2020
Harris Directory of
Kansas
Businesses

MERGENT

Exclusive Provider of
Dun & Bradstreet Library Solutions

dun & bradstreet

HOOVERS™ First Research® HARRIS INFOSOURCE™

Published April 2020 next update April 2021

WARNING: Purchasers and users of this directory may not use this directory to compile mailing lists, other marketing aids and other types of data, which are sold or otherwise provided to third parties. Such use is wrongful, illegal and a violation of the federal copyright laws.

CAUTION: Because of the many thousands of establishment listings contained in this directory and the possibilities of both human and mechanical error in processing this information, Mergent Inc. cannot assume liability for the correctness of the listings or information on which they are based. Hence, no information contained in this work should be relied upon in any instance where there is a possibility of any loss or damage as a consequence of any error or omission in this volume.

Publisher
Mergent Inc.
444 Madison Ave
New York, NY 10022

2020 Mergent Business Press
ISSN 1080-2614
ISBN 978-1-64141-614-6

MERGENT
BUSINESS PRESS
by FTSE Russell

TABLE OF CONTENTS

SUMMARY OF CONTENTS

Number of Companies 16,196
Number of Decision Makers.................................... 33,678
Minimum Number of Employees (Services)................. 10
Minimum Number of Employees (Manufacturers)........ 5

EXPLANATORY NOTES

How to Cross-Reference in This Directory

Sequential Entry Numbers. Each establishment in the Geographic Section is numbered sequentially (G-0000). The number assigned to each establishment is referred to as its "entry number." To make cross-referencing easier, each listing in the Geographic, SIC, Alphabetic and Product Sections includes the establishment's entry number. To facilitate locating an entry in the Geographic Section, the entry numbers for the first listing on the left page and the last listing on the right page are printed at the top of the page next to the city name.

Source Suggestions Welcome

Although all known sources were used to compile this directory, it is possible that companies were inadvertently omitted. Your assistance in calling attention to such omissions would be greatly appreciated. A special form on the facing page will help you in the reporting process.

Analysis

Every effort has been made to contact all firms to verify their information. The one exception to this rule is the annual sales figure, which is considered by many companies to be confidential information. Therefore, estimated sales have been calculated by multiplying the nationwide average sales per employee for the firm's major SIC/NAICS code by the firm's number of employees. Nationwide averages for sales per employee by SIC/NAICS codes are provided by the U.S. Department of Commerce and are updated annually. All sales—sales (est)—have been estimated by this method. The exceptions are parent companies (PA), division headquarters (DH) and headquarter locations (HQ) which may include an actual corporate sales figure—sales (corporate-wide) if available.

Types of Companies

Descriptive and statistical data are included for companies in the entire state. These comprise manufacturers, machine shops, fabricators, assemblers and printers. Also identified are corporate offices in the state.

Employment Data

The employment figure shown in the Products & Services Section includes male and female employees and embraces all levels of the company. This directory includes manufacturing companies with 5 or more employees and service companies with 10 or more employees. This figure is for the facility listed and does not include other plants or offices. It should be recognized that these figures represent an approximate year-round average. These employment figures are broken into codes A through F and used in the Alphabetic and Geographic Sections to further help you in qualifying a company. Be sure to check the footnotes at the bottom of the page for the code breakdowns.

Standard Industrial Classification (SIC)

The Standard Industrial Classification (SIC) system used in this directory was developed by the federal government for use in classifying establishments by the type of activity they are engaged in. The SIC classifications used in this directory are from the 1987 edition published by the U.S. Government's Office of Management and Budget. The SIC system separates all activities into broad industrial divisions (e.g., manufacturing, mining, retail trade). It further subdivides each division. The range of manufacturing industry classes extends from two-digit codes (major industry group) to four-digit codes (product).

For example:

Industry Breakdown	Code	Industry, Product, etc.
*Major industry group	20	Food and kindred products
Industry group	203	Canned and frozen foods
*Industry	2033	Fruits and vegetables, etc.

*Classifications used in this directory

Only two-digit and four-digit codes are used in this directory.

Arrangement

1. The **Geographic Section** contains complete in-depth corporate data. This section is sorted by cities listed in alphabetical order and companies listed alphabetically within each city. A County/City Index for referencing cities within counties precedes this section.

2. The **Standard Industrial Classification (SIC) Section** lists companies under approximately 500 four-digit SIC codes. An alphabetical and a numerical index precedes this section. A company can be listed under several codes. The codes are in numerical order with companies listed alphabetically under each code.

3. The **Alphabetic Section** lists all companies with their full physical or mailing addresses and telephone number.

4. The **Product & Services Section** lists companies under unique Harris categories. An index precedes this section. Companies can be listed under several categories.

USER'S GUIDE TO LISTINGS

GEOGRAPHIC SECTION

ANYTOWN
Any County

(G-1723)
READY MOVERS (HQ) ✪
Storage Division
Also Called RMI
704 Lawrence Rd (99999-9999)
PO Box 6 (99999-9999)
PHONE 999 999-9999
TOLL FREE: 800 999-9999
FAX: 999 999-9999
Jack Van Hulst, *President*
H L Gordon, *V P Marketing*
R T Bigelow, *General Mgr*
Ed Locke, *Purch Agent*
◆ **EMP**: 50 **EST**: 1992
SQ FT: 100,000
SALES (est.): $1MM-$4.9MM **Privately Held**
SALES (corporate-wide): 1.45B
WEB: www.readymovers.com
SIC: **4214** 4212 4222 Local moving & storage service
HQ: Intl Trucking Co
500 5th Ave
New York, NY 10001
212 800-4800

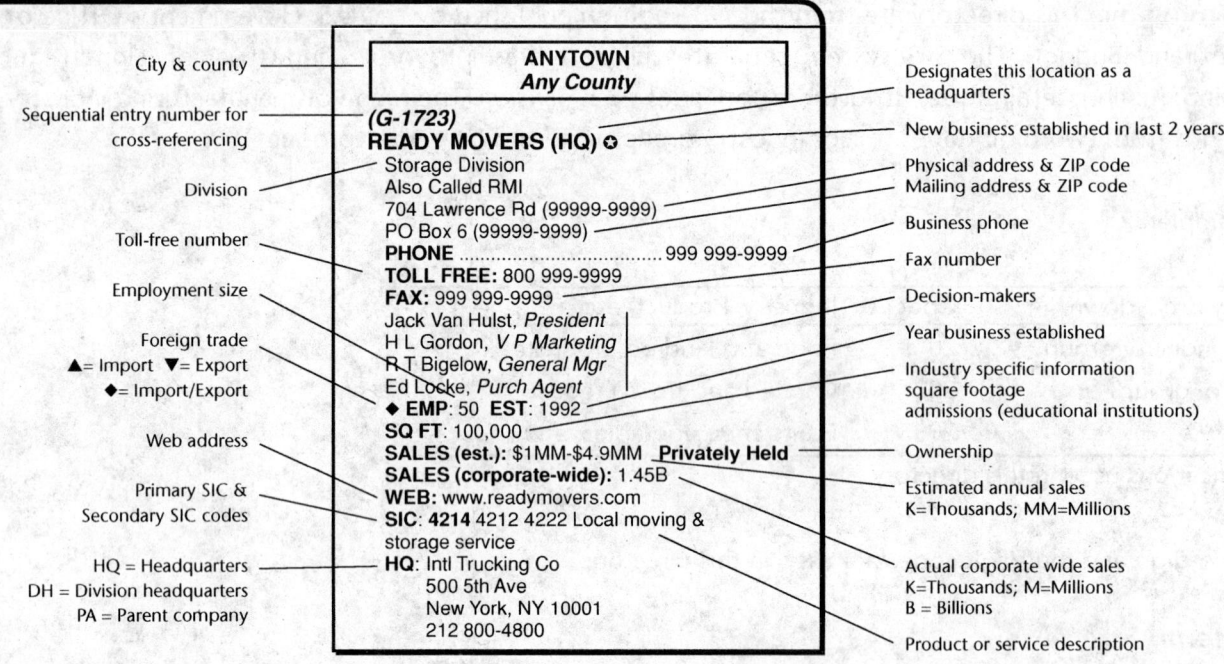

City & county
Sequential entry number for cross-referencing
Division
Toll-free number
Employment size
Foreign trade
▲= Import ▼= Export
◆= Import/Export
Web address
Primary SIC & Secondary SIC codes
HQ = Headquarters
DH = Division headquarters
PA = Parent company

Designates this location as a headquarters
New business established in last 2 years
Physical address & ZIP code
Mailing address & ZIP code
Business phone
Fax number
Decision-makers
Year business established
Industry specific information
square footage
admissions (educational institutions)
Ownership
Estimated annual sales
K=Thousands; MM=Millions
Actual corporate wide sales
K=Thousands; M=Millions
B = Billions
Product or service description

SIC SECTION

4214-Local Trucking, with Storage
Affordable Inds .... **D**...999 999-9999
Yourtown ***(G-54)***
◆ **Ready Movers** .... **E**...999 999-9999
Anytown ***(G-1723)***

4-digit SIC number & description
Foreign trade
▲= Import ▼= Export
◆= Import/Export
City

Indicates approximate employment figure
A = over 500 employees, B = 251–500
C = 101–250, D = 51–100, E = 20–50
F = 10-19, G = 1–9
Business phone
Geographic Section entry number where full company information appears

ALPHABETIC SECTION

R & R Manufacturing (HQ) 999 999-9999
651 Tally Blvd, Yourtown (99999) ***(G-1710)***
Ready Movers 999 999-9999
704 Lawrence Rd, Anytown (99999) ***(G-1723)***
Rendall Transportation, Anytown *Also Called RTI* ***(G-1730)***

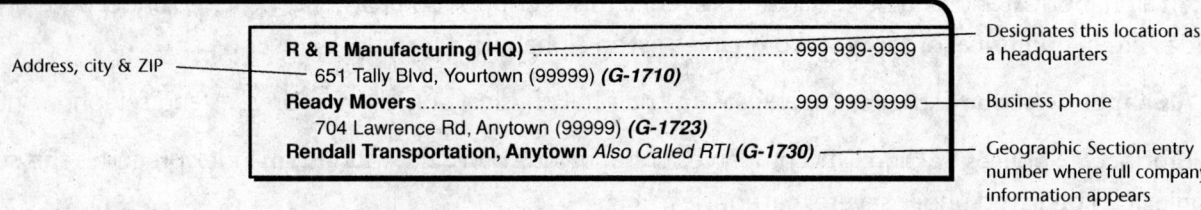

Address, city & ZIP

Designates this location as a headquarters
Business phone
Geographic Section entry number where full company information appears

PRODUCTS & SERVICES SECTION

TRUCKING & STORAGE: Local
Edgar & Son Trucking ....**C**...999 999-9999
Yourtown ***(G-522)***
Ready Movers ....**E**...999 999-9999
Anytown ***(G-1723)***
TUBING: Steel
Best Steel Tubes Inc ....**B**...999 999-9999
Yourtown ***(G-198)***

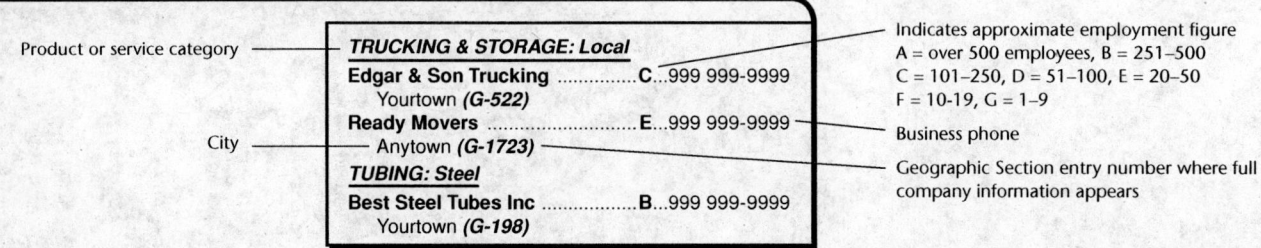

Product or service category
City

Indicates approximate employment figure
A = over 500 employees, B = 251–500
C = 101–250, D = 51–100, E = 20–50
F = 10-19, G = 1–9
Business phone
Geographic Section entry number where full company information appears

GEOGRAPHIC SECTION

Companies sorted by city in alphabetical order

In-depth company data listed

STANDARD INDUSTRIAL CLASSIFICATIONS

Alphabetical index of classifcation descriptions

Numerical index of classifcation descriptions

Companies sorted by SIC product groupings

ALPHABETIC SECTION

Company listings in alphabetical order

PRODUCTS & SERVICES INDEX

Products & Services categories listed in alphabetical order

PRODUCTS & SERVICES SECTION

Companies sorted by product & service classifications

Kansas
County Map

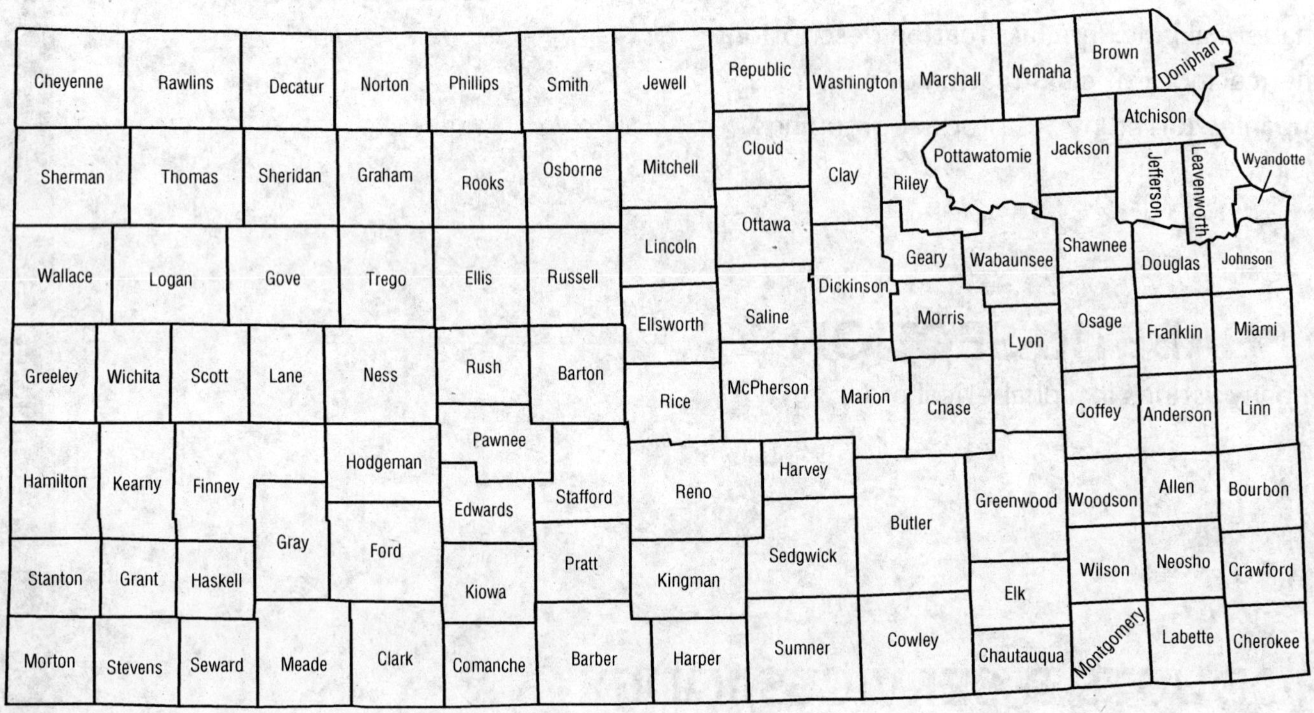

COUNTY/CITY CROSS-REFERENCE INDEX

ENTRY#

Linn
Blue Mound .... (G-532)
La Cygne .... (G-4640)
Linn Valley .... (G-6414)
Mound City .... (G-7169)
Parker .... (G-9656)
Pleasanton .... (G-9995)
Prescott .... (G-10166)

Logan
Oakley .... (G-7471)

Lyon
Allen .... (G-60)
Americus .... (G-76)
Emporia .... (G-1692)
Hartford .... (G-2726)
Olpe .... (G-8166)
Reading .... (G-10198)

Marion
Burns .... (G-646)
Durham .... (G-1474)
Florence .... (G-1929)
Goessel .... (G-2458)
Hillsboro .... (G-3040)
Marion .... (G-6866)
Peabody .... (G-9758)
Ramona .... (G-10189)

Marshall
Axtell .... (G-350)
Beattie .... (G-417)
Blue Rapids .... (G-533)
Bremen .... (G-581)
Frankfort .... (G-2021)
Home .... (G-3118)
Marysville .... (G-6878)
Summerfield .... (G-12214)
Waterville .... (G-13472)

Mcpherson
Canton .... (G-679)
Conway .... (G-1133)
Galva .... (G-2092)
Inman .... (G-3581)
Lindsborg .... (G-6391)
Marquette .... (G-6877)
Mc Pherson .... (G-6930)
McPherson .... (G-6931)
Moundridge .... (G-7178)
Roxbury .... (G-10257)
Smolan .... (G-12045)
Windom .... (G-16112)

Meade
Fowler .... (G-2019)
Meade .... (G-7046)
Plains .... (G-9973)

Miami
Bucyrus .... (G-593)
Hillsdale .... (G-3059)
Louisburg .... (G-6435)
Osawatomie .... (G-8191)
Paola .... (G-9539)

Mitchell
Beloit .... (G-469)
Cawker City .... (G-688)
Glen Elder .... (G-2424)
Scottsville .... (G-10838)
Tipton .... (G-12247)

Montgomery
Caney .... (G-664)
Cherryvale .... (G-800)
Coffeyville .... (G-907)
Havana .... (G-2728)
Independence .... (G-3497)
Tyro .... (G-13276)

Morris
Council Grove .... (G-1157)
White City .... (G-13567)

Morton
Elkhart .... (G-1617)
Rolla .... (G-10232)

Nemaha
Bern .... (G-520)
Centralia .... (G-697)
Sabetha .... (G-10304)
Seneca .... (G-10856)
Wetmore .... (G-13566)

Neosho
Chanute .... (G-700)
Erie .... (G-1856)
Galesburg .... (G-2091)
Saint Paul .... (G-10378)
Stark .... (G-12112)
Thayer .... (G-12246)

Ness
Brownell .... (G-589)
Ness City .... (G-7251)
Ransom .... (G-10192)
Utica .... (G-13334)

Norton
Almena .... (G-67)
Lenora .... (G-6243)
Norton .... (G-7440)

Osage
Burlingame .... (G-622)
Carbondale .... (G-684)
Lyndon .... (G-6476)
Melvern .... (G-7077)
Osage City .... (G-8181)
Overbrook .... (G-8322)
Quenemo .... (G-10178)
Scranton .... (G-10839)
Vassar .... (G-13371)

Osborne
Alton .... (G-74)
Downs .... (G-1468)
Natoma .... (G-7231)
Osborne .... (G-8207)
Portis .... (G-10006)

Ottawa
Bennington .... (G-512)
Delphos .... (G-1216)
Minneapolis .... (G-7113)
Tescott .... (G-12244)

Pawnee
Burdett .... (G-621)
Garfield .... (G-2367)
Larned .... (G-4694)
Rozel .... (G-10258)

Phillips
Logan .... (G-6420)
Long Island .... (G-6427)
Phillipsburg .... (G-9776)
Prairie View .... (G-10011)

Pottawatomie
Belvue .... (G-506)
Havensville .... (G-2739)
Louisville .... (G-6470)
Olsburg .... (G-8168)
Onaga .... (G-8171)
Saint George .... (G-10346)
Saint Marys .... (G-10358)
Wamego .... (G-13402)
Westmoreland .... (G-13546)

Pratt
Cullison .... (G-1185)
Iuka .... (G-3640)
Pratt .... (G-10090)
Sawyer .... (G-10794)

Rawlins
Atwood .... (G-281)

Reno
Buhler .... (G-614)
Haven .... (G-2729)
Hutchinson .... (G-3189)
Langdon .... (G-4664)
Nickerson .... (G-7431)
Pretty Prairie .... (G-10168)
South Hutchinson .... (G-12055)
Sylvia .... (G-12221)
Turon .... (G-13275)
Yoder .... (G-16196)

Republic
Belleville .... (G-450)
Courtland .... (G-1179)
Munden .... (G-7229)
Republic .... (G-10200)
Scandia .... (G-10798)

Rice
Alden .... (G-58)
Bushton .... (G-652)
Chase .... (G-782)
Geneseo .... (G-2393)
Little River .... (G-6418)
Lyons .... (G-6479)
Sterling .... (G-12113)

Riley
Leonardville .... (G-6249)
Manhattan .... (G-6525)
Randolph .... (G-10191)
Riley .... (G-10205)

Rooks
Palco .... (G-9537)
Plainville .... (G-9979)
Stockton .... (G-12181)

Rush
La Crosse .... (G-4633)
Otis .... (G-8240)
Rush Center .... (G-10259)

Russell
Bunker Hill .... (G-620)
Dorrance .... (G-1464)
Gorham .... (G-2492)
Lucas .... (G-6471)
Russell .... (G-10263)

Saline
Assaria .... (G-200)
Carlton .... (G-686)
Falun .... (G-1928)
New Cambria .... (G-7269)
Salina .... (G-10387)

Scott
Scott City .... (G-10803)

Sedgwick
Andale .... (G-77)
Bel Aire .... (G-425)
Cheney .... (G-787)
Clearwater .... (G-887)
Colwich .... (G-1090)
Derby .... (G-1218)
Eastborough .... (G-1476)
Garden Plain .... (G-2321)
Goddard .... (G-2429)
Haysville .... (G-2933)
Kechi .... (G-4566)
Maize .... (G-6507)
Mount Hope .... (G-7202)
Mulvane .... (G-7211)
Park City .... (G-9598)
Valley Center .... (G-13336)
Viola .... (G-13378)
Wichita .... (G-13576)

Seward
Kismet .... (G-4630)
Liberal .... (G-6272)

Shawnee
Auburn .... (G-293)
Berryton .... (G-525)
Lecompton .... (G-5610)
Rossville .... (G-10251)
Silver Lake .... (G-12028)
Tecumseh .... (G-12238)
Topeka .... (G-12274)
Wakarusa .... (G-13384)

Sheridan
Hoxie .... (G-3135)
Selden .... (G-10855)

Sherman
Goodland .... (G-2459)
Kanorado .... (G-3773)

Smith
Athol .... (G-273)
Kensington .... (G-4574)
Smith Center .... (G-12031)

Stafford
Hudson .... (G-3146)
Macksville .... (G-6499)
Saint John .... (G-10349)
Stafford .... (G-12104)

Stanton
Johnson .... (G-3651)

Stevens
Hugoton .... (G-3147)
Moscow .... (G-7167)

Sumner
Argonia .... (G-138)
Belle Plaine .... (G-445)
Caldwell .... (G-655)
Conway Springs .... (G-1136)
Oxford .... (G-9532)
Peck .... (G-9763)
Wellington .... (G-13488)

Thomas
Brewster .... (G-582)
Colby .... (G-987)
Levant .... (G-6265)
Rexford .... (G-10201)

Trego
WA Keeney .... (G-13382)
Wakeeney .... (G-13385)

Wabaunsee
Alma .... (G-61)
Alta Vista .... (G-69)
Eskridge .... (G-1865)
Maple Hill .... (G-6862)
Paxico .... (G-9756)

Wallace
Sharon Springs .... (G-10894)

Washington
Clifton .... (G-900)
Greenleaf .... (G-2667)
Haddam .... (G-2694)
Hanover .... (G-2709)
Linn .... (G-6407)
Mahaska .... (G-6505)
Palmer .... (G-9538)
Washington .... (G-13459)

Wichita
Leoti .... (G-6250)
Modoc .... (G-7153)

Wilson
Altoona .... (G-75)
Buffalo .... (G-613)
Coyville .... (G-1182)
Fredonia .... (G-2025)
Neodesha .... (G-7234)

Woodson
Piqua .... (G-9801)
Yates Center .... (G-16195)

Wyandotte
Bonner Springs .... (G-538)
Edwardsville .... (G-1495)
Kansas City .... (G-3774)

GEOGRAPHIC SECTION

ANYTOWN
Any County

(G-1723)
READY BOX CO (HQ) ✪
Storage Division
Also Called RBC
704 Lawrence Rd (99999-9999)
P.O. Box 6 (99999-9999)
PHONE......................999 999-9999
TOLL FREE: 800 999-9999
FAX: 999 999-9999
Paul Smith, *President*
Cliff Smith, *VP Marketing*
C T House, *Plant Manager*
▲ **EMP:** 50 **EST:** 1992
SQ FT: 11,000
SALES (est): 17.2MM **Publicly Held**
SALES (corp-wide): 1.2B
WEB: www.readybox.com
SIC: 2657 2675 2679 Folding paperboard boxes; die cutting
HQ: Intl Box Co
500 5th Ave
New York, NY 10001
212 800-4800

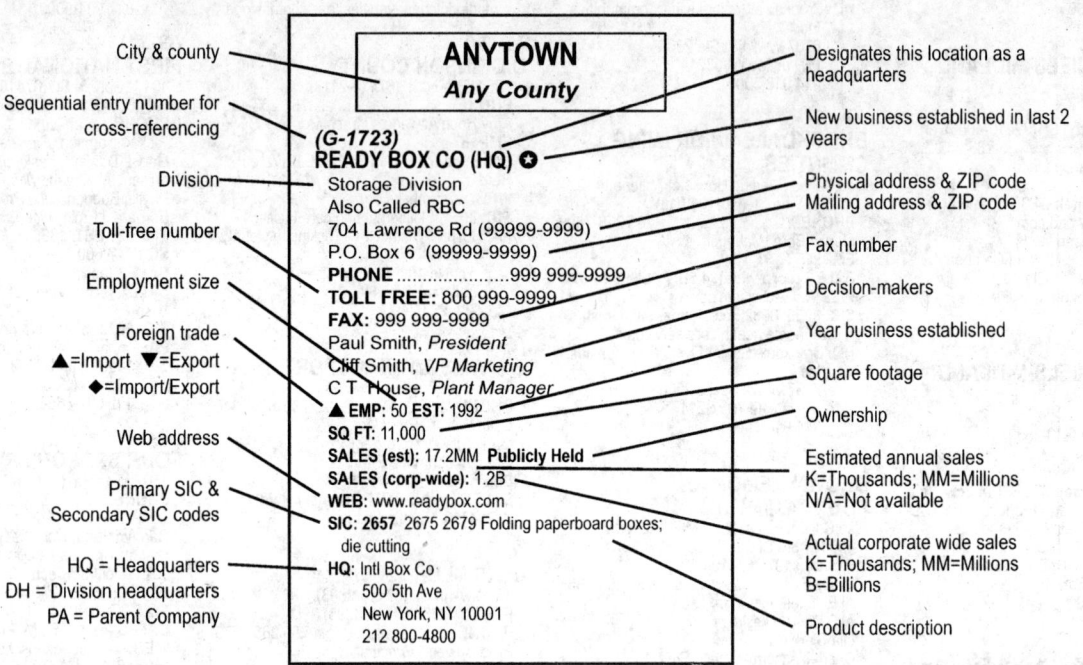

City & county
Sequential entry number for cross-referencing
Division
Toll-free number
Employment size
Foreign trade
▲=Import ▼=Export
◆=Import/Export
Web address
Primary SIC & Secondary SIC codes
HQ = Headquarters
DH = Division headquarters
PA = Parent Company

Designates this location as a headquarters
New business established in last 2 years
Physical address & ZIP code
Mailing address & ZIP code
Fax number
Decision-makers
Year business established
Square footage
Ownership
Estimated annual sales
K=Thousands; MM=Millions
N/A=Not available
Actual corporate wide sales
K=Thousands; MM=Millions
B=Billions
Product description

See footnotes for symbols and codes identification.

- This section is in alphabetical order by city.
- Companies are sorted alphabetically under their respective cities.
- To locate cities within a county refer to the County/City Cross Reference Index.

IMPORTANT NOTICE: It is a violation of both federal and state law to transmit an unsolicited advertisement to a facsimile machine. Any user of this product that violates such laws may be subject to civil and criminal penalties which may exceed $500 for each transmission of an unsolicited facsimile. Harris InfoSource provides fax numbers for lawful purposes only and expressly forbids the use of these numbers in any unlawful manner.

Abilene
Dickinson County

(G-1)
ABILENE ANIMAL HOSPITAL PA (PA)
320 Ne 14th St (67410-1928)
PHONE..................................785 263-2301
Frank R Jordan, *Partner*
Dr Michael L Whitehair, *Corp Secy*
Dr Steven C Henry, *Vice Pres*
Shelli Gugler, *Pharmacist*
Jon Gose, *Med Doctor*
EMP: 25 **EST:** 1945
SQ FT: 3,500
SALES (est): 1.9MM **Privately Held**
WEB: www.aahpa.com
SIC: 0741 0742 Animal hospital services, livestock; animal hospital services, pets & other animal specialties

(G-2)
ABILENE CHILDCARE LEARNING CTR
504 S Campbell St (67410-3108)
PHONE..................................785 263-1799
Pat Lacey, *Director*
Bruce Hattenbach, *Director*
George Welborn, *Director*
EMP: 11
SQ FT: 2,900
SALES: 316K **Privately Held**
SIC: 8351 Preschool center

(G-3)
ABILENE COUNTRY CLUB
1705 Country Club Ln (67410-6931)
PHONE..................................785 263-3811
Trudy Adams, *Manager*
EMP: 20
SALES: 230.7K **Privately Held**
SIC: 7997 Country club, membership; golf club, membership; swimming club, membership; tennis club, membership

(G-4)
ABILENE FAMILY PHYSICIANS PA
511 Ne 10th St (67410-2153)
PHONE..................................785 263-7190
Gary Coleman, *President*
Kathi Hoerner, *Principal*
J Steven Schwarting, *Admin Sec*
EMP: 16
SALES (est): 1.3MM **Privately Held**
SIC: 8011 Clinic, operated by physicians; general & family practice, physician/surgeon; physicians' office, including specialists

(G-5)
ABILENE HOUSING INC
Also Called: Frontier Estates
601 N Buckeye Ave (67410-2255)
PHONE..................................785 263-1080
Duane Facklam, *Principal*
EMP: 11 **EST:** 1976
SQ FT: 50,000
SALES: 505.5K **Privately Held**
WEB: www.abilenehousing.com
SIC: 6513 Retirement hotel operation

(G-6)
ABILENE PHYSCL THRPY & SPRTS
103 Nw 15th St (67410-1547)
PHONE..................................785 263-3519
Tonya Mills, *Owner*
EMP: 11
SALES (est): 597.5K **Privately Held**
SIC: 8049 Physiotherapist; physical therapist

(G-7)
ABILENE PRINTING CO INC
Also Called: Abilene Printing & Office Pdts
207 Ne 3rd St (67410-2501)
P.O. Box 188 (67410-0188)
PHONE..................................785 263-2330
Ralph Hilton, *President*
Judy Hilton, *Vice Pres*
EMP: 5
SQ FT: 5,000
SALES (est): 649K **Privately Held**
SIC: 2752 2759 2796 Commercial printing, offset; letterpress printing; engraving on copper, steel, wood or rubber: printing plates

(G-8)
ABILENE RFLCTOR CHRONICLE PUBG
Also Called: Central Market Place
303 N Broadway St (67410-2616)
PHONE..................................785 263-1000
Carmage Lee Walls Sr, *President*
Yvonne Walls, *Corp Secy*
Carmage Lee Walls Jr, *Vice Pres*
EMP: 20
SQ FT: 7,000
SALES (est): 1.1MM **Privately Held**
SIC: 2711 2741 Newspapers: publishing only, not printed on site; shopping news: publishing & printing

(G-9)
ABILENE SUPER EIGHT
Also Called: Super 8 Motel
2207 N Buckeye Ave (67410-1508)
PHONE..................................785 263-4545
Linda Franco, *Manager*
EMP: 12
SALES (est): 429.3K **Privately Held**
SIC: 7011 Hotels & motels

(G-10)
ABRASIVE BLAST SYSTEMS INC
Also Called: ABS
418 Ne 14th St (67410-1820)
P.O. Box 307 (67410-0307)
PHONE..................................785 263-3786
Sam Browning, *President*
EMP: 20
SQ FT: 15,000
SALES: 1.5MM **Privately Held**
SIC: 3569 8711 Blast cleaning equipment, dustless; consulting engineer

(G-11)
ADM MILLING CO
210 Ne 3rd St (67410-2502)
P.O. Box 338 (67410-0338)
PHONE..................................785 263-1631
Steve Storniolo, *General Mgr*
EMP: 30
SALES (corp-wide): 64.3B **Publicly Held**
WEB: www.admmilling.com
SIC: 2041 5153 Grain mills (except rice); grain elevators

HQ: Adm Milling Co.
8000 W 110th St Ste 300
Overland Park KS 66210
913 491-9400

(G-12)
ARCHER-DANIELS-MIDLAND COMPANY
Also Called: ADM
1000 N Washington St (67410-4006)
PHONE..................................785 263-2260
Keith Bartley, *Branch Mgr*
EMP: 30
SALES (corp-wide): 64.3B **Publicly Held**
WEB: www.admworld.com
SIC: 2048 Prepared feeds
PA: Archer-Daniels-Midland Company
77 W Wacker Dr Ste 4600
Chicago IL 60601
312 634-8100

(G-13)
ARCHER-DANIELS-MIDLAND COMPANY
ADM
210 Ne 3rd St (67410-2502)
PHONE..................................785 263-2260
EMP: 30
SALES (corp-wide): 67.7B **Publicly Held**
SIC: 4221 2041 Farm Product Warehousing Mfg Flour/Grain Mill Prooducts
PA: Archer-Daniels-Midland Company
77 W Wacker Dr Ste 4600
Chicago IL 60601
312 634-8100

(G-14)
BERT AND WETTA SALES INC
Also Called: Bert & Wetta Abilene
509 Se 4th St (67410)
P.O. Box 128 (67410-0128)
PHONE..................................785 263-2258
Stan Foltz, *Opers-Prdtn-Mfg*
EMP: 22
SALES (corp-wide): 8MM **Privately Held**
WEB: www.usalfalfa.net
SIC: 2048 5191 Alfalfa or alfalfa meal, prepared as animal feed; animal feeds
PA: Bert And Wetta Sales, Inc.
1230 Ne Trail St
Larned KS 67550
620 285-7777

(G-15)
BEVERLY ENTERPRISES-KANSAS LLC
Also Called: Beverly Healthcare
705 N Brady St (67410-2113)
PHONE..................................785 263-1431
Annie Hoch-Altwagg, *Principal*
EMP: 60
SALES (corp-wide): 393.8MM **Privately Held**
SIC: 8051 Convalescent home with continuous nursing care
HQ: Beverly Enterprises-Kansas, Llc
1 1000 Beverly Way
Fort Smith AR 72919
479 201-2000

(G-16)
BRIERTON ENGINEERING INC
1200 S Buckeye Ave (67410-6386)
P.O. Box 217 (67410-0217)
PHONE..................................785 263-7711
Mike Brierton, *President*
Theresa Brierton, *Corp Secy*
▲ **EMP:** 22
SQ FT: 21,000
SALES (est): 3.3MM **Privately Held**
WEB: www.brietoneng.com
SIC: 7539 3714 3537 3462 Axle straightening, automotive; axles, motor vehicle; industrial trucks & tractors; iron & steel forgings

(G-17)
BROOKDALE SENIOR LIVING COMMUN
Also Called: Sterling House of Abilene I
1100 N Vine St Ofc (67410-4022)
PHONE..................................785 263-7400
Stefanie Silmon, *Director*
EMP: 18
SALES (corp-wide): 4.5B **Publicly Held**
WEB: www.assisted.com
SIC: 8051 Skilled nursing care facilities
HQ: Brookdale Senior Living Communities, Inc.
6737 W Wa St Ste 2300
Milwaukee WI 53214
414 918-5000

(G-18)
BROOKDALE SNIOR LVING CMMNTIES
Also Called: Sterling House of Abilene II
1102 N Vine St (67410-4015)
PHONE..................................785 263-7800
Maryjo Berg, *Manager*
EMP: 15
SALES (corp-wide): 4.5B **Publicly Held**
WEB: www.assisted.com
SIC: 8059 8082 Rest home, with health care; home health care services
HQ: Brookdale Senior Living Communities, Inc.
6737 W Wa St Ste 2300
Milwaukee WI 53214
414 918-5000

(G-19)
BROWN MEMORIAL FOUNDATION
Also Called: BROWN MEMORIAL HOME
409 Nw 3rd St Ste G (67410-2639)
P.O. Box 187 (67410-0187)
PHONE..................................785 263-2351
Al P Jones, *President*
Al P Davis, *President*
Lila Clark, *Corp Secy*
Charles A Norman, *Vice Pres*
EMP: 43
SALES: 1.3MM **Privately Held**
SIC: 8361 Home for the aged

(G-20)
CONCORDIA TRACTOR INC
Also Called: John Deere Authorized Dealer
1300 S Buckeye Ave (67410-6383)
PHONE..................................785 263-3051
Harley Adams, *General Mgr*
Ann Adams, *Technology*
EMP: 19
SALES (est): 236.3K
SALES (corp-wide): 1.3MM **Privately Held**
WEB: www.westernstarag.com
SIC: 5083 5261 Agricultural machinery & equipment; lawnmowers & tractors
PA: Western Star Ag Resources, Inc
834 E Prescott Rd
Salina KS 67401
785 823-3794

(G-21)
COUNTY OF DICKINSON
Also Called: Highway Dept
408 Se 2nd St (67410-2920)
PHONE..................................785 263-3193
EMP: 15 **Privately Held**
SIC: 1611 Highway Maintenance
PA: County Of Dickinson
109 E 1st St Ste 201
Abilene KS
785 263-3093

(G-22)
CROP SERVICE CENTER INC (PA)
1123 Eden Rd (67410-6652)
PHONE..................................785 479-2204
Dale C Koop, *President*
Mona Koop, *Corp Secy*
Mike Kleiber, *Vice Pres*
EMP: 13
SQ FT: 1,200
SALES (est): 5.7MM **Privately Held**
WEB: www.cropservicecenter.com
SIC: 0721 Crop spraying services

(G-23)
CROWN TL INC
Also Called: Crown Cabinets
210 N Brady St (67410-2810)
PHONE..................................785 263-7061
Ryan Johnson, *President*
EMP: 7
SQ FT: 15,000
SALES (est): 1.2MM **Privately Held**
WEB: www.crowncabinetry.com
SIC: 5712 2434 Cabinets, except custom made: kitchen; vanities, bathroom: wood

(G-24)
DICKINSON COUNTY
705 N Brady St (67410-2113)
PHONE..................................785 263-1431
Amy Hoch Altwegg, *Branch Mgr*
EMP: 87
SALES (corp-wide): 34.2MM **Privately Held**
WEB: www.mhsks.org
SIC: 8051 Skilled nursing care facilities
PA: Hospital District 1 Of Dickinson County, Kansas
511 Ne 10th St
Abilene KS 67410
785 263-2100

(G-25)
E S WILSON TRANSPORT INC
1120 S Buckeye Ave (67410-6380)
PHONE..................................785 263-9845
Evan Wilson, *President*
Mark Wilson, *Corp Secy*
Greg Wilson, *Vice Pres*
EMP: 16
SALES (est): 2.8MM **Privately Held**
SIC: 4213 Contract haulers

(G-26)
ELKS CLUB
417 Nw 4th St (67410-2603)
P.O. Box 695 (67410-0695)
PHONE..................................785 263-1675
Brad Cowers, *Principal*
EMP: 16
SALES (est): 222.2K **Privately Held**
SIC: 8699 Charitable organization

(G-27)
EMMANUEL UNITED METHODIST CH
Also Called: Emmanuel Church
1300 N Vine St (67410-4014)
P.O. Box 534 (67410-0534)
PHONE..................................785 263-3342
Mike Eurit, *Pastor*
Phil Watson, *Maintence Staff*
EMP: 12
SALES (est): 505.7K **Privately Held**
SIC: 8661 8322 Methodist Church; youth center

(G-28)
EVERETTS INC
205 S Van Buren St (67410-3711)
PHONE..................................785 263-4172
Dennis L Everett, *President*
Ronald D Everett, *Vice Pres*
Gerald E Everett, *Treasurer*
EMP: 11
SALES (est): 2.2MM **Privately Held**
WEB: www.everetts.net
SIC: 4213 4212 Trucking, except local; dump truck haulage

(G-29)
EVERGY KANSAS CENTRAL INC
209 Olive St (67410)
P.O. Box 86 (67410-0086)
PHONE..................................785 263-2023
Gary Myrick, *Manager*
EMP: 12
SALES (corp-wide): 4.2B **Publicly Held**
SIC: 4911 Distribution, electric power
HQ: Evergy Kansas Central, Inc.
818 S Kansas Ave
Topeka KS 66612
785 575-6300

(G-30)
FAMILY VIDEO MOVIE CLUB INC
409 N Buckeye Ave (67410-2529)
PHONE..................................785 263-3853
Tammy Holub, *Branch Mgr*
EMP: 26
SALES (corp-wide): 189.9MM **Privately Held**
SIC: 7841 Video disk/tape rental to the general public
HQ: Family Video Movie Club Inc.
2500 Lehigh Mt Ave
Glenview IL 60026
847 904-9000

(G-31)
FIRST NATIONAL BANK INC (HQ)
401 N Spruce St (67410-2643)
P.O. Box 669 (67410-0669)
PHONE..................................785 263-1090
Rick Williamson, *President*
Gary L Donley, *President*
William W Altman, *Vice Pres*
Phyllis Budden, *Vice Pres*
Barbara J Emig, *Vice Pres*
EMP: 21 **EST:** 1885
SQ FT: 7,600
SALES (est): 5.3MM
SALES (corp-wide): 282.8MM **Privately Held**
SIC: 6022 State commercial banks
PA: Pinnacle Bancorp, Inc.
18081 Burt St Fl 3
Elkhorn NE 68022
402 697-8666

(G-32)
FOUR SEASONS RV ACRES INC
2502 Mink Rd (67410-7245)
PHONE..................................785 598-2221
Darell Fenn, *President*
Carolyn Fenn, *Corp Secy*
Diana Irvine, *Sales Dir*
Josh Abel, *Info Tech Dir*
EMP: 25 **EST:** 1975
SQ FT: 30,000
SALES (est): 6.6MM **Privately Held**
WEB: www.4seasonsrv.com
SIC: 5561 5411 7033 7538 Campers (pickup coaches) for mounting on trucks; convenience stores, independent; campgrounds; recreational vehicle repairs

(G-33)
GAVILON GRAIN LLC
513 W 1st St (67410-3009)
P.O. Box 544 (67410-0544)
PHONE..................................785 263-7275
Fax: 785 263-3203
EMP: 11
SALES (corp-wide): 65.8B **Privately Held**
SIC: 6221 Commodity Contract Broker
HQ: Gavilon Grain, Llc
1331 Capitol Ave
Omaha NE 68102
402 889-4000

(G-34)
GREAT PLAINS MANUFACTURING INC
Land Pride
1100 Nw 8th St (67410-2363)
PHONE..................................785 263-2486
Dana Dulahery, *Plant Mgr*
Jim Stroda, *Maint Spvr*
Steve Janssen, *Engineer*
Delia Treffer, *Manager*
Dana Dulohery, *Executive*
EMP: 130 **Privately Held**
WEB: www.greatplainsmfg.com
SIC: 3523 3524 3423 Farm machinery & equipment; lawn & garden equipment; hand & edge tools
HQ: Great Plains Manufacturing Incorporated
1525 E North St
Salina KS 67401
785 823-3276

(G-35)
GREYHOUND HALL OF FAME
407 S Buckeye Ave (67410-2925)
PHONE..................................785 263-3000
Vey Weaver, *President*
Kathryn Lounsbury, *Director*
EMP: 17
SQ FT: 27,000
SALES: 128.3K **Privately Held**
WEB: www.greyhoundhalloffame.com
SIC: 8412 Museum

(G-36)
H & P INC
Also Called: Abilene Concrete & Supply
1101 Portland Ave (67410-1553)
PHONE..................................785 263-4183

Michael Parsons, *President*
John Eichman, *Vice Pres*
Rob Eichman, *Admin Sec*
EMP: 7 **EST:** 1945
SQ FT: 22,500
SALES (est): 915.9K **Privately Held**
SIC: 3273 5085 Ready-mixed concrete; industrial supplies

(G-37)
HEARTLAND CLINIC
511 Ne 10th St (67410-2153)
PHONE....785 263-4131
Dr M Chantel Long, *Partner*
Doug Shernn, *Partner*
Dr William Short, *Partner*
Brian Holmes, *Principal*
EMP: 16
SALES (est): 2.1MM **Privately Held**
SIC: 8011 General & family practice, physician/surgeon

(G-38)
HOLIDAY INN EX HT & SUITES
110 E Lafayette Ave (67410-7285)
PHONE....785 263-4049
Mukul Ghosh Hajra, *President*
EMP: 20
SALES (est): 901.7K **Privately Held**
SIC: 7011 Hotels & motels

(G-39)
HOSPITAL DISTRICT 1 OF DCKNSN
Also Called: Hope Hlth Hspice Dckinson Cnty
1111 N Brady St (67410-1804)
P.O. Box 69 (67410-0069)
PHONE....785 263-6630
Mark Miller, *Branch Mgr*
EMP: 11
SALES (est): 355.5K
SALES (corp-wide): 34.2MM **Privately Held**
SIC: 8082 Home health care services
PA: Hospital District 1 Of Dickinson County, Kansas
511 Ne 10th St
Abilene KS 67410
785 263-2100

(G-40)
HOSPITAL DST 1 DCKNSON CNTY KA (PA)
Also Called: Memorial Health System
511 Ne 10th St (67410-2153)
P.O. Box 69 (67410-0069)
PHONE....785 263-2100
Reginald Harold Courtois, *CEO*
Elgin Glanzer, *CFO*
EMP: 250
SQ FT: 86,000
SALES: 34.2MM **Privately Held**
WEB: www.mhsks.org
SIC: 8062 Hospital, affiliated with AMA residency

(G-41)
HUSQVARNA CHAIN SAWS & PWR EQP
1701 W 1st St (67410-3501)
PHONE....785 263-7668
Sarah Picking, *President*
EMP: 5
SALES (est): 311.4K **Privately Held**
SIC: 3546 Saws & sawing equipment

(G-42)
INTERNATIONAL ASSN LIONS CLUBS
623 3300 Ave (67410-7502)
PHONE....785 388-2764
Myron Lady, *President*
EMP: 23
SALES (corp-wide): 63.7MM **Privately Held**
WEB: www.iaopc.com
SIC: 8641 Civic associations
PA: The International Association Of Lions Clubs Incorporated
300 W 22nd St
Oak Brook IL 60523
630 571-5466

(G-43)
KENNY LIVINGSTON TRUCKING INC
1375 Highway 18 (67410-6043)
PHONE....785 598-2493
Kenny Livingston, *President*
EMP: 12
SALES: 2.3MM **Privately Held**
SIC: 4213 Contract haulers

(G-44)
LAST CHANCE GRAPHICS INC
201 N Broadway St (67410-2648)
P.O. Box 184 (67410-0184)
PHONE....785 263-4470
Alan Iezek, *President*
Michelle Iezek, *Vice Pres*
EMP: 5
SQ FT: 2,000
SALES: 350K **Privately Held**
SIC: 7336 2759 Graphic arts & related design; screen printing

(G-45)
LOVES TRAVEL STOPS
2322 Fair Rd (67410-6941)
PHONE....785 263-3390
EMP: 13
SALES (corp-wide): 4.6B **Privately Held**
SIC: 4724 Travel agencies
PA: Love's Travel Stops & Country Stores, Inc.
10601 N Pennsylvania Ave
Oklahoma City OK 73120
405 302-6500

(G-46)
MEMORIAL HOSPITAL FITNESS CTR
418 N Broadway St (67410-2619)
PHONE....785 263-3888
Raelyn Whitehair, *Director*
EMP: 10
SALES (est): 125.1K **Privately Held**
SIC: 7991 Physical fitness facilities

(G-47)
NATIONAL ARCHIVES AND REC ADM
Also Called: Dwight D Eisenhower Library
200 Se 4th St (67410-2900)
P.O. Box 339 (67410-0339)
PHONE....785 263-6700
Daniel Holt, *Director*
EMP: 60 **Publicly Held**
WEB: www.nationalarchives.com
SIC: 8231 8412 Libraries; museum
HQ: National Archives And Records Administration
8601 Adelphi Rd Ste 4200
College Park MD 20740
301 837-2000

(G-48)
NATIONAL GREYHOUND ASSOCIATION
729 Old 40 (67410-6664)
P.O. Box 543 (67410-0543)
PHONE....785 263-4660
Tim Horan, *Principal*
Gary Guccione, *Director*
EMP: 11 **EST:** 1906
SQ FT: 4,600
SALES: 3.4MM **Privately Held**
WEB: www.agcouncil.com
SIC: 7361 0752 Registries; animal specialty services

(G-49)
PROSCAPE INC
955 2440 Ln (67410-7289)
PHONE....785 263-7104
Mike Houlton, *President*
Mike Holton, *President*
Marsha Holton, *Corp Secy*
Marsha Houlton, *Corp Secy*
EMP: 10
SALES (est): 660.8K **Privately Held**
SIC: 0782 Landscape contractors

(G-50)
RAWHIDE PORTABLE CORRAL INC
900 N Washington St (67410-3606)
PHONE....785 263-3436
John McDonald, *Owner*
Mary McDonald, *Co-Owner*
EMP: 30
SALES (est): 2.9MM **Privately Held**
SIC: 0751 Cattle services

(G-51)
ROBSON OIL CO INC
1302 Portland Ave (67410-1586)
P.O. Box 694 (67410-0694)
PHONE....785 263-2470
W Patrick Robson, *President*
Sue Robson, *Corp Secy*
Anita Williams, *Office Mgr*
EMP: 15
SQ FT: 1,800
SALES (est): 3.2MM **Privately Held**
SIC: 5541 5171 4213 Filling stations, gasoline; petroleum bulk stations; trucking, except local; liquid petroleum transport, non-local

(G-52)
RUSSELL STOVER CHOCOLATES LLC
Also Called: Russell Stover 109
1993 Caramel Blvd (67410)
P.O. Box 579 (67410-0579)
PHONE....785 263-0463
Bob O'Neil, *Purch Mgr*
Greg Stuber, *Plant Engr*
Tracy Leach, *Branch Mgr*
EMP: 29
SALES (corp-wide): 4.4B **Privately Held**
WEB: www.russell-stover.com
SIC: 5441 2657 2066 Candy; folding paperboard boxes; chocolate & cocoa products
HQ: Russell Stover Chocolates, Llc
4900 Oak St
Kansas City MO 64112
816 842-9240

(G-53)
RYAN FARMS INC
2231 Deer Rd (67410-6933)
PHONE....785 263-1613
Don Ryan, *President*
Deanna Ryan, *Admin Sec*
EMP: 11
SALES (est): 1.7MM **Privately Held**
SIC: 0279 Domestic animal farms

(G-54)
THUNDER STRUCK INC
401 Cottage Ave (67410-2849)
PHONE....785 200-6680
Casen Brown, *President*
Dale Jones, *Vice Pres*
EMP: 35
SALES (est): 6.8MM **Privately Held**
SIC: 3714 Motor vehicle engines & parts

(G-55)
UMB BANK NATIONAL ASSOCIATION
400 N Broadway St (67410-2619)
PHONE....785 263-1130
Daryl Roney, *Branch Mgr*
Kristy Engle, *Manager*
EMP: 14
SALES (corp-wide): 1.1B **Publicly Held**
WEB: www.umbwebsolutions.com
SIC: 6021 National commercial banks
HQ: Umb Bank, National Association
1010 Grand Blvd Fl 3
Kansas City MO 64106
816 842-2222

(G-56)
WADDELL & REED INC
203 Nw 15th St (67410-1579)
P.O. Box 84 (67410-0084)
PHONE....785 263-7496
April Barker, *Branch Mgr*
EMP: 10 **Publicly Held**
SIC: 6282 Investment counselors
HQ: Waddell & Reed, Inc.
6300 Lamar Ave
Shawnee Mission KS 66202
913 236-2000

(G-57)
WAYNE R WARD & ASSOCIATES
2205 N Buckeye Ave Ste C (67410-1508)
P.O. Box 487 (67410-0487)
PHONE....785 263-7272
Julia Ann Ward, *Owner*
Kim Colburn, *Admin Sec*
EMP: 12
SALES (est): 242K **Privately Held**
SIC: 0279 Kennels, breeding & raising own stock

Alden
Rice County

(G-58)
FREDERICK HARVESTING
301 N Pioneer St (67512-9362)
P.O. Box 187 (67512-0187)
PHONE....620 534-2211
Lance Frederick, *Owner*
EMP: 10
SALES (est): 1.2MM **Privately Held**
WEB: www.frederickharvesting.com
SIC: 0722 Crop harvesting

(G-59)
STERLING TRUCKING INC
9 Pioneer St (67512-9330)
PHONE....620 534-2461
Kyle Kopfmann, *President*
Ann Kopfmann, *Corp Secy*
EMP: 10 **EST:** 1994
SALES: 1.5MM **Privately Held**
SIC: 1389 Haulage, oil field

Allen
Lyon County

(G-60)
2I FEEDERS LLC
884 Road 350 (66833-9401)
PHONE....620 528-3740
Lacie Schumann, *Admin Sec*
EMP: 10
SALES (est): 630.4K **Privately Held**
SIC: 0211 Beef cattle feedlots

Alma
Wabaunsee County

(G-61)
ALMA FOODS LLC
110 E 1st St (66401-9831)
PHONE....785 765-3396
Carl Haga, *Owner*
EMP: 19
SALES (est): 5.8MM
SALES (corp-wide): 9.5B **Publicly Held**
WEB: www.hormel.com
SIC: 2013 Sausages & other prepared meats
PA: Hormel Foods Corporation
1 Hormel Pl
Austin MN 55912
507 437-5611

(G-62)
BANK OF FLINT HILLS
408 Missouri Ave (66401-9822)
PHONE....785 765-2220
Dennis Hadley, *Vice Pres*
Bill Johnston, *Branch Mgr*
EMP: 19
SALES (corp-wide): 12.2MM **Privately Held**
SIC: 6021 National commercial banks
PA: Bank Of The Flint Hills
806 5th St
Wamego KS 66547
785 456-2221

(G-63)
GRANDMA HOERNERS FOODS INC
31862 Thompson Rd (66401-9091)
PHONE..................................785 765-2300
Duane McCoy, *President*
Regina McCoy, *Vice Pres*
Fuller Brenda, *Opers Mgr*
Jim Holcomb, *Plant Engr*
Brad Voth, *Info Tech Mgr*
EMP: 40
SQ FT: 45,000
SALES: 15MM **Privately Held**
WEB: www.grandmahoerners.com
SIC: 2033 5149 Apple sauce: packaged in cans, jars, etc.; sauces

(G-64)
IRISH EXPRESS INC
32750 Wabaunsee Rd (66401-8800)
PHONE..................................785 765-2500
Patrick Shannon, *President*
Mike Shannon, *Vice Pres*
EMP: 35
SALES: 9.1MM **Privately Held**
WEB: www.irishexpressinc.com
SIC: 4213 Trucking, except local

(G-65)
MIDWEST HEALTH SERVICES INC
Also Called: Alma Manor
234 Manor Cir (66401-8891)
P.O. Box 127 (66401-0127)
PHONE..................................785 765-3318
Erica Smith, *Manager*
EMP: 50
SALES (corp-wide): 32.7MM **Privately Held**
WEB: www.halsteadhealthrehab.com
SIC: 8051 8059 Extended care facility; nursing home, except skilled & intermediate care facility
PA: Midwest Health, Inc
3024 Sw Wanamaker Rd # 300
Topeka KS 66614
785 272-1535

(G-66)
WAB CO ROAD & BRIDGE
215 Kansas Ave (66401-9797)
P.O. Box 278 (66401-0278)
PHONE..................................785 765-3432
Rodney Allan, *Commissioner*
EMP: 12
SALES: 3.6MM **Privately Held**
SIC: 4959 Road, airport & parking lot maintenance services

Almena
Norton County

(G-67)
CALVERT CORPORATION
22850 Kansas 383 (67622)
PHONE..................................785 877-5221
Dean Kruse, *Manager*
EMP: 7
SALES (est): 463.8K **Privately Held**
SIC: 3295 Minerals, ground or treated

(G-68)
PRAIRIE DOG PRESS
523 Main St (67622-9652)
P.O. Box 3 (67622-0003)
PHONE..................................785 669-2009
Laura Craig, *Chairman*
Howard Vandewege, *Treasurer*
Marge Kate, *Admin Sec*
EMP: 18
SALES (est): 710.1K **Privately Held**
SIC: 2711 Newspapers

Alta Vista
Wabaunsee County

(G-69)
ALTA VISTA STATE BANK
619 Main St (66834-9768)
P.O. Box 249 (66834-0249)
PHONE..................................785 499-6304
Fred R Clark, *President*
EMP: 11 **EST:** 1900
SALES: 738K **Privately Held**
SIC: 6022 State commercial banks

(G-70)
K CONSTRUCTION INC
515 Main St (66834)
P.O. Box 276 (66834-0276)
PHONE..................................785 499-5296
Joseph H Kormanik, *President*
Carla A Kormanik, *Corp Secy*
Ben Kormanik, *Vice Pres*
Joe Kormanik, *Vice Pres*
Carla Kormanik, *Treasurer*
EMP: 10
SALES: 1.6MM **Privately Held**
SIC: 1542 Commercial & office building, new construction

(G-71)
PERFECTION II MASONRY INC
223 S 1000 Rd (66834-9407)
PHONE..................................785 499-6307
Charles M Lillich, *President*
William L Stephenson, *Admin Sec*
EMP: 10
SQ FT: 3,000
SALES (est): 790.1K **Privately Held**
SIC: 1741 Bricklaying

Altamont
Labette County

(G-72)
COUNTY OF LABETTE
Also Called: Labette County Highway Dept
901 S Huston St (67330-9229)
P.O. Box 301 (67330-0301)
PHONE..................................620 784-5391
Sandy Krider, *Manager*
Sandra Krider, *Software Engr*
EMP: 42 **Privately Held**
WEB: www.labettecounty.com
SIC: 1611 Highway & street maintenance
PA: County Of Labette
501 Merchant St
Oswego KS 67356
620 795-2138

(G-73)
TWIN VALLEY ELECTRIC COOP
501 S Huston St (67330-7006)
P.O. Box 368 (67330-0368)
PHONE..................................620 784-5500
Dan Peterson, *President*
Kelly Walker, *CFO*
Rebecca Hanigan, *Finance*
Jennifer Winters, *Admin Asst*
EMP: 13 **EST:** 1946
SQ FT: 3,500
SALES: 6.5MM **Privately Held**
SIC: 4911 Distribution, electric power

Alton
Osborne County

(G-74)
PROGRESSIVE CARE PROF HM CARE
513 Mill St (67623-9211)
PHONE..................................785 984-2290
Donna Gregory, *Owner*
EMP: 40 **EST:** 1994
SALES (est): 368.6K **Privately Held**
SIC: 8082 Home health care services

Altoona
Wilson County

(G-75)
APPLEWOOD REHABILATION INC
20526 1700 Rd (66710-8576)
PHONE..................................620 431-7300
Fax: 620 431-2127
EMP: 35
SALES (est): 1.9MM **Privately Held**
SIC: 8361 8059 Residential Care Services Nursing/Personal Care

Americus
Lyon County

(G-76)
G S INC OF KANSAS
562 Locust St (66835-9780)
P.O. Box 25 (66835-0025)
PHONE..................................620 443-5121
Larry Grimsley, *President*
Jack Grimsley, *Vice Pres*
Wanda Grimsley, *Treasurer*
Joyce Grimsley, *Admin Sec*
EMP: 6
SQ FT: 5,000
SALES (est): 966.2K **Privately Held**
SIC: 3567 Industrial furnaces & ovens

Andale
Sedgwick County

(G-77)
ANDALE READY MIX CENTRAL INC
430 2nd St (67001-7000)
P.O. Box 156 (67001-0156)
PHONE..................................316 832-0063
James H Molitor, *President*
Lucinda Molitor, *Corp Secy*
EMP: 10
SQ FT: 1,500
SALES (est): 2.6MM **Privately Held**
SIC: 3273 Ready-mixed concrete

(G-78)
KANZA COOPERATIVE ASSOCIATION
220 N Main St (67001-7051)
PHONE..................................316 444-2141
EMP: 42
SALES (corp-wide): 300MM **Privately Held**
SIC: 5153 5191 5984 5251 Grains; feed; seeds: field, garden & flower; fertilizer & fertilizer materials; liquefied petroleum gas, delivered to customers' premises; hardware; grain elevator, storage only
PA: Kanza Cooperative Association
102 N Main St
Iuka KS 67066
620 546-2231

Andover
Butler County

(G-79)
AMERICAN MECHANICAL INC
1608 E Us Highway 54 (67002-8014)
PHONE..................................316 262-1100
Brian Pinkston, *President*
Richard Caywood, *Vice Pres*
Joe Clark, *Manager*
Aron Schroeder, *Manager*
EMP: 20
SQ FT: 3,500
SALES (est): 3.7MM **Privately Held**
SIC: 1711 Plumbing contractors; mechanical contractor

(G-80)
ANDOVER HEALTH CARE CENTER
621 W 21st St (67002-8498)
PHONE..................................316 448-4041
Laura Richardson, *Director*
Fred Davenport, *Director*
EMP: 155
SQ FT: 48,000
SALES (est): 3.4MM **Privately Held**
SIC: 8051 Extended care facility

(G-81)
ANDOVER SPINE & HEALTH CTR
149 S Andover Rd Ste 400 (67002-7935)
PHONE..................................316 733-9555
Jamie Stinemetz, *Owner*
EMP: 11
SALES (est): 419.4K **Privately Held**
SIC: 8062 General medical & surgical hospitals

(G-82)
ANDOVER STATE BANK (PA)
511 N Andover Rd (67002)
P.O. Box 278 (67002-0278)
PHONE..................................316 733-1375
Harriet McConachie, *Ch of Bd*
Brian Chamberlin, *President*
Kirk McConachie, *Chairman*
Mac Carter Sr, *Vice Pres*
Allison M Grace, *Vice Pres*
EMP: 18 **EST:** 1916
SQ FT: 10,000
SALES: 4.2MM **Privately Held**
WEB: www.andoverstatebank.com
SIC: 6022 State trust companies accepting deposits, commercial

(G-83)
ASM ENGINEERING CONS LLC
202 E Rhondda Ave Ste C (67002-8893)
P.O. Box 460, Benton (67017-0460)
PHONE..................................316 260-5895
Derek Hake, *Project Engr*
Micky McCune, *Office Mgr*
Ryan McCune, *Mng Member*
Shana Mitchell, *Admin Asst*
EMP: 11
SALES (est): 2.1MM **Privately Held**
SIC: 8711 Civil engineering

(G-84)
BANK AMERICA NATIONAL ASSN
329 S Andover Rd (67002-7918)
PHONE..................................316 529-6730
EMP: 15
SALES (corp-wide): 110.5B **Publicly Held**
WEB: www.bofa.com
SIC: 6021 National commercial banks
HQ: Bank Of America, National Association
100 S Tryon St
Charlotte NC 28202
704 386-5681

(G-85)
CAREGIVER COMPANY LLC
Also Called: Caregiver Bed, The
541 S Riverview St (67002-9426)
PHONE..................................316 247-4005
Hal Maccoy Sr, *CEO*
Chris McCoy, *President*
Jim Foulston, *COO*
Russ Meyer III, *Senior VP*
Terry Freund, *CFO*
EMP: 10
SALES (est): 1.4MM **Privately Held**
SIC: 2599 Hospital beds

(G-86)
CEDAR SURGICAL LLC
2237 Keystone Cir (67002-8742)
PHONE..................................316 616-6272
Janice McGreevy, *Office Mgr*
Badr Idbeis,
Robert Fleming,
Nicole Revoal, *Assistant*
EMP: 10
SALES (est): 710K **Privately Held**
WEB: www.kansasveincenter.com
SIC: 8011 Cardiologist & cardio-vascular specialist

(G-87)
COUNTRY ACCENTS INC
16328 Sw 123rd Ter (67002-8610)
PHONE..................................316 440-1343
Chad Joachims, *President*
Kimberly Joachims, *Corp Secy*
EMP: 6
SQ FT: 7,000
SALES (est): 555.1K **Privately Held**
WEB: www.countryaccentsinc.com
SIC: 2499 Decorative wood & woodwork

(G-88)
COUNTRYSIDE PET CLINIC PA
1936 N Andover Rd (67002-8301)
PHONE..................................316 733-8433
Kevin Cederberg, *President*
EMP: 20
SQ FT: 6,000
SALES: 500K **Privately Held**
SIC: 0742 3999 0752 Animal hospital services, pets & other animal specialties; pet supplies; training services, pet & animal specialties (not horses)

(G-89)
DESIGNER PALMS INC
12631 Sw Frontr Trail St (67002-8211)
PHONE..................................316 733-2284
Wendell Turner, *President*
Helen Turner, *Corp Secy*
EMP: 14
SQ FT: 5,200
SALES (est): 2.1MM **Privately Held**
WEB: www.designerpalms.com
SIC: 3446 Ornamental metalwork

(G-90)
DEWALD ENTERPRISES
Also Called: Dewalt Interprises.
224 Cory Dr (67002-8514)
PHONE..................................316 655-1155
Steven Dewald, *Owner*
EMP: 5
SALES (est): 299.9K **Privately Held**
SIC: 3589 Car washing machinery

(G-91)
EVERIDGE LLC
International Cold Storage
215 E 13th St (67002-9329)
PHONE..................................316 733-1385
Kevin Wilson, *Branch Mgr*
EMP: 150 **Privately Held**
WEB: www.icsco.com
SIC: 3585 Refrigeration & heating equipment
PA: Everidge Llc
15600 37th Ave N Ste 100
Minneapolis MN 55446

(G-92)
FAMILY PHYSICIANS KANSAS LLC
Also Called: Hartley, James M
524 N Andover Rd (67002-9712)
PHONE..................................316 733-4500
James M Hartley,
Kimberly Allman,
Stanley J Mosier,
EMP: 11
SQ FT: 5,695
SALES: 1.1MM **Privately Held**
SIC: 8011 General & family practice, physician/surgeon

(G-93)
FLINT HILLS NATIONAL GOLF CLUB
Also Called: Maintanence Shop
12400 Sw Butler Rd (67002-8662)
PHONE..................................316 733-4131
Thomas Dowler, *President*
EMP: 72 **Privately Held**
WEB: www.flinthillsnational.com
SIC: 7992 7997 Public golf courses; golf club, membership
PA: Flint Hills National Golf Club
1 S Flint Hills Nat Blvd
Andover KS 67002

(G-94)
HOWELL MATTHEW D DR DDS PA
Also Called: Andover Family Dentistry PA
1145 N Andover Rd Ste 101 (67002-8902)
PHONE..................................316 260-6220
Matthew D Howell, *Principal*
EMP: 10
SALES (est): 217.9K **Privately Held**
SIC: 8021 8011 Dentists' office; offices & clinics of medical doctors

(G-95)
INTRUST BANK NA
308 W Central Ave (67002-9616)
P.O. Box 335 (67002-0335)
PHONE..................................316 383-3350
Matt Childers, *Manager*
EMP: 10
SALES (corp-wide): 134.2MM **Privately Held**
WEB: www.intrustbank.com
SIC: 6021 National trust companies with deposits, commercial
HQ: Intrust Bank National Association
105 N Main St
Wichita KS 67202
316 383-1111

(G-96)
J & H TRANSPORTATION INC (PA)
1534 N Main St (67002-9554)
P.O. Box 131 (67002-0131)
PHONE..................................316 733-8200
John Blickenstaff, *President*
Bud Cooper, *Principal*
EMP: 19
SQ FT: 5,000
SALES (est): 8.4MM **Privately Held**
WEB: www.jhtrucking.com
SIC: 4731 Truck transportation brokers

(G-97)
KANSAS MEDICAL ASSOC INC
943 N Andover Rd (67002-9795)
P.O. Box 550 (67002-0550)
PHONE..................................316 733-4747
Richard Miller, *Director*
EMP: 10
SALES (est): 610.1K **Privately Held**
SIC: 8099 Health & allied services

(G-98)
KIMBERLY A ALLMAN LLC
524 N Andover Rd (67002-9712)
PHONE..................................316 733-3003
Kimberly A Allman, *Principal*
EMP: 15
SALES (est): 122.7K **Privately Held**
SIC: 8011 General & family practice, physician/surgeon

(G-99)
KINDERCARE EDUCATION LLC
836 N Andover Rd (67002-9527)
P.O. Box 725 (67002-0725)
PHONE..................................316 733-2066
Annette Hendrix, *Manager*
EMP: 20
SALES (corp-wide): 963.9MM **Privately Held**
WEB: www.knowledgelearning.com
SIC: 8351 Group day care center
PA: Kindercare Education Llc
650 Ne Holladay St # 1400
Portland OR 97232
503 872-1300

(G-100)
KINDERCARE LEARNING CTRS LLC
836 N Andover Rd (67002-9527)
P.O. Box 725 (67002-0725)
PHONE..................................316 733-2066
Tero McFarland, *Principal*
EMP: 19
SALES (corp-wide): 963.9MM **Privately Held**
SIC: 8351 Group day care center
HQ: Kindercare Learning Centers, Llc
650 Ne Holladay St # 1400
Portland OR 97232
503 872-1300

(G-101)
KIWANIS INTERNATIONAL INC
722 S Daisy Ln (67002-7829)
PHONE..................................316 733-4984
Linn Heath, *Admin Sec*
EMP: 14
SALES (corp-wide): 23.6MM **Privately Held**
WEB: www.kfne.org
SIC: 8641 Civic associations
PA: Kiwanis International, Inc.
3636 Woodview Trce
Indianapolis IN 46268
317 875-8755

(G-102)
LATOUR MANAGEMENT INC
Also Called: Latour At Terradyne
1400 Terradyne Dr (67002-7939)
PHONE..................................316 733-1922
Craig Smith, *Owner*
EMP: 15
SALES (corp-wide): 7MM **Privately Held**
WEB: www.chelseasbarandgrill.com
SIC: 8741 5812 Management services; eating places
PA: Latour Management, Inc.
2949 N Rock Rd Ste 100
Wichita KS 67226
316 524-2290

(G-103)
LIFE CARE CENTERS AMERICA INC
Also Called: Life Care Center of Andover
621 W 21st St (67002-8498)
P.O. Box 100 (67002-0100)
PHONE..................................316 733-5376
Janet Garreson, *Administration*
EMP: 25
SQ FT: 33,000
SALES (corp-wide): 144MM **Privately Held**
SIC: 8051 Convalescent home with continuous nursing care
PA: Life Care Centers Of America, Inc.
3570 Keith St Nw
Cleveland TN 37312
423 472-9585

(G-104)
MEDI-WEIGHTLOSS CLINICS LLC
1145 N Andover Rd Ste 109 (67002-8902)
PHONE..................................316 733-8505
Jeanine Cobb, *Owner*
EMP: 21 **Privately Held**
SIC: 8093 Weight loss clinic, with medical staff
PA: Medi-Weightloss Clinics, Llc
509 S High Park Ave
Tampa FL 33606

(G-105)
PMA ANDOVER
308 E Central Ave (67002-5605)
P.O. Box 10 (67002-0010)
PHONE..................................316 733-1331
Stephen Lemons, *President*
Sam Williams, *Manager*
EMP: 50
SALES (est): 1.2MM **Privately Held**
SIC: 8011 Medical centers

(G-106)
PREFERRED MEDICAL ASSOCIATES
Also Called: Barclay, Andrew M
308 E Central Ave (67002-5605)
P.O. Box 10 (67002-0010)
PHONE..................................316 733-1331
Stephen F Lemons MD, *Partner*
Paul Huser, *Partner*
EMP: 50
SALES (est): 1.8MM **Privately Held**
SIC: 8011 Physicians' office, including specialists

(G-107)
PREMIER LANDSCAPING INC
Also Called: Premier Landscape
12739 Sw Butler Rd (67002-8608)
PHONE..................................316 733-4773
Marian Stuhslatz, *President*
EMP: 18
SALES (est): 1.1MM **Privately Held**
SIC: 0782 4971 Landscape contractors; irrigation systems

(G-108)
SOUTH CNTL MNTAL HLTH CNSELING
Also Called: Suicide Prvntion For Btlr Cnty
217 W Ira Ct (67002-9469)
PHONE..................................316 733-5047
Judy Lowmaster, *Human Res Mgr*
Ron Fisher, *Manager*
Julie Marshall, *Nurse*
EMP: 11
SALES (est): 431.3K **Privately Held**
SIC: 8322 Emergency social services

(G-109)
SUPERCUTS INC
229 N Andover Rd Ste 500 (67002-2005)
PHONE..................................316 218-1400
David Duntz, *Branch Mgr*
EMP: 10
SALES (corp-wide): 1B **Publicly Held**
WEB: www.supercuts.com
SIC: 7231 Unisex hair salons
HQ: Supercuts, Inc.
7201 Metro Blvd
Minneapolis MN 55439
952 947-7777

(G-110)
TERRADYNE COUNTRY CLUB LLC
1400 Terradyne Dr (67002-7939)
PHONE..................................316 733-2582
Greg Bray, *General Mgr*
Ryan Bourne, *Superintendent*
Curtis Schriever, *Superintendent*
Andrea Kelly, *Director*
EMP: 40
SQ FT: 60,000
SALES (est): 2.9MM **Privately Held**
SIC: 7997 Country club, membership; golf club, membership

(G-111)
TREE-RIFIC LANDSCAPING INC
13594 Sw Us Highway 54 (67002-8341)
PHONE..................................316 733-0900
Robert Kubish, *President*
EMP: 10
SALES (est): 778.1K **Privately Held**
SIC: 0782 Landscape contractors

(G-112)
TREESCAPE INC
Also Called: Treescapes
1202 N Andover Rd (67002-9706)
PHONE..................................316 733-6388
David Martine, *President*
Schana Martine, *Corp Secy*
EMP: 25
SALES (est): 1.8MM **Privately Held**
SIC: 0782 5261 5199 5083 Garden planting services; nurseries & garden centers; Christmas trees, including artificial; lawn & garden machinery & equipment; lighting fixtures; landscape planning services

(G-113)
VIA CHRISTI CLINIC PA
612 N Andover Rd (67002-9778)
PHONE..................................316 733-6618
Fax: 316 733-5299
EMP: 10
SALES (corp-wide): 2.2B **Privately Held**
SIC: 8011 Medical Doctor's Office
HQ: Via Christi Clinic, P.A.
3311 E Murdock St
Wichita KS 67208
316 689-9111

(G-114)
VICTORIA FLLS SKLLD CRE & RHAB
224 E Central Ave (67002-8580)
PHONE..................................316 733-0654
Rebecca Murray, *Principal*
Ashley Russell, *Director*
EMP: 11
SALES (est): 455.7K **Privately Held**
SIC: 8351 Child day care services

(G-115)
VORNADO AIR LLC
415 E 13th St (67002-9313)
PHONE..................................316 733-0035
Bill Philips, *CEO*
Drew Jones, *Principal*
Randy Brillhart, *COO*
Kay Reed, *CFO*
David Mercer, *Marketing Staff*
◆ **EMP:** 60
SQ FT: 112,000
SALES (est): 17.1MM
SALES (corp-wide): 87.7MM **Privately Held**
WEB: www.vornado.com
SIC: 3634 5064 3564 3433 Fans, electric: floor; fans, household: electric; blowers & fans; heating equipment, except electric
PA: Merchsource, Llc
7755 Irvine Center Dr
Irvine CA 92618
800 374-2744

(G-116)
WALGREEN CO
Also Called: Walgreens
440 N Andover Rd (67002-9508)
PHONE..................................316 218-0819
Sara Hornecker, *Manager*
EMP: 30
SALES (corp-wide): 136.8B **Publicly Held**
WEB: www.walgreens.com
SIC: 5912 7384 Drug stores; photofinishing laboratory
HQ: Walgreen Co.
200 Wilmot Rd
Deerfield IL 60015
800 925-4733

(G-117)
WINGATE INNS INTERNATIONAL INC
600 S Allen St (67002-7938)
PHONE..................................316 733-8833
Tim Johnson, *Manager*
EMP: 24 **Publicly Held**
WEB: www.wingateatlanta.com
SIC: 7011 Hotels & motels
HQ: Wingate Inns International, Inc.
339 Jefferson Rd
Parsippany NJ 07054
973 753-8000

(G-118)
YOUNG MENS CHRISTIAN ASSOCIA
Also Called: Andover YMCA
1115 E Us Highway 54 (67002-8044)
PHONE..................................316 733-9622
Corey Ratzlaff, *Personnel*
Shane Loy, *Director*
Bree Bolin, *Director*
Shannan Broughton, *Director*
Ben Gerber, *Director*
EMP: 135
SALES (corp-wide): 44.6MM **Privately Held**
SIC: 8641 Youth organizations
PA: The Young Men's Christian Association Of Wichita Kansas
402 N Market St
Wichita KS 67202
316 219-9622

Anthony
Harper County

(G-119)
ANTHONY FRMRS COOP ELEV CMPNYS (PA)
519 W Main St (67003-2726)
P.O. Box 111 (67003-0111)
PHONE..................................620 842-5181
Dan Cashier, *General Mgr*
EMP: 15
SQ FT: 5,000
SALES: 14MM **Privately Held**
SIC: 5999 5153 5541 4221 Feed & farm supply; grains; gasoline service stations; grain elevator, storage only

(G-120)
ANTHONY LIVESTOCK SALES CO
624 S Jennings Ave (67003-2548)
P.O. Box 393 (67003-0393)
PHONE..................................620 842-3757
Jay Gates, *President*
EMP: 13 **EST:** 1974
SQ FT: 5,000
SALES (est): 2.9MM **Privately Held**
SIC: 5154 Auctioning livestock

(G-121)
BANCCENTRAL NATIONAL ASSN
203 W Main St (67003-2723)
P.O. Box 484 (67003-0484)
PHONE..................................620 842-1000
Kyle Hughbanks, *Manager*
EMP: 10
SALES (corp-wide): 21MM **Privately Held**
SIC: 6021 National commercial banks
PA: Banccentral, National Association
604 Flynn St
Alva OK 73717
580 327-1122

(G-122)
CENTRAL ELECTROPOLISHING INC
Also Called: Celco
103 N Lawrence Ave (67003-2804)
PHONE..................................620 842-3701
Kenneth Bellesine, *CEO*
Steve Bellesine, *President*
Joyce Bellesine, *Treasurer*
▲ **EMP:** 28
SQ FT: 30,000
SALES (est): 3.3MM **Privately Held**
WEB: www.celcoinc.com
SIC: 3471 Finishing, metals or formed products

(G-123)
CITY OF ANTHONY
Also Called: Anthony Police Department
202 S Bluff Ave (67003-2514)
PHONE..................................620 842-5123
John Blevins, *Chief*
EMP: 5 **Privately Held**
WEB: www.anthonykansas.org
SIC: 9221 2711 ; newspapers
PA: City Of Anthony
124 S Bluff Ave
Anthony KS 67003

(G-124)
CONRADY WESTERN INC (PA)
501 W Main St (67003-2726)
P.O. Box 151 (67003-0151)
PHONE..................................620 842-5137
Thomas L Conrady, *President*
Marc Conrady, *Vice Pres*
Michael Williams, *Vice Pres*
EMP: 28
SQ FT: 26,000
SALES (est): 10MM **Privately Held**
WEB: www.conradys.com
SIC: 5083 Agricultural machinery & equipment

(G-125)
COUNTRY LIVING INC
420 N 5th Ave (67003-2134)
PHONE..................................620 842-5858
E Wyckoff, *Principal*
EMP: 15
SALES: 672.1K **Privately Held**
SIC: 8361 Rest home, with health care incidental

(G-126)
COUNTY OF HARPER
Also Called: Harper County Engineer
201 N Jennings Ave (67003-2748)
PHONE..................................620 842-5240
John McClure, *Manager*
EMP: 40 **Privately Held**
WEB: www.harpercountyks.gov
SIC: 8711 Engineering services
PA: County Of Harper
201 N Jennings Ave
Anthony KS 67003
620 842-6007

(G-127)
HARPER HOSPITAL DISTRICT 5 (PA)
485 N Ks Hwy 2 (67003-2526)
PHONE..................................620 896-7324
Loretta Kerschen, *General Mgr*
Arlene Gomez, *Director*
Kaitlyn Zomlot, *Director*
Amy Rhodes, *Business Dir*
Wendy Booker, *Phys Thrpy Dir*
EMP: 108
SALES: 7.6MM **Privately Held**
WEB: www.harperhospital.com
SIC: 8062 General medical & surgical hospitals

(G-128)
HOSPITAL DST 6 HARPER CNTY
Also Called: Patterson Health Center
485 N Ks Hwy 2 (67003-2526)
PHONE..................................620 914-1200
Pat Patton, *CEO*
Lori Allen, *COO*
Tom Hornbeck, *Engineer*
Sandra Owen, *CFO*
Beverly Hendrick, *Manager*
EMP: 166
SQ FT: 20,864
SALES: 6.5MM **Privately Held**
WEB: www.amcks.org
SIC: 8062 General medical & surgical hospitals

(G-129)
M & S TRUCKS INC
632 S Jennings Ave (67003-2548)
P.O. Box 361 (67003-0361)
PHONE..................................620 842-3764
Mike Francis, *President*
EMP: 12
SALES (est): 476.4K **Privately Held**
SIC: 4214 Local trucking with storage

(G-130)
NANCE MANUFACTURING INC
396 W Highway 2 (67003-9014)
PHONE..................................620 842-3761
Jim McMurry, *Manager*
EMP: 30
SALES (corp-wide): 10.6MM **Privately Held**
WEB: www.nancemanufacturing.com
SIC: 3728 3599 3523 Aircraft parts & equipment; machine shop, jobbing & repair; farm machinery & equipment
PA: Nance Manufacturing, Inc.
2005 S West St
Wichita KS 67213
316 942-8671

(G-131)
PARK HILL LANES
Hwy 14 (67003)
PHONE..................................620 842-5571
EMP: 10
SQ FT: 6,000
SALES (est): 300K **Privately Held**
SIC: 7933 Bowling Center

(G-132)
PLP INC
Also Called: John Deere Authorized Dealer
501 W Main St (67003-2726)
P.O. Box 151 (67003-0151)
PHONE..................................620 842-5137
Land Praire, *Principal*
EMP: 32
SALES (corp-wide): 66.9MM **Privately Held**
SIC: 5999 5082 Farm equipment & supplies; construction & mining machinery
PA: Plp, Inc
811 E 30th Ave Ste F
Hutchinson KS 67502
620 664-5860

(G-133)
PRAIRIE BELTING INC
396 W State Road 2 (67003-9014)
P.O. Box 564 (67003-0564)
PHONE..................................620 842-5147
James McMurry, *President*
Cary Fox, *General Mgr*
Jim McMurry, *Principal*
Chet Barber, *Opers Staff*
Teresa Wilcox, *Sales Mgr*
▲ **EMP:** 35
SQ FT: 50,000
SALES (est): 8.3MM
SALES (corp-wide): 10.6MM **Privately Held**
WEB: www.prairiebelting.com
SIC: 3052 Rubber belting
PA: Nance Manufacturing, Inc.
2005 S West St
Wichita KS 67213
316 942-8671

(G-134)
RUSTY S BAITS & LURES
Also Called: Rusty's Channel Cat Baits
213 E Main St (67003-2721)
P.O. Box 465 (67003-0465)
PHONE..................................620 842-5301
Vernon Ryan, *Owner*
EMP: 17
SQ FT: 7,500
SALES (est): 1.3MM **Privately Held**
SIC: 3949 Bait, artificial: fishing; lures, fishing: artificial

(G-135)
SECURITY 1ST TITLE LLC
110 N Jennings Ave (67003-2709)
PHONE..................................620 842-3333
EMP: 21 **Privately Held**
SIC: 6541 Title & trust companies
PA: Security 1st Title Llc
727 N Waco Ave Ste 300
Wichita KS 67203

Antonino
Ellis County

(G-136)
PA HAYS ANESTHESIOLOGIST ASSOC
2220 Canterbury Dr (67601-2370)
P.O. Box 821, Hays (67601-0821)
PHONE..................................785 628-8300
EMP: 15
SALES (est): 1MM **Privately Held**
SIC: 8011 Anesthesiologist

Arcadia
Crawford County

(G-137)
MACQUARIE INFRASTRUCTURE
1150 E 700th Ave (66711-4092)
P.O. Box 7 (66711-0007)
PHONE..................................620 638-4339
Matt Sanders, *Branch Mgr*
EMP: 200
SALES (corp-wide): 116.7MM **Privately Held**
SIC: 4953 Garbage: collecting, destroying & processing
PA: Macquarie Infrastructure Partners Ii International, L.P.
125 W 55th St
New York NY 10019
212 231-1310

Argonia
Sumner County

(G-138)
KISER MANUFACTURING CO INC
601 E Us Highway 160 (67004-8818)
P.O. Box 315 (67004-0315)
PHONE..................................620 435-6981
Jerry L Kiser, *President*
Debbie Kiser, *Vice Pres*
EMP: 18 **EST:** 1996
SQ FT: 10,000
SALES (est): 3.2MM **Privately Held**
SIC: 3599 Machine shop, jobbing & repair

▲ = Import ▼=Export
◆ =Import/Export

Arkansas City
Cowley County

(G-139)
ADM MILLING CO
1200 S Mill Rd (67005-3764)
P.O. Box 958 (67005-0958)
PHONE..................................620 442-6200
Doug Goff, *Manager*
EMP: 90
SALES (corp-wide): 64.3B **Publicly Held**
WEB: www.admmilling.com
SIC: **2041** 4221 Grain mills (except rice); grain elevator, storage only
HQ: Adm Milling Co.
8000 W 110th St Ste 300
Overland Park KS 66210
913 491-9400

(G-140)
ADM MILLING CO
309 W Madison Ave (67005-2845)
P.O. Box 958 (67005-0958)
PHONE..................................620 442-5500
Doug Goff, *Manager*
EMP: 40
SALES (corp-wide): 64.3B **Publicly Held**
WEB: www.admmilling.com
SIC: **2041** Flour mills, cereal (except rice); grain mills (except rice)
HQ: Adm Milling Co.
8000 W 110th St Ste 300
Overland Park KS 66210
913 491-9400

(G-141)
ALDERBROOK VILLAGE
402 E Windsor Rd (67005-3894)
PHONE..................................620 442-4400
K Ziegler, *Exec Dir*
Kathy Ziegler, *Exec Dir*
EMP: 18
SALES: 604.7K **Privately Held**
SIC: **8322** Old age assistance

(G-142)
AMERICAN NATIONAL RED CROSS
Also Called: ARC
110 W Bryant Rd (67005-4053)
PHONE..................................620 446-0966
EMP: 40
SALES (corp-wide): 2.6B **Privately Held**
SIC: **8322** Individual & family services
PA: The American National Red Cross
430 17th St Nw
Washington DC 20006
202 737-8300

(G-143)
ARK CITY CLINIC P A
510 W Radio Ln (67005-4098)
PHONE..................................620 442-2100
David Schmeidler, *President*
David Schmeizler, *Vice Pres*
Andrea Crawford, *Info Tech Mgr*
Coney Ruyle, *Administration*
Valerie Albin, *Physician Asst*
EMP: 50
SALES (est): 5.2MM **Privately Held**
WEB: www.arkcityclinic.com
SIC: **8011** Clinic, operated by physicians; medical insurance plan

(G-144)
ARK CITY WAREHOUSE TRUCKLINE
Also Called: A C W Truckline
1105 W Madison Ave (67005-3008)
P.O. Box 493 (67005-0493)
PHONE..................................620 442-7305
Donna Sybrant, *President*
Jim Sybrant, *President*
EMP: 10
SALES (est): 1.1MM **Privately Held**
SIC: **4213** Refrigerated products transport

(G-145)
ARK VALLEY DISTRIBUTING INC
7748 2nd Ave (67005)
P.O. Box 1051 (67005-1051)
PHONE..................................620 221-6500
Mike Morgan, *President*
Patricia Morgan, *Treasurer*
EMP: 12
SALES (est): 2.6MM **Privately Held**
SIC: **5181** Beer & other fermented malt liquors

(G-146)
ARK VETERINARY ASSOCIATES PA
907 E Kansas Ave (67005-6686)
P.O. Box 694 (67005-0694)
PHONE..................................620 442-3306
Steve White, *President*
Patsy White, *Treasurer*
EMP: 10
SALES (est): 541.1K **Privately Held**
SIC: **0742** Veterinarian, animal specialties; animal hospital services, pets & other animal specialties

(G-147)
ARKANSAS CITY PRESBT MANOR INC
1711 N 4th St (67005-1607)
PHONE..................................620 442-8700
Lynne Lawrence, *President*
Sarah Griggs, *Exec Dir*
Bryan Bailey, *Director*
Shannon Grose, *Admin Asst*
EMP: 10
SALES: 6.9MM **Privately Held**
SIC: **8051** Skilled nursing care facilities

(G-148)
BNSF RAILWAY COMPANY
Also Called: Burlington Northern
520 E Central Ave (67005-2663)
PHONE..................................620 441-2276
Larry Trimble, *Branch Mgr*
EMP: 46
SALES (corp-wide): 225.3B **Publicly Held**
WEB: www.billpurdy.com
SIC: **4011** Railroads, line-haul operating
HQ: Bnsf Railway Company
2650 Lou Menk Dr
Fort Worth TX 76131
800 795-2673

(G-149)
COMFORT MANAGEMENT INC
Also Called: Waldorf-Riley
1705 N Summit St (67005-3920)
PHONE..................................620 442-5610
Fax: 620 221-9259
EMP: 14 **EST**: 1997
SALES (est): 1.4MM **Privately Held**
SIC: **1711** Plumbing/Heating/Air Cond Contractor

(G-150)
COWLEY COLLEGE & AREA
Also Called: Post-Secondary Education
125 S 2nd St (67005-2662)
PHONE..................................620 442-0430
Eric Nitsche, *Admin Sec*
Julie Rhoads, *Education*
EMP: 300
SALES (est): 702.5K **Privately Held**
SIC: **8211** 7371 Secondary school; computer software development & applications

(G-151)
COWLEY COUNTY JOINT BOARD HLTH
Also Called: County Health Department
115 E Radio Ln (67005-3914)
PHONE..................................620 442-3260
Kelli Waggoner, *Nutritionist*
David Bravil, *Manager*
EMP: 10
SALES (corp-wide): 2.2MM **Privately Held**
SIC: **8093** 9431 Specialty outpatient clinics;
PA: Cowley County Joint Board Of Health
320 E 9th Ave Ste 2
Winfield KS 67156
620 221-1430

(G-152)
CREEKSTONE FARM PREM
604 Goff Industrial Pk Rd (67005-8880)
PHONE..................................620 741-3100
Dennis Buhlke, *CEO*
Leon Trautwein, *CFO*
◆ **EMP**: 700
SALES (est): 118.1MM **Privately Held**
SIC: **2011** Beef products from beef slaughtered on site
HQ: Cfpb Holdings Llc
604 Goff Industrial Pk Rd
Arkansas City KS 67005
620 741-3100

(G-153)
DOROTHY RUSH REALTY INC
206 N Summit St (67005-2260)
P.O. Box 1187 (67005-1187)
PHONE..................................620 442-7851
Dorothy Rush, *President*
EMP: 11
SQ FT: 1,800
SALES (est): 690K **Privately Held**
SIC: **6531** 6411 Real estate agent, residential; insurance agents

(G-154)
DR NICK ROGERS
1939 N 11th St (67005-1799)
PHONE..................................620 442-5660
Nick Rogers, *Owner*
EMP: 10
SALES (est): 541.8K **Privately Held**
SIC: **8021** Dentists' office

(G-155)
EVERGY KANSAS SOUTH INC
3113 N Summit St (67005-8821)
PHONE..................................620 441-2427
Rex Erving, *Branch Mgr*
EMP: 38
SALES (corp-wide): 4.2B **Publicly Held**
SIC: **4911** Generation, electric power
HQ: Evergy Kansas South, Inc.
120 E 1st St N
Wichita KS

(G-156)
FIRST INTERMARK CORPORATION
Also Called: Follow Up Sales Systems
400 S Summit St (67005-2851)
PHONE..................................620 442-2460
Kasha Kelley, *CEO*
Greg Kelley, *President*
Diana Kelley, *Vice Pres*
Scott Margolius, *Vice Pres*
Steve Bruce, *Manager*
EMP: 45
SQ FT: 76,000
SALES: 3MM **Privately Held**
WEB: www.fussinc.com
SIC: **8742** Retail trade consultant

(G-157)
GE ENGINE SERVICES LLC
7577 4th Ave (67005)
P.O. Box 797 (67005-0797)
PHONE..................................316 264-4741
Mike Bluffington, *Sales/Mktg Mgr*
EMP: 700
SALES (corp-wide): 121.6B **Publicly Held**
SIC: **7699** 3724 Aircraft & heavy equipment repair services; aircraft engines & engine parts
HQ: Ge Engine Services, Llc
1 Neumann Way
Cincinnati OH 45215
513 243-2000

(G-158)
H J BORN STONE INC (PA)
30994 141st Rd (67005-6150)
P.O. Box 332 (67005-0332)
PHONE..................................316 838-7788
Sharon Born, *President*
Todd J Born, *Vice Pres*
Nancy Countryman, *Admin Sec*
EMP: 13 **EST**: 1946
SQ FT: 230,000
SALES (est): 1.2MM **Privately Held**
WEB: www.bornstone.com
SIC: **3281** Cut stone & stone products

(G-159)
HAWKS FUNERAL HOME INC (PA)
906 W Kansas Ave (67005-1863)
PHONE..................................620 442-0220
Mike Hylton, *Director*
EMP: 14
SALES (est): 1.8MM **Privately Held**
WEB: www.hawksfuneralhome.com
SIC: **6553** 6311 Cemeteries, real estate operation; funeral insurance

(G-160)
HNB CORPORATION
Also Called: Home National Bank
126 S Summit St (67005-2625)
P.O. Box 1047 (67005-1047)
PHONE..................................620 442-4040
Trent Brown, *President*
Roger Brown, *Chairman*
John Hoback, *Exec VP*
Lisa Kessler, *Exec VP*
Diane Morrow, *Vice Pres*
EMP: 80
SQ FT: 50,000 **Privately Held**
SIC: **6712** Bank holding companies

(G-161)
JET AIRWERKS LLC
3015 N Summit St (67005-8819)
PHONE..................................620 442-3625
Katelyn Edwards, *Sales Staff*
Keith Humphrey, *Mng Member*
EMP: 25
SALES (est): 3.8MM **Privately Held**
WEB: www.jetairwerks.com
SIC: **4581** Aircraft maintenance & repair services

(G-162)
KNIGHTS OF COLUMBUS
29731 41st Rd (67005-5412)
PHONE..................................620 442-7264
Barry K Leavitt, *Branch Mgr*
EMP: 12
SALES (corp-wide): 2.3B **Privately Held**
SIC: **8641** Fraternal associations
PA: Knights Of Columbus
1 Columbus Plz Ste 1700
New Haven CT 06510
203 752-4000

(G-163)
KUHN MECHANICAL INC
1001 E Kansas Ave (67005-6687)
P.O. Box 551 (67005-0551)
PHONE..................................620 441-9339
Dustin P Schuetz, *President*
EMP: 18 **EST**: 1999
SALES: 1.5MM **Privately Held**
SIC: **1711** Mechanical contractor

(G-164)
LG PIKE CONSTRUCTION CO INC
Also Called: L G Pike Shtmtl Mar Fbrication
815 W Madison Ave (67005-3035)
P.O. Box 912 (67005-0912)
PHONE..................................620 442-9150
Lawrence G Pike, *President*
Angie Bruce, *Principal*
Ted Biggs, *Vice Pres*
Carlla J Pike, *Treasurer*
EMP: 55
SQ FT: 30,000
SALES: 12.6MM **Privately Held**
WEB: www.lgpike.kscoxmail.com
SIC: **4789** 1761 Railroad maintenance & repair services; roofing, siding & sheet metal work

(G-165)
MEDICALODGES INC
Also Called: Medicalodges Arkansas City
203 E Osage Ave (67005-1255)
PHONE..................................620 442-9300
Mattews Stephenson, *Manager*
EMP: 70
SALES (corp-wide): 100.2MM **Privately Held**
WEB: www.medicalodges.com
SIC: **8051** 8052 Convalescent home with continuous nursing care; intermediate care facilities

GEOGRAPHIC

PA: Medicalodges, Inc.
201 W 8th St
Coffeyville KS 67337
620 251-6700

(G-166)
MIKE GROVES OIL INC
Also Called: U-Haul
801 E Madison Ave (67005-8954)
P.O. Box 735 (67005-0735)
PHONE..................................620 442-0480
Mike Groves, *President*
Judith E Groves, *Corp Secy*
EMP: 15
SALES (est): 1.6MM **Privately Held**
SIC: 7513 5171 7519 Truck rental & leasing, no drivers; petroleum bulk stations; trailer rental

(G-167)
MORRIS COMMUNICATIONS CO LLC
Also Called: Arkansas City Traveler
200 E 5th Ave (67005-2606)
P.O. Box 988 (67005-0988)
PHONE..................................620 442-4200
Kim Benedict, *Manager*
EMP: 30 **Privately Held**
WEB: www.morris.com
SIC: 2721 2711 Periodicals; newspapers
HQ: Morris Communications Company Llc
725 Broad St
Augusta GA 30901
706 724-0851

(G-168)
ORSCHELN FARM AND HOME LLC
Also Called: Orschelin Farm and Home 40
2715 N Summit St (67005-8813)
PHONE..................................620 442-5760
Kenton Gibbs, *Manager*
EMP: 11
SALES (corp-wide): 822.7MM **Privately Held**
WEB: www.orschelnfarmhome.com
SIC: 5191 5251 5699 Farm supplies; hardware; work clothing
PA: Orscheln Farm And Home Llc
1800 Overcenter Dr
Moberly MO 65270
800 577-2580

(G-169)
PARMAN TNNER SOULE JACKSON CPA (PA)
110 S 1st St (67005-2626)
P.O. Box 758 (67005-0758)
PHONE..................................620 442-3700
Elliot Jackson, *Partner*
John Parman, *Partner*
EMP: 10
SQ FT: 6,600
SALES (est): 1.1MM **Privately Held**
SIC: 8721 Accounting services, except auditing; auditing services

(G-170)
PRESBYTERIAN MANORS INC
Also Called: Presbyterian Manor Arkansas Cy
1711 N 4th St (67005-1699)
PHONE..................................620 442-8700
Sarah Griggs, *Exec Dir*
EMP: 80
SQ FT: 101,300
SALES (corp-wide): 8.6MM **Privately Held**
SIC: 8051 Convalescent home with continuous nursing care
HQ: Presbyterian Manors, Inc.
2414 N Woodlawn Blvd
Wichita KS 67220
316 685-1100

(G-171)
RAKIES OIL LLC
302 N Summit St (67005-2296)
PHONE..................................620 442-2210
Daniel McGowan, *Mng Member*
EMP: 15
SQ FT: 2,000
SALES (est): 2MM **Privately Held**
WEB: www.eddymcgowan.com
SIC: 5541 5171 5531 5014 Filling stations, gasoline; petroleum bulk stations; automotive tires; automobile tires & tubes; carwash, self-service

(G-172)
RAYMOND JAMES FINCL SVCS INC
118 W Chestnut Ave (67005-2426)
PHONE..................................620 442-1198
Clinton R Combs, *Manager*
Lillie Pankaskie, *Manager*
EMP: 11
SALES (corp-wide): 8B **Publicly Held**
SIC: 6211 Brokers, security
HQ: Raymond James Financial Services, Inc.
880 Carillon Pkwy
Saint Petersburg FL 33716
727 567-1000

(G-173)
RCB BANK SERVICE INC
601 N Summit St (67005-2229)
P.O. Box 1047 (67005-1047)
PHONE..................................620 442-4040
Dave Schaller, *President*
EMP: 62
SALES (corp-wide): 22MM **Privately Held**
WEB: www.homenational.com
SIC: 6021 National trust companies with deposits, commercial
HQ: Rcb Bank Service, Inc.
300 W Patti Page Blvd
Claremore OK 74017
918 341-6150

(G-174)
REEDY FORD INC
Also Called: Reedy Ford
3319 N Summit St (67005-8875)
PHONE..................................620 442-4800
Richard Reedy, *President*
Tim Milby, *Principal*
Rodney Reedy, *Vice Pres*
Wilma Reedy, *Vice Pres*
Donna Kunkel, *Comptroller*
▼ **EMP:** 22
SQ FT: 16,000
SALES (est): 9.3MM **Privately Held**
WEB: www.reedyford.com
SIC: 5511 7538 Automobiles, new & used; general automotive repair shops

(G-175)
ROB CARROLLS SNDBLST & PNTG
12046 292nd Rd (67005-6209)
P.O. Box 646 (67005-0646)
PHONE..................................620 442-1361
Rob Carroll, *President*
Shawn Williams, *Superintendent*
Janet Carroll, *Corp Secy*
EMP: 25
SALES (est): 2.4MM **Privately Held**
SIC: 1721 1799 Industrial painting; sandblasting of building exteriors

(G-176)
RPPG INC
1409 W Madison Ave (67005-3056)
PHONE..................................620 705-5100
Nathan Biddle, *President*
Ken Capps, *Treasurer*
Clayton Biggerstaff, *Admin Sec*
EMP: 20
SQ FT: 1,000
SALES (est): 3.2MM **Privately Held**
WEB: www.rppginc.com
SIC: 3444 Sheet metalwork
HQ: Zeeco, Inc.
22151 E 91st St S
Broken Arrow OK 74014
918 258-8551

(G-177)
RURAL WATER DST 3 COWLEY CNTY
10972 286th Rd (67005-6290)
PHONE..................................620 442-7131
James Crow, *Manager*
April Walker, *Manager*
EMP: 12
SALES (est): 1MM **Privately Held**
SIC: 4941 Water supply

(G-178)
SECURITY 1ST TITLE LLC
111 N Summit St (67005-2257)
PHONE..................................620 442-7029
Terry Wright, *Branch Mgr*
EMP: 16 **Privately Held**
SIC: 6541 Title abstract offices
PA: Security 1st Title Llc
727 N Waco Ave Ste 300
Wichita KS 67203

(G-179)
SIGN SOLUTIONS
Also Called: Rob Caroll Sandblasting & Pntg
12046 292nd Rd (67005-6209)
P.O. Box 646 (67005-0646)
PHONE..................................620 442-5649
Janet Carroll, *Owner*
EMP: 12
SALES (est): 714.1K **Privately Held**
SIC: 3993 2759 Signs & advertising specialties; commercial printing

(G-180)
SKYLINE CORPORATION
Also Called: Homette
315 W Skyline Rd (67005-4023)
P.O. Box 719 (67005-0719)
PHONE..................................620 442-9060
Roy Pepper, *Manager*
EMP: 60
SALES (corp-wide): 1.3B **Publicly Held**
WEB: www.skylinecorp.com
SIC: 2451 Mobile homes, except recreational
PA: Skyline Champion Corporation
200 Nibco Pkwy Ste 200 # 200
Elkhart IN 46516
574 294-6521

(G-181)
SOUTH CNTL KANS RGONAL MED CTR
Also Called: South Central Kansas Med Ctr
6401 Patterson Pkwy (67005-5701)
P.O. Box 1107 (67005-1107)
PHONE..................................620 442-2500
Vigil Watson, *CEO*
Lance Niles, *Treasurer*
Kamran Shahzada, *Persnl Dir*
Perry Lin, *Med Doctor*
Jane Campbell, *Manager*
EMP: 182
SQ FT: 62,500
SALES: 25.9MM **Privately Held**
WEB: www.sckrmc.com
SIC: 8062 General medical & surgical hospitals

(G-182)
SPARKS MUSIC CO
315 S Summit St (67005-2892)
PHONE..................................620 442-5030
Roger Sparks, *Owner*
EMP: 13
SQ FT: 25,000
SALES (est): 1.1MM **Privately Held**
WEB: www.sparksmusic.com
SIC: 5736 5731 7841 Musical instrument stores; television sets; high fidelity stereo equipment; video tape rental

(G-183)
TWIN RIVERS DEVELOPMENTAL SUPP
22179 D St (67005)
P.O. Box 133 (67005-0133)
PHONE..................................620 402-6395
Lara McGrew, *CEO*
Linda Byerley, *COO*
Brady Dutton, *CFO*
Joni Barnes, *Manager*
EMP: 75 **EST:** 1976
SALES (est): 3.7MM **Privately Held**
WEB: www.twinrivers.com
SIC: 8361 Home for the mentally handicapped

(G-184)
TWIN RVERS DVLPMENTAL SUPPORTS
Also Called: CCDS
4th St (67005)
P.O. Box 133 (67005-0133)
PHONE..................................620 442-3575
Tammy Powell, *Bookkeeper*
Joni Barnes, *Manager*
Martha Crane, *Exec Dir*
EMP: 65 **EST:** 1976
SQ FT: 37,500
SALES: 3.4K **Privately Held**
WEB: www.twinriversdevelopmental.com
SIC: 8331 Vocational rehabilitation agency

(G-185)
TWO RIVERS CONSUMERS COOP ASSN (PA)
210 S D St (67005-2772)
P.O. Box 1087 (67005-1087)
PHONE..................................620 442-2360
Kevin Kelly, *Principal*
Mark Fuchs, *Controller*
Eddie Crittenden, *Manager*
EMP: 26
SQ FT: 6,000
SALES (est): 10.1MM **Privately Held**
SIC: 5191 5153 5411 Feed; fertilizer & fertilizer materials; grains; co-operative food stores

(G-186)
UNION STATE BANK (HQ)
127 S Summit St (67005-2679)
P.O. Box 928 (67005-0928)
PHONE..................................620 442-5200
Eric Kurtz, *President*
Jeanna Breech, *President*
Lance Niles, *President*
David Marshall, *Exec VP*
Dan Biddle, *Vice Pres*
EMP: 36 **EST:** 1908
SALES: 15.3MM **Privately Held**
SIC: 6022 State trust companies accepting deposits, commercial

(G-187)
UNITED AGENCY INC
Also Called: Allstate
726 N Summit St (67005-2299)
P.O. Box 817 (67005-0817)
PHONE..................................620 442-0400
Stephen Ross, *President*
Fred Bunting, *Vice Pres*
Dan Deener, *Treasurer*
Brooke Padgett, *Accounts Mgr*
Mary Bowlby, *Agent*
EMP: 24
SALES (est): 4.3MM **Privately Held**
WEB: www.arkcityks.net
SIC: 6411 6531 Insurance agents, brokers & service; real estate brokers & agents

Arma
Crawford County

(G-188)
ARMA CARE CENTER LLC
605 E Melvin St (66712-4100)
P.O. Box 789 (66712-0789)
PHONE..................................620 347-4103
Jon Robertson, *President*
Jodee Valley, *Director*
Dana Dugger, *Administration*
EMP: 43
SALES (est): 2.5MM **Privately Held**
SIC: 8051 Skilled nursing care facilities
PA: Deseret Health Group, Llc.
190 S Main St
Bountiful UT 84010

(G-189)
CLELAND MASONRY INC
728 E 640th Ave (66712-9516)
P.O. Box 117 (66712-0117)
PHONE..................................620 347-8546
John P Cleland, *President*
EMP: 10
SALES (est): 583.4K **Privately Held**
SIC: 1741 Bricklaying

(G-190)
ROLL OUT INC
232 N 230th St (66712-3902)
PHONE.................................620 347-4753
Charles Kukovich, *President*
Matthew Belo, *Vice Pres*
EMP: 5
SALES (est): 513.4K **Privately Held**
WEB: www.rollout.net
SIC: 3714 Motor vehicle parts & accessories

(G-191)
STRESS PANEL MANUFACTURERS
104 S Industrial Dr (66712-9405)
PHONE.................................620 347-8200
Gene Goff, *President*
EMP: 6
SQ FT: 43,000
SALES (est): 1MM **Privately Held**
WEB: www.stresspanel.com
SIC: 2899 Insulating compounds

(G-192)
TOBYS CARNIVAL INC
503 N West St (66712-8100)
P.O. Box 978 (66712-0978)
PHONE.................................620 235-6667
Daniel Yarnell, *President*
EMP: 30
SALES: 500K **Privately Held**
SIC: 7999 Carnival operation

Ashland
Clark County

(G-193)
ASHLAND FEED & SEED CO (PA)
S Main & Santa Fe St (67831)
P.O. Box 635 (67831-0635)
PHONE.................................620 635-2856
Neil Kay, *President*
Betty Kay, *Corp Secy*
Jeff Kay, *Vice Pres*
EMP: 7
SQ FT: 50,000
SALES (est): 1.5MM **Privately Held**
SIC: 2048 Livestock feeds

(G-194)
GARDINER ANGUS RANCH
2605 Cr 13 (67831-3136)
PHONE.................................620 635-2932
Henry Gardiner, *CEO*
Mark Gardiner, *President*
EMP: 10
SALES (est): 5.1MM **Privately Held**
SIC: 0212 Beef cattle except feedlots

(G-195)
GODLY PLAY RESOURCES INC
122 W 8th Ave (67831-3200)
P.O. Box 563 (67831-0563)
PHONE.................................620 635-4018
Jerome Berryman, *President*
Tom Berryman, *General Mgr*
Teresa Arnold, *Manager*
EMP: 6
SALES (est): 617.7K **Privately Held**
WEB: www.godlyplay.com
SIC: 2499 Decorative wood & woodwork

(G-196)
HOSPITAL DISTRICT 3 CLARK CNTY (PA)
Also Called: Ashland Health Center
625 S Kentucky Ashland (67831)
P.O. Box 188 (67831-0188)
PHONE.................................620 635-2241
Randall Spare, *Chairman*
Rachel Rogers, *Council Mbr*
Jan Endicott, *Admin Sec*
Debbie Silson, *Administration*
EMP: 70
SALES (est): 4.3MM **Privately Held**
SIC: 8062 General medical & surgical hospitals

(G-197)
PRATT FEEDERS LLC
Also Called: Ashland Feeders
2590 County Rd L (67831)
PHONE.................................620 635-2213
Dave Latta, *General Mgr*
Nick Sharp, *Branch Mgr*
EMP: 14
SALES (corp-wide): 5.8MM **Privately Held**
WEB: www.prattfeeders.com
SIC: 0211 Beef cattle feedlots
PA: Pratt Feeders, L.L.C.
40010 Nw 20th Ave
Pratt KS 67124
620 672-3401

(G-198)
SHAW FEEDYARD INC
2428 Cr 15 (67831-3140)
P.O. Box 655 (67831-0655)
PHONE.................................620 635-2670
William Shaw, *President*
EMP: 10 **EST:** 1963
SQ FT: 1,500
SALES (est): 1.3MM **Privately Held**
SIC: 0751 Cattle services

(G-199)
STOCKGROWERS STATE BANK (HQ)
622 Main St (67831)
P.O. Box 458 (67831-0458)
PHONE.................................800 772-2265
Jhon T Fellers, *President*
Keith Randal, *Vice Pres*
Frank York, *Vice Pres*
EMP: 40 **EST:** 1885
SALES: 5.1MM **Privately Held**
WEB: www.stockgrowersbank.com
SIC: 6022 State trust companies accepting deposits, commercial

Assaria
Saline County

(G-200)
D J INC
Also Called: Donna Jean's Unique Gift Shop
6737 S Tamara Ln (67416-8825)
PHONE.................................785 667-4651
Donna Sinnett, *President*
EMP: 16
SALES (est): 884.7K **Privately Held**
SIC: 3999 5945 Bric-a-brac; arts & crafts supplies

(G-201)
DYNAMOLD CORPORATION
706 E Salemsborg Rd (67416-5018)
P.O. Box 91 (67416-0091)
PHONE.................................785 667-4626
Jim Markle, *President*
Larry Shackelford, *Vice Pres*
EMP: 10 **EST:** 1969
SQ FT: 16,000
SALES: 1.4MM **Privately Held**
SIC: 3559 Concrete products machinery

Atchison
Atchison County

(G-202)
ACHIEVEMENT SVCS FOR NE KANS (PA)
215 N 5th St (66002-2412)
P.O. Box 186 (66002-0186)
PHONE.................................913 367-2432
Jerry Henry, *Director*
Lois Reid, *Director*
EMP: 35
SQ FT: 11,000
SALES: 1.7MM **Privately Held**
SIC: 8331 Sheltered workshop

(G-203)
AMERICINN MOTEL & SUITES
500 Us Hwy 73 S (66002-3175)
PHONE.................................913 367-4000
Deb Ashby, *Manager*
Mike Harris, *Manager*
EMP: 16 **EST:** 2000
SALES (est): 707.8K **Privately Held**
SIC: 7011 Hotels & motels

(G-204)
AMSTED RAIL COMPANY INC
2604 Industrial Rd (66002-9455)
PHONE.................................913 367-7200
Jeff Hewitt, *Branch Mgr*
EMP: 50
SALES (corp-wide): 2.4B **Privately Held**
SIC: 3743 Railroad equipment
HQ: Amsted Rail Company, Inc.
311 S Wacker Dr Ste 5300
Chicago IL 60606

(G-205)
AMSTED RAIL COMPANY INC
2604 Industry St (66002)
PHONE.................................800 621-8442
Evan Bryant, *Branch Mgr*
EMP: 12
SALES (corp-wide): 2.4B **Privately Held**
SIC: 3643 Rail bonds, electric: for propulsion & signal circuits
HQ: Amsted Rail Company, Inc.
311 S Wacker Dr Ste 5300
Chicago IL 60606

(G-206)
ATCHISON AREA CHAMBER COMMERCE
200 S 10th St (66002-2772)
P.O. Box 126 (66002-0126)
PHONE.................................913 367-2427
Bridgette Bise, *President*
Mike Julo, *Principal*
EMP: 12
SQ FT: 5,000
SALES: 564.6K **Privately Held**
WEB: www.atchisonkansas.net
SIC: 8611 Chamber of Commerce

(G-207)
ATCHISON CHILD CARE ASSN
Also Called: Acca
1326 Kansas Ave (66002-2250)
PHONE.................................913 367-6441
Frances Strieby, *Exec Dir*
Carrie Sowers, *Director*
EMP: 12
SALES: 655.3K **Privately Held**
WEB: www.atchchildcare.org
SIC: 8351 Group day care center

(G-208)
ATCHISON COUNTY AUCTION CO
16971 286th Rd (66002-4521)
PHONE.................................913 367-5278
Ron Estes, *President*
Steven Estes, *Vice Pres*
Katherine Estes, *Treasurer*
EMP: 20 **EST:** 1946
SALES (est): 3MM **Privately Held**
SIC: 5154 Auctioning livestock

(G-209)
ATCHISON HOSPITAL ASSOCIATION (PA)
800 Ravenhill Dr (66002-9204)
PHONE.................................913 367-2131
John Jacobson, *CEO*
D Mark Windsor, *Chairman*
Robert M Adrian, *Vice Pres*
Jan Branson, *Opers Staff*
Teresa Zacharias, *Buyer*
EMP: 270
SQ FT: 100,000
SALES: 38.1MM **Privately Held**
SIC: 8062 General medical & surgical hospitals

(G-210)
ATCHISON HOSPITALITY GROUP LLC
Also Called: Holiday Inn
401 Main St (66002-2839)
PHONE.................................913 674-0033
Terri Canterbury, *Site Mgr*
Debbie Applebaugh, *Manager*
William Michaud,
EMP: 18
SALES (est): 119.3K **Privately Held**
SIC: 7011 Hotels & motels

(G-211)
B & D EQUIPMENT CO INC
17526 286th Rd (66002-4526)
P.O. Box 401 (66002-0401)
PHONE.................................913 367-1744
Mike Barton, *President*
Rosemary Barton, *Vice Pres*
EMP: 15 **EST:** 1962
SALES (est): 2.9MM **Privately Held**
WEB: www.bdequipmentco.com
SIC: 5083 7699 Agricultural machinery & equipment; farm machinery repair

(G-212)
BAKER SERVICES INC
1699 Highway 59 (66002-2671)
PHONE.................................913 367-1657
Jeffrey R Baker, *President*
Anthony W Baker, *Vice Pres*
EMP: 12
SQ FT: 8,000
SALES (est): 1.5MM **Privately Held**
SIC: 0711 0721 Fertilizer application services; crop thinning (chemical) services

(G-213)
BELLEVUE GOLF AND COUNTRY CLUB
Also Called: Bellevue Country Club
1713 Country Club Rd (66002-1505)
PHONE.................................913 367-3022
Dave Farris, *CEO*
John Kujawa, *Vice Pres*
EMP: 25
SQ FT: 4,000
SALES (est): 879.3K **Privately Held**
SIC: 7997 Country club, membership; golf club, membership; swimming club, membership; tennis club, membership

(G-214)
BERGER COMPANY (PA)
104 N 6th St Ste 10 (66002-2440)
P.O. Box 187 (66002-0187)
PHONE.................................913 367-3700
Richard N Berger, *Chairman*
Bob Adrian, *Exec VP*
◆ **EMP:** 10
SQ FT: 54,000
SALES (est): 22.8MM **Privately Held**
WEB: www.bergercompany.com
SIC: 5199 5131 Leather goods, except footwear, gloves, luggage, belting; binding, textile; piece goods & other fabrics

(G-215)
BERGER COMPANY
Also Called: Atchison Leather
316 Commercial St Ste 10 (66002-2519)
P.O. Box 187 (66002-0187)
PHONE.................................913 367-3700
Richard Berger, *President*
EMP: 60
SALES (corp-wide): 22.8MM **Privately Held**
WEB: www.bergercompany.com
SIC: 4225 General warehousing & storage
PA: Berger Company
104 N 6th St Ste 10
Atchison KS 66002
913 367-3700

(G-216)
BLAIR MILLING & ELEV CO INC
Also Called: Blair Feeds
1000 Main St (66002-2712)
P.O. Box 437 (66002-0437)
PHONE.................................913 367-2310
Bill Blair, *Ch of Bd*
Tom Bishop, *President*
Pam Blair, *Vice Pres*
Wes Blair, *Vice Pres*
▲ **EMP:** 22 **EST:** 1867
SQ FT: 10,000
SALES: 2.5MM **Privately Held**
WEB: www.blairfeeds.com
SIC: 2048 Livestock feeds

(G-217)
BLISH-MIZE CO (PA)
223 S 5th St (66002-2801)
P.O. Box 249 (66002-0249)
PHONE.................................913 367-1250

GEOGRAPHIC

Jonathan Mize, *CEO*
Jonathan D Mize, *President*
Lydia Funk, *Exec VP*
Greg Lutz, *Senior VP*
Amy Hennis, *Vice Pres*
EMP: 40
SQ FT: 125,000
SALES (est): 112.8MM **Privately Held**
WEB: www.blishmize.com
SIC: 5072 Builders' hardware

(G-218)
BLISH-MIZE CO
2606 Industrial Rd (66002-9455)
PHONE..................................913 367-1250
Greg Lutz, *Vice Pres*
EMP: 110
SQ FT: 450,000
SALES (corp-wide): 112.8MM **Privately Held**
WEB: www.blishmize.com
SIC: 5072 5198 Hardware; paints
PA: Blish-Mize Co.
223 S 5th St
Atchison KS 66002
913 367-1250

(G-219)
BOTTORFF CONSTRUCTION INC
8001 Industrial Park Ln (66002-9539)
PHONE..................................913 874-5681
Justin Bottorff, *President*
Leslie Chew, *Manager*
EMP: 70
SQ FT: 20,000
SALES (est): 9.9MM **Privately Held**
WEB: www.bottorffconstruction.com
SIC: 1771 Foundation & footing contractor

(G-220)
BRADKEN INC
Bradken-Atchison Facility
400 S 4th St (66002-2886)
PHONE..................................913 367-2121
Jeff Woolston, *Production*
Mary Brant, *Engineer*
Tom Armstrong, *Manager*
Malcolm Griffin, *Manager*
Wayne Braun, *Director*
EMP: 100 **Privately Held**
SIC: 3325 3321 3312 Steel foundries; gray & ductile iron foundries; blast furnaces & steel mills
HQ: Bradken, Inc.
12200 N Ambassador Dr # 647
Kansas City MO 64163
816 270-0701

(G-221)
BUNGE MILLING INC
16755 274th Rd (66002-9202)
P.O. Box 29061, Hot Springs AR (71903-9061)
PHONE..................................913 367-3251
Dean Hughes, *Principal*
Tom Bartlett, *Warehouse Mgr*
EMP: 110 **Privately Held**
WEB: www.bungemilling.com
SIC: 5153 Grains
HQ: Bunge Milling, Inc.
1391 Timberlake Manor Pkw
Chesterfield MO 63017
314 292-2000

(G-222)
CGB ENTERPRISES INC
812 Skyway Hwy (66002-2752)
PHONE..................................913 367-5450
EMP: 27 **Privately Held**
SIC: 6331 Federal crop insurance corporation
PA: Cgb Enterprises, Inc.
1127 Hwy 190 E Service Rd
Covington LA 70433

(G-223)
COUNTY OF ATCHISON
Also Called: Atchison Senior Village
1419 N 6th St (66002-1244)
PHONE..................................913 367-1905
Peggy House, *Branch Mgr*
EMP: 50 **Privately Held**
SIC: 8052 Personal care facility
PA: County Of Atchison
423 N 5th St
Atchison KS 66002
913 367-4400

(G-224)
DIRECT MOP SALES INC
7700 Schuele Rd (66002-4203)
PHONE..................................913 367-3087
Mike Jewel Jr, *CEO*
Mike Julo, *Facilities Mgr*
Lisa Tseng, *Assistant*
▲ **EMP:** 20
SALES: 4MM **Privately Held**
SIC: 2392 Mops, floor & dust

(G-225)
DOOLEY CENTER
801 S 8th St (66002-2724)
PHONE..................................913 360-6200
Anne Shepard, *Owner*
EMP: 36 **EST:** 2009
SALES (est): 966.6K **Privately Held**
SIC: 8059 Personal care home, with health care

(G-226)
E-Z INFO INC
Also Called: Brms
801 Atchison St (66002-2352)
PHONE..................................913 367-5020
Daniel J Growney MD, *Vice Pres*
Mark Growney, *Project Mgr*
John T Growney, *Treasurer*
Sheila Growney, *Director*
EMP: 10
SQ FT: 1,400
SALES (est): 1.1MM **Privately Held**
WEB: www.ez-info.com
SIC: 3993 3953 Signs, not made in custom sign painting shops; marking devices

(G-227)
EXCHANGE NATIONAL BANK & TR CO (HQ)
600 Commercial St (66002-2405)
P.O. Box 189 (66002-0189)
PHONE..................................913 367-6000
Paul H Adair, *Ch of Bd*
Richard R Dickason, *President*
Sharon Baldridge, *Vice Pres*
Janice Goodlet, *Vice Pres*
Russ McCort, *Vice Pres*
EMP: 38 **EST:** 1857
SQ FT: 20,000
SALES: 18MM
SALES (corp-wide): 16.6MM **Privately Held**
SIC: 6021 National trust companies with deposits, commercial
PA: Exchange National Bank And Trust Company
600 Commercial St
Atchison KS 66002
913 833-5560

(G-228)
EXCHANGE NATIONAL BANK & TR CO (PA)
600 Commercial St (66002-2405)
P.O. Box 189 (66002-0189)
PHONE..................................913 833-5560
Richard R Dickason, *President*
Paul H Adair, *Chairman*
Chuck Swinford, *Exec VP*
Christy Brull, *Assistant VP*
Joe Penning, *Assistant VP*
EMP: 52 **EST:** 1857
SQ FT: 500
SALES: 16.6MM **Privately Held**
SIC: 6022 State commercial banks

(G-229)
GATEHOUSE MEDIA INC
Also Called: Atchison Globe
308 Commercial St (66002-2519)
P.O. Box 247 (66002-0247)
PHONE..................................913 367-0583
Joe Warren, *Principal*
EMP: 9
SQ FT: 10,000
SALES (corp-wide): 1.5B **Publicly Held**
WEB: www.gatehousemedia.com
SIC: 2711 Newspapers: publishing only, not printed on site
HQ: Gatehouse Media, Llc
175 Sullys Trl Fl 3
Pittsford NY 14534
585 598-0030

(G-230)
GBW RAILCAR SERVICES LLC
Also Called: Grs
Hwy 59 W (66002)
PHONE..................................866 785-4082
Don Walsh, *Branch Mgr*
EMP: 37
SALES (corp-wide): 3B **Publicly Held**
SIC: 4789 Railroad car repair
HQ: Gbw Railcar Services, L.L.C.
4350 Nw Front Ave
Portland OR 97210

(G-231)
GOLDEN STAR INC
7712 Industrial Park Ln (66002-9538)
P.O. Box 531 (66002-0531)
PHONE..................................913 874-2178
Joe Julo, *Branch Mgr*
Meredith Scherer, *Admin Asst*
EMP: 87
SALES (corp-wide): 39.1MM **Privately Held**
WEB: www.goldenstar.com
SIC: 2299 2273 2392 Yarns & thread, made from non-fabric materials; carpets & rugs; household furnishings
PA: Golden Star Inc.
6445 Metcalf Ave
Overland Park KS 66202
816 842-0233

(G-232)
GRACE MANAGEMENT INC
1301 N 4th St (66002-1207)
PHONE..................................913 367-2655
EMP: 1758
SALES (corp-wide): 20.5MM **Privately Held**
SIC: 8051 Skilled nursing care facilities
PA: Grace Management, Inc.
6900 Wedgwood Rd N # 300
Maple Grove MN 55311
763 544-9934

(G-233)
GUIDANCE CENTER
201 Main St (66002-2828)
PHONE..................................913 367-1593
Keith Rickard, *Director*
EMP: 30
SALES (corp-wide): 8.1MM **Privately Held**
WEB: www.theguidance-ctr.org
SIC: 8093 9111 8322 8069 Mental health clinic, outpatient; county supervisors' & executives' offices; social worker; alcoholism rehabilitation hospital; clinical psychologist
PA: The Guidance Center
500 Limit St
Leavenworth KS
913 682-5118

(G-234)
HENRY SCHERER CROP INSURANCE
Also Called: Crop Risk Management Services
14225 318th Rd (66002-3249)
PHONE..................................785 847-6843
Henry Scherer, *Owner*
EMP: 13
SALES (est): 1.1MM **Privately Held**
SIC: 6411 Insurance agents

(G-235)
HIGH PLAINS INC
Also Called: High Plains Distlery
1700 Rooks Rd (66002-6106)
PHONE..................................913 773-5780
Seth Fox, *President*
EMP: 6
SQ FT: 7,500
SALES (est): 57.6K **Privately Held**
SIC: 2085 Distilled & blended liquors

(G-236)
INCLUSION TECHNOLOGIES LLC
1145 Main St (66002-2751)
PHONE..................................913 370-8070
Jansen Christopher, *Principal*
Christopher Jansen, *Principal*
EMP: 17 **EST:** 2014
SALES (est): 2.9MM **Privately Held**
SIC: 2043 Coffee substitutes, made from grain

(G-237)
INTERNTIONAL FOREST FRIENDSHIP
913 Main St (66002-2706)
PHONE..................................913 367-1419
Kay Baker, *Admin Sec*
EMP: 22
SALES: 36.5K **Privately Held**
SIC: 8641 Civic associations

(G-238)
KEARNEY CONSTRUCTION INC
6199 Osage Rd (66002-9255)
PHONE..................................913 367-1200
Gary Kearnet Jr, *President*
EMP: 10
SALES (est): 2.1MM **Privately Held**
SIC: 1542 Commercial & office buildings, renovation & repair

(G-239)
KEIMIG BODY SHOP
Also Called: Redneck Street Rods
300 Main St (66002-2840)
PHONE..................................913 367-0184
Wayne Keimig, *Owner*
EMP: 10
SALES (est): 631.5K **Privately Held**
WEB: www.redneckstreetrods.com
SIC: 7532 Body shop, automotive

(G-240)
KING LUMINAIRE COMPANY INC
14503 Wallick Rd (66002-8500)
PHONE..................................913 255-3112
Matt Lacey, *Manager*
EMP: 9
SALES (corp-wide): 27.4MM **Privately Held**
WEB: www.stresscrete3.com
SIC: 3272 Concrete products
HQ: King Luminaire Company, Inc.
1153 State Route 46 N
Jefferson OH 44047
440 576-9073

(G-241)
LOCKWOOD COMPANY INC (PA)
Also Called: Lockwood Business Forms
8191 Pratt Rd (66002-4551)
P.O. Box 128 (66002-0128)
PHONE..................................913 367-0110
Patricia Lockwood-Snowden, *Ch of Bd*
Buck Snowden, *President*
James Wietharn, *Corp Secy*
Jim Weithern, *Vice Pres*
EMP: 24 **EST:** 1903
SQ FT: 33,000
SALES (est): 3.2MM **Privately Held**
WEB: www.lockwoodcoinc.com
SIC: 2752 Commercial printing, offset

(G-242)
MARLATT CONSTRUCTION CO INC
17588 274th Rd (66002-5196)
PHONE..................................913 367-3342
Lester Marlatt, *President*
Ruthanna Marlatt, *Corp Secy*
Steven Marlatt, *Vice Pres*
Thomas Marlatt, *Vice Pres*
EMP: 13
SALES: 1.1MM **Privately Held**
SIC: 1794 1799 1795 Excavation & grading, building construction; building site preparation; demolition, buildings & other structures

(G-243)
MEDICALODGES INC
1635 Riley St (66002-1518)
PHONE..................................913 367-2077
Cathy W Fisher, *CFO*
EMP: 71

SALES (corp-wide): 100.2MM **Privately Held**
WEB: www.medicalodge.com
SIC: 6513 Retirement hotel operation
PA: Medicalodges, Inc.
201 W 8th St
Coffeyville KS 67337
620 251-6700

(G-244)
MEDICALODGES INC
1637 Riley St (66002-1598)
PHONE..................................913 367-6066
Kathaleen Fuelling, *Principal*
EMP: 104
SALES (corp-wide): 100.2MM **Privately Held**
WEB: www.medicalodges.com
SIC: 8051 Convalescent home with continuous nursing care
PA: Medicalodges, Inc.
201 W 8th St
Coffeyville KS 67337
620 251-6700

(G-245)
MGP INGREDIENTS INC (PA)
100 Commercial St (66002-2514)
P.O. Box 130 (66002-0130)
PHONE..................................913 367-1480
Karen L Seaberg, *Ch of Bd*
Augustus C Griffin, *President*
Michael Buttshaw, *Vice Pres*
Stephen J Glaser, *Vice Pres*
Mike Templin, *Plant Mgr*
◆ **EMP:** 102 **EST:** 1941
SQ FT: 18,000
SALES: 376MM **Publicly Held**
SIC: 2085 2041 Distillers' dried grains & solubles & alcohol; flour & other grain mill products

(G-246)
MGP INGREDIENTS INC
1300 Main St (66002-2666)
PHONE..................................913 367-1480
Laidacker Seaberg, *CEO*
Shanae Randolph, *Manager*
EMP: 13
SALES (corp-wide): 376MM **Publicly Held**
SIC: 2041 Flour & other grain mill products
PA: Mgp Ingredients, Inc.
100 Commercial St
Atchison KS 66002
913 367-1480

(G-247)
MGPI PROCESSING INC (HQ)
100 Commercial St (66002-2514)
P.O. Box 130 (66002-0130)
PHONE..................................913 367-1480
Gus Griffin, *President*
Scott B Phillips, *Vice Pres*
Randy M Schrick, *Vice Pres*
Tom Pigott, *CFO*
◆ **EMP:** 48
SQ FT: 18,000
SALES (est): 93.5MM
SALES (corp-wide): 376MM **Publicly Held**
WEB: www.midwestgrain.com
SIC: 2085 2041 Distilled & blended liquors; flour & other grain mill products
PA: Mgp Ingredients, Inc.
100 Commercial St
Atchison KS 66002
913 367-1480

(G-248)
MGPI PROCESSING INC
1300 Main St (66002-2666)
PHONE..................................913 367-1480
Ladd Seaburg, *Branch Mgr*
EMP: 7
SALES (corp-wide): 376MM **Publicly Held**
SIC: 2085 Distilled & blended liquors
HQ: Mgpi Processing, Inc.
100 Commercial St
Atchison KS 66002
913 367-1480

(G-249)
MICHAEL S HUNDLEY CNSTR INC
1900 Main St (66002-2110)
PHONE..................................913 367-7059
Mike Hundley, *President*
Shane M Hundley, *Vice Pres*
Ashley Hundley, *Treasurer*
Deborah S Hundley, *Admin Sec*
EMP: 16
SQ FT: 5,000
SALES (est): 1.3MM **Privately Held**
SIC: 7389 1521 1542 Interior design services; single-family housing construction; nonresidential construction

(G-250)
MO-KAN TRANSIT MIX INC
1503 Highway 59 (66002-2689)
PHONE..................................913 367-1332
Stephen Betts, *President*
Debrah Betts, *Treasurer*
EMP: 7
SQ FT: 2,000
SALES (est): 1.1MM **Privately Held**
SIC: 3273 Ready-mixed concrete

(G-251)
NEK CAP INC
Also Called: Atchison County Headstart
751 S 8th St Rm 101 (66002-2783)
PHONE..................................913 367-7848
Joan Hockeneargar, *Director*
EMP: 18
SALES (corp-wide): 10.1MM **Privately Held**
SIC: 8351 Head start center, except in conjunction with school
PA: Nek Cap, Inc.
1260 220th St
Hiawatha KS 66434
785 742-2222

(G-252)
OPERATIONS MANAGEMENT INTL INC
515 Kansas Ave (66002-2424)
PHONE..................................913 367-5563
Mike Mattews, *Manager*
EMP: 22
SALES (corp-wide): 12.7B **Publicly Held**
WEB: www.omiinc.com
SIC: 4952 Sewerage systems
HQ: Operations Management International, Inc.
9193 S Jamaica St Ste 400
Englewood CO 80112
303 740-0019

(G-253)
OREILLY AUTOMOTIVE STORES INC
Also Called: O'Reilly Auto Parts
819 Main St (66002-2710)
PHONE..................................913 367-4138
Mario Underwood, *Manager*
EMP: 15 **Publicly Held**
WEB: www.oreillyauto.com
SIC: 5013 5531 Automotive supplies & parts; automotive parts
HQ: O'reilly Automotive Stores, Inc.
233 S Patterson Ave
Springfield MO 65802
417 862-2674

(G-254)
ORSCHELN FARM AND HOME LLC
Also Called: Orschelin Farm and Home 80
605 S 10th St (66002-2782)
PHONE..................................913 367-2261
Dale Herrman, *Manager*
EMP: 12
SALES (corp-wide): 822.7MM **Privately Held**
WEB: www.orschelnfarmhome.com
SIC: 5191 5251 5699 5084 Farm supplies; hardware; work clothing; engines, gasoline
PA: Orscheln Farm And Home Llc
1800 Overcenter Dr
Moberly MO 65270
800 577-2580

(G-255)
PATRICK S KEARNEY
16083 262nd Rd (66002-9265)
PHONE..................................913 367-3161
Patrick Kearney, *Managing Prtnr*
Tesea Kearney, *Managing Prtnr*
EMP: 14
SALES (est): 810.8K **Privately Held**
SIC: 1522 Residential construction

(G-256)
PROGRESS RAIL SERVICES
2604 Indul Rd (66002)
PHONE..................................256 593-1260
Rob Turner, *Engineer*
Joe Balich, *Sales Dir*
Rick Wilburn, *Manager*
EMP: 17 **EST:** 2016
SALES (est): 2.8MM **Privately Held**
SIC: 8748 Business consulting

(G-257)
PROJECT CONCERN INC
504 Kansas Ave (66002-2420)
PHONE..................................913 367-4655
Bill Thorton, *President*
Keith Allison, *Vice Pres*
Lois Wohletz, *Administration*
EMP: 10
SALES: 414.7K **Privately Held**
SIC: 8399 Council for social agency

(G-258)
RIVERBEND RGNAL HLTHCARE FNDTI
Also Called: ATCHSION HOSPITAL
800 Ravenhill Dr (66002-9204)
PHONE..................................913 367-2131
John Jacobson, *CEO*
Eugene Hegarty, *Chairman*
Marty Zumbrunn, *Opers Staff*
Lisa Feil, *Director*
Brandi Oom, *Director*
EMP: 300
SALES: 1.2MM **Privately Held**
SIC: 8062 8011 General medical & surgical hospitals; psychiatrist

(G-259)
SAINT FRANCIS ACDMY INC ATCHSN (PA)
19137 258th Rd (66002-3186)
PHONE..................................913 367-5005
Rev Phillip J Rapp, *President*
Rev Ora A Calhoun, *Exec Dir*
Javier Perez, *Director*
EMP: 50
SQ FT: 56,000
SALES: 1MM **Privately Held**
SIC: 7033 8093 Campsite; mental health clinic, outpatient

(G-260)
SAINT JOSEPH ONCOLOGY INC
Also Called: Rangineni, Raj MD
104 N 6th St Ste 15 (66002-2440)
PHONE..................................913 367-9175
Raj Rangineni, *President*
EMP: 10
SALES (est): 239.5K **Privately Held**
SIC: 8011 Oncologist

(G-261)
STEINLITE CORPORATION
121 N 4th St (66002-2508)
P.O. Box C (66002-0178)
PHONE..................................913 367-3945
Martin J Clements, *President*
▼ **EMP:** 25
SQ FT: 16,875
SALES (est): 3MM **Privately Held**
SIC: 3825 Electrical power measuring equipment

(G-262)
STEINLITE CORPORATION
1015 Main St (66002-2711)
P.O. Box C (66002-0178)
PHONE..................................913 367-3945
Martin J Clements, *President*
EMP: 10
SQ FT: 16,875
SALES (est): 1.8MM **Privately Held**
WEB: www.steinlite.com
SIC: 3825 Electron tube test equipment

(G-263)
STONE INVESTMENT INC
216 S 10th St (66002-2772)
PHONE..................................913 367-0276
Tammy Schuler, *President*
EMP: 21
SALES: 500K **Privately Held**
SIC: 6799 Investors

(G-264)
STRESSCRETE INC
14503 Wallick Rd (66002-8500)
PHONE..................................913 255-3112
Matt Lacey, *Plant Mgr*
Daris Calhoon, *Human Resources*
Royce Fawcett, *Manager*
EMP: 14
SALES (est): 2.3MM **Privately Held**
SIC: 3272 Concrete products

(G-265)
SUPERNOVA PAINTING LLC
1419 Santa Fe St (66002-2234)
PHONE..................................785 850-0158
EMP: 11
SALES (est): 330K **Privately Held**
SIC: 1721 Painting/Paper Hanging Contractor

(G-266)
UMB BANK NATIONAL ASSOCIATION
320 Commercial St (66002-2519)
PHONE..................................913 360-6060
Kent Wohlgemuth, *Branch Mgr*
EMP: 12
SALES (corp-wide): 1.1B **Publicly Held**
SIC: 6021 National commercial banks
HQ: Umb Bank, National Association
1010 Grand Blvd Fl 3
Kansas City MO 64106
816 842-2222

(G-267)
UNION STATE BANK OF EVEREST
Also Called: Bank of Atchison
701 Kansas Ave (66002-2436)
PHONE..................................913 367-2700
Cheryl Lanter, *Manager*
EMP: 20 **Privately Held**
WEB: www.mybankusb.com
SIC: 6022 6141 State commercial banks; personal credit institutions
HQ: The Union State Bank Of Everest
545 Main St
Everest KS 66424
785 548-7521

(G-268)
UNITED STEELWORKERS
Also Called: Uswa
625 Commercial St Ste 2 (66002-2458)
PHONE..................................913 674-5067
Greg Welch, *President*
EMP: 25
SALES (corp-wide): 4.9MM **Privately Held**
WEB: www.uswa.org
SIC: 8631 Labor union
PA: United Steelworkers
60 Bolevard Of The Allies
Pittsburgh PA 15222
412 562-2400

(G-269)
VALLEY HOPE ASSOCIATION
1816 N 2nd St (66002-1004)
P.O. Box 312 (66002-0312)
PHONE..................................913 367-1618
Jack Selberg, *Branch Mgr*
Amy Welker, *Director*
EMP: 45
SALES (corp-wide): 46.7MM **Privately Held**
WEB: www.valleyhope.com
SIC: 8093 8069 Alcohol clinic, outpatient; drug addiction rehabilitation hospital
PA: Valley Hope Association
103 S Wabash Ave
Norton KS 67654
785 877-2421

(G-270)
WE-MAC MANUFACTURING CO
11016 Us Highway 59 (66002-9214)
PHONE..................................913 367-3778
Harold Slimer, *Manager*
EMP: 18
SALES (corp-wide): 5.3MM **Privately Held**
WEB: www.wemactanks.com
SIC: 3443 5039 Tanks, standard or custom fabricated: metal plate; septic tanks
PA: We-Mac Manufacturing Co.
326 E 14th Ave
Kansas City MO 64116
800 444-3218

(G-271)
WEISHAAR ADAPTATION
7237 Elm Dr (66002-3093)
PHONE..................................913 367-6299
Pamela J Weishaar, *Owner*
EMP: 30
SALES: 950K **Privately Held**
SIC: 8611 Business associations

(G-272)
YOUNG MENS CHRISTIAN ASSOC AT
Also Called: Y M C A
321 Commercial St (66002-2518)
PHONE..................................913 367-4948
Lorin Affield, *President*
Linda Keebler, *Real Est Agnt*
Jessica Norris, *Real Est Agnt*
EMP: 55
SQ FT: 60,000
SALES (est): 1.2MM **Privately Held**
SIC: 8322 8661 Individual & family services; religious organizations

Athol
Smith County

(G-273)
CENTRAL PLANES COOP (PA)
205 Railway (66932-1516)
PHONE..................................785 695-2216
Ron Griffith, *President*
EMP: 12 **EST:** 1963
SALES (est): 4.1MM **Privately Held**
SIC: 5153 5191 Grain elevators; feed; seeds: field, garden & flower; fertilizer & fertilizer materials; insecticides

Atlanta
Cowley County

(G-274)
GP TRAPS LLC
2711 Se 190th St (67008-9307)
PHONE..................................620 394-2341
Frank Miller, *Vice Pres*
Brent Fleming,
EMP: 5
SQ FT: 3,000
SALES (est): 479.9K **Privately Held**
WEB: www.gptraps.com
SIC: 3949 Trap racks (clay targets)

Attica
Harper County

(G-275)
ATTICA ENGINEERING LLC
201 N Main St (67009-9111)
P.O. Box 375 (67009-0375)
PHONE..................................620 254-7070
R Eugene Wyatt, *Principal*
Carolyn Wyatt, *Treasurer*
EMP: 12
SALES: 950K **Privately Held**
SIC: 8711 Engineering services

(G-276)
ATTICA HOSPITAL DISTRICT 1
Also Called: Attica Long Term Care
302 N Botkin St (67009-9032)
PHONE..................................620 254-7253
Holly Noble, *Director*
EMP: 75 **EST:** 1956
SQ FT: 29,632
SALES (est): 4.6MM **Privately Held**
SIC: 8052 Intermediate care facilities

(G-277)
ECK AGENCY INC (PA)
Also Called: Kemper Insurance
123 N Main St (67009-9103)
P.O. Box 377 (67009-0377)
PHONE..................................620 254-7222
P John Eck, *President*
Kathy Eck, *Admin Sec*
EMP: 27
SQ FT: 1,500
SALES (est): 5.2MM **Privately Held**
WEB: www.eckagency.com
SIC: 6411 Insurance agents

(G-278)
R & B OIL & GAS INC
111 N Blaine St (67009-9106)
P.O. Box 195 (67009-0195)
PHONE..................................620 254-7251
Randell J Newberry, *President*
Becky Newberry, *Corp Secy*
EMP: 10
SQ FT: 3,000
SALES (est): 1.8MM **Privately Held**
SIC: 1381 Drilling oil & gas wells

(G-279)
SHAWNEE WELL SERVICE INC
Miles N Of Hwy 160 (67009)
P.O. Box 333 (67009-0333)
PHONE..................................620 254-7893
Jeff Capps, *President*
Marvin Capps, *President*
EMP: 13
SALES (est): 920K **Privately Held**
SIC: 1381 Service well drilling

(G-280)
TRUE SPEC FINISHES LLC
121 N Harper St (67009-9035)
P.O. Box 195 (67009-0195)
PHONE..................................620 254-7733
EMP: 5
SALES (est): 406.6K **Privately Held**
SIC: 3471 Plating/Polishing Service

Atwood
Rawlins County

(G-281)
BEAVER VALLEY SUPPLY CO INC (PA)
Also Called: Great Outdoors
21366 Highway 36 (67730-3315)
P.O. Box 419 (67730-0419)
PHONE..................................800 982-1280
Frank A Chvatal, *President*
Scott Chvatal, *Vice Pres*
Theresa Chvatal, *Treasurer*
Kevin Chvatal, *Sales Associate*
Joe Kanak, *Marketing Staff*
▲ **EMP:** 50
SQ FT: 12,400
SALES: 54MM **Privately Held**
SIC: 5083 5191 Farm implements; farm supplies

(G-282)
CARLSONS CHOKE TUBE/NW ARMS
720 S 2nd St (67730-2114)
PHONE..................................785 626-3078
Scott Carlson, *Owner*
▲ **EMP:** 11
SQ FT: 6,500
SALES (est): 1.4MM **Privately Held**
WEB: www.choketube.com
SIC: 3484 3949 Guns (firearms) or gun parts, 30 mm. & below; sporting & athletic goods

(G-283)
DEVELOPMENTAL SVCS NW KANS INC
Also Called: Prairie Developmental Center
208 S 4th St (67730-1924)
PHONE..................................785 626-3688
Roger Predeaux, *Manager*
EMP: 28
SALES (corp-wide): 14.4MM **Privately Held**
SIC: 8331 Vocational rehabilitation agency
PA: Developmental Services Of Northwest Kansas, Inc.
2703 Hall St Ste B10
Hays KS 67601
785 625-5678

(G-284)
EVANGELICAL LUTHERAN
Also Called: Good Samaritan Soc - Atwood
650 Lake Rd (67730-1535)
P.O. Box 5038, Sioux Falls SD (57117-5038)
PHONE..................................785 626-9015
Rodney Dill, *Director*
EMP: 80 **Privately Held**
WEB: www.good-sam.com
SIC: 8059 Nursing home, except skilled & intermediate care facility
HQ: The Evangelical Lutheran Good Samaritan Society
4800 W 57th St
Sioux Falls SD 57108
866 928-1635

(G-285)
FARMERS BANK & TRUST (PA)
Also Called: RAWLINS BANCSHARES
101 S 4th St (67730-1951)
P.O. Box 279 (67730-0279)
PHONE..................................785 626-3233
Barnabas Horton, *President*
EMP: 11 **EST:** 1987
SALES: 3.4MM **Privately Held**
SIC: 6022 State trust companies accepting deposits, commercial

(G-286)
FINLEY CONSTRUCTION & RDYMX
Also Called: Finley Auto Spa
N Hwy 25 (67730)
PHONE..................................785 626-3282
Steven Finley, *President*
Anita Finley, *Admin Sec*
EMP: 5 **EST:** 1946
SQ FT: 30,000
SALES (est): 563.4K **Privately Held**
SIC: 7542 3272 3273 1542 Washing & polishing, automotive; concrete products, precast; ready-mixed concrete; commercial & office building, new construction; agricultural building contractors; concrete work

(G-287)
J D SKILES INC
Also Called: Skiles Industries
101 Grant St (67730-1539)
P.O. Box 157 (67730-0157)
PHONE..................................785 626-9338
Jerry D Skiles, *President*
▲ **EMP:** 10
SQ FT: 25,000
SALES (est): 2.3MM **Privately Held**
WEB: www.jdskiles.com
SIC: 3523 Fertilizing machinery, farm

(G-288)
RAWLINS CNTY DNTL CLINIC FUND
515 State St (67730-1930)
P.O. Box 177 (67730-0177)
PHONE..................................785 626-8290
Heidi S Hueftle, *CEO*
Heidi Hueftle, *CEO*
Tammi Engel, *Dental Hygenist*
EMP: 13
SALES: 800K **Privately Held**
SIC: 8021 Dental clinic

(G-289)
RAWLINS COUNTY HEALTH CENTER
707 Grant St (67730-1526)
P.O. Box 47 (67730-0047)
PHONE..................................785 626-3211
Ryan Marvin, *Safety Dir*
Tara Bowles, *Empl Rel Dir*
Mary Clark, *Director*
Deanna Freeman, *Administration*
EMP: 80
SQ FT: 30,000
SALES (est): 8.2MM **Privately Held**
WEB: www.rchc.us
SIC: 8062 General medical & surgical hospitals

(G-290)
RAWLINS COUNTY SQ DEAL PUBG
Also Called: Square Deal Newspaper
114 S 4th St (67730-1922)
P.O. Box 371 (67730-0371)
PHONE..................................785 626-3600
Rosalie Ross, *President*
EMP: 9
SALES (est): 469.4K **Privately Held**
SIC: 2711 Newspapers, publishing & printing

(G-291)
ROTARY INTERNATIONAL
305 S 4th St (67730-2009)
PHONE..................................785 626-9444
Thos Marks, *Branch Mgr*
EMP: 12
SALES (corp-wide): 503.3MM **Privately Held**
WEB: www.rotary5340.org
SIC: 8641 Fraternal associations
PA: Rotary International
1 Rotary Ctr
Evanston IL 60201
847 866-3000

(G-292)
SUREFIRE AG SYSTEMS INC (PA)
9904 Highway 25 (67730-3217)
PHONE..................................785 626-3670
Matthew W Wolters, *Partner*
Josh Wolters, *Corp Secy*
Blaine Ginther, *Vice Pres*
Jason Bergling, *Purch Mgr*
Cedric Green, *Engineer*
EMP: 35
SALES (est): 4.7MM **Privately Held**
WEB: www.surefireag.com
SIC: 0711 Fertilizer application services

Auburn
Shawnee County

(G-293)
AUBURN ANIMAL CLINIC INC
8370 Sw Auburn Rd (66402-9553)
P.O. Box 239 (66402-0239)
PHONE..................................785 256-2476
Norbert Zander, *President*
Dallas D Caster, *Partner*
Dallas Caster,
EMP: 15
SALES (est): 606.9K **Privately Held**
SIC: 0741 0742 Veterinarian, livestock; veterinarian, animal specialties

(G-294)
COAL CREEK CONSTRUCTION CO
8248 Sw 77th St (66402-9520)
P.O. Box 118 (66402-0118)
PHONE..................................785 256-7171
Michael W Tindell, *President*
EMP: 12
SALES (est): 2.6MM **Privately Held**
SIC: 1542 Commercial & office buildings, renovation & repair

(G-295)
HAAG INC (PA)
Also Called: AAMCO Transmissions
7233 Sw 85th St (66402-9732)
PHONE..................................785 256-2311
Thomas Haag, *President*
Ida Haag, *Corp Secy*
Ernie Haag, *Vice Pres*
EMP: 76
SALES (est): 2.4MM **Privately Held**
SIC: 7537 Automotive transmission repair shops

(G-296)
MIDWEST TURF & LANDSCAPE LLC
9748 Sw Hoch Rd (66402-9453)
P.O. Box 89 (66402-0089)
PHONE....................................785 383-7839
Derrick Keim,
EMP: 10
SALES (est): 950K **Privately Held**
SIC: 0781 Landscape services

(G-297)
STAUFFER LAWN AND LDSCP LLC
1150 Washington St (66402-9209)
PHONE....................................785 256-7300
Pete Stauffer, *Mng Member*
EMP: 14
SALES (est): 1.1MM **Privately Held**
WEB: www.staufferlawn.com
SIC: 0782 Lawn care services

(G-298)
VALLEY SPRINGS
280 Valley Springs Dr (66402-9464)
PHONE....................................785 256-7100
Renessa Ullery, *Manager*
EMP: 19 **EST:** 2000
SALES: 250K **Privately Held**
SIC: 8052 Intermediate care facilities

Augusta
Butler County

(G-299)
4PC LLC
Also Called: 4pc Security Technologies
415 State St (67010-1105)
PHONE....................................316 833-6906
Coby Hayes, *Mng Member*
EMP: 9 **EST:** 2013
SALES (est): 1.2MM **Privately Held**
SIC: 1731 3699 Safety & security specialization; security control equipment & systems

(G-300)
APAC-KANSAS INC
11221 Sw Us Highway 54 (67010-8900)
PHONE....................................316 775-7639
Bob Philipi, *Manager*
EMP: 22
SALES (corp-wide): 29.7B **Privately Held**
SIC: 1611 Highway & street construction
HQ: Apac-Kansas, Inc.
9660 Legler Rd
Lenexa KS 66219

(G-301)
AUGUSTA COUNTRY CLUB
1610 Fairway Dr (67010-2247)
PHONE....................................316 775-7281
Henry Marburger, *General Mgr*
Rusty Patterson, *Principal*
EMP: 23
SALES (est): 727.7K **Privately Held**
SIC: 7997 7992 Country club, membership; public golf courses

(G-302)
AUGUSTA CRIME STOPPERS INC
2100 Ohio St (67010-2175)
P.O. Box 131 (67010-0131)
PHONE....................................316 775-0055
Tayler Brewer, *Director*
EMP: 40
SALES (est): 742.7K **Privately Held**
SIC: 8322 Hotline

(G-303)
AUGUSTA ELECTRIC PLANT 2
Also Called: City of Agusta
615 12th Ave (67010)
P.O. Box 489 (67010-0489)
PHONE....................................316 775-4527
Bill Webster, *Director*
EMP: 10 **EST:** 2000
SALES (est): 2.1MM **Privately Held**
SIC: 4911 Generation, electric power

(G-304)
AUGUSTA FAMILY DENTISTRY PA
401 State St (67010-1105)
P.O. Box 567 (67010-0567)
PHONE....................................316 775-2482
Paul F Mitsch III, *President*
EMP: 17
SQ FT: 3,800
SALES (est): 1.4MM **Privately Held**
WEB: www.afdmitsch.com
SIC: 8021 Dentists' office

(G-305)
AUGUSTA FAMILY PRACTICE PA
1306 State St (67010-1126)
PHONE....................................316 775-9191
Michael A Rausch, *Principal*
EMP: 26 **EST:** 1999
SALES (est): 3.5MM **Privately Held**
SIC: 8011 General & family practice, physician/surgeon

(G-306)
AUGUSTA HEAD START
730 Cliff Dr (67010-1349)
PHONE....................................316 775-3421
EMP: 10 **EST:** 2010
SALES (est): 250K **Privately Held**
SIC: 8351 Child Day Care Services

(G-307)
AUGUSTA L LAKEPOINT L C (PA)
Also Called: LAKE POINT NURSING CENTER
901 Lakepoint Dr (67010-2423)
PHONE....................................316 775-6333
Stephanie Dunlap, *Director*
Eric Ohlson, *Director*
Dori Smith, *Director*
Twila Jones, *Social Dir*
Peter Pelas, *Food Svc Dir*
EMP: 100
SALES: 8.3MM **Privately Held**
SIC: 8051 Convalescent home with continuous nursing care

(G-308)
AUGUSTA RENTAL INC
9965 Sw Santa Fe Lake Rd (67010-8189)
PHONE....................................316 775-5050
Christopher Kuhlmann,
EMP: 12 **EST:** 2007
SALES (est): 1.6MM **Privately Held**
SIC: 5211 7359 Concrete & cinder block; lawn & garden equipment rental

(G-309)
AUGUSTA WHITE EAGLE CREDIT UN (PA)
2830 Ohio St (67010-2361)
P.O. Box 86 (67010-0086)
PHONE....................................316 775-5747
Richard G Blue, *Manager*
EMP: 25
SALES: 4.7MM **Privately Held**
WEB: www.awecu.com
SIC: 6061 Federal credit unions

(G-310)
AUSTIN TRUCKING
1782 Sw 92nd Ter (67010-8296)
PHONE....................................316 323-0313
Dale Alan Austin, *Owner*
EMP: 13 **EST:** 1989
SALES (est): 900.3K **Privately Held**
SIC: 4213 Trucking, except local

(G-311)
BEAVERS PLUMBING L L C
231 N Walnut St (67010-1031)
PHONE....................................316 619-6119
Jason Beavers, *President*
Kelly Beavers, *Partner*
EMP: 10 **EST:** 2008
SALES: 900K **Privately Held**
SIC: 1711 Plumbing contractors

(G-312)
BNSF RAILWAY COMPANY
301 E 5th Ave (67010-1013)
PHONE....................................316 708-4472
EMP: 46
SALES (corp-wide): 225.3B **Publicly Held**
WEB: www.billpurdy.com
SIC: 4011 Railroads, line-haul operating
HQ: Bnsf Railway Company
2650 Lou Menk Dr
Fort Worth TX 76131
800 795-2673

(G-313)
CHUCK KRTE RLTY EST AUCTN SVCS
Also Called: Prudential Dinning Beard
420 N Walnut St (67010-1036)
PHONE....................................316 775-2201
Charles Korte, *President*
Deann Korte, *Vice Pres*
EMP: 20
SALES (est): 943.2K **Privately Held**
WEB: www.chuckkorte.com
SIC: 6531 Real estate brokers & agents

(G-314)
COMMUNITY NATIONAL BANK
645 State St (67010-1109)
PHONE....................................316 775-6068
Eric Grooms, *President*
EMP: 13 **Privately Held**
SIC: 6021 National commercial banks
HQ: Community National Bank & Trust
14 N Lincoln Ave
Chanute KS 66720

(G-315)
COTTONWOOD POINT INC
100 Cottonwood Point Ln (67010-2169)
PHONE....................................316 775-0368
Bob Hirschfeld, *President*
Donna Poage, *Corp Secy*
Bill Morris, *Vice Pres*
Sharla Keller, *Director*
EMP: 12
SALES: 815.6K **Privately Held**
WEB: www.cottonwoodpoint.com
SIC: 8361 Residential care

(G-316)
D-J ENGINEERING INC (PA)
219 W 6th Ave (67010-1251)
P.O. Box 278 (67010-0278)
PHONE....................................316 775-1212
Rezaul Chowdhury, *President*
Ryan Hernandez, *Vice Pres*
Rob Short, *Vice Pres*
Raymond Tuschhoff, *Vice Pres*
Jeff Brown, *Opers Mgr*
▲ **EMP:** 170
SQ FT: 206,000
SALES (est): 69.8MM **Privately Held**
WEB: www.djgrp.com
SIC: 3728 Aircraft assemblies, subassemblies & parts

(G-317)
DINNING BEARD INC
420 N Walnut St (67010-1036)
PHONE....................................316 775-2201
Jennifer Hudson, *Manager*
EMP: 11
SALES (corp-wide): 62.9B **Publicly Held**
WEB: www.prugo.com
SIC: 6531 Real estate agent, residential
HQ: Dinning Beard Inc
12021 E 13th St N Ste 100
Wichita KS 67206
316 636-1115

(G-318)
EMPRISE BANK
1700 Ohio St (67010-2144)
PHONE....................................316 775-4233
EMP: 11
SALES (corp-wide): 80MM **Privately Held**
SIC: 6022 State trust companies accepting deposits, commercial
HQ: Emprise Bank
257 N Broadway Ave
Wichita KS 67202
316 383-4400

(G-319)
GLOBAL PARTS INC (HQ)
Also Called: Global Parts Aero
901 Industrial Rd (67010-9565)
PHONE....................................316 733-9240
Troy Palmer, *President*
Malissa Nesmith, *Vice Pres*
Scott Toom, *Opers Staff*
Shannon McDaniel, *Purchasing*
Khelifa Inchekel, *QC Mgr*
◆ **EMP:** 78
SQ FT: 99,500
SALES (est): 38.3MM
SALES (corp-wide): 41.1MM **Privately Held**
WEB: www.globalparts.com
SIC: 5088 Aircraft & parts
PA: Global Parts Group, Inc.
901 Industrial Rd
Augusta KS 67010
316 733-9240

(G-320)
GLOBAL PARTS AERO MFG
901 Industrial Rd (67010-9565)
PHONE....................................316 775-9292
Troy Palmer, *President*
EMP: 45 **EST:** 2012
SALES (est): 328.8K
SALES (corp-wide): 41.1MM **Privately Held**
SIC: 4581 Aircraft maintenance & repair services
HQ: Global Parts, Inc.
901 Industrial Rd
Augusta KS 67010
316 733-9240

(G-321)
GLOBAL PARTS GROUP INC (PA)
901 Industrial Rd (67010-9565)
PHONE....................................316 733-9240
Troy Palmer, *President*
Malissa Nesmith, *COO*
EMP: 60 **EST:** 2013
SALES (est): 41.4MM
SALES (corp-wide): 41.1MM **Privately Held**
SIC: 4581 Aircraft maintenance & repair services

(G-322)
H & R BLOCK TAX SERVICES LLC
299 W 7th Ave (67010-1305)
PHONE....................................316 775-7331
Karen Strassburg, *Principal*
EMP: 12
SALES (corp-wide): 3B **Publicly Held**
SIC: 7291 Tax return preparation services
HQ: H & R Block Tax Services Llc
1 H And R Block Way
Kansas City MO 64105

(G-323)
HARDER FAMILY PRACTICE PA
2820 Ohio St (67010-2361)
PHONE....................................316 775-7500
Scott N Harder, *Owner*
EMP: 14
SALES (est): 2.7MM **Privately Held**
SIC: 8011 General & family practice, physician/surgeon

(G-324)
HEARTLAND PLASTICS INC
930 West St (67010-1334)
PHONE....................................316 775-2199
Marvin Ellington, *President*
Melanie L Budda, *Director*
Marsha Ellington, *Admin Sec*
EMP: 9
SQ FT: 10,000
SALES (est): 1.4MM **Privately Held**
WEB: www.heartlandplastics.net
SIC: 3089 Injection molding of plastics

(G-325)
HOMESTEAD OF AUGUSTA
1611 Fairway Dr (67010-2246)
PHONE....................................316 775-1000
Michael Tryon, *Principal*
EMP: 83

SALES (est): 156K
SALES (corp-wide): 32.7MM **Privately Held**
SIC: 8051 Skilled nursing care facilities
PA: Midwest Health, Inc
3024 Sw Wanamaker Rd # 300
Topeka KS 66614
785 272-1535

(G-326)
HUNN LEATHER PRODUCTS INC
900 Industrial Rd (67010-9565)
PHONE..................................316 775-6300
Robert Hunn, *President*
EMP: 10
SQ FT: 6,000
SALES: 750K **Privately Held**
SIC: 5191 Equestrian equipment

(G-327)
INSURANCE GUYS LLC
416 State St (67010-1106)
P.O. Box 611 (67010-0611)
PHONE..................................316 775-0606
Brent Leedom, *Mng Member*
Joe Williams,
EMP: 10 **EST:** 2005
SALES (est): 966.9K **Privately Held**
SIC: 6411 Insurance agents, brokers & service

(G-328)
INTRUST BANK NA
112 W 7th Ave (67010-1302)
PHONE..................................316 383-3340
Nicole Corbin, *Branch Mgr*
EMP: 16
SALES (corp-wide): 134.2MM **Privately Held**
WEB: www.intrustbank.com
SIC: 6021 National trust companies with deposits, commercial
HQ: Intrust Bank National Association
105 N Main St
Wichita KS 67202
316 383-1111

(G-329)
KANSAS MUSEUM OF MLTRY HISTRY
135 N Walnut St (67010-1212)
PHONE..................................316 775-1425
Brad Wise, *Treasurer*
Lisa Lazareva, *Director*
EMP: 14 **EST:** 1991
SALES (est): 273.1K **Privately Held**
SIC: 8412 Museum

(G-330)
KGJ QUARTER HORSES
4278 Sw 100th St (67010-8261)
PHONE..................................316 775-0954
Kathryn James, *Owner*
EMP: 10 **EST:** 1989
SALES (est): 210K **Privately Held**
WEB: www.kgjquarterhorses.com
SIC: 0272 0752 Horse farm; animal specialty services

(G-331)
KINDERCARE EDUCATION LLC
Also Called: A B C Nursery Schl & Day Camp
1300 State St (67010-1126)
PHONE..................................316 775-7503
Karen M Busch, *Manager*
Karen Busch, *Manager*
EMP: 14
SALES (corp-wide): 963.9MM **Privately Held**
WEB: www.knowledgelearning.com
SIC: 8351 Group day care center
PA: Kindercare Education Llc
650 Ne Holladay St # 1400
Portland OR 97232
503 872-1300

(G-332)
LAKEPOINT CORPORATE
2101 Dearborn St (67010-2116)
PHONE..................................316 990-6792
Paul F Good, *Administration*
EMP: 10
SALES (est): 299.7K **Privately Held**
SIC: 8748 Business consulting

(G-333)
MARK H ARMFIELD DDS
Also Called: Armfield Dentistry
2814 Ohio St (67010-2361)
PHONE..................................316 775-5451
Mark H Armfield DDS, *Owner*
Melody Armfield, *Co-Owner*
EMP: 12
SQ FT: 1,600
SALES (est): 571.5K **Privately Held**
SIC: 8021 Dentists' office

(G-334)
MARTIN MARIETTA MATERIALS INC
Also Called: Augusta Quarry
7160 Sw Diamond Rd (67010-8046)
PHONE..................................316 775-5458
Mike Jantz, *Branch Mgr*
EMP: 20 **Publicly Held**
WEB: www.martinmarietta.com
SIC: 1429 Igneous rock, crushed & broken-quarrying
PA: Martin Marietta Materials Inc
2710 Wycliff Rd
Raleigh NC 27607

(G-335)
PAGE CORPORATION
Also Called: Roof-Techs International
6333 Sw Santa Fe Lake Rd (67010-7526)
P.O. Box 780122, Wichita (67278-0122)
PHONE..................................316 262-7200
Kyle Howard, *President*
Michael Page, *Chairman*
Colt Page, *Info Tech Mgr*
Mike Page, *Exec Dir*
Paula Page, *Admin Sec*
EMP: 10
SQ FT: 2,000
SALES (est): 2.3MM **Privately Held**
SIC: 1542 1521 Commercial & office building, new construction; commercial & office buildings, renovation & repair; single-family housing construction; single-family home remodeling, additions & repairs

(G-336)
PARKER PEST CONTROL INC
1002 Wirth St (67010-1444)
PHONE..................................316 524-4311
Larry Courtney, *President*
Tim Dahl, *Controller*
EMP: 16
SALES (est): 60K **Privately Held**
SIC: 7342 Pest control services

(G-337)
PATTERSON RACING INC
920 Industrial Rd (67010-9565)
P.O. Box 338 (67010-0338)
PHONE..................................316 775-7771
Alan Patterson, *President*
Todd Patterson, *Vice Pres*
Barbara Patterson, *Finance*
EMP: 10
SQ FT: 16,000
SALES (est): 2.2MM **Privately Held**
WEB: www.pattersonracing.com
SIC: 5013 7948 Automotive supplies & parts; race car drivers

(G-338)
PK SAFETY SERVICES INC
5351 Sw 100th St (67010-7707)
P.O. Box 336 (67010-0336)
PHONE..................................316 260-4141
Kevin Purpin, *CEO*
Kenny Purpin, *COO*
Brian Purpin, *CFO*
EMP: 75
SALES (est): 2.5MM **Privately Held**
SIC: 8999 Search & rescue service

(G-339)
PRO-KLEEN INC (PA)
Also Called: Pk Industrial Pk Industries
5351 Sw 100th St (67010-7707)
P.O. Box 336 (67010-0336)
PHONE..................................316 775-6898
Kevin Turpin, *President*
Kenny Turpin, *COO*
Brian Turpin, *CFO*
Brady Reed, *Manager*
EMP: 38 **EST:** 1997
SALES (est): 15.2MM **Privately Held**
WEB: www.prokleenindustries.com
SIC: 1799 3479 1721 Sandblasting of building exteriors; painting of metal products; industrial painting

(G-340)
PRO-KLEEN INC
Pk Industrial
10886 Sw Ohio Street Rd (67010-8403)
PHONE..................................316 253-7556
Brian Turpin, *Principal*
EMP: 14
SALES (corp-wide): 15.2MM **Privately Held**
SIC: 1799 Sandblasting of building exteriors
PA: Pro-Kleen, Inc.
5351 Sw 100th St
Augusta KS 67010
316 775-6898

(G-341)
RANDY JOHNSON
10426 Sw Eagle Rd (67010-7904)
P.O. Box 55 (67010-0055)
PHONE..................................316 775-6786
Randy Johnson, *Owner*
EMP: 10
SALES (est): 510K **Privately Held**
SIC: 1742 Drywall

(G-342)
SATCHELL CREEK EXPRESS INC
508 State St (67010-1108)
PHONE..................................316 775-1300
Susan Williams, *President*
EMP: 21
SALES (est): 2.3MM **Privately Held**
SIC: 4212 Local trucking, without storage

(G-343)
SECOND HAND ENTERPRISES INC
P.O. Box 780688, Wichita (67278-0688)
PHONE..................................316 775-7627
EMP: 18
SALES (est): 181.5K **Privately Held**
SIC: 7299 Misc Personal Services

(G-344)
SECURITY 1ST TITLE LLC
703 State St (67010-1111)
PHONE..................................316 260-5634
Angela Engels, *Branch Mgr*
EMP: 21 **Privately Held**
SIC: 6541 Title & trust companies
PA: Security 1st Title Llc
727 N Waco Ave Ste 300
Wichita KS 67203

(G-345)
SIGMA TEK INC (PA)
1001 Industrial Rd (67010-9500)
PHONE..................................316 775-6373
Harris Chandler, *President*
Randy Castleberry, *Exec VP*
Debbie Micgnius, *Purch Mgr*
David Baugher, *Electrical Engi*
Roxann Heit, *Human Res Mgr*
EMP: 40
SQ FT: 42,500
SALES (est): 7.8MM **Privately Held**
WEB: www.sigmatek.com
SIC: 3728 3812 Aircraft parts & equipment; search & navigation equipment

(G-346)
SOUTH CENTRAL MNTL HLTH CN
Also Called: Counseling Ctr For Butlr Cnty
520 E Augusta Ave (67010-2100)
PHONE..................................316 775-5491
Brad Base, *Manager*
EMP: 12
SALES (corp-wide): 1.9MM **Privately Held**
SIC: 8322 8069 Individual & family services; drug addiction rehabilitation hospital
PA: South Central Mental Health Counseling Center
524 N Main St
El Dorado KS 67042
316 321-6036

(G-347)
SOUTH WEST BUTLER QUARRY LLC
9423 Sw 165th St (67010-7833)
PHONE..................................316 775-1737
Daren Bannon,
Ronnie A Bannon,
EMP: 11
SQ FT: 250
SALES (est): 125K **Privately Held**
SIC: 1429 5032 Igneous rock, crushed & broken-quarrying; stone, crushed or broken

(G-348)
STM INC
Also Called: Seeber Thermoforming & Mfg
1000 Industrial Rd (67010-9510)
P.O. Box 38 (67010-0038)
PHONE..................................316 775-2223
Thomas Peterie, *President*
Brian Mattingly, *Plant Mgr*
▲ **EMP:** 25 **EST:** 1966
SQ FT: 35,000
SALES (est): 4.7MM **Privately Held**
WEB: www.botanicawatergardens.com
SIC: 3089 Molding primary plastic; injection molding of plastics; blow molded finished plastic products

(G-349)
TRIPLE J MACHINING LLC
204 E 5th Ave Ste C (67010-1012)
P.O. Box 146 (67010-0146)
PHONE..................................316 214-2414
Jason Rohr,
EMP: 11
SALES: 500K **Privately Held**
SIC: 1081 Metal mining services

Axtell
Marshall County

(G-350)
AXTELL TRUSS MANUFACTURING INC
2828 Pony Express Hwy (66403-9016)
P.O. Box 213 (66403-0213)
PHONE..................................785 736-2291
Brian Deters, *President*
Sharon Deters, *Corp Secy*
EMP: 9
SQ FT: 14,000
SALES (est): 1.1MM **Privately Held**
SIC: 2439 Trusses, wooden roof

(G-351)
NEMAHA-MARSHALL ELECTRIC
402 Prairie St (66403-9625)
P.O. Box O (66403-0235)
PHONE..................................785 736-2345
Kathleen A Brinker, *Manager*
EMP: 13 **EST:** 1938
SQ FT: 4,500
SALES: 6.5MM **Privately Held**
SIC: 4911 Distribution, electric power

Baldwin City
Douglas County

(G-352)
A & H AC & HTG INC
1717 College St (66006-4037)
PHONE..................................785 594-3357
Bill Harmon, *President*
Alan Wright, *Vice Pres*
EMP: 13
SALES (est): 2.6MM **Privately Held**
WEB: www.ah-air.com
SIC: 1711 Warm air heating & air conditioning contractor

(G-353)
AMERICAN DESIGN INC (PA)
1015 Firetree Ave (66006-4173)
P.O. Box 935 (66006-0935)
PHONE..................................785 766-0409
Darren Othick, *President*
Meghan Othick, *Vice Pres*
EMP: 10

▲ = Import ▼=Export
◆ =Import/Export

SALES: 185K **Privately Held**
SIC: 7374 Data processing & preparation

(G-354)
APPLIED ECOLOGICAL SVCS INC
224 E 1260th Rd (66006-8240)
PHONE..................................785 594-2245
Steve Applebaum, *Branch Mgr*
EMP: 18
SALES (corp-wide): 26.8MM **Privately Held**
SIC: 8748 Environmental consultant
PA: Applied Ecological Services, Inc.
17921 W Smith Rd
Brodhead WI 53520
608 897-8641

(G-355)
BALDWIN STATE BANK
721 High St (66006-3015)
P.O. Box 46 (66006-0046)
PHONE..................................785 594-6421
Donald O Nutt, *Ch of Bd*
Ivan Huntoon, *COO*
Jay Randels, *Vice Pres*
Bryan Butel, *Manager*
Brent Sherwood, *Administration*
EMP: 20 **EST:** 1892
SQ FT: 6,000
SALES: 2.9MM **Privately Held**
WEB: www.baldwinstatebank.com
SIC: 6022 State commercial banks

(G-356)
BLACK JACK TREE LAWN AND LDSCP
311 Baker St (66006-3084)
PHONE..................................785 865-8536
David Cavender, *President*
EMP: 5
SALES: 240K **Privately Held**
SIC: 2411 Logging

(G-357)
COMMUNITY LVING OPPRTNTIES INC
2084 N 600 Rd Unit B (66006-7264)
PHONE..................................785 979-1889
EMP: 28
SALES (corp-wide): 22.5MM **Privately Held**
SIC: 8361 Home for the mentally handicapped
PA: Community Living Opportunities, Inc.
11627 W 79th St
Lenexa KS 66214
913 341-9316

(G-358)
CUSTOM MOBILE EQUIPMENT INC
439 E High St (66006-3071)
PHONE..................................785 594-7475
Gary Dick, *President*
▲ **EMP:** 24
SQ FT: 21,000
SALES (est): 12.7MM **Privately Held**
WEB: www.versa-lift.com
SIC: 5084 Industrial machine parts; materials handling machinery

(G-359)
EAC AUDIT INC
Rr 3 (66006)
PHONE..................................785 594-6707
Ronald Haskey, *President*
Janet Haskey, *Corp Secy*
EMP: 10
SQ FT: 1,500
SALES (est): 757.1K **Privately Held**
SIC: 8742 8748 Banking & finance consultant; environmental consultant

(G-360)
FINCH SIGN COMPANY INC
1459 N 300th Rd (66006-7225)
P.O. Box 528 (66006-0528)
PHONE..................................785 423-3213
Charles Duane Finch, *President*
Melaine Finch, *Vice Pres*
EMP: 6
SALES: 180K **Privately Held**
SIC: 3993 1799 Signs & advertising specialties; sign installation & maintenance

(G-361)
FRONTIER FARM CREDIT
1270 N 300th Rd (66006-7223)
PHONE..................................785 594-2900
Bob Rhoton, *Branch Mgr*
Aaron Lueger, *Officer*
EMP: 17
SALES (corp-wide): 12.1MM **Privately Held**
SIC: 0191 General farms, primarily crop
PA: Frontier Farm Credit
9370 E Us Highway 24
Manhattan KS
785 776-6931

(G-362)
GENESIS HEALTHCARE CORPORATION
1223 Orchard Ln (66006-4011)
PHONE..................................785 594-6492
EMP: 10 **Publicly Held**
SIC: 8051 Skilled nursing care facilities
HQ: Genesis Healthcare Corporation
101 E State St
Kennett Square PA 19348
610 444-6350

(G-363)
HERITAGE TRACTOR INC (PA)
Also Called: John Deere Authorized Dealer
915 Industrial Park Rd (66006)
PHONE..................................785 594-6486
Ken Wagner, *CEO*
Tim Deneke, *Vice Pres*
Kevin Harper, *Vice Pres*
Jeremy Knuth, *Vice Pres*
Darren Zerr, *Vice Pres*
▲ **EMP:** 83
SQ FT: 32,000
SALES (est): 66.3MM **Privately Held**
WEB: www.heritagetractor.com
SIC: 5083 Farm & garden machinery

(G-364)
HOWARD STULTZ CONSTRUCTION
983 E 1700 Rd (66006-7353)
PHONE..................................785 842-4796
Howard Stultz, *Owner*
Stephen Mazza, *Professor*
Taylor Larue, *Internal Med*
EMP: 15
SALES: 850K **Privately Held**
SIC: 1742 Drywall

(G-365)
LODGE
502 Ames St (66006-5089)
PHONE..................................785 594-0574
Ted Madl, *Owner*
EMP: 15
SALES (est): 676.1K **Privately Held**
SIC: 7011 Motels

(G-366)
MCFARLANE AVIATION INC
Also Called: McFarlane Aviation Products
696 E 1700 Rd (66006-7351)
PHONE..................................785 594-2741
David McFarlane, *President*
Cheryl Kurtz, *Treasurer*
Daniel McFarlane, *Admin Sec*
EMP: 62
SQ FT: 25,866
SALES (est): 13.7MM **Privately Held**
WEB: www.mcfarlaneaviation.com
SIC: 3728 5088 Aircraft parts & equipment; transportation equipment & supplies

(G-367)
RICE PRECISION MFG INC
401 E High St (66006-3071)
PHONE..................................785 594-2670
Bryan Rice, *President*
EMP: 22
SALES (est): 776.2K **Privately Held**
SIC: 3599 0723 1761 1799 Custom machinery; feed milling custom services; flour milling custom services; grain milling, custom services; architectural sheet metal work; sheet metalwork; welding on site; consulting engineer

(G-368)
SANTA FE MARKET INC
309 Ames St (66006-3001)
PHONE..................................785 594-7466
EMP: 10
SALES (est): 1.2MM **Privately Held**
SIC: 5411 7513 Ret Groceries Truck Rental/Leasing

(G-369)
VINLAND AERODROME INC
696 E 1700 Rd (66006-7351)
PHONE..................................785 594-2741
David McFarlane, *President*
Cheryl McFarlane, *Treasurer*
Phyllis McFarlane, *Admin Sec*
EMP: 5
SALES (est): 366.1K **Privately Held**
SIC: 3728 Aircraft parts & equipment

Bartlett
Labette County

(G-370)
1ST DUE ER RESPONSE SOLUTNS LL
Also Called: 1st Due E.R.S.
1728 7000 Rd (67332-9305)
PHONE..................................620 226-3566
Leighton Davis, *CFO*
Denise Davis,
EMP: 10
SALES: 840K **Privately Held**
SIC: 7389 Fire protection service other than forestry or public

(G-371)
BARTLETT COOPERATIVE ASSN (PA)
4th Main St (67332)
PHONE..................................620 226-3311
Kit Houston, *President*
EMP: 38 **EST:** 1950
SQ FT: 2,000
SALES: 67MM **Privately Held**
SIC: 5153 5191 5171 5541 Grain elevators; farm supplies; feed; fertilizer & fertilizer materials; chemicals, agricultural; petroleum bulk stations; gasoline service stations

Basehor
Leavenworth County

(G-372)
ANGEL LITTLE LEARNING CTR INC
Also Called: LITTLE ANGEL CHRISTIAN CENTER
1206 N 155th St (66007-9389)
PHONE..................................913 724-4442
David Delladio, *President*
EMP: 22
SALES: 826.2K **Privately Held**
SIC: 8351 Group day care center

(G-373)
COMMUNITY NATIONAL BANK
15718 Pinehurst Dr (66007-8228)
P.O. Box 437 (66007-0437)
PHONE..................................913 724-9901
Debbie Adair, *Vice Pres*
Jamie Smith, *Vice Pres*
David Haverkamp, *Marketing Staff*
Steve Kettler, *Branch Mgr*
EMP: 10
SALES (corp-wide): 21.4MM **Privately Held**
WEB: www.communitynationalbank.net
SIC: 6021 National commercial banks
PA: Community National Bank
210 Main St
Seneca KS 66538
785 336-6143

(G-374)
EARL BRYANT ENTERPRISES INC
Also Called: Earl, Bryant Heating & AC
15280 Briar Rd (66007-5141)
PHONE..................................913 724-4100
David Bryant, *President*
Eileen Bryant, *Treasurer*
Donna Bryant, *Admin Sec*
EMP: 12
SQ FT: 7,000
SALES (est): 2.6MM **Privately Held**
SIC: 1711 Warm air heating & air conditioning contractor

(G-375)
ELITE ELECTRIC INC
2211 N 145th Ter (66007-5197)
P.O. Box 368 (66007-0368)
PHONE..................................913 724-1645
Marshall Hockersmith, *President*
Shawn Stevens, *Treasurer*
EMP: 40 **EST:** 1996
SQ FT: 5,600
SALES (est): 3.9MM **Privately Held**
WEB: www.eliteelectrickc.com
SIC: 1731 General electrical contractor

(G-376)
FALCON LAKES GOLF LLC
4605 Clubhouse Dr (66007-9100)
PHONE..................................913 724-4653
Dean Ralston, *Manager*
Dan Baker, *Business Dir*
EMP: 40
SALES (est): 1.8MM **Privately Held**
SIC: 7992 5812 Public golf courses; eating places

(G-377)
FALCON LAKES MAINTENANCE
Also Called: Falcon Golf Management
14011 Hollingsworth Rd (66007-3083)
PHONE..................................913 724-4460
Ruston Ferzandi, *Owner*
EMP: 50
SALES (est): 1.1MM **Privately Held**
SIC: 7992 Public golf courses

(G-378)
FIRST STATE BANK & TRUST
15506 Pinehurst Dr (66007-3402)
PHONE..................................913 724-2121
A Kaminski Ashley Crane, *Manager*
Deanne Schurer, *Retailers*
EMP: 13 **Privately Held**
WEB: www.firststateks.com
SIC: 6022 State trust companies accepting deposits, commercial
HQ: First State Bank & Trust
400 S Bury St
Tonganoxie KS 66086
913 845-2500

(G-379)
INTEGRATED BEHAVIORAL TECH INC
Also Called: NON PROFIT
1106 N 155th St Ste B (66007-7100)
P.O. Box 252, Tonganoxie (66086-0252)
PHONE..................................913 662-7071
Linda H Powell, *President*
Christopher Powell, *CFO*
Linda Heitzman-Powell, *Train & Dev Mgr*
Paige Boydston, *Consultant*
Ali Heidebrecht, *Consultant*
EMP: 70
SALES: 1.3MM **Privately Held**
SIC: 8093 8082 8351 Mental health clinic, outpatient; home health care services; child day care services

(G-380)
INTEGRATED BEHAVIORAL TECH INC
Also Called: For Profit
1106 N 155th St (66007-7100)
PHONE..................................913 662-7071
Edna Heitzman, *General Mgr*
Linda Heitzman-Powell, *Exec Dir*
EMP: 20
SALES (est): 590K **Privately Held**
SIC: 8082 8093 Home health care services; mental health clinic, outpatient

(G-381)
JED INSTALLATION LLC
2722 N 155th St (66007-9253)
PHONE.................................913 724-4600
Dennis Mertz, *Mng Member*
Joe Parizek,
EMP: 20 **EST:** 2000
SQ FT: 2,500
SALES: 820K **Privately Held**
WEB: www.jedinstallation.com
SIC: 1799 Office furniture installation

(G-382)
K C CONSTRUCTION INC
1211 158th St (66007-7344)
P.O. Box 264 (66007-0264)
PHONE.................................913 724-1474
David K Breuer, *President*
Cheryl Breuer, *Treasurer*
Todd Breuer, *Admin Sec*
EMP: 18
SQ FT: 6,400
SALES (est): 3.1MM **Privately Held**
SIC: 1623 Underground utilities contractor

(G-383)
KIWANIS INTERNATIONAL INC
3707 N 155th St (66007-9205)
PHONE.................................913 724-1120
John Klinkenbert, *Owner*
EMP: 14
SALES (corp-wide): 23.6MM **Privately Held**
WEB: www.kfne.org
SIC: 8641 Civic associations
PA: Kiwanis International, Inc.
3636 Woodview Trce
Indianapolis IN 46268
317 875-8755

(G-384)
MILES EXCAVATING INC
15063 State Ave (66007-3024)
P.O. Box 458 (66007-0458)
PHONE.................................913 724-1934
Steve M Miles, *President*
Darla Miles, *Corp Secy*
EMP: 180
SQ FT: 1,200
SALES: 27.2MM **Privately Held**
SIC: 1794 1611 1771 Excavation & grading, building construction; general contractor, highway & street construction; concrete work

(G-385)
ORSCHELN FARM AND HOME LLC
Also Called: Orscheln Farm Home
15256 Wolfcreek Pkwy (66007-6221)
PHONE.................................913 728-2014
Steve Collins, *Branch Mgr*
EMP: 26
SALES (corp-wide): 822.7MM **Privately Held**
SIC: 5191 Farm supplies
PA: Orscheln Farm And Home Llc
1800 Overcenter Dr
Moberly MO 65270
800 577-2580

(G-386)
OTL LOGISTICS INC
14500 Parallel Rd Ste A (66007-3001)
P.O. Box 4 (66007-0004)
PHONE.................................816 918-7688
David O'Bryan, *President*
EMP: 60
SQ FT: 1,500
SALES (est): 891.2K **Privately Held**
SIC: 7513 4119 Truck leasing, without drivers; local passenger transportation

(G-387)
REECE & NICHOLS REALTORS INC
Also Called: Reece & Nichols Premier Realty
15510 State Ave Ste 7 (66007-7102)
PHONE.................................913 351-5600
Shirley Keller, *Manager*
EMP: 34
SALES (corp-wide): 225.3B **Publicly Held**
WEB: www.reece-nichols.com
SIC: 6531 Real estate brokers & agents
HQ: Reece & Nichols Realtors, Inc.
11601 Granada St
Leawood KS 66211
913 491-1001

(G-388)
RON STIERLY FLOOR SERVICES
14428 Parallel Rd (66007-3005)
P.O. Box 376 (66007-0376)
PHONE.................................913 724-4822
Ron Stierly, *President*
EMP: 10
SQ FT: 3,600
SALES (est): 729K **Privately Held**
SIC: 1752 Wood floor installation & refinishing

(G-389)
STEPPING STONES DAY CARE CTR
15515 Elm St (66007-9211)
PHONE.................................913 724-7700
Cindy Harvey, *Owner*
EMP: 10
SALES (est): 223.9K **Privately Held**
SIC: 8351 Child day care services

(G-390)
VEE VILLAGE PARTS INC (PA)
15145 Sweetbriar Dr (66007-3029)
PHONE.................................816 421-6441
Thomas Athon, *President*
Dennis Melvin, *Vice Pres*
EMP: 10
SALES (est): 2.4MM **Privately Held**
WEB: www.veevillage.com
SIC: 5531 7538 7539 5013 Automotive parts; general automotive repair shops; brake services; automotive supplies & parts

(G-391)
WHITE WILLIAM & SONS CNSTR CO
15427 Stoneridge Dr (66007-5247)
PHONE.................................913 375-9161
Pleda White, *President*
Gary White, *Vice Pres*
James White, *Treasurer*
EMP: 60
SQ FT: 5,000
SALES (est): 3.9MM **Privately Held**
SIC: 1771 Concrete work

Baxter Springs
Cherokee County

(G-392)
AMERICA CARE QUAKER HILL MANOR
8675 Se 72nd Ter (66713-3186)
PHONE.................................620 848-3797
Michael Hammond, *Administration*
EMP: 47
SALES (est): 2.6MM **Privately Held**
SIC: 8051 Skilled nursing care facilities

(G-393)
AMERICAN BANK BAXTER SPRINGS (HQ)
1201 Military Ave (66713-2739)
P.O. Box 597 (66713-0597)
PHONE.................................620 856-2301
Joyce Cure, *President*
Mandy Hudson, *Vice Pres*
Rosanne Suckley, *Officer*
EMP: 15 **EST:** 1917
SQ FT: 9,375
SALES: 3.6MM
SALES (corp-wide): 3.3MM **Privately Held**
WEB: www.americanbank.com
SIC: 6022 State commercial banks
PA: American Bancshares, Inc.
1201 Military Ave
Baxter Springs KS 66713
620 856-2301

(G-394)
ATEC STEEL LLC
Also Called: Atec Steel Fabrication & Cnstr
1000 W 5th St (66713-2545)
PHONE.................................877 457-5352
Rick Clifton, *Vice Pres*
Joshua Tippit, *Project Mgr*
Jeff Schroeder, *Foreman/Supr*
Cindy Dunnic, *Purchasing*
Eric Malone, *Engineer*
EMP: 140
SQ FT: 10,000
SALES (est): 56.7MM **Privately Held**
WEB: www.atecsteel.com
SIC: 3795 Tanks & tank components

(G-395)
BAGCRAFTPAPERCON I LLC
3400 Bagcraft Blvd (66713-2964)
PHONE.................................620 856-4615
Jim Jaroszski, *Branch Mgr*
Tony Pendleton, *Manager*
Gary Burr, *Director*
EMP: 200
SALES (corp-wide): 2.9B **Privately Held**
WEB: www.packaging-dynamics.com
SIC: 2671 2674 2673 5162 Packaging paper & plastics film, coated & laminated; paper bags: made from purchased materials; bags: plastic, laminated & coated; plastics materials; coated & laminated paper
HQ: Bagcraftpapercon I, Llc
3900 W 43rd St
Chicago IL 60632
620 856-2800

(G-396)
BAXTER DRUG INC
1000 Military Ave (66713-1547)
PHONE.................................620 856-5858
Terry L Martin, *President*
EMP: 5
SQ FT: 2,500
SALES (est): 550.2K **Privately Held**
SIC: 2834 Pharmaceutical preparations

(G-397)
BAXTER STATE BANK (PA)
1401 Military Ave (66713-2799)
P.O. Box 71 (66713-0071)
PHONE.................................620 856-2323
Jim Hoskins, *CEO*
EMP: 15
SQ FT: 20,000
SALES: 1.3MM **Privately Held**
WEB: www.baxterstatebank.com
SIC: 6022 State commercial banks

(G-398)
BAXTER VAULT COMPANY INC
1325 Grant Ave (66713-1930)
P.O. Box 508 (66713-0508)
PHONE.................................620 856-3441
George Moss, *President*
Lonnie Allen, *Corp Secy*
Betty Moss, *Office Mgr*
EMP: 11
SQ FT: 20,000
SALES (est): 1.6MM **Privately Held**
SIC: 8748 Business consulting

(G-399)
BLAYLOCK DIESEL SERVICE INC
Also Called: Blaylock Turbo
3100 Military Ave (66713)
PHONE.................................620 856-5227
Jim Blaylock, *President*
Diana Blaylock, *Treasurer*
▲ **EMP:** 10
SQ FT: 17,500
SALES (est): 1.4MM **Privately Held**
WEB: www.blaylock-turbo.com
SIC: 3714 5531 Motor vehicle parts & accessories; automotive parts

(G-400)
BRAD CARSON (PA)
Also Called: Autumn Place
120 Aaron Ln (66713-1298)
PHONE.................................620 856-3999
Brad Carson, *Owner*
EMP: 13
SQ FT: 55,000
SALES (est): 1MM **Privately Held**
SIC: 8361 Home for the aged

(G-401)
BROCK MAGGARD
Also Called: Players Choice Mounds
2011 Fairview Ave (66713-2264)
PHONE.................................417 793-7790
Brock Maggard, *Owner*
EMP: 10
SALES: 700K **Privately Held**
SIC: 5941 7389 Sporting goods & bicycle shops;

(G-402)
CHEROKEE COUNTY AMBULANCE
311 Military Ave (66713-1258)
P.O. Box 137 (66713-0137)
PHONE.................................620 856-2561
Wilfredo Diaz, *Principal*
EMP: 15
SQ FT: 4,800
SALES (est): 709.8K **Privately Held**
WEB: www.cherokeecounty-ks.gov
SIC: 4119 Ambulance service

(G-403)
COMMUNITY HEALTH CENTER OF SOU
2990 Military Ave (66713-2331)
PHONE.................................620 856-2900
Douglas Stuckey, *Branch Mgr*
EMP: 12
SALES (corp-wide): 25MM **Privately Held**
SIC: 8021 Dental clinic
PA: Community Health Center Of Southeast Kansas, Inc.
3011 N Michigan St
Pittsburg KS 66762
620 231-9873

(G-404)
DIVERSIFIED SPORTS TECH LLC
Also Called: Pro Ice
140 E 10th St (66713-1519)
PHONE.................................949 466-2393
Dan Greenberg,
◆ **EMP:** 9 **EST:** 2009
SALES (est): 304.7K **Privately Held**
SIC: 7941 2834 Sports clubs, managers & promoters; medicines, capsuled or ampuled

(G-405)
EMPIRE DISTRICT ELECTRIC CO
905 Ottawa Ave (66713-1445)
PHONE.................................620 856-2121
Ann Butts, *Manager*
EMP: 15
SALES (corp-wide): 1.6B **Privately Held**
WEB: www.empiredistrict.com
SIC: 4911 Distribution, electric power
HQ: The Empire District Electric Company
602 S Joplin Ave
Joplin MO 64801
417 625-5100

(G-406)
FARMERS COOPERATIVE ASSN
10th & Railroad (66713)
PHONE.................................620 856-2365
Steve Scott, *Manager*
EMP: 14
SALES (corp-wide): 40MM **Privately Held**
SIC: 5153 Grain elevators
PA: Farmers Cooperative Association Inc
402 E Country Rd
Columbus KS 66725
620 429-2296

(G-407)
FILE A GEM INC
120 W 11th St (66713-1508)
P.O. Box 138 (66713-0138)
PHONE.................................620 856-3800
Bob D Sirratt, *President*
Doris Sirratt, *Vice Pres*
EMP: 9
SQ FT: 1,000

▲ = Import ▼=Export
◆ =Import/Export

SALES (est): 1.1MM Privately Held
SIC: 3993 5944 Displays & cutouts, window & lobby; jewelry stores

(G-408)
HELPING HANDS SERVICES-KANSAS
1001 Grant Ave (66713-1534)
PHONE....................417 438-6102
James R Case, *President*
EMP: 50
SQ FT: 4,000
SALES (est): 719.2K Privately Held
SIC: 7349 Cleaning service, industrial or commercial

(G-409)
HUTCHINSON SALT COMPANY INC
136 W 12th St (66713-2732)
PHONE....................620 856-3332
Marilyn Taber, *Branch Mgr*
EMP: 6
SALES (corp-wide): 6MM Privately Held
SIC: 2899 Salt
PA: Hutchinson Salt Company, Inc.
40 Sw Grove Rd
Baxter Springs KS 66713
620 662-3345

(G-410)
JIM WOODS MARKETING INC
2308 Sunset Ave (66713-2341)
P.O. Box 108 (66713-0108)
PHONE....................620 856-3554
Jim Woods, *Chairman*
M Theresia Forgey, *Corp Secy*
EMP: 16
SQ FT: 15,000
SALES (est): 11.7MM Privately Held
SIC: 5171 5541 Petroleum bulk stations; gasoline service stations

(G-411)
PRIDE AMUSEMENTS LLC
1202 W 12th St (66713-1905)
P.O. Box 128, Galena (66739-0128)
PHONE....................417 529-3810
Andrew Burlingame, *Owner*
Betty Burlingame, *Co-Owner*
EMP: 20
SALES (est): 347.7K Privately Held
SIC: 7999 Amusement ride

(G-412)
SHARON MILLER
Also Called: H & R Block
2321 Military Ave (66713-2324)
PHONE....................620 856-3377
Sharon Miller, *Owner*
EMP: 10
SALES (est): 275.1K Privately Held
SIC: 7291 Tax return preparation services

(G-413)
SHOW ME BIRDS HUNTING RESORT
2400 Quaker Rd (66713-4120)
PHONE....................620 674-8863
Kim Shira, *Owner*
EMP: 12
SALES (est): 750K Privately Held
WEB: www.showmebirds.com
SIC: 0971 7032 7011 Hunting services; hunting camp; resort hotel

(G-414)
STAR LUBE AUTO EX CARE INC
1510 Military Ave (66713-2721)
PHONE....................620 856-4281
Artheu Martin, *CEO*
EMP: 13
SQ FT: 5,000
SALES: 1.1MM Privately Held
SIC: 7538 General automotive repair shops

(G-415)
WILLIAMS DIVERSIFIED MTLS INC
2903 Military Ave (66713-2356)
P.O. Box 660 (66713-0660)
PHONE....................620 679-9810
Larry Bingham, *President*
EMP: 25 EST: 1950
SQ FT: 20,000
SALES (est): 6.2MM Privately Held
SIC: 5032 Sand, construction; gravel

(G-416)
YRC INC
Also Called: Yellow Transportation
2600 Powell Rd (66713-2362)
P.O. Box 638 (66713-0638)
PHONE....................620 856-2161
Susan Carter, *Finance Spvr*
Tom Budimlija, *Manager*
EMP: 325
SALES (corp-wide): 5B Publicly Held
WEB: www.roadway.com
SIC: 4213 Contract haulers
HQ: Yrc Inc.
10990 Roe Ave
Overland Park KS 66211
913 696-6100

Beattie
Marshall County

(G-417)
ANNA M KRAMER
2014 Granite Rd (66406-8634)
PHONE....................785 353-2205
Anna Kramer, *Owner*
EMP: 8 EST: 2015
SALES (est): 88.7K Privately Held
SIC: 7692 Welding repair

(G-418)
BEATTIE FARMERS UN COOP ASSN (PA)
203 Hamilton St (66406)
P.O. Box 79 (66406-0079)
PHONE....................785 353-2237
Larry Preuss, *General Mgr*
Ralph Suther, *Chairman*
Steve Moser, *Vice Pres*
John D Dummermuth, *Director*
John Fangman, *Director*
EMP: 42 EST: 1915
SQ FT: 3,000
SALES (est): 48.3MM Privately Held
SIC: 5153 5191 Grains; grain elevators; farm supplies; feed

(G-419)
SMART TRUCK LINE INC
511 Hamilton St (66406-9770)
P.O. Box 95 (66406-0095)
PHONE....................785 353-2411
David Byers, *President*
Kathi Byers, *Corp Secy*
EMP: 15
SQ FT: 1,200
SALES (est): 2.3MM Privately Held
SIC: 4213 Contract haulers

(G-420)
STUDER TRUCK LINE INC
309 Center St (66406)
P.O. Box 37 (66406-0037)
PHONE....................785 353-2241
Paul Studer, *President*
EMP: 10 EST: 1935
SQ FT: 1,200
SALES (est): 450K Privately Held
SIC: 4212 4213 Petroleum haulage, local; trucking, except local

(G-421)
TWIN VLY DVELOPMENTAL SVCS INC
307 Whiting St (66406-9742)
PHONE....................785 353-2347
Frances Richard, *Manager*
EMP: 30
SALES (corp-wide): 4.8MM Privately Held
SIC: 8361 Group foster home
PA: Twin Valley Developmental Services, Inc.
413 Commercial St
Greenleaf KS 66943
785 747-2611

(G-422)
TWIN VLY DVELOPMENTAL SVCS INC
Also Called: Twin Valley Dev Srvs
811 Oak St (66406-8646)
P.O. Box 63 (66406-0063)
PHONE....................785 353-2347
Frances Richards, *Manager*
EMP: 30
SALES (corp-wide): 4.8MM Privately Held
SIC: 8361 Group foster home
PA: Twin Valley Developmental Services, Inc.
413 Commercial St
Greenleaf KS 66943
785 747-2611

(G-423)
TWIN VLY DVELOPMENTAL SVCS INC
1109 Main St (66406-9747)
PHONE....................785 353-2226
Francis Richards, *Manager*
EMP: 11
SALES (corp-wide): 4.8MM Privately Held
SIC: 8361 Group foster home
PA: Twin Valley Developmental Services, Inc.
413 Commercial St
Greenleaf KS 66943
785 747-2611

Beaver
Barton County

(G-424)
BEAVER GRAIN CORPORATION INC (PA)
1905 Main St (67525-9229)
PHONE....................620 587-3417
N R Weber, *President*
Steve Major, *General Mgr*
EMP: 18 EST: 1958
SQ FT: 1,200
SALES (est): 1.5MM Privately Held
SIC: 4221 5191 Grain elevator, storage only; fertilizer & fertilizer materials; feed

Bel Aire
Sedgwick County

(G-425)
ACCEL CONSTRUCTION LLC
4015 N Woodlawn Ct Ste 1 (67220-3877)
PHONE....................316 866-2885
Doug Bird, *Project Mgr*
Tony Caputo,
Karen Nielsen, *Admin Asst*
W L Shafer,
EMP: 25
SQ FT: 2,000
SALES: 20.5MM Privately Held
SIC: 1542 Commercial & office building, new construction

(G-426)
ADVANCE CATASTROPHE TECH INC
Also Called: Advanced Catastrophe Tech
3835 N Hillcrest St Ste 4 (67220-3879)
PHONE....................316 262-9992
Christian Wiley, *President*
Keith Mesler, *Director*
Brad Squires, *Director*
EMP: 25
SQ FT: 9,000
SALES (est): 2.7MM
SALES (corp-wide): 3.8MM Privately Held
WEB: www.cwcon.net
SIC: 8322 Disaster service
PA: Cwc Inc
3835 N Hillcrest St Ste 4
Bel Aire KS 67220
888 747-1515

(G-427)
ADVANCED TECHNOLOGIES INC
4278 Westlake Dr (67220-1752)
PHONE....................316 744-2285
Skip Nelson, *CEO*
Sharonlyn Nelson, *President*
Brian Sundberg, *Treasurer*
◆ EMP: 5
SQ FT: 900
SALES: 500K Privately Held
WEB: www.ati-inc.net
SIC: 3641 3645 3646 3648 Electric lamps; residential lighting fixtures; commercial indusl & institutional electric lighting fixtures; lighting equipment

(G-428)
CATHOLIC CARE CENTER INC
6700 E 45th St N (67226-8817)
PHONE....................316 744-8651
Courtney Wolfe, *President*
Thomas Church, *Principal*
Laurel Alkire, *Principal*
Gerard Brungardt, *Principal*
Joan Felts, *Principal*
EMP: 256
SQ FT: 186,500
SALES: 23.2MM
SALES (corp-wide): 45.5MM Privately Held
WEB: www.cdowk.org
SIC: 8051 Convalescent home with continuous nursing care
PA: Catholic Diocese Of Wichita Inc
424 N Broadway Ave
Wichita KS 67202
316 269-3900

(G-429)
CATHOLIC DIOCESE OF WICHITA
Catholic Care Center
6700 E 45th St N (67226-8817)
PHONE....................316 744-2020
Theresa Knoff, *Manager*
EMP: 350
SALES (corp-wide): 45.5MM Privately Held
WEB: www.cdowk.org
SIC: 8051 Convalescent home with continuous nursing care
PA: Catholic Diocese Of Wichita Inc
424 N Broadway Ave
Wichita KS 67202
316 269-3900

(G-430)
CENTURY MANUFACTURING INC
9750 E 50th St N (67226-8804)
PHONE....................316 636-5423
James V Laubach, *Ch of Bd*
Gary Kemnitz, *President*
Sharon Laubach, *Corp Secy*
▲ EMP: 200
SALES (est): 26.5MM Privately Held
WEB: www.centurymfg.com
SIC: 3089 Novelties, plastic

(G-431)
CREATIVE DESIGN TS INC
3835 N Hillcrest St Ste 2 (67220-3879)
PHONE....................316 681-1868
Anne Wille, *President*
Janelle Caylor, *Sales Staff*
EMP: 10
SQ FT: 2,500
SALES (est): 1.3MM Privately Held
WEB: www.creativedesigntees.com
SIC: 2759 Screen printing

(G-432)
EPIC SPORTS
9750 E 53rd St N (67226-8718)
PHONE....................316 612-0150
Gary Proctor, *President*
Ron Knackstedt, *Warehouse Mgr*
Tiffany Lesperance, *Purch Agent*
Cody Patton, *Office Mgr*
William Davis, *Prgrmr*
◆ EMP: 120
SQ FT: 170,000

SALES: 47.2MM **Privately Held**
WEB: www.epicsoccer.com
SIC: 5941 5699 3949 5611 Playground equipment; customized clothing & apparel; team sports equipment; clothing, sportswear, men's & boys'

(G-433)
GOLDEN KEY SALON
4023 Clarendon St (67220-1905)
PHONE..................................316 744-0230
Cynthia Biggs, *Owner*
EMP: 10
SALES (est): 220K **Privately Held**
SIC: 7231 Unisex hair salons

(G-434)
GRANITE TRNSFRMTION WCHITA LLC
6254 E 37th St N Ste 130 (67220-2054)
P.O. Box 28, Kechi (67067-0028)
PHONE..................................316 681-1900
Darrin Murray,
Clay Morris,
EMP: 11
SALES (est): 962.8K **Privately Held**
SIC: 1799 Counter top installation

(G-435)
HEARTLAND ANIMAL HOSPITAL
4100 N Woodlawn Blvd (67220-3846)
PHONE..................................316 744-8160
Gary Breault, *Owner*
EMP: 12
SQ FT: 3,200
SALES (est): 641.4K **Privately Held**
SIC: 0742 Animal hospital services, pets & other animal specialties

(G-436)
MSI AUTOMATION INC
4065 N Woodlawn Ct Ste 4 (67220-3871)
PHONE..................................316 681-3566
Dave Brinkerhoff, *President*
EMP: 10
SQ FT: 10,000
SALES (est): 1.7MM **Privately Held**
WEB: www.msiautomation.com
SIC: 3567 3545 8733 Induction heating equipment; calipers & dividers; machine tool attachments & accessories; medical research

(G-437)
OTIS ELEVATOR COMPANY
3979 N Woodlawn Ct Ste 1 (67220-1996)
PHONE..................................316 682-6886
Ben Boeson, *Manager*
EMP: 15
SALES (corp-wide): 66.5B **Publicly Held**
WEB: www.otis.com
SIC: 5084 1796 Elevators; elevator installation & conversion
HQ: Otis Elevator Company
1 Carrier Pl
Farmington CT 06032
860 674-3000

(G-438)
PPG INDUSTRIES INC
Also Called: PPG 4631
6334 Crestmark St (67220-3868)
PHONE..................................316 262-2456
Kerry Albrechik, *Branch Mgr*
EMP: 24
SALES (corp-wide): 15.3B **Publicly Held**
WEB: www.ppg.com
SIC: 2851 Paints & allied products
PA: Ppg Industries, Inc.
1 Ppg Pl
Pittsburgh PA 15272
412 434-3131

(G-439)
RETAIL SERVICES WIS CORP
4065 N Woodlawn Ct Ste 1 (67220-3871)
PHONE..................................316 683-3289
Jeff Hunter, *Branch Mgr*
EMP: 40
SQ FT: 500
SALES (corp-wide): 69.5MM **Privately Held**
WEB: www.wisusa.com
SIC: 7389 Inventory computing service
HQ: Retail Services Wis Corporation
9265 Sky Park Ct Ste 100
San Diego CA 92123
858 565-8111

(G-440)
SOUTH CENTRAL KANSAS
Also Called: Sckedd
9730 E 50th St N (67226-8804)
PHONE..................................316 262-7035
Sherdeill Breathett, *President*
Cheryl Adelhardt, *Principal*
Ronald Hirst, *Principal*
Daniel Bass, *Controller*
EMP: 30
SALES: 2.9MM **Privately Held**
SIC: 8748 Economic consultant

(G-441)
TOTAL INSTALLATION MANAGEMENT
3919 N Hillcrest St Ste 2 (67220-3881)
P.O. Box 780471, Wichita (67278-0471)
PHONE..................................316 267-0584
Timothy L Bishop, *President*
Kim Bishop, *Corp Secy*
Mabry Morrison, *Accounts Mgr*
David Di Marino, *Consultant*
EMP: 12
SQ FT: 12,000
SALES (est): 1.6MM **Privately Held**
WEB: www.totalinstallation.biz
SIC: 1799 Office furniture installation

(G-442)
UFCW DISTRICT UNION LOCAL 2 (PA)
3951 N Woodlawn Ct (67220-1991)
PHONE..................................816 842-4086
Tom Price, *President*
EMP: 20
SQ FT: 3,000
SALES: 7.4MM **Privately Held**
SIC: 8631 Labor union

(G-443)
WICHITA CHAPTER OF LINKS INC
4819 N Harding St (67220-1437)
P.O. Box 8843, Wichita (67208-0843)
PHONE..................................316 744-7873
EMP: 12
SALES: 161.4K **Privately Held**
SIC: 8641 Civic associations

(G-444)
WICHITA HOOPS LLC
5260 N Toler Dr (67226-6632)
PHONE..................................316 440-4990
Justin Jarman, *General Mgr*
EMP: 10 **EST:** 2014
SALES (est): 368.1K **Privately Held**
SIC: 7941 Basketball club

Belle Plaine
Sumner County

(G-445)
CURB APPEAL OF KANSAS INC
402 N Merchant St (67013-9104)
PHONE..................................620 488-5214
Marrk Calbeck, *President*
EMP: 30 **EST:** 2010
SALES (est): 1.1MM **Privately Held**
SIC: 5039 Exterior flat glass: plate or window

(G-446)
FORMING SPECIALISTS INC
631 Industrial Park Rd (67013-8527)
P.O. Box 548 (67013-0548)
PHONE..................................620 488-3243
Becky J Wilson, *President*
Terrance Wilson, *Treasurer*
EMP: 5
SQ FT: 18,000
SALES (est): 574.7K **Privately Held**
SIC: 3728 Aircraft assemblies, subassemblies & parts

(G-447)
METAL FORMING INCORPORATED
305 S Farmer St (67013-8525)
P.O. Box 487 (67013-0487)
PHONE..................................620 488-3930
Eldon Gould, *President*
Deanne Gould, *President*
Walt Gould, *Prdtn Mgr*
EMP: 14
SQ FT: 10,700
SALES: 1.2MM **Privately Held**
WEB: www.metalforminginc.com
SIC: 3728 Bodies, aircraft

(G-448)
MORLEY BANCSHARES CORPORATION
Also Called: Valley State Bank The
502 N Merchant St (67013-9700)
P.O. Box 428 (67013-0428)
PHONE..................................620 488-2211
Douglas M Morley, *President*
EMP: 62 **EST:** 1990
SALES (est): 4.7MM **Privately Held**
WEB: www.valleybancshares.com
SIC: 6022 State commercial banks

(G-449)
VALLEY STATE BANK
Also Called: VALLEY STATE BANK THE
502 N Merchant St (67013-9700)
P.O. Box 428 (67013-0428)
PHONE..................................620 488-2211
Douglas M Morley, *President*
Matt Canfield, *Vice Pres*
Stacey Clark, *CFO*
Jim Randall, *Bookkeeper*
EMP: 31 **EST:** 1897
SQ FT: 6,300
SALES: 5.9MM **Privately Held**
SIC: 6022 State trust companies accepting deposits, commercial

Belleville
Republic County

(G-450)
ARBUTHNOTS INC
Also Called: Arbuthnot Drug
1806 M St (66935-2206)
P.O. Box 567 (66935-0567)
PHONE..................................785 527-2146
J Robert Arbuthnot, *President*
EMP: 24
SQ FT: 5,000
SALES (est): 4.9MM **Privately Held**
WEB: www.arbuthnotdrug.com
SIC: 5912 5947 8082 Drug stores; gift shop; home health care services

(G-451)
BELLEVILLE MEDICAL CLINIC P A
Also Called: Wheeler, Sean MD
2337 G St Ste 100 (66935-2462)
PHONE..................................785 527-2217
Duane L Scott, *President*
Duane D Scott, *Med Doctor*
EMP: 13
SALES (est): 1.6MM **Privately Held**
SIC: 8011 Clinic, operated by physicians

(G-452)
BELLEVILLE SUPER 8 MOTEL
1410 28th St (66935-2610)
PHONE..................................785 527-2112
Paul Dahia, *President*
EMP: 10
SALES (est): 516.5K **Privately Held**
SIC: 7011 Hotels & motels

(G-453)
BEST WEST FABRICATION LLC
1817 E Frontage Rd (66935-2332)
PHONE..................................785 527-2450
Mike Kasel, *Mng Member*
EMP: 5
SALES (est): 412.9K **Privately Held**
SIC: 3499 Fire- or burglary-resistive products

(G-454)
BESTIFOR HAY CO
1817 E Frontage Rd (66935-2332)
PHONE..................................785 527-2450
Thyne Larson, *Owner*
EMP: 10
SALES (est): 540.4K **Privately Held**
SIC: 0723 5191 Hay baling services; alfalfa

(G-455)
CENTRAL PLINS RSPRTORY MED LLC
1331 18th St (66935-2209)
PHONE..................................785 527-8727
Deanna Morris,
EMP: 10 **EST:** 2015
SALES (est): 1.2MM **Privately Held**
SIC: 5047 Medical equipment & supplies

(G-456)
COUNTY OF REPUBLIC
Also Called: Highway Dept
702 K St (66935-1520)
PHONE..................................785 527-2235
Charles Joy, *Administration*
EMP: 31 **Privately Held**
SIC: 8711 Construction & civil engineering
PA: County Of Republic
1815 M St Ste 1
Belleville KS 66935
785 527-7231

(G-457)
HAARSLEV INC
Haarslev Industries
537 28th St (66935-2401)
P.O. Box 98 (66935-0098)
PHONE..................................785 527-5641
Rick Jennings, *Purch Mgr*
Dani Isaacson, *Admin Sec*
EMP: 15
SALES (corp-wide): 1.1MM **Privately Held**
SIC: 3523 3541 Cattle feeding, handling & watering equipment; milling machines
HQ: Haarslev, Inc.
9700 Nw Conant Ave
Kansas City MO 64153
816 799-0808

(G-458)
KANSAS DEPARTMENT TRNSP
Also Called: Belleville Construction
1652 Us Highway 81 (66935-8138)
PHONE..................................785 527-2520
Jeff Woodward, *Manager*
EMP: 10 **Privately Held**
WEB: www.nwwichitabypass.com
SIC: 8711 9621 Engineering services; regulation, administration of transportation;
HQ: Kansas Department Of Transportation
700 Sw Harrison St # 500
Topeka KS 66603
785 296-3501

(G-459)
LAMBERT VET SUPPLY LLC
Also Called: Lambrier Vet Supply
814 K St (66935-1522)
PHONE..................................785 527-2209
Doug Lambert, *Branch Mgr*
Erica Leipold, *Manager*
EMP: 18
SALES (corp-wide): 122.5MM **Privately Held**
SIC: 0752 Boarding services, kennels
PA: Lambert Vet Supply, Llc
714 5th St
Fairbury NE 68352
402 729-3044

(G-460)
LOS PRIMOS INC (PA)
Also Called: Johnson Monument & Trigard
630 M St (66935-1548)
P.O. Box 461 (66935-0461)
PHONE..................................785 527-5535
Maurice Gieber, *President*
Dean Esslinger, *Principal*
Linda Esslinger, *Principal*
Mark Gieber, *Vice Pres*
EMP: 8
SQ FT: 9,600

SALES (est): 1.4MM **Privately Held**
SIC: 5999 3272 3281 Monuments, finished to custom order; burial vaults, concrete or precast terrazzo; cut stone & stone products

(G-461)
LSL OF KANSAS LLC
Also Called: BELLEVILLE HEALTHCARE CENTER
2626 Wesleyan Dr (66935-2440)
PHONE..................................785 527-5636
Michael A Marshall, *Principal*
Amanda Jeardoe, *Administration*
EMP: 34
SALES: 4.1MM **Privately Held**
SIC: 8059 Nursing home, except skilled & intermediate care facility

(G-462)
POLANSKY SEED INC
2729 M St (66935-2645)
P.O. Box 306 (66935-0306)
PHONE..................................785 527-2271
Adrian Polansky, *Owner*
EMP: 10
SALES (est): 1MM **Privately Held**
WEB: www.polanskyseed.com
SIC: 5261 5191 Nursery stock, seeds & bulbs; seeds: field, garden & flower

(G-463)
REINKE MANUFACTURING CO INC
1207 H St (66935-9782)
PHONE..................................785 527-8024
EMP: 5
SALES (corp-wide): 76.8MM **Privately Held**
SIC: 3711 Chassis, motor vehicle
HQ: Reinke Manufacturing Co., Inc.
1040 Road 5300
Deshler NE 68340
402 365-7251

(G-464)
REPUBLIC COUNTY EMS
Also Called: County Ambulance Service
2405 F St (66935-2434)
PHONE..................................785 527-7149
Jeremy Morris, *Psychologist*
David Stranad, *Director*
EMP: 15
SALES (est): 75K **Privately Held**
SIC: 4119 Ambulance service

(G-465)
REPUBLIC COUNTY FAMILY
2337 G St Ste 100 (66935-2462)
PHONE..................................785 527-2237
Robert E Holt, *Owner*
EMP: 10
SALES (est): 855.1K **Privately Held**
SIC: 8011 Clinic, operated by physicians

(G-466)
SCOTT SPECIALTIES INC (PA)
Also Called: Sport Aid, Rebound, Scott
512 M St (66935-1546)
P.O. Box 508 (66935-0508)
PHONE..................................785 527-5627
Wilson H Scott, *CEO*
Jim McDonald, *President*
EMP: 115
SQ FT: 50,000
SALES (est): 17.4MM **Privately Held**
WEB: www.scottspecialties.com
SIC: 3842 Orthopedic appliances

(G-467)
TELESCOPE INC
Also Called: Belleville Telescope
1805 N St (66935-2247)
P.O. Box 349 (66935-0349)
PHONE..................................785 527-2244
Mark Miller, *President*
Merle M Miller, *President*
EMP: 10 **EST:** 1936
SQ FT: 5,000
SALES (est): 914.1K **Privately Held**
WEB: www.highbanks.org
SIC: 2711 2752 Newspapers: publishing only, not printed on site; lithographing on metal

(G-468)
TRIGARD VAULTS (PA)
630 M St (66935-1548)
P.O. Box 461 (66935-0461)
PHONE..................................785 527-5595
John Trigard, *Owner*
EMP: 10
SALES (est): 1.2MM **Privately Held**
SIC: 1711 Septic system construction

Beloit
Mitchell County

(G-469)
ACKERMAN SUPPLY INC (PA)
Also Called: True Value
3147 Us 24 Hwy (67420-1577)
PHONE..................................785 738-5733
Henry J Ackerman, *President*
Gloria Ackerman, *Treasurer*
EMP: 11
SQ FT: 16,000
SALES (est): 1.7MM **Privately Held**
SIC: 5251 5191 Hardware; farm supplies

(G-470)
AGCO CORPORATION
3154 Hallie Trl (67420-3175)
PHONE..................................785 738-2261
Tim Kresky, *Controller*
Sam Depaulis, *Accountant*
Ron Harris, *Manager*
Tom Draper, *Manager*
William Polly, *Manager*
EMP: 300
SALES (corp-wide): 9.3B **Publicly Held**
WEB: www.agcocorp.com
SIC: 3523 Plows, agricultural: disc, moldboard, chisel, listers, etc.
PA: Agco Corporation
4205 River Green Pkwy
Duluth GA 30096
770 813-9200

(G-471)
AGMARK LLC (PA)
118 W Main St (67420-2745)
P.O. Box 444 (67420-0444)
PHONE..................................785 738-9641
Toll Free:..888 -
Farmway Co-Op,
Jeff Bechard,
Cloud County Co-Op,
Randall Co-Op,
Robert Johnson,
EMP: 10
SQ FT: 2,500
SALES: 387.3MM **Privately Held**
WEB: www.agmarkllc.com
SIC: 5153 Grain elevators

(G-472)
ALL THINGS EXTERIOR INC
Also Called: Direct Wholesale
3075 Us 24 Hwy (67420-1506)
PHONE..................................785 738-5015
Curtis R Farwell, *President*
Curtis Farwell, *President*
EMP: 20
SALES (est): 2.2MM **Privately Held**
SIC: 1521 Single-family home remodeling, additions & repairs

(G-473)
ANCIENT FREE & ACCPTD MASONS
Also Called: Mount Vernon Lodge
965 Kansas 14 Hwy (67420-1958)
PHONE..................................785 738-5095
Joseph Brown, *President*
Eric Harvey, *Warden*
Stanley Crietz, *Admin Sec*
EMP: 89
SALES (est): 809K **Privately Held**
SIC: 8641 Fraternal associations

(G-474)
BELL MEMORIALS LLC (PA)
Also Called: Victorian Glass
301 S River St (67420-3532)
PHONE..................................785 738-2257
James P Bell,
Ruth Bell,
EMP: 14
SQ FT: 7,500
SALES (est): 3.3MM **Privately Held**
SIC: 5099 5999 5231 Monuments & grave markers; monuments, finished to custom order; glass

(G-475)
BELOIT CALL
119 E Main St (67420-3234)
P.O. Box 366 (67420-0366)
PHONE..................................785 738-3537
Brad Lowell, *President*
EMP: 5
SALES (est): 224.7K **Privately Held**
SIC: 2711 Newspapers: publishing only, not printed on site

(G-476)
BELOIT COUNTRY CLUB INC
3167 Hallie Trl (67420-3175)
P.O. Box 84 (67420-0084)
PHONE..................................785 738-3163
Bob Miller, *President*
Dave Pruitt, *Vice Pres*
Lynne Vossman, *Treasurer*
Vickie Mears, *Admin Sec*
EMP: 25
SQ FT: 3,000
SALES: 333.5K **Privately Held**
SIC: 7997 Country club, membership; golf club, membership

(G-477)
BELOIT MEDICAL CENTER P A (PA)
1005 N Lincoln Ave (67420-1215)
P.O. Box 587 (67420-0587)
PHONE..................................785 738-2246
Martin Klenda, *President*
Craig Concannon MD, *Treasurer*
Kris G Kimple, *Med Doctor*
Carl L Fugate MD, *Admin Sec*
EMP: 35
SALES (est): 6MM **Privately Held**
SIC: 8011 Internal medicine, physician/surgeon

(G-478)
BELOIT READY MIX INCORPORATED (PA)
2936 K Rd (67420-3152)
PHONE..................................785 738-4683
Blaine Engelbert, *President*
Michael Vlass, *Vice Pres*
Angela Engelbert, *Admin Sec*
EMP: 6
SALES (est): 745K **Privately Held**
SIC: 3273 Ready-mixed concrete

(G-479)
BOETTCHER SUPPLY INC (PA)
118 W Court St (67420-3132)
PHONE..................................785 738-5781
Jarold W Boettcher, *Ch of Bd*
Blake Miller, *President*
▲ **EMP:** 25 **EST:** 1937
SQ FT: 8,500
SALES: 7.1MM **Privately Held**
WEB: www.boettchersupply.com
SIC: 5083 5013 5074 5063 Mowers, power; automotive engines & engine parts; plumbing fittings & supplies; electrical supplies

(G-480)
CARRICO IMPLEMENT CO INC (PA)
Also Called: John Deere Authorized Dealer
3160 Us 24 Hwy (67420-1577)
PHONE..................................785 738-5744
Ronald Ellenz, *President*
Joan Ellenz, *Exec VP*
Brandy Goddard, *Human Res Mgr*
Cherie Eck, *Sales Mgr*
Kevin Moore, *Sales Staff*
EMP: 55
SALES: 58.8MM **Privately Held**
WEB: www.carricoimplement.com
SIC: 5083 Farm implements

(G-481)
CENTRAL VALLEY AG COOPERATIVE
204 E Court St (67420-3242)
PHONE..................................785 738-2241
Allen Eilert, *Chairman*
EMP: 121 **Privately Held**
SIC: 5153 5191 5541 5172 Grain elevators; farm supplies; feed; fertilizer & fertilizer materials; gasoline service stations; engine fuels & oils
PA: Central Valley Ag Cooperative
2803 N Nebraska Ave
York NE 68467

(G-482)
COUNTY OF MITCHELL
Also Called: Mitchell County Hospital
400 W 8th St (67420-1605)
P.O. Box 399 (67420-0399)
PHONE..................................785 738-2266
Phyllis Oetting, *Vice Pres*
Cindy Taylor, *Opers Staff*
David Dick, *Manager*
Nate Richards, *Info Tech Dir*
Mitch Wing, *IT/INT Sup*
EMP: 18 **Privately Held**
SIC: 8051 Skilled nursing care facilities
PA: County Of Mitchell
114 S Hersey Ave
Beloit KS 67420
785 738-3652

(G-483)
FARMWAY CREDIT UNION (PA)
200 S Hersey Ave (67420-3233)
P.O. Box 446 (67420-0446)
PHONE..................................785 738-2224
Joe Deneke, *Manager*
EMP: 35
SALES: 4MM **Privately Held**
WEB: www.farmwaycu.com
SIC: 6061 Federal credit unions

(G-484)
FIRST NAT BNKSHARES BELOIT INC
101 E Main St (67420-3234)
P.O. Box 600 (67420-0600)
PHONE..................................785 738-2251
Robert L Lampeart, *President*
Robert Meats, *Senior VP*
David Dubbert, *Vice Pres*
Stephanie Chancelor, *Info Tech Dir*
EMP: 17 **EST:** 1884
SQ FT: 7,500
SALES: 2.8MM **Privately Held**
WEB: www.fnbbeloit.com
SIC: 6021 National commercial banks

(G-485)
GUARANTY STATE BNK TR BLOIT KA (HQ)
201 S Mill St (67420-3238)
P.O. Box 607 (67420-0607)
PHONE..................................785 738-3501
Doug Johnson, *President*
EMP: 20 **EST:** 1922
SALES: 14.1MM **Privately Held**
WEB: www.guarantystate.com
SIC: 6022 State trust companies accepting deposits, commercial

(G-486)
HEINEKEN ELECTRIC CO INC (PA)
3121b Us 24 Hwy (67420-1595)
P.O. Box 236 (67420-0236)
PHONE..................................785 738-3831
Kyle Heineken, *President*
EMP: 46
SQ FT: 4,000
SALES (est): 3.8MM **Privately Held**
WEB: www.heinekenelectric.com
SIC: 1731 General electrical contractor

(G-487)
HILLTOP LODGE
815 N Independence Ave (67420-1639)
P.O. Box 467 (67420-0467)
PHONE..................................785 738-2509
Harold Heidrick, *President*
Patricia Heidrick, *Corp Secy*
EMP: 140

SALES: 5.8MM Privately Held
SIC: 8051 7011 Convalescent home with continuous nursing care; hotels & motels

(G-488)
ICON INDUSTRIES INC
1600 W 8th St (67420-1660)
PHONE 785 738-3547
Don Llando, *President*
Dan Caffrey, *Vice Pres*
EMP: 25 EST: 1977
SQ FT: 40,000
SALES (est): 4.9MM Privately Held
WEB: www.iconindinc.com
SIC: 3531 Blades for graders, scrapers, dozers & snow plows

(G-489)
KRIERS AUTO PARTS INC
Also Called: Carquest Auto Parts
223 N Mill St (67420-2345)
PHONE 785 738-3526
Douglas J Krier, *President*
Mike Krier, *Opers Staff*
Gregory Krier, *Accounting Staf*
EMP: 6
SQ FT: 6,400
SALES (est): 962.2K Privately Held
SIC: 5531 3599 7694 Automotive parts; machine shop, jobbing & repair; electric motor repair

(G-490)
LANDOLL CORPORATION
1600 W 8th St (67420-1660)
PHONE 785 738-6613
Ron McKain, *Branch Mgr*
EMP: 30
SALES (corp-wide): 110.5MM Privately Held
SIC: 3479 3799 5599 7539 Hot dip coating of metals or formed products; trailers & trailer equipment; utility trailers; trailer repair
PA: Landoll Corporation
1900 North St
Marysville KS 66508
785 562-5381

(G-491)
LIMESTONE FEEDERS LLC
3575 Jazmine Trl (67420-3171)
P.O. Box 465 (67420-0465)
PHONE 402 770-4118
Bill Westering, *Partner*
EMP: 20
SQ FT: 2,500
SALES: 20MM Privately Held
SIC: 3523 Cattle feeding, handling & watering equipment

(G-492)
MCGRATH PUBLISHING COMPANY
Also Called: Waconda Trader
221 S Mill St (67420-3238)
P.O. Box 445 (67420-0445)
PHONE 785 738-2424
Harry McGrath Jr, *Owner*
Stacy Stausser, *Manager*
Joe Sporleder, *CIO*
EMP: 7
SQ FT: 2,200
SALES (est): 775.5K Privately Held
SIC: 2741 2711 Shopping news: publishing only, not printed on site; newspapers

(G-493)
MITCHELL COUNT HOSPI HEALT SYS
400 W 8th St (67420-1605)
P.O. Box 399 (67420-0399)
PHONE 785 738-2266
David Dick, *CEO*
Eldon Koepke, *CFO*
Deb Beam, *Agent*
Janelle Budke, *Director*
Amber Krier, *Director*
EMP: 300 EST: 2005
SALES: 24.3MM Privately Held
SIC: 8062 General medical & surgical hospitals

(G-494)
MITCHELL COUNTY FARM BUR ASSN
Also Called: Insurance Services
1674 Kansas 14 Hwy (67420-3454)
P.O. Box 423 (67420-0423)
PHONE 785 738-2551
Ron Tice, *Vice Pres*
Greg Shamburg, *Treasurer*
Lindy Lindblad, *Manager*
EMP: 13
SQ FT: 1,400
SALES (est): 1.5MM Privately Held
SIC: 6411 Insurance agents, brokers & service

(G-495)
NCK WELLNESS CENTER INC
3033 Us 24 Hwy (67420-1591)
P.O. Box 66 (67420-0066)
PHONE 785 738-3995
Lori May, *Director*
EMP: 35
SALES: 416.3K Privately Held
SIC: 7991 Physical fitness clubs with training equipment

(G-496)
NORTH CENTL KANS HM HLTH AGCY
310 W 8th St (67420-1603)
PHONE 785 738-5175
Patricia Dowlin, *Director*
EMP: 13
SALES (est): 234.8K Privately Held
SIC: 8082 Home health care services

(G-497)
O K THOMPSONS TIRE INC (PA)
1015 N Independence Ave (67420-2101)
P.O. Box 563 (67420-0563)
PHONE 785 738-2283
Michael Thompson, *President*
Phillip Thompson, *Treasurer*
▲ EMP: 21
SQ FT: 11,800
SALES: 18.3MM Privately Held
SIC: 5014 5531 7534 5999 Tires & tubes; automotive tires; tire recapping; alcoholic beverage making equipment & supplies

(G-498)
OCCK INC
501 W 7th St (67420-2107)
PHONE 785 738-3490
Barbara Wise, *Branch Mgr*
EMP: 35
SALES (corp-wide): 14.7MM Privately Held
WEB: www.occk.net
SIC: 8331 8361 8322 3993 Job training services; job counseling; residential care for the handicapped; children's home; individual & family services; signs & advertising specialties
PA: Occk, Inc.
1710 W Schilling Rd
Salina KS 67401
785 827-9383

(G-499)
ONEOK INC
Also Called: Kansas Gas Service
701 W 8th St (67420-1610)
PHONE 785 738-9700
Clayton Peterson, *Manager*
EMP: 15
SALES (corp-wide): 12.5B Publicly Held
WEB: www.oneok.com
SIC: 4924 Natural gas distribution
PA: Oneok, Inc.
100 W 5th St Ste Ll
Tulsa OK 74103
918 588-7000

(G-500)
RIDLEY USA INC
Also Called: Hubbard Feeds
3154 Us Highway 24 (67420-1577)
PHONE 785 738-2215
Derreck McChesney, *Manager*
EMP: 20
SALES (corp-wide): 1.6B Privately Held
WEB: www.hubbardfeeds.net
SIC: 2048 Prepared feeds
HQ: Ridley Usa Inc.
111 W Cherry St Ste 500
Mankato MN 56001
507 388-9400

(G-501)
ROLLING HILLS ELECTRIC COOP (PA)
3075b Us Highway 24 (67420-1506)
P.O. Box 339 (67420-0339)
PHONE 785 534-1601
Gene Mietler, *President*
Lionel J Overmiller, *Vice Pres*
Bernard Bohnen, *Treasurer*
Kevin Weber, *Technology*
Kevin Cromwell, *Admin Sec*
EMP: 17 EST: 1937
SQ FT: 9,500
SALES: 27.6MM Privately Held
SIC: 4911 5999 5984 Distribution, electric power; electronic parts & equipment; propane gas, bottled

(G-502)
SCHNELL & PESTINGER INC
108 S Mill St (67420-3237)
PHONE 785 738-3624
Mike Pestinger, *President*
Karen Pestinger, *Corp Secy*
EMP: 10
SQ FT: 6,000
SALES (est): 1.4MM Privately Held
SIC: 5712 5722 1711 Furniture stores; electric household appliances, major; warm air heating & air conditioning contractor

(G-503)
SOLOMON VALLEY FEEDERS LLC
3575 Jazmine Trl (67420-3171)
PHONE 785 738-2263
Duane Zortman,
EMP: 18 EST: 1970
SQ FT: 1,500
SALES: 35MM Privately Held
SIC: 0211 Beef cattle feedlots

(G-504)
SUPER 8 MOTEL OF BELOIT
3018 Us 24 Hwy (67420-1514)
PHONE 785 738-4300
Jeanette Riemus, *Manager*
EMP: 12
SALES (est): 418.9K Privately Held
SIC: 7011 Hotels & motels

Belpre
Edwards County

(G-505)
F G HOLL COMPANY LLC
Also Called: Prairie Pipe Line
Corner Of Hwy 15 And 9 (67519)
P.O. Box 158 (67519-0158)
PHONE 620 995-3171
Rob Long, *Branch Mgr*
EMP: 13
SALES (corp-wide): 1.5MM Privately Held
SIC: 1311 Crude petroleum production; natural gas production
PA: F G Holl Company Llc
9431 E Central Ave # 100
Wichita KS 67206
316 684-8481

Belvue
Pottawatomie County

(G-506)
KANSAS HARDWOODS INC
22620 Highway 24 (66407-5006)
P.O. Box 118 (66407-0118)
PHONE 785 456-8141
James Rutschmann, *President*
EMP: 10
SALES (est): 1.7MM Privately Held
SIC: 2421 2448 Sawmills & planing mills, general; pallets, wood

(G-507)
NEMAHA COUNTY COOPERATIVE ASSN
305 Noble Ave (66407-5208)
P.O. Box 147 (66407-0147)
PHONE 785 456-6924
Ben Zimmerman, *Manager*
EMP: 10
SALES (est): 394.6K
SALES (corp-wide): 108.6MM Privately Held
SIC: 0191 4221 5261 General farms, primarily crop; grain elevator, storage only; fertilizer
PA: The Nemaha County Cooperative Association
223 E Main St
Seneca KS 66538
785 336-6153

(G-508)
ONYX COLLECTION INC
202 Broadway St (66407-9600)
P.O. Box 37 (66407-0037)
PHONE 785 456-8604
Robert Awerkamp Jr, *President*
Louise Awerkamp, *Corp Secy*
Francis Awerkamp, *Vice Pres*
Robert J Awerkamp, *CFO*
Francis Awercamp, *Finance Mgr*
EMP: 450
SQ FT: 200,000
SALES (est): 73MM Privately Held
WEB: www.onyxtop.com
SIC: 3088 Plastics plumbing fixtures

(G-509)
TRADITIONAL TRUCKING CORP
202 Broadway St (66407-9600)
P.O. Box 37 (66407-0037)
PHONE 785 456-8604
Robert J Awerkamp, *President*
Francis Awerkamp, *Vice Pres*
Louise Awerkamp, *Treasurer*
EMP: 64
SALES: 8.8MM Privately Held
SIC: 4213 Trucking, except local

Bendena
Doniphan County

(G-510)
BENDENA STATE BANK (PA)
933 Friendship Rd (66008-8130)
P.O. Box 147 (66008-0147)
PHONE 785 988-4453
Mark Twombly, *President*
Linda Gaither, *Exec VP*
Josh Falk, *Branch Mgr*
EMP: 12 EST: 1904
SQ FT: 2,000
SALES: 2.8MM Privately Held
SIC: 6022 State trust companies accepting deposits, commercial

(G-511)
CONSUMER OIL COMPANY INC (PA)
Also Called: Conoco
209 Commercial St (66008)
P.O. Box 216 (66008-0216)
PHONE 785 988-4459
Kathleen Jones, *President*
Charles M Franken, *Vice Pres*
EMP: 13
SQ FT: 5,000
SALES (est): 5.9MM Privately Held
SIC: 5171 5984 Petroleum bulk stations; liquefied petroleum gas, delivered to customers' premises

Bennington
Ottawa County

(G-512)
BENNINGTON AMBULANCE SERVICE
584 N 180th Rd (67422-9438)
P.O. Box 116 (67422-0116)
PHONE..................................785 488-3768
Brandon Cochran, *Director*
Robert Boss, *Director*
EMP: 11
SALES (est): 310K **Privately Held**
SIC: 4119 Ambulance service

(G-513)
BENNINGTON STATE BANK
104 W Washington St (67422-5025)
P.O. Box 308 (67422-0308)
PHONE..................................785 488-3344
Kent Berkley, *President*
EMP: 16
SALES (corp-wide): 33.3MM **Privately Held**
SIC: 6022 State commercial banks
PA: Bennington State Bank
2130 S Ohio St
Salina KS 67401
785 827-5522

Benton
Butler County

(G-514)
CENTRAL PAVING INC
1250 N Main St (67017-8716)
P.O. Box 476 (67017-0476)
PHONE..................................316 778-1194
Merle Edson, *President*
Toni L Edson, *Vice Pres*
Bryan Edson, *Treasurer*
EMP: 35
SALES (est): 3.9MM **Privately Held**
SIC: 1611 Surfacing & paving

(G-515)
CENTURION MANUFACTURING
701 N Main St (67017-8761)
P.O. Box 306 (67017-0306)
PHONE..................................316 210-3504
Steven Coltrane, *President*
EMP: 6
SALES (est): 548.4K **Privately Held**
SIC: 3999 Manufacturing industries

(G-516)
KEYSTONE CONSTRUCTION INC
Also Called: Keystone Solid Surfaces
1250 N Main St (67017-8716)
P.O. Box 118 (67017-0118)
PHONE..................................316 778-1566
Danny R Smith, *President*
EMP: 12
SQ FT: 12,000
SALES: 1.8MM **Privately Held**
SIC: 2541 1542 Counter & sink tops; commercial & office buildings, renovation & repair

(G-517)
KEYSTONE FINANCIAL LLC
1250 N Main St (67017-8716)
P.O. Box 325 (67017-0325)
PHONE..................................620 757-3593
Cyle Barnwell, *Principal*
EMP: 17
SQ FT: 8,500
SALES (est): 701.8K **Privately Held**
SIC: 2541 Counter & sink tops; table or counter tops, plastic laminated

(G-518)
LITTLE CREEK TRUCKING INC
13457 Sw 20th St (67017-9029)
PHONE..................................316 778-1873
Jerry Roths, *President*
EMP: 18
SALES (est): 1.5MM **Privately Held**
SIC: 4213 Trucking, except local

(G-519)
MACK PICKENS GENERAL CONT
207 N Main St (67017-4506)
PHONE..................................316 778-1131
Mack Pickens, *Owner*
EMP: 30
SALES: 1.9MM **Privately Held**
SIC: 1521 General remodeling, single-family houses

Bern
Nemaha County

(G-520)
BERN BANCSHARES INC (PA)
Also Called: State Bank
402 Main St (66408-9783)
P.O. Box 123 (66408-0123)
PHONE..................................785 336-6121
William Sheik, *President*
Gary Sparling, *Vice Pres*
EMP: 10
SALES: 3.2MM **Privately Held**
SIC: 6022 State commercial banks

(G-521)
BERN MEAT PLANT INCORPORATED
411 Main St (66408-9783)
P.O. Box 97 (66408-0097)
PHONE..................................785 336-2165
Terry Miller, *President*
Nancy Miller, *Vice Pres*
EMP: 10 **EST:** 1961
SQ FT: 5,000
SALES (est): 696K **Privately Held**
SIC: 5421 5451 5147 5143 Meat markets, including freezer provisioners; cheese; meats, fresh; cheese; meat meal & tankage: prepared as animal feed

(G-522)
FLINT HILLS POWERSPORTS INC (PA)
Also Called: Duffers Repair & Supply
423 Main St (66408-9783)
P.O. Box 9 (66408-0009)
PHONE..................................785 336-3901
Eldon Kaster, *CEO*
EMP: 6
SQ FT: 3,600
SALES (est): 839K **Privately Held**
WEB: www.duffersrepair.com
SIC: 3799 7699 All terrain vehicles (ATV); motorcycle repair service; engine repair & replacement, non-automotive

(G-523)
HAVERKAMP BROTHERS INC
2964 L4 Rd (66408-8029)
PHONE..................................785 858-4457
Robert G Haverkamp, *President*
Mark Haverkamp, *Vice Pres*
Leon Haverkamp, *Treasurer*
Alan Haverkamp, *Admin Sec*
EMP: 60
SALES (est): 2.6MM **Privately Held**
WEB: www.haverkampbros.com
SIC: 0213 Hogs

(G-524)
TIMBERVIEW FARM
1732 208th Rd (66408-8062)
PHONE..................................785 336-2399
Clinton Strahm, *General Ptnr*
EMP: 12
SALES (est): 1.1MM **Privately Held**
SIC: 0191 General farms, primarily crop

Berryton
Shawnee County

(G-525)
AIR CARE SYSTEMS HVAC INC
4140 Se 61st St (66409-9731)
PHONE..................................360 403-9939
Robert S Sivik Jr, *President*
EMP: 11
SALES (est): 1.2MM **Privately Held**
SIC: 8711 Heating & ventilation engineering

(G-526)
E4 EXCAVATING INC
1452 E 1st Rd (66409-9000)
PHONE..................................785 379-5111
Robin Edmonds, *President*
Jane Edmonds, *Corp Secy*
EMP: 10
SALES (est): 940K **Privately Held**
SIC: 1794 Excavation work

(G-527)
JC AUTO
1645 Se 77th St (66409-9698)
PHONE..................................785 266-1300
James Christenberry, *Principal*
EMP: 10
SALES (est): 621.6K **Privately Held**
SIC: 7538 General automotive repair shops

(G-528)
PAW PRINTS ANIMAL HOSPITAL
4144 Se 45th St (66409-9707)
PHONE..................................785 267-1918
Robert D Johnson, *Owner*
Robert Johnson, *Owner*
EMP: 12
SQ FT: 300
SALES (est): 645.9K **Privately Held**
SIC: 0742 Animal hospital services, pets & other animal specialties

Bird City
Cheyenne County

(G-529)
BIRD CITY DAIRY LLC
1440 Road 32 (67731-4001)
PHONE..................................785 734-2295
Laura Bussen,
Michael McCarty,
EMP: 20
SALES (est): 1.6MM **Privately Held**
SIC: 0241 Dairy farms

(G-530)
FRONTIER AG INC
W Hwy 36 (67731)
P.O. Box 99 (67731-0099)
PHONE..................................785 734-2331
Ray Magnani, *Manager*
EMP: 12 **Privately Held**
SIC: 5153 5172 Grain elevators; diesel fuel
PA: Frontier Ag, Inc.
415 W 2nd St
Oakley KS 67748

Bloom
Clark County

(G-531)
MINNEOLA HOSPITAL DISTRICT 2
Also Called: Minneola Community Clinic
222 Main St (67865-8511)
P.O. Box 127, Minneola (67865-0127)
PHONE..................................620 885-4202
Deborah Bruner, *CEO*
EMP: 17
SALES (corp-wide): 8.9MM **Privately Held**
SIC: 8062 8011 General medical & surgical hospitals; general & family practice, physician/surgeon
PA: Minneola Hospital District 2
212 Main St
Bloom KS 67865

Blue Mound
Linn County

(G-532)
FARMERS STATE BANK BLUE MOUND (PA)
205 S 5th (66010)
P.O. Box 158 (66010-0158)
PHONE..................................913 756-2221
Dale Sprague, *President*
Janice Sprague, *Senior VP*
EMP: 20 **EST:** 1913
SALES: 2.3MM **Privately Held**
SIC: 6022 State commercial banks

Blue Rapids
Marshall County

(G-533)
BLUE RAPIDS GREENHOUSE INC
805 Pomeroy St (66411-1218)
P.O. Box 215 (66411-0215)
PHONE..................................785 363-7300
Nikolas Lockhart, *President*
Amanda Lockhart, *Vice Pres*
EMP: 26
SALES (est): 2MM **Privately Held**
SIC: 0182 0181 5992 Vegetable crops grown under cover; flowers: grown under cover (e.g. greenhouse production); florists

(G-534)
BLUE VALLEY HEALTH CARE (PA)
Also Called: Blue Valley Nursing Home
710 Western Ave (66411-1236)
PHONE..................................785 363-7777
Paul Worth, *Principal*
Tina Wilson, *Chf Purch Ofc*
Jeannie Zidek, *Office Mgr*
EMP: 20
SQ FT: 600
SALES (est): 1MM **Privately Held**
SIC: 8051 Convalescent home with continuous nursing care

(G-535)
COMMUNITY MEMORIAL HEALTHCARE
Also Called: Blue Rapids Medical Clinic
607 Lincoln St (66411-1419)
P.O. Box 127 (66411-0127)
PHONE..................................785 363-7202
Tammy Holle, *Manager*
EMP: 16
SALES (corp-wide): 21.5MM **Privately Held**
SIC: 8062 8011 General medical & surgical hospitals; general & family practice, physician/surgeon
PA: Community Memorial Healthcare Inc
708 N 18th St
Marysville KS 66508
785 562-2311

(G-536)
GEORGIA-PACIFIC LLC
2127 Us Highway 77 (66411-8695)
PHONE..................................785 363-7767
Fred Anson, *Manager*
EMP: 115
SALES (corp-wide): 40.6B **Privately Held**
WEB: www.gp.com
SIC: 3275 5031 Gypsum products; lumber: rough, dressed & finished
HQ: Georgia-Pacific Llc
133 Peachtree St Nw
Atlanta GA 30303
404 652-4000

(G-537)
SHARP MANUFACTURING LLC
608 Main St (66411-1440)
PHONE..................................785 363-7336
Rob Swearingen,
EMP: 10
SQ FT: 8,000

GEOGRAPHIC

SALES (est): 1.6MM **Privately Held**
WEB: www.sharpmanufacturing.com
SIC: 3715 Truck trailers

Bonner Springs
Wyandotte County

(G-538)
A STEP ABOVE ACADEMY-WYANDOTTE
Also Called: Little Learners
600 N 118th St (66012-9027)
PHONE..................................913 721-3770
Aaron Wegnar, *Owner*
EMP: 12
SALES (est): 78.2K **Privately Held**
SIC: 8351 Child day care services

(G-539)
ALCOHOLICS ANONYMS BNNR SPRNGS
144 N Nettleton Ave (66012-1467)
P.O. Box 149 (66012-0149)
PHONE..................................913 441-3277
EMP: 10
SALES (est): 470K **Privately Held**
SIC: 8069 Specialty Hospital

(G-540)
BERKEL & COMPANY CONTRS INC (PA)
2649 S 142nd St (66012-9459)
P.O. Box 335 (66012-0335)
PHONE..................................913 422-5125
Alan R Roach, *President*
Randy Jones, *Superintendent*
Chris Miller, *Superintendent*
Art Rhodes, *Superintendent*
Chris Chinopulos, *Regional Mgr*
▼ **EMP:** 60
SQ FT: 18,000
SALES (est): 209MM **Privately Held**
WEB: www.berkelandcompany.com
SIC: 1771 1741 Foundation & footing contractor; concrete repair; foundation & retaining wall construction

(G-541)
BERNING TIRE INC
306 Oak St (66012-1031)
P.O. Box 107 (66012-0107)
PHONE..................................913 422-3033
Thomas E Berning, *President*
Judith A Berning, *Vice Pres*
EMP: 12
SQ FT: 9,000
SALES (est): 1.5MM **Privately Held**
SIC: 5531 7538 Automotive tires; general automotive repair shops

(G-542)
BONNER SPRINGS HEAD START
402 N Neconi Ave (66012-1551)
PHONE..................................913 441-2828
Pat Likins, *President*
Naomi Mills, *Director*
EMP: 18
SALES (est): 590K **Privately Held**
SIC: 8351 Child day care services

(G-543)
BRUCES WOODWORKS LLC
Also Called: Moon Marble Company
600 E Front St (66012-1122)
PHONE..................................913 441-1432
Bruce Breslow, *Mng Member*
Lynda Sproules, *Mng Member*
EMP: 10
SQ FT: 8,500
SALES (est): 664.5K **Privately Held**
WEB: www.moonmarble.com
SIC: 5947 3944 5945 Gift shop; marbles (toys); toys & games

(G-544)
BYERS GLASS & MIRROR INC
11685 Kaw Dr (66012)
P.O. Box 291 (66012-0291)
PHONE..................................913 441-8717
Danny Byers, *President*
Brenda Byers, *Admin Sec*
▲ **EMP:** 20
SQ FT: 4,000
SALES (est): 4.9MM **Privately Held**
SIC: 1793 Glass & glazing work

(G-545)
CLC BONNER SPRINGS
520 E Morse Ave (66012-1911)
PHONE..................................913 441-2515
Dean Caldwell, *Administration*
EMP: 60
SALES (est): 812.1K **Privately Held**
SIC: 8051 Skilled nursing care facilities

(G-546)
CSM BAKERY SOLUTIONS LLC
Also Called: Best Brands
2410 Scheidt Ln (66012-1379)
PHONE..................................913 441-7216
Scott Humphrey, *Principal*
Gordon Brest, *Maintence Staff*
EMP: 179
SALES (corp-wide): 177.9K **Privately Held**
WEB: www.bestbrandscorp.com
SIC: 5149 Bakery products
HQ: Csm Bakery Solutions Llc
1912 Montreal Rd
Tucker GA 30084
404 478-5400

(G-547)
D JS FOUNDATION & FLATWORK
16160 174th St (66012-7299)
PHONE..................................913 441-1909
Danny Maxwell, *President*
EMP: 12
SALES (est): 1MM **Privately Held**
SIC: 1771 Concrete work

(G-548)
DELICH ROTH & GOODWILLIE PA (PA)
913 Sheidley Ave Ste 110 (66012-9500)
PHONE..................................913 441-1100
Joseph Roth, *Ch of Bd*
Christopher Burns, *President*
Carl Reed, *Vice Pres*
Kirby Demott, *Treasurer*
Craig Mitchell, *Asst Treas*
EMP: 13
SQ FT: 3,200
SALES (est): 2.5MM **Privately Held**
WEB: www.drgengineers.com
SIC: 8711 Consulting engineer

(G-549)
DELICH ROTH & GOODWILLIE PA
913 Sheidley Ave Ste 110 (66012-9500)
PHONE..................................913 441-1100
Craig Mitchell, *Branch Mgr*
EMP: 11
SALES (corp-wide): 2.5MM **Privately Held**
WEB: www.drgengineers.com
SIC: 8711 Consulting engineer
PA: Delich, Roth & Goodwillie, P.A.
913 Sheidley Ave Ste 110
Bonner Springs KS 66012
913 441-1100

(G-550)
DR WILLIAM E HARTMAN ASSOC PA
13031 Kansas Ave (66012-9206)
PHONE..................................913 441-1600
William E Hartman, *President*
EMP: 16
SQ FT: 3,200
SALES (est): 1.3MM **Privately Held**
SIC: 8021 Dentists' office

(G-551)
DS BUS LINES INC
313 E Front St (66012-1008)
PHONE..................................913 384-1190
Donald Kincaid, *CEO*
Dale Bohn, *Vice Pres*
EMP: 99
SQ FT: 1,500
SALES (est): 974.3K **Privately Held**
SIC: 4111 Bus transportation

(G-552)
E D BISHOP LUMBER MUNCIE INC
Also Called: Vesta Lee Lumber Company
2300 S 138th St (66012-1629)
P.O. Box 392 (66012-0392)
PHONE..................................913 441-2691
James L Bishop, *President*
EMP: 12
SQ FT: 1,000
SALES (est): 3.1MM **Privately Held**
SIC: 5211 5031 Lumber products; lumber, plywood & millwork

(G-553)
FESTIVAL GROGS INC
Also Called: Kansas City Renaissance
628 N 126th St (66012-9045)
PHONE..................................913 721-2110
James Peterson, *President*
Karla Taylor, *Director*
EMP: 12
SALES (est): 361.1K **Privately Held**
WEB: www.kcrenfest.com
SIC: 7999 Festival operation

(G-554)
H C DAVIS SONS MFG CO
Also Called: Davis Manufacturing
416 E Front St (66012-1010)
P.O. Box 395 (66012-0395)
PHONE..................................913 422-3000
Thomas McPherson, *President*
H Davis, *Founder*
Frank E Stransky, *Purchasing*
Mark C Walker, *Engineer*
Debra Davis-Mcpherson, *Controller*
▼ **EMP:** 14
SQ FT: 14,385
SALES (est): 3.3MM **Privately Held**
WEB: www.hcdavis.com
SIC: 3523 3531 Farm machinery & equipment; mixers: ore, plaster, slag, sand, mortar, etc.

(G-555)
INFUSION DESIGN INCORPORATED (PA)
110 W 3rd St (66012-1032)
PHONE..................................913 422-0317
Sean Elsner, *President*
EMP: 20
SALES (est): 1.6MM **Privately Held**
SIC: 7389 7336 Design, commercial & industrial; graphic arts & related design

(G-556)
INTER-STATE STUDIO & PUBG CO
144 N Nettleton Ave (66012-1467)
PHONE..................................913 745-6700
EMP: 52
SALES (corp-wide): 44.3MM **Privately Held**
SIC: 7221 Photographic studios, portrait
PA: Inter-State Studio & Publishing Co.
3500 Snyder Ave
Sedalia MO 65301
660 826-1764

(G-557)
JONES & JONES DEVELOPMENT LLC
2527 S 142nd St (66012-9458)
PHONE..................................913 422-9477
EMP: 11
SALES (est): 1.1MM **Privately Held**
SIC: 6552 Subdivider/Developer

(G-558)
KANSAS CY RENAISSANCE FESTIVAL
628 N 126th St (66012-9045)
PHONE..................................913 721-2110
James Peterson, *President*
Karla Taylor, *Director*
EMP: 12
SALES (est): 613.8K **Privately Held**
SIC: 7999 Tourist attractions, amusement park concessions & rides

(G-559)
LEGAL PRINTING COMPANY INC
Also Called: Powerhouse Graphics
15591 Cedar Ln (66012)
P.O. Box 508, Tonganoxie (66086-0508)
PHONE..................................913 369-1623
Russ Wesley, *President*
Nia-Ying Wesley, *Vice Pres*
EMP: 7 **EST:** 1975
SQ FT: 1,600
SALES (est): 750K **Privately Held**
WEB: www.legalprintinginc.com
SIC: 2752 Commercial printing, lithographic

(G-560)
LITTLE JOES ASPHALT INC
610 N 134th St (66012-9109)
P.O. Box 516 (66012-0516)
PHONE..................................913 721-3261
Theresa A Buehler, *President*
Joseph L Buehler, *Vice Pres*
Don Bruns, *Project Mgr*
EMP: 16
SALES (est): 3.1MM **Privately Held**
SIC: 1771 Blacktop (asphalt) work

(G-561)
LONE STAR INDUSTRIES INC
Also Called: Buzzi Uncem USA
12200 Kaw Dr (66012-7118)
P.O. Box 297 (66012-0297)
PHONE..................................913 422-1050
Melissa Wild, *Opers-Prdtn-Mfg*
EMP: 12
SALES (corp-wide): 356.1MM **Privately Held**
SIC: 3241 Portland cement
HQ: Lone Star Industries Inc
10401 N Meridian St # 120
Indianapolis IN 46290
317 706-3314

(G-562)
MIDWEST BUS SALES INC (PA)
313 E Front St (66012-1008)
PHONE..................................913 422-1000
Graydon J Kincaid Jr, *President*
Kenny Haydon, *General Mgr*
Patricia Kincaid, *Vice Pres*
Gene Dutton, *Opers Mgr*
Justin Lott, *Parts Mgr*
EMP: 22
SQ FT: 6,000
SALES (est): 30.6MM **Privately Held**
WEB: www.midwestbussales.com
SIC: 5012 7513 Buses; truck rental & leasing, no drivers

(G-563)
MILLERS SIGN SHOPPE LLC
Also Called: Miller Sign Shoppe
15146 174th St (66012-7869)
PHONE..................................913 441-6883
Kimberly Miller,
EMP: 8
SQ FT: 3,200
SALES (est): 1.1MM **Privately Held**
WEB: www.millersignshoppe.com
SIC: 3993 Signs, not made in custom sign painting shops

(G-564)
MUTUAL SAVINGS ASSOCIATION
229 Oak St (66012-1028)
PHONE..................................913 441-5555
Erin Lansing, *Manager*
EMP: 12
SALES (est): 1.2MM
SALES (corp-wide): 9.6MM **Privately Held**
SIC: 6035 Federal savings & loan associations
PA: Mutual Savings Association
100 S 4th St
Leavenworth KS 66048
913 682-3491

(G-565)
NATIONAL AG CTR & HALL FAME
Also Called: AG HALL OF HAME
630 N 126th St (66012-9045)
PHONE..................................913 721-1075

Robert Carlson, *President*
EMP: 17
SQ FT: 1,200
SALES: 168.8K **Privately Held**
WEB: www.aghalloffame.com
SIC: **8412** Museum

(G-566)
NATIONAL COLD STORAGE INC
12755 Loring Dr (66012)
P.O. Box 72 (66012-0072)
PHONE..................................913 422-4050
Hurshel Surritt, *Branch Mgr*
EMP: 25 **Privately Held**
SIC: **4225** General warehousing & storage
PA: National Cold Storage, Inc.
3020 Ne 40th Ct
Fort Lauderdale FL 33308

(G-567)
NATIONAL COLD STORAGE KC INC
12755 Loring Dr (66012)
P.O. Box 72 (66012-0072)
PHONE..................................913 422-4050
Amir Minoofar, *President*
EMP: 35
SQ FT: 995,000
SALES (est): 2.5MM **Privately Held**
SIC: **4225** General warehousing & storage

(G-568)
OLDCASTLE APG MIDWEST INC
P.O. Box 8 (66012-0008)
PHONE..................................913 667-1792
Brad Smith, *General Mgr*
EMP: 35
SALES (corp-wide): 29.7B **Privately Held**
SIC: **8712** Architectural services
HQ: Oldcastle Apg Midwest, Inc.
3 Glenlake Pkwy Fl 12
Atlanta GA 30328

(G-569)
OVERLAND CABINET COMPANY INC
13933 Leavenworth St (66012-1646)
PHONE..................................913 441-1985
Ron Coleman, *President*
Kala Coleman, *Vice Pres*
EMP: 15 **EST:** 1958
SQ FT: 5,000
SALES (est): 1.7MM **Privately Held**
WEB: www.overlandcabinet.com
SIC: **2434** Wood kitchen cabinets

(G-570)
PERFORMANCE GLASS INC
15955 Linwood Rd (66012-7167)
P.O. Box 277 (66012-0277)
PHONE..................................913 441-1290
Bob Atchison, *President*
Nathan Foster, *Project Mgr*
Paula Broadbent, *Treasurer*
EMP: 15
SALES (est): 2.6MM **Privately Held**
SIC: **1793** 5231 Glass & glazing work; glass

(G-571)
PINNACLE HLTH FCLTIES XVIII LP
Also Called: Bonner Springs Nrsng & Rehab
520 E Morse Ave (66012-1911)
PHONE..................................913 441-2515
Michael Adams, *Administration*
EMP: 51 **Privately Held**
SIC: **8051** 8059 Skilled nursing care facilities; convalescent home
PA: Pinnacle Health Facilities Xviii, Lp
5420 W Plano Pkwy
Plano TX 75093

(G-572)
SERVIMSTER PROF RSTORATION CLG
18730 174th St (66012)
PHONE..................................785 832-0055
Kurt Young, *Owner*
EMP: 15
SALES (est): 203.3K **Privately Held**
SIC: **7349** Building maintenance services

(G-573)
SOUTHWEST STL FABRICATION LLC
Also Called: Southwest Steel Fabricators
2520 Scheidt Ln (66012-1381)
P.O. Box 275 (66012-0275)
PHONE..................................913 422-5500
Nicholas McLean,
Thomas Sanford,
EMP: 35
SALES (est): 1.5MM **Privately Held**
SIC: **3441** 3449 3446 Expansion joints (structural shapes), iron or steel; bars, concrete reinforcing: fabricated steel; gratings, open steel flooring

(G-574)
SOUTHWEST STL FABRICATORS INC (PA)
2520 Scheidt Ln (66012-1381)
P.O. Box 275 (66012-0275)
PHONE..................................913 422-5500
Richard J Teahan, *Ch of Bd*
Thomas Sanford, *President*
Craig T Nelsen, *President*
Kirk Nelsen, *Vice Pres*
Kevin Scott, *Vice Pres*
EMP: 40
SQ FT: 200,000
SALES (est): 7.1MM **Privately Held**
SIC: **3449** Miscellaneous metalwork

(G-575)
SUNFLOWER HILLS GOLF COURSE
122 Riverview Rd (66012)
PHONE..................................913 721-2727
Mike Yadrich, *Superintendent*
EMP: 18
SALES (est): 730K **Privately Held**
SIC: **7992** Public golf courses

(G-576)
SUPER 8 MOTEL
13041 Ridge Dr (66012-1868)
PHONE..................................913 721-3877
David Block, *Executive Asst*
EMP: 10 **EST:** 2009
SALES (est): 435.9K **Privately Held**
SIC: **7011** Hotels & motels

(G-577)
TIGER TOW & TRANSPORT INC
2914 Loring Dr (66012-9483)
P.O. Box 571 (66012-0571)
PHONE..................................913 422-7300
Philip Layton Smith, *President*
Margaret Smith, *Vice Pres*
EMP: 10
SQ FT: 7,000
SALES (est): 507.4K **Privately Held**
SIC: **7549** Towing service, automotive; towing services

(G-578)
TRIMAC INDUSTRIAL SYSTEMS LLC
12601 Kaw Dr Ste C (66012-7104)
PHONE..................................913 441-0043
Martha Sawyer,
EMP: 20
SALES (est): 5.4MM **Privately Held**
SIC: **3567** 7699 Industrial furnaces & ovens; industrial equipment cleaning

(G-579)
VFS ACQUISITION CORP
Also Called: Valley Feed & Supply Co.
600 W 2nd St (66012-1252)
P.O. Box 322 (66012-0322)
PHONE..................................913 422-4088
Matthew Laipple, *Principal*
EMP: 10
SALES (est): 449.9K **Privately Held**
SIC: **6799** Investors

(G-580)
WAGNER AUTO BODY & SALES INC
Also Called: Wagner's Auto Body & Sales
741 E Front St (66012-1123)
PHONE..................................913 422-1955
Willie Wagner, *President*
Willie G Wagner, *President*
Barbara Wagner, *Corp Secy*
EMP: 12 **EST:** 1968
SQ FT: 18,000
SALES: 4.2MM **Privately Held**
SIC: **7532** 5521 Body shop, automotive; automobiles, used cars only; antique automobiles

Bremen
Marshall County

(G-581)
BREMEN FARMERS MUTUAL INSUR CO
201 Brenneke St (66412-8623)
P.O. Box 98 (66412-0098)
PHONE..................................785 337-2203
Curtis Holle, *President*
Gary Holle, *Vice Pres*
Whitney Meyer, *Underwriter*
EMP: 14
SQ FT: 3,920
SALES (est): 6.6MM **Privately Held**
WEB: www.bfmic.com
SIC: **6331** Fire, marine & casualty insurance & carriers

Brewster
Thomas County

(G-582)
ARCHER-DANIELS-MIDLAND COMPANY
Also Called: ADM
410 Railroad Ave (67732-8701)
P.O. Box 218 (67732-0218)
PHONE..................................785 694-2286
Jeff Mettlen, *Branch Mgr*
EMP: 7
SALES (corp-wide): 64.3B **Publicly Held**
WEB: www.admworld.com
SIC: **2041** 5191 5261 Flour & other grain mill products; fertilizers & agricultural chemicals; fertilizer
PA: Archer-Daniels-Midland Company
77 W Wacker Dr Ste 4600
Chicago IL 60601
312 634-8100

(G-583)
FRONTIER AG INC
428 Kansas Ave (67732-8676)
P.O. Box 69 (67732-0069)
PHONE..................................785 694-2281
Bruce Ferguson, *Manager*
EMP: 13 **Privately Held**
SIC: **5999** 5191 5261 Feed & farm supply; feed; fertilizer & fertilizer materials; flower & field bulbs; fertilizer
PA: Frontier Ag, Inc.
415 W 2nd St
Oakley KS 67748

(G-584)
INTERNATIONAL ASSN LIONS CLUBS
320 Illinois Ave (67732-8621)
P.O. Box 159 (67732-0159)
PHONE..................................785 694-2278
Mike Baughn, *Principal*
EMP: 27
SALES (est): 193.8K **Privately Held**
SIC: **8641** Civic associations

(G-585)
PRAISE NETWORK INC
Also Called: Kgcr Radio
3410 Road 66 (67732-8907)
P.O. Box 9 (67732-0009)
PHONE..................................785 694-2877
James Claassen, *Manager*
EMP: 10
SALES (corp-wide): 1.1MM **Privately Held**
WEB: www.kgrd.org
SIC: **4832** 7313 Radio broadcasting stations; radio advertising representative
PA: The Praise Network Inc
128 S 4th St
Oneill NE 68763
402 336-3886

(G-586)
S & T TELEPHONE COOP ASSN (PA)
320 Kansas Ave (67732-8674)
PHONE..................................785 694-2256
Steve Richards, *CEO*
Dale Hudson, *President*
Zack Odell, *Principal*
Mitch Moomaw, *Corp Secy*
Ben Cramer, *Vice Pres*
EMP: 24 **EST:** 1952
SQ FT: 6,500
SALES (est): 19MM **Privately Held**
WEB: www.sttelcom.com
SIC: **4841** 4813 Cable television services;

Bronson
Bourbon County

(G-587)
RAINBOW ORGANIC FARMS CO
1976 55th St (66716-9131)
PHONE..................................620 939-4933
Diana Endicott, *President*
Betty Endicott, *Corp Secy*
Gary Endicott, *Manager*
EMP: 10
SALES (est): 782K **Privately Held**
SIC: **0182** 0211 Hydroponic crops grown under cover; beef cattle feedlots

(G-588)
RIG 6 DRILLING INC
Rr 3 (66716)
P.O. Box 227, Iola (66749-0227)
PHONE..................................620 365-6294
Raymond K Sifers, *President*
John Barker, *Vice Pres*
EMP: 6
SALES (est): 400K **Privately Held**
SIC: **1381** Drilling oil & gas wells

Brownell
Ness County

(G-589)
RESOURCE MANAGEMENT CO INC
25656 160 Rd (67521-2528)
PHONE..................................785 398-2240
Twylia Sekavec, *President*
Marvin Sekavec, *Principal*
EMP: 18
SQ FT: 6,700
SALES: 2.2MM **Privately Held**
SIC: **4953** Recycling, waste materials

Bucklin
Ford County

(G-590)
BUCKLIN HOSPITAL DISTRICT INC
Also Called: Hilltop House
505 W Elm St (67834-3461)
P.O. Box 248 (67834-0248)
PHONE..................................620 826-3202
Judy Kregar, *Administration*
EMP: 45 **EST:** 1966
SQ FT: 10,000
SALES: 1.8MM **Privately Held**
SIC: **8052** Personal care facility

(G-591)
BUCKLIN TRACTOR & IMPT CO INC (PA)
Also Called: John Deere Authorized Dealer
115 W Railroad St (67834-3410)
P.O. Box 127 (67834-0127)
PHONE..................................620 826-3271
Kelly Estes, *President*
Mike Estes, *General Mgr*

GEOGRAPHIC

Sherry M Smith, *Exec VP*
Marc A Howze, *Vice Pres*
Mary K Jones, *Vice Pres*
EMP: 30
SQ FT: 21,000
SALES (est): 44.7MM **Privately Held**
WEB: www.gti-bti.com
SIC: 5083 5999 Tractors, agricultural; farm equipment & supplies

(G-592)
FARMERS STATE BANK OF BUCKLIN
111 N Main St (67834-3443)
P.O. Box 187 (67834-0187)
PHONE..................................620 826-3231
Kim Ellis, *Vice Pres*
Stuart Kirk, *Officer*
EMP: 10 **EST:** 1909
SALES: 1.6MM **Privately Held**
WEB: www.fsbbucklin.com
SIC: 6022 State trust companies accepting deposits, commercial

Bucyrus
Miami County

(G-593)
ACTUARIUS LLC
18283 Melrose Dr (66013-9081)
PHONE..................................913 908-2830
Jason Harrell,
EMP: 13
SALES (est): 224.1K **Privately Held**
SIC: 8721 Accounting, auditing & bookkeeping

(G-594)
BOLIVAR CONTRACTING INC
20924 Floyd St (66013-9102)
PHONE..................................913 533-2240
Mike McCown, *President*
EMP: 31 **EST:** 2009
SALES (est): 9.9MM **Privately Held**
SIC: 1542 Agricultural building contractors

(G-595)
CTI FREIGHT SYSTEMS INC
4530 W 207th St (66013-9649)
PHONE..................................913 236-7400
Chris Mnichowski, *President*
EMP: 10
SALES (est): 2.1MM **Privately Held**
SIC: 4111 Passenger rail transportation

(G-596)
DOVER SOD FARMS INC
10886 W 239th St (66013-9217)
PHONE..................................913 897-2336
Gary Dover, *President*
Ronny Dover, *Vice Pres*
Carol Dover, *Admin Sec*
EMP: 15
SALES (est): 864.9K **Privately Held**
SIC: 0782 0181 Sodding contractor; sod farms

(G-597)
GRASS PAD INC
Also Called: Grass Pad Warehouse
8160 W 199th St (66013-9419)
PHONE..................................913 681-8948
Corby Predmoore, *Manager*
EMP: 20
SALES (corp-wide): 40.8MM **Privately Held**
WEB: www.grasspad.com
SIC: 5261 0782 Nursery stock, seeds & bulbs; sodding contractor
PA: Grass Pad, Inc.
425 N Rawhide Dr
Olathe KS 66061
913 764-4100

(G-598)
H & R LAWN & LANDSCAPE INC
6735 W 207th St (66013-9252)
PHONE..................................913 897-9705
Robin Milliken, *President*
Jackie Milliken, *Corp Secy*
Michael Nemeth, *CFO*
EMP: 60
SQ FT: 5,500
SALES (est): 5.1MM **Privately Held**
WEB: www.handrlawn.com
SIC: 0782 1711 Landscape contractors; irrigation sprinkler system installation

(G-599)
HAYES BROS CONST CO INC
20745 Foster Ct (66013-9080)
PHONE..................................913 685-3636
Ronald Hayes, *President*
EMP: 15
SALES (est): 2.7MM **Privately Held**
SIC: 1794 Excavation work

(G-600)
INLAND INDUSTRIES INC (PA)
19841 Benson St (66013-8201)
PHONE..................................913 492-9050
Jack D Burton, *President*
Brian D Murray, *Chairman*
Beau Campbell, *Vice Pres*
Craig R Murray, *Vice Pres*
Michael C Murray, *Vice Pres*
EMP: 8
SQ FT: 64,000
SALES (est): 20.8MM **Privately Held**
SIC: 5084 2711 2893 5999 Printing trades machinery, equipment & supplies; newspapers, publishing & printing; letterpress or offset ink; art & architectural supplies; tourist camps, cabins, cottages & courts; commercial & industrial building operation

(G-601)
KANSAS ASPHALT INC (PA)
Also Called: Kai Total Pavement Management
7000 W 206th St (66013-9610)
PHONE..................................877 384-2280
Jane Jeffries, *President*
Charles Jeffries, *COO*
Pam Peckinpaugh, *Exec VP*
Jenna Beckett, *Vice Pres*
Andy Jeffries, *Vice Pres*
EMP: 63
SQ FT: 14,000
SALES: 41.4MM **Privately Held**
SIC: 1611 8744 8741 Highway & street paving contractor; grading; base maintenance (providing personnel on continuing basis); construction management

(G-602)
MCCOWN MARKETING LLC
20924 Floyd St (66013-9102)
PHONE..................................913 284-5584
Lindsay McCown, *Principal*
EMP: 10
SALES: 500K **Privately Held**
SIC: 2325 Shorts (outerwear): men's, youths' & boys'

(G-603)
MEYERS TURF FARMS INC
12390 W 215th St (66013-9200)
P.O. Box 69, Stilwell (66085-0069)
PHONE..................................913 533-2456
John W Meyers Jr, *President*
Thomas L Meyer, *Treasurer*
William H Meyers, *Admin Sec*
EMP: 100
SQ FT: 1,800
SALES (est): 2.5MM **Privately Held**
SIC: 0181 Sod farms

(G-604)
MILLER PLUMBING CO INC
20625 Metcalf Ave (66013-9101)
P.O. Box 393, Stilwell (66085-0393)
PHONE..................................913 851-1333
Patrick Brian Miller, *President*
Leann M Miller, *Treasurer*
EMP: 16
SQ FT: 6,000
SALES (est): 3.8MM **Privately Held**
SIC: 1711 Plumbing contractors

(G-605)
NORAG LLC (PA)
20710 Foster Ct Bucyrus (66013)
P.O. Box 412, Stilwell (66085-0412)
PHONE..................................913 851-7200
Randy R Osmundson, *President*
Lori A Osmundson, *Admin Sec*
EMP: 51
SALES (est): 5.6MM **Privately Held**
SIC: 0722 0723 4221 Cash grains, machine harvesting services; cash grain crops market preparation services; grain elevator, storage only

(G-606)
OVERLAND PARK ARBORETM & BTNCL
8909 W 179th St (66013-9084)
PHONE..................................913 685-3604
Karen Kerkhoff, *Manager*
Kristin Marema, *Director*
EMP: 35
SALES (est): 635.3K **Privately Held**
SIC: 8422 Botanical garden

(G-607)
RINGS AND CAGES INC
315 Main St (66013-9210)
PHONE..................................816 945-7772
Chad Sullivan, *President*
EMP: 5
SALES (est): 606.8K **Privately Held**
SIC: 3949 Sporting & athletic goods

(G-608)
RON WEERS CONSTRUCTION INC
20765 Foster Ct (66013-9080)
PHONE..................................913 681-5575
Ronald G Weers, *President*
EMP: 29 **EST:** 1973
SALES: 1MM **Privately Held**
SIC: 1794 1623 Excavation & grading, building construction; sewer line construction; water main construction

(G-609)
SOD SHOP INC
4855 W 231st St (66013-9088)
PHONE..................................913 814-0044
Wade Wilbure, *President*
EMP: 10
SALES: 900K **Privately Held**
SIC: 0782 Sodding contractor

(G-610)
SPARKER INDUSTRIES INC
8802 W 193rd Ter (66013-9671)
PHONE..................................913 963-5261
Stephanie Parker, *Principal*
EMP: 6
SALES (est): 298.7K **Privately Held**
SIC: 3999 Manufacturing industries

(G-611)
TOPPS PRODUCTS INC (PA)
20105 Metcalf Ave (66013-9276)
P.O. Box 1632, Canton MS (39046-1632)
PHONE..................................913 685-2500
Arlan Koppel, *President*
John Fry, *Chairman*
Larry Roe, *Accounts Mgr*
William B Schmidt, *Admin Sec*
▼ **EMP:** 12
SQ FT: 8,500
SALES (est): 2.1MM **Privately Held**
WEB: www.toppsproducts.com
SIC: 3069 Roofing, membrane rubber

(G-612)
YOUNG MANAGEMENT CORPORATION (PA)
22602 State Line Rd (66013-9733)
PHONE..................................913 947-3134
Willam G Young, *President*
Dave E Lundgren, *Vice Pres*
Linda Krizmanic, *Accountant*
Carla Schubert, *Manager*
Jean Stauch, *Manager*
EMP: 10
SQ FT: 12,000
SALES (est): 5.8MM **Privately Held**
SIC: 8742 Management consulting services

Buffalo
Wilson County

(G-613)
MICRO-LITE LLC
Micro Lite St (66717)
P.O. Box 45 (66717-0045)
PHONE..................................620 537-7025
Bill Beck, *Vice Pres*
EMP: 10
SALES (corp-wide): 2.7MM **Privately Held**
WEB: www.micro-litellc.com
SIC: 2048 Feed supplements
PA: Micro-Lite, L.L.C
3731 S Santa Fe Ave
Chanute KS 66720
620 431-0530

Buhler
Reno County

(G-614)
BUHLER SUNSHINE HOME INC
Also Called: SUNSHINE MEADOWS RETIREMENT CO
400 S Buhler Rd (67522-8133)
PHONE..................................620 543-2251
Keith Pankratz, *CEO*
Dana Weast, *Food Svc Dir*
Debi Weast, *Executive*
Nathan Spencer, *Admin Sec*
EMP: 90
SALES (est): 5.5MM **Privately Held**
WEB: www.sunshinemeadows.org
SIC: 8052 8051 Personal care facility; skilled nursing care facilities

(G-615)
DALTON L HUNT DDS
Also Called: Family Dentistry PA
115 N Main St (67522-9809)
P.O. Box 571 (67522-0571)
PHONE..................................620 543-2768
Dalton L Hunt, *CEO*
EMP: 10
SQ FT: 3,000
SALES (est): 615.8K **Privately Held**
SIC: 8021 Dentists' office

(G-616)
GAEDDERT FARMS SWEET CORN INC
13209 E 82nd Ave (67522-9004)
PHONE..................................620 543-2473
Julie Gaeddert, *President*
Tonya Martisko, *Vice Pres*
Jason Gaeddert, *Admin Sec*
EMP: 35
SALES (est): 292.8K **Privately Held**
WEB: www.kansassweetcorn.com
SIC: 0161 Corn farm, sweet

(G-617)
IDEATEK TELECOM LLC
111 Old Mill St (67522-2228)
P.O. Box 407 (67522-0407)
PHONE..................................620 543-2580
Daniel Friesen, *CEO*
Ivan Kuhn, *Marketing Staff*
Tyler Radi, *Manager*
Kent Hoskinson, *CIO*
Peter Gustaf, *Security Dir*
EMP: 23
SALES (est): 2.9MM **Privately Held**
SIC: 4813

(G-618)
MIKES EQUIPMENT COMPANY
9716 E 82nd Ave (67522-9101)
P.O. Box 287 (67522-0287)
PHONE..................................620 543-2535
Michael E Prieb, *President*
David Hiebert, *Cust Mgr*
▲ **EMP:** 12
SALES: 1.8MM **Privately Held**
WEB: www.mikesequipment.com
SIC: 5083 5013 Harvesting machinery & equipment; truck parts & accessories

(G-619)
WILDFLOWER INTERNET LLC
102 N Main St (67522-9810)
PHONE..................................620 543-2580
Daniel P Friesen, *Mng Member*
EMP: 20
SALES (est): 1.6MM **Privately Held**
SIC: 4813

Bunker Hill
Russell County

(G-620)
SMOKY HILLS PUBLIC TV CORP
Also Called: Kdck/Channel 21
604 Elm St (67626)
P.O. Box 9 (67626-0009)
PHONE..................................785 483-6990
Dawn J Gabel, *CEO*
Kelli King, *General Mgr*
Terry Cutler, *Chief Engr*
Callie Kolacny, *Mktg Dir*
Malinda Walker, *Director*
EMP: 17
SQ FT: 9,000
SALES: 1.6MM **Privately Held**
WEB: www.shptv.org
SIC: 4833 Television broadcasting stations

Burdett
Pawnee County

(G-621)
DELANEY IMPLEMENT CO INC
502 Broadway Ave (67523-8517)
P.O. Box 198 (67523-0198)
PHONE..................................620 525-6221
Howard Delaney, *President*
Jeff Delaney, *Corp Secy*
James Delaney, *Vice Pres*
EMP: 12
SQ FT: 18,000
SALES (est): 3.2MM **Privately Held**
SIC: 5083 Agricultural machinery & equipment

Burlingame
Osage County

(G-622)
BURLINGAME HISTORICAL PRESERVA
Also Called: BURLINGAME SCHUYLER MUSEUM
117 S Dacotah St (66413-1225)
P.O. Box 74 (66413-0074)
PHONE..................................785 654-3561
Carolyn Strohm, *President*
Kathy Smith, *Vice Pres*
Linda Fagan, *Treasurer*
Kathy Kraus, *Admin Sec*
EMP: 100
SALES: 137.9K **Privately Held**
WEB: www.burlingamehistorical.org
SIC: 8412 Historical society

(G-623)
FIRST STATE BANK (INC)
115 S Topeka Ave (66413-1213)
P.O. Box 5 (66413-0005)
PHONE..................................785 654-2421
David Fowler, *President*
Steve Dworht, *Vice Pres*
EMP: 26 **EST:** 1941
SALES (est): 3.9MM **Privately Held**
WEB: www.firststatebank.net
SIC: 6022 State trust companies accepting deposits, commercial

(G-624)
OSAGE GRAPHICS
223 W Hall Ave (66413-1407)
P.O. Box 47 (66413-0047)
PHONE..................................785 654-3939
Claudia Lynn, *President*
EMP: 10
SQ FT: 5,500
SALES (est): 712.8K **Privately Held**
WEB: www.osagegraphics.com
SIC: 2752 Commercial printing, lithographic

Burlington
Coffey County

(G-625)
B&B COOPERATIVE VENTURES LLC
1044 Us Highway 75 (66839-9061)
PHONE..................................620 364-1311
Edward E Birk,
Laura Birk, *Admin Sec*
EMP: 20
SALES (est): 2.9MM **Privately Held**
SIC: 1389 Oil field services

(G-626)
CHARLOMA INC
Also Called: Burlington Division
1290 10th Rd (66839-9097)
PHONE..................................620 364-2701
Mark Hight, *Sales Executive*
Justin Marchant, *Manager*
EMP: 25
SALES (corp-wide): 32.4MM **Privately Held**
WEB: www.charloma.com
SIC: 3088 3089 Shower stalls, fiberglass & plastic; tubs (bath, shower & laundry), plastic; bathroom fixtures, plastic; boats, nonrigid: plastic
HQ: Charloma, Inc.
727 N Liberty St
Cherryvale KS 67335
620 336-2124

(G-627)
COF TRAINING SERVICES INC
1415 S 6th St (66839-8967)
PHONE..................................620 364-2151
Sid Meeker, *Branch Mgr*
EMP: 30
SALES (corp-wide): 8.3MM **Privately Held**
SIC: 8331 Sheltered workshop
PA: Cof Training Services, Inc.
1516 N Davis Ave
Ottawa KS 66067
785 242-5035

(G-628)
COFFEY COUNTY HOSPITAL (PA)
Also Called: Coffey County Medical Center
801 N 4th St (66839-2602)
PHONE..................................620 364-5655
Karen Smith, *CFO*
Juanita White, *CFO*
Craig Stukey, *Accountant*
EMP: 200
SQ FT: 31,000
SALES: 21.4MM **Privately Held**
SIC: 8062 General medical & surgical hospitals

(G-629)
COFFEY COUNTY HOSPITAL
Also Called: Meadows, The
1201 Martindale St (66839-2400)
PHONE..................................620 364-8861
Elaine Seaman Birk, *Manager*
EMP: 24
SALES (corp-wide): 21.4MM **Privately Held**
SIC: 8062 8082 General medical & surgical hospitals; home health care services
PA: Coffey County Hospital
801 N 4th St
Burlington KS 66839
620 364-5655

(G-630)
COFFEY COUNTY HOSPITAL
Also Called: Coffey County Medical Center
309 Sanders St (66839-2616)
P.O. Box 289 (66839-0289)
PHONE..................................620 364-5395
Dennis George, *Director*
EMP: 35
SALES (corp-wide): 21.4MM **Privately Held**
SIC: 8062 8011 General medical & surgical hospitals; clinic, operated by physicians
PA: Coffey County Hospital
801 N 4th St
Burlington KS 66839
620 364-5655

(G-631)
COFFEY COUNTY TRNSP INC
520 Cross St (66839-1108)
PHONE..................................620 364-1935
Susan Mueller, *President*
Sharon Hall, *Vice Pres*
Charles Huff, *Vice Pres*
Kent Hoyt, *Treasurer*
Kara Reynolds, *Exec Dir*
EMP: 16
SQ FT: 2,100
SALES: 544.1K **Privately Held**
SIC: 4121 Taxicabs

(G-632)
COFFEY HEALTH SYSTEMS
801 N 4th St (66839-2602)
PHONE..................................620 364-5118
Cindy McKerrigan, *Officer*
EMP: 99
SALES (est): 4.4MM **Privately Held**
SIC: 8062 General medical & surgical hospitals

(G-633)
CSD7 SOCIAL MEDAL
1016 S 6th St (66839-2078)
PHONE..................................620 203-0477
Christopher Dobyns, *Principal*
EMP: 99
SALES: 950K **Privately Held**
SIC: 7389 Business services

(G-634)
FAIMON PUBLICATIONS INC
Also Called: Coffey County Republican
324 Hudson St (66839-1327)
P.O. Box A (66839-0218)
PHONE..................................620 364-5325
Christopher Faimon, *President*
EMP: 15
SALES (est): 1.1MM **Privately Held**
SIC: 2711 5044 Newspapers, publishing & printing; office equipment

(G-635)
FIRST NATIONAL BANK OF KANSAS
600 N 4th St (66839-1284)
P.O. Box 228 (66839-0228)
PHONE..................................785 733-2564
Craig A Meader, *CEO*
Barbara Burk, *President*
Tom AST, *Vice Pres*
Craig Stukey, *Real Est Agnt*
EMP: 12
SQ FT: 3,000
SALES: 3.2MM **Privately Held**
WEB: www.fnbofks.com
SIC: 6021 National commercial banks

(G-636)
FITTINGS EXPORT LLC
3916 4th St (66839-8979)
PHONE..................................620 364-2930
Doug Hauff, *Mng Member*
EMP: 5
SALES (est): 200K **Privately Held**
SIC: 3089 5199 Fittings for pipe, plastic; art goods & supplies

(G-637)
HOOVER STORES INC
Also Called: Hoovers
314 Cross St (66839-1189)
PHONE..................................620 364-5444
Tamara K Salava, *President*
Ronald D Hoover, *Corp Secy*
EMP: 70
SQ FT: 194,000
SALES (est): 5.9MM **Privately Held**
SIC: 5411 4724 Grocery stores, independent; travel agencies

(G-638)
LIFE CARE CENTER BURLINGTON
Also Called: BURLINGTON HEALTHCARE CENTER
601 Cross St (66839-1105)
PHONE..................................620 364-2117
Brian Warren, *President*
EMP: 85
SALES: 4.8MM **Privately Held**
SIC: 8051 Skilled nursing care facilities

(G-639)
LIFE CARE CENTERS AMERICA INC
Also Called: Burlington Health Care Ctr
601 Cross St (66839-1105)
PHONE..................................620 364-2117
Mike Pelzer, *Branch Mgr*
Peter Mungai, *Exec Dir*
EMP: 75
SALES (corp-wide): 144MM **Privately Held**
SIC: 8051 8052 Convalescent home with continuous nursing care; intermediate care facilities
PA: Life Care Centers Of America, Inc.
3570 Keith St Nw
Cleveland TN 37312
423 472-9585

(G-640)
MENARD INCORPORATED
Also Called: Kan-Seal
1905 Us Highway 75 (66839-8952)
P.O. Box 453 (66839-0453)
PHONE..................................620 364-3600
Christopher Menard, *President*
Erin Menard, *Sales Staff*
EMP: 13
SQ FT: 3,400
SALES (est): 5MM **Privately Held**
WEB: www.kanseal.com
SIC: 5085 Industrial supplies

(G-641)
PRESCRIPTION CENTRE
312 Cross St (66839-1189)
PHONE..................................620 364-5523
Dan Salava, *President*
Tammy Salava, *Vice Pres*
EMP: 5
SALES (est): 432.4K **Privately Held**
SIC: 5999 2834 Toiletries, cosmetics & perfumes; medicines, capsuled or ampuled

(G-642)
RESELLERS EDGE LLC
615 N 4th St (66839-1285)
PHONE..................................620 364-3398
Tammy Baumann, *Vice Pres*
Mike Baumann,
▲ **EMP:** 12
SALES (est): 790K **Privately Held**
SIC: 2759 Promotional printing

(G-643)
THRIVENT FINANCIAL FOR LUTHERA
1020 Osborne St (66839-1150)
PHONE..................................620 364-2177
EMP: 23
SALES (corp-wide): 9B **Privately Held**
WEB: www.thrivent.com
SIC: 6411 Insurance agents, brokers & service
PA: Thrivent Financial For Lutherans Foundation
625 4th Ave S
Minneapolis MN 55415
800 847-4836

(G-644)
TRUSTPOINT SERVICES INC
Also Called: Nationwide
800 N 4th St Ste 101 (66839-2618)
PHONE..................................620 364-5665
Angela Trimble, *President*
Janet Payne, *Vice Pres*
EMP: 15
SQ FT: 4,000

SALES (est): 4.5MM **Privately Held**
WEB: www.trustpointinsurance.net
SIC: 6411 6531 Insurance agents; real estate brokers & agents

(G-645)
WOLF CREEK NUCLEAR OPER CORP
Also Called: Wcnoc
1550 Oxen Ln (66839-9127)
P.O. Box 411 (66839-0411)
PHONE..................................620 364-4141
Matt Sunseri, *President*
Lance Link, *Superintendent*
Bruce Barrett, *Principal*
Travis Moerer, *QC Mgr*
Alex Alahmed, *Engineer*
▲ **EMP:** 1003
SQ FT: 90,000
SALES (est): 4.2B **Privately Held**
SIC: 4911 ; generation, electric power

Burns
Marion County

(G-646)
GOODWIN INDUSTRIES INC
215 W Broadway St (66840-8912)
P.O. Box 127 (66840-0127)
PHONE..................................620 726-5281
Larry Goodwin, *President*
Teresa Goodwin, *Treasurer*
EMP: 6
SALES (est): 667.5K **Privately Held**
SIC: 3599 Machine shop, jobbing & repair

(G-647)
HADLEY TRANSIT LLC
12287 Nw Boyer Rd (66840-8848)
PHONE..................................620 726-5853
Joanna Hadley, *Principal*
EMP: 11
SALES (est): 1.4MM **Privately Held**
SIC: 4213 Trucking, except local

Burrton
Harvey County

(G-648)
GREAT PLAINS MOBILE HM MOVERS
209 N Burrton Ave (67020-2007)
P.O. Box 608 (67020-0608)
PHONE..................................620 463-2420
Fax: 620 463-2813
EMP: 10
SALES (est): 610K **Privately Held**
SIC: 4213 Trucking Operator-Nonlocal

(G-649)
HARDWOOD MANUFACTURING LLC
202 E Dean St (67020-2002)
PHONE..................................620 463-2663
Steven C Lang, *Mng Member*
Steve Lang, *Mng Member*
EMP: 10
SALES (est): 1.1MM **Privately Held**
SIC: 2431 Millwork

(G-650)
SOUTHWEST AND ASSOCIATES INC
100 N Reno Ave (67020-2000)
P.O. Box 547 (67020-0547)
PHONE..................................620 463-5631
Kim Corcoran, *Principal*
Clinton Hageman, *Vice Pres*
Pat Cooper, *Sales Staff*
EMP: 55
SQ FT: 28,000
SALES (est): 14.6MM **Privately Held**
WEB: www.southwestassociates.com
SIC: 1796 1791 3441 3444 Elevator installation & conversion; storage tanks, metal: erection; fabricated structural metal; sheet metalwork

(G-651)
STINGER LTD
302 E Dean St (67020-2092)
PHONE..................................620 465-2683
Larry W Matlack, *Partner*
Betty Matlack, *Partner*
Melissa Matlack, *Partner*
William L Matlack, *Partner*
Bobbie J Oneal, *Office Mgr*
▲ **EMP:** 25
SQ FT: 16,000
SALES (est): 6.3MM **Privately Held**
WEB: www.stingerltd.com
SIC: 3523 Farm machinery & equipment

Bushton
Rice County

(G-652)
BUSHTON MANUFACTURING LLC
Also Called: Hawk Woodworking Tools
319 S Main St (67427-3217)
P.O. Box 127 (67427-0127)
PHONE..................................620 562-3557
Loren Orth,
Nilus Orth,
EMP: 9
SALES (est): 740K **Privately Held**
SIC: 3423 Edge tools for woodworking: augers, bits, gimlets, etc.

(G-653)
HOELSCHER INC
312 S Main St (67427-3217)
P.O. Box 195 (67427-0195)
PHONE..................................620 562-3575
Darrel G Hoelscher, *President*
Marc Cannon, *Sales Staff*
EMP: 13
SQ FT: 22,000
SALES (est): 2.2MM **Privately Held**
WEB: www.hoelscherinc.com
SIC: 3523 Haying machines: mowers, rakes, stackers, etc.

(G-654)
ONEOK INC
Also Called: Oneok Field Services
777 Avenue Y (67427-9502)
PHONE..................................620 562-4205
Kevin Willt, *Branch Mgr*
EMP: 42
SALES (corp-wide): 12.5B **Publicly Held**
WEB: www.oneok.com
SIC: 1321 1311 Natural gas liquids; crude petroleum & natural gas
PA: Oneok, Inc.
100 W 5th St Ste Ll
Tulsa OK 74103
918 588-7000

Caldwell
Sumner County

(G-655)
CALDWELL AREA CHAMBE
24 N Main St (67022-1530)
P.O. Box 42 (67022-0042)
PHONE..................................620 845-6914
Lu Ann Jamison, *Exec Dir*
EMP: 16
SALES (est): 375.3K **Privately Held**
SIC: 8611 Chamber of Commerce

(G-656)
CALDWELL COMMUNICARE
601 S Osage St (67022-1654)
PHONE..................................620 845-6492
Virgil Watson, *Manager*
EMP: 85
SALES (est): 660.7K **Privately Held**
SIC: 8082 Home health care services

(G-657)
CALDWELL SNIOR CTIZENS CTR INC
428 N Chisholm St (67022-1020)
PHONE..................................620 845-6926
Beverly Walta, *President*
Barbara Jenista, *Admin Sec*
Diana Mata, *Admin Asst*
EMP: 12
SQ FT: 3,000
SALES (est): 57.5K **Privately Held**
SIC: 8641 Community membership club

(G-658)
FARMERS COOPERATIVE GRAIN CO
102 N Arapahoe St (67022-1508)
P.O. Box 191 (67022-0191)
PHONE..................................620 845-6441
Robert W Johnston, *President*
EMP: 18 **EST:** 1920
SQ FT: 2,000
SALES: 3.1MM **Privately Held**
SIC: 5153 5191 Grain elevators; feed; fertilizer & fertilizer materials; seeds: field, garden & flower; chemicals, agricultural

(G-659)
KANOKLA COMMUNICATIONS LLC (HQ)
Also Called: Kanokla Networks
100 Kanokla Ave (67022-1040)
P.O. Box 111 (67022-0111)
PHONE..................................620 845-5682
Dana Pierce, *CEO*
Scott Bannister, *President*
Alysia Keller, *Accountant*
Lacy Turek, *Bookkeeper*
Ryan Schmidt, *Technology*
EMP: 60
SQ FT: 50,000
SALES: 1.5MM
SALES (corp-wide): 21.6MM **Privately Held**
WEB: www.kskc.net
SIC: 4813 Local & long distance telephone communications
PA: Kanokla Telephone Association
100 Kanokla Ave
Caldwell KS 67022
620 845-5682

(G-660)
KANOKLA TELEPHONE ASSOCIATION (PA)
Also Called: Kanokla Networks
100 Kanokla Ave (67022-1040)
P.O. Box 111 (67022-0111)
PHONE..................................620 845-5682
Dana Pierce, *CEO*
Scott Bannister, *President*
Harold Lavalley, *Vice Pres*
Carol Peterson, *Treasurer*
Melinda Karns, *Bookkeeper*
EMP: 39
SQ FT: 9,800
SALES: 21.6MM **Privately Held**
SIC: 5065 1731 5045 7378 Telephone & telegraphic equipment; communications specialization; computers; computer peripheral equipment repair & maintenance; computer related consulting services; voice telephone communications

(G-661)
STOCK EXCHANGE BANK
103 S Main St (67022-1607)
P.O. Box 273 (67022-0273)
PHONE..................................620 442-2400
C Gage Overall, *President*
Tricia Cook, *President*
Lesly Blosser, *Admin Asst*
EMP: 13 **EST:** 1881
SALES: 2.6MM **Privately Held**
SIC: 6021 National commercial banks

(G-662)
SUMNER COUNTY HOSPITAL DST 1
601 S Osage St (67022-1698)
P.O. Box 42 (67022-0042)
PHONE..................................620 845-6492
Joe Halling, *Director*
Peggy Miller, *Lab Dir*
Joyce Marcrum, *Food Svc Dir*
Tom Henton, *Administration*
EMP: 67
SQ FT: 17,000
SALES: 3.6MM **Privately Held**
WEB: www.schd1.com
SIC: 8062 General medical & surgical hospitals

Cambridge
Cowley County

(G-663)
FERGUSON RANCH
9203 327th Rd (67023-9322)
PHONE..................................620 467-2265
William Ferguson III, *Owner*
EMP: 10
SALES: 300K **Privately Held**
WEB: www.fergusonranch.com
SIC: 0212 Beef cattle except feedlots

Caney
Montgomery County

(G-664)
AGRA AXE INTERNATIONAL INC
Also Called: Midland Industrial Group
166e Industrial Park Hwy (67333)
P.O. Box 250 (67333-0250)
PHONE..................................620 879-5858
Josef Barbi, *President*
EMP: 20 **EST:** 1999
SALES (est): 2.3MM **Privately Held**
SIC: 3421 Shears, hand

(G-665)
ARROW VALVE CO INC
201 N Foreman St (67333-1329)
P.O. Box 343 (67333-0343)
PHONE..................................620 879-2126
Monroe Robertson, *President*
Kathy Alani, *Corp Secy*
EMP: 9
SQ FT: 120,000
SALES: 400K **Privately Held**
SIC: 3494 3491 Pipe fittings; industrial valves

(G-666)
ARVEST BANK
301 W 4th Ave (67333-1463)
P.O. Box 36 (67333-0036)
PHONE..................................620 879-5811
Connie Kirkpatrick, *Branch Mgr*
EMP: 15
SALES (corp-wide): 2.3B **Privately Held**
SIC: 6022 State trust companies accepting deposits, commercial
HQ: Arvest Bank
103 S Bloomington St
Lowell AR 72745
479 575-1000

(G-667)
ENGINEERED SYSTEMS & EQP INC
106 C Industrial Park (67333)
PHONE..................................620 879-5841
Josef W Barbi, *President*
▼ **EMP:** 100
SQ FT: 50,000
SALES (est): 11.6MM **Privately Held**
WEB: www.midlandindustrialgroup.com
SIC: 3556 Dairy & milk machinery

(G-668)
GARY GORBY
Also Called: G & G Dozer
Hwy 75 N (67333)
P.O. Box 6 (67333-0006)
PHONE..................................620 879-5243
Gary Gorby, *Owner*
EMP: 50
SALES (est): 3.6MM **Privately Held**
SIC: 1794 1389 Excavation work; oil field services

(G-669)
GOOD NEWS PUBLISHING CO INC
124 N State St (67333-1334)
P.O. Box 1317, Independence (67301-1317)
PHONE..................................620 879-5460
Kirk Clinsclaes, *President*
Penny Coy, *Vice Pres*
June Friensberg, *Treasurer*
Sara Shivley, *Admin Sec*
EMP: 37
SALES (est): 3MM **Privately Held**
WEB: www.goodnewspress.com
SIC: 2721 2741 Magazines: publishing only, not printed on site; miscellaneous publishing

(G-670)
GUEST HOME ESTATES
Also Called: Lightning Creek
400 S Mcgee St (67333-1601)
PHONE..................................620 879-5199
Doug Matics, *Branch Mgr*
EMP: 20
SALES (corp-wide): 1.6MM **Privately Held**
SIC: 8059 Personal care home, with health care
PA: Guest Home Estates
1910 E Centennial Dr
Pittsburg KS 66762
620 431-7115

(G-671)
KOPCO INC (PA)
Hwy 166 E (67333)
P.O. Box 69 (67333-0069)
PHONE..................................620 879-2117
Kenneth K George Sr, *CEO*
Kenneth George Jr, *President*
Reba J George, *Corp Secy*
Robert Sower, *Purch Mgr*
Joel Dodson, *Manager*
EMP: 100 **EST:** 1960
SQ FT: 65,000
SALES (est): 27.2MM **Privately Held**
WEB: www.kopcoinc.com
SIC: 2752 2791 2789 Commercial printing, offset; typesetting; bookbinding & related work

(G-672)
MONTGOMERY COUNTY CHRONICLE
Also Called: Caney Chronicle
202 W 4th Ave (67333-1462)
P.O. Box 186 (67333-0186)
PHONE..................................620 879-2156
Rudy Taylor, *President*
Andy Taylor, *Editor*
Kathy Taylor, *Corp Secy*
Heather Brown, *Regional*
EMP: 8 **EST:** 1888
SQ FT: 2,500
SALES (est): 377.6K **Privately Held**
SIC: 2711 Newspapers: publishing only, not printed on site

(G-673)
SPEARS CANEY INC
Also Called: Spears Manufacturing
1609 Cr 1900 (67333-8588)
PHONE..................................620 879-2131
Wayne Spears, *President*
▲ **EMP:** 250 **EST:** 1984
SALES (est): 45.3MM
SALES (corp-wide): 1.5B **Privately Held**
WEB: www.spearsmfg.com
SIC: 3089 Fittings for pipe, plastic
PA: Spears Manufacturing Co.
15853 Olden St
Sylmar CA 91342
818 364-1611

(G-674)
SPEARS MANUFACTURING CO
Hwy 166 (67333)
PHONE..................................620 879-2131
Geoff Collins, *Manager*
EMP: 350
SALES (corp-wide): 1.5B **Privately Held**
WEB: www.spearsmfg.com
SIC: 3089 3498 Fittings for pipe, plastic; fabricated pipe & fittings
PA: Spears Manufacturing Co.
15853 Olden St
Sylmar CA 91342
818 364-1611

(G-675)
THORNTON AIR ROTARY LLC
2186 Us Highway 166 (67333-8505)
PHONE..................................620 879-2073
EMP: 7
SALES (est): 480K **Privately Held**
SIC: 1389 Oil/Gas Field Services

(G-676)
TOMS DITCHING & BACKHOE INC
1876 Us Highway 75 (67333-8507)
PHONE..................................620 879-2215
Thomas C Scimeca, *President*
Toni Z Scimeca, *Vice Pres*
EMP: 14
SALES (est): 1.8MM **Privately Held**
SIC: 1623 1629 1731 Pipeline construction; trenching contractor; fiber optic cable installation

(G-677)
TRUCKING BY GEORGE INC
Ind Pk Hwy 166 E (67333)
PHONE..................................620 879-2117
Kenneth K George, *President*
Reba George, *Corp Secy*
EMP: 10
SQ FT: 600
SALES: 1MM
SALES (corp-wide): 27.2MM **Privately Held**
WEB: www.kopcoinc.com
SIC: 4213 Trucking, except local
PA: Kopco, Inc.
Hwy 166 E
Caney KS 67333
620 879-2117

(G-678)
WE-MAC MANUFACTURING CO
Industrial Park (67333)
P.O. Box 12378, Kansas City MO (64116-0378)
PHONE..................................620 879-2187
Mike Mravunac, *Sales Staff*
EMP: 14
SALES (corp-wide): 5.3MM **Privately Held**
SIC: 3443 Fabricated plate work (boiler shop)
PA: We-Mac Manufacturing Co.
326 E 14th Ave
Kansas City MO 64116
800 444-3218

Canton
Mcpherson County

(G-679)
AMERICAN ENERGIES GAS SVC LLC
136 S Main St (67428-8939)
PHONE..................................620 628-4424
Steve Moore, *Manager*
EMP: 15 **EST:** 2002
SALES (est): 844.7K **Privately Held**
SIC: 1623 4925 Pipeline construction; gas production and/or distribution

(G-680)
CYCLONE WELL SERVICE INC
1504 27th Ave (67428-8800)
P.O. Box 522 (67428-0522)
PHONE..................................620 628-4428
Terry Bandy, *President*
EMP: 7 **EST:** 1971
SALES: 258.8K **Privately Held**
SIC: 1389 Servicing oil & gas wells; oil field services

(G-681)
SCHULZ WELDING SERVICE INC
Also Called: Schulz Oil & Gas
114 S Main St (67428-8939)
P.O. Box 515 (67428-0515)
PHONE..................................620 628-4431
Roger A Schulz, *President*
Roger A Swaultz, *President*
Chris Schulz, *Vice Pres*
Mitchell Schulz, *Treasurer*
Rodney Schulz, *Admin Sec*
EMP: 11
SQ FT: 5,000
SALES (est): 500K **Privately Held**
SIC: 1389 7692 Oil & gas wells: building, repairing & dismantling; cracked casting repair

(G-682)
SPRING VALLEY WOODWORKS INC
2592 Chisholm Rd (67428-8857)
PHONE..................................620 345-8330
Brenda Traffas, *President*
Don Swank, *General Mgr*
Stephen Klepacki, *Admin Sec*
EMP: 8
SQ FT: 7,000
SALES (est): 608.1K **Privately Held**
WEB: www.springvalleywood.com
SIC: 2511 5712 Wood household furniture; furniture stores

(G-683)
STATE BANK OF CANTON
103 S Main St (67428-8939)
P.O. Box 66 (67428-0066)
PHONE..................................620 628-4425
Douglas D Loewen, *President*
EMP: 14 **EST:** 1989
SALES: 903K **Privately Held**
SIC: 6022 State trust companies accepting deposits, commercial

Carbondale
Osage County

(G-684)
MERCER BUS SERVICE
1252 W 141st St (66414-9463)
PHONE..................................785 836-7174
James Mercer, *Owner*
EMP: 18
SALES: 580K **Privately Held**
SIC: 4141 Local bus charter service

(G-685)
STORMONT-VAIL HEALTHCARE INC
Also Called: Osage County Clinic
211 Main St (66414-9714)
P.O. Box 309 (66414-0309)
PHONE..................................785 836-7111
Dida Lewis, *Manager*
EMP: 12
SALES (corp-wide): 719MM **Privately Held**
SIC: 8062 8011 General medical & surgical hospitals; general & family practice, physician/surgeon
PA: Stormont-Vail Healthcare, Inc.
1500 Sw 10th Ave
Topeka KS 66604
785 354-6000

Carlton
Saline County

(G-686)
CROMWELL BUILDERS MFG
Also Called: Jc.net/Cromwell/Builders
665 Eden Rd (67448)
PHONE..................................785 949-2433
James A Cromwell, *President*
EMP: 15
SQ FT: 14,000
SALES: 600K **Privately Held**
WEB: www.cromwellbuildersltd.com
SIC: 3714 3799 3312 3443 Axles, motor vehicle; trailers & trailer equipment; hot-rolled iron & steel products; farm storage tanks, metal plate

Cassoday
Butler County

(G-687)
DATA SOURCE OF KANSAS LLC
17000 Ne State Road 177 (66842-9005)
PHONE..................................620 735-4353
Allan Smith, *Owner*
Alan Smith,
Becky Smith,
EMP: 10
SALES (est): 740K **Privately Held**
SIC: 8732 Market analysis or research

Cawker City
Mitchell County

(G-688)
CAWKER CITY SENIOR CENTER
521 Wisconson St (67430)
P.O. Box 301 (67430-0301)
PHONE..................................785 781-4763
Colleen Eberle, *Vice Pres*
Marge Schultz, *Manager*
EMP: 15
SALES (est): 478.1K **Privately Held**
SIC: 8322 Senior citizens' center or association

(G-689)
S&K FUELS LLC
Also Called: Bob's Fuel
605 Wisconsin St (67430-9795)
PHONE..................................785 454-6219
Sam Bowles, *Mng Member*
EMP: 5
SALES (est): 249.4K **Privately Held**
SIC: 2869 Fuels

(G-690)
SMC CONCRETE AND CNSTR LLC
1417 Locust St (67430-9716)
PHONE..................................785 545-5186
Skyler M Wise, *Mng Member*
Skyler Wise, *Mng Member*
EMP: 12
SALES: 1MM **Privately Held**
SIC: 1771 Concrete work

(G-691)
WISE CONSTRUCTION INC
604 Wisconsin St (67430-9795)
P.O. Box 17 (67430-0017)
PHONE..................................785 781-4383
Richard Wise, *President*
Susan Wise, *Corp Secy*
EMP: 15
SALES (est): 3.5MM **Privately Held**
WEB: www.wiseconstruction.com
SIC: 1542 1771 Commercial & office buildings, prefabricated erection; concrete work

Cedar Vale
Chautauqua County

(G-692)
CANEY VALLEY ELC COOP ASSN
401 Lawrence St (67024-9156)
P.O. Box 308 (67024-0308)
PHONE..................................620 758-2262
Allen Zadorozny, *General Mgr*
Bonnie Campbell, *Executive*
EMP: 19 **EST:** 1940
SQ FT: 4,000
SALES: 9.6MM **Privately Held**
WEB: www.caneyvalley.com
SIC: 4911 Distribution, electric power

(G-693)
CEDAR VALE RURAL HEALTH CLINIC
Also Called: Cedar Vale Rural Hlth Clinics
501 Walnut St (67024)
P.O. Box 578 (67024-0578)
PHONE....................620 758-2221
Fay Milton, *Manager*
EMP: 10
SALES (est): 610.4K **Privately Held**
SIC: 8011 Offices & clinics of medical doctors

(G-694)
FULSOM BROTHERS INC
980 Kansas Rd (67024-9029)
P.O. Box 522 (67024-0522)
PHONE....................620 758-2828
Paul J Fulsom, *President*
EMP: 10 **EST:** 2010
SALES (est): 906.8K **Privately Held**
SIC: 1611 Highway & street construction

(G-695)
WESTERN FEED MILLS INC
403 Sale Barn Rd (67024)
PHONE....................620 758-2283
Fred Raybourn, *President*
EMP: 20
SALES (est): 5.4MM **Privately Held**
SIC: 2048 7389 Prepared feeds;

Centerville
Anderson County

(G-696)
RICK SAUCEDA TRUCKING LLC
3348 W 1200 Ln (66014-9133)
PHONE....................913 231-8584
Richard Sauceda,
Sara Sauceda,
EMP: 11 **EST:** 2016
SALES (est): 345.4K **Privately Held**
SIC: 4212 Local trucking, without storage

Centralia
Nemaha County

(G-697)
CENTRLIA CMMMITY HLTH CARE SVC
Also Called: East Ridge
604 1st St (66415-9637)
PHONE....................785 857-3388
Pam Bachman, *Director*
EMP: 55
SALES (est): 1.7MM **Privately Held**
SIC: 8052 Intermediate care facilities

(G-698)
D KOHAKE
677 120th Rd (66415-8013)
PHONE....................785 857-3854
EMP: 48
SALES (est): 1.3MM **Privately Held**
SIC: 8322 Individual/Family Services

(G-699)
FIRST HERITAGE BANK (PA)
Also Called: FIRST NATIONAL BANK
620 4th St (66415-9661)
P.O. Box 188 (66415-0188)
PHONE....................785 857-3341
Bruce Bachman, *President*
Matthew Bachman, *Vice Pres*
Teresa Harris, *Admin Sec*
EMP: 12 **EST:** 1882
SQ FT: 3,000
SALES: 6.4MM **Privately Held**
WEB: www.fnbcentralia.com
SIC: 6021 National commercial banks

Chanute
Neosho County

(G-700)
2R TOOL & MACHINE INC
915 W Ash St (66720-1584)
PHONE....................620 902-5151
Roger Roseberry, *President*
Virginia Roseberry, *Vice Pres*
Harold Roseberry, *Admin Sec*
EMP: 7
SQ FT: 20,000
SALES (est): 631.7K **Privately Held**
SIC: 3599 Machine & other job shop work

(G-701)
A-1 ELECTRIC INC
414 E Main St (66720-1839)
P.O. Box 663 (66720-0663)
PHONE....................620 431-7500
Lyle Bruenger, *President*
Diana Bruenger, *Vice Pres*
EMP: 13
SQ FT: 20,000
SALES (est): 1.8MM **Privately Held**
SIC: 1711 5075 5063 Warm air heating & air conditioning contractor; warm air heating equipment & supplies; air conditioning & ventilation equipment & supplies; electrical apparatus & equipment

(G-702)
ADVANCED SYSTEMS HOMES INC
4711 S Santa Fe Ave (66720-5409)
PHONE....................620 431-3320
Darin Luebbering, *President*
Scott Luebbering, *Vice Pres*
Doug Luebbering, *Director*
Stanley Luebbering, *Director*
EMP: 41
SQ FT: 35,000
SALES (est): 3.5MM **Privately Held**
WEB: www.advancedsystemshomes.com
SIC: 1521 2452 Prefabricated single-family house erection; prefabricated wood buildings

(G-703)
ASH GROVE CEMENT COMPANY
Also Called: Chanute Plant
1801 N Santa Fe Ave (66720-1383)
P.O. Box 519 (66720-0519)
PHONE....................620 433-3500
James D Shea, *Opers-Prdtn-Mfg*
Sandy Hand, *Buyer*
Tim Heenan, *Human Res Mgr*
Tom Erickson, *Supervisor*
Brad Larue, *Maintence Staff*
EMP: 45
SALES (corp-wide): 29.7B **Privately Held**
WEB: www.ashgrove.com
SIC: 3241 5032 Cement, hydraulic; cement
HQ: Ash Grove Cement Company
11011 Cody St Ste 300
Overland Park KS 66210
913 451-8900

(G-704)
B & G CONSTRUCTION
3914 S Santa Fe Ave (66720-5402)
PHONE....................620 431-0849
David Petersen, *President*
EMP: 15
SALES (est): 1MM **Privately Held**
SIC: 1542 School building construction

(G-705)
BANK OF COMMERCE (HQ)
Also Called: SOUTHEAST CHECK PRINTING
101 W Main St (66720-1750)
P.O. Box 538 (66720-0538)
PHONE....................620 431-1400
Virgil Lair, *Ch of Bd*
Mark Lair, *President*
Sallie Knapp, *Vice Pres*
Patti Slansky, *Opers Staff*
EMP: 37
SALES: 6.3MM **Privately Held**
SIC: 6022 State trust companies accepting deposits, commercial

(G-706)
BARNHARTS EXCAVATION LLC
2082 W 21st St (66720-6110)
P.O. Box 835 (66720-0835)
PHONE....................620 431-0959
Ervin Barnhart,
Wendy Barnhart,
EMP: 10
SALES (est): 1.4MM **Privately Held**
SIC: 1629 1794 Land clearing contractor; excavation work

(G-707)
BIG CREEK INVESTMENT CORP INC
Also Called: Big Creek Sound
10280 210th Rd (66720-6425)
PHONE....................620 431-3445
David Orr, *CEO*
Cheryl Orr, *Principal*
Terri Phillips, *Comptroller*
Deshon Orr, *Director*
EMP: 5
SQ FT: 32,000
SALES (est): 430K **Privately Held**
SIC: 6799 3713 3599 8742 Investors; truck bodies & parts; utility truck bodies; machine & other job shop work; sales (including sales management) consultant; sales promotion

(G-708)
CANCER CENTER OF KANSAS PA
505 S Plummer Ave (66720-1950)
PHONE....................620 431-7580
Dennis F Moore, *Med Doctor*
Michael Cannon, *Director*
EMP: 10
SALES (corp-wide): 24.4MM **Privately Held**
SIC: 8011 Oncologist
PA: Cancer Center Of Kansas, P.A.
818 N Emporia St Ste 403
Wichita KS 67214
316 262-4467

(G-709)
CANEY GUEST HOME INC
Also Called: Ozark Country Home
7440 220th Rd (66720-6409)
PHONE....................620 431-7115
Loretta Walker, *Manager*
EMP: 13 **Privately Held**
SIC: 8361 Residential care
PA: Caney Guest Home Inc
111 W 4th Ave
Caney KS

(G-710)
CFT LLC
Also Called: Chanute Fintube
500 W 21st St (66720-5101)
P.O. Box 599 (66720-0599)
PHONE....................620 431-0885
Jerry Pruit, *Manager*
EMP: 20 **Privately Held**
WEB: www.carpetfabrictech.com
SIC: 3469 Tube fins, stamped metal
PA: Cft Llc
5727 S Lewis Ave Ste 600
Tulsa OK

(G-711)
CHANUTE ART GALLERY
17 N Lincoln Ave (66720-1818)
PHONE....................620 431-7807
Elly Mc Coy, *Director*
EMP: 12
SALES (est): 217.9K **Privately Held**
SIC: 7999 5999 Art gallery, commercial; art dealers

(G-712)
CHANUTE PUBLISHING COMPANY
Also Called: Chanute Tribune
15 N Evergreen Ave (66720)
PHONE....................620 431-4100
Bruce Bucanan, *President*
EMP: 700
SQ FT: 15,000
SALES (est): 21.2MM
SALES (corp-wide): 1.5B **Publicly Held**
WEB: www.chanute.com
SIC: 2711 2741 2752 Newspapers: publishing only, not printed on site; shopping news: publishing only, not printed on site; commercial printing, lithographic
HQ: Harris Enterprises, Inc.
1 N Main St Ste 616
Hutchinson KS
620 694-5830

(G-713)
CHANUTE RECREATION COMMISSION
400 S Highland Ave Ste 2 (66720-2425)
PHONE....................620 431-4199
Mark Sthoemehl, *Director*
EMP: 79
SALES (est): 1.7MM **Privately Held**
SIC: 7999 Recreation center

(G-714)
CHASE CONTRACTORS INC
800 W 35th Pkwy (66720-5299)
PHONE....................620 431-2142
Mike Chase, *President*
Charlotte Chase, *Corp Secy*
EMP: 8
SALES (est): 929.7K **Privately Held**
SIC: 1623 1381 Cable television line construction; service well drilling

(G-715)
CHERRY STREET YOUTH CENTER (PA)
710 N Forest Ave (66720-1725)
P.O. Box 414 (66720-0414)
PHONE....................620 431-0818
Barbara Prier, *Director*
EMP: 12
SQ FT: 3,900
SALES: 785.6K **Privately Held**
WEB: www.cherrystreetyouthcenter.org
SIC: 8322 Youth center

(G-716)
CITY OF CHANUTE
Also Called: Electric Dept Power Plant
1415 S Garfield St (66720)
P.O. Box 907 (66720-0907)
PHONE....................620 431-5270
Larry Gaets, *Superintendent*
James Hutchison, *Principal*
Jim Hutchison, *Principal*
EMP: 17 **Privately Held**
SIC: 4911 ; generation, electric power
PA: City Of Chanute
101 S Lincoln Ave
Chanute KS 66720
620 431-5768

(G-717)
COBANK ACB
Also Called: Farm Credit Services
725 W Cherry St (66720-1576)
P.O. Box 727 (66720-0727)
PHONE....................620 431-0240
Fax: 620 431-4373
EMP: 10
SALES (corp-wide): 2.7B **Privately Held**
SIC: 6111 Federal Land Bank
PA: Cobank Acb
6340 S Fiddlers Green Cir
Greenwood Village CO 80111
303 740-6527

(G-718)
COMFORT CONTRACTORS INC
215 N Lincoln Ave (66720-1821)
P.O. Box 643 (66720-0643)
PHONE....................620 431-4780
Mark Sigler, *President*
Linda Sigler, *Corp Secy*
Melanie Leistikow, *Officer*
EMP: 25
SQ FT: 6,000
SALES (est): 3.3MM **Privately Held**
SIC: 1711 1731 Warm air heating & air conditioning contractor; plumbing contractors; general electrical contractor

(G-719)
COMMERCIAL BANK
1315 S Santa Fe Ave (66720-3054)
P.O. Box 558 (66720-0558)
PHONE..................................620 431-3200
Tim Fairchild, *Manager*
EMP: 10
SALES (corp-wide): 30.2MM **Publicly Held**
SIC: 6022 6159 State commercial banks; agricultural credit institutions
HQ: Commercial Bank
1901 Main St
Parsons KS 67357
620 423-0770

(G-720)
COMMUNITY NATIONAL BANK
Also Called: Chanute First Street Drive Up
115 E 1st St (66720-2303)
P.O. Box 628 (66720-0628)
PHONE..................................620 431-2265
Rob Snyder, *Branch Mgr*
EMP: 13 **Privately Held**
SIC: 6141 Personal credit institutions
HQ: Community National Bank & Trust
14 N Lincoln Ave
Chanute KS 66720

(G-721)
COMMUNITY NATIONAL BANK & TR (HQ)
14 N Lincoln Ave (66720-1833)
P.O. Box 628 (66720-0628)
PHONE..................................620 431-2265
Daniel Mildfelt, *President*
Phillip Eastep, *Chairman*
Jim Kelly, *Exec VP*
Dean Kennedy, *Exec VP*
Tom Strickler, *Exec VP*
EMP: 42
SALES: 56.9MM **Privately Held**
SIC: 6022 State commercial banks

(G-722)
CONSOLIDATED OIL WELL SER
1322 S Grant Ave (66720-2854)
P.O. Box 884 (66720-0884)
PHONE..................................620 431-9217
Edsel Noland, *Principal*
EMP: 18
SALES (est): 917.2K **Privately Held**
SIC: 1389 Well logging

(G-723)
CUSTOM CAMPERS INC
3701 S Johnson Rd (66720-4003)
P.O. Box 965 (66720-0965)
PHONE..................................620 431-3990
Michael S Mitchell, *CEO*
Neil Ford, *President*
EMP: 200 **EST:** 1969
SQ FT: 57,000
SALES: 31.2MM
SALES (corp-wide): 40.1MM **Privately Held**
WEB: www.nuwa.com
SIC: 3792 Trailer coaches, automobile
PA: Nu-Wa Industries, Inc
3939 S Ross Ln
Chanute KS 66720
620 431-2088

(G-724)
DIVERSICARE LEASING CORP
Also Called: Diversicare of Chanute
530 W 14th St (66720-2877)
PHONE..................................620 431-4940
EMP: 13
SALES (corp-wide): 563.4MM **Publicly Held**
SIC: 8051 Skilled nursing care facilities
HQ: Diversicare Leasing Corp.
1621 Galleria Blvd
Brentwood TN 37027

(G-725)
ENTERPRISE BANK & TRUST
Also Called: First Commerical
17 S Lincoln Ave (66720-2429)
PHONE..................................620 431-7070
Connie Schoolcy, *Vice Pres*
EMP: 10 **Publicly Held**
WEB: www.enterprisefinancial.com
SIC: 6022 State trust companies accepting deposits, commercial
HQ: Enterprise Bank & Trust
150 N Meramec Ave Ste 300
Saint Louis MO 63105
314 725-5500

(G-726)
ESSLINGER MANUFACTURING
22165 Harper Rd (66720-5391)
PHONE..................................620 431-4338
David Esslinger, *Owner*
EMP: 6
SALES (est): 429.3K **Privately Held**
SIC: 3089 Injection molding of plastics

(G-727)
EVERBRITE ELECTRONICS INC
720 W Cherry St (66720-1577)
PHONE..................................620 431-7383
William J Fritz, *President*
Greg Harruff, *Vice Pres*
Rob Mathson, *Vice Pres*
Trudy Witten, *Plant Mgr*
Cody Kesich, *Project Mgr*
▲ **EMP:** 70
SQ FT: 20,000
SALES (est): 13.1MM
SALES (corp-wide): 244.9MM **Privately Held**
WEB: www.everbrite.com
SIC: 3612 Specialty transformers
PA: Everbrite, Llc
4949 S 110th St
Greenfield WI 53228
414 529-3500

(G-728)
FMS MIDWEST DIALYSIS CTRS LLC
Also Called: Renal Care Group Chanute
703 S Plummer Ave (66720-2552)
PHONE..................................620 431-1239
Carol Hamilton, *Manager*
EMP: 10
SALES (corp-wide): 18.3B **Privately Held**
WEB: www.bamap.com
SIC: 8092 Kidney dialysis centers
HQ: Fms Midwest Dialysis Centers, Llc
920 Winter St
Waltham MA 02451
781 699-9000

(G-729)
FOUNDATION OF NEOSHO MEMORIAL
629 S Plummer Ave (66720-1928)
P.O. Box 426 (66720-0426)
PHONE..................................620 431-4000
Murray L Brown, *CEO*
Stephanie Byers, *Marketing Staff*
Brian W Kueser, *Med Doctor*
Kathy Greve, *Manager*
Holly Norris, *Manager*
EMP: 41
SALES: 49.7MM **Privately Held**
SIC: 8062 General medical & surgical hospitals

(G-730)
HBD INDUSTRIES INC
Also Called: Chanute Operations
201 N Allen Ave (66720-1428)
P.O. Box 728 (66720-0728)
PHONE..................................620 431-9100
Roger Prather, *COO*
Roger N Prather, *Opers-Prdtn-Mfg*
Jerry Adams, *Engineer*
R Dean Hibbs, *Engineer*
Jim Culp, *Sales Staff*
EMP: 81
SALES (corp-wide): 260.7MM **Privately Held**
WEB: www.hbdelgin.com
SIC: 3052 3443 2295 Rubber & plastics hose & beltings; ducting, metal plate; coated fabrics, not rubberized
PA: Hbd Industries Inc
5200 Upper Metro
Dublin OH 43017
614 526-7000

(G-731)
HEALTH MANAGEMENT OF KANSAS
Also Called: Windsor Home Care
324 E Main St Ste A (66720-1837)
PHONE..................................620 431-7474
Jewel Ware, *Manager*
EMP: 80 **Privately Held**
SIC: 8741 8082 Nursing & personal care facility management; home health care services
PA: Health Management Of Kansas, Inc
104 W 8th St
Coffeyville KS 67337

(G-732)
HOLIDAY INN EXPRESS & SUITES
3401 Blue Comet Dr (66720-7201)
PHONE..................................620 431-0817
Kurt Boerner, *Principal*
EMP: 20
SQ FT: 80,000
SALES (est): 132.1K **Privately Held**
SIC: 7011 Hotels & motels

(G-733)
HOME SAVINGS BANK
214 N Lincoln Ave (66720-1822)
P.O. Box 467 (66720-0467)
PHONE..................................620 431-1100
J Michael Reid, *CEO*
Jerry Herron, *Exec VP*
EMP: 11
SQ FT: 3,000
SALES: 3.1MM **Privately Held**
SIC: 6022 State commercial banks

(G-734)
JOHNSON MORTUARY INC
Also Called: Penwell Gabel Funeral Home
101 N Highland Ave (66720-1814)
PHONE..................................620 431-1220
James Earl, *Manager*
Michael Benedick, *Director*
EMP: 12
SQ FT: 10,000
SALES: 333.6K **Privately Held**
SIC: 7261 Funeral home

(G-735)
KEPLEY WELL SERVICE LLC
19245 Ford Rd (66720-5498)
PHONE..................................620 431-9212
Ivy Kepley,
Michael Kent Kepley,
EMP: 10
SALES (est): 225K **Privately Held**
SIC: 1381 1389 Reworking oil & gas wells; well plugging & abandoning, oil & gas; fishing for tools, oil & gas field; pumping of oil & gas wells; servicing oil & gas wells

(G-736)
KUSTOM SIGNALS INC
1010 W Chestnut St (66720-1429)
P.O. Box 947 (66720-0947)
PHONE..................................620 431-2700
Joan Vitt, *CEO*
Kelly Nickels, *Purch Agent*
Jeff Wade, *Manager*
EMP: 105
SQ FT: 45,000
SALES (corp-wide): 2.9B **Privately Held**
WEB: www.kustomsignals.com
SIC: 3812 3663 3651 3823 Radar systems & equipment; radio broadcasting & communications equipment; video cassette recorders/players & accessories; industrial instrmnts msrmnt display/control process variable
HQ: Kustom Signals, Inc.
9652 Loiret Blvd
Lenexa KS 66219
913 492-1400

(G-737)
LANG DIESEL INC
201 35th Pkwy (66720-5514)
PHONE..................................620 431-6700
John Stewart, *Branch Mgr*
EMP: 13
SALES (corp-wide): 7.8MM **Privately Held**
SIC: 5083 Agricultural machinery & equipment
PA: Lang Diesel, Inc.
2818 Plaza Ave
Hays KS 67601
785 301-2426

(G-738)
LARUE MACHINE INC
Also Called: Econo-Larue Machine
220 W 14th St (66720-2891)
PHONE..................................620 431-3303
Ron Larue, *President*
Rhonda Larue, *Corp Secy*
EMP: 11
SQ FT: 6,800
SALES (est): 1MM **Privately Held**
SIC: 3599 3312 7692 3544 Machine shop, jobbing & repair; tool & die steel; welding repair; special dies, tools, jigs & fixtures

(G-739)
LIL TOLEDO LODGE LLC
Also Called: Lil' Toledo Lodge
10600 170th Rd (66720-6485)
PHONE..................................620 244-5668
Ronald L King, *Owner*
EMP: 20
SQ FT: 40,000
SALES (est): 866.6K **Privately Held**
WEB: www.liltoledo.com
SIC: 7997 Hunting club, membership

(G-740)
MAGNA TECH INC
Also Called: Magna Transportation
4331 S Johnson Rd (66720-4015)
P.O. Box 647 (66720-0647)
PHONE..................................620 431-3490
David G Orr, *President*
Deshon Orr, *Vice Pres*
Dan A Call, *Production*
Scotty S Bunch, *Director*
EMP: 20
SQ FT: 34,800
SALES (est): 1.4MM **Privately Held**
WEB: www.magnatechinc.com
SIC: 3799 3441 4212 5013 Towing bars & systems; recreational vehicles; fabricated structural metal; local trucking, without storage; automotive servicing equipment

(G-741)
MAIN STREET CHANUTE INC
4 E Elm St (66720)
P.O. Box 22 (66720-0022)
PHONE..................................620 431-0056
Sharon Stirewalt, *Exec Dir*
EMP: 17
SALES: 47.5K **Privately Held**
SIC: 1542 Commercial & office buildings, renovation & repair

(G-742)
MARK RANDOLF
Also Called: Super 8 Motel
3502 S Santa Fe Ave (66720-3239)
PHONE..................................620 431-7788
Taylor Collins, *General Mgr*
EMP: 15 **EST:** 2001
SALES (est): 525.9K **Privately Held**
SIC: 7011 Hotels & motels

(G-743)
MID-WEST FERTILIZER INC
Also Called: W G Fertilizer-Chanute
1971 S Country Club Rd (66720-6133)
PHONE..................................620 431-3430
Greg Semred, *Manager*
EMP: 7
SALES (corp-wide): 73.8MM **Privately Held**
SIC: 2874 5191 Phosphatic fertilizers; fertilizers & agricultural chemicals
PA: Mid-West Fertilizer, Inc.
1105 Baptiste Dr
Paola KS 66071
913 294-5555

GEOGRAPHIC

(G-744)
N & B ENTERPRISES INC
Also Called: Noland, Edsel
1302 S Henry St (66720-2887)
P.O. Box 812 (66720-0812)
PHONE..................................620 431-6424
Richard Burris, *President*
Ed Nolan, *Corp Secy*
Edsel E Noland, *Treasurer*
EMP: 7
SALES: 600K **Privately Held**
SIC: 1311 Crude petroleum & natural gas

(G-745)
NATIONAL HEALTHCARE CORP
Also Called: Park Pl Healthcare & Rehab Ctr
530 W 14th St (66720-2877)
PHONE..................................620 431-4940
Randy Alsup, *Branch Mgr*
Janice Jones, *Director*
EMP: 100
SALES (corp-wide): 980.3MM **Publicly Held**
WEB: www.healthcarebenefits.com
SIC: 8051 Convalescent home with continuous nursing care
PA: National Healthcare Corporation
100 E Vine St
Murfreesboro TN 37130
615 890-2020

(G-746)
NHI OF CHANUTE LLC
530 W 14th St (66720-2877)
PHONE..................................620 431-4940
EMP: 54
SALES (est): 436.6K
SALES (corp-wide): 144.5MM **Privately Held**
SIC: 8051 Nursing Care
PA: N H C O P Lp
100 E Vine St
Murfreesboro TN 37130
615 890-2020

(G-747)
NOAHS ARK CHRISTIAN DAY CARE
Also Called: NOAHS ARK CACFP
208 N Lincoln Ave (66720-1822)
P.O. Box 626 (66720-0626)
PHONE..................................620 431-1832
Mary Kay Barclay, *Exec Dir*
Ralph Barclay, *Director*
EMP: 15
SQ FT: 3,200
SALES: 2.9MM **Privately Held**
SIC: 8322 Children's aid society

(G-748)
NU-WA INDUSTRIES INC (PA)
3939 S Ross Ln (66720-4021)
PHONE..................................620 431-2088
Michael S Mitchell, *CEO*
Neil Ford, *President*
Orv Breiner, *Marketing Staff*
Ginger Lycnh, *Executive*
Kiz Porter, *Admin Asst*
EMP: 200 **EST:** 1958
SALES (est): 40.1MM **Privately Held**
WEB: www.nuwa.com
SIC: 3792 Travel trailers & campers

(G-749)
OIL PATCH PUMP AND SUPPLY INC (PA)
3290 S Plummer Ave (66720-8700)
P.O. Box 591 (66720-0591)
PHONE..................................620 431-1890
Robert F Manley II, *President*
Ronald Wiltse, *Vice Pres*
EMP: 13 **EST:** 1965
SQ FT: 2,000
SALES (est): 4.8MM **Privately Held**
SIC: 5084 5983 Oil well machinery, equipment & supplies; fuel oil dealers

(G-750)
OPTIMIZED PROCESS FURNACES INC
3995 S Santa Fe Ave (66720-5402)
P.O. Box 706 (66720-0706)
PHONE..................................620 431-1260
Rob Phillips, *President*
▲ **EMP:** 18
SQ FT: 6,500
SALES: 21.5MM **Privately Held**
WEB: www.firedheater.com
SIC: 3443 3567 3559 Heat exchangers, condensers & components; industrial furnaces & ovens; refinery, chemical processing & similar machinery

(G-751)
OPTIMUS INDUSTRIES LLC
Also Called: Chanute Manufacturing
1700 S Washington Ave (66720-6138)
P.O. Box 599 (66720-0599)
PHONE..................................620 431-3100
Clint Isaac, *General Mgr*
Jim Scheiper, *Vice Pres*
Dustin Stanley, *Project Mgr*
Pam Viscuso, *Sr Project Mgr*
Elmer Roush, *Manager*
EMP: 175
SALES (corp-wide): 40MM **Privately Held**
WEB: www.optimus-tulsa.com
SIC: 3443 8711 Pipe, large diameter: metal plate; engineering services
PA: Optimus Industries Llc
5727 S Lewis Ave Ste 600
Tulsa OK 74105
918 491-9191

(G-752)
ORIZON AROSTRUCTURES - NKC LLC
615 W Cherry St (66720-1516)
PHONE..................................620 431-4037
EMP: 35
SALES (corp-wide): 18.9MM **Privately Held**
SIC: 3728 Manufactures Aircraft Parts/Equipment
PA: Orizon Aerostructures - Nkc, Llc
3515 Ne 33rd Ter
Kansas City MO 66061
816 788-7800

(G-753)
ORIZON ARSTRCTRES - CHNUTE INC
2522 W 21st St (66720-6132)
PHONE..................................816 788-7800
Charles Newell, *CEO*
EMP: 86 **EST:** 2016
SQ FT: 74,000
SALES (est): 4.1MM
SALES (corp-wide): 74.6MM **Privately Held**
SIC: 3728 Fuselage assembly, aircraft
PA: Orizon Aerostructures, Llc
1200 Main St Ste 4000
Kansas City MO 64105
816 788-7800

(G-754)
ORIZON ARSTRUCTURES - PROC INC
2526 W 21st St (66720)
PHONE..................................620 305-2402
Charlie Newell, *CEO*
Henry Newell, *President*
Scott Underwood, *COO*
Mark Deuel, *CFO*
EMP: 40
SQ FT: 102,000
SALES (est): 1.5MM
SALES (corp-wide): 74.6MM **Privately Held**
SIC: 3812 Acceleration indicators & systems components, aerospace
PA: Orizon Aerostructures, Llc
1200 Main St Ste 4000
Kansas City MO 64105
816 788-7800

(G-755)
POPUP INDUSTRIES INC
220 W 14th St (66720-2891)
PHONE..................................620 431-9196
Bernard Dick, *President*
EMP: 35
SALES (est): 4.8MM **Privately Held**
SIC: 3441 5013 Fabricated structural metal; automotive servicing equipment

(G-756)
POSTROCK ENERGY CORPORATION
4402 S Johnson Rd (66720-4016)
PHONE..................................620 432-4200
EMP: 13 **Publicly Held**
SIC: 1382 Oil & gas exploration services
PA: Postrock Energy Corporation
210 Park Ave Ste 2750
Oklahoma City OK 73102

(G-757)
Q CONSLDATED OIL WELL SVCS LLC (HQ)
1322 S Grant Ave (66720-2854)
P.O. Box 884 (66720-0884)
PHONE..................................620 431-9210
Steve Stanfield,
EMP: 6
SALES: 138.6MM
SALES (corp-wide): 1.1B **Privately Held**
SIC: 1389 Oil field services
PA: Quintana Energy Services Lp
1415 La St Ste 2900
Houston TX 77002
832 518-4094

(G-758)
QES PRESSURE PUMPING LLC (HQ)
1322 S Grant Ave (66720-2854)
P.O. Box 884 (66720-0884)
PHONE..................................620 431-9210
S D Stanfield, *President*
Stephen D Stanfield, *President*
Ron Calaway, *Engineer*
Vicki Carlson, *Controller*
EMP: 25 **EST:** 1956
SQ FT: 8,000
SALES: 45MM
SALES (corp-wide): 1.1B **Privately Held**
SIC: 1389 Oil field services; cementing oil & gas well casings; acidizing wells
PA: Quintana Energy Services Lp
1415 La St Ste 2900
Houston TX 77002
832 518-4094

(G-759)
RAVIN PRINTING LLC
1526 S Santa Fe Ave (66720-3221)
PHONE..................................620 431-5830
Kevin D Krokstrom, *Mng Member*
Randy Galemore, *Mng Member*
EMP: 7
SQ FT: 5,600
SALES: 500K **Privately Held**
WEB: www.ravinprinting.com
SIC: 2752 Commercial printing, offset

(G-760)
RENTAL STATION LLC
2029 S Santa Fe Ave (66720-3245)
PHONE..................................620 431-7368
Jim Eden, *Manager*
Eldon E Cleaver,
Cathryn Cleaver,
EMP: 35
SALES (est): 2.1MM **Privately Held**
WEB: www.rentalstation.com
SIC: 7359 Rental store, general

(G-761)
SCHELL ELECTRONICS INC
120 N Lincoln Ave (66720-1896)
PHONE..................................620 431-2350
Jerry L Schell, *President*
Janice E Schell, *Corp Secy*
EMP: 6
SQ FT: 10,000
SALES (est): 1.3MM **Privately Held**
WEB: www.schellelectronics.net
SIC: 3679 3663 Electronic circuits; receiver-transmitter units (transceiver)

(G-762)
SKYLINE MOTEL
1216 W Main St (66720-1414)
PHONE..................................620 431-1500
Shirley Mangine, *Owner*
EMP: 13
SALES (est): 292K **Privately Held**
SIC: 7011 Motels

(G-763)
SOUTHEAST BANCSHARES INC (PA)
Also Called: Southeast Check Printing
101 W Main St (66720-1750)
P.O. Box 538 (66720-0538)
PHONE..................................620 431-1400
Mark Lair, *President*
Virgil Lair, *Chairman*
Ken Lickteig, *Vice Pres*
EMP: 50
SALES: 6.7MM **Privately Held**
SIC: 6022 8111 State commercial banks; general practice attorney, lawyer

(G-764)
SOUTHEAST KANS MENTAL HLTH CTR
402 S Kansas Ave (66720-2107)
P.O. Box 335 (66720-0335)
PHONE..................................620 431-7890
Robert Chase, *Director*
EMP: 15
SALES (est): 643.8K
SALES (corp-wide): 8.3MM **Privately Held**
SIC: 8093 Mental health clinic, outpatient
PA: Southeast Kansas Mental Health Center
1106 S 9th St
Humboldt KS 66748
620 473-2241

(G-765)
SOUTHEAST KS AR AG AGING
1 W Ash St (66720-1700)
PHONE..................................620 431-2980
Cindy Lane, *Exec Dir*
EMP: 60 **EST:** 1976
SALES: 2.8MM **Privately Held**
SIC: 8322 8082 Old age assistance; home health care services

(G-766)
SUPPORTED EMPLOYMENT SERVICES
222 W Main St Ste C (66720-1760)
PHONE..................................620 431-1805
Bob Chase, *Exec Dir*
EMP: 11
SALES (est): 275.1K **Privately Held**
SIC: 7361 Employment agencies

(G-767)
TAYLOR MIH WOMENS CLINIC
1409 W 7th St (66720-2550)
P.O. Box 426 (66720-0426)
PHONE..................................620 431-0340
Kathy Taylor, *Owner*
Larry Taylor, *Owner*
EMP: 10
SALES (est): 280.3K **Privately Held**
SIC: 8062 General medical & surgical hospitals

(G-768)
TFI FAMILY SERVICES INC
424 W 14th St (66720-2878)
PHONE..................................620 431-0312
EMP: 14
SALES (corp-wide): 20.7MM **Privately Held**
SIC: 8361 Foster Care
PA: Tfi Family Services, Inc.
618 Commercial St Ste C
Emporia KS 66801
620 342-2239

(G-769)
THERMOVAC INC
1120 W Beech St (66720-1177)
PHONE..................................620 431-3270
Todd Taylor, *President*
Brian Taylor, *Vice Pres*
EMP: 9
SQ FT: 25,000
SALES: 1MM **Privately Held**
SIC: 3089 Thermoformed finished plastic products

(G-770)
TIOGA TERRITORY LTD
502 E Main St (66720-1841)
PHONE..................................620 431-2479
Debbie Hughes, *President*

Georgia Wille, *President*
Kim Bartlett, *Graphic Designe*
EMP: 15
SQ FT: 12,500
SALES (est): 1.3MM **Privately Held**
WEB: www.tiogaterritory.com
SIC: 2395 5611 5621 2759 Embroidery products, except schiffli machine; clothing, sportswear, men's & boys'; women's sportswear; screen printing

(G-771)
TOP IT
401 W Cherry Ave (66720-1685)
PHONE..................................620 431-1866
Kerry Henson, *Principal*
EMP: 5
SALES (est): 666K **Privately Held**
SIC: 2541 Counter & sink tops

(G-772)
TRANSCARE OF KS LLC
113 W 2nd St (66720-2206)
PHONE..................................620 431-6300
Jerry Hughes, *General Mgr*
Marty D Hughes, *Principal*
EMP: 26 **EST:** 2009
SALES (est): 639.9K **Privately Held**
SIC: 4119 Ambulance service

(G-773)
W-W PRODUCTION CO
1150 Highway 39 (66720-5215)
PHONE..................................620 431-4137
Michael Wimsett, *Owner*
EMP: 7
SALES (est): 467.2K **Privately Held**
SIC: 1311 1381 Crude petroleum production; drilling oil & gas wells

(G-774)
YOUNGS PRODUCTS LLC
Also Called: Popup Towing Products
4330 S Johnson Rd (66720-4014)
PHONE..................................620 431-2199
Harvey Young, *President*
Derrick Bruenger, *Sales Staff*
EMP: 60
SQ FT: 165,000
SALES (est): 3.3MM
SALES (corp-wide): 14.1MM **Privately Held**
SIC: 3714 Frames, motor vehicle
PA: Young's Welding, Inc.
4115 S Johnson Rd
Chanute KS 66720
620 431-2199

(G-775)
ZIMMERMAN ELECTRIC SERVICE
1202 W Beech St (66720-1178)
P.O. Box 533 (66720-0533)
PHONE..................................620 431-2260
R Max Zimmerman, *President*
John R Zimmerman, *Corp Secy*
EMP: 7 **EST:** 1966
SQ FT: 9,500
SALES (est): 972.2K **Privately Held**
SIC: 1731 7694 General electrical contractor; rebuilding motors, except automotive

Chapman
Dickinson County

(G-776)
AGRI TRAILS COOP INC
1754 Quail Rd (67431-9325)
PHONE..................................785 479-5870
EMP: 89
SALES (corp-wide): 160MM **Privately Held**
SIC: 5191 Fertilizer & fertilizer materials
PA: Agri Trails Coop, Inc.
508 N Main St
Hope KS 67451
785 366-7213

(G-777)
CHAPMAN ADULT CARE HOMES INC
Also Called: CHAPMAN VALLEY MANOR
1009 N Marshall Ave (67431-8821)
P.O. Box 219 (67431-0219)
PHONE..................................785 922-6525
Pam Sheets, *Director*
EMP: 60
SQ FT: 20,000
SALES: 2.5MM **Privately Held**
SIC: 8051 Convalescent home with continuous nursing care

(G-778)
FLINT HILLS ROOF SERVICE
2206 Vane Rd (67431-8909)
P.O. Box 3032, Junction City (66441-6032)
PHONE..................................785 238-8609
Cliff Hutchinson, *Owner*
EMP: 12
SALES (est): 489.3K **Privately Held**
SIC: 1761 Roofing contractor

(G-779)
GENESIS SOLUTION LLC
205 E 2nd St (67431-9571)
P.O. Box 458 (67431-0458)
PHONE..................................785 317-5710
EMP: 10
SALES (est): 410K **Privately Held**
SIC: 1721 1711 1521 Painting And Paper Hanging

(G-780)
L BLIXT CONSTRUCTION INC
2646 Sage Rd (67431-8823)
PHONE..................................785 922-6180
Leroy Blixt, *President*
Jeff Blixt, *Vice Pres*
EMP: 15
SALES (est): 2.3MM **Privately Held**
SIC: 1794 1795 1629 Excavation & grading, building construction; demolition, buildings & other structures; earthmoving contractor; waterway construction; land clearing contractor

(G-781)
WILDCAT SERVICES INC
2175 Old Hwy 40 (67431)
P.O. Box 583 (67431-0583)
PHONE..................................785 922-6466
Tyler Kuntz, *President*
Cole Krinhop, *Vice Pres*
Karen Michael, *Office Mgr*
EMP: 10
SALES (est): 968.3K **Privately Held**
SIC: 1542 1522 Nonresidential construction; residential construction

Chase
Rice County

(G-782)
CAL-MAINE FOODS INC
625 Avenue K (67524-9408)
PHONE..................................620 938-2300
John Miller, *Manager*
Keith Marcelle, *Manager*
EMP: 70
SALES (corp-wide): 1.3B **Publicly Held**
WEB: www.calmainefoods.com
SIC: 5144 2015 Poultry & poultry products; poultry slaughtering & processing
PA: Cal-Maine Foods, Inc.
3320 W Woodrow Wilson Ave
Jackson MS 39209
601 948-6813

(G-783)
JAYHAWK PIPELINE LLC
1390 10th Rd (67524-9400)
PHONE..................................620 938-2971
Keith Rush, *Branch Mgr*
EMP: 20
SALES (corp-wide): 31.9B **Publicly Held**
WEB: www.jayhawkpl.com
SIC: 4612 Crude petroleum pipelines
HQ: Jayhawk Pipeline, L.L.C.
2000 S Main St
Mcpherson KS 67460
620 241-9270

(G-784)
KIZZAR WELL SERVICING INC
320 Frontage Rd (67524)
P.O. Box 346 (67524-0346)
PHONE..................................620 938-2555
Doug Kizzar, *President*
EMP: 12
SALES: 100K **Privately Held**
SIC: 1389 Running, cutting & pulling casings, tubes & rods

(G-785)
MIKES TESTING & SALVAGE INC
1125 S Main St (67524)
P.O. Box 467 (67524-0467)
PHONE..................................620 938-2943
Mike Kelso, *President*
EMP: 16
SQ FT: 1,000
SALES (est): 2.4MM **Privately Held**
SIC: 1389 Servicing oil & gas wells

(G-786)
POWERLINE MACHINE WORKS INC
791 5th Rd (67524-9487)
PHONE..................................620 824-6204
Darrel Hoelscher, *President*
EMP: 11
SQ FT: 6,350
SALES (est): 1.6MM **Privately Held**
SIC: 3491 Industrial valves

Cheney
Sedgwick County

(G-787)
AERO INTERIOR MAINTENANCE INC
2120 S 343rd St W (67025-9189)
PHONE..................................316 990-5088
Barbara Laverentz, *President*
Edward Laverentz, *General Mgr*
Ed Laverentz, *Principal*
EMP: 13
SALES (est): 1.1MM **Privately Held**
SIC: 4581 Aircraft servicing & repairing

(G-788)
ALBERS FINSHG & SOLUTIONS LLC
38628 W 15th St S (67025-8202)
PHONE..................................316 542-0405
Bret Albers, *President*
Craig Albers, *Vice Pres*
EMP: 10 **EST:** 2014
SALES (est): 240.8K **Privately Held**
SIC: 1721 Industrial painting

(G-789)
CHENEY GOLDEN AGE HOME INC
724 N Main St (67025-9059)
P.O. Box 370 (67025-0370)
PHONE..................................316 540-3691
Theresa Achilles, *Administration*
EMP: 70
SQ FT: 12,000
SALES: 3.5MM **Privately Held**
WEB: www.cheneygoldenage.com
SIC: 8051 Skilled nursing care facilities

(G-790)
CHENEY LANES INC
Also Called: D Marios
1635 S Cheney Rd (67025)
PHONE..................................316 542-3126
Dorothy Albers, *President*
Ken Winter, *Chief*
Donald R Albers, *Corp Secy*
Bret Albers, *Manager*
Jeff Albers, *Manager*
EMP: 16
SALES (est): 555K **Privately Held**
SIC: 5812 7933 Pizzeria, independent; bowling centers

(G-791)
CITIZENS STATE BANK
306 N Main St (67025-2526)
PHONE..................................316 542-3142
Roger S Brown, *President*
John Mies, *Exec VP*
Donna Rausch, *Admin Sec*
EMP: 15 **EST:** 1884
SALES: 15.8MM **Privately Held**
SIC: 6022 State commercial banks
PA: Citizens State Bancshares, Inc.
306 N Main St
Cheney KS 67025

(G-792)
GIGOT AGRA SERVICES INC (PA)
8105 S 295th St W (67025-9120)
PHONE..................................620 276-8444
Gerald Gigot, *President*
Nancy Garner, *Treasurer*
EMP: 10
SQ FT: 10,000
SALES: 1.2MM **Privately Held**
SIC: 5083 Irrigation equipment

(G-793)
MANUFACTURING DEVELOPMENT INC
Also Called: M D I
37515 W 15th St S (67025-8828)
P.O. Box 550 (67025-0550)
PHONE..................................316 542-0182
Marcia Mies, *President*
Matthew R Mies, *COO*
Pat Brost, *Mktg Dir*
Dnarda Collins, *Contract Mgr*
Charles Dick, *Manager*
EMP: 25
SQ FT: 36,000
SALES (est): 5.6MM **Privately Held**
WEB: www.mdicheney.com
SIC: 3728 3444 Aircraft assemblies, subassemblies & parts; sheet metalwork

(G-794)
MCLAUGHLIN LEASING INC
Also Called: McLaughlin Equipment
15775 Se 20 St (67025-8575)
PHONE..................................316 542-0303
Steve McLaughlin, *President*
Irene McLaughlin, *Vice Pres*
EMP: 12
SALES (est): 3.5MM **Privately Held**
WEB: www.mclaughlinequip.com
SIC: 7699 5083 5084 Laboratory instrument repair; farm implements; materials handling machinery

(G-795)
REFRIGERATION TECHNOLOGIES
38121 W 55th St S (67025-8759)
P.O. Box 549 (67025-0549)
PHONE..................................316 542-0397
Fax: 316 542-0424
EMP: 12
SQ FT: 3,000
SALES (est): 1.8MM **Privately Held**
SIC: 5078 Whol Refrigeration Equipment/Supplies

(G-796)
SEDGWICK COUNTY ELC COOP ASSN
1355 S 383rd St W (67025-9087)
P.O. Box 220 (67025-0220)
PHONE..................................316 542-3131
John Hillman, *President*
Cindy Foster, *Principal*
Don Metzen, *Principal*
Stan Theis, *Principal*
Eugene Scheer, *Vice Pres*
EMP: 18 **EST:** 1937
SQ FT: 1,200
SALES: 16.6MM **Privately Held**
SIC: 4911 Distribution, electric power

(G-797)
TIMES SENTINEL NEWSPAPERS
Also Called: Time-Sentinel, The
125 N Main St (67025-8844)
P.O. Box 544 (67025-0544)
PHONE..................................316 540-0500
Paul Rhodes, *Owner*
EMP: 6
SQ FT: 1,300
SALES (est): 336.6K **Privately Held**
SIC: 2711 Newspapers: publishing only, not printed on site

(G-798)
WEST WICHITA GAS GATHERING LLC
13521 Ne 10 St (67025-8410)
PHONE.................................970 764-6653
Michael Lafferty, *Branch Mgr*
EMP: 12 **Privately Held**
SIC: 4922 Natural gas transmission
HQ: West Wichita Gas Gathering, Llc
4200 E Skelly Dr Ste 760
Tulsa OK 74135

Cherokee
Crawford County

(G-799)
BSJ POWER SERVICES INC
441 W 520th Ave (66724-5066)
PHONE.................................417 850-1707
Britt Commons, *Principal*
EMP: 12
SALES: 650K **Privately Held**
SIC: 1623 Water, sewer & utility lines

Cherryvale
Montgomery County

(G-800)
ALLIED WASTE INDS ARIZ INC
Also Called: Allied Waste Svcs Cherryvale
4237 Cr 5300 (67335-8829)
PHONE.................................620 336-3678
Don Cartwright, *Manager*
EMP: 13
SALES (corp-wide): 10B **Publicly Held**
SIC: 4953 Refuse collection & disposal services
HQ: Allied Waste Industries (Arizona), Inc.
15880 N Greenway
Scottsdale AZ 85260
480 627-2700

(G-801)
CHARLOMA INC (HQ)
727 N Liberty St (67335-1246)
P.O. Box 367 (67335-0367)
PHONE.................................620 336-2124
Charles O Fink, *President*
Wendell Wells, *Principal*
Ryan Rexwinkle, *Warehouse Mgr*
Tom Ward, *Purch Mgr*
Janice Bell, *Human Res Dir*
▲ **EMP:** 25 **EST:** 1969
SQ FT: 150,000
SALES (est): 32.4MM **Privately Held**
WEB: www.charloma.com
SIC: 3089 Plastic kitchenware, tableware & houseware; plastic processing
PA: The Molding Company Inc
1601 Airpark Dr
Farmington MO 63640
573 760-1227

(G-802)
CHERRYVALE ALUMNI COMMNTY/EDUC
404 N Liberty St (67335-1229)
P.O. Box 65 (67335-0065)
PHONE.................................620 336-3198
Billie J Ott, *President*
EMP: 15 **EST:** 1997
SALES (est): 165.7K **Privately Held**
SIC: 8641 Alumni association

(G-803)
COMMUNITY NATIONAL BANK & TR
Also Called: Cherryvale Banking Center
333 W Main St (67335-1231)
P.O. Box 307 (67335-0307)
PHONE.................................620 336-2145
Chuck Goad, *Manager*
EMP: 15 **Privately Held**
SIC: 6021 National commercial banks
HQ: Community National Bank & Trust
14 N Lincoln Ave
Chanute KS 66720

(G-804)
CORNEJO & SONS LLC
Rural Route 1
PHONE.................................620 336-3534
Steve Sloan, *Branch Mgr*
EMP: 20
SALES (corp-wide): 2.1B **Publicly Held**
WEB: www.midwestminerals.com
SIC: 1422 Crushed & broken limestone
HQ: Cornejo & Sons, L.L.C.
2060 E Tulsa St
Wichita KS 67216
316 522-5100

(G-805)
COYSON TRANSPORTATION LLC
929 N Liberty St (67335-1247)
P.O. Box 454, S Coffeyville OK (74072-0454)
PHONE.................................620 336-2846
Charles Sink, *Owner*
Shannon Noble, *Manager*
EMP: 20
SALES (est): 5MM **Privately Held**
SIC: 5012 Automobiles

(G-806)
FEDEX FREIGHT CORPORATION
1017 N Liberty St (67335-1245)
PHONE.................................800 752-0045
Brandon Rector, *Manager*
EMP: 15
SALES (corp-wide): 69.6B **Publicly Held**
SIC: 4213 Less-than-truckload (LTL) transport
HQ: Fedex Freight Corporation
1715 Aaron Brenner Dr
Memphis TN 38120

(G-807)
GLENCARE/CHERRYVALE CA LTD PT
Also Called: Cherryvale Medi-Lodge
1001 W Main St (67335-1104)
PHONE.................................620 336-2102
Temmie Hokins, *Branch Mgr*
EMP: 24
SALES (est): 1.7MM **Privately Held**
SIC: 8051 Skilled nursing care facilities
PA: Glencare/Cherryvale, A California Limited Partnership
1640 School St
Moraga CA 94556

(G-808)
GRANDVIEW PRODUCTS CO
Also Called: Grandview Pdts Cherryville Div
200 N Galveston St (67335-1408)
PHONE.................................620 336-2309
Rod Fleming, *Manager*
Pam Armbruster, *Executive*
EMP: 78
SALES (corp-wide): 34MM **Privately Held**
WEB: www.grandviewcabinets.com
SIC: 2434 2431 Wood kitchen cabinets; millwork
HQ: Grandview Products Co., Inc.
1601 Superior Dr
Parsons KS 67357
620 421-6950

(G-809)
H&R BLOCK INC
Also Called: H & R Block
308c E Main St (67335-1414)
PHONE.................................620 336-2750
Margie Tetens, *Owner*
EMP: 12
SALES (corp-wide): 3B **Publicly Held**
SIC: 7291 Tax return preparation services
PA: H&R Block, Inc.
1 H&R Block Way
Kansas City MO 64105
816 854-3000

(G-810)
K&J OUTDOOR PRODUCTS LLC
5306 Cr 6200 (67335-6201)
PHONE.................................816 769-6060
Kevin Redford, *Administration*
EMP: 13
SALES (est): 139.4K **Privately Held**
SIC: 7822 Motion picture & tape distribution

(G-811)
NEWTONS INC
Also Called: True Value Hardware
116 W Main St (67335-1322)
PHONE.................................620 336-2276
Joe Long, *President*
Barbara E Long, *Corp Secy*
EMP: 12
SQ FT: 4,800
SALES: 1MM **Privately Held**
SIC: 5251 1711 1731 Hardware; plumbing, heating, air-conditioning contractors; electrical work

(G-812)
REPUBLIC SERVICES INC
4237 Cr 5300 (67335-8829)
PHONE.................................620 336-3678
Jim Melton, *Branch Mgr*
EMP: 34
SALES (corp-wide): 10B **Publicly Held**
SIC: 4953 Refuse collection & disposal services
PA: Republic Services, Inc.
18500 N Allied Way # 100
Phoenix AZ 85054
480 627-2700

(G-813)
SOUTH KANSAS AND OKLA RR INC
123 N Depot St (67335-1336)
PHONE.................................620 336-2291
Rick Webb, *Branch Mgr*
EMP: 25
SALES (corp-wide): 997.9MM **Privately Held**
SIC: 4011 4013 Railroads, line-haul operating; switching & terminal services
HQ: South Kansas And Oklahoma Railroad, Inc.
315 W 3rd St
Pittsburg KS 66762

(G-814)
VISION WOODWORKS LLC
111 E Main St (67335-1409)
PHONE.................................620 336-2158
Jack Ellison, *Mng Member*
Evelyn Ellison,
EMP: 15
SQ FT: 5,500
SALES (est): 600K **Privately Held**
SIC: 2434 Wood kitchen cabinets

(G-815)
WATCO COMPANIES LLC
123 N Depot St (67335-1336)
PHONE.................................620 336-2291
Richard B Webb, *President*
EMP: 56
SALES (corp-wide): 997.9MM **Privately Held**
WEB: www.watcocompanies.com
SIC: 4011 Railroads, line-haul operating
PA: Watco Companies, L.L.C.
315 W 3rd St
Pittsburg KS 66762
575 745-2329

Chetopa
Labette County

(G-816)
BARTLETT COOPERATIVE ASSN
508 S 3rd St (67336-8863)
PHONE.................................620 236-7143
Fred Goddard, *Principal*
EMP: 39
SALES (corp-wide): 67MM **Privately Held**
SIC: 8699 Athletic organizations
PA: Bartlett Cooperative Association
4th Main St
Bartlett KS 67332
620 226-3311

(G-817)
FAULKNER GRAIN INC (PA)
9904 Sw Falcon Ln (67336-8568)
PHONE.................................620 597-2636
Virginia Overman, *President*
EMP: 10 **EST:** 1948
SQ FT: 1,000
SALES (est): 2.9MM **Privately Held**
SIC: 5191 5153 Farm supplies; grain elevators

(G-818)
WOODWORTH ENTERPRISES INC
Also Called: Heritage House
814 Walnut St (67336-8990)
PHONE.................................620 236-7248
Donald Woodworth, *President*
EMP: 41
SALES (corp-wide): 2.4MM **Privately Held**
SIC: 8052 Personal care facility
PA: Woodworth Enterprises Inc
1217 S 15th St
Parsons KS

(G-819)
WOODWORTH INTERNATIONAL INC
Also Called: CHETOPA MANOR
814 Walnut St (67336-8990)
P.O. Box 167 (67336-0167)
PHONE.................................620 236-7248
Don Woodworth, *President*
EMP: 28
SALES: 2.1MM **Privately Held**
SIC: 8059 Convalescent home; nursing home, except skilled & intermediate care facility

Cimarron
Gray County

(G-820)
CARL LEATHERWOOD INC
215 S Main St (67835-8545)
P.O. Box 788 (67835-0788)
PHONE.................................620 855-3850
Carl Leatherwood, *President*
Michelle Leatherwood, *Corp Secy*
EMP: 25
SALES (est): 1.5MM **Privately Held**
SIC: 5191 Hay

(G-821)
CIMARRON WELDING INC
112 N Main St113 # 113 (67835)
P.O. Box 1105 (67835-1105)
PHONE.................................620 855-3582
Curt Adams, *President*
Chris Adams, *Vice Pres*
EMP: 6
SQ FT: 6,000
SALES: 1MM **Privately Held**
SIC: 7692 Welding repair

(G-822)
CIMARRON WIND ENERGY LLC
10001 Rd 19 (67835)
PHONE.................................561 691-7171
John W Ketchum, *Principal*
EMP: 6
SALES (est): 325.9K
SALES (corp-wide): 16.7B **Publicly Held**
SIC: 3621 Windmills, electric generating
HQ: Cimarron Wind Energy Holdings, Llc
700 Universe Blvd
Juno Beach FL 33408
561 691-7171

(G-823)
DM & M FARMS INC (PA)
220 S Main St (67835)
P.O. Box 668 (67835-0668)
PHONE.................................620 855-3934
Daniel D Miller, *President*
Janice M McNiece, *Corp Secy*
Michael J McNiece, *Vice Pres*
EMP: 20 **EST:** 1980
SQ FT: 8,000

▲ = Import ▼=Export
◆ =Import/Export

SALES (est): 3.4MM Privately Held
WEB: www.dmfarms.com
SIC: 5153 0211 Grain elevators; beef cattle feedlots

(G-824)
DUKE ENERGY CORPORATION
Also Called: Cimarron Wind Power 2
8502 State Road 23 (67835-9008)
PHONE....620 855-6830
Duke Energy, *Owner*
EMP: 13
SALES (corp-wide): 24.5B Publicly Held
SIC: 4911 4924 4931 Electric services; natural gas distribution; electric & other services combined
PA: Duke Energy Corporation
550 S Tryon St
Charlotte NC 28202
704 382-3853

(G-825)
FIRST NATIONAL BANK (PA)
Also Called: 1ST NATIONAL BANK IN CIMARRON
121 N Main St (67835)
P.O. Box 129 (67835-0129)
PHONE....620 855-3416
Dave Long, *President*
Max Knopp, *Vice Pres*
Shelly Mowry, *Vice Pres*
Kara Lock, *Manager*
EMP: 21
SALES: 4MM Privately Held
SIC: 6021 National commercial banks

(G-826)
GENERAL PEST CONTROL LLC
15609 State Rd 23 (67835)
PHONE....620 855-7768
Kyle Litton, *Partner*
EMP: 15
SQ FT: 1,200
SALES (est): 1MM Privately Held
SIC: 7342 Pest control in structures

(G-827)
GOLDEN PLAINS PUBLISHERS INC (PA)
Also Called: Jacksonian Newspaper
101 N Main (67835)
P.O. Box 528 (67835-0528)
PHONE....620 855-3902
Mark Anderson, *President*
Gerald Anderson, *Vice Pres*
EMP: 7
SQ FT: 7,500
SALES (est): 1.5MM Privately Held
SIC: 2711 5943 Commercial printing & newspaper publishing combined; office forms & supplies

(G-828)
GRAY COUNTY PRINTERS
Also Called: Golden Plains Publishing
101 N Main St (67835)
P.O. Box 528 (67835-0528)
PHONE....620 855-2467
Mark Anderson, *Owner*
EMP: 6
SALES (est): 315.2K Privately Held
SIC: 2759 Commercial printing

(G-829)
GRAYCO OVER 50
221 S Main St (67835)
P.O. Box 236 (67835-0236)
PHONE....620 855-3711
Hazel Flowers, *President*
EMP: 10
SALES (est): 217K Privately Held
SIC: 8322 Senior citizens' center or association

(G-830)
IRSIK & DOLL FEED SERVICES INC (PA)
104 W Ave A (67835)
P.O. Box 847 (67835-0847)
PHONE....620 855-3747
John Petz, *President*
Ernie Massoth, *Treasurer*
Tyler Siek, *Manager*
EMP: 13 EST: 1969
SQ FT: 2,400
SALES (est): 62.5MM Privately Held
WEB: www.irsikanddoll.com
SIC: 5153 4221 0211 Grains; grain elevator, storage only; beef cattle feedlots

(G-831)
IRSIK & DOLL FEED SERVICES INC
Also Called: Gray County Feed Yard
23405 State Road 23 (67835-8520)
PHONE....620 855-3486
David AST, *Manager*
EMP: 23
SALES (corp-wide): 62.5MM Privately Held
WEB: www.irsikanddoll.com
SIC: 0211 Beef cattle feedlots
PA: Irsik & Doll Feed Services, Inc.
104 W Ave A
Cimarron KS 67835
620 855-3747

(G-832)
POWERLINE DAIRY LLC
Also Called: Forget-Me-Not-farms
22502 R Rd (67835-8638)
P.O. Box 1240 (67835-1240)
PHONE....620 855-2844
Ted Boersma,
EMP: 60
SQ FT: 10,000
SALES: 10MM Privately Held
SIC: 0241 Dairy farms

(G-833)
PREMIER CATTLE CO LLC
13745 16 Rd (67835-8860)
P.O. Box 349 (67835-0349)
PHONE....620 855-3162
David Freelove, *Branch Mgr*
EMP: 10
SALES (corp-wide): 2.6MM Privately Held
SIC: 0211 Beef cattle feedlots
PA: Premier Cattle Co., L.L.C.
State Lake Rd
Syracuse KS 67878
620 384-5711

(G-834)
PRO TECH SPRAYING SERVICE INC
E Hwy 50 (67835)
P.O. Box 969 (67835-0969)
PHONE....620 855-7793
Kyle Litton, *Owner*
EMP: 15
SQ FT: 2,500
SALES (est): 887.2K Privately Held
SIC: 0782 0721 Lawn care services; crop spraying services

(G-835)
R AND P CALF RANCH LLC
17502 19th Rd (67835)
P.O. Box 364 (67835-0364)
PHONE....620 855-2550
Rusty Woods,
Philipp Woods,
EMP: 10 EST: 1995
SALES: 6MM Privately Held
SIC: 5154 Auctioning livestock

(G-836)
SHEPHERD OF PLAINS FOUNDATION
Also Called: SHEPHERD CENTER
101 E Cedar Ridge Dr (67835-9031)
P.O. Box 843 (67835-0843)
PHONE....620 855-3498
Lori Litton, *Director*
Jean Bryant, *Administration*
EMP: 45
SALES: 1.8MM Privately Held
SIC: 8051 Skilled nursing care facilities

(G-837)
STEVE HILKER TRUCKING INC
602 E Ave A (67835)
P.O. Box 152 (67835-0152)
PHONE....620 855-3257
Steve Hilker, *President*
EMP: 20
SALES (est): 1.6MM Privately Held
SIC: 4212 Dump truck haulage

Circleville
Jackson County

(G-838)
FARMERS STATE BANKSHARES INC (PA)
205 Lincoln St (66416-9406)
P.O. Box 465, Holton (66436-0465)
PHONE....785 924-3311
James M Meyer, *President*
Beth Mitchell, *Assistant VP*
Anita Schafer, *Vice Pres*
EMP: 22 EST: 1900
SALES: 2.7MM Privately Held
SIC: 6022 State trust companies accepting deposits, commercial

Claflin
Barton County

(G-839)
BRACKEEN LINE CLEANING INC
Also Called: Leiker Propane
101 S 6th St (67525-2526)
P.O. Box 434 (67525-0434)
PHONE....620 587-3351
Darrin Smith, *President*
EMP: 10 EST: 1948
SQ FT: 10,000
SALES (est): 823.6K Privately Held
SIC: 1389 Oil field services

(G-840)
CLAFLIN AMBULANCE SERVICE ASSN
309 W Front St (67525)
P.O. Box 387 (67525-0387)
PHONE....620 587-3498
Doug Hubbard, *Director*
EMP: 22 EST: 1961
SQ FT: 6,300
SALES: 104.4K Privately Held
SIC: 4119 Ambulance service

(G-841)
CLASSIC WELL SERVICE INC
510 W Hamilton St (67525-9275)
P.O. Box 539 (67525-0539)
PHONE....620 587-3402
Fred Beck, *President*
EMP: 12
SALES (est): 2.6MM Privately Held
SIC: 5084 Oil well machinery, equipment & supplies

Clay Center
Clay County

(G-842)
AG GROWTH INTERNATIONAL INC
Also Called: Hutchinson Mayrath
514 W Crawford St (67432-2345)
P.O. Box 629 (67432-0629)
PHONE....785 632-2161
Cliff Williams, *Branch Mgr*
Sharon Evans, *Exec Dir*
EMP: 175
SALES (corp-wide): 704.1MM Privately Held
WEB: www.globalindinc.com
SIC: 3444 3556 3532 Metal housings, enclosures, casings & other containers; food products machinery; mining machinery
PA: Ag Growth International Inc
198 Commerce Dr
Winnipeg MB R3P 0
204 489-1855

(G-843)
BIG LKES DEVELOPMENTAL CTR INC
Also Called: Clay Center Office
302 Lincoln Ave (67432-2806)
PHONE....785 632-5357
Gail Habluetzel, *Manager*
EMP: 22
SALES (corp-wide): 8.7MM Privately Held
WEB: www.biglakes.org
SIC: 8249 8361 8331 8093 Vocational schools; residential care; sheltered workshop; rehabilitation center, outpatient treatment; furniture repair & maintenance
PA: Big Lakes Developmental Center, Inc.
1416 Hayes Dr
Manhattan KS 66502
785 776-9201

(G-844)
BLUESTEM ELECTRIC COOPERATIVE
524 Dexter St (67432-2535)
P.O. Box 513 (67432-0513)
PHONE....785 632-3111
Kenneth Maginley, *Branch Mgr*
EMP: 20
SALES (corp-wide): 17.1MM Privately Held
WEB: www.bluestemelectric.com
SIC: 4911 Distribution, electric power
PA: Bluestem Electric Cooperative, Inc.
614 E Hwy 24
Wamego KS 66547
785 456-2212

(G-845)
BRUNA BROTHERS IMPLEMENT LLC
Also Called: Bruna Implement Company
1798 18th Rd (67432-7408)
PHONE....785 632-5621
Tony Bruna, *Sales Staff*
Toby Bruna, *Manager*
EMP: 15
SALES (corp-wide): 26.5MM Privately Held
WEB: www.brunaimplementco.com
SIC: 5083 5191 Agricultural machinery & equipment; farm supplies
PA: Bruna Brothers Implement, Llc
1128 Pony Express Hwy
Marysville KS 66508
785 562-5304

(G-846)
BUDS TIRE SERVICE INC
410 Court St (67432-2532)
PHONE....785 632-2135
Benny Wallace, *President*
Larry W Wallace, *President*
Helen M Wallace, *Corp Secy*
EMP: 11
SQ FT: 15,000
SALES (est): 1.4MM Privately Held
SIC: 5531 5941 5014 Automotive tires; sporting goods & bicycle shops; automobile tires & tubes

(G-847)
CALLAWAY ELECTRIC
Also Called: Republican Valley Irrigation
1803 Limestone Rd (67432-8108)
PHONE....785 632-5588
Bill Callaway, *Owner*
William Callaway, *Owner*
EMP: 6
SALES (est): 427.2K Privately Held
SIC: 1731 5084 5083 5074 Electrical work; pumps & pumping equipment; irrigation equipment; pipes & fittings, plastic; pipe fittings, fabricated from purchased pipe; trenching contractor

(G-848)
CENTRAL OFFICE SVC & SUP INC
421 Lincoln Ave (67432-2907)
PHONE....785 632-2177
Steven C McMahan, *President*
Steve Wickersham, *Vice Pres*
Arlyss Vathauer, *Treasurer*
EMP: 13
SQ FT: 6,200
SALES (est): 3.4MM Privately Held
WEB: www.centralofficesupply.com
SIC: 5044 5943 5947 Office equipment; office forms & supplies; gift shop

GEOGRAPHIC

(G-849)
CITY OF CLAY CENTER
427 Court St (67432-2531)
P.O. Box 117 (67432-0117)
PHONE....................................785 632-2139
Susan Carlson, *Manager*
Donoban Direrking, *Manager*
Otto Straub, *Manager*
Billy Callaway, *Exec Dir*
EMP: 35 **Privately Held**
SIC: 4931 Electric & other services combined
PA: City Of Clay Center
427 Court St
Clay Center KS 67432
785 632-2137

(G-850)
CLAY CENTER FAMILY DENTISTRY (PA)
Also Called: Kolterman & Hammel DDS
714 Liberty St (67432-1529)
PHONE....................................785 632-3126
Rick Hammel DDS, *Owner*
Nancy V Hammel, *Office Mgr*
EMP: 15
SALES (est): 1.1MM **Privately Held**
SIC: 8021 Dentists' office

(G-851)
CLAY CENTER FMLY PHYSICIANS PA (PA)
Also Called: Ccfp
609 Liberty St (67432-1564)
P.O. Box 520 (67432-0520)
PHONE....................................785 632-2181
Tim Penner MD, *CEO*
Cary Murphy, *Vice Pres*
Kent E Erickson MD, *Admin Sec*
Cindy Affolter,
EMP: 49
SALES (est): 3.3MM **Privately Held**
WEB: www.ccfp.net
SIC: 8011 General & family practice, physician/surgeon

(G-852)
CLAY CENTER PUBLISHING CO INC
Also Called: Dispatch, The
805 5th St (67432-2502)
P.O. Box 519 (67432-0519)
PHONE....................................785 632-2127
Harry E Valentine Jr, *President*
Lory Reidon, *Manager*
EMP: 9
SQ FT: 5,000
SALES (est): 762.5K **Privately Held**
WEB: www.claycenter.com
SIC: 2711 Commercial printing & newspaper publishing combined

(G-853)
CLAY COUNTY CHILD CARE CTR INC (PA)
Also Called: HEAD START
314 Court St (67432-2420)
PHONE....................................785 632-2195
Vicki Justice, *Human Res Dir*
Lisa Stonehouse, *Exec Dir*
Amy Morrison, *Exec Dir*
EMP: 28
SQ FT: 8,069
SALES: 2.9MM **Privately Held**
SIC: 8351 Group day care center; head start center, except in conjunction with school

(G-854)
CLAY COUNTY CHILD CARE CTR INC
1021 4th St (67432-2501)
PHONE....................................785 632-5399
Marsha Habluetzel, *Manager*
EMP: 15
SALES (corp-wide): 2.9MM **Privately Held**
SIC: 8351 Head start center, except in conjunction with school
PA: Clay County Child Care Center, Inc.
314 Court St
Clay Center KS 67432
785 632-2195

(G-855)
CLEANING BY LAMUNYON INC
Also Called: Lamunyon Restoration
1541 18th Rd (67432-7600)
PHONE....................................785 632-1259
Michael E Lamunyon, *President*
Arlene Lamunyon, *Admin Sec*
EMP: 15
SALES: 2MM **Privately Held**
WEB: www.lamunyon.com
SIC: 1799 8744 5169 1742 Post-disaster renovations; coating, caulking & weather, water & fireproofing; ; specialty cleaning & sanitation preparations; acoustical & insulation work

(G-856)
CONCORDIA TRACTOR INC
Also Called: CTI
1181 18th Rd (67432-7839)
PHONE....................................785 632-3181
Harley Adams, *President*
Lisa Canfield, *Asst Supt*
EMP: 23 **EST:** 1999
SALES (est): 2.1MM **Privately Held**
SIC: 5261 5082 Lawnmowers & tractors; construction & mining machinery

(G-857)
COUNTRY PLACE SENIOR LIVING
722 Liberty St (67432-1575)
PHONE....................................785 632-5052
Ann Bearden, *Opers Staff*
Ray Frigon, *Director*
Debbie Rethman, *Director*
EMP: 13
SALES (est): 340.8K **Privately Held**
SIC: 8052 Personal care facility

(G-858)
COUNTY OF CLAY
Also Called: Clay County Ambulance Service
603 4th St (67432-2924)
PHONE....................................785 632-2166
Marvin Vanblaricon, *Director*
EMP: 30
SQ FT: 8,000 **Privately Held**
WEB: www.courts.addresses.com
SIC: 4119 Ambulance service
PA: County Of Clay
712 5th St Ste 102
Clay Center KS 67432
785 632-2800

(G-859)
COUNTY OF CLAY
Also Called: Clay County Health Department
820 Spellman Cir (67432-7492)
PHONE....................................785 632-3193
Janet Schwab, *Manager*
EMP: 20 **Privately Held**
WEB: www.courts.addresses.com
SIC: 8082 9111 Home health care services; county supervisors' & executives' offices
PA: County Of Clay
712 5th St Ste 102
Clay Center KS 67432
785 632-2800

(G-860)
DIECKS INC
Also Called: Clay Center Locker
212 6th St (67432-3312)
PHONE....................................785 632-5550
Brad Dieckmann, *President*
EMP: 20
SQ FT: 6,000
SALES (est): 1.7MM **Privately Held**
SIC: 2011 8611 2013 Meat packing plants; business associations; sausages & other prepared meats

(G-861)
EARLY HEAD START CLAY COUNTY
1021 4th St (67432-2501)
PHONE....................................877 688-5454
Dawn Thorn, *Director*
Dawn Ghoin, *Director*
EMP: 14
SALES (est): 330.1K **Privately Held**
SIC: 8351 Head start center, except in conjunction with school

(G-862)
ESPI LLC
6030 Lincoln Ave (67432)
PHONE....................................785 777-2707
Kyle Bauer, *CFO*
▲ **EMP:** 10
SALES (est): 1.2MM **Privately Held**
SIC: 3629 Battery chargers, rectifying or nonrotating

(G-863)
FARMERS UNION COOP ASSN
Also Called: Farmer Union Co Op
625 W Court St (67432-2335)
P.O. Box 524 (67432-0524)
PHONE....................................785 632-5632
Mike Crimmis, *Manager*
EMP: 10
SALES (corp-wide): 5MM **Privately Held**
SIC: 2041 5261 5153 2875 Flour & other grain mill products; fertilizer; grain elevators; fertilizers, mixing only
PA: The Farmers Union Co-Operative Association
803 3rd St
Clay Center KS
785 632-5632

(G-864)
FRATERNAL ORDER EAGLES INC
Also Called: Foe 3650
419 Lincoln Ave (67432-2907)
P.O. Box 82 (67432-0082)
PHONE....................................785 632-3521
Larry Drummond, *President*
EMP: 24
SALES (corp-wide): 5.7MM **Privately Held**
WEB: www.fraternalorderofeagles.tribe.net
SIC: 8641 Fraternal associations
PA: Fraternal Order Of Eagles, Bryan Aerie
2233 Of Bryan, Ohio
221 S Walnut St
Bryan OH 43506
419 636-7812

(G-865)
GIBSONS ACE HARDWARE
Also Called: Ace Hardware
728 W Crawford St (67432-2338)
PHONE....................................785 632-3147
Thomas F Jones, *President*
Mark Jones, *Vice Pres*
Scott Jones, *Treasurer*
Letty Jones, *Admin Sec*
EMP: 30
SQ FT: 30,000
SALES (est): 2.7MM **Privately Held**
SIC: 5251 5199 Hardware; variety store merchandise

(G-866)
GIRTON PROPANE SERVICE INC
1156 Bridge St (67432-3607)
P.O. Box 606 (67432-0606)
PHONE....................................785 632-6273
Barry Girton, *President*
Brad Girton, *Vice Pres*
EMP: 80
SQ FT: 2,500
SALES (est): 56.6MM **Privately Held**
SIC: 5172 4212 Gases, liquefied petroleum (propane); liquid transfer services

(G-867)
GT MFG INC
324 5th St (67432-2935)
P.O. Box 525 (67432-0525)
PHONE....................................785 632-2151
Dennis M Pedersen, *President*
Kevin Pedersen, *Purchasing*
James Sampson, *Treasurer*
Lori Carter, *Accountant*
▼ **EMP:** 27
SQ FT: 160,000
SALES: 6.7MM **Privately Held**
WEB: www.gtmfg.com
SIC: 3523 Loaders, farm type: manure, general utility

(G-868)
HUTCHINSON/MAYRATH
514 W Crawford St (67432-2345)
PHONE....................................785 632-2161
Cliff Williams, *President*
Scott Rickley, *Purch Mgr*
Mike Walker, *QC Mgr*
David Hicks, *Engineer*
Darla Coffman, *Sales Staff*
▲ **EMP:** 25
SALES (est): 5.2MM **Privately Held**
SIC: 3523 Farm machinery & equipment

(G-869)
KANEQUIP INC
615 W Court St (67432-2335)
P.O. Box 310, Wamego (66547-0310)
PHONE....................................785 632-3441
Jim Meinhard, *President*
EMP: 14
SALES (corp-wide): 117MM **Privately Held**
WEB: www.kanequip.com
SIC: 5083 7359 5571 5261 Irrigation equipment; stores & yards equipment rental; all terrain vehicle parts and accessories; lawnmowers & tractors; contractors' materials; saws & sawing equipment
PA: Kanequip, Inc.
18035 E Us Highway 24
Wamego KS 66547
785 456-2041

(G-870)
LAMUNYON CLG & RESTORATION
1541 18th Rd (67432-7600)
PHONE....................................785 632-1259
Mike E Lamunyon, *President*
EMP: 10 **EST:** 2011
SALES (est): 296.3K **Privately Held**
SIC: 8322 1799 7349 Disaster service; post-disaster renovations; air duct cleaning

(G-871)
MEDICALODGES INC
Also Called: Medicalodge Clay Center
715 Liberty St (67432-1528)
P.O. Box 517 (67432-0517)
PHONE....................................785 632-5696
Christina Cunningham, *Manager*
EMP: 70
SALES (corp-wide): 100.2MM **Privately Held**
WEB: www.medicalodges.com
SIC: 8051 Convalescent home with continuous nursing care
PA: Medicalodges, Inc.
201 W 8th St
Coffeyville KS 67337
620 251-6700

(G-872)
MELS PUMP & PLUMBING
208 S 6th St (67432-3315)
PHONE....................................785 632-3392
Mel M Anderson, *Owner*
EMP: 10
SQ FT: 770
SALES (est): 786.2K **Privately Held**
SIC: 1711 1623 Plumbing contractors; water & sewer line construction

(G-873)
MICHAEL W RYAN ATTY
Also Called: Ryan and Mullin
509 Court St (67432-2504)
P.O. Box 205 (67432-0205)
PHONE....................................785 632-5666
Michael Ryan, *President*
Micheal Ryan, *President*
Dustin Mullin, *Principal*
EMP: 13 **EST:** 2001
SALES (est): 968.5K **Privately Held**
SIC: 8111 Specialized law offices, attorneys

(G-874)
OETINGER-LLOYD CONSTRUCTION
1819 Meadowlark Rd (67432-8201)
PHONE....................................785 632-2106
Bill Oetinger, *President*
Grace Oetinger, *Vice Pres*

EMP: 15
SQ FT: 7,000
SALES: 2.5MM Privately Held
SIC: 1542 1521 Commercial & office building, new construction; new construction, single-family houses

(G-875)
PARONTO MALL CONSTRUCTION INC
223 6th St (67432-3327)
P.O. Box 172 (67432-0172)
PHONE..................................785 632-2484
Durwin Mall, *President*
EMP: 10
SQ FT: 5,000
SALES: 500K Privately Held
SIC: 1794 1541 1771 1711 Excavation & grading, building construction; renovation, remodeling & repairs: industrial buildings; sidewalk contractor; septic system construction

(G-876)
PRESBYTERIAN MANORS INC
924 8th St (67432-2620)
PHONE..................................785 632-5646
Mike Derousseau, *Director*
EMP: 75
SALES (corp-wide): 8.6MM Privately Held
SIC: 8059 8052 8051 Nursing home, except skilled & intermediate care facility; intermediate care facilities; skilled nursing care facilities
HQ: Presbyterian Manors, Inc.
2414 N Woodlawn Blvd
Wichita KS 67220
316 685-1100

(G-877)
PRINTERY INC (PA)
Also Called: Workman Printing Co
411 Court St (67432-2531)
PHONE..................................785 632-5501
Scott Trautwein, *President*
Robert Maigatter, *Controller*
Daryl Braun, *Accounts Exec*
Heidi Johnson, *Assistant*
EMP: 12
SQ FT: 1,240
SALES (est): 1.5MM Privately Held
SIC: 2752 2759 7336 2796 Commercial printing, offset; letterpress printing; silk screen design; creative services to advertisers, except writers; platemaking services; typesetting; bookbinding & related work

(G-878)
ROTHFUSS MOTELS (PA)
Also Called: Cedar Court Motel
905 Crawford St (67432-2203)
PHONE..................................785 632-2148
Mike Rothfuss, *President*
Sandy Rothfuss, *Corp Secy*
EMP: 13 EST: 1958
SQ FT: 5,000
SALES (est): 638.1K Privately Held
SIC: 7011 Motels

(G-879)
ROTHFUSS MOTELS
Also Called: Sunrise Motel
1136 Crawford St (67432-2208)
PHONE..................................785 632-5611
Mike Rothfuss, *Manager*
EMP: 10
SALES (corp-wide): 638.1K Privately Held
SIC: 7011 Motels
PA: Rothfuss Motels
905 Crawford St
Clay Center KS 67432
785 632-2148

(G-880)
RYAN CONDRAY AND WENGER LLC
509 Court St (67432-2504)
P.O. Box 205 (67432-0205)
PHONE..................................785 632-5666
Micheal W Ryan, *Mng Member*
Dustin Mullin,
EMP: 11
SALES (est): 500.2K Privately Held
SIC: 8111 Legal services

(G-881)
SCOTT SPECIALTIES INC
1827 Meadowlark Rd (67432-8201)
P.O. Box 508, Belleville (66935-0508)
PHONE..................................785 632-3161
Kay Beaver, *Manager*
EMP: 32
SALES (est): 994.7K
SALES (corp-wide): 17.4MM Privately Held
WEB: www.scottspecialties.com
SIC: 3842 5999 Surgical appliances & supplies; orthopedic & prosthesis applications
PA: Scott Specialties, Inc.
512 M St
Belleville KS 66935
785 527-5627

(G-882)
TASTY PASTRY BAKERY
511 Court St (67432-2504)
PHONE..................................785 632-2335
Joshua Macy, *Owner*
EMP: 25
SQ FT: 1,680
SALES (est): 660K Privately Held
SIC: 5461 5149 Bakeries; bakery products

(G-883)
TAYLOR COMMUNICATIONS INC
Also Called: K. C. L. Y. FM
1815 Meadowlark Rd (67432-8201)
PHONE..................................785 632-5661
Kyle Bauer, *President*
Angie Komar, *Exec VP*
Rod Keen, *Opers Mgr*
Clay Dalquest, *Sales Staff*
Robin Sherbert, *Advt Staff*
EMP: 20 EST: 1975
SQ FT: 5,000
SALES (est): 1.7MM Privately Held
WEB: www.kfrm.com
SIC: 4832 Radio broadcasting stations, music format

(G-884)
TSI KANSAS INC
612 W Court St (67432-2313)
PHONE..................................785 632-5183
Jason Hall, *President*
Bill Hickman, *Principal*
Linda Hickman, *Vice Pres*
Sandy Link, *Director*
Rita Speltz, *Assistant*
EMP: 24
SALES (est): 3.5MM Privately Held
SIC: 4213 Contract haulers

(G-885)
UNION STATE BANK (PA)
701 5th St (67432-2936)
P.O. Box 518 (67432-0518)
PHONE..................................785 632-3122
Daniel L Heeren, *President*
James E Beck, *Vice Pres*
Brandon Lee, *Vice Pres*
EMP: 23
SALES: 5.4MM Privately Held
WEB: www.usbcc.com
SIC: 6022 State commercial banks

(G-886)
WARDCRAFT HOMES INC
614 Maple St (67432-3418)
P.O. Box B (67432)
PHONE..................................785 632-5664
Roberta Holz, *Transportation*
Jane Schenck, *Human Res Mgr*
Zach Jones, *Manager*
Tim Mayo, *Info Tech Mgr*
EMP: 80
SALES (corp-wide): 34.1MM Privately Held
WEB: www.wardcraft.com
SIC: 1521 2452 New construction, single-family houses; prefabricated wood buildings
PA: Wardcraft Homes, Inc.
4800 Baseline Rd
Boulder CO 80303
970 542-1700

Clearwater
Sedgwick County

(G-887)
CHARLES ENGINEERING INC
10400 S 119th St W (67026-8822)
P.O. Box 369 (67026-0369)
PHONE..................................620 584-2381
Jim Charles, *President*
David Hutchinson, *Vice Pres*
Tim McCulley, *Engineer*
Darla Loger, *Finance Mgr*
EMP: 38
SQ FT: 41,500
SALES: 6MM Privately Held
WEB: www.chaseng.com
SIC: 3728 8711 Aircraft parts & equipment; industrial engineers

(G-888)
CLEARWATER CABLE VISION INC
Also Called: Skit
112 S Lee St (67026-7810)
P.O. Box 800 (67026-0800)
PHONE..................................620 584-2077
Kendall Mikesell, *President*
Donna Van Allen, *Sales Executive*
Dick Croft, *Adjutant*
EMP: 50 EST: 1979
SALES (est): 5.2MM Privately Held
SIC: 4841 Cable television services

(G-889)
CLEARWTER NRSING RHABILITATION
620 E Wood St (67026-9757)
PHONE..................................620 584-2271
Danielle Reicks, *Manager*
EMP: 11
SALES: 4.9MM Privately Held
SIC: 8051 Skilled nursing care facilities

(G-890)
CLONMEL COMMUNITY CLUB INC
Also Called: Clonmel Hall
6101 S 167th St W (67026-9044)
PHONE..................................620 545-7136
Greg Simon, *President*
Bill Meczen, *Vice Pres*
Jim Armour, *Treasurer*
Jerry Klausmeyer, *Admin Sec*
EMP: 30
SALES (est): 1.3MM Privately Held
WEB: www.clonmel.ie
SIC: 6512 Auditorium & hall operation

(G-891)
EMPRISE BANK
201 E Ross St (67026-7825)
PHONE..................................620 584-2201
Rae Gibbs, *Manager*
EMP: 13
SALES (corp-wide): 80MM Privately Held
WEB: www.firststateks.com
SIC: 6022 State commercial banks
HQ: Emprise Bank
257 N Broadway Ave
Wichita KS 67202
316 383-4400

(G-892)
FCG INC
6315 S 151st St W (67026-9037)
PHONE..................................620 545-8300
Fred F Gorges, *President*
EMP: 13
SALES (est): 675.6K Privately Held
SIC: 4789 7389 Transportation services;

(G-893)
HEALY BIODIESEL INC
11130 W 47th St S (67026-9055)
PHONE..................................620 545-7800
Benjamin Healy, *President*
Rachel Bowyer, *Office Mgr*
EMP: 15
SALES: 250K Privately Held
SIC: 4953 Liquid waste, collection & disposal

(G-894)
MARTIN WELDING
16401 W 55th St S (67026-8560)
PHONE..................................620 545-7311
Gary Martin, *Owner*
EMP: 5
SALES (est): 359.6K Privately Held
SIC: 1799 7692 Welding on site; welding repair

(G-895)
RONALD G HIGGINS
Also Called: Clearwater Dental Office
136 N Gorin St (67026-7802)
P.O. Box 519 (67026-0519)
PHONE..................................620 584-2223
Ronald G Higgins, *Owner*
EMP: 10
SQ FT: 2,500
SALES (est): 629.2K Privately Held
SIC: 8021 Dentists' office

(G-896)
SHACKELFORD MACHINE INC
116 S Tracy St (67026-7830)
P.O. Box 670 (67026-0670)
PHONE..................................620 584-2436
Carl Shackelford, *Co-Owner*
Jay Shackelford, *Co-Owner*
EMP: 24
SQ FT: 10,000
SALES (est): 3.4MM Privately Held
WEB: www.fast411.com
SIC: 3599 Machine shop, jobbing & repair

(G-897)
SOUTH CENTL KS EDUCATN SVC CTR (PA)
Also Called: Orion Education and Training
13939 W Diagonal Rd (67026-9413)
P.O. Box 160 (67026-0160)
PHONE..................................620 584-3300
Earl Guoit, *Manager*
Lori Jensen, *Consultant*
Brad Pepper, *Exec Dir*
Deanne Hersche, *Director*
Kay Higaearger, *Director*
EMP: 15
SALES (est): 1.9MM Privately Held
WEB: www.sckesc.org
SIC: 8621 Education & teacher association

(G-898)
SOUTHERN KANSAS TELE CO INC (PA)
Also Called: Business Systems Division
112 S Lee St (67026-7810)
P.O. Box 800 (67026-0800)
PHONE..................................620 584-2255
Gordon G Mikesell, *CEO*
Kendall Mikesell, *President*
Donna Allen, *Director*
Donna Van Allen, *Director*
Edwin Mikesell, *Shareholder*
EMP: 45 EST: 1940
SQ FT: 4,000
SALES (est): 19MM Privately Held
WEB: www.sktbcs.com
SIC: 4813 5065 Local telephone communications; long distance telephone communications; communication equipment

(G-899)
SOUTHERN KANSAS TELE CO INC
128 N Gorin St (67026-7802)
P.O. Box 800 (67026-0800)
PHONE..................................620 584-2255
Gordon G Mikesell, *CEO*
Jill Mc Millan, *Admin Sec*
EMP: 35
SALES (corp-wide): 19MM Privately Held
WEB: www.sktbcs.com
SIC: 5065 4813 Communication equipment; telephone communication, except radio
PA: The Southern Kansas Telephone Company Inc
112 S Lee St
Clearwater KS 67026
620 584-2255

Clifton
Washington County

(G-900)
COMMUNITY CARE INC
310 Strand St (66937-9629)
PHONE..................................785 455-3522
Howard Bowman, *President*
Marcia Ryan, *Corp Secy*
Eugene Leblanc, *Vice Pres*
Mike Kantack, *Director*
Alvin Veesart, *Director*
EMP: 25
SQ FT: 10,000
SALES: 793.9K **Privately Held**
SIC: 8052 Intermediate care facilities

(G-901)
K C PORK INC
451 3rd Rd (66937-8861)
PHONE..................................785 455-3410
Kent F Condray, *President*
EMP: 10
SQ FT: 22,576
SALES (est): 482.3K **Privately Held**
SIC: 0213 Hogs

(G-902)
NORTHERN NATURAL GAS COMPANY
2930 Gas City Rd (66937-5201)
P.O. Box 160 (66937-0160)
PHONE..................................785 455-3311
Jon Werrenette, *Manager*
EMP: 34
SALES (corp-wide): 225.3B **Publicly Held**
SIC: 4226 4922 Special warehousing & storage; natural gas transmission
HQ: Northern Natural Gas Company
1111 S 103rd St
Omaha NE 68124

(G-903)
XCEL NDT LLC
104 Avon St (66937-9602)
P.O. Box 146 (66937-0146)
PHONE..................................785 455-2027
Cole Morehead, *President*
Chris Schropp, *Vice Pres*
Grant Cain, *Office Mgr*
Karah Standridge, *Office Mgr*
Barrett Winter, *Office Mgr*
EMP: 29 **EST:** 2012
SALES: 2.1MM
SALES (corp-wide): 19.6MM **Privately Held**
SIC: 8748 Testing services
PA: Crossbridge Compliance, Llc
2755 State Highway 322
Longview TX 75603
903 643-7304

Clyde
Cloud County

(G-904)
BUDREAU CONSTRUCTION INC
132 S Railroad Ave (66938-9649)
PHONE..................................785 446-3665
Mark Budreau, *President*
Trish Budreau, *Admin Sec*
EMP: 10 **EST:** 1994
SALES (est): 1MM **Privately Held**
SIC: 1521 Single-family housing construction

(G-905)
CLAY CENTER FMLY PHYSICIANS PA
Also Called: Family Practice
815 Campbell Ave (66938-9428)
PHONE..................................785 446-2226
Lance Haller, *Manager*
EMP: 10
SALES (est): 280.2K
SALES (corp-wide): 3.3MM **Privately Held**
WEB: www.ccfp.net
SIC: 8062 General medical & surgical hospitals
PA: Clay Center Family Physicians Pa, Inc
609 Liberty St
Clay Center KS 67432
785 632-2181

(G-906)
CLYDE DEVELOPMENT INC
Also Called: PARK VILLA NURSING HOME
114 S High St (66938-9472)
PHONE..................................785 446-2818
Joe Cassady, *Administration*
EMP: 37
SALES: 1.8MM **Privately Held**
WEB: www.clydekansas.org
SIC: 8059 Nursing home, except skilled & intermediate care facility

Coffeyville
Montgomery County

(G-907)
ACME FOUNDRY INC (PA)
1502 Spruce St (67337-5321)
P.O. Box 908 (67337-0908)
PHONE..................................620 251-6800
Thomas A Tatman, *President*
Drew Cantrell, *Traffic Mgr*
Mark Stallsmith, *Maint Spvr*
Robbie Cook, *Production*
Robert L Shepard, *CFO*
▲ **EMP:** 382 **EST:** 1914
SQ FT: 250,000
SALES: 46.3MM **Privately Held**
SIC: 3321 Gray iron castings

(G-908)
ACME FOUNDRY INC
Magic Circle Division
1209 Buckeye St (67337-3711)
P.O. Box 657 (67337-0657)
PHONE..................................620 251-4920
Mark Stallsmith, *Maint Spvr*
Jim Tatman, *Manager*
EMP: 30
SALES (corp-wide): 46.3MM **Privately Held**
SIC: 3599 3321 Machine shop, jobbing & repair; gray & ductile iron foundries
PA: Acme Foundry, Inc.
1502 Spruce St
Coffeyville KS 67337
620 251-6800

(G-909)
ALDERMAN ACRES MFG INC
623 Union St (67337-6019)
PHONE..................................620 251-4095
Carmen Jo Alderman, *President*
Tom Alderman, *Vice Pres*
Donald Alderman, *Treasurer*
EMP: 16
SQ FT: 17,000
SALES (est): 2.1MM **Privately Held**
WEB: www.aldermanacres.com
SIC: 2541 2591 2391 Partitions for floor attachment, prefabricated: wood; curtain & drapery rods, poles & fixtures; curtains & draperies

(G-910)
BARTLETT MILLING COMPANY LP
1307 Maple St (67337-5233)
PHONE..................................620 251-4650
Rod Geiger, *Principal*
John Gilquist, *Principal*
Beth Edgar, *Manager*
EMP: 50
SALES (corp-wide): 1B **Privately Held**
SIC: 2041 Wheat flour
HQ: Bartlett Milling Company, L.P.
4900 Main St Ste 1200
Kansas City MO 64112
816 753-6300

(G-911)
BERRY HOLDINGS LP
714 Maple St (67337-4913)
PHONE..................................620 251-4400
Lonney Bay, *Principal*
EMP: 440
SALES (corp-wide): 432.6MM **Privately Held**
SIC: 1541 Industrial buildings & warehouses
PA: Berry Holdings, Lp
1414 Corn Product Rd
Corpus Christi TX 78409
361 693-2100

(G-912)
BEST WESTERN BRICKTOWN LODGE
605 Northeast St (67337-7212)
P.O. Box 250, Oologah OK (74053-0250)
PHONE..................................620 251-3700
Ande Harmon, *Partner*
EMP: 12
SALES (est): 498.6K **Privately Held**
SIC: 7011 Hotels & motels

(G-913)
BOBS SUPER SAVER INC
Also Called: Country Mart West
1000 Hall St (67337-3621)
PHONE..................................620 251-6820
Kay Littlepage, *Manager*
EMP: 92
SALES (corp-wide): 14.6MM **Privately Held**
SIC: 5411 2051 5461 Supermarkets, chain; bread, cake & related products; bakeries
PA: Bobs Super Saver Inc
15621 W 87th Street Pkwy
Lenexa KS 66219
913 856-6610

(G-914)
BROOKDALE SENIOR LIVING COMMUN
Also Called: Sterling House Asbury Village
3800 Asbury Dr (67337-9153)
PHONE..................................620 251-6270
Ginger Bellm, *Manager*
EMP: 14
SALES (corp-wide): 4.5B **Publicly Held**
WEB: www.assisted.com
SIC: 8059 Rest home, with health care
HQ: Brookdale Senior Living Communities, Inc.
6737 W Wa St Ste 2300
Milwaukee WI 53214
414 918-5000

(G-915)
CITY OF COFFEYVILLE
Also Called: Coffeyville Power & Light Dept
605 Santa Fe St (67337-6343)
P.O. Box 1629 (67337-8029)
PHONE..................................620 252-6180
Tony Lawson, *Superintendent*
EMP: 18 **Privately Held**
WEB: www.coffeyville.com
SIC: 4911 Distribution, electric power; generation, electric power; transmission, electric power
PA: City Of Coffeyville
102 W 7th St
Coffeyville KS 67337
620 252-6114

(G-916)
CLOUGH OIL COMPANY INC
104 E 4th St (67337-6008)
P.O. Box 1356 (67337-5656)
PHONE..................................620 251-0521
Charles G Clough, *President*
Jacquelyne Clough, *Treasurer*
EMP: 13
SALES (est): 6.6MM **Privately Held**
SIC: 5171 Petroleum bulk stations

(G-917)
CLOUGH OIL COMPANY INC
1106 Oak St (67337-6500)
P.O. Box 1356 (67337-5656)
PHONE..................................620 251-0103
Charles G Clough, *President*
EMP: 23
SALES (est): 3.6MM **Privately Held**
SIC: 5172 Petroleum products

(G-918)
COFFEYVILLE COUNTRY CLUB
1322 Englewood (67337)
P.O. Box 265 (67337-0265)
PHONE..................................620 251-5236
John Isaac, *President*
EMP: 25
SQ FT: 11,000
SALES: 729.4K **Privately Held**
SIC: 5813 7997 Bar (drinking places); swimming club, membership

(G-919)
COFFEYVILLE DOCTORS CLINIC P A
801 W 8th St (67337-4109)
P.O. Box 1057 (67337-2057)
PHONE..................................620 251-7500
Paul Sandhu MD, *President*
EMP: 30
SQ FT: 11,000
SALES (est): 4.4MM **Privately Held**
SIC: 8011 Offices & clinics of medical doctors

(G-920)
COFFEYVILLE PRINTING CENTER
707 Walnut St (67337-4910)
P.O. Box 203 (67337-0203)
PHONE..................................620 251-6040
Alicia Yates, *President*
EMP: 6
SALES: 300K **Privately Held**
SIC: 2759 Commercial printing

(G-921)
COFFEYVILLE RESOURCES LLC
701 E Martin St (67337-1911)
P.O. Box 1566 (67337-7866)
PHONE..................................620 252-4781
Keith Osborn, *Branch Mgr*
Terry Smith, *Manager*
EMP: 15 **Publicly Held**
SIC: 2911 Gasoline
HQ: Coffeyville Resources, Llc
2277 Plaza Dr Ste 500
Sugar Land TX 77479
281 207-3200

(G-922)
COFFEYVILLE SEKTAM INC
509 Cline Rd (67337-3026)
PHONE..................................620 251-3880
Steve Cornell, *President*
Jack S Cornell, *Vice Pres*
Earl Grove, *Engineer*
Barbara Schroeder, *Finance*
EMP: 100
SQ FT: 45,000
SALES: 19MM **Privately Held**
SIC: 3599 Machine shop, jobbing & repair

(G-923)
COFFEYVLLE FMLY PRCTICE CLINIC
209 W 7th St (67337-4954)
P.O. Box 564 (67337-0564)
PHONE..................................620 251-1100
Allen Gillis, *Partner*
James Christensen, *Partner*
EMP: 28
SQ FT: 4,000
SALES (est): 1.7MM **Privately Held**
SIC: 8031 8011 Offices & clinics of osteopathic physicians; general & family practice, physician/surgeon

(G-924)
COFFEYVLLE RGIONAL MED CTR INC
1400 W 4th St (67337-3306)
PHONE..................................620 251-1200
Brian Lawrence, *CEO*
Lori Rexwinkle, *Principal*
John Smith, *Principal*
Cheryl Batchelor, *CFO*
William Page, *CFO*
EMP: 380
SQ FT: 112,962

SALES: 40.2MM Privately Held
WEB: www.crmcinc.com
SIC: 8062 General medical & surgical hospitals

(G-925)
COFFEYVLLE RSRCES REF MKTG LLC
701 E North St (67337-1926)
PHONE....620 251-4000
EMP: 55 Publicly Held
SIC: 2873 Ammonium nitrate, ammonium sulfate; anhydrous ammonia
HQ: Coffeyville Resources Refining & Marketing, Llc
2277 Plaza Dr Ste 500
Sugar Land TX 77479
281 207-3200

(G-926)
COFFEYVLLE RSRCES REF MKTG LLC
400 N Linden St (67337-1900)
PHONE....620 251-4252
EMP: 100 Publicly Held
SIC: 2911 Petroleum refining
HQ: Coffeyville Resources Refining & Marketing, Llc
2277 Plaza Dr Ste 500
Sugar Land TX 77479
281 207-3200

(G-927)
COFFEYVLLE UNFIED SCHL DST 445
Also Called: Coffeyville Recreation Comm
508 Park St (67337-7136)
P.O. Box 307 (67337-0307)
PHONE....620 251-5910
Jim Cadwell, *Director*
EMP: 20
SQ FT: 12,000
SALES (corp-wide): 29.9MM Privately Held
SIC: 8211 7999 Public elementary & secondary schools; recreation center
PA: Coffeyville Unified School District 445
615 Ellis St
Coffeyville KS 67337
620 252-6400

(G-928)
COMMUNITY STATE BANK (PA)
1414 W 11th St (67337-3610)
P.O. Box 219 (67337-0219)
PHONE....620 251-1313
Mike Ewy, *President*
Chris Cook, *Assistant VP*
Kim Hearson, *Assistant VP*
Jeff Stewart, *Vice Pres*
Tom Swanson, *Vice Pres*
EMP: 15
SALES: 6.6MM Privately Held
WEB: www.bankcommunitystate.com
SIC: 6022 State trust companies accepting deposits, commercial

(G-929)
CONDON NATIONAL BANK (PA)
814 Walnut St (67337-5826)
P.O. Box 219 (67337-0219)
PHONE....620 251-5500
Ron Levis, *President*
Janie C Houston, *Vice Pres*
EMP: 28
SALES: 3.6MM Privately Held
WEB: www.condonbank.com
SIC: 6021 National trust companies with deposits, commercial

(G-930)
COOK PUMP COMPANY
1400 W 12th St (67337)
PHONE....620 251-0880
John Carmack, *President*
EMP: 25
SQ FT: 40,000
SALES (est): 4.7MM Privately Held
WEB: www.cookpumpingjacks.com
SIC: 3561 3441 7699 Pumps, oil well & field; fabricated structural metal; pumps & pumping equipment repair

(G-931)
CORNEJO & SONS LLC
Also Called: Coffeyville Concrete
206 N Linden St (67337-1904)
PHONE....620 251-1690
William Feess, *Branch Mgr*
EMP: 8
SALES (corp-wide): 2.1B Publicly Held
WEB: www.midwestminerals.com
SIC: 3273 Ready-mixed concrete
HQ: Cornejo & Sons, L.L.C.
2060 E Tulsa St
Wichita KS 67216
316 522-5100

(G-932)
DARWIN INDUSTRIES INC
Also Called: John Deere Authorized Dealer
5184 E Industrial Rd B (67337-6409)
P.O. Box 251 (67337-0251)
PHONE....620 251-8438
Cary D Pitts, *President*
Steve G Pitts, *Corp Secy*
Carl M Pitts, *Vice Pres*
Robert Folk, *Engineer*
Jackie Everitt, *Sales Staff*
EMP: 10
SQ FT: 32,000
SALES (est): 3.9MM Privately Held
WEB: www.darwinindustries.com
SIC: 5084 Pumps & pumping equipment

(G-933)
DECKER CONSTRUCTION INC (PA)
1215 E 8th St (67337-7254)
P.O. Box 254 (67337-0254)
PHONE....620 251-7693
Ronald McVey, *President*
Ronald Mc Vey, *President*
EMP: 50 EST: 1970
SQ FT: 4,000
SALES (est): 8.9MM Privately Held
WEB: www.dci.kscoxmail.com
SIC: 1541 1542 Industrial buildings & warehouses; commercial & office building, new construction

(G-934)
DM ROOFING
502 Highland Rd (67337-2615)
PHONE....620 515-0015
David Leander, *Owner*
EMP: 15
SALES: 1MM Privately Held
SIC: 1761 Roofing contractor

(G-935)
EAGLE SECURITY SERVICES
2444 Cr 4500 (67337-7915)
PHONE....620 251-0085
Gene Tucker, *Owner*
EMP: 57
SALES (est): 746.5K Privately Held
SIC: 7381 Security guard service

(G-936)
EMERALD TRANSFORMER KANSAS LLC
2474 N Us Highway 169 (67337-9231)
PHONE....620 251-6380
Shane Willis, *Principal*
EMP: 45
SALES (est): 1.4MM Privately Held
SIC: 3612 Transformers, except electric

(G-937)
EMERALD TRANSFORMER PPM LLC
2474 N Us Highway 169 (67337-9231)
PHONE....620 251-6380
Bonnie Martin, *Technical Staff*
EMP: 50
SALES (corp-wide): 247.7MM Privately Held
SIC: 4953 5983 Hazardous waste collection & disposal; fuel oil dealers
HQ: Emerald Transformer Ppm Llc
9820 Westpoint Dr Ste 300
Indianapolis IN 46256

(G-938)
FIRST STUDENT INC
204 N Central St (67337-1418)
PHONE....620 251-8441
Fax: 620 251-2331
EMP: 20
SALES (corp-wide): 9.2B Privately Held
SIC: 4142 Bus Charter Service-Nonlocal
HQ: First Student, Inc.
600 Vine St Ste 1400
Cincinnati OH 45202
513 241-2200

(G-939)
FOUR CNTY MENTAL HLTH CTR INC
Also Called: Coffeyville
813 Union St (67337-5823)
PHONE....620 251-8180
Greg Hennen, *Director*
EMP: 111
SALES (corp-wide): 15.9MM Privately Held
SIC: 8322 8069 8093 Individual & family services; drug addiction rehabilitation hospital; specialty outpatient clinics
PA: Four County Mental Health Center, Inc.
3751 W Main St
Independence KS 67301
620 331-1748

(G-940)
FOUR STATE MAINTENANCE SUP INC
503 N Cline Rd (67337-1104)
P.O. Box 591 (67337-0591)
PHONE....620 251-7033
Tim Roberts, *President*
Mike Hayes, *Vice Pres*
Tom Tipton, *Vice Pres*
Dakota Deivernois, *Warehouse Mgr*
Jeff Garton, *Warehouse Mgr*
EMP: 27
SQ FT: 26,000
SALES (est): 7.6MM Privately Held
WEB: www.4statemaint.com
SIC: 5087 Janitors' supplies

(G-941)
FRITO-LAY NORTH AMERICA INC
2209 W 8th St (67337-2936)
PHONE....620 251-4367
S Chittum, *Manager*
EMP: 25
SALES (corp-wide): 64.6B Publicly Held
WEB: www.fritolay.com
SIC: 5145 Potato chips; snack foods
HQ: Frito-Lay North America, Inc.
7701 Legacy Dr
Plano TX 75024

(G-942)
GBW RAILCAR SERVICES LLC
1604 Spruce St (67337-5323)
PHONE....844 364-7403
Dion Wilkens, *Principal*
EMP: 35
SALES (corp-wide): 3B Publicly Held
WEB: www.watcocompanies.com
SIC: 4789 Railroad car repair
HQ: Gbw Railcar Services, L.L.C.
4350 Nw Front Ave
Portland OR 97210

(G-943)
HARTLEY SHEET METAL CO INC
405 Walnut St (67337-4816)
P.O. Box 471 (67337-0471)
PHONE....620 251-4330
Glenn Storm, *President*
Kathern Wise, *Vice Pres*
Vicki Storm, *Treasurer*
EMP: 11
SALES (est): 1.6MM Privately Held
SIC: 1711 1761 Warm air heating & air conditioning contractor; sheet metalwork

(G-944)
HEALTH MANAGEMENT OF KANSAS
Also Called: Windsor Place Home Care Div
106 Tyler Blvd (67337-2425)
PHONE....620 251-1866
Jenny Hendrix, *Administration*
EMP: 100 Privately Held
SIC: 8741 8082 Nursing & personal care facility management; home health care services
PA: Health Management Of Kansas, Inc
104 W 8th St
Coffeyville KS 67337

(G-945)
HEALTH MANAGEMENT OF KANSAS
Also Called: Windsor Place
2921 W 1st St (67337-2441)
PHONE....620 251-5190
Monte Coffman, *Human Res Dir*
Lisa Barron, *Food Svc Dir*
EMP: 180 Privately Held
SIC: 8741 8051 8052 Nursing & personal care facility management; skilled nursing care facilities; intermediate care facilities
PA: Health Management Of Kansas, Inc
104 W 8th St
Coffeyville KS 67337

(G-946)
HEALTH MANAGEMENT OF KANSAS (PA)
Also Called: Windsor Place
104 W 8th St (67337-5806)
PHONE....620 251-6545
Charles W Wurth, *President*
Charlene Merriman, *Bookkeeper*
Mike Coltharp, *Technology*
EMP: 91
SALES (est): 15.5MM Privately Held
SIC: 8741 Nursing & personal care facility management

(G-947)
HOSPICE INCORPORATED
2404 W 8th St (67337-2931)
PHONE....620 251-1640
EMP: 28
SALES (corp-wide): 18.1MM Privately Held
SIC: 8052 Personal care facility
PA: Hospice, Incorporated
313 S Market St
Wichita KS 67202
316 265-9441

(G-948)
INTERNATIONAL UNION UNITED AU
900 Hall St Ste 107 (67337-3504)
P.O. Box 1404 (67337-6704)
PHONE....620 251-2022
Kenneth Vest, *Branch Mgr*
Jerry Gregory, *Branch Mgr*
EMP: 170
SALES (corp-wide): 237MM Privately Held
SIC: 8631 Labor union
PA: International Union, United Automobile, Aerospace And Agricultural Implement Workers Of Am
8000 E Jefferson Ave
Detroit MI 48214
313 926-5000

(G-949)
J GRAHAM CONSTRUCTION INC
1306 Elm St (67337-5215)
PHONE....620 252-2395
Jeff Graham, *Principal*
Stephen Graham, *Principal*
EMP: 25
SALES (est): 226.9K Privately Held
SIC: 1521 New construction, single-family houses

(G-950)
JACKS GENUINE MFG INC
1629 Cr 3700 (67337-9417)
PHONE....620 948-3000
EMP: 14 EST: 2007
SALES (est): 2.7MM Privately Held
SIC: 3561 Mfg Pumps/Pumping Equipment

(G-951)
JOHN DERE CFFEYVILLE WORKS INC
2624 N Us Highway 169 (67337-9235)
PHONE....620 251-3400
Rob Chopp, *President*
Kevin Allen, *Engineer*
Jeff Parker, *Engineer*
Dale Kowalski, *Manager*

GEOGRAPHIC

▲ **EMP:** 450
SQ FT: 270,000
SALES (est): 57.3MM
SALES (corp-wide): 39.2B **Publicly Held**
WEB: www.deere.com
SIC: **5531** 3714 Automobile & truck equipment & parts; power transmission equipment, motor vehicle
PA: Deere & Company
1 John Deere Pl
Moline IL 61265
309 765-8000

(G-952)
KGGF K U S N BROADCASTING STN (PA)
Also Called: Kggf AM 690
306 W 8th St (67337-5829)
PHONE..................................620 251-3800
Robert Mahaffey, *President*
Paul Cooper, *Manager*
John Leonard, *Manager*
EMP: 15 **EST:** 1947
SQ FT: 3,600
SALES (est): 2.2MM **Privately Held**
SIC: **4832** Radio broadcasting stations

(G-953)
KRINA CORPORATION
Also Called: Regal Inn
1215 E 3rd St 166169n (67337-7013)
P.O. Box 373 (67337-0373)
PHONE..................................620 251-1034
James D Cook, *President*
Pam Wall, *Principal*
EMP: 10
SQ FT: 8,250
SALES (est): 581.7K **Privately Held**
SIC: **7011** Hotel, franchised

(G-954)
LABETTE HEALTH FOUNDATION INC
Also Called: Chetopa Medical Clinic
575 2000 Rd (67337-7720)
P.O. Box 285, Chetopa (67336-0285)
PHONE..................................620 922-3838
Fax: 620 236-7323
EMP: 12
SALES (corp-wide): 163.5K **Privately Held**
SIC: **8062** 8011 General Hospital Medical Doctor's Office
PA: Labette Health Foundation, Inc.
1902 S Us Highway 59
Parsons KS 67357
620 421-4881

(G-955)
LEE SHAFER RICKY
Also Called: R.I.C. Construction
1272 Cr 4500 (67337-9453)
P.O. Box 488 (67337-0488)
PHONE..................................620 252-9126
Ricky Shafer, *Owner*
EMP: 20
SALES (est): 1.5MM **Privately Held**
SIC: **1541** 1611 7389 Industrial buildings & warehouses; general contractor, highway & street construction;

(G-956)
LIEBERT BROTHERS ELECTRIC CO (PA)
Also Called: L B Supply Company
313 W 8th St 315 (67337-5828)
PHONE..................................620 251-0299
Robert L Liebert, *President*
Albert C Liebert, *Chairman*
Tim F Vannoster, *Vice Pres*
Ann Marie Vannoster, *Treasurer*
Janice Land, *Admin Sec*
EMP: 12 **EST:** 1911
SQ FT: 15,200
SALES (est): 1.5MM **Privately Held**
SIC: **1731** 1711 5722 5063 General electrical contractor; refrigeration contractor; warm air heating & air conditioning contractor; household appliance stores; electrical supplies

(G-957)
MCCARTYS
Also Called: McCartys Office Machines
214 W 9th St (67337-5812)
PHONE..................................620 251-6169
Jim McCarty, *President*
Jim Bogner, *Manager*
EMP: 7
SQ FT: 5,000
SALES (est): 832K **Privately Held**
SIC: **5112** 5021 2759 Office supplies; office furniture; commercial printing

(G-958)
MEDICALODGES INC (PA)
201 W 8th St (67337-5807)
P.O. Box 509 (67337-0509)
PHONE..................................620 251-6700
Garen Cox, *President*
Richard Butler, *Chairman*
Fred Benjamin, *COO*
Clifford Fischer, *COO*
Cathy Fisher, *Vice Pres*
EMP: 70 **EST:** 1961
SQ FT: 21,000
SALES: 100.2MM **Privately Held**
WEB: www.medicalodges.com
SIC: **8051** Convalescent home with continuous nursing care

(G-959)
MEDICALODGES INC
Also Called: Medicalodges of Coffeyville
720 W 1st St (67337-3854)
PHONE..................................620 251-3705
Deann Christenson, *Administration*
EMP: 39
SALES (corp-wide): 100.2MM **Privately Held**
WEB: www.medicalodges.com
SIC: **8051** 8059 Convalescent home with continuous nursing care; rest home, with health care
PA: Medicalodges, Inc.
201 W 8th St
Coffeyville KS 67337
620 251-6700

(G-960)
MEDICALODGES INC
Also Called: Medicalodge Construction Div
201 W 8th St (67337-5807)
P.O. Box 509 (67337-0509)
PHONE..................................620 251-6700
Larry Fisher, *Manager*
EMP: 71
SALES (corp-wide): 100.2MM **Privately Held**
WEB: www.medicalodges.com
SIC: **8051** Convalescent home with continuous nursing care
PA: Medicalodges, Inc.
201 W 8th St
Coffeyville KS 67337
620 251-6700

(G-961)
MEDICALODGES CNSTR CO INC
Also Called: Home Equipment Co
201 W 8th St (67337-5807)
P.O. Box 509 (67337-0509)
PHONE..................................620 251-6700
S Arthur Hann, *Ch of Bd*
Garen Cox, *President*
Larry Fischer, *President*
J D Feller, *Principal*
Allen Ediger, *Vice Pres*
EMP: 13 **EST:** 1969
SALES (est): 927.6K
SALES (corp-wide): 100.2MM **Privately Held**
WEB: www.medicalodges.com
SIC: **8742** Maintenance management consultant
PA: Medicalodges, Inc.
201 W 8th St
Coffeyville KS 67337
620 251-6700

(G-962)
MESSER LLC
210 Cedar St (67337-6127)
PHONE..................................620 251-9190
Randy Post, *Branch Mgr*
EMP: 7
SALES (corp-wide): 1.4B **Privately Held**
SIC: **2813** Nitrogen; oxygen, compressed or liquefied
HQ: Messer Llc
200 Somerset Corp Blvd # 7000
Bridgewater NJ 08807
908 464-8100

(G-963)
MIDLAND THEATER FOUNDATION INC
214 W 8th St (67337-5808)
P.O. Box 545 (67337-0545)
PHONE..................................901 501-6832
Haylie Bagwell, *President*
Darrel Harbaugh, *Vice Pres*
EMP: 15
SALES: 25K **Privately Held**
SIC: **6512** Theater building, ownership & operation

(G-964)
MULLER CONSTRUCTION INC
204 N Central St (67337-1499)
P.O. Box 1235 (67337-5135)
PHONE..................................620 251-1110
Larry Muller, *President*
Mark Muller, *Vice Pres*
Fred Muller, *Treasurer*
EMP: 20 **EST:** 1935
SQ FT: 3,000
SALES (est): 2.8MM **Privately Held**
WEB: www.mullerconstruction.com
SIC: **1794** Excavation work

(G-965)
MULTIMEDIA CABLEVISION
Also Called: Cox Communications
102 W 11th St (67337-5902)
P.O. Box 189 (67337-0189)
PHONE..................................620 251-6610
Fax: 620 251-4064
EMP: 14
SALES (corp-wide): 7.4B **Privately Held**
SIC: **4841** Cable/Pay Television Service
HQ: Multimedia Cablevision Of Chicago Ridge, Inc.
901 S George Wash Blvd
Wichita KS 67211

(G-966)
O K ELECTRIC WORK INC
10 E North St (67337-1899)
PHONE..................................620 251-2270
Dale Hamlin, *President*
Tom Moley, *Vice Pres*
Patricia Hamlin, *Treasurer*
Terry Moley, *Admin Sec*
EMP: 7
SQ FT: 2,950
SALES: 350K **Privately Held**
SIC: **6514** 7694 7539 Residential building, four or fewer units: operation; electric motor repair; automotive repair shops

(G-967)
OREILLY AUTOMOTIVE STORES INC
Also Called: O'Reilly Auto Parts
611 W 11th St (67337-5025)
PHONE..................................620 251-5280
Paul Reynolds, *Manager*
EMP: 12 **Publicly Held**
WEB: www.oreillyauto.com
SIC: **5013** 5531 Automotive supplies & parts; automotive parts
HQ: O'reilly Automotive Stores, Inc.
233 S Patterson Ave
Springfield MO 65802
417 862-2674

(G-968)
ORSCHELN FARM AND HOME LLC
Also Called: Orschelin Farm and Home 36
1702 W 11th St (67337-3115)
PHONE..................................620 251-2950
Daryl Cook, *Manager*
EMP: 10
SALES (corp-wide): 822.7MM **Privately Held**
WEB: www.orschelnfarmhome.com
SIC: **5191** 5251 5699 Farm supplies; hardware; work clothing
PA: Orscheln Farm And Home Llc
1800 Overcenter Dr
Moberly MO 65270
800 577-2580

(G-969)
PARMAC LLC
201 E 12th St (67337-6607)
P.O. Box 1149 (67337-4349)
PHONE..................................620 251-5000
Steve Braschler, *Chief Engr*
Richard J Feldstein, *Treasurer*
R L Shadwick, *Controller*
Derrick Morris, *Mng Member*
EMP: 20 **EST:** 1898
SQ FT: 145,000
SALES (est): 4.8MM **Privately Held**
WEB: www.parmacbrake.com
SIC: **3533** Oil field machinery & equipment

(G-970)
PENWELL GBL FRL WLF BRNS CHPL
2405 Woodland Ave (67337-1131)
PHONE..................................620 251-3100
Ren Newcomer, *President*
EMP: 14
SQ FT: 10,000
SALES (est): 473.7K **Privately Held**
SIC: **7261** Funeral home

(G-971)
PEPSI-COLA METRO BTLG CO INC
2406 N 169 (67337)
PHONE..................................620 251-2890
Bob Slader, *Branch Mgr*
EMP: 30
SALES (corp-wide): 64.6B **Publicly Held**
WEB: www.joy-of-cola.com
SIC: **2086** Carbonated soft drinks, bottled & canned
HQ: Pepsi-Cola Metropolitan Bottling Company, Inc.
1111 Westchester Ave
White Plains NY 10604
914 767-6000

(G-972)
PERL AUTO CENTER INC
806 W 8th St (67337-4110)
PHONE..................................620 251-4050
John W Schmid, *President*
Paul Schmid, *Admin Sec*
EMP: 10 **EST:** 1976
SALES (est): 112.8K **Privately Held**
SIC: **7538** 5511 General automotive repair shops; new & used car dealers

(G-973)
ROBINSON SUPPLY LLC
2804 Walnut St (67337-6928)
P.O. Box 246 (67337-0246)
PHONE..................................620 251-0490
David Cook,
Larry Rhoden,
EMP: 5 **EST:** 2001
SALES (est): 342.3K **Privately Held**
SIC: **1321** 5251 Natural gasoline production; pumps & pumping equipment

(G-974)
S & H INC
Also Called: Brass Hat Lawn Maintenance
204 W 1st St (67337-5518)
PHONE..................................620 251-4422
Jim Schoonover, *President*
Eva Schoonover, *Corp Secy*
EMP: 15
SALES (est): 333.7K **Privately Held**
SIC: **7349** Building maintenance services

(G-975)
SAFEHOUSE INC
Also Called: Safehouse Satellite Ofc
1317 W 8th St (67337-3507)
PHONE..................................620 251-0030
Rebecca Reedy, *Director*
EMP: 16
SALES (est): 283.1K **Privately Held**
SIC: **8322** Crisis center

(G-976)
SEK READY MIX INC
2453 N Us Highway 169 (67337-9253)
P.O. Box 1084 (67337-2084)
PHONE..................................620 252-8699
Sean O'Brien, *President*
EMP: 30
SALES: 1MM **Privately Held**
SIC: 3273 Ready-mixed concrete

(G-977)
SIEMENS INDUSTRY INC
400 N Linden St (67337-1900)
PHONE..................................620 252-4223
Roy Wolff, *Manager*
EMP: 21
SALES (corp-wide): 96.9B **Privately Held**
SIC: 4953
HQ: Siemens Industry, Inc.
1000 Deerfield Pkwy
Buffalo Grove IL 60089
847 215-1000

(G-978)
SLEEP INN AND SUITE
202 E 11th St (67337-6512)
PHONE..................................620 688-6400
Lori Etherton, *Principal*
EMP: 17 **EST:** 2009
SALES (est): 635.6K **Privately Held**
SIC: 7011 Hotels & motels

(G-979)
STAR PIPE USA LLC
Also Called: Sp Foundy
1004 W 14th St (67337-4406)
PHONE..................................281 558-3000
Ramesh Bhutada,
EMP: 175 **Privately Held**
SIC: 3321 3561 3713 3533 Gray & ductile iron foundries; pumps, oil well & field; pumps, domestic: water or sump; pump jacks & other pumping equipment; truck beds; oil & gas field machinery; sheet metalwork
HQ: Star Pipe Usa, Llc
4018 Westhollow Pkwy
Houston TX 77082
620 251-5700

(G-980)
STAR PIPE USA LLC (HQ)
Also Called: Sp Foundry
1004 W 14th St (67337-4406)
P.O. Box 1509 (67337-7809)
PHONE..................................620 251-5700
Diana Knisley, *Treasurer*
Ramesh Bhutada, *Mng Member*
Navin K Bharagava,
Kiran Bhutada,
Daniel McCutchen,
EMP: 67
SALES: 12MM
SALES (corp-wide): 68.5MM **Privately Held**
WEB: www.jencast.com
SIC: 3321 Gray & ductile iron foundries
PA: Star Pipe, L.L.C.
4018 Westhollow Pkwy
Houston TX 77082
281 558-3000

(G-981)
TAYLOR CRANE & RIGGING INC (PA)
1211 W 12th St (67337-3701)
PHONE..................................620 251-1530
James C Taylor Jr, *President*
Larry Shufeldt, *Vice Pres*
Alan Munson, *CFO*
Jenny Taylor, *Marketing Staff*
EMP: 54
SQ FT: 240,000
SALES: 10.7MM **Privately Held**
WEB: www.taylorcrane.com
SIC: 7389 4214 1796 4226 Child restraint seat, automotive: rental; local trucking with storage; machine moving & rigging; millwright; special warehousing & storage; trucking, except local; local trucking, without storage

(G-982)
TESSENDERLO KERLEY INC
515 N Laurel St (67337-1852)
PHONE..................................620 251-3111
Ed Golden, *Branch Mgr*
EMP: 15 **Privately Held**
WEB: www.mprserve.com
SIC: 5052 4613 Sulfur; gasoline pipelines (common carriers)
HQ: Tessenderlo Kerley, Inc.
2255 N 44th St Ste 300
Phoenix AZ 85008
602 889-8300

(G-983)
THOMPSON BROS SUPPLIES INC (PA)
Also Called: Thompson Bros Eqp & Wldg Sups
2319 W 8th St (67337-2928)
P.O. Box 995 (67337-0995)
PHONE..................................620 251-1740
Katherine R Thompson, *Ch of Bd*
Rick Thompson, *President*
Sondra K McGuire, *Corp Secy*
James McGuire, *Vice Pres*
Nick Thompson, *Vice Pres*
EMP: 22
SQ FT: 20,000
SALES (est): 9.7MM **Privately Held**
WEB: www.tbswelds.com
SIC: 5084 Welding machinery & equipment

(G-984)
W CARTER ORVIL INC (PA)
Also Called: Carter Automotive Warehouse
105 W 11th St Unit 111 (67337)
PHONE..................................620 251-4700
Debbie Carter, *President*
Deborah A Carter, *President*
Dave Pal, *Vice Pres*
EMP: 25
SQ FT: 11,400
SALES (est): 11.7MM **Privately Held**
SIC: 5013 5531 Automotive supplies; automotive supplies & parts; automotive parts; automotive accessories

(G-985)
WEBER MANUFACTURING LLC
1300 E 3rd St (67337-7000)
P.O. Box 156 (67337-0156)
PHONE..................................620 251-9800
Kevin Weber, *Vice Pres*
Jim Cook,
▲ **EMP:** 17
SQ FT: 25,000
SALES (est): 4.9MM **Privately Held**
SIC: 5084 Industrial machinery & equipment

(G-986)
WRIGHT REDDEN & ASSOCIATES LLC
Also Called: Wright, Larry CPA
109 W 7th St (67337-4901)
P.O. Box 669 (67337-0669)
PHONE..................................620 251-6204
Larry Wright, *Owner*
EMP: 13
SALES (est): 1MM **Privately Held**
SIC: 8721 Accounting services, except auditing

Colby
Thomas County

(G-987)
101ST EARTHBORN ENVMTL TECH LP
1065 Taylor Ave (67701-9054)
PHONE..................................785 691-8918
Linda Taylor, *Principal*
EMP: 5 **EST:** 2011
SALES (est): 414.9K **Privately Held**
SIC: 3471 Cleaning & descaling metal products

(G-988)
BANDY ENTERPRISES INC (PA)
Also Called: Commercial Sign Company
1185 Zelfer Ave (67701-4101)
P.O. Box 897 (67701-0897)
PHONE..................................785 462-3361
Bruce Bandy, *President*
Kaylene Gabel, *Graphic Designe*
EMP: 13
SALES (est): 1.3MM **Privately Held**
SIC: 3993 Signs & advertising specialties

(G-989)
BANKWEST OF KANSAS
295 N Franklin Ave (67701-2321)
P.O. Box 327 (67701-0327)
PHONE..................................785 462-7557
Linda Goodwin, *Vice Pres*
Kris Cameron, *Manager*
Shelly Thompson, *Officer*
EMP: 10 **Privately Held**
SIC: 6153 6035 Short-term business credit; savings institutions, federally chartered
PA: Bankwest Of Kansas
924 Main Ave
Goodland KS 67735

(G-990)
BEVERLY ENTERPRISES-KANSAS LLC
Also Called: Lantern Park Manor
105 E College Dr (67701-3701)
PHONE..................................785 462-6721
Monty Montgomery, *Principal*
EMP: 50
SALES (corp-wide): 393.8MM **Privately Held**
SIC: 8051 Convalescent home with continuous nursing care
HQ: Beverly Enterprises-Kansas, Llc
1 1000 Beverly Way
Fort Smith AR 72919
479 201-2000

(G-991)
BRISTOL HOTEL & RESORTS INC
645 W Willow Ave (67701-4023)
PHONE..................................785 462-8787
Tammy Horn, *Manager*
EMP: 25 **Privately Held**
WEB: www.bristolhotels.com
SIC: 8741 7011 Hotel or motel management; hotels
HQ: Bristol Hotel & Resorts Inc.
3 Ravinia Dr Ste 100
Atlanta GA 30346

(G-992)
CENTRAL PWR SYSTEMS & SVCS LLC
Also Called: Detroit Diesel
1920 Thielen Ave (67701-4105)
PHONE..................................785 462-8211
James Brown, *Branch Mgr*
EMP: 12
SALES (corp-wide): 80MM **Privately Held**
SIC: 5084 Engines & parts, diesel
PA: Central Power Systems & Services, Llc
9200 Liberty Dr
Pleasant Valley MO 64068
816 781-8070

(G-993)
CHAD BRINEY
Also Called: C B Heating & Air Conditioning
1730 W 4th St (67701-1547)
PHONE..................................785 462-2445
Chad Briney, *Owner*
EMP: 14
SALES: 900K **Privately Held**
SIC: 1711 Warm air heating & air conditioning contractor

(G-994)
CITIZENS MEDICAL CENTER INC
100 E College Dr (67701-3799)
PHONE..................................785 462-7511
Greg Unruh, *CEO*
Vern Schwanke, *Ch of Bd*
Sheila Frahm S, *Vice Ch Bd*
Jaime Liudahl, *Buyer*
Lisa Stoll, *QA Dir*
EMP: 301
SALES: 30.2MM **Privately Held**
WEB: www.nwkshealthcare.com
SIC: 8062 General medical & surgical hospitals

(G-995)
COLBY A G CENTER LLC
Also Called: Kubota Authorized Dealer
305 E Horton Ave (67701-3900)
P.O. Box 568 (67701-0568)
PHONE..................................785 462-6132
Wanda Brown, *Office Mgr*
Gerald W Heim,
Larry Ummel,
EMP: 14
SQ FT: 10,000
SALES (est): 4.9MM **Privately Held**
WEB: www.colbyag.com
SIC: 5083 7699 5261 Farm implements; agricultural equipment repair services; lawnmowers & tractors

(G-996)
COLBY BOWL
Also Called: Colby Bowl and Fun Center
1175 S Range Ave Ste 3 (67701-3540)
P.O. Box 612 (67701-0612)
PHONE..................................785 460-2672
Charles Schwanke, *Partner*
Vernon Schwanke, *Partner*
EMP: 15
SQ FT: 16,000
SALES (est): 407K **Privately Held**
SIC: 7933 Ten pin center

(G-997)
COLBY CONVENTION CENTER
2227 S Range Ave (67701-4017)
PHONE..................................785 460-0131
Julie Saddler, *Director*
EMP: 25
SALES (est): 712.2K **Privately Held**
SIC: 7389 Convention & show services; tourist information bureau

(G-998)
COLBY LIVESTOCK AUCTION
125 S Country Club Dr (67701-3817)
PHONE..................................785 460-3231
Leland Wilson, *Owner*
EMP: 16 **EST:** 1955
SQ FT: 3,500
SALES (est): 1.3MM **Privately Held**
SIC: 5154 Auctioning livestock

(G-999)
COLBY SUPPLY & MFG CO
Also Called: Colby Canvas Co
285 E 3rd St (67701-2406)
P.O. Box 793 (67701-0793)
PHONE..................................785 462-3981
Stevan J Molstad, *Owner*
J Steven Molstad, *Managing Prtnr*
David B Molstad, *Partner*
Stanley G Molstad, *Partner*
EMP: 11 **EST:** 1958
SQ FT: 8,500
SALES: 1MM **Privately Held**
WEB: www.colbycanvas.com
SIC: 3496 5999 2394 Conveyor belts; canvas products; tarpaulins, fabric: made from purchased materials

(G-1000)
CORNERSTONE AG LLC
2148 County Road Q (67701-9123)
P.O. Box 468 (67701-0468)
PHONE..................................785 462-3354
Eric Sperber, *Mng Member*
EMP: 17
SALES (est): 12.5MM **Privately Held**
SIC: 5153 Grains; grain elevators

(G-1001)
COUNTY OF THOMAS
Also Called: Ambulance Service
1275 S Franklin Ave (67701-3718)
PHONE..................................785 460-4585
Thomas Krueger, *Director*
EMP: 30 **Privately Held**
SIC: 4119 9111 Ambulance service; county supervisors' & executives' offices
PA: County Of Thomas
300 N Court Ave
Colby KS 67701
785 460-4548

GEOGRAPHIC

(G-1002)
CUMMINS CENTRAL POWER LLC
Also Called: Cummins Mid-America
1880 S Range Ave (67701-4018)
PHONE....................................785 462-3945
Jim Mayhan, *Branch Mgr*
EMP: 11
SALES (corp-wide): 23.7B **Publicly Held**
SIC: 7538 5084 3519 Diesel engine repair: automotive; engines & parts, diesel; internal combustion engines
HQ: Cummins Central Power, Llc
10088 S 136th St
Omaha NE 68138
402 551-7678

(G-1003)
FAMILY CENTER FOR HEALTH CARE
Also Called: Citizens Medical Center
310 E College Dr (67701-3716)
PHONE....................................785 462-6184
Greg Unruh, *CEO*
Scott Focke, *Manager*
Brenda Kopriva, *Surgeon*
Daniel Kuhlman, *Family Practiti*
Jenny Niblock, *Nurse Practr*
EMP: 50
SALES (est): 3.1MM **Privately Held**
SIC: 8011 General & family practice, physician/surgeon

(G-1004)
FARM & RANCH REALTY INC
1420 W 4th St (67701-1541)
P.O. Box 947 (67701-0947)
PHONE....................................785 462-3904
Don Hazlett, *President*
Donald L Hazlett, *Corp Secy*
Mike Bailey, *Sales Staff*
Cindy Hake, *Office Mgr*
EMP: 10
SQ FT: 3,500
SALES (est): 1MM **Privately Held**
WEB: www.farmandranchrealty.com
SIC: 6531 Selling agent, real estate; appraiser, real estate

(G-1005)
FARM CREDIT OF WESTERN KANSAS (PA)
Also Called: Farm Credit Wstn KS PCA/Ffca
1190 S Range Ave (67701-3503)
P.O. Box 667 (67701-0667)
PHONE....................................785 462-6714
Larry Barrett, *Chairman*
Vernon Roemer, *Vice Pres*
Larry Maxwell, *Branch Mgr*
Chad Hendricks, *Director*
Kyle Kennedy, *Director*
EMP: 21
SQ FT: 4,300
SALES (est): 8.4MM **Privately Held**
SIC: 6159 Agricultural credit institutions

(G-1006)
FARM CREDIT OF WESTERN KANSAS
1055 S Range Ave (67701-3505)
PHONE....................................785 462-6714
Larry Maxwell, *Branch Mgr*
EMP: 22
SALES (corp-wide): 8.4MM **Privately Held**
SIC: 6029 Commercial banks
PA: Farm Credit Of Western Kansas
1190 S Range Ave
Colby KS 67701
785 462-6714

(G-1007)
FARMERS & MERCHANTS BANK COLBY
240 W 4th St (67701-2239)
P.O. Box 170, Scott City (67871-0170)
PHONE....................................785 460-3321
Bret Wiedeman, *President*
Sondra Stephens, *Credit Staff*
Lisa Wilson, *Advisor*
EMP: 21
SQ FT: 11,000
SALES: 10.1MM **Privately Held**
WEB: www.fmbcolby.com
SIC: 6021 6022 National commercial banks; state commercial banks
PA: Security Bancshares, Inc
506 S Main St
Scott City KS

(G-1008)
G H K FARMS
Also Called: Colby Fertilizer
1580 Highway K25 (67701-9120)
PHONE....................................785 462-6440
Glen Kersenbrock, *Owner*
EMP: 11
SQ FT: 7,500
SALES (est): 690K **Privately Held**
SIC: 0211 0115 0119 0111 Beef cattle feedlots; corn; sunflower farm; milo farm; wheat; gases, liquefied petroleum (propane)

(G-1009)
GOLDEN PLAINS AG TECH
650 E Pine St (67701-3804)
P.O. Box 307 (67701-0307)
PHONE....................................785 462-6753
Andy Davis, *President*
EMP: 5
SQ FT: 54,000
SALES (est): 818K **Privately Held**
SIC: 3523 5083 Fertilizing machinery, farm; farm equipment parts & supplies

(G-1010)
HAMPTON INN
1000 E Willow Ave (67701-4001)
PHONE....................................785 460-2333
Yvonne Covelli, *Controller*
Maryann Downing, *Manager*
EMP: 12
SALES (est): 574.3K **Privately Held**
SIC: 7011 Hotels & motels

(G-1011)
HAYNES PUBLISHING CO
Also Called: Colby Free Press
155 W 5th St (67701-2312)
PHONE....................................785 462-3963
Sharon Friedlander, *Branch Mgr*
EMP: 10
SQ FT: 5,000
SALES (est): 504.4K
SALES (corp-wide): 3.3MM **Privately Held**
SIC: 2711 Newspapers, publishing & printing
PA: Haynes Publishing Co
170 S Penn Ave
Oberlin KS 67749
785 475-2206

(G-1012)
HI PLAINS COOPERATIVE ASSN (PA)
Also Called: Hi-Plains Co-Op
405 E 4th St (67701-2526)
P.O. Box 429 (67701-0429)
PHONE....................................785 462-3351
John Strecker, *President*
EMP: 13 **EST:** 1949
SALES (est): 39.4MM **Privately Held**
WEB: www.hi-plainscoop.com
SIC: 5153 5191 Grain elevators; feed; fertilizer & fertilizer materials; chemicals, agricultural

(G-1013)
HI-PLAINS DOOR SYSTEMS INC
1120 S Country Club Dr (67701-3602)
P.O. Box 821 (67701-0821)
PHONE....................................785 462-6352
Steve Alwin, *President*
Marc Alwin, *General Mgr*
Mark Alwin, *General Mgr*
Sean Youngman, *Opers Staff*
EMP: 11 **EST:** 2014
SALES (est): 460.2K **Privately Held**
SIC: 5211 1751 Door & window products; window & door installation & erection

(G-1014)
HIGH PLAINS MENTAL HEALTH CTR
750 S Range Ave (67701-2905)
PHONE....................................785 462-6774
Gene Garrison, *Manager*
EMP: 23
SALES (corp-wide): 9.5MM **Privately Held**
SIC: 8052 8322 Home for the mentally retarded, with health care; family counseling services
PA: High Plains Mental Health Center
208 E 7th St
Hays KS 67601
785 628-2871

(G-1015)
HIGH PLAINS PRINTING
680 N Riddle Ave (67701-1833)
PHONE....................................785 460-6350
Cynthia F Black, *Owner*
EMP: 5
SALES: 250K **Privately Held**
SIC: 2752 Commercial printing, lithographic

(G-1016)
J R GALLEY INC
1175 S Range Ave (67701-3539)
P.O. Box 228, Grainfield (67737-0228)
PHONE....................................785 938-8024
Jarrold Gallentine, *President*
Amanda Gallentine, *Admin Sec*
EMP: 10 **EST:** 2016
SALES (est): 71.9K **Privately Held**
SIC: 7997 Lawn bowling club, membership

(G-1017)
JIMS ELECTRIC INC
210 E 2nd St (67701-2438)
PHONE....................................785 460-2844
Marilyn Unger, *President*
Jeff Unger, *Corp Secy*
EMP: 10
SQ FT: 5,750
SALES: 850K **Privately Held**
SIC: 1731 5719 1794 General electrical contractor; lighting fixtures; excavation work

(G-1018)
K D SULLIVAN INVESTMENTS LLC
1979 W 4th St (67701-1550)
PHONE....................................785 460-0170
Dustin Sullivan, *Mng Member*
Katrina N Sullivan,
EMP: 11
SALES: 900K **Privately Held**
SIC: 5521 5712 7999 Automobiles, used cars only; furniture stores; gymnastic instruction, non-membership

(G-1019)
K YOUNG INC
Also Called: K & K Motors
105 W Horton Ave (67701-3748)
PHONE....................................785 475-3888
Kirk Young, *President*
Holly Young, *Vice Pres*
EMP: 10
SQ FT: 13,200
SALES (est): 2.7MM **Privately Held**
WEB: www.semitruck.com
SIC: 5521 5084 5999 5511 Used car dealers; trucks, industrial; farm machinery; pickups, new & used; trailer rental

(G-1020)
KANSAS DEPT FOR CHLDREN FMLIES
Also Called: Kansas St of Scl & Rehab Srvc
180 W 5th St (67701-2313)
PHONE....................................785 462-6769
Jeanne Daniels, *Administration*
EMP: 30 **Privately Held**
SIC: 8322 9441 Child related social services;
HQ: Kansas Department For Children And Families
555 S Kansas Ave
Topeka KS 66603
785 368-6358

(G-1021)
KIWANIS INTERNATIONAL INC
1025 Villa Vista Dr (67701-3533)
PHONE....................................785 462-6007
Douglas Munderloh, *Branch Mgr*
EMP: 14
SALES (corp-wide): 23.6MM **Privately Held**
WEB: www.kfne.org
SIC: 8641 Civic associations
PA: Kiwanis International, Inc.
3636 Woodview Trce
Indianapolis IN 46268
317 875-8755

(G-1022)
L & C HOME HEALTH AGENCY INC
1175 S Range Ave Ste 1 (67701-3540)
PHONE....................................785 465-7444
Elizabeth Horney, *Vice Pres*
Tony Bice, *CFO*
Lisa Bice, *Administration*
Phyllis Cheney, *Admin Sec*
Jennifer Griffin,
EMP: 12
SALES: 547.1K **Privately Held**
SIC: 8399 Health systems agency

(G-1023)
L & M STEEL & MFG
1130 Plains Ave (67701-3608)
P.O. Box 533 (67701-0533)
PHONE....................................785 462-8216
Larry Oren, *Owner*
Mary Lee Oren, *Co-Owner*
EMP: 5 **EST:** 1980
SALES: 200K **Privately Held**
SIC: 5051 3599 3448 Steel; machine & other job shop work; prefabricated metal components

(G-1024)
LANG DIESEL INC
1280 S Country Club Dr (67701-3719)
PHONE....................................785 462-2412
Dan Koon, *Manager*
EMP: 10
SALES (corp-wide): 7.8MM **Privately Held**
SIC: 3523 5999 Cabs, tractors & agricultural machinery; farm equipment & supplies
PA: Lang Diesel, Inc.
2818 Plaza Ave
Hays KS 67601
785 301-2426

(G-1025)
LAXMINARAYAN LODGING LLC
1950 S Range Ave (67701-4020)
PHONE....................................785 462-3933
Mahek Patel, *Mng Member*
EMP: 10
SALES (est): 248.8K **Privately Held**
SIC: 7011 Hotels & motels

(G-1026)
LIVEWELL NORTHWEST KANSAS INC
Also Called: Northwest Abuse
460 N Garfield Ave (67701-2026)
PHONE....................................785 460-8177
Sue Evans, *Director*
EMP: 12
SALES: 666.7K **Privately Held**
SIC: 8069 Drug addiction rehabilitation hospital

(G-1027)
M ROCKING RADIO INC
Also Called: Krdq-FM
1065 S Range Ave (67701-3505)
PHONE....................................785 460-3306
Sacha Sanguinitti, *Branch Mgr*
EMP: 10
SALES (corp-wide): 3.1MM **Privately Held**
SIC: 4832 Radio broadcasting stations
PA: M Rocking Radio Inc
1707 Thomas Cir Ste A
Manhattan KS 66502
785 565-0406

(G-1028)
MIDWEST ENERGY INC
1125 S Range Ave (67701-3506)
P.O. Box 766 (67701-0766)
PHONE....................................785 462-8251
Phil Draper, *Principal*
EMP: 30

SALES (corp-wide): 219.6MM **Privately Held**
WEB: www.mwenergy.com
SIC: 4911 1711 Distribution, electric power; heating & air conditioning contractors
PA: Midwest Energy, Inc.
1330 Canterbury Dr
Hays KS 67601
785 625-3437

(G-1029)
MINGO CUSTOM WOODS
1965 W 4th St (67701-1550)
PHONE..................................785 462-2200
Craig Myers, *Owner*
EMP: 5
SQ FT: 2,400
SALES (est): 456.1K **Privately Held**
WEB: www.mingocustomwoods.com
SIC: 2434 2511 Wood kitchen cabinets; wood household furniture

(G-1030)
MORRISON OPTOMETRIC ASSOC PA (PA)
Also Called: Vision Source of Colby
1005 S Range Ave Ste 100 (67701-3538)
PHONE..................................785 462-8231
Jeffrey Morrison, *President*
Mark Wahlmeier, *Vice Pres*
EMP: 18
SQ FT: 5,800
SALES (est): 1.9MM **Privately Held**
SIC: 8042 5995 Specialized optometrists; optical goods stores

(G-1031)
MURFIN DRILLING COMPANY INC
675 E College Dr (67701-3750)
P.O. Box 661 (67701-0661)
PHONE..................................785 462-7541
David Murfin, *CEO*
Martin Ruda, *Manager*
EMP: 10 **Privately Held**
SIC: 1381 1311 Directional drilling oil & gas wells; crude petroleum production; natural gas production
HQ: Murfin Drilling Company, Inc.
250 N Water St Ste 300
Wichita KS 67202
316 267-3241

(G-1032)
OFFICE WORKS LLC
960 S Range Ave (67701-3501)
P.O. Box 706 (67701-0706)
PHONE..................................785 462-2222
Doug Tittel, *Mng Member*
Ted Domsch,
Dwight Focke,
Eugene Wieland,
EMP: 10
SQ FT: 2,400
SALES: 2MM **Privately Held**
SIC: 5112 5044 5021 Office supplies; office equipment; office furniture

(G-1033)
ORSCHELN FARM AND HOME LLC
1915 S Range Ave (67701-4014)
PHONE..................................785 460-1551
Dennis Owens, *Branch Mgr*
EMP: 10
SALES (corp-wide): 822.7MM **Privately Held**
WEB: www.orschelnfarmhome.com
SIC: 5191 Farm supplies
PA: Orscheln Farm And Home Llc
1800 Overcenter Dr
Moberly MO 65270
800 577-2580

(G-1034)
PRIDE OF PRAIRIE ORCHESTRA INC
1255 S Range Ave (67701-4007)
PHONE..................................785 460-5518
Karen Larmer, *Exec Dir*
Pat Ziegelmeier, *Director*
EMP: 45
SALES (est): 320.9K **Privately Held**
SIC: 7929 Orchestras or bands

(G-1035)
RED RIVER COMMODITIES INC
1320 E College Dr (67701-9018)
PHONE..................................785 462-3911
Dee Olson, *Finance*
Brad Thompson, *Manager*
EMP: 25
SALES (corp-wide): 836.8MM **Privately Held**
WEB: www.redriv.com
SIC: 0723 2068 Seed cleaning; salted & roasted nuts & seeds
HQ: Red River Commodities, Inc.
501 42nd St N
Fargo ND 58102
701 282-2600

(G-1036)
ROOFMASTERS ROOFING CO INC
425 E Hill St (67701-3631)
PHONE..................................785 462-6642
Susan Haines, *President*
Fred Haines, *Corp Secy*
EMP: 30
SQ FT: 1,200
SALES (est): 4MM **Privately Held**
WEB: www.roofmastersroofing.net
SIC: 1761 1541 Roofing contractor; steel building construction

(G-1037)
RURAL HEALTH DEVELOPMENT INC
Also Called: Prairie Senior Living Complex
1625 S Franklin Ave (67701-3722)
PHONE..................................785 462-8295
Angela McArthur, *Exec Dir*
Teresa Tarman, *Records Dir*
EMP: 60 **Privately Held**
WEB: www.rhdconsult.com
SIC: 8052 Intermediate care facilities
PA: Rural Health Development Inc
115 Nasby St
Cambridge NE 69022

(G-1038)
S & T TELEPHONE COOP ASSN
755 Davis Ave (67701-9000)
PHONE..................................785 460-7300
Steve Richards, *CEO*
Brian Siegfried, *Opers Staff*
Alicia Moore, *Marketing Mgr*
Malinda Bradstreet, *Branch Mgr*
EMP: 17
SALES (corp-wide): 19MM **Privately Held**
WEB: www.sttelcom.com
SIC: 4813 8243 7372 5734 Telephone communication, except radio; data processing schools; prepackaged software; computer & software stores; cable & other pay television services
PA: S & T Telephone Cooperative Association
320 Kansas Ave
Brewster KS 67732
785 694-2256

(G-1039)
SAINT FRANCIS CMNTY SVCS INC
Also Called: Saint Francis Academy
180 W 5th St (67701-2313)
PHONE..................................785 462-6679
Jamie Heskett, *Branch Mgr*
EMP: 109
SALES (corp-wide): 108.2MM **Privately Held**
SIC: 8322 Individual & family services
PA: Saint Francis Community Services, Inc.
509 E Elm St
Salina KS 67401
785 825-0541

(G-1040)
SERVICE OIL COMPANY (HQ)
Also Called: Golden Plains Motel
285 E 4th St (67701-2408)
P.O. Box 446 (67701-0446)
PHONE..................................785 462-3441
Tom Waldschmidt, *President*
Kevin Taylor, *Vice Pres*
Tim Moeder, *Treasurer*
Richard Garvey, *Shareholder*
Warren Sweat, *Shareholder*
EMP: 10
SQ FT: 2,500
SALES (est): 9.4MM
SALES (corp-wide): 13.6MM **Privately Held**
WEB: www.goldenplainsmotel.com
SIC: 5171 7011 Petroleum bulk stations; motels
PA: Jagee Holdings, Llp
2918 Wingate St
Fort Worth TX 76107
817 335-5881

(G-1041)
SIX CONTINENTS HOTELS INC
Also Called: Holiday Inn
645 W Willow Ave (67701-4023)
P.O. Box 365 (67701-0365)
PHONE..................................785 462-8787
Martha Brewer, *Manager*
EMP: 25 **Privately Held**
WEB: www.sixcontinenthotels.com
SIC: 7011 8741 Hotels & motels; hotel or motel management
HQ: Six Continents Hotels, Inc.
3 Ravinia Dr Ste 100
Dunwoody GA 30346
770 604-2000

(G-1042)
SUNFLOWER PARTNERS INC
Also Called: Quality Inn
1950 S Range Ave (67701-4020)
P.O. Box 487 (67701-0487)
PHONE..................................785 462-3933
Everett Robert, *Manager*
EMP: 25
SALES (est): 898.7K **Privately Held**
SIC: 7011 Hotels & motels
PA: Sunflower Partners Inc
846 S Market St
Wichita KS

(G-1043)
SUPER 8 HOTEL IN COLBY KANSAS
Also Called: Super 8 Motel
1040 Zelfer Ave 223-224 (67701-4107)
PHONE..................................785 462-8248
Bernie Zalasney, *Owner*
EMP: 13
SALES (est): 675.1K **Privately Held**
SIC: 7011 Hotels & motels

(G-1044)
SWARTZ VETERINARY HOSPITAL
1775 W 4th St (67701-1546)
PHONE..................................785 460-1078
Tammy Swartz, *Owner*
Cory Swartz, *Co-Owner*
EMP: 12
SALES (est): 460K **Privately Held**
SIC: 0742 Animal hospital services, pets & other animal specialties

(G-1045)
TARBET CONSTRUCTION CO INC
Also Called: Tarbet Ready Mix
1055 Plains Ave (67701-3605)
P.O. Box 142 (67701-0142)
PHONE..................................785 462-7432
Stan Orth, *Manager*
EMP: 5
SALES (corp-wide): 8MM **Privately Held**
WEB: www.tarbertdrilling.com
SIC: 1771 3273 Concrete work; ready-mixed concrete
PA: Tarbet Construction Co Inc
303 S Road I
Ulysses KS 67880
620 356-2110

(G-1046)
THOMAS COUNTY FEEDERS INC
1762 Us Highway 83 (67701-9305)
P.O. Box 1506, Great Bend (67530-1506)
PHONE..................................785 462-3947
Lee Borck, *President*
Roger Murphy, *Vice Pres*
EMP: 25
SQ FT: 2,000
SALES (est): 704.8K
SALES (corp-wide): 31.2MM **Privately Held**
WEB: www.thomascountyfeeders.com
SIC: 0212 Beef cattle except feedlots
PA: Innovative Livestock Services, Inc.
2006 Broadway Ave Ste 2c
Great Bend KS 67530
620 793-9200

(G-1047)
WAITT MEDIA INC
Also Called: Kxxx Kqls
1065 S Range Ave (67701-3505)
PHONE..................................785 462-3305
Joe Munsell, *Principal*
EMP: 12
SALES (corp-wide): 70.2MM **Privately Held**
WEB: www.kqky.com
SIC: 4833 Television broadcasting stations
PA: Waitt Media, Inc.
1125 S 103rd St Ste 425
Omaha NE 68124
402 697-8000

(G-1048)
WESTERN SPRINKLERS INC (PA)
1100 S Range Ave (67701-3503)
P.O. Box 488 (67701-0488)
PHONE..................................785 462-6755
Louis T Hines, *President*
Douglas Bell, *Vice Pres*
Melissa Johnson, *Treasurer*
EMP: 18
SQ FT: 5,000
SALES (est): 5.1MM **Privately Held**
WEB: www.westernsprinklers.com
SIC: 5083 Irrigation equipment

(G-1049)
WOOFTER CNSTR & IRRIGATION INC (PA)
Also Called: Woofter Cnstr & Irrigation
1965 Thielen Ave (67701-4111)
P.O. Box 526 (67701-0526)
PHONE..................................785 462-8653
Michael D Woofter, *President*
EMP: 25 **EST**: 1975
SQ FT: 12,000
SALES (est): 12.1MM **Privately Held**
SIC: 1542 8741 5083 Commercial & office building, new construction; farm building construction; construction management; irrigation equipment

(G-1050)
WOOFTER WOOFTER STUPKA INC
Also Called: Comfort Inn
1110 Plains Ave Ste 1 (67701-3665)
PHONE..................................785 460-6683
Michael Woofter, *President*
EMP: 31
SALES (est): 890.5K **Privately Held**
SIC: 7011 Hotels & motels

Coldwater
Comanche County

(G-1051)
BEREXCO INCORPORATED
401 S Leavenworth Ave (67029-6401)
P.O. Box 697 (67029-0697)
PHONE..................................620 582-2575
Kameron Wilson, *Manager*
EMP: 5
SALES (est): 276.6K **Privately Held**
SIC: 1311 Crude petroleum production

(G-1052)
COMANCHE CNTY HOSP MED CLINIC
202 S Frisco St (67029-9101)
PHONE..................................620 582-2144
Nancy Zimmerman, *Administration*
EMP: 29
SALES (est): 2.2MM **Privately Held**
SIC: 8062 General medical & surgical hospitals

(G-1053)
COMANCHE COUNTY
Also Called: Commanche County Med Clinic
301 S Washington St (67029-9758)
P.O. Box 778 (67029-0778)
PHONE..................................620 582-2136
Nancy Zimmerman, *Director*
EMP: 10 **Privately Held**
WEB: www.comanchecounty.com
SIC: 8011 Clinic, operated by physicians
PA: Comanche County
201 S New York Ave
Coldwater KS 67029
620 582-2182

(G-1054)
COMANCHE COUNTY
Also Called: Road and Bridge Department
401 S Philadelphia St (67029)
P.O. Box 685 (67029-0685)
PHONE..................................620 582-2933
Dennis Hernandez, *Principal*
EMP: 14 **Privately Held**
WEB: www.comanchecounty.com
SIC: 9121 0721 Legislative bodies, state & local; weed control services after planting
PA: Comanche County
201 S New York Ave
Coldwater KS 67029
620 582-2182

(G-1055)
COMANCHE COUNTY
202 S Frisco St (67029-9101)
PHONE..................................620 582-2144
Nancy Zimmerman, *Director*
EMP: 43 **Privately Held**
WEB: www.comanchecounty.com
SIC: 8062 General medical & surgical hospitals
PA: Comanche County
201 S New York Ave
Coldwater KS 67029
620 582-2182

(G-1056)
PEOPLES BANK
101 E Main St (67029-9701)
P.O. Box 727 (67029-0727)
PHONE..................................620 582-2166
Wynn Alexander, *President*
EMP: 11 **EST:** 1905
SQ FT: 1,500
SALES: 2.2MM **Privately Held**
WEB: www.peoplesbankcoldwater.com
SIC: 6022 6411 State trust companies accepting deposits, commercial; insurance agents, brokers & service

(G-1057)
PIONEER COMMUNITY CARE INC
Also Called: Pioneer Lodge
300 W 3rd St (67029-2900)
P.O. Box 487 (67029-0487)
PHONE..................................620 582-2123
D Thompson, *Exec Dir*
Diana Thompson, *Exec Dir*
EMP: 40
SALES: 1.6MM **Privately Held**
SIC: 8059 Nursing home, except skilled & intermediate care facility

(G-1058)
UNRUH SAND & GRAVEL
P.O. Box 462 (67029-0462)
PHONE..................................620 582-2774
Randy Unruh, *Principal*
EMP: 6
SALES (est): 555.6K **Privately Held**
SIC: 1442 Construction sand & gravel

Columbus
Cherokee County

(G-1059)
ADVANTAGE METALS RECYCLING LLC
2466 Nw Highway 7 (66725-1279)
PHONE..................................620 674-3800
Steph Watson, *Manager*
EMP: 70
SALES (corp-wide): 25B **Publicly Held**
SIC: 5093 Metal scrap & waste materials
HQ: Advantage Metals Recycling Llc
510 Walnut St Ste 300
Kansas City MO 64106
816 861-2700

(G-1060)
B-3 CONSTRUCTION INC
1106 S Highschool Ave (66725-1679)
PHONE..................................620 479-2323
Robert D Burgan, *President*
Mary Pat Burgan, *Treasurer*
EMP: 12
SALES (est): 1.9MM **Privately Held**
SIC: 1795 Demolition, buildings & other structures

(G-1061)
BNSF RAILWAY COMPANY
Also Called: Burlington Northern
400 N Tennessee Ave (66725-1259)
PHONE..................................620 429-3850
Jeff Schmitt, *Principal*
EMP: 60
SALES (corp-wide): 225.3B **Publicly Held**
WEB: www.billpurdy.com
SIC: 4011 Railroads, line-haul operating
HQ: Bnsf Railway Company
2650 Lou Menk Dr
Fort Worth TX 76131
800 795-2673

(G-1062)
BRAD CARSON
Also Called: Autum Place, The
311 S East Ave (66725-2181)
PHONE..................................620 429-1011
Connie Bennett, *Manager*
Penny McKinney, *Director*
EMP: 18 **Privately Held**
SIC: 8361 Residential care
PA: Brad Carson
120 Aaron Ln
Baxter Springs KS 66713

(G-1063)
BUTTERBALL LLC
6410 Sw Hallowell Rd (66725-3080)
PHONE..................................620 597-2800
Phillip Harmon, *Manager*
EMP: 133
SALES (corp-wide): 1.8B **Privately Held**
SIC: 0751 Poultry services
PA: Butterball, Llc
1 Butterball Ln
Garner NC 27529
919 255-7900

(G-1064)
CALIBRATED FORMS
537 N East Ave (66725-1323)
P.O. Box 191 (66725-0191)
PHONE..................................620 429-1120
Richard Miller, *General Mgr*
Terry Blancett, *CTO*
▲ **EMP:** 140
SQ FT: 25,000
SALES (est): 25.7MM
SALES (corp-wide): 400.7MM **Publicly Held**
WEB: www.calforms.com
SIC: 2761 Computer forms, manifold or continuous
PA: Ennis, Inc.
2441 Presidential Pkwy
Midlothian TX 76065
972 775-9801

(G-1065)
CHEROKEE CNTY AMBULANCE & ASSN
800 W Powrachute Way (66725-9701)
P.O. Box 307 (66725-0307)
PHONE..................................620 429-3018
Doug Mogle, *Director*
Ralph White,
EMP: 27
SALES: 992.2K **Privately Held**
SIC: 4119 Ambulance service

(G-1066)
CLASS LTD (PA)
1200 E Merle Evans Dr (66725-9698)
P.O. Box 266 (66725-0266)
PHONE..................................620 429-1212
Jan Bolin, *President*
Tom Hardy, *Vice Chairman*
Gretchen Andrews, *Vice Pres*
Cliff Sperry, *Vice Pres*
Cyndie Howell, *CFO*
EMP: 170 **EST:** 1975
SALES: 9.8MM **Privately Held**
SIC: 8331 8361 Job training & vocational rehabilitation services; rehabilitation center, residential: health care incidental

(G-1067)
COLUMBUS TELEPHONE COMPANY (PA)
224 S Kansas Ave (66725-1799)
PHONE..................................620 429-3132
James Dahmen, *CEO*
Wes Houser, *President*
Gene Hamilton, *Plant Mgr*
Joe Schibi, *Engineer*
Patricia Beaty, *Director*
EMP: 12 **EST:** 1905
SQ FT: 3,000
SALES (est): 2.3MM **Privately Held**
WEB: www.columbus-ks.com
SIC: 4813 Local telephone communications

(G-1068)
COMMERCE BANK
137 W Maple St (66725-1703)
P.O. Box 269 (66725-0269)
PHONE..................................620 429-2515
Jane Rhinehart, *Manager*
EMP: 15
SALES (corp-wide): 1.3B **Publicly Held**
SIC: 6022 State commercial banks
HQ: Commerce Bank
1000 Walnut St Fl 700
Kansas City MO 64106
816 234-2000

(G-1069)
COMMUNITY HEALTH CENTER OF SOU
Also Called: Columbus Clinic
120 W Pine St (66725-1705)
PHONE..................................620 429-2101
Jamie Schaffer, *Office Mgr*
EMP: 10
SALES (est): 301.2K
SALES (corp-wide): 25MM **Privately Held**
SIC: 8011 Clinic, operated by physicians
PA: Community Health Center Of Southeast Kansas, Inc.
3011 N Michigan St
Pittsburg KS 66762
620 231-9873

(G-1070)
COUNTY OF CHEROKEE
Also Called: Cherokee County Highway Dept
509 E Country Rd (66725)
PHONE..................................620 429-3954
Mike Barnett, *Branch Mgr*
EMP: 40 **Privately Held**
WEB: www.cherokeecounty-ks.gov
SIC: 4959 Road, airport & parking lot maintenance services
PA: County Of Cherokee
110 W Maple St Rm 220
Columbus KS 66725
620 429-2042

(G-1071)
CROSSLAND CONSTRUCTION CO INC (PA)
833 S East Ave (66725-2307)
P.O. Box 45 (66725-0045)
PHONE..................................620 429-1414
Ivan E Crossland Jr, *CEO*
Bennie L Crossland, *President*
John Balsters, *Superintendent*
Tim Carson, *Superintendent*
Bud Howard, *Superintendent*
▲ **EMP:** 220 **EST:** 1978
SQ FT: 16,000
SALES (est): 567.9MM **Privately Held**
SIC: 1542 Commercial & office building, new construction

(G-1072)
CROSSLAND HEAVY CONTRS INC (PA)
833 S East Ave (66725-2307)
P.O. Box 350 (66725-0350)
PHONE..................................620 429-1410
Mark Sell, *President*
Tim Heitkamp, *Superintendent*
Chance Tucker, *Superintendent*
Ivan E Crossland, *Corp Secy*
Darrel Moorman, *Vice Pres*
EMP: 100
SQ FT: 3,000
SALES (est): 64.2MM **Privately Held**
SIC: 1622 Bridge construction

(G-1073)
CROSSLAND PREFAB LLC
501 S East Ave (66725-2375)
P.O. Box 17 (66725-0017)
PHONE..................................620 429-1414
Jerry Duncan, *General Mgr*
EMP: 26
SALES (est): 1MM
SALES (corp-wide): 567.9MM **Privately Held**
SIC: 1791 Precast concrete structural framing or panels, placing of
PA: Crossland Construction Company, Inc.
833 S East Ave
Columbus KS 66725
620 429-1414

(G-1074)
DAVIS CONSTRUCTION LLC
2143 Ne Highway 7 (66725-2093)
PHONE..................................620 674-3100
Michael Davis,
EMP: 10 **EST:** 1991
SALES (est): 1.1MM **Privately Held**
SIC: 1542 Commercial & office building contractors

(G-1075)
DETACORP INC LLC
3600 Nw 74th St (66725-1773)
PHONE..................................620 597-2552
Clive Whiteside,
EMP: 30
SALES (est): 4.1MM
SALES (corp-wide): 6MM **Privately Held**
WEB: www.slurryexplosive.com
SIC: 2892 Explosives
PA: I Chemex Corporation
5700 N Portland Ave # 301
Oklahoma City OK 73112
405 947-0764

(G-1076)
GOOD SHEPHERD CHILD CARE CTR
128 W Elm St (66725-1797)
PHONE..................................620 429-4611
Brett Weary, *Director*
EMP: 12
SALES: 120K **Privately Held**
SIC: 8351 Group day care center

(G-1077)
HALLOWELL MANUFACTURING LLC
3600 Nw 74th St (66725-1773)
PHONE..................................620 597-2552
Jim Mitchell, *Principal*
▲ **EMP:** 17
SALES (est): 5.7MM **Privately Held**
SIC: 3561 Pumps & pumping equipment

(G-1078)
HEALTH MANAGEMENT OF KANSAS
111 S Pennsylvania Ave (66725-1710)
PHONE..................................620 429-3803
Monte Coffman, *Administration*
EMP: 79 **Privately Held**
WEB: www.windsorplace.net
SIC: 8741 8082 Nursing & personal care facility management; home health care services

PA: Health Management Of Kansas, Inc
104 W 8th St
Coffeyville KS 67337

(G-1079)
JAY HATFIELD MOBILITY LLC (PA)
200 S East Ave (66725-1955)
P.O. Box 270 (66725-0270)
PHONE..................................620 429-2636
Jay F Hatfield, *Mng Member*
EMP: 14
SALES: 1MM **Privately Held**
SIC: 5047 Medical equipment & supplies

(G-1080)
JESSEE TRUCKING INCORPORATED
6878 Se Highway 160 (66725-2387)
PHONE..................................620 389-2546
Rick Jessee, *President*
Brent Jessee, *Vice Pres*
Becky Beck, *Admin Sec*
EMP: 24
SQ FT: 300
SALES: 2.1MM **Privately Held**
SIC: 4213 Trucking, except local

(G-1081)
MEDICALODGES INC
101 Lee Ave (66725-1021)
PHONE..................................620 429-4317
Cathy W Fisher, *CFO*
EMP: 71
SALES (corp-wide): 100.2MM **Privately Held**
SIC: 8051 Skilled nursing care facilities
PA: Medicalodges, Inc.
201 W 8th St
Coffeyville KS 67337
620 251-6700

(G-1082)
MEDICALODGES INC
Also Called: Medicalodges of Columbus
101 Lee Ave (66725-1021)
PHONE..................................620 429-2134
Deanna Fitz, *Director*
Dana Dougger, *Administration*
EMP: 70
SALES (corp-wide): 100.2MM **Privately Held**
WEB: www.medicalodges.com
SIC: 8052 8051 Intermediate care facilities; skilled nursing care facilities
PA: Medicalodges, Inc.
201 W 8th St
Coffeyville KS 67337
620 251-6700

(G-1083)
MERCY HOSPITAL COLUMBUS
220 N Pennsylvania Ave (66725-1110)
PHONE..................................620 429-2545
Scott Reynolds, *Principal*
EMP: 17 **EST:** 2011
SALES: 5.1MM **Privately Held**
SIC: 8062 General medical & surgical hospitals

(G-1084)
MID WEST COLOR GRAPHICS INC
Also Called: Midwest Color Graphics
500 S Railroad Ave (66725-1963)
P.O. Box 74 (66725-0074)
PHONE..................................620 429-1088
Dave Soper, *President*
Chris Green, *Vice Pres*
Dewayne Soper, *Vice Pres*
Jack Soper, *Treasurer*
EMP: 21
SQ FT: 4,000
SALES: 1.6MM **Privately Held**
SIC: 2752 2796 2791 Commercial printing, offset; color separations for printing; typesetting

(G-1085)
PILGRIMS PRIDE CORPORATION
6410 Sw Hallowell Rd (66725-3080)
PHONE..................................620 597-2820
Tony Ewing, *Manager*
EMP: 38 **Publicly Held**
WEB: www.pilgrimspride.com
SIC: 2015 Chicken, slaughtered & dressed
HQ: Pilgrim's Pride Corporation
1770 Promontory Cir
Greeley CO 80634
970 506-8000

(G-1086)
SPECIALTY PROJECTS CORP INC
500 S Railroad Ave (66725-1963)
P.O. Box 147 (66725-0147)
PHONE..................................620 429-1086
Dave Soper, *President*
Dewayne Soper, *Vice Pres*
EMP: 6
SQ FT: 6,000
SALES (est): 350K **Privately Held**
SIC: 2752 Commercial printing, lithographic

(G-1087)
ST JHNS MAUDE NORTON MEM HOSP
220 N Pennsylvania Ave (66725-1110)
PHONE..................................620 429-2545
Cynthia Neely, *CFO*
EMP: 60
SALES (est): 2.8MM **Privately Held**
WEB: www.chi-national.org
SIC: 8062 General medical & surgical hospitals
PA: Commonspirit Health
444 W Lake St Ste 2500
Chicago IL 60606

(G-1088)
TAMKO BUILDING PRODUCTS INC
600 Ne Bethlehem Rd (66725-2349)
PHONE..................................620 429-1800
Erin Hobart, *Branch Mgr*
EMP: 67
SALES (corp-wide): 510.4MM **Privately Held**
WEB: www.tamko.com
SIC: 2952 Roofing materials
PA: Tamko Building Products, Inc.
198 Four States Dr
Galena KS 66739
800 641-4691

(G-1089)
TEAM THREADS
119 W Maple St (66725-1703)
PHONE..................................620 429-4402
Kim Brown, *President*
EMP: 9 **EST:** 2011
SALES (est): 472.3K **Privately Held**
SIC: 5699 2284 T-shirts, custom printed; embroidery thread

Colwich
Sedgwick County

(G-1090)
4G EXPRESS INC
549 Homestead Ct (67030-9217)
PHONE..................................316 619-3888
Vince Grady, *President*
EMP: 18
SALES (est): 285.6K **Privately Held**
SIC: 4789 Transportation services

(G-1091)
ABENGOA BNERGY HYBRID KANS LLC
523 E Union Ave (67030-9723)
PHONE..................................316 796-1234
Javier S Leirado,
EMP: 15
SALES (est): 1.2MM **Privately Held**
SIC: 2869 Industrial organic chemicals

(G-1092)
COLWICH FINANCIAL CORP (PA)
Also Called: Legacy Bank
240 W Wichita Ave (67030-9794)
P.O. Box 68 (67030-0068)
PHONE..................................316 796-1221
Frank A Suellentrop, *President*
Larry Eck, *Assistant VP*
Brad Yaeger, *Vice Pres*
Sandy Ring, *Credit Staff*
Gene Suellentrop, *Shareholder*
EMP: 28
SQ FT: 4,000
SALES (est): 18.8MM **Privately Held**
SIC: 6022 State trust companies accepting deposits, commercial

(G-1093)
CUSHMAN WKEFIELD SOLUTIONS LLC
Also Called: Quality Solutions, Inc.
128 N 1st St (67030-9637)
PHONE..................................316 721-3656
Eric Crabb, *CEO*
Tiffany Bridwell, *Project Mgr*
Urban Eck, *Project Mgr*
Luke Mackinnon, *Project Mgr*
Brooklyn Marcik, *Project Mgr*
EMP: 130
SQ FT: 50,000
SALES (est): 31.8MM
SALES (corp-wide): 8.2B **Privately Held**
WEB: www.qsifacilities.com
SIC: 8741 Business management
HQ: Cushman & Wakefield U.S., Inc.
225 W Wacker Dr Ste 3000
Chicago IL 60606
312 424-8000

(G-1094)
ERI SOLUTIONS INC
125 N 1st St (67030-9637)
PHONE..................................316 927-4290
Nathan Vander Griend, *President*
Bruce Pearson, *Senior VP*
Jay Beckel, *Vice Pres*
EMP: 20 **EST:** 2007
SQ FT: 2,500
SALES (est): 2.4MM **Privately Held**
SIC: 8748 Systems analysis & engineering consulting services

(G-1095)
EVERGY KANSAS CENTRAL INC
Also Called: Murray Gill Energy Center
6001 N 151st St W (67030-9738)
PHONE..................................316 291-8626
Dean Schowalter, *Branch Mgr*
EMP: 50
SALES (corp-wide): 4.2B **Publicly Held**
SIC: 4911 Generation, electric power
HQ: Evergy Kansas Central, Inc.
818 S Kansas Ave
Topeka KS 66612
785 575-6300

(G-1096)
EVERGY KANSAS CENTRAL INC
Also Called: K P L Gas Service
6001 N 151st St W (67030-9738)
P.O. Box 189 (67030)
PHONE..................................316 291-8612
John Bridson, *Branch Mgr*
EMP: 42
SALES (corp-wide): 4.2B **Publicly Held**
SIC: 4911 Distribution, electric power
HQ: Evergy Kansas Central, Inc.
818 S Kansas Ave
Topeka KS 66612
785 575-6300

(G-1097)
ICM INC (PA)
310 N 1st St (67030-9655)
P.O. Box 397 (67030-0397)
PHONE..................................316 796-0900
David Vander Griend, *CEO*
Dan Linton, *Superintendent*
Jesse Loya, *Superintendent*
Ryan Mass, *Business Mgr*
Shirley Anderson, *Counsel*
EMP: 148
SQ FT: 30,000
SALES (est): 149.2MM **Privately Held**
WEB: www.icminc.com
SIC: 8748 8711 Energy conservation consultant; consulting engineer; construction & civil engineering

(G-1098)
MARICK INC
13915 W 53rd St N (67030-9409)
PHONE..................................316 941-9575
Mark Thornton, *Branch Mgr*
EMP: 28
SALES (corp-wide): 18.7MM **Privately Held**
SIC: 1711 Refrigeration contractor
PA: Marick, Inc.
138 Jefferson Ave
Des Moines IA 50314
515 243-8288

(G-1099)
MIES & SONS TRUCKING INC
19620 W 85th St N (67030-9624)
PHONE..................................316 796-0186
Gerald Mies, *President*
Catherine Mies, *Corp Secy*
EMP: 42
SQ FT: 1,500
SALES (est): 6MM **Privately Held**
SIC: 4213 Trucking, except local

Concordia
Cloud County

(G-1100)
ABC PHONES NORTH CAROLINA INC
Also Called: Z Wireless
1578 Lincoln St (66901-4830)
PHONE..................................785 243-4099
EMP: 25
SALES (corp-wide): 149.7MM **Privately Held**
SIC: 4812 Cellular telephone services
PA: Abc Phones Of North Carolina, Inc.
8510 Colonnade Center Dr
Raleigh NC 27615
252 317-0388

(G-1101)
ALSOP SAND CO INC (PA)
E Hwy 9 (66901)
PHONE..................................785 243-4249
Henry Barclay, *President*
Lisa Lynn, *Admin Sec*
EMP: 25
SQ FT: 1,000
SALES (est): 2.7MM **Privately Held**
SIC: 3273 1442 Ready-mixed concrete; construction sand mining; gravel mining

(G-1102)
ANGEL SQUARE
517 Washington St (66901-2116)
PHONE..................................785 534-1080
Jolene Carter, *Owner*
Russell Carter, *Co-Owner*
EMP: 11
SALES (est): 197.8K **Privately Held**
SIC: 8361 Residential care for the handicapped

(G-1103)
BLADE EMPIRE PUBLISHING CO
510 Washington St (66901-2117)
P.O. Box 309 (66901-0309)
PHONE..................................785 243-2424
J Bradley Lowell, *President*
James B Lowell, *President*
EMP: 30 **EST:** 1920
SQ FT: 10,000
SALES (est): 2MM **Privately Held**
SIC: 2711 2752 5943 5112 Commercial printing & newspaper publishing combined; commercial printing, lithographic; office forms & supplies; office supplies

(G-1104)
C & C TRUCK LINE
611 E 1st St (66901-1605)
PHONE..................................785 243-3719
Adolph R Charbonneau, *President*
Elizabeth Charbonneau, *Corp Secy*
EMP: 15
SQ FT: 10,000
SALES (est): 2MM **Privately Held**
SIC: 4213 4212 Heavy hauling; light haulage & cartage, local

(G-1105)
CHAMPLIN TIRE RECYCLING INC
301 Cedar St (66901-1717)
P.O. Box 445 (66901-0445)
PHONE..................................785 243-3345
Ronald Champlin, *President*
Corey Champlin, *Treasurer*
Gary Champlin, *Admin Sec*
EMP: 23
SQ FT: 15,000
SALES (est): 4.6MM **Privately Held**
WEB: www.champlintirerecycling.com
SIC: 4953 Recycling, waste materials

(G-1106)
CLOUD COUNTY HEALTH CENTER INC
Also Called: CCHC
1100 Highland Dr (66901-3923)
PHONE..................................785 243-1234
Cherri Waites, *President*
Betty Wallace, *Purch Mgr*
Kent Anderson, *Treasurer*
Charles Zimmerman, *Treasurer*
Kris Topple, *Manager*
EMP: 158
SQ FT: 78,000
SALES: 15.3MM **Privately Held**
WEB: www.cchc.com
SIC: 8062 General medical & surgical hospitals

(G-1107)
COCA-COLA COMPANY
Hwy 81 & 148 Jct (66901)
PHONE..................................785 243-1071
EMP: 15
SALES (corp-wide): 46.8B **Publicly Held**
SIC: 5149 Whol Groceries
PA: The Coca-Cola Company
1 Coca Cola Plz Nw
Atlanta GA 30313
404 676-2121

(G-1108)
CONCORDIA TECHNOLOGIES LLC
1830 E 6th St (66901-2620)
P.O. Box 333 (66901-0333)
PHONE..................................785 262-4066
Roy Applequist, *Ch of Bd*
Jay Reynolds, *President*
Cass Reynolds, *Vice Pres*
EMP: 27
SALES (est): 4.7MM **Privately Held**
SIC: 3312 3499 Primary finished or semi-finished shapes; strapping, metal

(G-1109)
DUIS MEAT PROCESSING INC (PA)
1991 E 6th St (66901-2621)
PHONE..................................785 243-7850
Keith Duis, *CEO*
Ron Duis, *President*
Susan Duis, *Corp Secy*
Toby Duis, *Vice Pres*
EMP: 15
SQ FT: 3,200
SALES (est): 1.5MM **Privately Held**
SIC: 5421 5147 2011 Meat markets, including freezer provisioners; meats, fresh; beef products from beef slaughtered on site

(G-1110)
FARM MANAGEMENT SERVICES INC
310 Washington St (66901-1716)
P.O. Box 622 (66901-0622)
PHONE..................................785 243-1854
Quentin Smith, *President*
A S Olsen, *Treasurer*
Brian Kemling,
EMP: 10
SALES (est): 601.4K **Privately Held**
WEB: www.ksfmsi.com
SIC: 8721 Accounting, auditing & bookkeeping

(G-1111)
FRONTIER LODGING CONCORDIA LLC
Also Called: Holiday Inn Express
2175 Lincoln St (66901-5317)
PHONE..................................785 243-2700
Jacquie Haytes, *Principal*
EMP: 12
SALES (est): 617.1K **Privately Held**
SIC: 7011 Hotels & motels

(G-1112)
G H C ASSOCIATES INC
Also Called: Century 21
201 W 6th St (66901-2816)
P.O. Box 472 (66901-0472)
PHONE..................................785 243-1555
Kim Wiesner, *President*
EMP: 12
SQ FT: 2,200
SALES (est): 470K **Privately Held**
SIC: 6531 6411 Real estate agent, residential; insurance agents

(G-1113)
GE STEAM POWER INC
1830 E 6th St (66901-2620)
PHONE..................................785 243-3300
Tim Curran, *President*
EMP: 5
SALES (corp-wide): 121.6B **Publicly Held**
SIC: 3463 Pump, compressor, turbine & engine forgings, except auto
HQ: Ge Steam Power, Inc.
175 Addison Rd
Windsor CT 06095
866 257-8664

(G-1114)
GEISLER ROOFING INC
908 E 6th St (66901-3106)
PHONE..................................785 243-7298
Steve Geisler, *President*
Karen Geisler, *Vice Pres*
Tyler Hasenbank, *Sales Associate*
Linda Leclair, *Office Mgr*
EMP: 16
SALES (est): 1.8MM **Privately Held**
WEB: www.geislerroofing.com
SIC: 1761 Roofing contractor

(G-1115)
GENERAL FINANCE INCORPORATED
Also Called: Cloud Ceramics Div
1716 Quail Rd (66901-6806)
P.O. Box 369 (66901-0369)
PHONE..................................785 243-1284
Gene Kindel, *Manager*
EMP: 54
SALES (corp-wide): 8.7MM **Privately Held**
WEB: www.cloudceramics.com
SIC: 3251 Structural brick & blocks
PA: General Finance Incorporated
1716 Quail Rd
Concordia KS 66901
785 243-1284

(G-1116)
GERARD TANK & STEEL INC
1540 E 11th St (66901-6800)
P.O. Box 513 (66901-0513)
PHONE..................................785 243-3895
Joe Gerard, *President*
Delores Gerard, *Corp Secy*
EMP: 30
SQ FT: 27,500
SALES (est): 6.5MM **Privately Held**
WEB: www.gerardtank.com
SIC: 1623 1791 7353 Water, sewer & utility lines; structural steel erection; cranes & aerial lift equipment, rental or leasing

(G-1117)
HEARTLAND COCA-COLA BTLG LLC
439 Us Hwy 81 (66901)
PHONE..................................785 243-1071
EMP: 3433
SALES (corp-wide): 23.9B **Privately Held**
SIC: 5149 2086 Beverages, except coffee & tea; carbonated beverages, nonalcoholic: bottled & canned
PA: Heartland Coca-Cola Bottling Company Llc
9000 Marshall Dr
Lenexa KS

(G-1118)
HOOD HTG AIR PLG ELECTRIC INC
2201 E 6th St (66901-2606)
PHONE..................................785 243-1489
John Hood, *President*
Joyce Hood, *Corp Secy*
EMP: 15
SQ FT: 14,000
SALES: 2MM **Privately Held**
SIC: 1711 1731 Warm air heating & air conditioning contractor; heating & air conditioning contractors; process piping contractor; electrical work

(G-1119)
KANSASLAND TIRE INC
1721 Lincoln St (66901-4801)
PHONE..................................785 243-2706
Bob Mikefell, *Branch Mgr*
EMP: 12
SALES (corp-wide): 94.3MM **Privately Held**
WEB: www.nktiregroup.com
SIC: 5531 7538 Automotive tires; general automotive repair shops
HQ: Kansasland Tire, Inc.
2904 S Spruce St
Wichita KS 67216
316 522-5434

(G-1120)
KNCK INC
Also Called: Am-Knck
1391 W 11th St (66901-3935)
P.O. Box 629 (66901-0629)
PHONE..................................785 243-1414
Joseph Jindra, *President*
EMP: 12
SQ FT: 1,600
SALES (est): 655.4K **Privately Held**
SIC: 4832 Radio broadcasting stations

(G-1121)
KUDERX LLC
302 E 13th St (66901-4902)
PHONE..................................785 760-2298
EMP: 15
SALES (est): 209K **Privately Held**
SIC: 8082 Home Health Care Services

(G-1122)
KVCO
2221 Campus Dr (66901-5305)
PHONE..................................785 243-4444
John Chapin, *Director*
EMP: 25
SALES (est): 1.4MM **Privately Held**
WEB: www.kvco.com
SIC: 4832 Radio broadcasting stations

(G-1123)
MARQUIS PLACE CONCORDIA LLC
205 W 21st St (66901-5205)
PHONE..................................785 243-2255
Brian Warren, *Mng Member*
Sonia Deruseau, *Administration*
Kim Brownell,
EMP: 30
SALES (est): 942.8K **Privately Held**
SIC: 8361 Residential care

(G-1124)
N C K COMMERCIAL LAUNDRY INC
217 W 3rd St (66901-1708)
P.O. Box 328 (66901-0328)
PHONE..................................785 243-4432
Melvern D Giersch, *President*
EMP: 15
SQ FT: 7,100
SALES (est): 759K **Privately Held**
SIC: 7218 7213 Industrial launderers; linen supply

(G-1125)
OCCK INC
1502 Lincoln St (66901-4830)
PHONE..................................785 243-1977
James Quillen, *Branch Mgr*
EMP: 30
SALES (corp-wide): 14.7MM **Privately Held**
WEB: www.occk.net
SIC: 8331 8361 8322 7331 Job training services; job counseling; residential care for the handicapped; children's home; individual & family services; direct mail advertising services
PA: Occk, Inc.
1710 W Schilling Rd
Salina KS 67401
785 827-9383

(G-1126)
ORSCHELN FARM AND HOME LLC
Also Called: Orschelin Farm and Home 127
1620 Lincoln St (66901-4832)
PHONE..................................785 243-6071
Scott Cartledge, *Manager*
EMP: 10
SALES (corp-wide): 822.7MM **Privately Held**
WEB: www.orschelnfarmhome.com
SIC: 5191 Farm supplies
PA: Orscheln Farm And Home Llc
1800 Overcenter Dr
Moberly MO 65270
800 577-2580

(G-1127)
RODS FOOD STORES INC
Also Called: Rod's Thriftway
307 W 6th St (66901-2818)
PHONE..................................785 243-2035
Rodney Imhoff, *President*
Katherine Imhoff, *Corp Secy*
Fr Larry Latourneau, *Vice Pres*
EMP: 30 **EST:** 1982
SQ FT: 15,000
SALES: 2.5MM **Privately Held**
SIC: 5411 5199 Grocery stores, independent; ice, manufactured or natural

(G-1128)
SAINT FRANCIS CMNTY SVCS INC
904 Broadway (66901-3502)
PHONE..................................785 243-4215
EMP: 87
SALES (corp-wide): 108.2MM **Privately Held**
SIC: 8399 8361 8322 Community development groups; group foster home; individual & family services
PA: Saint Francis Community Services, Inc.
509 E Elm St
Salina KS 67401
785 825-0541

(G-1129)
SCOTT SPECIALTIES INC
1820 E 7th St (66901-2609)
PHONE..................................785 243-2594
Vicki Menard, *Manager*
EMP: 41
SALES (corp-wide): 17.4MM **Privately Held**
WEB: www.scottspecialties.com
SIC: 5999 7372 Orthopedic & prosthesis applications; prepackaged software
PA: Scott Specialties, Inc.
512 M St
Belleville KS 66935
785 527-5627

(G-1130)
SERVICEMASTER NORTH CENTL KANS
610 Industrial Rd (66901)
P.O. Box 336 (66901-0336)
PHONE..................................785 243-1965
Dennis Smith, *Co-Owner*
Nancy Smith, *Co-Owner*
EMP: 15
SALES (est): 381.9K **Privately Held**
SIC: 7349 7217 Building maintenance services; carpet & upholstery cleaning on customer premises

(G-1131)
SUNSET HOME INC
620 2nd Ave (66901-2799)
PHONE..................................785 243-2720
Larry Blocklinger, *Administration*
Larry Blochlinger, *Administration*
EMP: 100
SQ FT: 30,000
SALES: 3.6MM **Privately Held**
SIC: 8052 8051 6513 Intermediate care facilities; skilled nursing care facilities; retirement hotel operation

(G-1132)
SUPER 8 MOTEL OF CONCORDIA
1320 Lincoln St (66901-4842)
PHONE..................................785 243-4200
Pat Patel, *Owner*
EMP: 15
SALES (est): 622.9K **Privately Held**
SIC: 7011 Hotels & motels

Conway
Mcpherson County

(G-1133)
BROOKDALE SENIOR LIVING COMMUN
Also Called: Sterling House of McPherson
1460 N Main St (67460-1902)
PHONE..................................620 241-6600
Patty Soden, *Manager*
EMP: 15
SALES (corp-wide): 4.5B **Publicly Held**
WEB: www.assisted.com
SIC: 8051 Skilled nursing care facilities
HQ: Brookdale Senior Living Communities, Inc.
6737 W Wa St Ste 2300
Milwaukee WI 53214
414 918-5000

(G-1134)
KOCH PIPELINE COMPANY LP
1299 8th Ave (67460-6049)
PHONE..................................620 834-2309
EMP: 18
SALES (corp-wide): 31.2B **Privately Held**
SIC: 4612 Crude Petroleum Pipeline
HQ: Koch Pipeline Company, L.P.
4111 E 37th St N
Wichita KS 67220
316 828-5511

(G-1135)
ONEOK HYDROCARBON LP
462 Hwy 56 (67460-6129)
PHONE..................................620 834-2204
Steve Tatum, *Branch Mgr*
EMP: 9
SALES (corp-wide): 12.5B **Publicly Held**
SIC: 3999 Barber & beauty shop equipment
HQ: Oneok Hydrocarbon, L.P.
1910 S Broadacres Rd
Hutchinson KS 67501
620 669-3759

Conway Springs
Sumner County

(G-1136)
CITY OF CONWAY SPRINGS
Also Called: City Clerks Office
208 W Spring Ave (67031-8288)
P.O. Box 187 (67031-0187)
PHONE..................................620 456-2345
Daniel Pettegrew, *Mayor*
Jim Brozovich, *Director*
Spanky Brooks, *Maintence Staff*
EMP: 50 **Privately Held**
SIC: 4941 Water supply
PA: City Of Conway Springs
210 W Spring Ave
Conway Springs KS 67031

(G-1137)
CONWAY BANK (PA)
124 W Spring Ave (67031-3100)
P.O. Box 8 (67031-0008)
PHONE..................................620 456-2255
Robert G Wall, *President*
Jodi Guillemette, *Director*
EMP: 38
SALES: 5MM **Privately Held**
WEB: www.conwaybank.net
SIC: 6021 National commercial banks

(G-1138)
D-J ENGINEERING INC
723 E Spring Ave (67031-8128)
PHONE..................................620 456-3211
Kenny Zoglmann, *Manager*
EMP: 6
SALES (corp-wide): 69.8MM **Privately Held**
SIC: 3728 Aircraft parts & equipment
PA: D-J Engineering, Inc.
219 W 6th Ave
Augusta KS 67010
316 775-1212

(G-1139)
D-J EXTRUDING LLC
723 E Spring Ave (67031-8128)
PHONE..................................620 456-3211
Rezaul Chowdhury,
EMP: 25
SQ FT: 15,000
SALES: 1.6MM **Privately Held**
SIC: 3354 Aluminum extruded products

(G-1140)
DOLL TRUCK LINE
824 E Saint Louis St (67031-8051)
PHONE..................................620 456-2519
Ivan Doll, *President*
Cynthia Doll, *Corp Secy*
Darrin Doll, *Vice Pres*
EMP: 11 **EST:** 1975
SALES: 1.2MM **Privately Held**
SIC: 4213 Contract haulers

(G-1141)
FARMERS COOP GRN ASSN INC (PA)
524 E Parallel St (67031-8002)
PHONE..................................620 456-2222
Pat Lies, *President*
EMP: 10 **EST:** 1954
SQ FT: 7,500
SALES: 32.7MM **Privately Held**
SIC: 5153 5191 4221 Grains; farm supplies; grain elevator, storage only

(G-1142)
KDOLL KOATINGS INC
751 E Spring Ave (67031-8128)
PHONE..................................620 456-2588
Gina Doll, *President*
Mike May, *Business Mgr*
Kevin Doll, *Manager*
EMP: 5
SQ FT: 40,000
SALES: 3MM **Privately Held**
SIC: 3441 1799 1721 Fabricated structural metal; sandblasting of building exteriors; painting & paper hanging

(G-1143)
LANGE COMPANY LLC
205 S Highland St (67031-8243)
PHONE..................................620 456-2996
Greg Lange,
Jeff Lange,
Steve Lange,
EMP: 11
SQ FT: 1,000
SALES: 13.5MM **Privately Held**
SIC: 5153 0711 5191 Grain & field beans; fertilizer application services; fertilizers & agricultural chemicals

(G-1144)
RURAL WATER DIST 5 SUMNER CNTY
202 W Spring Ave (67031-3113)
PHONE..................................620 456-2350
Steve Van Alen, *Chairman*
EMP: 11 **EST:** 2014
SALES (est): 269.7K **Privately Held**
SIC: 8699 Charitable organization

(G-1145)
SPRING VIEW MANOR INC
412 S 8th St (67031-8252)
P.O. Box 98 (67031-0098)
PHONE..................................620 456-2285
Donna Devlin, *President*
Paul Winter, *President*
Virginia C Winter, *Treasurer*
EMP: 30 **EST:** 1964
SALES: 1.9MM **Privately Held**
WEB: www.springviewmanorinc.com
SIC: 8052 Personal care facility

Coolidge
Hamilton County

(G-1146)
MILK PALACE DAIRY LLC
12701 Sw County Road 32 (67836)
PHONE..................................620 372-2021
Michael Spinni, *Mng Member*
EMP: 30 **EST:** 1998
SALES: 10MM **Privately Held**
SIC: 0241 Dairy farms

(G-1147)
SCOULAR COMPANY
12501 W Hwy 50 (67836-1110)
P.O. Box 126 (67836-0126)
PHONE..................................620 372-8611
Jim Foltz, *General Mgr*
EMP: 11
SALES (corp-wide): 4.2B **Privately Held**
WEB: www.scoular.com
SIC: 5153 Wheat
PA: The Scoular Company
2027 Dodge St Ste 200
Omaha NE 68102
402 342-3500

Copeland
Gray County

(G-1148)
ARCHER-DANIELS-MIDLAND COMPANY
Also Called: ADM
2502 Hwy 56 (67837)
P.O. Box 185 (67837-0185)
PHONE..................................620 675-8520
Lee Mason, *Branch Mgr*
EMP: 12
SALES (corp-wide): 64.3B **Publicly Held**
WEB: www.admworld.com
SIC: 5153 Grain elevators
PA: Archer-Daniels-Midland Company
77 W Wacker Dr Ste 4600
Chicago IL 60601
312 634-8100

(G-1149)
JIES LLC
2134 70th Rd (67837-7026)
PHONE..................................620 668-5585
Lynn Johnson, *Mng Member*
Lance Johnson,
EMP: 10
SALES (est): 840.6K **Privately Held**
SIC: 7699 5083 7389 Agricultural equipment repair services; irrigation equipment;

(G-1150)
MAST TRUCKING INC
31800 2 Rd (67837-8022)
P.O. Box 62 (67837-0062)
PHONE..................................620 668-5121
Leroy Mast, *President*
Breanna Mast, *Vice Pres*
EMP: 10
SQ FT: 8,400
SALES: 2.5MM **Privately Held**
SIC: 4213 Contract haulers

Cottonwood Falls
Chase County

(G-1151)
BEAVER DAM HEALTH CARE CENTER
Also Called: Golden Living Centre
612 Walnut St (66845-9798)
PHONE..................................620 273-6369
Judy Boyce, *Manager*
EMP: 30
SALES (corp-wide): 393.8MM **Privately Held**
WEB: www.goldenven.com
SIC: 8051 Skilled nursing care facilities
PA: Beaver Dam Health Care Center
5220 Tennyson Pkwy # 400
Plano TX 75024
972 372-6300

(G-1152)
CHASE COUNTY EMS
130 Broadway St (66845-2885)
P.O. Box 568 (66845-0568)
PHONE..................................620 273-6590
Robert Burright, *Director*
EMP: 15
SALES: 100K **Privately Held**
SIC: 4119 Ambulance service

(G-1153)
EXCHANGE NATIONAL BANK INC
235 Broadway St (66845-9728)
P.O. Box 310 (66845-0310)
PHONE..................................620 273-6389
Steve Mermis, *President*
Thomas Bell, *Vice Pres*
EMP: 11 **EST:** 1888
SQ FT: 5,000
SALES: 1.4MM **Privately Held**
WEB: www.exchangenationalbank.com
SIC: 6021 National commercial banks

(G-1154)
GRAND CENTRAL HOTEL CORP
Also Called: Grand Central Hotel & Grill
215 Broadway St (66845-9728)
P.O. Box 506 (66845-0506)
PHONE..................................620 273-6763
Suzan Barnes, *President*
Tom Cernich, *Vice Pres*
EMP: 28
SQ FT: 8,000
SALES (est): 1.2MM **Privately Held**
WEB: www.grandcentralhotel.com
SIC: 7011 5812 Hotels; eating places

(G-1155)
KANSAS GRAPHICS INC
418 N Walnut St (66845-2843)
P.O. Box 340 (66845-0340)
PHONE..................................620 273-6111
Marvin L Adcock, *President*
Ronald Scott, *Corp Secy*
EMP: 8
SQ FT: 6,000
SALES (est): 1.3MM **Privately Held**
WEB: www.kansasgraphics.com
SIC: 2752 3993 2396 Commercial printing, offset; signs & advertising specialties; automotive & apparel trimmings

(G-1156)
SHC HOLDINGS LLC
200 N Walnut St (66845-8001)
P.O. Box 130 (66845-0130)
PHONE..................................620 273-6900
Donald Linn, *Mng Member*
Ken Stambler,
EMP: 10 **EST:** 2013
SALES (est): 1.6MM **Privately Held**
SIC: 8742 Marketing consulting services

Council Grove
Morris County

(G-1157)
A/C ENTERPRISES INC
Also Called: Dreamsteamer
510 Spencer St (66846-1264)
PHONE..................................620 767-5695
Jeff Allen, *President*
Scott Allen, *Exec VP*
Gayle Allen, *Admin Sec*
EMP: 9
SALES (est): 920.9K **Privately Held**
WEB: www.thedreamsteamer.com
SIC: 3433 Steam heating apparatus

(G-1158)
BUILDING BLOCKS CHILD CARE CTR
300 N Union St Ste A (66846-1233)
PHONE..................................620 767-8029
Julie Hower, *President*
Holly Edwards, *Director*
EMP: 19
SALES: 191.7K **Privately Held**
SIC: 8351 Group day care center

(G-1159)
COTTAGE HOUSE HOTEL AND MOTEL
25 N Neosho St (66846-1633)
P.O. Box 235 (66846-0235)
PHONE..................................620 767-6828
Connie Essington, *President*
EMP: 15
SALES (est): 870.1K **Privately Held**
WEB: www.cottagehousehotel.com
SIC: 7011 5947 Motels; gift shop

(G-1160)
COUNCIL GROVE AREA FOUNDATION
315 W Main St (66846-1706)
P.O. Box 137 (66846-0137)
PHONE..................................620 767-6653
Julie Hower, *President*
EMP: 15
SALES: 143.2K **Privately Held**
SIC: 8699 Charitable organization

(G-1161)
COUNCIL GROVE REPUBLICAN
Also Called: Concil Grove Publishing
302 W Main St (66846-1707)
P.O. Box 237 (66846-0237)
PHONE..................................620 767-5123
Craig McNeal, *President*
Marci McNeal, *Corp Secy*
Michael McNeal, *Vice Pres*
EMP: 5
SALES (est): 435.9K **Privately Held**
SIC: 2711 Newspapers, publishing & printing

(G-1162)
DANNY AXE
Also Called: Custom Fabricators
1040 N Union St (66846-9359)
P.O. Box 296 (66846-0296)
PHONE..................................620 767-5211
Danny Axe, *Owner*
EMP: 20 **EST:** 1998
SALES (est): 3.6MM **Privately Held**
WEB: www.axeequipment.com
SIC: 3441 Fabricated structural metal

(G-1163)
DIVERSICARE LEASING CORP
Also Called: Diversicare of Council Grove
400 Sunset Dr (66846-1554)
PHONE..................................620 767-5172
EMP: 15
SALES (corp-wide): 563.4MM **Publicly Held**
SIC: 8051 Skilled nursing care facilities
HQ: Diversicare Leasing Corp.
1621 Galleria Blvd
Brentwood TN 37027

(G-1164)
EMPRISE BANK
20 S Mission St (66846-1841)
PHONE..................................620 767-5128
C Rein, *Manager*
EMP: 11
SALES (corp-wide): 80MM **Privately Held**
SIC: 6022 State commercial banks
HQ: Emprise Bank
257 N Broadway Ave
Wichita KS 67202
316 383-4400

(G-1165)
FAMILY HEALTH CTR MORRIS CNTY
604 N Washington St (66846-1422)
PHONE..................................620 767-5126
Lora Siegal, *Partner*
Ron Christenson, *CFO*
Bill Lauer, *CIO*
EMP: 12
SALES (est): 1.5MM **Privately Held**
SIC: 8011 Clinic, operated by physicians

(G-1166)
FARMERS & DROVERS BANK (PA)
Also Called: FARMERS INSURANCE
201 W Main St (66846-1704)
P.O. Box C (66846-0620)
PHONE..................................620 767-2265
John H White, *President*
Henry A White Jr, *Senior VP*
Marjorie Buchman, *Assistant VP*
Alan Lierz, *Vice Pres*
Leland Loquist, *Vice Pres*
EMP: 24 **EST:** 1882
SQ FT: 12,500
SALES: 6.8MM **Privately Held**
WEB: www.farmersanddrovers.com
SIC: 6411 Insurance agents, brokers & service

(G-1167)
FLINT HLLS RUR ELC COOP ASSN I (PA)
1564 S 1000 Rd (66846-8703)
P.O. Box B (66846-0610)
PHONE..................................620 767-5144
Robert Reece, *President*
Gina Muhlig, *Manager*
Chuck Goeckel, *Asst Mgr*
Sharon Brooks, *Admin Sec*
Roger Zimmerman,
EMP: 21
SQ FT: 5,000
SALES: 11.5MM **Privately Held**
WEB: www.flinthillsrec.com
SIC: 4911 Distribution, electric power

(G-1168)
GEO BIT EXPLORATION INC
Also Called: Dugas
100 Blue Heron Pt (66846-8410)
PHONE..................................940 888-3134
Day Carlin, *President*
Glenda Carlin, *Vice Pres*
EMP: 13 **EST:** 1961
SQ FT: 1,500
SALES (est): 1.2MM **Privately Held**
WEB: www.dugas.com
SIC: 5984 5172 Butane gas, bottled; gases, liquefied petroleum (propane)

(G-1169)
HARTMAN MASONRY LLC
Also Called: PIONEER MOBILE HOME VILLAGE
204 N 8th St (66846-1106)
PHONE..................................620 767-5286
Victor Hartman,
Sandra Hartman,
EMP: 40
SQ FT: 40,000
SALES: 2.1MM **Privately Held**
SIC: 1741 Concrete block masonry laying

(G-1170)
LEXINET CORPORATION
701 N Union St (66846-9358)
PHONE..................................620 767-6346
Lisa Boyer, *President*
Jan Lerner, *Vice Pres*
Stewart Cindy, *Opers Mgr*
Lucas Ziegenhirt, *Sales Mgr*
Katherine Johnson, *Marketing Staff*
EMP: 50
SQ FT: 24,000
SALES (est): 7.3MM **Privately Held**
WEB: www.lexinet.net
SIC: 7331 7371 Mailing service; computer software development

(G-1171)
MONARCH MOLDING INC
120 Liberty St (66846-1218)
P.O. Box 279 (66846-0279)
PHONE..................................620 767-5115
Judy D Scott, *President*
H Pete Dehoff, *Treasurer*
Denise Chaney, *Admin Sec*
EMP: 9
SQ FT: 23,000
SALES (est): 1.5MM **Privately Held**
SIC: 3089 Injection molding of plastics; casting of plastic

(G-1172)
MOONLITE TRUCKING INC
1126 Old Us Highway 56 (66846-8301)
P.O. Box 254 (66846-0254)
PHONE..................................620 767-5499
Oscar Ochella, *Principal*
EMP: 11
SALES (est): 1.1MM **Privately Held**
SIC: 4212 Local trucking, without storage

(G-1173)
NATIONAL HEALTHCARE CORP
Also Called: Council Grove Healthcare
400 Sunset Dr (66846-1554)
PHONE..................................620 767-5172
Paula Gant, *Manager*
EMP: 100
SALES (corp-wide): 980.3MM **Publicly Held**
WEB: www.healthcarebenefits.com
SIC: 8051 Convalescent home with continuous nursing care
PA: National Healthcare Corporation
100 E Vine St
Murfreesboro TN 37130
615 890-2020

(G-1174)
NEOSHO GARDENS LLC
601 N Union St (66846-9357)
P.O. Box 172 (66846-0172)
PHONE..................................620 767-6920
Eric Nelson, *General Ptnr*
Maureen Adams, *Manager*
Evan Nelson, *Manager*
▲ **EMP:** 40
SQ FT: 2,000
SALES (est): 2.6MM **Privately Held**
SIC: 0181 Bedding plants, growing of; plants, potted: growing of

(G-1175)
QUALITY PROFILE SERVICES INC
701 Donnon St (66846-1181)
P.O. Box 256 (66846-0256)
PHONE..................................620 767-6757
John True, *President*
Steven Shephard, *Vice Pres*
Nicole Shepard, *QC Mgr*
EMP: 45
SQ FT: 40,000
SALES (est): 7.7MM **Privately Held**
WEB: www.qualityprofile.com
SIC: 3089 Extruded finished plastic products

(G-1176)
REX MATERIALS OF KANSAS INC
Also Called: Rex Roto
1000 N Union St (66846-9359)
P.O. Box 160 (66846-0160)
PHONE..................................620 767-5119
David D Rex, *President*
Barry Wessel, *Safety Mgr*
Ray Schmick, *Admin Sec*
▲ **EMP:** 85
SQ FT: 76,000
SALES (est): 10.4MM **Privately Held**
SIC: 3297 Heat resistant mixtures

(G-1177)
STINGER BY AXE
Also Called: Under Axe Equipment
1040 N Union St (66846-9359)
P.O. Box 296 (66846-0296)
PHONE..................................620 767-7555
Danny Axe, *Owner*
EMP: 10 **EST:** 2000
SALES (est): 833.8K **Privately Held**
WEB: www.stingerlifts.com
SIC: 3559 Automotive maintenance equipment

(G-1178)
TRI-COUNTY TELEPHONE ASSN INC
Also Called: Council Grove Telephone Co
1568 S 1000 Rd (66846-8703)
P.O. Box 299 (66846-0299)
PHONE..................................785 366-7000
Dale Jones, *President*
Rhonda Bebe, *Principal*
EMP: 51
SQ FT: 12,000
SALES (est): 11.7MM **Privately Held**
SIC: 4813 Local telephone communications; local & long distance telephone communications

Courtland
Republic County

(G-1179)
C & W FARM SUPPLY INC
518 Main St (66939-3013)
P.O. Box 257 (66939-0257)
PHONE..................................785 374-4521
Beverly Sothers, *President*
Kaylene Clark, *Corp Secy*
Jeffery Sothers, *Vice Pres*
Karen Sothers, *Shareholder*
EMP: 13
SQ FT: 6,000
SALES (est): 1.8MM **Privately Held**
SIC: 5083 Farm equipment parts & supplies; farm implements

(G-1180)
DEPOT MARKET
1101 30 Rd (66939-8050)
PHONE..................................785 374-4255
Daniel Kuhn, *Owner*
Kathryn Kuhn, *Co-Owner*
EMP: 15
SQ FT: 3,000
SALES (est): 87.8K **Privately Held**
SIC: 0175 5431 5148 Deciduous tree fruits; fruit & vegetable markets; fresh fruits & vegetables

(G-1181)
ZOLTENKO FARMS INC
2980 Cedar Rd (66939-8076)
PHONE..................................785 278-5405
James Zoltenko, *President*
Sherryl Zoltenko, *Vice Pres*
Lannin Zoltenko, *Sales Dir*
EMP: 40
SALES (est): 6MM **Privately Held**
WEB: www.zfistud.com
SIC: 0213 Hogs

Coyville
Wilson County

(G-1182)
A LERT CORP (PA)
401 N 6th St (66736-1306)
PHONE..................................620 378-4153
Terry Evans, *Principal*
EMP: 16
SALES (est): 5.6MM **Privately Held**
SIC: 1521 Single-family housing construction

(G-1183)
NATIONAL ASSN LTR CARRIERS
602 N 6th St (66736-1310)
PHONE..................................620 378-3263
Eldon McGinnis, *Branch Mgr*

▲ = Import ▼=Export
◆ =Import/Export

EMP: 20
SALES (corp-wide): 1B **Privately Held**
WEB: www.nalc.org
SIC: 8631 Labor union
PA: National Association Of Letter Carriers
100 Indana Ave Nw Ste 709
Washington DC 20001
202 393-4695

Crestline
Cherokee County

(G-1184)
PBI-GORDON CORPORATION
69 Alternate Hwy (66728)
P.O. Box 78 (66728-0078)
PHONE..................................620 848-3849
Ms Tommie Bottorff, *Production*
Tommie Bottorss, *Manager*
EMP: 40
SALES (corp-wide): 31.9MM **Privately Held**
WEB: www.pbigordon.com
SIC: 2879 2875 Fungicides, herbicides; fertilizers, mixing only
PA: Pbi-Gordon Corporation
22701 W 68th Ter
Shawnee KS 66226
816 421-4070

Cullison
Pratt County

(G-1185)
ELLIS KINNEY SWIMMING POOL
Also Called: Pratt Swimming Pool
201 S Haskell St (67124)
PHONE..................................620 672-7724
Mike Harvey, *Owner*
EMP: 20
SALES (est): 145.6K **Privately Held**
SIC: 7999 Swimming pool, non-membership

Cummings
Atchison County

(G-1186)
CARGILL INCORPORATED
15662 258th Rd (66016-8901)
PHONE..................................913 367-3579
Tom Hotlez, *Opers-Prdtn-Mfg*
EMP: 11
SALES (corp-wide): 113.4B **Privately Held**
WEB: www.cargill.com
SIC: 4221 5153 Grain elevator, storage only; grain elevators
PA: Cargill, Incorporated
15407 Mcginty Rd W
Wayzata MN 55391
952 742-7575

Cunningham
Kingman County

(G-1187)
HILLTOP MANOR INC
403 S Valley St (67035-8120)
P.O. Box 8 (67035-0008)
PHONE..................................620 298-2781
Joe Strong, *President*
Gary Wegger, *Corp Secy*
EMP: 105
SQ FT: 20,000
SALES: 3MM **Privately Held**
SIC: 8052 Intermediate care facilities

(G-1188)
NORTHERN NATURAL GAS COMPANY
20307 Ne 150th Ave (67035-9123)
P.O. Box 178 (67035-0178)
PHONE..................................620 298-5111
Dean Hallowell, *Branch Mgr*
EMP: 20
SALES (corp-wide): 225.3B **Publicly Held**
SIC: 4226 4922 Special warehousing & storage; natural gas transmission
HQ: Northern Natural Gas Company
1111 S 103rd St
Omaha NE 68124

(G-1189)
SKYLAND GRAIN LLC
100 Cairo Main St (67035-9101)
PHONE..................................620 672-3961
Ed Laing, *Manager*
EMP: 10
SALES (corp-wide): 20.9MM **Privately Held**
SIC: 5153 5191 5541 Grains; fertilizer & fertilizer materials; filling stations, gasoline
PA: Skyland Grain, L.L.C.
304 E Highland
Johnson KS 67855
620 492-2126

Danville
Harper County

(G-1190)
PROGRESSIVE AG COOP ASSN
420 Ryan Ave (67036-8800)
PHONE..................................620 962-5238
Derek Lumley, *Manager*
EMP: 12
SALES (corp-wide): 24.8MM **Privately Held**
SIC: 5191 Fertilizers & agricultural chemicals
PA: Progressive Ag Cooperative Association
9011 N A St
Wellington KS 67152
620 326-7496

De Soto
Johnson County

(G-1191)
AIRTEX INC
Also Called: Engineered Air
32050 W 83rd St (66018-9693)
PHONE..................................913 583-3181
Ric Rambacher, *President*
EMP: 99
SALES (est): 13.4MM **Privately Held**
SIC: 3585 Refrigeration & heating equipment

(G-1192)
AIRTEX MANUFACTURING LLLP (DH)
Also Called: Engineered Air
32050 W 83rd St (66018-9693)
P.O. Box 650 (66018-0650)
PHONE..................................913 583-3181
Richard Rambacher, *Partner*
Brian Bosch, *Partner*
Rick Purifoy, *Division Mgr*
Rob Boicey, *Engineer*
Kelly Hajash, *Hum Res Coord*
▲ **EMP:** 200
SQ FT: 130,000
SALES (est): 81.5MM
SALES (corp-wide): 3.3MM **Privately Held**
SIC: 3585 5075 3564 3433 Air conditioning units, complete: domestic or industrial; air conditioning & ventilation equipment & supplies; blowers & fans; heating equipment, except electric
HQ: Airtex Manufacturing Partnership
1401 Hastings Cres Se Suite 1421
Calgary AB T2G 4
403 287-2590

(G-1193)
BDAY PARTIES (PA)
32605 W 82nd St (66018-8002)
PHONE..................................913 961-1857
Amy Kremer, *Principal*
EMP: 14 **EST:** 2010
SALES (est): 783.8K **Privately Held**
SIC: 7299 Costume rental

(G-1194)
BETTYS TRUCKING INCORPORATED
9455 Lexington Ave (66018-9037)
P.O. Box 706 (66018-0706)
PHONE..................................913 583-3666
Betty Cannon, *President*
EMP: 11
SQ FT: 3,600
SALES: 700K **Privately Held**
SIC: 4212 Dump truck haulage

(G-1195)
BIODESIX INC
Also Called: Oncimmune
8960 Commerce Dr Bldg 6 (66018-8433)
PHONE..................................913 583-9000
EMP: 20 **Privately Held**
SIC: 8731 8071 Medical research, commercial; blood analysis laboratory
PA: Biodesix, Inc.
2970 Wilderness Pl # 120
Boulder CO 80301

(G-1196)
CLEARVIEW CITY INC
36000 W 103rd St (66018-8432)
PHONE..................................913 583-1451
David Rhodes, *President*
EMP: 15
SALES: 1MM **Privately Held**
WEB: www.clearviewcity.com
SIC: 6531 Rental agent, real estate

(G-1197)
COMMERCIAL FLOORS
9055 Hillview Dr (66018-9415)
PHONE..................................913 583-3525
Sandra Holden, *President*
EMP: 21
SALES (est): 1.1MM **Privately Held**
SIC: 1752 Floor laying & floor work

(G-1198)
CUSTOM FOODS INC
9101 Commerce Dr (66018-8410)
PHONE..................................913 585-1900
John Khoury, *President*
Joseph J Bisogno, *Owner*
Jamie Droegemeier, *Accountant*
EMP: 40
SQ FT: 48,000
SALES (est): 9.6MM **Privately Held**
WEB: www.customfoodsinc.com
SIC: 2038 2041 2053 Frozen specialties; pizza dough, prepared; frozen bakery products, except bread

(G-1199)
FINUCANE ENTERPRISES INC
32565 Lexington Ave Ste A (66018-8461)
PHONE..................................913 829-5665
EMP: 11
SQ FT: 10,000
SALES (est): 1.6MM **Privately Held**
SIC: 5047 Whol Medical Equipment

(G-1200)
GREAT AMERICAN BANK (HQ)
33050 W 83rd St (66018-8051)
P.O. Box 429 (66018-0429)
PHONE..................................913 585-1131
Arlen Gabriel, *President*
Cathy McGivern, *President*
EMP: 11 **EST:** 1901
SQ FT: 3,700
SALES: 8MM **Privately Held**
WEB: www.greatambank.com
SIC: 6022 State trust companies accepting deposits, commercial

(G-1201)
HILLSIDE VILLAGE LLC
Also Called: Hillside Village of De Soto
33600 W 85th St (66018-8118)
PHONE..................................913 583-1266
R Haynes, *Partner*
Frank Chastain, *Maintenance Dir*
Brenda Hernandez, *Director*
Todd Simpson, *Administration*
Robert Haynes,
EMP: 70
SQ FT: 40,000
SALES (est): 3.5MM **Privately Held**
SIC: 8051 Convalescent home with continuous nursing care

(G-1202)
HUHTAMAKI INC (HQ)
9201 Packaging Dr (66018-8600)
PHONE..................................913 583-3025
Jukka Moisio, *CEO*
Clay Dunn, *President*
Jacob Cats, *General Mgr*
James Lightfoot, *Business Mgr*
Olli Koponen, *Exec VP*
◆ **EMP:** 400 **EST:** 1994
SQ FT: 480,000
SALES (est): 1B
SALES (corp-wide): 3.4B **Privately Held**
SIC: 3565 2656 Labeling machines, industrial; ice cream containers: made from purchased material
PA: Huhtamaki Oyj
Revontulenkuja 1
Espoo 02100
106 867-000

(G-1203)
HUHTAMAKI AMERICAS INC
9201 Packaging Dr (66018-8600)
PHONE..................................913 583-3025
Jukka Moisio, *CEO*
Norman Botwinik, *Principal*
Steve Lyons, *Principal*
Clay Dunn, *Exec VP*
Suresh Gupta, *Exec VP*
▲ **EMP:** 400
SALES (est): 123.1MM
SALES (corp-wide): 145.2MM **Privately Held**
SIC: 3089 Plastic containers, except foam
HQ: Huhtamaki Beheer V B.V.
Wegalaan 8
Hoofddorp 2132
235 679-988

(G-1204)
HUHTAMAKI FILMS INC
9201 Packaging Dr (66018-8600)
PHONE..................................913 583-3025
Clay Dunn, *CEO*
John Odea, *Vice Pres*
Earlene A Sells, *Treasurer*
Rochelle Stringer, *Admin Sec*
◆ **EMP:** 647
SALES (est): 81.6MM
SALES (corp-wide): 3.4B **Privately Held**
SIC: 3089 7389 5963 Plastic containers, except foam; packaging & labeling services; food services, direct sales
PA: Huhtamaki Oyj
Revontulenkuja 1
Espoo 02100
106 867-000

(G-1205)
KANSAS TRUCKING LLC
9620 Lexington Ave (66018-9022)
PHONE..................................913 586-5911
EMP: 15
SALES (est): 2.6MM **Privately Held**
SIC: 4212 Local Trucking Operator

(G-1206)
LUMBER ONE LLC
9800 Sunflower Rd (66018-9023)
PHONE..................................913 583-9889
Rex Allen, *Principal*
Corey Bomhoff, *Principal*
Todd Joeckel, *Principal*
Scott McDaniel, *Principal*
Don Parr, *Principal*
EMP: 29
SALES (est): 15.4MM **Privately Held**
SIC: 5099 Timber products, rough

(G-1207)
MARTIN MARIETTA MATERIALS INC
Also Called: Sunflower Quarry
34135 W 95th St (66018)
P.O. Box 715 (66018-0715)
PHONE..................................913 583-3311
James Nicholson, *Manager*
EMP: 18 **Publicly Held**
WEB: www.martinmarietta.com
SIC: 1422 Crushed & broken limestone

GEOGRAPHIC

PA: Martin Marietta Materials Inc
2710 Wycliff Rd
Raleigh NC 27607

(G-1208)
MERCK SHARP & DOHME CORP
35500 W 91st St (66018-7103)
PHONE..................................913 422-6001
Scott Dormann, *Vice Pres*
Kevin Jennings, *Production*
Wayne Katt, *Supervisor*
Tommy Zerse, *Director*
EMP: 78
SALES (corp-wide): 42.2B **Publicly Held**
SIC: 2834 Pharmaceutical preparations
HQ: Merck Sharp & Dohme Corp.
2000 Galloping Hill Rd
Kenilworth NJ 07033
908 740-4000

(G-1209)
MR GOODCENTS FRANCHISE SYSTEMS
8997 Commerce Dr (66018-8428)
PHONE..................................913 583-8400
Joe Bosogno, *President*
EMP: 30
SALES (est): 5MM **Privately Held**
SIC: 6794 5812 Franchises, selling or licensing; sandwiches & submarines shop

(G-1210)
PROFIT PLUS BUS SOLUTIONS LLC
8997 Commerce Dr (66018-8428)
PHONE..................................913 583-8440
Farrellynn Wolf,
EMP: 12
SALES (est): 966.1K **Privately Held**
SIC: 8741 Business management

(G-1211)
REHRIG PACIFIC COMPANY
8875 Commerce Dr (66018-8423)
PHONE..................................913 585-1175
Benjamin Troja, *QC Mgr*
Garrett Forsythe, *Engineer*
Chris Gab, *Engineer*
Justin Stryker, *Engineer*
Steve Trieb, *Engineer*
EMP: 50 **Privately Held**
SIC: 3089 Plastic processing
HQ: Rehrig Pacific Company
4010 E 26th St
Vernon CA 90058
323 262-5145

(G-1212)
RL DUNCAN CNSTR CO INC
9560 Lexington Ave (66018-9038)
P.O. Box 225 (66018-0225)
PHONE..................................913 583-1160
Russell L Duncan, *President*
Paula Rhodes, *Corp Secy*
Thurman L Duncan, *Vice Pres*
EMP: 65
SQ FT: 6,000
SALES (est): 8.4MM **Privately Held**
SIC: 1794 Excavation work

(G-1213)
SPECPRO ENVIRONMENTAL SVCS LLC
35425 W 103rd St (66018)
P.O. Box 549 (66018-0549)
PHONE..................................913 583-3000
Terry Dunavin, *Branch Mgr*
EMP: 10
SALES (corp-wide): 1.3B **Privately Held**
WEB: www.specproenv.com
SIC: 8748 Environmental consultant
HQ: Specpro Environmental Services, Llc
1006 Floyd Culler Ct
Oak Ridge TN 37830
865 481-7837

(G-1214)
TRACKER DOOR SYSTEMS LLC
35000 W 95th St (66018-9193)
PHONE..................................913 585-3100
Cynthia Johannsen,
Glen Johannsen,
EMP: 8
SALES (est): 1.1MM **Privately Held**
WEB: www.trackerdoor.com
SIC: 5211 3537 3442 2431 Door & window products; garage doors, sale & installation; loading docks: portable, adjustable & hydraulic; shutters, door or window: metal; fire doors, metal; garage doors, overhead: wood

(G-1215)
TRICENTURY BANK (PA)
33485 Lexington Ave (66018-8270)
P.O. Box 329 (66018-0329)
PHONE..................................913 648-8010
L Travis Hicks, *Administration*
EMP: 12
SALES: 4.9MM **Privately Held**
SIC: 6021 National commercial banks

Delphos
Ottawa County

(G-1216)
DELPHOS COOPERATIVE ASSN
413 W 1st St (67436-4041)
P.O. Box 308 (67436-0308)
PHONE..................................785 523-4213
Dennis Ablard, *Ch of Bd*
EMP: 22
SQ FT: 3,000
SALES (est): 18.1MM **Privately Held**
SIC: 5153 5191 Grain elevators; feed; seeds: field, garden & flower; fertilizer & fertilizer materials; chemicals, agricultural

(G-1217)
ROKENN ENTERPRISES INC
137 N 110th Rd (67436-9315)
PHONE..................................785 523-4251
Robert Smith, *President*
EMP: 7
SALES (est): 491.9K **Privately Held**
SIC: 3999 5999 Pet supplies; pets

Derby
Sedgwick County

(G-1218)
ATWOOD DISTRIBUTING LP
333 W Red Powell Dr (67037-2629)
PHONE..................................316 789-1800
Gary Atwood, *Branch Mgr*
EMP: 20
SALES (corp-wide): 266.6MM **Privately Held**
SIC: 5191 Farm supplies
PA: Atwood Distributing, L.P.
500 S Garland Rd
Enid OK 73703
580 233-3702

(G-1219)
AUTO MASTERS LLC
945 N K 15 Hwy (67037-1832)
PHONE..................................316 789-8540
Jeff Erickson, *Manager*
EMP: 10
SALES (est): 794.8K
SALES (corp-wide): 3MM **Privately Held**
SIC: 7533 7537 7538 7539 Auto exhaust system repair shops; automotive transmission repair shops; general automotive repair shops; wheel alignment, automotive
PA: Auto Masters Llc
945 N K 15 Hwy
Derby KS 67037
316 789-8540

(G-1220)
AUTO MASTERS LLC (PA)
Also Called: Auto Masters Service Center
945 N K 15 Hwy (67037-1832)
PHONE..................................316 789-8540
Larry Greider,
EMP: 20
SQ FT: 10,800
SALES: 3MM **Privately Held**
SIC: 7549 7537 7542 7539 High performance auto repair & service; automotive transmission repair shops; washing & polishing, automotive; wheel alignment, automotive

(G-1221)
AVITA ASSISTED LIVING AT DERBY
731 N Klein Cir (67037-7011)
PHONE..................................316 260-4447
Albert Coccetella,
EMP: 13
SALES (est): 522.7K **Privately Held**
SIC: 8051 Skilled nursing care facilities

(G-1222)
BANK AMERICA NATIONAL ASSN
201 N Baltimore Ave (67037-1601)
PHONE..................................316 788-2811
Bert Barrett, *Principal*
EMP: 15
SALES (corp-wide): 110.5B **Publicly Held**
WEB: www.bofa.com
SIC: 6021 National commercial banks
HQ: Bank Of America, National Association
100 S Tryon St
Charlotte NC 28202
704 386-5681

(G-1223)
BECK ROOFING & CONSTRUCTION
400 N River St (67037-1521)
P.O. Box 836 (67037-0836)
PHONE..................................316 684-7663
Lawrence J Beck, *President*
EMP: 10
SALES (est): 820.4K **Privately Held**
SIC: 1761 Roofing contractor

(G-1224)
BRANSTETTER & ASSOCIATES
Also Called: Branstetter & Sparks
1105 N Buckner St (67037-2719)
P.O. Box 326 (67037-0326)
PHONE..................................316 788-9290
Laura Branstetter, *Owner*
Rebecca Sparks, *Bd of Directors*
EMP: 13
SALES (est): 801.2K **Privately Held**
WEB: www.branstettersparks.com
SIC: 8042 5995 Contact lense specialist optometrist; contact lenses, prescription

(G-1225)
BRG PRECISION PRODUCTS INC
600 N River St (67037-1536)
PHONE..................................316 788-2000
John Bode, *President*
Linda Bode, *Vice Pres*
◆ **EMP:** 50
SQ FT: 80,000
SALES (est): 10.1MM **Privately Held**
WEB: www.brgproducts.com
SIC: 3663 3873 Digital encoders; watches, clocks, watchcases & parts

(G-1226)
BROOKDALE SENIOR LIVING COMMUN
Also Called: Brookdale Derby
1709 E Walnut Grove Rd (67037-3580)
PHONE..................................316 788-0370
Christie Underwood, *Director*
EMP: 15
SALES (corp-wide): 4.5B **Publicly Held**
WEB: www.assisted.com
SIC: 8361 Residential care
HQ: Brookdale Senior Living Communities, Inc.
6737 W Wa St Ste 2300
Milwaukee WI 53214
414 918-5000

(G-1227)
BRYTAM MANUFACTURING INC
229 S Water St (67037-1514)
PHONE..................................316 788-3300
Tammy Reed, *President*
Bryon Reed, *Vice Pres*
Jennifer Reed, *Admin Asst*
EMP: 7
SQ FT: 3,000
SALES: 826K **Privately Held**
WEB: www.brytammfg.com
SIC: 3599 Machine shop, jobbing & repair

(G-1228)
CELLCO PARTNERSHIP
Also Called: Verizon Wireless
2100 N Rock Rd Ste 100 (67037-3774)
PHONE..................................316 789-9911
Scot Jacobson, *Branch Mgr*
EMP: 12
SALES (corp-wide): 130.8B **Publicly Held**
SIC: 5999 5065 4812 Mobile telephones & equipment; telephone & telegraphic equipment; cellular telephone services
HQ: Cellco Partnership
1 Verizon Way
Basking Ridge NJ 07920

(G-1229)
CITIZENS BANK OF KANSAS NA
1033 N Buckner St (67037-1824)
PHONE..................................316 788-1111
EMP: 17 **Privately Held**
SIC: 6021 National commercial banks
HQ: Citizens Bank Of Kansas
300 N Main St
Kingman KS 67068
620 532-5162

(G-1230)
CLEARWATER ENGINEERING INC
301 N River St (67037-1528)
PHONE..................................316 425-0202
Diane Cool, *CEO*
David N Cool, *President*
Kevin Elliott, *VP Opers*
▲ **EMP:** 24
SQ FT: 10,000
SALES (est): 7.6MM **Privately Held**
WEB: www.clearwateren.com
SIC: 3728 Aircraft assemblies, subassemblies & parts

(G-1231)
COLLISION WORKS LLC
910 N Nelson Dr (67037-1859)
PHONE..................................316 788-5722
Jake Nossaman, *Mng Member*
EMP: 22
SALES (corp-wide): 2.5MM **Privately Held**
SIC: 7532 Collision shops, automotive
PA: Collision Works Llc
3224 Se 29th St
Oklahoma City OK 73115
405 670-2500

(G-1232)
CONFEDERATED BUILDERS SUPPLY
503 N Buckner St (67037-1696)
PHONE..................................316 788-3913
Charles E Powell, *President*
Geneva Wilkes, *Corp Secy*
EMP: 25
SQ FT: 2,500
SALES (est): 9.4MM **Privately Held**
SIC: 5031 1542 Building materials, exterior; building materials, interior; commercial & office building, new construction; restaurant construction; religious building construction

(G-1233)
DCS INC
2300 N Nelson Dr Unit 13 (67037-2578)
PHONE..................................316 806-4899
Stephen F Timmermeyer, *President*
Josh Scott, *General Mgr*
EMP: 8
SALES: 520K **Privately Held**
SIC: 3724 Aircraft engines & engine parts

(G-1234)
DENNIS C MCALLISTER DDS PA
Also Called: Tanglewood Family Dentistry
1700 E James St (67037-3543)
P.O. Box 207 (67037-0207)
PHONE..................................316 788-3736
Dennis McAllister DDS, *President*

▲ = Import ▼=Export
◆ =Import/Export

EMP: 45
SALES (est): 1.2MM Privately Held
SIC: 8021 Dentists' office

(G-1235)
DERBY DENTAL CARE
1120 N Rock Rd Ste 100 (67037-3587)
PHONE....316 789-9999
Brent Nelson, *Owner*
EMP: 20
SALES (est): 429.8K Privately Held
SIC: 8021 Dental clinic

(G-1236)
DERBY HOTEL INC
Also Called: Hampton Inn Derby
1701 E Cambridge St (67037-3782)
P.O. Box 570 (67037-0570)
PHONE....316 425-7900
Mj Tarmar, *General Mgr*
EMP: 16 EST: 2010
SALES (est): 764.5K Privately Held
SIC: 7011 Hotels & motels

(G-1237)
DERBY PUBLIC SCHOOLS
Also Called: Derby School Service Center
120 N Westview Dr (67037-3201)
PHONE....316 788-8450
Tony Digregorio, *Principal*
EMP: 100
SALES (corp-wide): 82.9MM Privately Held
WEB: www.derbyschools.net
SIC: 4151 School buses
PA: Derby Public Schools
120 E Washington St
Derby KS 67037
316 788-8400

(G-1238)
DERBY RECREATION COMM USD 260
801 E Market St (67037-2200)
P.O. Box 324 (67037-0324)
PHONE....316 788-3781
Frank Sietz, *President*
Frank Seitz, *Superintendent*
Roberts Janet, *Bookkeeper*
Caryn Greenstreet, *Manager*
Rob McDonald, *Info Tech Dir*
EMP: 75
SQ FT: 20,000
SALES (est): 3.4MM Privately Held
WEB: www.derbyrec.com
SIC: 7999 Recreation services; recreation center

(G-1239)
DERBY TRAILER TECHNOLOGIES LLC
Also Called: Derby Steel Technologies
449 N Water St (67037-1510)
P.O. Box 610 (67037-0610)
PHONE....316 788-3331
Larry Spikes, *Mng Member*
Kathy Andrews, *Manager*
EMP: 14
SALES (est): 3.4MM Privately Held
WEB: www.derbytrailer.com
SIC: 3441 Fabricated structural metal

(G-1240)
DON HATTAN DERBY INC
2518 N Rock Rd (67037-3816)
PHONE....316 744-1275
Jill Hattan, *President*
Benjamin Thomas, *Vice Pres*
EMP: 28
SALES (est): 2.1MM Privately Held
SIC: 5511 7538 Automobiles, new & used; general automotive repair shops

(G-1241)
E BRENT NELSON
1120 N Rock Rd Ste 100 (67037-3587)
PHONE....316 789-9999
Brent Nelson, *Principal*
EMP: 14 EST: 2001
SALES (est): 343K Privately Held
SIC: 8021 Dentists' office

(G-1242)
EDWARD J LIND II
1101 N Rock Rd Ste 100 (67037-3750)
PHONE....316 788-6963
Edward J Lind II, *Owner*
EMP: 30
SALES (est): 907K Privately Held
SIC: 8011 8049 General & family practice, physician/surgeon; offices of health practitioner

(G-1243)
EL PASO ANIMAL CLINIC
Also Called: Herod, Jeff J Dvm
841 N Buckner St (67037-1494)
PHONE....316 788-1561
Gary D Oehnke, *Owner*
EMP: 16
SALES (est): 658.8K Privately Held
SIC: 0742 5999 3999 0752 Animal hospital services, pets & other animal specialties; pet food; pet supplies; boarding services, kennels

(G-1244)
ENCO OF KANSAS INC
3701 E Haven Dr (67037-7041)
PHONE....316 788-4143
David George, *President*
Brian Ramseyer, *Opers Mgr*
EMP: 66
SQ FT: 34,000
SALES (est): 10MM Privately Held
SIC: 3559 Automotive related machinery

(G-1245)
ENCOBOTICS INC
3701 E Haven Dr (67037-7041)
PHONE....316 788-5656
David George, *President*
Diana George, *Corp Secy*
EMP: 5
SALES (est): 700.4K Privately Held
SIC: 3549 Assembly machines, including robotic

(G-1246)
FAITH EVANGELICAL LUTHERAN CH
Also Called: Faith Lutheran School
208 S Derby Ave (67037-1443)
PHONE....316 788-1715
Karen Boettcher, *Principal*
Thomas Johnson, *Pastor*
EMP: 20
SALES (est): 1MM Privately Held
SIC: 8661 8351 Lutheran Church; child day care services

(G-1247)
FRAZIER ENTERPRISES INC (PA)
Also Called: Derby Bowl
444 S Baltimore Ave (67037-1408)
PHONE....316 788-0263
Earnest D Frazier, *President*
Tanya Frazier, *Manager*
EMP: 10
SQ FT: 7,000
SALES (est): 1.1MM Privately Held
SIC: 7933 Ten pin center

(G-1248)
GOODWILL INDUSTRIES EA
1247 N Rainbow Dr (67037-3783)
PHONE....316 789-8804
Jonathan Young, *Branch Mgr*
EMP: 31
SALES (corp-wide): 10.8MM Privately Held
SIC: 8331 Vocational rehabilitation agency
PA: Goodwill Industries Easter Seal Society Of Kansas, Inc.
3636 N Oliver St
Wichita KS
316 744-9291

(G-1249)
GRACE CONSTRUCTION & ASSOC INC
102 Reyer St (67037)
P.O. Box 155, Rose Hill (67133-0155)
PHONE....316 617-1729
Dave Jones, *President*
Ashley Jones, *Admin Sec*
EMP: 10
SALES: 120K Privately Held
SIC: 1521 1542 General remodeling, single-family houses; commercial & office building contractors

(G-1250)
GREEN MEADOWS LAWN LANDSCAPING
7800 E Lyons Cir (67037-9437)
PHONE....316 788-0282
David Dittmer, *President*
EMP: 10
SALES (est): 480.2K Privately Held
SIC: 0782 1799 Lawn services; swimming pool construction

(G-1251)
HONEYWELL INTERNATIONAL INC
306 S Brook Forest Rd (67037-2068)
PHONE....316 204-5503
EMP: 694
SALES (corp-wide): 41.8B Publicly Held
SIC: 3724 Aircraft engines & engine parts
PA: Honeywell International Inc.
300 S Tryon St
Charlotte NC 28202
973 455-2000

(G-1252)
INTRUST BANK NA
1501 N Rock Rd (67037-3729)
PHONE....316 383-1767
Anna Warren, *Branch Mgr*
EMP: 16
SALES (corp-wide): 134.2MM Privately Held
WEB: www.intrustbank.com
SIC: 6021 National commercial banks
HQ: Intrust Bank National Association
105 N Main St
Wichita KS 67202
316 383-1111

(G-1253)
J & A RENTALS INC (PA)
Also Called: Colortyme
1600 E Patriot Ave (67037-8760)
P.O. Box 287 (67037-0287)
PHONE....316 788-4540
John Prothro, *President*
EMP: 10
SALES (est): 4MM Privately Held
SIC: 7359 Equipment rental & leasing

(G-1254)
J P WEIGAND & SONS INC
1121 N College Park St # 700 (67037-3666)
PHONE....316 788-5581
Kimberly Brace, *Manager*
EMP: 25
SALES (est): 800.3K
SALES (corp-wide): 10.6MM Privately Held
WEB: www.jpweigand.com
SIC: 6531 Real estate agent, residential; real estate managers
PA: J P Weigand & Sons Inc
150 N Market St
Wichita KS 67202
316 686-3773

(G-1255)
JAKUBS LADDER INC
330 N Valley Stream Dr (67037-8726)
P.O. Box 572 (67037-0572)
PHONE....316 214-8932
Danny Jakub, *Exec Dir*
EMP: 5
SALES (est): 100K Privately Held
SIC: 1521 1522 1389 Single-family housing construction; multi-family dwellings, new construction; construction, repair & dismantling services

(G-1256)
KINDERCARE LEARNING CTRS LLC
Also Called: Kindercare Child Care Network
1720 E Walnut Grove Rd (67037-3527)
PHONE....316 788-5925
EMP: 12
SALES (corp-wide): 1B Privately Held
SIC: 8351 Child Day Care Services
HQ: Kindercare Learning Centers, Llc
650 Ne Holladay St # 1400
Portland OR 97232
503 872-1300

(G-1257)
KUHN CO LLC (PA)
Also Called: Big Tool Store
4640 E 63rd St S (67037-9162)
P.O. Box 44 (67037-0044)
PHONE....316 788-6500
Dale V Kuhn, *Managing Prtnr*
Shelly Dunnegan, *Partner*
Jeff Kuhn, *Partner*
Patricia Kuhn, *Partner*
Dennis Laird, *General Mgr*
EMP: 29
SQ FT: 18,000
SALES (est): 6MM Privately Held
WEB: www.kuhncompany.com
SIC: 4225 6512 5251 5085 Miniwarehouse, warehousing; commercial & industrial building operation; tools, power; tools, hand; industrial tools; welding supplies

(G-1258)
LINDSEY MANAGEMENT CO INC
Also Called: Derby Golf & Country Club
2600 N Triple Creek Dr (67037-9454)
PHONE....316 788-3070
Adrian Harper, *Branch Mgr*
EMP: 19 Privately Held
SIC: 7997 Golf club, membership
PA: Lindsey Management Co., Inc.
1200 E Joyce Blvd
Fayetteville AR 72703

(G-1259)
LOWES HOME CENTERS LLC
424 W Patriot Ave (67037-8758)
PHONE....316 206-0000
Danny Whimberly, *Manager*
EMP: 150
SALES (corp-wide): 71.3B Publicly Held
SIC: 5211 5031 5722 5064 Home centers; building materials, exterior; building materials, interior; household appliance stores; electrical appliances, television & radio
HQ: Lowe's Home Centers, Llc
1605 Curtis Bridge Rd
Wilkesboro NC 28697
336 658-4000

(G-1260)
LSL OF DERBY KS LLC
Also Called: WESTVIEW MANOR
445 N Westview Dr (67037-2228)
PHONE....316 788-3739
Arien Reeves, *Administration*
EMP: 70
SALES: 3.3MM Privately Held
SIC: 8051 Skilled nursing care facilities

(G-1261)
MERITRUST CREDIT UNION
1257 N Buckner St (67037-2721)
PHONE....316 219-7614
Amy Cleine, *Manager*
EMP: 12
SALES (corp-wide): 53.9MM Privately Held
WEB: www.bwcu.org
SIC: 6062 6163 State credit unions, not federally chartered; loan brokers
PA: Meritrust Credit Union
8710 E 32nd St N
Wichita KS 67226
316 683-1199

(G-1262)
MID CONTINENT CONTROLS INC
901 N River St (67037-1534)
PHONE....316 789-0088
Rick A Hemphill, *President*
Michelle Hemphill, *Prdtn Mgr*
Mike Alumbaugh, *Opers Staff*
Tim Bynum, *QC Mgr*
Tom Zamudio, *QC Mgr*
EMP: 42
SQ FT: 22,000

GEOGRAPHIC

SALES (est): 8MM **Privately Held**
WEB: www.midcontinentcontrols.com
SIC: 3728 Aircraft parts & equipment

(G-1263)
MOCKRY & SONS MACHINE CO INC
621 N River St (67037-1533)
PHONE..................................316 788-7878
Michael Mockry, *President*
Anthony Mockry, *Vice Pres*
Russell Varner, *Administration*
EMP: 21
SQ FT: 3,000
SALES: 2MM **Privately Held**
SIC: 3728 3542 3599 Aircraft parts & equipment; machine tools, metal forming type; machine shop, jobbing & repair

(G-1264)
P A FAMILY MEDCENTERS
Also Called: Derby Family Medcenter
1101 N Rock Rd Stop 1 (67037-3705)
PHONE..................................316 771-9999
EMP: 140
SALES (est): 17.6MM **Privately Held**
SIC: 8011 Medical Doctor's Office

(G-1265)
PRIM AND POLISHED LLC
1030 E Splitwood Way St (67037-8784)
PHONE..................................316 516-2537
Tavane Donesay, *President*
EMP: 10
SALES (est): 48.7K **Privately Held**
SIC: 7231 Manicurist, pedicurist

(G-1266)
PRO CARWASH SYSTEMS INC
3019 N Oliver St (67037-8791)
PHONE..................................316 788-9933
Troy L Wayman, *President*
Judy Wayman, *Shareholder*
EMP: 12
SQ FT: 3,500
SALES (est): 1.2MM **Privately Held**
SIC: 1799 5087 5084 Service station equipment installation, maintenance & repair; carwash equipment & supplies; cleaning equipment, high pressure, sand or steam

(G-1267)
RAEANNS FANCY FOOTWORK
949 N K 15 Hwy (67037-1832)
PHONE..................................316 788-4499
Raeann Gaulin, *President*
EMP: 16
SALES (est): 280.7K **Privately Held**
SIC: 7911 7999 Dance studio & school; gymnastic instruction, non-membership

(G-1268)
RENAL TRTMNT CENTERS-WEST INC
Also Called: Renal Treatment Ctrs - Derby
250 W Red Powell Dr (67037-2626)
PHONE..................................316 788-2899
James K Hilger,
EMP: 14 **Publicly Held**
WEB: www.davita.com
SIC: 8092 Kidney dialysis centers
HQ: Renal Treatment Centers-West, Inc.
2000 16th St
Denver CO 80202

(G-1269)
RIVERSIDE INDUSTRIES LLC
Also Called: Derby Machine
3701 E Haven Dr (67037-7041)
PHONE..................................316 788-4428
Mike Turner, *Opers Mgr*
Diana George,
EMP: 8
SALES (est): 1MM **Privately Held**
WEB: www.derbymachine.com
SIC: 3599 Machine shop, jobbing & repair

(G-1270)
ROGERS DUNCAN DILLEHAY DDS PA (PA)
1821 E Madison Ave (67037-2357)
PHONE..................................316 683-6518
Ken Dillehay, *President*
Carol Latan, *Corp Secy*
Kari L Miller, *Administration*
EMP: 13 **EST:** 1970
SALES (est): 1MM **Privately Held**
SIC: 8021 8011 Orthodontist; offices & clinics of medical doctors

(G-1271)
SHELTON COLLISION REPAIR INC
Also Called: Shelton Body Shop
325 W Patriot Ave (67037-8757)
PHONE..................................316 788-1528
Brad Shelton, *President*
Tracie Shelton, *Principal*
Don Cook, *Prdtn Mgr*
Kenny Thompson, *Manager*
EMP: 10
SQ FT: 8,600
SALES (est): 1.6MM **Privately Held**
WEB: www.sheltoncollision.com
SIC: 7532 Body shop, automotive

(G-1272)
SHIRTS PLUS INC
703 N Buckner St (67037-1635)
PHONE..................................316 788-1550
Kevin Cardwell, *President*
Cheryl Cardwell, *Vice Pres*
EMP: 10
SQ FT: 3,500
SALES (est): 957.6K **Privately Held**
WEB: www.shirtsplusderby.com
SIC: 2759 5699 2395 2396 Screen printing; sports apparel; embroidery products, except schiffli machine; automotive & apparel trimmings

(G-1273)
TANGLEWOOD FAMILY MED CTR PA
606 N Mulberry Rd (67037-3532)
PHONE..................................316 788-3787
Roger Thomas, *President*
Glen Patton, *Vice Pres*
Catherine Mitchell, *Admin Sec*
Joshua Wigdahl, *Physician Asst*
EMP: 27
SALES (est): 1.8MM **Privately Held**
SIC: 8011 Clinic, operated by physicians

(G-1274)
TANGLEWOOD FAMILY MEDICAL CTR
606 N Mulberry Rd (67037-3532)
PHONE..................................316 788-3787
Fax: 316 788-2618
EMP: 26
SALES (est): 1.7MM **Privately Held**
SIC: 8011 Medical Doctor's Office

(G-1275)
TENDERCARE LAWN AND LANDSCAPE
219 S Water St (67037-1514)
P.O. Box 352 (67037-0352)
PHONE..................................316 788-5416
Kevin Payne, *President*
EMP: 13
SALES (est): 1.5MM **Privately Held**
WEB: www.tendercarelandscape.com
SIC: 0782 Landscape contractors; lawn care services

(G-1276)
TOMMY J KEMP
Also Called: Kemp Construction Company
612 N Mulberry Rd (67037-3532)
PHONE..................................316 522-7255
Tom Kemp, *Owner*
EMP: 20
SQ FT: 3,500
SALES (est): 5.3MM **Privately Held**
WEB: www.kempconst.com
SIC: 1521 1542 1522 Single-family housing construction; nonresidential construction; multi-family dwellings, new construction

(G-1277)
TWIN FIDDLE INVESTMENT CO LLC
Also Called: T.F.I.
6020 S Greenwich Rd (67037-9205)
PHONE..................................316 788-2855
Lee Johnson, *Top Exec*
Graham Dorian, *Mng Member*
EMP: 20
SQ FT: 15,000
SALES (est): 616.8K **Privately Held**
SIC: 7992 5941 7999 5812 Public golf courses; golf goods & equipment; golf driving range; snack bar

(G-1278)
USP TECHNICAL SERVICES
7311 E 58th St S (67037-9359)
PHONE..................................310 517-1800
Leonard Van Snow III, *President*
Leslie Way, *CFO*
EMP: 14
SQ FT: 32,000
SALES (est): 845.1K **Privately Held**
SIC: 7363 3629 Engineering help service; electronic generation equipment

(G-1279)
VBC ENTERPRISES LLC
Also Called: Derby Plaza Theaters
1300 N Nelson Dr (67037-2649)
PHONE..................................316 789-0114
Cecil Boone, *Owner*
Beth Abel, *VP Opers*
Lori Armstrong,
EMP: 25
SALES (est): 1.3MM **Privately Held**
WEB: www.derbyplazatheaters.com
SIC: 7832 Motion picture theaters, except drive-in

(G-1280)
VIA CHRISTI CLINIC PA
Also Called: Palacio, Camilo H
1720 E Osage Rd (67037-2090)
PHONE..................................316 789-8222
Terry Peters, *Branch Mgr*
Camilo Palacio, *Med Doctor*
EMP: 16
SALES (corp-wide): 25.3B **Privately Held**
SIC: 8011 General & family practice, physician/surgeon; internal medicine, physician/surgeon
HQ: Via Christi Clinic, P.A.
3311 E Murdock St
Wichita KS 67208
316 689-9111

(G-1281)
WESTVIEW MNOR HEALTHCARE ASSOC
Also Called: Westview of Derby
445 N Westview Dr (67037-2228)
PHONE..................................316 788-3739
John Nicholas, *Administration*
EMP: 60
SALES (est): 3.5MM **Privately Held**
SIC: 8052 Intermediate care facilities

Dighton
Lane County

(G-1282)
1ST NATIONAL BANK OF DIGHTON
Also Called: FIRST NATIONAL BANK
105 E Long St (67839-5434)
P.O. Box 727 (67839-0727)
PHONE..................................620 397-5324
Mark Von Leonard, *President*
Harold W Hall Jr, *Chairman*
EMP: 11 **EST:** 1910
SALES: 2.2MM **Privately Held**
SIC: 6021 National commercial banks
PA: Dighton National Bancshares, Inc.
105 E Long St
Dighton KS 67839

(G-1283)
BRETZ INC
640 W Long St (67839)
P.O. Box 577 (67839-0577)
PHONE..................................620 397-5329
Russell Bretz, *President*
Martha Bretz, *Corp Secy*
Connie Bretz, *Vice Pres*
EMP: 10
SQ FT: 12,800
SALES: 1.4MM **Privately Held**
SIC: 5083 Agricultural machinery & equipment

(G-1284)
DIGHTON HERALD
113 E Long St (67839-5434)
P.O. Box 426 (67839-0426)
PHONE..................................620 397-5347
Jim Gardner, *Owner*
Barbara Gardner, *COO*
EMP: 5 **EST:** 1950
SQ FT: 2,500
SALES (est): 168.1K **Privately Held**
SIC: 2711 Newspapers, publishing & printing

(G-1285)
FEED-LOT MAGAZINE INC
Also Called: Feed-Lot Magazine Main Ofc
116 E Long St (67839-5434)
P.O. Box 850 (67839-0850)
PHONE..................................620 397-2838
Gregory Strong, *President*
Greg Strong, *Exec VP*
EMP: 5
SALES (est): 566.9K **Privately Held**
WEB: www.feedlotmagazine.com
SIC: 2721 Magazines: publishing & printing

(G-1286)
LANE COUNTY FEEDERS INC
16 W Road 230 (67839-5050)
P.O. Box 607 (67839-0607)
PHONE..................................620 397-5341
Larry Jasper, *President*
EMP: 50
SQ FT: 8,000
SALES (est): 6.6MM **Privately Held**
WEB: www.lanecountyfeeders.com
SIC: 0211 Beef cattle feedlots

(G-1287)
LANE COUNTY HOSPITAL (PA)
235 W Vine St (67839-5089)
P.O. Box 969 (67839-0969)
PHONE..................................620 397-5321
Donna Mc Gowan, *CEO*
EMP: 65
SQ FT: 46,673
SALES: 4.5MM **Privately Held**
SIC: 8062 8051 General medical & surgical hospitals; skilled nursing care facilities

Dodge City
Ford County

(G-1288)
ACCOUNT RCVERY SPECIALISTS INC
200 W Wyatt Earp Blvd (67801-4448)
PHONE..................................620 227-8510
Kecia Kesler, *Branch Mgr*
Terry Skinner, *Info Tech Mgr*
EMP: 15
SALES (corp-wide): 5.7MM **Privately Held**
SIC: 7322 Collection agency, except real estate
PA: Account Recovery Specialists, Inc.
3505 N Topeka St
Wichita KS 67219
620 227-8510

(G-1289)
ADM MILLING CO
1901 E Wyatt Earp Blvd (67801-7090)
P.O. Box 400 (67801-0400)
PHONE..................................620 227-8101
Ken Bailey, *Manager*
EMP: 23
SALES (corp-wide): 64.3B **Publicly Held**
WEB: www.admmilling.com
SIC: 2041 5153 Grain mills (except rice); grain elevators
HQ: Adm Milling Co.
8000 W 110th St Ste 300
Overland Park KS 66210
913 491-9400

(G-1290)
ADVANCED ORTHPDCS & SPRTS MED
2300 N 14th Ave Ste 104 (67801-2367)
PHONE..................................620 225-7744
Alexander Neel, *Owner*
EMP: 10
SALES (est): 468.7K **Privately Held**
WEB: www.docneel.com
SIC: 8011 Orthopedic physician

(G-1291)
AL MORRIS
Also Called: Wardrobe Cleaners
801 N 2nd Ave (67801-4412)
PHONE..................................620 225-5611
Al Morris, *Owner*
Jamie Morris, *Principal*
EMP: 10
SALES (est): 315K **Privately Held**
WEB: www.wardrobecleaners.com
SIC: 7216 Drycleaning collecting & distributing agency

(G-1292)
ALS MARSHFIELD LLC
3201 E Trail St (67801-9004)
P.O. Box 340 (67801-0340)
PHONE..................................620 225-4172
Zachary Taylor, *Branch Mgr*
EMP: 16 **Privately Held**
SIC: 8734 Food testing service
HQ: Als Marshfield, Llc
1000 N Oak Ave
Marshfield WI 54449

(G-1293)
APAC-KANSAS INC
11188 56th Byp (67801)
P.O. Box 668 (67801-0668)
PHONE..................................620 227-6908
Steve Collins, *Manager*
EMP: 27
SALES (corp-wide): 29.7B **Privately Held**
SIC: 1794 Excavation work
HQ: Apac-Kansas, Inc.
9660 Legler Rd
Lenexa KS 66219

(G-1294)
APPRAISAL OFFICE FORD COUNTY
100 Gunsmoke St (67801-4401)
PHONE..................................620 227-4570
Nancy Slattery, *Director*
EMP: 16
SALES (est): 517.9K **Privately Held**
SIC: 6531 Appraiser, real estate

(G-1295)
APRIA HEALTHCARE LLC
2600 Central Ave Ste 7 (67801-6211)
PHONE..................................949 616-2606
Jacquie Miller, *Branch Mgr*
EMP: 11 **Privately Held**
WEB: www.apria.com
SIC: 5047 Hospital equipment & furniture
HQ: Apria Healthcare Llc
26220 Enterprise Ct
Lake Forest CA 92630
949 639-2000

(G-1296)
ARROWHEAD WEST INC
231 San Jose (67801-2712)
PHONE..................................620 225-4061
Liz Demuth, *Manager*
Christopher Konda, *Technical Staff*
EMP: 25
SALES (corp-wide): 13.9MM **Privately Held**
SIC: 8331 Vocational rehabilitation agency
PA: Arrowhead West, Inc.
1100 E Wyatt Earp Blvd
Dodge City KS 67801
620 227-8803

(G-1297)
ARROWHEAD WEST INC (PA)
1100 E Wyatt Earp Blvd (67801-5337)
P.O. Box 1417 (67801-1417)
PHONE..................................620 227-8803
Steve Mead, *Ch of Bd*
Lori Pendergast, *President*
EMP: 20
SQ FT: 4,800
SALES: 13.9MM **Privately Held**
SIC: 8331 Vocational rehabilitation agency; sheltered workshop

(G-1298)
ARROWHEAD WEST INC
401 Edgemore St (67801-2456)
PHONE..................................620 225-5177
Jennifer Tasset, *Manager*
EMP: 10
SALES (corp-wide): 13.9MM **Privately Held**
SIC: 8331 8322 Vocational rehabilitation agency; individual & family services
PA: Arrowhead West, Inc.
1100 E Wyatt Earp Blvd
Dodge City KS 67801
620 227-8803

(G-1299)
B & B MOVIE THEATRES LLC
2601 Central Ave (67801-6200)
PHONE..................................620 227-8100
EMP: 18
SALES (corp-wide): 64.1MM **Privately Held**
SIC: 7832 Motion picture theaters, except drive-in
PA: B & B Theatres Operating Company, Inc.
2700 Ne Kendallwood Pkwy
Gladstone MO 64119
816 883-2170

(G-1300)
B&B WELDING
2945 E Trail St Lot 203 (67801-9059)
PHONE..................................620 253-1023
Melchor Baeza, *Principal*
EMP: 8
SALES (est): 88.7K **Privately Held**
SIC: 7692 Welding repair

(G-1301)
BANGERTER REBEIN PA
810 W Frontview St (67801-2231)
P.O. Box 1147 (67801-1147)
PHONE..................................620 227-8126
David Rebein, *Partner*
EMP: 11
SALES (est): 1MM **Privately Held**
SIC: 8111 General practice attorney, lawyer; corporate, partnership & business law; criminal law

(G-1302)
BANK AMERICA NATIONAL ASSN
619 N 2nd Ave (67801-4441)
PHONE..................................316 261-4242
Frank Garcia, *Branch Mgr*
EMP: 19
SALES (corp-wide): 110.5B **Publicly Held**
SIC: 6021 National commercial banks
HQ: Bank Of America, National Association
100 S Tryon St
Charlotte NC 28202
704 386-5681

(G-1303)
BANK OF WEST
400 W Frontview St (67801-2211)
PHONE..................................620 225-4147
Roberta Stauth, *Manager*
EMP: 10
SALES (corp-wide): 2.7B **Privately Held**
SIC: 6022 State trust companies accepting deposits, commercial
HQ: Bank Of The West
180 Montgomery St # 1400
San Francisco CA 94104
415 765-4800

(G-1304)
BATH & BODY WORKS LLC
2601 Central Ave Ste 2a (67801-6295)
PHONE..................................620 338-8409
Nita Walter, *Manager*
EMP: 17
SALES (corp-wide): 13.2B **Publicly Held**
WEB: www.bath-and-body.com
SIC: 5999 7231 Perfumes & colognes; facial salons
HQ: Bath & Body Works, Llc
7 Limited Pkwy E
Reynoldsburg OH 43068

(G-1305)
BECK SALES COMPANY
Also Called: P & R Supply Co
10860 Us Highway 50 (67801-6538)
P.O. Box 1735 (67801-1735)
PHONE..................................620 225-1770
Pat Beck, *President*
Patrick A Beck, *President*
Roxie Beck, *Vice Pres*
EMP: 7
SQ FT: 20,000
SALES (est): 1MM **Privately Held**
SIC: 3523 Barn, silo, poultry, dairy & livestock machinery

(G-1306)
BELL AND CARLSON INCORPORATED
101 Allen Rd (67801-7073)
PHONE..................................620 225-6688
Harold Dunn Jr, *General Mgr*
Dustin Agan, *Prdtn Mgr*
EMP: 35
SALES (est): 3.3MM **Privately Held**
WEB: www.bellandcarlson.com
SIC: 2426 5941 3484 Gun stocks, wood; sporting goods & bicycle shops; small arms

(G-1307)
BEST WSTN CNTRY INN & SUITES
506 N 14th Ave (67801-4000)
PHONE..................................620 225-7378
Bill Cunningham, *Owner*
EMP: 14
SALES (est): 606.1K **Privately Held**
SIC: 7011 Hotels & motels

(G-1308)
BHCMC LLC
Also Called: Boot Hill Casino and Resort
4000 W Comanche St (67801-8106)
P.O. Box 1497 (67801-1497)
PHONE..................................620 682-7777
Diane Giardine, *General Mgr*
Elsie Holz, *Purchasing*
Kari Casterline, *Marketing Mgr*
Jessi Rabe, *Marketing Staff*
Clark Stewart, *Mng Member*
EMP: 300
SALES (est): 17.8MM
SALES (corp-wide): 58.7MM **Publicly Held**
SIC: 7011 7999 Casino hotel; gambling & lottery services
PA: Butler National Corporation
19920 W 161st St
Olathe KS 66062
913 780-9595

(G-1309)
BLACK HILLS/KANSAS GAS
Also Called: Black Hills Energy
11142 Kliesen St (67801-7071)
PHONE..................................605 721-1700
EMP: 16
SALES (corp-wide): 1.7B **Publicly Held**
SIC: 4924 Natural gas distribution
HQ: Black Hills/Kansas Gas Utility Company, Llc
7001 Mount Rushmore Rd
Rapid City SD 57702

(G-1310)
BNSF RAILWAY COMPANY
804 E Trail St (67801-9003)
PHONE..................................620 227-5977
EMP: 50
SALES (corp-wide): 225.3B **Publicly Held**
WEB: www.billpurdy.com
SIC: 4011 Railroads, line-haul operating
HQ: Bnsf Railway Company
2650 Lou Menk Dr
Fort Worth TX 76131
800 795-2673

(G-1311)
BRAK-HARD CONCRETE CNSTR CO
Also Called: Brak-Hard Concrete Cnstr
10744 Marshall Rd (67801-6723)
P.O. Box 423 (67801-0423)
PHONE..................................620 225-1957
Lowell A Brakey,
EMP: 14
SQ FT: 3,400
SALES: 1.5MM **Privately Held**
WEB: www.brakhard.com
SIC: 1771 Concrete work

(G-1312)
BROCE MANUFACTURING CO INC
Also Called: Broce Manufacturing Fab Div
1460 S 2nd Ave (67801-6623)
PHONE..................................620 227-8811
Matt McMamara, *Manager*
EMP: 7
SALES (corp-wide): 15.2MM **Privately Held**
WEB: www.brocebroom.com
SIC: 3711 3531 3523 Motor vehicles & car bodies; aggregate spreaders; farm machinery & equipment
PA: Broce Manufacturing Co., Inc.
1460 S 2nd Ave
Dodge City KS 67801
620 227-8811

(G-1313)
BROOKDALE SENIOR LIVING COMMUN
Also Called: Sterling House of Dodge City
2400 N 14th Ave Ofc (67801-2370)
PHONE..................................620 225-7555
Connie Watkins, *Manager*
EMP: 23
SALES (corp-wide): 4.5B **Publicly Held**
WEB: www.assisted.com
SIC: 8051 Skilled nursing care facilities
HQ: Brookdale Senior Living Communities, Inc.
6737 W Wa St Ste 2300
Milwaukee WI 53214
414 918-5000

(G-1314)
BUILDING SOLUTIONS LLC
11106 Saddle Rd (67801-7353)
PHONE..................................620 225-1199
Brian Marshall, *Managing Prtnr*
Jordin Scott, *Controller*
Ryan Scott, *Manager*
Nancy Marshall,
EMP: 19
SALES: 950K **Privately Held**
WEB: www.bldgsolutions.net
SIC: 1522 1791 5211 7375 Residential construction; structural steel erection; roofing material; on-line data base information retrieval

(G-1315)
BUSTER CRUST INC (PA)
2300 E Trail St (67801)
PHONE..................................620 227-7106
Donald Hornung, *CEO*
Wayne Daubert, *Vice Pres*
Walter Ludt, *Officer*
EMP: 100 **EST:** 1959
SQ FT: 100,000
SALES (est): 14.6MM **Privately Held**
SIC: 3523 Farm machinery & equipment

(G-1316)
C & S MEDICAL CLINIC PA
2200 Summerlon Cir Ste A (67801-2905)
PHONE..................................620 408-9700
Marcia Snodgrass, *President*
EMP: 42
SALES (est): 3MM **Privately Held**
SIC: 8011 Clinic, operated by physicians

(G-1317)
CARGILL MEAT SOLUTIONS CORP
Also Called: Excel Beef
3201 E Hwy 154 (67801)
PHONE..................................620 225-2610
Dan Schnitker, *Branch Mgr*
EMP: 20

SALES (corp-wide): 113.4B **Privately Held**
WEB: www.excelmeats.com
SIC: 2011 Meat packing plants
HQ: Cargill Meat Solutions Corp
151 N Main St Ste 900
Wichita KS 67202
316 291-2500

(G-1318)
CARGILL MT LGSTICS SLTIONS INC
3201 E Hwy 400 (67801-8207)
P.O. Box 1060 (67801-1060)
PHONE..................................620 225-2610
Dan Snickster, *Manager*
EMP: 11
SALES (corp-wide): 113.4B **Privately Held**
WEB: www.exceltransportationinc.com
SIC: 4213 2013 2011 Contract haulers; sausages & other prepared meats; meat packing plants
HQ: Cargill Meat Logistics Solutions, Inc.
250 N Water St
Wichita KS 67202
877 596-4062

(G-1319)
CATHOLIC CHARITIES OF SOUTHWES
906 Central Ave (67801-4905)
PHONE..................................620 227-1562
Rebecca Ford, *Marketing Staff*
Kate Schieferecke, *Case Mgr*
Debbie Smith, *Exec Dir*
Marci Smith, *Director*
Gina Pack, *Admin Asst*
EMP: 11 **EST:** 1965
SALES: 1.1MM **Privately Held**
SIC: 8322 8699 Adoption services; charitable organization

(G-1320)
CENTERA BANK
2200 N 14th Ave (67801-2309)
PHONE..................................620 227-6370
Susan Otterstein, *President*
EMP: 10
SALES (corp-wide): 11.1MM **Privately Held**
WEB: www.centerabank.com
SIC: 6021 National commercial banks
PA: Centera Bank
119 S Inman St
Sublette KS 67877
620 675-8611

(G-1321)
CENTRAL STATION CLUB & GR
207 E Wyatt Earp Blvd (67801-4938)
PHONE..................................620 225-1176
Lee Mackey, *Principal*
EMP: 12
SALES (est): 333K **Privately Held**
SIC: 7997 Membership sports & recreation clubs

(G-1322)
CITY OF DODGE CITY
Also Called: Water Department
705 W Trail St (67801-5420)
P.O. Box 880 (67801-0880)
PHONE..................................620 225-8176
Corey Keller, *Branch Mgr*
EMP: 18 **Privately Held**
SIC: 4941 Water supply
PA: City Of Dodge City
806 N 2nd Ave
Dodge City KS 67801
620 225-8100

(G-1323)
CITY OF DODGE CITY
400 W Wyatt Earp Blvd (67801-4348)
PHONE..................................620 225-8186
Walter Hamm, *Branch Mgr*
EMP: 43 **Privately Held**
SIC: 4724 Travel agencies
PA: City Of Dodge City
806 N 2nd Ave
Dodge City KS 67801
620 225-8100

(G-1324)
CLARK SECURITY SERVICE
1701 Avenue C (67801-4516)
PHONE..................................620 225-6577
Jeff B Clark, *Owner*
EMP: 15
SALES: 150K **Privately Held**
SIC: 7381 Security guard service

(G-1325)
COAKE FEEDING CO INC
Also Called: Coake Feed Yards
1406 Highland Ter (67801-2362)
PHONE..................................620 227-2673
Richard Koenke, *President*
Stephanie Koenke, *Treasurer*
EMP: 10
SALES (est): 75K **Privately Held**
SIC: 0211 Beef cattle feedlots

(G-1326)
COMMUNITY FNDTION STHWEST KANS
208 W Wyatt Earp Blvd (67801-4427)
P.O. Box 1313 (67801-1313)
PHONE..................................620 225-0959
Pat Hamit, *Exec Dir*
EMP: 14
SALES: 2MM **Privately Held**
SIC: 6732 Charitable trust management

(G-1327)
COMMUNITY LIVING SERV
1100 E Wyatt Earp Blvd (67801-5337)
P.O. Box 1417 (67801-1417)
PHONE..................................620 227-8803
Lorie Tendergast, *President*
EMP: 216 **EST:** 2001
SQ FT: 4,000
SALES: 94.3K
SALES (corp-wide): 13.9MM **Privately Held**
SIC: 8322 Social services for the handicapped
PA: Arrowhead West, Inc.
1100 E Wyatt Earp Blvd
Dodge City KS 67801
620 227-8803

(G-1328)
COMPASS BEHAVIORAL HEALTH
Also Called: Area Mntl Hlth Cmnty Sprt Svc
3000 N 14th Ave (67801-2376)
PHONE..................................620 227-5040
Jim Kellie, *Managing Prtnr*
EMP: 24
SALES (corp-wide): 10MM **Privately Held**
SIC: 8093 8011 8099 Mental health clinic, outpatient; psychiatric clinic; medical services organization
PA: Compass Behavioral Health
531 Campus View St
Garden City KS 67846
620 276-6470

(G-1329)
COMPASS BEHAVIORAL HEALTH
Hwy 50 Byp (67801)
PHONE..................................620 227-8566
Michael Denton, *Manager*
EMP: 25
SALES (corp-wide): 10MM **Privately Held**
SIC: 8093 8322 8069 8049 Mental health clinic, outpatient; crisis intervention center; alcoholism rehabilitation hospital; clinical psychologist; psychiatric clinic
PA: Compass Behavioral Health
531 Campus View St
Garden City KS 67846
620 276-6470

(G-1330)
CONANT CONSTRUCTION LLC
10562 Us Highway 50 (67801-6526)
PHONE..................................620 408-6784
Quentin Conant, *Principal*
Craig Carson, *Project Mgr*
EMP: 10
SALES (est): 1.1MM **Privately Held**
SIC: 8742 Construction project management consultant

(G-1331)
COOPER ENTERPRISES (PA)
Also Called: South Drive In
911 S 2nd Ave (67801-5902)
P.O. Box 195 (67801-0195)
PHONE..................................620 225-4347
Ronald E Cooper, *Owner*
EMP: 17
SQ FT: 3,000
SALES (est): 1.1MM **Privately Held**
WEB: www.southdrivein.com
SIC: 7833 7832 Drive-in motion picture theaters; motion picture theaters, except drive-in

(G-1332)
COUNTY OF FORD
Also Called: Ford County Communications
100 Gunsmoke St Ste 38 (67801-4456)
PHONE..................................620 227-4556
Linda Smith, *Manager*
EMP: 18 **Privately Held**
SIC: 4119 Ambulance service
PA: County Of Ford
100 Gunsmoke St Ste 35
Dodge City KS 67801
620 227-4550

(G-1333)
COX COMMUNICATIONS INC
2012 1st Ave (67801-2623)
PHONE..................................620 227-3361
Pam Veatch, *Manager*
EMP: 12
SALES (corp-wide): 29.2B **Privately Held**
SIC: 4841 8748 5731 Cable television services; communications consulting; antennas, satellite dish
HQ: Cox Communications, Inc.
6205 B Pchtree Dnwody Rd
Atlanta GA 30328

(G-1334)
CRISIS CENTER OF DODGE CITY
605 Central Ave (67801-4942)
P.O. Box 1173 (67801-1173)
PHONE..................................620 225-6987
Tammie West, *Exec Dir*
Betsy Morin, *Director*
EMP: 10
SALES: 373.4K **Privately Held**
SIC: 8322 Crisis intervention center

(G-1335)
CROP QUEST INC (PA)
Also Called: CROP QUEST AGRONOMIC SERVICES
1204 W Frontview St (67801-2039)
P.O. Box 1715 (67801-1715)
PHONE..................................620 225-2233
Ron O' Hanlon, *President*
Kent Davis, *Division Mgr*
Tracy Smith, *COO*
Dwight Koops, *Vice Pres*
Chris McInteer, *Treasurer*
EMP: 11
SQ FT: 3,000
SALES: 14.6MM **Privately Held**
WEB: www.cropquest.com
SIC: 8748 Agricultural consultant

(G-1336)
CROTTS AIRCRAFT SERVICE INC
102 Airport Rd (67801-9350)
PHONE..................................620 227-3553
Leigh Crotts, *President*
Neil Crotts, *Vice Pres*
Patty Robler, *Treasurer*
EMP: 15
SQ FT: 40,000
SALES: 2MM **Privately Held**
WEB: www.crottsaircraft.com
SIC: 4581 Airport terminal services; aircraft servicing & repairing

(G-1337)
CRUSTBUSTER/SPEED KING INC (PA)
2300 E Trail St (67801)
P.O. Box 526, Spearville (67876-0526)
PHONE..................................620 227-7106
Donald Hornung, *President*
Wayne Daubert, *Vice Pres*
Christian Hornung, *Safety Mgr*
Jennifer Toland, *Purch Agent*
Walter Ludt, *Treasurer*
EMP: 100
SQ FT: 115,000
SALES (est): 40.6MM **Privately Held**
WEB: www.crustbuster.com
SIC: 5083 Farm equipment parts & supplies; agricultural machinery & equipment

(G-1338)
CURTIS MACHINE COMPANY INC
Also Called: Manufacturing
4209 Jayhawk Dr (67801-7008)
P.O. Box 700 (67801-0700)
PHONE..................................620 227-7164
Betty Jane Curtis, *CEO*
EMP: 70
SALES (est): 25.3MM **Privately Held**
SIC: 3566 3568 Gears, power transmission, except automotive; power transmission equipment

(G-1339)
DAVE TARTER
Also Called: H & R Block
710 3rd Ave (67801-4321)
P.O. Box 1148 (67801-1148)
PHONE..................................620 227-8031
Dave Tarter, *Owner*
EMP: 10
SALES (est): 369.2K **Privately Held**
SIC: 7291 Tax return preparation services

(G-1340)
DEE JAYS ENTERPRISES
Also Called: Artz Dee Jay Insurance Agency
10764 Us Highway 50 (67801-6528)
P.O. Box 787 (67801-0787)
PHONE..................................620 227-3126
Dee Jay Artz, *President*
EMP: 15 **EST:** 1981
SQ FT: 3,200
SALES (est): 2.1MM **Privately Held**
SIC: 6411 5094 5046 Insurance agents; jewelry; restaurant equipment & supplies

(G-1341)
DILLON COMPANIES INC
Also Called: Dillon's 00001
1700 N 14th Ave (67801-3413)
PHONE..................................620 225-6130
Moe Lang, *Branch Mgr*
EMP: 150
SALES (corp-wide): 121.1B **Publicly Held**
WEB: www.dillons.com
SIC: 5411 7384 5992 5461 Supermarkets, chain; photofinish laboratories; florists; bakeries
HQ: Dillon Companies, Inc.
2700 E 4th Ave
Hutchinson KS 67501
620 665-5511

(G-1342)
DODGE CITY BREWING CO LLC
701 3rd Ave (67801-4336)
PHONE..................................620 338-7247
Larry Cook, *Mng Member*
Sheri Cook,
EMP: 7
SQ FT: 3,888
SALES (est): 254.7K **Privately Held**
SIC: 2082 Beer (alcoholic beverage)

(G-1343)
DODGE CITY CONCRETE INC
1105 E Wyatt Earp Blvd (67801-5338)
PHONE..................................620 227-3041
George Tyler, *President*
Lyndell Mosley, *Treasurer*
EMP: 13
SQ FT: 2,400
SALES: 2MM **Privately Held**
SIC: 3273 5211 Ready-mixed concrete; masonry materials & supplies

(G-1344)
DODGE CITY COOPERATIVE EXCH (PA)
Also Called: Pride AG Resources
710 W Trail St (67801-5419)
PHONE..................................620 225-4193
Scott McNair, *President*

Larry Scott, *Corp Secy*
Tony Bleumer, *Vice Pres*
Matt Stafford, *Store Mgr*
Pat Vest, *Store Mgr*
EMP: 24 **EST:** 1915
SQ FT: 2,400
SALES (est): 41MM **Privately Held**
WEB: www.dodgecitycoop.com
SIC: 5251 5541 4221 5153 Hardware; filling stations, gasoline; grain elevator, storage only; grains; general automotive repair shops

(G-1345)
DODGE CITY COOPERATIVE EXCH
708 W Trail St (67801-5419)
PHONE....................620 227-8671
Gerald Kemmerer, *Manager*
EMP: 10
SALES (corp-wide): 41MM **Privately Held**
WEB: www.dodgecitycoop.com
SIC: 5191 5261 Farm supplies; fertilizer
PA: Dodge City Cooperative Exchange
710 W Trail St
Dodge City KS 67801
620 225-4193

(G-1346)
DODGE CITY COUNTRY CLUB
1900 Country Club Dr (67801-6402)
P.O. Box 879 (67801-0879)
PHONE....................620 225-5231
Leslee Lomas, *President*
Renee Ricke-, *General Mgr*
Ethan Swartzman, *Superintendent*
EMP: 35 **EST:** 1916
SALES: 978.4K **Privately Held**
WEB: www.dccountryclub.com
SIC: 7997 Country club, membership; golf club, membership; swimming club, membership; tennis club, membership

(G-1347)
DODGE CITY DENTAL
2300 N 14th Ave Ste 202 (67801-2367)
PHONE....................620 225-2650
Bruce Johnston DDS, *Partner*
EMP: 17
SALES (est): 1.2MM **Privately Held**
SIC: 8021 Dentists' office

(G-1348)
DODGE CITY INTERNATIONAL INC (PA)
2201 E Wyatt Earp Blvd (67801-7016)
P.O. Box 1719 (67801-1719)
PHONE....................620 225-4177
Jim Kerschen, *President*
Mark Holderness, *Vice Pres*
EMP: 25
SQ FT: 22,000
SALES (est): 9.9MM **Privately Held**
WEB: www.dodgecityinternational.com
SIC: 5511 5531 7538 4785 Trucks, tractors & trailers: new & used; automobile & truck equipment & parts; general truck repair; inspection services connected with transportation

(G-1349)
DODGE CITY MED CTR CHARTERED (PA)
2020 Central Ave (67801-6411)
P.O. Box 1000 (67801-1000)
PHONE....................620 227-8506
Dr Mladen Perak, *President*
Alok Shah, *President*
Amy Guhr, *Technology*
Arthur Dole, *Admin Sec*
Jean Dole, *Administration*
EMP: 125 **EST:** 1990
SQ FT: 60,000
SALES (est): 14.3MM **Privately Held**
SIC: 8011 Clinic, operated by physicians

(G-1350)
DODGE CITY PUBLIC LIBRARY
1001 N 2nd Ave (67801-4416)
PHONE....................620 225-0248
Frank Shipps, *Facilities Mgr*
Cathy Reeves, *Director*
Rosanne Goble, *Director*
Diedre Lemon, *Director*
EMP: 35
SALES (est): 1.1MM **Privately Held**
WEB: www.trails.net
SIC: 8231 8999 Public library; information bureau

(G-1351)
DODGE CITY SAND COMPANY INC
801 Lulu Ave (67801-9050)
P.O. Box 430 (67801-0430)
PHONE....................620 227-6091
Jim Coffin, *Owner*
EMP: 11 **EST:** 1945
SALES (est): 1.2MM **Privately Held**
SIC: 1442 Construction sand & gravel

(G-1352)
DODGE CITY VETERINARY CLINIC
1920 E Trail St (67801-9017)
P.O. Box 938 (67801-0938)
PHONE....................620 227-8651
Chad Kerr, *Partner*
Brock Kerr, *Partner*
Nels Lindberg, *Partner*
EMP: 11
SALES (est): 1.1MM **Privately Held**
SIC: 0741 0742 0752 Veterinary services for livestock; animal hospital services, pets & other animal specialties; boarding services, kennels

(G-1353)
DODGE CY HEALTHCARE GROUP LLC
Also Called: Western Plains Medical Complex
3001 Avenue A (67801-2270)
PHONE....................620 225-8401
William M Gracey, *Principal*
EMP: 13 **EST:** 2011
SALES (est): 370.6K
SALES (corp-wide): 713.4MM **Privately Held**
SIC: 8082 Home health care services
HQ: Legacy Lifepoint Health, Inc.
330 Seven Springs Way
Brentwood TN 37027
615 920-7000

(G-1354)
DODGE CY UNIFIED SCHL DST 443
Also Called: Usd 443
1000 N 2nd Ave (67801-4415)
PHONE....................620 227-1614
Rebecca Hermocillo, *Director*
EMP: 70
SALES (corp-wide): 60.8MM **Privately Held**
WEB: www.usd443.org
SIC: 8351 Head start center, except in conjunction with school
PA: Unified School District 443
1000 N 2nd Ave
Dodge City KS 67801
620 371-1028

(G-1355)
DODGE CY UNIFIED SCHL DST 443
2601 Central Ave Frnt (67801-6200)
PHONE....................620 227-7771
Barbara Wilson, *Manager*
EMP: 75
SALES (corp-wide): 60.8MM **Privately Held**
WEB: www.usd443.org
SIC: 8211 8071 Public elementary & secondary schools; X-ray laboratory, including dental
PA: Unified School District 443
1000 N 2nd Ave
Dodge City KS 67801
620 371-1028

(G-1356)
DODGE ENTEPRISE INC
Also Called: Travel Lodge
1510 W Wyatt Earp Blvd (67801-3351)
PHONE....................620 227-2125
Ying Ou, *Owner*
EMP: 25
SQ FT: 30,000
SALES (est): 970K **Privately Held**
SIC: 7011 5812 5813 Hotels & motels; restaurant, family: independent; night clubs

(G-1357)
EMBERHOPE INC
11200 Lariat Way (67801-7328)
PHONE....................620 225-0276
Michael Hoar, *Managing Dir*
EMP: 100
SALES (corp-wide): 8MM **Privately Held**
SIC: 8641 8322 8361 Youth organizations; youth center; residential care for children
PA: Emberhope, Inc.
900 W Broadway St
Newton KS 67114
316 529-9100

(G-1358)
ERVS BODY SHOP INC
1409 W Mcartor Rd (67801-6095)
PHONE....................620 225-4015
Ervie Smith, *President*
Leland Smith, *Assistant VP*
Robert Smith, *Assistant VP*
EMP: 12 **EST:** 1963
SQ FT: 6,000
SALES (est): 1.1MM **Privately Held**
SIC: 7532 7549 Body shop, automotive; towing service, automotive

(G-1359)
FIDELITY STATE BNK TR DDGE CY (HQ)
510 N 2nd Ave (67801-4438)
P.O. Box 1120 (67801-1120)
PHONE....................620 227-8586
Ben Zimmerman III, *President*
John Eisler, *Vice Pres*
Noel Gaucin, *Assoc VP*
Larry G Stoppel, *CFO*
Rhonda Ratts, *Technology*
EMP: 26
SQ FT: 26,000
SALES: 5.9MM
SALES (corp-wide): 899K **Privately Held**
SIC: 6022 State commercial banks
PA: The Fidelity Bank Corporation Dodge City Ks
510 N 2nd Ave
Dodge City KS 67801
620 227-8586

(G-1360)
FIRST DENTAL
2306 1st Ave (67801-2527)
PHONE....................620 225-5154
Paul Lemhkuhler, *Owner*
EMP: 25 **EST:** 2016
SALES (est): 133.5K **Privately Held**
SIC: 8021 Specialized dental practitioners

(G-1361)
FOLEY EQUIPMENT COMPANY
Also Called: Caterpillar Authorized Dealer
1600 E Wyatt Earp Blvd (67801-7003)
PHONE....................620 225-4121
Larry Cummings, *Sales Staff*
John Mullen, *Sales Staff*
Ken Davis, *Manager*
EMP: 50
SALES (corp-wide): 124.2MM **Privately Held**
SIC: 5082 General construction machinery & equipment
HQ: Foley Equipment Company
1550 S West St
Wichita KS 67213
316 943-4211

(G-1362)
FOSTER UNRUH INC
Also Called: John Deere Authorized Dealer
11311 Us Highway 50 (67801-7081)
PHONE....................620 227-2165
Dan Cammack, *President*
Bill Wall, *Treasurer*
Jeff Kippes, *Director*
EMP: 27
SQ FT: 63,500
SALES (est): 5.7MM **Privately Held**
SIC: 5083 5261 5571 Farm implements; farm equipment parts & supplies; irrigation equipment; lawn & garden equipment; all terrain vehicle parts and accessories

(G-1363)
FRONTLINE MANAGEMENT
Also Called: Trinity Manor
510 W Frontview St (67801-2213)
P.O. Box 788 (67801-0788)
PHONE....................620 227-8551
Babara Whitney, *Manager*
Kyle Hager, *Director*
Amy Lopez, *Director*
Angie Scott, *Nursing Dir*
Shawn Williams, *Food Svc Dir*
EMP: 80
SQ FT: 22,000
SALES (corp-wide): 8.5MM **Privately Held**
SIC: 8052 8051 Intermediate care facilities; skilled nursing care facilities
PA: Frontline Management
2668 Northpark Dr Ste 220
Lafayette CO 80026
303 952-9216

(G-1364)
GARCIA AND ANTOSH LLP
1401 Central Ave (67801-4604)
PHONE....................620 225-7400
Jesse Garcia, *Partner*
Peter Antosh, *Partner*
Morgan Koon, *Partner*
EMP: 10
SALES (est): 774.8K **Privately Held**
SIC: 8111 8748 General practice law office; business consulting

(G-1365)
GLAZERS BEER AND BEVERAGE LLC
1409 W Wyatt Earp Blvd (67801-4040)
PHONE....................620 227-8168
Bennett Glazer, *Branch Mgr*
EMP: 42
SQ FT: 1,500
SALES (corp-wide): 122.7MM **Privately Held**
SIC: 5181 Beer & other fermented malt liquors
PA: Glazer's Beer And Beverage, Llc
14911 Quorum Dr Ste 200
Dallas TX 75254
972 392-8090

(G-1366)
GOSSEN LIVINGSTON ASSOCIATES
100 Military Ave Ste 126 (67801-4916)
PHONE....................620 225-3300
William Livingston, *President*
EMP: 60
SALES (est): 2MM **Privately Held**
SIC: 8712 Architectural services

(G-1367)
GREAT WESTERN TIRE OF DODGE CY
200 W Frontview St (67801-2207)
PHONE....................620 225-1343
Dennis Schulte, *President*
Virginia Shulte, *Vice Pres*
Chris Shelt, *Manager*
EMP: 10
SQ FT: 4,500
SALES (est): 2.5MM **Privately Held**
SIC: 5511 7538 5014 Automobiles, new & used; general automotive repair shops; automobile tires & tubes

(G-1368)
GWALTNEY INC (PA)
Also Called: Diamond Roofing
100 E Mcartor St (67801-6631)
P.O. Box 37 (67801-0037)
PHONE....................620 225-2622
Kevin Gwaltney, *President*
EMP: 70
SQ FT: 15,000
SALES: 15MM **Privately Held**
WEB: www.gwaltney.com
SIC: 1761 Roofing contractor

(G-1369)
HARDROCK SAND & GRAVEL LLC
11170 106 Rd (67801-6752)
PHONE.................................620 408-4030
Kolt Huber,
EMP: 7 **EST:** 2004
SALES (est): 756.1K **Privately Held**
SIC: 1442 Construction sand & gravel

(G-1370)
HARRYS MACHINE WORKS INC
407 W Mcartor Rd (67801-6019)
PHONE.................................620 227-2201
Daniel Hubbell, *President*
Dan Cammack, *Vice Pres*
J B Galasco, *Vice Pres*
Bill Wall, *Vice Pres*
EMP: 9
SQ FT: 13,000
SALES (est): 919.1K **Privately Held**
SIC: 3599 7538 Machine shop, jobbing & repair; engine rebuilding: automotive

(G-1371)
HEFNER MACHINE INC
1108 S 14th Ave (67801-6120)
PHONE.................................620 225-4999
Wes Hefner, *President*
Cheryle Hefner, *Corp Secy*
EMP: 7
SQ FT: 1,500
SALES (est): 844.9K **Privately Held**
SIC: 3599 Machine shop, jobbing & repair

(G-1372)
HIGH PLAINS PUBLISHERS INC (PA)
Also Called: High Plains Journal
1500 E Wyatt Earp Blvd (67801-7001)
P.O. Box 760 (67801-0760)
PHONE.................................620 227-7171
Fax: 620 227-7171
EMP: 75 **EST:** 1945
SQ FT: 36,000
SALES (est): 14.5MM **Privately Held**
SIC: 2711 Newspapers-Publishing/Printing

(G-1373)
HILAND DAIRY FOODS COMPANY LLC
Also Called: Hiland/Steffen Dairy Foods Co
1103 E Trail St (67801-9062)
PHONE.................................620 225-4111
Rick Mongole, *Manager*
EMP: 11
SALES (corp-wide): 1.7B **Privately Held**
SIC: 5143 0241 Dairy products, except dried or canned; milk production
HQ: Hiland Dairy Foods Company., Llc
1133 E Kearney St
Springfield MO 65803
417 862-9311

(G-1374)
HIPLAINS FARM EQUIPMENT INC
1509 S 2nd Ave (67801-6626)
PHONE.................................620 225-0064
Kenneth Schulte, *President*
Robert Schnewiess, *Treasurer*
Kenneth Rueb, *Admin Sec*
EMP: 12
SQ FT: 8,400
SALES (est): 2.6MM **Privately Held**
WEB: www.hiplainsfarm.com
SIC: 5083 Agricultural machinery & equipment

(G-1375)
HOSPICE OF THE PRAIRIE INC
Also Called: HOSPICE OF THE PRAIRIE AND HOM
200 4th Cir (67801-2400)
P.O. Box 1298 (67801-1298)
PHONE.................................620 227-7209
Leah Friedrick, *Treasurer*
Julie Pinkerton, *Exec Dir*
EMP: 22
SALES: 2.5MM **Privately Held**
WEB: www.hospiceoftheprairie.com
SIC: 8052 Personal care facility

(G-1376)
HOWELL COUNTRY FEEDERS LLC
10256 Us Highway 50 (67801-6561)
P.O. Box 1661 (67801-1661)
PHONE.................................620 227-6612
Mark Fischer, *Mng Member*
EMP: 22
SQ FT: 864
SALES (est): 2.6MM **Privately Held**
SIC: 0211 Beef cattle feedlots

(G-1377)
HUFFORD HOUSE
11200 Lariat Way (67801-7328)
PHONE.................................620 225-0276
Michael Hoar, *President*
Randy Wilson, *Principal*
EMP: 65
SALES (est): 441.1K **Privately Held**
SIC: 8361 Residential care for children

(G-1378)
INN HAMPTON AND SUITES
4002 W Comanche St (67801-8106)
P.O. Box 1421 (67801-1421)
PHONE.................................620 225-0000
Amee Shah, *General Mgr*
EMP: 15
SALES (est): 796.4K **Privately Held**
SIC: 7011 Hotels & motels

(G-1379)
J & J POWERLINE CONTRACTORS
2716 Butter And Egg Rd (67801-9048)
P.O. Box 861 (67801-0861)
PHONE.................................620 227-2467
James A Abel, *President*
Jennifer Abel, *Corp Secy*
EMP: 21
SALES (est): 1.9MM **Privately Held**
SIC: 1623 Electric power line construction; telephone & communication line construction

(G-1380)
J-A-G CONSTRUCTION COMPANY (PA)
11257 109 Rd (67801-6730)
P.O. Box 1493 (67801-1493)
PHONE.................................620 225-0061
James A Coffin, *President*
Meggan Starks, *General Mgr*
Mark Green, *Vice Pres*
Scott Reiderer, *Vice Pres*
Ken Braley, *Manager*
EMP: 140
SQ FT: 23,520
SALES (est): 32.8MM **Privately Held**
WEB: www.jagconstruction.com
SIC: 1542 3273 Commercial & office building, new construction; ready-mixed concrete

(G-1381)
J-A-G CONSTRUCTION COMPANY
Also Called: J A G II Construction
108 N 14th Ave Ste E (67801-5547)
P.O. Box 1087 (67801-1087)
PHONE.................................620 225-0061
Brian Marshall, *Manager*
EMP: 45
SALES (corp-wide): 32.8MM **Privately Held**
WEB: www.jagconstruction.com
SIC: 1542 3273 Nonresidential construction; ready-mixed concrete
PA: J-A-G Construction Company
11257 109 Rd
Dodge City KS 67801
620 225-0061

(G-1382)
JANKI INC
Also Called: La Quinta
2400 W Wyatt Earp Blvd (67801-3042)
PHONE.................................620 225-7373
Kanti Patel, *Treasurer*
Wilson Marmar, *Admin Sec*
EMP: 15
SALES (est): 698.1K **Privately Held**
SIC: 7011 5812 Hotels; ethnic food restaurants

(G-1383)
JOHNS BODY SHOP INC
110 W Beeson Rd (67801-5910)
PHONE.................................620 225-2213
John Trabert, *President*
Shirley Trabert, *Systems Mgr*
EMP: 18
SQ FT: 90,000
SALES (est): 1.6MM **Privately Held**
WEB: www.johnsbodyshop.net
SIC: 7532 5521 Body shop, automotive; automobiles, used cars only

(G-1384)
KANEQUIP INC
Also Called: Ford County Equipment
1451 S 2nd Ave (67801-6624)
P.O. Box 1176 (67801-1176)
PHONE.................................620 225-0016
Carl Horning, *General Mgr*
EMP: 12
SALES (corp-wide): 117MM **Privately Held**
SIC: 5083 5261 Farm implements; lawnmowers & tractors
PA: Kanequip, Inc.
18035 E Us Highway 24
Wamego KS 66547
785 456-2041

(G-1385)
KANSAS FEEDS INC (PA)
1110 E Trail St (67801-9062)
P.O. Box 1555 (67801-1555)
PHONE.................................620 225-3500
John Synar, *President*
EMP: 19
SQ FT: 1,872
SALES (est): 6MM **Privately Held**
WEB: www.kansasfeeds.net
SIC: 2048 Chicken feeds, prepared

(G-1386)
KANSAS GENEALOGICAL SOCIE
2601 Central Ave Ste 17b (67801-6212)
PHONE.................................620 225-1951
Betty Herrman, *Director*
EMP: 20 **EST:** 1996
SALES (est): 281.1K **Privately Held**
SIC: 8412 Historical society

(G-1387)
KANSAS LEGAL SERVICES INC
701 E Comanche Ln Ste F (67801-4500)
PHONE.................................620 227-7349
Shirley Calvin, *Director*
EMP: 33
SALES (corp-wide): 7MM **Privately Held**
SIC: 8111 Legal aid service
PA: Kansas Legal Services, Inc
712 S Kansas Ave Ste 200
Topeka KS 66603
785 354-8531

(G-1388)
KELLY S HENRICHS DDS
Also Called: Medical Heights Dental Center
100 W Ross Blvd Ste 2c (67801-7217)
PHONE.................................620 225-6555
Kelly Henrichs, *Owner*
EMP: 11
SALES (est): 696.3K **Privately Held**
SIC: 8021 Dentists' office

(G-1389)
KENNEDY MC KEE AND COMPANY LLP
Also Called: McKee, Richard W CPA
1100 W Frontview St (67801-2037)
P.O. Box 1477 (67801-1477)
PHONE.................................620 227-3135
Dick Mc Kee, *Partner*
James Kennedy, *Partner*
Robert Niedart, *Partner*
Rick Shirley, *Partner*
Amanda Wasson, *Accountant*
EMP: 16
SALES (est): 1.3MM **Privately Held**
WEB: www.kmc-cpa.com
SIC: 8721 Payroll accounting service; certified public accountant

(G-1390)
KEY OFFICE PRODUCTS INC (PA)
108 W Plaza Ave (67801-2513)
P.O. Box 1393 (67801-1393)
PHONE.................................620 227-2101
Kelly King, *President*
EMP: 5
SALES (est): 2.1MM **Privately Held**
SIC: 5112 2752 5044 Office supplies; commercial printing, lithographic; copying equipment

(G-1391)
KINDSVATER INC
Also Called: Kindsvater Truck Lines
2301 E Trail St (67801-9023)
P.O. Box 1027 (67801-1027)
PHONE.................................620 227-6191
Thomas Kindsvater, *President*
Dennis Kindsvater, *Vice Pres*
EMP: 60 **EST:** 1960
SALES (est): 10.3MM **Privately Held**
WEB: www.kindsvater.com
SIC: 4213 Trucking, except local

(G-1392)
KIRBY MEAT CO INC
2501 E Wyatt Earp Blvd (67801-7038)
P.O. Box 1700 (67801-1700)
PHONE.................................620 225-0031
Tim Kirby, *President*
Linda Kirby, *Admin Sec*
EMP: 8
SQ FT: 9,500
SALES (est): 811K **Privately Held**
SIC: 2011 Beef products from beef slaughtered on site

(G-1393)
KITCHENS INC
2301 W Frontview St (67801-9586)
P.O. Box 876 (67801-0876)
PHONE.................................620 225-0208
Scott Bogner, *President*
Karen Konnesky, *Corp Secy*
EMP: 12 **EST:** 1973
SQ FT: 12,600
SALES (est): 1.8MM **Privately Held**
SIC: 2434 Wood kitchen cabinets

(G-1394)
KOCH FERTILIZER LLC
11559 Us Highway 50 (67801-7010)
PHONE.................................620 227-8631
Steve Packebush,
EMP: 27
SALES (corp-wide): 40.6B **Privately Held**
SIC: 2873 5169 2813 Nitrogenous fertilizers; chemicals & allied products; industrial gases
HQ: Koch Fertilizer, Llc
4111 E 37th St N
Wichita KS 67220
316 828-5010

(G-1395)
KOCH INDUSTRIES INC
11559 Us Highway 50 (67801-7010)
PHONE.................................620 227-8631
Gary Lerock, *Systems Staff*
EMP: 41
SALES (corp-wide): 40.6B **Privately Held**
WEB: www.kochind.com
SIC: 5191 5261 2873 Fertilizers & agricultural chemicals; fertilizer; nitrogenous fertilizers
PA: Koch Industries, Inc.
4111 E 37th St N
Wichita KS 67220
316 828-5500

(G-1396)
LEGENDS PRINTING & GRAPHICS
901 N 2nd Ave (67801-4414)
P.O. Box 1563 (67801-1563)
PHONE.................................620 225-0020
Robert Hughes, *President*
Sonya Hughes, *Corp Secy*
EMP: 8 **EST:** 1981
SQ FT: 6,100

SALES (est): 570K Privately Held
WEB: www.legendsofdodgecity.com
SIC: 2752 7336 Commercial printing, offset; graphic arts & related design

(G-1397)
LEISURE HOTEL CORPORATION
Also Called: Super 8 Motel
1708 W Wyatt Earp Blvd (67801-3256)
PHONE....620 225-3924
Ana Bhuyia, *Manager*
EMP: 16
SALES (corp-wide): 6.9MM Privately Held
SIC: 7011 7021 Hotels & motels; lodging house, except organization
PA: Leisure Hotel Corporation
8725 Rosehill Rd Ste 300
Lenexa KS 66215
913 905-1460

(G-1398)
LEISURE HOTEL CORPORATION
Also Called: Holiday Inn
2320 W Wyatt Earp Blvd (67801-3040)
PHONE....620 227-5000
Joe Schaid, *Manager*
EMP: 20
SALES (corp-wide): 6.9MM Privately Held
SIC: 7011 7389 7299 Hotels & motels; convention & show services; banquet hall facilities
PA: Leisure Hotel Corporation
8725 Rosehill Rd Ste 300
Lenexa KS 66215
913 905-1460

(G-1399)
LIBEL & RIPPLE DVM
Also Called: Veterinary Hospital
1007 E Trail St (67801-9013)
PHONE....620 227-2751
Davi Ripple, *Partner*
David Repple, *Partner*
EMP: 10 EST: 2001
SALES: 350K Privately Held
SIC: 0742 Animal hospital services, pets & other animal specialties

(G-1400)
M ROCKING RADIO INC
Also Called: K X X
2601 Central Ave Ste C (67801-6212)
PHONE....620 225-8080
Fax: 620 225-6935
EMP: 70 EST: 2007
SALES (est): 3.5MM Privately Held
SIC: 4832 Radio Broadcast Station

(G-1401)
MAUPIN TRUCK PARTS INC
Also Called: Maupin Western Star
Hwy 283 (67801)
P.O. Box 490 (67801-0490)
PHONE....620 225-4433
Jay Maupin, *President*
Dian Maupin, *Principal*
EMP: 50
SQ FT: 8,000
SALES (est): 8.2MM Privately Held
WEB: www.maupins.com
SIC: 5531 5013 Truck equipment & parts; truck parts & accessories

(G-1402)
MAX RE PROFESSIONAL INC
1206 W Frontview St # 202 (67801-2016)
PHONE....620 227-3629
Linda Casterline, *President*
EMP: 10 EST: 1992
SALES (est): 377.7K Privately Held
WEB: www.dodge.kscoxmail.com
SIC: 6531 Real estate agent, residential

(G-1403)
MEDICAL HEIGHTS MEDICAL CENTER
Also Called: Kye, Win
100 W Ross Blvd Ste 2a (67801-7217)
PHONE....620 227-3141
Aye M Win, *President*
EMP: 20
SALES (est): 2.4MM Privately Held
SIC: 8011 Medical centers

(G-1404)
MERRILL R CONANT MD
Also Called: Family Prctice Assoc Wstn Kans
120 W Ross Blvd (67801-2131)
PHONE....620 227-6550
Merrill Conant MD, *Partner*
R C Trotter, *Partner*
EMP: 20
SALES (est): 2.3MM Privately Held
SIC: 8011 General & family practice, physician/surgeon

(G-1405)
MIDWEST MIXER SERVICE LLC
1501 S 2nd Ave (67801-6626)
P.O. Box 1300 (67801-1300)
PHONE....620 225-7150
Andy Brown, *Partner*
Jody Klein,
EMP: 11
SALES (est): 1.9MM Privately Held
SIC: 3523 Farm machinery & equipment

(G-1406)
MIDWEST STAR EQUITIES LLC
Also Called: Nendels Inn
2523 E Wyatt Earp Blvd (67801-7038)
PHONE....620 225-3000
Dave Benneth,
EMP: 15
SQ FT: 35,000
SALES: 400K Privately Held
SIC: 7011 Hotels

(G-1407)
MORRIS COMMUNICATIONS CO LLC
Also Called: Dodge City Daily Globe
705 N 2nd Ave (67801-4410)
PHONE....620 225-4151
Debbie Eddy, *Branch Mgr*
EMP: 47 Privately Held
WEB: www.morris.com
SIC: 2711 2752 Newspapers, publishing & printing; commercial printing, lithographic
HQ: Morris Communications Company Llc
725 Broad St
Augusta GA 30901
706 724-0851

(G-1408)
MURPHY TRACTOR & EQP CO INC
Also Called: John Deere Authorized Dealer
10893 112 Rd (67801-6585)
P.O. Box 1760 (67801-1760)
PHONE....620 227-3139
Thomas Udland, *President*
Terry Stefan, *Manager*
EMP: 15 Privately Held
WEB: www.murphytractor.com
SIC: 5082 General construction machinery & equipment
HQ: Murphy Tractor & Equipment Co., Inc.
5375 N Deere Rd
Park City KS 67219
855 246-9124

(G-1409)
MURPHY USA INC
1907 N 14th Ave (67801-2304)
PHONE....620 227-5607
EMP: 16 Publicly Held
SIC: 5541 5411 2911 Gasoline service stations; convenience stores; petroleum refining
PA: Murphy Usa Inc.
200 E Peach St
El Dorado AR 71730

(G-1410)
NATIONAL BEEF PACKING CO LLC
2000 E Trail St (67801-9018)
P.O. Box 539 (67801-0539)
PHONE....620 227-7135
Carey Hoskinson, *Manager*
Scott Kellenberger, *Manager*
Gary Hersh, *Director*
EMP: 75 Privately Held
WEB: www.nationalbeef.com
SIC: 2011 2013 Meat packing plants; sausages & other prepared meats
HQ: National Beef Packing Company, L.L.C.
12200 N Ambassador Dr # 5
Kansas City MO 64163
800 449-2333

(G-1411)
NATIONAL WEATHER SERVICE
104 Airport Rd (67801-9350)
PHONE....620 225-6514
Larry Ruthi, *Branch Mgr*
EMP: 33 Publicly Held
SIC: 8999 9611 Weather forecasting; administration of general economic programs;
HQ: National Weather Service
1325 E West Hwy
Silver Spring MD 20910

(G-1412)
NEW CHANCE INC (PA)
Also Called: NEW CHANGE
2500 E Wyatt Earp Blvd (67801-7037)
P.O. Box 43 (67801-0043)
PHONE....620 225-0476
Dorise Unruh, *President*
Joan McCarthy, *CTO*
Peggy Cecil, *Exec Dir*
EMP: 32
SALES: 1.5MM Privately Held
WEB: www.newchance.org
SIC: 8093 8069 Rehabilitation center, outpatient treatment; alcoholism rehabilitation hospital; drug addiction rehabilitation hospital

(G-1413)
NICHOLSON VENTURES
11089 Whirlwind Rd (67801-6751)
PHONE....620 225-4637
Deketa Schuckman, *CFO*
EMP: 10
SALES (est): 847.1K Privately Held
SIC: 0191 General farms, primarily crop

(G-1414)
NORSE LLC
1009 E Trail St (67801-9013)
PHONE....620 225-0778
Chris Trayler, *Owner*
EMP: 27 EST: 2012
SALES (est): 1.2MM Privately Held
SIC: 1731 General electrical contractor

(G-1415)
O K TIRE OF DODGE CITY INC
1808 W Wyatt Earp Blvd (67801-3298)
PHONE....620 225-0204
Jeff Koehn, *President*
Michelle Koehn, *Treasurer*
EMP: 11
SQ FT: 7,500
SALES (est): 1.9MM Privately Held
SIC: 5014 7538 Tires & tubes; general automotive repair shops

(G-1416)
ORSCHELN FARM AND HOME LLC
Also Called: Orschelin Farm and Home 34
1701 N 14th Ave Ste D (67801-3494)
PHONE....620 227-8700
Eldon Glenn, *Manager*
EMP: 13
SALES (corp-wide): 822.7MM Privately Held
WEB: www.orschelnfarmhome.com
SIC: 5191 Farm supplies
PA: Orscheln Farm And Home Llc
1800 Overcenter Dr
Moberly MO 65270
800 577-2580

(G-1417)
PARKER HAFKINS INSURANCE INC
1712 Central Ave (67801-4507)
P.O. Box 176 (67801-0176)
PHONE....620 225-2888
Madonna Hafkins, *President*
EMP: 10
SALES (est): 705.5K Privately Held
SIC: 6411 Insurance agents, brokers & service

(G-1418)
PATRICK FRIESS LLP
1100 W Frontview St (67801-2037)
P.O. Box 1477 (67801-1477)
PHONE....620 227-3135
Patrick Friess, *CPA*
EMP: 12 EST: 2013
SALES (est): 38.5K Privately Held
SIC: 8721 Certified public accountant

(G-1419)
PEPSI-COLA METRO BTLG CO INC
811 E Wyatt Earp Blvd (67801-5332)
P.O. Box 1178 (67801-1178)
PHONE....620 227-8123
Terry Buehne, *Manager*
EMP: 21
SALES (corp-wide): 64.6B Publicly Held
WEB: www.joy-of-cola.com
SIC: 5149 Soft drinks
HQ: Pepsi-Cola Metropolitan Bottling Company, Inc.
1111 Westchester Ave
White Plains NY 10604
914 767-6000

(G-1420)
POS-T-VAC LLC
Also Called: Pos-T-Vac Medical
2111 W Wyatt Earp Blvd (67801-3143)
P.O. Box 1436 (67801-1436)
PHONE....800 279-7434
Andy Gesek, *President*
Debbie Roybal, *Credit Mgr*
Tina Giebler, *Director*
EMP: 17
SQ FT: 3,000
SALES: 2.2MM
SALES (corp-wide): 8.4MM Privately Held
SIC: 3842 Surgical appliances & supplies
PA: Fort Washington Pharma Llc
500 Office Center Dr # 400
Fort Washington PA 19034
800 279-7434

(G-1421)
PRESBYTERIAN MANORS INC
Also Called: Manor of The Plains
200 Campus Dr Ofc Ofc (67801-2706)
PHONE....620 225-4474
Charlotte Rathke, *Manager*
EMP: 26
SALES (corp-wide): 8.6MM Privately Held
SIC: 8051 Skilled nursing care facilities
HQ: Presbyterian Manors, Inc.
2414 N Woodlawn Blvd
Wichita KS 67220
316 685-1100

(G-1422)
PRIDE AG RESOURCES
708 W Trail St (67801-5419)
PHONE....620 227-8671
Gerald Kemmerer, *Owner*
EMP: 14
SALES (est): 1.9MM Privately Held
SIC: 5153 5052 Grain elevators; coal

(G-1423)
RELEVIUM LABS INC
500 Park St (67801-5409)
PHONE....614 568-7000
EMP: 13
SALES (corp-wide): 2.5MM Privately Held
SIC: 5047 5999 3845 Electro-medical equipment; medical apparatus & supplies; electromedical apparatus
PA: Relevium Labs, Inc.
4663 Katie Ln Ste O
Oxford OH 45056
614 568-7000

(G-1424)
RIDDLES GROUP INC
2601 Central Ave Ste 8 (67801-6212)
PHONE....620 371-6284
EMP: 79
SALES (corp-wide): 186MM Privately Held
SIC: 7631 5944 Jewelry repair services; jewelry stores

PA: Riddle's Group, Inc.
2707 Mount Rushmore Rd
Rapid City SD 57701
605 343-2226

(G-1425)
ROTO-MIX LLC (PA)
2205 E Wyatt Earp Blvd (67801-7016)
P.O. Box 1724 (67801-1724)
PHONE..................................620 225-1142
Rodney Neier, *President*
Brant Law, *General Mgr*
Mark Cooksey, *Vice Pres*
Myron Ricke, *Foreman/Supr*
Andrew Featherstone, *Project Engr*
◆ **EMP:** 70
SQ FT: 100,000
SALES (est): 21.5MM **Privately Held**
WEB: www.rotomix.com
SIC: 3523 Cattle feeding, handling & watering equipment

(G-1426)
SALLEE INC
Also Called: Dodge City Express
1201 E Trail St (67801-9069)
PHONE..................................620 227-3320
Martin Keim, *President*
Richard Schilling, *Vice Pres*
Jeff Rouse, *Manager*
Denis Cowley, *Admin Sec*
EMP: 75
SALES (est): 6.5MM **Privately Held**
WEB: www.salleeinc.com
SIC: 4212 4213 Local trucking, without storage; trucking, except local

(G-1427)
SALVATION ARMY
1100 Avenue E (67801-4844)
P.O. Box 14 (67801-0014)
PHONE..................................620 225-4871
Joaquin Rangel, *Branch Mgr*
EMP: 12
SALES (corp-wide): 2.2B **Privately Held**
WEB: www.salarmychicago.org
SIC: 8661 8699 Non-church religious organizations; charitable organization
HQ: The Salvation Army
5550 Prairie Stone Pkwy # 130
Hoffman Estates IL 60192
847 294-2000

(G-1428)
SENATE UNITED STATES
100 Military Ave Ste 203 (67801-4945)
PHONE..................................620 227-2244
EMP: 10 **Publicly Held**
SIC: 9199 8661 2711 ; Methodist Church; newspapers, publishing & printing
HQ: Senate, United States
111 Russell Senate Bldg
Washington DC 20510

(G-1429)
SERVI TECH INC (PA)
Also Called: Servi-Tech Laboratories
1816 E Wyatt Earp Blvd (67801-7091)
P.O. Box 1397 (67801-1397)
PHONE..................................620 227-7509
Greg Ruehle, *President*
Jeffrey McDaniel, *Business Mgr*
Dominic Hernandez, *Maint Spvr*
Jeff McDaniel, *CFO*
Monica Springer, *Corp Comm Staff*
EMP: 200
SQ FT: 20,000
SALES (est): 24.2MM **Privately Held**
WEB: www.servitechlabs.com
SIC: 8748 0721 0711 8731 Agricultural consultant; crop disease control services; irrigation system operation, not providing water; soil testing services; commercial physical research; medical research, commercial

(G-1430)
SHOROEDERS JIM SFTWR & VIDEO
Also Called: Schroeder's
1410 Circle Lake Dr (67801-2977)
PHONE..................................620 227-7628
Jim Schroeder, *Owner*
EMP: 14
SQ FT: 3,200
SALES (est): 1.6MM **Privately Held**
SIC: 5045 7379 Computer software; data processing consultant

(G-1431)
SOUTHWEST KS AGENCY ON AGING (PA)
236 San Jose (67801-2732)
P.O. Box 1636 (67801-1636)
PHONE..................................620 225-8230
Carol Klein, *Case Mgr*
Dave Geist, *Exec Dir*
David Geist, *Exec Dir*
EMP: 17
SQ FT: 3,000
SALES: 4.9MM **Privately Held**
WEB: www.swkaaa.org
SIC: 8322 Senior citizens' center or association

(G-1432)
SOUTHWEST KS COORD TRANS COUNC
1100 E Wyatt Earp Blvd (67801-5337)
P.O. Box 1417 (67801-1417)
PHONE..................................620 227-8803
Angelica Avila-Ochoa, *Treasurer*
EMP: 45
SALES: 879.4K
SALES (corp-wide): 13.9MM **Privately Held**
SIC: 4111 Local & suburban transit
PA: Arrowhead West, Inc.
1100 E Wyatt Earp Blvd
Dodge City KS 67801
620 227-8803

(G-1433)
SPARE TYME LLC
Also Called: Fun Center 24 Bowl
11150 Kliesen St (67801-7071)
PHONE..................................620 225-2695
Brenda Webb,
Dave Hewes,
Bob Pfannenstiel,
EMP: 16 **EST:** 1978
SALES (est): 777K **Privately Held**
SIC: 7933 Ten pin center

(G-1434)
SPECIAL TEE GRAPHICS
503 N 2nd Ave (67801-4439)
PHONE..................................620 227-8160
Steve Phannenstiel, *Manager*
EMP: 8
SALES: 500K **Privately Held**
SIC: 2759 Screen printing

(G-1435)
STATE OF KANSAS
100 Military Ave Ste 220 (67801-4945)
PHONE..................................620 225-4804
EMP: 411 **Privately Held**
SIC: 8742 Human resource consulting services
PA: State Of Kansas
300 Sw 10th Ave Ste 222s
Topeka KS 66612
785 354-1388

(G-1436)
SUNFLOWER BANK INC
2408 1st Ave (67801-2562)
P.O. Box 1240 (67801-1240)
PHONE..................................620 225-0086
Pat Harbert, *President*
Anita J Williams, *Exec VP*
Marlyn Redetzke, *Senior VP*
Kirk Manion, *Vice Pres*
Elaine Trenkamp, *Loan Officer*
EMP: 40
SALES (est): 6.9MM
SALES (corp-wide): 52.4MM **Privately Held**
SIC: 6021 National commercial banks
PA: Sunflower Holdings, Inc.
2090 S Ohio St
Salina KS 67401
785 827-5564

(G-1437)
SUPERIOR HOME IMPROVEMENTS LLC
11164 Kliesen St (67801-7071)
PHONE..................................620 225-3560
Gene Kirby,
EMP: 5
SQ FT: 10,000
SALES (est): 1.1MM **Privately Held**
SIC: 5211 2952 Siding; siding, insulating: impregnated, from purchased materials

(G-1438)
SWAIM FUNERAL HOME INC
1901 6th Ave (67801-2652)
PHONE..................................620 227-2136
Kevin S Morin, *President*
Kyle Kistler, *Director*
EMP: 12
SQ FT: 8,000
SALES (est): 941.6K **Privately Held**
SIC: 7261 Funeral home; funeral director

(G-1439)
TRACTOR SUPPLY COMPANY
2612 Central Ave (67801-6209)
PHONE..................................620 408-9119
EMP: 10
SALES (corp-wide): 7.9B **Publicly Held**
SIC: 5191 Farm supplies
PA: Tractor Supply Company
5401 Virginia Way
Brentwood TN 37027
615 440-4000

(G-1440)
TRUCK SALES INC
1305 Rath Ave (67801-6630)
P.O. Box 490 (67801-0490)
PHONE..................................620 225-4155
Kenny Snook, *President*
EMP: 10
SALES (est): 510K **Privately Held**
SIC: 7539 Automotive repair shops

(G-1441)
TUCSON TRANSFORMER & APPA
11075 Quaker Rd (67801-6731)
PHONE..................................620 227-5100
EMP: 17
SALES (est): 881.5K **Privately Held**
SIC: 8999 Services-Misc

(G-1442)
UNITED COMMUNICATIONS ASSN INC
1107 W Mcartor Rd (67801-6031)
P.O. Box 117 (67801-0117)
PHONE..................................620 227-8645
Todd Haufman, *President*
Jene Linnebur, *Manager*
EMP: 32
SQ FT: 8,000
SALES (est): 1.1MM
SALES (corp-wide): 11.2MM **Privately Held**
SIC: 4841 4813 Cable television services;
PA: United Telephone Association, Inc.
1107 W Mcartor Rd
Dodge City KS 67801
620 227-8641

(G-1443)
UNITED TELEPHONE ASSN INC (PA)
Also Called: United Wireless Communications
1107 W Mcartor Rd (67801-6031)
P.O. Box 117 (67801-0117)
PHONE..................................620 227-8641
Todd Houseman, *CEO*
Kendall Hopp, *General Mgr*
Jennifer Pachner, *CFO*
Mike Salmans, *Info Tech Mgr*
Elizabeth Neuschafer, *Telecomm Mgr*
EMP: 49 **EST:** 1952
SQ FT: 8,000
SALES (est): 11.2MM **Privately Held**
SIC: 4813 Telephone communication, except radio

(G-1444)
UNITED WEST COMMUNITY CR UN (PA)
1200 W Frontview St (67801-2039)
P.O. Box 1028 (67801-1028)
PHONE..................................620 227-7181
Tom Armstrong, *CEO*
Adrianne Melendez, *Opers Mgr*
Maribel Ultreras, *Loan Officer*
Betty Konrade, *Manager*
EMP: 19
SQ FT: 3,000
SALES: 3.5MM **Privately Held**
WEB: www.cudodge.com
SIC: 6061 Federal credit unions

(G-1445)
UNITED WRLESS CMMNICATIONS INC
1107 W Mcartor Rd (67801-6031)
P.O. Box 117 (67801-0117)
PHONE..................................620 227-8127
Craig Mock, *General Mgr*
Jeff Renner, *Manager*
EMP: 40
SALES (est): 1.6MM **Privately Held**
SIC: 4812 Cellular telephone services

(G-1446)
UNITED WRLSS ARINA MGRK CONF C
4100 W Comanche St (67801-8109)
PHONE..................................620 371-7390
Brett Hoffman, *Opers Staff*
Nancy Mooradian, *Sales Dir*
Steven Giannino, *Manager*
Lisa Killion, *Manager*
Sonja Streeter, *Manager*
EMP: 11
SALES (est): 703.9K **Privately Held**
SIC: 6512 4812 Nonresidential building operators; cellular telephone services

(G-1447)
VICTORY ELECTRIC COOP ASSN INC
Also Called: Victory Elc Cooperative Mkec
3230 N 14th Ave (67801)
P.O. Box 1335 (67801-1335)
PHONE..................................620 227-2139
Shane Laws, *Principal*
Ryan Miller, *Opers Staff*
Angela Unruh, *CFO*
Jessica Garcia, *Accountant*
Jerri Imgarten, *Marketing Staff*
EMP: 94 **EST:** 1945
SQ FT: 25,000
SALES: 68.9MM **Privately Held**
WEB: www.victoryelectric.net
SIC: 4911 Distribution, electric power

(G-1448)
WAITT MEDIA INC
Also Called: Kgno-Am/Kols-fm
2601 Central Ave Ste C (67801-6200)
PHONE..................................620 225-8080
George Demarco, *Manager*
EMP: 15
SALES (corp-wide): 70.2MM **Privately Held**
WEB: www.kqky.com
SIC: 4832 7313 Radio broadcasting stations; radio advertising representative
PA: Waitt Media, Inc.
1125 S 103rd St Ste 425
Omaha NE 68124
402 697-8000

(G-1449)
WASTE CONNECTIONS US INC
Also Called: Northend Disposal Service
1108 E Trail St (67801-9062)
PHONE..................................620 227-3371
Shawn Anderson, *Manager*
EMP: 26
SALES (corp-wide): 4.6B **Privately Held**
WEB: www.wcnx.org
SIC: 4953 Garbage: collecting, destroying & processing
HQ: Waste Connections Us, Inc.
3 Waterway Square Pl # 110
The Woodlands TX 77380

(G-1450)
WATER SPT RCREATION CAMPGROUND
500 Cherry St Ofc (67801-5626)
PHONE..................................620 225-9003
Pat Morgison, *Owner*
EMP: 10
SALES (est): 380K **Privately Held**
SIC: 7033 Campgrounds; recreational vehicle parks

▲ = Import ▼=Export
◆ =Import/Export

(G-1451)
WATERS INC
Also Called: True Value
310 W Frontview St (67801-2209)
PHONE..................................620 227-2900
Mike Kohler, *Branch Mgr*
EMP: 27
SALES (corp-wide): 49.8MM **Privately Held**
SIC: 5251 0781 0181 0811 Hardware; landscape services; nursery stock, growing of; tree farm; paint, glass & wallpaper
PA: Waters, Inc.
3213 Arnold Ave
Salina KS 67401
785 825-7309

(G-1452)
WEBER REFRIGERATION & HTG INC (PA)
11154 Kliesen St (67801-7087)
PHONE..................................620 225-7700
Michael Weber, *President*
Diana Weber, *Vice Pres*
Fred Stewart, *Admin Sec*
EMP: 15
SALES: 7.3MM **Privately Held**
SIC: 1711 Refrigeration contractor; warm air heating & air conditioning contractor

(G-1453)
WESSEL IRON & SUPPLY INC
803 E Trail St (67801)
P.O. Box 1149 (67801-1149)
PHONE..................................620 225-0568
John Wessel, *President*
Nancy Bogel, *Vice Pres*
Linda Burke, *Treasurer*
EMP: 15
SQ FT: 22,000
SALES: 5MM **Privately Held**
SIC: 5051 5093 Steel; ferrous metal scrap & waste

(G-1454)
WESTERN BEVERAGE INC
301 E Wyatt Earp Blvd (67801-5322)
P.O. Box 124 (67801-0124)
PHONE..................................620 227-7641
John Boegner, *President*
Joe Bogner, *President*
EMP: 50
SQ FT: 8,640
SALES (est): 11.8MM **Privately Held**
SIC: 5181 Beer & other fermented malt liquors

(G-1455)
WESTERN PLINS RGIONAL HOSP LLC
Also Called: Western Plains Home Health Ctr
3001 A Ave 334 (67801)
PHONE..................................620 225-8700
Norma Noland, *Manager*
EMP: 12
SALES (corp-wide): 713.4MM **Privately Held**
WEB: www.westernplainsmc.com
SIC: 8741 Hospital management
HQ: Western Plains Regional Hospital, Llc
3001 Avenue A
Dodge City KS 67801

(G-1456)
WESTERN PLINS RGIONAL HOSP LLC (DH)
Also Called: Western Plains Medical Complex
3001 Avenue A (67801-2270)
P.O. Box 1478 (67801-1478)
PHONE..................................620 225-8400
Scott Smith, *CEO*
Shawna Culver, *MIS Dir*
Amy Dunn, *Director*
Lisa Akers, *Hlthcr Dir*
Jennifer Imel,
EMP: 271
SALES: 42.7MM
SALES (corp-wide): 713.4MM **Privately Held**
WEB: www.westernplainsmc.com
SIC: 8062 General medical & surgical hospitals
HQ: Historic Lifepoint Hospitals, Inc.
330 Seven Springs Way
Brentwood TN 37027
615 372-8500

(G-1457)
WILROADS FEED YARD LLC
Also Called: Finest Beef
11449 Lariat Way (67801-6694)
PHONE..................................620 225-3960
Keith Bowman, *Mng Member*
Laura Bowman, *Mng Member*
EMP: 25
SALES: 1MM **Privately Held**
SIC: 0211 Beef cattle feedlots

(G-1458)
WILSON TRAILER SALES KANS INC
2730 E Trail St (67801-9041)
P.O. Box 297 (67801-0297)
PHONE..................................620 225-6220
Terry Summers, *Manager*
EMP: 11
SALES (est): 913.4K
SALES (corp-wide): 5.1MM **Privately Held**
SIC: 5012 5599 5511 Trailers for trucks, new & used; utility trailers; trucks, tractors & trailers: new & used
PA: Wilson Trailer Sales Of Kansas, Inc.
332 Deframe Ct
Golden CO 80401
303 278-1767

(G-1459)
WINNER CIR FEEDYARD DODGE LLC
11995 Quaker Rd (67801-6679)
PHONE..................................620 227-2246
Gene Carson, *Mng Member*
EMP: 10
SALES (est): 1.3MM **Privately Held**
SIC: 0211 Beef cattle feedlots

(G-1460)
WINTER FEED YARD INC
Ft Dodge Rd (67801)
P.O. Box 115 (67801-0115)
PHONE..................................620 225-4128
Kenneth Winter, *President*
Kathleen Winter, *Vice Pres*
EMP: 30
SQ FT: 7,000
SALES (est): 3.5MM **Privately Held**
WEB: www.winterfeedyard.com
SIC: 0211 Beef cattle feedlots

(G-1461)
WINTER LIVESTOCK INC
1414 E Trail St (67801-9014)
PHONE..................................620 225-4159
Brian Winter, *CFO*
EMP: 10
SALES (corp-wide): 27MM **Privately Held**
WEB: www.winterlivestock.com
SIC: 5154 Auctioning livestock
PA: Winter Livestock Inc
1028 W Cherry Ave
Enid OK 73703
580 237-4600

(G-1462)
WKI OPERATIONS INC
1301 Minneola Rd (67801-6608)
PHONE..................................316 838-0867
EMP: 14
SALES (est): 3.5MM **Privately Held**
SIC: 5511 5084 6159 Trucks, tractors & trailers: new & used; lift trucks & parts; finance leasing, vehicles: except automobiles & trucks

(G-1463)
WOLF & HATFIELD INC
2520 N 14th Ave (67801-2315)
PHONE..................................620 227-3071
David L Wolf Od, *President*
Robert Hatfield Od, *Vice Pres*
EMP: 13
SALES (est): 546.9K **Privately Held**
SIC: 8042 Contact lense specialist optometrist

Dorrance
Russell County

(G-1464)
GENERAL ELECTRIC COMPANY
19797 Winterset Ln (67634-9404)
PHONE..................................785 666-4244
Mark Feist, *Manager*
EMP: 1800
SALES (corp-wide): 121.6B **Publicly Held**
SIC: 8071 X-ray laboratory, including dental
PA: General Electric Company
5 Necco St
Boston MA 02210
617 443-3000

(G-1465)
PRO-BOUND SPORTS LLC
428 Hwy 40 (67634)
P.O. Box 44 (67634-0044)
PHONE..................................785 666-4207
Heddy Mahoney, *CFO*
Tom Mahoney,
EMP: 15
SALES (est): 1.2MM **Privately Held**
WEB: www.proboundsports.com
SIC: 3949 Basketball equipment & supplies, general

Douglass
Butler County

(G-1466)
DOUGLASS MEDICALODGES
619 S Us Highway 77 (67039-8321)
P.O. Box 458, Oxford (67119-0458)
PHONE..................................316 747-2157
Janice Baldridge, *Administration*
EMP: 40 **EST:** 2011
SALES: 1.7MM **Privately Held**
SIC: 8361 8093 8052 Residential care; rehabilitation center, outpatient treatment; intermediate care facilities

(G-1467)
MM DISTRIBUTION LLC
Also Called: Asphalt Sealcoating Direct.com
519 E 1st St (67039-9313)
P.O. Box 194, Lakeview AR (72642-0194)
PHONE..................................800 689-2098
Bradley Morris, *Principal*
▼ **EMP:** 5
SALES (est): 598.6K **Privately Held**
SIC: 2951 2952 Asphalt paving mixtures & blocks; asphalt felts & coatings

Downs
Osborne County

(G-1468)
BEVERLY ENTERPRISES-KANSAS LLC
Also Called: Downs Nursing Center
1218 Kansas St 2 (67437-1404)
PHONE..................................785 454-3321
Dave Hardy, *Branch Mgr*
EMP: 52
SALES (corp-wide): 393.8MM **Privately Held**
SIC: 8051 Skilled nursing care facilities
HQ: Beverly Enterprises-Kansas, Llc
1 1000 Beverly Way
Fort Smith AR 72919
479 201-2000

(G-1469)
BRUSH ART CORPORATION (PA)
343 W Highway 24 (67437-8800)
P.O. Box 217 (67437-0217)
PHONE..................................785 454-3415
Tim Brush, *CEO*
Douglas C Brush, *Ch of Bd*
Thomas Brush, *Vice Pres*
Heidi Doane, *Vice Pres*
EMP: 44 **EST:** 1962
SQ FT: 15,000
SALES: 11.5MM **Privately Held**
WEB: www.brushart.com
SIC: 7311 Advertising consultant

(G-1470)
BRUSH GROUP LLC
Also Called: Donlevy Lthograph/Sun Graphics
343 W Highway 24 (67437-8800)
P.O. Box 217 (67437-0217)
PHONE..................................785 454-3383
Ila Kay Brush,
Thomas Brush,
Timothy Brush,
Heidi Doane,
EMP: 56
SQ FT: 65,000
SALES: 11MM **Privately Held**
SIC: 2752 Commercial printing, lithographic

(G-1471)
DOWNS SENIOR CITIZENS INC
514 Morgan Ave (67437-2019)
PHONE..................................785 454-6228
Elinor Fink, *President*
Ida Niles, *Vice Pres*
Joan Garey, *Treasurer*
Florence Walter, *Admin Sec*
EMP: 11
SALES (est): 280K **Privately Held**
SIC: 8322 Senior citizens' center or association

(G-1472)
MILLER WELDING INC
354 W Highway 24 (67437-8800)
PHONE..................................785 454-3425
Dwayne Miller, *President*
Kathy Miller, *Treasurer*
EMP: 10
SALES: 100K **Privately Held**
SIC: 7692 7539 5599 5084 Welding repair; trailer repair; utility trailers; welding machinery & equipment; tractors, agricultural; welding on site

(G-1473)
THOMAS AND SONS TRUCKING LLC
240 Morgan Ave (67437-2008)
P.O. Box 4 (67437-0004)
PHONE..................................785 454-3839
Dallason Thomas,
Dawn Thomas,
EMP: 20
SALES: 4.2MM **Privately Held**
SIC: 4212 4213 Local trucking, without storage; refrigerated products transport

Durham
Marion County

(G-1474)
DONAHUE CORPORATION
946 290th (67438)
P.O. Box 126 (67438-0126)
PHONE..................................620 924-5500
James C Donahue, *President*
Joan M Donahue, *Treasurer*
Carol Klenda, *Admin Sec*
EMP: 20
SALES (est): 3.7MM **Privately Held**
SIC: 3523 Cabs, tractors & agricultural machinery; trailers & wagons, farm

(G-1475)
DONAHUE MANUFACTURING LLC
946 290th (67438)
P.O. Box 126 (67438-0126)
PHONE..................................620 732-2665
Doug Kjellin,
EMP: 13
SQ FT: 37,000
SALES (est): 2.2MM **Privately Held**
SIC: 3523 Trailers & wagons, farm

GEOGRAPHIC

Eastborough
Sedgwick County

(G-1476)
MARC GORGES
Also Called: Gorges Motor Co
15 N High Dr (67206-2018)
PHONE..................................316 630-0689
Marc Gorges, *Owner*
EMP: 40
SQ FT: 14,000
SALES (est): 852.5K **Privately Held**
SIC: 6512 7359 Commercial & industrial building operation; equipment rental & leasing

(G-1477)
MEDIA PARTNERS INC
15 E Douglas Ave (67207-1046)
P.O. Box 789762, Wichita (67278-9762)
PHONE..................................316 652-2210
Susan Bowers, *President*
Meghan Hageman, *Graphic Designe*
EMP: 13
SALES (est): 1.6MM **Privately Held**
WEB: www.mpiwichita.com
SIC: 7311 Advertising consultant

Easton
Leavenworth County

(G-1478)
COUNTRY CARE INC
515 Dawson St (66020-9200)
P.O. Box 279 (66020-0279)
PHONE..................................913 773-5517
Martha Hegarty, *President*
Tamara K O'Donnell, *Vice Pres*
Richard Whitlow, *Director*
EMP: 54
SALES: 2.6MM **Privately Held**
SIC: 8052 Personal care facility

Edgerton
Johnson County

(G-1479)
ARROWHEAD INTERMODAL SVCS LLC
32355 W 191st St (66021-9794)
PHONE..................................816 509-0746
Joshua Cooley, *Principal*
EMP: 10
SALES (est): 1.3MM
SALES (corp-wide): 9.4MM **Privately Held**
SIC: 8742 Management consulting services
PA: Illinois Transport, Inc.
20012 W South Arsenal Rd
Wilmington IL 60481
708 333-7510

(G-1480)
BNSF RAILWAY COMPANY
32880 W 191st St (66021-9715)
PHONE..................................913 893-4295
EMP: 59
SALES (corp-wide): 225.3B **Publicly Held**
SIC: 4011 Railroads, line-haul operating
HQ: Bnsf Railway Company
2650 Lou Menk Dr
Fort Worth TX 76131
800 795-2673

(G-1481)
CENTRAL BANK OF MIDWEST
405 E Nelson St (66021-2150)
PHONE..................................913 893-6049
EMP: 82
SALES (corp-wide): 4.1MM **Privately Held**
SIC: 6022 State commercial banks
PA: Central Bank Of The Midwest
609 Ne State Route 291
Lees Summit MO 64086
816 525-5754

(G-1482)
CLASSIC HEATING AND COOLG LLC
20944 Spooncreek Rd (66021-9477)
P.O. Box 3 (66021-0003)
PHONE..................................913 238-1036
Kent W Moritz, *Principal*
EMP: 10
SALES (est): 1.7MM **Privately Held**
SIC: 3585 Parts for heating, cooling & refrigerating equipment

(G-1483)
COLDPOINT LOGISTICS LLC
31301 W 181st St (66021-4506)
PHONE..................................816 888-7380
Heather Pfender,
EMP: 50 **EST:** 2016
SALES (est): 2MM **Privately Held**
SIC: 4731 Freight transportation arrangement

(G-1484)
HOME READERS INC
Also Called: Toll Free 1 877 841 7323
604 W Hulett St (66021-2312)
P.O. Box 336 (66021-0336)
PHONE..................................913 893-6900
Kathy Eble, *President*
EMP: 14
SALES (est): 599K **Privately Held**
SIC: 8322 Association for the handicapped

(G-1485)
INTERMODAL ACQUISITION LLC
Also Called: In-Terminal Services
32880 W 191st St (66021-9715)
P.O. Box 9019, Lawrence (66044-1919)
PHONE..................................708 225-2400
EMP: 266 **Privately Held**
SIC: 4789 Cargo loading & unloading services
PA: Intermodal Acquisition, Llc
8205 Cass Ave Ste 115
Darien IL 60561

(G-1486)
KUBOTA TRACTOR CORPORATION
30901 W 191st St (66030-8536)
PHONE..................................913 215-5298
Mike Jacobson, *Manager*
EMP: 13 **Privately Held**
SIC: 5083 4225 Tractors, agricultural; general warehousing & storage
HQ: Kubota Tractor Corporation
1000 Kubota Dr
Grapevine TX 76051
817 756-1171

(G-1487)
LANESFIELD SCHL HISTORIC SITE
18745 Dillie Rd (66021-9786)
PHONE..................................913 893-6645
Mindi Love, *Director*
EMP: 10
SALES (est): 169.8K **Privately Held**
SIC: 8412 Museum

(G-1488)
NETWORK CONSULTING INC
20265 Peppertree Rd (66021-9700)
PHONE..................................913 893-4150
Larry Alsup, *President*
EMP: 11
SALES: 900K **Privately Held**
WEB: www.ncikc.com
SIC: 8748 Telecommunications consultant

(G-1489)
SMART WAREHOUSING LLC (PA)
18905 Kill Creek Rd (66021-4501)
PHONE..................................913 888-3222
K Van Keppel, *Principal*
Erin Essman, *Business Mgr*
Traci Patterson, *Business Mgr*
Ed Hickert, *Vice Pres*
Tony Wasinger, *Vice Pres*
▲ **EMP:** 25
SQ FT: 800,000
SALES (est): 30.9MM **Privately Held**
WEB: www.smartwarehousing.com
SIC: 4225 General warehousing

(G-1490)
SPECTRUM BRANDS INC
31100 W 196th St (66021-4503)
PHONE..................................949 279-4099
EMP: 5
SALES (corp-wide): 3.8B **Publicly Held**
SIC: 3692 Primary batteries, dry & wet
HQ: Spectrum Brands, Inc.
3001 Deming Way
Middleton WI 53562
608 275-3340

(G-1491)
TRIUMPH STRCTRES - KANS CY INC (HQ)
31800 W 196th St (66021-4505)
PHONE..................................913 882-7200
Richard Moraski, *President*
Michael Deshaies, *President*
John M McMahon, *Director*
EMP: 73
SQ FT: 100,000
SALES (est): 20MM **Publicly Held**
WEB: www.ntihc.com
SIC: 3724 3769 Aircraft engines & engine parts; guided missile & space vehicle parts & auxiliary equipment

Edna
Labette County

(G-1492)
COMMUNITY NATIONAL BANK
Also Called: Edna Banking Center
100 Delware Ave (67342)
P.O. Box 250 (67342-0250)
PHONE..................................620 922-3294
Dave Jones, *Manager*
EMP: 15 **Privately Held**
SIC: 6021 National commercial banks
HQ: Community National Bank & Trust
14 N Lincoln Ave
Chanute KS 66720

(G-1493)
FIRST STATE BANK OF EDNA INC
100 N Delaware St (67342-4215)
PHONE..................................620 922-3294
Gary Cotterill, *President*
J David Jones, *Exec VP*
Jane Rhodes, *Vice Pres*
EMP: 21 **EST:** 1985
SALES (est): 3.9MM **Privately Held**
SIC: 6022 State trust companies accepting deposits, commercial

(G-1494)
JMAR CONSTRUCTION INC
627 7000 Rd (67342-9368)
PHONE..................................620 922-3690
Jim Maritt, *President*
EMP: 12
SALES (est): 764.9K **Privately Held**
SIC: 1521 1629 General remodeling, single-family houses; trenching contractor

Edwardsville
Wyandotte County

(G-1495)
BEAVER DAM HEALTH CARE CENTER
Also Called: Golden Living Center
749 Blake St (66111-1338)
PHONE..................................913 422-5952
Cindy Susienka, *CEO*
EMP: 99
SALES (corp-wide): 393.8MM **Privately Held**
SIC: 8051 Skilled nursing care facilities
PA: Beaver Dam Health Care Center
5220 Tennyson Pkwy # 400
Plano TX 75024
972 372-6300

(G-1496)
BEVERLY ENTERPRISES-KANSAS LLC
750 Blake St (66111-1339)
PHONE..................................913 422-5832
Glenn Hagen, *Manager*
EMP: 40
SALES (corp-wide): 393.8MM **Privately Held**
SIC: 8051 Convalescent home with continuous nursing care
HQ: Beverly Enterprises-Kansas, Llc
1 1000 Beverly Way
Fort Smith AR 72919
479 201-2000

(G-1497)
EARP MEAT COMPANY
Also Called: Earp Distribution
2730 S 98th St (66111-3507)
PHONE..................................913 287-3311
Donald C Earp, *President*
Thom Bear, *COO*
Vince Meighen, *Transptn Dir*
Scott Dreiling, *Project Mgr*
Doug Hudson, *Warehouse Mgr*
EMP: 250
SQ FT: 102,900
SALES (est): 204.6MM **Privately Held**
WEB: www.earpdistribution.com
SIC: 5142 5141 5113 Packaged frozen goods; groceries, general line; industrial & personal service paper

(G-1498)
EDWARDSLLE UNTD MTHDST DAYCARE
Also Called: Edwardsville United Methdst Ch
302 N 4th St (66111-1316)
PHONE..................................913 422-5384
Wayne Morrison, *Pastor*
Charles Munson, *Vice Pres*
EMP: 10
SALES (est): 234.6K **Privately Held**
SIC: 8661 8351 Religious organizations; child day care services

(G-1499)
EVAPTECH INC
2644 S 96th St (66111-3483)
PHONE..................................913 322-5165
Bill Bartley, *CEO*
John Ahern, *President*
Bret Calkins, *Business Mgr*
Robert King, *Business Mgr*
Darryl Miller, *Business Mgr*
▲ **EMP:** 52
SQ FT: 7,000
SALES (est): 50MM
SALES (corp-wide): 382.7MM **Privately Held**
WEB: www.evaptechinc.com
SIC: 3443 Cooling towers, metal plate
PA: Evapco, Inc.
5151 Allendale Ln
Taneytown MD 21787
410 756-2600

(G-1500)
FEDEX FREIGHT CORPORATION
9140 Woodend Rd (66111-1714)
PHONE..................................800 872-7028
EMP: 250
SALES (corp-wide): 69.6B **Publicly Held**
SIC: 4213 Contract haulers
HQ: Fedex Freight Corporation
1715 Aaron Brenner Dr
Memphis TN 38120

(G-1501)
GOLDEN LC EDWARDSVILL
751 Blake St (66111-1338)
PHONE..................................913 441-1900
Eric Hosler, *Principal*
EMP: 20 **EST:** 2010
SALES (est): 751.5K **Privately Held**
SIC: 8051 Skilled nursing care facilities

(G-1502)
HERFF JONES LLC
2525 Midpoint Dr (66111-8800)
P.O. Box D (66113)
PHONE..................................913 432-8100
John McNown, *Manager*
EMP: 100

SALES (corp-wide): 1.1B **Privately Held**
SIC: 2741 Yearbooks: publishing & printing
HQ: Herff Jones, Llc
4501 W 62nd St
Indianapolis IN 46268
800 419-5462

(G-1503)
ILLINOIS AUTO ELECTRIC CO
Also Called: Midwest Engine Warehouse
9630 Woodend Rd (66111-1704)
PHONE..................................913 543-7600
Bradley Day, *Branch Mgr*
EMP: 13
SALES (est): 895.3K
SALES (corp-wide): 110.5MM **Privately Held**
WEB: www.iaeco.net
SIC: 4225 Warehousing, self-storage
PA: Illinois Auto Electric Co.
2115 Diehl Rd
Aurora IL 60502
630 862-3300

(G-1504)
INX INTERNATIONAL INK CO
2647 S 96th St (66111-3484)
PHONE..................................913 441-0057
Matt Morrow, *Maint Spvr*
Chris Tusker, *Manager*
EMP: 51 **Privately Held**
SIC: 2893 5085 Printing ink; ink, printers'
HQ: Inx International Ink Co.
150 N Martingale Rd # 700
Schaumburg IL 60173
630 382-1800

(G-1505)
K C WOOD PRODUCTS
10651 Kaw Dr Ste 700 (66111-1128)
P.O. Box 13284 (66113-0284)
PHONE..................................913 422-3320
Steve Jones, *Owner*
EMP: 16
SALES (est): 708.6K **Privately Held**
SIC: 1751 Cabinet building & installation

(G-1506)
KINCAID COACH LINES INC (PA)
9207 Woodend Rd (66111-1769)
PHONE..................................913 441-6200
Currie Myers, *CEO*
Gary Callahan, *General Mgr*
Fran Tucker, *Manager*
EMP: 80
SQ FT: 4,500
SALES (est): 14.2MM **Privately Held**
SIC: 4131 Interstate bus line

(G-1507)
LANDWORKS INC
9317 Woodend Rd (66111-1709)
PHONE..................................913 422-9300
Courtney Welch, *President*
Jeffrey S Welch, *Vice Pres*
EMP: 40
SALES: 2.4MM **Privately Held**
WEB: www.landworks-inc.com
SIC: 0782 Landscape contractors; lawn services

(G-1508)
M H P MANAGEMENT SERVICES
10011 Woodend Rd (66111-1763)
PHONE..................................913 441-0194
Thomas J Horner Jr, *President*
Dana Horner, *Manager*
Deborah A Horner, *Admin Sec*
EMP: 30
SALES: 2MM **Privately Held**
SIC: 6531 Real estate managers

(G-1509)
MWI VETERINARY SUPPLY CO
2450 Midpoint Dr (66111-8803)
PHONE..................................913 422-3900
Jon Turner, *Branch Mgr*
EMP: 18
SALES (corp-wide): 179.5B **Publicly Held**
SIC: 5047 Veterinarians' equipment & supplies
HQ: Mwi Veterinary Supply Co.
3041 W Pasadena Dr
Boise ID 83705
208 955-8930

(G-1510)
NBH BANK
Also Called: Bank Midwest
110 S 4th St (66111-1306)
P.O. Box 13246 (66113-0246)
PHONE..................................913 441-6800
Lollie Davis, *Manager*
EMP: 13 **Publicly Held**
WEB:
www.bankmw.com+%22bank+midwest%22+%22lexington
SIC: 6022 State commercial banks
HQ: Nbh Bank
7800 E Orchard Rd
Greenwood Village CO 80111
720 554-6680

(G-1511)
OFFICEMAX INCORPORATED
2401 Midpoint Dr (66111-8803)
PHONE..................................913 667-5300
Pam Mask, *Branch Mgr*
EMP: 25
SALES (corp-wide): 11B **Publicly Held**
SIC: 5112 5021 Office supplies; office & public building furniture
HQ: Officemax Incorporated
6600 N Military Trl
Boca Raton FL 33496
630 438-7800

(G-1512)
OKONITE COMPANY
2631 S 96th St (66111-3484)
PHONE..................................913 441-4465
Bob Ryan, *District Mgr*
EMP: 10
SALES (corp-wide): 407MM **Privately Held**
WEB: www.okonite.com
SIC: 5063 Wire & cable
PA: The Okonite Company Inc
102 Hilltop Rd
Ramsey NJ 07446
201 825-0300

(G-1513)
PROTEC CONSTRUCTION & SUP LLC
108 S 9th St (66111-1327)
P.O. Box 13271 (66113-0271)
PHONE..................................913 441-2121
Jerry Q Lamberd, *Mng Member*
Ashley Milka, *Admin Sec*
EMP: 25
SALES (est): 1.8MM **Privately Held**
SIC: 1761 5033 Roofing contractor; roofing, asphalt & sheet metal

(G-1514)
S JACKSON SERVICE CENTER INC
10635 Kaw Dr (66111-1170)
PHONE..................................913 422-7438
Gary Jackson, *President*
Jane Jackson, *Vice Pres*
Scott Jackson, *Manager*
EMP: 17
SQ FT: 5,000
SALES (est): 2MM **Privately Held**
SIC: 5541 5411 7538 Filling stations, gasoline; convenience stores, independent; general automotive repair shops

(G-1515)
SOUTHERN GLAZER SPI KS
Also Called: Sgws of KS
1100 Blake St (66111-3824)
PHONE..................................913 745-2900
Jim Dorsey, *President*
David Zaudke, *Vice Pres*
Rian Watts, *Director*
▲ **EMP:** 140
SQ FT: 100,000
SALES (est): 29.6MM
SALES (corp-wide): 12.3B **Privately Held**
SIC: 5182 5181 Wine & distilled beverages; beer & other fermented malt liquors
PA: Southern Glazer's Wine And Spirits, Llc
1600 Nw 163rd St
Miami FL 33169
305 625-4171

(G-1516)
STANDARD MOTOR PRODUCTS INC
Champ Service Item Div
845 S 9th St (66111-1354)
PHONE..................................913 441-6500
Thom Norberry, *Principal*
Greg White, *Purchasing*
EMP: 375
SALES (corp-wide): 1B **Publicly Held**
WEB: www.smpcorp.com
SIC: 5013 3694 4226 4225 Automotive supplies & parts; automotive electrical equipment; automobile dead storage; general warehousing; motor vehicle parts & accessories; nonferrous wiredrawing & insulating
PA: Standard Motor Products, Inc.
3718 Northern Blvd # 600
Long Island City NY 11101
718 392-0200

(G-1517)
TOTAL ELECTRIC CONSTRUCTION CO
109 S 4th St (66111-1305)
P.O. Box 13247 (66113-0247)
PHONE..................................913 441-0192
Jim Leonard, *President*
EMP: 13
SQ FT: 10,000
SALES (est): 1.5MM **Privately Held**
SIC: 1731 General electrical contractor

(G-1518)
TOTAL ELECTRIC CONTRACTORS
9247 Woodend Rd (66111-1711)
P.O. Box 13247 (66113-0247)
PHONE..................................913 441-0192
Jim Leonard, *President*
EMP: 13
SALES: 1.5MM **Privately Held**
SIC: 1731 Electrical work

(G-1519)
TRUCK INSURANCE MART INC (PA)
10027 Woodend Rd (66111-1763)
PHONE..................................913 441-0349
Lucy Harrity, *CEO*
Donald F Beilman, *President*
John Stalder, *Production*
Pete Pomerenke, *Producer*
Betty Lockridge, *Admin Sec*
EMP: 17 **EST:** 1969
SQ FT: 5,200
SALES (est): 6.3MM **Privately Held**
WEB: www.truck-insurance-mart.com
SIC: 6411 Insurance agents; property & casualty insurance agent

(G-1520)
VAN BOOVEN LAWN & LANDSCAPING
10021 Woodend Rd (66111-1763)
P.O. Box 9377, Shawnee Mission (66201-2077)
PHONE..................................913 722-3275
Greg Van Booven, *Owner*
EMP: 10
SALES (est): 579.4K **Privately Held**
WEB: www.vanbooventree.com
SIC: 0782 Lawn services

(G-1521)
WHITE LAWN AND LANDSCAPE LLC
10953 Kaw Dr (66111-1147)
P.O. Box 11072, Kansas City (66111-0072)
PHONE..................................913 709-1472
Garrett White, *President*
EMP: 10
SQ FT: 5,000
SALES: 950K **Privately Held**
SIC: 0781 Landscape services

(G-1522)
WRAP FACTORY
10933 Kaw Dr (66111-1183)
PHONE..................................913 667-3010
EMP: 5
SALES (est): 434K **Privately Held**
SIC: 3993 Signs & advertising specialties

Effingham
Atchison County

(G-1523)
EXCHANGE NATIONAL BANK & TR CO
423 Main St (66023-4084)
P.O. Box 249 (66023-0249)
PHONE..................................913 833-5560
Brian Handke, *Branch Mgr*
EMP: 13
SALES (corp-wide): 16.6MM **Privately Held**
SIC: 6029 6022 6021 Commercial banks; state commercial banks; national commercial banks
HQ: Exchange National Bank & Trust Co
600 Commercial St
Atchison KS 66002
913 367-6000

(G-1524)
WHEATLAND CONTRACTING LLC
6204 246th Rd (66023-5151)
PHONE..................................913 833-2304
Stacie M Coder,
EMP: 10
SALES (est): 539.6K **Privately Held**
SIC: 1711 Plumbing contractors

El Dorado
Butler County

(G-1525)
ACKLIN CONSTRUCTION
3720 Ne 4th St (67042-8668)
PHONE..................................316 321-6648
Red Acklin, *Owner*
EMP: 10
SALES: 500K **Privately Held**
SIC: 1521 New construction, single-family houses; general remodeling, single-family houses

(G-1526)
AJ INVESTORS LLC
Also Called: Grizzly Bowl
307 S Haverhill Rd (67042-3220)
PHONE..................................316 321-0580
Wade Wilkinson, *CEO*
Kim Smith, *Director*
EMP: 18
SQ FT: 14,000
SALES (est): 928.4K **Privately Held**
SIC: 3949 Bowling alleys & accessories

(G-1527)
ALBERT G HOGOBOOM
Also Called: Hogoboom Oilfield Trckg Svcs
767 Oil Hill Rd (67042-3361)
PHONE..................................316 321-1397
Kathy Jack, *Owner*
Missy Jack, *Office Mgr*
EMP: 35 **EST:** 1956
SQ FT: 2,500
SALES (est): 5MM **Privately Held**
SIC: 4213 1389 Heavy hauling; oil field services

(G-1528)
APAC-KANSAS INC
5143 Sw Hwy 254 (67042)
PHONE..................................316 321-3221
John Thompson, *Branch Mgr*
EMP: 20
SALES (corp-wide): 29.7B **Privately Held**
SIC: 1751 Carpentry work
HQ: Apac-Kansas, Inc.
9660 Legler Rd
Lenexa KS 66219

(G-1529)
ASSOCIATED HOMECARE INC
113 S Main St (67042-3403)
PHONE..................................316 320-0473
Laurena Klein, *President*
EMP: 200
SALES (est): 2.4MM **Privately Held**
WEB: www.associatedoffices.com
SIC: 8082 8049 Home health care services; nurses, registered & practical

(G-1530)
ASSURED OCCUPATIONAL SOLUTIONS
111 W Ash Ave (67042-3401)
P.O. Box 783 (67042-0783)
PHONE..................................316 321-3313
Mike King, *Owner*
Monica Ross, *Director*
EMP: 10
SALES (est): 499.9K **Privately Held**
SIC: 8099 Health screening service; physical examination & testing services

(G-1531)
AUGUSTA L LAKEPOINT L C
1313 S High St (67042-3751)
PHONE..................................316 320-4140
EMP: 25
SALES (est): 1.1MM
SALES (corp-wide): 8.3MM **Privately Held**
SIC: 8051 Convalescent home with continuous nursing care
PA: Augusta L Lakepoint L C
901 Lakepoint Dr
Augusta KS 67010
316 775-6333

(G-1532)
AUTOMOTIVE SPECIALISTS INC
2150 W Central Ave (67042-3203)
PHONE..................................316 321-5130
Mitch Wolfe, *Owner*
EMP: 10
SALES (est): 500K **Privately Held**
WEB: www.automotivespecialists.com
SIC: 7549 7532 5521 Automotive maintenance services; body shop, automotive; pickups & vans, used

(G-1533)
B SCOTT STUDIO INC
1717 W Towanda Ave (67042-2353)
PHONE..................................316 321-1225
Scott Haines, *President*
Lisa Haines, *Corp Secy*
EMP: 5
SALES: 182K **Privately Held**
SIC: 8999 2759 Artist's studio; screen printing

(G-1534)
BARTON SOLVENTS INC
2601 Pioneer Dr (67042-4805)
P.O. Box 711 (67042-0711)
PHONE..................................316 321-1540
Dave Williams, *Branch Mgr*
EMP: 17
SALES (corp-wide): 157MM **Privately Held**
WEB: www.barsol.com
SIC: 5169 5172 5084 Industrial chemicals; lubricating oils & greases; printing trades machinery, equipment & supplies
PA: Barton Solvents, Inc.
1920 Ne 46th Ave
Des Moines IA 50313
515 265-7998

(G-1535)
BEAVER DAM HEALTH CARE CENTER
Also Called: Golden Living Centers
900 Country Club Ln (67042-4206)
PHONE..................................316 321-4444
Sheldon Klassen, *Branch Mgr*
EMP: 60
SALES (corp-wide): 393.8MM **Privately Held**
WEB: www.goldenven.com
SIC: 8051 Skilled nursing care facilities
PA: Beaver Dam Health Care Center
5220 Tennyson Pkwy # 400
Plano TX 75024
972 372-6300

(G-1536)
BEST CORPORATION INC
Also Called: ServiceMaster
225 N Main St (67042-2019)
P.O. Box 48639, Wichita (67201-8639)
PHONE..................................316 687-1895
Sam Lazarus, *Vice Pres*
EMP: 20
SALES (est): 266.7K **Privately Held**
SIC: 7349 Building maintenance services
PA: Best Corporation Inc
729 E Boston St
Wichita KS 67211

(G-1537)
BG PRODUCTS INCORPORATED
2415 Pioneer Dr (67042-4813)
PHONE..................................316 265-2686
EMP: 140
SALES (corp-wide): 76.3MM **Privately Held**
SIC: 2992 Lubricating oils & greases
PA: Bg Products, Incorporated
740 S Wichita St
Wichita KS 67213
316 265-2686

(G-1538)
BLACKBURN CONSTRUCTION INC
2200 W 6th Ave (67042-3177)
PHONE..................................316 321-5358
Bradley Clites, *President*
Terry Clites, *Vice Pres*
Scott Vanpatten, *Safety Mgr*
Brian Clites, *Treasurer*
John Hammer, *Manager*
EMP: 150
SQ FT: 3,000
SALES: 12.8MM **Privately Held**
SIC: 1629 Chemical plant & refinery construction
PA: C-Tech Industrial Group, Inc.
2200 W 6th Ave
El Dorado KS 67042

(G-1539)
BUCKEYE CORPORATION (PA)
Also Called: Aztec Oil Division
625 S Main St (67042-3519)
P.O. Box 1020 (67042-1020)
PHONE..................................316 321-1060
Charles V Cross, *Ch of Bd*
Rick Cross, *President*
Matthew Cross, *Corp Secy*
Barry Cross, *Vice Pres*
Lewis Jackson, *Buyer*
EMP: 8
SQ FT: 3,200
SALES (est): 8.9MM **Privately Held**
SIC: 5082 1311 Oil field equipment; crude petroleum production

(G-1540)
BUTLER COUNTY HEALTH SERVICES
Also Called: Lake Point Nursing & Rehab
1313 S High St (67042-3751)
PHONE..................................316 320-4140
Elizabeth L Heinrich, *Principal*
Warner Harrison, *Principal*
Kevin Unrein, *Principal*
Larry Wilkerson, *Principal*
Kari Einerson, *Human Res Dir*
EMP: 90
SQ FT: 12,000
SALES (est): 1.9MM **Privately Held**
SIC: 8051 8069 Convalescent home with continuous nursing care; specialty hospitals, except psychiatric

(G-1541)
BUTLER RURAL ELC COOP ASSN INC
216 S Vine St (67042-3424)
P.O. Box 1242 (67042-1242)
PHONE..................................316 321-9600
Richard Jimenez, *President*
Sarah Madden, *General Mgr*
Jeff Adams, *Vice Pres*
Ben Whiteside, *Vice Pres*
Cheryl Martin, *Opers Staff*
EMP: 31 **EST:** 1938
SQ FT: 12,000
SALES: 18.9MM **Privately Held**
SIC: 4911 Distribution, electric power

(G-1542)
C-TECH INDUSTRIAL GROUP INC (PA)
2200 W 6th Ave (67042-3166)
PHONE..................................316 321-5358
Bradley Clites, *President*
Brian Clites, *Corp Secy*
Terry Clites, *Vice Pres*
Tracy Clites, *Vice Pres*
Steve Springer, *Project Mgr*
EMP: 19
SQ FT: 6,000
SALES (est): 32.8MM **Privately Held**
SIC: 1629 Oil refinery construction

(G-1543)
CARLISLE HEATING & AC
1100 N Main St (67042-4336)
PHONE..................................316 321-6230
John Grange, *President*
Nancy Grange, *Corp Secy*
EMP: 10
SQ FT: 8,000
SALES (est): 1.4MM **Privately Held**
WEB: www.carlisleinc.net
SIC: 1711 1731 Warm air heating & air conditioning contractor; general electrical contractor

(G-1544)
CD&H INC
Also Called: Petro Chem Ref Pipeline Indust
2510 W 6th Ave (67042-3071)
P.O. Box 845 (67042-0845)
PHONE..................................316 320-7187
Colleen Harris, *Principal*
Michael Harris, *Opers Mgr*
EMP: 14 **EST:** 2014
SALES (est): 3MM **Privately Held**
SIC: 4212 1629 Garbage collection & transport, no disposal; dams, waterways, docks & other marine construction

(G-1545)
CDH ENTERPRISES
2000 W 6th Ave (67042-3119)
PHONE..................................316 320-7187
Colleen Harris, *Owner*
Darwin Harris, *Co-Owner*
EMP: 17
SALES (est): 870K **Privately Held**
SIC: 1521 Single-family housing construction

(G-1546)
COMMERCE BANK
100 N Main St (67042-2092)
P.O. Box 777 (67042-0777)
PHONE..................................316 321-1250
Stephen C Funk, *President*
Mark Utech, *Manager*
EMP: 50
SALES (corp-wide): 1.3B **Publicly Held**
SIC: 6022 State commercial banks
HQ: Commerce Bank
1000 Walnut St Fl 700
Kansas City MO 64106
816 234-2000

(G-1547)
COMMUNITY NAT BNK OF EL DORADO
301 N Main St (67042-2021)
P.O. Box 223 (67042-0223)
PHONE..................................316 320-2265
Colin Rowell, *President*
Stephen L Waite, *President*
EMP: 12
SALES (est): 1.2MM **Privately Held**
WEB: www.communitynational.net
SIC: 6111 Federal & federally sponsored credit agencies

(G-1548)
CONFAB INC
Also Called: Blackbird Maintenance
2200 W 6th Ave (67042-3166)
PHONE..................................316 321-5358
Tracy Clites, *President*
Bradley Clites, *President*
Brian Clites, *Corp Secy*
Terri Clites, *Vice Pres*
EMP: 20
SQ FT: 11,000
SALES: 2.3MM **Privately Held**
SIC: 1791 Structural steel erection

(G-1549)
CONSOCIATES GROUP LLC
116 W Pine Ave Ste 105 (67042-3457)
P.O. Box 352 (67042-0352)
PHONE..................................316 321-7500
Greg Chestnut, *Manager*
Michael Ward,
EMP: 12 **EST:** 2001
SALES (est): 450K **Privately Held**
WEB: www.consociates.com
SIC: 7349 Building maintenance services

(G-1550)
CONTINENTAL AMERICAN CORP
Also Called: Pioneer Balloon Company
2400 Pioneer Dr (67042-4812)
P.O. Box 251 (67042-0251)
PHONE..................................316 321-4551
Matt Wallsmith, *General Mgr*
Tom Douglas, *General Mgr*
Ned Zacharias, *Project Engr*
Shelli Bump, *Human Res Mgr*
Shelli Lewis, *Executive*
EMP: 200
SALES (corp-wide): 228.7MM **Privately Held**
WEB: www.qualatex.com
SIC: 3069 5092 3087 Balloons, advertising & toy: rubber; toy novelties & amusements; custom compound purchased resins
PA: Continental American Corporation
5000 E 29th St N
Wichita KS 67220
316 685-2266

(G-1551)
CORRECTIONS KANSAS DEPARTMENT
Also Called: El Dorado Correctional Fcilty
1737 Se Hwy 54 (67042)
P.O. Box 311 (67042-0311)
PHONE..................................316 321-7284
EMP: 71 **Privately Held**
SIC: 8744 9223 Correctional facility;
HQ: Kansas Department Of Corrections
714 Sw Jackson St Fl 3
Topeka KS 66603
785 296-3317

(G-1552)
COUNSELING CTR FOR BUTLR CNTY
Also Called: S Central Mental Health
524 N Main St (67042-2024)
PHONE..................................316 776-2007
Bill Johnston, *Manager*
EMP: 55
SALES (est): 2.2MM **Privately Held**
SIC: 8322 8069 Individual & family services; drug addiction rehabilitation hospital

(G-1553)
COUNTY OF BUTLER
Also Called: County Attorney
201 W Pine Ave Ste 104 (67042-2911)
PHONE..................................316 322-4130
Jan Satterfield, *Manager*
EMP: 14 **Privately Held**
WEB: www.andoverks.com
SIC: 8111 General practice attorney, lawyer
PA: County Of Butler
205 W Central Ave
El Dorado KS 67042
316 322-4300

(G-1554)
CURBS PLUS INC
205 Metcalf Rd (67042-3140)
PHONE..................................888 639-2872
Steve Rodman, *Vice Pres*
Darren Ehrlich, *Branch Mgr*
Wendy Jones, *Payroll Mgr*
EMP: 40 **Privately Held**

SIC: 3444 Sheet metalwork
PA: Curbs Plus, Inc.
8767 Alabama Hwy
Ringgold GA 30736

(G-1555)
DAVY HARKINS DVM
Also Called: El Dorado Animal Clinic
111 E Locust Ave (67042-3506)
PHONE..................................316 321-1050
Davy Harkins Dvm, *Owner*
Eric Del Mar, *Med Doctor*
EMP: 17
SALES: 554K **Privately Held**
WEB: www.eldoradoanimalclinic.com
SIC: 0742 Animal hospital services, pets & other animal specialties; veterinarian, animal specialties

(G-1556)
DEMO SALES INC
Also Called: Best Beverage
202 W 5th Ave (67042-1931)
P.O. Box 113 (67042-0113)
PHONE..................................316 320-6670
Donna Demo, *President*
Donald Demo, *President*
Daniel Demo, *COO*
Diana Dean, *Admin Sec*
Dianna Dean, *Admin Sec*
EMP: 11
SQ FT: 12,000
SALES (est): 2.2MM **Privately Held**
WEB: www.innovativeretailserv.com
SIC: 5181 Beer & other fermented malt liquors

(G-1557)
EL DORADO CLINIC PA
700 W Central Ave Ste 205 (67042-2186)
PHONE..................................316 321-2010
R W Proctor MD, *President*
EMP: 25
SQ FT: 1,500
SALES: 1.7MM **Privately Held**
WEB: www.eldoradoclinic.com
SIC: 8011 Clinic, operated by physicians

(G-1558)
EL DORADO INTRNAL MEDICINE LLC
700 W Central Ave Ste 201 (67042-2186)
PHONE..................................316 321-2100
H Richard Kuhns Jr, *President*
EMP: 15
SALES (est): 1.3MM **Privately Held**
SIC: 8011 Internal medicine, physician/surgeon

(G-1559)
EL DORADO LIVESTOCK AUCTION
Also Called: El Dorado Sales Company
2595 Se Us Highway 54 (67042-8614)
PHONE..................................316 320-3212
Billy Wyly, *President*
Jacqueline T Seeley, *Treasurer*
EMP: 25
SALES (est): 3.4MM **Privately Held**
SIC: 5154 Auctioning livestock

(G-1560)
EVERGY KANSAS CENTRAL INC
700 N Star St (67042-3937)
PHONE..................................800 383-1183
EMP: 12
SALES (corp-wide): 4.2B **Publicly Held**
SIC: 4911 Distribution, electric power
HQ: Evergy Kansas Central, Inc.
818 S Kansas Ave
Topeka KS 66612
785 575-6300

(G-1561)
FASTENAL COMPANY
2502 W Central Ave (67042-3278)
PHONE..................................316 320-2223
Travis Miller, *Branch Mgr*
EMP: 10
SALES (corp-wide): 4.9B **Publicly Held**
WEB: www.fastenal.com
SIC: 5085 Fasteners, industrial: nuts, bolts, screws, etc.
PA: Fastenal Company
2001 Theurer Blvd
Winona MN 55987
507 454-5374

(G-1562)
FLINTHILLS SERVICES INC (PA)
505 S Walnut Valley Dr (67042-9001)
PHONE..................................316 321-2325
Kathy Walter, *Exec Dir*
Gayle Tharp, *Exec Dir*
Seth Nesmith, *Director*
Amy Peterson, *Director*
EMP: 58
SALES: 3.9MM **Privately Held**
WEB: www.flinthills.kscoxmail.com
SIC: 8322 Social services for the handicapped

(G-1563)
FRIGIQUIP INTERNATIONAL INC
Also Called: Spikes Spider
3910 W Central Ave (67042-3476)
P.O. Box 813 (67042-0813)
PHONE..................................316 321-2400
George Lawson, *President*
▲ **EMP:** 9 **EST:** 1976
SALES (est): 1.5MM **Privately Held**
WEB: www.spikes-spiderusa.com
SIC: 5075 3714 3713 Automotive air conditioners; motor vehicle parts & accessories; truck & bus bodies

(G-1564)
GATEHUSE MDIA KANS HLDINGS INC
Also Called: El Dorado Times, The
114 N Vine St (67042-2028)
PHONE..................................316 321-6136
Ken Serota, *President*
EMP: 15 **EST:** 1919
SQ FT: 20,000
SALES (est): 1MM **Privately Held**
WEB: www.eldoradotimes.com
SIC: 2711 2752 2741 Newspapers, publishing & printing; commercial printing, lithographic; shopping news: publishing only, not printed on site

(G-1565)
H & R BLOCK
1430 W Central Ave (67042-2201)
PHONE..................................316 321-6960
Kristy Randall, *President*
Kristy A Randall, *Site Mgr*
EMP: 13
SALES (est): 287.3K **Privately Held**
SIC: 7291 Tax return preparation services

(G-1566)
HOLIDAY INN EXPRESS AND SUITES
3100 El Dorado Ave (67042-8014)
PHONE..................................316 322-7275
Sharon Wilkinson, *Owner*
Kim Smith, *General Mgr*
EMP: 15
SALES (est): 664.9K **Privately Held**
SIC: 7011 Hotels & motels

(G-1567)
HOLLYFRNTIER EL DORADO REF LLC
1401 Douglas Rd (67042-3674)
P.O. Box 1121 (67042-1121)
PHONE..................................316 321-2200
Michael C Jennings, *CEO*
Jeffrey Lewellen, *Superintendent*
Paul Luck, *Opers Staff*
Jason Lund, *Engineer*
Christopher Gammon, *Project Engr*
▲ **EMP:** 400
SALES (est): 175.7MM
SALES (corp-wide): 17.7B **Publicly Held**
SIC: 2911 Petroleum refining
HQ: Frontier Refining & Marketing, Llc
8055 E Tufts Ave Ste 525
Denver CO 80237
303 694-0025

(G-1568)
HOWARD ELECTRONIC INSTRS INC
974 Se Pioneer Rd (67042-8601)
PHONE..................................316 321-2800
Jerry Howard, *President*
Barbara Howard, *Corp Secy*
▲ **EMP:** 5
SQ FT: 3,000
SALES (est): 847.2K **Privately Held**
WEB: www.heinc.com
SIC: 3825 3669 Internal combustion engine analyzers, to test electronics; indicating instruments, electric; emergency alarms

(G-1569)
HYDROCHEM LLC
Also Called: Hydrochempsc
703 N Taylor St (67042-3912)
PHONE..................................316 321-7541
Robin Balman, *Manager*
EMP: 26
SALES (corp-wide): 546.7MM **Privately Held**
WEB: www.hydrochem.com
SIC: 7349 5084 Chemical cleaning services; cleaning equipment, high pressure, sand or steam
HQ: Hydrochem Llc
900 Georgia Ave
Deer Park TX 77536
713 393-5600

(G-1570)
INDUSTRIAL INSULATION SVCS INC
2200 W 6th Ave (67042-3166)
PHONE..................................316 321-5358
Bradley Clites, *President*
Brian Clites, *Corp Secy*
Terry Clites, *Vice Pres*
Tracy Clites, *Vice Pres*
EMP: 100
SALES: 2.3MM **Privately Held**
SIC: 1799 Insulation of pipes & boilers
PA: C-Tech Industrial Group, Inc.
2200 W 6th Ave
El Dorado KS 67042

(G-1571)
INSURANCE CENTER INC (PA)
Also Called: I C I
120 W Central Ave (67042-2138)
PHONE..................................316 321-5600
Thomas Murry, *CEO*
Sharlene Stewart, *Opers Mgr*
Dusty Davis, *Treasurer*
Lonnie Currier, *Broker*
Rebecca Anderson, *Personnel*
EMP: 23
SQ FT: 4,000
SALES (est): 5.6MM **Privately Held**
WEB: www.insurancehome.com
SIC: 6411 Insurance agents

(G-1572)
INTERNAL MEDICINE
700 W Central Ave Ste 201 (67042-2186)
PHONE..................................316 321-2100
Amy Seeber, *Principal*
EMP: 30
SALES (est): 950.5K **Privately Held**
SIC: 8011 Internal medicine practitioners

(G-1573)
INTRUST BANK NA
100 S Main St (67042-3402)
P.O. Box 1349 (67042-1349)
PHONE..................................316 321-1640
Matt Childers, *Manager*
EMP: 16
SALES (corp-wide): 134.2MM **Privately Held**
WEB: www.intrustbank.com
SIC: 6021 National trust companies with deposits, commercial
HQ: Intrust Bank National Association
105 N Main St
Wichita KS 67202
316 383-1111

(G-1574)
ITGS SHIPPING
420 N Industrial Rd (67042-9121)
PHONE..................................316 322-3000
Sean Riley,
EMP: 20
SALES (est): 358.4K **Privately Held**
SIC: 4953 Refuse systems

(G-1575)
KANSAS DEPARTMENT TRNSP
Also Called: KS Dept Trnsp Dist 5 Area 2
205 Oil Hill Rd (67042-3351)
PHONE..................................316 321-3370
Mike Longshaw, *Principal*
EMP: 34 **Privately Held**
WEB: www.nwwichitabypass.com
SIC: 1611 9621 General contractor, highway & street construction; highway & street maintenance; regulation, administration of transportation;
HQ: Kansas Department Of Transportation
700 Sw Harrison St # 500
Topeka KS 66603
785 296-3501

(G-1576)
KANSAS SECURED TITLE (DH)
220 W Central Ave (67042-2101)
P.O. Box 393 (67042-0393)
PHONE..................................316 320-2410
Randall Waldorf, *President*
Lori Turner, *Vice Pres*
Kathryn Waldorf, *Treasurer*
EMP: 10
SALES (est): 1.6MM
SALES (corp-wide): 22MM **Privately Held**
SIC: 6541 8748 Title & trust companies; business consulting
HQ: Title Midwest, Inc.
4400 Shawnee Mission Pkwy # 208
Fairway KS 66205
785 232-9110

(G-1577)
KANSAS TURNPIKE AUTHORITY
Rr 4 (67042)
PHONE..................................316 321-0631
Steve Hewitt, *Branch Mgr*
EMP: 40
SALES (corp-wide): 124.8MM **Privately Held**
WEB: www.ksturnpike.com
SIC: 4785 Toll road operation
PA: Kansas Turnpike Authority
9401 E Kellogg Dr
Wichita KS 67207
316 682-4537

(G-1578)
KELLY MACLASKEY
105 N Industrial Rd (67042-9133)
P.O. Box 222 (67042-0222)
PHONE..................................316 321-9011
Michael Traylor, *Manager*
EMP: 40
SALES (corp-wide): 11.9MM **Privately Held**
SIC: 5172 1389 Crude oil; servicing oil & gas wells
PA: Kelly Maclaskey Oil Field Services, Inc.
5900 W Carlsbad Hwy
Hobbs NM
575 393-1016

(G-1579)
KNOX ELECTRONIC LTD
3910 W Central Ave (67042-3476)
P.O. Box 813 (67042-0813)
PHONE..................................316 321-2400
George L Lawson, *President*
Scott Meyer, *Vice Pres*
◆ **EMP:** 10
SALES (est): 1MM **Privately Held**
WEB: www.knoxelectronicusa.com
SIC: 3577 Computer peripheral equipment

(G-1580)
KOCH INDUSTRIES INC
35 Se 20th St (67042)
PHONE..................................316 321-6380
Jack Brurleson, *Branch Mgr*
EMP: 10
SALES (corp-wide): 40.6B **Privately Held**
WEB: www.kochind.com
SIC: 4613 Refined petroleum pipelines
PA: Koch Industries, Inc.
4111 E 37th St N
Wichita KS 67220
316 828-5500

GEOGRAPHIC

(G-1581)
KUHNS H RICHARD JR MD EL
700 W Central Ave Ste 201 (67042-2186)
PHONE..................................316 320-1917
H R Kuhns Jr, *Owner*
EMP: 22 **EST:** 2001
SALES (est): 469.1K **Privately Held**
SIC: 8011 Internal medicine, physician/surgeon

(G-1582)
KYLE TIPTON MD LLC
700 W Central Ave Ste 201 (67042-2186)
PHONE..................................316 321-2100
Cindy Carson MD, *Principal*
Kyle M Tipton, *Med Doctor*
EMP: 27
SALES (est): 581.2K **Privately Held**
SIC: 8011 Internal medicine, physician/surgeon

(G-1583)
LEROY COOK
Also Called: Traf-O-Teria System
121 W Ash Ave (67042-3401)
P.O. Box 103 (67042-0103)
PHONE..................................316 321-0844
Leroy Cook, *Owner*
EMP: 8
SQ FT: 2,400
SALES (est): 742.1K **Privately Held**
SIC: 2759 2752 Letterpress printing; commercial printing, offset

(G-1584)
M6 CONCRETE ACCESSORIES CO INC
933 Oil Hill Rd (67042-3377)
PHONE..................................316 452-5466
Marvin Linville, *Branch Mgr*
EMP: 5
SALES (corp-wide): 15.5MM **Privately Held**
WEB: www.conacc.com
SIC: 3272 Concrete products
PA: M6 Concrete Accessories Company, Inc.
1040 S West St
Wichita KS 67213
316 263-7251

(G-1585)
MAGELLAN PIPELINE COMPANY LP
1309 Sunset Rd (67042-3676)
PHONE..................................316 321-3730
Pat Skinner, *Manager*
EMP: 10
SALES (corp-wide): 2.8B **Publicly Held**
SIC: 4613 Refined petroleum pipelines
HQ: Magellan Pipeline Company, L.P.
1 Williams Ctr
Tulsa OK 74172
918 574-7000

(G-1586)
NUSTAR PIPELINE OPER PARTNR LP
Also Called: Kaneb Services
1624 Sunset Rd (67042-4701)
PHONE..................................316 321-3500
Dale Smith, *Engineer*
Darcy Williams, *Manager*
EMP: 10 **Publicly Held**
WEB: www.kanebpipeline.com
SIC: 4613 Refined petroleum pipelines
HQ: Nustar Pipeline Operating Partnership Lp
2608 E Highway 50
Yankton SD 57078
605 665-4764

(G-1587)
ONEOK INC
700 N Star St (67042-3937)
PHONE..................................316 322-8131
John Gardner, *Manager*
EMP: 15
SALES (corp-wide): 12.5B **Publicly Held**
WEB: www.oneok.com
SIC: 4922 Natural gas transmission
PA: Oneok, Inc.
100 W 5th St Ste Ll
Tulsa OK 74103
918 588-7000

(G-1588)
OREILLY AUTOMOTIVE STORES INC
Also Called: O'Reilly Auto Parts
1816 W Central Ave (67042-2263)
PHONE..................................316 321-4371
Curt Profitt, *Manager*
EMP: 12 **Publicly Held**
WEB: www.oreillyauto.com
SIC: 5531 5063 Automotive parts; storage batteries, industrial
HQ: O'reilly Automotive Stores, Inc.
233 S Patterson Ave
Springfield MO 65802
417 862-2674

(G-1589)
ORSCHELN FARM AND HOME LLC
Also Called: Orschelin Farm and Home 69
2354 W Central Ave (67042-3207)
PHONE..................................316 321-4004
Scott Taylor, *Manager*
EMP: 14
SALES (corp-wide): 822.7MM **Privately Held**
WEB: www.orschelnfarmhome.com
SIC: 5191 5251 5699 Farm supplies; hardware; work clothing
PA: Orscheln Farm And Home Llc
1800 Overcenter Dr
Moberly MO 65270
800 577-2580

(G-1590)
PHILLIPS WELL SERVICE INC
315 N Industrial Rd (67042)
P.O. Box 1263 (67042-1263)
PHONE..................................316 321-6650
Terry Phillips, *President*
Glenda Phillips, *Corp Secy*
EMP: 8
SQ FT: 1,000
SALES: 480K **Privately Held**
SIC: 1389 Oil & gas wells: building, repairing & dismantling

(G-1591)
PIONEER AUTOMATION TECHNOLOGY
1220 N Haverhill Rd (67042-4810)
P.O. Box 114 (67042-0114)
PHONE..................................316 322-0123
Ted Blamis, *Owner*
EMP: 17
SALES (est): 1.7MM **Privately Held**
WEB: www.pioneerautomation.com
SIC: 1796 8742 Machinery installation; automation & robotics consultant

(G-1592)
PKHLS ARCHITECTURE PA
Also Called: T K H L Architects
101 S Star St (67042-2932)
PHONE..................................316 321-4774
Vince Haines, *President*
Lester Limone, *Principal*
David Stewart, *Principal*
EMP: 10
SQ FT: 1,100
SALES (est): 1.1MM **Privately Held**
SIC: 8712 Architectural engineering

(G-1593)
PRAIRIE TRAILS GOLF CNTRY CLB
1100 Country Club Ln (67042-4208)
PHONE..................................316 321-4114
Kevin Wishart, *Ch of Bd*
Derald Ted Dankert, *Vice Pres*
EMP: 20
SQ FT: 6,500
SALES (est): 598.1K **Privately Held**
WEB: www.prairietrails.com
SIC: 7997 Country club, membership; golf club, membership; swimming club, membership; tennis club, membership

(G-1594)
PROFESSIONAL SALES SVCS INC
410 N Industrial Rd (67042-9121)
PHONE..................................316 941-4542
Dennis E Daugherty, *President*
EMP: 18
SQ FT: 3,000
SALES (est): 9.5MM **Privately Held**
WEB: www.pssks.com
SIC: 5085 Industrial tools

(G-1595)
RAILSERVE INC
Ameritrack Rail
304 E 12th Ave (67042-4323)
PHONE..................................316 321-3816
Mark Berrus, *Branch Mgr*
EMP: 45
SALES (corp-wide): 225.3B **Publicly Held**
SIC: 4789 Railroad maintenance & repair services
HQ: Railserve, Inc.
1691 Phoenix Blvd Ste 250
Atlanta GA 30349

(G-1596)
RECOVERY FOR ALL FOUNDATION
226 W Central Ave (67042-2153)
P.O. Box 47361, Wichita (67201-7361)
PHONE..................................316 322-7057
EMP: 10
SALES (est): 323.3K **Privately Held**
SIC: 8322 Individual And Family Services, Nsk

(G-1597)
RED COACH INN
Also Called: Best Western
2525 W Central Ave (67042-3289)
P.O. Box 526 (67042-0526)
PHONE..................................316 321-6900
John Tyle, *President*
EMP: 20
SQ FT: 60,000
SALES (est): 1MM **Privately Held**
SIC: 7011 5812 Hotels & motels; eating places

(G-1598)
REGIONAL MEDIA CORPORATION INC
Also Called: Powwwer Net
216 S Vine St (67042-3424)
P.O. Box 1242 (67042-1242)
PHONE..................................316 320-1120
Dale Short, *President*
Ben Whiteside, *Vice Pres*
Sarah Madden, *Accountant*
EMP: 10
SALES (est): 716.4K **Privately Held**
WEB: www.regionalmedia.com
SIC: 4813

(G-1599)
ROADSAFE TRAFFIC SYSTEMS INC
1224 W 6th Ave (67042-1524)
PHONE..................................316 778-2112
John Paul Kollsitka, *Branch Mgr*
EMP: 95 **Privately Held**
SIC: 7389 Flagging service (traffic control)
PA: Roadsafe Traffic Systems, Inc.
3015 E Illini St
Phoenix AZ 85040

(G-1600)
ROADSAFE TRAFFIC SYSTEMS INC
2504 Enterprise Ave (67042-3230)
PHONE..................................316 322-3070
Adam Brenton, *Branch Mgr*
EMP: 23 **Privately Held**
SIC: 7389 1721 Flagging service (traffic control); pavement marking contractor
PA: Roadsafe Traffic Systems, Inc.
3015 E Illini St
Phoenix AZ 85040

(G-1601)
SECURITY 1ST TITLE LLC
114 E Central Ave (67042-2128)
PHONE..................................316 322-8164
Trisha Powell, *Branch Mgr*
EMP: 16 **Privately Held**
SIC: 6541 Title abstract offices
PA: Security 1st Title Llc
727 N Waco Ave Ste 300
Wichita KS 67203

(G-1602)
SHADY CREEK SALES INC
1000 Ne Marina Rd (67042)
P.O. Box 287 (67042-0287)
PHONE..................................316 321-0943
Mike Morgan, *President*
EMP: 10
SQ FT: 13,000
SALES (est): 2.2MM **Privately Held**
WEB: www.shadycreek.com
SIC: 5551 7699 Boat dealers; boat repair

(G-1603)
SOROPTIMIST INTERNATIONAL
737 Harvard Ave (67042-4309)
PHONE..................................316 321-0433
Bonnie Buckman, *Principal*
EMP: 30
SALES (est): 960K **Privately Held**
WEB: www.soroptimistinternational.net
SIC: 8641 Civic associations

(G-1604)
SOUTH CNTL MNTAL HLTH CNSLING (PA)
524 N Main St (67042-2024)
PHONE..................................316 321-6036
Ron Fischer, *President*
Pete Lawlor, *President*
Darrell R Whitney, *Vice Pres*
Wallace Davis, *Treasurer*
Amanda Parsons, *Finance Dir*
EMP: 30
SQ FT: 3,000
SALES (est): 1.9MM **Privately Held**
SIC: 8093 8063 Mental health clinic, outpatient; hospital for the mentally ill

(G-1605)
SUNSET INN
1901 W Central Ave (67042-2299)
PHONE..................................316 321-9172
Rick Johannas, *Partner*
Wanda Price, *Manager*
EMP: 10
SALES (est): 328.6K **Privately Held**
SIC: 7011 Hotels

(G-1606)
SURFACE PROTECTION SVCS LLC
2012 W 6th Ave (67042-3119)
P.O. Box 870 (67042-0870)
PHONE..................................316 322-5135
Andy Waller,
Russell Waller,
EMP: 12
SALES (est): 2MM **Privately Held**
SIC: 1611 1771 Highway & street maintenance; concrete work; blacktop (asphalt) work

(G-1607)
SUSAN B ALLEN MEMORIAL HOSP (PA)
720 W Central Ave (67042-2112)
PHONE..................................316 322-4510
Jim Wilson, *President*
Gayle Arnett, *Vice Pres*
Lisa Vandusen, *Agent*
Karen Hockett, *Supervisor*
Mark Rooker, *Technology*
EMP: 410
SQ FT: 156,125
SALES: 47.1MM **Privately Held**
WEB: www.sbamh.com
SIC: 8062 8051 General medical & surgical hospitals; skilled nursing care facilities

(G-1608)
THAIRAPY SALON
625 N Washington St (67042-1862)
PHONE..................................316 321-6263
Ada Wedel, *Owner*
EMP: 11
SALES (est): 145.7K **Privately Held**
SIC: 7231 Beauty shops

(G-1609)
THRASHER BSMNT FOUNDATION REPR (PA)
804 N Haverhill Rd (67042-4803)
PHONE..................................316 320-1853
Dave Tinsman, *Sales Associate*
Kathleen Morrow, *Admin Sec*

EMP: 65
SQ FT: 15,000
SALES (est): 7.6MM **Privately Held**
SIC: 1771 Foundation & footing contractor

(G-1610)
TRAIL WOOD COMPANY INC
Also Called: Realty Executives
615 N Main St (67042-2027)
PHONE..................................316 321-6500
Eddie Dean, *President*
EMP: 12
SQ FT: 5,000
SALES (est): 1.3MM **Privately Held**
SIC: 6531 Real estate agent, residential

(G-1611)
VALMONT INDUSTRIES INC
955 N Haverhill Rd (67042-4806)
PHONE..................................316 321-1201
Meryl McGonigle, *Manager*
EMP: 100
SALES (corp-wide): 2.7B **Publicly Held**
WEB: www.valmont.com
SIC: 3441 Fabricated structural metal
PA: Valmont Industries, Inc.
1 Valmont Plz Ste 500
Omaha NE 68154
402 963-1000

(G-1612)
VINTAGE GROUP INC
Also Called: Vintage Place Assistant Living
1650 E 12th Ave (67042-4300)
PHONE..................................316 321-7777
Susan Zukel, *Branch Mgr*
EMP: 27
SALES (corp-wide): 2MM **Privately Held**
SIC: 8051 8361 Skilled nursing care facilities; home for the aged
PA: Vintage Group Inc
550 N 159th St E Ste 101
Wichita KS 67230
316 733-0690

(G-1613)
WALNUT VALLEY PACKING LLC
1000 S Main St (67042-9764)
PHONE..................................866 421-3595
Dave Nixon, *Principal*
EMP: 8
SALES (est): 909.4K **Privately Held**
SIC: 2011 Meat packing plants

(G-1614)
WILLIAM BARNES
Also Called: Midwest Turf
1975 Jamaica St (67042-4144)
PHONE..................................316 321-3094
William Barnes, *Owner*
EMP: 11 **EST:** 1995
SALES (est): 679.9K **Privately Held**
SIC: 0782 Lawn care services

(G-1615)
WYNNE TRANSPORT SERVICE INC
805 N Haverhill Rd (67042-4804)
P.O. Box 749 (67042-0749)
PHONE..................................316 321-3900
Dixie Collans, *Manager*
EMP: 25
SALES (corp-wide): 32.4MM **Privately Held**
WEB: www.wynnetr.com
SIC: 4212 4213 Petroleum haulage, local; liquid petroleum transport, non-local
PA: Wynne Transport Service, Inc.
2222 N 11th St
Omaha NE 68110
402 342-4001

(G-1616)
YOUNG MENS CHRISTIAN ASSOCIA
Also Called: El Dorado YMCA
300 N Main St (67042-2020)
PHONE..................................316 320-9622
Jessica Ralo, *Branch Mgr*
EMP: 87
SALES (corp-wide): 44.6MM **Privately Held**
SIC: 7991 8351 8641 7032 Physical fitness facilities; child day care services; youth organizations; sporting camps; individual & family services
PA: The Young Men's Christian Association Of Wichita Kansas
402 N Market St
Wichita KS 67202
316 219-9622

Elkhart
Morton County

(G-1617)
AMERICAN IMPLEMENT INC
Also Called: John Deere Authorized Dealer
364 Us Hgwy 56 (67950)
P.O. Box 1400 (67950-1400)
PHONE..................................620 697-2182
Albert Waugh, *Manager*
EMP: 20
SALES (corp-wide): 6.6MM **Privately Held**
SIC: 5083 Farm implements
PA: American Implement Inc
1104 W Hwy 24
Goodland KS
785 890-7575

(G-1618)
COUNTY OF MORTON
Also Called: Road Dept
1 2 Mile S Of Wilburton16 (67950)
PHONE..................................620 593-4288
Charles McKinley, *Manager*
EMP: 20 **Privately Held**
SIC: 1611 9111 Highway & street maintenance; county supervisors' & executives' offices
PA: County Of Morton
1025 Morton St
Elkhart KS 67950
620 697-2157

(G-1619)
ELKHART COOP EQUITY EXCHNGE (PA)
840 N Border Ave (67950-5052)
P.O. Box 210 (67950-0210)
PHONE..................................620 697-2135
Harry Minns, *Ch of Bd*
Kelly Pike, *Principal*
Kent Cruise, *Vice Pres*
Joel Mc Clure, *Admin Sec*
EMP: 40 **EST:** 1917
SQ FT: 30,000
SALES: 44.9MM **Privately Held**
SIC: 5153 5999 Grain elevators; feed & farm supply

(G-1620)
ELKHART TELEPHONE COMPANY INC
610 S Cosmos St (67950)
P.O. Box 817 (67950-0817)
PHONE..................................620 697-2111
Trent Boalden, *President*
Bob Boaldin, *President*
Morgan Walls, *Opers Mgr*
Margaret Grice, *Sales Executive*
Dianna Boaldin, *Admin Sec*
EMP: 33 **EST:** 1956
SQ FT: 5,000
SALES (est): 2.8MM
SALES (corp-wide): 10.5MM **Privately Held**
WEB: www.epictouch.com
SIC: 4813 Local telephone communications
PA: Epic Touch Co.
610 S Cosmos St
Elkhart KS 67950
620 697-2111

(G-1621)
FIRST NATIONAL BANK ELKHART (PA)
601 Morton St (67950-5017)
P.O. Box 1000 (67950-1000)
PHONE..................................620 697-2777
Robert Elder, *President*
Shane Haynes, *President*
Moe Hautz, *Vice Pres*
Moe Houtz, *Vice Pres*
Daniel Smith, *Vice Pres*
EMP: 19
SALES: 4.4MM **Privately Held**
WEB: www.fnbelkhart.com
SIC: 6022 State commercial banks

(G-1622)
MITCHELL FARMS
Hwy 95 S (67950)
P.O. Box 427 (67950-0427)
PHONE..................................580 696-4568
Kenneth Mitchell, *Partner*
Brent Mitchell, *Partner*
Brian Mitchell, *Partner*
Roy Mitchell, *Partner*
Kendra Ramsey, *Partner*
EMP: 15
SALES (est): 1.3MM **Privately Held**
SIC: 0111 0115 0119 Wheat; corn; milo farm

(G-1623)
MORTON COUNTY HOSPITAL (PA)
Also Called: Morton County Health System
445 Hilltop Ave (67950)
P.O. Box 937 (67950-0937)
PHONE..................................620 697-2141
Steve May, *Safety Mgr*
Jeff Weaver, *CFO*
Roxanna Fullerton, *Med Doctor*
Gail Horner, *Manager*
Leonard Hernandez, *Administration*
EMP: 225
SQ FT: 44,932
SALES: 7.5MM **Privately Held**
WEB: www.mchswecare.com
SIC: 8062 8052 General medical & surgical hospitals; personal care facility

(G-1624)
MORTON COUNTY HOSPITAL
Also Called: Iway, Olivia N MD
411 Sunset St (67950-5001)
P.O. Box 460 (67950-0460)
PHONE..................................620 697-2175
Jeff Weaver, *Manager*
EMP: 14
SALES (corp-wide): 7.5MM **Privately Held**
WEB: www.mchswecare.com
SIC: 8011 Psychiatrist
PA: Morton County Hospital
445 Hilltop Ave
Elkhart KS 67950
620 697-2141

(G-1625)
NUSSER OIL COMPANY INC
570 Border Ave (67950-5011)
P.O. Box 670 (67950-0670)
PHONE..................................620 697-4624
John F Nusser, *President*
Karen S Nusser, *Corp Secy*
EMP: 26
SQ FT: 26,920
SALES (est): 13.2MM **Privately Held**
SIC: 5171 5984 5541 Petroleum bulk stations; propane gas, bottled; gasoline service stations

Ellinwood
Barton County

(G-1626)
A R SYSTEMS INC
Also Called: Private Business Data Systems
13 N Main St Lowr Level (67526-1637)
PHONE..................................620 564-3790
Monty Strecker, *President*
Catherine Strecker, *Corp Secy*
EMP: 30
SALES (est): 1.8MM **Privately Held**
SIC: 7379 Data processing consultant

(G-1627)
BARTON COUNTY FEEDERS INC
1164 Se 40 Rd (67526-9276)
PHONE..................................620 564-2200
Crokett A Profitt, *President*
Alan Pohlnan, *General Mgr*
Mitch Mulch, *Corp Secy*
Kenneth Knight, *Vice Pres*
Jack Schlessiger, *Vice Pres*
EMP: 27
SQ FT: 4,000
SALES (est): 3MM **Privately Held**
WEB: www.bartoncountyfeeders.com
SIC: 0211 Beef cattle feedlots

(G-1628)
CITY OF ELLINWOOD
Also Called: City Maintenance Shop
505 E Santa Fe Blvd (67526-1726)
PHONE..................................620 564-3046
Darryle Nielsen, *General Mgr*
EMP: 10 **Privately Held**
WEB: www.cityofellinwood.com
SIC: 7539 9111 Automotive repair shops; mayors' offices
PA: City Of Ellinwood
104 E 2nd St
Ellinwood KS 67526
620 564-3161

(G-1629)
DICKS ENGINE & MACHINE SERVICE
803 E Santa Fe Blvd (67526-2602)
PHONE..................................620 564-2238
Jack Wise, *President*
Sandra Wise, *Corp Secy*
Andy Wise, *Vice Pres*
EMP: 15 **EST:** 1951
SALES (est): 1.2MM **Privately Held**
SIC: 7699 5084 3599 Engine repair & replacement, non-automotive; oil well machinery, equipment & supplies; machine shop, jobbing & repair

(G-1630)
ELLINWOOD TANK SERVICE INC (PA)
601 E Santa Fe Blvd (67526-1738)
P.O. Box 366, Chase (67524-0366)
PHONE..................................620 793-0246
Anita Sheridan, *President*
EMP: 5 **EST:** 1965
SQ FT: 2,250
SALES: 450K **Privately Held**
SIC: 1389 Oil field services; haulage, oil field

(G-1631)
ERNSTINGS INCORPORATED
Also Called: Ernsting's Radiator
180a Se 100 Ave (67526-9257)
PHONE..................................620 564-2793
Guy Ernsting, *President*
Shelly Churchill, *Office Mgr*
EMP: 7 **EST:** 1971
SALES (est): 928.9K **Privately Held**
SIC: 3533 7699 7539 3433 Oil field machinery & equipment; industrial machinery & equipment repair; radiator repair shop, automotive; heating equipment, except electric

(G-1632)
FIVE STAR QUALITY CARE-KS LLC
Also Called: Woodhaven Care Center
510 W 7th St (67526-1101)
PHONE..................................620 564-2337
Bruce J Mackey Jr, *President*
EMP: 63
SALES (est): 530.9K **Publicly Held**
WEB: www.fivestarqualitycare.com
SIC: 8051 Skilled nursing care facilities
PA: Five Star Senior Living Inc.
400 Centre St
Newton MA 02458

(G-1633)
GRADY BOLDING CORPORATION
114 N Main St (67526-1640)
P.O. Box 486 (67526-0486)
PHONE..................................620 564-2240
Grady Bolding, *President*
Lyle Gunn, *Treasurer*
EMP: 6
SQ FT: 2,200
SALES (est): 580.9K **Privately Held**
SIC: 1311 Crude petroleum production

GEOGRAPHIC

(G-1634)
GREAT PLAINS ELLINWOOD INC
Also Called: Ellinwood District Hospital
605 N Main St (67526-1440)
PHONE..................................620 564-2548
Steve Carlson, *Ch of Bd*
James Teri, *General Mgr*
Cheri Doll, *Materials Mgr*
Chris Robl, *Human Res Dir*
Karen Riggs, *Manager*
EMP: 29
SALES (est): 203.2K
SALES (corp-wide): 112.9MM **Privately Held**
SIC: 8082 Home health care services
PA: Great Plains Health Alliance, Inc.
625 3rd St
Phillipsburg KS 67661
785 543-2111

(G-1635)
KIMPLE INC
Also Called: Kimple Furniture & Gifts
113 N Main St (67526-1639)
P.O. Box 246 (67526-0246)
PHONE..................................620 564-2300
Richard F Kimple, *President*
Linda Kimple, *Corp Secy*
EMP: 11
SQ FT: 5,500
SALES: 769.3K **Privately Held**
WEB: www.kimple.com
SIC: 5712 5713 5714 5999 Furniture stores; floor covering stores; drapery & upholstery stores; monuments & tombstones; funeral service & crematories

(G-1636)
SCHWABS TINKER SHOP INTL INC
110 W D St (67526-1815)
P.O. Box 248 (67526-0248)
PHONE..................................620 564-2547
Duane Schwab, *Branch Mgr*
EMP: 5
SALES (corp-wide): 1.2MM **Privately Held**
SIC: 3533 Oil & gas field machinery
PA: Schwab's Tinker Shop International, Inc.
430 Rollie Rd
Liberal KS 67901
620 624-7611

(G-1637)
SNELL HARVESTING INC
509 W 6th St (67526-1318)
PHONE..................................620 564-3312
Thomas Snell, *President*
EMP: 15
SALES (est): 2.5MM **Privately Held**
SIC: 4213 Trucking, except local

(G-1638)
SOUTHWIND DRILLING INC
8 N Main St (67526-1638)
P.O. Box 276 (67526-0276)
PHONE..................................620 564-3800
Leroy Holt, *CEO*
Chris Batchman, *Vice Pres*
Todd Morgensteon, *Vice Pres*
EMP: 55
SALES (est): 7.5MM **Privately Held**
SIC: 1381 Directional drilling oil & gas wells

(G-1639)
ST JOHNS CHILD DEV CTR LLC
512 N Wilhelm Ave (67526-1345)
PHONE..................................620 564-2044
Christopher Ringwald, *Principal*
EMP: 16
SALES (est): 154.5K **Privately Held**
SIC: 8351 Child day care services

(G-1640)
YARCO COMPANY INC
Also Called: Ellinwood Heights Apartments
511 S Bismark Ave 515 (67526-1917)
PHONE..................................620 564-2180
EMP: 177
SALES (corp-wide): 129.3MM **Privately Held**
SIC: 6513 Apartment Building Operator
PA: Yarco Company, Inc.
7920 Ward Pkwy
Kansas City MO 64114
816 561-4240

Ellis
Ellis County

(G-1641)
COMMUNITY FOUNDATION OF ELLIS
820 Washington St (67637-2221)
PHONE..................................785 726-2660
Sylvia Kinderknecht, *Chairman*
EMP: 10
SALES: 74.9K **Privately Held**
SIC: 8748 8322 Urban planning & consulting services; outreach program

(G-1642)
EARLY CHLDHOOD CNNECTION/PRE K
Also Called: Washington Gradeschool
100 E 13th St (67637-1721)
PHONE..................................785 726-2413
John Befort, *Principal*
EMP: 25
SALES (est): 199.6K **Privately Held**
SIC: 8351 Head start center, except in conjunction with school

(G-1643)
ELITE PIPE TESTING
1305 Maple St (67637-1840)
PHONE..................................785 726-4366
Paul Fisher, *Owner*
EMP: 6
SALES (est): 419.2K **Privately Held**
SIC: 1389 Oil field services

(G-1644)
EVANGELICAL LUTHERAN
Also Called: Good Samaritan Society - Ellis
1101 Spruce St (67637-1757)
P.O. Box 5038, Sioux Falls SD (57117-5038)
PHONE..................................785 726-3101
Sharon Leuenberger, *Branch Mgr*
EMP: 77 **Privately Held**
WEB: www.good-sam.com
SIC: 8059 Nursing home, except skilled & intermediate care facility
HQ: The Evangelical Lutheran Good Samaritan Society
4800 W 57th St
Sioux Falls SD 57108
866 928-1635

(G-1645)
FISCHER PIPE TESTING INC
1858 Ellis Ave (67637-9272)
P.O. Box 273 (67637-0273)
PHONE..................................785 726-3411
Donald Fisher, *President*
Viola Fischer, *Admin Sec*
EMP: 16
SALES: 900K **Privately Held**
SIC: 1389 Oil field services

(G-1646)
GOLDEN BELT COOP ASSN INC
917 Monroe St (67637-1752)
P.O. Box 138 (67637-0138)
PHONE..................................785 726-3115
Robert A Redger, *President*
Brandon Pfeifer, *Chairman*
EMP: 15 **EST:** 1905
SQ FT: 5,000
SALES (est): 9.9MM **Privately Held**
SIC: 5153 5191 5172 5541 Grain elevators; grains; farm supplies; feed; fertilizer & fertilizer materials; engine fuels & oils; filling stations, gasoline

(G-1647)
HORIZON PIPE TESTING INC
301 W 2nd Street Ter (67637-2022)
P.O. Box 163 (67637-0163)
PHONE..................................785 726-3773
John Fischer, *President*
EMP: 5
SALES (est): 615.3K **Privately Held**
SIC: 1389 Pipe testing, oil field service; oil field services

(G-1648)
KELLER BROS HARVESTING & TRCKG
Rr 2 Box 107a (67637)
PHONE..................................785 726-3555
Duane Keller, *President*
EMP: 10
SALES (est): 619.6K **Privately Held**
WEB: www.kellerbrosharvesting.com
SIC: 0722 Crop harvesting

(G-1649)
LOVES TRAVEL STOPS
200 Washington St (67637-2130)
PHONE..................................785 726-2561
Todd Turner, *Opers Staff*
Wendy Reedy, *Branch Mgr*
EMP: 26
SALES (corp-wide): 4.6B **Privately Held**
SIC: 8699 Travel club
PA: Love's Travel Stops & Country Stores, Inc.
10601 N Pennsylvania Ave
Oklahoma City OK 73120
405 302-6500

(G-1650)
MARLENE SCHOENBERGER
Also Called: Schoenberger Nursing Agency
106 W 10th St (67637-1624)
P.O. Box 54 (67637-0054)
PHONE..................................785 625-8189
Marlene Schoenberger, *Owner*
EMP: 50
SALES (est): 617.7K **Privately Held**
SIC: 8082 Home health care services

(G-1651)
RAYES INC (PA)
Also Called: W O K
204 W 2nd St (67637-2026)
P.O. Box 320 (67637-0320)
PHONE..................................785 726-4885
Willard L Frickey, *President*
Tracy Frickey, *CFO*
Tracy Hudson, *CFO*
Jackie Frickey, *Admin Sec*
▲ **EMP:** 70
SQ FT: 37,000
SALES (est): 13.1MM **Privately Held**
WEB: www.rayes.com
SIC: 3842 Wheelchairs

(G-1652)
SIZEWISE RENTALS LLC
204 W 2nd St (67637-2026)
PHONE..................................800 814-9389
Willard Frickey, *Branch Mgr*
EMP: 12 **Privately Held**
SIC: 7359 Equipment rental & leasing
PA: Sizewise Rentals, L.L.C.
8601 Monrovia St
Lenexa KS 66215

(G-1653)
SIZEWISE RENTALS LLC
210 Jefferson St (67637)
P.O. Box 320 (67637-0320)
PHONE..................................785 726-4371
Mike Legleiter, *Branch Mgr*
EMP: 30 **Privately Held**
SIC: 5047 Medical & hospital equipment
PA: Sizewise Rentals, L.L.C.
8601 Monrovia St
Lenexa KS 66215

(G-1654)
SUNFLOWER MEDICAL LLC
206 Jefferson St (67637-9208)
P.O. Box 276 (67637-0276)
PHONE..................................785 726-2486
Brian K Frickey, *Principal*
▲ **EMP:** 17
SQ FT: 15,000
SALES (est): 3MM **Privately Held**
WEB: www.sunflowermedical.com
SIC: 5046 Commercial equipment

(G-1655)
WOLF MEMORIAL CO INC
Also Called: Kansas Granite Industries
205 W 9th St (67637-2207)
P.O. Box 206 (67637-0206)
PHONE..................................785 726-4430
Brian Wolf, *President*
James C Wolf, *Corp Secy*
▲ **EMP:** 13
SALES: 455K **Privately Held**
SIC: 5999 5099 Monuments, finished to custom order; monuments & grave markers

Ellsworth
Ellsworth County

(G-1656)
AMERICAN ASSN UNIV WOMEN
Also Called: Aauw Ellsworth
606 Webb St (67439-4250)
PHONE..................................785 472-5737
Diane Oconnor, *President*
Leslie Brooks, *Treasurer*
EMP: 16
SALES (est): 362.4K **Privately Held**
SIC: 8621 Education & teacher association

(G-1657)
B & B PLUMBING HEATING & AC
814 Stanberry St (67439-2230)
PHONE..................................785 472-5239
Bruce Bowie, *President*
Jane Kohls, *Manager*
Alan Byerley, *Admin Sec*
EMP: 10
SALES: 1.5MM **Privately Held**
SIC: 1711 Plumbing contractors; warm air heating & air conditioning contractor

(G-1658)
CARRICO IMPLEMENT CO INC
Also Called: John Deere Authorized Dealer
1104 E 8th St (67439-2511)
PHONE..................................785 472-4400
Ron Allens, *President*
Rodger Budke, *Sales Mgr*
Tom Thiessen, *Sales Staff*
EMP: 11
SALES (est): 994K
SALES (corp-wide): 58.8MM **Privately Held**
WEB: www.carricoimplement.com
SIC: 5083 Farm implements
PA: Carrico Implement Co., Inc.
3160 Us 24 Hwy
Beloit KS 67420
785 738-5744

(G-1659)
CASHCO INC (PA)
607 W 15th St (67439-1624)
P.O. Box 6 (67439-0006)
PHONE..................................785 472-4461
Clint Rogers, *President*
Jerome H Soukup, *CFO*
Lee Perry III, *Director*
Harold M Miller Jr, *Admin Sec*
◆ **EMP:** 140
SQ FT: 118,327
SALES: 25.1MM **Privately Held**
WEB: www.cashco.com
SIC: 3491 Process control regulator valves; regulators (steam fittings)

(G-1660)
CITIZENS STATE BNK TR ELLSWRTH (HQ)
203 N Douglas Ave (67439-3215)
P.O. Box 128 (67439-0128)
PHONE..................................785 472-3141
David Brownback, *President*
Dawn Olson, *Admin Asst*
EMP: 20 **EST:** 1901
SQ FT: 12,000
SALES: 8.4MM **Privately Held**
WEB: www.csbanc.com
SIC: 6022 State trust companies accepting deposits, commercial

(G-1661)
CITY PLUMBING HEATING & AC INC
120 N Lincoln Ave (67439-3312)
P.O. Box 25 (67439-0025)
PHONE....................785 472-3001
Rick Kempke, *President*
Mary Wires, *Corp Secy*
EMP: 10
SQ FT: 6,000
SALES (est): 1MM **Privately Held**
SIC: 1711 Warm air heating & air conditioning contractor; plumbing contractors

(G-1662)
CLUBINE & RETTELE
Also Called: Langley, Jay D
118 N Lincoln Ave (67439-3312)
P.O. Box 104 (67439-0104)
PHONE....................785 472-3915
Jay D Langley, *Partner*
EMP: 25
SALES (est): 971.2K **Privately Held**
SIC: 8721 Certified public accountant

(G-1663)
COACH AND FOUR BOWLING LANES
203213 N Main (67439)
P.O. Box 174 (67439-0174)
PHONE....................785 472-5571
Gail Shanele, *President*
Abby Seiler, *Treasurer*
EMP: 14
SQ FT: 6,000
SALES (est): 559.1K **Privately Held**
SIC: 5812 7933 Pizzeria, chain; ten pin center

(G-1664)
COUNSELING INC
525 E 3rd St (67439-3618)
P.O. Box 84 (67439-0084)
PHONE....................785 472-4300
Steven Steinhauz, *Owner*
EMP: 10
SALES (est): 211.6K
SALES (corp-wide): 430.4K **Privately Held**
SIC: 8322 Family counseling services
PA: Counseling Inc
102 N Neshoba St
Tishomingo OK 73460
580 371-3551

(G-1665)
COUNTY OF ELLSWORTH
Also Called: Post Rock Rual Water District
103 N Douglas Ave (67439-3213)
PHONE....................785 472-4486
David Bailey, *Branch Mgr*
EMP: 10 **Privately Held**
WEB: www.postrockrwd.com
SIC: 4941 9111 Water supply; county supervisors' & executives' offices
PA: County Of Ellsworth
210 N Kansas Ave
Ellsworth KS 67439
785 472-4052

(G-1666)
DOUBRAVA WOODWORKING INC
1375 1/2 Avenue K (67439-8697)
PHONE....................785 472-4204
Ralph Doubrava, *President*
Venicia Doubrava, *Principal*
EMP: 6
SALES (est): 634.9K **Privately Held**
SIC: 1751 2431 Cabinet & finish carpentry; millwork

(G-1667)
ELLSWORTH COOP (PA)
100 N Kansas Ave (67439-3116)
P.O. Box 397 (67439-0397)
PHONE....................785 472-3261
Alan Doubrava, *President*
Mary Peppiatt, *Office Mgr*
EMP: 12
SQ FT: 3,000
SALES: 12.7MM **Privately Held**
SIC: 5153 5191 5541 4221 Grains; farm supplies; feed; seeds: field, garden & flower; chemicals, agricultural; filling stations, gasoline; grain elevator, storage only

(G-1668)
ELLSWORTH COUNTY AMBULANCE
1107 Evans St (67439-2553)
PHONE....................785 472-3454
Michelle Maze, *Director*
EMP: 33
SALES (est): 300K **Privately Held**
SIC: 4119 8099 Ambulance service; medical rescue squad

(G-1669)
ELLSWORTH COUNTY HIGHWAY DEPT
408 W 15th St (67439-1623)
PHONE....................785 472-4182
Rick Nondorf, *Superintendent*
EMP: 21 **EST:** 1800
SALES (est): 1MM **Privately Held**
SIC: 0782 Highway lawn & garden maintenance services

(G-1670)
ELLSWORTH COUNTY MEDICAL CTR
1604 Aylward Ave (67439-2541)
P.O. Box 87 (67439-0087)
PHONE....................785 472-3111
Roger A Masse, *CEO*
Teresa McHenry, *Engineer*
Cecelia Askren, *Accountant*
Teresa Sauvain, *Human Resources*
Beth Vallier, *Corp Comm Staff*
EMP: 175
SQ FT: 28,000
SALES: 12.9MM **Privately Held**
WEB: www.ellsworth.hpmin.com
SIC: 8062 General medical & surgical hospitals

(G-1671)
ELLSWORTH MEDICAL CLINIC INC
Also Called: Rural Health Clinic
1604 Aylward Ave (67439-2541)
PHONE....................785 472-3277
Geneva Schneider, *Treasurer*
Roger Pierson, *Administration*
EMP: 30
SQ FT: 1,200
SALES (est): 532.4K **Privately Held**
WEB: www.ewmed.com
SIC: 8011 Physicians' office, including specialists

(G-1672)
ELLSWORTH REPORTER INC
304 N Douglas Ave (67439-3218)
PHONE....................785 472-5085
Landa Denning, *President*
EMP: 9 **EST:** 1971
SALES (est): 581.1K
SALES (corp-wide): 285.7MM **Privately Held**
WEB: www.ellsworthinderep.com
SIC: 2711 Commercial printing & newspaper publishing combined; newspapers, publishing & printing
PA: Morris Multimedia, Inc.
27 Abercorn St
Savannah GA 31401
912 233-1281

(G-1673)
ELLSWRTH KNPLIS CHMBER CMMERCE
114 N Douglas Ave (67439-3231)
P.O. Box 315 (67439-0315)
PHONE....................785 472-4071
Anita Hoffhines, *President*
Ken Arnhold, *Vice Pres*
Peter Eck, *Treasurer*
Megan Muchow, *Admin Sec*
EMP: 10
SALES: 66.5K **Privately Held**
SIC: 8611 Chamber of Commerce

(G-1674)
EVANGELICAL LUTHERAN
Also Called: Good Smrtan Soc - Ellswrth Vlg
1156 Highway 14 (67439-8661)
P.O. Box 5038, Sioux Falls SD (57117-5038)
PHONE....................785 472-3167
Lynette Ammerman, *Sales & Mktg St*
Bobbie Tripp, *Director*
EMP: 91 **Privately Held**
WEB: www.good-sam.com
SIC: 8052 8059 8051 6513 Intermediate care facilities; nursing home, except skilled & intermediate care facility; skilled nursing care facilities; apartment building operators
HQ: The Evangelical Lutheran Good Samaritan Society
4800 W 57th St
Sioux Falls SD 57108
866 928-1635

(G-1675)
GREAT PLAINS MANUFACTURING INC
1607 State St (67439-1628)
PHONE....................785 472-3508
Jeff Haassey, *Manager*
EMP: 9 **Privately Held**
SIC: 3523 Farm machinery & equipment
HQ: Great Plains Manufacturing Incorporated
1525 E North St
Salina KS 67401
785 823-3276

(G-1676)
KANEQUIP INC
704 Kunkle Dr (67439-2338)
P.O. Box 189 (67439-0189)
PHONE....................785 472-3114
Don Lamstch, *Branch Mgr*
Terry Robl, *Branch Mgr*
EMP: 22
SALES (corp-wide): 117MM **Privately Held**
SIC: 5083 Farm & garden machinery
PA: Kanequip, Inc.
18035 E Us Highway 24
Wamego KS 66547
785 456-2041

(G-1677)
MAICO INDUSTRIES INC
936 Highway 14 (67439-8715)
P.O. Box 24 (67439-0024)
PHONE....................785 472-5390
Paul MAI, *President*
Rex Muchow, *Purchasing*
Chris Pfeiffer, *Shareholder*
Gwen Bunch, *Executive Asst*
EMP: 55
SQ FT: 50,000
SALES (est): 17.4MM **Privately Held**
WEB: www.maicoind.com
SIC: 3312 3441 Structural shapes & pilings, steel; fabricated structural metal

(G-1678)
MICHAEL KIRKHAM & ASSOC INC
217 N Douglas Ave (67439-3215)
PHONE....................785 472-3163
Jon Halbgewathx, *Manager*
EMP: 30
SALES (corp-wide): 21.2MM **Privately Held**
SIC: 8712 8711 Architectural engineering; consulting engineer
HQ: Michael Kirkham & Associates Inc
12700 W Dodge Rd
Omaha NE 68154
402 393-5630

(G-1679)
MOSAIC
117 N Douglas Ave (67439-3213)
P.O. Box 169 (67439-0169)
PHONE....................785 472-4081
Deena Duesberg, *Branch Mgr*
EMP: 40
SALES (corp-wide): 257.7MM **Privately Held**
WEB: www.mosaicinfo.org
SIC: 8741 8059 Hospital management; nursing & personal care facility management; home for the mentally retarded, exc. skilled or intermediate
PA: Mosaic
4980 S 118th St
Omaha NE 68137
402 896-3884

(G-1680)
ROLLING HILLS ELECTRIC COOP
208 W 1st St (67439-3104)
P.O. Box 339, Beloit (67420-0339)
PHONE....................785 472-4021
Doug Jackson, *General Mgr*
Mark Martin, *Safety Mgr*
EMP: 48
SALES (corp-wide): 27.6MM **Privately Held**
WEB: www.rollinghills.coop
SIC: 4911 Distribution, electric power
PA: Rolling Hills Electric Cooperative, Inc
3075b Us Highway 24
Beloit KS 67420
785 534-1601

(G-1681)
SURVEYS INC
111 W North Main St (67439-3229)
P.O. Box 250 (67439-0250)
PHONE....................785 472-4456
Norman Peterson, *President*
Ruth Place, *President*
George Place, *Corp Secy*
EMP: 24
SQ FT: 2,000
SALES (est): 1.7MM **Privately Held**
SIC: 8713 Surveying services

(G-1682)
TK & COMPANY INC OF KANSAS
312 Kunkle Dr (67439-2306)
PHONE....................785 472-3226
Theresa Kyler, *President*
EMP: 10 **EST:** 1996
SALES (est): 328.3K **Privately Held**
SIC: 7349 7389 Janitorial service, contract basis;

Elsmore
Allen County

(G-1683)
NEW ENGLAND LIFE INSURANCE CO
391 3800th St (66732-4030)
PHONE....................620 754-3725
Todd Lhuiller, *Branch Mgr*
EMP: 23
SALES (corp-wide): 67.9B **Publicly Held**
WEB: www.thehoovercompanies.com
SIC: 6282 Investment advice
HQ: The New England Life Insurance Company
501 Boylston St Ste 500
Boston MA 02116
617 578-2000

Elwood
Doniphan County

(G-1684)
DONIPAN CNTY SVCS & WORKSKILLS
Also Called: DONIPHAN COUNTY SERVICES & WOR
203 Roseport Rd (66024)
P.O. Box 588 (66024-0588)
PHONE....................913 365-5561
Mark Long, *President*
Linda Whittaker, *General Mgr*
Lisa Simerly, *Exec Dir*
EMP: 27

SALES: 540.7K Privately Held
SIC: 8322 Social services for the handicapped

(G-1685)
DUNNING EXPRESS INC
1910 Roseport Rd (66024)
P.O. Box 419 (66024-0419)
PHONE....................785 806-3915
Tara Dunning, *President*
Mike Dunning, *Vice Pres*
EMP: 20 EST: 2010
SALES: 1MM Privately Held
SIC: 3715 Truck trailers

(G-1686)
EDWARDS CHEMICALS INC (PA)
1504 Roseport Rd (66024)
P.O. Box 488 (66024-0488)
PHONE....................913 365-5158
Bettie Edwards, *CEO*
Todd Edwards, *Vice Pres*
EMP: 15 EST: 1976
SQ FT: 22,000
SALES (est): 6.8MM Privately Held
SIC: 5169 5087 Industrial chemicals; janitors' supplies

(G-1687)
FAIRVIEW MILLS LLC
217 S 7th St (66024)
PHONE....................785 336-2148
Brant Clary, *Branch Mgr*
EMP: 10
SALES (corp-wide): 108.6MM Privately Held
SIC: 2041 Grain mills (except rice)
HQ: Fairview Mills, Llc
604 Nemaha St
Seneca KS 66538
785 336-2148

(G-1688)
KANSAS AUTO AUCTION INC (PA)
Also Called: Poodle & Steve's Auto Auction
1507 Roseport Rd (66024)
PHONE....................913 365-0460
Gregg Boswell, *President*
Lloyd Wall, *Shareholder*
EMP: 22
SALES (est): 3.1MM Privately Held
SIC: 5012 Automobile auction

(G-1689)
PRO-DIG LLC
1604 Roseport Rd (66024)
P.O. Box 289 (66024-0289)
PHONE....................785 856-2661
Michael A Charlton, *President*
◆ EMP: 10
SQ FT: 22,000
SALES: 3MM Privately Held
SIC: 3462 5039 Gears, forged steel; prefabricated structures

(G-1690)
ROCK RIDGE STEEL COMPANY LLC
901 Woodsdale Rd (66024)
P.O. Box 455 (66024-0455)
PHONE....................913 365-5200
Dan Riley,
EMP: 10
SALES (est): 3.8MM Privately Held
SIC: 5051 Metals service centers & offices

(G-1691)
ST JOE CONCRETE PRODUCTS (PA)
1807 Roseport Rd (66024)
P.O. Box 2001, Saint Joseph MO (64502-2001)
PHONE....................913 365-7281
Dean Ellenberger, *President*
Kevin Ellenberger, *Vice Pres*
Beverly Ellenberger, *Treasurer*
EMP: 24
SQ FT: 30,000
SALES: 1.5MM Privately Held
WEB: www.stjoeconcreteproducts.com
SIC: 3272 Concrete products, precast; concrete stuctural support & building material; precast terrazo or concrete products

Emporia
Lyon County

(G-1692)
ADVANTAGE METALS RECYCLING LLC
302 Graham St (66801-4402)
PHONE....................620 342-1122
EMP: 44
SALES (corp-wide): 25B Publicly Held
SIC: 5093 Ferrous metal scrap & waste; metal scrap & waste materials
HQ: Advantage Metals Recycling Llc
510 Walnut St Ste 300
Kansas City MO 64106
816 861-2700

(G-1693)
AGLER AND GAEDDERT CHARTERED (PA)
1225 W 6th Ave Ste A (66801-2576)
PHONE....................620 342-7641
D Thomas, *President*
Raymond Meyer, *Vice Pres*
Kreston Norris, *Treasurer*
Lucille Hinderliter, *Admin Sec*
EMP: 24
SQ FT: 4,500
SALES (est): 1.9MM Privately Held
SIC: 8721 Accounting services, except auditing; auditing services; billing & bookkeeping service; certified public accountant

(G-1694)
ALEXANDER CAMP
1783 Road P5 (66801-8140)
PHONE....................620 342-1386
EMP: 20
SALES: 288.5K Privately Held
SIC: 7032 Sport/Recreation Camp

(G-1695)
APAC-KANSAS INC
302 Peyton St (66801-3720)
PHONE....................620 342-2047
Dean McDaniel, *Branch Mgr*
EMP: 30
SALES (corp-wide): 29.7B Privately Held
SIC: 1611 Highway & street construction
HQ: Apac-Kansas, Inc.
9660 Legler Rd
Lenexa KS 66219

(G-1696)
AT HOME SUPPORT CARE INC
417 Commercial St Ste 1 (66801-4080)
PHONE....................620 341-9350
Tresa Hullocker, *Owner*
EMP: 40
SALES: 96K Privately Held
SIC: 8082 Home health care services

(G-1697)
AUSEMUS STNLEY R ESQ CHARTERED
413 Commercial St (66801-4038)
P.O. Box 1083 (66801-1083)
PHONE....................620 342-8717
Stanley R Ausemus, *President*
EMP: 10
SALES (est): 1MM Privately Held
SIC: 8111 General practice attorney, lawyer

(G-1698)
AUSPISION LLC
1211 Stanton St (66801-6158)
PHONE....................620 343-3685
Melody Gryner, *Office Mgr*
Kimberly Reynolds, *Supervisor*
Matthew Reynolds,
Roy Lingenfelter,
EMP: 20
SQ FT: 4,000
SALES (est): 1.1MM Privately Held
WEB: www.auspision.com
SIC: 8322 Rehabilitation services

(G-1699)
B & B MOVIE THEATRES LLC
1614 Industrial Rd (66801-6222)
PHONE....................620 342-0900
John Dickinson, *Branch Mgr*
EMP: 18
SALES (corp-wide): 64.1MM Privately Held
SIC: 7832 Motion picture theaters, except drive-in
PA: B & B Theatres Operating Company, Inc.
2700 Ne Kendallwood Pkwy
Gladstone MO 64119
816 883-2170

(G-1700)
B P E INC
890 Road 160 (66801-7700)
PHONE....................620 343-3783
Robert L Finlay, *President*
Marian L Finlay, *Corp Secy*
▼ EMP: 6
SQ FT: 13,000
SALES (est): 740.8K Privately Held
SIC: 3949 3229 3089 Archery equipment, general; level vials for instruments, glass; plastic containers, except foam

(G-1701)
BALL-MCCOLM POST NO 5 INC
Also Called: MCCOLM POST 5
2921 W 12th Ave (66801-6203)
PHONE....................620 342-1119
John Sanderson, *Pt Cmdr*
Bill Gardner, *Adjutant*
EMP: 20
SQ FT: 8,000
SALES: 103.2K Privately Held
SIC: 8641 Veterans' organization

(G-1702)
BARDEN AND THOMPSON LLC
2518 W 15th Ave (66801-6102)
PHONE....................620 343-8000
Ronald Barden, *Partner*
Kerri Thompson DDS, *Partner*
EMP: 10
SALES (est): 672.2K Privately Held
SIC: 8021 Dentists' office

(G-1703)
BETTER LIFE TECHNOLOGY LLC
1219 Hatcher St (66801-6205)
PHONE....................620 343-2212
David Jamison, *Manager*
EMP: 20
SALES (corp-wide): 25.5MM Privately Held
WEB: www.bltlc.com
SIC: 1752 Floor laying & floor work
PA: Better Life Technology Llc
9736 Legler Rd
Lenexa KS 66219
913 894-0403

(G-1704)
BLI RENTALS LLC
1554 Road 175 (66801-8127)
P.O. Box 992 (66801-0992)
PHONE....................620 342-7847
Jennifer Dalton, *CFO*
Brian Dorsey, *Sales Staff*
Brian Haag, *Manager*
Ashley Foraker, *Executive Asst*
Will Symmonds, *Legal Staff*
EMP: 25 EST: 2008
SALES (est): 3.3MM Privately Held
SIC: 7359 Rental store, general

(G-1705)
BLUESTEM FARM AND RNCH SUP INC
Also Called: Ace Hardware
2611 W Us Highway 50 (66801-6352)
P.O. Box 1064 (66801-1064)
PHONE....................620 342-5502
Lee E Nelson, *CEO*
Kenny Bruner, *President*
Bruce Burenheide, *Manager*
EMP: 70
SQ FT: 50,000
SALES (est): 24.1MM Privately Held
WEB: www.bluestemfarmandranch.com
SIC: 5191 Animal feeds

(G-1706)
BNSF RAILWAY COMPANY
1112 W South Ave (66801-4513)
PHONE....................620 203-2586
Harry Hesterman, *Branch Mgr*
EMP: 200
SALES (corp-wide): 225.3B Publicly Held
WEB: www.billpurdy.com
SIC: 4011 Railroads, line-haul operating
HQ: Bnsf Railway Company
2650 Lou Menk Dr
Fort Worth TX 76131
800 795-2673

(G-1707)
BRAUMSS
2120 Industrial Rd (66801-6612)
PHONE....................620 340-8169
EMP: 5
SALES (est): 165.6K Privately Held
SIC: 2024 Ice cream & frozen desserts

(G-1708)
BROOKDALE SENIOR LIVING COMMUN
Also Called: Sterling House of Emporia
1200 W 12th Ave Ofc (66801-2557)
PHONE....................620 342-1000
Donna Mayer, *Manager*
EMP: 24
SALES (corp-wide): 4.5B Publicly Held
WEB: www.assisted.com
SIC: 8051 Skilled nursing care facilities
HQ: Brookdale Senior Living Communities, Inc.
6737 W Wa St Ste 2300
Milwaukee WI 53214
414 918-5000

(G-1709)
BROWING GAYLA
Also Called: Crawdad Construction
1731 Whittier St (66801-5214)
PHONE....................620 343-2274
Gayla Browing, *Owner*
EMP: 22
SALES (est): 799.9K Privately Held
SIC: 1799 Fence construction

(G-1710)
BRUCE DAVIS CONSTRUCTION LLC
1201 Graphic Arts Rd (66801-6232)
P.O. Box 1924 (66801-1924)
PHONE....................620 342-5001
Bruce Davis,
EMP: 20
SALES (est): 956.5K Privately Held
SIC: 1771 Concrete work

(G-1711)
BUNGE NORTH AMERICA INC
701 E 6th Ave (66801-3405)
P.O. Box 518 (66801-0518)
PHONE....................620 342-7270
Kevin Collins, *Branch Mgr*
EMP: 70 Privately Held
WEB: www.bungenorthamerica.com
SIC: 5153 Barley
HQ: Bunge North America, Inc.
1391 Tmberlake Manor Pkwy
Chesterfield MO 63017
314 292-2000

(G-1712)
BURNAP BROS INC
Also Called: BATH EXPRESSIONS
722 Commercial St (66801-2912)
PHONE....................620 342-2645
David J Cole, *President*
Steve Moore, *Vice Pres*
Mike Cole, *Treasurer*
Kenneth L Martell, *Admin Sec*
EMP: 13 EST: 1904
SQ FT: 6,250
SALES: 4.4MM Privately Held
SIC: 1711 Plumbing contractors

(G-1713)
BURNHAM BUILDERS
314 Neosho St (66801-4160)
PHONE..................................620 343-2047
Max Burnham, *Owner*
EMP: 12
SALES: 800K **Privately Held**
WEB: www.burnhambuilders.com
SIC: 6411 Insurance agents, brokers & service

(G-1714)
C B C S INC
Also Called: Cbcs Collections
105 W 5th Ave (66801-4037)
P.O. Box 428 (66801-0428)
PHONE..................................620 343-6220
Barry Owens, *Manager*
Barry Owen, *Manager*
EMP: 10
SALES (est): 709.4K **Privately Held**
SIC: 7322 7323 Collection agency, except real estate; credit bureau & agency

(G-1715)
CAMSO MANUFACTURING USA LTD
1601 E South Ave (66801-3627)
PHONE..................................620 340-6500
EMP: 24
SALES (corp-wide): 992.7MM **Privately Held**
SIC: 5014 Tires & tubes
HQ: Camso Manufacturing Usa, Ltd.
1 Martina Cir
Plattsburgh NY 12901
518 561-7528

(G-1716)
CAPITOL FEDERAL SAVINGS BANK
Also Called: Capital Federal
602 Commercial St (66801-3996)
PHONE..................................620 342-0125
Delores Heins, *Branch Mgr*
Dolris Hienz, *Manager*
EMP: 10
SALES (corp-wide): 351.9MM **Publicly Held**
WEB: www.capfed.com
SIC: 6035 Federal savings banks
HQ: Capitol Federal Savings Bank
700 S Kansas Ave Fl 1
Topeka KS 66603
785 235-1341

(G-1717)
CARGILL ANIMAL NUTRITION
841 Graphic Arts Rd (66801-5128)
PHONE..................................620 342-1650
Scott Steele, *Manager*
Rick Lovelady, *Manager*
EMP: 42
SALES (est): 7.5MM **Privately Held**
SIC: 5191 Animal feeds

(G-1718)
CBI-KANSAS INC
Also Called: Commerce Bank & Trust
1440 Industrial Rd (66801-6200)
PHONE..................................620 341-7420
Brad Yount, *Branch Mgr*
EMP: 10
SALES (corp-wide): 1.3B **Publicly Held**
SIC: 6022 State commercial banks
HQ: Cbi-Kansas, Inc.
1000 Walnut St Fl 700
Kansas City MO

(G-1719)
CHESTER PRESS INC
2 S Commercial St (66801-7203)
PHONE..................................620 342-8792
Phillip Edwardson, *CEO*
Carla Edwardson, *Vice Pres*
Marie Hammond, *Office Mgr*
EMP: 9
SQ FT: 18,000
SALES: 750K **Privately Held**
SIC: 2752 Commercial printing, offset

(G-1720)
CITY OF EMPORIA
Also Called: Emporia Public Works Dept
1220 Hatcher St (66801-6206)
PHONE..................................620 340-6339
Ronald Childers, *Exec Dir*
EMP: 45 **Privately Held**
SIC: 9511 8641 Waste management agencies; civic social & fraternal associations
PA: City Of Emporia
522 Mechanic St
Emporia KS 66801
620 343-4260

(G-1721)
CLINE AUTO SUPPLY INC
Also Called: NAPA Auto Parts
810 Industrial Rd (66801-5191)
PHONE..................................620 343-6000
Rob Woodruff, *President*
EMP: 20
SQ FT: 12,000
SALES (est): 2.3MM **Privately Held**
SIC: 5531 5013 Automobile & truck equipment & parts; automotive supplies & parts; automotive batteries

(G-1722)
COBANK ACB
Also Called: Farm Credit Services
1221 E 12th Ave (66801-3321)
P.O. Box L (66801-7350)
PHONE..................................620 342-0138
Perry Briggs, *Manager*
EMP: 12
SALES (corp-wide): 4.3B **Privately Held**
WEB: www.usagbank.com
SIC: 6111 Federal Land Banks
PA: Cobank, Acb
6340 S Fiddlers Green Cir
Greenwood Village CO 80111
303 740-6527

(G-1723)
COCA-COLA BOTTLING EMPORIA INC
2931 W 15th Ave (66801-6296)
PHONE..................................239 444-1746
Laurent C De Bauge, *President*
Jeff De Bauge, *Corp Secy*
Barbara De Bauge, *Vice Pres*
Andre Debauge, *Shareholder*
EMP: 22
SQ FT: 21,000
SALES (est): 2.9MM **Privately Held**
WEB: www.emporiacoke.com
SIC: 2086 Bottled & canned soft drinks

(G-1724)
COFFELT SIGN CO INC
18 S Commercial St (66801-4624)
P.O. Box 985 (66801-0985)
PHONE..................................620 343-6411
Nelson Coffelt, *President*
Daisi Hamman, *Vice Pres*
EMP: 7
SQ FT: 3,600
SALES (est): 520K **Privately Held**
SIC: 3993 1799 Electric signs; sign installation & maintenance

(G-1725)
COREFIRST BANK & TRUST
1440 Industrial Rd (66801-6200)
PHONE..................................620 341-7420
Brad Yount, *Branch Mgr*
EMP: 19
SALES (corp-wide): 48MM **Privately Held**
SIC: 6022 State trust companies accepting deposits, commercial
HQ: Corefirst Bank & Trust
3035 Sw Topeka Blvd
Topeka KS 66611
785 267-8900

(G-1726)
CORRECTIONS KANSAS DEPARTMENT
Also Called: Emporia Parole Office
430 Commercial St Bsmnt (66801)
PHONE..................................620 341-3294
Nancy Borthwick, *Director*
EMP: 26 **Privately Held**
WEB: www.kdoc.dc.state.ks.us
SIC: 8322 9223 Parole office; correctional institutions;
HQ: Kansas Department Of Corrections
714 Sw Jackson St Fl 3
Topeka KS 66603
785 296-3317

(G-1727)
DAVES PUMPING SERVICE INC
Also Called: Dave Holland Portable Toilets
1257 Road 137 (66801-7516)
PHONE..................................620 343-3081
David Hollond, *President*
Kim Hollond, *Vice Pres*
EMP: 11
SALES (est): 820.5K **Privately Held**
SIC: 7699 Septic tank cleaning service

(G-1728)
DEER TRAIL IMPLEMENT INC
1744 Road F (66801-7638)
P.O. Box 2023 (66801-2023)
PHONE..................................620 342-5000
EMP: 24
SALES (est): 2.8MM **Privately Held**
SIC: 5083 Whol Farm/Garden Machinery

(G-1729)
DETROIT DIESEL REMANUFACTURING
840 Overlander Rd (66801-8900)
PHONE..................................620 343-3790
David Uschwald, *Vice Pres*
Brian Lewallen, *Vice Pres*
William H Nichols, *Treasurer*
Joline O'Neal, *Admin Sec*
◆ **EMP:** 170
SQ FT: 68,000
SALES (est): 28.1MM
SALES (corp-wide): 185.6B **Privately Held**
SIC: 3519 Diesel engine rebuilding
HQ: Detroit Diesel Remanufacturing Llc
100 Lodestone Way
Tooele UT 84074

(G-1730)
DOT GREEN BIOPLASTICS INC (PA)
Also Called: Green DOT
527 Commercial St Ste 310 (66801-4081)
PHONE..................................620 273-8919
Mark Remmert, *CEO*
Mark Mahoney, *Principal*
Kevin Ireland, *Comms Mgr*
Mike Parker, *Manager*
EMP: 10
SALES: 3MM **Privately Held**
SIC: 2821 Plastics materials & resins

(G-1731)
DOUBLE T ENTERPRISES
Also Called: Thomas Property Management
906 E 6th Ave (66801-3204)
P.O. Box 1023 (66801-1023)
PHONE..................................620 342-2655
Kenneth B Thomas Sr, *Partner*
Della L Thomas, *Partner*
Jerry Thomas, *Partner*
Nancy J Thomas, *Partner*
EMP: 18
SQ FT: 46,000
SALES (est): 1.2MM **Privately Held**
SIC: 6513 Apartment building operators

(G-1732)
DPP MANUFACTURING LLC
886 Road 160 (66801-7700)
P.O. Box 247 (66801-0247)
PHONE..................................620 340-7200
EMP: 5
SALES (est): 388.3K **Privately Held**
SIC: 3599 Machine shop, jobbing & repair

(G-1733)
DRS PRICE YOUNG ODLE HORSCH PA
512 Commercial St (66801-4006)
PHONE..................................620 343-7120
Gilan L Cockrell Od, *Partner*
EMP: 30 **EST:** 2001
SALES (est): 904.7K **Privately Held**
SIC: 8042 Contact lense specialist optometrist

(G-1734)
DYNAMIC DISCS LLC (PA)
912 Commercial St (66801-2917)
PHONE..................................620 208-3472
Bradley Crow, *General Mgr*
Kris Edson, *Opers Mgr*
Denise Cameron, *Buyer*
Jamie Rusco, *Sales Staff*
Jacob Torkelson, *Art Dir*
▲ **EMP:** 13
SALES (est): 3.7MM **Privately Held**
SIC: 5941 7999 Golf goods & equipment; golf professionals

(G-1735)
EAGEL TRANSIT INC
4245 W Us Highway 50 (66801-7666)
PHONE..................................620 343-3444
Ronald W McCoy, *President*
EMP: 32
SALES (est): 2MM **Privately Held**
SIC: 4213 Trucking, except local

(G-1736)
EMPORIA COLD STORAGE CO
2601 W 6th Ave (66801-6333)
PHONE..................................620 343-8010
Kim Howe, *Manager*
EMP: 11
SALES (est): 540.1K **Privately Held**
SIC: 4222 Warehousing, cold storage or refrigerated

(G-1737)
EMPORIA COMMUNITY DAYCARE CTR (PA)
802 Commercial St (66801-3407)
P.O. Box 545 (66801-0545)
PHONE..................................620 343-2888
Deb Crowl, *Manager*
Dennise Wilson, *Manager*
EMP: 14
SALES: 836.1K **Privately Held**
SIC: 8351 Group day care center

(G-1738)
EMPORIA CONSTRUCTION & RMDLG
306 Market St (66801-3930)
PHONE..................................620 341-3131
Paul Challender, *President*
Chris Walker, *Editor*
Lisa Stueve, *Sales Dir*
EMP: 20
SQ FT: 2,400
SALES (est): 2MM **Privately Held**
SIC: 1771 1542 1521 Concrete work; commercial & office building, new construction; commercial & office buildings, renovation & repair; general remodeling, single-family houses

(G-1739)
EMPORIA COUNTRY CLUB INC
1801 Rural St (66801-5451)
P.O. Box 744 (66801-0744)
PHONE..................................620 342-0343
Darrell Brock, *President*
Jon Pool, *Corp Secy*
EMP: 30
SALES: 639.7K **Privately Held**
WEB: www.emporiacc.org
SIC: 7997 Country club, membership

(G-1740)
EMPORIA ORTHODONTICS
919 W 12th Ave Ste A (66801-5584)
PHONE..................................620 343-7275
Stephen Haught, *Owner*
EMP: 10
SALES (est): 396.9K **Privately Held**
WEB: www.emporiaorthodontics.com
SIC: 8021 Orthodontist

(G-1741)
EMPORIA PET PRODUCTS INC
Also Called: Emporia Pet Foods
841 Graphic Arts Rd (66801-5128)
PHONE..................................620 342-1650
Barbara Wry, *Plant Mgr*
EMP: 35

SALES (est): 4.7MM
SALES (corp-wide): 400MM **Privately Held**
WEB: www.anibrands.com
SIC: 2047 Dog food
PA: American Nutrition, Inc.
2813 Wall Ave
Ogden UT 84401
801 394-3477

(G-1742)
EMPORIA PHYSICAL THERAPY
1024 W 12th Ave Ste B (66801-5553)
PHONE..................................620 342-4100
Greg Bachman, *Owner*
EMP: 10
SALES (est): 270.3K **Privately Held**
SIC: 8062 General medical & surgical hospitals

(G-1743)
EMPORIA PRSBT MNOR OF MID AMER
2300 Industrial Rd (66801-6635)
PHONE..................................620 412-2019
Roger Clossen, *Director*
EMP: 70
SQ FT: 91,500
SALES: 6.1MM **Privately Held**
SIC: 6513 8051 Retirement hotel operation; convalescent home with continuous nursing care

(G-1744)
EMPORIA STATE FEDERAL CR UN
310 W 12th Ave (66801-5026)
PHONE..................................620 342-2336
Dusty Eubanks, *Loan Officer*
Bill Huth, *Loan Officer*
Angela Miller, *Manager*
Josh Hubler, *Producer*
Ron Hanson, *Director*
EMP: 20
SALES: 3MM **Privately Held**
WEB: www.emporiastatefederalcreditunion.com
SIC: 6061 Federal credit unions

(G-1745)
EMPORIA STATE UNIV FNDTION INC
1500 Highland St (66801-5018)
PHONE..................................620 341-5440
Ed Bashaw, *Dean*
Lynn Hobson, *Dean*
Catherine Bergman, *Manager*
Boyce Baumgardner, *Exec Dir*
James Willingham, *Director*
EMP: 18
SALES: 12.1MM **Privately Held**
SIC: 8641 Alumni association

(G-1746)
EMPORIA VETERINARY HOSPITAL
710 Anderson St (66801-6394)
PHONE..................................620 342-6515
Dr Scott A Gordon, *Owner*
Bryan Barr, *Partner*
Dr Duane M Henrikson, *Partner*
Scott Gordon, *Manager*
EMP: 10
SQ FT: 7,000
SALES (est): 462.9K **Privately Held**
SIC: 0741 0742 Animal hospital services, livestock; animal hospital services, pets & other animal specialties

(G-1747)
EMPORIA WHOLESALE COFFEE CO (PA)
Also Called: Evco
309 Merchant St (66801-7207)
P.O. Box D (66801-7343)
PHONE..................................620 343-7000
Charles Evans, *President*
Janet K Evans, *Vice Pres*
Kirk Massmann, *Vice Pres*
Mark Kosec, *Opers Mgr*
Jenny Gibbs, *Buyer*
EMP: 155
SQ FT: 90,000
SALES: 1.5MM **Privately Held**
WEB: www.evcofoods.com
SIC: 5141 5087 Food brokers; janitors' supplies

(G-1748)
EMPORIA WINERY LLC
Also Called: Twin Rvers Wine Gourmet Shoppe
627 Commercial St (66801-3901)
PHONE..................................620 481-7129
Justin Ogleby,
Melissa Ogleby,
Harlan Smith Jr,
Rebecca Smith,
Casey Woods,
EMP: 5
SQ FT: 9,750
SALES (est): 247.8K **Privately Held**
SIC: 2084 Wine cellars, bonded: engaged in blending wines

(G-1749)
EMPORIAS RADIO STATIONS INC
Also Called: K V O E FM
1420 C Of E Dr Ste 200 (66801-2556)
P.O. Box 968 (66801-0968)
PHONE..................................620 342-1400
Steve Sauder, *President*
Ron Thomas, *General Mgr*
Susan Grother, *Corp Secy*
Steve Inwood, *Sales Staff*
Scott Hayes, *Program Dir*
EMP: 18 **EST:** 1957
SALES (est): 1.4MM **Privately Held**
SIC: 4832 Radio broadcasting stations

(G-1750)
ENTERTAINMENT SPECIALTIES
Also Called: Rollers
701 Graham St (66801-5183)
PHONE..................................620 342-3322
Terry W Maxfield, *President*
Peggy L Maxfield, *Treasurer*
Cody Maxfield, *Sales Mgr*
EMP: 15
SALES (est): 1.8MM **Privately Held**
WEB: www.audiolite.com
SIC: 1731 7999 Sound equipment specialization; lighting contractor; voice, data & video wiring contractor; roller skating rink operation

(G-1751)
ESB FINANCIAL (PA)
801 Merchant St (66801-2811)
P.O. Box 807 (66801-0807)
PHONE..................................620 342-3454
James C Wayman, *President*
Howard Gunkel, *Chairman*
Mike Sykes, *Exec VP*
Kenneth Buchele, *Senior VP*
Craig Black, *Vice Pres*
EMP: 40 **EST:** 1901
SQ FT: 8,000
SALES: 11.1MM **Privately Held**
WEB: www.esbtrust.com
SIC: 6022 State trust companies accepting deposits, commercial

(G-1752)
EVERGREEN DESIGN BUILD LLC
813 Graham St (66801-5110)
PHONE..................................620 342-6622
John Mallon, *President*
Justin Mallon, *Vice Pres*
EMP: 40
SQ FT: 2,000
SALES: 7MM **Privately Held**
SIC: 1541 Industrial buildings & warehouses

(G-1753)
EVERGY KANSAS CENTRAL INC
Also Called: K P L Gas Service
210 E 2nd Ave (66801-3906)
PHONE..................................620 341-7020
Bill Heins, *Opers Staff*
EMP: 53
SALES (corp-wide): 4.2B **Publicly Held**
SIC: 4911 Electric services
HQ: Evergy Kansas Central, Inc.
818 S Kansas Ave
Topeka KS 66612
785 575-6300

(G-1754)
FAMILY LIFE SERVICES EMPORIA
615 Congress St (66801-2819)
P.O. Box 748 (66801-0748)
PHONE..................................620 342-2244
Cindy Rhudy, *Principal*
Carol Alderman, *Director*
EMP: 11
SALES: 103.1K **Privately Held**
SIC: 8322 Social service center

(G-1755)
FAMILY VIDEO MOVIE CLUB INC
1012 Commercial St (66801-2919)
PHONE..................................620 342-4659
Shannon Hill, *Manager*
EMP: 12
SALES (corp-wide): 189.9MM **Privately Held**
WEB: www.familyvideo.net
SIC: 7841 Video disk/tape rental to the general public
HQ: Family Video Movie Club Inc.
2500 Lehigh Mt Ave
Glenview IL 60026
847 904-9000

(G-1756)
FIRST START RENTL SLS SVC INC
2026 W 6th Ave (66801-6463)
PHONE..................................620 343-0983
Scott William Grimmett, *CEO*
EMP: 5
SALES: 1.2MM **Privately Held**
SIC: 3524 0782 Lawn & garden equipment; lawn & garden services

(G-1757)
FLINT HILLS CARE CENTER
1620 Wheeler St (66801-6146)
PHONE..................................620 342-3280
Margaret Edlund, *Administration*
EMP: 70
SALES: 3.2MM **Privately Held**
SIC: 8051 Skilled nursing care facilities

(G-1758)
FLINT HILLS CMNTY HLTH CTR INC
420 W 15th Ave (66801-5367)
PHONE..................................620 342-4864
Liz Conrade, *CEO*
Betty Murrell, *CFO*
Stephanie Ringgold, *CFO*
Seresa Howe, *Accountant*
Tabatha Tafoya, *Human Res Dir*
EMP: 75
SQ FT: 38,307
SALES: 9.8MM **Privately Held**
WEB: www.flinthillshealth.org
SIC: 8011 Clinic, operated by physicians

(G-1759)
FLINT HILLS MALL LLC
1632 Industrial Rd (66801-6222)
PHONE..................................620 342-4631
Jose L Feliciano, *Mng Member*
EMP: 12
SALES (est): 899.2K **Privately Held**
SIC: 6512 Shopping center, property operation only

(G-1760)
FLINTELLS EYECARE
Also Called: Reimer, Paul E
512 Commercial St (66801-4006)
PHONE..................................620 343-7120
Od Gilan Cockrell, *Partner*
EMP: 20
SQ FT: 8,000
SALES (est): 1MM **Privately Held**
SIC: 5995 8042 Contact lenses, prescription; offices & clinics of optometrists

(G-1761)
GENESIS HLTH CLUBS EMPORIA LLC
1007 Commercial St (66801-2918)
PHONE..................................620 343-6034
Ryan Brooks, *CFO*
EMP: 330
SALES: 12MM **Privately Held**
SIC: 7991 Health club

(G-1762)
GLACIER PETROLEUM INC
825 Commercial St (66801-2914)
P.O. Box 577 (66801-0577)
PHONE..................................620 342-1148
EMP: 10 **EST:** 1969
SQ FT: 1,800
SALES (est): 1.6MM **Privately Held**
SIC: 1311 1389 Crude petroleum production; servicing oil & gas wells

(G-1763)
GLENDO LLC
Also Called: Grs
900 Overlander Rd (66801-8916)
P.O. Box 1153 (66801-1153)
PHONE..................................620 343-1084
Kim A Pember, *President*
Kim Pember, *General Mgr*
Steve Willhite, *Mfg Staff*
David Mackay, *IT/INT Sup*
Janice Stone, *Executive*
▼ **EMP:** 50
SQ FT: 48,158
SALES: 13MM **Privately Held**
SIC: 3559 Jewelers' machines

(G-1764)
GOODWILL INDUSTRIES EA
904 E 12th Ave (66801-3238)
PHONE..................................620 343-3564
EMP: 31
SALES (corp-wide): 10.8MM **Privately Held**
SIC: 8331 Vocational rehabilitation agency
PA: Goodwill Industries Easter Seal Society Of Kansas, Inc.
3636 N Oliver St
Wichita KS
316 744-9291

(G-1765)
GRIMMETT MASONRY INC
Also Called: Grimmett Scott Masonry
2026 W 6th Ave (66801-6463)
PHONE..................................620 342-6582
Scott Grimmett, *President*
Lory Grimmet, *Admin Sec*
EMP: 12
SQ FT: 18,000
SALES (est): 1.1MM **Privately Held**
SIC: 1741 Masonry & other stonework

(G-1766)
HAND IN HAND & HOSPICE
1201 W 12th Ave (66801-2504)
PHONE..................................620 340-6177
Andrea Elwood, *Exec Dir*
EMP: 16
SALES (est): 368.4K **Privately Held**
SIC: 8082 Home health care services

(G-1767)
HANNAH & OLTJEN
Also Called: Hannah J Joseph
3021 Eaglecrest Dr Ste A (66801-6193)
PHONE..................................620 343-3000
Judy Beran, *Manager*
EMP: 12
SALES (corp-wide): 1.9MM **Privately Held**
SIC: 8021 Orthodontist
PA: Hannah & Oltjen
1441 E 151st St
Olathe KS 66062
913 829-2244

(G-1768)
HEADSTART PROGRAM
Also Called: Maynard Early Childhood Center
19 Constitution St (66801-4078)
PHONE..................................620 341-2260
Keva Scheib, *Principal*
Mary Rodriguez, *Director*
Shari Meade, *Teacher*

EMP: 20
SALES (est): 237.7K **Privately Held**
SIC: 8351 Preschool center

(G-1769)
HERTZ CORPORATION
602 State St (66801-2714)
PHONE..................................620 342-6322
Susan Blubaugh, *Branch Mgr*
EMP: 45
SALES (corp-wide): 9.5B **Publicly Held**
WEB: www.hertz.com
SIC: 7514 7513 Rent-a-car service; truck rental, without drivers
HQ: The Hertz Corporation
8501 Williams Rd
Estero FL 33928
239 301-7000

(G-1770)
HERTZ CORPORATION
3105 W 6th Ave (66801-5172)
PHONE..................................620 341-9656
Daniel Switzer, *Owner*
EMP: 23
SALES (corp-wide): 9.5B **Publicly Held**
SIC: 7514 Rent-a-car service
HQ: The Hertz Corporation
8501 Williams Rd
Estero FL 33928
239 301-7000

(G-1771)
HETLINGER DVLOPMENTAL SVCS INC
707 S Commercial St (66801-8804)
P.O. Box 2204 (66801-2204)
PHONE..................................620 342-1087
Bev Gilligan, *Principal*
Trudy Hutchinson, *Exec Dir*
Sara Pearson, *Administration*
EMP: 26
SQ FT: 30,000
SALES: 1.5MM **Privately Held**
WEB: www.hetlinger.org
SIC: 8331 Sheltered workshop

(G-1772)
HILLS PET NUTRITION INC
400 S Weaver St (66801-7590)
PHONE..................................620 340-6920
Tim Braue, *President*
EMP: 100
SALES (corp-wide): 15.5B **Publicly Held**
SIC: 2048 Canned pet food (except dog & cat)
HQ: Hill's Pet Nutrition, Inc.
400 Sw 8th Ave Ste 101
Topeka KS 66603
800 255-0449

(G-1773)
HOLIDAY HEALTHCARE LLC (PA)
2700 W 30th Ave (66801-9100)
PHONE..................................620 343-9285
Michael Fry, *President*
EMP: 21
SQ FT: 46,500
SALES (est): 6.9MM **Privately Held**
SIC: 8361 Rest home, with health care incidental

(G-1774)
HOOVER BACHMAN & ASSOC INC
Also Called: Emporia Fitness
2812 W 12th Ave (66801-6202)
PHONE..................................620 342-2348
Greg Bachman, *CEO*
EMP: 12
SALES (est): 512.9K **Privately Held**
SIC: 7991 Health club

(G-1775)
HOPKINS MANUFACTURING CORP (PA)
428 Peyton St (66801-3722)
P.O. Box 1157 (66801-1157)
PHONE..................................620 342-7320
Brad Kraft, *President*
David Moore, *Senior VP*
Rick Stempien, *Vice Pres*
Curtis Strong, *Vice Pres*
Mark Turgyan, *Vice Pres*
◆ **EMP:** 350
SQ FT: 310,000
SALES (est): 213.5MM **Privately Held**
WEB: www.hopkinsdev.com
SIC: 3714 Motor vehicle parts & accessories

(G-1776)
HOSTESS BRANDS LLC
1525 Industrial Rd (66801-6219)
PHONE..................................620 342-6811
Todd Crook, *VP Mfg*
EMP: 7
SALES (corp-wide): 850.3MM **Publicly Held**
SIC: 2051 Bakery: wholesale or wholesale/retail combined
HQ: Hostess Brands, Llc
1 E Armour Blvd
Kansas City MO 64111
816 701-4600

(G-1777)
INNWORKS INC
Also Called: Super 8 Motel
2913 W Us Highway 50 (66801-5140)
PHONE..................................620 342-7567
Mariyln Patterson, *Principal*
EMP: 12 **Privately Held**
WEB: www.innworks.com
SIC: 7011 Hotels & motels
PA: Innworks Inc
1611 County Road B W # 200
Saint Paul MN

(G-1778)
INTERNAL MEDICINE ASSOCIATES
1301 W 12th Ave Ste 202 (66801-2589)
P.O. Box 907 (66801-0907)
PHONE..................................620 342-2521
James M Geitz, *Partner*
James A Barnett MD, *Partner*
W Brock Kretsinger Do, *Partner*
EMP: 35
SALES (est): 4.2MM **Privately Held**
SIC: 8011 Internal medicine, physician/surgeon

(G-1779)
JACK JONES INC
1620 Road 210 (66801-7968)
PHONE..................................620 342-4221
EMP: 16
SALES (est): 860K **Privately Held**
SIC: 7336 Commercial Art/Graphic Design

(G-1780)
JOHN C PATTON DDS
1507 W 12th Ave (66801-2457)
PHONE..................................620 342-0673
John C Patton DDS, *President*
EMP: 12
SALES (est): 1MM **Privately Held**
SIC: 8021 Dentists' office

(G-1781)
JONES FOUNDATION
2501 W 18th Ave Ste D (66801-6195)
PHONE..................................620 342-1714
Sharon Tidwell, *Exec Dir*
EMP: 10
SALES: 2.2MM **Privately Held**
WEB: www.jonesfdn.org
SIC: 8322 Individual & family services

(G-1782)
K & S EASTSIDE AMOCO INC
1102 Whittier St (66801-3359)
PHONE..................................620 342-3565
Kim Nelson, *President*
Sherry Nelson, *Treasurer*
EMP: 15
SQ FT: 2,500
SALES (est): 2.5MM **Privately Held**
SIC: 5541 5411 7513 Filling stations, gasoline; convenience stores, independent; truck rental, without drivers

(G-1783)
KAN FAB INC
623 Graham St (66801-5107)
PHONE..................................620 342-5669
John Chester Mast, *President*
James Mast, *Vice Pres*
EMP: 5
SALES: 118.1K **Privately Held**
SIC: 7692 3499 3599 Automotive welding; fire- or burglary-resistive products; crankshafts & camshafts, machining

(G-1784)
KANSAS ASSISTIVE TECH CORP (PA)
Also Called: Katco
215 W 6th Ave Ste 205 (66801-4007)
PHONE..................................620 341-9002
Basil Kessler PHD, *Director*
Mary Ann Newton, *Director*
EMP: 42
SALES (est): 559.7K **Privately Held**
SIC: 6163 Loan agents

(G-1785)
KANSAS CHILDRENS SERVICE LEAG
402 Commercial St (66801-4082)
P.O. Box 1103 (66801-1103)
PHONE..................................620 340-0408
EMP: 15
SALES (corp-wide): 15MM **Privately Held**
SIC: 8322 Adoption services
PA: Kansas Children's Service League
1365 N Custer St
Wichita KS 67203
316 942-4261

(G-1786)
KANSAS CONTINENTAL EXPRESS INC
Also Called: K C X
709 Industrial Rd (66801-5121)
P.O. Box 1448 (66801-1448)
PHONE..................................620 343-7100
Jim Sanborn, *Natl Sales Mgr*
EMP: 12
SQ FT: 2,500
SALES: 10MM **Privately Held**
WEB: www.kcxi.com
SIC: 4213 Trucking, except local

(G-1787)
LYON COUNTY STATE BANK (PA)
902 Merchant St (66801-2814)
P.O. Box 488 (66801-0488)
PHONE..................................620 342-3523
Tom Thompson, *President*
Yovana Weller, *Credit Staff*
Lisa Hill, *Human Res Mgr*
Mike Tovar, *Manager*
EMP: 24 **EST:** 1913
SALES: 6.2MM **Privately Held**
WEB: www.lyoncountybank.com
SIC: 6022 State trust companies accepting deposits, commercial

(G-1788)
LYON COUNTY STATE BANK
527 Commercial St (66801-4027)
PHONE..................................620 343-4444
EMP: 15
SALES (corp-wide): 6.4MM **Privately Held**
SIC: 6022 State Commercial Bank
PA: Lyon County State Bank
902 Merchant St
Emporia KS 66801
620 342-3523

(G-1789)
MALLON FAMILY LLC
813 Graham St (66801-5110)
PHONE..................................620 342-6622
John J Mallon, *Mng Member*
John Mallon, *Mng Member*
EMP: 10
SALES (est): 680K **Privately Held**
SIC: 6512 Commercial & industrial building operation

(G-1790)
MASONIC TEMPLE
424 Merchant St (66801-4059)
P.O. Box 179 (66801-0179)
PHONE..................................620 342-3913
William E Gardner, *Principal*
EMP: 11
SALES (est): 410K **Privately Held**
SIC: 8641 Fraternal associations

(G-1791)
MEDICAL ARTS CLNIC A PROF ASSN
1301 W 12th Ave Ste 401 (66801-2591)
PHONE..................................620 343-2900
Cotton O'Niel, *President*
H R Bradley, *President*
Todd Detwiler, *Vice Pres*
▲ **EMP:** 27 **EST:** 1957
SALES (est): 2.4MM **Privately Held**
SIC: 8011 Clinic, operated by physicians

(G-1792)
MELS TIRE LLC
915 Graham St (66801-5112)
PHONE..................................620 342-8473
Dj Eidman, *Mng Member*
Allen Mize,
Joe Dreier,
Steven Preisner,
EMP: 14
SQ FT: 15,000
SALES (est): 2.8MM **Privately Held**
SIC: 5531 7539 Automotive tires; brake services; wheel alignment, automotive

(G-1793)
MEMORIAL UNION CORP EMPORIA
1200 Coml St Pmb 4066 4066 Pmb (66801)
PHONE..................................620 341-5901
Lynn Hobson, *Director*
Blythe Hendricks, *Director*
David Hendricks, *Director*
Greg Larsen, *Director*
EMP: 72 **EST:** 1922
SQ FT: 168,000
SALES: 2MM **Privately Held**
SIC: 7993 5962 Amusement machine rental, coin-operated; food vending machines

(G-1794)
MENTAL HLTH CTR OF EST-CNTRAL (PA)
1000 Lincoln St (66801-2449)
PHONE..................................620 343-2211
Anne Fritz, *President*
Jayne Mudge, *Vice Pres*
Bill Persinger, *Exec Dir*
EMP: 46
SQ FT: 12,000
SALES: 1.8K **Privately Held**
SIC: 8093 Mental health clinic, outpatient; alcohol clinic, outpatient; rehabilitation center, outpatient treatment

(G-1795)
MIDAS TOUCH GOLDEN TANS
2918 W Us Highway 50 F (66801-5149)
PHONE..................................620 340-1011
Darrell Ringler, *Owner*
EMP: 10
SALES (est): 275.5K **Privately Held**
WEB: www.midastouchtans.com
SIC: 7299 Tanning salon

(G-1796)
MITCHELL-MARKOWITZ CNSTR
414 Graham St (66801-4404)
PHONE..................................620 343-6840
John Markowitz, *President*
Rick Mitchell, *Vice Pres*
EMP: 23
SQ FT: 2,400
SALES: 4MM **Privately Held**
SIC: 1542 1521 1522 Commercial & office building, new construction; general remodeling, single-family houses; new construction, single-family houses; multi-family dwellings, new construction

(G-1797)
MODERN AIR CONDITIONING INC
106 Commercial St (66801-4096)
PHONE..................................620 342-7577
Jim Kessler, *Partner*
Robert Burenheide, *Vice Pres*
Charles Haag, *Vice Pres*
R J Kuhlmann, *Vice Pres*
Travis Sullivan, *Vice Pres*
EMP: 22 **EST:** 1968
SQ FT: 22,000

SALES (est): 2.8MM **Privately Held**
WEB: www.modernairconditioning.com
SIC: 1711 1761 Warm air heating & air conditioning contractor; refrigeration contractor; sheet metalwork
PA: Modern Air Conditioner
106 Commercial St
Emporia KS 66801

(G-1798)
MOTEL 6 OPERATING LP
2630 W 18th Ave (66801-6108)
PHONE....620 343-1240
Patricia Gordon, *Manager*
EMP: 15
SALES (corp-wide): 579.1MM **Privately Held**
WEB: www.motel6.com
SIC: 7011 Hotels & motels
HQ: Motel 6 Operating L.P.
4001 Intl Pkwy Ste 500
Carrollton TX 75007
972 360-9000

(G-1799)
MUCKENTHALER INCORPORATED (PA)
308 Commercial St (66801-4011)
PHONE....620 342-5653
John E Muckenthaler, *President*
James F Muckenthaler, *Vice Pres*
Joe E Muckenthaler, *Treasurer*
Joe Muckenthaler, *Treasurer*
Theresa Muckenthaler, *Train & Dev Mgr*
EMP: 13 **EST:** 1970
SQ FT: 15,000
SALES: 6MM **Privately Held**
WEB: www.muckenthaler.com
SIC: 5046 5719 Restaurant equipment & supplies; kitchenware

(G-1800)
NAVRATS INC (PA)
Also Called: Office Products
728 Mechanic St (66801-2955)
P.O. Box N (66801-7352)
PHONE....620 342-2092
Richard Duncan, *President*
Monica Duncan, *Treasurer*
Rusty Smiley, *Treasurer*
Kent Schnakenberg, *VP Human Res*
Jack Call, *Sales Staff*
EMP: 18 **EST:** 1945
SQ FT: 18,000
SALES: 5.9MM **Privately Held**
WEB: www.navrats.com
SIC: 2752 5021 5112 2789 Commercial printing, offset; office furniture; business forms; bookbinding & related work; commercial printing; automotive & apparel trimmings

(G-1801)
NEW DIMENSION PDTS EMPORIA INC
1015 Scott St (66801-5160)
PHONE....620 342-6412
EMP: 26
SALES (est): 2.3MM **Privately Held**
SIC: 1521 Remodeling Contractor Of Single-Family Homes

(G-1802)
NEWMAN MEM HOSP FOUNDATION
1301 W 12th Ave Ste 301 (66801-2590)
PHONE....620 342-2521
EMP: 34
SALES (corp-wide): 1MM **Privately Held**
SIC: 8011 General & family practice, physician/surgeon
PA: Newman Memorial Hospital Foundation
1201 W 12th Ave
Emporia KS 66801
620 343-6800

(G-1803)
NEWMAN MEM HOSP FOUNDATION (PA)
Also Called: Newman Regional Health
1201 W 12th Ave (66801-2504)
PHONE....620 343-6800
Robert Wright, *CEO*
John Rossseld, *CEO*
Nancy Wells, *Principal*
Shirley Hogan, *Project Mgr*
Tyson Allen, *Purch Dir*
EMP: 500
SQ FT: 379,000
SALES (est): 1MM **Privately Held**
WEB: www.newmanrh.org
SIC: 8062 5047 8011 Hospital, medical school affiliated with nursing & residency; medical & hospital equipment; clinic, operated by physicians

(G-1804)
NEWMAN MEM HOSP FOUNDATION
Newman Medical Eqp & Sups
1015 Industrial Rd (66801-5127)
PHONE....620 343-1800
Allen Tyson, *Branch Mgr*
EMP: 15
SALES (corp-wide): 1MM **Privately Held**
SIC: 5047 Medical & hospital equipment
PA: Newman Memorial Hospital Foundation
1201 W 12th Ave
Emporia KS 66801
620 343-6800

(G-1805)
NEWMAN MEM HOSP FOUNDATION
Also Called: Newman Home Health
1201 W 12th Ave (66801-2504)
PHONE....620 340-6161
Vicki Fell, *Manager*
EMP: 21
SALES (corp-wide): 1MM **Privately Held**
WEB: www.newmanrh.org
SIC: 8082 Home health care services
PA: Newman Memorial Hospital Foundation
1201 W 12th Ave
Emporia KS 66801
620 343-6800

(G-1806)
NONPROFIT SOLUTIONS INC
618 Commercial St Ste B (66801-3970)
P.O. Box 2224 (66801-2224)
PHONE....620 343-6111
Dale Bell, *CEO*
Richard Wright, *CFO*
Angela Westcott, *Finance Mgr*
Eric Huggard, *Director*
EMP: 90
SQ FT: 14,000
SALES: 2.9MM **Privately Held**
SIC: 8742 Administrative services consultant

(G-1807)
NORFOLK IRON & METAL CO
1701 E South Ave (66801-9788)
P.O. Box 1467 (66801-1467)
PHONE....620 342-9202
Jeff Beckmer, *President*
EMP: 200
SALES (est): 46.9MM **Privately Held**
SIC: 5051 Steel

(G-1808)
O S S INC
25 W 5th Ave (66801-4035)
P.O. Box 1191 (66801-1191)
PHONE....620 343-8799
Connie Cahoone, *Exec Dir*
Susan Moran, *Director*
EMP: 43
SALES: 1.6MM **Privately Held**
WEB: www.soswww.com
SIC: 8322 Emergency shelters

(G-1809)
OLPE LOCKER
1530 Williby Ave (66801-5759)
PHONE....620 475-3375
Rex Turner, *Partner*
Connie Turner, *Partner*
EMP: 5 **EST:** 1956
SQ FT: 4,400
SALES (est): 431.9K **Privately Held**
SIC: 2011 4222 Meat packing plants; storage, frozen or refrigerated goods

(G-1810)
ONEOK INC
Also Called: Kansas Gas Service
220 Mechanic St (66801-3940)
PHONE....620 341-7054
Terry Ellis, *Manager*
EMP: 13
SALES (corp-wide): 12.5B **Publicly Held**
WEB: www.oneok.com
SIC: 4922 Natural gas transmission
PA: Oneok, Inc.
100 W 5th St Ste Ll
Tulsa OK 74103
918 588-7000

(G-1811)
PARAGON HOLDINGS LC
Also Called: Paragon Laser Systems
3700 Oakes Dr (66801-5132)
PHONE....620 343-0920
Jerry Waddell,
▼ **EMP:** 46
SQ FT: 64,000
SALES (est): 3.9MM **Privately Held**
WEB: www.paragonlasersystems.com
SIC: 3699 Laser systems & equipment

(G-1812)
PLP INC
Also Called: John Deere Authorized Dealer
1744 Road F (66801-7638)
P.O. Box 2023 (66801-2023)
PHONE....620 342-5000
Richard Garber, *Branch Mgr*
EMP: 30
SALES (corp-wide): 66.9MM **Privately Held**
SIC: 5999 5082 Farm equipment & supplies; construction & mining machinery
PA: Plp, Inc
811 E 30th Ave Ste F
Hutchinson KS 67502
620 664-5860

(G-1813)
PROFESSIONAL PRINTING KANS INC
315 Constitution St (66801-4045)
P.O. Box 427 (66801-0427)
PHONE....620 343-7125
William Henry, *President*
Aaron Marcum, *Finance*
EMP: 15
SQ FT: 23,500
SALES: 1.2MM **Privately Held**
WEB: www.proprintusa.com
SIC: 7331 2759 Direct mail advertising services; commercial printing

(G-1814)
QUEST SERVICES INC
2608 W 12th Ave (66801-6312)
PHONE....620 208-6180
Brenda Sherwood, *President*
Phil Moore, *Treasurer*
Marlin Johnson, *Admin Sec*
EMP: 183
SALES (est): 6.4MM **Privately Held**
SIC: 8399 Health systems agency

(G-1815)
RED LINE INC
Also Called: Refrigerated Express Delivery
2805 Bel Aire Dr (66801-4417)
PHONE....620 343-1000
Kevin Nelson, *President*
Don Nelson, *Chairman*
EMP: 10
SQ FT: 3,500
SALES (est): 2.7MM **Privately Held**
SIC: 4213 Refrigerated products transport

(G-1816)
REEBLE INC (PA)
Also Called: Price Chopper
1020 Merchant St (66801-2816)
PHONE....620 342-0404
Arnold Graham, *President*
Carol Strickland, *Exec Dir*
EMP: 55
SQ FT: 22,000
SALES (est): 13.2MM **Privately Held**
WEB: www.reeble.com
SIC: 6798 Real estate investment trusts

(G-1817)
RPS INC
Also Called: Midwest Business Service
1224 Frontier Way (66801-6110)
PHONE....620 342-3026
EMP: 16
SQ FT: 20,000
SALES (est): 2.2MM **Privately Held**
SIC: 2752 Lithographic Commercial Printing

(G-1818)
S&S QUALITY MEATS LLC
Also Called: Fanestil Meats
1542 S Highway 99 (66801-7765)
P.O. Box 629 (66801-0629)
PHONE....620 342-6354
Jay Woerz, *Vice Pres*
Damon Clopton, *Plant Mgr*
Tracy Eastman, *Controller*
Dan Smoots,
EMP: 65 **EST:** 1942
SQ FT: 25,000
SALES: 110MM **Privately Held**
WEB: www.fanestils.com
SIC: 2011 2013 Meat packing plants; sausages & other prepared meats

(G-1819)
SADY VIJAY INC
Also Called: Econo Lodge
2511 W 18th Ave (66801-6105)
PHONE....620 343-7750
Ramesh Patel, *Principal*
EMP: 10
SALES (est): 517.2K **Privately Held**
SIC: 7011 Hotels & motels

(G-1820)
SALON X
Also Called: Details Intimate Apparel
518 Commercial St (66801-4006)
PHONE....620 343-8634
EMP: 12 **EST:** 1990
SQ FT: 3,256
SALES (est): 240K **Privately Held**
SIC: 7231 5632 Beauty Salon & Ret Women's Lingerie

(G-1821)
SALVATION ARMY
520 Constitution St (66801-4049)
PHONE....620 343-3166
Deb Thompson, *Branch Mgr*
EMP: 12
SALES (corp-wide): 5.8MM **Privately Held**
WEB: www.salvationarmykc.org
SIC: 8661 8399 8699 8322 Churches, temples & shrines; community development groups; charitable organization; individual & family services
PA: The Salvation Army
1351 E 10th St
Kansas City MO 64106
816 421-5434

(G-1822)
SANA HOSPITALITY CORP
Also Called: Super 8 Motel
2913 W Us Highway 50 (66801-5140)
PHONE....620 342-7567
Mish Bhakta, *General Mgr*
EMP: 10 **EST:** 2009
SALES (est): 187.2K **Privately Held**
SIC: 7011 Hotels & motels

(G-1823)
SAUDER CUSTOM FABRICATION INC
220 Weaver St (66801-3500)
P.O. Box 1158 (66801-1158)
PHONE....620 342-2550
Dale K Davis, *President*
Frederick J Pimple, *Exec VP*
Robert A Laflen, *Senior VP*
Sandra R Moore, *CFO*
Melissa Carson, *Controller*
▲ **EMP:** 80
SQ FT: 140,000
SALES (est): 21.8MM **Privately Held**
WEB: www.saudercf.com
SIC: 3443 Process vessels, industrial: metal plate

(G-1824)
SCHELLERS INC
401 S Prairie St (66801-4491)
PHONE....620 342-3990
Michael R Scheller, *President*
Melvin Scheller, *Principal*
EMP: 13

SQ FT: 3,000
SALES: 650K **Privately Held**
SIC: 1799 0782 Parking lot maintenance; lawn care services

(G-1825)
SERVICES OFFERING SAFETY
25 W 5th Ave (66801-4035)
P.O. Box 1191 (66801-1191)
PHONE..................................620 343-8799
Susan Moran, *Director*
Tara Schnakenberg, *Director*
EMP: 30
SALES (est): 258K **Privately Held**
WEB: www.soskansas.com
SIC: 8322 Emergency social services

(G-1826)
SHEAR DESIGNERS
2607 W 18th Ave (66801-6107)
PHONE..................................620 342-5393
Sue Bahm, *Owner*
EMP: 10
SQ FT: 1,100
SALES (est): 90.4K **Privately Held**
SIC: 7231 5621 Cosmetologist; ready-to-wear apparel, women's

(G-1827)
SHEMAR INC
Also Called: H & R Block
729 W 6th Ave (66801-2601)
PHONE..................................620 342-5787
Marcy Trear, *President*
Sheila Burenheide, *Vice Pres*
EMP: 15
SALES: 330K **Privately Held**
SIC: 7291 Tax return preparation services

(G-1828)
SIMMONS PET FOOD INC
1400 E Logan Ave (66801-6822)
PHONE..................................620 342-1323
Todd Simmons, *CEO*
EMP: 190
SALES (corp-wide): 540MM **Privately Held**
SIC: 2047 Dog & cat food
PA: Simmons Pet Food, Inc.
601 N Hico St
Siloam Springs AR 72761
479 524-8151

(G-1829)
SIMMONS PREPARED FOODS INC
417 Warren Way (66801-4629)
PHONE..................................479 524-8151
Todd Simmons, *CEO*
EMP: 157
SALES (corp-wide): 800MM **Privately Held**
SIC: 2015 Poultry slaughtering & processing
PA: Simmons Prepared Foods, Inc.
601 N Hico St
Siloam Springs AR 72761
479 524-8151

(G-1830)
STORMONT-VAIL HEALTHCARE INC
Also Called: Medical Arts Clinic-Emporia
1301 W 12th Ave (66801-2587)
PHONE..................................620 343-2900
Pam Harrison, *Med Doctor*
Robert Stewart, *Family Practiti*
EMP: 383
SALES (corp-wide): 719MM **Privately Held**
SIC: 8062 General medical & surgical hospitals
PA: Stormont-Vail Healthcare, Inc.
1500 Sw 10th Ave
Topeka KS 66604
785 354-6000

(G-1831)
STRAWDER SECURITY SERVICE
926 Dove Run (66801-4964)
PHONE..................................620 343-8392
Fred Strawder, *Owner*
EMP: 12
SALES (est): 213.4K **Privately Held**
SIC: 7381 Security guard service

(G-1832)
SUMMIT DRILLING CO INC
Also Called: Summitt Drilling
825 Commercial St (66801-2914)
P.O. Box 2004 (66801-2004)
PHONE..................................620 343-3278
Jeff Hawes, *President*
Mac Knighton, *Treasurer*
EMP: 18
SQ FT: 500
SALES (est): 1.5MM **Privately Held**
SIC: 1311 Crude petroleum & natural gas

(G-1833)
SUMMIT HOTEL PROPERTIES LLC
Also Called: Holiday Inn
2921 W 18th Ave (66801-6198)
PHONE..................................620 341-9393
EMP: 18 **Privately Held**
SIC: 7011 Hotels And Motels

(G-1834)
TFI FAMILY SERVICES INC (PA)
618 Commercial St Ste C (66801-3970)
P.O. Box 2224 (66801-2224)
PHONE..................................620 342-2239
Dale W Bell, *President*
Richard T Wright, *CFO*
Shanna Shearer, *MIS Staff*
Michael A Partrick, *Exec Dir*
EMP: 60
SQ FT: 4,200
SALES: 20.7MM **Privately Held**
WEB: www.the-farm.org
SIC: 8361 Residential care for children; juvenile correctional home; group foster home; self-help group home

(G-1835)
TFI FAMILY SERVICES INC
Also Called: T F I Family Services
618 Commercial St Ste A (66801-3970)
P.O. Box 2224 (66801-2224)
PHONE..................................620 342-2239
Richard Todd Wright, *Branch Mgr*
EMP: 19
SALES (corp-wide): 20.7MM **Privately Held**
WEB: www.the-farm.org
SIC: 8361 Residential care for children; juvenile correctional home; group foster home; self-help group home
PA: Tfi Family Services, Inc.
618 Commercial St Ste C
Emporia KS 66801
620 342-2239

(G-1836)
TFI FAMILY SERVICES INC
618 Commercial St (66801-3969)
P.O. Box 2224 (66801-2224)
PHONE..................................620 342-2239
EMP: 102
SALES (corp-wide): 20.7MM **Privately Held**
SIC: 8699 Charitable organization
PA: Tfi Family Services, Inc.
618 Commercial St Ste C
Emporia KS 66801
620 342-2239

(G-1837)
THERMAL CERAMICS INC
Also Called: Morgan Advanced Materials
221 Weaver St (66801-3537)
P.O. Box 2128 (66801-2128)
PHONE..................................620 343-2308
Bobbie Duncan, *Sales Staff*
John Stang, *Branch Mgr*
EMP: 41
SALES (corp-wide): 1.3B **Privately Held**
WEB: www.thermalceramics.com
SIC: 3297 Nonclay refractories
HQ: Thermal Ceramics Inc.
2102 Old Savannah Rd
Augusta GA 30906
706 796-4200

(G-1838)
THOMAS TRANSFER & STOR CO INC (PA)
Also Called: United Van Lines
906 E 6th Ave (66801-3204)
P.O. Box 743 (66801-0743)
PHONE..................................620 342-2321
Kenneth B Thomas Sr, *Ch of Bd*
Jerid R Thomas, *President*
Nancy Thomas, *Treasurer*
▲ **EMP:** 55 **EST:** 1945
SQ FT: 46,000
SALES (est): 8MM **Privately Held**
WEB: www.thomasunited.com
SIC: 4213 4226 Trucking, except local; household goods, warehousing

(G-1839)
TOTAL RENAL CARE INC
Also Called: Emporia Dialysis
1616 Industrial Rd # 2004 (66801-6222)
PHONE..................................620 340-8043
James K Hilger,
EMP: 22 **Publicly Held**
SIC: 8092 Kidney dialysis centers
HQ: Total Renal Care, Inc.
2000 16th St
Denver CO 80202
303 405-2100

(G-1840)
TRINITY PROPERTY GROUP LLC
1105 Scott St (66801)
PHONE..................................620 342-8723
Rae Ann Warneke,
Phil Peacock,
EMP: 20
SALES (est): 1.1MM **Privately Held**
SIC: 6531 Real estate managers

(G-1841)
TURNBULL CORPORATION (PA)
Also Called: Roberts Blue Barnett
605 State St (66801-2713)
P.O. Box 175 (66801-0175)
PHONE..................................620 342-2134
Michael Turnbull, *President*
Diana Jones, *Manager*
EMP: 11 **EST:** 1977
SQ FT: 8,000
SALES (est): 488.8K **Privately Held**
SIC: 7261 Funeral home

(G-1842)
TYSON FOODS INC
2101 W 6th Ave (66801-6377)
PHONE..................................620 343-3640
Pat Costello, *Principal*
Glenn Lofdel, *Prdtn Mgr*
Nathan Rodriguez, *Engineer*
Jim Andrew, *Plant Engr*
Ron Kelsheimer, *Sales Executive*
EMP: 24
SALES (corp-wide): 42.4B **Publicly Held**
SIC: 2015 Chicken slaughtering & processing
PA: Tyson Foods, Inc.
2200 W Don Tyson Pkwy
Springdale AR 72762
479 290-4000

(G-1843)
TYSON FRESH MEATS INC
2101 W 6th Ave (66801-6377)
PHONE..................................620 343-3640
David Ranger, *Purch Mgr*
Art Tabares, *Human Res Dir*
Rodger Brownrigg, *Persnl Mgr*
Kim Howe, *Branch Mgr*
EMP: 8
SALES (corp-wide): 42.4B **Publicly Held**
SIC: 2011 Meat packing plants
HQ: Tyson Fresh Meats, Inc.
800 Stevens Port Dr
Dakota Dunes SD 57049
605 235-2061

(G-1844)
TYSON FRESH MEATS INC
Also Called: Trans Continental Cold Storage
2601 W 6th Ave (66801-6333)
PHONE..................................620 343-8010
Kim Howe, *Manager*
EMP: 25
SALES (corp-wide): 42.4B **Publicly Held**
SIC: 4213 Contract haulers
HQ: Tyson Fresh Meats, Inc.
800 Stevens Port Dr
Dakota Dunes SD 57049
605 235-2061

(G-1845)
VEKTEK LLC (PA)
1334 E 6th Ave (66801-3389)
P.O. Box 625 (66801-0625)
PHONE..................................620 342-7637
Troy Estes, *President*
Rodney E Nelson, *Vice Pres*
Chad Lee, *Mfg Spvr*
Carol Schoeck, *Purch Mgr*
Reese Johnson, *Design Engr*
▲ **EMP:** 104
SQ FT: 53,000
SALES (est): 22.3MM **Privately Held**
WEB: www.vektek.com
SIC: 3429 3593 3545 Manufactured hardware (general); fluid power cylinders & actuators; machine tool accessories

(G-1846)
VERNON ENTERPRISES
700 Overlander Rd (66801-8915)
PHONE..................................620 343-9111
Bud Vernon, *Owner*
EMP: 25
SALES (est): 1MM **Privately Held**
SIC: 4213 Trucking, except local

(G-1847)
VILLAGE ELEMENTARY SCHOOL PTO
2302 W 15th Ave (66801-6004)
PHONE..................................620 341-2282
Judith Stanley, *Principal*
EMP: 76
SALES: 11.8K **Privately Held**
SIC: 8641 Parent-teachers' association

(G-1848)
WAECHTER LLC
Also Called: J W Trucking
1761 Road G (66801)
P.O. Box 2123 (66801-2123)
PHONE..................................620 342-1080
John Waechter, *Mng Member*
Doreen Waechter, *Mng Member*
EMP: 25
SALES (est): 4.9MM **Privately Held**
SIC: 4731 Domestic freight forwarding

(G-1849)
WATERS INC
Also Called: True Value
2727 W Us Highway 50 (66801-6354)
PHONE..................................620 343-2800
Mark Shook, *Branch Mgr*
EMP: 25
SALES (corp-wide): 49.8MM **Privately Held**
SIC: 5251 0781 0181 0811 Hardware; landscape services; nursery stock, growing of; tree farm; paint, glass & wallpaper
PA: Waters, Inc.
3213 Arnold Ave
Salina KS 67401
785 825-7309

(G-1850)
WELLNITZ TREE CARE INC
310 Congress St (66801-4136)
PHONE..................................620 340-2484
Randy Wellnitz, *President*
Jacqulyn Wellnitz, *Info Tech Mgr*
Jacque Wellnitz, *Admin Sec*
EMP: 12
SALES (est): 184.6K **Privately Held**
SIC: 0783 Planting, pruning & trimming services

(G-1851)
WHITE CORPORATION INC
Also Called: Emporia Gazette
517 Merchant St Frnt (66801-7215)
P.O. Box D (66801-7343)
PHONE..................................620 342-4800
Paul David Walker, *President*
Ashley Walker, *Editor*
Barbara White Walker, *Vice Pres*
Margie McHaley, *Production*
Kathrine L Walker, *Treasurer*
EMP: 30 **EST:** 1890
SQ FT: 10,000

SALES (est): 1.7MM **Privately Held**
WEB: www.emporia.com
SIC: 2711 Newspapers, publishing & printing

(G-1852)
WILLIAMS AUTOMOTIVE INC
3105 W 6th Ave (66801-5172)
PHONE..................................620 343-0086
Rex Williams, *President*
Debbie Williams, *Vice Pres*
EMP: 17
SQ FT: 8,400
SALES (est): 1.1MM **Privately Held**
SIC: 7538 7549 7532 5013 General automotive repair shops; towing service, automotive; exterior repair services; radiators

Enterprise
Dickinson County

(G-1853)
ANR PIPELINE COMPANY
1615 Nail Rd (67441-9095)
PHONE..................................785 479-5814
Butch McAlexander, *Manager*
EMP: 11
SALES (corp-wide): 10.3B **Privately Held**
SIC: 4922 1623 Natural gas transmission; pipeline construction
HQ: Anr Pipeline Company
700 Louisiana St Ste 700 # 700
Houston TX 77002
832 320-2000

(G-1854)
ENTERPRISE CMNTY NURSING HM
Also Called: ENTERPRISE ESTATES NURSING CEN
602 Crestview Dr (67441-9124)
PHONE..................................785 263-8278
Maredith Bchard, *Administration*
EMP: 49
SQ FT: 19,650
SALES: 1.7MM **Privately Held**
SIC: 8051 Skilled nursing care facilities

(G-1855)
MIDCO PLASTICS INC
801 S Bluff St (67441-9112)
P.O. Box 416 (67441-0416)
PHONE..................................785 263-8999
Mike Carney, *President*
EMP: 30 **EST:** 1960
SQ FT: 30,800
SALES (est): 6MM **Privately Held**
WEB: www.midcoplastics.com
SIC: 2673 3081 Plastic bags: made from purchased materials; unsupported plastics film & sheet

Erie
Neosho County

(G-1856)
BEACHNER GRAIN INC
725 N Main St (66733-1021)
P.O. Box 55 (66733-0055)
PHONE..................................620 244-3277
Jeffrey Gard, *Branch Mgr*
EMP: 10
SALES (corp-wide): 112.2MM **Privately Held**
WEB: www.beachner.com
SIC: 4221 5261 1796 Grain elevator, storage only; nursery stock, seeds & bulbs; elevator installation & conversion
PA: Beachner Grain, Inc.
2600 Flynn Dr
Parsons KS 67357
620 820-8600

(G-1857)
CENTURION INDUSTRIES INC
Also Called: A-Lert Roof Systems
810 N Main St (66733-1062)
P.O. Box 79 (66733-0079)
PHONE..................................620 244-3201
Ethan Buche, *General Mgr*
Tom Rubin, *Manager*
EMP: 50
SALES (corp-wide): 162.4MM **Privately Held**
WEB: www.centurionind.com
SIC: 3444 Sheet metalwork
PA: Centurion Industries, Inc.
1107 N Taylor Rd
Garrett IN 46738
260 357-6665

(G-1858)
COOVER TRUCKING INC
17670 180th Rd (66733-4153)
PHONE..................................620 244-3572
Dave Coover, *President*
Rosie Coover, *Corp Secy*
EMP: 16
SQ FT: 4,800
SALES: 1.8MM **Privately Held**
SIC: 4213 Contract haulers

(G-1859)
JOHN F HAFNER LLC
Also Called: Green Environmental Services
608 E 2nd St (66733)
P.O. Box 17 (66733-0017)
PHONE..................................620 244-5393
John F Hafner, *Mng Member*
Joe Hafner,
EMP: 13
SALES: 1.8MM **Privately Held**
SIC: 4953 Garbage: collecting, destroying & processing

(G-1860)
NEOSHO COUNTY FAIR ASSN INC
600 W Canville St (66733-5037)
PHONE..................................620 433-0446
Rebecca Isle, *Principal*
EMP: 20
SALES (est): 85.1K **Privately Held**
SIC: 8699 Membership organizations

(G-1861)
NEOSHO COUNTY ROAD AND BRIDGE
515 E 4th St (66733-1459)
PHONE..................................620 244-3855
Kent Ford, *Supervisor*
Cyndi Cornett, *Admin Asst*
EMP: 27
SALES (est): 7.6MM **Privately Held**
SIC: 3531 Road construction & maintenance machinery

(G-1862)
NEOSHO SMALL PARTS LLC
301 S Broadway St (66733-1429)
P.O. Box 201 (66733-0201)
PHONE..................................620 244-3263
Keith Kyser, *MIS Staff*
Crissy Kyser,
C Keith Kyser,
EMP: 11
SQ FT: 11,975
SALES (est): 890K **Privately Held**
SIC: 3469 3544 3599 Stamping metal for the trade; special dies, tools, jigs & fixtures; machine shop, jobbing & repair

(G-1863)
NMRMC EMS
515 Power Dr (66733-4226)
PHONE..................................620 244-3522
EMP: 30
SALES (est): 341.8K **Privately Held**
SIC: 4119 Ambulance service

(G-1864)
R & F FARM SUPPLY INC
10200 Highway 59 (66733-5152)
PHONE..................................620 244-3275
David Harris, *President*
Lori Jensen, *Principal*
Richard Beck, *Vice Pres*
EMP: 15 **EST:** 1972
SQ FT: 2,750
SALES (est): 6.2MM **Privately Held**
SIC: 5083 5191 Farm implements; farm supplies

Eskridge
Wabaunsee County

(G-1865)
BEVERLY ENTERPRISES-KANSAS LLC
Also Called: Heritage Village of Eskridge
505 N Main St (66423-9646)
P.O. Box 248 (66423-0248)
PHONE..................................785 449-2294
Theresa Foster, *Branch Mgr*
EMP: 40
SALES (corp-wide): 393.8MM **Privately Held**
SIC: 8051 8741 Convalescent home with continuous nursing care; nursing & personal care facility management
HQ: Beverly Enterprises-Kansas, Llc
1 1000 Beverly Way
Fort Smith AR 72919
479 201-2000

(G-1866)
FLINT HILLS BANK (PA)
103 1/2 N Main St (66423-9218)
P.O. Box 5 (66423-0005)
PHONE..................................785 449-2266
Patrick J Wiederholt, *CEO*
Mat Colt, *Ch of Bd*
Rick Bryan, *President*
Mark Hoelting, *Vice Pres*
Sara C Colt, *Director*
EMP: 20 **EST:** 1985
SALES: 5.2MM **Privately Held**
WEB: www.flinthillsbankofeskridge.com
SIC: 6022 State commercial banks

(G-1867)
GOLDEN LIVINGCENTER - ESKRIDGE
505 N Main St (66423-9646)
PHONE..................................785 449-2294
Francy Keearns, *Administration*
EMP: 19
SALES (est): 791.4K **Privately Held**
SIC: 8051 Convalescent home with continuous nursing care

(G-1868)
LOGAN FARMS INC
20849 Massasoit Rd (66423-9082)
PHONE..................................785 256-6334
Rex H Logan, *President*
EMP: 20
SALES (est): 580K **Privately Held**
SIC: 0722 0191 Crop harvesting; general farms, primarily crop

Eudora
Douglas County

(G-1869)
AIR FILTER PLUS INC
1205 Cardinal Dr (66025-9566)
PHONE..................................785 542-3700
Bret Kay, *President*
Tom Kay, *COO*
Linda Kay, *Treasurer*
Scott Hanks, *Marketing Mgr*
Hal Schump, *Marketing Staff*
EMP: 26
SQ FT: 10,800
SALES: 2.7MM **Privately Held**
WEB: www.airfilterplus.com
SIC: 7699 5085 3564 Filter cleaning; filters, industrial; filters, air: furnaces, air conditioning equipment, etc.

(G-1870)
BENCHMARK CONSTRUCTION LLC
1006 Ash St (66025-9558)
PHONE..................................785 862-0340
Timothy Bruce, *CEO*
Aaron West, *COO*
Beth Quinn, *CFO*
EMP: 15
SQ FT: 4,000
SALES (est): 1.4MM **Privately Held**
WEB: www.benchmarkconstructionks.com
SIC: 1521 8711 1542 Single-family housing construction; construction & civil engineering; commercial & office building contractors

(G-1871)
BLUEJCKET CRSSING VNYRD WINERY
1969 N 1250th Rd (66025-8122)
PHONE..................................785 542-1764
Selvan Kandaya, *Owner*
EMP: 5 **EST:** 2007
SALES (est): 374.7K **Privately Held**
SIC: 2084 Wines

(G-1872)
C-HAWKK CONSTRUCTION INC (PA)
527 Main St (66025-9469)
P.O. Box 449 (66025-0449)
PHONE..................................785 542-1800
Henrietta Shelton, *President*
Kara Latessa, *Vice Pres*
Kevin Shelton, *Treasurer*
Alvis Shelton, *Admin Sec*
EMP: 13
SQ FT: 2,000
SALES (est): 3.1MM **Privately Held**
SIC: 7359 1721 Work zone traffic equipment (flags, cones, barrels, etc.); pavement marking contractor

(G-1873)
EUDORA ANIMAL HOSPITAL INC
1905 Elm St (66025-9102)
P.O. Box 710 (66025-0710)
PHONE..................................785 542-3265
Dr G Schreiner Dvm, *President*
Dr George Schreiner, *President*
EMP: 15
SALES (est): 877K **Privately Held**
SIC: 0741 0742 Veterinarian, livestock; veterinarian, animal specialties

(G-1874)
EUDORA LION CLUB FOUNDATION
1135 Locust St 31 (66025-9551)
P.O. Box 31 (66025-0031)
PHONE..................................785 542-2315
Earl R Slapar, *Admin Sec*
EMP: 18
SALES (est): 105.2K **Privately Held**
SIC: 8641 Civic associations

(G-1875)
EUROT VERTI FLIGH SOLUT LLC
Also Called: Eurotec Vfs
1040 Ocl Pkwy (66025-9565)
PHONE..................................785 331-2220
Shane Koch, *Opers Staff*
Tina Decker, *CFO*
Annie Hadl, *Human Resources*
Rhiannon Hadl, *Human Resources*
Brenna Winder, *Sales Associate*
▲ **EMP:** 7
SQ FT: 4,000
SALES (est): 1.2MM **Privately Held**
SIC: 3724 Aircraft engines & engine parts

(G-1876)
KAW VALLEY INDUSTRIAL INC
2218 N 1400th Rd (66025-9291)
PHONE..................................785 841-9751
Mark Lauber, *President*
Rick Lauber, *Vice Pres*
EMP: 6
SQ FT: 6,000
SALES: 900K **Privately Held**
SIC: 5571 5261 7699 5084 Motorcycles; all-terrain vehicles; motorcycle parts & accessories; lawn & garden equipment; motorcycle repair service; engines, gasoline; saws & sawing equipment

(G-1877)
KAW VALLEY STATE BANK
739 Main St (66025-9471)
P.O. Box 702 (66025-0702)
PHONE..................................785 542-4200
James Hoover, *President*
David Becker, *Vice Pres*

Renae Cowley, *Vice Pres*
Rhonda Shepard, *Manager*
EMP: 15 **EST:** 1899
SQ FT: 3,200
SALES: 2.3MM **Privately Held**
WEB: www.kawvalleystatebank.com
SIC: 6022 State trust companies accepting deposits, commercial

(G-1878)
KINGSTON PRINTING & DESIGN INC
1030 Ocl Pkwy (66025-9565)
PHONE..................................785 690-7222
Lawson Johnson, *President*
Dan Fagan, *Sales Staff*
Bill Rogers, *Manager*
EMP: 13
SQ FT: 7,000
SALES (est): 3.6MM **Privately Held**
SIC: 2759 Commercial printing

(G-1879)
RAGLAND SPECIALTY PRINTING
Also Called: Ragland Specialty Prtg & Mfg
1499 E 2300 Rd (66025-9276)
P.O. Box 609 (66025-0609)
PHONE..................................785 542-3058
John Ragland, *President*
Sheryl Ragland, *Vice Pres*
EMP: 45
SQ FT: 25,000
SALES (est): 5.2MM **Privately Held**
SIC: 2759 5085 2396 Promotional printing; bottler supplies; automotive & apparel trimmings

(G-1880)
STERLING READINESS ROUNDS LLC
112 E 10th St (66025-9511)
P.O. Box 612 (66025-0612)
PHONE..................................785 542-1405
Donald E Death, *CEO*
Melisa Lynn, *Office Mgr*
EMP: 15
SQ FT: 4,000
SALES: 1.5MM **Privately Held**
WEB: www.readinessrounds.com
SIC: 8742 Business consultant

(G-1881)
SUPERIOR DISPOSAL SERVICE INC
2114 N 1300th Rd (66025-8129)
PHONE..................................913 406-9460
Glen Smith, *Branch Mgr*
EMP: 14
SALES (corp-wide): 8.6MM **Privately Held**
SIC: 4953 Refuse collection & disposal services
PA: Superior Disposal Service, Inc.
447 N Cherry St
Gardner KS 66030
913 938-4552

Eureka
Greenwood County

(G-1882)
COUNTY OF GREENWOOD
Also Called: Greenwood County Road & Bridge
510 S Jefferson St (67045-2207)
PHONE..................................620 583-8112
Evan Casey, *Supervisor*
EMP: 30 **Privately Held**
SIC: 1622 Bridge construction
PA: County Of Greenwood
311 N Main St Ste 3
Eureka KS 67045
620 583-8121

(G-1883)
DAYSTAR PETROLEUM INC
522 N Main St (67045-1316)
P.O. Box 560 (67045-0560)
PHONE..................................620 583-5527
Matthew Osborne, *Principal*
EMP: 5
SALES (est): 458.1K **Privately Held**
SIC: 1311 Crude petroleum production

(G-1884)
ELITE CEMENTING ACIDIZING
810 E 7th St (67045-1624)
P.O. Box 92 (67045-0092)
PHONE..................................620 583-5561
Rene Wiggins, *Principal*
EMP: 9 **EST:** 2014
SALES (est): 814K **Privately Held**
SIC: 1389 Acidizing wells

(G-1885)
EUREKA FOUNDATION
416 E 5th St (67045-1714)
P.O. Box 247 (67045-0247)
PHONE..................................620 583-8630
Matt Wilson, *President*
Marvin Steele, *Vice Pres*
EMP: 12
SALES: 27.6K **Privately Held**
SIC: 8748 Urban planning & consulting services

(G-1886)
EUREKA GREENHOUSES INC
420 N Pine St (67045-1430)
PHONE..................................620 583-8676
Keith Moots, *President*
Eric Moots, *Vice Pres*
Virginia Moots, *Treasurer*
EMP: 13
SQ FT: 50,000
SALES (est): 612.2K **Privately Held**
SIC: 5193 5992 Flowers, fresh; flowers, fresh

(G-1887)
GRAN VILLA
1820 E River St (67045-2156)
PHONE..................................620 583-7473
Polly Vines, *Manager*
EMP: 14
SALES (est): 271.2K
SALES (corp-wide): 100.2MM **Privately Held**
WEB: www.medicalodges.com
SIC: 8361 Residential care
PA: Medicalodges, Inc.
201 W 8th St
Coffeyville KS 67337
620 251-6700

(G-1888)
GREENWOOD CNTY HOSP FOUNDATION
100 W 16th St (67045-1064)
PHONE..................................620 583-5909
Lisa Ramsay, *CFO*
Melissa Bogle, *Director*
Ashley Boles, *Nurse*
Melinda Mitchell, *Nurse*
EMP: 140
SALES (est): 10.3MM **Privately Held**
WEB: www.gwch.org
SIC: 8062 General medical & surgical hospitals

(G-1889)
GREENWOOD CNTY RUR WTR DST 1
106 E 3rd St (67045-1747)
P.O. Box 2 (67045-0002)
PHONE..................................620 583-7181
John Cills, *President*
John Cilla, *President*
EMP: 12
SALES (est): 906.3K **Privately Held**
SIC: 4941 Water supply

(G-1890)
GULICK DRILLING
910 E 7th St (67045-1626)
PHONE..................................620 583-5804
Ron Gulick, *Owner*
EMP: 10
SALES (est): 753K **Privately Held**
WEB: www.gulickdrilling.com
SIC: 1781 Water well drilling

(G-1891)
HOME BANK AND TRUST COMPANY (PA)
217 N Main St (67045-1303)
P.O. Box 620 (67045-0620)
PHONE..................................620 583-5516
R D Rucker, *President*
Keith Ball, *President*
Brad Rucker, *President*
MAI Schendel, *Vice Pres*
EMP: 17 **EST:** 1904
SALES: 5.5MM **Privately Held**
WEB: www.homebank-trust.com
SIC: 6022 State trust companies accepting deposits, commercial

(G-1892)
INVENA CORPORATION
416 E 5th St (67045-1714)
P.O. Box 148 (67045-0148)
PHONE..................................620 583-8630
Matthew E Wilson, *President*
EMP: 35 **EST:** 1998
SQ FT: 3,200
SALES (est): 6MM **Privately Held**
WEB: www.invena.com
SIC: 8999 7699 5084 3533 Inventor; industrial equipment services; industrial machinery & equipment; oil & gas field machinery

(G-1893)
KANSAS DEPARTMENT TRNSP
1308 E 7th St (67045-1602)
PHONE..................................620 583-5661
Teresa Gulick, *Branch Mgr*
EMP: 79 **Privately Held**
SIC: 1611 9621 Highway & street maintenance;
HQ: Kansas Department Of Transportation
700 Sw Harrison St # 500
Topeka KS 66603
785 296-3501

(G-1894)
MEDICALODGES INC
Also Called: Medicalodges of Eureka
1020 N School St (67045-1106)
P.O. Box 94c (67045)
PHONE..................................620 583-7418
Peggy Hackett, *Opers-Prdtn-Mfg*
EMP: 100
SALES (corp-wide): 100.2MM **Privately Held**
WEB: www.medicalodges.com
SIC: 8052 8051 Intermediate care facilities; skilled nursing care facilities
PA: Medicalodges, Inc.
201 W 8th St
Coffeyville KS 67337
620 251-6700

(G-1895)
MIDWEST MILL MODERNIZATION
1206 E River St (67045-2102)
P.O. Box 30 (67045-0030)
PHONE..................................620 583-6883
Charles Lew Bitler, *President*
Barbara Beitz, *Corp Secy*
Dan Bitler, *Exec VP*
Jim Beitz, *Vice Pres*
EMP: 12
SALES (est): 2.2MM **Privately Held**
SIC: 1541 3523 Grain elevator construction; industrial buildings, new construction; farm machinery & equipment; elevators, farm

(G-1896)
NEW BEGINNINGS ENTERPRISE
219 N Main St (67045-1303)
PHONE..................................620 583-6835
Joe O'Rouke, *CEO*
EMP: 10
SALES (corp-wide): 1.7MM **Privately Held**
SIC: 8331 Job training & vocational rehabilitation services
PA: New Beginnings Enterprise, Inc
1001 Wilson St
Neodesha KS 66757
620 325-3333

(G-1897)
ORSCHELN FARM AND HOME LLC
501 Us Highway 54 (67045-4327)
PHONE..................................620 583-5043
Joe Hampton, *President*
EMP: 52
SALES (corp-wide): 822.7MM **Privately Held**
SIC: 5251 0191 Hardware; general farms, primarily crop
PA: Orscheln Farm And Home Llc
1800 Overcenter Dr
Moberly MO 65270
800 577-2580

(G-1898)
RANCH-AID INC
304 E 9th St (67045-1141)
P.O. Box 389 (67045-0389)
PHONE..................................620 583-5585
George W Aicher, *President*
Maribelle Aicher, *Corp Secy*
Frances A Lewis, *Vice Pres*
EMP: 14 **EST:** 1886
SQ FT: 6,000
SALES: 2.6MM **Privately Held**
SIC: 2048 5191 Prepared feeds; fertilizer & fertilizer materials; grass seed; chemicals, agricultural

(G-1899)
WITCHITA CLINIC INC
Also Called: Bluestem Medical Clinic, P.A.
100 W 16th St (67045-1064)
PHONE..................................620 583-7436
Terry Morris, *Partner*
Mike McClintick, *Treasurer*
EMP: 12
SQ FT: 4,800
SALES (est): 844.2K **Privately Held**
SIC: 8031 Offices & clinics of osteopathic physicians

Everest
Brown County

(G-1900)
K-W MANUFACTURING LLC
404 Locust St (66424-9057)
PHONE..................................785 548-7454
Weldon Gullickson, *Mng Member*
EMP: 10 **EST:** 1996
SALES: 1.2MM **Privately Held**
SIC: 5072 3452 Bolts, nuts & screws; bolts, nuts, rivets & washers

(G-1901)
RAINBOW COMMUNICATIONS LLC
608 Main St (66424-9136)
P.O. Box 147 (66424-0147)
PHONE..................................785 548-7511
Jason Smith, *President*
Rob Hoerntlein, *Manager*
EMP: 34
SALES: 9MM **Privately Held**
SIC: 4841 Cable television services

(G-1902)
RAINBOW TELECOM ASSN INC
Also Called: R.T.C.A.
608 Main St (66424-9136)
P.O. Box 147 (66424-0147)
PHONE..................................785 548-7511
Dennis Anderson, *President*
James Lednicky, *Principal*
EMP: 12 **EST:** 1955
SQ FT: 4,500
SALES: 4.6MM **Privately Held**
WEB: www.rainbowtel.net
SIC: 4813 Telephone communication, except radio

(G-1903)
UNION STATE BANK OF EVEREST (HQ)
545 Main St (66424-9157)
P.O. Box 105 (66424-0105)
PHONE..................................785 548-7521
Steven J Handke, *President*
Jane E Bruning, *Exec VP*
Jane Bruning, *Exec VP*
EMP: 12 **EST:** 1901
SQ FT: 2,600
SALES: 15.5MM **Privately Held**
WEB: www.mybankusb.com
SIC: 6022 State trust companies accepting deposits, commercial

Fairview
Brown County

(G-1904)
HOLTHAUS AUTOHAUS LLC
720 W Oak St (66425-9530)
PHONE....785 467-3101
Joe Hackney, *Mng Member*
Joni Hackney,
EMP: 7
SQ FT: 500
SALES: 3.5MM **Privately Held**
SIC: 3751 Motorcycles & related parts

Fairway
Johnson County

(G-1905)
BITUMINOUS CASUALTY CORP
4330 Shawnee Mission Pkwy
(66205-2522)
PHONE....913 262-4664
Diana Mayfield, *Vice Pres*
EMP: 17
SALES (corp-wide): 6B **Publicly Held**
SIC: 6331 6411 Automobile insurance; insurance agents, brokers & service
HQ: Bituminous Casualty Corporation
3700 Market Square Cir
Davenport IA 52807
309 786-5401

(G-1906)
COMPRESULTS LLC
4330 Shawnee Mission Pkwy # 221
(66205-2522)
PHONE....913 310-9800
James Weir,
Michael McTeer,
EMP: 18
SALES (est): 1.1MM **Privately Held**
WEB: www.compresults.com
SIC: 8399 Health systems agency

(G-1907)
FIRSTRUST MORTGAGE INC
4400 Shawnee Mission Pkwy # 208
(66205-2518)
PHONE....913 312-2000
Mark A McDougald, *President*
Patty Shoenewe, *Vice Pres*
EMP: 30
SQ FT: 4,800
SALES (est): 3.9MM **Privately Held**
WEB: www.getahomeloan.com
SIC: 6162 Mortgage bankers & correspondents

(G-1908)
GDM ENTERPRISES LLC
Also Called: Lano Company, The
3505 Shawnee Mission Pkwy
(66205-2709)
PHONE....816 753-2900
Miranda Coggins, *President*
Layne Coggins, *Vice Pres*
▲ **EMP:** 10
SALES (est): 257.6K **Privately Held**
WEB: www.thelanocompany.com
SIC: 5122 5999 Cosmetics; cosmetics

(G-1909)
HAAS WILKERSON & WOHLBERG INC (PA)
Also Called: Haas & Wilkerson Insurange
4300 Shawnee Mission Pkwy
(66205-2519)
PHONE....913 432-4400
William R Wilkerson III, *Ch of Bd*
William Wilkerson III, *President*
J Philip Coulson, *President*
Mitch Castor, *Treasurer*
Kim Carter, *Accounts Mgr*
EMP: 31 **EST:** 1965
SQ FT: 6,000
SALES (est): 7.3MM **Privately Held**
SIC: 6411 Insurance agents, brokers & service

(G-1910)
HIRES GAGE DVM
Also Called: Fairway Animal Hospital
6000 Mission Rd (66205-3248)
PHONE....913 432-7611
Hires Gage Dvm, *Owner*
EMP: 20
SALES (est): 1.1MM **Privately Held**
SIC: 0742 Animal hospital services, pets & other animal specialties

(G-1911)
JOHNSON COUNTY PNTG & HM REPR (PA)
Also Called: Johnson County Pntg
5839 Mission Rd (66205-3167)
PHONE....913 631-5252
Ron Duck, *Owner*
EMP: 20
SALES (est): 921.5K **Privately Held**
SIC: 1721 Residential painting

(G-1912)
LAW OFFICE OF PTER A JOURAS JR
Also Called: Jouras, Peter A Jr
4330 Shawnee Mission Pkwy # 205
(66205-2522)
PHONE....913 677-1999
Peter Jouras Jr, *Owner*
EMP: 10
SALES (est): 604.2K **Privately Held**
SIC: 8111 General practice law office

(G-1913)
MCINNES GROUP INC (PA)
4300 Shawnee Mission Pkwy # 100
(66205-2526)
PHONE....913 831-0999
Duncan Innes, *Owner*
Bill Stoddart, *Vice Pres*
Sunny Foutes, *CFO*
Carol Daunis, *Accounts Mgr*
Jane Limbach, *Accounts Mgr*
EMP: 18
SALES (est): 7MM **Privately Held**
SIC: 6411 Insurance agents

(G-1914)
MEREDITH CORPORATION
Also Called: Kctv5
4500 Shawnee Mission Pkwy
(66205-2509)
PHONE....913 677-5555
Chuck Poduska, *Vice Pres*
Mike Sulzman, *Engineer*
Bernie Erber, *Persnl Mgr*
John Rhodes, *Persnl Mgr*
Chris Oberholtz, *Manager*
EMP: 150
SALES (corp-wide): 3.1B **Publicly Held**
SIC: 4833 Television broadcasting stations
PA: Meredith Corporation
1716 Locust St
Des Moines IA 50309
515 284-3000

(G-1915)
OLD MISSION UNITED METHDST CH
Also Called: Old Mission United Methdist Ch
5519 State Park Rd (66205-2664)
PHONE....913 262-1040
Amy Hernandez-Zoell, *Corp Comm Staff*
Betty Leonard, *Director*
Sarah Hill, *Director*
Mike Ott, *Art Dir*
EMP: 14
SALES (est): 913.7K **Privately Held**
SIC: 8351 Preschool center

(G-1916)
PERKINS SMART & BOYD INC (PA)
4330 Shawnee Mission Pkwy # 204
(66205-2522)
PHONE....800 344-1621
F Scott Perkins, *President*
Robert L Smart, *Chairman*
EMP: 19
SALES (est): 2.8MM **Privately Held**
SIC: 6211 Stock brokers & dealers

(G-1917)
PLATFORM TECHNOLOGIES LLC
4220 Shawnee Mission Pkwy
(66205-2532)
PHONE....816 285-3874
Max Hoffmeier, *Mng Member*
EMP: 30
SALES (est): 516.5K **Privately Held**
SIC: 7371 Computer software development & applications

(G-1918)
ROLF PERRIN & ASSOCIATES PC
4210 Shawnee Mission Pkwy 202a
(66205-2527)
PHONE....913 671-8600
John Rolf, *President*
Matt Radetic, *Vice Pres*
Cindy Kueck, *Tax Mgr*
Hayley Harman, *Auditor*
EMP: 13
SALES (est): 1MM **Privately Held**
WEB: www.rolfperrin.com
SIC: 8721 Certified public accountant

(G-1919)
SECURITY BANK OF KANSAS CITY
2701 Shawnee Mission Pkwy
(66205-1773)
PHONE....913 384-3300
Theresa Flynn, *Branch Mgr*
EMP: 17
SALES (corp-wide): 100MM **Privately Held**
SIC: 6022 State trust companies accepting deposits, commercial
HQ: Security Bank Of Kansas City
701 Minnesota Ave
Kansas City KS 66101
913 281-3165

(G-1920)
TITLE MIDWEST INC (HQ)
4400 Shawnee Mission Pkwy # 208
(66205-2518)
PHONE....785 232-9110
John Stauffer Jr, *CEO*
Keith Love, *President*
Lora Carlson, *Treasurer*
EMP: 12
SQ FT: 4,000
SALES: 22MM **Privately Held**
SIC: 6541 Title & trust companies
PA: Tm Holdings, Inc.
4400 Shawnee Mission Pkwy
Fairway KS 66205
785 232-9110

(G-1921)
TM HOLDINGS INC (PA)
4400 Shawnee Mission Pkwy
(66205-2525)
PHONE....785 232-9110
John Stauffer, *CEO*
Bill Mosimann, *President*
Jim Humphrey, *COO*
Craig Weingartner, *CFO*
Lora Carlson, *Treasurer*
EMP: 12
SALES (est): 22MM **Privately Held**
WEB: www.titlemidwest.com
SIC: 6541 Title & trust companies

(G-1922)
TRIAD CAPITAL ADVISORS INC (PA)
Also Called: Triad Mortgage
4400 Shawnee Mission Pkwy # 209
(66205-2525)
PHONE....816 561-7000
John Parker, *President*
Tom Anderson, *Exec VP*
Mark Reichter, *Vice Pres*
EMP: 10
SQ FT: 4,000
SALES (est): 2MM **Privately Held**
WEB: www.triadmortgage.com
SIC: 6162 Mortgage bankers

(G-1923)
TRUSTEES INDIANA UNIVERSITY
Also Called: Brandt, Kenneth MD
5755 Windsor Dr (66205-3342)
PHONE....913 499-6661
Rafael Graund, *Manager*
EMP: 20
SALES (corp-wide): 2.2B **Privately Held**
WEB: www.iupui.edu
SIC: 8011 8221 Rheumatology specialist, physician/surgeon; university
PA: Trustees Indiana University
Bryan Hall 107 S Ind Ave St Bryan Ha
Bloomington IN 47405
812 855-4848

(G-1924)
UNIVERSITY OF KANSAS
Also Called: Clinical Research Center
4350 Shawnee Mission Pkwy
(66205-2528)
PHONE....913 677-1590
Willis Chuck, *Director*
EMP: 933
SALES (corp-wide): 1.2B **Privately Held**
SIC: 8011 Medical centers
PA: University Of Kansas
1450 Jayhawk Blvd Rm 225
Lawrence KS 66045
785 864-4868

(G-1925)
UNIVERSITY OF KS MEDCL (DH)
Also Called: KUMC RESEARCH INTITUTE
4330 Shawnee Mission Pkwy
(66205-2522)
PHONE....913 588-1261
Paul F Terranova, *President*
Timothy Siskey, *CFO*
Sherilyn Laduke, *Personnel*
Jamie Caldwell, *Exec Dir*
Kelly Robertson, *Executive Asst*
EMP: 28
SALES: 429.4K
SALES (corp-wide): 1.2B **Privately Held**
SIC: 8733 Research institute
HQ: The University Of Kansas Medical Center
3901 Rainbow Blvd
Kansas City KS 66160
913 588-1443

Fall River
Greenwood County

(G-1926)
CORPS OF ENGINEERS FALL RIVER
2453 Lake Rd (67047-8366)
PHONE....620 658-4445
Lloyed Linton, *Manager*
Susan Couch, *Manager*
EMP: 12 **EST:** 2000
SALES (est): 611.7K **Privately Held**
SIC: 8711 Engineering services

(G-1927)
FLINT OAK
Also Called: Flint Oak
2639 Quail (67047-4904)
PHONE....620 658-4401
Chris Jarvis, *Partner*
EMP: 40
SQ FT: 140,000
SALES (est): 2.7MM **Privately Held**
WEB: www.flintoak.com
SIC: 0279 0971 7999 5812 Dog farm; game preserve; shooting range operation; skeet shooting facility; restaurant, family: independent; vacation lodges

Falun
Saline County

(G-1928)
PIHL REPAIR & FABRICATION LLC
8625 S Lightville Rd (67442)
PHONE....785 668-2014

▲ = Import ▼=Export
◆ =Import/Export

Roger Pihl,
Kendall Pihl,
Kevin Pihl,
EMP: 5
SALES (est): 441.2K **Privately Held**
SIC: 1799 7692 Welding on site; automotive welding

Florence
Marion County

(G-1929)
LUDWIG TRUCK LINE INC
1164 Hwy 77 (66851)
P.O. Box 6 (66851-0006)
PHONE..................................620 878-4243
EMP: 20
SQ FT: 961
SALES (est): 3.2MM **Privately Held**
SIC: 4213 Over-The-Road Trucking

(G-1930)
WILLIAMS SERVICE INC
1101 Main St (66851-1164)
P.O. Box 147 (66851-0147)
PHONE..................................620 878-4225
Rodney Williams, *President*
Stanton Williams, *Vice Pres*
Stephanie Williams, *Vice Pres*
Twilah L Williams, *Treasurer*
EMP: 22
SQ FT: 18,000
SALES (est): 8.3MM **Privately Held**
WEB: www.williamsservice.com
SIC: 5511 5531 5013 7538 Trucks, tractors & trailers: new & used; truck equipment & parts; truck parts & accessories; general truck repair

Ford
Ford County

(G-1931)
FORD CATTLE COMPANY INC
12466 Us Highway 400 (67842-9420)
PHONE..................................620 369-2252
George Herrman, *President*
Danny Herrman, *President*
EMP: 50
SALES: 15.7MM
SALES (corp-wide): 3MM **Privately Held**
WEB: www.fordedgeforum.com
SIC: 0211 Beef cattle feedlots
PA: Ford Holding Company Inc
12466 Us Highway 400
Ford KS 67842
620 369-2252

(G-1932)
FORD COUNTY FEED YARD INC
12466 Us Highway 400 (67842-9420)
PHONE..................................620 369-2252
George Herrmann, *President*
Ron Herrmann, *Vice Pres*
Karen Fravel, *Admin Asst*
EMP: 59
SQ FT: 5,000
SALES (est): 6.7MM
SALES (corp-wide): 3MM **Privately Held**
WEB: www.fordedgeforum.com
SIC: 0211 Beef cattle feedlots
PA: Ford Holding Company Inc
12466 Us Highway 400
Ford KS 67842
620 369-2252

(G-1933)
HERRMANN LAND & CATTLE CO
12466 Us Highway 400 (67842-9420)
PHONE..................................620 369-2252
EMP: 10
SALES (est): 607K
SALES (corp-wide): 3MM **Privately Held**
SIC: 0119 Cash grains
PA: Ford Holding Company Inc
12466 Us Highway 400
Ford KS 67842
620 369-2252

Fort Leavenworth
Leavenworth County

(G-1934)
ARMED FORCES BANK NAT ASSN (DH)
320 Kansas Ave (66027-1139)
P.O. Box 26158, Kansas City MO (64196-6158)
PHONE..................................913 682-9090
Rick L Smalley, *Ch of Bd*
Robert Arter, *Vice Ch Bd*
Don Giles, *President*
EMP: 258 **EST:** 1907
SALES: 86.2MM **Privately Held**
WEB: www.afbca.com
SIC: 6021 National commercial banks
HQ: Dickinson Financial Corp
1111 Main St Ste 1600
Kansas City MO 64105
816 472-5244

(G-1935)
ARMED FORCES BANK NAT ASSN
330 Kansas Ave Bldg 700 (66027-1139)
PHONE..................................913 651-2992
Cathey Boney, *Manager*
EMP: 10 **Privately Held**
WEB: www.afbca.com
SIC: 6021 National commercial banks
HQ: Armed Forces Bank, National Association
320 Kansas Ave
Fort Leavenworth KS 66027
913 682-9090

(G-1936)
COMMAND AND GENERAL STAFF
Also Called: Cgsc Foundation
100 Stimson Ave Ste 1149 (66027-2301)
PHONE..................................913 651-0624
Doug Tystad, *CEO*
Michael D Hockley, *Chairman*
Thomas A Dials, *Treasurer*
Douglass J Adair, *Admin Sec*
EMP: 11
SALES: 511.2K **Privately Held**
SIC: 8621 Education & teacher association

(G-1937)
DLA DOCUMENT SERVICES
290 Grant Ave Bldg 77 (66027-1254)
PHONE..................................913 684-5591
Rodney Day, *Branch Mgr*
EMP: 5 **Publicly Held**
SIC: 2752 9711 Commercial printing, lithographic; national security;
HQ: Dla Document Services
5450 Carlisle Pike Bldg 9
Mechanicsburg PA 17050
717 605-2362

(G-1938)
FORT LEAVENWORTH CREDIT UNION (PA)
301 Kansas Ave (66027-1140)
P.O. Box 3032 (66027-0032)
PHONE..................................913 651-6575
William Hauber, *President*
Tina Wardlow, *Loan Officer*
EMP: 24
SQ FT: 5,000
SALES: 5.5MM **Privately Held**
SIC: 6062 State credit unions, not federally chartered

(G-1939)
FORT LEAVENWORTH FRONTIER
220 Hancock Ave (66027-1329)
P.O. Box 3387 (66027-0387)
PHONE..................................913 682-6300
Deb Healy, *Director*
EMP: 16
SALES (est): 1.8MM **Privately Held**
SIC: 6513 Apartment building operators

(G-1940)
NORTHROP GRUMMAN SYSTEMS CORP
530 Organ Ave Bldg 222 (66027-1390)
PHONE..................................913 651-8311
Barbara Evans, *Manager*
Richard Gonzalez, *Manager*
EMP: 320 **Publicly Held**
WEB: www.logicon.com
SIC: 8711 8732 7374 Engineering services; research services, except laboratory; data processing & preparation
HQ: Northrop Grumman Systems Corporation
2980 Fairview Park Dr
Falls Church VA 22042
703 280-2900

(G-1941)
REST EASY LLC
214 Grant Ave Bldg 695 (66027-1247)
PHONE..................................913 684-4091
Shirley Dickson, *General Mgr*
EMP: 36 **Privately Held**
SIC: 7011 Hotels & motels
PA: Rest Easy Llc
1201 Demonbreun St # 800
Nashville TN 37203

(G-1942)
UNITED STATES DEPT OF ARMY
Also Called: Hro Fort Stewart
821 Mcclellan Ave (66027-1361)
PHONE..................................913 684-2747
Joe Osborne, *Director*
EMP: 319 **Publicly Held**
SIC: 8011 9711 Offices & clinics of medical doctors; Army
HQ: United States Department Of The Army
101 Army Pentagon
Washington DC 20310

(G-1943)
UNITED STATES DEPT OF ARMY
Also Called: Munson Army Health Center
550 Pope Ave (66027-2332)
PHONE..................................913 684-6000
Ryan Heart, *Principal*
EMP: 300 **Publicly Held**
SIC: 8062 9711 General medical & surgical hospitals; Army;
HQ: United States Department Of The Army
101 Army Pentagon
Washington DC 20310

(G-1944)
UNITED STATES DEPT OF ARMY
Also Called: Personnel Services
821 Mcclellan Ave (66027-1361)
PHONE..................................913 684-2151
Joe Osborne, *Director*
EMP: 20 **Publicly Held**
SIC: 8741 9711 Personnel management; Army
HQ: United States Department Of The Army
101 Army Pentagon
Washington DC 20310

Fort Riley
Geary County

(G-1945)
ARMY & AIR FORCE EXCHANGE SVC
Also Called: Custer Hill Bowling Center
7485 Fort Riley Campus (66442)
PHONE..................................785 239-4366
Dennis O Connell, *Branch Mgr*
EMP: 20 **Publicly Held**
WEB: www.aafes.com
SIC: 7933 9711 Ten pin center; Army;
HQ: Army & Air Force Exchange Service
3911 S Walton Walker Blvd
Dallas TX 75236
214 312-2011

(G-1946)
CONTRACT SERVICES INC
Supply Division
7920 Apennines Dr (66442-4392)
PHONE..................................785 239-9069
EMP: 85
SALES (corp-wide): 9.7MM **Privately Held**
SIC: 8744 7349 Facilities Support Services Building Maintenance Services
PA: Contract Services, Inc.
801 W 6th St Ste C
Junction City KS 85086
785 762-6161

(G-1947)
CORVIAS MILITARY LIVING LLC
2460 G St Ste A (66442-2701)
PHONE..................................785 717-2200
Susan McKenzie, *Principal*
EMP: 11
SALES (corp-wide): 192.6MM **Privately Held**
SIC: 6552 Subdividers & developers
HQ: Corvias Military Living, Llc
1405 S County Trl Ste 510
East Greenwich RI 02818
401 228-2800

(G-1948)
FSIG LLC
Also Called: Riley Food Services
265 Stewart Ave (66442-7003)
P.O. Box 2713 (66442-0713)
PHONE..................................785 784-2566
Stephen Linn, *General Mgr*
EMP: 80
SALES (est): 242.3K **Privately Held**
SIC: 1711 7349 Plumbing, heating, air-conditioning contractors; janitorial service, contract basis

(G-1949)
RILEY COMMUNITIES LLC
211 Custer Ave (66442-4020)
PHONE..................................785 717-2210
Picerne John, *Mng Member*
John Picerne, *Mng Member*
Jennifer Chamrin, *Manager*
EMP: 100
SQ FT: 20,000
SALES (est): 3.9MM **Privately Held**
SIC: 6514 1521 Residential building, four or fewer units: operation; single-family housing construction

(G-1950)
SKOOKUM EDUCATIONAL PROGRAMS
Also Called: Skookum Contract Services
315 Marshall Ave (66442-7005)
PHONE..................................785 307-8180
Howard Whittaker, *Manager*
EMP: 119 **Privately Held**
SIC: 8744 Base maintenance (providing personnel on continuing basis)
PA: Skookum Educational Programs Inc
4525 Auto Center Way
Bremerton WA 98312

(G-1951)
UNITED STATES DEPT OF ARMY
Also Called: Fort Riley Recycle Center
407 Pershing Ct (66442-7026)
PHONE..................................785 239-2385
Jill Dalton, *Branch Mgr*
EMP: 20 **Publicly Held**
SIC: 4953 9711 Refuse systems; Army;
HQ: United States Department Of The Army
101 Army Pentagon
Washington DC 20310

(G-1952)
UNITED STATES DEPT OF ARMY
Miccftriley-W800a8
7920 Apennines Dr (66442-4392)
PHONE..................................785 240-0308
Donald Abbott, *IT/INT Sup*
EMP: 57 **Publicly Held**
SIC: 9711 7371 Army; computer software development & applications
HQ: United States Department Of The Army
101 Army Pentagon
Washington DC 20310

(G-1953)
UNITED STATES DEPT OF ARMY
Also Called: Irwin Army Community Hospital
650 Huebner Rd (66442-4030)
PHONE..................................785 239-7000
J Thomas Hardy, *Branch Mgr*
EMP: 720 **Publicly Held**

GEOGRAPHIC

SIC: 8062 9711 General medical & surgical hospitals; Army;
HQ: United States Department Of The Army
101 Army Pentagon
Washington DC 20310

Fort Scott
Bourbon County

(G-1954)
AMERICAN BOTTLING COMPANY
425 Marble Rd (66701-8639)
P.O. Box 182 (66701-0182)
PHONE..................................620 223-6166
Daniel Bouch, *Manager*
EMP: 14
SQ FT: 40,000 **Publicly Held**
WEB: www.cs-americas.com
SIC: 5149 Soft drinks
HQ: The American Bottling Company
5301 Legacy Dr
Plano TX 75024

(G-1955)
ANODIZING INC
Also Called: Extrusions
2401 S Main St (66701-3027)
P.O. Box 430 (66701-0430)
PHONE..................................620 223-1111
Matthew Ida, *President*
Billie Ida Parker, *Corp Secy*
Ja Ida, *Director*
EMP: 100
SQ FT: 100,000
SALES (est): 9.2MM
SALES (corp-wide): 19.5MM **Privately Held**
SIC: 3354 Aluminum extruded products
PA: Extrusions, Inc.
2401 S Main St
Fort Scott KS 66701
620 223-1111

(G-1956)
CARDINAL LOGISTICS
4805 Campbell Dr (66701-8646)
PHONE..................................620 223-4903
Terry Gerrond, *Vice Pres*
Joanna Rench, *Transportation*
Nancy Miller, *Human Res Mgr*
Susan Robertson, *Security Mgr*
Steve Deaktor, *Manager*
EMP: 25
SALES (est): 145.2K **Privately Held**
SIC: 4789 Transportation services

(G-1957)
CARE 4 ALL HOME MEDICAL EQP
2 W 18th St (66701-3177)
PHONE..................................620 223-4141
Kimberly Phillips, *President*
Glenn Pearson, *President*
Joy Pearson, *Admin Sec*
EMP: 9
SALES (est): 1.2MM **Privately Held**
SIC: 3845 Electromedical equipment

(G-1958)
CEQUEL COMMUNICATIONS LLC
Also Called: Suddenlink Communications
14 E 2nd St (66701-2040)
PHONE..................................620 223-1804
Charles Hembree, *Manager*
EMP: 34
SALES (corp-wide): 4.6MM **Privately Held**
SIC: 4841 Cable television services
HQ: Cequel Communications, Llc
3015 S Southeast Loop 323
Tyler TX 75701
314 965-2020

(G-1959)
CITIZENS BANK NA (HQ)
200 S Main St (66701-2064)
P.O. Box 899 (66701-0899)
PHONE..................................620 223-1200
Randall Edge, *CEO*
H Dean Mann, *Ch of Bd*
Ellis Spencer, *President*
James S Womeldorff, *Senior VP*
Carrie Allen, *Vice Pres*
EMP: 49
SQ FT: 18,000
SALES (est): 17.5MM **Privately Held**
SIC: 6021 National commercial banks

(G-1960)
CITY STATE BANK
202 Scott Ave (66701-2054)
P.O. Box 231 (66701-0231)
PHONE..................................620 223-1600
William Thompson, *Branch Mgr*
EMP: 11
SALES (corp-wide): 1.8MM **Privately Held**
WEB: www.citysb.com
SIC: 6022 State trust companies accepting deposits, commercial
HQ: The City State Bank
1012 Highway 69
Fort Scott KS 66701

(G-1961)
CITY STATE BANK (HQ)
1012 Highway 69 (66701-8718)
P.O. Box 231 (66701-0231)
PHONE..................................620 223-1600
Bill Thompson, *President*
Vickie Chaplin, *Opers Mgr*
EMP: 10
SALES: 1.9MM
SALES (corp-wide): 1.8MM **Privately Held**
SIC: 6022 State trust companies accepting deposits, commercial

(G-1962)
COURTLAND DAY SPA
121 E 1st St (66701-1406)
PHONE..................................620 223-0098
Cheryl Adamson, *President*
EMP: 10
SALES (est): 190.7K **Privately Held**
WEB: www.courtlandhotel.com
SIC: 7231 7299 Beauty shops; massage parlor & steam bath services

(G-1963)
CST OIL & GAS CORPORATION (PA)
1690 155th St (66701-8346)
PHONE..................................620 829-5307
Steven A Tedesco, *President*
Christine T Tedesco, *Corp Secy*
Tedesco Christine T, *Director*
EMP: 5
SQ FT: 3,500
SALES (est): 996.4K **Privately Held**
SIC: 1382 Oil & gas exploration services

(G-1964)
DIEHL BANWART BOLTON JARRED (PA)
7 1/2 E Wall St (66701-1422)
P.O. Box 469 (66701-0469)
PHONE..................................620 223 4300
EMP: 20
SALES (est): 2.8MM **Privately Held**
SIC: 8721 Certified Public Accountants

(G-1965)
ENNIS INC
2920 Richards Rd (66701-2911)
PHONE..................................620 223-6500
Sherri Clark, *Manager*
EMP: 100
SALES (corp-wide): 400.7MM **Publicly Held**
WEB: www.ennis.com
SIC: 2761 5112 Manifold business forms; business forms
PA: Ennis, Inc.
2441 Presidential Pkwy
Midlothian TX 76065
972 775-9801

(G-1966)
ENNIS BUSINESS FORMS OF KANSAS
2920 Richards Rd (66701-2911)
P.O. Box 310 (66701-0310)
PHONE..................................620 223-6500
Charles Ray, *President*
Harve Cathey, *Corp Secy*
EMP: 100
SQ FT: 54,000
SALES (est): 18.3MM
SALES (corp-wide): 400.7MM **Publicly Held**
WEB: www.ennis.com
SIC: 2761 5112 Manifold business forms; business forms
PA: Ennis, Inc.
2441 Presidential Pkwy
Midlothian TX 76065
972 775-9801

(G-1967)
EXTRUSIONS INC (PA)
2401 S Main St (66701-3027)
PHONE..................................620 223-1111
Matt Ida, *President*
Brian McGowen, *General Mgr*
Billie Ida-Williamson, *Treasurer*
EMP: 78 **EST:** 1963
SQ FT: 120,000
SALES (est): 19.5MM **Privately Held**
WEB: www.winventwindows.com
SIC: 3354 Aluminum extruded products

(G-1968)
FIRSTSOURCE SOLUTIONS USA INC
4500 Campbell Dr (66701-8636)
PHONE..................................620 223-8200
Nancy A Maze, *Vice Pres*
Martin Miner, *Branch Mgr*
EMP: 11
SALES (corp-wide): 1B **Privately Held**
SIC: 8741 Financial management for business
HQ: Firstsource Solutions Usa Inc
205 Bryant Woods S
Buffalo NY 14228

(G-1969)
FORT SCOTT COUNTRY CLUB INC
2414 Horton St (66701-3170)
PHONE..................................620 223-5060
Mark McMoy, *President*
EMP: 18
SALES (est): 407.8K **Privately Held**
SIC: 7997 Country club, membership

(G-1970)
FORT SCOTT LIVESTOCK MARKET
Old Hwy 54 (66701)
P.O. Box 270 (66701-0270)
PHONE..................................620 223-4600
Larry Martin, *President*
EMP: 50
SALES (est): 7.4MM **Privately Held**
WEB: www.fslivestock.com
SIC: 5154 Auctioning livestock

(G-1971)
FORT SCOTT PRESBYTERIAN VLG
2401 Horton St (66701-3178)
PHONE..................................620 223-5550
Dinger Nance, *Exec Dir*
EMP: 30
SALES (est): 792.9K **Privately Held**
SIC: 8322 Adult day care center

(G-1972)
FORT SCOTT TRUCK & TRACTOR
2595 Quail Rd (66701-1897)
PHONE..................................620 223-6506
Tom C Gorman, *President*
J David Gorman, *Corp Secy*
EMP: 10
SQ FT: 13,500
SALES (est): 1.4MM **Privately Held**
SIC: 5083 7699 Agricultural machinery & equipment; farm machinery repair

(G-1973)
FREEDOM READY MIX INC
1740 Highway 54 (66701-8338)
P.O. Box 225 (66701-0225)
PHONE..................................620 224-2800
Jason Marbery, *President*
Lane Cutler, *Vice Pres*
Glinda Cutler, *Treasurer*
EMP: 8
SALES (est): 630K **Privately Held**
SIC: 3273 Ready-mixed concrete

(G-1974)
GP EXPRESS INC
103 W 19th St (66701-3110)
P.O. Box 646 (66701-0646)
PHONE..................................620 223-1244
Greg Post, *President*
EMP: 15
SQ FT: 2,400
SALES (est): 1.5MM **Privately Held**
SIC: 4213 Contract haulers

(G-1975)
GUEST HOME ESTATES VI
737 Heylman St (66701-2421)
P.O. Box 936 (66701-0936)
PHONE..................................620 223-1620
Cynthia Lipe, *Director*
EMP: 25
SALES (est): 457.5K **Privately Held**
SIC: 8361 Geriatric residential care

(G-1976)
JOHN C GROSS III (PA)
Also Called: Gross Real Estate
18 S National Ave (66701-1309)
PHONE..................................620 223-2550
John C Gross III, *President*
EMP: 14 **EST:** 1913
SQ FT: 1,500
SALES (est): 2.5MM **Privately Held**
WEB: www.grossrealestate.com
SIC: 6411 6531 Insurance agents; real estate brokers & agents

(G-1977)
KANSAS TEACHERS CMNTY CR UN
24 S National Ave (66701-1309)
PHONE..................................620 223-1475
Justin Webb, *Manager*
EMP: 11 **Privately Held**
SIC: 6141 6061 Personal credit institutions; federal credit unions
PA: Kansas Teachers Community Credit Union
416 N Broadway St
Pittsburg KS 66762

(G-1978)
KEURIG DR PEPPER INC
425 Marble Rd (66701)
PHONE..................................620 223-6166
Dave Gillen, *Branch Mgr*
EMP: 99 **Publicly Held**
SIC: 2086 Soft drinks: packaged in cans, bottles, etc.
PA: Keurig Dr Pepper Inc.
53 South Ave
Burlington MA 01803

(G-1979)
KEY INDUSTRIES INC
400 Marble Rd (66701-8639)
PHONE..................................620 223-2000
Chris Barnes, *President*
William K Pollock, *Chairman*
▲ **EMP:** 45
SQ FT: 130,000
SALES (est): 22.3MM **Privately Held**
WEB: www.keyindustriesinc.com
SIC: 5136 Men's & boys' outerwear

(G-1980)
LABCONCO CORPORATION
2500 Liberty Bell Rd (66701-3004)
PHONE..................................620 223-5700
Tammy Phillips, *Traffic Mgr*
Mike Lakeman, *Manager*
Kevin Gilkison, *Director*
EMP: 40
SALES (corp-wide): 41.3MM **Privately Held**
WEB: www.labconco.com
SIC: 3444 3821 Hoods, range: sheet metal; laboratory apparatus & furniture
PA: Labconco Corporation
8811 Prospect Ave
Kansas City MO 64132
816 333-8811

(G-1981)
LIBERTY LABELS LLC
2146 Native Rd (66701-8380)
PHONE..................................620 223-2208
Chris Middleton, *Office Mgr*
Dennis Stewart,
EMP: 9
SQ FT: 10,000
SALES (est): 1.7MM **Privately Held**
WEB: www.libertylabels.com
SIC: 3565 Labeling machines, industrial

(G-1982)
M C M RESTORATION COMPANY INC (PA)
2 N Main St (66701-1435)
P.O. Box 1117 (66701-1117)
PHONE..................................620 223-6602
Craig M McKenny, *President*
Patrick Mc Kenny, *Vice Pres*
Tim McKenny, *Treasurer*
EMP: 20
SQ FT: 4,500
SALES (est): 3.7MM **Privately Held**
WEB: www.mcmrestoration.com
SIC: 1799 Waterproofing

(G-1983)
MADISON BROTHERS CONCRETE INC
Also Called: Rogers & Son Concrete
2461 Quail Rd (66701-1797)
PHONE..................................620 224-6098
Bill Madison, *President*
Frank Madison, *Vice Pres*
EMP: 13 **EST:** 1975
SQ FT: 3,200
SALES (est): 1.1MM **Privately Held**
SIC: 1771 Concrete pumping

(G-1984)
MEDICALODGES INC
Also Called: Community Care Connection
120 E Wall St (66701-1425)
P.O. Box 565 (66701-0565)
PHONE..................................620 223-5085
Helen Pherry, *Manager*
EMP: 140
SALES (corp-wide): 100.2MM **Privately Held**
WEB: www.medicalodges.com
SIC: 8051 8322 8082 Convalescent home with continuous nursing care; individual & family services; home health care services
PA: Medicalodges, Inc.
201 W 8th St
Coffeyville KS 67337
620 251-6700

(G-1985)
MEDICALODGES INC
Also Called: Medicalodge of Fort Scott
915 Horton St (66701-2437)
P.O. Box 510 (66701-0510)
PHONE..................................620 223-0210
Karen Brown, *Manager*
EMP: 90
SALES (corp-wide): 100.2MM **Privately Held**
WEB: www.medicalodges.com
SIC: 8052 8051 Intermediate care facilities; skilled nursing care facilities
PA: Medicalodges, Inc.
201 W 8th St
Coffeyville KS 67337
620 251-6700

(G-1986)
MERCY HEALTH
401 Woodland Hills Blvd (66701-8797)
P.O. Box 829 (66701-0829)
PHONE..................................620 223-2200
Reta Baker, *Administration*
EMP: 439
SALES (corp-wide): 6.5B **Privately Held**
SIC: 8062 General medical & surgical hospitals
PA: Mercy Health
14528 South Outer 40 Rd # 100
Chesterfield MO 63017
314 579-6100

(G-1987)
MERCY HLTH FNDTION STHSTERN PA
Also Called: Mercy Physicans Group
710 W 8th St (66701-2404)
PHONE..................................620 223-2200
EMP: 19
SALES (corp-wide): 16.3B **Privately Held**
SIC: 6733 8011 Trust Management Medical Doctor's Office
HQ: Mercy Health Foundation Of Southeastern Pennsylvania
1 W Elm St Ste 100
Conshohocken PA 19428
610 567-6000

(G-1988)
MERCY HOME HEALTH
901 Horton St (66701)
PHONE..................................620 223-8090
Rebecca Davide, *Director*
EMP: 15
SALES (est): 339.2K **Privately Held**
SIC: 8082 Home health care services

(G-1989)
MERCY KANSAS COMMUNITIES INC (HQ)
Also Called: Mercy Hospital
401 Woodland Hills Blvd (66701-8797)
P.O. Box 829 (66701-0829)
PHONE..................................620 223-7075
John Woodrich, *President*
Rita Baker, *President*
Terri Del Chiaro, *CFO*
EMP: 450
SALES: 67.5MM
SALES (corp-wide): 6.5B **Privately Held**
WEB: www.mercykansas.com
SIC: 8062 8069 General medical & surgical hospitals; specialty hospitals, except psychiatric
PA: Mercy Health
14528 South Outer 40 Rd # 100
Chesterfield MO 63017
314 579-6100

(G-1990)
MID-CNTINENTAL RESTORATION INC (PA)
401 E Hudson St (66701-4611)
PHONE..................................620 223-3700
Frank J Halsey, *President*
Scott Halsey, *Exec VP*
Matt Deloney, *Vice Pres*
Steve Floyd, *CFO*
EMP: 140 **EST:** 1946
SQ FT: 30,000
SALES (est): 43.9MM **Privately Held**
SIC: 1741 Tuckpointing or restoration

(G-1991)
MIDLAND RESTORATION COMPANY
2159 Indian Rd (66701-8732)
P.O. Box 247 (66701-0247)
PHONE..................................620 223-6855
Russel Felt, *President*
Toni Felt, *Corp Secy*
EMP: 12
SALES: 750K **Privately Held**
WEB: www.midlandrestoration.com
SIC: 1542 1799 Commercial & office buildings, renovation & repair; waterproofing

(G-1992)
MY1STOP LLC
Also Called: My1stop.com
3200 Liberty Bell Rd (66701-8633)
PHONE..................................316 554-9700
Wendy Saldivar, *Sales Staff*
Roger Kraft,
Michael Del Chiaro,
EMP: 15
SALES (est): 2MM **Privately Held**
WEB: www.my1stop.com
SIC: 7389 Printers' services: folding, collating

(G-1993)
NEW GENERATION
1502 Scott Ave (66701-2768)
PHONE..................................620 223-1506
Elizabeth Nuss, *Treasurer*
Amy Boyd, *Director*
EMP: 16
SALES: 365.3K **Privately Held**
SIC: 8351 Child day care services

(G-1994)
NIECE PRODUCTS OF KANSAS INC
3904 Liberty Bell Rd (66701-8600)
PHONE..................................620 223-0340
E L Niece, *CEO*
Patrick Flanagan, *COO*
Renee Clark, *CFO*
Chuck Stewart, *CFO*
EMP: 42 **EST:** 2012
SALES (est): 6MM **Privately Held**
SIC: 3443 3429 Tanks for tank trucks, metal plate; manufactured hardware (general)

(G-1995)
NORVELL COMPANY INC
4002 Liberty Bell Rd (66701-8638)
PHONE..................................620 223-3110
Alan Hale, *President*
Randy L Sprague, *Engineer*
Andrea Bryant, *Sales Staff*
Julie Carpenter, *Sales Associate*
EMP: 30
SQ FT: 30,000
SALES (est): 4.6MM **Privately Held**
WEB: www.norvellco.com
SIC: 3556 Flour mill machinery

(G-1996)
OLD FORT GENEALGCL SOCTY SE KS
Also Called: Southeastern Kansas
3rd And National Ave (66701)
P.O. Box 786 (66701-0786)
PHONE..................................620 223-3300
Ken Lyon, *President*
Virginia Brown, *Principal*
Nancy Patterson, *Vice Pres*
Nolene Whiteside, *Treasurer*
Barbara Wood, *Admin Sec*
EMP: 10
SALES (est): 350K **Privately Held**
SIC: 7299 Genealogical investigation service

(G-1997)
PARRIS R DAVID MD
Also Called: Mercy Physicians Group
403 Woodland Hills Blvd (66701-8798)
PHONE..................................620 223-8045
David Parris MD, *Partner*
EMP: 50
SALES (est): 2.5MM **Privately Held**
SIC: 8011 Obstetrician

(G-1998)
PEERLESS PRODUCTS INC
2403 S Main St (66701-3027)
PHONE..................................620 223-4610
Bill Osbern, *President*
Coby Jones, *President*
Steve Cliffman, *Plant Mgr*
Justin Ebert, *Project Mgr*
Benjamin Gruver, *Production*
▲ **EMP:** 350 **EST:** 1952
SQ FT: 5,366
SALES: 51.1MM **Privately Held**
WEB: www.peerlessproducts.com
SIC: 3442 Window & door frames

(G-1999)
PRESBYTRIAN MNORS OF MD-MERICA
Also Called: Presbytrian Village
2401 Horton St Apt 121 (66701-2790)
PHONE..................................620 223-5550
G Dierksen Nance, *General Mgr*
EMP: 30
SQ FT: 58,000
SALES (corp-wide): 8.6MM **Privately Held**
SIC: 8361 Residential care
PA: Presbyterian Manors Of Mid-America Inc
2414 N Woodlawn Blvd
Wichita KS 67220
316 685-1100

(G-2000)
R & R EQUIPMENT INC
2355 Locust Rd (66701-8121)
PHONE..................................620 223-2450
Tom Riley Jr, *President*
EMP: 8
SALES: 3MM **Privately Held**
WEB: www.rrequipment.com
SIC: 3531 Construction machinery

(G-2001)
RAY SHEPHERD MOTORS INC
Also Called: Ford Lincoln Mercury
1819 S Main St (66701-3015)
P.O. Box 112 (66701-0112)
PHONE..................................620 644-2625
David Shepherd, *President*
Mary Shepherd, *Corp Secy*
EMP: 50
SALES (est): 13.8MM **Privately Held**
WEB: www.shepherdteam.com
SIC: 5511 7515 7514 Automobiles, new & used; passenger car leasing; passenger car rental

(G-2002)
RECREATION COMMISSION
735 Scott Ave (66701-2722)
PHONE..................................620 223-0386
EMP: 10
SALES (est): 75K **Privately Held**
SIC: 7997 Membership sports & recreation clubs

(G-2003)
SEKAN PRINTING COMPANY INC
Also Called: Sekan Occasion Shops
2210 S Main St (66701-3024)
P.O. Box 631 (66701-0631)
PHONE..................................620 223-5190
Donald D Banwart, *President*
Lonnie G Banwart, *Vice Pres*
Carol Carter, *Financial Exec*
Davin Reichard, *Comptroller*
Justin Banwart, *Manager*
EMP: 48
SQ FT: 120,000
SALES (est): 9.1MM **Privately Held**
WEB: www.sekan.com
SIC: 2752 5621 Commercial printing, offset; bridal shops

(G-2004)
SHORT GO INC
Also Called: Twister Trailer Manufacturing
400 N National Ave (66701-3628)
PHONE..................................620 223-2866
Steven Brent Mosing, *President*
EMP: 77
SALES: 8MM **Privately Held**
SIC: 3715 Trailers or vans for transporting horses

(G-2005)
SLEEP INN & SUITES
302 E Wall St (66701-1403)
PHONE..................................620 223-2555
EMP: 11 **EST:** 2014
SALES (est): 169.8K **Privately Held**
SIC: 7011 Hotels & motels

(G-2006)
SOUTHEAST KANS MENTAL HLTH CTR
212 State St (66701-2031)
P.O. Box 704 (66701-0704)
PHONE..................................620 223-5030
Kelly K Ferguson, *Psychologist*
Bob Chase, *Director*
EMP: 20
SALES (corp-wide): 8.3MM **Privately Held**
SIC: 8093 Mental health clinic, outpatient
PA: Southeast Kansas Mental Health Center
1106 S 9th St
Humboldt KS 66748
620 473-2241

(G-2007)
STEWART REALTY CO INC
1707 S National Ave (66701-3452)
P.O. Box 937 (66701-0937)
PHONE..................................620 223-6700

Donald L Stewart, *President*
EMP: 15
SALES (est): 1MM **Privately Held**
SIC: 6531 Real estate agent, residential

(G-2008)
TIMKEN SMO LLC
Also Called: Carlisle Belts
4505 Campbell Dr (66701-8636)
PHONE..................................620 223-0080
Kenneth Cameron, *Manager*
EMP: 340
SALES (corp-wide): 3.5B **Publicly Held**
WEB: www.grainware.com
SIC: 3451 3714 Screw machine products; air conditioner parts, motor vehicle
HQ: Timken Smo Llc
2601 W Battlefield St
Springfield MO 65807
866 773-2926

(G-2009)
TOWER METAL PRODUCTS LP
301 N Hill St (66701-1515)
P.O. Box 791 (66701-0791)
PHONE..................................620 215-2622
Audie Tand, *Branch Mgr*
EMP: 40
SALES (corp-wide): 4.1MM **Privately Held**
SIC: 3341 Aluminum smelting & refining (secondary)
PA: Tower Metal Products L.P.
1965 Pratt Blvd
Elk Grove Village IL 60007
847 806-7200

(G-2010)
TRACTOR SUPPLY COMPANY
Also Called: Tractor Supply 1277
2420 S Main St (66701-3028)
PHONE..................................620 223-4900
Joel Mayfield, *Branch Mgr*
EMP: 10
SALES (corp-wide): 7.9B **Publicly Held**
WEB: www.tractorsupplyco.com
SIC: 5191 Farm supplies
PA: Tractor Supply Company
5401 Virginia Way
Brentwood TN 37027
615 440-4000

(G-2011)
TRAINWRECK TEES LLC
Also Called: Train Wreck Promotion
108 Scott Ave (66701-1421)
P.O. Box 648 (66701-0648)
PHONE..................................620 224-2480
Dallas Smith, *Principal*
James Smith,
Paulette Smith,
EMP: 6 **EST:** 2007
SALES: 425K **Privately Held**
WEB: www.trainwrecktees.com
SIC: 2759 5632 5949 7319 Screen printing; millinery; sewing, needlework & piece goods; distribution of advertising material or sample services

(G-2012)
TRI-VALLEY DEVELOPMENTAL SVCS
4305 Campbell Dr (66701-8644)
P.O. Box 1052 (66701-1052)
PHONE..................................620 223-3990
Alene Jolly, *Finance Other*
Aimee Thompson, *Pub Rel Dir*
Valerie Frederick,
EMP: 67
SQ FT: 1,200
SALES (corp-wide): 5.2MM **Privately Held**
WEB: www.tvds.org
SIC: 4111 8361 8331 Local & suburban transit; home for the mentally handicapped; sheltered workshop
PA: Tri-Valley Developmental Services Inc
3740 S Santa Fe Ave
Chanute KS
620 431-7401

(G-2013)
UMB BANK NATIONAL ASSOCIATION
324 S National Ave (66701-1325)
P.O. Box B (66701)
PHONE..................................620 223-1255
Cynthia Bowman, *Manager*
EMP: 13
SALES (corp-wide): 1.1B **Publicly Held**
SIC: 6021 National commercial banks
HQ: Umb Bank, National Association
1010 Grand Blvd Fl 3
Kansas City MO 64106
816 842-2222

(G-2014)
VALU MERCHANDISERS COMPANY
4805 Campbell Dr (66701-8646)
PHONE..................................620 223-1313
Kevin Addington, *Owner*
EMP: 10
SALES (corp-wide): 9.7B **Privately Held**
SIC: 5199 General merchandise, non-durable
HQ: Valu Merchandisers Company
5000 Kansas Ave
Kansas City KS 66106

(G-2015)
VELOCITY MANUFACTURING CO LLC
523 E Wall St (66701-1534)
PHONE..................................620 223-1277
Robbie Forester, *General Mgr*
Tommy Guss, *Prdtn Mgr*
Greg Fess, *Branch Mgr*
▲ **EMP:** 12
SALES (est): 2.1MM **Privately Held**
SIC: 3482 Small arms ammunition

(G-2016)
W/K HOLDING COMPANY INC (PA)
2401 Cooper St (66701-3033)
PHONE..................................620 223-5500
Mark Tucker, *President*
Roger Davis, *General Mgr*
Phil Quick, *General Mgr*
Roger Kraft, *Principal*
Eastwood Jim, *Buyer*
▲ **EMP:** 10
SALES (est): 97.8MM **Privately Held**
SIC: 2754 Commercial printing, gravure

(G-2017)
WARD-KRAFT INC (HQ)
2401 Cooper St (66701-3033)
P.O. Box 938 (66701-0938)
PHONE..................................800 821-4021
Roger Kraft, *CEO*
Mark Tucker, *President*
Steve Sinn, *General Mgr*
Kevin Marquardt, *Vice Pres*
Don Gauthier, *Purch Mgr*
▲ **EMP:** 300
SQ FT: 230,610
SALES (est): 102.1MM
SALES (corp-wide): 97.8MM **Privately Held**
WEB: www.wardkraft.com
SIC: 2761 2672 Manifold business forms; labels (unprinted), gummed: made from purchased materials
PA: W/K Holding Company, Inc.
2401 Cooper St
Fort Scott KS 66701
620 223-5500

(G-2018)
WARD-KRAFT INC
Also Called: W/K-Short Run Division
2400 Liberty Bell Rd (66701-3043)
PHONE..................................620 223-1104
EMP: 50
SALES (corp-wide): 80.8MM **Privately Held**
SIC: 5111 Whol Printing/Writing Paper
HQ: Ward-Kraft, Inc.
2401 Cooper St
Fort Scott KS 66701
620 223-5500

Fowler
Meade County

(G-2019)
FOWLER FEEDERS LLC
5113 23 Rd (67844-9144)
PHONE..................................620 646-5269
Todd Seick, *Principal*
Boyd Orr, *Treasurer*
Rick Blattner, *Mng Member*
EMP: 12
SQ FT: 3,000
SALES (est): 6.5MM **Privately Held**
WEB: www.fowlerfeeders.com
SIC: 0211 Beef cattle feedlots

(G-2020)
FOWLER NURSING HOME
401 E 6th Ave (67844-4419)
PHONE..................................620 646-5215
Barbara Whitney, *Director*
EMP: 28
SQ FT: 3,000
SALES (est): 1.1MM **Privately Held**
SIC: 8052 8051 Intermediate care facilities; skilled nursing care facilities

Frankfort
Marshall County

(G-2021)
BOB HULL INC
710 N Elm St (66427-1503)
P.O. Box 202 (66427-0202)
PHONE..................................785 292-4790
Richard P Hull, *President*
Carlene H Hull, *Corp Secy*
David W Hull, *Vice Pres*
Rebecca Jane Dunlap, *Shareholder*
EMP: 20
SQ FT: 5,000
SALES (est): 3.4MM **Privately Held**
SIC: 1623 Underground utilities contractor

(G-2022)
FRANKFORT COMMUNITY CARE HOME
510 N Walnut St (66427-1446)
PHONE..................................785 292-4442
Everett Spunugle, *President*
Robert Myers, *Vice Pres*
Jay Peckham, *Treasurer*
Tish Outhet, *Nursing Dir*
Laura O'Neil, *Administration*
EMP: 55
SQ FT: 18,000
SALES: 2.4MM **Privately Held**
WEB: www.fcch.net
SIC: 8052 8051 Intermediate care facilities; skilled nursing care facilities

(G-2023)
SUTHER FEEDS INC (PA)
105 S Kansas Ave (66427-1346)
PHONE..................................785 292-4414
Jerry Suther, *President*
Pam A Suther, *Corp Secy*
Tim Suther, *Vice Pres*
Roy Kannenberg, *Plant Mgr*
Jeff Sleichter, *CFO*
EMP: 10
SQ FT: 11,200
SALES (est): 6MM **Privately Held**
WEB: www.sutherfeeds.com
SIC: 2833 2048 Animal based products; prepared feeds

(G-2024)
SUTHER FEEDS INC
Also Called: Suthers
105 S Kansas Ave (66427-1346)
PHONE..................................785 292-4415
Jerry Suther, *Manager*
EMP: 15
SALES (corp-wide): 6MM **Privately Held**
WEB: www.sutherfeeds.com
SIC: 4225 General warehousing & storage
PA: Suther Feeds, Inc.
105 S Kansas Ave
Frankfort KS 66427
785 292-4414

Fredonia
Wilson County

(G-2025)
A ADOPT FAMILY INC
1400 S Cement Plant Rd (66736-2068)
PHONE..................................620 378-4458
Anthony Decosmo, *Treasurer*
Don Braden, *Director*
Debbie Dean, *Admin Sec*
EMP: 16
SALES (est): 303K **Privately Held**
SIC: 8699 Charitable organization

(G-2026)
AERO SPACE MANUFACTURING CORP
1075 Fillmore St (66736-2103)
PHONE..................................620 378-4441
David Fink, *President*
Deanna Fink, *Corp Secy*
EMP: 17
SALES (est): 3.6MM **Privately Held**
SIC: 3728 3354 Aircraft parts & equipment; aluminum extruded products

(G-2027)
BROWNS PROCESSING
103 W Jefferson St (66736)
PHONE..................................620 378-2441
Ricky Brown, *Partner*
Jeff Walker, *Partner*
EMP: 5
SALES (est): 475.9K **Privately Held**
SIC: 4222 2011 Warehousing, cold storage or refrigerated; meat packing plants

(G-2028)
CENTURION INDUSTRIES INC
Also Called: A-Lert Construction Services
401 N 6th St (66736-1306)
P.O. Box 531 (66736-0531)
PHONE..................................620 378-4401
Randy Shinkle, *General Mgr*
EMP: 280
SALES (corp-wide): 162.4MM **Privately Held**
WEB: www.centurionind.com
SIC: 1796 3444 1761 Millwright; sheet metalwork; roofing contractor
PA: Centurion Industries, Inc.
1107 N Taylor Rd
Garrett IN 46738
260 357-6665

(G-2029)
CITY OF FREDONIA
Also Called: Madison Square Clubhouse
1701 Madison St (66736-1600)
PHONE..................................620 378-2802
Terry Deschaine, *Principal*
EMP: 15 **Privately Held**
WEB: www.fredoniaks.org
SIC: 2099 Food preparations
PA: City Of Fredonia
100 N 15th St
Fredonia KS 66736
620 378-2231

(G-2030)
DENISON INC (PA)
Also Called: Denison Weldings Supplies
405 Madison St (66736-1237)
PHONE..................................620 378-4148
Howard L Alger, *President*
Donna Ella Alger, *Treasurer*
EMP: 11
SQ FT: 8,000
SALES (est): 2.3MM **Privately Held**
SIC: 5084 5169 Welding machinery & equipment; oxygen

(G-2031)
EXCELL ART SIGN PRODUCTS LLC
1641 N 15th St (66736-2255)
PHONE..................................620 378-4477
EMP: 6

SALES (corp-wide): 1.3MM **Privately Held**
SIC: 3993 Mfg Of Aluminum Signs
PA: Excell Art Sign Products Llc
1654 S Lone Elm Rd
Olathe KS 66061
913 764-2364

(G-2032)
FIRST NAT BNCSHRES OF FREDONIA
730 Madison St (66736-1339)
P.O. Box 190 (66736-0190)
PHONE....................620 378-2151
M D Jeffers, *President*
Michael Douglas, *Exec VP*
Curtus Aylor, *Vice Pres*
Beverly Gaines, *Vice Pres*
Elizabeth Walker, *Bookkeeper*
EMP: 15
SQ FT: 4,500
SALES: 4.1MM **Privately Held**
WEB: www.fnbfredonia.com
SIC: 6712 6162 Bank holding companies; mortgage bankers & correspondents

(G-2033)
FREDONIA LIVESTOCK AUCTION LLC
360 W Madison St (66736-2050)
P.O. Box 385 (66736-0385)
PHONE....................620 378-2212
Cecil D Haun, *Mng Member*
Brad Haun,
Carole L Haun,
EMP: 25 **EST:** 1948
SALES (est): 1.4MM **Privately Held**
SIC: 5154 Auctioning livestock; hogs; sheep

(G-2034)
GOOD RIDDANCE CORPORATION
6983 200 Rd (66736-7693)
PHONE....................620 633-5222
Dovavon Knightingale, *Principal*
EMP: 7 **EST:** 2001
SALES (est): 725.5K **Privately Held**
SIC: 3089 Garbage containers, plastic

(G-2035)
HIGHTECH SOLUTIONS INC
Also Called: HI Tek Innovations
705 Cement Plant Rd (66736-7578)
PHONE....................620 228-2216
Hans Hazen, *President*
Julie Hazen, *Vice Pres*
EMP: 221 **EST:** 2013
SALES (est): 14.2MM **Privately Held**
SIC: 5734 7929 4812 Personal computers; entertainment service; cellular telephone services

(G-2036)
KOEHN CONSTRUCTION SVCS LLC
1111 N 2nd St (66736-2207)
P.O. Box 420 (66736-0420)
PHONE....................620 378-3002
Lyle Koehn, *Mng Member*
EMP: 25
SALES (est): 1MM **Privately Held**
SIC: 1542 Commercial & office building contractors

(G-2037)
LA DOW & SPOHN INC
433 Madison St (66736-1237)
P.O. Box 578 (66736-0578)
PHONE....................620 378-2541
Nancy Mahan, *President*
Monte Mahan, *Admin Sec*
EMP: 14
SQ FT: 20,000
SALES (est): 2.1MM **Privately Held**
SIC: 2752 Commercial printing, offset

(G-2038)
LAFARGE NORTH AMERICA INC
1400 S Cement Rd (66736)
PHONE....................620 378-4458
Horace Compton, *Opers-Prdtn-Mfg*
EMP: 100
SALES (corp-wide): 4.5B **Privately Held**
WEB: www.lafargenorthamerica.com
SIC: 3241 Cement, hydraulic
HQ: Lafarge North America Inc.
8700 W Bryn Mawr Ave
Chicago IL 60631
773 372-1000

(G-2039)
LMI AEROSPACE INC
1075 Fillmore St (66736-2103)
PHONE....................620 378-4441
EMP: 11 **Privately Held**
SIC: 3728 Aircraft parts & equipment
HQ: Lmi Aerospace, Inc.
411 Fountain Lakes Blvd
Saint Charles MO 63301
636 946-6525

(G-2040)
MIDWESTERN LITHO
Also Called: Twinmounds.com
321 N 6th St (66736-1304)
P.O. Box 31 (66736-0031)
PHONE....................620 378-2912
Delaine Pekrul, *President*
Kevin Pekrul, *Vice Pres*
Brian Sumner, *Purch Mgr*
Darla Tindle, *Personnel*
Hugh Runyan, *Sales Staff*
EMP: 6 **EST:** 1955
SQ FT: 3,500
SALES (est): 878.1K **Privately Held**
WEB: www.twinmounds.com
SIC: 2752 2791 2789 Commercial printing, offset; typesetting; bookbinding & related work

(G-2041)
QUALITY HEALTH CARE INC (PA)
Also Called: Sanctuary Unit The
1527 Madison St Fl 2 (66736-1751)
PHONE....................316 263-8880
Alan Chapman, *COO*
Courtney Vitamvas, *Human Res Dir*
Kellene Walker, *Director*
EMP: 11
SALES (est): 876.2K **Privately Held**
SIC: 8099 Blood related health services

(G-2042)
R PUCKETT FARMS INC
314 N 14th St (66736-1624)
PHONE....................620 378-3565
Raymond Puckett, *CEO*
Judy Puckett, *Corp Secy*
EMP: 22
SALES (est): 2.7MM **Privately Held**
SIC: 0191 1611 General farms, primarily crop; gravel or dirt road construction

(G-2043)
R PUCKETT FARMS INC
Also Called: Puckett Construction
1020 N 2nd St (66736)
PHONE....................620 378-3342
Fax: 620 378-2215
EMP: 15
SALES (est): 1.1MM **Privately Held**
SIC: 1794 0116 0111 5191 Excavation Work

(G-2044)
RADIANT ELECTRIC COOPERATIVE (PA)
100 N 15th St (66736-1628)
PHONE....................620 378-2161
Loren Dickens, *President*
Chuck Springer, *President*
Tom Ayers, *Treasurer*
EMP: 16 **EST:** 1941
SQ FT: 4,000
SALES: 11.9MM **Privately Held**
WEB: www.radiantec.coop
SIC: 4911 Distribution, electric power

(G-2045)
STATE BANK OF KANSAS (PA)
501 Madison St (66736-1327)
P.O. Box 480 (66736-0480)
PHONE....................620 378-2114
Jac Jensik, *CEO*
Alan Guthire, *President*
Lewis T Bambick, *Cashier*
EMP: 13
SQ FT: 5,000
SALES: 1.9MM **Privately Held**
SIC: 6022 State trust companies accepting deposits, commercial

(G-2046)
SYSTECH ENVIRONMENTAL CORP
1420 S Cement Plant Rd (66736-2068)
PHONE....................620 378-4451
Randy Robinson, *Principal*
Kent Short, *Technician*
EMP: 28
SALES (corp-wide): 4.5B **Privately Held**
SIC: 8748 Environmental consultant
HQ: Systech Environmental Corporation
3085 Woodman Dr Ste 300
Dayton OH 45420
800 888-8011

(G-2047)
TINDLE CONSTRUCTION INC
Also Called: TCI FABRICATION
933 Fillmore St (66736-2170)
PHONE....................620 378-2046
Barry Tindle, *CEO*
Brandon Tindle, *President*
Darla Tindle, *CFO*
Miranda Dinkel, *Admin Sec*
EMP: 70
SQ FT: 40,000
SALES: 9.1MM **Privately Held**
WEB: www.tcifabrication.com
SIC: 1629 3441 3446 Industrial plant construction; fabricated structural metal; architectural metalwork

(G-2048)
VALENT AEROSTRUCTURES LLC
1075 Fillmore St (66736-2103)
P.O. Box 558 (66736-0558)
PHONE....................620 378-4441
Josh Fink, *Branch Mgr*
EMP: 8 **Privately Held**
SIC: 3728 Aircraft parts & equipment
HQ: Valent Aerostructures Llc
11064 Strang Line Rd
Lenexa KS 66215
816 423-5600

(G-2049)
WILSON COUNTY CITIZEN INC
406 N 7th St (66736-1315)
PHONE....................620 378-4415
Joseph S Relph, *President*
Mina Deberry, *Principal*
Rita Relph, *Corp Secy*
EMP: 5
SQ FT: 4,800
SALES (est): 357.3K **Privately Held**
SIC: 2711 Newspapers: publishing only, not printed on site

Frontenac
Crawford County

(G-2050)
A1AIR HEATING & COOLING LLC
1035 N Highway 69 (66763-8100)
PHONE....................620 235-0600
Steve Chen,
John Indellicate,
EMP: 10
SALES: 500K **Privately Held**
SIC: 1711 Warm air heating & air conditioning contractor; heating & air conditioning contractors

(G-2051)
AINSWORTH PET NUTRITION LLC
1601 W Mckay St (66763-8136)
PHONE....................620 231-7779
Colin Terlip, *Branch Mgr*
EMP: 200
SALES (corp-wide): 7.8B **Publicly Held**
SIC: 2047 Dog & cat food
HQ: Ainsworth Pet Nutrition, Llc
18746 Mill St
Meadville PA 16335
814 724-7710

(G-2052)
ARTHUR DOGSWELL LLC
Also Called: Natural Life Pet Products
1601 W Mckay St (66763-8136)
PHONE....................620 231-7779
Kurt Terlip, *Branch Mgr*
EMP: 70
SALES (corp-wide): 24.5MM **Privately Held**
WEB: www.tripletwhitetails.com
SIC: 8741 Business management
PA: Arthur Dogswell, L.L.C.
11301 W Olympic Blvd
Los Angeles CA 90064
888 559-8833

(G-2053)
BARTOS ENTERPRISES INC (PA)
Also Called: Idle Hour Club
509 S Cayuga St (66763-2456)
PHONE....................620 232-9813
Carolyn Barto, *President*
Carla Barto, *President*
EMP: 18
SALES (est): 700K **Privately Held**
SIC: 5812 5813 6515 Steak restaurant; cocktail lounge; mobile home site operators

(G-2054)
EAGLE BEVERAGE CO INC
250 N Cayuga St (66763-2061)
P.O. Box 939 (66763-0939)
PHONE....................620 231-7970
Irene Menghini, *President*
Patricia Terlip, *Vice Pres*
Anthony J Menghini, *Treasurer*
Jenny Snow, *Office Mgr*
EMP: 18
SQ FT: 22,000
SALES (est): 6MM **Privately Held**
SIC: 5181 Beer & other fermented malt liquors

(G-2055)
HEALTH AND ENVMT KANS DEPT
Also Called: Surface Mining Section
4033 Parkview Dr (66763-2302)
PHONE....................620 231-8540
Murray Balk, *Manager*
EMP: 13 **Privately Held**
WEB: www.healthbookcorner.com
SIC: 1221 9511 Surface mining, lignite;
HQ: Kansas Department Of Health And Environment
1000 Sw Jackson St
Topeka KS 66612
785 296-1500

(G-2056)
JENNIFER BRUNETTI
214 E Mckay St (66763-2219)
P.O. Box 931 (66763-0931)
PHONE....................620 235-0100
Jennifer Brunetti, *Owner*
Kim Scott, *Admin Sec*
EMP: 65
SALES (est): 3.5MM **Privately Held**
SIC: 8111 Criminal law

(G-2057)
KIDS FIRST DAY CARE PRESCHOOL
102 S Cayuga St (66763-2408)
PHONE....................620 231-4994
Deloris Casey, *Director*
EMP: 20
SALES (est): 225.9K **Privately Held**
SIC: 8351 Group day care center

(G-2058)
LUSKER MASONRY
452 S 210th St (66763-8407)
PHONE....................620 231-9899
Adam Lusker, *Partner*
Lisa Lusker, *Partner*
EMP: 10 **EST:** 1997
SALES (est): 764.3K **Privately Held**
SIC: 1741 Stone masonry

(G-2059)
MEDICALODGES FRONTENAC
206 S Dittman St (66763-2253)
PHONE..................................620 231-0322
Scott L Hines, *CFO*
EMP: 14
SALES: 3.7MM **Privately Held**
SIC: 8051 Convalescent home with continuous nursing care

(G-2060)
MID AMRICA PRPTS PITTSBURG LLC
1035 N Highway 69 (66763-8100)
PHONE..................................620 232-1678
Norman Miller, *Owner*
EMP: 17
SALES (est): 2.5MM **Privately Held**
SIC: 6512 Nonresidential building operators

(G-2061)
OBRIEN ROCK COMPANY INC
O'Brien Ready-Mixed Con Co
791 E 590th Ave (66763-8406)
P.O. Box 597, Pittsburg (66762-0597)
PHONE..................................620 231-4940
Dwayne O'Brien, *Manager*
EMP: 5
SALES (corp-wide): 9.6MM **Privately Held**
SIC: 3273 Ready-mixed concrete
PA: O'brien Rock Company Inc
712 Central St
Saint Paul KS 66771
620 449-2257

(G-2062)
PALLUCCA AND SONS
Also Called: Pallucca & Sons Super Market
207 E Mckay St (66763-2222)
P.O. Box 1025 (66763-1025)
PHONE..................................620 231-7700
Richard J Pallucca, *Owner*
EMP: 15
SQ FT: 11,250
SALES (est): 1.3MM **Privately Held**
SIC: 5411 5141 Grocery stores, independent; groceries, general line

(G-2063)
PAYNES INC
Also Called: Payne's Truck Parts
806 W Mckay St (66763-2182)
PHONE..................................620 231-3170
James L Payne, *President*
Marla Payne, *Corp Secy*
EMP: 13
SALES (est): 880K **Privately Held**
WEB: www.paynesinc.kscoxmail.com
SIC: 3599 5531 5013 5521 Machine shop, jobbing & repair; truck equipment & parts; truck parts & accessories; trucks, tractors & trailers: used; truck rental & leasing, no drivers

(G-2064)
SUGAR CREEK PACKING CO
1600 W Mc Ky (66763)
P.O. Box 1019 (66763-1019)
PHONE..................................620 232-2700
Mike John, *Branch Mgr*
EMP: 170
SALES (corp-wide): 700MM **Privately Held**
WEB: www.sugarcreek.com
SIC: 2013 2011 Sausages from purchased meat; bacon, slab & sliced from meat slaughtered on site
PA: Sugar Creek Packing Co.
2101 Kenskill Ave
Wshngtn Ct Hs OH 43160
740 335-3586

(G-2065)
SUMMIT ROOFING & CONTG LLC
1035 N Highway 69 (66763-8100)
PHONE..................................417 873-9191
Mike Wyckoff,
EMP: 10
SQ FT: 1,040
SALES: 1MM **Privately Held**
SIC: 1761 Roofing contractor

(G-2066)
SUNSET MANOR INC
Also Called: Sunset Manor Nursing Home
206 S Dittman St (66763-2299)
PHONE..................................620 231-7340
Jo Ann Knaup, *President*
Raymond R Knaup, *Corp Secy*
EMP: 128
SQ FT: 57,000
SALES: 38K **Privately Held**
WEB: www.sunsetmanor.com
SIC: 8052 8051 Intermediate care facilities; skilled nursing care facilities

(G-2067)
WISEMAN DISCOUNT TIRE INC
4078 Parkview Dr (66763-2305)
PHONE..................................620 231-5291
Richard Wiseman, *President*
Anna L Wiseman, *Corp Secy*
Joe Wiseman, *Vice Pres*
Scott Wiseman, *Vice Pres*
EMP: 10
SQ FT: 12,920
SALES (est): 1.5MM **Privately Held**
SIC: 5531 7532 7538 Automotive tires; body shop, automotive; body shop, trucks; general automotive repair shops

Galena
Cherokee County

(G-2068)
ALLIED SERVICES LLC
Also Called: Site 393
1715 E Front St (66739-4206)
PHONE..................................620 783-5841
Peter Forst, *Manager*
EMP: 60
SALES (corp-wide): 10B **Publicly Held**
SIC: 4953 4212 Garbage: collecting, destroying & processing; local trucking, without storage
HQ: Allied Services, L.L.C.
15880 N Grnway Hyden Loop
Scottsdale AZ 85260
480 627-2700

(G-2069)
BENT TREE PARTNERS LLC
444 Four States Dr (66739-4324)
P.O. Box 2546, Joplin MO (64803-2546)
PHONE..................................417 206-7846
Joe Caputo, *Manager*
Joseph M Caputo, *Manager*
EMP: 10
SALES (est): 433.2K **Privately Held**
SIC: 6519 Real property lessors

(G-2070)
CELLTRON INC
1110 W 7th St (66739-1379)
P.O. Box 98 (66739-0098)
PHONE..................................620 783-1333
John McConnell, *President*
Kim Richards, *Purch Mgr*
Regina Westhoff, *Purch Mgr*
Shara Wyler, *Purch Mgr*
Larry Gollhofer, *Purchasing*
▲ **EMP:** 400
SQ FT: 70,000
SALES (est): 113.4MM **Privately Held**
WEB: www.celltron.com
SIC: 3679 Harness assemblies for electronic use: wire or cable

(G-2071)
CITY OF GALENA
Emergency Services
210 Turner Dr (66739-1253)
PHONE..................................620 783-5065
Garry Abram, *Branch Mgr*
EMP: 15 **Privately Held**
SIC: 4119 Ambulance service
PA: City Of Galena
211 W 7th St
Galena KS 66739
620 783-1991

(G-2072)
COMMUNITY BANK AND TRUST
215 E 7th St (66739-1230)
PHONE..................................620 783-1395
Kathy Anderson, *Vice Pres*
David Fuller, *Branch Mgr*
EMP: 10
SALES (corp-wide): 22.8MM **Privately Held**
WEB: www.communitybankandtrust.net
SIC: 6022 State trust companies accepting deposits, commercial
HQ: Community Bank And Trust
100 S Wood St
Neosho MO 64850

(G-2073)
GALENA MEDICAL PROPERTIES LLC
444 Four States Dr Ste 1 (66739-4325)
PHONE..................................620 783-4616
Joseph M Caputo, *Mng Member*
EMP: 10 **EST:** 2012
SALES (est): 851.2K **Privately Held**
SIC: 8059 Rest home, with health care

(G-2074)
GALENA SENTINEL TIMES
511 S Main St (66739-1292)
PHONE..................................620 783-5034
David Nelson, *Owner*
Barbara Nelson, *Co-Owner*
Frances Secrist, *Marketing Staff*
Machelle Smith, *Manager*
EMP: 9 **EST:** 1880
SALES (est): 338.6K **Privately Held**
WEB: www.sentineltimes.com
SIC: 2711 Newspapers: publishing only, not printed on site

(G-2075)
JAYHAWK FINE CHEMICALS CORP
8545 Jayhawk Dr (66739-4130)
PHONE..................................620 783-1321
Jeff Black, *President*
Jeff Dimmit, *Vice Pres*
Borys Schafran, *Vice Pres*
Scott Schulte, *Vice Pres*
◆ **EMP:** 123 **EST:** 1983
SQ FT: 3,920
SALES: 50MM
SALES (corp-wide): 35.5MM **Privately Held**
SIC: 2879 2899 Agricultural chemicals; chemical preparations
HQ: Permira Advisers Llc
320 Park Ave Fl 28
New York NY 10022
212 386-7480

(G-2076)
KEMLEE MANUFACTURING INC (PA)
Also Called: Kmi Metals
1404 Industrial Prk Rd (66739)
P.O. Box 215 (66739-0215)
PHONE..................................620 783-5035
Larry G Edie, *President*
Rick Roberts, *General Mgr*
Kendra Henderson, *Vice Pres*
Dan Lashley, *Sales Executive*
EMP: 52
SQ FT: 40,000
SALES (est): 9.8MM **Privately Held**
SIC: 3556 5051 3444 Food products machinery; metals service centers & offices; sheet metalwork

(G-2077)
OASIS CAR WASH SYSTEMS INC
1909 E 12th St (66739-4221)
PHONE..................................620 783-1355
Stephen D Wade, *President*
Curtis Wade, *Vice Pres*
David Eckhart, *Info Tech Mgr*
◆ **EMP:** 20
SQ FT: 30,000
SALES (est): 9.8MM **Privately Held**
WEB: www.oasiscarwashsystems.net
SIC: 5084 3559 Cleaning equipment, high pressure, sand or steam; boot making & repairing machinery

(G-2078)
ORTHO 4-STATES REAL ESTATE LLC
444 Four States Dr Ste 1 (66739-4325)
P.O. Box 2546, Joplin MO (64803-2546)
PHONE..................................417 206-7846
Joseph Caputo,
Joseph M Caputo,
EMP: 10
SALES (est): 1.1MM **Privately Held**
SIC: 8011 Orthopedic physician

(G-2079)
ORTHOPDIC SPCALISTS FOUR STATE
444 Four States Dr Ste 1 (66739-4325)
P.O. Box 2546, Joplin MO (64803-2546)
PHONE..................................620 783-4441
Brian Ipsen, *Partner*
Amanda Brown, *Manager*
Mark McNemar, *Orthopedist*
David Blancho, *Podiatrist*
Jonathan Grantham, *Surgeon*
EMP: 49 **EST:** 2010
SALES (est): 7.4MM **Privately Held**
SIC: 8011 Orthopedic physician

(G-2080)
PBI-GORDON CORPORATION
Also Called: J Hawk Plant
7530 Se Boston Mills Rd (66739)
P.O. Box 78, Crestline (66728-0078)
PHONE..................................620 848-3849
Vernon Ross III, *Branch Mgr*
EMP: 35
SALES (corp-wide): 31.9MM **Privately Held**
SIC: 2879 Pesticides, agricultural or household
PA: Pbi-Gordon Corporation
22701 W 68th Ter
Shawnee KS 66226
816 421-4070

(G-2081)
QUALITY INTRCNNECT SYSTEMS INC (PA)
1009 W 11th St (66739-1400)
P.O. Box 368 (66739-0368)
PHONE..................................620 783-5087
Ann K Turney, *CEO*
Clay Turney, *President*
EMP: 34
SQ FT: 10,000
SALES: 2.5MM **Privately Held**
SIC: 3679 Harness assemblies for electronic use: wire or cable; electronic circuits

(G-2082)
REPUBLIC SERVICES INC
Also Called: American Disposal Services
1715 E Front St (66739-4206)
PHONE..................................620 783-5841
Rory Stadt, *Branch Mgr*
EMP: 34
SALES (corp-wide): 10B **Publicly Held**
SIC: 4953 Refuse collection & disposal services
PA: Republic Services, Inc.
18500 N Allied Way # 100
Phoenix AZ 85054
480 627-2700

(G-2083)
RH MONTGOMERY PROPERTIES INC
Also Called: Galena Manor Nursing Center
1220 E 8th St (66739-1865)
PHONE..................................620 783-1383
Jeff Carter, *Administration*
EMP: 45
SQ FT: 10,000
SALES (corp-wide): 31.9MM **Privately Held**
SIC: 8051 Extended care facility
PA: Rh Montgomery Properties, Inc.
214 N Scott St
Sikeston MO 63801
573 471-1113

(G-2084)
SE KANSAS NTURE CTR SCHRMRHORN
3511 S Main St (66739-1503)
PHONE...................................620 783-5207
Linda Phipps, *President*
EMP: 40
SALES (est): 1.2MM **Privately Held**
SIC: 8748 8641 Environmental consultant; Boy Scout organization

(G-2085)
SHORT CREEK CONSTRUCTION
815 W 7th St (66739-1680)
P.O. Box 96 (66739-0096)
PHONE...................................620 783-2896
Nio Oglesby, *Owner*
Sarah Oglesby, *Co-Owner*
EMP: 10
SALES (est): 572K **Privately Held**
SIC: 1521 Single-family housing construction

(G-2086)
STATELINE SURGERY CENTER LLC
444 Four States Dr Ste 2 (66739-4325)
PHONE...................................620 783-4072
Maria Wilson, *Administration*
Jennifer L Morris, *Administration*
Echo Mills, *Nurse Practr*
EMP: 47
SALES (est): 4.8MM **Privately Held**
SIC: 8011 Orthopedic physician

(G-2087)
STERLING MANUFACTURING CO INC
1220 W 7th St (66739-1293)
P.O. Box 11, Riverton (66770-0011)
PHONE...................................620 783-5234
Stan Elston, *President*
Nancy Elston, *Vice Pres*
EMP: 5
SQ FT: 4,400
SALES (est): 1MM **Privately Held**
SIC: 3556 Poultry processing machinery

(G-2088)
SUNFLOWER SUPPLY COMPANY INC
1001 W 7th St (66739-1300)
P.O. Box 248 (66739-0248)
PHONE...................................620 783-5473
Gary L Hall, *President*
EMP: 35
SQ FT: 30,000
SALES (est): 17.4MM **Privately Held**
SIC: 5194 5113 Chewing tobacco; cigarettes; cigars; snuff; industrial & personal service paper; dishes, disposable plastic & paper; bags, paper & disposable plastic; cups, disposable plastic & paper

(G-2089)
WILLIAMS MACHINE AND TL CO INC
1009 Schermerhorn Rd (66739-4079)
P.O. Box 188 (66739-0188)
PHONE...................................620 783-5184
Denise Titus, *President*
Kelly Williams, *President*
Wanda J Williams, *Chairman*
Dennis Williams, *Corp Secy*
Brian Williams, *Vice Pres*
▼ **EMP:** 50
SQ FT: 42,000
SALES (est): 8.9MM **Privately Held**
WEB: www.wilmaco.com
SIC: 3599 Machine shop, jobbing & repair

(G-2090)
ZODIAC INDUSTRIES INC
724 W 7th St (66739)
P.O. Box 157 (66739-0157)
PHONE...................................620 783-5041
Gerald J Yeoman, *President*
EMP: 26
SQ FT: 15,450
SALES (est): 4.2MM **Privately Held**
WEB: www.zodiacindustries.com
SIC: 5012 5511 3716 Vans, commercial; vans, new & used; motor homes

Galesburg
Neosho County

(G-2091)
CVR MANUFACTURING INC
Also Called: Heatsource 1
6 Center St (66740)
P.O. Box 68 (66740-0068)
PHONE...................................620 763-2500
Kelly Coover, *CEO*
Bryan Coover, *Corp Secy*
EMP: 5 **EST:** 2000
SQ FT: 13,000
SALES: 500K **Privately Held**
SIC: 3433 3993 Stoves, wood & coal burning; signs & advertising specialties

Galva
Mcpherson County

(G-2092)
CHRISTS KIDS CHILDCARE
400 Northview Rd (67443-8896)
PHONE...................................620 654-4567
Sandy Bruton, *Director*
EMP: 12
SALES: 253.9K **Privately Held**
SIC: 8351 Preschool center

(G-2093)
HOME COMMUNICATIONS INC
211 S Main St (67443-4401)
P.O. Box 8 (67443-0008)
PHONE...................................620 654-3381
Carla Shearer, *President*
Tracy Minson, *Office Mgr*
Bryant Baldwin, *Technician*
Brett Williams, *Technician*
EMP: 15
SQ FT: 7,000
SALES (est): 803.1K **Privately Held**
SIC: 8999 Communication services

(G-2094)
HOME TELEPHONE CO INC
211 N Main St (67443-9500)
P.O. Box 8 (67443-0008)
PHONE...................................620 654-3381
Carla Shearei, *President*
EMP: 11
SQ FT: 2,800
SALES (est): 1.8MM **Privately Held**
WEB: www.hometelco.net
SIC: 4813 Local & long distance telephone communications

(G-2095)
QUALITY PRINTING & GIFT SHOP
1307 21st Ave (67443-8008)
PHONE...................................620 654-3487
Galen D Koehn, *Owner*
EMP: 5 **EST:** 1964
SALES: 275K **Privately Held**
WEB: www.earth-gallery.com
SIC: 2752 2759 5947 Commercial printing, offset; letterpress printing; gift shop; greeting cards

(G-2096)
TRUCK INSURANCE MART INC
245 W Highway 56 (67443-8000)
P.O. Box 650 (67443-0650)
PHONE...................................620 654-3921
Larry Tredway, *Manager*
EMP: 11
SALES (corp-wide): 6.3MM **Privately Held**
WEB: www.truck-insurance-mart.com
SIC: 6411 Insurance agents
PA: Truck Insurance Mart Inc
10027 Woodend Rd
Edwardsville KS 66111
913 441-0349

Garden City
Finney County

(G-2097)
ACCURATE CONSTRUCTION INC
3085 W Sagebrush Rd (67846-8983)
PHONE...................................620 275-0429
Charles Owings Jr, *President*
Jimmie Owings, *Treasurer*
EMP: 15 **EST:** 2007
SQ FT: 4,500
SALES: 999.6K **Privately Held**
SIC: 1799 Insulation of pipes & boilers

(G-2098)
AMERICAN IMPLEMENT INC (PA)
Also Called: John Deere Authorized Dealer
2611 W Jones Ave (67846-2514)
P.O. Box 855 (67846-0855)
PHONE...................................620 275-4114
Duane E Koster, *President*
Ben Boehs, *Parts Mgr*
Michael Borgmann, *Parts Mgr*
Emmett Averett, *CFO*
Bryce Kopper, *Controller*
EMP: 40
SQ FT: 10,000
SALES (est): 79.4MM **Privately Held**
WEB: www.americanimplement.com
SIC: 5083 Farm implements

(G-2099)
AMERICAN STATE BANK & TRUST CO
1901 E Mary St (67846-3654)
PHONE...................................620 271-0123
Ray Purdy, *Branch Mgr*
EMP: 10
SALES (corp-wide): 28.4MM **Privately Held**
SIC: 6022 State commercial banks
PA: American State Bank & Trust Company
1321 Main St Ste A
Great Bend KS 67530
620 793-5900

(G-2100)
AMERICOLD LOGISTICS LLC
2007 W Mary St (67846-2670)
P.O. Box 1967 (67846-1974)
PHONE...................................620 276-2304
Derik Elliot, *General Mgr*
Scott Zimmerman, *Opers Mgr*
EMP: 25
SALES (corp-wide): 1.6B **Publicly Held**
WEB: www.americoldlogistics.com
SIC: 4222 Warehousing, cold storage or refrigerated
HQ: Americold Logistics, Llc
10 Glenlake Pkwy Ste 324
Atlanta GA 30328
678 441-1400

(G-2101)
ANIMAL HEALTH INTL INC
Also Called: Lextron Animal Health
2103 W Jones Ave (67846-2543)
P.O. Box 895 (67846-0895)
PHONE...................................620 276-8289
Steve Cuttingham, *Branch Mgr*
EMP: 20
SALES (corp-wide): 5.5B **Publicly Held**
WEB: www.lextronanimalhealth.com
SIC: 5047 5083 Veterinarians' equipment & supplies; livestock equipment
HQ: Animal Health International, Inc.
822 7th St Ste 740
Greeley CO 80631
970 353-2600

(G-2102)
ARCTIC GLACIER INC
Also Called: Myers Ice Company
102 N 9th St (67846-5350)
PHONE...................................620 275-5751
Bob Ellis, *Branch Mgr*
EMP: 12
SQ FT: 5,370
SALES (corp-wide): 2.4B **Publicly Held**
SIC: 2097 Manufactured ice
HQ: Agi Ccaa Inc
625 Henry Ave
Winnipeg MB R3A 0
204 772-2473

(G-2103)
AT&T CORP
3104 E Kansas Ave (67846-6995)
PHONE...................................620 272-0383
Mary Martinez, *Branch Mgr*
EMP: 95
SALES (corp-wide): 170.7B **Publicly Held**
SIC: 4812 Cellular telephone services
HQ: At&T Corp.
1 At&T Way
Bedminster NJ 07921
800 403-3302

(G-2104)
BAKKEN WELL SERVICE INC
3210 W Jones Ave (67846-2564)
P.O. Box 297 (67846-0297)
PHONE...................................620 276-3442
Brian Post, *President*
EMP: 15
SALES (est): 693.4K **Privately Held**
SIC: 1389 Building oil & gas well foundations on site

(G-2105)
BEALMEAR BOWL TRREY HOCH REVES
Also Called: Torrey, David P Od
707 E Kansas Plz (67846-5866)
PHONE...................................620 276-3381
Randall Bowling, *President*
Robert Speckman, *Principal*
David Torrey, *Treasurer*
Robert Hock, *Admin Sec*
EMP: 25
SQ FT: 7,000
SALES (est): 1.3MM **Privately Held**
SIC: 8042 Offices & clinics of optometrists

(G-2106)
BECKER ALFALFA (PA)
Also Called: Becker, James
1602 N Van Dittie Dr (67846-6926)
PHONE...................................620 275-5567
James Becker, *Owner*
EMP: 6
SALES: 1.9MM **Privately Held**
SIC: 2048 Cereal-, grain-, & seed-based feeds; alfalfa or alfalfa meal, prepared as animal feed; alfalfa, cubed

(G-2107)
BENEVOLENT & P O OF ELKS 1404
905 E Kansas Plz (67846-5861)
PHONE...................................620 276-3732
EMP: 15
SALES: 79.5K **Privately Held**
SIC: 8641 Civic/Social Association

(G-2108)
BEREXCO LLC
808 S Us Hwy 83 Frntage (67846-6739)
PHONE...................................620 275-0320
Robert Beren, *President*
EMP: 12
SALES (corp-wide): 456.6MM **Privately Held**
SIC: 1382 Oil & gas exploration services
PA: Berexco Llc
2020 N Bramblewood St
Wichita KS 67206
316 265-3311

(G-2109)
BERRY COMPANIES INC
Berry Tractor and Equipment
3830 W Jones Ave (67846-9766)
P.O. Box 621 (67846-0621)
PHONE...................................620 277-2290
Clint Golay, *District Mgr*
Russell Crone, *Manager*
EMP: 19

GEOGRAPHIC

SALES (corp-wide): 181.7MM **Privately Held**
WEB: www.berrycompaniesinc.com
SIC: 5083 7359 5261 5084 Agricultural machinery & equipment; stores & yards equipment rental; lawnmowers & tractors; materials handling machinery; contractors' materials
PA: Berry Companies, Inc.
3223 N Hydraulic St
Wichita KS 67219
316 838-3321

(G-2110)
BILL HARMON
Also Called: Harmon & Miller
5550 N 16 Mile Rd (67846-9207)
PHONE..................................620 275-9597
Bill Harmon, *Owner*
EMP: 25
SALES (est): 4.1MM **Privately Held**
SIC: 5083 Harvesting machinery & equipment

(G-2111)
BIMBO BAKERIES USA INC
Also Called: Rainbo Bread
1130 Massey Ferguson Rd (67846-7115)
PHONE..................................620 276-6308
Larry Davis, *Manager*
EMP: 7 **Privately Held**
SIC: 2051 Bread, cake & related products
HQ: Bimbo Bakeries Usa, Inc
255 Business Center Dr # 200
Horsham PA 19044
215 347-5500

(G-2112)
BLACK HILLS/KANSAS GAS
Also Called: Black Hills Energy
1810 Buffalo Jones Ave (67846-4842)
PHONE..................................605 721-1700
EMP: 14
SALES (corp-wide): 1.7B **Publicly Held**
SIC: 4924 Natural gas distribution
HQ: Black Hills/Kansas Gas Utility Company, Llc
7001 Mount Rushmore Rd
Rapid City SD 57702

(G-2113)
BLICKS PHSPHATE CNVERSIONS LLC
401 N Campus Dr (67846-6124)
PHONE..................................800 932-5425
Steven Blickenstaff, *President*
EMP: 8
SALES (est): 1.1MM **Privately Held**
SIC: 2874 Phosphatic fertilizers

(G-2114)
BOGNER OIL FIELD SERVICE INC
606 E Thompson St (67846-3451)
PHONE..................................620 276-9453
Richard Bogner, *CEO*
Paul Bogner, *President*
EMP: 5
SALES (est): 441K **Privately Held**
SIC: 1389 Oil field services

(G-2115)
BONANZA BIOENERGY LLC
2830 E Us Highway 50 (67846-8528)
P.O. Box 1178, Liberal (67905-1178)
PHONE..................................620 276-4741
Thomas Willis, *CEO*
Dusty Turner, *COO*
Brian Obholz, *Maintence Staff*
EMP: 35
SALES (est): 10.1MM
SALES (corp-wide): 14.6MM **Privately Held**
SIC: 2869 Ethyl alcohol, ethanol
PA: Conestoga Energy Holdings, Llc
1701 N Kansas Ave Ste 101
Liberal KS 67901
620 624-2901

(G-2116)
BRADY FLUID SERVICE INC
3020 W Oller Rd (67846-9748)
P.O. Box 1713 (67846-1713)
PHONE..................................620 275-5827
Eilene Brady, *President*
EMP: 14
SALES (est): 1.5MM **Privately Held**
SIC: 4212 Liquid haulage, local

(G-2117)
BROOKOVER FEED YARDS INC (PA)
50 Grandview Dr (67846-9640)
PHONE..................................620 275-9206
E C Brookover Jr, *President*
EMP: 100
SQ FT: 7,000
SALES (est): 22.4MM **Privately Held**
SIC: 0211 Beef cattle feedlots

(G-2118)
BROOKOVER FEED YARDS INC
Also Called: Brookover Ranch Feedyard
3 1/2 Mile Se 5250 Brkver (67846)
P.O. Box 917 (67846-0917)
PHONE..................................620 275-0125
Brian Price, *Manager*
EMP: 30
SALES (est): 4.3MM
SALES (corp-wide): 22.4MM **Privately Held**
SIC: 0211 Beef cattle feedlots
PA: Brookover Feed Yards, Inc.
50 Grandview Dr
Garden City KS 67846
620 275-9206

(G-2119)
BROOKOVER LAND ENTERPRISES LP
50 Grandview Dr (67846-9640)
P.O. Box 917 (67846-0917)
PHONE..................................620 275-9206
Earl C Brookover Jr, *Partner*
Jane Cook, *Partner*
Mary Drussell, *Partner*
Sandra Kemper, *Partner*
EMP: 10 **EST:** 1975
SQ FT: 2,000
SALES: 1.4MM **Privately Held**
SIC: 0111 0212 Wheat; beef cattle except feedlots

(G-2120)
CALIHAN BRWN BURGRDT WURST
Also Called: Wurst, Wendel W
212 W Pine St (67846-5347)
P.O. Box 1016 (67846-1016)
PHONE..................................620 276-2381
Wendel Wurst, *Partner*
Brian K Dempsey,
EMP: 12
SALES (est): 1MM **Privately Held**
SIC: 8111 General practice attorney, lawyer

(G-2121)
CARGILL INCORPORATED
3680 W Jones Ave (67846-9708)
PHONE..................................620 277-2558
Fax: 620 277-2210
EMP: 20
SALES (corp-wide): 134.8B **Privately Held**
SIC: 2048 5191 Mfg Prepared Feeds Whol Farm Supplies
PA: Cargill, Incorporated
15407 Mcginty Rd W
Wayzata MN 55391
952 742-7575

(G-2122)
CELLCO PARTNERSHIP
Also Called: Verizon Wireless
3010 E Kansas Ave (67846-6816)
PHONE..................................620 276-6776
Ryan Powers, *Branch Mgr*
EMP: 71
SALES (corp-wide): 130.8B **Publicly Held**
SIC: 4812 Cellular telephone services
HQ: Cellco Partnership
1 Verizon Way
Basking Ridge NJ 07920

(G-2123)
CENTRAL CARE PA
Also Called: Central Care Cancer Center
410 E Spruce St (67846-5659)
PHONE..................................620 272-2579
EMP: 44 **Privately Held**
SIC: 8099 Blood related health services
PA: Central Care, Pa
2337 E Crawford St
Salina KS 67401

(G-2124)
CIRCLE LAND & CATTLE CORP
Also Called: C Dean Gigot Farms
955 S Circle Land Rd (67846-8909)
PHONE..................................620 275-6131
Clarence Dean Gigot, *President*
Gina Gigot, *Corp Secy*
Esther Gigot, *Vice Pres*
EMP: 15
SQ FT: 1,200
SALES (est): 2.6MM **Privately Held**
SIC: 0191 0211 6519 General farms, primarily crop; beef cattle feedlots; farm land leasing

(G-2125)
CITY OF GARDEN CITY
Also Called: Lee Richardson Zoo
312 Finnup Dr (67846-6561)
PHONE..................................620 276-1250
F K Sinclair, *Exec Dir*
Kristi Newlane, *Director*
EMP: 27 **Privately Held**
WEB: www.ficolec.org
SIC: 8422 Arboreta & botanical or zoological gardens
PA: City Of Garden City
301 N 8th St
Garden City KS 67846
620 276-1160

(G-2126)
CITY OF GARDEN CITY
Also Called: Garden City Water Department
106 S 11th St (67846)
PHONE..................................620 276-1291
David Glenn, *Superintendent*
EMP: 12 **Privately Held**
WEB: www.ficolec.org
SIC: 4941 Water supply
PA: City Of Garden City
301 N 8th St
Garden City KS 67846
620 276-1160

(G-2127)
CIVIL AIR PATROL INC
2708 N 7th St (67846-3150)
PHONE..................................620 275-6121
EMP: 20 **Privately Held**
SIC: 7381 Detective/Armored Car Services
PA: Civil Air Patrol, Inc.
105 S Hansell St Bldg 714
Maxwell Afb AL 36112
877 227-9142

(G-2128)
COBANK ACB
Also Called: Federal Land Bank
1606 E Kansas Ave (67846-6233)
P.O. Box 2509 (67846-8509)
PHONE..................................620 275-4281
Mark Anderson, *President*
EMP: 23
SALES (corp-wide): 4.3B **Privately Held**
WEB: www.usagbank.com
SIC: 6159 Agricultural credit institutions
PA: Cobank, Acb
6340 S Fiddlers Green Cir
Greenwood Village CO 80111
303 740-6527

(G-2129)
COMMERCE BANK
1111 Fleming St (67846-4706)
PHONE..................................620 276-5600
Richard Harp, *President*
Debra Berry, *Vice Pres*
EMP: 40
SALES (corp-wide): 1.3B **Publicly Held**
SIC: 6021 National commercial banks
HQ: Commerce Bank
1000 Walnut St Fl 700
Kansas City MO 64106
816 234-2000

(G-2130)
COMMUNITY DAY CARE CENTER 1
505 College Dr (67846-6168)
P.O. Box 2615 (67846-8632)
PHONE..................................620 275-5757
Debbie Gunderson, *Director*
EMP: 50
SQ FT: 1,500
SALES: 1MM **Privately Held**
SIC: 8351 Group day care center

(G-2131)
COMPASS BEHAVIORAL HEALTH (PA)
531 Campus View St (67846-7904)
P.O. Box 477 (67846-0477)
PHONE..................................620 276-6470
Ric Dalke, *Exec Dir*
EMP: 40
SQ FT: 9,000
SALES: 10MM **Privately Held**
SIC: 8052 8322 Home for the mentally retarded, with health care; community center

(G-2132)
COMPASS BEHAVIORAL HEALTH
1145 E Kansas Plz (67846-5870)
P.O. Box 1905 (67846-1905)
PHONE..................................620 275-0625
Sumar Stormont, *Human Res Dir*
Ric Dalke, *Branch Mgr*
Melissa Parker, *Manager*
EMP: 85
SALES (corp-wide): 10MM **Privately Held**
SIC: 8093 Mental health clinic, outpatient
PA: Compass Behavioral Health
531 Campus View St
Garden City KS 67846
620 276-6470

(G-2133)
COUNTY OF FINNEY
Also Called: District Dourt
425 N 8th St (67846-5302)
PHONE..................................620 271-6120
Christine Blake, *Principal*
EMP: 13 **Privately Held**
WEB: www.finneycounty.org
SIC: 8322 Child related social services
PA: County Of Finney
311 N 9th St
Garden City KS 67846
620 272-3575

(G-2134)
COUNTY OF FINNEY
Also Called: Health Department
919 W Zerr Rd (67846-2777)
PHONE..................................620 272-3600
Colleen Drees, *Director*
EMP: 30 **Privately Held**
WEB: www.finneycounty.org
SIC: 8011 Offices & clinics of medical doctors
PA: County Of Finney
311 N 9th St
Garden City KS 67846
620 272-3575

(G-2135)
COUNTY OF FINNEY
Also Called: Department of Public Works
201 W Maple St (67846-6470)
PHONE..................................620 272-3564
Max Morgan, *Director*
EMP: 60 **Privately Held**
WEB: www.finneycounty.org
SIC: 1611 9111 Concrete construction: roads, highways, sidewalks, etc.; county supervisors' & executives' offices
PA: County Of Finney
311 N 9th St
Garden City KS 67846
620 272-3575

(G-2136)
COUNTY OF FINNEY
Also Called: Waste Connections
1250 S Raceway Rd (67846-9425)
PHONE..................................620 275-4421
Chris Gromquist, *Manager*

EMP: 10 **Privately Held**
SIC: 4953 9199 Sanitary landfill operation;
PA: County Of Finney
311 N 9th St
Garden City KS 67846
620 272-3575

(G-2137)
COX COMMUNICATIONS INC
1109 College Dr (67846-4711)
PHONE..................................620 275-5552
Reynaldo Mesa, *Director*
EMP: 16
SALES (corp-wide): 29.2B **Privately Held**
SIC: 4841 Cable television services
HQ: Cox Communications, Inc.
6205 B Pchtree Dnwody Rd
Atlanta GA 30328

(G-2138)
CRAZY HOUSE INC (PA)
Also Called: C-Bar-H Farm & Home
3502 N Campus Dr (67846-6316)
P.O. Box 2440 (67846-8440)
PHONE..................................620 275-2153
Gregory H Shaw, *President*
Brian Shaw, *Vice Pres*
Valoyce Shaw, *Treasurer*
Tamera Shaw Halloran, *Admin Sec*
EMP: 18
SQ FT: 35,000
SALES (est): 3.5MM **Privately Held**
WEB: www.crazyhouse.com
SIC: 5399 5191 Country general stores; farm supplies

(G-2139)
CREDIT BUREAU SERVICES (PA)
1135 College Dr Ste L2 (67846-4774)
PHONE..................................620 276-7631
Roland Belcher, *President*
Scott Selzer, *Vice Pres*
Jill Belcher, *Treasurer*
EMP: 34
SALES (est): 2.5MM **Privately Held**
WEB: www.cbwichita.com
SIC: 7323 7322 Credit bureau & agency; adjustment bureau, except insurance

(G-2140)
CROSS BELL FARMS PARTNERS
2711 N Rowland Rd (67846-3249)
PHONE..................................620 275-1705
EMP: 27
SALES (est): 1.3MM **Privately Held**
SIC: 0191 General Crop Farm

(G-2141)
D V DOUGLASS ROOFING INC
1215 W Mary St (67846-2633)
P.O. Box 506 (67846-0506)
PHONE..................................620 276-7474
Steven Douglass, *President*
Mark Douglass, *Vice Pres*
Tim Douglass, *Vice Pres*
EMP: 24 **EST**: 1954
SQ FT: 1,200
SALES (est): 5MM **Privately Held**
SIC: 1761 1742 Roofing contractor; insulation, buildings

(G-2142)
DARLING INGREDIENTS INC
755 S Farmland Rd (67846-8320)
PHONE..................................620 276-7618
James Davis, *Division Mgr*
Dave Pace, *Treasurer*
EMP: 20
SQ FT: 2,160
SALES (corp-wide): 3.3B **Publicly Held**
WEB: www.darlingii.com
SIC: 2047 2077 Dog & cat food; rendering
PA: Darling Ingredients Inc.
5601 N Macarthur Blvd
Irving TX 75038
972 717-0300

(G-2143)
DARREN MILLER
407 N 7th St (67846-5524)
PHONE..................................620 276-4515
Ed Whittaker, *President*
Darren Miller, *Manager*
EMP: 12
SALES (est): 350.3K **Privately Held**
SIC: 8748 Telecommunications consultant

(G-2144)
DENTAL ASSOCIATES
1133 E Kansas Plz (67846-5870)
PHONE..................................620 276-7681
Jay Keltner, *President*
EMP: 16
SALES (est): 1.6MM **Privately Held**
SIC: 8621 Dental association

(G-2145)
DESIGN COURT
Also Called: Main Street Salon and Spa
523 N Main St (67846-5430)
PHONE..................................620 276-3019
Danna Greenlee, *Owner*
EMP: 10
SALES (est): 180K **Privately Held**
SIC: 7231 Beauty shops

(G-2146)
DESTINY SUPPORTS INC
2508 N John St (67846-2804)
PHONE..................................620 272-0564
Carol Galbrith, *President*
EMP: 12
SALES (est): 923.7K **Privately Held**
SIC: 8399 Health systems agency

(G-2147)
DICK CONSTRUCTION INC
1805 E Mary St Ste A (67846-3973)
P.O. Box 1215 (67846-1215)
PHONE..................................620 275-1806
Gary D Dick, *President*
EMP: 14
SALES (est): 3.4MM **Privately Held**
WEB: www.dickconstruction.com
SIC: 1542 7299 Commercial & office building, new construction; commercial & office buildings, renovation & repair; handyman service

(G-2148)
DILLON COMPANIES INC
Also Called: Dillons 60
1211 Buffalo Jones Ave (67846-4833)
PHONE..................................620 275-0151
Steve Avila, *Manager*
EMP: 100
SALES (corp-wide): 121.1B **Publicly Held**
WEB: www.dillons.com
SIC: 5411 5912 5141 Supermarkets, chain; drug stores; groceries, general line
HQ: Dillon Companies, Inc.
2700 E 4th Ave
Hutchinson KS 67501
620 665-5511

(G-2149)
DREILING CONSTRUCTION LLC
2917 W Mary St (67846-9782)
P.O. Box 1218 (67846-1218)
PHONE..................................620 275-9433
Donald A Dreiling, *Mng Member*
EMP: 17
SALES (est): 3.1MM **Privately Held**
SIC: 1623 Telephone & communication line construction

(G-2150)
E-Z SALSA INC
Also Called: El Zarape
1712 E Fulton Plz (67846-6164)
PHONE..................................620 521-9097
Miguel Rodriguez, *President*
Alin Rodriguez, *Vice Pres*
EMP: 5
SQ FT: 1,500
SALES (est): 150K **Privately Held**
SIC: 2032 Mexican foods: packaged in cans, jars, etc.

(G-2151)
EATHERLY CONSTRUCTORS INC (PA)
Also Called: Delta Supply
1810 Boots Rd (67846-7213)
P.O. Box 756 (67846-0756)
PHONE..................................620 276-6611
Robert J Eatherly, *President*
Jim Rogers, *Vice Pres*
Rocky Cook, *Treasurer*
Laura Eatherly, *Admin Sec*
EMP: 15
SQ FT: 10,000
SALES (est): 10.7MM **Privately Held**
SIC: 1623 Pipeline construction

(G-2152)
EHRESMAN PACKING CO
912 E Fulton St (67846-6042)
P.O. Box 403 (67846-0402)
PHONE..................................620 276-3791
Mike Plankenhorn, *Principal*
EMP: 10 **EST**: 2012
SALES (est): 906.9K **Privately Held**
SIC: 2011 Meat packing plants

(G-2153)
ESTES EXPRESS LINES
284 N Industrial Dr (67846-9695)
P.O. Box 67 (67846-0067)
PHONE..................................620 260-9580
Gary Rohr, *Branch Mgr*
EMP: 58
SALES (corp-wide): 3.1B **Privately Held**
WEB: www.estes-express.com
SIC: 4213 Contract haulers
PA: Estes Express Lines
3901 W Broad St
Richmond VA 23230
804 353-1900

(G-2154)
FAMILIES TOGETHER INC
1518 Taylor Plz E (67846-4055)
PHONE..................................620 276-6364
Tammy Schwindt, *Director*
Darla Nelson-Metzger,
EMP: 10 **Privately Held**
SIC: 8322 Individual & family services
PA: Families Together Inc
3033 W 2nd St N Ste 122
Wichita KS 67203

(G-2155)
FANDHILL ORTHPD & SPT MEDICINE
Also Called: Sandhill Orthpdic Spt Medicine
101 E Fulton St (67846-5455)
PHONE..................................620 275-8400
Harland Thompson, *Principal*
EMP: 10
SALES (est): 789.7K **Privately Held**
WEB: www.sandhillorthopaedic.com
SIC: 8011 8049 Clinic, operated by physicians; physical therapist

(G-2156)
FARM BUREAU CLAIMS
1707 E Maggie St (67846-3647)
PHONE..................................620 275-9195
Ken Hamilton, *Manager*
EMP: 12
SALES (est): 759.4K **Privately Held**
SIC: 6411 Insurance claim adjusters, not employed by insurance company

(G-2157)
FARM BUREAU MUTL INSUR CO INC
Also Called: Garden City Claims Office
1707 E Maggie St (67846-3647)
P.O. Box B (67846-0039)
PHONE..................................620 275-9195
Ken Hamilton, *Manager*
EMP: 13
SALES (corp-wide): 137.3MM **Privately Held**
SIC: 6411 Insurance agents, brokers & service
PA: The Farm Bureau Mutual Insurance Company Inc
2627 Kfb Plz
Manhattan KS 66503
785 587-6000

(G-2158)
FBO AIR - GARDEN CITY INC (HQ)
Also Called: Saker Aviation Services
2117 S Air Service Dr (67846-9100)
PHONE..................................620 275-5055
Ron Ricciardi, *President*
William Melendez, *Supervisor*
EMP: 11
SALES: 950K
SALES (corp-wide): 11.1MM **Publicly Held**
WEB: www.firstflight-llc.com
SIC: 5172 Aircraft fueling services
PA: Saker Aviation Services, Inc.
20 S St Pier 6 E Riv
New York NY 10004
212 776-4046

(G-2159)
FEED MERCANTILE TRANSPORT INC (PA)
1513 E Fulton Ter (67846-6165)
P.O. Box 1053 (67846-1053)
PHONE..................................620 275-4158
Earl C Brookover, *President*
EMP: 15
SALES (est): 1.2MM **Privately Held**
SIC: 4212 Local trucking, without storage

(G-2160)
FINNEY CNTY COMMITTEE ON AGING
Also Called: Senior Center
907 N 10th St (67846-5209)
PHONE..................................620 272-3626
Bonnie Burgardt, *Principal*
Barbara Jensen, *Exec Dir*
EMP: 40
SALES: 1.1MM **Privately Held**
SIC: 4111 Local & suburban transit

(G-2161)
FINNEY COUNTY ATTORNEYS OFFICE
409 N 9th St (67846-5314)
PHONE..................................620 272-3568
John Wheeler, *Principal*
Laura Bors, *Principal*
Tamara Hicks, *Principal*
Linda Lobmeyer, *Principal*
Sydney Thomas, *Principal*
EMP: 17
SALES (est): 858K **Privately Held**
SIC: 8111 8661 Specialized law offices, attorneys; religious organizations

(G-2162)
FINNEY COUNTY COMMUNITY HLTH
310 E Walnut St Ste 202 (67846-5560)
PHONE..................................620 765-1185
Deanna Berry, *Treasurer*
Callie Dyer, *Exec Dir*
Verna Weber, *Exec Dir*
Diane Garvey, *Director*
Lee Ann Shrader, *Administration*
EMP: 12
SALES (est): 473.4K **Privately Held**
SIC: 8099 Medical services organization

(G-2163)
FINNEY COUNTY EMERGENCY MED
Also Called: Finney County Ems
803 W Mary St (67846-2747)
PHONE..................................620 272-3822
Tyler Swords, *Principal*
EMP: 33
SALES (est): 647.3K **Privately Held**
SIC: 4119 Ambulance service

(G-2164)
FINNEY COUNTY FEED YARD INC
Also Called: Finney County Feedyard
4170 N Finney Feeders Rd (67846)
PHONE..................................620 275-7163
Robert Minter, *President*
James Danley, *Vice Pres*
Jeff George, *Manager*
Jeff Jones, *Asst Mgr*
Duane Koster, *Admin Sec*
▲ **EMP**: 29
SQ FT: 6,000
SALES (est): 5.5MM **Privately Held**
SIC: 0211 Beef cattle feedlots

(G-2165)
FIRST NAT BNK SYRACUSE INC
2414 E Kansas Ave (67846-6961)
PHONE..................................620 276-6971
Caleb Woods, *Assistant VP*

GEOGRAPHIC

Matt Benett, *Branch Mgr*
EMP: 14
SALES (corp-wide): 19MM **Privately Held**
SIC: 6021 National commercial banks
PA: First National Bank Of Syracuse Inc.
11 N Main St
Syracuse KS 67878
620 384-7441

(G-2166)
FRANCIS CASING CREWS INC
Industrial Dr (67846)
PHONE..................................620 275-0443
Steve Dellinger, *Manager*
EMP: 25
SALES (corp-wide): 3MM **Privately Held**
SIC: 1389 5082 Running, cutting & pulling casings, tubes & rods; oil field equipment
PA: Francis Casing Crews Inc
5810 Anchor Way
Great Bend KS 67530
620 793-9630

(G-2167)
FRY EYE ASSOCIATES (PA)
502 College Dr (67846-6183)
PHONE..................................620 275-7248
Luther Fry MD, *President*
Jennifer Teeter, *Vice Pres*
EMP: 34
SALES (est): 5.5MM **Privately Held**
WEB: www.fryeye.com
SIC: 8011 Ophthalmologist

(G-2168)
FRY EYE ASSOCIATES
411 N Campus Dr (67846-6124)
PHONE..................................620 276-7699
EMP: 10
SALES (corp-wide): 5.5MM **Privately Held**
SIC: 8011 Ophthalmologist
PA: Fry Eye Associates
502 College Dr
Garden City KS 67846
620 275-7248

(G-2169)
FRY EYE SURGERY CENTER LLC
411 N Campus Dr Ste 101 (67846-6195)
PHONE..................................620 276-7699
Debra K Olson, *Office Mgr*
Luther Fry MD,
Sandy Kirchoff,
Glori Hopkins,
EMP: 30
SALES (est): 1.5MM **Privately Held**
SIC: 8011 Eyes, ears, nose & throat specialist: physician/surgeon

(G-2170)
GARDEN CITY CO-OP INC (PA)
106 N 6th St (67846-5545)
P.O. Box 838 (67846-0838)
PHONE..................................620 275-6161
John McClelland, *President*
Elevatorsken Jameson, *Vice Pres*
Grain Jameson, *Vice Pres*
Brent McMillan, *Opers Mgr*
Abe Hamm, *Warehouse Mgr*
EMP: 15 **EST:** 1919
SQ FT: 4,000
SALES (est): 133.3MM **Privately Held**
WEB: www.gccoop.com
SIC: 6411 5191 5172 Insurance agents, brokers & service; feed; petroleum products

(G-2171)
GARDEN CITY CO-OP INC
1304 Massey Ferguson Rd (67846-7104)
P.O. Box 838 (67846-0838)
PHONE..................................620 276-8903
Rod Petty, *Vice Pres*
Ann Jackson, *Human Res Mgr*
EMP: 10
SALES (corp-wide): 133.3MM **Privately Held**
WEB: www.gccoop.com
SIC: 5984 8611 5172 Propane gas, bottled; business associations; diesel fuel
PA: The Garden City Co-Op Inc
106 N 6th St
Garden City KS 67846
620 275-6161

(G-2172)
GARDEN CITY FEED YARD LLC
1805 W Annie Scheer Rd (67846-8800)
PHONE..................................620 275-4191
EMP: 60
SQ FT: 2,800
SALES (est): 5.5MM
SALES (corp-wide): 188MM **Privately Held**
SIC: 0211 Beef Cattle Feedlot
PA: Aztx Cattle Co., Ltd.
311 E Park Ave
Hereford TX 79045
806 364-8871

(G-2173)
GARDEN CITY IRON & METAL
3710 W Jones Ave (67846-9762)
PHONE..................................620 277-0227
Von Fahrenbrulh, *Owner*
EMP: 16
SALES (est): 1MM **Privately Held**
SIC: 5093 Ferrous metal scrap & waste; metal scrap & waste materials

(G-2174)
GARDEN CITY KANSAS KENNEL CLUB
3460 N Farmland Rd (67846-9302)
PHONE..................................620 275-4739
Rachel Smith, *President*
EMP: 25
SALES (est): 270.3K **Privately Held**
SIC: 0752 Grooming services, pet & animal specialties

(G-2175)
GARDEN CITY PRODUCTION CR ASSN (PA)
Also Called: Farm Cr Grdn Cy P C A/F L C A
1606 E Kansas Ave (67846-6233)
PHONE..................................620 275-4281
Mark Anderson, *President*
Cynthia Johnson, *Vice Pres*
EMP: 27 **EST:** 1933
SQ FT: 1,800
SALES (est): 3.9MM **Privately Held**
WEB: www.fcswks.com
SIC: 6159 Agricultural credit institutions

(G-2176)
GARDEN CITY PUBLIC SCHOOLS
714 Ballinger St (67846-5918)
PHONE..................................620 275-0291
Kathleen Whitley, *Branch Mgr*
EMP: 27
SALES (corp-wide): 60MM **Privately Held**
SIC: 8351 8211 Child day care services; elementary & secondary schools
PA: Garden City Public Schools
1205 Fleming St
Garden City KS 67846
620 805-7000

(G-2177)
GARDEN CITY TELEGRAM
310 N 7th St (67846-5521)
P.O. Box 958 (67846-0958)
PHONE..................................620 275-8500
Dina Statler, *President*
Brett Riggs, *Loan Officer*
Dj Richmeier, *Mktg Dir*
EMP: 50 **EST:** 1932
SQ FT: 12,000
SALES (est): 3.1MM
SALES (corp-wide): 1.5B **Publicly Held**
WEB: www.gctelegram.com
SIC: 2711 Commercial printing & newspaper publishing combined; newspapers: publishing only, not printed on site
HQ: Harris Enterprises, Inc.
1 N Main St Ste 616
Hutchinson KS
620 694-5830

(G-2178)
GARDEN CITY TIRE CENTER INC (PA)
611 E Fulton St (67846-5761)
P.O. Box 1409 (67846-1409)
PHONE..................................620 276-7652
Duane Koster, *President*
Emil Krug, *Corp Secy*
EMP: 11
SQ FT: 8,000
SALES (est): 1.7MM **Privately Held**
SIC: 7534 5014 Tire retreading & repair shops; automobile tires & tubes

(G-2179)
GARDEN CITY TRAVEL PLAZA LLC
1265 Solar Ave (67846-8105)
PHONE..................................620 275-4404
Paul Schmieder, *Mng Member*
EMP: 50
SQ FT: 22,000
SALES (est): 6.7MM **Privately Held**
SIC: 5541 5812 5947 7538 Truck stops; restaurant, family: independent; gift shop; truck engine repair, except industrial; truck rental & leasing, no drivers

(G-2180)
GARDEN CY AMMONIA PROGRAM LLC
2405 E Fulton Plz (67846-6159)
P.O. Box 2336 (67846-2336)
PHONE..................................620 271-0037
Randy Williams, *Mng Member*
EMP: 15
SALES (est): 919.9K **Privately Held**
SIC: 8742 Industrial consultant

(G-2181)
GARDEN CY AREA CHMBER COMMERCE
1509 E Fulton Ter (67846-6165)
PHONE..................................620 276-3264
Paul Joseph, *President*
Angelica Hahn, *Vice Pres*
EMP: 18
SALES: 459K **Privately Held**
SIC: 8611 Chamber of Commerce

(G-2182)
GARDEN MEDICAL CLINIC PA
Also Called: Garden Medical Clinic Group
311 E Spruce St (67846-5614)
PHONE..................................620 275-3702
Sheldon D Roberts MD, *President*
Marc Rowe, *Principal*
James T Zauche MD, *Vice Pres*
Zeferino J Arroyo MD, *Treasurer*
Monica W Warnken, *Administration*
EMP: 146
SQ FT: 74,000
SALES (est): 3.1MM **Privately Held**
SIC: 8011 Clinic, operated by physicians

(G-2183)
GARDEN SURGICAL ASSOC
Also Called: Arroyo, Zeferino J
311 E Spruce St (67846-5614)
PHONE..................................620 275-3740
Sheldon D Roberts MD, *Principal*
EMP: 23
SALES (est): 640.4K **Privately Held**
SIC: 8011 General & family practice, physician/surgeon; urologist

(G-2184)
GARDEN VLY RETIREMENT VLG LLC
1505 E Spruce St (67846-6296)
P.O. Box 195, Longmont CO (80502-0195)
PHONE..................................620 275-9651
Mary Acker, *Food Svc Dir*
Ericka Boone, *Administration*
EMP: 150
SQ FT: 1,200
SALES: 7MM **Privately Held**
WEB: www.gardenvalleyretirementvillage.com
SIC: 8361 8082 8051 Home for the aged; home health care services; skilled nursing care facilities
PA: Frontier Management, Inc
2668 Northpark Dr Ste 220
Lafayette CO 80026
303 517-9245

(G-2185)
GARNAND FUNERAL HOME INC (PA)
Also Called: Garnand Funeral Chapel
412 N 7th St (67846-5594)
PHONE..................................620 276-3219
Darin Bradstreet, *President*
Craig Boomhower, *Vice Pres*
EMP: 11
SALES (est): 1.1MM **Privately Held**
SIC: 7261 Funeral home

(G-2186)
GERALD A WALLACE
Also Called: Wallace Electric
1803 Humphrey Rd (67846-7107)
PHONE..................................620 275-2484
Gerald A Wallace, *Principal*
EMP: 8
SALES (est): 1.3MM **Privately Held**
SIC: 2911 Petroleum refining

(G-2187)
GERES
3102 Vfw Rd (67846)
P.O. Box 1662 (67846-1662)
PHONE..................................620 276-6179
William Gere, *Owner*
EMP: 7
SALES (est): 1.2MM **Privately Held**
SIC: 1389 Oil field services

(G-2188)
GOLDEN PLAINS CREDIT UNION (PA)
1714 E Kansas Ave (67846-6235)
PHONE..................................620 275-8187
Eric Schaefer, *President*
Vic Deaver, *Exec VP*
Terry Bottorf, *Assistant VP*
Jeremy Curlo, *Vice Pres*
Roxana Koch, *Vice Pres*
EMP: 43
SQ FT: 17,000
SALES: 25MM **Privately Held**
SIC: 6062 7322 State credit unions, not federally chartered; adjustment bureau, except insurance

(G-2189)
GOLF CLUB AT SOUTHWIND LLC
77 Grandview Dr (67846-9640)
PHONE..................................620 275-2117
Luke Nickodemus, *General Mgr*
Ryan Martin, *Director*
EMP: 30
SALES (est): 1.7MM **Privately Held**
SIC: 7997 Golf club, membership

(G-2190)
GOODWILL INDUSTRIES EA
Also Called: Goodwill Inds Easter Seals Soc
2005 E Schulman Ave (67846-7801)
PHONE..................................620 275-1007
Randy Trout, *Manager*
EMP: 20
SALES (corp-wide): 10.8MM **Privately Held**
SIC: 8331 Vocational rehabilitation agency
PA: Goodwill Industries Easter Seal Society Of Kansas, Inc.
3636 N Oliver St
Wichita KS
316 744-9291

(G-2191)
HAMPTON INN
2505 E Crestway Dr (67846-6947)
PHONE..................................620 272-0454
Karli Mader, *Manager*
EMP: 12
SALES (est): 514.3K **Privately Held**
SIC: 7011 Hotels & motels

▲ = Import ▼=Export
◆ =Import/Export

(G-2192)
HEALTH AND ENVMT KANS DEPT
Also Called: City County Health Department
919 W Zerr Rd (67846-2777)
PHONE..................................620 272-3600
Ashley Goff, *Administration*
EMP: 30 **Privately Held**
SIC: 8322 9431 Individual & family services;
HQ: Kansas Department Of Health And Environment
1000 Sw Jackson St
Topeka KS 66612
785 296-1500

(G-2193)
HEART SPPORT GROUP FOR BTTRED
Also Called: FAMILY CRISIS SERVICES
106 W Fulton St (67846-5456)
PHONE..................................620 275-5911
Janine Radke, *Director*
EMP: 13
SALES: 666.7K **Privately Held**
SIC: 8322 Individual & family services

(G-2194)
HEARTLAND COCA-COLA BTLG LLC
4645 E Commerce Dr (67846-9085)
PHONE..................................620 276-3221
EMP: 3433
SALES (corp-wide): 23.9B **Privately Held**
SIC: 5149 2086 Beverages, except coffee & tea; carbonated beverages, nonalcoholic: bottled & canned
PA: Heartland Coca-Cola Bottling Company Llc
9000 Marshall Dr
Lenexa KS

(G-2195)
HELENA AGRI-ENTERPRISES LLC
1004 N Anderson Rd (67846-9280)
PHONE..................................620 275-9531
Mike Green, *Manager*
EMP: 33 **Privately Held**
WEB: www.helenachemical.com
SIC: 2875 5191 4226 Fertilizers, mixing only; fertilizers & agricultural chemicals; special warehousing & storage
HQ: Helena Agri-Enterprises, Llc
255 Schilling Blvd # 300
Collierville TN 38017
901 761-0050

(G-2196)
HI PLAINS FEED LLC
1650 N Sherlock Rd (67846-7023)
PHONE..................................620 277-2886
Troy Miller,
Ted Jackson,
EMP: 9
SQ FT: 30,000
SALES (est): 2.3MM **Privately Held**
SIC: 2048 Prepared feeds

(G-2197)
HOME DEPOT USA INC
Also Called: Home Depot, The
3110 E Kansas City (67846)
PHONE..................................620 275-5943
Mike Cason, *Branch Mgr*
EMP: 100
SALES (corp-wide): 108.2B **Publicly Held**
WEB: www.homerentalsdepot.com
SIC: 5211 7359 Home centers; tool rental
HQ: Home Depot U.S.A., Inc.
2455 Paces Ferry Ave
Atlanta GA 30339

(G-2198)
HOME TOWN REAL
1135 College Dr Ste A (67846-4774)
PHONE..................................620 271-9500
Ken Lawhon, *Principal*
EMP: 12
SALES (est): 492.3K **Privately Held**
SIC: 6519 6531 Real property lessors; real estate brokers & agents; real estate managers

(G-2199)
HOPKINS & HOPKINS
Also Called: Hopkins, George A
802 N Campus Dr (67846-6342)
PHONE..................................620 275-5375
George A Hopkins, *Partner*
EMP: 17
SALES (est): 1.5MM **Privately Held**
WEB: www.hopkinshopkins.com
SIC: 8042 5995 Specialized optometrists; contact lenses, prescription

(G-2200)
HUBER SAND COMPANY
395 N Industrial Dr (67846-8088)
P.O. Box 1359 (67846-1359)
PHONE..................................620 275-7601
Louis Huber, *Principal*
Robin Huber, *Principal*
EMP: 12
SALES (est): 3.3MM **Privately Held**
SIC: 1442 5032 Sand mining; gravel mining; pebble mining; aggregate

(G-2201)
HYDRO RSRCES - MID CNTNENT INC
3795 W Jones Ave (67846-8700)
P.O. Box 639 (67846-0639)
PHONE..................................620 277-2389
Alton Cherry, *President*
Mark McWatter, *Vice Pres*
EMP: 80 **EST:** 1939
SQ FT: 20,000
SALES (est): 11.6MM
SALES (corp-wide): 49.8MM **Privately Held**
WEB: www.henkledrilling.com
SIC: 1781 5084 Water well drilling; water pumps (industrial); pumps & pumping equipment
PA: Hydro Resources Holdings, Inc.
1 Sugar Creek Center Blvd # 400
Sugar Land TX 77478
713 622-4033

(G-2202)
INDUSTRIAL MFG & REPR SVC
Also Called: Industrial Mfg & Repair Svc
2805 W Mary St (67846-2693)
P.O. Box 1547 (67846-1547)
PHONE..................................620 275-0481
Larry Claar, *Owner*
Cathy Claar, *Treasurer*
EMP: 5
SALES (est): 527.2K **Privately Held**
SIC: 3599 1799 Machine shop, jobbing & repair; welding on site

(G-2203)
INGSTAD BROADCASTING INC
Also Called: Kbuf/Kkjq
1402 E Kansas Ave (67846-5806)
PHONE..................................620 276-2366
James Janda, *Program Mgr*
Rhonda Fisher, *Manager*
EMP: 28
SQ FT: 10,000
SALES (corp-wide): 8.2MM **Privately Held**
SIC: 4832 Radio broadcasting stations, music format
PA: Ingstad Broadcasting, Incorporated
2501 13th Ave S
Fargo ND 58103
701 237-4500

(G-2204)
INTERNATIONAL PAPER COMPANY
2502 E Us Highway 50 (67846-9648)
PHONE..................................620 272-8318
Don Sparaco, *Branch Mgr*
EMP: 83
SALES (corp-wide): 23.3B **Publicly Held**
WEB: www.tin.com
SIC: 2653 Boxes, corrugated: made from purchased materials
PA: International Paper Company
6400 Poplar Ave
Memphis TN 38197
901 419-9000

(G-2205)
IRSIK & DOLL FEED SERVICES INC
Also Called: Irsik & Doll Feed Yard
8220 E Us Highway 50 (67846-9071)
PHONE..................................620 275-7131
Mark Sebranek, *Manager*
EMP: 30
SALES (corp-wide): 62.5MM **Privately Held**
WEB: www.irsikanddoll.com
SIC: 0751 Livestock services, except veterinary
PA: Irsik & Doll Feed Services, Inc.
104 W Ave A
Cimarron KS 67835
620 855-3747

(G-2206)
IRSIK EQUITIES LP
3705 F Rd Ste Fm (67846)
PHONE..................................620 335-5454
Tami Meng, *Controller*
EMP: 10
SALES (est): 217.8K **Privately Held**
SIC: 0191 General farms, primarily crop

(G-2207)
J A G II INC
615 N Industrial Dr (67846)
PHONE..................................620 276-8409
James Coffin, *President*
Karl Ashe, *Corp Secy*
Marie Coffin, *Vice Pres*
EMP: 20
SQ FT: 5,000
SALES (est): 2.4MM **Privately Held**
SIC: 1542 Commercial & office building, new construction; commercial & office buildings, renovation & repair

(G-2208)
JACAM CHEMICALS LLC
2725 N Ray Rd (67846-2538)
P.O. Box 96, Sterling (67579-0096)
PHONE..................................620 275-1500
Donald Dietz, *Branch Mgr*
EMP: 10 **Privately Held**
SIC: 2899 Chemical supplies for foundries; rust resisting compounds
HQ: Jacam Chemicals, Llc
205 S Broadway Ave
Sterling KS 67579
620 278-3355

(G-2209)
JOHNNY SCHWINDT INC
Also Called: Daylight Donuts
201 E Kansas Ave (67846-5544)
PHONE..................................620 275-0633
Jhon Schwindt, *President*
EMP: 7
SALES (est): 308K **Privately Held**
SIC: 5461 2051 Doughnuts; doughnuts, except frozen

(G-2210)
K & L TANK TRUCK SERVICE INC
4940 E Us Highway 50 (67846)
P.O. Box 821 (67846-0821)
PHONE..................................620 277-0101
Scott Tremble, *President*
Barbara Brown, *Consultant*
Alfonso Martinez, *Executive*
EMP: 13 **EST:** 1970
SQ FT: 5,200
SALES (est): 1.5MM **Privately Held**
SIC: 4212 Liquid haulage, local

(G-2211)
K & S LLC
Also Called: Clarion Hotel
1911 E Kansas Ave (67846-6240)
P.O. Box 577 (67846-0577)
PHONE..................................620 275-7471
Samy Amro, *Mng Member*
EMP: 100
SALES: 5MM **Privately Held**
SIC: 7011 Hotels & motels

(G-2212)
KANAMAK HYDRAULICS INC
Also Called: Fluidpro
2218 W Mary St (67846-2659)
P.O. Box 575 (67846-0575)
PHONE..................................800 473-5843
Ken Madgwick, *President*
Rick Hardwick, *Principal*
Diane Woolwine, *Principal*
Stephen Madgwick, *Engineer*
Willis Campbell, *Sales Engr*
▲ **EMP:** 25
SQ FT: 9,600
SALES (est): 6MM **Privately Held**
WEB: www.kanamak.com
SIC: 3511 7699 5084 Hydraulic turbines; hydraulic turbine generator set units, complete; hydraulic equipment repair; hydraulic systems equipment & supplies

(G-2213)
KANSAS CHILDRENS SERVICE LEAG
Also Called: Head Start Western Kansas
2111 E Labrador Blvd (67846-3605)
PHONE..................................620 276-3232
Christie Reed, *Director*
EMP: 80
SALES (corp-wide): 15MM **Privately Held**
WEB: www.kcsl.org+kansas+childrens+service+garde
SIC: 8351 8322 Child day care services; individual & family services
PA: Kansas Children's Service League
1365 N Custer St
Wichita KS 67203
316 942-4261

(G-2214)
KANSAS STATE UNIVERSITY
Also Called: Southwest Research EXT Ctr
4500 E Mary St (67846-9132)
PHONE..................................620 275-9164
Robert Gillen, *Director*
EMP: 40
SALES (corp-wide): 637.6MM **Privately Held**
WEB: www.ksu.edu
SIC: 8731 9511 Agricultural research;
PA: Kansas State University
Anderson Hall 110 1301 Mi St Anderson Ha
Manhattan KS 66506
785 532-6011

(G-2215)
KARIS INC
1515 E Fulton Ter (67846-6165)
PHONE..................................620 260-9931
Sandra Weiderstein, *President*
Cheryl Sturdevant, *Treasurer*
EMP: 10
SALES (est): 562.3K **Privately Held**
WEB: www.karis.net
SIC: 5047 Medical & hospital equipment

(G-2216)
KCOE ISOM LLP
816 N Campus Dr Ste 100 (67846-6332)
PHONE..................................620 672-7476
Leroy Jones, *Chairman*
Becky Sweet, *Manager*
EMP: 10
SALES (corp-wide): 48MM **Privately Held**
WEB: www.kcoe.com
SIC: 8721 8748 Certified public accountant; agricultural consultant
PA: Kcoe Isom, Llp
3030 Courtland Cir
Salina KS
785 825-1561

(G-2217)
KELLER & MILLER CPAS LLP
Also Called: Clarke, Jeffrey A CPA
401 N Campus Dr (67846-6124)
PHONE..................................620 275-6883
Steven Keller, *Partner*
Jeffrey Clark, *Partner*
Susan Miller, *Partner*
EMP: 13

SALES (est): 1MM **Privately Held**
WEB: www.kellermiller.com
SIC: 8721 7291 Certified public accountant; tax return preparation services

(G-2218)
KELLER LEOPOLD INSURANCE LLC (PA)
Also Called: Allstate
302 Fleming St Ste 1 (67846-6162)
P.O. Box 517 (67846-0517)
PHONE..................................620 276-7671
Douglas Keller, *President*
Eric Keller, *Vice Pres*
Aaron Barnes, *Accounts Mgr*
Shawn Gallardo, *Accounts Mgr*
Nancy Urban, *Accounts Mgr*
EMP: 12
SALES (est): 2.5MM **Privately Held**
WEB: www.kellerleopold.com
SIC: 6411 6311 Insurance agents; life insurance

(G-2219)
KOERS-TURGEON CONSULTING SVC
2018 N Henderson Dr (67846-3524)
PHONE..................................620 272-9131
Max Vandament, *Manager*
EMP: 10
SALES (est): 313.9K **Privately Held**
SIC: 8748 Agricultural consultant

(G-2220)
KORTE TRUCKING INC
2180 N Anderson Rd (67846-9753)
PHONE..................................620 276-8873
Alvin Korte, *President*
Marilyn Korte, *Corp Secy*
Melinda Wallace, *Vice Pres*
EMP: 10
SALES: 650K **Privately Held**
SIC: 4213 4212 Contract haulers; local trucking, without storage

(G-2221)
L & L FLOOR COVERING INC
112 N Main St (67846-5458)
PHONE..................................620 275-0499
Larry Funk, *President*
EMP: 14
SQ FT: 14,000
SALES (est): 1.5MM **Privately Held**
WEB: www.llfloorcovering.com
SIC: 1752 5713 Carpet laying; ceramic floor tile installation; linoleum installation; carpets

(G-2222)
LEE CONSTRUCTION INC
1711 Eaman Rd (67846-7111)
PHONE..................................620 276-6811
Gail Lee, *President*
EMP: 39
SALES (corp-wide): 11.3MM **Privately Held**
WEB: www.leeconstructioninc.com
SIC: 1542 1541 3599 Commercial & office building contractors; industrial buildings & warehouses; machine shop, jobbing & repair
PA: Lee Construction, Inc.
413 N Campus Dr Ste 1
Garden City KS 67846
620 276-6811

(G-2223)
LEE ENTERPRISES INCORPORATED
204 E Fulton Ter (67846-6151)
PHONE..................................620 276-2311
Raphael Archilla, *Branch Mgr*
EMP: 5
SALES (corp-wide): 509.8MM **Publicly Held**
WEB: www.lee.net
SIC: 2711 Newspapers, publishing & printing
PA: Lee Enterprises, Incorporated
201 N Harrison St Ste 600
Davenport IA 52801
563 383-2100

(G-2224)
LEISURE HOTEL CORPORATION
Also Called: Holiday Inn
2502 E Kansas Ave (67846-6963)
PHONE..................................620 275-5900
Therese Cruz, *General Mgr*
EMP: 25
SALES (corp-wide): 6.9MM **Privately Held**
SIC: 7011 7389 7299 Hotels & motels; hotel & motel reservation service; banquet hall facilities
PA: Leisure Hotel Corporation
8725 Rosehill Rd Ste 300
Lenexa KS 66215
913 905-1460

(G-2225)
LEWIS HOOPER & DICK LLC (PA)
Also Called: Lewis Hoooper & Dick
405 N 6th St (67846-5506)
P.O. Box 699 (67846-0699)
PHONE..................................620 275-9267
Rodney Van Norden, *Partner*
Gary Schlappe, *Mng Member*
Charles Claar Jr,
David Hetrich,
Donald R Linville,
EMP: 40
SQ FT: 13,000
SALES (est): 3.9MM **Privately Held**
WEB: www.lhd.com
SIC: 8721 Certified public accountant

(G-2226)
LOCKHART GEOPHYSICAL KANS INC
2802 W Jones Ave (67846-2525)
P.O. Box 1195 (67846-1195)
PHONE..................................620 277-7771
EMP: 6 **EST:** 2018
SALES (est): 562.5K **Privately Held**
SIC: 1382 Oil & gas exploration services

(G-2227)
MAD DOG METAL INC
3005 W Mary St (67846-9737)
PHONE..................................620 275-9685
Ken Madgwick, *President*
EMP: 5
SALES: 278K **Privately Held**
SIC: 3499 Fire- or burglary-resistive products

(G-2228)
MARTIN MOBILE HOME PARK INC
Also Called: East Garden Village
4101 E Us Highway 50 Ofc (67846-8303)
PHONE..................................620 275-4722
Robert Martin, *President*
EMP: 11
SQ FT: 7,500
SALES (est): 827.2K **Privately Held**
SIC: 6515 Mobile home site operators

(G-2229)
MAURICES INCORPORATED
Also Called: Maurices 411
2206 E Kansas Ave Ste 9 (67846-6957)
PHONE..................................620 275-1210
Jennifer Espinosa, *Manager*
EMP: 20 **Privately Held**
WEB: www.maurices.com
SIC: 5621 5611 2329 Ready-to-wear apparel, women's; clothing, sportswear, men's & boys'; athletic (warmup, sweat & jogging) suits: men's & boys'
HQ: Maurices Incorporated
425 W Superior St
Duluth MN 55802
218 727-8431

(G-2230)
MEADOWLARK DAIRY NUTRITION LLC
330 S Us Highway 83 (67846-8758)
PHONE..................................620 765-7700
Vicky Christensen, *Finance*
Wes Clark, *Director*
EMP: 66
SALES (est): 2.7MM **Privately Held**
SIC: 0241 Dairy farms

(G-2231)
MICHAEL P HARRIS INC
218 E Fulton Ter (67846-6151)
PHONE..................................620 276-7623
Michael P Harris, *President*
Grant Harris, *Vice Pres*
Grant P Harris, *Fmly & Gen Dent*
EMP: 16
SALES (est): 1.2MM **Privately Held**
SIC: 8021 Dentists' office

(G-2232)
MID-AMERICA MILLWRIGHT SVC INC
2720 N 11th St (67846-2714)
P.O. Box 2243 (67846-2243)
PHONE..................................620 275-6796
Ken Green, *President*
EMP: 20
SQ FT: 16,000
SALES (est): 3.5MM **Privately Held**
SIC: 1796 Millwright

(G-2233)
MIDWEST HEALTH SERVICES INC
Also Called: Homestead Assisted Living
2414 N Henderson Dr (67846-7600)
PHONE..................................620 272-9800
Tim White, *Branch Mgr*
EMP: 28
SALES (corp-wide): 32.7MM **Privately Held**
SIC: 8052 8361 Intermediate care facilities; residential care
PA: Midwest Health, Inc
3024 Sw Wanamaker Rd # 300
Topeka KS 66614
785 272-1535

(G-2234)
MIDWEST HEALTH SERVICES INC
2308 N 3rd St (67846-3109)
PHONE..................................620 276-7643
EMP: 186
SALES (corp-wide): 32.7MM **Privately Held**
SIC: 8051 Skilled nursing care facilities
PA: Midwest Health, Inc
3024 Sw Wanamaker Rd # 300
Topeka KS 66614
785 272-1535

(G-2235)
MIDWEST PMS LLC
985 N Anderson Rd (67846-9279)
P.O. Box 1926 (67846-1926)
PHONE..................................620 276-0970
Kendall Adler, *Owner*
EMP: 8 **Privately Held**
SIC: 2048 Stock feeds, dry
PA: Midwest Pms Llc
11347 Business Park Cir
Firestone CO 80504

(G-2236)
MINI BUS SERVICE INC
907 N 10th St (67846-5209)
PHONE..................................620 272-3626
Norma Nichols, *Director*
EMP: 18
SALES (est): 367.4K **Privately Held**
SIC: 8322 Senior citizens' center or association

(G-2237)
MINTER-WILSON DRILLING CO INC (PA)
Also Called: Garden City Hilton Inn
2007 W Jones Ave (67846-2542)
P.O. Box A (67846-0020)
PHONE..................................620 276-8269
Robert L Minter, *President*
EMP: 13 **EST:** 1964
SQ FT: 8,000
SALES (est): 5.7MM **Privately Held**
SIC: 1781 7011 Water well drilling; hotel, franchised

(G-2238)
MINTER-WILSON DRILLING CO INC
Also Called: Garden City Plaza Inn, The
1911 E Kansas Ave (67846)
PHONE..................................620 275-7471
Robert L Minter, *Owner*
EMP: 23
SALES (corp-wide): 5.2MM **Privately Held**
SIC: 7011 5083 Hotels; irrigation equipment
PA: Minter-Wilson Drilling Co Inc
2007 W Jones Ave
Garden City KS 67846
620 276-8269

(G-2239)
MORTON BUILDINGS INC
4255 E Us Highway 50 (67846-9066)
P.O. Box 975 (67846-0975)
PHONE..................................620 275-4105
Lavern Durst, *Sales/Mktg Mgr*
EMP: 11
SALES (corp-wide): 463.7MM **Privately Held**
WEB: www.mortonbuildings.com
SIC: 1541 5039 Industrial buildings, new construction; prefabricated structures
PA: Morton Buildings, Inc.
252 W Adams St
Morton IL 61550
800 447-7436

(G-2240)
MOSAIC
2708 N 11th St (67846-2714)
PHONE..................................620 276-7972
Davis Jasper, *Exec Dir*
EMP: 120
SALES (corp-wide): 257.7MM **Privately Held**
WEB: www.mosaicinfo.org
SIC: 7389 Document & office record destruction
PA: Mosaic
4980 S 118th St
Omaha NE 68137
402 896-3884

(G-2241)
MOSS ENTERPRISES INC
Also Called: Peterbilt of Garden City
3255 W Jones Ave (67846-2565)
P.O. Box 1866 (67846-1866)
PHONE..................................620 277-2646
Mike Legleiter, *President*
Joe Moss, *Vice Pres*
Jim Moss, *Treasurer*
EMP: 27
SQ FT: 15,000
SALES (est): 7.4MM **Privately Held**
WEB: www.mossenterprises.com
SIC: 5012 Truck tractors

(G-2242)
NAAB ELECTRIC INC
2013 W Jones Ave (67846-2542)
P.O. Box 1112 (67846-1112)
PHONE..................................620 276-8101
Michael Gian, *President*
Frank Gian, *Treasurer*
Janis Gian, *Admin Sec*
EMP: 12
SQ FT: 13,000
SALES (est): 3.7MM **Privately Held**
SIC: 5063 7629 7694 Motors, electric; generators; motor controls, starters & relays: electric; electronic equipment repair; generator repair; electric motor repair

(G-2243)
NORDER SUPPLY INC
809 W Mary St (67846-2747)
PHONE..................................620 805-5972
Tim Norder, *Principal*
EMP: 30
SALES (corp-wide): 23.3MM **Privately Held**
SIC: 5099 Brass goods
PA: Norder Supply, Inc.
136 E Main St
Bruning NE 68322
402 353-6175

▲ = Import ▼=Export
◆ =Import/Export

(G-2244)
NUTRIEN AG SOLUTIONS INC
S Star Rte (67846)
P.O. Box 636 (67846-0636)
PHONE..................................620 275-4271
Wade Kromer, *Manager*
EMP: 25 **Privately Held**
WEB: www.cropproductionservices.com
SIC: 5191 Fertilizer & fertilizer materials
HQ: Nutrien Ag Solutions, Inc.
3005 Rocky Mountain Ave
Loveland CO 80538
970 685-3300

(G-2245)
PALETERIA TARAHUMARA
1101 N Taylor Ave (67846-4018)
PHONE..................................620 805-6509
Karina Ornelas, *Owner*
EMP: 5
SALES (est): 288.6K **Privately Held**
SIC: 2024 Ice cream & frozen desserts

(G-2246)
PALMER OIL INC
3118 Cummings Rd (67846-2403)
P.O. Box 399 (67846-0399)
PHONE..................................620 275-2963
Cecil O'Brate, *President*
EMP: 30
SALES (est): 968.3K **Privately Held**
SIC: 1389 Oil field services

(G-2247)
PANHANDLE STEEL ERECTORS INC
6800 E Us Highway 50 (67846-9121)
P.O. Box 1425 (67846-1425)
PHONE..................................620 271-9878
Mandrup Skeie, *President*
EMP: 10
SALES (corp-wide): 9.1MM **Privately Held**
SIC: 7359 1791 7389 7353 Equipment rental & leasing; structural steel erection; crane & aerial lift service; cranes & aerial lift equipment, rental or leasing
PA: Panhandle Steel Erectors, Inc
3805 S Fm 1258
Amarillo TX 79118
620 276-8809

(G-2248)
PAPER GRAPHICS INC
2006 E Schulman Ave (67846-7800)
PHONE..................................620 276-7641
Martin L Boyles, *President*
EMP: 6
SQ FT: 3,600
SALES (est): 520K **Privately Held**
SIC: 2759 2752 Letterpress printing; commercial printing, offset

(G-2249)
PEPSICO INC
355 Industrial Park (67846)
PHONE..................................620 275-5312
Jack Myers, *Manager*
EMP: 14
SALES (corp-wide): 64.6B **Publicly Held**
WEB: www.pepsico.com
SIC: 4226 Special warehousing & storage
PA: Pepsico, Inc.
700 Anderson Hill Rd
Purchase NY 10577
914 253-2000

(G-2250)
PERFORMIX HIGH PLAINS LLC
1650 N Sherlock Rd (67846-7023)
PHONE..................................620 225-0080
Ted Jackson, *Mng Member*
EMP: 28
SALES (est): 3.1MM **Privately Held**
SIC: 2048 Feed supplements

(G-2251)
PERFORMIX NUTRITION SYSTEMS
1650 N Sherlock Rd (67846-7023)
PHONE..................................620 277-2886
Ted Jackson, *Manager*
EMP: 42
SQ FT: 1,300
SALES (est): 3.1MM
SALES (corp-wide): 342.6MM **Privately Held**
SIC: 2048 Feed supplements
PA: Agri Beef Co.
1555 W Shoreline Dr # 320
Boise ID 83702
208 338-2500

(G-2252)
PETERSEN PRINTING INC
1002 N 4th St (67846-5630)
PHONE..................................620 275-7331
Drew Petersen, *President*
Brent Peterson, *Partner*
Drew Peterson, *Partner*
Brent Petersen, *Corp Secy*
EMP: 7
SQ FT: 1,750
SALES: 460K **Privately Held**
WEB: www.petersenprinting.com
SIC: 2752 Commercial printing, offset

(G-2253)
PETROSANTANDER (USA) INC
11130 E 7 Mile Rd (67846-9213)
PHONE..................................620 272-7187
Christopher Whyte, *CEO*
Ian Gollop, *Exec VP*
Victor Low, *Treasurer*
EMP: 13
SALES: 7.7MM **Privately Held**
SIC: 1311 Crude petroleum production
PA: Petrosantander Inc.
6363 Woodway Dr Ste 350
Houston TX 77057

(G-2254)
PHOENIX RESTORATION SERVICE
1612 Terminal Ave (67846-6612)
PHONE..................................620 276-6994
David Salas, *Owner*
Sonja Troy, *Controller*
Jaime Moore, *Marketing Mgr*
Brian Hauk, *Marketing Staff*
EMP: 22
SALES (est): 1.1MM **Privately Held**
WEB: www.phoenixrestoration.com
SIC: 7217 7389 7349 1799 Carpet & upholstery cleaning; air pollution measuring service; air duct cleaning; post-disaster renovations

(G-2255)
PILAND AUTO DISMANTLING
803 W Lake Ave (67846-6423)
PHONE..................................620 275-5506
Terry Piland, *Owner*
EMP: 10
SQ FT: 4,500
SALES: 30K **Privately Held**
SIC: 5015 Automotive parts & supplies, used

(G-2256)
PLANKENHORN INC
Also Called: Ehersman Packing Co
912 E Fulton St (67846-6042)
PHONE..................................620 276-3791
Mike Plankenhorn, *President*
Velda Plankenhorn, *Corp Secy*
EMP: 13
SQ FT: 5,000
SALES: 1.4MM **Privately Held**
SIC: 5421 5147 0751 2013 Meat markets, including freezer provisioners; meats, fresh; slaughtering: custom livestock services; sausages & other prepared meats; meat packing plants

(G-2257)
POST & MASTIN WELL SERVICE
3210 W Jones Ave (67846-2564)
P.O. Box 297 (67846-0297)
PHONE..................................620 276-3442
Brian Post, *President*
EMP: 16
SALES (est): 1MM **Privately Held**
SIC: 1389 Servicing oil & gas wells

(G-2258)
PREFERRED AG SERVICES INC
535 E Us Highway 50 Byp (67846-8024)
P.O. Box 972 (67846-0972)
PHONE..................................620 271-7366
Dustin Deines, *President*
EMP: 15
SALES (est): 10.2MM **Privately Held**
SIC: 5191 Fertilizer & fertilizer materials

(G-2259)
PREFERRED CARTAGE SERVICE INC (PA)
Also Called: Trek Trucking
1401 W Joe Mcgraw St (67846-2600)
P.O. Box 940, Greeley CO (80632-0940)
PHONE..................................620 276-8080
Jarrett McGraw, *President*
Brett McGraw, *Exec VP*
Marilee McGraw, *Treasurer*
EMP: 85
SQ FT: 1,500
SALES (est): 19.7MM **Privately Held**
WEB: www.preferredcartage.com
SIC: 4731 Agents, shipping

(G-2260)
PSSK LLC
Also Called: Best Wstn Plus Emrald Inn Stes
2412 E Kansas Ave (67846-6961)
PHONE..................................620 277-7100
P-Jay Patel, *Mng Member*
EMP: 15
SALES (est): 113K **Privately Held**
SIC: 7011 Hotels & motels

(G-2261)
R T SPORTING GOODS INC
1135 College Dr Ste E (67846-4774)
PHONE..................................620 275-5507
Steve E Spellman, *President*
Mary Beth Spellman, *Treasurer*
EMP: 10
SQ FT: 6,000
SALES: 1.2MM **Privately Held**
WEB: www.rtsportinggoods.com
SIC: 5091 5941 Athletic goods; specialty sport supplies

(G-2262)
R&R PALLET GARDEN CITY INC
2008 W Mary St (67846-2669)
P.O. Box 861 (67846-0861)
PHONE..................................620 275-2394
Walt Wadel, *President*
Rodney Wadel, *General Mgr*
Rod Wadel, *Vice Pres*
Rich Wadel, *Vice Pres*
Marilyn Wadel, *Treasurer*
▲ **EMP:** 38
SQ FT: 30,000
SALES: 8.5MM **Privately Held**
SIC: 2448 4213 Pallets, wood; trucking, except local

(G-2263)
RAYMIRE INC
Also Called: Hard Rock Lanes
1612 E Laurel St (67846-6110)
PHONE..................................620 275-4061
Ray Shearmire, *President*
Lilia Shearmire, *Treasurer*
EMP: 10 **EST:** 1977
SALES (est): 456.9K **Privately Held**
WEB: www.hardrocklanes.com
SIC: 7933 Ten pin center

(G-2264)
REEVE AGRI-ENERGY INC
5665 S Us Old Hwy 83 (67846)
P.O. Box 1036 (67846-1036)
PHONE..................................620 275-7541
Lee Reeve, *President*
EMP: 10
SQ FT: 27,000
SALES: 25MM **Privately Held**
SIC: 2869 2048 Ethyl alcohol, ethanol; livestock feeds

(G-2265)
REEVE CATTLE CO INC
7 Mi South Of Town (67846)
P.O. Box 1036 (67846-1036)
PHONE..................................620 275-0234
M P Reeve, *President*
Lee Reeve, *Corp Secy*
EMP: 15
SQ FT: 20,000
SALES (est): 2.9MM **Privately Held**
SIC: 0211 Beef cattle feedlots

(G-2266)
RENAL TRTMNT CENTERS-WEST INC
Also Called: Garden City Dialysis Center
2308 E Kansas Ave (67846-6959)
PHONE..................................620 260-9852
James K Hilger,
EMP: 15 **Publicly Held**
WEB: www.davita.com
SIC: 8092 Kidney dialysis centers
HQ: Renal Treatment Centers-West, Inc.
2000 16th St
Denver CO 80202

(G-2267)
RES-CARE INC
2102 E Spruce St (67846-6362)
PHONE..................................620 271-0176
Jared Nozzle, *Branch Mgr*
EMP: 48
SALES (corp-wide): 2B **Privately Held**
WEB: www.rescare.com
SIC: 8082 Home health care services
HQ: Res-Care, Inc.
805 N Whittington Pkwy
Louisville KY 40222
502 394-2100

(G-2268)
ROBINSON OIL CO INC
710 N Vfw Rd (67846-7008)
PHONE..................................620 275-4237
Charles D Robinson, *President*
EMP: 10 **EST:** 1970
SQ FT: 2,500
SALES (est): 6.8MM **Privately Held**
WEB: www.robinsonoil.com
SIC: 5172 5541 Lubricating oils & greases; filling stations, gasoline

(G-2269)
ROYAL FARMS DAIRY LLC
3705 F Rd (67846-9229)
PHONE..................................620 335-5704
Steve Irsik, *Mng Member*
EMP: 50 **EST:** 2000
SQ FT: 40,000
SALES (est): 13.1MM **Privately Held**
SIC: 0241 Dairy farms

(G-2270)
RUSSELL CHILD DEV CTR INC (PA)
2735 N Jennie Barker Rd (67846-9077)
PHONE..................................620 275-0291
Deanna Berry, *CEO*
Dave Ranney, *Editor*
Dana McNutt, *CFO*
EMP: 54
SQ FT: 15,000
SALES: 5.3MM **Privately Held**
SIC: 8351 Montessori child development center

(G-2271)
RUTTER CLINE ASSOCIATES INC
Also Called: Allstate
110 W Chestnut St (67846-5403)
P.O. Box 993 (67846-0993)
PHONE..................................620 276-8274
Ric Gudding, *President*
Rick Walz, *Corp Secy*
Dave Gilkensom, *Vice Pres*
Janet Kruleski, *Director*
Angela Reich, *Director*
EMP: 15
SQ FT: 4,000
SALES (est): 2.7MM **Privately Held**
WEB: www.rutterclineassoc.com
SIC: 6411 Insurance agents, brokers & service

(G-2272)
SAINT FRANCIS CMNTY SVCS INC
1110 J C St (67846-6345)
PHONE..................................620 276-4482
EMP: 109
SALES (corp-wide): 108.2MM **Privately Held**
SIC: 8741 8361 Hospital management; residential care

PA: Saint Francis Community Services, Inc.
509 E Elm St
Salina KS 67401
785 825-0541

(G-2273)
SALVATION ARMY
Also Called: Salvation Army Thrift Store
216 N 9th St (67846-5310)
PHONE..................................620 276-4027
Lt Jeff Curran, *Principal*
EMP: 17
SALES (corp-wide): 2.2B **Privately Held**
WEB: www.salvationarmykc.org
SIC: 8661 8322 Religious organizations; emergency social services
HQ: The Salvation Army
5550 Prairie Stone Pkwy # 130
Hoffman Estates IL 60192
847 294-2000

(G-2274)
SALVATION ARMY
203 N 8th St (67846-5338)
PHONE..................................620 276-6622
EMP: 21
SALES (corp-wide): 2.2B **Privately Held**
WEB: www.salarmychicago.org
SIC: 8661 8699 Non-church religious organizations; charitable organization
HQ: The Salvation Army
5550 Prairie Stone Pkwy # 130
Hoffman Estates IL 60192
847 294-2000

(G-2275)
SCHEOPNERS WATER COND LLC
2203 E Fulton Plz (67846-6187)
P.O. Box 721 (67846-0721)
PHONE..................................620 275-5121
Liz Scheopner,
Nethan Scheopner,
EMP: 15
SQ FT: 10,000
SALES: 1.4MM **Privately Held**
SIC: 7359 7389 5999 Home appliance, furniture & entertainment rental services; water softener service; water purification equipment

(G-2276)
SCHWARTZ INC
Also Called: Comfort Inn
1335 Hineman Dr (67846-3538)
PHONE..................................620 275-5800
Darrel Schwartz, *President*
Tim Schiffelbien, *General Mgr*
EMP: 14
SALES (est): 520K **Privately Held**
SIC: 7011 Hotels & motels

(G-2277)
SCHWIETERMAN INC (PA)
1616 E Kansas Ave (67846-6233)
P.O. Box 1196 (67846-1196)
PHONE..................................620 275-4100
Luke Schwieterman, *President*
Verena Schwieterman, *Corp Secy*
EMP: 12
SQ FT: 6,000
SALES (est): 5.3MM **Privately Held**
WEB: www.upthelimit.com
SIC: 6221 Commodity brokers, contracts

(G-2278)
SECURITY FARMS INC (PA)
911 N Main St (67846-5561)
PHONE..................................620 275-4200
Stan Fansher, *President*
Mary M Hopkins, *Corp Secy*
EMP: 10
SALES (est): 725.4K **Privately Held**
SIC: 0191 General farms, primarily crop

(G-2279)
SERVICEMASTER COMPANY LLC
3020 E Kansas Ave (67846-6816)
PHONE..................................620 260-9994
EMP: 17
SALES (corp-wide): 1.9B **Publicly Held**
SIC: 7349 Building maintenance services
HQ: The Servicemaster Company Llc
150 Peabody Pl
Memphis TN 38103
901 597-1400

(G-2280)
SKEETERS BODY SHOP INC
3104 W Jones Ave (67846-2566)
PHONE..................................620 275-7255
Larry Smith, *President*
EMP: 10
SALES (est): 1MM **Privately Held**
SIC: 7532 Body shop, automotive

(G-2281)
SLEEP INN AND SUITES 07
1931 E Kansas Ave (67846-6240)
PHONE..................................620 805-6535
Amaro Samy, *Owner*
EMP: 10
SALES (est): 394.9K **Privately Held**
SIC: 7011 Hotels & motels

(G-2282)
SMITH AUTO & TRUCK PARTS INC
402 E Burnside Dr (67846-6712)
P.O. Box 696 (67846-0696)
PHONE..................................620 275-9145
Larry L Smith, *President*
Lela R Smith, *Corp Secy*
Eldon Ford, *Vice Pres*
Brad Smith, *Vice Pres*
EMP: 14 **EST:** 1939
SQ FT: 14,000
SALES (est): 2MM **Privately Held**
WEB: www.smithauto-truck.com
SIC: 5531 5015 5013 Automotive parts; truck equipment & parts; automotive supplies, used; automotive supplies & parts

(G-2283)
SOCIAL AND REHABILITATION SERV
Also Called: SOCIAL AND REHABILITATION SERVICES, KANSAS DEPT OF
1710 Palace Dr (67846-6268)
PHONE..................................620 272-5800
Le-Ann Curtis, *Manager*
EMP: 80 **Privately Held**
SIC: 8322 9441 8331 Public welfare center; administration of social & manpower programs; ; job training & vocational rehabilitation services
HQ: Kansas Department For Children And Families
555 S Kansas Ave
Topeka KS 66603
785 368-6358

(G-2284)
SOUTHWEST PALLETS
Also Called: Southwest Pallets & Warehouse
50 S Farmland Rd (67846-9635)
PHONE..................................620 275-4343
Darren West, *President*
EMP: 6
SALES: 100K **Privately Held**
SIC: 2448 4225 Pallets, wood; general warehousing

(G-2285)
SOUTHWIND DEVELOPMENT CO
50 Grandview Dr (67846-9640)
P.O. Box 534 (67846-0534)
PHONE..................................620 275-2117
Bill Baxter, *Partner*
Brookover Land Enterprises, *General Ptnr*
EMP: 20
SALES (est): 1.8MM **Privately Held**
SIC: 6552 Subdividers & developers

(G-2286)
SPARKLE AUTO LLC
Also Called: Sparkleauto.com
163 N Campus Dr (67846-6603)
PHONE..................................620 272-9559
Vic Freeman, *President*
◆ **EMP:** 11
SQ FT: 5,400
SALES: 1.2MM **Privately Held**
SIC: 5531 5013 Automotive & home supply stores; automotive supplies & parts

(G-2287)
ST CATHERINE HOSPITAL
601 N Main St Ste B (67846-5468)
PHONE..................................620 272-2660
Peggy Taylor, *Branch Mgr*
EMP: 18
SALES (corp-wide): 466.6MM **Privately Held**
SIC: 8082 Home health care services
HQ: St. Catherine Hospital
401 E Spruce St
Garden City KS 67846
620 272-2222

(G-2288)
ST CATHERINE HOSPITAL (HQ)
401 E Spruce St (67846-5672)
PHONE..................................620 272-2222
Mark Steadham, *President*
Scott Taylor, *Principal*
John Yox, *Senior VP*
Margie Prewitt, *Vice Pres*
Amanda Vaughan, *CFO*
EMP: 465
SQ FT: 161,439
SALES: 92.8MM
SALES (corp-wide): 466.6MM **Privately Held**
SIC: 8062 General medical & surgical hospitals
PA: Centura Health Corporation
9100 E Mineral Cir
Centennial CO 80112
303 290-6500

(G-2289)
ST CATHERINE HOSPITAL
Also Called: Saint Catherine Home Care Svc
602 N 6th St (67846-5509)
PHONE..................................620 272-2519
Michelle Shull, *Branch Mgr*
EMP: 15
SALES (corp-wide): 466.6MM **Privately Held**
SIC: 8062 8051 General medical & surgical hospitals; skilled nursing care facilities
HQ: St. Catherine Hospital
401 E Spruce St
Garden City KS 67846
620 272-2222

(G-2290)
ST CATHRINE HOSP DEV FUNDATION
401 E Spruce St (67846-5679)
PHONE..................................620 272-2222
Thomas Koksal, *Chairman*
EMP: 10
SALES: 639.2K **Privately Held**
SIC: 8062 General medical & surgical hospitals

(G-2291)
STEAM ACTION RESTORATION
2116 W Mary St (67846-2648)
PHONE..................................620 276-0622
Dwayne Bomtrager, *Owner*
EMP: 13
SQ FT: 2,500
SALES: 200K **Privately Held**
WEB: www.steamactionrestoration.com
SIC: 7217 Carpet & furniture cleaning on location

(G-2292)
SUGARCAT HOSPITALITY INC
1335 Hineman Dr (67846-3538)
PHONE..................................620 275-5800
Devin McMillian, *Administration*
EMP: 11 **EST:** 2010
SALES (est): 403.5K **Privately Held**
SIC: 7011 Hotels & motels

(G-2293)
SUNFLOWER ELECTRIC POWER CORP
2075 Saint John St (67846-5071)
PHONE..................................620 275-0161
Keith Overland, *Engineer*
Bill Nolte, *Legal Staff*
EMP: 46 **Privately Held**
WEB: www.sunflower.net
SIC: 4911 Generation, electric power; transmission, electric power
HQ: Sunflower Electric Power Corporation
301 W 13th St
Hays KS 67601
785 628-2845

(G-2294)
SUNSHINE HORIZONS
2718 Cummings Rd Ste W (67846-2401)
PHONE..................................620 276-1787
Stacy Geil, *Principal*
EMP: 10
SALES (est): 173.5K **Privately Held**
SIC: 8082 Home health care services

(G-2295)
SUNSHINE NURSING AGENCY INC
Also Called: Sunshine's Nursing Horizons
2718 Cummings Rd Ste E (67846-2401)
PHONE..................................620 276-8868
Stacy Geil, *President*
John Geil, *Principal*
EMP: 30
SALES (est): 842.7K **Privately Held**
SIC: 8082 Home health care services

(G-2296)
TATRO PLUMBING CO INC (PA)
1285 Acraway St Ste 300 (67846-8096)
PHONE..................................620 277-2167
James H Johnson, *Ch of Bd*
Justin Sanchez, *President*
Terry Fowler, *President*
Donna Hageman, *Corp Secy*
Rl Kreutzer, *CFO*
EMP: 12
SQ FT: 5,000
SALES: 13MM **Privately Held**
WEB: www.tatroplumbing.com
SIC: 1711 Plumbing contractors

(G-2297)
TEETER IRRIGATION INC
2707 W Jones Ave (67846-2524)
PHONE..................................620 276-8257
Terry Winkelman, *Owner*
EMP: 11
SALES (corp-wide): 9.7MM **Privately Held**
WEB: www.teeterirrigation.com
SIC: 5083 5084 5051 Irrigation equipment; engines, gasoline; pipe & tubing, steel
PA: Teeter Irrigation, Inc.
2729 W Oklahoma Ave
Ulysses KS 67880
620 353-1111

(G-2298)
TEX-OK-KAN OIL FIELD SVCS LLC
2005 N Taylor Ave (67846-2683)
PHONE..................................620 271-7310
Leon Frazer, *CEO*
Stacy Farr,
EMP: 50
SALES (est): 48.2MM **Privately Held**
SIC: 5172 Crude oil

(G-2299)
TONYS PIZZA
220 Air Links Rd (67846-9428)
PHONE..................................620 275-4626
EMP: 10
SALES (est): 127.3K **Privately Held**
SIC: 8322 Individual/Family Services

(G-2300)
TRANS-PAK INC (PA)
4555 N Jennie Barker Rd (67846-9253)
PHONE..................................620 275-1758
Richard L Schilling, *President*
Denis E Cowley, *Corp Secy*
Roxann Schwertner, *CFO*
EMP: 10
SQ FT: 3,000
SALES (est): 1.5MM **Privately Held**
SIC: 5141 Food brokers

(G-2301)
TRIANGLE H
1955 W Plymell Rd (67846-8833)
PHONE..................................620 276-4004
Gregory Hands, *Partner*
Samuel Hands, *Partner*

▲ = Import ▼=Export
◆ =Import/Export

Tyler Hands, *Partner*
EMP: 19
SALES (est): 512.4K **Privately Held**
SIC: 0115 Corn

(G-2302)
TRIANGLE H GRAIN & CATTLE CO
1955 W Plymell Rd (67846-8833)
PHONE..................................620 276-4004
Greg Hands, *Partner*
Cedric Hands, *Partner*
Sam Hands, *Partner*
Tyler Hands, *Partner*
EMP: 12
SALES (est): 1.9MM **Privately Held**
WEB: www.trianglehfarm.com
SIC: 0211 0119 0115 Beef cattle feedlots; feeder grains; corn

(G-2303)
TRINITY FEEDYARD LLC
1805 W Annie Scheer Rd (67846-8800)
PHONE..................................620 275-4191
Betty Dew, *Manager*
Todd Tuls,
EMP: 25 **EST:** 2015
SALES (est): 499.8K **Privately Held**
SIC: 0211 Beef cattle feedlots
PA: Tuls Dairy - Butler County, Llc
2670 D Rd
Rising City NE 68658

(G-2304)
TUMBLEWEED FESTIVAL INC
1719 E Texas St (67846-3662)
P.O. Box 296 (67846-0296)
PHONE..................................620 275-9141
Dave Sweley, *President*
EMP: 13
SALES: 91.8K **Privately Held**
SIC: 7999 Festival operation

(G-2305)
UNDERGROUND SPECIALISTS INC
520 Airlinks Dr (67846)
P.O. Box 915 (67846-0915)
PHONE..................................620 276-3344
Ron D Leiker Jr, *President*
EMP: 10
SQ FT: 8,000
SALES (est): 4.1MM **Privately Held**
SIC: 5083 Lawn & garden machinery & equipment

(G-2306)
UNIFIRST CORPORATION
903 W Prospect Ave (67846-2757)
PHONE..................................620 275-0231
Todd Linder, *CTO*
EMP: 60
SALES (corp-wide): 1.8B **Publicly Held**
WEB: www.unifirst.com
SIC: 7218 Industrial uniform supply; work clothing supply; radiation protective garment supply
PA: Unifirst Corporation
68 Jonspin Rd
Wilmington MA 01887
978 658-8888

(G-2307)
UNITED METHODIST WESTERN KANSA (PA)
Also Called: Genesis Family Health
712 Saint John St (67846-5128)
P.O. Box 766 (67846-0766)
PHONE..................................620 275-1766
Julie Wright, *CEO*
Marcie Strine, *CFO*
Gerald Greene, *Treasurer*
Penney Schwab, *Exec Dir*
Thelma Miller, *Admin Sec*
EMP: 38
SQ FT: 3,000
SALES: 5.1MM **Privately Held**
SIC: 8322 Individual & family services

(G-2308)
WALMART INC
3101 E Kansas Ave Ste 7 (67846-6999)
PHONE..................................620 275-0775
Stephanie Sullivan, *Manager*
Sonia Castillo, *Manager*
EMP: 453
SQ FT: 205,187
SALES (corp-wide): 514.4B **Publicly Held**
WEB: www.walmartstores.com
SIC: 5311 5411 7221 5812 Department stores, discount; supermarkets, hypermarket; photographic studios, portrait; eating places; automotive & home supply stores
PA: Walmart Inc.
702 Sw 8th St
Bentonville AR 72716
479 273-4000

(G-2309)
WEBER REFRIGERATION & HTG INC
711 N Main St (67846-5474)
PHONE..................................580 338-7338
Mike Weber, *President*
EMP: 50
SALES (corp-wide): 7.3MM **Privately Held**
SIC: 1711 5719 5078 5075 Heating & air conditioning contractors; fireplace equipment & accessories; commercial refrigeration equipment; air conditioning & ventilation equipment & supplies
PA: Weber Refrigeration & Heating, Inc.
11154 Kliesen St
Dodge City KS 67801
620 225-7700

(G-2310)
WESTERN HYDRO LLC
3585c N Williams Rd (67846-9508)
PHONE..................................620 277-2132
Gary Elliot, *Manager*
EMP: 10
SALES (corp-wide): 1.3B **Publicly Held**
SIC: 5084 Pumps & pumping equipment
HQ: Western Hydro Llc
2034 Research Dr
Livermore CA 94550
559 275-3305

(G-2311)
WESTERN IRRIGATION INC
2990 Morton Rd (67846-8380)
PHONE..................................620 275-4033
Gale Louk, *President*
EMP: 20
SQ FT: 4,500
SALES (est): 3.3MM **Privately Held**
SIC: 1629 1711 Irrigation system construction; irrigation sprinkler system installation

(G-2312)
WESTERN TRANSPORT
100 N 7th St (67846-5547)
P.O. Box 838 (67846-0838)
PHONE..................................620 271-0540
Jan Hornett, *Principal*
EMP: 18
SALES (est): 223.5K **Privately Held**
SIC: 4789 Transportation services

(G-2313)
WHARTONS FOR EVERY
906 N 10th St (67846-5208)
PHONE..................................620 276-6000
George Wharton, *President*
James E Wharton, *Vice Pres*
Debbie Wharton, *Admin Sec*
EMP: 20
SQ FT: 10,000
SALES (est): 1.2MM **Privately Held**
SIC: 5992 5947 0181 Flowers, fresh; gift shop; flowers: grown under cover (e.g. greenhouse production)

(G-2314)
WHEATLAND ELECTRIC COOP INC
2005 W Fulton St (67846-9775)
P.O. Box 973 (67846-0973)
PHONE..................................620 275-0261
Stan Bieker, *Superintendent*
EMP: 30
SALES (corp-wide): 108.6MM **Privately Held**
WEB: www.weci.net
SIC: 4911 Distribution, electric power
PA: Wheatland Electric Cooperative, Inc.
101 N Main St
Scott City KS 67871
620 872-5885

(G-2315)
WILLIAMS INVESTIGATION & SEC
Also Called: Williams Security
4245 Chambers Dr (67846-9621)
P.O. Box 1313 (67846-1313)
PHONE..................................620 275-1134
Dale Williams, *President*
Susan Williams, *Corp Secy*
EMP: 27
SQ FT: 1,500
SALES (est): 1.9MM **Privately Held**
SIC: 5999 5063 7381 5065 Alarm & safety equipment stores; telephone & communication equipment; electric alarms & signaling equipment; guard services; private investigator; paging & signaling equipment; communication equipment; mobile telephone equipment

(G-2316)
WINDRIVER GRAIN LLC
2810 E Us Highway 50 (67846-8528)
PHONE..................................620 275-2101
Robert Tempel, *COO*
Robert A Tempel, *COO*
Kammi Hansen, *CFO*
EMP: 24 **EST:** 1997
SALES: 251.7MM **Privately Held**
SIC: 5153 Grain elevators

(G-2317)
WINFIELD SOLUTIONS LLC
4460 Jones Ave Ste B (67846-9727)
PHONE..................................620 277-2231
Michael Burch, *Manager*
EMP: 12
SALES (corp-wide): 6.8B **Privately Held**
SIC: 5191 Chemicals, agricultural
HQ: Winfield Solutions, Llc
1080 County Road F W
Saint Paul MN 55126

(G-2318)
WORTHINGTON CYLINDER CORP
2814 W Jones Ave (67846-2525)
PHONE..................................620 275-7461
EMP: 191
SALES (corp-wide): 3.7B **Publicly Held**
SIC: 3443 Cylinders, pressure: metal plate
HQ: Worthington Cylinder Corporation
200 W Old Wlson Bridge Rd
Worthington OH 43085
614 840-3210

(G-2319)
YOUNG MENS CHRISTIAN ASSN
1224 Center St (67846-4643)
PHONE..................................620 275-1199
Chad Knight, *Exec Dir*
EMP: 20
SALES: 2.8MM **Privately Held**
SIC: 8641 7991 8351 7032 Youth organizations; physical fitness facilities; child day care services; youth camps; individual & family services

(G-2320)
YOUNG MNS CHRSTN ASSN OF STHWE
1224 Center St (67846-4643)
PHONE..................................620 275-1199
Chad Knight, *Director*
Karla Springer, *Director*
Karen Berry, *Executive*
EMP: 45 **EST:** 1950
SQ FT: 36,000
SALES: 2.7MM **Privately Held**
SIC: 8641 Youth organizations

Garden Plain
Sedgwick County

(G-2321)
BECKER BROS INC
514 N Main St (67050-5005)
P.O. Box 66 (67050-0066)
PHONE..................................316 531-2264
John Garrison, *President*
Elizabeth Garrison, *Admin Sec*
EMP: 18 **EST:** 1971
SQ FT: 5,500
SALES: 1.9MM **Privately Held**
SIC: 1711 Warm air heating & air conditioning contractor

(G-2322)
STUHLSATZ SERVICE INC (PA)
Also Called: Garden Plain Service Center
29622 W Harry St (67050-5018)
P.O. Box 56 (67050-0056)
PHONE..................................316 531-2282
Kenneth Stuhlsatz, *President*
Clarence Stuhlsatz, *Shareholder*
EMP: 12
SALES (est): 2.1MM **Privately Held**
SIC: 5541 5171 Filling stations, gasoline; petroleum bulk stations

Gardner
Johnson County

(G-2323)
ALEA COMMUNICATIONS LLC
510 N Poplar St (66030-1825)
PHONE..................................913 439-7391
Jeffrey Leroy, *CEO*
EMP: 10
SALES: 1MM **Privately Held**
SIC: 1623 8748 1731 Transmitting tower (telecommunication) construction; telecommunications consultant; telephone & telephone equipment installation

(G-2324)
ALLIED BUSINESS SOLUTIONS INC
314 E Main St Ste 202 (66030-1486)
P.O. Box 246 (66030-0246)
PHONE..................................913 856-2323
Larry Alsup, *President*
EMP: 12
SALES (est): 721.4K **Privately Held**
SIC: 8748 Communications consulting

(G-2325)
ALTERNATIVE BUILDING TECH
Also Called: Trail West Hardware & Feed
711 S Sycamore St (66030-1479)
PHONE..................................913 856-4536
Rex E Cummings, *President*
Rex Cummings, *President*
EMP: 14
SALES: 1.4MM **Privately Held**
SIC: 5251 2048 5999 5261 Hardware; livestock feeds; pet supplies; nurseries & garden centers; pesticides; paint

(G-2326)
AMERICAN TELEPHONE INC
17540 Four Corners Rd (66030-9733)
PHONE..................................913 780-3166
Mignon Ephland, *President*
Mark Ephland, *Vice Pres*
Michael Pestano Sr, *Vice Pres*
EMP: 12
SQ FT: 2,500
SALES (est): 1.2MM **Privately Held**
WEB: www.americantelephoneinc.com
SIC: 4813 Local telephone communications

(G-2327)
ARVEST BANK
306 E Main St (66030-1314)
PHONE..................................913 279-3300
Mark Parman, *Branch Mgr*
EMP: 17

SALES (corp-wide): 2.3B **Privately Held**
WEB: www.solutionsbank.com
SIC: 6022 State trust companies accepting deposits, commercial
HQ: Arvest Bank
103 S Bloomington St
Fayetteville AR 72745
479 575-1000

(G-2328)
ASPEN PLACE APARTMENTS
101 Aspen St (66030-1533)
PHONE..................................913 856-8185
Sarah Pollard, *Manager*
Sara Pollard, *Manager*
EMP: 10
SALES (est): 547.8K **Privately Held**
SIC: 6513 Apartment building operators

(G-2329)
BCI MECHANICAL INC
Also Called: Honeywell Authorized Dealer
341 S Poplar St (66030-1118)
P.O. Box 441 (66030-0441)
PHONE..................................913 856-6747
Brian Livingston, *Corp Secy*
David Livingston, *Vice Pres*
EMP: 13
SALES (est): 3.4MM **Privately Held**
WEB: www.bcimechanical.biz
SIC: 1711 Mechanical contractor; heating & air conditioning contractors

(G-2330)
BRITTANY COURT INV PARTNER LP
153 Brittany Ct (66030-1800)
PHONE..................................816 300-0685
Krista Bazata, *Principal*
Jonathan Cohn, *Principal*
Robert Schock, *Principal*
EMP: 15
SALES (est): 447.7K **Privately Held**
SIC: 6799 Investors

(G-2331)
CENTRAL BANK OF MIDWEST
900 E Main St (66030-1510)
PHONE..................................913 856-7715
James Dean, *Senior VP*
EMP: 82
SALES (corp-wide): 4.1MM **Privately Held**
SIC: 6022 State trust companies accepting deposits, commercial
PA: Central Bank Of The Midwest
609 Ne State Route 291
Lees Summit MO 64086
816 525-5754

(G-2332)
CHAUDHRYS INVESTMENT GROUP
Also Called: Super 8 Gardner
2001 E Santa Fe St (66030-1503)
PHONE..................................913 856-8887
Ali Chaudhry, *President*
EMP: 15
SALES (est): 535.5K **Privately Held**
SIC: 7011 Hotels & motels

(G-2333)
CNC UNDERGROUND LLC
633 N Oak St (66030-1772)
PHONE..................................913 744-0485
Christina Wood,
EMP: 19
SALES: 350K **Privately Held**
SIC: 1731 Fiber optic cable installation

(G-2334)
CONTINENTAL POOLS INC
805 E Warren St (66030-1619)
PHONE..................................913 856-2841
John S Waage, *President*
Daniel Wayne Doll, *Admin Sec*
EMP: 10
SALES (est): 1.3MM **Privately Held**
SIC: 1799 Swimming pool construction

(G-2335)
CRAMER PRODUCTS INC
Active Ankle Systems
153 W Warren St (66030-1151)
PHONE..................................913 856-7511
Jim Patterson, *Principal*
EMP: 15
SALES (corp-wide): 132MM **Privately Held**
SIC: 3842 5047 Supports: abdominal, ankle, arch, kneecap, etc.; medical equipment & supplies
HQ: Cramer Products, Inc.
153 W Warren St
Gardner KS 66030
800 345-2231

(G-2336)
CURBYS LAWN & GARDEN LLC
14835 S Gardner Rd (66030-9319)
P.O. Box 301, Olathe (66051-0301)
PHONE..................................913 764-6159
William C Hughes, *Mng Member*
EMP: 15
SALES (est): 778.4K **Privately Held**
SIC: 0782 Lawn care services

(G-2337)
DD TRADERS INC
Also Called: Demdaco
31426 W 191st St (66030)
PHONE..................................913 402-6800
EMP: 10
SALES (est): 933.5K
SALES (corp-wide): 108.6MM **Privately Held**
WEB: www.demdaco.com
SIC: 4225 General warehousing
PA: Dd Traders, Inc.
5000 W 134th St
Leawood KS 66209
913 402-6800

(G-2338)
DISTRIBUTORCENTRAL LLC
1200 Energy Center Dr (66030-1599)
P.O. Box 489 (66030-0489)
PHONE..................................888 516-7401
Thomas Mertz, *CEO*
Angela Taylor, *Mktg Dir*
Amelia Madl, *Manager*
EMP: 10
SQ FT: 200
SALES (est): 859.2K **Privately Held**
WEB: www.distributorcentral.com
SIC: 7371 Computer software development

(G-2339)
DLLC - DUPREE LANDSCAP
791 E Warren St (66030-1629)
PHONE..................................913 856-0120
Lonnie Dupree, *President*
EMP: 12
SQ FT: 850,000
SALES: 550K **Privately Held**
SIC: 0781 Landscape services

(G-2340)
DVC TRAINING SPECIALISTS LLC
814 E Main St (66030-1287)
PHONE..................................913 908-3393
EMP: 7
SALES (est): 330.1K **Privately Held**
SIC: 3949 8742 Targets, archery & rifle shooting; training & development consultant

(G-2341)
EPIC LANDSCAPE PRODUCTIONS (PA)
23933 W 175th St (66030-9362)
PHONE..................................913 897-3858
John A Constant, *President*
Steve Nelson, *General Mgr*
Chad Wallerstedt, *Project Mgr*
Mike McGroder, *Accounts Mgr*
Saundra Tennison, *Admin Asst*
EMP: 10
SALES (est): 965.6K **Privately Held**
SIC: 0781 0782 Landscape services; landscape contractors

(G-2342)
EPIC LANDSCAPE PRODUCTIONS LC
23933 W 175th St (66030-9362)
PHONE..................................913 856-0113
Don Chapman, *Principal*
Andrew Stith, *Prdtn Mgr*
Anne Spachman, *Human Res Dir*
Joel Grogan, *Accounts Mgr*
Kurtis Wenger, *Accounts Mgr*
EMP: 10
SALES (est): 1.6MM **Privately Held**
SIC: 0782 Landscape contractors

(G-2343)
FAITH VILLAGE INC
Also Called: Faith Village II
123 E Colleen Dr (66030-1281)
PHONE..................................913 856-4607
Tony Jones, *Manager*
EMP: 60
SALES (corp-wide): 126.8MM **Privately Held**
SIC: 8361 Home for the mentally handicapped
HQ: Faith Village Inc
14150 W 113th St
Olathe KS 66215
913 906-5000

(G-2344)
FIRST POINT URGENT CARE INC
907 E Lincoln Ln (66030-3701)
PHONE..................................913 856-1369
Carmen Boulevard, *Manager*
EMP: 10
SALES (corp-wide): 798K **Privately Held**
SIC: 8011 Freestanding emergency medical center
PA: First Point Urgent Care Inc
8144 Nw Prairie View Rd
Kansas City MO 64151
816 505-3669

(G-2345)
FIRST STUDENT INC
19450 S Gardner Rd (66030-9133)
PHONE..................................913 856-5650
Susan Leihy, *Branch Mgr*
EMP: 12
SALES (corp-wide): 9.1B **Privately Held**
WEB: www.firststudentinc.com
SIC: 4151 School buses
HQ: First Student, Inc.
600 Vine St Ste 1400
Cincinnati OH 45202

(G-2346)
FLYOVER INNOVATIONS INC
Also Called: Blumoo
622 E Meadowlark Pl (66030-1831)
PHONE..................................913 827-2248
Jason Carman, *CEO*
▲ **EMP:** 6
SQ FT: 2,000
SALES: 1MM **Privately Held**
SIC: 3651 Household audio & video equipment

(G-2347)
GARDNER ANIMAL HOSPITAL PA
945 E Santa Fe St (66030 1550)
PHONE..................................913 856-6255
Eileen E Mertz Dvm, *President*
Marguerite Ermeling, *Director*
EMP: 12
SQ FT: 2,160
SALES (est): 986.4K **Privately Held**
SIC: 0742 Animal hospital services, pets & other animal specialties

(G-2348)
GARDNER DENTAL CARE
971 E Lincoln Ln (66030-3701)
PHONE..................................913 856-7123
Paul Mabe DDS, *Owner*
EMP: 17
SALES (est): 973.4K **Privately Held**
WEB: www.gardnerdentalcare.com
SIC: 8021 Dentists' office

(G-2349)
GARDNER HOSPITALITY LLC
Also Called: Hampton Inn Gdnr Cnference Ctr
151 S Cedar Niles Rd (66030-8418)
PHONE..................................913 856-2100
Deepak Parmar, *Mng Member*
EMP: 35
SALES (est): 550.3K **Privately Held**
SIC: 7011 Hotels & motels

(G-2350)
HEARTLAND PLUMBING INC
800 Creekside Dr (66030-8408)
P.O. Box 422 (66030-0422)
PHONE..................................913 856-5846
Curt Longanecker, *President*
EMP: 12
SQ FT: 3,200
SALES (est): 2.3MM **Privately Held**
WEB: www.heartlandplumbing.com
SIC: 1711 Plumbing contractors

(G-2351)
ILLINOIS TOOL WORKS INC
Also Called: ITW Labels
147 Cherokee St (66030-1456)
PHONE..................................913 856-2546
Robert Lester, *Branch Mgr*
EMP: 36
SALES (corp-wide): 14.7B **Publicly Held**
SIC: 2679 Building, insulating & packaging paper
PA: Illinois Tool Works Inc.
155 Harlem Ave
Glenview IL 60025
847 724-7500

(G-2352)
L & M OIL COMPANY (PA)
Also Called: Dee's Mini-Mart
20315 S Gardner Rd (66030-9138)
PHONE..................................913 856-8502
Larry Pearce, *Owner*
EMP: 12
SQ FT: 1,500
SALES (est): 2.1MM **Privately Held**
SIC: 5172 5541 5411 7542 Gasoline; filling stations, gasoline; convenience stores, independent; carwash, self-service

(G-2353)
L & M OIL COMPANY
Also Called: Dee's Mini Mart
20315 S Gardner Rd (66030-9138)
PHONE..................................913 893-9789
Piara Siengh, *Owner*
EMP: 11
SALES (corp-wide): 2.1MM **Privately Held**
SIC: 5172 Gasoline
PA: L & M Oil Company
20315 S Gardner Rd
Gardner KS 66030
913 856-8502

(G-2354)
LITTLE BLDG BLOCKS DAYCARE LLC
813 E Lincoln Ln (66030-1594)
PHONE..................................913 856-5633
Misty Eaton, *Director*
Marcia Booton,
EMP: 12 **EST:** 2008
SALES (est): 301.9K **Privately Held**
SIC: 8351 Group day care center

(G-2355)
MID AMERICA PRODUCTS INC
800 N Center St (66030-9321)
PHONE..................................913 856-6550
Patrick Fiene, *President*
EMP: 205
SQ FT: 83,000
SALES (est): 2.1MM **Privately Held**
SIC: 3089 3544 3083 Injection molding of plastics; special dies, tools, jigs & fixtures; laminated plastics plate & sheet

(G-2356)
OAKBROOK ANIMAL HOSPITAL INC
500 W Main St (66030-1194)
PHONE..................................913 884-8778
Thomas Buckley, *President*
EMP: 11
SALES (est): 675.6K **Privately Held**
WEB: www.oakbrookanimalhospital.com
SIC: 0742 Animal hospital services, pets & other animal specialties

(G-2357)
OLATHE FORD SALES INC
Also Called: Olathe Ford R V Sales
19310 S Gardner Rd (66030-9132)
PHONE..................................913 856-8145
James Frum, *Manager*
Daryn Anderson, *Manager*
EMP: 22
SALES (corp-wide): 99MM **Privately Held**
SIC: 5511 7538 Automobiles, new & used; recreational vehicle repairs
PA: Ford Olathe Sales Inc
1845 E Santa Fe St
Olathe KS 66062
913 782-0881

(G-2358)
OPEN ARMS LTHRAN CHILD DEV CTR
306 E Madison St (66030-1833)
PHONE..................................913 856-4250
Sonjia Hermistein, *Principal*
EMP: 20
SALES (est): 238.1K **Privately Held**
SIC: 8351 Preschool center

(G-2359)
POWERHOUSE ELECTRIC INC
123 W Warren St (66030-1151)
P.O. Box 534 (66030-0534)
PHONE..................................913 856-4141
Claude Alexander, *President*
David Devlin, *Vice Pres*
EMP: 8
SQ FT: 2,400
SALES: 850K **Privately Held**
SIC: 3625 Electric controls & control accessories, industrial

(G-2360)
ROMERO CUSTOM
126 Circle Dr (66030-1102)
PHONE..................................913 548-3852
EMP: 10
SALES (est): 420K **Privately Held**
SIC: 1743 Tile/Marble Contractor

(G-2361)
SAMS FANTASTIC
315 N Moonlight Rd (66030-1943)
PHONE..................................913 856-4247
Jason Nokes, *Owner*
EMP: 15
SALES (est): 181.3K **Privately Held**
SIC: 7231 Unisex hair salons

(G-2362)
SANTA FE AC & RFRGN INC
1100 E Santa Fe St (66030-1502)
PHONE..................................913 856-5801
Duane Wood, *President*
Cris Wood, *Principal*
Sara Hill, *Vice Pres*
EMP: 16
SQ FT: 4,000
SALES (est): 3.2MM **Privately Held**
WEB: www.santafeair.com
SIC: 1711 Warm air heating & air conditioning contractor; refrigeration contractor

(G-2363)
SIGN HERE INC
558 W Main St (66030-1367)
PHONE..................................913 856-0148
David Fesenmeyer, *President*
EMP: 7 **EST:** 2000
SQ FT: 5,250
SALES: 1MM **Privately Held**
WEB: www.signhere.com
SIC: 3993 Electric signs

(G-2364)
SUPERIOR DISPOSAL SERVICE INC (PA)
447 N Cherry St (66030-1728)
PHONE..................................913 938-4552
Glen Smith, *President*
EMP: 14 **EST:** 2005
SALES (est): 8.6MM **Privately Held**
SIC: 4953 Garbage: collecting, destroying & processing; refuse collection & disposal services

(G-2365)
TRADENET PUBLISHING INC
1200 Energy Center Dr (66030-1599)
PHONE..................................913 856-4070
Tom Mertz, *President*
Brandon Fixsen, *Vice Pres*
Connie Riley, *CFO*
Chris Schlemmer, *Info Tech Dir*
◆ **EMP:** 125
SQ FT: 98,000
SALES (est): 29.5MM **Privately Held**
WEB: www.tradenetonline.com
SIC: 3993 Signs & advertising specialties

(G-2366)
TRI-COUNTY NEWSPAPERS INC
Also Called: Gardner News
936 E Santa Fe St (66030-1549)
P.O. Box 303 (66030-0303)
PHONE..................................913 856-7615
Rhonda Humble, *President*
Mark Humble, *Admin Sec*
EMP: 13
SALES (est): 94.9K **Privately Held**
WEB: www.gardnernews.com
SIC: 2711 Newspapers: publishing only, not printed on site

Garfield
Pawnee County

(G-2367)
SHAWNS FOUNDATIONS
762 Us Highway 56 (67529-2955)
PHONE..................................316 214-1070
EMP: 13
SALES (est): 487.5K **Privately Held**
SIC: 8641 Civic social & fraternal associations

Garnett
Anderson County

(G-2368)
ANDERSON COUNTY COUNCIL
128 W 5th Ave (66032-1322)
PHONE..................................785 448-4237
Patricia Ransey, *Bookkeeper*
EMP: 18
SALES (est): 410.6K **Privately Held**
SIC: 4789 Transportation services

(G-2369)
ANDERSON COUNTY SALES CO
Hwy 59 (66032)
P.O. Box 266 (66032-0266)
PHONE..................................785 448-3811
Max Ratliff, *Partner*
EMP: 15
SALES (est): 1.4MM **Privately Held**
SIC: 5154 Livestock

(G-2370)
BS CVF INC
Also Called: Bauman's Cedar Valley Farms
24161 Nw Kentucky Rd (66032-8291)
PHONE..................................785 448-2239
John Bauman, *President*
Rosanna Bauman, *Admin Sec*
EMP: 18 **EST:** 2011
SALES (est): 552.7K **Privately Held**
SIC: 0254 0291 Poultry hatcheries; livestock farm, general

(G-2371)
C & R WELL SERVICE
424 W 10th Ave (66032-1734)
PHONE..................................785 448-8792
EMP: 5
SALES (est): 300.2K **Privately Held**
SIC: 1389 Servicing oil & gas wells

(G-2372)
EAST KANSAS AGRI-ENERGY LLC
1304 S Main St (66032-2450)
PHONE..................................785 448-2888
Scott A Burkdoll, *Ch of Bd*
William R Pracht, *President*
Robert Taylor, *Plant Mgr*
Thomas D Leitnaker, *CFO*
Jill A Zimmerman, *Admin Sec*
EMP: 50
SALES: 100MM **Privately Held**
WEB: www.ekaellc.com
SIC: 2869 Ethyl alcohol, ethanol

(G-2373)
GARNETT PUBLISHING INC
Also Called: Anderson Countian
112 W 6th Ave (66032-1402)
P.O. Box 409 (66032-0409)
PHONE..................................785 448-3121
Dane Hicks, *President*
EMP: 13 **EST:** 1956
SQ FT: 2,750
SALES (est): 834.8K **Privately Held**
WEB: www.garnett-ks.com
SIC: 2711 2759 Newspapers: publishing only, not printed on site; letterpress printing

(G-2374)
GENCO MANUFACTURING
29128 N Highway 59 (66032-9516)
P.O. Box 321 (66032-0321)
PHONE..................................785 448-2501
Pete Gencarelli, *President*
Michael Gencarelli, *VP Sales*
EMP: 8
SALES (est): 1.3MM **Privately Held**
SIC: 3441 Fabricated structural metal

(G-2375)
GOPPERT STATE SERVICE BANK (PA)
Also Called: GSSB
106 E 5th Ave (66032-1514)
P.O. Box 329 (66032-0329)
PHONE..................................785 448-3111
Dwight Nelson, *President*
Kimberly Wuertz, *Officer*
Josh Smith, *Asst Broker*
EMP: 21 **EST:** 1899
SALES: 7.4MM **Privately Held**
SIC: 6022 State trust companies accepting deposits, commercial

(G-2376)
HAWKINS INC
1202 E 2nd Ave (66032-2454)
PHONE..................................785 448-1610
Ronald Hawkins, *Branch Mgr*
EMP: 21
SALES (corp-wide): 556.3MM **Publicly Held**
SIC: 8999 Chemical consultant
PA: Hawkins, Inc.
2381 Rosegate
Roseville MN 55113
612 331-6910

(G-2377)
HAYESBRAND MOLDING INC
614 S Oak St (66032-1433)
PHONE..................................913 238-0424
Cheryl Hayes, *President*
Gary Hayes, *Principal*
Marci Forster, *Vice Pres*
Jessica Whitham, *Vice Pres*
EMP: 12
SALES (est): 1.4MM **Privately Held**
SIC: 3089 Injection molding of plastics

(G-2378)
HOLDERMAN PRINTING LLC (PA)
110 W 4th Ave (66032-1314)
P.O. Box 403 (66032-0403)
PHONE..................................913 557-6848
Richard Holderman, *President*
Lynn Holderman, *Treasurer*
EMP: 6
SALES (est): 555K **Privately Held**
SIC: 2752 Commercial printing, lithographic

(G-2379)
JARIT MANUFACTURING INC
29128 N Highway 59 (66032-9516)
P.O. Box 321 (66032-0321)
PHONE..................................785 448-2501
Jay C Waltermire, *President*
Rita K Waltermire, *Admin Sec*
EMP: 8
SALES (est): 570K **Privately Held**
SIC: 3441 Fabricated structural metal

(G-2380)
LAKE GARNETT SPORTING CLUB
432 E 1st Ave (66032-1115)
PHONE..................................785 448-5803
Bill Dick, *President*
Jim Buckley, *Vice Pres*
Jack Eden, *Treasurer*
Joyce Buckley, *Admin Sec*
EMP: 5
SALES (est): 223.7K **Privately Held**
SIC: 3949 Targets, archery & rifle shooting

(G-2381)
LYBARGER OIL INC (PA)
704 N Maple St (66032-1077)
P.O. Box 99 (66032-0099)
PHONE..................................785 448-5512
David Lybarger, *President*
Betty J Lybarger, *Corp Secy*
Dennis Swartz, *CFO*
EMP: 19
SQ FT: 7,700
SALES (est): 13.6MM **Privately Held**
WEB: www.lybargeroil.com
SIC: 5172 Petroleum products

(G-2382)
MANOR OF GARNETT INC
Also Called: Golden Heights Living Center
101 N Pine St (66032-1134)
PHONE..................................785 448-2434
John Covault, *President*
Eldora Vetter, *Treasurer*
EMP: 52
SQ FT: 18,000
SALES: 3MM **Privately Held**
WEB: www.goldenheightslivingcenter.com
SIC: 8051 Convalescent home with continuous nursing care

(G-2383)
MILLER CONSTRUCTION
19324 Nw Highway 31 (66032-8307)
PHONE..................................785 448-6788
Everett Miller, *Owner*
EMP: 10
SALES (est): 470K **Privately Held**
SIC: 1521 1542 New construction, single-family houses; commercial & office building, new construction

(G-2384)
NATIONAL SOCIETY DAUGHTERS REV
Also Called: 4 Winds Chapter
417 W 6th Ave (66032-1407)
PHONE..................................785 448-5959
Alice Walker, *President*
Juanita Kellerman, *Principal*
Ruth Allen, *Vice Pres*
Agnes Carr, *Treasurer*
Betty Penn, *Admin Sec*
EMP: 20
SALES (est): 213.7K **Privately Held**
SIC: 8641 Social associations

(G-2385)
R & S PIPE SUPPLY LLC
210 S Catalpa St (66032-1934)
PHONE..................................785 448-5401
Russel Rickerson,
EMP: 12
SALES: 700K **Privately Held**
SIC: 3312 Pipes, iron & steel

(G-2386)
RICKERSON PIPE LINING LLC
210 S Catalpa St (66032-1934)
PHONE..................................785 448-5401
Brock Rickerson, *Owner*
EMP: 11
SALES (est): 2.3MM **Privately Held**
SIC: 2679 3494 Pipes & fittings, fiber: made from purchased material; pipe fittings

(G-2387)
ROBERT GIGSTAD
Also Called: Gigstad Hay Company
27718 Nw Indiana Rd (66032-8207)
PHONE..................................785 448-6923

Robert Gigstad, *Owner*
EMP: 22
SALES: 1.8MM **Privately Held**
SIC: 0139 0211 Hay farm; beef cattle feedlots

(G-2388)
SAINT LUKES HOSP GARNETT INC (PA)
Also Called: Anderson County Hospital
421 S Maple St (66032-1334)
P.O. Box 309 (66032-0309)
PHONE..................................785 448-3131
Dennis A Hachenberg, *CEO*
Beth Anderson, *Principal*
Vicki Mills, *CFO*
Karen Gillespie, *Human Res Dir*
Kelly Johnson, *Manager*
EMP: 190
SQ FT: 40,000
SALES: 19.6MM **Privately Held**
SIC: 8062 8051 4119 General medical & surgical hospitals; skilled nursing care facilities; ambulance service

(G-2389)
SOUTHEAST KANS MENTAL HLTH CTR
519 S Elm St (66032-1420)
PHONE..................................785 448-6806
Bob Chase, *Exec Dir*
EMP: 10
SALES (corp-wide): 8.3MM **Privately Held**
SIC: 8093 Mental health clinic, outpatient
PA: Southeast Kansas Mental Health Center
1106 S 9th St
Humboldt KS 66748
620 473-2241

(G-2390)
TAYLOR FORGE ENGINEERED
1312 S Maple St (66032-1743)
PHONE..................................785 448-6803
EMP: 30
SALES (corp-wide): 56.1MM **Privately Held**
SIC: 3443 Mfg Fabricated Steel & Plate Products
PA: Taylor Forge Engineered Systems, Inc.
208 N Iron St
Paola KS 66071
785 867-2590

Gas
Allen County

(G-2391)
MID-AMERICA MAINTENANCE KANSAS
117 N Stanley St (66742)
PHONE..................................620 365-3872
Buzz Biezunski, *President*
Cynthia Biezunski, *Vice Pres*
EMP: 15
SALES: 200K **Privately Held**
SIC: 7217 Carpet & upholstery cleaning

(G-2392)
NELSON QUARRIES INC
1307 2000 St (66742)
P.O. Box 100 (66742-0100)
PHONE..................................620 496-2211
Kenneth L Nelson, *President*
Dorothy A Hess, *Corp Secy*
EMP: 45 **EST:** 1932
SQ FT: 1,200
SALES (est): 752.8K **Privately Held**
SIC: 1422 0191 Crushed & broken limestone; general farms, primarily crop

Geneseo
Rice County

(G-2393)
KRATZER INDUSTRIES
Also Called: Clean Sweep,
603 10th St (67444-9002)
P.O. Box 300 (67444-0300)
PHONE..................................620 824-6405
Don Kratzer, *President*
Judith Kratzer, *Vice Pres*
EMP: 5
SALES: 150K **Privately Held**
SIC: 3559 Clay working & tempering machines

Girard
Crawford County

(G-2394)
ADVANCED MACHINE SOLUTIONS LLC
Also Called: Thomas Mfg
414 S Cherokee St (66743-1702)
P.O. Box 39 (66743-0039)
PHONE..................................620 724-6220
Steve Adamson, *Mng Member*
Justin Payne, *Mng Member*
Susan Thomas, *Mng Member*
EMP: 12
SQ FT: 12,500
SALES: 1.1MM **Privately Held**
SIC: 3535 Unit handling conveying systems

(G-2395)
CARE 4 U INC
207 E Prairie Ave (66743-1563)
PHONE..................................620 223-1411
Glen Pearson, *President*
EMP: 39 **EST:** 2014
SALES (est): 478.3K **Privately Held**
SIC: 8082 Home health care services

(G-2396)
CHALLENGER CONSTRUCTION CORP
Also Called: Challenger Hydroseeding
415 E Saint John St (66743-1363)
P.O. Box 216 (66743-0216)
PHONE..................................316 680-3036
Kevin Huber, *President*
EMP: 10 **EST:** 2011
SQ FT: 18,000
SALES (est): 388.4K **Privately Held**
SIC: 0782 Landscape contractors; mulching services, lawn; sprigging services, lawn

(G-2397)
COMMUNITY MNTL HLTH CTR CRWFD
Also Called: Addictn Treatmnt Ctr SE Kansas
810 Cedar St (66743-2056)
P.O. Box 37 (66743-0037)
PHONE..................................620 724-8806
Stacy Kraez, *Director*
EMP: 30
SALES (est): 529.6K **Privately Held**
SIC: 8093 8069 Mental health clinic, outpatient; specialty hospitals, except psychiatric

(G-2398)
COMMUNITY NATIONAL BANK
Also Called: Girard Banking Center
606 W Saint John St (66743-2001)
P.O. Box 326 (66743-0326)
PHONE..................................620 724-4446
Tony Stonerock, *Branch Mgr*
EMP: 12 **Privately Held**
SIC: 6022 State commercial banks
HQ: Community National Bank & Trust
14 N Lincoln Ave
Chanute KS 66720

(G-2399)
CRAW-KAN TELEPHONE COOP INC (PA)
200 N Ozark St (66743-1323)
P.O. Box 100 (66743-0100)
PHONE..................................620 724-8235
Toll Free:..................................888 -
Jerry James, *General Mgr*
EMP: 67 **EST:** 1952
SQ FT: 10,000
SALES: 30.6MM **Privately Held**
WEB: www.ckt.net
SIC: 4813 Local telephone communications

(G-2400)
CRAWFORD CNTY ASSISTD LVNG COM
Also Called: Westridge Apartments
950 W Saint John St (66743-2051)
PHONE..................................620 724-6760
Roger Brenermen, *President*
John Shireman, *Vice Pres*
EMP: 17
SALES (est): 745.9K **Privately Held**
SIC: 8361 Home for the aged

(G-2401)
DELANGE SEED HOUSE INC (PA)
537 W 47 Hwy (66743-2059)
P.O. Box 7 (66743-0007)
PHONE..................................620 724-6223
Howard F De Lange, *President*
Darrin De Lange, *Corp Secy*
Jill Delange, *Office Mgr*
EMP: 35
SQ FT: 5,750
SALES (est): 8.7MM **Privately Held**
SIC: 5191 Seeds: field, garden & flower

(G-2402)
DENCO ALUMINUM INC
109 E Southern Blvd (66743)
P.O. Box 156 (66743-0156)
PHONE..................................620 724-6325
Charles Denham, *President*
Tyler Denham, *Vice Pres*
Mary Patricia Denham, *Admin Sec*
EMP: 10
SQ FT: 13,000
SALES: 1.5MM **Privately Held**
SIC: 3365 Aluminum & aluminum-based alloy castings

(G-2403)
ETCO SPECIALTY PRODUCTS INC
621 W Saint John St (66743-2002)
P.O. Box 346 (66743-0346)
PHONE..................................620 724-6463
Steve Thompson, *President*
▲ **EMP:** 36
SQ FT: 36,000
SALES (est): 8.5MM **Privately Held**
WEB: www.etcospecialtyproducts.com
SIC: 3089 3643 3444 Plastic hardware & building products; current-carrying wiring devices; sheet metalwork

(G-2404)
EXPRESS YOURSELF DIGITAL
1706 Carline Rd (66743-2180)
PHONE..................................620 724-8389
Mark Mahar, *President*
Donald Kluge, *Vice Pres*
EMP: 5
SQ FT: 2,500
SALES (est): 406.8K **Privately Held**
SIC: 2395 Pleating & stitching

(G-2405)
FIRST NATIONAL BANK OF GIRARD
205 S Summit St (66743-1540)
P.O. Box 6 (66743-0006)
PHONE..................................620 724-6111
John W Lehman, *President*
Randy Bogts, *Exec VP*
Norma Storey, *Senior VP*
Brian Blythe, *Assistant VP*
EMP: 15
SQ FT: 4,000
SALES: 3.3MM **Privately Held**
SIC: 6021 National commercial banks

(G-2406)
GIRARD ANIMAL HOSPITAL PA
207 E Southern Blvd (66743-1736)
PHONE..................................620 724-6068
EMP: 10
SQ FT: 2,000
SALES (est): 1MM **Privately Held**
SIC: 0741 0742 Livestock And Pet Veterinarian

(G-2407)
GIRARD MEDICAL CENTER
804 W Saint John St (66743-2005)
PHONE..................................620 724-7288
Mike Payne, *Branch Mgr*
EMP: 100
SALES (est): 579K
SALES (corp-wide): 18.5MM **Privately Held**
SIC: 8062 General medical & surgical hospitals
PA: Girard Medical Center
302 N Hospital Dr
Girard KS 66743
620 724-8291

(G-2408)
GIRARD MEDICAL CENTER (PA)
Also Called: Hospital Dst 1 Crawford Cnty
302 N Hospital Dr (66743-2000)
PHONE..................................620 724-8291
Cheryl Giefer, *COO*
Pat Holt, *Safety Mgr*
Alice Grotheer, *Controller*
Stephanie Cheney, *Manager*
Joyce Geier, *Manager*
EMP: 76
SALES (est): 18.5MM **Privately Held**
SIC: 8062 General medical & surgical hospitals

(G-2409)
GIRARD NATIONAL BANK (HQ)
100 E Forest Ave (66743-1311)
P.O. Box 67 (66743-0067)
PHONE..................................620 724-8223
Martin Schifferdecker, *President*
Mark Schifferdecker, *President*
Jeff Smith, *Vice Pres*
Scott Missy, *Auditor*
Alan Koehler, *Technology*
EMP: 10 **EST:** 1929
SALES: 30.7MM **Privately Held**
WEB: www.gn-bank.com
SIC: 6021 National commercial banks

(G-2410)
GIRARD TARPS INC
411 W Saint John St (66743-1212)
P.O. Box 344 (66743-0344)
PHONE..................................620 724-8909
Lisa Franklin, *President*
Jerry Franklin, *Corp Secy*
EMP: 6
SQ FT: 5,000
SALES: 270K **Privately Held**
SIC: 2394 7699 Tarpaulins, fabric: made from purchased materials; liners & covers, fabric: made from purchased materials; tent repair shop

(G-2411)
HEARTLAND RURAL ELC COOP INC (PA)
110 Enterprise St (66743-2058)
P.O. Box 40 (66743-0040)
PHONE..................................620 724-8251
Toll Free:..................................888 -
Dale Coomes, *CEO*
Robert Stainbrook, *President*
Donald Davied, *Corp Secy*
Harry Oehlert, *Vice Pres*
EMP: 25
SALES: 25.1MM **Privately Held**
WEB: www.heartland-rec.com
SIC: 4911 Distribution, electric power

(G-2412)
HOME HEALTH AGENCY HOSP DST
Also Called: Girard Medical Center
804 W Saint John St (66743-2005)
PHONE..................................620 724-8469

Kenny Boyd, *Director*
EMP: 15 **EST:** 2002
SALES (est): 490K **Privately Held**
SIC: 8082 Home health care services

(G-2413)
HOSPITAL DISTRICT 1
302 N Hospital Dr (66743-2000)
PHONE....................620 724-8291
Rev Eldor Meyer, *Principal*
EMP: 43
SALES: 41.8K **Privately Held**
SIC: 8062 General medical & surgical hospitals

(G-2414)
KANSAS BUSINESS FORMS LLC
300 N Summit St (66743-1345)
PHONE....................620 724-5234
Jim Powell, *Treasurer*
Dough Diskin, *Mng Member*
Rick Buckle, *Mng Member*
EMP: 27 **EST:** 2001
SQ FT: 8,500
SALES: 3MM **Privately Held**
SIC: 2621 2761 5112 Business form paper; continuous forms, office & business; strip forms (manifold business forms); stationery & office supplies

(G-2415)
PRODUCERS COOP ASSN GIRARD (PA)
300 E Buffalo St (66743-1553)
P.O. Box 323 (66743-0323)
PHONE....................620 724-8241
Monte Hicks, *President*
EMP: 30 **EST:** 1948
SQ FT: 3,000
SALES (est): 24.4MM **Privately Held**
WEB: www.girardcoop.com
SIC: 5153 5999 0722 Grains; feed & farm supply; crop harvesting

(G-2416)
QUALITY MILLING LLC
309 E Saint John St (66743-1328)
P.O. Box 1008, Carthage MO (64836-5008)
PHONE....................620 724-4900
Doug Thornton,
Melissa Thornton,
EMP: 10
SALES (est): 1.7MM **Privately Held**
SIC: 2048 Prepared feeds

(G-2417)
SOUTHAST KANS RGNAL JVNILE DTN
270 Enterprise St (66743-2057)
P.O. Box 218 (66743-0218)
PHONE....................620 724-4174
Pat Barone, *Ch of Bd*
Dick Work, *Chairman*
Tami Cooper, *Manager*
EMP: 26
SALES: 1.2MM **Privately Held**
SIC: 8744 Correctional facility

(G-2418)
SOUTHEAST KANS EDUCATN SVC CTR (PA)
Also Called: Greenbush
947 W 47 Hwy (66743-2347)
P.O. Box 189 (66743-0189)
PHONE....................620 724-6281
Dave De Moss, *CEO*
David Demoss, *Superintendent*
Cinda Holmes, *Purchasing*
Roz Mosier, *Treasurer*
Melody Cherry, *Manager*
EMP: 120
SALES (est): 20MM **Privately Held**
SIC: 8299 8748 8211 Educational service, nondegree granting: continuing educ.; business consulting; elementary & secondary schools

(G-2419)
SOUTHEAST KANSAS COMMUNITY (PA)
Also Called: SEK-CAP
401 N Sinnett St (66743-1913)
P.O. Box 128 (66743-0128)
PHONE....................620 724-8204
Steven Lohr, *CEO*
Jeff Ervin, *CFO*
EMP: 35
SQ FT: 10,000
SALES: 13.8MM **Privately Held**
WEB: www.sek-cap.com
SIC: 8399 Community action agency; community development groups

(G-2420)
T W G NURSING HOME INC
Also Called: Heritage Nursing Home
511 N Western Ave (66743-1152)
PHONE....................620 724-8288
John Twarog, *President*
David Twarog, *Vice Pres*
John Twarog Jr, *Office Mgr*
EMP: 80
SQ FT: 35,000
SALES (est): 2.3MM **Privately Held**
SIC: 8051 Convalescent home with continuous nursing care

(G-2421)
THOMAS MANUFACTURING INC
414 S Cherokee St (66743-1702)
P.O. Box 39 (66743-0039)
PHONE....................620 724-6220
Francis Thomas, *President*
Susan Thomas, *Corp Secy*
EMP: 10
SQ FT: 12,000
SALES (est): 4.1MM **Privately Held**
WEB: www.thomasmanufacturing.com
SIC: 3535 3599 Conveyors & conveying equipment; custom machinery

Glasco
Cloud County

(G-2422)
NATURAL GAS PIPELINE AMER LLC
687 Deer Rd (67445-9320)
PHONE....................785 568-2231
Norris Andersen, *Manager*
EMP: 5 **Publicly Held**
SIC: 4922 1311 Natural gas transmission; crude petroleum & natural gas
HQ: Natural Gas Pipeline Company Of America Llc
1001 Louisiana St
Houston TX 77002
713 369-9000

(G-2423)
NICOL HOME INC
303 E Buffalo St (67445-9386)
PHONE....................785 568-2251
Tom Cummings, *Administration*
EMP: 40
SALES: 1.9MM **Privately Held**
SIC: 8052 Personal care facility

Glen Elder
Mitchell County

(G-2424)
CUNNINGHAM COMMUNICATIONS INC
Also Called: Cunningham Tele & Cable Svc
220 W Main St (67446-9795)
P.O. Box 108 (67446-0108)
PHONE....................785 545-3215
David Cunningham, *President*
John Cunningham, *Vice Pres*
Brenda Cunningham, *Admin Sec*
EMP: 15
SQ FT: 1,000
SALES (est): 1.4MM
SALES (corp-wide): 2.8MM **Privately Held**
SIC: 4813 Local & long distance telephone communications
PA: Cunningham Telephone Company Inc
220 W Main St
Glen Elder KS 67446
785 545-3215

(G-2425)
CUNNINGHAM TELEPHONE COMPANY (PA)
Also Called: Cunningham Tele & Cable Co
220 W Main St (67446-9795)
P.O. Box 108 (67446-0108)
PHONE....................785 545-3215
David B Cunningham, *President*
Brenda Cunningham, *Corp Secy*
John D Cunningham, *Vice Pres*
EMP: 14 **EST:** 1930
SQ FT: 56,000
SALES (est): 2.8MM **Privately Held**
SIC: 4813 Local telephone communications; local & long distance telephone communications

(G-2426)
JM TRAN-SPORT LLC
2275 200 Rd (67446-9494)
PHONE....................785 545-3756
EMP: 6
SALES (est): 350K **Privately Held**
SIC: 3799 Mfg Transportation Equipment

(G-2427)
MITCHELL COUNTY RUR WTR DST 2
109 E Kansas St (67446)
P.O. Box 17 (67446-0017)
PHONE....................785 545-3341
Carl Graff, *Manager*
EMP: 12
SALES (est): 808.6K **Privately Held**
SIC: 4941 Water supply

(G-2428)
WINKEL MANUFACTURING CO
2225a 200 Rd (67446-9494)
PHONE....................785 545-3297
Dorothy Winkel, *President*
Alan Winkel, *Vice Pres*
Paul Winkel, *Shareholder*
Roy Winkel, *Admin Sec*
EMP: 15 **EST:** 1952
SALES: 2.5MM **Privately Held**
SIC: 3523 Cattle feeding, handling & watering equipment

Goddard
Sedgwick County

(G-2429)
AMERICAN UNDERWRITERS LF INSUR (PA)
1035 S 183rd St W (67052-9215)
P.O. Box 9510, Wichita (67277-0510)
PHONE....................316 794-2200
R Kell Hawkins, *President*
Norma J Hawkins, *Corp Secy*
Ron Kell Hawkins, *Exec VP*
Bruce Welner, *Vice Pres*
EMP: 64
SQ FT: 13,000
SALES (est): 8.7MM **Privately Held**
SIC: 6411 Life insurance agents

(G-2430)
C & H TRUCKING LLC
18333 W 39th St S (67052-8254)
PHONE....................316 794-8282
Vickie Berg, *Mng Member*
Don Klausmeyer,
EMP: 12
SALES (est): 828.9K **Privately Held**
SIC: 4212 4213 Local trucking, without storage; trucking, except local

(G-2431)
C BAR P TRUCKING INC
20707 W 21st St N (67052-9145)
PHONE....................316 722-2019
Chris Petz, *President*
EMP: 30
SALES (est): 2.4MM **Privately Held**
SIC: 4212 Local trucking, without storage

(G-2432)
CIRCLE C PAVING AND CNSTR LLC
630 Industrial Rd (67052-7009)
P.O. Box 361 (67052-0361)
PHONE....................316 794-5070
Chad Alexander, *Principal*
Chris Alexander, *Principal*
Rachel Correll, *Principal*
Chris Baalmann, *Project Mgr*
EMP: 32
SALES (est): 131.8K **Privately Held**
SIC: 1611 Surfacing & paving

(G-2433)
CONVERTING TECHNOLOGIES INC
Also Called: Contech
1756 S 151st St W (67052-9449)
PHONE....................316 722-6907
Debra Ogden, *President*
Max Ogden, *Vice Pres*
Mike Salsgiver, *Vice Pres*
Gary Wolfe, *Engineer*
George Olson, *Sales Engr*
▲ **EMP:** 19
SQ FT: 30,000
SALES (est): 5.9MM **Privately Held**
WEB: www.contechusa.com
SIC: 3549 3089 3559 Metalworking machinery; laminating of plastic; plastics working machinery

(G-2434)
CREATIVE PARADISE INC
415 Industrial Rd (67052-7008)
P.O. Box 734 (67052-0734)
PHONE....................316 794-8621
Stephanie O'Toole, *President*
▼ **EMP:** 14
SQ FT: 24,000
SALES (est): 1.1MM **Privately Held**
WEB: www.creativeparadise.com
SIC: 3544 Forms (molds), for foundry & plastics working machinery

(G-2435)
CUSTOM FLATWORK INC
18333 W 39th St S (67052-8254)
PHONE....................316 794-8282
Vicki Berg, *President*
EMP: 15
SALES (est): 1.4MM **Privately Held**
SIC: 1771 Concrete work

(G-2436)
DOVE ESTATES SENIOR LIVING
1400 S 83rd St W (67052)
PHONE....................316 550-6343
Dianne Jilby, *Mng Member*
Jill Steiner, *Mng Member*
EMP: 50
SQ FT: 73,000
SALES (est): 594.3K **Privately Held**
SIC: 8322 8361 Old age assistance; home for the aged

(G-2437)
EMPRISE BANK
701 N Goddard Rd (67052-8861)
PHONE....................316 794-2258
EMP: 11
SALES (corp-wide): 80MM **Privately Held**
SIC: 6022 State trust companies accepting deposits, commercial
HQ: Emprise Bank
257 N Broadway Ave
Wichita KS 67202
316 383-4400

(G-2438)
EPIC INSULATION INC
17600 W Highview Dr (67052-7701)
P.O. Box 253 (67052-0253)
PHONE....................316 500-1650
Cristy Goodwin, *Owner*
Jason Goodwin, *Owner*
EMP: 16
SALES: 1MM **Privately Held**
SIC: 1742 7389 Insulation, buildings; acoustical & insulation work;

GEOGRAPHIC

(G-2439)
GLOBAL ENGINEERING & TECH INC
1720 S 151st St W (67052-9449)
P.O. Box 780787, Wichita (67278-0787)
PHONE.................................316 729-9232
Delores A Nevin, *CEO*
Finley Nevin, *President*
Shawn Dixon, *Prdtn Mgr*
Bill Hudnall, *QC Mgr*
EMP: 145
SQ FT: 37,000
SALES (est): 25.6MM **Privately Held**
SIC: 3728 2434 7389 Aircraft parts & equipment; wood kitchen cabinets; design services

(G-2440)
GODDARD PUBLIC SCHOOLS
Also Called: Goddard Intermediate Lrng Ctr
335 N Walnut St (67052-9548)
P.O. Box 277 (67052-0277)
PHONE.................................316 794-2281
Jill Hackett, *Principal*
EMP: 40
SALES (corp-wide): 27.7MM **Privately Held**
SIC: 8211 8351 Public elementary & secondary schools; child day care services
PA: Goddard Public Schools
201 S Main St
Goddard KS 67052
316 794-4000

(G-2441)
GODDARD VETERINARY CLINIC
19912 W Kellogg Dr (67052-9300)
P.O. Box 735 (67052-0735)
PHONE.................................316 794-8022
Jack Reynolds, *Owner*
EMP: 15
SQ FT: 930
SALES (est): 521.1K **Privately Held**
SIC: 0741 0742 Veterinarian, livestock; animal hospital services, pets & other animal specialties

(G-2442)
HOLST MACHINE SHOP
18621 W 39th St S (67052-8215)
PHONE.................................316 794-8477
Carsten Holst, *Owner*
EMP: 12
SQ FT: 2,100
SALES (est): 1.1MM **Privately Held**
SIC: 3599 Machine shop, jobbing & repair

(G-2443)
INTER-AMERICAS INSURANCE CORP (PA)
1035 S 183rd St W (67052-9215)
P.O. Box 9510, Wichita (67277-0510)
PHONE.................................316 794-2200
R Kell Hawkins, *President*
Robert Kell Hawkins, *President*
Norma J Hawkins, *Corp Secy*
Ronald J Hawkins, *Exec VP*
Misti Davis, *Clerk*
EMP: 87
SQ FT: 13,000
SALES (est): 16.2MM **Privately Held**
WEB: www.cuicauto.com
SIC: 6411 Insurance agents

(G-2444)
KINGS CAMP & RETREAT CENTER
24401 W 39th St S (67052-8713)
P.O. Box 215 (67052-0215)
PHONE.................................316 794-2913
Fax: 316 794-2773
EMP: 50
SALES (est): 749.9K **Privately Held**
SIC: 7032 Sporting And Recreational Camps, Nsk

(G-2445)
LANDWEHR MACHINE
Also Called: I-Machine
2100 S 231st St W (67052-9189)
P.O. Box 442 (67052-0442)
PHONE.................................316 794-3390
Mike Landwehr, *Owner*
INA Landwehr, *Co-Owner*
EMP: 5
SQ FT: 3,600
SALES (est): 467.8K **Privately Held**
SIC: 3599 Machine shop, jobbing & repair

(G-2446)
MEDICALODGES INC
Also Called: Medicalodge of Goddard
501 Easy St (67052-9211)
PHONE.................................316 794-8635
Shannon Lager, *Branch Mgr*
EMP: 63
SALES (corp-wide): 100.2MM **Privately Held**
WEB: www.medicalodges.com
SIC: 8051 8052 Convalescent home with continuous nursing care; intermediate care facilities
PA: Medicalodges, Inc.
201 W 8th St
Coffeyville KS 67337
620 251-6700

(G-2447)
NELSON ELECTRIC INC
1200 N 199th St W (67052-8811)
P.O. Box 848 (67052-0848)
PHONE.................................316 794-8025
Phil Nelson, *Mng Member*
EMP: 12
SALES: 1.2MM **Privately Held**
SIC: 1731 Electric power systems contractors; general electrical contractor

(G-2448)
NORRIS COLLISION CENTER LLC
19918 W Kellogg Dr (67052-9300)
PHONE.................................316 794-1161
Jeremy Edwards, *Manager*
EMP: 10 **EST:** 2005
SALES (est): 1MM **Privately Held**
SIC: 7532 7536 Paint shop, automotive; automotive glass replacement shops

(G-2449)
NOWAK CONSTRUCTION CO INC
200 S Goddard Rd (67052-8923)
P.O. Box 218 (67052-0218)
PHONE.................................316 794-8898
Joe Nowak, *President*
John G Nowak, *Treasurer*
Jeff Murphy, *Manager*
Greg Post, *Manager*
EMP: 87
SQ FT: 6,000
SALES (est): 21.8MM **Privately Held**
WEB: www.nowakconstruction.com
SIC: 1623 Water main construction; sewer line construction; pipeline construction

(G-2450)
NOWAK PIPE REAMING INC
200 S Goddard Rd (67052-8923)
P.O. Box 218 (67052-0218)
PHONE.................................316 794-8898
John Nowak, *President*
EMP: 85 **EST:** 2001
SALES (est): 3MM **Privately Held**
WEB: www.pipereaming.com
SIC: 4619 Coal pipeline operation

(G-2451)
NUTRIEN AG SOLUTIONS INC
530 Industrial Rd (67052-7006)
PHONE.................................316 794-2231
Jason Trent, *Manager*
EMP: 10 **Privately Held**
WEB: www.cropproductionservices.com
SIC: 5191 Fertilizer & fertilizer materials
HQ: Nutrien Ag Solutions, Inc.
3005 Rocky Mountain Ave
Loveland CO 80538
970 685-3300

(G-2452)
PERINATAL CONSULTANTS PA
15315 W Hendryx St (67052-5205)
PHONE.................................785 354-5952
John Evans, *Owner*
EMP: 11
SALES (est): 484.7K **Privately Held**
SIC: 8748 Business consulting

(G-2453)
ROYAL FLUSH PLUMBING LLC
5500 S 231st St W (67052-8992)
P.O. Box 352 (67052-0352)
PHONE.................................316 794-2656
Jolene Hernden, *Corp Secy*
Mark Herndon,
EMP: 10
SALES: 1.2MM **Privately Held**
SIC: 1711 7629 Plumbing contractors; electrical household appliance repair

(G-2454)
S&S LIMOUSINE LLC
24401 W 39th St S (67052-8713)
PHONE.................................316 794-3340
EMP: 10
SALES (est): 260K **Privately Held**
SIC: 4119 Local Passenger Transportation

(G-2455)
UNIVERSAL PRODUCTS INC
521 Industrial Rd (67052-7002)
P.O. Box 332 (67052-0332)
PHONE.................................316 794-8601
Randy Morriss, *President*
Mark Wasinger, *Warehouse Mgr*
Missy Daley, *Production*
Deborah Morrison, *Treasurer*
Betty Danahy, *Sales Staff*
▲ **EMP:** 171 **EST:** 1977
SQ FT: 165,000
SALES (est): 31.6MM **Privately Held**
WEB: www.u-p.com
SIC: 2759 5113 Screen printing; industrial & personal service paper

(G-2456)
WALMART INC
18631 W Kellogg Dr (67052-9221)
PHONE.................................316 347-2092
Joey Ritchie, *Branch Mgr*
EMP: 283
SQ FT: 120,243
SALES (corp-wide): 514.4B **Publicly Held**
SIC: 5311 7384 Department stores, discount; photofinish laboratories
PA: Walmart Inc.
702 Sw 8th St
Bentonville AR 72716
479 273-4000

(G-2457)
XPRESSOTECH SOLUTIONS LLC
18500 W 2nd Cir N (67052-8708)
PHONE.................................316 993-9397
Tim Kerr,
EMP: 10
SALES (est): 239.3K **Privately Held**
SIC: 7371 Computer software development

Goessel
Marion County

(G-2458)
MENNONITE BETHESDA SOCIETY
Also Called: BETHESDA HOME
408 E Main St (67053-5302)
P.O. Box 37 (67053-0037)
PHONE.................................620 367-2291
Eric Schrag, *President*
Sally Thiesen, *QC Dir*
Vicki Conn, *VP Finance*
Gloria Rediger, *Marketing Staff*
Barb Abrahams, *Info Tech Mgr*
EMP: 80
SALES: 4.5MM **Privately Held**
WEB: www.bethesdahome.org
SIC: 8051 Skilled nursing care facilities

Goodland
Sherman County

(G-2459)
ADM TRUCKING INC
6425 Road 14 (67735-9023)
PHONE.................................785 899-6500
Steve Boshoff, *Branch Mgr*
EMP: 14
SALES (corp-wide): 64.3B **Publicly Held**
SIC: 4213 Trucking, except local
HQ: Adm Trucking, Inc.
2501 N Brush College Rd
Decatur IL 62526
217 424-5200

(G-2460)
AG POWER EQUIPMENT CO
124 W Hwy 24 (67735-9642)
P.O. Box 249, Sharon Springs (67758-0249)
PHONE.................................785 899-3432
Curt Parker, *General Mgr*
Alex Howard, *Parts Mgr*
Lynn Stover, *Branch Mgr*
EMP: 12
SALES (corp-wide): 7.8MM **Privately Held**
SIC: 5083 Agricultural machinery & equipment
PA: Ag Power Equipment Co
1385 Kansas 27
Sharon Springs KS 67758
785 852-4235

(G-2461)
AMERICAL INC
Also Called: Super 8 Motel
2520 Commerce Rd (67735-9747)
PHONE.................................785 890-7566
Jacquie Benessoni, *Manager*
EMP: 12
SALES (corp-wide): 2.2MM **Privately Held**
SIC: 7011 Hotels & motels
PA: Americal Inc
500 S Boyd St
Aberdeen SD 57401
605 226-3163

(G-2462)
ARCHER-DANIELS-MIDLAND COMPANY
Also Called: ADM
6425 Road 14 (67735-9023)
PHONE.................................785 899-3700
Steve Bosshoff, *Branch Mgr*
EMP: 50
SALES (corp-wide): 64.3B **Publicly Held**
WEB: www.admworld.com
SIC: 2041 0723 Flour & other grain mill products; crop preparation services for market
PA: Archer-Daniels-Midland Company
77 W Wacker Dr Ste 4600
Chicago IL 60601
312 634-8100

(G-2463)
BANKWEST OF KANSAS (PA)
924 Main Ave (67735-2941)
P.O. Box 499 (67735-0499)
PHONE.................................785 899-2342
Linda Goodland, *President*
Tom Murrphy, *Vice Pres*
Mel Pfau, *Vice Pres*
Michael Wiens, *Branch Mgr*
EMP: 45
SALES: 5.9MM **Privately Held**
SIC: 6022 State commercial banks

(G-2464)
CITY GOODLAND INSPECTION DEPT
204 W 11th St (67735-2840)
P.O. Box 59 (67735-0059)
PHONE.................................785 890-4500
Fax: 785 899-4532
EMP: 56
SALES (est): 66.5K **Privately Held**
SIC: 7389 Business Services

▲ = Import ▼=Export
◆ =Import/Export

(G-2465)
CITY OF GOODLAND
Also Called: Goodland Municipal Power Plant
1701 Cherry Ave (67735-3251)
P.O. Box 59 (67735-0059)
PHONE..................................785 890-4555
Chuck Luthers, *Manager*
EMP: 12 **Privately Held**
WEB: www.goodlandkansas.net
SIC: 4911 Electric services
PA: City Of Goodland
316 W 11th St
Goodland KS 67735
785 899-2318

(G-2466)
COLLINGWOOD GRAIN INC
17 Wyoming (67735)
PHONE..................................785 899-3636
Darel Pattey, *Manager*
EMP: 85 **EST:** 1995
SALES (est): 40.7MM
SALES (corp-wide): 64.3B **Publicly Held**
WEB: www.collingwoodgrain.com
SIC: 5172 Petroleum products
PA: Archer-Daniels-Midland Company
77 W Wacker Dr Ste 4600
Chicago IL 60601
312 634-8100

(G-2467)
COUNTY OF SHERMAN
Also Called: Goodland Regional Medical Ctr
220 W 2nd St (67735-1602)
PHONE..................................785 890-3625
Tracey Purvis, *Safety Dir*
Jennie Klinge, *Opers Staff*
Sara Townsend, *Purch Dir*
Marilyn Hanson, *Human Res Dir*
Heather Frisbie, *Anesthesiology*
EMP: 22 **Privately Held**
SIC: 8062 9431 General medical & surgical hospitals;
PA: County Of Sherman
813 Broadway Ave Ste 7
Goodland KS 67735
785 890-4810

(G-2468)
EAGLE MED INC
Also Called: Ballard Aviation
217 E 10th St (67735-3003)
PHONE..................................785 899-3810
Jim Ballard, *President*
EMP: 12
SALES (est): 558.4K **Privately Held**
SIC: 4522 Ambulance services, air

(G-2469)
EVANGELICAL LUTHERAN
Also Called: Good Smrtan Soc - Sherman Cnty
208 W 2nd St (67735-1660)
P.O. Box 5038, Sioux Falls SD (57117-5038)
PHONE..................................785 890-7517
Mary Callahan, *Chf Purch Ofc*
Anna Mannis, *Administration*
EMP: 60 **Privately Held**
WEB: www.good-sam.com
SIC: 8059 Nursing home, except skilled & intermediate care facility
HQ: The Evangelical Lutheran Good Samaritan Society
4800 W 57th St
Sioux Falls SD 57108
866 928-1635

(G-2470)
FEDEX FREIGHT CORPORATION
666 E 19th St (67735-9600)
PHONE..................................888 880-1320
EMP: 13
SALES (corp-wide): 69.6B **Publicly Held**
SIC: 4789 Freight car loading & unloading
HQ: Fedex Freight Corporation
1715 Aaron Brenner Dr
Memphis TN 38120

(G-2471)
FIRST NATIONAL BANK (HQ)
202 E 11th St (67735-3006)
P.O. Box 570 (67735-0570)
PHONE..................................785 890-2000
Lawrence L McCants, *President*
Kermit Bear, *Senior VP*
Peggy Hanke, *Senior VP*
Jim Lunsway, *Senior VP*
Janet Mehling, *Senior VP*
EMP: 55 **EST:** 1886
SQ FT: 5,000
SALES: 9.3MM **Privately Held**
WEB: www.fnb.com
SIC: 6021 National commercial banks

(G-2472)
FRONTIER AG INC
1201 W Us Highway 24 (67735-8700)
P.O. Box 998 (67735-0998)
PHONE..................................785 734-7011
Brad Cowan, *Branch Mgr*
EMP: 25 **Privately Held**
SIC: 5153 Grain elevators
PA: Frontier Ag, Inc.
415 W 2nd St
Oakley KS 67748

(G-2473)
GENESEE & WYOMING INC
1801 Main Ave (67735-2972)
PHONE..................................785 899-2307
Dan Lovelady, *Manager*
EMP: 10
SALES (corp-wide): 2.3B **Privately Held**
SIC: 4011 Railroads, line-haul operating
PA: Genesee & Wyoming Inc.
20 West Ave
Darien CT 06820
203 202-8900

(G-2474)
GOODLAND MACHINE & AUTO LLC
419 E 19th St (67735-9633)
PHONE..................................785 899-6628
Pam Mendelhall, *Office Mgr*
Terry Selbe, *Mng Member*
EMP: 6
SALES (est): 729.3K **Privately Held**
SIC: 5999 7538 3599 Farm equipment & supplies; engine rebuilding: automotive; machine shop, jobbing & repair

(G-2475)
HAYNES PUBLISHING CO
Also Called: Goodland Star News, The
1205 Main Ave (67735-2946)
PHONE..................................785 899-2338
Steve Haynes, *Manager*
EMP: 20
SALES (corp-wide): 3.3MM **Privately Held**
SIC: 2711 Newspapers, publishing & printing
PA: Haynes Publishing Co
170 S Penn Ave
Oberlin KS 67749
785 475-2206

(G-2476)
HELENA AGRI-ENTERPRISES LLC
6409 Road 25 (67735-8924)
PHONE..................................785 899-2391
Bob Stewart, *Manager*
EMP: 10 **Privately Held**
WEB: www.helenachemical.com
SIC: 5191 Fertilizers & agricultural chemicals
HQ: Helena Agri-Enterprises, Llc
255 Schilling Blvd # 300
Collierville TN 38017
901 761-0050

(G-2477)
HERITAGE HEALTHCARE MANAGEMENT
Also Called: Goodland Assisted Living
707 Wheat Ridge Cir Ofc (67735-2259)
PHONE..................................785 899-0100
David Beardsley, *President*
Judy Goodwin, *Manager*
EMP: 15
SALES (est): 402K **Privately Held**
SIC: 8059 Nursing home, except skilled & intermediate care facility

(G-2478)
HOLIDAY INN EXPRESS
2631 Enterprise Rd (67735-9700)
PHONE..................................785 890-9060
Mat Hughes, *Manager*
EMP: 19
SALES (est): 690.6K **Privately Held**
SIC: 7011 Hotels & motels

(G-2479)
KCOE ISOM LLP
520 Main Ave Ste 1 (67735-1855)
P.O. Box 187 (67735-0187)
PHONE..................................785 899-3676
Larry Lewis, *Partner*
Barbara Abbot, *Manager*
EMP: 16
SALES (corp-wide): 48MM **Privately Held**
WEB: www.kcoe.com
SIC: 8721 Certified public accountant
PA: Kcoe Isom, Llp
3030 Courtland Cir
Salina KS
785 825-1561

(G-2480)
NATIONAL WEATHER SERVICE
920 Armory Rd (67735-9273)
PHONE..................................785 899-2360
Scot Menszer, *Manager*
EMP: 21 **Publicly Held**
SIC: 8999 9611 Weather forecasting; administration of general economic programs;
HQ: National Weather Service
1325 E West Hwy
Silver Spring MD 20910

(G-2481)
ORSCHELN FARM AND HOME LLC
2021 Enterprise Rd (67735-9703)
PHONE..................................785 899-7132
Jerry Freeman, *Manager*
EMP: 10
SALES (corp-wide): 822.7MM **Privately Held**
WEB: www.orschelnfarmhome.com
SIC: 5191 Farm supplies
PA: Orscheln Farm And Home Llc
1800 Overcenter Dr
Moberly MO 65270
800 577-2580

(G-2482)
RES-CARE INC
Also Called: Golden West Community Services
1080 Aspen Rd (67735)
PHONE..................................785 899-2322
Meripat Bowman, *Manager*
EMP: 34
SALES (corp-wide): 2B **Privately Held**
WEB: www.rescare.com
SIC: 8082 Home health care services
HQ: Res-Care, Inc.
805 N Whittington Pkwy
Louisville KY 40222
502 394-2100

(G-2483)
RES-CARE KANSAS INC
108 Aspen Rd (67735-1508)
PHONE..................................785 728-7198
EMP: 49
SALES (corp-wide): 2B **Privately Held**
SIC: 8052 Intermediate care facilities
HQ: Res-Care Kansas, Inc.
5031 Matney Ave
Kansas City KS 66106
913 342-9426

(G-2484)
S & B MOTELS INC
Also Called: Comfort Inn
2519 Enterprise Rd (67735-9768)
PHONE..................................785 899-7181
Judy Siruta, *General Mgr*
Starla Kennedy, *Manager*
EMP: 20
SALES (est): 828.1K
SALES (corp-wide): 12MM **Privately Held**
SIC: 7011 Hotels & motels
PA: S & B Motels, Inc.
400 N Woodlawn St Ste 205
Wichita KS 67208
316 522-3864

(G-2485)
S & T TELEPHONE COOP ASSN
1318 Main Ave (67735-2949)
P.O. Box 90 (67735-0090)
PHONE..................................785 890-7400
Gary Slough, *Branch Mgr*
EMP: 20
SALES (corp-wide): 19MM **Privately Held**
SIC: 4813 Telephone communication, except radio
PA: S & T Telephone Cooperative Association
320 Kansas Ave
Brewster KS 67732
785 694-2256

(G-2486)
SCHLOSSER INC
Also Called: Schlosser Ready Mix
1301 W 25th (67735)
P.O. Box 635 (67735-0635)
PHONE..................................785 899-6535
Gary Schlosser, *President*
EMP: 8
SALES (corp-wide): 1.4MM **Privately Held**
WEB: www.schlosser.com
SIC: 3273 Ready-mixed concrete
PA: Schlosser Inc
755 Us Highway 385
Burlington CO 80807
719 346-8806

(G-2487)
SUGAR HILLS GOLF CLUB INC
6450 Road 16 (67735-9056)
PHONE..................................785 899-2785
Randy Topliss, *President*
Duane Harper, *Vice Pres*
Jackie Elliott, *Admin Sec*
EMP: 20 **EST:** 1968
SALES: 249.3K **Privately Held**
SIC: 7997 7992 Country club, membership; golf club, membership; public golf courses

(G-2488)
T-BONE FEEDERS INC
1751 Road 65 (67735-9052)
P.O. Box 733 (67735-0733)
PHONE..................................785 899-6551
Harlan D House, *President*
Cora House, *Shareholder*
EMP: 12
SQ FT: 1,000
SALES (est): 1.8MM **Privately Held**
WEB: www.t-bonefeeders.com
SIC: 0211 Beef cattle feedlots

(G-2489)
WALMART INC
2160 Commerce Rd (67735-9776)
PHONE..................................785 899-2111
Karen Isaac, *Human Res Mgr*
Laura Pope, *Manager*
EMP: 205
SQ FT: 111,696
SALES (corp-wide): 514.4B **Publicly Held**
WEB: www.walmartstores.com
SIC: 5311 5411 7384 Department stores, discount; supermarkets, hypermarket; photofinishing laboratory
PA: Walmart Inc.
702 Sw 8th St
Bentonville AR 72716
479 273-4000

(G-2490)
WEATHERCRAFT COMPANY N PLATTE
Also Called: Overhead Door Company NW Kans
716 W Hwy 24 (67735-9636)
P.O. Box 555 (67735-0555)
PHONE..................................785 899-3064
Randy Topliff, *Manager*
EMP: 7
SALES (corp-wide): 9.6MM **Privately Held**
SIC: 5211 3699 Door & window products; door opening & closing devices, electrical

PA: Weathercraft Company Of North Platte
2401 E 8th St
North Platte NE 69101
308 534-3480

(G-2491)
WESTERN STATE BANK
815 Center Ave (67735-2930)
P.O. Box 539 (67735-0539)
PHONE..................................785 899-2393
Stephen West, *Manager*
EMP: 11
SALES (corp-wide): 21.8MM **Privately Held**
WEB: www.wsbks.com
SIC: 6022 6162 State trust companies accepting deposits, commercial; mortgage bankers & correspondents
PA: Western State Bank
1500 E Kansas Ave
Garden City KS 67846
620 275-4128

Gorham
Russell County

(G-2492)
YOST ELECTRIC INC
4212 176th St (67640-9023)
P.O. Box 165 (67640-0165)
PHONE..................................785 637-5454
Chuck Yost, *President*
Terri Yost, *Treasurer*
EMP: 6 **EST:** 1978
SALES (est): 617.5K **Privately Held**
WEB: www.yostelectric.com
SIC: 1731 7694 General electrical contractor; armature rewinding shops

Gove
Gove County

(G-2493)
FAITH TECHNOLOGIES INC
Also Called: Smoky Hill Ranch
1164 County Road 54 (67736-6032)
PHONE..................................785 938-4499
Michelle Schwanke, *Branch Mgr*
EMP: 282
SALES (corp-wide): 773.3MM **Privately Held**
SIC: 1731 General electrical contractor
PA: Faith Technologies, Inc.
225 Main St
Menasha WI 54952
920 738-1500

Grainfield
Gove County

(G-2494)
B & B OIL TOOLS CO LLC
806 Main St (67737)
P.O. Box 166 (67737-0166)
PHONE..................................785 673-4828
Jerry Brown,
Debra Brown,
EMP: 5
SALES (est): 290K **Privately Held**
SIC: 1389 Oil field services

(G-2495)
M & A BARNETT TRUCKING INC
218 Main St (67737-3734)
P.O. Box 145 (67737-0145)
PHONE..................................785 673-4700
Rodney Haffner, *President*
Kay Haffner, *Admin Sec*
EMP: 17
SQ FT: 500
SALES (est): 1.7MM **Privately Held**
SIC: 4213 Trucking, except local

(G-2496)
SHAW MOTOR CO INC
Hwy Jct I 70 & K 23 (67737)
P.O. Box 178 (67737-0178)
PHONE..................................785 673-4228
Curtis Shaw, *President*
Herman Zerr, *President*
Dean Shaw, *Corp Secy*
EMP: 10
SQ FT: 2,000
SALES (est): 2.3MM **Privately Held**
SIC: 5511 5083 5541 Automobiles, new & used; pickups, new & used; agricultural machinery & equipment; gasoline service stations

Grantville
Jefferson County

(G-2497)
MC PHERSON WRECKING INC (PA)
2333 Barton Rd (66429-9246)
PHONE..................................785 246-3012
Virgil Mc Pherson, *President*
Scott McPherson, *Treasurer*
EMP: 17 **EST:** 1966
SQ FT: 7,500
SALES (est): 2.3MM **Privately Held**
SIC: 1795 Demolition, buildings & other structures

(G-2498)
START TO FINISH CELEBRATION
3736 South St (66429-9319)
PHONE..................................785 364-2257
Rose Souter, *Principal*
EMP: 10
SALES (est): 230K **Privately Held**
SIC: 8351 Child day care services

Great Bend
Barton County

(G-2499)
AARONS REPAIR & SUPPLY INC
170 Sw 40 Ave (67530-9737)
PHONE..................................620 792-5361
Aaron Maresch, *President*
EMP: 6 **EST:** 1978
SALES: 700K **Privately Held**
SIC: 3599 3559 Machine shop, jobbing & repair; plastics working machinery

(G-2500)
ADAMS BROWN BRAN BALL CHRTERED (PA)
2006 Broadway Ave (67530-4042)
P.O. Box J (67530-8010)
PHONE..................................620 549-3271
Terrance W Brown, *President*
Rex Ball, *Vice Pres*
Richard A Ball, *Vice Pres*
Kenneth Beren, *Vice Pres*
Kim Hullman, *Vice Pres*
EMP: 17
SALES (est): 9.4MM **Privately Held**
SIC: 8721 8111 Certified public accountant; legal services

(G-2501)
ADVANCED THERAPY & SPT MED LLC
Also Called: Advance Therapy & Spt Medicine
4801 10th St (67530-3252)
PHONE..................................620 792-7868
Kevyn Soupiset, *Mng Member*
EMP: 18
SALES: 3.2MM **Privately Held**
SIC: 8049 Physical therapist

(G-2502)
ALCOHOLICS ANONYMOUS
1620 Hubbard St (67530-4137)
PHONE..................................620 793-3962
Bud Arnold, *President*
EMP: 50
SALES (est): 527.4K **Privately Held**
SIC: 8322 Alcoholism counseling, nontreatment

(G-2503)
ALLIED OF KANSAS INC
N Main St (67530)
P.O. Box 628 (67530-0628)
PHONE..................................620 793-5861
Norman Dreiling, *Manager*
EMP: 6
SALES (corp-wide): 8.1MM **Privately Held**
SIC: 1389 Cementing oil & gas well casings
PA: Allied Of Kansas, Inc.
24 S Lincoln St
Russell KS 67665
785 483-2627

(G-2504)
ALLSTAFF CHARTERED
2000 Washington St (67530-2451)
PHONE..................................620 792-4643
Greg Allison, *President*
Diana Allison, *Vice Pres*
EMP: 50
SALES: 1.5MM **Privately Held**
SIC: 8049 Nurses, registered & practical

(G-2505)
AMERICAN FIRE SPRINKLER CORP
4901 8th St (67530-4667)
P.O. Box 1644 (67530-1644)
PHONE..................................620 792-1909
Ed Bulle, *Manager*
EMP: 18
SALES (corp-wide): 13.9MM **Privately Held**
SIC: 1711 Fire sprinkler system installation
PA: American Fire Sprinkler Corporation
6750 W 47th Ter
Shawnee Mission KS 66203
913 722-6900

(G-2506)
AMERICAN STATE BANK & TRUST CO (PA)
1321 Main St Ste A (67530-4400)
P.O. Box 1346 (67530-1346)
PHONE..................................620 793-5900
Don Lackamp, *President*
Genevieve Lamb, *Vice Pres*
EMP: 15
SALES: 28.4MM **Privately Held**
WEB: www.americanstatebankna.com
SIC: 6022 State commercial banks

(G-2507)
AMERICAS BEST VALUE INN
3500 10th St (67530-3539)
PHONE..................................620 793-8486
Theresa Fanders, *Owner*
EMP: 10
SALES (est): 366K **Privately Held**
SIC: 7011 Inns

(G-2508)
AMERINE UTILITIES CONSTRUCTION
252 Se 10 Ave (67530)
P.O. Box 1546 (67530-1546)
PHONE..................................620 792-1223
Glen Amerine, *President*
Patricia Amerine, *Corp Secy*
Craig Amerine, *Vice Pres*
Melissa Amerine, *Vice Pres*
Marcie Fross, *Vice Pres*
EMP: 25
SALES: 6.6MM **Privately Held**
SIC: 1623 Underground utilities contractor

(G-2509)
ANGUS INN BEST WESTERN MOTEL
2920 10th St (67530-4260)
PHONE..................................620 792-3541
Loren Unruh, *President*
EMP: 65 **EST:** 1970
SQ FT: 6,600
SALES (est): 2.5MM **Privately Held**
WEB: www.bwangus.com
SIC: 7011 7991 5812 Hotels & motels; physical fitness facilities; eating places

(G-2510)
ANIMAL MEDICAL CENTER LLC
622 Mckinley St (67530-4706)
PHONE..................................620 792-1265
Nels Lindberg, *Mng Member*
EMP: 10
SQ FT: 5,500
SALES (est): 932.3K **Privately Held**
SIC: 0742 Animal hospital services, pets & other animal specialties; veterinarian, animal specialties

(G-2511)
ARGONNA POST 180 AMERCN LEGION
Also Called: AMERICAN LEGION ARGONNE POST 1
1011 Kansas Ave (67530-4401)
P.O. Box 721 (67530-0721)
PHONE..................................620 793-5912
Comdr Leonard White, *Principal*
Leonard White, *Vice Pres*
Joe McLaughlin, *Commissioner*
Wayne McReynolds, *Admin Sec*
EMP: 13
SQ FT: 12,500
SALES: 186.6K **Privately Held**
SIC: 8641 Veterans' organization

(G-2512)
ARK VALLEY VETERINARY HOSPITAL
1205 Patton Rd (67530-3117)
PHONE..................................620 793-5457
Terry K Schmitt Dvm, *President*
Terry Turner Dvm, *Corp Secy*
EMP: 10
SQ FT: 3,240
SALES (est): 420.6K **Privately Held**
SIC: 0742 Animal hospital services, pets & other animal specialties

(G-2513)
BACHMAN PRODUCTION SPECIALTIES
307 C Ave (67530-9777)
PHONE..................................620 792-2549
J Michael Bachman, *President*
Harold L Smart, *Vice Pres*
Angela Bachman, *Admin Sec*
EMP: 11
SALES: 1.2MM
SALES (corp-wide): 1.4B **Publicly Held**
SIC: 1389 Chemically treating wells
HQ: The Bachman Services Inc
2220 S I 35 Service Rd
Oklahoma City OK 73129
405 677-8296

(G-2514)
BAKER PETROLITE LLC
Baker Hughes
5801 10th St (67530-3103)
PHONE..................................620 793-3546
Todd Ost, *Manager*
EMP: 56
SQ FT: 3,200
SALES (corp-wide): 22.8B **Publicly Held**
WEB: www.bakerpetrolite.com
SIC: 1389 5169 Oil field services; oil additives
HQ: Baker Petrolite Llc
12645 W Airport Blvd
Sugar Land TX 77478
281 276-5400

(G-2515)
BANK OF WEST
1200 Kansas Ave (67530-4406)
PHONE..................................620 792-1771
Shelley Jones, *Manager*
EMP: 10
SALES (corp-wide): 2.7B **Privately Held**
SIC: 6022 State trust companies accepting deposits, commercial
HQ: Bank Of The West
180 Montgomery St # 1400
San Francisco CA 94104
415 765-4800

(G-2516)
BARTON COUNTY CLUB INC
Also Called: Barton Golf Course
N Hwy 281 (67530)
P.O. Box 666 (67530-0666)
PHONE..................................620 653-4255
Randy Bonfeldt, *President*
EMP: 12
SALES: 228K **Privately Held**
SIC: 7997 Golf club, membership

(G-2517)
BAYLESS DRY CLEANING INC
1110 Kansas Ave (67530-4404)
PHONE..................................620 793-3576
Robert Bayless, *President*
David Bayless, *Treasurer*
EMP: 10
SQ FT: 5,000
SALES (est): 419.4K **Privately Held**
SIC: 7216 7219 Cleaning & dyeing, except rugs; fur garment cleaning, repairing & storage

(G-2518)
BCCC CHILD DEVELOPMENT CENTER
245 Ne 30 Rd (67530-9107)
PHONE..................................620 786-1131
Larissa Adams, *Director*
EMP: 37
SALES (est): 426.2K **Privately Held**
SIC: 8351 Child day care services

(G-2519)
BECKER TIRE & TREADING INC (PA)
904 Washington St (67530-4939)
P.O. Box 268 (67530-0268)
PHONE..................................620 793-5414
Gary Albright, *CEO*
Steven Burhenn, *President*
Willy Allen, *Vice Pres*
Paul Doll, *Vice Pres*
Jean Radke, *Admin Sec*
EMP: 100 **EST:** 1954
SQ FT: 100,000
SALES (est): 96.3MM **Privately Held**
WEB: www.beckertire.com
SIC: 5014 5531 Automobile tires & tubes; automotive tires

(G-2520)
BENEFIT MANAGEMENT LLC (HQ)
Also Called: Benefit Management Inc
2015 16th St (67530-4030)
P.O. Box 1090 (67530-1090)
PHONE..................................620 792-1779
Chad Somers, *President*
Kelli Glover, *Accounts Mgr*
Greg Cunningham, *Technical Staff*
EMP: 20
SALES (est): 7.5MM
SALES (corp-wide): 46.4MM **Privately Held**
WEB: www.benefitmanagementks.com
SIC: 6411 Medical insurance claim processing, contract or fee basis
PA: Nueterra Dc Holdings, Llc
11221 Roe Ave Ste 1a
Leawood KS 66211
913 387-0689

(G-2521)
BLIZZARD ENERGY INC
9015 8th St (67530-9713)
PHONE..................................620 796-2396
Franciska Sheppard, *President*
Nick Seib, *General Mgr*
EMP: 10 **EST:** 2013
SALES (est): 755.2K **Privately Held**
SIC: 7534 Rebuilding & retreading tires

(G-2522)
BROOKDALE SENIOR LIVING COMMUN
Also Called: Sterling House of Great Bend
1206 Patton Rd Ofc (67530-3191)
PHONE..................................620 792-7000
Gaiyla Nielsen, *Director*
EMP: 14
SALES (corp-wide): 4.5B **Publicly Held**
WEB: www.assisted.com
SIC: 8051 Skilled nursing care facilities
HQ: Brookdale Senior Living Communities, Inc.
6737 W Wa St Ste 2300
Milwaukee WI 53214
414 918-5000

(G-2523)
BRYANT-FUNERAL HOME
Also Called: Bryant Funeral Home
1425 Patton Rd (67530-3187)
PHONE..................................620 793-3525
Bill Nickelson, *President*
Bill Nicholson, *President*
EMP: 10 **EST:** 1936
SQ FT: 13,000
SALES (est): 394.8K **Privately Held**
SIC: 7261 Funeral home

(G-2524)
BURKEY RICHARD L DPM P A
3509 Forest Ave (67530-3607)
PHONE..................................620 793-7624
Richard L Burkey, *President*
Donna L Burkey, *Office Mgr*
EMP: 10
SALES (est): 983.1K **Privately Held**
SIC: 8011 Offices & clinics of medical doctors

(G-2525)
BUTTERFLY SUPPLY INC
Also Called: CNG Developments
5858 10th St (67530-3104)
P.O. Box 613, Lawrence (66044-0613)
PHONE..................................620 793-7156
David Evans, *President*
Gary Burk, *President*
EMP: 12
SQ FT: 450
SALES (est): 270.7K **Privately Held**
WEB: www.butterflysupplyinc.com
SIC: 5051 5084 1311 5999 Metals service centers & offices; oil well machinery, equipment & supplies; crude petroleum production; natural gas production; alcoholic beverage making equipment & supplies

(G-2526)
CENTER FOR COUNSELING & CNSLTN (PA)
5815 Broadway Ave (67530-3197)
PHONE..................................620 792-2544
Doug McMett, *Exec Dir*
EMP: 39
SQ FT: 5,000
SALES: 4.7MM **Privately Held**
WEB: www.thecentergb.org
SIC: 8093 8322 8069 8011 Mental health clinic, outpatient; general counseling services; alcoholism rehabilitation hospital; psychiatrist

(G-2527)
CENTRAL KANS FMLY PRACTICE PA
Also Called: Rose, Tom MD
1309 Polk St Ste C (67530-3652)
PHONE..................................620 792-5341
Donna Meyers, *Manager*
EMP: 25
SQ FT: 6,000
SALES (est): 2.6MM **Privately Held**
SIC: 8011 General & family practice, physician/surgeon

(G-2528)
CENTRAL KANS SURVEYING MAPPING
2344 Washington St (67530-2457)
PHONE..................................620 792-2873
Randy Anderson, *President*
Cathy Anderson, *Admin Sec*
EMP: 10
SQ FT: 2,100
SALES (est): 720.2K **Privately Held**
SIC: 8713 Surveying services

(G-2529)
CENTRAL KANSAS MEDICAL CENTER (HQ)
Also Called: St Rose Campus
3515 Broadway Ave (67530-3633)
PHONE..................................620 792-2511
Sharon Lind, *CEO*
Kathy Ceushing, *CFO*
Larry E Brown, *Director*
EMP: 500
SQ FT: 100,000
SALES: 8.1MM **Privately Held**
WEB: www.ckmc.org
SIC: 8062 General medical & surgical hospitals

(G-2530)
CENTRAL KANSAS MEDICAL CENTER
Golden Belt HM Hlth & Hospice
3515 Broadway Ave Ste 102 (67530-3657)
PHONE..................................620 792-8171
Donita Wolf, *Branch Mgr*
EMP: 18 **Privately Held**
WEB: www.ckmc.org
SIC: 8062 General medical & surgical hospitals
HQ: Central Kansas Medical Center Inc
3515 Broadway Ave
Great Bend KS 67530
620 792-2511

(G-2531)
CENTRAL KANSAS ORTHPD GROUP
Also Called: Central Kansas Orthepedics
1514 State Road 96 Ste A (67530-3012)
PHONE..................................620 792-4383
Leonard T Fleske, *President*
Randall Hilderbrand, *Vice Pres*
EMP: 17
SALES (est): 2.4MM **Privately Held**
SIC: 8011 Orthopedic physician

(G-2532)
CENTRAL KANSAS RENDERING INC
58 Se 20 Rd (67530)
P.O. Box 417 (67530-0417)
PHONE..................................620 792-2059
Ann Cedar, *President*
Bob Cedar, *Corp Secy*
EMP: 6
SALES (est): 417.5K **Privately Held**
SIC: 2077 Rendering

(G-2533)
CENTRAL KS MEDICAL PARK PA
1309 Polk St Ste C (67530-3652)
PHONE..................................620 793-5404
Perry Smith, *Partner*
Connie Blanton, *Technician*
EMP: 10
SALES (est): 683.4K **Privately Held**
SIC: 8071 X-ray laboratory, including dental

(G-2534)
CENTRAL PWR SYSTEMS & SVCS LLC
Also Called: Dda Sales/Service
625 10th St (67530-5601)
PHONE..................................620 792-1361
Adan Rowley, *Branch Mgr*
EMP: 24
SALES (corp-wide): 80MM **Privately Held**
SIC: 5531 7538 Truck equipment & parts; general automotive repair shops
PA: Central Power Systems & Services, Llc
9200 Liberty Dr
Pleasant Valley MO 64068
816 781-8070

(G-2535)
CHASE WELL SERVICE INC
5286 Timber Creek Rd (67530-6633)
PHONE..................................620 793-9556
Janice Link, *President*
EMP: 10
SALES (est): 699K **Privately Held**
SIC: 1389 Oil field services

(G-2536)
CHC MCPHERSON REFINERY INC
Also Called: N C R A
2421 10th St (67530-4354)
PHONE..................................620 793-3111
Bob Wiatt, *Manager*
EMP: 26
SALES (corp-wide): 31.9B **Publicly Held**
SIC: 4213 2911 5172 Contract haulers; petroleum refining; petroleum products
HQ: Chs Mcpherson Refinery Inc.
2000 S Main St
Mcpherson KS 67460
620 241-2340

(G-2537)
CHEMICAL SERVICES INC
32 Ne 40th Ave (67530)
P.O. Box 113 (67530-0113)
PHONE..................................620 792-6886
Rick Kirkpatrick, *President*
Kent Boles, *Vice Pres*
Terry Price, *Admin Sec*
EMP: 12
SALES: 2.4MM **Privately Held**
SIC: 5169 Industrial chemicals

(G-2538)
CHERRY VILLAGE BENEVOLENCE
Also Called: CHERRY VILLAGE RETIREMENT
1401 Cherry Ln (67530-3152)
PHONE..................................620 792-2165
Pamela Lewis, *Exec Dir*
EMP: 70
SALES: 3.3MM **Privately Held**
SIC: 8052 8059 Personal care facility; nursing home, except skilled & intermediate care facility

(G-2539)
CHERRY VLG ASSISTED SELF-CARE
Also Called: Cherry Village Nursing Home
5926 Eisenhower Ave Ofc (67530-3189)
PHONE..................................620 793-5765
Joe Hansen, *Owner*
EMP: 17 **EST:** 1997
SALES (est): 232.5K **Privately Held**
SIC: 8361 Home for the aged

(G-2540)
CITY OF GREAT BEND (PA)
1209 Williams St (67530-4446)
P.O. Box 1168 (67530-1168)
PHONE..................................620 793-4111
Mike Allison, *Mayor*
Scott Keeler, *Director*
Howard Parkington, *Administration*
EMP: 40 **Privately Held**
WEB: www.greatbendks.net
SIC: 9111 8611 ; business associations

(G-2541)
CITY OF GREAT BEND
Also Called: Great Bend, City of
2005 Kansas Ave (67530-2513)
PHONE..................................620 792-3906
Rozena Tomlin, *Director*
EMP: 15 **Privately Held**
WEB: www.greatbendks.net
SIC: 8322 9111 Senior citizens' center or association; mayors' offices
PA: City Of Great Bend
1209 Williams St
Great Bend KS 67530
620 793-4111

(G-2542)
CITY OF GREAT BEND
Also Called: Water Pollution Control Dept
200 Kiowa Rd (67530-6115)
P.O. Box 1168 (67530-1168)
PHONE..................................620 793-4170
Robert Schwartz, *Superintendent*
EMP: 15 **Privately Held**
WEB: www.greatbendks.net
SIC: 4941 9111 Water supply; mayors' offices
PA: City Of Great Bend
1209 Williams St
Great Bend KS 67530
620 793-4111

(G-2543)
CITY OF GREAT BEND
Also Called: Great Bend Coop, The
323 S Us Highway 281 (67530-9621)
PHONE..................................620 793-5031
Frank Reidl, *Manager*
EMP: 70 **Privately Held**

GEOGRAPHIC

WEB: www.greatbendks.net
SIC: 5191 Fertilizers & agricultural chemicals
PA: City Of Great Bend
1209 Williams St
Great Bend KS 67530
620 793-4111

(G-2544)
COMFORT INN
911 Grant St (67530-3571)
PHONE..................................620 793-9000
Gary Patel, *Owner*
EMP: 12 **EST:** 2008
SALES (est): 453.5K **Privately Held**
SIC: 7011 Hotels & motels

(G-2545)
CONCRETE SERVICE CO INC (PA)
221 Baker Ave (67530-5547)
P.O. Box 1205 (67530-1205)
PHONE..................................620 792-2558
Roy Westhoff, *President*
Dale Westhoff, *Vice Pres*
Marcia Westhoff, *Admin Sec*
EMP: 20 **EST:** 1963
SQ FT: 2,200
SALES (est): 3.2MM **Privately Held**
SIC: 3273 1611 Ready-mixed concrete; concrete construction: roads, highways, sidewalks, etc.

(G-2546)
CONCRETE VAULTS INC
Also Called: Wheatland Vaults
559 B St (67530-9315)
PHONE..................................620 792-6687
James Kasper, *Manager*
EMP: 7
SALES (corp-wide): 5.3MM **Privately Held**
WEB: www.concrete-vaults.com
SIC: 3272 Burial vaults, concrete or precast terrazzo
PA: Concrete Vaults, Inc.
901 Sharps Dr
Newton KS 67114
316 283-3790

(G-2547)
CORRECTIONS KANSAS DEPARTMENT
Also Called: Great Bend Parole Office
1806 12th St (67530-4500)
PHONE..................................620 792-3549
Lester L Harmon, *Director*
EMP: 10 **Privately Held**
WEB: www.kdoc.dc.state.ks.us
SIC: 8322 9223 Parole office; correctional institutions;
HQ: Kansas Department Of Corrections
714 Sw Jackson St Fl 3
Topeka KS 66603
785 296-3317

(G-2548)
COUNTY OF BARTON
Also Called: Probation Services
1806 12th St (67530-4500)
PHONE..................................620 793-1910
Sabrina Chism, *Manager*
EMP: 11 **Privately Held**
WEB: www.bartoncounty.org
SIC: 8322 Probation office
PA: County Of Barton
1400 Main St Ste 107
Great Bend KS 67530
620 793-1847

(G-2549)
CPI QUALIFIED PLAN CONS INC (DH)
Also Called: CUNA Mutl Retirement Solutions
1809 24th St (67530-2622)
P.O. Box 1167 (67530-1167)
PHONE..................................620 793-8473
Kevin S Thompson, *CEO*
Jon L Prescott, *President*
Dana C Miller, *COO*
Barb Boxberger, *Pastor*
Renee Dykes, *CFO*
EMP: 395
SQ FT: 122,800
SALES: 1.2MM
SALES (corp-wide): 3.5B **Privately Held**
WEB: www.cpiqpc.com
SIC: 6411 8742 Pension & retirement plan consultants; compensation & benefits planning consultant
HQ: Cmfg Life Insurance Company
5910 Mineral Point Rd
Madison WI 53705
800 356-2644

(G-2550)
CRAWFORD & COMPANY
1411 Harding St (67530-3311)
PHONE..................................913 323-0300
Bret D Malone, *Branch Mgr*
EMP: 11
SALES (corp-wide): 1.1B **Publicly Held**
WEB: www.crawfordandcompany.com
SIC: 6411 Insurance adjusters
PA: Crawford & Company
5335 Triangle Pkwy Ofc C
Peachtree Corners GA 30092
404 300-1000

(G-2551)
D S & W WELL SERVICING INC
1822 24th St (67530-2623)
PHONE..................................620 793-5838
Curtis Hitschmann, *President*
EMP: 20
SALES (est): 736.5K **Privately Held**
SIC: 1389 Oil field services

(G-2552)
DAMM PIPE TESTING LLC
5548 Oilcenter Rd S (67530-9724)
P.O. Box 1981 (67530-1981)
PHONE..................................620 617-8990
Bryan Kramer, *Mng Member*
EMP: 9
SALES: 750K **Privately Held**
SIC: 1389 Pipe testing, oil field service

(G-2553)
DELTA KAPPA GAMMA SOCIETY
2331 Garfield St (67530-7460)
PHONE..................................620 793-3977
Jari Marietta, *President*
Kay Krouse, *Principal*
EMP: 20 **EST:** 2001
SALES (est): 134.4K **Privately Held**
SIC: 8641 University club

(G-2554)
DOONAN SPECIALIZED TRAILER LLC
36 Ne Us Highway 156 B (67530-8827)
P.O. Box 1988 (67530-1988)
PHONE..................................620 792-6222
Kraig Miller, *Purch Agent*
Brad Kershner, *Engineer*
Kristy Rupe, *Sales Staff*
Jim Waitt, *Webmaster*
Elgen L Reynolds,
EMP: 30 **EST:** 2006
SQ FT: 72,000
SALES (est): 11.6MM **Privately Held**
WEB: www.doonan.com
SIC: 3715 Truck trailers

(G-2555)
DOONAN TRUCK & EQUIPMENT INC
Also Called: Doonan Peterbilt of Great Bend
Jct Hwy 56 & 156 (67530)
P.O. Box 1286 (67530-1286)
PHONE..................................620 792-2491
Kenneth M Doonan, *President*
Brent Doonan, *Vice Pres*
EMP: 35
SQ FT: 8,200
SALES (est): 7.9MM
SALES (corp-wide): 23.5B **Publicly Held**
WEB: www.paccar.com
SIC: 5012 Trucks, commercial; trailers for trucks, new & used
PA: Paccar Inc
777 106th Ave Ne
Bellevue WA 98004
425 468-7400

(G-2556)
DUKE DRILLING CO INC
5539 2nd St (67530-9739)
P.O. Box 823 (67530-0823)
PHONE..................................620 793-8366
Craig D Biggs, *Manager*
EMP: 90
SALES (corp-wide): 177.2MM **Privately Held**
SIC: 1381 Drilling oil & gas wells
PA: Duke Drilling Co., Inc.
100 S Main St Ste 410
Wichita KS
316 267-1331

(G-2557)
EAGLE COMMUNICATIONS INC
Also Called: Eagle Radio
1200 Baker Ave (67530-4523)
P.O. Box 609 (67530-0609)
PHONE..................................620 792-3101
Randy Georinge, *Manager*
EMP: 10
SALES (corp-wide): 71.7MM **Privately Held**
WEB: www.eaglecom.net
SIC: 4832 Radio broadcasting stations
PA: Eagle Communications, Inc.
2703 Hall St 15
Hays KS 67601
785 625-5910

(G-2558)
EDMISTON OIL COMPANY INC
231 S Us Highway 281 (67530-9658)
P.O. Box 232 (67530-0232)
PHONE..................................620 792-6924
Dale May, *Manager*
EMP: 6
SALES (corp-wide): 2.2MM **Privately Held**
SIC: 1382 Geophysical exploration, oil & gas field
PA: Edmiston Oil Company Inc
125 N Market St Ste 1420
Wichita KS 67202
316 265-5241

(G-2559)
ELDERCARE INC
Also Called: FRIENDSHIP MEALS
1121 Washington St Ste A (67530-4370)
P.O. Box 1364 (67530-1364)
PHONE..................................620 792-5942
Gaila Nielsen, *Exec Dir*
EMP: 180
SALES: 3MM **Privately Held**
SIC: 8322 8361 Senior citizens' center or association; geriatric residential care

(G-2560)
EVERGY KANSAS CENTRAL INC
1800 Kansas Ave (67530-2510)
P.O. Box 789 (67530-0789)
PHONE..................................620 793-3515
Conrad Koehler, *Manager*
EMP: 17
SALES (corp-wide): 4.2B **Publicly Held**
SIC: 4911 Electric services
HQ: Evergy Kansas Central, Inc.
818 S Kansas Ave
Topeka KS 66612
785 575-6300

(G-2561)
EVERGY MISSOURI WEST INC
Also Called: Aquila Networks
335 Nw 50 Ave (67530-9046)
P.O. Box 170 (67530-0170)
PHONE..................................620 793-1279
Tom Ford, *Branch Mgr*
EMP: 14
SALES (corp-wide): 833.9MM **Privately Held**
SIC: 4911 Generation, electric power; transmission, electric power; distribution, electric power
PA: Evergy Missouri West, Inc.
1200 Main St Fl 30
Kansas City MO 64105
816 556-2200

(G-2562)
FAMILY CRISIS CENTER INC
1924 Broadway Ave (67530-4010)
PHONE..................................620 793-9941
Laura Patzner, *Exec Dir*
EMP: 15
SALES: 1.1MM **Privately Held**
WEB: www.familycrisiscntr.org
SIC: 8361 8322 Residential care; emergency social services

(G-2563)
FARMERS BANK & TRUST (HQ)
1017 Harrison St (67530-4213)
P.O. Box 267 (67530-0267)
PHONE..................................620 792-2411
W R Robbins, *President*
Robert Rugan, *President*
EMP: 40 **EST:** 1907
SQ FT: 10,000
SALES: 34.9MM **Privately Held**
WEB: www.farmersbankna.com
SIC: 6022 State commercial banks
PA: Farmers Enterprises Inc
2001 Main St
Albert KS 67511
620 923-4212

(G-2564)
FEDEX FREIGHT CORPORATION
301 10th St (67530-6205)
PHONE..................................888 399-4737
EMP: 12
SALES (corp-wide): 69.6B **Publicly Held**
SIC: 4213 Less-than-truckload (LTL) transport
HQ: Fedex Freight Corporation
1715 Aaron Brenner Dr
Memphis TN 38120

(G-2565)
FIRST STEPS CHILDCARE AND LEAR
4531 Prairie Rose Dr (67530-7471)
PHONE..................................620 518-1532
Tara Haslouer, *CEO*
EMP: 10
SALES (est): 61.1K **Privately Held**
SIC: 8351 Child day care services

(G-2566)
FOLEY EQUIPMENT COMPANY
Also Called: Caterpillar Authorized Dealer
701 10th St (67530-5603)
PHONE..................................620 792-5246
Jay Wade, *Sales Staff*
Mike Keeler, *Manager*
EMP: 10
SALES (corp-wide): 124.2MM **Privately Held**
SIC: 5082 General construction machinery & equipment
HQ: Foley Equipment Company
1550 S West St
Wichita KS 67213
316 943-4211

(G-2567)
FRANCIS CASING CREWS INC (PA)
5810 Anchor Way (67530-6515)
P.O. Box 815 (67530-0815)
PHONE..................................620 793-9630
John Francis, *President*
EMP: 7
SQ FT: 2,000
SALES (est): 3MM **Privately Held**
SIC: 1389 Running, cutting & pulling casings, tubes & rods

(G-2568)
FULLER INDUSTRIES LLC
1 Fuller Way (67530-2466)
PHONE..................................620 792-1711
Mark Chalfant, *CEO*
Ellen Moran, *CFO*
◆ **EMP:** 134
SALES (est): 43.2MM **Privately Held**
SIC: 3589 Commercial cleaning equipment

(G-2569)
GBK VENTURES LLC
Also Called: Holiday Inn
3821 10th St (67530-3548)
PHONE..................................620 603-6565

Claudia Elsen, *Mng Member*
EMP: 16 **EST:** 2013
SALES (est): 284.6K **Privately Held**
SIC: 7011 Hotels & motels

(G-2570)
GLASS KING MANUFACTURING CO
211 N Us Highway 281 (67530-9735)
P.O. Box 614 (67530-0614)
PHONE..................................620 793-7838
Gerald Herrman, *President*
Leroy Herman, *Vice Pres*
EMP: 14 **EST:** 1970
SQ FT: 25,600
SALES (est): 2.6MM **Privately Held**
SIC: 3443 3089 Tanks, standard or custom fabricated: metal plate; plastic & fiberglass tanks

(G-2571)
GOLDEN BELT COUNTRY CLUB INC
Also Called: Stoneridge
1438 24th St (67530-2660)
PHONE..................................620 792-4303
Rick Ball, *Principal*
EMP: 40
SQ FT: 7,200
SALES (est): 1.1MM **Privately Held**
SIC: 7997 Country club, membership

(G-2572)
GOLDEN BELT PRINTING II LLC
1125 Us Highway 281 Byp (67530-5625)
PHONE..................................620 793-6351
Kenneth Vink, *Principal*
EMP: 10
SQ FT: 6,500
SALES (est): 1.8MM **Privately Held**
WEB: www.goldenbelt.com
SIC: 2752 Commercial printing, offset

(G-2573)
GREAT BEND CHILD DAY CARE ASSN
Also Called: Great Bend Childrens Lrng Ctr
1802 22nd St (67530-2650)
PHONE..................................620 792-2421
Jane Smith, *Treasurer*
Barbara Morris, *Manager*
Sue Detter, *Director*
Kelly Higgins, *Bd of Directors*
EMP: 14
SQ FT: 7,500
SALES: 489.8K **Privately Held**
SIC: 8351 Group day care center

(G-2574)
GREAT BEND CHILDRENS CLINIC PA
1021 Eisenhower Ave (67530-3213)
PHONE..................................620 792-5437
Marta Edmonds, *Partner*
Ryan M Williams, *Med Doctor*
EMP: 20
SALES (est): 1.2MM **Privately Held**
SIC: 8011 Clinic, operated by physicians; pediatrician

(G-2575)
GREAT BEND COMMISSION ON AGING
2005 Kansas Ave (67530-2513)
PHONE..................................620 792-3906
Rosina Tomlin, *Director*
EMP: 12
SALES (est): 145.9K **Privately Held**
SIC: 8322 Senior citizens' center or association

(G-2576)
GREAT BEND COOPERATIVE ASSN (PA)
606 Main St (67530-5406)
P.O. Box 68 (67530-0068)
PHONE..................................620 793-3531
Frank Riedl, *President*
Dennis Neeland, *Opers Mgr*
Sloan Folk, *Mktg Coord*
Jeff Cotten, *Manager*
Marvin Rose, *Manager*
EMP: 50 **EST:** 1959
SQ FT: 7,000
SALES: 146.7MM **Privately Held**
WEB: www.greatbendcoop.com
SIC: 5153 5191 5171 4221 Grains; feed; fertilizer & fertilizer materials; petroleum bulk stations; grain elevator, storage only

(G-2577)
GREAT BEND COOPERATIVE ASSN
2302 10th St (67530-4353)
PHONE..................................620 792-1281
Roland Nagel, *Manager*
EMP: 11
SALES (corp-wide): 146.7MM **Privately Held**
WEB: www.greatbendcoop.com
SIC: 5531 5541 7539 Automotive tires; gasoline service stations; wheel alignment, automotive
PA: The Great Bend Cooperative Association
606 Main St
Great Bend KS 67530
620 793-3531

(G-2578)
GREAT BEND FARM EQUIPMENT INC
Also Called: John Deere Authorized Dealer
3412 23rd St (67530-7555)
PHONE..................................620 793-3509
Les Hopkins, *President*
Cecil O'Brate, *Corp Secy*
Leslie O Hopkins, *Manager*
EMP: 17 **EST:** 1966
SQ FT: 16,000
SALES (est): 4.6MM **Privately Held**
WEB: www.gbfarm.com
SIC: 5083 Farm implements

(G-2579)
GREAT BEND FEEDING INC
355 Nw 30 Ave (67530-8554)
PHONE..................................620 792-2508
Andrew Murphy, *CEO*
EMP: 33
SQ FT: 1,200
SALES (est): 4.5MM
SALES (corp-wide): 31.2MM **Privately Held**
WEB: www.gbfeeding.com
SIC: 0211 0212 Beef cattle feedlots; beef cattle except feedlots
PA: Innovative Livestock Services, Inc.
2006 Broadway Ave Ste 2c
Great Bend KS 67530
620 793-9200

(G-2580)
GREAT BEND FOUNDATION INC
3720 10th St (67530-3543)
P.O. Box 365 (67530-0365)
PHONE..................................620 792-4217
EMP: 16
SALES: 102.3K **Privately Held**
SIC: 8641 Civic social & fraternal associations

(G-2581)
GREAT BEND INDUSTRIES INC
Also Called: Hampton Hydraulics
8701 6th St (67530-9702)
PHONE..................................620 792-4368
George Winchester, *General Mgr*
Jeff Alsup, *Plant Mgr*
EMP: 62
SALES: 15MM **Privately Held**
SIC: 3492 Valves, hydraulic, aircraft

(G-2582)
GREAT BEND INTERNISTS PA
Also Called: Central Camp Medical Center
3515 Broadway Ave Ste 107 (67530-3657)
PHONE..................................620 793-8429
Sharon Lind, *CEO*
Elizabeth Amnen, *Vice Pres*
EMP: 25
SALES: 1.9MM **Privately Held**
SIC: 8011 Internal medicine, physician/surgeon

(G-2583)
GREAT BEND MANOR
Also Called: GREAT BEND HEALTH AND REHAB
1560 State Road 96 (67530-3012)
PHONE..................................620 792-2448
Courtney Bailey, *Administration*
EMP: 95
SALES: 2.9MM **Privately Held**
SIC: 8051 Skilled nursing care facilities

(G-2584)
GREAT PLAINS INSPTN & LINING
5858 10th St (67530-3104)
PHONE..................................620 793-7090
Gary Burke, *President*
EMP: 12
SQ FT: 10,000
SALES (est): 836.5K **Privately Held**
WEB: www.greatplainsinspectioninc.com
SIC: 7389 Inspection & testing services

(G-2585)
GREAT WESTERN DINING SVC INC
Also Called: Barton County Cmnty College
245 Ne 30 Rd (67530-9251)
PHONE..................................620 792-9224
Warren Hunt, *Manager*
EMP: 15 **Privately Held**
SIC: 1521 5141 Single-family housing construction; groceries, general line
PA: Great Western Dining Service, Inc.
111 W Moniteau St
Tipton MO 65081

(G-2586)
H B LANDSCAPING & SEPTIC TANKS
323 N Washington Ave (67530-9064)
PHONE..................................620 793-3985
Howard Baker, *Owner*
EMP: 10
SALES (est): 229.1K **Privately Held**
SIC: 0782 Landscape contractors

(G-2587)
H&R BLOCK INC
Also Called: H & R Block
2023 Lakin Ave (67530-4427)
PHONE..................................620 793-9361
Rita Doan, *Manager*
EMP: 10
SALES (corp-wide): 3B **Publicly Held**
WEB: www.hrblock.com
SIC: 7291 Tax return preparation services
PA: H&R Block, Inc.
1 H&R Block Way
Kansas City MO 64105
816 854-3000

(G-2588)
H2 OIL FIELD SERVICES
705 Harrison St (67530-3569)
PHONE..................................620 792-7115
Richard Herzberger, *Principal*
EMP: 5
SALES (est): 409.2K **Privately Held**
SIC: 1389 Oil field services

(G-2589)
HAIR E CLIPS LTD
1914 Main St (67530-2550)
PHONE..................................620 793-9050
Pam Baize, *Partner*
Jan Moeder, *Partner*
Pat Straup, *Partner*
EMP: 11
SALES (est): 216K **Privately Held**
SIC: 7231 Unisex hair salons

(G-2590)
HAMPTON HYDRAULICS LLC
Also Called: Great Bend Industries
8701 6th St (67530-9702)
PHONE..................................620 792-4368
Mike Petz, *Branch Mgr*
EMP: 93
SALES (corp-wide): 501.5MM **Privately Held**
WEB: www.hampton-hydraulics.com
SIC: 3714 3471 3325 3593 Motor vehicle parts & accessories; plating & polishing; steel foundries; fluid power cylinders & actuators
HQ: Hampton Hydraulics, Llc.
712 1st St Nw
Hampton IA 50441
641 456-4871

(G-2591)
HIGHLAND LODGING LLC (PA)
Also Called: Aamia Enterprises
3017 10th St (67530-4261)
PHONE..................................620 792-2431
Ifhwar Patel, *Owner*
EMP: 11
SALES (est): 1.6MM **Privately Held**
WEB: www.highlandhotel-gb.com
SIC: 7011 Hotels & motels

(G-2592)
ILS FARM PARTNERSHIP
551a Sw 30 Rd (67530-9730)
PHONE..................................620 792-6166
Lee Borck, *Partner*
EMP: 18
SALES (est): 950K **Privately Held**
SIC: 0751 Cattle services

(G-2593)
INNOVATIVE LIVESTOCK SVCS INC (PA)
2006 Broadway Ave Ste 2c (67530-4043)
P.O. Box 1506 (67530-1506)
PHONE..................................620 793-9200
Lee Borck, *CEO*
Andrew Murphy, *COO*
Lori Skelton, *Accountant*
EMP: 70
SALES (est): 31.2MM **Privately Held**
WEB: www.ilsbeef.com
SIC: 0139 0211 Alfalfa farm; beef cattle feedlots

(G-2594)
JACK B KELLEY INC
Also Called: Terminal 18
Us Hwy 281 S (67530)
PHONE..................................620 792-8205
David Borgen, *Manager*
EMP: 60
SALES (corp-wide): 2.3B **Privately Held**
WEB: www.jackbkelley.com
SIC: 4213 4212 Trucking, except local; local trucking, without storage
HQ: Jack B. Kelley, Inc.
3700 S Fm 1258
Amarillo TX 79118
806 353-3553

(G-2595)
JOHN JACO INC
Also Called: Nationwide
820 Main St (67530-5013)
P.O. Box G (67530-8007)
PHONE..................................620 792-2541
John Jaco, *President*
Joanne C Estes, *Treasurer*
EMP: 14
SQ FT: 3,500
SALES (est): 2.7MM **Privately Held**
WEB: www.johnjacorealty.com
SIC: 6411 Insurance agents

(G-2596)
JOMAX CONSTRUCTION COMPANY INC (DH)
238 Se 10 Ave (67530-9624)
P.O. Box 701 (67530-0701)
PHONE..................................620 792-3686
M E Nichols, *President*
Bill Duryee, *Corp Secy*
EMP: 10 **EST:** 1974
SQ FT: 8,400
SALES: 227MM **Privately Held**
WEB: www.jomaxgb.com
SIC: 1623 Oil & gas pipeline construction
HQ: Api Group Inc.
1100 Old Highway 8 Nw
Saint Paul MN 55112
651 636-4320

(G-2597)
KANSAS DOOR INC
3708 17th St (67530-7403)
PHONE..................................620 793-7600
James R Holley, *President*
Kenton Lewis, *Vice Pres*
EMP: 10
SQ FT: 4,000
SALES (est): 1.4MM **Privately Held**
SIC: 5211 5031 Garage doors, sale & installation; doors, garage

(G-2598)
KANSOTA TRANSPORT INC
1910 Broadway Ave (67530-4010)
PHONE..................................620 792-9100
Sanford Hayson, *President*
EMP: 44
SQ FT: 2,000
SALES (est): 2.5MM **Privately Held**
SIC: 4731 Transportation agents & brokers

(G-2599)
KELLER RE & INSUR AGCY
Also Called: Nationwide
1101 Williams St (67530-4445)
P.O. Box 945 (67530-0945)
PHONE..................................620 792-2128
Kevin Keller, *President*
Jeffrey Keller, *Treasurer*
Connie Rathbun, *Accounts Mgr*
Brad Kuhn, *Agent*
Ashley McAtee, *Agent*
EMP: 13
SALES (est): 949.3K **Privately Held**
SIC: 6531 6411 Real estate brokers & agents; insurance agents, brokers & service

(G-2600)
L & M CONTRACTORS INC
1405 State Road 96 (67530-3335)
P.O. Box 1171 (67530-1171)
PHONE..................................620 793-8137
Curtis E Mauler, *President*
Edwin H Mauler, *Vice Pres*
EMP: 55 **EST:** 1971
SQ FT: 2,000
SALES: 5.9MM **Privately Held**
SIC: 1622 Bridge construction

(G-2601)
L D DRILLING INC
7 Sw 26 Ave (67530-6525)
P.O. Box 183 (67530-0183)
PHONE..................................620 793-3051
L D Davis, *President*
Bessie De Werff, *Corp Secy*
EMP: 35 **EST:** 1965
SQ FT: 1,500
SALES (est): 4.1MM **Privately Held**
SIC: 1311 1381 Crude petroleum production; natural gas production; drilling oil & gas wells

(G-2602)
LEIKER WELL SERVICE INC
1200 Main St (67530-4434)
P.O. Box 1902 (67530-1902)
PHONE..................................620 793-2336
David Leiker, *President*
Gary Klima, *Corp Secy*
Dennis Klima, *Vice Pres*
EMP: 7
SALES (est): 690K **Privately Held**
SIC: 1389 Servicing oil & gas wells

(G-2603)
LITTLE GIANT FITTINGS COMPANY
11 Ne 50 Ave (67530-9013)
P.O. Box 197 (67530-0197)
PHONE..................................620 793-5399
Craig Donecker, *President*
Jeff Donecker, *Vice Pres*
EMP: 5
SQ FT: 7,000
SALES (est): 500K **Privately Held**
SIC: 3494 3498 Valves & pipe fittings; fabricated pipe & fittings

(G-2604)
MAGNUS INC
800 Washington St (67530-4937)
P.O. Box 1877 (67530-1877)
PHONE..................................620 793-9222
Michael Sohm, *President*
▲ **EMP:** 6
SQ FT: 4,600
SALES (est): 801.7K **Privately Held**
WEB: www.archeryretailers.com
SIC: 3949 Archery equipment, general

(G-2605)
MAYBERRYS INC
Also Called: Walnut Bowl
3101 Washington St (67530-7009)
P.O. Box 924 (67530-0924)
PHONE..................................620 793-9400
Jim Mayberry, *President*
Linda Mayberry, *Corp Secy*
EMP: 15 **EST:** 1962
SQ FT: 25,600
SALES (est): 855.8K **Privately Held**
SIC: 7933 5812 7992 Ten pin center; grills (eating places); public golf courses

(G-2606)
MCDONALD TANK AND EQP CO INC
620 Morton St (67530-5435)
P.O. Box 1265 (67530-1265)
PHONE..................................620 793-3555
Lance Walters, *President*
Bob Weigel, *Vice Pres*
Dorothy Essmiller, *Admin Sec*
EMP: 28 **EST:** 1940
SQ FT: 4,000
SALES (est): 4.4MM **Privately Held**
SIC: 7699 5084 Tank repair; petroleum industry machinery; plastic products machinery

(G-2607)
MCDONALD TANK II
470 C Ave (67530-6539)
PHONE..................................620 792-3661
Lance Walters, *Owner*
EMP: 6
SALES (est): 843.9K **Privately Held**
SIC: 3089 Plastic & fiberglass tanks

(G-2608)
MCPHERSON & MCVEY LAW OFFICES
2109 12th St (67530-4426)
P.O. Box 1429 (67530-1429)
PHONE..................................620 793-3420
Brock McPherson, *Owner*
Brock Mc Pherson, *Owner*
EMP: 10
SALES (est): 510K **Privately Held**
SIC: 8111 General practice attorney, lawyer

(G-2609)
MID AMERICA ILS INC
251 Nw 10 Ave Lot 4 (67530-8570)
PHONE..................................620 792-1378
Jerry Anderson, *President*
Jane Anderson, *Admin Sec*
EMP: 11
SQ FT: 400
SALES (est): 2MM
SALES (corp-wide): 31.2MM **Privately Held**
WEB: www.midamericafeeders.com
SIC: 0211 Beef cattle feedlots
PA: Innovative Livestock Services, Inc.
2006 Broadway Ave Ste 2c
Great Bend KS 67530
620 793-9200

(G-2610)
MID CONTINENT TRANSPORTATION (PA)
3711 Main St (67530-6712)
P.O. Box 369 (67530-0369)
PHONE..................................620 793-3573
Richard W Dougherty Jr, *President*
Stacy Dougherty, *General Mgr*
EMP: 11 **EST:** 1947
SQ FT: 8,200
SALES (est): 1.7MM **Privately Held**
SIC: 4789 Cargo loading & unloading services

(G-2611)
MIDWEST ENERGY INC
1025 Patton Rd (67530-3113)
PHONE..................................620 792-1301
Michael Sadehi, *General Mgr*
EMP: 50
SALES (corp-wide): 219.6MM **Privately Held**
WEB: www.mwenergy.com
SIC: 4911 Distribution, electric power
PA: Midwest Energy, Inc.
1330 Canterbury Dr
Hays KS 67601
785 625-3437

(G-2612)
MOBILE RADIO SERVICE INC
156 S Us Highway 281 (67530-9659)
P.O. Box 340 (67530-0340)
PHONE..................................620 793-3231
John Harding, *President*
Donna S Petz, *Corp Secy*
Robert Jarmer, *Vice Pres*
Donna Petz, *Treasurer*
EMP: 10
SQ FT: 2,500
SALES: 1MM **Privately Held**
SIC: 7622 5731 Radio repair shop; radios, two-way, citizens' band, weather, shortwave, etc.

(G-2613)
MORRIS NEWSPAPER CORP KANSAS
Also Called: Great Bend Tribune
2012 Forest Ave (67530-4014)
P.O. Box 228 (67530-0228)
PHONE..................................620 792-1211
Charles Morris, *President*
Jim Misunas, *Editor*
Dale Hogg, *Manager*
EMP: 48
SQ FT: 10,000
SALES (est): 2.7MM
SALES (corp-wide): 285.7MM **Privately Held**
WEB: www.gbtribune.com
SIC: 2711 7261 Newspapers, publishing & printing; funeral service & crematories
PA: Morris Multimedia, Inc.
27 Abercorn St
Savannah GA 31401
912 233-1281

(G-2614)
MURPHY TRACTOR & EQP CO INC
Also Called: John Deere Authorized Dealer
325 S Us Highway 281 (67530-9621)
P.O. Box 1206 (67530-1206)
PHONE..................................620 792-2748
Kevin Rose, *Manager*
EMP: 10 **Privately Held**
WEB: www.murphytractor.com
SIC: 5082 General construction machinery & equipment
HQ: Murphy Tractor & Equipment Co., Inc.
5375 N Deere Rd
Park City KS 67219
855 246-9124

(G-2615)
NATURAL GAS PIPELINE AMER LLC
846 Nw 40 Rd (67530-9033)
PHONE..................................620 793-7118
Milton White, *Manager*
EMP: 12 **Publicly Held**
SIC: 4922 Pipelines, natural gas
HQ: Natural Gas Pipeline Company Of America Llc
1001 Louisiana St
Houston TX 77002
713 369-9000

(G-2616)
OFFICE PRODUCTS INC (PA)
Also Called: O P I
1204 Main St (67530-4434)
PHONE..................................620 793-8180
Terry L Vink, *President*
Kenneth Vink, *Corp Secy*
EMP: 32
SQ FT: 6,000
SALES: 4.5MM **Privately Held**
WEB: www.opiwireless.com
SIC: 5943 7629 5712 Office forms & supplies; business machine repair, electric; office furniture

(G-2617)
OLD DOMINION FREIGHT LINE INC
71 Sw 40 Ave (67530-9799)
PHONE..................................620 792-2006
Adam Rhodes, *Branch Mgr*
EMP: 12
SALES (corp-wide): 4B **Publicly Held**
WEB: www.odfl.com
SIC: 4213 Less-than-truckload (LTL) transport
PA: Old Dominion Freight Line Inc
500 Old Dominion Way
Thomasville NC 27360
336 889-5000

(G-2618)
ONEOK INC
1800 Kansas Ave (67530-2510)
PHONE..................................620 792-0603
Ron Seidel, *Manager*
EMP: 30
SALES (corp-wide): 12.5B **Publicly Held**
WEB: www.oneok.com
SIC: 4922 Natural gas transmission
PA: Oneok, Inc.
100 W 5th St Ste Ll
Tulsa OK 74103
918 588-7000

(G-2619)
ORSCHELN FARM AND HOME LLC
Also Called: Orschelin Farm and Home 31
5320 10th St (67530-3263)
PHONE..................................620 792-5480
Steve Titus, *Branch Mgr*
EMP: 10
SALES (corp-wide): 822.7MM **Privately Held**
WEB: www.orschelnfarmhome.com
SIC: 5191 Farm supplies
PA: Orscheln Farm And Home Llc
1800 Overcenter Dr
Moberly MO 65270
800 577-2580

(G-2620)
OVERSIZE WARNING PRODUCTS INC
Also Called: Www.oversizewarningproductscom
258 Se 20 Rd (67530-9664)
PHONE..................................620 792-5266
David Huddleston, *President*
Rachel Huttleson, *Vice Pres*
EMP: 9
SQ FT: 3,360
SALES (est): 671.1K **Privately Held**
SIC: 3993 Signs & advertising specialtics

(G-2621)
P & S ELC & ROUSTABOUT SVC INC
Also Called: P&S Electric
255 W Barton County Rd (67530-9348)
P.O. Box 1757 (67530-1757)
PHONE..................................620 792-7426
Paul Pack, *President*
Tia Pack, *Treasurer*
EMP: 13
SQ FT: 10,000
SALES (est): 3MM **Privately Held**
WEB: www.ps-electric.com
SIC: 1731 General electrical contractor

(G-2622)
PETL MANAGEMENT CORP INC
Also Called: Protective Equipment Testing
919 Adams St (67530-4817)
PHONE..................................620 792-1717
Michael L Harbaugh, *President*
EMP: 15
SALES (est): 1.3MM **Privately Held**
SIC: 8741 Management services

▲ = Import ▼=Export
◆ =Import/Export

(G-2623)
PICKRELL DRILLING CO INC
Also Called: C Dirt Services
Railroad Ave (67530)
PHONE.................................620 793-5742
Danny Biggs, *Vice Pres*
EMP: 30
SALES (est): 1.8MM
SALES (corp-wide): 10.4MM **Privately Held**
SIC: 1781 Water well drilling
PA: Pickrell Drilling Co, Inc
100 S Main St Ste 505
Wichita KS 67202
316 262-8427

(G-2624)
PRIMUS STERILIZER COMPANY LLC
175 N Us Highway 281 (67530-9773)
PHONE.................................620 793-7177
Jeff Spreier, *Branch Mgr*
EMP: 30
SALES (corp-wide): 73.1MM **Privately Held**
WEB: www.primus-sterilizer.com
SIC: 3842 Sterilizers, hospital & surgical
HQ: Primus Sterilizer Company, Llc
8719 S 135th St Ste 300
Omaha NE 68138

(G-2625)
PRYOR AUTMTC FIRE SPRNKLR INC
694c Harrison St (67530-3566)
P.O. Box 1243 (67530-1243)
PHONE.................................620 792-6400
Robert Pryor, *President*
Kevin Arnberger, *Vice Pres*
Shelly Arnberger, *Treasurer*
Mary Pryor, *Admin Sec*
EMP: 13
SALES: 2.3MM **Privately Held**
WEB: www.pryorautomatic.com
SIC: 1711 Fire sprinkler system installation

(G-2626)
PT KANSAS LLC
4110 Quail Creek Dr (67530-6824)
PHONE.................................620 791-7082
Kevyn Soupiset, *Principal*
EMP: 22
SALES (est): 369.6K **Privately Held**
SIC: 7389

(G-2627)
Q S NURSES KANSAS LLC
1117 Washington St (67530-4350)
PHONE.................................620 793-7262
Terry Whitlow, *Mng Member*
Lindi Clough, *Manager*
EMP: 80
SALES (est): 2.4MM **Privately Held**
WEB: www.qsnurses.com
SIC: 7361 Nurses' registry

(G-2628)
R & S DIGITAL SERVICES INC (PA)
1920 A 24th St (67530)
P.O. Box C (67530-8003)
PHONE.................................620 792-6171
Bruce Schneider, *President*
Jane Schneider, *Vice Pres*
EMP: 13
SALES (est): 1.8MM **Privately Held**
WEB: www.rsdigital.com
SIC: 7374 Computer graphics service

(G-2629)
RAY A CHEELY CHARTERED
809 S Patton Rd (67530-4625)
P.O. Box 24 (67530-0024)
PHONE.................................620 793-8436
EMP: 10
SQ FT: 5,600
SALES (est): 480K **Privately Held**
SIC: 8721 Accounting, Auditing, And Bookkeeping

(G-2630)
RES-CARE INC
2317 Washington St (67530-2456)
PHONE.................................620 793-8501
Larry Meeks, *Owner*
EMP: 48
SALES (corp-wide): 2B **Privately Held**
SIC: 8082 Home health care services
HQ: Res-Care, Inc.
805 N Whittington Pkwy
Louisville KY 40222
502 394-2100

(G-2631)
RES-CARE KANSAS INC
2317 Washington St (67530-2456)
PHONE.................................620 793-8501
Theada Clifton, *Branch Mgr*
EMP: 68
SALES (corp-wide): 2B **Privately Held**
SIC: 8052 8331 8361 Intermediate care facilities; job training & vocational rehabilitation services; home for the mentally handicapped
HQ: Res-Care Kansas, Inc.
5031 Matney Ave
Kansas City KS 66106
913 342-9426

(G-2632)
ROSENCRANTZ BEMIS ENTERPRISES (PA)
1105 Us Highway 281 Byp (67530)
P.O. Box 713 (67530-0713)
PHONE.................................620 792-2488
Fredia Dodson, *President*
Lora Alefs, *Treasurer*
EMP: 24
SQ FT: 2,500
SALES (est): 2.9MM **Privately Held**
SIC: 1629 1781 Irrigation system construction; geothermal drilling

(G-2633)
ROSEWOOD SERVICES INC
384 N Washington Ave (67530-9096)
P.O. Box 1321 (67530-1321)
PHONE.................................620 793-5888
Tammy Hammond, *President*
Melonie Myers, *Human Res Dir*
Jennifer Stoddard, *Director*
EMP: 45 **EST:** 1998
SALES (est): 4.7MM **Privately Held**
SIC: 8399 Community development groups

(G-2634)
SAINT FRNCIS ACDEMY GREAT BEND
1508 Main St (67530-4007)
PHONE.................................620 793-7454
Linda Arthington, *Director*
EMP: 23
SALES (est): 682.6K **Privately Held**
SIC: 8322 Child related social services

(G-2635)
SERVICE CORPS RETIRED EXECS
Also Called: S C O R E 0673
1400 Main St Ste 107 (67530-4037)
PHONE.................................620 793-3420
Rick Scheufler, *Branch Mgr*
EMP: 11
SALES (corp-wide): 13.1MM **Privately Held**
WEB: www.score199.mv.com
SIC: 8611 Business associations
PA: Service Corps Of Retired Executives Association
1175 Herndon Pkwy Ste 900
Herndon VA 20170
703 487-3612

(G-2636)
SIX CONTINENTS HOTELS INC
Also Called: Holiday Inn
3017 10th St (67530-4261)
PHONE.................................620 792-2431
Don Comstock, *Manager*
EMP: 75 **Privately Held**
WEB: www.sixcontinenthotels.com
SIC: 7011 Hotels & motels
HQ: Six Continents Hotels, Inc.
3 Ravinia Dr Ste 100
Dunwoody GA 30346
770 604-2000

(G-2637)
SOUTHARD CORPORATION (PA)
Also Called: Renewal By Andersen
1222 10th St (67530-5616)
P.O. Box 894 (67530-0894)
PHONE.................................620 793-5434
Mike Southard, *President*
R Joe Southard, *Chairman*
Shannon Donovan, *Vice Pres*
Jeff Fry, *Vice Pres*
Todd Wenberg, *Vice Pres*
EMP: 29 **EST:** 1951
SQ FT: 16,000
SALES: 25.9MM **Privately Held**
WEB: www.southardcorp.com
SIC: 5211 5031 Door & window products; windows

(G-2638)
SOUTHWEST DEVELOPMENTAL SVCS
Also Called: Sdsi
1105 Main St Ste D (67530-4471)
PHONE.................................620 793-7604
Mark Hinde, *CEO*
EMP: 10
SALES (est): 181.7K **Privately Held**
SIC: 8322 Community center

(G-2639)
STONE SAND CO INC
421 S Washington Ave (67530)
P.O. Box 872 (67530-0872)
PHONE.................................620 793-7864
Nelson Stone Jr, *President*
EMP: 22 **EST:** 1935
SALES (est): 4.8MM **Privately Held**
SIC: 1442 5032 Common sand mining; gravel mining; brick, stone & related material

(G-2640)
STRATA DRILLING INC
Also Called: Chase Well Service
5286 Timber Creek Rd (67530-6633)
PHONE.................................620 793-7971
Kenneth Link, *President*
Anita Barry, *Corp Secy*
Helen Steincamp, *Vice Pres*
Charles Stiencamp, *Treasurer*
EMP: 23 **EST:** 1955
SALES (est): 1MM **Privately Held**
SIC: 1311 Crude petroleum production; natural gas production

(G-2641)
STRAUB INTERNATIONAL INC (PA)
Also Called: Roth Equipment
200 S Patton Rd (67530-4614)
P.O. Box 1606 (67530-1606)
PHONE.................................620 792-5256
Larry Straub, *CEO*
Ronald Straub, *President*
Kathy Straub, *CFO*
EMP: 30 **EST:** 1971
SALES: 93MM **Privately Held**
WEB: www.straubint.com
SIC: 5083 5531 Agricultural machinery & equipment; truck equipment & parts

(G-2642)
STUEDER CONTRACTORS INC
3410 10th St (67530-3537)
PHONE.................................620 792-6044
Terry Stueder, *President*
Steve Wondra, *Sales Dir*
Gary Wondra, *Sales Staff*
Marla Poppelreiter, *Office Mgr*
EMP: 27
SQ FT: 4,000
SALES (est): 4.2MM **Privately Held**
WEB: www.stueders.com
SIC: 1711 5999 1731 Warm air heating & air conditioning contractor; plumbing contractors; architectural supplies; water purification equipment; electrical work

(G-2643)
SUNFLOWER DIVERSIFIED SVCS INC (PA)
8823 4th St (67530)
P.O. Box 838 (67530-0838)
PHONE.................................620 792-1321
James Johnson, *CEO*
EMP: 100 **EST:** 1971
SQ FT: 18,000
SALES: 115.3K **Privately Held**
WEB: www.sunflowerdiv.com
SIC: 8331 Vocational rehabilitation agency

(G-2644)
SUNFLOWER DIVERSIFIED SVCS INC
1312 Patton Rd (67530-3120)
PHONE.................................620 792-4087
Jim Johnson, *Branch Mgr*
EMP: 140
SALES (corp-wide): 115.3K **Privately Held**
SIC: 8331 Vocational rehabilitation agency
PA: Sunflower Diversified Services, Inc.
8823 4th St
Great Bend KS 67530
620 792-1321

(G-2645)
SUNFLOWER DIVERSIFIED SVCS INC
Also Called: Sunflower Early Education Ctr
1521 State Road 96 (67530-3011)
P.O. Box B (67530-8002)
PHONE.................................620 792-1325
Cathy Estes, *Principal*
EMP: 140
SALES (corp-wide): 115.3K **Privately Held**
WEB: www.sunflowerdiv.com
SIC: 8331 Job training & vocational rehabilitation services
PA: Sunflower Diversified Services, Inc.
8823 4th St
Great Bend KS 67530
620 792-1321

(G-2646)
T & C MFG & OPERATING INC
1020 Hoover St (67530-3498)
P.O. Box 225 (67530-0225)
PHONE.................................620 793-5483
Craig A Pangburn, *President*
Thomas H McGlinn, *Vice Pres*
Brian Schrader, *Controller*
Thomas McGlinn, *Executive*
EMP: 24
SQ FT: 4,000
SALES: 2.5MM **Privately Held**
WEB: www.tcmfg.com
SIC: 5083 8748 3069 1389 Irrigation equipment; environmental consultant; hard rubber & molded rubber products; oil field services; molding primary plastic; engineering services

(G-2647)
TIMOTHY R KEENAN
5260 Timber Creek Rd (67530-6633)
PHONE.................................620 793-7811
Timothy R Keenan, *Owner*
EMP: 15
SALES (est): 630K **Privately Held**
SIC: 8111 General practice law office

(G-2648)
TOWN & COUNTRY RACQUET CLUB
3806 Broadway Ave Ste 1 (67530-3688)
PHONE.................................620 792-1366
Kathleen Casey, *President*
Caron Zager, *Corp Secy*
Kevin Casey, *Vice Pres*
EMP: 32
SQ FT: 14,000
SALES (est): 984.4K **Privately Held**
SIC: 7997 Membership sports & recreation clubs

(G-2649)
TURNER TRUST PARTNERSHIP (PA)
Also Called: Turner Farms Partnership
551a Sw 30 Rd (67530-9730)
PHONE.................................620 792-6144
Stephanie Turner, *Partner*
Cynthia Latham, *Partner*
Fernanda Litt, *Partner*
Chase Turner, *Partner*
EMP: 27
SALES (est): 1.4MM **Privately Held**
SIC: 0191 General farms, primarily crop

(G-2650)
UKHS GREAT BEND LLC
Also Called: UNIVERSITY OF KANSAS MEDICAL C
514 Cleveland St (67530-3562)
PHONE..................................620 792-8833
Kerry Noble, *CEO*
Tim Latimer, *CFO*
EMP: 30
SQ FT: 14,348
SALES: 39.9MM
SALES (corp-wide): 708.6MM **Privately Held**
SIC: 8062 General medical & surgical hospitals
PA: The University Of Kansas Hospital Authority
4000 Cambridge St
Kansas City KS 66160
913 588-5000

(G-2651)
UNDERGRUND CVERN STBLZTION LLC (PA)
1020 Hoover St (67530-3415)
P.O. Box 225 (67530-0225)
PHONE..................................620 662-6367
Steve Pangburn,
Vicky Hester, *Admin Sec*
EMP: 10
SALES (est): 790.2K **Privately Held**
SIC: 0711 Soil preparation services

(G-2652)
USA GYM SUPPLY
Also Called: Great Bend Industrial Fabrics
1721 4th St (67530)
P.O. Box 844 (67530-0844)
PHONE..................................620 792-2800
Mark Ball, *Owner*
EMP: 12
SALES (corp-wide): 4.6MM **Privately Held**
WEB: www.usagymsupply.com
SIC: 2394 Tarpaulins, fabric: made from purchased materials
PA: Usa Gym Supply Inc.
319 Mckinley St
Great Bend KS 67530
620 792-2209

(G-2653)
USA GYM SUPPLY INC (PA)
319 Mckinley St (67530-5325)
P.O. Box 844 (67530-0844)
PHONE..................................620 792-2209
Mark Ball, *President*
Oleta Beckwith, *Corp Secy*
Bruce Ball, *Vice Pres*
EMP: 5
SQ FT: 6,880
SALES (est): 4.6MM **Privately Held**
WEB: www.usagymsupply.com
SIC: 5091 2394 Gymnasium equipment; tarpaulins, fabric: made from purchased materials

(G-2654)
VENTURE CORPORATION
214 S Us Highway 281 (67530-9660)
P.O. Box 1486 (67530-1486)
PHONE..................................620 792-5921
Orville Spray Jr, *Ch of Bd*
Orville Spray III, *Vice Pres*
Ron Wagoner, *Vice Pres*
Robert Holt, *Treasurer*
EMP: 60
SQ FT: 17,000
SALES (est): 15.1MM **Privately Held**
SIC: 1611 Highway & street paving contractor

(G-2655)
VULCAN MACHINE & REPAIR
247 E Us Highway 56 (67530-8800)
PHONE..................................620 796-2190
Gary L Mick, *Owner*
EMP: 8
SALES (est): 665.5K **Privately Held**
SIC: 3533 Oil field machinery & equipment

(G-2656)
WASHINGTON COMPANIES INC (PA)
828 10th St (67530-5606)
P.O. Box 1956 (67530-1956)
PHONE..................................620 792-2430
Charles E Carpenter, *President*
EMP: 15
SQ FT: 4,000
SALES: 1.7MM **Privately Held**
SIC: 1761 1742 Roofing contractor; insulation, buildings

(G-2657)
WATCO SUPPLY CHAIN SVCS LLC
9047 6th St (67530-9770)
PHONE..................................479 502-3658
Paul Williams, *Branch Mgr*
EMP: 18
SALES (corp-wide): 997.9MM **Privately Held**
SIC: 8741 Management services
HQ: Watco Supply Chain Services Llc
3905 Elliot Ave
Springdale AR 72762
479 715-8777

(G-2658)
WATKINS CALCARA RONDEAU FRIEDE
1321 Main St Ste 300 (67530-4400)
P.O. Box 1110 (67530-1110)
PHONE..................................620 792-8231
Mark Calcara, *President*
Dianna Cushenbery, *COO*
Earl Watkins, *Vice Pres*
Richard Friedeman, *Officer*
Allen G Glendenning,
EMP: 18
SQ FT: 3,500
SALES (est): 2MM **Privately Held**
WEB: www.wcrf.com
SIC: 8111 General practice law office

(G-2659)
WELLER TRACTOR SALVAGE INC
200 Sw 40 Ave (67530-9354)
PHONE..................................620 792-5243
David Weller, *CEO*
Ruth Weller, *Treasurer*
Becky Weller, *Marketing Staff*
Rebecca Weller, *Admin Sec*
▲ **EMP:** 16 **EST:** 1979
SALES (est): 3.1MM **Privately Held**
WEB: www.wellerparts.com
SIC: 7699 3531 5082 Construction equipment repair; blades for graders, scrapers, dozers & snow plows; graders, motor

(G-2660)
WESTERN AG ENTERPRISES INC
120 S Patton Rd (67530-4612)
PHONE..................................620 793-8355
Kevin Henderson, *Manager*
EMP: 20
SALES (corp-wide): 25.7MM **Privately Held**
SIC: 5191 Farm supplies
PA: Western Ag Enterprises, Inc.
8121 W Harrison St
Tolleson AZ 85353
623 907-4034

(G-2661)
WESTERN KANSAS AND SUPPLY
80 E Tents St (67530)
PHONE..................................620 792-4731
Wally Eldridge, *President*
Deanna Eldridge, *Vice Pres*
EMP: 14
SALES (est): 622.1K **Privately Held**
SIC: 1799 Fence construction

(G-2662)
WESTERN TRUCK EQUIPMENT CO
1310 10th St (67530-5618)
P.O. Box 828 (67530-0828)
PHONE..................................620 793-8464
Ray Moeder, *President*
Bernadine Moeder, *Vice Pres*
Ken Moeder, *Treasurer*
EMP: 10
SQ FT: 6,000
SALES: 1.3MM **Privately Held**
SIC: 3713 3715 5531 Truck beds; truck trailers; truck equipment & parts

(G-2663)
WHEATLAND ELECTRIC COOP INC
2300 Broadway Ave (67530-3920)
P.O. Box 1446 (67530-1446)
PHONE..................................620 793-4223
Chris Huber, *Branch Mgr*
EMP: 19
SALES (corp-wide): 108.6MM **Privately Held**
SIC: 4911 Distribution, electric power
PA: Wheatland Electric Cooperative, Inc.
101 N Main St
Scott City KS 67871
620 872-5885

(G-2664)
WYOMING CASING SERVICE INC
386 Sw 20 Ave (67530)
P.O. Box 815 (67530-0815)
PHONE..................................620 793-9630
Mary Barton, *Branch Mgr*
EMP: 12
SALES (corp-wide): 182.2MM **Privately Held**
SIC: 1389 Haulage, oil field
PA: Wyoming Casing Service, Inc.
198 40th St E
Dickinson ND 58601
701 225-8521

Greeley
Anderson County

(G-2665)
DONOHUE RANCH
Also Called: Greeley Seed Co
331 N Vine (66033-9778)
PHONE..................................785 867-2160
Joe Donohue, *Owner*
Roberta Donohue, *Co-Owner*
EMP: 10
SQ FT: 4,000
SALES (est): 1.3MM **Privately Held**
SIC: 5191 0212 0191 Seeds: field, garden & flower; beef cattle except feedlots; general farms, primarily crop

Green
Clay County

(G-2666)
ROTH FARM
1924 Valleyview Rd (67447-9100)
PHONE..................................785 944-3329
Ronald R Roth, *Partner*
John Roth, *Partner*
Robert Roth, *Partner*
EMP: 10 **EST:** 1948
SALES (est): 4MM **Privately Held**
SIC: 0111 0213 0211 Wheat; hogs; beef cattle feedlots

Greenleaf
Washington County

(G-2667)
CITIZENS NATIONAL BANK (PA)
417 Commercial St (66943-9755)
P.O. Box 309 (66943-0309)
PHONE..................................785 747-2261
Gary W Padgett, *CEO*
Judy Allen, *Senior VP*
Todd Engemoen, *CFO*
Virginia Rawlings, *Manager*
Janece Leduc, *CIO*
EMP: 77 **EST:** 1960
SALES: 7.7MM **Privately Held**
SIC: 6021 National commercial banks

(G-2668)
FARMERS COOPERATIVE ELEV ASSN (PA)
401 Commercial St (66943-9755)
P.O. Box 303 (66943-0303)
PHONE..................................785 747-2236
Pat Breeding, *President*
Leslie Gauby, *Chairman*
Larry Hauschel, *Admin Sec*
EMP: 12
SQ FT: 14,400
SALES (est): 2.7MM **Privately Held**
SIC: 5153 5191 Grains; feed

(G-2669)
GOLDEN SEA GRAPHICS INC
704 Main St (66943-9480)
P.O. Box 36 (66943-0036)
PHONE..................................785 747-2822
Tom Brabec, *President*
Jean Brabec, *Treasurer*
EMP: 6
SQ FT: 576
SALES (est): 758.1K **Privately Held**
SIC: 2396 5699 Printing & embossing on plastics fabric articles; T-shirts, custom printed; sports apparel

(G-2670)
TWIN VLY DVELOPMENTAL SVCS INC (PA)
Also Called: Twin Valley Laundry
413 Commercial St (66943-9755)
P.O. Box 42 (66943-0042)
PHONE..................................785 747-2611
Ed Henry, *CEO*
Edgar C Henry, *CEO*
EMP: 13
SQ FT: 12,000
SALES: 4.8MM **Privately Held**
SIC: 8361 Home for the physically handicapped; group foster home

Greensburg
Kiowa County

(G-2671)
ALLIANCE AG AND GRAIN LLC
311 N Main St (67054-1546)
PHONE..................................620 723-3351
Rod Craft, *Branch Mgr*
EMP: 16
SALES (corp-wide): 55.1MM **Privately Held**
SIC: 5153 5191 Grains; fertilizer & fertilizer materials
PA: Alliance Ag And Grain, Llc
313 N Main St
Spearville KS 67876
620 385-2898

(G-2672)
ANR PIPELINE COMPANY
15499 19th Ave (67054-6800)
PHONE..................................620 723-2381
Ron Banta, *Manager*
EMP: 11
SALES (corp-wide): 10.3B **Privately Held**
SIC: 4922 Natural gas transmission
HQ: Anr Pipeline Company
700 Louisiana St Ste 700 # 700
Houston TX 77002
832 320-2000

(G-2673)
COUNTY OF KIOWA
Also Called: Kiowa County Highway Dept
1002 S Grove St (67054-2105)
PHONE..................................620 723-2531
Travis Payne, *Manager*
EMP: 18 **Privately Held**
SIC: 1611 Highway & street maintenance
PA: County Of Kiowa
211 E Florida Ave
Greensburg KS
620 723-2156

(G-2674)
COUNTY OF KIOWA
Also Called: Kiowa County Memorial Hospital
501 S Walnut St (67054)
P.O. Box 77 (67054-0077)
PHONE..................................620 723-3341

Mary Sweet, *Manager*
EMP: 100 **Privately Held**
SIC: 8062 8082 General medical & surgical hospitals; home health care services
PA: County Of Kiowa
211 E Florida Ave
Greensburg KS
620 723-2156

(G-2675)
GREAT PLAINS HLTH ALIANCE INC
Also Called: Great Plains of Kiowa County
921 N Sycamore St (67054)
PHONE..................................620 723-3341
Mary Colclazier, *Branch Mgr*
EMP: 60
SALES (corp-wide): 112.9MM **Privately Held**
WEB: www.gpha.com
SIC: 8742 Productivity improvement consultant
PA: Great Plains Health Alliance, Inc.
625 3rd St
Phillipsburg KS 67661
785 543-2111

(G-2676)
GREAT PLAINS KIOWA CO INC (HQ)
Also Called: Kiowa County Memorial Hospital
721 W Kansas Ave (67054-1633)
PHONE..................................620 723-3341
Dave Dellesaga, *CEO*
Kelsey Hott, *President*
Mary Sweet, *Administration*
EMP: 90
SALES: 4.5MM
SALES (corp-wide): 112.9MM **Privately Held**
SIC: 8062 General medical & surgical hospitals
PA: Great Plains Health Alliance, Inc.
625 3rd St
Phillipsburg KS 67661
785 543-2111

(G-2677)
GREENSBURG FAMILY PRACTICE PA
721 W Kansas Ave (67054-1633)
PHONE..................................620 723-2127
Jane Oborny, *CFO*
Lori Young, *Manager*
Lavonda Cobb, *Director*
Susan West, *Nursing Dir*
Julie Keeton, *Business Dir*
EMP: 16
SALES (est): 541.7K **Privately Held**
SIC: 8099 Medical services organization

(G-2678)
GREENSBURG STATE BANK
240 S Main St (67054-1726)
P.O. Box 109 (67054-0109)
PHONE..................................620 723-2131
Thomas Corns, *President*
Chris Ballard, *Vice Pres*
William Chris Wirth, *Vice Pres*
EMP: 10 **EST:** 1924
SALES: 1.5MM **Privately Held**
WEB: www.bestbank.us
SIC: 6022 State commercial banks

(G-2679)
HEFT & SONS LLC (PA)
14081 I St (67054-6722)
P.O. Box 200 (67054-0200)
PHONE..................................620 723-2495
Dayle Heft, *Mng Member*
Kevin Heft,
Steve Heft,
EMP: 30
SQ FT: 1,000
SALES (est): 6.6MM **Privately Held**
SIC: 1442 3273 0119 0115 Construction sand mining; ready-mixed concrete; milo farm; corn; wheat; livestock services, except veterinary

(G-2680)
IROQUOIS CTR FOR HUMN DEV INC
610 E Grant Ave (67054-2708)
PHONE..................................620 723-2272
Sheldon Carpenter, *Exec Dir*
C S Carpenter, *Director*
EMP: 50
SALES: 2.5MM **Privately Held**
WEB: www.irqcenter.com
SIC: 8093 Mental health clinic, outpatient

(G-2681)
KIOWA COUNTY EMS
721 W Kansas Ave (67054-1633)
PHONE..................................620 723-3112
Rosa Spainhour, *Director*
EMP: 10
SALES (est): 466.2K **Privately Held**
SIC: 4119 Ambulance service

(G-2682)
L C CROSSFAITH
22259 183 Hwy (67054-4718)
PHONE..................................620 723-2626
Traci Gumtenberger, *Manager*
EMP: 20
SALES (est): 859.5K **Privately Held**
SIC: 0161 Rooted vegetable farms

(G-2683)
PANHANDLE EASTRN PIPE LINE LP
1 Mile W 3/4 N On Hwy 183 (67054)
PHONE..................................620 723-2185
Russell Hardman, *Superintendent*
EMP: 12
SALES (corp-wide): 54B **Publicly Held**
SIC: 4612 Crude petroleum pipelines
HQ: Panhandle Eastern Pipe Line Company, Lp
8111 Westchester Dr # 600
Dallas TX 75225
214 981-0700

(G-2684)
SAND AND SAGE FARM AND RANCH
22035 183 Hwy (67054-4719)
Rural Route R 1 Box 137 (67054)
PHONE..................................620 723-3052
EMP: 10
SALES (est): 432.2K **Privately Held**
SIC: 0191 General Farm

(G-2685)
VOLZ OIL COMPANY - KINSLEY INC
1001 E Kansas Ave (67054-2232)
PHONE..................................620 659-2979
Norman Volz, *President*
EMP: 10
SQ FT: 32,000
SALES: 12MM **Privately Held**
SIC: 5172 Petroleum products

Grenola
Elk County

(G-2686)
GRENOLA SENIOR CITIZENS
121 N Main St (67346)
P.O. Box 63 (67346-0063)
PHONE..................................620 358-3601
Carolyn Hill, *President*
EMP: 10
SALES (est): 189.4K **Privately Held**
SIC: 8322 Senior citizens' center or association

(G-2687)
KELLY MANUFACTURING COMPANY
311 N Cana St (67346-9764)
PHONE..................................620 358-3826
Chris Kelly, *Manager*
EMP: 11
SALES (est): 818.1K **Privately Held**
SIC: 3728 Aircraft parts & equipment
PA: Kelly Manufacturing Company
555 S Topeka Ave
Wichita KS 67202

Gridley
Coffey County

(G-2688)
COFFEY COUNTY DISTRICT 2
502 Main St (66852-9358)
P.O. Box 206 (66852-0206)
PHONE..................................620 836-4080
Mike Arndt, *Principal*
Dale John, *Chairman*
Vernon Barke, *Admin Sec*
EMP: 11
SALES (est): 851.4K **Privately Held**
SIC: 4941 Water supply

(G-2689)
COUNTERTOP TRENDS LLC
406 Main St (66852-9777)
P.O. Box 157 (66852-0157)
PHONE..................................620 836-2311
Jack Haynes, *Purch Agent*
Ryan Landis, *Purch Agent*
Kara Beyer, *Mng Member*
EMP: 50
SQ FT: 30,000
SALES: 4MM **Privately Held**
WEB: www.countertoptrends.com
SIC: 2542 Partitions & fixtures, except wood

(G-2690)
FCS MANUFACTURING
3430 Ee Rd (66852-9332)
PHONE..................................620 427-4200
Jay Luthi, *President*
Jane Luthi, *Corp Secy*
EMP: 5
SQ FT: 3,500
SALES: 410K **Privately Held**
SIC: 3441 Fabricated structural metal

(G-2691)
TRIMBLE & MACLASKEY OIL LLC
110 South St (66852)
PHONE..................................620 836-2000
Randall L Trimble,
EMP: 13
SALES (est): 1.8MM **Privately Held**
SIC: 7353 Oil well drilling equipment, rental or leasing

Grinnell
Gove County

(G-2692)
FRONTIER AG INC
100 Railroad Ave (67738)
P.O. Box 338 (67738-0338)
PHONE..................................785 824-3201
Mike Bucher, *Principal*
EMP: 50 **Privately Held**
SIC: 5153 5191 Grain elevators; feed; seeds: field, garden & flower; fertilizer & fertilizer materials; chemicals, agricultural
PA: Frontier Ag, Inc.
415 W 2nd St
Oakley KS 67748

(G-2693)
GRINNELL LOCKER PLANT INC
108 S Adams (67738-5701)
PHONE..................................785 824-3400
Brian Beckman, *President*
EMP: 14
SQ FT: 3,080
SALES (est): 1.3MM **Privately Held**
SIC: 5421 2013 4222 Meat markets, including freezer provisioners; sausages & other prepared meats; storage, frozen or refrigerated goods

Haddam
Washington County

(G-2694)
BROWN HONEY FARMS
428 Kent St (66944-9055)
PHONE..................................785 778-2002
Robert Brown, *Owner*
Donette Brown, *Co-Owner*
Donna Brown, *Co-Owner*
Jerry Brown, *Co-Owner*
Debra Brown, *Info Tech Mgr*
EMP: 5
SALES: 78K **Privately Held**
SIC: 2099 3312 Honey, strained & bottled; bouillon cubes; beehive coke oven products; electrometallurgical steel

(G-2695)
REVHONEY INC
1104 Main St (66944-9056)
PHONE..................................785 778-2006
Nathaniel J Brown, *Principal*
EMP: 13 **EST:** 2009
SALES (est): 1.6MM **Privately Held**
SIC: 2086 Bottled & canned soft drinks

Halstead
Harvey County

(G-2696)
BRYANT AND BRYANT CNSTR INC
703 Mcnair St (67056-2420)
PHONE..................................316 835-3322
Kaywin Bryant, *President*
Joseph Bryant, *Vice Pres*
EMP: 38
SQ FT: 1,500
SALES (est): 6.6MM **Privately Held**
SIC: 1771 Concrete work

(G-2697)
CITY OF HALSTEAD (PA)
303 Main St (67056-1914)
P.O. Box 312 (67056-0312)
PHONE..................................316 835-2286
William Ewert, *Mayor*
Dianne Muller, *Clerk*
EMP: 22
SQ FT: 3,300 **Privately Held**
WEB: www.halsteadks.com
SIC: 9111 8611 City & town managers' offices; business associations

(G-2698)
CITY OF HALSTEAD
103 Locust St (67056-1613)
PHONE..................................316 835-3492
Pat Adams, *Manager*
EMP: 25 **Privately Held**
WEB: www.halsteadks.com
SIC: 7349 Building maintenance services
PA: City Of Halstead
303 Main St
Halstead KS 67056
316 835-2286

(G-2699)
FARMERS COOPERATIVE ELEV CO (PA)
302 W 1st St (67056-1699)
PHONE..................................316 835-2261
Jack Queen, *President*
Randy Valentine, *Controller*
Carrie Bridges, *Director*
EMP: 15 **EST:** 1918
SQ FT: 2,000
SALES (est): 6.4MM **Privately Held**
WEB: www.farcoop.com
SIC: 5172 5191 5999 5983 Fuel oil; fertilizers & agricultural chemicals; feed & farm supply; fuel oil dealers; fertilizer

(G-2700)
HALSTD-BNTLEY UNFIED SCHL DST (PA)
521 W 6th St (67056-2111)
PHONE..................................316 835-2641
Cory Gibson, *Superintendent*

GEOGRAPHIC

Susan Sigwing, *Purch Dir*
Shawn Kohr,
EMP: 110
SALES (est): 8MM **Privately Held**
WEB: www.usd440.com
SIC: 8211 8351 Public elementary & secondary schools; child day care services

(G-2701)
HALSTEAD PLACE INC
Also Called: Halstead Place Assisted Living
715 W 6th St (67056-2173)
PHONE..................................316 830-2424
Brian Warren, *President*
EMP: 21 **EST:** 1999
SALES (est): 620.8K **Privately Held**
SIC: 8322 8052 Old age assistance; intermediate care facilities

(G-2702)
HARVEY COUNTY INDEPENDENT
Also Called: Heartman Publishing
220 Main St (67056-1913)
P.O. Box 340, Hesston (67062-0340)
PHONE..................................316 835-2235
Robb Reeves, *Owner*
Martha Reeves, *Co-Owner*
EMP: 7
SALES (est): 299.5K **Privately Held**
SIC: 2711 Newspapers: publishing only, not printed on site

(G-2703)
MIDWEST HEALTH SERVICES INC
Also Called: Halstead Hlth & Rehabilitation
915 Mcnair St (67056-2518)
PHONE..................................316 835-4810
Rebecca Wilson, *Manager*
EMP: 47
SALES (corp-wide): 32.7MM **Privately Held**
WEB: www.halsteadhealthrehab.com
SIC: 8051 8093 Convalescent home with continuous nursing care; rehabilitation center, outpatient treatment
PA: Midwest Health, Inc
3024 Sw Wanamaker Rd # 300
Topeka KS 66614
785 272-1535

(G-2704)
SENIOR CENTER
Also Called: Halstead Sixty Plus Club
523 Poplar St (67056-2129)
PHONE..................................316 835-2283
Josephine Unruh, *President*
Larry Smith, *Vice Pres*
Mary Joe Hall, *Treasurer*
Margaret Krisinger, *Admin Sec*
EMP: 20
SALES (est): 312.4K **Privately Held**
SIC: 8322 Social service center

(G-2705)
TRAIL WORTHY INC
312 E 1st St (67056-1700)
PHONE..................................316 337-5311
Todd Wooten, *Principal*
EMP: 6
SALES (est): 390.9K **Privately Held**
SIC: 3559 Wheel balancing equipment, automotive

(G-2706)
WEDGEWOOD GOLF COURSE
9007 W 1st St (67056-9125)
PHONE..................................316 835-2991
Sam Everly, *Superintendent*
EMP: 87
SALES (est): 952.8K **Privately Held**
SIC: 7992 Public golf courses

(G-2707)
WOOTEN ENTERPRISES LLC
312 E 1st St (67056-1700)
PHONE..................................316 830-2328
Kendall C Wooten, *President*
Amanda Hahn, *Director*
EMP: 6
SQ FT: 23,000
SALES (est): 1.1MM **Privately Held**
SIC: 2431 Millwork

Hamilton
Greenwood County

(G-2708)
SCHLOTTERBECK MACHINE SHOP
Also Called: SMS
2599 W Rd N (66853-9775)
PHONE..................................620 678-3210
Don Schlotterbeck, *President*
Barbara Schlotterbeck, *Treasurer*
Donna Schlotterbeck, *Admin Sec*
EMP: 7
SQ FT: 8,000
SALES (est): 520K **Privately Held**
SIC: 3599 7692 Machine shop, jobbing & repair; welding repair

Hanover
Washington County

(G-2709)
B & W ELECTRIC INC
107 W North St (66945-9065)
P.O. Box 96 (66945-0096)
PHONE..................................785 337-2598
Russell H Behrends, *President*
Diane Behrends, *Corp Secy*
EMP: 10
SQ FT: 1,800
SALES (est): 1.5MM **Privately Held**
SIC: 1711 1731 Plumbing contractors; warm air heating & air conditioning contractor; general electrical contractor

(G-2710)
BLUE VALLEY INSURANCE AGENCIES (PA)
Also Called: Mansfeild Agency
204 W North St (66945-9060)
P.O. Box 243, Greenleaf (66943-0243)
PHONE..................................785 337-2268
Dennis E Minge, *President*
Leslie Spence, *Corp Secy*
David Savage, *Vice Pres*
EMP: 11
SALES (est): 1.9MM **Privately Held**
SIC: 6411 Insurance agents

(G-2711)
HANOVER ELECTRIC INC
105 W Washington St (66945-8806)
P.O. Box 308 (66945-0308)
PHONE..................................785 337-2711
Ron D Schlabach, *CEO*
Marjorie Schlabach, *Vice Pres*
Ronald Schlabach, *Admin Sec*
EMP: 10 **EST:** 1949
SQ FT: 3,600
SALES (est): 880K **Privately Held**
SIC: 1731 1711 General electrical contractor; warm air heating & air conditioning contractor; plumbing contractors

(G-2712)
HANOVER HOSPITAL & CLINIC
Also Called: Hanover Home Healthcare
205 S Hanover St (66945-8924)
P.O. Box 38 (66945-0038)
PHONE..................................785 337-2214
Roger Warren, *Administration*
EMP: 83
SQ FT: 8,000
SALES: 3.5MM **Privately Held**
SIC: 8062 General medical & surgical hospitals

(G-2713)
MIDWEST MATERIALS BY MUELLER (PA)
Also Called: Mueller Sand & Gravel
203 W North St (66945-9060)
P.O. Box 396 (66945-0396)
PHONE..................................785 337-2252
Robert D Holle, *President*
Jay Holle, *Vice Pres*
EMP: 15 **EST:** 1948
SALES (est): 4.5MM **Privately Held**
SIC: 1442 3273 Construction sand mining; gravel mining; ready-mixed concrete

(G-2714)
WARREN CLINIC
205 S Hanover St (66945-8924)
P.O. Box 38 (66945-0038)
PHONE..................................785 337-2214
Linda Warren,
EMP: 80
SALES (est): 2.1MM **Privately Held**
SIC: 8011 General & family practice, physician/surgeon

Hanston
Hodgeman County

(G-2715)
WINTER LIVESTOCK INC
Also Called: Pawnee Valley
4 Mi East & 3 Mi St Mi Ea (67849)
PHONE..................................620 525-6271
Mark Winter, *Branch Mgr*
EMP: 20
SALES (corp-wide): 27MM **Privately Held**
SIC: 5154 Auctioning livestock
PA: Winter Livestock Inc
1028 W Cherry Ave
Enid OK 73703
580 237-4600

Harper
Harper County

(G-2716)
BNSF RAILWAY COMPANY
210 E 5th St (67058-1175)
PHONE..................................620 896-2096
EMP: 65
SALES (corp-wide): 223.6B **Publicly Held**
SIC: 4013 Rail Switching/Terminal Services
HQ: Bnsf Railway Company
2650 Lou Menk Dr
Fort Worth TX 76131
800 795-2673

(G-2717)
COBBLESTONER INN AND SUITES
899 Frontage Rd (67058-8056)
PHONE..................................620 896-2400
EMP: 10
SALES (est): 402.6K **Privately Held**
SIC: 7011 Hotels; inns

(G-2718)
COX MACHINE INC
949 N State Road 14 (67058-1928)
PHONE..................................316 943-1342
Rory Traffas, *Branch Mgr*
EMP: 60
SALES (corp-wide): 44.9MM **Privately Held**
SIC: 3599 3728 Machine shop, jobbing & repair; aircraft parts & equipment
PA: Cox Machine, Inc.
5338 W 21st St N Ste 100
Wichita KS 67205
316 943-1342

(G-2719)
DANVILLE INDUSTRIES
124 W Main St (67058-1227)
PHONE..................................620 896-7126
Floyd Ghere, *Partner*
Pam Mc Caslin, *Partner*
EMP: 5
SQ FT: 9,000
SALES: 250K **Privately Held**
SIC: 3524 Lawn & garden equipment

(G-2720)
ELCO MANUFACTURING INC
939 N State Road 14 (67058-1928)
P.O. Box 187 (67058-0187)
PHONE..................................620 896-7333
Rickey Pugh, *President*
Martha Mc Daniel, *Admin Sec*
EMP: 25
SQ FT: 40,000
SALES (est): 3.9MM **Privately Held**
SIC: 3442 5211 Metal doors, sash & trim; door & window products

(G-2721)
ELKHORN VALLEY PACKING CO
101 Central St (67058-8103)
PHONE..................................620 896-2300
Lynn D Grant, *President*
Bonnie Grant, *Vice Pres*
Felisha Ramirez, *Safety Mgr*
Dusty Grant, *Sales Mgr*
Maury Finuf, *Sales Staff*
EMP: 60
SALES (est): 11.1MM **Privately Held**
SIC: 2011 Beef products from beef slaughtered on site

(G-2722)
GREEN LINE INC
Also Called: Big G Manufacturing
851 N State Road 14 (67058-8024)
P.O. Box 434 (67058-0434)
PHONE..................................620 896-7372
Thomas W Wedman, *President*
Georgia Wedman, *Corp Secy*
▲ **EMP:** 10
SQ FT: 18,000
SALES (est): 2.1MM **Privately Held**
WEB: www.greenline.com
SIC: 3523 5211 Plows, agricultural: disc, moldboard, chisel, listers, etc.; prefabricated buildings

(G-2723)
HARPER INDUSTRIES INC
Also Called: Deweze Manufacturing
151 E Us Highway 160 (67058-8201)
PHONE..................................620 896-7381
Tim Penner, *CEO*
Corbin Hostetler, *Vice Pres*
Rita Polsley, *Vice Pres*
Heber Ramer, *Vice Pres*
Luke Thornton, *VP Opers*
▲ **EMP:** 84
SQ FT: 89,000
SALES (est): 29.6MM **Privately Held**
WEB: www.deweze.com
SIC: 3594 3524 3523 Fluid power pumps & motors; lawn & garden equipment; haying machines: mowers, rakes, stackers, etc.

(G-2724)
MIDWEST MACHINING INC
1100 W Main St (67058-2114)
P.O. Box 402 (67058-0402)
PHONE..................................620 896-5050
Larry Gaug, *President*
EMP: 10 **EST:** 1996
SQ FT: 28,000
SALES (est): 1.6MM **Privately Held**
SIC: 3599 Machine shop, jobbing & repair

(G-2725)
WELCH MACHINE INC
870 N State Road 14 (67058-8024)
PHONE..................................620 896-2764
Bob Welch, *President*
EMP: 5
SQ FT: 15,000
SALES: 500K **Privately Held**
SIC: 3599 Machine shop, jobbing & repair

Hartford
Lyon County

(G-2726)
APAC-KANSAS INC
669 County Road Z (66854)
PHONE..................................620 392-5771
Dwayne H Boyo, *President*
Phil Mott, *Manager*
EMP: 15
SALES (corp-wide): 29.7B **Privately Held**
SIC: 1423 Crushed & broken granite
HQ: Apac-Kansas, Inc.
9660 Legler Rd
Lenexa KS 66219

(G-2727)
BRECHEISENS STOP 2 SHOP INC
Also Called: Brecheisen Oil Company
108 E Plumb Ave (66854-9447)
P.O. Box 27 (66854-0027)
PHONE....620 392-5577
Ronnie W Brecheisen, *Owner*
EMP: 20
SQ FT: 2,400
SALES (est): 1.8MM **Privately Held**
SIC: 5541 5171 Filling stations, gasoline; petroleum bulk stations

Havana
Montgomery County

(G-2728)
INTERNATIONAL ASSN LIONS CLUBS
3121 Junction Rd (67347-9101)
PHONE....620 673-8081
Linda Moore, *Admin Sec*
EMP: 33
SALES (corp-wide): 63.7MM **Privately Held**
WEB: www.iaopc.com
SIC: 8641 Civic associations
PA: The International Association Of Lions Clubs Incorporated
300 W 22nd St
Oak Brook IL 60523
630 571-5466

Haven
Reno County

(G-2729)
D & A TRUCKING INC
9304 E Red Rock Rd (67543-8083)
PHONE....620 465-3370
David Borntrager, *President*
Annette Borntrager, *Corp Secy*
Bryan Nelson, *Vice Pres*
EMP: 12
SALES: 1MM **Privately Held**
SIC: 4213 4212 Contract haulers; local trucking, without storage

(G-2730)
FIRST NAT BNK OF HUTCHINSON
101 N Kansas St (67543-9251)
PHONE....620 465-2225
David D Newcomer, *President*
EMP: 23
SALES (corp-wide): 26.4MM **Privately Held**
SIC: 6021 National commercial banks
HQ: The First National Bank Of Hutchinson
1 N Main St Ste 320
Hutchinson KS 67501
620 663-1521

(G-2731)
HAVEN STEEL PRODUCTS INC
13206 S Willison Rd (67543-8580)
P.O. Box 430 (67543-0430)
PHONE....620 465-2573
Marlon Cohn, *President*
Steve Burt, *Engineer*
Steve Oker, *Treasurer*
Kevin Popp, *Sales Executive*
▼ **EMP:** 85
SQ FT: 31,200
SALES (est): 47MM **Privately Held**
WEB: www.havensteel.com
SIC: 3441 Fabricated structural metal

(G-2732)
IMPERIAL SLEEP PRODUCTS INC
Also Called: Restonic & Imperial Sleep Pdts
8819 E Industrial Rd (67543)
P.O. Box 450 (67543-0450)
PHONE....620 465-2242
Roland A Elpers, *President*
Stanley Elpers, *Vice Pres*
Mary Jane Elpers, *Admin Sec*
▲ **EMP:** 20
SQ FT: 31,000
SALES (est): 2.1MM **Privately Held**
SIC: 2515 Mattresses, innerspring or box spring

(G-2733)
KAUFFMAN SEEDS INC
Also Called: Mid Land Seed
7508 S Mayfield Rd (67543-8102)
PHONE....877 664-3526
Tom Clayman, *President*
Dustine Miller, *Vice Pres*
EMP: 15 **EST:** 1966
SQ FT: 15,930
SALES: 1.7MM **Privately Held**
SIC: 5191 0723 Seeds: field, garden & flower; seed cleaning

(G-2734)
MID-KANSAS COOPERATIVE ASSN
112 W 2nd St (67543-8202)
P.O. Box 469 (67543-0469)
PHONE....620 465-2292
Perry Stussy, *Manager*
EMP: 11
SALES (corp-wide): 371.5MM **Privately Held**
WEB: www.mkcoop.com
SIC: 5153 Grains
PA: Mid-Kansas Cooperative Association
307 W Cole St
Moundridge KS 67107
620 345-6328

(G-2735)
PANHANDLE EASTRN PIPE LINE LP
Also Called: Panhandle Eastern Pipeline
12610 S Kent Rd (67543-8006)
PHONE....620 465-2201
Mike Cox, *Enginr/R&D Mgr*
EMP: 25
SALES (corp-wide): 54B **Publicly Held**
SIC: 4922 Natural gas transmission
HQ: Panhandle Eastern Pipe Line Company, Lp
8111 Westchester Dr # 600
Dallas TX 75225
214 981-0700

(G-2736)
SCHMIDT HAVEN FORD SALES INC
121 S Kansas St (67543-9261)
P.O. Box G (67543-0229)
PHONE....620 465-2252
John H Schmidt, *President*
Marline Schmidt, *Corp Secy*
Leroy D Schmidt, *Vice Pres*
Mary Schmidt, *Treasurer*
EMP: 16 **EST:** 1980
SQ FT: 5,600
SALES: 2.5MM
SALES (corp-wide): 12.5MM **Privately Held**
WEB: www.schmidtinc.com
SIC: 5511 7538 Automobiles, new & used; general automotive repair shops
PA: John Schmidt & Sons, Inc.
12903 E Silver Lake Rd
Mount Hope KS 67108
316 445-2103

(G-2737)
SLEEP HAVEN INC
8819 E Industrial Dr (67543)
P.O. Box 450 (67543-0450)
PHONE....620 465-2242
Kevin Evenson, *President*
EMP: 10 **EST:** 2012
SALES (est): 2.3MM **Privately Held**
SIC: 2515 Mattresses & bedsprings

(G-2738)
WHEATLAND INVESTMENTS INC
Also Called: Bankhaven
101 N Kansas St (67543-9251)
P.O. Box A (67543-0136)
PHONE....620 465-2225
Dean W Fahrbach, *President*
David Newcomer, *President*
Timothy J Fahrbach, *Director*
Michael Fahrbach, *Admin Sec*
EMP: 13 **Privately Held**
SIC: 6712 Bank holding companies

Havensville
Pottawatomie County

(G-2739)
ANR PIPELINE COMPANY
19955 English Ridge Rd (66432-9715)
PHONE....785 948-2670
Steve Askren, *Plant Mgr*
Kenneth Switzer, *Manager*
EMP: 18
SALES (corp-wide): 10.3B **Privately Held**
SIC: 4922 Natural gas transmission
HQ: Anr Pipeline Company
700 Louisiana St Ste 700 # 700
Houston TX 77002
832 320-2000

Haviland
Kiowa County

(G-2740)
HAVILAND BANCSHARES INC (PA)
Also Called: HAVILAND STATE BANK
209 N Main St (67059-5902)
P.O. Box 348 (67059-0348)
PHONE....620 862-5222
Stephen Matthews, *Ch of Bd*
Trent Jacks, *Senior VP*
Stan Robertson, *Vice Pres*
EMP: 12
SQ FT: 2,500
SALES: 1.7MM **Privately Held**
WEB: www.havilandstatebank.com
SIC: 6022 State commercial banks

(G-2741)
HAVILAND TELEPHONE COMPANY INC (HQ)
106 N Main St (67059-9500)
P.O. Box 308 (67059-0308)
PHONE....620 862-5211
Gene Morris, *President*
Robert E Dolan, *Vice Pres*
John Cole, *Admin Sec*
EMP: 13
SQ FT: 3,400
SALES (est): 4.4MM
SALES (corp-wide): 392.6MM **Publicly Held**
SIC: 4813 Local telephone communications
PA: Lict Corporation
401 Theodore Fremd Ave
Rye NY 10580
914 921-8821

(G-2742)
SURVEY COMPANIES LLC
200 Main St (67059)
PHONE....620 862-5291
EMP: 38 **Privately Held**
SIC: 8051 Skilled nursing care facilities
PA: The Survey Companies Llc
3008 7th Ave S
Birmingham AL 35233

Hays
Ellis County

(G-2743)
A-1 SCAFFOLD MFG INC
590 Commerce Pkwy (67601-9320)
PHONE....785 621-5121
Dwight Allenbaugh, *President*
Sam Hull, *CFO*
Kandyce Kloeckner, *Sales Staff*
Brian Dube, *Technology*
▲ **EMP:** 40
SALES: 2MM **Privately Held**
SIC: 3315 Steel wire & related products

(G-2744)
ADAMS BROWN BRAN BALL CHRTERED
Also Called: Adams Brown Beran Ball
718 Main St Ste 224 (67601-4465)
P.O. Box 1186 (67601-1186)
PHONE....785 628-3046
Ken Beran, *Director*
Becky Graver, *Admin Asst*
EMP: 20
SALES (corp-wide): 9.4MM **Privately Held**
SIC: 8721 Certified public accountant
PA: Adams, Brown, Beran & Ball Chartered Inc
2006 Broadway Ave
Great Bend KS 67530
620 549-3271

(G-2745)
AMAZING GRACE STAFFING INC
2004 Hall St (67601-3140)
PHONE....785 432-2920
Isaac North, *CEO*
Kelly Ancar, *Chairman*
EMP: 30
SALES: 350K **Privately Held**
SIC: 7361 Registries

(G-2746)
AMERICAN BOTTLING COMPANY
723 E 6th St (67601-3914)
PHONE....785 625-4488
Tim Herman, *Branch Mgr*
EMP: 70 **Publicly Held**
SIC: 2086 Bottled & canned soft drinks
HQ: The American Bottling Company
5301 Legacy Dr
Plano TX 75024

(G-2747)
AMPHENOL ADRONICS INC
608 E 13th St (67601-3444)
PHONE....785 625-3000
Shirley Grecian, *Manager*
EMP: 75
SALES (est): 11.5MM
SALES (corp-wide): 8.2B **Publicly Held**
SIC: 3465 Body parts, automobile: stamped metal
PA: Amphenol Corporation
358 Hall Ave
Wallingford CT 06492
203 265-8900

(G-2748)
ANSWERNET INC
2000 E 13th St (67601-2664)
PHONE....785 301-2810
Dan Esmand, *Principal*
EMP: 15
SALES (corp-wide): 62.6MM **Privately Held**
SIC: 7389 5065 Telemarketing services; telephone & telegraphic equipment
PA: Answernet, Inc.
3930 Commerce Ave
Willow Grove PA 19090
800 411-5777

(G-2749)
APAC-KANSAS INC
820 Cantebury Rd (67601)
P.O. Box 190 (67601-0190)
PHONE....785 625-3459
Cheryl Rohleder, *Office Mgr*
Ken Johnson, *Manager*
EMP: 100
SALES (corp-wide): 29.7B **Privately Held**
SIC: 1611 Highway & street paving contractor
HQ: Apac-Kansas, Inc.
9660 Legler Rd
Lenexa KS 66219

(G-2750)
ARVEDA LLC
Also Called: Stromgren Supports
718 Main St Ste 201 (67601-4465)
P.O. Box 1001, Gardner (66030-1001)
PHONE....785 625-4674
Steve Arensdorf,
▲ **EMP:** 50

GEOGRAPHIC

SQ FT: 400,000
SALES (est): 5.2MM Privately Held
WEB: www.stromgren.com
SIC: 3842 Braces, orthopedic; elastic hosiery, orthopedic (support); hosiery, support

(G-2751)
AT&T CORP
126 W 11th St (67601-3606)
PHONE..................................785 625-0120
Bob Reiner, *Area Mgr*
EMP: 22
SALES (corp-wide): 170.7B Publicly Held
WEB: www.swbell.com
SIC: 4813 Telephone cable service, land or submarine
HQ: At&T Corp.
1 At&T Way
Bedminster NJ 07921
800 403-3302

(G-2752)
AUMAN CO INC
311 E 11th St (67601-3503)
PHONE..................................785 628-2833
William J Auman, *President*
Vicki Auman, *Corp Secy*
EMP: 10
SQ FT: 1,575
SALES (est): 1.4MM Privately Held
SIC: 1711 7623 Warm air heating & air conditioning contractor; plumbing contractors; heating systems repair & maintenance; air conditioning repair

(G-2753)
B & L MOTELS INC (PA)
Also Called: Comfort Inn
2810 Vine St (67601-1927)
PHONE..................................785 628-8008
Bruce Weilert, *President*
EMP: 15
SALES (est): 2.6MM Privately Held
SIC: 7011 Hotels & motels

(G-2754)
BAKER HGHES OLFLD OPRTIONS LLC
103 E 27th St (67601-2956)
PHONE..................................785 650-0182
Dan Pfannenstiel, *Accounts Mgr*
Dona Hughes, *Branch Mgr*
EMP: 106
SALES (corp-wide): 22.8B Publicly Held
SIC: 1389 Oil field services
HQ: Baker Hughes Oilfield Operations Llc
17021 Aldine Westfield Rd
Houston TX 77073
713 879-1000

(G-2755)
BANK AMERICA NATIONAL ASSN
1200 E 27th St (67601-2106)
PHONE..................................785 625-3413
Anne Zimmerman, *Manager*
EMP: 15
SALES (corp-wide): 110.5B Publicly Held
WEB: www.bofa.com
SIC: 6021 National commercial banks
HQ: Bank Of America, National Association
100 S Tryon St
Charlotte NC 28202
704 386-5681

(G-2756)
BANK OF HAYS (PA)
1000 W 27th St (67601-4825)
P.O. Box 640 (67601-0640)
PHONE..................................785 621-2265
Brandon Prough, *General Mgr*
Randy Walker, *Principal*
Michelle Rounsley, *Vice Pres*
Gary Wentling, *Vice Pres*
Josh Smith, *Officer*
EMP: 14
SALES: 10.5MM Privately Held
SIC: 6022 State trust companies accepting deposits, commercial

(G-2757)
BEREXCO LLC
800a Commerce Pkwy (67601-9322)
P.O. Box 723 (67601-0723)
PHONE..................................785 628-6101
Dennis Kirmer, *CFO*
EMP: 18
SALES (corp-wide): 456.6MM Privately Held
SIC: 1311 Crude petroleum production
PA: Berexco Llc
2020 N Bramblewood St
Wichita KS 67206
316 265-3311

(G-2758)
BIG DS RENT ALL
1110 E 22nd St (67601-2422)
PHONE..................................785 625-2443
Dale Staab, *Owner*
EMP: 14 EST: 2011
SALES (est): 2.3MM Privately Held
SIC: 7359 Rental store, general

(G-2759)
BLACK DIAMOND OIL INC
P.O. Box 641 (67601-0641)
PHONE..................................785 625-5891
Kenneth Vehige, *President*
EMP: 5
SQ FT: 1,000
SALES (est): 635.8K Privately Held
SIC: 1311 Crude petroleum production

(G-2760)
BOW CREEK OIL COMPANY LLC
1304 Eisenhower Rd (67601-2532)
PHONE..................................785 650-1738
EMP: 7
SALES: 3MM Privately Held
SIC: 1382 Oil/Gas Exploration Services

(G-2761)
BROOKDALE SENIOR LIVING COMMUN
Also Called: Sterling House of Hays
1801 E 27th St Ofc (67601-2128)
PHONE..................................785 628-1111
Beverly Hartsook, *Corp Comm Staff*
Lisa Leiker, *Manager*
EMP: 20
SALES (corp-wide): 4.5B Publicly Held
WEB: www.assisted.com
SIC: 8051 Skilled nursing care facilities
HQ: Brookdale Senior Living Communities, Inc.
6737 W Wa St Ste 2300
Milwaukee WI 53214
414 918-5000

(G-2762)
C & P ENTERPRISES INC
Also Called: ServiceMaster
808 Milner St (67601-4135)
P.O. Box 748 (67601-0748)
PHONE..................................785 628-6712
Cory J Munsch, *President*
Pam Munsch, *Vice Pres*
EMP: 25
SQ FT: 3,000
SALES (est): 722.2K Privately Held
SIC: 7349 1521 Building maintenance services; repairing fire damage, single-family houses

(G-2763)
C&J WELL SERVICES INC
Eli Wireline
1327 Noose Rd (67601-9744)
PHONE..................................785 628-6395
Fred Barber, *Branch Mgr*
EMP: 30 Privately Held
SIC: 1389 Oil field services
HQ: C&J Well Services, Inc.
3990 Rogerdale Rd
Houston TX 77042
713 325-6000

(G-2764)
CARE A LOT DAYCARE
401 Oak St (67601-4136)
PHONE..................................785 628-2563
EMP: 10 EST: 2010
SALES (est): 230K Privately Held
SIC: 8351 Child Day Care Services

(G-2765)
CARRICO IMPLEMENT CO INC
Also Called: John Deere Authorized Dealer
300 W 48th St (67601-9465)
PHONE..................................785 625-2219
Bryan Pekarek, *Manager*
Judy Gracey, *Info Tech Mgr*
EMP: 30
SALES (corp-wide): 58.8MM Privately Held
WEB: www.carricoimplement.com
SIC: 5083 5945 Farm implements; lawn machinery & equipment; garden machinery & equipment; hobby, toy & game shops
PA: Carrico Implement Co., Inc.
3160 Us 24 Hwy
Beloit KS 67420
785 738-5744

(G-2766)
CBI-KANSAS INC
Also Called: Commerce Bank
2200 Vine St (67601-2405)
P.O. Box 10 (67601-0010)
PHONE..................................785 625-6542
Tom Thomas, *Branch Mgr*
EMP: 36
SALES (corp-wide): 1.3B Publicly Held
SIC: 6021 National commercial banks
HQ: Cbi-Kansas, Inc.
1000 Walnut St Fl 700
Kansas City MO

(G-2767)
CERVS CONOCO & CONVENIENCE
2701 Vine St (67601-1925)
PHONE..................................785 625-7777
Russ Pfannenstiel, *Owner*
EMP: 15
SALES (est): 1.1MM Privately Held
SIC: 5411 5541 7999 Convenience stores; filling stations, gasoline; lottery tickets, sale of

(G-2768)
CHEM-TECH LLC
1023 Reservation Rd (67601-3982)
PHONE..................................785 625-1141
Bob Goodrow, *Principal*
EMP: 5 EST: 1996
SALES (est): 329K Privately Held
SIC: 1389 Oil field services

(G-2769)
CLASSIC ENTERPRISES INC
Also Called: Classic Quality Body Shop
2719 Plaza Ave (67601-1921)
PHONE..................................785 628-6700
Shelton J Renz, *President*
Shelton Renz, *President*
Nancy Pfeifer, *Manager*
EMP: 13
SQ FT: 6,000
SALES (est): 1.3MM Privately Held
SIC: 7514 Rent-a-car service

(G-2770)
CLAYTON J BEFORT
Also Called: Befort Harvest and Trucking
1177 Commerce Pkwy (67601-9300)
PHONE..................................785 625-7628
Clayton J Befort, *Owner*
EMP: 16
SALES (est): 3.1MM Privately Held
SIC: 0722 4212 Crop harvesting; animal & farm product transportation services

(G-2771)
CLEAN-RITE LLC
1307 Vine St (67601-3427)
PHONE..................................785 628-1945
Cristin Chester, *President*
EMP: 10 EST: 1968
SQ FT: 4,000
SALES: 1.5MM Privately Held
WEB: www.cleanritejanitorialsupply.com
SIC: 7349 5087 7217 Janitorial service, contract basis; janitors' supplies; carpet & furniture cleaning on location

(G-2772)
CLOUD STORAGE CORPORATION
1305 Canterbury Dr (67601-2707)
PHONE..................................785 621-4350
Shirley Liu, *President*
▲ EMP: 10
SQ FT: 12,000
SALES: 7MM Privately Held
SIC: 5045 Computer peripheral equipment

(G-2773)
COMMERCE BANK
2200 Vine St (67601-4445)
PHONE..................................785 625-6542
Lindsay Martin, *Accounting Mgr*
Kerry McQueen, *Branch Mgr*
EMP: 13
SALES (corp-wide): 1.3B Publicly Held
SIC: 6022 State commercial banks
HQ: Commerce Bank
1000 Walnut St Fl 700
Kansas City MO 64106
816 234-2000

(G-2774)
COMMERCIAL BUILDERS INC
2717 Canal Blvd Ste I (67601-1770)
PHONE..................................785 625-6272
Gary Weatherbee, *President*
Debra Weatherbee, *Treasurer*
EMP: 60
SQ FT: 1,100
SALES (est): 11.3MM Privately Held
SIC: 1542 Commercial & office building, new construction

(G-2775)
COMMERCIAL SIGN COMPANY HAY
Also Called: Company Commercial Sign
720 E 7th St (67601-3919)
PHONE..................................785 625-1765
Bruce Bandy, *Owner*
EMP: 12
SALES (est): 1.1MM Privately Held
SIC: 3993 Electric signs
PA: Bandy Enterprises Inc
1185 Zelfer Ave
Colby KS 67701

(G-2776)
CONCRETE SERVICE CO INC
Also Called: Ellis County Concrete Co
1648 230th Ave (67601-9739)
P.O. Box 69 (67601-0069)
PHONE..................................785 628-2100
Todd Jacobs, *Branch Mgr*
EMP: 6
SALES (corp-wide): 3.2MM Privately Held
SIC: 3273 1611 Ready-mixed concrete; concrete construction: roads, highways, sidewalks, etc.
PA: Concrete Service Co., Inc.
221 Baker Ave
Great Bend KS 67530
620 792-2558

(G-2777)
COUNTRYSIDE OF HAYS INC
Also Called: ARC
1000 Reservation Rd (67601-3981)
PHONE..................................785 625-6539
L Van Witthuhn, *President*
EMP: 9
SALES (est): 777K Privately Held
WEB: www.countrysidehays.com
SIC: 2452 Modular homes, prefabricated, wood

(G-2778)
COUNTY OF ELLIS
Also Called: Ellis County Highway Dept
1195 280th Ave (67601-9325)
P.O. Box 691 (67601-0691)
PHONE..................................785 628-9455
Bill Ring, *Superintendent*
EMP: 58 Privately Held
WEB: www.ellisco.net
SIC: 1622 9111 Bridge construction; county supervisors' & executives' offices

PA: County Of Ellis
718 Main St Ste 206
Hays KS 67601
785 628-9450

(G-2779)
CP PARTNERSHIPS INC
Also Called: T R'S Sportswear
1003 Main St (67601-3616)
PHONE..................................785 625-7388
Duane Kramer, *President*
Steve Pfannenstiel, *Vice Pres*
EMP: 16
SQ FT: 12,000
SALES: 1MM **Privately Held**
WEB: www.trsportswear.com
SIC: 2395 2261 Embroidery & art needlework; screen printing of cotton broadwoven fabrics

(G-2780)
CROSS MANUFACTURING INC
901 Canterbury Dr (67601-4518)
PHONE..................................785 625-2585
Greg Schmidt, *Production*
Doug Dinkel, *Purchasing*
Eric Schmidt, *Supervisor*
EMP: 64
SALES (est): 9.8MM
SALES (corp-wide): 21.3MM **Privately Held**
WEB: www.crossmfg.com
SIC: 3592 5084 3492 3594 Carburetors, pistons, rings, valves; hydraulic systems equipment & supplies; fluid power valves & hose fittings; fluid power pumps & motors; fluid power cylinders & actuators
PA: Cross Manufacturing, Inc.
11011 King St Ste 210
Overland Park KS 66210
913 451-1233

(G-2781)
DAMAR RESOURCES INC
234 W 11th St Ste A (67601-3805)
P.O. Box 70 (67601-0070)
PHONE..................................785 625-0020
Daniel F Schippers, *President*
Curtis R Longpine, *Treasurer*
EMP: 5
SQ FT: 2,000
SALES: 3.5MM **Privately Held**
SIC: 1311 1382 Crude petroleum production; oil & gas exploration services

(G-2782)
DAVID M KING & ASSOCIATES
Also Called: Raymond James
103 W 13th St Bsmt (67601-4774)
PHONE..................................319 377-4636
Harold Pierce, *Manager*
EMP: 10
SALES (corp-wide): 3.4MM **Privately Held**
SIC: 6211 6282 Brokers, security; investment advisory service
PA: King, David M & Associates Ltd
1425 Oread West St # 106
Lawrence KS 66049
785 841-9517

(G-2783)
DEBAKEY HEART CLINIC
2220 Canterbury Dr (67601-2370)
PHONE..................................785 625-4699
Sammy Minear, *Office Mgr*
EMP: 16
SALES (est): 770K **Privately Held**
SIC: 8011 Clinic, operated by physicians; cardiologist & cardio-vascular specialist

(G-2784)
DELTA OMEGA OF DELTA ZETA BLDG
410 W 6th St (67601-4695)
PHONE..................................785 625-3719
EMP: 50
SALES: 94.9K **Privately Held**
SIC: 7041 Membership-Basis Lodging

(G-2785)
DEVELOPMENTAL SVCS NW KANS INC (PA)
Also Called: Dsnwk
2703 Hall St Ste B10 (67601-1899)
P.O. Box 310 (67601-0310)
PHONE..................................785 625-5678
Gerard Michaud, *President*
Stephanie Pelkey, *Manager*
EMP: 32
SQ FT: 14,125
SALES: 14.4MM **Privately Held**
SIC: 8059 Home for the mentally retarded, exc. skilled or intermediate

(G-2786)
DEVELOPMENTAL SVCS NW KANS INC
Also Called: Dsnwk
317 W 13th St (67601-3703)
PHONE..................................785 625-2521
James Blume, *General Mgr*
EMP: 200
SALES (corp-wide): 14.4MM **Privately Held**
SIC: 8059 8322 Home for the mentally retarded, exc. skilled or intermediate; individual & family services
PA: Developmental Services Of Northwest Kansas, Inc.
2703 Hall St Ste B10
Hays KS 67601
785 625-5678

(G-2787)
DEVELOPMENTAL SVCS NW KANS INC
Also Called: Access Van Service
1205 E 22nd St (67601)
P.O. Box 1016 (67601-1016)
PHONE..................................785 621-2078
Ron Strait, *Manager*
EMP: 15
SALES (corp-wide): 14.4MM **Privately Held**
SIC: 4119 Local passenger transportation
PA: Developmental Services Of Northwest Kansas, Inc.
2703 Hall St Ste B10
Hays KS 67601
785 625-5678

(G-2788)
DISCOUNT SIDING SUPPLY LP
Also Called: Discount Sding Spply-Hys/Bloit
2706 Plaza Ave (67601-1922)
P.O. Box 718 (67601-0718)
PHONE..................................785 625-4619
James Fout, *Ltd Ptnr*
EMP: 15
SALES: 1.6MM **Privately Held**
WEB: www.discountsiding.net
SIC: 1761 1751 1799 5033 Siding contractor; window & door (prefabricated) installation; fence construction; roofing & siding materials; patio & deck construction & repair

(G-2789)
DISCOVERY DRILLING CO INC
1029 Reservation Rd (67601-3982)
P.O. Box 763 (67601-0763)
PHONE..................................785 623-2920
Thomas H Alm, *President*
Glenna Alm, *Treasurer*
EMP: 50
SALES: 3.5MM **Privately Held**
SIC: 1381 Drilling oil & gas wells

(G-2790)
DISCOVERY DRILLING SHOP
1029 Reservation Rd (67601-3982)
P.O. Box 763 (67601-0763)
PHONE..................................785 650-0029
Thomas Alm, *Owner*
EMP: 30
SALES (est): 1.1MM **Privately Held**
SIC: 1799 Core drilling & cutting

(G-2791)
DREILING OIL INC
1008 Cody Ave (67601-2431)
P.O. Box 550 (67601-0550)
PHONE..................................785 625-8327
John G Dreiling, *President*
Joe Hess, *Exec VP*
EMP: 5
SQ FT: 3,000
SALES: 300K **Privately Held**
SIC: 1389 1311 Servicing oil & gas wells; crude petroleum production

(G-2792)
EAGLE BRADBAND INVESTMENTS LLC
2703 Hall St Ste 15 (67601-1964)
P.O. Box 817 (67601-0817)
PHONE..................................785 625-5910
Rod Siemers,
EMP: 17
SALES (est): 163.2K
SALES (corp-wide): 209MM **Privately Held**
SIC: 4813
PA: Gtcr Llc
300 N La Salle Dr # 5600
Chicago IL 60654
312 382-2200

(G-2793)
EAGLE COMMUNICATIONS INC (PA)
Also Called: Eagle Radio
2703 Hall St 15 (67601-1964)
P.O. Box 817 (67601-0817)
PHONE..................................785 625-5910
Gary Shorman, *Ch of Bd*
Kurt David, *President*
Joe Jeter, *Corp Secy*
Curtis Longpine, *Vice Pres*
Mark Trotman, *Vice Pres*
EMP: 10 **EST:** 1946
SALES (est): 71.7MM **Privately Held**
WEB: www.eaglecom.net
SIC: 4832 4841 Radio broadcasting stations; cable television services

(G-2794)
EAGLE COMMUNICATIONS INC
Also Called: Ellis Cable TV Co
1007 W 27th St (67601-4818)
PHONE..................................785 726-3291
Rex Skiles, *Manager*
EMP: 12
SALES (corp-wide): 71.7MM **Privately Held**
WEB: www.eaglecom.net
SIC: 4832 7313 4813 4841 Radio broadcasting stations; television & radio time sales; ; cable & other pay television services
PA: Eagle Communications, Inc.
2703 Hall St 15
Hays KS 67601
785 625-5910

(G-2795)
EAGLE COMMUNICATIONS INC
Also Called: K H A Z FM Radio
2300 Hall St (67601-3062)
P.O. Box 6 (67601-0006)
PHONE..................................785 650-5349
Tanja Galander, *Partner*
Todd Nelson, *Manager*
EMP: 60
SALES (corp-wide): 71.7MM **Privately Held**
WEB: www.eaglecom.net
SIC: 4832 7313 Radio broadcasting stations; radio, television, publisher representatives
PA: Eagle Communications, Inc.
2703 Hall St 15
Hays KS 67601
785 625-5910

(G-2796)
EARLY CHILDHOOD CONNECTIONS
2501 E 13th St Ste 1 (67601-2764)
PHONE..................................785 623-2430
Donna Hudson-Hamilton, *Director*
EMP: 35
SALES (est): 407.9K **Privately Held**
WEB: www.haysheadstart.com
SIC: 8351 Child day care services

(G-2797)
ECONO LODGE
3503 Vine St (67601-1952)
PHONE..................................785 625-4839
Chuck Patel, *Owner*
Matesh Patel, *Principal*
EMP: 12
SALES (est): 641.7K **Privately Held**
SIC: 7011 1522 Hotels & motels; hotel/motel, new construction

(G-2798)
EMPRISE BANK NATIONAL ASSN (HQ)
1011 W 27th St (67601-4823)
PHONE..................................785 625-6595
Wayne Woofter, *President*
Coleen Tabor, *Exec VP*
Aaron K Veatch, *Exec VP*
Connie Bollig, *Vice Pres*
Michael Hessman, *Vice Pres*
EMP: 49
SQ FT: 51,000
SALES (est): 9.7MM
SALES (corp-wide): 80MM **Privately Held**
SIC: 6022 State commercial banks
PA: Emprise Financial Corporation
211 N Broadway Ave
Wichita KS 67202
316 264-8394

(G-2799)
ENERSYS
1 Enersys Rd (67601-9706)
PHONE..................................785 625-3355
David Hutchinson, *Manager*
Mason Younger, *IT Specialist*
EMP: 180
SALES (corp-wide): 2.8B **Publicly Held**
SIC: 3691 5063 Lead acid batteries (storage batteries); storage batteries, industrial
PA: Enersys
2366 Bernville Rd
Reading PA 19605
610 208-1991

(G-2800)
ERROL E ENGEL INC
Also Called: I-70 Truck Repair
5500 N Vine St (67601)
P.O. Box 921 (67601-0921)
PHONE..................................785 625-3195
Erroll E Engel, *President*
Nadine Engel, *Admin Sec*
EMP: 24
SQ FT: 16,000
SALES (est): 3.8MM **Privately Held**
SIC: 5013 7538 Truck parts & accessories; general automotive repair shops

(G-2801)
EVANGELICAL LUTHERAN
Also Called: Good Samaritan Society - Hays
2700 Canal Blvd (67601-1702)
P.O. Box 5038, Sioux Falls SD (57117-5038)
PHONE..................................785 625-7331
Noe Gillespie, *Branch Mgr*
EMP: 126 **Privately Held**
WEB: www.good-sam.com
SIC: 8059 Nursing home, except skilled & intermediate care facility
HQ: The Evangelical Lutheran Good Samaritan Society
4800 W 57th St
Sioux Falls SD 57108
866 928-1635

(G-2802)
EVANGELICAL LUTHERAN
Also Called: Good Samaritan Cntral KS
2703 Hall St Ste 6 (67601-1964)
PHONE..................................785 621-2499
Cherie Mattson, *Branch Mgr*
EMP: 116 **Privately Held**
SIC: 8051 8052 Convalescent home with continuous nursing care; intermediate care facilities
HQ: The Evangelical Lutheran Good Samaritan Society
4800 W 57th St
Sioux Falls SD 57108
866 928-1635

GEOGRAPHIC

(G-2803)
EYE SPECIALISTS
Also Called: Pokorny, John C MD
2214 Canterbury Dr # 312 (67601-2387)
PHONE..................................785 628-8218
Tom McDonald MD, *Partner*
John C Pokory MD, *Partner*
EMP: 11
SALES (est): 1.2MM **Privately Held**
SIC: 8011 Eyes, ears, nose & throat specialist: physician/surgeon

(G-2804)
FANCHON BALLROOM & SUPPER CLUB
2350 Old Hwy 40 (67601)
PHONE..................................785 628-8154
Alfred Linenberger, *Owner*
EMP: 10 **EST:** 1979
SQ FT: 14,000
SALES (est): 145K **Privately Held**
SIC: 7911 5812 Dance hall or ballroom operation; restaurant, family: independent

(G-2805)
FERGUSON PROPERTIES INC
Also Called: Fairfield Inn
377 W Mopar Dr (67601-9479)
PHONE..................................785 625-3344
Carol McCall, *Manager*
EMP: 22
SALES (est): 1.1MM **Privately Held**
WEB: www.fergusonproperties.com
SIC: 7011 Hotels & motels

(G-2806)
FIRST CALL FOR HELP ELLIS CNTY
607 E 13th St (67601-3443)
PHONE..................................785 623-2800
Shirley Green, *President*
Judy Caprez, *Vice Pres*
Walt Manteuffel, *Treasurer*
Pam Blau, *Exec Dir*
Jane Vanick, *Admin Sec*
EMP: 20 **EST:** 1995
SALES: 214.7K **Privately Held**
SIC: 8999 Information bureau

(G-2807)
FIRST CARE CLINIC INC
105 W 13th St (67601-3613)
PHONE..................................785 621-4990
Bryan Brady, *CEO*
Nancy Apel, *CFO*
EMP: 22
SALES: 4.8MM **Privately Held**
SIC: 8011 8021 Clinic, operated by physicians; dental clinics & offices

(G-2808)
FISCHER WELL SERVICE INC
1316 Central St (67601-9214)
P.O. Box 773 (67601-0773)
PHONE..................................785 628-3837
Donald A Fischer, *President*
EMP: 9
SALES (est): 852.9K **Privately Held**
SIC: 1389 7389 Oil field services;

(G-2809)
FISHING LIGHTS ETC LLC (PA)
2707 Vine St Ste 7 (67601-1907)
PHONE..................................785 621-2646
Thomas Payne, *Mng Member*
▲ **EMP:** 9
SALES (est): 864.5K **Privately Held**
SIC: 3648 3646 3645 Underwater lighting fixtures; fluorescent lighting fixtures, commercial; fluorescent lighting fixtures, residential; garden, patio, walkway & yard lighting fixtures: electric

(G-2810)
FIVE STAR SERVICE INC
Also Called: Five Star Amoco
1300 Vine St (67601-3454)
PHONE..................................785 625-9400
Greg Werth, *President*
Glen Werth, *Vice Pres*
Tim Werth, *Director*
EMP: 30
SALES: 3MM **Privately Held**
SIC: 7539 Automotive repair shops

(G-2811)
FORT HAYS STATE UNIVERSITY
Also Called: Sternberg Mseum Ntural History
3000 Sternberg Dr (67601-2006)
PHONE..................................785 628-4286
Jerry Choate, *Director*
EMP: 50
SALES (corp-wide): 81.3MM **Privately Held**
WEB: www.fhsu.edu
SIC: 8412 8221 Museum; university
PA: Fort Hays State University
600 Park St
Hays KS 67601
785 628-4000

(G-2812)
FRANK COMMUNICATIONS HAYS INC
1005 E 17th St (67601-2417)
PHONE..................................785 623-1500
Leon Frank, *President*
Janet Frank, *Vice Pres*
EMP: 8
SQ FT: 6,000
SALES: 1MM **Privately Held**
SIC: 3663 Radio & TV communications equipment

(G-2813)
FRESENIUS MED CARE W WLLOW LLC
2905 Canterbury Dr (67601-2152)
PHONE..................................785 625-0033
Sherry Brown, *Manager*
EMP: 12
SALES (corp-wide): 18.3B **Privately Held**
SIC: 8092 Kidney dialysis centers
HQ: Fresenius Medical Care West Willow, Llc
2201 W Plano Pkwy Ste 200
Plano TX 75075

(G-2814)
FRITO-LAY NORTH AMERICA INC
2000 Front St (67601)
PHONE..................................785 625-6581
Mike Palmer, *Director*
EMP: 16
SALES (corp-wide): 64.6B **Publicly Held**
WEB: www.fritolay.com
SIC: 5145 Snack foods
HQ: Frito-Lay North America, Inc.
7701 Legacy Dr
Plano TX 75024

(G-2815)
FUR IS FLYING LLC
700 E 8th St (67601-3923)
PHONE..................................785 621-7300
Bernadette Bowen, *Partner*
EMP: 5 **EST:** 2009
SALES (est): 376.9K **Privately Held**
SIC: 3999 Furs

(G-2816)
GLASSMAN BIRD POWELL LLP
200 W 13th St (67601-3702)
P.O. Box 727 (67601-0727)
PHONE..................................785 625-6919
John Bird, *Partner*
Todd Powell, *Partner*
EMP: 13
SALES (est): 1.4MM **Privately Held**
WEB: www.haysamerica.com
SIC: 8111 General practice attorney, lawyer

(G-2817)
GLASSMAN CORPORATION
900 Commerce Pkwy (67601-9342)
P.O. Box 218 (67601-0218)
PHONE..................................785 625-2115
Joseph Glassman, *President*
Dave Rupp, *Opers Staff*
Dave Stoecklein, *Purch Dir*
EMP: 65
SQ FT: 10,500
SALES: 10.7MM **Privately Held**
SIC: 1711 Plumbing contractors; warm air heating & air conditioning contractor

(G-2818)
GOLDEN BELT BANKING & SAV ASSN
Also Called: Golden Belt Bank F S A
1101 E 27th St (67601-2103)
P.O. Box 931 (67601-0931)
PHONE..................................785 625-7345
Ronald Wente, *President*
Wendy Richmeier, *Opers-Prdtn-Mfg*
EMP: 25
SALES (corp-wide): 11.6MM **Privately Held**
WEB: www.goldenbeltbank.com
SIC: 6036 6035 Savings & loan associations, not federally chartered; federal savings & loan associations
PA: Golden Belt Banking & Savings Association
901 Washington St
Ellis KS 67637
785 726-3157

(G-2819)
GOLDEN PLAINS CREDIT UNION
2720 Broadway Ave (67601-1928)
P.O. Box 99 (67601-0099)
PHONE..................................785 628-1007
Kim Rupp, *Manager*
EMP: 13
SALES (corp-wide): 25MM **Privately Held**
SIC: 6062 State credit unions, not federally chartered
PA: Golden Plains Credit Union
1714 E Kansas Ave
Garden City KS 67846
620 275-8187

(G-2820)
GONE LOGO SCREEN PRINTING
2717 Plaza Ave (67601-1921)
PHONE..................................785 625-3070
John Flynn, *Owner*
EMP: 7
SALES (est): 430K **Privately Held**
SIC: 2759 Screen printing

(G-2821)
GOODWIN SPORTING GOODS INC
109 W 11th St (67601-3605)
P.O. Box 1545 (67601-8545)
PHONE..................................785 625-2419
Terry T Bright, *President*
EMP: 7 **EST:** 1952
SQ FT: 3,500
SALES: 485K **Privately Held**
SIC: 2759 5941 Screen printing; sporting goods & bicycle shops

(G-2822)
H SCHWALLER & SONS INC
Also Called: General Hays Inn
1500 Vine St (67601-3455)
P.O. Box 855 (67601-0855)
PHONE..................................785 628-6162
Henry Schwaller Sr, *President*
Paula Harris, *Treasurer*
EMP: 10
SQ FT: 4,000
SALES (est): 833.3K **Privately Held**
SIC: 6531 7011 Real estate leasing & rentals; inns

(G-2823)
HABITAT FOR HMANITY ELLIS CNTY
1316 Donald Dr (67601-2609)
P.O. Box 44 (67601-0044)
PHONE..................................785 623-4200
Phil Ring, *CEO*
EMP: 12
SALES (est): 485K **Privately Held**
SIC: 7389 Fund raising organizations

(G-2824)
HAIR WEAR AND CO
Also Called: Haus of Sytle
2703 Hall St Ste A2 (67601-1899)
PHONE..................................785 625-2875
Shirley Steffen, *Owner*
Diane Wellberock, *Partner*
EMP: 11
SALES (est): 224.1K **Privately Held**
SIC: 7231 Hairdressers

(G-2825)
HAMPTON INN HAYS-NORTH I-70
4002 General Hays Rd (67601-6000)
PHONE..................................785 621-4444
Dianne Johnson, *General Mgr*
EMP: 13 **EST:** 1985
SALES (est): 672.3K **Privately Held**
SIC: 7011 Hotels & motels

(G-2826)
HAPPY AUTOS LLC
801 Main St (67601)
PHONE..................................785 621-4100
Mark Ottley,
Trever Ottley,
EMP: 14
SALES (est): 1.8MM **Privately Held**
SIC: 5511 7549 Automobiles, new & used; automotive maintenance services

(G-2827)
HAYS ACADEMY OF HAIR DESIGN
Also Called: Liberal Academy of Hair Design
1214 E 27th St (67601-2106)
PHONE..................................785 628-6624
Summer Melvin, *CEO*
Danielle Markley, *Partner*
Len Melvin, *Mktg Dir*
Randi Gerstner, *Hlthcr Dir*
EMP: 17
SQ FT: 7,500
SALES (est): 849.2K **Privately Held**
SIC: 7231 Beauty culture school; beauty schools

(G-2828)
HAYS AREA CHILDREN CENTER INC
94 Lewis Dr (67601-4020)
PHONE..................................785 625-3257
Susan Bowles, *Director*
EMP: 40
SQ FT: 10,000
SALES: 1.1MM **Privately Held**
WEB: www.hacc.info
SIC: 8322 8351 Child guidance agency; preschool center

(G-2829)
HAYS FAMILY PRACTICE CENTER
Also Called: Hay Medical Center
2509 Canterbury Dr (67601-2294)
PHONE..................................785 623-5095
Richard Rajewski, *Owner*
Mickey Myrick, *Principal*
Jodi Schmidt, *Vice Pres*
Tina Rohr, *Human Resources*
Gayla Wichman, *Marketing Staff*
EMP: 20 **EST:** 1976
SALES (est): 1.8MM **Privately Held**
SIC: 8011 General & family practice, physician/surgeon; physicians' office, including specialists

(G-2830)
HAYS FEEDER HOLDINGS LLC
1174 Feedlot Rd (67601-9728)
PHONE..................................785 625-3415
Scott Temple,
EMP: 14
SALES (est): 280.6K **Privately Held**
SIC: 0211 Beef cattle feedlots

(G-2831)
HAYS LIVESTOCK MARKET CENTER
Hwy 183 (67601)
P.O. Box 832 (67601-0832)
PHONE..................................785 628-8206
EMP: 30
SQ FT: 7,000
SALES (est): 4MM **Privately Held**
SIC: 5154 Livestock Auction

(G-2832)
HAYS MACK SALES AND SVC INC
451 240th Ave (67601-9669)
PHONE..................................785 625-7343
Richard Grabbe, *President*
Timothy Lang, *Vice Pres*

EMP: 15 **EST:** 1959
SQ FT: 12,000
SALES (est): 2.3MM **Privately Held**
WEB: www.haysmack.com
SIC: 5013 5012 Truck parts & accessories; truck tractors

(G-2833)
HAYS MEDICAL CENTER INC
Also Called: HMC Medical Oncology Services
2220 Canterbury Dr (67601-2370)
PHONE....................................785 623-5774
January Fields, *Manager*
Pam Mayers, *Director*
EMP: 19
SALES (corp-wide): 199.5MM **Privately Held**
SIC: 8062 8011 General medical & surgical hospitals; offices & clinics of medical doctors
PA: Hays Medical Center, Inc.
2220 Canterbury Dr
Hays KS 67601
785 623-5000

(G-2834)
HAYS MEDICAL CENTER INC (PA)
Also Called: Haysmed
2220 Canterbury Dr (67601-2370)
P.O. Box 8100 (67601-8100)
PHONE....................................785 623-5000
John H Jeter MD, *President*
Julie Fischer, *President*
Shawna North, *Business Mgr*
Bryce A Young, *COO*
Bryce Young, *COO*
EMP: 575
SQ FT: 130,000
SALES: 199.5MM **Privately Held**
SIC: 8062 8051 General medical & surgical hospitals; skilled nursing care facilities

(G-2835)
HAYS MEDICAL CENTER INC
Also Called: HMC Hays Psychological Assoc
2500 Canterbury Dr # 204 (67601-2247)
PHONE....................................785 623-6270
John Jeter, *CEO*
Wanda Augustine, *Sales Executive*
Pam Wong, *Manager*
Kelly Flaska, *Director*
EMP: 800
SALES (corp-wide): 199.5MM **Privately Held**
SIC: 8062 8322 General medical & surgical hospitals; family counseling services
PA: Hays Medical Center, Inc.
2220 Canterbury Dr
Hays KS 67601
785 623-5000

(G-2836)
HAYS ORTHOPEDIC CLINIC PA
Also Called: Woods, Gregory A MD
2500 Canterbury Dr # 112 (67601-2257)
PHONE....................................785 625-3012
Dr Gregory Woods, *Treasurer*
Gulraiz Cheema, *Surgeon*
Max De Carvalho, *Surgeon*
Timothy Wright, *Surgeon*
EMP: 34
SALES (est): 2MM **Privately Held**
SIC: 8011 Surgeon

(G-2837)
HAYS PATHOLOGY LABORATORIES PA (DH)
Also Called: Central Plains Laboratories
207 E 7th St A (67601-4133)
PHONE....................................785 650-2700
Vergil Minden, *President*
EMP: 40
SQ FT: 9,000
SALES (est): 4.1MM
SALES (corp-wide): 7.5B **Publicly Held**
WEB: www.labone.com
SIC: 8071 Medical laboratories
HQ: Labone, Inc.
10101 Renner Blvd
Lenexa KS 66219
913 888-1770

(G-2838)
HAYS PLANING MILL INC
1013 Elm St (67601-3821)
PHONE....................................785 625-6507
Charles Comeau, *Principal*
EMP: 9 **EST:** 1896
SQ FT: 2,400
SALES (est): 627.1K **Privately Held**
SIC: 2426 1751 2515 2511 Turnings, furniture: wood; cabinet building & installation; mattresses & bedsprings; wood household furniture; wood kitchen cabinets; millwork

(G-2839)
HAYS VETERINARY HOSP PROF ASSN
1016 E 8th St (67601-3929)
PHONE....................................785 625-2719
Steven R Mosier Dvm, *President*
EMP: 10
SALES (est): 443.1K **Privately Held**
SIC: 0742 7261 Animal hospital services, pets & other animal specialties; crematory

(G-2840)
HEARTLAND DERMATOLOGY CENTER (PA)
2707 Vine St Ste 10 (67601-1986)
PHONE....................................785 628-3231
Mathew Shaffer, *President*
Andrew Ratzlaff, *Human Res Dir*
Kayla Dortland, *Nurse Practr*
EMP: 20
SALES (est): 1.9MM **Privately Held**
WEB: www.heartland-derm.com
SIC: 8011 Dermatologist; surgeon

(G-2841)
HERTEL TANK SERVICE INC
704 E 12th St (67601-3440)
PHONE....................................785 628-2445
Al Hertel, *Director*
EMP: 5
SALES (corp-wide): 1.6MM **Privately Held**
SIC: 7538 5087 5084 3589 General automotive repair shops; cleaning & maintenance equipment & supplies; materials handling machinery; sewage treatment equipment; septic system construction; oil field services
PA: Hertel Tank Service Inc
704 E 12th St
Hays KS 67601
785 628-2445

(G-2842)
HESS MEDICAL SERVICES PA
Also Called: Hess Medical Services & Clinic
2201 Canterbury Dr (67601-2341)
PHONE....................................785 628-7495
Katrina Hess MD, *President*
EMP: 20
SALES (est): 2.2MM **Privately Held**
SIC: 8011 General & family practice, physician/surgeon

(G-2843)
HESS SERVICES INC
2670 E 9th St (67601)
P.O. Box 843 (67601-0843)
PHONE....................................785 625-9295
Dan Hess, *President*
Allyssa Weigel, *Principal*
Lisa Hess, *Vice Pres*
Leon Legleiter, *Manager*
EMP: 60
SQ FT: 21,000
SALES (est): 32.5MM **Privately Held**
SIC: 3443 Industrial vessels, tanks & containers

(G-2844)
HIGH PLAINS FARM CREDIT FLCA
2905 Vine St (67601-1929)
P.O. Box 836 (67601-0836)
PHONE....................................785 625-2110
Kevin Swayne, *Branch Mgr*
EMP: 12
SALES (corp-wide): 4.4MM **Privately Held**
SIC: 6162 Mortgage bankers & correspondents
PA: High Plains Farm Credit Flca
605 Main St
Larned KS 67550
620 285-6978

(G-2845)
HIGH PLAINS MACHINE WORKS INC
208 E 7th St (67601-4139)
PHONE....................................785 625-4672
Gene Gottschalk, *President*
Holly Gottschalk, *Admin Sec*
EMP: 16
SQ FT: 11,400
SALES (est): 2.3MM **Privately Held**
SIC: 7699 3715 Industrial machinery & equipment repair; agricultural equipment repair services; truck trailers

(G-2846)
HIGH PLAINS MENTAL HEALTH CTR (PA)
208 E 7th St (67601-4199)
PHONE....................................785 628-2871
Carl Grahs, *Manager*
Ken Loos, *Manager*
Walter Hill, *Exec Dir*
EMP: 202
SQ FT: 18,000
SALES: 9.5MM **Privately Held**
SIC: 8093 Mental health clinic, outpatient

(G-2847)
HIGH PLAINS MENTAL HEALTH CTR
Also Called: High Plains Mental Health Care
1412 E 29th St (67601-1930)
PHONE....................................785 625-2400
Gordon Kuntz, *Manager*
EMP: 11
SALES (corp-wide): 9.5MM **Privately Held**
SIC: 8052 8063 Home for the mentally retarded, with health care; psychiatric hospitals
PA: High Plains Mental Health Center
208 E 7th St
Hays KS 67601
785 628-2871

(G-2848)
HOLIDAY INN EXPRESS
4650 Roth Ave (67601-4704)
PHONE....................................785 625-8000
Marjorie Dansel, *Principal*
EMP: 17
SALES (est): 813K **Privately Held**
SIC: 7011 Hotels & motels

(G-2849)
HOME STL SIDING & WINDOWS LLC
1390 E 8th St Ste B (67601-3974)
P.O. Box 799 (67601-0799)
PHONE....................................785 625-8622
Timothy Kingsley,
EMP: 10
SQ FT: 2,360
SALES: 1.8MM **Privately Held**
SIC: 1761 5999 5031 2394 Gutter & downspout contractor; siding contractor; awnings; doors & windows; canvas awnings & canopies; window & door (prefabricated) installation; insulation, buildings

(G-2850)
HOMESTEAD OF HAYS
2929 Sternberg Dr (67601-2055)
PHONE....................................785 628-3200
EMP: 83
SALES (est): 270.9K
SALES (corp-wide): 32.7MM **Privately Held**
SIC: 8361 Residential care
PA: Midwest Health, Inc
3024 Sw Wanamaker Rd # 300
Topeka KS 66614
785 272-1535

(G-2851)
HUMANE SOC OF HIGH PLAINS
Also Called: HAYS HUMANE SOCIETY
2050 E Us Highway 40 (67601-9310)
P.O. Box 311 (67601-0311)
PHONE....................................785 625-5252
Wayne Asthwee, *Treasurer*
Teddy Hanson, *Office Mgr*
EMP: 10
SALES: 444.2K **Privately Held**
SIC: 8699 Animal humane society

(G-2852)
INFORMATION TECH INTL INC
3800 Post Rd (67601-9804)
PHONE....................................913 579-8079
Timothy Flax, *President*
EMP: 11
SQ FT: 3,000
SALES (est): 650K **Privately Held**
SIC: 7371 Computer software development

(G-2853)
INSURANCE PLANNING INC (PA)
Also Called: Ipi Financial Services
3006 Broadway Ave (67601-1916)
P.O. Box 100 (67601-0100)
PHONE....................................785 625-5605
Larry Caspers, *President*
Sherri Bergholz, *General Mgr*
Stan Jackson, *Senior VP*
James Braun, *Vice Pres*
Richard Kraemer, *Vice Pres*
EMP: 42
SQ FT: 8,000
SALES (est): 11.2MM **Privately Held**
WEB: www.insurance-planning.com
SIC: 6411 Insurance agents

(G-2854)
J CORP
1707 E 10th St (67601-4516)
P.O. Box 698 (67601-0698)
PHONE....................................785 628-8101
Jeanette Pfannenstiel, *President*
Tina Waddell, *Office Mgr*
EMP: 15 **EST:** 1999
SALES: 1.5MM **Privately Held**
SIC: 1771 1623 1611 Concrete work; water & sewer line construction; gravel or dirt road construction

(G-2855)
J L D J INC
Also Called: H & R Block
2707 Vine St Ste 12 (67601-1908)
PHONE....................................785 625-6316
Janet Ehrlich, *President*
EMP: 11
SALES (est): 265.7K **Privately Held**
SIC: 7291 8742 Tax return preparation services; compensation & benefits planning consultant

(G-2856)
JOE BOB OUTFITTERS LLC
4850 General Hays Rd (67601-6002)
PHONE....................................785 639-7121
Joseph Boeckner,
EMP: 15
SALES (est): 219.6K **Privately Held**
SIC: 3484 5091 5941 Guns (firearms) or gun parts, 30 mm. & below; firearms, sporting; firearms

(G-2857)
KANSAS ACID INC
2140 E 8th St (67601-4528)
PHONE....................................785 625-5599
Bob Harris, *President*
EMP: 5
SALES (est): 385.5K **Privately Held**
SIC: 1389 Oil field services

(G-2858)
KANSAS STATE UNIVERSITY
Also Called: AG Research Center- Hayes
1232 240th Ave (67601-9228)
PHONE....................................785 625-3425
Pat Coyne, *Principal*
Robert Gillen, *Dept Chairman*
EMP: 50

SALES (corp-wide): 637.6MM **Privately Held**
WEB: www.ksu.edu
SIC: 8733 8221 Research institute; university
PA: Kansas State University
Anderson Hall 110 1301 Mi St Anderson Ha
Manhattan KS 66506
785 532-6011

(G-2859)
KEVIN R MCDONALD
2214 Canterbury Dr # 308 (67601-2375)
PHONE..................................785 628-6014
Kevin R McDonald, *Executive*
EMP: 16 **EST:** 2001
SALES (est): 304K **Privately Held**
SIC: 8011 Offices & clinics of medical doctors

(G-2860)
KLAUS MASONRY LLC
1908 E 25th St (67601-2232)
P.O. Box 42 (67601-0042)
PHONE..................................785 650-3854
Mike Klaus,
Brad Klaus,
EMP: 15
SALES: 1.2MM **Privately Held**
SIC: 1741 Masonry & other stonework

(G-2861)
L-K WIRELINE INC
Also Called: L-K Acid
2480 E 8th St (67601-4500)
P.O. Box 1188 (67601-1188)
PHONE..................................785 625-6877
Randy K Longpine, *President*
Bill Longpipe, *Shareholder*
EMP: 6
SQ FT: 7,000
SALES (est): 1.3MM **Privately Held**
SIC: 1389 1311 Oil field services; acidizing wells; perforating well casings; well logging; crude petroleum production

(G-2862)
LARIO OIL & GAS COMPANY
2501 280th Ave (67601-9598)
P.O. Box 784 (67601-0784)
PHONE..................................785 625-5023
Tim Gillogly, *Manager*
EMP: 17
SALES (corp-wide): 63.6MM **Privately Held**
WEB: www.lario.net
SIC: 1311 Crude petroleum production
HQ: Lario Oil & Gas Company
301 S Market St
Wichita KS 67202
316 265-5611

(G-2863)
LEONS WELDING & FABRICATION
1027 E Us Highway 40 Byp (67601-3970)
PHONE..................................785 625-5736
Leon Pfannenstiel, *Managing Prtnr*
EMP: 13
SALES (est): 1.4MM **Privately Held**
SIC: 1799 7692 Welding on site; welding repair

(G-2864)
LINK INC
2401 E 13th St (67601-2663)
PHONE..................................785 625-6942
Angie Zimmerman, *Exec Dir*
Carol Boxberger, *Admin Asst*
EMP: 10
SALES: 4MM **Privately Held**
SIC: 8322 Social services for the handicapped

(G-2865)
LOCKHART GEOPHYSICAL COMPANY
1846 250th Ave (67601-9458)
P.O. Box 1195, Garden City (67846-1195)
PHONE..................................785 625-9175
Michael Comeau, *Branch Mgr*
EMP: 10
SALES (corp-wide): 172.2MM **Privately Held**
SIC: 1382 Oil & gas exploration services
PA: Lockhart Geophysical Company
1600 Broadway Ste 1660
Denver CO 80202
303 592-5220

(G-2866)
LOG-TECH INC
1011 240th Ave (67601-9601)
PHONE..................................785 625-3858
Glenn Schmeidler, *President*
EMP: 18
SALES (est): 1.3MM **Privately Held**
WEB: www.log-tech.com
SIC: 1389 Oil field services

(G-2867)
M & D EXCAVATING INC
1116 E 8th St (67601-3932)
PHONE..................................785 628-3169
Vauhn McMurtrie, *President*
EMP: 14
SALES (est): 1MM **Privately Held**
SIC: 1794 1629 1389 Excavation work; trenching contractor; oil field services

(G-2868)
M & D OF HAYS INCORPORATED
1116 E 8th St (67601-3932)
P.O. Box 184 (67601-0184)
PHONE..................................785 628-3169
Vaughn Mc Murtrie, *President*
Darrell Dreher, *Corp Secy*
EMP: 20
SALES (est): 3.3MM **Privately Held**
SIC: 1794 1711 Excavation work; irrigation sprinkler system installation

(G-2869)
MARY ELIZABETH MATERNITY HOME
204 W 7th St (67601-4402)
P.O. Box 132 (67601-0132)
PHONE..................................785 625-6800
C Nunnery, *Exec Dir*
Christin Nunnery, *Exec Dir*
EMP: 10
SALES: 150.1K **Privately Held**
WEB: www.maryelizabeth.net
SIC: 8069 Maternity hospital

(G-2870)
MASONIC ORDER
Also Called: Masonic Temple
107 W 11th St Fl 2 (67601-3605)
PHONE..................................785 625-3127
Dennis Jhonson, *Principal*
Richard Friendley,
EMP: 30
SALES (est): 176.3K **Privately Held**
SIC: 8641 7041 Fraternal associations; fraternity residential house

(G-2871)
MEDICAL SPECIALIST
2214 Canterbury Dr # 202 (67601-2386)
PHONE..................................785 623-2312
John Jeter, *CEO*
EMP: 20
SALES (est): 928K **Privately Held**
SIC: 8011 Internal medicine, physician/surgeon

(G-2872)
MERCURY WIRELINE
1023 Reservation Rd (67601-3982)
PHONE..................................785 625-1182
Larry Patterson, *Owner*
EMP: 5
SALES (est): 318.9K **Privately Held**
SIC: 1389 Oil field services

(G-2873)
MIDWEST ENERGY INC (PA)
1330 Canterbury Dr (67601-2708)
P.O. Box 898 (67601-0898)
PHONE..................................785 625-3437
Earnest A Lehman, *President*
Bonnie Augustine, *Vice Pres*
Bill Dowling, *Vice Pres*
Sharon Dreher, *Vice Pres*
Tim Flax, *Vice Pres*
EMP: 55
SQ FT: 40,000
SALES: 219.6MM **Privately Held**
WEB: www.mwenergy.com
SIC: 4911 8611 Generation, electric power; business associations

(G-2874)
MLR WELDING LLC
2409 280th Ave (67601-9464)
PHONE..................................785 203-1020
EMP: 7
SALES (est): 99.1K **Privately Held**
SIC: 7692 Welding repair

(G-2875)
MONSTER PUMP OPERATIONS INC
1515 Commerce Pkwy (67601-9331)
PHONE..................................785 623-4488
Jenny Baldwin, *Principal*
EMP: 5
SALES (est): 299.5K **Privately Held**
SIC: 1389 Oil field services

(G-2876)
NALCO COMPANY LLC
Also Called: Nalco Champion
1019 Reservation Rd (67601-3982)
P.O. Box 547 (67601-0547)
PHONE..................................785 625-3822
Chuck Stahl, *Branch Mgr*
EMP: 40
SALES (corp-wide): 14.6B **Publicly Held**
WEB: www.champ-tech.com
SIC: 5169 Chemicals & allied products
HQ: Nalco Company Llc
1601 W Diehl Rd
Naperville IL 60563
630 305-1000

(G-2877)
NEWS PUBLISHING CO INC
Also Called: Hays Daily News
507 Main St (67601-4228)
P.O. Box 857 (67601-0857)
PHONE..................................785 628-1081
John Montgomery, *President*
EMP: 70
SQ FT: 12,000
SALES (est): 3.4MM
SALES (corp-wide): 1.5B **Publicly Held**
WEB: www.hdnews.net
SIC: 2711 7011 Commercial printing & newspaper publishing combined; hotels & motels
HQ: Harris Enterprises, Inc.
1 N Main St Ste 616
Hutchinson KS
620 694-5830

(G-2878)
NEX-TECH LLC (HQ)
2418 Vine St (67601-2456)
P.O. Box 339 (67601-0339)
PHONE..................................785 625-7070
Jimmy Todd, *CEO*
Michael Pollock, *COO*
Rhonda Goddard, *CFO*
Melinda Bieker, *Accounting Mgr*
Diana Staab, *Financial Exec*
▲ **EMP:** 110
SQ FT: 3,500
SALES: 54.6MM
SALES (corp-wide): 174.9MM **Privately Held**
WEB: www.nextechdirectory.com
SIC: 4813 Telephone communication, except radio
PA: Rural Telephone Service Company, Inc.
145 N Main St
Lenora KS 67645
785 567-4281

(G-2879)
NEX-TECH WIRELESS LLC (DH)
3001 New Way (67601-3262)
PHONE..................................785 567-4281
Jon Lightle, *CEO*
Eian Wagner, *Sales Mgr*
Anne Erbert, *Manager*
Jeff Marshall, *Manager*
Larry E Sevier,
EMP: 57
SALES (est): 37.3MM
SALES (corp-wide): 174.9MM **Privately Held**
WEB: www.nextechdirectory.com
SIC: 4812 Cellular telephone services

(G-2880)
NORTHWEST AWARDS & SIGNS
131 W 8th St (67601-4432)
PHONE..................................785 621-2116
Marc Pechanec, *Owner*
EMP: 5
SALES (est): 542.2K **Privately Held**
SIC: 3993 2759 Signs, not made in custom sign painting shops; engraving

(G-2881)
NORTHWESTERN PRINTERS INC
114 W 9th St (67601-4435)
P.O. Box 1067 (67601-1067)
PHONE..................................785 625-1110
Marvin L Rack, *President*
EMP: 12
SQ FT: 7,500
SALES (est): 2MM **Privately Held**
SIC: 2752 Commercial printing, offset; business forms, lithographed; calendars, lithographed

(G-2882)
OLDHAM SALES INC
815 E 11th St (67601-3435)
P.O. Box 447 (67601-0447)
PHONE..................................785 625-2547
Delmar Dinkel, *President*
Lawrence Koirth, *Vice Pres*
Richard Bolig, *Treasurer*
EMP: 10 **EST:** 1948
SQ FT: 10,100
SALES (est): 1.6MM **Privately Held**
SIC: 5013 Automotive supplies & parts

(G-2883)
OPTIONS DOM & SEXUAL VIOLENC
2716 Plaza Ave (67601-1922)
PHONE..................................785 625-4202
Jennifer Hecker, *Exec Dir*
Katie Dorzweiler, *Admin Sec*
EMP: 17
SALES: 1MM **Privately Held**
SIC: 8322 Self-help organization; crisis intervention center

(G-2884)
ORSCHELN FARM AND HOME LLC
Also Called: Orschelin Farm and Home 58
2900 Broadway Ave (67601-1914)
PHONE..................................785 625-7316
Larry Zwickle, *Manager*
EMP: 10
SALES (corp-wide): 822.7MM **Privately Held**
WEB: www.orschelnfarmhome.com
SIC: 5191 5251 5699 5084 Farm supplies; hardware; work clothing; engines, gasoline
PA: Orscheln Farm And Home Llc
1800 Overcenter Dr
Moberly MO 65270
800 577-2580

(G-2885)
PAUL-WERTENBERGER CNSTR INC
1102 E 8th St (67601-3931)
P.O. Box 1311 (67601-1311)
PHONE..................................785 625-8220
Robert L Wertenberger, *President*
Josh Thoma, *Superintendent*
Steven L Paul, *Corp Secy*
Steve Paul, *Vice Pres*
Kyle Kinser, *Project Mgr*
EMP: 50
SQ FT: 15,000
SALES: 9.9MM **Privately Held**
SIC: 1542 1521 Commercial & office buildings, renovation & repair; new construction, single-family houses

▲ = Import ▼=Export
◆ =Import/Export

(G-2886)
PEPSI-COLA METRO BTLG CO INC
Also Called: Pepsico
2000 Front St (67601)
PHONE....................785 628-3024
Todd Lindhoff, *Branch Mgr*
EMP: 126
SALES (corp-wide): 64.6B **Publicly Held**
WEB: www.pbg.com
SIC: 5149 Soft drinks
HQ: Pepsi-Cola Metropolitan Bottling Company, Inc.
1111 Westchester Ave
White Plains NY 10604
914 767-6000

(G-2887)
PRAIRIE SPORTS INC
Also Called: Centennial Lanes
2400 Vine St (67601-2491)
PHONE....................785 625-2916
Bruce Herreman, *President*
Wayne Herreman, *Vice Pres*
Jill Herreman, *Admin Sec*
EMP: 15 **EST:** 1959
SQ FT: 18,900
SALES: 240K **Privately Held**
SIC: 7933 Ten pin center

(G-2888)
PRICE TRUCK LINE INC
1198 280th Ave (67601-9325)
PHONE....................785 625-2603
Dan Wolf, *Manager*
EMP: 16
SALES (est): 803.1K
SALES (corp-wide): 27MM **Privately Held**
SIC: 4213 4212 Contract haulers; local trucking, without storage
PA: Price Truck Line, Inc.
4931 S Victoria St
Wichita KS 67216
316 945-6915

(G-2889)
PRICELESS
2719 Plaza Ave (67601-1921)
PHONE....................785 625-7664
Sheloton Renz, *Owner*
EMP: 11
SALES (est): 370K **Privately Held**
SIC: 7514 Rent-a-car service

(G-2890)
PROFESSIONAL CARGO SVCS INC
724 E 7th St (67601-3919)
PHONE....................785 625-2249
Doug Mermis, *Manager*
EMP: 25
SALES (corp-wide): 4.4MM **Privately Held**
SIC: 4731 Freight transportation arrangement
PA: Professional Cargo Services, Inc.
3735 S West St
Wichita KS 67217
316 522-2224

(G-2891)
PROFESSIONAL HOME HEALTH SVCS
1307 Lawrence Dr (67601-2626)
PHONE....................785 625-0055
Thu MAI, *President*
Sandy Watchouse, *Vice Pres*
EMP: 17
SALES: 214.5K **Privately Held**
SIC: 8082 Home health care services

(G-2892)
PROFESSIONAL PULLING SVC LLC
1835 Nunjor Rd (67601)
P.O. Box 486 (67601-0486)
PHONE....................785 625-8928
Jeff Psannenstiel, *President*
Gerald Walker, *Vice Pres*
Gaylen Walker, *Admin Sec*
EMP: 12
SALES (est): 921.6K **Privately Held**
SIC: 1389 Oil field services

(G-2893)
Q GOLDEN BILLIARDS
Also Called: Golden-Q
809 Ash St (67601-4463)
PHONE....................785 625-6913
Danny Herman, *Owner*
Jenna Herman, *Principal*
EMP: 15
SQ FT: 3,500
SALES: 370K **Privately Held**
SIC: 5812 7999 Restaurant, family: independent; recreation center

(G-2894)
QUEST DIAGNOSTICS INCORPORATED
2501 Canterbury Dr Ste 1 (67601-2296)
PHONE....................785 621-4300
Chardell Parke, *Manager*
EMP: 12
SALES (corp-wide): 7.5B **Publicly Held**
SIC: 8071 Medical laboratories
PA: Quest Diagnostics Incorporated
500 Plaza Dr Ste G
Secaucus NJ 07094
973 520-2700

(G-2895)
R D H ELECTRIC INC
800 E 12th St (67601-3442)
PHONE....................785 625-3833
Robert D Herl, *President*
Ellen Herl, *Vice Pres*
Justin Herl, *Vice Pres*
EMP: 20
SQ FT: 2,500
SALES: 4.3MM **Privately Held**
SIC: 1731 1542 8741 General electrical contractor; commercial & office buildings, renovation & repair; construction management

(G-2896)
R P NIXON OPERATIONS INC
Also Called: Nixon, Dan A
207 W 12th St (67601-3810)
PHONE....................785 628-3834
Dan A Nixon, *President*
EMP: 5 **EST:** 1971
SQ FT: 1,250
SALES: 2MM **Privately Held**
SIC: 1311 Crude petroleum production

(G-2897)
RAYES INC
Also Called: Wheelchairs of Kansas
500 Commerce Pkwy (67601-9320)
PHONE....................785 726-4885
Willard Frickey, *President*
EMP: 55 **Privately Held**
SIC: 3842 Wheelchairs
PA: Raye's, Inc.
204 W 2nd St
Ellis KS 67637

(G-2898)
REGAL AUDIO VIDEO
124 W 9th St (67601-4435)
PHONE....................785 628-2700
Alan Kohl, *Owner*
EMP: 6
SQ FT: 7,000
SALES (est): 676.8K **Privately Held**
WEB: www.regalav.com
SIC: 3675 7841 Electronic capacitors; video tape rental

(G-2899)
REGIS CORPORATION
Also Called: Regis Salon
2938 Vine St (67601)
PHONE....................785 628-2111
Vallere Dohe, *Manager*
EMP: 12
SALES (corp-wide): 1B **Publicly Held**
WEB: www.regiscorp.com
SIC: 7231 Beauty shops
PA: Regis Corporation
7201 Metro Blvd
Edina MN 55439
952 947-7777

(G-2900)
RIEDEL GARDEN CENTER
1358 Us Highway 40 (67601-9221)
PHONE....................785 628-2877
Darran D Riedel, *Owner*
EMP: 12
SQ FT: 4,000
SALES: 1.3MM **Privately Held**
SIC: 0781 5261 Landscape services; garden supplies & tools

(G-2901)
ROME CORPORATION (PA)
Also Called: Western Well Service
1023 Reservation Rd (67601-3982)
PHONE....................785 625-1182
Larry Patterson, *CEO*
Martin Patterson, *President*
Deborah McKune, *Corp Secy*
Patrick Patterson, *Vice Pres*
EMP: 50
SALES (est): 3.8MM **Privately Held**
SIC: 1389 Servicing oil & gas wells

(G-2902)
ROYS CUSTOM CABINETS
821 E 11th St (67601-3435)
PHONE....................785 625-6724
Rodney Roy, *Owner*
Cristy Roy, *Principal*
EMP: 6
SQ FT: 4,000
SALES (est): 360K **Privately Held**
SIC: 1751 5211 5031 2499 Cabinet building & installation; cabinets, kitchen; kitchen cabinets; decorative wood & woodwork

(G-2903)
RULE PROPERTIES LLC
Also Called: Coffee Rules Lounge
1708 Copper Creek Ct (67601-2660)
PHONE....................785 621-8000
Jason Rule,
EMP: 12
SALES (est): 307.3K **Privately Held**
SIC: 5812 7389 Coffee shop; coffee service

(G-2904)
S & W SUPPLY COMPANY INC (HQ)
300 E 8th St (67601-4145)
P.O. Box 130 (67601-0130)
PHONE....................785 625-7363
Dg Bickle, *President*
Jan Stauth, *General Mgr*
Dg Bickle Sr, *Chairman*
Frank Appelhans, *Store Mgr*
Shelby Barnett, *Store Mgr*
EMP: 25
SQ FT: 900
SALES (est): 27.2MM **Privately Held**
SIC: 5531 5015 5013 Automotive parts; motor vehicle parts, used; motor vehicle supplies & new parts
PA: Warehouse, Inc.
320 E 8th St
Hays KS 67601
785 625-5611

(G-2905)
SAINT FRANCIS ACDMY INC ATCHSN
Also Called: Saint Francs Acdmy Bldng Fmls
105 W 13th St (67601-3613)
PHONE....................785 625-6651
Jerlee Taylor, *Director*
EMP: 12 **Privately Held**
SIC: 8322 Individual & family services
PA: The Saint Francis Academy Incorporated Atchison
19137 258th Rd
Atchison KS 66002

(G-2906)
SALON BRANDS
4325 Vine St Ste 30 (67601-9582)
PHONE....................785 301-2984
Amie Husted, *Principal*
EMP: 10
SALES (est): 99.6K **Privately Held**
SIC: 7231 5999 Unisex hair salons; toiletries, cosmetics & perfumes

(G-2907)
SALON TEN O SEVEN
1007 Main St (67601-3616)
PHONE....................785 628-6000
Dwight Allenbaugh, *President*
Tracer Giess, *Engineer*
EMP: 20
SALES (est): 248K **Privately Held**
SIC: 7231 Unisex hair salons

(G-2908)
SLEEP INN INN & SUITES
1011 E 41st St (67601-9495)
PHONE....................785 625-2700
Mitch Homburg, *Manager*
EMP: 11
SALES (est): 394.1K **Privately Held**
SIC: 7011 Hotels & motels

(G-2909)
SMOKY HILL COUNTRY CLUB INC
Also Called: SMOKY HILL PRO SHOP
3303 N Hall St (67601)
P.O. Box 204 (67601-0204)
PHONE....................785 625-4021
Tom Johanson, *President*
Carol Waggoner, *President*
Justin Vanek, *Superintendent*
Stella Kruse, *Office Mgr*
Shelby Doty, *Manager*
EMP: 30
SALES: 1.6MM **Privately Held**
SIC: 7997 Country club, membership

(G-2910)
ST JOHNS REST HOME INC (PA)
Also Called: Saint Jhns Vctria Nrsing Fclty
2225 Canterbury Dr (67601-2300)
PHONE....................785 735-2208
Theresa Barfield, *Project Mgr*
Chad Johnson, *Med Doctor*
Kenneth Harper, *Security Mgr*
David Karlin, *Director*
Bob Bethell, *Administration*
EMP: 55
SALES: 280.5MM **Privately Held**
SIC: 8361 Home for the aged

(G-2911)
ST JOHNS REST HOME INC
Also Called: St Johns of Hays
2401 Canterbury Dr (67601-2345)
PHONE....................785 628-3241
Jennifer Goehring, *Director*
Darla Anderson, *Admin Sec*
EMP: 80
SALES (corp-wide): 280.5MM **Privately Held**
SIC: 8051 Skilled nursing care facilities
PA: St Johns Rest Home Inc
2225 Canterbury Dr
Hays KS 67601
785 735-2208

(G-2912)
STECKLEIN ENTERPRISES LLC
Also Called: U-Save Pharmacy
2505 Canterbury Dr (67601-2233)
PHONE....................785 625-2529
Stephanie Stecklein, *Vice Pres*
Eric Moeder, *Pharmacist*
Karen Moeder, *Pharmacist*
Douglas Stecklein, *Mng Member*
EMP: 19
SQ FT: 5,000
SALES: 2MM **Privately Held**
SIC: 5122 5047 Pharmaceuticals; medical equipment & supplies

(G-2913)
STEEL FABRICATIONS INC
1640 E Us Highway 40 Byp (67601-4535)
PHONE....................785 625-3075
Ron Rome, *President*
Dennis Volbracht, *Vice Pres*
Carol Rome, *Treasurer*
EMP: 8
SQ FT: 11,200
SALES: 850.3K **Privately Held**
SIC: 7692 3441 3541 Welding repair; fabricated structural metal; machine tools, metal cutting type; lathes

(G-2914)
SUNFLOWER BANK NATIONAL ASSN
Also Called: First National Bank
1010 E 27th St (67601-2102)
PHONE....785 625-8888
Paul Ferguson, *Exec VP*
HUD Chapin, *Vice Pres*
Laura Frazier, *Vice Pres*
Cindy Starika, *Auditor*
Judy Parks, *Branch Mgr*
EMP: 24
SALES (corp-wide): 52.4MM **Privately Held**
WEB: www.sunflowerbank.com
SIC: 6021 National commercial banks
HQ: Sunflower Bank, National Association
1400 16th St Ste 250
Denver CO 80202
888 827-5564

(G-2915)
SUNFLOWER CHAPTER OF THE AMERI
Also Called: Sunflower Chapter of Ahsgr
2301 Canal Blvd (67601-3018)
PHONE....785 656-0329
Kevin D Rupp, *President*
Gerald Braun, *Treasurer*
EMP: 10
SALES (est): 114.5K **Privately Held**
SIC: 8412 Historical society

(G-2916)
SUNFLOWER ELECTRIC POWER CORP (HQ)
301 W 13th St (67601-3087)
P.O. Box 1020 (67601-1020)
PHONE....785 628-2845
Stuart Lowry, *President*
Jana Horsfall, *President*
Kyle Nelson, *Senior VP*
Bill Branch, *Vice Pres*
Gary Ratts, *Vice Pres*
EMP: 30 **EST:** 1957
SQ FT: 18,425
SALES (est): 183.5MM **Privately Held**
SIC: 4911 Generation, electric power; transmission, electric power

(G-2917)
SUNFLWER CHILD SPPORT SVCS LLC
205 E 7th St Ste 400a (67601-4851)
PHONE....785 623-4516
Lee Fisher,
EMP: 17
SALES (est): 478.4K **Privately Held**
SIC: 8111 Administrative & government law

(G-2918)
SUNSHINE CONNECTIONS INC
2517 Indian Trl Apt B (67601-2265)
P.O. Box 803 (67601-0803)
PHONE....785 625-2093
Kelly Horn, *Director*
EMP: 12
SALES: 1.5MM **Privately Held**
SIC: 8322 Child related social services

(G-2919)
TENGASCO INC
1327 Noose Rd (67601-9744)
P.O. Box 458 (67601-0458)
PHONE....785 625-6374
Linda Pfannenstiel, *Manager*
EMP: 20 **Publicly Held**
WEB: www.tengasco.com
SIC: 1382 1311 Oil & gas exploration services; crude petroleum & natural gas production
PA: Tengasco, Inc.
800 E Maplewood Ave # 130
Centennial CO 80121

(G-2920)
TOTAL LEASE SERVICE INC (PA)
1309 Toulon Ave (67601-9338)
PHONE....785 735-9520
Robert Boardman, *President*
Martha Boardman, *Corp Secy*
EMP: 7
SALES (est): 1.7MM **Privately Held**
SIC: 1389 1623 1794 4959 Roustabout service; oil & gas pipeline construction; water & sewer line construction; excavation work; snowplowing

(G-2921)
TRILOBITE TESTING INC (PA)
1515 Commerce Pkwy (67601-9331)
PHONE....785 625-4778
Paul Simpson, *President*
Tina Simpson, *Vice Pres*
EMP: 31
SALES (est): 7.2MM **Privately Held**
WEB: www.trilobitetesting.com
SIC: 1389 Oil field services; testing, measuring, surveying & analysis services

(G-2922)
UNITED PARCEL SERVICE INC
Also Called: UPS
1101 General Custer Rd (67601-2598)
PHONE....785 628-3253
Lane Lummus, *Business Mgr*
EMP: 158
SALES (corp-wide): 71.8B **Publicly Held**
SIC: 4215 Parcel delivery, vehicular
HQ: United Parcel Service, Inc.
55 Glenlake Pkwy
Atlanta GA 30328
404 828-6000

(G-2923)
VERNIES TRUX-N-EQUIP INC
Also Called: Toys-4-Trux
655 E 41st St (67601-9480)
P.O. Box 655 (67601-0655)
PHONE....785 625-5087
Darrell Unrein, *President*
Norene Unrein, *Corp Secy*
EMP: 6 **EST:** 1966
SQ FT: 22,500
SALES (est): 489.5K **Privately Held**
SIC: 7692 7532 5013 5511 Automotive welding; body shop, automotive; paint shop, automotive; truck parts & accessories; trucks, tractors & trailers: new & used; truck & bus bodies

(G-2924)
VETERANS FGN WARS POST 9076
2106 Vine St (67601-2854)
PHONE....785 625-9940
Chris Stegman, *Principal*
EMP: 15
SALES: 181.8K **Privately Held**
SIC: 8699 8641 Personal interest organization; veterans' organization

(G-2925)
VETERINARY RESEARCH AND CNSLT
4413 Larned Cir (67601-1670)
PHONE....785 324-9200
James Fox, *Exec Dir*
Miranda Fox,
EMP: 11
SALES (est): 280.8K **Privately Held**
SIC: 8742 8748 8999 8731 Management consulting services; agricultural consultant; scientific consulting; agricultural research

(G-2926)
VIA CHRISTI VILLAGE HAYS INC
2225 Canterbury Dr (67601-2300)
PHONE....785 628-3241
Betsy Schwien, *Principal*
Crystal Quint, *Food Svc Dir*
EMP: 180
SALES: 8.4MM **Privately Held**
SIC: 8059 Convalescent home

(G-2927)
VOLGA-CANAL HOUSING INC
2703 Hall St Ste 10 (67601-1964)
P.O. Box 310 (67601-0310)
PHONE....785 625-5678
Jerry Michaud, *President*
EMP: 33
SALES (est): 436.3K **Privately Held**
SIC: 8059 Convalescent home

(G-2928)
WALGREEN CO
Also Called: Walgreens
2600 Vine St (67601-2201)
PHONE....785 628-1767
Chandler Broman, *Branch Mgr*
EMP: 30
SALES (corp-wide): 136.8B **Publicly Held**
WEB: www.walgreens.com
SIC: 5912 7384 Drug stores; photofinishing laboratory
HQ: Walgreen Co.
200 Wilmot Rd
Deerfield IL 60015
800 925-4733

(G-2929)
WARREN DAVIDSON TRUCKING
200 W 38th St (67601-1655)
PHONE....785 625-5126
Warren Davidson, *Owner*
EMP: 12
SALES (est): 821.1K **Privately Held**
SIC: 4212 Local trucking, without storage

(G-2930)
WERTH HTG PLBG AIRCONDITIONING
516 E 8th St (67601-3967)
PHONE....785 628-8088
Stanley Werth, *Owner*
EMP: 13
SQ FT: 4,000
SALES: 1.7MM **Privately Held**
SIC: 1711 Plumbing, heating, air-conditioning contractors

(G-2931)
WESTERN ALUMINUM & GLASS CO
Also Called: ABC Seamless
1507 E 27th St (67601-2111)
PHONE....785 625-2418
Ed Neuburger, *President*
Olivia Becker, *Corp Secy*
EMP: 10
SQ FT: 11,000
SALES: 1.6MM **Privately Held**
SIC: 1761 3444 3442 Siding contractor; awnings, sheet metal; storm doors or windows, metal; sash, door or window: metal

(G-2932)
WESTERN BEVERAGE-HAYS
2100 E Us Hwy 40 Byp (67601)
P.O. Box 759 (67601-0759)
PHONE....785 625-3712
Joe Bogner, *Owner*
EMP: 12
SALES (est): 1.6MM **Privately Held**
SIC: 5181 Beer & other fermented malt liquors

Haysville
Sedgwick County

(G-2933)
A-ONE AUTO SALVAGE OF WICHITA (PA)
7335 S Broadway Ave (67060-1404)
PHONE....316 524-3273
Dale L Lehning, *President*
Sandra L Lehning, *Treasurer*
EMP: 14
SQ FT: 5,000
SALES (est): 2.4MM **Privately Held**
WEB: www.aoneautosalvage.com
SIC: 5531 5013 Automotive parts; automotive supplies & parts

(G-2934)
AAA AIR SUPPORT MFG LLC
205 Pirner Ste 1 (67060-1946)
PHONE....316 946-9299
Matt Kerster, *Mng Member*
Bob Smith,
Ted Mezzo,
EMP: 9
SALES (est): 978.4K **Privately Held**
SIC: 3728 Aircraft parts & equipment

(G-2935)
AIR PRODUCTS AND CHEMICALS INC
6601 S Ridge Rd (67060-7134)
PHONE....316 522-8181
Pamela Johnson, *Manager*
EMP: 23
SALES (corp-wide): 8.9B **Publicly Held**
WEB: www.airproducts.com
SIC: 2813 Industrial gases
PA: Air Products And Chemicals, Inc.
7201 Hamilton Blvd
Allentown PA 18195
610 481-4911

(G-2936)
ALTERNATIVE CHROME CREATIONS
8900 S Broadway Ave (67060-8004)
PHONE....316 680-1209
Larry Perkins, *Manager*
EMP: 5
SALES (est): 172.2K **Privately Held**
SIC: 3471 Chromium plating of metals or formed products

(G-2937)
ARMSTRONG CREATIVE SERVICES
Also Called: Armstrong Shank
7450 S Seneca St (67060-7642)
P.O. Box 16719, Wichita (67216-0719)
PHONE....316 522-3000
Susan Armstrong, *President*
Bruce Armstrong, *Corp Secy*
Zach Armstrong, *Accounts Exec*
Mark Chamberlin, *Mktg Dir*
Dayna Hoock, *Marketing Staff*
EMP: 10
SALES (est): 2MM **Privately Held**
WEB: www.as-marketingu.com
SIC: 7311 Advertising consultant

(G-2938)
CPB MATERIALS LLC
5114 W 87th St S (67060-7335)
PHONE....316 833-1146
Chad Bledsoe, *Mng Member*
EMP: 6
SALES: 2MM **Privately Held**
SIC: 2951 3531 Asphalt paving mixtures & blocks; pavers

(G-2939)
DIVERSICARE LEASING CORP
Also Called: Diversicare of Haysville
215 N Lamar Ave (67060-1266)
PHONE....316 524-3211
Danny Lasiter, *QC Dir*
Tammy Calvert, *Social Dir*
EMP: 18
SALES (corp-wide): 563.4MM **Publicly Held**
SIC: 8051 Skilled nursing care facilities
HQ: Diversicare Leasing Corp.
1621 Galleria Blvd
Brentwood TN 37027

(G-2940)
DME ELECTRONICS
170 Cain Dr (67060-2003)
PHONE....316 529-2441
Craig Williams, *President*
Lynn Williams, *Owner*
Lynn M Williams, *Treasurer*
EMP: 5
SQ FT: 3,000
SALES: 600K **Privately Held**
SIC: 3678 3544 Electronic connectors; industrial molds

(G-2941)
EMPRISE BANK
330 N Main St (67060-1153)
PHONE....316 522-2222
Deb Kanaga, *Manager*
EMP: 13
SALES (corp-wide): 80MM **Privately Held**
SIC: 6022 State commercial banks
HQ: Emprise Bank
257 N Broadway Ave
Wichita KS 67202
316 383-4400

(G-2942)
EVONIK CORPORATION
6601 S Ridge Rd (67060-7134)
P.O. Box 12291, Wichita (67277-2291)
PHONE..................................316 529-9670
EMP: 1000
SALES (corp-wide): 2.5B **Privately Held**
SIC: 3674 2891 Solar cells; adhesives & sealants
HQ: Evonik Corporation
299 Jefferson Rd
Parsippany NJ 07054
973 929-8000

(G-2943)
FARNEYS INC
Also Called: Farney's Distributing
280 Cain Dr (67060-2000)
P.O. Box 274 (67060-0274)
PHONE..................................316 522-7248
Fax: 316 522-6393
EMP: 10
SQ FT: 10,150
SALES: 1MM **Privately Held**
SIC: 5013 5172 Whol Auto Parts/Supplies Whol Petroleum Products

(G-2944)
FIRST ASSEMBLY GOD INC
Also Called: Kiddie Kollege
1100 E Grand Ave (67060-1425)
PHONE..................................316 524-4981
Stewart Mowry, *President*
EMP: 25
SALES (est): 718K **Privately Held**
SIC: 8351 8661 Child day care services; miscellaneous denomination church

(G-2945)
FORM SYSTEMS INC
330 Cain Dr (67060-2004)
P.O. Box 16923, Wichita (67216-0923)
PHONE..................................316 522-9285
Scott Ruud, *President*
Jennifer Ruud, *Train & Dev Mgr*
EMP: 10
SQ FT: 22,000
SALES (est): 2.3MM **Privately Held**
WEB: www.formsystems.com
SIC: 3271 Blocks, concrete: insulating; blocks, concrete or cinder: standard

(G-2946)
HAYSVILLE FAMILY MEDCENTER
7107 S Meridian St (67060-7678)
PHONE..................................316 858-4165
David W Niederee, *Principal*
EMP: 11
SALES (est): 784.3K **Privately Held**
SIC: 8011 Clinic, operated by physicians

(G-2947)
INTRUST BANK NATIONAL ASSN
107 S Wayne Ave (67060-1798)
P.O. Box 424 (67060-0424)
PHONE..................................316 524-3251
Pat Ferguson, *Branch Mgr*
EMP: 26
SALES (corp-wide): 134.2MM **Privately Held**
WEB: www.intrustbank.com
SIC: 6022 State commercial banks
HQ: Intrust Bank National Association
105 N Main St
Wichita KS 67202
316 383-1111

(G-2948)
ITRANSPORT & LOGISTICS INC
422 N Baughman Ave (67060-1300)
PHONE..................................316 665-7653
Michael Owen, *President*
Mary Owen, *Shareholder*
EMP: 24
SQ FT: 4,500
SALES (est): 2.5MM **Privately Held**
SIC: 4731 Freight transportation arrangement

(G-2949)
JENKINS BUILDING MAINTENANCE
7030 S Plaza Dr (67060-2602)
P.O. Box 17314, Wichita (67217-0314)
PHONE..................................316 529-1263
EMP: 18
SALES: 250K **Privately Held**
SIC: 7349 Janitorial Service

(G-2950)
JOJACS LANDSCAPE & MOWING
205 Cain Dr (67060-2001)
PHONE..................................316 945-3525
Steven C Dale, *Owner*
Brenda Dale, *Owner*
EMP: 10
SQ FT: 5,000
SALES (est): 962.5K **Privately Held**
SIC: 0782 4959 Landscape contractors; mowing services, lawn; snowplowing

(G-2951)
JTS TRANSPORTS INC
7426 S Broadway Ave (67060-2122)
PHONE..................................316 554-0706
Ted Oliphant, *CEO*
Laurie Rucker, *Bookkeeper*
EMP: 25
SALES (est): 3.3MM **Privately Held**
SIC: 4231 4731 Trucking terminal facilities; freight transportation arrangement

(G-2952)
NATIONAL HEALTHCARE CORP
Also Called: Haysville Healthcare
215 N Lamar Ave (67060-1266)
PHONE..................................316 524-3211
Monica Gibbson-Roe, *Manager*
EMP: 115
SALES (corp-wide): 980.3MM **Publicly Held**
WEB: www.healthcarebenefits.com
SIC: 8051 Convalescent home with continuous nursing care
PA: National Healthcare Corporation
100 E Vine St
Murfreesboro TN 37130
615 890-2020

(G-2953)
NATIONAL PUBLISHERS GROUP INC
Also Called: American Oil & Gas Reporter
1326 E 79th St S (67060-2217)
P.O. Box 343, Derby (67037-0343)
PHONE..................................316 788-6271
Charles E Cookson, *President*
Tim Castillo, *President*
Margaret Cookson, *Corp Secy*
EMP: 14
SALES (est): 1.3MM **Privately Held**
WEB: www.aogr.com
SIC: 2721 8611 Trade journals: publishing only, not printed on site; business associations

(G-2954)
PALMER FAMILY DENTISTRY
Also Called: Palmer DDS
1425 W Grand Ave Ste 101 (67060-1270)
PHONE..................................316 453-6918
Scott Palmer, *Owner*
EMP: 19 **EST:** 2001
SALES (est): 1.6MM **Privately Held**
WEB: www.scottpalmer.net
SIC: 8021 Dentists' office

(G-2955)
PREFERRED MORTUARY SVCS LLC
210 Cain Dr (67060-2000)
PHONE..................................316 522-7300
Kim Strohm, *Partner*
Jan Jacobs, *Director*
EMP: 20
SALES: 500K **Privately Held**
SIC: 7261 Funeral director

(G-2956)
PROFESSORS OF PEACE LLC
150 Stewart Ave (67060-1602)
PHONE..................................316 213-7233
Johnna Crawford, *CEO*
EMP: 11
SALES (est): 205.7K **Privately Held**
SIC: 8748 Business consulting

(G-2957)
R A RUUD & SON INC
7760 S Hydraulic St (67060-7845)
P.O. Box 16082, Wichita (67216-0082)
PHONE..................................316 788-5000
Robert S Ruud, *President*
Michael Lennox, *General Mgr*
Jennifer Ruud, *Corp Secy*
EMP: 15
SQ FT: 2,000
SALES (est): 4.8MM **Privately Held**
SIC: 3273 5032 Ready-mixed concrete; sand, construction

(G-2958)
ROGERS CONTRACTING
1912 E Diedrich St Ste A (67060-5406)
PHONE..................................316 613-2002
Bradley A Rogers, *Administration*
EMP: 11 **EST:** 2012
SALES (est): 1.5MM **Privately Held**
SIC: 5082 General construction machinery & equipment

(G-2959)
SENIORTRUST OF HAYSVILLE LLC
Also Called: Haysville Healthcare Center
215 N Lamar Ave (67060-1266)
PHONE..................................316 524-3211
Robert Webb,
EMP: 130
SALES (est): 4.3MM **Privately Held**
SIC: 8051 Skilled nursing care facilities; rehabilitation center, outpatient treatment

(G-2960)
SLEEP INN SUITE
Also Called: Choice Hotels
651 E 71st St S (67060-2103)
PHONE..................................316 425-6077
Ramona George, *Branch Mgr*
EMP: 10
SALES (est): 271.2K **Privately Held**
SIC: 7011 Hotels & motels

(G-2961)
TALENT ON PARADE
137 Pirner Ste 5 (67060-2607)
P.O. Box 535 (67060-0535)
PHONE..................................316 522-4836
Kimberly McClure, *Owner*
EMP: 12
SALES (est): 370K **Privately Held**
WEB: www.talentonparade.com
SIC: 7922 Agent or manager for entertainers

(G-2962)
TRACY ELECTRIC INC
8025 S Broadway St (67060-2331)
PHONE..................................316 522-8408
Mike Tracy, *President*
EMP: 42
SALES: 9.6MM **Privately Held**
WEB: www.tracyelectric.kscoxmail.com
SIC: 1731 General electrical contractor

(G-2963)
WATERSOURCE TECHNOLOGIES INC
952 E Grand Ave (67060-1421)
PHONE..................................316 927-2100
Darryl Lewson, *President*
EMP: 6 **EST:** 2008
SALES (est): 841.6K **Privately Held**
SIC: 3589 Water filters & softeners, household type

(G-2964)
WICHITA BODY & EQUIPMENT CO
6701 S Broadway Ave (67060-2115)
PHONE..................................316 522-1080
Tim Brockleman, *President*
Karla Brockleman, *Treasurer*
Terry Misak,
EMP: 7
SQ FT: 20,000
SALES (est): 1MM **Privately Held**
SIC: 3713 7539 3711 Bus bodies (motor vehicles); truck bodies (motor vehicles); van bodies; frame repair shops, automotive; motor vehicles & car bodies

Healy
Lane County

(G-2965)
DAY FARMS INC
6008 W Illinois (67850-5087)
P.O. Box 218 (67850-0218)
PHONE..................................620 398-2255
Dwight York, *President*
EMP: 10
SALES (est): 293.9K **Privately Held**
WEB: www.dayfarms.com
SIC: 0191 General farms, primarily crop

(G-2966)
HEALY COOPERATIVE ELEVATOR CO
Also Called: Farmers Store & Deli
225 S Dodge Rd (67850)
P.O. Box 110 (67850-0110)
PHONE..................................620 398-2211
Mike Scheuerman, *President*
Dale A Hollibaugh, *General Mgr*
EMP: 20 **EST:** 1916
SALES (est): 3.3MM **Privately Held**
SIC: 5153 5541 5211 5251 Grains; grain elevators; filling stations, gasoline; lumber & other building materials; hardware; grocery stores

(G-2967)
SHARP BROS SEED COMPANY (PA)
Also Called: Sharp Farms
1005 S Sycamore (67850-5100)
P.O. Box 140 (67850-0140)
PHONE..................................620 398-2231
Daniel Sharp, *President*
Gail Sharp, *Vice Pres*
▼ **EMP:** 40 **EST:** 1958
SALES (est): 20.3MM **Privately Held**
WEB: www.sharpseed.com
SIC: 5541 5191 Filling stations, gasoline; seeds: field, garden & flower

Heizer
Barton County

(G-2968)
STRECKER MACHINE INC
610 Bend Ave (67530-8503)
PHONE..................................620 793-7128
William F Strecker, *President*
Marilyn Strecker, *Vice Pres*
Rose Marie Lang, *Manager*
EMP: 6
SALES: 400K **Privately Held**
SIC: 3599 Machine shop, jobbing & repair

Herington
Dickinson County

(G-2969)
AGRI TRAILS COOP INC
500 N 7th St (67449-1515)
PHONE..................................785 258-2286
Thomas Remy, *Manager*
EMP: 10
SALES (corp-wide): 160MM **Privately Held**
SIC: 5191 4221 5153 Feed; grain elevator, storage only; grain elevators
PA: Agri Trails Coop, Inc.
508 N Main St
Hope KS 67451
785 366-7213

(G-2970)
ATMOS ENERGY CORPORATION
Colorado-Kansas Division
20 W Main St (67449-2244)
PHONE..................................785 258-2300

GEOGRAPHIC

Gregg Wolff, *Branch Mgr*
EMP: 16
SALES (corp-wide): 2.9B **Publicly Held**
WEB: www.atmosenergy.com
SIC: 4924 Natural gas distribution
PA: Atmos Energy Corporation
5430 Lyndon B Johnson Fwy
Dallas TX 75240
972 934-9227

(G-2971)
BARONDA SUPPLIES & SERVICE
1550 S 2700 Rd (67449-5073)
PHONE..................................785 466-2501
Leon Baronda, *President*
Marcia Baronda, *President*
EMP: 10
SALES: 450K **Privately Held**
SIC: 1522 Residential construction

(G-2972)
CHAMBER OF COMMERCE
Also Called: Herington Main Street Program
106 N Broadway Ste A (67449-2225)
PHONE..................................785 258-2115
Brenda Swinney, *President*
Dan Cook, *Vice Pres*
Jeff Mortensen, *Treasurer*
Shelly Idleman, *Admin Sec*
EMP: 10
SALES (est): 460K **Privately Held**
SIC: 8611 Chamber of Commerce

(G-2973)
CUSTOM METAL FABRICATORS INC
Also Called: CMF
3194 R Ave (67449-4043)
P.O. Box 286 (67449-0286)
PHONE..................................785 258-3744
Frank Meyer, *Ch of Bd*
Ben Meyer, *President*
Shirley Meyer, *Systems Staff*
EMP: 35
SQ FT: 36,000
SALES (est): 9.8MM **Privately Held**
SIC: 3535 3537 3523 3444 Bulk handling conveyor systems; industrial trucks & tractors; farm machinery & equipment; sheet metalwork; fabricated plate work (boiler shop); fabricated structural metal

(G-2974)
HERINGTON LIVESTOCK MARKET
502 E Lewerenz St (67449-1622)
PHONE..................................785 258-2205
Marcia Mathias, *President*
EMP: 30
SALES (est): 4.6MM **Privately Held**
SIC: 5154 Auctioning livestock

(G-2975)
HERINGTON OPCO LLC
2 E Ash St (67449-1662)
PHONE..................................785 789-4750
Kristi Depusoir,
EMP: 14
SALES (est): 133.6K **Privately Held**
SIC: 8051 Skilled nursing care facilities

(G-2976)
HODGDON POWDER COMPANY INC
Also Called: Pyrodex Division
1347 S 2600 Rd (67449-4016)
PHONE..................................785 258-3388
Brad Schick, *Manager*
EMP: 60
SALES (corp-wide): 16.1MM **Privately Held**
WEB: www.hodgdon.com
SIC: 2892 Explosives
PA: Hodgdon Powder Company, Inc.
6430 Vista Dr
Shawnee Mission KS 66218
913 362-9455

(G-2977)
J B TURNER SONS
620 W Main St (67449-2118)
P.O. Box 19525, Topeka (66619-0525)
PHONE..................................785 233-9603
John Turner, *President*
Randy Wilson, *Maintenance Dir*
EMP: 49
SALES (est): 2.4MM **Privately Held**
SIC: 1761 Roofing contractor

(G-2978)
LARRY LAWRENZ CONSTRUCTION
220 W Walnut St Ste 1 (67449-2482)
PHONE..................................785 258-2056
Larry Lawrenz, *Owner*
EMP: 15
SQ FT: 1,400
SALES (est): 731.6K **Privately Held**
SIC: 1741 Masonry & other stonework

(G-2979)
LAWRENZ MASONRY LLC
220 W Walnut St (67449-2482)
PHONE..................................785 366-0866
Nathan Lawrenz,
Joshua Lawrenz,
EMP: 25
SALES (est): 526.1K **Privately Held**
SIC: 1741 Masonry & other stonework

(G-2980)
OSWALD MANUFACTURING CO INC
450 S 5th St (67449-2907)
P.O. Box 446 (67449-0446)
PHONE..................................785 258-2877
Merlin Oswald, *President*
Beverly Oswald, *Treasurer*
EMP: 7
SQ FT: 10,000
SALES (est): 573.2K **Privately Held**
SIC: 3523 7699 3949 7629 Fertilizing machinery, farm; farm machinery repair; dumbbells & other weightlifting equipment; electrical repair shops; blast furnaces & steel mills

(G-2981)
SQUAD IT SERVICES LLC
1100 N Broadway Apt 119 (67449-1683)
PHONE..................................785 844-3114
Elizabeth Huann Braden,
EMP: 50
SALES (est): 998.8K **Privately Held**
SIC: 2741

(G-2982)
U S STONE INDUSTRIES LLC
2561 Q Ave (67449-4042)
PHONE..................................913 529-4154
Brent Bayer, *Mng Member*
Kyra Nistler, *Director*
Kent Barnow,
EMP: 130
SALES (est): 7.8MM **Privately Held**
WEB: www.usstoneindustries.com
SIC: 5032 3281 Limestone; limestone, cut & shaped

Hesston
Harvey County

(G-2983)
A G 1 SOURCE LLC
603 E Lincoln Blvd (67062-9165)
P.O. Box 784 (67062-0784)
PHONE..................................620 327-2205
Scott Wedel, *Partner*
Rick Rupp, *COO*
Mark Waschek, *Vice Pres*
Mike Smith, *Mng Member*
Elizabeth Weber, *Executive*
EMP: 30
SALES (est): 1.3MM **Privately Held**
SIC: 8748 Agricultural consultant

(G-2984)
AGCO CORPORATION
420 W Lincoln Blvd (67062-8807)
P.O. Box 4000 (67062-2094)
PHONE..................................620 327-6413
Ed Swenson, *Opers Mgr*
Andy Peterson, *Mfg Staff*
Jeff Baldauf, *Draft/Design*
Leslie Brown, *Engineer*
Kelly Franz, *Engineer*
EMP: 120
SALES (corp-wide): 9.3B **Publicly Held**
WEB: www.agcocorp.com
SIC: 3523 Haying machines: mowers, rakes, stackers, etc.
PA: Agco Corporation
4205 River Green Pkwy
Duluth GA 30096
770 813-9200

(G-2985)
BMG OF KANSAS INC
606 Commerce Dr (67062-8816)
P.O. Box 698 (67062-0698)
PHONE..................................620 327-4038
Joe Brenneman, *President*
Doug Brenneman, *Corp Secy*
Jim Brenneman, *Vice Pres*
Luke Logan, *CIO*
EMP: 55
SQ FT: 30,000
SALES (est): 11.2MM **Privately Held**
SIC: 3444 3443 3412 3354 Sheet metalwork; fabricated plate work (boiler shop); metal barrels, drums & pails; aluminum extruded products

(G-2986)
CITIZENS STATE BANK
201 N Main St (67062-9159)
P.O. Box 869 (67062-0869)
PHONE..................................620 327-4941
Richard Drake, *Branch Mgr*
Kyle Friesen, *Technology*
EMP: 14
SALES (corp-wide): 18MM **Privately Held**
SIC: 6022 State commercial banks
PA: The Citizens State Bank
201 S Christian Ave
Moundridge KS
620 345-6317

(G-2987)
CITY OF HESSTON
Also Called: Hesston Golf Course
520 Yost Dr (67062-9064)
PHONE..................................620 327-2331
Scott Welsh, *Manager*
EMP: 11 **Privately Held**
WEB: www.hesstonks.org
SIC: 7992 Public golf courses
PA: City Of Hesston
115 E Smith St
Hesston KS 67062
620 327-4412

(G-2988)
CROSSWIND CONFERENCE CENTER
8036 N Hoover Rd (67062-9322)
PHONE..................................620 327-2700
Milo Koffiman, *Director*
EMP: 25
SALES (est): 1.4MM **Privately Held**
SIC: 7389 Convention & show services

(G-2989)
EXCEL INDUSTRIES INC
Also Called: Excel Mower Sales
605 Commerce Dr (67062-9427)
PHONE..................................800 942-4911
Vance Truskett, *Branch Mgr*
EMP: 11
SALES (corp-wide): 196.7MM **Privately Held**
WEB: www.hustlerturfequipment.com
SIC: 5261 3523 Lawnmowers & tractors; turf equipment, commercial
PA: Excel Industries, Inc.
200 S Ridge Rd
Hesston KS 67062
620 327-4911

(G-2990)
EXCEL SALES INC
200 S Ridge Rd (67062-8808)
P.O. Box 7000 (67062-2097)
PHONE..................................620 327-4911
Roy Mullet, *Ch of Bd*
Paul Mullet, *President*
Bob Mullet, *Treasurer*
Byron Henson, *Systems Dir*
Vernon Nikkel, *Admin Sec*
EMP: 14
SQ FT: 10,000
SALES: 250K
SALES (corp-wide): 196.7MM **Privately Held**
SIC: 5261 7699 Lawn & garden equipment; lawn mower repair shop
PA: Excel Industries, Inc.
200 S Ridge Rd
Hesston KS 67062
620 327-4911

(G-2991)
GVL POLYMERS INC
8515 N Hesston Rd (67062-9284)
PHONE..................................320 693-8411
EMP: 10
SQ FT: 51,000
SALES (est): 1.5MM **Privately Held**
SIC: 3089 Molding primary plastic

(G-2992)
HESSTON RECORD
347 N Old Us Highway 81 (67062-9406)
P.O. Box 340 (67062-0340)
PHONE..................................620 327-4831
Robb Reeves, *Owner*
EMP: 5
SALES (est): 185.1K **Privately Held**
SIC: 2711 Commercial printing & newspaper publishing combined

(G-2993)
HESSTON UNIFIED SCHOOL DST 460
Also Called: Heston Recreation Commission
200 N Ridge Rd (67062-8810)
P.O. Box 2000 (67062-2092)
PHONE..................................620 327-2989
Larry Thompson, *Branch Mgr*
Lindsay Jaso, *Teacher*
EMP: 43
SALES (corp-wide): 7.5MM **Privately Held**
SIC: 8211 7999 Elementary & secondary schools; recreation center
PA: Hesston Unified School District 460
150 N Ridge Rd
Hesston KS 67062
620 327-4931

(G-2994)
INTERNATIONAL ASSOCIATION OF
421 N Streeter Ave (67062-8924)
P.O. Box 461 (67062-0461)
PHONE..................................620 327-4271
Dean Day, *Admin Sec*
EMP: 32
SALES (corp-wide): 63.7MM **Privately Held**
WEB: www.iaopc.com
SIC: 8641 Civic associations
PA: The International Association Of Lions Clubs Incorporated
300 W 22nd St
Oak Brook IL 60523
630 571-5466

(G-2995)
KING CONSTRUCTION COMPANY INC
301 N Lancaster Ave (67062-8985)
P.O. Box 849 (67062-0849)
PHONE..................................620 327-4251
Donald King, *President*
Craig Alexander, *Corp Secy*
EMP: 85 **EST:** 1950
SQ FT: 3,000
SALES (est): 11.5MM **Privately Held**
SIC: 1622 1611 Bridge construction; general contractor, highway & street construction; concrete construction: roads, highways, sidewalks, etc.

(G-2996)
L & J WOOD PRODUCTS INC
Also Called: Dry Creek Farms
9015 N Emma Creek Rd (67062-9271)
P.O. Box 10 (67062-0010)
PHONE..................................620 327-2183
Lowell Unruh, *President*
Ward Unruh, *Vice Pres*
Joseph Unruh, *Treasurer*
EMP: 8
SQ FT: 25,600

SALES (est): 1.4MM Privately Held
SIC: 5031 0191 2441 Lumber: rough, dressed & finished; general farms, primarily crop; shipping cases, wood: nailed or lock corner

(G-2997)
MID KANSAS FAMILY PRACTICE
Also Called: Mid Family Practice PA
705 E Randall St (67062-8806)
P.O. Box 609 (67062-0609)
PHONE....620 327-2440
Mark S Hall MD, *Owner*
EMP: 22
SALES (est): 1.1MM Privately Held
SIC: 8011 General & family practice, physician/surgeon

(G-2998)
O I C INC (PA)
Also Called: Office Installation Company
125 N Main St (67062-9143)
P.O. Box 608 (67062-0608)
PHONE....816 471-5400
Tom Reimer, *President*
Todd Banpelt, *General Mgr*
Joel Feiock, *Branch Mgr*
EMP: 21
SQ FT: 12,000
SALES: 3MM Privately Held
WEB: www.oicinstall.com
SIC: 1799 Office furniture installation

(G-2999)
PROVIMI NORTH AMERICA INC
Also Called: Sunglo Feeds
300 N Main St (67062-9160)
P.O. Box 789 (67062-0789)
PHONE....620 327-2280
Brooke Humphrey, *Marketing Staff*
Allen Schrag, *Branch Mgr*
Blaine Blackburn, *Director*
Terry Davies, *Director*
Mark Hulsebus, *Director*
EMP: 34
SALES (corp-wide): 113.4B Privately Held
WEB: www.vigortone.com
SIC: 2048 5191 Livestock feeds; animal feeds
HQ: Provimi North America, Inc.
10 Nutrition Way
Brookville OH 45309
937 770-2400

(G-3000)
SCHOWALTER VILLA
200 W Cedar St (67062-8100)
PHONE....620 327-0400
James Krehbiel, *President*
EMP: 33
SALES: 13.6MM Privately Held
SIC: 8361 Home for the aged

Hiawatha
Brown County

(G-3001)
AG PARTNERS COOPERATIVE INC (PA)
708 S 10th St (66434-8500)
PHONE....785 742-2196
Howard Elliott, *President*
Mitch Williams, *Principal*
Jason Taylor, *Vice Pres*
Mark Meyer, *Treasurer*
Ray Brintnall, *Controller*
EMP: 20 EST: 1956
SQ FT: 5,000
SALES (est): 47.2MM Privately Held
WEB: www.agpartnerscoop.com
SIC: 5153 Grains; grain elevators

(G-3002)
BANK OF BLUE VALLEY
7th & Delaware St (66434)
P.O. Box 200 (66434-0200)
PHONE....785 742-2121
Samuel Schuetz, *Manager*
EMP: 28 Publicly Held
SIC: 6022 State commercial banks
HQ: Bank Of Blue Valley
11935 Riley St
Overland Park KS 66213
913 338-1000

(G-3003)
BESTWAY INC
2021 Iowa St (66434-2267)
PHONE....785 742-2949
Dawn P Meenen, *President*
EMP: 35
SALES: 2.5MM Privately Held
SIC: 3523 Sprayers & spraying machines, agricultural

(G-3004)
BROWN CNTY DEVELOPMENTAL SVCS
400 S 12th St (66434-2552)
PHONE....785 742-2053
Linda Lock, *Exec Dir*
EMP: 40
SALES: 2.4MM Privately Held
SIC: 8322 8093 Social services for the handicapped; rehabilitation center, outpatient treatment

(G-3005)
BRUNA BROTHERS IMPLEMENT LLC
Also Called: Bruna Implement Company
201 E Miami St (66434-1810)
PHONE....785 742-2261
Alan Bruna, *Mng Member*
EMP: 18
SALES (corp-wide): 26.5MM Privately Held
WEB: www.brunaimplementco.com
SIC: 5083 7699 Agricultural machinery & equipment; agricultural equipment repair services
PA: Bruna Brothers Implement, Llc
1128 Pony Express Hwy
Marysville KS 66508
785 562-5304

(G-3006)
CITIZENS STATE BANK AND TR CO (PA)
610 Oregon St (66434-2231)
P.O. Box 360 (66434-0360)
PHONE....785 742-2101
Theadore Starr, *President*
Erik Madsen, *Assistant VP*
Cathy Henson, *Vice Pres*
Dan Hermesch, *Vice Pres*
Sara Knudson, *Vice Pres*
EMP: 26 EST: 1907
SQ FT: 1,500
SALES: 4MM Privately Held
WEB: www.csbkansas.com
SIC: 6022 0762 State trust companies accepting deposits, commercial; farm management services

(G-3007)
EVERGY KANSAS CENTRAL INC
1701 Oregon St (66434-8902)
P.O. Box 158 (66434-0158)
PHONE....785 742-2185
Beverly Sunderman, *Branch Mgr*
EMP: 32
SQ FT: 25,000
SALES (corp-wide): 4.2B Publicly Held
SIC: 4911 Generation, electric power
HQ: Evergy Kansas Central, Inc.
818 S Kansas Ave
Topeka KS 66612
785 575-6300

(G-3008)
GIRARD NATIONAL BANK
805 S 1st St (66434-2767)
P.O. Box 437 (66434-0437)
PHONE....785 742-7120
Cathy Dove, *Branch Mgr*
EMP: 12 Privately Held
WEB: www.gn-bank.com
SIC: 6021 National commercial banks
HQ: Girard National Bank
100 E Forest Ave
Girard KS 66743
620 724-8223

(G-3009)
HI-TECH INTERIORS INC
1651 Apache Ave (66434-8928)
PHONE....785 742-1766
Casey Willich, *Branch Mgr*
EMP: 57 Privately Held
SIC: 1742 Drywall
PA: Hi-Tech Interiors, Inc.
5006 Skyway Dr
Manhattan KS 66503

(G-3010)
HIAWATHA HOSPITAL ASSOCIATION
Also Called: Family Practice Clinic
300 Utah St (66434-2314)
PHONE....785 742-2161
Beth A Morrison, *Principal*
EMP: 10
SALES (corp-wide): 25.1MM Privately Held
SIC: 8062 8011 General medical & surgical hospitals; clinic, operated by physicians
PA: Hiawatha Hospital Association, Inc.
300 Utah St
Hiawatha KS 66434
785 742-2131

(G-3011)
JADE MILLWRIGHTS INC
2583 Prairie Rd (66434-9699)
PHONE....785 544-7771
Dale Elliott, *President*
Jeremiah Dolisi, *Vice Pres*
Nicole Dolisi, *Advt Staff*
Angel Elliot, *Admin Sec*
EMP: 25
SQ FT: 3,484,800
SALES (est): 3.5MM Privately Held
SIC: 1796 7699 Millwright; elevators: inspection, service & repair

(G-3012)
K N Z A INC (PA)
5 Onehalf Mi S Hiawatha H (66434)
P.O. Box 104 (66434-0104)
PHONE....785 547-3461
Greg Buser, *President*
Robert Hilton, *Treasurer*
EMP: 15
SQ FT: 2,000
SALES (est): 2.2MM Privately Held
SIC: 4832 News

(G-3013)
KEN BABCOCK SALES INC
Also Called: Babcock Sales & Service
105 S 1st St (66434-2603)
PHONE....785 544-6592
Kenneth Babcock, *President*
EMP: 12 EST: 1977
SALES (est): 3.7MM Privately Held
SIC: 1541 1542 Industrial buildings, new construction; agricultural building contractors

(G-3014)
KIWANIS INTERNATIONAL INC
100 S 2nd St (66434-2300)
P.O. Box 25 (66434-0025)
PHONE....785 742-2596
Janice Smith, *Admin Sec*
EMP: 28
SALES (corp-wide): 23.6MM Privately Held
WEB: www.kfne.org
SIC: 8641 Civic associations
PA: Kiwanis International, Inc.
3636 Woodview Trce
Indianapolis IN 46268
317 875-8755

(G-3015)
LAFAYETTE LIFE PLAN INC
Also Called: Maple Hts Nrsing Rhabilitation
302 E Iowa St (66434-9826)
PHONE....785 742-7465
Lisa Duryea, *Administration*
EMP: 80
SQ FT: 3,000
SALES (est): 3.6MM Privately Held
SIC: 8052 Intermediate care facilities

(G-3016)
LESLIE D BOECKNER
Also Called: Advantage Concrete
710 N 1st St (66434-1833)
PHONE....785 741-1036
Craig Boeckner, *Partner*
EMP: 10
SALES: 1MM Privately Held
SIC: 1771 Concrete work

(G-3017)
MEDICALODGES INC
Also Called: Gran Villas of Hiawatha
400 Kansas Ave (66434-1954)
PHONE....785 742-4566
Sue Korthanke, *Manager*
EMP: 14
SALES (corp-wide): 100.2MM Privately Held
WEB: www.medicalodges.com
SIC: 8051 Convalescent home with continuous nursing care
PA: Medicalodges, Inc.
201 W 8th St
Coffeyville KS 67337
620 251-6700

(G-3018)
MID WEST READY MIX & BLDG SUPS
1456 230th St (66434-8607)
PHONE....785 742-3678
Dennis Meyer, *Owner*
EMP: 5
SALES (corp-wide): 1.3MM Privately Held
SIC: 3273 Ready-mixed concrete
PA: Mid West Ready Mix And Building Supplies Inc
926 Grant St
Sabetha KS 66534
785 284-2911

(G-3019)
NEK CAP INC (PA)
Also Called: Ne KS Community Action Program
1260 220th St (66434-8923)
PHONE....785 742-2222
Carol Graves, *CFO*
Robert Grissom, *CFO*
Heather William, *Office Mgr*
Lu Hangley, *Exec Dir*
Jeanette Collier, *Exec Dir*
EMP: 50
SQ FT: 15,000
SALES (est): 10.1MM Privately Held
SIC: 8351 Head start center, except in conjunction with school

(G-3020)
NORTHAST KANS AREA AGCY ON AGI
1803 Oregon St (66434-2256)
PHONE....785 742-7152
Karen Wilson, *Exec Dir*
EMP: 10
SALES: 1.5MM Privately Held
SIC: 8322 Senior citizens' center or association

(G-3021)
PHYSICAL RSPRTORY THERAPY SVCS
Also Called: Hiawatha Hospital
300 Utah St (66434-2314)
PHONE....785 742-2131
Michele Schmitz, *Principal*
John Sharing, *Director*
EMP: 15
SALES (corp-wide): 617K Privately Held
WEB: www.hch-ks.org
SIC: 8093 8049 Respiratory therapy clinic; physical therapist
PA: Physical & Respiratory Therapy Services
204 S 6th St
Hiawatha KS

(G-3022)
PHYSICAL RSPRTORY THERAPY SVCS
Also Called: Prts
700 Oregon St (66434-2232)
PHONE....785 742-7606

David Nachtigal, *President*
EMP: 30
SALES (est): 1.6MM **Privately Held**
SIC: 8049 Physical therapist

(G-3023)
RHS INC
2021 Iowa St (66434-2267)
P.O. Box 394 (66434-0394)
PHONE..................................785 742-2949
Rick Heiniger, *CEO*
Dean Ryerson, *President*
Debbie Heiniger, *Corp Secy*
Bill Burdick, *Sales Mgr*
EMP: 46
SQ FT: 48,000
SALES (est): 21.1MM **Privately Held**
WEB: www.rhs-inc.com
SIC: 5083 3523 3535 Agricultural machinery; dusters, mechanical: agricultural; conveyors & conveying equipment

(G-3024)
SAINT JUDE HOSPICE
708 Oregon St (66434-2232)
PHONE..................................785 742-3823
Lisa Walder, *Principal*
EMP: 10
SALES (est): 426.9K **Privately Held**
SIC: 8052 Personal care facility

(G-3025)
STEVES QUICK LUBE
97 Sioux Ave (66434-2735)
PHONE..................................785 742-3500
Steve Schmidt, *Owner*
EMP: 10
SALES (est): 539K **Privately Held**
SIC: 7538 General automotive repair shops

(G-3026)
U-TEK CNC SOLUTIONS LLC
1322 260th St (66434-8382)
PHONE..................................888 317-6503
John Shane, *President*
Monte Unruh, *Vice Pres*
EMP: 10
SALES (est): 1.5MM **Privately Held**
SIC: 3444 Sheet metalwork

(G-3027)
VINTAGE PARK AT HIAWATHA LLC
400 Kansas Ave (66434-1954)
PHONE..................................785 742-4566
Sussan Jacobs, *Mng Member*
EMP: 19
SALES (est): 635.9K **Privately Held**
SIC: 8059 Nursing home, except skilled & intermediate care facility

(G-3028)
WILDE TOOL CO INC (PA)
1210 Pottawatomie St (66434)
P.O. Box 30 (66434-0030)
PHONE..................................785 742-7171
Martin Froeschl, *Ch of Bd*
Philip Froeschl Jr, *Corp Secy*
Matthew H Froeschl, *Vice Pres*
EMP: 43 **EST:** 1955
SQ FT: 100,000
SALES (est): 6.8MM **Privately Held**
WEB: www.wildetool.com
SIC: 3423 5085 3544 Hand & edge tools; industrial tools; special dies, tools, jigs & fixtures

Highland
Doniphan County

(G-3029)
HIGHLAND HEALTHCARE AND
402 S Avenue (66035-4162)
P.O. Box 117 (66035-0117)
PHONE..................................785 442-3217
Do Smith, *Director*
George V Hager Jr,
EMP: 40
SALES: 1MM **Publicly Held**
WEB: www.highlandcarecenter.net
SIC: 8051 Skilled nursing care facilities
HQ: Genesis Healthcare Llc
101 E State St
Kennett Square PA 19348

Hill City
Graham County

(G-3030)
CHS MCPHERSON REFINERY INC
Also Called: N C R A
721 W Main St (67642-1935)
PHONE..................................785 421-2157
Bob Wyatt, *Manager*
EMP: 11
SALES (corp-wide): 31.9B **Publicly Held**
SIC: 4221 Elevator storage
HQ: Chs Mcpherson Refinery Inc.
2000 S Main St
Mcpherson KS 67460
620 241-2340

(G-3031)
COUNTY OF GRAHAM
Also Called: Graham County Hospital
304 W Prout St (67642-1435)
P.O. Box 339 (67642-0339)
PHONE..................................785 421-5464
Fred J Meis, *Branch Mgr*
EMP: 50
SQ FT: 20,000 **Privately Held**
SIC: 8062 General medical & surgical hospitals
PA: County Of Graham
410 N Pomeroy Ave
Hill City KS 67642
785 421-2107

(G-3032)
DAWSON PLACE INC
208 W Prout St (67642-1434)
PHONE..................................785 421-3414
James Thompson, *President*
Nancy McGinnis, *Administration*
Janice Perkowski, *Administration*
EMP: 49
SQ FT: 13,000
SALES: 1.8MM **Privately Held**
SIC: 8059 Nursing home, except skilled & intermediate care facility

(G-3033)
DEVELOPMENTAL SVCS NW KANS INC
Also Called: Kobler Center
100 W Mcfarland St (67642-1624)
PHONE..................................785 421-2851
Susan Burd, *Director*
EMP: 33
SALES (corp-wide): 14.4MM **Privately Held**
SIC: 8331 Vocational rehabilitation agency
PA: Developmental Services Of Northwest Kansas, Inc.
2703 Hall St Ste B10
Hays KS 67601
785 625-5678

(G-3034)
FARMERS & MERCHANTS BANK HL CY (PA)
120 E Main St (67642-1922)
P.O. Box 338 (67642-0338)
PHONE..................................785 421-2131
Jerry Hanzlick, *President*
Fred Keener, *Vice Pres*
EMP: 13
SALES: 1.8MM **Privately Held**
SIC: 6022 State commercial banks

(G-3035)
HOSPICE OF GRAHAM COUNTY
Also Called: GRAHAM COUNTY HOSPITAL
304 W Prout St (67642-1435)
P.O. Box 339 (67642-0339)
PHONE..................................785 421-2121
Shawn Keef, *CEO*
Marsha Dinkel, *Materials Mgr*
Alfreda Lobmeyer, *QA Dir*
Jill Berland, *Human Res Dir*
Donna Schierkolk, *Exec Dir*
EMP: 108 **EST:** 1997
SALES: 6.1MM **Privately Held**
WEB: www.gchospital.org
SIC: 8051 8082 Skilled nursing care facilities; home health care services

(G-3036)
MURFIN DRILLING COMPANY INC
E Hwy 24 (67642)
P.O. Box 130 (67642-0130)
PHONE..................................785 421-2101
John Gerstner, *Branch Mgr*
EMP: 30 **Privately Held**
SIC: 1311 1381 Crude petroleum production; drilling oil & gas wells
HQ: Murfin Drilling Company, Inc.
250 N Water St Ste 300
Wichita KS 67202
316 267-3241

(G-3037)
NEX-TECH LLC
Also Called: Rural Telephone
118 W Main St (67642-1924)
PHONE..................................785 421-4197
Trela Miniun, *Principal*
Whitney Dubois, *Personnel Assit*
EMP: 10
SALES (corp-wide): 174.9MM **Privately Held**
WEB: www.nextechdirectory.com
SIC: 7389 4813 Telephone services; local telephone communications
HQ: Nex-Tech, Llc
2418 Vine St
Hays KS 67601

(G-3038)
WSI HOLDINGS LLC
Also Called: Wellhead Systems
710 W Mcvey St (67642-3000)
P.O. Box 129 (67642-0129)
PHONE..................................785 421-2255
Missy Balthazor, *Cust Mgr*
Charley Nelson, *Manager*
Dale J Goodeyon II,
Jessica Goodeyon,
EMP: 46 **EST:** 2012
SQ FT: 20,000
SALES (est): 6.9MM **Privately Held**
SIC: 3533 Oil field machinery & equipment

(G-3039)
X-PERT SERVICE TOOLS INC
310 Plum St (67642-2105)
P.O. Box 158 (67642-0158)
PHONE..................................785 421-5600
Clark Law, *President*
EMP: 8
SQ FT: 2,000
SALES (est): 2.3MM **Privately Held**
SIC: 1389 Oil field services

Hillsboro
Marion County

(G-3040)
AG-SERVICE INC (PA)
1830 Kanza (67063-8102)
PHONE..................................620 947-3166
Michael L Kleiber, *President*
Carolyn Kleiber, *Treasurer*
EMP: 15
SQ FT: 3,000
SALES (est): 17MM **Privately Held**
SIC: 5191 Fertilizer & fertilizer materials; chemicals, agricultural

(G-3041)
BAKER BROS PRINTING CO INC
113 S Main St (67063-1525)
PHONE..................................620 947-3520
James C Baker, *President*
Elaine Baker, *Corp Secy*
Michael Klaassen, *Graphic Designe*
EMP: 7 **EST:** 1963
SALES (est): 1.1MM **Privately Held**
SIC: 2759 2752 Commercial printing; commercial printing, lithographic

(G-3042)
BARKMAN HONEY LLC (PA)
120 Santa Fe St (67063-9688)
PHONE..................................620 947-3173
Dustin Miner, *Buyer*
Doug Weinbrenner, *CFO*
Jessica Cummings, *Mktg Dir*
Jacqueline Cusick, *Office Mgr*
Brian Butler, *CTO*
◆ **EMP:** 80 **EST:** 1940
SQ FT: 100,000
SALES (est): 18.1MM **Privately Held**
SIC: 2099 Honey, strained & bottled

(G-3043)
CAH ACQUISITION COMPANY 5 LLC
Also Called: Hillsboro Community Hospital
101 Industrial Rd (67063-9602)
PHONE..................................620 947-3114
Victoria Skarzynski, *Director*
Lawrence J Arthur,
EMP: 25
SALES: 5MM **Privately Held**
SIC: 8062 General medical & surgical hospitals

(G-3044)
CIRCLE D CORPORATION INC
613 N Ash St (67063-1104)
PHONE..................................620 947-2385
Wendell Dirks, *President*
Shelby Dirks, *Vice Pres*
EMP: 28
SQ FT: 33,000
SALES: 3.4MM **Privately Held**
WEB: www.circle-dtrailers.com
SIC: 3799 Trailers & trailer equipment

(G-3045)
CONCRETE PRODUCTS CO INC (PA)
209 S Cedar St (67063-1311)
P.O. Box 295 (67063-0295)
PHONE..................................620 947-5921
Terry Rhea, *President*
EMP: 14 **EST:** 1949
SQ FT: 5,000
SALES (est): 1.5MM **Privately Held**
SIC: 3273 Ready-mixed concrete

(G-3046)
CONTAINER SERVICES INC
Also Called: Csi
220 Santa Fe St (67063-9601)
P.O. Box 43 (67063-0043)
PHONE..................................620 947-2664
Darrell L Driggers, *President*
Thomas Leihy, *Prdtn Mgr*
Danny Spohn, *Supervisor*
EMP: 58
SALES: 12.5MM **Privately Held**
SIC: 3085 7389 Plastics bottles;

(G-3047)
COUNTRYSIDE FEED LLC (PA)
101 Santa Fe St (67063-9687)
PHONE..................................620 947-3111
Bill Fish, *Sales Mgr*
Luke Lindsey, *Mng Member*
EMP: 26
SQ FT: 6,400
SALES (est): 21MM **Privately Held**
WEB: www.countrysidefeed.com
SIC: 5191 5999 Feed; feed & farm supply

(G-3048)
FLINT HILLS INDUSTRIES INC
Also Called: Hillsboro Industries
220 Industrial Rd (67063-9651)
PHONE..................................620 947-3127
Rae Heitschmidt, *Principal*
EMP: 8
SALES (est): 81.4K **Privately Held**
SIC: 3715 Truck trailers

(G-3049)
HILLSBORO FORD INC
202 S Main St (67063-1532)
P.O. Box 268 (67063-0268)
PHONE..................................620 947-3134
Randy Hagen, *President*
Terry Hagen, *Vice Pres*
EMP: 32 **EST:** 1952
SQ FT: 7,500

SALES: 4.5MM Privately Held
SIC: 5511 7532 Automobiles, new & used; body shop, automotive

(G-3050)
HILLSBORO STATE BANK
200 N Main St (67063-1243)
P.O. Box 158 (67063-0158)
PHONE....................................620 947-3961
Carl Long, *President*
Cynthia Fleming, *President*
Linda Beltz, *Vice Pres*
Larry Payne, *Administration*
EMP: 11
SALES: 753K Privately Held
SIC: 6022 State commercial banks

(G-3051)
LANG DIESEL INC
603 N Ash St (67063-1104)
PHONE....................................620 947-3182
Arron Etlner, *Branch Mgr*
EMP: 10
SALES (corp-wide): 7.8MM Privately Held
SIC: 5083 Agricultural machinery & equipment
PA: Lang Diesel, Inc.
2818 Plaza Ave
Hays KS 67601
785 301-2426

(G-3052)
MII MANAGEMENT GROUP INC
207 S Lincoln St (67063-1712)
PHONE....................................620 947-3608
EMP: 60
SALES (est): 2.5MM Privately Held
SIC: 8741 Management Services

(G-3053)
PARKSIDE HOMES INC
200 Willow Rd Ofc (67063-1999)
PHONE....................................620 947-2301
Lu Janzen, *CEO*
Roblyn Regier, *Human Res Dir*
Melissa Arndt, *Director*
Craig Roble, *Director*
Judith Wineland, *Administration*
EMP: 100
SQ FT: 25,000
SALES: 4.4MM Privately Held
WEB: www.parksideks.org
SIC: 8059 8052 8051 Personal care home, with health care; personal care facility; skilled nursing care facilities

(G-3054)
PRAIRIE PRODUCTS
111 Commerce St (67063-9533)
P.O. Box 325 (67063-0325)
PHONE....................................620 947-3922
Rod Funk, *Owner*
Roger Hagen, *Manager*
EMP: 8
SQ FT: 12,000
SALES: 460K Privately Held
SIC: 3523 Cattle feeding, handling & watering equipment

(G-3055)
PRAIRIE VIEW INC
Also Called: Compeer of Prairie View
508 S Ash St (67063-1559)
PHONE....................................620 947-3200
Joy Robb, *Vice Pres*
Pam Burns, *Manager*
George Rogers III,
EMP: 20
SALES (corp-wide): 21.2MM Privately Held
WEB: www.pvi.org
SIC: 8063 8049 Psychiatric hospitals; clinical psychologist
PA: Prairie View, Inc.
1901 E 1st St
Newton KS 67114
316 284-6400

(G-3056)
PRINT SOURCE DIRECT LLC
Also Called: Hillsboro Free Press
116 S Main St (67063-1526)
PHONE....................................620 947-5702
Natalie Hoffman, *Adv Mgr*
Joel Klassen, *Mng Member*
Patty Decker, *Manager*
Don Ratzlaff,
EMP: 20 EST: 1995
SALES (est): 1.2MM Privately Held
SIC: 7389 Printing broker

(G-3057)
SALEM HOSPITAL INC
Also Called: SALEM HOME
704 S Ash St (67063-1506)
PHONE....................................620 947-2272
Kris Erickson, *CEO*
Allen Ediger, *CFO*
EMP: 85
SQ FT: 60,000
SALES: 2.7MM Privately Held
WEB: www.salemhospital.com
SIC: 8051 Skilled nursing care facilities

(G-3058)
WHEATBELT INC
300 Industrial Rd (67063-9694)
PHONE....................................620 947-2323
Roger Hofer, *President*
▼ EMP: 6
SQ FT: 13,000
SALES (est): 1.1MM Privately Held
WEB: www.rollupshutter.com
SIC: 3442 Shutters, door or window: metal; rolling doors for industrial buildings or warehouses, metal

Hillsdale
Miami County

(G-3059)
MAGNUM
Also Called: Bucyrus
209 Central St (66036)
P.O. Box 156 (66036-0156)
PHONE....................................913 783-4600
Gary Dover, *President*
Steven Dover, *Vice Pres*
Mark Hildreth, *Sales Staff*
Brent Vosika, *Sales Staff*
Carol Dover, *Admin Sec*
▲ EMP: 20
SALES (est): 5.7MM Privately Held
SIC: 3523 5083 Farm machinery & equipment; farm & garden machinery

Hoisington
Barton County

(G-3060)
CLARA BARTON HOSPITAL
Also Called: Clara Barton Surgical Services
351 W 10th St (67544-1715)
PHONE....................................620 653-4191
Deb Hawkins, *Principal*
EMP: 10
SALES (corp-wide): 19.4MM Privately Held
SIC: 8062 General medical & surgical hospitals
PA: Clara Barton Hospital Hoisington Kansas, The Inc
252 W 9th St
Hoisington KS 67544
620 653-2114

(G-3061)
CLARA BARTON HOSPITAL (PA)
Also Called: Russell Family Medical Care
252 W 9th St (67544-1725)
PHONE....................................620 653-2114
Sandy Ray, *Purchasing*
John Moshier, *Human Res Dir*
Curt Colson, *Branch Mgr*
Paula Hofmeister, *Manager*
Michelle Moshier, *Director*
EMP: 53
SQ FT: 32,000
SALES (est): 19.4MM Privately Held
WEB: www.clarabartonhospital.org
SIC: 8062 General medical & surgical hospitals

(G-3062)
CLARA BARTON HOSPITAL
250 W 9th St (67544-1799)
PHONE....................................620 653-2114
Jim Blackwell, *Administration*
EMP: 91
SALES (corp-wide): 19.4MM Privately Held
SIC: 8062 General medical & surgical hospitals
PA: Clara Barton Hospital Hoisington Kansas, The Inc
252 W 9th St
Hoisington KS 67544
620 653-2114

(G-3063)
ESSEX GROUP INC
75 E State Road 4 (67544-9200)
PHONE....................................620 653-2191
Brent Rensch, *Manager*
EMP: 275
SQ FT: 150,000 Privately Held
WEB: www.essexwire.com
SIC: 3357 Nonferrous wiredrawing & insulating
HQ: Essex Group, Inc.
1601 Wall St
Fort Wayne IN 46802
260 461-4000

(G-3064)
FIRST KANSAS BANK (PA)
101 N Main St (67544-2593)
PHONE....................................620 653-4921
Brad Titmen, *Exec VP*
Janet Hichmanan, *Vice Pres*
Paul Snapp, *Officer*
EMP: 24 EST: 1961
SQ FT: 4,000
SALES: 5.8MM Privately Held
WEB: www.firstkansasbank.com
SIC: 6022 State trust companies accepting deposits, commercial

(G-3065)
GPS KIDS CLUB
Also Called: GPS AFTER SCHOOL PROGRAM
352 W 12th St (67544-1501)
PHONE....................................620 282-2288
Debbie Stephens, *Administration*
EMP: 15
SQ FT: 3,000
SALES: 157.2K Privately Held
SIC: 8361 Residential care for children

(G-3066)
HOISINGTON HOMESTEAD
259 W 6th St (67544-2014)
PHONE....................................620 653-4121
Allanah Reed, *Manager*
EMP: 18
SALES (est): 418.8K Privately Held
SIC: 8011 Medical centers

(G-3067)
KAN COLO CREDIT UNION
216 N Maple St (67544-2342)
PHONE....................................620 653-4415
Allan Rose, *Chairman*
Joann Freeman, *Treasurer*
Tim McQuade, *Manager*
EMP: 12
SALES: 25.3K Privately Held
SIC: 6062 State credit unions

(G-3068)
KANSAS BRICK AND TILE CO INC
Also Called: Kansas Brick & Tile
767 N Us Highway 281 (67544-9037)
P.O. Box 450 (67544-0450)
PHONE....................................620 653-2157
Don Kling, *President*
Mike Kieser, *Vice Pres*
Kevin Burkey, *Sales Staff*
Andy Saken, *Admin Sec*
EMP: 50
SQ FT: 3,200
SALES (est): 5.4MM Privately Held
WEB: www.kansasbrick.com
SIC: 3251 Brick clay: common face, glazed, vitrified or hollow

(G-3069)
MANWEILER CHEVROLET CO INC
271 S Main St (67544-2703)
P.O. Box 390 (67544-0390)
PHONE....................................620 653-2121
Gene Manweiler, *President*
Larry M Manweiler, *Vice Pres*
Brenda Wetzel, *Manager*
EMP: 11
SQ FT: 9,800
SALES: 5.5MM Privately Held
WEB: www.mchevy.com
SIC: 5511 7538 7532 Automobiles, new & used; pickups, new & used; vans, new & used; general automotive repair shops; body shop, automotive

(G-3070)
ROTO-MIX LLC
558 S Main St (67544-9453)
PHONE....................................620 653-7323
Jim Bell, *Principal*
EMP: 40
SALES (corp-wide): 21.5MM Privately Held
WEB: www.rotomix.com
SIC: 3523 5083 3531 Cattle feeding, handling & watering equipment; livestock equipment; construction machinery
PA: Roto-Mix, Llc
2205 E Wyatt Earp Blvd
Dodge City KS 67801
620 225-1142

(G-3071)
SUPERIOR ESSEX INC
75 E State Road 4 (67544-9200)
PHONE....................................620 653-2191
Brent Rensch, *Branch Mgr*
EMP: 30 Privately Held
SIC: 3357 Nonferrous wiredrawing & insulating
HQ: Superior Essex Inc.
5770 Powers Ferry Rd # 300
Atlanta GA 30327
770 657-6000

(G-3072)
TOWN & COUNTRY SUPER MARKET
818 N Elm St (67544-1899)
PHONE....................................620 653-2330
Delores Deutsch, *President*
Randy Deutsch, *Vice Pres*
EMP: 38
SQ FT: 45,000
SALES (est): 3.6MM Privately Held
SIC: 5411 6531 1311 Grocery stores, independent; real estate agents & managers; crude petroleum & natural gas

(G-3073)
WILSON STATE BANK
201 N Main St (67544-2357)
PHONE....................................620 653-4113
Jim Carney, *Manager*
EMP: 12
SALES (corp-wide): 3.9MM Privately Held
SIC: 6021 National commercial banks
PA: Wilson State Bank
422 26th St
Wilson KS 67490
785 658-3441

Holcomb
Finney County

(G-3074)
EMPIRICAL TECHNOLOGY INC
3105 N Ibp Rd (67851-8902)
P.O. Box 1005 (67851-1005)
PHONE....................................620 277-2753
Craig Letch, *QA Dir*
Jeff Norton, *Manager*
EMP: 230
SALES (corp-wide): 151.8MM Privately Held
SIC: 2011 2013 Meat packing plants; sausages & other prepared meats

PA: Empirical Technology, Inc.
891 Two Rivers Dr
Dakota Dunes SD 57049
605 217-8000

(G-3075)
HOLCOMB RECREATION COMMISSION
106 Wiley St (67851-9175)
P.O. Box 78 (67851-0078)
PHONE..................................620 277-2152
Eric Jantz, *Director*
EMP: 60
SALES (est): 949.7K **Privately Held**
SIC: 7999 Recreation center

(G-3076)
NORTHERN NATURAL GAS COMPANY
P.O. Box 37 (67851-0037)
PHONE..................................620 277-2364
Walt Williams, *Branch Mgr*
EMP: 17
SALES (corp-wide): 225.3B **Publicly Held**
SIC: 4226 4924 Special warehousing & storage; natural gas distribution
HQ: Northern Natural Gas Company
1111 S 103rd St
Omaha NE 68124

(G-3077)
PREMIER HOUSING INC
Also Called: Premier Homes
7845 W Us Highway 50 (67851-8949)
PHONE..................................620 277-0707
Gary Greenlee, *President*
Danna Greenlee, *Vice Pres*
EMP: 22
SALES (est): 1.7MM **Privately Held**
WEB: www.premierhousingsolutions.com
SIC: 1521 New construction, single-family houses

(G-3078)
PREMIUM SOURCE AG LLC
3495 S Holcomb Ln (67851)
P.O. Box 10, Garden City (67846-0010)
PHONE..................................620 277-2009
Kevin Martin, *Manager*
Mark Linch,
EMP: 15
SALES (est): 2.2MM **Privately Held**
SIC: 0134 Irish potatoes

(G-3079)
RONS MARKET
106 N Jones Ave (67851-9075)
P.O. Box 289 (67851-0289)
PHONE..................................620 277-2073
Ron Leonard, *Owner*
EMP: 13
SQ FT: 4,000
SALES: 1.2MM **Privately Held**
SIC: 5411 5147 5541 Grocery stores, independent; meats, fresh; filling stations, gasoline

(G-3080)
SUNFLOWER ELECTRIC POWER CORP
2440 S Holcomb Ln (67851-9602)
P.O. Box 430 (67851-0430)
PHONE..................................620 277-2590
Royce Roemer, *Buyer*
Steven Mosf, *Enginr/R&D Mgr*
Robert Vigil, *Maintence Staff*
EMP: 150 **Privately Held**
SIC: 4911 ; generation, electric power; transmission, electric power
HQ: Sunflower Electric Power Corporation
301 W 13th St
Hays KS 67601
785 628-2845

(G-3081)
T L C TRUCKING LLC
3830 N Big Lowe Rd (67851)
P.O. Box 92 (67851-0092)
PHONE..................................620 277-0140
Troy Connsbutck, *Owner*
EMP: 12
SALES (est): 600K **Privately Held**
SIC: 4212 Local trucking, without storage

(G-3082)
TYSON FRESH MEATS INC
Also Called: I B P
3105 N Ibp Rd (67851-8902)
P.O. Box 149 (67851-0149)
PHONE..................................620 277-2614
Paul Karkiaimen, *Branch Mgr*
Luther Britton, *IT/INT Sup*
EMP: 60
SALES (corp-wide): 42.4B **Publicly Held**
SIC: 2011 2013 Meat packing plants; sausages & other prepared meats
HQ: Tyson Fresh Meats, Inc.
800 Stevens Port Dr
Dakota Dunes SD 57049
605 235-2061

Holton
Jackson County

(G-3083)
4-B PROPERTIES LLC
Also Called: Pennsylvania Place
925 Pennsylvania Ave (66436-1855)
PHONE..................................785 364-4643
Lee Jewel, *Manager*
EMP: 20
SALES (corp-wide): 600K **Privately Held**
SIC: 8059 Home for the mentally retarded, exc. skilled or intermediate
PA: 4-B Properties, L.L.C.
236 Main St
Uniontown KY 42461
270 822-4218

(G-3084)
AMERICAN WHOLESALE CORPORATION
24000 Us Highway 75 (66436-8116)
PHONE..................................785 364-4901
Don Armstrong, *President*
Gary Heideman, *Co-Owner*
Amanda Armstrong, *Vice Pres*
Data Armstrong, *Admin Sec*
EMP: 12
SQ FT: 20,000
SALES (est): 6.6MM **Privately Held**
SIC: 5031 5033 Building materials, exterior; roofing & siding materials

(G-3085)
BARROW TOOLING SYSTEMS INC
2000 Frontage Rd (66436-8055)
PHONE..................................785 364-4306
Troy Barrow, *President*
EMP: 5
SQ FT: 4,000
SALES (est): 1MM **Privately Held**
WEB: www.gladu.com
SIC: 5085 3425 7699 Industrial tools; saws, hand: metalworking or woodworking; industrial tool grinding

(G-3086)
COMMUNITY HEALTHCARE SYS INC
Also Called: Holton Family Health Clinic
1603 W 4th St (66436-1153)
PHONE..................................785 364-3205
Sharon Iverson, *Manager*
EMP: 20
SALES (corp-wide): 28.4MM **Privately Held**
SIC: 8062 8011 Hospital, affiliated with AMA residency; clinic, operated by physicians
PA: Community Healthcare System, Inc.
120 W 8th St
Onaga KS 66521
785 889-4274

(G-3087)
DEVELOPMENTAL SERVICES OF JACK
625 Vermont Ave (66436-2037)
P.O. Box 1011 (66436-1011)
PHONE..................................785 364-3534
Mary Nelson, *Ch of Bd*
Sandra Brucken, *Vice Ch Bd*
Mary Tessendorf, *President*
Evelyn Allen, *Treasurer*
EMP: 39 **EST:** 1983
SQ FT: 5,400
SALES: 1.3MM **Privately Held**
SIC: 8331 Vocational training agency

(G-3088)
EUBANKS CUSTOM WOODWORKS
310 New York Ave (66436-1740)
PHONE..................................785 364-4377
Mike Eubanks, *President*
EMP: 9
SQ FT: 8,100
SALES (est): 1MM **Privately Held**
SIC: 2426 2434 Turnings, furniture: wood; vanities, bathroom: wood

(G-3089)
FARMERS STATE BANKSHARES INC
209 Montana Ave (66436-1126)
P.O. Box 465 (66436-0465)
PHONE..................................785 364-4691
David Allen, *President*
Tarin Wray, *Officer*
Frida Kieffaber, *Receptionist*
EMP: 20
SALES (est): 5.1MM
SALES (corp-wide): 2.7MM **Privately Held**
SIC: 6022 State commercial banks
PA: Farmers State Bankshares Inc
205 Lincoln St
Circleville KS 66416
785 924-3311

(G-3090)
GARY BELL
Also Called: Bell Graphics
118 E 5th St (66436-1811)
PHONE..................................785 233-6677
Gary Bell, *Owner*
EMP: 8
SALES (est): 851.7K **Privately Held**
SIC: 2752 2791 2789 2759 Commercial printing, offset; typesetting; bookbinding & related work; commercial printing; coated & laminated paper

(G-3091)
GIANT COMMUNICATIONS INC
418 W 5th St Ste B (66436-1585)
P.O. Box 231 (66436-0231)
PHONE..................................785 362-9331
Gene Morris, *President*
EMP: 20
SALES (est): 3.7MM
SALES (corp-wide): 392.6MM **Publicly Held**
SIC: 4813 Local telephone communications;
PA: Lict Corporation
401 Theodore Fremd Ave
Rye NY 10580
914 921-8821

(G-3092)
GIANT KFN HOLDING COMPANY LLC
418 W 5th St (66436-1584)
PHONE..................................785 362-2532
Jean Moores, *Mng Member*
EMP: 20 **Privately Held**
SIC: 6719 Holding companies

(G-3093)
GRAN VILLAS OF HOLTON INC
Also Called: Medical Lodges
410 Juniper Dr (66436-1535)
PHONE..................................785 364-5051
Angela Hall, *Manager*
Lisa Walder, *Manager*
EMP: 14 **EST:** 1996
SALES (est): 335.3K **Privately Held**
SIC: 8051 Convalescent home with continuous nursing care

(G-3094)
HALLAUER OIL CO INC
Also Called: 66 Food Plaza
19425 P Rd (66436-8194)
PHONE..................................785 364-3140
Ray Hallauer, *President*
Marilyn Sue Hallauer, *Vice Pres*
Brian Hallauer, *Treasurer*
Troy Hallauer, *Shareholder*
EMP: 15
SQ FT: 3,000
SALES (est): 1.2MM **Privately Held**
SIC: 5411 5171 Convenience stores; petroleum bulk stations

(G-3095)
HAMMERSMITH MFG & SALES INC
1000 Vermont Ave (66436-2022)
PHONE..................................785 364-4140
John Hammersmith, *Manager*
EMP: 5
SALES (est): 771.3K
SALES (corp-wide): 21.5MM **Privately Held**
WEB: www.vailproducts.com
SIC: 3443 7692 Tanks, standard or custom fabricated: metal plate; welding repair
PA: Hammersmith Mfg. & Sales, Inc.
401 Central Ave
Horton KS 66439
785 486-2121

(G-3096)
HOLTON DENTAL
1100 Columbine Dr Ste B (66436-8839)
PHONE..................................785 364-3038
Alex C Gilliland, *Owner*
EMP: 10
SALES (est): 585.8K **Privately Held**
SIC: 8021 Dental clinic

(G-3097)
HOLTON LIVESTOCK EXCHANGE INC
13788 Highway K16 (66436-8381)
P.O. Box 227 (66436-0227)
PHONE..................................785 364-4114
Dan Harris, *President*
Melvina Harris, *Corp Secy*
EMP: 25 **EST:** 1951
SQ FT: 24,000
SALES (est): 3.9MM **Privately Held**
SIC: 5154 0291 Auctioning livestock; livestock farm, general

(G-3098)
HOLTON NATIONAL BANK (PA)
100 E 5th St (66436-1811)
P.O. Box 229 (66436-0229)
PHONE..................................785 364-2166
Kin Glennon, *President*
Kenneth Glennon, *Executive*
Sharol Callison, *Admin Sec*
EMP: 13
SQ FT: 15,000
SALES (est): 5.9MM **Privately Held**
SIC: 6022 State trust companies accepting deposits, commercial

(G-3099)
JACKSON COUNTY NURSING HOME
1121 W 7th St (66436-1123)
PHONE..................................785 364-3164
Mapu Lemnaua, *President*
Colleen Gutierrez, *Principal*
EMP: 60
SALES (est): 1.3MM **Privately Held**
SIC: 8051 Convalescent home with continuous nursing care

(G-3100)
JACKSON FARMERS INC (PA)
509 Lowell Ave (66436)
P.O. Box 191 (66436-0191)
PHONE..................................785 364-3161
Darla Lanter, *President*
Wally Edmonds, *Controller*
Matt Bloom, *Manager*
EMP: 17 **EST:** 1916
SQ FT: 4,000
SALES: 36.4MM **Privately Held**
WEB: www.jacksonfarmers.com
SIC: 5153 5191 5541 Grains; feed; seeds: field, garden & flower; fertilizer & fertilizer materials; filling stations, gasoline

(G-3101)
JBN TELEPHONE COMPANY INC
418 W 5th St Ste A (66436-1587)
P.O. Box 111 (66436-0111)
PHONE..................................785 362-3323
Gene Morris, *President*
Jan Charles, *Manager*
EMP: 17
SQ FT: 7,000
SALES (est): 3.2MM
SALES (corp-wide): 392.6MM **Publicly Held**
WEB: www.jbntelco.com
SIC: 4813 Local telephone communications
PA: Lict Corporation
401 Theodore Fremd Ave
Rye NY 10580
914 921-8821

(G-3102)
JOHNSONVILLE LLC
Also Called: Banner Creek
619 E 4th St (66436-2101)
PHONE..................................785 364-3126
Andrew Kaiser, *Engineer*
Tom Dorothy, *Manager*
EMP: 170
SALES (corp-wide): 656.1MM **Privately Held**
SIC: 2013 Sausages from purchased meat
PA: Johnsonville, Llc
N6928 Johnsonville Way
Sheboygan Falls WI 53085
920 453-6900

(G-3103)
KANSAS STATE BANK (HQ)
100 E 5th St (66436-1811)
P.O. Box 229 (66436-0229)
PHONE..................................785 364-2166
Kenneth Glennon, *President*
Clarence W Norris, *President*
John Morrissey, *Principal*
Eric Valaika, *COO*
Cindy Bechtold, *Assistant VP*
EMP: 22 **EST:** 1937
SALES (est): 5.2MM
SALES (corp-wide): 5.9MM **Privately Held**
SIC: 6022 State trust companies accepting deposits, commercial
PA: Holton National Bank
100 E 5th St
Holton KS 66436
785 364-2166

(G-3104)
MARKETING CONCEPTS
2007 Frontage Rd (66436-8055)
PHONE..................................785 364-4611
Denise Kathrens, *President*
Rick Jill, *Owner*
Jill Crouch, *Manager*
EMP: 10
SALES: 510K **Privately Held**
WEB: www.mar-con.com
SIC: 7331 Mailing service

(G-3105)
MILL CREEK LLC
19035 Us Highway 75 (66436-8101)
PHONE..................................785 364-2328
Jacob Wamego, *President*
Bobbie Jo, *CFO*
EMP: 14
SALES (est): 7.2MM
SALES (corp-wide): 6.7MM **Privately Held**
SIC: 1542 Commercial & office building contractors; commercial & office building, new construction; commercial & office buildings, renovation & repair
PA: Prairie Band, Llc
19035 Us Highway 75
Holton KS 66436
785 364-2463

(G-3106)
MORTON BUILDINGS INC
2006 Frontage Rd (66436-8055)
PHONE..................................785 364-4177
Darrel Meyer, *Manager*
EMP: 20
SALES (corp-wide): 463.7MM **Privately Held**
WEB: www.mortonbuildings.com
SIC: 3448 Farm & utility buildings
PA: Morton Buildings, Inc.
252 W Adams St
Morton IL 61550
800 447-7436

(G-3107)
NEK CAP INC
Also Called: Jackson County Head Start
130 S Iowa Ave (66436-1500)
PHONE..................................785 364-4798
Debra Davis, *Exec Dir*
EMP: 18
SALES (corp-wide): 10.1MM **Privately Held**
SIC: 8351 Head start center, except in conjunction with school
PA: Nek Cap, Inc.
1260 220th St
Hiawatha KS 66434
785 742-2222

(G-3108)
POWLS PUBLISHING COMPANY INC
Also Called: Holton Recorder
109 W 4th St (66436-1701)
P.O. Box 311 (66436-0311)
PHONE..................................785 364-3141
David Powls, *President*
EMP: 15
SALES (est): 869.8K **Privately Held**
WEB: www.sabethaks.com
SIC: 2711 Newspapers: publishing only, not printed on site

(G-3109)
PRAIRIE BAND LLC (PA)
19035 Us Highway 75 (66436-8101)
PHONE..................................785 364-2463
Jacob Wamego, *CEO*
Peggy Houston, *Vice Chairman*
William Evans, *Bd of Directors*
Tracy Stanhoff, *Bd of Directors*
Jona Rupnicki, *Admin Sec*
EMP: 14
SALES (est): 6.7MM **Privately Held**
SIC: 6719 Investment holding companies, except banks

(G-3110)
RURAL HLTH RSURCES JACKSON INC (PA)
Also Called: HOLTON COMMUNITY HOSPITAL
1110 Columbine Dr (66436-8824)
PHONE..................................785 364-2116
Carrie Saia, *CEO*
Elizabeth Schraer, *Purch Mgr*
Jason Woltje, *Info Tech Dir*
Dawna Smith, *Business Dir*
Rhea Bertulfo, *Lab Dir*
EMP: 140
SQ FT: 30,000
SALES: 16.4MM **Privately Held**
WEB: www.ruralhealthresearch.org
SIC: 8093 8062 Specialty outpatient clinics; general medical & surgical hospitals

(G-3111)
RURAL HLTH RSURCES JACKSON INC
Also Called: Family Practice Associates
1100 Columbine Dr Ste D (66436-8839)
PHONE..................................785 364-2126
Rachel Gross, *Manager*
EMP: 18
SALES (corp-wide): 16.4MM **Privately Held**
WEB: www.ruralhealthresearch.org
SIC: 8093 8011 Specialty outpatient clinics; general & family practice, physician/surgeon
PA: Rural Health Resources Of Jackson Co., Inc.
1110 Columbine Dr
Holton KS 66436
785 364-2116

(G-3112)
TECHS INC
Also Called: Jackson County Ems
300 W 4th St (66436-1605)
P.O. Box 109 (66436-0109)
PHONE..................................785 364-1911
Brent W Teter, *President*
Jay A Watkins, *Director*
EMP: 60
SALES (est): 1.2MM **Privately Held**
WEB: www.techs.com
SIC: 4119 Ambulance service

(G-3113)
TWO-BEE INC
Also Called: HOLTON FARM & HOME
925 W 6th St (66436-1221)
P.O. Box 390 (66436-0390)
PHONE..................................785 364-2162
Delbert Hawthorne, *President*
Julie Hawthorne, *Vice Pres*
EMP: 15
SQ FT: 12,000
SALES: 1.6MM **Privately Held**
SIC: 5191 5013 5722 5251 Feed; seeds: field, garden & flower; automotive supplies & parts; household appliance stores; hardware

Holyrood
Ellsworth County

(G-3114)
H & B CABLE SERVICE INC
Also Called: H & B Video
108 N Main St (67450-9690)
PHONE..................................785 252-4000
Robert A Koch, *President*
Del Jeane Nash, *Corp Secy*
Katherine Koch, *Vice Pres*
Donald Nash, *CFO*
EMP: 20
SALES (est): 1.2MM **Privately Held**
SIC: 4841 5731 Cable television services; radio, television & electronic stores

(G-3115)
H & B COMMUNICATIONS INC (PA)
108 N Main St (67450-9690)
PHONE..................................620 562-3598
Robert Koch, *President*
Del Jean Nash, *Corp Secy*
Katherine E Koch, *Vice Pres*
Donald Nash, *CFO*
John Radenberg, *Technician*
EMP: 19 **EST:** 1945
SQ FT: 10,000
SALES (est): 4.1MM **Privately Held**
WEB: www.hbcomm.net
SIC: 4813 Local telephone communications; long distance telephone communications

(G-3116)
HOLYROOD BANCSHARES INC
100 S Main St (67450-9688)
P.O. Box 128 (67450-0128)
PHONE..................................785 252-3239
Gerald Pauley, *President*
EMP: 15 **Privately Held**
SIC: 6712 Bank holding companies

(G-3117)
HUTCHENS CORPORATION
204 N County Rd (67450-9603)
PHONE..................................785 252-3423
EMP: 7
SALES (est): 350K **Privately Held**
SIC: 3229 Mfg Pressed/Blown Glass

Home
Marshall County

(G-3118)
BLUE VALLEY TELE-MARKETING
1555 Pony Express Hwy (66438-9000)
PHONE..................................785 799-3500
Troy Linkugel, *President*
Walter Peters, *Corp Secy*
Wesley Johnson, *Vice Pres*
EMP: 60
SQ FT: 10,000
SALES (est): 2.4MM
SALES (corp-wide): 20.9MM **Privately Held**
WEB: www.bluevalley.net
SIC: 7389 Telemarketing services
PA: Blue Valley Tele-Communications, Inc.
1559 Pony Express Hwy
Home KS 66438
785 799-3311

(G-3119)
BLUE VLY TL-COMMUNICATIONS INC (PA)
1559 Pony Express Hwy (66438-9000)
PHONE..................................785 799-3311
Terry Force, *President*
Candace Wright, *CFO*
EMP: 82 **EST:** 1956
SQ FT: 3,000
SALES: 20.9MM **Privately Held**
WEB: www.bluevalley.net
SIC: 4813 7389 Local telephone communications; telemarketing services

(G-3120)
SINCLAIR COMPANIES
402 3rd St (66438-9776)
PHONE..................................785 799-3116
EMP: 62
SALES (corp-wide): 3.9B **Privately Held**
SIC: 2911 Petroleum refining
PA: The Sinclair Companies
550 E South Temple
Salt Lake City UT 84102
801 524-2700

Hope
Dickinson County

(G-3121)
FIRST NATIONAL BANK (PA)
112 N Main St (67451-4001)
P.O. Box 67 (67451-0067)
PHONE..................................785 366-7225
Dan Coup, *President*
Danny E Emig, *Senior VP*
Patty Fells, *Vice Pres*
Linda Riedy, *Vice Pres*
Gary Coup, *Loan Officer*
EMP: 12 **EST:** 1923
SQ FT: 2,000
SALES: 4MM **Privately Held**
SIC: 6512 Bank building operation

Horton
Brown County

(G-3122)
BROWN-ATCHINSON ELC COOP ASSN (PA)
Also Called: Brown-Atchison Electric Co-Op
1712 Central Ave (66439-1217)
P.O. Box 230 (66439-0230)
PHONE..................................785 486-2117
Kevin Gigstad, *President*
Robert Perry, *General Mgr*
Jim Currie, *Superintendent*
John Carmody, *Governor*
Kevin Compton, *Vice Pres*
EMP: 15 **EST:** 1937
SALES: 6.8MM **Privately Held**
WEB: www.baelectric.com
SIC: 4911 Distribution, electric power

(G-3123)
GASKELL MACHINE & METAL INC
505 W 7th St (66439-1665)
PHONE..................................785 486-2674
Kirk Gaskell, *President*
Cindy Gaskell, *Vice Pres*
Shannon Scott, *Treasurer*
EMP: 10
SQ FT: 10,000

GEOGRAPHIC

SALES (est): 675.1K **Privately Held**
SIC: 3452 3599 Bolts, metal; nuts, metal; washers; machine shop, jobbing & repair

(G-3124)
GIRARD NATIONAL BANK
Also Called: Horton Main Branch
110 E 8th St (66439-1705)
PHONE....785 486-2124
Thomas Kidwell, *Branch Mgr*
EMP: 10 **Privately Held**
SIC: 6021 National commercial banks
HQ: Girard National Bank
100 E Forest Ave
Girard KS 66743
620 724-8223

(G-3125)
GOLDEN EAGLE CASINO
1121 Goldfinch Rd (66439-9537)
PHONE....785 486-6601
Toll Free:....888 -
Nancy Sumner, *Comptroller*
Gary Bontrager, *Marketing Mgr*
Martin Hale, *Manager*
Tonya Negonsott-Rodve, *Manager*
Jarrod Simon, *Manager*
EMP: 360
SQ FT: 70,000
SALES (est): 12.5MM **Privately Held**
WEB: www.goldeneaglecasino.com
SIC: 7999 5812 7011 5813 Gambling establishment; gambling machines, operation; eating places; casino hotel; drinking places

(G-3126)
HAMMERSMITH MFG & SALES INC (PA)
Also Called: Vail Products
401 Central Ave (66439-1739)
PHONE....785 486-2121
Edward A Hammersmith, *President*
Dennis Hammersmith, *Chairman*
Brian Young, *Engineer*
Aaron Weaver, *Design Engr*
Van Norris, *CFO*
▼ **EMP:** 90 **EST:** 1964
SQ FT: 3,000
SALES: 21.5MM **Privately Held**
WEB: www.vailproducts.com
SIC: 3443 7692 Industrial vessels, tanks & containers; welding repair

(G-3127)
HARVEST FUEL INC
Also Called: Sweetpro Feeds
1505 4th Ave E (66439-2055)
P.O. Box 69 (66439-0069)
PHONE....785 486-2626
Mark Hertzel, *QC Mgr*
Craig Wischropp, *Manager*
EMP: 5
SALES (corp-wide): 2.9MM **Privately Held**
WEB: www.sweetpro.com
SIC: 2048 Cereal-, grain-, & seed-based feeds
PA: Harvest Fuel, Inc.
207 14th St
Walhalla ND 58282
701 549-3450

(G-3128)
KANSAS DEPARTMENT TRNSP
1686 1st Ave E (66439-1246)
PHONE....785 486-2142
Leroy Koenhn, *Manager*
EMP: 40 **Privately Held**
WEB: www.nwwichitabypass.com
SIC: 1611 9621 Highway & street construction; regulation, administration of transportation;
HQ: Kansas Department Of Transportation
700 Sw Harrison St # 500
Topeka KS 66603
785 296-3501

(G-3129)
KICKAPOO NATION HEALTH CENTER
1117 Goldfinch Rd (66439-9537)
PHONE....785 486-2154
Debra Whiteberg, *Director*
Josephine Bellonger, *Director*
EMP: 12
SALES (est): 828.1K **Privately Held**
SIC: 8011 Clinic, operated by physicians

(G-3130)
KICKAPOO TRIBE IN KANSAS INC (PA)
824 111th Dr (66439-9502)
PHONE....785 486-2131
Brad Adden, *Principal*
Russell Bradley, *Principal*
Craig Wahwasuck, *Principal*
Steve Cadue, *Chairman*
EMP: 120 **EST:** 1981
SQ FT: 2,000
SALES (est): 7.4MM **Privately Held**
SIC: 5812 7011 8741 Eating places; casino hotel; administrative management

(G-3131)
MISSION VILLAGE LIVING CTR INC
1890 Euclid Ave Unit Frnt (66439-1247)
PHONE....785 486-2697
Patricia Raasch, *Administration*
EMP: 50
SQ FT: 33,000
SALES: 1.4MM **Privately Held**
SIC: 8052 Intermediate care facilities

(G-3132)
NATURES WAY INC
1374 Horned Owl Rd (66439-9519)
PHONE....785 486-3302
Dan Haverkamp, *President*
Maxine Haverkamp, *Corp Secy*
EMP: 5
SQ FT: 10,000
SALES (est): 517.4K **Privately Held**
SIC: 2048 2869 0711 Prepared feeds; enzymes; soil preparation services

(G-3133)
REGULATORY CONSULTANTS INC
Also Called: Rci
140 W 8th St (66439-1602)
PHONE....785 486-2882
Ron Demaray, *President*
Sam Germer, *COO*
Sandy Reese, *CFO*
Dave Powers, *VP Mktg*
Tim Boyer, *CIO*
EMP: 47
SQ FT: 6,200
SALES (est): 4.9MM
SALES (corp-wide): 22.2MM **Privately Held**
WEB: www.rci-safety.com
SIC: 8742 8748 7373 Hospital & health services consultant; environmental consultant; systems software development services
PA: Behavioral Science Technology, Inc.
1000 Town Center Dr # 600
Oxnard CA 93036
805 646-0166

Howard
Elk County

(G-3134)
HARRODS BLACKSMITH & WELDING
Also Called: Harrod's
436 W Washington St (67349)
P.O. Box 1080 (67349-1080)
PHONE....620 374-2323
Jerry Harrod, *Owner*
Mary Harrod, *Co-Owner*
EMP: 5 **EST:** 1969
SQ FT: 4,000
SALES: 460K **Privately Held**
SIC: 7692 7699 Welding repair; blacksmith shop

Hoxie
Sheridan County

(G-3135)
BAINTER CONSTRUCTION CO INC
844 Main St (67740)
P.O. Box 705 (67740-0705)
PHONE....785 675-3297
Wesley Bainter, *President*
▼ **EMP:** 27
SQ FT: 700
SALES (est): 6.7MM **Privately Held**
WEB: www.bainterconstruction.com
SIC: 3531 0211 Roofing equipment; beef cattle feedlots

(G-3136)
COUNTY OF SHERIDAN
Also Called: Sheridan County Health Complex
826 18th St (67740-4371)
P.O. Box 167 (67740-0167)
PHONE....785 675-3281
Teresa Poage, *QA Dir*
Rhonda Miller, *Lab Dir*
Dalene Babcock, *Food Svc Dir*
Joe Stratton, *Administration*
EMP: 10 **Privately Held**
SIC: 8062 General medical & surgical hospitals
PA: County Of Sheridan
925 9th St
Hoxie KS 67740
785 675-3361

(G-3137)
FIRST STATE BANK
801 Main St (67740)
P.O. Box 137 (67740-0137)
PHONE....785 675-3241
Keith Caldwell, *Vice Pres*
Marcella Cameron, *Vice Pres*
EMP: 15 **Privately Held**
SIC: 6022 State trust companies accepting deposits, commercial
PA: First State Bank
105 W Main St
Norton KS 67654

(G-3138)
FORMATION PLASTICS INC
2025 Sheridan Ave Apt 9 (67740-9627)
PHONE....785 754-3828
Galen Huffman, *CEO*
Brad Lovelady, *General Mgr*
EMP: 25
SALES (est): 2.6MM **Privately Held**
WEB: www.formationplastics.com
SIC: 3089 Thermoformed finished plastic products

(G-3139)
HOXIE IMPLEMENT CO INC
Also Called: Kubota Authorized Dealer
933 Oak Ave Hwy 23 & 24 (67740)
PHONE....785 675-3201
Gerald W Heim, *President*
Patrick Heim, *Vice Pres*
Edward Heim, *Treasurer*
Michael Heim, *Admin Sec*
▲ **EMP:** 30 **EST:** 1990
SQ FT: 35,000
SALES (est): 16.4MM **Privately Held**
SIC: 5083 Farm implements

(G-3140)
PSI TRANSPORT LLC
742 Us 24 (67740)
P.O. Box 605 (67740-0605)
PHONE....785 675-3881
Kyle Williams, *Mng Member*
EMP: 25
SALES (est): 290.8K **Privately Held**
SIC: 4789 Transportation services

(G-3141)
SCHIPPERS OIL FIELD SVCS LLC
1255 E Us Highway 24 (67740-4171)
PHONE....785 675-9991
Scott Schippers, *Mng Member*
EMP: 5
SALES: 2MM **Privately Held**
SIC: 1389 Servicing oil & gas wells

(G-3142)
STATE BANK (PA)
745 Main St (67740)
P.O. Box 77 (67740-0077)
PHONE....785 675-3261
Michael Mense, *CEO*
EMP: 14
SQ FT: 10,125
SALES: 7.6MM **Privately Held**
WEB: www.statebank-online.com
SIC: 6022 State commercial banks

(G-3143)
TAYLOR IMPLEMENT CO INC
451 W Highway 24 (67740-4284)
P.O. Box 725 (67740-0725)
PHONE....785 675-3272
Kory Taylor, *Treasurer*
EMP: 21
SALES (corp-wide): 1.6MM **Privately Held**
SIC: 7699 5083 3524 5531 Farm machinery repair; tractor repair; agricultural machinery & equipment; grass catchers, lawn mower; automotive parts
PA: Taylor Implement Co. Inc.
37525 State Highway 59
Yuma CO 80759
800 322-5830

(G-3144)
WOOFTER PUMP & WELL INC
1024 Oak Ave (67740-4442)
P.O. Box 689 (67740-0689)
PHONE....785 675-3991
Jay C Woofter, *President*
Dale Woofter, *Vice Pres*
Susan Woofter, *Treasurer*
Gladys Woofter, *Admin Sec*
EMP: 10
SQ FT: 2,500
SALES (est): 961.2K **Privately Held**
SIC: 1781 7699 Water well drilling; industrial machinery & equipment repair

Hoyt
Jackson County

(G-3145)
HOYT PALLET CO
11621 P4 Rd (66440-9142)
PHONE....785 986-6785
Mike Gordon, *President*
Jeremy Andrews, *Vice Pres*
EMP: 22
SALES (est): 2.8MM **Privately Held**
SIC: 2448 Pallets, wood

Hudson
Stafford County

(G-3146)
STAFFORD COUNTY FLOUR MILLS CO (PA)
108 S Church St (67545-9704)
PHONE....620 458-4121
Reuel Foote, *President*
Kenneth Spangenberg, *Treasurer*
EMP: 30 **EST:** 1905
SQ FT: 3,400
SALES (est): 9.9MM **Privately Held**
WEB: www.hudsoncream.com
SIC: 2041 5153 5191 Flour & other grain mill products; grain elevators; feed

Hugoton
Stevens County

(G-3147)
AMERICAN IMPLEMENT INC
Also Called: John Deere Authorized Dealer
843 E Highway 51 (67951)
P.O. Box 368 (67951-0368)
PHONE....620 544-4351
Joe Fort, *Principal*

EMP: 11
SALES (est): 1.4MM **Privately Held**
SIC: 5083 Farm implements

(G-3148)
ANADARKO PETROLEUM CORPORATION
P.O. Box 40 (67951-0040)
PHONE....620 544-4344
Terry Lewis, *Principal*
EMP: 32
SALES (corp-wide): 18.9B **Publicly Held**
WEB: www.anadarko.com
SIC: 1311 Crude petroleum production
HQ: Anadarko Petroleum Corporation
1201 Lake Robbins Dr
The Woodlands TX 77380
832 636-1000

(G-3149)
BULTMAN COMPANY INC MFG
Also Called: BCI Manufacturing
1550 W 10th St (67951-8900)
P.O. Box 966 (67951-0966)
PHONE....620 544-8004
Alan Bultman, *President*
▲ **EMP:** 18
SQ FT: 20,000
SALES (est): 1.8MM **Privately Held**
WEB: www.spadolly.com
SIC: 5531 3792 3088 3523 Automotive tires; travel trailers & campers; plastics plumbing fixtures; farm machinery & equipment

(G-3150)
CARING CONNECTIONS
516 Northeast Ave (67951-2560)
P.O. Box 278 (67951-0278)
PHONE....620 544-2050
Nicole Crites, *Owner*
Tamara Baehler, *Director*
EMP: 10
SALES (est): 139.6K **Privately Held**
SIC: 8351 Child day care services

(G-3151)
CIMARRON VALLEY IRRIGATION LLC
715 E 11th St (67951-2965)
P.O. Box 486 (67951-0486)
PHONE....620 544-7323
Jequita Kemp,
EMP: 13
SQ FT: 7,500
SALES (est): 1.2MM **Privately Held**
SIC: 1711 Irrigation sprinkler system installation

(G-3152)
CITIZENS STATE BANK
601 S Main St (67951-2419)
P.O. Box 728 (67951-0728)
PHONE....316 518-6621
Jack Rowden, *President*
Robin Sullivan, *Vice Chairman*
Kim Harper, *Senior VP*
Betty Lee, *Senior VP*
Janine Beltz, *Assistant VP*
EMP: 35 **EST:** 1913
SQ FT: 11,000
SALES: 5.7MM
SALES (corp-wide): 5.6MM **Privately Held**
SIC: 6022 6021 State trust companies accepting deposits, commercial; national commercial banks
PA: Hugoton Bancshares Inc

Hugoton KS 67951
620 544-4331

(G-3153)
CORRPRO COMPANIES INC
839 E 11th St (67951-2966)
PHONE....620 544-4411
EMP: 21
SALES (corp-wide): 1.3B **Publicly Held**
SIC: 3699 Electrical equipment & supplies
HQ: Corrpro Companies, Inc.
1055 W Smith Rd
Medina OH 44256
330 723-5082

(G-3154)
COUNTY OF STEVENS
Also Called: Street and Highway Dept
510 W 6th St (67951)
P.O. Box 668 (67951-0668)
PHONE....620 544-8782
Tony Marcus, *Principal*
EMP: 29 **Privately Held**
SIC: 1611 9111 Highway & street maintenance; county supervisors' & executives' offices
PA: County Of Stevens
200 E 6th St Ste 1
Hugoton KS 67951
620 544-4684

(G-3155)
COUNTY OF STEVENS
Also Called: Pioneer Manor
6th & Polk (67951)
P.O. Box 758 (67951-0758)
PHONE....620 544-2023
Linda Dalcup, *Administration*
EMP: 100 **Privately Held**
SIC: 8052 8051 Intermediate care facilities; skilled nursing care facilities
PA: County Of Stevens
200 E 6th St Ste 1
Hugoton KS 67951
620 544-4684

(G-3156)
COUNTY OF STEVENS
Stevens Cnty Emrgncy Med Svcs
109 Northwest Ave (67951-2144)
P.O. Box 94 (67951-0094)
PHONE....620 544-2562
Mike Schechter, *Director*
EMP: 30 **Privately Held**
SIC: 4119 9111 Ambulance service; county supervisors' & executives' offices
PA: County Of Stevens
200 E 6th St Ste 1
Hugoton KS 67951
620 544-4684

(G-3157)
CR INSPECTION INC
621 S Main St (67951-2419)
PHONE....620 544-2666
Cheryl Seiwald, *CEO*
Eric Seiwald, *Principal*
EMP: 100 **EST:** 2010
SQ FT: 3,000
SALES: 18MM **Privately Held**
SIC: 7389 Inspection & testing services

(G-3158)
CUSTOM RENOVATION
600 E 11th St (67951-2912)
PHONE....620 544-2653
Dwayne West, *Owner*
EMP: 12
SQ FT: 2,000
SALES (est): 710K **Privately Held**
SIC: 1521 5713 1752 5211 General remodeling, single-family houses; floor covering stores; carpets; linoleum; floor tile; carpet laying; linoleum installation; asphalt tile installation; windows, storm: wood or metal; doors, storm: wood or metal

(G-3159)
DILLCO FLUID SERVICE INC (HQ)
513 W 4th St (67951)
PHONE....620 544-2929
Bobby Talbert, *Principal*
EMP: 30
SQ FT: 10,000
SALES (est): 21.6MM
SALES (corp-wide): 46.9MM **Publicly Held**
SIC: 1389 Oil & gas wells: building, repairing & dismantling
PA: Enservco Corporation
999 18th St Ste 1925
Denver CO 80202
303 333-3678

(G-3160)
DONUT X-PRESS
406 W 11th St (67951-2949)
P.O. Box 145, Rolla (67954-0145)
PHONE....620 544-4700
Arlan Decker, *Principal*
EMP: 8
SALES (est): 438.1K **Privately Held**
SIC: 2051 Doughnuts, except frozen

(G-3161)
EARLY CHILDHOOD DEV CTR
Also Called: Ecdc
507 S Madison St (67951-2607)
PHONE....620 544-4334
Tiffany Boxun, *Principal*
EMP: 30
SALES (est): 213.9K **Privately Held**
SIC: 8351 8211 Preschool center; kindergarten

(G-3162)
FEDERAL LAND BANK ASSOC
Also Called: Farm Credit of Garden City
600 S Monroe St (67951-2728)
PHONE....620 544-4006
EMP: 15
SALES (est): 1MM **Privately Held**
SIC: 6111 Federal Credit Agency

(G-3163)
GHUMMS AUTO CENTER LLC
531 S Jackson St (67951-2133)
PHONE....620 544-7800
Jim Ghumms, *Mng Member*
EMP: 10
SALES (est): 580K **Privately Held**
SIC: 7538 5521 General automotive repair shops; used car dealers

(G-3164)
GREAT PLINS GAS CMPRESSION LLC
210 E 1st St (67951-2502)
P.O. Box 639 (67951-0639)
PHONE....620 544-3578
Jim Wilson, *President*
Terry McBride, *Principal*
Stacy Smith, *Vice Pres*
Derek Dillinger, *Opers Mgr*
Jeff Intres, *Purch Agent*
EMP: 131 **EST:** 2001
SALES (est): 50MM **Privately Held**
WEB: www.greatplainsgas.com
SIC: 1389 Gas compressing (natural gas) at the fields

(G-3165)
HUGOTON SWIMMING POOL
114 E 5th St (67951-2410)
PHONE....620 544-2793
EMP: 20
SALES (est): 205.2K **Privately Held**
SIC: 7999 Amusementrcrtnnec

(G-3166)
J & J MARTIN TRUCKING
101 N Jackson St (67951-2037)
PHONE....620 544-7976
Jeff Martin, *Owner*
Virginia Martin, *Co-Owner*
EMP: 15
SALES (est): 1.4MM **Privately Held**
SIC: 4213 Heavy hauling

(G-3167)
JAMES & SON FARMS
581 Road 24 (67951-5169)
PHONE....620 262-1512
Matthew James, *Principal*
Anthony James, *Principal*
Richard James, *Principal*
EMP: 10
SALES (est): 321.9K **Privately Held**
SIC: 0191 General farms, primarily crop

(G-3168)
KDI OPERATING COMPANY LLC
Also Called: Kansas Dairy Ingredients Plant
1010 E 10th St (67951-2908)
PHONE....620 544-4114
Mike Eshbaugh, *Branch Mgr*
EMP: 30
SALES (corp-wide): 40.7MM **Privately Held**
SIC: 0241 Dairy farms
PA: Kdi Operating Company, Llc
11050 Roe Ave Ste 211
Leawood KS 66211
620 453-1034

(G-3169)
KIWANIS INTERNATIONAL INC
Hc 1 Box 29 (67951)
PHONE....620 544-8445
Richardcli BR, *Manager*
EMP: 14
SALES (corp-wide): 23.6MM **Privately Held**
WEB: www.kfne.org
SIC: 8641 Civic associations
PA: Kiwanis International, Inc.
3636 Woodview Trce
Indianapolis IN 46268
317 875-8755

(G-3170)
KRAMER SEED FARMS
Also Called: High Plains Hybrids
1114 S Monroe St (67951-2934)
PHONE....620 544-4330
Jim Kramer, *Partner*
Kenneth Kramer, *Partner*
Richard Kramer, *Partner*
Wanda Kramer, *Partner*
EMP: 14
SALES (est): 1.1MM **Privately Held**
SIC: 0111 Wheat

(G-3171)
LEWIS WHEELER LEE WHEELER PTR
Also Called: L & L Farms
2044 Road H (67951-5184)
PHONE....620 544-8289
Lewis Wheeler, *Partner*
Lee Wheeler, *Partner*
EMP: 10
SALES (est): 752.8K **Privately Held**
SIC: 0119 0116 0111 0115 Sorghum farm; soybeans; wheat; corn

(G-3172)
MARTIN TRUCKING INC
1015 W City Limits St (67951-2344)
P.O. Box M (67951-1212)
PHONE....620 544-4920
Ronald E Martin, *President*
Douglas Martin, *Vice Pres*
Douglas E Martin, *Vice Pres*
William B Martin, *Treasurer*
James P Martin, *Admin Sec*
EMP: 35
SQ FT: 5,400
SALES: 10MM **Privately Held**
SIC: 4213 Trucking, except local

(G-3173)
MCBRIDE CONSTRUCTION INC
613 E 11th St (67951-2911)
PHONE....620 544-7146
Tony J McBride, *President*
Rhonda McBride, *Corp Secy*
Todd McBride, *Vice Pres*
EMP: 15
SQ FT: 4,000
SALES: 3.6MM **Privately Held**
WEB: www.mcbrideconstruction.com
SIC: 1521 1542 New construction, single-family houses; commercial & office building, new construction

(G-3174)
ONEOK FIELD SERVICES CO LLC
114 W 2nd St (67951-2004)
PHONE....620 544-2179
Jim Graves, *Manager*
EMP: 15
SALES (corp-wide): 12.5B **Publicly Held**
SIC: 4922 Natural gas transmission
HQ: Oneok Field Services Company, L.L.C.
100 W 5th St Ste Ll
Tulsa OK 74103

(G-3175)
PASSMORE BROS INC
E Hwy 51 (67951)
P.O. Box 297 (67951-0297)
PHONE....620 544-2189
Bobby Passmore, *President*
Carlis Passmore, *Vice Pres*
Lynda Passmore, *Treasurer*
Sandra K Passmore, *Admin Sec*
EMP: 20
SQ FT: 5,000

GEOGRAPHIC

SALES: 1.5MM **Privately Held**
SIC: 1389 4213 Roustabout service; heavy machinery transport

(G-3176)
SOUTHWEST EXPRESS INC
Also Called: Martin Southwest Trucking
1015 W City Limits St (67951-2344)
P.O. Box Q (67951-1216)
PHONE..................................620 544-7500
Ron Martin, *President*
Doug Martin, *Vice Pres*
EMP: 13
SQ FT: 11,250
SALES (est): 1.6MM **Privately Held**
SIC: 4213 Trucking, except local

(G-3177)
STEVENS COUNTY HOSPITAL
Also Called: Stevens County Clinic
1006 S Jackson St (67951-2858)
P.O. Box 10 (67951-0010)
PHONE..................................620 544-8511
Linda Stalcup, *CEO*
Dave Piper, *CFO*
Chad Kennedy, *Med Doctor*
David Piper, *CIO*
Larry Kiley, *Info Tech Dir*
EMP: 112
SQ FT: 37,000
SALES: 13.1MM **Privately Held**
SIC: 8062 General medical & surgical hospitals

(G-3178)
TRECO INC
823 E 11th St (67951-2966)
P.O. Box 493, Ulysses (67880-0493)
PHONE..................................620 544-2606
Vernon Norton, *Manager*
EMP: 20
SALES (corp-wide): 27.8MM **Privately Held**
WEB: www.treco-inc.com
SIC: 1389 Roustabout service
PA: Treco, Inc.
2871 W Oklahoma
Ulysses KS 67880
620 356-4785

(G-3179)
UNITED PRARIE AG
509 Northwest Ave (67951-2019)
PHONE..................................620 544-2017
Billy Clubb, *Manager*
EMP: 18
SALES (est): 1.2MM **Privately Held**
SIC: 4221 Grain elevator, storage only

(G-3180)
WTG HUGOTON LP
Also Called: West Texas Gas Hugoton
2272 Road Q (67951-5124)
PHONE..................................620 544-4381
James L Davis, *General Ptnr*
Richard Hatchett, *Ltd Ptnr*
EMP: 33
SQ FT: 5,000
SALES (est): 4MM
SALES (corp-wide): 117.5MM **Privately Held**
SIC: 4213 Liquid petroleum transport, non-local
PA: West Texas Gas, Inc.
211 N Colorado St
Midland TX 79701
432 682-4349

Humboldt
Allen County

(G-3181)
B & W CUSTOM TRUCK BEDS INC
Also Called: B & W Trailer Hitches
1216 Hawaii Rd (66748-1390)
P.O. Box 186 (66748-0186)
PHONE..................................800 810-4918
Joe W Works, *President*
Clay Garver, *Purchasing*
Bob Francis, *Engineer*
Taylor Jones, *Engineer*
Bryan Wolfe, *Sales Staff*
EMP: 181
SQ FT: 90,000
SALES (est): 63.2MM **Privately Held**
WEB: www.turnoverball.com
SIC: 3713 3714 5531 Truck beds; trailer hitches, motor vehicle; trailer hitches, automotive

(G-3182)
BROYLES INC (PA)
1303 N 9th St (66748-9767)
PHONE..................................620 473-3835
David N Broyles, *President*
Irene Broyles, *Corp Secy*
EMP: 10
SQ FT: 4,000
SALES (est): 4.7MM **Privately Held**
WEB: www.humboldtks.com
SIC: 1799 Service station equipment installation, maintenance & repair

(G-3183)
BROYLES PETROLEUM EQUIPMENT CO
1303 N 9th St (66748-9767)
PHONE..................................417 863-6800
Gregg Korte, *President*
Timothy Rear, *Manager*
EMP: 30 **EST**: 2012
SALES (est): 731.7K **Privately Held**
SIC: 7629 Electrical equipment repair services

(G-3184)
HERITAGE HOUSE ASSISTED LIVING
615 Franklin St (66748-1011)
PHONE..................................620 473-3456
Fax: 620 473-3803
EMP: 12
SALES (est): 160.7K **Privately Held**
SIC: 8051 Skilled Nursing Care Facility

(G-3185)
HOFER & HOFER & ASSOCIATES INC
1201 N 10th St (66748-1057)
P.O. Box 57 (66748-0057)
PHONE..................................620 473-3919
Michael A Hofer, *President*
Justin Wintjen, *Principal*
Frank Shoemaker, *Vice Pres*
Johnetta Hofer, *Treasurer*
EMP: 30
SQ FT: 3,000
SALES: 4.4MM **Privately Held**
SIC: 1542 Commercial & office building, new construction; commercial & office buildings, renovation & repair

(G-3186)
KANSAS CITY UROLOGY CARE
Also Called: Kansas City Urology Care PA
1314 S 8th St (66748-1782)
PHONE..................................913 831-1003
David Emmott MD, *President*
John Strickland MD, *Admin Sec*
EMP: 14
SQ FT: 3,045
SALES: 1MM **Privately Held**
SIC: 8011 Urologist

(G-3187)
MONARCH CEMENT COMPANY (PA)
449 1200th St (66748-1785)
P.O. Box 1000 (66748-0900)
PHONE..................................620 473-2222
Walter H Wulf Jr, *Ch of Bd*
Kent Webber, *President*
Robert M Kissick, *Vice Pres*
Dennis Osborn, *Opers Mgr*
Dusty Bartlett, *Maint Spvr*
▲ **EMP**: 115
SALES (est): 147MM **Publicly Held**
WEB: www.monarchcement.com
SIC: 3241 3273 Portland cement; ready-mixed concrete

(G-3188)
SOUTHEAST KANS MENTAL HLTH CTR (PA)
1106 S 9th St (66748-1934)
P.O. Box 39 (66748-0039)
PHONE..................................620 473-2241
Job Springer, *General Mgr*
Bob Chase, *Exec Dir*
Amanda Denton, *Nurse Practr*
Elizabeth Garton, *Nurse Practr*
EMP: 67
SQ FT: 5,400
SALES: 8.3MM **Privately Held**
SIC: 8093 Mental health clinic, outpatient

Hutchinson
Reno County

(G-3189)
ABSOLUTELY FLOWERS
1328 N Main St (67501-4002)
PHONE..................................620 728-0266
Mitzi Alexander, *Owner*
Karen Maness, *Co-Owner*
EMP: 12
SALES (est): 573K **Privately Held**
WEB: www.absolutelyflowers.biz
SIC: 5193 Flowers, fresh

(G-3190)
AD ASTRA PER ASPERA BROADCASTI
Also Called: Ksku-FM Knzs-FM Kxk-FM Kwhk-FM
10 E 5th Ave Ste 2 (67501-6201)
PHONE..................................620 665-5758
Cliff C Shank, *President*
Chris Shank, *Vice Pres*
Aaron Napier, *Opers Mgr*
Aaron West, *Manager*
EMP: 20
SQ FT: 3,750
SALES: 1.3MM **Privately Held**
SIC: 4832 Radio broadcasting stations, music format

(G-3191)
ADAMS BROWN BRAN BALL CHRTERED
1701 Landon St (67502-5663)
PHONE..................................620 663-5659
Richard A Ball, *President*
Grace Huxman, *Accountant*
Jeanie Rome, *Accountant*
Sophia Schippers, *Accountant*
Shelby Stucky, *Accountant*
EMP: 11
SALES (corp-wide): 9.4MM **Privately Held**
SIC: 8721 Certified public accountant
PA: Adams, Brown, Beran & Ball Chartered Inc
2006 Broadway Ave
Great Bend KS 67530
620 549-3271

(G-3192)
ADVANCE TERMITE & PEST CONTROL
2515 E 14th Ave (67501-2121)
PHONE..................................620 662-3616
Al Wells, *President*
Helen Wells, *Corp Secy*
Jeff Wells, *Vice Pres*
EMP: 14
SQ FT: 6,000
SALES: 900K **Privately Held**
WEB: www.advancepest.com
SIC: 7342 Pest control services; termite control; pest control in structures; exterminating & fumigating

(G-3193)
ADVANCED HOMECARE MGT INC
Also Called: Encompass Home Health
1300 N Main St Ste 3 (67501-4002)
PHONE..................................620 662-9238
Susan Simon, *Branch Mgr*
EMP: 50
SALES (corp-wide): 4.2B **Publicly Held**
SIC: 8082 Home health care services
HQ: Advanced Homecare Management, Inc.
6688 N Cntrl Expy # 1300
Dallas TX 75206
214 239-6500

(G-3194)
AG SERVICES LLC
1515 E 30th Ave (67502-1225)
P.O. Box 1747 (67504-1747)
PHONE..................................620 662-5406
Scott Anderson,
EMP: 12
SALES (est): 800.9K **Privately Held**
SIC: 1731 Safety & security specialization

(G-3195)
ALCOA INC
1501 Airport Rd (67501-1976)
PHONE..................................620 665-5281
Brian Urkiel, *Manager*
EMP: 122
SALES (corp-wide): 14B **Publicly Held**
SIC: 5051 Aluminum bars, rods, ingots, sheets, pipes, plates, etc.
PA: Arconic Inc.
201 Isabella St Ste 200
Pittsburgh PA 15212
412 553-1950

(G-3196)
ALLEN SAMUELS WACO D C J INC
Also Called: Allen Smels Ddge Chrysler Jeep
1421 E 30th Ave (67502-1235)
PHONE..................................620 860-1869
Dereck Tanksley, *Branch Mgr*
EMP: 34
SALES (corp-wide): 3.3MM **Privately Held**
SIC: 5511 7538 Automobiles, new & used; general automotive repair shops
PA: Allen Samuels Waco D C J, Inc.
201 W Loop 340
Waco TX 76712
888 498-1414

(G-3197)
ALPHA LAND SURVEYS INC
102 E 4th Ave (67501-6934)
PHONE..................................620 728-0012
Lloyd Dorzweiler, *President*
EMP: 10
SALES (est): 738.6K **Privately Held**
SIC: 8713 Surveying services

(G-3198)
AMERICAN GOLF CORPORATION
Also Called: Highlands Golf Club
922 Crazy Horse Rd (67502-8957)
PHONE..................................620 663-5301
Mark Ahrens, *General Mgr*
EMP: 35 **Publicly Held**
WEB: www.americangolf.com
SIC: 7997 Golf club, membership; country club, membership
HQ: American Golf Corporation
909 N Pacific Coast Hwy
El Segundo CA 90245
310 664-4000

(G-3199)
ANSWER LINK
107 W 1st Ave (67501-5235)
PHONE..................................620 662-4427
David Cow, *Owner*
EMP: 10
SALES (est): 666.4K **Privately Held**
SIC: 7389 7338 Telephone answering service; secretarial & typing service

(G-3200)
APAC-KANSAS INC
1600 N Lorraine St Ste 1 (67501-5600)
PHONE..................................620 662-3307
Bill Giard, *President*
Steve Ferland, *Plant Mgr*
Bradley Gover, *Safety Mgr*
EMP: 20
SALES (corp-wide): 29.7B **Privately Held**
SIC: 1611 7521 5032 General contractor, highway & street construction; airport runway construction; parking lots; stone, crushed or broken
HQ: Apac-Kansas, Inc.
9660 Legler Rd
Lenexa KS 66219

(G-3201)
APAC-KANSAS INC
5603 E 4th Ave (67501)
P.O. Box 1605 (67504-1605)
PHONE....................................785 625-3459
Bruce Almquise, *Manager*
EMP: 23
SALES (corp-wide): 29.7B **Privately Held**
SIC: 5032 5261 Brick, stone & related material; top soil
HQ: Apac-Kansas, Inc.
9660 Legler Rd
Lenexa KS 66219

(G-3202)
APAC-KANSAS INC
819 W 1st Ave (67501-5137)
P.O. Box 1605 (67504-1605)
PHONE....................................620 662-2112
Bob Ratley, *Branch Mgr*
EMP: 25
SALES (corp-wide): 29.7B **Privately Held**
SIC: 1611 Surfacing & paving
HQ: Apac-Kansas, Inc.
9660 Legler Rd
Lenexa KS 66219

(G-3203)
APPLE LANE ANIMAL HOSPITAL
2909 Apple Ln (67502-1919)
PHONE....................................620 662-0515
Gerald Schrater Dvm, *Owner*
EMP: 10
SALES (est): 665.7K **Privately Held**
WEB: www.apple.kscoxmail.com
SIC: 0742 Veterinarian, animal specialties; animal hospital services, pets & other animal specialties

(G-3204)
ARCHER-DANIELS-MIDLAND COMPANY
Also Called: ADM
1700 N Halstead St (67501-2148)
PHONE....................................620 663-7957
Tracy Spencer, *Manager*
EMP: 48
SALES (corp-wide): 64.3B **Publicly Held**
WEB: www.admworld.com
SIC: 2041 5153 Flour & other grain mill products; grain elevators
PA: Archer-Daniels-Midland Company
77 W Wacker Dr Ste 4600
Chicago IL 60601
312 634-8100

(G-3205)
ARCHER-DANIELS-MIDLAND COMPANY
Also Called: ADM
816 N Halstead St (67501-2043)
PHONE....................................620 663-7278
Tracy Spencer, *Superintendent*
EMP: 10
SALES (corp-wide): 64.3B **Publicly Held**
SIC: 2041 Flour & other grain mill products
PA: Archer-Daniels-Midland Company
77 W Wacker Dr Ste 4600
Chicago IL 60601
312 634-8100

(G-3206)
ARCONIC INC
1501 Airport Rd (67501-1976)
PHONE....................................620 665-2932
EMP: 8
SALES (est): 989.1K **Privately Held**
SIC: 2834 Pharmaceutical preparations

(G-3207)
ARTSTUDIO SIGNS & DESIGN
Also Called: Art Studio Signs & Design
3010 N Plum St (67502-2936)
PHONE....................................620 663-3950
Tammy Stanfield, *Owner*
EMP: 10
SALES (est): 580K **Privately Held**
SIC: 3993 Signs & advertising specialties

(G-3208)
ASTLE REALTY INC
Also Called: Plaza Astle Realty
224 E 30th Ave (67502-2488)
PHONE....................................620 662-0576
Karen Galliland, *President*
Terry Brigman, *Vice Pres*
Marilyn Johnson, *Broker*
Kelly Polson, *Agent*
Phyllis Agers, *Admin Sec*
EMP: 18
SQ FT: 2,800
SALES (est): 1.8MM **Privately Held**
SIC: 6531 Real estate agent, residential; rental agent, real estate; buying agent, real estate; selling agent, real estate

(G-3209)
AT&T CORP
2519 E 17th Ave (67501-1140)
PHONE....................................620 665-1946
Matthew Burkes, *Branch Mgr*
EMP: 69
SALES (corp-wide): 170.7B **Publicly Held**
SIC: 4813 Telephone communication, except radio
HQ: At&T Corp.
1 At&T Way
Bedminster NJ 07921
800 403-3302

(G-3210)
B & B HYDRAULICS INC (PA)
2400 Line Rd (67501-9542)
P.O. Box 2973 (67504-2973)
PHONE....................................620 662-2552
Maurice Penny, *President*
Alex W Macleod, *President*
EMP: 25
SQ FT: 12,600
SALES: 3MM **Privately Held**
SIC: 5084 7699 Hydraulic systems equipment & supplies; hydraulic equipment repair

(G-3211)
B & B MOVIE THEATRES LLC
1500 E 11th Ave (67501-3701)
PHONE....................................620 669-8510
Guy Tracy, *Branch Mgr*
EMP: 18
SALES (corp-wide): 64.1MM **Privately Held**
SIC: 7832 Motion picture theaters, except drive-in
PA: B & B Theatres Operating Company, Inc.
2700 Ne Kendallwood Pkwy
Gladstone MO 64119
816 883-2170

(G-3212)
BANK AMERICA NATIONAL ASSN
20 2nd (67501)
P.O. Box 1488 (67504-1488)
PHONE....................................620 694-4395
Pat Michaelis, *President*
Bardie Carna, *Vice Pres*
EMP: 82
SALES (corp-wide): 110.5B **Publicly Held**
WEB: www.bofa.com
SIC: 6021 National commercial banks
HQ: Bank Of America, National Association
100 S Tryon St
Charlotte NC 28202
704 386-5681

(G-3213)
BANK OF WEST
829 E 30th Ave (67502-4341)
PHONE....................................620 662-0543
Marian Miller, *Manager*
EMP: 12
SALES (corp-wide): 2.7B **Privately Held**
SIC: 6022 State trust companies accepting deposits, commercial
HQ: Bank Of The West
180 Montgomery St # 1400
San Francisco CA 94104
415 765-4800

(G-3214)
BANK SNB
100 E 30th Ave (67502-2407)
P.O. Box 1707 (67504-1707)
PHONE....................................620 728-3000
Mark Funke, *President*
EMP: 15
SALES (corp-wide): 824.5MM **Publicly Held**
WEB: www.bankofkansas.com
SIC: 6021 National commercial banks
HQ: Bank Snb
608 S Main St
Stillwater OK 74074
405 372-2230

(G-3215)
BARKER B&C INVESTMENTS LLC
Also Called: Leech Products
1430 W 4th Ave (67501-5035)
P.O. Box 2147 (67504-2147)
PHONE....................................620 669-0145
Brice Barker,
Carol Barker,
EMP: 11
SQ FT: 45,000
SALES: 3MM **Privately Held**
WEB: www.leechadhesives.com
SIC: 2891 Adhesives

(G-3216)
BLADON DIALYSIS LLC
Also Called: DIALYSIS CENTER OF HUTCHINSON
1901 N Waldron St (67502-1129)
P.O. Box 2037, Tacoma WA (98401-2037)
PHONE....................................620 728-0440
Darryl Serpan, *Principal*
EMP: 38 **EST:** 2007
SALES: 4.6MM **Publicly Held**
SIC: 8092 Kidney dialysis centers
PA: Davita Inc.
2000 16th St
Denver CO 80202

(G-3217)
BOLD LLC
1125 E 4th Ave (67501-7046)
PHONE....................................620 663-3300
Bob Peel, *Mng Member*
EMP: 10
SALES (est): 1.7MM **Privately Held**
SIC: 4225 General warehousing & storage

(G-3218)
BORNHOLDT PLANTLAND INC
1508 W 4th Ave (67501-5093)
PHONE....................................620 662-0544
Gary J Bornholdt, *President*
Charla Bornholdt, *Corp Secy*
EMP: 16
SQ FT: 200,000
SALES (est): 2MM **Privately Held**
SIC: 5261 0782 Nursery stock, seeds & bulbs; landscape contractors

(G-3219)
BOYS GIRLS CLUBS HUTHINSON INC
Also Called: Boys Grls CLB Htchnsn-Kids Aft
600 W 2nd Ave (67501-5107)
PHONE....................................620 665-7171
Skip Wilson, *Director*
EMP: 15
SALES (est): 137.6K **Privately Held**
WEB: www.bgchutch.com
SIC: 8641 Youth organizations
PA: Boys & Girls Clubs Of Huthinson, Inc.
600 W 2nd Ave
Hutchinson KS 67501

(G-3220)
BOYS GIRLS CLUBS HUTHINSON INC (PA)
Also Called: BOY & GIRLS CLUBS
600 W 2nd Ave (67501-5107)
P.O. Box 1967 (67504-1967)
PHONE....................................620 665-7171
Lisa Ward, *President*
Carl Cushinverry, *Vice Pres*
Lance Patterson, *Opers Staff*
Steve Richarson, *Treasurer*
Brenda Higginbotham, *Program Dir*
EMP: 60
SALES: 880.7K **Privately Held**
WEB: www.bgchutch.com
SIC: 8351 8322 Child day care services; youth center

(G-3221)
BRETZ & YOUNG LAW OFFICE
3 Compound Dr (67502-4349)
P.O. Box 1782 (67504-1782)
PHONE....................................620 662-3435
Matt Bretz, *Partner*
Melinda Young, *Partner*
EMP: 12
SALES (est): 810K **Privately Held**
SIC: 8111 General practice attorney, lawyer

(G-3222)
BRIAN STRANGE
Also Called: Grene Vision Group
2701 N Main St Ste A (67502-3480)
PHONE....................................620 663-8700
Brian Strange, *Owner*
EMP: 25
SALES (est): 1.6MM **Privately Held**
SIC: 8042 Offices & clinics of optometrists

(G-3223)
BRIGHTHOUSE INC
335 N Washington St # 240 (67501-4863)
PHONE....................................620 665-3630
Donna Davis, *President*
EMP: 20
SALES: 629.8K **Privately Held**
SIC: 8322 Crisis center; emergency shelters; hotline; temporary relief service

(G-3224)
BRISCOE RICHARD L DDS PA
1710 E 23rd Ave (67502-1114)
PHONE....................................620 669-1032
Richard L Briscoe DDS, *Owner*
EMP: 11
SALES (est): 509.5K **Privately Held**
SIC: 8021 Dentists' office

(G-3225)
BRISK TRANSPORTATION
Also Called: Greatwhite Logistics
2700 E 4th Ave (67501-1903)
PHONE....................................620 669-3481
Mike Hodgins, *Manager*
EMP: 22
SALES (est): 1.7MM **Privately Held**
SIC: 4213 Refrigerated products transport

(G-3226)
BURKHART ENTERPRISES INC
Also Called: ServiceMaster
808 W 1st Ave (67501-5103)
PHONE....................................620 662-8678
Robert Burkhart, *President*
Sheryl A Burkhart, *Corp Secy*
EMP: 42
SALES (est): 1.1MM **Privately Held**
SIC: 7349 Building maintenance services

(G-3227)
C2I INC
4108 Sherwood Dr (67502-1852)
PHONE....................................620 259-6610
Jerry Crabbs, *President*
EMP: 25 **EST:** 2007
SQ FT: 2,000
SALES (est): 1.6MM **Privately Held**
SIC: 1799 Coating of metal structures at construction site; welding on site

(G-3228)
CANCER COUNCIL OF RENO COUNTY
633 Hutchinson (67504)
P.O. Box 633 (67504-0633)
PHONE....................................620 665-5555
Cinda Wright, *President*
Lisa Barker, *Vice Pres*
Diane Ravstien, *Treasurer*
Mary Hall, *Director*
Marj Westsal, *Admin Sec*
EMP: 10 **EST:** 1998
SALES: 434.5K **Privately Held**
SIC: 8322 Individual & family services

(G-3229)
CARGILL INCORPORATED
609 E Avenue G (67501-7574)
P.O. Box 1403 (67504-1403)
PHONE....................................620 663-2141
Christopher Marshall, *Branch Mgr*
EMP: 100

SALES (corp-wide): 113.4B **Privately Held**
WEB: www.cargill.com
SIC: 2899 5149 Salt; salt, edible
PA: Cargill, Incorporated
15407 Mcginty Rd W
Wayzata MN 55391
952 742-7575

(G-3230)
CARGILL INCORPORATED
309 N Halstead St (67501-1832)
PHONE..................................620 663-4401
Jeff Handevidt, *Manager*
EMP: 20
SALES (corp-wide): 113.4B **Privately Held**
WEB: www.cargill.com
SIC: 5153 2076 Grains; vegetable oil mills
PA: Cargill, Incorporated
15407 Mcginty Rd W
Wayzata MN 55391
952 742-7575

(G-3231)
CENTRAL BANK AND TRUST CO
700 E 30th Ave (67502-8435)
P.O. Box 1366 (67504-1366)
PHONE..................................620 663-0666
Earl D Mc Vicker, *President*
Russell Reinert, *CFO*
EMP: 37 **EST:** 1915
SQ FT: 8,000
SALES: 11MM **Privately Held**
WEB: www.centralbank-kansas.com
SIC: 6022 State trust companies accepting deposits, commercial
PA: Cenwest Financial Corporation
101 W Avenue A
Hutchinson KS

(G-3232)
CENTRAL KANSAS CREDIT UNION (PA)
2616 N Main St (67502-3404)
PHONE..................................620 663-1566
Jacque Cully, *Manager*
EMP: 16
SQ FT: 11,000
SALES: 1.1MM **Privately Held**
SIC: 6061 Federal credit unions

(G-3233)
CENTRAL PRINTING & BINDING
107 W 1st Ave (67501-5235)
PHONE..................................620 665-7251
Steven J Conard, *President*
Joseph R Conard Jr, *Director*
EMP: 8
SALES (est): 101.5K **Privately Held**
SIC: 2752 2759 Commercial printing, offset; letterpress printing

(G-3234)
CENTRAL STATES RECOVERY INC
Also Called: Csr
1314 N Main St (67501-4002)
P.O. Box 3130 (67504-3130)
PHONE..................................620 663-8811
Robert C Capps, *President*
Kirby Quinn, *Corp Secy*
EMP: 36
SALES (est): 2.7MM **Privately Held**
WEB: www.csrecovery.com
SIC: 7322 Collection agency, except real estate

(G-3235)
CENTRAL WELDING & MACHINE LLC
218 N Whiteside St (67501-5133)
P.O. Box 1836 (67504-1836)
PHONE..................................620 663-9353
Scott Jewel, *Mng Member*
EMP: 10
SQ FT: 10,000
SALES: 500K **Privately Held**
SIC: 3599 7692 Machine shop, jobbing & repair; welding repair

(G-3236)
CHENEY DOOR CO INC
2701 E 17th Ave (67501-1144)
PHONE..................................620 669-9306
Keith Bomholt, *President*
Pat Bomholt, *Manager*
EMP: 15
SALES (corp-wide): 15.9MM **Privately Held**
WEB: www.cheneydoor.com
SIC: 5211 7699 3699 Door & window products; garage doors, sale & installation; door & window repair; door opening & closing devices, electrical
PA: Cheney Door Co., Inc.
136 S Lulu Ave
Wichita KS 67211
877 268-2098

(G-3237)
CHRISTS CARE PRE-SCHOOL
4290 N Monroe St (67502-2223)
PHONE..................................620 662-1283
Melissa Marcum, *Director*
EMP: 12
SALES (est): 86.5K **Privately Held**
SIC: 8351 8661 Preschool center; religious organizations

(G-3238)
CHS INC
Also Called: Legacy Foods
2701 E 11th Ave (67501-2141)
PHONE..................................620 663-5711
M Van Veldnuis, *Human Resources*
Mike Considine, *Branch Mgr*
EMP: 75
SALES (corp-wide): 31.9B **Publicly Held**
WEB: www.cenexharveststates.com
SIC: 5191 Farm supplies
PA: Chs Inc.
5500 Cenex Dr
Inver Grove Heights MN 55077
651 355-6000

(G-3239)
CITY BEVERAGE CO INC
2 S Kirby St (67501-1834)
PHONE..................................620 662-6271
Ann Bush, *President*
Bob Bush, *Principal*
EMP: 35 **EST:** 1959
SQ FT: 24,000
SALES (est): 5.1MM **Privately Held**
SIC: 5181 Beer & other fermented malt liquors

(G-3240)
CITY OF HUTCHINSON
Also Called: Building Inspection
125 E Avenue B (67501-7422)
P.O. Box 1567 (67504-1567)
PHONE..................................620 694-2632
John Deardoff, *Manager*
EMP: 400 **Privately Held**
WEB: www.hutchgov.com
SIC: 1711 Plumbing contractors
PA: City Of Hutchinson
125 E Avenue B
Hutchinson KS 67501
620 694-2611

(G-3241)
CITY OF HUTCHINSON
Also Called: Central Garage
1500 S Plum St (67501-7500)
P.O. Box 1567 (67504-1567)
PHONE..................................620 694-1970
John Deardoff, *Director*
EMP: 75 **Privately Held**
WEB: www.hutchgov.com
SIC: 7538 General automotive repair shops
PA: City Of Hutchinson
125 E Avenue B
Hutchinson KS 67501
620 694-2611

(G-3242)
COLLINS BUS CORPORATION (DH)
415 W 6th Ave (67505-1323)
P.O. Box 2946 (67504-2946)
PHONE..................................620 662-9000
John Becker, *Ch of Bd*
Dino Cusuano, *Vice Pres*
John Doswell, *Vice Pres*
Brandi Atha, *Production*
Tom Heinsen, *Treasurer*
◆ **EMP:** 105
SQ FT: 250,000
SALES: 120MM **Publicly Held**
WEB: www.collinsaav.com
SIC: 3711 Motor buses, except trackless trollies, assembly of
HQ: Collins Industries, Inc.
15 Compound Dr
Hutchinson KS 67502
620 663-5551

(G-3243)
COLLINS INDUSTRIES INC (HQ)
15 Compound Dr (67502-4349)
PHONE..................................620 663-5551
Kenneth Dabrowski, *Ch of Bd*
John Dreasher, *Vice Pres*
Ron Sorenson, *Vice Pres*
Hans Heinsen, *CFO*
EMP: 21
SQ FT: 5,000
SALES (est): 356.4MM **Publicly Held**
WEB: www.collinsind.com
SIC: 4522 Ambulance services, air

(G-3244)
CONCRETE ENTERPRISES INC (HQ)
2430 E 1st Ave (67501-1804)
P.O. Box 394, Kingman (67068-0394)
PHONE..................................620 662-1219
Walter H Wulf Jr, *President*
Ric Rush, *Vice Pres*
EMP: 15 **EST:** 1955
SQ FT: 15,000
SALES (est): 3.4MM
SALES (corp-wide): 147MM **Publicly Held**
WEB: www.monarchcement.com
SIC: 3273 Ready-mixed concrete
PA: The Monarch Cement Company
449 1200th St
Humboldt KS 66748
620 473-2222

(G-3245)
CONKLIN FANGMAN INVESTMENT CO (PA)
1400 E 11th Ave (67501-2712)
P.O. Box 628 (67504-0628)
PHONE..................................620 662-4467
Stuart Conklin Jr, *President*
Scott D Conklin, *Vice Pres*
Stuart Conklin III, *Vice Pres*
Joseph P Fangman, *Vice Pres*
EMP: 148
SALES: 120MM **Privately Held**
SIC: 5511 7538 5521 New & used car dealers; general automotive repair shops; used car dealers

(G-3246)
CONTAINERCRAFT INC
2507 E 14th Ave (67501)
P.O. Box 752 (67504-0752)
PHONE..................................620 663-1168
Bob Burgess, *President*
Mark Elzea, *Principal*
Brian Archer, *Vice Pres*
EMP: 10
SQ FT: 15,000
SALES: 2MM **Privately Held**
SIC: 2448 Cargo containers, wood; pallets, wood

(G-3247)
COSMOSPHERE INC (PA)
1100 N Plum St (67501-1418)
PHONE..................................620 662-2305
Dick Hollowell, *CEO*
Richard Hollowell, *COO*
Mimi Meredith, *Vice Pres*
Steve Barnum, *Opers Staff*
Bill Tucker, *Opers Staff*
▲ **EMP:** 42
SQ FT: 105,000
SALES: 4.8MM **Privately Held**
SIC: 5947 8412 Gift, novelty & souvenir shop; museum

(G-3248)
COUNTY OF RENO
Also Called: Land Fill
703 S Mohawk Rd (67501-9031)
PHONE..................................620 694-2587
Justin Bland, *Director*
EMP: 25 **Privately Held**
SIC: 4953 Sanitary landfill operation
PA: County Of Reno
206 W 1st Ave
Hutchinson KS 67501
620 694-2911

(G-3249)
COUNTY OF RENO
Also Called: Reno County Cmnty Corrections
115 W 1st Ave (67501-5235)
PHONE..................................620 665-7042
Derek Norrick, *Marketing Staff*
Debbie McCoy, *Manager*
EMP: 21 **Privately Held**
SIC: 9223 8322 ; probation office
PA: County Of Reno
206 W 1st Ave
Hutchinson KS 67501
620 694-2911

(G-3250)
COX COMMUNICATIONS
1510 E 17th Ave (67501-1113)
PHONE..................................620 474-4318
Lew Pearce, *Principal*
EMP: 17
SALES (corp-wide): 29.2B **Privately Held**
SIC: 4841 Cable television services
HQ: Cox Communications
6689 Fox Cntre Pkwy 109
Gloucester VA 23061
804 693-3535

(G-3251)
CROSSFAITH VENTURES LC
Also Called: Ramsey Oil
1101 W 4th Ave (67501-5018)
P.O. Box 3070 (67504-3070)
PHONE..................................620 662-8365
Linda Ringwald, *President*
Linda Wringwald, *President*
Michel Ringwald, *Vice Pres*
Patty Coon, *Controller*
EMP: 22
SALES (est): 15.7MM **Privately Held**
SIC: 5172 2992 5984 5983 Gases, liquefied petroleum (propane); lubricating oils & greases; liquefied petroleum gas dealers; fuel oil dealers

(G-3252)
CUSTOM HARVEST INSURANCE
1125 E 4th Ave 1 (67501-7046)
P.O. Box 1069 (67504-1069)
PHONE..................................620 259-6996
Mike Esau, *Principal*
EMP: 14
SALES (est): 1.1MM **Privately Held**
SIC: 0722 Crop harvesting

(G-3253)
DANDEE AIR INC
Also Called: Dan Dee Air
639 W 2nd Ave (67501-5141)
PHONE..................................620 663-4341
Richard Dauber, *President*
Jack Krehbiel, *Treasurer*
EMP: 17
SQ FT: 5,000
SALES (est): 2.4MM **Privately Held**
WEB: www.dandeeair.com
SIC: 3444 Metal ventilating equipment

(G-3254)
DANIKSCO OFFICE INTERIORS LLC
1125 E 4th Ave 11 (67501-7046)
PHONE..................................620 259-8009
Laurie Jones, *Branch Mgr*
EMP: 17
SALES (corp-wide): 43.9MM **Privately Held**
SIC: 5044 Typewriters
PA: Daniksco Office Interiors, Llc
6010 N Broadway Ave
Park City KS 67219
316 491-2607

(G-3255)
DATA CENTER INC (PA)
20 W 2nd Ave Ste 300 (67501-7189)
PHONE..................................620 694-6800
John Jones, *President*
Sarah Fankhauser, *Exec VP*
Gerald Rempe, *Senior VP*
Devin Brown, *Vice Pres*

James Kitson, *Vice Pres*
EMP: 220
SQ FT: 50,000
SALES: 28.8MM **Privately Held**
WEB: www.datacenterinc.com
SIC: 7374 Data processing service

(G-3256)
DATA CENTER INC
220 E Sherman St (67501-7132)
PHONE..................................620 694-6800
Jerry Rempe, *Manager*
EMP: 40
SALES (est): 3.6MM
SALES (corp-wide): 28.8MM **Privately Held**
SIC: 7374 Data processing service
PA: Data Center, Inc.
20 W 2nd Ave Ste 300
Hutchinson KS 67501
620 694-6800

(G-3257)
DAVES SERVICE & REPAIR INC
6005 S Broadacres Rd (67501-7817)
PHONE..................................620 662-8285
Dave Hevener, *President*
Marilyn Hevener, *Treasurer*
EMP: 8
SALES: 430K **Privately Held**
SIC: 1711 3432 Plumbing contractors; plastic plumbing fixture fittings, assembly

(G-3258)
DAYMON WORLDWIDE INC
1302 N Grand St (67501-2133)
PHONE..................................620 669-4200
Mitch Cramer, *Branch Mgr*
EMP: 15
SALES (corp-wide): 13B **Privately Held**
SIC: 8742 Marketing consulting services
HQ: Daymon Worldwide Inc.
333 Lundlow St Fl 4 Flr 4
Stamford CT 06902
203 352-7500

(G-3259)
DAYS INN SUITES HUTCHINSON LLC
1420 N Lorraine St (67501-6158)
PHONE..................................620 665-3700
D Barot, *Manager*
EMP: 10
SALES (est): 484.3K **Privately Held**
SIC: 7011 Hotels & motels

(G-3260)
DEERE & COMPANY
Also Called: Agris Hardware
1800 S Lorraine St (67501-2437)
P.O. Box 1667 (67504-1667)
PHONE..................................800 665-4620
Tom Tayor, *President*
Susan Pegg, *Marketing Mgr*
Kelly Jones, *Branch Mgr*
EMP: 26
SALES (corp-wide): 39.2B **Publicly Held**
WEB: www.deere.com
SIC: 5083 Farm & garden machinery
PA: Deere & Company
1 John Deere Pl
Moline IL 61265
309 765-8000

(G-3261)
DELMARVA PAD CO
Also Called: Winters Excelsior
406 S Obee Rd (67501-3447)
PHONE..................................620 665-9757
Dennis Myrick, *Manager*
EMP: 15 **Privately Held**
SIC: 2429 Excelsior, including pads & wrappers: wood
PA: Delmarva Pad Co.
Hwy 21
Mc Williams AL 36753

(G-3262)
DESERET HEALTH GROUP LLC
Also Called: Hutchinson Health Care
2301 N Severance St (67502-4301)
PHONE..................................620 662-0597
Jon Robertson, *Principal*
EMP: 339 **Privately Held**
SIC: 8741 Hospital management
PA: Deseret Health Group, Llc.
190 S Main St
Bountiful UT 84010

(G-3263)
DILLON COMPANIES INC
Also Called: Dillons 25
206 W 5th Ave (67501-4807)
PHONE..................................620 663-4464
David Streck, *Manager*
EMP: 175
SALES (corp-wide): 121.1B **Publicly Held**
WEB: www.dillons.com
SIC: 5411 5912 2051 Supermarkets, chain; drug stores; bread, cake & related products
HQ: Dillon Companies, Inc.
2700 E 4th Ave
Hutchinson KS 67501
620 665-5511

(G-3264)
DILLON CREDIT UNION
2704 N Lorraine St (67502-4257)
P.O. Box 2323 (67504-2323)
PHONE..................................620 669-8500
David Cleeves, *Ch of Bd*
Kim Gustafson, *Loan Officer*
Sherry Kent, *Loan Officer*
EMP: 11
SALES: 1.4MM **Privately Held**
WEB: www.dillonecu.com
SIC: 6062 State credit unions, not federally chartered

(G-3265)
DILLON NATURE CENTER
Also Called: Hutchinson Recreation Comm
3002 E 30th Ave (67502-1506)
PHONE..................................620 663-7411
Mary Clark, *General Mgr*
James Smith, *Director*
Jims M Smith, *Director*
EMP: 20
SALES: 151.5K **Privately Held**
SIC: 7996 7999 Theme park, amusement; recreation center

(G-3266)
DIRECTV GROUP INC
2314 N Wilson Rd (67502-9742)
PHONE..................................620 663-8132
EMP: 128
SALES (corp-wide): 170.7B **Publicly Held**
SIC: 4841 Direct broadcast satellite services (DBS)
HQ: The Directv Group Inc
2260 E Imperial Hwy
El Segundo CA 90245
310 964-5000

(G-3267)
DIVERSICARE OF HUTCHINSON
1202 E 23rd Ave (67502-5656)
PHONE..................................620 669-9393
Kelly J Gill, *CEO*
EMP: 13
SALES: 5.2MM **Privately Held**
SIC: 8051 Skilled nursing care facilities

(G-3268)
DONS CAR CARE & BODY SHOP INC
104 E 4th Ave (67501-6934)
PHONE..................................620 669-8178
Donald Strawn, *President*
Cris Dosch, *Corp Secy*
EMP: 15
SQ FT: 11,500
SALES (est): 1.2MM **Privately Held**
WEB: www.donscarcare.com
SIC: 7532 7549 7536 Body shop, automotive; towing service, automotive; automotive glass replacement shops

(G-3269)
DRYWALL INC
507 N Whiteside St (67501-1518)
PHONE..................................620 662-3454
James Strawn, *President*
James Spain, *Vice Pres*
EMP: 13
SQ FT: 700
SALES: 1MM **Privately Held**
SIC: 1742 Drywall; acoustical & ceiling work

(G-3270)
DUDLEY CONSTRUCTION CO INC
7311 N Halstead St Ste B (67502-8743)
PHONE..................................620 665-1166
Wayne Dudley, *President*
Sue Dudley, *Treasurer*
EMP: 10
SALES (est): 2.9MM **Privately Held**
WEB: www.dudleyconstruction.com
SIC: 1611 General contractor, highway & street construction

(G-3271)
E & M PLUMBING INC
Also Called: E & M Plbg Htg & A Conditionin
701 W 2nd Ave (67501-5142)
P.O. Box 357 (67504-0357)
PHONE..................................620 662-1281
Robert Nielsen, *President*
Linda Nielsen, *Corp Secy*
EMP: 18 **EST:** 1951
SQ FT: 3,000
SALES (est): 2.5MM **Privately Held**
SIC: 1711 Plumbing contractors

(G-3272)
EAGLE COMMUNICATIONS INC
Also Called: Khut & Kwbw
25 N Main St (67501-5216)
P.O. Box 1036 (67504-1036)
PHONE..................................620 662-4486
Dan Deming, *Manager*
EMP: 30
SQ FT: 3,000
SALES (corp-wide): 71.7MM **Privately Held**
WEB: www.eaglecom.net
SIC: 4832 Radio broadcasting stations
PA: Eagle Communications, Inc.
2703 Hall St 15
Hays KS 67601
785 625-5910

(G-3273)
EARL BARNES
Also Called: Smith's Market
211 S Main St (67501-5425)
PHONE..................................620 662-6761
Earl Barnes, *Owner*
EMP: 10 **EST:** 1950
SQ FT: 7,500
SALES (est): 1.7MM **Privately Held**
SIC: 5148 5431 Fruits, fresh; vegetables, fresh; fruit stands or markets; vegetable stands or markets

(G-3274)
EATON CORPORATION
3401 E 4th Ave (67501-1969)
PHONE..................................620 663-5751
Roger Basinger, *Engineer*
Ken Norris, *Branch Mgr*
EMP: 500
SQ FT: 700,000 **Privately Held**
WEB: www.eaton.com
SIC: 3593 5084 3561 3494 Fluid power cylinders, hydraulic or pneumatic; hydraulic systems equipment & supplies; pumps & pumping equipment; valves & pipe fittings; fabricated plate work (boiler shop)
HQ: Eaton Corporation
1000 Eaton Blvd
Cleveland OH 44122
440 523-5000

(G-3275)
EGBERT OIL OPERATIONS INC
500 N Monroe St Ste 1 (67501-1356)
PHONE..................................620 662-4533
Shirley Egbert, *President*
EMP: 18
SQ FT: 1,000
SALES (est): 1MM **Privately Held**
SIC: 1311 5921 5411 Crude petroleum production; wine & beer; hard liquor; convenience stores, independent

(G-3276)
ELECTREX INC
6 N Walnut St (67501-7105)
PHONE..................................620 662-4866
Peter L Ochs, *President*
Rodie Pierce, *CFO*
Lance Bonnensteel, *Manager*
Steve Krehbiel, *Administration*
EMP: 139
SQ FT: 50,000
SALES: 16MM **Privately Held**
WEB: www.electrexinc.com
SIC: 3694 3679 Engine electrical equipment; harness assemblies for electronic use: wire or cable

(G-3277)
ELLIOTT MORTUARY INC
1219 N Main St (67501-4595)
PHONE..................................620 663-3327
Thomas Elliott, *President*
Carolyn Elliott, *Corp Secy*
EMP: 16
SQ FT: 2,000
SALES (est): 1MM **Privately Held**
WEB: www.elliottmortuary.com
SIC: 7261 Funeral home; funeral director

(G-3278)
ELMDALE COMMUNITY CENTER
Also Called: Hutch Rec Comm
400 E Avenue E (67501-7721)
PHONE..................................620 663-6170
Ted Nelson, *Director*
EMP: 17
SALES (est): 360.9K **Privately Held**
WEB: www.hutchrec.com
SIC: 7999 Recreation services

(G-3279)
EMERITUS CORPORATION
Also Called: Elm Grove Esttes Rtrment Cmnty
2416 Brentwood St Ofc Ofc (67502-5029)
PHONE..................................620 663-9195
Michael Truman, *Director*
Vanessa Delgado, *Nursing Dir*
EMP: 80
SALES (corp-wide): 4.5B **Publicly Held**
WEB: www.emeraldestatesslc.com
SIC: 6513 Retirement hotel operation
HQ: Emeritus Corporation
3131 Elliott Ave Ste 500
Milwaukee WI 53214

(G-3280)
EVANGELICAL LUTHERAN
Also Called: Good Smrtan Soc - Htchnson Vlg
810 E 30th Ave (67502-4340)
P.O. Box 5038, Sioux Falls SD (57117-5038)
PHONE..................................620 663-1189
Debbie Fuller, *Director*
EMP: 128 **Privately Held**
WEB: www.good-sam.com
SIC: 8059 8051 Nursing home, except skilled & intermediate care facility; skilled nursing care facilities
HQ: The Evangelical Lutheran Good Samaritan Society
4800 W 57th St
Sioux Falls SD 57108
866 928-1635

(G-3281)
FAIRFELD INN SUITES HUTCHINSON
1111 N Lorraine St (67501-6168)
PHONE..................................620 259-8787
Amrutlal Patel, *Principal*
EMP: 11 **EST:** 2013
SALES (est): 444.4K **Privately Held**
SIC: 7011 Hotels & motels

(G-3282)
FAIRLAWN BURIAL PARK ASSN
Also Called: Fairlawn Burial Pk & Mausoleum
2401 Carey Blvd (67501-3947)
PHONE..................................620 662-3431
Sharon F McDonough, *President*
William Wright, *Vice Pres*
EMP: 10

GEOGRAPHIC

SALES (est): 390K **Privately Held**
SIC: 6553 3272 Cemeteries, real estate operation; burial vaults, concrete or precast terrazzo

(G-3283)
FEE INSURANCE GROUP INC
1 N Main St Ste 700 (67501-5252)
P.O. Box 976 (67504-0976)
PHONE....................620 662-2381
Allen Fee, *President*
Troy Hutton, *Exec VP*
Chelsea Barker, *Vice Pres*
Cheri Fahrbach, *Vice Pres*
Bob Fee, *Vice Pres*
EMP: 17 **EST:** 1883
SQ FT: 2,000
SALES (est): 1.8MM **Privately Held**
SIC: 6411 Insurance agents

(G-3284)
FEEDEX COMPANIES LLC
1616 E Wasp Rd (67501-8733)
PHONE....................620 500-5016
Bill Frazier,
EMP: 12
SALES (corp-wide): 2.7MM **Privately Held**
SIC: 2048 Stock feeds, dry
PA: Feedex Companies, Llc
500 N Main St
South Hutchinson KS 67505
620 662-0033

(G-3285)
FIRST NAT BNK OF HUTCHINSON (HQ)
1 N Main St Ste 320 (67501-5248)
P.O. Box 913 (67504-0913)
PHONE....................620 663-1521
R A Edwards, *Ch of Bd*
Greg Binns, *President*
Geni Woody, *Managing Dir*
Keith Hughes, *Exec VP*
Kent Baird, *Senior VP*
EMP: 92
SQ FT: 100,000
SALES: 36.2MM
SALES (corp-wide): 26.4MM **Privately Held**
WEB: www.fnbhutch.com
SIC: 6021 National commercial banks
PA: First Kansas Bancshares
1 N Main St Ste 320
Hutchinson KS 67501
620 663-1521

(G-3286)
FIRST NAT BNK OF HUTCHINSON
2500 N Main St Ste H (67502-3651)
PHONE....................620 662-7858
David Inskeep, *Branch Mgr*
EMP: 23
SALES (corp-wide): 26.4MM **Privately Held**
SIC: 6021 National commercial banks
HQ: The First National Bank Of Hutchinson
1 N Main St Ste 320
Hutchinson KS 67501
620 663-1521

(G-3287)
FIRST NAT BNK OF HUTCHINSON
2501 N Main St (67502-3640)
P.O. Box B (67504)
PHONE....................620 694-2304
Kathy Wagoner, *Branch Mgr*
EMP: 16
SALES (corp-wide): 26.4MM **Privately Held**
WEB: www.fnbhutch.com
SIC: 6021 National commercial banks
HQ: The First National Bank Of Hutchinson
1 N Main St Ste 320
Hutchinson KS 67501
620 663-1521

(G-3288)
FIRST NAT BNK OF HUTCHINSON
1 N Main St (67501-5229)
PHONE....................620 663-1521
R Edwards, *President*
EMP: 23
SALES (corp-wide): 26.4MM **Privately Held**
SIC: 6021 National commercial banks
HQ: The First National Bank Of Hutchinson
1 N Main St Ste 320
Hutchinson KS 67501
620 663-1521

(G-3289)
FIRST TEAM SPORTS INC
902 Corey Rd (67501-1980)
PHONE....................620 663-6080
Wayne Unruh, *President*
Jeff Roth, *Vice Pres*
Kerry Reimer, *Finance*
▲ **EMP:** 8 **EST:** 1996
SQ FT: 4,500
SALES (est): 1.1MM **Privately Held**
WEB: www.firstteaminc.com
SIC: 3949 Basketball equipment & supplies, general

(G-3290)
FOUR CORNERS CONSTRUCTION LLC
921 S Main St (67501-5315)
PHONE....................620 662-8163
Jason Bleything,
Adam Bleything,
Amy Mitchell,
EMP: 6
SQ FT: 15,000
SALES (est): 198.5K **Privately Held**
SIC: 2511 1521 1751 Wood household furniture; single-family home remodeling, additions & repairs; cabinet building & installation

(G-3291)
FRANCHISE DEVELOPMENT INC
Also Called: ServiceMaster
300 Hayes St (67501-5126)
P.O. Box 798 (67504-0798)
PHONE....................620 662-3283
David Cowles, *President*
Lu Anne Cowles, *Vice Pres*
EMP: 25
SQ FT: 2,400
SALES (est): 637.6K **Privately Held**
SIC: 7349 Building maintenance services

(G-3292)
FRANK COLLADAY HARDWARE CO
2516 E 14th Ave (67501-2100)
P.O. Box 766 (67504-0766)
PHONE....................620 663-4477
H Duane Banning, *President*
Mike Sutton, *Manager*
Leon Scott, *Admin Sec*
EMP: 16
SQ FT: 50,000
SALES (est): 3.8MM **Privately Held**
SIC: 5074 5083 5023 5072 Plumbing & hydronic heating supplies; garden machinery & equipment; home furnishings; builders' hardware

(G-3293)
FRATERNAL ORDER OF POLICE
210 W 1st Ave (67501-5204)
PHONE....................620 694-2830
Tyson Myer, *President*
EMP: 69
SALES: 51.3K **Privately Held**
SIC: 8641 Fraternal associations

(G-3294)
FREEMAN SUPPLY INC
221 W 3rd Ave (67501-5119)
P.O. Box 1096 (67504-1096)
PHONE....................620 662-2330
Cindy Freeman, *President*
Brett Mattison, *Admin Sec*
EMP: 15
SQ FT: 25,000
SALES: 1.6MM
SALES (corp-wide): 5.4MM **Privately Held**
SIC: 5075 Warm air heating equipment & supplies; air conditioning & ventilation equipment & supplies
PA: Decker & Mattison Company, Inc.
500 W 2nd Ave
Hutchinson KS
620 662-2339

(G-3295)
FREUND INVESTMENT INC
Also Called: Freund Construction
1201 N Halstead St (67501-2125)
PHONE....................620 669-9649
Rose Freund, *President*
Glenn Freund, *Treasurer*
EMP: 10
SQ FT: 10,000
SALES (est): 1.2MM **Privately Held**
SIC: 1521 New construction, single-family houses; general remodeling, single-family houses

(G-3296)
FRIENDS OF THE DEPARTMENT
1 N Main St Ste 804 (67501-5229)
PHONE....................620 694-2387
Brandon Thompson, *Vice Pres*
EMP: 15
SALES (est): 227.8K **Privately Held**
SIC: 0119 Milo farm

(G-3297)
GARBER SURVEYING SERVICE PA (PA)
2908 N Plum St Ste B (67502-8419)
PHONE....................620 665-7032
Daniel Garber, *President*
EMP: 40
SQ FT: 4,000
SALES (est): 4.1MM **Privately Held**
WEB: www.garbersurveying.com
SIC: 8713 Photogrammetric engineering

(G-3298)
GENESIS HEALTH CLUB INC
412 E 30th Ave (67502-2413)
PHONE....................620 663-9090
Rodney Stevens, *Branch Mgr*
EMP: 10
SALES (corp-wide): 5.8MM **Privately Held**
SIC: 7991 Health club
PA: Genesis Health Club, Inc.
3725 W 13th St N
Wichita KS 67203
316 945-8331

(G-3299)
GILLILAND & HAYES PA (PA)
20 W 2nd Ave Ste 200 (67501-5225)
P.O. Box 2977 (67504-2977)
PHONE....................620 662-0537
Gerald L Green, *Partner*
Kent G Voth, *Partner*
James R Gilliland, *Principal*
John F Hayes, *Principal*
Bruce B Waugh, *Principal*
EMP: 67
SALES: 6MM **Privately Held**
WEB: www.gillilandandhayes.com
SIC: 8111 General practice attorney, lawyer

(G-3300)
GIVENS INVESTMENTS LLC
1300 N Grand St (67501-2133)
PHONE....................620 662-1784
Brett Givens, *President*
EMP: 12
SALES (est): 1.2MM **Privately Held**
SIC: 1761 Sheet metalwork

(G-3301)
GLOBAL ENGINEERING AND TECH
1200 N Halstead St (67501-2109)
P.O. Box 780787, Wichita (67278-0787)
PHONE....................620 664-6268
Mike Luker, *Manager*
Darren Moore, *Manager*
Mindy Towns, *Executive*
EMP: 23
SALES (est): 1.5MM **Privately Held**
SIC: 4581 Aircraft maintenance & repair services

(G-3302)
GOOD SAMARITAN SOCIETY
810 E 30th Ave (67502-4340)
PHONE....................620 663-1189
Brenda Janda, *Administration*
EMP: 120
SALES: 7MM **Privately Held**
SIC: 8051 Skilled nursing care facilities

(G-3303)
GRAND PRAIRIE HT & CONVENTION
1400 N Lorraine St (67501-6158)
PHONE....................620 669-9311
Luis Rosado, *General Mgr*
Brian Anderson, *General Mgr*
EMP: 200
SALES (est): 3.8MM **Privately Held**
WEB: www.grandprairiehotel.com
SIC: 7011 5091 Hotel, franchised; water slides (recreation park)

(G-3304)
GRANT D RINGLER DDS INC
Also Called: Bill G Goble
3008 Garden Grove Pkwy (67502-4216)
PHONE....................620 669-0835
Grant D Ringler DDS, *Principal*
EMP: 12
SALES (est): 1MM **Privately Held**
SIC: 8021 Dentists' office

(G-3305)
GRAPHIC IMPRESSIONS INC
Also Called: Proforma
1101 N Halstead St (67501-2138)
P.O. Box 625 (67504-0625)
PHONE....................620 663-5939
Jeff Westfall, *President*
Thomas E Westfall, *President*
Carol S Westfall, *Admin Sec*
EMP: 25
SQ FT: 21,000
SALES (est): 8.5MM **Privately Held**
WEB: www.graphicimpressions1.com
SIC: 5112 2759 5999 2752 Stationery & office supplies; screen printing; decals; commercial printing, lithographic; automotive & apparel trimmings

(G-3306)
GUST OROTHONDTCS PA G MORRISON
1000 E 30th Ave (67502-4227)
PHONE....................620 662-3255
Sarah Maxwell, *Manager*
EMP: 11
SALES (est): 835.3K **Privately Held**
SIC: 8021 Orthodontist

(G-3307)
HADLEY DAY CARE CTR INC
Also Called: HADLEY DAY CARE CENTER
1010 E 5th Ave (67501-7001)
PHONE....................620 663-9622
Rebecca Eikleberry, *Director*
EMP: 25
SALES: 560.6K **Privately Held**
SIC: 8351 Group day care center

(G-3308)
HAYDENS SALON AND DAY SPA
13 E 2nd Ave (67501-7154)
PHONE....................620 663-2179
Hayden M Hitchcock, *President*
Karen Hitchcock, *Corp Secy*
EMP: 10
SQ FT: 2,500
SALES (est): 310K **Privately Held**
SIC: 7231 Beauty shops

(G-3309)
HEALTH CARE INC (PA)
Also Called: Promise Regional Medical Ctr
1701 E 23rd Ave (67502-9907)
PHONE....................620 665-2000
Kevin Miller, *President*
Kim Moore, *Principal*
Joyce Radke, *Principal*
Raleigh White, *Ch Radiology*
Duane Miller, *CFO*
EMP: 900

▲ = Import ▼=Export
◆ =Import/Export

SALES: 127.1MM Privately Held
WEB: www.hmhc.com
SIC: 8062 7352 6512 General medical & surgical hospitals; medical equipment rental; nonresidential building operators

(G-3310)
HEARTLAND CREDIT UNION (PA)
900 E 23rd Ave (67502-5648)
P.O. Box 1645 (67504-1645)
PHONE....620 669-0177
Garth Strand, *President*
Darren Werth, *President*
Dan Springer, *Exec VP*
Michelle Waln, *Vice Pres*
Ed Switzer, *Treasurer*
EMP: 20
SQ FT: 1,800
SALES: 12.2MM Privately Held
WEB: www.hutchinsoncreditunion.com
SIC: 6061 Federal credit unions

(G-3311)
HIEB & ASSOCIATES LLC
708 W 2nd Ave (67501-5108)
PHONE....620 663-9430
Jim Strawm,
Jeff Luke,
EMP: 12
SQ FT: 5,000
SALES (est): 2.6MM Privately Held
WEB: www.hieb.net
SIC: 1542 Commercial & office building, new construction

(G-3312)
HORIZONS MENTAL HEALTH CTR INC (PA)
1600 N Lorraine St # 202 (67501-5600)
PHONE....620 663-7595
Michael Garrett, *CEO*
Gary Halderman, *CFO*
EMP: 170
SALES: 13.1MM Privately Held
SIC: 8093 Mental health clinic, outpatient

(G-3313)
HOSPICE OF RENO COUNTY INC
1523 E 20th Ave (67502-4720)
PHONE....620 669-3773
Sheila Mc Grath, *Administration*
EMP: 18 Privately Held
SIC: 8051 Skilled nursing care facilities
PA: Hospice Of Reno County, Inc.
1600 N Lorraine St # 203
Hutchinson KS 67501

(G-3314)
HOSPICE OF RENO COUNTY INC (PA)
Also Called: Homecare of Hutchinson
1600 N Lorraine St # 203 (67501-5600)
PHONE....620 665-2473
Darla Wilson, *Director*
EMP: 50
SQ FT: 10,000
SALES: 5.3MM Privately Held
SIC: 8082 Visiting nurse service

(G-3315)
HUBCO INC
215 S Poplar St (67501-7456)
P.O. Box 1286 (67504-1286)
PHONE....620 663-8301
Merlin Preheim, *Ch of Bd*
Trey McPherson, *President*
Arthur J Collins III, *Vice Pres*
Fred Moore, *Vice Pres*
▲ EMP: 47 EST: 1919
SQ FT: 42,000
SALES: 7.3MM Privately Held
WEB: www.hubcoinc.com
SIC: 2393 Textile bags

(G-3316)
HUTCH GOOD SAMARITAN VILLAGE
810 E 30th Ave (67502-4340)
PHONE....620 663-1189
Brenda Jahnda, *Principal*
Jim Morford, *COO*
Ronda Worden, *Finance*
Debbie Landsdown, *Human Res Dir*
Sherry Leiker, *Human Res Dir*
EMP: 31
SALES (est): 676.4K Privately Held
SIC: 8051 Skilled nursing care facilities

(G-3317)
HUTCH SIGN
1325 A Half N Halstead St (67501)
P.O. Box 727 (67504-0727)
PHONE....620 663-6108
Tom Westfall, *Owner*
EMP: 5 EST: 1986
SALES (est): 186.4K Privately Held
WEB: www.hutchsign.net
SIC: 3993 Signs & advertising specialties

(G-3318)
HUTCHINSON CARE CENTER LLC
2301 N Severance St (67502-4301)
PHONE....620 662-0597
Rex Maris, *Administration*
Daniel Hames, *Administration*
EMP: 60
SALES (est): 1.8MM Privately Held
SIC: 8099 Medical services organization

(G-3319)
HUTCHINSON CLINIC PA (PA)
Also Called: Lyons Medical Center
2101 N Waldron St (67502-1197)
PHONE....620 669-2500
Michael Heck, *CEO*
Stanton Barker, *President*
Darryl Serpen, *COO*
Brian Voth, *COO*
Ginger Morrell, *Vice Pres*
EMP: 650
SQ FT: 120,000
SALES (est): 57.6MM
SALES (corp-wide): 63.4MM Privately Held
WEB: www.heartlandcancercenter.com
SIC: 8011 8071 5912 5999 Clinic, operated by physicians; radiologist; medical laboratories; drug stores & proprietary stores; hearing aids

(G-3320)
HUTCHINSON COMMUNITY COLLEGE
Also Called: Kent Hall HCC Girls Dormitory
1521 N Ford St (67501-5868)
PHONE....620 665-3500
Kyle Crookes, *Branch Mgr*
EMP: 16
SALES (corp-wide): 24.5MM Privately Held
SIC: 7021 8222 Rooming & boarding houses; junior colleges & technical institutes
PA: Hutchinson Community College
1300 N Plum St
Hutchinson KS 67501
620 665-3423

(G-3321)
HUTCHINSON HLTH CARE SVCS INC (HQ)
Also Called: Health- E-Quip
803 E 30th Ave (67502-4341)
PHONE....620 665-0528
Kevin Miller, *President*
James Mc Comas, *VP Opers*
EMP: 23
SQ FT: 10,400
SALES (est): 9.5MM
SALES (corp-wide): 127.1MM Privately Held
SIC: 5999 7352 Hospital equipment & supplies; medical equipment rental
PA: Health Care, Inc.
1701 E 23rd Ave
Hutchinson KS 67502
620 665-2000

(G-3322)
HUTCHINSON PUBLISHING CO
Also Called: Hutchinson News
300 W 2nd Ave (67501-5211)
P.O. Box 190 (67504-0190)
PHONE....620 694-5700
John Montgomery, *President*
Kimberly Cline, *District Mgr*
Bruce Buchanan, *Vice Pres*
Sarah Liebl, *Controller*
Heath Hensley, *IT Specialist*
EMP: 200 EST: 1933
SQ FT: 38,000
SALES (est): 11.1MM
SALES (corp-wide): 1.5B Publicly Held
WEB: www.hutchnews.com
SIC: 2711 Commercial printing & newspaper publishing combined; newspapers, publishing & printing
HQ: Harris Enterprises, Inc.
1 N Main St Ste 616
Hutchinson KS
620 694-5830

(G-3323)
HUTCHINSON RECREATION COMM
Also Called: Keller Leisure Arts Center
17 E 1st Ave (67501-7146)
PHONE....620 663-6179
John Gallagher, *Superintendent*
Thomas Cook, *Principal*
Bo Frondorf, *Finance*
EMP: 11
SALES (est): 537.7K Privately Held
SIC: 7999 Recreation center

(G-3324)
HUTCHINSON SALT COMPANY INC
3300 Carey Blvd (67501-9604)
PHONE....620 662-3341
Max Liby, *Plant Mgr*
Harold Mayo, *Plant Mgr*
EMP: 40
SALES (corp-wide): 6MM Privately Held
SIC: 1479 5149 2899 Salt (common) mining; salt, edible; salt
PA: Hutchinson Salt Company, Inc.
40 Sw Grove Rd
Baxter Springs KS 66713
620 662-3345

(G-3325)
HUTCHINSON SYMPHONY ASSN
10104 N Tobacco Rd (67502-9142)
P.O. Box 1241 (67504-1241)
PHONE....620 543-2511
Keith Temaat, *President*
Karen Anderson, *Vice Pres*
Diane Cannon, *Bd of Directors*
EMP: 17
SALES: 53.5K Privately Held
SIC: 7929 Symphony orchestras

(G-3326)
HUTCHINSON THEATRE GUILD
901 W 1st Ave (67501-5138)
P.O. Box 993 (67504-0993)
PHONE....620 662-9202
Todd Ray, *President*
Stephen Mills, *Treasurer*
Charles Johnston, *Director*
EMP: 10
SALES (est): 602.1K Privately Held
SIC: 1799 Special trade contractors

(G-3327)
HUTCHINSON USD 308
Also Called: Building Maintenance
815 W 4th Ave (67501-5008)
PHONE....620 615-5575
Bob Williams, *Principal*
EMP: 17
SALES (corp-wide): 62.3MM Privately Held
WEB: www.usd308.com
SIC: 4173 7349 Maintenance facilities for motor vehicle passenger transport; janitorial service, contract basis
PA: Hutchinson Usd 308
1520 N Plum St
Hutchinson KS 67501
620 615-4000

(G-3328)
HUTCHINSON VENDING COMPANY (PA)
24 Prairie Dunes Dr (67502-8766)
PHONE....620 662-6474
David Allen, *President*
Jeffrey Allen, *Treasurer*
Diane Hudson, *Shareholder*
EMP: 11 EST: 1941
SQ FT: 4,250
SALES (est): 688.6K Privately Held
SIC: 7933 5962 7993 Bowling centers; merchandising machine operators; coin-operated amusement devices

(G-3329)
HUTCHINSON/RENO COUNTY CHAMBER
117 N Walnut St (67501-7165)
P.O. Box 519 (67504-0519)
PHONE....620 662-3391
Jon Daveline, *President*
Marcy Kauffman, *Director*
EMP: 10 EST: 1919
SQ FT: 1,500
SALES: 1.3MM Privately Held
WEB: www.hutchchamber.com
SIC: 8611 Chamber of Commerce

(G-3330)
HUTCHNSON HOSP PSYCHIATRIC CTR
Also Called: New Choices Program
1701 E 23rd Ave (67502-9907)
PHONE....620 665-2364
Bunny Czarnopys, *Director*
EMP: 23
SALES: 1.4MM Privately Held
WEB: www.hutchinsonhospital.com
SIC: 8322 Individual & family services

(G-3331)
HUTCHNSON REGIONAL MED CTR INC
1701 E 23rd Ave (67502-1105)
PHONE....620 665-2000
Kendall Johnson, *CEO*
Michael Krach, *President*
Cassandra Dolen, *CFO*
Louise Mc Intire, *Director*
EMP: 1000
SQ FT: 330,000
SALES (est): 33.6MM
SALES (corp-wide): 127.1MM Privately Held
WEB: www.hmhc.com
SIC: 8062 General medical & surgical hospitals
PA: Health Care, Inc.
1701 E 23rd Ave
Hutchinson KS 67502
620 665-2000

(G-3332)
INEEDA LAUNDRY & DRY CLEANERS (PA)
Also Called: Ineeda Cleaners
1224 N Main St (67501-4501)
P.O. Box 486 (67504-0486)
PHONE....620 662-6450
Chris Nelson, *Owner*
Darla Neal, *Treasurer*
EMP: 75 EST: 1946
SALES (est): 2.3MM Privately Held
SIC: 7216 7213 Drycleaning plants, except rugs; uniform supply

(G-3333)
INEEDA LAUNDRY AND DRYCLEANERS
Also Called: Neal John E
1 Compound Dr 8 (67502-4349)
P.O. Box 486 (67504-0486)
PHONE....620 663-5688
John E Neal, *President*
EMP: 29
SALES (est): 560.6K Privately Held
SIC: 7216 Drycleaning plants, except rugs

(G-3334)
INTEGRATED SOLUTIONS GROUP INC (HQ)
Also Called: I S G
1632 E 23rd Ave (67502-4705)
P.O. Box 2044 (67504-2044)
PHONE....620 662-5796
Gary Hobbs, *President*
Carol Santangelo, *CFO*
Jay Humphrey, *Info Tech Dir*
John Mattie, *Technology*
Sandy Tucker, *Technical Staff*
EMP: 41
SQ FT: 16,000

GEOGRAPHIC

SALES (est): 10.1MM Privately Held
WEB: www.isg-inc.net
SIC: 7379 Computer related consulting services

(G-3335)
INTERIM HEALTHCARE INC
525 N Main St (67501-4820)
PHONE..................................620 663-2423
Tony Cornejo, *Manager*
EMP: 40
SALES (est): 1MM Privately Held
SIC: 7363 Temporary help service

(G-3336)
INTERNATIONAL FINCL SVCS INC
327 W 4th Ave (67501-4842)
P.O. Box 550 (67504-0550)
PHONE..................................620 665-7708
Richard E Smith, *President*
EMP: 25
SQ FT: 5,000
SALES (est): 2.2MM Privately Held
WEB: www.natcom.org
SIC: 7389 7322 Financial services; adjustment & collection services

(G-3337)
J & J DRAINAGE PRODUCTS CO
110 N Pershing St (67501-7125)
P.O. Box 829 (67504-0829)
PHONE..................................620 663-1575
Dale Smith, *CEO*
Margie Doeden, *President*
Ron Altvater, *Vice Pres*
Susan Corcoran, *Admin Sec*
EMP: 30
SQ FT: 2,000
SALES (est): 6MM Privately Held
WEB: www.jjdrainage.com
SIC: 3444 Culverts, sheet metal

(G-3338)
J P WEIGAND AND SONS INC
Also Called: JP Weigand
1009 N Main St (67501-4403)
PHONE..................................620 663-4458
Josie Thompson, *General Mgr*
EMP: 15
SALES (corp-wide): 22.7MM Privately Held
WEB: www.weigand.com
SIC: 6531 Real estate agent, residential
PA: J. P. Weigand And Sons, Inc.
150 N Market St
Wichita KS 67202
316 292-3991

(G-3339)
JACKSONS FROZEN FOOD CENTER
Also Called: Jackson Meats
13 W 6th Ave (67501-4650)
PHONE..................................620 662-4465
Michael Jackson, *President*
Howard Bill Jackson, *President*
Rosella Jackson, *Corp Secy*
Mark Daubert, *Treasurer*
EMP: 7 EST: 1946
SQ FT: 3,000
SALES (est): 1.8MM Privately Held
SIC: 5142 5147 2013 2011 Packaged frozen goods; meats, fresh; sausages & other prepared meats; meat packing plants

(G-3340)
JAMES GRUVER CONSTRUCTION INC
105 N Main St (67501-5218)
P.O. Box 3116 (67504-3116)
PHONE..................................620 663-7982
James Gruver, *President*
Debra Gruver, *Corp Secy*
EMP: 20
SALES (est): 1.4MM Privately Held
SIC: 1521 1542 General remodeling, single-family houses; nonresidential construction

(G-3341)
JAMES P GERTKEN DDS
Also Called: Dental Care Family
2901 N Lorraine St Ste A (67502-4276)
PHONE..................................620 669-0411
James P Gertken DDS, *Owner*
EMP: 10
SALES (est): 1MM Privately Held
SIC: 8021 Dentists' office

(G-3342)
JOHN D MESCHKE DDS PA (PA)
Also Called: Meschke, John D
2 Compound Dr (67502-4300)
PHONE..................................620 662-6667
John D Meschke DDS, *President*
John C Mescheke, *CPA*
EMP: 12
SALES (est): 1.2MM Privately Held
SIC: 8021 Orthodontist

(G-3343)
JOHN F DAHM DR
2411 N Main St (67502-3638)
PHONE..................................620 665-5582
John F Dahm, *Owner*
EMP: 11
SALES (est): 851.9K Privately Held
SIC: 8021 Offices & clinics of dentists

(G-3344)
K H U T F M COUNTRY MUSIC
1700 W 17th Ave (67501)
PHONE..................................620 662-4486
Mark Trotman, *Manager*
EMP: 25
SALES (est): 495.1K Privately Held
SIC: 4832 Radio broadcasting stations

(G-3345)
KANSAS FARM MGT ASSOC SC (PA)
1722 N Plum St (67502-5501)
PHONE..................................620 662-7868
Nick Steffen, *President*
Meredith Behnke, *Admin Sec*
EMP: 11
SALES: 574.3K Privately Held
SIC: 0762 Farm management services

(G-3346)
KANSAS LEGAL SERVICES INC
Also Called: Hutchnson Reno Cnty Legal Svcs
206 W 1st Ave (67501-5204)
PHONE..................................620 694-2955
Marilyn Harp, *Branch Mgr*
EMP: 10
SALES (corp-wide): 7MM Privately Held
SIC: 8111 Legal aid service
PA: Kansas Legal Services, Inc
712 S Kansas Ave Ste 200
Topeka KS 66603
785 354-8531

(G-3347)
KANSAS STATE COUNCIL OF FIRE
817 W 19th Ave (67502-4107)
PHONE..................................620 662-1808
Robert Wing, *Administration*
EMP: 12
SALES: 167.8K Privately Held
SIC: 8631 Labor union

(G-3348)
KAUFFMAN SEEDS INC
9218 S Halstead St (67501-8369)
PHONE..................................620 465-2245
Thomas Clayman, *President*
Dustin Miller, *Vice Pres*
EMP: 25
SALES (est): 328.6K Privately Held
SIC: 0119 Bean (dry field & seed) farm

(G-3349)
KCSC SPACE WORKS INC
1100 N Plum St (67501-1418)
PHONE..................................620 662-2305
Thaine Woolsey, *Ch of Bd*
Richard Robl, *Corp Secy*
Helene Kain, *Manager*
Marcie McKinnell, *Director*
Laura Page, *Director*
EMP: 27
SQ FT: 15,000
SALES (est): 792.9K
SALES (corp-wide): 4.8MM Privately Held
SIC: 7699 Aircraft & heavy equipment repair services
PA: Cosmosphere, Inc.
1100 N Plum St
Hutchinson KS 67501
620 662-2305

(G-3350)
KENNYS ELECTRICAL CO INC
1035 W 4th Ave (67501-5017)
PHONE..................................620 662-2359
Ronald E Barnhart, *President*
William E Barnhart, *Treasurer*
E Dexter Galloway, *Admin Sec*
EMP: 18 EST: 1959
SQ FT: 12,000
SALES (est): 2.6MM Privately Held
WEB: www.kennyselec.kscoxmail.com
SIC: 1731 General electrical contractor

(G-3351)
KOCH HYDROCARBON SOUTHWES
1910 S Broadacres Rd (67501-9627)
P.O. Box 2256, Wichita (67201-2256)
PHONE..................................620 662-6691
Jennifer Ramsey, *Principal*
EMP: 5
SALES (est): 540K Privately Held
SIC: 2911 Fractionation products of crude petroleum, hydrocarbons

(G-3352)
KOCH INDUSTRIES INC
1910 S Broadacres Rd (67501-9627)
PHONE..................................620 662-6691
Lowry Morris, *Branch Mgr*
EMP: 17
SALES (corp-wide): 40.6B Privately Held
WEB: www.kochind.com
SIC: 2869 2992 2899 Industrial organic chemicals; lubricating oils & greases; chemical preparations
PA: Koch Industries, Inc.
4111 E 37th St N
Wichita KS 67220
316 828-5500

(G-3353)
L L C OASIS OF HUTCHINSON
Also Called: Summit, The
1818 E 23rd Ave (67502-1106)
PHONE..................................620 663-4800
Gordon Funk, *Mng Member*
Terry Stofferson, *Mng Member*
John Fiebich, *Director*
Stephanie Stieben, *Physician Asst*
EMP: 50
SALES (est): 3.8MM Privately Held
SIC: 8721 Billing & bookkeeping service

(G-3354)
LINDBURG VOGEL PIERC FARIS CH (PA)
2301 N Halstead St (67502-1137)
P.O. Box 2047 (67504-2047)
PHONE..................................620 669-0461
Mike Evans, *President*
EMP: 45
SQ FT: 5,000
SALES (est): 4.1MM Privately Held
WEB: www.lv-cpas.com
SIC: 8721 Accounting services, except auditing; certified public accountant

(G-3355)
LIVING CENTER INC
1701 E 23rd Ave (67502-1105)
PHONE..................................620 665-2170
Tyler Lawrence, *Administration*
EMP: 85
SQ FT: 60,000
SALES: 551.4K Privately Held
WEB: www.dillonlivingcenter.com
SIC: 8052 6513 Intermediate care facilities; retirement hotel operation

(G-3356)
LONGFELLOW FOUNDATION INC (PA)
Also Called: Longfellow Foundations Nic
909 Corey Rd (67501-1982)
PHONE..................................620 662-1228
Mike Kemery, *President*
Jason Hoy, *Vice Pres*
▲ EMP: 14 EST: 1997
SALES (est): 5MM Privately Held
SIC: 1771 Foundation & footing contractor

(G-3357)
LOWEN CORPORATION
1501 N Halstead St (67501-2114)
PHONE..................................620 663-2161
Roger Borth, *Branch Mgr*
EMP: 5
SALES (corp-wide): 80.3MM Privately Held
SIC: 2752 Decals, lithographed
PA: Lowen Corporation
1111 Airport Rd
Hutchinson KS 67501
620 663-2161

(G-3358)
LOWEN CORPORATION (PA)
Also Called: Lowen Sign Company
1111 Airport Rd (67501-1983)
P.O. Box 1528 (67504-1528)
PHONE..................................620 663-2161
Matt T Lowen, *President*
James Mihm, *Business Mgr*
Doug Cook, *Senior VP*
Jeryl Hendricks, *Vice Pres*
Mary Purdue, *Plant Mgr*
▼ EMP: 284
SALES (est): 80.3MM Privately Held
WEB: www.lowencg.com
SIC: 2759 3993 5999 2679 Commercial printing; signs & advertising specialties; decals; labels, paper: made from purchased material; commercial printing, lithographic

(G-3359)
LOWES HOME CENTERS LLC
1930 E 17th Ave (67501-1105)
PHONE..................................620 513-2000
Tim Mulligan, *Branch Mgr*
EMP: 150
SALES (corp-wide): 71.3B Publicly Held
SIC: 5211 5031 5722 5064 Home centers; building materials, exterior; building materials, interior; household appliance stores; electrical appliances, television & radio
HQ: Lowe's Home Centers, Llc
1605 Curtis Bridge Rd
Wilkesboro NC 28697
336 658-4000

(G-3360)
LUMINOUS NEON INC (PA)
Also Called: Luminous Neon Art Sign Systems
1429 W 4th Ave (67501-5054)
PHONE..................................620 662-2363
Ron Sellers, *President*
Merl F Sellers, *Principal*
Mert Sellers, *Chairman*
Tom Sellers, *Exec VP*
Matt Brasel, *Vice Pres*
EMP: 80
SQ FT: 11,000
SALES (est): 11.6MM Privately Held
SIC: 3993 Electric signs

(G-3361)
MAA SANTOSHI LLC
Also Called: Hampton Inn
1401 E 11th Ave (67501-2750)
PHONE..................................620 665-9800
Ishwar Patel,
EMP: 23
SALES (est): 1.6MM Privately Held
SIC: 7011 Hotels & motels

(G-3362)
MAAS PAINT AND PAPER LLC
4616 E 69th Ave (67502-8229)
PHONE..................................785 643-4790
Andrea Maas, *Accounting Mgr*
Terri Maas, *Manager*
David Lawson,

▲ = Import ▼=Export ◆ =Import/Export

Jason Maas,
W Scott Maas,
EMP: 17 **EST:** 2011
SALES (est): 525.4K **Privately Held**
SIC: 1721 Commercial painting; residential painting; commercial wallcovering contractor; residential wallcovering contractor

(G-3363)
MANN & CO ARCHITECTS/ENGINEERS
1703 Landon St (67502-5663)
PHONE..................................620 662-4493
Lynn W Schwartzkopf, *President*
Mitchell A Brown, *Vice Pres*
Mark Schwartzkopf, *Info Tech Mgr*
EMP: 10
SQ FT: 1,800
SALES: 600K **Privately Held**
WEB: www.mannandcompany.com
SIC: 8712 Architectural engineering

(G-3364)
MARK BORECKY CONSTRUCTION
201 N Van Buren St (67501-5060)
PHONE..................................620 259-6655
Mark Borecky, *Principal*
EMP: 11 **EST:** 2009
SALES (est): 1.6MM **Privately Held**
SIC: 1521 General remodeling, single-family houses

(G-3365)
MARTINDELL SWEARER SHAFFER
20 Compound Dr (67502-4300)
PHONE..................................620 662-3331
John B Swearer, *Managing Prtnr*
Elwin F Cabbage, *Partner*
Jerry L Ricksecker, *Partner*
William B Swearer, *Partner*
John Caton, *Editor*
EMP: 26 **EST:** 1886
SALES (est): 2.6MM **Privately Held**
WEB: www.martindell-law.com
SIC: 8111 General practice law office; general practice attorney, lawyer

(G-3366)
MASONIC LODGE
Also Called: LODGE 124
1800 E 23rd Ave (67502-1106)
PHONE..................................620 662-7012
Garrlid Rodman, *Admin Sec*
EMP: 11
SALES: 23K **Privately Held**
SIC: 8641 7011 Social club, membership; vacation lodges

(G-3367)
MAXINES INC
Also Called: Webcon
2627 E 4th Ave (67501-1964)
PHONE..................................620 669-8189
Toll Free:..................................888 -
Maxine Webster, *President*
Thomas Webster, *Vice Pres*
EMP: 15
SALES (est): 1.7MM **Privately Held**
WEB: www.webconroof.com
SIC: 1761 Roofing contractor

(G-3368)
MEDICAL CENTER P A (PA)
Also Called: Davis, William D
104 Crescent Blvd (67502-5542)
PHONE..................................620 669-6690
Stephen C Mills, *Med Doctor*
Barbara Hanzlicek, *Administration*
EMP: 70
SQ FT: 40,000
SALES (est): 4.4MM **Privately Held**
SIC: 8099 Medical services organization

(G-3369)
MEDICAL CENTER P A
Also Called: Medical Center West
104 Crescent Blvd (67502-5542)
PHONE..................................620 669-9657
J Diehl, *Manager*
EMP: 25
SALES (corp-wide): 4.4MM **Privately Held**
SIC: 8099 8093 Medical services organization; specialty outpatient clinics
PA: Medical Center, P A
104 Crescent Blvd
Hutchinson KS 67502
620 669-6690

(G-3370)
MEGA MANUFACTURING INC (PA)
Also Called: Piranha Fabrication Equipment
1 N Main St Ste 604 (67501-5251)
P.O. Box 457 (67504-0457)
PHONE..................................620 663-1127
Robert Green, *President*
John P Claxton, *CFO*
Scott Donahy, *Manager*
▲ **EMP:** 35
SALES (est): 19.5MM **Privately Held**
WEB: www.piranhafab.com
SIC: 3542 Punching, shearing & bending machines

(G-3371)
MEGA MANUFACTURING INC
3310 E 4th Ave (67501-1962)
PHONE..................................620 663-1127
EMP: 28
SALES (corp-wide): 18.6MM **Privately Held**
SIC: 3542 3523 Mfg Metal Forming Machine Tools & Tillage Tools
PA: Mega Manufacturing, Inc.
1 N Main St Ste 604
Hutchinson KS 67501
620 663-1127

(G-3372)
MELVIN SIMON & ASSOCIATES INC
Also Called: Hutchinson Mall
1500 E 11th Ave Ste 400 (67501-3783)
PHONE..................................620 665-5307
Dan Flores, *Manager*
EMP: 58
SQ FT: 450,000
SALES (corp-wide): 7.5MM **Privately Held**
WEB: www.youseeontv.com
SIC: 6512 Shopping center, property operation only
PA: Melvin Simon & Associates Inc
225 W Washington St
Indianapolis IN 46204
317 636-1600

(G-3373)
MEMBERS MORTGAGE SERVICES LLC
200 E 1st Ave (67501-7110)
P.O. Box 1185 (67504-1185)
PHONE..................................620 665-7713
Todd Brunner, *President*
Michael Harms, *Vice Pres*
Paul Scofield, *QC Mgr*
Jim Dunleavy, *Sales Staff*
Brittany Shipley, *Manager*
EMP: 40
SQ FT: 16,000
SALES: 5.3MM **Privately Held**
SIC: 6211 Mortgages, buying & selling

(G-3374)
MENNONITE FRNDSHIP COMMUNITIES
Also Called: Center Court Assisted Living
606 Centre Ct (67505-1744)
PHONE..................................620 663-7175
Julie Graves, *Vice Pres*
Deb Cable, *Branch Mgr*
EMP: 125
SALES (corp-wide): 11.3MM **Privately Held**
SIC: 8052 Personal care facility
PA: Mennonite Friendship Communities, Inc
600 W Blanchard Ave
South Hutchinson KS 67505
620 663-7175

(G-3375)
MICHAEL E EVANS CPA
2301 N Halstead St (67502-1137)
P.O. Box 2047 (67504-2047)
PHONE..................................620 669-0461
Michael E Evans, *Principal*
Mike Evans, *Principal*
EMP: 21
SALES (est): 637.2K **Privately Held**
SIC: 8721 Certified public accountant

(G-3376)
MID KANSAS MARINE & RV INC (PA)
517 E 4th Ave (67501-6989)
PHONE..................................620 665-0396
Clarence Nolte, *President*
Susan Nolte, *Manager*
EMP: 14
SQ FT: 13,000
SALES (est): 3MM **Privately Held**
SIC: 5551 7699 Motor boat dealers; boat repair

(G-3377)
MID-AMERICA REDI-MIX INC (PA)
Also Called: Sterling Sand & Gravel
2510 W Blanchard Ave (67501-7807)
P.O. Box 2146 (67504-2146)
PHONE..................................620 663-1559
Marc Westhoff, *President*
Dale Westhoff, *Corp Secy*
Roy Westhoff, *Vice Pres*
EMP: 12
SALES (est): 2.2MM **Privately Held**
SIC: 3273 Ready-mixed concrete

(G-3378)
MIDWEST IRON & METAL CO INC (PA)
700 S Main St (67501-5312)
P.O. Box 70 (67504-0070)
PHONE..................................620 662-5663
Matt Mayo, *Principal*
Charlotte Galler, *Chairman*
Charlotte Gallere, *Chairman*
EMP: 47
SQ FT: 5,000
SALES (est): 11.1MM **Privately Held**
SIC: 5093 5051 Ferrous metal scrap & waste; junk & scrap; steel

(G-3379)
MIDWEST MALIBU CENTER INC
1180 Airport Rd (67501-1916)
PHONE..................................620 728-1356
Tony Beauchamp, *Principal*
EMP: 10
SALES (est): 1.1MM **Privately Held**
SIC: 4581 Aircraft maintenance & repair services

(G-3380)
MIDWEST PAIN MANAGEMENT
Also Called: Knudsen, John III MD
1708 E 23rd Ave (67502-1114)
PHONE..................................620 664-6724
Douglas Friezen, *Owner*
EMP: 15
SALES (est): 916.7K **Privately Held**
SIC: 8011 Primary care medical clinic

(G-3381)
MILLER HOMEBUILDERS INC
301 Hemlock St (67502-9659)
PHONE..................................620 662-1687
Wendell Miller, *President*
Kerri Miller, *Corp Secy*
Glenn Miller Jr, *Vice Pres*
EMP: 35
SQ FT: 1,100
SALES (est): 4.2MM **Privately Held**
SIC: 1521 1542 New construction, single-family houses; commercial & office building contractors

(G-3382)
MISSION PLACE LTD LP
3101 N Plum St (67502-2941)
PHONE..................................620 662-8731
L William Rudnick, *Partner*
EMP: 34
SALES: 712.4K **Privately Held**
WEB: www.missionplace.com
SIC: 6531 Real estate agents & managers

(G-3383)
ML NEVIUS BUILDERS INC
Also Called: Nevius, M L
1915 W 82nd Ave (67502-9453)
PHONE..................................620 662-7767
Micheal Nevius, *President*
EMP: 19
SQ FT: 3,000
SALES (est): 1.4MM **Privately Held**
SIC: 1741 Masonry & other stonework

(G-3384)
MOBILE PRODUCTS INC
15 Compound Dr (67502-4349)
PHONE..................................903 759-0610
Phillip Ford, *President*
EMP: 130
SALES (est): 14.8MM **Publicly Held**
WEB: www.collinsind.com
SIC: 3991 Street sweeping brooms, hand or machine
HQ: Collins Industries, Inc.
15 Compound Dr
Hutchinson KS 67502
620 663-5551

(G-3385)
MONTES DE AREIA LLC
Also Called: Crazy Hrse Spt CLB & Golf Crse
922 Crazy Horse Rd (67502-8957)
PHONE..................................620 663-5301
Jon Mollhagen,
EMP: 22
SALES (est): 113.2K **Privately Held**
SIC: 7997 Golf club, membership

(G-3386)
MURPHY USA INC
1903 E 17th Ave (67501-1103)
PHONE..................................620 664-9479
EMP: 13 **Publicly Held**
SIC: 5541 2911 Gasoline service stations; petroleum refining
PA: Murphy Usa Inc.
200 E Peach St
El Dorado AR 71730

(G-3387)
NATIONAL CREDIT ADJUSTERS LLC
327 W 4th Ave (67501-4842)
P.O. Box 3023 (67504-3023)
PHONE..................................888 768-0674
Mark Huston, *CFO*
Tyler Rempel, *Human Res Dir*
EMP: 200 **EST:** 2002
SQ FT: 14,000
SALES (est): 21.6MM **Privately Held**
SIC: 7322 Collection agency, except real estate

(G-3388)
NATIONAL EXPRESS LLC
Also Called: Durham School Services
1401 W 4th Ave (67501-5054)
PHONE..................................620 662-1299
Marilee Mayes, *Manager*
EMP: 30 **Privately Held**
SIC: 4151 4141 School buses; local bus charter service
HQ: National Express Llc
2601 Navistar Dr
Lisle IL 60532

(G-3389)
NETWORK MANAGEMENT GROUP INC
324 E 4th Ave (67501-6936)
P.O. Box 1343 (67504-1343)
PHONE..................................620 665-3611
Randolph P Johnston, *CEO*
Doug Elliott, *Principal*
Kenneth McClelland, *Principal*
Ben Evans, *Engineer*
Earl Bean, *Accounts Exec*
EMP: 30
SQ FT: 7,200
SALES: 6.8MM **Privately Held**
WEB: www.nmgi.com
SIC: 5734 7378 7379 Computer & software stores; computer maintenance & repair; data processing consultant

GEOGRAPHIC

(G-3390)
NEW BEGINNINGS INC
100 E 2nd Ave (67501-7103)
P.O. Box 2504 (67504-2504)
PHONE....620 966-0274
Shara Gonzales, *President*
EMP: 14
SALES: 768.4K **Privately Held**
SIC: 8322 Social service center

(G-3391)
NISLY BROTHERS INC
Also Called: Nisly Brothers Trash Service
5212 S Herren Rd (67501-9156)
PHONE....620 662-6561
Marvin Nisly, *President*
Steve Ellingboe, *Sales Mgr*
EMP: 20
SQ FT: 6,250
SALES (est): 3.6MM **Privately Held**
WEB: www.nislybrothers.com
SIC: 4953 7359 Garbage: collecting, destroying & processing; portable toilet rental

(G-3392)
OLDCASTLE INFRASTRUCTURE INC
1600 N Lorraine St Ste 1 (67501-5600)
PHONE....620 662-3307
EMP: 13
SALES (corp-wide): 29.7B **Privately Held**
SIC: 1611 Highway & street paving contractor
HQ: Oldcastle Infrastructure, Inc.
7000 Cntl Prkaway Ste 800
Atlanta GA 30328
470 602-2000

(G-3393)
ONEOK INC
110 W 2nd Ave (67501-5209)
PHONE....620 728-4303
Kelly Hagman, *Project Mgr*
Stan Parsons, *Branch Mgr*
EMP: 47
SALES (corp-wide): 12.5B **Publicly Held**
WEB: www.oneok.com
SIC: 4924 Natural gas distribution
PA: Oneok, Inc.
100 W 5th St Ste Ll
Tulsa OK 74103
918 588-7000

(G-3394)
ONEOK INC
4817 N Dean Rd (67502-9685)
PHONE....620 669-2300
Tracy Peterson, *Project Mgr*
EMP: 11
SALES (corp-wide): 12.5B **Publicly Held**
WEB: www.oneok.com
SIC: 4922 Natural gas transmission
PA: Oneok, Inc.
100 W 5th St Ste Ll
Tulsa OK 74103
918 588-7000

(G-3395)
ONEOK HYDROCARBON LP (DH)
1910 S Broadacres Rd (67501-9627)
PHONE....620 669-3759
Steve Tatum, *President*
Troy Reusser, *Vice Pres*
Terry Spencer, *Vice Pres*
Stephen H Mims, *VP Opers*
Elaine Daubert, *Treasurer*
EMP: 76
SALES (est): 21.5MM
SALES (corp-wide): 12.5B **Publicly Held**
WEB: www.kochhydrocarbon.com
SIC: 2911 Petroleum refining

(G-3396)
OREILLY AUTOMOTIVE STORES INC
Also Called: O'Reilly Auto Parts
1101 E 30th Ave (67502-4228)
PHONE....620 664-6800
Charlie O Reilly, *Owner*
EMP: 10 **Publicly Held**
SIC: 5013 5531 Automotive supplies & parts; automotive parts
HQ: O'reilly Automotive Stores, Inc.
233 S Patterson Ave
Springfield MO 65802
417 862-2674

(G-3397)
ORSCHELN FARM AND HOME LLC
Also Called: Orschelin Farm and Home 58
1500 E 11th Ave (67501-3799)
PHONE....620 662-8867
Paul Garden, *Manager*
EMP: 17
SALES (corp-wide): 822.7MM **Privately Held**
WEB: www.orschelnfarmhome.com
SIC: 5191 5251 5699 0291 Greenhouse equipment & supplies; hardware; work clothing; animal specialty farm, general
PA: Orscheln Farm And Home Llc
1800 Overcenter Dr
Moberly MO 65270
800 577-2580

(G-3398)
OSWALT ARNOLD OSWALD & HENRY
Also Called: Assoction Indvdual Prctitioners
330 W 1st Ave (67501-5205)
PHONE....620 662-5489
James Oswalt, *Owner*
Nick Oswald,
EMP: 10
SALES (est): 991.4K **Privately Held**
SIC: 8111 General practice attorney, lawyer

(G-3399)
PANKRATZ IMPLEMENT CO
Also Called: John Deere Implmnt Co
1800 S Lorraine St (67501-2437)
PHONE....620 662-8681
Darrell Pankratz, *President*
Linda Ratzlaff, *Treasurer*
Mary Pankratz, *Admin Sec*
EMP: 21
SQ FT: 18,500
SALES: 9MM **Privately Held**
WEB: www.pankratzimplement.com
SIC: 5083 5261 Farm implements; lawn & garden equipment

(G-3400)
PANTRY SHELF COMPANY
401 S Adams St (67501-5373)
P.O. Box 613 (67504-0613)
PHONE....620 662-9342
Fax: 620 662-9306
EMP: 5
SALES (est): 474.3K **Privately Held**
SIC: 2045 Mfg Prepared Flour Mixes/Doughs

(G-3401)
PEOPLES BANK & TRUST CO
6300 W Morgan Ave (67501-9023)
PHONE....620 662-6502
Richard Kollhoff, *Manager*
EMP: 62
SALES (corp-wide): 22.1MM **Privately Held**
WEB: www.peoplesbankonline.com
SIC: 6022 State commercial banks
PA: Peoples Bank & Trust Co (Inc)
101 S Main St
Mcpherson KS 67460
620 241-2100

(G-3402)
PEOPLES BANK & TRUST CO
601 E 30th Ave (67502-8432)
PHONE....620 669-0234
Don Keller, *Manager*
EMP: 38
SALES (corp-wide): 22.1MM **Privately Held**
WEB: www.peoplesbankonline.com
SIC: 6022 State commercial banks
PA: Peoples Bank & Trust Co (Inc)
101 S Main St
Mcpherson KS 67460
620 241-2100

(G-3403)
PEOPLES BANK & TRUST CO
1020 N Main St Ste 1 (67501-4477)
P.O. Box 99 (67504-0099)
PHONE....620 663-4000
Don Keller, *Manager*
EMP: 13
SALES (corp-wide): 22.1MM **Privately Held**
WEB: www.peoplesbankonline.com
SIC: 6022 State commercial banks
PA: Peoples Bank & Trust Co (Inc)
101 S Main St
Mcpherson KS 67460
620 241-2100

(G-3404)
PERRYS INC
Also Called: Reger Rental Sales & Service
615 N Main St (67501-4601)
P.O. Box 1284 (67504-1284)
PHONE....620 662-2375
Perry E Reger, *President*
Crhristina Reger, *Corp Secy*
Mary E Jenkins, *Vice Pres*
EMP: 10
SQ FT: 20,250
SALES: 650K **Privately Held**
WEB: www.perryshobbies.com
SIC: 7359 5999 Equipment rental & leasing; medical apparatus & supplies

(G-3405)
PETRONOMICS MFG GROUP INC
208 E 2nd Ave (67501-7118)
PHONE....620 663-8559
Gary Clark, *CEO*
Jan Clark, *Manager*
EMP: 20 **EST:** 1978
SQ FT: 36,000
SALES (est): 2.8MM **Privately Held**
SIC: 2992 Lubricating oils & greases

(G-3406)
PIPELINE TSTG CONSORTIUM INC
9 Compound Dr (67502-4349)
PHONE....620 669-8800
Vergi Geurian, *President*
Earlene Neuway, *Corp Secy*
Mike Neuway, *Vice Pres*
Jeremy Kocher, *Accounts Exec*
Bret Towell, *Accounts Exec*
EMP: 28
SQ FT: 12,000
SALES (est): 2.3MM **Privately Held**
WEB: www.pipelinetesting.com
SIC: 8071 8093 Testing laboratories; drug clinic, outpatient

(G-3407)
PIZZA RANCH
1805 E 17th Ave (67501-1102)
P.O. Box 2064 (67504-2064)
PHONE....620 662-2066
Rebekah Powell, *Principal*
EMP: 19
SALES (est): 526.1K **Privately Held**
SIC: 5812 0191 Pizzeria, chain; general farms, primarily crop

(G-3408)
PLP INC (PA)
Also Called: John Deere Authorized Dealer
811 E 30th Ave Ste F (67502-4308)
PHONE....620 664-5860
Darrell Pankratz, *President*
Mitch Guetterman, *Store Mgr*
Kelly Pitts, *Store Mgr*
Mike Ramsey, *Store Mgr*
Denis Robidou, *Parts Mgr*
EMP: 117 **EST:** 2008
SQ FT: 32,000
SALES (est): 66.9MM **Privately Held**
SIC: 5999 5082 Farm equipment & supplies; construction & mining machinery

(G-3409)
PORTFOLIO RECOVERY ASSOC LLC
500 W 1st Ave (67501-5222)
PHONE....620 662-2800
Macy Church, *President*
William O'Daire, *Principal*
Michele Slack, *Accounts Mgr*
EMP: 152
SALES (corp-wide): 908.2MM **Publicly Held**
SIC: 7322 Collection agency, except real estate
HQ: Portfolio Recovery Associates, Llc
120 Corporate Blvd
Norfolk VA 23502

(G-3410)
PRAIRIE HILLS NURSERY INC
Also Called: Prairie Hills Tree Nurs Ldscpg
2999 E 30th Ave (67502-1500)
PHONE....620 665-5500
Tom R Heintzman, *President*
EMP: 10
SQ FT: 1,100
SALES (est): 730K **Privately Held**
SIC: 5261 0782 Nurseries & garden centers; landscape contractors

(G-3411)
PRAIRIE IND LVING RESOURCE CTR (PA)
Also Called: P I L R
17 S Main St (67501-5421)
PHONE....620 663-3989
Christy Ireland, *Principal*
Heather Dean, *Manager*
Chris Owens, *Exec Dir*
Christine Owens, *Director*
Andy Reichart, *Asst Director*
EMP: 14
SALES: 975.4K **Privately Held**
WEB: www.pilr.com
SIC: 8322 Social services for the handicapped

(G-3412)
PRAIRIELAND PARTNERS LLC
811 E 30th Ave Ste F (67502-4308)
PHONE....620 664-6552
Darrell Pankratz,
Kyle Adams,
Curtis Beagley,
Drue Durst,
Jamie Gudeman,
EMP: 99
SALES (est): 24.2MM **Privately Held**
SIC: 5083 Agricultural machinery & equipment

(G-3413)
PRAIRIESTAR HEALTH CENTER INC
2700 E 30th Ave (67502-1242)
PHONE....620 663-8484
Sally Tesluk, *Exec Dir*
EMP: 13
SQ FT: 1,500
SALES: 6.1MM **Privately Held**
SIC: 8011 Clinic, operated by physicians

(G-3414)
PREFERRED SEAMLESS GUTTERING
11017 S Osage Rd (67501-8463)
PHONE....620 663-7600
Sergio Pineda, *Principal*
EMP: 5
SALES (est): 640.1K **Privately Held**
SIC: 3089 Gutters (glass fiber reinforced), fiberglass or plastic

(G-3415)
PROFESSIONAL DATA SERVICES (DH)
1632 E 23rd Ave (67502-4705)
P.O. Box 2044 (67504-2044)
PHONE....620 663-5282
Gary Mundhenke, *President*
Carol Santangelo, *Corp Secy*
Jim Harders, *Vice Pres*
Marc McCrary, *Controller*
Lana Hutchens, *Marketing Staff*
EMP: 19
SQ FT: 6,500
SALES: 1MM **Privately Held**
WEB: www.pdsmed.com
SIC: 7372 Business oriented computer software

HQ: Integrated Solutions Group, Inc.
1632 E 23rd Ave
Hutchinson KS 67502
620 662-5796

(G-3416)
PROVALUE COOPERATIVE INC (PA)
Also Called: Nationwide
1515 E 30th Ave (67502-1225)
P.O. Box 1747 (67504-1747)
PHONE....................................620 662-5406
Mitch Williams, *CEO*
EMP: 26
SQ FT: 7,500
SALES (est): 5.3MM **Privately Held**
WEB: www.kfsa.com
SIC: 8748 Business consulting

(G-3417)
PROVALUE INSURANCE LLC
1515 E 30th Ave (67502-1225)
P.O. Box 1747 (67504-1747)
PHONE....................................620 662-5406
Scott Anderson, *COO*
Jorden Olsen, *Accounts Mgr*
Shawnda Hembree, *Mng Member*
John Knipp, *Manager*
Scott Smith, *Manager*
EMP: 29
SALES (est): 272.6K
SALES (corp-wide): 5.3MM **Privately Held**
SIC: 6411 Insurance agents
PA: Provalue Cooperative, Inc.
1515 E 30th Ave
Hutchinson KS 67502
620 662-5406

(G-3418)
RADIO KANSAS
815 N Walnut St Ste 300 (67501-6389)
PHONE....................................620 662-6646
Ken Baker, *General Mgr*
Dave Horning, *General Mgr*
Doug Kaufman, *Engineer*
Rosemary Sayers, *Librarian*
JD Hershberger, *Director*
EMP: 22
SALES (est): 1.5MM **Privately Held**
WEB: www.radiokansas.org
SIC: 4832 Radio broadcasting stations

(G-3419)
RAILWAY CONSTRUCTION
1816 Tracy Ln (67501-2920)
P.O. Box 97 (67504-0097)
PHONE....................................620 663-9233
Lonnie Thiel, *Owner*
EMP: 13
SALES (est): 600K **Privately Held**
WEB: www.railwayconstruction.com
SIC: 1629 Railroad & railway roadbed construction

(G-3420)
RCB BANK
1330 E 17th Ave (67501-5611)
PHONE....................................620 860-7797
Michelle May, *Branch Mgr*
EMP: 12
SALES (corp-wide): 22MM **Privately Held**
SIC: 6022 State trust companies accepting deposits, commercial
HQ: Rcb Bank
300 W Patti Page Blvd
Claremore OK 74017

(G-3421)
RED HILLS RESOURCES INC
1304 W 24th Ave (67502-2526)
P.O. Box 132, Englewood (67840-0132)
PHONE....................................620 669-9996
Wallace G Mc Kinney, *President*
Joan S Mc Kinney, *Corp Secy*
EMP: 6
SALES: 272.5K **Privately Held**
SIC: 1311 Natural gas production

(G-3422)
REIB INC
201 E 2nd Ave Ste A (67501-7235)
P.O. Box 1622 (67504-1622)
PHONE....................................620 662-0583
Ron Gingerich, *President*
EMP: 10
SALES (est): 807.4K **Privately Held**
SIC: 6531 Real estate brokers & agents

(G-3423)
RENO COUNTY ABSTRACT & TITLE
Also Called: Rcat
408 N Main St (67501-4816)
PHONE....................................620 662-5455
Charles Brown, *President*
Todd Brown, *Vice Pres*
R Wayne Colburn, *Vice Pres*
EMP: 14
SALES: 700K **Privately Held**
WEB: www.rcathutch.com
SIC: 6541 Title & trust companies

(G-3424)
RENO COUNTY AMBULANCE SERVICE
1701 E 23rd Ave (67502-9907)
PHONE....................................620 665-2120
Randy Miller, *Director*
EMP: 35
SALES (est): 452.8K **Privately Held**
SIC: 4119 Ambulance service

(G-3425)
RENO COUNTY YOUTH SERVICES
Also Called: Bob Johnson Youth Shelter
219 W 2nd Ave (67501-5232)
PHONE....................................620 694-2500
Jeanne Kelly, *Principal*
Bill Hermes, *Director*
EMP: 46
SQ FT: 1,000
SALES (est): 1.4MM **Privately Held**
SIC: 8322 8361 Youth center; juvenile correctional facilities

(G-3426)
RENO FABRICATING & SLS CO INC
Also Called: Plus It View Home Improvement
6401 W Morgan Ave (67501-9024)
PHONE....................................620 663-1269
Norman Yutzy, *President*
Ken Yutzy, *Treasurer*
Shirley Nisly, *Director*
Vernon Wickey, *Admin Sec*
EMP: 20 **EST:** 1956
SQ FT: 36,500
SALES (est): 3.3MM **Privately Held**
WEB: www.pleasantviewkansas.com
SIC: 3442 1761 3354 Storm doors or windows, metal; siding contractor; aluminum extruded products

(G-3427)
REYNOLD FORK BERKL SUTER ROSE
Also Called: Berkley, Raymond F
129 W 2nd Ave Ste 200 (67501-5270)
P.O. Box 1868 (67504-1868)
PHONE....................................620 663-7131
Dan Forker, *Partner*
John Suter, *Partner*
EMP: 20
SALES (est): 1MM **Privately Held**
SIC: 8111 General practice law office

(G-3428)
ROBERTS HUTCH-LINE INC
413 E 3rd Ave (67501-6906)
P.O. Box 1363 (67504-1363)
PHONE....................................620 662-3356
Mike Lindt, *President*
Donald Lindt, *Chairman*
Amanda Parks, *Purchasing*
Bonna Reusser, *Manager*
Jim Postier, *CTO*
EMP: 25
SQ FT: 15,000
SALES (est): 4.7MM **Privately Held**
WEB: www.robertshutchline.com
SIC: 5943 2752 5021 Office forms & supplies; commercial printing, lithographic; office furniture

(G-3429)
ROGER D GAUSMAN DDS
Also Called: Pediatric Dentistry
1311 Wheatland Dr (67502-5667)
PHONE....................................620 663-5044
Roger Gausman DDS, *Owner*
Kricket Young, *Managing Prtnr*
Kricket C Young, *Fmly & Gen Dent*
EMP: 10
SALES (est): 527.9K **Privately Held**
SIC: 8021 Dentists' office

(G-3430)
RON D HANSEN OD INC
Also Called: Douglas E Bald
3120 N Plum St (67502-2918)
PHONE....................................620 662-2355
Ron D Hansen, *Partner*
Dr Douglas Bald, *Partner*
EMP: 11
SALES (est): 1.1MM **Privately Held**
SIC: 8042 5995 Specialized optometrists; contact lenses, prescription

(G-3431)
ROSAS DRYWALL CO
Also Called: Rosas Ezra
1519 Linwood Dr (67502-2606)
PHONE....................................620 665-6959
Ezra Rosas, *President*
Becky Rosas, *Corp Secy*
EMP: 13
SALES: 450K **Privately Held**
SIC: 1742 Drywall

(G-3432)
ROSE MOTOR SUPPLY INC
109 E Sherman St (67501-7194)
PHONE....................................620 662-1254
Keith W Rose, *President*
Barbara Rose, *Vice Pres*
EMP: 10
SQ FT: 3,200
SALES: 2.5MM **Privately Held**
SIC: 5013 5531 Automotive supplies & parts; automotive parts

(G-3433)
ROYER BROTHERS TREE SVC LLC
2401 S Lorraine St (67501-9606)
PHONE....................................620 899-7621
Mark Royer,
Jack Royer,
Jason Thomas,
EMP: 60
SALES (est): 1.2MM **Privately Held**
SIC: 0783 Ornamental shrub & tree services

(G-3434)
S N C INC
10021 Paganica Ct (67502-8326)
PHONE....................................620 665-6651
EMP: 42
SQ FT: 3,000
SALES: 4.4MM **Privately Held**
SIC: 7382 1731 7629 5999 Security Systems Services

(G-3435)
S S OF KANSAS INC
Also Called: Sirloin Stockade
1526 E 17th Ave (67501-1113)
PHONE....................................620 663-5951
Laura Davis, *Manager*
EMP: 40
SALES (corp-wide): 18.9MM **Privately Held**
SIC: 5812 7299 Restaurant, family: chain; banquet hall facilities
PA: S. S. Of Kansas Inc
335 N Washington St # 120
Hutchinson KS 67501
620 669-1194

(G-3436)
SAINT FRNCIS ACDEMY HUTCHINSON
501 N Monroe St (67501-1345)
PHONE....................................620 669-3734
Karen Showalter, *Manager*
EMP: 40
SALES (est): 688.7K **Privately Held**
SIC: 8322 Individual & family services

(G-3437)
SALVATION ARMY
700 N Walnut St (67501-6288)
P.O. Box 310 (67504-0310)
PHONE....................................620 663-3353
John McCarty, *Branch Mgr*
EMP: 10
SALES (corp-wide): 2.2B **Privately Held**
WEB: www.salarmychicago.org
SIC: 8661 8699 Non-church religious organizations; charitable organization
HQ: The Salvation Army
5550 Prairie Stone Pkwy # 130
Hoffman Estates IL 60192
847 294-2000

(G-3438)
SCKATS INC
1722 N Plum St (67502-5501)
PHONE....................................620 662-2368
Eric Allen, *CEO*
Clark Oswald, *Director*
EMP: 11
SALES (est): 270.8K **Privately Held**
SIC: 7291 Tax return preparation services

(G-3439)
SDK LABORATORIES INC
1000 Corey Rd (67501-1978)
P.O. Box 886 (67504-0886)
PHONE....................................620 665-5661
Dennis H Hogan, *President*
Shirley A Hogan, *Corp Secy*
Matt Hogan, *Vice Pres*
Dara Warthen, *Executive Asst*
EMP: 30 **EST:** 1952
SALES (est): 3.5MM **Privately Held**
WEB: www.sdklabs.com
SIC: 8734 0742 Veterinary testing; water testing laboratory; veterinary services, specialties

(G-3440)
SEAT KING LLC (PA)
6 N Walnut St (67501-7105)
PHONE....................................620 665-5464
Peter Ochs,
Nick Coulter,
EMP: 23
SALES (est): 4.5MM **Privately Held**
SIC: 2531 Seats, automobile

(G-3441)
SHIELD INDUSTRIES INC
Also Called: Shield Agricultural Equipment
950 Scott Blvd (67505)
P.O. Box 687 (67504-0687)
PHONE....................................620 662-7221
Mike Bergmeier, *President*
Angie Bergmeier, *Vice Pres*
Brenda Klug, *Buyer*
Andy Klamm, *Regl Sales Mgr*
▲ **EMP:** 42
SQ FT: 6,000
SALES (est): 7.4MM **Privately Held**
SIC: 5999 3523 Farm equipment & supplies; farm machinery & equipment

(G-3442)
SNC ALARM SERVICE
2611 E 17th Ave (67501-1142)
PHONE....................................620 665-6651
Ailiff Neel, *Owner*
EMP: 30
SALES (est): 870K **Privately Held**
SIC: 7922 3699 Theatrical producers & services; electrical equipment & supplies

(G-3443)
SONOCO PRODUCTS COMPANY
Sonoco-Hutchinson Mill
100 N Halstead St (67501-1800)
P.O. Box 1267 (67504-1267)
PHONE....................................620 662-2331
Jim Kicklighter, *Principal*
EMP: 115
SALES (corp-wide): 5.3B **Publicly Held**
WEB: www.sonoco.com
SIC: 2631 Paperboard mills
PA: Sonoco Products Company
1 N 2nd St
Hartsville SC 29550
843 383-7000

(G-3444)
SOUTHWIND EYECARE
3120 N Plum St (67502-2918)
PHONE.................................620 662-2355
Benjamin Whiteredge, *Managing Prtnr*
Ron Hansen, *Partner*
Benjamin Whittredge,
EMP: 12
SALES (est): 519.6K **Privately Held**
SIC: 5995 8042 Contact lenses, prescription; offices & clinics of optometrists

(G-3445)
SRD ENVIRONMENTAL SERVICES
315 W Blanchard Ave (67505-1531)
PHONE.................................620 665-5590
John Stutzman, *President*
EMP: 50
SALES (est): 1.8MM **Privately Held**
WEB: www.srdinc.net
SIC: 8748 Environmental consultant

(G-3446)
STERLING FOOD MART INC
114 Kisiwa Pkwy (67502-4458)
PHONE.................................620 278-3371
Diana Holliday, *Principal*
EMP: 5
SALES (est): 502.1K **Privately Held**
SIC: 5411 1389 3643 Convenience stores; processing service, gas; outlets, electric: convenience

(G-3447)
STEVEN D BRAUN
Also Called: Chalmers Cancer Treatment Ctr
1701 E 23rd Ave (67502-1105)
PHONE.................................620 662-1212
Steven D Braun, *Principal*
EMP: 10
SALES (est): 262.4K **Privately Held**
SIC: 8011 Physicians' office, including specialists

(G-3448)
STOCKADE COMPANIES LLC (PA)
Also Called: Montana Mike's Steakhouse
2908 N Plum St Ste A (67502-8419)
PHONE.................................620 669-9372
Ed Sadler, *Director*
Steven L Schmidt,
Tommy M Ford,
Doug Frieling,
Terry Harstad,
EMP: 95
SQ FT: 5,000
SALES (est): 2.8MM **Privately Held**
WEB: www.stockadecompanies.com
SIC: 5812 6794 Restaurant, family: chain; franchises, selling or licensing

(G-3449)
STRAIGHTLINE HDD INC
1816 E Wasp Rd (67501-8714)
PHONE.................................620 802-0200
Don Cary, *President*
Brent Milleville, *Purch Mgr*
Bob Buller, *Buyer*
Terry Beczak, *Design Engr*
Justin Dawkins, *Controller*
▲ **EMP:** 55
SALES (est): 12.2MM **Privately Held**
SIC: 3541 Drilling & boring machines

(G-3450)
STRANDS
2520 N Main St (67502-3641)
PHONE.................................620 663-6397
Amanda O'Dell, *Owner*
EMP: 10
SALES (est): 138.7K **Privately Held**
SIC: 7231 Unisex hair salons

(G-3451)
STRAUB INTERNATIONAL INC
1100 Wilbeck Dr (67505-8757)
PHONE.................................620 662-0211
Lonny Brummer, *Manager*
EMP: 16
SQ FT: 6,000
SALES (corp-wide): 93MM **Privately Held**
WEB: www.straubint.com
SIC: 5083 7699 Farm implements; agricultural equipment repair services
PA: Straub International, Inc.
200 S Patton Rd
Great Bend KS 67530
620 792-5256

(G-3452)
STROBERG EQUIPMENT CO INC
602 Urban Dr (67501-1538)
PHONE.................................620 662-7650
Bernadine Stroberg, *President*
EMP: 8 **EST:** 1954
SQ FT: 4,000
SALES (est): 1.3MM **Privately Held**
WEB: www.strobergequipment.com
SIC: 3523 Cattle feeding, handling & watering equipment

(G-3453)
STURDI-BILT STORAGE BARNS INC
Also Called: STURDI-BILT DOOR CO (DIV)
3909 Stacy Rd (67501-7828)
PHONE.................................620 663-5998
Gary Miller, *President*
Perry Miller, *Corp Secy*
Marvin Miller, *Sales Executive*
David Yoder, *Maintence Staff*
EMP: 30
SQ FT: 9,960
SALES: 8.7MM **Privately Held**
SIC: 1542 Garage construction

(G-3454)
STUTZMAN GREENHOUSE INC
Also Called: Stutzman Grnhse Grdn Ctr Gift
6709 W State Road 61 (67501-7855)
PHONE.................................620 662-0559
Ben Miller, *President*
Marlene Miller, *Corp Secy*
EMP: 50
SQ FT: 250,000
SALES (est): 7.4MM **Privately Held**
WEB: www.stutzmans.com
SIC: 5193 5261 Plants, potted; flowers, fresh; nursery stock, seeds & bulbs

(G-3455)
SUMMIT SURGICAL LLC
Also Called: SUMMIT, THE
1818 E 23rd Ave (67502-1106)
PHONE.................................620 663-4800
Nancy Corwin, *COO*
Kellie Chastain, *CFO*
Erik Severud, *Mng Member*
EMP: 20
SALES: 6.2MM **Privately Held**
SIC: 8069 8011 Orthopedic hospital; gynecologist

(G-3456)
SUN VALLEY INC
1601 E Blanchard Ave (67501-8107)
P.O. Box 1942 (67504-1942)
PHONE.................................620 662-0101
Keith Bauer, *President*
EMP: 24
SALES: 3.5MM **Privately Held**
SIC: 3715 Truck trailers

(G-3457)
SUNFLWER ELC SUP HTCHINSON INC (PA)
100 W 2nd Ave (67501-5209)
P.O. Box 828 (67504-0828)
PHONE.................................620 662-0531
Phillip E Miller, *President*
Leon J Morris, *Corp Secy*
EMP: 23
SQ FT: 50,000
SALES (est): 7.5MM **Privately Held**
SIC: 5063 Electrical supplies

(G-3458)
SUPERIOR HOLDING INC (PA)
3524 E 4th Ave (67501-1960)
PHONE.................................620 662-6693
John J Murphy, *President*
Carl Fry, *Vice Pres*
EMP: 18 **EST:** 1947
SQ FT: 39,000
SALES (est): 29.9MM **Privately Held**
SIC: 3443 Boiler & boiler shop work

(G-3459)
SURGERY CTR S CENTL KANS LLC
Also Called: Surgery Center S Centl Kans
1708 E 23rd St Ave (67502)
PHONE.................................620 663-7187
Christopher A Holden, *President*
Staci Pankratz, *Director*
EMP: 11
SALES (est): 1.2MM
SALES (corp-wide): 643.1MM **Privately Held**
WEB: www.amsurg.com
SIC: 8011 Ambulatory surgical center
HQ: Envision Healthcare Corporation
1a Burton Hills Blvd
Nashville TN 37215
615 665-1283

(G-3460)
T & E OIL COMPANY INC 1 (PA)
Also Called: Pantry
911 N Halstead St (67501-2008)
P.O. Box 1303 (67504-1303)
PHONE.................................620 663-3777
Kevin G Brown, *President*
Stanley E Brown, *Chairman*
Katherine M Brown, *Corp Secy*
Kent A Brown, *Exec VP*
EMP: 20
SQ FT: 11,000
SALES (est): 45.4MM **Privately Held**
WEB: www.teoil.com
SIC: 5541 5172 Filling stations, gasoline; petroleum products

(G-3461)
T O HAAS LLC
16 W Avenue A (67501-5403)
PHONE.................................620 662-0261
Kip Voss, *Manager*
Ann Graham, *Asst Mgr*
Randy Haas,
George Hullen,
EMP: 12 **EST:** 1960
SQ FT: 4,000
SALES (est): 936.7K **Privately Held**
SIC: 5531 5014 Automotive tires; tires & tubes

(G-3462)
TAKAKO AMERICA CO INC
715 Corey Rd (67501-1971)
P.O. Box 1642 (67504-1642)
PHONE.................................620 663-1790
Toshikatsu Ishikawa, *President*
Lisa Goering, *QC Mgr*
Vincent Kinast, *Human Res Mgr*
Don McKenzie, *Manager*
Bill Phipps, *Manager*
▲ **EMP:** 144
SQ FT: 80,000
SALES (est): 26.4MM **Privately Held**
WEB: www.tswproducts.com
SIC: 3545 3599 Precision tools, machinists'; machine shop, jobbing & repair
PA: Takako Co.,Ltd.
1-1-6, Shibuya
Shibuya-Ku TKY

(G-3463)
TECHNIQUE MANUFACTURING INC
614 E 1st Ave (67501-7114)
P.O. Box 1007 (67504-1007)
PHONE.................................620 663-6360
Ted A Robinson, *President*
Tom Goering, *Vice Pres*
EMP: 13
SQ FT: 32,000
SALES (est): 1.6MM **Privately Held**
SIC: 2431 2434 Doors, wood; trim, wood; wood kitchen cabinets

(G-3464)
THYSSENKRUPP MATERIALS NA INC
3001 E 11th Ave (67501-2143)
PHONE.................................620 802-0900
Mike Cave, *Principal*
EMP: 13
SALES (corp-wide): 46.8B **Privately Held**
SIC: 5051 Metals service centers & offices
HQ: Thyssenkrupp Materials Na, Inc.
22355 W 11 Mile Rd
Southfield MI 48033
248 233-5600

(G-3465)
TRACTOR SUPPLY COMPANY
1203 N Lorraine St (67501-6169)
PHONE.................................620 663-7607
Mike Lynn, *Branch Mgr*
EMP: 11
SALES (corp-wide): 7.9B **Publicly Held**
WEB: www.tractorsupplyco.com
SIC: 5999 5261 5531 5251 Feed & farm supply; lawn & garden equipment; lawn & garden supplies; truck equipment & parts; tools; work clothing; fence construction
PA: Tractor Supply Company
5401 Virginia Way
Brentwood TN 37027
615 440-4000

(G-3466)
TRAINING & EVALUATION CENTE
3000 E Avenue B (67501-1819)
P.O. Box 399 (67504-0399)
PHONE.................................620 663-2216
Aurie Workney, *Manager*
EMP: 45
SALES (corp-wide): 7.3MM **Privately Held**
SIC: 8322 Association for the handicapped
PA: Training And Evaluation Center Of Hutchinson, Inc
10 E 1st Ave
Hutchinson KS 67501
620 663-1596

(G-3467)
TRAINING & EVALUATION CENTE (PA)
Also Called: TECH
10 E 1st Ave (67501-7101)
P.O. Box 399 (67504-0399)
PHONE.................................620 663-1596
Brenda Maxey, *President*
Lacey Mills, *Marketing Staff*
EMP: 46
SQ FT: 37,500
SALES: 7.3MM **Privately Held**
SIC: 8322 Association for the handicapped; child guidance agency

(G-3468)
TRAINING & EVALUATION CENTE
Also Called: Early Education Center
303 E Bigger St (67501-7702)
PHONE.................................620 615-5850
Kaann Graham, *Principal*
EMP: 50
SALES (corp-wide): 7.3MM **Privately Held**
SIC: 8322 8351 Association for the handicapped; child day care services
PA: Training And Evaluation Center Of Hutchinson, Inc
10 E 1st Ave
Hutchinson KS 67501
620 663-1596

(G-3469)
TRESSES HAIR SALON
Also Called: Tresses Family Hair Salon
2901 N Lorraine St Ste B (67502-4276)
PHONE.................................620 662-2299
Richard Campbell, *Owner*
Linda Campbell, *Partner*
EMP: 12
SALES (est): 169.7K **Privately Held**
SIC: 7231 Beauty shops

(G-3470)
TWB INC
Also Called: Highland Golf Country Club
922 Crazy Horse Rd (67502-8957)
PHONE.................................620 663-8396
Fax: 620 663-4234
EMP: 30
SQ FT: 140,000

SALES (est): 1.8MM Privately Held
SIC: 7997 Membership Sport/Recreation Club

(G-3471)
TYSON FOODS INC
521 S Main St (67501-5307)
PHONE..........620 669-8761
Bill Woodward, *Manager*
Casey Cantrell, *Manager*
EMP: 125
SALES (corp-wide): 42.4B Publicly Held
SIC: 2015 Poultry, processed
PA: Tyson Foods, Inc.
2200 W Don Tyson Pkwy
Springdale AR 72762
479 290-4000

(G-3472)
UNDERGROUND VAULTS & STOR INC (PA)
Also Called: Record Center of Wichita
906 N Halstead St (67501-2044)
P.O. Box 1723 (67504-1723)
PHONE..........620 662-6769
David Murfin, *Ch of Bd*
Lee Spence, *President*
Mike Sipe, *Opers Mgr*
Jack Koelling, *Treasurer*
Brad Clifton, *Accounting Mgr*
EMP: 23 EST: 1959
SQ FT: 30,000
SALES (est): 18.8MM Privately Held
WEB: www.undergroundvaults.com
SIC: 4226 Document & office records storage

(G-3473)
UNDERGROUND VAULTS & STOR INC
3500 E Avenue G (67501-8284)
P.O. Box 1723 (67504-1723)
PHONE..........620 663-5434
Jeff Ollenburger, *Vice Pres*
Lee Spence, *Branch Mgr*
EMP: 50
SALES (corp-wide): 18.8MM Privately Held
WEB: www.undergroundvaults.com
SIC: 4226 Document & office records storage
PA: Underground Vaults & Storage, Inc.
906 N Halstead St
Hutchinson KS 67501
620 662-6769

(G-3474)
UNDERGRUND CVERN STBLZTION LLC
7513 S K 14 Hwy (67501-8893)
P.O. Box 225, Great Bend (67530-0225)
PHONE..........620 617-0302
Steve Pangburn, *General Mgr*
EMP: 8
SALES (corp-wide): 790.2K Privately Held
SIC: 2899 Drilling mud
PA: Underground Cavern Stabilization, Llc
1020 Hoover St
Great Bend KS 67530
620 662-6367

(G-3475)
UNION VALLEY PTO
2501 E 30th Ave (67502-1231)
PHONE..........620 662-4891
EMP: 11
SALES: 17.5K Privately Held
SIC: 8641 Parent-teachers' association

(G-3476)
UNITED PARCEL SERVICE INC
Also Called: UPS
2518 E 14th Ave (67501-2119)
PHONE..........620 662-5961
Randy Brooks, *Manager*
EMP: 60
SALES (corp-wide): 71.8B Publicly Held
WEB: www.upsscs.com
SIC: 4215 Parcel delivery, vehicular
HQ: United Parcel Service, Inc.
55 Glenlake Pkwy
Atlanta GA 30328
404 828-6000

(G-3477)
UNITED STATES CSTM HARVESTERS
Also Called: U S Custom Harvester
119 W Sherman St (67501-5431)
P.O. Box 124, Manley NE (68403-0124)
PHONE..........620 664-6297
EMP: 9
SALES: 967.1K Privately Held
SIC: 3523 Mfg Farm Machinery/Equipment

(G-3478)
V & M TRANSPORT INC
Also Called: Groendyke Transport
301 N Kirby St (67501-3133)
P.O. Box 536 (67504-0536)
PHONE..........620 662-7281
John Munds, *President*
EMP: 30
SQ FT: 4,000
SALES (est): 5.7MM Privately Held
SIC: 4213 Liquid petroleum transport, non-local

(G-3479)
VISION GREEN GROUP
1708 E 23rd Ave (67502-1114)
PHONE..........620 663-7187
Susan Wade, *President*
Sandra Jung, *Graphic Designe*
EMP: 20
SQ FT: 5,600
SALES (est): 1.5MM Privately Held
WEB: www.hutcheye.com
SIC: 8011 Ophthalmologist

(G-3480)
WAGGONERS INC
9316 S Halstead St (67501-8346)
P.O. Box 1037 (67504-1037)
PHONE..........620 662-0181
James Waggoner Jr, *President*
Robert Waggoner, *Vice Pres*
Sam Sanders, *Sales Staff*
Paul Waggoner, *Admin Sec*
EMP: 27
SALES: 3.5MM Privately Held
SIC: 2531 Church furniture

(G-3481)
WARREN CONSULTING INC
Also Called: Kingdom Cartridge
2005 N Adams St (67502-2818)
PHONE..........620 727-2468
Chuck Warren, *CEO*
EMP: 20
SALES: 950K Privately Held
SIC: 3999 Manufacturing industries

(G-3482)
WAYNES PRINTING & COPYING
26 S Main St (67501-5422)
PHONE..........620 662-4655
Wayne Strawder, *Owner*
EMP: 5
SQ FT: 3,125
SALES (est): 536.1K Privately Held
WEB: www.waynesprinting.com
SIC: 2752 Commercial printing, offset

(G-3483)
WELLS AIRCRAFT INC
800 Airport Rd (67501-1953)
PHONE..........620 663-1546
Don Rogers, *President*
Keri Cox, *Administration*
EMP: 21
SQ FT: 11,000
SALES (est): 3.4MM Privately Held
WEB: www.wellsac.com
SIC: 4581 Fixed base operator

(G-3484)
WELLS FARGO CLEARING SVCS LLC
Also Called: Wells Fargo Advisors
1 N Main St Ste 402 (67501-5250)
PHONE..........620 665-0659
Roger D Gatton, *Sales/Mktg Mgr*
EMP: 14
SALES (corp-wide): 101B Publicly Held
SIC: 6211 6221 Brokers, security; commodity brokers, contracts
HQ: Wells Fargo Clearing Services, Llc
1 N Jefferson Ave Fl 7
Saint Louis MO 63103
314 955-3000

(G-3485)
WESLEY TOWERS INC
Also Called: HOME HEATH BY WESLEY TOWERS
700 Monterey Pl Ofc (67502-2248)
PHONE..........620 663-9175
Ray Vernon, *CEO*
Cindy Kerschner, *IT/INT Sup*
Hope Jordan, *Director*
Shannon McPike, *Records Dir*
EMP: 260 EST: 1973
SQ FT: 101,700
SALES: 13.4MM Privately Held
WEB: www.wesleytowers.com
SIC: 6513 Retirement hotel operation

(G-3486)
WESTERN SUPPLY CO INC (PA)
2514 E 14th Ave (67501-2119)
P.O. Box 1686 (67504-1686)
PHONE..........620 663-9082
Jack Martin, *President*
Leann Knight, *Opers Dir*
Clint Long, *Store Mgr*
Lora Martin, *Treasurer*
Candace Winkel, *Credit Staff*
EMP: 25
SQ FT: 40,000
SALES (est): 12.1MM Privately Held
WEB: www.proseriespumps.com
SIC: 5075 5074 5083 Warm air heating equipment & supplies; plumbing & hydronic heating supplies; lawn machinery & equipment

(G-3487)
WESTFALL NEWCO LLC
1101 N Halstead St (67501-2138)
PHONE..........844 663-5939
Carol Westfall, *President*
Thomas Westfall, *Vice Pres*
EMP: 25
SQ FT: 20,500
SALES (est): 2.1MM Privately Held
SIC: 5111 Printing & writing paper

(G-3488)
WIENS & COMPANY CONSTRUCTION
219 N Whiteside St (67501-5159)
P.O. Box 490 (67504-0490)
PHONE..........620 665-1155
Sid Wiens, *President*
Troy Holgerson, *Project Mgr*
Tammy Wiens, *Treasurer*
EMP: 25
SQ FT: 15,000
SALES (est): 5.9MM Privately Held
SIC: 1542 Commercial & office building, new construction; commercial & office buildings, renovation & repair

(G-3489)
WIFCO STEEL PRODUCTS INC
8003 Medora Rd (67502-8618)
P.O. Box 1325 (67504-1325)
PHONE..........620 543-2827
Fred Ade, *CEO*
Josh Stubbs, *President*
Peter Atha, *Opers Staff*
Stephanie Domingo, *Controller*
Michelle Winiarski, *Human Resources*
EMP: 87
SQ FT: 75,000
SALES (est): 36.2MM Privately Held
WEB: www.wifcosp.com
SIC: 5051 3599 Steel; machine shop, jobbing & repair

(G-3490)
WILLIAM UNSDERFER MD
Also Called: Medical Center
104 Crescent Blvd (67502-5542)
PHONE..........620 669-6690
William Unsderfer MD, *Partner*
EMP: 20
SALES (est): 1.1MM Privately Held
SIC: 8011 Specialized medical practitioners, except internal

(G-3491)
WOMANS PLACE PA
Also Called: Hentzen, Page Ann MD
1818 E 23rd Ave (67502-1106)
PHONE..........620 662-2229
Lisa Echolls, *Manager*
Karlen Jones, *Administration*
EMP: 10 EST: 1999
SALES (est): 1MM Privately Held
SIC: 8011 Obstetrician

(G-3492)
WOODWORK MFG & SUP INC
403 S Adams St (67501-5373)
P.O. Box 1158 (67504-1158)
PHONE..........620 663-3393
E Jay Schrock, *President*
Connie Schrock, *Admin Sec*
EMP: 33
SQ FT: 91,300
SALES (est): 11.3MM Privately Held
WEB: www.woodworkmfg.com
SIC: 5031 2431 Millwork; moldings, wood: unfinished & prefinished

(G-3493)
WRAY & SONS ROOFING INC
229 E 3rd Ave (67501-6964)
PHONE..........620 663-7107
Jerry Wray, *President*
Greg Wray, *Vice Pres*
Clifford Wray, *Admin Sec*
EMP: 15
SQ FT: 29,000
SALES (est): 1.7MM Privately Held
SIC: 1761 Roofing contractor

(G-3494)
YMCA OF HUTCHINSON RENO CNTY
Also Called: Y M C A
716 E 13th Ave (67501-5896)
PHONE..........620 662-1203
Kirby Lift, *CEO*
EMP: 90
SQ FT: 48,000
SALES: 1.6MM Privately Held
WEB: www.hutchymca.org
SIC: 7997 8641 8351 7991 Swimming club, membership; youth organizations; child day care services; physical fitness facilities

(G-3495)
YODER SMOKERS INC
1816 E Wasp Rd (67501-8714)
PHONE..........620 802-0201
Don Cary, *President*
Joe Phillips, *Vice Pres*
Brent Milleville, *Project Mgr*
Greg Tyler, *Prdtn Mgr*
Jon Potter, *Buyer*
EMP: 100 EST: 2011
SALES: 6MM Privately Held
SIC: 3631 Barbecues, grills & braziers (outdoor cooking)

(G-3496)
ZENOR ELECTRIC COMPANY INC
1203 W 4th Ave (67501-5038)
PHONE..........620 662-4694
Dusty Moore, *President*
Christopher Groves, *Vice Pres*
EMP: 24
SQ FT: 3,000
SALES (est): 1.8MM Privately Held
WEB: www.zenorelectric.com
SIC: 1731 General electrical contractor

Independence
Montgomery County

(G-3497)
APPLE TREE INN
201 N 8th St (67301-3301)
PHONE..........620 331-5500
Jerry Schlegel, *Owner*
EMP: 18
SALES (est): 1MM
SALES (corp-wide): 770K Privately Held
SIC: 7011 Inns

PA: Apple Tree Inn
8325 N Armada Ave
Kansas City MO

(G-3498)
BANK AMERICA NATIONAL ASSN
501 N Penn Ave (67301-3000)
PHONE..................................620 331-4800
Charles W Goad, *Senior VP*
EMP: 32
SALES (corp-wide): 110.5B **Publicly Held**
WEB: www.bofa.com
SIC: 6021 National commercial banks
HQ: Bank Of America, National Association
100 S Tryon St
Charlotte NC 28202
704 386-5681

(G-3499)
BARTON KELLER SAWMILL LLC
2667 W Oak St (67301-8694)
PHONE..................................620 331-8206
Kent Keller, *Mng Member*
Laura Keller,
EMP: 7 **EST:** 1953
SALES: 1.2MM **Privately Held**
SIC: 2421 Lumber: rough, sawed or planed

(G-3500)
BEST BEVERAGE SALES INC
Also Called: Demo Distributors
709 N 20th St (67301-2621)
P.O. Box 924 (67301-0924)
PHONE..................................620 331-7100
Donald C Demo, *President*
Drew Demo, *Vice Pres*
EMP: 12
SQ FT: 16,000
SALES (est): 3.8MM **Privately Held**
WEB: www.bestbev.com
SIC: 5181 Beer & other fermented malt liquors

(G-3501)
BOOTH HOTEL LLC
201 W Main St (67301-3544)
PHONE..................................620 331-1704
Linda Grice,
EMP: 11
SALES (est): 425.5K **Privately Held**
SIC: 7011 Hotels

(G-3502)
CHILD SUPPORT ENFORCEMENT
301 N 8th St (67301-3303)
PHONE..................................620 331-7231
Linda Godbey, *Manager*
EMP: 15
SALES (est): 322.3K **Privately Held**
WEB: www.childsupportenforcement.com
SIC: 8322 Child related social services

(G-3503)
CLASS LTD
2801 W Main St Unit B (67301-8422)
PHONE..................................620 331-8604
Phillip Chappuie, *Director*
EMP: 40
SALES (corp-wide): 9.8MM **Privately Held**
SIC: 8322 Rehabilitation services
PA: Class Ltd
1200 E Merle Evans Dr
Columbus KS 66725
620 429-1212

(G-3504)
COLDWELL BANKER RE CORP
1921 N Penn Ave (67301-2140)
PHONE..................................620 331-2950
Sharon Leeseberg, *Branch Mgr*
EMP: 24 **Publicly Held**
SIC: 6531 Real estate agent, residential
HQ: Coldwell Banker Real Estate Corporation
175 Park Ave
Madison NJ 07940
973 407-2000

(G-3505)
COLDWELL BNKR PSTERNAK JOHNSON
2001 N Penn Ave (67301-2141)
PHONE..................................620 331-5510
Bob Pasternak, *Owner*
Debbie Johnson, *Co-Owner*
Sandra L Rollins, *Associate*
EMP: 12
SALES (est): 798.3K **Privately Held**
WEB: www.cbpj.com
SIC: 6531 Real estate agent, residential

(G-3506)
COMMERCIAL BANK
121 Peter Pan Rd (67301-7307)
PHONE..................................620 423-0750
Lisa Ward, *Manager*
EMP: 13
SALES (corp-wide): 30.2MM **Publicly Held**
SIC: 6022 State trust companies accepting deposits, commercial
HQ: Commercial Bank
1901 Main St
Parsons KS 67357
620 423-0770

(G-3507)
COMMERCIAL METALS COMPANY
Also Called: CMC Recycling
501 S 20th St (67301)
P.O. Box 402 (67301-0402)
PHONE..................................620 331-1710
David Rood, *Safety Mgr*
Brian Wright, *Manager*
EMP: 21
SALES (corp-wide): 5.8B **Publicly Held**
SIC: 4953 Recycling, waste materials
PA: Commercial Metals Company
6565 N Macarthur Blvd # 800
Irving TX 75039
214 689-4300

(G-3508)
CORNERSTONE RGNAL SRVEYING LLC
1921 N Penn Ave (67301-2140)
PHONE..................................620 331-6767
Gary Walker,
William A Booe,
Rick Kemp,
Curtis Lavine,
EMP: 32
SQ FT: 980
SALES (est): 2MM **Privately Held**
WEB: www.cornerstoneregionalsurveying.com
SIC: 8713 Surveying services

(G-3509)
DART CHEROKEE BASIN OPER LLC
211 W Myrtle St (67301-3318)
PHONE..................................620 331-7870
Michael Murphy, *Manager*
EMP: 5
SALES (est): 567.8K **Privately Held**
SIC: 1382 Oil & gas exploration services

(G-3510)
DAVIS CONTRACTING LP
4775 E Us Highway 160 (67301-7533)
P.O. Box 229 (67301-0229)
PHONE..................................620 331-3922
Harley Davis, *Partner*
Tricia Davis, *Partner*
EMP: 30
SALES: 500K **Privately Held**
SIC: 0782 Lawn services

(G-3511)
DAVITA INC
801 W Myrtle St (67301-3239)
PHONE..................................620 331-6117
Marge Beckman, *Principal*
EMP: 27 **Publicly Held**
SIC: 8092 Kidney dialysis centers
PA: Davita Inc.
2000 16th St
Denver CO 80202

(G-3512)
DURHAM SCHOOL SERVICES L P
1125 E Main St (67301-3755)
PHONE..................................620 331-7088
Janelle Johnson, *Manager*
EMP: 20 **Privately Held**
SIC: 4142 4111 4151 Bus charter service, except local; bus transportation; school buses
HQ: Durham School Services, L. P.
2601 Navistar Dr
Lisle IL 60532
630 836-0292

(G-3513)
EAGLE ESTATES INC
1354 Taylor Rd (67301-5400)
PHONE..................................620 331-1662
Ben Chism, *President*
Benjamin Chism, *Vice Pres*
David Chism, *Treasurer*
EMP: 20
SALES (est): 825.3K **Privately Held**
SIC: 8361 Home for the aged

(G-3514)
EARTH CARE PRODUCTS INC
800 N 21st St (67301-8635)
P.O. Box 787 (67301-0787)
PHONE..................................620 331-0090
Andrew Livingston, *President*
Vera Livingston, *Vice Pres*
Bijoy Thomas, *Engineer*
Tom Workman, *Engineer*
Lucas Livingston, *Marketing Mgr*
EMP: 12
SQ FT: 45,000
SALES (est): 2.1MM **Privately Held**
WEB: www.ecpisystems.com
SIC: 3629 Electrochemical generators (fuel cells)

(G-3515)
EPSILON SIGMA ALPHA INTL
3001 Terra Vista Dr (67301-1537)
PHONE..................................620 331-1063
Theresa McVey, *President*
EMP: 24
SALES (est): 212.5K **Privately Held**
SIC: 8641 University club

(G-3516)
EVERGY KANSAS CENTRAL INC
1101 E Main St (67301-3755)
PHONE..................................800 383-1183
Don Hill, *Principal*
EMP: 41
SALES (corp-wide): 4.2B **Publicly Held**
SIC: 4911 Distribution, electric power
HQ: Evergy Kansas Central, Inc.
818 S Kansas Ave
Topeka KS 66612
785 575-6300

(G-3517)
FIRST INDEPENDENCE CORPORATION (HQ)
Also Called: FIRST FEDERAL
112 E Myrtle St (67301-3718)
P.O. Box 947 (67301-0947)
PHONE..................................620 331-1660
Fax: 620 331-1600
EMP: 28
SALES: 6.5MM
SALES (corp-wide): 7.4MM **Privately Held**
SIC: 6035 Federal Savings Institution
PA: First Independence Corporation
112 E Myrtle St
Independence KS 67301
620 331-1660

(G-3518)
FIRST INDEPENDENCE CORPORATION (PA)
112 E Myrtle St (67301-3718)
P.O. Box 947 (67301-0947)
PHONE..................................620 331-1660
EMP: 10
SQ FT: 3,000
SALES (est): 7.4MM **Privately Held**
SIC: 6035 Federal Savings Institution

(G-3519)
FIRSTOAK BANK (PA)
113 N Penn Ave (67301-3523)
P.O. Box 868 (67301-0868)
PHONE..................................620 331-2265
Brad Oakes, *President*
Christy Mavers, *President*
John Thompson, *Exec VP*
Janet Blurton, *Assistant VP*
Debbie Worley, *Assistant VP*
EMP: 12 **EST:** 1881
SALES: 5.5MM **Privately Held**
WEB: www.bankindependence.com
SIC: 6021 National commercial banks

(G-3520)
FOUR CNTY MENTAL HLTH CTR INC (PA)
3751 W Main St (67301-8446)
P.O. Box 688 (67301-0688)
PHONE..................................620 331-1748
Tina Smith, *Vice Pres*
Greg Hennen, *CFO*
Lacie King, *Human Res Dir*
Blair Millemon, *Human Resources*
Michele Jimenez, *Manager*
EMP: 165 **EST:** 1964
SQ FT: 15,000
SALES: 15.9MM **Privately Held**
SIC: 8093 Mental health clinic, outpatient

(G-3521)
FOUR CNTY MENTAL HLTH CTR INC
Also Called: S.E.k Academy
220 E Chestnut St (67301-3132)
PHONE..................................620 331-0057
Mike Alford, *Director*
EMP: 17
SALES (est): 223.8K
SALES (corp-wide): 15.9MM **Privately Held**
SIC: 8093 Mental health clinic, outpatient
PA: Four County Mental Health Center, Inc.
3751 W Main St
Independence KS 67301
620 331-1748

(G-3522)
GANSEL HOUSE LLC
3768 Cr 5250 (67301-7939)
PHONE..................................620 331-7422
Beverly Zemlock, *Owner*
EMP: 10
SALES (est): 246.5K **Privately Held**
SIC: 8361 Geriatric residential care

(G-3523)
GLENWOOD ESTATE INC
621 S 2nd St (67301-4399)
PHONE..................................620 331-2260
Mary Pollock, *President*
EMP: 60
SALES (est): 2.6MM **Privately Held**
WEB: www.glenwoodestate.com
SIC: 6531 8052 Real estate brokers & agents; intermediate care facilities

(G-3524)
GREAT PLAINS FEDERAL CR UN
123 E Main St (67301-3797)
PHONE..................................620 331-4060
Carolyn Jump, *Manager*
EMP: 10
SALES (corp-wide): 7.1MM **Privately Held**
WEB: www.greatplainsfcu.com
SIC: 6061 6062 Federal credit unions; state credit unions
PA: Great Plains Federal Credit Union (Inc)
2306 S Range Line Rd
Joplin MO 64804
417 626-8500

(G-3525)
HEARTLAND CEMENT COMPANY
1765 Limestone Ln (67301-4547)
P.O. Box 428 (67301-0428)
PHONE..................................620 331-0200
Massimo Toso, *CEO*
Nancy Krial, *CFO*
David Howell, *Credit Mgr*
EMP: 10

SALES (est): 1.9MM
SALES (corp-wide): 356.1MM **Privately Held**
SIC: 3241 Masonry cement
HQ: Rc Lonestar Inc.
100 Brodhead Rd Ste 230
Bethlehem PA 18017

(G-3526)
HUGOS INDUSTRIAL SUPPLY INC
Also Called: Hugo's Mini Storage
2700 W Main St (67301-8414)
PHONE..................................620 331-4846
Terry P Hugo, *President*
Corey Hugo, *Owner*
EMP: 23
SQ FT: 3,000
SALES: 18MM **Privately Held**
SIC: 5087 Janitors' supplies

(G-3527)
INDEPENDENCE COUNTRY CLUB
Also Called: Country Club Restaurant
2824 Country Club Cir (67301-1608)
PHONE..................................620 331-1270
Ed Sak, *General Mgr*
Lester Stamps, *Principal*
EMP: 35
SQ FT: 35,000
SALES: 436.8K **Privately Held**
SIC: 7997 Country club, membership; bowling league or team; golf club, membership; swimming club, membership

(G-3528)
INDEPENDENCE MAIN STREET INC
109 E Main St (67301-3709)
P.O. Box 611 (67301-0611)
PHONE..................................620 331-2300
Tom Sewell, *Chairman*
Donna Dittmer, *Director*
EMP: 14
SALES: 117.2K **Privately Held**
SIC: 7999 Festival operation

(G-3529)
INDEPENDENCE READY MIX INC
915 N Penn Ave (67301-2500)
P.O. Box 528 (67301-0528)
PHONE..................................620 331-4150
Raymond H Woods, *President*
Mark Woods, *Treasurer*
Jon Viets, *Admin Sec*
EMP: 6
SQ FT: 19,000
SALES (est): 767.9K **Privately Held**
SIC: 3273 Ready-mixed concrete

(G-3530)
KANSAS AVI INDEPENDENCE LLC
Also Called: Kansas Aviation Independence
401 Freedom Dr (67301-8966)
P.O. Box 684 (67301-0684)
PHONE..................................620 331-7716
Toby Lavine, *President*
Matt Gillman, *Opers Mgr*
Randy Ballew, *Production*
Adam Watts, *Purchasing*
Jason Taylor, *QC Mgr*
EMP: 80
SALES (est): 57.5K
SALES (corp-wide): 697.2MM **Publicly Held**
WEB: www.kansasaviation.com
SIC: 3724 Aircraft engines & engine parts
HQ: Vse Aviation, Inc.
6348 Walker Ln
Alexandria VA 22310
703 328-4600

(G-3531)
KELLY MANUFACTURING COMPANY
55 S Topeka (67301)
PHONE..................................316 265-4271
Justin Kelly, *President*
EMP: 72 **Privately Held**
WEB: www.kellymfg.com
SIC: 3812 Aircraft control instruments
PA: Kelly Manufacturing Company
555 S Topeka Ave
Wichita KS 67202

(G-3532)
LANG BUILDERS LLC
2067 N 21st St (67301-8697)
PHONE..................................620 331-5850
Karl Lang,
EMP: 10
SALES: 750K **Privately Held**
SIC: 1522 Residential construction

(G-3533)
LITTLE HSE ON PRRIE MUSEUM INC
2507 Cr 3000 (67301-7265)
PHONE..................................559 202-8147
Jean Schodorf, *President*
Kristin Schodorf, *Exec Dir*
EMP: 10 **EST:** 2017
SALES: 96.3K **Privately Held**
SIC: 8732 Commercial sociological & educational research

(G-3534)
LOCKNCLIMB LLC
2500 W Laurel St (67301-8781)
PHONE..................................620 331-8247
Tammy Fairbanks, *Controller*
Jeffrey Green, *Branch Mgr*
EMP: 5
SALES (corp-wide): 103.9K **Privately Held**
SIC: 3499 Metal ladders
PA: Lock N Climb, Llc
24206 N 3962 Rd
Bartlesville OK
620 332-4198

(G-3535)
LR ENERGY
211 W Myrtle St (67301-3318)
PHONE..................................620 627-2499
Mike Taylor, *Principal*
EMP: 5
SALES (est): 466.8K **Privately Held**
SIC: 1382 Oil & gas exploration services

(G-3536)
MATSU MANUFACTURING INC
Also Called: Matcor Metal Fabrication
2400 W Laurel (67301)
PHONE..................................620 331-8737
Denise Crisler, *Branch Mgr*
EMP: 150
SALES (corp-wide): 97.2MM **Privately Held**
SIC: 3441 Fabricated structural metal
PA: Matsu Manufacturing Inc
7657 Bramalea Rd
Brampton ON L6T 5
905 291-5000

(G-3537)
MERCY HOSP FDN OF INDEPENDENCE
800 W Myrtle St (67301-3240)
P.O. Box 388 (67301-0388)
PHONE..................................620 331-2200
EMP: 15
SALES (est): 90.1K **Privately Held**
SIC: 8062 General Hospital

(G-3538)
MERCY KANSAS COMMUNITIES INC
422 W Main St (67301-3517)
PHONE..................................620 332-3215
Ronda Howerter, *Director*
Kathy Bennett, *Admin Sec*
EMP: 12
SALES (corp-wide): 6.5B **Privately Held**
WEB: www.mercykansas.com
SIC: 8071 Medical laboratories
HQ: Mercy Kansas Communities, Inc
401 Woodland Hills Blvd
Fort Scott KS 66701
620 223-7075

(G-3539)
MERCY KANSAS COMMUNITIES INC
Also Called: Mercy Hospital
800 W Myrtle St (67301-3240)
P.O. Box 388 (67301-0388)
PHONE..................................620 332-3264
Jerry Stevenson, *CEO*
Sharon Hinds, *Software Dev*
EMP: 300
SQ FT: 140,000
SALES (corp-wide): 6.5B **Privately Held**
WEB: www.mercykansas.com
SIC: 8062 General medical & surgical hospitals
HQ: Mercy Kansas Communities, Inc
401 Woodland Hills Blvd
Fort Scott KS 66701
620 223-7075

(G-3540)
MICROTEL INN & SUITES
2917 W Main St (67301-8439)
PHONE..................................620 331-0088
Don Comstock, *Owner*
EMP: 15
SALES (est): 522.7K **Privately Held**
SIC: 7011 Hotels & motels

(G-3541)
MONTGOMERY COUNTY MEDIA LLC
Also Called: Independence Daily Reporter
320 N 6th St (67301-3129)
PHONE..................................620 331-3550
Josh Umholtz, *Publisher*
Tracy Harder, *Business Mgr*
Nick Theodoran, *Prdtn Mgr*
Scott Wood,
Scott Wesner,
EMP: 30
SALES (est): 487.7K **Privately Held**
SIC: 2711 8748 7311 Newspapers: publishing only, not printed on site; publishing consultant; advertising agencies

(G-3542)
MUNCHKIN VILLAGE
500 S 9th St (67301)
PHONE..................................620 577-2440
EMP: 14
SALES (est): 370K **Privately Held**
SIC: 8351 8299 Child Day Care Services School/Educational Services

(G-3543)
NEWKIRK DENNIS & BUCKLES (PA)
Also Called: Nationwide
304 N Penn Ave (67301-3326)
P.O. Box 547 (67301-0547)
PHONE..................................620 331-3700
Doug Buckles, *President*
Meade T Smith, *Vice Pres*
David B Dennis Jr, *Treasurer*
Debbie Horst, *Agent*
Frank Laforge, *Bd of Directors*
EMP: 15
SQ FT: 4,600
SALES (est): 4.7MM **Privately Held**
WEB: www.ndb-insurance.com
SIC: 6411 Insurance agents

(G-3544)
NOAHS ARKADEMY
2246 S 10th St Unit D (67301-8909)
PHONE..................................620 331-7791
Princha Walls, *Director*
Shera Acuss, *Director*
EMP: 19
SALES (est): 313.1K **Privately Held**
SIC: 8351 Child day care services

(G-3545)
OREILLY AUTOMOTIVE STORES INC
Also Called: O'Reilly Auto Parts
224 W Main St (67301-3513)
PHONE..................................620 331-1018
Jason Simmons, *Manager*
EMP: 10 **Publicly Held**
WEB: www.oreillyauto.com
SIC: 5531 5013 Automotive parts; automotive supplies & parts
HQ: O'reilly Automotive Stores, Inc.
233 S Patterson Ave
Springfield MO 65802
417 862-2674

(G-3546)
ORSCHELN FARM AND HOME LLC
Also Called: Orschenlin Farm & Home 73
2900 W Main St (67301-8438)
PHONE..................................620 331-2551
Rick Wilson, *General Mgr*
EMP: 10
SALES (corp-wide): 822.7MM **Privately Held**
WEB: www.orschelnfarmhome.com
SIC: 5191 5251 5699 Feed; hardware; work clothing
PA: Orscheln Farm And Home Llc
1800 Overcenter Dr
Moberly MO 65270
800 577-2580

(G-3547)
PRECISION AVIATION CONTROLS
Also Called: A C I
101 Freedom Dr (67301-8962)
PHONE..................................620 331-8180
Jim Robertson, *President*
Iain Glendinning, *Treasurer*
Eddie Mason, *Controller*
June Portillo, *Asst Controller*
EMP: 65 **EST:** 2010
SQ FT: 26,000
SALES (est): 8MM
SALES (corp-wide): 33.5MM **Privately Held**
SIC: 3728 Aircraft parts & equipment
HQ: Pag Holding Corp.
495 Lake Mirror Rd Bldg 8
Atlanta GA 30349
404 768-9090

(G-3548)
PRECISION RAILWAY EQP CO LLC (PA)
825 S 19th St (67301-4124)
P.O. Box 1015 (67301-1015)
PHONE..................................817 737-5885
Scott Taylor, *President*
Harry Smith, *Vice Pres*
EMP: 15
SALES (est): 3MM **Privately Held**
SIC: 3621 Railway motors & control equipment, electric

(G-3549)
PRO CARPET BUILDING SVCS LLC
Also Called: Pro Carpet Plus
919 W Oak St (67301-2342)
P.O. Box 503 (67301-0503)
PHONE..................................620 331-4304
Ronnie K Ward,
Carolyn Ward,
Ron Ward,
EMP: 35
SQ FT: 8,000
SALES (est): 2.2MM **Privately Held**
WEB: www.procarpetplus.com
SIC: 7217 Carpet & upholstery cleaning

(G-3550)
REAL ESTATE CTR INDPNDENCE LLC
533 N Penn Ave (67301-3013)
PHONE..................................620 331-7550
Clayton Farlow, *President*
Clara Farlow, *Vice Pres*
EMP: 14
SALES (est): 750K **Privately Held**
SIC: 6531 Real estate brokers & agents

(G-3551)
REDBUD E&P INC
211 W Myrtle St (67301-3318)
PHONE..................................620 331-7870
Tom Kaetzer, *Vice Pres*
EMP: 25 **Privately Held**
SIC: 1382 Oil & gas exploration services
PA: Redbud E&P Inc.
16000 Stuebner Airline Rd # 320
Spring TX 77379

(G-3552)
REGAL ESTATE
1000 Mulberry St (67301-2026)
P.O. Box 627 (67301-0627)
PHONE.................................305 751-4257
Maryann Pollock, *Owner*
EMP: 50
SALES (est): 996K **Privately Held**
WEB: www.regalestate.com
SIC: 8052 Intermediate care facilities

(G-3553)
REMEDIATION SERVICES INC
Also Called: R S I
2735 S 10th St (67301-8954)
P.O. Box 587 (67301-0587)
PHONE.................................800 335-1201
Grant V Sherwood, *President*
John Gillman, *Vice Pres*
John R Gilman, *Vice Pres*
Wayne Holum, *Vice Pres*
Jack Denton, *Project Mgr*
EMP: 35
SQ FT: 4,500
SALES: 10.6MM **Privately Held**
WEB: www.bairsglass.com
SIC: 8744 1799 ; asbestos removal & encapsulation

(G-3554)
RENAL TRTMNT CENTERS-WEST INC
Also Called: Independence Dialysis Center
801 W Myrtle St (67301-3239)
PHONE.................................620 331-6117
James K Hilger,
EMP: 11 **Publicly Held**
WEB: www.davita.com
SIC: 8092 Kidney dialysis centers
HQ: Renal Treatment Centers-West, Inc.
2000 16th St
Denver CO 80202

(G-3555)
RESTORE IT SYSTEMS LLC (PA)
Also Called: Steam Way Restorations
1817 W Main St (67301-8407)
PHONE.................................620 331-3997
Linda Kirchoff, *Bookkeeper*
Douglas C Knapp,
Angela Knapp,
EMP: 14
SQ FT: 5,000
SALES (est): 454.3K **Privately Held**
SIC: 7349 Cleaning service, industrial or commercial

(G-3556)
ROMANS OUTDOOR POWER INC (PA)
Also Called: Kubota Authorized Dealer
3011 W Main St (67301-8495)
PHONE.................................620 331-2970
Randall Romans, *President*
EMP: 10
SALES (est): 6.6MM **Privately Held**
SIC: 5261 5083 Lawnmowers & tractors; farm & garden machinery

(G-3557)
SCA CONSTRUCTION INC
2500 W Laurel St (67301-8781)
P.O. Box 347 (67301-0347)
PHONE.................................620 331-8247
Jeffery Green, *President*
Rick Meigs, *Vice Pres*
EMP: 45
SQ FT: 4,000
SALES (est): 7.3MM **Privately Held**
SIC: 1542 Commercial & office building, new construction

(G-3558)
SEKTAM OF INDEPENDENCE INC
120 S 24th St (67301-8752)
PHONE.................................620 331-5480
Chris Moore, *President*
Curtis A Rexwinkle, *Vice Pres*
Brian Jabben, *Engineer*
Jeane Rexwinkle, *Treasurer*
Chrity Holmes, *Manager*
EMP: 12
SQ FT: 8,000
SALES: 2MM **Privately Held**
WEB: www.sektam-indy.com
SIC: 3544 3599 Industrial molds; machine shop, jobbing & repair

(G-3559)
SHARPER IMAGES COMPANY LLC
3345 W Main St (67301-8400)
PHONE.................................620 331-7646
Brian Yakshaw,
EMP: 12 **EST:** 1997
SALES (est): 1.3MM **Privately Held**
SIC: 1541 Renovation, remodeling & repairs: industrial buildings

(G-3560)
SHEPHERDS TRUCK & TRACTOR
3720 W Main St (67301-8441)
PHONE.................................620 331-2970
Randy Shepherd, *President*
Brian Shepherd, *Treasurer*
EMP: 12
SQ FT: 13,650
SALES (est): 2.1MM **Privately Held**
SIC: 5083 7699 Farm implements; tractor repair

(G-3561)
SOUTHEAST KANSAS LUTHERANS INC
Also Called: Penn Manor Apartments
601 S Penn Ave (67301-4200)
P.O. Box 355 (67301-0355)
PHONE.................................620 331-8010
Christy Dunan, *Manager*
Karla Clubine, *Manager*
EMP: 18
SALES: 397K **Privately Held**
SIC: 6513 Apartment building operators

(G-3562)
STANDARD MOTOR PRODUCTS INC
1300 W Oak St (67301-2347)
P.O. Box 788 (67301-0788)
PHONE.................................620 331-1000
Dave Peters, *Engineer*
Chris Romine, *Engineer*
Todd Taylor, *Plant Engr*
Mike Lewis, *Project Engr*
Tom Latimer, *Branch Mgr*
EMP: 400
SALES (corp-wide): 1B **Publicly Held**
WEB: www.smpcorp.com
SIC: 3559 3613 3714 Automotive maintenance equipment; switchboards & parts, power; motor vehicle parts & accessories
PA: Standard Motor Products, Inc.
3718 Northern Blvd # 600
Long Island City NY 11101
718 392-0200

(G-3563)
STEAM WAY CARPET RESTORATIONS (PA)
1817 W Main St (67301-8407)
PHONE.................................620 331-9553
Jerry Stover, *President*
EMP: 11
SALES (est): 265.5K **Privately Held**
SIC: 7217 7349 Carpet & furniture cleaning on location; air duct cleaning

(G-3564)
TEXTRON AVIATION INC
1 Cessna Blvd (67301-9060)
P.O. Box 1996 (67301-1996)
PHONE.................................620 332-0228
Terry Clark, *Manager*
EMP: 144
SALES (corp-wide): 13.9B **Publicly Held**
WEB: www.cessna.com
SIC: 3721 5088 Airplanes, fixed or rotary wing; transportation equipment & supplies
HQ: Textron Aviation Inc.
1 Cessna Blvd
Wichita KS 67215
316 517-6000

(G-3565)
TIMOTHY D WHITE
Also Called: Bill White Realty Co
411 N Penn Ave (67301-3011)
P.O. Box 703 (67301-0703)
PHONE.................................620 331-7060
Timothy D White, *Owner*
EMP: 12
SQ FT: 2,500
SALES (est): 478.7K **Privately Held**
WEB: www.billwhiterealty.com
SIC: 6531 6512 6514 Real estate brokers & agents; shopping center, property operation only; dwelling operators, except apartments

(G-3566)
TRANSWOOD INC
Also Called: Transwood Inc Mechanic
4158 County Rd 4200 (67301)
PHONE.................................620 331-5924
Fax: 620 331-5758
EMP: 30
SALES (corp-wide): 150MM **Privately Held**
SIC: 7538 General Auto Repair
HQ: Transwood, Inc.
2565 Saint Marys Ave
Omaha NE 68105
402 346-8092

(G-3567)
TRANSWOOD INC
810 Cement St (67301-4400)
P.O. Box 8625 MO (64054-0625)
PHONE.................................620 331-5699
EMP: 23
SALES (corp-wide): 150MM **Privately Held**
SIC: 4212 Local Trucking Operator
HQ: Transwood, Inc.
2565 Saint Marys Ave
Omaha NE 68105
402 346-8092

(G-3568)
TRANSYSTEMS CORPORATION
115 S 6th St Ste B (67301-3707)
PHONE.................................620 331-3999
Shawn Turner, *Branch Mgr*
EMP: 20
SALES (corp-wide): 174.5MM **Privately Held**
SIC: 8711 Consulting engineer
PA: Transystems Corporation
2400 Pershing Rd Ste 400
Kansas City MO 64108
816 329-8700

(G-3569)
TRI STAR UTILITIES INC
2109 W Maple St (67301-8426)
P.O. Box 903 (67301-0903)
PHONE.................................620 331-7159
Ben Chism, *President*
EMP: 10
SALES (est): 1.5MM **Privately Held**
SIC: 1623 Underground utilities contractor

(G-3570)
V & R MOTEL LLC
Also Called: Super 8 Motel
2800 W Main St (67301-8421)
PHONE.................................620 331-8288
Tom Van Stavern, *Principal*
B D Van Stavern,
EMP: 15
SALES (est): 649.4K **Privately Held**
SIC: 7011 Hotels & motels

(G-3571)
VT HACKNEY INC
Also Called: Hackney & Sons
300 N Hackney Ave (67301-8896)
P.O. Box 608 (67301-0608)
PHONE.................................620 331-6600
Kevin Sears, *Branch Mgr*
EMP: 125
SALES (corp-wide): 4.9B **Privately Held**
WEB: www.rescueleader.com
SIC: 3713 3715 Truck bodies (motor vehicles); truck trailers
HQ: Vt Hackney, Inc.
911 W 5th St
Washington NC 27889
252 946-6521

(G-3572)
WERNER PIPE SERVICE INC
Also Called: Seal Tite Div
4307 E Us Highway 160 (67301-7557)
P.O. Box 965 (67301-0965)
PHONE.................................620 331-7384
John Werner, *President*
Terry Werner, *Vice Pres*
Robert Werner, *Treasurer*
EMP: 15
SQ FT: 3,000
SALES (est): 2.2MM **Privately Held**
SIC: 3084 1389 3317 3312 Plastics pipe; pipe testing, oil field service; steel pipe & tubes; blast furnaces & steel mills

(G-3573)
WINDSOR PLACE AT-HOME CARE
201 N Penn Ave Ste 104 (67301-3357)
PHONE.................................620 331-3388
Toll Free:...866 -
Sonia Larimore, *Principal*
EMP: 30
SALES (est): 332.4K **Privately Held**
SIC: 8051 Skilled nursing care facilities

(G-3574)
WOODICH JOHN
Also Called: Mercy Hospital
800 W Laurel St (67301-3211)
P.O. Box 845 (67301-0845)
PHONE.................................620 332-3280
John Woodich, *CEO*
Rita Taylor, *Office Mgr*
EMP: 45
SALES (est): 2.7MM **Privately Held**
SIC: 8011 8062 Offices & clinics of medical doctors; general medical & surgical hospitals

(G-3575)
Y & M BUSINESS SERVICES LLC
208 E Laurel St (67301-3137)
P.O. Box 707 (67301-0707)
PHONE.................................620 331-4600
Dan Carroll, *Partner*
EMP: 10
SALES (est): 262.4K **Privately Held**
SIC: 7291 Tax return preparation services

Ingalls
Gray County

(G-3576)
INGALLS FEED YARD
10505 Us Highway 50 (67853-9202)
PHONE.................................620 335-5174
John Petz, *CEO*
EMP: 25 **EST:** 1961
SALES (est): 1.9MM **Privately Held**
SIC: 0211 Beef cattle feedlots

(G-3577)
IRSIK FAMILY PARTNERSHIP
5405 6 Rd (67853-9044)
PHONE.................................620 335-5363
EMP: 12 **EST:** 2009
SALES: 450K **Privately Held**
SIC: 0291 General Animal Farm

(G-3578)
J MARQUEZ TRUCKING
13909 M Rd (67853-9121)
P.O. Box 96 (67853-0096)
PHONE.................................620 335-5872
EMP: 12 **EST:** 2005
SALES: 100K **Privately Held**
SIC: 4213 Trucking Operator-Nonlocal

(G-3579)
MIDWEST FEEDERS INC
5013 13 Rd (67853-9023)
PHONE.................................620 335-5790
Jeffrey Sternberger, *President*
Robert Baker, *Shareholder*
Lee Brandt, *Shareholder*
Charles Lemaster, *Shareholder*
David Lemaster, *Shareholder*
EMP: 41
SALES (est): 3.8MM **Privately Held**
WEB: www.midwest-feeders.com
SIC: 0212 Beef cattle except feedlots

(G-3580)
STEPHEN JR & KAY IRSIK
5405 6 Rd (67853-9044)
PHONE..................................620 335-5363
EMP: 10 **EST:** 1972
SALES (est): 540K **Privately Held**
SIC: 0191 General Crop Farm

Inman
Mcpherson County

(G-3581)
FAB WORKS LLC
800 E Center St (67546-8027)
PHONE..................................620 585-2626
Jim Pacey, *President*
EMP: 7
SALES (est): 1.1MM **Privately Held**
SIC: 3441 Fabricated structural metal

(G-3582)
FUQUA CONSTRUCTION INC
118 S Main St (67546-9776)
P.O. Box 335 (67546-0335)
PHONE..................................620 585-2270
Max Fuqua, *President*
Ric Ratzlaff, *Superintendent*
Sandra Fuqua, *Contractor*
EMP: 10
SQ FT: 1,500
SALES: 3.5MM **Privately Held**
WEB: www.fuquabuilds.com
SIC: 1542 1521 Religious building construction; commercial & office building, new construction; general remodeling, single-family houses

(G-3583)
PENNER FEED & SUPPLY INC
778 Cherokee Rd (67546-8694)
P.O. Box 509 (67546-0509)
PHONE..................................620 585-6612
Fax: 620 585-6570
EMP: 17
SQ FT: 12,000
SALES (est): 1.2MM **Privately Held**
SIC: 4213 Over-The-Road Trucking

(G-3584)
PEOPLES BANK & TRUST CO
215 S Main St (67546-4611)
PHONE..................................620 585-2265
Bob Ratzlaff, *Manager*
EMP: 40
SALES (corp-wide): 22.1MM **Privately Held**
WEB: www.peoplesbankonline.com
SIC: 6021 National commercial banks
PA: Peoples Bank & Trust Co (Inc)
101 S Main St
Mcpherson KS 67460
620 241-2100

Iola
Allen County

(G-3585)
ADVANTAGE COMPUTER ENTPS INC
1000 W Miller Rd (66749-4003)
P.O. Box 385 (66749-0385)
PHONE..................................620 365-5156
Cheri D Clark, *President*
Kim Colgin, *CIO*
Danny Mattheis, *Technology*
Lynette Prasko, *Exec Dir*
EMP: 24
SQ FT: 9,000
SALES (est): 3.7MM **Privately Held**
WEB: www.jayhawksoftware.com
SIC: 7373 7371 Computer integrated systems design; custom computer programming services

(G-3586)
ALLEN COUNTY LODGING LLC
Also Called: Super 8 Motel
200 Bills Way (66749-3926)
PHONE..................................620 365-3030
Angela Robertson, *Manager*
EMP: 15
SALES (est): 506.1K **Privately Held**
SIC: 7011 Hotels & motels

(G-3587)
ANIXTER INC
502 N State St (66749-2202)
P.O. Box 137, Gas (66742-0137)
PHONE..................................620 365-7161
Timothy Hein, *Branch Mgr*
EMP: 12
SALES (corp-wide): 8.4B **Publicly Held**
SIC: 5063 Electrical apparatus & equipment
HQ: Anixter Inc.
2301 Patriot Blvd
Glenview IL 60026
800 323-8167

(G-3588)
BORENS ROOFING INC
306 N State St (66749-2306)
PHONE..................................620 365-7663
Ronald E Boren, *President*
Katheryn Boren, *Corp Secy*
EMP: 14 **EST:** 1954
SALES (est): 1.6MM **Privately Held**
SIC: 1761 Roofing contractor

(G-3589)
CASA OF THE THIRTY-FIRST JUDIC
1 N Washington Ave (66749-2802)
PHONE..................................620 365-1448
Cynthia Jacobson, *President*
EMP: 22
SALES: 116.4K **Privately Held**
SIC: 7389 8699 Fund raising organizations; charitable organization

(G-3590)
CATALYST ARTIFICIAL LIFT LLC (PA)
2702 N State St (66749-9403)
PHONE..................................620 365-7150
Josh Maier, *Manager*
Matthew Jendusa, *Manager*
EMP: 21
SALES (est): 4.5MM **Privately Held**
SIC: 7389 Crane & aerial lift service

(G-3591)
CENTRAL PUBLISHING CO INC
1811 East St (66749-3049)
P.O. Box 806 (66749-0806)
PHONE..................................620 365-2106
Harvey Collins, *President*
Harvey W Collins, *President*
Lillie M Collins, *President*
Linda Bass, *Corp Secy*
EMP: 8 **EST:** 1971
SQ FT: 5,000
SALES: 343.8K **Privately Held**
SIC: 2741 Directories: publishing only, not printed on site; maps: publishing only, not printed on site

(G-3592)
CHINA PALACE
110 N State St (66749-2818)
PHONE..................................620 365-3723
Paul Cheung, *Partner*
Sharon Cheung, *Partner*
P Poon, *Partner*
P N Soong, *Partner*
EMP: 10
SALES (est): 405.1K **Privately Held**
SIC: 5812 7299 Chinese restaurant; banquet hall facilities

(G-3593)
CITY OF IOLA
2 W Jackson Ave (66749-2832)
P.O. Box 308 (66749-0308)
PHONE..................................620 365-4900
Judith Brigham, *Administration*
Rhonda Fulton, *Admin Asst*
EMP: 110
SALES (est): 1.3MM **Privately Held**
SIC: 4939 Combination utilities
PA: City Of Iola
2 W Jackson Ave
Iola KS 66749
620 365-4910

(G-3594)
COLUMBIA METAL PRODUCTS CO
600 S State Fairgrnd & Ri (66749)
P.O. Box 507 (66749-0507)
PHONE..................................620 365-3166
Harlan Cleaver, *Manager*
EMP: 25
SALES (corp-wide): 3.9MM **Privately Held**
SIC: 3442 Storm doors or windows, metal
PA: Columbia Metal Products Company
1600 N Jackson Ave
Kansas City MO
816 241-5800

(G-3595)
COMMUNITY NATIONAL BANK & TR
Also Called: Iola Madison Banking Center
120 E Madison Ave (66749-3331)
P.O. Box 447 (66749-0447)
PHONE..................................620 365-6000
Ken Gilpin, *Manager*
EMP: 14 **Privately Held**
SIC: 6021 National commercial banks
HQ: Community National Bank & Trust
14 N Lincoln Ave
Chanute KS 66720

(G-3596)
COPY PRODUCTS INC
207 S Jefferson Ave (66749-2939)
PHONE..................................620 365-7611
Gloria Williams, *Accounts Mgr*
Mark Henry, *Manager*
EMP: 60
SALES (corp-wide): 21MM **Privately Held**
WEB: www.copyproductsinc.com
SIC: 5044 5045 5999 Photocopy machines; typewriters; computers; photocopy machines
PA: Copy Products, Inc.
2103 W Vista St
Springfield MO 65807
417 889-5665

(G-3597)
COUNTY OF ALLEN
Also Called: Alan County Magistrate
1 N Washington Ave Rm B (66749-2841)
PHONE..................................620 365-1425
Jennifer Barrow, *Manager*
EMP: 21 **Privately Held**
WEB: www.districtcourt.com
SIC: 8111 Legal services
PA: County Of Allen
410 N State St
Iola KS

(G-3598)
DIEBOLT LLC
Also Called: Do It Best
214 Sunflower Ln (66749-9041)
PHONE..................................620 496-2222
Don D Diebolt, *President*
Susan Diebolt, *Admin Sec*
▲ **EMP:** 25 **EST:** 1951
SQ FT: 10,000
SALES: 6.7MM **Privately Held**
WEB: www.dieboltlumber.com
SIC: 5251 5031 Hardware; lumber, plywood & millwork

(G-3599)
FAMILY PHYSICIANS MGT CORP
1408 East St Ste A (66749-4403)
P.O. Box 514 (66749-0514)
PHONE..................................620 365-3115
Glen Singer, *President*
Brian Wolfe, *Corp Secy*
Patty Haen, *Bookkeeper*
Charles Woodall, *Director*
EMP: 17
SQ FT: 3,600
SALES (est): 2.4MM **Privately Held**
WEB: www.dr.kscoxmail.com
SIC: 8011 Clinic, operated by physicians

(G-3600)
FEUERBORN FMLY FNRL SVC
Also Called: Waugh-Yokum & Friskel Memorial
1883 Us Highway 54 (66749-3059)
PHONE..................................620 365-2948
Paul Friskel, *President*
EMP: 10
SALES (est): 393.7K **Privately Held**
SIC: 7261 Funeral director

(G-3601)
FIREMANS RELIEF ASSOC INC
408 N Washington Ave (66749-2353)
PHONE..................................620 365-4972
Ronald Jenkins, *President*
Tim Thyer, *Vice Pres*
EMP: 16
SALES (est): 266.6K **Privately Held**
SIC: 8621 Professional membership organizations

(G-3602)
FOUNTAIN VILLA INC
2620 N Kentucky St (66749-1940)
PHONE..................................620 365-6002
Della Monsour, *CEO*
Anthony Monsour, *Principal*
Joe Monsour, *Administration*
EMP: 12
SALES: 500K **Privately Held**
SIC: 8361 Home for the aged

(G-3603)
GATES CORPORATION
1450 Montana Rd (66749-3995)
P.O. Box 606 (66749-0606)
PHONE..................................620 365-4100
Scott Day, *COO*
Jordan Rhi, *Administration*
Joshua Powell, *Technician*
EMP: 540
SALES (corp-wide): 3.3B **Publicly Held**
WEB: www.gates.com
SIC: 5085 Industrial supplies
HQ: The Gates Corporation
1144 15th St Ste 1400
Denver CO 80202
303 744-1911

(G-3604)
GENERAL REPAIR & SUPPLY INC
1008 N Industrial Rd (66749-2270)
P.O. Box 703 (66749-0703)
PHONE..................................620 365-5954
Rick Robb, *President*
Becky Robb, *Treasurer*
Es Robb, *Director*
EMP: 8 **EST:** 1891
SQ FT: 5,000
SALES: 300K **Privately Held**
WEB: www.generalrepairandsupply.com
SIC: 7692 3599 3444 Welding repair; machine shop, jobbing & repair; sheet metalwork

(G-3605)
GREAT SOUTHERN BANK
119 E Madison Ave (66749-3330)
P.O. Box 650 (66749-0650)
PHONE..................................620 365-3101
Billy Ohmie, *Branch Mgr*
EMP: 14
SALES (corp-wide): 242.1MM **Publicly Held**
SIC: 6022 State commercial banks
HQ: Great Southern Bank
1451 E Battlefield St
Springfield MO 65804
417 887-4400

(G-3606)
HALDEX BRAKE PRODUCTS CORP
2702 N State St (66749-9403)
PHONE..................................620 365-5275
EMP: 97
SALES (corp-wide): 582.4MM **Privately Held**
SIC: 3714 Mfg Motor Vehicle Parts/Accessories

HQ: Haldex Brake Products Corporation
10930 N Pomona Ave
Kansas City MO 64153
816 891-2470

(G-3607)
HCA HOLDINGS INC
826 E Madison Ave (66749-3555)
PHONE..................................620 365-1330
Songyoth Sakdisri, *Branch Mgr*
EMP: 100 **Publicly Held**
SIC: 8011 Obstetrician
HQ: Hca Inc.
1 Park Plz
Nashville TN 37203
615 344-9551

(G-3608)
HCA INC
Also Called: Allen County Hospital
3066 N Kentucky St (66749-1951)
P.O. Box 540 (66749-0540)
PHONE..................................620 365-1000
Paula Sell, *Human Res Dir*
Steve Hoelscher, *Branch Mgr*
Tina Spenser, *Manager*
Tina Spencer, *Info Tech Dir*
Judy Highberger, *Director*
EMP: 151
SQ FT: 30,000 **Publicly Held**
SIC: 8062 General medical & surgical hospitals
HQ: Hca Inc.
1 Park Plz
Nashville TN 37203
615 344-9551

(G-3609)
IOLA BROADCASTING INC
Also Called: Radio Station Kiks-AM
2221 S State St (66749-3083)
P.O. Box 710 (66749-0710)
PHONE..................................620 365-3151
Michael P Russell, *President*
Mike Russell, *General Mgr*
Lovetta R Russell, *Vice Pres*
EMP: 11
SQ FT: 2,500
SALES (est): 530.7K **Privately Held**
WEB: www.iolaradio.com
SIC: 4832 Radio broadcasting stations

(G-3610)
IOLA PRE SCHL FOR EXCPTNL CHLD
Also Called: Special Ed Coop
819 Kansas Dr (66749-2730)
PHONE..................................620 365-6730
EMP: 10
SALES (est): 160.3K **Privately Held**
SIC: 8351 Child Day Care Services

(G-3611)
IOLA REGISTER INC
302 S Washington Ave (66749-3255)
P.O. Box 767 (66749-0767)
PHONE..................................620 365-2111
Susan Lynn, *President*
EMP: 24 **EST:** 1939
SQ FT: 7,500
SALES (est): 1.7MM **Privately Held**
WEB: www.iolaregister.com
SIC: 2711 2759 2752 Newspapers, publishing & printing; commercial printing; commercial printing, lithographic

(G-3612)
IRRIGATION & TURF EQUIPMENT
2725 N State St (66749-9403)
P.O. Box 43 (66749-0043)
PHONE..................................620 365-2121
Kevin Pargman, *President*
EMP: 6
SQ FT: 10,000
SALES (est): 2MM **Privately Held**
SIC: 3523 Turf equipment, commercial; fertilizing machinery, farm

(G-3613)
J & J CONTRACTORS INC (PA)
1646 1600th St (66749)
P.O. Box 646 (66749-0646)
PHONE..................................620 365-5500
Jacqualin K Jensen, *President*
EMP: 10
SQ FT: 1,200
SALES (est): 3.5MM **Privately Held**
SIC: 1622 1611 Bridge construction; guardrail construction, highways

(G-3614)
J & W EQUIPMENT INC
2795 N State St (66749-9403)
P.O. Box 531 (66749-0531)
PHONE..................................620 365-2341
Gary W Witherspoon, *President*
Gerald H Jacobs, *Corp Secy*
EMP: 12
SQ FT: 14,000
SALES: 1.8MM **Privately Held**
WEB: www.jwequipment.com
SIC: 5083 5261 Farm implements; farm equipment parts & supplies; lawn & garden equipment

(G-3615)
JAYHAWK SOFTWARE
1000 W Miller Rd (66749-4003)
P.O. Box 385 (66749-0385)
PHONE..................................620 365-8065
Sheri Clark, *Owner*
Steve Prasko, *Co-Owner*
EMP: 5
SALES (est): 219K **Privately Held**
SIC: 7372 Business oriented computer software

(G-3616)
JMZ CORPORATION
Also Called: Kwikom Communications
800 W Miller Rd (66749-1604)
PHONE..................................620 365-7782
John V Vogel, *President*
Zachery Peres, *Vice Pres*
Dorothy Hass, *Treasurer*
John Vogel, *Manager*
Michael Peres, *Shareholder*
EMP: 21
SQ FT: 14,000
SALES: 750K **Privately Held**
SIC: 4899 Data communication services

(G-3617)
KIWANIS INTERNATIONAL INC
Also Called: Kiwanis Club of Iola
P.O. Box 503 (66749-0503)
PHONE..................................620 365-3925
Larry Nelson, *Branch Mgr*
EMP: 14
SALES (corp-wide): 23.6MM **Privately Held**
WEB: www.kfne.org
SIC: 8641 Civic associations
PA: Kiwanis International, Inc.
3636 Woodview Trce
Indianapolis IN 46268
317 875-8755

(G-3618)
KNEISLEY MANUFACTURING COMPANY
900 W Miller Rd (66749-1730)
PHONE..................................620 365-6628
Robert Bagby, *President*
Michael Hagan, *Vice Pres*
Eric Olson, *Vice Pres*
Bridgette Bagby, *Admin Sec*
EMP: 11
SALES: 500K **Privately Held**
WEB: www.sonicequipment.com
SIC: 5049 3677 Theatrical equipment & supplies; electronic coils, transformers & other inductors

(G-3619)
M & W MFG INC
129 N Kentucky St (66749-2525)
P.O. Box 861 (66749-0861)
PHONE..................................620 365-7456
Neil Westervelt, *President*
Joy Westervelt, *Corp Secy*
EMP: 17
SQ FT: 9,600
SALES (est): 2.7MM **Privately Held**
WEB: www.readybrake.com
SIC: 3599 Machine shop, jobbing & repair

(G-3620)
NSA RV PRODUCTS INC
445 W Lincoln Rd (66749-2263)
P.O. Box 861 (66749-0861)
PHONE..................................620 365-7714
Tod Westervelt, *President*
Stacey Westervelt, *Admin Sec*
▲ **EMP:** 5
SALES (est): 731.4K **Privately Held**
SIC: 3599 Machine shop, jobbing & repair

(G-3621)
ORSCHELN FARM AND HOME LLC
1918 N State St (66749-1639)
PHONE..................................620 365-7695
Jason Daughtery, *Manager*
EMP: 10
SALES (corp-wide): 822.7MM **Privately Held**
WEB: www.orschelnfarmhome.com
SIC: 5191 Farm supplies
PA: Orscheln Farm And Home Llc
1800 Overcenter Dr
Moberly MO 65270
800 577-2580

(G-3622)
PAYLESS CONCRETE PRODUCTS INC
802 N Industrial Rd (66749-2225)
P.O. Box 664 (66749-0664)
PHONE..................................620 365-5588
George B Rose, *President*
Audra Rose, *Vice Pres*
EMP: 10
SALES (est): 1.5MM **Privately Held**
SIC: 3273 Ready-mixed concrete

(G-3623)
PLAINS MARKETING LP
Old Hwy 169 (66749)
P.O. Box 537 (66749-0537)
PHONE..................................620 365-3208
Scott Muller, *Manager*
EMP: 12 **Publicly Held**
WEB: www.plainsmarketing.com
SIC: 4612 Crude petroleum pipelines
HQ: Plains Marketing, L.P.
333 Clay St Ste 1600
Houston TX 77002
713 646-4100

(G-3624)
PLAINS MARKETING LP
1170 Mississippi Rd (66749)
P.O. Box 537 (66749-0537)
PHONE..................................620 365-3208
Scott Mueller, *Manager*
EMP: 11 **Publicly Held**
WEB: www.plainsmarketing.com
SIC: 5172 Petroleum products
HQ: Plains Marketing, L.P.
333 Clay St Ste 1600
Houston TX 77002
713 646-4100

(G-3625)
PRECISION INTERNATIONAL
25 W Miller Rd (66749-1655)
P.O. Box 607 (66749-0607)
PHONE..................................620 365-7255
Mark Burris, *President*
◆ **EMP:** 57
SQ FT: 32,000
SALES (est): 23.1MM **Privately Held**
WEB: www.precisiondhpumps.com
SIC: 3533 Oil field machinery & equipment

(G-3626)
PREFERED MEDICAL ASSOCIATES
Also Called: Family Med Center
401 S Washington Ave (66749-3256)
P.O. Box 868 (66749-0868)
PHONE..................................620 365-6933
Fax: 620 365-8126
EMP: 20
SALES (est): 1.1MM **Privately Held**
SIC: 8011 Medical Doctor's Office

(G-3627)
PRICE TRUCK LINE INC
1421 S Washington Ave (66749-4311)
PHONE..................................620 365-6626
James McPoland, *Manager*
EMP: 10
SALES (est): 554.5K
SALES (corp-wide): 27MM **Privately Held**
SIC: 4213 Contract haulers
PA: Price Truck Line, Inc.
4931 S Victoria St
Wichita KS 67216
316 945-6915

(G-3628)
QUALITY CONNECTIONZ INC
449 W Lincoln Rd (66749)
PHONE..................................620 380-6262
John Westervelt, *President*
EMP: 8
SALES (est): 1MM **Privately Held**
SIC: 3533 Oil & gas field machinery

(G-3629)
R & S PIPE SUPPLY
503 W Lincoln Rd (66749-1805)
PHONE..................................620 365-8114
EMP: 6
SALES: 250K **Privately Held**
SIC: 1311 Oilfield Pipe Manufacturer

(G-3630)
R E B INC
Also Called: Sonic Equipment Co
900 W Miller Rd (66749-1730)
PHONE..................................620 365-5701
Bob Bagby, *President*
Paige Olson, *Purchasing*
▲ **EMP:** 25
SALES (est): 6.4MM **Privately Held**
SIC: 5043 Motion picture studio & theater equipment

(G-3631)
RVB TRUCKING INC
28 Davis St (66749-3103)
P.O. Box 613 (66749-0613)
PHONE..................................620 365-6823
Dennis Ringwald, *President*
Mary E Ringwald, *Corp Secy*
EMP: 50
SQ FT: 3,000
SALES (est): 5.8MM **Privately Held**
SIC: 4213 Contract haulers

(G-3632)
SNODGRASS DUNLAP & COMPANY PA (PA)
16 W Jackson Ave (66749-2832)
P.O. Box 768 (66749-0768)
PHONE..................................620 365-3125
Andrew Dunlap, *Senior Partner*
John Baker, *Partner*
Joseph Bambick, *Partner*
Stephen Richards, *Partner*
Max Snodgrass, *Partner*
EMP: 22
SQ FT: 1,000
SALES (est): 726.5K **Privately Held**
SIC: 8721 Certified public accountant

(G-3633)
SOUTHEAST KANS MENTAL HLTH CTR
304 N Jefferson Ave (66749-2327)
PHONE..................................620 365-5717
Bob Chaese, *Manager*
Becky Stanley, *Manager*
EMP: 20
SALES (corp-wide): 8.3MM **Privately Held**
SIC: 8322 8093 Individual & family services; alcohol clinic, outpatient
PA: Southeast Kansas Mental Health Center
1106 S 9th St
Humboldt KS 66748
620 473-2241

(G-3634)
SOUTHEAST KANSAS COMMUNITY
Also Called: Iola Head Start
223 S Sycamore St (66749-3317)
P.O. Box 514 (66749-0514)
PHONE..................................620 365-7189
Linda Broyles, *Director*
EMP: 17

▲ = Import ▼=Export
◆ =Import/Export

SALES (corp-wide): 13.8MM Privately Held
WEB: www.sek-cap.com
SIC: 8351 Head start center, except in conjunction with school
PA: Southeast Kansas Community Action Program, Incorporated
401 N Sinnett St
Girard KS 66743
620 724-8204

(G-3635)
ST MARYS HOSP OF BLUE SPRNG
101 S 1st St (66749-3505)
PHONE..................................816 523-4525
Diana Enna, *Branch Mgr*
EMP: 442 Privately Held
SIC: 8011 Cardiologist & cardio-vascular specialist
PA: St. Mary's Hospital Of Blue Springs, Inc
201 Nw R D Mize Rd
Blue Springs MO

(G-3636)
STORRER IMPLEMENT INC
Also Called: Kubota Authorized Dealer
1801 East St (66749-3049)
PHONE..................................620 365-5692
Robert Storrer, *President*
Stephen Frank, *Vice Pres*
▲ EMP: 10 EST: 1940
SQ FT: 11,400
SALES: 13MM Privately Held
WEB: www.storrerimplement.com
SIC: 5083 7699 Farm implements; agricultural equipment repair services

(G-3637)
TRI-VALLEY DEVELOPMENTAL SVCS
Also Called: Iola Community Support Office
405 N Jefferson Ave (66749-2328)
PHONE..................................620 365-3307
Bill Fiscus, *Branch Mgr*
EMP: 88
SALES (corp-wide): 5.2MM Privately Held
WEB: www.tvds.org
SIC: 8322 4111 8361 8331 Social services for the handicapped; local & suburban transit; home for the mentally handicapped; sheltered workshop
PA: Tri-Valley Developmental Services Inc
3740 S Santa Fe Ave
Chanute KS
620 431-7401

(G-3638)
WINDSOR PLACE
Also Called: WINDSOR PLACE AT IOLA
600 E Garfield St (66749-2034)
PHONE..................................620 251-6545
Chuck Worth, *Owner*
Linda Harrison, *Executive*
EMP: 60
SALES: 3.8MM Privately Held
SIC: 8051 Convalescent home with continuous nursing care

Isabel
Barber County

(G-3639)
FARMERS CO-OPERATIVE EQUITY CO (PA)
102 N Burr St (67065-6011)
PHONE..................................620 739-4335
Chris Boyd, *President*
Craig Rakin, *Vice Pres*
Charles Swayze, *Manager*
Phillp Hellman, *Admin Sec*
Len Messenger,
EMP: 11 EST: 1919
SQ FT: 3,000
SALES: 36.3MM Privately Held
SIC: 5153 5191 5171 5541 Grains; feed; seeds: field, garden & flower; fertilizer & fertilizer materials; petroleum bulk stations; filling stations, gasoline

Iuka
Pratt County

(G-3640)
KANZA COOPERATIVE ASSOCIATION (PA)
102 N Main St (67066-9401)
P.O. Box 175 (67066-0175)
PHONE..................................620 546-2231
Bruce Krehbiel, *CEO*
Jeff Bolen, *Vice Pres*
Bryan Nickelson, *Vice Pres*
Brad Riley, *CFO*
Mickaela Holmes, *Comptroller*
EMP: 18
SQ FT: 800
SALES: 300MM Privately Held
SIC: 5153 5191 5541 4221 Grains; farm supplies; fertilizer & fertilizer materials; chemicals, agricultural; filling stations, gasoline; grain elevator, storage only

(G-3641)
KANZA COOPERATIVE ASSOCIATION
Also Called: Iuka Coop Farm Supply
109 N Main St (67066)
P.O. Box 175 (67066-0175)
PHONE..................................620 546-2593
Bruce Krehbiel, *Manager*
EMP: 72
SALES (corp-wide): 300MM Privately Held
SIC: 5153 Grains
PA: Kanza Cooperative Association
102 N Main St
Iuka KS 67066
620 546-2231

Jamestown
Cloud County

(G-3642)
CHEYENNE LODGE INC
Also Called: CHEYENNE LODGE NURSING HOME
716 Cedar St (66948-3007)
P.O. Box 467, Beloit (67420-0467)
PHONE..................................785 439-6211
Harold L Hiedrick, *President*
Joe Fuentez, *Administration*
EMP: 45
SQ FT: 15,000
SALES: 102.7MM Privately Held
WEB: www.cheyennelodge.com
SIC: 8052 Intermediate care facilities

(G-3643)
JAMESTOWN STATE BANK (PA)
422 Walnut St (66948-9782)
P.O. Box 285 (66948-0285)
PHONE..................................785 439-6224
A J Herbin, *Ch of Bd*
Roger D Anderson, *Vice Pres*
Marvin L Dunlap, *Vice Pres*
EMP: 10 EST: 1898
SQ FT: 3,500
SALES: 584K Privately Held
SIC: 6022 State trust companies accepting deposits, commercial

Jennings
Decatur County

(G-3644)
VICTOR RITTER
Hc 1 (67643)
PHONE..................................785 678-2423
Victor Ritter, *Owner*
EMP: 11
SALES (est): 317.6K Privately Held
SIC: 0291 Livestock farm, general

Jetmore
Hodgeman County

(G-3645)
ARCHER-DANIELS-MIDLAND COMPANY
Also Called: ADM
1122 Main St (67854-9326)
P.O. Box 35 (67854-0035)
PHONE..................................620 357-8733
William Carr, *Branch Mgr*
EMP: 7
SALES (corp-wide): 64.3B Publicly Held
WEB: www.collingwoodgrain.com
SIC: 2041 5191 5541 Flour & other grain mill products; feed; fertilizer & fertilizer materials; filling stations, gasoline
PA: Archer-Daniels-Midland Company
77 W Wacker Dr Ste 4600
Chicago IL 60601
312 634-8100

(G-3646)
BOOTHILL FEEDERS INC
20041 Sw C Rd (67854-5518)
PHONE..................................620 227-8195
Connie Kuhlman, *General Mgr*
EMP: 14
SALES (est): 2.3MM Privately Held
SIC: 0211 Beef cattle feedlots

(G-3647)
HODGEMAN COUNTY HEALTH CENTER (PA)
809 W Bramley St (67854-9320)
P.O. Box 310 (67854-0310)
PHONE..................................620 357-8361
Ronnie Diehl, *Plant Mgr*
Phil Low, *Administration*
EMP: 105
SQ FT: 3,600
SALES: 7.2MM Privately Held
WEB: www.hchconline.org
SIC: 8062 8051 General medical & surgical hospitals; convalescent home with continuous nursing care

(G-3648)
STONE POST DAIRY LLC
33002 Se K Rd (67854-5403)
PHONE..................................620 357-8634
Donald E Barton, *Manager*
Jerry George,
Jan Moffberg,
Jerry Moffberg,
Randy Moffberg,
EMP: 26
SALES (est): 1.9MM Privately Held
SIC: 0241 Milk production

Jewell
Jewell County

(G-3649)
BOURBON TRUCKING LLC
864 Highway 14 (66949-1861)
PHONE..................................785 428-3030
Eric Bourbon, *Mng Member*
EMP: 25
SALES: 1MM Privately Held
SIC: 4212 Moving services

(G-3650)
JEWELL IMPLEMENT COMPANY INC
105 S Custer St (66949-9760)
P.O. Box 346 (66949-0346)
PHONE..................................785 428-3261
Bill Loomis, *President*
Becky Loomis, *Treasurer*
EMP: 10
SALES (est): 2.5MM Privately Held
SIC: 5083 Farm implements

Johnson
Stanton County

(G-3651)
BAXTER CMMDTS-DNTITY GRINS LLC
450 E Road 13 (67855)
P.O. Box 390 (67855-0390)
PHONE..................................620 492-4040
Pat Josserand, *Principal*
EMP: 16
SALES (est): 4.8MM Privately Held
SIC: 6221 Commodity brokers, contracts

(G-3652)
CHEM TILL SPRAY COMPANY INC
Also Called: Chem-Till
609 S Main St (67855)
P.O. Box 570 (67855-0570)
PHONE..................................620 492-2751
Robert Duran, *President*
Jesus Tarin, *Vice Pres*
EMP: 11 EST: 1941
SALES (est): 1.9MM Privately Held
SIC: 0111 0115 0119 0721 Wheat; corn; milo farm; crop spraying services

(G-3653)
FIRST NAT BNK SYRACUSE INC
509 N Main St (67855)
PHONE..................................620 492-1754
Chris Floyd, *Manager*
EMP: 10
SALES (corp-wide): 19MM Privately Held
WEB: www.fnb-windmill.com
SIC: 6021 National commercial banks
PA: First National Bank Of Syracuse Inc.
11 N Main St
Syracuse KS 67878
620 384-7441

(G-3654)
JOHNSON COOPERATIVE GRN CO INC (PA)
304 E Highland (67855-5509)
PHONE..................................620 492-6210
David Corn, *CEO*
Martie Floyd, *President*
Rodney Friesen, *CFO*
David Smith, *Manager*
EMP: 13
SQ FT: 2,400
SALES: 83.9MM Privately Held
WEB: www.johnsoncoop.com
SIC: 5153 5191 5172 Grain elevators; farm supplies; feed; fertilizer & fertilizer materials; seeds: field, garden & flower; petroleum products

(G-3655)
JOHNSON COOPERATIVE GRN CO INC
Also Called: AG Center
104 W Highland Rd (67855)
P.O. Box 280 (67855-0280)
PHONE..................................620 492-2297
David Smith, *Manager*
EMP: 10
SALES (corp-wide): 83.9MM Privately Held
WEB: www.johnsoncoop.com
SIC: 5153 Grain elevators
PA: Johnson Cooperative Grain Company, Inc.
304 E Highland
Johnson KS 67855
620 492-6210

(G-3656)
JOHNSON STATE BANK (PA)
202 S Main St (67855-4139)
PHONE..................................620 492-6200
Gregory Wartman, *President*
Darrell Cockrum, *Chairman*
EMP: 20 EST: 1913
SQ FT: 6,000
SALES: 3.1MM Privately Held
WEB: www.johnsonstatebank.com
SIC: 6022 State trust companies accepting deposits, commercial

GEOGRAPHIC

(G-3657)
JOHNSON STATE BANKSHARES INC
202 S Main St (67855-4139)
PHONE..................................620 492-6200
Darrell K Cockrum, *President*
Greg R Wartman, *Admin Sec*
EMP: 12
SQ FT: 5,000 **Privately Held**
SIC: 6712 Bank holding companies

(G-3658)
MELVIN WINGER
507 N Main (67855)
P.O. Box 914 (67855-0914)
PHONE..................................620 492-6214
Melvin Winger, *President*
Shawn Peterson, *Manager*
Mona Winger, *Admin Sec*
EMP: 10 **EST:** 1945
SALES: 133.6K **Privately Held**
SIC: 0212 0111 0115 Beef cattle except feedlots; wheat; corn

(G-3659)
PRIME FEEDERS LLC
4256 N Rd L (67855)
PHONE..................................620 492-6674
William Nicholas,
EMP: 10
SALES (est): 1MM **Privately Held**
SIC: 5191 Feed

(G-3660)
SKYLAND GRAIN LLC (PA)
304 E Highland (67855-5509)
P.O. Box 280 (67855-0280)
PHONE..................................620 492-2126
David Cron, *President*
Paul Sack, *Area Mgr*
Pete Goetzmann, *Vice Pres*
Ken Keller, *Vice Pres*
Wade Tucker, *Vice Pres*
EMP: 10
SALES (est): 20.9MM **Privately Held**
WEB: www.skylandgrain.com
SIC: 5191 5172 4221 Fertilizer & fertilizer materials; feed; petroleum products; grain elevator, storage only

(G-3661)
SOUTHWEST KANSAS COOP SVCS LLC
304 W Highland St (67855)
P.O. Box 280 (67855-0280)
PHONE..................................620 492-2126
Paul Sack,
EMP: 25 **EST:** 2007
SALES (est): 4.7MM **Privately Held**
SIC: 2911 Oils, fuel

(G-3662)
STANTON COUNTY HOSP AUX INC
Also Called: County Family Practice
404 N Chestnut St (67855)
P.O. Box 779 (67855-0779)
PHONE..................................620 492-6250
Jay Tusten, *CEO*
Rob Nahmensen, *CFO*
Camille Davidson, *Human Resources*
Mary Cockrum, *Manager*
Robin Kempke, *Manager*
EMP: 110
SQ FT: 30,600
SALES: 6.2MM **Privately Held**
SIC: 8062 8051 General medical & surgical hospitals; skilled nursing care facilities

(G-3663)
SUPERIOR CAR CARE CENTER LLC
608 S Main St (67855)
P.O. Box 176 (67855-0176)
PHONE..................................620 492-6856
Joe Wilson, *Mng Member*
Danny Navarro,
EMP: 10
SALES (est): 1.6MM **Privately Held**
SIC: 7534 5531 Tire repair shop; automotive tires

(G-3664)
WALTON SWATHING
6501 E Road 10 (67855-8825)
PHONE..................................620 492-6827
Jason Walton, *Owner*
EMP: 5
SALES (est): 678.4K **Privately Held**
SIC: 1389 Swabbing wells

(G-3665)
WESTERN FEED YARD INC
548 S Road I (67855-8812)
PHONE..................................620 492-6256
Roger Canny, *President*
EMP: 45 **EST:** 1968
SQ FT: 1,200
SALES: 12.5MM **Privately Held**
SIC: 0211 Beef cattle feedlots

(G-3666)
WINGER CATTLE CO INC
Also Called: Winger Seed
507 N Main St (67855-4158)
P.O. Box 914 (67855-0914)
PHONE..................................620 492-6214
Melvin Winger, *President*
EMP: 10 **EST:** 1963
SALES (est): 1MM **Privately Held**
SIC: 0211 0212 0111 0115 Beef cattle feedlots; beef cattle except feedlots; wheat; corn

Junction City
Geary County

(G-3667)
ARMED FORCES BANK NAT ASSN
429 W 18th St (66441-2221)
PHONE..................................785 238-2241
Ron Bramlage, *Branch Mgr*
EMP: 10 **Privately Held**
WEB: www.afbca.com
SIC: 6021 National commercial banks
HQ: Armed Forces Bank, National Association
320 Kansas Ave
Fort Leavenworth KS 66027
913 682-9090

(G-3668)
ARMED SERVICES YMCA OF USA
Also Called: Junction City Family YMCA
111 E 16th St (66441-2517)
P.O. Box 113 (66441-0113)
PHONE..................................785 238-2972
Ted Hayden, *Branch Mgr*
EMP: 16
SALES (corp-wide): 6.8MM **Privately Held**
WEB: www.camppendletonasymca.org
SIC: 8322 Social service center; family service agency
PA: Armed Services Ymca Of The U.S.A.
14040 Central Loop B
Woodbridge VA 22193
703 445-3986

(G-3669)
AUTO-CRAFT INC
220 E Chestnut St (66441-3549)
PHONE..................................785 579-5997
Blake Sterns, *Branch Mgr*
EMP: 20
SALES (corp-wide): 4.9MM **Privately Held**
SIC: 7542 7532 5231 Carwashes; paint shop, automotive; glass
PA: Auto-Craft, Inc.
1427 E 1st St N
Wichita KS 67214
316 265-6828

(G-3670)
B & K ENTERPRISES INC
Also Called: B & K Vending & Amusement
417 N Franklin St (66441-2864)
PHONE..................................785 238-3076
Karren Blanken, *President*
Robert L Blanken, *Corp Secy*
EMP: 10 **EST:** 1956
SQ FT: 10,000
SALES: 900K **Privately Held**
SIC: 7359 Coin-operated machine rental services

(G-3671)
BANK AMERICA NATIONAL ASSN
227 W 18th St (66441-2320)
PHONE..................................785 238-8012
Julie Allen-Murry, *Branch Mgr*
EMP: 15
SALES (corp-wide): 110.5B **Publicly Held**
WEB: www.bofa.com
SIC: 6021 National commercial banks
HQ: Bank Of America, National Association
100 S Tryon St
Charlotte NC 28202
704 386-5681

(G-3672)
BELL TAXI AND TRNSP INC (PA)
Also Called: Bell Taxi & K C I Roadrunner
1002 N Washington St (66441-2497)
PHONE..................................785 238-6161
Glenn D Puett Jr, *President*
Ann J Puett, *Vice Pres*
EMP: 14
SQ FT: 4,000
SALES (est): 3.4MM **Privately Held**
SIC: 4121 4111 Taxicabs; local & suburban transit

(G-3673)
BEN KITCHENS PAINTING CO INC
611 Country Club Ter (66441-3268)
PHONE..................................785 375-3288
Ben Kitchens, *Owner*
EMP: 16
SALES (est): 420.2K **Privately Held**
SIC: 1721 1751 Residential painting; finish & trim carpentry

(G-3674)
BENEVOLENT/PROTECTV ORDER ELKS
Also Called: Elk's Lodge 1037
723 S Washington St (66441-3754)
P.O. Box 1212 (66441-1212)
PHONE..................................785 762-2922
Wendell Wright,
EMP: 16
SALES (corp-wide): 28.1MM **Privately Held**
SIC: 8641 Fraternal associations
PA: Benevolent And Protective Order Of Elks
2750 N Lakeview Ave
Chicago IL 60614
773 755-4700

(G-3675)
BROOKDALE SENIOR LIVING COMMUN
Also Called: Sterling House Junction City
1022 Caroline Ave Ofc (66441-5235)
PHONE..................................785 762-3123
Gloria Lansbury, *Manager*
EMP: 20
SALES (corp-wide): 4.5B **Publicly Held**
WEB: www.assisted.com
SIC: 8059 Rest home, with health care
HQ: Brookdale Senior Living Communities, Inc.
6737 W Wa St Ste 2300
Milwaukee WI 53214
414 918-5000

(G-3676)
CENTRAL NATIONAL BANK (HQ)
Also Called: CENTRAL INVESTMENT SERVICES
802 N Washington St (66441-2447)
P.O. Box 700 (66441-0700)
PHONE..................................785 238-4114
Ed C Rolfs, *President*
Steve Barker, *Vice Pres*
Linda Barten, *Vice Pres*
Roger Dean, *Vice Pres*
Ed Mechams, *Vice Pres*
EMP: 37
SQ FT: 5,000
SALES: 53.9MM
SALES (corp-wide): 55.4MM **Privately Held**
WEB: www.centralnational.com
SIC: 6021 National commercial banks
PA: Central Of Kansas, Inc.
802 N Washington St
Junction City KS 66441
785 238-4114

(G-3677)
CENTRAL NATIONAL BANK
540 W 6th St (66441-3144)
P.O. Box 700 (66441-0700)
PHONE..................................785 238-4114
Rhonda Henry, *General Mgr*
EMP: 10
SALES (corp-wide): 55.4MM **Privately Held**
WEB: www.centralnational.com
SIC: 6021 National commercial banks
HQ: Central National Bank (Inc)
802 N Washington St
Junction City KS 66441
785 238-4114

(G-3678)
CENTRAL OF KANSAS INC (PA)
Also Called: Central Investment Services
802 N Washington St (66441-2447)
P.O. Box 700 (66441-0700)
PHONE..................................785 238-4114
Robert Munson, *President*
Ed J Rolfs, *Vice Pres*
EMP: 100
SALES (est): 55.4MM **Privately Held**
SIC: 6021 6411 7374 National commercial banks; insurance agents, brokers & service; data processing service

(G-3679)
CERTAINTEED GYPSUM MFG INC
3105 Industrial St (66441-8913)
PHONE..................................785 762-2994
Don Moses, *Principal*
EMP: 7
SALES (corp-wide): 209.1MM **Privately Held**
SIC: 3275 Gypsum products
HQ: Certainteed Gypsum Manufacturing, Inc.
750 E Swedesford Rd
Wayne PA 19087
813 286-3900

(G-3680)
CERTANTEED GYPS FNSHG PDTS INC (HQ)
3105 Industrial St (66441-8913)
PHONE..................................785 762-2994
Keith Campbell, *President*
▼ **EMP:** 11
SQ FT: 44,000
SALES (est): 2.7MM
SALES (corp-wide): 209.1MM **Privately Held**
SIC: 2891 Adhesives
PA: Compagnie De Saint-Gobain
Les Miroirs La Defense 3
Courbevoie 92400
140 880-316

(G-3681)
CITY CYCLE SALES
Also Called: City Cycle Sls Harley Davidson
1021 Goldenbelt Blvd (66441-3938)
P.O. Box 520 (66441-0520)
PHONE..................................785 238-3411
Wayne Daecke, *President*
EMP: 15
SQ FT: 6,000
SALES (est): 2.6MM **Privately Held**
WEB: www.citycyclesales.com
SIC: 5571 7699 Motorcycle dealers; motorcycle repair service

(G-3682)
CITY OF JUNCTION CITY
Public Works Dept
2324 N Jackson St (66441-2288)
PHONE..................................785 238-7142
Steve Hoambrecker, *Director*
EMP: 50 **Privately Held**
WEB: www.jcks.com
SIC: 1611 Highway & street construction

PA: City Of Junction City
700 N Jefferson St Ste B
Junction City KS 66441
785 238-7142

(G-3683)
CMT INC
1002 Perry St (66441-2733)
PHONE....785 762-4400
Marilyn Sliski, *CEO*
Chester Sliski, *President*
Todd Sliski, *President*
EMP: 120
SQ FT: 85,000
SALES: 5.5MM **Privately Held**
WEB: www.jcwh.com
SIC: 3641 3694 3613 Lead-in wires, electric lamp made from purchased wire; battery cable wiring sets for internal combustion engines; control panels, electric

(G-3684)
COUNTY OF GEARY
Also Called: Junction CT Geary Cnty Hlth De
1212 W Ash St (66441-3344)
P.O. Box 282 (66441-0282)
PHONE....785 762-5788
Patricia Hunter, *Director*
EMP: 24 **Privately Held**
WEB: www.gearycounty.org
SIC: 8099 8011 Health screening service; offices & clinics of medical doctors
PA: County Of Geary
200 E 8th St
Junction City KS 66441
785 238-4407

(G-3685)
COURT TRUSTEE DEPT
801 N Washington St Ste D (66441-2483)
P.O. Box 887 (66441-0885)
PHONE....785 762-2583
Audry Magana, *CEO*
EMP: 16 **EST:** 2001
SALES (est): 968.4K **Privately Held**
SIC: 8744 8322 Facilities support services; family service agency

(G-3686)
COX COMMUNICATIONS INC
140 W 8th St (66441-2461)
PHONE....785 238-6165
EMP: 76
SALES (corp-wide): 29.2B **Privately Held**
SIC: 4841 Cable television services
HQ: Cox Communications, Inc.
6205 B Pchtree Dnwody Rd
Atlanta GA 30328

(G-3687)
DICK EDWARDS FORD LINCOLN MERC (PA)
1825 Goldenbelt Blvd (66441-3935)
P.O. Box 368, Manhattan (66505-0368)
PHONE....785 320-4499
D I C K Edwards, *President*
Dick Edwards, *President*
Ken Schmelzle, *Corp Secy*
Eugene Huslig, *Sales Mgr*
Kenny Constable, *Sales Staff*
EMP: 100
SQ FT: 36,000
SALES (est): 39.3MM **Privately Held**
SIC: 5511 5521 7538 7532 Automobiles, new & used; used car dealers; general automotive repair shops; top & body repair & paint shops; automotive & home supply stores

(G-3688)
EXCHANGE BANK
702 N Washington St (66441-2922)
P.O. Box 348 (66441-0348)
PHONE....785 762-4121
James H Davis, *Branch Mgr*
EMP: 18
SALES (corp-wide): 41.7MM **Privately Held**
SIC: 6022 State trust companies accepting deposits, commercial
PA: Exchange Bank
14 Labarre St
Gibbon NE 68840
308 468-5741

(G-3689)
FAMILY VIDEO MOVIE CLUB INC
215 W 6th St (66441-3046)
PHONE....785 762-2377
Jason Sassatelli, *Manager*
EMP: 13
SALES (corp-wide): 189.9MM **Privately Held**
WEB: www.familyvideo.net
SIC: 7841 Video disk/tape rental to the general public
HQ: Family Video Movie Club Inc.
2500 Lehigh Mt Ave
Glenview IL 60026
847 904-9000

(G-3690)
FIRST NATIONAL BANK & TRUST CO
1038 W 6th St (66441-3231)
PHONE....785 762-4121
Tammy Ballard, *Manager*
EMP: 13
SALES (est): 1.1MM
SALES (corp-wide): 5.6MM **Privately Held**
SIC: 6022 State commercial banks
PA: First National Bank & Trust Co, Inc
702 N Washington St
Junction City KS

(G-3691)
GARAGE DOOR GROUP INC
Also Called: Peninsula Overhead Doors
1010 Cottonwood St (66441-4106)
PHONE....757 253-0522
Loiuse Dombek, *President*
Louise Dombek, *President*
EMP: 10
SALES: 1MM **Privately Held**
SIC: 1751 Garage door, installation or erection

(G-3692)
GEARY COMMUNITY HOSPITAL
Also Called: Gary Community Hosp Rur Clinic
1106 Saint Marys Rd # 310 (66441-4158)
PHONE....785 762-5437
Jimmy Jenkins, *Med Doctor*
Dennis Sewell, *Program Mgr*
EMP: 12
SALES (est): 1.3MM
SALES (corp-wide): 39.9MM **Privately Held**
SIC: 8011 Pediatrician
PA: Geary County Hospital
1102 Saint Marys Rd
Junction City KS 66441
785 238-4131

(G-3693)
GEARY CORRECTIONS CENTER
Also Called: 8th Jdcial Dst Cmnty Crrctions
801 N Washington St Ste E (66441-2483)
PHONE....785 762-4679
Mike Wederski, *Director*
EMP: 25
SALES (est): 952.7K **Privately Held**
SIC: 8322 Probation office

(G-3694)
GEARY COUNTY HOSPITAL (PA)
Also Called: Geary Community Hospital
1102 Saint Marys Rd (66441-4139)
P.O. Box 490 (66441-0490)
PHONE....785 238-4131
Mark Stenstrom, *Ch of Bd*
Melanie Griffin, *Business Mgr*
Jeff Kline, *Purch Dir*
Bill Jones, *Purch Agent*
Steve Doherty, *CFO*
EMP: 425
SQ FT: 76,900
SALES: 39.9MM **Privately Held**
SIC: 8062 General medical & surgical hospitals

(G-3695)
GEARY COUNTY PUBLIC WORKS
310 E 8th St (66441-2642)
PHONE....785 238-3612
Dennis Cox, *Administration*
EMP: 35
SALES (est): 3.2MM **Privately Held**
SIC: 8711 Civil engineering

(G-3696)
GEARY RHABILITATION FITNES CTR
104 S Washington St (66441-3557)
PHONE....785 238-3747
Justin Hoover, *President*
Matt Hoover, *Manager*
EMP: 25
SALES (est): 487.7K **Privately Held**
WEB: www.gearyrehab.com
SIC: 8049 7991 Physical therapist; physical fitness facilities

(G-3697)
GUSTAFSON CONCRETE INC
7115 Davis Creek Rd (66441-8026)
PHONE....785 238-7747
John Gustafson, *President*
Louise Gustafson, *Admin Sec*
EMP: 10
SALES (est): 850K **Privately Held**
SIC: 1771 Concrete work

(G-3698)
HAMPTON INN JUNCTION CITY
1039 S Washington St (66441-3807)
PHONE....785 579-4633
Nish Kharod, *Principal*
EMP: 15
SALES: 950K **Privately Held**
SIC: 7011 Hotels & motels

(G-3699)
HESS & SON SALVAGE INC
1209 Perry St (66441-2736)
P.O. Box 1263 (66441-1263)
PHONE....785 238-3382
Lanny Hess, *President*
Rick Hess, *Admin Sec*
EMP: 14
SQ FT: 3,024
SALES (est): 2.5MM **Privately Held**
WEB: www.hessandsonssalvage.com
SIC: 5015 Automotive supplies, used; automotive parts & supplies, used

(G-3700)
INTRUST BANK NA
121 N Washington St (66441-2906)
PHONE....785 761-2265
EMP: 11
SALES (corp-wide): 134.2MM **Privately Held**
SIC: 6022 State commercial banks
HQ: Intrust Bank National Association
105 N Main St
Wichita KS 67202
316 383-1111

(G-3701)
INTRUST BANK NATIONAL ASSN
121 N Washington St (66441-2906)
PHONE....785 238-1121
Robert Locke, *Branch Mgr*
EMP: 16
SALES (corp-wide): 134.2MM **Privately Held**
SIC: 6022 State commercial banks
HQ: Intrust Bank National Association
105 N Main St
Wichita KS 67202
316 383-1111

(G-3702)
J & K CONTRACTING LC
801 W 6th St Ste B (66441-3275)
P.O. Box 306 (66441-0306)
PHONE....785 238-3298
Shannon Locke,
EMP: 12
SALES (est): 2MM **Privately Held**
SIC: 8741 Construction management

(G-3703)
JUNCTION CITY BOWL INC
Also Called: Long Shots Bar
835 S Washington St (66441-3803)
PHONE....785 238-6813
Joseph R Ellison, *President*
EMP: 15
SQ FT: 15,000
SALES (est): 857.1K **Privately Held**
WEB: www.bigbowl.com
SIC: 7933 Ten pin center

(G-3704)
JUNCTION CITY FAMILY YMCA INC (PA)
1703 Mcfarland Rd (66441-3368)
P.O. Box 113 (66441-0113)
PHONE....785 762-4780
Ted Hayden, *Exec Dir*
EMP: 45
SALES: 764.7K **Privately Held**
WEB: www.junctioncityfamilyymca.com
SIC: 8641 7991 8351 7032 Youth organizations; physical fitness facilities; child day care services; youth camps; individual & family services

(G-3705)
JUNCTION CITY LODGING LLC
221 E Ash St (66441-1450)
PHONE....785 579-5787
Michael May, *Principal*
EMP: 20 **EST:** 2017
SALES (est): 109.1K **Privately Held**
SIC: 7011 Hotels & motels
PA: Mars Development, Llc
19284 Cottonwood Dr # 203
Parker CO 80138

(G-3706)
JUNCTION CITY WIRE HARNESS LLC
1002 Perry St (66441-2733)
PHONE....785 762-4400
EMP: 100 **EST:** 2011
SALES (est): 10.3MM
SALES (corp-wide): 26.3MM **Privately Held**
SIC: 3641 3694 3613 Lead-in wires, electric lamp made from purchased wire; battery cable wiring sets for internal combustion engines; control panels, electric
HQ: Sentral Assemblies Llc
595 Bond St
Lincolnshire IL 60069

(G-3707)
JUNCTION CT-FT RLY MHT TRNSINC
Also Called: Junction City Transportation
301 E 4th St (66441-2849)
P.O. Box 327 (66441-0327)
PHONE....785 762-2219
Dave Bruce, *President*
David R Bruce, *Principal*
Merle Deitrich, *Vice Pres*
EMP: 12 **EST:** 1938
SQ FT: 3,600
SALES (est): 602.1K **Privately Held**
WEB: www.jctransinc.com
SIC: 4151 School buses

(G-3708)
JUST FOR KIDS EXPRESS
Also Called: B & B Busing
2722 Gateway Ct (66441-3928)
P.O. Box 1425 (66441-1425)
PHONE....785 238-8555
Brian K Bennett, *Owner*
EMP: 18
SALES (est): 510K **Privately Held**
SIC: 4141 4142 Local bus charter service; bus charter service, except local

(G-3709)
K & K INDUSTRIES INC
9170 Clarks Creek Rd (66441-7466)
PHONE....906 293-5242
Keith Klaty, *President*
EMP: 40 **EST:** 1976
SALES (est): 9.7MM **Privately Held**
SIC: 1711 1731 5074 Plumbing contractors; electrical work; plumbing & hydronic heating supplies

(G-3710)
K C I ROADRUNNER EXPRESS INC
1002 N Washington St (66441-2452)
PHONE....785 238-6161
Glen D Puett Jr, *President*
Anne J Puett, *Vice Pres*

GEOGRAPHIC

EMP: 100
SALES (est): 7.8MM **Privately Held**
WEB: www.kciroadrunner.com
SIC: 4212 4724 4213 Local trucking, without storage; travel agencies; trucking, except local

(G-3711)
KANAS CATTLEMENS ASSOCIATE
725 N Washington St Ste B (66441-2996)
P.O. Box 1489 (66441-1489)
PHONE..................................785 238-1483
Perry Owens, *President*
Daryl Larson, *Bd of Directors*
Hal Luthi, *Bd of Directors*
Ken Winter, *Bd of Directors*
EMP: 11
SALES (est): 113.6K **Privately Held**
SIC: 8699 Charitable organization

(G-3712)
KANSAS 4-H FOUNDATION INC
Also Called: Conference Center
1168 K157 Hwy (66441)
PHONE..................................785 257-3221
Mike Sohn, *Manager*
Michael Brock, *Supervisor*
Chris Anderson, *Director*
William Biles, *Tech/Comp Coord*
EMP: 13
SALES (corp-wide): 3.5MM **Privately Held**
WEB: www.rocksprings.net
SIC: 7033 Campgrounds
PA: Kansas 4-H Foundation Inc
116 Umberger Hall
Manhattan KS
785 532-5881

(G-3713)
KANSAS KIDS DAYCARE PRESCHOOL
110 N Eisenhower Dr (66441-3314)
PHONE..................................785 762-4338
Linda Talley, *Owner*
EMP: 15
SQ FT: 4,700
SALES (est): 323K **Privately Held**
SIC: 8351 Preschool center

(G-3714)
KAW VALLEY ENGINEERING INC (PA)
2319 N Jackson St (66441-4724)
P.O. Box 1304 (66441-1304)
PHONE..................................785 762-5040
Leon Osbourn, *President*
Charles Sharp, *Treasurer*
Dana Bowles, *Admin Sec*
EMP: 46
SQ FT: 6,000
SALES (est): 24.8MM **Privately Held**
WEB: www.kveng.com
SIC: 8711 8713 0711 7389 Civil engineering; surveying services; soil testing services; inspection & testing services

(G-3715)
KINGS MOVING & STORAGE INC
Also Called: King's North Amercn Van Lines
906 Perry St (66441-2731)
P.O. Box 786 (66441-0786)
PHONE..................................785 238-7341
George Newby, *Manager*
EMP: 28
SALES (corp-wide): 14.8MM **Privately Held**
WEB: www.kingms.com
SIC: 4214 4212 Local trucking with storage; moving services
PA: King's Moving & Storage, Inc.
2111 E Industrial St
Wichita KS 67216
316 247-6528

(G-3716)
KIWANIS INTERNATIONAL INC
1407 Mcfarland Rd (66441-3308)
PHONE..................................785 238-4521
John Rosa, *Branch Mgr*
EMP: 14
SALES (corp-wide): 23.6MM **Privately Held**
WEB: www.kfne.org
SIC: 8641 Civic associations
PA: Kiwanis International, Inc.
3636 Woodview Trce
Indianapolis IN 46268
317 875-8755

(G-3717)
KONZA CONSTR CO INC
Also Called: Konza Construction & Sand
3107 N Highway K57 (66441-8397)
P.O. Box 563, Chapman (67431-0563)
PHONE..................................785 762-2995
John Musser, *President*
David Walker, *Shareholder*
▼ **EMP:** 55
SQ FT: 2,900
SALES: 10MM **Privately Held**
SIC: 1611 General contractor, highway & street construction

(G-3718)
KONZA PRAIRIE CMNTY HLTH CTR
361 Grant Ave (66441-4201)
PHONE..................................785 238-4711
Lee Wolf, *CEO*
Larry Schmidt, *President*
Ron Coryell, *Corp Secy*
Michael Dolan, *COO*
Waldo Berry, *Vice Pres*
EMP: 15
SALES: 9.1MM **Privately Held**
WEB: www.konzaprairiechc.com
SIC: 8011 General & family practice, physician/surgeon

(G-3719)
KS STATEBANK
539 W 6th St (66441-3143)
PHONE..................................785 762-5050
EMP: 24
SALES (corp-wide): 95MM **Privately Held**
SIC: 6022 State trust companies accepting deposits, commercial
HQ: Ks Statebank
1010 Westloop Pl
Manhattan KS 66502
785 587-4000

(G-3720)
LAS VILLAS DEL NORTE (PA)
Also Called: Las Villas Del Norte Hlth Ctr
416 W Spruce St (66441-3604)
PHONE..................................760 741-1046
Sharyl Ronan, *Director*
EMP: 90
SALES (est): 3MM **Privately Held**
SIC: 8361 8051 Geriatric residential care; skilled nursing care facilities

(G-3721)
LIFE CARE SERVICES LLC
Also Called: Valley Vista
1417 W Ash St (66441-3332)
PHONE..................................785 762-2162
Scott Steinmetz, *Administration*
EMP: 123
SALES (corp-wide): 54.8MM **Privately Held**
WEB: www.lcsnet.com
SIC: 8051 Skilled nursing care facilities
HQ: Life Care Services Llc
400 Locust St Ste 820
Des Moines IA 50309
515 875-4500

(G-3722)
LOVING ARMS DAYCARE CTRS INC
Also Called: Loving Arms Chldcare Preschool
1531 Saint Marys Rd Ste A (66441-4040)
PHONE..................................785 238-2767
Lafarris Risby, *Exec Dir*
EMP: 12
SQ FT: 9,000
SALES: 280K **Privately Held**
SIC: 8351 Group day care center; preschool center

(G-3723)
MANE THING
Also Called: Attitudes 902
902 W 7th St (66441-3250)
PHONE..................................785 762-2397
Rhonda Sharp, *Owner*
EMP: 22
SQ FT: 4,000
SALES (est): 429K **Privately Held**
SIC: 7231 7299 Hairdressers; manicurist, pedicurist; facial salons; massage parlor

(G-3724)
MANKO WINDOW SYSTEMS INC
Also Called: Interstate Jayhawk Glass Co
2005 N Jackson St (66441-4727)
P.O. Box 1344 (66441-1344)
PHONE..................................785 238-3188
Steve Edwards, *Natl Sales Mgr*
Art Leon, *Manager*
EMP: 12
SALES (est): 1MM
SALES (corp-wide): 221.8MM **Privately Held**
WEB: www.mankowindows.com
SIC: 5013 1799 Automobile glass; glass tinting, architectural or automotive
PA: Manko Window Systems, Inc.
800 Hayes Dr
Manhattan KS 66502
785 776-9643

(G-3725)
MERITRUST CREDIT UNION
343 E Chestnut St (66441-9466)
PHONE..................................785 579-5700
Shannon Watkins, *Branch Mgr*
EMP: 15
SALES (corp-wide): 53.9MM **Privately Held**
SIC: 6062 State credit unions, not federally chartered
PA: Meritrust Credit Union
8710 E 32nd St N
Wichita KS 67226
316 683-1199

(G-3726)
MILLENNIUM BANCSHARES INC
Also Called: Millennium Bank
121 N Washington St (66441-2906)
PHONE..................................785 761-2265
Maureen Gustafon, *President*
EMP: 10
SALES (est): 0 **Privately Held**
SIC: 6021 National commercial banks

(G-3727)
MONTGOMERY COMMUNICATIONS INC (PA)
Also Called: Junction City Daily Union
222 W 6th St (66441-5500)
PHONE..................................785 762-5000
John Montgomery, *President*
Calvin Pottberg, *Treasurer*
Penny Nelson, *Admin Sec*
EMP: 80 **EST:** 1888
SQ FT: 22,000
SALES (est): 3.9MM **Privately Held**
WEB: www.home-guide.net
SIC: 2711 4833 Newspapers; television broadcasting stations

(G-3728)
N CENTRAL KS REG JUVEN DETEN
820 N Monroe St (66441-2645)
PHONE..................................785 238-4549
Shawn Brand Mahl, *Director*
EMP: 15
SALES (est): 898.8K **Privately Held**
SIC: 8744 Correctional facility

(G-3729)
NEIGHBORHOOD LEARNING CTR LLC
227 W 7th St (66441-3052)
PHONE..................................785 238-2321
Susan Bowler, *Principal*
Susan Boller, *Principal*
EMP: 15
SALES (est): 451.2K **Privately Held**
SIC: 8351 Preschool center

(G-3730)
NEW DIRECTIONS EMRGNCY SHELTER
1115 W 14th St (66441-2041)
PHONE..................................785 223-0500
Cynthia Nixon, *Owner*
Barry Smith, *Director*
EMP: 30
SALES (est): 1MM **Privately Held**
SIC: 8322 Crisis intervention center

(G-3731)
NEW HORIZONS RV CORP
2401 Lacy Dr (66441-8035)
PHONE..................................785 238-7575
Brian Tillet, *President*
Karen Brokenicky, *Corp Secy*
Drew Brokenicky, *Vice Pres*
Erin Usher, *Sales Staff*
EMP: 40
SQ FT: 48,000
SALES (est): 9.5MM **Privately Held**
WEB: www.horizonsrv.com
SIC: 3711 Bus & other large specialty vehicle assembly

(G-3732)
NOGALES HOTEL COMPANY LLC
Also Called: Candlewood Suites
100 Hammons Dr (66441-4371)
PHONE..................................785 238-1454
Rajinder Bal,
Rajindr Bal,
Nirmal Nagra,
EMP: 25
SALES: 1MM **Privately Held**
SIC: 7011 Hotel, franchised

(G-3733)
ONEOK INC
1118 S Madison St (66441-3834)
PHONE..................................785 223-5408
Vernon Boltz, *Branch Mgr*
EMP: 13
SALES (corp-wide): 12.5B **Publicly Held**
WEB: www.oneok.com
SIC: 4922 Natural gas transmission
PA: Oneok, Inc.
100 W 5th St Ste Ll
Tulsa OK 74103
918 588-7000

(G-3734)
ORSCHELN FARM AND HOME LLC
Also Called: Orschelin Farm and Home 71
1023 S Washington St (66441-3807)
PHONE..................................785 762-4411
Reggie Oysterhaus, *Manager*
EMP: 13
SALES (corp-wide): 822.7MM **Privately Held**
WEB: www.orschelnfarmhome.com
SIC: 5191 5251 5699 Farm supplies; hardware; work clothing
PA: Orscheln Farm And Home Llc
1800 Overcenter Dr
Moberly MO 65270
800 577-2580

(G-3735)
PAWNEE MENTAL HEALTH SVCS INC
Also Called: Pmhs
814 Caroline Ave (66441-5210)
PHONE..................................785 762-5250
Mary Shane, *Manager*
EMP: 50
SALES (corp-wide): 16.5MM **Privately Held**
SIC: 8093 Mental health clinic, outpatient
PA: Pawnee Mental Health Services, Inc.
2001 Claflin Rd
Manhattan KS 66502
785 762-5250

(G-3736)
PAYAL HOTELS LLC
Also Called: Comfort Inn
221 E Ash St (66441-1450)
PHONE..................................785 579-5787
Chass Clark, *Principal*
Tracy Foster, *Principal*
EMP: 10 **EST:** 2011

SALES (est): 802.1K **Privately Held**
SIC: 7011 Hotels & motels

(G-3737)
PENN ENTERPRISES INC
1116 Grant Ave (66441-4224)
PHONE....785 762-3600
Michelle Gawrych, *Manager*
EMP: 25 **Privately Held**
SIC: 7218 7211 Industrial launderers; power laundries, family & commercial
PA: Penn Enterprises, Inc
5260 S Stonehaven Dr
Springfield MO 65809

(G-3738)
POTTBERG GSSMAN HFFMAN CHRTRED (PA)
816 N Washington St (66441-2447)
PHONE....785 238-5166
Calvin Pottberg, *President*
Dan Hoffman, *Admin Sec*
EMP: 15
SALES (est): 2.1MM **Privately Held**
WEB: www.pgh-cpa.com
SIC: 8721 Certified public accountant

(G-3739)
PRICE & YOUNG & ODLE
Also Called: Eye Doctors, The
1025 W 6th St (66441-3230)
PHONE....785 223-5777
Mary Polland, *Manager*
EMP: 11
SALES (corp-wide): 4.3MM **Privately Held**
SIC: 8042 5995 Contact lense specialist optometrist; opticians
PA: Price & Young & Odle
3012 Anderson Ave
Manhattan KS 66503
785 537-1118

(G-3740)
PRINTERY INC
Also Called: Printery, The
221 N Washington St (66441-2908)
PHONE....785 762-5112
Robin Gramm, *Branch Mgr*
EMP: 5
SALES (corp-wide): 1.5MM **Privately Held**
SIC: 2752 Commercial printing, offset
PA: Printery Inc
411 Court St
Clay Center KS 67432
785 632-5501

(G-3741)
PROFESSIONAL GROUP
2101 N Jackson St (66441-4729)
P.O. Box 686 (66441-0686)
PHONE....785 762-5855
Fax: 785 762-6178
EMP: 18 **EST:** 2007
SALES (est): 778.3K **Privately Held**
SIC: 8711 Engineering Services

(G-3742)
PROPANE CENTRAL
Also Called: Lovetts L P Gas & Fuel Service
2618 Central Dr (66441-9010)
PHONE....785 762-5160
Chris Ross, *Manager*
Jim Ray, *Manager*
EMP: 10
SQ FT: 2,976
SALES (est): 742.5K **Privately Held**
SIC: 5984 5172 Liquefied petroleum gas, delivered to customers' premises; gases, liquefied petroleum (propane)

(G-3743)
Q 1035 (PA)
Also Called: Kjck AM
1030 Southwind Ct (66441-2601)
P.O. Box 789 (66441-0789)
PHONE....785 762-5525
Mark Ediger, *General Mgr*
Ed Klimek, *General Mgr*
EMP: 18
SQ FT: 4,000
SALES (est): 1.4MM **Privately Held**
WEB: www.kjck.com
SIC: 4832 Radio broadcasting stations

(G-3744)
QUALITY INN
305 E Chestnut St (66441-9466)
PHONE....785 784-5106
Shiella Dickson, *Manager*
EMP: 14 **EST:** 2009
SALES (est): 757.9K **Privately Held**
SIC: 7011 Hotels & motels

(G-3745)
QUALITY TRUST INC
1906 Mcfarland Rd (66441-8847)
PHONE....785 375-6372
Larry Ruiz, *President*
Denna L Ruiz, *Vice Pres*
EMP: 30
SQ FT: 3,200
SALES: 1MM **Privately Held**
WEB: www.qualitytrustinc.com
SIC: 1542 1521 7532 Specialized public building contractors; commercial & office building contractors; new construction, single-family houses; body shop, automotive

(G-3746)
R & R DEVELOPERS INC
217 N Washington St (66441-2908)
P.O. Box 1204 (66441-1204)
PHONE....785 762-2255
Richard Rothfuss, *President*
Dale Rumbaugh, *Vice Pres*
Paul R Rothfuss, *Treasurer*
Darrell Rothfuss, *Admin Sec*
EMP: 11
SQ FT: 1,700
SALES: 5MM **Privately Held**
SIC: 1521 1522 1531 New construction, single-family houses; multi-family dwelling construction; speculative builder, multi-family dwellings; speculative builder, single-family houses

(G-3747)
R C KENNELS
Also Called: R C Kennels Boarding Grooming
12344 Kennel Dr (66441-7610)
PHONE....785 238-7000
Cathy Stopser, *Owner*
Ron Stopser, *Partner*
EMP: 15
SALES (est): 349.2K **Privately Held**
SIC: 0752 5999 Boarding services, kennels; pets & pet supplies

(G-3748)
REVOCABLE TRUST
Also Called: Courtyard By Marriott Jct Cy
310 Hammons Dr (66441-4368)
PHONE....785 210-1500
EMP: 312
SALES (corp-wide): 537.5MM **Privately Held**
SIC: 7011 Hotels & motels
PA: John Q Hammons Rvoc Tr 12281989
300 S John Q Hammons Pkwy # 9
Springfield MO 65806
417 864-4300

(G-3749)
SAINT FRANCIS CMNTY SVCS INC
Also Called: St. Francis Community Svc
1013 W 8th St Ste A (66441-2281)
PHONE....785 210-1000
Merta Litke, *Branch Mgr*
EMP: 44
SALES (corp-wide): 108.2MM **Privately Held**
SIC: 8741 Management services
PA: Saint Francis Community Services, Inc.
509 E Elm St
Salina KS 67401
785 825-0541

(G-3750)
SCREEN MACHINE LLC
Also Called: Screen Machine Sports
115 E 7th St (66441-2940)
PHONE....785 762-3081
Justin Hoover, *CEO*
Greg Bachman, *Partner*
Mary Hogan, *Partner*
EMP: 15
SQ FT: 1,700
SALES: 250K **Privately Held**
SIC: 2752 5999 5941 Offset & photolithographic printing; canvas products; sporting goods & bicycle shops

(G-3751)
SEA COAST DISPOSAL INC
2325 N Jackson St (66441-4724)
PHONE....785 784-5308
Mathew Bergains, *President*
EMP: 25
SALES (est): 428.6K **Privately Held**
SIC: 4953 Refuse systems

(G-3752)
SHADMEA MINISTRIES INC
2610 Strauss Blvd # 1106 (66441-2810)
P.O. Box 384 (66441-0384)
PHONE....912 332-0563
Faith Allen, *Principal*
Marcus Kambleh, *Principal*
Peter Diama, *Vice Pres*
Paulina Dolo, *Treasurer*
Jerry Smith, *Admin Sec*
EMP: 20
SALES (est): 342.9K **Privately Held**
SIC: 7389

(G-3753)
SHEILA M BURDETT AGENCY LLC
517 Wheatland Dr (66441-8968)
PHONE....785 762-2451
Sheila M Burdett, *CEO*
EMP: 10
SALES (est): 788.5K **Privately Held**
WEB: www.c21.kscoxmail.com
SIC: 6519 6531 Real property lessors; real estate agents & managers

(G-3754)
SIEMENS INDUSTRY INC
3200 Industrial St (66441)
PHONE....785 762-7814
Calvin Ince, *Manager*
EMP: 25
SALES (corp-wide): 96.9B **Privately Held**
SIC: 3589 Water treatment equipment, industrial
HQ: Siemens Industry, Inc.
1000 Deerfield Pkwy
Buffalo Grove IL 60089
847 215-1000

(G-3755)
SMITHFIELD DIRECT LLC
1920 Lacy Dr (66441-7559)
PHONE....785 762-3306
Derek Wik, *Principal*
EMP: 33 **Privately Held**
SIC: 5147 Meats, fresh
HQ: Smithfield Direct, Llc
4225 Naperville Rd # 600
Lisle IL 60532

(G-3756)
SMITHFIELD FOODS INC
1920 Lacy Dr (66441-7559)
PHONE....785 762-3306
EMP: 15 **Privately Held**
SIC: 2011 Meat packing plants
HQ: Smithfield Foods, Inc.
200 Commerce St
Smithfield VA 23430
757 365-3000

(G-3757)
SOONER OIL LLC
1626 Rivendell St (66441-4844)
PHONE....785 340-5602
Scott Bowen, *Principal*
EMP: 13
SALES (est): 222.1K **Privately Held**
SIC: 7389

(G-3758)
SUNFLOWER BANK NATIONAL ASSN
Also Called: First National Bank
510 N Jefferson St Ste 1 (66441-2978)
PHONE....785 238-3177
Gary Drake, *Manager*
EMP: 13
SALES (corp-wide): 52.4MM **Privately Held**
WEB: www.sunflowerbank.com
SIC: 6021 National trust companies with deposits, commercial
HQ: Sunflower Bank, National Association
1400 16th St Ste 250
Denver CO 80202
888 827-5564

(G-3759)
SYNGENTA SEEDS INC
11783 Ascher Rd (66441-7699)
PHONE....785 210-0218
Rollin Sears, *Manager*
EMP: 10
SALES (corp-wide): 63.3B **Privately Held**
SIC: 5191 Seeds: field, garden & flower
HQ: Syngenta Seeds, Llc
11055 Wayzata Blvd
Hopkins MN 55305
612 656-8600

(G-3760)
TUCSON HOTELS LP
310 Hammons Dr (66441-4368)
PHONE....785 210-1500
Karen Carroll, *Info Tech Mgr*
EMP: 157 **Privately Held**
SIC: 7011 Hotels & motels
PA: Tucson Hotels Lp
2711 Centerville Rd # 400
Wilmington DE 19808

(G-3761)
UPLAND MUTUAL INSURANCE INC
2220 Lacy Dr (66441-7574)
PHONE....785 762-4324
Wayne Gfeller, *Ch of Bd*
Chris Brown, *President*
Morris Edwards, *Vice Pres*
Ronald Koester, *CFO*
Trudy Britt, *Treasurer*
EMP: 14
SQ FT: 8,000
SALES: 15.4MM **Privately Held**
WEB: www.uplandmi.com
SIC: 6411 Insurance agents, brokers & service

(G-3762)
UPU INDUSTRIES INC
Also Called: Farmer's
3002 Indl St (66441)
PHONE....785 238-6990
Steve Orr, *Ch of Bd*
Phillip Orr, *President*
Alison Leathem, *Principal*
Brian Doyle, *CFO*
▲ **EMP:** 55
SQ FT: 110,000
SALES (est): 38.9MM **Privately Held**
WEB: www.upuindustries.com
SIC: 5083 Agricultural machinery

(G-3763)
VALLEY VIEW SENIOR LIFE LLC
1417 W Ash St (66441-3332)
PHONE....316 733-1144
Rachael Falls, *Human Res Dir*
Kelly Everson, *Marketing Staff*
Greg James, *Manager*
Bobbie Collette, *Director*
Deanna Shepard, *Director*
EMP: 99
SALES: 7.4MM **Privately Held**
SIC: 8051 Skilled nursing care facilities

(G-3764)
VENTRIA BIOSCIENCE INC
Also Called: Kansas Biomanufacturing Fcilty
2718 Industrial St (66441-8398)
PHONE....785 238-1101
Ron Backman, *Vice Pres*
Patrick Smith, *Facilities Mgr*
Lind Petrillo, *Controller*
Greg Unruh, *Branch Mgr*
EMP: 18
SALES (est): 364.6K **Privately Held**
SIC: 8733 Biotechnical research, noncommercial

(G-3765)
VEOLIA WATER NORTH AMERICA OPE
2101 N Jackson St (66441-4729)
P.O. Box 686 (66441-0686)
PHONE..................................785 762-5855
Dennis Taggart, *Manager*
EMP: 15
SALES (corp-wide): 582.1MM **Privately Held**
SIC: 4953 Recycling, waste materials
HQ: Veolia Water North America Operating Services, Llc
53 State St Ste 14
Boston MA 02109
617 849-6600

(G-3766)
WASTE MANAGEMENT OF KANSAS
2300 Elmdale Ave (66441-4502)
PHONE..................................785 238-3293
EMP: 11
SALES (corp-wide): 14.9B **Publicly Held**
SIC: 4953 Refuse systems
HQ: Waste Management Of Kansas, Inc
3611 Nw 16th St
Topeka KS 66618
785 233-3541

(G-3767)
WATERS INC
Also Called: True Value
129 E 6th St (66441-2937)
PHONE..................................785 238-3114
Jeff Hoss, *Branch Mgr*
EMP: 49
SALES (corp-wide): 49.8MM **Privately Held**
SIC: 5251 0781 0181 0811 Hardware; landscape services; nursery stock, growing of; tree farm
PA: Waters, Inc.
3213 Arnold Ave
Salina KS 67401
785 825-7309

(G-3768)
WEARY DAVIS LLC (PA)
Also Called: Weary Law Firm
819 N Washington St (66441-2446)
P.O. Box 187 (66441-0187)
PHONE..................................785 762-2210
Victor A Davis, *Partner*
Steve Struebing, *Partner*
David Troup, *Partner*
Kieth R Henry, *Principal*
Steven Struebing, *Principal*
EMP: 12
SALES (est): 1.4MM **Privately Held**
SIC: 8111 General practice attorney, lawyer

(G-3769)
WILLGRATTTEN PUBLICATIONS LLC
222 W 6th St (66441-5500)
PHONE..................................785 762-5000
Christopher Walker, *Principal*
Penny Nelson, *Principal*
EMP: 29
SQ FT: 13,000
SALES (est): 631K **Privately Held**
SIC: 2711 Newspapers, publishing & printing

(G-3770)
XXTRA CLEAN
10937 Clarks Creek Rd (66441-7814)
PHONE..................................785 210-5255
Keith Boller, *Manager*
EMP: 10
SALES: 76K **Privately Held**
SIC: 7349 Building maintenance services

Kalvesta
Gray County

(G-3771)
KALVESTA IMPLEMENT CO INC
32730 E State Road 156 (67835-9201)
P.O. Box 236, Cimarron (67835-0236)
PHONE..................................620 855-3567
Bruce Baldwin, *President*
▲ **EMP:** 15 **EST:** 1950
SQ FT: 5,400
SALES (est): 5.5MM **Privately Held**
SIC: 5083 Farm implements

Kanopolis
Ellsworth County

(G-3772)
INDEPENDENT SALT COMPANY
1126 20th Rd (67454-9560)
P.O. Box 36 (67454-0036)
PHONE..................................785 472-4421
Brian G Keener, *President*
Michelle Janssen, *Vice Pres*
Nadine B Keener, *Director*
EMP: 50 **EST:** 1913
SQ FT: 25,000
SALES (est): 18.7MM **Privately Held**
WEB: www.indsalt.com
SIC: 2899 Salt

Kanorado
Sherman County

(G-3773)
LIVENGOOD JL FARMS INC
6020 Road 3 (67741-9553)
PHONE..................................785 399-2251
Jim L Livengood, *President*
Tim Livengood, *Vice Pres*
EMP: 10
SALES (est): 474.5K **Privately Held**
SIC: 0212 0191 Beef cattle except feedlots; general farms, primarily crop

Kansas City
Wyandotte County

(G-3774)
1-800 RADIATOR & A/C
Also Called: Radiator Express
2820 Roe Ln Ste A (66103-1560)
PHONE..................................913 677-1799
Kevin Myers, *Branch Mgr*
EMP: 20
SALES (corp-wide): 42.9MM **Privately Held**
SIC: 5013 Radiators
PA: 1-800 Radiator & A/C
4401 Park Rd
Benicia CA 94510
707 747-7400

(G-3775)
7TH STREET CASINO
777 N 7th St (66101-3035)
PHONE..................................913 371-3500
Jim Nesvold, *General Mgr*
Erin Jones, *Principal*
Stephen Dow, *Controller*
Irene Siedler, *Human Res Mgr*
Jerrell Royal, *Marketing Mgr*
EMP: 29
SALES (est): 1.5MM **Privately Held**
SIC: 7011 Casino hotel

(G-3776)
A & K RAILROAD MATERIALS INC
2131 S 74th St (66106-4999)
PHONE..................................913 375-1810
Phillip Poce, *Manager*
EMP: 100
SALES (corp-wide): 150.1MM **Privately Held**
WEB: www.akrailroad.com
SIC: 5088 Railroad equipment & supplies
PA: A & K Railroad Materials, Inc.
1505 S Redwood Rd
Salt Lake City UT 84104
801 974-5484

(G-3777)
A 1 SEWER & SEPTIC SERVICE
1891 Merriam Ln (66106-4713)
PHONE..................................913 631-5201
Danielle McNeace, *President*
Mark L Mullin, *President*
Joyce Darlene Mullin, *Vice Pres*
EMP: 15
SALES (est): 2.5MM **Privately Held**
SIC: 7699 Sewer cleaning & rodding

(G-3778)
A M MECHANICAL SERVICE CO
225 S 65th St (66111-2202)
PHONE..................................913 829-5885
David Livingston, *President*
EMP: 13
SQ FT: 1,500
SALES (est): 1.1MM **Privately Held**
SIC: 1711 Warm air heating & air conditioning contractor

(G-3779)
ABRAHAM JACOB GORELICK
Also Called: Heart of America Police Supply
620 Minnesota Ave (66101-2806)
PHONE..................................913 371-0459
Abraham Jacob Gorelick, *Owner*
Nora Brown, *Coordinator*
EMP: 10
SQ FT: 32,000
SALES (est): 335K **Privately Held**
SIC: 5932 5331 5091 Pawnshop; variety stores; ammunition, sporting; firearms, sporting

(G-3780)
ACCENT ERECTION & MAINT CO INC
Also Called: Accent Sales and Service Co
501 S Valley St (66105-1133)
PHONE..................................913 371-1600
Ernest Sherrow, *CEO*
EMP: 18
SQ FT: 35,000
SALES (est): 5.5MM **Privately Held**
SIC: 5084 7699 Materials handling machinery; industrial machinery & equipment repair

(G-3781)
ACCORD SERVICES INC
4141 Fairbanks Ave (66106-1262)
P.O. Box 2346 (66110-0346)
PHONE..................................913 281-1879
Robert Banach, *President*
Bryan L Neal, *President*
James Sageser, *COO*
John Blake Hegeman, *Admin Sec*
EMP: 40
SQ FT: 2,000
SALES (est): 2.9MM **Privately Held**
SIC: 4213 Trucking, except local

(G-3782)
ACH FOAM TECHNOLOGIES INC
4001 Kaw Dr (66102-3716)
PHONE..................................913 321-4114
Ted Dann, *Principal*
EMP: 100 **Privately Held**
WEB: www.achfoam.com
SIC: 3545 5084 2821 3086 Cutting tools for machine tools; industrial machinery & equipment; plastics materials & resins; insulation or cushioning material, foamed plastic
HQ: Ach Foam Technologies, Inc.
8700 Turnpike Dr Ste 400
Westminster CO 80031
855 597-4427

(G-3783)
ACH FOAM TECHNOLOGIES INC
1400 N 3rd St (66101-1924)
PHONE..................................913 371-1973
Richard Nickloy, *Branch Mgr*
EMP: 15
SALES (corp-wide): 125.9MM **Privately Held**
SIC: 3086 Insulation or cushioning material, foamed plastic
PA: Ach Foam Technologies, Inc.
8700 Turnpike Dr Ste 400
Westminster CO 80031
855 597-4427

(G-3784)
ADAMS DENTAL GROUP PA
2119 Minnesota Ave (66102-4145)
PHONE..................................913 621-3113
Travis A Roberts DDS, *President*
Melissa Roberts, *Office Mgr*
EMP: 11
SALES (est): 1.2MM **Privately Held**
SIC: 8021 Dentists' office

(G-3785)
ADM GRAIN RIVER SYSTEM INC
10520 Wolcott Dr Ste 1 (66109-4091)
PHONE..................................913 788-7226
Robert Thomas, *Manager*
EMP: 11
SALES (corp-wide): 64.3B **Publicly Held**
SIC: 5153 2046 Grains; corn starch; high fructose corn syrup (HFCS)
HQ: Adm Grain River System, Inc.
4666 E Faries Pkwy
Decatur IL 62526
312 634-8100

(G-3786)
ADULT HEALTH SERVICES INC
1999 N 77th St (66112-2232)
PHONE..................................913 788-9896
Randall P Marquardt, *President*
EMP: 195
SALES: 3.3MM **Privately Held**
WEB: www.adultservices.com
SIC: 8082 8322 Home health care services; adult day care center

(G-3787)
ADVANCED MEDICAL DME LLC
2040 Hutton Rd (66109-4526)
PHONE..................................913 814-7464
Craig Meyer, *Mng Member*
EMP: 17
SALES (est): 3.5MM **Privately Held**
SIC: 5047 Medical equipment & supplies

(G-3788)
ADVANTAGE METALS RECYCLING LLC
1153 S 12th St (66105-1614)
PHONE..................................913 621-2711
Richard Galamba, *Branch Mgr*
EMP: 44
SALES (corp-wide): 25B **Publicly Held**
SIC: 5093 Metal scrap & waste materials
HQ: Advantage Metals Recycling Llc
510 Walnut St Ste 300
Kansas City MO 64106
816 861-2700

(G-3789)
ADVANTAGE METALS RECYCLING LLC
1015 S Packard St (66105-2128)
PHONE..................................913 321-3358
Brian Jacobs, *Branch Mgr*
EMP: 44
SALES (corp-wide): 25B **Publicly Held**
SIC: 5093 Ferrous metal scrap & waste; metal scrap & waste materials
HQ: Advantage Metals Recycling Llc
510 Walnut St Ste 300
Kansas City MO 64106
816 861-2700

(G-3790)
ADVANTAGE METALS RECYCLING LLC
201 N 2nd St (66118-1100)
PHONE..................................816 861-2700
EMP: 44

SALES (corp-wide): 25B **Publicly Held**
SIC: 5093 Metal scrap & waste materials
HQ: Advantage Metals Recycling Llc
510 Walnut St Ste 300
Kansas City MO 64106
816 861-2700

(G-3791)
AFFTON TRUCKING COMPANY INC
10 Shawnee Ave Ste C (66105-1401)
PHONE.....913 871-1315
Dan Karleskint, *Branch Mgr*
EMP: 13
SALES (corp-wide): 20.6MM **Privately Held**
SIC: 4731 Freight transportation arrangement
PA: Affton Trucking Company, Inc.
420 Gimblin Rd
Saint Louis MO 63147
314 942-6635

(G-3792)
AHERN RENTALS INC
350 N James St (66118-1141)
PHONE.....913 281-7555
Jimmy Mpbell, *Branch Mgr*
Jim Campbell, *Manager*
EMP: 20
SALES (corp-wide): 465.6MM **Privately Held**
WEB: www.ahernrentals.com
SIC: 7359 Tool rental
PA: Ahern Rentals, Inc.
1401 Mineral Ave
Las Vegas NV 89106
702 362-0623

(G-3793)
AHN MARKETING INCORPORATED (PA)
Also Called: Bunny's Beauty Supply
3748 State Ave (66102-3831)
PHONE.....913 342-2176
Scott Ahn, *President*
Kwang Ahn, *Admin Sec*
EMP: 15
SQ FT: 100,000
SALES (est): 5.5MM **Privately Held**
SIC: 5087 5999 Beauty parlor equipment & supplies; toiletries, cosmetics & perfumes

(G-3794)
AIRFIXTURE LLC
Also Called: Walnut Manufacturing
51 Kansas Ave Ste A (66105-1430)
PHONE.....913 312-1100
Kevin Pedrigi, *Manager*
William G Scott,
David Locke,
Michael McQueeny,
Jeff Otte,
◆ **EMP:** 28
SALES (est): 8.7MM **Privately Held**
SIC: 3647 Aircraft lighting fixtures

(G-3795)
ALA OPERATIONS LLC
Also Called: Piper, The
2300 N 113th Ter (66109-3786)
PHONE.....785 313-4059
Stephen Shields, *CEO*
EMP: 50 **EST:** 2014
SALES: 300K **Privately Held**
SIC: 8361 Home for the aged; rest home, with health care incidental

(G-3796)
ALL CITY TOW SERVICE
1015 S Bethany St (66105-1626)
PHONE.....913 371-1000
Ralph Richardson, *President*
EMP: 11
SALES (est): 603.2K **Privately Held**
SIC: 7549 Towing service, automotive; towing services

(G-3797)
ALL FREIGHT SYSTEMS INC (PA)
1134 S 12th St (66105-1615)
PHONE.....913 281-1203
Robert E Smith, *President*
Darrin Karley, *Vice Pres*
EMP: 50
SQ FT: 30,000
SALES (est): 10.2MM **Privately Held**
WEB: www.allfreightsystems.com
SIC: 4213 Contract haulers

(G-3798)
ALL SEASONS PARTY RENTAL INC
Also Called: Marquee Event Rentals
5050 Kansas Ave (66106-1135)
PHONE.....816 765-1444
▲ **EMP:** 105
SQ FT: 25,000
SALES (est): 16MM
SALES (corp-wide): 16MM **Privately Held**
WEB: www.allseasonstentrental.com
SIC: 7389 7359 Convention & show services; party supplies rental services
PA: Marquee Event Group, Inc.
9500 W 55th St Ste A
Countryside IL 60525
630 871-9999

(G-3799)
ALL SYSTEMS INC
3241 N 7th Street Trfy (66115-1105)
PHONE.....913 281-5100
Gary Venable, *CEO*
Gary Venable Jr, *President*
Richard Eberhardt, *Project Mgr*
Jason Lafferty, *Opers Mgr*
David Govro, *Manager*
EMP: 44 **EST:** 1974
SQ FT: 17,000
SALES: 7.2MM
SALES (corp-wide): 6.1MM **Privately Held**
SIC: 5065 7622 Communication equipment; communication equipment repair
PA: G E V Investment Inc
3241 N 7th Street Trfy
Kansas City KS 66115
913 677-5333

(G-3800)
ALL SYSTEMS DSGNED SLTIONS INC
3241 N 7th Street Trfy (66115-1105)
PHONE.....913 281-5100
Gary Venable Sr, *CEO*
Gary Venable Jr, *President*
Kourtney Govro, *Vice Pres*
David Govro, *Manager*
Holly Grohmann, *Manager*
EMP: 45
SQ FT: 18,000
SALES: 6.5MM **Privately Held**
WEB: www.allsystemsdesignedsolutions.com
SIC: 1731 Fire detection & burglar alarm systems specialization

(G-3801)
ALPH OMEGA GEOTECH INC
1701 State Ave (66102-4225)
PHONE.....913 371-0000
J Allan Bush, *President*
Shera Jay, *Office Mgr*
EMP: 30
SQ FT: 12,000
SALES (est): 5.4MM **Privately Held**
WEB: www.aogeotech.com
SIC: 8711 Consulting engineer

(G-3802)
ALS USA INC
Also Called: Als Tribology
935 Sunshine Rd (66115-1122)
PHONE.....913 281-9881
EMP: 25 **Privately Held**
SIC: 8734 Testing laboratories
HQ: Als Usa Inc.
4977 Energy Way
Reno NV 89502
775 356-5395

(G-3803)
AMERICAN BLDRS CONTRS SUP INC
Also Called: ABC Supply 6
1262 Southwest Blvd (66103-1902)
PHONE.....913 722-4747
Ray Beery, *Branch Mgr*
EMP: 60
SALES (corp-wide): 3.5B **Privately Held**
WEB: www.abcsupply.com
SIC: 5031 Building materials, exterior; windows
HQ: American Builders & Contractors Supply Co., Inc.
1 Abc Pkwy
Beloit WI 53511
608 362-7777

(G-3804)
AMERICAN CRANE & TRACTOR PARTS (PA)
Also Called: Actparts
2200 State Line Rd (66103-2187)
PHONE.....913 551-8223
Stacy Kenneth, *President*
Jerry Duxbury, *Plant Mgr*
Charles Yelton, *Opers Mgr*
Ron Brown, *Purchasing*
Jaime Pineiro, *Sales Mgr*
◆ **EMP:** 60
SQ FT: 60,000
SALES (est): 67.3MM **Privately Held**
SIC: 5082 Cranes, construction; tractors, construction

(G-3805)
AMERICAN MEDICAL RESPONSE INC
1902 Foxridge Dr (66106-4710)
PHONE.....913 227-0911
Steven Hoger, *Branch Mgr*
EMP: 106 **Privately Held**
SIC: 4119 Ambulance service
HQ: American Medical Response, Inc.
6363 S Fiddlers Green Cir # 1400
Greenwood Village CO 80111

(G-3806)
AMERIPURE WATER COMPANY
2704 W 43rd Ave (66103-3125)
PHONE.....913 825-6600
Dixie Williford, *Owner*
EMP: 18
SQ FT: 5,000
SALES (est): 2.9MM **Privately Held**
WEB: www.ameripurewater.com
SIC: 3589 Water purification equipment, household type

(G-3807)
AMINO BROS CO INC
8110 Kaw Dr (66111-1746)
P.O. Box 11277 (66111-0277)
PHONE.....913 334-2330
Mary Sullivan, *CEO*
Denise Janes, *President*
Albert K Seeman, *Vice Pres*
David Seeman, *Treasurer*
EMP: 200 **EST:** 1936
SQ FT: 3,800
SALES (est): 42.4MM **Privately Held**
SIC: 1611 General contractor, highway & street construction

(G-3808)
AMSTED RAIL COMPANY INC
7111 Griffin Rd (66111-2406)
PHONE.....913 299-2223
EMP: 13
SALES (corp-wide): 2.4B **Privately Held**
SIC: 5099 5088 1629 Brass goods; railroad equipment & supplies; railroad & railway roadbed construction
HQ: Amsted Rail Company, Inc.
311 S Wacker Dr Ste 5300
Chicago IL 60606

(G-3809)
ANDERSON & SONS TRUCKING INC
108 S 102nd St (66111-1268)
PHONE.....913 422-3171
George Anderson, *CEO*
Winfred Anderson, *President*
Darrell Anderson, *Treasurer*
Katie Anderson, *Admin Sec*
EMP: 24
SALES (est): 3.5MM **Privately Held**
SIC: 4212 Dump truck haulage; hazardous waste transport

(G-3810)
ANDERSON ERICKSON DAIRY CO
Also Called: Ae Farms
5341 Speaker Rd (66106-1055)
PHONE.....913 621-4801
Rich Redze, *General Mgr*
Mike Dorrian, *Manager*
EMP: 60
SALES (corp-wide): 112.1MM **Privately Held**
SIC: 5143 0241 Dairy products, except dried or canned; milk production
PA: Anderson Erickson Dairy Co.
2420 E University Ave
Des Moines IA 50317
515 265-2521

(G-3811)
ANDREWS AND ABBEY RILEY LLC
Also Called: Abbey-Riley Furniture Studio
4462 State Line Rd (66103-3512)
PHONE.....913 262-2212
Gary Boyce, *President*
Jim Pimenteo, *President*
James Pimentel, *Vice Pres*
Jimmie Sistrunk, *Treasurer*
Brad Boyce, *Mng Member*
EMP: 12
SQ FT: 24,000
SALES: 1.2MM **Privately Held**
WEB: www.genevaparks.com
SIC: 7641 2512 2391 Reupholstery; upholstery work; upholstered household furniture; curtains & draperies

(G-3812)
ANIXTER POWER SOLUTIONS INC
4600 Kansas Ave (66106-1127)
PHONE.....913 202-6945
Joe Guthrie, *Branch Mgr*
EMP: 12
SALES (corp-wide): 8.4B **Publicly Held**
SIC: 5063 Wire & cable
HQ: Anixter Power Solutions Inc.
2301 Patriot Blvd
Glenview IL 60026

(G-3813)
ANN BARBER
Also Called: Nguyen, Colleen A DDS
9501 State Ave Ste 7 (66111-1871)
PHONE.....913 788-0800
Ann Barber, *Owner*
EMP: 13
SALES (est): 526.6K **Privately Held**
SIC: 8021 Dentists' office

(G-3814)
ARC DOCUMENT SOLUTIONS INC
1100 W Cambrdg Cir Dr 300 (66103)
PHONE.....816 300-6600
Vince Pingel, *Branch Mgr*
EMP: 27
SALES (corp-wide): 400.7MM **Publicly Held**
SIC: 7334 Photocopying & duplicating services
PA: Arc Document Solutions, Inc.
12657 Alcosta Blvd # 200
San Ramon CA 94583
925 949-5100

(G-3815)
ARC DOCUMENT SOLUTIONS INC
1100 W Cambrdg Circl 300 (66103)
PHONE.....314 231-5025
EMP: 27
SALES (corp-wide): 400.7MM **Publicly Held**
SIC: 7334 Photocopying & duplicating services
PA: Arc Document Solutions, Inc.
12657 Alcosta Blvd # 200
San Ramon CA 94583
925 949-5100

GEOGRAPHIC

(G-3816)
ARCHDIOCESE KANSAS CY IN KANS
Also Called: Catholic Cmnty Svc HM Hlth Dp
2220 Central Ave (66102-4759)
PHONE....................................913 621-5090
Darlene Smikahl, *Director*
EMP: 39
SALES (corp-wide): 77.1MM **Privately Held**
WEB: www.archkck.org
SIC: 8082 8322 Home health care services; adoption services
PA: Archdiocese Of Kansas City In Kansas
12615 Parallel Pkwy
Kansas City KS 66109
913 721-1570

(G-3817)
ARCHER-DANIELS-MIDLAND COMPANY
Also Called: ADM
940 Kindleberger Rd (66115-1118)
P.O. Box 15036 (66115)
PHONE....................................913 321-1696
Phil Swearengin, *Manager*
EMP: 5
SALES (corp-wide): 64.3B **Publicly Held**
WEB: www.admworld.com
SIC: 2041 Flour & other grain mill products
PA: Archer-Daniels-Midland Company
77 W Wacker Dr Ste 4600
Chicago IL 60601
312 634-8100

(G-3818)
ARGENTINE SAVINGS AND LN ASSN (PA)
3004 Strong Ave (66106-2112)
P.O. Box 6269 (66106-0269)
PHONE....................................913 831-2004
Mark Rielley, *President*
Marvin Max, *Chairman*
Larry Radke, *Exec VP*
EMP: 10 **EST:** 1906
SQ FT: 7,500
SALES: 2MM **Privately Held**
SIC: 6035 Federal savings & loan associations

(G-3819)
ARMDAT INC
18 Central Ave (66118-1198)
PHONE....................................913 321-4287
David Tyler, *President*
Janet Tyler, *Treasurer*
EMP: 10 **EST:** 1969
SQ FT: 6,000
SALES: 930K **Privately Held**
SIC: 7699 Tank truck cleaning service

(G-3820)
ARTS MEXICAN PRODUCTS INC
615 Kansas Ave (66105-1311)
PHONE....................................913 371-2163
Robert Gutierrez, *President*
Rachel Kelly, *Vice Pres*
Angela Gutierrez, *Treasurer*
EMP: 19 **EST:** 1961
SQ FT: 17,250
SALES (est): 2.4MM **Privately Held**
WEB: www.artsmexican.com
SIC: 2099 5141 Tortillas, fresh or refrigerated; groceries, general line

(G-3821)
ASH GROVE CEMENT COMPANY
8440 Gibbs Rd (66111-2629)
PHONE....................................913 422-2523
EMP: 36
SALES (corp-wide): 29.7B **Privately Held**
SIC: 3241 Masonry cement
HQ: Ash Grove Cement Company
11011 Cody St Ste 300
Overland Park KS 66210
913 451-8900

(G-3822)
ASNER IRON AND METAL CO
34 N James St (66118-1148)
PHONE....................................913 281-4000
Labe Asner, *President*
Gloria Asner, *Admin Sec*
EMP: 10
SQ FT: 6,000
SALES (est): 2MM **Privately Held**
SIC: 5093 Ferrous metal scrap & waste; metal scrap & waste materials

(G-3823)
ASSOCIATED CYLINDER SE
1201 Douglas Ave (66103-1405)
PHONE....................................951 776-9915
Mark Olguin, *Principal*
EMP: 5 **EST:** 2013
SALES (est): 584.1K **Privately Held**
SIC: 3491 Compressed gas cylinder valves

(G-3824)
ASSOCIATED PODIATRIST PA
Also Called: Gentry, Donald A
8919 Parallel Pkwy # 550 (66112-1545)
PHONE....................................913 321-0522
Donald A Gentry DPM, *Partner*
Daniel Shead, *Podiatrist*
Gregory Folsom, *Surgeon*
EMP: 40
SALES (est): 1.5MM **Privately Held**
SIC: 8043 Offices & clinics of podiatrists

(G-3825)
ASSOCIATED WHOLESALE GROC INC (PA)
Also Called: Associated Grocers
5000 Kansas Ave (66106-1135)
PHONE....................................913 288-1000
Don Woods Jr, *Vice Ch Bd*
Jerry Garland, *President*
Bob Hufford, *Chairman*
Robert Dillard, *District Mgr*
Frances Puhl, *Senior VP*
◆ **EMP:** 850 **EST:** 1926
SQ FT: 990,000
SALES: 9.7B **Privately Held**
WEB: www.awginc.com
SIC: 4225 5143 5142 5147 General warehousing & storage; dairy products, except dried or canned; packaged frozen goods; meats & meat products; meats, fresh; fish, fresh; fish, frozen, unpackaged; fresh fruits & vegetables

(G-3826)
ASSOCIATED WHOLESALE GROC INC
Also Called: Awg
5000 Kansas Ave (66106-1135)
PHONE....................................913 319-8500
Gary Philips, *President*
EMP: 151
SALES (corp-wide): 9.7B **Privately Held**
WEB: www.awginc.com
SIC: 4225 General warehousing & storage
PA: Associated Wholesale Grocers, Inc.
5000 Kansas Ave
Kansas City KS 66106
913 288-1000

(G-3827)
ASSOCIATES FAMILY MEDICINE PA
Also Called: Jevons, Robert E
8940 State Ave (66112-1646)
PHONE....................................913 596-1313
David B Johnson, *President*
Patty Johnson, *Manager*
EMP: 30
SQ FT: 9,000
SALES: 1.5MM **Privately Held**
SIC: 8011 General & family practice, physician/surgeon

(G-3828)
ASSOCIATES FOR FEMALE CARE PA
9501 State Ave Ste 3 (66111-1871)
PHONE....................................913 299-2229
Larry Nibbelink, *President*
Charles Stubblefield, *President*
EMP: 11
SQ FT: 4,000
SALES (est): 910K **Privately Held**
WEB: www.whnobgyn.com
SIC: 8011 Gynecologist; obstetrician

(G-3829)
AT&T CORP
1813 Village West Pkwy (66111-1880)
PHONE....................................913 334-9615
Glen Cadle, *Manager*
Christie Eads, *Manager*
EMP: 12
SALES (corp-wide): 170.7B **Publicly Held**
SIC: 4812 Cellular telephone services
HQ: At&T Corp.
1 At&T Way
Bedminster NJ 07921
800 403-3302

(G-3830)
AVENUE OF LIFE INC
500 N 7th St (66101-3034)
P.O. Box 34495 MO (64116-0895)
PHONE....................................816 519-8419
Desiree Monize, *Exec Dir*
Andre Jones, *Director*
EMP: 23
SALES: 2MM **Privately Held**
SIC: 8322 Child related social services; emergency social services

(G-3831)
AWG ACQUISITION LLC
5000 Kansas Ave (66106-1192)
PHONE....................................913 288-1000
Gary L Phillips, *Director*
EMP: 610
SALES (est): 6.2MM
SALES (corp-wide): 9.7B **Privately Held**
SIC: 6799 Investors
PA: Associated Wholesale Grocers, Inc.
5000 Kansas Ave
Kansas City KS 66106
913 288-1000

(G-3832)
B & B DELIVERY ENTERPRISE LLC
Also Called: B & B Transfer
29 Woodswether Rd (66118-1132)
PHONE....................................913 541-9090
John Cockle,
Lynn Cockle,
EMP: 15
SALES (est): 1.8MM **Privately Held**
SIC: 4212 Delivery service, vehicular

(G-3833)
B & E INC
Also Called: Ranch West Bowling Center
8201 State Ave (66112-1840)
PHONE....................................913 299-1110
Robert Johannes, *President*
EMP: 19
SQ FT: 10,000
SALES (est): 505.1K **Privately Held**
SIC: 7933 5812 5941 7993 Ten pin center; snack bar; sporting goods & bicycle shops; coin-operated amusement devices

(G-3834)
B & H FREIGHT LINE INC
468 S 26th St (66105-1106)
P.O. Box 509, Harrisonville MO (64701-0509)
PHONE....................................913 621-1840
Paul Billings, *General Mgr*
Mike Morgan, *VP Sales*
EMP: 10
SALES (corp-wide): 7MM **Privately Held**
SIC: 4213 Contract haulers
PA: B & H Freight Line, Inc.
1700 Anaconda Rd
Harrisonville MO 64701
816 884-4054

(G-3835)
B & J FOOD SERVICE EQP INC (PA)
236 N 7th St (66101-3202)
PHONE....................................913 621-6165
Toll Free:....................................888 -
Nancy Mosburg, *CEO*
Bill Mosburg, *President*
Robert Pickering, *Senior VP*
Scott Mosburg, *Vice Pres*
Deb Davis, *Project Mgr*
EMP: 38
SQ FT: 40,000
SALES (est): 93MM **Privately Held**
WEB: www.bjfoodservice.com
SIC: 5046 Restaurant equipment & supplies

(G-3836)
BAADER LINCO INC (DH)
2955 Fairfax Trfy (66115-1317)
PHONE....................................913 621-3366
Ralph A Miller, *President*
Andrew Miller, *Principal*
Leslie Hughes, *Purch Agent*
Doug Barnett, *Engineer*
Joshua Cunningham, *Engineer*
▲ **EMP:** 30
SQ FT: 70,000
SALES (est): 21MM
SALES (corp-wide): 64.9MM **Privately Held**
WEB: www.baaderna.com
SIC: 3556 5084 Poultry processing machinery; industrial machinery & equipment
HQ: Baader North America Corporation
2955 Fairfax Trfy
Kansas City KS 66115
913 621-3366

(G-3837)
BAADER NORTH AMERICA CORP (HQ)
2955 Fairfax Trfy (66115-1317)
PHONE....................................913 621-3366
Thorir Einarsson, *CEO*
Andrew R Miller, *President*
Shawn Nicholas, *Corp Secy*
Dave Hargis, *Purch Agent*
Karen Brady, *CFO*
▲ **EMP:** 10
SALES (est): 21MM
SALES (corp-wide): 64.9MM **Privately Held**
SIC: 5084 3556 Food industry machinery; fish processing machinery, equipment & supplies; food products machinery
PA: Nordischer Maschinenbau Rud. Baader Gmbh + Co. Kg
Geniner Str. 249
Lubeck 23560
451 530-20

(G-3838)
BAGEL WORKS CAFE INC
Also Called: Bagel Works Bread Company
1523 S 45th St (66106-2572)
PHONE....................................913 789-7333
Steve Ellenberg, *President*
Enzo Di Pede, *Treasurer*
EMP: 18
SQ FT: 4,000
SALES: 1MM **Privately Held**
SIC: 5812 5149 Cafe; caterers; bakery products

(G-3839)
BANK AMERICA NATIONAL ASSN
7809 State Ave (66112-2416)
PHONE....................................816 979-8215
Amario Griffin, *Manager*
EMP: 15
SALES (corp-wide): 110.5B **Publicly Held**
WEB: www.bofa.com
SIC: 6021 National commercial banks
HQ: Bank Of America, National Association
100 S Tryon St
Charlotte NC 28202
704 386-5681

(G-3840)
BANK AMERICA NATIONAL ASSN
1314 N 38th St (66102-2231)
PHONE....................................816 979-8257
Steven Trader, *Branch Mgr*
EMP: 19
SALES (corp-wide): 110.5B **Publicly Held**
WEB: www.bofa.com
SIC: 6021 National commercial banks
HQ: Bank Of America, National Association
100 S Tryon St
Charlotte NC 28202
704 386-5681

(G-3841)
BANK OF LABOR
7354 State Ave (66112-3005)
PHONE....................................913 321-4242
Susan Cole, *Branch Mgr*

EMP: 25
SALES (corp-wide): 26.3MM **Privately Held**
SIC: 6022 State trust companies accepting deposits, commercial
HQ: Bank Of Labor
756 Minnesota Ave
Kansas City KS 66101
913 321-6800

(G-3842)
BANK OF LABOR
4431 Shawnee Dr (66106-3644)
PHONE..................................913 321-4242
Mary Moulin, *Manager*
EMP: 25
SALES (corp-wide): 26.3MM **Privately Held**
SIC: 6022 State trust companies accepting deposits, commercial
HQ: Bank Of Labor
756 Minnesota Ave
Kansas City KS 66101
913 321-6800

(G-3843)
BANK OF LABOR (HQ)
756 Minnesota Ave (66101-2704)
PHONE..................................913 321-6800
Cal Roberts, *President*
Susie Roberts, *President*
Bill Arnold, *Exec VP*
Fred Myers, *Exec VP*
David Duggins, *Senior VP*
EMP: 45
SQ FT: 20,000
SALES: 30.3MM
SALES (corp-wide): 26.3MM **Privately Held**
SIC: 6022 State trust companies accepting deposits, commercial
PA: Brotherhood Bancshares Inc
756 Minnesota Ave
Kansas City KS 66101
913 321-4242

(G-3844)
BANKERS AND INVESTORS CO
1300 N 78th St Ste G03 (66112-2406)
PHONE..................................913 299-5008
Jerrod Foresman, *Manager*
EMP: 15
SALES (est): 2.1MM **Privately Held**
WEB: www.bankersinvestors.com
SIC: 6411 Insurance brokers

(G-3845)
BARTLETT GRAIN COMPANY LP
1310 Fairfax Trfy (66115-1404)
PHONE..................................913 321-0900
Louis Barrack, *Branch Mgr*
Ken Day, *Manager*
EMP: 15
SALES (corp-wide): 1B **Privately Held**
SIC: 5153 Grains
HQ: Bartlett Grain Company, L.P.
4900 Main St Ste 1200
Kansas City MO 64112
816 753-6300

(G-3846)
BARTLETT GRAIN COMPANY LP
940 Kindleberger Rd (66115-1118)
PHONE..................................913 321-1696
Jeff Armstrong, *Manager*
EMP: 10
SALES (corp-wide): 1B **Privately Held**
SIC: 5153 Grains
HQ: Bartlett Grain Company, L.P.
4900 Main St Ste 1200
Kansas City MO 64112
816 753-6300

(G-3847)
BARTON SOLVENTS INC
901 S 66th Ter (66111-2348)
P.O. Box 11207 (66111-0207)
PHONE..................................913 287-5500
Andy Betts, *Marketing Staff*
John Guigli, *Analyst*
EMP: 19
SALES (corp-wide): 157MM **Privately Held**
WEB: www.barsol.com
SIC: 5169 5172 Industrial chemicals; lubricating oils & greases
PA: Barton Solvents, Inc.
1920 Ne 46th Ave
Des Moines IA 50313
515 265-7998

(G-3848)
BATLINER PAPER STOCK COMPANY
Also Called: Batliner Paper Converting
305 Sunshine Rd (66115-1230)
PHONE..................................913 233-1367
Kelly Ryan, *General Mgr*
EMP: 10
SALES (corp-wide): 48.7MM **Privately Held**
SIC: 5093 Waste paper
HQ: Batliner Paper Stock Company
2501 E Front St
Kansas City MO 64120
816 483-3343

(G-3849)
BAXTER MECHANICAL CONTRACTORS
Also Called: Honeywell Authorized Dealer
565 S 4th St (66105-1321)
P.O. Box 5102 (66119-0102)
PHONE..................................913 281-6303
John Martin, *CEO*
David Martin, *Opers Mgr*
EMP: 15
SALES (est): 1.5MM **Privately Held**
SIC: 1711 5082 Mechanical contractor; general construction machinery & equipment

(G-3850)
BEAUTY BRANDS LLC
6519 Nw Barry Rd (66106)
PHONE..................................816 505-2800
Tammy Fisher, *Manager*
EMP: 20 **Privately Held**
SIC: 7231 Beauty shops
PA: Beauty Brands Llc
15507 W 99th St
Lenexa KS 66219

(G-3851)
BEAVER DRILL & TOOL COMPANY
3995 Mission Rd (66103-2798)
PHONE..................................913 384-2400
Robert Vielhauer, *President*
Keith Taschler, *Vice Pres*
EMP: 13 **EST:** 1954
SQ FT: 6,000
SALES (est): 7MM **Privately Held**
WEB: www.beaverdrill.com
SIC: 5085 Industrial supplies

(G-3852)
BEELMAN TRUCK CO
51 Silver Ave (66103-2164)
PHONE..................................913 362-0553
EMP: 48
SALES (corp-wide): 110.6MM **Privately Held**
SIC: 4214 Local trucking with storage
PA: Beelman Truck Co.
1 Racehorse Dr
East Saint Louis IL 62205
618 646-5300

(G-3853)
BENNET ROGERS PIPE COATING
Also Called: Rota-Carrus
900 Kindleberger Rd (66115-1118)
PHONE..................................913 371-5288
Champ C Bennett, *President*
Grant Bennett III, *Vice Pres*
G G Bennett Jr, *Treasurer*
EMP: 12
SALES (est): 1.2MM **Privately Held**
SIC: 4213 Trucking, except local

(G-3854)
BENNETT RGERS PIPE COATING INC
900 Kindleberger Rd (66115-1118)
P.O. Box 15016 (66115-0016)
PHONE..................................913 371-3880
Champ Bennett, *President*
Champ C Bennett, *President*
Grant G Bennett Jr, *Chairman*
Grant Bennett III, *Vice Pres*
EMP: 20 **EST:** 1954
SQ FT: 4,200
SALES (est): 5MM **Privately Held**
SIC: 1623 3498 Water, sewer & utility lines; fabricated pipe & fittings

(G-3855)
BENNETT TOOL & DIE LLC
Also Called: A & E Custom Manufacturing
3150 Chrysler Rd (66115-1326)
PHONE..................................913 371-4641
John Jaixen, *Plant Mgr*
Mike Evans, *Sales Staff*
Joe Sheehan, *Mktg Dir*
Steven Hasty, *Executive*
Sue Hicks, *Administration*
EMP: 65
SALES (corp-wide): 47.1MM **Privately Held**
SIC: 3469 3544 3441 Stamping metal for the trade; special dies, tools, jigs & fixtures; fabricated structural metal
HQ: Bennett Tool & Die, Llc
1550 Airport Rd
Gallatin TN 37066
615 227-5291

(G-3856)
BEST HARVEST LLC
Also Called: Best Harvest Bakeries
530 S 65th St (66111-2324)
PHONE..................................913 287-6300
Angela Arteman, *Manager*
Chris Botticella, *Technology*
Edward F Honesty,
▲ **EMP:** 60
SQ FT: 32,000
SALES (est): 20.6MM **Privately Held**
WEB: www.bestharvest.com
SIC: 2051 Buns, bread type: fresh or frozen
PA: Beavers Holdings, Llc
3550 Hobson Rd Fl 3
Woodridge IL 60517

(G-3857)
BEST WSTN K C SPDWAY INN SITES
10401 France Family Dr (66111-1905)
PHONE..................................913 334-4440
Dave Hasvold, *Principal*
EMP: 14 **EST:** 2011
SALES (est): 556.8K **Privately Held**
SIC: 7011 Hotels & motels

(G-3858)
BETHEL NEIGHBORHOOD CENTER
14 S 7th St (66101-3831)
PHONE..................................913 371-8218
Lisa Harris, *Exec Dir*
Mang Sonna, *Exec Dir*
Matthew Sweden, *Director*
EMP: 12
SALES (est): 567.6K **Privately Held**
WEB: www.bethelcenter.org
SIC: 8322 Individual & family services

(G-3859)
BICHELMEYER MEATS A CORP
Also Called: Bichelmeyer's
704 Cheyenne Ave (66105-2010)
PHONE..................................913 342-5945
James N Bichelmeyer, *President*
Joseph M Bichelmeyer, *Vice Pres*
EMP: 18
SQ FT: 13,500
SALES: 3.2MM **Privately Held**
WEB: www.bichelmeyers.com
SIC: 5421 5147 Meat markets, including freezer provisioners; meats, fresh

(G-3860)
BIG W INDUSTRIES INC
200 S 5th St (66101-3828)
PHONE..................................913 321-2112
Charles Nickloy III, *President*
C Nickloy III, *President*
EMP: 24
SALES (est): 4MM **Privately Held**
WEB: www.big-w.com
SIC: 3634 5023 Waffle irons, electric; kitchenware

(G-3861)
BILLS TROPICAL GREENHOUSE
Also Called: Bill Tropical Greenhouse
2943 S 47th St (66106-3739)
P.O. Box 6127 (66106-0127)
PHONE..................................913 432-6383
William E Messmer, *President*
Juanita E Messmer, *Treasurer*
EMP: 12 **EST:** 1970
SQ FT: 10,000
SALES (est): 994.8K **Privately Held**
SIC: 0181 Ornamental nursery products

(G-3862)
BIMBO BAKERIES USA INC
7565 State Ave (66112-2815)
PHONE..................................913 328-1234
Linda Capper, *Manager*
EMP: 8 **Privately Held**
SIC: 2051 Bread, cake & related products
HQ: Bimbo Bakeries Usa, Inc
255 Business Center Dr # 200
Horsham PA 19044
215 347-5500

(G-3863)
BLACKBURNS ALL STAR ROOFING
902 Osage Ave (66105-1834)
PHONE..................................913 321-3456
Paul Blackburn, *President*
EMP: 20
SQ FT: 1,600
SALES (est): 1.8MM **Privately Held**
SIC: 1761 Roofing contractor

(G-3864)
BLACKFIN LLC
537 Central Ave (66101-3549)
PHONE..................................816 985-4850
John E Pauley,
John Pauley,
EMP: 10
SQ FT: 4,500
SALES (est): 1MM **Privately Held**
SIC: 6531 Real estate agents & managers

(G-3865)
BLACKJACK TIRE SUPPLIES INC
Also Called: Blackjack Manufacturing
3260 N 7th Street Trfy (66115-1106)
PHONE..................................816 872-1158
James Parker, *President*
Ron Castleman, *Admin Sec*
▲ **EMP:** 12
SQ FT: 9,000
SALES (est): 5MM **Privately Held**
WEB: www.fciautomotive.com
SIC: 5013 Automotive supplies & parts; automotive supplies

(G-3866)
BLACKS RETAIL LIQUOR LLC
Also Called: Black's Liquor Store
1014 Central Ave (66102-5315)
PHONE..................................913 281-1551
Harry Scherzer,
EMP: 10 **EST:** 1965
SQ FT: 3,000
SALES: 4MM **Privately Held**
SIC: 5921 5182 Hard liquor; wine & distilled beverages

(G-3867)
BLAKE & UHLIG P A (PA)
753 State Ave Ste 475 (66101-2510)
PHONE..................................913 321-8884
Martin Walter, *Managing Prtnr*
Richard L Calcara, *Treasurer*
Curtis G Barnhill,
Charles R Schwartz,
Robert L Uhlig,

GEOGRAPHIC

EMP: 30
SALES (est): 3.9MM **Privately Held**
SIC: 8111 General practice law office

(G-3868)
BNSF RAILWAY COMPANY
2525 Argentine Blvd (66106-1270)
PHONE..................................913 551-4882
Dan Davis, *Principal*
EMP: 13
SALES (corp-wide): 225.3B **Publicly Held**
WEB: www.billpurdy.com
SIC: 4011 Railroads, line-haul operating
HQ: Bnsf Railway Company
2650 Lou Menk Dr
Fort Worth TX 76131
800 795-2673

(G-3869)
BNSF RAILWAY COMPANY
Also Called: Burlington Northern
4515 Kansas Ave (66106-1124)
PHONE..................................913 551-2604
Carl Myers, *Manager*
EMP: 46
SALES (corp-wide): 225.3B **Publicly Held**
WEB: www.billpurdy.com
SIC: 4011 Railroads, line-haul operating
HQ: Bnsf Railway Company
2650 Lou Menk Dr
Fort Worth TX 76131
800 795-2673

(G-3870)
BOARD OF EDCATN OF KANS CY KS
Also Called: Morse Early Childhood Center
912 S Baltimore St (66105-1715)
PHONE..................................913 627-6550
Debi Apple, *Principal*
EMP: 25
SALES (corp-wide): 100.7MM **Privately Held**
WEB: www.kckps.k12.ks.us
SIC: 8211 8351 Public elementary school; preschool center
PA: Board Of Education Of Kansas City, Ks (Inc)
2010 N 59th St
Kansas City KS 66104
913 551-3200

(G-3871)
BOARD OF EDCATN OF KANS CY KS
Also Called: Nutritional Services
2112 N 18th St (66104-4706)
PHONE..................................913 627-3913
Carla Robinson, *Director*
EMP: 45
SALES (corp-wide): 100.7MM **Privately Held**
WEB: www.kckps.k12.ks.us
SIC: 8049 Dietician
PA: Board Of Education Of Kansas City, Ks (Inc)
2010 N 59th St
Kansas City KS 66104
913 551-3200

(G-3872)
BOWDEN CONTRACTING COMPANY INC
1030 Pawnee Ave (66105-1743)
PHONE..................................913 342-5112
Dan Bowden, *President*
EMP: 17
SQ FT: 12,800
SALES (est): 4.8MM **Privately Held**
WEB: www.bowdencontracting.com
SIC: 1542 Commercial & office building, new construction; commercial & office buildings, renovation & repair

(G-3873)
BOYS & GIRLS CLUBS OF AMERICA
Also Called: Boys Grls Clubs Grater Kans Ci
1240 Troup Ave (66104-5866)
PHONE..................................913 621-3260
Ross Jensby, *Corp Comm Staff*
Eunice Holmes, *Director*
EMP: 15
SALES (corp-wide): 141.3MM **Privately Held**
WEB: www.careerlaunch.net
SIC: 8641 Youth organizations
PA: Boys & Girls Clubs Of America
1275 Peachtree St Ne # 500
Atlanta GA 30309
404 487-5700

(G-3874)
BRACO SALES INC
Also Called: Braco Stone
3299 N 7th Street Trfy (66115-1105)
PHONE..................................816 471-5005
Graham Bray, *President*
Mark Bray, *Vice Pres*
Scott Bray, *Treasurer*
Mark Gray, *Manager*
EMP: 27
SALES: 5MM **Privately Held**
WEB: www.bracostone.com
SIC: 5032 3281 Granite building stone; marble building stone; altars, cut stone

(G-3875)
BRAHAM J GEHA
8800 State Line (66160-0001)
PHONE..................................913 383-9099
Braham Geha, *Principal*
EMP: 20 **EST**: 2001
SALES (est): 268.8K **Privately Held**
SIC: 8011 Offices & clinics of medical doctors

(G-3876)
BRANDSAFWAY SERVICES LLC
548 S 11th St (66105-1252)
PHONE..................................913 342-9000
Mike Legrande, *Manager*
EMP: 10
SALES (corp-wide): 2.1B **Privately Held**
WEB: www.safway.com
SIC: 5082 Scaffolding
HQ: Brandsafway Services Llc
1325 Cobb International D
Kennesaw GA 30152

(G-3877)
BRIDGESTONE RET OPERATIONS LLC
Also Called: Tires Plus Total Car Care
7815 State Ave (66112-2416)
PHONE..................................913 299-3090
John Schmalz, *Manager*
EMP: 10 **Privately Held**
WEB: www.tiresplus.com
SIC: 7534 Tire retreading & repair shops
HQ: Bridgestone Retail Operations, Llc
333 E Lake St Ste 300
Bloomingdale IL 60108
630 259-9000

(G-3878)
BRIDGESTONE RET OPERATIONS LLC
Also Called: Firestone
7717 State Ave (66112-2819)
PHONE..................................913 334-1555
Nicholas Harp, *Manager*
EMP: 30 **Privately Held**
WEB: www.bfis.com
SIC: 5531 7534 7539 Automotive tires; rebuilding & retreading tires; brake services
HQ: Bridgestone Retail Operations, Llc
333 E Lake St Ste 300
Bloomingdale IL 60108
630 259-9000

(G-3879)
BROWN STRAUSS INC
802 Kindleberger Rd (66115-1117)
PHONE..................................913 621-4000
Chris Gunderson, *Manager*
EMP: 25 **Privately Held**
SIC: 5051 Steel
PA: Brown Strauss, Inc.
2495 Uravan St
Aurora CO 80011

(G-3880)
BURKE INC (PA)
Also Called: Leisure-Lift
1800 Merriam Ln (66106-4778)
PHONE..................................913 722-5658
Du Wayne Kramer, *President*
Ron Kruse, *Vice Pres*
Brian White, *Vice Pres*
Thania Farrar, *Research*
Jerry Traylor, *Engineer*
EMP: 45
SQ FT: 28,000
SALES (est): 15.5MM **Privately Held**
WEB: www.pacesaver.com
SIC: 3751 3842 Motor scooters & parts; surgical appliances & supplies

(G-3881)
BURNS BOYS CO INC
6634 Kaw Dr (66111-2321)
PHONE..................................913 788-8654
Rex Burns, *President*
Shirley Burns, *Corp Secy*
EMP: 15
SALES (est): 2.9MM **Privately Held**
SIC: 1796 Millwright

(G-3882)
BUTLER TRANSPORT INC
347 N James St (66118-1140)
PHONE..................................913 321-0047
George M Butler, *President*
Judith L Butler, *Corp Secy*
Chris Ray, *Opers Staff*
Judy Butler, *Human Res Dir*
Pat Delperdang, *Manager*
EMP: 200
SQ FT: 150,000
SALES (est): 69.7MM **Privately Held**
WEB: www.butlertransport.com
SIC: 4213 4212 4731 Contract haulers; refrigerated products transport; local trucking, without storage; truck transportation brokers

(G-3883)
BYRDS DANCE & GYMNASTICS INC
2929 N 103rd Ter (66109-5014)
PHONE..................................913 788-9792
Susan Atwood, *President*
Carol Byrd, *Vice Pres*
EMP: 35
SALES (est): 322.8K **Privately Held**
SIC: 7911 7999 Dance studio & school; gymnastic instruction, non-membership

(G-3884)
C & W OPERATIONS LTD
Also Called: Fantastic Sams
8157 State Ave (66112-2421)
PHONE..................................913 299-8820
Denna Dogan, *Branch Mgr*
EMP: 10
SALES (est): 172.3K
SALES (corp-wide): 1.7MM **Privately Held**
WEB: www.fscw.com
SIC: 7231 Unisex hair salons
PA: C & W Operations, Ltd.
9108 Barton St
Shawnee Mission KS 66214
913 438-6400

(G-3885)
CAM-DEX CORPORATION (PA)
Also Called: CAM-Dex Security
10 Central Ave (66118-1114)
PHONE..................................913 621-6160
John R Krumme Jr, *CEO*
John R Krumme Sr, *Vice Pres*
Delores Krumme, *Admin Sec*
EMP: 11
SQ FT: 6,500
SALES (est): 3.3MM **Privately Held**
WEB: www.cam-dex.com
SIC: 7382 Security systems services

(G-3886)
CAMERON ASHLEY BLDG PDTS INC
2801 Fairfax Trfy (66115-1315)
PHONE..................................913 621-3111
Brad Harris, *Manager*
EMP: 10
SALES (corp-wide): 55.2MM **Privately Held**
WEB: www.cabp.com
SIC: 5033 Roofing, siding & insulation
HQ: Cameron Ashley Building Products, Inc.
979 Batesville Rd Ste A
Greer SC 29651

(G-3887)
CANADIAN WEST INC
Also Called: Century Roofing
6 S 59th St (66102-3340)
PHONE..................................913 422-0099
Graziano Cornolo, *President*
Breonna Keaton, *Opers Mgr*
Kevin Pratt, *CFO*
James Hinrichs, *Sales Associate*
EMP: 30
SQ FT: 5,000
SALES (est): 5.1MM **Privately Held**
SIC: 1761 Roofing contractor

(G-3888)
CAPITAL ELECTRIC CNSTR CO INC (HQ)
2801 Fairfax Trfy (66115-1315)
PHONE..................................816 472-9500
Michael A Wells, *President*
Mike Martin Sr, *Vice Pres*
David Bailey, *Project Mgr*
Keegan Mikessell, *Project Mgr*
Kevin Minor, *Project Mgr*
EMP: 50 **EST**: 1957
SQ FT: 14,000
SALES (est): 156.3MM
SALES (corp-wide): 4.5B **Publicly Held**
WEB: www.capitalelectric.com
SIC: 1731 General electrical contractor
PA: Mdu Resources Group, Inc.
1200 W Century Ave
Bismarck ND 58503
701 530-1000

(G-3889)
CAR CLINIC AUTO SALON
1270 Southwest Blvd (66103-1902)
PHONE..................................913 208-5478
Ray Henson, *Owner*
EMP: 12
SALES (est): 524.1K **Privately Held**
SIC: 7549 7542 Automotive services; washing & polishing, automotive

(G-3890)
CARGILL INCORPORATED
6833 Griffin Rd (66111-2405)
PHONE..................................913 299-2326
Patrick Fraley, *Branch Mgr*
EMP: 30
SALES (corp-wide): 113.4B **Privately Held**
WEB: www.propet.com
SIC: 2047 Dog & cat food
PA: Cargill, Incorporated
15407 Mcginty Rd W
Wayzata MN 55391
952 742-7575

(G-3891)
CARLSTAR GROUP LLC
2701 S 98th St (66111-3587)
PHONE..................................913 667-1000
EMP: 50
SALES (corp-wide): 1.4B **Privately Held**
SIC: 3011 Industrial tires, pneumatic
PA: The Carlstar Group Llc
725 Cool Springs Blvd
Franklin TN 37067
615 503-0220

(G-3892)
CARPET FACTORY OUTLET INC (PA)
Also Called: Rd Mann
3200 S 24th St (66106-4725)
PHONE..................................913 261-6800
Gaylord Johnson, *President*
Barbara Goodwin, *Vice Pres*
Sherman Johnson, *Vice Pres*
Fran Sulley, *Admin Sec*
EMP: 26
SQ FT: 40,000
SALES (est): 11.9MM **Privately Held**
WEB: www.mcintyremann.com
SIC: 5713 1743 5211 Carpets; tile installation, ceramic; tile, ceramic

(G-3893)
CARROLLS LLC
Also Called: National Tire Wholesale
625 S Adams St (66105-1402)
PHONE..................................913 321-2233
Bob Kotam, *Manager*
EMP: 16
SALES (corp-wide): 205.4MM **Privately Held**
WEB: www.tirecenters.com
SIC: 5014 Automobile tires & tubes
PA: Carroll's, Llc
4281 Old Dixie Hwy
Atlanta GA 30354
404 366-5476

(G-3894)
CATHOLIC CEMTERIES INC
Also Called: Catholic Cemeteries K C K
1150 N 38th St (66102-2227)
P.O. Box 2327 (66110-0327)
PHONE..................................913 371-4040
Terry Moulcare, *Director*
EMP: 23
SALES (est): 2.1MM **Privately Held**
SIC: 6553 Cemeteries, real estate operation

(G-3895)
CATHOLIC CHARITIES OF
Also Called: Archdiocese of Kansas City
12615 Parallel Pkwy (66109-3718)
PHONE..................................913 721-1570
James Keleher, *Publisher*
Kathy O'Hara, *Superintendent*
Ann Connor, *Asst Supt*
Amy Lanham, *Development*
Tom Tank, *Sales Executive*
EMP: 70
SALES (corp-wide): 182.1MM **Privately Held**
WEB: www.josephinum.org
SIC: 8322 Individual & family services
PA: Catholic Charities Of The Archdiocese Of Chicago
721 N La Salle Dr
Chicago IL 60654
312 655-7000

(G-3896)
CATHOLIC CHRTIES FNDTION NRTHA
Also Called: CATHOLIC COMMUNTY SERVICES
2220 Central Ave (66102-4759)
PHONE..................................913 621-1504
Jan Lewis, *Exec Dir*
EMP: 150
SALES: 3.3MM **Privately Held**
WEB: www.catholiccharitiesks.org
SIC: 8322 Individual & family services

(G-3897)
CATHOLIC CHRTIES NRTHAST KANS (PA)
2220 Central Ave (66102-4759)
PHONE..................................913 433-2100
Carleen Benson, *Principal*
Zena Weist, *Vice Pres*
Ryan Forshee, *Facilities Mgr*
Rachel Bonar, *Program Mgr*
Tracy Fuller, *Manager*
EMP: 73
SALES: 26.2MM **Privately Held**
SIC: 8322 Social service center

(G-3898)
CDI INDUSTRIAL MECH CONTRS INC
5621 Kansas Ave (66106-1146)
PHONE..................................913 287-0334
Ed Raby, *President*
Tracy Lehr, *Project Mgr*
Michael Pina, *Project Mgr*
EMP: 150
SQ FT: 15,000
SALES (est): 20.6MM **Privately Held**
SIC: 1629 3498 3441 1711 Industrial plant construction; fabricated pipe & fittings; fabricated structural metal; plumbing, heating, air-conditioning contractors; installing building equipment; structural steel erection

(G-3899)
CE WATER MANAGEMENT INC
3250 Brinkerhoff Rd (66115-1203)
PHONE..................................913 621-7047
Richard D Clark Jr, *President*
Alison Clark, *Vice Pres*
EMP: 9
SALES (est): 1.5MM **Privately Held**
SIC: 2819 Industrial inorganic chemicals

(G-3900)
CEMEX MATERIALS LLC
Also Called: Wilson Concrete Batch Plant
759 S 65th St (66111-2350)
PHONE..................................913 287-5725
Bruno Burgess, *Manager*
EMP: 75 **Privately Held**
WEB: www.rinkermaterials.com
SIC: 3271 3272 Concrete block & brick; concrete products
HQ: Cemex Materials Llc
1501 Belvedere Rd
West Palm Beach FL 33406
561 833-5555

(G-3901)
CENTRAL MAINTENANCE SYSTEM
401 Funston Rd (66115-1213)
P.O. Box 15071 (66115-0071)
PHONE..................................913 621-6545
Frank B Nobrega, *Ch of Bd*
Mark E Nobrega, *President*
Greg Kovac, *General Mgr*
Darrin Farmer, *Opers Staff*
Angela Coder, *Accountant*
EMP: 50
SQ FT: 28,000
SALES (est): 1.2MM **Privately Held**
SIC: 7349 Janitorial service, contract basis; window cleaning

(G-3902)
CENTRAL SOLUTIONS INC (PA)
401 Funston Rd (66115-1213)
PHONE..................................913 621-6542
Mark E Nobrega, *President*
Michael F Nobrega, *Vice Pres*
Roy Pierce, *Opers Staff*
Paul Nobrega, *Treasurer*
Ed Martin, *Personnel Exec*
▲ **EMP**: 31 **EST**: 1925
SQ FT: 12,000
SALES (est): 6.6MM **Privately Held**
WEB: www.centralsolutions.com
SIC: 2844 Shampoos, rinses, conditioners: hair

(G-3903)
CENTRAL STATES CONTG SVCS INC
610 S 78th St (66111-3101)
PHONE..................................913 788-1100
William J Szczygiel, *President*
Jason Szczygiel, *Vice Pres*
Karen A Szczygiel, *Vice Pres*
Mindy Rocha, *Sales Mgr*
EMP: 15
SQ FT: 4,800
SALES: 6.8MM **Privately Held**
SIC: 1711 Mechanical contractor

(G-3904)
CENTRAL TRANSPORT INTL INC
615 Miami Ave (66105-2111)
PHONE..................................913 371-7500
Chris Thompson, *Branch Mgr*
EMP: 30
SALES (corp-wide): 273.6MM **Privately Held**
SIC: 4213 Trucking, except local
HQ: Central Transport International, Inc.
12225 Stephens Rd
Warren MI 48089
586 467-0100

(G-3905)
CERNER GOVERNMENT SERVICES INC
10200 Abilities Way (66111-3402)
PHONE..................................816 201-2273
Kara Stinemetz, *Principal*
Zane Burke, *Principal*
Travis Dalton, *Principal*
Daniel Devers, *Principal*
Marc Elkins, *Principal*
EMP: 32
SALES (est): 1.8MM
SALES (corp-wide): 5.3B **Publicly Held**
SIC: 7373 Computer integrated systems design
PA: Cerner Corporation
2800 Rock Creek Pkwy
Kansas City MO 64117
816 201-1024

(G-3906)
CERTAINTEED CORPORATION
103 Funston Rd (66115-1309)
P.O. Box 15080 (66115)
PHONE..................................913 342-6624
Jim Zalanik, *Principal*
Steven Cassidy, *Div Sub Head*
John Dolan, *Purch Mgr*
Dave Senne, *Engineer*
Terry Heintzelman, *Sales Mgr*
EMP: 500
SALES (corp-wide): 209.1MM **Privately Held**
WEB: www.certainteed.net
SIC: 3296 Mineral wool
HQ: Certainteed Llc
20 Moores Rd
Malvern PA 19355
610 893-5000

(G-3907)
CG INVESTMENTS
421 N 82nd Ter (66112-1901)
PHONE..................................816 398-5862
Brad Crain, *Principal*
EMP: 50
SALES (est): 1.6MM **Privately Held**
SIC: 6799 Investors

(G-3908)
CHAMELEON DENTAL PRODUCTS
200 N 6th St (66101-3310)
P.O. Box 171458 (66117-0458)
PHONE..................................913 281-5552
Timothy Sigler, *President*
J Thomas Sigler, *Vice Pres*
EMP: 30
SQ FT: 26,000
SALES (est): 2.9MM
SALES (corp-wide): 3.7MM **Privately Held**
SIC: 3843 Denture materials
PA: Myron's Dental Laboratories Inc
200 N 6th St
Kansas City KS 66101
800 359-7111

(G-3909)
CHEM-TROL INC (PA)
Also Called: Vegetation Management Supply
411 S 42nd St (66106-1005)
PHONE..................................913 342-3006
Joseph A White, *President*
Joe White, *President*
Dean Beasley, *Vice Pres*
EMP: 15
SQ FT: 5,000
SALES (est): 7MM **Privately Held**
WEB: www.chem-trol.com
SIC: 0721 Weed control services after planting

(G-3910)
CHILDRENS MERCY HOME CARE
1900 N 47th St (66102)
PHONE..................................913 696-8999
Debbie Wesley, *Director*
EMP: 27
SALES (est): 318.4K **Privately Held**
SIC: 8082 Home health care services

(G-3911)
CHILDRENS MERCY HOSPITAL
Also Called: Children's Mercy West Clinic
4313 State Ave (66102-3734)
PHONE..................................913 287-8800
Dylane Cornelius, *Branch Mgr*
EMP: 35
SALES (corp-wide): 826.4MM **Privately Held**
SIC: 8062 General medical & surgical hospitals
PA: Mercy Children's Hospital
2401 Gillham Rd
Kansas City MO 64108
816 234-3000

(G-3912)
CITY OIL COMPANY INC
Also Called: Mystik Lubricants
2011 N 10th St (66104-5306)
P.O. Box 171655 (66117-0655)
PHONE..................................913 321-1764
Steve Shondell, *President*
EMP: 20
SQ FT: 20,000
SALES (est): 1.1MM **Privately Held**
SIC: 6512 Commercial & industrial building operation

(G-3913)
CITY WIDE SERVICE INC
Also Called: City Wide Heating & Cooling
2820 Roe Ln Ste G (66103-1560)
PHONE..................................913 927-6124
Tim Duval, *President*
Ted Duval, *Vice Pres*
EMP: 12
SQ FT: 4,000
SALES: 800.2K **Privately Held**
SIC: 1711 Warm air heating & air conditioning contractor

(G-3914)
CITY WIDE SHEET METAL INC
2824 Roe Ln (66103-1543)
PHONE..................................913 871-7464
Charles W Duval, *Ch of Bd*
Nicholas Duval, *President*
Douglas Duval, *Vice Pres*
Vivian Duval, *Shareholder*
EMP: 16 **EST**: 1949
SQ FT: 8,400
SALES (est): 2.2MM **Privately Held**
WEB: www.citywidesheetmetal.com
SIC: 1711 Mechanical contractor

(G-3915)
CJ INDUSTRIES LLC
610 S 78th St Ste 1 (66111-3101)
PHONE..................................913 788-1104
Melinda K Rocha, *President*
EMP: 10
SALES: 3.4MM **Privately Held**
SIC: 1711 Mechanical contractor

(G-3916)
CLARK-TIMMONS OIL COMPANY (PA)
445 Sunshine Rd (66115-1235)
PHONE..................................816 229-0228
EMP: 12
SQ FT: 1,000
SALES: 12.3MM **Privately Held**
SIC: 5171 Petroleum Bulk Station

(G-3917)
CLARKE ENTERPRISES LLC
3250 Brinkerhoff Rd (66115-1203)
PHONE..................................913 601-3830
Don Hugo, *Partner*
Richard D Clark,
EMP: 20
SQ FT: 40,000
SALES: 1.5MM **Privately Held**
SIC: 5169 Salts, industrial

(G-3918)
CLASSIC COLLISION CENTER
4835 Metropolitan Ave (66106-2343)
PHONE..................................913 287-9410
John Burdolski, *Owner*
Karmen White, *Manager*
EMP: 13
SQ FT: 15,000
SALES (est): 866K **Privately Held**
SIC: 7532 Collision shops, automotive

(G-3919)
CLEAN HARBORS WICHITA LLC
Also Called: Universal Oil
601 S 66th Ter (66111-2345)
PHONE..................................913 287-6880
Mike Hall, *COO*
Kevin Kelly, *COO*
Randall Wilson, *CFO*
Greg Van Stechelman, *Marketing Staff*
Mike Bernard, *Manager*

GEOGRAPHIC

EMP: 20 **Privately Held**
WEB: www.universallubes.com
SIC: 5172 Lubricating oils & greases
HQ: Clean Harbors Wichita, Llc
2808 N Ohio St
Wichita KS 67219
316 832-0151

(G-3920)
CLINICAL RADIOLOGY FOUNDATION
3901 Rainbow Blvd Rm 2162
(66160-8500)
PHONE....................................913 588-6830
Stanton Rosenthal, *President*
Louis H Wetzel, *Vice Pres*
EMP: 17
SALES: 91.2K **Privately Held**
WEB: www.ukans.edu
SIC: 8621 Medical field-related associations

(G-3921)
COALITION FOR INDEPENDENCE (PA)
626 Minnesota Ave Fl 2 (66101-2821)
PHONE....................................913 321-5140
Clarence Smith, *President*
Amber Thurston, *Principal*
Diane Heichel, *CFO*
Clarence T Smith, *Exec Dir*
EMP: 25
SALES: 7.3MM **Privately Held**
WEB: www.cfi-kc.org
SIC: 8322 Community center

(G-3922)
COFFEYVILLE ACQUISITION LLC
10 E Cambridge Circle Dr (66103-1334)
PHONE....................................913 982-0500
Jack Lipinski,
EMP: 40
SQ FT: 11,400
SALES (est): 3.5MM **Privately Held**
SIC: 2873 2911 Nitrogenous fertilizers; ammonia liquor; ammonium nitrate, ammonium sulfate; fractionation products of crude petroleum, hydrocarbons

(G-3923)
COFFEYVILLE RESOURCES LLC
Also Called: Coffeyville Refinery
10 E Cambridge Circle Dr # 250
(66103-1334)
PHONE....................................913 982-0500
Keith Osborne, *Branch Mgr*
Karen Gilliland, *Manager*
Brian Waltz, *Manager*
EMP: 20 **Publicly Held**
WEB: www.coffeyvillegroup.com
SIC: 2873 2911 Nitrogenous fertilizers; petroleum refining
HQ: Coffeyville Resources, Llc
2277 Plaza Dr Ste 500
Sugar Land TX 77479
281 207-3200

(G-3924)
COFFEYVLLE NTRGN FRTLIZERS INC
10 E Cambridge Circle Dr (66103-1334)
PHONE....................................913 982-0500
EMP: 207
SALES (est): 1.2MM
SALES (corp-wide): 11.7B **Publicly Held**
SIC: 2873 Nitrogenous fertilizers
HQ: Icahn Enterprises Holdings L.P.
767 5th Ave Ste 4700
New York NY 10153
212 702-4300

(G-3925)
COFFEYVLLE RSRCES REF MKTG LLC
10 E Cambrdge Cir Dr 250 (66103)
PHONE....................................913 982-0500
Bill Copeland, *Vice Pres*
EMP: 9 **Publicly Held**
SIC: 2911 Gasoline
HQ: Coffeyville Resources Refining & Marketing, Llc
2277 Plaza Dr Ste 500
Sugar Land TX 77479
281 207-3200

(G-3926)
COMFORT INN KANSAS CITY
234 N 78th St (66112-2902)
PHONE....................................913 299-5555
Steve Ranat, *Manager*
EMP: 15
SALES (est): 811.6K **Privately Held**
SIC: 7011 Hotels & motels

(G-3927)
COMMERCE BANK
4020 Rainbow Blvd (66103-2919)
PHONE....................................816 234-2000
Bridgette Bade, *Manager*
EMP: 13
SALES (corp-wide): 1.3B **Publicly Held**
SIC: 6021 National commercial banks
HQ: Commerce Bank
1000 Walnut St Fl 700
Kansas City MO 64106
816 234-2000

(G-3928)
COMMERCE BANK
1906 W 43rd Ave (66103-3396)
PHONE....................................816 234-2000
Kelly Collins, *Manager*
EMP: 18
SALES (corp-wide): 1.3B **Publicly Held**
SIC: 6022 State commercial banks
HQ: Commerce Bank
1000 Walnut St Fl 700
Kansas City MO 64106
816 234-2000

(G-3929)
COMMERCIAL FLTR SVC KNSAS CTY
1946 Foxridge Dr (66106-4710)
PHONE....................................913 384-5858
Justin Spolar, *President*
EMP: 5
SQ FT: 3,000
SALES (est): 863.4K **Privately Held**
SIC: 5075 5013 3564 Warm air heating & air conditioning; body repair or paint shop supplies, automotive; filters, air: furnaces, air conditioning equipment, etc.

(G-3930)
COMMERCIAL LANDSCAPERS INC
10800 Donahoo Rd (66109-3320)
PHONE....................................913 721-5455
Michael A Rhodes, *President*
EMP: 10
SALES (est): 1.3MM **Privately Held**
WEB: www.commerciallandscapers.net
SIC: 0782 Landscape contractors

(G-3931)
COMMUNITY HSING WYANDOTTE CNTY
Also Called: Chwc
2 S 14th St (66102-5041)
PHONE....................................913 342-7580
Donny Smith, *Exec Dir*
EMP: 13
SALES: 1.4MM **Privately Held**
SIC: 8748 Urban planning & consulting services

(G-3932)
COMPREHENSIVE LOGISTICS CO INC
Also Called: Cli- Kansas City
230 Kindleberger Rd (66115-1200)
PHONE....................................913 371-0770
Kurt Rohrer, *Branch Mgr*
EMP: 35 **Privately Held**
SIC: 4225 General warehousing
PA: Comprehensive Logistics, Co., Inc.
4944 Belmont Ave Ste 202
Youngstown OH 44505

(G-3933)
CONSPEC MARKETING AND MFG CO
636 S 66th Ter (66111-2344)
PHONE....................................913 287-1700
Elizabeth Maday, *Principal*
EMP: 1000
SQ FT: 40,000
SALES (est): 81.8MM
SALES (corp-wide): 42.9B **Publicly Held**
WEB: www.daytonsuperior.com
SIC: 2819 Industrial inorganic chemicals
HQ: Dayton Superior Corporation
1125 Byers Rd
Miamisburg OH 45342
937 866-0711

(G-3934)
CONSTRUCTION & GEN LABOR 1290 (PA)
2600 Merriam Ln (66106-4606)
PHONE....................................913 432-1903
Carlton Young, *President*
Mark Nidiffer, *Manager*
EMP: 12
SQ FT: 1,150
SALES (est): 1.6MM **Privately Held**
SIC: 8631 Labor union

(G-3935)
CONSTRUCTION DESIGN INC (PA)
Also Called: C D I
5621 Kansas Ave (66106-1146)
PHONE....................................913 287-0334
Edward L Raby, *President*
Dennis P Haist, *Admin Sec*
EMP: 200
SQ FT: 15,000
SALES (est): 14.2MM **Privately Held**
WEB: www.cdikc.com
SIC: 8711 Building construction consultant

(G-3936)
CONTRACT TRAILER SERVICE INC
47 Kansas Ave (66105-1428)
PHONE....................................913 281-2589
Larry Kratzberg, *President*
Carol Kratzberg, *Vice Pres*
EMP: 16
SQ FT: 20,000
SALES (est): 1.5MM **Privately Held**
WEB: www.contracttrailer.com
SIC: 7539 5012 Trailer repair; trailers for trucks, new & used

(G-3937)
CONVOY EQUIPMENT LEASING LLC (PA)
333 N James St (66118-1140)
PHONE....................................913 371-6500
Terry E Gruenewald,
Susan Gruenewald,
EMP: 80
SQ FT: 2,800
SALES (est): 9.2MM **Privately Held**
WEB: www.convoysystems.com
SIC: 4213 7513 Trucking, except local; truck leasing, without drivers

(G-3938)
CONVOY LEASING INC
333 N James St (66118-1140)
PHONE....................................913 371-6500
Terry E Gruenewald, *President*
Susan Gruenewald, *Vice Pres*
EMP: 12
SQ FT: 8,500
SALES (est): 2.7MM
SALES (corp-wide): 9.2MM **Privately Held**
WEB: www.convoysystems.com
SIC: 7513 Truck leasing, without drivers
PA: Convoy Equipment Leasing, L.L.C.
333 N James St
Kansas City KS 66118
913 371-6500

(G-3939)
COPART OF KANSAS INC
Also Called: Copart Kansas City Salv Pool
6211 Kansas Ave (66111-2124)
P.O. Box 12670 (66112-0670)
PHONE....................................913 287-6200
Donna Francis, *Ch of Bd*
James E Meeks, *COO*
A Jayson Adair, *Exec VP*
Marvin L Schmidt, *Senior VP*
Paul A Styer, *Senior VP*
▼ **EMP:** 13
SALES (est): 3.4MM
SALES (corp-wide): 2B **Publicly Held**
WEB: www.copart.com
SIC: 5012 Automobile auction
PA: Copart, Inc.
14185 Dallas Pkwy Ste 300
Dallas TX 75254
972 391-5000

(G-3940)
CORBIN BRONZE LIMITED
1166 Southwest Blvd (66103-1910)
PHONE....................................913 766-4012
Thomas Corbin, *President*
EMP: 5
SQ FT: 2,000
SALES (est): 420K **Privately Held**
WEB: www.corbinbronze.com
SIC: 2511 8999 3645 3446 Wood household furniture; sculptor's studio; residential lighting fixtures; architectural metalwork; metal household furniture

(G-3941)
CORE CARRIER CORPORATION
1020 Sunshine Rd (66115-1125)
PHONE....................................913 621-3434
Michael D Koch, *President*
EMP: 180
SALES (est): 21.8MM **Privately Held**
WEB: www.corecarrier.com
SIC: 4213 4231 Contract haulers; trucking terminal facilities

(G-3942)
CORESLAB STRUCTURES KANSAS INC
759 S 65th St (66111-2350)
PHONE....................................913 287-5725
Mark Simpson, *Vice Pres*
Ramon Aguilar, *Project Mgr*
Tom Trautman, *Project Mgr*
Michael Eilers, *Chief Engr*
Sal Simsek, *Controller*
EMP: 90
SALES (est): 18.6MM
SALES (corp-wide): 27.3MM **Privately Held**
SIC: 3272 Concrete products
HQ: Coreslab Structures (Ont) Inc
205 Coreslab Dr
Dundas ON L9H 0
905 689-3993

(G-3943)
COUNTRY CLUB BANK
11006 Parallel Pkwy (66109-4440)
PHONE....................................816 751-4270
Zoe Walsh, *Marketing Staff*
EMP: 17
SALES (corp-wide): 38MM **Privately Held**
SIC: 6029 Commercial banks
HQ: Country Club Bank
1 Ward Pkwy
Kansas City MO 64112

(G-3944)
CRANE SALES & SERVICE CO INC
Also Called: Finch Bayless Crane Sls & Svc
1025 S Mill St (66105-1925)
PHONE....................................913 621-7040
Chris Comer, *Sales Staff*
Hugh Murphy, *Manager*
EMP: 10 **Privately Held**
SIC: 5082 7353 7389 3531 General construction machinery & equipment; heavy construction equipment rental; crane & aerial lift service; backhoes, tractors, cranes, plows & similar equipment

▲ = Import ▼=Export
◆ =Import/Export

HQ: Crane Sales & Service Co., Inc.
5910 S 27th St
Omaha NE 68107
402 731-7484

(G-3945)
CREDIT MOTORS INC (PA)
1400 State Ave (66102-4398)
PHONE..................................913 621-1206
Thomas C Wood, *President*
Debbie S Freeman, *Vice Pres*
EMP: 17 **EST:** 1977
SALES (est): 2.9MM **Privately Held**
WEB: www.creditmotors.com
SIC: 5521 7538 Automobiles, used cars only; general automotive repair shops

(G-3946)
CROSS-LINES CMNTY OUTREACH INC
736 Shawnee Ave (66105-2025)
PHONE..................................913 281-3388
Susila Gabbert, *Manager*
Roberta Lindbeck, *Exec Dir*
EMP: 10
SALES: 1.3MM **Privately Held**
SIC: 8399 Council for social agency

(G-3947)
CS CAREY LLC
Also Called: Brush Reduction
6225 Kansas Ave (66111-2124)
PHONE..................................913 432-4877
Chris Carey, *President*
Philip Carey, *Vice Pres*
Jennifer Bustamante, *Project Mgr*
Kelly Carey, *Manager*
Drew Meylan, *Info Tech Dir*
EMP: 17
SQ FT: 8,000
SALES (est): 3.9MM **Privately Held**
WEB: www.cscarey.com
SIC: 1629 2499 Land clearing contractor; mulch, wood & bark

(G-3948)
CUSTOM CBNETS BY LWRENCE CNSTR
1427 Merriam Ln (66103-1528)
PHONE..................................913 208-9797
EMP: 15 **EST:** 2013
SALES (est): 2.2MM **Privately Held**
SIC: 2434 Wood kitchen cabinets

(G-3949)
CZ-USA
3341 N 7th Street Trfy (66115-1107)
P.O. Box 171073 (66117-0073)
PHONE..................................913 321-1811
Alice Poluchova, *CEO*
Chris Stumpenhaus, *Vice Pres*
Keith Lawton, *VP Opers*
Lynn Matthews, *CFO*
Sherri Goodwyn, *VP Sales*
▲ **EMP:** 72
SQ FT: 45,000
SALES (est): 18.8MM
SALES (corp-wide): 87.9K **Privately Held**
WEB: www.czusa.com
SIC: 3484 Guns (firearms) or gun parts, 30 mm. & below
HQ: Ceska Zbrojovka A.S.
Svat. Cecha 1283
Uherske Brod 68801
225 375-800

(G-3950)
D ROCKEY HOLDINGS INC
Also Called: Eagle Products
87 Shawnee Ave (66105-1418)
PHONE..................................816 474-9423
Dave Rockey, *President*
EMP: 50
SQ FT: 35,000
SALES: 6MM **Privately Held**
SIC: 2759 2395 Screen printing; embroidery & art needlework

(G-3951)
DADE CONSTRUCTION LLC
6352 County Line Rd (66106-5420)
P.O. Box 4090 (66104-0090)
PHONE..................................913 208-1968
Marlene Dade,
EMP: 10
SQ FT: 1,000
SALES (est): 1.2MM **Privately Held**
SIC: 1521 1751 General remodeling, single-family houses; new construction, single-family houses; carpentry work; cabinet & finish carpentry; finish & trim carpentry

(G-3952)
DAGOSTINO MECH CONTRS INC
4440 Oliver St (66106-3763)
PHONE..................................913 384-5170
John D'Agostino, *President*
Jerry Swanson, *Vice Pres*
Scott Miros, *Project Mgr*
Max Singer, *Treasurer*
Dorothy Magner, *Accountant*
EMP: 60
SQ FT: 12,000
SALES (est): 10.4MM **Privately Held**
WEB: www.dagmech.com
SIC: 1711 1761 Plumbing contractors; warm air heating & air conditioning contractor; roofing, siding & sheet metal work

(G-3953)
DAIRY FARMERS AMERICA INC (PA)
1405 N 98th St (66111-1865)
PHONE..................................816 801-6455
Rick Smith, *President*
Jim McIntire, *Superintendent*
David Rothfuss, *Regional Mgr*
Rose Charlotten, *Plant Mgr*
Diana Poettgen, *Opers Mgr*
▼ **EMP:** 350
SQ FT: 100,000
SALES: 13.6B **Privately Held**
WEB: www.dfamilk.com
SIC: 2023 2022 2021 2024 Condensed milk; powdered milk; natural cheese; processed cheese; creamery butter; ice cream & ice milk; dairy machinery & equipment; milk processing (pasteurizing, homogenizing, bottling)

(G-3954)
DAMAGE CTRL & RESTORATION INC
413 Division St (66103-1903)
PHONE..................................913 722-0228
Robert Sigler, *President*
Karen Davenport, *Office Mgr*
EMP: 20
SQ FT: 6,000
SALES: 7.4MM **Privately Held**
SIC: 1521 1542 1799 General remodeling, single-family houses; commercial & office buildings, renovation & repair; post-disaster renovations

(G-3955)
DANIEL AIRES MD
3901 Rainbow Blvd 2027 (66160-8500)
PHONE..................................913 588-6050
Daniel Aaron West, *Principal*
EMP: 22 **EST:** 2011
SALES (est): 704.1K **Privately Held**
SIC: 8011 Offices & clinics of medical doctors

(G-3956)
DARLING INGREDIENTS INC
685 S Adams St (66105-1402)
PHONE..................................913 321-9328
William Fosdick, *General Mgr*
EMP: 38
SALES (corp-wide): 3.3B **Publicly Held**
WEB: www.darlingii.com
SIC: 2077 Animal & marine fats & oils
PA: Darling Ingredients Inc.
5601 N Macarthur Blvd
Irving TX 75038
972 717-0300

(G-3957)
DARLING INGREDIENTS INC
229 N James St (66118-1142)
P.O. Box 171366 (66117-0366)
PHONE..................................913 371-7083
William Perkins, *Sales/Mktg Mgr*
EMP: 9
SQ FT: 30,000
SALES (corp-wide): 3.3B **Publicly Held**
WEB: www.darlingii.com
SIC: 2077 5191 Stearin, animal: inedible; animal feeds
PA: Darling Ingredients Inc.
5601 N Macarthur Blvd
Irving TX 75038
972 717-0300

(G-3958)
DAVINCI REPROGRAPHICS
1140 Adams St (66103-1307)
PHONE..................................913 371-0014
EMP: 10
SALES (est): 82.9K **Privately Held**
SIC: 7336 Commercial art & graphic design

(G-3959)
DAYTON SUPERIOR CORPORATION
4226 Kansas Ave (66106-1119)
PHONE..................................913 279-4800
Rick Zimmerman, *CEO*
Nick Lynn, *Sales Mgr*
Jim Sanderson, *Manager*
EMP: 30
SALES (corp-wide): 42.9B **Publicly Held**
WEB: www.daytonsuperior.com
SIC: 5039 Prefabricated structures
HQ: Dayton Superior Corporation
1125 Byers Rd
Miamisburg OH 45342
937 866-0711

(G-3960)
DAYTON SUPERIOR CORPORATION
Dayton Superior Specialty Chem
636 S 66th Ter (66111-2344)
PHONE..................................913 596-9784
Kevin Humphrey, *Branch Mgr*
EMP: 65
SALES (corp-wide): 42.9B **Publicly Held**
WEB: www.daytonsuperior.com
SIC: 3272 2899 Concrete products; chemical preparations
HQ: Dayton Superior Corporation
1125 Byers Rd
Miamisburg OH 45342
937 866-0711

(G-3961)
DB2 SERVICES INC
508 S 14th St (66105-1102)
PHONE..................................913 677-2408
Sabina Boyle, *President*
Kyle Hanks, *Superintendent*
Terry Lemon, *Superintendent*
Danny Boyle, *Vice Pres*
David Heffner, *Foreman/Supr*
EMP: 15
SALES (est): 4.9MM **Privately Held**
SIC: 3444 Sheet metalwork

(G-3962)
DDI HOLDINGS INC (PA)
640 Miami Ave (66105-2122)
PHONE..................................913 371-2200
Steven E Cole, *President*
Gary W Strub, *Vice Pres*
Russ Sanders, *Warehouse Mgr*
Tony Costa, *Representative*
▲ **EMP:** 28 **EST:** 1979
SQ FT: 75,000
SALES (est): 9.6MM **Privately Held**
WEB: www.dedicateddistribution.com
SIC: 5047 Medical equipment & supplies

(G-3963)
DE HOFF TOOL & MFG CO INC
1021 S Pyle St (66105-2034)
PHONE..................................913 342-2212
Kim Dehoff, *President*
Mary Dehoff, *Chairman*
EMP: 14 **EST:** 1967
SQ FT: 19,000
SALES (est): 1.9MM **Privately Held**
SIC: 3599 3544 Machine shop, jobbing & repair; special dies & tools

(G-3964)
DE LEON FURNITURE INC
1142 Minnesota Ave (66102-4455)
PHONE..................................913 342-9446
Anolad Deleon, *President*
Anolad De Leon, *President*
Anola De Leon, *Principal*
Albert De Leon, *Vice Pres*
Jose De Leon, *Treasurer*
EMP: 10
SQ FT: 5,000
SALES (est): 461.7K **Privately Held**
SIC: 7641 5712 Reupholstery; furniture repair & maintenance; furniture refinishing; furniture stores

(G-3965)
DEFFENBAUGH INDUSTRIES INC (HQ)
Also Called: Waste Management
2601 Midwest Dr (66111-8801)
P.O. Box 3220, Shawnee Mission (66203-0220)
PHONE..................................913 631-3300
Jim Donahue, *President*
John King, *Vice Pres*
Doug Sheldrick, *Safety Mgr*
Sylvia Bedolla, *Opers Spvr*
Kenny Hulshof, *Opers Staff*
EMP: 1200
SALES (est): 509.9MM
SALES (corp-wide): 14.9B **Publicly Held**
WEB: www.deffenbaughindustries.com
SIC: 4212 4953 Garbage collection & transport, no disposal; sanitary landfill operation; refuse collection & disposal services
PA: Waste Management, Inc.
1001 Fannin St Ste 4000
Houston TX 77002
713 512-6200

(G-3966)
DELAWARE HGHLNDS ASSISTD LVNG
12600 Delaware Pkwy (66109-8509)
PHONE..................................913 721-1400
Ketti Dawson, *Principal*
Tom Walker, *Director*
EMP: 11
SALES (est): 1.2MM **Privately Held**
SIC: 8011 Group health association

(G-3967)
DELTA INNOVATIVE SERVICES INC
508 S 14th St (66105-1102)
PHONE..................................913 371-7100
Sabina R Boyle, *President*
Brian Plake, *Superintendent*
Danny Boyle Jr, *Vice Pres*
Tom Ruzicka, *Safety Dir*
Louis Lambert, *Project Mgr*
EMP: 90
SQ FT: 10,000
SALES (est): 18.4MM **Privately Held**
SIC: 1761 Roofing contractor

(G-3968)
DEMPSEY INC
Also Called: Dempsey Foundery
72 Central Ave (66118-1155)
PHONE..................................913 371-3107
Michael Dempsey, *President*
EMP: 9 **EST:** 1946
SQ FT: 5,000
SALES: 400K **Privately Held**
WEB: www.dempseyinc.com
SIC: 3363 3364 Aluminum die-castings; brass & bronze die-castings

(G-3969)
DESIGN MATERIALS INC (PA)
241 S 55th St (66106-1013)
PHONE..................................913 342-9796
Marty Wessinger, *President*
Don Fields, *Corp Secy*
Jim Fields, *Vice Pres*
Rick Fields, *Vice Pres*
Tom Fields, *Vice Pres*
◆ **EMP:** 29
SQ FT: 35,000
SALES: 11MM **Privately Held**
WEB: www.dmikc.com
SIC: 5023 5198 Floor coverings; wallcoverings

(G-3970)
DESIGN MECHANICAL INC
Also Called: HONEYWELL AUTHORIZED DEALER
100 Greystone Ave (66103-1326)
PHONE..................................913 281-7200
William Iler, *President*

GEOGRAPHIC

Daryl Cox, *Vice Pres*
William Pointer, *CFO*
Patty Neville, *Sales Staff*
Valerie Mussett, *Manager*
EMP: 115
SQ FT: 25,000
SALES: 58.5MM **Privately Held**
WEB: www.dmi-kc.com
SIC: 1711 Mechanical contractor

(G-3971)
DGS-RE LLC
5000 Kansas Ave (66106-1135)
PHONE..................................913 288-1000
Betty Welch,
EMP: 35
SALES (est): 473.7K
SALES (corp-wide): 9.7B **Privately Held**
SIC: 5141 Groceries, general line
PA: Associated Wholesale Grocers, Inc.
5000 Kansas Ave
Kansas City KS 66106
913 288-1000

(G-3972)
DISCOUNT TOBACCO & CELLULAR
1017 N 18th St (66102-4229)
PHONE..................................913 281-3067
Ssalixind Lachmi, *Owner*
EMP: 17
SALES (est): 560.3K **Privately Held**
SIC: 4812 Cellular telephone services

(G-3973)
DISH NETWORK CORPORATION
4701 Parallel Pkwy (66104-3241)
PHONE..................................816 256-5622
EMP: 58
SALES (corp-wide): 15B **Publicly Held**
SIC: 4841 Cable/Pay Television Service
PA: Dish Network Corporation
9601 S Meridian Blvd
Englewood CO 80112
303 723-1000

(G-3974)
DISPLAY STUDIOS INC
5420 Kansas Ave (66106-1143)
PHONE..................................913 305-5948
John McCoy, *President*
Vern Jensen, *Treasurer*
Jim Kelly, *Admin Sec*
EMP: 21
SQ FT: 150,000
SALES (est): 3.5MM **Privately Held**
SIC: 7389 Exhibit construction by industrial contractors

(G-3975)
DORMAKABA USA INC
301 Southwest Blvd (66103-2149)
PHONE..................................913 831-3001
Katherine Hunter, *Branch Mgr*
EMP: 16
SALES (corp-wide): 2.8B **Privately Held**
WEB: www.doorcontrolsinc.com
SIC: 3429 Builders' hardware
HQ: Dormakaba Usa Inc.
100 Dorma Dr
Reamstown PA 17567
717 336-3881

(G-3976)
DOWNTOWN SHAREHOLDERS
726 Armstrong Ave Ste 201 (66101-2710)
PHONE..................................913 371-0705
Edward Linnebur, *Exec Dir*
EMP: 20
SALES: 562.2K **Privately Held**
SIC: 8641 Civic associations

(G-3977)
DRAGNET ENTERPRISES
2507 S 42nd St (66106-3607)
PHONE..................................913 362-8378
Charles Gay, *Co-Owner*
Nancy L Gay, *Co-Owner*
EMP: 10
SQ FT: 1,500
SALES: 700K **Privately Held**
SIC: 3669 Metal detectors

(G-3978)
EAGLE CASE MANAGEMENT LLC
7345 Leavenworth Rd (66109-1221)
PHONE..................................913 334-9035
Patrick Nwanguzo,
Morris Egon,
EMP: 30
SALES (est): 1.1MM **Privately Held**
SIC: 8741 Business management

(G-3979)
EAGLE SECURITY INC
5340 N 109th St (66109-4721)
PHONE..................................913 721-1360
Lloyd Beth, *President*
EMP: 73
SALES (est): 690.6K **Privately Held**
SIC: 7381 Security guard service

(G-3980)
ECONOMIC OPPRTUNITY FOUNDATION (PA)
950 Quindaro Blvd (66101-1228)
PHONE..................................913 371-7800
Douglas Stangler, *President*
Rita Adams, *Exec Dir*
Ladora Jackson, *Exec Dir*
Julia Price, *Exec Dir*
EMP: 20
SQ FT: 4,000
SALES: 8.1MM **Privately Held**
SIC: 8322 Social service center

(G-3981)
EIDSONS FLORIST
Also Called: Eidson's Florist & Tuxedo
2420 N 131st St (66109-3325)
PHONE..................................913 721-2775
Terry W Eidson, *Partner*
Aileen C Eidson, *Partner*
EMP: 10
SQ FT: 7,200
SALES (est): 427.8K **Privately Held**
WEB: www.eidsonsflorist.com
SIC: 5992 4724 Flowers, fresh; plants, potted; travel agencies

(G-3982)
EL CENTRO INC (PA)
Also Called: WWW.ELCENTROINC.COM
650 Minnesota Ave Fl 1 (66101-2800)
PHONE..................................913 677-0100
Mary Lou Jaramillo, *President*
EMP: 15
SQ FT: 24,000
SALES: 2.4MM **Privately Held**
WEB: www.elcentroinc.com
SIC: 8322 Senior citizens' center or association; refugee service; offender rehabilitation agency

(G-3983)
EL CENTRO INC
Also Called: Academy of Children
1330 S 30th St (66106-2135)
PHONE..................................913 677-1115
Della Muzquiz, *Director*
EMP: 11
SALES (corp-wide): 2.4MM **Privately Held**
WEB: www.elcentroinc.com
SIC: 8322 8748 Individual & family services; educational consultant
PA: El Centro Inc
650 Minnesota Ave Fl 1
Kansas City KS 66101
913 677-0100

(G-3984)
EL TAQUITO INC
Also Called: El Taquito Manufacturing Plant
640 Reynolds Ave (66101-3466)
PHONE..................................913 371-0452
Chris Medina, *President*
Enrique Chaurand, *Vice Pres*
Mike Casey, *Treasurer*
EMP: 8
SQ FT: 6,250
SALES: 500K **Privately Held**
SIC: 2099 5411 Tortillas, fresh or refrigerated; grocery stores

(G-3985)
EM SALES LLC
Also Called: Pickel Gear
1949 Foxridge Dr (66106-4733)
PHONE..................................913 486-6762
Eric Medved, *Mng Member*
EMP: 10
SALES (est): 515K **Privately Held**
SIC: 4822 Electronic mail

(G-3986)
EMCO SPECIALTY PRODUCTS INC
408 Miami Ave (66105-2116)
PHONE..................................913 281-4555
Gary Metzger, *CEO*
Bob Metzger, *President*
Linda Metzger, *Vice Pres*
Hans Weding, *Sales Mgr*
EMP: 5 **EST:** 1996
SQ FT: 8,500
SALES: 1MM **Privately Held**
WEB: www.emcospi.com
SIC: 3999 3315 Figures, wax; steel wire & related products

(G-3987)
EMPIRE CANDLE CO LLC
2900 Fairfax Trfy (66115-1318)
PHONE..................................913 621-4555
EMP: 9 **Privately Held**
SIC: 3999 Candles
PA: Empire Candle Co., Llc
2925 Fairfax Trfy
Kansas City KS 66115

(G-3988)
EMPIRE CANDLE CO LLC
3100 Fairfax Trfy (66115-1306)
PHONE..................................913 621-4555
Mike Rainen, *Chairman*
EMP: 14 **Privately Held**
SIC: 3999 Candles
PA: Empire Candle Co., Llc
2925 Fairfax Trfy
Kansas City KS 66115

(G-3989)
EMPIRE CANDLE CO LLC (PA)
Also Called: Langley/Empire Candle
2925 Fairfax Trfy (66115-1317)
PHONE..................................913 621-4555
Richard W Langley Jr, *President*
Mike Rainen, *Chairman*
Chet Stone, *CFO*
Tracie Koppers, *Human Res Dir*
Fred Rutherford, *VP Sales*
◆ **EMP:** 181
SQ FT: 282,000
SALES (est): 45.6MM **Privately Held**
WEB: www.empirecandle.com
SIC: 3999 Candles

(G-3990)
ENVIRONMENTAL VIEW LLC
Also Called: Environmental View Landscaping
1044 Merriam Ln (66103-1650)
P.O. Box 1617, Shawnee Mission (66222-0617)
PHONE..................................913 432-5011
Dave Heinen, *Principal*
Michael Mc Vey, *Principal*
EMP: 15
SALES (est): 731.9K **Privately Held**
WEB: www.environmentalview.com
SIC: 0781 Landscape services

(G-3991)
ENVISION INC
925 Sunshine Rd (66115-1122)
PHONE..................................316 267-2244
Glen Coy, *Branch Mgr*
EMP: 28
SQ FT: 25,000
SALES (corp-wide): 207.3MM **Privately Held**
WEB: www.envisionus.com
SIC: 2673 2676 Plastic bags: made from purchased materials; towels, paper: made from purchased paper
PA: Envision, Inc.
610 N Main St Ste 400
Wichita KS 67203
316 440-1500

(G-3992)
EPI HOLDINGS INC
87 Shawnee Ave (66105-1418)
PHONE..................................816 474-9423
Dave Rockey, *President*
William Morris, *General Mgr*
Scott Richmond, *Products*
EMP: 50 **EST:** 1966
SQ FT: 35,000
SALES: 2MM **Privately Held**
WEB: www.bearwhiz.com
SIC: 2759 Screen printing

(G-3993)
EPOXY COATING SPECIALISTS INC
Also Called: E C S
3940 S Ferree St (66103-1717)
PHONE..................................913 362-4141
David A Schloegel, *President*
Paul Budenbender, *Vice Pres*
Steve Trave, *Opers Mgr*
Deborah Lee, *Controller*
Teresa Lee, *Accountant*
EMP: 50
SQ FT: 40,000
SALES: 10MM **Privately Held**
SIC: 1799 Epoxy application

(G-3994)
EQUITY BANK NA
650 Kansas Ave (66105-1328)
PHONE..................................913 371-1242
EMP: 22 **Publicly Held**
SIC: 6022 State commercial banks
HQ: Equity Bank, N.A.
7701 E Kellogg Dr Ste 300
Wichita KS 67207
316 612-6000

(G-3995)
ERGON ASPHALT & EMULSIONS INC
10520 Wolcott Dr (66109-4000)
PHONE..................................913 788-5300
EMP: 8
SALES (corp-wide): 997.6MM **Privately Held**
SIC: 2951 Asphalt paving mixtures & blocks
HQ: Ergon Asphalt & Emulsions Inc
2829 Lakeland Dr Ste 2000
Flowood MS 39232
601 933-3000

(G-3996)
ERMAN CORPORATION INC
6600 Thorn Dr (66106-5039)
PHONE..................................913 287-4800
Rob Roth, *Manager*
EMP: 27
SALES (corp-wide): 18.1MM **Privately Held**
SIC: 5093 3341 Ferrous metal scrap & waste; secondary nonferrous metals
HQ: Erman Corporation, Inc.
21 N Skokie Hwy Ste 101
Lake Bluff IL 60044
847 615-1020

(G-3997)
ESTES EXPRESS LINES INC
4601 Speaker Rd (66106-1035)
PHONE..................................913 281-1723
Max Thierer, *Manager*
Ken Warren, *Manager*
EMP: 100
SALES (corp-wide): 3.1B **Privately Held**
WEB: www.estes-express.com
SIC: 4213 Contract haulers
PA: Estes Express Lines
3901 W Broad St
Richmond VA 23230
804 353-1900

(G-3998)
EXCEL LIGHTING LLC
735 Southwest Blvd Ste B (66103-1931)
PHONE..................................816 461-4694
Dustan Fankhauser, *Principal*
EMP: 5 **EST:** 2008
SALES (est): 620K **Privately Held**
SIC: 3993 Signs & advertising specialties

▲ = Import ▼=Export
◆ =Import/Export

(G-3999)
EXCEL LINEN SUPPLY
501 Funston Rd (66115-1215)
PHONE..................................816 842-6565
Joe Brancato, *Principal*
Dominic Brancato, *Vice Pres*
EMP: 23 **EST:** 2013
SALES (est): 2MM **Privately Held**
SIC: 7213 Uniform supply

(G-4000)
EXIDE TECHNOLOGIES
GNB Brand Products
3001 Fairfax Trfy (66115-1319)
PHONE..................................913 321-3561
Paul Zahner, *QC Mgr*
C J Dimarco, *Branch Mgr*
EMP: 240
SALES (corp-wide): 2.3B **Privately Held**
WEB: www.exideworld.com
SIC: 3691 3692 3629 Storage batteries; primary batteries, dry & wet; battery chargers, rectifying or nonrotating
PA: Exide Technologies
13000 Drfeld Pkwy Bldg 20
Milton GA 30004
678 566-9000

(G-4001)
EXIDE TECHNOLOGIES
Also Called: GNB Industrial
501 Kindleberger Rd (66115-1226)
PHONE..................................913 321-4600
Brian Rooney, *Branch Mgr*
EMP: 6
SALES (corp-wide): 2.3B **Privately Held**
WEB: www.exideworld.com
SIC: 3625 3629 Truck controls, industrial battery; battery chargers, rectifying or nonrotating
PA: Exide Technologies
13000 Drfeld Pkwy Bldg 20
Milton GA 30004
678 566-9000

(G-4002)
FAGAN COMPANY
Also Called: Emcor Services Fagan
3125 Brinkerhoff Rd (66115-1201)
PHONE..................................913 621-4444
William Adams, *President*
William C Fagan, *Exec VP*
EMP: 150
SQ FT: 24,000
SALES (est): 33.2MM
SALES (corp-wide): 8.1B **Publicly Held**
SIC: 1711 Warm air heating & air conditioning contractor; refrigeration contractor
PA: Emcor Group, Inc.
301 Merritt 7 Fl 6
Norwalk CT 06851
203 849-7800

(G-4003)
FAIRBANKS MORSE PUMP CORP (HQ)
P.O. Box 6999 (66106-0999)
PHONE..................................630 859-7000
John Kucharik, *President*
Dave Angelo, *Vice Pres*
Jeff Darbut, *Vice Pres*
◆ **EMP:** 300
SQ FT: 300,000
SALES (est): 101.5MM
SALES (corp-wide): 1.5B **Publicly Held**
SIC: 3561 Pumps & pumping equipment
PA: Spx Corporation
13320a Balntyn Corp Pl
Charlotte NC 28277
980 474-3700

(G-4004)
FAIRBANKS MORSE PUMP CORP
3601 Fairbanks Ave (66106-1200)
PHONE..................................913 371-5000
Jim Sexton, *Research*
Greg Gutwein, *Engineer*
Barry Jongsma, *Engineer*
Dave Angelo, *Manager*
Scott McKerlie, *MIS Staff*
EMP: 14
SALES (corp-wide): 1.5B **Publicly Held**
SIC: 3561 Pumps & pumping equipment
HQ: Fairbanks Morse Pump Corporation
Kansas City KS 66106
630 859-7000

(G-4005)
FAMILY CONSERVANCY INC (PA)
444 Minnesota Ave Ste 200 (66101-2900)
PHONE..................................913 342-1110
Betsy Vandervelde, *President*
Carolyn Hathaway, *COO*
Kristin Graue, *Vice Pres*
Jocelyn Mourning, *Vice Pres*
Lois Carr, *Accountant*
EMP: 56
SALES: 12MM **Privately Held**
WEB: www.thefamilyconservancy.org
SIC: 8322 Family (marriage) counseling; senior citizens' center or association

(G-4006)
FAMILY CONSERVANCY INC
5424 State Ave (66102-3446)
PHONE..................................913 287-1300
Marla Baldwin, *General Mgr*
Paula Neth, *Vice Pres*
EMP: 15
SALES (corp-wide): 12MM **Privately Held**
WEB: www.thefamilyconservancy.org
SIC: 8322 Family (marriage) counseling
PA: The Family Conservancy Inc
444 Minnesota Ave Ste 200
Kansas City KS 66101
913 342-1110

(G-4007)
FAMILY MEDICAL GROUP PA
8101 Parallel Pkwy # 100 (66112-2067)
PHONE..................................913 299-9200
Michael Parra MD, *President*
Sabrina Markese, *Family Practiti*
EMP: 20
SALES (est): 2.2MM **Privately Held**
SIC: 8011 General & family practice, physician/surgeon

(G-4008)
FAMILY PRACTICE ASSOCIATES (PA)
1150 N 75th Pl Ste 200 (66112-2466)
PHONE..................................913 299-2100
Vicente C Palmeri MD, *President*
Maria Palmeri, *Vice Pres*
EMP: 16
SALES (est): 1.5MM **Privately Held**
SIC: 8011 General & family practice, physician/surgeon; internal medicine, physician/surgeon

(G-4009)
FERGUSON DRY WALL COMPANY INC
Also Called: Ferguson Drywall Co Inc
224 N 72nd St (66112-3108)
PHONE..................................913 334-5658
Steven D Ferguson, *President*
EMP: 20 **EST:** 1974
SQ FT: 900
SALES (est): 1.7MM **Privately Held**
SIC: 1742 Drywall

(G-4010)
FIRST BANCSHARES INC
Also Called: First State Bank
650 Kansas Ave (66105-1328)
P.O. Box 5188 (66119-0188)
PHONE..................................913 371-1242
David Spehar, *CEO*
Jack Brozman, *Vice Chairman*
EMP: 20
SQ FT: 10,000
SALES: 1.2MM **Privately Held**
SIC: 6022 State trust companies accepting deposits, commercial

(G-4011)
FIRST FEDERAL BANK KANSAS CITY
711 Minnesota Ave (66101-2703)
PHONE..................................913 233-6100
Richard Merker, *Branch Mgr*
EMP: 13
SALES (corp-wide): 35.7MM **Privately Held**
WEB: www.isfedkc.com
SIC: 6035 Federal savings & loan associations
PA: First Federal Bank Of Kansas City
6900 Executive Dr
Kansas City MO 64120
816 241-7800

(G-4012)
FLEX-N-GATE MISSOURI LLC
900 S 68th St (66111-2334)
PHONE..................................913 387-3857
Dave Ekblad, *President*
Flex-N-Gate Corporation, *Mng Member*
EMP: 80
SALES: 1MM **Privately Held**
SIC: 5063 Motors, electric

(G-4013)
FLUEBROTHERS LLC
Also Called: Fluesbrothers Chimney Service
1701 Southwest Blvd (66103-1750)
PHONE..................................913 236-7141
Jeremy S Biswell, *Principal*
Brandi Biswell, *Vice Pres*
Aubrey Leiter, *Marketing Staff*
EMP: 10
SALES (est): 185.1K **Privately Held**
SIC: 7349 Chimney cleaning

(G-4014)
FOLEY GROUP INC (PA)
333 N 6th St (66101-3356)
P.O. Box 171256 (66117-0256)
PHONE..................................913 342-3336
Fred Denney, *President*
Andy Matlock, *Sales Staff*
Gary Meier, *Sales Staff*
EMP: 13 **EST:** 1961
SALES (est): 4.2MM **Privately Held**
WEB: www.foley-group.com
SIC: 5063 5075 Electrical supplies; warm air heating & air conditioning

(G-4015)
FONTASTIK INC
1851 Merriam Ln Ste C (66106-4723)
PHONE..................................816 474-4366
Darrell Olberding, *President*
EMP: 7
SQ FT: 3,100
SALES: 750K **Privately Held**
WEB: www.fontastik.com
SIC: 2759 2741 Commercial printing; miscellaneous publishing

(G-4016)
FOR WYANDOT CENTER
2205 W 36th Ave (66103-2107)
PHONE..................................913 362-0393
EMP: 72
SALES (corp-wide): 11.1MM **Privately Held**
SIC: 8322 8093 Crisis intervention center; mental health clinic, outpatient
PA: Wyandot Center For Community Behavioral Healthcare, Inc.
757 Armstrong Ave
Kansas City KS 66101
913 233-3300

(G-4017)
FOR WYANDOT CENTER
7840 Washington Ave (66112-2152)
P.O. Box 12005 (66112-0005)
PHONE..................................913 328-4600
Tonja Speer, *Vice Pres*
Gary Sparks, *Branch Mgr*
Tonya Briggs, *Case Mgr*
Sherrie Alvey, *Manager*
Joy Rannebeck, *Director*
EMP: 163
SALES (corp-wide): 11.1MM **Privately Held**
WEB: www.wmhci.org
SIC: 8093 Mental health clinic, outpatient
PA: Wyandot Center For Community Behavioral Healthcare, Inc.
757 Armstrong Ave
Kansas City KS 66101
913 233-3300

(G-4018)
FRIENDS OF YATES INC
1418 Garfield Ave (66104-5815)
PHONE..................................913 321-1566
Dwight Townsend, *President*
Rasmita Patro, *Manager*
Ladora Lattimore, *Director*
EMP: 25
SALES: 1.5MM **Privately Held**
WEB: www.friendsofyates.org
SIC: 8322 Crisis intervention center

(G-4019)
FSW SUBTECH HOLDINGS LLC
236 N 7th St (66101-3202)
PHONE..................................816 795-9955
Jason Scarborough, *Vice Pres*
Anthony Kelley, *Controller*
EMP: 14
SALES (est): 604.2K **Privately Held**
SIC: 5046 Restaurant equipment & supplies; coffee brewing equipment & supplies; commercial cooking & food service equipment; ovens, microwave: commercial

(G-4020)
FUCHS LUBRICANTS CO
2140 S 88th St (66111-1756)
PHONE..................................913 422-4022
Jeff Meloy, *Vice Pres*
David Clark, *Manager*
James Butler, *Supervisor*
Steve Mills, *IT/INT Sup*
EMP: 100
SALES (corp-wide): 2.8B **Privately Held**
WEB: www.fuchs.com
SIC: 2992 5172 Oils & greases, blending & compounding; lubricating oils & greases
HQ: Fuchs Lubricants Co.
17050 Lathrop Ave
Harvey IL 60426
708 333-8901

(G-4021)
FUJIFILM NORTH AMERICA CORP
Also Called: Fujifilm Graphic Systems
1101 W Cambridge Cir Dr (66103-1311)
PHONE..................................816 914-5942
Gretchen Tosatto, *Purch Agent*
Neil Clark, *Accounts Mgr*
Ron Peterson, *Manager*
EMP: 12 **Privately Held**
SIC: 5043 5169 5045 5084 Photographic equipment & supplies; chemicals & allied products; computers, peripherals & software; printing trades machinery, equipment & supplies
HQ: Fujifilm North America Corporation
200 Summit Lake Dr Fl 2
Valhalla NY 10595
914 789-8100

(G-4022)
FUJIFILM SERICOL USA INC
Also Called: Graphic Systems Division
1101 W Cambridge Dr (66103)
PHONE..................................913 342-4060
Ryutaro Hosoda, *CEO*
Merle D Arthur, *President*
Sam Ota, *President*
Moriho Atsumi, *Chairman*
Mitch Bode, *Vice Pres*
◆ **EMP:** 160
SQ FT: 49,544
SALES (est): 33.7MM **Privately Held**
WEB: www.sericol.com
SIC: 2893 5085 5084 Printing ink; ink, printers'; industrial machinery & equipment
HQ: Fujifilm Corporation
9-7-3, Akasaka
Minato-Ku TKY 107-0

(G-4023)
FULL FAITH CHURCH OF LOVE
Also Called: Maranatha Kinderprep
2737 S 42nd St (66106-3950)
PHONE..................................913 262-3145
Fax: 913 262-3268
EMP: 10
SALES (corp-wide): 4.1MM **Privately Held**
SIC: 8351 Child Day Care Services

PA: Full Faith Church Of Love
6824 Lackman Rd
Shawnee Mission KS 66217
913 631-1100

(G-4024)
G E V INVESTMENT INC (PA)
3241 N 7th Street Trfy (66115-1105)
PHONE..................................913 677-5333
Gary Venable, *President*
Jan Venable, *Treasurer*
EMP: 46
SQ FT: 7,200
SALES: 6.1MM **Privately Held**
SIC: 5065 7622 1731 Communication equipment; security control equipment & systems; communication equipment repair; communications specialization

(G-4025)
GARSITE PROGRESS LLC (PA)
539 S 10th St (66105-1201)
PHONE..................................913 342-5600
Peter Buffkin, *Vice Pres*
Amy Young, *Buyer*
John George, *Mng Member*
Steve Barron, *Maintence Staff*
▼ **EMP:** 80
SQ FT: 300,000
SALES (est): 25MM **Privately Held**
WEB: www.garsite.com
SIC: 3724 7699 Aircraft engines & engine parts; aircraft & heavy equipment repair services

(G-4026)
GATEWAY HOUSING LP
Also Called: Gateway Plaza Townhomes
1430 N 4th St (66101-2304)
PHONE..................................913 621-3840
JD Lakhani, *Partner*
Cathy Feriend, *Principal*
EMP: 20
SALES (est): 1MM **Privately Held**
SIC: 6513 Apartment building operators

(G-4027)
GATEWAY PLAZA WEST LTD
1430 N 4th St (66101-2304)
PHONE..................................913 621-3840
J D Lakheni, *Partner*
EMP: 10
SALES: 110K **Privately Held**
SIC: 8748 Business consulting

(G-4028)
GEAR HEADQUARTERS INC
3012 S 24th St (66106-4798)
PHONE..................................913 831-1700
James N Timble, *Ch of Bd*
Michael J Gricus, *Vice Pres*
Robert W Singer, *Admin Sec*
EMP: 16 **EST:** 1900
SQ FT: 20,000
SALES (est): 2.8MM
SALES (corp-wide): 162.5MM **Privately Held**
WEB: www.gearheadquarters.com
SIC: 3462 3599 Gears, forged steel; machine shop, jobbing & repair
PA: Headco Industries, Inc.
2601 Parkes Dr
Broadview IL 60155
708 681-4400

(G-4029)
GEIGER READY-MIX CO INC
4303 Speaker Rd (66106-1029)
PHONE..................................913 281-0111
E W Geiger, *Owner*
EMP: 30
SALES (corp-wide): 37.5MM **Privately Held**
SIC: 3273 Ready-mixed concrete
PA: Geiger Ready-Mix Co., Inc.
1333 S 2nd St
Leavenworth KS 66048
913 772-4010

(G-4030)
GENERAL DELIVERY INC
1601 Fairfax Trfy (66115-1432)
PHONE..................................913 281-6580
James O Neighbors, *President*
Franklin D Reiss, *Corp Secy*
EMP: 10
SALES: 1.5MM **Privately Held**
SIC: 3537 Trucks: freight, baggage, etc.: industrial, except mining

(G-4031)
GENERAL MOTORS LLC
3201 Fairfax Trfy (66115-1307)
P.O. Box 15278 (66115)
PHONE..................................913 573-7981
Melissa Churning, *District Mgr*
William Kulhanek, *Plant Mgr*
Joshua Manger, *Safety Mgr*
Sagnik Banerjee, *Engineer*
William Humphreys, *Engineer*
EMP: 2390 **Publicly Held**
SIC: 5511 3711 Automobiles, new & used; motor vehicles & car bodies
HQ: General Motors Llc
300 Renaissance Ctr L1
Detroit MI 48243

(G-4032)
GFG AG SERVICES LLC
501 S Coy St (66105-1303)
PHONE..................................913 233-0001
Lupe Casaraes, *Manager*
Laura Perry, *Manager*
EMP: 15
SALES (corp-wide): 16.8MM **Privately Held**
SIC: 5153 Grains
PA: Gfg Ag Services, Llc
117 N Alanthus Ave
Stanberry MO 64489
660 783-2700

(G-4033)
GGNSC HOLDINGS LLC
750 Blake St (66111-1339)
PHONE..................................913 422-5832
EMP: 10
SALES (corp-wide): 2.6B **Privately Held**
SIC: 8051 Skilled nursing care facilities
HQ: Ggnsc Holdings Llc
5220 Tennyson Pkwy # 400
Plano TX 75024
972 372-6300

(G-4034)
GIBBS TECHNOLOGY COMPANY
1212 W Cambridge Cir Dr (66103-1314)
PHONE..................................913 621-2424
John Hauck, *Sales Mgr*
Andrea Paul, *Administration*
EMP: 34
SALES (corp-wide): 69.8MM **Privately Held**
SIC: 5044 Office equipment
PA: Gibbs Technology Company
12163 Prichard Farm Rd
Maryland Heights MO 63043
314 997-6300

(G-4035)
GJO INC
5320 Speaker Rd (66106-1050)
PHONE..................................913 621-6611
Greg Ohmes, *President*
Larry McKinney, *Treasurer*
Amy Weber, *Human Res Mgr*
Kevin Grefsas, *Marketing Staff*
Liz Smith, *Clerk*
EMP: 30
SQ FT: 5,000
SALES (est): 7.9MM **Privately Held**
SIC: 1731 General electrical contractor

(G-4036)
GJO HOLDINGS INC
5320 Speaker Rd (66106-1050)
PHONE..................................913 621-6611
Greg Ohmes,
EMP: 25
SALES (corp-wide): 8.5MM **Privately Held**
SIC: 6719 Investment holding companies, except banks
PA: Pro Power Electric, Llc
5320 Speaker Rd
Kansas City KS 66106
913 621-6611

(G-4037)
GLANTZ HOLDINGS INC
Also Called: Glantz, N & Son
1921 Foxridge Dr (66106-4733)
PHONE..................................913 722-1000
Scott Patten, *Branch Mgr*
EMP: 15
SQ FT: 6,400
SALES (corp-wide): 118.9MM **Privately Held**
WEB: www.glantz.net
SIC: 5085 Signmaker equipment & supplies
PA: Glantz Holdings Inc
16 Court St Ste 3000
Brooklyn NY 11241
502 271-5560

(G-4038)
GLEN-GERY CORPORATION
336 S 42nd St (66106-1004)
PHONE..................................913 281-2800
Gary Watkins, *Manager*
EMP: 7
SALES (corp-wide): 1.2MM **Privately Held**
WEB: www.glengerybrick.com
SIC: 5032 5932 5083 3272 Brick, except refractory; building materials, secondhand; landscaping equipment; concrete products, precast
HQ: Glen-Gery Corporation
1166 Spring St
Reading PA 19610
610 374-4011

(G-4039)
GOLDEN OAKS HEALTHCARE INC
Also Called: Healthcare Resort of Kansas Cy
8900 Parallel Pkwy (66112-1637)
PHONE..................................913 788-2100
Soon Burnam, *Treasurer*
Lisa Kolman, *Exec Dir*
EMP: 79
SALES: 8.1MM
SALES (corp-wide): 2B **Publicly Held**
SIC: 8051 Mental retardation hospital
PA: The Ensign Group Inc
29222 Rncho Vejo Rd Ste 1
San Juan Capistrano CA 92675
949 487-9500

(G-4040)
GORYDZ INC
2636 N Early St (66101-1242)
PHONE..................................913 486-1665
Dale McDaniel, *CEO*
EMP: 10
SQ FT: 1,567
SALES (est): 217.5K **Privately Held**
SIC: 7371 7373 4121 Computer software development & applications; computer software development; systems software development services; systems integration services; taxicabs

(G-4041)
GOURMET SPECIALTIES INC
111 Southwest Blvd (66103-2132)
PHONE..................................913 432-5228
Joe R Polo Sr, *President*
Josh Popejoy, *Business Mgr*
Thomas Clark, *Vice Pres*
Christine Polo, *Office Mgr*
◆ **EMP:** 70
SQ FT: 60,000
SALES (est): 14.4MM **Privately Held**
SIC: 2035 Pickles, sauces & salad dressings

(G-4042)
GRABILL PLUMBING INC
3121 Merriam Ln Ste G (66106-4624)
PHONE..................................913 432-9660
Kevin Grabill, *President*
EMP: 25
SALES (est): 2.2MM **Privately Held**
SIC: 1711 Plumbing contractors

(G-4043)
GRACE ANGELS FAMILY SERVICE
1220 Troup Ave Ste B (66104-5853)
PHONE..................................913 233-2944
Wanda Bibbs, *Director*
EMP: 12 **EST:** 2010
SALES (est): 455.4K **Privately Held**
SIC: 8351 Child day care services

(G-4044)
GRAIN CRAFT INC
56 Silver Ave (66103-2164)
PHONE..................................913 262-1779
Charlie Jackson, *Opers-Prdtn-Mfg*
EMP: 25
SALES (corp-wide): 288.5MM **Privately Held**
WEB: www.cerealfood.com
SIC: 2041 Grain mills (except rice)
PA: Grain Craft, Inc.
201 W Main St Ste 203
Chattanooga TN 37408
423 265-2313

(G-4045)
GRANITE CITY FOOD & BREWRY LTD
1701 Village West Pkwy (66111-1879)
PHONE..................................913 334-2255
Grant Lowe, *Manager*
EMP: 100
SALES (corp-wide): 358.6MM **Privately Held**
SIC: 5812 2082 Family restaurants; beer (alcoholic beverage)
HQ: Granite City Food & Brewery Ltd.
3600 American Blvd W # 400
Bloomington MN 55431
952 215-0660

(G-4046)
GREAT PLAINS ROOFG SHTMTL INC
2820 Roe Ln Ste O (66103-1560)
PHONE..................................913 677-4679
J R Harrington, *President*
EMP: 100
SALES (est): 16.1MM **Privately Held**
WEB: www.greatplainsroofing.com
SIC: 1761 Roofing contractor

(G-4047)
GREAT WOLF KANSAS SPE LLC
Also Called: Great Wolf Kansas City
10401 Cabela Dr (66111-1954)
PHONE..................................913 299-7001
Jim Calder,
Craig Stark,
EMP: 300
SALES (est): 12.2MM
SALES (corp-wide): 1.6B **Privately Held**
SIC: 7011 7999 Resort hotel; tourist attractions, amusement park concessions & rides
HQ: Great Wolf Resorts Holdings, Inc.
1255 Fourier Dr Ste 201
Madison WI 53717
608 662-4700

(G-4048)
GREAT WOLF LODGE KANSAS CY LLC
10401 Cabela Dr (66111-1954)
PHONE..................................913 299-7001
Karina Addari, *Manager*
EMP: 13
SALES (est): 250.3K **Privately Held**
SIC: 7011 Resort hotel

(G-4049)
GREEN EXPECTATIONS LDSCPG INC
1910 S 74th St (66106-4902)
PHONE..................................913 897-8076
Thomas Bunker, *President*
Nancy Bunker, *Corp Secy*
EMP: 15
SALES (est): 411.2K **Privately Held**
SIC: 0782 8748 5063 Landscape contractors; lighting consultant; lighting fixtures

(G-4050)
GREENBRIER RAILCAR LLC
1109 S 12th St (66105-1614)
PHONE..................................913 342-0010
Tina Muolo, *Purch Dir*
Bonnie Pittman, *Branch Mgr*
EMP: 40

SALES (corp-wide): 3B **Publicly Held**
SIC: 4789 Railroad car repair
HQ: Greenbrier Railcar Llc
1 Centerpointe Dr Ste 200
Lake Oswego OR 97035
503 684-7000

(G-4051)
GREG KETZNER
7860 Washington Ave (66112-2193)
PHONE.................................913 334-6770
Greg Ketzner, *Principal*
EMP: 20 **EST:** 2001
SALES (est): 273.1K **Privately Held**
SIC: 0742 Veterinarian, animal specialties

(G-4052)
GREG SMITH ENTERPRISES INC
Also Called: G S Enterprises
2540 S 88th St (66111-1764)
P.O. Box 13286, Edwardsville (66113-0286)
PHONE.................................913 543-7614
Greg Smith, *President*
Gloria Saucedo, *COO*
Janet Price, *Vice Pres*
Synthia Smith, *Vice Pres*
EMP: 20
SALES (est): 4.4MM **Privately Held**
SIC: 4213 Trucking, except local

(G-4053)
GREGORY A SCOTT INC
Also Called: Midwest Sales
6320 Kansas Ave (66111-2127)
P.O. Box 11058 (66111-0058)
PHONE.................................913 677-0414
Greg A Scott, *President*
EMP: 20
SQ FT: 16,000
SALES: 1.7MM **Privately Held**
SIC: 2395 2759 Embroidery & art needlework; screen printing

(G-4054)
GRIFFIN WHEEL COMPANY
7111 Griffin Rd (66111-2497)
PHONE.................................913 299-2223
Robert W Reum, *President*
Eldon McDonald, *Project Mgr*
Michael Decola, *Opers Mgr*
Aaron McCrady, *Opers Mgr*
Linda Olderman, *Safety Mgr*
EMP: 34
SALES (est): 934.4K
SALES (corp-wide): 2.4B **Privately Held**
SIC: 3462 5015 Iron & steel forgings; automotive parts & supplies, used
PA: Amsted Industries Incorporated
180 N Stetson Ave # 1800
Chicago IL 60601
312 645-1700

(G-4055)
GROENDYKE TRANSPORT INC
299 E Donovan Rd (66115-1426)
PHONE.................................913 621-2200
Brian James, *Manager*
EMP: 50
SALES (corp-wide): 292.7MM **Privately Held**
WEB: www.groendyke.com
SIC: 4213 Contract haulers
PA: Groendyke Transport Inc.
2510 Rock Island Blvd
Enid OK 73701
580 234-4663

(G-4056)
GROSS PHD JUDITH M S
2737 N 68th St (66109-1845)
PHONE.................................913 645-2437
Judith M S Gross PHD, *Owner*
EMP: 12
SALES (est): 146.6K **Privately Held**
SIC: 8221 7389 Colleges universities & professional schools;

(G-4057)
GS ENTERPRISES INC
51 Osage Ave (66105-1412)
P.O. Box 13286, Edwardsville (66113-0286)
PHONE.................................913 543-7614
Greg Smith, *Principal*
EMP: 10
SALES (est): 1.5MM **Privately Held**
SIC: 4213 Automobiles, transport & delivery

(G-4058)
GULFSIDE SUPPLY INC
5660 Inland Dr (66106-1316)
PHONE.................................913 384-9610
Brad Rash, *Owner*
EMP: 14
SALES (corp-wide): 642.5MM **Privately Held**
SIC: 5033 Roofing, asphalt & sheet metal
PA: Gulfside Supply, Inc.
2900 E 7th Ave Ste 100
Tampa FL 33605
813 636-9808

(G-4059)
GUNTER CONSTRUCTION COMPANY
520 Division St (66103-1904)
PHONE.................................913 362-7844
Christina Gunter, *President*
EMP: 15 **EST:** 2009
SALES (est): 2.8MM **Privately Held**
SIC: 8741 1611 1795 1771 Construction management; concrete construction: roads, highways, sidewalks, etc.; general contractor, highway & street construction; concrete breaking for streets & highways; curb & sidewalk contractors

(G-4060)
H&R BLOCK INC
Also Called: H & R Block
5008 State Ave 5010 (66102-3460)
PHONE.................................913 788-7779
David Young, *Manager*
EMP: 20
SALES (corp-wide): 3B **Publicly Held**
WEB: www.hrblock.com
SIC: 7291 Tax return preparation services
PA: H&R Block, Inc.
1 H&R Block Way
Kansas City MO 64105
816 854-3000

(G-4061)
H&R BLOCK INC
Also Called: H & R Block
7616 State Ave (66112)
PHONE.................................913 788-5222
David Young, *Manager*
EMP: 12
SALES (corp-wide): 3B **Publicly Held**
WEB: www.hrblock.com
SIC: 7291 Tax return preparation services
PA: H&R Block, Inc.
1 H&R Block Way
Kansas City MO 64105
816 854-3000

(G-4062)
HAMMEL SCALE KANSAS CITY INC (PA)
612 Kansas Ave (66105-1312)
P.O. Box 5065 (66119-0065)
PHONE.................................913 321-5428
John R Hammel, *President*
Michael G Lewis, *Vice Pres*
Ralph Taylor, *Train & Dev Mgr*
Karin Super, *Admin Asst*
James Vandiver, *Technician*
EMP: 15
SQ FT: 10,000
SALES (est): 2.9MM **Privately Held**
SIC: 5046 7699 Scales, except laboratory; scale repair service

(G-4063)
HAMPEL OIL INC
2920 Fairfax Trfy (66115-1318)
PHONE.................................913 321-0139
William Hampel, *President*
Brian Williams, *Opers Mgr*
Staci Terstriep, *Branch Mgr*
EMP: 25 **EST:** 1994
SQ FT: 40,000
SALES (est): 16MM
SALES (corp-wide): 135.4MM **Privately Held**
WEB: www.hampeloilinc.com
SIC: 5171 Petroleum bulk stations
PA: Hampel Oil Distributors, Inc.
3727 S West St
Wichita KS 67217
316 529-1162

(G-4064)
HAMPTON INN
1400 Village West Pkwy (66111-1876)
PHONE.................................913 328-1400
Daniel Nawokawiski, *General Mgr*
EMP: 22
SALES (est): 1.1MM **Privately Held**
SIC: 7011 Hotels & motels

(G-4065)
HANGER PROSTHETICS &
Also Called: Hanger Clinic
3914 Rainbow Blvd (66103-2918)
PHONE.................................913 588-6548
Sam Liang, *President*
Matthew Luecke, *Manager*
Matt Luetke, *Manager*
EMP: 5
SALES (corp-wide): 1B **Publicly Held**
SIC: 5047 3842 Artificial limbs; limbs, artificial
HQ: Hanger Prosthetics & Orthotics East, Inc.
33 North Ave Ste 101
Tallmadge OH 44278

(G-4066)
HAPPY HEARTS LEARNING CTR LLC
1901 N 63rd Dr (66102-1101)
PHONE.................................913 334-3331
Matt Popilek, *Mng Member*
EMP: 12
SALES: 300K **Privately Held**
SIC: 8351 Child day care services

(G-4067)
HARBOUR CONSTRUCTION INC
2717 S 88th St (66111-1757)
PHONE.................................913 441-2555
Robert W Harbour Jr, *President*
Pat Harbour, *Corp Secy*
EMP: 15 **EST:** 1961
SALES: 4MM **Privately Held**
SIC: 1611 1221 Highway & street paving contractor; bituminous coal & lignite-surface mining

(G-4068)
HARCROS CHEMICALS INC (PA)
5200 Speaker Rd (66106-1048)
PHONE.................................913 321-3131
Kevin Mirner, *CEO*
Wade Christensen, *Regional Mgr*
Rich Wingo, *Regional Mgr*
Jim Grady, *District Mgr*
Doug Gwatney, *District Mgr*
◆ **EMP:** 150
SQ FT: 225,000
SALES (est): 512.6K **Privately Held**
WEB: www.harcroschem.com
SIC: 5169 2869 Industrial gases; industrial organic chemicals

(G-4069)
HARCROS CHEMICALS INC
Tech Center
5200 Speaker Rd (66106-1048)
PHONE.................................913 621-7721
Joel Zillner, *Branch Mgr*
EMP: 150
SALES (corp-wide): 512.6K **Privately Held**
WEB: www.harcroschem.com
SIC: 2819 Industrial inorganic chemicals
PA: Harcros Chemicals Inc.
5200 Speaker Rd
Kansas City KS 66106
913 321-3131

(G-4070)
HARVEST MEAT COMPANY INC
1301 Argentine Blvd (66105-1569)
PHONE.................................913 371-2333
Mike Leavy, *General Mgr*
EMP: 16
SALES (corp-wide): 292.7MM **Privately Held**
WEB: www.harvestmeat.com
SIC: 5147 Meats, fresh
HQ: Harvest Meat Company, Inc.
1000 Bay Marina Dr
National City CA 91950

(G-4071)
HD SUPPLY INC
4600 Kansas Ave (66106-1127)
PHONE.................................816 283-3687
Nicole Wright, *President*
EMP: 43 **Publicly Held**
SIC: 5031 Building materials, exterior
HQ: Hd Supply, Inc.
3400 Cumberland Blvd Se
Atlanta GA 30339
770 852-9000

(G-4072)
HEADCO INDUSTRIES INC
Also Called: Bearing Headquarters Co
3010 S 24th St (66106-4707)
PHONE.................................913 831-1444
Robert Sullivan, *Vice Pres*
Greg Dovel, *Sales Staff*
William Beebe, *Manager*
EMP: 13
SALES (corp-wide): 162.5MM **Privately Held**
WEB: www.his-tech.com
SIC: 5085 5063 Bearings; power transmission equipment, electric
PA: Headco Industries, Inc.
2601 Parkes Dr
Broadview IL 60155
708 681-4400

(G-4073)
HEALTH OPTIONS THAT MATTER
340 Southwest Blvd (66103-2150)
PHONE.................................913 722-3100
Sharon Lee, *CEO*
Kevin Dennis, *COO*
EMP: 20
SALES: 125K **Privately Held**
SIC: 8011 Primary care medical clinic

(G-4074)
HEART AMERICA SURGERY CTR LLC
Also Called: Heart America Surgery Center
8935 State Ave (66112-1645)
PHONE.................................913 334-8935
Sharon K Wetterberg, *Office Mgr*
Phyllis Steer,
Dwight Hendricks,
EMP: 40
SALES (est): 4.3MM **Publicly Held**
WEB: www.hoasc1.com
SIC: 8093 Specialty outpatient clinics
HQ: Midamerica Division, Inc.
903 E 104th St Ste 500
Kansas City MO 64131
816 508-4000

(G-4075)
HEARTLAND HBTAT FOR HMNITY INC
155 S 18th St Ste 120 (66102-5644)
PHONE.................................913 342-3047
Thomas J Lally, *Exec Dir*
Doris Gordon, *Administration*
EMP: 11
SALES: 3MM **Privately Held**
SIC: 8399 1522 Social change association; residential construction

(G-4076)
HEARTLAND IMAGING COMPANIES
Also Called: Lawrence Photo-Graphic
1211 W Cambridge Cir Dr (66103-1313)
PHONE.................................913 621-1211
Robert J Gourley, *Chairman*
Vernon Vogel, *Vice Pres*
Thomas M Prater, *Treasurer*
Elizabeth M Gourley, *Admin Sec*
EMP: 373
SQ FT: 17,000
SALES: 141MM **Privately Held**
WEB: www.heartlandimaging.com
SIC: 5043 Printing apparatus, photographic

(G-4077)
HEARTLAND PRIMARY CARE PA
2040 Hutton Rd Ste 102 (66109-4566)
PHONE..................................913 299-3700
William F Taylor, *President*
EMP: 40
SQ FT: 6,200
SALES (est): 4.4MM **Privately Held**
WEB: www.heartlandprimarycare.com
SIC: 8011 Pediatrician

(G-4078)
HEIMEN LDSCP & IRRIGATION LLC
1044 Merriam Ln (66103-1650)
PHONE..................................913 432-5011
David Heimen, *Owner*
EMP: 20 **EST:** 1986
SALES (est): 670K **Privately Held**
SIC: 0782 Landscape contractors

(G-4079)
HIGHTECH SIGNS LLC
2338 Merriam Ln (66106-4719)
PHONE..................................913 894-4422
Dick Robinson, *Partner*
Mike Rhodes, *Partner*
EMP: 33
SALES (est): 4.1MM **Privately Held**
SIC: 3993 5999 Signs, not made in custom sign painting shops; banners

(G-4080)
HILLVIEW CHURCH OF GOD INC
Also Called: Hillview Christian Center
701 N 78th St (66112-2803)
PHONE..................................913 299-4406
Dexter White, *Pastor*
EMP: 15
SQ FT: 6,000
SALES (est): 650K **Privately Held**
WEB: www.hillviewcog.org
SIC: 8661 8351 Christian Reformed Church; preschool center

(G-4081)
HILTON GARDEN INN 23930
Also Called: Hilton Hotels
520 Minnesota Ave (66101-2930)
PHONE..................................913 342-7900
Kurt Mayo, *General Mgr*
Ron Johnson, *Director*
EMP: 80
SALES (est): 3.5MM **Privately Held**
SIC: 7011 Hotels & motels

(G-4082)
HIT INC
Also Called: Haskin Incorporated Transfer
29 Woodswether Rd (66118-1132)
PHONE..................................913 281-4040
Rob Patterson, *President*
Krista Ward, *Marketing Staff*
Crystal Jewell, *Manager*
EMP: 30
SQ FT: 8,000
SALES (est): 3.9MM **Privately Held**
WEB: www.coreyhaskin.com
SIC: 4212 Local trucking, without storage

(G-4083)
HMONG MANUFACTURING INC
1900 Osage Ave (66105-1567)
PHONE..................................913 371-2752
Her Vang, *CEO*
EMP: 40
SQ FT: 10,000
SALES (est): 5.5MM **Privately Held**
SIC: 3993 Signs & advertising specialties

(G-4084)
HOLIDAY INN EXPRESS VILLAGE W
1931 Prairie Crossing St (66111-1210)
PHONE..................................913 328-1024
Renee Hadley, *General Mgr*
EMP: 19
SALES (est): 1MM **Privately Held**
SIC: 7011 Hotels & motels

(G-4085)
HOSPITAL LINEN SERVICES INC
611 S 4th St (66105-1431)
PHONE..................................913 621-2228
John Gotfredson, *General Mgr*
EMP: 85
SQ FT: 60,000
SALES: 7.7MM **Privately Held**
WEB: www.ntlkc.com
SIC: 7213 Uniform supply

(G-4086)
HOUSE OF ROCKS INC
1725 Merriam Ln (66106-4743)
PHONE..................................913 432-5990
Jack L Robinson, *President*
EMP: 20
SQ FT: 3,000
SALES (est): 2.9MM **Privately Held**
SIC: 5999 5032 Rock & stone specimens; stone, crushed or broken

(G-4087)
HUB CAP & WHEEL STORE INC
2810 S 44th St (66106-3717)
PHONE..................................913 432-0002
Tony Rice, *President*
Julie Rice, *Vice Pres*
EMP: 10
SQ FT: 15,000
SALES (est): 1.3MM **Privately Held**
WEB: www.hubcapwheelstore.com
SIC: 5531 5013 Automotive & home supply stores; automotive supplies & parts

(G-4088)
HUBERGROUP USA INC
3008 S 44th St (66106-3719)
PHONE..................................913 262-2510
Kevin Blake, *Owner*
EMP: 17
SALES (corp-wide): 355.8K **Privately Held**
SIC: 2893 Printing ink
HQ: Hubergroup Usa, Inc.
1701 Golf Rd Ste 3-201
Rolling Meadows IL 60008
815 929-9293

(G-4089)
HUGHES DEVELOPMENT COMPANY INC (PA)
1021 N 7th St Ste 106 (66101-2886)
PHONE..................................913 321-2262
Robert L Hughes Jr, *President*
Angela Chico, *Vice Pres*
Verona M Hughes, *Treasurer*
EMP: 12 **EST:** 1966
SQ FT: 3,000
SALES (est): 1.8MM **Privately Held**
SIC: 6531 Real estate managers

(G-4090)
HYDEMAN COMPANY INC
3300 Rainbow Ext (66103-2026)
PHONE..................................913 384-2620
Douglass Hydeman, *President*
Gary McClintock, *Sales Executive*
EMP: 8
SQ FT: 1,500
SALES (est): 1.8MM **Privately Held**
SIC: 3575 3596 3496 Computer terminals; scales & balances, except laboratory; miscellaneous fabricated wire products

(G-4091)
I B S INDUSTRIES INC
500 State Ave Rm 176 (66101-2409)
PHONE..................................913 281-0787
Dean Lynn, *Manager*
EMP: 14
SALES (est): 196.1K **Privately Held**
SIC: 7349 Janitorial service, contract basis

(G-4092)
IAA INC
Also Called: Iaa 527
2663 S 88th St (66111-1767)
PHONE..................................913 422-9303
Steve Crouper, *Manager*
EMP: 16 **Publicly Held**
SIC: 5012 Automobile auction
HQ: Insurance Auto Auctions, Inc.
2 Westbrook Corporate Ctr # 1000
Westchester IL 60154
708 492-7000

(G-4093)
IBT INC
Also Called: Ibt Aerospace
3003 Power Dr (66106-4720)
PHONE..................................913 428-4958
Bob W McGinnis, *Branch Mgr*
EMP: 10
SALES (corp-wide): 161.7MM **Privately Held**
WEB: www.ibtinc.com
SIC: 5085 Bearings
PA: Ibt, Inc.
9400 W 55th St
Shawnee Mission KS 66203
913 677-3151

(G-4094)
ICARE USA INC
100 Abbie Ave (66103-1304)
PHONE..................................919 624-9095
John Floyd, *President*
Lorine Nemes, *Accounting Mgr*
Seth Rogers, *Manager*
EMP: 11
SALES: 13MM
SALES (corp-wide): 526.7K **Privately Held**
SIC: 8099 Medical services organization
HQ: Icare Finland Oy
Ayritie 22
Vantaa 01510

(G-4095)
IDEALEASE OF MO-KAN INC
Also Called: Diamond Idealease
346 N James St (66118-1141)
PHONE..................................785 379-2300
Mike Rissler, *Manager*
EMP: 18
SALES (corp-wide): 78.2MM **Privately Held**
SIC: 7513 Truck leasing, without drivers; truck rental, without drivers
HQ: Idealease Of Mo-Kan, Inc.
7700 Ne 38th St
Kansas City MO 64161

(G-4096)
IN TERMINAL CONSOLIDATION CO
Also Called: Kansas City Piggy Back
4010 Argentine Blvd (66106-1936)
PHONE..................................913 671-7755
David Nickell, *Owner*
EMP: 20
SALES (corp-wide): 16.2MM **Privately Held**
WEB: www.kcpiggy.com
SIC: 4731 Freight consolidation
PA: Terminal Consolidation Company
3600 Ne Great Midwest Dr
Kansas City MO 64161
816 453-5101

(G-4097)
INDEPENDENT ELECTRIC MCHY CO (PA)
4425 Oliver St (66106-3764)
PHONE..................................913 362-1155
David B Launder Sr, *President*
Bernard Favaloro, *Exec VP*
Tyler Burks, *Sales Staff*
Scott Hamilton, *Sales Staff*
Jeanie Jones, *Sales Staff*
EMP: 36 **EST:** 1908
SQ FT: 60,000
SALES: 9MM **Privately Held**
WEB: www.iemco.com
SIC: 7629 5063 3599 7692 Electrical equipment repair services; electrical apparatus & equipment; machine shop, jobbing & repair; welding repair

(G-4098)
INDUSTRIAL COATINGS INC
200 S 5th St (66101-3828)
PHONE..................................913 321-2116
Charles H Nickloy, *CEO*
EMP: 5
SALES (est): 640.2K **Privately Held**
SIC: 2952 Roofing felts, cements or coatings

(G-4099)
INDUSTRIAL STATE BANK (HQ)
3201 Strong Ave (66106-2115)
P.O. Box 171297 (66117-0297)
PHONE..................................913 831-2000
Clay Corburn Jr, *President*
EMP: 30 **EST:** 1917
SALES: 6.6MM
SALES (corp-wide): 100MM **Privately Held**
WEB: www.industrialbankkck.com
SIC: 6022 State trust companies accepting deposits, commercial
PA: Valley View Bancshares, Inc
7500 W 95th St
Shawnee Mission KS 66212
913 381-3311

(G-4100)
INFINITY TENTS INC
Also Called: All Seasons Tent Sales
5050 Kansas Ave (66106-1135)
PHONE..................................913 820-3700
Scott Berk, *President*
Seth Berk, *Corp Secy*
EMP: 20
SALES (est): 437K **Privately Held**
SIC: 5999 2394 Tents; tents: made from purchased materials

(G-4101)
INNOVATIVE ADHESIVES COMPANY (PA)
450 Funston Rd (66115-1214)
PHONE..................................913 371-8555
William Kugler, *CEO*
Bernard Blake, *Ch of Bd*
Richard Paradise, *President*
EMP: 15
SQ FT: 55,000
SALES (est): 1.8MM **Privately Held**
SIC: 2952 Roof cement: asphalt, fibrous or plastic

(G-4102)
INSYSIV LLC
9850 Meek Rd (66109-3264)
PHONE..................................816 694-9397
Justin Strelow, *Mng Member*
David Goode,
Jason Hester,
David Strelow,
EMP: 10 **EST:** 2011
SALES (est): 336.6K **Privately Held**
SIC: 7374 7389 Computer processing services;

(G-4103)
INTERNATIONAL BROTHERHOOD (PA)
753 State Ave Ste 570 (66101-2511)
PHONE..................................913 371-2640
Newton B Jones, *President*
Mark Keffeler, *Business Mgr*
J Tom Baca, *Vice Pres*
Warren Fairley, *Vice Pres*
David Haggerty, *Vice Pres*
EMP: 42
SQ FT: 224,097
SALES (est): 25MM
SALES (corp-wide): 26.3MM **Privately Held**
SIC: 8631 Labor union

(G-4104)
INTERNATIONAL BROTHERHOOD
Blacksmith Forgers and Helpers
753 State Ave Ste 800 (66101-2514)
PHONE..................................913 281-5036
Bill Palmisno, *Owner*
EMP: 10
SALES (corp-wide): 26.3MM **Privately Held**
SIC: 8631 Collective bargaining unit
PA: International Brotherhood Of Boilermakers Archives, Inc.
753 State Ave Ste 570
Kansas City KS 66101
913 371-2640

(G-4105)
INTERNATIONAL BROTHERHOOD OF
753 State Ave Ste 565 (66101-2511)
PHONE..................................913 371-2640
Newton B Jones, *President*
EMP: 10
SALES (est): 449.2K **Privately Held**
SIC: 8631 Labor unions & similar labor organizations

(G-4106)
INTERNATIONAL EX TRCKG INC (HQ)
Also Called: I X T
3359 Brinkerhoff Rd (66115-1248)
PHONE..................................913 621-1525
Karen Duff, *President*
EMP: 20
SQ FT: 10,000
SALES (est): 7.6MM **Privately Held**
WEB: www.ixtkc.com
SIC: 4213 Trailer or container on flat car (TOFC/COFC)

(G-4107)
INTERNATIONAL FOOD PDTS CORP
Also Called: International Food Group
6721 Griffin Rd (66111-2319)
P.O. Box 11014 (66111-0014)
PHONE..................................913 788-7720
Charles Lillich, *Opers-Prdtn-Mfg*
EMP: 10
SALES (corp-wide): 65.8MM **Privately Held**
SIC: 5149 Sugar, refined
PA: International Food Products Corporation
150 Lrkin Wllams Indus Ct
Fenton MO 63026
636 717-2100

(G-4108)
INTERNATIONAL TRANS LOGIS INC
701 S 38th St (66106-1292)
PHONE..................................913 621-2750
EMP: 16
SALES (corp-wide): 15MM **Privately Held**
SIC: 4785 Inspection & fixed facilities
PA: International Transload Logistics, Inc.
3675 Darlene Ct Ste E
Aurora IL 60504
866 883-9402

(G-4109)
INTERNATIONAL UNION UNITED AU
Also Called: U A W Local 31
500 Kindleberger Rd (66115-1227)
PHONE..................................913 342-7330
Jeff Manning, *President*
EMP: 2600
SALES (corp-wide): 237MM **Privately Held**
SIC: 8631 Labor union
PA: International Union, United Automobile, Aerospace And Agricultural Implement Workers Of Am
8000 E Jefferson Ave
Detroit MI 48214
313 926-5000

(G-4110)
INTERSTATE FLOORING LLC (PA)
Also Called: ISC Surfaces
5100 Kansas Ave (66106-1137)
PHONE..................................913 573-0600
Len Farrell, *CFO*
▲ **EMP:** 150
SALES (est): 74.5MM **Privately Held**
SIC: 5032 5023 Ceramic wall & floor tile; home furnishings

(G-4111)
INVENTORY SALES CO
2949 Chrysler Rd (66115-1323)
PHONE..................................913 371-7002
Howard Bellamy, *Branch Mgr*
EMP: 20
SALES (corp-wide): 64MM **Privately Held**
WEB: www.inventorysales.com
SIC: 5085 Industrial supplies
PA: Inventory Sales Co.
9777 Reavis Rd
Saint Louis MO 63123
314 776-6200

(G-4112)
IRIS DATA SERVICES INC (DH)
501 Kansas Ave (66105-1309)
PHONE..................................913 937-0590
Tom Olofson, *CEO*
Brad Scott, *COO*
John Stanton, *Vice Pres*
Adam Gross, *Engineer*
Karin-Joyce Tjon Sien Fat, *CFO*
EMP: 60
SQ FT: 3,600
SALES (est): 41.4MM
SALES (corp-wide): 589.6MM **Privately Held**
SIC: 7374 7378 4813 Data processing service; computer & data processing equipment repair/maintenance;
HQ: Epiq Systems, Inc.
2 Ravinia Dr Ste 850
Atlanta GA 30346
913 621-9500

(G-4113)
J & D EQUIPMENT INC
Also Called: American Equipment
3250 Harvester Rd (66115-1109)
PHONE..................................913 342-1450
Douglas Keith, *President*
Kent Yahne, *General Mgr*
Chris Little, *Parts Mgr*
Luanne Keith, *Admin Sec*
EMP: 21 **EST:** 1930
SQ FT: 14,000
SALES (est): 8.8MM **Privately Held**
WEB: www.americanequipmentco.com
SIC: 5012 Trucks, commercial

(G-4114)
J & S TOOL AND FASTENER INC
Also Called: Southern Fastening Systems
3040 S 44th St (66106-3719)
PHONE..................................913 677-2000
David Kasten, *President*
Ed Murphy, *Vice Pres*
EMP: 19 **EST:** 1980
SQ FT: 12,000
SALES (est): 2.8MM **Privately Held**
SIC: 5072 5251 Miscellaneous fasteners; builders' hardware

(G-4115)
J J MARTINY CONCRETE CO
7350 Douglas Ave (66106-5002)
PHONE..................................913 268-7775
Vic Martiny, *President*
J J Martiny, *President*
Jay Martiny Jr, *Corp Secy*
Kirk Martiny, *Vice Pres*
EMP: 56
SQ FT: 7,600
SALES (est): 5.3MM **Privately Held**
SIC: 1611 Concrete construction: roads, highways, sidewalks, etc.

(G-4116)
JACK COOPER TRANSPORT CO INC
Also Called: Fairfax Terminal
200 E Marley Rd (66115-1400)
PHONE..................................913 321-8500
Greg Endecott, *Finance*
Ronald Lewis, *Branch Mgr*
Andi Berg, *Director*
Alex Meza, *Director*
EMP: 140
SQ FT: 10,000
SALES (corp-wide): 667.8MM **Privately Held**
WEB: www.jackcooper.com
SIC: 4213 4212 Contract haulers; local trucking, without storage
HQ: Jack Cooper Transport Company, Inc.
1100 Walnut St Ste 2400
Kansas City MO 64106
816 983-4000

(G-4117)
JAKOBE FURNITURE LLC
450 S 55th St (66106-1018)
PHONE..................................913 371-8900
Nicholas King, *Project Mgr*
Jeff Gray,
Brian Georgie,
▼ **EMP:** 80
SQ FT: 110,000
SALES (est): 31.2MM **Privately Held**
SIC: 5021 Furniture

(G-4118)
JAY MAA AMBE LLC
10401 France Family Dr (66111-1905)
PHONE..................................785 554-1044
Dilip G Patel, *Principal*
EMP: 34 **EST:** 2012
SALES (est): 1.7MM **Privately Held**
SIC: 7011 Hotels & motels

(G-4119)
JAY MCCONNELL CONSTRUCTION INC
5721 Georgia Ave (66104-2937)
PHONE..................................913 492-9300
EMP: 10
SQ FT: 2,500
SALES (est): 1.7MM **Privately Held**
SIC: 1542 Nonresidential Construction

(G-4120)
JAYHAWK MLLWRIGHT ERECTORS INC
811 S Coy St (66105-2015)
PHONE..................................913 371-5212
Phillip Heavelow, *President*
EMP: 25 **EST:** 1974
SQ FT: 3,750
SALES: 6.2MM **Privately Held**
SIC: 1796 Millwright

(G-4121)
JC NICHOLS DNTON RBRTS RLTORS
Also Called: JC Nichols Denton & Roberts
2100 Hutton Rd (66109-4524)
PHONE..................................913 299-1600
Clay Roberts Jr, *Owner*
EMP: 10
SQ FT: 1,300
SALES (est): 526.8K **Privately Held**
SIC: 6531 Real estate agent, residential; real estate brokers & agents

(G-4122)
JERRYS NURSERY AND LDSCPG INC
5319 N 139th St (66109-3818)
PHONE..................................913 721-1444
Danny Jones, *President*
Nancy Jones, *Corp Secy*
EMP: 10
SQ FT: 7,000
SALES (est): 1.1MM **Privately Held**
SIC: 5261 5193 Nurseries; lawn & garden supplies; nursery stock

(G-4123)
JESSE INC
Also Called: Acro Dishwashing Service
940 Miami Ave (66105-1840)
PHONE..................................913 342-4282
Terry Heinz, *President*
▲ **EMP:** 11
SALES (est): 1.6MM **Privately Held**
WEB: www.jesse.com
SIC: 3589 Dishwashing machines, commercial

(G-4124)
JGS AUTO WRECKING
Also Called: Jgs Auto Wrecking & Tow
1128 Pawnee Ave (66105-1656)
PHONE..................................913 321-2716
Christina Smith, *Owner*
EMP: 10
SALES (est): 490K **Privately Held**
SIC: 7549 Towing services

(G-4125)
JOCKEY INTERNATIONAL GLOBL INC
1811 Village West Pkwy (66111-1849)
PHONE..................................913 334-4455
Patty Rogers, *Branch Mgr*
EMP: 5
SALES (corp-wide): 581.5MM **Privately Held**
SIC: 2211 Underwear fabrics, cotton
HQ: Jockey International Global, Inc.
2300 60th St
Kenosha WI 53140

(G-4126)
JOHN ROHRER CONTRACTING CO INC (PA)
Also Called: JOHN RORHER CONTRACTING
2820 Roe Ln (66103-1543)
PHONE..................................913 236-5005
John Rohrer, *President*
Analee Lanio, *Corp Secy*
Bill Henry, *Senior VP*
Brandon McMullen, *Vice Pres*
Curtis Barkley, *Project Mgr*
EMP: 50 **EST:** 1922
SQ FT: 18,800
SALES: 14.3MM **Privately Held**
WEB: www.johnrohrercontracting.com
SIC: 1771 Concrete repair

(G-4127)
JOHNSON FOOD EQUIPMENT INC
2955 Fairfax Trfy (66115-1317)
P.O. Box 15300 (66115-0300)
PHONE..................................913 621-3366
Shawn Nicholas, *President*
▲ **EMP:** 20
SALES (est): 3.6MM **Privately Held**
SIC: 3556 Food products machinery

(G-4128)
JUNIPER GARDENS CHILDRENS PRJ
444 Minnesota Ave Fl 3 (66101-2914)
PHONE..................................913 321-3143
Charles Greenwood PHD, *Principal*
Howard Wills, *Research*
EMP: 72
SALES (est): 3.2MM
SALES (corp-wide): 1.2B **Privately Held**
SIC: 8732 Educational research
PA: University Of Kansas
1450 Jayhawk Blvd Rm 225
Lawrence KS 66045
785 864-4868

(G-4129)
JUPITER ESOURCES LLC (DH)
501 Kansas Ave (66105-1309)
PHONE..................................405 488-3886
Michael A Bickford,
Mike Mathews,
Roy Nuttall,
EMP: 16
SALES (est): 1.6MM
SALES (corp-wide): 589.6MM **Privately Held**
SIC: 7371 7374 Computer software development; data processing service
HQ: Epiq Systems, Inc.
2 Ravinia Dr Ste 850
Atlanta GA 30346
913 621-9500

(G-4130)
JUST IN TIME ADULT CARE
3227 Georgia Ave (66104-4132)
PHONE..................................913 371-3391
Gayle Harlin, *President*
EMP: 10
SALES (est): 335.5K **Privately Held**
SIC: 8059 Nursing & personal care

(G-4131)
K C ABRASIVE CO LLC
Also Called: K C Abrasive Company
3140 Dodge Rd (66115-1208)
PHONE..................................913 342-2900
Jared Barncord, *Plant Mgr*
Ken Clark, *Plant Mgr*
Ronald L Barncord,
Jim Hale,

▲ **EMP:** 21 **EST:** 1942
SQ FT: 73,000
SALES: 3.5MM **Privately Held**
WEB: www.kcabrasive.com
SIC: 3291 Aluminum oxide (fused) abrasives

(G-4132)
K C FREIGHTLINER BODY SHOP
Also Called: Kansas Freightlines & Sales
11 N James St (66118-1193)
PHONE..................................913 342-4269
Terry Freeman, *Manager*
EMP: 17
SALES (est): 1.2MM **Privately Held**
SIC: 7532 7538 Body shop, automotive; general automotive repair shops

(G-4133)
K C K ANIMAL CONTROL
3301 Park Dr (66102-4586)
PHONE..................................913 321-1445
Gil Angel, *Director*
EMP: 10 **EST:** 1971
SQ FT: 18,000
SALES (est): 280K **Privately Held**
SIC: 0752 Shelters, animal

(G-4134)
KANSAS CITY BD PUB UTILITIES (PA)
Also Called: BPU
540 Minnesota Ave (66101-2930)
PHONE..................................913 573-9000
David Alvey, *President*
Don L Gray, *Principal*
Dan Jaksa, *Engineer*
Jerry Schrick, *Engineer*
Brian Knowles, *Senior Engr*
▲ **EMP:** 135 **EST:** 1909
SQ FT: 96,000
SALES: 256.1MM **Privately Held**
WEB: www.kcbpu.com
SIC: 4931 4941 Electric & other services combined; water supply

(G-4135)
KANSAS CITY BD PUB UTILITIES
Also Called: Nearman Water Plant
4301 Brenner Dr (66104-1164)
P.O. Box 4066 (66104-0066)
PHONE..................................913 573-9280
Don Gray, *General Mgr*
EMP: 30
SALES (corp-wide): 256.1MM **Privately Held**
WEB: www.kcbpu.com
SIC: 4941 Water supply
PA: Kansas City Board Of Public Utilities
540 Minnesota Ave
Kansas City KS 66101
913 573-9000

(G-4136)
KANSAS CITY BD PUB UTILITIES
Also Called: Board of Pension Trustees
540 Minnesota Ave (66101-2930)
PHONE..................................913 573-9000
EMP: 140
SALES (corp-wide): 256.1MM **Privately Held**
SIC: 4931 Electric & other services combined
PA: Kansas City Board Of Public Utilities
540 Minnesota Ave
Kansas City KS 66101
913 573-9000

(G-4137)
KANSAS CITY BD PUB UTILITIES
Also Called: Quindaro Power Station
3601 N 12th St (66104-5102)
PHONE..................................913 573-9300
Darrell Dorsey, *Superintendent*
EMP: 80
SALES (corp-wide): 256.1MM **Privately Held**
WEB: www.kcbpu.com
SIC: 4931 4941 Electric & other services combined; water supply
PA: Kansas City Board Of Public Utilities
540 Minnesota Ave
Kansas City KS 66101
913 573-9000

(G-4138)
KANSAS CITY BD PUB UTILITIES
Also Called: Electric Operations
6742 Riverview Ave (66102-3043)
PHONE..................................913 573-9556
Stephen Rehm, *Manager*
Julia Ford, *Supervisor*
EMP: 216
SALES (corp-wide): 256.1MM **Privately Held**
WEB: www.kcbpu.com
SIC: 4931 4911 Electric & other services combined; electric services
PA: Kansas City Board Of Public Utilities
540 Minnesota Ave
Kansas City KS 66101
913 573-9000

(G-4139)
KANSAS CITY BD PUB UTILITIES
Also Called: Bpu
380 S 11th St (66102-5555)
PHONE..................................913 573-9675
Scott Hiatt, *Principal*
Steve Green, *Director*
EMP: 110
SALES (corp-wide): 256.1MM **Privately Held**
WEB: www.kcbpu.com
SIC: 4911 Electric services
PA: Kansas City Board Of Public Utilities
540 Minnesota Ave
Kansas City KS 66101
913 573-9000

(G-4140)
KANSAS CITY BD PUB UTILITIES
Also Called: Nearman Creek Power Plant
4240 N 55th St (66104-1275)
P.O. Box 4088 (66104-0088)
PHONE..................................913 573-9700
Dong Quach, *Manager*
EMP: 66
SALES (corp-wide): 256.1MM **Privately Held**
WEB: www.kcbpu.com
SIC: 4941 Water supply
PA: Kansas City Board Of Public Utilities
540 Minnesota Ave
Kansas City KS 66101
913 573-9000

(G-4141)
KANSAS CITY BD PUB UTILITIES
Also Called: Bpu
540 Minnesota Ave (66101-2930)
PHONE..................................913 573-9143
Don Gray, *Manager*
EMP: 650
SALES (corp-wide): 256.1MM **Privately Held**
WEB: www.kcbpu.com
SIC: 4931 4941 4911 Electric & other services combined; water supply; electric services
PA: Kansas City Board Of Public Utilities
540 Minnesota Ave
Kansas City KS 66101
913 573-9000

(G-4142)
KANSAS CITY BD PUB UTILITIES
Also Called: Board of Public Utlities
312 N 65th St (66102-3027)
PHONE..................................913 573-6810
Larry Adair, *Branch Mgr*
EMP: 20
SALES (corp-wide): 256.1MM **Privately Held**
WEB: www.kcbpu.com
SIC: 4911 Distribution, electric power
PA: Kansas City Board Of Public Utilities
540 Minnesota Ave
Kansas City KS 66101
913 573-9000

(G-4143)
KANSAS CITY CANCER CENTER LLC
8919 Parallel Pkwy # 326 (66112-1636)
PHONE..................................913 788-8883
Stephanie Bycraft, *Branch Mgr*
EMP: 13
SALES (corp-wide): 7.5MM **Privately Held**
SIC: 8011 8099 Oncologist; medical services organization
PA: Kansas City Cancer Center, Llc
9200 Indian Creek Pkwy # 300
Overland Park KS 66210
913 541-4600

(G-4144)
KANSAS CITY COML WHSNG CO
1021 Pacific Ave (66102-5535)
PHONE..................................913 287-3800
Monica Miller, *President*
EMP: 30
SQ FT: 180,000
SALES (est): 2.3MM **Privately Held**
WEB: www.kansascitystorage.com
SIC: 4225 4212 General warehousing; local trucking, without storage

(G-4145)
KANSAS CITY HYDRAULICS INC
944 Osage Ave (66105-1848)
PHONE..................................913 371-6151
Christopher Collene, *President*
Eric Moore, *Vice Pres*
Judith Moore, *Treasurer*
EMP: 5
SQ FT: 2,500
SALES: 425K **Privately Held**
SIC: 7699 3471 Hydraulic equipment repair; cleaning, polishing & finishing

(G-4146)
KANSAS CITY IMAGING CENTER
Also Called: Kcic
11011 Haskell Ave (66109-8500)
PHONE..................................913 667-5600
Michael Parsa, *Owner*
EMP: 15
SALES (est): 1MM **Privately Held**
SIC: 8011 Radiologist

(G-4147)
KANSAS CITY MECHANICAL INC
6822 Kansas Ave (66111-2407)
PHONE..................................913 334-1101
Cathy Hotujac, *President*
Paul Hotujac Jr, *Vice Pres*
Brian Eikenbary, *Treasurer*
Fred Burroughs, *Supervisor*
Michael Tanner, *Admin Sec*
EMP: 38
SQ FT: 1,900
SALES: 10.7MM **Privately Held**
SIC: 1711 Warm air heating & air conditioning contractor; plumbing contractors

(G-4148)
KANSAS CITY PETERBILT INC (PA)
8915 Woodend Rd (66111-1717)
PHONE..................................913 441-2888
Leon C Geis, *President*
Dwight Mann, *Parts Mgr*
Randy Zeller, *Cust Mgr*
Josh Beck, *Sales Staff*
Ken McWhorter, *Sales Staff*
EMP: 90
SQ FT: 24,000
SALES (est): 40.9MM **Privately Held**
WEB: www.kcpete.com
SIC: 5012 Trucks, commercial

(G-4149)
KANSAS CITY POWER PRODUCTS INC
80 S James St (66118-1128)
PHONE..................................913 321-7040
James H Brazeal, *President*
Catherine Ann Brazeal, *Corp Secy*
▲ **EMP:** 11
SQ FT: 19,000
SALES (est): 4.3MM **Privately Held**
WEB: www.kcpp.com
SIC: 5084 Engines, gasoline

(G-4150)
KANSAS CITY RAILCAR SVC INC (PA)
1147 S 14th St (66105-1657)
PHONE..................................913 621-0326
Greg Eighmey, *President*
EMP: 36
SQ FT: 2,000
SALES (est): 2.7MM **Privately Held**
WEB: www.kcrailcar.com
SIC: 4789 Railroad car repair

(G-4151)
KANSAS CITY TSTG & ENGRG LLC
1308 Adams St (66103-1359)
PHONE..................................913 321-8100
Scott Martens, *Vice Pres*
Elisabeth R Decoursey, *Mng Member*
EMP: 23
SALES: 2MM **Privately Held**
SIC: 8711 Construction & civil engineering

(G-4152)
KANSAS CITY WINNELSON CO
1529 Lake Ave (66103-1732)
P.O. Box 3359 (66103-0359)
PHONE..................................913 262-6868
Joseph W Deseure, *President*
Gregory D Shelby, *Admin Sec*
EMP: 11 **EST:** 1961
SQ FT: 21,000
SALES (est): 5.7MM
SALES (corp-wide): 4.5B **Privately Held**
SIC: 5074 Plumbing & hydronic heating supplies
PA: Winsupply Inc.
3110 Kettering Blvd
Moraine OH 45439
937 294-5331

(G-4153)
KANSAS CNTY DST ATTYS ASSOCIAT
4601 State Ave Unit 58 (66102-3608)
PHONE..................................785 232-5822
EMP: 57 **Privately Held**
SIC: 9211 8621 Courts; professional membership organizations

(G-4154)
KANSAS ENTERTAIMENT LLC
Also Called: Hollywood Casino
777 Hollywood Casino Blvd (66111-8102)
PHONE..................................913 288-9300
Sheila Reichert, *President*
EMP: 21
SALES (est): 1MM **Privately Held**
SIC: 7011 Casino hotel

(G-4155)
KANSAS FMLY MDICINE FOUNDATION
3901 Rainbow Blvd # 4010 (66160-8500)
PHONE..................................913 588-1900
Joshua Freeman, *President*
Mark Meyer, *Director*
EMP: 25
SALES: 1.2MM **Privately Held**
SIC: 8011 General & family practice, physician/surgeon

(G-4156)
KANSAS LEGAL SERVICES INC
Also Called: Wyandtt-Leavenworth Legal Svcs
400 State Ave Ste 1015 (66101-2420)
PHONE..................................913 621-0200
Leland Cox, *Manager*
EMP: 15
SALES (corp-wide): 7MM **Privately Held**
WEB: www.kansaslegalservices.org
SIC: 8111 Legal aid service
PA: Kansas Legal Services, Inc
712 S Kansas Ave Ste 200
Topeka KS 66603
785 354-8531

(G-4157)
KANSAS SPEEDWAY CORPORATION
Also Called: I S C
400 Speedway Blvd (66111-1200)
PHONE..................................913 328-3300

Lesa France Kennedy, *CEO*
James C France, *Ch of Bd*
John Saunders, *President*
Pat Warren, *Principal*
W Garrett Crotty, *Senior VP*
EMP: 45 **EST:** 1996
SALES (est): 4.2MM
SALES (corp-wide): 675MM **Privately Held**
WEB: www.kansasspeedway.com
SIC: 7948 Automotive race track operation
HQ: International Speedway Corporation
1 Daytona Blvd
Daytona Beach FL 32114
386 254-2700

(G-4158)
KANSAS UNIV PHYSICIANS INC (PA)
Also Called: University of Kansas
3901 Rainbow Blvd (66160-8500)
PHONE....................913 362-2128
Jim Albertson, *CEO*
Jennifer Preston, *Human Res Dir*
Michelle Swisher, *IT/INT Sup*
Steve Alvarez, *Maintence Staff*
Katrina Rothrock, *Teacher*
EMP: 108
SALES: 346.3MM **Privately Held**
SIC: 8011 Clinic, operated by physicians

(G-4159)
KAW VALLEY CENTER
4300 Brenner Dr (66104-1163)
PHONE....................913 334-0294
Jackie Suttinpon, *Principal*
EMP: 11
SALES (est): 656.8K **Privately Held**
SIC: 8093 Mental health clinic, outpatient

(G-4160)
KAW VALLEY COMPANIES INC (PA)
Also Called: Kaw Valley Sand & Gravel
5600 Kansas Ave (66106-1147)
PHONE....................913 281-9950
Joey Kates, *CEO*
Tim Kates, *President*
Brad George, *General Mgr*
Jason Jacobson, *Vice Pres*
Bill Leonhart, *CFO*
EMP: 130
SALES (est): 33.6MM **Privately Held**
SIC: 5032 1611 1795 1794 Sand, construction; highway & street construction; demolition, buildings & other structures; excavation work

(G-4161)
KAW VALLEY COMPANIES INC
5622 Kansas Ave (66106-1147)
PHONE....................913 596-9752
Tim Kates, *Manager*
EMP: 15
SALES (corp-wide): 33.6MM **Privately Held**
SIC: 7389 Packaging & labeling services
PA: Kaw Valley Companies, Inc.
5600 Kansas Ave
Kansas City KS 66106
913 281-9950

(G-4162)
KAW VALLEY SAND AND GRAVEL INC (HQ)
5600 Kansas Ave (66106-1147)
PHONE....................913 281-9950
Ben Kates, *President*
Dan Hays, *Sales Staff*
EMP: 25
SQ FT: 3,000
SALES (est): 31MM
SALES (corp-wide): 33.6MM **Privately Held**
SIC: 5032 Sand, construction; gravel
PA: Kaw Valley Companies, Inc.
5600 Kansas Ave
Kansas City KS 66106
913 281-9950

(G-4163)
KC BLIND ALL-STARS FOUNDATION
1100 State Ave (66102-4411)
PHONE....................913 281-3308
Kelly Myers, *President*
Madeleine Burkindine, *Vice Pres*
Della Molloy, *Treasurer*
EMP: 10
SALES: 50.7K **Privately Held**
SIC: 7389 Fund raising organizations

(G-4164)
KC BOWL INC
8201 State Ave (66112-1840)
PHONE....................913 299-1110
Robert Johannes, *Principal*
EMP: 18
SALES (est): 584.7K **Privately Held**
SIC: 7933 Ten pin center

(G-4165)
KC PRESORT
2820 Roe Ln Ste U (66103-1560)
PHONE....................913 432-0866
Judy Parker, *Principal*
EMP: 15
SALES (est): 1.7MM **Privately Held**
SIC: 7331 Mailing service

(G-4166)
KCAI LP
Also Called: Chateau Avalon
701 Village West Pkwy (66111-1883)
PHONE....................913 596-6000
Cheryl Vaught, *Manager*
EMP: 30
SQ FT: 35,000
SALES (est): 1.7MM **Privately Held**
SIC: 7011 7389 Tourist camps, cabins, cottages & courts; advertising, promotional & trade show services

(G-4167)
KCG INC
Rew Materials
1136 Southwest Blvd (66103-1910)
PHONE....................913 236-4909
John Thomas, *Marketing Staff*
Shannon Doherty, *Manager*
Don Harris, *Manager*
EMP: 45
SALES (corp-wide): 263.4MM **Privately Held**
WEB: www.kcg-inc.com
SIC: 5032 Drywall materials
PA: Kcg, Inc.
15720 W 108th St Ste 100
Lenexa KS 66219
913 438-4142

(G-4168)
KEEBLER COMPANY
801 Sunshine Rd (66115-1121)
PHONE....................913 342-2300
Larry R Jobe, *Branch Mgr*
EMP: 72
SALES (corp-wide): 13.5B **Publicly Held**
WEB: www.keebler.com
SIC: 2051 2052 Biscuits, baked: baking powder & raised; cookies & crackers
HQ: Keebler Company
1 Kellogg Sq
Battle Creek MI 49017
269 961-2000

(G-4169)
KELLER FIRE & SAFETY INC (HQ)
1129 Scott Ave (66105-1229)
PHONE....................913 371-8494
Craig Schraad, *President*
Darrell Clark, *Sales Staff*
Kevin Vanbuskirk, *Sales Staff*
Warren Howe, *Technician*
Nicki Goldring,
EMP: 78
SQ FT: 15,000
SALES: 17MM
SALES (corp-wide): 351.7MM **Privately Held**
WEB: www.kellerfire.com
SIC: 5087 5099 Sprinkler systems; fire extinguishers
PA: The Fike Corporation
704 Sw 10th St
Blue Springs MO 64015
816 229-3405

(G-4170)
KEMPER AUCTION GROUP
5629 Pawnee Ave (66106-1538)
PHONE....................913 287-3207
Robert A Kemper, *Owner*
EMP: 10
SALES (est): 477K **Privately Held**
SIC: 7389 Auction, appraisal & exchange services

(G-4171)
KESTERS MDSG DISPLAY INTL
400 Funston Rd (66115-1214)
PHONE....................913 281-4200
Will Kester, *President*
Alan Morton, *Sr Corp Ofcr*
Walter Morton, *Manager*
EMP: 45
SQ FT: 50,000
SALES (est): 6MM **Privately Held**
SIC: 2541 Wood partitions & fixtures

(G-4172)
KEY EQUIPMENT & SUPPLY CO
6716 Berger Ave (66111-2311)
P.O. Box 11035 (66111-0035)
PHONE....................913 788-2546
Jeff Miles, *Sales/Mktg Mgr*
EMP: 15
SALES (est): 2MM
SALES (corp-wide): 23.8MM **Privately Held**
WEB: www.keyequipment.com
SIC: 5084 Materials handling machinery
PA: Key Equipment & Supply Co.
13507 Nw Industrial Dr
Bridgeton MO 63044
314 298-8330

(G-4173)
KEYSTONE AUTO HOLDINGS INC
90 Shawnee Ave (66105-1421)
PHONE....................913 371-3249
Eusebio Gonzalez, *Manager*
EMP: 17
SALES (corp-wide): 11.8B **Publicly Held**
SIC: 5013 Automotive supplies & parts
HQ: Keystone Automotive Holdings, Inc.
44 Tunkhannock Ave
Exeter PA 18643

(G-4174)
KEYSTONE AUTOMOTIVE INDS INC
Also Called: Lkq Keystone
555 River Park Dr (66105-1411)
PHONE....................816 921-8929
Buch Henry, *Branch Mgr*
EMP: 45
SALES (corp-wide): 11.8B **Publicly Held**
WEB: www.kool-vue.com
SIC: 5013 Automotive supplies & parts
HQ: Keystone Automotive Industries, Inc.
5846 Crossings Blvd
Antioch TN 37013
615 781-5200

(G-4175)
KIDDI KOLLEGE INC
Also Called: Kiddi Kollege 3
7502 Nebraska Ave (66112-2467)
PHONE....................913 788-7060
Heidi Carroll, *Director*
EMP: 15
SALES (corp-wide): 2.5MM **Privately Held**
SIC: 8351 Group day care center
PA: Kiddi Kollege Inc
340 N Lindenwood Dr
Olathe KS 66062
913 764-4423

(G-4176)
KLEMP ELECTRIC MACHINERY CO
Also Called: AC Blower Wheels Motors & Fans
739 Central Ave (66101-3544)
PHONE....................913 371-4330
Henry H Klemp, *President*
Helen R Klemp, *Corp Secy*
EMP: 10 **EST:** 1929
SQ FT: 28,000
SALES (est): 4.4MM **Privately Held**
SIC: 5063 7694 Motors, electric; electric motor repair

(G-4177)
KNIGHT-SWIFT TRNSP HLDINGS INC
9000 Woodend Rd (66111-1716)
PHONE....................913 535-5155
Mike Taylor, *Branch Mgr*
Casey Ireland, *Maintence Staff*
EMP: 80
SALES (corp-wide): 5.3B **Publicly Held**
SIC: 4213 Contract haulers
PA: Knight-Swift Transportation Holdings Inc.
20002 N 19th Ave
Phoenix AZ 85027
602 269-2000

(G-4178)
KNIT-RITE INC (PA)
Also Called: Therafirm
120 Osage Ave (66105-1415)
PHONE....................913 279-6310
Mark W L Smith, *Ch of Bd*
Chris H Vering, *COO*
Ron Hercules, *Exec VP*
Evan McGill, *Exec VP*
Pat Meikel, *Controller*
▲ **EMP:** 80
SQ FT: 60,000
SALES (est): 19.8MM **Privately Held**
WEB: www.knitrite.com
SIC: 3842 Orthopedic appliances; prosthetic appliances; elastic hosiery, orthopedic (support)

(G-4179)
KONRADYS LDSCP WINTER SVC INC
4512 Speaker Rd (66106-1034)
P.O. Box 2534, Shawnee Mission (66201-2534)
PHONE....................913 647-0286
Dana Gordon, *President*
Charisse Konrady, *President*
EMP: 10
SALES (est): 247.1K **Privately Held**
SIC: 0782 Garden maintenance services

(G-4180)
KRAFT LEASING LLC (PA)
320 Kindleberger Rd (66115-1204)
PHONE....................913 601-6999
Spencer Kraft, *CEO*
EMP: 20
SALES (est): 3.3MM **Privately Held**
SIC: 7359 Equipment rental & leasing

(G-4181)
KU CHILDRENS CTR FOUNDATION (PA)
Also Called: Administration Dept
3901 39th And Rnbow 2026 (66160-0001)
PHONE....................913 588-6301
Chet Johnson MD, *Chairman*
Cheng T Cho, *Vice Pres*
Robert Trueworthy, *Treasurer*
Martha Barnard, *Admin Sec*
Dr Michael Rapoff, *Admin Sec*
EMP: 45
SALES: 5.7MM **Privately Held**
SIC: 8011 Pediatrician

(G-4182)
KU PHYSICIANS INC
3901 Rainb Blvd Mails 401 (66160-0001)
P.O. Box 410389 MO (64141-0389)
PHONE....................913 588-3243
James Albertson, *CEO*
William F Gabrielli, *Principal*
EMP: 11
SALES: 8.2MM **Privately Held**
SIC: 8011 Pediatrician

(G-4183)
KU WOMENS HLTH SPECIALTY CTRS (PA)
Also Called: Kansas University Physicians
3901 Rainbow Blvd (66160-8500)
PHONE....................913 588-6200
Julia Chapman, *Principal*
John Calkins, *Chairman*
Paul Wiener, *Chairman*

Christophe W Crenner MD, *Med Doctor*
Rajib Bhattacharya, *Diabetes*
EMP: 14 **EST:** 1974
SALES: 216.6MM **Privately Held**
WEB: www.kuphysicians.com
SIC: 8011 Gynecologist; obstetrician

(G-4184)
KUPI RPRDCTIVE ENDCRNOLOGY LAB
3901 Rainbow Blvd (66160-8500)
PHONE..................................913 588-6377
Chester Gillmore, *VP Mfg*
EMI Watanabe, *Engineer*
Scott Brunton, *Sales Staff*
Kathy Roby, *Director*
EMP: 20
SALES (est): 1.4MM **Privately Held**
SIC: 8071 Medical laboratories

(G-4185)
KUSHS PAINTING
1401 Minnesota Ave (66102-4309)
PHONE..................................913 888-0230
Raymond Kush, *Owner*
EMP: 14
SALES (est): 376.6K **Privately Held**
SIC: 1721 Painting & paper hanging

(G-4186)
KVC HEALTH SYSTEMS INC
4300 Brenner Dr (66104-1163)
PHONE..................................913 621-5753
Anne Roberts, *Branch Mgr*
Vishral Adma, *Director*
Stacy Manbeck, *Director*
Ryan Speier, *Officer*
EMP: 57 **Privately Held**
SIC: 8093 Mental health clinic, outpatient
PA: Kvc Health Systems, Inc.
21350 W 153rd St
Olathe KS 66061

(G-4187)
L & L MANUFACTURING INC
3130 Brinkerhoff Rd (66115-1202)
PHONE..................................816 257-8411
Chris A Pugh, *President*
Marion Naylor, *Materials Mgr*
EMP: 20
SALES: 2MM **Privately Held**
SIC: 2732 Book printing

(G-4188)
L G BARCUS AND SONS INC (PA)
1430 State Ave (66102-4469)
PHONE..................................913 621-1100
Douglas G Barcus, *Ch of Bd*
Lawrence G Barcus, *Vice Ch Bd*
Richard W Hoener, *President*
David Grossman, *Vice Pres*
Todd Kalwei, *Vice Pres*
▼ **EMP:** 70
SQ FT: 5,000
SALES (est): 73.5MM **Privately Held**
WEB: www.barcus.com
SIC: 1629 1622 Pile driving contractor; bridge construction

(G-4189)
L G EVERIST INCORPORATED
2101 S 86th St (66111)
P.O. Box 11145 (66111-0145)
PHONE..................................913 302-5394
Jeff Pierce, *Branch Mgr*
EMP: 15
SALES (corp-wide): 343.3MM **Privately Held**
WEB: www.lgeverist.com
SIC: 1422 Cement rock, crushed & broken-quarrying
PA: L. G. Everist, Incorporated
350 S Main Ave Ste 400
Sioux Falls SD 57104
712 552-1347

(G-4190)
L M C C INC
Also Called: Langley Muehlberger Con Cnstr
54 N 10th St (66102-5368)
PHONE..................................913 371-1070
Dennis Langley, *President*
EMP: 25
SALES (est): 2.8MM **Privately Held**
SIC: 1771 Blacktop (asphalt) work

(G-4191)
LA NENA TORTILLERIA ROSTISERIA
1200 Minnesota Ave (66102-4457)
PHONE..................................913 281-8993
Nena Smith, *Principal*
EMP: 6
SALES (est): 482K **Privately Held**
SIC: 2099 Tortillas, fresh or refrigerated

(G-4192)
LAFARGE NORTH AMERICA INC
317 S 3rd St (66118-1109)
PHONE..................................816 365-9143
Thomas McLaughlin, *Principal*
EMP: 24
SALES (corp-wide): 4.5B **Privately Held**
SIC: 3241 3273 Cement, hydraulic; ready-mixed concrete
HQ: Lafarge North America Inc.
8700 W Bryn Mawr Ave
Chicago IL 60631
773 372-1000

(G-4193)
LAKHANI COMMERCIAL CORP (PA)
6828 Kaw Dr (66111-2410)
PHONE..................................913 677-1100
Hanif Lakhani, *President*
Kenneth Collyard, *Broker*
George Jump, *Broker*
Jim Thome, *Sales Staff*
Joe Gardenhire, *Associate*
EMP: 100
SALES (est): 8.3MM **Privately Held**
SIC: 5541 7542 Gasoline service stations; carwashes

(G-4194)
LAMINATE WORKS INC
1200 S 5th St (66105-2130)
PHONE..................................913 281-7474
EMP: 49
SALES (corp-wide): 22MM **Privately Held**
SIC: 2493 Particleboard, plastic laminated
PA: Laminate Works, Inc.
15900 College Blvd # 200
Lenexa KS 66219
913 800-8263

(G-4195)
LAMINATE WORKS KANSAS CITY LLC
1200 S 5th St (66105-2130)
PHONE..................................913 281-7474
EMP: 5
SALES (est): 467.9K **Privately Held**
SIC: 2493 Particleboard, plastic laminated

(G-4196)
LAYNE CHRISTENSEN COMPANY
Also Called: Layne-Western
620 S 38th St (66106-1263)
PHONE..................................913 321-5000
Joe Harvison, *Manager*
EMP: 30
SALES (corp-wide): 3.3B **Publicly Held**
WEB: www.laynechristensen.com
SIC: 1781 7699 Water well drilling; pumps & pumping equipment repair
HQ: Layne Christensen Company
9303 New Trils Dr Ste 200
Spring TX 77381
281 475-2600

(G-4197)
LAYNE CHRISTENSEN COMPANY
Layne Western
620 S 38th St (66106-1263)
PHONE..................................913 321-5000
Joe Harvison, *Manager*
EMP: 15
SALES (corp-wide): 3.3B **Publicly Held**
WEB: www.laynechristensen.com
SIC: 5084 1781 Pumps & pumping equipment; water well servicing
HQ: Layne Christensen Company
9303 New Trils Dr Ste 200
Spring TX 77381
281 475-2600

(G-4198)
LED DIRECT LLC
735 Southwest Blvd Ste B (66103-1931)
PHONE..................................913 912-3760
Dustan Fankhauser,
EMP: 5
SALES (est): 358.2K **Privately Held**
SIC: 3641 Electric light bulbs, complete

(G-4199)
LED2 LIGHTING INC (PA)
600 Minnesota Ave (66101-2806)
PHONE..................................816 912-2180
Yangtian Martin Zhang, *CEO*
EMP: 7
SALES: 2.7MM **Privately Held**
SIC: 5063 3648 8748 Lighting fixtures, commercial & industrial; lighting equipment; business consulting

(G-4200)
LEES PRINTING COMPANY INC
804 Central Ave (66101-3504)
PHONE..................................913 371-0569
Earl Wm Price, *President*
Crystal Lee, *Admin Sec*
EMP: 7
SQ FT: 3,000
SALES: 1MM **Privately Held**
SIC: 2752 Commercial printing, lithographic

(G-4201)
LIBERTY BANK AND TRUST COMPANY
1314 N 5th St (66101-2300)
PHONE..................................913 321-7200
Castina Cooper, *Branch Mgr*
EMP: 18 **Privately Held**
WEB: www.libertybank.net
SIC: 6022 State commercial banks
HQ: Liberty Bank And Trust Company
6600 Plaza Dr Ste 310
New Orleans LA 70127
504 240-5100

(G-4202)
LIBERTY FRUIT COMPANY INC
1247 Argentine Blvd (66105-1508)
PHONE..................................913 281-5200
John McClelland, *CEO*
Allen Caviar, *President*
Jennifer Lee, *Business Mgr*
Reade Sievert, *Exec VP*
Mike Logan, *VP Opers*
▲ **EMP:** 351 **EST:** 1965
SQ FT: 126,000
SALES (est): 151.2MM **Privately Held**
WEB: www.libertyfruit.com
SIC: 5148 Fruits, fresh; vegetables, fresh

(G-4203)
LIFT INC
5525 Kaw Dr (66102-3367)
P.O. Box 2432 (66110-0432)
PHONE..................................913 287-4343
Joel Foterburg, *President*
Gary Foderberg, *Admin Sec*
EMP: 15
SQ FT: 9,000
SALES (est): 1MM **Privately Held**
SIC: 1791 Structural steel erection

(G-4204)
LINDSEY MASONRY CO INC
4623 N 123rd Ter (66109-3114)
PHONE..................................913 721-2458
Jon R Lindsey, *President*
Joan L Lindsey, *Treasurer*
EMP: 10
SQ FT: 3,200
SALES (est): 790K **Privately Held**
SIC: 1741 Bricklaying; stone masonry; concrete block masonry laying

(G-4205)
LITTLE TOTS MONTESSORI CORP (PA)
3001 N 115th St (66109-4840)
PHONE..................................913 602-7923
Jodie Murphy, *Principal*
EMP: 11
SALES (est): 680.4K **Privately Held**
SIC: 8351 Montessori child development center

(G-4206)
LOCAMP LLC
1333 Meadowlark Ln # 103 (66102-1249)
PHONE..................................913 287-4400
Lucky Omorobion,
EMP: 12
SALES (est): 325K **Privately Held**
SIC: 8082 Home health care services

(G-4207)
LOWES HOME CENTERS LLC
6920 State Ave (66102-3023)
PHONE..................................913 328-7170
Dave Trevarrow, *Manager*
EMP: 150
SALES (corp-wide): 71.3B **Publicly Held**
SIC: 5211 5031 5722 5064 Home centers; building materials, exterior; building materials, interior; household appliance stores; electrical appliances, television & radio
HQ: Lowe's Home Centers, Llc
1605 Curtis Bridge Rd
Wilkesboro NC 28697
336 658-4000

(G-4208)
LSI INTERNATIONAL INC
640 Miami Ave (66105-2122)
PHONE..................................913 894-4493
Mark Glass, *CEO*
Mark Reiter, *Senior VP*
EMP: 20
SQ FT: 19,800
SALES (est): 2.8MM **Privately Held**
SIC: 3842 3845 3844 Surgical appliances & supplies; electromedical equipment; therapeutic X-ray apparatus & tubes

(G-4209)
LVT TRUCKING INC
1401 Fairfax Traffic Way (66115)
PHONE..................................913 233-2111
Larry Vanderhoff, *Branch Mgr*
EMP: 13 **Privately Held**
SIC: 4213 Trucking, except local
PA: Lvt Trucking Inc
11609 W Sheriac St
Wichita KS 67209

(G-4210)
LYNN TAPE & LABEL
11551 Kaw Dr (66111-1111)
P.O. Box 6261 (66106-0261)
PHONE..................................913 422-0484
Rod Dixon, *Owner*
EMP: 10
SALES (est): 580K **Privately Held**
SIC: 2759 2679 Labels & seals: printing; labels, paper: made from purchased material

(G-4211)
MACS FENCE INC
6037 Speaker Rd (66111-2235)
PHONE..................................913 287-6173
Chad Bell, *CEO*
John Bell, *Vice Pres*
Frances Bell, *Admin Sec*
EMP: 25
SALES (est): 14.3MM **Privately Held**
WEB: www.macsfence.com
SIC: 5031 5211 Fencing, wood; fencing

(G-4212)
MADERAK CONSTRUCTION CO INC
Also Called: Maderak, J A Construction Co
220 S 74th St (66111-2618)
PHONE..................................913 299-3929
Mike Maderak, *President*
John Maderak, *Treasurer*
EMP: 15 **EST:** 1952
SQ FT: 2,000
SALES (est): 1.2MM **Privately Held**
SIC: 1741 Masonry & other stonework

(G-4213)
MAGELLAN PIPELINE COMPANY LP
401 E Donovan Rd (66115-1401)
PHONE..................................913 647-8400
Bryan Middendorf, *Buyer*
John Martin, *Manager*
EMP: 25

SALES (corp-wide): 2.8B **Publicly Held**
SIC: 4612 Crude petroleum pipelines
HQ: Magellan Pipeline Company, L.P.
1 Williams Ctr
Tulsa OK 74172
918 574-7000

(G-4214)
MAGELLAN PIPELINE COMPANY LP
1090a Sunshine Rd (66115-1125)
PHONE....913 647-8504
Rod Lawrence, *Owner*
EMP: 12
SALES (corp-wide): 2.8B **Publicly Held**
SIC: 4612 Crude petroleum pipelines
HQ: Magellan Pipeline Company, L.P.
1 Williams Ctr
Tulsa OK 74172
918 574-7000

(G-4215)
MAIL CONTRACTORS OF AMERICA
250 S 59th Ln (66111-2102)
PHONE....913 287-9811
Rich Clair, *President*
David Widener, *Vice Pres*
Belinda Notgrass, *Admin Sec*
EMP: 100
SQ FT: 2,000
SALES (est): 5.8MM **Privately Held**
WEB: www.mcalogistics.com
SIC: 4212 Mail carriers, contract

(G-4216)
MANNA PRO PRODUCTS LLC
3158 N 7th Street Trfy (66115-1104)
PHONE....913 621-2355
Rick Sweeney, *Manager*
Bryan Martin, *Info Tech Dir*
EMP: 30
SALES (corp-wide): 85MM **Privately Held**
SIC: 2048 5191 Feeds, specialty: mice, guinea pig, etc.; animal feeds
PA: Manna Pro Products, Llc
707 Spirit 40 Park Dr # 150
Chesterfield MO 63005
636 681-1700

(G-4217)
MARATHON REPROGRAPHICS INC
Also Called: Mysmartplans
901 N 8th St (66101-2706)
PHONE....816 221-7881
Dominick Armato, *CEO*
Shelley Armato, *President*
EMP: 15 **EST:** 2006
SQ FT: 10,000
SALES (est): 2.1MM **Privately Held**
SIC: 7334 7371 Blueprinting service; computer software development

(G-4218)
MARKETING TECHNOLOGIES INC
Also Called: Martech
550 Stanley Rd (66115-1221)
PHONE....913 342-9111
Sam Schembri, *President*
Chris Schembri, *President*
EMP: 80
SQ FT: 17,000
SALES (est): 10.4MM **Privately Held**
SIC: 2759 7375 7331 Commercial printing; information retrieval services; direct mail advertising services

(G-4219)
MARTEN TRANSPORT LTD
2519 S 88th St (66111-1765)
PHONE....913 535-5255
Rachel Lubeck, *Accounts Mgr*
Seth Reda, *Branch Mgr*
Erin Rickert, *Manager*
EMP: 277
SALES (corp-wide): 787.5MM **Publicly Held**
SIC: 4213 Automobiles, transport & delivery
PA: Marten Transport, Ltd.
129 Marten St
Mondovi WI 54755
715 926-4216

(G-4220)
MARTEN TRANSPORT LTD
10020 Woodend Rd (66111-1705)
PHONE....913 535-5259
Seth Reba, *Branch Mgr*
EMP: 50
SALES (corp-wide): 787.5MM **Publicly Held**
SIC: 4213 Trucking, except local
PA: Marten Transport, Ltd.
129 Marten St
Mondovi WI 54755
715 926-4216

(G-4221)
MARY CARR
Also Called: Carr Trucking
2531 S 53rd St (66106-2236)
PHONE....913 207-0900
Mary Carr, *Owner*
EMP: 22
SALES (est): 856.5K **Privately Held**
SIC: 4212 1794 Dump truck haulage; excavation & grading, building construction

(G-4222)
MC COY COMPANY INC
Also Called: Mc Coy Sales
3130 Brinkerhoff Rd (66115-1202)
PHONE....913 342-1653
Joseph Mc Coy, *President*
Bill Mc Coy, *Vice Pres*
James B Mc Coy, *Vice Pres*
John Mc Coy, *Vice Pres*
Clay Reeder, *Treasurer*
EMP: 120
SQ FT: 10,000
SALES (est): 26.5MM
SALES (corp-wide): 1.5B **Publicly Held**
SIC: 5074 3084 3432 Plumbing fittings & supplies; plastics pipe; plumbing fixture fittings & trim
HQ: Orion Enterprises, Inc.
1600 Osgood St Ste 2005
North Andover MA 01845
913 342-1653

(G-4223)
MC ELECTRIC
2701 S 96th St (66111-3486)
PHONE....913 721-2988
Bob May, *President*
EMP: 30 **EST:** 2007
SALES (est): 1.8MM **Privately Held**
SIC: 1731 General electrical contractor

(G-4224)
MCANANY VAN CLEAVE & PHILLIPS
10 E Cambridge Circle Dr # 300
(66103-1342)
PHONE....913 371-3838
Fredrick Greenbaum, *President*
Eric Lanham, *Managing Prtnr*
EMP: 18 **EST:** 2010
SALES (est): 2.4MM **Privately Held**
SIC: 8111 General practice attorney, lawyer

(G-4225)
MCANANY VAN CLEAVE PHILLIPS PA (PA)
10 E Cambridge Circle Dr # 300
(66103-1342)
P.O. Box 171300 (66117-0300)
PHONE....913 371-3838
Fredrick Greenbaum, *President*
Neely Holland, *President*
Rebecca Moran, *President*
John J Jurcyk, *Managing Prtnr*
Patricia Musick, *Managing Prtnr*
EMP: 51
SALES (est): 12.9MM **Privately Held**
WEB: www.mvplaw.com
SIC: 8111 General practice law office; general practice attorney, lawyer

(G-4226)
MCCRAY LUMBER COMPANY
Also Called: Pioneer Wood Products
3200 Mccormick Rd (66115-1113)
P.O. Box 15058 (66115-0058)
PHONE....913 321-8840
Dave Warlick, *Principal*
Tony Denoon, *Sales Staff*
Cassandra Johnston, *Sales Staff*
Crawford Scott, *Sales Staff*
Chad Wastler, *Sales Staff*
EMP: 75
SALES (corp-wide): 71.1MM **Privately Held**
WEB: www.mccraylumber.com
SIC: 5211 5031 2431 Planing mill products & lumber; lumber, plywood & millwork; millwork
PA: Mccray Lumber Company
10741 El Monte St
Shawnee Mission KS 66211
913 341-6900

(G-4227)
MEDART INC
Also Called: Medart Engines Division
9630 Woodend Rd (66111-1704)
PHONE....636 282-2300
Wayne Taake, *Purchasing*
Chuck Hartbauer, *Manager*
Brian Jones, *Education*
EMP: 10
SALES (corp-wide): 129.1MM **Privately Held**
WEB: www.medartinc.com
SIC: 5013 4226 5084 Automotive supplies & parts; special warehousing & storage; engines, gasoline
PA: Medart, Inc.
124 Manufacturers Dr
Arnold MO 63010
636 282-2300

(G-4228)
MEDICAL ADMINISTRATIVE K U MED
3901 Rainbow Blvd (66160-8500)
PHONE....913 588-8400
Toby Bruce, *Principal*
EMP: 29 **Privately Held**
SIC: 8011 Orthopedic physician
PA: Jayhawk Primary Care, Inc.
2330 Shawnee Mission Pkwy
Westwood KS 66205

(G-4229)
MEDICAL POSITIONING INC
1146 Booth St (66103-1310)
PHONE....816 474-1555
Laura Brady, *CEO*
Ruben Salinas, *President*
Michael G Falbo, *Vice Pres*
John Gordon, *Vice Pres*
▲ **EMP:** 25
SQ FT: 15,000
SALES (est): 7.3MM **Privately Held**
WEB: www.medicalpositioning.com
SIC: 5047 3826 Medical equipment & supplies; diagnostic equipment, medical; analytical instruments

(G-4230)
MEDICAL-SURGICAL EYE CARE PA
8919 Parallel Pkwy # 226 (66112-1636)
PHONE....913 299-8800
Karl D Hendricks MD, *President*
Brian Stephens Od, *Principal*
Sujote David MD, *Corp Secy*
EMP: 20 **EST:** 1971
SALES (est): 199.9K **Privately Held**
SIC: 8011 Ophthalmologist

(G-4231)
MEDICALODGES OF KANSAS CITY
Also Called: Medicalodges Post Center
6500 Greeley Ave (66104-2647)
PHONE....913 334-0200
Cindy Frakes, *Administration*
EMP: 32
SALES (est): 2.2MM **Privately Held**
SIC: 8051 Convalescent home with continuous nursing care

(G-4232)
MEL STEVENSON & ASSOCIATES INC (PA)
Also Called: Spec Roofing Contractors Sup
2840 Roe Ln (66103-1543)
PHONE....913 262-0505
Mel Stevenson, *President*
Michael Tucker, *General Mgr*
Matt Grant, *District Mgr*
Brook Benge, *COO*
Steve Wright, *Senior VP*
▼ **EMP:** 100
SQ FT: 50,000
SALES (est): 277.2MM **Privately Held**
SIC: 5033 5082 5023 Roofing, asphalt & sheet metal; siding, except wood; general construction machinery & equipment; window covering parts & accessories

(G-4233)
MEL STEVENSON & ASSOCIATES INC
Also Called: Spec Roofers Wholeseller
2840 Roe Ln (66103-1543)
PHONE....913 262-0505
Mike Beyersdorfer, *Manager*
EMP: 10
SALES (corp-wide): 277.2MM **Privately Held**
SIC: 5033 Roofing, siding & insulation
PA: Mel Stevenson & Associates, Inc.
2840 Roe Ln
Kansas City KS 66103
913 262-0505

(G-4234)
MENTAL HEALTH ASSOCIATION
Also Called: Mental Health Amr
739 Minnesota Ave (66101-2703)
PHONE....913 281-2221
Susan C Lewis, *President*
Janet Cook, *Principal*
James Glenn, *Senior VP*
Richard Brumbaugh, *CFO*
EMP: 21
SQ FT: 14,900
SALES: 735.3K **Privately Held**
SIC: 8093 Mental health clinic, outpatient

(G-4235)
MERCY & TRUTH MED MISSIONS INC (PA)
721 N 31st St (66102-3962)
PHONE....913 248-9965
Elizabeth McGhee, *Vice Pres*
Cynthia Moore, *Vice Pres*
Bart Schubert, *Vice Pres*
John Vandewahle, *Vice Pres*
Tim Walla, *Vice Pres*
EMP: 12 **EST:** 1995
SALES: 749.8K **Privately Held**
WEB: www.mercyandtruth.com
SIC: 8062 General medical & surgical hospitals

(G-4236)
METAL PANELS INC
Also Called: M P I
8341 Ruby Ave (66111-3007)
PHONE....913 766-7200
Mitchell Hentkowski, *President*
Jennifer Hentkowski, *Treasurer*
Brad McCready, *Controller*
EMP: 32
SQ FT: 34,000
SALES (est): 5.4MM **Privately Held**
WEB: www.metlpanels.com
SIC: 3444 5211 Metal roofing & roof drainage equipment; roofing material

(G-4237)
METRO PARK WAREHOUSES INC
251 S 55th St (66106-1013)
PHONE....913 621-3116
Bob Banach, *President*
EMP: 22
SALES (est): 1.9MM
SALES (corp-wide): 51.3MM **Privately Held**
WEB: www.mpw-inc.com
SIC: 4225 General warehousing

PA: Metro Park Warehouses, Inc.
6920 Executive Dr
Kansas City MO 64120
816 231-0777

(G-4238)
METRO PARK WAREHOUSES INC
4141 Fairbanks Ave (66106-1262)
P.O. Box 2346 (66110-0346)
PHONE..................................913 342-8141
Jim Sagester, *COO*
Charlie Thompson, *Manager*
John Cushing, *Supervisor*
Michael Dacy, *Supervisor*
Roger Turner, *Info Tech Mgr*
EMP: 35
SALES (corp-wide): 51.3MM **Privately Held**
WEB: www.mpw-inc.com
SIC: 4225 General warehousing
PA: Metro Park Warehouses, Inc.
6920 Executive Dr
Kansas City MO 64120
816 231-0777

(G-4239)
METRO PARK WAREHOUSES INC
5020 Swartz Rd (66106-1766)
PHONE..................................913 287-7366
Eric Fardellman, *Manager*
EMP: 22
SALES (est): 1.4MM
SALES (corp-wide): 51.3MM **Privately Held**
WEB: www.mpw-inc.com
SIC: 4225 General warehousing
PA: Metro Park Warehouses, Inc.
6920 Executive Dr
Kansas City MO 64120
816 231-0777

(G-4240)
MGES LLC
640 Southwest Blvd (66103-1921)
PHONE..................................913 334-6333
Mitchell Waldberg,
EMP: 5
SALES (est): 216K **Privately Held**
SIC: 3646 Commercial indusl & institutional electric lighting fixtures

(G-4241)
MI RANCHO TEQUILA USA INC
11005 Northridge Dr (66109-4905)
PHONE..................................913 530-7260
Michael Dean, *Ch of Bd*
EMP: 7
SALES (est): 210.5K **Privately Held**
SIC: 2085 Distillers' dried grains & solubles & alcohol

(G-4242)
MID AMERICA CRDIOLGY ASSOC PC (PA)
3901 Rainbow Blvd G600 (66160-8500)
PHONE..................................913 588-9600
Randy Genton, *President*
Peter Tadros, *Principal*
EMP: 20
SQ FT: 4,000
SALES (est): 13.5MM **Privately Held**
WEB: www.mac.md
SIC: 8011 Cardiologist & cardio-vascular specialist

(G-4243)
MID-AMERICA MNFCT HSNG CMMNTS
10011 Woodend Rd (66111-1763)
PHONE..................................913 441-0194
Thomas J Horner Jr, *President*
EMP: 54
SALES (est): 2.9MM **Privately Held**
SIC: 6515 Mobile home site operators

(G-4244)
MID-AMERICA PUMP LLC
Also Called: Letts Vankirk and Associates
5600 Inland Dr (66106-1316)
PHONE..................................913 287-3900
Jack Letts, *President*
Richard V Kirk, *Sales Mgr*
Rick Van Kirk, *Sales Mgr*
Brad Saul, *Manager*
Don Kirby, *Administration*
EMP: 17
SQ FT: 10,000
SALES (est): 9.6MM **Privately Held**
WEB: www.midamericapump.com
SIC: 5085 3599 Industrial supplies; machine shop, jobbing & repair

(G-4245)
MID-AMRCAN DSTRBTRS/JYHAWK RAD
8022 Leavenworth Rd (66109-1503)
PHONE..................................913 321-9664
Curtis D Lash Sr, *President*
Curtis Lash Jr, *Vice Pres*
Michael Lash, *Treasurer*
EMP: 10
SQ FT: 14,000
SALES (est): 1.3MM **Privately Held**
SIC: 5013 7539 5531 Radiators; heaters, motor vehicle; radiator repair shop, automotive; automotive air conditioning repair; automobile air conditioning equipment, sale, installation; automotive parts

(G-4246)
MID-SOUTH MILLING COMPANY INC
213 Central Ave (66118-1117)
PHONE..................................913 621-5442
Jack Starkey, *Manager*
EMP: 25
SALES (corp-wide): 14.9MM **Privately Held**
WEB: www.msmilling.com
SIC: 2048 Feed premixes
PA: Mid-South Milling Company, Inc.
710 Oakleaf Office Ln
Memphis TN 38117
901 767-0071

(G-4247)
MID-WEST CONVEYOR COMPANY
2601 S 90th St (66111-1760)
PHONE..................................734 288-4400
Fax: 913 441-2125
EMP: 207
SALES (corp-wide): 28.6MM **Privately Held**
SIC: 3535 3536 5084 3537 Mfg Conveyors/Equipment Mfg Hoist/Crane/Monorail Whol Industrial Equip Mfg Indstl Truck/Tractor
PA: Mid-West Conveyor Company
8245 Nieman Rd Ste 123
Lenexa KS 66214
913 384-9950

(G-4248)
MIDPOINT NATIONAL INC
Also Called: Funzee Limited
1263 Southwest Blvd (66103-1901)
P.O. Box 414176 MO (64141-4176)
PHONE..................................913 362-7400
Ron Freund, *President*
Angie Buehler, *Accounts Mgr*
EMP: 20
SQ FT: 75,000
SALES (est): 2.9MM **Privately Held**
WEB: www.midpt.com
SIC: 7331 4225 Mailing service; general warehousing

(G-4249)
MIDTOWN SIGNS LLC
2416 S 8th St (66103-1804)
PHONE..................................816 561-7446
Dennis Baughman, *Mng Member*
EMP: 15
SALES (est): 590.7K **Privately Held**
WEB: www.midtownsigns.com
SIC: 3993 Signs & advertising specialties

(G-4250)
MIDWEST CAST STONE KANSAS INC
1610 State Ave (66102-4224)
PHONE..................................913 371-3300
Sarah Mathews, *President*
Sean Gaeta, *Vice Pres*
Tom Waldschmidt, *Sales Staff*
EMP: 43
SQ FT: 12,000
SALES (est): 5.8MM **Privately Held**
WEB: www.midwestcaststone.com
SIC: 3272 5211 Stone, cast concrete; masonry materials & supplies

(G-4251)
MIDWEST DISTRIBUTORS CO INC
6501 Kansas Ave (66111-2396)
PHONE..................................913 287-2020
Gary Marvine, *President*
Tom White, *Vice Pres*
▲ **EMP:** 55
SQ FT: 90,000
SALES (est): 21MM **Privately Held**
WEB: www.midwestdistributorsco.com
SIC: 5181 Beer & other fermented malt liquors

(G-4252)
MIDWEST FUELS LLC
300 N 78th St (66112-2924)
PHONE..................................913 299-3331
Mahfooz Azam, *Owner*
EMP: 5
SALES (est): 626.5K **Privately Held**
SIC: 2869 Fuels

(G-4253)
MIDWEST GLASS & GLAZING LLC
3909 Mission Rd (66103-2749)
PHONE..................................913 768-6778
Tim Carson, *Project Mgr*
John Davis,
Greg Hirleman,
Joe Hirleman,
EMP: 20
SALES (est): 4MM **Privately Held**
SIC: 1793 Glass & glazing work

(G-4254)
MIDWEST MOTORSPORTS INC
Also Called: Motorsports of Kansas City
6285 State Ave (66102-3151)
PHONE..................................913 334-0477
Brad Harrison, *Manager*
EMP: 24
SALES (corp-wide): 4.2MM **Privately Held**
WEB: www.midwestmotorsportsinc.com
SIC: 5531 3711 Speed shops, including race car supplies; automobile assembly, including specialty automobiles
PA: Midwest Motorsports, Inc.
1905 Se Hulsizer Rd
Ankeny IA 50021
515 233-5503

(G-4255)
MIDWEST REFRIGERATED SVCS LLC
1601 Fairfax Trfy (66115-1432)
PHONE..................................913 621-1111
Dane E Bear,
Lindsey Kaberlein,
EMP: 16
SQ FT: 62,000
SALES (est): 2.2MM **Privately Held**
SIC: 4222 Warehousing, cold storage or refrigerated

(G-4256)
MIDWEST REGIONAL CREDIT UNION (PA)
7240 State Ave (66112-3003)
P.O. Box 12217 (66112-0217)
PHONE..................................913 755-2127
Lloyd D Nugent, *CEO*
Thad Jones, *Vice Pres*
Beth Silvey, *Loan Officer*
Teresa Spear, *VP Human Res*
Melissa Douglas, *Loan*
EMP: 16
SQ FT: 5,000
SALES: 1.9MM **Privately Held**
WEB: www.mrcu.com
SIC: 6062 State credit unions, not federally chartered

(G-4257)
MIDWEST SERVICES & TOWING INC
Also Called: Midwest Tow Service
400 Kansas Ave (66105-1308)
PHONE..................................913 281-1003
Sam Sails, *President*
Gary O'Kelley, *Corp Secy*
EMP: 50
SQ FT: 10,000
SALES (est): 5.8MM **Privately Held**
WEB: www.midwestts.com
SIC: 7549 7538 5012 Towing service, automotive; general truck repair; trucks, commercial

(G-4258)
MIDWEST SIGN COMPANY LLC
550 Stanley Rd (66115-1221)
PHONE..................................913 568-7552
Tony Russell, *Opers Mgr*
Jason Yeager, *Mng Member*
EMP: 15
SQ FT: 4,000
SALES: 1MM **Privately Held**
SIC: 3993 Signs & advertising specialties

(G-4259)
MIDWEST TRNSPT SPECIALISTS INC
400 Kansas Ave (66105-1308)
PHONE..................................913 281-1003
Sam Sales, *President*
Dave Snuffer, *Director*
EMP: 58
SQ FT: 7,500
SALES (est): 12.5MM **Privately Held**
SIC: 4214 4213 Local trucking with storage; trucking, except local

(G-4260)
MILLER - STAUCH CNSTR CO INC
Also Called: Miller Stauch Construction
32 N 6th St (66101-3404)
PHONE..................................913 599-1040
Duane Dean, *President*
Jay Henderson, *Superintendent*
Gene Dean, *Vice Pres*
Randy Dean, *Vice Pres*
EMP: 50 **EST:** 1958
SQ FT: 10,000
SALES: 195.1K **Privately Held**
WEB: www.millerstauch.com
SIC: 1542 1541 Commercial & office building, new construction; industrial buildings, new construction

(G-4261)
MILLER PAVING & CNSTR LLC
7150 Kaw Dr (66111-2428)
PHONE..................................913 334-5579
Kevin James, *Mng Member*
Charlie James,
EMP: 250
SQ FT: 10,000
SALES (est): 21MM **Privately Held**
SIC: 1623 Underground utilities contractor

(G-4262)
MINI ADVENTURES
545 S 94th St (66111-1462)
PHONE..................................913 334-6008
Sarah Gibson, *Manager*
EMP: 12
SALES (est): 337.2K **Privately Held**
SIC: 8351 Group day care center

(G-4263)
MISSOURI-KANSAS SUPPLY CO INC
Also Called: Mks Pipe & Valve
1202 Adams St (66103-1322)
P.O. Box 412553 MO (64141-2553)
PHONE..................................816 842-6513
Patrick M Adam, *President*
Ejay Cahill, *Business Mgr*
Kyle Smiddy, *Business Mgr*
Steven Adams, *Exec VP*
Skip Shepherd, *Vice Pres*
◆ **EMP:** 49 **EST:** 1946
SALES: 23.8MM **Privately Held**
SIC: 5085 Valves & fittings

(G-4264)
MKT COMMUNITY DEVELOPMENT INC
Also Called: Crestwood Apartments
2100 N 57th St (66104-2930)
PHONE..................................913 596-7310
Candy Williams, *Manager*
EMP: 10
SALES (est): 199.6K **Privately Held**
SIC: 6513 Apartment building operators

(G-4265)
MM PROPERTY MGT & RMDLG LLC
Also Called: Mm Companyies
912 Minnesota Ave (66101-2611)
PHONE..................................913 871-6867
Miguel Benitez, *President*
Guillermo Lopez, *Vice Pres*
Maria Lopez, *Vice Pres*
Paul Hurd, *Sales Staff*
Alejandra Corona, *Manager*
EMP: 15
SALES (est): 2.7MM **Privately Held**
SIC: 1521 1542 1522 7389 General remodeling, single-family houses; commercial & office building contractors; remodeling, multi-family dwellings; styling of fashions, apparel, furniture, textiles, etc.; kitchen & bathroom remodeling

(G-4266)
MOBILE FX INC
Also Called: Loud & Clear
5237 State Ave (66102-3463)
PHONE..................................913 287-1556
Tom Dinkel, *President*
Donnie Martin, *Vice Pres*
EMP: 10
SQ FT: 1,500
SALES (est): 1MM **Privately Held**
SIC: 7539 Automotive sound system service & installation

(G-4267)
MOSAIC
8047 Parallel Pkwy Ste 9 (66112-2078)
PHONE..................................913 788-8400
Stan House, *General Mgr*
EMP: 50
SALES (corp-wide): 257.7MM **Privately Held**
WEB: www.mosaicinfo.org
SIC: 8741 Administrative management
PA: Mosaic
4980 S 118th St
Omaha NE 68137
402 896-3884

(G-4268)
MOUNT ST SCHOLASTICA INC
2220 Central Ave (66102-4759)
PHONE..................................913 906-8990
EMP: 148
SALES (corp-wide): 4.5MM **Privately Held**
SIC: 8322 Adult day care center
PA: Mount St. Scholastica, Inc.
801 S 8th St
Atchison KS 66002
913 360-6200

(G-4269)
MRG HOLDINGS INC
Also Called: Midwest Pallet
1161 S 12th St (66105-1614)
PHONE..................................913 371-3555
Mike Gunter, *President*
EMP: 16
SALES (est): 2MM **Privately Held**
SIC: 2448 Pallets, wood

(G-4270)
MT CARMEL REDEVELOPMENT CORP (PA)
1130 Troup Ave (66104-5883)
PHONE..................................913 621-4111
Ervin Sams, *Pastor*
Ondra Penn, *Facilities Mgr*
Belita Baskin, *Manager*
EMP: 10
SALES: 415.6K **Privately Held**
SIC: 8399 Community development groups

(G-4271)
MULTIPRENS USA INC (PA)
20 Ohio Ave (66118-1129)
PHONE..................................913 371-6999
Debra Shaumeyer, *President*
Joe Shaumeyer, *Plant Supt*
Dianne Johnson, *Manager*
Nancee Wilk, *Executive Asst*
▲ **EMP:** 25
SQ FT: 30,000
SALES (est): 5.2MM **Privately Held**
WEB: www.multiprensusa.com
SIC: 3499 Stabilizing bars (cargo), metal

(G-4272)
MULTISPECIALTY KANZA GROUP PA
8919 Parallel Pkwy # 555 (66112-1636)
PHONE..................................913 788-7099
James Appelbaum, *Partner*
Donna Burton, *Manager*
EMP: 30
SALES (est): 1.1MM **Privately Held**
SIC: 8011 Dermatologist

(G-4273)
MURPHY & SONS ROOFING (PA)
1010 N 54th St (66102-3416)
PHONE..................................913 287-2116
Larry Murphy, *Owner*
Chris Murphy, *Sales Mgr*
Angel Murphy, *Office Mgr*
EMP: 11 **EST:** 1957
SQ FT: 3,800
SALES (est): 2.4MM **Privately Held**
WEB: www.murphyroofing.com
SIC: 1761 Roofing contractor

(G-4274)
MURPHY-HOFFMAN COMPANY
Also Called: Midwest Carrier Transicold
2700 S 88th St (66111-1739)
PHONE..................................913 441-6300
Allan Guin, *General Mgr*
Todd Harrington, *VP Bus Dvlpt*
Melinda Keim, *Analyst*
EMP: 18
SALES (corp-wide): 1B **Privately Held**
SIC: 7623 5511 Refrigeration service & repair; pickups, new & used
PA: Murphy-Hoffman Company
11120 Tomahawk Creek Pkwy
Leawood KS 66211
816 483-6444

(G-4275)
MYRON INTERNATIONAL INC
200 N 6th St (66101-3310)
P.O. Box 171458 (66117-0458)
PHONE..................................913 281-5552
Timothy Sigler, *President*
EMP: 10
SQ FT: 26,000
SALES (est): 788.8K
SALES (corp-wide): 3.7MM **Privately Held**
WEB: www.miragecdp.com
SIC: 6794 Patent buying, licensing, leasing
PA: Myron's Dental Laboratories Inc
200 N 6th St
Kansas City KS 66101
800 359-7111

(G-4276)
MYRONS DENTAL LABORATORIES (PA)
200 N 6th St (66101-3310)
P.O. Box 171458 (66117-0458)
PHONE..................................800 359-7111
Timothy Sigler, *President*
J Thomas Sigler, *Vice Pres*
EMP: 35 **EST:** 1935
SQ FT: 26,000
SALES (est): 3.7MM **Privately Held**
SIC: 8072 3843 6794 Crown & bridge production; dental materials; patent buying, licensing, leasing

(G-4277)
N T S LLC
801 Armourdale Pkwy (66105-2103)
PHONE..................................913 281-5353
Bill Willhite Jr, *President*
Kathy Willhite, *Principal*
Brandon McNeely, *Sales Staff*
Blake Willhite, *Sales Staff*
Shaun Helm, *Technology*
EMP: 25
SQ FT: 5,000
SALES (est): 3.3MM **Privately Held**
WEB: www.ntstrucking.com
SIC: 4212 4213 Delivery service, vehicular; trucking, except local

(G-4278)
NATIO ASSOC FOR THE ADVAN OF
Also Called: Natrional Assoc Advncmnt Color
7103 Waverly Ave (66109-2532)
PHONE..................................913 334-0366
Charles Jean, *Manager*
EMP: 60
SALES (corp-wide): 26.6MM **Privately Held**
WEB: www.detroitnaacp.org
SIC: 8641 Social associations
PA: National Association For The Advancement Of Colored People
4805 Mount Hope Dr
Baltimore MD 21215
410 580-5777

(G-4279)
NATIONAL FABRIC CO INC
901 S 7th St (66105-2092)
PHONE..................................913 281-1833
Daniel K West, *President*
Debra H West, *Vice Pres*
EMP: 12
SQ FT: 32,000
SALES (est): 2.3MM **Privately Held**
SIC: 5199 Automobile fabrics
PA: Wescorp Ltd
901 S 7th St
Kansas City KS 66105
913 281-1833

(G-4280)
NATIONAL FIBER SUPPLY LLC
Also Called: National Fiber Supply Co
3210 N 7th Street Trfy (66115-1106)
PHONE..................................913 321-0066
Gary Inselman, *Principal*
EMP: 15
SALES (corp-wide): 41.2MM **Privately Held**
WEB: www.nationalfibersupply.com
SIC: 5093 5113 4953 Waste paper & cloth materials; waste paper; industrial & personal service paper; recycling, waste materials
PA: National Fiber Supply L.L.C.
303 W Madison St Ste 1650
Chicago IL 60606
312 346-4800

(G-4281)
NATIONAL GOLF PROPERTIES LLC
Also Called: Dubs Dread Golf Course
12601 Hollingsworth Rd (66109-3822)
PHONE..................................913 721-1333
Joe Nugent, *General Mgr*
EMP: 35 **Privately Held**
WEB: www.nationalgolfproperties.com
SIC: 7997 7992 5941 Golf club, membership; public golf courses; golf goods & equipment
PA: National Golf Properties Llc
2951 28th St Ste 3000
Santa Monica CA 90405

(G-4282)
NBH BANK
Also Called: Bank Midwest
4600 Shawnee Dr (66106-3649)
PHONE..................................913 831-4184
Naomi Goodnight, *Vice Pres*
Jon Walker, *Vice Pres*
EMP: 10 **Publicly Held**
WEB:
www.bankmw.com+%22bank+midwest%22+%22lexington
SIC: 6022 State commercial banks
HQ: Nbh Bank
7800 E Orchard Rd
Greenwood Village CO 80111
720 554-6680

(G-4283)
NBH BANK
Also Called: Bank Midwest
7804 State Ave (66112-2417)
P.O. Box 12188 (66112-0188)
PHONE..................................913 299-9700
D Nill, *Branch Mgr*
EMP: 15 **Publicly Held**
WEB:
www.bankmw.com+%22bank+midwest%22+%22lexington
SIC: 6022 State commercial banks
HQ: Nbh Bank
7800 E Orchard Rd
Greenwood Village CO 80111
720 554-6680

(G-4284)
NEBRASKA TRANSPORT CO INC
Also Called: N T C
6125 Speaker Rd (66111-2215)
PHONE..................................913 281-9991
Brent Holiday, *CEO*
EMP: 33
SALES (corp-wide): 70.9MM **Privately Held**
SIC: 4789 Pipeline terminal facilities, independently operated
PA: Nebraska Transport Co., Inc.
1225 Country Club Rd
Gering NE 69341
308 635-1214

(G-4285)
NEFF SALES CO INC
Also Called: Neff Packaging Systems
555 Sunshine Rd (66115-1239)
P.O. Box 15056 (66115-0056)
PHONE..................................913 371-0777
John R Latenser, *President*
Dave Ralston, *Marketing Staff*
▲ **EMP:** 14 **EST:** 1982
SQ FT: 30,000
SALES (est): 6.3MM **Privately Held**
SIC: 5199 Packaging materials

(G-4286)
NESCO HOLDINGS INC
Also Called: Truck Utilities Kansas City
5320 Kansas Ave (66106-1141)
PHONE..................................913 287-0001
Marian Noah, *Manager*
EMP: 8
SALES (corp-wide): 114.8MM **Publicly Held**
SIC: 3713 7532 7353 5082 Truck bodies (motor vehicles); body shop, trucks; cranes & aerial lift equipment, rental or leasing; cranes, construction; backhoes, tractors, cranes, plows & similar equipment; hoists, cranes & monorails
PA: Nesco Holdings, Inc.
6714 Pointe Inverness Way # 220
Fort Wayne IN 46804
800 252-0043

(G-4287)
NEW WAVE ENTERPRISES INC
6320 Kansas Ave (66111-2127)
PHONE..................................913 287-7671
Max Pinney Jr, *President*
EMP: 15
SQ FT: 16,000
SALES (est): 1.6MM **Privately Held**
SIC: 2261 2759 Screen printing of cotton broadwoven fabrics; screen printing

(G-4288)
NILL BROTHERS SILKSCREEN INC
Also Called: Nilk Brothers Sporting Goods
2814 S 44th St (66106-3717)
PHONE..................................913 384-4242
W Randall Nill, *President*
W Stanley Nill, *Vice Pres*
EMP: 15
SQ FT: 1,500
SALES (est): 1MM **Privately Held**
SIC: 2396 Screen printing on fabric articles

(G-4289)
NORDIC FOODS INC
4747 Speaker Rd (66106-1037)
PHONE..................................913 281-1167

Jason Hall, *CEO*
Ted Jovanovic, *President*
Lazar Jovanocic, *Vice Pres*
Melody Hoffman, *Plant Mgr*
Jerry Lumianski, *Treasurer*
EMP: 55
SQ FT: 47,000
SALES (est): 9.6MM **Privately Held**
WEB: www.nordicfoods.com
SIC: 2011 2013 Meat packing plants; sausages & other prepared meats

(G-4290)
NRA-UKMC KANSAS LLC
Also Called: University Physcans Dlysis Ctr
6401 Parallel Pkwy (66102-1042)
PHONE....................................913 299-1044
Cimmeron Jeffries, *Branch Mgr*
EMP: 19
SALES (corp-wide): 623.2K **Privately Held**
SIC: 8092 Kidney dialysis centers
PA: Nra-Ukmc, Kansas, Llc
920 Winter St
Waltham MA 02451
781 699-9000

(G-4291)
NTS LLC
51 Osage Ave (66105-1412)
PHONE....................................913 321-3838
Bill Willhite,
EMP: 20 **EST:** 1995
SALES (est): 540.1K **Privately Held**
SIC: 4212 Local trucking, without storage

(G-4292)
OAK RIDGE YOUTH DEV CORP
9301 Parallel Pkwy (66112-1530)
PHONE....................................913 788-5657
Ricky Turner, *Pastor*
EMP: 40
SALES: 196.7K **Privately Held**
SIC: 6732 Trusts: educational, religious, etc.

(G-4293)
OMEGA CONCRETE SYSTEMS INC
Also Called: Manufacture Precst-Prestrssed
5525 Kaw Dr (66102-3367)
P.O. Box 2443 (66110-0443)
PHONE....................................913 287-4343
Gary Foderberg, *CEO*
Joel Foderberg, *President*
Keith Jensen, *Vice Pres*
Andy Downs, *Plant Mgr*
EMP: 25
SQ FT: 50,000
SALES (est): 5MM **Privately Held**
WEB: www.omegaconcrete.net
SIC: 3272 Concrete products, precast

(G-4294)
ON DEMAND EMPLOYMENT SVCS LLC
Also Called: Labor On Demand
1718 Central Ave B (66102-4945)
PHONE....................................913 371-3212
Barton Nelson IV, *Principal*
Barton Nelson Iiii,
Benjamin Keip,
EMP: 10 **EST:** 1998
SQ FT: 2,000
SALES (est): 1.4MM **Privately Held**
SIC: 7363 Temporary help service

(G-4295)
ONEOK INC
Also Called: Kansas Gas Service
1421 N 3rd St (66101-1923)
P.O. Box 171254 (66117-0254)
PHONE....................................800 794-4780
Marty Brownfield, *Branch Mgr*
EMP: 10
SALES (corp-wide): 12.5B **Publicly Held**
SIC: 4924 Natural gas distribution
PA: Oneok, Inc.
100 W 5th St Ste Ll
Tulsa OK 74103
918 588-7000

(G-4296)
OREILLY AUTOMOTIVE STORES INC
Also Called: O'Reilly Auto Parts
4700 Parallel Pkwy (66104-3240)
P.O. Box 1156, Springfield MO (65801-1156)
PHONE....................................913 287-2409
Allen Beard, *Manager*
EMP: 11 **Publicly Held**
WEB: www.oreillyauto.com
SIC: 7539 5013 Automotive repair shops; motor vehicle supplies & new parts
HQ: O'reilly Automotive Stores, Inc.
233 S Patterson Ave
Springfield MO 65802
417 862-2674

(G-4297)
OREILLY AUTOMOTIVE STORES INC
Also Called: O'Reilly Auto Parts 170
2901 State Ave (66102-3917)
PHONE....................................913 621-6939
David Penn, *Branch Mgr*
EMP: 15 **Publicly Held**
WEB: www.oreillyauto.com
SIC: 5013 5531 Automotive supplies & parts; automotive & home supply stores
HQ: O'reilly Automotive Stores, Inc.
233 S Patterson Ave
Springfield MO 65802
417 862-2674

(G-4298)
ORRICK TRAILER SERVICES LLC
600 Sunshine Rd (66115-1234)
PHONE....................................913 321-0400
Dan Orrick,
Tom Ryan,
David Snell,
EMP: 10 **EST:** 1999
SALES: 470K **Privately Held**
SIC: 7539 Trailer repair

(G-4299)
ORTHOPEDIC PROFESSIONAL ASSN (PA)
8919 Parallel Pkwy # 270 (66112-1636)
PHONE....................................913 788-7111
Rhon Cowherd Wright, *Principal*
Kelly White, *Administration*
EMP: 14
SQ FT: 5,200
SALES (est): 2MM **Privately Held**
SIC: 8011 Orthopedic physician

(G-4300)
OTIS ELEVATOR COMPANY
1100 W Cambridg Cir (66103)
PHONE....................................913 621-8800
Todd Boever, *Branch Mgr*
EMP: 33
SALES (corp-wide): 66.5B **Publicly Held**
WEB: www.otis.com
SIC: 5084 Elevators
HQ: Otis Elevator Company
1 Carrier Pl
Farmington CT 06032
860 674-3000

(G-4301)
OTOLARYNGIC HEAD/NECK SURGRY
Also Called: EAR NOSE AND THROAT CLINIC
3901 Rainbow Blvd (66160-8500)
PHONE....................................913 588-6700
Douglas Girod, *Director*
EMP: 36
SALES: 0 **Privately Held**
SIC: 8011 Eyes, ears, nose & throat specialist: physician/surgeon

(G-4302)
OUR LADYS MONTESSORI SCHOOL
3020 S 7th St (66103-2602)
PHONE....................................913 403-9550
Angeline Rasoamialy, *Principal*
Janelle Hilger, *Director*
EMP: 14
SALES: 279.3K **Privately Held**
SIC: 8351 Preschool center

(G-4303)
OVERLAND PARK GARDEN CTR INC (PA)
Also Called: Family Tree Nursery
5430 N 97th St (66109-3015)
PHONE....................................913 788-7974
Eric Nelson, *President*
Beverly Nelson, *Admin Sec*
EMP: 20
SALES (est): 11.1MM **Privately Held**
SIC: 5193 Flowers, fresh; plants, potted

(G-4304)
OWENS CORNING SALES LLC
3201 Mccormick Rd (66115-1112)
PHONE....................................913 281-9495
Danny Perkins, *Manager*
EMP: 22 **Publicly Held**
WEB: www.owenscorning.com
SIC: 3296 Mineral wool
HQ: Owens Corning Sales, Llc
1 Owens Corning Pkwy
Toledo OH 43659
419 248-8000

(G-4305)
OWENS CORNING SALES LLC
300 Sunshine Rd (66115-1231)
PHONE....................................419 248-8000
Rick Copp, *Manager*
EMP: 475 **Publicly Held**
WEB: www.owenscorning.com
SIC: 3296 Fiberglass insulation
HQ: Owens Corning Sales, Llc
1 Owens Corning Pkwy
Toledo OH 43659
419 248-8000

(G-4306)
PACES WYANDOT CTR YOUTH SVCS
1620 S 37th St (66106-2704)
PHONE....................................913 956-3420
Sherry Sullivant, *Principal*
EMP: 30 **EST:** 2008
SALES (est): 368.8K **Privately Held**
SIC: 8322 Child related social services

(G-4307)
PACIFIC DENTAL SERVICES LLC
10818 Parallel Pkwy (66109-3649)
PHONE....................................913 299-8860
EMP: 23 **Privately Held**
SIC: 8021 Dental clinics & offices
PA: Pacific Dental Services, Llc
17000 Red Hill Ave
Irvine CA 92614

(G-4308)
PANDARAMA PRSCHOOL TODDLER CTR (PA)
1118 N 7th St (66101-2102)
P.O. Box 171050 (66117-0050)
PHONE....................................913 342-9692
Morris Sipple, *President*
EMP: 18
SQ FT: 2,000
SALES (est): 877.8K **Privately Held**
SIC: 8351 Preschool center

(G-4309)
PANEL SYSTEMS PLUS INC
3255 Harvester Rd (66115-1108)
PHONE....................................913 321-0111
Douglas Porter, *President*
Porter Denise, *Vice Pres*
Denise Porter, *Vice Pres*
Scott Cassidy, *Sales Staff*
EMP: 40
SQ FT: 47,000
SALES (est): 4.4MM **Privately Held**
WEB: www.panelsystemsplus.com
SIC: 1799 7641 Office furniture installation; office furniture repair & maintenance

(G-4310)
PARALLEL PKWY EMRGNCY PHYSCANS
8929 Parallel Pkwy (66112-1689)
PHONE....................................913 596-4000
Mark J Slepin, *Owner*
Sean Richardson, *COO*
EMP: 25 **EST:** 2011
SALES (est): 648.6K
SALES (corp-wide): 3.5B **Privately Held**
SIC: 8011 Clinic, operated by physicians
HQ: Prime Healthcare Services Inc
3480 E Guasti Rd
Ontario CA 91761

(G-4311)
PARAMOUNT LANDSCAPE INC
7756 Holliday Dr (66106-4948)
PHONE....................................913 375-1697
Karl Schottler II, *President*
EMP: 10
SALES: 900K **Privately Held**
SIC: 0781 Landscape services

(G-4312)
PAREDES CONSTRUCTION INC
Also Called: M & A Construction
1407 N 79th St (66112-2105)
PHONE....................................913 334-9662
Mark Paredes, *President*
EMP: 10
SALES: 650K **Privately Held**
SIC: 1742 Plastering, drywall & insulation

(G-4313)
PARKER OIL CO INC
6601 Kansas Ave (66111-2314)
PHONE....................................316 529-4343
Pat Clubb, *Manager*
EMP: 15
SALES (est): 2.9MM **Privately Held**
SIC: 5172 Lubricating oils & greases

(G-4314)
PARKER OIL COMPANY INC
6601 Kansas Ave (66111-2314)
PHONE....................................913 596-6247
Pat Clubb, *Manager*
EMP: 13
SALES (corp-wide): 18.4MM **Privately Held**
WEB: www.parkeroilco.com
SIC: 5172 Lubricating oils & greases
PA: Parker Oil Co., Inc.
4343 S West St
Wichita KS 67217
316 529-4343

(G-4315)
PARSONS CORPORATION
104 Greystone Ave (66103-1355)
PHONE....................................913 233-3100
Sam Conner, *Manager*
EMP: 15
SALES (corp-wide): 3.5B **Publicly Held**
SIC: 8711 Consulting engineer
PA: The Parsons Corporation
5875 Trinity Pkwy Ste 300
Centreville VA 20120
703 988-8500

(G-4316)
PARTNERS IN PRIMARY CARE
7527 State Ave (66112-2815)
PHONE....................................913 335-6986
Jose Garza, *Manager*
EMP: 23 **Privately Held**
SIC: 8011 Offices & clinics of medical doctors
PA: Partners In Primary Care, P.C.
401 Route 73 N Ste 201
Marlton NJ 08053

(G-4317)
PBI-GORDON CORPORATION
300 S 3rd St (66118-1110)
PHONE....................................816 421-4070
Ed Bianchi, *Manager*
EMP: 50
SALES (corp-wide): 31.9MM **Privately Held**
WEB: www.pbigordon.com
SIC: 2879 2899 2875 2869 Pesticides, agricultural or household; chemical preparations; fertilizers, mixing only; industrial organic chemicals
PA: Pbi-Gordon Corporation
22701 W 68th Ter
Shawnee KS 66226
816 421-4070

(G-4318)
PEERLESS CONVEYOR AND MFG CORP
201 E Quindaro Blvd (66115-1424)
PHONE..................................913 342-2240
William S Walker, *President*
▼ **EMP:** 18
SQ FT: 42,000
SALES (est): 7.3MM
SALES (corp-wide): 92.1MM **Privately Held**
WEB: www.peerlessconveyor.com
SIC: 3531 3535 5084 Construction machinery; conveyors & conveying equipment; conveyor systems
PA: The G W Van Keppel Company
5800 E Bannister Rd
Kansas City MO 64134
913 281-4800

(G-4319)
PENTAIR FLOW TECHNOLOGIES LLC
Pentair Pump Group
3601 Fairbanks Ave (66106-1200)
P.O. Box 6999 (66106-0999)
PHONE..................................913 371-5000
Gary James, *Sales Staff*
Dave Angelo, *Branch Mgr*
Steve Wilson, *Manager*
Mike Wiley, *Director*
EMP: 243
SALES (corp-wide): 18.3B **Publicly Held**
WEB: www.aurorapump.com
SIC: 3589 5084 Water purification equipment, household type; power plant machinery
HQ: Pentair Flow Technologies, Llc
1101 Myers Pkwy
Ashland OH 44805
419 289-1144

(G-4320)
PGW AUTO GLASS LLC
Also Called: Pgw Autoglass
555 River Park Dr (66105-1411)
PHONE..................................913 927-2753
Shawn Niederwerder, *Branch Mgr*
EMP: 11
SALES (corp-wide): 11.8B **Publicly Held**
SIC: 5013 Automotive supplies & parts; automobile glass
HQ: Pgw Auto Glass, Llc
51 Dutilh Rd Ste 310
Cranberry Township PA 16066
878 208-4001

(G-4321)
PHOENIX CORPORATION
Also Called: Phoenix Metals
201 E Donovan Rd (66115-1426)
PHONE..................................913 321-5200
Thomas Hudgins, *Production*
John Dallas, *Credit Staff*
Sam Lavalleur, *Sales Staff*
Aaron Schilb, *Sales Staff*
Roger Spiezio, *Sales Staff*
EMP: 37
SALES (corp-wide): 11.5B **Publicly Held**
SIC: 5051 Steel
HQ: Phoenix Corporation
4685 Buford Hwy
Peachtree Corners GA 30071
770 447-4211

(G-4322)
PICTURE & FRAME INDUSTRIES INC
35 Southwest Blvd (66103-2192)
PHONE..................................913 384-3751
Chris Funk, *President*
Jack Britton, *Vice Pres*
Missy Walsh, *Office Mgr*
Reed Wintering, *Admin Sec*
▲ **EMP:** 40
SQ FT: 33,000
SALES (est): 5.7MM **Privately Held**
WEB: www.pictureandframe.com
SIC: 5023 Frames & framing, picture & mirror

(G-4323)
PIONEER INDUSTRIES INTL INC
305 Sunshine Rd (66115-1230)
PHONE..................................913 233-1368
EMP: 23
SALES (corp-wide): 14.2MM **Privately Held**
SIC: 7389 Personal service agents, brokers & bureaus
PA: Pioneer Industries International, Inc.
500 Park Blvd Ste 250
Itasca IL 60143
630 543-7676

(G-4324)
PLASTIC OMNIUM AUTO INERGY
220 Kindleberger Rd (66115-1200)
PHONE..................................913 370-6081
EMP: 13
SALES (est): 1.9MM **Privately Held**
SIC: 7538 General automotive repair shops

(G-4325)
PLASTIC PACKAGING TECH LLC (DH)
Also Called: P P T
750 S 65th St (66111-2301)
PHONE..................................913 287-3383
David Staker, *CEO*
Deena Stous, *CFO*
Shari Frank, *Human Res Dir*
John Kennedy, *Manager*
▲ **EMP:** 131 **EST:** 1967
SQ FT: 64,000
SALES (est): 26.2MM
SALES (corp-wide): 614.5MM **Privately Held**
SIC: 2673 Bags: plastic, laminated & coated
HQ: Ppt Holdings Llc
750 S 65th St
Kansas City KS 66111
913 287-3383

(G-4326)
POMPS TIRE SERVICE INC
Also Called: Cross Midwest Tire
401 S 42nd St (66106-1005)
PHONE..................................913 621-5200
William Jolly, *Branch Mgr*
EMP: 17
SALES (corp-wide): 611.8MM **Privately Held**
SIC: 5014 7539 Truck tires & tubes; wheel alignment, automotive
PA: Pomp's Tire Service, Inc.
1123 Cedar St
Green Bay WI 54301
920 435-8301

(G-4327)
POWER EQUIPMENT SALES CO
1507 Lake Ave (66103-1732)
P.O. Box 3134 (66103-0134)
PHONE..................................913 384-3848
R T Weeks, *President*
Tim Weeks, *Owner*
William Miller, *Vice Pres*
Kelly Hoss, *Sales Staff*
Mendel Lightfoot, *Sales Staff*
EMP: 10 **EST:** 1964
SQ FT: 21,000
SALES (est): 1.8MM **Privately Held**
WEB: www.powerequipsales.com
SIC: 5063 Electrical supplies

(G-4328)
PPT HOLDINGS LLC (HQ)
750 S 65th St (66111-2301)
PHONE..................................913 287-3383
Wayne Kocourek,
Mike Kocourek,
Donald F Piazza,
EMP: 6
SALES (est): 26.2MM
SALES (corp-wide): 614.5MM **Privately Held**
SIC: 2673 Bags: plastic, laminated & coated
PA: Mid Oaks Investments Llc
750 W Lake Cook Rd # 460
Buffalo Grove IL 60089
847 215-3475

(G-4329)
PQ CORPORATION
Also Called: P Q
1700 Kansas Ave (66105-1198)
PHONE..................................913 371-3020
Fax: 913 371-0646
EMP: 70
SALES (corp-wide): 3.8B **Publicly Held**
SIC: 2819 2899 Mfg Industrial Inorganic Chemicals Mfg Chemical Preparations
HQ: Pq Corporation
300 Lindenwood Dr
Malvern PA 19355
610 651-4429

(G-4330)
PREMIER CONTRACTING INC
Also Called: Premier Equipment
3940 S Ferree St (66103-1717)
PHONE..................................913 362-4141
Michael Budenbender, *President*
Debbie Budenbender, *Vice Pres*
Barbara Langley, *Human Res Mgr*
Matt Sole, *Sales Staff*
EMP: 75
SQ FT: 40,000
SALES (est): 14MM **Privately Held**
WEB: www.premiercontractinginc.com
SIC: 1761 4953 Roofing contractor; refuse collection & disposal services

(G-4331)
PREMIER CUSTOM FOODS LLC
756 Pawnee Ave (66105-2053)
PHONE..................................913 225-9505
Shanon Gray, *President*
Teri Lesman, *CFO*
Patrick Williams, *Treasurer*
EMP: 60
SQ FT: 34,000
SALES: 28.5MM **Privately Held**
SIC: 2099 Sandwiches, assembled & packaged: for wholesale market

(G-4332)
PREMIER MECHANICAL PDTS LLC
3016 S 24th St (66106-4707)
PHONE..................................913 271-5002
Ashley Tumberger,
EMP: 10
SQ FT: 10,500
SALES (est): 1.6MM **Privately Held**
SIC: 3498 3296 Fabricated pipe & fittings; fiberglass insulation

(G-4333)
PRESBYTERIAN MANORS INC
Also Called: Kansas City Presbyterian Manor
7850 Freeman Ave (66112-2198)
PHONE..................................913 334-3666
Bob Richard, *Branch Mgr*
EMP: 62
SALES (corp-wide): 8.6MM **Privately Held**
SIC: 8059 8052 8051 Nursing home, except skilled & intermediate care facility; intermediate care facilities; skilled nursing care facilities
HQ: Presbyterian Manors, Inc.
2414 N Woodlawn Blvd
Wichita KS 67220
316 685-1100

(G-4334)
PRETECH CORPORATION
8934 Woodend Rd (66111-1718)
PHONE..................................913 441-4600
William Bundschuh, *President*
Jason Rew, *Plant Mgr*
Ryan Adams, *Sales Staff*
Lance Stegman, *Sales Staff*
Larry Mauk, *Marketing Staff*
▲ **EMP:** 45
SQ FT: 116,000
SALES (est): 13.3MM **Privately Held**
SIC: 3272 Precast terrazo or concrete products

(G-4335)
PRICE TRUCK LINE INC
5510 Kansas Ave (66106-1145)
PHONE..................................913 596-9779
James Toon, *Branch Mgr*
EMP: 31
SALES (est): 1.8MM
SALES (corp-wide): 27MM **Privately Held**
SIC: 4213 Contract haulers
PA: Price Truck Line, Inc.
4931 S Victoria St
Wichita KS 67216
316 945-6915

(G-4336)
PRIDE/CHAPTER INTL ASSOC
Also Called: Pride-International Assn Black
1726 Quindaro Blvd (66104-5456)
PHONE..................................913 321-2733
Jehrome B Randolph, *President*
James Johnson, *Vice Pres*
EMP: 27
SQ FT: 10,000
SALES (est): 298.4K **Privately Held**
SIC: 8699 8641 Personal interest organization; fraternal associations

(G-4337)
PRIME HEALTHCARE SERVICES INC
Also Called: Providence Medical Center
8929 Parallel Pkwy (66112-1689)
PHONE..................................913 596-4000
Randall Nyp, *CEO*
Pat McBratney, *Marketing Mgr*
Lisa Shipley, *Manager*
Karen Orr, *Ch Nursing Ofcr*
EMP: 1000
SALES (corp-wide): 3.5B **Privately Held**
SIC: 8062 8051 General medical & surgical hospitals; skilled nursing care facilities
HQ: Prime Healthcare Services Inc
3480 E Guasti Rd
Ontario CA 91761

(G-4338)
PRINCIPAL LANDSCAPE GROUP LLC
3065 Merriam Ln (66106-4613)
PHONE..................................913 362-0089
EMP: 12
SALES: 500K **Privately Held**
SIC: 0781 Landscape planning services

(G-4339)
PRINGLE AUTO BODY & SALES INC
2720 S 34th St (66106-4262)
PHONE..................................913 432-6361
Steve Pringle, *President*
Marsha Pringle, *Vice Pres*
Carol Pringle, *Admin Sec*
EMP: 12
SQ FT: 8,400
SALES (est): 902.8K **Privately Held**
SIC: 7532 5521 Body shop, automotive; automobiles, used cars only

(G-4340)
PRO ELECTRIC LC
5320 Speaker Rd (66106-1050)
PHONE..................................913 621-6611
Gregory J Ohmes,
EMP: 110
SQ FT: 13,200
SALES (est): 8.2MM **Privately Held**
WEB: www.proelectriclc.com
SIC: 1731 General electrical contractor

(G-4341)
PROCTER & GAMBLE MFG CO
1900 Kansas Ave (66105-1126)
PHONE..................................913 573-0200
M Schweider, *Branch Mgr*
Jeff Ager, *Manager*
Rhonda Stout, *Telecomm Mgr*
EMP: 300
SALES (corp-wide): 67.6B **Publicly Held**
SIC: 2841 Detergents, synthetic organic or inorganic alkaline
HQ: The Procter & Gamble Manufacturing Company
1 Procter And Gamble Plz
Cincinnati OH 45202
513 983-1100

(G-4342)
PROFESSIONAL EXPRESS INC
835 S Saint Paul St (66105-2123)
PHONE..................................913 722-6060

GEOGRAPHIC

Jim Brown, *Principal*
EMP: 15
SALES (est): 750K **Privately Held**
WEB: www.kcproexpress.com
SIC: 7389 Courier or messenger service

(G-4343)
PROFESSIONAL SERVICE INDS INC
Also Called: Intertech PSI
1211 W Cambridge Cir Dr (66103-1313)
PHONE..................................913 310-1600
Kelly Rotert, *Vice Pres*
EMP: 50
SALES (corp-wide): 3.6B **Privately Held**
SIC: 8748 8711 1799 Environmental consultant; professional engineer; lead burning
HQ: Professional Service Industries, Inc.
545 E Algonquin Rd
Arlington Heights IL 60005
630 691-1490

(G-4344)
PROGRESSIVE CASUALTY INSUR CO
Also Called: Progressive Insurance
1930 S 45th St Ste 150 (66106-2501)
PHONE..................................913 202-6600
Roger Thimmesch, *Branch Mgr*
Megan Bowers, *Associate*
EMP: 17
SALES (corp-wide): 31.9B **Publicly Held**
WEB: www.progressinsurance.com
SIC: 6331 6351 Fire, marine & casualty insurance; credit & other financial responsibility insurance
HQ: Progressive Casualty Insurance Company
6300 Wilson Mills Rd
Mayfield Village OH 44143
440 461-5000

(G-4345)
PROJECT EAGLE
Also Called: Head Start
444 Minnesota Ave Ste 100 (66101-2939)
PHONE..................................913 281-2648
Martha Staker, *Director*
Kim Bavit, *Director*
EMP: 47
SALES (est): 1.6MM **Privately Held**
SIC: 8322 Community center

(G-4346)
PROPAK LOGISTICS INC
4600 Kansas Ave (66106-1127)
PHONE..................................913 213-3896
EMP: 83 **Privately Held**
SIC: 4789 Pipeline terminal facilities, independently operated
PA: Propak Logistics, Inc.
1100 Garrison Ave
Fort Smith AR 72901

(G-4347)
PROVIDENCE MEDICAL CENTER (DH)
Also Called: PROVIDENCE-MEDICAL CENTER GIFT SHOP
8929 Parallel Pkwy (66112-3607)
PHONE..................................913 596-4870
Randy Nyp, *CEO*
Lori Wiskochil, *Business Mgr*
Heather L Allred, *Counsel*
Jennifer Staley, *Project Dir*
Doug Dremann, *Opers Staff*
EMP: 10
SQ FT: 1,000
SALES: 146.5MM
SALES (corp-wide): 3.5B **Privately Held**
SIC: 8062 General medical & surgical hospitals

(G-4348)
PROVIDENCE PLACE INC
8909 Parallel Pkwy (66112-1685)
PHONE..................................913 596-4200
Michael Warren, *Administration*
Mike Warren, *Administration*
EMP: 18
SQ FT: 30,000
SALES (est): 1.8MM
SALES (corp-wide): 3.5B **Privately Held**
WEB: www.cprvip.com
SIC: 8051 Skilled nursing care facilities
HQ: Prime Healthcare Services Inc
3480 E Guasti Rd
Ontario CA 91761

(G-4349)
PURPOSE PRODUCTIONS
1804 N 78th Pl (66112-2053)
PHONE..................................913 620-3508
Julian Vaughn, *Principal*
EMP: 10
SALES (est): 125.1K **Privately Held**
SIC: 7822 Motion picture & tape distribution

(G-4350)
QINS INTERNATIONAL INC
Also Called: Queen Foods
844 S 14th St (66105-1526)
PHONE..................................913 342-4488
David W Qin, *President*
Jennifer Qin, *Treasurer*
EMP: 22
SQ FT: 60,000
SALES (est): 15.9MM **Privately Held**
SIC: 5146 5147 5431 5499 Seafoods; meats & meat products; vegetable stands or markets; dried fruit

(G-4351)
QUALITY CARRIERS INC
20 Central Ave (66118-1155)
PHONE..................................913 281-0901
John Owens, *Manager*
EMP: 15 **Privately Held**
WEB: www.qualitycarriers.com
SIC: 4213 4212 Contract haulers; local trucking, without storage
HQ: Quality Carriers, Inc.
1208 E Kennedy Blvd
Tampa FL 33602
800 282-2031

(G-4352)
QUALITY LITHO INC
4627 Mission Rd (66103-3999)
PHONE..................................913 262-5341
James Muiller, *President*
Donna Muiller, *Corp Secy*
EMP: 26
SQ FT: 8,000
SALES: 1.3MM **Privately Held**
SIC: 2752 2789 2759 Commercial printing, offset; bookbinding & related work; commercial printing

(G-4353)
QUEST DIAGNOSTICS INCORPORATED
10940 Parallel Pkwy (66109-4434)
PHONE..................................913 299-8538
Billie Woods, *Sales Staff*
Carolyn Hazard, *Branch Mgr*
EMP: 17
SALES (corp-wide): 7.5B **Publicly Held**
SIC: 8071 Testing laboratories
PA: Quest Diagnostics Incorporated
500 Plaza Dr Ste G
Secaucus NJ 07094
973 520-2700

(G-4354)
QUICKSILVER EX COURIER OF MO
1126 Adams St (66103-1306)
PHONE..................................913 321-5959
Michael Crary, *President*
Becky Wagner, *Treasurer*
Curt Sloan, *Admin Sec*
EMP: 75
SQ FT: 6,500
SALES (est): 6.7MM
SALES (corp-wide): 59.8MM **Privately Held**
WEB: www.qec.com
SIC: 4212 7389 Delivery service, vehicular; courier or messenger service
PA: Quicksilver Express Courier, Inc.
203 Little Canada Rd E
Saint Paul MN 55117
651 484-1111

(G-4355)
QUIKRETE COMPANIES INC
Also Called: Quikrete of Kansas City
2424 S 88th St (66111-1750)
PHONE..................................913 441-6525
John Mitchel, *Manager*
EMP: 30 **Privately Held**
WEB: www.quikrete.com
SIC: 3273 5211 3274 3272 Ready-mixed concrete; masonry materials & supplies; lime; concrete products; brick, stone & related material
HQ: The Quikrete Companies Llc
5 Concourse Pkwy Ste 1900
Atlanta GA 30328
404 634-9100

(G-4356)
QUIVIRA COUNTRY CLUB INC
100 Crescent Blvd (66106)
PHONE..................................913 631-4820
John Miller, *President*
EMP: 50
SALES (est): 426.8K **Privately Held**
SIC: 7997 Country club, membership

(G-4357)
R F FISHER HOLDINGS INC (PA)
1707 W 39th Ave (66103-1727)
P.O. Box 3110 (66103-0110)
PHONE..................................913 384-1500
Gary Seeley, *President*
Jay Natzke, *Vice Pres*
EMP: 200
SQ FT: 6,000
SALES (est): 23.9MM **Privately Held**
WEB: www.rffisher.com
SIC: 1731 General electrical contractor

(G-4358)
RADIATION ONCOLOGY
3901 Rainbow Blvd (66160-8500)
PHONE..................................913 588-3600
Eashwer Redy, *Chairman*
Leela Krishnan, *Director*
EMP: 32
SALES: 11.1MM **Privately Held**
SIC: 3829 8069 8011 Nuclear radiation & testing apparatus; cancer hospital; offices & clinics of medical doctors

(G-4359)
RAILROAD GROUP
2131 S 74th St (66106-4905)
PHONE..................................913 375-1157
Michael Van Wagnor, *President*
EMP: 6
SALES (est): 669.2K **Privately Held**
WEB: www.railroadgroup.com
SIC: 3743 Railroad equipment

(G-4360)
RAINBOW CAR WASH INC
4604 Rainbow Blvd (66103-3431)
PHONE..................................913 432-1116
Michael McKee, *President*
EMP: 12
SQ FT: 3,000
SALES: 760K **Privately Held**
SIC: 7542 5541 Carwash, automatic; filling stations, gasoline

(G-4361)
RAINBOW VILLAGE MANAGEMENT
Also Called: Best Western
501 Southwest Blvd (66103-1917)
PHONE..................................913 677-3060
Robert L Woodbury, *President*
EMP: 30
SQ FT: 60,000
SALES (est): 945.9K **Privately Held**
WEB: www.bwinnandconferencecenter.com
SIC: 7011 6512 Hotels & motels; shopping center, property operation only

(G-4362)
RAVEN LINING SYSTEMS INC
686 S Adams St (66105-1403)
PHONE..................................918 615-0020
EMP: 18
SALES (est): 7.2MM **Privately Held**
WEB: www.cohesant.com
SIC: 2851 Epoxy coatings
PA: Cohesant Inc.
3601 Green Rd Ste 308
Beachwood OH 44122

(G-4363)
REARDON PALLET COMPANY INC
100 Funston Rd (66115-1310)
P.O. Box 171583 (66117-0583)
PHONE..................................816 221-3300
Dan Reardon, *President*
Daniel Reardon, *Vice Pres*
Gail Reardon, *Treasurer*
Jason Kane, *Accounts Exec*
EMP: 35
SQ FT: 137,000
SALES: 7MM **Privately Held**
WEB: www.reardonpallet.com
SIC: 2448 Pallets, wood

(G-4364)
RECONSERVE OF KANSAS INC
Also Called: International Trnsp Svcs
41 N James St (66118-1146)
PHONE..................................913 621-5619
Myer Luskin, *President*
Rida Hamed, *Admin Sec*
EMP: 25 **EST:** 2001
SALES (est): 4.2MM
SALES (corp-wide): 203.7MM **Privately Held**
SIC: 4959 4953 Sanitary services; recycling, waste materials
PA: Scope Industries
2811 Wilshire Blvd # 410
Santa Monica CA 90403
310 458-1574

(G-4365)
RECORD PUBLICATIONS
Also Called: Record Newspaper
3414 Strong Ave (66106-2047)
P.O. Box 6197 (66106-0197)
PHONE..................................913 362-1988
Jon Males, *Owner*
EMP: 5
SALES (est): 239.6K **Privately Held**
WEB: www.recordnews.com
SIC: 2711 Newspapers, publishing & printing

(G-4366)
REDMON MICHAEL LAW OFFICE
831 Armstrong Ave (66101-2604)
PHONE..................................913 342-5917
Michael Redmon, *Owner*
EMP: 10
SALES (est): 812.8K **Privately Held**
SIC: 8111 General practice attorney, lawyer

(G-4367)
REGIONAL PRVNTION CTR WYNDOTTE
7250 State Ave Ste 33-31 (66112-3003)
PHONE..................................913 288-7685
Linda Stewart, *Administration*
EMP: 10
SALES (est): 142.4K **Privately Held**
SIC: 8999 Personal services

(G-4368)
REINTJES & HITER CO INC
101 Sunshine Rd (66115-1396)
PHONE..................................913 371-1872
G Forrest Reintjes, *President*
Christine Sparks, *Vice Pres*
Dennis Hill, *Sales Staff*
Garnett M Reintjes, *Admin Sec*
EMP: 15 **EST:** 1957
SQ FT: 25,000
SALES (est): 8.4MM **Privately Held**
SIC: 5084 3498 Hydraulic systems equipment & supplies; fabricated pipe & fittings

(G-4369)
RELIABLE CONCRETE PRODUCTS
615 Scott Ave (66105-1396)
P.O. Box 5095 (66119-0095)
PHONE..................................913 321-8108
Marneal Porter, *CEO*
Matt Porter, *President*
EMP: 9 **EST:** 1971

▲ = Import ▼=Export
◆ =Import/Export

SQ FT: 6,000
SALES (est): 1.4MM **Privately Held**
SIC: 3272 Concrete products, precast

(G-4370)
REPAIRS UNLIMITED INC (PA)
Also Called: Rui Contracting
1940 Merriam Ln (66106-4739)
PHONE..................................913 262-6937
Emory F James III, *President*
Sean Szarwinski, *Business Mgr*
Steve Galey, *Exec VP*
Craig Conner, *Vice Pres*
Todd Wertev, *Vice Pres*
EMP: 13
SQ FT: 3,000
SALES: 15.9MM **Privately Held**
WEB: www.repairs-unlimited.com
SIC: 1799 1521 Post-disaster renovations; repairing fire damage, single-family houses; general remodeling, single-family houses

(G-4371)
RES-CARE INC
132 S 17th St (66102-5704)
PHONE..................................913 281-1161
Penn Sloane, *Manager*
EMP: 48
SALES (corp-wide): 2B **Privately Held**
SIC: 8082 Home health care services
HQ: Res-Care, Inc.
805 N Whittington Pkwy
Louisville KY 40222
502 394-2100

(G-4372)
RES-CARE KANSAS INC (DH)
Also Called: RES Care
5031 Matney Ave (66106-3402)
PHONE..................................913 342-9426
Litha Farwell, *President*
EMP: 10
SQ FT: 44,000
SALES (est): 2.7MM
SALES (corp-wide): 2B **Privately Held**
SIC: 8052 8331 Home for the mentally retarded, with health care; job training & vocational rehabilitation services
HQ: Res-Care, Inc.
805 N Whittington Pkwy
Louisville KY 40222
502 394-2100

(G-4373)
RESTORTION WTR PROOFING CONTRS
901 Scott Ave (66105-1219)
PHONE..................................913 321-6226
Al Hanks, *Branch Mgr*
EMP: 20
SALES: 6.5MM **Privately Held**
SIC: 1799 Waterproofing

(G-4374)
REW MATERIALS INC
Also Called: Rew Acoustical Products
1136 Southwest Blvd (66103-1910)
P.O. Box 3360 (66103-0360)
PHONE..................................913 236-4909
Rick Rew, *President*
John Wier, *Vice Pres*
Paul Perrin, *Credit Staff*
Shannon Doherty, *Sales Executive*
Jt Thomas, *Marketing Staff*
EMP: 60 **EST:** 1966
SQ FT: 10,000
SALES (est): 14.5MM **Privately Held**
SIC: 5032 5211 Drywall materials; lumber & other building materials

(G-4375)
REYES MEDIA GROUP INC
1701 S 55th St (66106-2241)
PHONE..................................913 287-1480
Clara Reyes, *President*
EMP: 20
SALES (est): 1MM **Privately Held**
SIC: 4832 Radio broadcasting stations

(G-4376)
RHINO BUILDERS INC
1040 Merriam Ln (66103-1650)
PHONE..................................913 722-4353
Terry E Skilling, *President*
Doreen Skilling, *Vice Pres*
EMP: 11
SQ FT: 2,400
SALES (est): 1.8MM **Privately Held**
WEB: www.rhinobuilders.com
SIC: 1521 1799 1761 1542 General remodeling, single-family houses; kitchen & bathroom remodeling; siding contractor; commercial & office buildings, renovation & repair

(G-4377)
RI HERITAGE INN OF KC LLC
Also Called: Residnce Inn Kans Cy At Lgends
1875 Village West Pkwy (66111-1880)
PHONE..................................913 788-5650
Michael McFarland, *General Mgr*
EMP: 25
SALES (est): 241.8K **Privately Held**
SIC: 7011 Hotels

(G-4378)
RIGDON FLOOR COVERINGS INC
Also Called: Rigdon Carpet & Flooring
3015 Merriam Ln (66106-4613)
PHONE..................................913 362-9829
Bob Rigdon, *President*
EMP: 23
SQ FT: 3,700
SALES (est): 4.5MM **Privately Held**
SIC: 5023 5713 Carpets; resilient floor coverings: tile or sheet; rugs; carpets; floor tile; linoleum; rugs

(G-4379)
RITE-MADE PAPER CONVERTERS LLC
2600 Bi State Dr (66103-1309)
P.O. Box 843736 MO (64184-3736)
PHONE..................................913 621-5000
Craig Gunckel, *CEO*
Todd Whitaker, *President*
Fred Brown, *Vice Pres*
Brian Burns, *Vice Pres*
Clayton Campbel, *Vice Pres*
◆ **EMP:** 140
SALES (est): 72.8MM
SALES (corp-wide): 2.9B **Privately Held**
WEB: www.ritemade.com
SIC: 2679 Telegraph, teletype & adding machine paper; adding machine rolls, paper: made from purchased material; paper products, converted
HQ: Iconex, Llc
3237 Satellite Blvd # 550
Duluth GA 30096
800 543-8130

(G-4380)
RIVERSIDE TRANSPORT INC (PA)
5400 Kansas Ave (66106-1143)
PHONE..................................913 233-5500
Bill Grojean, *President*
Sean Tulipana, *Opers Staff*
Chris Shomaker, *Manager*
Brian Hedge, *Info Tech Dir*
Lisa Schermerhorn, *Director*
EMP: 74
SQ FT: 6,000
SALES (est): 98.5MM **Privately Held**
SIC: 4212 4213 Local trucking, without storage; trucking, except local

(G-4381)
RJ CRMAN DERAILMENT SVCS LLC
5380 Speaker Rd (66106-1050)
PHONE..................................913 371-1537
Kevin Klenklen, *Manager*
EMP: 12
SALES (corp-wide): 250.2MM **Privately Held**
SIC: 4013 Railroad switching
HQ: R.J. Corman Derailment Services, Llc
101 Rj Corman Dr
Nicholasville KY 40356
859 881-7521

(G-4382)
RMVK ENTERPRISES INC
Also Called: Steves Mobile Maintenance Svc
30 Osage Ave (66105-1413)
PHONE..................................913 321-1915
Steve Herman, *President*
Rose Herman, *Vice Pres*
EMP: 21
SALES (est): 3.2MM **Privately Held**
SIC: 7539 7699 Trailer repair; industrial truck repair

(G-4383)
ROAD BUILDERS MCHY & SUP CO
1103 S Mill St (66105-1927)
PHONE..................................913 371-3822
EMP: 14
SALES (corp-wide): 111.7MM **Privately Held**
SIC: 5082 General construction machinery & equipment
PA: Road Builders Machinery & Supply Co Inc
1001 S 7th St
Kansas City KS 66105
913 371-3822

(G-4384)
ROAD BUILDERS MCHY & SUP CO (PA)
1001 S 7th St (66105-2007)
P.O. Box 5125 (66119-0125)
PHONE..................................913 371-3822
Bryan Mc Coy, *President*
M Nicole Argard, *Corp Secy*
Gerry Buser, *Senior VP*
Bryan McCoy, *Vice Pres*
Tom Everett, *Foreman/Supr*
▼ **EMP:** 62
SQ FT: 38,000
SALES: 111.7MM **Privately Held**
SIC: 5082 7353 7699 General construction machinery & equipment; heavy construction equipment rental; construction equipment repair

(G-4385)
ROBINSONS DELIVERY SERVICE
1 Shawnee Ave (66105-1420)
P.O. Box 171154 (66117-0154)
PHONE..................................913 281-4952
Fax: 913 281-5169
EMP: 26
SQ FT: 5,500
SALES: 2MM **Privately Held**
SIC: 4212 Local Trucking Operator

(G-4386)
RODRIGUEZ MECH CONTRS INC
541 S 11th St (66105-1254)
PHONE..................................913 281-1814
Paul Rodriguez, *President*
Ronnie McGarrah, *Project Mgr*
Dave Scaggs, *Project Mgr*
Gerald Thrasher, *Project Mgr*
Brian Turner, *Project Mgr*
EMP: 75
SQ FT: 2,000
SALES (est): 16.3MM **Privately Held**
WEB: www.rmckc.com
SIC: 1711 1623 Plumbing contractors; mechanical contractor; water main construction; sewer line construction

(G-4387)
ROLLING MEADOWS LANDSCAPE
901 N 10th St (66101-2619)
PHONE..................................913 839-0229
Kenneth Rau, *Branch Mgr*
EMP: 14 **Privately Held**
SIC: 0781 Landscape services
PA: Rolling Meadows Landscape
12501 W 151st St
Olathe KS 66062

(G-4388)
ROOFING SUP GRUP-KANSAS CY LLC
200 S 42nd St (66106-1002)
PHONE..................................913 281-4300
Mike Lyle, *Branch Mgr*
EMP: 18
SALES (corp-wide): 7.1B **Publicly Held**
SIC: 5033 Roofing, siding & insulation
HQ: Roofing Supply Group-Kansas City, Llc
505 Huntmar Park Dr # 300
Herndon VA 20170
570 323-3939

(G-4389)
ROSEDALE DEVELOPMENT ASSN INC
1403 Southwest Blvd (66103-1828)
PHONE..................................913 677-5097
Heidi Holliday, *Exec Dir*
EMP: 19
SALES: 269.4K **Privately Held**
SIC: 8641 Social associations; neighborhood association

(G-4390)
ROTARY INTERNATIONAL
7938 Greeley Ave (66109-2245)
PHONE..................................913 299-0466
James Knight, *Manager*
EMP: 12
SALES (corp-wide): 503.3MM **Privately Held**
WEB: www.rotary5340.org
SIC: 8641 Civic associations
PA: Rotary International
1 Rotary Ctr
Evanston IL 60201
847 866-3000

(G-4391)
RUSSELL STEEL PRODUCTS INC (PA)
2221 Metropolitan Ave (66106-2952)
P.O. Box 6409 (66106-0409)
PHONE..................................913 831-4600
Perry D Rainey Jr, *President*
David Rainey, *Vice Pres*
EMP: 40
SQ FT: 14,000
SALES (est): 5.3MM **Privately Held**
WEB: www.russellsteel.net
SIC: 3423 Hand & edge tools

(G-4392)
RYDER TRUCK RENTAL INC
5500 State Ave (66102-3485)
PHONE..................................913 573-2119
EMP: 15
SALES (corp-wide): 7.3B **Publicly Held**
SIC: 7513 Truck Rental/Leasing
HQ: Ryder Truck Rental, Inc.
11690 Nw 105th St
Medley FL 33178
305 500-3726

(G-4393)
RYDER TRUCK RENTAL INC
37 S James St (66118-1126)
PHONE..................................913 621-3300
Fred Manning, *Branch Mgr*
EMP: 27
SALES (corp-wide): 8.4B **Publicly Held**
SIC: 7513 Truck rental, without drivers
HQ: Ryder Truck Rental, Inc.
11690 Nw 105th St
Medley FL 33178
305 500-3726

(G-4394)
RYLIE EQUIPMENT & CONTG CO
913 S Boeke St (66105-1893)
P.O. Box 5145 (66119-0145)
PHONE..................................913 621-2725
George Shaw, *Exec VP*
Tom Howard, *Manager*
David Jensen, *Software Engr*
EMP: 93
SALES (est): 11.5MM
SALES (corp-wide): 15MM **Privately Held**
SIC: 1623 1542 1541 Underground utilities contractor; nonresidential construction; industrial buildings & warehouses
PA: Rylie Equipment & Contracting Company
1521 W Anna St
Grand Island NE 68801
308 382-8362

(G-4395)
SACRED HEART HOME CARE
13021 Meadow Ln (66109-1473)
PHONE..................................913 299-4515
Robert Blevins, *Director*
EMP: 11
SALES (est): 226.3K **Privately Held**
SIC: 8082 Home health care services

(G-4396)
SAINT LUKES SOUTH HOSPITAL INC
12300 Metcalf Ave (66103)
PHONE....................................913 317-7514
Julie Quirin, *CEO*
EMP: 22
SALES (corp-wide): 138MM **Privately Held**
SIC: 8062 General medical & surgical hospitals
PA: Saint Luke's South Hospital, Inc.
12300 Metcalf Ave
Shawnee Mission KS 66213
913 317-7000

(G-4397)
SALVATION ARMY
6711 State Ave (66102-3020)
PHONE....................................913 232-5400
EMP: 11
SALES (corp-wide): 2.2B **Privately Held**
WEB: www.salarmychicago.org
SIC: 8322 Emergency shelters
HQ: The Salvation Army
5550 Prairie Stone Pkwy # 130
Hoffman Estates IL 60192
847 294-2000

(G-4398)
SALVATION ARMY
7623 State Ave (66112)
PHONE....................................913 232-5400
Major Jeffrey Smith, *President*
EMP: 99
SALES (est): 1.8MM **Privately Held**
SIC: 8361 Residential care

(G-4399)
SALVATION ARMY NATIONAL CORP
1331 N 75th Pl (66112-2498)
PHONE....................................913 299-4822
Judy Forney, *Manager*
EMP: 19
SALES (corp-wide): 2.2B **Privately Held**
WEB: www.salvationarmyusa.org
SIC: 8322 Senior citizens' center or association
PA: The Salvation Army National Corporation
615 Slaters Ln
Alexandria VA 22314
703 684-5500

(G-4400)
SAND DOLLAR HOSPITALITY 2 LLC
Also Called: Country Suites By Carlson
1805 N 110th St (66111-1903)
PHONE....................................913 299-4700
Jason Shove, *Branch Mgr*
Steven Kluvers,
EMP: 21
SALES (corp-wide): 4.6MM **Privately Held**
SIC: 7011 Hotels & motels
PA: Sand Dollar Hospitality 2, Llc
4765 Lilac Dr
West Fargo ND 58078
832 250-2709

(G-4401)
SARA LEE CORP
4612 Speaker Rd (66106-1036)
PHONE....................................913 233-3200
Sean Connelly, *CEO*
Michiel Herkemij, *Exec VP*
Bob Bridges, *Manager*
EMP: 8
SALES (est): 597.9K **Privately Held**
SIC: 2051 Bakery: wholesale or wholesale/retail combined

(G-4402)
SCAVUZZOS INC
6550 Kansas Ave (66111-2313)
PHONE....................................816 231-1517
Pam M Scavuzzo, *President*
Santo Scavuzzo, *General Mgr*
Amy Scavuzzo, *Corp Secy*
Craig Jordison, *COO*
Amalia Nichols, *Vice Pres*
EMP: 70
SQ FT: 55,000
SALES (est): 42.9MM **Privately Held**
WEB: www.scavuzzos.com
SIC: 5142 Frozen fish, meat & poultry

(G-4403)
SCHMUHL BROTHERS INC
1134 S 12th St (66105-1615)
P.O. Box 860490, Shawnee (66286-0490)
PHONE....................................913 422-1111
Ty Schmuhl, *President*
Ryan Schmuhl, *Vice Pres*
EMP: 50
SALES (est): 8.1MM **Privately Held**
SIC: 4214 4213 Local trucking with storage; trucking, except local

(G-4404)
SCHROER MANUFACTURING COMPANY (PA)
Also Called: Shor-Line
511 Osage Ave (66105-2115)
PHONE....................................913 281-1500
Joseph A Schroer, *President*
Brian Gomen, *General Mgr*
Karl J Donahue, *Vice Pres*
John Walczuk, *Vice Pres*
Micky Merritt, *Mfg Staff*
◆ **EMP:** 115 **EST:** 1927
SQ FT: 300,000
SALES (est): 25.1MM **Privately Held**
WEB: www.shor-line.com
SIC: 3821 3841 3596 3523 Laboratory apparatus & furniture; surgical & medical instruments; scales & balances, except laboratory; farm machinery & equipment; metal stampings

(G-4405)
SCHULER HEATING AND COOLING
3400 Shawnee Dr (66106-3900)
PHONE....................................913 262-2969
Steve Schuler, *President*
EMP: 10 **EST:** 1964
SQ FT: 7,500
SALES (est): 1.5MM **Privately Held**
SIC: 1711 Warm air heating & air conditioning contractor

(G-4406)
SCHULTZ BROTHERS ELC CO INC
Also Called: Mid America Cabling Comm
3030 S 24th St Ste A (66106-4707)
PHONE....................................913 321-8338
Roger Schultz Jr, *President*
Heinz Maurer, *Project Mgr*
Ann Cothran, *Office Mgr*
Sarah Schultz, *Graphic Designe*
EMP: 35
SQ FT: 8,000
SALES (est): 5.5MM **Privately Held**
WEB: www.schultzpower.com
SIC: 8748 1731 Telecommunications consultant; electrical work; general electrical contractor

(G-4407)
SCIENTIFIC PLASTICS CO INC
1016 Southwest Blvd (66103-1908)
P.O. Box 171177 (66117-0177)
PHONE....................................913 432-0322
Patricia Bartley, *President*
▲ **EMP:** 25
SQ FT: 40,000
SALES (est): 5.2MM **Privately Held**
SIC: 3089 Plastic & fiberglass tanks

(G-4408)
SCRAP MANAGEMENT LLC
Also Called: Rivers Edge Scrap Management
836 S 26th St (66106-1241)
PHONE....................................913 573-1000
Kay Kates, *CEO*
Tim Kates, *Vice Pres*
EMP: 12
SQ FT: 20,000
SALES (est): 3.8MM **Privately Held**
SIC: 5093 Metal scrap & waste materials

(G-4409)
SCRIPTPRO LLC
10911 Georgia Ave (66109-4418)
PHONE....................................913 403-5260
Shafi U Shilad, *Vice Pres*
Lenka Brown, *Branch Mgr*
Aaron James, *Software Engr*
EMP: 83 **Privately Held**
SIC: 3559 Sewing machines & hat & zipper making machinery
PA: Scriptpro Llc
5828 Reeds Rd
Shawnee Mission KS 66202

(G-4410)
SEALY INC
435 River Park Dr (66105-1419)
PHONE....................................913 321-3677
Ronald L Jones, *President*
Greg Mason, *General Mgr*
EMP: 175
SALES (corp-wide): 2.7B **Publicly Held**
SIC: 2515 Mattresses, innerspring or box spring
HQ: Sealy Mattress Company
1 Office Parkway Rd
Trinity NC 27370
336 861-3500

(G-4411)
SEALY MATTRESS CO KANS CY INC
435 River Park Dr (66105-1419)
PHONE....................................913 321-3677
Ronald L Jones, *President*
Ronald Stolle, *Treasurer*
EMP: 100 **EST:** 1930
SQ FT: 120,000
SALES (est): 11.7MM
SALES (corp-wide): 2.7B **Publicly Held**
SIC: 2515 Mattresses, containing felt, foam rubber, urethane, etc.; box springs, assembled
HQ: Sealy Mattress Company
1 Office Parkway Rd
Trinity NC 27370
336 861-3500

(G-4412)
SECURITY BANK OF KANSAS CITY (HQ)
701 Minnesota Ave (66101-2703)
P.O. Box 2924, Shawnee Mission (66201-1324)
PHONE....................................913 281-3165
James S Lewis, *President*
Jason Brown, *COO*
John Klinedinst, *COO*
Steve Lynn, *Exec VP*
Amber Vonderbruegge, *Exec VP*
EMP: 80 **EST:** 1933
SQ FT: 200,000
SALES: 123.2MM
SALES (corp-wide): 100MM **Privately Held**
SIC: 6022 State trust companies accepting deposits, commercial
PA: Valley View Bancshares, Inc
7500 W 95th St
Shawnee Mission KS 66212
913 381-3311

(G-4413)
SECURITY BANK OF KANSAS CITY
8155 Parallel Pkwy (66112-2010)
P.O. Box 171297 (66117-0297)
PHONE....................................913 621-8423
Ed Loomis, *President*
EMP: 12
SALES (corp-wide): 100MM **Privately Held**
SIC: 6022 State trust companies accepting deposits, commercial
HQ: Security Bank Of Kansas City
701 Minnesota Ave
Kansas City KS 66101
913 281-3165

(G-4414)
SECURITY BANK OF KANSAS CITY
1901 Central Ave (66102-4812)
P.O. Box 171297 (66117-0297)
PHONE....................................913 621-8465
Valorie Harlan, *Manager*
Alison Petterson, *Manager*
Carol Sprague, *Admin Sec*
EMP: 15
SALES (corp-wide): 100MM **Privately Held**
SIC: 6022 State trust companies accepting deposits, commercial
HQ: Security Bank Of Kansas City
701 Minnesota Ave
Kansas City KS 66101
913 281-3165

(G-4415)
SECURITY BANK OF KANSAS CITY
7364 State Ave (66112-3055)
PHONE....................................913 621-8462
Rodger Gilbert, *Manager*
EMP: 14
SALES (corp-wide): 100MM **Privately Held**
SIC: 6022 State trust companies accepting deposits, commercial
HQ: Security Bank Of Kansas City
701 Minnesota Ave
Kansas City KS 66101
913 281-3165

(G-4416)
SECURITY BANK OF KANSAS CITY
1300 N 78th St Ste 100 (66112-2406)
PHONE....................................913 299-6200
David Spehar, *President*
EMP: 52
SALES (corp-wide): 100MM **Privately Held**
SIC: 6022 State trust companies accepting deposits, commercial
HQ: Security Bank Of Kansas City
701 Minnesota Ave
Kansas City KS 66101
913 281-3165

(G-4417)
SERGEANTS PET CARE PDTS INC
16 Kansas Ave (66105-1429)
PHONE....................................913 627-1245
Roger Schmidt, *Manager*
EMP: 7
SALES (corp-wide): 528.6MM **Publicly Held**
SIC: 2046 Corn & other vegetable starches
HQ: Sergeant's Pet Care Products, Llc
10077 S 134th St
Omaha NE 68138

(G-4418)
SERVICE CORP INTERNATIONAL
Also Called: SCI
701 N 94th St (66112-1511)
PHONE....................................913 334-3366
Joel Brinkly, *General Mgr*
Joel Brinkley, *Site Mgr*
EMP: 20
SALES (corp-wide): 3.1B **Publicly Held**
WEB: www.sci-corp.com
SIC: 6553 7261 Cemeteries, real estate operation; crematory
PA: Service Corporation International
1929 Allen Pkwy
Houston TX 77019
713 522-5141

(G-4419)
SHANNAHAN CRANE & HOIST INC
10901 Kaw Dr (66111-1174)
PHONE....................................816 746-9822
Todd Leeber, *Manager*
EMP: 10
SALES (corp-wide): 7.7MM **Privately Held**
WEB: www.shannahancrane.com
SIC: 7389 7699 5084 3531 Crane & aerial lift service; industrial equipment services; hoists; backhoes, tractors, cranes, plows & similar equipment
PA: Shannahan Crane & Hoist, Inc.
11695 Lkeside Crossing Ct
Saint Louis MO 63146
314 965-2800

▲ = Import ▼=Export
◆ =Import/Export

(G-4420)
SHARON LEE FAMILY HEALTH CARE
340 Southwest Blvd (66103-2150)
PHONE..................................913 722-3100
James Wing, *President*
Sharon Lee, *Director*
EMP: 60
SALES: 2.1MM **Privately Held**
SIC: 8011 8111 General & family practice, physician/surgeon; legal aid service

(G-4421)
SILVER CITY CMNTY RESOURCE CTR
2332 Birch Dr (66106-2996)
PHONE..................................913 362-3367
Carolyn Holland, *Principal*
EMP: 10
SALES (est): 191.5K **Privately Held**
SIC: 8322 Community center

(G-4422)
SISTERS OF CHARITY OF LEAVENWO
Also Called: Providence
8919 Parallel Pkwy # 118 (66112-1636)
PHONE..................................913 825-0500
Sister Marie Damian Glatt, *President*
Michael Meurer, *Med Doctor*
Marlena Blackwell, *Analyst*
EMP: 30
SALES (corp-wide): 2.7B **Privately Held**
WEB: www.sclhsc.org
SIC: 8011 8062 Health maintenance organization; general medical & surgical hospitals
PA: Sisters Of Charity Of Leavenworth Health System, Inc.
500 Eldorado Blvd # 6300
Broomfield CO 80021
303 813-5000

(G-4423)
SISTERS SERVANTS OF MARY
Also Called: Servants of Mary Ministers
800 N 18th St (66102-4214)
PHONE..................................913 371-3423
Carmela Sanz, *Relg Ldr*
EMP: 38 **EST**: 1917
SALES (est): 1.3MM **Privately Held**
SIC: 8082 Home health care services

(G-4424)
SKYMARK REFUELERS LLC (PA)
Also Called: Flowmark Vacuum Trucks
610 S Adams St (66105-1403)
PHONE..................................913 653-8100
Steven Paul, *President*
Melvyn Paul, *Vice Pres*
Mike Ellis,
Douglas E Moskowitz,
◆ **EMP**: 88 **EST**: 2013
SQ FT: 50,000
SALES: 64MM **Privately Held**
SIC: 3713 5511 Truck & bus bodies; trucks, tractors & trailers: new & used

(G-4425)
SMALLWOOD LOCK SUPPLY INC (PA)
Also Called: Smallwood Locksmiths
1008 N 18th St (66102-4294)
PHONE..................................913 371-5678
Michael Smallwood, *President*
Matt Smallwood, *Purchasing*
Ken Lierz, *Sales Staff*
Julia Smallwood, *Office Mgr*
EMP: 13 **EST**: 1912
SQ FT: 8,500
SALES: 2.2MM **Privately Held**
WEB: www.smallwoodlock.com
SIC: 5072 7699 Security devices, locks; locksmith shop

(G-4426)
SMART HOME INNOVATIONS LLC
1136 Adams St (66103-1306)
PHONE..................................913 339-8641
Gary Gilfry, *President*
Jeremy Goeller, *Vice Pres*
Jay Ray, *CFO*
EMP: 16
SALES: 4MM **Privately Held**
SIC: 1521 General remodeling, single-family houses

(G-4427)
SMITH TRANSPORTATION INC
2540 S 88th St (66111-1764)
P.O. Box 13286, Edwardsville (66113-0286)
PHONE..................................913 543-7614
Gregory Smith, *President*
Janet Price, *Vice Pres*
Greg McLeod, *Manager*
EMP: 12
SALES (est): 1.9MM **Privately Held**
SIC: 4213 Trucking, except local

(G-4428)
SMITHS INTRCNNECT AMERICAS INC
Also Called: Smiths Connectors
5101 Richland Ave (66106-1019)
PHONE..................................913 342-5544
Vadim Radunsky, *President*
EMP: 6
SALES (corp-wide): 3.1B **Privately Held**
SIC: 3679 Microwave components
HQ: Smiths Interconnect Americas, Inc.
5101 Richland Ave
Kansas City KS 66106
913 342-5544

(G-4429)
SMITHS INTRCNNECT AMERICAS INC (DH)
Also Called: Synergetix
5101 Richland Ave (66106-1019)
PHONE..................................913 342-5544
Dom Matos, *President*
Khee Hong, *General Mgr*
Thad Sketers, *Regional Mgr*
Pete Galdin, *Business Mgr*
Kim Hause, *Business Mgr*
▲ **EMP**: 175
SQ FT: 47,000
SALES (est): 104.2MM
SALES (corp-wide): 3.1B **Privately Held**
WEB: www.idinet.com
SIC: 3679 3825 3643 3625 Microwave components; instruments to measure electricity; current-carrying wiring devices; relays & industrial controls
HQ: Smiths Interconnect Group Limited
130 Centennial Park
Borehamwood HERTS
208 450-8033

(G-4430)
SPANISH GARDENS FOOD MFG CO
2301 Metropolitan Ave (66106-5599)
PHONE..................................913 831-4242
Norma Jean Miller, *President*
Grace Silva, *Corp Secy*
EMP: 19 **EST**: 1948
SQ FT: 20,000
SALES (est): 2.6MM **Privately Held**
WEB: www.spanishgardens.com
SIC: 2032 Ethnic foods: canned, jarred, etc.

(G-4431)
SPECCHEM LLC
444b Richmond Ave (66101-2343)
PHONE..................................913 371-8705
Greg Maday, *CEO*
EMP: 10 **Privately Held**
SIC: 2891 Adhesives & sealants
PA: Specchem, Llc
1511 Baltimore Ave # 600
Kansas City MO 64108

(G-4432)
SPECCHEM LLC
444 Richmond Ave (66101-2343)
PHONE..................................816 968-5600
Troy Robinett, *Regl Sales Mgr*
David Swain, *Sales Staff*
Greg Maday, *Mng Member*
EMP: 20
SALES (est): 934.8K **Privately Held**
SIC: 1771 Concrete work

(G-4433)
SPECTRUM HEALTH FOUNDATION INC
Also Called: SPECTRUM HOME HEALTH AGENCY
2915 Strong Ave (66106-2144)
P.O. Box 6070 (66106-0070)
PHONE..................................913 831-2979
Leonard Rewert, *President*
Stacey Baker, *Vice Pres*
Mari Maybrier, *Sales Executive*
Vivian Crawford, *Executive*
Marilyn Appl, *Admin Sec*
EMP: 60
SQ FT: 5,000
SALES: 125.8K **Privately Held**
WEB: www.spectrumhomehealth.com
SIC: 8082 Home health care services

(G-4434)
SPECTRUM MEDICAL EQUIPMENT INC
2915 Strong Ave (66106-2144)
P.O. Box 6070 (66106-0070)
PHONE..................................913 831-2979
Cory Appl, *President*
Francisco Lopez, *Corp Secy*
EMP: 14
SALES: 950K **Privately Held**
SIC: 5047 Medical equipment & supplies

(G-4435)
SPICIN FOODS INC
Also Called: Original Juan Specialty Foods
111 Southwest Blvd (66103-2132)
PHONE..................................913 432-5228
Scott Morse, *CEO*
Valerie Lewellen, *Vice Pres*
Jason Erickson, *Purch Mgr*
Travis Barnes, *Controller*
Stephanie Hoopes, *Sales Staff*
EMP: 80
SQ FT: 60,000
SALES (est): 9MM **Privately Held**
SIC: 2033 Tomato products: packaged in cans, jars, etc.; barbecue sauce: packaged in cans, jars, etc.; spaghetti & other pasta sauce: packaged in cans, jars, etc.; chili sauce, tomato: packaged in cans, jars, etc.

(G-4436)
SPORTS NUTZ OF KANSAS INC
1803 Vlg West Pkwy M137 (66111-1855)
PHONE..................................913 400-7733
Stephen T Housh, *President*
EMP: 12
SQ FT: 4,500
SALES (est): 1.3MM **Privately Held**
SIC: 3949 Sporting & athletic goods

(G-4437)
SR FOOD AND BEVERAGE CO INC
Also Called: Woodlands
9700 Leavenworth Rd (66109)
P.O. Box 385, Saint Joseph MO (64502-0385)
PHONE..................................913 299-9797
Bill Grace, *President*
EMP: 90
SALES (est): 3.3MM **Privately Held**
SIC: 8741 Management services

(G-4438)
STANION WHOLESALE ELC CO INC
2040 S 45th St (66106-2530)
PHONE..................................913 342-1177
Mary Oberhotz, *Sales Staff*
Tony Flakus, *Branch Mgr*
EMP: 12
SALES (corp-wide): 97.6MM **Privately Held**
WEB: www.stanion.com
SIC: 5063 Electrical supplies
PA: Stanion Wholesale Electric Co., Inc.
812 S Main St
Pratt KS 67124
620 672-5678

(G-4439)
STARDUST CORPORATION
Also Called: Imprints Wholesale
9525 Woodend Rd (66111-1707)
PHONE..................................913 894-1966
Todd Highfill, *Manager*
EMP: 12
SALES (corp-wide): 21.6MM **Privately Held**
SIC: 5136 5137 Sportswear, men's & boys'; sportswear, women's & children's
HQ: Stardust Corporation
515 Commerce Pkwy
Verona WI
608 845-5600

(G-4440)
STERICYCLE INC
3140 N 7th St (66115-1104)
PHONE..................................913 321-3928
Chad Bergman, *General Mgr*
EMP: 10
SALES (corp-wide): 3.4B **Publicly Held**
WEB: www.stericycle.com
SIC: 4953 Medical waste disposal
PA: Stericycle, Inc.
2355 Waukegan Rd Ste 300
Bannockburn IL 60015
847 367-5910

(G-4441)
STOUSE LLC
Also Called: Magna-Plus
2828 S 44th St (66106-3717)
PHONE..................................913 384-0014
Clay Davis, *Branch Mgr*
EMP: 40
SALES (corp-wide): 56MM **Privately Held**
SIC: 3499 Magnets, permanent: metallic
PA: Stouse, Llc
300 New Century Pkwy
New Century KS 66031
913 764-5757

(G-4442)
STURGIS MATERIALS INC
550 S Packard St 552 (66105-1318)
P.O. Box 5133 (66119-0133)
PHONE..................................913 371-7757
Marc Lonesk, *President*
Matthew Lonesk, *Vice Pres*
Edward N Walsh, *Vice Pres*
Jeff Bolton, *Mktg Coord*
EMP: 35 **EST**: 1976
SQ FT: 15,000
SALES (est): 7.6MM **Privately Held**
WEB: www.sturgismaterials.com
SIC: 5211 5032 Paving stones; sand & gravel; sand, construction; stone, crushed or broken

(G-4443)
SUB-TECHNOLOGIES INC (PA)
Also Called: Subtech USA
236 N 7th St (66101-3202)
PHONE..................................816 795-9955
John Wells, *CEO*
Adam West, *COO*
Anthony Kelley, *Controller*
◆ **EMP**: 30
SALES: 10MM **Privately Held**
SIC: 5046 Restaurant equipment & supplies

(G-4444)
SUBSTANCE ABUSE CNTR E KANSAS (PA)
2005 Washington Blvd (66102-2756)
PHONE..................................913 362-0045
Roy Young, *Treasurer*
Erma E Cunningham Embry, *Exec Dir*
Erma Cunningham Embry, *Director*
Jackie Middelcamp, *Admin Sec*
EMP: 25
SALES: 3K **Privately Held**
SIC: 8361 Rehabilitation center, residential: health care incidental

GEOGRAPHIC

(G-4445)
SUCCESS TRUCK LEASING INC (PA)
Also Called: NationaLease
77 S James St (66118-1126)
P.O. Box 2346 (66110-0346)
PHONE....................................913 321-1716
John Malinee, *President*
Dolores Wedlan, *Vice Pres*
Kay Carlile, *Site Mgr*
Christina Lanfranca, *Sales Executive*
David Wedlan, *Admin Sec*
EMP: 34
SQ FT: 14,000
SALES (est): 9.1MM **Privately Held**
SIC: 7513 Truck rental, without drivers; truck leasing, without drivers

(G-4446)
SUNBURST SYSTEMS INC
Also Called: Classifiedkits.com
807 Armourdale Pkwy (66105-2103)
PHONE....................................913 383-9309
Beth Dowell, *President*
William Weigel, *Vice Pres*
EMP: 10 **EST:** 1998
SQ FT: 1,600
SALES (est): 1.7MM **Privately Held**
WEB: www.sunburstsystems.com
SIC: 2499 5099 Signboards, wood; signs, except electric

(G-4447)
SUPERIOR DOOR SERVICE INC
106 Greystone Ave (66103-1355)
PHONE....................................913 381-1767
Mike Nikolas, *President*
Mike Nicholas, *President*
Lori Nikolas, *Vice Pres*
EMP: 10
SQ FT: 6,000
SALES (est): 3.2MM **Privately Held**
SIC: 5031 5211 Doors, garage; garage doors, sale & installation

(G-4448)
SUPERIOR MOBILE WASH INC
Also Called: Action Mobile Wash
1839 N 10th St (66104-5303)
PHONE....................................913 915-9642
Jeffrey Schuler, *President*
Tamara Schuler, *Corp Secy*
EMP: 15
SQ FT: 10,000
SALES (est): 853.5K **Privately Held**
SIC: 7542 3559 Truck wash; degreasing machines, automotive & industrial

(G-4449)
SUPERIOR SHEET METAL CO INC
3940 S Ferree St (66103-1717)
PHONE....................................913 831-9900
Tina Considine, *President*
Troy Holck, *President*
Richard Harmes, *Vice Pres*
Nornam Waters, *Treasurer*
Chris Boland, *Admin Sec*
EMP: 15
SALES (est): 2.5MM **Privately Held**
WEB: www.superiorsheetmetal.com
SIC: 1761 Roofing, siding & sheet metal work

(G-4450)
SUPERVAN SERVICE CO INC
511 Miami Ave (66105-2109)
PHONE....................................913 281-4044
Don Wilson, *Branch Mgr*
EMP: 20
SALES (corp-wide): 11MM **Privately Held**
SIC: 4212 Delivery service, vehicular
PA: Supervan Service Co., Inc.
121 Bremen Ave
Saint Louis MO 63147
314 231-8444

(G-4451)
SWAMI INVESTMENT INC
Also Called: Candlewood Suites
10920 Parallel Pkwy (66109-4431)
PHONE....................................913 788-9929
Arvind Patel, *President*
Robert Ortiz, *General Mgr*
EMP: 15
SALES: 950K **Privately Held**
SIC: 7011 Hotel, franchised

(G-4452)
SWAN ENGINEERING & SUP CO INC
1132 Adams St (66103-1306)
P.O. Box 5158 (66119-0158)
PHONE....................................913 371-7425
W Kurt Gagel, *President*
Dan Mercer, *Vice Pres*
Michael Saysoff, *Vice Pres*
Kevin Kieffer, *Admin Sec*
EMP: 18
SQ FT: 10,000
SALES: 4.9MM **Privately Held**
WEB: www.swanengineering.net
SIC: 5085 3492 Hose, belting & packing; industrial fittings; packing, industrial; seals, industrial; hose & tube couplings, hydraulic/pneumatic

(G-4453)
SWOPE HEALTH SERVICES
21 N 12th St Ste 400 (66102-5172)
PHONE....................................816 922-7600
Verneda Robinson, *Branch Mgr*
EMP: 19
SALES (corp-wide): 3.7MM **Privately Held**
SIC: 8062 General medical & surgical hospitals
HQ: Swope Health Services
3801 Blue Pkwy
Kansas City MO 64130
816 923-5800

(G-4454)
T KENNEL SYSTEMS INC
Also Called: T-Kennels Systems
415 Osage Ave (66105-2113)
PHONE....................................816 668-8995
Richard A Donahue, *President*
Jack Donahue, *President*
Richard E Donahue II, *Vice Pres*
Joseph Schroer, *Vice Pres*
▲ **EMP:** 60
SQ FT: 20,000
SALES (est): 9.6MM
SALES (corp-wide): 25.1MM **Privately Held**
WEB: www.shor-line.com
SIC: 3821 Laboratory apparatus & furniture
PA: Schroer Manufacturing Company
511 Osage Ave
Kansas City KS 66105
913 281-1500

(G-4455)
T-BONES BASEBALL CLUB LLC
Also Called: Kansas City T-Bones
1800 Village West Pkwy (66111-1825)
PHONE....................................913 328-2255
John Ehlert,
EMP: 14
SALES (est): 1.5MM **Privately Held**
SIC: 7941 Baseball club, professional & semi-professional

(G-4456)
T2 HOLDINGS LLC
Also Called: Proshred Security
3052 S 24th St (66106-4707)
PHONE....................................913 327-8889
Brenda Fletcher, *Consultant*
Tricia McCullough,
Todd McCullough,
EMP: 18
SQ FT: 24,150
SALES (est): 650K **Privately Held**
WEB: www.proshred.com
SIC: 7389 Document & office record destruction

(G-4457)
TABCO INCORPORATED
1323 S 59th St (66106-1598)
P.O. Box 6246 (66106-0246)
PHONE....................................913 287-3333
Eugene Kubicki Jr, *President*
John Kubicki, *Vice Pres*
Dennis Shannon, *VP Bus Dvlpt*
EMP: 43 **EST:** 1957
SQ FT: 29,000
SALES (est): 9.9MM **Privately Held**
WEB: www.tabcoinc.com
SIC: 2759 2672 2675 Flexographic printing; labels (unprinted), gummed: made from purchased materials; die-cut paper & board

(G-4458)
TARTAN MANUFACTURING INC
Also Called: Wholesale Sheet Metal
800 Southwest Blvd (66103-1926)
P.O. Box 3153 (66103-0153)
PHONE....................................913 432-7100
Pat Chilen, *President*
Jerry Ragsdale, *Vice Pres*
EMP: 107
SQ FT: 60,000
SALES (est): 7.6MM
SALES (corp-wide): 35.1MM **Privately Held**
WEB: www.wsmkc.com
SIC: 3444 3312 Sheet metal specialties, not stamped; blast furnaces & steel mills
PA: Wholesale Sheet Metal, Inc.
800 Southwest Blvd
Kansas City KS 66103
913 432-7100

(G-4459)
TAYLOR MADE VISIONS LLC
4101 S Minnie St (66103-3015)
PHONE....................................913 210-0699
Linda Taylor, *CEO*
EMP: 14
SALES (est): 517.9K **Privately Held**
SIC: 8699 Charitable organization

(G-4460)
TC INDUSTRIES INC
101 Central Ave (66118-1115)
PHONE....................................913 371-7922
Terry K Cheyney, *President*
Mary O Cheyney, *Treasurer*
EMP: 10 **EST:** 1980
SQ FT: 5,000
SALES: 700K **Privately Held**
SIC: 3369 Nonferrous foundries

(G-4461)
TEAM CAR CARE LLC
Also Called: Jiffy Lube
1010 N 78th St (66112-2812)
PHONE....................................913 334-5950
Kevin Rogers, *Manager*
EMP: 10 **Privately Held**
SIC: 7549 Lubrication service, automotive
PA: Team Car Care, Llc
105 Decker Ct Ste 900
Irving TX 75062

(G-4462)
TECH GURUS LLC
5434 Webster Ave (66104-2147)
PHONE....................................913 299-8700
Michael Vazquez,
EMP: 10
SALES (est): 688.4K **Privately Held**
SIC: 7378 Computer maintenance & repair

(G-4463)
TENDER HEARTS INC
2035 N 82nd St (66109-2283)
PHONE....................................913 788-2273
Christine Strub, *Exec Dir*
Mary Highman, *Director*
EMP: 12
SALES (est): 372.9K **Privately Held**
SIC: 8351 Group day care center

(G-4464)
TERRELL PUBLISHING CO
Also Called: Onpoint Specialty Products
1310 Adams St (66103-1359)
PHONE....................................913 948-8226
Edward W Armstrong, *Ch of Bd*
Jake Shaffer, *President*
Jacob W Shaffer, *Principal*
▲ **EMP:** 5
SQ FT: 5,400
SALES (est): 949.3K
SALES (corp-wide): 13.1MM **Privately Held**
WEB: www.terrellpublishing.com
SIC: 5099 2731 7336 Souvenirs; books: publishing & printing; graphic arts & related design
PA: Mccormick-Armstrong Co., Incorporated
1501 E Douglas Ave
Wichita KS 67211
316 264-1363

(G-4465)
TERRY TRUCKING & WRECKING LLC
3645 N 85th St (66109-4633)
PHONE....................................913 281-3854
Cliff Terry, *Principal*
EMP: 13
SQ FT: 5,000
SALES (est): 1.2MM **Privately Held**
SIC: 4212 Local trucking, without storage

(G-4466)
TEST AND MEASUREMENT INC
1304 Adams St (66103-1359)
PHONE....................................913 233-2724
Beth Karriker, *President*
Larry McDonald, *Vice Pres*
Lee Nguyen, *Vice Pres*
Bill Embry, *Sales Staff*
Ben Embry Jr, *Shareholder*
EMP: 16
SQ FT: 3,500
SALES (est): 1.4MM **Privately Held**
WEB: www.testandmeasurement.com
SIC: 7629 Electrical measuring instrument repair & calibration

(G-4467)
TFT GLOBAL INC
5300 Kansas Ave (66106-1141)
PHONE....................................519 842-4540
Kim Parker, *Opers Mgr*
EMP: 10
SALES (corp-wide): 109.6MM **Privately Held**
SIC: 4225 8742 General warehousing; quality assurance consultant
HQ: Tft Global Inc
25 Townline Rd Suite 200
Tillsonburg ON N4G 2
519 842-4540

(G-4468)
THOMPSON PUMP CO
504 S 70th St (66111-2433)
PHONE....................................913 788-2583
Bill Thompson, *President*
Dale Conway, *Vice Pres*
John Farell, *Vice Pres*
Doug French, *Vice Pres*
Majid Tabakloi, *Vice Pres*
EMP: 20
SALES (est): 4.1MM **Privately Held**
SIC: 5084 Pumps & pumping equipment

(G-4469)
TNO LLC
2405 Merriam Ln (66106-4601)
PHONE....................................913 278-1911
Michael Jones, *CEO*
Todd Stone, *COO*
Tonia Chambers, *Manager*
EMP: 40
SQ FT: 3,000
SALES (est): 621.6K **Privately Held**
SIC: 0782 Lawn & garden services

(G-4470)
TOTAL RENAL CARE INC
Also Called: Wyandotte County Dialysis
5001 State Ave (66102-3459)
PHONE....................................913 287-5724
Cindy Kramer, *Branch Mgr*
EMP: 24 **Publicly Held**
WEB: www.davita.com
SIC: 8092 Kidney dialysis centers
HQ: Total Renal Care, Inc.
2000 16th St
Denver CO 80202
303 405-2100

(G-4471)
TOTAL TOOL SUPPLY INC
275 Southwest Blvd (66103-2147)
PHONE....................................913 722-7879
Mike Wilson, *Principal*
EMP: 18

SALES (corp-wide): 65.3MM **Privately Held**
SIC: 5085 7699 Industrial tools; professional instrument repair services
PA: Total Tool Supply, Inc.
315 Pierce St N Ste A
Saint Paul MN 55104
651 646-4055

(G-4472)
TRAFTEC INC
Also Called: Contractors Traffic Protection
1428 Kansas Ave (66105-1116)
PHONE..................................913 621-2919
Mickey Kanan, *President*
Bernard D Kanan Jr, *President*
W K Kanan, *Vice Pres*
Roseann Smallwood, *Admin Sec*
EMP: 10
SQ FT: 17,700
SALES (est): 1.3MM **Privately Held**
WEB: www.traftec.com
SIC: 7359 5099 Signs, except electric; work zone traffic equipment (flags, cones, barrels, etc.)

(G-4473)
TRANSWOOD EDWARDSVILLE66
8907 Woodend Rd (66111-1717)
PHONE..................................913 745-1773
Jimmy Hancock, *General Mgr*
EMP: 30
SALES (est): 1.1MM **Privately Held**
SIC: 4213 4212 Trucking, except local; local trucking, without storage

(G-4474)
TRIEB SHEET METAL CO
1642 S 45th St (66106-2573)
P.O. Box 6797 (66106-0797)
PHONE..................................913 831-1166
Steve Tomberger, *Owner*
EMP: 31
SQ FT: 15,000
SALES (est): 4.3MM **Privately Held**
SIC: 3444 Sheet metal specialties, not stamped

(G-4475)
TROOSTWOOD GARAGE & BODY SHOP
1516 N 13th St (66102-2939)
PHONE..................................816 444-3800
EMP: 20 **EST:** 1940
SQ FT: 12,000
SALES (est): 2.3MM **Privately Held**
SIC: 7538 7532 General Automotive Repair

(G-4476)
TRUE NORTH OUTDOOR LLC
3909 Mission Rd (66103-2749)
PHONE..................................913 322-1340
Greg Hirleman,
Brenda Reedy, *Executive Asst*
EMP: 26
SALES (est): 6.1MM **Privately Held**
SIC: 4959 Snowplowing

(G-4477)
TURNER CERAMIC TILE INC
11535 Kaw Dr (66111-1111)
PHONE..................................913 441-6161
Molly Turner, *President*
Marshall Kidd, *Engineer*
Amanda Free, *Treasurer*
Kevin Long, *Supervisor*
▲ **EMP:** 11
SQ FT: 15,000
SALES: 3MM **Privately Held**
SIC: 1743 Tile installation, ceramic

(G-4478)
TURNER HOUSE CLINIC INC
Also Called: Vibrant Health
21 N 12th St Ste 300 (66102-5105)
PHONE..................................913 342-2552
Patrick Sallee, *CEO*
Andrea Woodward, *Office Mgr*
Sara Adams, *Director*
Ruth Becker, *Bd of Directors*
Karla Garcia, *Bd of Directors*
EMP: 50
SQ FT: 9,500
SALES: 5.6MM **Privately Held**
WEB: www.thcckc.org
SIC: 8011 8021 8063 Medical centers; dental clinics & offices; hospital for the mentally ill

(G-4479)
TURNER RECREATION COMMISSION
831 S 55th St (66106-1307)
PHONE..................................913 287-2111
Skyler Rorabaugh, *Principal*
EMP: 70
SALES (est): 3.6MM **Privately Held**
SIC: 7389 Personal service agents, brokers & bureaus

(G-4480)
TWIN TRAFFIC MARKING CORP
626 N 47th St (66102-3449)
PHONE..................................913 428-2575
James R Francis, *President*
William Francis, *Vice Pres*
Brian Francis, *Shareholder*
EMP: 27
SQ FT: 10,000
SALES (est): 2.5MM **Privately Held**
SIC: 1721 Pavement marking contractor

(G-4481)
U-HAUL CO OF KANSAS INC (DH)
5200 State Ave (66102-3498)
PHONE..................................913 287-1327
Gary Wittkopp, *President*
Chad Lawson, *Sales Executive*
EMP: 78 **EST:** 1952
SQ FT: 60,000
SALES (est): 7.5MM
SALES (corp-wide): 3.7B **Publicly Held**
SIC: 7513 7359 7353 Truck rental & leasing, no drivers; equipment rental & leasing; heavy construction equipment rental
HQ: U-Haul International, Inc.
2727 N Central Ave
Phoenix AZ 85004
602 263-6011

(G-4482)
ULTRA-TECH AEROSPACE INC
3000 Power Dr (66106-4721)
PHONE..................................913 262-7009
Keith Mills, *President*
EMP: 22
SQ FT: 28,000
SALES: 7.7MM
SALES (corp-wide): 161.7MM **Privately Held**
WEB: www.ultratechkc.com
SIC: 3599 Machine shop, jobbing & repair
PA: Ibt, Inc.
9400 W 55th St
Shawnee Mission KS 66203
913 677-3151

(G-4483)
UMB BANK NATIONAL ASSOCIATION
909 N 6th St (66101-2843)
PHONE..................................913 621-8002
Andrew Morris, *Site Mgr*
Andy Morris, *Manager*
EMP: 15
SALES (corp-wide): 1.1B **Publicly Held**
WEB: www.umbwebsolutions.com
SIC: 6021 National commercial banks
HQ: Umb Bank, National Association
1010 Grand Blvd Fl 3
Kansas City MO 64106
816 842-2222

(G-4484)
UNBOUND (PA)
1 Elmwood Ave (66103-2118)
P.O. Box 219114 MO (64121-9114)
PHONE..................................913 384-6500
Scott Wasserman, *President*
EMP: 120 **EST:** 1981
SQ FT: 100,000
SALES: 123.5MM **Privately Held**
WEB: www.cfcausa.org
SIC: 8699 Charitable organization

(G-4485)
UNIFIED GVRNMENT CMNTY CORECTN
812 N 7th St Fl 3 (66101-3049)
PHONE..................................913 573-4180
Phillip L Lockman, *Director*
Ashli Johnson, *Officer*
EMP: 45
SALES (est): 1.2MM **Privately Held**
WEB: www.ugcc.state.ks.us
SIC: 8744 Correctional facility

(G-4486)
UNION MACHINE & TOOL WORKS INC
1141 S 12th St (66105-1614)
PHONE..................................913 342-6000
Charles Schleicher, *President*
EMP: 17 **EST:** 1948
SQ FT: 25,000
SALES (est): 2.2MM **Privately Held**
SIC: 3599 Machine shop, jobbing & repair

(G-4487)
UNITED MEDICAL GROUP LLC
5701 State Ave Ste 100 (66102-1281)
PHONE..................................913 287-7800
Pratip Patel MD, *Treasurer*
Mahendra Rupani-MD,
EMP: 140
SQ FT: 20,000
SALES (est): 11MM **Privately Held**
WEB: www.umghealth.com
SIC: 8011 Internal medicine, physician/surgeon

(G-4488)
UNITED PARCEL SERVICE INC
Also Called: UPS
233 N James St (66118)
PHONE..................................913 573-4701
EMP: 158
SALES (corp-wide): 71.8B **Publicly Held**
WEB: www.upsscs.com
SIC: 4215 Parcel delivery, vehicular
HQ: United Parcel Service, Inc.
55 Glenlake Pkwy
Atlanta GA 30328
404 828-6000

(G-4489)
UNITED STATES COURTS ADM
Also Called: Probation Satellite Office
500 State Ave Rm M35 (66101-2400)
PHONE..................................913 735-2242
Kristin Tourtillott, *Branch Mgr*
EMP: 62 **Publicly Held**
SIC: 8322 Probation office
HQ: The United States Courts Administrative Office Of
1 Columbus Cir Ne
Washington DC 20544
202 502-3800

(G-4490)
UNITED STATES SYSTEMS INC
1028 Scott Ave (66105-1222)
P.O. Box 5218 (66119-0218)
PHONE..................................913 281-1010
Greg A Hawkins, *President*
EMP: 10
SQ FT: 10,000
SALES (est): 4.1MM **Privately Held**
WEB: www.unitedstatessystems.com
SIC: 3535 Pneumatic tube conveyor systems

(G-4491)
UNITED WATER WORKS CO
6636 Berger Ave (66111-2310)
PHONE..................................913 287-1280
Harv Newlin, *Owner*
Chris Antos, *Co-Owner*
Ryan Miller, *Manager*
EMP: 30
SQ FT: 10,000
SALES (est): 1.9MM **Privately Held**
SIC: 5082 Contractors' materials

(G-4492)
UNITED WAY OF WYANDOTTE COUNTY
434 Minnesota Ave (66101-2993)
P.O. Box 171042 (66117-0042)
PHONE..................................913 371-3674
Wendell Maddox, *President*
Grace Freeman, *Manager*
Pam Edvalds, *Admin Sec*
EMP: 21
SALES: 3.4MM **Privately Held**
WEB: www.unitedway-wyco.org
SIC: 8399 Fund raising organization, non-fee basis

(G-4493)
UNIVAR SOLUTIONS USA INC
Also Called: Nexeo Solutions Kansas City
5420 Speaker Rd (66106-1052)
PHONE..................................913 621-7494
EMP: 10
SALES (corp-wide): 8.6B **Publicly Held**
SIC: 5169 5162 Industrial chemicals; plastics materials & basic shapes
HQ: Univar Solutions Usa Inc.
3075 Highland Pkwy # 200
Downers Grove IL 60515
331 777-6000

(G-4494)
UNIVERSAL CONSTRUCTION CO INC (PA)
Also Called: Ucc
1615 Argentine Blvd (66105-1511)
PHONE..................................913 342-1150
Steve Smith, *President*
Archie Smith, *Exec VP*
John Shortall, *Vice Pres*
David Saheb, *Safety Dir*
Gary Walker, *Project Mgr*
EMP: 25 **EST:** 1931
SQ FT: 20,000
SALES: 15MM **Privately Held**
WEB: www.universalconstruction.net
SIC: 1542 1541 8741 Hospital construction; industrial buildings & warehouses; construction management

(G-4495)
UNIVERSAL MANAGEMENT INC (PA)
1021 N 7th St Ste 106 (66101-2823)
PHONE..................................913 321-3521
Robert Hughes Jr, *President*
Angela Agustin, *CFO*
Jan Kennedy, *Director*
EMP: 22 **EST:** 1997
SQ FT: 1,200
SALES (est): 1.5MM **Privately Held**
SIC: 6531 Real estate managers

(G-4496)
UNIVERSITY OF KANSAS
Also Called: Dept of Rehab Medicine
3901 Rainbow Blvd (66160-8500)
PHONE..................................913 588-6798
George Varghese, *Ch of Bd*
EMP: 30
SALES (corp-wide): 1.2B **Privately Held**
WEB: www.ukans.edu
SIC: 8361 8011 Rehabilitation center, residential: health care incidental; cardiologist & cardio-vascular specialist
PA: University Of Kansas
1450 Jayhawk Blvd Rm 225
Lawrence KS 66045
785 864-4868

(G-4497)
UNIVERSITY OF KANSAS
Also Called: Child Development Unit
3901 Rainbow Blvd (66160-8500)
PHONE..................................913 588-5900
Debra Schlobohm, *Manager*
EMP: 40
SALES (corp-wide): 1.2B **Privately Held**
WEB: www.ukans.edu
SIC: 8011 8221 Medical centers; university
PA: University Of Kansas
1450 Jayhawk Blvd Rm 225
Lawrence KS 66045
785 864-4868

(G-4498)
UNIVERSITY OF KANSAS
Also Called: Kansas Cancer Institute
3901 Rainbow Blvd (66160-8500)
PHONE..................................913 588-4718
William Jewell, *Branch Mgr*
EMP: 2004

SALES (corp-wide): 1.2B **Privately Held**
SIC: 8733 8221 Research institute; colleges universities & professional schools
PA: University Of Kansas
1450 Jayhawk Blvd Rm 225
Lawrence KS 66045
785 864-4868

(G-4499)
UNIVERSITY OF KANSAS
Also Called: University Kans Med Ctr Police
115 Support Services Bldg (66106)
PHONE..................................913 588-5133
Richard Johnson, *Chief*
EMP: 45
SALES (corp-wide): 1.2B **Privately Held**
WEB: www.ukans.edu
SIC: 8062 8221 Hospital, medical school affiliation; colleges universities & professional schools
PA: University Of Kansas
1450 Jayhawk Blvd Rm 225
Lawrence KS 66045
785 864-4868

(G-4500)
UNIVERSITY OF KANSAS
University Kans Hosp & Med Ctr
3901 Rainbow Blvd (66160-8500)
P.O. Box 928, Lawrence (66044-0928)
PHONE..................................913 588-5000
Irene Cummings, *Branch Mgr*
Nancy Baker, *Info Tech Mgr*
Mary E Kondrat, *Professor*
EMP: 126
SALES (corp-wide): 1.2B **Privately Held**
WEB: www.ukans.edu
SIC: 8062 8221 General medical & surgical hospitals; university
PA: University Of Kansas
1450 Jayhawk Blvd Rm 225
Lawrence KS 66045
785 864-4868

(G-4501)
UNIVERSITY OF KANSAS
University Kansas Medical Ctr
3901 Rainbow Blvd (66160-8500)
PHONE..................................913 588-1443
Barbara Atkinson, *Principal*
Lisa Chrisman, *Research*
Kristi Jones, *Research*
Marisa Jones, *Research*
Trisha Steele, *Research*
EMP: 2500
SALES (corp-wide): 1.2B **Privately Held**
WEB: www.ukans.edu
SIC: 8011 8221 Medical centers; university
PA: University Of Kansas
1450 Jayhawk Blvd Rm 225
Lawrence KS 66045
785 864-4868

(G-4502)
UNIVERSITY OF KANSAS
Also Called: University of Kansas Mdcl Ctr
3901 Rainbow Blvd (66160-8500)
PHONE..................................913 588-5436
Gregory Kopf, *Director*
EMP: 2500
SALES (corp-wide): 1.2B **Privately Held**
WEB: www.ukans.edu
SIC: 6732 Charitable trust management
PA: University Of Kansas
1450 Jayhawk Blvd Rm 225
Lawrence KS 66045
785 864-4868

(G-4503)
UNIVERSITY OF KANSAS
Also Called: Lab Animal Resources
2010 W 39th Ave (66103)
PHONE..................................913 588-7015
David Pinson Dvm, *Manager*
EMP: 30
SALES (corp-wide): 430.3K **Privately Held**
WEB: www.kumc.edu
SIC: 0742 Veterinary services, specialties
PA: University Of Kansas Medical Center Auxiliary, Inc.
3901 Rainbow Blvd
Kansas City KS 66160
913 588-5495

(G-4504)
UNIVERSITY OF KANSAS
Also Called: Department of Preventive
4004 Robinson Hall Mail (66160-0001)
PHONE..................................913 588-2720
Jasjit Ahluwalia, *Chairman*
EMP: 60
SALES (corp-wide): 1.2B **Privately Held**
SIC: 8011 Internal medicine practitioners
PA: University Of Kansas
1450 Jayhawk Blvd Rm 225
Lawrence KS 66045
785 864-4868

(G-4505)
UNIVERSITY OF KANSAS
Also Called: Internal Medicine Foundation
3901 Rainbow Blvd (66160-8500)
PHONE..................................913 588-6000
Justin Lawing, *Branch Mgr*
EMP: 849
SALES (corp-wide): 1.2B **Privately Held**
SIC: 8011 Internal medicine, physician/surgeon
PA: University Of Kansas
1450 Jayhawk Blvd Rm 225
Lawrence KS 66045
785 864-4868

(G-4506)
UNIVERSITY OF KANSAS HOSP AUTH (PA)
Also Called: University Kansas Health Sys
4000 Cambridge St (66160-8501)
PHONE..................................913 588-5000
Bob Page, *CEO*
Angela Cook, *Principal*
Linsey Gregory, *Principal*
Shirley Lefever, *Dean*
Charlie Walker, *Department Mgr*
EMP: 12
SALES (est): 708.6MM **Privately Held**
WEB: www.kumed.com
SIC: 8062 General medical & surgical hospitals

(G-4507)
UNIVERSITY OF KANSAS HOSPITAL
Also Called: Ku Eye Center - Miller Clinic
3901 Rainbow Blvd (66160-8500)
PHONE..................................913 588-5000
Irene Cumming, *CEO*
EMP: 186
SALES (corp-wide): 708.6MM **Privately Held**
WEB: www.ukans.edu
SIC: 8011 8221 Medical centers; university
PA: The University Of Kansas Hospital Authority
4000 Cambridge St
Kansas City KS 66160
913 588-5000

(G-4508)
UNIVERSITY OF KANSAS MED CTR
Also Called: Pediatric Cardiology Dept
3901 Rainbow Blvd # 4004 (66160-8500)
PHONE..................................913 588-6311
Martin Olaughlin, *Principal*
EMP: 12
SALES (corp-wide): 1.2B **Privately Held**
SIC: 8062 8011 Hospital, medical school affiliation; cardiologist & cardio-vascular specialist
HQ: The University Of Kansas Medical Center
3901 Rainbow Blvd
Kansas City KS 66160
913 588-1443

(G-4509)
UNIVERSITY OF KANSAS MED CTR
Also Called: Radiology Department
3901 Rainbow Blvd (66160-8500)
PHONE..................................913 588-6805
Solomon Batnitzky, *Principal*
EMP: 12
SALES (corp-wide): 1.2B **Privately Held**
WEB: www.ukans.edu
SIC: 8062 Hospital, medical school affiliation
HQ: The University Of Kansas Medical Center
3901 Rainbow Blvd
Kansas City KS 66160
913 588-1443

(G-4510)
UPS GROUND FREIGHT INC
3800 Kansas Ave (66106-1251)
PHONE..................................913 281-0055
Jeff Wry, *Branch Mgr*
Mark Ironsmith, *Manager*
EMP: 13
SALES (corp-wide): 71.8B **Publicly Held**
SIC: 4213 Trucking, except local
HQ: Ups Ground Freight, Inc.
1000 Semmes Ave
Richmond VA 23224
866 372-5619

(G-4511)
US BOATWORKS INC
930 Osage Ave (66105-1850)
PHONE..................................913 342-0011
Mike Tracy, *President*
Beth Tracy, *Accounting Mgr*
EMP: 10
SALES (est): 1.3MM **Privately Held**
WEB: www.boatengine.com
SIC: 7699 Boat repair

(G-4512)
USF HOLLAND LLC
Also Called: USFreightways
9711 State Ave (66111-1811)
PHONE..................................913 287-1770
Steven Emahiser, *Manager*
EMP: 250
SALES (corp-wide): 5B **Publicly Held**
WEB: www.usfc.com
SIC: 4213 Less-than-truckload (LTL) transport
HQ: Usf Holland Llc
700 S Waverly Rd
Holland MI 49423
616 395-5000

(G-4513)
VALU MERCHANDISERS COMPANY (HQ)
Also Called: Always Fresh
5000 Kansas Ave (66106-1135)
P.O. Box 2932 (66110-2932)
PHONE..................................913 319-8500
Dan Funk, *President*
John Lane, *Vice Pres*
Joe Bush, *Treasurer*
Alex Valverde, *Accounts Mgr*
▲ **EMP:** 41
SQ FT: 40,000
SALES (est): 275.3MM
SALES (corp-wide): 9.7B **Privately Held**
WEB: www.awginc.com
SIC: 5199 General merchandise, non-durable
PA: Associated Wholesale Grocers, Inc.
5000 Kansas Ave
Kansas City KS 66106
913 288-1000

(G-4514)
VELOCITI INC
120 Kansas Ave (66105-1409)
P.O. Box 5205 (66119-0205)
PHONE..................................913 233-7230
Donald Soetaert, *Branch Mgr*
EMP: 23
SALES (corp-wide): 34.4MM **Privately Held**
WEB: www.cstk.com
SIC: 5078 7623 5084 5063 Refrigeration units, motor vehicles; refrigeration repair service; engines & transportation equipment; generators
HQ: Velociti Inc.
4780 Nw 41st St Ste 500
Riverside MO 64150
913 551-0113

(G-4515)
VENTRA KANSAS LLC
900 S 68th St (66111-2334)
PHONE..................................913 334-0614
David Ekblad, *CFO*
▲ **EMP:** 100
SALES (est): 29.4MM
SALES (corp-wide): 3.1B **Privately Held**
SIC: 3089 Automotive parts, plastic
PA: Flex-N-Gate Llc
1306 E University Ave
Urbana IL 61802
217 384-6600

(G-4516)
VERITIV OPERATING COMPANY
Also Called: Xpedx
2552 S 98th St (66111-3509)
PHONE..................................913 667-1500
Scott Huddlestun, *Sales Staff*
Greg Traen, *Branch Mgr*
EMP: 150
SQ FT: 5,000
SALES (corp-wide): 8.7B **Publicly Held**
WEB: www.internationalpaper.com
SIC: 5084 Processing & packaging equipment; printing trades machinery, equipment & supplies
HQ: Veritiv Operating Company
1000 Abernathy Rd Bldg 4
Atlanta GA 30328
770 391-8200

(G-4517)
VERITIV OPERATING COMPANY
Southwest Market Area
10960 Lakeview Ave (66101)
P.O. Box 14688, Shawnee Mission (66285-4688)
PHONE..................................913 492-5050
Darryl Stotts, *Opers Mgr*
Mike Elliott, *Manager*
EMP: 54
SALES (corp-wide): 8.7B **Publicly Held**
WEB: www.unisourcelink.com
SIC: 5113 5111 Industrial & personal service paper; printing & writing paper
HQ: Veritiv Operating Company
1000 Abernathy Rd Bldg 4
Atlanta GA 30328
770 391-8200

(G-4518)
VERNON L GOEDECKE COMPANY INC
1413 Osage Ave (66105-1524)
PHONE..................................913 621-1284
Darren Golesmith, *Sales/Mktg Mgr*
EMP: 25
SALES (corp-wide): 93.6MM **Privately Held**
WEB: www.vlgoedecke.com
SIC: 3531 Construction machinery
PA: Vernon L. Goedecke Company, Inc.
812 E Taylor Ave
Saint Louis MO 63147
314 652-1810

(G-4519)
VERSAFLEX INC (PA)
686 S Adams St (66105-1403)
P.O. Box 32226 MO (64171-5226)
PHONE..................................913 321-9000
David Cerchie, *President*
Matt Spiller, *Regional Mgr*
Jeff Downing, *Vice Pres*
Joe Haydu, *Vice Pres*
Art Weiss, *Vice Pres*
▲ **EMP:** 40
SQ FT: 30,000
SALES (est): 15.3MM **Privately Held**
SIC: 2851 Polyurethane coatings

(G-4520)
VICTORY HILL RETIREMENT CMNTY
1900 N 70th St Ofc (66102-1094)
PHONE..................................913 299-1166
Jan Thayer, *President*
Bruce Irving, *Manager*
Lynn Dodge, *Exec Dir*
EMP: 23
SALES (est): 1.3MM **Privately Held**
SIC: 8051 Skilled nursing care facilities

(G-4521)
VISTA MANUFACTURING COMPANY
1307 Central Ave (66102-5098)
PHONE..................................913 342-4939
Andy Gredell, *President*

Rebecca Gredell, *President*
◆ **EMP:** 25
SQ FT: 27,000
SALES: 2.4MM **Privately Held**
WEB: www.vista-mfg.com
SIC: 3444 3672 Sheet metal specialties, not stamped; printed circuit boards

(G-4522)
VITAL SIGN CENTER
3410 Gibbs Rd (66106-3808)
PHONE....................913 262-4447
Betty McGill, *Owner*
EMP: 5
SALES: 200K **Privately Held**
SIC: 3993 Signs & advertising specialties

(G-4523)
VVF INTERVEST LLC (HQ)
1705 Kansas Ave (66105-1121)
PHONE....................913 281-7444
Kurussh Amrolia, *President*
Curt Konrardy, *Vice Pres*
Phil Ishmael, *Controller*
Rebecca Belmer, *Sales Staff*
Hector Terriquez, *Manager*
▲ **EMP:** 10
SQ FT: 900,000
SALES (est): 2.8MM **Privately Held**
SIC: 2841 Detergents, synthetic organic or inorganic alkaline

(G-4524)
VVF KANSAS LLC
1705 Kansas Ave (66105-1121)
PHONE....................913 281-7444
Brad Davison, *Warehouse Mgr*
Sharon Horvat, *Engineer*
Steven Byrd, *Sales Staff*
Kurussh Amrolia, *Mng Member*
Curt Konrardy, *Mng Member*
▲ **EMP:** 34
SQ FT: 900,000
SALES (est): 10.2MM **Privately Held**
SIC: 2841 Detergents, synthetic organic or inorganic alkaline

(G-4525)
VVF KANSAS SERVICES LLC
1705 Kansas Ave (66105-1121)
PHONE....................913 529-2292
Matthew King, *Engineer*
Kurussh Amrolia,
Curt Konrardy,
▲ **EMP:** 165
SALES (est): 54.2MM **Privately Held**
SIC: 2841 Soap & other detergents
PA: V V F Limited
Plot No-109, Opp Sion Fort Garden,
Mumbai MH 40002

(G-4526)
W CARTER & ASSOC GLAZING LLC
Also Called: W Carter and Glass
1938 Foxridge Dr (66106-4710)
PHONE....................913 543-2600
William P Carter, *President*
Charlene C Carter, *Mng Member*
EMP: 20
SQ FT: 9,000
SALES: 1.1MM **Privately Held**
SIC: 1793 Glass & glazing work

(G-4527)
WABASH NATIONAL CORPORATION
539 S 10th St (66105-1201)
PHONE....................913 621-7298
EMP: 102
SALES (corp-wide): 2.2B **Publicly Held**
SIC: 3715 Truck trailers
PA: Wabash National Corporation
1000 Sagamore Pkwy S
Lafayette IN 47905
765 771-5300

(G-4528)
WAGNER INTERIOR SYSTEMS INC
3411 Brinkerhoff Rd (66115-1242)
PHONE....................913 647-6622
Mick Wagner, *President*
EMP: 40
SALES (est): 3.7MM **Privately Held**
SIC: 1742 Solar reflecting insulation film

(G-4529)
WAGNER INTR SUP KANS CY INC (PA)
3411 Brinkerhoff Rd (66115-1242)
PHONE....................913 647-6622
Vincent Wagner Jr, *President*
Joseph Wagner, *Vice Pres*
EMP: 17
SQ FT: 26,000
SALES (est): 21.8MM **Privately Held**
SIC: 5039 Ceiling systems & products

(G-4530)
WALLIS OIL COMPANY
Also Called: Wallis Lubricant
445 Sunshine Rd (66115-1235)
PHONE....................913 621-6521
Joe Fears, *Branch Mgr*
EMP: 15
SALES (corp-wide): 266MM **Privately Held**
WEB: www.mail.wallisco.com
SIC: 5172 5984 Lubricating oils & greases; liquefied petroleum gas dealers
PA: Wallis Oil Company
106 E Washington St
Cuba MO 65453
573 885-2277

(G-4531)
WASTE MANAGEMENT OF KANSAS
2601 Midwest Dr (66111-8801)
PHONE....................913 631-3300
Jim Fish, *Branch Mgr*
EMP: 99
SALES (corp-wide): 14.9B **Publicly Held**
SIC: 4953 Refuse systems
HQ: Waste Management Of Kansas, Inc
3611 Nw 16th St
Topeka KS 66618
785 233-3541

(G-4532)
WATER DST NO1 JHNSON CNTY KANS
Also Called: Hansen Water Treatment Plant
7601 Holliday Dr (66106-4945)
PHONE....................913 895-5800
Tom Schrempp, *Branch Mgr*
EMP: 100
SALES (corp-wide): 117.1MM **Privately Held**
WEB: www.waterone.com
SIC: 4941 Water supply
PA: Water District No1 Of Johnson County Kansas
10747 Renner Blvd
Lenexa KS 66219
913 895-5500

(G-4533)
WELBORN ANIMAL HOSPITAL
Also Called: Welborn Pet Hospital
7860 Washington Ave (66112-2193)
PHONE....................913 334-6770
Curtis Bock, *Owner*
James Swanson, *Co-Owner*
Lindsay Bray, *Office Mgr*
EMP: 30
SQ FT: 2,500
SALES (est): 1MM **Privately Held**
WEB: www.welbornpet.com
SIC: 0741 0742 Animal hospital services, livestock; animal hospital services, pets & other animal specialties

(G-4534)
WESCORP LTD (PA)
901 S 7th St (66105-2005)
PHONE....................913 281-1833
Daniel West, *President*
Debra West, *Vice Pres*
EMP: 19
SQ FT: 32,000
SALES (est): 2.3MM **Privately Held**
SIC: 5013 Automotive supplies & parts

(G-4535)
WESTERN ENTERPRISE INC
956 Osage Ave (66105-1848)
PHONE....................913 342-0505
Ronald Stremming, *President*
EMP: 16
SALES (est): 1.7MM **Privately Held**
SIC: 1711 Plumbing contractors

(G-4536)
WESTERN ROOFING CO SERVICES
2820 Roe Ln Ste O (66103-1560)
PHONE....................816 931-1075
Marcus B Manson, *President*
Jane Parsons, *Corp Secy*
Lauren Goering, *Vice Pres*
EMP: 30 **EST:** 1893
SALES (est): 3.7MM **Privately Held**
SIC: 1761 Roofing contractor

(G-4537)
WESTERN STATES FIRE PROTECTION
Also Called: National Fire Suppression
501 Sunshine Rd (66115-1239)
PHONE....................913 321-9208
Joe Depriest, *Branch Mgr*
EMP: 65
SQ FT: 40,000 **Privately Held**
SIC: 1711 Fire sprinkler system installation
HQ: Western States Fire Protection Company Inc
7026 S Tucson Way
Centennial CO 80112
303 792-0022

(G-4538)
WESTERN TRAILER SERVICE INC
3550 Fairbanks Ave (66106-1202)
PHONE....................913 281-2226
Scott Wilde, *President*
Debra Green, *Office Mgr*
EMP: 24 **EST:** 1970
SQ FT: 9,000
SALES: 2MM **Privately Held**
SIC: 7539 5012 Trailer repair; trailers for trucks, new & used

(G-4539)
WESTPRO CONSTRUCTION SOLUTIONS (PA)
2850 Fairfax Trfy (66115-1316)
PHONE....................816 561-7667
A L Bontrager, *President*
Tim Parks, *Exec VP*
EMP: 12
SQ FT: 2,000
SALES (est): 12.7MM **Privately Held**
WEB: www.westernfireproofing.com
SIC: 1761 Roofing, siding & sheet metal work

(G-4540)
WESTROCK CP LLC
5050 Kansas Ave (66106-1135)
PHONE....................816 746-0403
Joe Lockwood, *Manager*
EMP: 151
SALES (corp-wide): 18.2B **Publicly Held**
WEB: www.smurfit-stone.com
SIC: 2653 Boxes, corrugated: made from purchased materials
HQ: Westrock Cp, Llc
1000 Abernathy Rd
Atlanta GA 30328

(G-4541)
WHITEWAY INC
Also Called: Excel Linen Supply
501 Funston Rd (66115-1215)
PHONE....................816 842-6565
Joseph F Brancato, *President*
Dominick S Brancato, *Vice Pres*
Anthony Brancato, *Shareholder*
Joseph V Brancato, *Shareholder*
EMP: 90
SQ FT: 34,000
SALES (est): 3.1MM **Privately Held**
WEB: www.excellinen.com
SIC: 7213 Uniform supply

(G-4542)
WHOLESALE BATTERIES INC (PA)
605 Kansas Ave (66105-1311)
PHONE....................913 342-0113
Randy Powell, *President*
Steve Anderson, *General Mgr*
Rich Richeson, *Vice Pres*
Stephen Anderson, *Treasurer*
Bob Worthley, *Sales Staff*
▲ **EMP:** 15 **EST:** 1977
SQ FT: 14,000
SALES (est): 7MM **Privately Held**
WEB: www.wholesalebatteries.net
SIC: 5013 5531 Automotive batteries; batteries, automotive & truck

(G-4543)
WHOLESALE SHEET METAL INC (PA)
800 Southwest Blvd (66103-1926)
P.O. Box 3153 (66103-0153)
PHONE....................913 432-7100
Pat Chilen, *President*
EMP: 107
SQ FT: 60,000
SALES (est): 35.1MM **Privately Held**
WEB: www.wsmkc.com
SIC: 5051 3444 Sheets, metal; sheet metalwork

(G-4544)
WILLIAMS-CARVER COMPANY INC
4001 Mission Rd (66103-2750)
PHONE....................913 236-4949
Richard Carver, *President*
Bradley Carver, *President*
Lee Messinger, *Sales Staff*
Steven Carver, *Sales Executive*
Gwen Carver, *Admin Sec*
EMP: 20 **EST:** 1955
SQ FT: 8,000
SALES: 8.5MM **Privately Held**
WEB: www.williamscarver.com
SIC: 1711 3556 Refrigeration contractor; food products machinery

(G-4545)
WILLIAMSON & CUBBISON
Also Called: Jeserich, Gerald N
748 Ann Ave (66101-3014)
PHONE....................913 371-1930
M Warren McCamish, *Owner*
Timothy P Mc Carthy, *Partner*
John Peterson, *Co-Owner*
Phillip P Ashley,
David W Boal,
EMP: 16 **EST:** 1930
SQ FT: 1,500
SALES (est): 1.2MM **Privately Held**
WEB: www.jpci.com
SIC: 8111 General practice attorney, lawyer

(G-4546)
WILSON IELAH
Also Called: D&M Construction
2503 N 91st St (66109-1906)
PHONE....................913 954-9798
Ielah C Wilson, *Owner*
EMP: 15
SALES (est): 569.9K **Privately Held**
SIC: 1761 Roofing, siding & sheet metal work

(G-4547)
WINAVIE LLC
Also Called: O'Neal Electric Service
3073 Merriam Ln (66106-4613)
PHONE....................913 789-8169
Rebecca Mock, *Manager*
Winnie Root,
EMP: 50
SALES (est): 3.7MM **Privately Held**
WEB: www.oeskc.com
SIC: 1731 Electrical work

(G-4548)
WOLSKI & ASSOCIATES
753 State Ave Ste 370 (66101-2518)
PHONE....................913 281-3233
Susan L Wolski, *CEO*
EMP: 10
SALES: 560K **Privately Held**
WEB: www.kckcpa.com
SIC: 8721 Certified public accountant

(G-4549)
WOOD VIEW APARTMENTS LLC
3124 Woodview Ridge Dr (66103-3601)
PHONE....................913 262-8733

Kristen Wendel, *Manager*
EMP: 10
SQ FT: 5,000 **Privately Held**
SIC: 6513 Apartment building operators
PA: Wood View Apartments Llc
6375 Riverside Dr Ste 220
Dublin OH

(G-4550)
WYANDOT CENTER FOR COMMUNITY B (PA)
757 Armstrong Ave (66101-2701)
PHONE..................................913 233-3300
Cathryn Carter, *Train & Dev Mgr*
Linnea Cullumber, *Train & Dev Mgr*
Christine Swenson, *Manager*
Tonja Speer, *Exec Dir*
Erin Pullen, *Director*
EMP: 40
SQ FT: 18,000
SALES: 11.1MM **Privately Held**
SIC: 8093 Mental health clinic, outpatient

(G-4551)
WYANDOT INC
757 Armstrong Ave (66101-2701)
PHONE..................................913 233-3300
Mayra Flores, *Manager*
EMP: 19
SALES: 4.6MM **Privately Held**
SIC: 8093 Mental health clinic, outpatient

(G-4552)
WYANDOTTE CENTRAL DIALYSIS LLC
3737 State Ave (66102-3830)
PHONE..................................913 233-0536
Lauren Hosford, *President*
Judy Piper, *Principal*
EMP: 12
SALES: 5.9MM **Publicly Held**
WEB: www.davita.com
SIC: 8092 Kidney dialysis centers
PA: Davita Inc.
2000 16th St
Denver CO 80202

(G-4553)
WYANDOTTE COUNTY SPORTS ASSN
10100 Leavenworth Rd (66109-3010)
P.O. Box 12231 (66112-0231)
PHONE..................................913 299-9197
Brenda Bennett, *Manager*
EMP: 12
SQ FT: 10,000
SALES: 205.6K **Privately Held**
WEB: www.wycosports.com
SIC: 7999 Recreation center

(G-4554)
WYANDTTE CNTY UNFIED GVERNMENT
Also Called: Public Works Dept
5033 State Ave (66102-3491)
PHONE..................................913 573-8300
Mike Tobin, *Branch Mgr*
EMP: 30 **Privately Held**
SIC: 1611 Highway & street maintenance
PA: Unified Government Of Wyandotte County
701 N 7th St
Kansas City KS 66101
913 573-5000

(G-4555)
WYANDTTE CNTY UNFIED GVERNMENT
Also Called: K C Kansas Housing Authority
1124 N 9th St (66101-2120)
PHONE..................................913 281-3300
Thomas Stibal, *Principal*
EMP: 120 **Privately Held**
SIC: 7349 Building maintenance services
PA: Unified Government Of Wyandotte County
701 N 7th St
Kansas City KS 66101
913 573-5000

(G-4556)
WYANDTTE CNTY UNFIED GVERNMENT
Also Called: Engineering Dept
701 N 7th St (66101-3035)
PHONE..................................913 573-5700
Fred Backus, *Administration*
EMP: 19 **Privately Held**
SIC: 8711 Engineering services
PA: Unified Government Of Wyandotte County
701 N 7th St
Kansas City KS 66101
913 573-5000

(G-4557)
WYANDTTE OCCPATIONAL HLTH SVCS
Also Called: Ku Medical Occupational Health
4810 State Ave (66102-1748)
PHONE..................................913 945-9740
Sherry Dorsam, *Administration*
▲ **EMP:** 12
SALES (est): 525.7K **Privately Held**
WEB: www.corporatehealthpartners.com
SIC: 8011 Occupational & industrial specialist, physician/surgeon

(G-4558)
WYNNEWOOD REFINING COMPANY LLC
10 E Cambridge Circle Dr (66103-1334)
PHONE..................................913 982-0500
John J Lipinski, *President*
John R Walter, *Senior VP*
Susan M Ball, *CFO*
Martin J Power, *Ch Credit Ofcr*
EMP: 80
SALES (est): 11.8MM **Publicly Held**
SIC: 2911 Petroleum refining
HQ: Cvr Refining, Llc
2277 Plaza Dr Ste 500
Sugar Land TX 77479
281 207-3200

(G-4559)
XENOTECH LLC
Also Called: Sekisui-Xenotech
1101 W Cambridge Cir Dr (66103-1311)
PHONE..................................913 438-7450
Nicholas Hatfield, *Production*
Katherine Wellemeyer, *Production*
Joshua Swift, *QC Mgr*
Steve Berryman, *Research*
Sadaff Ejaz, *Research*
EMP: 110
SQ FT: 20,000
SALES (est): 27.7MM **Privately Held**
WEB: www.xenotechllc.com
SIC: 2836 8733 Biological products, except diagnostic; biotechnical research, noncommercial
HQ: Sekisui America Corporation
333 Meadowlands Pkwy
Secaucus NJ 07094
201 423-7960

(G-4560)
XPO LOGISTICS FREIGHT INC
234 E Donovan Rd (66115-1416)
PHONE..................................913 281-3535
Mike Pajak, *Sales Staff*
Paul Moneymaker, *Branch Mgr*
EMP: 62
SALES (corp-wide): 17.2B **Publicly Held**
WEB: www.con-way.com
SIC: 4213 Contract haulers
HQ: Xpo Logistics Freight, Inc.
2211 Old Earhart Rd # 100
Ann Arbor MI 48105
800 755-2728

(G-4561)
XPO STACKTRAIN LLC
2663 S 88th St (66111-1767)
PHONE..................................913 422-6400
Francis Fatool, *General Mgr*
EMP: 10
SALES (corp-wide): 17.2B **Publicly Held**
WEB: www.pacerstack.com
SIC: 4731 Freight transportation arrangement
HQ: Xpo Stacktrain, Llc
5165 Emerald Pkwy
Dublin OH 43017
925 887-1400

(G-4562)
YACO PRODUCTIONS
2900 S 63rd St (66106-5439)
PHONE..................................913 669-7380
Vashti Goracke, *Principal*
EMP: 10
SALES (est): 147.8K **Privately Held**
SIC: 7822 Motion picture & tape distribution

(G-4563)
YARCO COMPANY INC
Also Called: Mt. Carmel Apartments
1130 Troup Ave (66104-5883)
PHONE..................................913 225-8733
EMP: 177
SALES (corp-wide): 129.3MM **Privately Held**
SIC: 6531 Real Estate Agent/Manager
PA: Yarco Company, Inc.
7920 Ward Pkwy
Kansas City MO 64114
816 561-4240

(G-4564)
YOUNG MENS CHRISTIAN ASSOCIA (PA)
Also Called: YMCA of Greater Kansas City
900 N 8th St (66101-2707)
PHONE..................................913 321-9622
David Wallace, *Director*
EMP: 22
SQ FT: 500,000
SALES (est): 880.8K **Privately Held**
SIC: 7991 Physical fitness facilities

(G-4565)
YRC INC
Also Called: Roadway Express
233 S 42nd St (66106-1001)
PHONE..................................913 696-6100
Brain Krystensen, *Sales/Mktg Mgr*
Julie Berry, *Executive*
EMP: 300
SALES (corp-wide): 5B **Publicly Held**
WEB: www.roadway.com
SIC: 4213 4212 Contract haulers; local trucking, without storage
HQ: Yrc Inc.
10990 Roe Ave
Overland Park KS 66211
913 696-6100

Kechi
Sedgwick County

(G-4566)
CILLESSEN EQUIPMENT CO LLC
2300 E Tigua St (67067-8920)
P.O. Box 9 (67067-0009)
PHONE..................................316 682-2400
Robert Cillessen,
Paula Cillessen,
EMP: 14
SALES (est): 3.3MM **Privately Held**
SIC: 7353 Heavy construction equipment rental

(G-4567)
F & H ABATEMENT SERVICES INC
5003 E 61st St N (67067-9001)
P.O. Box 250 (67067-0250)
PHONE..................................316 264-2208
John R Pfister, *President*
Mark Rossillon, *Vice Pres*
Tom Patten, *Admin Sec*
Mike Emmett, *Training Spec*
EMP: 200
SQ FT: 15,000
SALES (est): 19.5MM **Privately Held**
WEB: www.f-hcompanies.com
SIC: 1742 1799 Insulation, buildings; asbestos removal & encapsulation

(G-4568)
FH COMPANIES INC
5003 E 61st St N (67067-9001)
P.O. Box 250 (67067-0250)
PHONE..................................316 264-2208
John R Pfister, *President*
Mark Rossillon, *Vice Pres*
Thomas F Patten, *Treasurer*
Richard Yust, *Controller*
EMP: 130
SQ FT: 10,000
SALES (est): 11.7MM **Privately Held**
SIC: 1742 1791 Insulation, buildings; plaster & drywall work; acoustical & insulation work; exterior wall system installation

(G-4569)
HARMAN HUFFMAN CNSTR GROUP INC (PA)
5615 Huffman Dr (67067-9054)
PHONE..................................316 744-2081
Gregory L Harman, *President*
Paul E Huffman, *Vice Pres*
Paul Huffman, *Vice Pres*
Vickie Wiggins, *Admin Asst*
Patty Wells, *Assistant*
EMP: 38
SQ FT: 2,400
SALES (est): 13.5MM **Privately Held**
SIC: 1542 Commercial & office building, new construction; commercial & office buildings, renovation & repair; school building construction

(G-4570)
K & F DISTRIBUTORS INC
1303 E Kechi Rd Ste C (67067-9072)
PHONE..................................316 213-2030
Robyn Heitfield, *Principal*
EMP: 10
SALES (est): 1.1MM **Privately Held**
SIC: 5199 Nondurable goods

(G-4571)
KARG ART GLASS
111 N Oliver St (67067-9059)
PHONE..................................316 744-2442
Patricia Karg, *Owner*
Rollin Karg, *Partner*
▲ **EMP:** 20
SQ FT: 3,300
SALES (est): 2.3MM **Privately Held**
WEB: www.rkarg.com
SIC: 3229 Glassware, art or decorative

(G-4572)
METER ENGINEERS INC
1600 E Tigua St (67067-8922)
P.O. Box 129 (67067-0129)
PHONE..................................316 721-4214
William R Young Jr, *President*
Deb Jacobs, *General Mgr*
Rita K Young, *Treasurer*
John Gradziel, *Manager*
EMP: 10
SQ FT: 7,200
SALES (est): 6.6MM **Privately Held**
WEB: www.meterengineers.com
SIC: 5063 Electrical apparatus & equipment

(G-4573)
NEALS FOUNDATIONS INC
5515 Huffman Dr (67067-9003)
P.O. Box 396 (67067-0396)
PHONE..................................316 744-0064
Steve Neal, *President*
EMP: 45
SQ FT: 4,000
SALES (est): 3.6MM **Privately Held**
SIC: 1522 Residential construction

Kensington
Smith County

(G-4574)
DESERET HEALTH GROUP
Also Called: Deseret Hlth Rhab At Knsington
613 N Main St (66951-8000)
PHONE..................................785 476-2623
Jon Robertson, *Branch Mgr*
EMP: 18

▲ = Import ▼=Export
◆ =Import/Export

SALES (est): 697.1K **Privately Held**
SIC: 8051 Skilled nursing care facilities
PA: Deseret Health Group
190 S Main St
Bountiful UT 84010

(G-4575)
FERGUSON ZY FARMS INC
1062 120 Rd (66951-5510)
PHONE..................................785 476-2297
Roy Ferguson, *President*
Desiree Ferguson, *Principal*
EMP: 12
SALES (est): 960K **Privately Held**
SIC: 0191 General farms, primarily crop

(G-4576)
K & D FERGUSON PARTNERSHIP
2051 120 Rd (66951-6028)
PHONE..................................785 476-2657
Kerry Lynn Ferguson, *Partner*
EMP: 15
SALES (est): 288.8K **Privately Held**
SIC: 8748 Agricultural consultant

(G-4577)
KENSINGTON LOCKERS INC
218 W Highway 36 (66951-9792)
PHONE..................................785 476-2834
Wayne Beckman, *President*
Jolene Beckman, *Corp Secy*
EMP: 15
SQ FT: 6,000
SALES (est): 870K **Privately Held**
SIC: 2011 4222 Meat packing plants; storage, frozen or refrigerated goods

(G-4578)
KENSINGTON SENIOR CMNTY CTR
102 E Pne (66951)
P.O. Box 164 (66951-0164)
PHONE..................................785 476-2224
Carman Rice, *President*
Darlene Miller, *Vice Pres*
Lucinda Migalski, *Treasurer*
EMP: 15
SALES (est): 438.9K **Privately Held**
SIC: 8322 Senior citizens' center or association

(G-4579)
PRO AG MARKETING
228 S Main St (66951-9785)
PHONE..................................785 476-2211
Dennis Graf, *President*
EMP: 14
SALES (est): 1.5MM **Privately Held**
SIC: 8742 Marketing consulting services

(G-4580)
SAINT FRANCIS CMNTY SVCS INC
129 S Main St (66951-9804)
PHONE..................................785 476-3234
Janine Howell, *Manager*
EMP: 87
SALES (corp-wide): 108.2MM **Privately Held**
SIC: 8999 Artists & artists' studios
PA: Saint Francis Community Services, Inc.
509 E Elm St
Salina KS 67401
785 825-0541

Kincaid
Anderson County

(G-4581)
STINNETT TIMBERS LLC
30213 Se Highway 31 (66039-4006)
PHONE..................................620 363-4757
Vicki Stinnett,
EMP: 7
SQ FT: 15,000
SALES (est): 961.2K **Privately Held**
SIC: 2448 Wood pallets & skids

Kingman
Kingman County

(G-4582)
AP ROOFING SPECIALTY CODINGS
602 N Defonte St (67068-1016)
PHONE..................................620 532-1076
Aaron Parsons, *Owner*
EMP: 15
SALES (est): 100.8K **Privately Held**
SIC: 1721 7319 Residential painting; distribution of advertising material or sample services

(G-4583)
BHAKTA LLC
Also Called: Copa Motel
1113 E Us Highway 54 (67068-1820)
PHONE..................................620 532-3118
Ronald Ranck, *Manager*
EMP: 15
SALES (est): 617.5K
SALES (corp-wide): 777.6K **Privately Held**
WEB: www.southernrailleasing.com
SIC: 7011 Motels
PA: Bhakta Llc
300 E Highway 24
Moberly MO 65270
660 263-8862

(G-4584)
C5 MANUFACTURING LLC
1005 E Us Highway 54 (67068-1818)
PHONE..................................620 532-3675
EMP: 20
SALES (est): 2.5MM **Privately Held**
SIC: 2879 Insecticides, agricultural or household

(G-4585)
CANNONBALL ENGINEERING LLC (PA)
1005 E Us Highway 54 (67068-1818)
P.O. Box 289 (67068-0289)
PHONE..................................620 532-3675
Terry Schrag, *Owner*
Jeff Neighbors, *Principal*
Andrew Schrag, *Principal*
Debora Schrag,
▲ **EMP**: 19
SQ FT: 20,000
SALES (est): 4.1MM **Privately Held**
WEB: www.cannonballengineering.com
SIC: 3523 Planting, haying, harvesting & processing machinery

(G-4586)
CITIZENS BANK OF KANSAS (HQ)
300 N Main St (67068-1303)
P.O. Box 436 (67068-0436)
PHONE..................................620 532-5162
Jane Deterding, *Ch of Bd*
Mark Keeny, *President*
Brian Wilborn, *Vice Pres*
Kelly Woods, *Loan Officer*
Jacey Bedore, *Manager*
EMP: 22 **EST**: 1886
SQ FT: 15,000
SALES: 11.5MM **Privately Held**
SIC: 6022 State commercial banks

(G-4587)
CONCRETE ENTERPRISES INC
319 E Sherman St (67068)
PHONE..................................620 532-1165
Walter Wuff, *President*
EMP: 22
SALES (corp-wide): 147MM **Publicly Held**
SIC: 3273 Ready-mixed concrete
HQ: Concrete Enterprises, Inc.
2430 E 1st Ave
Hutchinson KS 67501
620 662-1219

(G-4588)
COUNTY OF KINGMAN
Also Called: Kingman County Highway Dept
823 E A Ave (67068-1725)
P.O. Box 474 (67068-0474)
PHONE..................................620 532-5241
Charles Arensdorf, *Branch Mgr*
EMP: 16 **Privately Held**
SIC: 4785 Highway bridge operation
PA: County Of Kingman
130 N Spruce St
Kingman KS 67068
620 532-2521

(G-4589)
EVERGY KANSAS CENTRAL INC
990 Sw 70 Ave (67068-8159)
PHONE..................................620 532-2782
Chris Mader, *Manager*
EMP: 11
SALES (corp-wide): 4.2B **Publicly Held**
SIC: 4911 Distribution, electric power
HQ: Evergy Kansas Central, Inc.
818 S Kansas Ave
Topeka KS 66612
785 575-6300

(G-4590)
FABPRO ORIENTED POLYMERS LLC
100 Fabpro Way (67068-1701)
PHONE..................................620 532-5141
EMP: 18
SALES (est): 3.2MM **Privately Held**
SIC: 3089 Plastic processing

(G-4591)
GREAT LAKES POLYMER TECH LLC (PA)
Also Called: Glpt
701 E A Ave (67068-1723)
P.O. Box 517 (67068-0517)
PHONE..................................620 532-5141
Mark Eaton, *President*
Dennis Gyolai, *CFO*
Bikash Gupta, *Financial Analy*
▲ **EMP**: 245
SALES (est): 82.6MM **Privately Held**
SIC: 2298 Twine, cord & cordage

(G-4592)
GREAT LAKES POLYMER TECH LLC
100 Fabpro Way (67068-1701)
PHONE..................................507 320-7000
Tim Mason, *Mng Member*
EMP: 175
SALES (est): 4.7MM
SALES (corp-wide): 82.6MM **Privately Held**
SIC: 2298 Cordage & twine
PA: Great Lakes Polymer Technologies Llc
701 E A Ave
Kingman KS 67068
620 532-5141

(G-4593)
GREAT LAKES POLYMER TECH LLC
100 Fabpro Way (67068-1701)
P.O. Box 517 (67068-0517)
PHONE..................................208 324-2120
Dwight Osborn, *Branch Mgr*
EMP: 35
SALES (corp-wide): 82.6MM **Privately Held**
WEB: www.bridoncordage.com
SIC: 2298 5085 Binder & baler twine; cordage
PA: Great Lakes Polymer Technologies Llc
701 E A Ave
Kingman KS 67068
620 532-5141

(G-4594)
GREAT LKES PLYMERS HLDNGS CORP (HQ)
Also Called: Great Lakes Polymer Tech
100 Fabpro Way (67068-1701)
PHONE..................................507 320-7000
Mark Eaton, *President*
Dennis Gyolai, *CFO*
EMP: 17 **EST**: 2014
SALES (est): 3.2MM
SALES (corp-wide): 2.1MM **Privately Held**
SIC: 2298 Hard fiber cordage & twine
PA: Great Lakes Steel Holdings Corporation
1010 Clarke Rd
London ON N5V 3
519 455-0770

(G-4595)
HORIZONS MENTAL HEALTH CTR INC
760 W D Ave Ste 1 (67068-1211)
PHONE..................................620 532-3895
Michael Garrett, *Administration*
EMP: 12
SALES (corp-wide): 13.1MM **Privately Held**
SIC: 8093 8322 8069 8049 Mental health clinic, outpatient; family counseling services; drug addiction rehabilitation hospital; clinical psychologist
PA: Horizons Mental Health Center, Inc.
1600 N Lorraine St # 202
Hutchinson KS 67501
620 663-7595

(G-4596)
KANZA BANK (PA)
151 N Main St (67068-1333)
P.O. Box 313 (67068-0313)
PHONE..................................620 532-5821
John Boyer IV, *Ch of Bd*
Clark E Boyer, *President*
Vicky Knapic, *President*
Todd Loescher, *Senior VP*
Jason Bollman, *Assistant VP*
EMP: 27 **EST**: 1905
SQ FT: 12,000
SALES: 9.6MM **Privately Held**
SIC: 6022 State trust companies accepting deposits, commercial

(G-4597)
KING BANCSHARES INC (PA)
300 N Main St (67068-1303)
PHONE..................................620 532-5162
Jane Deterding, *Ch of Bd*
Theodore J Mc Vay, *Corp Secy*
EMP: 20
SALES (est): 11.5MM **Privately Held**
WEB: www.citizensbankofkansas.com
SIC: 6022 State commercial banks

(G-4598)
KINGMAN CNTY ECNMIC DEV CNCIL
324 N Main St (67068-1303)
P.O. Box 28 (67068-0028)
PHONE..................................620 532-3694
Daniel Shea, *CEO*
EMP: 521
SALES: 104K **Privately Held**
SIC: 8732 7389 Economic research; brokers, business: buying & selling business enterprises

(G-4599)
KINGMAN COUNTY RETIREMENT ASSN
Also Called: WHEATLANDS HEALTH CARE CENTER,
750 W Washington Ave (67068-2000)
PHONE..................................620 532-5801
Nikki Schmitz, *Nursing Dir*
Sharon Rinke, *Administration*
EMP: 73
SQ FT: 200
SALES: 3.8MM **Privately Held**
SIC: 8051 8052 Convalescent home with continuous nursing care; intermediate care facilities

(G-4600)
KINGMAN DRUG INC (PA)
Also Called: Kingman Pharmacy
211 N Main St (67068-1396)
PHONE..................................620 532-5113
Merlin McFarland, *President*
John Nixon, *Broker*
Greg Heikes, *Pharmacist*
EMP: 12 **EST**: 1937
SQ FT: 2,500

SALES (est): 3.1MM **Privately Held**
SIC: 5912 7352 5947 Drug stores; invalid supplies rental; gift shop

(G-4601)
KINGMAN EMERGENCY MEDICAL SVCS
332 N Main St (67068-1303)
PHONE..................................620 532-5624
Zach Bieghler, *Director*
EMP: 30
SALES (est): 770K **Privately Held**
SIC: 4119 Ambulance service

(G-4602)
KINGMAN LEADER COURIER
140 N Main St (67068-1301)
P.O. Box 353 (67068-0353)
PHONE..................................620 532-3151
Robert L McQuin, *Owner*
Beverly McQuin, *Co-Owner*
EMP: 7 **EST:** 1947
SQ FT: 7,000
SALES (est): 385.7K **Privately Held**
SIC: 2711 5044 Commercial printing & newspaper publishing combined; office equipment

(G-4603)
KLAVER CONSTRUCTION CO INC
701 E Ave D (67068)
P.O. Box 9163, Wichita (67277-0163)
PHONE..................................620 532-3183
James Klaver, *President*
Howard Sherwood, *Vice Pres*
Tim Thimesch, *Manager*
Roy Elam, *IT/INT Sup*
EMP: 100
SQ FT: 10,000
SALES: 11MM
SALES (corp-wide): 2MM **Privately Held**
SIC: 1622 1771 Bridge construction; concrete work
PA: Klaver Construction Products Llc
245 E Sherman Ave
Kingman KS 67068
620 532-3661

(G-4604)
KLAVER CONSTRUCTION PDTS LLC (PA)
Also Called: K C P
245 E Sherman Ave (67068-1906)
PHONE..................................620 532-3661
Josh Smith, *Sales Executive*
Bill Klaver,
Mark Arensdorf,
EMP: 20
SALES: 2MM **Privately Held**
SIC: 3273 Ready-mixed concrete

(G-4605)
LDB INC
1040 E Us Highway 54 (67068-1817)
P.O. Box 247 (67068-0247)
PHONE..................................620 532-2236
Leland D Brown, *President*
Jeffery L Brown, *Corp Secy*
EMP: 7
SQ FT: 20,000
SALES: 300K **Privately Held**
SIC: 3523 Soil preparation machinery, except turf & grounds

(G-4606)
MESSENGER PETROLEUM INC
525 S Main St (67068-1968)
PHONE..................................620 532-5400
Jon F Messenger, *President*
Gayla Messenger, *Vice Pres*
EMP: 6
SALES (est): 360K **Privately Held**
WEB: www.messengerpetroleum.com
SIC: 8711 1311 Petroleum, mining & chemical engineers; crude petroleum & natural gas production

(G-4607)
MIZE & CO INC
Also Called: Mize Wire Products
2020 N Koch Industrial St (67068-8088)
P.O. Box 516 (67068-0516)
PHONE..................................620 532-3191
Max Mize, *President*
Patrick Robinson, *President*
▲ **EMP:** 23 **EST:** 1936
SQ FT: 57,000
SALES (est): 6MM **Privately Held**
WEB: www.mizeandcompany.com
SIC: 3714 5085 3643 3357 Automotive wiring harness sets; industrial fittings; current-carrying wiring devices; nonferrous wiredrawing & insulating

(G-4608)
NEVILLE WELDING INC
Also Called: Neville Cstm Bilt Smi-Trailers
5581 Sw 50 St (67068-8695)
PHONE..................................620 532-3487
Richard Neville, *President*
Marvin Neville, *Vice Pres*
Jill Neville, *Treasurer*
Janice Neville, *Admin Sec*
▲ **EMP:** 45
SQ FT: 49,000
SALES (est): 10.8MM **Privately Held**
WEB: www.nevillebuilt.com
SIC: 3523 7692 Trailers & wagons, farm; haying machines: mowers, rakes, stackers, etc.; welding repair

(G-4609)
PARSONS AARON PAINTING LLC
1113 S High St (67068-8607)
PHONE..................................620 532-1076
Aaron Parsons, *Owner*
Ericca Parson, *Co-Owner*
EMP: 7
SALES (est): 413.2K **Privately Held**
SIC: 1721 2952 Exterior residential painting contractor; roofing materials

(G-4610)
PLP INC
Also Called: John Deere Authorized Dealer
1202 E Us Highway 54 (67068-1821)
PHONE..................................620 532-3106
Gerard K Seiler, *Branch Mgr*
EMP: 32
SALES (corp-wide): 66.9MM **Privately Held**
SIC: 5999 5261 5083 Feed & farm supply; lawnmowers & tractors; tractors, agricultural
PA: Plp, Inc
811 E 30th Ave Ste F
Hutchinson KS 67502
620 664-5860

(G-4611)
POLYMER GROUP INC
Also Called: P G I Oriented Polymer Div
701 E A Ave (67068-1723)
P.O. Box 517 (67068-0517)
PHONE..................................620 532-5141
Jean Lamb, *Branch Mgr*
EMP: 120 **Publicly Held**
WEB: www.polymergroupinc.com
SIC: 2297 2296 Nonwoven fabrics; tire cord & fabrics
HQ: Avintiv Specialty Materials Inc.
9335 Harris Corners Pkwy
Charlotte NC 28269

(G-4612)
POLYMER GROUP INC
Also Called: P G I Oriented Polymers Div
100 Fabpro Way (67068-1701)
P.O. Box 517 (67068-0517)
PHONE..................................620 532-4000
Ron Mechling, *Vice Pres*
Ed Evans, *Manager*
Linda Roark, *Manager*
Catherine Saunders, *Manager*
EMP: 200 **Publicly Held**
WEB: www.polymergroupinc.com
SIC: 2282 2298 Manmade & synthetic fiber yarns: twisting, winding, etc.; cordage & twine
HQ: Avintiv Specialty Materials Inc.
9335 Harris Corners Pkwy
Charlotte NC 28269

(G-4613)
RIDGE ENTERPRISES LLC
2120 N Koch Industrial St (67068)
PHONE..................................620 491-2141
Jeffry Base, *CEO*
Cari Jo Base, *CFO*
Jeff L Base, *Administration*
EMP: 8 **EST:** 2010
SALES (est): 1.1MM **Privately Held**
SIC: 3533 Oil field machinery & equipment

Kinsley
Edwards County

(G-4614)
ARCHER-DANIELS-MIDLAND COMPANY
Also Called: ADM
Hwy 56 & Colony Ave (67547)
P.O. Box 187 (67547-0187)
PHONE..................................620 659-2099
Darrel Pettay, *Branch Mgr*
EMP: 12
SALES (corp-wide): 64.3B **Publicly Held**
WEB: www.admworld.com
SIC: 5153 Grains
PA: Archer-Daniels-Midland Company
77 W Wacker Dr Ste 4600
Chicago IL 60601
312 634-8100

(G-4615)
ARENSMAN SERVICES
1003 Briggs Ave (67547-1521)
PHONE..................................620 430-1106
Ben Arensman III, *Owner*
EMP: 12
SALES (est): 300K **Privately Held**
SIC: 0781 Landscape services

(G-4616)
EDWARDS COUNTY HOSPITAL
620 W 8th St (67547-2329)
P.O. Box 99 (67547-0099)
PHONE..................................620 659-2732
Connie McLean, *Chairman*
Brad Eustace, *Chairman*
Larry Myers, *Corp Secy*
Anna Fulls, *Facilities Mgr*
Alisha Herrmann, *Info Tech Dir*
EMP: 60
SQ FT: 25,000
SALES: 8.4MM **Privately Held**
SIC: 8062 General medical & surgical hospitals

(G-4617)
ESLINGER CONSTRUCTION & RDYMX
1321 90th Ave (67547-4707)
PHONE..................................620 659-2371
Edward O Eslinger, *President*
EMP: 10
SALES (est): 1.1MM **Privately Held**
SIC: 1771 3273 5211 Concrete pumping; ready-mixed concrete; sand & gravel

(G-4618)
GOLDEN BELT FEEDERS INC
1278 P Rd (67547-4763)
PHONE..................................620 659-2111
Kyle Kaiser, *Opers Mgr*
Jeff George, *Branch Mgr*
Shane Haselhorst, *Manager*
EMP: 35
SALES (corp-wide): 8.7MM **Privately Held**
WEB: www.goldenbeltfeeders.com
SIC: 0211 Beef cattle feedlots
PA: Golden Belt Feeders, Inc.
1149 Nw 10th Ave
Saint John KS 67576
620 549-3241

(G-4619)
MEDICALODGES INC
Also Called: Medicalodges of Kinsley
620 Winchester Ave (67547-2348)
PHONE..................................620 659-2156
Tammy Castaneda, *Executive*
Carie Perez, *Administration*
EMP: 50
SALES (corp-wide): 100.2MM **Privately Held**
WEB: www.medicalodges.com
SIC: 8051 8052 8322 Convalescent home with continuous nursing care; intermediate care facilities; adult day care center
PA: Medicalodges, Inc.
201 W 8th St
Coffeyville KS 67337
620 251-6700

(G-4620)
MIDWAY MANUFACTURING INC
400 Winchester Ave (67547-2346)
P.O. Box 251 (67547-0251)
PHONE..................................620 659-3631
Daniel R Woolard, *President*
Robert Mike Schnoebelen, *Vice Pres*
EMP: 25
SQ FT: 10,000
SALES (est): 3.2MM **Privately Held**
WEB: www.midwaymfg.com
SIC: 7699 Hydraulic equipment repair

(G-4621)
STRATE CONSTRUCTION INC
220 W 10th St (67547-2215)
PHONE..................................620 659-2251
Russell Strate, *President*
Margaret Strate, *Corp Secy*
EMP: 10 **EST:** 1950
SQ FT: 7,000
SALES (est): 1.6MM **Privately Held**
SIC: 1542 1521 Commercial & office building, new construction; farm building construction; new construction, single-family houses

(G-4622)
WESTERN UNION
615 Niles Ave (67547-1135)
PHONE..................................800 325-6000
EMP: 14 **EST:** 2017
SALES (est): 3MM **Privately Held**
SIC: 6099 Functions related to deposit banking

Kiowa
Barber County

(G-4623)
CUSTOM ROPE A DIV WILLIAMS
436 Campbell St (67070-1322)
P.O. Box 446 (67070-0446)
PHONE..................................620 825-4196
Donna Williams, *President*
EMP: 20
SALES (est): 5.1MM **Privately Held**
WEB: www.customrope.com
SIC: 5085 2298 Rope, except wire rope; cordage & twine

(G-4624)
KIOWA DISTRICT HOSPITAL
Also Called: Kiowa Hospital District Manor
1020 Main St (67070-1421)
PHONE..................................620 825-4117
Alden Van De Veer, *Administration*
EMP: 30
SALES (corp-wide): 4.5MM **Privately Held**
SIC: 8051 Convalescent home with continuous nursing care
PA: Kiowa District Hospital (Inc)
1002 S 4th St
Kiowa KS 67070
620 825-4131

(G-4625)
KIOWA DISTRICT HOSPITAL (PA)
1002 S 4th St (67070-1825)
P.O. Box 184 (67070-0184)
PHONE..................................620 825-4131
Steve Ashcraft, *CEO*
EMP: 52
SALES: 4.5MM **Privately Held**
SIC: 8062 Hospital, affiliated with AMA residency

(G-4626)
KIOWA LOCKER SYSTEM LLC
Also Called: Chiefton Brand Meats
128 S 6th St (67070-1509)
PHONE..................................620 825-4538
Rick Hitchcock, *Partner*
Bill Hitchcock, *Partner*
EMP: 10
SQ FT: 15,000

SALES (est): 885.8K **Privately Held**
SIC: 0751 5147 2013 2011 Slaughtering: custom livestock services; meats, fresh; sausages & other prepared meats; meat packing plants

(G-4627)
KNIGHTS OF COLUMBUS
1218 Main St (67070-1408)
P.O. Box 92 (67070-0092)
PHONE..................................620 825-4378
Carl Helfrich, *Principal*
EMP: 13
SALES (corp-wide): 2.3B **Privately Held**
WEB: www.kofc.org
SIC: 8641 Fraternal associations
PA: Knights Of Columbus
1 Columbus Plz Ste 1700
New Haven CT 06510
203 752-4000

(G-4628)
O K COOP GRN & MERC CO (PA)
130 Main St (67070-1400)
P.O. Box 144 (67070-0144)
PHONE..................................620 825-4212
Steve Inslee, *General Mgr*
EMP: 12 **EST:** 1917
SQ FT: 800
SALES (est): 12.8MM **Privately Held**
SIC: 5191 4221 5153 Feed; fertilizer & fertilizer materials; grain elevator, storage only; grains

(G-4629)
RADIOFRQUENCY SAFTEY INTL CORP
543 Main St (67070-1405)
PHONE..................................620 825-4600
Miranda Allan, *CEO*
Steve Walz, *CEO*
Greg Kechter, *COO*
Gary Jacobs, *CFO*
EMP: 25
SQ FT: 7,000
SALES (est): 2.7MM **Privately Held**
WEB: www.rsicorp.com
SIC: 7389 Safety inspection service

Kismet
Seward County

(G-4630)
GREEN PLAINS CATTLE CO LLC
Also Called: Supreme Cattle Feeders Div
19016 Road I (67859-6026)
PHONE..................................620 624-6296
Todd A Becker, *President*
Jeff S Briggs, *COO*
Jerry L Peters, *CFO*
EMP: 60 **EST:** 1998
SALES (est): 6.3MM
SALES (corp-wide): 3.8B **Publicly Held**
SIC: 0211 5153 Beef cattle feedlots; grain & field beans
PA: Green Plains Inc.
1811 Aksarben Dr
Omaha NE 68106
402 884-8700

(G-4631)
NORTHERN NATURAL GAS COMPANY
Rr 1 Box 17 (67859)
PHONE..................................620 675-2239
Randy Rice, *Branch Mgr*
EMP: 25
SALES (corp-wide): 225.3B **Publicly Held**
SIC: 4226 4922 Special warehousing & storage; natural gas transmission
HQ: Northern Natural Gas Company
1111 S 103rd St
Omaha NE 68124

(G-4632)
S W AGRO CENTER
Also Called: SW Agro Center
303 Main St (67859-9612)
PHONE..................................620 563-7264
Rock Ormiston, *President*
EMP: 10
SALES (est): 1MM **Privately Held**
SIC: 0115 Corn

La Crosse
Rush County

(G-4633)
FLAME ENGINEERING INC
230 Highway 4 (67548-4852)
P.O. Box 577 (67548-0577)
PHONE..................................785 222-2873
R Mike Pivonka, *CEO*
Jason Pivonka, *Vice Pres*
EMP: 47
SQ FT: 20,200
SALES (est): 8.9MM **Privately Held**
WEB: www.flameeng.com
SIC: 3728 3648 Aircraft parts & equipment; lighting equipment

(G-4634)
LA CROSSE LIVESTOCK MARKET
P.O. Box 657 (67548-0657)
PHONE..................................785 222-2586
Frank Seidel, *President*
Howard Delaney, *Principal*
Jack Delaney, *Principal*
Ron Wilson, *Principal*
EMP: 23
SQ FT: 20,000
SALES (est): 3.4MM **Privately Held**
WEB: www.lacrosselivestock.com
SIC: 5154 Auctioning livestock

(G-4635)
LACROSSE FURNITURE CO
1215 Oak St (67548-9770)
P.O. Box 99 (67548-0099)
PHONE..................................785 222-2541
Chris Podschun, *CEO*
Edmond Oborny, *Chairman*
Richard Byrne, *Vice Pres*
Don Manhart, *CFO*
▲ **EMP:** 70
SQ FT: 103,440
SALES (est): 10MM **Privately Held**
WEB: www.lacrossefurniture.com
SIC: 2512 Couches, sofas & davenports: upholstered on wood frames; chairs: upholstered on wood frames

(G-4636)
MILLER TRUCKING LTD
1st & Peace St (67548)
P.O. Box 283 (67548-0283)
PHONE..................................785 222-3170
Michael Miller, *President*
Leland Miller, *Principal*
Tillie Miller, *Corp Secy*
EMP: 24
SALES (est): 4MM **Privately Held**
WEB: www.millertrucking.net
SIC: 4213 Trucking, except local

(G-4637)
RUSH COUNTY MEMORIAL HOSPITAL
801 Locust St (67548-9673)
P.O. Box 520 (67548-0520)
PHONE..................................785 222-2545
Duane Fields, *CFO*
Brenda Leglieter, *Director*
Terri Deuel, *Administration*
EMP: 61
SQ FT: 41,000
SALES: 4.8MM **Privately Held**
SIC: 8062 General medical & surgical hospitals

(G-4638)
RUSH COUNTY NURSING HOME SOC
701 W 6th St (67548-9738)
PHONE..................................785 222-2574
Charlotte Rathke, *Principal*
EMP: 12
SALES: 3.5MM **Privately Held**
SIC: 8051 Skilled nursing care facilities

(G-4639)
SKILLETT & SONS INCORPORATED
2309 Highway 183 (67548-4801)
P.O. Box 196, Rush Center (67575-0196)
PHONE..................................785 222-3611
Garold Skillett, *President*
Rob Skillett, *Corp Secy*
EMP: 30
SQ FT: 2,100
SALES (est): 5MM **Privately Held**
WEB: www.skillettandsons.com
SIC: 4213 Contract haulers

La Cygne
Linn County

(G-4640)
EVERGY METRO INC
Also Called: La Cygne Station
Rr 1 (66040)
PHONE..................................913 757-4451
Dana Crawford, *Manager*
EMP: 130
SALES (corp-wide): 4.2B **Publicly Held**
WEB: www.kcpl.com
SIC: 4911 Generation, electric power
HQ: Evergy Metro, Inc.
1200 Main St
Kansas City MO 64105
816 556-2200

(G-4641)
PEOPLES TELECOMMUNICATIONS LLC
208 N Broadway St (66040-4135)
P.O. Box 450 (66040-0450)
PHONE..................................913 757-2500
Kathy Faircloth, *General Mgr*
EMP: 11 **EST:** 1914
SQ FT: 6,800
SALES (est): 1.3MM **Privately Held**
WEB: www.peoplestelecom.net
SIC: 4813 Local telephone communications

(G-4642)
REED MINERAL DIVISION
18730 E 2150 Rd (66040-7500)
P.O. Box 37 (66040-0037)
PHONE..................................913 757-4561
Jeremey Boatman, *Principal*
EMP: 7
SALES (est): 714.9K
SALES (corp-wide): 1.7B **Publicly Held**
SIC: 3295 Minerals, ground or treated
PA: Harsco Corporation
350 Poplar Church Rd
Camp Hill PA 17011
717 763-7064

(G-4643)
TANGLEWOOD LK OWNERS ASSN INC
610 Sw Lakeside Dr (66040-4203)
PHONE..................................913 795-2286
Brian McQuay, *President*
EMP: 10
SALES (est): 371.1K **Privately Held**
SIC: 8641 Homeowners' association

(G-4644)
THOELE FOUNDATIONS LLC
23319 Querry Rd (66040-6088)
PHONE..................................913 757-2317
Jeff Thoele,
Sheila Thoele,
EMP: 30
SALES (est): 2.2MM **Privately Held**
SIC: 1771 Concrete work

(G-4645)
US MINERALS INC
911 Linnco Dr (66040)
PHONE..................................219 798-5472
Nick Cimesa, *Plant Mgr*
EMP: 5
SALES (corp-wide): 33.2MM **Privately Held**
SIC: 3291 Abrasive products
PA: U.S. Minerals, Inc.
18635 West Creek Dr Ste 2
Tinley Park IL 60477
708 623-1935

(G-4646)
WADE AGRICULTURAL PRODUCTS INC (PA)
Also Called: Wade Quarries
23096 E 2400 Rd (66040-9175)
P.O. Box 38 (66040-0038)
PHONE..................................913 757-2255
Ron Wade, *President*
Barbara L Wade, *President*
Gwen Gooding, *Corp Secy*
Craig Gooding, *Vice Pres*
EMP: 9 **EST:** 1975
SALES (est): 3.6MM **Privately Held**
SIC: 1422 1611 Crushed & broken limestone; resurfacing contractor

La Harpe
Allen County

(G-4647)
ALLEN CNTY ANMAL RSCUE FNDTION
305 E Highway 54 (66751-1206)
PHONE..................................620 496-3647
Viriginia Hawk, *Treasurer*
EMP: 10
SALES: 187.5K **Privately Held**
SIC: 8699 Animal humane society

Lakin
Kearny County

(G-4648)
COLORADO INTERSTATE GAS CO LLC
W Hwy 50 (67860)
PHONE..................................620 355-7955
Jesse Espinoza, *Manager*
EMP: 14 **Publicly Held**
WEB: www.dsirestoration.org
SIC: 4922 Pipelines, natural gas
HQ: Colorado Interstate Gas Company Llc
1001 La St Ste 1000
Houston TX 77002
713 369-9000

(G-4649)
COUNTY OF KEARNY
Also Called: Family Health Center
506 E Thorpe St Ste 355 (67860-9625)
PHONE..................................620 355-7501
Erick Sandstorm, *Principal*
EMP: 18 **Privately Held**
SIC: 8011 General & family practice, physician/surgeon
PA: County Of Kearny
304 N Main St
Lakin KS 67860
620 355-7358

(G-4650)
KEARNY COUNTY BANK
221 N Main St (67860-9482)
P.O. Box 67 (67860-0067)
PHONE..................................620 355-6222
Gary Beymer, *President*
Robert Beymer, *Vice Pres*
Michael Dykstra, *Vice Pres*
EMP: 24 **EST:** 1888
SQ FT: 2,500
SALES (est): 2MM
SALES (corp-wide): 10.8MM **Privately Held**
WEB: www.kearnycountybank.com
SIC: 6022 State commercial banks
PA: Lakin Bancshares, Inc.
221 N Main St
Lakin KS 67860
620 355-6222

(G-4651)
KEARNY COUNTY FEEDERS LLC
1544 Rd 180 (67860)
P.O. Box 109 (67860-0109)
PHONE....................................620 355-6630
Stewart Stabel,
EMP: 18
SQ FT: 5,000
SALES (est): 2.1MM **Privately Held**
SIC: 0211 Beef cattle feedlots

(G-4652)
KEARNY COUNTY HOME FOR AGED
Also Called: High Plains Retirement Village
607 Court Pl (67860-9704)
P.O. Box 1041 (67860-1041)
PHONE....................................620 355-7836
Drew Escamilla, *Director*
Tina Vincent, *Executive*
John Loebl, *Administration*
EMP: 40
SALES (est): 1.7MM **Privately Held**
SIC: 8361 Home for the aged

(G-4653)
KEARNY COUNTY HOSPITAL (PA)
500 E Thorpe St (67860-9625)
PHONE....................................620 355-7111
Kendal Carswell, *Principal*
Marley Koons, *Accountant*
Julie Munson, *Med Doctor*
Kimberly Meyer, *Director*
Benjamin Anderson, *Administration*
EMP: 106 **EST:** 1952
SQ FT: 100,000
SALES: 17.3MM **Privately Held**
SIC: 8062 Hospital, affiliated with AMA residency

(G-4654)
LAKIN BANCSHARES INC (PA)
Also Called: KEARNY COUNTY BANK
221 N Main St (67860-9482)
P.O. Box 67 (67860-0067)
PHONE....................................620 355-6222
Gary Beymer, *President*
Robert K Beymer, *Vice Pres*
Michael Dykstra, *Corp Comm Staff*
Todd Dauber, *Branch Mgr*
Brick Beymer, *Trust Officer*
EMP: 30
SQ FT: 2,500
SALES: 10.8MM **Privately Held**
WEB: www.kearnycountybank.com
SIC: 6022 State commercial banks

(G-4655)
LAKIN DAIRY
771 Road R (67860-6138)
P.O. Box 389 (67860-0389)
PHONE....................................620 355-6640
Fred Ritzama, *Partner*
Yoka Rodenhuis, *Partner*
EMP: 20
SALES (est): 732K **Privately Held**
SIC: 0241 Dairy farms

(G-4656)
MID STATES HAY INC
River Rd (67860)
P.O. Box 1090 (67860-1090)
PHONE....................................620 355-7976
Darrel Kuhn, *President*
Linda Kuhn, *Vice Pres*
EMP: 20
SALES (est): 1.9MM **Privately Held**
SIC: 0139 Hay farm

(G-4657)
PAPPAS CONCRETE INC (PA)
Also Called: Rok-Hard Ready-Mix
2104 Road 140 (67860-6224)
PHONE....................................620 277-2127
Ivan Nolde, *President*
Tammie L Nolde, *Vice Pres*
EMP: 27 **EST:** 1959
SQ FT: 696,960
SALES (est): 2.5MM **Privately Held**
SIC: 3272 3273 Precast terrazo or concrete products; ready-mixed concrete

(G-4658)
RAMON E GUARDIOLA
Also Called: R & D Transports
1007 Kendall Ave (67860-9742)
P.O. Box 515 (67860-0515)
PHONE....................................620 355-4266
EMP: 10 **EST:** 2007
SALES (est): 470K **Privately Held**
SIC: 4212 Local Trucking Operator

(G-4659)
REGENCY GAS SERVICES LLC
1473 Us Highway 50 (67860)
P.O. Box U (67860-0950)
PHONE....................................620 355-7905
Connie Hougland, *Vice Pres*
Gerald Daugherty, *Manager*
EMP: 11
SALES (est): 1.2MM **Privately Held**
SIC: 8748 Business consulting

(G-4660)
TALLGRASS ENERGY PARTNERS LP
2089 Road 130 (67860-6215)
PHONE....................................620 355-7122
Tab Bailor, *Branch Mgr*
EMP: 11
SALES (corp-wide): 793.2MM **Publicly Held**
SIC: 4922 Natural gas transmission
HQ: Tallgrass Energy Partners, Lp
4200 W 115th St Ste 350
Leawood KS 66211
913 928-6060

(G-4661)
TRIPLE T FARMS
101 N Main St (67860-9474)
P.O. Box 69 (67860-0069)
PHONE....................................620 355-6707
George Tate, *Partner*
Bradner Tate, *Partner*
Bret Tate, *Partner*
Victor Tate, *Partner*
EMP: 15
SQ FT: 8,000
SALES (est): 571.8K **Privately Held**
WEB: www.tripletbordercollies.com
SIC: 0762 Farm management services

(G-4662)
XTO ENERGY INC
805 Highway 25 S (67860)
P.O. Box 383 (67860-0383)
PHONE....................................620 355-7838
Wayne King, *Manager*
EMP: 55
SALES (corp-wide): 290.2B **Publicly Held**
SIC: 1311 Crude petroleum & natural gas
HQ: Xto Energy Inc.
110 W 7th St
Fort Worth TX 76102

Lane
Franklin County

(G-4663)
SNOW INC
Also Called: Show Engraving
703 6th St (66042-2500)
P.O. Box 41 (66042-0041)
PHONE....................................785 869-2021
Robert L Snow, *President*
Charlene Snow, *Corp Secy*
EMP: 7 **EST:** 1995
SALES (est): 550K **Privately Held**
SIC: 3953 Embossing seals & hand stamps

Langdon
Reno County

(G-4664)
SHEROW CATTLE CO
22703 W Castleton Rd (67583-9074)
PHONE....................................620 596-2813
Michael B Sherow, *Owner*
EMP: 10
SALES (est): 539K **Privately Held**
SIC: 0211 Beef cattle feedlots

Lansing
Leavenworth County

(G-4665)
A DEERE PLACE INC
1104 Industrial St (66043-5000)
PHONE....................................913 727-5437
Debbie Deere, *Owner*
EMP: 12 **EST:** 2009
SALES (est): 415.1K **Privately Held**
SIC: 8351 Preschool center

(G-4666)
AMERICAN ENERGY PRODUCTS INC
1105 Industrial St (66043-5001)
PHONE....................................913 351-3388
Gail Watson, *President*
Michael R Perez, *Vice Pres*
EMP: 6
SQ FT: 10,000
SALES (est): 862.5K **Privately Held**
SIC: 5999 3443 Plumbing & heating supplies; fabricated plate work (boiler shop)

(G-4667)
ARAMARK UNF & CAREER AP LLC
123 American Ave (66043-1349)
PHONE....................................913 351-3534
Dave Mancini, *Branch Mgr*
EMP: 45 **Publicly Held**
WEB: www.aramark-uniform.com
SIC: 7213 Linen supply
HQ: Aramark Uniform & Career Apparel, Llc
115 N First St Ste 203
Burbank CA 91502
818 973-3700

(G-4668)
ASSOCIATE IN FAMILY HLTH CARE
712 1st Ter Ste A (66043-1735)
PHONE....................................913 727-1018
Missy Medill, *Office Mgr*
Joyce Stoughton, *Manager*
Bob Cole, *Director*
EMP: 50
SALES (est): 4.3MM **Privately Held**
SIC: 8011 Internal medicine, physician/surgeon; general & family practice, physician/surgeon

(G-4669)
BEVERLY ENTERPRISES-KANSAS LLC
Also Called: Colonial Manor of Lansing
210 N Plaza Dr (66043-1381)
P.O. Box 250 (66043-0250)
PHONE....................................913 351-1284
Angela King, *Administration*
EMP: 40
SALES (corp-wide): 393.8MM **Privately Held**
SIC: 8051 8741 Convalescent home with continuous nursing care; nursing & personal care facility management
HQ: Beverly Enterprises-Kansas, Llc
1 1000 Beverly Way
Fort Smith AR 72919
479 201-2000

(G-4670)
CARAWAY PRINTING COMPANY INC
204 N Main St Ste B (66043-1333)
P.O. Box 57 (66043-0057)
PHONE....................................913 727-5223
Harold Poe, *President*
EMP: 5
SQ FT: 3,000
SALES (est): 370K **Privately Held**
SIC: 2752 Commercial printing, offset

(G-4671)
CITIZENS NATIONAL BANK
601 N Main St (66043-1371)
PHONE....................................913 727-3266
Chuck Pederson, *Vice Pres*
Chuck Peterson, *Branch Mgr*
EMP: 12
SALES (corp-wide): 7.7MM **Privately Held**
SIC: 6021 National commercial banks
PA: The Citizens National Bank
417 Commercial St
Greenleaf KS 66943
785 747-2261

(G-4672)
CORRECTIONS KANSAS DEPARTMENT
Also Called: Lansing Correctional Facility
301 E Kansas St (66043-1619)
P.O. Box 2 (66043-0002)
PHONE....................................913 727-3235
Sam Klien, *Warden*
EMP: 71 **Privately Held**
SIC: 8744 9223 Correctional facility;
HQ: Kansas Department Of Corrections
714 Sw Jackson St Fl 3
Topeka KS 66603
785 296-3317

(G-4673)
FLANNER & MC BRATNEY MDS PA
1004 Progress Dr Ste 200 (66043-6323)
PHONE....................................913 651-3111
Kathleen McBratney MD, *Partner*
Nicholas Brockert, *Family Practiti*
Valerie L Duff, *Family Practiti*
EMP: 17
SALES (est): 2.5MM **Privately Held**
SIC: 8011 General & family practice, physician/surgeon

(G-4674)
GOLDEN LIVING CENTER
210 N Plaza Dr (66043-1381)
P.O. Box 250 (66043-0250)
PHONE....................................913 727-1284
James Brockenborough, *Director*
EMP: 15
SALES (est): 567.1K **Privately Held**
SIC: 8051 Skilled nursing care facilities

(G-4675)
HOLIDAY INN EXPRESS
120 Express Ln (66043-1382)
PHONE....................................913 250-1000
Celeste Gammon, *General Mgr*
Heather Garton, *Manager*
EMP: 15
SALES (est): 749.1K **Privately Held**
SIC: 7011 Hotels & motels

(G-4676)
KANSAS CARDIOVASCULAR ASSOC
712 1st Ter Ste C (66043-1735)
PHONE....................................913 682-6950
Ashwani Mehta, *President*
EMP: 15
SALES (est): 623.8K **Privately Held**
SIC: 8011 Medical centers

(G-4677)
KINDERCARE LEARNING CTRS LLC
Also Called: Kindercare Child Care Network
100 E Mary St (66043-1631)
PHONE....................................913 727-6267
Kelly Dougan, *Branch Mgr*
Lynette Vinzant, *Branch Mgr*
EMP: 12
SALES (corp-wide): 963.9MM **Privately Held**
WEB: www.kindercare.com
SIC: 8351 Group day care center
HQ: Kindercare Learning Centers, Llc
650 Ne Holladay St # 1400
Portland OR 97232
503 872-1300

(G-4678)
KIWANIS INTERNATIONAL INC
Also Called: Lansing Kiwanis Club
203 Emile St (66043-1324)
PHONE....................................913 727-1039
EMP: 17
SALES (corp-wide): 15.1MM **Privately Held**
SIC: 8641 Civic/Social Association

PA: Kiwanis International, Inc.
3636 Woodview Trce
Indianapolis IN 46268
317 875-8755

(G-4679)
LANSING CARE RHBLTTION CTR LLC
210 N Plaza Dr (66043-1381)
PHONE....913 727-1284
Joseph Schwartz, *Principal*
Susan Bowers, *Principal*
EMP: 60
SALES (est): 1.2MM **Privately Held**
SIC: 8051 Skilled nursing care facilities

(G-4680)
LANSING UNIFIED SCHL DST 469
1102 Industrial St (66043-5000)
P.O. Box 2 (66043-0002)
PHONE....913 250-0749
Jim Slapper, *Director*
EMP: 26
SALES (corp-wide): 8.5MM **Privately Held**
SIC: 8299 4111 Arts & crafts schools; bus transportation
PA: Lansing Unified School District 469
401 S 2nd St
Lansing KS 66043
913 727-1100

(G-4681)
LEAVCON II INC
108 American Ave (66043-1350)
P.O. Box 26 (66043-0026)
PHONE....913 351-1430
Glen A Leintz, *President*
Bruce A Leintz, *Vice Pres*
Bruce Leintz, *Vice Pres*
Mike Corriston, *Foreman/Supr*
Tamara Bradshaw, *Controller*
EMP: 50
SQ FT: 5,000
SALES (est): 7.6MM **Privately Held**
WEB: www.leavcon.com
SIC: 1771 1542 1541 Concrete work; nonresidential construction; industrial buildings & warehouses

(G-4682)
LEAVENWORTH COUNTRY CLUB
455 W Eisenhower Rd (66043-2200)
PHONE....913 727-6600
Jason Reheis, *General Mgr*
Mike Boaz, *Manager*
EMP: 50
SQ FT: 5,500
SALES: 221.2K **Privately Held**
WEB: www.leavenworthcountryclub.com
SIC: 7997 Country club, membership

(G-4683)
LEAVENWORTH COUNTY COOP ASSN (PA)
Also Called: Leavenworth County Co-Op
1101 Industrial St (66043-5001)
PHONE....913 727-1900
Brenda Bennett, *General Mgr*
Gary Oberdiek, *Chairman*
Janette Hightower, *Manager*
Brian Potter, *Director*
Scott Johnson, *Admin Sec*
EMP: 15
SALES (est): 20.5MM **Privately Held**
SIC: 5191 5541 5171 Feed; seeds: field, garden & flower; filling stations, gasoline; petroleum bulk stations

(G-4684)
LEAVENWORTH FAMILY HEALTH CTR
720 1st Ter (66043-1704)
PHONE....913 682-5588
Laura Jobe, *Principal*
EMP: 10
SALES (est): 846.9K **Privately Held**
SIC: 8011 General & family practice, physician/surgeon

(G-4685)
LEISURE HOTEL CORPORATION
120 Express Ln (66043-1382)
PHONE....913 250-1000
Barbara Myracle, *Director*
EMP: 25
SALES (corp-wide): 6.9MM **Privately Held**
SIC: 7011 Motels
PA: Leisure Hotel Corporation
8725 Rosehill Rd Ste 300
Lenexa KS 66215
913 905-1460

(G-4686)
LINAWEAVER CONSTRUCTION INC (PA)
719 E Gilman Rd (66043-6261)
PHONE....913 351-3474
Betty Linaweaver, *President*
Jerry Linaweaver, *Vice Pres*
EMP: 10
SALES (est): 3.3MM **Privately Held**
SIC: 1794 1623 Excavation & grading, building construction; water & sewer line construction

(G-4687)
M R I OF ROCK CREEK
Also Called: Rock Creek Open M R I
712 1st Ter Ste B (66043-1735)
PHONE....913 351-4674
Missy Medill, *Treasurer*
EMP: 30 **EST**: 2002
SALES (est): 2.2MM **Privately Held**
SIC: 3845 Magnetic resonance imaging device, nuclear

(G-4688)
MIDWEST HEALTH SERVICES INC
657 W Eisenhower Rd (66043-2204)
PHONE....913 727-6100
EMP: 372
SALES (corp-wide): 32.7MM **Privately Held**
SIC: 8051 Convalescent home with continuous nursing care
PA: Midwest Health, Inc
3024 Sw Wanamaker Rd # 300
Topeka KS 66614
785 272-1535

(G-4689)
PERSONALIZED LAWN CARE INC
1410 Corey Ln (66043-6274)
P.O. Box 310 (66043-0310)
PHONE....913 727-3977
EMP: 10 **EST**: 2009
SALES (est): 220K **Privately Held**
SIC: 0782 Lawn/Garden Services

(G-4690)
PETER J CRISTIANO DR
Also Called: Lansing Lvnworth Fmly Hlth Ctr
720 1st Ter (66043-1704)
PHONE....913 682-5588
Dr Peter J Cristiano, *Owner*
EMP: 14
SALES (est): 1.1MM **Privately Held**
SIC: 8011 General & family practice, physician/surgeon

(G-4691)
REIMERS FURNITURE MFG INC
Also Called: Rfm Preferred Seating
1213 136th St (66043-6322)
PHONE....913 727-5100
Mike Tuten, *Branch Mgr*
Jeff O'Dell, *Manager*
EMP: 7
SALES (est): 743.7K
SALES (corp-wide): 7.9MM **Privately Held**
SIC: 2521 2512 Upholstered household furniture; chairs, office: padded, upholstered or plain: wood
PA: Reimers Furniture Mfg., Inc.
619 Sw Wood St
Hillsboro OR 97123
503 648-6121

(G-4692)
SIEMENS INDUSTRY INC
1001 N 8th St (66043-1134)
PHONE....913 683-9787
EMP: 34
SALES (corp-wide): 96.9B **Privately Held**
SIC: 3589 Water treatment equipment, industrial
HQ: Siemens Industry, Inc.
1000 Deerfield Pkwy
Buffalo Grove IL 60089
847 215-1000

(G-4693)
ST LUKES HEALTH CORPORATION
Also Called: Saint Lkes Med Group - Lansing
1004 Progress Dr Ste 220 (66043-6327)
PHONE....913 250-1244
Joyce Gonzales, *Office Mgr*
EMP: 130
SALES (corp-wide): 471MM **Privately Held**
SIC: 8062 General medical & surgical hospitals
PA: St. Luke's Health Corporation
232 S Woods Mill Rd
Chesterfield MO 63017
314 434-1500

Larned
Pawnee County

(G-4694)
B&B QUALITY MEATS LLC
508 Broadway St (67550-3042)
P.O. Box 346 (67550-0346)
PHONE....620 285-8988
Carroll Bennette, *Principal*
EMP: 6 **EST**: 2012
SALES (est): 515.1K **Privately Held**
SIC: 2011 Meat packing plants

(G-4695)
BERT & WETTA LARNED INC
1416 Us Highway 56 (67550)
P.O. Box 130 (67550-0130)
PHONE....620 285-7777
Bert Carlton, *President*
Shari Bert, *Admin Sec*
EMP: 20
SQ FT: 2,500
SALES (est): 1.5MM **Privately Held**
SIC: 0191 2048 General farms, primarily crop; alfalfa or alfalfa meal, prepared as animal feed

(G-4696)
BERT AND WETTA SALES INC (PA)
1230 Ne Trail St (67550)
P.O. Box 130 (67550-0130)
PHONE....620 285-7777
Carlton Bert, *President*
Rachel Jane Bert, *Corp Secy*
Raymond Bert, *Vice Pres*
▼ **EMP**: 20 **EST**: 1946
SQ FT: 2,500
SALES (est): 8MM **Privately Held**
WEB: www.usalfalfa.net
SIC: 2048 Alfalfa or alfalfa meal, prepared as animal feed

(G-4697)
CARR AUCTION & REALESTATE
909 Auction Ave (67550)
P.O. Box 300 (67550-0300)
PHONE....620 285-3148
Jim Froetschner, *Owner*
Jim Tammy Froetschner, *Owner*
EMP: 20
SQ FT: 10,000
SALES (est): 1.7MM **Privately Held**
WEB: www.carrauction.com
SIC: 7389 6531 Auctioneers, fee basis; real estate brokers & agents

(G-4698)
CHAD EAKIN CONCRETE
111 Main St (67550-3917)
PHONE....620 285-2097
Chad Eakin, *Owner*
Anna Connell, *Officer*
EMP: 11
SALES: 1.5MM **Privately Held**
SIC: 1771 Concrete work

(G-4699)
CORRECTIONS KANSAS DEPARTMENT
Larned Jvnile Crrctonal Fcilty
1301 K264 Hwy (67550-5353)
PHONE....620 285-0300
Leo Herman, *Superintendent*
EMP: 163 **Privately Held**
WEB: www.jjaco.wpo.state.ks.us
SIC: 8361 9223 Juvenile correctional facilities; correctional institutions;
HQ: Kansas Department Of Corrections
714 Sw Jackson St Fl 3
Topeka KS 66603
785 296-3317

(G-4700)
COUNTY OF PAWNEE
Also Called: Pawnee County Highway Dept
615 E 10th St (67550-2653)
PHONE....620 285-6141
Gary Schneiders, *Director*
EMP: 21 **Privately Held**
WEB: www.pawnee.kscoxmail.com
SIC: 1611 9111 Highway & street construction; county supervisors' & executives' offices
PA: County Of Pawnee
615 E 10th St
Larned KS 67550
620 285-6141

(G-4701)
DIVERSICARE OF LARNED LLC
1114 W 11th St (67550-1939)
PHONE....620 285-6914
Jennifer Kennon, *Executive*
Kelly Gill,
James McKnight,
Brenda Wimsatt,
EMP: 69
SALES (est): 1.6MM **Privately Held**
SIC: 8051 Skilled nursing care facilities

(G-4702)
FARMERS BANK & TRUST
102 W 6th St (67550-3044)
PHONE....620 285-3177
B Kent Moffat, *Branch Mgr*
EMP: 14
SALES (corp-wide): 34.9MM **Privately Held**
SIC: 6022 State commercial banks
HQ: Farmers Bank & Trust
1017 Harrison St
Great Bend KS 67530
620 792-2411

(G-4703)
FIRST STATE BNK TR OF LARNED (HQ)
116 W 6th St (67550-9900)
PHONE....620 285-6931
Reed A Peters, *CEO*
Jack Galle, *Senior VP*
Sharon Lessard, *Vice Pres*
James White, *Vice Pres*
EMP: 16 **EST**: 1896
SQ FT: 10,000
SALES: 6.3MM **Privately Held**
WEB: www.bankkansas.com
SIC: 6022 State trust companies accepting deposits, commercial

(G-4704)
HAYNES ELECTRIC INC
321 W 14th St (67550-2107)
P.O. Box 497 (67550-0497)
PHONE....620 285-2242
Jim Haynes, *President*
Suzan Haynes, *Vice Pres*
EMP: 27 **EST**: 1963
SQ FT: 5,600
SALES: 6MM **Privately Held**
WEB: www.hayneselectricinc.com
SIC: 1731 General electrical contractor

GEOGRAPHIC

(G-4705)
HIGH PLAINS FARM CREDIT FLCA (PA)
Also Called: Flca of Hays
605 Main St (67550-3034)
P.O. Box 67 (67550-0067)
PHONE..................................620 285-6978
Doug Thurman, *President*
Travis Holdeman, *President*
James Dibble, *Senior VP*
Kristen Windscheffel, *Vice Pres*
EMP: 21
SALES (est): 4.4MM **Privately Held**
SIC: 6162 Mortgage bankers & correspondents

(G-4706)
KANSAS DEPT FOR AGING & DISABI
Also Called: Larned State Hospital
1301 Ks Highway 264 (67550-5353)
PHONE..................................620 285-2131
Bill Rein, *Superintendent*
Angela Burcham, *Psychologist*
Rebecca Farr, *Psychologist*
Robin Karp, *Psychologist*
Michael Burke, *Psychiatry*
EMP: 66 **Privately Held**
SIC: 8063 Psychiatric hospitals
HQ: Kansas Department For Aging And Disability Services
503 S Kansas Ave
Topeka KS 66603

(G-4707)
NATIONAL HEALTHCARE CORP
Also Called: Larned Healthcare & Living Ctr
1114 W 11th St (67550-1939)
PHONE..................................620 285-6914
Mike Velder, *Administration*
EMP: 70
SALES (corp-wide): 980.3MM **Publicly Held**
WEB: www.healthcarebenefits.com
SIC: 8051 Convalescent home with continuous nursing care
PA: National Healthcare Corporation
100 E Vine St
Murfreesboro TN 37130
615 890-2020

(G-4708)
NATIONAL PARK SERVICE
Also Called: Fort Larned Nat Historic Site
1767 Ks Highway 156 (67550-5357)
PHONE..................................620 285-6911
Betty Boyko, *Superintendent*
EMP: 13 **Publicly Held**
WEB: www.nps.gov
SIC: 1799 Parking facility equipment installation; rigging, theatrical
HQ: National Park Service
1849 C St Nw
Washington DC 20240

(G-4709)
PAWNEE COUNTY HUMANE SOC INC
1406 M5 Rd (67550-5360)
PHONE..................................620 285-8510
Lois Eye, *President*
EMP: 10
SALES: 46.1K **Privately Held**
SIC: 8699 Animal humane society

(G-4710)
PAWRNEE VALLEY SCOUTS INC
Also Called: Central STS Scout Museum
109 E 15th St (67550-1702)
PHONE..................................620 285-6427
Charles Sherman, *President*
Kent Converse, *Vice Pres*
Jack Dipman, *Vice Pres*
Grace Fancia, *Treasurer*
EMP: 10
SALES: 20K **Privately Held**
SIC: 8412 Museum

(G-4711)
SANTA FE TRAIL ASSOCIATION
1349 K156 Hwy (67550-5347)
PHONE..................................620 285-2054
Larry Justice, *President*
Larry Short, *Vice Pres*
Ruth Peters, *Treasurer*
Joanne Van Coevern, *Manager*
Shirley Coupal, *Admin Sec*
EMP: 16
SQ FT: 500
SALES: 253.9K **Privately Held**
WEB: www.santafetrail.org
SIC: 8412 Museum

(G-4712)
SEBES HAY LLC
1175 Morris Ave (67550-1930)
PHONE..................................620 285-6941
Mike Sebes, *Mng Member*
EMP: 25
SALES (est): 415K **Privately Held**
SIC: 7363 0139 Truck driver services; hay farm

(G-4713)
STAR COMMUNICATION CORPORATION
Also Called: Tiller & Toiler Newspaper
115 W 5th St (67550-3016)
P.O. Box 206 (67550-0206)
PHONE..................................620 285-3111
John Settle, *President*
EMP: 17
SALES (est): 851.3K **Privately Held**
SIC: 2711 Commercial printing & newspaper publishing combined

(G-4714)
STATE THEATRE
617 Broadway St (67550-3050)
PHONE..................................620 285-3535
Susan Haynes, *President*
EMP: 50
SALES (est): 958.7K **Privately Held**
WEB: www.statetheatre.com
SIC: 7832 Motion picture theaters, except drive-in

(G-4715)
WARD FEED YARD INC
1190 100th Ave (67550)
P.O. Box H (67550-0380)
PHONE..................................620 285-2183
Lee Borck, *President*
Chris Burris, *Vice Pres*
John Skelton, *Treasurer*
Aaron Spanier, *Human Resources*
Kimi Buwnin, *Admin Sec*
EMP: 40 **EST:** 1962
SQ FT: 1,600
SALES (est): 7.8MM
SALES (corp-wide): 31.2MM **Privately Held**
WEB: www.wardfeedyard.com
SIC: 0211 0139 Beef cattle feedlots; alfalfa farm
PA: Innovative Livestock Services, Inc.
2006 Broadway Ave Ste 2c
Great Bend KS 67530
620 793-9200

(G-4716)
WILLIAM G WOODS
1041 K19 Hwy S (67550-5210)
PHONE..................................620 285-6971
William G Woods, *Owner*
EMP: 10
SALES: 100K **Privately Held**
SIC: 5191 Feed

Lawrence
Douglas County

(G-4717)
A & M TOWING & RECOVERY INC
529 Maple St (66044-5451)
P.O. Box 254 (66044-0254)
PHONE..................................785 331-3100
Andrew W Moon, *President*
Andrew Moon, *President*
EMP: 10
SALES (est): 429.3K **Privately Held**
SIC: 7549 Towing service, automotive

(G-4718)
ACTION PLUMBING OF LAWRENCE
801 Comet Ln Ste D (66049-3262)
P.O. Box 1051 (66044-8051)
PHONE..................................785 843-5670
Kevin Hoppe, *President*
Dina Bahnmaier, *Manager*
EMP: 11
SQ FT: 800
SALES (est): 1.8MM **Privately Held**
SIC: 1711 5999 1542 Plumbing contractors; plumbing & heating supplies; commercial & office buildings, renovation & repair

(G-4719)
ADO STAFFING INC
100 E 9th St (66044-2623)
PHONE..................................785 842-1515
Shirley Smith, *Branch Mgr*
EMP: 15
SALES (corp-wide): 26.4B **Privately Held**
WEB: www.adeccona.com
SIC: 7363 Temporary help service
HQ: Ado Staffing, Inc.
175 Broadhollow Rd
Melville NY 11747
631 844-7800

(G-4720)
ADT LLC
Also Called: Protection One Alarm Mnitoring
1035 N 3rd St Ste 101 (66044-1491)
PHONE..................................785 856-5500
Valerie Dugan, *Accounts Mgr*
George Green, *Sales Staff*
Tim Whall, *Branch Mgr*
Rosalinda Hernandez, *Manager*
Derick Rogers, *Manager*
EMP: 2870
SALES (corp-wide): 4.5B **Publicly Held**
SIC: 7382 Burglar alarm maintenance & monitoring
HQ: Adt Llc
1501 W Yamato Rd
Boca Raton FL 33431
561 988-3600

(G-4721)
ADVANCED CHIROPRACTIC SVCS PA (PA)
1605 Wakarusa Dr (66047-1805)
PHONE..................................785 842-4181
Christopher Wertin, *President*
EMP: 12
SALES (est): 943.5K **Privately Held**
SIC: 8041 8049 Offices & clinics of chiropractors; acupuncturist

(G-4722)
ADVANTAGE MEDICAL GROUP
1104 E 23rd St (66046-5004)
PHONE..................................785 749-0130
James T Brady, *Owner*
Celeste Chiang, *Manager*
EMP: 10
SALES (est): 530.3K **Privately Held**
SIC: 8041 8742 8093 Offices & clinics of chiropractors; hospital & health services consultant; rehabilitation center, outpatient treatment

(G-4723)
ADVANTAGE METALS RECYCLING LLC
1545 N 3rd St (66044-9182)
PHONE..................................785 841-0396
EMP: 44
SALES (corp-wide): 25B **Publicly Held**
SIC: 5093 Metal scrap & waste materials
HQ: Advantage Metals Recycling Llc
510 Walnut St Ste 300
Kansas City MO 64106
816 861-2700

(G-4724)
AG SOURCE INC (PA)
4910 Corp Centre Dr # 110 (66047-1000)
PHONE..................................785 841-1315
Troy Bird, *President*
Steve Spencer, *Division Mgr*
Brad Bird, *Vice Pres*
Todd Bird, *Treasurer*
EMP: 14
SQ FT: 2,000
SALES (est): 7MM **Privately Held**
SIC: 4731 Brokers, shipping

(G-4725)
ALL OF E SOLUTIONS LLC
Also Called: Allofe Studio
2510 W 6th St (66049-2442)
PHONE..................................785 832-2900
Jordan Kane, *Project Mgr*
Tracy Kemp, *Purchasing*
Drew Manderfeld, *Senior Mgr*
Amit Guha,
Sash Guha,
EMP: 25
SQ FT: 15,000
SALES (est): 2.5MM **Privately Held**
SIC: 7371 Computer software development

(G-4726)
ALL-N-1 LANDSCAPE LLC
411 N Iowa St (66044-9617)
PHONE..................................785 856-5296
Troy Karlin,
EMP: 11
SALES: 1MM **Privately Held**
WEB: www.all-n-1landscape.com
SIC: 0781 Landscape services

(G-4727)
ALL-PRO SERVICES INC
757 Highway 40 (66049-4174)
PHONE..................................785 842-1402
Rodney Eisenbarger, *President*
Kelly Eisenbarger, *Corp Secy*
EMP: 16
SALES: 600K **Privately Held**
WEB: www.all-proinc.com
SIC: 7217 7389 Carpet & upholstery cleaning; water softener service

(G-4728)
ALLEN K KELLEY DDS PA
Also Called: Heck, Brian W DDS
4900 Legends Dr (66049-3886)
PHONE..................................785 841-5590
Allen K Kelley DDS, *Owner*
Brian Heck DDS, *Co-Owner*
Brian W Heck, *Fmly & Gen Dent*
Allen Kelley, *Fmly & Gen Dent*
EMP: 13
SALES (est): 721.6K **Privately Held**
SIC: 8021 Dentists' office

(G-4729)
ALLEN PRESS INC (PA)
810 E 10th St (66044-3018)
P.O. Box 368 (66044-0368)
PHONE..................................785 843-1234
Gerald Lillian, *CEO*
▼ **EMP:** 100 **EST:** 1935
SQ FT: 170,000
SALES (est): 41MM **Privately Held**
SIC: 2721 8741 Magazines: publishing & printing; trade journals: publishing & printing; management services

(G-4730)
ALLIED BODY SHOP INCORPORATED
Also Called: Allied Auto Body Carstar
800 E 23rd St (66046-4910)
PHONE..................................785 841-3672
Ron Glenn, *President*
John Kramer, *Admin Sec*
EMP: 10
SQ FT: 4,800
SALES (est): 645.9K **Privately Held**
SIC: 7532 7539 Body shop, automotive; wheel alignment, automotive

(G-4731)
ALPHA CHI OMEGA
1500 Sigma Nu Pl (66044-2524)
PHONE..................................785 843-7600
Janet Williams, *President*
Ann Cunnigan, *Admin Sec*
EMP: 10
SALES (est): 302.1K **Privately Held**
SIC: 8641 7041 Alumni association; fraternal associations; fraternities & sororities

(G-4732)
ALVAMAR INC (PA)
Also Called: Alvamar Golf and Country Club
1809 Crossgate Dr (66047-3533)
PHONE..................................785 842-2929
Richard A Stuntz, *President*
Wes Lynch, *General Mgr*
EMP: 20
SQ FT: 10,000
SALES (est): 5.4MM **Privately Held**
WEB: www.alvamar.com
SIC: 7997 5812 7992 6552 Country club, membership; eating places; public golf courses; subdividers & developers; golf goods & equipment; tennis goods & equipment

(G-4733)
ALVAMAR INC
Alvamar Realty
1611 Saint Andrews Dr (66047-1701)
P.O. Box 3726 (66046-0726)
PHONE..................................785 843-0196
B S-Billings, *Manager*
EMP: 20
SALES (corp-wide): 5.4MM **Privately Held**
WEB: www.alvamar.com
SIC: 7997 Membership sports & recreation clubs
PA: Alvamar, Inc.
1809 Crossgate Dr
Lawrence KS 66047
785 842-2929

(G-4734)
AMERICAN EQUIPMENT SALES INC
1723 E 1500 Rd (66044-9305)
PHONE..................................785 843-4500
Clay Heine, *President*
EMP: 15
SALES (est): 3.9MM **Privately Held**
SIC: 5511 5084 Trucks, tractors & trailers: new & used; lift trucks & parts

(G-4735)
ANDERSON RENTALS INC
1312 W 6th St (66044-2219)
PHONE..................................785 843-2044
Bill Anderson, *President*
Mary Anderson, *Treasurer*
Hazel Anderson, *Admin Sec*
EMP: 15 **EST:** 1946
SQ FT: 24,000
SALES (est): 1.5MM **Privately Held**
WEB: www.andersonrental.com
SIC: 7359 Tool rental; dishes, silverware, tables & banquet accessories rental

(G-4736)
ANIMAL HOSPITAL OF LAWRENCE
Also Called: Bayouth, William Dr
701 Michigan St (66044-2347)
PHONE..................................785 842-0609
Dr William Bayouth, *Owner*
Marsha Heeb, *Manager*
EMP: 10
SALES (est): 342.6K **Privately Held**
SIC: 0742 Veterinarian, animal specialties; animal hospital services, pets & other animal specialties

(G-4737)
API AMERICAS INC (DH)
Also Called: API Foils
3841 Greenway Cir (66046-5444)
PHONE..................................732 382-6800
Brad Mueller, *President*
Scott Lewis, *Vice Pres*
William Piercey, *Treasurer*
▲ **EMP:** 75
SQ FT: 47,000
SALES: 35MM **Privately Held**
WEB: www.apifoils.com
SIC: 3497 1761 Metal foil & leaf; sheet metalwork
HQ: Api Group Limited
Second Avenue
Stockport SK12
162 585-8700

(G-4738)
ASK ASSOCIATES INC
1201 Wakarusa Dr Ste C1 (66049-3889)
P.O. Box 3885 (66046-0885)
PHONE..................................785 841-8194
Sheila A Martinez, *CEO*
Bridget Walmsley, *President*
Kim Long, *Exec VP*
Kenneth Martinez, *Vice Pres*
Aimee Martinez, *Bd of Directors*
EMP: 25
SQ FT: 6,000
SALES: 5MM **Privately Held**
WEB: www.askusa.com
SIC: 8742 7379 Business planning & organizing services; computer related consulting services

(G-4739)
ASSOCIATES GOULD-EVENS
706 Massachusetts St (66044-2333)
PHONE..................................785 842-3800
Robert Gould, *Partner*
David Evans, *Partner*
Robert Gould, *Partner*
EMP: 23
SQ FT: 2,000
SALES (est): 1.1MM **Privately Held**
WEB: www.gouldevans.com
SIC: 8712 6512 Architectural engineering; nonresidential building operators

(G-4740)
ASSOCIATES IN DENTISTRY
Also Called: Kincaid, Paul D D S
306 E 23rd St (66046-4801)
P.O. Box 3745 (66046-0745)
PHONE..................................785 843-4333
Charles L Kincaid, *President*
David Brown, *Fmly & Gen Dent*
EMP: 15
SALES (est): 1MM **Privately Held**
WEB: www.charleskincaid.com
SIC: 8021 Dentists' office

(G-4741)
ASTHMA & ALLERGY ASSOCIATES PA
4601 W 6th St Ste B (66049-4129)
PHONE..................................785 842-3778
Ronald Weiner, *Owner*
EMP: 12
SALES (est): 65.5K **Privately Held**
SIC: 8011 Allergist

(G-4742)
AT&T CORP
3310 Iowa St Ste A (66046-5237)
PHONE..................................785 832-2700
Jason Ward, *President*
EMP: 46
SALES (corp-wide): 170.7B **Publicly Held**
SIC: 4812 Cellular telephone services
HQ: At&T Corp.
1 At&T Way
Bedminster NJ 07921
800 403-3302

(G-4743)
AT&T CORP
547 E 19th St (66046-3101)
PHONE..................................785 749-7155
EMP: 36
SALES (corp-wide): 170.7B **Publicly Held**
WEB: www.swbell.com
SIC: 4813 Local & long distance telephone communications
HQ: At&T Corp.
1 At&T Way
Bedminster NJ 07921
800 403-3302

(G-4744)
AUTOBODY OF LAWRENCE
Also Called: Briggs Chrysler Jeep Dodge Ram
2101 W 29th Ter (66047-3163)
PHONE..................................785 843-3055
Steve Puryear, *Principal*
▲ **EMP:** 50
SQ FT: 45,000
SALES (est): 10MM **Privately Held**
WEB: www.jimclarkmotors.com
SIC: 5511 7538 Automobiles, new & used; general automotive repair shops

(G-4745)
AVIS BUDGET GROUP INC
Also Called: Budget Truck Rental Service
2201 Saint James Ct (66046-5130)
PHONE..................................785 331-0658
Emma Stan, *Manager*
EMP: 10
SALES (corp-wide): 9.1B **Publicly Held**
WEB: www.cendant.com
SIC: 7514 Rent-a-car service
PA: Avis Budget Group, Inc.
6 Sylvan Way Ste 1
Parsippany NJ 07054
973 496-4700

(G-4746)
AVIS RENTAL CAR SYSTEMS
1216 E 23rd St (66046-5006)
PHONE..................................785 749-1464
Mark Viki, *Branch Mgr*
EMP: 264
SALES (corp-wide): 61.7MM **Privately Held**
SIC: 7514 Rent-a-car service
PA: Avis Rental Car Systems
6 Sylvan Way Ste 1
Parsippany NJ 07054
973 496-3000

(G-4747)
B A GREEN CONSTRUCTION CO INC
1207 Iowa St (66044-1923)
P.O. Box 8 (66044-0008)
PHONE..................................785 843-5277
Tracy Green, *President*
Timothy Green, *Corp Secy*
Michael Green, *Vice Pres*
EMP: 30 **EST:** 1947
SQ FT: 2,000
SALES (est): 7.2MM **Privately Held**
SIC: 1542 Commercial & office building, new construction; commercial & office buildings, renovation & repair

(G-4748)
B G CONSULTANTS INC
1405 Wakarusa Dr (66049-3832)
PHONE..................................785 749-4474
Brian Kingsley, *Vice Pres*
Dan Harden, *Project Engr*
Cecil Kingsley, *Manager*
EMP: 15
SALES (est): 1.3MM
SALES (corp-wide): 10.6MM **Privately Held**
WEB: www.bgcons.com
SIC: 8711 Consulting engineer
PA: B G Consultants, Inc
4806 Vue Du Lac Pl
Manhattan KS 66503
785 537-7448

(G-4749)
BANK AMERICA NATIONAL ASSN
Also Called: Bank of America Lawrence
900 Ohio St (66044-2847)
PHONE..................................785 842-1000
Rick Godsil, *Manager*
EMP: 15
SALES (corp-wide): 110.5B **Publicly Held**
WEB: www.bofa.com
SIC: 6021 National commercial banks
HQ: Bank Of America, National Association
100 S Tryon St
Charlotte NC 28202
704 386-5681

(G-4750)
BANK AMERICA NATIONAL ASSN
900 Ohio St (66044-2847)
PHONE..................................785 235-1532
S K Alexander III, *Branch Mgr*
EMP: 23
SALES (corp-wide): 110.5B **Publicly Held**
WEB: www.bofa.com
SIC: 6021 National commercial banks
HQ: Bank Of America, National Association
100 S Tryon St
Charlotte NC 28202
704 386-5681

(G-4751)
BATH & BODY WORKS LLC
Also Called: Bath Body Works 2038
3140 Iowa St Ste 105 (66046-5777)
PHONE..................................785 749-0214
Diane Lagesse, *Manager*
EMP: 17
SALES (corp-wide): 13.2B **Publicly Held**
WEB: www.bath-and-body.com
SIC: 5999 7231 Toiletries, cosmetics & perfumes; cosmetology & personal hygiene salons
HQ: Bath & Body Works, Llc
7 Limited Pkwy E
Reynoldsburg OH 43068

(G-4752)
BEAM-WARD KRUSE WILSON WRIGHT
10 E 9th St Ste E (66044-2600)
PHONE..................................785 865-1558
Charles Schimmel, *Manager*
EMP: 12
SALES (est): 441.7K **Privately Held**
SIC: 8111 General practice law office

(G-4753)
BEAR COMMUNICATIONS LLC
725 N 2nd St Ste M (66044-1475)
PHONE..................................785 856-3333
Brett Niles, *CEO*
EMP: 250 **EST:** 2004
SALES: 5MM **Privately Held**
SIC: 4899 Data communication services

(G-4754)
BERRY GLOBAL INC
2401 Lakeview Rd (66044)
PHONE..................................800 777-3080
EMP: 127 **Publicly Held**
SIC: 3089 3081 Bottle caps, molded plastic; unsupported plastics film & sheet
HQ: Berry Global, Inc.
101 Oakley St
Evansville IN 47710
812 424-2904

(G-4755)
BERT NASH CMNTY MNTAL HLTH CTR
200 Maine St Ste A (66044-1396)
PHONE..................................785 843-9192
David Johnson, *CEO*
EMP: 200
SQ FT: 12,000
SALES: 12.7MM **Privately Held**
WEB: www.bertnash.org
SIC: 8093 Mental health clinic, outpatient

(G-4756)
BETA THETA PHI
1425 Tennessee St (66044-3481)
PHONE..................................785 843-9188
Trey Anderson, *Principal*
EMP: 10
SALES (est): 215.6K **Privately Held**
SIC: 7041 Fraternities & sororities

(G-4757)
BIG HEART PET BRANDS
Also Called: Del Monte Foods
727 N Iowa St (66044-9000)
P.O. Box 1120 (66044-8120)
PHONE..................................785 312-3662
Eric Hirt, *Opers Mgr*
Taylor Yoest, *Opers Mgr*
Steve Allen, *Warehouse Mgr*
Jennifer Wolken, *Human Res Mgr*
Rod Marshall, *Branch Mgr*
EMP: 160
SALES (corp-wide): 7.8B **Publicly Held**
SIC: 2047 Cat food; dog food
HQ: Big Heart Pet Brands, Inc.
1 Maritime Plz Fl 2
San Francisco CA 94111
415 247-3000

(G-4758)
BISEL INC
Also Called: Minuteman Press
1404 E 24th St Ste B (66046-5354)
PHONE..................................785 842-2656
Dee Bisel, *President*
Ronald Bisel, *Vice Pres*
Kristi Burgess, *Treasurer*
Deanna D Bisel, *Officer*
Ryan Bisel, *Admin Sec*
EMP: 7
SQ FT: 2,800
SALES (est): 1.3MM **Privately Held**
WEB: www.minutemanlawrence.com
SIC: 2752 Commercial printing, lithographic

(G-4759)
BLACK HILLS/KANSAS GAS
Also Called: Black Hills Energy
601 N Iowa St (66044-9643)
PHONE..................................605 721-1700
Craig Allensworth, *President*
EMP: 26
SALES (corp-wide): 1.7B **Publicly Held**
SIC: 4924 Natural gas distribution
HQ: Black Hills/Kansas Gas Utility Company, Llc
7001 Mount Rushmore Rd
Rapid City SD 57702

(G-4760)
BLACK STAG BREWERY LLC
623 Massachusetts St (66044-2235)
PHONE..................................785 764-1628
Kathryn D Myers,
John Hampton,
EMP: 60
SQ FT: 12,000
SALES (est): 407K **Privately Held**
SIC: 5813 5084 Bar (drinking places); brewery products manufacturing machinery, commercial

(G-4761)
BLUESTREAK ENTERPRISES INC
Also Called: Stanley Steemer Carpet Cleaner
808 Lynn St (66044-4341)
PHONE..................................785 550-8179
Patrick Budenbender, *President*
Johnica Budenbender, *Vice Pres*
EMP: 10 **EST:** 1991
SALES: 850K **Privately Held**
SIC: 7217 Carpet & furniture cleaning on location

(G-4762)
BOYER INDUSTRIES CORPORATION (PA)
Also Called: Prosoco
3741 Greenway Cir (66046-5441)
PHONE..................................785 865-4200
Gerald E Boyer, *CEO*
David W Boyer, *President*
John Bourne, *Vice Pres*
Bruce Boyer, *Vice Pres*
Keith Donner, *Treasurer*
EMP: 70
SALES (est): 87.7MM **Privately Held**
SIC: 2899 Waterproofing compounds

(G-4763)
BOYS GRLS CLB LWRNCE LWRNCE K
Also Called: Boys & Girls of Lawrence
2910 Haskell Ave (66046-4942)
P.O. Box 748 (66044-0748)
PHONE..................................785 841-5672
James Lawrence, *Human Res Dir*
Alissa Bauer, *Marketing Staff*
Kenita Jarrett, *Marketing Staff*
Lindsay Simms, *Program Mgr*
Cody Wilson, *Director*
EMP: 80
SQ FT: 5,808
SALES: 3.6MM **Privately Held**
SIC: 8641 8322 7999 Youth organizations; youth center; recreation center

(G-4764)
BRAD H ALLEN ROOFING INC
776 Grant St (66044-5428)
P.O. Box 3221 (66046-0221)
PHONE..................................785 423-3861
Brad Allen, *President*
Susan Allen, *Admin Sec*
EMP: 12
SQ FT: 2,000
SALES: 1.5MM **Privately Held**
SIC: 1761 Roofing contractor

(G-4765)
BRADLEY ANIMAL HOSPITAL
935 E 23rd St (66046-4913)
PHONE..................................785 843-9533
John Bradley, *Owner*
EMP: 15
SALES (est): 1MM **Privately Held**
SIC: 0742 0752 Animal hospital services, pets & other animal specialties; grooming services, pet & animal specialties

(G-4766)
BRANDON WOODS RETIREMENT CMNTY
1501 Inverness Dr Ofc (66047-1834)
PHONE..................................785 838-8000
Teresa Prochaska, *Human Res Dir*
Jan Maddox, *Marketing Staff*
Taira Metcalf, *Office Mgr*
Jason Kohler, *Exec Dir*
Jason Koehler, *Exec Dir*
EMP: 250
SALES (est): 4.5MM **Privately Held**
SIC: 8361 8052 8051 Home for the aged; intermediate care facilities; skilled nursing care facilities

(G-4767)
BRIDGE HVEN MMORY CARE RSDENTS
1701 Research Park Dr (66047-3883)
PHONE..................................785 856-1630
R Wilson, *Exec Dir*
Sarah Randolph, *Exec Dir*
Robert Wilson, *Exec Dir*
EMP: 25 **EST:** 2011
SALES (est): 580.7K **Privately Held**
SIC: 8361 Residential care

(G-4768)
BRITE ENERGY SOLAR INC
1035 N 3rd St Ste 101 (66044-1491)
PHONE..................................785 856-9936
Tim Whall, *CEO*
Dan Bresingham, *CFO*
EMP: 50
SALES (est): 2.8MM
SALES (corp-wide): 209MM **Privately Held**
SIC: 1711 Solar energy contractor
PA: Gtcr Llc
300 N La Salle Dr # 5600
Chicago IL 60654
312 382-2200

(G-4769)
BROOKDALE SNIOR LVING CMMNTIES
Also Called: Sterling House of Lawrence
3220 Peterson Rd (66049-1963)
PHONE..................................785 832-9900
Amy Homer, *Manager*
EMP: 15
SALES (corp-wide): 4.5B **Publicly Held**
WEB: www.assisted.com
SIC: 8059 Rest home, with health care
HQ: Brookdale Senior Living Communities, Inc.
6737 W Wa St Ste 2300
Milwaukee WI 53214
414 918-5000

(G-4770)
BROWN INDUSTRIES LLC (PA)
Also Called: Brown Specialty Vehicles
807 E 29th St (66046-4925)
PHONE..................................785 842-6506
David Price, *President*
Dane Jennison, *President*
Brett Agnew, *General Mgr*
W Dane Jennison, *Vice Pres*
Jeremiah Lahm, *Opers Staff*
EMP: 85 **EST:** 1946
SQ FT: 62,000
SALES (est): 27.6MM **Privately Held**
WEB: www.bcvi.com
SIC: 3312 3711 3715 5012 Rails, steel or iron; truck & tractor truck assembly; bus trailers, tractor type; trailers for passenger vehicles

(G-4771)
BUCKINGHAM PALACE INC
Also Called: Buckingham Palace House Clg
2441 W 6th St (66049-2557)
PHONE..................................785 842-6264
Jennifer Lutz, *President*
EMP: 60
SALES (est): 1.6MM **Privately Held**
SIC: 7349 Janitorial service, contract basis

(G-4772)
CALLAHAN CREEK INC (PA)
805 New Hampshire St A (66044-2774)
PHONE..................................785 838-4774
Cynthia Maude, *CEO*
Chris Marshall, *President*
Tom Tholen, *President*
Jan Anderson, *Vice Pres*
Sarah Etzel, *Vice Pres*
EMP: 58
SALES (est): 14.2MM **Privately Held**
WEB: www.callahancreek.com
SIC: 7311 8732 Advertising agencies; market analysis or research

(G-4773)
CALLED TO GREATNESS MINISTRIES
5836 Robinson Dr (66049-5007)
PHONE..................................785 749-2100
Brooke Waters, *Exec Dir*
Burton Gepford, *Director*
Wayne Katie Simien, *Director*
EMP: 38
SALES: 116.4K **Privately Held**
SIC: 8699 Charitable organization

(G-4774)
CALVIN EDDY & KAPPELMAN INC (PA)
Also Called: Nationwide
1011 Westdale Rd (66049-2638)
PHONE..................................785 843-2772
Joe Baker, *President*
Allan Hack, *Corp Secy*
Mark Tomes, *Vice Pres*
EMP: 20
SQ FT: 3,000
SALES (est): 3.9MM **Privately Held**
WEB: www.cek-insurance.com
SIC: 6411 Insurance agents

(G-4775)
CAPITOL FEDERAL SAVINGS BANK
11th & Vermont Sts (66044)
PHONE..................................785 749-9100
Deborah Johnston, *Manager*
EMP: 11
SALES (corp-wide): 351.9MM **Publicly Held**
WEB: www.capfed.com
SIC: 6035 Federal savings & loan associations
HQ: Capitol Federal Savings Bank
700 S Kansas Ave Fl 1
Topeka KS 66603
785 235-1341

(G-4776)
CASCADE DENTAL CARE
1425 Wakarusa Dr (66049-3832)
PHONE..................................785 841-3311
Thomas A Rainbolt DDS, *Owner*
Shari Duff, *Manager*
EMP: 12
SALES (est): 1.3MM **Privately Held**
SIC: 8021 Dentists' office

(G-4777)
CAVE INN LLC
Also Called: Country Suites By Carlson
2176 E 23rd St (66046-5602)
PHONE..................................785 749-6010
Doug Wildeman,
EMP: 20
SALES (est): 109.1K **Privately Held**
SIC: 7011 Hotels & motels

(G-4778)
CEK REAL ESTATE INC
Also Called: C E K Real Estte
1501 Kasold Dr (66047-1601)
PHONE..................................785 843-2055
Patrick Flavin, *President*
EMP: 13
SALES (est): 606.5K **Privately Held**
SIC: 6531 Real estate agent, residential

(G-4779)
CENTRAL NATIONAL BANK
3140 Nieder Rd (66047-1950)
PHONE..................................785 838-1960
Kindal Ware, *Branch Mgr*
EMP: 10
SALES (corp-wide): 55.4MM **Privately Held**
SIC: 6021 National commercial banks
HQ: Central National Bank (Inc)
802 N Washington St
Junction City KS 66441
785 238-4114

(G-4780)
CENTRAL NATIONAL BANK
711 Wakarusa Dr (66049-3751)
PHONE..................................785 838-1893
Stephanie Rasys, *Manager*
EMP: 12
SALES (corp-wide): 55.4MM **Privately Held**
WEB: www.centralnational.com
SIC: 6021 National commercial banks
HQ: Central National Bank (Inc)
802 N Washington St
Junction City KS 66441
785 238-4114

(G-4781)
CENTRAL SOYFOODS
710 E 22nd St Ste C (66046-3118)
P.O. Box 581 (66044-0581)
PHONE..................................785 312-8638
William Mackie, *General Mgr*
EMP: 12
SQ FT: 1,800
SALES (est): 1.5MM **Privately Held**
WEB: www.centralsoyfoods.com
SIC: 2099 5153 Tofu, except frozen desserts; grain & field beans

(G-4782)
CENTURY SCHOOL INC
816 Kentucky St (66044-2648)
PHONE..................................785 832-0101
Don Bushell, *President*
EMP: 30
SALES: 566.5K **Privately Held**
WEB: www.centuryschool.org
SIC: 8351 8211 Preschool center; private elementary school

(G-4783)
CHADA SALES INC
815 E 12th St Ste A (66044-3372)
PHONE..................................785 842-1199
Christine Copp, *President*
Robert Palmateer, *Sales Staff*
EMP: 10
SQ FT: 5,000
SALES (est): 3.6MM **Privately Held**
WEB: www.chadasales.com
SIC: 5085 Industrial supplies

(G-4784)
CHEMTRADE PHOSPHOROUS SPC LLC
440 N 9th St (66044-5424)
PHONE..................................785 843-2290
Mark Davis, *CEO*
Leon Aarts, *Vice Pres*
Rohit Bhardwaj, *Vice Pres*
Douglas Cadwell, *Vice Pres*
Tab McCullough, *Vice Pres*
EMP: 28
SALES (est): 5.3MM **Privately Held**
SIC: 2899 Chemical preparations

(G-4785)
CHEMTRADE REFINERY SVCS INC (HQ)
Also Called: Chemtrade Phosphorous Spc
440 N 9th St (66044-5424)
PHONE..................................785 843-2290

Mark Davis, *CEO*
Michael Boyce, *Ch of Bd*
Paul Ferrall, *President*
Drew Fleming, *Plant Mgr*
Ken Graham, *Maint Spvr*
EMP: 70
SALES (est): 70.3MM
SALES (corp-wide): 1.2B **Privately Held**
SIC: 2819 Sulfuric acid, oleum
PA: Chemtrade Logistics Income Fund
155 Gordon Baker Rd Suite 300
North York ON M2H 3
416 496-5856

(G-4786)
CHILDRENS LEARNING CENTER INC
205 N Michigan St (66044-1036)
PHONE..................................785 841-2185
Tara Glanton, *Director*
Becky Sullivan, *Director*
EMP: 33
SALES: 718.5K **Privately Held**
SIC: 8351 Child day care services

(G-4787)
CHIPS INC
2220 Harper St (66046-3244)
PHONE..................................785 842-6921
David Vaughn, *President*
EMP: 10
SALES (est): 372K **Privately Held**
SIC: 4932 Gas & other services combined

(G-4788)
CHRISTIAN PSYCHOLOGICAL SVCS (PA)
3500 Westridge Dr (66049-2258)
PHONE..................................785 843-2429
Mac Harnden, *Exec Dir*
Barrie Arachtingi, *Exec Dir*
EMP: 12
SALES: 672.8K **Privately Held**
SIC: 8322 8049 Family counseling services; clinical psychologist

(G-4789)
CITY OF LAWRENCE
110 Riverfront Rd (66044-1476)
PHONE..................................785 832-7700
Scott McCullough, *Principal*
EMP: 15 **Privately Held**
SIC: 9199 7389 ; building inspection service
PA: City Of Lawrence
6 E 6th St
Lawrence KS 66044
785 832-3123

(G-4790)
CITY OF LAWRENCE
Also Called: Eagle Bend Golf Course
1250 E 902nd Rd (66047)
P.O. Box 708 (66044-0708)
PHONE..................................785 748-0600
Jim Kane, *Manager*
EMP: 12 **Privately Held**
WEB: www.lawrence.lib.ks.us
SIC: 7992 Public golf courses
PA: City Of Lawrence
6 E 6th St
Lawrence KS 66044
785 832-3123

(G-4791)
CITY OF LAWRENCE
Also Called: Wastewater Treatment Facility
1400 E 8th St (66044-2690)
P.O. Box 708 (66044-0708)
PHONE..................................785 832-7840
Dave King, *Superintendent*
Dave Wagner, *Branch Mgr*
EMP: 50 **Privately Held**
WEB: www.lawrence.lib.ks.us
SIC: 4941 9511 Water supply; waste management agencies
PA: City Of Lawrence
6 E 6th St
Lawrence KS 66044
785 832-3123

(G-4792)
CLEANSWEEP JANITORIAL INC
Also Called: ServiceMaster Cleansweep Jantr
423 Hutton Cir (66049-4843)
PHONE..................................785 856-8617
Julie Mitchell, *President*
Jackson Mitchell, *Principal*
EMP: 10
SALES: 125K **Privately Held**
SIC: 7349 Building maintenance services

(G-4793)
CLINTON MARINA INC
1329 E 800 Rd (66046)
P.O. Box 3427 (66046-0427)
PHONE..................................785 749-3222
Megan Hiebert, *President*
EMP: 20
SALES (est): 857.1K **Privately Held**
SIC: 4493 Boat yards, storage & incidental repair

(G-4794)
CLINTON PARKWAY ANIMAL HOSP
4340 Clinton Pkwy (66047-2009)
PHONE..................................785 841-3131
Gary Olson, *Owner*
Thomas Liebl, *Co-Owner*
Netta George, *Office Mgr*
Tom Liebl, *Med Doctor*
Miranda Lyon, *Med Doctor*
EMP: 32
SALES (est): 1.1MM **Privately Held**
SIC: 0742 0752 Animal hospital services, pets & other animal specialties; boarding services, kennels

(G-4795)
CLOUDS HEATING AND AC
920 E 28th St (66046-4922)
P.O. Box 3569 (66046-0569)
PHONE..................................785 842-2258
Sharla Cloud, *President*
Douglas W Cloud, *President*
Sharla Huntington, *President*
Shannon C Cloud, *Admin Sec*
EMP: 21 **EST:** 1971
SQ FT: 19,000
SALES (est): 3.5MM **Privately Held**
WEB: www.cloudhvac.com
SIC: 1711 Warm air heating & air conditioning contractor; refrigeration contractor

(G-4796)
COBALT IRON INC
Also Called: Cobalt Iron Vault
1421 Res Pk Dr Ste 2c (66049)
PHONE..................................888 584-4766
Richard R Spurlock, *CEO*
Mary Spurlock, *Vice Pres*
Brian Smith, *VP Opers*
Randy Jones, *VP Engrg*
Michael Mesarchik, *Sales Staff*
EMP: 23 **EST:** 2013
SQ FT: 7,300
SALES (est): 10.8MM **Privately Held**
SIC: 5045 Computer software

(G-4797)
COLLECTION OF LAWRENCE INC
303 W 11th St (66044-3311)
PHONE..................................785 843-4210
Lynann L Chance, *President*
John R Haase, *Treasurer*
John Haase, *Admin Sec*
EMP: 20
SQ FT: 3,500
SALES (est): 1.2MM **Privately Held**
SIC: 7323 Credit bureau & agency

(G-4798)
COLLIERS INTL NENG LLC
805 New Hampshire St (66044-2739)
PHONE..................................785 865-5100
EMP: 24
SALES (corp-wide): 2.8B **Privately Held**
SIC: 6531 Real estate agent, commercial
HQ: Colliers International New England, Llc
160 Federal St Fl 11
Boston MA 02110
617 330-8000

(G-4799)
COMMERCE BANK
955 Iowa St (66044-1836)
PHONE..................................785 865-4799
Miller Cathy, *Branch Mgr*
EMP: 13
SALES (corp-wide): 1.3B **Publicly Held**
SIC: 6021 National commercial banks
HQ: Commerce Bank
1000 Walnut St Fl 700
Kansas City MO 64106
816 234-2000

(G-4800)
COMMERCE BANK
1015 W 23rd St (66046-4412)
PHONE..................................816 234-2000
Judy Demorest, *Branch Mgr*
EMP: 13
SALES (corp-wide): 1.3B **Publicly Held**
SIC: 6022 State commercial banks
HQ: Commerce Bank
1000 Walnut St Fl 700
Kansas City MO 64106
816 234-2000

(G-4801)
COMMERCE BANK
1321 Oread Ave (66045-3125)
PHONE..................................816 234-2000
Jennifer Cook, *Manager*
EMP: 13
SALES (corp-wide): 1.3B **Publicly Held**
SIC: 6021 National commercial banks
HQ: Commerce Bank
1000 Walnut St Fl 700
Kansas City MO 64106
816 234-2000

(G-4802)
COMMERCIAL RE WOMEN NETWRK
Also Called: Crew Network
1201 Wakarusa Dr Ste D1 (66049-1892)
PHONE..................................785 832-1808
Gail Ayers, *CEO*
Bill Beck, *General Mgr*
Matthew Hicks, *General Mgr*
Bruce Holder, *General Mgr*
Larry Long, *General Mgr*
EMP: 17
SQ FT: 3,000
SALES: 348.3K **Privately Held**
SIC: 8742 Management consulting services

(G-4803)
COMMUNITY CHILDRENS CENTER INC
Also Called: Head Start
925 Vermont St (66044-2864)
PHONE..................................785 842-2515
Carolyn Kelly, *Store Dir*
EMP: 18
SALES: 501.9K **Privately Held**
SIC: 8351 Head start center, except in conjunction with school

(G-4804)
COMMUNITY LVING OPPRTNTIES INC
Also Called: Clo
2113 Delaware St (66046-3149)
PHONE..................................785 865-5520
Jamie Price, *COO*
Dorothy Lind, *Manager*
Mike Strauss, *Exec Dir*
Connie Keeling, *Director*
Michelle Ray, *Director*
EMP: 225
SALES (corp-wide): 22.5MM **Privately Held**
WEB: www.clokansas.com
SIC: 8361 8322 Home for the mentally handicapped; individual & family services
PA: Community Living Opportunities, Inc.
11627 W 79th St
Lenexa KS 66214
913 341-9316

(G-4805)
COMMUNITY LVING OPPRTNTIES INC
Also Called: Monterey Way House
1121 Monterey Way (66049-3503)
PHONE..................................785 832-2332
Mike Glazes, *Manager*
EMP: 11
SALES (corp-wide): 22.5MM **Privately Held**
WEB: www.clokansas.com
SIC: 8361 8059 Home for the mentally handicapped; home for the mentally retarded, exc. skilled or intermediate
PA: Community Living Opportunities, Inc.
11627 W 79th St
Lenexa KS 66214
913 341-9316

(G-4806)
COMMUNITY LVING OPPRTNTIES INC
Also Called: Terrace House
1311 E 21st Ter Ste 4 (66046-3269)
PHONE..................................785 843-7072
Michael Strous, *Manager*
EMP: 35
SALES (corp-wide): 22.5MM **Privately Held**
WEB: www.clokansas.com
SIC: 8361 8059 Home for the mentally handicapped; home for the mentally retarded, exc. skilled or intermediate
PA: Community Living Opportunities, Inc.
11627 W 79th St
Lenexa KS 66214
913 341-9316

(G-4807)
COMPUTRZED ASSSSMENTS LRNG LLC
Also Called: Cal
1202 E 23rd St Ste D (66046-4103)
PHONE..................................785 856-1034
Amanda Sterling, *Project Mgr*
Peter Toth, *Project Mgr*
Paula Schumacher, *Business Anlyst*
Patrick Wilbur, *Business Anlyst*
Doug Glasnip PHD, *Mng Member*
EMP: 10
SALES (est): 1.4MM
SALES (corp-wide): 1.3B **Publicly Held**
SIC: 8748 Testing service, educational or personnel
PA: Educational Testing Service Inc
660 Rosedale Rd
Princeton NJ 08540
609 921-9000

(G-4808)
CONCRETE INC
791 E 1500 Rd (66046-8212)
PHONE..................................785 594-4838
Toll Free:..................................888 -
John N Stevens, *President*
Karen Steven, *Corp Secy*
EMP: 10 **EST:** 1997
SALES (est): 934.3K **Privately Held**
SIC: 1771 Concrete work

(G-4809)
CONNECTION AT LAWRENCE
3100 Ousdahl Rd (66046-4367)
PHONE..................................785 842-3336
Wendy Huggins, *Principal*
EMP: 20
SALES (est): 810K **Privately Held**
SIC: 6531 Rental agent, real estate

(G-4810)
CONNEX INTERNATIONAL INC
1800 E 23rd St (66046-5107)
PHONE..................................785 749-9500
Dominic Mercurio, *General Mgr*
Patrick Hole, *Opers Mgr*
Ruthann Krohn, *Accounts Mgr*
Jeff Toohey, *Supervisor*
Cindy Blais, *Executive Asst*
EMP: 107
SALES (est): 2.7MM
SALES (corp-wide): 78.2MM **Privately Held**
WEB: www.connexintl.com
SIC: 4813
PA: Connex International, Inc.
46 Federal Rd Ste F
Danbury CT 06810
203 731-5400

(G-4811)
COPY CO CORPORATION
Also Called: Copy Co of Lawrence
540 Fireside Ct (66049-2300)
PHONE..................................785 832-2679

GEOGRAPHIC

Ryan Irwin, *Manager*
EMP: 7
SALES (est): 948.4K **Privately Held**
WEB: www.wwwebservice.net
SIC: 8742 2759 7334 Management consulting services; invitations: printing; blueprinting service
PA: Copy Co Corporation
2346 Planet Ave
Salina KS 67401

(G-4812)
COTTONWOOD INCORPORATED
2801 W 31st St (66047-3050)
PHONE..................................785 842-0550
Sharon Spratt, *CEO*
Gay Quinn, *Engineer*
Nina Schmus, *Sales Mgr*
JRC Condra, *Marketing Staff*
Drew Diedel, *Case Mgr*
EMP: 239
SQ FT: 64,000
SALES: 19.7MM **Privately Held**
SIC: 8331 Vocational rehabilitation agency

(G-4813)
COUNTY OF DOUGLAS
Also Called: Noxious Weeds
711 23rd (66046)
PHONE..................................785 331-1330
Harold Starkebaum, *Director*
EMP: 30 **Privately Held**
WEB: www.douglas-county.com
SIC: 0711 Weed control services before planting
PA: County Of Douglas
1100 Mkschstts St Ste 200
Lawrence KS 66044
785 832-5268

(G-4814)
COUNTY OF DOUGLAS
Also Called: Public Work Dept
3755 E 25th St (66046-5674)
PHONE..................................785 832-5293
Keith Browning, *Superintendent*
Keith Brownie, *Director*
EMP: 50 **Privately Held**
WEB: www.douglas-county.com
SIC: 1611 9121 General contractor, highway & street construction;
PA: County Of Douglas
1100 Mkschstts St Ste 200
Lawrence KS 66044
785 832-5268

(G-4815)
COYOTE INVESTMENT & NETWORKING
2011 Hogan Dr (66047-2043)
PHONE..................................785 550-6028
Dr Dan Bloom, *Principal*
EMP: 50
SALES (est): 1.5MM **Privately Held**
SIC: 1521 Single-family housing construction

(G-4816)
COYOTES INC
1003 E 23rd St (66046-5003)
PHONE..................................785 842-2295
EMP: 25
SALES (est): 990K **Privately Held**
SIC: 6512 7997 Nonresidential Building Operator Membership Sport/Recreation Club

(G-4817)
CRITITECH INC
1849 E 1450 Rd (66044-9452)
P.O. Box 442280 (66044-1280)
PHONE..................................785 841-7120
Matthew McClorey, *President*
Jahna Espinosa, *Director*
EMP: 13
SQ FT: 10,000
SALES (est): 1.2MM **Privately Held**
WEB: www.crititech.com
SIC: 8733 Research institute

(G-4818)
CRITITECH PARTICLE ENGG
1849 E 1450 Rd (66044-9452)
PHONE..................................785 841-7120
Matthew McClorey,
Neal Gapinski,
Jeffrey Morrison,
EMP: 15 **EST:** 2017
SQ FT: 10,000
SALES (est): 1MM **Privately Held**
SIC: 2834 Powders, pharmaceutical; druggists' preparations (pharmaceuticals); solutions, pharmaceutical; tablets, pharmaceutical

(G-4819)
CSL PLASMA INC
816 W 24th St (66046-4417)
PHONE..................................785 749-5750
Wayne Sharp, *Manager*
EMP: 20 **Privately Held**
WEB: www.zlbplasma.com
SIC: 8099 2836 Plasmapherous center; blood derivatives
HQ: Csl Plasma Inc.
900 Broken Sound Pkwy Nw # 400
Boca Raton FL 33487
561 981-3700

(G-4820)
CUSTOM FABRICATION LLC
1017 N 1156 Rd (66047-9439)
PHONE..................................785 331-9460
Stephen Wendland, *Principal*
EMP: 5
SALES (est): 282.8K **Privately Held**
SIC: 3499 Novelties & giftware, including trophies

(G-4821)
CUTLER REPAVING INC (PA)
921 E 27th St (66046-4917)
PHONE..................................785 843-1524
Bob Veskerna, *CEO*
Charles Robert Veskerna, *President*
Judith K Coffman, *Corp Secy*
Douglas Cutler, *Exec VP*
John Miles, *Vice Pres*
EMP: 100
SQ FT: 3,000
SALES (est): 42.9MM **Privately Held**
WEB: www.cutlerrepaving.com
SIC: 1611 Resurfacing contractor

(G-4822)
CYDEX PHARMACEUTICALS INC
2029 Becker Dr (66047-1620)
PHONE..................................913 685-8850
John L Higgins, *President*
Jose L Rodriguez, *Vice Pres*
Allen K Roberson, *CFO*
EMP: 17
SQ FT: 19,500
SALES (est): 2.4MM
SALES (corp-wide): 251.4MM **Publicly Held**
WEB: www.cydexinc.com
SIC: 2834 Druggists' preparations (pharmaceuticals)
PA: Ligand Pharmaceuticals Incorporated
3911 Sorrento Valley Blvd # 110
San Diego CA 92121
858 550-7500

(G-4823)
D & D TIRE INC
1000 Vermont St (66044-2983)
PHONE..................................785 843-0191
Phillip D Dwyer, *President*
Daryl D Dwyer, *Vice Pres*
Norma J Dwyer, *Admin Sec*
EMP: 10
SQ FT: 3,000
SALES (est): 2.1MM **Privately Held**
SIC: 5531 5014 Automotive tires; tires & tubes

(G-4824)
DALE P DENNING MD FACS
1130 W 4th St Ste 2051 (66044-1336)
PHONE..................................785 856-8346
Dale Denning, *Principal*
EMP: 10
SALES (est): 104.2K **Privately Held**
SIC: 8011 Surgeon

(G-4825)
DANCE GALLERY
4940 Legends Dr (66049-3886)
PHONE..................................785 838-9100
Karen Fender, *Owner*
Tim Flattery, *Director*
EMP: 15
SALES (est): 365.8K **Privately Held**
SIC: 7911 Dance instructor & school services

(G-4826)
DATATEAM SYSTEMS INC
4911 Legends Dr (66049-5800)
PHONE..................................785 843-8150
Roger B Haack, *President*
Craig McCollam, *Vice Pres*
Beth Senn, *Vice Pres*
EMP: 21
SQ FT: 6,200
SALES (est): 1.4MM **Privately Held**
WEB: www.datateam.com
SIC: 7372 7371 Prepackaged software; custom computer programming services

(G-4827)
DAVID M KING & ASSOCIATES (PA)
1425 Oread West St # 106 (66049-4087)
PHONE..................................785 841-9517
Roger Schenewerk, *President*
EMP: 13
SQ FT: 4,800
SALES (est): 3.4MM **Privately Held**
SIC: 6211 Brokers, security

(G-4828)
DCCCA INC
Also Called: Deca Outpatient
1739 E 23rd St (66046-5017)
PHONE..................................785 830-8238
Lisa Carter, *Manager*
EMP: 10 **Privately Held**
SIC: 8093 8322 Alcohol clinic, outpatient; individual & family services
PA: Dccca, Inc.
3312 Clinton Pkwy
Lawrence KS

(G-4829)
DCCCA INC
Also Called: First Step House
3015 W 31st St (66047-3042)
PHONE..................................785 843-9262
Lisa Carter, *Director*
EMP: 25 **Privately Held**
SIC: 8093 Alcohol clinic, outpatient
PA: Dccca, Inc.
3312 Clinton Pkwy
Lawrence KS

(G-4830)
DECIPHERA PHARMACEUTICALS LLC
643 Msschsetts St Ste 200 (66044)
PHONE..................................785 830-2100
Michael D Taylor, *CEO*
Mike Kaufman, *Vice Pres*
Bryan Smith, *Research*
Susan E McElwain, *Finance*
Jama Jameson Pitman, *Manager*
EMP: 10
SQ FT: 8,000
SALES (est): 1.9MM **Privately Held**
SIC: 8731 Biotechnical research, commercial

(G-4831)
DELTA GAMMA
1015 Emery Rd (66044-2514)
PHONE..................................785 830-9945
Andrea Hadel, *President*
EMP: 12
SALES: 340.3K **Privately Held**
SIC: 8641 7041 University club; boarding house, fraternity & sorority

(G-4832)
DELTA TAU DELTA SOCIETY
Also Called: Delta Tau Delta of Lawrence
1111 W 11th St (66044-2903)
PHONE..................................785 843-6866
Andy Chatman, *President*
Billy Budnovitch, *Vice Pres*
EMP: 13
SALES: 337.8K **Privately Held**
SIC: 8641 University club

(G-4833)
DESIGN ANALYSIS AND RES CORP
Also Called: Darcorporation
910 E 29th St (66046-4926)
PHONE..................................785 832-0434
Willem Anemaat, *President*
Maryjo Anemaat, *Vice Pres*
EMP: 17
SALES (est): 2.2MM **Privately Held**
WEB: www.darcorp.com
SIC: 7373 8748 5192 8711 Computer systems analysis & design; business consulting; books; engineering services

(G-4834)
DEW - DRINK EAT WELL LLC
2205 Haskell Ave (66046-3253)
PHONE..................................785 856-3399
Hilary Brown, *President*
Lydia Butler, *President*
Becky Harpstrite, *Prdtn Mgr*
EMP: 35
SALES (est): 7MM **Privately Held**
SIC: 2038 Frozen specialties

(G-4835)
DEYNO LLC
925 Iowa St Ste K (66044-1801)
PHONE..................................785 551-8949
Derric Wheeler,
EMP: 12
SALES (est): 1.1MM **Privately Held**
SIC: 2337 2326 5699 Uniforms, except athletic: women's, misses' & juniors'; work uniforms; medical & hospital uniforms, men's; uniforms

(G-4836)
DOUGLAS COUNTY BANK (PA)
300 W 9th St (66044-2889)
P.O. Box 429 (66044-0429)
PHONE..................................785 865-1000
Ross Beach, *CEO*
Ted Haggart, *President*
Patrick Slabough, *Exec VP*
Doug Gaston, *Vice Pres*
Judy Mulford, *Vice Pres*
EMP: 75 **EST:** 1951
SALES: 11.9MM **Privately Held**
WEB: www.douglascountybank.com
SIC: 6022 State trust companies accepting deposits, commercial

(G-4837)
DOUGLAS COUNTY BANK
Also Called: Knights of Kentucky
1501 Inverness Dr Ofc (66047-1834)
PHONE..................................785 865-1022
Ted Haggert, *Manager*
EMP: 28
SALES (corp-wide): 11.9MM **Privately Held**
WEB: www.douglascountybank.com
SIC: 6022 State commercial banks
PA: Douglas County Bank
300 W 9th St
Lawrence KS 66044
785 865-1000

(G-4838)
DOUGLAS COUNTY CHILD DEV ASSN
Also Called: Positive Bright Start
1900 Delaware St (66046-3172)
PHONE..................................785 842-9679
Anna Jenny, *Exec Dir*
EMP: 16
SALES: 1.4MM **Privately Held**
WEB: www.dccda.org
SIC: 8322 Children's aid society

(G-4839)
DOUGLAS COUNTY DNTL CLINIC INC
4920 Bob Billings Pkwy (66049-3855)
PHONE..................................785 312-7770
Julie Branstrom, *Exec Dir*
Elizabeth Mitchell, *Assistant*
EMP: 11
SQ FT: 1,500
SALES: 1.2MM **Privately Held**
SIC: 8021 Dental surgeon

(G-4840)
DOUGLAS COUNTY HISTORICAL SOC
Also Called: WATKINS COMMUNITY MUSEUM OF HI
1047 Massachusetts St (66044-2961)
PHONE..................................785 841-4109
John Jewell, *Business Mgr*
Sarah Bell, *Manager*
Brittany Keegan, *Manager*
Steve Nowak, *Exec Dir*
Steven Nowak, *Director*
EMP: 10
SALES: 743.3K **Privately Held**
SIC: 8412 Historical society; museum

(G-4841)
DRS DOBBINS & LETOURNEAU
Also Called: Dobbins, Kent E
831 Vermont St (66044-2665)
PHONE..................................785 843-5665
Charles Pohl, *Partner*
Kent Dobbins, *Partner*
EMP: 15
SALES (est): 1.1MM **Privately Held**
SIC: 8042 8011 5995 Specialized optometrists; offices & clinics of medical doctors; contact lenses, prescription

(G-4842)
DUNCO INC
1729 Bullene Ave (66044-4322)
PHONE..................................785 594-7137
Wayne Duncan, *Principal*
EMP: 13
SALES (est): 1.7MM **Privately Held**
WEB: www.dunco.com
SIC: 3585 Heating & air conditioning combination units

(G-4843)
E STATE MANAGEMENT LLC
1311 George Ct (66044-2272)
PHONE..................................785 312-9945
Steven George, *Mng Member*
EMP: 10 **EST:** 2007
SALES (est): 371.1K **Privately Held**
SIC: 6514 Dwelling operators, except apartments

(G-4844)
EAGLE TRAILER COMPANY INC
920 E 30th St (66046-4928)
PHONE..................................785 841-3200
Kevin Fredrickson, *President*
EMP: 5
SQ FT: 3,900
SALES (est): 1MM **Privately Held**
WEB: www.usatrailers.com
SIC: 3715 7539 5599 5051 Truck trailers; trailer repair; utility trailers; steel; trailers & trailer equipment

(G-4845)
EDGE ENTERPRISES INC
708 W 9th St Ste 107 (66044-2846)
P.O. Box 1304 (66044-8304)
PHONE..................................785 749-1473
Jean Schumaker, *President*
Donald Deshler, *Vice Pres*
EMP: 20
SQ FT: 2,000
SALES (est): 1.7MM **Privately Held**
WEB: www.edgeenterprisesinc.com
SIC: 8733 Educational research agency

(G-4846)
EDR LAWRENCE LTD PARTNERSHIP
Also Called: Reserve On West 31st St, The
2511 W 31st St (66047-2073)
PHONE..................................785 842-0032
Ciara Roberts, *Manager*
EMP: 17 **EST:** 2011
SALES (est): 886.7K **Privately Held**
SIC: 6513 Apartment building operators

(G-4847)
EDWARDS & WILSON PERIODONTIDES
Also Called: Wilson, Angela DDS Ms
4830 Quail Crest Pl Ste A (66049-3842)
PHONE..................................785 843-4076
Mark Edwards DDS, *Partner*
Angela Wilson DDS, *Partner*
EMP: 12
SALES (est): 542.1K **Privately Held**
SIC: 8021 Periodontist

(G-4848)
EICHHORN HOLDINGS LLC
Also Called: Rueschhoff Lsmith SEC Systems
3727 W 6th St (66049-3250)
PHONE..................................785 843-1426
Warren White, *General Mgr*
Don Stowe,
EMP: 15
SALES: 2MM **Privately Held**
SIC: 7382 7699 Security systems services; locksmith shop

(G-4849)
ELDRIDGE HOLDING LLC
701 Massachusetts St (66044-2345)
PHONE..................................785 749-5011
Michelle Crowell,
EMP: 12 **Privately Held**
SIC: 6719 Holding companies

(G-4850)
ELDRIDGE HOUSE INVEST LTD PTNR
701 Massachusetts St (66044-2345)
PHONE..................................785 749-5011
Robert Phillips, *Partner*
EMP: 40
SQ FT: 50,000
SALES (est): 1.5MM **Privately Held**
WEB: www.eldridgehotel.com
SIC: 7011 7299 5812 Hotels; banquet hall facilities; caterers

(G-4851)
ELIZABETH B BALLARD COMM CTR
708 Elm St (66044-5434)
P.O. Box 7 (66044-0007)
PHONE..................................785 842-0729
Dianne Ensminger, *CEO*
EMP: 15
SQ FT: 7,500
SALES: 751.1K **Privately Held**
SIC: 8351 8322 Child day care services; individual & family services; emergency shelters

(G-4852)
EMPRISE BANK
1121 Wakarusa Dr (66049-3864)
PHONE..................................785 838-2001
Cynthia Yulich, *Manager*
EMP: 12
SALES (corp-wide): 80MM **Privately Held**
WEB: www.emprisebank.com
SIC: 6022 6162 State trust companies accepting deposits, commercial; mortgage bankers & correspondents
HQ: Emprise Bank
257 N Broadway Ave
Wichita KS 67202
316 383-4400

(G-4853)
EMR-PCG CONSTRUCTION GROUP
2110 Delaware St Ste B (66046-3112)
PHONE..................................406 249-7730
Marvin Yakos,
EMP: 25
SALES (est): 1.1MM **Privately Held**
SIC: 1542 7389 Commercial & office building, new construction;

(G-4854)
EVERGY KANSAS CENTRAL INC
Also Called: Kpl Gas Service
1250 N 1800 Rd (66049-9025)
PHONE..................................785 331-4700
John Bridson, *Director*
EMP: 120
SALES (corp-wide): 4.2B **Publicly Held**
SIC: 4911 Electric services
HQ: Evergy Kansas Central, Inc.
818 S Kansas Ave
Topeka KS 66612
785 575-6300

(G-4855)
FAIRWAY INDEPENDENT MRTG CORP
2701 W 6th St (66049-4306)
PHONE..................................785 841-4434
Diane Fry, *Branch Mgr*
EMP: 15 **Privately Held**
SIC: 6162 Mortgage bankers & correspondents
PA: Fairway Independent Mortgage Corporation
4750 S Biltmore Ln
Madison WI 53718

(G-4856)
FAMILY MEDICINE ASSOCIATES PA
4921 W 18th St (66047-2090)
PHONE..................................785 830-0100
Dan G Severa MD, *Owner*
Jean Schrader, *Med Doctor*
EMP: 15
SALES (est): 2.3MM **Privately Held**
SIC: 8011 General & family practice, physician/surgeon

(G-4857)
FAMILY THERAPY INST MIDWEST
2619 W 6th St Ste B (66049-4300)
PHONE..................................785 830-8299
Greg Tentari, *Principal*
Wes Crenshaw, *Director*
David Barnum PHD, *Director*
Wes Cirenshaw, *Director*
Mary L Egidy, *Director*
EMP: 10 **EST:** 2001
SALES (est): 661.8K **Privately Held**
SIC: 8322 8049 Family counseling services; psychotherapist, except M.D.

(G-4858)
FEET ON GROUND MARKETING INC
1301 Louisiana St (66044-3427)
PHONE..................................913 242-5558
Conner Howell, *Principal*
EMP: 10
SALES (est): 215.7K **Privately Held**
SIC: 7319 8742 Advertising; marketing consulting services

(G-4859)
FIRST CONSTRUCTION LLC
901 New Hampshire St (66044-3043)
P.O. Box 1797 (66044-8797)
PHONE..................................785 749-0006
Shannon Abrahamson, *CFO*
Douglas Compton, *Mng Member*
EMP: 25
SQ FT: 40,000
SALES: 800K **Privately Held**
SIC: 1542 Commercial & office building, new construction

(G-4860)
FIRST MANAGEMENT INC (PA)
901 New Hampshire St # 201 (66044-3085)
P.O. Box 1797 (66044-8797)
PHONE..................................785 749-0006
Robert Green, *President*
Doug Compton, *President*
Amanda Habiger, *Manager*
Carolyn Leary, *Manager*
EMP: 77
SQ FT: 18,000
SALES (est): 23.3MM **Privately Held**
WEB: www.firstmanagementinc.com
SIC: 8742 Management consulting services

(G-4861)
FIRST MED PA
Also Called: First Medical Walk-In
2323 Ridge Ct (66046-3956)
PHONE..................................785 865-5300
Ronald J Burt MD, *President*
Mary L Tawadros, *Principal*
Nancy Burt, *Admin Sec*
EMP: 30
SALES (est): 3.1MM **Privately Held**
SIC: 8011 General & family practice, physician/surgeon

(G-4862)
FIRST SERVE TENNIS
5200 Clinton Pkwy (66047-8910)
PHONE..................................785 749-3200
Mike Elwell, *President*
EMP: 85
SALES (est): 578.2K **Privately Held**
SIC: 7997 Tennis club, membership

(G-4863)
FIRST STATE BANK & TRUST
3901 W 6th St (66049-3601)
PHONE..................................785 749-0400
Megan Richardson, *Site Mgr*
David Hooper, *Branch Mgr*
EMP: 20 **Privately Held**
SIC: 6022 State trust companies accepting deposits, commercial
HQ: First State Bank & Trust
400 S Bury St
Tonganoxie KS 66086
913 845-2500

(G-4864)
FIRST STUDENT INC
1548 E 23rd St Ste C (66046-5117)
PHONE..................................785 841-3594
Wayne Bachary, *Branch Mgr*
EMP: 150
SALES (corp-wide): 9.1B **Privately Held**
WEB: www.leag.com
SIC: 4151 School buses
HQ: First Student, Inc.
600 Vine St Ste 1400
Cincinnati OH 45202

(G-4865)
FREE STATE BREWING CO INC
636 Massachusetts St (66044-2236)
PHONE..................................785 843-4555
Chuck Magerl, *President*
Brad Taylor, *Purch Dir*
Donald Dunhaupt, *Admin Sec*
Eric McClelland, *Maintence Staff*
EMP: 90
SQ FT: 7,000
SALES (est): 14MM **Privately Held**
WEB: www.freestatebrewing.com
SIC: 2082 5812 7299 Beer (alcoholic beverage); eating places; banquet hall facilities

(G-4866)
FUNDAMENTAL TECHNOLOGIES LLC
2411 Ponderosa Dr Ste A (66046-5057)
PHONE..................................785 840-0800
Thomas Armstrong, *Managing Prtnr*
Heather Mull, *Sales Staff*
Jerry W Manweiler, *Manager*
Janette Armstrong,
EMP: 12
SALES (est): 986.3K **Privately Held**
WEB: www.ftecs.com
SIC: 7371 Computer software systems analysis & design, custom

(G-4867)
G I P INC (PA)
Also Called: Professional Glass Installers
3000 Four Wheel Dr Ste B (66047-3146)
PHONE..................................785 749-0005
Harry Carpenter, *President*
EMP: 12
SALES (est): 806.2K **Privately Held**
SIC: 7536 7532 Automotive glass replacement shops; top & body repair & paint shops; van conversion

(G-4868)
GANNETT CO INC
Also Called: U S A Today
609 New Hampshire St (66044-2243)
P.O. Box 888 (66044-0888)
PHONE..................................785 832-6319
Ann L Gardner, *Regional Mgr*
Ralph Gage, *COO*
EMP: 150
SALES (corp-wide): 1.5B **Publicly Held**
WEB: www.gannett.com
SIC: 2711 Newspapers
HQ: Gannett Media Corp.
7950 Jones Branch Dr
Mc Lean VA 22102
703 854-6000

GEOGRAPHIC

(G-4869)
GCB HOLDINGS LLC
643 Massachusetts St (66044-2235)
P.O. Box 906 (66044-0906)
PHONE..................................785 841-5185
Tim Fritzel, *Principal*
EMP: 70
SALES (est): 2.3MM **Privately Held**
SIC: 6512 Nonresidential building operators

(G-4870)
GCSAA
1421 Research Park Dr (66049-3858)
PHONE..................................800 832-4410
Mollie Qualseth, *Principal*
Megan Hirt, *Editor*
Rafael Barajas, *Vice Pres*
Brett Iliff, *Accounts Mgr*
Andrew Hartsock, *Manager*
EMP: 17
SALES (est): 1.2MM **Privately Held**
SIC: 8611 Trade associations

(G-4871)
GENERAL DYNAMICS INFO TECH INC
3833 Greenway Dr (66046-5502)
PHONE..................................785 832-0207
Mark Andrews, *Branch Mgr*
EMP: 30
SALES (corp-wide): 36.1B **Publicly Held**
SIC: 3577 2761 7372 7374 Optical scanning devices; computer forms, manifold or continuous; application computer software; tabulating service; optical scanning data service; information retrieval services
HQ: General Dynamics Information Technology, Inc.
3150 Frview Pk Dr Ste 100
Falls Church VA 22042
703 995-8700

(G-4872)
GENTLE CARE ANIMAL HOSPITAL
601 Kasold Dr Ste D105 (66049-3236)
PHONE..................................785 841-1919
H Marguerite Ermeling, *President*
Darren Rausch, *Med Doctor*
EMP: 15
SALES (est): 996.9K **Privately Held**
WEB: www.gntlcareanimalhospital.com
SIC: 0742 0752 Animal hospital services, pets & other animal specialties; grooming services, pet & animal specialties

(G-4873)
GLOBALCOM SOLUTIONS LLC
850 N 1663 Rd (66049-4786)
PHONE..................................785 832-8101
Scott W Robinson,
EMP: 15
SQ FT: 2,500
SALES: 10MM **Privately Held**
WEB: www.callcenterprojects.com
SIC: 8742 Business consultant

(G-4874)
GOLF CRSE SUPERINTENDENTS AMER
1421 Research Park Dr (66049-3858)
PHONE..................................785 841-2240
J Rhett Evans, *CEO*
Rhett Evans, *President*
Richard Konzem, *COO*
Cameron Oury, *CFO*
EMP: 85
SALES: 18.2MM **Privately Held**
SIC: 8699 Professional golf association

(G-4875)
GOODWILL WSTN MO & EASTRN KANS
Also Called: Goodwill Store 5
2200 W 31st St (66047-3171)
PHONE..................................785 331-3908
Brett Spurlock, *Manager*
EMP: 12
SALES (corp-wide): 21.3MM **Privately Held**
WEB: www.mokangoodwill.org
SIC: 5932 7349 8331 3444 Clothing, secondhand; furniture, secondhand; janitorial service, contract basis; job training services; sheet metalwork; fabricated structural metal
PA: Goodwill Of Western Missouri & Eastern Kansas
800 E 18th St
Kansas City MO 64108
816 220-1779

(G-4876)
GOOGOLS OF LEARNING
500 Rockledge Rd (66049-2561)
PHONE..................................785 856-6002
Amy Gottschaner, *Owner*
EMP: 28
SALES (est): 291.4K **Privately Held**
SIC: 8351 Preschool center

(G-4877)
GPW & ASSOCIATES LLC
1001 New Hampshire St (66044-3045)
PHONE..................................785 865-2332
Gina P Watson,
EMP: 18
SQ FT: 7,962
SALES: 1.6MM **Privately Held**
WEB: www.gpwassociates.com
SIC: 8712 8711 Architectural services; engineering services

(G-4878)
GQ INC
Also Called: Images Hairstyling
511 W 9th St (66044-2807)
PHONE..................................785 843-2138
Rocky Browning, *President*
EMP: 16
SALES (est): 224.7K **Privately Held**
SIC: 7231 Beauty shops

(G-4879)
GRANADA THEATER
1020 Massachusetts St (66044-2922)
PHONE..................................785 842-1390
Brett Mossman, *Owner*
EMP: 12
SALES (est): 340.1K **Privately Held**
SIC: 7922 Legitimate live theater producers

(G-4880)
GREAT AMERICAN BANK (HQ)
888 New Hampshire St A (66044-2791)
P.O. Box 4530 (66046-1530)
PHONE..................................785 838-9704
Les J Dreiling, *CEO*
Terry Sutcliffe, *President*
Vickie Knight, *Exec VP*
David M Clark, *Senior VP*
Derek Bailey, *Vice Pres*
EMP: 12
SALES: 11.1MM **Privately Held**
WEB: www.lawrencebank.com
SIC: 6022 State commercial banks

(G-4881)
GREAT AMERICAN INSURANCE CO
4910 Corp Centre Dr # 200 (66047-1000)
P.O. Box 7016 (66044-7003)
PHONE..................................785 840-1100
Chris Fisher, *Branch Mgr*
Brent Dorsey, *Manager*
EMP: 55 **Publicly Held**
SIC: 6331 Fire, marine & casualty insurance
HQ: Great American Insurance Company
301 E 4th St Fl 24
Cincinnati OH 45202
513 369-5000

(G-4882)
GREAT PLAINS FINANCIAL GROUP
3310 Mesa Way Ste 101 (66049-2602)
PHONE..................................785 843-7070
Rich Lorenzo, *Partner*
Don Burman, *Partner*
EMP: 11 **EST:** 2001
SALES (est): 1.4MM **Privately Held**
SIC: 6211 Brokers, security

(G-4883)
GSR CONSTRUCTION INC
932 Msschsetts St Ste 304 (66044)
PHONE..................................785 749-1770
Gregory S Randel, *President*
EMP: 10
SALES (est): 6MM **Privately Held**
SIC: 1541 Industrial buildings, new construction

(G-4884)
H & R BLOCK TAX SERVICES LLC
2104 W 25th St (66047-2968)
PHONE..................................785 749-1649
Dave Anderson, *Principal*
EMP: 12
SALES (corp-wide): 3B **Publicly Held**
SIC: 7291 Tax return preparation services
HQ: H & R Block Tax Services Llc
1 H And R Block Way
Kansas City MO 64105

(G-4885)
HAIR EXPERTS DESIGN TEAM
Also Called: Hair Experts Salon & Spa
529 Sandpiper Dr (66044-9483)
PHONE..................................785 841-6886
Brenda Peterson, *President*
EMP: 18
SALES (est): 360.6K **Privately Held**
SIC: 7241 7231 Barber shops; beauty shops

(G-4886)
HALLMARK CARDS INCORPORATED
101 Mcdonald Dr (66044-1056)
P.O. Box 99 (66044-0099)
PHONE..................................785 843-9050
Karmen Huyser, *Division Mgr*
Sherita Clifton, *Safety Mgr*
Diane Waltho, *Production*
Gene Petrie, *Engineer*
Larry Elder, *Manager*
EMP: 26
SALES (corp-wide): 11B **Privately Held**
WEB: www.hallmark.com
SIC: 2771 Greeting cards
PA: Hallmark Cards, Incorporated
2501 Mcgee St
Kansas City MO 64108
816 274-5111

(G-4887)
HANDS 2 HELP
401 Cattleman Ct (66049-2242)
PHONE..................................785 832-2515
EMP: 65
SALES: 1MM **Privately Held**
SIC: 8082 Home Health Care Services

(G-4888)
HAPPY SHIRT PRINTING CO LLC
608 N 2nd St (66044-1406)
PHONE..................................785 371-1660
Justin Shiney, *Mng Member*
EMP: 8
SQ FT: 3,000
SALES (est): 1.1MM **Privately Held**
SIC: 2752 Commercial printing, offset

(G-4889)
HARDISTER PAINTING AND DCTG
Also Called: Hardister Painting & Dctg Svc
1081 E 1200 Rd (66047-9447)
PHONE..................................785 842-2832
EMP: 10
SQ FT: 3,200
SALES: 550K **Privately Held**
SIC: 1721 Commercial Painting Contractor

(G-4890)
HARRIS COMPUTER SYSTEMS
4911 Legends Dr (66049-5800)
PHONE..................................785 843-8150
Roger B Haack, *Branch Mgr*
EMP: 65
SALES (corp-wide): 3B **Privately Held**
SIC: 7373 Systems software development services
HQ: N. Harris Computer Corporation
1 Antares Dr Suite 400
Nepean ON K2E 8
613 226-5511

(G-4891)
HARTZLER LORENDA
Also Called: Body Boutique
2330 Yale Rd (66049-2650)
PHONE..................................785 749-2424
Lorenda Hartzler, *Owner*
EMP: 35
SQ FT: 2,000
SALES (est): 1.2MM **Privately Held**
SIC: 7991 7299 Health club; tanning salon

(G-4892)
HASKELL FOUNDATION
155 Indian Ave (66046-4817)
PHONE..................................785 749-8425
Joe Clote, *President*
Brittany Hall, *Business Mgr*
Lara Waits, *Vice Pres*
Patty Battese, *Treasurer*
Ruth Harjo, *Admin Sec*
EMP: 11
SQ FT: 3,000
SALES: 560.8K **Privately Held**
SIC: 7389 Fund raising organizations

(G-4893)
HAWK WASH WINDOW CLEANING
2113 E 28th St (66046-5608)
P.O. Box 3717 (66046-0717)
PHONE..................................785 749-0244
Jackie Bird, *Owner*
EMP: 10
SALES (est): 362.9K **Privately Held**
SIC: 7349 Janitorial service, contract basis; window cleaning

(G-4894)
HEARTLAND MEDICAL CLINIC INC
Also Called: Heartland Community Health Ctr
346 Maine St Ste 150 (66044-1393)
PHONE..................................785 841-7297
Jon Stewart, *CEO*
EMP: 10
SALES: 3.9MM **Privately Held**
SIC: 8011 Clinic, operated by physicians

(G-4895)
HERBS & MORE INC
Also Called: Rejuvene Day Spa
2108 W 27th St Ste D (66047-3168)
PHONE..................................785 865-4372
Marsha Butell, *Owner*
EMP: 15
SALES (est): 538.8K **Privately Held**
SIC: 5499 7299 Health & dietetic food stores; massage parlor

(G-4896)
HETRICK AIR SERVICES INC
1930 N Airport Rd (66044-9419)
PHONE..................................785 842-0000
Lloyd Hetrick, *President*
Jeanie Hetrick, *Treasurer*
Janice Turner, *Office Mgr*
EMP: 15
SALES (est): 2.1MM **Privately Held**
WEB: www.hetrickairservices.com
SIC: 4581 Aircraft servicing & repairing

(G-4897)
HILLTOP CHILD DEVELOPMENT CTR
1605 Irving Hill Rd (66045-7592)
PHONE..................................785 864-4940
Jack Del Rio Jr, *Top Exec*
Machaela V Whelan, *Sls & Mktg Exec*
Jeremy Fite, *Exec Dir*
Chris Hotvedt, *Admin Asst*
Dalene Andrews, *Education*
EMP: 43
SALES: 2.4MM **Privately Held**
SIC: 8351 Preschool center

(G-4898)
HIPER TECHNOLOGY INC
Also Called: Pro Advantage
2920 Haskell Ave Ste 300 (66046-4905)
PHONE..................................785 749-6011

Fax: 785 749-4760
◆ **EMP:** 17
SQ FT: 40,000
SALES (est): 4.6MM **Privately Held**
SIC: **5013** 3624 Whol Auto Parts/Supplies Mfg Carbon/Graphite Products

(G-4899)
HITE COLLISION REPAIR CTR INC
3401 W 6th St (66049-3200)
PHONE..................................785 843-8991
David Buller, *President*
Julie Buller, *Vice Pres*
EMP: 12
SQ FT: 6,500
SALES (est): 300K **Privately Held**
WEB: www.hitecollision.com
SIC: **7532** Body shop, automotive

(G-4900)
HOME DEPOT USA INC
Also Called: Home Depot, The
1910 W 31st St (66046-5511)
PHONE..................................785 749-2074
Alex Poole, *Manager*
EMP: 135
SALES (corp-wide): 108.2B **Publicly Held**
WEB: www.homerentalsdepot.com
SIC: **5211** 7359 Home centers; tool rental
HQ: Home Depot U.S.A., Inc.
2455 Paces Ferry Ave
Atlanta GA 30339

(G-4901)
HONEY CREEK DISPOSAL SERVICE
26195 Linwood Rd (66044-9426)
P.O. Box 1, Tonganoxie (66086-0001)
PHONE..................................913 369-8999
Kevin Weldon, *President*
EMP: 17 **EST:** 1999
SALES (est): 1.5MM **Privately Held**
SIC: **4953** Garbage: collecting, destroying & processing

(G-4902)
HORIZONPSI INC
1101 Horizon Dr (66046-4951)
PHONE..................................785 842-1299
Wes Kohl, *President*
Dave Nutter, *Vice Pres*
Doug Kirkpatrick, *CFO*
Dennis Long, *Director*
EMP: 60
SQ FT: 50,000
SALES (est): 14.3MM **Privately Held**
WEB: www.horizonsystemsinc.com
SIC: **3535** Pneumatic tube conveyor systems

(G-4903)
HOSPICE PREFERRED CHOICE INC
Also Called: Aseracare Hospice
411 N Iowa St Ste A (66044-9617)
PHONE..................................785 840-0820
Holly Rasmussenjones, *Branch Mgr*
EMP: 24
SALES (corp-wide): 2.6B **Privately Held**
SIC: **8082** Home health care services
HQ: Hospice Preferred Choice Inc
1000 Fianna Way
Fort Smith AR 72919

(G-4904)
HOSS AND BROWN ENGINEERS INC (PA)
4910 Corporate Centre Dr # 177 (66047-1002)
PHONE..................................785 832-1105
Pete Laughlin, *President*
Laura Blanchard, *Vice Pres*
Jim Lord, *Project Mgr*
Matthew Bunyard, *Engineer*
Matt Murrell, *Engineer*
EMP: 20
SQ FT: 1,700
SALES (est): 3.1MM **Privately Held**
WEB: www.hbengineerstk.com
SIC: **8711** Mechanical engineering; electrical or electronic engineering

(G-4905)
HOUSEKEEPING UNLIMITED
1611 Saint Andrews Dr (66047-1701)
P.O. Box B (66044-8996)
PHONE..................................785 842-2444
Linda Kelly, *Owner*
Laurie Wilson, *General Mgr*
EMP: 25
SALES (est): 656.1K **Privately Held**
WEB: www.housekeepingunlimited.com
SIC: **7349** 7363 Maid services, contract or fee basis; domestic help service

(G-4906)
HULSING HOTELS KANSAS INC (PA)
Also Called: Doubltree By Hlton Ht Lawrence
200 Mcdonald Dr (66044-1057)
PHONE..................................785 841-7077
Dennis Hulsing, *President*
Stephen Horton, *General Mgr*
Jillana Hulsing, *Vice Pres*
EMP: 95
SALES (est): 10.7MM **Privately Held**
SIC: **7011** Hotels & motels

(G-4907)
HUXTABLE & ASSOCIATES INC
2151 Haskell Ave Blgd1 (66046-3251)
PHONE..................................785 843-2910
Smitty G Belcher, *President*
Joyce Jacob, *Admin Sec*
EMP: 240 **EST:** 1927
SQ FT: 24,000
SALES (est): 13.9MM
SALES (corp-wide): 243.8MM **Privately Held**
WEB: www.p1group.com
SIC: **1711** 1731 Mechanical contractor; general electrical contractor
PA: P1 Group, Inc.
13605 W 96th Ter
Lenexa KS 66215
913 529-5000

(G-4908)
IDENTIGEN NORTH AMERICA INC
2029 Becker Dr (66047-1620)
PHONE..................................785 856-8800
Ronan Loftus, *CEO*
EMP: 10
SALES (est): 1.7MM
SALES (corp-wide): 485.3K **Privately Held**
SIC: **8734** Testing laboratories
HQ: Identigen Limited
2 Blackrock Business Park
Blackrock

(G-4909)
IMAGES SALON & DAY SPA
511 W 9th St (66044-2807)
PHONE..................................785 843-2138
Rocky Browning, *Owner*
EMP: 16
SALES (est): 142.6K **Privately Held**
SIC: **7231** 7299 Manicurist, pedicurist; massage parlor & steam bath services

(G-4910)
INDEPENDENCE INC
2001 Haskell Ave (66046-3249)
P.O. Box 3607 (66046-0607)
PHONE..................................785 841-0333
Joyce Ward, *Payroll Mgr*
Daniel Brown, *Program Mgr*
Alisa Snyder, *Manager*
Jill Enyart, *Exec Dir*
Bob Mikesic, *Deputy Dir*
EMP: 26
SQ FT: 14,400
SALES: 2.5MM **Privately Held**
SIC: **8082** 8322 Home health care services; social services for the handicapped

(G-4911)
INDIAN HILLS HARDWARE INC
4309 Quail Pointe Rd (66047-1966)
PHONE..................................785 841-1479
Douglas Paul, *President*
EMP: 25
SALES (est): 2.2MM **Privately Held**
SIC: **5072** Hardware

(G-4912)
INTERNAL MEDICINE GROUP PA
4525 W 6th St Ste 100 (66049-7700)
PHONE..................................785 843-5160
Thomas F Frist Jr, *Vice Ch Bd*
David T Vandewater, *COO*
Christopher Penn, *Safety Mgr*
Ellen Herman, *Exec Dir*
EMP: 32
SQ FT: 3,300
SALES (est): 1MM **Publicly Held**
SIC: **8011** Internal medicine, physician/surgeon
HQ: Hca Inc.
1 Park Plz
Nashville TN 37203
615 344-9551

(G-4913)
INTERNATIONAL ASSOCIATION
218 Arizona St (66049-2109)
PHONE..................................785 760-5005
Dr Jennifer M McKinley, *Principal*
K Gerald Van Den Boogaart, *Principal*
Guillaume Caumon, *Principal*
Qiuming Cheng, *Principal*
David Collins, *Principal*
EMP: 10
SALES: 182K **Privately Held**
SIC: **8699** Membership organizations

(G-4914)
INTERNATIONAL ASSOCIATION OF
Also Called: Lawrence Lions Club
1005 N 1116 Rd (66047-9431)
PHONE..................................785 842-8847
Ken Rowen, *Admin Sec*
EMP: 25
SALES (corp-wide): 63.7MM **Privately Held**
WEB: www.iaopc.com
SIC: **8641** Civic associations
PA: The International Association Of Lions Clubs Incorporated
300 W 22nd St
Oak Brook IL 60523
630 571-5466

(G-4915)
INTRUST BANK NATIONAL ASSN
901 Vermont St (66044-2864)
PHONE..................................785 830-2600
Denise Kissinger, *Principal*
EMP: 12
SALES (corp-wide): 134.2MM **Privately Held**
WEB: www.intrustbank.com
SIC: **6021** National commercial banks
HQ: Intrust Bank National Association
105 N Main St
Wichita KS 67202
316 383-1111

(G-4916)
ISP TECHNOLOGIES INC (PA)
4225 Wimbledon Dr (66047-2034)
PHONE..................................785 760-1572
Ray Sawyer, *CEO*
Lynda Shafer, *President*
EMP: 7
SALES (est): 1.3MM **Privately Held**
SIC: **2873** Fertilizers: natural (organic), except compost

(G-4917)
J A PETERSON REALTY CO INC
Also Called: Park Twenty-Five Apartments
2401 W 25th St Apt 9a3 (66047-2939)
PHONE..................................785 842-1455
Linda Love, *Manager*
EMP: 10
SALES (corp-wide): 11.8MM **Privately Held**
WEB: www.petersoncompanies.com
SIC: **6513** Apartment building operators
HQ: J. A. Peterson Realty Co. Inc.
10000 W 75th St Ste 100
Shawnee Mission KS 66204
913 384-3800

(G-4918)
JACK WILSON & ASSOCIATES INC
Also Called: Jwavideo
901 Kentucky St Ste 106 (66044-2853)
P.O. Box 1895 (66044-8895)
PHONE..................................785 856-4546
John R Wilson, *CEO*
EMP: 10
SALES: 300K **Privately Held**
SIC: **7812** Motion picture & video production

(G-4919)
JAYHAWK BOWLING SUP & EQP INC
355 N Iowa St (66044-9625)
P.O. Box 685 (66044-0685)
PHONE..................................785 842-3237
John A Hardman, *President*
Gerry Keslar, *Admin Sec*
▼ **EMP:** 13
SQ FT: 18,000
SALES: 3.8MM **Privately Held**
WEB: www.jayhawkbowling.com
SIC: **5091** 3949 Bowling equipment; bowling equipment & supplies

(G-4920)
JAYHAWK PLUMBING INC
3009 Four Wheel Dr Ste A (66047-3259)
PHONE..................................785 865-5225
Harrison Starks, *Owner*
EMP: 13
SQ FT: 5,000
SALES (est): 1MM **Privately Held**
SIC: **1711** 1542 Plumbing contractors; commercial & office buildings, renovation & repair

(G-4921)
JAYHAWK TROPHY COMPANY INC
3341 W 6th St (66049-3105)
P.O. Box 1621 (66044-8621)
PHONE..................................785 843-3900
Monty Hobbs, *President*
EMP: 7
SQ FT: 3,000
SALES (est): 945.7K **Privately Held**
WEB: www.jayhawktrophy.com
SIC: **5999** 3479 5094 Trophies & plaques; engraving jewelry silverware, or metal; trophies

(G-4922)
JEFF GOLDMAN
Also Called: Signature Cleaning
1420 N 3rd St (66044-9128)
PHONE..................................785 842-0351
Jeff Goldman, *Owner*
EMP: 11
SALES (est): 220K **Privately Held**
WEB: www.pds-spc.com
SIC: **7349** Cleaning service, industrial or commercial

(G-4923)
JNN LLC
Also Called: Best Western
2309 Iowa St (66046-3939)
PHONE..................................785 843-9100
Nitin B Patel, *Mng Member*
EMP: 23
SALES (est): 1.3MM **Privately Held**
SIC: **7011** Hotels & motels

(G-4924)
JOE BARNS
Also Called: J C Nichols Residential
1127 Iowa St (66044-1921)
PHONE..................................785 842-2772
Joe Barns, *Owner*
EMP: 10
SALES (est): 272.4K **Privately Held**
SIC: **6531** Real estate agents & managers

(G-4925)
JOEL FRITZEL CONSTRUCTION CO (PA)
1616 New Hampshire St (66044-4262)
PHONE..................................785 843-0566
Joel Fritzel, *President*
Brenda R Childers, *Corp Secy*
Dennis L Gisel, *COO*

GEOGRAPHIC

EMP: 25
SQ FT: 2,000
SALES (est): 4.4MM **Privately Held**
WEB: www.joelfritzel.com
SIC: 1542 1521 Commercial & office building, new construction; new construction, single-family houses; general remodeling, single-family houses

(G-4926)
JOHN H HAY DDS
10 E 9th St Ste D (66044-2600)
PHONE..................................785 749-2525
John H Hay DDS, *Owner*
EMP: 11
SALES (est): 260.7K **Privately Held**
SIC: 8021 Offices & clinics of dentists

(G-4927)
JOHN P GRAVINO DO
Also Called: My Oread Family Practice
3510 Clinton Pl Ste 200 (66047-2178)
PHONE..................................785 842-5070
William Stueve, *Owner*
Barb Karr, *Director*
EMP: 18 **EST:** 2008
SALES (est): 343.1K **Privately Held**
SIC: 8011 Physicians' office, including specialists

(G-4928)
K J H K 907 FM
1301 Jayhawk Blvd 4274f (66045-7593)
PHONE..................................785 864-4745
Thomas Johnson, *General Mgr*
Tom Johnson, *General Mgr*
Kaitlin Brennan, *Manager*
Zach Beaseley, *Manager*
EMP: 20
SALES (est): 574.4K **Privately Held**
SIC: 4832 Radio broadcasting stations

(G-4929)
K U ENDOWMENT ASSOCIATION (PA)
1891 Constant Ave (66047-3743)
PHONE..................................785 830-7600
Andy Morrison, *President*
Jennifer Berry, *Principal*
Susan Burton, *Assistant VP*
Bridget Ite, *Assistant VP*
Jeff Davis, *Vice Pres*
EMP: 11
SALES (est): 456.7K **Privately Held**
SIC: 8611 Business associations

(G-4930)
KANSAS ATHLETICS INCORPORATED
1651 Naismith Dr (66045-4069)
PHONE..................................785 864-7050
Jeff Long, *Director*
Sheahon Zenger, *Director*
Lorretta Zachary, *Admin Asst*
EMP: 434
SALES: 104.4MM
SALES (corp-wide): 1.2B **Privately Held**
WEB: www.ukans.edu
SIC: 8699 Athletic organizations
PA: University Of Kansas
1450 Jayhawk Blvd Rm 225
Lawrence KS 66045
785 864-4868

(G-4931)
KANSAS BIG BROS BIG SSTERS INC
536 Fireside Ct Ste B (66049-2365)
PHONE..................................785 843-7359
Keith Wood, *Exec Dir*
EMP: 11
SALES (corp-wide): 4.1MM **Privately Held**
SIC: 8322 Helping hand service (Big Brother, etc.)
PA: Kansas Big Brothers Big Sisters, Inc.
310 E 2nd St N
Wichita KS 67202
316 263-3300

(G-4932)
KANSAS BIOLOGICAL SURVEY
2101 Constant Ave (66047-3759)
PHONE..................................785 864-1505
Patrice Baker, *Dean*
Susan Stover, *Manager*
Edward Martinko, *Exec Dir*
EMP: 38
SALES (est): 1.4MM **Privately Held**
SIC: 8713 Surveying services

(G-4933)
KANSAS INVESTMENT CORPORATION
Also Called: Virginia Inn Motel
2903 W 6th St (66049-4533)
PHONE..................................785 843-6611
Kenny D Liu, *President*
Deborah C Liu, *Corp Secy*
EMP: 13
SALES: 800K **Privately Held**
SIC: 7011 Motels

(G-4934)
KANSAS LALECHE LEAGUE INC
807 W 28th Ter (66046-4627)
PHONE..................................785 865-5919
Jane Tuttle, *Representative*
EMP: 14 **EST:** 1999
SALES (est): 289.7K **Privately Held**
SIC: 8322 Individual & family services

(G-4935)
KANSAS MANUFACTURING COMPANY
201 Perry St (66044-1558)
P.O. Box 614 (66044-0614)
PHONE..................................785 843-2892
Adrian M Burns, *Partner*
Richard Martin, *Partner*
EMP: 7 **EST:** 1945
SQ FT: 8,000
SALES: 500K **Privately Held**
WEB: www.kansasmfg.com
SIC: 3599 Machine shop, jobbing & repair

(G-4936)
KANSAS SCHOLASTIC PRESS ASSOC
2063 Dale Ctr (66045-0001)
PHONE..................................785 864-7612
Kathy Habiger, *Principal*
EMP: 16
SALES (est): 102.1K **Privately Held**
SIC: 8641 Civic social & fraternal associations

(G-4937)
KANSAS STATEWIDE HOMELESS
2001 Haskell Ave Ste 207 (66046-3249)
PHONE..................................785 354-4990
Diane Etzel-Wise, *Exec Dir*
EMP: 12
SALES (est): 121.3K **Privately Held**
SIC: 8322 Individual & family services

(G-4938)
KASTL PLUMBING INC
4920 Legends Dr Ste 100 (66049-3840)
PHONE..................................785 841-2112
Howard Kastl, *President*
EMP: 20
SALES: 3MM **Privately Held**
SIC: 1711 Plumbing contractors

(G-4939)
KEA ADVISORS
3320 Mesa Way Ste D (66049-2367)
PHONE..................................913 832-6099
Keith Ely, *Owner*
EMP: 15
SALES (est): 857.1K **Privately Held**
SIC: 8742 Business consultant

(G-4940)
KELTECH SOLUTIONS LLC
Also Called: UNI Computers
4920 Legends Dr Ste 200 (66049-3840)
PHONE..................................785 841-4611
Amin Emami, *General Mgr*
Keith Keltner, *General Mgr*
Lance Keltner,
Keith Kelner,
Brent Keltner,
EMP: 11
SALES (est): 1.5MM **Privately Held**
WEB: www.unicomputers.com
SIC: 5734 5045 7378 Personal computers; computers & accessories, personal & home entertainment; computer peripheral equipment repair & maintenance

(G-4941)
KEMIRA WATER SOLUTIONS INC
Also Called: Kemiron Customer Service Ctr
3211 Clinton Parkway Ct # 1 (66047-2654)
PHONE..................................785 842-7424
Tammy Yergey, *Branch Mgr*
EMP: 13
SALES (corp-wide): 2.8B **Privately Held**
WEB: www.kemiron.com
SIC: 8742 Sales (including sales management) consultant
HQ: Kemira Water Solutions, Inc.
1000 Parkwood Cir Se # 500
Atlanta GA 30339
770 436-1542

(G-4942)
KENNEDY GLASS INC
730 New Jersey St (66044-2790)
P.O. Box 681 (66044-0681)
PHONE..................................785 843-4416
Gary Kennedy, *President*
John Kennedy, *Vice Pres*
Jerry Townsend, *Project Mgr*
Martin Kennedy, *Treasurer*
EMP: 29
SQ FT: 15,000
SALES (est): 5.8MM **Privately Held**
WEB: www.kennedyglassinc.com
SIC: 1793 7536 5231 Glass & glazing work; automotive glass replacement shops; glass

(G-4943)
KERMIT COTTRELL ALLSTATE AGCY
2233 Louisiana St Ste H2 (66046-3010)
PHONE..................................785 843-2532
Kermit Cottrell, *Owner*
EMP: 34
SALES: 214K **Privately Held**
SIC: 6411 Insurance agents, brokers & service

(G-4944)
KEVIN J STUEVER MD
4525 W 6th St Ste 100 (66049-7700)
PHONE..................................785 843-5160
Kevin J Stuever MD, *Owner*
EMP: 50
SALES (est): 647.8K **Privately Held**
SIC: 8011 Physicians' office, including specialists

(G-4945)
KIEFS CDS & TAPES
2429 Iowa St Ste D (66046-4075)
PHONE..................................785 842-1544
John Kiefer, *Owner*
EMP: 20
SALES (est): 969.4K **Privately Held**
WEB: www.kiefs.com
SIC: 5099 Compact discs

(G-4946)
KNIGHT ENTERPRISES LTD
4840 Bob Billings Pkwy # 1000
(66049-3876)
PHONE..................................785 843-5511
James T Knight, *President*
Scott McKinney, *Vice Pres*
Michelle Knight, *Treasurer*
EMP: 20
SQ FT: 5,000
SALES (est): 1.6MM **Privately Held**
SIC: 7331 8741 Direct mail advertising services; management services

(G-4947)
KNOLOGY INC
Also Called: Sunflower Broadband
1 Riverfront Plz (66044-2293)
PHONE..................................785 841-2100
EMP: 200
SALES (corp-wide): 1.1B **Publicly Held**
SIC: 4813 Telephone Communications
HQ: Knology, Inc.
1241 Og Skinner Dr
West Point GA 31833
334 644-2611

(G-4948)
KOHLMAN SYSTEMS RESEARCH INC
5916 Longleaf Dr (66049-5801)
PHONE..................................785 843-4099
Terry Marshall, *President*
Walt Willmert, *CPA*
EMP: 15
SALES (est): 2.5MM **Privately Held**
WEB: www.kohlmansystems.com
SIC: 3829 Measuring & controlling devices

(G-4949)
KU WORKGROUP FOR COMMUNITY HEA
1000 Sunnysde Av R4082 Fl (66045-0001)
PHONE..................................785 864-0533
EMP: 20
SALES (est): 408.9K **Privately Held**
SIC: 8399 Social Services

(G-4950)
KUGLERS VINEYARD
1235 N 1100 Rd (66047-9427)
PHONE..................................785 843-8516
Tony Kugler, *Principal*
EMP: 7
SALES (est): 354K **Privately Held**
SIC: 2084 Wines

(G-4951)
LA PETITE ACADEMY INC
3211 W 6th St (66049-3103)
PHONE..................................785 843-5703
Brittany Farthing, *Director*
EMP: 15
SALES (corp-wide): 164MM **Privately Held**
WEB: www.lapetite.com
SIC: 8351 Preschool center
HQ: La Petite Academy, Inc.
21333 Haggerty Rd Ste 300
Novi MI 48375
877 861-5078

(G-4952)
LA PETITE ACADEMY INC
3200 Clinton Parkway Ct (66047-2626)
PHONE..................................785 843-6445
Kristen Lewis, *Sales/Mktg Dir*
EMP: 16
SALES (corp-wide): 164MM **Privately Held**
WEB: www.lapetite.com
SIC: 8351 Preschool center
HQ: La Petite Academy, Inc.
21333 Haggerty Rd Ste 300
Novi MI 48375
877 861-5078

(G-4953)
LAMBDA CHI ALPHA FRTERNITY INC
2005 Stewart Ave (66046-2510)
PHONE..................................785 843-1172
EMP: 67
SALES (corp-wide): 5.3MM **Privately Held**
SIC: 8641 Civic/Social Association
PA: Lambda Chi Alpha Fraternity Incorporated
11711 N Penn St Ste 250
Carmel IN 46032
317 872-8000

(G-4954)
LANDPLAN ENGINEERING PA (PA)
Also Called: L P E
1310 Wakarusa Dr Ste 100 (66049-3854)
PHONE..................................785 843-7530
Philip Struble, *President*
EMP: 54
SQ FT: 5,000
SALES (est): 5.1MM **Privately Held**
WEB: www.landplan-pa.com
SIC: 8711 8713 0781 Sanitary engineers; surveying services; landscape architects

(G-4955)
LARSEN & ASSOCIATES INC
1311 E 25th St Ste B (66046-5010)
PHONE....................785 841-8707
Lisa Larsen, *President*
Catherine S Clark, *Admin Sec*
EMP: 10
SQ FT: 750
SALES (est): 1.4MM **Privately Held**
WEB: www.larsenenvironmental.com
SIC: 8748 Environmental consultant

(G-4956)
LASER RECYCLING COMPANY
Also Called: Discount Toner and Ink
4724 Killarney Cir (66047-2064)
PHONE....................785 865-4075
Timothy Arnold, *Owner*
EMP: 11
SQ FT: 2,000
SALES (est): 638.4K **Privately Held**
WEB: www.laserrecycle.com
SIC: 4953 Recycling, waste materials

(G-4957)
LAWRENC-DOUGLAS CNTY HLTH DEPT
200 Maine St Ste B (66044-1396)
PHONE....................785 843-3060
Gary Johnson, *Ch of Bd*
Dan Partridge, *Director*
Kay Kent, *Officer*
Andrew Stull, *Officer*
Jennie Henault, *Executive*
EMP: 44
SALES (est): 4MM **Privately Held**
SIC: 8093 Family planning & birth control clinics

(G-4958)
LAWRENCE ANAESTHESIA PA
613 N 2nd St (66044-1407)
P.O. Box 545 (66044-0545)
PHONE....................785 842-7026
Thomas Nique, *Principal*
Michael Lange, *Vice Pres*
EMP: 18
SALES: 3.4MM **Privately Held**
SIC: 8011 Offices & clinics of medical doctors

(G-4959)
LAWRENCE CANCER CENTER
330 Arkansas St Ste 120 (66044-1485)
PHONE....................785 749-3600
Karen Wesbecker, *Manager*
EMP: 15
SALES (est): 1.3MM **Privately Held**
SIC: 8011 Oncologist

(G-4960)
LAWRENCE CITY VEHICLE MAINT
1141 Haskell Ave (66044-3345)
P.O. Box 708 (66044-0708)
PHONE....................785 832-3020
Steve Steward, *Director*
EMP: 15
SALES: 2MM **Privately Held**
SIC: 7549 Automotive maintenance services

(G-4961)
LAWRENCE CLLSION SPCALISTS LLC
Also Called: Carstar
800 E 23rd St (66046-4910)
PHONE....................785 841-3672
Ron Glenn,
EMP: 12
SALES: 1.1MM **Privately Held**
SIC: 7532 Body shop, automotive

(G-4962)
LAWRENCE COMMUNITY SHELTER
3701 Franklin Park Cir (66046-8224)
PHONE....................785 832-8864
Loring Henderson, *Director*
EMP: 11 **EST:** 1996
SALES: 1MM **Privately Held**
SIC: 8322 Emergency shelters

(G-4963)
LAWRENCE COUNTRY CLUB
Also Called: LAWRENCE COUNTRY CLUB POOL
400 Country Club Ter (66049-2445)
PHONE....................785 842-0592
Megan McGee, *Office Mgr*
Terry Schmidt, *Manager*
EMP: 60
SQ FT: 18,000
SALES: 2.9MM **Privately Held**
WEB: www.lawrencecountryclub.com
SIC: 7997 Country club, membership

(G-4964)
LAWRENCE EYECARE ASSOCIATES
Also Called: Lawrence Eye Care Optical
1112 W 6th St Ste 214 (66044-2279)
PHONE....................785 841-2280
R A Orchard MD, *Owner*
Mary Lange MD,
Lynn O Neal MD,
EMP: 15
SALES (est): 1MM **Privately Held**
WEB: www.lawrenceeyecare.org
SIC: 8042 Offices & clinics of optometrists

(G-4965)
LAWRENCE FAMILY PRACTICE CTR
4951 W 18th St (66047-2090)
PHONE....................785 841-6540
Mary Vernon, *Partner*
Rodney J Barnes MD, *Partner*
Brad Phipps MD, *Partner*
Carla Phipps MD, *Partner*
Steven T Thompson MD, *Partner*
EMP: 45 **EST:** 1976
SALES (est): 5.9MM **Privately Held**
SIC: 8011 Clinic, operated by physicians; general & family practice, physician/surgeon

(G-4966)
LAWRENCE FEED & FARM SUP INC
Also Called: Great Western Pet Supply
545 Wisconsin St (66044-6700)
PHONE....................785 843-4311
Roger Tuckel, *President*
EMP: 10
SQ FT: 2,000
SALES (est): 1.1MM **Privately Held**
SIC: 5999 5191 5199 Feed & farm supply; pet supplies; farm supplies; animal feeds; seeds: field, garden & flower; fertilizer & fertilizer materials; pets & pet supplies

(G-4967)
LAWRENCE FUNERAL CHAPEL INC
3821 W 6th St (66049-3252)
PHONE....................785 841-3822
Chris Hutton, *Owner*
EMP: 10
SALES (est): 259.3K **Privately Held**
SIC: 7261 Funeral home

(G-4968)
LAWRENCE GYMNASTICS ACADEMY
4930 Legends Dr (66049-3886)
PHONE....................785 865-0856
EMP: 30 **EST:** 1994
SALES (est): 686.6K **Privately Held**
SIC: 7999 7299 Amusement/Recreation Services Misc Personal Services

(G-4969)
LAWRENCE HOME BUILDERS ASSN
604 N 600th Rd (66047-9527)
P.O. Box 3490 (66046-0490)
PHONE....................785 748-0612
James Myers, *President*
EMP: 10
SALES: 163.3K **Privately Held**
WEB: www.lhba.net
SIC: 8611 Contractors' association

(G-4970)
LAWRENCE INTERNAL MEDICINE PA
1440 Wakarusa Dr Ste 300 (66049-3879)
PHONE....................785 842-7200
Jon F Barr, *Partner*
Rodney Bishop, *Partner*
Steven Dillon, *Partner*
EMP: 21
SQ FT: 7,200
SALES (est): 2.3MM **Privately Held**
WEB: www.lawrenceintmed.com
SIC: 8011 Internal medicine, physician/surgeon

(G-4971)
LAWRENCE LANDSCAPE
608 Lincoln Ct (66044-5322)
PHONE....................785 749-7554
Glen Westervelt, *Owner*
Dan Newsom, *General Mgr*
EMP: 20
SALES (est): 379.7K **Privately Held**
SIC: 0781 Landscape services

(G-4972)
LAWRENCE LANDSCAPE INC
600 Lincoln St (66044-5349)
PHONE....................785 843-4370
Glen Westervelt, *President*
Skip Foster, *Manager*
Terri Kilburn, *Manager*
EMP: 35
SQ FT: 3,000
SALES (est): 12.3MM **Privately Held**
WEB: www.lawrencelandscape.com
SIC: 5083 0781 0782 Lawn & garden machinery & equipment; landscape planning services; landscape contractors

(G-4973)
LAWRENCE MEMORIAL HOSPITAL (PA)
Also Called: L M H
325 Maine St (66044-1360)
PHONE....................785 505-5000
Gene Meyer, *President*
Sheryle D Amico, *Vice Pres*
Carolyn Bowmer, *Vice Pres*
Janice Early, *Vice Pres*
Dana Hale, *Vice Pres*
EMP: 45
SALES: 293.7MM **Privately Held**
SIC: 8062 General medical & surgical hospitals

(G-4974)
LAWRENCE MEMORIAL HOSPITAL END (HQ)
Also Called: Lmh
330 Arkansas St Ste 201 (66044-1335)
PHONE....................785 505-3315
Gene Meyer, *CEO*
Eugene W Meyer, *President*
Deborah Thomson, *President*
Sheryle D Amico, *Vice Pres*
Carolyn Bowmer, *Vice Pres*
EMP: 1000
SQ FT: 250,000
SALES: 3.4MM **Privately Held**
SIC: 8051 8062 Skilled nursing care facilities; general medical & surgical hospitals

(G-4975)
LAWRENCE MEMORIAL HOSPITAL END
Also Called: Lawrence Mem Occupational Hlth
325 Maine St (66044-1360)
PHONE....................785 840-3114
Greg Windholz, *Director*
EMP: 11 **Privately Held**
SIC: 8062 General medical & surgical hospitals
HQ: Lawrence Memorial Hospital Endowment Association
330 Arkansas St Ste 201
Lawrence KS 66044
785 505-3315

(G-4976)
LAWRENCE MEMORIAL HOSPITAL END
Also Called: Kreider Rehab South
3500 Clinton Pkwy (66047-2145)
PHONE....................785 505-3780
Gene Myers, *CEO*
EMP: 12 **Privately Held**
SIC: 8062 General medical & surgical hospitals
HQ: Lawrence Memorial Hospital Endowment Association
330 Arkansas St Ste 201
Lawrence KS 66044
785 505-3315

GEOGRAPHIC

(G-4977)
LAWRENCE MUNICIPAL AIRPORT-LWC
1930 N Airport Rd (66044-9419)
PHONE....................785 842-0000
Steve Bennett, *Principal*
Charles Soules, *Principal*
Janice Turner, *Admin Sec*
EMP: 19 **EST:** 2011
SALES (est): 841.3K **Privately Held**
SIC: 4581 Airport

(G-4978)
LAWRENCE OCCPATIONAL HLTH SVCS
Also Called: Lawrence Prompt Care
3511 Clinton Pl Ste B (66047-2213)
PHONE....................785 838-1500
Micheal Gies, *Owner*
Darin J Elo, *Med Doctor*
EMP: 15
SALES (est): 1.1MM **Privately Held**
SIC: 8011 Clinic, operated by physicians; general & family practice, physician/surgeon

(G-4979)
LAWRENCE ORAL SURGERY
Also Called: Lawrence Oral Maxillofacial Sg
308 Maine St (66044-1359)
PHONE....................785 843-5490
Joseph Harvey, *Partner*
Jeffrey Armstrong, *Partner*
Philip Gaus, *Partner*
EMP: 13
SALES (est): 1.6MM **Privately Held**
SIC: 8021 Maxillofacial specialist; dental surgeon

(G-4980)
LAWRENCE ORTHPAEDIC SURGERY PA
Also Called: Lawrence Orthopedic Surgery
1112 W 6th St Ste 124 (66044-2249)
PHONE....................785 843-9125
Richard G Wendt MD, *President*
Ken Wertzberger MD, *Corp Secy*
William Bailey MD, *Vice Pres*
EMP: 45
SALES: 500K **Privately Held**
SIC: 8011 Orthopedic physician

(G-4981)
LAWRENCE OTLRYNGOLOGY ASSOC PA (PA)
Also Called: Segebrecht, Stephen L MD
1112 W 6th St Ste 216 (66044-2249)
PHONE....................620 343-6600
Stephen Segebrecht, *President*
Dr Robert Dinsdale, *Treasurer*
Renee Pettijohn, *Manager*
Dynelle Kessler, *Admin Asst*
EMP: 15
SALES (est): 1.9MM **Privately Held**
WEB: www.lawoto.com
SIC: 8011 8049 5999 Ears, nose & throat specialist: physician/surgeon; audiologist; hearing aids

(G-4982)
LAWRENCE PAPER COMPANY (PA)
2801 Lakeview Rd (66049-8950)
PHONE....................785 843-8111
Justin D Hill, *President*
Shane Old, *Plant Supt*
Kevin Bryant, *Prdtn Mgr*
David Wiese, *Prdtn Mgr*

Kevin Payne, *Maint Spvr*
▲ **EMP:** 212 **EST:** 1882
SQ FT: 800,000
SALES (est): 92.3MM **Privately Held**
WEB: www.lpco.net
SIC: 5199 Packaging materials

(G-4983)
LAWRENCE PEDIATRICS PA
3310 Clinton Parkway Ct (66047-2629)
PHONE..................................785 856-9090
Kirsten E Evans, *Principal*
EMP: 12
SALES (est): 825.2K **Privately Held**
SIC: 8011 Pediatrician

(G-4984)
LAWRENCE PRINTING AND DESIGN
2317 Ponderosa Dr (66046-5055)
P.O. Box 608 (66044-0608)
PHONE..................................785 843-4600
John Kaslaitis, *President*
Charlane Kimbell, *Manager*
EMP: 10
SQ FT: 5,400
SALES (est): 1.1MM **Privately Held**
SIC: 2752 Commercial printing, offset

(G-4985)
LAWRENCE PUBLIC LIB FOUNDATION
Also Called: Lawrence Public Lib Foundation
707 Vermont St (66044-2371)
PHONE..................................785 843-3833
Denise Berkley, *President*
Kathleen Morgan, *General Mgr*
Karen Allen, *Executive*
EMP: 86
SALES: 620.2K **Privately Held**
SIC: 8641 Civic social & fraternal associations

(G-4986)
LAWRENCE REALTY ASSOCIATES
4321 W 6th St (66049-3692)
PHONE..................................785 841-2727
John Bush, *CEO*
Patrick Flavin, *President*
Wanda Hughes, *Vice Pres*
EMP: 52 **EST:** 2000
SALES (est): 1.8MM **Privately Held**
SIC: 6531 Real estate agent, residential

(G-4987)
LAWRENCE SURGERY CENTER LLC
1112 W 6th St Ste 220 (66044-2249)
PHONE..................................785 832-0588
Thomas A Nique, *Medical Dir*
EMP: 20
SALES (est): 3.9MM **Privately Held**
SIC: 8011 Ambulatory surgical center

(G-4988)
LAWRENCE THEATRE INC
4660 Bauer Farm Dr (66049-9084)
PHONE..................................785 843-7469
Donny Slough, *President*
Mary Dovton, *Exec Dir*
Neal Barbour, *Education*
EMP: 11
SALES: 861.1K **Privately Held**
SIC: 7922 Legitimate live theater producers

(G-4989)
LAWRENCE WMENS TRNSTNAL CRE S
Also Called: WTCS
2518 Ridge Ct (66046-5852)
P.O. Box 633 (66044-0633)
PHONE..................................785 865-3956
Sarah Terwelp, *Director*
EMP: 14
SALES: 690.3K **Privately Held**
SIC: 8322 Individual & family services

(G-4990)
LBUBS 2003-C5 NISMITH HALL LLC
1800 Naismith Dr (66045-4072)
PHONE..................................785 832-8676
Leonard Edmond, *General Mgr*
EMP: 19
SQ FT: 120,000
SALES (est): 2.8MM **Privately Held**
SIC: 7021 Dormitory, commercially operated

(G-4991)
LEANDER HEALTH TECH INC
315 Ne Industrial Ln A (66044-1472)
PHONE..................................785 856-7474
Dennis Anthony, *President*
EMP: 11
SALES (est): 927.7K **Privately Held**
WEB: www.leandertables.org
SIC: 2522 Office desks & tables: except wood

(G-4992)
LEGENDS DRIVE DENTAL CTR LLC
4900 Legends Dr (66049-3886)
PHONE..................................785 841-5590
Ryan Brittingham, *Manager*
Ryan Drittingham,
EMP: 11
SALES (est): 700K **Privately Held**
SIC: 8072 Dental laboratories

(G-4993)
LENEXA HOTEL LP (PA)
Also Called: Crowne Plaza Hotel
730 New Hampshire St # 206 (66044-2736)
PHONE..................................785 841-3100
Stephen J Craig, *President*
Carol Childers, *Admin Asst*
EMP: 644 **EST:** 1971
SQ FT: 1,800
SALES (est): 9.9MM **Privately Held**
WEB: www.radissonlenexa.com
SIC: 7011 Hotels & motels

(G-4994)
LIBERTY HALL INC
Also Called: Liberty Hall Video
642 Massachusetts St (66044-2236)
PHONE..................................785 749-1972
Rob Fitzgerald, *Manager*
EMP: 12
SQ FT: 10,000
SALES (est): 399.4K **Privately Held**
WEB: www.libertyhall.net
SIC: 7922 7841 7299 Entertainment promotion; legitimate live theater producers; video tape rental; banquet hall facilities

(G-4995)
LIBERTY HALL INC
644 Massachusetts St (66044-2236)
PHONE..................................785 749-1972
David Millstein, *President*
EMP: 20
SALES (est): 1.1MM **Privately Held**
WEB: www.libertyhall.com
SIC: 7841 7922 7832 Video tape rental; concert management service; motion picture theaters, except drive-in

(G-4996)
LIGAND PHARMACEUTICALS INC
2029 Becker Dr (66047-1620)
PHONE..................................785 856-2346
EMP: 5
SALES (corp-wide): 251.4MM **Publicly Held**
SIC: 2834 Pharmaceutical preparations
PA: Ligand Pharmaceuticals Incorporated
3911 Sorrento Valley Blvd # 110
San Diego CA 92121
858 550-7500

(G-4997)
LILKEN LLLP
Also Called: Holiday Inn
3411 S Iowa St (66046-5231)
P.O. Box 4345 (66046-1345)
PHONE..................................785 749-7555
Ellen Troeltzsch, *Supervisor*
EMP: 20
SALES: 1,000K
SALES (corp-wide): 7.9MM **Privately Held**
SIC: 7011 Hotels & motels
PA: Hall Equities Group
1855 Olympic Blvd Ste 300
Walnut Creek CA
925 933-4000

(G-4998)
LINUX NEW MEDIA USA LLC
2721 W 6th St Ste D (66049-4302)
PHONE..................................785 856-3080
Brian Osborn, *Mng Member*
EMP: 6
SQ FT: 1,150
SALES (est): 176.1K **Privately Held**
SIC: 2741 Technical manuals: publishing & printing

(G-4999)
LITTLE & MILLER CHARTERED INC
Also Called: Miller, Chris
645 Country Club Ter (66049-2450)
PHONE..................................785 841-6245
Christopher Miller, *Principal*
Miller Chris,
EMP: 11
SALES (est): 696.1K **Privately Held**
SIC: 8111 General practice attorney, lawyer

(G-5000)
LODGIAN INC
Also Called: Holiday Inn
200 Mcdonald Dr (66044-1098)
PHONE..................................785 841-7077
Bruce Pham, *Branch Mgr*
EMP: 45 **Privately Held**
SIC: 7011 5813 5812 Hotels & motels; drinking places; eating places
HQ: Lodgian, Inc.
2002 Summit Blvd Ste 300
Brookhaven GA 30319
404 364-9400

(G-5001)
LRM INDUSTRIES INC (PA)
Also Called: Lawrence Ready Mix
4705 Cherry Hills Ct (66047-9655)
PHONE..................................785 843-1688
Stephen E Glass, *President*
Howard Hasler, *Vice Pres*
Laura A Glass, *Admin Sec*
EMP: 26
SALES (est): 9.5MM **Privately Held**
WEB: www.lrmindust.com
SIC: 3273 1611 1629 4212 Ready-mixed concrete; highway & street paving contractor; earthmoving contractor; local trucking, without storage; water, sewer & utility lines; recycling, waste materials

(G-5002)
LUMINOUS NEON INC
Also Called: Luminous Neon Art Sign Systems
801 E 23rd St (66046-4911)
PHONE..................................785 842-4930
John Motush, *Branch Mgr*
EMP: 8
SALES (corp-wide): 11.6MM **Privately Held**
SIC: 3993 1799 Signs & advertising specialties; sign installation & maintenance
PA: Luminous Neon, Inc.
1429 W 4th Ave
Hutchinson KS 67501
620 662-2363

(G-5003)
LYNN ELC & COMMUNICATIONS INC
725 N 2nd St Ste K (66044-1442)
PHONE..................................785 843-5079
George F Grieb, *President*
EMP: 25
SQ FT: 5,000
SALES (est): 5.1MM **Privately Held**
SIC: 1731 General electrical contractor

(G-5004)
LYNN W ONEAL
Also Called: Oneal Lynn W
1112 W 6th St Ste 214 (66044-2249)
PHONE..................................785 841-2280
Lynn W O Neal MD, *Partner*
EMP: 16
SALES (est): 1MM **Privately Held**
SIC: 8042 Offices & clinics of optometrists

(G-5005)
M P M SERVICES INC
Also Called: All Service Maint & Rmdlg
600 Lawrence Ave Ste 2d (66049-4235)
PHONE..................................785 841-5797
Michael Jacobson, *President*
Mary Pat Jacobson, *Vice Pres*
EMP: 12
SQ FT: 1,450
SALES (est): 1MM **Privately Held**
WEB: www.mpmservices.com
SIC: 6513 7299 Apartment building operators; apartment locating service

(G-5006)
MAGERS LODGINGS INC
Also Called: Hampton Inn
2300 W 6th St (66049-2554)
PHONE..................................785 841-4994
Derek Feltch, *Manager*
EMP: 20
SALES (corp-wide): 5MM **Privately Held**
WEB: www.magerslodgings.com
SIC: 7011 Hotels & motels
PA: Magers Lodgings Inc
2776 S Campbell Ave
Springfield MO 65807
417 882-9397

(G-5007)
MAINSTREET CREDIT UNION
901 Iowa St Ste A (66044-1803)
PHONE..................................785 856-5200
EMP: 10
SALES (corp-wide): 16.9MM **Privately Held**
SIC: 6061 Federal Credit Union
PA: Mainstreet Credit Union
13001 W 95th St
Lenexa KS 66215
913 599-1010

(G-5008)
MAINSTREET FEDERAL CREDIT UN
901 Iowa St (66044-1836)
PHONE..................................785 856-5200
David Collins, *CFO*
EMP: 23
SALES (corp-wide): 14.7MM **Privately Held**
SIC: 6061 Federal credit unions
PA: Mainstreet Federal Credit Union
13001 W 95th St
Lenexa KS 66215
913 599-1010

(G-5009)
MAINSTREET FEDERAL CREDIT UN
1001 E 23rd St (66046-5003)
PHONE..................................785 842-5657
Marlo Hultgren, *President*
EMP: 13
SALES (corp-wide): 14.7MM **Privately Held**
SIC: 6061 Federal credit unions
PA: Mainstreet Federal Credit Union
13001 W 95th St
Lenexa KS 66215
913 599-1010

(G-5010)
MAR LAN CONSTRUCTION LC
1008 Nh St Ste 200 (66044)
P.O. Box 4001 (66046-1001)
PHONE..................................785 749-2647
Gale Lantis,
Brian Lantis,
Kevin Markley,
EMP: 15
SQ FT: 3,000
SALES (est): 4.4MM **Privately Held**
SIC: 1542 Commercial & office building, new construction; commercial & office building contractors

(G-5011)
MARCHE ASSOCIATES INC
123 W 8th St Ste 200 (66044-2687)
PHONE..................................785 749-2925
Stephen Lang, *President*
EMP: 15

SQ FT: 3,000
SALES: 1MM **Privately Held**
WEB: www.marchedesign.com
SIC: 8711 3679 Engineering services; electronic circuits

(G-5012)
MARTIN-LOGAN LTD
2001 Delaware St (66046-3175)
PHONE..................................785 749-0133
Sean Bennett, *Sales Staff*
Keith Riley, *Manager*
EMP: 58
SALES (corp-wide): 25.9MM **Privately Held**
WEB: www.martinlogan.com
SIC: 3651 Loudspeakers, electrodynamic or magnetic
PA: Martin-Logan, Ltd.
2101 Delaware St
Lawrence KS 66046
785 749-0133

(G-5013)
MASTERCRAFT CORPORATION
Also Called: Mastercraft Agency
2601 Dover Sq (66049-4305)
PHONE..................................785 842-4455
James D Schwada, *President*
Russell Tuckell Jr, *Vice Pres*
EMP: 20
SQ FT: 10,000
SALES (est): 1MM **Privately Held**
SIC: 6531 1522 1542 Real estate managers; multi-family dwelling construction; commercial & office building, new construction

(G-5014)
MAYHEW ENVMTL TRAINING ASSOC
Also Called: Meta
2200 W 25th St (66047-2956)
P.O. Box 786 (66044-0786)
PHONE..................................800 444-6382
Brad Mayhew, *President*
Teresa Wilson, *General Mgr*
Belinda Hoover, *Principal*
EMP: 25
SQ FT: 1,900
SALES (est): 3MM **Privately Held**
SIC: 8748 Testing services

(G-5015)
MC GREW REALESTATE INC (PA)
Also Called: Caldwell Banker Mc Grew RE
1501 Kasold Dr (66047-1601)
PHONE..................................785 843-2055
Mike Mc Grew, *CEO*
Lisa Kavanaugh, *President*
Nick McCann, *President*
Jamie Price, *COO*
Jamie Prescott, *Pastor*
EMP: 10
SQ FT: 7,000
SALES (est): 5.3MM **Privately Held**
WEB: www.coldwellbankermcgrew.com
SIC: 6531 Real estate agent, residential; real estate agent, commercial

(G-5016)
MCCONNELL MACHINERY CO INC (PA)
Also Called: Kubota Authorized Dealer
1111 E 23rd St (66046-5005)
PHONE..................................785 843-2676
Doris McConnell, *President*
Daren McConnell, *Vice Pres*
Linda Erlacher, *Treasurer*
Greg Purdon, *Marketing Staff*
Phil Gabriel, *Manager*
EMP: 11
SQ FT: 11,000
SALES (est): 5MM **Privately Held**
WEB: www.mcconnellmachineryco.com
SIC: 5083 5261 Tractors, agricultural; agricultural machinery; farm equipment parts & supplies; lawn & garden equipment

(G-5017)
MCDANIEL KNUTSON INC
Also Called: McDaniel Kntson Fincl Partners
2500 W 31st St Ste B (66047-3051)
PHONE..................................785 841-4664
Wayne McDaniel, *President*
Peter Knutson, *Vice Pres*
EMP: 12
SALES (est): 1.1MM **Privately Held**
WEB: www.mcdanielfinancial.com
SIC: 8742 6282 Financial consultant; investment advisory service

(G-5018)
MCKEE POOL & LANDSCAPING INC
600 Lincoln St (66044-5349)
PHONE..................................785 843-9119
Bruce McKee, *President*
Nancy McKee, *Corp Secy*
EMP: 13
SALES (est): 850K **Privately Held**
SIC: 1799 0781 Swimming pool construction; landscape counseling & planning

(G-5019)
MCNISH FOUNDATIONS INC
1643 N 1300 Rd (66046-9248)
PHONE..................................785 865-2413
Dennis McNish, *President*
EMP: 15 **EST:** 1999
SALES: 500K **Privately Held**
SIC: 1771 Foundation & footing contractor

(G-5020)
MEADOWBROOK APARTMENTS
2601 Dover Sq (66049-4305)
PHONE..................................785 842-4200
Burt Wickersham, *Manager*
Kaitlen Darnell, *Consultant*
EMP: 23 **EST:** 1970
SQ FT: 2,000
SALES (est): 950K **Privately Held**
WEB: www.meadowbrookapartments.net
SIC: 6513 Apartment building operators

(G-5021)
MEDICAL ASSISTANCE PROGRA
303 W 11th St (66044-3311)
PHONE..................................785 842-0726
Lyn Chance, *President*
EMP: 10 **EST:** 1991
SALES (est): 164.2K **Privately Held**
WEB: www.haaseandlong.com
SIC: 8322 Individual & family services

(G-5022)
MERITRUST CREDIT UNION
Also Called: Bwcu
650 Congressional Dr A (66049-4869)
PHONE..................................785 856-7878
Pat Wildeman, *Principal*
EMP: 10
SALES (corp-wide): 53.9MM **Privately Held**
WEB: www.bwcu.org
SIC: 6061 Federal credit unions
PA: Meritrust Credit Union
8710 E 32nd St N
Wichita KS 67226
316 683-1199

(G-5023)
MERRY MAIDS LTD PARTNERSHIP
2201 W 25th St Ste D (66047-2957)
PHONE..................................785 842-2410
Stanton Hinkly, *Owner*
EMP: 15
SALES (corp-wide): 1.9B **Publicly Held**
WEB: www.merrymaids.com
SIC: 7349 7363 Maid services, contract or fee basis; domestic help service
HQ: Merry Maids Limited Partnership
150 Peabody Pl Ste 100
Memphis TN 38103
901 597-8100

(G-5024)
MICROTECH COMPUTERS INC
Also Called: Atipa Technologies
4921 Legends Dr (66049-5800)
PHONE..................................785 841-9513
Mike Y Zheng, *President*
Dana Chang, *Vice Pres*
◆ **EMP:** 20
SQ FT: 32,000
SALES (est): 16.6MM **Privately Held**
WEB: www.microtechkansas.com
SIC: 5045 Computer peripheral equipment

(G-5025)
MIDCONTINENT COMMUNICATIONS
Also Called: Wow
1 Riverfront Plz (66044-2293)
PHONE..................................785 841-2100
Patrick McAdaragh, *Partner*
EMP: 238
SALES (corp-wide): 355.6MM **Privately Held**
SIC: 4813
PA: Midcontinent Communications
3600 Minnesota Dr Ste 700
Minneapolis MN 55435
952 844-2600

(G-5026)
MIDLAND PROFESSIONAL SERVICES (PA)
Also Called: Midland Group The
1310 Wakarusa Dr Ste A (66049-3854)
PHONE..................................785 840-9676
Roger McAllister, *President*
Jeanne Thomsen, *Vice Pres*
Jenifer Janousek, *Opers Staff*
Steve Frederickson, *CFO*
Steve Fredrickson, *CFO*
EMP: 40
SQ FT: 2,800
SALES (est): 3.4MM **Privately Held**
WEB: www.midlandgroup.com
SIC: 8742 Hospital & health services consultant

(G-5027)
MIL-SPEC SECURITY GROUP LLC
520 E 22nd Ter Ste A (66046-3109)
P.O. Box 1636 (66044-8636)
PHONE..................................785 832-1351
Derek Spain,
EMP: 15
SALES (est): 1.7MM **Privately Held**
SIC: 6211 Floor traders, security

(G-5028)
MILES AUTOMOTIVE INC
Also Called: Crown Toyota
3400 Iowa St (66046)
PHONE..................................785 843-7700
Miles E Schnaer, *President*
Paul Blake, *Controller*
Brenda Roberts, *Bookkeeper*
Randy Habiger, *Sales Mgr*
Dave Williamson, *Manager*
EMP: 100
SALES (est): 27.1MM **Privately Held**
WEB: www.crownautomotive.com
SIC: 5511 7538 Automobiles, new & used; general automotive repair shops

(G-5029)
MILLER & MIDYETT REALTOR INC
Also Called: Century 21
1045 E 23rd St (66046-5343)
PHONE..................................785 843-8566
Larry Midyett, *President*
Sherry Heart, *Admin Sec*
EMP: 17
SQ FT: 2,300
SALES (est): 1.2MM **Privately Held**
SIC: 6531 Real estate agent, residential

(G-5030)
MIZE HOUSER & COMPANY PA
211 E 8th St Ste A (66044-2771)
P.O. Box 488 (66044-0488)
PHONE..................................785 842-8844
Natalie Saffle, *Accountant*
Loren Kingsdury, *Manager*
EMP: 10
SALES (corp-wide): 23.3MM **Privately Held**
SIC: 8699 Athletic organizations
PA: Mize Houser & Company P.A.
534 S Kansas Ave Ste 700
Topeka KS 66603
785 233-0536

(G-5031)
MORGAN CONCRETE SERVICES INC
1201 E 24th St (66046-5128)
P.O. Box 3545 (66046-0545)
PHONE..................................785 842-1686
Robert J Morgan, *President*
Gregory Thrasher, *Vice Pres*
Beverly Morgan, *Treasurer*
EMP: 25
SALES (est): 1.9MM **Privately Held**
SIC: 1771 Concrete work

(G-5032)
MORGAN STANLEY & CO LLC
1429 Oread West St # 100 (66049-5205)
PHONE..................................785 749-1111
Kent Tomlinson, *Sales/Mktg Mgr*
EMP: 11
SALES (corp-wide): 50.1B **Publicly Held**
WEB: www.msvp.com
SIC: 6211 Investment bankers
HQ: Morgan Stanley & Co. Llc
1585 Broadway
New York NY 10036
212 761-4000

(G-5033)
MOTIVATED RE SOLUTIONS LLC
3227 Huntington Rd (66049-5207)
PHONE..................................785 842-3530
Patrick Brown,
EMP: 53
SALES (est): 671.2K **Privately Held**
SIC: 7389

(G-5034)
MV TRANSPORTATION INC
Also Called: Lawrence Transit System
1260 Timberedge Rd (66049-8904)
PHONE..................................785 312-7054
Mike Sweetin, *Branch Mgr*
EMP: 50
SALES (corp-wide): 916.6MM **Privately Held**
WEB: www.mvtransit.com
SIC: 4111 Local & suburban transit
PA: Mv Transportation, Inc.
2711 N Haskell Ave # 1500
Dallas TX 75204
972 391-4600

(G-5035)
N R HAMM QUARRY INC
Also Called: Hamm Sanitary Landfill
16984 3rd St (66044-8300)
P.O. Box 17, Perry (66073-0017)
PHONE..................................785 842-3236
Jeremy Sedlock, *Manager*
EMP: 40
SALES (corp-wide): 2.1B **Publicly Held**
SIC: 4953 Sanitary landfill operation
HQ: Hamm, Inc.
609 Perry Pl
Perry KS 66073
785 597-5111

(G-5036)
NB REMODELING LLC
Also Called: Natural Breeze Remodeling
1440 Wakarusa Dr Ste 800 (66049-1713)
PHONE..................................785 749-1855
Terry Finton,
EMP: 11
SALES (est): 829.3K **Privately Held**
SIC: 1521 General remodeling, single-family houses

(G-5037)
NBH BANK
Also Called: Bank Midwest
4831 W 6th St (66049-5201)
P.O. Box 1795 (66044-8795)
PHONE..................................785 842-4300
Pete Cipolla, *Opers Staff*
Matt Whitlow, *Sales Mgr*
Michael Meyer, *Sales Staff*
Warner Lewis, *Marketing Staff*
Kevin Kajy, *Branch Mgr*
EMP: 13 **Publicly Held**
SIC: 6022 State commercial banks
HQ: Nbh Bank
7800 E Orchard Rd
Greenwood Village CO 80111
720 554-6680

G E O G R A P H I C

(G-5038)
NEW CINGULAR WIRELESS SVCS INC
520 W 23rd St Ste H (66046-4700)
PHONE..................................785 832-2700
Mark Turner, *Branch Mgr*
EMP: 19
SALES (corp-wide): 170.7B **Publicly Held**
SIC: 4812 Cellular telephone services
HQ: New Cingular Wireless Services, Inc.
7277 164th Ave Ne
Redmond WA 98052

(G-5039)
NEW MEDIA SAMURAI LLC
Also Called: Nms3
123 W 8th St Ste 302 (66044-2687)
P.O. Box 1487 (66044-8487)
PHONE..................................785 856-6673
Kimberly Millsap, *Mng Member*
Kris Millsap, *Creative Dir*
EMP: 10
SALES (est): 522.4K **Privately Held**
SIC: 7319 Advertising

(G-5040)
NIEDER CONTRACTING INC
Also Called: Jayhawk Guttering
692 N 1610 Rd (66049-9008)
PHONE..................................785 842-0094
Mike Nieder, *President*
Sheri Nieder, *Vice Pres*
EMP: 20
SALES: 1MM **Privately Held**
SIC: 1761 1542 Gutter & downspout contractor; commercial & office buildings, renovation & repair

(G-5041)
NIEHOFF HEATING & AIR INC
Also Called: Niehoff Dunco Heating & Coolg
1729 Bullene Ave Unit D (66044-4322)
PHONE..................................785 594-7137
Wayne Duncan, *President*
EMP: 20
SALES (est): 2.3MM **Privately Held**
WEB: www.niehoffdunco.com
SIC: 1711 Warm air heating & air conditioning contractor

(G-5042)
NORTHWIND MERCHANT COMPANY
1705 Haskell Ave Ste A (66044-4302)
PHONE..................................785 856-1183
Chuck Wargin, *Partner*
EMP: 11
SALES (est): 2.3MM **Privately Held**
SIC: 4731 Agents, shipping

(G-5043)
OLIVER ELECTRIC CNSTR INC
3104 Haskell Ave Ste A (66046-4901)
P.O. Box 3529 (66046-0529)
PHONE..................................785 748-0777
Diedre K Oliver, *CEO*
Merissa Kokhanovsky, *Accounting Mgr*
Todd Hockenbury, *Manager*
EMP: 27
SQ FT: 900
SALES: 4.5MM **Privately Held**
SIC: 1731 General electrical contractor

(G-5044)
OMALLEY BEVERAGE OF KANSAS
2050 Packer Ct (66044-8600)
PHONE..................................785 843-8816
Kevin O'Malley, *President*
EMP: 25
SALES (est): 6.2MM **Privately Held**
WEB: www.omalleybeverage.com
SIC: 5181 Beer & other fermented malt liquors

(G-5045)
ONE OF KIND PROGRESSIVE CHLD C
4640 W 27th St (66047-3346)
PHONE..................................785 830-9040
Stephanie Brosa, *President*
Amy Risley, *Vice Pres*
Cindy Leutz, *Treasurer*
Shanna Steadham, *Director*
Melissa Schiesser, *Director*
EMP: 40 **EST:** 2001
SALES: 698.5K **Privately Held**
SIC: 8351 Preschool center

(G-5046)
OREAD HOTEL
1200 Oread Ave (66044-3142)
PHONE..................................785 843-1200
EMP: 33
SALES (est): 1.9MM **Privately Held**
SIC: 7011 Resort hotel

(G-5047)
OREAD ORTHODONTICS
1425 Wakarusa Dr (66049-3832)
PHONE..................................785 856-2483
EMP: 10
SALES (est): 388.9K **Privately Held**
SIC: 8021 Dentist's Office

(G-5048)
OREILLY AUTOMOTIVE STORES INC
Also Called: O'Reilly Auto Parts
1008 W 23rd St (66046-4411)
PHONE..................................785 842-9800
Dave Peck, *Manager*
Justin Cook, *Manager*
EMP: 18 **Publicly Held**
WEB: www.oreillyauto.com
SIC: 5531 5013 Automotive parts; automotive supplies & parts
HQ: O'reilly Automotive Stores, Inc.
233 S Patterson Ave
Springfield MO 65802
417 862-2674

(G-5049)
OREILLY AUTOMOTIVE STORES INC
Also Called: O'Reilly Auto Parts
906 N 2nd St (66044-1412)
PHONE..................................785 832-0408
Joe Senske, *Manager*
EMP: 11 **Publicly Held**
WEB: www.oreillyauto.com
SIC: 5013 5531 Automotive supplies & parts; automotive parts
HQ: O'reilly Automotive Stores, Inc.
233 S Patterson Ave
Springfield MO 65802
417 862-2674

(G-5050)
ORSCHELN FARM AND HOME LLC
Also Called: Orschelin Farm and Home 48
1541 E 23rd St (66046-5013)
PHONE..................................785 838-3184
Nick Koso, *Branch Mgr*
EMP: 10
SALES (corp-wide): 822.7MM **Privately Held**
WEB: www.orschelnfarmhome.com
SIC: 5191 5251 5699 Farm supplies; hardware; work clothing
PA: Orscheln Farm And Home Llc
1800 Overcenter Dr
Moberly MO 65270
800 577-2580

(G-5051)
ORTHOKANSAS PA
1112 W 6th St (66044-2215)
PHONE..................................785 843-9125
Jeffrey C Randall, *Principal*
Karen Healy, *Technician*
EMP: 29
SALES (est): 4MM **Privately Held**
SIC: 8011 Internal medicine, physician/surgeon

(G-5052)
OVERFIELD CORPORATION
Also Called: Midwest Digital
1915 W 24th St (66046-3932)
P.O. Box 4246 (66046-1246)
PHONE..................................785 843-3434
Scott Overfield, *President*
Kathrine Overfield, *Treasurer*
EMP: 12
SQ FT: 3,000
SALES: 728.8K **Privately Held**
SIC: 1731 5999 7382 5063 Fire detection & burglar alarm systems specialization; telephone & communication equipment; telephone equipment & systems; security systems services; burglar alarm systems; cellular telephone services; radio broadcasting & communications equipment

(G-5053)
P A THERAPYWORKS INC
Also Called: Therapyworks Wellness Center
1311 Wakarusa Dr Ste 1000 (66049-1741)
PHONE..................................785 749-1300
Cynthia Johnson, *President*
EMP: 40
SALES (est): 1.2MM **Privately Held**
SIC: 8049 8093 7991 Physical therapist; rehabilitation center, outpatient treatment; aerobic dance & exercise classes

(G-5054)
P1 GROUP INC
2151 Haskell Ave Bldg 1 (66046-3209)
PHONE..................................785 843-2910
Bruce Belcher, *Principal*
EMP: 100
SALES (corp-wide): 243.8MM **Privately Held**
WEB: www.p1group.com
SIC: 1711 1731 Mechanical contractor; electrical work
PA: P1 Group, Inc.
13605 W 96th Ter
Lenexa KS 66215
913 529-5000

(G-5055)
PACKERWARE LLC
2330 Packer Rd (66049-8900)
P.O. Box 219 (66044-0219)
PHONE..................................785 331-4236
Roberto Buaron, *President*
Martin Imbler, *President*
James Kratochvil, *Exec VP*
Jon Rich, *CFO*
Mike Putnam, *Finance Dir*
▲ **EMP:** 700
SALES (est): 128.5MM **Publicly Held**
WEB: www.packerware.com
SIC: 3089 Injection molding of plastics
HQ: Berry Global, Inc.
101 Oakley St
Evansville IN 47710
812 424-2904

(G-5056)
PARKWAY 4000 LP
4001 Parkway Cir (66047-2001)
PHONE..................................785 749-2555
Lelon Capps, *Partner*
EMP: 16
SALES (est): 1MM **Privately Held**
SIC: 6513 Apartment hotel operation

(G-5057)
PATCHEN ELECTRIC & INDUS SUP
602 E 9th St (66044-2633)
P.O. Box 1060 (66044-8060)
PHONE..................................785 843-4522
Tommy E Patchen Jr, *President*
Clarice Patchen, *Corp Secy*
David Patchen, *Vice Pres*
Sandra Patchen, *Shareholder*
EMP: 7
SQ FT: 12,000
SALES (est): 1.5MM **Privately Held**
SIC: 7694 5251 1781 Electric motor repair; tools, power; pumps & pumping equipment; water well drilling

(G-5058)
PAUL DAVIS RESTORATIO OF GREAT
1420 N 3rd St (66044-9128)
PHONE..................................785 842-0351
Jeff Goldman, *President*
EMP: 23
SQ FT: 8,500
SALES (est): 4.7MM **Privately Held**
SIC: 1521 1541 Repairing fire damage, single-family houses; renovation, remodeling & repairs: industrial buildings

(G-5059)
PAWSH WASH
1520 Wakarusa Dr Ste C (66047-2255)
PHONE..................................785 856-7297
Nichele Nickel, *Owner*
Amber Nickle, *Co-Owner*
EMP: 12
SALES (est): 220.6K **Privately Held**
SIC: 0752 5999 Grooming services, pet & animal specialties; pet food; pet supplies

(G-5060)
PENNINGTON CO FUNDRAISING LLC
501 Gateway Dr Ste A (66049-2342)
PHONE..................................785 843-1661
Patrick Alderdice, *President*
Rod Barleen, *Vice Pres*
Jerry Cooper, *Vice Pres*
Matt Ellis, *Vice Pres*
Mary Dillon, *Treasurer*
EMP: 43
SALES (est): 5.6MM **Privately Held**
WEB: www.penningtonco.com
SIC: 7389 8743 8742 Fund raising organizations; public relations services; business planning & organizing services
PA: Omega Financial, Llc
1242 6th Ave
Columbus GA 31901

(G-5061)
PERIMETER SOLUTIONS LP
440 N 9th St (66044-5424)
PHONE..................................785 749-8100
Karen Schuyler, *Branch Mgr*
EMP: 160 **Privately Held**
SIC: 2819 Industrial inorganic chemicals.
HQ: Perimeter Solutions Lp
8000 Maryland Ave Ste 350
Saint Louis MO 63105
314 983-7500

(G-5062)
PERSONAL MEMBERSHIP
617 E 1450 Rd (66046-9294)
PHONE..................................785 979-7812
Ron Lawrenz, *Principal*
EMP: 10
SALES (est): 1.1MM **Privately Held**
SIC: 4911 Electric services

(G-5063)
PI KAPPA PHI HOUSE MOTHER
1537 Tennessee St (66044-4173)
PHONE..................................785 856-1400
Shari Head, *Principal*
EMP: 72
SALES (est): 278K **Privately Held**
SIC: 8641 University club

(G-5064)
PINE HOWARD GRDN CTR & GRNHSE
1320 N 3rd St (66044-9106)
PHONE..................................785 749-0302
Gerald Pine, *Owner*
EMP: 25 **EST:** 1963
SALES (est): 400K **Privately Held**
SIC: 0721 0182 0181 8422 Planting services; food crops grown under cover; tomatoes grown under cover; flowers: grown under cover (e.g. greenhouse production); botanical garden

(G-5065)
PINES INTERNATIONAL INC
1992 E 1400 Rd (66044-9303)
P.O. Box 927 (66044-0927)
PHONE..................................800 697-4637
Steve D Malone, *CEO*
Ron Seibold, *President*
EMP: 24 **EST:** 1977
SALES (est): 4.5MM **Privately Held**
WEB: www.wheatgrass.com
SIC: 2034 0139 Vegetables, dried or dehydrated (except freeze-dried); herb or spice farm

(G-5066)
PINNACLE TECHNOLOGY INC
2721 Oregon St (66046-4947)
PHONE..................................785 832-8866
Donna A Johnson, *President*
David A Johnson, *Vice Pres*

Seth Gabbert, *Senior Engr*
Shaheen Latif, *Sales Staff*
David E Scott, *Sales Associate*
EMP: 26
SQ FT: 8,300
SALES (est): 2.9MM **Privately Held**
WEB: www.pinnaclet.com
SIC: 8711 3826 3823 Consulting engineer; analytical instruments; dust sampling & analysis equipment; blood testing apparatus; industrial instrmnts msrmnt display/control process variable

(G-5067)
PIONEER RIDGE IND LIVING
650 Congressional Dr D (66049-4869)
PHONE..................................785 749-6785
EMP: 10 **EST:** 2017
SALES (est): 192.6K **Privately Held**
SIC: 8051 Skilled nursing care facilities

(G-5068)
PIONEER RIDGE RETIREMENT CMNTY
4851 Harvard Rd (66049-3964)
PHONE..................................785 344-1100
Marie Vogel, *Director*
EMP: 102
SALES: 6.6MM
SALES (corp-wide): 32.7MM **Privately Held**
WEB: www.pioneer-ridge.com
SIC: 8051 Skilled nursing care facilities
PA: Midwest Health, Inc
3024 Sw Wanamaker Rd # 300
Topeka KS 66614
785 272-1535

(G-5069)
PLASTIKON HEALTHCARE LLC
3780 Greenway Cir (66046-5440)
P.O. Box 667 (66044-0667)
PHONE..................................785 330-7100
Fred Soofer, *President*
Sandra Dixon, *General Mgr*
John A Emerson, *Principal*
John Low, *CFO*
EMP: 34 **EST:** 2010
SQ FT: 45,000
SALES (est): 7.9MM
SALES (corp-wide): 118.9MM **Privately Held**
SIC: 2835 In vitro & in vivo diagnostic substances
PA: Plastikon Industries, Inc.
688 Sandoval Way
Hayward CA 94544
510 400-1010

(G-5070)
PLASTIKON INDUSTRIES INC
3780 Greenway Cir (66046-5440)
PHONE..................................785 749-1630
Fred Soofer, *Branch Mgr*
EMP: 11
SALES (corp-wide): 118.9MM **Privately Held**
SIC: 3089 Injection molding of plastics
PA: Plastikon Industries, Inc.
688 Sandoval Way
Hayward CA 94544
510 400-1010

(G-5071)
POWELL ELECTRICAL SYSTEMS INC
4218 Tamarisk Ct (66047-2022)
PHONE..................................785 856-5863
David Dingus, *Branch Mgr*
EMP: 12
SALES (corp-wide): 517.1MM **Publicly Held**
SIC: 4911 Electric services
HQ: Powell Electrical Systems, Inc.
8550 Mosley Rd
Houston TX 77075
713 944-6900

(G-5072)
PRAIRIE PATCHES INC
1327 Covington Ct (66049-3806)
PHONE..................................785 749-4565
Cinda Garrison, *President*
EMP: 8
SALES (est): 540.7K **Privately Held**
SIC: 5947 5199 2395 Gift shop; gifts & novelties; embroidery & art needlework

(G-5073)
PREMIUM VENTURES LLC (PA)
Also Called: En- Tire Car Care Center
1801 W 31st St (66046-4339)
PHONE..................................785 842-5500
Jeff Tucker, *Manager*
EMP: 10
SQ FT: 7,000
SALES: 1MM **Privately Held**
SIC: 7538 3011 General automotive repair shops; automobile tires, pneumatic

(G-5074)
PRESBYTERIAN MANORS INC
Also Called: Lawrence Presbyterian Manor
1429 Kasold Dr (66049-3429)
PHONE..................................785 841-4262
Dorothy Devlin, *Director*
EMP: 80
SALES (corp-wide): 8.6MM **Privately Held**
SIC: 8051 8361 Convalescent home with continuous nursing care; residential care
HQ: Presbyterian Manors, Inc.
2414 N Woodlawn Blvd
Wichita KS 67220
316 685-1100

(G-5075)
PRIME COMMUNICATIONS LP
4821 W 6th St Ste M (66049-4827)
PHONE..................................785 371-4990
EMP: 10
SALES (corp-wide): 280MM **Privately Held**
SIC: 4813 Local & long distance telephone communications
PA: Prime Communications, L.P.
12550 Reed Rd Ste 100
Sugar Land TX 77478
281 240-7800

(G-5076)
PRIME SEC SVCS BORROWER LLC
1035 N 3rd St Ste 101 (66044-1491)
PHONE..................................630 410-0662
Leon Black, *CEO*
EMP: 11
SALES (est): 4.3B
SALES (corp-wide): 4.5B **Publicly Held**
SIC: 6799 7382 3699 7381 Investors; security systems services; protective devices, security; security devices; detective & armored car services; security guard service
PA: Adt Inc.
1501 W Yamato Rd
Boca Raton FL 33431
561 988-3600

(G-5077)
PRINTING SOLUTIONS KANSAS INC
725 N 2nd St Ste W (66044-1475)
P.O. Box 3588 (66046-0588)
PHONE..................................785 841-8336
John Hutton, *President*
Terry Jacobsen, *Corp Secy*
Shelle Arnold, *Director*
Tom Hutton, *Director*
Julianna Falls, *Executive Asst*
EMP: 7
SQ FT: 10,000
SALES (est): 2MM **Privately Held**
WEB: www.printing-solutions.com
SIC: 2752 Commercial printing, lithographic

(G-5078)
PROFESSIONAL MOVING & STORAGE
431 N Iowa St (66044-9617)
PHONE..................................785 842-1115
Bobby Jones, *President*
EMP: 20
SALES (est): 1.4MM **Privately Held**
SIC: 4214 Local trucking with storage

(G-5079)
PROFESSIONAL RENEWAL CENTER PA
1421 Res Pk Dr Ste 3b (66049)
PHONE..................................785 842-9772
Betsy Williams, *Principal*
EMP: 10
SALES (est): 688.2K **Privately Held**
WEB: www.prckansas.org
SIC: 8093 Rehabilitation center, outpatient treatment

(G-5080)
PROPRINT INCORPORATED
4931 W 6th St Ste 104 (66049-4831)
PHONE..................................785 842-3610
Don Grantham, *President*
EMP: 21
SALES (est): 1.6MM
SALES (corp-wide): 2.4MM **Privately Held**
WEB: www.proprintks.com
SIC: 2752 2791 2789 Commercial printing, offset; typesetting; bookbinding & related work
PA: Proprint Incorporated
1033 Sw Gage Blvd Ste 200
Topeka KS 66604
785 272-0070

(G-5081)
PROSOCO INC (HQ)
3741 Greenway Cir (66046-5441)
PHONE..................................785 865-4200
David W Boyer, *President*
Doug Barron, *Vice Pres*
John Bourne, *Vice Pres*
Bruce Boyer, *Vice Pres*
Brian Koenings, *Vice Pres*
EMP: 65 **EST:** 1939
SQ FT: 80,000
SALES (est): 87.5MM **Privately Held**
WEB: www.prosoco.com
SIC: 5169 2891 2851 2842 Chemicals & allied products; adhesives & sealants; paints & allied products; specialty cleaning, polishes & sanitation goods; soap & other detergents; waterproofing compounds

(G-5082)
PUR-O-ZONE INC
345 N Iowa St (66044-9625)
P.O. Box 727 (66044-0727)
PHONE..................................785 843-0771
Joseph P Bosco, *President*
Mike Lockhart, *Mfg Dir*
Michael Lane, *VP Sales*
Dennis O'Hagan, *Sales Mgr*
Tyrone Duckworth, *Sales Staff*
EMP: 45
SQ FT: 20,000
SALES (est): 15.7MM **Privately Held**
WEB: www.purozone.com
SIC: 5169 2842 Specialty cleaning & sanitation preparations; sanitation preparations

(G-5083)
QUALITY ELC DOUGLAS CNTY INC
1011 E 31st St (66046-5103)
PHONE..................................785 843-9211
Mike Hutton, *President*
EMP: 25
SQ FT: 6,000
SALES (est): 4.5MM **Privately Held**
SIC: 1731 General electrical contractor

(G-5084)
R & H CONCRETE INC
1887 E 1450 Rd (66044-9452)
P.O. Box 489 (66044-0489)
PHONE..................................785 286-0335
Robert Haag, *CEO*
Randy Haag, *President*
Ron Haag, *President*
Delores Haag, *Corp Secy*
EMP: 20
SALES (est): 2MM **Privately Held**
SIC: 1771 Foundation & footing contractor

(G-5085)
R D JOHNSON EXCAVATING CO INC
1705 N 1399 Rd (66046-9256)
PHONE..................................785 842-9100
Roger Johnson, *President*
Tim Hertach, *Controller*
Dustin Baker, *Director*
EMP: 38
SQ FT: 2,000
SALES (est): 7.3MM **Privately Held**
SIC: 1794 1611 1623 Excavation & grading, building construction; highway & street construction; water, sewer & utility lines

(G-5086)
RADIOLOGIC PROF SVCS PA
1112 W 6th St Ste 10 (66044-2249)
P.O. Box 29191, Shawnee Mission (66201-9191)
PHONE..................................785 841-3211
Scott Pattrick, *President*
EMP: 14
SQ FT: 2,500
SALES (est): 3.8MM **Privately Held**
SIC: 8011 Radiologist

(G-5087)
RAY BECHARD INC
275 Parrott Athletic Ctr (66045-0001)
PHONE..................................785 864-5077
Ray Bechard, *Principal*
EMP: 20
SALES (est): 2.2MM **Privately Held**
SIC: 5131 Sewing supplies & notions

(G-5088)
RAYMOND JAMES FINCL SVCS INC
711 Wakarusa Dr (66049-3751)
PHONE..................................785 383-1893
Raymond Lewman, *Branch Mgr*
EMP: 11
SALES (corp-wide): 8B **Publicly Held**
SIC: 6211 Brokers, security
HQ: Raymond James Financial Services, Inc.
880 Carillon Pkwy
Saint Petersburg FL 33716
727 567-1000

(G-5089)
RE MAX PROFESSIONALS L L C
Also Called: Re/Max
545 Columbia Dr (66049-2363)
PHONE..................................785 843-9393
EMP: 18
SALES (est): 1.1MM **Privately Held**
SIC: 6531 Real estate agent, residential

(G-5090)
RE/MAX EXCEL
1420 Wakarusa Dr Ste 203 (66049-3810)
PHONE..................................785 856-8484
Mary Northrop, *Owner*
Beth Pine, *Business Mgr*
Kristin Allan, *Broker*
Cal Lantis, *Broker*
Maggie Stonecipher, *Broker*
EMP: 10
SALES (est): 350K **Privately Held**
SIC: 6531 Real estate agent, residential

(G-5091)
REED DILLON & ASSOCIATES
1213 E 24th St (66046-5128)
PHONE..................................785 832-0083
Reed Dillon, *President*
Justin Swisher, *Division Mgr*
Nic Dannevik, *Project Mgr*
EMP: 11
SQ FT: 2,500
SALES (est): 652.3K **Privately Held**
SIC: 0781 0782 Landscape architects; landscape contractors

(G-5092)
RELAX INVESTMENTS INC
Also Called: Baymont Inn & Suites
740 Iowa St (66044-1741)
PHONE..................................785 838-4242
Arvind Patel, *President*
EMP: 10

GEOGRAPHIC

SALES (est): 810.7K **Privately Held**
SIC: 7011 Inns

(G-5093)
RESOLUTION SERVICES LLC
900 Msschsetts St Ste 380 (66044)
PHONE..................................785 843-1638
Amy Whalen Risley,
EMP: 23 **EST:** 1999
SALES (est): 1.7MM **Privately Held**
WEB: www.resolutionserv.com
SIC: 8748 Business consulting

(G-5094)
REUTER ORGAN CO INC
1220 Timberedge Rd (66049-8904)
PHONE..................................785 843-2622
Albert Neutel Jr, *President*
William Klimas, *Vice Pres*
Dorothy Schaake, *Exec Sec*
▼ **EMP:** 25
SQ FT: 75,000
SALES (est): 4.2MM **Privately Held**
WEB: www.reuterorgan.com
SIC: 3931 5736 Organs, all types: pipe, reed, hand, electronic, etc.; musical instrument stores

(G-5095)
RICHARD A ORCHARDS MD
1112 W 6th St Ste 214 (66044-2249)
PHONE..................................785 841-2280
Richard A Orchards MD, *President*
EMP: 17
SALES (est): 287.3K **Privately Held**
SIC: 8011 Ophthalmologist

(G-5096)
RICHARD F SOSINSKI
Also Called: Internal Medicine Group
4525 W 6th St Ste 100 (66049-7700)
PHONE..................................785 843-5160
Richard F Sosinski, *Owner*
EMP: 40
SALES (est): 2.6MM **Privately Held**
SIC: 8011 Internal medicine, physician/surgeon; general & family practice, physician/surgeon

(G-5097)
ROARK & ASSOCIATES PA
3504 Westridge Dr (66049-2258)
P.O. Box 123 (66044-0123)
PHONE..................................785 842-3431
Mike Roark, *President*
Jeff Miller, *Accountant*
Debbie Filkins, *Admin Asst*
Chris Seratte, *Administration*
EMP: 15
SALES (est): 1MM **Privately Held**
SIC: 8721 Certified public accountant

(G-5098)
RUESCHHOFF COMMUNICATIONS
Also Called: Rueschhoff Locksmith
3727 W 6th St Ste A (66049-3260)
PHONE..................................785 841-0111
David Rueschhoff, *President*
Heath Cummings, *Division Mgr*
Lisa Reuschhoff, *Vice Pres*
EMP: 21
SQ FT: 2,500
SALES (est): 2.9MM **Privately Held**
WEB: www.rueschhoffs.com
SIC: 5999 5251 7699 7389 Alarm signal systems; builders' hardware; locksmith shop; safety inspection service

(G-5099)
RUMSEY-YOST FUNERAL INC
Also Called: Rumsey-Yost Fnrl HM Crematory
601 Indiana St (66044-2329)
P.O. Box 1260 (66044-8260)
PHONE..................................785 843-5111
Bart Yost, *President*
Fleda Ann Yost, *Corp Secy*
EMP: 12 **EST:** 1946
SQ FT: 4,216
SALES (est): 770.5K **Privately Held**
WEB: www.rumsey-yost.com
SIC: 7261 5999 Funeral director; monuments & tombstones

(G-5100)
SALON DIMARCO AND DAY SPA
733 Massachusetts St (66044-2345)
PHONE..................................785 843-0044
Alex Fiori, *Owner*
Mark Willingham, *Co-Owner*
EMP: 12
SALES (est): 207.2K **Privately Held**
WEB: www.sdimarco.com
SIC: 7991 Spas

(G-5101)
SALVATION ARMY
946 New Hampshire St (66044-3098)
PHONE..................................785 843-1716
Rich Forney, *Manager*
EMP: 22
SALES (corp-wide): 2.2B **Privately Held**
WEB: www.salarmychicago.org
SIC: 8661 8699 Religious organizations; charitable organization
HQ: The Salvation Army
5550 Prairie Stone Pkwy # 130
Hoffman Estates IL 60192
847 294-2000

(G-5102)
SCANNING AMERICA INC (PA)
1440 N 3rd St (66044-9128)
PHONE..................................785 749-7471
Timothy Hunsinger, *President*
Michael Brock, *Production*
Lee Embrey, *Sales Mgr*
Terry Borovitcky, *Sales Staff*
Roger Long, *Manager*
EMP: 65
SQ FT: 12,000
SALES (est): 10.5MM **Privately Held**
WEB: www.scanningamerica.com
SIC: 7334 Photocopying & duplicating services

(G-5103)
SCHLUMBERGER TECHNOLOGY CORP
Lawrence Product Center
2400 Packer Rd (66049-8903)
PHONE..................................785 841-5610
Chris Von Fange, *Design Engr*
Barry Landon, *Sales/Mktg Mgr*
Kemp Webb, *Accounts Mgr*
EMP: 150 **Publicly Held**
SIC: 1389 3561 3357 Servicing oil & gas wells; pumps & pumping equipment; nonferrous wiredrawing & insulating
HQ: Schlumberger Technology Corp
300 Schlumberger Dr
Sugar Land TX 77478
281 285-8500

(G-5104)
SCHURLE SIGNS INC
1837 E 1450 Rd (66044-9452)
P.O. Box 514 (66044-0514)
PHONE..................................785 832-9897
Janet Schurle, *Branch Mgr*
EMP: 7
SALES (est): 828K
SALES (corp-wide): 2.3MM **Privately Held**
SIC: 3993 Signs & advertising specialties
PA: Schurle Signs, Inc.
7555 Falcon Rd
Riley KS 66531
785 485-2885

(G-5105)
SCOTCH INDUSTRIES INC
Also Called: Scotch Fabric Care Services
611 Florida St (66044-1721)
PHONE..................................785 843-8585
Shelly Wright, *Branch Mgr*
EMP: 20
SALES (corp-wide): 4.7MM **Privately Held**
SIC: 7211 7219 7216 Power laundries, family & commercial; garment alteration & repair shop; curtain cleaning & repair
PA: Scotch Industries Inc
1029 Nh St Apt B
Lawrence KS 66044
785 843-0037

(G-5106)
SCOTT MESLER
Also Called: Mesler Roofing Co
1628 Highway 40 (66044-9476)
PHONE..................................785 749-0462
Scott Mesler, *Owner*
EMP: 15
SQ FT: 4,000
SALES (est): 989.6K **Privately Held**
WEB: www.meslerroofingco.com
SIC: 1761 5033 Roofing contractor; roofing, siding & insulation

(G-5107)
SCREEN-IT GRPHICS LAWRENCE INC
Also Called: Grandstand Glassware and AP
3840 Greenway Cir (66046-5443)
PHONE..................................785 843-8888
Chris Piper, *President*
Chad Bryan, *Opers Mgr*
Chad Plueger, *Opers Staff*
Jennifer Gimlin, *Purch Mgr*
Tom Boyle, *Treasurer*
◆ **EMP:** 183
SQ FT: 20,000
SALES (est): 19.7MM **Privately Held**
WEB: www.egrandstand.com
SIC: 2759 2396 Screen printing; screen printing on fabric articles

(G-5108)
SENIOR RSRCE CTR FOR DGLAS CNT
Also Called: SENIOR SERVICES
745 Vermont St (66044-2371)
PHONE..................................785 842-0543
John Glassman, *Director*
EMP: 15
SALES: 916.7K **Privately Held**
SIC: 8322 Senior citizens' center or association

(G-5109)
SHARKS INVESTMENT INC
Also Called: Shark's Surf Shop
813 Massachusetts St (66044-2657)
P.O. Box 51, Overbrook (66524-0051)
PHONE..................................785 841-8289
Chris Cox, *President*
EMP: 12
SQ FT: 6,000
SALES (est): 1.5MM **Privately Held**
SIC: 5661 5699 7299 Shoe stores; sports apparel; tanning salon

(G-5110)
SHREEJI INVESTMENTS INC
Also Called: Baymont Inn & Suites
740 Iowa St (66044-1741)
PHONE..................................785 838-4242
Arvind Patel, *General Mgr*
EMP: 10 **Privately Held**
SIC: 7011 Inns
PA: Shreeji Investments, Inc.
1716 Jefferson St
Jefferson City MO 65109

(G-5111)
SJH FAMILY CORP
2400 Franklin Rd Ste A (66046-8227)
P.O. Box 161, Ursa IL (62376-0161)
PHONE..................................785 856-5296
EMP: 10
SALES (est): 887.2K **Privately Held**
SIC: 7389 Business Services

(G-5112)
SKY BLUE INC
2110 Delaware St Ste B (66046-3112)
PHONE..................................785 842-9013
EMP: 64 **EST:** 2015
SALES (est): 1MM **Privately Held**
SIC: 8711 1542 8744 Engineering Services Nonresidential Construction Facilities Support Services

(G-5113)
SOD SHOP INC
1783 E 1500 Rd Ste B (66044-9305)
P.O. Box 362 (66044-0362)
PHONE..................................913 814-0044
Wade Wilbur, *President*
Tony Wilbur, *Corp Secy*
Ted Wilbur, *Vice Pres*
EMP: 15
SQ FT: 300
SALES: 2.2MM **Privately Held**
SIC: 0181 Sod farms

(G-5114)
SPATIAL DATA RESEARCH INC
Also Called: Sdr
1220 Timberedge Rd (66049-8904)
P.O. Box 684, Olathe (66051-0684)
PHONE..................................314 705-0772
Susan Cunningham, *President*
Matthew Knight, *Vice Pres*
Kathleen Stahlman, *Admin Sec*
EMP: 15
SQ FT: 1,300
SALES (est): 1.2MM **Privately Held**
WEB: www.sdrmaps.com
SIC: 7371 Software programming applications

(G-5115)
SPIRIT INDUSTRIES INC
1021 E 31st St (66046-5103)
PHONE..................................913 749-5858
Thomas L Wilkerson, *President*
Rosann Wilkerson, *Treasurer*
EMP: 10
SQ FT: 15,000
SALES (est): 828K **Privately Held**
SIC: 2261 5131 Printing of cotton broadwoven fabrics; piece goods & other fabrics

(G-5116)
SRH MECHANICAL CONTRACTORS INC
Also Called: Superior Refrigeration and Htg
12612 246th St (66044-7334)
PHONE..................................785 842-0301
EMP: 15
SQ FT: 1,500
SALES (est): 1.6MM **Privately Held**
SIC: 1711 Refrigeration Heating Air Conditioning Hydronics & Water Process Piping Contractor

(G-5117)
STANDARD BEVERAGE CORPORATION
Also Called: Lawrence Distribution Center
2300 Lakeview Rd (66049-8942)
PHONE..................................800 999-8797
Bruce Alexander, *President*
Trent Glass, *Vice Pres*
Alex Brophy, *Sales Staff*
Joshua Jensen, *Sales Staff*
EMP: 128
SALES (corp-wide): 71.3MM **Privately Held**
SIC: 5182 Liquor
PA: Standard Beverage Corporation
2526 E 36th Cir N
Wichita KS 67219
316 838-7707

(G-5118)
STANION WHOLESALE ELC CO INC
2958 Four Wheel Dr (66047-3144)
PHONE..................................785 841-8420
Adam Didde, *Branch Mgr*
John Keller, *Branch Mgr*
Bill Alexander, *Manager*
EMP: 19
SALES (corp-wide): 97.6MM **Privately Held**
WEB: www.stanion.com
SIC: 5063 Electrical supplies
PA: Stanion Wholesale Electric Co., Inc.
812 S Main St
Pratt KS 67124
620 672-5678

(G-5119)
STAR SIGNS LLC
801 E 9th St (66044-2675)
PHONE..................................785 842-4892
Robert Terry, *Mng Member*
EMP: 47
SALES (est): 5.5MM **Privately Held**
SIC: 1799 Sign installation & maintenance

▲ = Import ▼=Export
◆ =Import/Export

(G-5120)
STAR SIGNS & GRAPHICS INC (PA)
801 E 9th St (66044-2675)
PHONE..................................785 842-2881
Mike Vickers, *President*
Shelley Rosdahl, *Admin Sec*
EMP: 40 **EST:** 1979
SQ FT: 14,000
SALES (est): 2.8MM **Privately Held**
WEB: www.starsigngraphics.com
SIC: 3993 Electric signs; neon signs

(G-5121)
STARFIRE ENTERPRISES INC
2029 Becker Dr (66047-1620)
PHONE..................................785 842-1111
Colette M Spurlock, *Principal*
Andrew Spurlock, *Principal*
Mary Spurlock, *Principal*
Richard Spurlock, *Principal*
EMP: 19
SALES (est): 646.7K **Privately Held**
SIC: 7363 Help supply services

(G-5122)
STEPHENS REALESTATE INC (PA)
Also Called: Stephen Commercial
2701 W 6th St (66049-4306)
PHONE..................................785 841-4500
Chris Earl, *Owner*
Pat McCanbless, *Co-Owner*
Lisa Stofac, *Marketing Staff*
Caitlin Fisher, *Receptionist*
Stephanie Harris, *Real Est Agnt*
EMP: 67
SALES (est): 4.2MM **Privately Held**
WEB: www.stephensre.com
SIC: 6531 6411 Real estate brokers & agents; insurance agents

(G-5123)
STEPPING STONES INC
Also Called: STEPPING STONES DAY CARE CENTE
1100 Wakarusa Dr (66049-3863)
PHONE..................................785 843-5919
Shelly Platz, *President*
EMP: 54
SALES: 977.2K **Privately Held**
SIC: 8351 Preschool center

(G-5124)
STERLING CENTRECORP INC
Also Called: Days Inn
730 Iowa St Ste 200 (66044-1741)
PHONE..................................785 841-6500
Dana Graham, *Branch Mgr*
EMP: 20
SALES (corp-wide): 15.8MM **Privately Held**
WEB: www.villagerlodgeflorence.com
SIC: 7011 Hotels & motels
HQ: Sterling Centrecorp Inc
1 N Clematis St Ste 305
West Palm Beach FL 33401

(G-5125)
STEVENS & BRAND LLP (PA)
Us Bank Tower Ste 500900 (66044)
P.O. Box 189 (66044-0189)
PHONE..................................785 843-0811
Bradley Finkeldei, *Managing Prtnr*
Colleen Smalley, *Chairman*
Laura Wywadis, *Legal Staff*
April Ramsey, *Receptionist*
EMP: 20
SALES (est): 3.5MM **Privately Held**
WEB: www.stevensbrand.com
SIC: 8111 General practice attorney, lawyer

(G-5126)
SUMMERS & SPENCER COMPANY
Also Called: S S & C Business & Tax Svcs
3320 Clinton Parkway Ct # 220 (66047-2629)
PHONE..................................785 838-4484
Blake Schuster, *Editor*
Gary Summers, *Manager*
Mary Baker, *Associate*
EMP: 12
SALES (est): 735.8K
SALES (corp-wide): 4MM **Privately Held**
WEB: www.ssccpas.com
SIC: 8721 8711 Certified public accountant; consulting engineer
PA: Summers & Spencer Company
5825 Sw 29th St Ste 101
Topeka KS 66614
785 272-4484

(G-5127)
SUN CREATIONS INC
2000 Delaware St (66046-3174)
PHONE..................................785 830-0403
Gene Wayenberg, *President*
EMP: 20
SQ FT: 20,000
SALES (est): 2.4MM **Privately Held**
WEB: www.suncreations.com
SIC: 2261 2262 2396 2397 Screen printing of cotton broadwoven fabrics; screen printing: manmade fiber & silk broadwoven fabrics; screen printing on fabric articles; schiffli machine embroideries

(G-5128)
SUNFLOWER BANK NATIONAL ASSN
4831 Quail Crest Pl (66049-3839)
PHONE..................................785 312-7274
Justin Hinkle, *Vice Pres*
Glynn Sheridan, *Branch Mgr*
EMP: 16
SALES (corp-wide): 52.4MM **Privately Held**
SIC: 6021 National trust companies with deposits, commercial
HQ: Sunflower Bank, National Association
1400 16th St Ste 250
Denver CO 80202
888 827-5564

(G-5129)
SUNFLOWER PAVING INC
Also Called: Sunflower Concrete
1457 N 1823 Rd (66044-9100)
PHONE..................................785 856-4590
Jeff J Engroff, *President*
Mike Rice, *Vice Pres*
EMP: 100
SALES: 15MM **Privately Held**
SIC: 1611 Surfacing & paving

(G-5130)
SUNLITE SCIENCE & TECHNOLOGY
4811 Quail Crest Pl (66049-3839)
PHONE..................................785 832-8818
Jeff Chen, *President*
Greg Divilbiss, *President*
Fong Suo, *Accounts Mgr*
Nathan Weipert, *Sales Engr*
Jim Haller, *Sales Staff*
▲ **EMP:** 5
SQ FT: 10,000
SALES (est): 600K **Privately Held**
WEB: www.sunlitest.com
SIC: 3826 Electrolytic conductivity instruments

(G-5131)
T & J HOLDINGS INC
Also Called: Midwest Property Management
1203 Iowa St (66044-1923)
PHONE..................................785 841-4935
John Salvino, *President*
EMP: 15
SQ FT: 1,100
SALES (est): 1.7MM **Privately Held**
WEB: www.masterplanmanagement.com
SIC: 6531 7299 Real estate managers; apartment locating service

(G-5132)
TEAM CAR CARE LLC
Also Called: Jiffy Lube
914 W 23rd St (66046-4409)
PHONE..................................785 749-1599
Nate Schmidt, *Branch Mgr*
EMP: 10 **Privately Held**
SIC: 7549 Lubrication service, automotive
PA: Team Car Care, Llc
105 Decker Ct Ste 900
Irving TX 75062

(G-5133)
TELLERS
746 Massachusetts St (66044-2344)
P.O. Box 1637 (66044-8637)
PHONE..................................785 843-4111
Brad Nelson, *Owner*
EMP: 85
SQ FT: 4,500
SALES (est): 1.5MM **Privately Held**
WEB: www.tellers.com
SIC: 5812 5813 7299 Pizza restaurants; drinking places; banquet hall facilities

(G-5134)
TEMPORARY EMPLOYMENT CORP (PA)
Also Called: Manpower
3300 Bob Billings Pkwy # 4 (66049-2926)
PHONE..................................785 749-2800
Frank Summerson, *President*
Jacki Summerson, *Vice Pres*
EMP: 24
SQ FT: 2,000
SALES (est): 4.4MM **Privately Held**
WEB: www.technicalrecruiting.itstaffrecruiter.c
SIC: 7363 Manpower pools

(G-5135)
TFMCOMM INC
910 E 28th St (66046-4922)
PHONE..................................785 841-2924
Randy Smith, *Manager*
EMP: 5
SALES (corp-wide): 2.1MM **Privately Held**
WEB: www.tfmcomm.com
SIC: 3663 Radio broadcasting & communications equipment
PA: Tfmcomm Inc.
125 Sw Jackson St
Topeka KS 66603
785 233-2343

(G-5136)
THOMPSON RAMSDELL QUALSETH PA
333 W 9th St (66044-3167)
PHONE..................................785 841-4554
Todd Thompson, *Partner*
Shon Qualson, *Partner*
Robert Ramsdell, *Partner*
EMP: 11
SALES (est): 1.1MM **Privately Held**
SIC: 8111 General practice law office

(G-5137)
TINS INC
Also Called: Royal Crest Lanes
933 Iowa St (66044-1836)
PHONE..................................785 842-1234
Larry Burton, *Principal*
Wayne Martin, *Principal*
EMP: 27 **EST:** 1958
SQ FT: 20,000
SALES (est): 1.1MM **Privately Held**
SIC: 7933 5812 Ten pin center; family restaurants

(G-5138)
TITLE BOXING CLUB
1520 Wakarusa Dr Ste J (66047-2255)
PHONE..................................785 856-2696
Jim Thomas, *CEO*
EMP: 15 **EST:** 2011
SALES (est): 215.1K **Privately Held**
SIC: 7997 Membership sports & recreation clubs

(G-5139)
TJK INC (PA)
Also Called: Keller & Associates
120 E 9th St Ste 201 (66044-2692)
PHONE..................................785 841-0110
Timothy J Keller, *President*
Judith Keller, *Treasurer*
Linda Griffin, *Accountant*
Jeff Botkin, *Manager*
Brian Klahr, *Director*
EMP: 12
SALES (est): 2MM **Privately Held**
SIC: 6531 7389 Appraiser, real estate; auction, appraisal & exchange services

(G-5140)
TOPEKA LUTHERAN SCHL CNTR FOR
1732 Sw Gage Blvd Ste 3a9 (66044)
PHONE..................................785 272-1704
Jane Jones, *Administration*
EMP: 24
SALES (est): 274.4K **Privately Held**
SIC: 8351 Preschool center

(G-5141)
TOPEKA SERVICES INC (PA)
Also Called: Manpower
3300 Bob Billings Pkwy # 4 (66049-2949)
PHONE..................................785 228-7800
Frank T Summerson, *President*
Jackie Summerson, *Vice Pres*
EMP: 12
SQ FT: 7,500
SALES (est): 9.2MM **Privately Held**
SIC: 7363 Manpower pools

(G-5142)
TOSHIBA AMER BUS SOLUTIONS INC
711 W 23rd St (66046-4405)
PHONE..................................785 242-4942
Mike Shoup, *Branch Mgr*
EMP: 20 **Privately Held**
SIC: 5044 Copying equipment
HQ: Toshiba America Business Solutions, Inc.
25530 Commercentre Dr
Lake Forest CA 92630
949 462-6000

(G-5143)
TOTAL RENAL CARE INC
Also Called: Lawrence Home Training
3510 Clinton Pkwy Ste 110 (66047-2145)
PHONE..................................785 841-0490
James K Hilger,
EMP: 22 **Publicly Held**
SIC: 8092 Kidney dialysis centers
HQ: Total Renal Care, Inc.
2000 16th St
Denver CO 80202
303 405-2100

(G-5144)
TOTAL RENAL CARE INC
Also Called: Lawrence Dialysis
330 Arkansas St Ste 100 (66044-1394)
PHONE..................................785 843-2000
James K Hilger,
Susie Mercer, *Administration*
EMP: 15 **Publicly Held**
SIC: 8092 Kidney dialysis centers
HQ: Total Renal Care, Inc.
2000 16th St
Denver CO 80202
303 405-2100

(G-5145)
TREANORHL INC (PA)
1040 Vermont St (66044-2920)
PHONE..................................785 842-4858
Daniel Rowe, *President*
Patty Weaver, *General Mgr*
Steve Malin, *Principal*
Matthew Murphy, *Principal*
Timothy Reynolds, *Principal*
EMP: 30
SALES (est): 14.6MM **Privately Held**
WEB: www.treanorarchitects.com
SIC: 8712 Architectural engineering

(G-5146)
TRINITY IN-HOME CARE INC
2201 W 25th St Ste Q (66047-2957)
PHONE..................................785 842-3159
Kelly Evans, *Principal*
Teresa Martell, *Principal*
EMP: 194
SALES: 973.3K **Privately Held**
WEB: www.trinityinhomecare.com
SIC: 8082 Home health care services

(G-5147)
TRUITY CREDIT UNION
Also Called: Ku Credit Union
3400 W 6th St (66049-3215)
P.O. Box 562 (66044-0562)
PHONE..................................785 749-2224
Lee McDougan, *Marketing Staff*

GEOGRAPHIC

Ginger Wehner, *Manager*
Gabe Gutierrez, *Business Dir*
EMP: 10
SALES (corp-wide): 32.6MM **Privately Held**
SIC: 6061 6062 Federal credit unions; state credit unions
PA: Truity Credit Union
501 S Johnstone Ave
Bartlesville OK 74003
785 749-2224

(G-5148)
ULTIMATE TAN
2449 Iowa St Ste O (66046-5715)
PHONE..................................785 842-4949
Jannah Laing, *Owner*
EMP: 15
SALES (est): 258.6K **Privately Held**
SIC: 7299 5099 Tanning salon; tanning salon equipment & supplies

(G-5149)
ULTRASOUND FOR WOMEN LLC (PA)
4500 Woodland Dr (66049-3748)
PHONE..................................785 331-4160
Diana Franklin,
EMP: 25
SALES (est): 1.3MM **Privately Held**
SIC: 8011 8071 Gynecologist; medical laboratories

(G-5150)
UMB BANK NATIONAL ASSOCIATION
1441 Wakarusa Dr (66049-3832)
PHONE..................................785 838-2500
Brad Johnson, *Manager*
EMP: 10
SALES (corp-wide): 1.1B **Publicly Held**
SIC: 6021 National commercial banks
HQ: Umb Bank, National Association
1010 Grand Blvd Fl 3
Kansas City MO 64106
816 842-2222

(G-5151)
UNITED PARCEL SERVICE INC
Also Called: UPS
331 Ne Industrial Ln (66044-1472)
PHONE..................................785 843-6530
Kevin Strark, *Manager*
EMP: 60
SALES (corp-wide): 71.8B **Publicly Held**
WEB: www.upsscs.com
SIC: 4215 Parcel delivery, vehicular
HQ: United Parcel Service, Inc.
55 Glenlake Pkwy
Atlanta GA 30328
404 828-6000

(G-5152)
UNITED PTRIOT ABTMENT SVCS LLC
4000 W 6th St Ste B341 (66049-3204)
PHONE..................................785 856-1349
Roger Gibson,
EMP: 12
SALES (est): 1.4MM **Privately Held**
SIC: 6099 Check clearing services

(G-5153)
UNITED RENTALS NORTH AMER INC
930 E 30th St (66046-4928)
PHONE..................................785 838-4110
Josh E Briscoe, *Manager*
EMP: 14
SALES (corp-wide): 8B **Publicly Held**
SIC: 7359 Rental store, general
HQ: United Rentals (North America), Inc.
100 Frederick St 700
Stamford CT 06902
203 622-3131

(G-5154)
UNIVERSITY DAILY KANSAN
120 Stauffer Flint Hall (66045-0001)
PHONE..................................785 864-4358
Malcolm Gibson, *General Mgr*
Nicole Asbury, *Editor*
Omar Sanchez, *Editor*
Maddy Tannahill, *Editor*
Nichola McDowell, *Chief*
EMP: 120
SQ FT: 5,000
SALES: 1MM **Privately Held**
WEB: www.kansan.com
SIC: 2711 Newspapers, publishing & printing

(G-5155)
UNIVERSITY KANSAS ALUMNI ASSN
Also Called: KU ALUMNI ASSOCIATION
1266 Oread Ave (66045-3100)
PHONE..................................785 864-4760
Heath Peterson, *President*
Bradley Eland, *Vice Pres*
Bryan Greve, *Vice Pres*
EMP: 45
SQ FT: 33,000
SALES: 5.8MM **Privately Held**
SIC: 8641 Alumni association

(G-5156)
UNIVERSITY KANSAS MEM CORP (PA)
Also Called: KU MEMORIAL UNIONS
1301 Jayhawk Blvd (66045-7593)
PHONE..................................785 864-4651
David Weakley, *General Mgr*
Rachel Barnes, *Production*
Angela Bollinger, *Controller*
David Mucci, *Director*
EMP: 88
SQ FT: 200,000
SALES: 44.4MM **Privately Held**
WEB: www.kubookstore.com
SIC: 5942 5812 7389 College book stores; cafeteria; coffee shop;

(G-5157)
UNIVERSITY NAT BNK OF LAWRENCE
1400 Kasold Dr (66049-3424)
P.O. Box 1777 (66044-8777)
PHONE..................................785 841-1988
Todd Sutherland, *President*
Tyler Rockers, *Assistant VP*
Jordan Sedlacek, *Assistant VP*
David Bennett, *Vice Pres*
Joylynn Harlow, *Vice Pres*
EMP: 25
SQ FT: 9,600
SALES: 3.7MM **Privately Held**
WEB: www.unbank.com
SIC: 6021 National commercial banks

(G-5158)
UNIVERSITY OF KANSAS
Also Called: Counseling & Psychological Svc
2100 Watkins Health Ctr (66045-0001)
PHONE..................................785 864-2277
Michael Maestas, *Branch Mgr*
Michael Lynch Maestas, *Director*
EMP: 27
SALES (corp-wide): 1.2B **Privately Held**
WEB: www.ukans.edu
SIC: 8011 8221 Offices & clinics of medical doctors; university
PA: University Of Kansas
1450 Jayhawk Blvd Rm 225
Lawrence KS 66045
785 864-4868

(G-5159)
UNIVERSITY OF KANSAS
Also Called: Watkins Memorial Health Center
1200 Schwegler Dr (66045-7558)
PHONE..................................785 864-9520
Dr Douglas Dechairo, *Director*
Tammie Brooks, *Admin Asst*
Betsy Craft, *Admin Asst*
Pamela Williams, *Admin Asst*
Robert Brown, *Professor*
EMP: 90
SALES (corp-wide): 1.2B **Privately Held**
SIC: 8999 Artists & artists' studios
PA: University Of Kansas
1450 Jayhawk Blvd Rm 225
Lawrence KS 66045
785 864-4868

(G-5160)
UNIVERSITY OF KANSAS
Also Called: Watson Library Acquisitions
1425 Jayhawk Blvd Rm 210s (66045-7594)
PHONE..................................785 864-8885
Lois Bauer, *Manager*
Rory Lee White, *Supervisor*
Kenneth Chris Beard, *Director*
Angela Perryman, *Director*
Lawrence L Brady, *Admin Asst*
EMP: 100
SALES (corp-wide): 1.2B **Privately Held**
WEB: www.ukans.edu
SIC: 7389 8221 Purchasing service; university
PA: University Of Kansas
1450 Jayhawk Blvd Rm 225
Lawrence KS 66045
785 864-4868

(G-5161)
UNIVERSITY OF KANSAS
Also Called: Kansas Biological Survey
Constant Ave (66047)
PHONE..................................785 864-1500
W D Kettle, *Research*
Ed Martinko, *Director*
Debra Baker, *Asst Director*
EMP: 54
SALES (corp-wide): 1.2B **Privately Held**
SIC: 8221 8731 University; environmental research
PA: University Of Kansas
1450 Jayhawk Blvd Rm 225
Lawrence KS 66045
785 864-4868

(G-5162)
UNIVERSITY OF KANSAS
Also Called: Center For Research & Learning
1122 W Campus Rd (66045-3101)
PHONE..................................785 864-4780
Ronda Consolver, *Opers Staff*
Janis Bulgren, *Research*
Donald Deshler, *Director*
Tom Krieshok, *Professor*
John Rury, *Professor*
EMP: 300
SALES (corp-wide): 1.2B **Privately Held**
WEB: www.ukans.edu
SIC: 8731 Commercial physical research
PA: University Of Kansas
1450 Jayhawk Blvd Rm 225
Lawrence KS 66045
785 864-4868

(G-5163)
UNIVERSITY OF KANSAS
Also Called: Life Span Institute
1000 Sunnyside Ave (66045-7599)
PHONE..................................785 864-2700
Carla Ramirez, *Facilities Mgr*
Nancy Brady, *Research*
Ashley Coles, *Research*
Justin Goetting, *Accountant*
Dave Gardner, *Director*
EMP: 126
SALES (corp-wide): 1.2B **Privately Held**
WEB: www.ukans.edu
SIC: 8062 8221 General medical & surgical hospitals; university
PA: University Of Kansas
1450 Jayhawk Blvd Rm 225
Lawrence KS 66045
785 864-4868

(G-5164)
UNIVERSITY OF KANSAS
Also Called: Museum of Anthropology
Spooner Hall 1430 Jy Hawk (66045-0001)
PHONE..................................785 864-2451
Kris Deltis, *Admin Sec*
Carly Michele Froyum, *Admin Asst*
Virginia L Sayler, *Assoc Prof*
EMP: 126
SALES (corp-wide): 1.2B **Privately Held**
SIC: 8412 8221 Museum; university
PA: University Of Kansas
1450 Jayhawk Blvd Rm 225
Lawrence KS 66045
785 864-4868

(G-5165)
UNIVERSITY OF KANSAS
Also Called: Helen Frsman Spence Museum Art
1301 Mississippi St (66045-7595)
PHONE..................................785 864-4710
Linda Stone-Ferrier, *Ch of Bd*
Sofia Liu, *Manager*
Saralyn Reece Hardy, *Director*
Marsha Haufler, *Professor*
David Cateforis, *Assoc Prof*
EMP: 51
SALES (corp-wide): 1.2B **Privately Held**
WEB: www.ukans.edu
SIC: 8412 8221 Museum; university
PA: University Of Kansas
1450 Jayhawk Blvd Rm 225
Lawrence KS 66045
785 864-4868

(G-5166)
UNIVERSITY OF KANSAS
Also Called: University Press
2502 Westbrooke Cir (66045-4444)
PHONE..................................785 864-4154
Fred Woodward, *Director*
EMP: 25
SALES (corp-wide): 1.2B **Privately Held**
WEB: www.ukans.edu
SIC: 2731 8221 Book publishing; university
PA: University Of Kansas
1450 Jayhawk Blvd Rm 225
Lawrence KS 66045
785 864-4868

(G-5167)
UNIVERSITY OF KANSAS
Also Called: Ku Natural History Museum
1345 Jayhawk Blvd (66045-7593)
PHONE..................................785 864-4540
Krishtalka Leonard, *Director*
Virginia Harper Ho, *Professor*
EMP: 200
SALES (corp-wide): 1.2B **Privately Held**
WEB: www.ukans.edu
SIC: 8412 8221 Museums & art galleries; university
PA: University Of Kansas
1450 Jayhawk Blvd Rm 225
Lawrence KS 66045
785 864-4868

(G-5168)
UNIVERSITY PRESS OF KANSAS
2502 Westbrooke Cir (66045-4444)
PHONE..................................785 864-4155
Charles Myers, *Director*
EMP: 20
SALES (est): 1.3MM **Privately Held**
SIC: 2731 Book publishing

(G-5169)
URBAN OUTFITTERS INC
1013 Massachusetts St (66044-2923)
PHONE..................................785 331-2885
EMP: 40
SALES (corp-wide): 3.5B **Publicly Held**
SIC: 5621 5611 5632 5661 Ret Misc Apparel/Accessories
PA: Urban Outfitters, Inc.
5000 S Broad St
Philadelphia PA 19112
215 454-5500

(G-5170)
US BANK NATIONAL ASSOCIATION
Also Called: US Bank
2701 Iowa St (66046-4155)
PHONE..................................785 312-5280
Julie Zule, *Principal*
EMP: 11
SALES (corp-wide): 25.7B **Publicly Held**
WEB: www.firstar.com
SIC: 6021 National commercial banks
HQ: U.S. Bank National Association
425 Walnut St Fl 14
Cincinnati OH 45202
513 632-4234

(G-5171)
US BANK NATIONAL ASSOCIATION
Also Called: US Bank
3500 W 6th St (66049-3245)
PHONE..................................785 312-5060
Terri Pippert, *Manager*
EMP: 10
SALES (corp-wide): 25.7B **Publicly Held**
WEB: www.firstar.com
SIC: 6021 National commercial banks

HQ: U.S. Bank National Association
425 Walnut St Fl 14
Cincinnati OH 45202
513 632-4234

(G-5172)
US BANK NATIONAL ASSOCIATION
Also Called: US Bank
1807 W 23rd St (66046-2747)
PHONE..................................785 312-6880
Ginny Sattler, *Manager*
EMP: 11
SALES (corp-wide): 25.7B **Publicly Held**
WEB: www.firstar.com
SIC: 6021 National commercial banks
HQ: U.S. Bank National Association
425 Walnut St Fl 14
Cincinnati OH 45202
513 632-4234

(G-5173)
VENTURA HOTEL CORP
730 New Hampshire St # 206
(66044-2736)
PHONE..................................785 841-3100
Stephen J Craig, *President*
Kristin Cain, *Vice Pres*
Timothy Peterson, *Admin Sec*
EMP: 150
SALES (est): 776.5K **Privately Held**
SIC: 7011 Hotels

(G-5174)
VINTAGE GREENMARK CNSTR INC
790 N 2nd St (66044-1408)
P.O. Box 442011 (66044-2011)
PHONE..................................785 843-2700
Owen Lehnann, *President*
EMP: 13
SQ FT: 2,000
SALES: 2MM **Privately Held**
SIC: 1771 Concrete work

(G-5175)
VISITING NURSES ASSOCIATION
200 Maine St Ste C (66044-1396)
PHONE..................................785 843-3738
Cynthia Lewis, *CEO*
Lori McSorley, *Business Mgr*
Janice White, *Human Res Mgr*
Janice J White, *Human Res Mgr*
EMP: 100
SQ FT: 6,000
SALES (est): 6.5MM **Privately Held**
WEB: www.vna.lawrence.ks.us
SIC: 8361 8082 7021 Residential care; home health care services; rooming & boarding houses

(G-5176)
WAKARUSA VETERINARY HOSPITAL
1825 Wakarusa Dr (66047-1809)
PHONE..................................785 843-5577
Christy Rowland, *President*
Kristi Bradley, *Vice Pres*
EMP: 15
SQ FT: 3,500
SALES (est): 1.1MM **Privately Held**
SIC: 0742 0752 Animal hospital services, pets & other animal specialties; boarding services, kennels

(G-5177)
WALDORF ASSOCIATION LAWRENCE
Also Called: PRAIRIE MOON WALDORF SCHOOL
1853 E 1600 Rd (66044-9458)
PHONE..................................785 841-8800
Richard Mitchell, *President*
David Eichler, *Treasurer*
EMP: 10
SALES: 530.7K **Privately Held**
SIC: 8699 Membership organizations

(G-5178)
WALGREEN CO
Also Called: Walgreens
3421 W 6th St (66049-3200)
P.O. Box 4024 (66046-1024)
PHONE..................................785 841-9000
A R Trupp, *Manager*
Roberta Mize, *Assistant*
EMP: 25
SALES (corp-wide): 136.8B **Publicly Held**
WEB: www.walgreens.com
SIC: 5912 7384 Drug stores; photofinishing laboratory
HQ: Walgreen Co.
200 Wilmot Rd
Deerfield IL 60015
800 925-4733

(G-5179)
WALGREEN CO
Also Called: Walgreens
400 W 23rd St (66046-4706)
PHONE..................................785 832-8388
D A Alvarez, *Manager*
EMP: 25
SALES (corp-wide): 136.8B **Publicly Held**
WEB: www.walgreens.com
SIC: 5912 7384 Drug stores; photofinishing laboratory
HQ: Walgreen Co.
200 Wilmot Rd
Deerfield IL 60015
800 925-4733

(G-5180)
WARREN MCELWAIN MORTUARY LLC
120 W 13th St (66044-3402)
PHONE..................................785 843-1120
Terry Cavanaugh, *Director*
Lisa Manley, *Director*
Larry McElwain,
Phil Patten,
EMP: 15
SQ FT: 3,300
SALES: 580K **Privately Held**
WEB: www.warrenmcelwain.com
SIC: 7261 Funeral home

(G-5181)
WAXMAN CANDLES INC (PA)
609 Massachusetts St (66044-2235)
PHONE..................................785 843-8593
Robert F Werts, *President*
EMP: 9
SQ FT: 14,000
SALES (est): 1.2MM **Privately Held**
SIC: 3999 5961 5999 Candles; mail order house; candle shops

(G-5182)
WESTERN INTERNATIONAL INC
701 E 22nd St (66046-3133)
P.O. Box 564 (66044-0564)
PHONE..................................785 856-1840
Lisa M Polasek, *President*
Shirley Fritz, *Corp Secy*
EMP: 15
SALES (est): 2.8MM **Privately Held**
WEB: www.yourbooksource.com
SIC: 5192 Books

(G-5183)
WESTHEFFER COMPANY INC
921 N 1st St (66044-1400)
P.O. Box 363 (66044-0363)
PHONE..................................785 843-1633
Samih Staitieh, *President*
EMP: 30 **EST:** 1958
SQ FT: 19,000
SALES (est): 8.8MM **Privately Held**
WEB: www.westheffer.com
SIC: 3523 5085 3563 Sprayers & spraying machines, agricultural; turf equipment, commercial; fertilizing machinery, farm; industrial supplies; air & gas compressors

(G-5184)
WESTMORE DRILLING COMPANY INC
4801 Innsbrook Dr (66047-1985)
PHONE..................................785 749-3712
Gordon Penny, *President*
Linda Penny, *Vice Pres*
EMP: 6
SALES: 2.5MM **Privately Held**
SIC: 1311 Crude petroleum production; natural gas production

(G-5185)
WILKERSON ANDERSON & ANDERSON
831 Vermont St Ste 1 (66044-2620)
PHONE..................................785 843-6060
Brian Wilkerson, *Partner*
Jeston Anderson, *Partner*
Michelle Anderson, *Partner*
EMP: 20
SALES (est): 1.4MM **Privately Held**
SIC: 8021 Dentists' office

(G-5186)
WILLOWRIDGE LANDSCAPE INC
1453 E 800th Rd (66049-9133)
PHONE..................................785 842-7022
Ron Baker, *President*
Kathy Baker, *Co-Owner*
Maria Gibson, *Manager*
EMP: 18 **EST:** 1974
SQ FT: 804
SALES (est): 2.4MM **Privately Held**
WEB: www.willowridgelandscape.com
SIC: 0782 1711 4959 Lawn care services; irrigation sprinkler system installation; snowplowing

(G-5187)
WINBURY GROUP OF KC LLC
Also Called: Grubb Ellis/The Winbury Group
805 New Hampshire St C (66044-2774)
PHONE..................................785 865-5100
Marilyn Bittendender, *Manager*
Kelvin Heck, *Manager*
EMP: 10
SALES (corp-wide): 2.8B **Privately Held**
WEB: www.winbury.com
SIC: 6531 Real estate brokers & agents; real estate managers
HQ: The Winbury Group Of K C Llc
4520 Main St Ste 1000
Kansas City MO 64111

(G-5188)
WINDSOR OF LAWRENCE
3220 Peterson Rd (66049-1963)
PHONE..................................785 832-9900
Amy Homer, *Director*
Lynn Dodge, *Director*
EMP: 25
SALES (est): 1.1MM **Privately Held**
WEB: www.windsorsl.com
SIC: 8051 Convalescent home with continuous nursing care

(G-5189)
WOMEN IN TRNSTION TOGETHER INC
1307 W 27th St (66046-4509)
P.O. Box 142 (66044-0142)
PHONE..................................785 424-7516
Kristy McManness, *Principal*
EMP: 15
SALES (est): 248.6K **Privately Held**
SIC: 7389

(G-5190)
WOMENS HEALTH CARE GROUP
3510 Clinton Pl Ste 310 (66047-2178)
PHONE..................................816 589-2121
R Tony Moulton, *Obstetrician*
Dr Hal Younglove, *Director*
EMP: 12
SALES (est): 1.1MM
SALES (corp-wide): 6.7MM **Privately Held**
SIC: 8011 Gynecologist
PA: The Women's Health Care Group
10600 Quivira Rd Ste 200
Lenexa KS 66215
913 438-0018

(G-5191)
WORK COMP SPECIALTY ASSOCIATES
4840 Bob Billings Pkwy # 1000
(66049-4092)
PHONE..................................785 841-7751
James Knight, *President*
Sarah Lober, *Manager*
EMP: 20
SALES (est): 1.2MM **Privately Held**
SIC: 7372 8111 Prepackaged software; legal services

(G-5192)
WORLDWEST LTD LIABILITY CO (PA)
Also Called: Steamboat Pilot/Today, The
609 New Hampshire St (66044-2243)
P.O. Box 688 (66044-0688)
PHONE..................................785 843-1000
Holly Hunter, *Office Mgr*
Julia Hebard, *Director*
Ralph D Gage Jr,
Dan C Simons,
Dolph C Simons III,
EMP: 110
SQ FT: 22,000
SALES (est): 6.5MM **Privately Held**
WEB: www.news-bulletin.com
SIC: 2711 Commercial printing & newspaper publishing combined

(G-5193)
ZIEGLER CORPORATION
1513 Brink Ct (66047-1868)
PHONE..................................785 841-4250
Sid Ziegler, *President*
EMP: 10
SALES: 4MM **Privately Held**
WEB: www.zieglercorporation.com
SIC: 8742 Construction project management consultant

(G-5194)
ZIMMER RADIO GROUP
Also Called: Klwn-AM Radio
3125 W 6th St (66049-3101)
PHONE..................................785 843-1320
Ron Covert, *Manager*
Han K Booth, *Manager*
Cheryl Chavez, *Manager*
EMP: 40 **EST:** 1951
SQ FT: 4,800
SALES (est): 2.5MM **Privately Held**
SIC: 4832 Radio broadcasting stations, music format

Le Roy
Coffey County

(G-5195)
ARNOLDS GREENHOUSE INC
Also Called: Wholesale AR
1430 Highway 58 (66857-9661)
PHONE..................................620 964-2463
Rita Arnold, *President*
George Arnold, *Vice Pres*
EMP: 12
SQ FT: 80,000
SALES (est): 759K **Privately Held**
WEB: www.arnoldsgreenhouse.com
SIC: 0181 5193 5992 Bedding plants, growing of; plants, potted; plants, potted

(G-5196)
LEROY COOPERATIVE ASSN INC (PA)
505 E 6th St (66857-9668)
P.O. Box 248 (66857-0248)
PHONE..................................620 964-2225
Rick Crooks, *President*
Janelle Wilson, *General Mgr*
Darren Specht, *Opers Staff*
EMP: 21 **EST:** 1960
SQ FT: 3,750
SALES: 53.7MM **Privately Held**
SIC: 5153 5191 5531 5541 Grain elevators; farm supplies; automotive tires; gasoline service stations; fertilizers, mixing only

(G-5197)
LUTHERS SMOKEHOUSE INC
Also Called: Luthers Jerky USA
98 W 6th St (66857-9450)
PHONE..................................620 964-2222
Martin Luther, *President*
Shirley Luther, *Corp Secy*
EMP: 9
SQ FT: 12,000
SALES (est): 620K **Privately Held**
WEB: www.jerkyusa.com
SIC: 2013 Beef, dried: from purchased meat

(G-5198)
MAME INC
815 E 6th St (66857-9451)
PHONE..................................620 964-2156
EMP: 11
SALES (est): 703.3K **Privately Held**
SIC: 7699 Industrial machinery & equipment repair

(G-5199)
MID-AMERICAN MACHINE & EQP INC (PA)
Also Called: M A M
815 E 6th St (66857-9451)
PHONE..................................620 964-2156
Shane Sutherland, *President*
John Mars, *General Mgr*
Johnny Guy, *Exec VP*
Jeremy Blair, *Project Engr*
Robin McNutt, *Admin Asst*
▲ **EMP:** 10 **EST:** 1997
SQ FT: 1,700
SALES (est): 11.1MM **Privately Held**
SIC: 7699 Industrial machinery & equipment repair

Leavenworth
Leavenworth County

(G-5200)
AH TANNERY INC
Also Called: Celsius Tannery, The
2212 S 4th St (66048-4509)
PHONE..................................913 772-1111
Suzanne Habbee, *Manager*
EMP: 13
SALES (corp-wide): 784.4K **Privately Held**
SIC: 7299 Tanning salon
PA: Ah Tannery Inc
13212 State Line Rd
Leawood KS 66209
913 544-6102

(G-5201)
AMERICAN ROOFING INC
2500 S 2nd St (66048-4542)
PHONE..................................913 772-1776
Michael Greenamyre, *President*
Daniel Greenamyre, *Principal*
Jeremy Greenamyre, *Principal*
Dale Morrison, *Data Proc Staff*
EMP: 30 **EST:** 1973
SQ FT: 46,000
SALES (est): 4.8MM **Privately Held**
SIC: 1761 Roofing contractor

(G-5202)
ANCILLA CENTER FOR CHILDREN
4100 S 4th St (66048-5082)
PHONE..................................913 758-6113
Sharon Bedeke, *Director*
EMP: 14
SALES (est): 159.1K **Privately Held**
SIC: 8351 8211 Kindergarten; preschool center

(G-5203)
ANDREA CLARK
Also Called: Women of Divine Wisdom
200 Osage St (66048-2038)
PHONE..................................913 683-3061
Andrea Clark, *Owner*
Kc Clark Jr, *Administration*
Tanya Cobbe, *Administration*
EMP: 75
SALES (est): 1.3MM **Privately Held**
SIC: 8322 Individual & family services

(G-5204)
ARMED FORCES INSURANCE EXHANGE
Also Called: Nationwide
550 Eisenhower Rd (66048-6205)
PHONE..................................913 651-5000
Lieut Gen Garry L Parks, *Ch of Bd*
Kurt Seelbach, *President*
Thomas Dials, *President*
David Wolk, *Facilities Mgr*
Carroll D Haverkamp, *Treasurer*
EMP: 210
SQ FT: 60,000
SALES: 69MM **Privately Held**
SIC: 6331 Fire, marine & casualty insurance

(G-5205)
B C C BUSINESS SERVICES INC
Also Called: Bushman & Associates Cpa's
121 Cherokee St (66048-2816)
PHONE..................................913 682-4548
Dinese Peterson, *President*
EMP: 12
SQ FT: 1,500
SALES (est): 513.8K **Privately Held**
SIC: 8721 Accounting services, except auditing

(G-5206)
BAKER CONSTRUCTION INC
Also Called: Keith Baker Construction
714 Oak St (66048-2577)
PHONE..................................913 682-6302
Keith Baker, *President*
EMP: 21
SALES: 1.2MM **Privately Held**
SIC: 1542 Commercial & office building contractors

(G-5207)
BELLA VITA SALON & DAY SPA INC
4516 S 4th St (66048-5041)
PHONE..................................913 651-6161
Lyndsay Metsker, *President*
EMP: 23
SALES (est): 439.2K **Privately Held**
SIC: 7231 7991 Beauty shops; spas

(G-5208)
BESHENICH MUIR & ASSOC LLC (PA)
Also Called: BMA
117 Cherokee St (66048-2816)
PHONE..................................913 904-1880
Sam McNully, *General Mgr*
Jim Ruth, *Counsel*
Tina Rader, *Opers Mgr*
Cedrick Dunham, *Sales Staff*
Lloyd Coley, *Program Mgr*
EMP: 15
SALES (est): 3.9MM **Privately Held**
SIC: 8742 Management consulting services

(G-5209)
BETA THETA PHI
P.O. Box 116 (66048-0116)
PHONE..................................785 843-4711
EMP: 80 **EST:** 2004
SALES (est): 1.9MM **Privately Held**
SIC: 8641 Civic/Social Association

(G-5210)
BILLY MURPHY & ASSOCIATES LLC
1011 Metropolitan Ave (66048-1370)
PHONE..................................913 306-0381
Jeff Hendren, *Principal*
Jeffrey Hendren,
EMP: 10
SALES: 450K **Privately Held**
SIC: 8748 Systems engineering consultant, ex. computer or professional

(G-5211)
BIRTHRIGHT INC
221 Delaware St Ste A (66048-2874)
P.O. Box 98363, Atlanta GA (30359-2063)
PHONE..................................913 682-2700
Margaret McNamee, *Director*
EMP: 30
SALES (corp-wide): 45.5MM **Privately Held**
WEB: www.birthright.net
SIC: 8322 8093 Crisis center; family planning clinic
HQ: Birthright, Inc
3424 Hardee Ave
Atlanta GA 30341
770 451-6336

(G-5212)
BKM CONSTRUCTION LLC
501 S 5th St (66048-2610)
PHONE..................................913 297-0049
Brent Motley,
EMP: 10
SALES: 750K **Privately Held**
SIC: 7389 1522 1541 8744 Interior design services; inventory stocking service; residential construction; industrial buildings, new construction; prefabricated building erection, industrial; renovation, remodeling & repairs: industrial buildings; facilities support services; single-family housing construction; plumbing, heating, air-conditioning contractors

(G-5213)
BOOZ ALLEN HAMILTON INC
1122 N 2nd St (66048-1559)
PHONE..................................913 682-5300
Tom Vogt, *Manager*
Andrew Fowler, *Associate*
EMP: 75 **Publicly Held**
WEB: www.bah.com
SIC: 8742 Management consulting services
HQ: Booz Allen Hamilton Inc.
8283 Greensboro Dr # 700
Mc Lean VA 22102
703 902-5000

(G-5214)
CARRIAGE SERVICES INC
Also Called: Belden Larkin Funeral Home
707 S 6th St (66048-2622)
PHONE..................................913 682-2820
Kurt Pocolson, *Manager*
EMP: 16 **Publicly Held**
WEB: www.carriageservices.com
SIC: 7261 Funeral home
PA: Carriage Services, Inc.
3040 Post Oak Blvd # 300
Houston TX 77056

(G-5215)
CENTRAL BAG COMPANY (PA)
4901 S 4th St (66048-5003)
P.O. Box 37, Lansing (66043-0037)
PHONE..................................913 250-0325
Chris Klimek, *President*
Jeff Chalabi, *Vice Pres*
Terry Braden, *Treasurer*
Doug Cross, *Sales Staff*
Daryl Augustine, *Admin Sec*
▲ **EMP:** 24
SQ FT: 250,000
SALES (est): 21.7MM **Privately Held**
WEB: www.centralbagcompany.com
SIC: 5113 2393 Bags, paper & disposable plastic; textile bags

(G-5216)
CENTURY VAN LINES INC
211 Marion St (66048-4530)
PHONE..................................913 651-3600
Jeffrey Klemp, *CEO*
Jeff Klent, *President*
Charles Scurlock, *Sales Mgr*
EMP: 25
SQ FT: 96,000
SALES: 1MM **Privately Held**
SIC: 4214 4213 Local trucking with storage; trucking, except local

(G-5217)
CEREAL INGREDIENTS INC (PA)
4720 S 13th St (66048-5585)
PHONE..................................913 727-3434
Robert Hatch, *CEO*
Bennett French, *Senior VP*
Amanda Fountaine, *Research*
Jack Waldron, *CFO*
Toby Wegner, *CFO*
◆ **EMP:** 55
SQ FT: 40,000
SALES (est): 21.5MM **Privately Held**
WEB: www.cerealingredients.com
SIC: 2051 2087 2064 Bakery: wholesale or wholesale/retail combined; flavoring extracts & syrups; candy & other confectionery products

(G-5218)
CITIZENS SAVINGS & LOAN ASSN (PA)
5151 S 4th St (66048-5050)
P.O. Box 489 (66048-0489)
PHONE..................................913 727-1040
Randall Baker, *CEO*
Karen Woodward, *Controller*
Karen Depriest, *Loan Officer*
Chuck Mason, *Loan*
EMP: 30
SQ FT: 6,000
SALES: 6.3MM **Privately Held**
WEB: www.citizensfsb.com
SIC: 6035 8699 Federal savings & loan associations; charitable organization

(G-5219)
CITY OF LEAVENWORTH
Also Called: Leavenworth Maintenance Dept
401 S 3rd St (66048-2871)
PHONE..................................913 684-1560
Mathew Dedeke, *Director*
EMP: 14 **Privately Held**
SIC: 7349 Building maintenance services
PA: Leavenworth, City Of (Inc)
100 N 5th St
Leavenworth KS 66048
913 682-9201

(G-5220)
CITY OF LEAVENWORTH
Also Called: Leavenwrth Rverfront Cmnty Ctr
123 N Esplanade St (66048-2028)
PHONE..................................913 651-2132
Tammy Metzger, *Manager*
EMP: 21 **Privately Held**
SIC: 7999 Recreation center
PA: Leavenworth, City Of (Inc)
100 N 5th St
Leavenworth KS 66048
913 682-9201

(G-5221)
CITY OF LEAVENWORTH
Also Called: Water Pollution Control Div
1800 S 2nd St (66048)
PHONE..................................913 682-1090
Tim Guardado, *Asst Supt*
Timothy Flora, *Branch Mgr*
EMP: 15 **Privately Held**
SIC: 4952 9221 Sewerage systems; police protection
PA: Leavenworth, City Of (Inc)
100 N 5th St
Leavenworth KS 66048
913 682-9201

(G-5222)
CITY OF LEAVENWORTH
Also Called: Water Department
601 Cherokee St (66048-2627)
P.O. Box 576 (66048-0576)
PHONE..................................913 682-1513
John Kaufmann, *Engrg Dir*
EMP: 35 **Privately Held**
SIC: 4941 Water supply
PA: Leavenworth, City Of (Inc)
100 N 5th St
Leavenworth KS 66048
913 682-9201

(G-5223)
COLLATERAL SERVICES INC
530 Delaware St (66048-2643)
PHONE..................................913 680-1015
Chris Thiele, *President*
Kelly Handke, *Admin Sec*
EMP: 12
SQ FT: 6,000
SALES (est): 1MM **Privately Held**
SIC: 8742 Financial consultant

(G-5224)
COMMERCE BANK
2830 S 4th St (66048-4519)
PHONE..................................913 682-8282
William Petrie, *President*
EMP: 18
SALES (corp-wide): 1.3B **Publicly Held**
SIC: 6022 State commercial banks
HQ: Commerce Bank
1000 Walnut St Fl 700
Kansas City MO 64106
816 234-2000

(G-5225)
CORECIVIC INC
Also Called: Leavenworth Detention Center
100 Highway Ter (66048-5021)
PHONE..................................913 727-3246
Fredrick Lawrence, *Warden*
Mindy Graham, *Administration*

EMP: 200
SALES (corp-wide): 1.8B **Publicly Held**
WEB: www.correctionscorp.com
SIC: 8744 Correctional facility
PA: Corecivic, Inc.
5501 Virginia Way Ste 110
Brentwood TN 37027
615 263-3000

(G-5226)
COUNTRY CLUB BANK
Also Called: MidAmerican Bank & Trust Co
401 Delaware St (66048-2732)
P.O. Box 410889, Kansas City MO (64141-0889)
PHONE..................................913 682-0001
Tim Byers, *Senior VP*
Charles Hill, *Senior VP*
Paul Thompson, *Officer*
EMP: 46
SALES (est): 6.1MM **Privately Held**
SIC: 6021 National commercial banks

(G-5227)
COUNTRY CLUB BANK
2310 S 4th St (66048-4574)
PHONE..................................913 682-2300
Michelle Bishop, *Manager*
EMP: 12
SALES (corp-wide): 38MM **Privately Held**
SIC: 6021 National commercial banks
HQ: Country Club Bank
1 Ward Pkwy
Kansas City MO 64112

(G-5228)
COUNTY OF LEAVENWORTH
Also Called: Leavenworth County Hwy Dept
23690 187th St (66048-8321)
PHONE..................................913 727-1800
Michael Spickelmier, *Director*
EMP: 56 **Privately Held**
WEB: www.leavenworthcounty.com
SIC: 1611 Highway & street construction
PA: County Of Leavenworth
300 Walnut St Ste 106
Leavenworth KS 66048
913 684-0422

(G-5229)
CRYSTAL HOSPITALITY LLC
Also Called: Hampton Inn By Hlton Lvenworth
405 Choctaw St (66048-2728)
PHONE..................................913 680-1500
Sanjay Koshiya, *Vice Pres*
EMP: 20
SQ FT: 55,000
SALES (est): 360.9K **Privately Held**
SIC: 7011 Hotels & motels

(G-5230)
CVS PHARMACY INC
390 Limit St (66048-4525)
PHONE..................................913 651-2323
Steve Montgomery, *Manager*
EMP: 20
SALES (corp-wide): 194.5B **Publicly Held**
WEB: www.cvsedi.com
SIC: 5912 7384 Drug stores; photofinishing laboratory
HQ: Cvs Pharmacy, Inc.
1 Cvs Dr
Woonsocket RI 02895
401 765-1500

(G-5231)
DEBRA L HEIDGEN
3550 S 4th St Ste 120 (66048-5061)
PHONE..................................913 772-6046
Fax: 913 758-0500
EMP: 11
SALES (est): 452.4K **Privately Held**
SIC: 8011 Medical Doctor's Office

(G-5232)
DEMARANVILLE & ASSOC CPAS LLC
121 Cherokee St (66048-2816)
PHONE..................................913 682-4548
Sherry Demaranville, *Manager*
EMP: 12
SALES (est): 231.5K **Privately Held**
SIC: 8721 Certified public accountant

(G-5233)
DEVELOPMENT INC
2500 S 2nd St (66048-4542)
PHONE..................................913 651-9717
Michael Greenamyre, *President*
Michael Greenamyer, *President*
Jeremy Greenamyre, *Vice Pres*
EMP: 15 **EST:** 1962
SQ FT: 160,000
SALES: 2.5MM **Privately Held**
SIC: 7349 6531 Building maintenance services; real estate leasing & rentals

(G-5234)
DR VERNON A MILLS
3550 S 4th St Ste 120 (66048-5061)
PHONE..................................913 772-6046
Vernon Mills, *Owner*
Debra Heidgen, *Manager*
EMP: 11 **EST:** 1983
SALES (est): 862.6K **Privately Held**
SIC: 8011 Pediatrician

(G-5235)
EASTON BUS SERVICE INC
1320 Ottawa St (66048-1748)
PHONE..................................913 682-2244
Jeffery Kincaid, *President*
Joe Heincker, *Admin Sec*
EMP: 88 **EST:** 1959
SQ FT: 2,500
SALES (est): 3.4MM **Privately Held**
SIC: 4151 School buses

(G-5236)
EQH - LEAVENWORTH LLC
Also Called: Home2 Suites By Hilton
120 Delaware St (66048)
PHONE..................................913 651-8600
Greg Mullinex,
Mike Mullinex,
EMP: 16
SALES: 1.9MM **Privately Held**
SIC: 7011 Hotels & motels

(G-5237)
FAMILY FIRST CENTER FOR AUTISM
1719 Metropolitan Ave (66048-1124)
PHONE..................................913 250-5634
EMP: 20
SALES (est): 84.5K **Privately Held**
SIC: 8322 Child related social services

(G-5238)
FEDERAL PRISON INDUSTRIES
1300 Metropolitan Ave (66048-1254)
P.O. Box 1000 (66048-1000)
PHONE..................................913 682-8700
Eric Wilson, *Branch Mgr*
EMP: 69 **Publicly Held**
WEB: www.unicor.gov
SIC: 2531 2759 3552 2761 Public building & related furniture; commercial printing; textile machinery; manifold business forms; commercial printing, lithographic; correctional institutions;
HQ: Federal Prison Industries, Inc
320 1st St Nw
Washington DC 20534
202 305-3500

(G-5239)
FIRST COMMAND FINCL PLG INC
Also Called: Uspa
417 S 2nd St (66048-2805)
PHONE..................................913 651-6820
Lannie Bowman, *District Mgr*
Nicholas Gilewitch, *Advisor*
EMP: 11
SALES (corp-wide): 467.4MM **Privately Held**
SIC: 6282 Investment advice
HQ: First Command Financial Planning, Inc.
1 Firstcomm Plz
Fort Worth TX 76109
817 731-8621

(G-5240)
FREDERICK EXCAVATING INC
19406 High Prairie Rd (66048-7570)
PHONE..................................913 772-0225
Virgil Frederick Jr, *President*
Mike Frederick, *Vice Pres*
Chris Frederick, *Admin Sec*
EMP: 10
SQ FT: 1,000
SALES (est): 1MM **Privately Held**
SIC: 1794 Excavation work

(G-5241)
GATEHOUSE MEDIA LLC
Also Called: Leavenwrth Tms/Chrncle Shopper
422 Seneca St (66048-1910)
PHONE..................................913 682-0305
David L Thompson, *Manager*
EMP: 60
SALES (corp-wide): 1.5B **Publicly Held**
SIC: 2711 Newspapers, publishing & printing
HQ: Gatehouse Media, Llc
175 Sullys Trl Fl 3
Pittsford NY 14534
585 598-0030

(G-5242)
GATEHOUSE MEDIA LLC
Leavenworth Times, The
422 Seneca St (66048-1910)
P.O. Box 144 (66048-0144)
PHONE..................................913 682-0305
Sandy Hattock, *General Mgr*
Alan Dale, *Editor*
Ray McConiga, *Engineer*
Beckie Mitchell, *Human Res Dir*
Barbara Daniels, *Chief Mktg Ofcr*
EMP: 38
SALES (corp-wide): 1.5B **Publicly Held**
WEB: www.gatehousemedia.com
SIC: 2711 Newspapers, publishing & printing
HQ: Gatehouse Media, Llc
175 Sullys Trl Fl 3
Pittsford NY 14534
585 598-0030

(G-5243)
GEIGER READY-MIX CO INC (PA)
1333 S 2nd St (66048-3508)
P.O. Box 50 (66048-0050)
PHONE..................................913 772-4010
Steve McDonald, *President*
E W Geiger III, *Principal*
Bill Geiger, *Chairman*
Todd Geiger, *Vice Pres*
Jim Van Veghte, *Plant Mgr*
EMP: 33 **EST:** 1949
SQ FT: 2,500
SALES (est): 37.5MM **Privately Held**
SIC: 3273 Ready-mixed concrete

(G-5244)
GENERAL DYNAMICS INFO TECH INC
1100 N 2nd St (66048-1559)
PHONE..................................913 684-5770
Allen Walker, *Project Mgr*
Gary Phillips, *IT/INT Sup*
EMP: 52
SALES (corp-wide): 36.1B **Publicly Held**
SIC: 7379 Computer related maintenance services
HQ: General Dynamics Information Technology, Inc.
3150 Frview Pk Dr Ste 100
Falls Church VA 22042
703 995-8700

(G-5245)
GENOA HEALTHCARE MASS LLC
500 Limit St (66048-4435)
PHONE..................................913 680-1652
EMP: 23
SALES (corp-wide): 226.2B **Publicly Held**
SIC: 8742 5912 Hospital & health services consultant; drug stores & proprietary stores
HQ: Genoa Healthcare Of Massachusetts, Llc
707 S Grady Way Ste 700
Renton WA 98057
800 519-1139

(G-5246)
GREAT CLIPS
1110 Eisenhower Rd (66048-5515)
PHONE..................................913 727-1917
Carrie Alam, *President*
Carrie Aoum, *Owner*
EMP: 12
SALES (est): 239.7K **Privately Held**
SIC: 7231 Unisex hair salons

(G-5247)
GREAT WESTERN MFG CO INC
2017 S 4th St (66048-3928)
P.O. Box 149 (66048-0149)
PHONE..................................913 682-2291
Jim Schroeder, *President*
Ken Burge, *Engineer*
Richard Pitts, *Engineer*
Jeff Seeger, *Engineer*
Michael Bell, *CFO*
◆ **EMP:** 84
SQ FT: 52,500
SALES (est): 21.4MM **Privately Held**
WEB: www.gwmfg.com
SIC: 3556 Flour mill machinery

(G-5248)
GREENAMYRE CONSTRUCTION LLC
2500 S 2nd St (66048-4542)
PHONE..................................913 772-1776
Rita Greenamyre,
EMP: 15
SALES (est): 693.2K **Privately Held**
SIC: 1521 Single-family housing construction

(G-5249)
GREENAMYRE RENTALS INC
2500 S 2nd St (66048-4542)
PHONE..................................913 651-9717
Mike Greenamyre, *President*
Dale Morrison, *Corp Secy*
Jeremy Greenamyre, *Vice Pres*
EMP: 15 **EST:** 1965
SALES (est): 1.3MM **Privately Held**
WEB: www.greenamyrerentals.com
SIC: 6514 6512 Residential building, four or fewer units: operation; commercial & industrial building operation

(G-5250)
HEARTLAND DENTAL GROUP
Also Called: Heartland Dental Care
3507 S 4th St (66048-5013)
PHONE..................................913 682-1000
Mark Ernzen, *Manager*
EMP: 18
SALES (est): 1.2MM
SALES (corp-wide): 265.1K **Privately Held**
SIC: 8021 Dentists' office
PA: Heartland Dental Group
104 N 6th St
Atchison KS 66002
913 367-2245

(G-5251)
HEARTLAND DENTAL GROUP PA
Also Called: Grigsby, Keith M DDS
3507 S 4th St (66048-5013)
PHONE..................................913 682-1000
Keith Grigsby, *President*
Dr Paul Hund, *Vice Pres*
Dr Darren Haun, *Treasurer*
Dr F Robert Burns, *Shareholder*
Dr John Zillman, *Shareholder*
▲ **EMP:** 53
SQ FT: 10,500
SALES (est): 2.7MM **Privately Held**
SIC: 8021 8011 Group & corporate practice dentists; clinic, operated by physicians

(G-5252)
HEATRON INC (HQ)
3000 Wilson Ave (66048-4637)
PHONE..................................913 651-4420
H B Turner, *President*
David Simpson, *Regional Mgr*
Laurie Boyd, *Vice Pres*
Laurie Harrod, *Vice Pres*
Bob Martter, *Vice Pres*
▲ **EMP:** 190

GEOGRAPHIC

SQ FT: 54,900
SALES (est): 50MM
SALES (corp-wide): 2.3B **Privately Held**
WEB: www.heatron.com
SIC: 3567 Radiant heating systems, industrial process
PA: Nibe Industrier Ab
Jarnvagsgatan 40
Markaryd 285 3
433 730-00

(G-5253)
HELP HOUSING CORPORATION
700 N 3rd St (66048-1512)
PHONE..................................913 651-6810
Karen Baker, *Director*
David Price, *Director*
EMP: 57
SQ FT: 2,500
SALES: 67.6K **Privately Held**
SIC: 8361 Home for the physically handicapped; self-help group home

(G-5254)
HENKE MANUFACTURING CORP (HQ)
3070 Wilson Ave (66048-4637)
PHONE..................................913 682-9000
Douglas Metcalf, *President*
Randy Wolf, *Engineer*
Michelle Perrin, *Accountant*
Robert Madison, *VP Sales*
Richard Deka, *Regl Sales Mgr*
EMP: 180
SQ FT: 70,000
SALES (est): 30.5MM
SALES (corp-wide): 1B **Publicly Held**
WEB: www.henkemfg.com
SIC: 3711 Snow plows (motor vehicles), assembly of
PA: Alamo Group Inc.
1627 E Walnut St
Seguin TX 78155
830 379-1480

(G-5255)
JACK JILL PRSCHL-EXTENDED CARE
130 N 6th St (66048-1921)
PHONE..................................913 682-1222
Joyce Dachcel, *Director*
Amy Andrews, *Asst Director*
EMP: 12
SALES (est): 368.6K **Privately Held**
SIC: 8351 Group day care center; preschool center

(G-5256)
JAMES B STDDARD TRNSF STOR INC
201 Commercial St (66048-5076)
PHONE..................................913 727-3627
Henria Campbell, *President*
John Campbell, *President*
EMP: 40 **EST**: 1931
SQ FT: 70,000
SALES (est): 4.9MM **Privately Held**
SIC: 4214 4213 Household goods moving & storage, local; household goods transport

(G-5257)
JF DENNEY INC
Also Called: Honeywell Authorized Dealer
76 Ash St (66048-5106)
P.O. Box 272 (66048-0272)
PHONE..................................913 772-8994
Joey Denney, *President*
EMP: 42 **EST**: 1952
SQ FT: 12,000
SALES: 4.8MM **Privately Held**
SIC: 1711 Plumbing contractors; warm air heating & air conditioning contractor

(G-5258)
JIFFY LUBE INTERNATIONAL INC
3120 S 4th St (66048-5006)
PHONE..................................913 682-7020
Jeff Diekman, *Manager*
EMP: 10
SALES (corp-wide): 388.3B **Privately Held**
WEB: www.jiffylube.com
SIC: 7549 Lubrication service, automotive
HQ: Jiffy Lube International, Inc.
700 Milam St
Houston TX 77002
713 546-1400

(G-5259)
JULIUS KAAZ CNSTR CO INC
716 Cherokee St (66048-2467)
PHONE..................................913 682-3550
Jody M Kaaz, *President*
Jeffrey D Kaaz, *Vice Pres*
Jody Kaaz, *Vice Pres*
Matt Kaaz, *Vice Pres*
Geri Wilburn, *Admin Asst*
EMP: 20
SQ FT: 15,000
SALES: 18.4MM **Privately Held**
SIC: 1542 1611 1541 Commercial & office building, new construction; commercial & office buildings, renovation & repair; resurfacing contractor; industrial buildings & warehouses

(G-5260)
KANSAS DEPARTMENT OF LABOR
Also Called: Leavenworth Job Service Center
515 Limit St Ste 200 (66048-4590)
PHONE..................................913 680-2200
Dennis Sutter, *Manager*
EMP: 10
SQ FT: 1,000 **Privately Held**
WEB: www.ethics.ks.gov
SIC: 7361 9441 6411 Employment agencies; administration of social & manpower programs; ; insurance brokers
HQ: Kansas Department Of Labor
401 Sw Topeka Blvd
Topeka KS 66603

(G-5261)
KANSAS DEPT FOR CHLDREN FMLIES
515 Limit St Ste 100 (66048-4590)
PHONE..................................913 651-6200
M J Vldham, *Branch Mgr*
EMP: 121 **Privately Held**
SIC: 8322 9441 General counseling services; social service center; administration of social & manpower programs;
HQ: Kansas Department For Children And Families
555 S Kansas Ave
Topeka KS 66603
785 368-6358

(G-5262)
KENS GARAGE INC
Also Called: Kens' Road & Field Service
108 Shawnee St (66048-2059)
PHONE..................................913 651-2433
Kenneth Sculley, *President*
Mary Sculley, *Treasurer*
EMP: 10
SALES (est): 990.1K **Privately Held**
SIC: 7538 General automotive repair shops

(G-5263)
KRAMER & ASSOCIATES CPAS LLC
2050 Spruce St (66048-2144)
PHONE..................................913 680-1690
Joseph J Wood, *CPA*
Anthony B Kramer,
EMP: 12
SALES (est): 701.6K **Privately Held**
WEB: www.dkcpas.org
SIC: 8721 7291 Accounting services, except auditing; tax return preparation services

(G-5264)
LARKIN EXCAVATING, INC.
13575 Gilman Rd (66048-6206)
P.O. Box 233, Lansing (66043-0233)
PHONE..................................913 727-3772
EMP: 65
SALES (est): 18MM **Privately Held**
WEB: www.larkinexc.com
SIC: 1794 Excavation work

(G-5265)
LEAVENWORTH EXCVTG EQP CO INC
5037 S 4th St (66048-5030)
PHONE..................................913 727-1234
Greg D Kaaz, *President*
Matt Kaaz, *Vice Pres*
Geri Wilburn, *Admin Asst*
EMP: 40 **EST**: 1959
SQ FT: 1,500
SALES (est): 5.3MM **Privately Held**
SIC: 1794 Excavation & grading, building construction

(G-5266)
LEAVENWORTH TECHNICAL SERVICES
4501 Commercial Pl (66048-5083)
PHONE..................................913 351-3344
Richard C Gervasini, *Principal*
EMP: 5
SALES: 250K **Privately Held**
SIC: 3577 Computer peripheral equipment

(G-5267)
LEES ENERGY CONNECTION
211 N 5th St (66048-1913)
PHONE..................................913 682-3782
Donna Lee, *Partner*
Danny Lee, *Partner*
EMP: 15
SALES (est): 430K **Privately Held**
SIC: 7991 Physical fitness facilities

(G-5268)
MCCANN PLUMBING & HEATING INC
4500 Brewer Pl (66048-5000)
P.O. Box 549 (66048-0549)
PHONE..................................913 727-6225
Francis L McCann, *Ch of Bd*
Michael D McCann, *President*
Helen McCann, *Corp Secy*
Daniel S McCann, *Vice Pres*
EMP: 25
SQ FT: 7,000
SALES (est): 2.3MM **Privately Held**
SIC: 1711 Plumbing contractors; warm air heating & air conditioning contractor

(G-5269)
MEDICALODGES INC
Also Called: Medical Lodge Adult Care
1503 Ohio St (66048-2999)
PHONE..................................913 772-1844
Cathleen Feeling, *Director*
Helen Riley, *Food Svc Dir*
EMP: 100
SALES (corp-wide): 100.2MM **Privately Held**
WEB: www.medicalodges.com
SIC: 8051 Convalescent home with continuous nursing care
PA: Medicalodges, Inc.
201 W 8th St
Coffeyville KS 67337
620 251-6700

(G-5270)
MEYER VETERINARY HOSPITAL
3525 S 4th St (66048-5013)
PHONE..................................913 682-6000
Stephen Meyer Dvm, *Owner*
EMP: 10 **EST**: 1979
SALES (est): 137.7K **Privately Held**
SIC: 0742 Animal hospital services, pets & other animal specialties

(G-5271)
MITRE CORPORATION
401 Delaware St (66048-2732)
PHONE..................................913 946-1900
EMP: 33
SALES (corp-wide): 1.1B **Privately Held**
SIC: 8733 Noncommercial research organizations
PA: The Mitre Corporation
202 Burlington Rd
Bedford MA 01730
781 271-2000

(G-5272)
MUTUAL SAVINGS ASSOCIATION (PA)
100 S 4th St (66048-2702)
P.O. Box 949 (66048-9049)
PHONE..................................913 682-3491
Davis Hoppes, *President*
Dru Wheatcroft, *Manager*
EMP: 60 **EST**: 1888
SALES: 9.6MM **Privately Held**
WEB: www.mutualwave.com
SIC: 6035 Federal savings & loan associations

(G-5273)
NATIONAL CEMETERY ADM
Also Called: Leavenworth National Cmtry 897
150 Muncie Rd (66048-5501)
PHONE..................................913 758-4105
Jeff Barnes, *Branch Mgr*
EMP: 16 **Publicly Held**
SIC: 6553 9451 Cemetery subdividers & developers; administration of veterans' affairs;
HQ: National Cemetery Administration
810 Vrmont Ave Nw Ste 427
Washington DC 20420

(G-5274)
NATIONAL CEMETERY ADM
Also Called: Fort Leavenworth Nat Cmtry 887
150 Muncie Rd (66048-5501)
PHONE..................................913 758-4105
Jeff S Barnes, *Director*
EMP: 16 **Publicly Held**
SIC: 6553 9451 Cemetery subdividers & developers; administration of veterans' affairs;
HQ: National Cemetery Administration
810 Vrmont Ave Nw Ste 427
Washington DC 20420

(G-5275)
NAVY FEDERAL CREDIT UNION
301 Cheyenne St (66048-1598)
PHONE..................................888 842-6328
EMP: 122
SALES (corp-wide): 5.3B **Privately Held**
SIC: 6061 Federal credit unions
PA: Navy Federal Credit Union
820 Follin Ln Se
Vienna VA 22180
703 255-8000

(G-5276)
NEK CAP INC
Also Called: Leavenworth County Headstart
2940 Ralph Bunch Dr (66048-5104)
PHONE..................................913 651-5692
Sherri Bridgette, *Manager*
Bridget Larabee, *Director*
EMP: 12
SALES (corp-wide): 10.1MM **Privately Held**
SIC: 8351 Head start center, except in conjunction with school
PA: Nek Cap, Inc.
1260 220th St
Hiawatha KS 66434
785 742-2222

(G-5277)
NORRIS & KELLY DRS
Also Called: Family Eyecare Center
2301 10th Ave (66048-4214)
PHONE..................................913 682-2929
Mark Norris, *Partner*
Kyle Kelly, *Partner*
EMP: 15
SALES (est): 1.3MM **Privately Held**
WEB: www.drsnorrisandkelly.com
SIC: 8042 Specialized optometrists

(G-5278)
P-AYR PRODUCTS
719 Delaware St (66048-2472)
P.O. Box 2040, Kyle TX (78640-1803)
PHONE..................................913 651-5543
Fax: 913 651-2084
EMP: 10
SALES (est): 540K **Privately Held**
SIC: 3711 Mfg Plastic Automotive Products

(G-5279)
PRESTIGE HOME CARE OF KANSAS
109 Delaware St (66048-2822)
PHONE..................................913 680-0493
Geri Martin, *Principal*
EMP: 12 **EST:** 2007
SALES (est): 407K **Privately Held**
SIC: 8082 Home health care services

(G-5280)
PRIME HEALTH SERVI-SAINT JOHN
3500 S 4th St (66048-5043)
PHONE..................................913 680-6000
Janet Geising, *Manager*
EMP: 15
SALES (corp-wide): 3.5B **Privately Held**
SIC: 8062 General medical & surgical hospitals
HQ: Prime Healthcare Services - Saint John Leavenworth, Llc
3500 S 4th St
Ontario CA 91761
913 680-6000

(G-5281)
PRIME HEALTHCARE SERVICES INC
Also Called: Saint John Home Health Center
3500 S 4th St (66048-5043)
PHONE..................................913 651-3542
Randall Nyp, *CEO*
EMP: 30
SALES (corp-wide): 3.5B **Privately Held**
SIC: 8062 General medical & surgical hospitals
HQ: Prime Healthcare Services Inc
3480 E Guasti Rd
Ontario CA 91761

(G-5282)
R & R BUILDERS INC
608 Delaware St (66048-2645)
P.O. Box 9 (66048-0009)
PHONE..................................913 682-1234
Jerome H Reilly, *President*
Darol E Rodrock, *Vice Pres*
J Reilly, *Treasurer*
EMP: 100
SQ FT: 7,000
SALES (est): 5.2MM **Privately Held**
SIC: 1521 6351 6531 New construction, single-family houses; warranty insurance, home; rental agent, real estate

(G-5283)
REIFSCHNEIDER EYE CENTER PC
1001 6th Ave Ste 100 (66048-3248)
PHONE..................................913 682-2900
John Reifschneider, *President*
EMP: 11
SQ FT: 4,200
SALES (est): 1.6MM **Privately Held**
SIC: 8011 Ophthalmologist

(G-5284)
REILLY COMPANY LLC
Also Called: Coldwell Banker
608 Delaware St (66048-2645)
P.O. Box 9 (66048-0009)
PHONE..................................913 682-1234
Jerome H Reilly, *President*
Edward F Reilly, *Principal*
J R Reilly, *Treasurer*
J Reilly, *Treasurer*
Shon Morsey, *Controller*
EMP: 55
SQ FT: 7,000
SALES (est): 4.7MM **Privately Held**
WEB: www.reillyandsons.com
SIC: 6531 6411 Real estate agent, residential; insurance agents, brokers & service

(G-5285)
RICHARD ALLEN CULTURAL CENTER
412 Kiowa St (66048-1551)
PHONE..................................913 682-8772
Phyllis Bass, *President*
EMP: 21
SALES: 53.6K **Privately Held**
SIC: 8412 Museum

(G-5286)
RIVERFRONT COMMUNITY CENTER
Also Called: Riverfront Park Campground
123 N Esplanade St (66048-2028)
PHONE..................................913 651-2132
Bill Katzenberger, *Director*
EMP: 25
SALES: 600K **Privately Held**
SIC: 7999 Recreation center

(G-5287)
RIVERSIDE RESOURCES INC
700 N 3rd St (66048-1512)
PHONE..................................913 651-6810
Karen Baker, *Director*
EMP: 53
SQ FT: 20,000
SALES: 2.1MM **Privately Held**
WEB: www.riversideresources.org
SIC: 8331 8361 Vocational rehabilitation agency; residential care for the handicapped

(G-5288)
SAINT LUKES CUSHING HOSPITAL (PA)
Also Called: Cushing Memorial Hospital
711 Marshall St (66048-3235)
PHONE..................................913 684-1100
Adele Ducharme, *CEO*
Jill Guenther, *Director*
John Shook, *Bd of Directors*
Robert Katzenberger, *Business Dir*
Gwendolyn Arnett, *Radiology Dir*
EMP: 285
SQ FT: 190,000
SALES: 38MM **Privately Held**
WEB: www.cushinghospital.org
SIC: 8062 General medical & surgical hospitals

(G-5289)
SMILE CENTRE
309 S 2nd St (66048-2803)
PHONE..................................913 651-9800
Paul E Kittle, *Partner*
Terri Greene, *Principal*
Alisha McAnelly, *Principal*
EMP: 18
SALES (est): 2MM **Privately Held**
SIC: 8021 Offices & clinics of dentists; dentists' office

(G-5290)
SPECTRUM MGT HOLDG CO LLC
Also Called: Time Warner American Cablvsn
541 Mcdonald Rd (66048-4873)
PHONE..................................913 682-2113
Gina Madox, *Principal*
EMP: 10
SALES (corp-wide): 43.6B **Publicly Held**
WEB: www.kcmetrosports.com
SIC: 4841 Cable television services
HQ: Spectrum Management Holding Company, Llc
400 Atlantic St
Stamford CT 06901
203 905-7801

(G-5291)
STERLING CENTRECORP INC
Also Called: Days Inn
3211 S 4th St Ste 200 (66048-5007)
PHONE..................................913 651-6000
Raman Patel, *Manager*
EMP: 20
SALES (corp-wide): 15.8MM **Privately Held**
WEB: www.villagerlodgeflorence.com
SIC: 7011 Hotels & motels
HQ: Sterling Centrecorp Inc
1 N Clematis St Ste 305
West Palm Beach FL 33401

(G-5292)
STRATGIC KNWLDGE SOLUTIONS INC
2524 Kensington Pl (66048-5080)
P.O. Box 896 (66048-1099)
PHONE..................................913 682-2002
Holly Baxter, *CEO*
Mike Prevou, *President*
EMP: 12
SALES (est): 1MM **Privately Held**
SIC: 8742 8732 8748 General management consultant; human resource consulting services; corporation organizing; educational research; business consulting

(G-5293)
STUDDARD MOVING & STORAGE INC (PA)
Also Called: Studdard Group
201 Commercial St (66048-5076)
PHONE..................................913 341-4600
John Campbell, *President*
Meegan Campbell, *Vice Pres*
EMP: 40
SQ FT: 100,000
SALES (est): 6.7MM **Privately Held**
WEB: www.studdardmoving.com
SIC: 4213 4214 Household goods transport; local trucking with storage

(G-5294)
STUDDARD RELOCATION SVCS LLC
201 Commercial St (66048-5076)
PHONE..................................816 524-2772
Tim Austin, *Opers Staff*
John Campbell, *Mng Member*
John H Campbell, *Mng Member*
EMP: 25 **EST:** 1999
SQ FT: 14,000
SALES (est): 2MM **Privately Held**
WEB: www.studdardrelo.com
SIC: 4214 Local trucking with storage

(G-5295)
SUNFLWER PCEMAKERS QUILT GUILD
18502 Tonganoxie Dr (66048-6397)
PHONE..................................913 727-1870
Pat McLoud, *Vice Pres*
EMP: 60
SALES (est): 3.4MM **Privately Held**
SIC: 2395 2396 Quilted fabrics or cloth; automotive & apparel trimmings

(G-5296)
SUPERIOR PRINTING CO
602 Grand Ave (66048-2396)
PHONE..................................913 682-3313
Curt Gilfert, *Owner*
Carl Gifert, *Owner*
EMP: 6
SQ FT: 2,500
SALES: 130K **Privately Held**
SIC: 2754 2752 Job printing, gravure; commercial printing, lithographic

(G-5297)
THORMAN ENTERPRISES LLC
Also Called: SERVPRO
629 Delaware St (66048-2644)
PHONE..................................913 772-1818
Daniel Thorman,
Heidi Thorman,
EMP: 14
SALES (est): 726.9K **Privately Held**
SIC: 7349 Building maintenance services

(G-5298)
TIRE TOWN INC (PA)
1825 S 4th St (66048-3932)
P.O. Box 87 (66048-0087)
PHONE..................................913 682-3201
Nancy Becker, *Admin Sec*
EMP: 27 **EST:** 1973
SQ FT: 168,000
SALES (est): 6.8MM **Privately Held**
WEB: www.tiretown.com
SIC: 5014 5531 Tires & tubes; automotive tires

(G-5299)
TPS LEAVENWORTH LP
Also Called: Towne Place Suites Leavenworth
1001 N 4th St (66048-1523)
PHONE..................................913 297-5400
Michael Watson, *General Mgr*
EMP: 25
SALES (est): 278K **Privately Held**
SIC: 7011 Hotel, franchised

(G-5300)
TRAINING TECH & SUPPORT INC
1931 Woodridge Dr (66048-2084)
PHONE..................................913 682-7048
Douglas J Lee, *President*
Douglas Lee, *General Mgr*
Terry Lee, *Vice Pres*
EMP: 23
SALES (est): 73.2K **Privately Held**
SIC: 8742 Training & development consultant

(G-5301)
TRI-COUNTY TITLE & ABSTRACT CO
360 Santa Fe St (66048-4537)
PHONE..................................913 682-8911
Carol Beall, *President*
EMP: 10
SALES (est): 840K **Privately Held**
SIC: 6411 6541 Insurance agents; title & trust companies

(G-5302)
TRIDEUM CORPORATION
1000 S 4th St Ste C (66048-3453)
PHONE..................................913 364-5900
Van Sullivan, *Branch Mgr*
EMP: 41
SALES (corp-wide): 11.8MM **Privately Held**
SIC: 8711 Engineering services
PA: Trideum Corporation
655 Discovery Dr Nw # 100
Huntsville AL 35806
256 704-6100

(G-5303)
UNIVERSITY OF KANSAS HOSPITAL
Also Called: Mid America Cardiology
3601 S 4th St Ste 1 (66048-5046)
PHONE..................................913 682-6950
EMP: 42
SALES (corp-wide): 708.6MM **Privately Held**
SIC: 8011 Cardiologist & cardio-vascular specialist; physicians' office, including specialists
PA: The University Of Kansas Hospital Authority
4000 Cambridge St
Kansas City KS 66160
913 588-5000

(G-5304)
VALIANT GLOBAL DEF SVCS INC
426 Delaware St Ste C3 (66048-2744)
PHONE..................................913 651-9782
John Harris, *Opers Staff*
Robert Forman, *Branch Mgr*
EMP: 75
SALES (corp-wide): 398MM **Privately Held**
SIC: 8611 7371 3699 Contractors' association; computer software systems analysis & design, custom; electrical equipment & supplies
HQ: Valiant Global Defense Services Inc.
3940 Ruffin Rd Ste C
San Diego CA 92123

(G-5305)
WESLEY MANAGEMENT INC
Also Called: Wesley Property Management
823 Miami St (66048-1815)
PHONE..................................913 682-6844
Jerry Wesley, *President*
EMP: 10
SALES (est): 795.8K **Privately Held**
SIC: 6531 Real estate managers

(G-5306)
WILLIAM O BROEKER ENTERPRISES
Also Called: Leavenworth Floral
701 Delaware St (66048-2472)
PHONE..................................913 682-2022
Janis Broeker, *President*
Abigail Howe, *Treasurer*
EMP: 22 **EST:** 1930
SQ FT: 16,000

GEOGRAPHIC

SALES (est): 911.6K **Privately Held**
SIC: 5992 5193 5947 Flowers, fresh; plants, potted; flowers, fresh; plants, potted; gift shop

(G-5307)
WOMENS CLINIC ASSOC PA
Also Called: Lorenzetti, Lisa A
3550 S 4th St Ste 150 (66048-5156)
PHONE..................................913 788-9797
Albert Liu, *President*
Luellen Hull, *Principal*
Lisa Lorenzetti, *Principal*
EMP: 12
SALES (est): 830K **Privately Held**
WEB: www.wcababy.com
SIC: 8011 Gynecologist; obstetrician

(G-5308)
WOMENS COMMUNITY Y
520 S Broadway St (66048-2526)
PHONE..................................913 682-6404
Pat Barnhardt, *Director*
EMP: 16
SALES: 270.5K **Privately Held**
SIC: 8351 Group day care center

(G-5309)
YOUNG HOINS SERVICE GROUP LLC
Also Called: Yesco
326 Choctaw St (66048-2736)
PHONE..................................913 772-0708
Christopher Hoins,
EMP: 10
SQ FT: 20,000
SALES (est): 811.1K **Privately Held**
SIC: 3993 Neon signs; electric signs

(G-5310)
YOUNG SIGN CO- INC
326 Choctaw St (66048-2736)
PHONE..................................913 651-5432
Ann Hoins, *President*
Christopher Hoins, *Vice Pres*
John Hoins IV, *Treasurer*
EMP: 22
SQ FT: 23,000
SALES: 2.5MM **Privately Held**
WEB: www.youngsigncompany.com
SIC: 3993 Signs & advertising specialties

Leawood
Johnson County

(G-5311)
A/R ALLEGIANCE GROUP LLC
6900 College Blvd Ste 550 (66211-1596)
P.O. Box 7401, Shawnee Mission (66207-0401)
PHONE..................................913 338-4790
Keith Lilek, *CEO*
EMP: 12 **EST:** 2006
SALES (est): 1MM **Privately Held**
SIC: 7322 Adjustment & collection services

(G-5312)
ADKORE STAFFING GROUP LLC (PA)
4200 W 115th St Ste 300 (66211-2728)
PHONE..................................913 402-8031
Robert Thayer, *Mng Member*
EMP: 16
SALES: 950K **Privately Held**
SIC: 7363 Temporary help service

(G-5313)
ADVANCED RESOURCES LLC
5400 W 133rd Pl Apt 221 (66209-4257)
PHONE..................................913 207-9998
Faaon Mitchell, *Principal*
EMP: 20
SALES (est): 338.7K **Privately Held**
SIC: 8742 Business planning & organizing services

(G-5314)
AGSPRING LLC (PA)
5101 College Blvd (66211-1614)
PHONE..................................913 333-3035
Randal Linville,
Jennifer Mick, *Executive Asst*
Dennis Krause,
EMP: 20
SALES (est): 163.4MM **Privately Held**
SIC: 0191 8748 General farms, primarily crop; agricultural consultant

(G-5315)
AGSPRING IDAHO LLC (HQ)
Also Called: Thresher Artisan Wheat
5101 College Blvd (66211-1614)
PHONE..................................952 956-6720
Randal Linville, *CEO*
Donald Wille, *COO*
EMP: 19 **EST:** 2014
SALES (est): 135.6MM
SALES (corp-wide): 163.4MM **Privately Held**
SIC: 5153 Grain elevators
PA: Agspring, Llc
5101 College Blvd
Leawood KS 66211
913 333-3035

(G-5316)
ALLEGIANT NETWORKS LLC
10983 Granada Ln 300 (66211-1401)
PHONE..................................913 599-6900
Bryan Dancer, *CEO*
Emily Martin, *Project Mgr*
Patty Massie, *Project Mgr*
Russ Bohn, *Sales Staff*
Zachary Coffman, *Marketing Staff*
EMP: 35
SQ FT: 8,000
SALES (est): 6.3MM **Privately Held**
WEB: www.allegiantnetworks.com
SIC: 4813 7373 ; systems software development services

(G-5317)
AMC ENTERTAINMENT HOLDINGS INC (DH)
1 Amc Way 11500 Ash St (66211)
PHONE..................................913 213-2000
Julie King, *CEO*
Lin Zhang, *Ch of Bd*
Adam M Aron, *President*
Nadiyrah Amatul-Malik, *General Mgr*
Darmecia Conners, *General Mgr*
EMP: 65
SALES: 5.4B
SALES (corp-wide): 7.3MM **Publicly Held**
SIC: 7832 Motion picture theaters, except drive-in

(G-5318)
AMC ENTERTAINMENT INC (DH)
11500 Ash St (66211-7804)
PHONE..................................913 213-2000
Lin Zhang, *Ch of Bd*
Gerardo I Lopez, *President*
Greg Brewton, *General Mgr*
Daniel Huffines, *General Mgr*
Kevin M Connor, *Senior VP*
EMP: 10
SALES: 2.9B
SALES (corp-wide): 7.3MM **Publicly Held**
WEB: www.amctheatres.com
SIC: 7832 Exhibitors, itinerant: motion picture

(G-5319)
AMERICAN ACDEMY FMLY PHYSCIANS (PA)
Also Called: Aafp
11400 Tomahawk Creek Pkwy (66211-2680)
P.O. Box 11210, Shawnee Mission (66207-1210)
PHONE..................................913 906-6000
Douglas E Henley, *CEO*
John S Cullen, *President*
John Meigs Jr, *President*
Michael L Munger, *President*
Wanda Filer, *Principal*
EMP: 350
SQ FT: 180,000
SALES: 100.5MM **Privately Held**
WEB: www.aafp.org
SIC: 8621 Health association

(G-5320)
AMERICAN GVRNMENT SLUTIONS LLC
5251 W 116th Pl Ste 200 (66211-2011)
PHONE..................................913 428-2550
Donald Ring, *CEO*
EMP: 17
SQ FT: 1,000
SALES (est): 1.1MM **Privately Held**
SIC: 7373 7374 7371 8732 Computer integrated systems design; calculating service (computer); computer software systems analysis & design, custom; market analysis, business & economic research; new business start-up consultant

(G-5321)
AMERICAN MULTI-CINEMA INC
Also Called: AMC
11701 Nall Ave (66211-2025)
PHONE..................................913 498-8696
Rob Kim, *Manager*
Katrina Wilcott, *Manager*
EMP: 60
SALES (corp-wide): 7.3MM **Publicly Held**
WEB: www.arrowheadtownecenter.com
SIC: 7832 Exhibitors, itinerant: motion picture
HQ: American Multi-Cinema, Inc.
1 Amc Way
Leawood KS 66211
913 213-2000

(G-5322)
AMERICAN MULTI-CINEMA INC (DH)
Also Called: AMC
1 Amc Way (66211)
PHONE..................................913 213-2000
Gerardo Lopez, *CEO*
Terry Crawford, *President*
Robert J Lenihan, *President*
Kevin M Connor, *Senior VP*
Chris A Cox, *Senior VP*
EMP: 250 **EST:** 1947
SQ FT: 75,000
SALES (est): 916.3MM
SALES (corp-wide): 7.3MM **Publicly Held**
WEB: www.arrowheadtownecenter.com
SIC: 7832 5812 8741 Motion picture theaters, except drive-in; concessionaire; management services
HQ: Amc Entertainment Inc.
11500 Ash St
Leawood KS 66211
913 213-2000

(G-5323)
AMERIPRISE FINANCIAL INC
5700 W 112th St Ste 130 (66211-1749)
PHONE..................................913 239-8140
Jean St Pierre, *Principal*
Jean Stpierre, *Agent*
EMP: 22
SALES (corp-wide): 12.8B **Publicly Held**
SIC: 8742 Financial consultant
PA: Ameriprise Financial, Inc.
55 Ameriprise Fincl Ctr
Minneapolis MN 55474
612 671-3131

(G-5324)
AMERIPRISE FINCL AMERIPRISE
Also Called: Ameriprise Financial Services
4550 W 109th St Ste 200 (66211-1354)
PHONE..................................913 451-2811
Vestana Ahlen, *Agent*
Michael Brun, *Agent*
Cole Dimond, *Agent*
Michael Ward, *Agent*
Dave Mehrer, *Advisor*
EMP: 14
SALES (est): 3MM **Privately Held**
SIC: 6282 Investment advice

(G-5325)
AMTRUST AG INSURANCE SVCS LLC
11300 Tomahwk Crk Pkwy # 300 (66211-2610)
PHONE..................................844 350-2767
Mark Raymie, *President*
Stuart Hollander, *Vice Pres*
Barry Moses, *Vice Pres*
Harry Schlachter, *Treasurer*
EMP: 80 **EST:** 2014
SALES (est): 6.2MM **Privately Held**
SIC: 6331 Agricultural insurance
HQ: Producers Ag Insurance Group, Inc.
2025 S Hughes St
Amarillo TX 79109

(G-5326)
ANSWER MEDIA LLC
2020 W 89th St Ste 200 (66206-1930)
PHONE..................................816 984-8853
Casey Murawski, *Vice Pres*
Michael Weber, *CFO*
Eric Hazen,
EMP: 10
SQ FT: 1,500
SALES (est): 985K **Privately Held**
SIC: 7313 Electronic media advertising representatives

(G-5327)
ANTHEM MEDIA LLC (PA)
Also Called: Anthem Media Group
4303 W 119th St (66209-1515)
PHONE..................................913 894-6923
Brian Weaver, *CEO*
Tom Pokorny, *President*
Erin Calvin, *Vice Pres*
Andre Player, *Vice Pres*
Dave Alverson, *CFO*
EMP: 25
SALES (est): 16.5MM **Privately Held**
WEB: www.anthemmotorsports.com
SIC: 2741 8748 7311 Miscellaneous publishing; business consulting; advertising agencies

(G-5328)
ANTHEM MOTORSPORTS INC
Also Called: Supercar Life
4303 W 119th St (66209-1515)
PHONE..................................913 894-6923
Brian Weaver, *President*
EMP: 18
SALES (est): 883.3K **Privately Held**
SIC: 2721 Magazines: publishing only, not printed on site

(G-5329)
ARATANA THERAPEUTICS INC (HQ)
11400 Tomahawk Creek Pkwy # 340 (66211-2730)
PHONE..................................913 353-1000
Wendy L Yarno, *Ch of Bd*
Craig Tooman, *President*
Brent Standridge, *COO*
Rhonda Hellums, *CFO*
EMP: 66
SQ FT: 17,600
SALES: 35.4MM
SALES (corp-wide): 3B **Publicly Held**
SIC: 2834 2836 Pharmaceutical preparations; veterinary biological products
PA: Elanco Animal Health Incorporated
2500 Innovation Way N
Greenfield IN 46140
877 352-6261

(G-5330)
ARVEST BANK
Also Called: Leawood Branch
10685 Mission Rd (66206-2700)
PHONE..................................913 953-4070
Cole Schwanke, *Branch Mgr*
EMP: 17
SALES (corp-wide): 2.3B **Privately Held**
SIC: 6022 State trust companies accepting deposits, commercial
HQ: Arvest Bank
103 S Bloomington St
Lowell AR 72745
479 575-1000

(G-5331)
ASCEND LEARNING LLC (HQ)
11161 Overbrook Rd (66211-2299)
PHONE..................................855 856-7705
Greg Sebasky, *CEO*
Thomas Morse, *Chief*
Christine O'Connor, *Counsel*
Christine Oconnor, *Counsel*
Rebecca Schuster, *Counsel*
EMP: 280 **EST:** 2010
SALES: 330MM **Privately Held**
SIC: 8742 Management consulting services

PA: Ascend Learning Holdings, Llc
11161 Overbrook Rd
Leawood KS 66211
800 667-7531

(G-5332)
ASCEND LEARNING HOLDINGS LLC (PA)
11161 Overbrook Rd (66211-2299)
PHONE..................................800 667-7531
Greg Sebasky, *CEO*
Bob Lyons, *Exec VP*
June Gary, *Vice Pres*
Mark Williams-Abrams, *Vice Pres*
David Williams, *Senior Engr*
EMP: 11
SALES (est): 330MM **Privately Held**
SIC: 7011 Hotels & motels

(G-5333)
ASE GROUP INC
6600 College Blvd Ste 310 (66211-1522)
PHONE..................................913 339-9333
Bonnie Siegel, *President*
Rameka Sahadeo, *President*
Jennifer Bryant, *Partner*
Suzanne Pearson, *Accounting Mgr*
Jonathan Schwartzbard, *Director*
EMP: 15
SQ FT: 5,900
SALES (est): 2.8MM **Privately Held**
WEB: www.ase-group.com
SIC: 7299 Party planning service

(G-5334)
ASSESSMENT TECH INST LLC
Also Called: ATI Nursing Education
11161 Overbrook Rd (66211-2299)
PHONE..................................800 667-7531
Rick Willett, *CEO*
Ashley Dixon, *Partner*
Betsy Malpass, *Partner*
Kandice D Shields, *Partner*
Russell Stibitz, *Partner*
EMP: 350
SQ FT: 3,000
SALES (est): 34.8MM
SALES (corp-wide): 330MM **Privately Held**
WEB: www.atitesting.com
SIC: 8748 8249 Testing service, educational or personnel; medical training services
HQ: Ascend Learning, Llc
11161 Overbrook Rd
Leawood KS 66211
855 856-7705

(G-5335)
ASSET MGT ANALIS GROUP LLC
5016 W 108th Ter Apt 517 (66211-1257)
PHONE..................................803 270-0996
Denice Pickett, *President*
EMP: 21
SQ FT: 1,600
SALES (est): 1.2MM **Privately Held**
WEB: www.amag.net
SIC: 8711 8742 Engineering services; management consulting services

(G-5336)
ASURION LLC
11460 Tomahwk Crk Pkwy # 300 (66211-7819)
PHONE..................................816 237-3000
Kevin M Taweel, *President*
EMP: 921
SALES (corp-wide): 6.7B **Privately Held**
SIC: 7549 Road service, automotive
HQ: Asurion, Llc
648 Grassmere Park # 300
Nashville TN 37211
615 837-3000

(G-5337)
AUTOMATED CONTROL SYSTEMS CORP
Also Called: ACS
5251 W 116th Pl Ste 200 (66211-2011)
PHONE..................................913 766-2336
Charles Olsen, *President*
Bob Rodriguez, *Vice Pres*
Robert Rodriguez, *Vice Pres*
Tom Schorn, *Sales Staff*
Tom Garrison, *Manager*
EMP: 52
SQ FT: 10,000
SALES (est): 26.6MM **Privately Held**
WEB: www.acs-1.com
SIC: 5075 1711 7623 Air conditioning & ventilation equipment & supplies; warm air heating equipment & supplies; plumbing, heating, air-conditioning contractors; refrigeration service & repair

(G-5338)
BALDWIN LLC (PA)
Also Called: Standard Style In Baldwin
6601 College Blvd Ste 140 (66211-1504)
PHONE..................................913 312-2375
Ashley Hight, *Pub Rel Staff*
Emily Baldwin, *Mng Member*
Lori Johnson, *Executive Asst*
Matt Baldwin,
▼ **EMP:** 10
SALES (est): 11.4MM **Privately Held**
WEB: www.standardstyle.com
SIC: 5621 5137 Women's clothing stores; women's & children's clothing

(G-5339)
BELL/KNOTT AND ASSOCIATES C (PA)
12730 State Line Rd (66209-1619)
PHONE..................................913 378-1600
Kerry L Knott, *President*
John C Bell, *Vice Pres*
EMP: 24
SQ FT: 5,000
SALES: 4MM **Privately Held**
WEB: www.bellknot.com
SIC: 8712 Architectural engineering

(G-5340)
BLACK KNIGHT FINCL SVCS INC
4400 College Blvd (66211-2341)
PHONE..................................913 693-0000
EMP: 5
SALES (corp-wide): 1.1B **Publicly Held**
SIC: 7372 Prepackaged software
HQ: Black Knight Financial Services, Inc.
601 Riverside Ave
Jacksonville FL 32204
904 854-5100

(G-5341)
BLUE INFOTECH INC
5251 W 116th Pl Ste 200 (66211-2011)
PHONE..................................816 945-2583
Dave Hetal, *Principal*
EMP: 10
SALES (est): 200.3K **Privately Held**
SIC: 8748 7375 7372 Business consulting; information retrieval services; prepackaged software

(G-5342)
BOTTARO MOREFIELD & KUBIN LC
11300 Tomahawk Creek Pkwy (66211-2610)
PHONE..................................913 948-8200
Kipp Kuban, *Principal*
Patrick Bottaro, *Principal*
Richard Morefield, *Principal*
EMP: 12 **EST:** 1996
SALES (est): 1.2MM **Privately Held**
WEB: www.kc-lawyers.com
SIC: 8111 Criminal law; specialized law offices, attorneys

(G-5343)
BROOKDALE SNIOR LVING CMMNTIES
4400 W 115th St (66211-2684)
PHONE..................................913 491-3681
T Andy Smith, *Branch Mgr*
EMP: 24
SALES (corp-wide): 4.5B **Publicly Held**
SIC: 8059 8011 Rest home, with health care; clinic, operated by physicians
HQ: Brookdale Senior Living Communities, Inc.
6737 W Wa St Ste 2300
Milwaukee WI 53214
414 918-5000

(G-5344)
BUKATY COMPANIES (PA)
4601 College Blvd Ste 100 (66211-1664)
PHONE..................................913 345-0440
Carol Woebbecke, *President*
Scott Dooley, *Vice Pres*
Jesse Edwards, *Accounts Mgr*
Krystle Lorigan, *Accounts Mgr*
Chris Stitt, *Accounts Mgr*
EMP: 35
SALES (est): 18.7MM **Privately Held**
WEB: www.bukaty.com
SIC: 6371 6411 Pension, health & welfare funds; insurance agents, brokers & service

(G-5345)
CALIFORNIA CASUALTY MGT CO
Also Called: California Casualty Svc Ctr
4000 W 114th St Ste 300 (66211-2622)
PHONE..................................913 266-3000
Pat Lynch, *Vice Pres*
Sharilyn Barteld, *Branch Mgr*
Claire Stevenson, *IT/INT Sup*
EMP: 99
SALES (corp-wide): 239.8MM **Privately Held**
SIC: 6331 Reciprocal interinsurance exchanges: fire, marine, casualty
HQ: California Casualty Management Company
1875 S Grant St Ste 800
San Mateo CA 94402
650 574-4000

(G-5346)
CAPITAL PERFORMANCE MGT LLC (PA)
11835 Roe Ave 236 (66211-2607)
PHONE..................................913 381-1481
Steven Jackson, *Project Mgr*
Tracy Canchola, *Office Mgr*
Robert L Black Jr, *Mng Member*
David Berthiaume, *Manager*
Brian Kidwell, *Manager*
EMP: 25
SQ FT: 1,800
SALES (est): 1.9MM **Privately Held**
WEB: www.cpmworks.com
SIC: 8741 Construction management

(G-5347)
CAREFUSION 213 LLC
11400 Tomahawk Creek Pkwy (66211-2680)
PHONE..................................800 523-0502
Lee Kim, *Director*
EMP: 475
SALES (corp-wide): 15.9B **Publicly Held**
SIC: 2834 Pharmaceutical preparations
HQ: Carefusion 213, Llc
3750 Torrey View Ct
San Diego CA 92130

(G-5348)
CARMIKE CINEMAS LLC (DH)
11500 Ash St (66211-7804)
PHONE..................................913 213-2000
Adam M Aron, *President*
A Dale Mayo, *President*
Craig R Ramsey, *CFO*
EMP: 17 **EST:** 1930
SQ FT: 48,500
SALES: 804.3MM
SALES (corp-wide): 7.3MM **Publicly Held**
WEB: www.carmike.com
SIC: 7832 Exhibitors, itinerant: motion picture

(G-5349)
CARMIKE REVIEWS HOLDINGS LLC
11500 Ash St (66211-7804)
PHONE..................................913 213-2000
EMP: 18 **EST:** 2014
SALES (est): 714.3K
SALES (corp-wide): 7.3MM **Publicly Held**
SIC: 7832 Exhibitors, itinerant: motion picture
HQ: Carmike Cinemas, Llc
11500 Ash St
Leawood KS 66211
913 213-2000

(G-5350)
CBIZ BENEFITS & INSUR SVCS INC
11440 Tomahawk Creek Pkwy (66211-2672)
PHONE..................................913 234-1000
David Katzman, *Managing Dir*
Bobby Svoboda, *Managing Dir*
Christian Schechinger, *Business Mgr*
Nancy M Mellard, *Exec VP*
Carolyn Watley, *Vice Pres*
EMP: 12 **Publicly Held**
SIC: 6411 Insurance agents, brokers & service
HQ: Cbiz Benefits & Insurance Services, Inc.
225 W Wacker Dr Ste 2000
Chicago IL 60606
312 602-6745

(G-5351)
CHICAGO TITLE AND TRUST CO
6700 College Blvd Ste 300 (66211-1511)
PHONE..................................913 451-1200
Jean Rogers, *Branch Mgr*
EMP: 10
SALES (corp-wide): 7.5B **Publicly Held**
SIC: 6361 6541 Real estate title insurance; title abstract offices
HQ: Chicago Title And Trust Company
10 S La Salle St Ste 3100
Chicago IL 60603
312 223-2000

(G-5352)
CITYWIDE PAINTING & RMDLG LLC
4904 W 114th St (66211-2005)
PHONE..................................913 238-9749
James Hardie, *Principal*
EMP: 12 **EST:** 2009
SALES (est): 577.1K **Privately Held**
SIC: 1721 Residential painting

(G-5353)
CLASSIC MOTOR FREIGHT LLC
10777 Barkley St Ste 210 (66211-1162)
PHONE..................................913 586-5911
Alexander Glenn,
EMP: 20
SALES (est): 491K **Privately Held**
SIC: 4212 Local trucking, without storage

(G-5354)
CLIENT ONE SECURITIES LLC
11460 Tomahwk Crk Pkwy # 200 (66211-7810)
PHONE..................................913 814-6097
Michael C Tuma, *Principal*
Allison Ryan, *Supervisor*
EMP: 11
SALES (est): 2.4MM **Privately Held**
SIC: 6211 Security brokers & dealers

(G-5355)
COMMERCE BANK
11405 Nall Ave (66211-1894)
PHONE..................................816 234-2000
Marjorie Valentine, *Vice Pres*
Kent Hatesohl, *Manager*
EMP: 13
SALES (corp-wide): 1.3B **Publicly Held**
SIC: 6022 State commercial banks
HQ: Commerce Bank
1000 Walnut St Fl 700
Kansas City MO 64106
816 234-2000

(G-5356)
COMMUNICATION CABLE COMPANY (DH)
Also Called: Comm Solutions
6130 Sprint Pkwy Ste 400 (66211-1155)
PHONE..................................610 644-5155
Paul S Black, *CEO*
John T Black, *President*
William Buckalew, *COO*
Jeff Rokicki, *Finance*
Vince Vevea, *Sr Ntwrk Engine*
EMP: 55
SQ FT: 10,400

GEOGRAPHIC

SALES (est): 19.4MM
SALES (corp-wide): 4.8B **Privately Held**
WEB: www.commcable.com
SIC: 7379 5045 Computer related consulting services; computer peripheral equipment
HQ: Optiv Security Inc.
1144 15th St Ste 2900
Denver CO 80202
303 298-0600

(G-5357)
COMPLETE MUSIC INC
Also Called: Complete Music Disc Jockey Svc
6363 W 110th St (66211-1509)
PHONE..................................913 432-1111
Wade Nelson, *Manager*
EMP: 25
SALES (corp-wide): 4.2MM **Privately Held**
SIC: 7929 7922 6512 Disc jockey service; theatrical talent & booking agencies; auditorium & hall operation
PA: Complete Music, Inc
110 N 9th St
Omaha NE 68102
402 339-3535

(G-5358)
CONTINENTAL CONSULTING INC
9000 State Line Rd (66206-1922)
PHONE..................................913 642-6642
Philip D Gibbs, *President*
Dave Lotz, *Engineer*
Kathleen Gibbs, *Admin Sec*
Brett Haugland, *Admin Sec*
Andrew Talkin, *Internal Med*
EMP: 25
SALES (est): 2.8MM **Privately Held**
WEB: www.ccengineers.com
SIC: 8711 Consulting engineer

(G-5359)
CONTINUA HOME HEALTH LLC
13002 State Line Rd (66209-1756)
PHONE..................................913 905-0255
Cynthia D Miller, *Principal*
Sandra Silva, *Exec Dir*
EMP: 19 **EST**: 2005
SALES: 3.7MM **Privately Held**
SIC: 8082 Visiting nurse service

(G-5360)
COUNTRY CLUB BANK
13451 Briar Dr Ste 100 (66209-3426)
PHONE..................................816 931-4060
Sean Doherty, *Exec VP*
Nina Strathmann, *Vice Pres*
Tai Le, *Technology*
EMP: 17
SALES (corp-wide): 38MM **Privately Held**
SIC: 6029 Commercial banks
HQ: Country Club Bank
1 Ward Pkwy
Kansas City MO 64112

(G-5361)
COUNTRY CLUB BANK
11181 Overbrook Rd (66211-2299)
PHONE..................................816 751-4251
EMP: 13
SALES (corp-wide): 38MM **Privately Held**
SIC: 7389 6061 Finishing services; federal credit unions
HQ: Country Club Bank
1 Ward Pkwy
Kansas City MO 64112

(G-5362)
COVERALL NORTH AMERICA INC
Also Called: Coverall Cleaning Concepts
8700 State Line Rd # 105 (66206-1500)
PHONE..................................913 888-5009
James Wilson, *General Mgr*
Kevin Morse, *Business Mgr*
Christopher Gilbert, *Sales Staff*
Sal Guerrera, *Sales Staff*
Gary Shafer, *Sales Staff*
EMP: 10
SALES (corp-wide): 255.9MM **Privately Held**
WEB: www.coverall.com
SIC: 7349 6794 Building maintenance services; franchises, selling or licensing
HQ: Coverall North America, Inc.
350 Sw 12th Ave
Deerfield Beach FL 33442
561 922-2500

(G-5363)
CREATIVE ONE MARKETING CORP
Also Called: Creative Marketing
11460 Tomahawk Creek Pkwy (66211-7810)
PHONE..................................913 814-0510
Mike Tripses, *CEO*
Mike Gripses, *President*
Phil Poje, *Exec VP*
Robb Edward, *Vice Pres*
Will Moneymaker, *CFO*
EMP: 106
SQ FT: 10,872
SALES (est): 33.3MM **Privately Held**
WEB: www.cmickc.com
SIC: 6411 Insurance agents, brokers & service

(G-5364)
CROSSFIRST BANK
11440 Tomahawk Creek Pkwy (66211-2672)
PHONE..................................913 312-6800
EMP: 202
SALES (est): 377.2K
SALES (corp-wide): 162.9MM **Publicly Held**
SIC: 6099 Functions related to deposit banking
PA: Crossfirst Bankshares, Inc.
11440 Tomahawk Creek Pkwy
Leawood KS 66211
913 312-6822

(G-5365)
CULTURE INDEX LLC
10200 State Ln Rd 102 (66206)
PHONE..................................816 361-7575
Gary W Walstrom, *Ch of Bd*
EMP: 10
SALES (est): 215.3K **Privately Held**
SIC: 8742 Planning consultant

(G-5366)
CURTIS KLAASSEN
Also Called: Mid-America Toxicology Course
2617 W 112th St (66211-2950)
PHONE..................................913 661-4616
Curtis Klaassen, *President*
EMP: 12
SALES (est): 224.3K **Privately Held**
SIC: 8331 Job training services; skill training center

(G-5367)
CUSTOM RDO COMMUNICATIONS LTD
Also Called: Solvenet Solutions
6600 College Blvd Ste 317 (66211-1522)
PHONE..................................816 561-4100
Alicia Foss, *President*
Greg Foss, *Vice Pres*
EMP: 14
SQ FT: 8,312
SALES (est): 2.9MM **Privately Held**
WEB: www.crcltd.com
SIC: 5064 5731 7622 Radios, motor vehicle; radios, two-way, citizens' band, weather, short-wave, etc.; radio & television repair

(G-5368)
DALMARK MANAGEMENT GROUP LLC
12220 State Line Rd (66209-1217)
PHONE..................................816 272-0041
Jim Nichols,
EMP: 18
SQ FT: 2,400
SALES (est): 2.1MM **Privately Held**
WEB: www.dalmarkgroup.com
SIC: 8741 Management services

(G-5369)
DANIEL J GEHA MD
Also Called: Geha, Daniel J
8800 State Line Rd (66206-1553)
PHONE..................................913 383-9099
Daniel Geha, *Principal*
EMP: 20
SALES (est): 982.3K **Privately Held**
SIC: 8011 General & family practice, physician/surgeon

(G-5370)
DATACO DEREX INC (PA)
6217 W 127th Ter (66209-3657)
PHONE..................................913 438-2444
Lee Pearlmutter, *President*
EMP: 18
SQ FT: 37,000
SALES (est): 2.5MM **Privately Held**
WEB: www.dataco.com
SIC: 5734 7378 2759 5045 Computer & software stores; printers & plotters: computers; computer peripheral equipment; computer maintenance & repair; computer peripheral equipment repair & maintenance; commercial printing; printers, computer

(G-5371)
DAVID B LYON MD
11261 Nall Ave (66211-1669)
PHONE..................................913 261-2020
Nelson Sabates MD, *Director*
▲ **EMP**: 30 **EST**: 2001
SALES (est): 2.1MM **Privately Held**
WEB: www.sabateseye.com
SIC: 8011 Ophthalmologist

(G-5372)
DAVIDSON & ASSOCIATES INC
12701 El Monte St (66209-2312)
PHONE..................................913 271-6859
Paul Biersmith, *President*
John Biersmith, *CFO*
Meghan Biersmith, *Admin Sec*
EMP: 22 **EST**: 1994
SQ FT: 5,000
SALES: 2.1MM **Privately Held**
WEB: www.davidsonassociatesinc.com
SIC: 8712 8741 8711 1542 Architectural engineering; construction management; engineering services; heating & ventilation engineering; commercial & office building, new construction

(G-5373)
DAVIS KETCHMARK MCCREIGHT
11161 Overbrook Rd (66211-2299)
PHONE..................................816 842-1515
Michael Ketchmark, *President*
EMP: 10 **EST**: 2011
SALES (est): 1.2MM **Privately Held**
SIC: 8111 General practice law office

(G-5374)
DAVIS KTCHMARK ESCHENS MCCRGHT
11161 Overbrook Rd # 210 (66211-2299)
PHONE..................................816 842-1515
Michael Ketchmark, *Managing Prtnr*
EMP: 11
SALES (est): 597.8K **Privately Held**
SIC: 8111 General practice attorney, lawyer

(G-5375)
DAYS INN OF OVERLAND PARK
6800 W 108th St (66211-1147)
PHONE..................................913 341-0100
EMP: 10
SALES (est): 261.8K **Privately Held**
SIC: 7011 Hotels & motels

(G-5376)
DD TRADERS INC (PA)
Also Called: Demdaco
5000 W 134th St (66209-7806)
PHONE..................................913 402-6800
Lawrence W Hart, *President*
Christine Lien, *President*
David Kiersznowski, *Chairman*
Steve Fowler, *COO*
Peter Friedmann, *Vice Pres*
◆ **EMP**: 285
SQ FT: 60,000
SALES (est): 108.6MM **Privately Held**
WEB: www.demdaco.com
SIC: 5199 Gifts & novelties

(G-5377)
DELTA DENTAL OF KANSAS INC
11300 Tomahwk Crk Pkwy # 350 (66211-2610)
PHONE..................................913 381-4928
Dean Newton, *Vice Pres*
EMP: 19
SALES (corp-wide): 305.3MM **Privately Held**
SIC: 6324 Dental insurance
PA: Delta Dental Of Kansas, Inc.
1619 N Waterfront Pkwy
Wichita KS 67206
316 264-4511

(G-5378)
DIAGNOSTIC IMAGING CENTERS PA
6650 W 110th St (66211-1501)
PHONE..................................913 319-8450
Ed Moore, *CEO*
Barbara Mautino, *Credit Mgr*
EMP: 200
SALES (est): 15.5MM **Privately Held**
SIC: 8011 Radiologist

(G-5379)
DO GOOD PRODUCTIONS INC
12000 Aberdeen Rd (66209-1007)
PHONE..................................913 400-3416
Nancy Seelen, *Principal*
EMP: 13
SALES: 10.5K **Privately Held**
SIC: 7822 Motion picture & tape distribution

(G-5380)
DUNES RESIDENTIAL SERVICES INC
4707 College Blvd Ste 203 (66211-2081)
PHONE..................................913 955-2900
Ward A Katz, *President*
Elisa L Edwards, *Senior VP*
Gina Johnson, *Vice Pres*
Liz Pence, *Vice Pres*
Trisha Stout, *Manager*
EMP: 35
SALES (est): 2.8MM **Privately Held**
SIC: 6531 Real estate managers

(G-5381)
E-CONSULTSUSA LLC
8900 State Line Rd Ste 50 (66206-1960)
PHONE..................................913 696-1001
Fred Church,
EMP: 10 **EST**: 2011
SALES (est): 4MM **Privately Held**
SIC: 7371 Computer software development

(G-5382)
EASTWYNN THEATRES INC (DH)
11500 Ash St (66211-7804)
PHONE..................................913 213-2000
Michael Duran, *Treasurer*
Michael Durant, *Treasurer*
Lee Champion, *Admin Sec*
EMP: 25
SQ FT: 48,500
SALES (est): 5.8MM
SALES (corp-wide): 7.3MM **Publicly Held**
WEB: www.carmike.com
SIC: 7832 Motion picture theaters, except drive-in
HQ: Carmike Cinemas, Llc
11500 Ash St
Leawood KS 66211
913 213-2000

(G-5383)
EASY CASH ASAP LLC
8900 State Line Rd # 230 (66206-1940)
PHONE..................................913 291-1134
Timothy Robbins, *Mng Member*
Michael Rametta, *Mng Member*
EMP: 38
SALES (est): 790.3K **Privately Held**
SIC: 6141 Personal credit institutions

▲ = Import ▼=Export
◆ =Import/Export

(G-5384)
EHLERS INDUSTRIES INC
Also Called: North Star Gifts
10217 Howe Dr (66206-2418)
PHONE.................................913 381-7884
William A Ehlers, *President*
Susan Ehlers, *Vice Pres*
EMP: 20
SQ FT: 90,000
SALES (est): 2.5MM **Privately Held**
SIC: 5094 Jewelry

(G-5385)
EIGHTEEN CAPITAL GROUP
11615 Rosewood St Ste 100 (66211-2017)
PHONE.................................866 799-5157
EMP: 16
SALES (est): 3.6MM **Privately Held**
SIC: 6799 Investors

(G-5386)
EMERGENT CARE PLUS LLC
4800 W 135th St (66224-8720)
PHONE.................................913 428-8000
Rob Kutch, *Manager*
EMP: 42
SALES (corp-wide): 4.8MM **Privately Held**
SIC: 0782 Lawn care services
PA: Emergent Care Plus, L.L.C.
2741 Ne Mcbaine Dr
Lees Summit MO 64064
816 554-2600

(G-5387)
ENVIRONMENTAL SYSTEMS RESEARCH
8700 State Line Rd (66206-1572)
PHONE.................................913 383-8235
Ed Crane, *Branch Mgr*
EMP: 76
SALES (corp-wide): 1.1B **Privately Held**
SIC: 5045 Computer software
PA: Environmental Systems Research Institute, Inc.
380 New York St
Redlands CA 92373
909 793-2853

(G-5388)
EPAY NORTH AMERICA
3500 College Blvd (66211-1901)
PHONE.................................913 327-4200
Tony Westlake, *CFO*
EMP: 17
SALES (est): 2.1MM **Publicly Held**
SIC: 7389 Personal service agents, brokers & bureaus
PA: Euronet Worldwide, Inc.
3500 College Blvd
Leawood KS 66211

(G-5389)
EURONET WORLDWIDE INC (PA)
3500 College Blvd (66211-1901)
PHONE.................................913 327-4200
Michael J Brown, *Ch of Bd*
Jason C Thompson, *Managing Dir*
Miro I Bergman, *COO*
Jeffrey B Newman, *Exec VP*
Rick Weller, *Exec VP*
EMP: 69
SALES: 2.5B **Publicly Held**
WEB: www.euronetworldwide.com
SIC: 6099 7372 4813 Automated teller machine (ATM) network; business oriented computer software; telephone communications broker

(G-5390)
EXAMFX INC
11161 Overbrook Rd (66211-2299)
PHONE.................................800 586-2253
Rick Wilett, *CEO*
Derek Bridges, *General Mgr*
Roger Bell, *Business Mgr*
Shelley Bell, *Business Mgr*
Paige Johnson, *Business Mgr*
EMP: 40 **EST:** 1996
SQ FT: 12,000
SALES (est): 4.9MM **Privately Held**
WEB: www.examsimulator.com
SIC: 7372 8243 Educational computer software; software training, computer

(G-5391)
EXECUTIVE HILLS MANAGEMENT
5000 College Blvd Ste 400 (66211-1726)
PHONE.................................913 451-9000
Larry Bridges, *President*
EMP: 51 **EST:** 1992
SALES (est): 5.3MM **Privately Held**
SIC: 6531 Real estate agents & managers

(G-5392)
EYE CARE PC
11500 Granada St (66211-1453)
PHONE.................................816 478-4400
EMP: 40
SALES (corp-wide): 21.5MM **Privately Held**
SIC: 8011 Ophthalmologist
PA: Eye Care, P.C.
4801 S Cliff Ave Ste 100
Independence MO 64055
816 478-1230

(G-5393)
EZ2 TECHNOLOGIES INC
6520 W 110th St Ste 205 (66211-1592)
PHONE.................................913 498-8872
Aruna Masireddy, *President*
Vimalnath Munuswamy, *Branch Mgr*
EMP: 35
SALES (corp-wide): 4.9MM **Privately Held**
SIC: 8731 Commercial physical research
PA: Ez2 Technologies, Inc.
12000 Westheimer Rd # 308
Houston TX 77077
913 944-4554

(G-5394)
FAIRWAYS OF IRONHORSE
5241 W 151st Ter (66224-9721)
PHONE.................................913 396-7931
EMP: 62
SALES (est): 75.1K
SALES (corp-wide): 32.7MM **Privately Held**
SIC: 6531 Real estate agents & managers
PA: Midwest Health, Inc
3024 Sw Wanamaker Rd # 300
Topeka KS 66614
785 272-1535

(G-5395)
FARMOBILE INC
4001 W 114th St Ste 300 (66211-2604)
PHONE.................................844 337-2255
Jason Tatge, *CEO*
Jessi Kingsbury, *COO*
Kristen Brown, *Human Res Mgr*
Jon Carenza, *Web Dvlpr*
EMP: 10 **EST:** 2015
SALES (est): 613.5K **Privately Held**
SIC: 7374 Data processing service

(G-5396)
FAVORITE HLTHCARE STAFFING INC
8700 State Line Rd # 330 (66206-1567)
PHONE.................................913 648-6563
Stephanie Render, *Branch Mgr*
EMP: 910
SALES (corp-wide): 447.6MM **Privately Held**
SIC: 7363 Temporary help service
PA: Favorite Healthcare Staffing, Inc.
7255 W 98th Ter Ste 150
Overland Park KS 66212
913 383-9733

(G-5397)
FEDERATED MUTUAL INSURANCE CO
6900 College Blvd Ste 700 (66211-1842)
PHONE.................................913 906-9363
Steve Luzenski, *Manager*
Jim Sodomka, *Director*
EMP: 60
SALES (corp-wide): 1.2B **Privately Held**
SIC: 6331 6321 Fire, marine & casualty insurance; accident & health insurance
PA: Federated Mutual Insurance Company
121 E Park Sq
Owatonna MN 55060
507 455-5200

(G-5398)
FIDELITY INVESTMENTS INSTITUTI
5400 College Blvd (66211-1607)
PHONE.................................913 345-8079
Mark Kistler, *Vice Pres*
Theresa Bishop, *Branch Mgr*
EMP: 22
SALES (corp-wide): 13.2B **Privately Held**
SIC: 6282 Investment advisory service
HQ: Fidelity Investments Institutional Operations Company, Inc.
245 Summer St
Boston MA 02210
617 563-7000

(G-5399)
FIDELITY NATIONAL FINCL INC
Also Called: Chicago Title Insurance Co
6700 College Blvd Ste 300 (66211-1511)
PHONE.................................913 422-5122
Garry Wright, *Branch Mgr*
EMP: 14
SALES (corp-wide): 7.5B **Publicly Held**
SIC: 6541 6099 Title & trust companies; escrow institutions other than real estate
PA: Fidelity National Financial, Inc.
601 Riverside Ave Fl 4
Jacksonville FL 32204
904 854-8100

(G-5400)
FINANCIAL BENEFITS OF KANSAS
11350 Tomahawk Creek Pkwy # 200 (66211-2727)
PHONE.................................913 385-7000
Bob Nonemaker, *President*
EMP: 12
SQ FT: 800
SALES (est): 490K **Privately Held**
WEB: www.finbenkc.com
SIC: 7389 6411 Personal service agents, brokers & bureaus; insurance agents, brokers & service

(G-5401)
FINANCIAL COUNSELORS INC (PA)
5901 College Blvd Ste 110 (66211-1814)
PHONE.................................816 329-1500
Robert Hunter, *President*
Grahm Hunt, *Chairman*
EMP: 13
SALES (est): 4.3MM **Privately Held**
WEB: www.fciadvisors.com
SIC: 6282 Investment advisory service

(G-5402)
FIRST BUSINESS BANK (HQ)
11300 Tomahwk Crk Pkwy # 100 (66211-2700)
PHONE.................................913 681-2223
Pam Berneking, *CEO*
Robert Barker, *Exec VP*
Deborah Eldridge, *Opers Staff*
Angela Jennings, *Opers Staff*
Doug Hoelscher, *CFO*
EMP: 12 **EST:** 1892
SALES (est): 8.9MM
SALES (corp-wide): 109.4MM **Publicly Held**
WEB: www.1stfinbank.com
SIC: 6022 State trust companies accepting deposits, commercial
PA: First Business Financial Services, Inc.
401 Charmany Dr
Madison WI 53719
608 238-8008

(G-5403)
FIRST BUSINESS BANK
11300 Tomahawk Creek Pkwy # 100 (66211-2700)
PHONE.................................913 681-2223
Brandy Strock, *Branch Mgr*
EMP: 10
SALES (corp-wide): 109.4MM **Publicly Held**
SIC: 6022 State commercial banks
HQ: First Business Bank
11300 Tomahwk Crk Pkwy # 100
Leawood KS 66211
913 681-2223

(G-5404)
FIRST STATE BNK OF ST CHARLES
6800 College Blvd (66211-1556)
PHONE.................................913 469-5400
Julie Breault, *Officer*
EMP: 12
SALES (corp-wide): 29.7MM **Privately Held**
SIC: 7381 Guard services
HQ: First State Bank Of St Charles (Inc)
206 N 5th St
Saint Charles MO 63301
636 940-5555

(G-5405)
FISHNET SECURITY
6130 Sprint Pkwy (66211-1156)
PHONE.................................816 701-3315
EMP: 13
SALES (est): 303.2K **Privately Held**
SIC: 7381 Guard services

(G-5406)
FIVE STAR SENIOR LIVING INC
Also Called: Forum At Overland Park
3501 W 95th St (66206-2063)
PHONE.................................913 648-4500
Bruce Mackey, *Branch Mgr*
Gail Schunck, *Exec Dir*
EMP: 63 **Publicly Held**
WEB: www.fivestarqualitycare.com
SIC: 8051 Skilled nursing care facilities
PA: Five Star Senior Living Inc.
400 Centre St
Newton MA 02458

(G-5407)
FOR WOMEN ONLY INC
4550 W 109th St Ste 130 (66211-1354)
PHONE.................................913 541-9495
James Mirabile MD, *President*
EMP: 12
SALES (est): 800K **Privately Held**
WEB: www.forwomenonlyob.com
SIC: 8011 8049 Obstetrician; gynecologist; midwife

(G-5408)
FORESTERS FINANCIAL SVCS INC
6900 College Blvd Ste 800 (66211-1873)
PHONE.................................913 310-0435
David Iannetto, *Branch Mgr*
EMP: 25
SALES (corp-wide): 2.1MM **Privately Held**
SIC: 6282 Investment advisory service
HQ: Foresters Financial Services, Inc.
40 Wall St Fl 10
New York NY 10005
212 858-8000

(G-5409)
FSS PSYCHIATRIC LLC
10711 Barkley St (66211-1161)
P.O. Box 7086, Overland Park (66207-0086)
PHONE.................................913 677-0500
Sandip Sen, *Principal*
Janice Scott, *Med Doctor*
EMP: 11
SALES (est): 574.7K **Privately Held**
SIC: 8049 Clinical psychologist

(G-5410)
GEORGE G KERASOTES CORPORATION
11500 Ash St (66211-7804)
P.O. Box 391, Columbus GA (31902-0391)
PHONE.................................913 213-2000
Beth Kerasotes, *President*
Jeff Cole, *Exec VP*
Marge Kerasotes, *Exec VP*
EMP: 1000
SALES (est): 2.3MM
SALES (corp-wide): 7.3MM **Publicly Held**
SIC: 7832 Exhibitors, itinerant: motion picture
HQ: Carmike Cinemas, Llc
11500 Ash St
Leawood KS 66211
913 213-2000

(G-5411)
GEORGIA KENWORTH INC (HQ)
Also Called: Mhc Kenworth - Savannah
11120 Tomahawk Creek Pkwy
(66211-2695)
PHONE..................................816 483-6444
Timothy R Murphy, *CEO*
Lee Sikes, *Principal*
Jeffrey W Johnson, *CFO*
EMP: 30
SQ FT: 17,000
SALES (est): 49.8MM
SALES (corp-wide): 1B **Privately Held**
WEB: www.kenworthofsavannah.com
SIC: 5511 5531 7538 7532 Trucks, tractors & trailers: new & used; truck equipment & parts; general automotive repair shops; truck painting & lettering
PA: Murphy-Hoffman Company
11120 Tomahawk Creek Pkwy
Leawood KS 66211
816 483-6444

(G-5412)
GKC MICHIGAN THEATRES INC
11500 Ash St (66211-7804)
P.O. Box 391, Columbus GA (31902-0391)
PHONE..................................913 213-2000
George G Kerasotes, *Ch of Bd*
Beth Kerasotes, *President*
Roger Ford, *Exec VP*
Ed Schuerman, *Exec VP*
Marge Kerasotes, *Vice Pres*
EMP: 268
SQ FT: 5,329
SALES (est): 1.8MM
SALES (corp-wide): 7.3MM **Publicly Held**
SIC: 7832 Motion picture theaters, except drive-in
HQ: Carmike Cinemas, Llc
11500 Ash St
Leawood KS 66211
913 213-2000

(G-5413)
GLOBAL CONNECTIONS INC (PA)
Also Called: Global Vacations
5360 College Blvd Ste 200 (66211-1641)
PHONE..................................913 498-0960
Tom Lyons, *President*
Frank Zawojski, *COO*
Dave Dawson, *Vice Pres*
Melanie Gring, *Vice Pres*
Cathy Wunder, *Vice Pres*
EMP: 43
SQ FT: 6,500
SALES (est): 31.3MM **Privately Held**
WEB: www.networkdirect.com
SIC: 4724 Tourist agency arranging transport, lodging & car rental

(G-5414)
GLOBAL SERVICES INC
Also Called: Personal Savings Network
5360 College Blvd Ste 200 (66211-1641)
PHONE..................................913 451-0960
Bill Clayton, *President*
Norman Jacobs, *Treasurer*
EMP: 75
SQ FT: 6,500
SALES: 7.5MM **Privately Held**
SIC: 8699 Travel club

(G-5415)
GOODY TICKETS LLC
7007 College Blvd Ste 100 (66211-2446)
PHONE..................................913 231-2674
Jeff Goodman, *President*
Heather Goodman, *Vice Pres*
Michael Goodman, *Vice Pres*
Mike Goodman, *Vice Pres*
Zoe Wright, *Admin Asst*
EMP: 12 **EST:** 2011
SALES: 20MM **Privately Held**
SIC: 7999 Ticket sales office for sporting events, contract

(G-5416)
GRACE GRDNS ASSISTD LVNG FCLTY
5201 W 143rd St (66224-9562)
PHONE..................................913 685-4800
Mark O'Hara, *Principal*
EMP: 19
SALES (est): 2.7MM **Privately Held**
SIC: 8051 Skilled nursing care facilities

(G-5417)
GRAIN CRAFT INC
4400 W 109th St Ste 200 (66211-1319)
PHONE..................................913 890-6300
Paul Myers, *Controller*
EMP: 367
SALES (corp-wide): 288.5MM **Privately Held**
SIC: 2041 Grain mills (except rice)
PA: Grain Craft, Inc.
201 W Main St Ste 203
Chattanooga TN 37408
423 265-2313

(G-5418)
HALLBROOK COUNTRY CLUB
11200 Overbrook Rd (66211-2957)
P.O. Box 7206, Shawnee Mission (66207-0206)
PHONE..................................913 345-9292
Mike Glazier, *President*
Bill Martin, *General Mgr*
Mike Fleming, *Vice Pres*
Karen Whallon, *Controller*
Karen Whalon, *Controller*
EMP: 70
SALES: 9.2MM **Privately Held**
WEB: www.hallbrookcc.org
SIC: 7997 Country club, membership

(G-5419)
HARRIS BMO BANK NATIONAL ASSN
Also Called: Bmo Harris Bank
8840 State Line Rd (66206-1553)
PHONE..................................913 693-1600
Sondra Weber, *Branch Mgr*
EMP: 11
SALES (corp-wide): 17.7B **Privately Held**
WEB: www.uhb-fl.com
SIC: 6022 State trust companies accepting deposits, commercial
HQ: Harris Bmo Bank National Association
111 W Monroe St Ste 1200
Chicago IL 60603
312 461-2323

(G-5420)
HEAD & NECK SURGERY KANS CY PA
5370 College Blvd Ste 100 (66211-1891)
PHONE..................................913 599-4800
Robert F Thompson, *President*
Sherry Scanlon, *Office Mgr*
Steven Ellis, *Med Doctor*
Robert Thompson, *Med Doctor*
EMP: 20
SALES (est): 3MM **Privately Held**
SIC: 8011 5999 Surgeon; hearing aids

(G-5421)
HEAD & NECK SURGICAL ASSOC
5701 W 119th St Ste 425 (66209-3755)
PHONE..................................913 663-5100
Mark Maslan, *President*
Thomas P Eyen, *Otolaryngology*
EMP: 15
SQ FT: 2,900
SALES (est): 3.1MM **Privately Held**
SIC: 8011 Ears, nose & throat specialist: physician/surgeon

(G-5422)
HEALTH AND BENEFIT SYSTEMS LLC
Also Called: Benefit Comm Insourcing
6363 College Blvd Ste 500 (66211-1887)
PHONE..................................913 642-1666
Don Morris, *President*
Ken Sigman, *President*
Jeanne Buchanan, *QC Mgr*
Sam Wilkerson, *QC Mgr*
Matthew Metzinger, *Engineer*
EMP: 25
SQ FT: 2,900
SALES (est): 8.1MM **Privately Held**
WEB: www.healthandbenefits.com
SIC: 6411 6321 Insurance agents; accident & health insurance

(G-5423)
HEALTHSTAFF DENTAL LLC
14109 Overbrook Rd Ste E (66224-4519)
PHONE..................................913 402-4334
Toni Erickson,
John Haas,
Mark Haas,
EMP: 99 **EST:** 2000
SALES: 750K **Privately Held**
WEB: www.healthstaffkc.com
SIC: 7361 Placement agencies

(G-5424)
HEARTLAND CSTMER SOLUTIONS LLC (DH)
14206 Overbrook Rd (66224-4536)
PHONE..................................913 685-8855
Patrick J Cocherl Jr, *President*
EMP: 118
SALES (est): 2.4MM **Privately Held**
SIC: 7699 7379 Camera repair shop; computer related maintenance services
HQ: Panasonic Corporation Of North America
2 Riverfront Plz Ste 200
Newark NJ 07102
201 348-7000

(G-5425)
HEARTLAND HOSPICE SERVICES LLC
Also Called: Heartland HM Hlth Care Hospice
4601 College Blvd Ste 160 (66211-1678)
PHONE..................................913 362-0044
Jason Lancaster, *Branch Mgr*
EMP: 10
SALES (corp-wide): 8.2B **Privately Held**
SIC: 8082 Home health care services
HQ: Heartland Hospice Services, Llc
333 N Summit St
Toledo OH 43604

(G-5426)
HEARTLAND MULTIPLE LI
11150 Overbrook Rd # 125 (66211-2237)
PHONE..................................913 661-1600
Diane Ruggiero, *CEO*
EMP: 18
SQ FT: 9,000
SALES (est): 2.1MM **Privately Held**
WEB: www.heartlandmlsweb.com
SIC: 6531 Real estate brokers & agents

(G-5427)
HEARTLAND SERVICES INC
14212 Overbrook Rd (66224-4536)
PHONE..................................913 685-8855
Patrick Cocheral, *CEO*
Deveney Kate, *Administration*
EMP: 29
SALES (corp-wide): 7.7MM **Privately Held**
SIC: 7629 Business machine repair, electric
PA: Heartland Services, Inc.
14206 Overbrook Rd
Leawood KS 66224
913 685-8855

(G-5428)
HEARTLAND SERVICES INC (PA)
14206 Overbrook Rd (66224-4536)
PHONE..................................913 685-8855
Patrick J Cocherl Jr, *President*
Shannon McHone, *Vice Pres*
Brian Deveney, *Manager*
Gary Weimar, *Info Tech Mgr*
Reca Hanna, *Technology*
▲ **EMP:** 45
SQ FT: 7,000
SALES (est): 7.7MM **Privately Held**
WEB: www.heartlandsi.com
SIC: 7629 Business machine repair, electric

(G-5429)
HOEFER WYSOCKI ARCHITECTS LLC (PA)
11460 Tomahawk Creek Pkwy
(66211-7810)
PHONE..................................913 307-3700
Mitchell R Hoefer, *CEO*
Robert Welker, *General Mgr*
Tim Devine, *Vice Pres*
Peter O'Connor, *Vice Pres*
Christopher Staus, *Vice Pres*
EMP: 100
SQ FT: 24,500
SALES: 17MM **Privately Held**
WEB: www.hwa.net
SIC: 8712 Architectural engineering

(G-5430)
HOKANSON LEHMAN & STEVENS
3400 College Blvd Ste 100 (66211-1940)
PHONE..................................913 338-2525
David F Hokanson, *President*
Jeanne Hokanson, *Vice Pres*
EMP: 18
SALES (est): 2.2MM **Privately Held**
SIC: 6211 6411 Security brokers & dealers; insurance information & consulting services

(G-5431)
HOLMAN HANSEN AND COLVILE PC (PA)
6900 College Blvd Ste 700 (66211-1842)
P.O. Box 7490, Overland Park (66207-0490)
PHONE..................................913 648-7272
Eric L Hansen, *President*
Linda Higdon, *Admin Sec*
Joseph Y Holman,
Robert J Rayburn III,
EMP: 20
SALES (est): 2.1MM **Privately Held**
WEB: www.hhc-law.com
SIC: 8111 Legal services

(G-5432)
HOWMEDICA OSTEONICS CORP
6600 College Blvd Ste 100 (66211-1610)
PHONE..................................913 491-3505
Joe Litizzette, *Branch Mgr*
EMP: 35
SALES (corp-wide): 13.6B **Publicly Held**
SIC: 5047 Orthopedic equipment & supplies; artificial limbs
HQ: Howmedica Osteonics Corp.
325 Corporate Dr
Mahwah NJ 07430
201 831-5000

(G-5433)
ICG INC
11401 Linden St (66211-2004)
P.O. Box 7609, Shawnee Mission (66207-0609)
PHONE..................................913 461-8759
Rasool Ahmed, *President*
EMP: 40 **EST:** 2001
SALES: 1.8MM **Privately Held**
SIC: 7349 1799 7389 Building maintenance services; parking lot maintenance;

(G-5434)
III INVESTMENTS INC (PA)
11313 El Monte St (66211-1744)
PHONE..................................913 262-6500
Robert W Spachman, *President*
Perry Puccetti, *Vice Pres*
Bonnie Brown, *Admin Sec*
EMP: 80
SQ FT: 8,000
SALES (est): 3.5MM **Privately Held**
WEB: www.triple-i.net
SIC: 8742 Management consulting services

(G-5435)
IN2ITIVE BUS SOLUTIONS LLC
6330 Sprint Pkwy Ste 425 (66211-1194)
PHONE..................................913 344-7002
Tracey Erbert, *President*
Nancy Bradley, *Manager*
Becky Slone, *Manager*
Elsa Stilwell, *Manager*
Mary Watson, *Manager*
EMP: 40
SQ FT: 60,019
SALES: 3.6MM **Privately Held**
SIC: 8721 Billing & bookkeeping service

(G-5436)
INFINITY INSUR SOLUTIONS LLC
10707 Barkley St Ste B (66211-1166)
PHONE..................................913 338-3200
EMP: 44
SALES (est): 2.4MM
SALES (corp-wide): 12.6MM **Privately Held**
SIC: 8713 6211 Surveying Services Security Broker/Dealer
HQ: Patriot Underwriters, Inc.
401 E Las Olas Blvd
Fort Lauderdale FL 33301
954 670-2900

(G-5437)
INFORMTION CMMUNICATIONS GROUP
4701 College Blvd Ste 110 (66211-1608)
PHONE..................................913 469-6767
Darlene Campbell, *President*
Kathy Stratman, *Office Mgr*
EMP: 28
SQ FT: 2,800
SALES (est): 2.1MM **Privately Held**
WEB: www.metromessageservices.com
SIC: 7389 4812 Telephone services; courier or messenger service; radio telephone communication; paging services

(G-5438)
INSTALLATION AND SVC TECH INC
Also Called: Ist
8340 Mission Rd Ste B4 (66206-1362)
PHONE..................................913 652-7000
Jacob Horwitz, *President*
Jeremy Felton, *Regional Mgr*
Carlos Fernandez, *Regional Mgr*
Tyler Parlet, *Regional Mgr*
Rob Stevens, *Regional Mgr*
EMP: 150
SALES (est): 16.1MM **Privately Held**
SIC: 7378 Computer maintenance & repair

(G-5439)
INTERIM HEALTHCARE KANSAS CITY
Also Called: Interim Health Care Services
10977 Granada Ln Ste 205 (66211-1433)
PHONE..................................913 381-3100
Jerry M Hess, *President*
Charles L Grewell, *General Mgr*
EMP: 50
SQ FT: 2,300
SALES (est): 3.1MM **Privately Held**
SIC: 7363 8082 Temporary help service; home health care services

(G-5440)
IOWA KENWORTH INC (HQ)
11120 Tomahawk Creek Pkwy (66211-2695)
PHONE..................................816 483-6444
Timothy Murphy, *CEO*
Mike Murphy, *President*
Jeff Johnson, *CFO*
EMP: 24
SQ FT: 9,000
SALES (est): 33.4MM
SALES (corp-wide): 1B **Privately Held**
SIC: 5012 7539 Trucks, commercial; trucks, noncommercial; automotive repair shops
PA: Murphy-Hoffman Company
11120 Tomahawk Creek Pkwy
Leawood KS 66211
816 483-6444

(G-5441)
JAY E SUDDRETH & ASSOCIATES
2127 W 116th St (66211-2954)
PHONE..................................913 451-5820
Jay E Suddreth, *President*
Ellen Suddreth, *Admin Sec*
EMP: 22 **EST:** 1976
SQ FT: 1,200
SALES (est): 1MM **Privately Held**
WEB: www.suddrethreporting.com
SIC: 7338 Court reporting service

(G-5442)
JEWISH HERITAGE FNDTN GREATER
5801 W 115th St Ste 104 (66211-1800)
PHONE..................................913 981-8866
Marylin Berenbom, *President*
Ellen K Kort, *Exec Dir*
EMP: 27
SALES (est): 3.3MM **Privately Held**
WEB: www.jhf-kc.org
SIC: 8733 Noncommercial research organizations

(G-5443)
JOHN KNOX VILLAGE
Also Called: John Knox Village HM Hlth Agcy
6600 College Blvd Ste 300 (66211-1869)
PHONE..................................913 403-8343
Jill Guenther, *Branch Mgr*
EMP: 15
SALES (corp-wide): 69MM **Privately Held**
SIC: 8051 8082 Convalescent home with continuous nursing care; home health care services
PA: John Knox Village
400 Nw Murray Rd Ofc
Lees Summit MO 64081

(G-5444)
KANSAS CITY ORTHOPED
Also Called: Dixon Dively Orthopedics
3651 College Blvd Ste 210 (66211-1910)
PHONE..................................913 338-4100
Charles Rhoades MD, *President*
EMP: 140
SALES (est): 5.3MM **Privately Held**
SIC: 8062 General medical & surgical hospitals

(G-5445)
KANSAS CITY REGIONAL
11150 Overbrook Rd # 100 (66211-2235)
PHONE..................................913 661-1600
Lee McClelland, *President*
Alison Trevor, *Education*
Lynn McGee,
Angela Sherman,
EMP: 13
SALES: 3.9MM **Privately Held**
SIC: 8699 Membership organizations

(G-5446)
KC IRRIGATION SPECIALIST
3315 W 92nd St (66206-1763)
PHONE..................................913 406-0670
Jeff Pankewich, *General Mgr*
Gregory Jones, *Principal*
EMP: 12
SALES (est): 912.5K **Privately Held**
SIC: 4971 Irrigation systems

(G-5447)
KDC CONSTRUCTION INC
12205 Buena Vista St (66209-1510)
PHONE..................................913 677-1920
Janene Ervin, *President*
Frank Perry, *Vice Pres*
Christopher Brown, *Project Mgr*
Ryan Ferris, *Manager*
Cheryl Perry, *Officer*
EMP: 10
SALES (est): 3.4MM **Privately Held**
WEB: www.kawdevelopment.com
SIC: 1542 1522 6552 Commercial & office building, new construction; residential construction; subdividers & developers

(G-5448)
KDI OPERATING COMPANY LLC (PA)
Also Called: Kansas Dairy Ingredients
11050 Roe Ave Ste 211 (66211-1200)
PHONE..................................620 453-1034
EMP: 20
SALES (est): 40.7MM **Privately Held**
SIC: 5143 Dairy products, except dried or canned

(G-5449)
KEYBANK REAL ESTATE
11501 Outlook St (66211-1811)
PHONE..................................216 813-4756
Clay Sublett, *Principal*
Craig Younggren, *Senior VP*
Diane C Haislip, *Vice Pres*
Andrew Lindenman, *Vice Pres*
Ken Schroeder, *Vice Pres*
EMP: 14
SALES (est): 1.4MM **Privately Held**
SIC: 6531 Real estate brokers & agents

(G-5450)
KING LOUIE AMERICA LC (PA)
Also Called: King Louie
6740 W 121st St Ste 100 (66209-2042)
PHONE..................................913 338-5212
T Fisher, *Controller*
McMillan John, *VP Sales*
Tanya Fisher, *Cust Svc Dir*
Michael Lerner, *Mng Member*
EMP: 13
SALES (est): 1.9MM **Privately Held**
SIC: 2211 Apparel & outerwear fabrics, cotton

(G-5451)
KNOPKE COMPANY LLC
Also Called: Knopke Contracting Services
2804 W 132nd St (66209-1675)
PHONE..................................816 231-1001
Mark Knopke, *Vice Pres*
Don Knopke, *Mng Member*
David Knopke, *Mng Member*
Matt Knopke, *Mng Member*
EMP: 30
SQ FT: 17,000
SALES: 9MM **Privately Held**
SIC: 1711 Mechanical contractor

(G-5452)
KOEHLER BORTNICK TEAM LLC
Also Called: Reece and Nchls The Koehlr BRT
5000 W 136th (66209)
PHONE..................................913 239-2069
Kathy Koehler, *President*
Kristi Soligo, *COO*
Monte Summers, *Sales Staff*
Fran Keal, *Sales Associate*
Rachel Ellibee, *Office Mgr*
EMP: 25
SALES (est): 7.6MM **Privately Held**
WEB: www.koehlerbortnick.com
SIC: 6361 Real estate title insurance

(G-5453)
LEAWOOD FAMILY CARE PA
11301 Ash St (66211-1643)
PHONE..................................913 338-4515
John Horton, *Principal*
Evelyn Nwaomah, *Administration*
EMP: 15
SALES (est): 3MM **Privately Held**
SIC: 8011 Ophthalmologist

(G-5454)
LEAWOOD PEDIATRICS LLC
5401 College Blvd Ste 101 (66211-1617)
PHONE..................................913 825-3627
Mary Hamm,
EMP: 15 **EST:** 2011
SALES (est): 2.1MM **Privately Held**
SIC: 8011 Pediatrician

(G-5455)
LEE & ASSOCIATES KANSAS CY LLC
8700 State Line Rd (66206-1572)
PHONE..................................913 890-2000
Eric Alfrey, *Manager*
Jason Kraft, *Manager*
Connie Smith, *Office Admin*
Nathan Anderson, *Admin Mgr*
David Armstrong, *Exec Dir*
EMP: 12
SALES (est): 755.4K **Privately Held**
SIC: 6531 Real estate agent, commercial
PA: Lee & Associates Inc.
3200 E Camelback Rd # 100
Phoenix AZ 85018

(G-5456)
LEGACY FINANCIAL STRATEGY LLC
11300 Tomahawk Creek Pkwy # 190 (66211-2693)
PHONE..................................913 403-0600
Gretchen Vosburgh, *COO*
Lynn Lutz, *Marketing Staff*
Nancy Clendening, *Office Mgr*
Michael Lutz, *Mng Member*
Ruth Patterson, *Manager*
EMP: 11
SALES (est): 1.9MM **Privately Held**
SIC: 6282 Investment advice

(G-5457)
LG ELCTRNICS MBILECOMM USA INC
6363 College Blvd Ste 220 (66211-1883)
PHONE..................................913 234-3701
Robert Stoddart, *Principal*
Soomin Schmeltz, *Software Dev*
EMP: 50 **Privately Held**
SIC: 5065 3663 Mobile telephone equipment; radio & TV communications equipment
HQ: Lg Electronics Mobilecomm U.S.A., Inc.
1000 Sylvan Ave
Englewood Cliffs NJ 07632

(G-5458)
LIVESTOCK MARKETING ASSN (PA)
Also Called: Nationwide
11501 Outlook St Ste 250 (66211-1807)
PHONE..................................816 891-0502
Dan Harris, *President*
Ivan Harder Jr, *President*
Lindsay G Runft, *Marketing Staff*
Lindsay Runft, *Marketing Staff*
Nora Lierz, *Administration*
EMP: 31
SALES: 2.4MM **Privately Held**
SIC: 6399 Deposit insurance

(G-5459)
LORD OF LIFE LUTHERAN CHURCH
Also Called: Lord of Life Pre School
3105 W 135th St (66224-7503)
PHONE..................................913 681-5167
Bert Gardwood, *Pastor*
EMP: 25
SALES (est): 614.7K **Privately Held**
WEB: www.lordlife.com
SIC: 8661 8351 Lutheran Church; preschool center

(G-5460)
LPL FINANCIAL
6800 College Blvd Ste 200 (66211-1534)
PHONE..................................913 345-2908
Kara Walters, *Accounts Mgr*
Brett Lange, *Accounts Exec*
Don Clark, *Accounts Exec*
Stephanie Gantt, *Advisor*
Sorouch Haddad, *Advisor*
EMP: 11
SALES (est): 604.5K **Privately Held**
SIC: 8742 Financial consultant

(G-5461)
LYNNE M SCHOPPER DDS PA
Also Called: Schopper, Lynne M
11313 Ash St (66211-1643)
PHONE..................................913 451-2929
Lynne Schopper DDS, *President*
EMP: 10
SALES (est): 626.2K **Privately Held**
SIC: 8021 Dentists' office

(G-5462)
MADDEN-MCFARLAND INTERIORS LTD (PA)
Also Called: International Design Guild
1903 W 135th St (66224-7606)
PHONE..................................913 681-2821
Bernie Madden, *CEO*
Patrick Madden, *President*
Mary Madden Bryson, *Vice Pres*
Paul Madden, *Opers Staff*
Jacqueline A Madden, *Treasurer*
EMP: 25 **EST:** 1920
SQ FT: 5,500
SALES (est): 6MM **Privately Held**
WEB: www.maddenmcfarland.com
SIC: 5713 5714 7389 Floor covering stores; draperies; interior design services

(G-5463)
MAISON DE NAISSANCE FOUNDATION
5000 W 134th St (66209-7806)
PHONE..................................913 402-6800
Heather Ehlert, *Exec Dir*
EMP: 12
SALES: 475K **Privately Held**
SIC: 8322 Individual & family services

(G-5464)
MANILDRA MILLING CORPORATION (DH)
4501 College Blvd Ste 310 (66211-2303)
PHONE..................................913 362-0777
Neal Bassi, *President*
Gerry Degnan, *President*
John T Honan, *Chairman*
Keval Bassi, *Vice Pres*
Paul Mall, *Treasurer*
◆ **EMP**: 11
SQ FT: 7,000
SALES (est): 20.5MM **Privately Held**
WEB: www.manildrausa.com
SIC: 5149 Groceries & related products
HQ: Honan Holdings U.S.A., Inc.
4501 College Blvd Ste 310
Leawood KS 66211
913 362-0777

(G-5465)
MARINER LLC (PA)
Also Called: Mariner Wealth Advisors
5700 W 112th St Ste 200 (66211-1759)
PHONE..................................913 647-9700
Marty Bichknell, *CEO*
Rosario Ruffino, *Managing Prtnr*
Jeff Couch, *Exec VP*
Kevin W Corbett, *Senior VP*
Chad Hamilton, *Vice Pres*
EMP: 41
SALES (est): 19.5MM **Privately Held**
SIC: 6282 Investment advisory service

(G-5466)
MARINO & ASSOCIATES INC
11221 Roe Ave (66211-1922)
PHONE..................................816 478-1122
Jasper Marino, *President*
Jennifer Marino, *Treasurer*
Leslie Zornes, *Admin Sec*
EMP: 12
SQ FT: 3,600
SALES: 1.3MM **Privately Held**
SIC: 6411 Insurance brokers

(G-5467)
MARSH & MCLENNAN AGENCY LLC
4300 W 133rd St (66209-3306)
PHONE..................................913 451-3900
EMP: 97
SALES (corp-wide): 14.9B **Publicly Held**
SIC: 6411 Insurance brokers
HQ: Marsh & Mclennan Agency Llc
360 Hamilton Ave Ste 930
White Plains NY 10601

(G-5468)
MASSMAN CONSTRUCTION CO (PA)
4400 W 109th St Ste 300 (66211-1319)
PHONE..................................913 291-2600
H J Massman IV, *President*
Henry Massman IV, *Principal*
Robert Roble, *Business Mgr*
Joseph T Kopp, *Vice Pres*
William G Praderio, *Vice Pres*
▲ **EMP**: 20 **EST**: 1908
SQ FT: 11,600
SALES (est): 119.3MM **Privately Held**
WEB: www.massman.net
SIC: 1629 1622 Dam construction; bridge construction

(G-5469)
MBB INC
Also Called: MBB Advertising
5250 W 116th Pl Ste 200 (66211-7826)
PHONE..................................816 531-1992
Jim Brown, *CEO*
John Muller, *President*
Garrett Street, *Vice Pres*
Danielle Larson, *Buyer*
Denny Meier, *CFO*
EMP: 45
SALES: 12.5MM **Privately Held**
SIC: 7311 7336 Advertising agencies; art design services

(G-5470)
MEARA WELCH BROWNE PC
2020 W 89th St Ste 300 (66206-1947)
PHONE..................................816 561-1400
John W Meara, *President*
Steve Brown, *Principal*
Julie Welch, *Vice Pres*
EMP: 20
SALES (est): 9.6K **Privately Held**
WEB: www.meara.com
SIC: 8721 Certified public accountant

(G-5471)
MEDICAL EQP SOLUTIONS INC
14116 Fontana St (66224-1155)
PHONE..................................816 241-3334
Michael Carr, *Branch Mgr*
EMP: 18 **Privately Held**
SIC: 5047 Medical & hospital equipment
PA: Medical Equipment Solutions, Inc.
1220 Vernon St
North Kansas City MO 64116

(G-5472)
MEGAFORCE LLC (PA)
4200 W 115th St Ste 300 (66211-2728)
PHONE..................................913 402-0800
Robert Thayer, *President*
Lisa Elling-White, *Supervisor*
Rob Thayer,
EMP: 75
SALES (est): 5.6MM **Privately Held**
WEB: www.megaforceusa.com
SIC: 7374 Data processing service

(G-5473)
MENUFYCOM LLC (PA)
6900 College Blvd Ste 500 (66211-1889)
PHONE..................................913 738-9399
Sharmil Desai, *CEO*
Tony Chang, *Opers Staff*
Ashishh Desai, *Accounts Exec*
EMP: 30 **EST**: 2009
SALES (est): 8.8MM **Privately Held**
SIC: 7379 8742 ; sales (including sales management) consultant

(G-5474)
MERCHANTS AUTOMOTIVE GROUP INC
6300 College Blvd (66211-1506)
PHONE..................................913 901-9900
Chris Brock, *Branch Mgr*
EMP: 24
SALES (corp-wide): 153.3MM **Privately Held**
SIC: 7515 5521 Passenger car leasing; automobiles, used cars only
PA: Merchants Automotive Group, Inc.
14 Central Park Dr Fl 1
Hooksett NH 03106
603 669-4100

(G-5475)
MERRILL LYNCH PIERCE FENNER
3401 College Blvd (66211-1912)
P.O. Box 7901, Overland Park (66207-0901)
PHONE..................................913 906-5200
Joe Lowery, *Manager*
David Klinginsmith, *Agent*
Joe Gilgus, *Advisor*
Jared Gudenkauf, *Advisor*
Donna Helm, *Advisor*
EMP: 60
SALES (corp-wide): 110.5B **Publicly Held**
WEB: www.merlyn.com
SIC: 6211 Security brokers & dealers
HQ: Merrill Lynch, Pierce, Fenner & Smith Incorporated
111 8th Ave
New York NY 10011
800 637-7455

(G-5476)
MERSOFT CORPORATION
7007 College Blvd Ste 450 (66211-2440)
PHONE..................................913 871-6200
Ronald E Sloop, *President*
T Isaacs, *President*
Jeff Smith, *Vice Pres*
Jeff Weiner, *Vice Pres*
Eric Groves, *Engineer*
EMP: 27
SQ FT: 4,600
SALES: 1.8MM **Privately Held**
SIC: 7372 7373 Business oriented computer software; computer integrated systems design

(G-5477)
MHC TRUCK LEASING INC (HQ)
11120 Tomahawk Creek Pkwy (66211-2695)
PHONE..................................816 483-0604
David Stroop, *President*
David Douglas, *Vice Pres*
Scott Jones, *Controller*
Kelly Kendall, *Sales Staff*
Aaron Ledesma, *Sales Staff*
EMP: 17
SQ FT: 10,000
SALES (est): 20.3MM
SALES (corp-wide): 1B **Privately Held**
SIC: 7513 Truck leasing, without drivers
PA: Murphy-Hoffman Company
11120 Tomahawk Creek Pkwy
Leawood KS 66211
816 483-6444

(G-5478)
MICHAEL J RANDALL
Also Called: Cornerstone Endodontics
4601 W 109th St Ste 250 (66211-1314)
PHONE..................................913 498-3636
Michael J Randall, *Partner*
Jake McGuire, *Partner*
James Randall, *Fmly & Gen Dent*
EMP: 10 **EST**: 2002
SALES (est): 991.6K **Privately Held**
WEB: www.cornerstoneendodontics.com
SIC: 8021 Endodontist

(G-5479)
MID AMERICA UROLOGY PC (PA)
Also Called: Uriolgist Center of Olthe
6740 W 121st St Ste 300 (66209-2017)
PHONE..................................913 948-8365
Keith Abercrombie, *President*
Bradley Connett, *Principal*
EMP: 10
SALES (est): 1.5MM **Privately Held**
WEB: www.mamcurology.com
SIC: 8011 Urologist

(G-5480)
MID-AMRCA KDNY STN ASSCTN LLC
Also Called: Maksa
10983 Granada Ln 110 (66211-1401)
P.O. Box 803341, Kansas City MO (64180-0001)
PHONE..................................913 766-1860
Shawn Woolery, *General Mgr*
Frank Albani MD,
Robert Bieber MD,
Calvin Lentz MD,
EMP: 13
SALES (est): 1.2MM **Privately Held**
SIC: 8011 Internal medicine, physician/surgeon

(G-5481)
MIDWEST ANESTHESIA ASSOC PA
6720 W 121st St 103 (66209-2002)
PHONE..................................913 642-4900
Don Rickter MD, *President*
John Robertson, *Corp Secy*
EMP: 40
SALES: 11MM **Privately Held**
SIC: 8011 Anesthesiologist

(G-5482)
MIDWEST BIOSCIENCE RES PK LLC
Also Called: MIDWEST TRUST
5901 College Blvd Ste 100 (66211-1834)
PHONE..................................913 319-0300
Bradley Bergman, *CEO*
Brad Beets, *Senior VP*
Bryan Allee, *Vice Pres*
Shellie Billau, *Vice Pres*
Dana Blackmon, *Vice Pres*
EMP: 24
SALES: 2.6K **Privately Held**
SIC: 8111 8741 6798 General practice attorney, lawyer; management services; real estate investment trusts

(G-5483)
MIDWEST DYNAMICS INC (PA)
Also Called: Midas Auto Repair
10342 Dateline (66206)
PHONE..................................913 383-9320
Jim Smith, *President*
EMP: 15
SQ FT: 5,000
SALES (est): 2.6MM **Privately Held**
WEB: www.midwestdynamics.com
SIC: 7533 7539 7549 Muffler shop, sale or repair & installation; brake repair, automotive; front end repair, automotive; automotive maintenance services

(G-5484)
MIDWEST HEALTH SERVICES INC
12720 State Line Rd (66209-1619)
PHONE..................................913 663-3351
Jackie Reed, *Director*
EMP: 20
SALES (corp-wide): 32.7MM **Privately Held**
SIC: 8051 Skilled nursing care facilities
PA: Midwest Health, Inc
3024 Sw Wanamaker Rd # 300
Topeka KS 66614
785 272-1535

(G-5485)
MILLER GROUP
6363 College Blvd Ste 400 (66211-1882)
PHONE..................................816 333-3000
Dale Gebauer, *Vice Pres*
Ben Williams, *Vice Pres*
Gaye Golden, *Accounts Mgr*
Lynda Williamson, *Accounts Mgr*
Susan Stasi, *Accounts Exec*
EMP: 15 **EST**: 2011
SALES (est): 1MM **Privately Held**
SIC: 8742 Financial consultant

(G-5486)
MISSION ROAD ANIMAL CLINIC
9420 Mission Rd (66206-2042)
PHONE..................................913 649-0552
Ken Winters, *Owner*
Gib Benschoter, *Co-Owner*
Jenny Tate,
EMP: 10
SALES (est): 333.1K **Privately Held**
SIC: 0742 Animal hospital services, pets & other animal specialties

(G-5487)
MISSOURI HOSPICE HOLDINGS LLC
Also Called: Continua Hospice
13002 State Line Rd (66209-1756)
PHONE..................................913 905-0255
Bobbi Blankenship, *Branch Mgr*
EMP: 16
SALES (corp-wide): 660.1K **Privately Held**
SIC: 8082 Home health care services
PA: Missouri Hospice Holdings, Llc
9001 Stateline Rd
Kansas City MO 64114
816 444-2273

(G-5488)
MISSOURI LIVESTOCK MKTG ASSN (PA)
11501 Outlook St 250 (66211-1811)
PHONE..................................816 891-0502
Leon Caselman, *President*
EMP: 35
SALES: 2.9MM **Privately Held**
SIC: 6411 8611 Insurance agents; trade associations

(G-5489)
MITCHELL CAPITAL MANAGEMENT CO
11460 Tomahawk Creek Pkwy (66211-7810)
PHONE..................................913 428-3222

▲ = Import ▼=Export
◆ =Import/Export

Kenneth Green, *President*
Frederick Mitchell, *President*
Rich Jones, *Vice Pres*
Christen Dusselier, *Portfolio Mgr*
Craig Beach, *Director*
EMP: 10
SQ FT: 2,000
SALES (est): 1.3MM **Privately Held**
WEB: www.mitchcap.com
SIC: 6282 Investment advisory service

(G-5490)
MOBILE HEALTH CLINICS LLC
6227 W 126th Ter (66209-2530)
PHONE..................................913 383-0991
Conrad Francis Dobler, *President*
Stephen Dobler, *Vice Pres*
EMP: 62
SALES: 2.5MM **Privately Held**
SIC: 7363 6411 Modeling service; medical insurance claim processing, contract or fee basis

(G-5491)
MORGAN STANLEY
11161 Overbrook Rd # 225 (66211-2203)
PHONE..................................913 402-5200
Phil Hall, *Manager*
EMP: 10
SALES (corp-wide): 50.1B **Publicly Held**
SIC: 6211 Security brokers & dealers
PA: Morgan Stanley
1585 Broadway
New York NY 10036
212 761-4000

(G-5492)
MURPHY-HOFFMAN COMPANY (PA)
11120 Tomahawk Creek Pkwy (66211-2695)
PHONE..................................816 483-6444
Timothy R Murphy, *President*
Clint Rogers, *General Mgr*
Matt McGinley, *District Mgr*
Brandon Watkins, *District Mgr*
Joseph Frey, *Business Mgr*
EMP: 50
SQ FT: 9,000
SALES (est): 1B **Privately Held**
SIC: 5511 7513 7538 6159 Automobiles, new & used; truck leasing, without drivers; general truck repair; truck finance leasing

(G-5493)
MUVE HEALTH LLC
11221 Roe Ave Ste 210 (66211-1878)
PHONE..................................303 862-9215
P Marshall Maran, *CEO*
Elaine Purvis, *COO*
EMP: 10 **EST:** 2015
SALES (est): 109K **Privately Held**
SIC: 8082 Home health care services

(G-5494)
MWH GLOBAL INC
11835 Roe Ave Ste 242 (66211-2607)
PHONE..................................913 383-2086
EMP: 10
SALES (corp-wide): 3.2B **Privately Held**
WEB: www.mwh-inc.com
SIC: 8711 Engineering services
HQ: Mwh Global, Inc.
370 Interlocken Blvd # 300
Broomfield CO 80021

(G-5495)
MYFREIGHTWORLD TECH INC (PA)
7007 College Blvd Ste 150 (66211-2415)
PHONE..................................913 677-6691
Kevin C Childress, *President*
Drew White, *COO*
EMP: 25
SALES: 17.8MM **Privately Held**
SIC: 4731 Transportation agents & brokers

(G-5496)
NAI HEARTLAND CO
4400 College Blvd Ste 170 (66211-2335)
PHONE..................................913 362-1000
Carl Lasala, *President*
Raymond W Sonnenberg, *Exec VP*
Caroline Peck, *Mktg Dir*
Raymond Sonnenberg, *Manager*
Ben Boyd, *Associate*
EMP: 12
SQ FT: 4,300
SALES (est): 1.7MM **Privately Held**
WEB: www.lasala-sonnenberg.com
SIC: 6552 Subdividers & developers

(G-5497)
NASB FINANCIAL INC
10950 El Monte St (66211-1474)
PHONE..................................913 327-2000
Bruce Thielen, *Branch Mgr*
Bill Moffitt, *Consultant*
Carlos Carter, *Loan*
Jason REA, *Loan*
EMP: 30
SALES (corp-wide): 125.9MM **Publicly Held**
SIC: 6282 Investment advice
PA: Nasb Financial, Inc.
12498 S Us Highway 71
Grandview MO 64030
816 765-2200

(G-5498)
NATIONAL ALMNM-BRASS FNDRY INC
12509 Juniper St (66209-3140)
PHONE..................................816 833-4500
Wes Kagay, *CEO*
EMP: 30
SQ FT: 34,000
SALES (est): 6.7MM **Privately Held**
WEB: www.nabfoundry.com
SIC: 3365 3364 3643 3369 Aluminum foundries; brass & bronze die-castings; current-carrying wiring devices; nonferrous foundries; copper foundries

(G-5499)
NATIONAL HEALTHCAREER ASSN
11161 Overbrook Rd (66211-2299)
PHONE..................................800 499-9092
Diane Riffel, *President*
Devin Ellis, *Partner*
Mike Dahir, *General Mgr*
Kalyn Carpenter, *Accounts Mgr*
Stacy Jones, *Marketing Mgr*
EMP: 31
SALES: 3MM **Privately Held**
SIC: 8621 Health association

(G-5500)
NATIONAL RURAL HEALTH ASSN
4501 College Blvd Ste 225 (66211-1921)
PHONE..................................913 220-2997
Alan Morgan, *CEO*
EMP: 15
SQ FT: 3,500
SALES: 4.6MM **Privately Held**
SIC: 8621 8399 Health association; health & welfare council

(G-5501)
NEW YORK LIFE INSURANCE CO
11400 Tomahwk Crk Pkwy # 540 (66211-2681)
PHONE..................................913 906-4000
Brad Clauser, *Vice Pres*
Kimberly Kent, *Vice Pres*
Taylor Aubree, *Business Anlyst*
John Beglay, *Manager*
Matt Bronson, *Associate*
EMP: 80
SALES (corp-wide): 10.8B **Privately Held**
WEB: www.newyorklife.com
SIC: 6311 Life insurance
PA: New York Life Insurance Company
51 Madison Ave Bsmt 1b
New York NY 10010
212 576-7000

(G-5502)
NICHOLS ENTERPRISES INC
4500 W 139th St (66224-1112)
PHONE..................................913 706-4581
Kathy Nichols, *Principal*
EMP: 16
SALES (est): 2MM **Privately Held**
SIC: 2673 Wardrobe bags (closet accessories): from purchased materials

(G-5503)
NORTH CAROLINA KENWORTH INC (HQ)
Also Called: Mhc Kenworth- Durham
11120 Tomahawk Creek Pkwy (66211-2695)
PHONE..................................816 483-6444
Timothy Murphy, *CEO*
Mike Murphy, *President*
John Oliver, *Parts Mgr*
Darren Harwood, *Buyer*
Jeff Johnson, *CFO*
EMP: 23
SALES (est): 58.9MM
SALES (corp-wide): 1B **Privately Held**
SIC: 5012 Trucks, commercial; trucks, noncommercial
PA: Murphy-Hoffman Company
11120 Tomahawk Creek Pkwy
Leawood KS 66211
816 483-6444

(G-5504)
NUEHEALTH MANAGEMENT SVCS LLC (HQ)
Also Called: Nueterra Healthcare MGT LLC
11221 Roe Ave Ste 300 (66211-1941)
PHONE..................................913 387-0510
Kevin Standefer, *Exec VP*
Mark Ackley, *Vice Pres*
Vickie Sanders, *Vice Pres*
Brandon Tasset, *Vice Pres*
Dan Tasset, *Mng Member*
EMP: 100
SALES (est): 5.1MM
SALES (corp-wide): 46.4MM **Privately Held**
SIC: 8011 Health maintenance organization
PA: Nueterra Dc Holdings, Llc
11221 Roe Ave Ste 1a
Leawood KS 66211
913 387-0689

(G-5505)
NUESYNERGY INC
4601 College Blvd Ste 280 (66211-1650)
PHONE..................................913 396-0884
Michael Bukaty, *CEO*
Josh Collins, *President*
Michelle King, *Opers Staff*
EMP: 12 **EST:** 2012
SQ FT: 3,000
SALES: 100K **Privately Held**
SIC: 8742 Banking & finance consultant

(G-5506)
NUETERRA DC HOLDINGS LLC (PA)
Also Called: Nueterra Healthcare
11221 Roe Ave Ste 1a (66211-1878)
PHONE..................................913 387-0689
Dan Tasset, *Chairman*
Melinda Welch, *Manager*
Lee Harper, *Director*
Brandon Stembach, *Director*
Francesca Williams, *Regional*
EMP: 30
SQ FT: 6,000
SALES (est): 46.4MM **Privately Held**
WEB: www.findlaysurgerycenter.com
SIC: 8741 Hospital management

(G-5507)
OBJECT TECH SOLUTIONS INC (PA)
6363 College Blvd Ste 230 (66211-1938)
PHONE..................................913 345-9080
Narasimha Gondi, *President*
Imtiaz Ali, *Technology*
David Frazier, *Business Dir*
Srikanth Gampa, *Recruiter*
EMP: 74
SQ FT: 4,000
SALES (est): 35.4MM **Privately Held**
WEB: www.otsi-usa.com
SIC: 7371 8742 Computer software development & applications; management consulting services

(G-5508)
OILPURE TECHNOLOGIES INC
13104 Falmouth St (66209-1790)
P.O. Box 483976, Kansas City MO (64148-3976)
PHONE..................................913 906-0400
Vichai Srimongkolkul, *President*
EMP: 6
SQ FT: 2,944
SALES (est): 500K **Privately Held**
WEB: www.oilpure.com
SIC: 3533 Oil & gas field machinery

(G-5509)
ORTHODONICS THOMPSON PC (PA)
4851 W 134th St Ste A (66209-7825)
PHONE..................................913 681-8300
Jeffrey Thompson DDS, *President*
Doug Thompson DDS, *Vice Pres*
EMP: 12
SQ FT: 2,894
SALES (est): 996.6K **Privately Held**
SIC: 8021 Orthodontist

(G-5510)
ORTHOPDIC SPT MDICINE CONS LLC
3651 College Blvd 100b (66211-1910)
PHONE..................................913 319-7534
Thomas Rasmussen, *Partner*
Mark Rasmussen, *Partner*
Randy Johnson, *Administration*
EMP: 25 **EST:** 1992
SALES (est): 5MM **Privately Held**
SIC: 8011 Orthopedic physician

(G-5511)
ORTHOPEDIC & SPO
Also Called: Osmckc
3651 College Blvd 100a (66211-1910)
PHONE..................................913 319-7546
Jon Browne, *President*
Dr Chris Barnthouse, *Vice Pres*
EMP: 15
SALES (est): 246.8K **Privately Held**
SIC: 8011 Orthopedic physician

(G-5512)
OVERLAND PARK SMILES
6700 W 121st St Ste 104 (66209-2028)
PHONE..................................913 851-8400
Richard Willits, *Partner*
Dave Woltkamp, *Partner*
EMP: 10
SALES (est): 764.4K **Privately Held**
SIC: 8021 Dentists' office

(G-5513)
P A SELECT HEALTHCARE
12140 Nall Ave Ste 305 (66209-2501)
PHONE..................................913 948-6400
Alexander Davis MD, *President*
Michael E Manoco MD, *Vice Pres*
EMP: 10
SQ FT: 3,000
SALES: 1MM **Privately Held**
SIC: 7389 Personal service agents, brokers & bureaus

(G-5514)
PARKINSONS EXERCISE AND
Also Called: Rock Study Boxing Kansas City
3665 W 95th St (66206-2034)
PHONE..................................913 276-4665
Sarrisa Curry, *President*
David Curry, *Admin Sec*
EMP: 12
SALES (est): 69.8K **Privately Held**
SIC: 8699 Charitable organization

(G-5515)
PARNELL CORPORATE SVCS US INC
7015 College Blvd Ste 600 (66211-1579)
PHONE..................................913 274-2100
Robert Joseph, *CEO*
Meagen Rankin, *Human Resources*
Nick Iles, *Marketing Staff*
EMP: 30
SALES (est): 8.1MM **Privately Held**
SIC: 2834 Pharmaceutical preparations

(G-5516)
PARS CONSULTING ENGINEERS INC (PA)
14109 Cambridge (66224-7500)
PHONE..................................913 432-0107
Rafie Hamidpour PHD, *President*
Iraj Pourmirza, *Opers Staff*
EMP: 20
SQ FT: 5,033
SALES: 1MM **Privately Held**
WEB: www.pars-engineers.com
SIC: 8711 Industrial engineers; electrical or electronic engineering

(G-5517)
PAYCHEX INC
5901 College Blvd Ste 400 (66211-1861)
PHONE..................................913 814-7776
Richard Cassidy, *Manager*
Missy Jones, *Supervisor*
Matteo Polo, *Analyst*
EMP: 65
SALES (corp-wide): 3.7B **Publicly Held**
WEB: www.paychex.com
SIC: 8721 Payroll accounting service
PA: Paychex, Inc.
911 Panorama Trl S
Rochester NY 14625
585 385-6666

(G-5518)
PAYSPOT LLC
Also Called: Epay North America
3500 College Blvd (66211-1901)
PHONE..................................913 327-4200
Kevin J Caponecchi, *President*
Sarah Herdman, *Accounts Mgr*
Tricia Greinert, *Manager*
Martin L Bruckner, *CTO*
Paul Kettley, *Technology*
EMP: 59
SQ FT: 8,000
SALES (est): 8MM **Publicly Held**
WEB: www.payspot.com
SIC: 4813 Telephone communication, except radio
PA: Euronet Worldwide, Inc.
3500 College Blvd
Leawood KS 66211

(G-5519)
PENN MUTUAL LIFE INSURANCE CO
4000 W 114th St Ste 180 (66211-2622)
PHONE..................................913 322-9177
Matthew Walker, *Branch Mgr*
EMP: 13
SALES (corp-wide): 2.8B **Privately Held**
WEB: www.thepfggroup.com
SIC: 6311 Life insurance
PA: The Penn Mutual Life Insurance Co
600 Dresher Rd
Horsham PA 19044
215 956-8000

(G-5520)
PEXCO COMPANY LLC
6731 W 121st St 216 (66209-2003)
PHONE..................................913 907-5022
Russell N Pilshaw,
Patricia A Pilshaw,
EMP: 29
SALES (est): 3.5MM **Privately Held**
SIC: 1629 Blasting contractor, except building demolition

(G-5521)
PFIZER INC
12744 Granada Ln (66209-2301)
PHONE..................................913 897-3054
David Hanson, *Principal*
EMP: 225
SALES (corp-wide): 53.6B **Publicly Held**
SIC: 2834 Pharmaceutical preparations
PA: Pfizer Inc.
235 E 42nd St Rm 107
New York NY 10017
212 733-2323

(G-5522)
PITTSBURG STEEL & MFG CO INC
10511 Mission Rd Unit 207 (66206-2702)
PHONE..................................620 231-8100
Kirk Nelsen, *President*
Richard J Teahan, *Treasurer*
Craig T Nelsen, *Admin Sec*
EMP: 14 **EST:** 1965
SQ FT: 50,000
SALES (est): 2.9MM
SALES (corp-wide): 7.1MM **Privately Held**
SIC: 3441 Fabricated structural metal
PA: Southwest Steel Fabricators, Inc.
2520 Scheidt Ln
Bonner Springs KS 66012
913 422-5500

(G-5523)
PLEX PLUS
6370 College Blvd (66211-1506)
PHONE..................................913 888-6223
Kenneth Petersen, *Owner*
EMP: 6
SQ FT: 5,000
SALES (est): 390K **Privately Held**
SIC: 3089 Cases, plastic; closures, plastic

(G-5524)
POLLEN INC
Also Called: C2fo
2020 W 89th St Ste 200 (66206-1930)
PHONE..................................877 465-4045
Alexander C Kemper, *CEO*
Chris Dark, *President*
Sandy Kemper, *Principal*
John E Kill, *Senior VP*
Matt Kerr, *Vice Pres*
EMP: 100
SALES (est): 19.3MM **Privately Held**
SIC: 6153 Working capital financing; direct working capital financing

(G-5525)
PREFERRED CONTG SYSTEMS CO
2012 W 104th St (66206-2647)
PHONE..................................913 341-0111
Michael Mulich, *President*
Katie Petty, *Director*
EMP: 15
SQ FT: 1,800
SALES (est): 2.2MM **Privately Held**
WEB: www.preferredcontracting.com
SIC: 1521 1542 1799 General remodeling, single-family houses; commercial & office building contractors; post-disaster renovations

(G-5526)
PREVAIL STRATEGIES LLC
Also Called: Prevail Innvtive Wlth Strtgies
4745 W 136th St (66224-5923)
PHONE..................................913 295-9500
Kerry Lawing, *CEO*
Andrew Stafford, *President*
Marcia Vanderwal, *Exec Officer*
Brad Lawing, *Vice Pres*
Heather Renfro, *Vice Pres*
EMP: 27
SALES (est): 1.1MM **Privately Held**
SIC: 6411 Advisory services, insurance

(G-5527)
PRIME LENDING
7101 College Blvd Ste 520 (66211)
PHONE..................................913 327-5507
David Curry, *General Mgr*
EMP: 20
SALES (est): 1.8MM **Privately Held**
SIC: 6162 Mortgage bankers & correspondents

(G-5528)
PRINT TIME INC
6700 W 121st St Ste 300 (66209-2028)
PHONE..................................913 345-8900
EMP: 23
SALES (corp-wide): 20MM **Privately Held**
SIC: 2759 7334 2791 2789 Commercial Printing Photocopying Service Typesetting Services Bookbinding/Related Work Lithographic Coml Print
PA: Print Time, Inc.
6700 W 121st St Ste 300
Leawood KS 64108
913 345-8900

(G-5529)
PRO PARTNERS MD HOLBROOK
4501 College Blvd Ste 300 (66211-2340)
PHONE..................................913 451-4776
Troy Burns, *Owner*
Vonda Accurso, *Office Mgr*
Genelle Slagle, *Family Practiti*
EMP: 20
SALES (est): 1.3MM **Privately Held**
SIC: 8011 General & family practice, physician/surgeon

(G-5530)
PROGRESSIVE MANUFACTURING CO
9217 Lee Blvd (66206-1821)
PHONE..................................913 383-2239
V Paul Schmeltz, *President*
Lawrence R Alton, *Vice Pres*
Robin Foster, *Admin Sec*
EMP: 10 **EST:** 1954
SQ FT: 46,000
SALES: 1.5MM **Privately Held**
SIC: 3444 7692 Sheet metalwork; welding repair

(G-5531)
QUINN PLASTIC SURGERY CTR LLC
6920 W 121st St Ste 102 (66209-2022)
PHONE..................................913 492-3443
John Quinn MD Facs, *Mng Member*
Jerri Harris, *Practice Mgr*
EMP: 10
SALES (est): 1.5MM **Privately Held**
SIC: 8011 Plastic surgeon

(G-5532)
RAM METAL PRODUCTS INC
6 S 59th Ln (66206)
PHONE..................................913 422-0099
Nash Medlock, *President*
EMP: 5
SALES (est): 657.9K **Privately Held**
SIC: 3399 3499 Iron ore recovery from open hearth slag; aerosol valves, metal

(G-5533)
RBC CAPITAL MARKETS LLC
4001 W 114th St Ste 200 (66211-2604)
PHONE..................................913 451-3500
Mark Borcherding, *Vice Pres*
Tom Talkington, *Vice Pres*
Mark Boreherbing, *Manager*
Dennis Salzman, *Representative*
EMP: 19
SALES (corp-wide): 21.4B **Privately Held**
WEB: www.hough.com
SIC: 6211 Brokers, security
HQ: Rbc Capital Markets, Llc
60 S 6th St Ste 700
Minneapolis MN 55402
612 371-2711

(G-5534)
REECE & NICHOLS REALTORS INC
15133 Rosewood Dr (66224-3503)
PHONE..................................913 851-8082
Susan R Kitzsteiner, *Broker*
Susan Kitzsteiner, *Manager*
Linda Hueffmeier, *Real Est Agnt*
EMP: 100
SALES (corp-wide): 225.3B **Publicly Held**
WEB: www.reece-nichols.com
SIC: 6531 Real estate agent, residential
HQ: Reece & Nichols Realtors, Inc.
11601 Granada St
Leawood KS 66211
913 491-1001

(G-5535)
REECE & NICHOLS REALTORS INC (DH)
Also Called: J D Reece Realtors
11601 Granada St (66211-1455)
PHONE..................................913 491-1001
Mike Frazier, *President*
Linda Vaughan, *Chairman*
Bess S Athan, *Vice Pres*
Shannon Belzer, *Broker*
Susan Lopez, *Broker*
EMP: 45
SQ FT: 8,500
SALES (est): 8MM
SALES (corp-wide): 225.3B **Publicly Held**
WEB: www.reece-nichols.com
SIC: 6531 Real estate brokers & agents
HQ: Homeservices Of America, Inc.
333 S 7th St Fl 27
Minneapolis MN 55402
612 336-5900

(G-5536)
REECE AND NICHOLS REALTORS INC
11601 Granada St Fl 2 (66211-1455)
PHONE..................................913 945-3704
Jerry Reece, *CEO*
Shirley Fuller, *Treasurer*
David Gentry, *Sales Staff*
Ruth Wroten, *Sales Staff*
Lynne Collinsworth, *Sales Associate*
EMP: 300
SQ FT: 30,000
SALES (est): 17.2MM
SALES (corp-wide): 225.3B **Publicly Held**
SIC: 6531 6351 Real estate brokers & agents; mortgage guarantee insurance
HQ: Homeservices Of America, Inc.
333 S 7th St Fl 27
Minneapolis MN 55402
612 336-5900

(G-5537)
REGAL CINEMAS INC
Also Called: Deer Valley Plaza 16
11500 Ash St (66211-7804)
PHONE..................................925 757-0466
Steven Chu, *General Mgr*
EMP: 30 **Privately Held**
WEB: www.regalcinemas.com
SIC: 7832 Motion picture theaters, except drive-in
HQ: Regal Cinemas, Inc.
101 E Blount Ave Ste 100
Knoxville TN 37920
865 922-1123

(G-5538)
RESOURCES INV ADVISORS INC
4860 College Blvd Ste 100 (66211-1676)
PHONE..................................913 338-5300
Vincent L Morris, *President*
EMP: 35
SALES (est): 192K
SALES (corp-wide): 18.7MM **Privately Held**
SIC: 6799 Investors
PA: Bukaty Companies
4601 College Blvd Ste 100
Leawood KS 66211
913 345-0440

(G-5539)
RISENOW LLC
4901 W 136th St Ste 101 (66224-5926)
P.O. Box 11233, Overland Park (66207-1233)
PHONE..................................913 948-7405
Tina McCarthy, *Controller*
Dave Bryan,
Linda Johnson,
Matt Stewart,
EMP: 16
SALES: 4.5MM **Privately Held**
SIC: 7379 Computer related consulting services

(G-5540)
ROBERT E MILLER INSURANCE AGCY (PA)
Also Called: Nationwide
6363 College Blvd Ste 400 (66211-1882)
PHONE..................................816 333-3000
Matthew J Miller, *President*
Sean R Miller, *Chairman*
Greg Smart, *COO*
Mark Lambertz, *Empl Benefits*
Tammy Doherty, *Accounts Mgr*
EMP: 40 **EST:** 1961
SQ FT: 12,000
SALES (est): 9.2MM **Privately Held**
SIC: 6411 8721 Insurance agents; certified public accountant

(G-5541)
ROCKHILL WOMENS CARE INC
5701 W 119th St Ste 225 (66209-3721)
PHONE..................................816 942-3339
Julie Katzfey, *Branch Mgr*
EMP: 20
SALES (corp-wide): 4MM **Privately Held**
SIC: 8011 Gynecologist
PA: Rockhill Womens Care Inc
20 Ne Saint Lukes Blvd # 310
Lees Summit MO 64086
816 942-3339

(G-5542)
ROCKIES EXPRESS PIPELINE LLC
4200 W 115th St Ste 350 (66211-2733)
PHONE..................................913 928-6060
Mark Kissel, *President*
Deborah Adams, *Vice Pres*
Carl L Brooks, *Vice Pres*
Dwayne Burton, *Vice Pres*
John Eagleton, *Vice Pres*
▲ **EMP:** 11
SALES (est): 1MM
SALES (corp-wide): 371MM **Privately Held**
SIC: 4922 Pipelines, natural gas
HQ: Tallgrass Operations Llc
4200 W 115th St Ste 350
Leawood KS 66211
913 928-6060

(G-5543)
ROOT LABORATORY INC
5201 College Blvd Ste 290 (66211-1624)
PHONE..................................913 491-3555
Daniel L Root, *President*
Rebecca Campbell, *Accountant*
EMP: 135
SQ FT: 10,000
SALES (est): 7.4MM **Privately Held**
SIC: 8072 Crown & bridge production

(G-5544)
SA CONSUMER PRODUCTS INC (PA)
3305 W 132nd St (66209-4118)
PHONE..................................888 792-4264
Thomas Fimmen, *President*
EMP: 8
SALES (est): 1.1MM **Privately Held**
SIC: 3499 Locks, safe & vault: metal

(G-5545)
SABATES EYE CENTERS PC
11261 Nall Ave (66211-1669)
PHONE..................................913 261-2020
EMP: 16
SALES (corp-wide): 4.3MM **Privately Held**
SIC: 8011 Ophthalmologist
PA: Sabates Eye Centers P.C.
11261 Nall Ave Ste 100
Shawnee Mission KS 66211
913 261-2020

(G-5546)
SALON ONE 19 & SPA
4581 W 119th St (66209-1503)
PHONE..................................913 451-7119
Lisa Amador, *Owner*
EMP: 13
SALES (est): 252.3K **Privately Held**
SIC: 7991 7231 Spas; cosmetology & personal hygiene salons

(G-5547)
SANDMEYER HENTHORN AND COMPANY
6500 W 110th St Ste 102 (66211-1539)
PHONE..................................913 951-2010
Fred Sandmeyer, *President*
EMP: 10
SQ FT: 2,400
SALES: 1.5MM **Privately Held**
SIC: 8711 Mechanical engineering; electrical or electronic engineering

(G-5548)
SAS CHILDCARE INC
Also Called: Primrose School of Leawood
4820 W 137th St (66224-5912)
PHONE..................................913 897-8900
Fax: 913 897-9010
EMP: 33 **EST:** 2012
SALES (est): 308.3K **Privately Held**
SIC: 8351 Child Day Care Services

(G-5549)
SCOR GLOBL LF USA REINSURANCE (HQ)
11625 Rosewood St Ste 300 (66211-2000)
P.O. Box 419076, Kansas City MO (64141-6076)
PHONE..................................913 901-4600
Edward Ritter, *CEO*
Bill Crouch, *Senior VP*
Terry Dickinson, *Senior VP*
Jay Kinnimon, *Senior VP*
Robin Fisher, *Assistant VP*
EMP: 36
SQ FT: 50,000
SALES (est): 86.1MM
SALES (corp-wide): 1.2B **Privately Held**
SIC: 6311 6321 Life reinsurance; reinsurance carriers, accident & health
PA: Scor Se
Scor Immeuble Scor
Paris 75116
158 447-000

(G-5550)
SERVICE USA INC
4745 W 136th St Ste 77 (66224-5923)
PHONE..................................913 543-3844
Will McCusker, *CEO*
Judy Thomas, *President*
EMP: 20
SALES (est): 272K **Privately Held**
SIC: 8999 Services

(G-5551)
SIGNAL KIT LLC
15023 Ash St (66224-3758)
PHONE..................................866 297-7585
Anthony Noll, *CEO*
Bill Noll, *COO*
EMP: 10
SALES: 1.4MM **Privately Held**
SIC: 7371 Computer software development

(G-5552)
SMITH NED E JR DDS MS CHARTER
10325 Mohawk Rd (66206-2588)
PHONE..................................913 383-3233
Ned E Smith Jr DDS, *President*
EMP: 10
SALES (est): 823.1K **Privately Held**
SIC: 8021 Dentists' office

(G-5553)
SNYDER LAW FIRM LLC
13401 Mission Rd (66209-1755)
PHONE..................................913 685-3900
Paul Hentzen, *Principal*
EMP: 10
SALES (est): 1MM **Privately Held**
SIC: 8111 General practice law office

(G-5554)
SOMA BY CHICOS LLC
5032 W 119th St (66209-1525)
PHONE..................................913 317-8566
Tonya Batson, *Principal*
EMP: 10
SALES (est): 299.5K **Privately Held**
SIC: 0179 Fruits & tree nuts

(G-5555)
SOUTHWEST STERLING INC (HQ)
Also Called: M H C Sterling
11120 Tomahawk Creek Pkwy (66211-2695)
PHONE..................................816 483-6444
Timothy Murphy, *CEO*
Ron Morton, *Vice Pres*
EMP: 34
SQ FT: 86,000
SALES (est): 8.9MM
SALES (corp-wide): 1B **Privately Held**
WEB: www.southweststerling.com
SIC: 5511 5531 7538 Trucks, tractors & trailers: new & used; truck equipment & parts; general truck repair; diesel engine repair: automotive
PA: Murphy-Hoffman Company
11120 Tomahawk Creek Pkwy
Leawood KS 66211
816 483-6444

(G-5556)
SPECIALTY FERTILIZER PDTS LLC (HQ)
Also Called: S F P
11550 Ash St Ste 220 (66211-7811)
PHONE..................................913 956-7500
Larry Sanders, *President*
▼ **EMP:** 12
SQ FT: 12,000
SALES (est): 22.4MM
SALES (corp-wide): 131.5MM **Privately Held**
WEB: www.specialtyfertilizer.com
SIC: 5191 2879 Fertilizer & fertilizer materials; agricultural chemicals
PA: Verdesian Life Sciences, Llc
1001 Winstead Dr Ste 480
Cary NC 27513
919 825-1901

(G-5557)
SPENCER REED GROUP LLC (PA)
5700 W 112th St Ste 100 (66211-1747)
PHONE..................................913 663-4400
William T Solon, *CEO*
James F Williams, *President*
Michele Sorrels, *Senior VP*
Chad Bly, *CFO*
Janine Bedora, *Manager*
EMP: 205
SQ FT: 12,000
SALES (est): 24.4MM **Privately Held**
WEB: www.spencerreed.com
SIC: 7361 7363 Executive placement; temporary help service

(G-5558)
SPINAL SIMPLICITY LLC
6600 College Blvd Ste 220 (66211-1522)
PHONE..................................913 451-4414
Karen Brown, *Principal*
Jonathan Hess, *Vice Pres*
Kelly Smith, *Cust Svc Dir*
Todd Moseley, *Mng Member*
EMP: 13
SALES (est): 974.3K **Privately Held**
SIC: 5047 Medical equipment & supplies

(G-5559)
SQUADBUILDERS INC
Also Called: PNS
10310 State Line Rd # 100 (66206-2671)
PHONE..................................913 649-4401
Kathy Vaughan, *CEO*
Steven Vaughan, *Vice Pres*
Ryan Vaughan, *Director*
EMP: 100
SALES: 600K **Privately Held**
SIC: 7361 7363 Nurses' registry; help supply services

(G-5560)
STACKIFY LLC
8900 State Line Rd # 100 (66206-1948)
PHONE..................................816 888-5055
Darin Howard, *Engineer*
Daniel Gidman, *Senior Engr*
Matt Watson,
Adam Shimmens, *Representative*
EMP: 15 **EST:** 2012
SALES (est): 1.6MM **Privately Held**
SIC: 7371 Computer software development

(G-5561)
STAR FUEL CENTERS INC (PA)
11161 Overbrook Rd # 150 (66211-2204)
PHONE..................................913 652-9400
David A Selph, *President*
Lincoln O Clifton, *Vice Pres*
Dan Engle, *CFO*
Kenneth Kestle, *Supervisor*
Rick L Ross,
EMP: 30
SQ FT: 12,000
SALES (est): 35.8MM **Privately Held**
SIC: 5541 7542 5411 Filling stations, gasoline; carwashes; convenience stores

(G-5562)
STATE LINE ANIMAL HOSPITAL
2009 W 104th St (66206-2646)
PHONE..................................913 381-3272
Vern Otte, *President*
EMP: 14
SALES (est): 1.2MM **Privately Held**
SIC: 0742 Animal hospital services, pets & other animal specialties

(G-5563)
SUMMIT CARE INC
6830 W 121st Ct (66209-2021)
PHONE..................................913 239-8777
Amy W Parise, *Principal*
EMP: 21 **EST:** 2007
SALES (est): 1.7MM **Privately Held**
SIC: 8322 Rehabilitation services

(G-5564)
SUNRISE SENIOR LIVING LLC
Also Called: Sunrise of Leawood
11661 Granada St (66211-1473)
PHONE..................................913 906-0200
Laurie Krenke, *Branch Mgr*
Michele Tonkin, *Hlthcr Dir*
EMP: 58
SALES (corp-wide): 4.7B **Publicly Held**
WEB: www.sunrise.com
SIC: 8051 Skilled nursing care facilities
HQ: Sunrise Senior Living, Llc
7902 Westpark Dr
Mc Lean VA 22102

(G-5565)
TALLGRASS DEVELOPMENT LP (PA)
4200 W 115th St Ste 350 (66211-2733)
PHONE..................................513 941-0500
Jacob Soliday, *Principal*
EMP: 20
SALES (est): 371MM **Privately Held**
SIC: 4922 Pipelines, natural gas

(G-5566)
TALLGRASS ENERGY LP (PA)
4200 W 115th St Ste 350 (66211-2733)
PHONE..................................913 928-6060
David G Dehaemers Jr, *President*
William R Moler, *COO*
EMP: 11 **EST:** 2015
SALES: 793.2MM **Publicly Held**
SIC: 4922 Natural gas transmission

(G-5567)
TALLGRASS ENERGY PARTNERS LP (HQ)
4200 W 115th St Ste 350 (66211-2733)
PHONE..................................913 928-6060
David G Dehaemers Jr, *President*
Tallgrass Mlp GP, *General Ptnr*
William R Moler, *COO*
Mike Callahan, *Counsel*
Mustafa Ostrander, *Counsel*
◆ **EMP:** 50 **EST:** 2013
SALES: 655.9MM
SALES (corp-wide): 793.2MM **Publicly Held**
SIC: 4923 4922 Gas transmission & distribution; pipelines, natural gas
PA: Tallgrass Energy, Lp
4200 W 115th St Ste 350
Leawood KS 66211
913 928-6060

(G-5568)
TALLGRASS INTERSTATE GAS TRANS
4200 W 115th St Ste 350 (66211-2733)
PHONE..................................913 928-6060
John Eagleton, *Mng Member*
EMP: 15
SALES (est): 1MM
SALES (corp-wide): 793.2MM **Publicly Held**
SIC: 4922 Natural gas transmission
HQ: Tallgrass Energy Partners, Lp
4200 W 115th St Ste 350
Leawood KS 66211
913 928-6060

GEOGRAPHIC

(G-5569)
TALLGRASS OPERATIONS LLC (HQ)
Also Called: Tallgrass Energy Partners
4200 W 115th St Ste 350 (66211-2733)
PHONE....913 928-6060
David Dehaemers, *CEO*
Mitch Meyer, *Principal*
EMP: 41 **EST:** 2008
SALES: 371MM **Privately Held**
SIC: **4922** Pipelines, natural gas
PA: Tallgrass Development, Lp
4200 W 115th St Ste 350
Leawood KS 66211
513 941-0500

(G-5570)
TEAM CAR CARE LLC
Also Called: Jiffy Lube
10300 State Line Rd (66206-2658)
PHONE....913 381-1005
Adoria Richardson, *Branch Mgr*
EMP: 10 **Privately Held**
SIC: **7549** Lubrication service, automotive
PA: Team Car Care, Llc
105 Decker Ct Ste 900
Irving TX 75062

(G-5571)
TENNESSEE KENWORTH INC (HQ)
11120 Tomahawk Creek Pkwy
(66211-2695)
PHONE....816 483-6444
Timothy R Murphy, *CEO*
EMP: 50
SALES (est): 59.4MM
SALES (corp-wide): 1B **Privately Held**
SIC: **5012** 5013 Trucks, commercial; truck parts & accessories
PA: Murphy-Hoffman Company
11120 Tomahawk Creek Pkwy
Leawood KS 66211
816 483-6444

(G-5572)
TERACRUNCH LLC
2913 W 112th St (66211-3088)
PHONE....214 405-7158
Tapan Bhatt, *Principal*
EMP: 12
SALES (est): 535.2K **Privately Held**
SIC: **7374** 7389 Data processing & preparation;

(G-5573)
TEVA NEUROSCIENCE INC (HQ)
11100 Nall Ave (66211-1205)
PHONE....913 777-3000
Larry Downey, *President*
Brandy Padberg, *Sales Staff*
Thomas Devine, *Executive*
EMP: 72 **EST:** 1995
SQ FT: 5,000
SALES (est): 63.1MM
SALES (corp-wide): 5.4B **Privately Held**
WEB: www.teva.co.il
SIC: **2834** Drugs acting on the central nervous system & sense organs
PA: Teva Pharmaceutical Industries Limited
5 Bazel
Petah Tikva 49510
392 672-67

(G-5574)
TEVA PHARMACEUTICALS
11100 Nall Ave (66211-1205)
PHONE....610 727-6055
Marguerite Brooker, *Principal*
Jim Genatone, *Sales Mgr*
Sarah Stultz, *Sales Mgr*
Ron Springston, *Regl Sales Mgr*
Barbara Fidler, *Manager*
EMP: 6 **EST:** 2011
SALES (est): 710.1K **Privately Held**
SIC: **2834** Pharmaceutical preparations

(G-5575)
TIEHEN GROUP
Also Called: Tehan Maintenance
3401 College Blvd Ste 250 (66211-1911)
PHONE....913 648-1188
Jim Tehan, *Mng Member*
EMP: 17
SALES (est): 279K **Privately Held**
SIC: **6513** Apartment building operators

(G-5576)
TIEHEN GROUP INC
3401 College Blvd Ste 250 (66211-1911)
PHONE....913 648-1188
James Tiehen, *President*
Kathleen Hartman, *Vice Pres*
EMP: 17
SALES (est): 1.4MM **Privately Held**
WEB: www.tiehengroup.com
SIC: **6531** Real estate agent, commercial; real estate managers

(G-5577)
TORCH RESEARCH LLC
4303 W 119th St (66209-1515)
PHONE....913 955-2738
Brian Weaver, *CEO*
EMP: 26
SALES (est): 461.4K **Privately Held**
SIC: **7371** Computer software development & applications

(G-5578)
TORTOISE CAPITAL ADVISORS LLC
11550 Ash St Ste 300 (66211-7811)
PHONE....913 981-1020
Jerry Polacek, *Managing Dir*
Michael J Kelnosky, *Vice Pres*
Jennifer Lester, *Vice Pres*
Prashanth Prakash, *Vice Pres*
Vincent Rupp, *Vice Pres*
EMP: 29
SALES (est): 6.4MM **Privately Held**
SIC: **6282** Investment advisory service
PA: Mariner Wealth Advisors, Llc
5700 W 112th St Ste 500
Overland Park KS 66211

(G-5579)
TORTOISE ENERGY CAPITAL CORP
11550 Ash St Ste 300 (66211-7811)
PHONE....913 981-1020
Terry Clyde Matlack, *CEO*
EMP: 13
SALES (est): 2.2MM **Privately Held**
SIC: **6722** Mutual fund sales, on own account

(G-5580)
TORTOISE ENERGY INDEPENDENC
Also Called: Tortoise Capital Advisors
11550 Ash St Ste 300 (66211-7811)
PHONE....913 981-1020
Zachary Hamel, *Principal*
EMP: 50
SALES (est): 3.3MM **Privately Held**
SIC: **6722** Money market mutual funds

(G-5581)
TOWN CENTER PLAZA LLC
5000 W 119th St (66209-1525)
PHONE....913 498-1111
Chuck Oglescy,
EMP: 10
SQ FT: 400,000
SALES (est): 550K **Privately Held**
SIC: **6512** 5621 Shopping center, property operation only; women's clothing stores

(G-5582)
TRAILBLAZER PIPELINE CO LLC
4200 W 115th St Ste 350 (66211-2733)
PHONE....913 928-6060
Frank Strong, *Mng Member*
EMP: 16
SALES (est): 987K
SALES (corp-wide): 793.2MM **Publicly Held**
SIC: **4613** Refined petroleum pipelines
HQ: Tallgrass Energy Partners, Lp
4200 W 115th St Ste 350
Leawood KS 66211
913 928-6060

(G-5583)
TRANSWEB LLC
11501 Outlook St Ste 100 (66211-1810)
PHONE....856 205-1313
Kumar Ogale, *Vice Pres*
Vicki Lane, *CFO*
Richard Granville, *Mng Member*
Paul Kaiser, *Mng Member*
Jim Mourlas,
▲ **EMP:** 50
SQ FT: 20,000
SALES: 11MM
SALES (corp-wide): 14.3B **Publicly Held**
WEB: www.trnsweb.com
SIC: **3564** Filters, air: furnaces, air conditioning equipment, etc.
HQ: Clarcor Inc.
840 Crescent Centre Dr # 600
Franklin TN 37067
615 771-3100

(G-5584)
TRI-COM TECHNICAL SERVICES LLC
11115 Ash St (66211-1763)
PHONE....913 652-0600
Matt Sharples, *Partner*
Carol Bruce, *Controller*
Erik Lyke, *Accounts Exec*
Melissa Russo, *Technical Staff*
Doug Washington, *Director*
EMP: 110
SQ FT: 5,000
SALES (est): 12.1MM **Privately Held**
WEB: www.tricomts.com
SIC: **7371** Computer software development & applications

(G-5585)
TRIPLE-I CORPORATION
4200 W 115th St Ste 300 (66211-2728)
PHONE....913 563-7227
Perry Puccetti, *President*
Robert Spachman, *Chairman*
Frank Russo, *Vice Pres*
Pat Hoyes, *VP Opers*
Linda Courtney, *Info Tech Mgr*
EMP: 75
SQ FT: 8,000
SALES: 7.7MM
SALES (corp-wide): 3.5MM **Privately Held**
WEB: www.triplei.com
SIC: **7373** Systems integration services
PA: Iii Investments, Inc.
11313 El Monte St
Leawood KS 66211
913 262-6500

(G-5586)
TRUIST BANK
BB&T
4501 College Blvd Ste 320 (66211-2328)
PHONE....913 491-6700
Bonnie Hodges, *Branch Mgr*
EMP: 35
SALES (corp-wide): 13B **Publicly Held**
SIC: **6021** National commercial banks
HQ: Truist Bank
200 W 2nd St
Winston Salem NC 27101
336 733-2000

(G-5587)
U S TOY CO INC
Also Called: Constructive Playthings
2008 W 103rd Ter (66206-2643)
PHONE....913 642-8247
Brian Fairbanks, *Branch Mgr*
EMP: 26
SALES (corp-wide): 74.6MM **Privately Held**
WEB: www.ustoy.com
SIC: **5945** 7299 5947 5199 Children's toys & games, except dolls; costume rental; gifts & novelties; carnival supplies; novelties, durable; school supplies
PA: U. S. Toy Co., Inc.
13201 Arrington Rd
Grandview MO 64030
816 761-5900

(G-5588)
UBS SECURITIES LLC
11150 Overbrook Rd (66211-2240)
PHONE....913 345-3200
Randy Marsh, *General Mgr*
EMP: 31
SALES (corp-wide): 29.9B **Privately Held**
SIC: **6211** Brokers, security
HQ: Ubs Securities Llc
677 Washington Blvd
Stamford CT 06901

(G-5589)
UNION BANK AND TRUST COMPANY
11460 Tomahawk Creek Pkwy # 120
(66211-7810)
PHONE....913 491-0909
Carla Selmon, *Branch Mgr*
Jan Radcliff, *Branch Mgr*
Mitchell Heather, *Supervisor*
Danielle Miller, *Training Spec*
EMP: 93
SALES (corp-wide): 258.8MM **Privately Held**
SIC: **6022** State commercial banks
PA: Union Bank And Trust Company
3643 S 48th St
Lincoln NE 68506
402 323-1235

(G-5590)
UNIVERSAL MECHANICAL LLC
Also Called: Universal Comfort Systems
2804 W 132nd St (66209-1675)
PHONE....573 636-8373
EMP: 20
SALES: 950K **Privately Held**
SIC: **1711** Plumbing/Heating/Air Cond Contractor

(G-5591)
UPG SOLUTIONS LLC
Also Called: Rfp360
8700 State Line Rd 250 (66206-1572)
PHONE....844 737-0365
Bryce Gilman, *Sales Engr*
Amanda Boude, *Sales Staff*
David Hulsen, *Mng Member*
Natalie Berigan, *Associate*
EMP: 11
SALES (est): 466.5K **Privately Held**
SIC: **7371** Computer software development

(G-5592)
US BANK NATIONAL ASSOCIATION
Also Called: US Bank
3700 W 95th St (66206-2037)
PHONE....913 383-2126
EMP: 12
SALES (corp-wide): 25.7B **Publicly Held**
SIC: **6021** National commercial banks
HQ: U.S. Bank National Association
425 Walnut St Fl 14
Cincinnati OH 45202
513 632-4234

(G-5593)
WADDELL & REED INC
4000 W 114th St Ste 310 (66211-2641)
PHONE....913 491-9202
Frederick Funke, *Manager*
Rick Funke, *Admin Mgr*
EMP: 18 **Publicly Held**
SIC: **6411** 8742 6211 Insurance agents, brokers & service; financial consultant; mutual funds, selling by independent salesperson
HQ: Waddell & Reed, Inc.
6300 Lamar Ave
Shawnee Mission KS 66202
913 236-2000

(G-5594)
WADDELL & REED INV MGT CO
4000 W 114th St Ste 310 (66211-2641)
PHONE....913 491-9202
Rick H Funke, *Branch Mgr*
EMP: 20 **Publicly Held**
SIC: **6282** 8742 6211 Investment advisory service; financial consultant; mutual funds, selling by independent salesperson
HQ: Waddell & Reed Investment Management Co.
6300 Lamar Ave
Shawnee Mission KS 66202

(G-5595)
WANDA AMERICA INV HOLDG CO LTD
11500 Ash St (66211-7804)
PHONE..................................913 213-2000
Adam M Aron, *President*
EMP: 37236
SALES (est): 98.4MM
SALES (corp-wide): 7.3MM **Publicly Held**
SIC: 7382 Security systems services
HQ: Dalian Wanda Group Co., Ltd.
No.539, Changjiang Rd., Xigang Dist.
Dalian 11601

(G-5596)
WELLS FARGO BANK NATIONAL ASSN
Also Called: Leawood Branch
2000 W 103rd St (66206-2369)
PHONE..................................913 341-4774
Melissa Oropeza, *Manager*
EMP: 15
SALES (corp-wide): 101B **Publicly Held**
SIC: 6021 National commercial banks
HQ: Wells Fargo Bank, National Association
101 N Phillips Ave
Sioux Falls SD 57104
605 575-6900

(G-5597)
WESTERN FIRST AID & SAFETY LLC (HQ)
5360 College Blvd Ste 200 (66211-1641)
PHONE..................................316 263-0687
Tom Lyons, *CEO*
Jim Riggs, *President*
Corey Coker, *Regional Mgr*
Rick Washburn, *CFO*
EMP: 15
SALES (est): 1.7MM
SALES (corp-wide): 31.3MM **Privately Held**
SIC: 8322 First aid service
PA: Global Connections, Inc.
5360 College Blvd Ste 200
Leawood KS 66211
913 498-0960

(G-5598)
WHEATLAND ENTERPRISES INC (PA)
Also Called: Overland Limousine Service
2017 W 104th St (66206-2646)
PHONE..................................913 381-3504
Diane Forgy, *President*
Joel Freisner, *Warehouse Mgr*
Maria Marsh, *Mktg Coord*
Kathryn Ramirez-Young, *Supervisor*
EMP: 26
SQ FT: 2,000
SALES: 444MM **Privately Held**
WEB: www.kclimo.com
SIC: 4119 Limousine rental, with driver

(G-5599)
WHEATLAND ENTERPRISES INC
Also Called: Plaza Limousine
2017 W 104th St (66206-2646)
PHONE..................................816 756-1700
Lisa Herndon, *Manager*
EMP: 35
SALES (corp-wide): 444MM **Privately Held**
WEB: www.kclimo.com
SIC: 4119 4111 Limousine rental, with driver; airport transportation
PA: Wheatland Enterprises, Inc.
2017 W 104th St
Leawood KS 66206
913 381-3504

(G-5600)
WOMENS CLINIC JOHNSON COUNTY (PA)
5525 W 119th St (66209-3724)
PHONE..................................913 491-4020
Dr Laura Kenny, *Director*
EMP: 15
SALES (est): 3MM **Privately Held**
WEB: www.wcjcobgyn.com
SIC: 8011 Clinic, operated by physicians; gynecologist

(G-5601)
WOMENS HEALTH SVCS KANS CY PC
2104 W 119th Ter (66209-1108)
PHONE..................................816 941-2700
Paul V Niewrzel MD, *Principal*
EMP: 12
SQ FT: 5,000
SALES (est): 740K **Privately Held**
SIC: 8011 Obstetrician; gynecologist

(G-5602)
WW KC METCALF LLC
Also Called: Waterwalk Overland Park
11200 Glenwood St (66211-1516)
PHONE..................................913 956-0234
Jack Deboer,
EMP: 13 **EST:** 2018
SALES (est): 118.5K **Privately Held**
SIC: 7011 Hotels

(G-5603)
XIPHIUM HAIR SALON
10589 Mission Rd (66206-2522)
PHONE..................................913 696-1616
Vilma Subel, *Owner*
EMP: 15
SALES (est): 388.1K **Privately Held**
WEB: www.xiphium.com
SIC: 7231 Manicurist, pedicurist

(G-5604)
ZILLOW GROUP INC
Also Called: Mortgage Lenders America
10975 El Monte St (66211-1407)
PHONE..................................913 491-4299
Philip Kneibert, *General Mgr*
Joe Cunningham, *Officer*
EMP: 42
SALES (corp-wide): 1.3B **Publicly Held**
SIC: 6163 Mortgage brokers arranging for loans, using money of others
PA: Zillow Group, Inc.
1301 2nd Ave Fl 31
Seattle WA 98101
206 470-7000

Lebo
Coffey County

(G-5605)
4 RIVERS ELECTRIC COOP INC
2731 Milo Ter (66856-9285)
PHONE..................................620 364-2116
Dennis Svanes, *Principal*
Roger Cole, *Principal*
Robert Converse, *Principal*
A Eugene Hutson, *Principal*
David Kunkel, *Principal*
EMP: 45
SALES (est): 1MM **Privately Held**
SIC: 1731 General electrical contractor

(G-5606)
HODGES FARMS & DREDGING LLC
501 N West St (66856-9322)
PHONE..................................620 343-0513
Jeff Hodges,
EMP: 15
SALES (est): 1.4MM **Privately Held**
SIC: 0711 4953 Fertilizer application services; soil testing services; liquid waste, collection & disposal

(G-5607)
KNIGHT TRUCKING LLC
2424 Fauna Rd (66856-9269)
P.O. Box 33 (66856-0033)
PHONE..................................620 256-6525
Terry Knight,
Jeffery Knight,
Jesse Knight,
EMP: 40
SALES (est): 4.7MM **Privately Held**
WEB: www.knighttrucking.com
SIC: 4212 Local trucking, without storage

(G-5608)
PEDRO LOPEZ CO INC
2775 Us Highway 75 (66856-9292)
PHONE..................................785 220-1509
Kirk Williams, *President*
EMP: 15
SQ FT: 18,000
SALES: 1.3MM **Privately Held**
WEB: www.engroffcater.com
SIC: 5812 2032 Caterers; Mexican foods: packaged in cans, jars, etc.

(G-5609)
T & T FLATWORKS INC
32015 S Wanamaker Rd (66856-9187)
P.O. Box 306, Burlington (66839-0306)
PHONE..................................620 794-0619
Charles Totty, *President*
EMP: 42
SALES (est): 5.4MM **Privately Held**
SIC: 1611 1771 Surfacing & paving; highway & street paving contractor; concrete work

Lecompton
Shawnee County

(G-5610)
BIG SPRINGS SPORTS CENTER
1895 E 56th Rd (66050-4074)
PHONE..................................785 887-6700
Chad Price,
EMP: 25 **EST:** 2011
SALES (est): 1.3MM **Privately Held**
SIC: 5085 Springs

(G-5611)
LECOMPTON HISTORICAL SOC INC
640 E Woodson Ave (66050-3078)
P.O. Box 68 (66050-0068)
PHONE..................................785 887-6260
Paul Bahnmaier, *President*
Elaine Boose, *Admin Sec*
EMP: 12
SALES: 239.1K **Privately Held**
SIC: 8412 Museum

(G-5612)
LONE PINE AG SERVICES INC
1557 E 100 Rd (66050-4007)
PHONE..................................785 887-6559
David Wulfkuhle, *President*
Carolyn Wulfkuhle, *Corp Secy*
Shelly Wulfkuhle, *Vice Pres*
Julie Kirkwood, *Manager*
EMP: 12
SALES: 1.6MM **Privately Held**
SIC: 5191 Seeds & bulbs; fertilizer & fertilizer materials; chemicals, agricultural

(G-5613)
PREFERRED LAWN SERVICE
1895 E 56th Rd (66050-4074)
PHONE..................................785 887-9900
EMP: 40
SALES (est): 766.8K **Privately Held**
SIC: 0782 Lawn/Garden Services

(G-5614)
WOODEN STUFF CABINETS INC
515 E Woodson Ave (66050-3077)
P.O. Box 61 (66050-0061)
PHONE..................................785 887-6003
David Powell, *President*
EMP: 10 **EST:** 1981
SALES (est): 1.1MM **Privately Held**
SIC: 2434 Wood kitchen cabinets

Lenexa
Johnson County

(G-5615)
1&1 INTERNET INC
10950 Strang Line Rd (66215-2322)
PHONE..................................816 621-4795
Thorsten Ziegler, *Manager*
EMP: 13
SQ FT: 55,000
SALES (corp-wide): 5.6B **Privately Held**
SIC: 4813 4822 7374 ; electronic mail; computer graphics service
HQ: 1&1 Ionos Inc.
701 Lee Rd Ste 300
Chesterbrook PA 19087
877 461-2631

(G-5616)
A D J-HUX SERVICE INC
Also Called: P1 Group
13605 W 96th Ter (66215-1253)
PHONE..................................913 529-5200
Smitty G Belcher, *President*
EMP: 86
SQ FT: 8,000
SALES (est): 6.7MM
SALES (corp-wide): 243.8MM **Privately Held**
WEB: www.p1group.com
SIC: 1711 1731 Mechanical contractor; electrical work
PA: P1 Group, Inc.
13605 W 96th Ter
Lenexa KS 66215
913 529-5000

(G-5617)
AAA PARTY RENTAL INC
10900 Mid America Dr (66219-1235)
PHONE..................................816 333-1767
Robert Johnson, *President*
Leslee Johnson, *Principal*
Kelly Capper, *Office Mgr*
EMP: 15
SQ FT: 17,000
SALES (est): 1.9MM **Privately Held**
WEB: www.aaapartyrental.com
SIC: 7359 5947 Party supplies rental services; party favors

(G-5618)
ABB MOTORS AND MECHANICAL INC
Also Called: Baldor Shour & Associates
9810 Industrial Blvd (66215-1218)
P.O. Box 802738, Kansas City MO (64180-2738)
PHONE..................................816 587-0272
Henry Majchar, *Manager*
John Schuh, *Manager*
EMP: 13
SALES (corp-wide): 36.7B **Privately Held**
WEB: www.baldor.com
SIC: 5063 5999 Motors, electric; engine & motor equipment & supplies
HQ: Abb Motors And Mechanical Inc.
5711 Rs Boreham Jr St
Fort Smith AR 72901
479 646-4711

(G-5619)
ABSECON SW HOTEL INC
9903 Pflumm Rd (66215-1222)
PHONE..................................913 345-2111
Linda Smith, *Corp Secy*
EMP: 25
SQ FT: 90,000
SALES (est): 150.1K **Privately Held**
SIC: 7011 Resort hotel, franchised

(G-5620)
ACCESS INFO MGT SHRED SVCS LLC
Also Called: Access Information Protected
17501 W 98th St (66219-1704)
PHONE..................................913 492-4581
EMP: 25 **Privately Held**
SIC: 4226 Document & office records storage
PA: Access Information Management Shared Services, Llc
500 Unicorn Park Dr # 503
Woburn MA 01801

(G-5621)
ACCESSIBLE TECHNOLOGIES INC (PA)
Also Called: Procharger
14801 W 114th Ter (66215-4884)
PHONE..................................913 338-2886
Dan Jones, *President*
Glen Roderique, *Principal*
Ken Jones, *Vice Pres*
Dean Rohr, *Prdtn Mgr*
Randy Erteld, *Inv Control Mgr*
EMP: 60

GEOGRAPHIC

SALES (est): 12.3MM **Privately Held**
WEB: www.procharger.com
SIC: 3511 5531 3732 3714 Turbines & turbine generator sets & parts; automotive parts; boat building & repairing; motor vehicle parts & accessories

(G-5622)
ACCREDO HEALTH GROUP INC
11411 Strang Line Rd (66215-4047)
PHONE..................................913 339-7100
Marion Huet, *Manager*
EMP: 28
SALES (corp-wide): 141.6B **Publicly Held**
WEB: www.accredotx.com
SIC: 8051 Skilled nursing care facilities
HQ: Accredo Health Group, Inc.
1640 Century Center Pkwy # 110
Memphis TN 38134
877 222-7336

(G-5623)
ACI CNCRETE PLACEMENT KANS LLC (PA)
25412 W 95th Ln Unit 1710 (66227-7360)
PHONE..................................913 281-3700
Larry Kaminsky, *Mng Member*
Stephanie Fields, *Administration*
Matt Kaminsky,
▲ **EMP:** 34
SALES (est): 7.8MM **Privately Held**
SIC: 1771 Concrete pumping

(G-5624)
ACME FLOOR COMPANY INC
10100 Marshall Dr (66215-1220)
PHONE..................................913 888-3200
Robert T Kenney II, *President*
Barbara Kenney, *Corp Secy*
Brian Kenney, *Vice Pres*
Emily Kenney-Moore, *Vice Pres*
▲ **EMP:** 100 **EST:** 1926
SQ FT: 24,000
SALES: 13MM **Privately Held**
WEB: www.acme-floor.com
SIC: 1752 5713 Wood floor installation & refinishing; floor covering stores

(G-5625)
ACS ELECTRONIC SYSTEMS INC
7856 Barton St (66214-3403)
PHONE..................................913 248-8828
Charles Olsen, *President*
Connie Goodman, *Accountant*
EMP: 30 **EST:** 2008
SALES (est): 3.8MM **Privately Held**
SIC: 7382 Security systems services

(G-5626)
ACSYS LASERTECHNIK US INC
8224 Nieman Rd (66214-1507)
PHONE..................................847 468-5302
Gerhard Kimmel, *Ch of Bd*
Andreas Plauschin, *COO*
EMP: 6
SQ FT: 2,300
SALES (est): 620.1K
SALES (corp-wide): 27.3MM **Privately Held**
SIC: 3541 7699 Machine tools, metal cutting type; industrial machinery & equipment repair
PA: Acsys Lasertechnik Gmbh
Leibnizstr 9
Kornwestheim 70806
715 480-8750

(G-5627)
AD ASTRA SELECTIONS LLC
9892 Pflumm Rd (66215-1208)
PHONE..................................913 307-0272
Josu Galdos, *Vice Pres*
Jeff Miller, *Sales Mgr*
Luke Lawlor, *Mng Member*
Sam Littler, *Manager*
EMP: 7 **EST:** 2012
SALES: 510K **Privately Held**
SIC: 2084 Wines

(G-5628)
ADAMS CABLE EQUIPMENT INC
Also Called: A C E
9635 Widmer Rd (66215-1290)
P.O. Box 25687, Overland Park (66225-5687)
PHONE..................................913 888-5100
Christian Adams, *CEO*
Mike Adams, *COO*
Leslie Washington, *Vice Pres*
Jay Widman, *Controller*
George Dean, *Accounting Mgr*
◆ **EMP:** 50
SQ FT: 75,000
SALES: 31MM **Privately Held**
SIC: 5065 Communication equipment

(G-5629)
ADEMCO INC
Also Called: ADI Global Distribution
8055 Flint St (66214-3335)
PHONE..................................913 438-1111
Steven Serrioz, *Manager*
EMP: 7
SALES (corp-wide): 4.8B **Publicly Held**
WEB: www.honeywell.com
SIC: 5063 3669 3822 Electrical apparatus & equipment; emergency alarms; air conditioning & refrigeration controls
HQ: Ademco Inc.
1985 Douglas Dr N
Golden Valley MN 55422
800 468-1502

(G-5630)
ADF LLC
11042 Strang Line Rd (66215-2113)
PHONE..................................913 825-7400
Matt Duffield, *CEO*
EMP: 21 **EST:** 2011
SALES (est): 2.2MM **Privately Held**
SIC: 3599 Machine shop, jobbing & repair

(G-5631)
ADVANCE SYSTEMS INTERNATIONAL
9801 Renner Blvd Ste 250 (66219-9718)
PHONE..................................913 888-3578
Monty G Anderson, *CEO*
Doug Able, *Ch of Bd*
Pamela S Anderson, *President*
Shawn G Anderson, *COO*
Steve Stoskopf, *Admin Sec*
EMP: 20
SALES (est): 2.4MM **Privately Held**
WEB: www.advancedinfraredsystems.com
SIC: 3812 3699 4785 7382 Infrared object detection equipment; security control equipment & systems; inspection services connected with transportation; security systems services
PA: Advanced Infrared Systems Corp
9324 Greenway Ln
Lenexa KS 66215
913 888-3578

(G-5632)
ADVANCED FOOD SERVICES INC
9729 Lackman Rd (66219-1207)
PHONE..................................913 888-8088
Raju Shah, *President*
Vivek Soni, *Accounts Mgr*
EMP: 30
SQ FT: 22,150
SALES: 35MM **Privately Held**
SIC: 2099 Food preparations

(G-5633)
ADVANCED INFRARED SYSTEMS (PA)
9324 Greenway Ln (66215-3172)
PHONE..................................913 888-3578
Monty Anderson, *President*
Shawn Anderson, *Corp Secy*
Pamela Anderson, *Vice Pres*
EMP: 6
SQ FT: 2,400
SALES (est): 2.4MM **Privately Held**
WEB: www.advancedinfraredsystems.com
SIC: 4785 3699 7382 Inspection services connected with transportation; security control equipment & systems; security systems services

(G-5634)
ADVANTAGE SALES & MKTG LLC
Sunflower Group, The
14001 Marshall Dr (66215-1227)
PHONE..................................913 890-0900
Patrick Carr, *Vice Pres*
Sally Reid, *Research*
Angela Finn, *Accounts Exec*
Wade Dewerff, *Software Dev*
Whitney Ray, *Director*
EMP: 10
SALES (corp-wide): 11.7B **Privately Held**
SIC: 8742 Marketing consulting services
HQ: Advantage Sales & Marketing Llc
2201 E 6th St
Austin TX 78702
949 797-2900

(G-5635)
ADVISORY ASSOCIATES INC
14904 W 87th Street Pkwy (66215-4159)
PHONE..................................913 829-7323
Robert Wagner, *President*
EMP: 21
SALES (est): 787.3K **Privately Held**
SIC: 8742 Business consultant

(G-5636)
AEROTEK INC
Also Called: Aerotek 964
15200 Santa Fe Dr Ste 100 (66219)
PHONE..................................913 981-1970
Scott Green, *Accounts Exec*
Russ Koziol, *Branch Mgr*
Carter Arnett, *Recruiter*
Jake Plegge, *Recruiter*
EMP: 22
SALES (corp-wide): 13.4B **Privately Held**
SIC: 7363 Temporary help service
HQ: Aerotek, Inc.
7301 Parkway Dr
Hanover MD 21076
410 694-5100

(G-5637)
AFFINITY MORTGAGE LLC
8725 Rosehill Rd Ste 109 (66215-4611)
PHONE..................................913 469-0777
Justin Rabin, *Consultant*
Matt McDowell,
EMP: 14
SQ FT: 900
SALES (est): 185K **Privately Held**
WEB: www.affinityhomeloan.com
SIC: 6162 6163 Mortgage bankers & correspondents; loan brokers

(G-5638)
ALENCO INC (HQ)
Also Called: Alenco Materials Company
16201 W 110th St (66219-1313)
PHONE..................................913 438-1902
Allen Erskine, *President*
Abe Eller, *General Mgr*
Molly Bechtold, *Production*
Adam Brewer, *Sales Staff*
John Oneill, *Sales Staff*
EMP: 20
SQ FT: 14,000
SALES (est): 104.3MM
SALES (corp-wide): 5.9B **Publicly Held**
WEB: www.alencohomeimprovement.com
SIC: 1521 1751 1761 General remodeling, single-family houses; single-family home remodeling, additions & repairs; new construction, single-family houses; window & door (prefabricated) installation; siding contractor
PA: Encana Corporation
500 Centre St Se
Calgary AB T2G 1
403 645-2000

(G-5639)
ALERT 360
Also Called: Central Security Group
11635 W 83rd Ter (66214-1538)
PHONE..................................913 599-3439
EMP: 103
SALES (corp-wide): 90.6MM **Privately Held**
SIC: 7381 Guard services
PA: Alert 360
2448 E 81st St Ste 4300
Tulsa OK 74137
918 491-3151

(G-5640)
ALIXA RX LLC
11286 Renner Blvd (66219-9605)
PHONE..................................913 307-8150
Nicole Satterlee, *Supervisor*
EMP: 8
SALES (corp-wide): 96MM **Privately Held**
SIC: 2834 Solutions, pharmaceutical
HQ: Alixa Rx Llc
6400 Pinecrest Dr Ste 200
Plano TX 75024
214 778-0300

(G-5641)
ALLEN COMMERCIAL CLG SVCS LLC
8194 Nieman Rd (66214-1506)
PHONE..................................913 322-2900
Dennis Allen, *Mng Member*
EMP: 20 **EST:** 2011
SQ FT: 4,000
SALES (est): 2.1MM **Privately Held**
SIC: 7699 Cleaning services

(G-5642)
ALORICA CUSTOMER CARE INC
95 Metcalf Sq Bldg J (66219)
PHONE..................................215 441-2323
EMP: 563
SALES (corp-wide): 5.4B **Privately Held**
SIC: 7389 Telemarketing services
HQ: Alorica Customer Care, Inc.
5085 W Park Blvd Ste 300
Plano TX

(G-5643)
ALTURA INCORPORATED
Also Called: Sweet Art Company
8411 Renner Blvd Apt 1309 (66219-5802)
PHONE..................................913 492-3701
EMP: 5
SQ FT: 4,600
SALES: 800K **Privately Held**
WEB: www.sweetart.com
SIC: 3556 Bakery machinery

(G-5644)
AMBS AND ASSOCIATES INC
Also Called: A.M.B.S. Marketing
9209 Quivira Rd (66215-3905)
PHONE..................................913 599-5939
EMP: 5
SALES (est): 792.6K **Privately Held**
SIC: 3449 5032 2851 Mfg Misc Structural Mtl Whol Brick/Stone Matrls Mfg Paints/Allied Prdts

(G-5645)
AMERICAN BOTTLING COMPANY
9960 Lakeview Ave (66219-2502)
P.O. Box 15904, Shawnee Mission (66285-5904)
PHONE..................................913 894-6777
Larry Young, *CEO*
Jeff Angold, *Principal*
EMP: 125 **Publicly Held**
WEB: www.cs-americas.com
SIC: 2086 5149 Bottled & canned soft drinks; groceries & related products
HQ: The American Bottling Company
5301 Legacy Dr
Plano TX 75024

(G-5646)
AMERICAN COLLEGE OF CLINICAL (PA)
Also Called: ACCP
13000 W 87th Street Pkwy # 100 (66215-4634)
PHONE..................................913 492-3311
Chelsea Earhart, *Project Mgr*
Renee Hultgren, *Project Mgr*
Michael Maddux, *Exec Dir*
Kathy Pham, *Director*
Sheldon Holstad, *Admin Sec*
EMP: 23

SALES: 8.3MM **Privately Held**
WEB: www.accp.com
SIC: 8621 Medical field-related associations

(G-5647)
AMERICAN CONSTRUCTION SVCS LLC
Also Called: ACS
11000 Lakeview Ave (66219-1311)
PHONE..................................913 754-3777
Jerri L Whetstone,
EMP: 11
SALES (est): 1.8MM **Privately Held**
SIC: 1542 Nonresidential construction

(G-5648)
AMERICAN DRECT PROCUREMENT INC (PA)
11000 Lakeview Ave (66219-1311)
PHONE..................................913 677-5588
Byron W Whetstone, *President*
Andy Metz, *Project Mgr*
Rod Beason, *CFO*
Destri Brown, *Controller*
Mark Turnbull, *Sales Staff*
EMP: 183
SQ FT: 15,000
SALES (est): 155.5MM **Privately Held**
WEB: www.americandirectco.com
SIC: 5031 Doors & windows

(G-5649)
AMERICAN HOMEPATIENT INC
11427 Strang Line Rd (66215-4047)
PHONE..................................913 495-9545
Lauren Milton, *Branch Mgr*
EMP: 24 **Privately Held**
SIC: 7352 Medical equipment rental
HQ: American Homepatient, Inc.
5213 Linbar Dr Ste 408
Nashville TN 37211
615 221-8884

(G-5650)
AMERICAN MARKING SYSTEMS INC
14609 W 106th St (66215-2013)
PHONE..................................913 492-6028
Lloyd H Roatch, *President*
Sharon Roatch, *CFO*
EMP: 7
SQ FT: 5,300
SALES (est): 1MM **Privately Held**
WEB: www.americanmarkingsystems.com
SIC: 3577 Bar code (magnetic ink) printers; optical scanning devices

(G-5651)
AMERICAN METALS SUPPLY CO INC
15201 W 101st Ter (66219-1458)
PHONE..................................913 754-0616
Christine Nardini, *Manager*
EMP: 25
SALES (corp-wide): 69.7MM **Privately Held**
WEB: www.americanmetalssupply.com
SIC: 5075 5051 1761 Warm air heating equipment & supplies; steel; roofing, siding & sheet metal work
PA: American Metals Supply Co., Inc.
1617 Park 370 Ct
Hazelwood MO 63042
217 483-5511

(G-5652)
AMERICAN NATIONAL RED CROSS
Also Called: American Red Cross
8053 Bond St (66214-1593)
PHONE..................................913 245-3565
EMP: 39
SALES (corp-wide): 2.6B **Privately Held**
SIC: 8322 Emergency social services
PA: The American National Red Cross
430 17th St Nw
Washington DC 20006
202 737-8300

(G-5653)
AMERIPATH INC
10101 Renner Blvd A (66219-9752)
PHONE..................................816 412-7003
Kenneth Watson, *Branch Mgr*
EMP: 20
SALES (corp-wide): 7.5B **Publicly Held**
SIC: 8071 Medical laboratories
HQ: Ameripath, Inc.
7111 Fairway Dr Ste 101
Palm Beach Gardens FL 33418
561 712-6200

(G-5654)
ANDERSEN CORPORATION
8180 Nieman Rd (66214-1506)
PHONE..................................913 385-1300
David Rever, *Branch Mgr*
EMP: 15
SALES (corp-wide): 2.8B **Privately Held**
SIC: 1751 Window & door installation & erection
PA: Andersen Corporation
100 4th Ave N
Bayport MN 55003
651 264-5150

(G-5655)
ANOTHER DAY HOMECARE INC
11802 W 77th St (66214-1456)
PHONE..................................913 599-2221
Lorraine Dold, *COO*
Cathye Olson, *Exec Dir*
EMP: 14
SALES (est): 777.1K **Privately Held**
SIC: 8082 Visiting nurse service

(G-5656)
ANTHONY INC
Also Called: Anthony Plumbing Htg & Coolg
15203 W 99th St (66219-1253)
PHONE..................................913 384-4440
Steve Burbridge, *President*
Kent Gurske, *Opers Mgr*
Kim Westhoff, *Marketing Staff*
Cecil Davis, *Manager*
Jamie Carpenter, *Recruiter*
EMP: 50
SALES (est): 10MM **Privately Held**
WEB: www.anthonyinc.com
SIC: 1711 Warm air heating & air conditioning contractor; heating & air conditioning contractors

(G-5657)
APEX CONSTRUCTION INC
13315 W 91st St (66215-3624)
PHONE..................................913 341-3688
Ron King, *President*
Jim Flemington, *Vice Pres*
EMP: 25
SALES (est): 3.9MM **Privately Held**
SIC: 1521 Single-family housing construction

(G-5658)
APRIA HEALTHCARE LLC
16815 College Blvd (66219-1309)
P.O. Box 60906, Saint Louis MO (63160-0906)
PHONE..................................913 492-2212
Robb Eaton, *Branch Mgr*
EMP: 266 **Privately Held**
WEB: www.apria.com
SIC: 5047 Hospital equipment & furniture
HQ: Apria Healthcare Llc
26220 Enterprise Ct
Lake Forest CA 92630
949 639-2000

(G-5659)
ARCADIS US INC
Rosehill Offc Pk 1 (66215)
PHONE..................................913 492-4156
Lindy Peters, *Manager*
EMP: 30
SALES (corp-wide): 6.4MM **Privately Held**
WEB: www.arcadis-us.com
SIC: 8748 Environmental consultant
HQ: Arcadis U.S., Inc.
630 Plaza Dr Ste 200
Highlands Ranch CO 80129
720 344-3500

(G-5660)
ARG CONTRACTING LLC
8167 Cole Pkwy (66227-2714)
P.O. Box 861140, Shawnee (66286-1140)
PHONE..................................913 441-1992
EMP: 14 **EST**: 2010
SALES (est): 1.5MM **Privately Held**
SIC: 1799 Trade Contractor

(G-5661)
ARJ INFUSION SERVICES INC (PA)
7930 Marshall Dr (66214-1562)
PHONE..................................913 451-8804
Lisa Sackuvich, *President*
Andy Copeland, *Vice Pres*
Brett Martin, *Opers Mgr*
Jim Ford, *Accounts Mgr*
Tracey Englert, *Regl Sales Mgr*
EMP: 28
SALES (est): 9.8MM **Privately Held**
WEB: www.arjinfusion.com
SIC: 8082 Home health care services

(G-5662)
ARROW ACQUISITION LLC
Also Called: Arrow Material Handling Pdts
16000 W 108th St (66219-1335)
PHONE..................................913 495-4869
Terry Melvin, *CEO*
Ross T Gault, *President*
Ross T Gault Jr, *Vice Pres*
Annette Vasser, *CFO*
Rusty Hardin, *Sales Staff*
▲ **EMP**: 68
SQ FT: 716,000
SALES (est): 32MM **Privately Held**
WEB: www.arrowforklift.com
SIC: 5084 Lift trucks & parts

(G-5663)
ARROW FORK LIFT PARTS INC
16000 W 108th St (66219-1335)
PHONE..................................816 231-4410
Mary Nicodelus, *Principal*
Annette Vesser, *CFO*
Robert Antes, *Info Tech Dir*
EMP: 6 **EST**: 2015
SALES (est): 128.7K **Privately Held**
SIC: 3599 5046 Air intake filters, internal combustion engine, except auto; balances, excluding laboratory

(G-5664)
ARROWHEAD CONTRACTING INC
10981 Eicher Dr (66219-2601)
PHONE..................................913 814-9994
Curt Koutelas, *President*
Steve Engley, *Vice Pres*
G Bryant Kroutch, *Vice Pres*
Greg Wallace, *Vice Pres*
EMP: 100
SQ FT: 4,950
SALES (est): 10.8MM **Privately Held**
SIC: 1541 1542 1799 Industrial buildings & warehouses; commercial & office building, new construction; asbestos removal & encapsulation

(G-5665)
ARTCO CASKET CO INC (PA)
16023 W 99th St (66219-1293)
P.O. Box 15808 (66285-5808)
PHONE..................................913 438-2655
Roger W Sevedge, *President*
Keith Sevedge, *Vice Pres*
Pat Duckers, *Sales Mgr*
Marty Adams, *Sales Staff*
Rick Newcomer, *Sales Staff*
EMP: 21 **EST**: 1951
SQ FT: 26,100
SALES (est): 17.3MM **Privately Held**
WEB: www.artcocasket.com
SIC: 5087 Caskets

(G-5666)
ASAP TRANSPORT SOLUTIONS LLC
11248 Strang Line Rd (66215-4039)
PHONE..................................800 757-1178
Christopher Steele, *President*
Ryan Beck,
EMP: 20
SALES: 200K **Privately Held**
SIC: 4731 Transportation agents & brokers

(G-5667)
ASI COMPUTER TECHNOLOGIES INC
Also Called: A S I Kansas
15000 W 106th St (66215-2052)
PHONE..................................913 888-8843
Jimmy Cheng, *Branch Mgr*
EMP: 40
SALES (corp-wide): 434.8MM **Privately Held**
WEB: www.asipartner.com
SIC: 5045 Disk drives; keying equipment; printers, computer; terminals, computer
PA: Asi Computer Technologies Inc
48289 Fremont Blvd
Fremont CA 94538
510 226-8000

(G-5668)
ASPLUNDH TREE EXPERT LLC
10575 Widmer Rd (66215-2096)
PHONE..................................913 469-5440
Ed Bradshew, *Branch Mgr*
Paul Snethen, *Supervisor*
EMP: 650
SALES (corp-wide): 4.5B **Privately Held**
WEB: www.asplundh.com
SIC: 0783 Planting, pruning & trimming services
PA: Asplundh Tree Expert, Llc
708 Blair Mill Rd
Willow Grove PA 19090
215 784-4200

(G-5669)
ASSEMBLY COMPONENT SYSTEMS INC (DH)
14621 W 112th St (66215-4096)
PHONE..................................913 492-9500
Jim Deegan, *President*
▲ **EMP**: 30
SQ FT: 135,000
SALES (est): 26.9MM
SALES (corp-wide): 1.6B **Publicly Held**
WEB: www.assemblycomponentsystems.com
SIC: 5072 Bolts, nuts & screws
HQ: Supply Technologies Llc
6065 Parkland Blvd Ste 2
Cleveland OH 44124
440 947-2100

(G-5670)
ASSOCIATED AIR PRODUCTS INC (PA)
Also Called: A A P
14900 W 107th St (66215-4018)
P.O. Box 7646, Overland Park (66207-0646)
PHONE..................................913 894-5600
Rex Mustaine, *President*
Paul Johnson, *Principal*
Mike Wixson, *Principal*
William Wilson, *Engineer*
Michael G Wixson, *Engineer*
EMP: 14
SQ FT: 1,900
SALES (est): 18MM **Privately Held**
WEB: www.aap-kc.com
SIC: 5084 Industrial machinery & equipment

(G-5671)
ASSOCIATED EQP SLS CO LLC
14535 W 96th Ter (66215-1165)
PHONE..................................913 894-4455
Roxanne West, *Project Mgr*
Sharla Dean, *Accountant*
Keith Hanson, *Sales Engr*
Jeff Davis, *Sales Staff*
Adam Koontz, *Sales Staff*
EMP: 15
SALES (est): 9.1MM **Privately Held**
WEB: www.aeskc.com
SIC: 5084 Industrial machinery & equipment

(G-5672)
ASSOCIATED ORTHOPEDICS P A
12200 W 106th St Ste 400 (66215-2305)
PHONE..................................913 541-8897
John Romito MD, *President*
Mark Humphrey, *Principal*
Joanne Turano, *Principal*

GEOGRAPHIC

EMP: 12
SALES (est): 1.5MM **Privately Held**
SIC: 8011 Orthopedic physician

(G-5673)
AT&T INC
10636 Lackman Rd (66219-1226)
PHONE..................................913 676-1136
Christopher Gustafson, *Manager*
EMP: 11
SALES (corp-wide): 170.7B **Publicly Held**
SIC: 4812 2741 4813 3661 Cellular telephone services; miscellaneous publishing; telephone communication, except radio; telephone & telegraph apparatus; radio & TV communications equipment
PA: At&T Inc.
208 S Akard St
Dallas TX 75202
210 821-4105

(G-5674)
ATRONIC ALARMS INC (PA)
Also Called: Honeywell Authorized Dealer
8220 Melrose Dr (66214-1626)
PHONE..................................913 432-4545
Perry Atha, *President*
John Erickson, *Treasurer*
Nick Hysom, *Consultant*
Nick Macaluso, *Supervisor*
Yabin Clemoens, *Technical Staff*
EMP: 26
SQ FT: 6,512
SALES (est): 40.2MM **Privately Held**
WEB: www.atronicalarms.com
SIC: 5063 5999 1731 Electric alarms & signaling equipment; fire alarm systems; alarm signal systems; access control systems specialization

(G-5675)
AUTOMATIC DATA PROCESSING INC
Also Called: ADP
16011 College Blvd # 110 (66219-1366)
PHONE..................................913 492-4200
Lori Burchfield, *Manager*
EMP: 10
SALES (corp-wide): 14.1B **Publicly Held**
SIC: 7374 Data processing service
PA: Automatic Data Processing, Inc.
1 Adp Blvd Ste 1 # 1
Roseland NJ 07068
973 974-5000

(G-5676)
AVATAR ENGINEERING INC
14360 W 96th Ter (66215-4708)
PHONE..................................913 897-6757
Jack Ward, *President*
Julie Baughman, *Office Mgr*
EMP: 18
SQ FT: 8,900
SALES (est): 3.9MM **Privately Held**
WEB: www.avatar-eng.com
SIC: 3672 8711 Printed circuit boards; engineering services

(G-5677)
AVI SYSTEMS INC
8019 Bond St (66214-1593)
PHONE..................................913 495-9494
Tom Madson, *Branch Mgr*
EMP: 35
SALES (corp-wide): 250.2MM **Privately Held**
WEB: www.avisystems.com
SIC: 5065 7622 7812 5999 Video equipment, electronic; communication equipment repair; audio-visual program production; audio-visual equipment & supplies
PA: Avi Systems, Inc.
9675 W 76th St Ste 200
Eden Prairie MN 55344
952 949-3700

(G-5678)
AXELACARE HOLDINGS INC (PA)
Also Called: Axelacare Health Care
15529 College Blvd (66219-1351)
PHONE..................................877 342-9352
Nancy Davenport, *General Mgr*
Tanya Menefee, *General Mgr*
Stacey Jensen, *Vice Pres*
Scott Murphy, *Vice Pres*
Andrew Pyrih, *Vice Pres*
EMP: 115
SALES (est): 65.9MM **Privately Held**
SIC: 8082 Home health care services

(G-5679)
B C A /FRY-WAGNER INC
Also Called: Fry-Wagner Mid MO Mvg & Stor
15850 Santa Fe Trail Dr (66219-9643)
PHONE..................................573 499-0000
Patrick Davidson, *Manager*
EMP: 50
SALES (corp-wide): 66.8MM **Privately Held**
SIC: 4213 Trucking, except local
HQ: B C A /Fry-Wagner Inc
15850 Santa Fe Trail Dr
Lenexa KS 66219
913 541-0020

(G-5680)
B F ASCHER & COMPANY INC
15501 W 109th St (66219-1307)
P.O. Box 717, Shawnee Mission (66201-0717)
PHONE..................................913 888-1880
James J Ascher, *Ch of Bd*
Christopher J Ascher, *President*
James J Ascher Jr, *President*
Sarah Powell, *Purch Agent*
Aaron Bengston, *Accountant*
▲ **EMP:** 40 **EST:** 1949
SQ FT: 34,000
SALES (est): 13MM **Privately Held**
WEB: www.bfascher.com
SIC: 2834 Pharmaceutical preparations

(G-5681)
B/E AEROSPACE INC
Also Called: Galley Products Group
10800 Pflumm Rd (66215-4061)
PHONE..................................913 338-9800
JP Foulon, *Vice Pres*
Chuck Robinson, *Vice Pres*
RAO Tella, *Vice Pres*
Linda Goodwin, *Purchasing*
Sebastien Ramus, *Engineer*
EMP: 100
SALES (corp-wide): 66.5B **Publicly Held**
WEB: www.beaerospace.com
SIC: 3728 Aircraft parts & equipment
HQ: B/E Aerospace, Inc.
1400 Corporate Center Way
Wellington FL 33414
561 791-5000

(G-5682)
BALANCE INNOVATIONS LLC
11011 Eicher Dr (66219-2604)
PHONE..................................913 599-1177
Darren Knipp, *President*
Todd Shutts, *President*
Aaron McKee, *Exec VP*
Tracy Transmeier, *Vice Pres*
James Hill, *Engineer*
EMP: 100
SALES (est): 6.7MM **Privately Held**
SIC: 7373 Systems software development services

(G-5683)
BALDWIN AMERICAS CORPORATION
14600 W 106th St (66215-2045)
PHONE..................................913 310-3258
Karl Puehringer, *President*
William Gegenheimer, *Partner*
John Favat, *Executive*
▲ **EMP:** 5
SQ FT: 1,000
SALES (est): 20.7MM **Privately Held**
SIC: 3555 Printing trade parts & attachments
HQ: Baldwin Technology Company, Inc.
8040 Forsyth Blvd
Saint Louis MO 63105
314 726-2152

(G-5684)
BALLYHOO BANNERS
8022 Monrovia St (66215-2727)
PHONE..................................913 385-5050
Curtis Heaton, *President*
EMP: 5
SALES (est): 424.9K **Privately Held**
SIC: 6162 5099 3993 Mortgage bankers & correspondents; signs, except electric; signs & advertising specialties

(G-5685)
BANK AMERICA NATIONAL ASSN
7747 Quivira Rd (66216-3406)
PHONE..................................816 979-8219
EMP: 15
SALES (corp-wide): 110.5B **Publicly Held**
WEB: www.bofa.com
SIC: 6021 National commercial banks
HQ: Bank Of America, National Association
100 S Tryon St
Charlotte NC 28202
704 386-5681

(G-5686)
BARBER FINANCIAL GROUP INC (PA)
Also Called: Comprehensive Fincl Plg Svcs
13550 W 95th St (66215-3302)
PHONE..................................913 393-1000
Dean Barber, *President*
Courtney Roberts, *Opers Staff*
Nanette Marx, *Admin Asst*
EMP: 19
SALES (est): 2.9MM **Privately Held**
SIC: 8742 8111 Financial consultant; legal services

(G-5687)
BARNES & DODGE INC
17135 W 116th St (66219-9607)
PHONE..................................913 321-6444
Roland R Phelps, *CEO*
Roger A Phelps, *President*
Russell Phelps, *General Mgr*
Russell D Phelps, *Vice Pres*
Zella M Phelps, *Treasurer*
EMP: 50
SQ FT: 25,000
SALES: 8.2MM **Privately Held**
WEB: www.barnesanddodge.com
SIC: 1761 1711 3444 Sheet metalwork; warm air heating & air conditioning contractor; ventilation & duct work contractor; sheet metalwork

(G-5688)
BARTLESVILLE SW HOTEL INC
Also Called: Hilton Garden In
9903 Pflumm Rd (66215-1222)
PHONE..................................913 345-2111
Donald E Culbertson, *President*
Barry Erautman, *Vice Pres*
Linda Smith, *Admin Sec*
EMP: 60
SALES (est): 1.2MM **Privately Held**
SIC: 7011 Hotels & motels

(G-5689)
BASYS PROCESSING INC
15423 W 100th Ter (66219-1289)
PHONE..................................800 386-0711
Carolynne Holden, *Technical Staff*
EMP: 20
SALES (est): 2.3MM **Privately Held**
WEB: www.bayspro.com
SIC: 7389 Credit card service

(G-5690)
BATS TRADING INC (DH)
8050 Marshall Dr Ste 120 (66214-1572)
PHONE..................................913 815-7000
Joe Ratterman, *President*
William O'Brien, *President*
Chris Isaacson, *COO*
Jill Bier, *Counsel*
Chris Solgan, *Counsel*
EMP: 76
SALES (est): 20.1MM **Publicly Held**
WEB: www.batstrading.com
SIC: 6211 Security brokers & dealers

(G-5691)
BE SMITH INC
8801 Renner Ave (66219-9717)
PHONE..................................913 341-9116
John Doug Smith, *CEO*
Lisa Carr, *Senior VP*
Colleen Chapp, *Senior VP*
Brian Christianson, *Senior VP*
Mark Madden, *Senior VP*
EMP: 271 **EST:** 1980
SQ FT: 24,000
SALES (est): 41.3MM
SALES (corp-wide): 2.1B **Publicly Held**
WEB: www.besmith.com
SIC: 8748 Business consulting
PA: Amn Healthcare Services, Inc.
12400 High Bluff Dr
San Diego CA 92130
866 871-8519

(G-5692)
BEACON SALES ACQUISITION INC
15500 W 108th St (66219-1304)
PHONE..................................913 871-1949
Rhian Cooper, *Sales Mgr*
Patrick Everson, *Sales Staff*
Dylan Baker, *Manager*
EMP: 15
SALES (corp-wide): 7.1B **Publicly Held**
WEB: www.shelterdistribution.com
SIC: 5033 Roofing, siding & insulation
HQ: Beacon Sales Acquisition, Inc.
50 Webster Ave
Somerville MA 02143
877 645-7663

(G-5693)
BEAR COMMUNICATIONS LLC
21987 W 83rd St (66227-3133)
PHONE..................................913 441-3355
EMP: 50
SALES (est): 5.6MM **Privately Held**
SIC: 1796 1731 Installing Building Equipment

(G-5694)
BEAUTY BRANDS LLC
Also Called: Beauty Brnds Slon Spa Sprstore
9570 Quivira Rd (66215-1670)
PHONE..................................913 492-7900
Marie Molle, *Manager*
EMP: 50 **Privately Held**
SIC: 5999 7231 Toiletries, cosmetics & perfumes; beauty shops
PA: Beauty Brands Llc
15507 W 99th St
Lenexa KS 66219

(G-5695)
BEAUTY BRANDS LLC (PA)
Also Called: Beauty Brnds Slon Spa Sprstore
15507 W 99th St (66219-1254)
PHONE..................................816 531-2266
Lyn Kirby, *CEO*
Rich Bos, *President*
Nicole Argo, *Marketing Staff*
Caryn Lerner,
EMP: 50
SQ FT: 6,000
SALES (est): 429.6MM **Privately Held**
SIC: 5999 7231 Cosmetics; hairdressers

(G-5696)
BEDESCHI MID-WEST CONVEYOR LLC
8245 Nieman Rd Ste 123 (66214-1509)
PHONE..................................913 384-9950
Rino Bedeschi, *CEO*
Larry Harp, *President*
Gerald Cohen, *Vice Pres*
Mike Ostradick, *Vice Pres*
Nancy Burriss, *Controller*
EMP: 25
SQ FT: 24,538
SALES (est): 916.2K **Privately Held**
SIC: 5084 Conveyor systems

(G-5697)
BEDROCK INTERNATIONAL LLC (HQ)
9929 Lackman Rd (66219-1211)
PHONE..................................913 438-7625
Byron Dougherty, *President*
Caryn Smith, *General Mgr*
Wanessa Dougherty, *COO*
Lalo Herrera, *Foreman/Supr*
Gatoff Brett, *Sales Staff*
▲ **EMP:** 28 **EST:** 2000
SQ FT: 20,000

SALES (est): 19.5MM
SALES (corp-wide): 489.7MM **Publicly Held**
WEB: www.kcstone.com
SIC: 5032 Granite building stone
PA: Select Interior Concepts, Inc.
400 Galleria Pkwy Se # 17
Atlanta GA 30339
714 701-4200

(G-5698)
BELTMANN GROUP INCORPORATED
8101 Lenexa Dr Ste B (66214-1633)
P.O. Box 14728, Shawnee Mission (66285-4728)
PHONE....913 888-9105
James Piasso, *General Mgr*
EMP: 21 **Privately Held**
WEB: www.beltmann.com
SIC: 4214 Local trucking with storage
HQ: Beltmann Group Incorporated
2480 Long Lake Rd
Saint Paul MN 55113
651 639-2800

(G-5699)
BETTER LIFE TECHNOLOGY LLC (PA)
9736 Legler Rd (66219-1282)
PHONE....913 894-0403
Brett Sneed,
Don Sneed,
▲ **EMP:** 10
SQ FT: 170,000
SALES (est): 25.5MM **Privately Held**
WEB: www.bltlc.com
SIC: 3081 Floor or wall covering, unsupported plastic

(G-5700)
BETWEEN LNES ELITE SPT ACADEMY
8259 Hedge Lane Ter (66227)
PHONE....913 422-1221
Robert Jones, *Mng Member*
Rusty Jones,
EMP: 10
SALES: 350K **Privately Held**
SIC: 7999 Baseball instruction school

(G-5701)
BHJLLC INC (PA)
14105 Marshall Dr (66215-1300)
PHONE....913 888-8028
Dennis Birkestrand, *CEO*
Rodney Holsapple, *President*
Bjorn Birkestrand, *Division Mgr*
Brian Drecktrah, *Division Mgr*
Suzanne Birkestrand, *Vice Pres*
EMP: 100
SQ FT: 84,000
SALES (est): 22.3MM **Privately Held**
WEB: www.kcfda.com
SIC: 5064 5087 5063 Electrical appliances, major; vacuum cleaning systems; electric alarms & signaling equipment

(G-5702)
BIG BLOCK INC
8167 Cole Pkwy (66227-2714)
P.O. Box 861140, Shawnee (66286-1140)
PHONE....913 927-2135
David Vanlerberg, *President*
Mark Decoursdy, *Vice Pres*
EMP: 10
SALES: 2MM **Privately Held**
WEB: www.bigblockinc.com
SIC: 3271 Concrete block & brick

(G-5703)
BINGHAM CANYON CORPORATION (PA)
10457 W 84th Ter (66214-1641)
PHONE....913 353-4560
Brett D Mayer, *President*
John W Peters, *Corp Secy*
EMP: 6
SQ FT: 650
SALES: 266.1K **Publicly Held**
SIC: 3822 Auto controls regulating residntl & coml environmt & applncs

(G-5704)
BIO-MICROBICS INC (PA)
16002 W 110th St (66219-1328)
PHONE....913 422-0707
Robert J Rebori, *President*
James Bell, *Vice Pres*
Robert Robori, *Vice Pres*
Steve Grant, *Comptroller*
Jennifer Cisneros, *Marketing Staff*
◆ **EMP:** 25
SALES (est): 6.7MM **Privately Held**
WEB: www.biomicrobics.com
SIC: 3589 Water treatment equipment, industrial

(G-5705)
BIOMED KANSAS INC (DH)
Also Called: Soleo Health
10633 Rene St (66215-4052)
PHONE....913 661-0100
Drew Walk, *CEO*
John Ginzler, *CFO*
EMP: 9
SALES (est): 1.1MM **Privately Held**
SIC: 2834 5912 Druggists' preparations (pharmaceuticals); drug stores & proprietary stores
HQ: Biomed Healthcare, Inc.
950 Calcon Hook Rd Ste 19
Sharon Hill PA 19079
888 244-2340

(G-5706)
BIOMUNE COMPANY
Also Called: Ceva Biomune
8735 Rosehill Rd (66215-4610)
PHONE....913 894-0230
EMP: 13
SALES (corp-wide): 5.4MM **Privately Held**
SIC: 2836 Vaccines
HQ: Biomune Company
8906 Rosehill Rd
Lenexa KS 66215

(G-5707)
BIOMUNE COMPANY (DH)
8906 Rosehill Rd (66215-3514)
PHONE....913 894-0230
Marc Prikarsky, *President*
Philppe Du-Mesnil, *Chairman*
Joan D Leonard, *Vice Pres*
Dennis Chong, *Manager*
Pierre Revel-Mourcz, *Director*
◆ **EMP:** 85
SQ FT: 18,000
SALES (est): 26.7MM
SALES (corp-wide): 5.4MM **Privately Held**
WEB: www.biomunecompany.com
SIC: 2836 Vaccines
HQ: Ceva Sante Animale
Zone Industrielle
Libourne 33500
963 045-235

(G-5708)
BLOCK REAL ESTATE SERVICES LLC
10411 W 84th Ter (66214-1641)
PHONE....816 412-8409
Ron Fredericks, *Principal*
EMP: 31 **Privately Held**
SIC: 6531 Real estate agents & managers
PA: Block Real Estate Services, Llc
700 W 47th St Ste 200
Kansas City MO 64112

(G-5709)
BOYCE BYNUM PATHOLOGY LABS PC
8550 Marshall Dr (66214-1505)
PHONE....816 813-2792
EMP: 36
SALES (corp-wide): 30.4MM **Privately Held**
SIC: 8071 Medical laboratories
PA: Boyce & Bynum Pathology Laboratories, P.C.
200 Portland St
Columbia MO 65201
573 886-4600

(G-5710)
BOYER-KANSAS INC
Also Called: Shred It Kansas City
10000 Lackman Rd (66219-1214)
PHONE....913 307-9400
Robert Boyer, *President*
David Foster, *Manager*
EMP: 30
SALES (est): 2.4MM **Privately Held**
SIC: 7389 Personal service agents, brokers & bureaus; document & office record destruction

(G-5711)
BRAD VIGNATELLI
Also Called: Blue Chip Copy & Print
17501 W 98th St Spc 1855 (66219-1703)
PHONE....913 541-9777
Brad Vignatelli, *President*
EMP: 7
SALES (est): 849.8K **Privately Held**
SIC: 2752 Commercial printing, lithographic

(G-5712)
BRIDGE CAPITAL MANAGEMENT LLC
16829 W 116th St (66219-9603)
PHONE....913 283-7804
Daniel Brewer,
EMP: 11
SALES: 50MM **Privately Held**
SIC: 6726 Management investment funds, closed-end

(G-5713)
BRIGHTMARKS LLC
9900 Pflumm Rd Ste 29 (66215-1231)
PHONE....913 338-1131
David Hutchison, *CEO*
Ashley Hutchison, *Controller*
Adam Murphy, *Sales Associate*
Connie Hutchison,
▲ **EMP:** 23
SQ FT: 15,000
SALES (est): 3.6MM **Privately Held**
WEB: www.brightmarks.com
SIC: 2759 Commercial printing

(G-5714)
BRIGHTVIEW LANDSCAPES LLC
12421 Santa Fe Trail Dr (66215-3597)
PHONE....913 371-2661
Lance Schelhammer, *Manager*
EMP: 36
SALES (corp-wide): 2.4B **Publicly Held**
SIC: 0781 Landscape services
HQ: Brightview Landscapes, Llc
980 Jolly Rd Ste 300
Blue Bell PA 19422
484 567-7204

(G-5715)
BRIGHTWELL DISPENSERS INC
9567 Alden St (66215-1164)
PHONE....913 956-4909
Stephen Woolmer, *President*
Andy Lewis, *Vice Pres*
EMP: 8
SALES (est): 103.4K **Privately Held**
SIC: 3999 Soap dispensers
HQ: Brightwell Dispensers Limited
1 Rich Industrial Estate
Newhaven E SUSSEX BN9 0
127 351-3566

(G-5716)
BRIOVARX LLC (HQ)
11142 Renner Blvd (66219-9621)
PHONE....913 307-9900
Robert Wamble, *Principal*
EMP: 17
SALES (est): 4.1MM
SALES (corp-wide): 226.2B **Publicly Held**
SIC: 5047 Medical & hospital equipment
PA: Unitedhealth Group Incorporated
9900 Bren Rd E Ste 300w
Minnetonka MN 55343
952 936-1300

(G-5717)
BRIOVARX INFUSION SVCS 305 LLC (DH)
15529 College Blvd (66219-1351)
PHONE....913 747-3700
Ted Kramm, *CEO*
Kathee Kramm, *President*
Dan Buning, *COO*
Joe Zavalishin, *Exec VP*
Larry Freni, *CFO*
EMP: 80 **EST:** 2015
SALES (est): 59.4MM
SALES (corp-wide): 226.2B **Publicly Held**
SIC: 5122 Pharmaceuticals

(G-5718)
BRODERSON MANUFACTURING CORP (DH)
14741 W 106th St (66215-2015)
P.O. Box 88638, Chicago IL (60680-1638)
PHONE....913 888-0606
Jeffry D Bust, *CEO*
Bill Baker, *President*
Stephen Burton, *President*
Bob Bailey, *Buyer*
Michael Holmes, *Engineer*
◆ **EMP:** 68
SQ FT: 62,000
SALES (est): 22.7MM
SALES (corp-wide): 181.8MM **Privately Held**
WEB: www.bmccranes.com
SIC: 3594 3546 3536 3531 Fluid power pumps & motors; power-driven handtools; hoists, cranes & monorails; cranes
HQ: Mi-Jack Products Inc.
3111 167th St
Hazel Crest IL 60429
708 596-5200

(G-5719)
BROWNS MEDICAL IMAGING
Also Called: B M I
9880 Pflumm Rd (66215-1208)
PHONE....913 888-6710
Dan Brown, *Owner*
EMP: 12
SALES (est): 1MM **Privately Held**
WEB: www.brownsmedicalimaging.com
SIC: 5047 X-ray machines & tubes

(G-5720)
BSE STRUCTURAL ENGINEERS LLC
Also Called: Busey Schmidtberger Engrg
11320 W 79th St (66214-1401)
PHONE....913 492-7400
Ryan Shafer, *VP Mktg*
Amy Boehringer, *Mktg Dir*
Nora Henderson, *Office Mgr*
Steve Busey, *Mng Member*
Cassie Barger, *Technician*
EMP: 20
SQ FT: 3,000
SALES (est): 1MM **Privately Held**
WEB: www.bse-dec.com
SIC: 8711 Consulting engineer

(G-5721)
BURLINGTON NTHRN SANTA FE LLC
8310 Nieman Rd (66214-1510)
PHONE....913 577-5521
Ralph Young, *Principal*
EMP: 100
SALES (corp-wide): 225.3B **Publicly Held**
SIC: 4011 Railroads, line-haul operating
HQ: Burlington Northern Santa Fe, Llc
2650 Lou Menk Dr
Fort Worth TX 76131

(G-5722)
BYRNE CUSTOM WOOD PRODUCTS INC
17501 W 98th St Spc 2862 (66219-1737)
PHONE....913 894-4777
Ian Byrne, *President*
Donovan Mumma, *General Mgr*
Kathy Byrne, *Vice Pres*
EMP: 15
SALES (est): 2.1MM **Privately Held**
WEB: www.byrnecustomwood.com
SIC: 1751 Cabinet building & installation

GEOGRAPHIC

(G-5723)
C & C GROUP OF COMPANIES
10012 Darnell St (66215-1151)
PHONE..................................913 492-8414
Michael Cillessen, *President*
Michael Scherrer, *VP Finance*
EMP: 80
SQ FT: 20,000
SALES (est): 2.6MM **Privately Held**
SIC: 1711 Heating & air conditioning contractors

(G-5724)
C A TITUS INC (PA)
Also Called: Zimmer Titus Associates
9545 Alden St (66215-1164)
PHONE..................................913 888-1024
Craig A Titus, *President*
Bill McCarrick, *Director*
EMP: 90 **EST:** 1959
SQ FT: 12,700
SALES: 80MM **Privately Held**
SIC: 5047 Orthopedic equipment & supplies; surgical equipment & supplies

(G-5725)
CALVERTS AUTO EXPRESS
11490 Strang Line Rd (66215-4046)
PHONE..................................913 631-9995
EMP: 21
SALES (est): 2.3MM **Privately Held**
SIC: 7538 General automotive repair shops

(G-5726)
CALVERTS EXPRESS AUTO S (PA)
11490 Strang Line Rd (66215-4046)
PHONE..................................913 631-9995
Gary Calvert, *CEO*
Keith Conner, *Warehouse Mgr*
EMP: 26
SALES (est): 13.2MM **Privately Held**
SIC: 7539 7538 Automotive repair shops; general automotive repair shops

(G-5727)
CAMCORP INC
9732 Pflumm Rd (66215-1206)
PHONE..................................913 831-0740
Tony Thill, *President*
Tracy Janssen, *Vice Pres*
Ted E Metz, *Vice Pres*
Michael J Milberger, *Vice Pres*
EMP: 14
SALES (est): 3.7MM **Privately Held**
SIC: 8711 Construction & civil engineering

(G-5728)
CAPTIFY HEALTH INC
13321 W 98th St (66215-1374)
PHONE..................................913 951-2600
Tom Sanders, *President*
John Bradberry, *CFO*
Johnny Lim, *CTO*
EMP: 40 **EST:** 2012
SALES (est): 302.3K
SALES (corp-wide): 23.2MM **Privately Held**
SIC: 8011 Offices & clinics of medical doctors
PA: Continuum Health Alliance, Llc
402 Lippincott Dr
Marlton NJ 08053
856 782-3300

(G-5729)
CAREER ATHLETES LLC
Also Called: Athlete Network
10000 Marshall Dr (66215-1244)
PHONE..................................913 538-6259
Chris Smith, *President*
Dirk Ochs, *COO*
Eli Fisher, *Vice Pres*
Benjamin McCabe, *Vice Pres*
Dj Washington, *Vice Pres*
EMP: 21
SALES (est): 1.8MM **Privately Held**
SIC: 7363 Help supply services

(G-5730)
CARGILL INCORPORATED
15405 College Blvd # 200 (66219-1324)
PHONE..................................913 752-1200
Kerrie Lindburg, *Branch Mgr*
EMP: 50
SALES (corp-wide): 113.4B **Privately Held**
SIC: 5159 Bristles
PA: Cargill, Incorporated
15407 Mcginty Rd W
Wayzata MN 55391
952 742-7575

(G-5731)
CASEY ASSOCIATES INC
Also Called: Scanneddocs.com
8307 Melrose Dr (66214-1629)
PHONE..................................913 276-3200
F Mark Casey, *President*
Fredric Casey, *General Mgr*
Mark Casey, *Vice Pres*
EMP: 15
SQ FT: 13,000
SALES: 1.2MM **Privately Held**
WEB: www.caseyinc.net
SIC: 7374 5734 7389 Data processing service; software, business & non-game; microfilm recording & developing service

(G-5732)
CAT CLINIC OF JOHNSON COUNTY
Also Called: Cat Clinic of Johnson, The
9421 Pflumm Rd A (66215-3307)
PHONE..................................913 541-0478
Irene Schuomacker, *Principal*
Irene Schomacker,
EMP: 10
SALES (est): 962.6K **Privately Held**
WEB: www.catclinicofjc.com
SIC: 0742 Animal hospital services, pets & other animal specialties

(G-5733)
CATAPULT INTERNATIONAL LLC (HQ)
Also Called: Catapult, A Mercator Company
13632 W 95th St (66215-3304)
PHONE..................................913 232-2389
Matthew Motsick, *CEO*
Virgil Ferreira, *President*
Bryan E Luttrell, *COO*
EMP: 26
SALES (est): 6.3MM **Privately Held**
SIC: 4731 7371 Freight transportation arrangement; computer software development & applications

(G-5734)
CATES HEATING & AC SVC CO
Also Called: Cates Service Co
14361 W 96th Ter (66215-4709)
PHONE..................................913 888-4470
James A Kiekel, *President*
Jeffrey V Kiekel, *Vice Pres*
Margaret G Kiekel, *Treasurer*
Derek Larm, *Director*
EMP: 25
SQ FT: 5,000
SALES: 5MM **Privately Held**
WEB: www.catesservice.com
SIC: 1711 Warm air heating & air conditioning contractor; heating & air conditioning contractors; heating systems repair & maintenance

(G-5735)
CB&I ENVMTL INFRASTRUCTURE INC
11206 Thompson Ave (66219-2303)
PHONE..................................913 451-1224
EMP: 37
SALES (corp-wide): 10.6B **Privately Held**
SIC: 8748 Environmental Services
HQ: Cb&I Environmental & Infrastructure, Inc.
4171 Essen Ln
Baton Rouge LA 70809
225 932-2500

(G-5736)
CBOE BATS LLC (HQ)
8050 Marshall Dr (66214-1524)
PHONE..................................913 815-7000
Edward T Tilly, *CEO*
Chris Concannon, *President*
James Arrante, *Business Mgr*
Chris Isaacson, *Exec VP*
Eric Swanson, *Exec VP*
EMP: 38
SALES (est): 1.6B **Publicly Held**
SIC: 6231 Security & commodity exchanges

(G-5737)
CC PRODUCTS LLC
Also Called: Ccpi
9700 Commerce Pkwy (66219-2402)
PHONE..................................913 693-3200
John Fryer, *President*
EMP: 400
SALES: 160MM
SALES (corp-wide): 6.8B **Publicly Held**
SIC: 2329 2339 Men's & boys' sportswear & athletic clothing; men's & boys' leather, wool & down-filled outerwear; men's & boys' athletic uniforms; women's & misses' athletic clothing & sportswear; athletic clothing: women's, misses' & juniors'; uniforms, athletic: women's, misses' & juniors'
HQ: Gfsi, Llc
9700 Commerce Pkwy
Lenexa KS 66219
913 693-3200

(G-5738)
CENTENE CORPORATION
8325 Lenexa Dr (66214-1654)
PHONE..................................913 599-3078
Kelley Cramm, *Branch Mgr*
EMP: 98 **Publicly Held**
SIC: 6324 Health maintenance organization (HMO), insurance only
PA: Centene Corporation
7700 Forsyth Blvd Ste 800
Saint Louis MO 63105

(G-5739)
CENTRINEX LLC
10310 W 84th Ter (66214-1638)
PHONE..................................913 827-9600
Bart N Miller, *Owner*
EMP: 12 **EST:** 2006
SALES (est): 1.4MM **Privately Held**
SIC: 8741 Management services

(G-5740)
CENTURY BUILDING SOLUTIONS INC
9800 Legler Rd (66219-1263)
P.O. Box 15376 (66285-5376)
PHONE..................................913 422-5555
Roger H Neighbors, *President*
Nancy Neighbors, *Vice Pres*
Jean Degreave, *Controller*
EMP: 10
SALES: 13.1MM
SALES (corp-wide): 76.9MM **Privately Held**
WEB: www.neighborsconstruction.com
SIC: 5031 Lumber: rough, dressed & finished; building materials, exterior; building materials, interior
PA: Neighbors Construction Co., Inc.
15226 W 87th Street Pkwy
Lenexa KS 66219
913 422-5555

(G-5741)
CENTURY CONSTRUCTION SUP LLC
9600 Dice Ln (66215-1152)
PHONE..................................913 438-3366
William You, *Manager*
EMP: 10
SQ FT: 1,000
SALES (est): 331.6K **Privately Held**
SIC: 8741 8742 Construction management; materials mgmt. (purchasing, handling, inventory) consultant

(G-5742)
CENTURY MARKETING INC
14631 W 95th St (66215-5216)
PHONE..................................913 696-9758
Phil Steinly, *President*
Troy Coup, *President*
John Ogilvie, *Prdtn Mgr*
Amanda Webster, *Production*
EMP: 16
SALES (est): 2MM **Privately Held**
WEB: www.centurypublications.com
SIC: 2721 Periodicals

(G-5743)
CERTTECH LLC
14425 College Blvd # 140 (66215-2002)
PHONE..................................913 814-9770
Sam Jarrell, *CEO*
EMP: 30
SALES (est): 6.9MM **Privately Held**
SIC: 7371 Computer software development

(G-5744)
CEVA ANIMAL HEALTH LLC (DH)
8735 Rosehill Rd Ste 300 (66215-4612)
PHONE..................................800 999-0297
Emily Umphrey, *Accountant*
Andrew Long, *Sales Mgr*
Jody Donohue, *Comms Mgr*
Ashley Bailes, *Mktg Coord*
Brad Bulter, *Mng Member*
EMP: 62
SALES (est): 14.2MM
SALES (corp-wide): 5.4MM **Privately Held**
WEB: www.summitvetpharm.com
SIC: 2048 0742 Canned pet food (except dog & cat); veterinary services, specialties
HQ: Ceva Sante Animale
Zone Industrielle
Libourne 33500
963 045-235

(G-5745)
CEVA ANIMAL HEALTH LLC
8906 Rosehill Rd (66215-3514)
PHONE..................................913 894-0230
Craige Wallce, *CEO*
Lopez Jose, *Research*
Didier Calkmejane, *CFO*
Jennifer Harlow, *Human Res Dir*
Edward Koronowski, *Manager*
▲ **EMP:** 179
SALES (est): 13.1MM **Privately Held**
SIC: 0742 Veterinary services, specialties

(G-5746)
CEVA BIOMUNE
8735 Rosehill Rd (66215-4610)
PHONE..................................913 894-0230
EMP: 21 **EST:** 2013
SALES (est): 5.1MM **Privately Held**
SIC: 2836 Biological products, except diagnostic

(G-5747)
CEVA US HOLDINGS INC
8906 Rosehill Rd (66215-3514)
PHONE..................................913 894-0230
Craig Wallace, *CEO*
Linda Jackson, *Regional Mgr*
Olivier Cazeaux, *CFO*
Greg Furstner, *Human Resources*
Mike Malone, *Manager*
EMP: 10
SQ FT: 2,500
SALES (est): 1.5MM
SALES (corp-wide): 5.4MM **Privately Held**
SIC: 8741 Business management
HQ: Ceva Sante Animale
Zone Industrielle
Libourne 33500
963 045-235

(G-5748)
CEVA USA INC
8735 Rosehill Rd (66215-4610)
PHONE..................................800 999-0297
Tandy Frank, *Facilities Mgr*
Carina Kornspan, *Purch Mgr*
Mark Vanbuskirk, *Sales Staff*
Jennifer Brisbin, *Manager*
Rene Cerra, *Manager*
EMP: 22
SALES (est): 1.9MM **Privately Held**
SIC: 2048 Dry pet food (except dog & cat)

(G-5749)
CHALLENGER SPORTS CORP (PA)
8263 Flint St (66214-1500)
PHONE..................................913 599-4884
Peter Arch, *CEO*
Andy Bennett, *Senior VP*

▲ = Import ▼=Export ◆ =Import/Export

Alan Jones, *Senior VP*
Derrik Shore, *Senior VP*
Nathan Hill, *Opers Staff*
▲ **EMP:** 40 **EST:** 1997
SQ FT: 20,000
SALES (est): 28MM **Privately Held**
SIC: 7999 7941 7997 Instruction schools, camps & services; sports clubs, managers & promoters; membership sports & recreation clubs

(G-5750)
CHALLENGER SPORTS TEAMWEAR LLC
8263 Flint St (66214-1500)
PHONE..................................913 599-4884
Paul Lawrence, *Principal*
Matt Bowman, *Director*
Dan Growcott, *Director*
Simon Wigley, *Director*
Mike Blumenthal,
▲ **EMP:** 40
SALES: 6MM **Privately Held**
SIC: 2339 2329 Uniforms, athletic: women's, misses' & juniors'; men's & boys' athletic uniforms

(G-5751)
CHAMPION WINDOW CO KANS CY INC
Also Called: Champion Win Sding Patio Rooms
9050 Quivira Rd (66215-3902)
PHONE..................................913 541-8282
Don Seabaugh, *President*
EMP: 21
SALES (est): 3.7MM
SALES (corp-wide): 517.2MM **Privately Held**
SIC: 3442 3444 5211 3231 Storm doors or windows, metal; awnings, sheet metal; lumber & other building materials; products of purchased glass
PA: Champion Opco, Llc
12121 Champion Way
Cincinnati OH 45241
513 327-7338

(G-5752)
CHANNELVIEW SW HOTEL INC
9903 Pflumm Rd (66215-1222)
PHONE..................................913 345-2111
Linda Smith, *Treasurer*
EMP: 20
SQ FT: 53,000
SALES (est): 428.7K **Privately Held**
SIC: 8741 Hotel or motel management

(G-5753)
CHILD HEALTH CORP AMERICA
Also Called: Childrens Hospital Association
16011 College Blvd # 250 (66219-9877)
PHONE..................................913 262-1436
Mark Wietecha, *CEO*
Amy Knight, *COO*
Brian Humphreys, *Vice Pres*
Kory Kittle, *Vice Pres*
David Spizman, *Vice Pres*
EMP: 120
SQ FT: 33,516
SALES (est): 26.1MM
SALES (corp-wide): 6.6MM **Privately Held**
SIC: 8621 Professional membership organizations
PA: National Association Of Children's Hospitals, Inc.
600 13th St Nw Ste 500
Washington DC 20005
202 753-5500

(G-5754)
CHOICECARE LLC
Also Called: Comfort Care
12345 W 95th St Ste 215 (66215-3837)
PHONE..................................913 906-9880
Chad Trondson, *Owner*
EMP: 70
SALES (est): 497K **Privately Held**
SIC: 8082 Home health care services

(G-5755)
CITY OF LENEXA
Also Called: Lenexa Community Center
17201 W 87th St (66219-9721)
PHONE..................................913 541-0209
Igor Sinyavskiy, *Facilities Mgr*
Bill Nixks, *Director*
Katie Williams, *Officer*
EMP: 90 **Privately Held**
WEB: www.lenexafd.net
SIC: 8322 9111 Community center; mayors' offices
PA: City Of Lenexa
17101 W 87th St
Lenexa KS 66219
913 477-7500

(G-5756)
CITY WIDE FRANCHISE CO INC
15447 W 100th Ter (66219-1289)
PHONE..................................913 888-5700
Jeffery Oddo, *President*
Frank Oddo, *Principal*
Erin Blair, *Controller*
EMP: 21
SQ FT: 7,572
SALES (est): 168.2K **Privately Held**
SIC: 7349 Building maintenance services

(G-5757)
CITY WIDE HOLDING COMPANY INC (PA)
15447 W 100th Ter (66219-1289)
PHONE..................................913 888-5700
Elizabeth A Oddo, *President*
Rick Oddo, *Vice Pres*
Sandro Romero, *Facilities Mgr*
Brad Oddo, *Treasurer*
Mike Sawicki, *Sales Executive*
EMP: 148
SQ FT: 21,000
SALES (est): 48.6MM **Privately Held**
SIC: 7349 1522 5087 Janitorial service, contract basis; multi-family dwelling construction; janitors' supplies

(G-5758)
CITY WIDE MAINTENANCE CO INC
15447 W 100th Ter (66219-1289)
PHONE..................................913 888-5700
Jeff Oddo, *President*
Casey McDowell, *President*
Scott Brown, *Principal*
Rob Ellis, *Principal*
Frank Oddo, *Principal*
EMP: 147
SALES (est): 8.6MM
SALES (corp-wide): 48.6MM **Privately Held**
SIC: 7349 Janitorial service, contract basis
PA: City Wide Holding Company, Inc.
15447 W 100th Ter
Lenexa KS 66219
913 888-5700

(G-5759)
CITY WIDE WINDOW WASHING INC
15447 W 100th Ter (66219-1289)
PHONE..................................913 888-5700
Jeff Oddo, *President*
Rick Oddo, *Vice Pres*
Gary Howell, *CFO*
Brad Oddo, *Treasurer*
Elizabeth Oddo, *Admin Sec*
EMP: 10 **EST:** 1980
SALES: 650K **Privately Held**
SIC: 3589 Floor washing & polishing machines, commercial

(G-5760)
CLEAN AIR MANAGEMENT CO INC
9732 Pflumm Rd (66215-1206)
PHONE..................................913 831-0740
Frank Handwork, *President*
EMP: 30
SQ FT: 5,000
SALES (est): 5.3MM **Privately Held**
SIC: 3535 3822 Conveyors & conveying equipment; hardware for environmental regulators

(G-5761)
CLEANING UP LLC
11386 Strang Line Rd (66215-4041)
P.O. Box 3736, Olathe (66063-3736)
PHONE..................................913 327-7226
Melanie McGreevy,
EMP: 50
SALES: 850K **Privately Held**
SIC: 7349 Janitorial service, contract basis

(G-5762)
CLINICAL ASSOCIATES
8629 Bluejacket St # 100 (66214-1604)
PHONE..................................913 677-3553
Bruce Michael Cappo, *Owner*
Quinn Eggesiecker, *Psychologist*
Stella Fernandez, *Psychologist*
Joseph Wilner, *Psychologist*
Wayne Witcher, *Psychologist*
EMP: 26 **EST:** 2001
SALES (est): 331.8K **Privately Held**
SIC: 8049 Clinical psychologist

(G-5763)
CLINICAL ASSOCIATES PA (PA)
8629 Bluejacket St # 100 (66214-1604)
PHONE..................................913 677-3553
Bruce Cappo, *President*
Tracey Litwin, *Psychologist*
Seth Wescott, *Director*
EMP: 12
SALES (est): 1.1MM **Privately Held**
SIC: 8049 Clinical psychologist

(G-5764)
CLINICAL REFERENCE LAB INC
11711 W 83rd Ter (66214-1513)
PHONE..................................913 492-3652
EMP: 10
SALES (corp-wide): 53.8MM **Privately Held**
SIC: 7389 Automobile recovery service
PA: Clinical Reference Laboratory, Inc.
8433 Quivira Rd
Lenexa KS 66215
913 492-3652

(G-5765)
CLINICAL REFERENCE LAB INC (PA)
Also Called: Crl
8433 Quivira Rd (66215-2802)
PHONE..................................913 492-3652
Timothy Sotos, *Ch of Bd*
Tim Sotos, *Ch of Bd*
Jonathan Oberg, *President*
Robert Stout, *President*
Tracy Knox, *Superintendent*
EMP: 365
SQ FT: 80,000
SALES (est): 53.8MM **Privately Held**
WEB: www.crlcorp.com
SIC: 8071 8734 8731 6311 Testing laboratories; blood analysis laboratory; urinalysis laboratory; testing laboratories; commercial physical research; life insurance

(G-5766)
CLORE AUTOMOTIVE LLC (PA)
8735 Rosehill Rd Ste 220 (66215-4612)
PHONE..................................913 310-1050
James Chasm, *CEO*
Charles Valinotti, *President*
Kirk Clore, *Vice Pres*
Paul Zainea, *VP Opers*
Robin Decker, *Production*
◆ **EMP:** 45
SQ FT: 8,000
SALES (est): 20.7MM **Privately Held**
WEB: www.cloreautomotive.com
SIC: 3714 3629 Booster (jump-start) cables, automotive; electronic generation equipment

(G-5767)
CMS MECHANICAL SERVICES LLC
14843 W 95th St (66215-5220)
PHONE..................................321 473-0488
Robert Bo, *Principal*
EMP: 35
SALES (corp-wide): 67.5MM **Privately Held**
SIC: 7623 Air conditioning repair
HQ: Cms Mechanical Services, Llc
445 West Dr Ste 101
Melbourne FL 32904

(G-5768)
COCA-COLA COMPANY
9000 Marshall Dr (66215-3842)
PHONE..................................913 492-8100
Judy Weiss, *Manager*
EMP: 10
SALES (corp-wide): 31.8B **Publicly Held**
WEB: www.cocacola.com
SIC: 2086 Bottled & canned soft drinks
PA: The Coca-Cola Company
1 Coca Cola Plz Nw
Atlanta GA 30313
404 676-2121

(G-5769)
COLLEGE PARK FMLY CARE CTR INC
12200 W 106th St Ste 235 (66215-2368)
PHONE..................................913 492-8686
Andrea Yag, *Director*
EMP: 58
SALES (corp-wide): 25.8MM **Privately Held**
SIC: 8011 Physicians' office, including specialists
PA: College Park Family Care Center Inc.
11725 W 112th St
Shawnee Mission KS 66210
913 469-5579

(G-5770)
COMBAT BRANDS LLC
Also Called: Ringside
15850 W 108th St (66219-1340)
PHONE..................................913 689-2300
Doug Skeems, *President*
Gary Patrick, *President*
Barbara Yoksh, *VP Human Res*
Stan Washington, *Executive*
◆ **EMP:** 38
SALES: 140.9K **Privately Held**
SIC: 5961 3949 5091 Fitness & sporting goods, mail order; gloves, sport & athletic: boxing, handball, etc.; sharpeners, sporting goods

(G-5771)
COMFORCARE SENIOR SERVICES
12345 W 95th St Ste 215 (66215-3837)
PHONE..................................913 906-9880
David Minick, *President*
Chad Tromdson, *Principal*
EMP: 30
SALES: 150K **Privately Held**
SIC: 8082 Home health care services

(G-5772)
COMMAND ALKON INCORPORATED
Jws
12351 W 96th Ter Ste 300 (66215-4410)
PHONE..................................913 384-0880
James Wilson, *General Mgr*
EMP: 40
SALES (corp-wide): 96.9MM **Privately Held**
WEB: www.commandalkon.com
SIC: 7371 Computer software development
PA: Command Alkon Incorporated
1800 Intl Pk Dr Ste 400
Birmingham AL 35243
205 879-3282

(G-5773)
COMMERCE BANK
8700 Monrovia St Ste 100 (66215-3500)
P.O. Box 419248, Kansas City MO (64141-6248)
PHONE..................................913 888-0700
Pat Olney, *Manager*
EMP: 10
SALES (corp-wide): 1.3B **Publicly Held**
SIC: 6022 State commercial banks
HQ: Commerce Bank
1000 Walnut St Fl 700
Kansas City MO 64106
816 234-2000

(G-5774)
COMMERCIAL CAPITAL COMPANY LLC
8215 Melrose Dr (66214-1625)
PHONE..................................913 341-0053

GEOGRAPHIC

Larry Rice, *President*
Mitch Rice, *Vice Pres*
Mark Boylan, *VP Sales*
Chad Duckers, *Sales Executive*
Debbie George, *Sales Executive*
EMP: 25
SQ FT: 7,500
SALES: 5.2MM **Privately Held**
SIC: 7359 6159 Equipment rental & leasing; machinery & equipment finance leasing

(G-5775)
COMMERCIAL HOTEL MANAGEMENT CO
11944 W 95th St (66215-3801)
PHONE..................................913 642-0160
EMP: 25
SALES (est): 1.9MM **Privately Held**
SIC: 8741 Management Services

(G-5776)
COMMUNICATION LINK LLC
16309 W 108th Cir (66219-1372)
PHONE..................................913 681-5400
Mary Willis, *President*
Marry Willis, *President*
Matt Willis, *Vice Pres*
EMP: 18
SQ FT: 3,000
SALES (est): 1.7MM **Privately Held**
WEB: www.protectivegrounding.com
SIC: 7629 Telecommunication equipment repair (except telephones)

(G-5777)
COMMUNITY LVING OPPRTNTIES INC (PA)
11627 W 79th St (66214-1488)
P.O. Box 14395 (66285-4395)
PHONE..................................913 341-9316
Mike C Strouse, *CEO*
James Sherman, *President*
Jan Sheldon, *Vice Pres*
Edward Frizell JC, *Treasurer*
Tanya Root, *Accountant*
EMP: 45
SQ FT: 5,000
SALES: 22.5MM **Privately Held**
WEB: www.clokansas.com
SIC: 8361 Home for the mentally handicapped

(G-5778)
COMMUNITYAMERICA CREDIT UNION (PA)
9777 Ridge Dr (66219-9746)
PHONE..................................913 905-7000
Lisa Ginter, *CEO*
Trevor Gunther, *President*
Julie Kerr, *President*
Katie Douglass, *Principal*
Todd Karnatz, *Principal*
EMP: 240
SQ FT: 94,000
SALES: 81.9MM **Privately Held**
WEB: www.cacu.com
SIC: 6062 6163 State credit unions, not federally chartered; loan brokers

(G-5779)
COMPASS CONTROLS MFG INC
14343 W 100th St (66215-1235)
PHONE..................................913 213-5748
Russell C Engel, *President*
EMP: 30
SALES (est): 6.1MM **Privately Held**
SIC: 3672 Printed circuit boards

(G-5780)
COMPASSIONATE FAMILY CARE LLC
15900 College Blvd # 100 (66219-1326)
PHONE..................................913 744-4300
Laura N Ray,
Jack Gonzenbach, *Admin Sec*
EMP: 10 **EST:** 2011
SALES (est): 1MM **Privately Held**
SIC: 8011 Offices & clinics of medical doctors

(G-5781)
COMPUTER CABLE CONNECTION INC
11227 Strang Line Rd (66215-4040)
PHONE..................................913 390-5141
Dave Borth, *Manager*
EMP: 25
SALES (corp-wide): 19.6MM **Privately Held**
SIC: 1731 Telephone & telephone equipment installation
PA: Computer Cable Connection Inc
2810 Harlan Dr
Bellevue NE 68005
402 291-9500

(G-5782)
COMPUTER INSTRUMENTS INC
10591 Widmer Rd (66215-2096)
P.O. Box 2472, Shawnee Mission (66201-2472)
PHONE..................................913 307-8850
Paul L Herring, *President*
Chris Herring, *Exec VP*
Cale Herring, *Vice Pres*
Allen Prince, *Vice Pres*
Jason Springer, *Accounts Mgr*
EMP: 20
SQ FT: 6,500
SALES (est): 2.3MM **Privately Held**
WEB: www.instruments.com
SIC: 7371 8243 Computer software development; software training, computer

(G-5783)
CONCENTRA MEDICAL CENTERS
14809 W 95th St (66215-5220)
PHONE..................................913 894-6601
Chuck Rice, *Branch Mgr*
EMP: 12
SALES (corp-wide): 5B **Publicly Held**
SIC: 8011 Medical centers
HQ: Concentra Medical Centers
26185 Greenfield Rd
Southfield MI 48076
248 569-2040

(G-5784)
CONTINENTAL COMPONENTS LLC
15941 W 108th St (66219-1343)
PHONE..................................816 547-8325
Katie Gurske, *President*
Richard J Schwind Jr, *Manager*
EMP: 7
SALES (est): 318.9K **Privately Held**
SIC: 3599 Machine & other job shop work

(G-5785)
CONTINUITY OPERATION PLG LLC (PA)
Also Called: Cavein Techonolgy
17501 W 98th St Spc 2632 (66219-1736)
PHONE..................................913 227-0660
Peter Clune, *CEO*
John M Clune, *President*
EMP: 11
SQ FT: 6,000
SALES: 2MM **Privately Held**
SIC: 8322 Disaster service

(G-5786)
CONTOURMD MARKETING GROUP LLC
15550 W 109th St (66219-1308)
PHONE..................................913 541-9200
Richard M Orr, *President*
Julie Smith, *COO*
Sean Orr, *Vice Pres*
EMP: 22
SALES (est): 5.6MM **Privately Held**
WEB: www.awmed.com
SIC: 5047 Medical equipment & supplies

(G-5787)
CORBION AMERICA HOLDINGS INC
Also Called: CSM Bakery Supplies North Amer
7905 Quivira Rd (66215-2732)
PHONE..................................913 890-5500
Tjerk De Ruiter, *CEO*
Eddy Van Rhede Van Der Kloot, *CFO*
Sven Thormahlen, *CFO*
◆ **EMP:** 100
SQ FT: 10,000
SALES (est): 415.5MM
SALES (corp-wide): 994.7MM **Privately Held**
WEB: www.csmnv.com
SIC: 2819 2869 2041 2023 Industrial inorganic chemicals; industrial organic chemicals; flour mixes; ice cream mix, unfrozen: liquid or dry
PA: Corbion N.V.
Piet Heinkade 127
Amsterdam
205 906-911

(G-5788)
CORE CASHLESS LLC
Also Called: Paydia
14803 W 95th St (66215-5220)
PHONE..................................913 529-8200
Dan Owen, *CEO*
EMP: 25 **EST:** 2007
SALES (est): 11MM **Privately Held**
SIC: 6099 7999 Electronic funds transfer network, including switching; card & game services

(G-5789)
CORPORATE ENTERPRISE SEC INC (PA)
11900 W 87th Street Pkwy # 120 (66215-2807)
PHONE..................................913 422-0410
Scott Roe, *President*
EMP: 15
SALES (est): 2.4MM **Privately Held**
SIC: 8742 8748 Management consulting services; systems analysis & engineering consulting services

(G-5790)
COUNTRY CLUB BANK
9100 Park St (66215-3353)
PHONE..................................913 438-5660
James K Frazier, *CEO*
EMP: 17
SALES (corp-wide): 38MM **Privately Held**
SIC: 6029 Commercial banks
HQ: Country Club Bank
1 Ward Pkwy
Kansas City MO 64112

(G-5791)
CRAZY GIRLS LLC
Also Called: Whole Child Development Center
9740 Rosehill Rd (66215-1414)
PHONE..................................913 495-9797
Susie Cox, *Partner*
Carla Luginbill, *Partner*
EMP: 16
SQ FT: 8,100
SALES: 650K **Privately Held**
SIC: 8351 Group day care center

(G-5792)
CREDIT RESTART LLC
8700 Monrovia St Ste 310 (66215-3500)
PHONE..................................888 670-7709
Lamonica Wallace, *CEO*
EMP: 12 **EST:** 2017
SQ FT: 1,100
SALES (est): 574K **Privately Held**
SIC: 7323 Credit reporting services

(G-5793)
CRO MAGNON REPAST LLC
Also Called: Evolve Paleo Chef
8428 Melrose Dr (66214-1646)
PHONE..................................913 747-5559
EMP: 11
SALES (est): 539.6K **Privately Held**
SIC: 5812 8742 Caterers; restaurant & food services consultants

(G-5794)
CROSSMARK INC
11900 W 87th Street Pkwy # 120 (66215-4614)
PHONE..................................913 338-1133
Todd Herrenbruck, *Manager*
EMP: 20 **Privately Held**
WEB: www.crossmark.com
SIC: 5141 Food brokers
PA: Crossmark, Inc.
5100 Legacy Dr
Plano TX 75024

(G-5795)
CROWN EQUIPMENT CORPORATION
Also Called: Crown Lift Trucks
9500 Widmer Rd (66215-1281)
PHONE..................................913 888-9777
Chris Strong, *Branch Mgr*
EMP: 27
SALES (corp-wide): 4.2B **Privately Held**
SIC: 3537 Lift trucks, industrial: fork, platform, straddle, etc.
PA: Crown Equipment Corporation
44 S Washington St
New Bremen OH 45869
419 629-2311

(G-5796)
CULLOR PROPERTY MANAGEMENT LLC
P.O. Box 14763 (66285-4763)
PHONE..................................913 324-5900
Gary Cullor, *CEO*
EMP: 15
SALES (est): 529K **Privately Held**
SIC: 8741 Management services

(G-5797)
CUMMINS - ALLISON CORP
8851 Long St (66215-3523)
PHONE..................................913 894-2266
Jeffrey Day, *Manager*
EMP: 7
SALES (corp-wide): 390.1MM **Privately Held**
WEB: www.gsb.com
SIC: 3579 3578 3519 Perforators (office machines); change making machines; internal combustion engines
PA: Cummins-Allison Corp
852 Feehanville Dr
Mount Prospect IL 60056
800 786-5528

(G-5798)
CUSTOM COLOR CORP
14320 W 101st Ter (66215-1123)
PHONE..................................913 730-3100
Matthew Keith, *President*
Jason Milbourne, *Vice Pres*
Brett Saunders, *CFO*
EMP: 47
SALES (est): 6.8MM **Privately Held**
WEB: www.focusprintinggroup.com
SIC: 2759 Commercial printing

(G-5799)
DAB OF LENEXA KS I LLC
Also Called: Lenexa Candlewood Suites
9630 Rosehill Rd (66215-1347)
PHONE..................................605 275-9499
Kerry Boekelheide, *Principal*
EMP: 25
SALES (est): 1.1MM **Privately Held**
SIC: 7011 Hotels & motels

(G-5800)
DAB OF LENEXA KS II LLC
Also Called: Lenexa Holiday Inn Express
9620 Rosehill Rd (66215-1347)
PHONE..................................913 492-4516
Kerry Boekelheide, *Principal*
EMP: 25 **EST:** 2016
SALES (est): 136.5K **Privately Held**
SIC: 7011 Hotels

(G-5801)
DARK HORSE DISTILLERY LLC
11740 W 86th Ter (66214-1520)
PHONE..................................913 492-3275
Eric Garcia, *General Mgr*
Damian Garcia, *Director*
EMP: 19
SALES (est): 2.1MM **Privately Held**
SIC: 2085 Distillers' dried grains & solubles & alcohol

(G-5802)
DATA CENTER INC
10051 Lakeview Ave (66219-2501)
PHONE..................................913 492-2468
Devin Brown, *Manager*

EMP: 14
SALES (est): 779.9K
SALES (corp-wide): 28.8MM **Privately Held**
WEB: www.datacenterinc.com
SIC: 7374 Data processing service
PA: Data Center, Inc.
20 W 2nd Ave Ste 300
Hutchinson KS 67501
620 694-6800

(G-5803)
DATA MAX OF KANSAS CITY
8030 Flint St Bldg 26 (66214-3334)
PHONE..................................913 752-2200
Toll Free:..888 -
David Rhodes, *President*
EMP: 37
SQ FT: 17,000
SALES (est): 7MM **Privately Held**
WEB: www.datamaxkc.com
SIC: 5045 3571 Printers, computer; electronic computers

(G-5804)
DAVINCI ROOFSCAPES LLC
13890 W 101st St (66215-1200)
PHONE..................................913 599-0766
Ray Rosewall, *CEO*
Michael Cobb, *Vice Pres*
Mark Hansen, *Vice Pres*
Bryan Ward, *VP Opers*
Eric Salvesen, *Technical Mgr*
▼ **EMP:** 20
SALES (est): 6.6MM **Privately Held**
WEB: www.davinciroofscapes.com
SIC: 1761 3069 2952 Roofing contractor; tile, rubber; roofing materials

(G-5805)
DAVITA INC
8922 Millstone Dr (66220-2559)
PHONE..................................913 660-8881
EMP: 29 **Publicly Held**
SIC: 8092 Kidney dialysis centers
PA: Davita Inc.
2000 16th St
Denver CO 80202

(G-5806)
DB FLOORING LLC
Also Called: Regents Flooring
9555 Alden St (66215-1164)
PHONE..................................913 663-9922
Julie Farrell, *President*
Karen Vogt, *Vice Pres*
EMP: 40
SALES (est): 1.4MM **Privately Held**
SIC: 1752 Carpet laying; vinyl floor tile & sheet installation; resilient floor laying; linoleum installation

(G-5807)
DBI INC (PA)
Also Called: Doing Better Inspections
15440 W 109th St (66219-1306)
PHONE..................................913 888-2321
Jeffrey D Hilfiker, *President*
Jeffrey K Morrow, *Shareholder*
EMP: 35
SQ FT: 1,600
SALES: 20MM **Privately Held**
WEB: www.dbindt.com
SIC: 8734 Testing laboratories

(G-5808)
DELMAR GARDENS LENEXA OPER LLC
9701 Monrovia St (66215-1564)
PHONE..................................913 492-1130
Jim Drozda, *Administration*
EMP: 99
SALES: 950K **Privately Held**
SIC: 8051 Skilled nursing care facilities

(G-5809)
DELMAR GARDENS OF LENEXA INC (PA)
Also Called: GARDEN VILLAS
9701 Monrovia St (66215-1564)
PHONE..................................913 492-1130
Henry Grossberg, *President*
Yetra Goldberg, *Treasurer*
Jim Drozda, *Manager*
Keith Wilhelm, *Food Svc Dir*
Barbara Grossberg, *Admin Sec*
EMP: 235
SQ FT: 84,000
SALES: 12.9MM **Privately Held**
SIC: 8051 6513 Skilled nursing care facilities; retirement hotel operation

(G-5810)
DELUXE CORPORATION
Also Called: Deluxe Check Printers
16505 W 113th St (66219-1383)
PHONE..................................913 888-3801
Izabel Gray, *Partner*
Rebecca Her, *Editor*
Zach Gouldsmith, *Accounts Mgr*
Lori Kurovski, *Sales Staff*
Lindsay Jones, *Branch Mgr*
EMP: 248
SALES (corp-wide): 2B **Publicly Held**
WEB: www.dlx.com
SIC: 2782 2791 2789 2759 Checkbooks; typesetting; bookbinding & related work; commercial printing; commercial printing, lithographic
PA: Deluxe Corporation
3680 Victoria St N
Shoreview MN 55126
651 483-7111

(G-5811)
DENTEC SAFETY SPECIALISTS (PA)
8101 Lenexa Dr Ste D (66214-1633)
PHONE..................................905 953-9946
Claudio Dentec, *President*
EMP: 10
SALES (est): 1.9MM **Privately Held**
SIC: 3842 Respiratory protection equipment, personal

(G-5812)
DENTEK INC
8056 Reeder Rd (66214)
PHONE..................................913 262-1717
Alexander Sokolovsky, *President*
Amanda Gasper, *Manager*
Dirk Vandermerwe, *Manager*
EMP: 35
SALES (est): 3.2MM **Privately Held**
WEB: www.denteklab.com
SIC: 8072 Dental laboratories

(G-5813)
DESIGN SOURCE FLOORING LLC (PA)
10645 Lackman Rd (66219-1225)
PHONE..................................913 387-5858
Dan Lawson, *General Mgr*
Corinne Espinoza, *Human Res Mgr*
Tim Blanchard, *Sales Staff*
Justin Lawson, *Sales Staff*
Daniel Lawson,
EMP: 35
SALES (est): 8.1MM **Privately Held**
SIC: 1752 1721 7217 Floor laying & floor work; commercial painting; carpet & upholstery cleaning

(G-5814)
DEVLIN PARTNERS LLC
Also Called: Papa John's
15617 W 87th St (66219-1435)
PHONE..................................913 894-1300
Rollie Textor, *Manager*
EMP: 15
SALES (est): 281.1K
SALES (corp-wide): 13.7MM **Privately Held**
SIC: 5812 6531 Pizzeria, chain; real estate agents & managers
PA: Devlin Partners Llc
1313 N Webb Rd Ste 100
Wichita KS 67206
316 634-1800

(G-5815)
DG BUSINESS SOLUTIONS INC
11008 Rene St (66215-2040)
PHONE..................................913 766-0163
Domenick Presa, *President*
Ganesh Venkatraman, *Vice Pres*
EMP: 12
SALES: 300K **Privately Held**
WEB: www.dgbsinc.com
SIC: 8742 7371 Management consulting services; computer software systems analysis & design, custom

(G-5816)
DIGITAL ALLY INC
9705 Loiret Blvd (66219-2409)
PHONE..................................913 814-7774
Stanton E Ross, *Ch of Bd*
Thomas J Heckman, *CFO*
Edward Brown, *Sales Staff*
Derek Butler, *Sales Staff*
Les Pingel, *Technology*
▲ **EMP:** 95
SQ FT: 33,776
SALES: 11.2MM **Privately Held**
WEB: www.digitalallyinc.com
SIC: 3663 3824 7372 Radio & TV communications equipment; speed indicators & recorders, vehicle; prepackaged software

(G-5817)
DIGITAL PRINTING SERVICES INC
13309 W 98th St (66215-1374)
PHONE..................................913 492-1500
A P Singh, *President*
Dan Riley, *Managing Prtnr*
Eric Amundson, *Opers Staff*
EMP: 13
SALES: 500K **Privately Held**
WEB: www.dpskc.com
SIC: 5111 7379 Printing & writing paper; computer related consulting services

(G-5818)
DIGITAL SIMPLISTICS INC
14207 W 95th St (66215-5208)
PHONE..................................913 643-2445
Ronald L Davis, *President*
Heath Reynolds, *President*
Sally Deweese, *Corp Secy*
Alan Arthur, *Technology*
Charles D Welch Jr, *Executive*
EMP: 21
SQ FT: 10,480
SALES (est): 4.3MM **Privately Held**
WEB: www.speedscript.com
SIC: 5045 Computers; computer software

(G-5819)
DIGITAL SOUND SYSTEMS INC (PA)
9721 Loiret Blvd (66219-2409)
PHONE..................................913 492-5775
Jeremy G Dixon, *President*
Joel Stone, *Vice Pres*
EMP: 20
SQ FT: 50,000
SALES (est): 3.5MM **Privately Held**
SIC: 7389 7812 Convention & show services; audio-visual program production

(G-5820)
DIMENSION GRAPHICS INC
Also Called: Dgi Print Solutions
13915 W 107th St (66215-2043)
PHONE..................................913 469-6800
Clifton E Pummill, *President*
EMP: 100
SQ FT: 70,000
SALES (est): 13.6MM **Privately Held**
WEB: www.magazineprinter.com
SIC: 2752 Calendar & card printing, lithographic

(G-5821)
DITEQ CORPORATION (HQ)
Also Called: Diamond Tools & Equipment
9876 Pflumm Rd (66215-1208)
PHONE..................................816 246-5515
Sung Gyu Kim, *CEO*
Young Chan Park, *COO*
Joon Koh, *CFO*
▲ **EMP:** 20
SQ FT: 1,100
SALES (est): 18.9MM **Privately Held**
WEB: www.diteq.com
SIC: 5085 3425 3531 3546 Industrial tools; saw blades & handsaws; road construction & maintenance machinery; surfacers, concrete grinding; drills & drilling tools; saws & sawing equipment

(G-5822)
DON JULIAN BUILDERS INC
15521 W 110th St (66219-1317)
PHONE..................................913 894-6300
Donald Julian, *Corp Secy*
Ruby Reeves, *Corp Secy*
Linda A Julian, *Vice Pres*
Travis Booth, *Project Mgr*
Teri Stolz, *Manager*
EMP: 21 **EST:** 1971
SQ FT: 5,000
SALES (est): 3.6MM **Privately Held**
SIC: 1521 New construction, single-family houses

(G-5823)
DOTS PRETZELS LLC
16286 W 110th St (66219-1312)
PHONE..................................913 274-1705
Kent Schmitberger, *Branch Mgr*
EMP: 70
SALES (corp-wide): 11.6MM **Privately Held**
SIC: 2052 Pretzels
HQ: Dot's Pretzels, Llc
3475 56th St S Ste 201
Fargo ND 58104
701 566-8520

(G-5824)
DR VERNON ROWE
Also Called: Consultants In Neurology
8550 Marshall Dr Ste 100 (66214-9836)
PHONE..................................913 894-1500
Vernon Rowe MD, *Owner*
EMP: 45
SALES (est): 1.8MM **Privately Held**
SIC: 8049 Offices of health practitioner

(G-5825)
DRAKE & ASSOC OPTOMETRISTS
Also Called: Customeyes
15601 W 87th Street Pkwy (66219-1435)
PHONE..................................913 894-2020
Linda Drake, *Owner*
Scott Drake, *Co-Owner*
EMP: 12
SALES (est): 168.1K **Privately Held**
SIC: 8042 Specialized optometrists

(G-5826)
DREXEL TECHNOLOGIES INC (PA)
10840 W 86th St (66214-1632)
PHONE..................................913 371-4430
Deron Taylor, *President*
Doug Lanman, *Vice Pres*
Kelly Stires, *Production*
Brenda Dreiling, *Supervisor*
Kevin Desmarteau, *Technology*
EMP: 45 **EST:** 1946
SQ FT: 9,800
SALES (est): 10.6MM **Privately Held**
SIC: 2759 5734 Commercial printing; printers & plotters: computers

(G-5827)
DXP ENTERPRISES INC
Also Called: Pump & Power Equipment
11691 W 85th St (66214-1515)
PHONE..................................913 888-0108
Bill Byron, *Manager*
EMP: 14 **Publicly Held**
SIC: 5074 5084 Water purification equipment; pumps & pumping equipment
PA: Dxp Enterprises, Inc.
5301 Hollister St Ste 400
Houston TX 77040

(G-5828)
EATON CORPORATION
11305 Strang Line Rd (66215-4042)
PHONE..................................913 451-6314
Greg Hausman, *Engineer*
Ron Evans, *Branch Mgr*
EMP: 27 **Privately Held**
WEB: www.eaton.com
SIC: 5063 Electrical apparatus & equipment
HQ: Eaton Corporation
1000 Eaton Blvd
Cleveland OH 44122
440 523-5000

(G-5829)
ECS INC INTERNATIONAL
15351 W 109th St (66219-1201)
PHONE..................................913 782-7787
Bradford R Slatten, *President*

Dan Kelly, *President*
David Meaney, *Vice Pres*
Eric Slatten, *Vice Pres*
Marty Rosa, *Engineer*
EMP: 15 **EST:** 1979
SQ FT: 10,000
SALES (est): 18MM **Privately Held**
WEB: www.ecsxtal.com
SIC: 3825 Frequency meters: electrical, mechanical & electronic

(G-5830)
ELANCO KC
10850 Lakeview Ave (66219-1330)
PHONE..................................816 442-4114
Corey Jones, *Sr Associate*
EMP: 12
SALES (est): 1.3MM **Privately Held**
SIC: 7389 Telephone services

(G-5831)
ELECTRONIC FUNDS TRANSFER INC
Also Called: Universal Money Center
15301 W 87th St Ste 220 (66219-1425)
PHONE..................................913 831-2055
Dave Bonsal, *Ch of Bd*
Pamela Glenn, *Vice Pres*
EMP: 30
SQ FT: 12,851
SALES (est): 5.7MM
SALES (corp-wide): 8MM **Privately Held**
WEB: www.electronicfundstransfer.com
SIC: 6099 Automated teller machine (ATM) network
PA: Universal Money Centers, Inc.
15301 W 87th Street Pkwy
Lenexa KS 66219
913 831-2055

(G-5832)
ELEVATED LIVING LLC
14909 W 90th Ter (66215-2927)
PHONE..................................316 619-7690
Parker Whitney,
EMP: 10
SALES: 1MM **Privately Held**
SIC: 0781 Landscape services

(G-5833)
ENCOMPASS MEDICAL GROUP PA (PA)
8550 Marshall Dr Ste 200 (66214-9836)
PHONE..................................913 495-2000
MD Kevin Fitzmaurice, *President*
Bonnie Barrett, *Office Mgr*
Kevin J Fitzmaurice, *Med Doctor*
Lila Iyer, *Med Doctor*
Kristen Duncan, *Technician*
EMP: 45 **EST:** 2000
SALES (est): 8.7MM **Privately Held**
WEB: www.encompassmed.com
SIC: 8011 Primary care medical clinic

(G-5834)
ENTERPRISE BUS SOLUTIONS LLC
11320 W 79th St (66214-1401)
PHONE..................................913 529-4350
Thomas Jenkins, *Partner*
Scott Jenkins, *Mng Member*
Joel Morris,
EMP: 16
SQ FT: 7,500
SALES (est): 1.9MM **Privately Held**
SIC: 8742 Construction project management consultant

(G-5835)
ENVIRONMENTAL PROTECTION AGCY
11201 Renner Blvd (66219-9601)
PHONE..................................913 551-7118
Karl Brooks, *Regional Mgr*
EMP: 350 **Publicly Held**
SIC: 9511 5093 Environmental protection agency, government; oil, waste
HQ: Environmental Protection Agency
1200 Pennsylvania Ave Nw
Washington DC 20460
202 564-4700

(G-5836)
ESA P PRTFOLIO OPER LESSEE LLC
Also Called: Extended Stay America, Inc.
9775 Lenexa Dr (66215-1345)
PHONE..................................913 541-4000
Mary Overby, *Branch Mgr*
EMP: 12
SALES (corp-wide): 1.2B **Publicly Held**
WEB: www.weddingbells.net
SIC: 7011 Hotels & motels
HQ: Esa P Portfolio Operating Lessee, Llc
11525 N Community House R
Charlotte NC 28277
980 345-1600

(G-5837)
EVANS MEDIA GROUP
15621 W 87th Street Pkwy # 223 (66219-1435)
PHONE..................................913 489-7364
Sara Paxton, *Principal*
EMP: 11
SALES (est): 364.4K **Privately Held**
SIC: 4899 Communication services

(G-5838)
EVERGY METRO INC
Also Called: Overland Park Commercial Off
16215 W 108th St (66219-1347)
PHONE..................................913 894-3000
Steve Gilkey, *Manager*
EMP: 75
SALES (corp-wide): 4.2B **Publicly Held**
WEB: www.kcpl.com
SIC: 4911 Generation, electric power
HQ: Evergy Metro, Inc.
1200 Main St
Kansas City MO 64105
816 556-2200

(G-5839)
EVOLOGIC LLC
17501 W 98th St Spc 1859 (66219-1736)
PHONE..................................913 599-5292
Gary Bicknell, *Principal*
Sandy Vetsch, *Business Mgr*
Trish Allenbrand, *Mng Member*
Chris McCormack, *Mng Member*
EMP: 20
SALES (est): 2.8MM **Privately Held**
SIC: 1799 Office furniture installation

(G-5840)
EXAMONE WORLD WIDE INC (DH)
10101 Renner Blvd (66219-9752)
PHONE..................................913 888-1770
Troy Hartman, *President*
Betsy Sears, *Exec VP*
Janice Jones, *Vice Pres*
Don Hess, *Manager*
EMP: 50
SALES (est): 10.6MM
SALES (corp-wide): 7.5B **Publicly Held**
SIC: 8099 Health screening service
HQ: Labone, Inc.
10101 Renner Blvd
Lenexa KS 66219
913 888-1770

(G-5841)
EXCEL TOOL AND MFG INC
14344 W 96th Ter (66215-4708)
PHONE..................................913 894-6415
Karin Kelter, *President*
Tom Kelter, *Senior VP*
Eric Kelter, *Vice Pres*
Jacob Rollheiser, *Manager*
EMP: 37
SALES (est): 7.4MM **Privately Held**
WEB: www.exceltool.com
SIC: 3544 Special dies & tools

(G-5842)
EXECUTIVE AIRSHARE LLC (PA)
Also Called: Executive Flight Services
8345 Lenexa Dr Ste 120 (66214-1654)
PHONE..................................816 221-7200
Keith Plumb, *CEO*
Bob Taylor, *Chairman*
Ben Clouse, *Vice Pres*
Michael McMillan, *Vice Pres*
Troy Welch, *Vice Pres*
EMP: 19
SALES (est): 19.3MM **Privately Held**
WEB: www.execairshare.com
SIC: 4522 Air passenger carriers, non-scheduled

(G-5843)
EXPRESS AUTO SERVICE INC (PA)
Also Called: Express Auto Service & Tire
11490 Strang Line Rd (66215-4046)
PHONE..................................816 373-9995
Gary Calvert, *President*
EMP: 21
SQ FT: 6,000
SALES: 6.5MM **Privately Held**
SIC: 7538 7539 General automotive repair shops; automotive repair shops

(G-5844)
EXPRESS SCALE PARTS INC
14560 W 99th St (66215-1105)
PHONE..................................913 441-4787
Michael Simmons, *President*
Barry Newkirk, *General Mgr*
Kelly Young, *Business Mgr*
Sarah J Bolander, *Purchasing*
▲ **EMP:** 23
SQ FT: 25,000
SALES: 4MM **Privately Held**
WEB: www.jemesp.com
SIC: 3523 3535 5046 7699 Farm machinery & equipment; conveyors & conveying equipment; scales, except laboratory; scale repair service; scales & balances, except laboratory; packaging materials

(G-5845)
FABRICLEAN SUPPLY KANSAS LC (HQ)
Also Called: Dry Cleaning and Laundry Sups
14400 W 97th Ter (66215-1140)
PHONE..................................913 492-1743
Jim Hericks, *CEO*
Robert Witcher, *President*
Lindon Ford, *CFO*
▲ **EMP:** 11
SQ FT: 8,000
SALES (est): 6.9MM
SALES (corp-wide): 8MM **Privately Held**
SIC: 5087 Laundry equipment & supplies
PA: Fabriclean Supply Of Oklahoma Limited Partnership
201 N Ann Arbor Ave
Oklahoma City OK 73127
405 232-9289

(G-5846)
FACILITY MGMT SVS GRP OF KC
14720 W 105th St (66215-4414)
PHONE..................................913 888-7600
Mark Wilson, *Principal*
EMP: 99
SALES (est): 3.1MM **Privately Held**
SIC: 6531 Real estate agents & managers

(G-5847)
FAITH TECHNOLOGIES INC
11086 Strang Line Rd (66215-2113)
PHONE..................................913 541-4700
Ed Crafton, *Superintendent*
Rocky Rowlett, *Vice Pres*
Sean Collins, *Project Mgr*
Jason Grant, *Project Mgr*
Jeff Neathery, *Project Mgr*
EMP: 58
SALES (corp-wide): 773.3MM **Privately Held**
SIC: 1731 General electrical contractor
PA: Faith Technologies, Inc.
225 Main St
Menasha WI 54952
920 738-1500

(G-5848)
FAMILY PRACTICE ASSOCIATES
Also Called: Carlos Palmeri
8760 Monrovia St (66215-3537)
PHONE..................................913 438-2226
Chris Getz, *Manager*
EMP: 15
SALES (corp-wide): 1.5MM **Privately Held**
SIC: 8011 General & family practice, physician/surgeon
PA: Family Practice Associates
1150 N 75th Pl Ste 200
Kansas City KS 66112
913 299-2100

(G-5849)
FEDERATED RURAL ELC MGT CORP (HQ)
7725 Renner Rd (66217-9414)
P.O. Box 15147 (66285-5147)
PHONE..................................913 541-0150
Philip Irwin, *President*
Michael Bird, *Vice Pres*
Richard Burns, *Vice Pres*
Chad Ogren, *Vice Pres*
Susan Olander, *Vice Pres*
EMP: 31
SQ FT: 26,500
SALES: 112.5MM **Privately Held**
WEB: www.federatedrural.com
SIC: 4911 Electric services
PA: Federated Rural Electric Insurance Exchange
7725 Renner Rd
Shawnee KS 66217
913 541-0150

(G-5850)
FEDEX OFFICE & PRINT SVCS INC
13450 W 87th Street Pkwy (66215-2816)
PHONE..................................913 894-2010
Dominic Lilly, *Store Mgr*
EMP: 20
SALES (corp-wide): 69.6B **Publicly Held**
WEB: www.kinkos.com
SIC: 7334 Photocopying & duplicating services
HQ: Fedex Office And Print Services, Inc.
7900 Legacy Dr
Plano TX 75024
800 463-3339

(G-5851)
FERGUSON ENTERPRISES LLC
9301 Rosehill Rd (66215-3762)
PHONE..................................913 752-5660
Aaron Starkey, *Sales Staff*
Scott Raven, *Branch Mgr*
Steven Fallon, *Manager*
EMP: 100
SALES (corp-wide): 20.7B **Privately Held**
WEB: www.ferguson.com
SIC: 5074 5399 Plumbing fittings & supplies; catalog showrooms
HQ: Ferguson Enterprises, Llc
12500 Jefferson Ave
Newport News VA 23602
757 874-7795

(G-5852)
FINANCIAL PRINTING RESOURCE
Also Called: Island Financial Printing
15009 W 101st Ter (66215-1162)
PHONE..................................913 599-6979
Claude R Soto Jr, *President*
Stephen Bamberger, *Vice Pres*
Karen Carter, *Treasurer*
EMP: 13
SQ FT: 12,000
SALES (est): 1.6MM **Privately Held**
WEB: www.fpr.net
SIC: 2752 Commercial printing, offset

(G-5853)
FIRE CNSLTING CASE REVIEW INTL
Also Called: Fcii
13415 W 98th St (66215-1363)
P.O. Box 15233 (66285-5233)
PHONE..................................913 262-5200
Donna Ingram, *Opers Staff*
Jennifer White, *Office Admin*
EMP: 10
SALES (est): 216.8K **Privately Held**
SIC: 8748 Environmental consultant

▲ = Import ▼=Export
◆ =Import/Export

(G-5854)
FIRELAKE-ARROWHEAD
14217 W 95th St (66215-5208)
PHONE..................................913 312-9540
Jack Foley, *CEO*
Jackie Foley, *CEO*
Lashana Hunt, *Manager*
EMP: 60 **EST:** 2016
SQ FT: 4,500
SALES (est): 2.1MM **Privately Held**
SIC: 1542 Commercial & office building contractors

(G-5855)
FIRELK-DIVERSIFIED JOINT VENTR
14217 W 95th St (66215-5208)
PHONE..................................913 312-9540
Jackie Foley, *CEO*
EMP: 30
SQ FT: 4,500
SALES (est): 1.3MM **Privately Held**
SIC: 1542 1711 1794 Commercial & office building contractors; commercial & office buildings, renovation & repair; plumbing, heating, air-conditioning contractors; mechanical contractor; excavation & grading, building construction

(G-5856)
FIRST BIOMEDICAL INC (HQ)
11130 Strang Line Rd (66215-2122)
PHONE..................................800 962-9656
Tom Creal, *President*
Tom Ruiz, *Vice Pres*
Kirsten Maher, *VP Sales*
Tan Phan, *Manager*
Larry Schifsky, *Technician*
EMP: 30
SQ FT: 28,733
SALES (est): 6.3MM **Publicly Held**
WEB: www.firstbiomed.com
SIC: 7352 5047 Medical equipment rental; medical equipment & supplies

(G-5857)
FIRST STUDENT INC
8020 Monticello Ter (66227-2646)
PHONE..................................913 422-8501
Roxanne Sanford, *Branch Mgr*
EMP: 71
SALES (corp-wide): 9.1B **Privately Held**
SIC: 4111 Local & suburban transit
HQ: First Student, Inc.
600 Vine St Ste 1400
Cincinnati OH 45202

(G-5858)
FLOWERS BAKING CO LENEXA LLC
8960 Marshall Dr (66215-3841)
PHONE..................................913 564-1100
Paul Frankum, *President*
EMP: 200
SQ FT: 15,000
SALES (est): 447.1K
SALES (corp-wide): 3.9B **Publicly Held**
SIC: 2051 Buns, bread type: fresh or frozen
PA: Flowers Foods, Inc.
1919 Flowers Cir
Thomasville GA 31757
229 226-9110

(G-5859)
FLUIDTECH LLC (HQ)
10940 Eicher Dr (66219-2600)
PHONE..................................913 492-3300
Dees Joe, *Opers Mgr*
Chris Harris,
Carole Hartman,
Rori Matters,
EMP: 24
SQ FT: 36,000
SALES (est): 16.1MM
SALES (corp-wide): 3.4B **Publicly Held**
WEB: www.fluidtech.net
SIC: 5084 Hydraulic systems equipment & supplies
PA: Applied Industrial Technologies, Inc.
1 Applied Plz
Cleveland OH 44115
216 426-4000

(G-5860)
FLUIDTECH LLC
Also Called: Fluidtech 0079
10940 Eicher Dr (66219-2600)
PHONE..................................913 492-3300
Dave Watson, *Branch Mgr*
EMP: 26
SALES (corp-wide): 3.4B **Publicly Held**
SIC: 5084 Hydraulic systems equipment & supplies
HQ: Fluidtech, Llc
10940 Eicher Dr
Lenexa KS 66219
913 492-3300

(G-5861)
FLUIDTECH LLC
Also Called: Mach V 0082
10940 Eicher Dr (66219-2600)
PHONE..................................913 492-3300
Ken Norvell, *Branch Mgr*
EMP: 15
SALES (corp-wide): 3.4B **Publicly Held**
SIC: 5084 Hydraulic systems equipment & supplies
HQ: Fluidtech, Llc
10940 Eicher Dr
Lenexa KS 66219
913 492-3300

(G-5862)
FMC TECHNOLOGIES INC
8040 Nieman Rd (66214-1523)
PHONE..................................913 214-4300
Rick Burch, *Manager*
Richard Chaplin, *Manager*
Tony Matute, *Sr Software Eng*
Victor Buller, *Software Dev*
Michael Terry, *Software Dev*
EMP: 26
SALES (corp-wide): 12.6B **Privately Held**
SIC: 3533 Oil & gas field machinery
HQ: Fmc Technologies, Inc.
11740 Katy Fwy Enrgy Twr
Houston TX 77079
281 591-4000

(G-5863)
FORMUFIT LC
17501 W 98th St Spc 1843 (66219-1714)
PHONE..................................913 782-0444
Joseph Cushing, *President*
Amy Cushing, *Treasurer*
▲ **EMP:** 6
SQ FT: 5,000
SALES: 70K **Privately Held**
SIC: 3088 3084 3089 Plastics plumbing fixtures; plastics pipe; fittings for pipe, plastic

(G-5864)
FOUNTAIN GLASS INC
15815 W 110th St (66219-1323)
PHONE..................................913 764-6014
David De Lafuente, *President*
Bonnie De Lafuente, *Corp Secy*
Julie Kessler, *Controller*
▲ **EMP:** 25
SQ FT: 7,500
SALES (est): 3.9MM **Privately Held**
SIC: 1793 Glass & glazing work

(G-5865)
FREEMAN CONCRETE CNSTR LLC
8357 Monticello Rd # 100 (66227-3120)
PHONE..................................913 825-0744
Mike Martin, *Project Mgr*
Dana N Knop, *Mng Member*
Monty Freeman,
EMP: 50
SQ FT: 2,000
SALES (est): 6.5MM **Privately Held**
SIC: 1771 Concrete work

(G-5866)
FRENCH-GERLEMAN ELECTRIC CO
Also Called: French Gerleman
9735 Commerce Pkwy (66219-2403)
PHONE..................................314 569-3122
Colleen Post, *Sales Staff*
Jim Talbot, *Manager*
EMP: 25
SALES (corp-wide): 184.5MM **Privately Held**
WEB: www.frenchgerleman.com
SIC: 5063 Electrical apparatus & equipment
PA: French-Gerleman Electric Company
2023 Westport Center Dr
Saint Louis MO 63146
314 569-3122

(G-5867)
FRY-WAGNER SYSTEMS INC
Also Called: Fry-Wagner Systems Dist Ctr
11550 Lakeview Dr (66219-1404)
P.O. Box 14851 (66285-4851)
PHONE..................................913 438-2925
Larry Fry, *Branch Mgr*
Jeff Matlock, *Manager*
EMP: 100
SALES (corp-wide): 66.8MM **Privately Held**
SIC: 4213 Trucking, except local
PA: Fry-Wagner Systems, Inc.
3700 Rider Trl S
Earth City MO
314 291-4100

(G-5868)
GARDNER BANCSHARES INC (HQ)
13423 W 92nd St (66215-3636)
P.O. Box 429, Gardner (66030-0429)
PHONE..................................855 856-0233
Ralph Leno, *President*
EMP: 35
SALES: 4.5MM
SALES (corp-wide): 3.1MM **Privately Held**
WEB: www.gardnernational.com
SIC: 6021 National commercial banks
PA: Small Business Bank
13423 W 92nd St
Lenexa KS 66215
913 856-7199

(G-5869)
GBA ARCHITECTS INC
9801 Renner Blvd Ste 300 (66219-8117)
PHONE..................................913 492-0400
Wilbur A Copenhafer, *Principal*
Paul Bertrand, *Vice Pres*
Neale Shour, *Accounts Mgr*
EMP: 23
SALES: 37.4MM
SALES (corp-wide): 66.8MM **Privately Held**
WEB: www.gbutler.com
SIC: 8712 8711 Architectural engineering; mechanical engineering
PA: George Butler Associates, Inc.
9801 Renner Blvd Ste 300
Lenexa KS 66219
913 492-0400

(G-5870)
GBA BUILDERS LLC
9801 Renner Blvd Ste 300 (66219-8117)
PHONE..................................913 492-0400
Dan Abitz, *Vice Pres*
Sandra Bachamp, *Senior Engr*
Kent Dyck, *Senior Engr*
Daniel L Abitz, *Mng Member*
Heidi Thummel, *Manager*
◆ **EMP:** 25
SALES: 31.3MM
SALES (corp-wide): 66.8MM **Privately Held**
SIC: 8741 8711 1522 1541 Construction management; engineering services; hotel/motel & multi-family home construction; industrial buildings, new construction
PA: George Butler Associates, Inc.
9801 Renner Blvd Ste 300
Lenexa KS 66219
913 492-0400

(G-5871)
GENERAL ELECTRIC COMPANY
10500 Lackman Rd (66219-1224)
PHONE..................................913 541-1839
EMP: 67
SALES (corp-wide): 121.6B **Publicly Held**
SIC: 1731 Electrical work
PA: General Electric Company
5 Necco St
Boston MA 02210
617 443-3000

(G-5872)
GENEX SERVICES LLC
11900 W 87th Street Pkwy # 210 (66215-4505)
PHONE..................................913 310-0303
Kara Green, *Branch Mgr*
EMP: 20 **Privately Held**
SIC: 6411 Advisory services, insurance
HQ: Genex Services, Llc
440 E Swedesford Rd Ste 1
Wayne PA 19087
610 964-5100

(G-5873)
GENTLE DENTAL SERVICE CORP
13100 W 87th Street Pkwy (66215-4532)
PHONE..................................913 248-8880
Ashley Jurkovich, *Branch Mgr*
EMP: 20 **Privately Held**
SIC: 8021 Dental clinic; orthodontist
HQ: Gentle Dental Service Corporation
9800 S La Cienega Blvd # 2
Inglewood CA 90301

(G-5874)
GFSI INC
9700 Lackman Rd (66219-1208)
PHONE..................................913 693-3200
John Fryer, *President*
Natalie Sowers, *Supervisor*
Ron Bishop, *Administration*
Katherine Sutphen, *Graphic Designe*
EMP: 15
SALES (corp-wide): 6.8B **Publicly Held**
SIC: 2339 2329 Sportswear, women's; men's & boys' sportswear & athletic clothing
HQ: Gfsi, Llc
9700 Commerce Pkwy
Lenexa KS 66219
913 693-3200

(G-5875)
GFSI LLC (DH)
Also Called: Gear For Sports
9700 Commerce Pkwy (66219-2402)
PHONE..................................913 693-3200
Larry D Graveel, *President*
Jim Malseed, *President*
Anita Carter, *Business Mgr*
Mike Gary, *Exec VP*
Lori Dunn, *Plant Mgr*
◆ **EMP:** 460
SQ FT: 250,000
SALES (est): 160MM
SALES (corp-wide): 6.8B **Publicly Held**
WEB: www.gearforsports.com
SIC: 2339 2329 2396 2395 Sportswear, women's; men's & boys' sportswear & athletic clothing; automotive & apparel trimmings; pleating & stitching
HQ: Gfsi Holdings Llc
9700 Commerce Pkwy
Winston Salem NC 27105
336 519-8080

(G-5876)
GILL BEBCO LLC
10800 Lackman Rd (66219-1230)
PHONE..................................816 942-3100
Paul Lage, *President*
Jamie Fain, *Vice Pres*
Debra Hoerl, *Vice Pres*
Judy Brown, *Accountant*
▲ **EMP:** 41
SQ FT: 284,000
SALES (est): 9.9MM
SALES (corp-wide): 68.6MM **Privately Held**
SIC: 2752 Advertising posters, lithographed
PA: Gill Studios, Inc.
10800 Lackman Rd
Shawnee Mission KS 66219
913 888-4422

(G-5877)
GLOBL ADAMS COMMUNICATIONS LLC
Also Called: AGC
9635 Widmer Rd (66215-1290)
PHONE..................................913 402-4499
Kenneth A Chymiak, *Chairman*
Scott Francis, *CFO*
▲ **EMP:** 20
SALES (est): 6.2MM
SALES (corp-wide): 55.1MM **Publicly Held**
SIC: 4841 Cable & other pay television services
PA: Addvantage Technologies Group, Inc.
13757 N Stemmons Fwy
Farmers Branch TX 75234
918 251-9121

(G-5878)
GOOD LIFE SNACKS INC
9900 Pflumm Rd Ste 46 (66215-1231)
PHONE..................................913 220-2117
Dominique Colantuoni, *Principal*
EMP: 8
SQ FT: 7,152
SALES (est): 454.3K **Privately Held**
SIC: 2034 Dried & dehydrated fruits

(G-5879)
GRAM ENTERPRISES INC (PA)
Also Called: Massage Envy
13224 W 87th Street Pkwy (66215-4534)
PHONE..................................913 888-3689
Ronald Garffie, *President*
Misti Garffie, *Vice Pres*
EMP: 31
SQ FT: 3,558
SALES: 1.2MM **Privately Held**
SIC: 7299 7231 5999 Massage parlor; facial salons; cosmetics

(G-5880)
GRANITE TRANSFORMATION KANS CY
14125 Marshall Dr (66215-1300)
PHONE..................................913 492-7600
Paul Whittaker, *Owner*
EMP: 13
SALES (est): 1MM **Privately Held**
WEB: www.gtkc.com
SIC: 1799 Counter top installation

(G-5881)
GRAPEVINE DESIGNS LLC (PA)
8406 Melrose Dr (66214-1646)
PHONE..................................913 307-0225
Jane Gaunce, *CEO*
Jane Beth McCarthy, *Exec VP*
Libby Carter, *Warehouse Mgr*
Brian Casey, *Warehouse Mgr*
Sarah Fath, *Production*
▲ **EMP:** 26
SQ FT: 10,850
SALES (est): 4.3MM **Privately Held**
WEB: www.gvinedesigns.com
SIC: 7389 Advertising, promotional & trade show services

(G-5882)
GRAYBEAL CONSTRUCTION CO INC
8700 Pine St (66220-3366)
PHONE..................................785 232-1033
EMP: 20
SALES (est): 2MM **Privately Held**
SIC: 1771 Concrete Contractor

(G-5883)
GREAT CLIPS FOR HAIR
14904 W 87th Street Pkwy (66215-4159)
PHONE..................................913 888-7447
Surriya Khan, *Owner*
EMP: 13
SALES (est): 127.8K **Privately Held**
SIC: 7231 Unisex hair salons

(G-5884)
GREG ORSCHELN TRNSP CO
9220 Marshall Dr (66215-3844)
PHONE..................................913 371-1260
Jeff Johnson, *President*
Sherry Michael, *Controller*
Verna Surham, *Accounts Mgr*
EMP: 22
SQ FT: 5,000
SALES (est): 8.3MM **Privately Held**
WEB: www.gotransportation.com
SIC: 4731 8742 Truck transportation brokers; business planning & organizing services

(G-5885)
H W LOCHNER INC
16105 W 113th St Ste 107 (66219-2304)
PHONE..................................816 945-5840
Steve Hileman, *Vice Pres*
Jeff Drees, *Engineer*
EMP: 100
SQ FT: 9,000
SALES (corp-wide): 91.2MM **Privately Held**
SIC: 8711 8712 Consulting engineer; architectural services
PA: H. W. Lochner, Inc.
225 W Washington St # 1200
Chicago IL 60606
312 372-7346

(G-5886)
HAIRUWEAR INC (PA)
Also Called: Hair U Wear
14865 W 105th St (66215-2007)
PHONE..................................954 835-2200
Norman L Levine, *CEO*
Michael Napolitano, *President*
▲ **EMP:** 49 **EST:** 1968
SALES (est): 24MM **Privately Held**
WEB: www.virtualrealityhair.com
SIC: 5199 Wigs

(G-5887)
HALLCON CORPORATION (PA)
Also Called: Hallcon Crew Transport
14325 W 95th St (66215-5210)
PHONE..................................913 890-6105
John R Stoiber, *President*
Jonathan Pero, *Manager*
EMP: 15
SALES (est): 4MM **Privately Held**
SIC: 4789 Transportation services

(G-5888)
HANDCRAFTED WINES LLC (PA)
Also Called: Handcrafted Wines of Kansas
17501 W 98th St Spc 46-27 (66219-1720)
PHONE..................................913 829-4500
Donald Brain, *CEO*
Greg Cantu, *Business Mgr*
Pj Angell, *Sales Mgr*
Greg Falk, *Sales Mgr*
Bryant Bickel, *Accounts Mgr*
EMP: 10
SQ FT: 7,500
SALES (est): 1.2MM **Privately Held**
WEB: www.handcraftedwines.net
SIC: 5182 Wine

(G-5889)
HARBISONWALKER INTL INC
9734 Pflumm Rd (66215-1206)
PHONE..................................913 888-0425
Garrett Childs, *Branch Mgr*
EMP: 22
SALES (corp-wide): 633.5MM **Privately Held**
WEB: www.hwr.com
SIC: 3255 Clay refractories
HQ: Harbisonwalker International, Inc.
1305 Cherrington Pkwy # 100
Moon Township PA 15108

(G-5890)
HAREN & LAUGHLIN CNSTR CO INC
Also Called: Haren Laughlin Construction
8035 Nieman Rd (66214-1544)
PHONE..................................913 495-9558
C Wells Haren III, *President*
Wells Haren III, *President*
Jeff Wasinger, *VP Opers*
Henry Specht, *Project Mgr*
Mj Lewis, *Controller*
EMP: 45 **EST:** 1932
SQ FT: 11,300
SALES (est): 31.4MM **Privately Held**
WEB: www.harenlaughlin.com
SIC: 1542 1541 6552 Commercial & office building, new construction; industrial buildings & warehouses; subdividers & developers

(G-5891)
HARPENAU POWER & PROCESS INC
11370 Strang Line Rd (66215-4041)
PHONE..................................913 451-2227
Patt Harpenau, *President*
Len Harpenau, *Sales Staff*
EMP: 5 **EST:** 1998
SALES (est): 550.8K **Privately Held**
SIC: 3612 Transformers, except electric

(G-5892)
HARRINGTON INDUSTRIAL PLAS LLC
Also Called: Harrington Pure Indus Plas
14401 W 100th St (66215-1156)
PHONE..................................816 400-9438
John D'Arco, *Branch Mgr*
EMP: 11
SQ FT: 15,000
SALES (corp-wide): 7MM **Privately Held**
SIC: 5074 Pipes & fittings, plastic
HQ: Harrington Industrial Plastics Llc
14480 Yorba Ave
Chino CA 91710
909 597-8641

(G-5893)
HCI ENERGY LLC
7923 Nieman Rd (66214-1565)
PHONE..................................913 283-8855
Tim Tierney, *Vice Pres*
Ray Ansari,
EMP: 12
SQ FT: 1,000
SALES: 500K **Privately Held**
SIC: 3621 Generating apparatus & parts, electrical

(G-5894)
HEALTHCARE ALLIANCE GROUP LLC
10053 Lakeview Ave (66219-2501)
PHONE..................................913 956-2080
Marcheta Bowlin,
EMP: 10
SALES (est): 1.2MM **Privately Held**
SIC: 6321 Health insurance carriers

(G-5895)
HEART TO HEART INTL INC (PA)
11550 Renner Blvd (66219-9600)
P.O. Box 15566 (66285-5566)
PHONE..................................913 764-5200
Jim Mitchum, *CEO*
Jim Kerr, *Ch of Bd*
Gary Morsch, *President*
Kim Carroll, *COO*
Dan Neal, *Vice Pres*
▼ **EMP:** 27
SQ FT: 6,031
SALES: 138.4MM **Privately Held**
SIC: 8399 Health systems agency

(G-5896)
HEARTLAND COCA-COLA BTLG LLC
10001 Industrial Blvd (66215-1209)
PHONE..................................913 599-9142
Clark Teneca, *QC Mgr*
EMP: 3433
SALES (corp-wide): 23.9B **Privately Held**
SIC: 5149 2086 Beverages, except coffee & tea; carbonated beverages, nonalcoholic: bottled & canned
PA: Heartland Coca-Cola Bottling Company Llc
9000 Marshall Dr
Lenexa KS

(G-5897)
HEARTLAND HEALTH LABS INC (PA)
10435 Lackman Rd (66219-1221)
PHONE..................................913 599-3636
David Clay, *Vice Pres*
EMP: 80
SALES (est): 4.3MM **Privately Held**
SIC: 8071 Testing laboratories

(G-5898)
HEARTLAND POOL & SPA SVC INC
14810 W 89th St (66215-2906)
PHONE..................................913 438-2909
Wade Wasinger, *Owner*
EMP: 13
SALES (est): 501.7K **Privately Held**
SIC: 7991 Spas

(G-5899)
HENDERSON BLDG SOLUTIONS LLC
8345 Lenexa Dr Ste 110 (66214-1654)
PHONE..................................913 894-9720
Drew Rimmer, *Vice Pres*
David Debiasse,
EMP: 18
SALES (est): 2.4MM **Privately Held**
SIC: 8741 Construction management

(G-5900)
HENDERSON ENGINEERS INC (PA)
8345 Lenexa Dr Ste 300 (66214-1777)
PHONE..................................913 742-5000
Duane Henderson, *CEO*
Richard Smith, *President*
David Haake, *COO*
Dana Kettle, *Senior VP*
Phil Miller, *Senior VP*
EMP: 330
SQ FT: 51,378
SALES (est): 93.7MM **Privately Held**
WEB: www.hei-eng.com
SIC: 8711 Professional engineer; electrical or electronic engineering

(G-5901)
HERMES CO INC (PA)
Also Called: Hermey Landscaping
13030 W 87th Street Pkwy # 100 (66215-4633)
PHONE..................................913 888-2413
Dalton Hermes, *Principal*
Hermes Landscaping, *Maintence Staff*
EMP: 28
SALES (est): 17.6MM **Privately Held**
WEB: www.hermeslandscaping.com
SIC: 0782 1711 0181 Landscape contractors; lawn services; irrigation sprinkler system installation; nursery stock, growing of

(G-5902)
HERTZ CORPORATION
13750 W 108th St (66215-2026)
PHONE..................................913 696-0003
Mark Hertz, *Branch Mgr*
EMP: 23
SALES (corp-wide): 9.5B **Publicly Held**
SIC: 7514 Rent-a-car service
HQ: The Hertz Corporation
8501 Williams Rd
Estero FL 33928
239 301-7000

(G-5903)
HI-TECH WELD OVERLAY GROUP LLC
14720 W 99th St Ste B (66215-1103)
P.O. Box 295, Greenwood MO (64034-0295)
PHONE..................................816 524-9010
Paul O'Donald, *President*
Kent Lamfer, *Vice Pres*
Jim Jenkins, *Project Mgr*
Dennis Henderson, *CFO*
Theresa Cassidy, *Admin Sec*
EMP: 25
SALES: 25MM **Privately Held**
SIC: 3548 3589 Resistance welders, electric; commercial cooking & foodwarming equipment

(G-5904)
HOBART SALES AND SERVICE INC
10631 Summit St (66215-2051)
PHONE..................................913 469-9600
Robert Wilson, *Manager*
EMP: 21

SALES (corp-wide): 14.7B **Publicly Held**
WEB: www.hobartcorp.com
SIC: 5046 Restaurant equipment & supplies
HQ: Hobart Sales And Service, Inc.
701 S Ridge Ave
Troy OH 45373
937 332-3000

(G-5905)
HOLLIDAY SAND & GRAVEL CO LLC
9660 Legler Rd (66219-1291)
P.O. Box 23910, Overland Park (66283-0910)
PHONE..................................913 492-5920
Charles Clark, *CEO*
EMP: 43
SALES (est): 106.4K
SALES (corp-wide): 29.7B **Privately Held**
SIC: 1442 Construction sand & gravel
HQ: Oldcastle Building Products, Inc.
3 Glenlake Pkwy
Atlanta GA 30328

(G-5906)
HUGHES MACHINERY COMPANY (DH)
14400 College Blvd (66215-2063)
PHONE..................................913 492-0355
Tim Powell, *President*
Jill Peterson, *CFO*
Greg Ferro, *Sales Staff*
Steve Stocker, *Sales Staff*
Mike Winkelmann, *Sales Staff*
EMP: 46 **EST:** 1924
SQ FT: 37,000
SALES (est): 27.4MM
SALES (corp-wide): 3.4B **Publicly Held**
WEB: www.hughesmachinery.com
SIC: 5084 5074 Industrial machinery & equipment; boilers, power (industrial)
HQ: Fcx Performance, Inc
3000 E 14th Ave
Columbus OH 43219
614 324-6050

(G-5907)
HUSSMANN CORPORATION
10542 Lackman Rd (66219-1224)
PHONE..................................816 373-1274
Dan Harjes, *Manager*
EMP: 30 **Privately Held**
WEB: www.hussmann.com
SIC: 3585 Refrigeration & heating equipment
HQ: Hussmann Corporation
12999 St Charles Rock Rd
Bridgeton MO 63044
314 291-2000

(G-5908)
HYLAND HOLDINGS LLC (DH)
8900 Renner Blvd (66219)
PHONE..................................913 227-7000
Bill Premier, *CEO*
Bob Bodine, *Vice Pres*
David Conley, *Vice Pres*
Rick Cummins, *Vice Pres*
Patrick Kearney, *Vice Pres*
EMP: 28
SALES (est): 81MM
SALES (corp-wide): 461.8MM **Privately Held**
SIC: 7372 Prepackaged software

(G-5909)
IDEXX LABORATORIES INC
11250 Strang Line Rd (66215-4039)
PHONE..................................913 339-4550
EMP: 100
SALES (corp-wide): 2.2B **Publicly Held**
SIC: 8734 Testing laboratories
PA: Idexx Laboratories, Inc.
1 Idexx Dr
Westbrook ME 04092
207 556-0300

(G-5910)
IMAGE FLOORING LLC
14720 W 105th St (66215-4414)
PHONE..................................314 432-3000
Melissa Miller, *President*
Jim Wilkinson, *Vice Pres*
Cathy Wilkinson, *Treasurer*
EMP: 99
SQ FT: 2,500
SALES (est): 24.5MM **Privately Held**
SIC: 5023 Carpets

(G-5911)
INDEPENDENCE ANESTHESIA INC
8725 Rosehill Rd (66215-4610)
PHONE..................................913 707-5294
Robert Bowser, *President*
Marc Turner, *Vice Pres*
Bruce Lerner, *Treasurer*
EMP: 14
SQ FT: 900
SALES (est): 566.7K **Privately Held**
WEB: www.independenceanesthesia.com
SIC: 8011 Anesthesiologist; physicians' office, including specialists

(G-5912)
INDUCTION DYNAMICS LLC (PA)
Also Called: MSE Audio
10661 Rene St (66215-4052)
PHONE..................................913 663-5600
Christopher E Combest, *President*
Shanielle Wenzl, *Exec VP*
Dave Staley, *VP Engrg*
Gary Looney, *Sales Staff*
Andy Lopez, *Sales Staff*
▲ **EMP:** 15
SALES (est): 2MM **Privately Held**
WEB: www.inductiondynamics.com
SIC: 3651 Speaker systems

(G-5913)
INDUSTRIAL FUMIGANT COLLC (HQ)
Also Called: I F C
13420 W 99th St (66215-1365)
PHONE..................................913 782-7600
Gary Rollins, *President*
Austin Mueller, *President*
Gary Cunningham, *Area Mgr*
Randi Hromas, *Area Mgr*
Robert Blachly, *Exec VP*
EMP: 40
SQ FT: 14,000
SALES (est): 33MM
SALES (corp-wide): 1.8B **Publicly Held**
WEB: www.irishfreedomcommittee.net
SIC: 7342 Exterminating & fumigating; pest control services
PA: Rollins, Inc.
2170 Piedmont Rd Ne
Atlanta GA 30324
404 888-2000

(G-5914)
INFINITY FASTENERS INC (PA)
11028 Strang Line Rd (66215-2113)
PHONE..................................913 438-8547
Franklin Gaeta, *Ch of Bd*
Bob Stoddard, *President*
Randy Gaeta, *Vice Pres*
Steve Hengeli, *Vice Pres*
Rob Stoddard, *QC Mgr*
▲ **EMP:** 21
SQ FT: 15,000
SALES: 12.5MM **Privately Held**
WEB: www.infinityfast.com
SIC: 5072 Nuts (hardware); bolts; screws

(G-5915)
INNOTECH LLC
9600 Dice Ln Ste 214 (66215-1152)
PHONE..................................913 888-4646
William You,
EMP: 5
SALES (est): 450K **Privately Held**
SIC: 2431 Exterior & ornamental woodwork & trim

(G-5916)
INNOVTIVE CINEMA SOLUTIONS LLC
13610 W 107th St (66215-2060)
PHONE..................................855 401-4567
Tom Ostermann, *VP Sales*
Pamela Ostermann, *Mng Member*
EMP: 15 **EST:** 2013
SALES (est): 933.9K **Privately Held**
SIC: 7832 Motion picture theaters, except drive-in

(G-5917)
INTERCITY DIRECT LLC
13202 W 98th St (66215-1359)
PHONE..................................913 647-7550
Stephan Haynes, *Broker*
Michael McMahon,
EMP: 11
SALES (est): 4.8MM **Privately Held**
SIC: 4213 Trucking, except local

(G-5918)
INTERDENT INC
Also Called: Advantage Dental
13100 W 87th Street Pkwy (66215-4532)
P.O. Box 21840, Oklahoma City OK (73156-1840)
PHONE..................................913 248-8880
Stacey Lareau, *Manager*
EMP: 20
SALES (corp-wide): 115.2MM **Privately Held**
SIC: 8021 8072 Dentists' office; dental laboratories
HQ: Interdent, Inc.
9800 S La Cienega Blvd # 800
Inglewood CA 90301
310 765-2400

(G-5919)
INTERNATIONAL ELECTRIC INC
21973 W 83rd St (66227-3133)
PHONE..................................913 451-8458
Clifton Dodge, *Owner*
Gary Suess, *Vice Pres*
Chad Dodge, *CFO*
Paul Werle, *Manager*
EMP: 97
SQ FT: 1,500
SALES (est): 8.7MM **Privately Held**
WEB: www.internationalelectric.com
SIC: 1731 Electrical work

(G-5920)
INTERNTNAL MTR COACH GROUP INC
Also Called: I N G
12351 W 96th Ter Ste 101 (66215-4410)
PHONE..................................913 906-0111
Steve Klika, *President*
Terri Phillips, *Office Admin*
EMP: 15
SQ FT: 1,400
SALES (est): 1.4MM **Privately Held**
WEB: www.imgcoach.com
SIC: 8741 4789 Management services; cargo loading & unloading services

(G-5921)
INTERSTATE FLOORING LLC
9801 Commerce Pkwy (66219-2401)
PHONE..................................913 541-9700
David Koenig, *Branch Mgr*
▲ **EMP:** 12
SALES (corp-wide): 74.5MM **Privately Held**
SIC: 1771 Flooring contractor
PA: Interstate Flooring, L.L.C.
5100 Kansas Ave
Kansas City KS 66106
913 573-0600

(G-5922)
IQ GROUP INC
9641 Inspiration St (66227-7300)
PHONE..................................913 722-6700
Sean Clouse, *President*
Stephen Clouse, *Vice Pres*
Eric Simon, *Vice Pres*
EMP: 10
SQ FT: 2,500
SALES (est): 1MM **Privately Held**
WEB: www.theiqgroup.com
SIC: 7371 4813 7374 Computer software development; ; computer graphics service

(G-5923)
IRIS STRGC MKTG SUPPORT INC
10801 Lakeview Ave (66219-1329)
PHONE..................................913 232-4825
Tiffany Kotz, *CEO*
Paul Kotz, *President*
Rachel Elvin, *Business Mgr*
Kate Hogard, *Business Mgr*
Kimberley Lee, *Business Mgr*
EMP: 20
SALES (est): 1.9MM **Privately Held**
SIC: 8742 2759 5045 5199 Marketing consulting services; menus: printing; computer software; advertising specialties

(G-5924)
IVY ANIMAL HEALTH INC (HQ)
Also Called: Vetlife
10850 Lakeview Ave (66219-1330)
PHONE..................................913 310-7900
Stephen H Jenison, *President*
EMP: 50
SALES (est): 12.4MM
SALES (corp-wide): 24.5B **Publicly Held**
SIC: 2834 3841 Veterinary pharmaceutical preparations; surgical & medical instruments
PA: Eli Lilly And Company
Lilly Corporate Ctr
Indianapolis IN 46285
317 276-2000

(G-5925)
IVY ANIMAL HEALTH INC
10850 Lakeview Ave (66219-1330)
PHONE..................................913 888-2192
Mark Whatley, *Branch Mgr*
EMP: 10
SALES (corp-wide): 24.5B **Publicly Held**
SIC: 2833 Animal based products
HQ: Ivy Animal Health, Inc.
10850 Lakeview Ave
Lenexa KS 66219
913 310-7900

(G-5926)
J S TRANSPORTATION LLC
21306 W 82nd St (66220-2579)
PHONE..................................816 651-1827
Jaswinder Singh, *Vice Pres*
EMP: 30
SALES: 8.5MM **Privately Held**
SIC: 4212 Local trucking, without storage

(G-5927)
J-CON REPROGRAPHICS INC
14324 W 96th Ter (66215-4708)
PHONE..................................913 859-0800
Connie Morris, *President*
Bill Morris, *Exec VP*
John H Flucke Jr, *Manager*
EMP: 11
SQ FT: 15,000
SALES (est): 1.7MM **Privately Held**
SIC: 2752 2791 2789 Commercial printing, offset; typesetting; bookbinding & related work

(G-5928)
JASPER INVESTMENTS INC
Also Called: UPS Store 4657
11944 W 95th St (66215-3801)
PHONE..................................913 599-0899
Jerry Amaro, *President*
EMP: 10 **EST:** 2007
SALES (est): 770.6K **Privately Held**
SIC: 7389 4731 4783 Mailbox rental & related service; brokers, shipping; packing goods for shipping

(G-5929)
JOHN A MARSHALL COMPANY (PA)
10930 Lackman Rd (66219-1232)
PHONE..................................913 599-4700
John E Marshall, *CEO*
William C Marshall, *Principal*
Mark Sneed, *Principal*
Mark J Donnelly, *Chairman*
James S Gutschow, *CFO*
▼ **EMP:** 101 **EST:** 1923
SQ FT: 83,100
SALES (est): 12MM **Privately Held**
WEB: www.jamarshall.com
SIC: 7363 5712 Temporary help service; office furniture

(G-5930)
JOHNSON CONTROLS
11019 Strang Line Rd (66215-2181)
PHONE..................................913 894-0010
Kelli Lane, *Sales Staff*
Shane Adams, *Branch Mgr*
EMP: 5 **Privately Held**
WEB: www.simplexgrinnell.com

GEOGRAPHIC

SIC: 3669 Emergency alarms
HQ: Johnson Controls Fire Protection Lp
6600 Congress Ave
Boca Raton FL 33487
561 988-7200

(G-5931)
JOHNSON COUNTY DEV SUPPORT (PA)
10501 Lackman Rd (66219-1223)
PHONE..................................913 826-2626
Karla J Gravenstein, *Principal*
EMP: 18
SALES (est): 1.4MM **Privately Held**
SIC: 8361 Residential care for the handicapped

(G-5932)
JORBAN-RISCOE ASSOCIATES INC (PA)
9808 Alden St (66215-1131)
PHONE..................................913 438-1244
Mark Riscoe, *President*
Brandy Whitaker, *Principal*
Kevin Harre, *Vice Pres*
Kurt Harre, *Vice Pres*
Mike Lorenz, *Vice Pres*
EMP: 29
SQ FT: 30,000
SALES (est): 21MM **Privately Held**
SIC: 5075 3542 3433 Warm air heating equipment & supplies; machine tools, metal forming type; heating equipment, except electric

(G-5933)
JS WESTHOFF & COMPANY INC
14006 W 107th St (66215-2005)
PHONE..................................913 663-9900
Joseph S Westhoff, *President*
Gerry Paden, *Project Mgr*
Connie Westhoff, *Treasurer*
EMP: 17 **EST:** 1999
SALES (est): 2.7MM **Privately Held**
SIC: 8711 Professional engineer

(G-5934)
JVF ENTERPRISES INC
Also Called: Avant Acoustics
14827 W 95th St (66215-5220)
PHONE..................................913 888-9111
Andrew Siebert, *President*
EMP: 11
SQ FT: 5,500
SALES (est): 1MM **Privately Held**
WEB: www.cfaconsulting.com
SIC: 8748 8711 Business consulting; acoustical engineering

(G-5935)
KANDARPAM HOTELS LLC
Also Called: Holiday Inn
25900 W 96th St (66227-7354)
PHONE..................................785 762-4200
S V Rangarajan,
EMP: 20
SALES (est): 900.3K **Privately Held**
SIC: 7011 Hotels & motels

(G-5936)
KANSAS CITY ELECTRICAL SUP CO (PA)
14851 W 99th St (66215-1110)
PHONE..................................913 563-7002
Kaylin Crain, *President*
John Owens, *Treasurer*
Greg Hanna, *Sales Staff*
EMP: 34 **EST:** 1927
SQ FT: 24,000
SALES: 41.2MM **Privately Held**
WEB: www.kcelectricalsupply.com
SIC: 5063 Electrical supplies

(G-5937)
KANSAS COMMUNICATIONS INC
Also Called: Allegiant
14641 W 95th St (66215-5216)
PHONE..................................913 402-2200
Bryan Dancer, *President*
Emily Martin, *Project Mgr*
Russ Bohn, *Sales Staff*
EMP: 20
SQ FT: 3,000
SALES (est): 1.4MM **Privately Held**
WEB: www.kansascomm.com
SIC: 7629 Telecommunication equipment repair (except telephones)

(G-5938)
KANSAS COUNSELORS KANS CY INC
8725 Rosehill Rd Ste 411 (66215-4610)
PHONE..................................913 541-9704
Clarence G White, *President*
EMP: 40
SALES (est): 3MM **Privately Held**
SIC: 7322 Adjustment & collection services

(G-5939)
KC CABINETWRIGHT INC
9837 Lackman Rd (66219-1209)
PHONE..................................913 825-6555
Kenny Jianhui Feng, *President*
▲ **EMP:** 40 **EST:** 2011
SALES (est): 4.3MM **Privately Held**
SIC: 3553 5031 Cabinet makers' machinery; kitchen cabinets

(G-5940)
KC DIGICAL
15504 College Blvd (66219-1350)
PHONE..................................913 541-2688
Libbie Bodde, *Managing Prtnr*
EMP: 5
SALES (est): 469.4K **Privately Held**
SIC: 2679 2759 Tags & labels, paper; labels & seals: printing

(G-5941)
KC GRANITE & CABINETRY LLC
10045 Lackman Rd (66219-1213)
PHONE..................................913 888-0003
Kenny Feng,
▲ **EMP:** 25
SALES (est): 2.7MM **Privately Held**
SIC: 1799 Counter top installation

(G-5942)
KCG INC (PA)
Also Called: Rew Materials
15720 W 108th St Ste 100 (66219-1338)
P.O. Box 19415, Shawnee Mission (66285-9415)
PHONE..................................913 438-4142
Rick J Rew, *President*
James W Bedsworth Sr, *President*
Kim Gray, *COO*
Jeff Butts, *Vice Pres*
David Clay, *Vice Pres*
▲ **EMP:** 30
SQ FT: 9,000
SALES (est): 263.4MM **Privately Held**
WEB: www.kcg-inc.com
SIC: 5032 2992 Drywall materials; lubricating oils & greases

(G-5943)
KCG INC
Also Called: Sierra Gypsum
15740 W 108th St (66219-1338)
P.O. Box 15868, Shawnee Mission (66285-5868)
PHONE..................................913 888-0882
Mark Parot, *Manager*
EMP: 6
SALES (corp-wide): 263.4MM **Privately Held**
WEB: www.kcg-inc.com
SIC: 5032 2992 Drywall materials; lubricating oils & greases
PA: Kcg, Inc.
15720 W 108th St Ste 100
Lenexa KS 66219
913 438-4142

(G-5944)
KCOE ISOM LLP
8801 Renner Ave Ste 100 (66219-9704)
PHONE..................................913 643-5000
Robert J Schuster, *Manager*
Robert Schuster,
EMP: 11
SALES (corp-wide): 48MM **Privately Held**
WEB: www.kcoe.com
SIC: 8721 Certified public accountant
PA: Kcoe Isom, Llp
3030 Courtland Cir
Salina KS
785 825-1561

(G-5945)
KENNETH R JOHNSON INC
Also Called: K R Johnson
13851 W 101st St (66215-1211)
PHONE..................................913 599-1133
John J McQueeney, *President*
▲ **EMP:** 20 **EST:** 1974
SQ FT: 6,000
SALES (est): 11MM **Privately Held**
WEB: www.krjohnson.com
SIC: 5085 Valves & fittings

(G-5946)
KEURIG DR PEPPER INC
7 Up/Snapple
9960 Lakeview Ave (66219-2502)
PHONE..................................913 894-6777
Norm Burke, *President*
Todd Lindhoff, *Sales Executive*
EMP: 100 **Publicly Held**
SIC: 2086 Soft drinks: packaged in cans, bottles, etc.
PA: Keurig Dr Pepper Inc.
5301 Legacy Dr
Plano TX 01803

(G-5947)
KEYWEST TECHNOLOGY INC
14563 W 96th Ter (66215-1165)
PHONE..................................913 492-4666
Koytt Nichols, *President*
Wes Dixson, *Vice Pres*
Wes Dixon, *CIO*
EMP: 15
SQ FT: 8,000
SALES (est): 3.1MM **Privately Held**
WEB: www.keywesttechnology.com
SIC: 3651 Household video equipment

(G-5948)
KIEWIT CORPORATION
Kiewit Power
9401 Renner Blvd (66219-9707)
PHONE..................................913 928-7000
Mark Young, *Area Mgr*
Dave Freeman, *Vice Pres*
Scott A Schmidt, *Vice Pres*
Tim Carrizales, *Project Mgr*
Neil Dublinske, *Project Mgr*
EMP: 100
SALES (corp-wide): 16.2B **Privately Held**
SIC: 1542 Commercial & office building contractors
HQ: Kiewit Corporation
3555 Farnam St Ste 1000
Omaha NE 68131
402 342-2052

(G-5949)
KIEWIT ENGINEERING GROUP INC (DH)
9401 Renner Blvd (66219-9707)
PHONE..................................402 943-1465
Bruce Grewcock, *CEO*
James K Needham, *President*
David A Flickinger, *Exec VP*
Thomas S Shelby, *Exec VP*
John R Burns, *Senior VP*
EMP: 241
SALES (est): 34.7MM
SALES (corp-wide): 16.2B **Privately Held**
WEB: www.bibb.com
SIC: 8712 8711 Architectural services; consulting engineer
HQ: Kiewit Corporation
3555 Farnam St Ste 1000
Omaha NE 68131
402 342-2052

(G-5950)
KIEWIT POWER CONSTRUCTORS CO (DH)
9401 Renner Blvd (66219-9707)
P.O. Box 452500, Omaha NE (68145-2500)
PHONE..................................913 928-7800
Dave Flickinger, *President*
Andre Aube, *Area Mgr*
Michael Nolte, *Manager*
EMP: 105 **EST:** 1982
SALES (est): 82.8MM
SALES (corp-wide): 16.2B **Privately Held**
SIC: 1611 Highway & street construction
HQ: Kiewit Corporation
3555 Farnam St Ste 1000
Omaha NE 68131
402 342-2052

(G-5951)
KIEWIT POWER GROUP INC
9401 Renner Blvd (66219-9707)
PHONE..................................913 227-3600
John Jennings, *President*
James K Needham, *Senior VP*
Steven J Brewer, *Vice Pres*
Jason Dedrickson, *Vice Pres*
John W Kruse, *Vice Pres*
EMP: 10
SALES (est): 1MM
SALES (corp-wide): 16.2B **Privately Held**
SIC: 1629 1731 Power plant construction; electrical work
HQ: Kiewit Corporation
3555 Farnam St Ste 1000
Omaha NE 68131
402 342-2052

(G-5952)
KIEWIT POWER NUCLEAR CO
9401 Renner Blvd (66219-9707)
PHONE..................................913 928-7800
Robert R Rausch, *President*
Michael J Piechoski, *Vice Pres*
Stephen S Thomas, *Treasurer*
Michael F Norton, *Admin Sec*
EMP: 12
SALES (est): 1.3MM **Privately Held**
SIC: 1799 Nuclear power refueling

(G-5953)
KLEINFELDER INC
11529 W 79th St Bldg 21 (66214-1410)
PHONE..................................913 962-0909
Bryan Johnson, *Manager*
EMP: 60
SALES (corp-wide): 249.4MM **Privately Held**
SIC: 8711 8748 Building construction consultant; environmental consultant
HQ: Kleinfelder, Inc.
550 W C St Ste 1200
San Diego CA 92101
619 831-4600

(G-5954)
KNIGHT TRENCHING & EXCVTG INC
14168 Santa Fe Trail Dr (66215-1237)
PHONE..................................913 599-6999
Pamela Knight, *President*
EMP: 22
SQ FT: 4,500
SALES (est): 3.9MM **Privately Held**
WEB: www.knightexcavating.com
SIC: 1794 Excavation & grading, building construction

(G-5955)
KOCHER + BECK USA LP (PA)
Also Called: K B
15850 W 99th St (66219-2905)
PHONE..................................913 529-4336
Lars Beck, *Partner*
Rolf Beck, *Principal*
Erich Kocher, *Principal*
David Morris, *Vice Pres*
Markus Seeger, *Vice Pres*
◆ **EMP:** 60 **EST:** 1999
SALES (est): 15.9MM **Privately Held**
SIC: 3544 Special dies & tools

(G-5956)
KOCHER + BECK USA LP
15850 W 99th St (66219-2905)
PHONE..................................913 529-4336
Lars Beck, *Principal*
EMP: 40
SALES (corp-wide): 15.9MM **Privately Held**
SIC: 3544 Special dies & tools
PA: Kocher + Beck Usa Lp
15850 W 99th St
Lenexa KS 66219
913 529-4336

(G-5957)
KOLLER ENTERPRISES INC
Also Called: Churchill Container
14601 W 99th St (66215-1106)
P.O. Box 718, Fenton MO (63026-0718)
PHONE.................................913 422-2027
Elijah Corbin, *General Mgr*
Dennis Milford, *General Mgr*
Alois J Koller Jr, *Principal*
Kevin Brady, *Plant Mgr*
Cheryl Huffman, *Personnel*
EMP: 100
SALES (corp-wide): 84MM **Privately Held**
WEB: www.koller-craft.com
SIC: 3089 5085 5162 2752 Injection molding of plastics; plastic bottles; plastics products; commercial printing, lithographic; automotive & apparel trimmings
PA: Koller Enterprises, Inc.
1400 S Old Highway 141
Fenton MO 63026
636 343-9220

(G-5958)
KONICA MINOLTA BUSINESS SOLUTI
14300 W 105th St (66215-2049)
PHONE.................................913 563-1800
Julie Sibala, *Sales Mgr*
Monique Penn, *Marketing Staff*
Carl Little, *Branch Mgr*
Adam Peterson, *Prgrmr*
Brian Tomlinson, *Executive*
EMP: 50 **Privately Held**
WEB: www.konicabt.com
SIC: 5044 Photocopy machines
HQ: Konica Minolta Business Solutions U.S.A., Inc.
100 Williams Dr
Ramsey NJ 07446
201 825-4000

(G-5959)
L KCP
16215 W 108th St (66219-1347)
PHONE.................................913 894-3009
EMP: 12
SALES (est): 992.5K **Privately Held**
SIC: 4911 Electric Services

(G-5960)
LA PETITE ACADEMY INC
15039 W 86th St (66215-4183)
PHONE.................................913 492-4183
Jami Johnson, *Director*
EMP: 11
SALES (corp-wide): 164MM **Privately Held**
WEB: www.lapetite.com
SIC: 8351 Preschool center
HQ: La Petite Academy, Inc.
21333 Haggerty Rd Ste 300
Novi MI 48375
877 861-5078

(G-5961)
LABONE INC (HQ)
Also Called: Quest Diagnostics
10101 Renner Blvd (66219-9752)
PHONE.................................913 888-1770
Barry Bauer, *President*
Teri Leibson, *Regional Mgr*
Pat Graham, *Area Mgr*
Melissa Wilson, *Area Mgr*
Joseph Benage, *Vice Pres*
▲ **EMP:** 800
SQ FT: 258,000
SALES (est): 75.1MM
SALES (corp-wide): 7.5B **Publicly Held**
SIC: 8071 6411 Testing laboratories; blood analysis laboratory; urinalysis laboratory; insurance information & consulting services
PA: Quest Diagnostics Incorporated
500 Plaza Dr Ste G
Secaucus NJ 07094
973 520-2700

(G-5962)
LAKEVIEW VILLAGE INC
Also Called: Lakeview Vlg Retirement Cmnty
9100 Park St (66215-3353)
PHONE.................................913 888-1900
Robert Clausen, *CEO*
Tedrick Housh, *Ch of Bd*
Mary Schworer, *COO*
Matt Nierman, *Facilities Mgr*
Carl Werkowitch, *Controller*
EMP: 550
SQ FT: 1,000,000
SALES: 44MM **Privately Held**
SIC: 6513 8052 Retirement hotel operation; intermediate care facilities; personal care facility

(G-5963)
LAMINATE WORKS INC (PA)
15900 College Blvd # 200 (66219-1334)
PHONE.................................913 800-8263
Bert Clothier, *President*
Kirk Uffelman, *General Mgr*
Gretchen Clothier, *Corp Secy*
Jason Aldrich, *Opers Mgr*
Gary Fenton, *CFO*
EMP: 70
SQ FT: 100,000
SALES: 22MM **Privately Held**
WEB: www.laminateworks.com
SIC: 2493 Particleboard, plastic laminated

(G-5964)
LANDIS+GYR INC
11146 Thompson Ave (66219-2301)
PHONE.................................913 312-4710
Jeff Wamboldt, *Sales Staff*
Saundra Harris, *Office Mgr*
Dennis Su, *Supervisor*
Vaishali Patil, *Database Admin*
James Packard, *IT/INT Sup*
EMP: 9
SALES (corp-wide): 1.7B **Privately Held**
SIC: 3825 Meters: electric, pocket, portable, panelboard, etc.
HQ: Landis+Gyr Llc
30000 Mill Creek Ave # 100
Alpharetta GA 30022
678 258-1500

(G-5965)
LEGACY HOME INSPECTIONS
15301 W 87th St Ste 220 (66219-1425)
PHONE.................................913 484-4157
Robert Ladd, *Owner*
EMP: 25
SALES (est): 115.9K **Privately Held**
SIC: 7389 Inspection & testing services

(G-5966)
LEISURE HOTEL CORPORATION (PA)
Also Called: Leisure Hotel Group Companies
8725 Rosehill Rd Ste 300 (66215-4625)
PHONE.................................913 905-1460
Steve Olson, *CEO*
Christine Mraz, *General Mgr*
Fran Jabara, *Corp Secy*
Gary Endicott, *Exec VP*
Jim Cook, *Vice Pres*
EMP: 65
SQ FT: 7,500
SALES (est): 6.9MM **Privately Held**
WEB: www.hotels.leisurehotel.com
SIC: 7011 8741 Hotels & motels; hotel or motel management

(G-5967)
LEISURE HOTELS LLC
8725 Rosehill Rd Ste 300 (66215-4625)
PHONE.................................913 905-1460
Brent Jaynes, *Managing Prtnr*
Jan Splitt, *Opers-Prdtn-Mfg*
Steve Olsen, *Mng Member*
Clarke Henning, *Technology*
EMP: 10
SALES (est): 664.4K
SALES (corp-wide): 6.9MM **Privately Held**
SIC: 8742 General management consultant
PA: Leisure Hotel Corporation
8725 Rosehill Rd Ste 300
Lenexa KS 66215
913 905-1460

(G-5968)
LENEXA CITY CENTER HOTEL CORP (PA)
Also Called: Hyatt Place Lenexa City Center
8741 Ryckert St (66219-7801)
PHONE.................................913 742-7777
Richard H Wiens, *CEO*
EMP: 36
SALES: 150K **Privately Held**
SIC: 7011 Hotels & motels

(G-5969)
LENEXA FDA OC LLC
11510 W 80th St (66214-3338)
PHONE.................................913 894-9735
Cameron Johnson, *Director*
EMP: 99
SALES (est): 2.2MM **Privately Held**
SIC: 6531 Real estate agents & managers

(G-5970)
LENEXA HOTEL LP
Also Called: Clarion Hotel Kansas
12601 W 95th St (66215-3810)
PHONE.................................913 217-1000
Stephen Craig, *General Mgr*
EMP: 75
SALES (est): 3.1MM
SALES (corp-wide): 9.9MM **Privately Held**
WEB: www.radissonlenexa.com
SIC: 7011 5813 5812 Motels; drinking places; eating places
PA: Lenexa Hotel, L.P.
730 New Hampshire St # 206
Lawrence KS 66044
785 841-3100

(G-5971)
LIFE TIME FITNESS INC
16851 W 90th St (66219-2716)
PHONE.................................913 492-4781
EMP: 141
SALES (corp-wide): 773.5MM **Privately Held**
SIC: 7991 Health club
HQ: Life Time, Inc.
2902 Corporate Pl
Chanhassen MN 55317

(G-5972)
LIFESOURCE INC
10606 Widmer Rd (66215-2072)
PHONE.................................913 660-9275
Sean Squire, *CEO*
EMP: 5
SQ FT: 2,500
SALES: 1.2MM **Privately Held**
SIC: 3845 Respiratory analysis equipment, electromedical

(G-5973)
LINCARE INC
14333 W 95th St (66215-5210)
PHONE.................................913 438-8200
Daisy Thompson, *Branch Mgr*
EMP: 20 **Privately Held**
SIC: 5047 Medical & hospital equipment
HQ: Lincare Inc.
19387 Us Highway 19 N
Clearwater FL 33764
727 530-7700

(G-5974)
LIONSHARE MARKETING INC
7830 Barton St (66214-3403)
PHONE.................................913 631-8400
Laura Lee Jones, *President*
Lori Holt, *Business Mgr*
Daniel Quinn, *Director*
Rachel Rottinghaus, *Executive Asst*
EMP: 18
SQ FT: 20,000
SALES (est): 3MM **Privately Held**
WEB: www.lionsharemarketing.com
SIC: 7331 8742 8732 Mailing service; marketing consulting services; market analysis, business & economic research; market analysis or research

(G-5975)
LITHKO CONTRACTING LLC
10800 Lakeview Ave (66219-1330)
PHONE.................................913 281-2700
Ted Strom, *Branch Mgr*
EMP: 15
SALES (corp-wide): 163.7MM **Privately Held**
SIC: 1771 Exterior concrete stucco contractor; concrete repair; flooring contractor; foundation & footing contractor
PA: Lithko Contracting, Llc
2958 Crescentville Rd
West Chester OH 45069
513 564-2000

(G-5976)
LMI AEROSPACE INC
11064 Strang Line Rd (66215-2113)
PHONE.................................913 469-6400
Dane Peck, *President*
EMP: 10 **Privately Held**
SIC: 3728 Aircraft parts & equipment
HQ: Lmi Aerospace, Inc.
411 Fountain Lakes Blvd
Saint Charles MO 63301
636 946-6525

(G-5977)
LMI LENEXA
11064 Strang Line Rd (66215-2113)
PHONE.................................913 491-6975
EMP: 5 **EST:** 2015
SALES (est): 428.9K **Privately Held**
SIC: 3728 Aircraft parts & equipment

(G-5978)
LONG MOTOR CORPORATION (PA)
Also Called: Victoria British
14600 W 107th St (66215-4015)
P.O. Box 14991, Shawnee Mission (66285-4991)
PHONE.................................913 541-1525
Rebecca Hanrahan, *President*
Janet Long, *Vice Pres*
Andy Scholler, *Facilities Mgr*
Aaron Hammond, *Production*
Kristi Huston, *Production*
◆ **EMP:** 105 **EST:** 1981
SQ FT: 336,000
SALES (est): 59.7MM **Privately Held**
WEB: www.longmotor.net
SIC: 5961 5013 Automotive supplies & equipment, mail order; automotive supplies & parts

(G-5979)
LONG MOTOR CORPORATION
15450 W 108th St (66219-1302)
PHONE.................................913 541-1525
Becky Hanrahan, *Vice Pres*
EMP: 140
SALES (corp-wide): 59.7MM **Privately Held**
SIC: 5961 5013 Catalog & mail-order houses; motor vehicle supplies & new parts
PA: Long Motor Corporation
14600 W 107th St
Lenexa KS 66215
913 541-1525

(G-5980)
LQ MANAGEMENT LLC
Also Called: La Quinta Inn
9461 Lenexa Dr (66215-3836)
PHONE.................................913 492-5500
David Berends, *Branch Mgr*
EMP: 20 **Publicly Held**
WEB: www.neubayern.net
SIC: 7011 Hotels & motels
HQ: Lq Management L.L.C.
909 Hidden Rdg Ste 600
Irving TX 75038
214 492-6600

(G-5981)
MAGTEK INC
9913 Pflumm Rd (66215-1222)
PHONE.................................913 451-1151
Dan Willard, *President*
Susan Willard, *CFO*
EMP: 10
SQ FT: 11,000
SALES: 1.5MM **Privately Held**
WEB: www.magtek.net
SIC: 5099 3695 Video & audio equipment; magnetic & optical recording media

(G-5982)
MAINSTREET FEDERAL CREDIT UN (PA)
13001 W 95th St (66215-3726)
PHONE.................................913 599-1010
John D Beverlin, *President*
Lee Patrick, *Exec VP*

GEOGRAPHIC

Doug Bankson, *Vice Pres*
David Collins, *CFO*
Collins Dave, *CFO*
EMP: 60
SALES: 14.7MM **Privately Held**
WEB: www.cujc.com
SIC: 6061 Federal credit unions

(G-5983)
MAJESTIC FRANCHISING INC
Also Called: Jani-King
14821 W 95th St (66215-5220)
PHONE..................................913 385-1440
Debbie Sinopoli, *President*
Barbison Sinopoli, *Vice Pres*
Shari Narde, *Opers Staff*
EMP: 10
SQ FT: 5,000
SALES (est): 526.9K **Privately Held**
WEB: www.janikingkc.com
SIC: 7349 6794 Janitorial service, contract basis; franchises, selling or licensing

(G-5984)
MAPS INC
Also Called: Mid America Peripheral Support
11630 W 85th St (66214-1541)
PHONE..................................913 599-0500
Darrel Yoder, *CEO*
Kent Reed, *Vice Pres*
EMP: 28
SQ FT: 10,000
SALES (est): 3.4MM **Privately Held**
WEB: www.mapsweb.com
SIC: 7378 Computer maintenance & repair

(G-5985)
MAR-BECK APPLIANCE SVC CO INC (PA)
17501 W 98th St Spc 17-56 (66219-1721)
PHONE..................................913 322-4022
Robert Wheeler, *President*
Robert G Wheeler, *President*
Ray Taurus, *Vice Pres*
Charles Wallace, *Opers Mgr*
EMP: 30
SALES (est): 5.9MM **Privately Held**
WEB: www.mar-beck.com
SIC: 7629 5722 Electrical household appliance repair; electric household appliances, small

(G-5986)
MAREL INC (HQ)
8145 Flint St (66214-3301)
PHONE..................................913 888-9110
Einar Einarsson, *President*
Diego Lages, *Managing Dir*
Larry Campbell, *Vice Pres*
Troels Svendsen, *Vice Pres*
David Whitem, *Vice Pres*
▲ **EMP:** 39
SALES (est): 65.6MM
SALES (corp-wide): 1.3B **Privately Held**
WEB: www.marelusa.com
SIC: 5046 Commercial cooking & food service equipment
PA: Marel Hf.
Austurhrauni 9
Gardabae 210
563 800-0

(G-5987)
MARLEN RESEARCH CORP
9202 Barton St (66214-1721)
PHONE..................................913 888-3333
▲ **EMP:** 19
SALES (est): 2.3MM **Privately Held**
SIC: 5084 Whol Industrial Equipment

(G-5988)
MASS MEDICAL STORAGE LLC
Also Called: Medical Design Systems
7848 Barton St (66214-3403)
PHONE..................................913 438-8835
Aubrey Guezuraga, *CEO*
Linda Dodson, *Controller*
Khayyam Burns, *Sales Staff*
Tandi Dietz, *Manager*
David Guezuraga, *Manager*
EMP: 11
SQ FT: 22,000
SALES (est): 2.6MM **Privately Held**
WEB: www.masscabinets.com
SIC: 4226 Special warehousing & storage

(G-5989)
MASTHEAD INTERNATIONAL INC (HQ)
11145 Thompson Ave (66219-2302)
PHONE..................................913 888-8600
William P Massey, *President*
Craig D Davis, *Principal*
Daniel J Hefferon, *CFO*
Charles F William, *Admin Sec*
EMP: 50
SALES (est): 9.5MM
SALES (corp-wide): 1.1B **Privately Held**
SIC: 1796 Machinery installation; machine moving & rigging
PA: Performance Contracting Group, Inc.
11145 Thompson Ave
Lenexa KS 66219
800 255-6886

(G-5990)
MCAFEE HENDERSON SOLUTIONS INC (PA)
15700 College Blvd # 202 (66219-1344)
PHONE..................................913 888-4647
Joseph McAfee, *President*
Matthew Henderson, *Vice Pres*
Ben Ellis, *Systs Prg Mgr*
Kim Turk, *Admin Asst*
EMP: 15
SQ FT: 3,750
SALES: 1.3MM **Privately Held**
WEB: www.mhs-eng.com
SIC: 8711 8713 Civil engineering; photogrammetric engineering

(G-5991)
MCAFEE HENDERSON SOLUTIONS INC
15700 College Blvd # 202 (66219-1373)
PHONE..................................913 888-4647
Matthew Henderson, *Branch Mgr*
EMP: 13
SALES (corp-wide): 1.3MM **Privately Held**
WEB: www.mhs-eng.com
SIC: 8711 8713 Civil engineering; surveying services
PA: Mcafee Henderson Solutions, Inc.
15700 College Blvd # 202
Lenexa KS 66219
913 888-4647

(G-5992)
MCLANE FOODSERVICE INC
8200 Monticello Rd (66227-2617)
PHONE..................................913 422-6100
Tim McKee, *Manager*
EMP: 159
SALES (corp-wide): 225.3B **Publicly Held**
SIC: 5141 Groceries, general line
HQ: Mclane Foodservice, Inc.
2085 Midway Rd
Carrollton TX 75006
972 364-2000

(G-5993)
MEDICARE ADVISORS 365 LLC
8523 Caenen Lake Ct (66215-4551)
PHONE..................................866 956-0745
Bruce Dahlquist, *Mng Member*
EMP: 10
SALES (est): 442.5K **Privately Held**
SIC: 6321 Accident & health insurance

(G-5994)
MER-SEA & CO LLC
Also Called: Mer Sea
14832 W 107th St (66215-4002)
PHONE..................................816 974-3115
Lina Dickinson, *Mng Member*
Melanie Bolin,
▲ **EMP:** 20
SQ FT: 12,000
SALES: 5.2MM **Privately Held**
SIC: 5199 Gifts & novelties

(G-5995)
METRO AIR CONDITIONING CO
8151 Mccoy St (66227-2644)
PHONE..................................913 888-3991
Gregory Mealy, *President*
Joe Bret, *Senior VP*
Justin Gunter, *Vice Pres*
Matt Kelso, *Vice Pres*
Greg Mealy, *Vice Pres*
EMP: 65
SQ FT: 12,000
SALES (est): 15.2MM **Privately Held**
SIC: 1711 Warm air heating & air conditioning contractor

(G-5996)
METRO TILE CONTRACTORS INC
10577 Widmer Rd (66215-2096)
PHONE..................................913 381-7770
John Kinney, *President*
Ken Dutro, *Vice Pres*
EMP: 50
SQ FT: 6,000
SALES (est): 5.5MM **Privately Held**
WEB: www.metrotilekc.com
SIC: 1743 5211 Tile installation, ceramic; marble installation, interior; tile, ceramic

(G-5997)
METRO TITLE SERVICES LLC
8033 Flint St (66214-3335)
PHONE..................................913 236-9923
Barry Kaseff, *President*
Eric Kaseff, *Vice Pres*
EMP: 60
SALES (est): 1.3MM
SALES (corp-wide): 92.6MM **Privately Held**
WEB: www.transtitle.com
SIC: 6541 Title & trust companies
HQ: Acertus
1111 Alderman Dr Ste 350
Alpharetta GA 30005
770 442-0222

(G-5998)
MID AMERICA CREDIT BUREAU LLC
13021 W 95th St Ste A (66215-3700)
PHONE..................................913 307-0551
Seth Shoemaker,
Chris Shoemaker,
EMP: 30
SQ FT: 40,000
SALES (est): 962.9K **Privately Held**
SIC: 7322 Collection agency, except real estate

(G-5999)
MIDAS LENEXA LLC
Also Called: Springhill Suites
17190 W 87th St (66219)
PHONE..................................913 225-9955
Katie O'Connor, *General Mgr*
EMP: 69
SALES (est): 210K
SALES (corp-wide): 64.8MM **Privately Held**
SIC: 7011 Hotels & motels
PA: Midas Hospitality, Llc
1804 Borman Circle Dr # 100
Saint Louis MO 63146
314 692-0100

(G-6000)
MIDWEST CARDIOLOGY ASSOCIATES
12200 W 106th St Ste 320 (66215-2305)
PHONE..................................913 894-9015
Zahra Raki, *COO*
Gary Brown, *Manager*
Ujjaval Patel, *Cardiology*
EMP: 16
SALES (corp-wide): 5.2MM **Privately Held**
WEB: www.midwestcardiology.com
SIC: 8011 Cardiologist & cardio-vascular specialist
PA: Midwest Cardiology Associates Inc
5701 W 119th St Ste 430
Shawnee Mission KS 66209
913 253-3045

(G-6001)
MIDWEST EXPRESS CORPORATION (PA)
9220 Marshall Dr (66215-3844)
◆ **PHONE**..................................913 573-1400
Jack Flores, *Business Mgr*
Jeff Johnson, *Vice Pres*
Ted Glickley, *Officer*
EMP: 15
SQ FT: 4,333
SALES (est): 15.9MM **Privately Held**
SIC: 4213 Contract haulers

(G-6002)
MIDWEST HEALTH SERVICES INC
8740 Caenen Lake Rd (66215-2069)
PHONE..................................913 894-0014
EMP: 25
SALES (corp-wide): 32.7MM **Privately Held**
SIC: 8051 Skilled nursing care facilities
PA: Midwest Health, Inc
3024 Sw Wanamaker Rd # 300
Topeka KS 66614
785 272-1535

(G-6003)
MIDWEST PRECISION INC
9900 Pflumm Rd U1112 (66215-1278)
PHONE..................................913 307-0211
Scott Smith, *President*
EMP: 10
SALES (est): 1.2MM **Privately Held**
SIC: 3545 Machine tool accessories

(G-6004)
MIDWEST SPORTS PRODUCTIONS LLC
21967 W 83rd St (66227-3133)
PHONE..................................913 543-6116
Jeremy McDowell, *Mng Member*
EMP: 23
SALES (est): 1.1MM **Privately Held**
SIC: 7822 Motion picture & tape distribution

(G-6005)
MINI MAID JOCO INCORPORATED
13100 W 95th St Ste 4c (66215-3795)
PHONE..................................913 894-2200
Betty Stewart, *President*
EMP: 18
SALES (est): 585.1K **Privately Held**
SIC: 7349 1711 Maid services, contract or fee basis; plumbing, heating, air-conditioning contractors

(G-6006)
MIRACORP INC
15317 W 95th St (66219-1262)
PHONE..................................913 322-8000
Lane Goebel, *Owner*
EMP: 9
SALES (est): 722.2K **Privately Held**
SIC: 2741 Music book & sheet music publishing

(G-6007)
MITEL (DELAWARE) INC
16201 W 95th St Ste 210 (66219-1216)
PHONE..................................913 752-9100
Melissa Higgins, *Branch Mgr*
EMP: 15
SALES (corp-wide): 1B **Privately Held**
WEB: www.inter-tel.com
SIC: 8999 Communication services
HQ: Mitel (Delaware). Inc.
1146 N Alma School Rd
Mesa AZ 85201
480 449-8900

(G-6008)
MITEL TECHNOLOGIES INC
16201 W 95th St Ste 210 (66219-1216)
PHONE..................................913 752-9100
Jason Spainhour, *Branch Mgr*
EMP: 44
SALES (corp-wide): 987.6MM **Privately Held**
SIC: 5065 Electronic parts & equipment
HQ: Mitel Technologies, Inc.
1146 N Alma School Rd
Mesa AZ 85201
480 449-8900

(G-6009)
MKC GOLF 3 LLC
8409 Nieman Rd (66214-1528)
PHONE..................................913 526-3312
John F Mathews,
EMP: 8

▲ = Import ▼=Export
◆ =Import/Export

SALES (est): 235K **Privately Held**
SIC: 3999 Barber & beauty shop equipment

(G-6010)
MOBILE REASONING INC
15737 W 100th Ter (66219-1285)
PHONE..................................913 888-2600
Scott Bublin, *President*
EMP: 5
SALES (est): 436.2K **Privately Held**
WEB: www.mobilereasoning.com
SIC: 7371 7372 Software programming applications; application computer software

(G-6011)
MONARCH INVENTORIES SERVICES
9716 Rosehill Rd (66215-1414)
PHONE..................................913 541-0645
Jeanette Paikowski, *President*
EMP: 30
SQ FT: 1,200
SALES (est): 1.8MM **Privately Held**
SIC: 7389 Inventory computing service

(G-6012)
MORE FLOODS INC
14804 W 114th Ter (66215-4883)
PHONE..................................913 469-9464
Cliff Cole, *President*
EMP: 6
SALES (est): 823.8K **Privately Held**
SIC: 2273 Carpets & rugs

(G-6013)
MOXIE SERVICES LLC
Also Called: Joshua's Pest Control
14635 W 101st Ter (66215-1122)
PHONE..................................913 416-1205
Kacey Swensen,
Casey Swensen,
Jason Walton,
EMP: 29
SQ FT: 4,500
SALES: 3.5MM **Privately Held**
SIC: 7342 Pest control in structures

(G-6014)
MS ELECTRONICS LLC
Also Called: MSE Audio
10661 Rene St (66215-4052)
PHONE..................................913 233-8518
Joe Vierra, *Manager*
EMP: 16
SALES (corp-wide): 8.6MM **Privately Held**
SIC: 5065 Sound equipment, electronic
PA: Ms Electronics Llc
10661 Rene St
Lenexa KS 66215
866 663-9770

(G-6015)
MS ELECTRONICS LLC (PA)
10661 Rene St (66215-4052)
PHONE..................................866 663-9770
Chris Combest,
EMP: 15
SALES (est): 8.6MM **Privately Held**
SIC: 3651 Loudspeakers, electrodynamic or magnetic

(G-6016)
MW BUILDERS INC (HQ)
13725 W 109th St (66215-4137)
PHONE..................................913 469-0101
Todd Whitterman, *President*
Jason Evelyn, *President*
Peter Kelley, *President*
David Cimpl, *CFO*
David Burt, *Treasurer*
EMP: 150
SQ FT: 16,000
SALES (est): 75.7MM
SALES (corp-wide): 440.7MM **Privately Held**
WEB: www.mmc.com
SIC: 1542 Commercial & office building contractors
PA: Mmc Corp
10955 Lowell Ave Ste 350
Overland Park KS 66210
913 469-0101

(G-6017)
NABHOLZ CONSTRUCTION CORP
17300 W 116th St (66219-9612)
PHONE..................................913 393-6500
Jon Pahl, *Vice Pres*
EMP: 70
SALES (corp-wide): 604.4MM **Privately Held**
WEB: www.nabholz.com
SIC: 1542 Commercial & office building, new construction
PA: Nabholz Construction Corporation
612 Garland St
Conway AR 72032
501 505-5800

(G-6018)
NATIONAL COMMERCIAL BLDRS INC
10555 Rene St (66215-4054)
PHONE..................................913 599-0200
James Reed, *Principal*
Frank Lightfoot, *Principal*
EMP: 10 **EST:** 2009
SQ FT: 3,500
SALES (est): 3.9MM **Privately Held**
SIC: 1542 Commercial & office building, new construction

(G-6019)
NEEDHAM & ASSOCIATES INC (PA)
Also Called: Design Build Steel
15950 College Blvd (66219-1369)
PHONE..................................913 385-5300
Jeffrey R Needham, *President*
David Mittendorf, *Vice Pres*
EMP: 7
SALES: 5MM **Privately Held**
WEB: www.needhamcompanies.com
SIC: 8711 8748 3441 Structural engineering; business consulting; fabricated structural metal

(G-6020)
NEIGHBORHOOD NETWORK LLC
11627 W 79th St (66214-1488)
PHONE..................................913 341-9316
Michael Strouse,
EMP: 40
SALES (est): 126.8K **Privately Held**
SIC: 8699 Charitable organization

(G-6021)
NEIGHBORS CONSTRUCTION CO INC (PA)
15226 W 87th Street Pkwy (66219-1429)
PHONE..................................913 422-5555
Roger H Neighbors, *President*
Aaron Neighbors, *Vice Pres*
Nancy L Neighbors, *Vice Pres*
EMP: 50
SALES: 76.9MM **Privately Held**
WEB: www.neighborsconstruction.com
SIC: 1522 5031 Residential construction; lumber, plywood & millwork

(G-6022)
NELSON HARMON KAPLN WMS MD
Also Called: Nelson, John B
10550 Quivira Rd Ste 335 (66215-2378)
PHONE..................................913 599-3800
John B Nelson MD, *Partner*
Gary Harmon MD, *Partner*
James Kaplan MD, *Partner*
Wade Williams, *Partner*
EMP: 10
SALES (est): 795.6K **Privately Held**
SIC: 8011 General & family practice, physician/surgeon

(G-6023)
NEUROSURGERY KANSAS CITY PA
12200 W 106th St Ste 400e (66215-2305)
PHONE..................................913 299-9507
Robert Beatty, *President*
EMP: 11
SALES (est): 650K **Privately Held**
SIC: 8011 Neurosurgeon

(G-6024)
NIFAST CORPORATION
9733 Lackman Rd (66219-1207)
PHONE..................................913 888-9344
Brett Fossnight, *Manager*
EMP: 16 **Privately Held**
SIC: 5072 Bolts; nuts (hardware); screws
HQ: Nifast Corporation
815 Carol Ct
Carol Stream IL 60188
630 539-0097

(G-6025)
NO SPILL INC
9808 Pflumm Rd (66215-1208)
PHONE..................................913 888-9200
Tom Cray, *President*
▲ **EMP:** 5
SQ FT: 5,000
SALES (est): 777.3K **Privately Held**
SIC: 3411 Oil cans, metal

(G-6026)
NORBROOK INC
9733 Loiret Blvd (66219-2409)
PHONE..................................913 599-5777
Kent Mick, *Principal*
Mackenzie Davis, *Regl Sales Mgr*
Robert Barron, *Manager*
Scott Egbert, *Manager*
Shane Hawthorne, *Manager*
◆ **EMP:** 32
SALES (est): 7.1MM **Privately Held**
SIC: 2834 Veterinary pharmaceutical preparations

(G-6027)
NORTHWEST HARDWOODS INC
15720 W 108th St (66219-1338)
PHONE..................................913 894-9790
Todd Walker, *Manager*
EMP: 36 **Privately Held**
SIC: 5031 Lumber: rough, dressed & finished
HQ: Northwest Hardwoods, Inc.
1313 Broadway Ste 300
Tacoma WA 98402

(G-6028)
NOVATECH LLC
Also Called: Orion Utility Automation
13555 W 107th St (66215-2019)
PHONE..................................913 451-1880
Alan Staatz, *Vice Pres*
EMP: 43
SALES (corp-wide): 44.6MM **Privately Held**
WEB: www.novatech-llc.com
SIC: 3699 Cleaning equipment, ultrasonic, except medical & dental
PA: Novatech, L.L.C.
1720 Molasses Way
Quakertown PA 18951
484 812-6000

(G-6029)
NOVATION IQ LLC
9806 Lackman Rd (66219-1210)
PHONE..................................913 492-6000
Cliff Illig,
Dawn Marriott, *Executive Asst*
EMP: 25 **EST:** 2001
SQ FT: 25,000
SALES (est): 16.1MM **Privately Held**
WEB: www.vertexfoam.com
SIC: 5199 3069 3086 5999 Foam rubber; sponge rubber & sponge rubber products; plastics foam products; padding, foamed plastic; foam & foam products; plastic finished products, laminated

(G-6030)
NUVIDIA LLC
10575 Widmer Rd (66215-2096)
PHONE..................................913 599-5200
Tom Doyle,
Stephen McComas,
EMP: 14
SALES (est): 2MM **Privately Held**
WEB: www.nuvidia.com
SIC: 3695 7812 Video recording tape, blank; motion picture & video production

(G-6031)
O RING SALES AND SERVICE INC
15019 W 95th St (66215-5229)
PHONE..................................913 310-0001
Doug A Johnson, *President*
Judy Johnson, *Vice Pres*
Dennis Ogran, *Sales Engr*
Jake Groff, *Sales Staff*
EMP: 16
SALES: 4MM **Privately Held**
SIC: 5085 Industrial supplies

(G-6032)
OAK PARK VILLAGE
Also Called: Resource Residential
9670 Halsey St (66215-1607)
PHONE..................................913 888-1500
Harold Grinstoon, *Owner*
EMP: 15
SALES (est): 746K **Privately Held**
WEB: www.bentleyplaceapartments.com
SIC: 6513 Apartment hotel operation

(G-6033)
OCONNOR COMPANY INC (HQ)
16910 W 116th St (66219-9604)
PHONE..................................913 894-8788
Greg Borr, *Principal*
EMP: 30
SQ FT: 25,000
SALES: 90MM
SALES (corp-wide): 116.3MM **Privately Held**
WEB: www.oconnor-hvac.com
SIC: 5075 Air conditioning & ventilation equipment & supplies
PA: Munch's Supply Llc
1901 Ferro Dr
New Lenox IL 60451
815 723-1111

(G-6034)
OLATHE MEDICAL SERVICES INC
Also Called: Walk In Health Care
14425 College Blvd # 100 (66215-2002)
PHONE..................................913 782-3798
Jeannette O'Harrah, *Manager*
EMP: 15 **Privately Held**
SIC: 8011 General & family practice, physician/surgeon
PA: Olathe Medical Services, Inc
15435 W 134th Pl
Olathe KS 66062

(G-6035)
OLATHE MILLWORK COMPANY (PA)
16002 W 110th St (66219-1328)
PHONE..................................913 894-5010
Keith North, *President*
Bentley Klingensmith, *Corp Secy*
Gary Klingensmith, *Vice Pres*
Brian North, *Vice Pres*
▲ **EMP:** 42
SQ FT: 30,000
SALES (est): 7.9MM **Privately Held**
SIC: 5031 Millwork

(G-6036)
ON CALL MOBILE THERAPIES LLC
15621 W 87th Street Pkwy # 356 (66219-1435)
PHONE..................................913 449-1679
Tom Feiden, *President*
Carl Hanks, *Principal*
Drew Phillips, *Vice Pres*
EMP: 25
SALES (est): 909.1K **Privately Held**
SIC: 8062 General medical & surgical hospitals

(G-6037)
ONLINE VEND MCH SLS & SVC INC
14408 W 90th Ter (66215-2918)
P.O. Box 14644 (66285-4644)
PHONE..................................913 492-1097
Michael H Hanna, *President*
Michael Hanna, *President*
Michael Jay Hanna, *General Mgr*
Carmen Hanna, *Vice Pres*

EMP: 5
SALES: 350K **Privately Held**
WEB: www.onlinevending.com
SIC: 7699 3581 Vending machine repair; automatic vending machines

(G-6038)
ORKIN LLC
Also Called: Orkin Pest Control 791
8605 Quivira Rd (66215-2804)
PHONE..................................913 492-4029
Jim Bailey, *Branch Mgr*
EMP: 14
SALES (corp-wide): 1.8B **Publicly Held**
WEB: www.orkin.com
SIC: 7342 Pest control services
HQ: Orkin, Llc
2170 Piedmont Rd Ne
Atlanta GA 30324
404 888-2000

(G-6039)
P/STRADA LLC
12401 W 82nd Ter (66215-2740)
PHONE..................................816 256-4577
Patrice Manual, *President*
EMP: 15
SQ FT: 1,500
SALES (est): 1.9MM **Privately Held**
WEB: www.pstrada.com
SIC: 8748 Business consulting

(G-6040)
P1 GROUP INC (PA)
13605 W 96th Ter (66215-1253)
PHONE..................................913 529-5000
Smitty Belcher, *CEO*
Dave Beebe, *Vice Pres*
Glenn Shain, *Vice Pres*
Stuart Sherrow, *Vice Pres*
Stephen Smith, *Vice Pres*
EMP: 300
SQ FT: 120,000
SALES (est): 243.8MM **Privately Held**
WEB: www.p1group.com
SIC: 1731 1796 Electrical work; machinery installation

(G-6041)
P1 GROUP INTERNATIONAL INC
Also Called: A. D. Jacobson Company, Inc.
13605 W 96th Ter (66215-1253)
PHONE..................................913 529-5000
James Gathen, *CEO*
Charles Brandon, *President*
Mike Yarbrough, *Project Engr*
EMP: 200
SQ FT: 55,000
SALES (est): 13.6MM
SALES (corp-wide): 243.8MM **Privately Held**
WEB: www.p1group.com
SIC: 1711 Mechanical contractor; warm air heating & air conditioning contractor; plumbing contractors; process piping contractor
PA: P1 Group, Inc.
13605 W 96th Ter
Lenexa KS 66215
913 529-5000

(G-6042)
PACE ANALYTICAL SERVICES INC
9608 Loiret Blvd (66219-2406)
PHONE..................................913 599-5665
Dave Neal, *Manager*
Tariq Mehmood, *Info Tech Mgr*
EMP: 51
SALES (corp-wide): 65.2MM **Privately Held**
WEB: www.pacelabs.com
SIC: 8734 Hazardous waste testing
HQ: Pace Analytical Services, Llc
1800 Elm St Se
Minneapolis MN 55414

(G-6043)
PARSONS BRNCKRHOFF HLDINGS INC
16201 W 95th St (66219-1220)
PHONE..................................913 310-9943
EMP: 37
SALES (corp-wide): 307MM **Privately Held**
SIC: 8742 Transportation consultant
PA: Parsons Brinckerhoff Holdings Inc.
1 Penn Plz
New York NY 10119
212 465-5000

(G-6044)
PARTNERS KAN-VERTING LLC
17501 W 98th St Unit 1439 (66219-1704)
PHONE..................................913 894-2700
Bryan Barlow, *Partner*
Philip Houston, *Partner*
EMP: 8
SQ FT: 35,000
SALES (est): 1.2MM **Privately Held**
SIC: 2679 Paper products, converted

(G-6045)
PATTERSON DENTAL SUPPLY INC
Also Called: Patterson Dental 230
11280 Renner Blvd (66219-9605)
PHONE..................................913 492-6100
Tony Count, *Manager*
EMP: 30
SALES (corp-wide): 5.5B **Publicly Held**
WEB: www.pattersondentalsupply.com
SIC: 5047 Dental equipment & supplies
HQ: Patterson Dental Supply, Inc.
1031 Mendota Heights Rd
Saint Paul MN 55120
651 686-1600

(G-6046)
PEARSON KENT MCKINLEY RAAF ENG (PA)
Also Called: Pkmr Engineers
13300 W 98th St (66215-1373)
PHONE..................................913 492-2400
Will Kent, *Principal*
Scott McKinley, *Principal*
Jerot Pearson, *Principal*
Pete Christiansen, *Engineer*
Steve Tobin, *Senior Engr*
EMP: 40
SQ FT: 9,000
SALES (est): 4.6MM **Privately Held**
SIC: 8711 Consulting engineer; mechanical engineering; heating & ventilation engineering; professional engineer

(G-6047)
PEAVEY CORPORATION
Also Called: Lynn Peavey Company
11042 Strang Line Rd (66215-2113)
P.O. Box 14100, Shawnee Mission (66285-4100)
PHONE..................................913 888-0600
Buck Peavey, *Co-President*
Doug Peavey, *Co-President*
Skip Peavey, *COO*
Lue Straub, *Controller*
Greg Ebeling, *Regl Sales Mgr*
EMP: 65
SQ FT: 19,000
SALES (est): 12.5MM **Privately Held**
WEB: www.peaveycorp.com
SIC: 3999 2672 5047 5199 Fingerprint equipment; tape, pressure sensitive: made from purchased materials; medical equipment & supplies; advertising specialties; search & navigation equipment; chemical preparations

(G-6048)
PELLA PRODUCTS KANSAS CITY INC (PA)
11333 Strang Line Rd (66215-4042)
PHONE..................................913 492-7927
Chan Lundy, *President*
Randy Petersen, *Opers Mgr*
Devin Brady, *Sales Staff*
Ali Daifallah, *Sales Staff*
John Morgan, *Sales Staff*
EMP: 40
SQ FT: 36,000
SALES (est): 21MM **Privately Held**
SIC: 5031 Windows; doors; skylights, all materials

(G-6049)
PERFECT SMILES DENTAL CARE PA
8650 Candlelight Ln Ste 1 (66215-6008)
PHONE..................................913 631-2677
Kelly D Bridenstine, *President*
Tracy Boldry, *Principal*
Beverly Moon, *Principal*
EMP: 15
SALES (est): 1.5MM **Privately Held**
SIC: 8021 Dental clinic

(G-6050)
PERFORMANCE ABATEMENT SVCS INC (DH)
Also Called: P A S
11145 Thompson Ave (66219-2302)
P.O. Box 2198, Shawnee Mission (66201-1198)
PHONE..................................913 888-8600
Darrel Bailey, *President*
Daniel Hefferon, *Treasurer*
Ron Eisenhauer, *Admin Sec*
Suzanne McNair, *Asst Sec*
EMP: 100
SQ FT: 9,000
SALES (est): 81.1MM
SALES (corp-wide): 1.1B **Privately Held**
SIC: 1799 Asbestos removal & encapsulation
HQ: Performance Contracting, Inc.
11145 Thompson Ave
Lenexa KS 66219
913 888-8600

(G-6051)
PERFORMANCE CONTRACTING INC (HQ)
Also Called: Issd
11145 Thompson Ave (66219-2302)
PHONE..................................913 888-8600
William P Massey, *President*
Clark Reynolds, *Superintendent*
Darrel Bailey, *Senior VP*
Charles F Williams, *Senior VP*
Stephen Barnes, *Vice Pres*
▲ EMP: 2900
SQ FT: 12,000
SALES (est): 1B
SALES (corp-wide): 1.1B **Privately Held**
SIC: 1742 8711 Insulation, buildings; building construction consultant
PA: Performance Contracting Group, Inc.
11145 Thompson Ave
Lenexa KS 66219
800 255-6886

(G-6052)
PERFORMANCE CONTRACTING INC
Engineered Systems Group
16407 110th (66219)
PHONE..................................913 928-2832
Jeff O'Neal, *General Mgr*
Chris Alonzo, *Superintendent*
Mike Metcalf, *Counsel*
Jon McCleary, *Vice Pres*
Robert Henderson, *Project Mgr*
EMP: 26
SALES (corp-wide): 1.1B **Privately Held**
SIC: 8711 3449 Machine tool design; miscellaneous metalwork
HQ: Performance Contracting, Inc.
11145 Thompson Ave
Lenexa KS 66219
913 888-8600

(G-6053)
PERFORMANCE CONTRACTING INC
Also Called: PCI Knsas Cy Pntg Coating Svcs
16047 W 110th St (66219-1327)
PHONE..................................913 928-2850
EMP: 26
SALES (corp-wide): 1.1B **Privately Held**
SIC: 1721 Industrial painting
HQ: Performance Contracting, Inc.
11145 Thompson Ave
Lenexa KS 66219
913 888-8600

(G-6054)
PERFORMANCE CONTRACTING INC
PCI Metal Fabrication
16047 W 110th St (66219-1327)
PHONE..................................913 928-2800
EMP: 20
SALES (corp-wide): 1.1B **Privately Held**
SIC: 3449 Miscellaneous metalwork
HQ: Performance Contracting, Inc.
11145 Thompson Ave
Lenexa KS 66219
913 888-8600

(G-6055)
PETE & MACS RECREATIONAL RESO
8809 Monrovia St (66215-3540)
PHONE..................................913 888-8889
C Wesley Remington,
Stephanie Remington,
EMP: 27
SALES (est): 1.1MM **Privately Held**
SIC: 0752 Grooming services, pet & animal specialties

(G-6056)
PHYTOTECH LABS INC
14610 W 106th St (66215-2045)
PHONE..................................913 341-5343
Ben Travis, *CEO*
James Schmalz, *General Mgr*
EMP: 19
SQ FT: 30,000
SALES (est): 811.4K **Privately Held**
SIC: 2836 3821 2869 Culture media; chemical laboratory apparatus; laboratory chemicals, organic

(G-6057)
PHYTOTECHNOLOGY LABS LLC
14610 W 106th St (66215-2045)
P.O. Box 12205, Shawnee Mission (66282-2205)
PHONE..................................913 341-5343
Kenneth C Torres, *President*
Janet S Torres, *Vice Pres*
Dustin Banbury, *Manager*
▲ EMP: 16
SQ FT: 14,500
SALES (est): 5MM **Privately Held**
WEB: www.phytotechlab.com
SIC: 2836 Culture media

(G-6058)
PIPING ALLOYS INC (PA)
13899 W 101st St (66215-1211)
PHONE..................................913 677-3833
William G Wilt, *President*
Ron Josey, *Manager*
Vicki Wilt, *Admin Sec*
▲ EMP: 42 EST: 1979
SQ FT: 25,000
SALES (est): 19.9MM **Privately Held**
WEB: www.pipingalloys.com
SIC: 5051 Pipe & tubing, steel

(G-6059)
PISHNY REAL ESTATE SERVICES
Also Called: Pishny Restoration Services
12202 W 88th St (66215-4607)
PHONE..................................913 227-0251
Julie Pishny, *Sales Executive*
Dean Pishny,
EMP: 15
SALES (est): 1.7MM **Privately Held**
SIC: 1799 1721 Athletic & recreation facilities construction; painting & paper hanging

(G-6060)
PIVOT INTERNATIONAL INC (PA)
11030 Strang Line Rd (66215-2113)
P.O. Box 15269 (66285-5269)
PHONE..................................913 312-6900
Mark Dohnalek, *President*
J Kirkland Douglass, *President*
Edwin Ching, *Corp Secy*
Elton Ching, *Vice Pres*
Kirk Douglass, *Vice Pres*
▲ EMP: 20
SQ FT: 80,000
SALES (est): 59.1MM **Privately Held**
WEB: www.pivotint.com
SIC: 3625 3679 8732 Timing devices, electronic; electronic circuits; market analysis or research

(G-6061)
PKC CONSTRUCTION CO
7802 Barton St (66214-3403)
PHONE..................................913 782-4646

▲ = Import ▼=Export
◆ =Import/Export

Perry Kessler, *CEO*
Eric Turner, *President*
Joe Shanafelt, *CFO*
Jason Goertzen, *Treasurer*
Miles Brown, *Manager*
EMP: 25
SQ FT: 8,000
SALES (est): 10.8MM **Privately Held**
WEB: www.pkcc.com
SIC: 1542 Commercial & office building, new construction

(G-6062)
POLYNOVA (USA) LLC
9810 Pflumm Rd (66215-1208)
PHONE..................................913 309-6977
Owez Nanjee, *President*
EMP: 5
SALES (est): 172.1K **Privately Held**
SIC: 5112 2671 Stationery & office supplies; packaging paper & plastics film, coated & laminated

(G-6063)
POWER SALES AND ADVERTISING (PA)
9909 Lakeview Ave (66219-2503)
PHONE..................................913 324-4900
David Roberts, *President*
Trent Bernard, *Vice Pres*
Toni Evans, *Credit Mgr*
▲ **EMP:** 55
SQ FT: 18,000
SALES (est): 41.2MM **Privately Held**
WEB: www.psarewards.com
SIC: 5199 Advertising specialties

(G-6064)
PQ CORPORATION
Also Called: CC Account
15200 Santa Fe Dr (66219)
PHONE..................................913 744-2056
EMP: 15
SALES (est): 1.5MM **Privately Held**
SIC: 8721 Accounting/Auditing/Bookkeeping

(G-6065)
PQ CORPORATION
15200 Santa Fe Trail Dr # 101 (66219-9609)
PHONE..................................913 227-0561
Scott Bollinger, *Director*
EMP: 14
SALES (corp-wide): 1.6B **Publicly Held**
SIC: 3231 2819 Products of purchased glass; sodium silicate, water glass
HQ: Pq Corporation
300 Lindenwood Dr
Malvern PA 19355
610 651-4200

(G-6066)
PRA INTERNATIONAL
9755 Ridge Dr (66219-9746)
PHONE..................................913 410-2000
Pat Donnelly, *Principal*
David Dockhorn, *Vice Pres*
Tami Klerr-Naivar, *Vice Pres*
Colleen Mullenix, *Project Mgr*
Diana Soto, *Project Mgr*
EMP: 73
SALES (est): 12MM **Privately Held**
WEB: www.praint.com
SIC: 8731 Commercial physical research

(G-6067)
PRA INTERNATIONAL LLC
10836 Strang Line Rd (66215-2206)
PHONE..................................913 345-5754
Jason Neat, *Manager*
EMP: 12
SALES (corp-wide): 2.8B **Publicly Held**
SIC: 8731 Biotechnical research, commercial
HQ: Pra International, Llc
4130 Parklake Ave Ste 400
Raleigh NC 27612
919 786-8200

(G-6068)
PRAIRIE POINT
12116 W 95th St (66215-3805)
PHONE..................................913 322-1222
Carol Kirchhoff, *Owner*
Vonda Sinha, *Owner*
EMP: 25
SALES (est): 1.5MM **Privately Held**
WEB: www.prairiepoint.com
SIC: 2395 5949 Quilting & quilting supplies; fabric stores piece goods

(G-6069)
PRAXAIR DISTRIBUTION INC
9725 Alden St (66215-1128)
PHONE..................................913 492-1551
Nicholas Morrison, *Branch Mgr*
EMP: 44 **Privately Held**
SIC: 2813 5084 Industrial gases; industrial machinery & equipment
HQ: Praxair Distribution, Inc.
10 Riverview Dr
Danbury CT 06810
203 837-2000

(G-6070)
PRINTING SERVICES INC
13309 W 98th St (66215-1374)
PHONE..................................913 492-1500
Eric Amundson, *CEO*
EMP: 5
SALES (est): 103K **Privately Held**
SIC: 7313 2732 2759 2752 Printed media advertising representatives; books: printing & binding; stationery: printing; commercial printing, lithographic

(G-6071)
PRIORITY ENVELOPE INC
17501 W 98th St Spc 1742 (66219-1736)
PHONE..................................913 859-9710
Dan Trowbridge, *Plant Supt*
Jay Battenberg, *Opers Staff*
Bob Drass, *Manager*
EMP: 31 **Privately Held**
WEB: www.priorityenv.com
SIC: 2759 Commercial printing
PA: Priority Envelope, Inc.
2920 Northwest Blvd # 160
Plymouth MN 55441

(G-6072)
PROFESSIONAL HAIRSTYLING
12243 W 87th Pkwy (66215)
PHONE..................................913 888-3536
Bob Salmons, *Partner*
Randy Cunningham, *Partner*
EMP: 11
SALES (est): 157.6K **Privately Held**
SIC: 7241 7231 Barber shops; manicurist, pedicurist

(G-6073)
PROFESSNAL TURF PDTS LTD PRTNR
10935 Eicher Dr (66219-2601)
PHONE..................................913 599-1449
Brad Davison, *Accounts Exec*
Dianna Hildreth, *Office Mgr*
EMP: 20 **Privately Held**
SIC: 5083 Irrigation equipment
PA: Professional Turf Products, Limited Partnership
1010 N Industrial Blvd
Euless TX 76039

(G-6074)
PROGENE BIOMEDICAL INC
Also Called: I B T Reference Laboratory
11274 Renner Blvd (66219-9605)
PHONE..................................913 492-2224
John F Halsey PHD, *President*
Sandra Halsey, *Exec VP*
EMP: 15
SQ FT: 26,552
SALES (est): 1MM **Privately Held**
WEB: www.ibtreflab.com
SIC: 8071 2835 Testing laboratories; in vitro & in vivo diagnostic substances

(G-6075)
PROGREEN WINDOW CLEANING INC
8215 Melrose Dr Ste 100 (66214-1617)
PHONE..................................913 387-3210
EMP: 10
SALES (est): 254K **Privately Held**
SIC: 7349 Janitorial service, contract basis; window cleaning

(G-6076)
PROMOTIONAL HEADWEAR INTL INC
Also Called: Sportsman Cap
17740 College Blvd (66219-1341)
PHONE..................................913 541-0901
Dan Saferstein, *President*
Caroline Saferstein, *Vice Pres*
Harvey Saferstein, *Vice Pres*
Diane Wilcox, *Controller*
▲ **EMP:** 13
SALES (est): 7.5MM **Privately Held**
WEB: www.promotionalheadwear.com
SIC: 5136 Caps, men's & boys'

(G-6077)
PROSSER WILBERT CNSTR INC
13730 W 108th St (66215-2026)
PHONE..................................913 906-0104
Andy Prosser, *President*
Harold Cooper, *Superintendent*
Lance Flory, *Superintendent*
Rick Ryan, *Superintendent*
Dennis Wilbert, *Exec VP*
EMP: 14
SQ FT: 14,000
SALES (est): 6.2MM **Privately Held**
WEB: www.prosserwilbert.com
SIC: 1542 Commercial & office buildings, renovation & repair

(G-6078)
PUBLISHERS DELIVERY SOLUT
10973 Eicher Dr (66219-2601)
PHONE..................................913 894-1299
Jason Green, *President*
EMP: 10
SALES (est): 684.7K **Privately Held**
SIC: 7389 Courier or messenger service

(G-6079)
PULSE DESIGN GROUP INC
8207 Melrose Dr Ste 145 (66214-1624)
PHONE..................................913 438-9095
Richard Embers, *President*
Mary Moore, *Mktg Dir*
EMP: 28
SALES (est): 2.9MM **Privately Held**
SIC: 7389 Design services

(G-6080)
PULSE NEEDLEFREE SYSTEMS INC
8210 Marshall Dr (66214-1537)
PHONE..................................913 599-1590
Edward S Stevens, *President*
Michael H Dutcher, *Vice Pres*
EMP: 15 **EST:** 2000
SQ FT: 7,500
SALES (est): 4.8MM **Privately Held**
WEB: www.feltonint.com
SIC: 5047 Medical equipment & supplies

(G-6081)
PURAC AMERICA INC (HQ)
Also Called: Corbion-Purac
8250 Flint St (66214-1500)
PHONE..................................913 890-5500
Eddy Van Rhede, *President*
Gerrit Vreeman, *President*
Peter Kooijman, *Vice Pres*
Curtis Landherr, *Admin Sec*
◆ **EMP:** 45
SALES (est): 195.3MM
SALES (corp-wide): 994.7MM **Privately Held**
WEB: www.puracamerica.com
SIC: 2869 Industrial organic chemicals
PA: Corbion N.V.
Piet Heinkade 127
Amsterdam
205 906-911

(G-6082)
QC HOLDINGS INC (PA)
8208 Melrose Dr (66214-1626)
PHONE..................................866 660-2243
Don Early, *Ch of Bd*
Mary Lou Early, *Vice Ch Bd*
Darrin J Andersen, *President*
Darrin Andersen, *COO*
Matthew J Wiltanger, *Vice Pres*
EMP: 114
SQ FT: 39,000
SALES (est): 194.2MM **Publicly Held**
SIC: 7389 6141 Financial services; personal finance licensed loan companies, small

(G-6083)
QUAD/GRAPHICS INC
14900 W 99th St (66215-1113)
PHONE..................................816 936-8536
Jennifer Wojcik, *Manager*
EMP: 406
SALES (corp-wide): 4.1B **Publicly Held**
SIC: 2752 Commercial printing, offset
PA: Quad/Graphics Inc.
N61w23044 Harrys Way
Sussex WI 53089
414 566-6000

(G-6084)
QUALITY PRINTING AND OFF SUPS
Also Called: Quality Printing and Off Sups
13610 W 107th St (66215-2060)
P.O. Box 3167, Olathe (66063-1167)
PHONE..................................913 491-6366
Teresa J Chien, *President*
Beverly Graham, *Treasurer*
▲ **EMP:** 10
SQ FT: 1,300
SALES (est): 880K **Privately Held**
SIC: 2752 5943 Photo-offset printing; office forms & supplies

(G-6085)
QUALITY STEEL & WIRE PDTS CO
9802 Widmer Rd (66215-1240)
PHONE..................................913 888-2929
Martin Isnert, *Principal*
EMP: 8
SQ FT: 9,000
SALES (est): 1.4MM **Privately Held**
SIC: 3496 5063 Miscellaneous fabricated wire products; wire & cable
PA: Wright & Associates Inc
9802 Widmer Rd
Lenexa KS

(G-6086)
QUIVIRA ATHLETIC CLUB L C
Also Called: Quivira Sports Clubs
7880 Quivira Rd (66216-3322)
PHONE..................................913 268-3633
Hal Edwards, *Principal*
Six One Two Plaza Corporation,
Lora Edwards,
EMP: 65
SQ FT: 30,000
SALES (est): 941K **Privately Held**
SIC: 7991 8049 Health club; dietician

(G-6087)
R P M SMITH CORPORATION
Also Called: Smith Pressroom Products
15019 W 95th St (66215-5229)
P.O. Box 12205, Overland Park (66282-2205)
PHONE..................................913 888-0695
Janette Schumm, *CEO*
Dennis Schupp, *President*
Dennis Fritz, *President*
▲ **EMP:** 15 **EST:** 1964
SQ FT: 29,349
SALES (est): 2.6MM **Privately Held**
WEB: www.smithrpm.com
SIC: 3555 3444 Printing trades machinery; sheet metalwork

(G-6088)
RA KNAPP CONSTRUCTION INC
12209 W 88th St (66215-4608)
PHONE..................................913 287-8700
Ronald A Knapp, *President*
Richard Knapp, *Vice Pres*
Ronald S Knapp, *Vice Pres*
Ronda Thompson, *Controller*
Maxine Knapp, *Admin Sec*
EMP: 35
SQ FT: 1,500
SALES: 6.2MM **Privately Held**
SIC: 1622 1623 Bridge, tunnel & elevated highway; water main construction; sewer line construction

(G-6089)
RAILCREW XPRESS LLC
9867 Widmer Rd (66215-1239)
PHONE..................................913 928-5000
Brian Ohara, *CEO*
Andrew Blott, *Chairman*
Sandy Walker, *Vice Pres*
Tara Johnson, *Human Res Dir*
Danielle Powers, *Human Resources*
EMP: 4500
SALES (est): 91.1MM **Privately Held**
SIC: 4131 Intercity & rural bus transportation

(G-6090)
RAUDIN MCCORMICK INC
15729 College Blvd (66219-1360)
PHONE..................................913 928-5000
Grady Riggs, *President*
EMP: 120
SALES (est): 10.6MM **Privately Held**
SIC: 4731 Transport clearinghouse

(G-6091)
RAY OMO INC
19204 W 98th Ter (66220-9749)
PHONE..................................620 227-3101
Terri Omo-Schmidt, *President*
Tim Wheaton, *Treasurer*
EMP: 20 **EST:** 1934
SALES (est): 2.4MM **Privately Held**
WEB: www.omoinc.kscoxmail.com
SIC: 1711 1761 Warm air heating & air conditioning contractor; plumbing contractors; sheet metalwork

(G-6092)
RC SPORTS INC (PA)
17501 W 98th St Spc 1851 (66219-1791)
PHONE..................................913 894-5177
Ronald J Creten, *Ch of Bd*
▲ **EMP:** 20
SQ FT: 20,000
SALES (est): 11.5MM **Privately Held**
WEB: www.rcsports.com
SIC: 5091 5941 Sporting & recreation goods; sporting goods & bicycle shops

(G-6093)
RD2RX LLC
16825 W 116th St (66219-9603)
PHONE..................................816 754-8047
Himanshu Sud, *CEO*
EMP: 10
SALES (est): 409.5K **Privately Held**
SIC: 2834 Druggists' preparations (pharmaceuticals)

(G-6094)
RDCS INC
14304 W 99th St (66215-1102)
PHONE..................................913 238-5377
Melanie D Green, *President*
EMP: 11
SALES (est): 1.2MM **Privately Held**
SIC: 1521 Single-family housing construction

(G-6095)
REDEMPTION PLUS LLC
9829 Commerce Pkwy (66219-2401)
PHONE..................................913 563-4331
Ron L Hill, *CEO*
Anthony Boyer, *Accounts Exec*
Brandt Hill, *Mng Member*
Ron Matsch, *Mng Member*
Matt Czugala, *Info Tech Mgr*
▲ **EMP:** 70
SQ FT: 75,000
SALES (est): 36MM **Privately Held**
WEB: www.redemption-plus.com
SIC: 5199 General merchandise, non-durable

(G-6096)
REGAL DISTRIBUTING CO (PA)
17201 W 113th St (66219-1337)
PHONE..................................913 894-8787
Gregory Kopulos, *CEO*
Dean Kopulos, *President*
Alex Kopulos, *Vice Pres*
Stu Lovejoy, *Vice Pres*
Maricela Toral, *Purchasing*
EMP: 35
SQ FT: 125,000
SALES: 69MM **Privately Held**
WEB: www.getregal.com
SIC: 5199 General merchandise, non-durable

(G-6097)
REGAN MARKETING INC (PA)
10934 Strang Line Rd (66215-2322)
PHONE..................................816 531-5111
Gary Regan, *President*
EMP: 12
SQ FT: 5,000
SALES (est): 3.4MM **Privately Held**
WEB: www.reganmarketing.com
SIC: 5141 8742 Food brokers; management consulting services

(G-6098)
REGENTS FLOORING CO INC
10035 Lakeview Ave (66219-2501)
PHONE..................................913 663-9922
Courtney Williams, *President*
Jeff Farrell, *Vice Pres*
Rich Greenstreet, *Vice Pres*
Stephen Williams, *Vice Pres*
Karen Vogt, *Sales Mgr*
EMP: 11
SQ FT: 2,000
SALES (est): 2.2MM **Privately Held**
SIC: 1752 Floor laying & floor work

(G-6099)
REIT MANAGEMENT & RESEARCH
15737 College Blvd (66219-1360)
PHONE..................................913 492-4375
Gyla Martin, *Principal*
EMP: 13
SALES (est): 1.6MM **Privately Held**
SIC: 8741 Business management

(G-6100)
RELLEC APPAREL GRAPHICS LLC
10618 Summit St (66215-2050)
PHONE..................................913 707-5249
Jerod Eller, *Mng Member*
Jennifer Eller, *Manager*
EMP: 5
SQ FT: 4,000
SALES (est): 57.7K **Privately Held**
SIC: 7389 3231 Apparel designers, commercial; products of purchased glass

(G-6101)
REMEL
17501 W 98th St Spc 3060 (66219-1737)
PHONE..................................913 895-4362
Joan Maxwell, *Mktg Coord*
EMP: 8
SALES (est): 1.1MM **Privately Held**
SIC: 2835 In vitro & in vivo diagnostic substances

(G-6102)
REMEL INC (DH)
Also Called: Thermo Fsher Scntfic Rmel Pdts
12076 Santa Fe Trail Dr (66215-3594)
PHONE..................................800 255-6730
Susanne Garay, *President*
John Schueler, *Vice Pres*
Peter Shearstone, *Vice Pres*
Sylvia McDonnell, *Site Mgr*
Tom Davis, *Mfg Spvr*
◆ **EMP:** 505 **EST:** 1997
SQ FT: 116,200
SALES (est): 326.4MM
SALES (corp-wide): 24.3B **Publicly Held**
WEB: www.remel.com
SIC: 2836 Culture media
HQ: Fisher Scientific International Llc
81 Wyman St
Waltham MA 02451
781 622-1000

(G-6103)
RENSEN HOUSE OF LIGHTS INC
9212 Marshall Dr (66215-3844)
PHONE..................................913 888-0888
Tom Rensenhouse, *President*
Gary Burgard, *Principal*
Marla Cooper, *Principal*
James Brink, *Vice Pres*
Ron A Thomas, *Vice Pres*
EMP: 30
SQ FT: 24,000
SALES (est): 5.4MM **Privately Held**
WEB: www.rensenhouseoflights.com
SIC: 5722 5719 5063 5064 Fans, electric; lighting fixtures; lighting fixtures; fans, household: electric

(G-6104)
RENZENBERGER INC (HQ)
14325 W 95th St (66215-5210)
P.O. Box 14610 (66285-4610)
PHONE..................................913 631-0450
William M Smith, *President*
Phil Simco, *Vice Pres*
O N Auer, *Admin Sec*
EMP: 150
SQ FT: 4,800
SALES (est): 111MM
SALES (corp-wide): 585.4MM **Privately Held**
WEB: www.renzenberger.com
SIC: 4131 4119 Intercity & rural bus transportation; local passenger transportation
PA: Peterson Manufacturing Company
4200 E 135th St
Grandview MO 64030
816 765-2000

(G-6105)
REPAIR SHACK INC
14021 W 95th St (66215-5206)
PHONE..................................913 732-0514
Brandon Cady, *President*
EMP: 35
SALES (est): 967.7K **Privately Held**
SIC: 7378 7622 7629 Computer maintenance & repair; television repair shop; electrical household appliance repair; circuit board repair

(G-6106)
RESEARCH CONCEPTS INC
Also Called: Rci
9501 Dice Ln (66215-1158)
PHONE..................................913 422-0210
Steven Mikinski, *President*
James Ronnau, *Vice Pres*
Marty Bolt, *Manager*
Kahlen Jones, *IT/INT Sup*
EMP: 10
SQ FT: 2,000
SALES (est): 2.4MM **Privately Held**
WEB: www.researchconcepts.com
SIC: 8711 3674 Electrical or electronic engineering; designing: ship, boat, machine & product; microprocessors

(G-6107)
RESOURCE SERVICE SOLUTIONS LLC
16309 W 108th Cir (66219-1372)
P.O. Box 4767, Olathe (66063-4767)
PHONE..................................913 338-5050
Kristine Ward,
Catherine Richardson,
EMP: 23
SQ FT: 12,128
SALES (est): 2MM **Privately Held**
WEB: www.resourceservicesolutions.com
SIC: 8741 1799 1711 7349 Management services; construction site cleanup; warm air heating & air conditioning contractor; building & office cleaning services; building cleaning service; carpet & upholstery cleaning

(G-6108)
RHYTHM ENGINEERING LLC
11228 Thompson Ave (66219-2303)
PHONE..................................913 227-0603
Jim Clark, *Engineer*
Sukumar Anekar, *Project Engr*
Amir Khezerzadeh, *Project Engr*
Steve Tubbert, *VP Finance*
Morgan Kyle, *Accountant*
EMP: 45
SQ FT: 2,900
SALES (est): 4.2MM **Privately Held**
WEB: www.proengg.com
SIC: 8748 7371 7373 Systems analysis & engineering consulting services; custom computer programming services; computer integrated systems design

(G-6109)
RICHARD NACHBAR PLUMBING INC
9053 Cottonwood Canyon Pl (66219-8174)
PHONE..................................913 268-9488
Richard Nachbar, *Owner*
EMP: 14
SALES (est): 2.1MM **Privately Held**
SIC: 1711 Plumbing contractors

(G-6110)
ROBBIE TRANSCONTINENTAL INC
Also Called: Robbie Flexibles
10810 Mid America Dr (66219-1245)
PHONE..................................913 492-3400
Doug Larson, *President*
Pepper Stokes, *President*
Irv Robinson, *Principal*
Angel Fox, *Production*
Michele Norris, *Production*
▲ **EMP:** 180 **EST:** 1970
SQ FT: 112,000
SALES (est): 70.8MM
SALES (corp-wide): 2.2B **Privately Held**
SIC: 5199 Packaging materials
PA: Transcontinental Inc
1 Place Ville-Marie Bureau 3240
Montreal QC H3B 0
514 954-4000

(G-6111)
ROCKWELL AUTOMATION INC
8047 Bond St (66214-1593)
PHONE..................................913 577-2500
Rob Schlimme, *Principal*
Brian Koscielski, *Manager*
Rick Moffet, *Manager*
EMP: 18 **Publicly Held**
SIC: 3625 Relays & industrial controls
PA: Rockwell Automation, Inc.
1201 S 2nd St
Milwaukee WI 53204

(G-6112)
RODROCK HOMES LLC
9550 Dice Ln (66215-1157)
PHONE..................................913 851-0347
Karen Long, *Project Mgr*
Bryan Rodrock, *Mng Member*
EMP: 15
SALES (est): 3MM **Privately Held**
SIC: 1521 New construction, single-family houses

(G-6113)
RONANS ROOFING INC
14122 W 107th St (66215-4034)
PHONE..................................913 384-0901
Michael T Ronan, *President*
Thomas Ronan, *Admin Sec*
EMP: 44
SQ FT: 10,000
SALES (est): 2.8MM **Privately Held**
SIC: 1761 Roofing contractor

(G-6114)
RYDER TRUCK RENTAL INC
10003 Lackman Rd (66219-1213)
PHONE..................................913 492-4420
Wayne Umschied, *Manager*
EMP: 30
SALES (corp-wide): 8.4B **Publicly Held**
SIC: 7513 7359 Truck rental, without drivers; truck leasing, without drivers; stores & yards equipment rental
HQ: Ryder Truck Rental, Inc.
11690 Nw 105th St
Medley FL 33178
305 500-3726

(G-6115)
RYKO SOLUTIONS INC
14058 W 107th St (66215-2066)
PHONE..................................913 451-3719
EMP: 10
SALES (corp-wide): 2.3B **Privately Held**
SIC: 5087 5084 Whol Service Establishment Equipment Whol Industrial Equipment
HQ: Ryko Solutions, Inc.
1500 Se 37th St
Grimes IA 50111
515 986-3700

(G-6116)
SAFC BIOSCIENCES INC (DH)
Also Called: Safc Biosciences Lenexa
13804 W 107th St (66215-2008)
PHONE....................................913 469-5580
Rod Kelley, *President*
Mark Radke, *Business Mgr*
Misa Gray, *Research*
Ryan Barnhart, *Sales Staff*
Eric Kern, *Sales Staff*
◆ **EMP:** 50
SQ FT: 80,000
SALES (est): 161MM
SALES (corp-wide): 16.4B **Privately Held**
WEB: www.jrhbio.com
SIC: 2836 Culture media
HQ: Sigma-Aldrich Corporation
3050 Spruce St
Saint Louis MO 63103
314 771-5765

(G-6117)
SANDS LEVEL AND TOOL COMPANY
Also Called: Unell Manufacturing Co
8325 Hedge Lane Ter (66227-3544)
PHONE....................................989 428-4141
EMP: 13
SALES (corp-wide): 5.6MM **Privately Held**
SIC: 3221 Mfg Glass Containers
PA: Sands Level And Tool Company Inc
1250 Tank Ave
Neodesha KS 66757
620 325-2687

(G-6118)
SAVAGE HOLDINGS INC
11364 Strang Line Rd (66215-4041)
PHONE....................................913 583-1007
Kasey Norris, *President*
Anne Kohlmeyer, *Office Mgr*
EMP: 10
SALES (est): 198.3K **Privately Held**
SIC: 4813 Telephone communication, except radio

(G-6119)
SCOTT HELLER TRUCKING
17210 W 84th St (66219-8124)
PHONE....................................816 591-1638
Scott Heller, *Owner*
EMP: 25
SALES (est): 1.1MM **Privately Held**
SIC: 4212 1771 1795 Local trucking, without storage; curb construction; sidewalk contractor; driveway contractor; demolition, buildings & other structures

(G-6120)
SCP DISTRIBUTORS LLC
Also Called: South Central Pool 20
14792 W 99th St (66215-1109)
PHONE....................................913 660-0061
Gerald Younger, *Branch Mgr*
EMP: 12 **Publicly Held**
WEB: www.atyourservicepools.com
SIC: 5091 5999 Swimming pools, equipment & supplies; swimming pool chemicals, equipment & supplies
HQ: Scp Distributors Llc
109 Northpark Blvd
Covington LA 70433
985 892-5521

(G-6121)
SCP SPECIALTY INFUSION LLC
9801 Renner Blvd Ste 275 (66219-8146)
PHONE....................................913 747-3700
Edward Kramm, *CEO*
EMP: 389
SALES (est): 21.4MM **Privately Held**
SIC: 5122 Drugs, proprietaries & sundries
PA: Axelacare Holdings, Inc.
15529 College Blvd
Lenexa KS 66219

(G-6122)
SECUREAIRE LTD LIABILITY CO
14900 W 107th St (66215-4018)
PHONE....................................813 766-0400
EMP: 17
SALES (corp-wide): 2.6MM **Privately Held**
SIC: 8731 Commercial physical research
PA: Secureaire Limited Liability Company
1968 Byshore Blvd Ste 207
Dunedin FL 34698
813 300-6077

(G-6123)
SELECT BRANDS INC (PA)
10817 Renner Blvd (66219-9608)
PHONE....................................913 663-4500
William Endres, *President*
Deborah Endres, *Vice Pres*
Eric Endres, *Vice Pres*
▲ **EMP:** 25
SALES (est): 5.4MM **Privately Held**
SIC: 3634 Electric household cooking appliances

(G-6124)
SERVICE PAK INC
Also Called: Service Pak Group
17501 W 98th St Spc 1761 (66219-1710)
PHONE....................................913 438-3500
Mary Wilkerson, *President*
Lon Wilkerson Sr, *Vice Pres*
EMP: 61
SQ FT: 56,000
SALES (est): 10.3MM **Privately Held**
WEB: www.servicepakgroup.com
SIC: 7336 Graphic arts & related design

(G-6125)
SEVO SYSTEMS INC
14335 W 97th Ter (66215-1150)
PHONE....................................913 677-1112
Jon P Flamm, *President*
◆ **EMP:** 20
SALES (est): 7MM **Privately Held**
SIC: 5099 Fire extinguishers

(G-6126)
SHAFER KLINE & WARREN INC (PA)
11250 Corporate Ave (66219-1392)
PHONE....................................913 888-7800
Ronald D Petering, *President*
Larry Graham, *Corp Secy*
Gerald Johnson, *Exec VP*
Allan Cooksey, *Vice Pres*
David Hamilton, *Vice Pres*
EMP: 45
SQ FT: 18,000
SALES: 38MM **Privately Held**
WEB: www.skw-inc.com
SIC: 8713 8711 8712 Surveying services; electrical or electronic engineering; civil engineering; mechanical engineering; structural engineering; architectural services

(G-6127)
SHASTA BEVERAGES INC
Also Called: Shasta Midwest
9901 Widmer Rd (66215-1282)
PHONE....................................913 888-6777
Dan Penrod, *Plant Mgr*
Steve Muckenthaler, *VP Engrg*
Rick Reynolds, *Manager*
EMP: 60
SQ FT: 100,000
SALES (corp-wide): 1B **Publicly Held**
SIC: 2086 Soft drinks: packaged in cans, bottles, etc.
HQ: Shasta Beverages, Inc.
26901 Indl Blvd
Hayward CA 94545
954 581-0922

(G-6128)
SHASTA MIDWEST INC
9901 Widmer Rd (66215-1282)
PHONE....................................913 888-6777
Nick A Caporella, *President*
Rick Reynolds, *Plant Mgr*
EMP: 50
SALES (est): 7.2MM
SALES (corp-wide): 1B **Publicly Held**
SIC: 5149 2086 Beverage concentrates; bottled & canned soft drinks
HQ: Newbevco, Inc.
1 N University Dr
Plantation FL 33324

(G-6129)
SHAUGHNSY-KNP-HW-PPR CO ST
Also Called: Shaughnessy Paper
14449 W 100th St (66215-1156)
PHONE....................................913 541-0080
Steve Radcliff, *Manager*
Steve R Ratcliff, *Manager*
EMP: 25
SALES (corp-wide): 854.2MM **Privately Held**
SIC: 5113 Industrial & personal service paper
HQ: Shaughnessy-Kniep-Hawe-Paper Company
2355 Ball Dr
Saint Louis MO 63146

(G-6130)
SHAWNEE BISCUIT INC (PA)
13851 W 101st St (66215-1211)
PHONE....................................913 441-7306
Ralph P D'Anza, *President*
Patricia E D'Anza, *Corp Secy*
EMP: 30
SQ FT: 1,500
SALES (est): 2.4MM **Privately Held**
SIC: 5149 5145 Cookies; candy

(G-6131)
SHAWNEE HEATING AND COOLING
10666 Widmer Rd (66215-2073)
PHONE....................................913 492-0824
Kevin Ellis, *President*
Stacey Moore, *Admin Sec*
EMP: 10
SQ FT: 15,000
SALES (est): 895.8K **Privately Held**
SIC: 1711 Warm air heating & air conditioning contractor

(G-6132)
SHORE TIRE CO INC
9300 Marshall Dr (66215-3845)
PHONE....................................913 541-9300
Christopher Shore, *President*
Jamie Heddings, *Manager*
Keith Carr, *Admin Sec*
▲ **EMP:** 47
SQ FT: 68,000
SALES (est): 13.8MM **Privately Held**
WEB: www.shoretire.com
SIC: 5014 5531 Tires & tubes; automotive tires

(G-6133)
SHRI RAM CORP
Also Called: Knights Inn
8601 Candlelight Ln (66215-6032)
PHONE....................................248 477-3200
Danny Patel, *President*
Michael Patel, *Vice Pres*
EMP: 12
SQ FT: 24,782
SALES: 1MM **Privately Held**
SIC: 7011 Hotels & motels

(G-6134)
SID BDEKER SAFETY SHOE SVC INC
Also Called: Hy-Test Boots & Shoes
14501 W 101st Ter # 1104 (66215-1144)
PHONE....................................913 599-6463
Roger Brezibine, *Branch Mgr*
EMP: 6
SALES (corp-wide): 17.4MM **Privately Held**
SIC: 3021 Protective footwear, rubber or plastic
PA: Sid Boedeker Safety Shoe Service, Inc.
6822 Hazelwood Ave
Saint Louis MO 63134
314 522-8180

(G-6135)
SILVERCREST AT COLLEGE VIEW SR
13600 W 110th Ter Apt 214 (66215-4084)
PHONE....................................913 915-6041
EMP: 10
SALES (est): 323.4K **Privately Held**
SIC: 8361 Residential care

(G-6136)
SKUTOUCH SOLUTIONS LLC
8226 Nieman Rd (66214-1507)
PHONE....................................913 538-5165
Terry Obershaw,
Douglas Obershaw,
EMP: 10
SALES (est): 1.2MM **Privately Held**
SIC: 8742 Distribution channels consultant; transportation consultant; business planning & organizing services; management information systems consultant

(G-6137)
SKYLINE E3 INC
9511 Legler Rd (66219-1227)
PHONE....................................913 599-4787
Duane Williams, *President*
Adam Cox, *Technical Staff*
EMP: 10
SQ FT: 6,000
SALES (est): 1.7MM **Privately Held**
WEB: www.skylinedisplayskc.com
SIC: 7389 Trade show arrangement; advertising, promotional & trade show services

(G-6138)
SLEEPCAIR INC
Also Called: Sleepcair Pharmacy
14333 W 95th St (66215-5210)
PHONE....................................913 438-8200
John Blevins, *President*
Virginia Blevins, *Vice Pres*
EMP: 32
SQ FT: 23,000
SALES (est): 1.5MM **Privately Held**
SIC: 8082 Home health care services

(G-6139)
SMALL BUSINESS BANK (PA)
13423 W 92nd St (66215-3636)
PHONE....................................913 856-7199
Ralph Leno, *President*
EMP: 20
SALES: 3.1MM **Privately Held**
SIC: 6021 National commercial banks

(G-6140)
SORELLA GROUP INC
14844 W 107th St (66215-4002)
PHONE....................................913 390-9544
Sheila Ohrenberg, *President*
Cara Rhoades, *Manager*
EMP: 10
SQ FT: 3,400
SALES (est): 5.3MM **Privately Held**
WEB: www.sorellagroupinc.com
SIC: 5046 Store fixtures; lockers, not refrigerated; shelving, commercial & industrial; partitions

(G-6141)
SOUNDTUBE ENTERTAINMENT INC
13720 W 109th St (66215-4137)
PHONE....................................913 233-8520
EMP: 15
SALES (corp-wide): 4.2MM **Privately Held**
SIC: 3651 Speaker systems
PA: Soundtube Entertainment, Inc.
8005 W 110th St Ste 208
Overland Park KS 66210
435 647-9555

(G-6142)
SOUTHERN STAR CENTRAL GAS PIPE
8195 Cole Pkwy (66227-2714)
PHONE....................................913 422-6304
Bob Bath, *Branch Mgr*
EMP: 21
SALES (corp-wide): 216.1MM **Privately Held**
SIC: 4924 Natural gas distribution
HQ: Southern Star Central Gas Pipeline, Inc.
4700 Highway 56
Owensboro KY 42301
270 852-5000

(G-6143)
SPACES INC (PA)
14950 W 86th St (66215-6037)
PHONE.....913 894-8900
Chris McCormack, *President*
Shelby Buttron, *Project Mgr*
Shawn Ornce, *Project Mgr*
Garett Miller, *Manager*
Amy Huke, *Director*
EMP: 22
SQ FT: 7,400
SALES (est): 17.6MM **Privately Held**
WEB: www.spaces.com
SIC: 5712 5021 Office furniture; office furniture

(G-6144)
SPARHAWK LABORATORIES INC (PA)
12340 Santa Fe Trail Dr (66215-3587)
PHONE.....913 888-7500
Bert Hughes, *CEO*
Burt Hughes, *CEO*
John Bascom, *Vice Pres*
Kristal Pekarek, *Manager*
Janis Strella, *Executive*
EMP: 64
SQ FT: 155,000
SALES (est): 17.2MM **Privately Held**
WEB: www.sparhawklabs.com
SIC: 2834 Pharmaceutical preparations

(G-6145)
SPARTAN INSTALLATION REPR LLC
Also Called: Spartan Foundation Repair
9010 Rosehill Rd (66215-3516)
P.O. Box 26052, Overland Park (66225-6052)
PHONE.....816 237-0017
Andrew Vleisides, *Owner*
Jennifer Spencer, *Sales Staff*
EMP: 10
SQ FT: 8,000
SALES (est): 778.9K **Privately Held**
SIC: 1522 1542 Residential construction; commercial & office building, new construction

(G-6146)
SPECIAL PRODUCT COMPANY
8540 Hedge Lane Ter (66227-3200)
PHONE.....972 208-1460
Tracey Patch, *Accounting Mgr*
Jim Houchens, *Manager*
EMP: 50
SALES (corp-wide): 42.2MM **Privately Held**
WEB: www.spc.net
SIC: 3669 3661 Intercommunication systems, electric; telephone & telegraph apparatus
PA: Special Product Company
8540 Hedge Lane Ter
Shawnee KS 66227
913 491-8088

(G-6147)
SPECTRAGRAPHICS INC
14701 W 106th St (66215-2015)
PHONE.....913 888-6828
Ted Williams, *CEO*
Kevin Briggs, *Vice Pres*
Jim Freeman, *Opers Mgr*
Marqus Dawson, *Production*
Patti Lindstrom, *Sls & Mktg Exec*
EMP: 30
SQ FT: 18,000
SALES (est): 5.6MM **Privately Held**
WEB: www.spectralabel.com
SIC: 2759 2672 Flexographic printing; coated & laminated paper

(G-6148)
SPLINTEK INC
Also Called: Sleepright
15555 W 108th St (66219-1303)
PHONE.....816 531-1900
Thomas W Brown, *CEO*
▼ **EMP:** 25
SALES (est): 5.2MM **Privately Held**
WEB: www.splintek.com
SIC: 3843 3634 2392 Dental materials; vaporizers, electric: household; cushions & pillows

(G-6149)
SPORTSGEAR OUTDOOR PRODUCTS
14308 W 96th Ter (66215-4708)
PHONE.....913 888-0379
Kevin Qu, *President*
▲ **EMP:** 5
SALES (est): 563.2K **Privately Held**
SIC: 2899 Rifle bore cleaning compounds

(G-6150)
SPSI INC
7943 Flint St (66214-3333)
PHONE.....913 541-8304
Sandy Reopelle, *Branch Mgr*
EMP: 11
SALES (corp-wide): 16.6MM **Privately Held**
SIC: 5084 Textile & leather machinery
PA: Spsi Inc
9825 85th Ave N Ste 100
Maple Grove MN 55369
763 391-7390

(G-6151)
STADIUM CHAIR COMPANY LLC
9824 Pflumm Rd (66215-1208)
P.O. Box 4172, Midland TX (79704-4172)
PHONE.....432 682-4682
Carl Wilhite,
▲ **EMP:** 30
SALES: 5.5MM **Privately Held**
SIC: 2531 Chairs, portable folding

(G-6152)
STANDARD BEVERAGE CORPORATION
14415 W 106th St (66215-2009)
PHONE.....913 888-7200
Fred Nachbar, *Vice Pres*
Mikael Barnheart, *Opers Mgr*
Ross Schimmels, *Manager*
EMP: 35
SALES (corp-wide): 71.3MM **Privately Held**
WEB: www.beverage-news.com
SIC: 5182 Liquor
PA: Standard Beverage Corporation
2526 E 36th Cir N
Wichita KS 67219
316 838-7707

(G-6153)
STERICYCLE INC
Also Called: Shred-It Kansas City
10000 Lackman Rd (66219-1214)
PHONE.....913 307-9400
David Foster, *Branch Mgr*
EMP: 27
SALES (corp-wide): 3.4B **Publicly Held**
SIC: 7389 Document & office record destruction
PA: Stericycle, Inc.
2355 Waukegan Rd Ste 300
Bannockburn IL 60015
847 367-5910

(G-6154)
STEVEN G MITCHELL DDS
Also Called: Oak Park Dental Group
12148 W 95th St (66215-3805)
PHONE.....913 492-9660
Steven Mitchell, *Owner*
Hiep Huynh, *Associate*
EMP: 13
SALES (est): 835.3K **Privately Held**
SIC: 8021 Dentists' office

(G-6155)
STREAMLINE BENEFITS GROUP LLC
Also Called: Streamline Insurance Group
10053 Lakeview Ave (66219-2501)
PHONE.....913 744-2900
Marcheta Bowlin,
Austin Bell,
Stephanie Bowlin,
EMP: 15
SALES (est): 2.9MM **Privately Held**
SIC: 6321 Indemnity plans health insurance, except medical service

(G-6156)
SUN MARBLE LLC
9600 Dice Ln (66215-1152)
PHONE.....913 438-3366
William You, *Mng Member*
William Wu,
▲ **EMP:** 12
SQ FT: 200,000
SALES: 2.3MM **Privately Held**
WEB: www.sunmarble.com
SIC: 5032 Marble building stone; granite building stone

(G-6157)
SUNFLOWER ELEC SYSTEMS LLC
17501 W 98th St (66219-1704)
PHONE.....913 894-1442
Greg Towsley, *General Mgr*
Gregory Towsley, *Mng Member*
Angela Charlton,
Robert Cummings,
EMP: 5 **EST:** 2008
SQ FT: 3,000
SALES: 797.1K **Privately Held**
SIC: 3643 Electric connectors

(G-6158)
SUNFLOWER HILLS INC
Also Called: Sunflower Food Company
14612 W 106th St (66215-2045)
PHONE.....913 894-2233
Brian Chisam, *President*
EMP: 11
SALES: 3MM **Privately Held**
SIC: 2096 2064 Potato chips & similar snacks; candy & other confectionery products

(G-6159)
SUNFLOWER VEGETABLE OIL INC
9880 Widmer Rd (66215-1240)
PHONE.....913 541-8882
Karen Lo, *President*
Ty Trieu, *Vice Pres*
Kyle Crandall, *Project Mgr*
▲ **EMP:** 8
SQ FT: 8,000
SALES (est): 2.5MM **Privately Held**
SIC: 2079 Vegetable refined oils (except corn oil)

(G-6160)
SUNRISE SENIOR LIVING INC
Also Called: Sunrise of Lenexa
15055 W 87th Street Pkwy (66215-5372)
PHONE.....913 307-0665
Patti Cady, *Manager*
EMP: 83
SALES (corp-wide): 4.7B **Publicly Held**
WEB: www.sunrise.com
SIC: 8051 Skilled nursing care facilities
HQ: Sunrise Senior Living, Llc
7902 Westpark Dr
Mc Lean VA 22102

(G-6161)
SUPPLY TECHNOLOGIES LLC
14621 W 112th St (66215-4096)
PHONE.....913 982-4016
James Anderson, *Cust Mgr*
EMP: 21
SALES (corp-wide): 1.6B **Publicly Held**
SIC: 5085 Fasteners, industrial: nuts, bolts, screws, etc.
HQ: Supply Technologies Llc
6065 Parkland Blvd Ste 2
Cleveland OH 44124
440 947-2100

(G-6162)
SUREWEST COMMUNICATIONS
14859 W 95th St (66215-5220)
PHONE.....913 825-2882
Jeremy Sperling, *Principal*
EMP: 12
SALES (corp-wide): 1.4B **Publicly Held**
SIC: 4813 Telephone communication, except radio
HQ: Surewest Communications
211 Lincoln St
Roseville CA 95678
916 786-6141

(G-6163)
SUREWEST KANS CONNECTIONS LLC (HQ)
14859 W 95th St (66215-5220)
PHONE.....913 890-4483
Ken N Johnson,
EMP: 75
SALES (est): 43.2MM
SALES (corp-wide): 1.4B **Publicly Held**
WEB: www.everestkc.com
SIC: 4813 Local & long distance telephone communications
PA: Consolidated Communications Holdings, Inc.
121 S 17th St
Mattoon IL 61938
217 235-3311

(G-6164)
SYSTEMAIR MFG INC
Also Called: System Air
10048 Indl Blvd (66215)
PHONE.....913 752-6000
Wettergren Ola, *President*
Hunt Douglas, *CFO*
◆ **EMP:** 29
SALES (est): 9.8MM
SALES (corp-wide): 901.1MM **Privately Held**
SIC: 3444 Metal ventilating equipment
PA: Systemair Ab
Industrivagen 3
Skinnskatteberg 739 3
222 440-00

(G-6165)
SYSTEMS BUILDING SERVICES LLC
Also Called: System Building Services
15950 College Blvd (66219-1369)
PHONE.....913 385-1496
Thomas Gallup,
EMP: 20
SALES (est): 756.1K **Privately Held**
SIC: 7372 Prepackaged software

(G-6166)
TANGENT RAIL ENERGY INC
15700 College Blvd # 300 (66219-1344)
PHONE.....913 948-9478
William Donley, *President*
EMP: 100 **EST:** 1994
SQ FT: 3,000
SALES (est): 4.8MM
SALES (corp-wide): 1.6B **Privately Held**
SIC: 1629 Railroad & subway construction
HQ: Tangent Rail Corporation
603 Stanwix St Ste 1000
Pittsburgh PA 15222
412 325-0202

(G-6167)
TANN ELECTRIC INC
13216 W 99th St (66215-1357)
PHONE.....913 236-7337
John Tann, *President*
Matt Breese, *Accounts Mgr*
Jason Brozen, *Master*
EMP: 18
SQ FT: 2,000
SALES (est): 2.4MM **Privately Held**
SIC: 1731 Electrical work

(G-6168)
TDB COMMUNICATIONS INC
10901 W 84th Ter Ste 105 (66214-1649)
PHONE.....913 327-7400
Thomas A Duckenfield III, *CEO*
Donna Divine, *CFO*
EMP: 198
SQ FT: 3,500
SALES (est): 12.9MM **Privately Held**
WEB: www.tdbcommunications.com
SIC: 7363 7361 Help supply services; employment agencies

(G-6169)
TEAGUE ELECTRIC CNSTR INC (PA)
12425 W 92nd St (66215-3869)
PHONE.....913 529-4600
Pat Shelley, *President*
Paul Saunders, *Vice Pres*
Arlin Saville, *Vice Pres*
Chance Pouncil, *Foreman/Supr*

Will Grogan, *Security Dir*
▲ **EMP:** 140 **EST:** 1977
SQ FT: 18,000
SALES (est): 20.9MM **Privately Held**
SIC: 1731 General electrical contractor

(G-6170)
TEAGUE ELECTRIC COMPANY INC
12425 W 92nd St (66215-3869)
PHONE..................................913 529-4600
David Saunders, *President*
Ryan Bealmear, *Vice Pres*
Paul Saunders, *Vice Pres*
Arlin Saville, *Vice Pres*
Suzy Fales, *Safety Dir*
EMP: 100
SQ FT: 10,000
SALES (est): 15.5MM
SALES (corp-wide): 20.9MM **Privately Held**
SIC: 1731 General electrical contractor
PA: Teague Electric Construction, Inc.
12425 W 92nd St
Lenexa KS 66215
913 529-4600

(G-6171)
TECH INC (PA)
Also Called: Tech Supply
10601 Lackman Rd (66219-1225)
PHONE..................................913 492-6440
Jack C Clifford Jr, *President*
Robert J Bjorseth, *COO*
Adam Roberts, *Sales Staff*
Anita Haufler, *Manager*
Jerry Ledoux, *Manager*
▲ **EMP:** 25 **EST:** 1954
SQ FT: 18,000
SALES (est): 17.4MM **Privately Held**
WEB: www.techinc.biz
SIC: 5014 Tire & tube repair materials

(G-6172)
TECHNOLOGY GROUP SOLUTIONS LLC
Also Called: T G S
8551 Quivira Rd (66215-2803)
PHONE..................................913 451-9900
Lenora Payne, *President*
Tammi Young, *Materials Mgr*
Heath Schwartz, *VP Sales*
Toby Muninger, *Accounts Exec*
Frank Martin, *Sales Staff*
EMP: 63
SQ FT: 267,000
SALES: 82MM **Privately Held**
WEB: www.tgs-kc.com
SIC: 7379

(G-6173)
TECNET INTERNATIONAL INC
11535 W 83rd Ter (66214-1532)
PHONE..................................913 859-9515
Scott H Ahn, *CEO*
Steve Koch, *Natl Sales Mgr*
Jeff Gordanier, *Technical Staff*
▲ **EMP:** 14
SALES (est): 2.5MM **Privately Held**
SIC: 3679 5065 Electronic circuits; electronic parts & equipment

(G-6174)
TED SYSTEMS LLC
Also Called: Total Elctrnic Dsgned Slutions
9745 Widmer Rd (66215-1260)
PHONE..................................913 677-5771
Jon Gann, *Business Mgr*
Jesse Weber, *Engineer*
Jerry Thorsen, *Sales Staff*
Brent Klusman, *Info Tech Mgr*
Herb Farnsworth,
EMP: 20
SALES (est): 9.7MM **Privately Held**
WEB: www.tedsystems.com
SIC: 5063 Fire alarm systems

(G-6175)
TELEDATA COMMUNICATIONS LLC
10620 Widmer Rd (66215-2072)
PHONE..................................913 663-2010
Cindy Deane, *President*
Joe Verebely, *Vice Pres*
EMP: 30
SQ FT: 1,000
SALES (est): 3MM **Privately Held**
WEB: www.teledata.com
SIC: 4813 5065 7622 1623 Data telephone communications; telephone equipment; communication equipment repair; communication line & transmission tower construction; telephone equipment & systems

(G-6176)
TERMINIX INTL CO LTD PARTNR
10623 Rene St (66215-4052)
PHONE..................................913 696-0351
Mike Gohannea, *Manager*
EMP: 35
SALES (corp-wide): 1.9B **Publicly Held**
SIC: 7342 Pest control services
HQ: The Terminix International Company Limited Partnership
150 Peabody Pl
Memphis TN 38103
901 766-1400

(G-6177)
TERRACON CONSULTANTS INC
Also Called: Terracon Consultants 2
13910 W 96th Ter (66215-1228)
PHONE..................................913 492-7777
Cale Wilson, *Branch Mgr*
EMP: 120
SALES (corp-wide): 751.7MM **Privately Held**
SIC: 8711 Consulting engineer
HQ: Terracon Consultants, Inc.
10841 S Ridgeview Rd
Olathe KS 66061
913 599-6886

(G-6178)
THERMO FISHER SCIENTIFIC INC
Also Called: Thermo Fsher Scntfic Rmel Pdts
12076 Santa Fe Dr (66215)
P.O. Box 14428 (66285-4428)
PHONE..................................800 255-6730
Paul Craig, *Principal*
Jim Bilger, *Vice Pres*
Valerie Bressler-Hill, *Vice Pres*
Gary Galluzzi, *Vice Pres*
Larry McDowell, *Vice Pres*
EMP: 53
SALES (corp-wide): 24.3B **Publicly Held**
SIC: 3826 Analytical instruments
PA: Thermo Fisher Scientific Inc.
168 3rd Ave
Waltham MA 02451
781 622-1000

(G-6179)
THRIVER SERVICES LLC
11320 W 79th St (66214-1401)
PHONE..................................913 955-2555
Lance Focht, *President*
EMP: 15
SALES (est): 280.7K **Privately Held**
SIC: 8322 8059 Old age assistance; personal care home, with health care

(G-6180)
THRULINE MARKETING INC (PA)
Also Called: Keypath Education
15500 W 113th St Ste 200 (66219-5106)
PHONE..................................913 254-6000
Dave Admire, *CEO*
Steve Fireng, *CEO*
Vince Giambalvo, *President*
Michael Platt, *President*
Lori Turec, *President*
EMP: 108
SALES (est): 59.5MM **Privately Held**
WEB: www.plattformad.com
SIC: 8742 Marketing consulting services

(G-6181)
TIMKEN COMPANY
14871 W 99th St (66215-1110)
PHONE..................................913 492-4848
Nichole Jones, *Principal*
EMP: 12
SALES (corp-wide): 3.5B **Publicly Held**
SIC: 5085 Bearings
PA: The Timken Company
4500 Mount Pleasant St Nw
North Canton OH 44720
234 262-3000

(G-6182)
TITLE BOXING LLC
Also Called: Title Boxing Club
14711 W 112th St (66215-4098)
PHONE..................................913 438-4427
David Hanson,
Tony J Carbajo,
Tom Lyons,
Joe H Wally,
◆ **EMP:** 125
SQ FT: 56,000
SALES (est): 11.8MM **Privately Held**
WEB: www.titleboxing.com
SIC: 7997 3949 Membership sports & recreation clubs; boxing equipment & supplies, general

(G-6183)
TK METALS INC
8115 Monticello Ter (66227-2604)
PHONE..................................913 667-3055
Troy Krentzel, *President*
Jacob Scott, *Project Mgr*
Anthony Eve, *Supervisor*
EMP: 9
SALES (est): 1.6MM **Privately Held**
SIC: 3444 Sheet metal specialties, not stamped

(G-6184)
TOO CUTE TOTES
8339 Monticello Rd (66227-3120)
PHONE..................................775 423-5907
Karen Scott, *President*
EMP: 5
SALES (est): 634.2K **Privately Held**
SIC: 3171 Handbags, women's

(G-6185)
TOP NOTCH INC
23754 W 82nd Ter (66227-2709)
PHONE..................................913 441-8900
Bruce Millon, *President*
Joan Millon, *Vice Pres*
Mary Talbott, *Manager*
EMP: 15
SQ FT: 2,500
SALES (est): 2.5MM **Privately Held**
WEB: www.topnotchheatingandair.com
SIC: 1711 Warm air heating & air conditioning contractor

(G-6186)
TOTAL RENOVATION GROUP INC
10680 Widmer Rd (66215-2073)
PHONE..................................913 491-5000
Gregory M Strand, *President*
Pat Strand, *Vice Pres*
EMP: 10
SQ FT: 2,000
SALES (est): 1.2MM **Privately Held**
SIC: 1761 1721 1521 Roofing contractor; painting & paper hanging; general remodeling, single-family houses

(G-6187)
TOUCHNET INFO SYSTEMS INC
15520 College Blvd (66219-1353)
PHONE..................................913 599-6699
Daniel J Toughey, *President*
Scott Martin, *General Mgr*
Elizabeth Mendez-Gilmore, *Business Mgr*
Brian Prosser, *Business Mgr*
Chad Elstun, *Vice Pres*
EMP: 60
SQ FT: 15,000
SALES (est): 11.4MM
SALES (corp-wide): 3.3B **Publicly Held**
WEB: www.touchnet.com
SIC: 7372 Business oriented computer software
HQ: Heartland Payment Systems, Llc
10 Glenlake Pkwy Ste 324
Atlanta GA 30328
609 683-3831

(G-6188)
TRADEWIND ENERGY INC (DH)
16105 W 113th St Ste 105 (66219-2307)
PHONE..................................913 888-9463
Rob H Freeman, *CEO*
Frank Costanza, *Exec VP*
Geoff Coventry, *Senior VP*
Joe ARB, *Vice Pres*
Matt Gilhousen, *VP Opers*
EMP: 45
SALES (est): 11.4MM
SALES (corp-wide): 42.1MM **Privately Held**
SIC: 3829 Wind direction indicators; solarimeters
HQ: Enel Green Power North America, Inc.
100 Brickstone Sq Ste 300
Andover MA 01810
978 681-1900

(G-6189)
TRANE US INC
11211 Lakeview Ave (66219-1399)
PHONE..................................417 863-2110
Nathan Whitney, *Project Mgr*
Tre Fruge, *Branch Mgr*
Daniel Ketelle, *Manager*
Robert Colombe, *Consultant*
EMP: 150 **Privately Held**
SIC: 3585 Refrigeration & heating equipment
HQ: Trane U.S. Inc.
3600 Pammel Creek Rd
La Crosse WI 54601
608 787-2000

(G-6190)
TRANSITIONS GROUP INC
Also Called: Furniture Options
10900 Pflumm Rd (66215-4027)
PHONE..................................913 327-0700
Karen Osman, *Manager*
EMP: 10
SALES (corp-wide): 26.6MM **Privately Held**
WEB: www.transitionsgroup.net
SIC: 7359 5712 Furniture rental; furniture stores
PA: Transitions Group, Inc.
116 N Cleveland Ave
Wichita KS 67214
316 262-9100

(G-6191)
TRENDSTONE LLC
10821 Lakeview Ave (66219-1329)
PHONE..................................913 599-5492
Greg Kivett,
Ted Liebig,
EMP: 8
SALES: 1.8MM **Privately Held**
WEB: www.trendstone.net
SIC: 1411 Granite dimension stone

(G-6192)
TRU HOME SOLUTIONS LLC
9601 Legler Rd (66219-1292)
PHONE..................................913 219-7547
Andrew Duncan, *Vice Pres*
Ann Morgan, *Vice Pres*
Bob Wolfe, *Vice Pres*
Chris Diltz, *Loan Officer*
Nic Hasselwander, *Loan Officer*
EMP: 24
SQ FT: 7,500
SALES (est): 4.2MM **Privately Held**
WEB: www.truhomesolutions.com
SIC: 6162 Mortgage companies, urban

(G-6193)
TRUGREEN LIMITED PARTNERSHIP
Also Called: Tru Green-Chemlawn
8420 Cole Pkwy (66227-3129)
PHONE..................................785 267-4121
Tom Wilhoit, *Branch Mgr*
EMP: 20
SALES (corp-wide): 3.2B **Privately Held**
SIC: 0782 Lawn care services
HQ: Trugreen Limited Partnership
1790 Kirby Pkwy
Memphis TN 38138
866 417-7866

(G-6194)
TURF DESIGN INC (PA)
23770 W 81st Ter (66227-2701)
P.O. Box 860303, Shawnee (66286-0303)
PHONE..................................913 764-6531
Adam Breidenthal, *President*

Lindsey Richardson, *Project Mgr*
EMP: 55
SALES (est): 6.7MM **Privately Held**
SIC: 0781 Landscape services

(G-6195)
TWA LLC
Also Called: Nuvidia
10575 Widmer Rd (66215-2096)
PHONE..................................913 599-5200
Thomas P Doyle,
EMP: 20
SALES (est): 1MM **Privately Held**
SIC: 7819 Video tape or disk reproduction

(G-6196)
TYTAN INTERNATIONAL LLC (PA)
16240 W 110th St (66219-1312)
PHONE..................................913 492-3222
Michelle Conley, *Vice Pres*
Steve Murphy, *Sales Staff*
Kert D Prez, *Sales Staff*
Will Bumgarner, *Sales Associate*
Scott Clay, *Mng Member*
▲ **EMP:** 18
SQ FT: 23,000
SALES (est): 21MM **Privately Held**
WEB: www.tytaninternational.com
SIC: 5199 Packaging materials

(G-6197)
U PRIORITY INC
14111 W 95th St (66215-5207)
PHONE..................................913 712-8524
Terrence Dueringer, *President*
Jolene Dueringer, *Vice Pres*
EMP: 10
SQ FT: 5,000
SALES: 1.2MM **Privately Held**
SIC: 1711 Plumbing, heating, air-conditioning contractors

(G-6198)
U S CENTRAL CREDIT UNION (PA)
9701 Renner Blvd (66219-8126)
PHONE..................................913 227-6000
Francis Lee, *President*
Francois Henriquez, *Vice Pres*
EMP: 270
SQ FT: 30,000
SALES (est): 31.4MM **Privately Held**
WEB: www.uscentralonline.net
SIC: 6062 State credit unions, not federally chartered

(G-6199)
U S X-RAY LLC
11201 Strang Line Rd (66215-4040)
PHONE..................................913 652-0550
Robert Bechard, *Principal*
EMP: 16
SQ FT: 1,300
SALES (est): 627K **Privately Held**
SIC: 8099 Physical examination & testing services

(G-6200)
UNION HORSE DISTILLING CO LLC
11740 W 86th Ter (66214-1520)
PHONE..................................913 492-3275
Eric Garcia,
EMP: 19
SALES (est): 738.2K **Privately Held**
SIC: 2085 Distillers' dried grains & solubles & alcohol

(G-6201)
UNITED PARCEL SERVICE INC
Also Called: UPS
14650 Santa Fe Trail Dr (66215-2017)
PHONE..................................913 541-3700
Dow Dameron, *Branch Mgr*
Stephanie Babcock, *Manager*
EMP: 49
SALES (corp-wide): 71.8B **Publicly Held**
SIC: 7389 Mailbox rental & related service
HQ: United Parcel Service, Inc.
55 Glenlake Pkwy
Atlanta GA 30328
404 828-6000

(G-6202)
UNITED PARCEL SERVICE INC
Also Called: UPS
16200 W 110th St (66219-1312)
PHONE..................................913 894-0255
James France, *Manager*
Darrell Ables, *Manager*
EMP: 75
SALES (corp-wide): 71.8B **Publicly Held**
WEB: www.upsscs.com
SIC: 4215 Parcel delivery, vehicular
HQ: United Parcel Service, Inc.
55 Glenlake Pkwy
Atlanta GA 30328
404 828-6000

(G-6203)
UNITED ROTARY BRUSH CORP (PA)
15607 W 100th Ter (66219-1362)
PHONE..................................913 888-8450
Rodney Olson, *CEO*
Rod Savage, *President*
Richard Savage, *Chairman*
Harry Vegter, *Vice Pres*
Mike Lutz, *CFO*
▲ **EMP:** 75
SQ FT: 73,000
SALES (est): 47.1MM **Privately Held**
WEB: www.united-rotary.com
SIC: 3991 Brushes, household or industrial

(G-6204)
UNIVERSAL MONEY CENTERS INC (PA)
15301 W 87th Street Pkwy (66219-9851)
PHONE..................................913 831-2055
David Bonsal, *Ch of Bd*
Pamela Glenn, *Vice Pres*
Leslie Doolin, *Project Mgr*
Amy Reynolds, *Controller*
Erin Winkler, *VP Finance*
EMP: 35
SQ FT: 12,851
SALES (est): 8MM **Privately Held**
WEB: www.universalmoney.com
SIC: 6099 7374 Electronic funds transfer network, including switching; automated teller machine (ATM) network; computer processing services

(G-6205)
US FOODS INC
16805 College Blvd (66219-1309)
PHONE..................................913 894-6161
Brett Schreiber, *Accounts Exec*
Kevin Craig, *Branch Mgr*
EMP: 150 **Publicly Held**
WEB: www.usfoodservice.com
SIC: 5141 Food brokers
HQ: Us Foods, Inc.
9399 W Higgins Rd Ste 500
Rosemont IL 60018

(G-6206)
US HEALTHWORKS MEDICAL GROUP
15319 W 95th St (66219-1262)
PHONE..................................913 495-9905
EMP: 23 **Privately Held**
SIC: 8011 Occupational & industrial specialist, physician/surgeon
PA: U.S. Healthworks Medical Group
25124 Springfield Ct
Valencia CA 91355

(G-6207)
VALENT AEROSTRUCTURES LLC (DH)
11064 Strang Line Rd (66215-2113)
PHONE..................................816 423-5600
Ed Dickinson, *CEO*
Henry Newell, *CEO*
Lawrence E Dickinson, *President*
Mark Deuel, *CFO*
▲ **EMP:** 25 **EST:** 2010
SALES: 123MM **Privately Held**
SIC: 3728 Aircraft parts & equipment
HQ: Lmi Aerospace, Inc.
411 Fountain Lakes Blvd
Saint Charles MO 63301
636 946-6525

(G-6208)
VANBERG SPECIALIZED COATINGS
10705 Cottonwood St (66215-2032)
PHONE..................................913 948-9825
EMP: 5
SALES (est): 575.8K **Privately Held**
SIC: 2851 Paints & allied products

(G-6209)
VANGUARD SHRINK FILMS INC
16945 W 116th St (66219-9604)
PHONE..................................913 599-1111
Scott Powell, *General Mgr*
Lee Powell, *Vice Pres*
◆ **EMP:** 10
SQ FT: 20,000
SALES (est): 1.5MM **Privately Held**
WEB: www.okura-usa.com
SIC: 3081 Unsupported plastics film & sheet

(G-6210)
VERTICAL 1 INC
19906 W 99th St (66220-2630)
PHONE..................................913 829-8100
Randy Akings, *President*
EMP: 31
SQ FT: 3,900
SALES (est): 1.3MM **Privately Held**
SIC: 7361 Placement agencies

(G-6211)
VETERAN FDSRVICE SOLUTIONS LLC
8811 Long St (66215-3585)
PHONE..................................913 307-9922
Randall Crawford,
G Hampton Oliver,
Garold Sokolenko,
EMP: 12
SALES (est): 938.1K
SALES (corp-wide): 8MM **Privately Held**
SIC: 5046 Commercial cooking & food service equipment
PA: Aegis Business Solutions, Llc
14453 Shady Bend Rd
Olathe KS 66061
913 307-9922

(G-6212)
VHC VAN HOECKE CONTRACTING INC
Also Called: V H C Van Hoecke Htg & Coolg
14150 Santa Fe Trail Dr (66215-1237)
PHONE..................................913 888-0036
Patricia Vanhoecke, *President*
EMP: 50
SQ FT: 10,000
SALES (est): 8MM **Privately Held**
SIC: 1711 7623 Warm air heating & air conditioning contractor; ventilation & duct work contractor; air conditioning repair

(G-6213)
VIAVI SOLUTIONS LLC
14408 W 105th St (66215-2316)
P.O. Box 9, New Century (66031)
PHONE..................................913 764-2452
Glenda Lantz-Kirk, *Prdtn Mgr*
Guy Hill, *Branch Mgr*
EMP: 130
SALES (corp-wide): 1.1B **Publicly Held**
SIC: 3825 3827 Test equipment for electronic & electric measurement; optical test & inspection equipment
HQ: Viavi Solutions Llc
10200 W York St
Wichita KS 67215
316 522-4981

(G-6214)
VICTORIAN PAPER COMPANY (PA)
Also Called: Victorian Trading Company
15600 W 99th St (66219-2900)
PHONE..................................913 438-3995
Randy Rolston, *President*
Melissa Rolston, *Vice Pres*
Erin Hornbaker, *Purch Dir*
Carrie Baumann, *Purch Mgr*
Heather McCoskey, *CFO*
▲ **EMP:** 100
SQ FT: 54,000
SALES (est): 23.1MM **Privately Held**
WEB: www.victoriantrading.com
SIC: 5961 5199 Cards, mail order; gifts & novelties

(G-6215)
VITALOGRAPH INC
13310 W 99th St (66215-1349)
PHONE..................................913 888-4221
Barbe Garbe, *CEO*
Michael Brown, *Business Mgr*
Robeth Martinez, *Vice Pres*
Rich Rosenthal, *Vice Pres*
Kevin Moore, *Director*
EMP: 30
SQ FT: 20,000
SALES (est): 5.5MM
SALES (corp-wide): 28.7MM **Privately Held**
WEB: www.vitalograph.com
SIC: 5047 Medical equipment & supplies
HQ: Vitalograph Limited
Maids Moreton House
Buckingham BUCKS MK18
128 082-7110

(G-6216)
VITAS HEALTHCARE CORPORATION
8527 Bluejacket St (66214-1656)
PHONE..................................913 722-1631
Noemi Howell, *Principal*
EMP: 30
SALES (corp-wide): 1.7B **Publicly Held**
WEB: www.vitasinnovativehospicecare.com
SIC: 8082 8051 Home health care services; skilled nursing care facilities
HQ: Vitas Healthcare Corporation
201 S Biscayne Blvd # 400
Miami FL 33131
305 374-4143

(G-6217)
VORONA LLC
9600 Dice Ln Ste 213 (66215-1152)
PHONE..................................913 888-4646
William You,
EMP: 5 **EST:** 2013
SALES (est): 418.9K **Privately Held**
SIC: 3131 Counters

(G-6218)
VOS DESIGN INC
13731 W 108th St (66215-2025)
PHONE..................................913 825-6556
Brad Sanders, *President*
Mary Jane Gruchala, *Finance*
EMP: 10
SALES (est): 830.1K **Privately Held**
SIC: 7371 Computer software development

(G-6219)
WACHTER INC (PA)
16001 W 99th St (66219-1293)
PHONE..................................913 541-2500
Brian Sloan, *CEO*
Greg Gosling, *General Mgr*
Brad Botteron, *Chairman*
Ken Hennings, *Business Mgr*
Greg K Sloan, *Senior VP*
EMP: 190
SQ FT: 27,000
SALES: 240.6MM **Privately Held**
SIC: 1731 8748 General electrical contractor; voice, data & video wiring contractor; business consulting; systems analysis or design

(G-6220)
WACHTER TECH SOLUTIONS INC (HQ)
16001 W 99th St (66219-1293)
PHONE..................................856 222-0643
Brian Sloan, *CEO*
Brad Botteron, *Ch of Bd*
Greg Sloan, *Senior VP*
Deanna Gillett, *CFO*
EMP: 51

SALES: 10MM
SALES (corp-wide): 240.6MM Privately Held
SIC: 1731 8748 7373 Telephone & telephone equipment installation; safety & security specialization; voice, data & video wiring contractor; business consulting; systems analysis or design; computer integrated systems design
PA: Wachter, Inc.
16001 W 99th St
Lenexa KS 66219
913 541-2500

(G-6221)
WALLABYS INC
Also Called: Wallaby's Grill and Pub
9562 Lackman Rd (66219-1204)
PHONE....913 541-9255
Mike Wall, *CEO*
EMP: 15
SQ FT: 2,000
SALES (est): 1.1MM Privately Held
SIC: 7389 Restaurant reservation service

(G-6222)
WATER DST NO1 JHNSON CNTY KANS (PA)
Also Called: WATERONE
10747 Renner Blvd (66219-9624)
PHONE....913 895-5500
Jason Beyer, *Editor*
Brenda Cherpitel, *Chairman*
Sean McGraw, *Safety Mgr*
Curt Vogel, *Opers Staff*
Randy Bartel, *Engineer*
EMP: 250
SQ FT: 22,247
SALES: 117.1MM Privately Held
WEB: www.waterone.com
SIC: 4941 Water supply

(G-6223)
WDS INC
15007 W 95th St (66215-5229)
PHONE....913 894-1881
Ramey Millett, *CFO*
EMP: 94 Privately Held
SIC: 1541 5199 7319 Industrial buildings & warehouses; advertising specialties; shopping news, advertising & distributing service
PA: Wds, Inc.
9640 Windygap Rd
Charlotte NC 28278

(G-6224)
WEBER CARPET INC (PA)
Also Called: Joe's Carpet
11400 Rogers Rd (66215-4031)
PHONE....913 469-5430
Mark Weber, *President*
Brett Bales, *General Mgr*
Dave Sinclair, *CFO*
Jose Garcia, *Wholesale*
Julie Baker, *Sales Staff*
▼ EMP: 190
SQ FT: 75,000
SALES (est): 78.5MM Privately Held
SIC: 5023 5713 Floor coverings; carpets; floor covering stores; carpets

(G-6225)
WELLNESS SERVICES INC (DH)
9724 Legler Rd (66219-1282)
PHONE....913 894-6600
Roger Crain, *President*
Janet Brooks, *President*
Judith Vogelsmeier, *Admin Sec*
EMP: 250
SALES (est): 9MM Publicly Held
SIC: 8011 Offices & clinics of medical doctors
HQ: Hca Inc.
1 Park Plz
Nashville TN 37203
615 344-9551

(G-6226)
WEST COAST EQUIPMENT INC
15607 W 100th Ter (66219-1362)
PHONE....623 842-0978
Phillop Prohroff, *President*
Lissa Haprov, *Admin Sec*
▲ EMP: 12
SQ FT: 8,000
SALES (est): 1.6MM Privately Held
WEB: www.westcoastequip.com
SIC: 3991 Brushes, household or industrial

(G-6227)
WESTDALE ASSET MANAGEMENT LTD
8730 Bourgade St (66219-1440)
PHONE....913 307-5900
EMP: 87 Privately Held
SIC: 8741 Financial management for business
PA: Westdale Asset Management, Ltd.
2550 Pacific Ave Ste 1600
Dallas TX 75226

(G-6228)
WHITING HOUSE GROUP LLC
16820 W 89th St (66219-4800)
PHONE....816 272-4496
Nicholas Kresz,
Michael Cantu,
EMP: 15
SALES (est): 526.3K Privately Held
SIC: 7379 Computer related consulting services

(G-6229)
WILKE RESOURCES INC (PA)
Also Called: Wilke International
14321 W 96th Ter (66215-4709)
PHONE....913 438-5544
Donovan Smith, *President*
Jim France, *General Mgr*
Christina Young, *Principal*
John Veazey, *CFO*
Michelle Johnson,
▲ EMP: 13 EST: 1997
SQ FT: 6,000
SALES (est): 5.8MM Privately Held
SIC: 5169 Food additives & preservatives

(G-6230)
WILKERSON CRANE RENTAL INC
9131 Noland Rd (66215-3644)
P.O. Box 12554, Kansas City (66112-0554)
PHONE....913 238-7030
Deanea Boydston, *Finance Mgr*
Fred Holt, *Sales Mgr*
Diana Holt, *Director*
EMP: 27
SALES (est): 10.5MM Privately Held
SIC: 5082 1799 7699 7353 Cranes, construction; welding on site; aircraft & heavy equipment repair services; cranes & aerial lift equipment, rental or leasing; cranes, industrial; cranes, industrial plant

(G-6231)
WILLIAMS FOODS INC (HQ)
13301 W 99th St (66215-1348)
PHONE....913 888-4343
Scott Petty Jr, *Ch of Bd*
Dale Tremblay, *President*
Brett Alvheim, *Vice Pres*
Thomas McRae, *Vice Pres*
▲ EMP: 130
SQ FT: 60,000
SALES (est): 44.1MM
SALES (corp-wide): 689.5MM Privately Held
WEB: www.williamsfoods.com
SIC: 2099 2051 5961 2035 Seasonings: dry mixes; gravy mixes, dry; sauces: dry mixes; dips, except cheese & sour cream based; bread, cake & related products; bread, all types (white, wheat, rye, etc): fresh or frozen; food, mail order; pickles, sauces & salad dressings
PA: C.H. Guenther & Son Llc
2201 Broadway St
San Antonio TX 78215
210 227-1401

(G-6232)
WINNING STREAK SPORTS LLC
9821 Widmer Rd (66215-1239)
PHONE....913 768-8868
Lauren Larson, *President*
Mark Towster, *CFO*
Jay Chaffee, *Sales Mgr*
Eric Bartley, *Sales Staff*
Nick Kormann, *Sales Staff*
▲ EMP: 10
SQ FT: 10,000
SALES (est): 1.3MM Privately Held
SIC: 2399 Banners, pennants & flags

(G-6233)
WOMENS HEALTH CARE GROUP (PA)
Also Called: Women's Healthcare Group The
10600 Quivira Rd Ste 200 (66215-2311)
PHONE....913 438-0018
Hal Younglove, *Owner*
Dana Crisp, *Department Mgr*
R Anthony Moulton, *Obstetrician*
Jennifer Tyson, *Administration*
EMP: 30
SALES (est): 6.7MM Privately Held
SIC: 8011 Gynecologist; obstetrician

(G-6234)
WORLDWIDE ENERGY INC
10413 W 84th Ter (66214-1641)
P.O. Box 14982 (66285-4982)
PHONE....913 310-0705
Gaylen Davenport, *CEO*
EMP: 12
SALES (est): 1.9MM Privately Held
SIC: 8748 5211 Energy conservation consultant; energy conservation products

(G-6235)
WRIGHT LANDSCAPING LLC
8113 Parkhill St (66215-2626)
PHONE....816 225-1050
Mechelle Wright, *Mng Member*
Dan Wright, *Mng Member*
EMP: 15
SALES (est): 654.2K Privately Held
SIC: 0782 Landscape contractors

(G-6236)
WSM INDUSTRIES INC
Also Called: All American Supply Co
9755 Lackman Rd (66219-1207)
PHONE....913 492-9299
Michael Legero, *Manager*
EMP: 25
SALES (corp-wide): 65MM Privately Held
WEB: www.wsm-industries.com
SIC: 3531 Construction machinery
HQ: Wsm Industries, Inc.
1601 S Sheridan St
Wichita KS 67213
316 942-9412

(G-6237)
WW GRAINGER INC
Also Called: Grainger 409
14790 W 99th St (66215-1109)
PHONE....913 492-8550
Tim Mitts, *Branch Mgr*
EMP: 20
SQ FT: 27,000
SALES (corp-wide): 11.2B Publicly Held
WEB: www.grainger.com
SIC: 5063 5084 5075 5078 Motors, electric; motor controls, starters & relays: electric; power transmission equipment, electric; generators; fans, industrial; pumps & pumping equipment; compressors, except air conditioning; pneumatic tools & equipment; warm air heating equipment & supplies; air conditioning equipment, except room units; refrigeration equipment & supplies; electric tools; power tools & accessories; hand tools
PA: W.W. Grainger, Inc.
100 Grainger Pkwy
Lake Forest IL 60045
847 535-1000

(G-6238)
X TEC REPAIR INC
Also Called: Xtec
10602 Lackman Rd (66219-1226)
PHONE....913 829-3773
Scott Martell, *President*
Kevin Jordan, *Software Dev*
EMP: 22
SQ FT: 30,000
SALES (est): 3.6MM Privately Held
WEB: www.xteconline.com
SIC: 7629 Electronic equipment repair

(G-6239)
YAEGER ARCHITECTURE INC
8655 Penrose Ln Ste 300 (66219-8118)
PHONE....913 742-8000
Carl Yaeger, *President*
Matthew Turner, *Vice Pres*
Jay Watters, *Project Mgr*
Katie Gall, *Marketing Staff*
Dominic Griffin, *Technology*
EMP: 35
SALES (est): 3.8MM Privately Held
WEB: www.bdyarchitects.net
SIC: 7389 8742 8712 Interior decorating; construction project management consultant; architectural services

(G-6240)
ZELL-METALL USA INC
10908 Strang Line Rd (66215-2322)
PHONE....913 327-0300
Patrick Pheffer, *President*
EMP: 13
SALES: 5MM Privately Held
SIC: 2821 Polystyrene resins; polyvinyl chloride resins (PVC); polypropylene resins; polyethylene resins
PA: Zl-Central Engineering Plastics, Inc.
10908 Strang Line Rd
Lenexa KS 66215

(G-6241)
ZILLNER MKTG CMMUNICATIONS INC
8725 Rosehill Rd (66215-4610)
PHONE....913 599-3230
Ronda Zillner, *Principal*
EMP: 33
SALES (est): 5MM Privately Held
SIC: 4899 Communication services

(G-6242)
ZIMMER INC
Also Called: Zimmer Titus Associates
9545 Alden St (66215-1164)
PHONE....913 888-1024
Stephanie Ebright, *Purchasing*
Nathan Gordon, *Engineer*
Steven Maxon, *Branch Mgr*
Susan Thomas, *Technician*
EMP: 5
SALES (corp-wide): 7.9B Publicly Held
WEB: www.zimmer.com
SIC: 3842 Orthopedic appliances
HQ: Zimmer, Inc.
1800 W Center St
Warsaw IN 46580
800 348-9500

Lenora
Norton County

(G-6243)
HACHMEISTER SERVICE CENTER LLC
22623 Road W6 (67645-9670)
PHONE....785 567-4818
Jay Hachmeister, *Principal*
EMP: 10
SALES (est): 957.7K Privately Held
SIC: 7538 General automotive repair shops

(G-6244)
JILLS HELPING HANDS INC
27438 Us Highway 283 (67645-9677)
PHONE....785 622-4254
Jill Edgett, *President*
Tom Edgett, *Vice Pres*
EMP: 60
SALES (est): 1MM Privately Held
SIC: 8082 Visiting nurse service

(G-6245)
RURAL TELEPHONE SERVICE CO INC (PA)
Also Called: Nex-Tech
145 N Main St (67645)
PHONE....785 567-4281
Jimmy Todd, *CEO*
F C Brungardt, *President*
Jim Harries, *President*
Jan Jackson, *General Mgr*

Michael Pollock, *COO*
EMP: 90 **EST:** 1951
SQ FT: 3,500
SALES (est): 174.9MM **Privately Held**
SIC: 4813 5734 5045 Local & long distance telephone communications; computer peripheral equipment; computers, peripherals & software

Leon
Butler County

(G-6246)
CLINTON L WILLIAMS
Also Called: Williams Farms & Trucking
10756 Se Stchell Creek Rd (67074-8345)
PHONE....................................316 775-1300
Clinton L Williams, *Owner*
EMP: 25
SQ FT: 2,400
SALES: 3.6MM **Privately Held**
SIC: 4213 Trucking, except local

(G-6247)
FLEMING FEED & GRAIN INC (PA)
Also Called: Fleming Feed & Seed
309 S Main St (67074-7403)
P.O. Box 66 (67074-0066)
PHONE....................................316 742-3411
Gick Fleming, *President*
Debbie Fleming, *Treasurer*
EMP: 20 **EST:** 1971
SQ FT: 15,000
SALES (est): 27.9MM **Privately Held**
WEB: www.flemingag.com
SIC: 5153 5191 5172 Grains; chemicals, agricultural; fertilizer & fertilizer materials; feed; seeds: field, garden & flower; gasoline

Leona
Brown County

(G-6248)
WILBUR-ELLIS COMPANY LLC
1299 Ash Point Rd (66532-9548)
PHONE....................................785 359-6569
Wilbur Bindel, *Branch Mgr*
EMP: 10
SALES (corp-wide): 2.6B **Privately Held**
SIC: 5999 5191 5169 Feed & farm supply; chemicals, agricultural; fertilizer & fertilizer materials; animal feeds; industrial chemicals
HQ: Wilbur-Ellis Company Llc
345 California St Fl 27
San Francisco CA 94104
415 772-4000

Leonardville
Riley County

(G-6249)
LEONARDVILLE NURSING HOME INC
409 W Barton Rd (66449-2023)
P.O. Box 148 (66449-0148)
PHONE....................................785 468-3661
Ed Johnson, *Ch of Bd*
Sandra Hageman, *Administration*
EMP: 55
SALES: 3.6MM **Privately Held**
WEB: www.leonardvillenh.org
SIC: 8052 Intermediate care facilities

Leoti
Wichita County

(G-6250)
ARCHER-DANIELS-MIDLAND COMPANY
Also Called: ADM
505 N 4th St (67861-9601)
P.O. Box 808 (67861-0808)
PHONE....................................620 375-4811
Michael Hernandez, *Branch Mgr*
EMP: 9
SQ FT: 1,000
SALES (corp-wide): 64.3B **Publicly Held**
WEB: www.admworld.com
SIC: 2041 5191 Flour & other grain mill products; feed; seeds: field, garden & flower; fertilizer & fertilizer materials
PA: Archer-Daniels-Midland Company
77 W Wacker Dr Ste 4600
Chicago IL 60601
312 634-8100

(G-6251)
C & W FARMS
116 S 4th St (67861-7032)
P.O. Box 327 (67861-0327)
PHONE....................................620 375-4429
Brad Whitham, *Owner*
EMP: 12
SALES (est): 648.7K **Privately Held**
SIC: 0191 General farms, primarily crop

(G-6252)
GREEN PLAINS INC
Also Called: Cargill
857 N Highway 25 (67861-6179)
PHONE....................................620 375-2255
Todd Allen, *Branch Mgr*
EMP: 70
SALES (corp-wide): 3.8B **Publicly Held**
WEB: www.cargill.com
SIC: 0211 Beef cattle feedlots
PA: Green Plains Inc.
1811 Aksarben Dr
Omaha NE 68106
402 884-8700

(G-6253)
HELENA CHEMICAL COMPANY
207 S Hwy 25 (67861)
PHONE....................................620 375-2073
Andy Snarsh, *Branch Mgr*
EMP: 5 **Privately Held**
SIC: 2819 5191 Chemicals, high purity: refined from technical grade; fertilizers & agricultural chemicals
HQ: Helena Agri-Enterprises, Llc
255 Schilling Blvd # 300
Collierville TN 38017
901 761-0050

(G-6254)
HI-PLAINS MOTEL & RESTAURANT
312 E Broadway (67861-5016)
P.O. Box 577 (67861-0577)
PHONE....................................620 375-4438
Bruce Endorf, *Owner*
EMP: 15
SALES (est): 425.2K **Privately Held**
SIC: 7011 5812 Hotels & motels; eating places

(G-6255)
LEOTI GREENTECH INCORPORATED
232 Kansas 96 (67861)
P.O. Box L (67861-0319)
PHONE....................................620 375-2621
Jeffery H Bieber, *President*
Jeffrey H Bieber, *President*
Martha A Bieber, *Corp Secy*
Mark Budde, *Vice Pres*
EMP: 16
SQ FT: 10,000
SALES (est): 3MM **Privately Held**
SIC: 5083 Farm implements

(G-6256)
MARK C JONES
Also Called: Jones Construction
612 E Orange St (67861-6289)
P.O. Box 338 (67861-0338)
PHONE....................................620 375-2357
Mark C Jones, *Owner*
EMP: 10
SALES (est): 588.6K **Privately Held**
SIC: 1521 Single-family housing construction

(G-6257)
SEABOARD FEED MILL
132 N County Road 14 (67861-6190)
P.O. Box 1583 (67861-1583)
PHONE....................................620 375-3300
Brian Bybee, *President*
John Williamson, *Project Mgr*
Janelle Gulotta, *Export Mgr*
Shaun Huls, *QC Mgr*
Jeff Sherbondy, *Controller*
EMP: 45
SALES (est): 286K **Privately Held**
SIC: 5191 Feed

(G-6258)
SEABOARD FOODS LLC
211 N 4th St (67861-9769)
P.O. Box 547 (67861-0547)
PHONE....................................620 375-4523
Stephen Prewit, *Manager*
EMP: 40
SALES (corp-wide): 6.5B **Publicly Held**
WEB: www.seaboardpork.com
SIC: 0213 Hogs
HQ: Seaboard Foods Llc
9000 W 67th St Ste 200
Shawnee Mission KS 66202
913 261-2600

(G-6259)
SEABOARD FOODS LLC
108 E Broadway (67861)
P.O. Box 547 (67861-0547)
PHONE....................................620 375-4431
Chris Conard, *Branch Mgr*
EMP: 20
SALES (corp-wide): 6.5B **Publicly Held**
WEB: www.seaboardpork.com
SIC: 0213 Hogs
HQ: Seaboard Foods Llc
9000 W 67th St Ste 200
Shawnee Mission KS 66202
913 261-2600

(G-6260)
WHITHAM FARMS FEEDYARD INC
902 Broadway Plz (67861-9009)
Rr # 2 Box 200 (67861-6267)
PHONE....................................620 375-4684
Fax: 620 375-2264
EMP: 25
SALES (est): 1.1MM **Privately Held**
SIC: 0211 Cattle Feed Lot

(G-6261)
WHITHAM FRANK E TRUST 2
Also Called: Whitco Petroleum
2nd & Broadway (67861)
PHONE....................................620 375-2229
Stewart Whitham, *Principal*
Barth E Whitham, *Principal*
EMP: 15
SALES (est): 526.9K **Privately Held**
SIC: 6733 1381 Trusts; service well drilling

(G-6262)
WICHITA CNTY LONG TERM REST HM
Also Called: Golden Acres Nursing Home
211 E Earl St (67861-9620)
P.O. Box 2 (67861-0002)
PHONE....................................620 375-4600
Vicki Vernming, *Manager*
Ed Finley, *Administration*
EMP: 65
SALES: 200.7K **Privately Held**
SIC: 8052 8051 Intermediate care facilities; skilled nursing care facilities

(G-6263)
WICHITA COUNTY HEALTH CENTER
211 E Earl St (67861-9620)
PHONE....................................620 375-2233
Janice Campas, *Manager*
Victoria Hahn, *Administration*
EMP: 90
SQ FT: 19,400
SALES (est): 2.3MM **Privately Held**
SIC: 8062 General medical & surgical hospitals

(G-6264)
WICHITA COUNTY HEALTH CENTER
211 E Earl St (67861-9620)
PHONE....................................620 375-2233
Victoria Han, *CEO*
Janice Campas, *CFO*
Janis Campas, *CFO*
Becky Miller, *Manager*
Heather Price, *Manager*
EMP: 99
SALES: 6.5MM **Privately Held**
SIC: 8062 General medical & surgical hospitals

Levant
Thomas County

(G-6265)
ROADRUNER MANUFACTURING LLC
1130 County Road R (67743-9012)
PHONE....................................785 586-2228
Bradley Skolout, *Mng Member*
EMP: 9
SALES (est): 1.7MM **Privately Held**
SIC: 3715 Truck trailers

Lewis
Edwards County

(G-6266)
CROSS BRAND FEED & ALFALFA INC
Hwy 50 E (67552)
PHONE....................................620 324-5571
Ann Derley, *President*
Antonio Morales, *Vice Pres*
Terry Powers, *Vice Pres*
Schianne Hornbaker, *Admin Sec*
▲ **EMP:** 20
SQ FT: 19,900
SALES (est): 2.6MM **Privately Held**
SIC: 2048 Alfalfa or alfalfa meal, prepared as animal feed

(G-6267)
CROSS BRAND OFFICE INC (PA)
Also Called: Cross Brand Feed
Hwy 50 S (67552)
PHONE....................................620 324-5571
James W Adair, *President*
Antonio Morales, *Vice Pres*
Ann Derley, *Admin Sec*
EMP: 20
SQ FT: 19,900
SALES: 4.5MM **Privately Held**
SIC: 2048 5999 Alfalfa or alfalfa meal, prepared as animal feed; feed & farm supply

(G-6268)
CROSS MANUFACTURING INC
100 James H Blvd (67552)
P.O. Box 67 (67552-0067)
PHONE....................................620 324-5525
Darren Bennett, *Engineer*
Jama Hommertzheim, *Personnel*
Bob Besser, *Manager*
EMP: 150
SALES (corp-wide): 21.3MM **Privately Held**
WEB: www.crossmfg.com
SIC: 3714 5013 5084 Motor vehicle parts & accessories; automotive supplies & parts; hydraulic systems equipment & supplies

▲ = Import ▼=Export
◆ =Import/Export

PA: Cross Manufacturing, Inc.
11011 King St Ste 210
Overland Park KS 66210
913 451-1233

(G-6269)
MICHAEL L SEBES
1975 Us Highway 50 (67552-5134)
PHONE..................................620 324-5509
Michael L Sebes, *Owner*
EMP: 11
SALES (est): 1MM **Privately Held**
SIC: 5154 Cattle

(G-6270)
SOUTHERN PLAINS CO-OP AT LEWIS (PA)
Also Called: Alliance AG and Grain
100 N Main St (67552-5300)
P.O. Box 128 (67552-0128)
PHONE..................................620 324-5536
Ron Gruber, *General Mgr*
EMP: 23 **EST:** 1902
SQ FT: 2,000
SALES: 58.9MM **Privately Held**
SIC: 5153 5191 6221 4213 Grain elevators; farm supplies; commodity brokers, contracts; trucking, except local; petroleum products

(G-6271)
TDN FARMS
1566 210th Ave (67552-5264)
PHONE..................................620 324-5296
Troy Nelson, *Partner*
Aurelia Denise Nelson, *Partner*
EMP: 22 **EST:** 1995
SQ FT: 16,000
SALES (est): 91.6K **Privately Held**
SIC: 0212 0191 Beef cattle except feedlots; general farms, primarily crop

Liberal
Seward County

(G-6272)
A S ESCORT
1431 Road F (67901-5711)
PHONE..................................620 655-6613
Cysom Ansley, *Owner*
EMP: 10
SALES (est): 639.9K **Privately Held**
SIC: 7389 Pilot car escort service

(G-6273)
AIR PRODUCTS AND CHEMICALS INC
2701 Road G (67901-5359)
PHONE..................................620 624-8151
Rick Prater, *Manager*
EMP: 25
SQ FT: 13,000
SALES (corp-wide): 8.9B **Publicly Held**
WEB: www.airproducts.com
SIC: 5169 5084 Chemicals & allied products; welding machinery & equipment
PA: Air Products And Chemicals, Inc.
7201 Hamilton Blvd
Allentown PA 18195
610 481-4911

(G-6274)
AIR PRODUCTS AND CHEMICALS INC
2525 N Country Ests (67901-2294)
PHONE..................................620 626-7062
John Hernandez, *Manager*
EMP: 13
SALES (corp-wide): 8.9B **Publicly Held**
WEB: www.airproducts.com
SIC: 2813 3443 Helium; cryogenic tanks, for liquids & gases
PA: Air Products And Chemicals, Inc.
7201 Hamilton Blvd
Allentown PA 18195
610 481-4911

(G-6275)
AIR PRODUCTS AND CHEMICALS INC
12412 Road R (67901-2405)
PHONE..................................620 626-5700
Tony Werner, *Branch Mgr*
EMP: 52
SALES (corp-wide): 8.9B **Publicly Held**
WEB: www.airproducts.com
SIC: 2813 Industrial gases
PA: Air Products And Chemicals, Inc.
7201 Hamilton Blvd
Allentown PA 18195
610 481-4911

(G-6276)
ALLIED OF KANSAS INC
712 N Country Estates Rd (67901-5317)
PHONE..................................620 624-5937
Kenny Baesa, *Branch Mgr*
EMP: 12
SALES (corp-wide): 8.1MM **Privately Held**
SIC: 1389 Construction, repair & dismantling services
PA: Allied Of Kansas, Inc.
24 S Lincoln St
Russell KS 67665
785 483-2627

(G-6277)
ALPHA SERVICES AND PRODUCTION
2511 Hwy 83 (67901)
P.O. Box 2162 (67905-2162)
PHONE..................................620 624-8318
Mark Anderson, *President*
Jim Anderson, *President*
EMP: 5 **EST:** 1970
SQ FT: 4,000
SALES (est): 473.4K **Privately Held**
SIC: 1389 Oil field services

(G-6278)
ANDRADE AUTO SALES INC
Also Called: Andrade Window Tinting
153 W Pancake Blvd (67901-4030)
PHONE..................................620 624-2400
Mike Andrade, *President*
EMP: 10
SQ FT: 4,400
SALES (est): 1.8MM **Privately Held**
SIC: 5521 7549 Automobiles, used cars only; pickups & vans, used; glass tinting, automotive

(G-6279)
ARKALON ENERGY LLC
300 N Lincoln Ave (67901-3334)
P.O. Box 1178 (67905-1178)
PHONE..................................620 624-2901
Nick Hatcher,
Rock Orminston,
Dusty Turner,
EMP: 35
SALES (est): 4.8MM **Privately Held**
SIC: 2869 Ethyl alcohol, ethanol

(G-6280)
AT&T CORP
111 E Tucker Rd (67901-2191)
PHONE..................................620 626-5168
EMP: 97
SALES (corp-wide): 170.7B **Publicly Held**
SIC: 4812 Cellular telephone services
HQ: At&T Corp.
1 At&T Way
Bedminster NJ 07921
800 403-3302

(G-6281)
BANK AMERICA NATIONAL ASSN
300 N Kansas Ave (67901-3328)
PHONE..................................316 261-4242
Kiran Thomas, *President*
EMP: 15
SALES (corp-wide): 110.5B **Publicly Held**
WEB: www.bofa.com
SIC: 6021 National commercial banks
HQ: Bank Of America, National Association
100 S Tryon St
Charlotte NC 28202
704 386-5681

(G-6282)
BANK AMERICA NATIONAL ASSN
1325 N Kansas Ave (67901-2443)
PHONE..................................316 261-4242
Diane Pomeroy, *Manager*
EMP: 15
SALES (corp-wide): 110.5B **Publicly Held**
WEB: www.bofa.com
SIC: 6021 National commercial banks
HQ: Bank Of America, National Association
100 S Tryon St
Charlotte NC 28202
704 386-5681

(G-6283)
BASIC ENERGY SERVICES LLC
1700 S Country Estates Rd (67901-5313)
PHONE..................................620 624-2277
Mark Krupicka, *President*
Keith Miller, *President*
Jordan Conklin, *Office Mgr*
EMP: 7
SALES (est): 900K **Privately Held**
SIC: 1389 Oil field services

(G-6284)
BLACK HILLS/KANSAS GAS
Also Called: Black Hills Energy
1600 General Welch Blvd (67901-5106)
PHONE..................................605 721-1700
EMP: 16
SALES (corp-wide): 1.7B **Publicly Held**
SIC: 4924 Natural gas distribution
HQ: Black Hills/Kansas Gas Utility Company, Llc
7001 Mount Rushmore Rd
Rapid City SD 57702

(G-6285)
BOB THORNTON
Also Called: H&R Block
11 Village Plz (67901-2762)
P.O. Box 1181 (67905-1181)
PHONE..................................620 624-7691
Bob Thornton, *Owner*
EMP: 22
SALES (est): 291.2K **Privately Held**
SIC: 7291 Tax return preparation services

(G-6286)
BRANDING IRON RESTAURANT & CLB
Also Called: Liberal Inn
603 E Pancake Blvd (67901-4317)
P.O. Box 1821 (67905-1821)
PHONE..................................620 624-7254
Kenneth McElvain, *President*
EMP: 22
SALES (est): 436.2K **Privately Held**
SIC: 7011 Motels

(G-6287)
BRIANS HOT OIL SERVICE LLC
P.O. Box 888 (67905-0888)
PHONE..................................620 629-5933
Brian Riddle,
EMP: 7 **EST:** 1998
SQ FT: 4,000
SALES (est): 590K **Privately Held**
SIC: 1389 Oil field services

(G-6288)
BYRON G BIRD ASSOC CHARTERED
Also Called: Byron Bird & Assoc Chartered
224 N Lincoln Ave (67901-3332)
PHONE..................................620 624-1994
Linda Billings, *CEO*
EMP: 10
SALES (est): 700K **Privately Held**
SIC: 8721 Accounting services, except auditing

(G-6289)
C B H CONSULTANTS INC
Also Called: Holiday Inn
1550 N Lincoln Ave (67901-5208)
PHONE..................................620 624-9700
Rikky Carrasco, *Branch Mgr*
EMP: 28
SALES (corp-wide): 1.2MM **Privately Held**
SIC: 7011 Hotels & motels
PA: C B H Consultants Inc
100 Pacifica Ste 470
Irvine CA 92618
949 387-9400

(G-6290)
CANCER CENTER OF KANSAS PA
315 W 15th St (67901-2455)
PHONE..................................620 629-6727
David Johnson, *Branch Mgr*
EMP: 17
SALES (corp-wide): 24.4MM **Privately Held**
SIC: 8011 Oncologist
PA: Cancer Center Of Kansas, P.A.
818 N Emporia St Ste 403
Wichita KS 67214
316 262-4467

(G-6291)
CENTRAL CARE PA
305 W 15th St Ste 203 (67901-2455)
PHONE..................................620 624-4700
Stacy Cloyd, *Branch Mgr*
EMP: 29 **Privately Held**
SIC: 8011 General & family practice, physician/surgeon
PA: Central Care, Pa
2337 E Crawford St
Salina KS 67401

(G-6292)
CITY OF LIBERAL
Also Called: Liberal Street & Alley
405 N Pennsylvania Ave (67901-3420)
P.O. Box 2199 (67905-2199)
PHONE..................................620 626-0135
Toby Miller, *Manager*
EMP: 26 **Privately Held**
WEB: www.liberalpd.com
SIC: 1611 Highway & street maintenance
PA: City Of Liberal
324 N Kansas Ave
Liberal KS 67901
620 626-2201

(G-6293)
CITY OF LIBERAL
Also Called: Water Department
1401 E Pine St (67901-5632)
P.O. Box 2199 (67905-2199)
PHONE..................................620 626-0138
Calvin Burke, *Trustee*
Burnard Kitten, *Director*
EMP: 15 **Privately Held**
WEB: www.liberalpd.com
SIC: 1629 Waste water & sewage treatment plant construction
PA: City Of Liberal
324 N Kansas Ave
Liberal KS 67901
620 626-2201

(G-6294)
CLINGAN TIRES INCORPORATED (PA)
Also Called: Clingan Tires Service Center
314 S Kansas Ave (67901-3797)
PHONE..................................620 624-5649
Robert W Clingan Sr, *Ch of Bd*
Jim Wills, *President*
Margaret Clingan, *Treasurer*
Robbie W Clingan Jr, *Shareholder*
Melinda K Clingan-Wills, *Admin Sec*
EMP: 42
SQ FT: 21,000
SALES (est): 5MM **Privately Held**
SIC: 5014 5531 Automobile tires & tubes; automotive tires

(G-6295)
COMET 1 H R CLEANERS INC
Also Called: Bose Bude
2361 N Kansas Ave (67901-2055)
PHONE..................................620 626-8100
Yvonne Hawkins, *President*
David Hawkins, *Vice Pres*
EMP: 10
SALES (est): 500K **Privately Held**
SIC: 7216 5087 7219 Drycleaning plants, except rugs; laundry equipment & supplies; garment alteration & repair shop

(G-6296)
COMMUNITY BANK
2320 N Kansas Ave (67901-2056)
PHONE..................................620 624-6898
Mark Schepers, *President*
EMP: 16
SALES: 5.7MM **Privately Held**
SIC: 6022 State trust companies accepting deposits, commercial
PA: Light Bancshares Corporation
2320 N Kansas Ave
Liberal KS 67901

(G-6297)
COUNTY OF SEWARD
Also Called: 911 Emergency Management
501 N Washington Ave # 101 (67901-3484)
PHONE..................................620 626-0198
Bill McBryde, *Sheriff*
Frank Simmons, *Director*
EMP: 10 **Privately Held**
WEB: www.cbasin.com
SIC: 8322 Hotline
PA: County Of Seward
515 N Washington Ave
Liberal KS 67901
620 309-3200

(G-6298)
COUNTY OF SEWARD
Also Called: Seward County Landfill
89th St Hwy 54 (67901)
PHONE..................................620 626-3266
Mike Tabber, *Manager*
EMP: 14 **Privately Held**
WEB: www.cbasin.com
SIC: 9111 4953 County supervisors' & executives' offices; sanitary landfill operation
PA: County Of Seward
515 N Washington Ave
Liberal KS 67901
620 309-3200

(G-6299)
COUNTY OF SEWARD
Also Called: Seward County Emrgncy Med Svc
320 W 18th St (67901-2466)
PHONE..................................620 626-3275
John Rolston, *Director*
EMP: 31 **Privately Held**
WEB: www.cbasin.com
SIC: 7363 Medical help service
PA: County Of Seward
515 N Washington Ave
Liberal KS 67901
620 309-3200

(G-6300)
CROWN CONSULTING INC
150 Plaza Dr Ste 103 (67901-2779)
P.O. Box 1816 (67905-1816)
PHONE..................................620 624-0156
David E Rice, *President*
Pam K Schartz, *Vice Pres*
Pam Schartz, *Vice Pres*
EMP: 11
SQ FT: 2,000
SALES (est): 1MM **Privately Held**
SIC: 1389 1381 1311 Oil consultants; drilling oil & gas wells; crude petroleum & natural gas

(G-6301)
DCP OPERATING COMPANY LP
7635 Road 3 (67901-5147)
PHONE..................................620 626-1201
Clay Butterfield, *General Mgr*
Ron Griffin, *Manager*
EMP: 35
SALES (corp-wide): 9.8B **Publicly Held**
SIC: 4925 4923 Gas production and/or distribution; gas transmission & distribution
HQ: Dcp Operating Company, Lp
370 17th St Ste 2500
Denver CO 80202
303 595-3331

(G-6302)
DCS SANITATION MANAGEMENT INC
1406 N Western Ave (67901-2212)
PHONE..................................620 624-5533
Roger Alvarez, *Principal*
EMP: 150
SALES (corp-wide): 38.1MM **Privately Held**
SIC: 5084 7349 Cleaning equipment, high pressure, sand or steam; building maintenance services
PA: Dcs Sanitation Management, Inc.
7864 Camargo Rd
Cincinnati OH 45243
513 891-4980

(G-6303)
DENNIS KNUDSEN DR
222 W 15th St (67901-2448)
P.O. Box 2529 (67905-2529)
PHONE..................................620 624-3811
Dennis Knudsen, *Owner*
Janell Knudsen, *Manager*
EMP: 13
SALES (est): 311.7K **Privately Held**
SIC: 8011 Obstetrician

(G-6304)
DIAMOND ETHANOL LLC
1701 N Kansas Ave (67901-2000)
PHONE..................................620 626-2026
EMP: 5
SALES (corp-wide): 4.3MM **Privately Held**
SIC: 3915 Diamond cutting & polishing
HQ: Diamond Ethanol, Llc
103 S Fm 2646
Levelland TX 79336
806 897-0911

(G-6305)
DISCO MACHINE LIBERAL COMPANY
2161 N Grant Ave (67901-2080)
P.O. Box 1888 (67905-1888)
PHONE..................................620 624-0179
Doug Heathman, *Manager*
EMP: 20
SALES (corp-wide): 10MM **Privately Held**
SIC: 3599 3471 Machine shop, jobbing & repair; cleaning, polishing & finishing
PA: Disco Machine Of Liberal Company
103 Texas St
Borger TX 79007
806 274-2214

(G-6306)
EARL RESSE WELDING
1441 General Welch Blvd (67901-5120)
PHONE..................................620 624-6141
Earl Feese, *Owner*
EMP: 5
SALES (est): 250.8K **Privately Held**
SIC: 1799 7692 Welding on site; welding repair

(G-6307)
EQUITY BANK NA
1700 N Lincoln Ave (67901-5210)
PHONE..................................620 624-1971
EMP: 53 **Publicly Held**
SIC: 6021 National commercial banks
HQ: Equity Bank, N.A.
7701 E Kellogg Dr Ste 300
Wichita KS 67207
316 612-6000

(G-6308)
EVANGELICAL LUTHERAN
Also Called: Good Samaritan Soc - Liberal
2160 Zinnia Ln (67901-2042)
P.O. Box 5038, Sioux Falls SD (57117-5038)
PHONE..................................620 624-3832
Richard Parra, *Branch Mgr*
EMP: 87 **Privately Held**
WEB: www.good-sam.com
SIC: 8059 8051 Nursing home, except skilled & intermediate care facility; skilled nursing care facilities
HQ: The Evangelical Lutheran Good Samaritan Society
4800 W 57th St
Sioux Falls SD 57108
866 928-1635

(G-6309)
FOLEY EQUIPMENT COMPANY
1701 E 5th St (67901-5320)
PHONE..................................620 626-6555
Doug Baringer, *Manager*
Bryan Garcia, *Manager*
EMP: 58
SALES (corp-wide): 124.2MM **Privately Held**
SIC: 5082 Construction & mining machinery
HQ: Foley Equipment Company
1550 S West St
Wichita KS 67213
316 943-4211

(G-6310)
FRONTIER LODGING LIBERAL LLC
Also Called: Holiday Inn
1550 N Lincoln Ave (67901-5208)
PHONE..................................620 624-9700
Paul Darling,
EMP: 20
SALES (est): 935.8K
SALES (corp-wide): 2.2MM **Privately Held**
SIC: 7011 Hotels & motels
PA: Americal Inc
500 S Boyd St
Aberdeen SD 57401
605 226-3163

(G-6311)
GATEWAY INN
720 E Pancake Blvd (67901-4327)
PHONE..................................620 624-0242
J Douglas Miller, *Owner*
EMP: 60
SALES (est): 1.2MM **Privately Held**
SIC: 7011 Motels

(G-6312)
GILMORE SHELLENBERGER & MAXWEL
500 N Kansas Ave (67901-3304)
PHONE..................................620 624-5599
Grant Shellenberg, *Owner*
Linda Gilmore, *Partner*
Jason Maxwell, *Partner*
EMP: 10 **EST:** 2000
SALES (est): 963.8K **Privately Held**
WEB: www.gsmpa.com
SIC: 8111 General practice attorney, lawyer

(G-6313)
GILMORES ROUSTABOUT SERVICE
1540 N Fairview Ave (67901-2223)
PHONE..................................620 624-0452
EMP: 15
SALES (est): 1.3MM **Privately Held**
SIC: 1389 Oilfield Roustabout Service

(G-6314)
GOLDEN PLAINS CREDIT UNION
21 Medical Dr (67901-5205)
P.O. Box 786 (67905-0786)
PHONE..................................620 624-8491
Jana Jantzen, *Director*
EMP: 15
SALES (corp-wide): 25MM **Privately Held**
SIC: 6062 State credit unions, not federally chartered
PA: Golden Plains Credit Union
1714 E Kansas Ave
Garden City KS 67846
620 275-8187

(G-6315)
GREENLEAF & BROOKS SMITH
400 N Washington Ave (67901-3444)
P.O. Box 2827 (67905-2827)
PHONE..................................620 624-6266
Eugene L Smith, *Partner*
Michael Allen, *Partner*
Steven L Brooks, *Partner*
Peter Olson, *Partner*
EMP: 11
SQ FT: 1,200
SALES (est): 424.2K **Privately Held**
SIC: 8111 General practice attorney, lawyer

(G-6316)
HAMPTON INN SUITES
508 Hotel Dr (67901-4232)
PHONE..................................620 604-0699
Claudia Garcia, *General Mgr*
EMP: 14
SALES (est): 709.2K **Privately Held**
SIC: 7011 Hotels & motels

(G-6317)
HARBISON-FISCHER INC
Also Called: Harbison-Fischer Sales
1470 General Welch Blvd (67901-5120)
P.O. Box 796 (67905-0796)
PHONE..................................620 624-9042
Gil Applehan, *Manager*
EMP: 5
SALES (corp-wide): 1.2B **Publicly Held**
WEB: www.hfpumps.com
SIC: 3533 3443 5084 Oil field machinery & equipment; tanks, lined: metal plate; oil well machinery, equipment & supplies
HQ: Harbison-Fischer, Inc.
901 N Crowley Rd
Crowley TX 76036
817 297-2211

(G-6318)
HARVEY & SON ELECTRIC
E Hwy 54 (67901)
PHONE..................................620 624-3688
Joe Harvey, *President*
EMP: 15
SQ FT: 2,500
SALES: 850K **Privately Held**
SIC: 1731 General electrical contractor

(G-6319)
HATCHER LAND & CATTLE COMPANY
1701 N Kansas Ave Ste 102 (67901-2000)
PHONE..................................620 624-1186
Nick Hatcher, *Partner*
Charlotte Hatcher, *Partner*
Lisa Hatcher, *Partner*
EMP: 11
SQ FT: 2,000
SALES (est): 214.5K **Privately Held**
SIC: 0211 0115 0131 Beef cattle feedlots; corn; cotton

(G-6320)
HAY & RICE ASSOC CHARTERED (PA)
21 Plaza Dr Ste 6 (67901-2790)
PHONE..................................620 624-8471
Darrell Hay, *President*
Craig Hay, *Corp Secy*
EMP: 17 **EST:** 1973
SQ FT: 5,600
SALES (est): 1.9MM **Privately Held**
SIC: 8721 Certified public accountant

(G-6321)
HOG SLAT INCORPORATED
1000 W Pancake Blvd (67901-3893)
PHONE..................................580 338-5003
Fritz Richards, *Manager*
EMP: 13
SALES (corp-wide): 553.2MM **Privately Held**
WEB: www.hogslat.com
SIC: 1542 5083 Farm building construction; livestock equipment
PA: Hog Slat, Incorporated
206 Fayetteville St
Newton Grove NC 28366
800 949-4647

(G-6322)
IAN F YEATS MD CHARTERED
1411 W 15th St Ste 102 (67901-2285)
PHONE..................................620 624-0142
Ian F Yeats MD, *Owner*
EMP: 12
SALES (est): 289.6K **Privately Held**
SIC: 8011 Offices & clinics of medical doctors

(G-6323)
INTERNTNAL PNCK DAY LIBERAL INC
318 N Lincoln Ave (67901-3334)
P.O. Box 665 (67905-0665)
PHONE..................................620 624-6423
Gary Callsen, *Chairman*
EMP: 20
SALES: 3.8K **Privately Held**
SIC: 8699 Charitable organization

(G-6324)
J-W OPERATING COMPANY
Also Called: J W Power Co
1480 General Welch Blvd (67901-5120)
P.O. Box 1068 (67905-1068)
PHONE....................620 626-7243
Fax: 620 626-4822
EMP: 11 **Privately Held**
SIC: 1311 5084 Crude Petroleum/Natural Gas Production Whol Industrial Equipment
HQ: J-W Operating Company
15505 Wright Brothers Dr B
Addison TX 75001
972 233-8191

(G-6325)
JIM OGRADY TRUCKING
720 W 2nd St (67901-3636)
P.O. Box 2910 (67905-2910)
PHONE....................620 624-5343
James Ogrady, *Owner*
Cindy Ogrady, *Co-Owner*
EMP: 15
SALES (est): 1.3MM **Privately Held**
SIC: 4213 Trucking, except local

(G-6326)
KANSAS CHILDRENS SERVICE LEAG
Also Called: Head Start
150 Plaza Dr Ste B (67901-2793)
PHONE....................620 626-5339
Julie Wright, *Director*
EMP: 15
SALES (corp-wide): 15MM **Privately Held**
WEB: www.kcsl.org+kansas+childrens+service+garde
SIC: 8322 Individual & family services
PA: Kansas Children's Service League
1365 N Custer St
Wichita KS 67203
316 942-4261

(G-6327)
KEATING TRACTOR & EQP INC
Also Called: John Deere Authorized Dealer
1900 W 2nd St (67901-5324)
P.O. Box 219 (67905-0219)
PHONE....................620 624-1668
Russ Keating, *President*
Julie Parsons, *Corp Secy*
Marlene Keating, *Vice Pres*
Stevie Headrick, *Parts Mgr*
Gene Sallee, *Sales Staff*
EMP: 20 **EST:** 1958
SQ FT: 4,500
SALES (est): 8.7MM **Privately Held**
WEB: www.keatingtractor.com
SIC: 5083 Farm equipment parts & supplies

(G-6328)
KENAI DRILLING LIMITED
2007 W 7th St (67901-5327)
PHONE....................805 937-7871
Robert Thacker, *Manager*
EMP: 248
SALES (corp-wide): 224.5MM **Privately Held**
SIC: 1781 Water well drilling
PA: Kenai Drilling Limited
6430 Cat Canyon Rd
Santa Maria CA 93454
805 937-7871

(G-6329)
KING ENTERPRISES INC
Also Called: King Excavating
1924 W 2nd St (67901-5324)
P.O. Box 1097 (67905-1097)
PHONE....................620 624-3332
Wayne King, *President*
Rodney King, *Vice Pres*
Tracy King, *Vice Pres*
EMP: 12 **EST:** 1949
SALES: 2.4MM **Privately Held**
SIC: 1731 1711 1794 General electrical contractor; plumbing contractors; warm air heating & air conditioning contractor; excavation work

(G-6330)
L & D OILFIELD SERVICE INC
11130 Hwy 54 (67901)
P.O. Box 1242 (67905-1242)
PHONE....................620 624-3329
Dale Scheuerman, *President*
Jessica Collins, *Corp Secy*
EMP: 5
SALES (est): 698.4K **Privately Held**
SIC: 1389 Oil field services; gas field services

(G-6331)
LIBERAL AREA RAPE CRISIS
Also Called: Larc Dvs
111 E 2nd St (67901-3855)
P.O. Box 1872 (67905-1872)
PHONE....................620 624-3079
Lori Hensley, *Exec Dir*
EMP: 10
SALES: 510.5K **Privately Held**
WEB: www.larcdvs.org
SIC: 8322 Crisis intervention center

(G-6332)
LIBERAL COUNTRY CLUB ASSN
339 W 18th St (67901-2465)
PHONE....................620 624-3992
Mike O'Kane, *President*
EMP: 27
SQ FT: 3,000
SALES: 657.4K **Privately Held**
SIC: 7997 Country club, membership

(G-6333)
LIBERAL GASKET MFG CO
15 W 5th St (67901-3323)
P.O. Box 2555 (67905-2555)
PHONE....................620 624-4921
Bill Griggs, *President*
Billy W Griggs, *President*
Greg W Griggs, *Vice Pres*
Joan Griggs, *Admin Sec*
EMP: 8
SQ FT: 14,000
SALES (est): 672K **Privately Held**
WEB: www.liberalgasket.com
SIC: 3053 Gaskets, all materials

(G-6334)
LIBERAL OFFICE MACHINES CO
Also Called: OFFICE OUTFITTERS
1015 N Kansas Ave (67901-2644)
PHONE....................620 624-5653
Larry D Wells, *President*
Gregory Wells, *Vice Pres*
EMP: 9
SQ FT: 3,000
SALES: 779.2K **Privately Held**
SIC: 2752 5943 5999 7699 Commercial printing, offset; office forms & supplies; typewriters; typewriter repair, including electric; office furniture

(G-6335)
LIBERAL SCHOOL DISTRICT
Educational Service Center
624 N Grant Ave (67901-3215)
PHONE....................620 604-2400
Lynn Ahrens, *Systems Dir*
Vicki Adams, *Administration*
EMP: 20
SALES (corp-wide): 31.6K **Privately Held**
SIC: 8211 8741 Public elementary & secondary schools; administrative management
PA: Liberal School District
401 N Kansas Ave
Liberal KS 67901
620 604-1010

(G-6336)
LIBERAL SUPER 8 MOTEL
747 E Pancake Blvd (67901-4320)
PHONE....................620 624-8880
Lynn Smith, *Manager*
EMP: 20
SALES (est): 499.9K **Privately Held**
SIC: 7011 Hotels & motels

(G-6337)
LONE STAR SERVICES LLC
6116 Old Hwy 54 (67901)
P.O. Box 499 (67905-0499)
PHONE....................620 626-7100
Larry Romme,
Kelley Romme, *Ch of Bd*
EMP: 30 **EST:** 2000
SQ FT: 6,000
SALES: 5MM **Privately Held**
SIC: 1389 4213 Oil field services; trucking, except local

(G-6338)
LYDDON AERO CENTER INC
757 Terminal Rd (67901-5117)
P.O. Box 945 (67905-0945)
PHONE....................620 624-1646
Jennifer Mannel, *Ch of Bd*
Steve Lyddon, *President*
William Lyddon, *Vice Pres*
EMP: 16
SQ FT: 44,000
SALES (est): 8.8MM **Privately Held**
WEB: www.lyddonaerocenter.com
SIC: 5172 4581 7359 8299 Aircraft fueling services; aircraft servicing & repairing; aircraft rental; flying instruction; flying charter service

(G-6339)
MANOR OF LIBERAL INC
1501 S Holly Dr (67901-2156)
PHONE....................620 624-0130
Mitchele Townsend, *Administration*
EMP: 60
SALES (est): 578.9K **Privately Held**
SIC: 8051 Skilled nursing care facilities

(G-6340)
MAS COW DAIRY LLC
1699 Rd 20 (67901)
PHONE....................620 626-7151
Bryan Hemann, *Mng Member*
Pete Tols,
EMP: 25 **EST:** 2013
SALES (est): 400.4K **Privately Held**
SIC: 0241 Dairy farms

(G-6341)
MERIT ENERGY COMPANY LLC
1900 W 2nd St (67901-5324)
P.O. Box 1293 (67905-1293)
PHONE....................620 629-4200
John Nichols, *Manager*
EMP: 20
SALES (corp-wide): 3.9B **Privately Held**
SIC: 1389 4911 Construction, repair & dismantling services; electric services
PA: Merit Energy Company, Llc
13737 Noel Rd Ste 1200
Dallas TX 75240
972 701-8377

(G-6342)
MIDWESTERN OILFIELD SVCS LLC
2461 Lilac Dr (67901-4942)
PHONE....................620 309-7027
Zachary Brown,
EMP: 5 **EST:** 2013
SALES (est): 211.9K **Privately Held**
SIC: 1389 Pipe testing, oil field service

(G-6343)
MIDWESTERN WELL SERVICE INC
341 S Country Estates Rd (67901-5314)
P.O. Box 263 (67905-0263)
PHONE....................620 624-8203
Cindy Bauer, *President*
EMP: 35
SQ FT: 1,500
SALES: 3MM **Privately Held**
SIC: 1389 Cleaning wells

(G-6344)
MIKES PIPE INSPECTION INC
417 E Oak St (67901-3857)
P.O. Box 218, Woodward OK (73802-0218)
PHONE....................620 624-9245
Fax: 620 624-1317
EMP: 25
SALES (est): 1.3MM
SALES (corp-wide): 536.3MM **Publicly Held**
SIC: 1389 Oil/Gas Field Services
PA: L. B. Foster Company
415 Holiday Dr Ste 1
Pittsburgh PA 15220
412 928-3400

(G-6345)
MOSAIC
441 Industrial Park Ave (67901-5107)
PHONE....................620 624-3817
David Jasper, *Director*
EMP: 65
SALES (corp-wide): 257.7MM **Privately Held**
WEB: www.mosaicinfo.org
SIC: 8093 Rehabilitation center, outpatient treatment
PA: Mosaic
4980 S 118th St
Omaha NE 68137
402 896-3884

(G-6346)
MYRIAD MACHINE CO
5 S Cntry Estates Rd (67901)
P.O. Box 1056 (67905-1056)
PHONE....................620 624-2962
Garret Van Vleet, *President*
Sheila Van Vleet, *Admin Sec*
EMP: 13
SQ FT: 15,000
SALES (est): 1.6MM **Privately Held**
SIC: 3599 Machine shop, jobbing & repair

(G-6347)
NALCO COMPANY
Also Called: Nalco Champion
1541 W Beckett St (67901)
PHONE....................620 624-1594
Fax: 620 624-0673
EMP: 5
SALES (corp-wide): 13.5B **Publicly Held**
SIC: 2819 Mfg Industrial Inorganic Chemicals
HQ: Nalco Company Llc
1601 W Diehl Rd
Naperville IL 60563
630 305-1000

(G-6348)
NATIONAL BEEF PACKING CO LLC
1501 E 8th St (67901-2879)
P.O. Box 978 (67905-0978)
PHONE....................800 449-2333
Randy Johnston, *Vice Pres*
Dean Aragon, *Purch Mgr*
Terry Gilbert, *Controller*
Dale Robertson, *Credit Mgr*
Karl Ulibarri, *Human Res Dir*
EMP: 14 **Privately Held**
SIC: 2011 Beef products from beef slaughtered on site
HQ: National Beef Packing Company, L.L.C.
12200 N Ambassador Dr # 5
Kansas City MO 64163
800 449-2333

(G-6349)
NATIONAL BEEF PACKING CO LLC
1501 E 8th St (67901-2879)
PHONE....................620 624-1851
John Miller, *Branch Mgr*
EMP: 157 **Privately Held**
WEB: www.nationalbeef.com
SIC: 2011 2015 Meat packing plants; poultry slaughtering & processing
HQ: National Beef Packing Company, L.L.C.
12200 N Ambassador Dr # 5
Kansas City MO 64163
800 449-2333

(G-6350)
NICHOLS WATER SVC AN OKLA CORP
Also Called: Nichols Fluid Service
316 Industrial Park Ave (67901-5104)
PHONE....................620 624-5582
Danny Slater, *Manager*
EMP: 18
SALES (corp-wide): 5.2MM **Privately Held**
WEB: www.nicoletwater.com
SIC: 4212 1389 Local trucking, without storage; oil field services

GEOGRAPHIC

PA: Nichols Water Service Inc An Oklahoma Corporation
E Hwy 64
Forgan OK 73938
580 487-3454

(G-6351)
OXY INC
1701 N Kansas Ave (67901-2000)
PHONE..................................620 629-4200
Del Olver, *Branch Mgr*
EMP: 13
SALES (corp-wide): 18.9B **Publicly Held**
SIC: 1311 Crude petroleum production
HQ: Oxy Inc.
5 Greenway Plz Ste 2400
Houston TX 77046
713 215-7000

(G-6352)
PANHANDLE EASTRN PIPE LINE LP
Also Called: Panhandle Eastern Pipeline
2330 N Kansas Ave (67901-2372)
PHONE..................................620 624-8661
John Kelly, *Partner*
EMP: 30
SALES (corp-wide): 54B **Publicly Held**
SIC: 4612 Crude petroleum pipelines
HQ: Panhandle Eastern Pipe Line Company, Lp
8111 Westchester Dr # 600
Dallas TX 75225
214 981-0700

(G-6353)
PANHANDLE EASTRN PIPE LINE LP
610 W 2nd St (67901-3612)
PHONE..................................620 624-7241
Ron Griffin, *Enginr/R&D Mgr*
EMP: 21
SALES (corp-wide): 54B **Publicly Held**
SIC: 1321 Natural gas liquids
HQ: Panhandle Eastern Pipe Line Company, Lp
8111 Westchester Dr # 600
Dallas TX 75225
214 981-0700

(G-6354)
PANHANDLE EASTRN PIPE LINE LP
13 1/2 E Us Highway 54 (67901)
PHONE..................................620 624-8661
Everett Tomilson, *Superintendent*
EMP: 27
SALES (corp-wide): 54B **Publicly Held**
SIC: 1389 Processing service, gas
HQ: Panhandle Eastern Pipe Line Company, Lp
8111 Westchester Dr # 600
Dallas TX 75225
214 981-0700

(G-6355)
PARK WHEATRIDGE CARE CENTER
Also Called: HERITAGE OF GERING
1501 S Holly Dr (67901-2156)
PHONE..................................620 624-0130
Jack Vetter, *President*
Steve McGill, *Corp Secy*
Bernard Dana, *Vice Pres*
Eldora Vetter, *Vice Pres*
EMP: 50
SQ FT: 800
SALES: 4.6MM
SALES (corp-wide): 60.6MM **Privately Held**
WEB: www.wheatridgepark.com
SIC: 8052 Personal care facility
PA: Vetter Health Services, Inc.
20220 Harney St
Elkhorn NE 68022
402 895-3932

(G-6356)
PEACHWAVE
1033 N Kansas Ave (67901-2644)
PHONE..................................620 624-2045
Caroline Archuleta, *Principal*
EMP: 5 **EST:** 2013
SALES (est): 285K **Privately Held**
SIC: 2024 Ice cream, bulk

(G-6357)
PEPSI-COLA METRO BTLG CO INC
212 S Virginia Ave (67901-3872)
PHONE..................................620 624-0287
Fax: 620 624-9106
EMP: 15
SALES (corp-wide): 63B **Publicly Held**
SIC: 5149 Whol Groceries
HQ: Pepsi-Cola Metropolitan Bottling Company, Inc.
1111 Westchester Ave
White Plains NY 10604
914 767-6000

(G-6358)
RAWHIDE WELL SERVICE LLC
1661 W 7th St (67901-5348)
P.O. Box 1988, Cody WY (82414-1988)
PHONE..................................620 624-2902
Jared T Nix,
A Dean Goedeker,
Kirchner Irrevokable Trust,
EMP: 40
SALES (est): 3MM **Privately Held**
SIC: 1389 Servicing oil & gas wells

(G-6359)
REHRIG PENN LOGISTICS INC
1620 W Pancake Blvd (67901-3879)
PHONE..................................620 624-5171
EMP: 9 **Privately Held**
SIC: 2842 Mfg Polish/Sanitation Goods
HQ: Rehrig Penn Logistics, Inc.
7800 100th St
Pleasant Prairie WI 53158
262 947-0032

(G-6360)
RES-CARE INC
418 S Washington Ave (67901-3830)
PHONE..................................620 624-5117
Terri Kaus, *Branch Mgr*
Annette Young, *Executive*
EMP: 48
SALES (corp-wide): 2B **Privately Held**
WEB: www.rescare.com
SIC: 8082 Home health care services
HQ: Res-Care, Inc.
805 N Whittington Pkwy
Louisville KY 40222
502 394-2100

(G-6361)
RONALD CARLILE
Also Called: Economy Storage
2240w Pine St (67901)
P.O. Box 2617 (67905-2617)
PHONE..................................620 624-2632
Ronald Carlile, *Owner*
EMP: 10
SQ FT: 3,900
SALES (est): 753.7K **Privately Held**
SIC: 4212 4225 0212 Local trucking, without storage; warehousing, self-storage; beef cattle except feedlots

(G-6362)
SANDHILL ORTHOPAEDIC
2132 N Kansas Ave Ste B (67901-2099)
PHONE..................................620 624-7400
Mariana E Lucero, *Principal*
EMP: 10
SALES (est): 451.5K **Privately Held**
SIC: 8099 Health & allied services

(G-6363)
SCHWABS TINKER SHOP INTL INC (PA)
430 Rollie Rd (67901)
P.O. Box 2764 (67905-2764)
PHONE..................................620 624-7611
John Schwab, *President*
Duane G Schwab, *Vice Pres*
▲ **EMP:** 5
SQ FT: 5,000
SALES (est): 1.2MM **Privately Held**
SIC: 3533 7699 Oil field machinery & equipment; industrial machinery & equipment repair

(G-6364)
SEWARD COUNTY BROADCASTING CO
Also Called: Kscb-Am-Fm Radio Station
1410 N Western Ave (67901-2212)
PHONE..................................620 624-3891
John C Landon, *President*
Stuart Melchert, *Corp Secy*
Lilia Sanchez, *Clerk*
EMP: 15
SALES (est): 1.3MM **Privately Held**
WEB: www.kscb.net
SIC: 4832 Radio broadcasting stations

(G-6365)
SEWARD COUNTY COUNCIL ON AGING
Also Called: SENIOR CITIZENS CENTER
701 N Grant Ave (67901-3216)
P.O. Box 376 (67905-0376)
PHONE..................................620 624-2511
Susan Roberts, *Exec Dir*
EMP: 23
SQ FT: 8,591
SALES: 459.9K **Privately Held**
SIC: 8322 Senior citizens' center or association

(G-6366)
SEWARD COUNTY HISTORICAL SOC
Also Called: DOROTHY'S HOUSE
567 E Cedar St (67901-3865)
PHONE..................................620 624-7624
Sherry Taylor, *Director*
EMP: 21
SQ FT: 3,900
SALES: 198.8K **Privately Held**
SIC: 8412 Museum

(G-6367)
SEWARD COUNTY PUBLISHING LLC
Also Called: High Plains Daily Leader
16 S Kansas Ave (67901-3732)
P.O. Box 889 (67905-0889)
PHONE..................................620 626-0840
Denasa Rice, *Office Mgr*
Earl Watts,
Rodger Crossman,
Jason Ett,
EMP: 28
SALES (est): 1.6MM **Privately Held**
WEB: www.hpleader.com
SIC: 2711 Commercial printing & newspaper publishing combined

(G-6368)
SHARP MCQUEEN MCKINLEY MORA
419 N Kansas Ave (67901-3329)
P.O. Box 2619 (67905-2619)
PHONE..................................620 624-2548
Kerry E McQueen, *President*
Kerry E Mc Queen, *President*
Shirla R McQueen,
Noel Nels,
Charles T Schimmel,
EMP: 20
SQ FT: 5,500
SALES (est): 1.5MM **Privately Held**
WEB: www.sharpmcqueen.com
SIC: 8111 General practice attorney, lawyer

(G-6369)
SOUTHWEST GLASS & DOOR INC
115 W 2nd St Ste 1 (67901-3768)
PHONE..................................620 626-7400
Jeff Mitchell, *President*
Jacki Mitchell, *Office Mgr*
EMP: 10
SQ FT: 15,800
SALES (est): 1.3MM **Privately Held**
SIC: 1793 7536 5211 Glass & glazing work; automotive glass replacement shops; garage doors, sale & installation

(G-6370)
SOUTHWEST GUIDANCE CENTER
333 W 15th St (67901-2455)
PHONE..................................620 624-8171
Rhonda McAdams, *Technology*
Jim Karlan, *Exec Dir*
EMP: 15
SALES (est): 1.7MM **Privately Held**
SIC: 8322 8011 Individual & family services; offices & clinics of medical doctors

(G-6371)
SOUTHWEST GUIDANCE CTR
21 Plaza Dr Ste 5 (67901-2790)
P.O. Box 2945 (67905-2945)
PHONE..................................620 624-0280
Mindy Martines, *Human Resources*
Jim Carlen, *Exec Dir*
EMP: 12
SALES: 1.8MM **Privately Held**
SIC: 8322 Child related social services

(G-6372)
SOUTHWEST MEDICAL CENTER (PA)
Also Called: Swmc
315 W 15th St (67901-2455)
P.O. Box 1340 (67905-1340)
PHONE..................................620 624-1651
William Ermann, *President*
Michele Gillespie, *Vice Pres*
EMP: 44
SQ FT: 145,500
SALES (est): 52.3MM **Privately Held**
SIC: 8062 8051 General medical & surgical hospitals; skilled nursing care facilities

(G-6373)
SUMMITT REST CARE LLC
2281 N Grant Ave (67901-2190)
PHONE..................................620 624-5117
Terri Kaus, *Partner*
EMP: 12
SALES (est): 347.5K **Privately Held**
SIC: 8093 Rehabilitation center, outpatient treatment

(G-6374)
SUNFLOWER BANK NATIONAL ASSN
711 N Kansas Ave (67901-3307)
PHONE..................................620 624-2063
Kayla Coleman, *Hum Res Coord*
Rick Harnden, *Branch Mgr*
Sarah Benoit, *Branch Mgr*
Jessica Determan, *Manager*
Bill Smellage, *Manager*
EMP: 10
SALES (corp-wide): 52.4MM **Privately Held**
SIC: 6021 National trust companies with deposits, commercial
HQ: Sunflower Bank, National Association
1400 16th St Ste 250
Denver CO 80202
888 827-5564

(G-6375)
TULS DAIRY FARMS LLC
12541 Road C (67901-5394)
PHONE..................................620 624-6455
Pete Tuls, *Partner*
Brian Hemann, *Partner*
EMP: 25
SQ FT: 2,000
SALES (est): 3.6MM **Privately Held**
SIC: 0241 Dairy farms

(G-6376)
U S WEATHERFORD L P
1401 E Pine St (67901-5632)
PHONE..................................620 624-9324
EMP: 12 **Privately Held**
SIC: 3533 Mfg Oil/Gas Field Machinery
HQ: U S Weatherford L P
2000 Saint James Pl
Houston TX 70395
713 693-4000

(G-6377)
U S WEATHERFORD L P
1500 General Welch Blvd (67901)
PHONE..................................620 624-6273
Les Franklin, *Manager*
EMP: 60 **Privately Held**
WEB: www.gaslift.com
SIC: 7359 7353 5082 Equipment rental & leasing; oil well drilling equipment, rental or leasing; oil field equipment

▲ = Import ▼=Export
◆ =Import/Export

HQ: U S Weatherford L P
179 Weatherford Dr
Schriever LA 70395
985 493-6100

(G-6378)
YOXALL ANTRIM & YOXALL
101 W 4th St (67901-3224)
PHONE..................................620 624-8444
Jim Yoxall, *Partner*
Nathanial Foreman, *Manager*
EMP: 10
SALES (est): 1.2MM **Privately Held**
SIC: 8111 General practice attorney, lawyer

Lincoln
Lincoln County

(G-6379)
APAC-KANSAS INC
1160 N Highway 14 (67455-9103)
P.O. Box 97 (67455-0097)
PHONE..................................785 524-4413
Rick White, *Manager*
EMP: 36
SALES (corp-wide): 29.7B **Privately Held**
SIC: 1429 Quartzite, crushed & broken-quarrying
HQ: Apac-Kansas, Inc.
9660 Legler Rd
Lenexa KS 66219

(G-6380)
COUNTY OF LINCOLN
Also Called: Lincoln Medical Clinic
313 E Franklin St (67455-1751)
PHONE..................................785 524-4474
Rita Peterson, *Manager*
Larry Dragone, *Osteopathy*
EMP: 11 **Privately Held**
SIC: 8011 Primary care medical clinic
PA: County Of Lincoln
216 E Lincoln Ave Ste D
Lincoln KS 67455
785 524-4757

(G-6381)
ENEL GREEN POWER N AMER INC
223 N Highway 14 (67455-9249)
PHONE..................................785 524-4900
EMP: 10
SALES (corp-wide): 42.1MM **Privately Held**
SIC: 4911 Generation, electric power
HQ: Enel Green Power North America, Inc.
100 Brickstone Sq Ste 300
Andover MA 01810
978 681-1900

(G-6382)
FINCH THEATRES
122 E Lincoln Ave (67455-2051)
P.O. Box 45 (67455-0045)
PHONE..................................785 524-4350
Deirdre Mahin, *Manager*
EMP: 14
SALES: 61.9K **Privately Held**
SIC: 7832 Motion picture theaters, except drive-in

(G-6383)
LINCOLN COUNTY HOSPITAL
624 N 2nd St (67455-1738)
PHONE..................................785 524-4403
Steve Granzow, *CEO*
Steven Granzow, *CEO*
Tawnya Seitz, *CFO*
EMP: 99
SALES (est): 8.6MM **Privately Held**
WEB: www.gpha.com
SIC: 8051 8062 Convalescent home with continuous nursing care; general medical & surgical hospitals

(G-6384)
LINCOLN SENTINEL REPUBLICAN
141 W Lincoln Ave (67455-1917)
P.O. Box 67 (67455-0067)
PHONE..................................785 524-4200
John Baetz, *Owner*
Bree Baetz, *Co-Owner*
EMP: 6
SALES (est): 361.4K **Privately Held**
WEB: www.lincolnsentinel.com
SIC: 2711 Newspapers, publishing & printing

(G-6385)
R & R STREET PLBG HTG & ELEC
Also Called: R & R Plumbing & Heating
2009 E Highway 18 (67455-9277)
P.O. Box 309 (67455-0309)
PHONE..................................785 524-4551
Mike Street, *President*
Ray Stauffer, *President*
Richard Gawith, *Vice Pres*
EMP: 10 **EST:** 1968
SQ FT: 2,394
SALES (est): 925.8K **Privately Held**
SIC: 1711 7623 7699 Plumbing contractors; warm air heating & air conditioning contractor; air conditioning repair; boiler & heating repair services

(G-6386)
RAPCO INC
365 N Highway 14 (67455-9250)
PHONE..................................785 524-4232
Richard Plinsky, *President*
EMP: 12
SALES: 1.5MM **Privately Held**
SIC: 8711 7389 Petroleum engineering; drafting service, except temporary help

(G-6387)
S & S AUTO BODY
229 W Lincoln Ave (67455-1919)
PHONE..................................785 524-4641
Jared Spear, *Owner*
EMP: 10 **EST:** 2010
SALES (est): 364.1K **Privately Held**
SIC: 7532 Body shop, automotive; body shop, trucks

(G-6388)
SALINE VALLEY FARM INC
2019 E Lark Dr (67455-9201)
PHONE..................................785 524-4562
Douglas Wilson, *CEO*
EMP: 10
SALES (est): 353.5K **Privately Held**
SIC: 0191 0291 7389 General farms, primarily crop; general farms, primarily animals;

(G-6389)
US TOWER CORP (PA)
702 E North St (67455-8926)
P.O. Box 285 (67455-0285)
PHONE..................................785 524-9966
Bruce Kopitar, *President*
Chuck Diehl, *Vice Pres*
Josh Wollberg, *Safety Mgr*
Ronnie Wood, *Program Mgr*
Dee Wenger, *Executive*
▲ **EMP:** 30
SQ FT: 175,000
SALES: 19.1MM **Privately Held**
WEB: www.ustower.com
SIC: 3441 Tower sections, radio & television transmission

(G-6390)
WALKER PRODUCTS COMPANY INC (PA)
414 S 6th St (67455-2505)
P.O. Box 349 (67455-0349)
PHONE..................................785 524-4107
Craig Walker, *President*
EMP: 18 **EST:** 1954
SQ FT: 2,500
SALES: 8MM **Privately Held**
SIC: 5153 3273 Grain elevators; ready-mixed concrete

Lindsborg
Mcpherson County

(G-6391)
BANK AMERICA NATIONAL ASSN
118 N Main St (67456-2227)
PHONE..................................785 227-3344
Kathlyn Wilhof, *Branch Mgr*
EMP: 15
SALES (corp-wide): 110.5B **Publicly Held**
WEB: www.bofa.com
SIC: 6021 National commercial banks
HQ: Bank Of America, National Association
100 S Tryon St
Charlotte NC 28202
704 386-5681

(G-6392)
BANK OF TESCOTT
202 N Main St (67456-2229)
PHONE..................................785 227-8830
Jenny Gotti, *President*
EMP: 11
SALES (corp-wide): 18.7MM **Privately Held**
SIC: 6022 State trust companies accepting deposits, commercial
PA: The Bank Of Tescott
104 S Main St
Tescott KS 67484
785 283-4217

(G-6393)
BETHANY COLLEGE
424 N 1st St (67456-1832)
PHONE..................................785 227-3380
Shwndra Fauchier, *Coordinator*
Kristin Van Tassel, *Assoc Prof*
EMP: 68
SALES (corp-wide): 163.2K **Privately Held**
WEB: www.bethanylb.edu
SIC: 7011 8221 Hostels; college, except junior
PA: Bethany College
335 E Swensson Ave
Lindsborg KS 67456
785 227-3311

(G-6394)
BETHANY HM ASSN LINDSBORG KANS
321 N Chestnut St (67456-1904)
PHONE..................................785 227-2334
Marlin Johnson, *President*
Shelley Conner, *Info Tech Mgr*
Deb Farres, *Director*
Delwin Koons, *Director*
Sara Anderson, *Nursing Dir*
EMP: 186
SQ FT: 25,000
SALES: 9.9MM **Privately Held**
SIC: 8051 8049 Skilled nursing care facilities; speech therapist; physical therapist; occupational therapist

(G-6395)
BETHANY HOME COTTAGE COMPLEX
321 N Chestnut St (67456-1999)
PHONE..................................785 227-2721
Karen Carlson, *QC Dir*
Jennifer Cantrell, *Marketing Staff*
Patricia Roraback, *Office Mgr*
Shiela Boyers, *Director*
Deb Farres, *Director*
EMP: 11
SALES: 160.2K **Privately Held**
SIC: 8051 6513 Convalescent home with continuous nursing care; apartment building operators

(G-6396)
COLUMBIA INDUSTRIES INC
Also Called: Columbia Glass Window
429 E Mcpherson St (67456-2839)
P.O. Box 429 (67456-0429)
PHONE..................................785 227-3351
Roy Rogers, *Opers Staff*
Ken Krueger, *Branch Mgr*
EMP: 20
SALES (est): 2.9MM
SALES (corp-wide): 3.2MM **Privately Held**
SIC: 3442 1751 2431 Storm doors or windows, metal; window & door (prefabricated) installation; millwork
PA: Columbia Industries Inc
1600 N Jackson Ave
Kansas City MO 64120
785 227-3087

(G-6397)
EAGLE CARE INC
840 N 2nd St (67456-1608)
PHONE..................................785 227-2304
John A Meyers, *President*
Bradley V Beckman, *Treasurer*
Greg K Diamonds, *Admin Sec*
EMP: 12
SALES (est): 477K **Privately Held**
SIC: 8051 Skilled nursing care facilities

(G-6398)
ERIK J PETERSON DDS
Also Called: Lindsborg Family Dental Care
101 N Harrison St (67456-2204)
P.O. Box 311 (67456-0311)
PHONE..................................785 227-2299
Erik J Peterson MD, *Owner*
EMP: 12
SALES (est): 644.2K **Privately Held**
SIC: 8021 Dentists' office

(G-6399)
HEMSLOJD INC
Also Called: Scandinavian Gifts
201 N Main St (67456-2228)
P.O. Box 152 (67456-0152)
PHONE..................................785 227-2983
Kenneth Swisher, *President*
Virginia Swisher, *Admin Sec*
EMP: 6
SQ FT: 5,000
SALES (est): 540.1K **Privately Held**
WEB: www.hemslojd.com
SIC: 5947 2499 5719 5961 Gift shop; decorative wood & woodwork; glassware; gift items, mail order

(G-6400)
LINDSBORG COMMUNITY HOSP ASSN
605 W Lincoln St (67456-2399)
PHONE..................................785 227-3308
Greg Lundstrom, *Administration*
Larry Van Der Wege, *Administration*
EMP: 83
SQ FT: 29,974
SALES: 11.9MM **Privately Held**
SIC: 8062 General medical & surgical hospitals

(G-6401)
LINDSBORG HOUSE 2
Also Called: Lindsborg II House
127 W Mcpherson St (67456-2717)
P.O. Box 408 (67456-0408)
PHONE..................................785 227-3652
Diedre Scott, *Manager*
Laura Williams, *Administration*
EMP: 12
SALES (est): 377.2K **Privately Held**
SIC: 8052 Intermediate care facilities

(G-6402)
MALM CONSTRUCTION CO
530 E State St Ste 269 (67456-2241)
P.O. Box 269 (67456-0269)
PHONE..................................785 227-3190
Deloris Malm, *Ch of Bd*
Paul K Malm, *President*
Kenneth Malm, *Vice Pres*
Terry Malm, *Vice Pres*
Elizabeth Palmquist, *Treasurer*
EMP: 15
SQ FT: 5,000
SALES: 1.5MM **Privately Held**
SIC: 1794 Excavation & grading, building construction

(G-6403)
MID-KANSAS COOPERATIVE ASSN
320 E Grant St (67456-2405)
P.O. Box 390 (67456-0390)
PHONE..................................785 227-3361

Steve Peterson, *Manager*
EMP: 12
SALES (corp-wide): 371.5MM **Privately Held**
WEB: www.mkcoop.com
SIC: 5541 0711 Filling stations, gasoline; fertilizer application services
PA: Mid-Kansas Cooperative Association
307 W Cole St
Moundridge KS 67107
620 345-6328

(G-6404)
MID-KANSAS COOPERATIVE ASSN
321 E Lincoln St (67456-2409)
P.O. Box 390 (67456-0390)
PHONE..................................785 227-3343
Steve Peterson, *Sales/Mktg Mgr*
EMP: 11
SALES (corp-wide): 371.5MM **Privately Held**
WEB: www.mkcoop.com
SIC: 5172 Gasoline
PA: Mid-Kansas Cooperative Association
307 W Cole St
Moundridge KS 67107
620 345-6328

(G-6405)
MULTI COMMUNITY DIVERSFD SVCS
Also Called: Lindsborg House
218 N Mckinley St (67456-2240)
PHONE..................................785 227-2712
Laura Willems, *Manager*
EMP: 13
SALES (corp-wide): 6.5MM **Privately Held**
WEB: www.cartridgekingks.com
SIC: 8052 Personal care facility
PA: Multi Community Diversified Services, Inc
2107 Industrial Dr
Mcpherson KS 67460
620 241-6693

(G-6406)
SWEDISH COUNTRY INN
112 W Lincoln St (67456-2319)
PHONE..................................785 227-2985
Carl Anderson, *Owner*
Becky Anderson, *Co-Owner*
EMP: 11
SALES (est): 350K **Privately Held**
WEB: www.swedishcountryinn.com
SIC: 7011 5947 Hotels; gift shop

Linn
Washington County

(G-6407)
JACKS FOOD MARKET
303 5th St (66953-9000)
P.O. Box 245 (66953-0245)
PHONE..................................785 348-5411
Jackie L Dieckmann, *Owner*
EMP: 8
SQ FT: 5,200
SALES: 850K **Privately Held**
SIC: 5411 3411 Supermarkets; tin cans

(G-6408)
LINN COMMUNITY NURSING HOME
612 3rd St (66953-9052)
P.O. Box 325 (66953-0325)
PHONE..................................785 348-5551
Kate Rieth, *Director*
Janell Wohler, *Administration*
EMP: 85 **EST:** 1971
SALES: 3.3MM **Privately Held**
SIC: 8052 8051 Intermediate care facilities; skilled nursing care facilities

(G-6409)
LINN POST & PIPE INC (PA)
711 Horizon Cir (66953-9043)
P.O. Box 276 (66953-0276)
PHONE..................................785 348-5526
Mike Peters, *President*
Mildred A Peters, *Corp Secy*
EMP: 48 **EST:** 1974
SQ FT: 28,800
SALES (est): 16.6MM **Privately Held**
WEB: www.linnpost.com
SIC: 5083 3523 Livestock equipment; farm machinery & equipment

(G-6410)
LITTLE CREEK DAIRY
1510 10th Rd (66953-9262)
PHONE..................................785 348-5576
Lee Holtmeier, *CEO*
EMP: 20
SALES (est): 1MM **Privately Held**
SIC: 6531 0241 Real estate brokers & agents; milk production

(G-6411)
OHLDES DAIRY INC
1814 9th Rd (66953-9288)
PHONE..................................785 348-5697
Steve Ohlde, *President*
EMP: 14
SALES (est): 2.2MM **Privately Held**
SIC: 0241 Dairy farms

(G-6412)
TITAN WEST INC
203 5th St (66953-9016)
P.O. Box 8 (66953-0008)
PHONE..................................785 348-5660
Dan Smerchek, *President*
Dave Smerchek, *President*
Linda Smerchek, *Corp Secy*
EMP: 35
SQ FT: 1,400
SALES (est): 8.6MM **Privately Held**
WEB: www.titanwestinc.com
SIC: 3523 Cattle feeding, handling & watering equipment

(G-6413)
WHOLMOOR AMRCN LGION POST 237
100 5th St (66953-9021)
P.O. Box 321 (66953-0321)
PHONE..................................785 348-5370
Jolene Parrack, *Manager*
EMP: 15
SALES: 131.8K **Privately Held**
SIC: 8641 Veterans' organization

Linn Valley
Linn County

(G-6414)
LINN VALLEY LAKE PROPERTY ASSN
9 Linn Valley Ave (66040-6147)
PHONE..................................913 757-4591
Pam McCoy, *General Mgr*
EMP: 25
SALES (est): 1.2MM **Privately Held**
SIC: 7041 Residence club, organization

Linwood
Leavenworth County

(G-6415)
ALEX R MASSON INC (PA)
12819 198th St (66052-4646)
P.O. Box 170 (66052-0170)
PHONE..................................913 301-3281
Alexander Masson, *Ch of Bd*
Deanna Fitch, *CFO*
▲ **EMP:** 68 **EST:** 1919
SQ FT: 5,000
SALES (est): 37.8MM **Privately Held**
SIC: 5193 Plants, potted

(G-6416)
CHRISTIAN CH OF GRATER KANS CY
Also Called: Tall Oaks Conf Ctr
12778 189th St (66052-4535)
PHONE..................................913 301-3004
Raymond Fancher, *Manager*
EMP: 10 **Privately Held**
SIC: 7389 Convention & show services
PA: The Christian Church Of Greater Kansas City
5700 Broadmoor St
Shawnee Mission KS 66202

(G-6417)
OLD WORLD CABINETS INC
322 Main St (66052-4363)
P.O. Box 140 (66052-0140)
PHONE..................................913 723-3740
Robert Hilt, *President*
EMP: 9
SQ FT: 4,000
SALES: 687K **Privately Held**
SIC: 2434 2521 Wood kitchen cabinets; cabinets, office: wood

Little River
Rice County

(G-6418)
GALYON LUMBER INC
798 26th Rd (67457-9120)
PHONE..................................620 897-6290
Philip Galyon, *President*
Dennis Galyon, *Vice Pres*
Alex Galyon, *Treasurer*
Chris Galyon, *Admin Sec*
EMP: 10
SQ FT: 1,800
SALES: 2MM **Privately Held**
SIC: 5031 Lumber: rough, dressed & finished

(G-6419)
HOSPITAL DISTRICT 2 RICE CNTY
Also Called: Sandstone Heights Nursing Home
440 State St (67457-9107)
PHONE..................................620 897-6266
Karen Halbert, *Partner*
John Gaines, *Director*
EMP: 65
SALES (est): 2.9MM **Privately Held**
SIC: 8051 Skilled nursing care facilities

Logan
Phillips County

(G-6420)
BAIRD OIL CO INC
113 W Main St (67646-5152)
P.O. Box 428 (67646-0428)
PHONE..................................785 689-7456
Jim R Baird, *President*
Robert Hartman, *Exec VP*
EMP: 5
SALES (est): 900K **Privately Held**
SIC: 1311 1382 Crude petroleum production; oil & gas exploration services

(G-6421)
CITY OF LOGAN
302 W Logan St (67646-5117)
PHONE..................................785 689-4227
Nancy Conyac, *Branch Mgr*
EMP: 60 **Privately Held**
SIC: 8051 Skilled nursing care facilities
PA: City Of Logan
105 W Main St
Logan KS 67646
785 689-4865

(G-6422)
CITY OF LOGAN
Also Called: Logan Manor Nursing Home
108 S Adams St (67646-5115)
P.O. Box 308 (67646-0308)
PHONE..................................785 689-4201
Teresa McComb, *Supervisor*
Theresa McComb, *Director*
EMP: 46 **Privately Held**
SIC: 8051 Convalescent home with continuous nursing care
PA: City Of Logan
105 W Main St
Logan KS 67646
785 689-4865

(G-6423)
DANE G HANSEN MEMORIAL M
110 W Main St (67646-5152)
PHONE..................................785 689-4848
Shirley Henrickson, *Director*
EMP: 13
SALES: 200K **Privately Held**
SIC: 8412 Museum

(G-6424)
GODDARD MANUFACTURING INC
107 S Mill St (67646-5112)
P.O. Box 502 (67646-0502)
PHONE..................................785 689-4341
Jerry Goddard, *President*
Ruth Goddard, *Vice Pres*
▼ **EMP:** 8
SQ FT: 10,000
SALES: 350K **Privately Held**
WEB: www.spiral-staircases.com
SIC: 3446 2431 Stairs, staircases, stair treads: prefabricated metal; staircases & stairs, wood

(G-6425)
KISER AG SERVICE LLC (PA)
305 S Douglas St (67646-5116)
P.O. Box 188 (67646-0188)
PHONE..................................785 689-4292
Randy Kiser,
EMP: 7
SALES (est): 954K **Privately Held**
SIC: 3523 Sprayers & spraying machines, agricultural

(G-6426)
LOGAN FUNERAL HOME
Also Called: Great Plains Funeral Service
102 E Church St (67646-5061)
P.O. Box 217 (67646-0217)
PHONE..................................785 689-4211
Ronald Boeve, *Owner*
Darlene Garman, *Office Mgr*
EMP: 12
SALES: 273.7K **Privately Held**
SIC: 7261 Funeral home

Long Island
Phillips County

(G-6427)
HUSKY HOGS LLC
1271 W Fox Rd (67647-9637)
P.O. Box 8 (67647-0008)
PHONE..................................785 854-7666
Terry Nelson, *Owner*
Bradley Hopkins, *Mng Member*
Norman T Nelson,
EMP: 50
SALES (est): 4.4MM **Privately Held**
SIC: 0213 Hogs

(G-6428)
LONG ISLAND GRAIN CO INC
Hwy 383 N Of Town (67647)
P.O. Box 97 (67647-0097)
PHONE..................................785 854-7431
Gary Hammond, *President*
Craig Hammond, *Vice Pres*
EMP: 10 **EST:** 1964
SQ FT: 2,000
SALES (est): 3.1MM **Privately Held**
SIC: 5153 4212 5191 2041 Grain elevators; local trucking, without storage; fertilizer & fertilizer materials; feed; seeds: field, garden & flower; chemicals, agricultural; flour & other grain mill products

(G-6429)
VALLEY FEEDS INC
2 1/2 Mile W (67647)
P.O. Box 38 (67647-0038)
PHONE..................................785 854-7611
N T Nelson, *President*
EMP: 28
SALES (est): 1.7MM **Privately Held**
SIC: 0211 Beef cattle feedlots

▲ = Import ▼=Export
◆ =Import/Export

Longford
Clay County

(G-6430)
HENRYS LTD
822 6th Rd (67458-9371)
PHONE..................................785 388-2480
Roy J Henry, *President*
Mary Wade, *Corp Secy*
S C Henry, *Vice Pres*
Linda Henry, *Treasurer*
EMP: 16
SALES (est): 1.7MM **Privately Held**
WEB: www.henrys.com
SIC: 0213 0191 Hogs; general farms, primarily crop

(G-6431)
LONGFORD RODEO LLC
Rodeo Grounds (67458)
PHONE..................................785 388-2330
Lyle Perry,
EMP: 60
SALES (est): 271K **Privately Held**
SIC: 7999 Rodeo operation

(G-6432)
LONGFORD WATER COMPANY LLC
108 Main St (67458)
P.O. Box 158 (67458-0158)
PHONE..................................785 388-2233
Kim Kramer, *Mng Member*
Wava Kramer,
EMP: 6
SQ FT: 1,500
SALES (est): 160.9K **Privately Held**
WEB: www.kiowata.com
SIC: 3069 Water bottles, rubber

Lorraine
Ellsworth County

(G-6433)
MOLY MANUFACTURING INC
Also Called: Silencer
2435 10th Rd (67459-9338)
PHONE..................................785 472-3388
Jon D Mollhagen, *President*
Patricia L Mollhagen, *Corp Secy*
▲ **EMP**: 40
SALES (est): 10.1MM **Privately Held**
WEB: www.molysilencerchutes.com
SIC: 3523 Cattle feeding, handling & watering equipment

(G-6434)
PRAXAIR INC
2486 8th Rd (67459-9302)
PHONE..................................620 562-4500
John Hill, *Principal*
EMP: 20 **Privately Held**
SIC: 2813 Industrial gases
HQ: Praxair, Inc.
10 Riverview Dr
Danbury CT 06810
203 837-2000

Louisburg
Miami County

(G-6435)
ACENTRIC LLC
26025 Metcalf Rd (66053-6206)
PHONE..................................913 787-4856
Debbie Akins, *Mng Member*
Debra Rau,
EMP: 10
SALES (est): 353.8K **Privately Held**
SIC: 0782 1711 Landscape contractors; irrigation sprinkler system installation

(G-6436)
AGAPE MORTGAGE PARTNERS CORP (PA)
105 E Amity St Ste 8 (66053-4076)
PHONE..................................913 871-7377
EMP: 18
SALES (est): 3.3MM **Privately Held**
SIC: 6163 Mortgage Broker

(G-6437)
ALAN GROVE COMPONENTS INC
27070 Metcalf Rd (66053-6202)
PHONE..................................913 837-4368
Alan Grove, *President*
EMP: 5
SQ FT: 4,500
SALES (est): 603.7K **Privately Held**
WEB: www.alangrovecomponents.com
SIC: 3465 Body parts, automobile: stamped metal

(G-6438)
ANN N HOGAN LLC
Also Called: Matcalf Ridge Golf Club
6302 W 295th St (66053-5121)
P.O. Box 699 (66053-0699)
PHONE..................................913 271-7440
David Welch,
EMP: 30
SALES (est): 794.4K **Privately Held**
SIC: 7997 Golf club, membership

(G-6439)
APPLE ELECTRIC INC
209 N Broadway St (66053-3536)
P.O. Box 626 (66053-0626)
PHONE..................................913 837-5285
Gary Schleicher, *President*
Patton Apple, *Vice Pres*
Deborah L Apple, *Treasurer*
EMP: 11
SQ FT: 4,000
SALES (est): 1.5MM **Privately Held**
SIC: 1731 General electrical contractor

(G-6440)
BAZIN SAWING & DRILLING LLC
30790 Switzer Rd (66053-5903)
PHONE..................................913 764-0843
Mary Bazin, *Owner*
EMP: 16 **EST**: 2008
SALES (est): 2.2MM **Privately Held**
SIC: 3546 3541 Drills & drilling tools; machine tools, metal cutting type; drilling & boring machines

(G-6441)
BOBCAT OIL FIELD SERVICE INC
27260 Normandy Rd (66053-5244)
PHONE..................................913 980-3858
Robert Eberhart II, *Partner*
EMP: 16
SALES (est): 200K **Privately Held**
SIC: 1311 Crude petroleum production

(G-6442)
CERTIFIED LIFE SAFETY LLC
5880 W 319th St (66053-6188)
PHONE..................................913 837-5319
Gail Brown, *Principal*
EMP: 6
SALES (est): 528.6K **Privately Held**
SIC: 3669 Fire alarm apparatus, electric

(G-6443)
CIRCLE C COUNTRY SUPPLY INC (PA)
204 N Broadway St (66053-3536)
P.O. Box 103, Bazine (67516-0103)
PHONE..................................785 398-2571
Chris Corsair, *President*
Nicole Corsair, *Vice Pres*
EMP: 10
SALES (est): 4.2MM **Privately Held**
WEB: www.circlecsupply.com
SIC: 6531 Real estate agent, commercial

(G-6444)
CROWN REALTY OF KANSAS INC
100 Crestview Cir Ste 101 (66053-6472)
PHONE..................................913 837-5155
Michael S Miller, *Partner*
Tammy Waterman, *Office Mgr*
Doug Bowes, *Branch Mgr*
Dara Stambaugh, *Agent*
Joe Hannon, *Associate*
EMP: 24
SALES (corp-wide): 10MM **Privately Held**
SIC: 6531 Real estate agent, residential; real estate brokers & agents
PA: Crown Realty Of Kansas Inc
102 S Silver St
Paola KS
913 557-4333

(G-6445)
CUTTING EDGE TRUCKING INC
8 S 4th St (66053-4099)
P.O. Box 597 (66053-0597)
PHONE..................................913 837-2249
Dough Teuser, *President*
EMP: 20
SALES: 2MM **Privately Held**
SIC: 4212 Local trucking, without storage

(G-6446)
ELLIOTT INSURANCE INC (PA)
278 Fairlane Dr (66053-4598)
PHONE..................................913 294-2110
Rick Elliott, *President*
Del McCullough, *Vice Pres*
Brock Elliott, *Producer*
EMP: 17
SALES (est): 6.4MM **Privately Held**
SIC: 6411 Insurance agents

(G-6447)
ENERGY TECH UNLIMITED LLC
306 Broadmoor Dr (66053-6439)
PHONE..................................913 837-4616
Thomas Overbay, *COO*
Tom Overbay, *COO*
EMP: 5
SALES (est): 528K **Privately Held**
SIC: 2869 Fuels

(G-6448)
FIRST NATIONAL BANK LOUISBURG (PA)
1201 W Amity St (66053-4121)
PHONE..................................913 837-5191
George C Karnaze, *President*
Joseph A Mc Liney, *Chairman*
Robert Nauman, *Vice Pres*
EMP: 10
SQ FT: 5,500
SALES: 4.5MM **Privately Held**
WEB: www.fnblouisburg.com
SIC: 6021 National commercial banks

(G-6449)
G-B CONSTRUCTION LLC
30790 Switzer Rd (66053-5903)
P.O. Box 1305 (66053-1305)
PHONE..................................913 837-5240
George Bazin,
EMP: 23
SALES (est): 2.7MM **Privately Held**
SIC: 1521 Single-family housing construction

(G-6450)
GRACE AGAPES INC
2 S Mulberry St (66053-6429)
PHONE..................................913 837-5885
Susan Juarez, *Exec Dir*
EMP: 26 **EST**: 2010
SALES (est): 900K **Privately Held**
SIC: 7389

(G-6451)
GRANNYS
201 Crestview Cir (66053-3582)
PHONE..................................913 837-5222
Sondra Gilmore, *Owner*
EMP: 25 **EST**: 1997
SALES: 275.4K **Privately Held**
SIC: 8351 Group day care center

(G-6452)
JEM INDUSTRIES INC
Also Called: Bomar Designs
208 S 1st St (66053-6312)
P.O. Box 10 (66053-0010)
PHONE..................................913 837-3202
Ed Semple, *President*
EMP: 8 **EST**: 1997
SQ FT: 5,000
SALES (est): 550K **Privately Held**
WEB: www.bomardesigns.com
SIC: 3089 Molding primary plastic

(G-6453)
KING WOOD PRODUCTS INC
609 S Metcalf Rd (66053-4035)
P.O. Box 703 (66053-0703)
PHONE..................................913 837-5300
Sam King, *President*
Cliff King, *Vice Pres*
Melissa King, *Treasurer*
Lianghua Wang, *Human Res Dir*
Delbert King, *Admin Sec*
EMP: 13
SQ FT: 6,500
SALES (est): 1.1MM **Privately Held**
SIC: 1751 Cabinet building & installation

(G-6454)
LA MESA MEXICAN RESTAURANT
116 Harvest Dr (66053-4081)
PHONE..................................913 837-3455
Oracio Palomino, *Branch Mgr*
EMP: 15 **Privately Held**
SIC: 5499 5812 7299 Gourmet food stores; Mexican restaurant; banquet hall facilities
PA: La Mesa Mexican Restaurant
1405 Fort Crook Rd S
Bellevue NE 68005

(G-6455)
LANDGENUITY LLC
1001 N 2nd St E (66053-6409)
P.O. Box 1471 (66053-1471)
PHONE..................................913 594-1845
Lara Justesen, *Mng Member*
EMP: 50
SALES (est): 655.3K **Privately Held**
SIC: 0781 Landscape architects

(G-6456)
LARRY BAIR EXCAVATING INC
Also Called: Bair Products
2785 W 247th St (66053-7225)
PHONE..................................913 947-7222
Larry Bair, *President*
Shane Bair, *Vice Pres*
Tonya Bair, *Vice Pres*
Shawn Shipps, *Supervisor*
Karen Bair, *Admin Sec*
EMP: 20
SALES (est): 4.6MM **Privately Held**
SIC: 1794 Excavation & grading, building construction

(G-6457)
LOUISBURG CHAMBER OF COMMERCE
16 S Broadway St (66053-3613)
P.O. Box 245 (66053-0245)
PHONE..................................913 837-2826
Julie Baalmann, *President*
Sue Knop, *President*
Patsy Bortner, *Exec Dir*
Steve Ward, *Director*
Cathy Johns, *Admin Sec*
EMP: 13
SALES: 19.1K **Privately Held**
WEB: www.louisburgkansas.com
SIC: 8611 Chamber of Commerce

(G-6458)
MOKAN DIAL INC
112 S Broadway St (66053-4082)
P.O. Box 429 (66053-0429)
PHONE..................................913 837-2219
Larry Townes, *President*
EMP: 12 **EST**: 1961
SQ FT: 1,500
SALES (est): 1.5MM
SALES (corp-wide): 25.4MM **Privately Held**
WEB: www.mokandial.com
SIC: 4813 Local & long distance telephone communications
PA: Townes Tele-Communications, Inc.
120 E 1st St
Lewisville AR 71845
870 921-4224

(G-6459)
NATE APPLE CONCRETE INC
7840 W 255th St (66053-6282)
PHONE..................................913 837-3022
Nate Apple, *President*
Sue Apple, *Treasurer*

EMP: 25
SALES (est): 2.6MM **Privately Held**
SIC: 1771 Curb & sidewalk contractors; driveway contractor; parking lot construction; foundation & footing contractor

(G-6460)
NATIONAL EXPRESS LLC
Also Called: Durham School Services
7420 W 68 Hwy (66053)
P.O. Box 940 (66053-0940)
PHONE..................................913 837-4470
Larry Pence, *Manager*
EMP: 20 **Privately Held**
SIC: 4151 4141 School buses; local bus charter service
HQ: National Express Llc
2601 Navistar Dr
Lisle IL 60532

(G-6461)
PANHANDLE EASTRN PIPE LINE LP
29115 Metcalf Rd (66053-8313)
PHONE..................................913 837-5163
Dan Corpening, *Enginr/R&D Mgr*
EMP: 26
SALES (corp-wide): 54B **Publicly Held**
SIC: 4922 Natural gas transmission
HQ: Panhandle Eastern Pipe Line Company, Lp
8111 Westchester Dr # 600
Dallas TX 75225
214 981-0700

(G-6462)
PENNYS CONCRETE INC
7905 W 247th St (66053-7311)
PHONE..................................913 441-8781
William Penny, *Owner*
EMP: 30
SALES (corp-wide): 43.9MM **Privately Held**
SIC: 3273 Ready-mixed concrete
PA: Penny's Concrete, Inc.
23400 W 82nd St
Shawnee Mission KS 66227
913 441-8781

(G-6463)
RABBIT CREEK PRODUCTS INC
903 N Broadway St (66053-3541)
P.O. Box 1059 (66053-1059)
PHONE..................................913 837-3073
Donna A Cook, *President*
EMP: 18
SQ FT: 4,000
SALES (est): 2.7MM **Privately Held**
WEB: www.rabbitcreekgourmet.com
SIC: 2034 2099 Dried & dehydrated soup mixes; seasonings & spices

(G-6464)
RANDOLPH CARTER ENTPS INC
Also Called: Randolf Carter Trucking
5 S Peoria St Ste 213 (66053-6440)
PHONE..................................913 837-3955
Keith O Randolph, *President*
EMP: 18
SQ FT: 250
SALES (est): 2.5MM **Privately Held**
SIC: 4212 Delivery service, vehicular

(G-6465)
RH MONTGOMERY PROPERTIES INC
Also Called: Louisburg Residential Care Ctr
1200 S Broadway St (66053-3607)
P.O. Box 339 (66053-0339)
PHONE..................................913 837-2916
Denise German, *Manager*
EMP: 60
SALES (corp-wide): 31.9MM **Privately Held**
SIC: 8051 Skilled nursing care facilities
PA: Rh Montgomery Properties, Inc.
214 N Scott St
Sikeston MO 63801
573 471-1113

(G-6466)
ROMANS OUTDOOR POWER INC
Also Called: Kubota Authorized Dealer
203 Crestview Cir (66053-3582)
PHONE..................................913 837-5225
Tim Kinder, *President*
EMP: 30
SALES (corp-wide): 6.6MM **Privately Held**
SIC: 7699 5531 5261 5083 Motorcycle repair service; automotive & home supply stores; lawnmowers & tractors; tractors, agricultural
PA: Romans Outdoor Power Inc
3011 W Main St
Independence KS 67301
620 331-2970

(G-6467)
SOUTHVIEW HOMECARE (PA)
107 S Broadway St Ste D (66053-4082)
PHONE..................................913 837-5121
Edward Lewis, *President*
Carrie Guresey, *Manager*
EMP: 12
SALES (est): 853.8K **Privately Held**
WEB: www.southviewhomecare.com
SIC: 8082 Home health care services

(G-6468)
VINTAGE PRK ASSISTD LVNG RSDNC
202 S Rogers Rd (66053-4064)
PHONE..................................913 837-5133
Tom Reddy, *President*
David O Smith, *Vice Pres*
Denise German, *Treasurer*
EMP: 19
SQ FT: 10,000
SALES: 700K **Privately Held**
SIC: 6513 Residential hotel operation

(G-6469)
WESTERN METAL COMPANY INC (PA)
1202 S Metcalf Rd (66053-4180)
P.O. Box 880 (66053-0880)
PHONE..................................913 681-8787
Doug Furnell, *President*
EMP: 10
SQ FT: 1,000
SALES (est): 1.5MM **Privately Held**
SIC: 5039 Metal buildings

Louisville
Pottawatomie County

(G-6470)
PROCKISH TRUCKING & EXCAVATING
409 E Hickory St (66547-7024)
PHONE..................................785 456-7320
Eugene Prockish, *Owner*
Jean Prockish, *Partner*
EMP: 16
SALES (est): 600K **Privately Held**
SIC: 4212 1794 Dump truck haulage; excavation & grading, building construction

Lucas
Russell County

(G-6471)
GREAT PLAINS MANUFACTURING INC
Also Called: Landpride
240 S Greeley Ave (67648-8823)
P.O. Box 407 (67648-0407)
PHONE..................................785 525-6128
Les Schneider, *Manager*
EMP: 50 **Privately Held**
WEB: www.greatplainsmfg.com
SIC: 3523 Farm machinery & equipment
HQ: Great Plains Manufacturing Incorporated
1525 E North St
Salina KS 67401
785 823-3276

(G-6472)
HEARTLAND HAY
1237 N 13th Rd (67648-9600)
PHONE..................................785 525-6331
Gene Mietler, *Owner*
EMP: 13
SQ FT: 1,000
SALES (est): 1.7MM **Privately Held**
SIC: 5191 Hay

(G-6473)
LUCAS ARTS HMNTIES COUNCIL INC
Also Called: GRASSROOTS ART CENTER
213 S Main St (67648-9718)
P.O. Box 304 (67648-0304)
PHONE..................................785 525-6118
Charlie Litchfield, *Technology*
Rosslyn Schultz, *Director*
EMP: 12
SALES: 177.1K **Privately Held**
SIC: 8412 Arts or science center

(G-6474)
MARTIN JAMES
Also Called: Martin & Son Logging
354 W 290th Dr (67648-9103)
PHONE..................................785 525-7761
James Martin, *Owner*
Susan Martin, *CFO*
EMP: 6
SALES (est): 165K **Privately Held**
SIC: 2411 5099 Logging camps & contractors; firewood

(G-6475)
UNITED AG SERVICE INC
300 W S Harvest St (67648)
PHONE..................................785 525-6455
Joel Brown, *General Mgr*
EMP: 12
SALES (corp-wide): 37.5MM **Privately Held**
SIC: 5153 Grain elevators
PA: United Ag Service Inc
129 Clifford St
Gorham KS 67640
785 637-5481

Lyndon
Osage County

(G-6476)
COUNTY OF OSAGE
Also Called: Osage Co Hwy Dept
1215 Washington (66451)
P.O. Box 281 (66451-0281)
PHONE..................................785 828-4444
Glen Tyson, *Principal*
EMP: 15 **Privately Held**
WEB: www.osageco.org
SIC: 4959 9111 Road, airport & parking lot maintenance services; county supervisors' & executives' offices
PA: County Of Osage
717 Topeka Ave
Lyndon KS 66451
785 828-3124

(G-6477)
LYNDON STATE BANK (PA)
817 Topeka Ave (66451-9864)
P.O. Box 518 (66451-0518)
PHONE..................................785 828-4411
Clyde Burns, *Ch of Bd*
Chris Cole, *Vice Pres*
David Thornburgh, *Vice Pres*
Willa Mishler, *Opers-Prdtn-Mfg*
Kathy Zabel, *Cashier*
EMP: 25 **EST:** 1901
SQ FT: 5,500
SALES: 3.8MM **Privately Held**
WEB: www.lyndonstatebank.com
SIC: 6022 State trust companies accepting deposits, commercial

(G-6478)
OSAGE CNTY ECNMIC DEV CORP INC
P.O. Box 226 (66451-0226)
PHONE..................................785 828-3242
Stephanie Watson, *Manager*
EMP: 99
SALES (est): 5.4MM **Privately Held**
SIC: 8741 Management services

Lyons
Rice County

(G-6479)
BAR K BAR TRUCKING INC
Also Called: Branson Truck Line
1700 E Us Highway 56 (67554-8813)
PHONE..................................620 257-5118
Kenny Knight, *President*
EMP: 15 **EST:** 1952
SALES (est): 1MM **Privately Held**
WEB: www.artguildbinders.com
SIC: 4213 Trucking, except local

(G-6480)
COMPASS MINERALS AMERICA INC
1662 Avenue N (67554-9201)
PHONE..................................620 257-2324
Mike Chisam, *Plant Mgr*
EMP: 125
SALES (corp-wide): 1.4B **Publicly Held**
SIC: 2819 Industrial inorganic chemicals
HQ: Compass Minerals America Inc
9900 W 109th St Ste 600
Overland Park KS 66210
913 344-9100

(G-6481)
CORNERSTONE DAY CARE PRESCHOOL
803 S Dinsmore Ave (67554-3632)
PHONE..................................620 257-5622
Yvonna Nave, *Exec Dir*
EMP: 10 **EST:** 2009
SALES (est): 247.7K **Privately Held**
SIC: 8351 Preschool center

(G-6482)
EAGLE BAR RANCH INC
1768 Avenue J (67554-8805)
PHONE..................................620 257-5106
Kenneth Knight, *President*
EMP: 30
SALES (est): 1.4MM **Privately Held**
SIC: 0211 Beef cattle feedlots

(G-6483)
EVANGELICAL LUTHERAN
Also Called: Good Samaritan Society - Lyons
1311 S Douglas Ave (67554-3704)
PHONE..................................620 257-5163
Lesa Dechant, *Branch Mgr*
EMP: 65 **Privately Held**
WEB: www.good-sam.com
SIC: 8059 Nursing home, except skilled & intermediate care facility
HQ: The Evangelical Lutheran Good Samaritan Society
4800 W 57th St
Sioux Falls SD 57108
866 928-1635

(G-6484)
HOSPITAL DISTRICT 1 RICE CNTY
Also Called: Rice Community Healthcare
619 S Clark Ave (67554-3003)
P.O. Box 828 (67554-0828)
PHONE..................................620 257-5173
George Scover, *Principal*
Terry Pound, *CFO*
EMP: 145
SQ FT: 60,000
SALES: 110.8K **Privately Held**
SIC: 8062 General medical & surgical hospitals

(G-6485)
HOSPITAL DST 1 OF RICE CNTY (PA)
Also Called: Lyons Hospital
619 S Clark Ave (67554-3003)
P.O. Box 828 (67554-0828)
PHONE..................................620 257-5173
Darren Bottom, *Safety Dir*
Janet Bruce, *Opers Staff*
Kim Williams, *Human Res Mgr*
Lana Brown, *Director*

Sharon Mead, *Director*
EMP: 56 **EST:** 1959
SQ FT: 42,000
SALES: 13.6MM **Privately Held**
WEB: www.rch-lyons.com
SIC: 8062 8361 General medical & surgical hospitals; geriatric residential care

(G-6486)
INDEPENDENT ELECTRIC MCHY CO
456 Wabash Ave (67554-1624)
PHONE..................................620 257-5375
David Launder, *Branch Mgr*
EMP: 8
SALES (corp-wide): 9MM **Privately Held**
SIC: 7694 Electric motor repair
PA: Independent Electric Machinery Company
4425 Oliver St
Kansas City KS 66106
913 362-1155

(G-6487)
KANSAS ETHANOL LLC
1630 Avenue Q (67554-8881)
PHONE..................................620 257-2300
Michael Chisam, *President*
Bob Obermite, *Manager*
EMP: 51
SALES (est): 13.1MM **Privately Held**
SIC: 2869 Ethyl alcohol, ethanol

(G-6488)
KNIGHT FARMS INC
2648 Ave J (67554)
PHONE..................................620 257-5106
Kenneth E Knight, *President*
Donald S Knight, *Corp Secy*
EMP: 12
SALES (est): 1MM **Privately Held**
SIC: 0191 General farms, primarily crop

(G-6489)
LYONS DAILY NEWS
Also Called: Star Communication
210 W Commercial St (67554-2716)
P.O. Box 768 (67554-0768)
PHONE..................................620 257-2368
Paul E Jones, *President*
David Settle, *Principal*
EMP: 7 **EST:** 1906
SQ FT: 4,800
SALES (est): 451.2K **Privately Held**
WEB: www.ldn.kscoxmail.com
SIC: 2711 Newspapers: publishing only, not printed on site

(G-6490)
LYONS FEDERAL SAVINGS ASSN (PA)
Also Called: LYON'S FEDERAL SAVINGS
200 East Ave S (67554-2722)
P.O. Box 58 (67554-0058)
PHONE..................................620 257-2316
Kevin McClure, *President*
Joan Burton, *Vice Pres*
Miles Craig, *Vice Pres*
Shane Edwards, *Vice Pres*
Brett Hille, *Vice Pres*
EMP: 16
SQ FT: 3,800
SALES: 5.3MM **Privately Held**
WEB: www.lyonsfed.com
SIC: 6035 Federal savings & loan associations

(G-6491)
LYONS MANUFACTURING CO INC
711 E Main St (67554-2111)
PHONE..................................620 257-2331
Allen Hale, *President*
Tammy Mullins, *Purch Mgr*
Dana Nelson, *Treasurer*
EMP: 25 **EST:** 1959
SQ FT: 50,000
SALES (est): 4.5MM **Privately Held**
WEB: www.lyonsmfg.com
SIC: 3728 3812 Aircraft assemblies, subassemblies & parts; search & navigation equipment

(G-6492)
LYONS SALT COMPANY
Also Called: Central Salt
1660 Avenue N (67554-9201)
PHONE..................................620 257-5626
Ken Grimm, *President*
EMP: 75
SQ FT: 1,100
SALES (est): 44.6MM
SALES (corp-wide): 5MM **Privately Held**
SIC: 5169 Chemicals & allied products
HQ: B.S.C. Holding, Inc.
10955 Lowell Ave Ste 500
Overland Park KS 66210
913 262-7263

(G-6493)
LYONS STATE BANK
101 E Main St (67554-2002)
PHONE..................................620 257-3775
Daniel Snyder, *President*
H H Snyder, *President*
Darlene McAllaster, *Vice Pres*
Kim Miller, *Vice Pres*
Karen Snyder, *Manager*
EMP: 25 **EST:** 1938
SQ FT: 7,500
SALES: 4.7MM **Privately Held**
WEB: www.lyonsstatebank.com
SIC: 6022 State trust companies accepting deposits, commercial

(G-6494)
MC KINNES IRON & METAL INC
316 N State St (67554-2027)
PHONE..................................620 257-3821
Donald McKinnes, *President*
EMP: 6
SQ FT: 1,250
SALES (est): 749.8K **Privately Held**
SIC: 5093 3446 Ferrous metal scrap & waste; architectural metalwork

(G-6495)
NATIONAL ASSN LTR CARRIERS
513 S Bell Ave (67554-3301)
PHONE..................................620 257-3934
Larry D Sewell, *Manager*
EMP: 20
SALES (corp-wide): 1B **Privately Held**
WEB: www.nalc.org
SIC: 8631 Labor union
PA: National Association Of Letter Carriers
100 Indana Ave Nw Ste 709
Washington DC 20001
202 393-4695

(G-6496)
PALLETON OF KANSAS INC (PA)
103 Industrial Dr (67554-1601)
P.O. Box 148, Exeter MO (65647-0148)
PHONE..................................620 257-3571
Ray Portrey, *President*
Cynthia Portrey, *Treasurer*
Larry Meyer, *Director*
EMP: 17
SQ FT: 9,800
SALES (est): 1.5MM **Privately Held**
SIC: 2448 Pallets, wood

(G-6497)
SELLERS FARMS INC
Also Called: Sellers Feedlot
1420 Avenue N (67554-9029)
PHONE..................................620 257-5144
Steve Sellers, *President*
EMP: 14
SQ FT: 3,000
SALES (est): 2.5MM **Privately Held**
WEB: www.sellersfeedlot.com
SIC: 0211 0111 0115 Beef cattle feedlots; wheat; corn

(G-6498)
SOUTHERN STAR CENTRAL GAS PIPE
455 Wabash Ave (67554-1600)
PHONE..................................620 257-7800
Bill Whitehead, *Supervisor*
EMP: 12
SALES (corp-wide): 216.1MM **Privately Held**
WEB: www.sscgp.com
SIC: 4923 Gas transmission & distribution
HQ: Southern Star Central Gas Pipeline, Inc.
4700 Highway 56
Owensboro KY 42301
270 852-5000

Macksville
Stafford County

(G-6499)
CLARK FLYING SERVICE INC
102 Nw 120th Ave (67557-9415)
PHONE..................................620 348-2685
Jim Clark, *President*
EMP: 10 **EST:** 1949
SQ FT: 600
SALES (est): 1.8MM **Privately Held**
SIC: 0721 Crop spraying services

Madison
Greenwood County

(G-6500)
FORUM ENERGY TECNHOLOGIES
Also Called: Abz Valve
113 W Main St (66860-9568)
P.O. Box 157 (66860-0157)
PHONE..................................620 437-2440
Wayne McClelland, *President*
Todd Pyle, *Engineer*
Diane Harrison, *Manager*
◆ **EMP:** 53
SALES (est): 10.3MM
SALES (corp-wide): 1B **Publicly Held**
WEB: www.abzvalve.com
SIC: 3491 Industrial valves
PA: Forum Energy Technologies, Inc.
10344 Sam Houston Park Dr
Houston TX 77064
281 949-2500

(G-6501)
HURRICANE SERVICES INC
3613a Y Rd (66860-8561)
P.O. Box 265 (66860-0265)
PHONE..................................620 437-2661
Joe Samuels, *Manager*
EMP: 50
SALES (corp-wide): 12.1MM **Privately Held**
SIC: 1381 Reworking oil & gas wells
PA: Hurricane Services, Inc.
250 N Water St Ste 200
Wichita KS 67202
316 303-9515

(G-6502)
KANSAS MAID INC
2369 Ks 58 Hwy (66860-8002)
PHONE..................................620 437-2958
Tom Knobloch, *President*
Jeri Knobloch, *Corp Secy*
EMP: 7
SALES (est): 420K **Privately Held**
WEB: www.kansas-city.homeconnections.com
SIC: 2051 2053 2045 Bread, cake & related products; frozen bakery products, except bread; prepared flour mixes & doughs

(G-6503)
LEISER CONSTRUCTION LLC
1927 365th St (66860-8567)
PHONE..................................620 437-2747
Sandra Leiser,
Lloyd Leiser,
EMP: 15 **EST:** 1998
SALES (est): 1.3MM **Privately Held**
SIC: 1791 Structural steel erection

(G-6504)
SCHANKIE WELL SERVICE INC
1006 Sw Blvd (66860-8048)
P.O. Box 397 (66860-0397)
PHONE..................................620 437-2595
Wallace Schankie, *President*
Clifford Schankie, *Vice Pres*
Randall Schankie, *Treasurer*
EMP: 6 **EST:** 1965
SALES (est): 747.8K **Privately Held**
SIC: 1389 Oil field services

Mahaska
Washington County

(G-6505)
LAMBRIARS INC
Also Called: Lambriar Kennels
113 N Pine St (66955-9226)
PHONE..................................785 245-3231
Roger E Lambert, *President*
Darlene Lambert, *Corp Secy*
Michelle Pachta, *Vice Pres*
EMP: 70
SQ FT: 6,000
SALES (est): 6.5MM **Privately Held**
WEB: www.lambriar.com
SIC: 5199 Cats; dogs

(G-6506)
LIVINGSTON ENTERPRISES INC
Also Called: State Line Swine
56265 702nd Rd (66955-8804)
PHONE..................................402 247-3323
Bruce Livingston, *President*
EMP: 23 **EST:** 1984
SALES: 3MM **Privately Held**
SIC: 0259 0213 Pigeon farm; hogs

Maize
Sedgwick County

(G-6507)
AERO-TECH ENGINEERING INC
Also Called: A Tei
5555 N 119th St W (67101-9512)
PHONE..................................316 942-8604
Tom Simon, *President*
Rick Jaso, *Corp Secy*
James Pryor, *Vice Pres*
Michael Osborn,
EMP: 70
SQ FT: 32,800
SALES (est): 12.6MM **Privately Held**
WEB: www.aerotecheng.org
SIC: 3728 Aircraft parts & equipment

(G-6508)
AVIATION CNSLTING ENGRG SLTONS
202 N Park St (67101-6736)
P.O. Box 411 (67101-0411)
PHONE..................................316 265-8335
Kevin Campbell, *President*
EMP: 9 **EST:** 1999
SQ FT: 15,000
SALES (est): 907.6K **Privately Held**
SIC: 8711 8071 3829 3826 Consulting engineer; testing laboratories; fatigue testing machines, industrial: mechanical; tensile strength testing equipment; environmental testing equipment

(G-6509)
CARLSON PRODUCTS LLC
4601 N Tyler Rd (67101-8734)
P.O. Box 429 (67101-0429)
PHONE..................................316 722-0265
Austin Peterson, *President*
Cathy Markey, *CFO*
Andy Gribble, *Sales Staff*
EMP: 80
SQ FT: 100,000
SALES (est): 18.2MM
SALES (corp-wide): 233MM **Privately Held**
SIC: 3499 3442 3469 Doors, safe & vault: metal; metal doors, sash & trim; boxes: tool, lunch, mail, etc.: stamped metal
HQ: The Vollrath Company L L C
21st St And Superior
Sheboygan WI 53081

(G-6510)
COUNTRY CHILD CARE INC
404 W Irma St (67101-9543)
P.O. Box 385 (67101-0385)
PHONE..................................316 722-4500
Nedra Jordan, *President*
EMP: 30

GEOGRAPHIC

SALES (est): 971.6K Privately Held
SIC: 8351 Preschool center

(G-6511)
CRANMER GRASS FARMS INC
6121 N 119th St W (67101-9597)
PHONE..................................316 722-7230
David D Cranmer, *President*
EMP: 20
SQ FT: 6,000
SALES (est): 2.7MM Privately Held
WEB: www.cranmergrass.com
SIC: 0181 0782 Sod farms; lawn & garden services

(G-6512)
DAVITA HEALTHCARE PARTNERS INC
10001 W Grady Ave (67101-3747)
PHONE..................................316 773-1400
EMP: 25 Publicly Held
SIC: 8092 Kidney dialysis centers
PA: Davita Inc.
2000 16th St
Denver CO 80202

(G-6513)
EVANS BUILDING CO INC
7700 W 53rd St N (67101-9183)
P.O. Box 12086, Wichita (67277-2086)
PHONE..................................316 524-0103
William Johnson, *President*
James Crabtree, *Project Mgr*
Lori Wigner, *Bookkeeper*
Karla Fimple, *Office Mgr*
J Johnson, *Manager*
EMP: 35 EST: 1962
SALES (est): 9.3MM Privately Held
WEB: www.evansbldg.com
SIC: 1542 Commercial & office building, new construction

(G-6514)
JAMES VOEGELI CONSTRUCTION
Also Called: Voegeli Concrete Construction
9325 W 53rd St N (67101-9101)
P.O. Box 520 (67101-0520)
PHONE..................................316 721-6800
James Voegeli, *President*
Mary Lou Voegeli, *Treasurer*
EMP: 25
SALES (est): 3.1MM Privately Held
SIC: 1771 Concrete work

(G-6515)
KEARNEY EQUIPMENT LLC (PA)
Also Called: Maice
5820 N 119th St W (67101-9569)
P.O. Box 476 (67101-0476)
PHONE..................................316 722-8710
Stanley Grube, *General Mgr*
James Kickman, *General Mgr*
Kevin Kaff, *Mng Member*
Branden Stitt, *Officer*
Anne Kaff,
EMP: 12
SQ FT: 12,850
SALES (est): 6.6MM Privately Held
WEB: www.maizecorporation.com
SIC: 5083 3469 Farm implements; machine parts, stamped or pressed metal

(G-6516)
MARROQUIN EXPRESS INC
6045 N Maize Rd (67101-9489)
PHONE..................................316 295-0595
Manual Marroquin Sr, *President*
EMP: 14
SALES (est): 1.7MM Privately Held
SIC: 4212 4213 Animal & farm product transportation services; trucking, except local

(G-6517)
MICHAEL DOWNEY
Also Called: Contractors Waterproofing
4958 N Maize Rd (67101-9625)
P.O. Box 176, Cheney (67025-0176)
PHONE..................................316 540-6166
Michael Downey, *Owner*
EMP: 18 EST: 1996
SQ FT: 10,000
SALES (est): 1.1MM Privately Held
WEB: www.michaeldowneyphoto.com
SIC: 1799 4213 Waterproofing; sandblasting of building exteriors; heavy hauling

(G-6518)
REIFENHAUSER INCORPORATED
12260 W 53rd St N (67101-9509)
P.O. Box 489 (67101-0489)
PHONE..................................316 260-2122
Holger Schumacher, *CEO*
▲ EMP: 17
SALES (est): 3.3MM
SALES (corp-wide): 549.1MM Privately Held
SIC: 3089 Extruded finished plastic products
HQ: Reifenhauser Blown Film Gmbh
Cornelius-Heyl-Str. 49
Worms 67547
624 190-20

(G-6519)
SHUTTLE AEROSPACE INC
12550 W 53rd St N (67101-9515)
PHONE..................................316 832-0210
Clovis S Ribas, *President*
Clovis Ribas, *General Mgr*
Sueli Ribas, *Vice Pres*
EMP: 7 EST: 1998
SALES (est): 1.2MM Privately Held
SIC: 3599 Machine shop, jobbing & repair

(G-6520)
SIMS INSURANCE SERVICES I
4621 N Maize Rd (67101-9514)
P.O. Box 369 (67101-0369)
PHONE..................................316 722-9977
Dee Sims, *President*
Christy Haynes, *Personnel*
Stephanie McFaul, *Commercial*
EMP: 10
SALES (est): 761.3K Privately Held
SIC: 6411 Insurance agents

(G-6521)
STOVERS RESTORATION INC
112 E Albert St (67101-6704)
P.O. Box 398 (67101-0398)
PHONE..................................316 686-5005
Phillip Stover, *CEO*
Trace Stover, *President*
Phil Stover, *General Mgr*
EMP: 18
SQ FT: 10,000
SALES (est): 1.5MM Privately Held
SIC: 7217 7349 7216 1799 Carpet & upholstery cleaning on customer premises; air duct cleaning; curtain cleaning & repair; post-disaster renovations

(G-6522)
U HAUL CO INDEPENDENT DEALERS
Also Called: U-Haul
4160 N Maize Rd (67101-9598)
PHONE..................................316 722-0216
Gerald Woodard, *Owner*
Leslie Woodard, *Co-Owner*
EMP: 10
SALES (est): 851K Privately Held
SIC: 7513 Truck rental & leasing, no drivers

(G-6523)
WORTHINGTON CYLINDER CORP
5605 N 119th St W (67101-9566)
P.O. Box 300 (67101-0300)
PHONE..................................316 529-6950
Andrew Billman, *President*
Jeff Anderson, *Office Mgr*
EMP: 191
SALES (corp-wide): 3.7B Publicly Held
SIC: 3443 Cylinders, pressure: metal plate
HQ: Worthington Cylinder Corporation
200 W Old Wlson Bridge Rd
Worthington OH 43085
614 840-3210

Manchester
Dickinson County

(G-6524)
HENRY STECKMAN PLUMBING
Also Called: Plumbing & Hvac
3266 Dove Rd (67410-7538)
PHONE..................................785 388-2782
Henry Steckman, *Owner*
EMP: 10
SALES: 800K Privately Held
SIC: 1711 Plumbing, heating, air-conditioning contractors

Manhattan
Riley County

(G-6525)
17TH STREET PROPERTIES LLC
Also Called: Parkwood Inn and Suites
505 S 17th St (66502-4213)
PHONE..................................785 320-5440
Allie Webb, *Sales Mgr*
Douglas R Maryott,
EMP: 16
SALES (est): 271.5K Privately Held
SIC: 7011 Hotels

(G-6526)
9 LINE MEDICAL SOLUTIONS LLC
620 Zeandale Rd (66502-6930)
PHONE..................................402 470-1696
Brandon Bailey, *Branch Mgr*
EMP: 15
SALES (corp-wide): 3.5MM Privately Held
SIC: 4119 Ambulance service
PA: 9 Line Medical Solutions, Llc
6720 E Sedona St
Derby KS 67037
402 480-6474

(G-6527)
A SCAMPIS BAR & GRILL
Also Called: Holiday Inn
530 Richards Dr (66502-3143)
PHONE..................................785 539-5311
Fax: 785 539-7428
EMP: 25
SALES (est): 443.4K Privately Held
SIC: 7011 5812 Hotel/Motel Operation & Restaurant

(G-6528)
A1 BONDING
700 Rosencutter Rd (66502-8496)
PHONE..................................785 539-3950
David Stuckman, *Owner*
EMP: 56
SALES (est): 2MM Privately Held
SIC: 7389 Bondsperson

(G-6529)
ABBOTT ALUMINUM INC (PA)
Also Called: Abbott Workholding Products
430 Mccall Rd (66502-5086)
PHONE..................................785 776-8555
Carl Reed, *President*
Joyce Graham, *Vice Pres*
Dixie Reed, *Vice Pres*
David Davis, *Prdtn Mgr*
▲ EMP: 45 EST: 1954
SQ FT: 47,000
SALES (est): 10.6MM Privately Held
WEB: www.abbottworkholding.com
SIC: 3545 3599 3443 Machine tool attachments & accessories; machine shop, jobbing & repair; fabricated plate work (boiler shop)

(G-6530)
ABC PHONES NORTH CAROLINA INC
Also Called: A Wireless
202 Nw 2nd St (66502)
PHONE..................................785 263-3553
EMP: 26
SALES (corp-wide): 149.7MM Privately Held
SIC: 4812 Cellular telephone services
PA: Abc Phones Of North Carolina, Inc.
8510 Colonnade Center Dr
Raleigh NC 27615
252 317-0388

(G-6531)
ACEWARE SYSTEMS INC
7480 Dyer Rd (66502-8309)
PHONE..................................785 537-2937
Chuck Havlicek, *President*
Sharon Brookshire, *Vice Pres*
Barbara Havlicek, *Vice Pres*
Matthew Olson, *Prgrmr*
Cheryl Scott, *Comp Tech*
EMP: 11
SQ FT: 2,300
SALES (est): 1.4MM Privately Held
WEB: www.aceware.com
SIC: 7371 Computer software systems analysis & design, custom; computer software development & applications

(G-6532)
ACRES INC
Also Called: N-Zone Sportswear
613 Pecan Cir (66502-8146)
PHONE..................................785 776-3234
Patrick Lee, *CEO*
Anndee Biltoft, *Sales Staff*
Addie Bunnell, *Sales Staff*
▲ EMP: 18
SQ FT: 12,500
SALES (est): 5.7MM Privately Held
WEB: www.n-zonesportswear.com
SIC: 5137 5136 Women's & children's clothing; men's & boys' clothing

(G-6533)
ADVANCED DERMATOLOGY AND SKIN
Also Called: Adams, John R MD
2735 Pembrook Pl (66502-7482)
PHONE..................................785 537-4990
John R Adams, *Owner*
April Kientz, *Nurse*
EMP: 26
SQ FT: 9,000
SALES (est): 2.7MM Privately Held
SIC: 8011 Dermatologist

(G-6534)
ADVANCED MANUFACTURING INST
510 Mccall Rd (66502-7017)
PHONE..................................785 532-7044
Tyler Jelinek, *Engineer*
Bradley Kramer, *Exec Dir*
Brad Kramer, *Director*
EMP: 25
SALES (est): 2.5MM Privately Held
WEB: www.amisuccess.com
SIC: 8748 8711 Business consulting; engineering services; consulting engineer

(G-6535)
AERO-MOD INCORPORATED
7927 E Us Highway 24 (66502-8166)
PHONE..................................785 537-4995
John McNellis, *CEO*
Brooks Newbry, *Regional Mgr*
Todd Steinbach, *Vice Pres*
Marvin Brown, *Project Mgr*
Retzlaff Robert, *Project Mgr*
▲ EMP: 30 EST: 1970
SQ FT: 12,000
SALES: 10MM Privately Held
WEB: www.aeromod.net
SIC: 3589 Water treatment equipment, industrial

(G-6536)
AG PRESS INC
Also Called: Grass & Grain
1531 Yuma St (66502-4257)
P.O. Box 1009 (66505-1009)
PHONE..................................785 539-7558
Verlla Coughenour, *Ch of Bd*
Dean Coughenour, *Corp Secy*
EMP: 60 EST: 1958
SQ FT: 42,000

SALES (est): 4.5MM **Privately Held**
WEB: www.grassandgrain.com
SIC: 2711 2752 Newspapers, publishing & printing; commercial printing, lithographic

(G-6537)
AIB INTERNATIONAL INC (HQ)
1213 Bakers Way (66502-4555)
P.O. Box 3999 (66505-3999)
PHONE..................................785 537-4750
Andre Biane, *CEO*
Salena Sauber, *Editor*
Paul Klover, *Corp Secy*
Tony Parish, *Controller*
Tania Arevalo, *Manager*
EMP: 100
SQ FT: 80,000
SALES: 17MM
SALES (corp-wide): 13.4MM **Privately Held**
WEB: www.aibinternational.com
SIC: 8742 Training & development consultant
PA: American Institute Of Baking
1213 Bakers Way
Manhattan KS 66502
785 537-4750

(G-6538)
ALAN CLARK BODY SHOP INC
2160 Pillsbury Dr (66502-9603)
PHONE..................................785 776-5333
Donald Howard, *President*
Pat Keating, *Vice Pres*
EMP: 12
SQ FT: 10,000
SALES: 1MM **Privately Held**
WEB: www.alanclarkbodyshop.com
SIC: 7532 7549 7536 Body shop, automotive; towing service, automotive; automotive glass replacement shops

(G-6539)
ALFRED BENESCH & COMPANY
3226 Kimball Ave (66503-2157)
PHONE..................................785 539-2202
Stephen Roth, *Sr Project Mgr*
Buck Driggs, *Manager*
EMP: 11
SQ FT: 5,000
SALES (corp-wide): 111MM **Privately Held**
WEB: www.hws.com
SIC: 8711 Consulting engineer
PA: Alfred Benesch & Company
35 W Wacker Dr Ste 3300
Chicago IL 60601
312 565-0450

(G-6540)
AMERICAN BOTTLING COMPANY
Also Called: 7 Up Snapple Group
613 Pecan Cir (66502-8146)
PHONE..................................785 537-2100
William Trebilcock, *Branch Mgr*
EMP: 22 **Publicly Held**
WEB: www.cs-americas.com
SIC: 2086 Soft drinks: packaged in cans, bottles, etc.
HQ: The American Bottling Company
5301 Legacy Dr
Plano TX 75024

(G-6541)
AMERICAN INSTITUTE OF BAKING (PA)
Also Called: A I B
1213 Bakers Way (66502-4576)
P.O. Box 3999 (66505-3999)
PHONE..................................785 537-4750
Andre Biane, *President*
Virgil Smail, *President*
Paul E Klover, *Vice Pres*
Kimberly Marquardt, *Accountant*
EMP: 80 **EST:** 1919
SQ FT: 73,200
SALES: 13.4MM **Privately Held**
SIC: 8299 8731 Cooking school; food research

(G-6542)
AMERICAN RSDNTIAL CMMNTIES LLC
Also Called: Riverchase
3050 Tuttle Creek Blvd (66502-7115)
PHONE..................................785 776-4440
EMP: 10 **Privately Held**
SIC: 6531 6515 Real Estate Agent/Manager Mobile Home Site Operator
PA: American Residential Communities, Llc
2 N Riverside Plz Ste 800
Chicago IL 60606

(G-6543)
APPLETECH DESIGN & CNSTR INC
240 Levee Dr Ste 1 (66502-5076)
PHONE..................................785 776-3530
George Lauppe, *President*
Anette Lauppe, *Vice Pres*
EMP: 14
SALES (est): 2.2MM **Privately Held**
WEB: www.appletechconstruction.com
SIC: 1521 General remodeling, single-family houses; single-family home remodeling, additions & repairs

(G-6544)
ARLA JEAN GENSTLER MD PA
1502 Browning Pl (66502-7479)
PHONE..................................785 537-3400
Helen Mathews, *Branch Mgr*
EMP: 10
SALES (corp-wide): 1.7MM **Privately Held**
SIC: 8011 Ophthalmologist
PA: Arla Jean Genstler, M.D., P.A.
3630 Sw Fairlawn Rd
Topeka KS 66614
785 273-8080

(G-6545)
ART CRAFT PRINTERS & DESIGN
317 Houston St Ste B (66502-8512)
PHONE..................................785 776-9151
Carolyn Arand, *President*
David Harmas, *Vice Pres*
Janice Flanary, *Treasurer*
EMP: 6
SALES (est): 794.5K **Privately Held**
SIC: 2752 2791 2759 Commercial printing, offset; typesetting; screen printing

(G-6546)
ARTHUR GREEN LLP
801 Poyntz Ave (66502-6054)
PHONE..................................785 537-1345
Derrick Roberson, *Partner*
Charles Arthur III, *Partner*
William Bahr, *Partner*
Derrick Boberson, *Partner*
John D Conderman, *Partner*
EMP: 10
SALES (est): 1MM **Privately Held**
WEB: www.arthur-green.com
SIC: 8111 General practice attorney, lawyer

(G-6547)
ASSOCIATED ENVIRONMENTAL INC
404 Pottawatomie Ave (66502-6412)
PHONE..................................785 776-7755
Brad Johnson, *President*
Dee Jonhson, *Corp Secy*
EMP: 12
SQ FT: 1,800
SALES (est): 1.9MM **Privately Held**
WEB: www.associatedenvironmental.com
SIC: 1381 8748 Drilling oil & gas wells; environmental consultant

(G-6548)
ASSOCIATED INSULATION INC (PA)
701 Pecan Cir (66502-8164)
PHONE..................................785 776-0145
Ronald Tacha, *President*
Karolyn Tacha, *Corp Secy*
EMP: 60 **EST:** 1978
SQ FT: 4,000
SALES (est): 5MM **Privately Held**
SIC: 1799 1742 Asbestos removal & encapsulation; lead burning; insulation, buildings

(G-6549)
ASSOCIATED UROLOGIST P A
1133 College Ave Ste G100 (66502-2756)
PHONE..................................785 537-8710
Fred A Freeman, *President*
Dr Don Devine, *Vice Pres*
Suelyn Hall, *Med Doctor*
EMP: 10
SQ FT: 1,500
SALES (est): 770K **Privately Held**
SIC: 8011 Urologist

(G-6550)
AT HOME ASSISTED CARE INC
400 Poyntz Ave (66502-6039)
PHONE..................................785 473-7007
Cindy Birnbaum, *Owner*
EMP: 11
SALES (est): 382.4K **Privately Held**
SIC: 8082 Home health care services

(G-6551)
B G CONSULTANTS INC (PA)
4806 Vue Du Lac Pl (66503-8688)
PHONE..................................785 537-7448
Stephen Berland, *President*
Tom Arpin, *Vice Pres*
Thomas Bennett, *Vice Pres*
Cecil Kingsley, *Vice Pres*
David Hamby, *Engineer*
EMP: 25
SQ FT: 5,000
SALES (est): 10.6MM **Privately Held**
WEB: www.bgcons.com
SIC: 8711 8712 8713 Civil engineering; architectural services; surveying services

(G-6552)
BANK OF FLINT HILLS
Also Called: First National Bank
7860 E Us Highway 24 (66502-8659)
PHONE..................................785 539-8322
Cathy Scauffer, *Manager*
EMP: 11
SALES (corp-wide): 12.2MM **Privately Held**
SIC: 6022 State commercial banks
PA: Bank Of The Flint Hills
806 5th St
Wamego KS 66547
785 456-2221

(G-6553)
BAYER CONSTRUCTION COMPANY INC
120 Deep Creek Rd (66502-9305)
P.O. Box 889 (66505-0889)
PHONE..................................785 776-8839
Neil Horton, *CEO*
Kelly Briggs, *President*
EMP: 145
SQ FT: 10,000
SALES: 22.5MM **Privately Held**
WEB: www.bayerconst.com
SIC: 1422 1623 1794 Crushed & broken limestone; water & sewer line construction; excavation work

(G-6554)
BAYSTONE FINANCIAL GROUP (PA)
2627 Kfb Plz Ste 202e (66503-8136)
PHONE..................................785 587-4050
H Evan Howe, *President*
H Phillip Howe, *Chairman*
Aaron Lindsten, *VP Sales*
David P Howe, *Shareholder*
EMP: 18
SALES (est): 1.5MM **Privately Held**
WEB: www.baystone.net
SIC: 6163 Mortgage brokers arranging for loans, using money of others

(G-6555)
BENCHMARK ENTERPRISES
1181 Rock Springs Ln (66502-1550)
PHONE..................................785 537-4447
Roger A Seymour, *Owner*
Connie Seymour, *Co-Owner*
EMP: 12
SALES (est): 604.8K **Privately Held**
SIC: 1521 1542 Single-family home remodeling, additions & repairs; nonresidential construction

(G-6556)
BEST WESTERN OF MANHATTAN
601 Poyntz Ave (66502-6006)
PHONE..................................785 537-8300
Dilit Patel, *Owner*
EMP: 10
SALES (est): 473.9K **Privately Held**
SIC: 7011 Hotels & motels

(G-6557)
BHS CONSTRUCTION INC
727 S Juliette Ave (66502-6406)
P.O. Box 1328 (66505-1328)
PHONE..................................785 537-2068
Wayne Sloan, *President*
Andrew Gerth, *Project Mgr*
Bobi Hoover, *Treasurer*
Cindy Sloan, *Admin Sec*
EMP: 20
SQ FT: 2,650
SALES: 16.3MM **Privately Held**
SIC: 1542 1541 Commercial & office building, new construction; industrial buildings & warehouses

(G-6558)
BIG LKES DEVELOPMENTAL CTR INC (PA)
1416 Hayes Dr (66502-5066)
PHONE..................................785 776-9201
Lori Feldkamp, *President*
Kathy Carlin, *Vice Pres*
Phillip Korenek, *Treasurer*
John Kaberlein, *Info Tech Dir*
Jan Lange, *Admin Sec*
EMP: 75
SALES: 8.7MM **Privately Held**
WEB: www.biglakes.org
SIC: 8361 8249 Home for the physically handicapped; vocational schools

(G-6559)
BIG LKES DEVELOPMENTAL CTR INC
515 Colorado St Ste 517 (66502-6229)
PHONE..................................785 776-7748
EMP: 12
SALES (corp-wide): 8.5MM **Privately Held**
SIC: 8249 8361 Sheltered Workshop
PA: Big Lakes Developmental Center, Inc.
1416 Hayes Dr
Manhattan KS 66502
785 776-9201

(G-6560)
BIG LKES DEVELOPMENTAL CTR INC
Also Called: Butternut Home
2304 Butternut Ln (66502-7628)
PHONE..................................785 776-0777
Patty Rourke, *Branch Mgr*
EMP: 14
SALES (corp-wide): 8.7MM **Privately Held**
WEB: www.biglakes.org
SIC: 8249 8361 Vocational schools; residential care
PA: Big Lakes Developmental Center, Inc.
1416 Hayes Dr
Manhattan KS 66502
785 776-9201

(G-6561)
BIRD MUSIC & AMUSEMENT SVCS
5104 Skyway Dr (66503-9710)
PHONE..................................785 537-2930
David Ptacek, *President*
Anton L Ptacek Jr, *Principal*
Anna Ptacek, *Corp Secy*
George Ptacek, *Vice Pres*
EMP: 20
SQ FT: 33,000
SALES (est): 1.1MM **Privately Held**
WEB: www.bird.com
SIC: 7993 Coin-operated amusement devices

GEOGRAPHIC

(G-6562)
BLACK HAWK INC
Also Called: Black Hawkins
2104 Tamarron Ter (66502-1957)
PHONE..................................785 539-8240
Briam Lamberson, *CEO*
Brian Lamberson, *Owner*
Celia Lamberson, *Treasurer*
EMP: 23
SALES (est): 1.5MM **Privately Held**
SIC: 1541 Grain elevator construction

(G-6563)
BLECHA ENTERPRISES LLC
6130 Tuttle Ter (66503-8685)
PHONE..................................785 539-6640
EMP: 12
SQ FT: 675
SALES (est): 1.2MM **Privately Held**
SIC: 1521 6519 Single-Family House Construction Real Property Lessor

(G-6564)
BOBBY TS BAR & GRILL INC
Also Called: Bobby T'S Restaurant & Bar
3236 Kimball Ave (66503-2157)
PHONE..................................785 537-8383
Fax: 785 537-8885
EMP: 10
SALES (est): 350K **Privately Held**
SIC: 7997 5812 7299 Membership Sport/Recreation Club Eating Place Misc Personal Services

(G-6565)
BOBS PLUMBING & HEATING INC (PA)
5281 Tuttle Creek Blvd (66502-8813)
PHONE..................................785 539-4155
Randall Steiner, *President*
Cathy Steiner, *Corp Secy*
Victor Steiner, *Vice Pres*
EMP: 13
SQ FT: 5,000
SALES: 2MM **Privately Held**
SIC: 1711 Plumbing contractors; warm air heating & air conditioning contractor

(G-6566)
BOCKERS TWO CATERING INC
Also Called: Bocker's Two Catering Service
1108 Laramie St 1106 (66502-5312)
P.O. Box 849 (66505-0849)
PHONE..................................785 539-9431
Robert Limbocker, *President*
Alycia Limbocker, *Co-Owner*
EMP: 10
SALES (est): 357.8K **Privately Held**
WEB: www.bockers2catering.com
SIC: 5812 7299 Caterers; banquet hall facilities

(G-6567)
BOYS & GIRLS CLB MANHATTAN INC
220 S 5th St (66502-6116)
P.O. Box 1294 (66505-1294)
PHONE..................................785 539-1947
Pamela Nealey, *Opers Staff*
Michelle Allison, *Human Res Mgr*
Junnae Campbell, *Exec Dir*
Lexi Ellenbecker, *Director*
Catherine Robson, *Education*
EMP: 60
SALES: 1.6MM **Privately Held**
SIC: 8641 Youth organizations

(G-6568)
BRIGGS AUTO GROUP INC
2500 Stagg Hill Rd (66502-3128)
PHONE..................................785 776-7799
EMP: 130
SALES (corp-wide): 51.3MM **Privately Held**
SIC: 5012 Automobiles & other motor vehicles
PA: Briggs Auto Group, Inc.
2312 Stagg Hill Rd
Manhattan KS 66502
785 776-7799

(G-6569)
BRIGGS AUTO GROUP INC
Also Called: Briggs Jeep Eagle Isuzu
2312 Stagg Hill Rd (66502-3157)
PHONE..................................785 776-3677
Russell Briggs, *Manager*
EMP: 20
SALES (corp-wide): 51.3MM **Privately Held**
SIC: 5511 7539 5521 7532 Automobiles, new & used; automotive repair shops; used car dealers; body shop, automotive; automobiles
PA: Briggs Auto Group, Inc.
2312 Stagg Hill Rd
Manhattan KS 66502
785 776-7799

(G-6570)
BRIGGS AUTO GROUP INC
2312 Stagg Hill Rd (66502-3157)
P.O. Box 249 (66505-0249)
PHONE..................................785 537-8330
Michelle Clark, *Mktg Dir*
James Dean, *Manager*
EMP: 130
SALES (corp-wide): 51.3MM **Privately Held**
SIC: 5012 5521 Automobiles & other motor vehicles; antique automobiles
PA: Briggs Auto Group, Inc.
2312 Stagg Hill Rd
Manhattan KS 66502
785 776-7799

(G-6571)
BUILT-SO-WELL
1210 Pottawatomie Ave (66502-4335)
PHONE..................................785 537-5166
Scott Sowell, *Owner*
Debbie Sowell, *Co-Owner*
EMP: 8
SQ FT: 13,000
SALES (est): 280K **Privately Held**
WEB: www.builtsowell.com
SIC: 7692 5531 Welding repair; automobile & truck equipment & parts

(G-6572)
BURNETT AUTOMOTIVE INC (PA)
400 Mccall Rd (66502-5032)
PHONE..................................785 539-8970
John K Stallman, *President*
William W Burnett, *Vice Pres*
David Rogers, *Vice Pres*
Jamie Pride, *Manager*
Thomas G Burnett, *Officer*
EMP: 16 **EST:** 1962
SQ FT: 6,000
SALES (est): 37.4MM **Privately Held**
SIC: 5013 5531 5014 Automotive supplies & parts; automotive tires; automotive parts; tires & tubes

(G-6573)
BUSCO INC
Also Called: Arrow Stage Lines
425 Mccall Rd (66502-5001)
PHONE..................................816 453-8727
Chuck Gunnels, *Branch Mgr*
EMP: 11
SALES (corp-wide): 77.6MM **Privately Held**
SIC: 4142 Bus charter service, except local
PA: Busco, Inc.
4220 S 52nd St
Omaha NE 68117
402 731-1900

(G-6574)
CANDLEWOOD MEDICAL GROUP PA
Also Called: Candlewood Medical Center
1133 College Ave Ste D200 (66502-2776)
PHONE..................................785 539-0800
Dane E Ditto, *President*
Sarla R Ditto, *Admin Sec*
EMP: 14
SALES (est): 1.5MM **Privately Held**
SIC: 8011 Urologist

(G-6575)
CAPITOL FEDERAL SAVINGS BANK
705 Commons Pl (66503-3002)
PHONE..................................785 539-9976
Krystal Dekat, *Site Mgr*
Penny Nelson, *Manager*
EMP: 15
SALES (corp-wide): 351.9MM **Publicly Held**
SIC: 6035 Federal savings banks
HQ: Capitol Federal Savings Bank
700 S Kansas Ave Fl 1
Topeka KS 66603
785 235-1341

(G-6576)
CAPSTONE MGT & DEV GROUP INC
Also Called: Prairiewood
1083 Wildcat Creek Rd (66503-9765)
P.O. Box 1427 (66505-1427)
PHONE..................................785 341-2494
Kail Kapzenmeier, *President*
Leah Graves, *Vice Pres*
EMP: 17
SALES (est): 767K **Privately Held**
SIC: 8741 Management services

(G-6577)
CARSON MOBILE HM PK SEWER DST
6215 Tuttle Creek Blvd (66503-9013)
PHONE..................................785 537-6330
Julie Winter, *Manager*
Leon Hobson, *Director*
EMP: 99
SALES (est): 554.8K **Privately Held**
SIC: 4952 7389 Sewerage systems;

(G-6578)
CB GRDUATION ANNOUNCEMENTS LLC (PA)
Also Called: CB Announcement Balfour
2316 Skyvue Ln (66502-3178)
P.O. Box 781 (66505-0781)
PHONE..................................785 776-5018
William C Barr, *Mng Member*
Chris Parrr, *Mng Member*
Mary Lipnitz, *Manager*
EMP: 20
SQ FT: 3,000
SALES (est): 3.2MM **Privately Held**
SIC: 2759 Invitation & stationery printing & engraving

(G-6579)
CBS MANHATTAN LLC (PA)
9130 Green Valley Dr (66502-1465)
PHONE..................................785 537-4935
Thom Howell, *General Mgr*
Josh Gleason, *Project Mgr*
Derek Resenbeck, *Project Mgr*
Jim Sutton, *Mng Member*
Tom Richard, *Mng Member*
EMP: 14
SALES (est): 10.7MM **Privately Held**
SIC: 5072 Hardware

(G-6580)
CELLCO PARTNERSHIP
Also Called: Verizon Wireless
100 Bluemont Ave Ste H (66502-5059)
PHONE..................................785 537-6159
EMP: 13
SALES (corp-wide): 130.8B **Publicly Held**
SIC: 5065 4813 4812 Telephone & telegraphic equipment; long distance telephone communications; cellular telephone services
HQ: Cellco Partnership
1 Verizon Way
Basking Ridge NJ 07920

(G-6581)
CENTRAL MECH CNSTR CO INC (HQ)
631 Pecan Cir (66502-8146)
P.O. Box 1063 (66505-1063)
PHONE..................................785 537-2437
John Lonker, *President*
EMP: 127 **EST:** 1963
SQ FT: 10,000
SALES (est): 24.3MM
SALES (corp-wide): 8.1B **Publicly Held**
SIC: 1711 Mechanical contractor
PA: Emcor Group, Inc.
301 Merritt 7 Fl 6
Norwalk CT 06851
203 849-7800

(G-6582)
CENTRAL MECH SVCS MNHATTAN INC
1131 Hayes Dr (66502-5017)
PHONE..................................785 776-9206
Trever Berry, *President*
EMP: 18 **EST:** 1973
SQ FT: 3,600
SALES: 1.4MM **Privately Held**
SIC: 1711 Plumbing contractors; warm air heating & air conditioning contractor

(G-6583)
CENTURY BUSINESS SYSTEMS INC (PA)
415 Houston St (66502-6135)
P.O. Box 1383 (66505-1383)
PHONE..................................785 776-0495
Mike Lierz, *President*
Jean Rowe, *General Mgr*
Mark Healy, *Accounts Exec*
Nathan Hylton, *Accounts Exec*
Jason Wolters, *Manager*
EMP: 14 **EST:** 1985
SQ FT: 3,800
SALES: 2.4MM **Privately Held**
WEB: www.cbssalina.com
SIC: 5044 7629 Photocopy machines; business machine repair, electric

(G-6584)
CHARLSON & WILSON BONDED ABSTR
111 N 4th St (66502-6013)
PHONE..................................785 565-4800
Roy H Worthington, *President*
Todd A Sheppard, *Vice Pres*
Lee S Taylor, *Vice Pres*
S Lee Taylor, *Vice Pres*
EMP: 16
SQ FT: 3,300
SALES (est): 2.6MM **Privately Held**
WEB: www.charlsonandwilson.com
SIC: 6411 Insurance agents

(G-6585)
CHARLSON WILSIN INSURANCE AGCY
555 Poyntz Ave Ste 205 (66502-0126)
P.O. Box 1989 (66505-1989)
PHONE..................................785 537-1600
Charles Hostetler, *President*
Mike Widman, *Vice Pres*
Mariah Rosso, *Personnel*
Jace Bailey, *Accounts Mgr*
Brooke Steiner, *Accounts Mgr*
EMP: 12
SALES (est): 2.1MM **Privately Held**
WEB: www.charlsonwilson.com
SIC: 6411 Insurance agents

(G-6586)
CHASE MANHATTAN APARTMENT
1409 Chase Pl (66502-4649)
PHONE..................................785 776-3663
Shana Berry, *Agent*
EMP: 10 **EST:** 1998
SALES (est): 432.6K **Privately Held**
SIC: 6513 7299 Apartment building operators; apartment locating service

(G-6587)
CITY OF MANHATTAN
Also Called: Parks & Recreation Dept
2333 Oak St (66502-3824)
PHONE..................................785 587-2737
Scott Schoemaker, *Director*
Cassie Anderson, *Program Dir*
Nicole Wade, *Education*
EMP: 25 **Privately Held**
WEB: www.manhattan.lib.ks.us
SIC: 7999 9512 Zoological garden, commercial; recreational program administration, government;

PA: City Of Manhattan
1101 Poyntz Ave
Manhattan KS 66502
785 587-2489

(G-6588)
CITY OF MANHATTAN
Also Called: Wastewater Treatment
7408 E Us Hwy 24 (66502)
PHONE..................................785 587-4555
Gary Dickinson, *Manager*
EMP: 11 **Privately Held**
WEB: www.manhattan.lib.ks.us
SIC: 4953 9511 ; water control & quality agency, government;
PA: City Of Manhattan
1101 Poyntz Ave
Manhattan KS 66502
785 587-2489

(G-6589)
CIVICPLUS LLC
Also Called: Networks Plus
2627 Kfb Plz Ste 206w (66503-8136)
P.O. Box 5311, Topeka (66605-0311)
PHONE..................................785 267-6800
Ward Morgan, *Director*
EMP: 10 **Privately Held**
WEB: www.civicplus.com
SIC: 4813
PA: Civicplus, Llc
302 S 4th St Ste 500
Manhattan KS 66502

(G-6590)
CIVICPLUS LLC (PA)
302 S 4th St Ste 500 (66502-6410)
PHONE..................................888 228-2233
Ward Morgan, *CEO*
Cole Cheever, *President*
Connie Casper, *Exec VP*
Deb McNew, *Vice Pres*
Sascha Ohler, *Vice Pres*
EMP: 160
SQ FT: 6,000
SALES (est): 46.8MM **Privately Held**
WEB: www.civicplus.com
SIC: 7374 Computer graphics service

(G-6591)
CLAFLIN BOOKS & COPIES
Also Called: Claflin Academic Publishing
103 N 4th St (66502-6013)
PHONE..................................785 776-3771
Stormy Kennedy, *Owner*
EMP: 10
SALES (est): 590K **Privately Held**
SIC: 2721 5942 Periodicals; book stores

(G-6592)
COLEMAN AMERICAN MOVING SVCS
5925 Corp Dr Section B (66503)
P.O. Box 960, Midland City AL (36350-0960)
PHONE..................................785 537-7284
William Brakefield III, *CEO*
James F Coleman, *Ch of Bd*
Joyce Farish, *CFO*
EMP: 10
SALES: 1,000K **Privately Held**
SIC: 4212 Moving services

(G-6593)
COLEMAN AMERICAN MVG SVCS INC
5925b Corporate Dr (66503-9675)
P.O. Box 202 (66505-0202)
PHONE..................................785 537-7284
Michael Tatum, *Manager*
EMP: 20 **Privately Held**
SIC: 4214 Household goods moving & storage, local
HQ: Coleman American Moving Services, Inc.
12905 Shwnee Mission Pkwy
Shawnee Mission KS 66216
913 631-1440

(G-6594)
COLLEGE PARK UNIV XING FULLY
2215 College Ave (66502-0509)
PHONE..................................785 539-0500
Anna Flores, *Principal*
EMP: 18 **EST:** 2007
SALES (est): 1.3MM **Privately Held**
SIC: 7021 Dormitory, commercially operated

(G-6595)
COLORADO PLAZA MANAGEMENT
420 Colorado St Apt 5o (66502-6279)
PHONE..................................785 776-7994
George Proctor, *Partner*
Ed Deveblis, *Partner*
Darold Proctor, *Partner*
Robert Proctor, *Partner*
EMP: 10
SQ FT: 34,500
SALES (est): 498.8K **Privately Held**
SIC: 6513 Apartment building operators

(G-6596)
COMMERCE BANK
727 Point Ave (66502)
PHONE..................................785 532-3500
Sue Strattman, *Manager*
EMP: 13
SALES (corp-wide): 1.3B **Publicly Held**
SIC: 6021 National commercial banks
HQ: Commerce Bank
1000 Walnut St Fl 700
Kansas City MO 64106
816 234-2000

(G-6597)
COMMERCE BANK
2740 Claflin Rd (66502-2718)
PHONE..................................785 587-1696
Tom Giller, *Manager*
EMP: 13
SALES (corp-wide): 1.3B **Publicly Held**
SIC: 6022 State commercial banks
HQ: Commerce Bank
1000 Walnut St Fl 700
Kansas City MO 64106
816 234-2000

(G-6598)
COMMERCE BANK
727 Poyntz Ave Ste 100 (66502-0120)
P.O. Box 1087 (66505-1087)
PHONE..................................785 537-1234
Tom Giller, *President*
Sue Strattman, *Manager*
EMP: 50
SALES (corp-wide): 1.3B **Publicly Held**
SIC: 6021 National commercial banks
HQ: Commerce Bank
1000 Walnut St Fl 700
Kansas City MO 64106
816 234-2000

(G-6599)
COMMUNITY FIRST NATIONAL BANK (HQ)
215 S Seth Child Rd (66502-3089)
PHONE..................................785 323-1111
Rob Stitt, *President*
Pat Dembkowski, *Vice Pres*
Neal Farmer, *Vice Pres*
Jay Terrill, *Vice Pres*
Curt Herrman, *Info Tech Dir*
EMP: 28
SALES: 20.6MM **Privately Held**
WEB: www.cfnbmanhattan.com
SIC: 6022 State commercial banks

(G-6600)
COMPLETE OUTDOORS INC
600 Zeandale Rd (66502-6930)
PHONE..................................785 565-4077
Doug Holden, *President*
Dana Holden, *Vice Pres*
EMP: 23
SALES (est): 1.8MM **Privately Held**
WEB: www.completeoutdoorsinc.com
SIC: 0782 Landscape contractors

(G-6601)
COMPONENT FABRICATORS INC
5107 Murray Rd (66503-9702)
PHONE..................................785 776-5081
William Avery, *President*
EMP: 5
SQ FT: 7,500
SALES (est): 627.5K **Privately Held**
SIC: 2439 Trusses, wooden roof

(G-6602)
COUNTY OF RILEY
Also Called: Riley County Senior Svc Ctr
301 N 4th St (66502-6170)
PHONE..................................785 537-4040
Jamie Ramsey, *Director*
EMP: 10 **Privately Held**
SIC: 8322 Individual & family services
PA: County Of Riley
110 Courthouse Plz
Manhattan KS 66502
785 537-6330

(G-6603)
COUNTY OF RILEY
Also Called: Riley County Emrgncy Med Svcs
2011 Claflin Rd (66502-3415)
PHONE..................................785 539-3535
Dave Adams, *Director*
EMP: 27 **Privately Held**
SIC: 8062 General medical & surgical hospitals
PA: County Of Riley
110 Courthouse Plz
Manhattan KS 66502
785 537-6330

(G-6604)
COUNTY OF RILEY
Also Called: Riley County Appraisers
110 Courthouse Plz B302 (66502-0125)
PHONE..................................785 537-6310
Sam Schmidt, *Manager*
EMP: 18 **Privately Held**
SIC: 6531 Appraiser, real estate
PA: County Of Riley
110 Courthouse Plz
Manhattan KS 66502
785 537-6330

(G-6605)
COX COMMUNICATIONS INC
900 Hayes Dr Ste B (66502-4394)
PHONE..................................785 236-1606
EMP: 78
SALES (corp-wide): 29.2B **Privately Held**
SIC: 4813 Telephone communication, except radio
HQ: Cox Communications, Inc.
6205 B Pchtree Dnwody Rd
Atlanta GA 30328

(G-6606)
CRISIS CENTER INC
423 Houston St (66502-6169)
P.O. Box 1526 (66505-1526)
PHONE..................................785 539-7935
Judy Davis, *Exec Dir*
Lorrie Gfeller, *Director*
EMP: 30
SALES: 1.2MM **Privately Held**
SIC: 8322 Crisis center

(G-6607)
CSL PLASMA INC
1130 Garden Way (66502-1786)
PHONE..................................785 776-9177
Darren Wildman, *Manager*
Stacy Teske, *Manager*
EMP: 19 **Privately Held**
WEB: www.zlbplasma.com
SIC: 8099 2836 Plasmapherous center; blood derivatives
HQ: Csl Plasma Inc.
900 Broken Sound Pkwy Nw # 400
Boca Raton FL 33487
561 981-3700

(G-6608)
D & R CONSTRUCTION INC
210 Southwind Pl Ste 2c (66503-3184)
PHONE..................................785 776-1087
Donald Crubel, *President*
Tracy Crubel, *Vice Pres*
Sylvia Crubel, *Treasurer*
John Crubel, *Admin Sec*
EMP: 20
SQ FT: 650
SALES (est): 2.9MM **Privately Held**
SIC: 1521 1542 New construction, single-family houses; general remodeling, single-family houses; nonresidential construction

(G-6609)
D J CARPENTER BUILDING SYSTEMS
709 Pecan Cir Ste B (66502-8135)
PHONE..................................785 537-9789
David Carpenter, *President*
EMP: 10
SQ FT: 5,000
SALES (est): 2.3MM **Privately Held**
SIC: 1542 Commercial & office buildings, prefabricated erection; commercial & office buildings, renovation & repair; agricultural building contractors

(G-6610)
D&K PAINTING INC
3986 Foxridge Dr (66502-8703)
PHONE..................................785 537-4779
David Cooper, *President*
EMP: 10
SALES: 500K **Privately Held**
SIC: 1721 Painting & paper hanging

(G-6611)
DELL ANN UPP
Also Called: Straight Upp
1223 Moro St (66502-5352)
PHONE..................................785 473-7001
Dell Ann Upp, *Owner*
EMP: 10
SALES (est): 175.8K **Privately Held**
SIC: 8999 Artist's studio

(G-6612)
DENTAL ASSOCIATES
Also Called: Hughes, C W Dntst
1133 College Ave Ste D202 (66502-2964)
PHONE..................................785 539-7401
Rick Fulton, *President*
Nancy Snyder, *Vice Pres*
EMP: 24
SALES (est): 2.3MM **Privately Held**
SIC: 8021 Dentists' office

(G-6613)
DESIGNER CONSTRUCTION INC
2716 Eureka Ter (66503-8507)
PHONE..................................785 776-9878
Galen Washington, *President*
Diane Washington, *Corp Secy*
Shannon Butler, *Manager*
EMP: 57
SQ FT: 1,800
SALES (est): 6MM **Privately Held**
SIC: 1771 Concrete work

(G-6614)
DIRECT VET MARKETING INC
Also Called: Vets First Choice
512 Poyntz Ave (66502-6040)
PHONE..................................888 280-2221
Lori Martin, *Branch Mgr*
EMP: 25
SALES (corp-wide): 292.5MM **Publicly Held**
SIC: 0741 Veterinary services for livestock
HQ: Direct Vet Marketing, Inc.
7 Custom House St Ste 5
Portland ME 04101
888 280-2221

(G-6615)
DLABAL & FELLNER GEN DENISTRY
Also Called: Dlabal J Dennis Dntst
1834 Claflin Rd Ste A (66502-3467)
PHONE..................................785 537-8484
Dennis J Dlabal DDS, *Partner*
Britt Fellner, *Partner*
EMP: 10
SQ FT: 2,300
SALES (est): 263.1K **Privately Held**
SIC: 8021 Dentists' office

(G-6616)
DPRA INCORPORATED
121 S 4th St Ste 202 (66502-6100)
PHONE..................................785 539-3565
Mary Carter, *CFO*
Ron Osborne, *IT/INT Sup*
Jonathan Kemper, *Administration*
Shilpa Dipin, *Analyst*
Craig Simons, *Sr Associate*
EMP: 15

GEOGRAPHIC

SALES (corp-wide): 21.8MM **Privately Held**
SIC: 8748 8732 Environmental consultant; economic research
PA: Dpra Incorporated
10215 Tech Dr Ste 201
Knoxville TN 37932
865 777-3772

(G-6617)
DRY CLEAN CITY
Also Called: Bob Boyd
427 E Poyntz Ave (66502-5045)
PHONE..................................785 776-1515
Sky Harbor, *Owner*
EMP: 10
SALES (est): 278.4K **Privately Held**
SIC: 7216 Drycleaning plants, except rugs

(G-6618)
EAGLE COMMUNICATIONS INC
301 S 4th St Ste 130 (66502-6233)
P.O. Box 789, Junction City (66441-0789)
PHONE..................................785 587-0103
Jeff Olasky, *Branch Mgr*
EMP: 12
SALES (corp-wide): 71.7MM **Privately Held**
SIC: 4832 7313 Radio broadcasting stations; radio advertising representative
PA: Eagle Communications, Inc.
2703 Hall St 15
Hays KS 67601
785 625-5910

(G-6619)
EASTSIDE MKT WESTSIDE MKT LLC
219 E Poyntz Ave (66502-3954)
PHONE..................................785 532-8686
Phesa Petty, *Manager*
EMP: 5
SQ FT: 3,000
SALES (corp-wide): 1.5MM **Privately Held**
SIC: 5431 5261 2033 5149 Fruit stands or markets; vegetable stands or markets; garden supplies & tools; Christmas trees (natural); nursery stock, seeds & bulbs; jams, jellies & preserves: packaged in cans, jars, etc.; honey; cheese
PA: Eastside Market & Westside Market Llc
521 Richards Dr
Manhattan KS 66502
785 539-7281

(G-6620)
ENDACOTT LIGHTING INC
511 Fort Riley Blvd (66502-6349)
P.O. Box 1224 (66505-1224)
PHONE..................................785 776-4472
Jeffrey H Endacott, *President*
Susan E Sayson, *Corp Secy*
EMP: 11 **EST:** 1949
SQ FT: 6,900
SALES (est): 2.3MM **Privately Held**
SIC: 5063 5719 Lighting fixtures, commercial & industrial; light bulbs & related supplies; lighting fittings & accessories; lighting, lamps & accessories

(G-6621)
ENVIRONMENTAL MFG INC
8887 Green Valley Dr (66502-1443)
PHONE..................................785 587-0807
Ben Brunner, *President*
Terry Wickham, *Plant Mgr*
Sherry Nelson, *Info Tech Mgr*
Patrick Keting, *Admin Sec*
EMP: 23
SQ FT: 20,000
SALES (est): 7.3MM **Privately Held**
SIC: 5082 Wellpoints (drilling equipment)

(G-6622)
EPIC HOMES OF KANSAS INC
101 Waterbridge Rd (66503-7591)
PHONE..................................785 537-3773
Rodney C Harms, *President*
EMP: 23
SALES (est): 1.4MM **Privately Held**
SIC: 1522 1542 Residential construction; commercial & office building, new construction

(G-6623)
ESB FINANCIAL
224 E Poyntz Ave (66502-5041)
P.O. Box 1920 (66505-1920)
PHONE..................................785 539-3553
Brad Wayman, *Branch Mgr*
Larie Schoap, *Loan*
EMP: 10
SALES (corp-wide): 11.1MM **Privately Held**
SIC: 6282 Investment advice
PA: Esb Financial
801 Merchant St
Emporia KS 66801
620 342-3454

(G-6624)
EVERGY KANSAS CENTRAL INC
225 S Seth Child Rd (66502-3089)
PHONE..................................785 587-2350
Brad Kesl, *Branch Mgr*
EMP: 53
SALES (corp-wide): 4.2B **Publicly Held**
SIC: 4911 Generation, electric power
HQ: Evergy Kansas Central, Inc.
818 S Kansas Ave
Topeka KS 66612
785 575-6300

(G-6625)
FARM BUREAU MUTL INSUR CO INC (PA)
Also Called: Farm Bureau Insurance
2627 Kfb Plz (66503-8116)
PHONE..................................785 587-6000
Steve Baccus, *President*
Michael D Wilds, *Exec VP*
Marty Orth, *Vice Pres*
Ron Koester, *Treasurer*
Dennis E Rice, *Admin Sec*
EMP: 180
SQ FT: 200,000
SALES: 137.3MM **Privately Held**
SIC: 6411 Insurance agents, brokers & service

(G-6626)
FEDERAL EXPRESS CORPORATION
Also Called: Fedex
809m Levee Dr (66502-5056)
PHONE..................................800 463-3339
EMP: 10
SALES (corp-wide): 69.6B **Publicly Held**
SIC: 4213 Trucking, except local
HQ: Federal Express Corporation
3610 Hacks Cross Rd
Memphis TN 38125
901 369-3600

(G-6627)
FEDEX OFFICE & PRINT SVCS INC
1329 Anderson Ave (66502-4002)
PHONE..................................785 537-7340
EMP: 15
SALES (corp-wide): 69.6B **Publicly Held**
WEB: www.kinkos.com
SIC: 7334 Photocopying & duplicating services
HQ: Fedex Office And Print Services, Inc.
7900 Legacy Dr
Plano TX 75024
800 463-3339

(G-6628)
FIRST COMMAND FINCL PLG INC
Also Called: First Command Financial Plg
1121 Hudson Ave Ste B (66503-9921)
PHONE..................................785 537-0497
Scott Hallock, *Manager*
Dan Seemann, *Advisor*
EMP: 12
SALES (corp-wide): 467.4MM **Privately Held**
SIC: 6282 Investment advice
HQ: First Command Financial Planning, Inc.
1 Firstcomm Plz
Fort Worth TX 76109
817 731-8621

(G-6629)
FIRST MANHATTAN BANCORPORATION (PA)
Also Called: First Savings Bank
701 Poyntz Ave (66502-6052)
PHONE..................................785 537-0200
Larry Heyka, *CEO*
Charles Hostetler, *Ch of Bd*
Cynthia Hostetler, *President*
EMP: 50
SQ FT: 25,700
SALES (est): 28.4MM **Privately Held**
WEB: www.firstbank1.com
SIC: 6035 Federal savings banks

(G-6630)
FLINT HILLS AREA TRNSP AGCY BD
5815 Marlatt Ave (66503-8125)
PHONE..................................787 537-6345
Derek Jackson, *President*
Stephanie Peterson, *Vice Pres*
Melanie Tuttle, *Finance*
Anne Smith, *Exec Dir*
EMP: 65
SALES (est): 860.9K **Privately Held**
SIC: 4789 Transportation services

(G-6631)
FLINT HILLS BEVERAGE LLC
5900 Corporate Dr (66503-9675)
PHONE..................................785 776-2337
Dean R Campbell Sr, *President*
D Robert Campbell Jr, *Corp Secy*
Terry Dow,
EMP: 15
SQ FT: 21,000
SALES (est): 6MM **Privately Held**
WEB: www.fhb.kscoxmail.com
SIC: 5181 Beer & other fermented malt liquors

(G-6632)
FLINT HILLS FORD INC
Also Called: Flint Hills Auto
7920 E Us Highway 24 (66502-8600)
PHONE..................................785 776-4004
Joe Bowers, *Principal*
Danny Benites, *Principal*
Andrew Olson, *Administration*
EMP: 40
SALES (est): 3.6MM **Privately Held**
SIC: 5511 7389 Automobiles, new & used; automobile recovery service

(G-6633)
FLINT HILLS HEART VASCULAR
3905 Vanesta Dr Ste A (66503-2002)
PHONE..................................785 320-5858
Raymond Dattilo,
EMP: 10
SALES (est): 1.7MM **Privately Held**
SIC: 8011 Cardiologist & cardio-vascular specialist

(G-6634)
FLINT HILLS HOSPITALITY LLC
Also Called: Candlewood Suites
210 Blue Earth Pl (66502-6346)
PHONE..................................785 320-7995
Beth Lohman, *General Mgr*
EMP: 17
SALES (est): 1.1MM **Privately Held**
SIC: 7011 Hotels

(G-6635)
FLINT HLLS AREA TRNSP AGCY INC
Also Called: ATA BUS
5815 Marlatt Ave (66503-8125)
PHONE..................................785 537-6345
Anne Smith, *Exec Dir*
Sandi Harper, *Officer*
Vicky McCallum, *Admin Asst*
EMP: 40
SQ FT: 11,250
SALES: 3.1MM **Privately Held**
SIC: 4111 Local & suburban transit

(G-6636)
FLORENCE CORPORATION KANSAS (HQ)
Also Called: Florence Manufacturing Company
5935 Corporate Dr (66503-9675)
P.O. Box 712993, Cincinnati OH (45271-2993)
PHONE..................................785 323-4400
John Altstadt, *President*
Kevin Fee, *Vice Pres*
Stacy Kohlmeier, *Vice Pres*
Steve Penn-Berkeley, *Vice Pres*
Kerri Winter, *Vice Pres*
▲ **EMP:** 175 **EST:** 1934
SQ FT: 85,000
SALES (est): 60MM
SALES (corp-wide): 1B **Publicly Held**
WEB: www.auth-florence.com
SIC: 3469 Boxes: tool, lunch, mail, etc.: stamped metal
PA: Gibraltar Industries, Inc.
3556 Lake Shore Rd # 100
Buffalo NY 14219
716 826-6500

(G-6637)
FOLEY EQUIPMENT COMPANY
Also Called: Caterpillar Authorized Dealer
5104 Skyway Dr (66503-9710)
PHONE..................................785 537-2101
Fred Coble, *Manager*
EMP: 70
SALES (corp-wide): 124.2MM **Privately Held**
SIC: 5084 7353 Industrial machinery & equipment; heavy construction equipment rental
HQ: Foley Equipment Company
1550 S West St
Wichita KS 67213
316 943-4211

(G-6638)
FOREST CITY ENTERPRISES INC
100 Manhattan Town Ctr (66502-6001)
PHONE..................................785 539-3500
Allen Raynor, *Manager*
EMP: 50
SALES (corp-wide): 513.4MM **Privately Held**
WEB: www.fceinc.com
SIC: 6512 Shopping center, property operation only
HQ: Forest City Enterprises, L.P.
127 Public Sq Ste 3200
Cleveland OH 44114
216 621-6060

(G-6639)
FOUR POINTS BY SHERATON
530 Richards Dr Ste B (66502-3146)
PHONE..................................785 539-5311
Jenn Alley, *Principal*
EMP: 13
SALES (est): 581.9K **Privately Held**
SIC: 7011 Hotels & motels

(G-6640)
FOX COMPUTER INC
Also Called: Fox Business Systems
531 Fort Riley Blvd (66502-6349)
PHONE..................................785 776-1452
James Lund, *President*
Cathy Lund, *Corp Secy*
EMP: 20
SQ FT: 4,000
SALES (est): 2.8MM **Privately Held**
SIC: 5734 7378 Computer peripheral equipment; computer maintenance & repair

(G-6641)
FRONTIER FARM CREDIT ACA
Also Called: Frontier Farm Credit, Flca
2009 Vanesta Pl (66503-0368)
P.O. Box 188 (66505-0188)
PHONE..................................785 776-6955
Parry Briggs, *President*
Tony English, *Principal*
Jim Aylward, *Principal*
Janet Bartel, *Principal*
Doug Hofbauer, *Principal*
EMP: 150

SALES (est): 10.7MM **Privately Held**
SIC: 6719 6159 Investment holding companies, except banks; agricultural credit institutions; agricultural loan companies

(G-6642)
G F ENTERPRISES
1810 Poyntz Ave (66502-3948)
PHONE..................................785 539-7113
Don Younkin, *Owner*
EMP: 6
SALES (est): 113K **Privately Held**
SIC: 7629 7692 7539 0782 Electrical repair shops; welding repair; automotive repair shops; cemetery upkeep services

(G-6643)
GAIA INC
Also Called: Gaia Salon
421 Poyntz Ave (66502-0115)
PHONE..................................785 539-2622
Ralph Diav, *Owner*
EMP: 15
SALES (est): 331.6K **Privately Held**
WEB: www.gaiasalon.com
SIC: 7231 5087 Unisex hair salons; beauty salon & barber shop equipment & supplies

(G-6644)
GENERAL ELECTRIC COMPANY
2627 Kfb Plz Ste 401e (66503-8123)
PHONE..................................785 320-2350
Brad Sonner, *Manager*
EMP: 60
SALES (corp-wide): 121.6B **Publicly Held**
SIC: 4581 Aircraft maintenance & repair services
PA: General Electric Company
5 Necco St
Boston MA 02210
617 443-3000

(G-6645)
GET AFTER IT LLC
Also Called: 9round
1620 Fort Riley Blvd (66502-4231)
PHONE..................................402 885-0964
EMP: 12
SALES (corp-wide): 1.4MM **Privately Held**
SIC: 7991 Physical fitness facilities
PA: Get After It, Llc
2800 N 83rd St Ste C
Lincoln NE 68507
402 885-0964

(G-6646)
GREY MOUNTAIN PARTNERS LLC
1822 Fair Ln (66502-3910)
PHONE..................................785 776-9482
Jason Spreer, *Branch Mgr*
EMP: 38
SALES (corp-wide): 462.1MM **Privately Held**
SIC: 1793 Glass & glazing work
PA: Grey Mountain Partners, Llc
1470 Walnut St Ste 400
Boulder CO 80302
303 449-5692

(G-6647)
GRIFFITH LUMBER COMPANY INC (PA)
Also Called: Griffith Lumber & Hardware
820 Levee Dr (66502-5012)
P.O. Box 457 (66505-0457)
PHONE..................................785 776-4104
Neal K Helmick, *President*
Eleanor G Stolzer, *Corp Secy*
Kathy Kohler, *Purchasing*
EMP: 25
SQ FT: 18,000
SALES (est): 15.3MM **Privately Held**
WEB: www.griffithlumber.com
SIC: 5031 5211 2522 Lumber: rough, dressed & finished; lumber & other building materials; cabinets, office: except wood

(G-6648)
GWALTNEY INC
Also Called: Diamond Roofing
9300 E Us Highway 24 (66502-8719)
PHONE..................................785 537-8008
Jason Kellner, *General Mgr*
Dwight Gwaltney III, *Branch Mgr*
EMP: 30
SALES (corp-wide): 15MM **Privately Held**
WEB: www.gwaltney.com
SIC: 1761 Roofing contractor
PA: Gwaltney, Inc.
100 E Mcartor St
Dodge City KS 67801
620 225-2622

(G-6649)
H&R BLOCK INC
Also Called: H & R Block
634 Tuttle Creek Blvd (66502-5854)
P.O. Box 163 (66505-0163)
PHONE..................................785 776-7531
Tammie Judy, *Manager*
EMP: 18
SALES (corp-wide): 3B **Publicly Held**
WEB: www.hrblock.com
SIC: 7291 Tax return preparation services
PA: H&R Block, Inc.
1 H&R Block Way
Kansas City MO 64105
816 854-3000

(G-6650)
HAIR EXPERTS
Also Called: Hair Experts Design Team
1323 Anderson Ave (66502-4002)
PHONE..................................785 776-4455
Debbie McCoullough, *Owner*
EMP: 20
SQ FT: 440
SALES (est): 505.4K **Privately Held**
WEB: www.hairexpertssalonandspa.com
SIC: 7231 Hairdressers

(G-6651)
HAYNES SALON AND SUPPLY INC
718 N Manhattan Ave (66502-5335)
PHONE..................................785 539-5512
Ira C Haynes II, *President*
Kathi Haynes, *Vice Pres*
EMP: 10
SQ FT: 4,400
SALES (est): 175.3K **Privately Held**
SIC: 7231 5087 Unisex hair salons; beauty parlor equipment & supplies

(G-6652)
HEARTLAND PLANT INNOVATIONS
1990 Kimball Ave (66502-3323)
PHONE..................................785 320-4300
Forrest Chumley, *CEO*
Dusti Gallagher, *President*
Kenneth L Audus, *Principal*
Rob Berard, *CFO*
EMP: 10
SALES: 1MM **Privately Held**
SIC: 8731 Biotechnical research, commercial

(G-6653)
HEINEKEN ELECTRIC COMPANY INC
2151 Fort Riley Blvd F (66502-3873)
P.O. Box 236, Beloit (67420-0236)
PHONE..................................785 539-7400
Dalen Meyer, *General Mgr*
EMP: 17
SALES (corp-wide): 3.8MM **Privately Held**
SIC: 1731 General electrical contractor
PA: Heineken Electric Co., Inc.
3121b Us 24 Hwy
Beloit KS 67420
785 738-3831

(G-6654)
HENTON PLUMBING & AC INC
Also Called: Henton Plumbing & AC
8838 Quail Ln (66502-1439)
PHONE..................................785 776-5548
Steve Kirby, *President*
Debbie Kirby, *Corp Secy*
EMP: 11
SQ FT: 800
SALES (est): 980K **Privately Held**
SIC: 1711 Warm air heating & air conditioning contractor; plumbing contractors

(G-6655)
HERITAGE BUILDERS INC
217 S 4th St (66502-6111)
PHONE..................................785 776-6011
Kenton Glasscock, *President*
EMP: 14
SALES (est): 1.1MM **Privately Held**
SIC: 1521 New construction, single-family houses

(G-6656)
HI-TECH INTERIORS INC (PA)
5006 Skyway Dr (66503-9778)
PHONE..................................785 539-7266
Frederick Willich, *President*
Martin Baumgard, *Superintendent*
Jarrod Willich, *Vice Pres*
Jeremy Houghton, *Controller*
EMP: 21
SQ FT: 3,000
SALES: 18MM **Privately Held**
WEB: www.hitechinteriors.com
SIC: 1742 Drywall

(G-6657)
HILAND DAIRY FOODS COMPANY LLC
Steffen's Dairy
2710 Amherst Ave (66502-2936)
PHONE..................................785 539-7541
Rick Clark, *Manager*
EMP: 13
SQ FT: 5,000
SALES (corp-wide): 1.7B **Privately Held**
SIC: 5143 0241 Dairy products, except dried or canned; milk production
HQ: Hiland Dairy Foods Company., Llc
1133 E Kearney St
Springfield MO 65803
417 862-9311

(G-6658)
HILL INVESTMENT & RENTAL CO
625 Pebblebrook Cir (66503-9841)
PHONE..................................785 537-9064
Mike Hill, *Owner*
EMP: 10
SALES (est): 794.9K **Privately Held**
WEB: www.hillinvestandrental.com
SIC: 6513 Apartment building operators

(G-6659)
HOPE PLANTING INTL INC
3310 Germann Dr (66503-8457)
PHONE..................................785 776-8523
Floyd Dowell, *Principal*
EMP: 13
SALES: 109.3K **Privately Held**
SIC: 8099 8699 9721 Nutrition services; charitable organization; foreign missions

(G-6660)
HOWIES ENTERPRISES LLC
Also Called: Howie's Trash Service
625 S 10th St (66502-5553)
PHONE..................................785 776-8352
Greg Wilson, *President*
Howard Wilson, *Vice Pres*
Jay Anderson, *Manager*
EMP: 17
SALES (est): 1.7MM **Privately Held**
SIC: 3639 4953 Trash compactors, household; waste materials, disposal at sea

(G-6661)
HOWL-A-DAYZ INN LLC
530 Mccall Rd Ste 150 (66502-5054)
PHONE..................................785 539-7849
Tyler Wolfe,
EMP: 10 **EST:** 2013
SALES (est): 219.8K **Privately Held**
SIC: 0752 Animal boarding services

(G-6662)
HULSING HOTELS KANSAS INC
Also Called: Clarion Hotel
530 Richards Dr Ste B (66502-3146)
PHONE..................................785 539-5311
Jessica Miner, *Branch Mgr*
EMP: 99
SALES (corp-wide): 10.7MM **Privately Held**
SIC: 7011 7299 5812 5813 Hotels & motels; banquet hall facilities; caterers; drinking places
PA: Hulsing Hotels Kansas, Inc.
200 Mcdonald Dr
Lawrence KS 66044
785 841-7077

(G-6663)
I 70 TAX SERVICES LLC
Also Called: Liberty Tax
100 Bluemont Ave Ste G (66502-5059)
PHONE..................................785 539-5240
Jay Copeland, *Principal*
EMP: 11
SALES (est): 207K **Privately Held**
SIC: 7291 Tax return preparation services

(G-6664)
IDEA CENTER INC
301 S 4th St Ste 200 (66502-6233)
PHONE..................................785 320-2400
Ken Ryalls, *President*
Karen Bryant, *Manager*
Jake Glover, *Consultant*
David Goodman, *Software Dev*
Joonsuk Lee, *Software Dev*
EMP: 14
SQ FT: 5,000
SALES: 3MM **Privately Held**
SIC: 8713 8221 Surveying services; colleges universities & professional schools

(G-6665)
INTRUST BANK NA
630 Humboldt St (66502-6045)
PHONE..................................785 565-5400
Colby Reynolds, *Manager*
EMP: 10
SALES (corp-wide): 134.2MM **Privately Held**
WEB: www.intrustbank.com
SIC: 6021 National trust companies with deposits, commercial
HQ: Intrust Bank National Association
105 N Main St
Wichita KS 67202
316 383-1111

(G-6666)
ITS GREEK TO ME INC (HQ)
Also Called: Champion Teamwear
520 Mccall Rd (66502-5034)
P.O. Box 8 (66505-0008)
PHONE..................................800 336-4486
Gerald Evans, *CEO*
Adam Glendening, *CFO*
John Strawn, *CIO*
▲ **EMP:** 121
SQ FT: 110,000
SALES (est): 237.4MM
SALES (corp-wide): 6.8B **Publicly Held**
WEB: www.kstategear.com
SIC: 5136 5699 5137 5947 Sportswear, men's & boys'; sports apparel; sportswear, women's & children's; gift shop; screen printing
PA: Hanesbrands Inc.
1000 E Hanes Mill Rd
Winston Salem NC 27105
336 519-8080

(G-6667)
JS SIGN & AWNING LLC
2726 Amherst Ave Ste A (66502-2956)
PHONE..................................785 776-8860
John Stroh, *Mng Member*
EMP: 5
SQ FT: 1,000
SALES: 1MM **Privately Held**
SIC: 3993 Signs, not made in custom sign painting shops

(G-6668)
K STATE RABIES LABORATORY
2005 Research Park Cir (66502-5020)
PHONE..................................785 532-4472
Ralph Richardson, *Ch of Bd*
EMP: 15
SALES (est): 1.2MM **Privately Held**
SIC: 2835 8734 Veterinary diagnostic substances; veterinary testing

(G-6669)
K-STATE DIAGNOSTIC & ANALYTICL
Also Called: VETERINARY DIAGNOSTIC LABORATO
1800 Denison Ave (66506-5611)
PHONE..................................785 532-3294
Gary Anderson, *Exec Dir*
EMP: 135
SALES: 10.1MM **Privately Held**
SIC: 8734 Testing laboratories

(G-6670)
K-STATE HRTCLTURE NTRAL RSRCES
1712 Claflin Rd (66506-4825)
PHONE..................................785 532-6170
Candice Shoemaker, *Director*
EMP: 50
SALES (est): 862.8K **Privately Held**
SIC: 0782 Lawn & garden services

(G-6671)
K-STATE UNION CORPORATION
Also Called: K-State Student Union
918 N 17th St (66506-3419)
PHONE..................................785 532-6575
Michala Langlois, *Nutritionist*
Irma Rosas, *Nutritionist*
Anna Wolff, *Nutritionist*
Matt McKernan, *Agent*
William Smriga, *Exec Dir*
EMP: 110 **EST:** 1956
SQ FT: 263,000
SALES: 5.1MM **Privately Held**
SIC: 5942 7999 7359 College book stores; recreation center; vending machine rental

(G-6672)
KA-COMM INC
2321 Skyvue Ln Ste A (66502-3169)
PHONE..................................785 776-8177
Scott L Fischer, *Manager*
Scott Fischer, *Manager*
EMP: 7
SALES (corp-wide): 7.1MM **Privately Held**
SIC: 7622 4812 3663 Communication equipment repair; cellular telephone services; radio broadcasting & communications equipment
PA: Ka-Comm., Inc
326 S Clark St
Salina KS 67401
785 827-8555

(G-6673)
KANGOLF INC
Also Called: Wildcat Creek Sports Center
800 Anneberg Cir (66503-7595)
PHONE..................................785 539-7529
Kevin Fateley, *President*
Beth Fateley, *Corp Secy*
EMP: 10
SALES (est): 684K **Privately Held**
SIC: 7992 7999 7993 Public golf courses; baseball batting cage; miniature golf course operation; golf driving range; arcades

(G-6674)
KANSAS AIR CENTER INC (PA)
1705 S Airport Rd (66503-9795)
PHONE..................................785 776-1991
Ronald K Nordt, *President*
EMP: 17
SALES: 1.2MM **Privately Held**
WEB: www.kansasair.com
SIC: 4522 4581 8299 Flying charter service; aircraft servicing & repairing; flying instruction

(G-6675)
KANSAS CROP IMPROVEMENT ASSN
2000 Kimball Ave (66502-3354)
PHONE..................................785 532-6118
Bob Bunck, *President*
Ardyce Kuhn, *Manager*
Daryl Strouts, *Director*
EMP: 10
SQ FT: 8,400
SALES: 619.2K **Privately Held**
SIC: 7389 Inspection & testing services

(G-6676)
KANSAS RGNRTIVE MDCINE CTR LLC
4809 Vue Du Lac Pl (66503-8673)
PHONE..................................785 320-4700
Kenneth A Woods Jr, *President*
Loraine S Farley, *Principal*
Kate Farley, *Marketing Staff*
Meghan Flanigan, *Admin Asst*
EMP: 12
SALES (est): 1MM **Privately Held**
SIC: 8011 Medical centers

(G-6677)
KANSAS STATE UNIV ALUMNI ASSN
Also Called: K-State Alumni Association
1720 Anderson Ave (66506-1001)
PHONE..................................785 532-6260
Amy Button Renz, *President*
Glenn Hoover, *Asst Director*
EMP: 35
SALES: 4.7MM **Privately Held**
WEB: www.k-statealumni.com
SIC: 8641 Alumni association

(G-6678)
KANSAS STATE UNIV FEDERAL CR (PA)
Also Called: K-STATE UNIVERSITY FEDERAL CR
2600 Anderson Ave (66502-2802)
PHONE..................................785 776-3003
Larae J Kraemer, *CEO*
Terri Vipond, *Vice Pres*
EMP: 15 **EST:** 2007
SALES: 3.3MM **Privately Held**
SIC: 6061 Federal credit unions

(G-6679)
KANSAS STATE UNIV FOUNDATION
Also Called: Ksu Foundation
1800 Kimball Ave Ste 200 (66502-3373)
PHONE..................................785 532-6266
Gary Hellebust, *CEO*
Fred Scholick, *CEO*
Jordan Tilley, *Business Mgr*
Pat Bosco, *Vice Pres*
John Morris, *Vice Pres*
EMP: 100
SQ FT: 38,500
SALES: 112.6MM **Privately Held**
WEB: www.ksuwildcats.com
SIC: 7389 Fund raising organizations

(G-6680)
KANSAS STATE UNIVERSITY
Also Called: Marianna Kstler Bch Museum Art
701 Beach Ln (66506-0600)
PHONE..................................785 532-7718
Lorne Render, *Director*
EMP: 25
SALES (corp-wide): 637.6MM **Privately Held**
WEB: www.ksu.edu
SIC: 8412 8221 Museum; university
PA: Kansas State University
Anderson Hall 110 1301 Mi St Anderson Ha
Manhattan KS 66506
785 532-6011

(G-6681)
KANSAS STATE UNIVERSITY
Also Called: KS St U Dept of Housing D
104 Pittman Building (66506-4600)
PHONE..................................785 532-6376
Chuck Werring, *Director*
EMP: 500
SALES (corp-wide): 637.6MM **Privately Held**
WEB: www.ksu.edu
SIC: 7021 8221 Dormitory, commercially operated; university
PA: Kansas State University
Anderson Hall 110 1301 Mi St Anderson Ha
Manhattan KS 66506
785 532-6011

(G-6682)
KANSAS STATE UNIVERSITY
Also Called: Athletic Department Bus Off
1800 College Ave (66502-3308)
PHONE..................................785 539-4971
Robert Krause, *Director*
EMP: 1092
SALES (corp-wide): 637.6MM **Privately Held**
WEB: www.ksu.edu
SIC: 8699 8221 Athletic organizations; university
PA: Kansas State University
Anderson Hall 110 1301 Mi St Anderson Ha
Manhattan KS 66506
785 532-6011

(G-6683)
KANSAS STATE UNIVERSITY
Also Called: Ksu/Land Arch/ Reg Co
302 Seaton Hall (66506-2900)
PHONE..................................785 532-5961
Steffani Rolley, *Director*
EMP: 25
SALES (corp-wide): 637.6MM **Privately Held**
WEB: www.ksu.edu
SIC: 0781 8221 Landscape planning services; university
PA: Kansas State University
Anderson Hall 110 1301 Mi St Anderson Ha
Manhattan KS 66506
785 532-6011

(G-6684)
KANSAS STATE UNIVERSITY
Also Called: Beef Cattle Institute
1320 Research Park Dr (66502-5000)
PHONE..................................785 564-7459
Kelly Oliver, *Branch Mgr*
EMP: 10
SALES (corp-wide): 637.6MM **Privately Held**
SIC: 0751 Breeding services, livestock
PA: Kansas State University
Anderson Hall 110 1301 Mi St Anderson Ha
Manhattan KS 66506
785 532-6011

(G-6685)
KANSAS STATE UNIVERSITY
Also Called: Recreational Service Ksu
101 Recreation Complex (66506)
PHONE..................................785 532-6980
Steve Martini, *Director*
EMP: 13
SALES (corp-wide): 637.6MM **Privately Held**
WEB: www.ksu.edu
SIC: 8221 7991 University; physical fitness facilities
PA: Kansas State University
Anderson Hall 110 1301 Mi St Anderson Ha
Manhattan KS 66506
785 532-6011

(G-6686)
KANSAS STATE UNIVERSITY
116 Cardwell Hall (66506-2600)
PHONE..................................785 532-6011
Jon Wefald, *President*
Dan Boyle, *Professor*
John Briggs, *Professor*
EMP: 100
SALES (corp-wide): 637.6MM **Privately Held**
WEB: www.ksu.edu
SIC: 8733 8221 Scientific research agency; colleges universities & professional schools
PA: Kansas State University
Anderson Hall 110 1301 Mi St Anderson Ha
Manhattan KS 66506
785 532-6011

(G-6687)
KANSAS STATE UNIVERSITY
Also Called: Athletic Department
1800 College Ave (66502-3308)
PHONE..................................785 532-7600
Tim Weizer, *Manager*
EMP: 45
SALES (corp-wide): 637.6MM **Privately Held**
WEB: www.ksu.edu
SIC: 6512 8221 Property operation, auditoriums & theaters; university
PA: Kansas State University
Anderson Hall 110 1301 Mi St Anderson Ha
Manhattan KS 66506
785 532-6011

(G-6688)
KANSAS STATE UNIVERSITY
Veterinary Diagnostic Lab
1800 Denison Ave (66506-5611)
PHONE..................................785 532-5650
Dr M M Chengappa, *Manager*
EMP: 100
SALES (corp-wide): 637.6MM **Privately Held**
WEB: www.ksu.edu
SIC: 8071 8221 Medical laboratories; university
PA: Kansas State University
Anderson Hall 110 1301 Mi St Anderson Ha
Manhattan KS 66506
785 532-6011

(G-6689)
KANSAS STATE UNIVERSITY
Also Called: Animal Resource Falicity
1600 Denison Ave Ste 103 (66506-5605)
PHONE..................................785 532-5640
Marilyn Land, *Manager*
EMP: 21
SALES (corp-wide): 637.6MM **Privately Held**
WEB: www.ksu.edu
SIC: 0742 8221 Veterinary services, specialties; university
PA: Kansas State University
Anderson Hall 110 1301 Mi St Anderson Ha
Manhattan KS 66506
785 532-6011

(G-6690)
KANSAS STATE UNIVERSITY
Also Called: Extension Agricultural Engrg
237 Seaton Hall (66506-2900)
PHONE..................................785 532-5813
James Murphy, *Principal*
EMP: 13
SALES (corp-wide): 637.6MM **Privately Held**
WEB: www.ksu.edu
SIC: 8748 8221 Educational consultant; university
PA: Kansas State University
Anderson Hall 110 1301 Mi St Anderson Ha
Manhattan KS 66506
785 532-6011

(G-6691)
KANSAS STATE UNIVERSITY
108 Edwards Hall (66506-4800)
PHONE..................................785 532-6412
Ronnie Grice, *Director*
EMP: 35
SALES (corp-wide): 637.6MM **Privately Held**
WEB: www.ksu.edu
SIC: 7381 8221 Protective services, guard; university
PA: Kansas State University
Anderson Hall 110 1301 Mi St Anderson Ha
Manhattan KS 66506
785 532-6011

(G-6692)
KANSAS STATE UNIVERSITY
Also Called: Career P& Employment Svc
100 Holtz Hall (66506-1700)
PHONE..................................785 532-6506
Tracey Fraser, *Director*
EMP: 25
SALES (corp-wide): 637.6MM **Privately Held**
WEB: www.ksu.edu
SIC: 7361 8221 Employment agencies; university

PA: Kansas State University
Anderson Hall 110 1301 Mi St Anderson Ha
Manhattan KS 66506
785 532-6011

(G-6693)
KANSAS STATE UNIVERSITY
Also Called: Ksu Animal Science
139 Call Hall (66506)
PHONE.....................................785 532-5654
Jack Riley, *Principal*
EMP: 200
SALES (corp-wide): 637.6MM **Privately Held**
WEB: www.ksu.edu
SIC: 0742 8221 Veterinary services, specialties; university
PA: Kansas State University
Anderson Hall 110 1301 Mi St Anderson Ha
Manhattan KS 66506
785 532-6011

(G-6694)
KANSAS STATE UNIVERSITY
Also Called: NISTAC
2005 Research Park Cir (66502-5020)
PHONE.....................................785 532-3900
Kent Glasscock, *President*
Victoria Appelhans, *Vice Pres*
Bret Ford, *Associate*
EMP: 11
SALES: 1.4MM **Privately Held**
SIC: 8748 Urban planning & consulting services

(G-6695)
KANSAS STATE UNIVERSITY
Also Called: Pre-Awards Services
2 Fairchild Hall (66506)
PHONE.....................................785 532-6804
Paul Lowe, *Director*
Socorro Herrera, *Director*
Debra Stryker, *Administration*
Lester Loschky, *Assoc Prof*
EMP: 12
SALES (corp-wide): 637.6MM **Privately Held**
WEB: www.ksu.edu
SIC: 8748 8221 Business consulting; university
PA: Kansas State University
Anderson Hall 110 1301 Mi St Anderson Ha
Manhattan KS 66506
785 532-6011

(G-6696)
KANSAS STATE UNIVERSITY
Also Called: Family Center
100 Justin Hall (66506-1400)
PHONE.....................................785 532-6984
Dr Stephan Boleman, *Director*
EMP: 36
SALES (corp-wide): 637.6MM **Privately Held**
WEB: www.ksu.edu
SIC: 8322 8221 Family counseling services; university
PA: Kansas State University
Anderson Hall 110 1301 Mi St Anderson Ha
Manhattan KS 66506
785 532-6011

(G-6697)
KANSAS STATE UNIVERSITY GOLF C
Also Called: Ksugcmrf
5200 Colbert Hills Dr (66503-9687)
PHONE.....................................785 776-6475
Bernard Haney, *Exec Dir*
EMP: 35
SALES (est): 165.8K **Privately Held**
SIC: 7992 Public golf courses

(G-6698)
KEATING & ASSOCIATES INC (PA)
1011 Poyntz Ave (66502-5458)
PHONE.....................................785 537-0366
Patrick J Keating, *President*
Gregory Hill, *Vice Pres*
Ryan Mann, *Vice Pres*
Libby Paul, *Project Mgr*
Mary Bartlett, *Opers Staff*
EMP: 20
SQ FT: 4,500
SALES (est): 3.1MM **Privately Held**
WEB: www.keatinginc.com
SIC: 8748 6411 Employee programs administration; insurance agents & brokers

(G-6699)
KINDERCARE LEARNING CTRS LLC
Also Called: Kindercare Child Care Network
1205 Hylton Heights Rd (66502-2823)
PHONE.....................................785 539-7540
Lisa Richards, *Exec Dir*
Lisa Phillips, *Director*
EMP: 15
SALES (corp-wide): 963.9MM **Privately Held**
WEB: www.kindercare.com
SIC: 8351 Group day care center
HQ: Kindercare Learning Centers, Llc
650 Ne Holladay St # 1400
Portland OR 97232
503 872-1300

(G-6700)
KRUSE CORPORATION
8971 Green Valley Dr # 1 (66502-9008)
PHONE.....................................785 320-7990
Josh McHugh, *Branch Mgr*
Cheri Lee, *Administration*
EMP: 30 **Privately Held**
SIC: 1711 Warm air heating & air conditioning contractor
PA: Kruse Corporation
3636 N Topeka St
Wichita KS 67219

(G-6701)
KS STATEBANK
8803 E Us Highway 24 (66502-1430)
PHONE.....................................785 587-4000
EMP: 24
SALES (corp-wide): 95MM **Privately Held**
SIC: 6022 State commercial banks
HQ: Ks Statebank
1010 Westloop Pl
Manhattan KS 66502
785 587-4000

(G-6702)
KS STATEBANK
Also Called: Downtown Branch
555 Poyntz Ave (66502-6085)
PHONE.....................................785 587-4000
Susan Walley, *Manager*
EMP: 24
SALES (corp-wide): 95MM **Privately Held**
SIC: 6022 State trust companies accepting deposits, commercial
HQ: Ks Statebank
1010 Westloop Pl
Manhattan KS 66502
785 587-4000

(G-6703)
KSU DPRTMENT OF CLNCAL SCIENCE
1800 Denison Ave (66506-5611)
PHONE.....................................785 532-5690
Roger Fingland, *Director*
EMP: 75
SALES (est): 1.6MM **Privately Held**
SIC: 8071 Medical laboratories

(G-6704)
KSU FOOTBALL OPERATION
2201 Kimball Ave (66502-3314)
PHONE.....................................785 532-6832
Tim Wiser, *Exec Dir*
Jim Epps, *Director*
Laua Tietjan, *Director*
EMP: 75
SALES (est): 1MM **Privately Held**
WEB: www.ksufootball.com
SIC: 7941 Football club

(G-6705)
KSU NATIONAL GAS MACHINERY LAB
245 Levee Dr (66502-5005)
PHONE.....................................785 532-2617
Kirby Chapman, *Director*
Joe Prockish, *Director*
Kimberly Elliott, *Admin Asst*
Uwe Thumm, *Professor*
Brian Washburn, *Professor*
EMP: 10
SALES (est): 735.9K **Privately Held**
SIC: 8734 Testing laboratories

(G-6706)
KXBZ B 104 7 FM
Also Called: K X B Z-104.7 F M
2414 Casement Rd (66502-6633)
PHONE.....................................785 539-1047
Seaton Stations, *Owner*
Cheri Marstall, *Business Mgr*
Andrea Besthorn, *Sales Mgr*
Richard Wartell, *Manager*
EMP: 40
SALES (est): 1.8MM **Privately Held**
SIC: 4832 Radio broadcasting stations

(G-6707)
LABORATORY CORPORATION AMERICA
1133 College Ave Bldg E (66502-2770)
PHONE.....................................785 539-2537
Jeff Roeser, *Branch Mgr*
EMP: 25 **Publicly Held**
SIC: 8071 Testing laboratories
HQ: Laboratory Corporation Of America
358 S Main St Ste 458
Burlington NC 27215
336 229-1127

(G-6708)
LANDMARK BANCORP INC (PA)
701 Poyntz Ave (66502-6052)
PHONE.....................................785 565-2000
Michael E Scheopner, *President*
Patrick L Alexander, *Chairman*
Mark A Herpich, *CFO*
Sandra Moll, *Director*
Sarah Hill-Nelson, *Bd of Directors*
EMP: 19
SALES: 48.7MM **Publicly Held**
SIC: 6021 National commercial banks

(G-6709)
LANDMARK NATIONAL BANK (HQ)
701 Poyntz Ave (66502-0100)
P.O. Box 1437, Dodge City (67801-1437)
PHONE.....................................620 225-1745
Patrick Alexander, *President*
Mark Herpich, *CFO*
Jeff Oliphant, *Loan Officer*
Joe Kennedy, *Marketing Staff*
Colby Neiswender, *Branch Mgr*
EMP: 62
SQ FT: 7,500
SALES: 42.2MM
SALES (corp-wide): 48.7MM **Publicly Held**
SIC: 6021 National commercial banks
PA: Landmark Bancorp, Inc.
701 Poyntz Ave
Manhattan KS 66502
785 565-2000

(G-6710)
LARSON CONSTRUCTION INC
2616 Eureka Ter (66503-8490)
P.O. Box 1411 (66505-1411)
PHONE.....................................785 537-0160
Robert W Rogers, *President*
Tamara Rogers, *Admin Sec*
EMP: 25 **EST:** 1951
SQ FT: 2,200
SALES: 8.6MM **Privately Held**
SIC: 1623 Underground utilities contractor

(G-6711)
LEE CONSTRUCTION CO
Also Called: Heritage Ridge Apts
3108 Heritage Ct Apt 45 (66503-2254)
PHONE.....................................785 539-7961
Mildred E Lee, *Partner*
Janice Lee, *Partner*
EMP: 11
SALES: 400K **Privately Held**
SIC: 6513 Apartment building operators

(G-6712)
LEISZLER OIL CO INC (PA)
Also Called: Short Stop
8228 Southport Dr (66502-8116)
PHONE.....................................785 632-5648
Charles Arthur III, *President*
Roger Bertsche, *Area Mgr*
Samantha Liby, *Exec VP*
Alison R Leiszler, *Vice Pres*
Traci Jacob, *Area Spvr*
EMP: 20
SQ FT: 3,000
SALES (est): 125.5MM **Privately Held**
WEB: www.leiszleroil.com
SIC: 5171 5411 5541 Petroleum bulk stations; grocery stores; gasoline service stations

(G-6713)
LIBERTY INC (PA)
8872 Green Valley Dr (66502-1560)
PHONE.....................................785 770-8788
B L Harris Jr, *Vice Pres*
Thomas Grieshaber, *Manager*
Darlaine Champaigne, *Manager*
EMP: 65
SQ FT: 5,000
SALES: 8.5MM **Privately Held**
WEB: www.travalong.com
SIC: 3523 5083 Trailers & wagons, farm; livestock equipment

(G-6714)
LITTLE APPLE BREWING COMPANY
1110 Westloop Pl (66502-2838)
PHONE.....................................785 539-5500
Galen Fink, *President*
James Gordon, *Treasurer*
Paul Miller, *Officer*
David Burchfield, *Admin Sec*
EMP: 125
SALES (est): 4.4MM **Privately Held**
WEB: www.littleapplebrewery.com
SIC: 5813 5812 7299 2082 Bar (drinking places); American restaurant; banquet hall facilities; malt beverages

(G-6715)
LITTLE APPLE LANES
515 Richards Dr (66502-3142)
PHONE.....................................785 539-0371
Robert Regan, *President*
EMP: 15
SALES (est): 834.8K **Privately Held**
SIC: 7933 Bowling centers

(G-6716)
M ROCKING RADIO INC (PA)
1707 Thomas Cir Ste A (66502-4635)
PHONE.....................................785 565-0406
Candice Thomas, *Business Mgr*
Christopher D Miller, *Vice Pres*
Monte Miller, *Executive*
EMP: 15
SALES (est): 3.1MM **Privately Held**
SIC: 4832 Radio broadcasting stations

(G-6717)
MAID SERVICES INC
Also Called: Merry Maids
2049 Fort Riley Ln (66502-3967)
PHONE.....................................785 537-6243
Sharon Hoffman, *President*
Corinna Ruckert, *Treasurer*
EMP: 20
SQ FT: 1,500
SALES: 720K **Privately Held**
SIC: 7359 7349 Home cleaning & maintenance equipment rental services; building maintenance services

(G-6718)
MANHATTAN BROADCASTING CO INC
Also Called: K-Rock
2414 Casement Rd (66502-6633)
PHONE.....................................785 776-1350
Corey Reeves, *General Mgr*
Rich Wartell, *General Mgr*
EMP: 33 **EST:** 1947
SQ FT: 3,600
SALES (est): 3.3MM **Privately Held**
WEB: www.z963.com
SIC: 4832 Radio broadcasting stations

(G-6719)
MANHATTAN CHAMBER OF COMMERCE
Also Called: MANHATTAN VISITORS BUREAU
501 Poyntz Ave (66502-6005)
PHONE.................................785 776-8829
John Pagen, *Vice Pres*
Lyle Butler, *Director*
Sydni Baker, *Admin Asst*
EMP: 12
SALES: 5.5MM **Privately Held**
SIC: 8611 Chamber of Commerce

(G-6720)
MANHATTAN COUNTRY CLUB INC
1531 N 10th St (66502-4607)
P.O. Box 1026 (66505-1026)
PHONE.................................785 539-7501
William Elliott, *General Mgr*
Dan Doerge, *General Mgr*
Dave Kelley, *General Mgr*
Christina Hodges, *Marketing Staff*
Katrina Brooks, *Director*
EMP: 100
SQ FT: 20,000
SALES: 2.1MM **Privately Held**
WEB: www.countryclub.com
SIC: 7997 Country club, membership

(G-6721)
MANHATTAN DAY CARE & LRNG CTR (PA)
Also Called: Manhattan Day Care Association
612 Poyntz Ave (66502-6041)
PHONE.................................785 776-5071
Fax: 785 776-8981
EMP: 13
SALES: 48.6K **Privately Held**
SIC: 8351 Day Care Center

(G-6722)
MANHATTAN EMRGNCY SHELTER INC
416 S 4th St (66502-6212)
PHONE.................................785 537-3113
Mandy C Semple, *Exec Dir*
EMP: 13
SALES: 1.2MM **Privately Held**
SIC: 8322 Social service center

(G-6723)
MANHATTAN MARTIN LUTHER KING J
Also Called: James Spencer
3418 Treesmill Cir (66503-2189)
PHONE.................................785 410-4599
Ben Hopper, *Treasurer*
EMP: 20
SALES (est): 77.1K **Privately Held**
SIC: 8641 Civic social & fraternal associations

(G-6724)
MANHATTAN MEDICAL CENTER INC
1133 College Ave (66502-2770)
PHONE.................................785 537-2651
Rick Fisher MD, *President*
EMP: 17
SQ FT: 100,000
SALES (est): 1.5MM **Privately Held**
SIC: 6512 Nonresidential building operators

(G-6725)
MANHATTAN ORAL SURGERY &
4201 Anderson Ave Ste E (66503-7603)
PHONE.................................785 477-4038
Mohammad Nomani, *President*
EMP: 11 **EST:** 2014
SQ FT: 4,200
SALES: 400K **Privately Held**
SIC: 8021 Dental surgeon

(G-6726)
MANHATTAN RADIOLOGY LLP
1133 College Ave Ste C143 (66502-2751)
PHONE.................................785 539-7641
Dr Frank Lyons, *Partner*
Dr Stanford Kruger, *Partner*
Dr Michael Sheffield, *Partner*
H William Volkmann, *Partner*
Dr Greg Welle, *Partner*
EMP: 14
SALES (est): 1.8MM **Privately Held**
SIC: 8011 Radiologist

(G-6727)
MANHATTAN RTRMENT FNDATION INC
Also Called: Meadowlark Hills
2121 Meadowlark Rd (66502-4521)
PHONE.................................785 537-4610
Jon Bechtel, *Project Mgr*
Dave Prockish, *Purchasing*
Chris Nelson, *Controller*
Jon Thompson, *Accountant*
Annie Peace, *Human Res Dir*
EMP: 300
SQ FT: 150,000
SALES (est): 21.3MM **Privately Held**
WEB: www.meadowlark.org
SIC: 8051 Skilled nursing care facilities

(G-6728)
MANHATTAN TRENCHING INC
805 Willard Pl (66502-2929)
PHONE.................................785 537-2330
EMP: 22
SQ FT: 1,500
SALES: 2.3MM **Privately Held**
SIC: 1794 Excavation Contractor

(G-6729)
MANHATTAN-CITY
Also Called: MANHATTAN COMMUNITY FOUNDATION
555 Poyntz Ave Ste 269 (66502-0127)
P.O. Box 1127 (66505-1127)
PHONE.................................785 587-8995
William Frost, *Partner*
Elaine Dhuyvetter, *Vice Pres*
Marla Brandon, *Finance Mgr*
EMP: 10 **EST:** 1945
SALES: 228.3K **Privately Held**
WEB: www.manhattancf.org
SIC: 8111 Specialized law offices, attorneys

(G-6730)
MANKO WINDOW SYSTEMS INC (PA)
800 Hayes Dr (66502-5087)
P.O. Box 1403 (66505-1403)
PHONE.................................785 776-9643
Gary Jones, *President*
Joe Jones, *Corp Secy*
J C Abernathy, *Vice Pres*
Kevin Dix, *Vice Pres*
Steve Jones, *Vice Pres*
▲ **EMP:** 375
SQ FT: 175,000
SALES (est): 221.8MM **Privately Held**
WEB: www.mankowindows.com
SIC: 5039 1799 3442 Glass construction materials; glass tinting, architectural or automotive; store fronts, prefabricated, metal

(G-6731)
MARK HUNGERFORD MD
Also Called: Family & Implant Dentistry
1305 Westloop Pl (66502-2841)
PHONE.................................785 539-5949
Mark Hungerford MD, *Owner*
EMP: 16
SALES (est): 800K **Privately Held**
SIC: 8021 Dentists' office

(G-6732)
MARTIN DYSART ENTERPRISES INC
Also Called: Sir Speedy
1668 Hayes Dr (66502-5070)
PHONE.................................785 776-6731
Randy Martin, *President*
Anne Oswald, *Vice Pres*
Mary Oswald, *Supervisor*
EMP: 7
SQ FT: 6,000
SALES: 750K **Privately Held**
SIC: 2752 Commercial printing, lithographic

(G-6733)
MASTER TEACHER INC (PA)
Also Called: Educational Publishers
2600 Leadership Ln (66502)
P.O. Box 1207 (66505-1207)
PHONE.................................785 539-0555
Robert L Debruyn, *Ch of Bd*
Tracey Debruyn, *President*
Niki Miller, *Vice Pres*
Nikki Warnick, *Vice Pres*
Brenda Schneider, *Sales Dir*
▲ **EMP:** 50 **EST:** 1970
SQ FT: 45,000
SALES: 9.1MM **Privately Held**
WEB: www.paraeducator.net
SIC: 2741 Miscellaneous publishing

(G-6734)
MATHESON TRI-GAS INC
Also Called: Linweld
511 E Poyntz Ave (66502-5047)
P.O. Box 682 (66505-0682)
PHONE.................................785 537-0395
Russty Booth, *Manager*
EMP: 11 **Privately Held**
WEB: www.linweld.net
SIC: 5084 5169 Welding machinery & equipment; industrial gases
HQ: Matheson Tri-Gas, Inc.
150 Allen Rd Ste 302
Basking Ridge NJ 07920
908 991-9200

(G-6735)
MCCALL PATTERN COMPANY
Also Called: Mc Call Pattern Co
615 Mccall Rd (66502-5084)
PHONE.................................785 776-4041
John Kobiskie, *CFO*
EMP: 288
SALES (corp-wide): 382.2MM **Publicly Held**
WEB: www.mccallpattern.com
SIC: 2741 2721 2731 Patterns, paper: publishing only, not printed on site; magazines: publishing only, not printed on site; pamphlets: publishing only, not printed on site
HQ: Mccall Pattern Company
120 Broadway Fl 34
New York NY 10271
212 465-6800

(G-6736)
MCCULLOUGH DEVELOPEMENT INC
Also Called: Wildcat Inns A Gen Partnerhip
2700 Amherst Ave (66502-2936)
P.O. Box 1088 (66505-1088)
PHONE.................................785 776-3010
EMP: 20
SALES (est): 815.6K **Privately Held**
SIC: 6513 Apartment building operators

(G-6737)
MCCULLOUGH DEVELOPMENT INC (PA)
Also Called: McCullough Property Management
210 N 4th St Ste C (66502-6056)
P.O. Box 1088 (66505-1088)
PHONE.................................888 776-3010
Charlie Busch, *President*
Tim Trubey, *Vice Pres*
EMP: 25
SQ FT: 4,000
SALES (est): 13.5MM **Privately Held**
SIC: 6531 1542 1521 6552 Real estate brokers & agents; real estate managers; commercial & office building, new construction; new construction, single-family houses; subdividers & developers; management consulting services

(G-6738)
MCGHEE AND ASSOCIATES LLC
417 Firethorn Dr (66503-8210)
PHONE.................................785 341-2550
Kimberly McGhee,
EMP: 45
SALES (est): 488.9K **Privately Held**
SIC: 7361 Employment agencies

(G-6739)
MEDICAL ASSOC MANHATTAN PA
Also Called: Medical Associates Manhattan
1133 College Ave Ste E110 (66502-2813)
PHONE.................................785 537-2651
Palmer F Meek, *Owner*
Roger Reitz MD, *Vice Pres*
Mark Wetzel MD, *Vice Pres*
EMP: 50
SALES (est): 5.4MM **Privately Held**
SIC: 8011 Internal medicine, physician/surgeon

(G-6740)
MERITRUST CREDIT UNION
104 Mccall Rd (66502-5026)
PHONE.................................785 320-7222
EMP: 15
SALES (corp-wide): 53.9MM **Privately Held**
SIC: 6062 State credit unions
PA: Meritrust Credit Union
8710 E 32nd St N
Wichita KS 67226
316 683-1199

(G-6741)
MID-AMERICAN WATER & PLBG INC
5009 Murray Rd (66503-9782)
PHONE.................................785 537-1072
Robert Cansler, *President*
Bruce Ewing, *Principal*
Dane Boyd, *Vice Pres*
Pat Heptig, *Manager*
Robert Skip, *Master*
EMP: 45
SALES (est): 24MM **Privately Held**
WEB: www.mawp.us
SIC: 5074 1711 Water softeners; plumbing contractors

(G-6742)
MID-KANSAS COOPERATIVE ASSN
3384 Excel Rd (66502-8721)
PHONE.................................785 776-9467
Rob Ashburn, *Branch Mgr*
EMP: 13
SALES (corp-wide): 371.5MM **Privately Held**
SIC: 5153 5191 Grain elevators; farm supplies
PA: Mid-Kansas Cooperative Association
307 W Cole St
Moundridge KS 67107
620 345-6328

(G-6743)
MIDLAND EXTERIORS LLC (PA)
8226 Southport Dr (66502-8116)
PHONE.................................785 537-5130
Jamie Musa, *Mng Member*
EMP: 12
SALES (est): 2.7MM **Privately Held**
SIC: 1521 5211 General remodeling, single-family houses; door & window products

(G-6744)
MIDSTATE MECHANICAL INC
230 Levee Dr (66502-5004)
PHONE.................................785 537-4343
Alvin Lovgren, *President*
Kurtis Lovgren, *Vice Pres*
Tom Jensen, *Administration*
EMP: 10
SQ FT: 3,890
SALES (est): 1.5MM **Privately Held**
SIC: 1711 Plumbing contractors; warm air heating & air conditioning contractor

(G-6745)
MIDWAY SALES & DISTRG INC
603 Pecan Cir (66502-8146)
PHONE.................................785 537-4665
Scott McFall, *Manager*
EMP: 15

SALES (corp-wide): 78.3MM **Privately Held**
WEB: www.midwaywholesale.com
SIC: **5033** 5031 5211 5082 Roofing & siding materials; building materials, interior; building materials, exterior; door & window products; general construction machinery & equipment; window & door (prefabricated) installation
PA: Midway Sales & Distributing Inc.
218 Se Branner St
Topeka KS 66607
785 233-7406

(G-6746)
MIDWEST CONCRETE MATERIALS INC
701 S 4th St (66502-6426)
P.O. Box 668 (66505-0668)
PHONE....................................785 776-8811
Robert Eichman, *President*
Richard Shermoen, *Corp Secy*
Christopher Eichman, *Vice Pres*
John Pendry, *Sales Staff*
Michael V Vleet, *Sales Staff*
EMP: 203
SQ FT: 4,000
SALES (est): 44.1MM **Privately Held**
WEB: www.4mcm.com
SIC: **3273** 1422 1794 3271 Ready-mixed concrete; crushed & broken limestone; excavation work; concrete block & brick; local trucking, without storage

(G-6747)
MIDWEST EDUCATIONAL CENTER
Also Called: WONDER WORKSHOP
1006 Leavenworth St (66502-5435)
PHONE....................................785 776-1234
Richard Pitts, *Exec Dir*
EMP: 16
SQ FT: 2,500
SALES: 98.8K **Privately Held**
WEB: www.wonderworkshop.org
SIC: **8412** Museum

(G-6748)
MIDWEST HEALTH SERVICES INC
Also Called: Stoneybrook Assisted Living
2029 Little Kitten Ave (66503-7545)
PHONE....................................785 537-1065
Sindey Washington, *Director*
EMP: 30
SALES (corp-wide): 32.7MM **Privately Held**
WEB: www.halsteadhealthrehab.com
SIC: **8051** 8052 Extended care facility; intermediate care facilities
PA: Midwest Health, Inc
3024 Sw Wanamaker Rd # 300
Topeka KS 66614
785 272-1535

(G-6749)
MIDWEST HEALTH SERVICES INC
Also Called: Stoneybrook Retirement Cmnty
2025 Little Kitten Ave (66503-7545)
PHONE....................................785 776-0065
Rick Jensen, *Manager*
EMP: 90
SALES (corp-wide): 32.7MM **Privately Held**
WEB: www.halsteadhealthrehab.com
SIC: **8051** Skilled nursing care facilities
PA: Midwest Health, Inc
3024 Sw Wanamaker Rd # 300
Topeka KS 66614
785 272-1535

(G-6750)
MIDWEST HEALTH SERVICES INC
Also Called: Homestead Assted Lving Rsdnce
1923 Little Kitten Ave (66503-7583)
PHONE....................................785 776-1772
Joe Braun, *Manager*
EMP: 20
SALES (corp-wide): 32.7MM **Privately Held**
SIC: **8361** 8052 Residential care; intermediate care facilities
PA: Midwest Health, Inc
3024 Sw Wanamaker Rd # 300
Topeka KS 66614
785 272-1535

(G-6751)
MOSIER MOSIER FMLY PHYSICIANS
Also Called: Mosier Mosier Fmly Physicians
2900 Amherst Ave Ste A (66503-3046)
PHONE....................................785 539-8700
Mike Mosier, *Partner*
Steve Mosier, *Partner*
EMP: 15
SALES (est): 844.9K **Privately Held**
SIC: **8042** 8011 Offices & clinics of optometrists; clinic, operated by physicians

(G-6752)
MOTEL 6 OPERATING LP
510 Tuttle Creek Blvd (66502-5853)
PHONE....................................785 537-1022
EMP: 16
SALES (corp-wide): 579.1MM **Privately Held**
WEB: www.motel6.com
SIC: **7011** Hotels & motels
HQ: Motel 6 Operating L.P.
4001 Intl Pkwy Ste 500
Carrollton TX 75007
972 360-9000

(G-6753)
MR PS PARTY OUTLET INC (PA)
3039 Conrow Dr (66503-2460)
PHONE....................................785 537-1804
Walt Pesaresi, *President*
Dorothy Pesaresi, *Admin Sec*
EMP: 10
SQ FT: 3,500
SALES (est): 997.9K **Privately Held**
SIC: **5947** 7389 2759 Gifts & novelties; souvenirs; party favors; balloons, novelty & toy; invitations: printing

(G-6754)
MRIGLOBAL - KANSAS LLC
2005 Research Park Cir (66502-5020)
PHONE....................................816 753-7600
Tom Bowser, *Ch of Bd*
Thomas M Sack, *President*
Linda D Evans, *Vice Pres*
Roger Harris, *Vice Pres*
Jefferson Tester, *Vice Pres*
EMP: 585
SALES (est): 4.6MM
SALES (corp-wide): 90.6MM **Privately Held**
SIC: **8731** 6794 Biological research; patent owners & lessors
PA: Mriglobal
425 Volker Blvd
Kansas City MO 64110
816 753-7600

(G-6755)
MTC DEVELOPMENT LLC
Also Called: Manhattan Town Center
100 Manhattan Town Ctr # 480 (66502-6001)
PHONE....................................785 539-3500
Jim Hansen, *Regional Mgr*
Allen Raynor,
EMP: 40 **EST:** 1984
SALES (est): 2.7MM **Privately Held**
WEB: www.manhattantowncenter.com
SIC: **6512** Shopping center, property operation only

(G-6756)
NACADA THE GLBL COMM FOR ACDM
2323 Anderson Ave Ste 225 (66502-2912)
PHONE....................................785 532-3398
Charlie Nutt, *Director*
Margaret Goe,
EMP: 20
SALES: 4.5MM **Privately Held**
SIC: **8641** Educator's association

(G-6757)
NATIONAL ENGRAVING
1712 Westbank Way (66503-7517)
PHONE....................................785 776-5757
Chris Barr, *CEO*
EMP: 40
SALES (est): 1.6MM **Privately Held**
SIC: **2759** Engraving

(G-6758)
NELSON POULTRY FARMS INC (PA)
8530 E Us Highway 24 (66502-8663)
P.O. Box 1285 (66505-1285)
PHONE....................................785 587-0399
Gregory B Nelson, *President*
L Wilburn Nelson, *Chairman*
James C Nelson, *Vice Pres*
Karla Carrender, *Treasurer*
▲ **EMP:** 16 **EST:** 1940
SQ FT: 10,000
SALES (est): 9.9MM **Privately Held**
SIC: **5144** 0254 Poultry products; poultry hatcheries

(G-6759)
NETWORKS PLUS (PA)
2627 Kfb Plz Ste 206w (66503-8136)
PHONE....................................785 825-0400
Ward Morgan, *Owner*
Adam Boyle, *Consultant*
EMP: 22
SALES (est): 5MM **Privately Held**
SIC: **1731** 5734 7371 7373 Computer installation; computer software & accessories; software programming applications; systems integration services

(G-6760)
NEW BOSTON CREATIVE GROUP LLC
315 Houston St Ste E (66502-6172)
PHONE....................................785 587-8185
Paige Burton-Argo, *Corp Comm Staff*
Chrissie Alquinta, *Marketing Staff*
Tanner Lucas, *Branch Mgr*
Lisa A Sisley, *Manager*
Jami Weisbender, *Director*
EMP: 11
SALES (est): 821.4K **Privately Held**
SIC: **8742** Marketing consulting services

(G-6761)
NEW PARADIGM SOLUTIONS INC
4130 Taneil Dr (66502-8800)
PHONE....................................785 313-0946
William Novotny, *CEO*
Doug Frihart, *Vice Pres*
EMP: 10
SALES (est): 866.9K **Privately Held**
SIC: **8742** Management consulting services

(G-6762)
NORTH CENTRAL FLINT HILLS AREA (PA)
401 Houston St (66502-6135)
PHONE....................................785 323-4300
Lashawna Simonsen, *CFO*
Kelsey Pfannenstiel, *Manager*
Juli Walter, *Exec Dir*
Julie Govert Walter, *Director*
EMP: 30
SQ FT: 3,400
SALES: 6.4MM **Privately Held**
WEB: www.ncfhaaa.com
SIC: **8322** Old age assistance; senior citizens' center or association

(G-6763)
NUETERRA HOLDINGS LLC
Also Called: Manhattan Surgical Center
1829 College Ave (66502-3381)
PHONE....................................785 776-5100
Moyer Bunting, *Branch Mgr*
EMP: 30
SALES (corp-wide): 46.4MM **Privately Held**
WEB: www.findlaysurgerycenter.com
SIC: **8062** General medical & surgical hospitals
PA: Nueterra Dc Holdings, Llc
11221 Roe Ave Ste 1a
Leawood KS 66211
913 387-0689

(G-6764)
OLSSON INC
302 S 4th St Ste 110 (66502-6410)
PHONE....................................785 539-6900
Jeff Jenkins, *CFO*
EMP: 15
SALES (corp-wide): 198MM **Privately Held**
WEB: www.oaconsulting.com
SIC: **8711** Consulting engineer
PA: Olsson, Inc.
601 P St Ste 200
Lincoln NE 68508
417 781-0643

(G-6765)
ORAZEM & SCALORA ENGRG PA
2312 Anderson Ave (66502-2903)
PHONE....................................785 537-2553
Thomas Orazem, *President*
Gerit Garman, *Principal*
Bradley Ross, *Principal*
Hillary Velasco, *Engineer*
David Griffith, *Treasurer*
EMP: 12
SQ FT: 3,600
SALES: 1.3MM **Privately Held**
SIC: **8711** Consulting engineer

(G-6766)
ORSCHELN FARM AND HOME LLC
Also Called: Orschelin Farm and Home 39
530 Mccall Rd (66502-5046)
PHONE....................................785 776-1476
Larry Monehan, *Manager*
EMP: 20
SALES (corp-wide): 822.7MM **Privately Held**
WEB: www.orschelnfarmhome.com
SIC: **5191** 5251 5699 Farm supplies; hardware; work clothing
PA: Orscheln Farm And Home Llc
1800 Overcenter Dr
Moberly MO 65270
800 577-2580

(G-6767)
ORTHOPDIC SPT MEDICINE CTR LLP
1600 Charles Pl (66502-2750)
PHONE....................................785 537-4200
Richard Baker MD, *Principal*
James McAtee, *Vice Pres*
Adam J Chase, *Med Doctor*
Daren Badura, *Physician Asst*
EMP: 40
SALES (est): 3.9MM **Privately Held**
WEB: www.kansasortho.com
SIC: **8011** Orthopedic physician

(G-6768)
PARKER-HANNIFIN CORPORATION
Also Called: Hose Products Division
1501 Hayes Dr (66502-5042)
PHONE....................................785 537-4181
Kendra Cox, *Plant Mgr*
Tim Donohoue, *Buyer*
Clem Suther, *Engineer*
Lonnie Gallup, *Branch Mgr*
Mohamed Al Tamimi, *Manager*
EMP: 200
SALES (corp-wide): 14.3B **Publicly Held**
WEB: www.parker.com
SIC: **5085** Hose, belting & packing
PA: Parker-Hannifin Corporation
6035 Parkland Blvd
Cleveland OH 44124
216 896-3000

(G-6769)
PAWNEE MENTAL HEALTH SVCS INC (PA)
2001 Claflin Rd (66502-3415)
P.O. Box 747 (66505-0747)
PHONE....................................785 762-5250
Bob Hanson, *COO*
Jelane Cook, *Facilities Mgr*
Ardyce Kuhn, *Manager*
Pamela Miller, *Manager*
Tyrone Tatum, *Manager*
EMP: 250
SQ FT: 15,000
SALES: 16.5MM **Privately Held**
SIC: **8093** 8322 Mental health clinic, outpatient; individual & family services

(G-6770)
PAWNEE MENTAL HEALTH SVCS INC
425 Houston St (66502-6169)
P.O. Box 747 (66505-0747)
PHONE..................................785 587-4344
Robin Cole, *CEO*
EMP: 40
SALES (corp-wide): 16.5MM **Privately Held**
SIC: 8093 8322 8069 Mental health clinic, outpatient; individual & family services; drug addiction rehabilitation hospital
PA: Pawnee Mental Health Services, Inc.
2001 Claflin Rd
Manhattan KS 66502
785 762-5250

(G-6771)
PEARCE KELLER AMERICAN LEGION
114 Mccall Rd (66502-5026)
PHONE..................................785 776-4556
David Fiser, *Principal*
EMP: 13
SALES (est): 127.3K **Privately Held**
SIC: 8641 Veterans' organization

(G-6772)
PENSKE TRUCK LEASING CO LP
1927 Fort Riley Ln (66502-3966)
PHONE..................................785 776-3139
Tom Atwood, *Manager*
EMP: 10
SALES (corp-wide): 9.6B **Privately Held**
WEB: www.pensketruckleasing.com
SIC: 7513 Truck rental & leasing, no drivers
HQ: Penske Truck Leasing Co., L.P.
2675 Morgantown Rd
Reading PA 19607
610 775-6000

(G-6773)
PEPSI-COLA BTLG MARYSVILLE INC
Also Called: Pepsico
703 Levee Dr (66502-5085)
PHONE..................................785 537-4730
Terry Francis, *Manager*
EMP: 20
SALES (corp-wide): 23.4MM **Privately Held**
WEB: www.fivestarvend.com
SIC: 2086 Carbonated soft drinks, bottled & canned
PA: Pepsi-Cola Bottling Company Of Marysville, Inc.
604 Center St
Marysville KS
785 562-5334

(G-6774)
PETERSON LABORATORY SVCS PA
1133 College Ave Bldg B (66502-2770)
PHONE..................................785 539-5363
Peggy S Peterson, *President*
Jeff Jaqua, *COO*
Dr John F Bambara, *Vice Pres*
Peggy Peterson, *Vice Pres*
Susan L Speaks, *Vice Pres*
EMP: 72
SQ FT: 8,000
SALES (est): 6MM **Privately Held**
WEB: www.petersonlab.com
SIC: 8071 Pathological laboratory

(G-6775)
PHI KAPPA THETA
1965 College Heights Rd (66502-3597)
PHONE..................................785 539-7491
EMP: 10
SALES (est): 72.5K **Privately Held**
SIC: 8641 Civic/Social Association

(G-6776)
PI BETA PHI HOUSE INC
1819 Todd Rd (66502-3497)
PHONE..................................785 539-1818
Claudine Miller, *President*
Marsha Dryden, *Treasurer*
Suzy Ball, *Admin Sec*
EMP: 12
SALES: 258.9K **Privately Held**
SIC: 8641 University club

(G-6777)
PIONEER HI-BRED INTL INC
3400 Wood Green Ct (66503-0336)
PHONE..................................785 776-1335
Mark David, *Principal*
EMP: 14
SALES (corp-wide): 30.6B **Publicly Held**
SIC: 5191 Seeds: field, garden & flower
HQ: Pioneer Hi-Bred International, Inc.
7100 Nw 62nd Ave
Johnston IA 50131
515 535-3200

(G-6778)
PRAIRIE CLEANING SERVICE
532 Pillsbury Dr (66502-7005)
P.O. Box 21 (66505-0021)
PHONE..................................785 539-4997
Robert Bliven, *Owner*
EMP: 23
SQ FT: 400
SALES (est): 593.4K **Privately Held**
SIC: 7349 Janitorial service, contract basis

(G-6779)
PRICE & YOUNG & ODLE (PA)
Also Called: Eye Doctors, The
3012 Anderson Ave (66503-2888)
PHONE..................................785 537-1118
Ron Price, *Partner*
Sam Odle MD, *Partner*
Gary Young MD, *Partner*
Maria Noa, *Train & Dev Mgr*
David Stormer, *Info Tech Mgr*
EMP: 30
SQ FT: 3,000
SALES (est): 4.3MM **Privately Held**
SIC: 8042 Contact lense specialist optometrist

(G-6780)
PRIMARY CARE PHYSCANS MNHATTAN
Also Called: Gardner, James Dixon MD
1133 College Ave Ste D200 (66502-2776)
PHONE..................................785 537-4940
James Gardner MD, *Partner*
Karen Fagan, *Partner*
Barbara Taylor MD, *Partner*
EMP: 22
SALES (est): 1.8MM **Privately Held**
WEB: www.pcpman.com
SIC: 8011 Internal medicine, physician/surgeon; general & family practice, physician/surgeon

(G-6781)
PRIME PLACE LLC
1532 College Ave Apt F19 (66502-2890)
PHONE..................................785 317-5265
Ben Brown, *Vice Pres*
Chris Elsei, *Mng Member*
EMP: 11
SALES: 2MM **Privately Held**
SIC: 1521 Single-family housing construction

(G-6782)
PROFESSIONAL ORTHC & PROSTHTC
260 Johnson Rd Unit A (66502-1516)
PHONE..................................785 375-7458
Brandon Smith,
EMP: 25
SALES (est): 121.2K **Privately Held**
SIC: 8082 Home health care services

(G-6783)
PURPLE WAVE AUCTION
825 Levee Dr (66502-5012)
PHONE..................................785 537-5057
Aaron McKee, *Owner*
Aaron Traffas, *Vice Pres*
Lea Briscoe, *Controller*
Sheila Fahey, *Accounting Dir*
Lea Cieslak, *Accounting Mgr*
EMP: 70
SALES (est): 3.6MM **Privately Held**
SIC: 7389 Auctioneers, fee basis

(G-6784)
QUALITY INN
150 E Poyntz Ave (66502-5040)
PHONE..................................785 770-8000
Jessie Baer, *Property Mgr*
EMP: 11
SALES (est): 543.4K **Privately Held**
SIC: 7011 Hotels & motels

(G-6785)
R M BARIL GENERAL CONTR INC
1600 Fair Ln (66502-4221)
PHONE..................................785 537-2190
Fax: 785 537-2193
EMP: 20
SQ FT: 4,500
SALES: 4.4MM **Privately Held**
SIC: 1542 1541 Nonresidential Construction Industrial Building Construction

(G-6786)
RANDAL J STEINER
Also Called: Bobs Plumbing
5281 Tuttle Creek Blvd (66502-8813)
PHONE..................................785 539-4155
Randal J Steiner, *Partner*
Victor Steiner, *Partner*
EMP: 18
SALES (est): 1.2MM **Privately Held**
SIC: 1711 Plumbing contractors; heating & air conditioning contractors

(G-6787)
RAYMOND JAMES FINCL SVCS INC
1011 Poyntz Ave (66502-5458)
PHONE..................................785 537-0366
Patrick Keating, *Owner*
Mark Queen, *Teacher*
EMP: 20
SALES (corp-wide): 8B **Publicly Held**
WEB: www.raymondjames.com
SIC: 6211 Brokers, security
HQ: Raymond James Financial Services, Inc.
880 Carillon Pkwy
Saint Petersburg FL 33716
727 567-1000

(G-6788)
REDI SYSTEMS INC
1601 Tuttle Creek Blvd (66502-4514)
PHONE..................................785 587-9100
Sean Ruth, *President*
Chris Lemman, *Opers Staff*
Marsha Jarvis, *Executive*
EMP: 10
SALES: 1.3MM **Privately Held**
SIC: 5731 1731 High fidelity stereo equipment; electronic controls installation

(G-6789)
REID PLUMBING HEATING & AC INC
8964 Green Valley Dr (66502-1466)
PHONE..................................785 537-2869
Tony Reid, *President*
Dawn Reid, *Corp Secy*
EMP: 15
SALES (est): 2.7MM **Privately Held**
SIC: 7699 1711 Sewer cleaning & rodding; heating & air conditioning contractors

(G-6790)
RELIABLE TRANSFER & STORAGE (PA)
1600 S 16th St (66502)
PHONE..................................785 776-4887
Dennie Bayer, *President*
Jo Ann Bayer, *Corp Secy*
Warren Bayer, *Vice Pres*
EMP: 15 **EST:** 1931
SQ FT: 8,000
SALES (est): 1.4MM **Privately Held**
SIC: 4214 Household goods moving & storage, local

(G-6791)
RF CONSTRUCTION INC
Also Called: Rf Benchmark
4361 S Dam Rd (66502-8621)
PHONE..................................785 776-8855
Tim Bruce, *CEO*
Aaron West, *Vice Pres*
Beth Quinn, *CFO*
EMP: 40 **EST:** 1994
SQ FT: 3,000
SALES: 20MM **Privately Held**
WEB: www.rfcms.com
SIC: 8741 1542 1521 Construction management; nonresidential construction; single-family housing construction

(G-6792)
RHW MANAGEMENT INC
Also Called: Manhattan Hampton Inn
501 E Poyntz Ave (66502-5047)
PHONE..................................785 776-8829
Teresa Morris, *Branch Mgr*
EMP: 27
SALES (corp-wide): 16MM **Privately Held**
SIC: 7011 Hotels & motels
PA: Rhw Management, Inc.
6704 W 121st St
Shawnee Mission KS 66209
913 451-1222

(G-6793)
RILEY HOTEL SUITES LLC
Also Called: Fairfield Inn
300 Colorado St (66502-6226)
PHONE..................................785 539-2400
Brad Everett, *Principal*
EMP: 30 **EST:** 1998
SALES (est): 2.4MM **Privately Held**
SIC: 7011 7389 Hotels & motels; office facilities & secretarial service rental

(G-6794)
ROGER L STEVENS DENTIST
1110 Westport Dr (66502-2859)
PHONE..................................785 539-2314
Roger Stevens, *Owner*
EMP: 10 **EST:** 2007
SALES (est): 366.4K **Privately Held**
SIC: 8021 Dentists' office

(G-6795)
ROTHWELL LANDSCAPE INC
1607 Fair Ln (66502-4220)
P.O. Box 1131 (66505-1131)
PHONE..................................785 238-2647
Jason Rothwell, *President*
EMP: 50 **EST:** 1986
SQ FT: 2,100
SALES (est): 4.2MM **Privately Held**
WEB: www.rothwelllandscape.com
SIC: 0781 Landscape services

(G-6796)
SAINT FRANCIS CMNTY SVCS INC
222 Southwind Pl (66503-3123)
PHONE..................................785 587-8818
Shannon Horton, *President*
EMP: 218
SALES (corp-wide): 108.2MM **Privately Held**
SIC: 8361 Group foster home
PA: Saint Francis Community Services, Inc.
509 E Elm St
Salina KS 67401
785 825-0541

(G-6797)
SCHWAB-EATON PA (PA)
4361 S Dam Rd (66502-1756)
PHONE..................................785 539-4687
Brad Fagan, *President*
Jeff Goering, *Chief*
Chris Cox, *Vice Pres*
Ian Reekie, *Engineer*
EMP: 50 **EST:** 1956
SALES (est): 4.3MM **Privately Held**
WEB: www.schwab-eaton.com
SIC: 8713 Surveying services

(G-6798)
SEATON PUBLISHING CO INC (PA)
Also Called: Manhattan Mercury
318 N 5th St (66502-5910)
P.O. Box 787 (66505-0787)
PHONE..................................785 776-2200
Edward L Seaton, *President*
Josh Dockendorf, *Advt Staff*
Mary Phelps, *Manager*
EMP: 80
SQ FT: 15,000

SALES (est): 27.7MM Privately Held
WEB: www.themercury.com
SIC: 2711 4832 2752 Commercial printing & newspaper publishing combined; radio broadcasting stations; commercial printing, lithographic

(G-6799)
SERVICMMBER AG VCATION EDUCATN
Also Called: Save
212 S 4th St Ste 130 (66502-6611)
PHONE..................................785 537-7493
Susan Metzger, *Ch of Bd*
Gary Lagrange, *President*
EMP: 20
SALES: 244.5K Privately Held
SIC: 0191 General farms, primarily crop

(G-6800)
SHILLING CONSTRUCTION CO INC
9620 E Us Highway 24 (66502-8709)
P.O. Box 1568 (66505-1568)
PHONE..................................785 776-5077
Mike Shilling, *President*
Steve Altobello, *CFO*
Douglas Shilling, *Treasurer*
EMP: 50 EST: 1964
SQ FT: 1,700
SALES (est): 16.9MM Privately Held
WEB: www.shilconst.com
SIC: 1611 Highway & street paving contractor

(G-6801)
SINK GORDON & ASSOCIATES LLP
727 Poyntz Ave Ste 601 (66502-0124)
PHONE..................................785 537-0190
Roger Sink, *Partner*
Glen Gillmore, *Partner*
James Gordon, *Partner*
Justin Minchow, *Managing Dir*
Thomas Martin, *Accountant*
EMP: 40
SALES (est): 2.8MM Privately Held
SIC: 8721 Certified public accountant

(G-6802)
SMH CONSULTANTS PA
2017 Vanesta Pl Ste 110 (66503-0445)
PHONE..................................785 776-0541
Timothy Sloan, *President*
Jeffrey Hancock, *Vice Pres*
Lesli Hanson, *Accountant*
EMP: 16
SQ FT: 2,500
SALES (est): 1.4MM Privately Held
WEB: www.sloanandmeier.com
SIC: 8711 Consulting engineer

(G-6803)
SOCIAL SECURITY EMPLOYEES
Also Called: Social Security Administration
1121a Hudson Ave Ste A (66503-2570)
PHONE..................................877 840-5741
Tenny Emmele, *Manager*
EMP: 13
SALES (corp-wide): 18.1MM Privately Held
WEB: www.ssaeaa.org
SIC: 8699 Athletic organizations
PA: Social Security Employees' Activities Association Service Corporation, Incorporated
6401 Security Blvd
Baltimore MD 21235
410 965-4587

(G-6804)
SPRINT SPECTRUM LP
707 Commons Pl (66503-3002)
PHONE..................................785 537-3500
John Workman, *Branch Mgr*
EMP: 13 Publicly Held
SIC: 5999 4813 4812 Telephone & communication equipment; telephone communication, except radio; cellular telephone services
HQ: Sprint Spectrum L.P.
6800 Sprint Pkwy
Overland Park KS 66251

(G-6805)
STAG HILL GOLF CLUB INC
Also Called: Stagg Hill Golf Club
4441 Riley Blvd (66502)
PHONE..................................785 539-1041
Marcia Roets, *President*
EMP: 10
SALES (est): 244.3K Privately Held
SIC: 7992 Public golf courses

(G-6806)
STAGG HILL GOLF CLUB INC
4441 Fort Riley Blvd (66502-9790)
PHONE..................................785 539-1041
Marsha Roats, *President*
Britt Feltner, *President*
Jim Gregory, *President*
Mark McKain, *Superintendent*
Orin Bell, *Treasurer*
EMP: 11
SALES (est): 722K Privately Held
SIC: 7997 Golf club, membership

(G-6807)
STANDARD PLUMBING INC
609 Pecan Cir (66502-9924)
PHONE..................................785 776-5012
Rod Frank, *CEO*
EMP: 15 EST: 1923
SQ FT: 5,000
SALES: 615K Privately Held
SIC: 1711 Plumbing contractors; warm air heating & air conditioning contractor

(G-6808)
STANION WHOLESALE ELC CO INC
Also Called: Stanion Whl Elc Co Str 6
2305 Skyvue Ln (66502-3179)
PHONE..................................785 537-4600
Camron Rymer, *Branch Mgr*
EMP: 12
SALES (corp-wide): 97.6MM Privately Held
WEB: www.stanion.com
SIC: 5063 Electrical supplies
PA: Stanion Wholesale Electric Co., Inc.
812 S Main St
Pratt KS 67124
620 672-5678

(G-6809)
STEEL AND PIPE SUPPLY CO INC (HQ)
555 Poyntz Ave Ste 122 (66502-0126)
P.O. Box 1688 (66505-1688)
PHONE..................................785 587-5100
Matthew Crocker, *CEO*
Dennis Mullin, *Ch of Bd*
Trevor Jensen, *Business Mgr*
Dirk Daveline, *Senior VP*
John Conley, *Vice Pres*
◆ EMP: 110 EST: 1948
SQ FT: 15,000
SALES (est): 409.8MM Privately Held
SIC: 5051 Steel
PA: Sps Companies, Inc.
6363 Highway 7
Minneapolis MN 55416
952 929-1377

(G-6810)
STEEL VENTURES LLC
Also Called: Exltube
555 Poyntz Ave Ste 122 (66502-0126)
PHONE..................................785 587-5100
Matthew Crocker, *CEO*
Bill Snyder, *President*
EMP: 100
SALES (est): 5.1MM
SALES (corp-wide): 409.8MM Privately Held
SIC: 3312 Pipes & tubes
HQ: Steel And Pipe Supply Company, Inc.
555 Poyntz Ave Ste 122
Manhattan KS 66502
785 587-5100

(G-6811)
STEVE PRIDDLE
1620 Charles Pl (66502-2750)
PHONE..................................785 776-1400
Steve Priddle, *Partner*
Nicole Stroh, *Human Res Mgr*
EMP: 35 EST: 2001
SALES (est): 400.9K Privately Held
SIC: 8011 Surgeon

(G-6812)
STICKELS INC
Also Called: Aggie Lounge
714 N 12th St (66502-5330)
PHONE..................................785 539-5722
Anthony Gieber, *President*
Brian Gieber, *Manager*
EMP: 24
SALES (est): 1.1MM Privately Held
SIC: 7216 5813 Curtain cleaning & repair; tavern (drinking places)

(G-6813)
STONECREEK FAMILY PHYSICIANS
Also Called: Hinkin, Douglas P MD
4101 Anderson Ave (66503-7588)
PHONE..................................785 587-4101
Sue Pfannenstiel, *Manager*
Jennifer Haefke, *Administration*
Keith Wright, *Family Practiti*
EMP: 30
SALES (est): 5.3MM Privately Held
SIC: 8011 General & family practice, physician/surgeon

(G-6814)
STORMONT-VAIL HEALTHCARE INC
Also Called: Medical Associates Manhattan
1133 College Ave Ste E110 (66502-2813)
PHONE..................................785 537-2651
Palmer F Meek, *President*
EMP: 383
SALES (corp-wide): 719MM Privately Held
SIC: 8062 General medical & surgical hospitals
PA: Stormont-Vail Healthcare, Inc.
1500 Sw 10th Ave
Topeka KS 66604
785 354-6000

(G-6815)
STREETER ENTERPRISES LLC
Also Called: Streeter Concessions
1911 Tuttle Creek Blvd (66502-4548)
PHONE..................................785 537-0100
Karen Streeter, *Principal*
EMP: 10
SQ FT: 2,500
SALES (est): 1.4MM Privately Held
SIC: 5141 5113 5812 Groceries, general line; industrial & personal service paper; soft drink stand

(G-6816)
SUMMER SNOW LLC
700 Pecan Cir (66502-8164)
P.O. Box 1206 (66505-1206)
PHONE..................................785 706-1003
Jeremy Bryant, *CEO*
EMP: 23
SALES (est): 777.9K Privately Held
SIC: 1799 Parking lot maintenance

(G-6817)
SUNFLOWER BANK NATIONAL ASSN
Also Called: First National Bank
2710 Anderson Ave (66502-2800)
PHONE..................................785 537-0550
Barb Bruna, *Manager*
EMP: 10
SALES (corp-wide): 52.4MM Privately Held
WEB: www.sunflowerbank.com
SIC: 6021 6035 National trust companies with deposits, commercial; savings institutions, federally chartered
HQ: Sunflower Bank, National Association
1400 16th St Ste 250
Denver CO 80202
888 827-5564

(G-6818)
SUNSET ZOOLOGICAL PK WILDLIFE
Also Called: CONSERVATION TRUST
2333 Oak St (66502-3824)
PHONE..................................785 587-2737
Scott Shoemaker, *Director*
EMP: 30
SALES: 441.7K Privately Held
SIC: 7999 5947 8351 Zoological garden, commercial; gift shop; child day care services

(G-6819)
T & M ELECTRONICS
3360 Excel Rd (66502-8721)
P.O. Box 395 (66505-0395)
PHONE..................................785 537-1455
Mike Mitchell, *Owner*
EMP: 5
SALES: 500K Privately Held
SIC: 3651 Home entertainment equipment, electronic

(G-6820)
T2 WIRELESS INC
711 Commons Pl (66503-3002)
PHONE..................................785 537-8034
Tate Fisher, *Principal*
EMP: 12
SALES (est): 596.7K Privately Held
SIC: 4812 Cellular telephone services

(G-6821)
TALLGRASS BREWING COMPANY
5960 Dry Hop Cir (66503-9815)
PHONE..................................785 537-1131
Jeff Gill, *President*
Jeffery D Gill, *Principal*
EMP: 20
SALES (est): 5.9MM Privately Held
SIC: 2082 Beer (alcoholic beverage)

(G-6822)
TERRACON CONSULTANTS INC
Also Called: Terracon Consultants C6
1120 Hostetler Dr (66502-5062)
PHONE..................................785 539-9099
Jamie Klein, *Branch Mgr*
EMP: 25
SALES (corp-wide): 751.7MM Privately Held
SIC: 8711 Consulting engineer
HQ: Terracon Consultants, Inc.
10841 S Ridgeview Rd
Olathe KS 66061
913 599-6886

(G-6823)
THAI NOODLE
1126 Laramie St (66502-5312)
PHONE..................................785 320-2899
EMP: 5
SALES (est): 276.9K Privately Held
SIC: 2098 Noodles (e.g. egg, plain & water), dry

(G-6824)
THERMAL COMFORT AIR INC (PA)
705 Pecan Cir (66502-8164)
PHONE..................................785 537-2436
Bob Bramhall, *President*
Kenneth Ziegler, *Vice Pres*
C Shane Good, *Admin Sec*
EMP: 35
SQ FT: 3,200
SALES (est): 6.4MM Privately Held
WEB: www.thermalcomfortair.com
SIC: 1711 7623 Heating systems repair & maintenance; air conditioning repair

(G-6825)
THOMAS OUTDOOR ADVERTISING INC
902 Fair Ln (66502-5545)
PHONE..................................785 537-2010
Jim Wells, *Admin Sec*
EMP: 8
SALES (est): 266.5K Privately Held
SIC: 3993 Signs & advertising specialties

(G-6826)
THUNDERHEAD ENGRG CONS INC
403 Poyntz Ave Ste B (66502-6081)
PHONE..................................785 770-8511
Brian Hardeman, *President*
Charles Thornton, *Vice Pres*
Kyle Perkuhn, *Engineer*
Daniel Swenson, *Treasurer*

Richard O'Konski, *Admin Sec*
EMP: 10
SQ FT: 1,500
SALES: 300K **Privately Held**
WEB: www.thunderheadeng.com
SIC: 8711 7372 7373 Consulting engineer; prepackaged software; computer integrated systems design

(G-6827)
TIMBERLINE CABINETRY MLLWK LLC
3475 Crown C Cir (66502-8131)
PHONE..................................785 323-0206
Tony Buessing, *Sales Staff*
Teresa Roberts, *Sales Staff*
Kent Swinson, *Manager*
EMP: 5
SALES (est): 724.2K **Privately Held**
SIC: 2434 Wood kitchen cabinets

(G-6828)
TPCKS INC
Also Called: Phone Connection of Kansas
322 Houston St Ste 110 (66502-6497)
PHONE..................................785 776-4429
Ward Morgan, *CEO*
Tom Boller, *President*
Leon Klaus, *Manager*
Corey Bohl, *Supervisor*
EMP: 15 **EST:** 2004
SQ FT: 3,000
SALES (est): 2.2MM **Privately Held**
SIC: 5999 7629 Telephone equipment & systems; telephone set repair

(G-6829)
TRACTOR SUPPLY COMPANY
Also Called: Tractor Supply 1179
8110 Southport Rd (66502-8122)
PHONE..................................785 587-8949
Brett Perkins, *Manager*
EMP: 10
SALES (corp-wide): 7.9B **Publicly Held**
WEB: www.tractorsupplyco.com
SIC: 5191 Farm supplies
PA: Tractor Supply Company
5401 Virginia Way
Brentwood TN 37027
615 440-4000

(G-6830)
TRADEHOME SHOE STORES INC
Also Called: Trade Home Shoes Stores
100 Manhattan Town Ctr # 670
(66502-6001)
PHONE..................................785 539-4003
Tony Hamburge, *Buyer*
Austin Marshall, *Manager*
EMP: 6
SALES (corp-wide): 118.6MM **Privately Held**
WEB: www.tradehome.com
SIC: 5661 2252 Shoes, orthopedic; socks
PA: Tradehome Shoe Stores, Inc.
8300 97th St S
Cottage Grove MN 55016
651 459-8600

(G-6831)
TRU8 SOLUTIONS LLC (PA)
1107 N 5th St (66502-5616)
PHONE..................................678 451-0264
Joshua Reid, *Mng Member*
Jay Reid,
EMP: 13 **EST:** 2014
SQ FT: 4,000
SALES (est): 1.7MM **Privately Held**
SIC: 8742 Business consultant

(G-6832)
TRUST COMPANY OF MANHATTAN
800 Poyntz Ave (66502-6055)
P.O. Box 1806 (66505-1806)
PHONE..................................785 537-7200
Mark Knackendoffel, *Principal*
Chuck Lyman, *Exec VP*
Eli Sallman, *Assistant VP*
Michael Carlisle, *Vice Pres*
Anne Lewis-Smith, *Vice Pres*
EMP: 13
SALES (est): 1.8MM **Privately Held**
WEB: www.thetrustco.com
SIC: 6282 8742 Investment advisory service; financial consultant

(G-6833)
TURF MANAGEMENT LLC
1012 Sedam Ave (66502-9374)
P.O. Box 724 (66505-0724)
PHONE..................................785 410-0394
Aaron Avery,
EMP: 10
SALES (est): 234.5K **Privately Held**
SIC: 0782 4959 Mowing services, lawn; fertilizing services, lawn; snowplowing

(G-6834)
U S ARMY CORPS OF ENGINEERS
5040 Tuttle Creek Blvd (66502-8812)
PHONE..................................785 537-7392
EMP: 76 **Publicly Held**
SIC: 9711 8711 Army; consulting engineer
HQ: U.S. Army Corps Of Engineers
441 G St Nw
Washington DC 20314
202 761-0001

(G-6835)
ULTRA ELECTRONICS ICE INC
2700 Amherst Ave (66502-2936)
PHONE..................................785 776-6423
Randy O'Boyle, *President*
Michael Casey, *Exec VP*
Mike Casey, *Vice Pres*
Ben Ketley, *Opers Staff*
John Buchanan, *Engineer*
▼ **EMP:** 68
SQ FT: 14,000
SALES (est): 16.2MM
SALES (corp-wide): 1B **Privately Held**
WEB: www.ice-ks.com
SIC: 3625 3728 Control equipment, electric; research & dev by manuf., aircraft parts & auxiliary equip
PA: Ultra Electronics Holdings Plc
417 Bridport Road
Greenford MIDDX UB6 8
208 813-4567

(G-6836)
UMB BANK NATIONAL ASSOCIATION
529 Humboldt St Ste 1 (66502-6073)
PHONE..................................785 776-9400
Larry Parker, *President*
EMP: 30
SALES (corp-wide): 1.1B **Publicly Held**
WEB: www.umbwebsolutions.com
SIC: 6021 6282 National commercial banks; investment advice
HQ: Umb Bank, National Association
1010 Grand Blvd Fl 3
Kansas City MO 64106
816 842-2222

(G-6837)
UNIFIED SCHOOL DISTRICT 383
Also Called: Manhattan Warehouse
1112 Hayes Dr (66502-5018)
PHONE..................................785 587-2850
EMP: 84
SALES (corp-wide): 111.6MM **Privately Held**
SIC: 8211 4225 Public elementary & secondary schools; general warehousing
PA: Unified School District 383
2031 Poyntz Ave
Manhattan KS 66502
785 587-2000

(G-6838)
UNIFIED SCHOOL DISTRICT 383
1120 Hayes Dr (66502-5018)
PHONE..................................785 587-2190
Doug Messer, *Director*
EMP: 95
SALES (corp-wide): 111.6MM **Privately Held**
SIC: 4151 School buses
PA: Unified School District 383
2031 Poyntz Ave
Manhattan KS 66502
785 587-2000

(G-6839)
USD 383 MNHTTAN OGDEN SCHL DST
Also Called: Maintenance Department
2031 Casement Rd (66502-4933)
PHONE..................................785 587-2180
Matt Davis, *Director*
EMP: 90
SALES (est): 6.7MM **Privately Held**
SIC: 8744 Base maintenance (providing personnel on continuing basis)

(G-6840)
V & V ELECTRIC COMPANY INC
629 Pecan Cir (66502-8146)
PHONE..................................785 539-1975
Victor Olson Jr, *President*
EMP: 22
SALES: 1,000K **Privately Held**
SIC: 1731 General electrical contractor

(G-6841)
VARNEY & ASSOCIATES CPAS LLC (PA)
120 N Juliette Ave (66502-6024)
PHONE..................................785 537-2202
Michael V Rogers, *CEO*
Gary D Burnett, *Corp Secy*
Richard A Boomer, *Vice Pres*
Janice Marks, *Vice Pres*
Josie Mitchell, *Accountant*
EMP: 35
SQ FT: 9,000
SALES (est): 3.8MM **Privately Held**
WEB: www.varney.com
SIC: 8721 8742 Certified public accountant; financial consultant

(G-6842)
VIA CHRISTI VLG MANHATTAN INC
Also Called: MOUNT ST MARY'S CONVENT
2800 Willow Grove Rd (66502-2096)
PHONE..................................785 539-7671
Cheyenne Strunk, *Exec Dir*
Doug Frihart, *Administration*
EMP: 120
SQ FT: 30,000
SALES: 8.4MM
SALES (corp-wide): 16.8MM **Privately Held**
SIC: 8051 8052 8093 Convalescent home with continuous nursing care; intermediate care facilities; rehabilitation center, outpatient treatment
HQ: Sisters Of St Joseph Of Wichita, Kansas
3700 E Lincoln St
Wichita KS 67218
316 686-7171

(G-6843)
VISTA FRANCHISE INC
Also Called: Vista Drive Inn
1911 Tuttle Creek Blvd (66502-4548)
PHONE..................................785 537-0100
Bradley Streeter, *President*
Andy Streeter, *General Mgr*
Karen Streeter, *Corp Secy*
EMP: 30
SQ FT: 2,500
SALES: 2MM **Privately Held**
SIC: 6794 6512 Franchises, selling or licensing; nonresidential building operators

(G-6844)
WADDELL & REED INC
Waddell & Reed Office 1603-00
555 Poyntz Ave Ste 280 (66502-0107)
PHONE..................................785 537-4505
Kenneth Ebert, *Branch Mgr*
EMP: 20 **Publicly Held**
SIC: 6311 8742 6211 Life insurance; financial consultant; mutual funds, selling by independent salesperson
HQ: Waddell & Reed, Inc.
6300 Lamar Ave
Shawnee Mission KS 66202
913 236-2000

(G-6845)
WALSON INK INC
610 S Delaware Ave (66502-3902)
PHONE..................................785 537-7370
Bret Williamson, *President*
Monty Williamson, *Treasurer*
EMP: 6
SALES (est): 469.6K **Privately Held**
SIC: 2759 2395 Textile printing rolls: engraving; embroidery products, except schiffli machine

(G-6846)
WALTERS-MORGAN CNSTR INC
2616 Tuttle Creek Blvd (66502-4479)
PHONE..................................785 539-7513
Scott Mueller, *CEO*
Dan Ellis, *Vice Pres*
Dick Green, *Vice Pres*
David W Levering, *Vice Pres*
Doug Kinney, *CFO*
EMP: 80 **EST:** 1938
SQ FT: 4,500
SALES (est): 29MM **Privately Held**
WEB: www.waltersmorgan.com
SIC: 1629 Waste water & sewage treatment plant construction

(G-6847)
WATERS INC
Also Called: True Value
338 N Seth Child Rd Ste A (66502-3034)
PHONE..................................785 537-1340
Jamie Pride, *Manager*
EMP: 34
SALES (corp-wide): 49.8MM **Privately Held**
SIC: 5251 0781 0181 0811 Hardware; landscape services; nursery stock, growing of; tree farm
PA: Waters, Inc.
3213 Arnold Ave
Salina KS 67401
785 825-7309

(G-6848)
WEDDLE AND SONS INC (PA)
2601 Anderson Ave 200a (66502-2809)
PHONE..................................785 532-8347
Allyn Weddle, *President*
Eric Weddle, *Treasurer*
EMP: 20
SALES: 5.3MM **Privately Held**
SIC: 1761 Roofing contractor

(G-6849)
WEISBENDER CONTRACTING INC
1812 Fair Ln (66502-3910)
PHONE..................................785 776-5034
Tim Weisbender, *President*
Russel Weisbender, *President*
Sheila Jennings, *General Mgr*
EMP: 5
SQ FT: 3,600
SALES (est): 759.7K **Privately Held**
SIC: 2431 2439 1521 Millwork; structural wood members; general remodeling, single-family houses

(G-6850)
WELLS FARGO HOME MORTGAGE INC
2601 Anderson Ave Ste 202 (66502-2809)
PHONE..................................785 565-2900
Jeff Carter, *Branch Mgr*
Carlin Murphy, *Branch Mgr*
EMP: 20
SALES (corp-wide): 101B **Publicly Held**
SIC: 6021 National commercial banks
HQ: Wells Fargo Home Mortgage Inc
1 Home Campus
Des Moines IA 50328
515 324-3707

(G-6851)
WESBANCO INC
224 E Poyntz Ave (66502-5041)
PHONE..................................785 539-3553
David Urban, *Branch Mgr*
EMP: 56
SALES (corp-wide): 515.2MM **Publicly Held**
SIC: 6282 Investment advice
PA: Wesbanco, Inc.
1 Bank Plz
Wheeling WV 26003
304 234-9000

(G-6852)
WEST SIDE MECHANICAL INC
424 Stone Grove Dr (66503-8785)
PHONE....................................913 788-1800
Renee Standish, *President*
Phillip Standish, *Vice Pres*
EMP: 10
SQ FT: 1,500
SALES (est): 1.1MM **Privately Held**
SIC: 1711 Mechanical contractor

(G-6853)
WESTSIDE VET CLNIC MNHATTAN PA
Also Called: Westside Veterinary Clinic
3130 Anderson Ave (66503-2865)
PHONE....................................785 539-7922
Richard Lewis, *Owner*
Cheryl Lewis, *Office Mgr*
EMP: 11
SALES: 750K **Privately Held**
SIC: 0742 Animal hospital services, pets & other animal specialties

(G-6854)
WIDGETS FAMILY FUN CENTER
8232 Southport Dr (66502-8116)
PHONE....................................785 320-5099
EMP: 11 **EST:** 2017
SALES (est): 450K **Privately Held**
SIC: 7996 Amusement parks

(G-6855)
WILDCAT GTTERING EXTERIORS INC
6116 Summit Dr (66503-9033)
PHONE....................................785 485-2194
Tony M Siebold, *President*
Tony Siebold, *President*
EMP: 10
SQ FT: 2,000
SALES (est): 970K **Privately Held**
SIC: 1761 1799 Siding contractor; gutter & downspout contractor; awning installation

(G-6856)
WOMENS HEALTH GROUP PA
Also Called: Ob-Gyn Office
1133 College Ave Bldg E (66502-2770)
PHONE....................................785 776-1400
Rudy Hugh MD, *Partner*
Rex R Fischer MD, *Partner*
Rudy Haun, *Partner*
Bonnie Patterson MD, *Partner*
Anne Wigglesworth, *Partner*
EMP: 20
SALES (est): 2.4MM **Privately Held**
SIC: 8011 Physical medicine, physician/surgeon

(G-6857)
YORGENSEN-MELOAN INC
Also Called: Yorgensn-Mloan-Londeen Fnrl HM
1616 Poyntz Ave (66502-4149)
PHONE....................................785 539-7481
Douglas Meloan, *President*
Eric Londeen, *Vice Pres*
EMP: 10
SQ FT: 6,000
SALES (est): 1MM **Privately Held**
WEB: www.ymlfuneralhome.com
SIC: 7261 Funeral home

Mankato
Jewell County

(G-6858)
JEWELL COUNTY EMS
510 E North St (66956-1832)
PHONE....................................785 378-3069
Shannon Meier, *Director*
EMP: 24
SALES (est): 448.6K **Privately Held**
SIC: 4119 Ambulance service

(G-6859)
JEWELL COUNTY HOSPITAL
100 Crestvue Ave (66956-2407)
PHONE....................................785 378-3137
Deanna Freeman, *Administration*
EMP: 90
SALES: 4.2MM **Privately Held**
SIC: 8062 8011 General medical & surgical hospitals; offices & clinics of medical doctors

(G-6860)
MANKATO LIVESTOCK INC
Also Called: Mankato Livestock Comm Co
810 N Commercial St (66956-1519)
P.O. Box 381 (66956-0381)
PHONE....................................785 378-3283
Scott Greene, *President*
Jon Russell, *Vice Pres*
Kelly Bouray, *Treasurer*
Bill Logan, *Admin Sec*
EMP: 20
SQ FT: 5,000
SALES (est): 2.8MM **Privately Held**
SIC: 5154 Auctioning livestock

(G-6861)
SCHUEMAN TRANSFER
10 Frontase St (66956)
P.O. Box 292 (66956-0292)
PHONE....................................785 378-3114
Thomas Walker, *Branch Mgr*
EMP: 40
SALES (corp-wide): 7.3MM **Privately Held**
SIC: 4212 Local trucking, without storage
PA: Schueman Transfer
108 Freeman St
Oakland IA 51560
712 482-6612

Maple Hill
Wabaunsee County

(G-6862)
ADAMS CATTLE COMPANY
Also Called: Xit Ranch
1 Mile Ne Of Town (66507)
PHONE....................................785 256-4200
Raymond E Adams Jr, *Owner*
EMP: 15
SALES (est): 757K **Privately Held**
WEB: www.adamscattlecompany.com
SIC: 0191 0212 0211 General farms, primarily crop; beef cattle except feedlots; beef cattle feedlots

(G-6863)
COUNTRY CARPET INC
14969 Wterman Crossing Rd (66507-8862)
P.O. Box 450 (66507-0450)
PHONE....................................785 256-4800
Jon D Ross, *President*
Gary L Ross, *Vice Pres*
Marcia A Ross, *Treasurer*
Denise Queen, *Admin Sec*
EMP: 18
SQ FT: 10,000
SALES (est): 5.8MM **Privately Held**
SIC: 5023 5713 Carpets; floor covering stores

(G-6864)
STOCKGROWERS STATE BANK (PA)
225 Main St (66507-8901)
P.O. Box 8 (66507-0008)
PHONE....................................785 256-4241
Steve Niemack, *CEO*
Max Fuller, *CEO*
James Stallbaumer, *President*
Beth Tarbutton, *Vice Pres*
Dick Poovey, *Manager*
EMP: 15 **EST:** 1906
SALES: 3.8MM **Privately Held**
SIC: 6022 State trust companies accepting deposits, commercial

(G-6865)
TOWER METAL WORKS INC
29273 Windy Hill Rd (66507-8551)
PHONE....................................785 256-4281
Charles H Willsey Jr, *President*
Beverly Willsey, *Vice Pres*
Robert Willsey, *Sales Mgr*
Renee Larson, *Office Mgr*
EMP: 35
SQ FT: 25,000
SALES (est): 8.5MM **Privately Held**
WEB: www.towermetalworksinc.com
SIC: 3444 3599 Sheet metal specialties, not stamped; machine shop, jobbing & repair

Marion
Marion County

(G-6866)
BRADBURY CO INC
Also Called: Marion Die & Fixture
421 W Main St (66861-1730)
P.O. Box 177 (66861-0177)
PHONE....................................620 382-3775
Don Bredemeier, *General Mgr*
Sarah Houser, *Accountant*
Jim Stork, *Sales Staff*
Kevin Neufeld, *Supervisor*
Mario Gallegos, *Technician*
EMP: 26
SALES (corp-wide): 141.4MM **Privately Held**
SIC: 3599 Machine shop, jobbing & repair
PA: The Bradbury Co Inc
1200 E Cole St
Moundridge KS 67107
620 345-6394

(G-6867)
CAREGIVER SUPPORT SYSTEM
306 S Roosevelt St (66861-1354)
PHONE....................................214 207-7273
Jere Reiser, *Owner*
EMP: 30
SALES (est): 1.6MM **Privately Held**
WEB: www.caregiversupport.com
SIC: 8051 Skilled nursing care facilities

(G-6868)
CENTRAL NATIONAL BANK
231 E Main St (66861-1627)
P.O. Box 256 (66861-0256)
PHONE....................................620 382-2129
Shawn Geis, *Branch Mgr*
EMP: 12
SALES (corp-wide): 55.4MM **Privately Held**
WEB: www.centralnational.com
SIC: 6021 National commercial banks
HQ: Central National Bank (Inc)
802 N Washington St
Junction City KS 66441
785 238-4114

(G-6869)
FLAMINGS PLUMBING HEATING & AC (PA)
113 S 2nd St (66861-1609)
PHONE....................................620 382-2181
Merle Flaming, *President*
Eva Flaming, *Treasurer*
EMP: 13
SQ FT: 4,800
SALES (est): 1.9MM **Privately Held**
SIC: 1711 Warm air heating & air conditioning contractor

(G-6870)
FLINT HILLS CLAY WORKS INC
Also Called: Flinthills Clay Works
126 W Main St (66861-1712)
PHONE....................................620 382-3620
Leslie Byer, *President*
Celia Byer, *Vice Pres*
EMP: 10
SQ FT: 4,000
SALES (est): 1.4MM **Privately Held**
SIC: 5032 3269 Tile & clay products; art & ornamental ware, pottery

(G-6871)
HETT CONSTRUCTION
1212 Pawnee Rd (66861)
PHONE....................................620 382-2236
David Hett, *Owner*
EMP: 10
SALES (est): 580K **Privately Held**
SIC: 1771 Concrete work

(G-6872)
HOCH PUBLISHING CO INC
Also Called: Hillsboro Star-Journal
117 S 3rd St (66861-1621)
P.O. Box 278 (66861-0278)
PHONE....................................620 382-2165
Eric Meyer, *President*
Jean Stuchlik, *Business Mgr*
Joan Meyer, *Vice Pres*
Melvin Honeyfield, *Prdtn Dir*
Donna Bernhardt, *Treasurer*
EMP: 9 **EST:** 1948
SQ FT: 4,750
SALES (est): 681.3K **Privately Held**
WEB: www.marionkansas.com
SIC: 2711 Newspapers, publishing & printing

(G-6873)
HOSPITAL DST 1 MARION CNTY
Also Called: MARION COUNTY HOME CARE
535 S Freeborn St (66861-1256)
PHONE....................................620 382-2177
Jeremy Armstrong, *CEO*
Hillary Dolbee, *CFO*
EMP: 110
SALES: 11.7MM **Privately Held**
WEB: www.slhmarion.org
SIC: 8062 General medical & surgical hospitals

(G-6874)
MARION MANUFACTURING INC
201 S Coble St (66861-1137)
PHONE....................................620 382-3751
David Richmond, *President*
Kayleah Kukuk, *Corp Secy*
Timothy Richmond, *Vice Pres*
Tim Richmond, *Sales Executive*
Mike Carroll, *Prgrmr*
EMP: 28 **EST:** 1979
SQ FT: 32,000
SALES (est): 6.1MM **Privately Held**
WEB: www.marionmanufacturing.com
SIC: 3547 3599 3542 Rolling mill machinery; machine shop, jobbing & repair; machine tools, metal forming type

(G-6875)
PLP INC
Also Called: John Deere Authorized Dealer
902 N Cedar St (66861-9524)
PHONE....................................620 382-3794
John Deere, *Partner*
Chad Gormley, *Manager*
EMP: 30
SALES (corp-wide): 66.9MM **Privately Held**
SIC: 5999 5082 Farm equipment & supplies; construction & mining machinery
PA: Plp, Inc
811 E 30th Ave Ste F
Hutchinson KS 67502
620 664-5860

(G-6876)
SHAWMAR OIL & GAS CO INC (PA)
1116 E Main St (66861-1230)
P.O. Box 9 (66861-0009)
PHONE....................................620 382-2932
James M Cloutier, *President*
Beau Cloutier, *Vice Pres*
EMP: 27 **EST:** 1962
SQ FT: 1,500
SALES (est): 3.6MM **Privately Held**
WEB: www.shawmar.com
SIC: 1311 Crude petroleum production; natural gas production

Marquette
Mcpherson County

(G-6877)
RIVERVIEW ESTATES INC
202 S Washington St (67464-9775)
P.O. Box 158 (67464-0158)
PHONE....................................785 546-2211
Ken Hedberg, *President*
Courtney Bailey, *Administration*
Carla Dunigan, *Administration*
EMP: 50

SQ FT: 10,000
SALES: 2.3MM **Privately Held**
SIC: 8052 Intermediate care facilities

Marysville
Marshall County

(G-6878)
ADVOCATE PUBLISHING CO INC
Also Called: Marysville Advocate
107 S 9th St (66508-1825)
P.O. Box 271 (66508-0271)
PHONE..................................785 562-2317
Howard Kessinger, *President*
Sarah Kessinger, *Principal*
Sharon Kessinger, *Treasurer*
EMP: 20
SQ FT: 3,000
SALES (est): 1.1MM **Privately Held**
SIC: 2711 2752 2721 Commercial printing & newspaper publishing combined; commercial printing, lithographic; periodicals

(G-6879)
ASTRO 3 THEATRE
Also Called: Astro Theatre
820 Center St (66508-1702)
P.O. Box 88 (66508-0088)
PHONE..................................785 562-3715
Mike Wilkinson, *President*
EMP: 10
SALES (est): 291.1K **Privately Held**
SIC: 7832 Exhibitors, itinerant: motion picture

(G-6880)
BOSS MOTORS INC
Also Called: Boss Mtrs-Ford Mercury Lincoln
605 Broadway (66508-1839)
P.O. Box 126 (66508-0126)
PHONE..................................785 562-3696
Jim Boss, *President*
Greg Boss, *Vice Pres*
EMP: 10 **EST:** 1936
SQ FT: 9,600
SALES: 1.5MM **Privately Held**
SIC: 5511 5561 7538 Automobiles, new & used; travel trailers: automobile, new & used; general automotive repair shops

(G-6881)
BRUNA BROTHERS IMPLEMENT LLC (PA)
Also Called: Bruna Implement Company
1128 Pony Express Hwy (66508-8647)
P.O. Box 390 (66508-0390)
PHONE..................................785 562-5304
Toby Bruna, *Finance Mgr*
Alan Bruna, *Mng Member*
Tom Bruna, *Mng Member*
Skid Steers, *Products*
Brian Bruna,
EMP: 19 **EST:** 1948
SQ FT: 13,500
SALES (est): 26.5MM **Privately Held**
WEB: www.brunaimplementco.com
SIC: 5083 7699 Farm implements; agricultural equipment repair services

(G-6882)
CITIZENS STATE BANK (HQ)
800 Broadway (66508-1803)
P.O. Box 388 (66508-0388)
PHONE..................................785 562-2186
Kirk Bradford, *CEO*
Lynn Mayer, *President*
EMP: 32 **EST:** 1907
SALES: 16.2MM
SALES (corp-wide): 1.7MM **Privately Held**
WEB: www.csbmarysville.com
SIC: 6022 State commercial banks
PA: Community Bancshares Of Marysville, Inc.
800 Broadway
Marysville KS 66508
785 562-2186

(G-6883)
COMMUNITY MEMORIAL HEALTHCARE
805 Broadway (66508-1802)
PHONE..................................785 562-4062
Jan White, *Director*
EMP: 23
SALES (corp-wide): 21.5MM **Privately Held**
SIC: 8099 Blood related health services
PA: Community Memorial Healthcare Inc
708 N 18th St
Marysville KS 66508
785 562-2311

(G-6884)
COMMUNITY MEMORIAL HEALTHCARE (PA)
708 N 18th St (66508-1338)
PHONE..................................785 562-2311
Curtis R Hawkinson, *CEO*
Colette Ottens, *Principal*
Janet Wassenberg, *Opers Staff*
Linda Schmidt, *Purchasing*
Therese Landoll, *CFO*
EMP: 190
SQ FT: 58,000
SALES: 21.5MM **Privately Held**
SIC: 8062 General medical & surgical hospitals

(G-6885)
COMMUNITY MEMORIAL HEALTHCARE
Also Called: Community Physicians Clinic
1902 May St (66508-1200)
PHONE..................................785 562-3942
EMP: 34
SALES (corp-wide): 21.5MM **Privately Held**
SIC: 8011 Medical centers
PA: Community Memorial Healthcare Inc
708 N 18th St
Marysville KS 66508
785 562-2311

(G-6886)
COMMUNITY MEMORIAL HOSPITAL
1172 11th Rd (66508-8643)
PHONE..................................785 562-2311
Randall Brown, *Principal*
EMP: 21
SALES (est): 1.9MM **Privately Held**
SIC: 8011 Physicians' office, including specialists

(G-6887)
COMMUNITY PHYSICIANS CLINIC
1902 May St (66508-1200)
PHONE..................................785 562-3942
Curtis Hawkinson, *CEO*
Jay Cancer, *CEO*
EMP: 16
SALES (est): 1MM **Privately Held**
SIC: 8011 Clinic, operated by physicians

(G-6888)
FARMERS DREAM INC
Also Called: Marysville Super 8
1155 Pony Express Hwy (66508-8501)
PHONE..................................785 562-5588
Lynn Bruna, *President*
Renea Bruna, *Vice Pres*
Doug G Bruna, *Treasurer*
Alan Bruna, *Admin Sec*
EMP: 18
SALES (est): 998.6K **Privately Held**
SIC: 7011 Hotels

(G-6889)
FIRST COMMERCE BANK
902 Broadway (66508-1805)
P.O. Box 70 (66508-0070)
PHONE..................................785 562-5558
Marc Degenhardt, *President*
Max Searcey, *Exec VP*
Jean Frerking, *Manager*
EMP: 13
SALES: 4.6MM **Privately Held**
SIC: 6022 State trust companies accepting deposits, commercial

(G-6890)
HALL BROTHERS INC (PA)
Also Called: Blue River Sand and Gravel Co
1196 Pony Express Hwy (66508-8647)
P.O. Box 166 (66508-0166)
PHONE..................................785 562-2386
Dick Kistner, *President*
Rob Lauer, *Vice Pres*
Julio Franco, *Director*
EMP: 10 **EST:** 1947
SQ FT: 3,000
SALES (est): 18.1MM **Privately Held**
WEB: www.hallbros.net
SIC: 1611 General contractor, highway & street construction

(G-6891)
KANEQUIP INC
1152 Pony Express Hwy (66508-8647)
P.O. Box 431 (66508-0431)
PHONE..................................785 562-2377
James B Meinhardt, *Branch Mgr*
EMP: 15
SALES (corp-wide): 117MM **Privately Held**
SIC: 5083 7699 Farm implements; agricultural equipment repair services
PA: Kanequip, Inc.
18035 E Us Highway 24
Wamego KS 66547
785 456-2041

(G-6892)
KANEQUIP INC
Also Called: Kubota Authorized Dealer
1152 Pony Express Hwy (66508-8647)
P.O. Box 431 (66508-0431)
PHONE..................................785 562-2377
James Meinhardt, *CEO*
Randal Bobbitt, *Manager*
Michael Brown, *Manager*
EMP: 167 **EST:** 1999
SQ FT: 21,000
SALES: 117MM **Privately Held**
SIC: 5046 5083 Commercial equipment; farm & garden machinery
PA: Kanequip, Inc.
18035 E Us Highway 24
Wamego KS 66547
785 456-2041

(G-6893)
LANDOLL CORPORATION (PA)
1900 North St (66508-1271)
P.O. Box 111 (66508-0111)
PHONE..................................785 562-5381
Donald Landoll, *President*
Steve Nieto, *District Mgr*
David L Roesch, *Vice Pres*
Deanna Wurtz, *Senior Buyer*
Jessica Leis, *Buyer*
◆ **EMP:** 415
SQ FT: 390,000
SALES (est): 110.5MM **Privately Held**
WEB: www.landoll.com
SIC: 3728 3715 3523 3537 Deicing equipment, aircraft; truck trailers; plows, agricultural: disc, moldboard, chisel, listers, etc.; forklift trucks

(G-6894)
LANDOLL CORPORATION
1104 Pony Express Hwy (66508-8647)
PHONE..................................785 562-4780
Don Landoll, *Branch Mgr*
EMP: 15
SALES (corp-wide): 110.5MM **Privately Held**
SIC: 3715 Trailer bodies
PA: Landoll Corporation
1900 North St
Marysville KS 66508
785 562-5381

(G-6895)
MARSHALL COUNTY AGCY ON AGING
111 S 8th St (66508-1899)
PHONE..................................785 562-5522
Heather Ruhkamp, *Director*
EMP: 10
SALES (est): 450.1K **Privately Held**
SIC: 8322 Individual & family services

(G-6896)
MARYSVILLE CHAMBER COMMERCE
Also Called: Marysville Ambulance Service
410 N 6th St (66508-1528)
PHONE..................................785 562-2359
Donna Tinman, *Principal*
EMP: 10
SALES (corp-wide): 46.6K **Privately Held**
SIC: 4119 Ambulance service
PA: Marysville Chamber Of Commerce
101 N 10th St
Marysville KS 66508
785 562-3101

(G-6897)
MARYSVILLE CHAMBER COMMERCE (PA)
101 N 10th St (66508-1739)
P.O. Box 16 (66508-0016)
PHONE..................................785 562-3101
Jerry Coleman, *President*
Brenda Staggenborg, *Admin Sec*
EMP: 10
SALES: 46.6K **Privately Held**
SIC: 8611 Chamber of Commerce

(G-6898)
MARYSVILLE CLINIC
1902 May St (66508-1200)
PHONE..................................785 562-2744
Fax: 785 562-2034
EMP: 10 **EST:** 1958
SALES (est): 490K **Privately Held**
SIC: 8011 Doctor's Office

(G-6899)
MARYSVILLE HEALTH CORPORATION
Also Called: Blue Valley Health Care
1100 N 16th St (66508-1126)
PHONE..................................785 562-2424
Paul Wurth, *President*
Lynda Bruna, *Office Mgr*
Iris Turnbull, *Director*
EMP: 90
SQ FT: 300
SALES (est): 4.7MM **Privately Held**
SIC: 8052 8051 Intermediate care facilities; skilled nursing care facilities

(G-6900)
MARYSVILLE LIVESTOCK INC
1180 Us Highway 77 (66508-8656)
P.O. Box 67 (66508-0067)
PHONE..................................785 562-1015
EMP: 16
SALES (corp-wide): 2.1MM **Privately Held**
SIC: 5154 Auctioning livestock
PA: Marysville Livestock Inc
17360 Godlove Rd
Onaga KS

(G-6901)
MARYSVILLE MUTUAL INSURANCE CO
1001 Broadway (66508-1814)
P.O. Box 151 (66508-0151)
PHONE..................................785 562-2379
Trent Moser, *President*
Harold Dorssom, *President*
Ugene Holz, *Chairman*
Donald McDowell, *Vice Pres*
Donald Kramer, *Treasurer*
EMP: 12 **EST:** 1888
SQ FT: 12,000
SALES: 127K **Privately Held**
WEB: www.marysvillemutual.com
SIC: 6411 Insurance agents

(G-6902)
MARYSVILLE SCHOOL DISTRICT
Also Called: Marysville High
1011 Walnut St (66508-1960)
PHONE..................................785 562-5386
Darren Schroeder, *Principal*
EMP: 75
SALES (corp-wide): 5.1MM **Privately Held**
WEB: www.marysvilleschools.org
SIC: 8211 8351 Public elementary & secondary schools; child day care services
PA: Marysville School District
211 S 10th St
Marysville KS 66508
785 562-5308

(G-6903)
MARYSVLLE AREA CMNTY THTRE INC
Also Called: M-Act
2401 North St (66508-8641)
P.O. Box 1 (66508-0001)
PHONE..................................785 268-0420
Mandy Cook, *Principal*
EMP: 60
SALES: 31.3K **Privately Held**
SIC: 7922 Theatrical producers & services

(G-6904)
OAK TREE AND PENNYS DINER
Also Called: Oak Tree Inn
1127 Pony Ex Hwy Ste A (66508)
PHONE..................................785 562-1234
Myrna Stirn, *General Mgr*
EMP: 11
SALES (est): 244.1K **Privately Held**
SIC: 5812 7011 Diner; hotels

(G-6905)
OREGON TRAIL EQUIPMENT LLC
Also Called: John Deere Authorized Dealer
553 Pony Express Hwy (66508-8831)
P.O. Box 517, Beatrice NE (68310-0517)
PHONE..................................785 562-2346
Richard Bennett, *Mng Member*
EMP: 11
SALES (est): 2.3MM **Privately Held**
SIC: 5083 Farm implements

(G-6906)
ORSCHELN FARM AND HOME LLC
Also Called: Orscheln Farm & Home 98
1095 Pony Express Hwy (66508-8649)
PHONE..................................785 562-2459
Rowdy Grabowski, *Manager*
EMP: 11
SALES (corp-wide): 822.7MM **Privately Held**
SIC: 5191 Feed
PA: Orscheln Farm And Home Llc
1800 Overcenter Dr
Moberly MO 65270
800 577-2580

(G-6907)
OTT ELECTRIC INC
810 Broadway (66508-1897)
P.O. Box 167 (66508-0167)
PHONE..................................785 562-2641
Alan Feldhausen, *President*
Sheree Feldhausen, *Corp Secy*
EMP: 12 **EST:** 1928
SQ FT: 2,000
SALES (est): 2MM **Privately Held**
WEB: www.ottelectric.com
SIC: 5722 7629 Electric household appliances; electrical household appliance repair

(G-6908)
ROADY TRUCKING
1203 8th Rd (66508-8834)
PHONE..................................785 562-1221
Warren Roady, *Principal*
EMP: 10 **EST:** 2008
SALES (est): 1MM **Privately Held**
SIC: 4212 Local trucking, without storage

(G-6909)
RSVP OF NORTHEAST KANSAS INC
813 Broadway (66508-1802)
PHONE..................................785 562-2154
Joanie Spellmeier, *Exec Dir*
EMP: 250
SALES: 92.4K **Privately Held**
SIC: 8399 Community development groups

(G-6910)
TEMPS DISPOSAL SERVICE INC
Also Called: Temps Waste Systems
783 Jayhawk Rd (66508-8811)
PHONE..................................785 562-5360
Richard Temps, *President*
H Richard Temps, *President*
Jane Ann Temps, *Corp Secy*
EMP: 11
SALES (est): 930K **Privately Held**
SIC: 4953 Garbage: collecting, destroying & processing

(G-6911)
TENSION ENVELOPE CORPORATION
1601 Spring St (66508-2073)
P.O. Box 350 (66508-0350)
PHONE..................................785 562-2307
Robert Griswold, *Mfg Staff*
Deborha Schuler, *Human Res Mgr*
EMP: 54
SALES (corp-wide): 234MM **Privately Held**
WEB: www.tension.com
SIC: 2677 5112 Envelopes; envelopes
PA: Tension Envelope Corporation
819 E 19th St
Kansas City MO 64108
816 471-3800

(G-6912)
UNITED BANK & TRUST (PA)
2333 Broadway (66508)
P.O. Box 311 (66508-0311)
PHONE..................................785 562-4330
Allen Myer, *President*
Judith Starr, *Assistant VP*
Donna Scheele, *Vice Pres*
Connie Holthaus, *Opers Staff*
EMP: 33
SALES: 26.1MM **Privately Held**
SIC: 6022 State trust companies accepting deposits, commercial

Mayetta
Jackson County

(G-6913)
1ST NATION PAINTING INC
207 S 4th St (66509-9201)
P.O. Box 67 (66509-0067)
PHONE..................................785 966-2935
Tony Wahweotten, *President*
EMP: 10
SALES (est): 393.5K **Privately Held**
SIC: 1721 Painting & paper hanging

(G-6914)
B & H MOTOR SPORTS (PA)
Also Called: Thunderhills Speedway
14212 142nd Rd (66509-8755)
PHONE..................................785 966-2575
Mike Henry, *Partner*
Kenneth Blair, *Partner*
EMP: 40 **EST:** 1998
SALES (est): 446.8K **Privately Held**
SIC: 7948 Race track operation

(G-6915)
LITTLE SOLDIER
14187 N1 Rd (66509-8835)
PHONE..................................785 845-1987
Keirsten Hale, *Partner*
Adrian Hale, *Partner*
EMP: 10
SALES (est): 190K **Privately Held**
SIC: 7929 7389 Entertainers & entertainment groups;

(G-6916)
PRAIRIE BAND CASINO AND RESORT
12305 150th Rd (66509-8815)
PHONE..................................785 966-7777
David Albrecht, *General Mgr*
Kimberly Schimmel, *Purch Mgr*
Corey Mzhickteno, *Treasurer*
Lisa Demint, *Controller*
Lisa Wamego, *Controller*
EMP: 800
SALES (est): 49.4MM **Privately Held**
SIC: 7011 Casino hotel
PA: Prairie Band Potawatomi Nation
16281 Q Rd
Mayetta KS 66509
785 966-2255

(G-6917)
PRAIRIE BAND POTAWATOMI BINGO
16277 Q Rd (66509-8970)
PHONE..................................785 966-4000
Dustin Haverkamp, *Principal*
EMP: 50
SQ FT: 12,500
SALES (est): 962.5K **Privately Held**
SIC: 7999 Bingo hall

(G-6918)
PRAIRIE BEND PTWTOMI CHILDCARE
Also Called: Prairie Bend Potawamtomi Early
15380 K Rd (66509-9092)
PHONE..................................785 966-2707
Philip Pfannenstiel, *Buyer*
Hope Abame, *Director*
EMP: 34
SALES (est): 705.2K **Privately Held**
SIC: 8351 Child day care services

(G-6919)
THUNDER HILL SPEEDWAY LLC
11995 142nd Rd (66509)
PHONE..................................785 313-2922
Patricia Conkwright, *Manager*
EMP: 25
SALES (est): 488.3K **Privately Held**
SIC: 7948 Automotive race track operation

Mc Cune
Crawford County

(G-6920)
MCCUNE FARMERS UNION COOP
708 Main St (66753)
P.O. Box 58 (66753-0058)
PHONE..................................620 632-4226
Russ Smith, *President*
EMP: 10 **EST:** 1941
SQ FT: 29,000
SALES: 5.5MM **Privately Held**
SIC: 5153 5191 5171 Grain elevators; fertilizer & fertilizer materials; chemicals, agricultural; petroleum bulk stations

(G-6921)
R P 3 INC
8519 Nw 50th St (66753-4079)
PHONE..................................620 827-6136
Roe Parsons III, *President*
EMP: 12 **EST:** 1976
SALES (est): 1MM **Privately Held**
SIC: 1711 Fire sprinkler system installation

(G-6922)
S NOBLE TRUCKING INC
113 Main St (66753-4005)
PHONE..................................620 704-0886
Steven C Noble, *President*
EMP: 13
SALES: 1.5MM **Privately Held**
SIC: 4212 Local trucking, without storage

(G-6923)
WIENEKE CONSTRUCTION CO INC
954 S 87th St (66753-6125)
PHONE..................................620 632-4529
David Wieneke, *President*
Brad Wieneke, *Vice Pres*
Todd Wieneke, *Admin Sec*
EMP: 15
SALES: 800K **Privately Held**
SIC: 1771 1522 Driveway contractor; residential construction

Mc Louth
Jefferson County

(G-6924)
AAF FLEET SERVICE INC
P.O. Box 358 (66054-0358)
PHONE..................................913 683-3816
Raymond I Alloway Jr, *Principal*
EMP: 15
SALES (est): 3.1MM **Privately Held**
SIC: 7353 Heavy construction equipment rental

(G-6925)
BUCK CONSTRUCTION CO
18345 46th St (66054-4184)
PHONE..................................913 796-6510
Emery Buck, *Owner*
EMP: 15
SALES (est): 850K **Privately Held**
SIC: 1794 Excavation work

(G-6926)
EARTH RISING INC
25110 235th St (66054-3040)
PHONE..................................913 796-2141
Jefpus David, *Principal*
David Jefpus, *Principal*
EMP: 12 **EST:** 1992
SALES: 103K **Privately Held**
SIC: 7032 7011 Sporting & recreational camps; tourist camps, cabins, cottages & courts

(G-6927)
FREESTATE ELECTRIC COOP INC
507 N Union St (66054)
PHONE..................................913 796-6111
Christopher Parr, *Manager*
EMP: 40
SALES (corp-wide): 40MM **Privately Held**
SIC: 4911 Electric services
PA: Freestate Electric Cooperative, Inc.
1100 Sw Auburn Rd
Topeka KS 66615
800 794-1989

(G-6928)
KLM EXPLORATION CO INC
600 E Lake St (66054-5205)
P.O. Box 151 (66054-0151)
PHONE..................................913 796-6763
Reid Scofield, *President*
Larry Alex, *Manager*
EMP: 10
SQ FT: 4,200
SALES (est): 1.2MM **Privately Held**
SIC: 1382 Oil & gas exploration services

(G-6929)
SERVICE AUTO GLASS INC (PA)
1580 W Ogden Ave Unit 140 (66054)
PHONE..................................630 628-0398
Ken Meyer, *President*
EMP: 11 **EST:** 1978
SQ FT: 2,000
SALES (est): 238.4K **Privately Held**
SIC: 7536 Automotive glass replacement shops

Mc Pherson
Mcpherson County

(G-6930)
AERO TRANSPORTATION PDTS INC
Also Called: Atp
1330 N 81 Byp (67460)
PHONE..................................620 241-7010
Todd Krahl, *Manager*
EMP: 55
SALES (corp-wide): 4.3B **Publicly Held**
SIC: 3743 Railroad equipment
HQ: Aero Transportation Products, Inc.
3300 E Geospace Dr
Independence MO 64056
816 257-5450

McPherson
Mcpherson County

(G-6931)
ADAMS BROWN BRAN BALL CHRTERED
200 S Main St (67460-4844)
P.O. Box 864 (67460-0864)
PHONE..................................620 241-2090

Michelle Schneider, *CFO*
Chris Keith, *Manager*
Kamran Faruqi, *CIO*
EMP: 16
SALES (corp-wide): 9.4MM **Privately Held**
SIC: 8721 8111 Certified public accountant; legal services
PA: Adams, Brown, Beran & Ball Chartered Inc
2006 Broadway Ave
Great Bend KS 67530
620 549-3271

(G-6932)
ADVANCED EXTRUSIONS CO LLC
404 N Chestnut St (67460)
PHONE..................................620 241-2006
Douglas A Schulz,
Tom Depperschmidt,
Doug Unruh,
EMP: 15
SQ FT: 40,000
SALES (est): 2.2MM **Privately Held**
WEB: www.advanced-extrusion.com
SIC: 3089 Injection molding of plastics

(G-6933)
AMERICAN LEGION
Also Called: HARRY B. DORST POST NO 24
401 N Main St (67460-3403)
P.O. Box 209 (67460-0209)
PHONE..................................620 241-0343
Wayne Blue, *Principal*
Roy Walsh, *Principal*
Gerald Garcia, *Commander*
EMP: 11
SALES: 161.7K **Privately Held**
SIC: 8641 Veterans' organization

(G-6934)
AMERICAN MAPLAN CORPORATION
Also Called: Battenfeld-Cincinnati USA
823 S Us Highway 81 Byp (67460-6031)
P.O. Box 832 (67460-0832)
PHONE..................................620 241-6843
Paul Godwin, *President*
Peter Hammer, *Vice Pres*
Arthur Day, *Senior Buyer*
Barry Weaver, *Controller*
Tiffany Bebermeyer, *Accounts Mgr*
◆ **EMP:** 51
SQ FT: 5,000
SALES (est): 46.9MM
SALES (corp-wide): 1MM **Privately Held**
WEB: www.maplan.com
SIC: 3559 8742 Plastics working machinery; industry specialist consultants
HQ: Battenfeld-Cincinnati Germany Gmbh
Gruner Weg 9
Bad Oeynhausen 32547
573 124-20

(G-6935)
ANGEL ARMS
Also Called: Angel Arms Home Health
318 N Main St (67460-4308)
PHONE..................................620 245-0848
Dawnelle Atcock, *Partner*
EMP: 15 **EST:** 1998
SALES (est): 499.9K **Privately Held**
SIC: 8052 Intermediate care facilities

(G-6936)
ANGEL ARMS
Also Called: ANGEL ARMS HOME HEALTH
110 S Main St (67460-4852)
PHONE..................................620 241-1074
Dawnelle Adcock, *Partner*
EMP: 12
SALES: 2.4MM **Privately Held**
SIC: 8082 Home health care services

(G-6937)
ARCHROCK INC
1404 Mohawk Rd (67460-8000)
P.O. Box 187 (67460-0187)
PHONE..................................620 241-8740
Hewitt Kay, *Project Mgr*
Lee Sumrall, *Branch Mgr*
EMP: 28 **Publicly Held**
WEB: www.exterran.com
SIC: 1389 4225 Gas compressing (natural gas) at the fields; general warehousing
PA: Archrock Inc.
9807 Katy Fwy Ste 100
Houston TX 77024

(G-6938)
BILLS OUTDOOR SPORTS
835 S Us Highway 81 Byp (67460-6031)
PHONE..................................620 241-7130
William Pendlay, *Owner*
EMP: 12
SQ FT: 2,000
SALES (est): 848.2K **Privately Held**
SIC: 5091 5941 Fishing tackle; fishing equipment

(G-6939)
BRUCE OIL CO LLC
1704 Limestone Rd (67460-6500)
PHONE..................................620 241-2938
Betty Koehn, *Partner*
Lonny Bruce,
Jerry Bruce,
Tommy Bruce,
EMP: 5
SALES (est): 432.2K **Privately Held**
SIC: 1381 8721 Drilling oil & gas wells; accounting services, except auditing

(G-6940)
CARGILL INCORPORATED
2025 E 1st St (67460-3963)
PHONE..................................620 241-5120
Mark Lacey, *Manager*
EMP: 15
SALES (corp-wide): 113.4B **Privately Held**
WEB: www.cargill.com
SIC: 2048 Prepared feeds
PA: Cargill, Incorporated
15407 Mcginty Rd W
Wayzata MN 55391
952 742-7575

(G-6941)
CARTRIDGE KING OF KANSAS (PA)
2107 Industrial Dr (67460-8128)
PHONE..................................620 241-7746
Cheryl Anderson, *Financial Exec*
Doug Wisby, *Director*
Sherry Plenat, *Director*
Mike Pruett, *Executive*
EMP: 20
SALES: 805.6K **Privately Held**
SIC: 2893 Printing ink

(G-6942)
CEDARS INC (PA)
Also Called: CEDARS HEALTH CARE CENTER
1021 Cedars Dr (67460-2700)
PHONE..................................620 241-0919
Carma Wall, *CEO*
Lamonte Rothrock, *Vice Pres*
Laurie Castor, *Consultant*
Carlene Dickson, *Director*
Katrina Westcott, *Director*
EMP: 200
SQ FT: 55,000
SALES: 11.7MM **Privately Held**
WEB: www.thecedars.org
SIC: 8052 6513 8059 8051 Personal care facility; retirement hotel operation; convalescent home; skilled nursing care facilities

(G-6943)
CEDARS INC
Also Called: Cedars Courts The
1071 Darlow Dr (67460-2741)
PHONE..................................620 241-7959
Mike Harold, *Vice Pres*
Kelly Schlehuber, *Manager*
Carol Yost, *Food Svc Dir*
EMP: 20
SALES (est): 261.6K
SALES (corp-wide): 11.7MM **Privately Held**
WEB: www.thecedars.org
SIC: 8361 Home for the aged
PA: The Cedars Inc
1021 Cedars Dr
Mcpherson KS 67460
620 241-0919

(G-6944)
CENTRAL STATES MKTG & MFG INC
1320 N Us Highway 81 Byp (67460-6005)
PHONE..................................620 245-9955
Charles Singleton, *President*
Chad French, *Manager*
Kim Clark, *Technician*
EMP: 32
SQ FT: 42,000
SALES (est): 4.7MM **Privately Held**
SIC: 8742 Marketing consulting services

(G-6945)
CERTAINTEED CORPORATION
873 N Hickory St (67460-3106)
PHONE..................................316 554-9638
Jim Van Derweide, *Manager*
EMP: 150
SALES (corp-wide): 209.1MM **Privately Held**
WEB: www.certainteed.net
SIC: 3089 Injection molded finished plastic products
HQ: Certainteed Llc
20 Moores Rd
Malvern PA 19355
610 893-5000

(G-6946)
CERTAINTEED LLC
Also Called: Vinyl Building Prod Div
500 W 1st St (67460-3218)
PHONE..................................620 241-5511
Penni Allen, *Vice Pres*
Tim Miller, *Plant Mgr*
John Razo, *Purch Agent*
Shane Baird, *Controller*
Kathy Boas, *Human Resources*
EMP: 40
SALES (corp-wide): 209.1MM **Privately Held**
WEB: www.certainteed.net
SIC: 3496 Miscellaneous fabricated wire products
HQ: Certainteed Llc
20 Moores Rd
Malvern PA 19355
610 893-5000

(G-6947)
CHEMSTAR PRODUCTS COMPANY
Also Called: McPherson Custom Products
503 W Hayes St (67460-5218)
PHONE..................................620 241-2611
Tim Scott, *Branch Mgr*
EMP: 42
SQ FT: 9,500
SALES (corp-wide): 8.6MM **Privately Held**
WEB: www.chemstar.com
SIC: 2046 Industrial starch
PA: Chemstar Products Company
3232 E 40th St
Minneapolis MN 55406
612 722-0079

(G-6948)
CHS INC
Also Called: C H S
1384 Iron Horse Rd (67460-6013)
PHONE..................................620 241-4247
Clinton Janzen, *Engineer*
Calvin Helm, *Manager*
Jeffrey Fields, *Administration*
EMP: 70
SALES (corp-wide): 31.9B **Publicly Held**
WEB: www.cenexharveststates.com
SIC: 2075 5153 2041 1311 Soybean oil, cake or meal; grain & field beans; semolina flour; crude petroleum production; gasoline; refined petroleum pipelines
PA: Chs Inc.
5500 Cenex Dr
Inver Grove Heights MN 55077
651 355-6000

(G-6949)
CHS MCPHERSON REFINERY INC (HQ)
Also Called: N C R A
2000 S Main St (67460-9402)
PHONE..................................620 241-2340
Shirley Cunningham, *Exec VP*
Lisa Zell, *Exec VP*
Zachary Crane, *Purchasing*
Timothy Skidmore, *CFO*
Jason Beckman, *Info Tech Mgr*
EMP: 415
SQ FT: 30,000
SALES (est): 164.1MM
SALES (corp-wide): 31.9B **Publicly Held**
WEB: www.NCRA.Coop
SIC: 4213 4612 2911 Liquid petroleum transport, non-local; crude petroleum pipelines; gasoline
PA: Chs Inc.
5500 Cenex Dr
Inver Grove Heights MN 55077
651 355-6000

(G-6950)
CITY OF MCPHERSON
Also Called: Crime Stoppers Hotline
1177 W Woodside St (67460-3256)
PHONE..................................620 241-1122
Dennis Shaw, *Director*
Catheryn McEachern, *Admin Asst*
EMP: 14 **Privately Held**
SIC: 8322 Hotline
PA: City Of Mcpherson
400 E Kansas Ave
Mcpherson KS 67460
620 245-2535

(G-6951)
COMPLETE AUTOMOTIVE LLC
1306 N Us Highway 81 Byp (67460-6005)
PHONE..................................620 245-0600
Bret Chapman, *Owner*
EMP: 32 **EST:** 2009
SALES: 750K **Privately Held**
SIC: 7538 General automotive repair shops

(G-6952)
COUNTY OF MCPHERSON
Also Called: County of Mc Pherson
1115 W Avenue A (67460-5241)
PHONE..................................620 241-0466
Tom Kramer, *Branch Mgr*
EMP: 44 **Privately Held**
WEB: www.machealth.org
SIC: 2951 9532 Asphalt paving mixtures & blocks; county planning & development agency, government
PA: County Of Mcpherson
117 N Maple St Ste 1
Mcpherson KS 67460
620 241-3656

(G-6953)
CREATIVE HAIRLINES INC
Also Called: Creative Hairlines Salon & Spa
207 S Main St (67460-4843)
PHONE..................................620 241-3535
Bonnie Kaufman, *President*
Kathy Gifford, *Manager*
EMP: 20
SALES (est): 604.8K **Privately Held**
WEB: www.creativehairlines.com
SIC: 7231 Hairdressers

(G-6954)
CULVER FISH FARM INC
1432 Ranch Rd (67460-1818)
P.O. Box 354 (67460-0354)
PHONE..................................620 241-5200
Brent H Culver, *President*
Brent Culver, *President*
EMP: 7
SALES: 500K **Privately Held**
SIC: 0921 2091 Fish hatcheries; fish: packaged in cans, jars, etc.

(G-6955)
DACUS LLC
Also Called: Dacus Autobody
2088 E South Front St (67460-7087)
PHONE..................................620 241-6054
Chris Dacus, *Mng Member*
EMP: 15
SALES (est): 124.1K **Privately Held**
SIC: 7532 Top & body repair & paint shops

(G-6956)
DAVIES COMMUNICATIONS INC
Also Called: The Ledger
411 E Euclid St (67460-4417)
P.O. Box 1069 (67460-1069)
PHONE..................................620 241-1504
Jerry Davies, *President*
Joe Johnston, *Manager*
▲ **EMP:** 10
SQ FT: 15,000
SALES (est): 581.2K **Privately Held**
WEB: www.midkansasmedia.com
SIC: 4832 7319 2759 2741 Radio broadcasting stations; shopping news, advertising & distributing service; commercial printing; newspapers: printing; shopping news: publishing & printing

(G-6957)
DISABLTY SPPRTS OF THE GRT PLN
501 E Northview Ave (67460-1941)
P.O. Box 843 (67460-0843)
PHONE..................................620 241-8411
Richard Staab, *President*
Steve Reed, *Maintence Staff*
EMP: 115 **EST:** 1996
SQ FT: 7,000
SALES: 8.3MM **Privately Held**
WEB: www.dsgp.org
SIC: 8322 Social services for the handicapped; association for the handicapped

(G-6958)
EMPRISE BANK
Also Called: McPherson Branch
109 N Main St (67460-4303)
PHONE..................................620 241-7113
EMP: 11
SALES (corp-wide): 80MM **Privately Held**
SIC: 6022 State commercial banks
HQ: Emprise Bank
257 N Broadway Ave
Wichita KS 67202
316 383-4400

(G-6959)
ENGQUIST TRACTOR SERVICE INC
1788 17th Ave (67460-8086)
PHONE..................................620 654-3651
Richard Engquist, *President*
Dee Ann Engquist, *Corp Secy*
EMP: 22 **EST:** 1980
SALES: 1.6MM **Privately Held**
SIC: 7538 3519 5084 Diesel engine repair: automotive; diesel engine rebuilding; engines & parts, diesel

(G-6960)
ESTHER V RETTIG
901 N Main St (67460-2841)
PHONE..................................620 245-0556
Esther V Rettig, *Owner*
EMP: 10
SALES (est): 480K **Privately Held**
SIC: 8011 Ophthalmologist

(G-6961)
EXCALIBUR PRODUCTION CO INC (PA)
1016 N Main St (67460-2852)
P.O. Box 278 (67460-0278)
PHONE..................................620 241-1265
Jinefer Kinzel, *President*
Jennifer Kinzel, *President*
Lucy Walline, *President*
Karen Mendoza, *CFO*
EMP: 6
SQ FT: 3,000
SALES (est): 882.6K **Privately Held**
SIC: 1311 Crude petroleum production; natural gas production

(G-6962)
FAMILY PRACTICE ASSOCIATES
1000 Hospital Dr (67460-2326)
PHONE..................................620 241-7400
Gregory Thomas, *Partner*
David Buller, *Partner*
Richard Ferree, *Partner*
Sheila Gorman, *Med Doctor*
EMP: 30
SALES (est): 3.6MM **Privately Held**
SIC: 8011 General & family practice, physician/surgeon

(G-6963)
FARMERS ALLIANCE MUTL INSUR CO (PA)
Also Called: Alliance Insurance Co
1122 N Main St (67460-2846)
P.O. Box 1401 (67460-1401)
PHONE..................................620 241-2200
Keith Birkhead, *Ch of Bd*
Dick Foulke, *Vice Pres*
Kara Lang, *Vice Pres*
Natalie Collins, *Project Mgr*
Jeff Collins, *Facilities Mgr*
EMP: 630 **EST:** 1888
SQ FT: 20,000
SALES (est): 159.2MM **Privately Held**
WEB: www.alliance-ins.com
SIC: 6411 Insurance agents, brokers & service

(G-6964)
FEMCO INC
1132 W 1st St (67460-3248)
P.O. Box 149 (67460-0149)
PHONE..................................620 241-3513
Rodney Borman, *President*
Doug Borman, *Admin Sec*
▲ **EMP:** 60 **EST:** 1965
SQ FT: 115,000
SALES (est): 18.6MM **Privately Held**
WEB: www.femcomfg.com
SIC: 3449 3559 Fabricated bar joists & concrete reinforcing bars; plastics working machinery

(G-6965)
FERGUSON PRODUCTION INC
2130 Industrial Dr (67460-8126)
PHONE..................................620 241-2400
Norlan Ferguson, *President*
Scott Ferguson, *Senior VP*
▲ **EMP:** 140
SQ FT: 66,350
SALES: 18.5MM **Privately Held**
WEB: www.fergusonproduction.com
SIC: 3089 Injection molding of plastics

(G-6966)
FRANK BLACK PIPE & SUPPLY CO
1375 17th Ave (67460-7080)
P.O. Box 325 (67460-0325)
PHONE..................................620 241-2582
Brent L Moore, *President*
Roger T Hall, *Vice Pres*
Lori Moore, *Treasurer*
EMP: 10
SQ FT: 14,800
SALES (est): 3.2MM **Privately Held**
WEB: www.blackravenpipeband.net
SIC: 5051 Steel

(G-6967)
GARBER SURVEYING SERVICE PA
115 E Marlin St Ste 102 (67460-4300)
PHONE..................................620 241-4441
Daniel Garber, *Branch Mgr*
EMP: 17
SALES (corp-wide): 4.1MM **Privately Held**
SIC: 8713 Surveying services
PA: Garber Surveying Service Pa
2908 N Plum St Ste B
Hutchinson KS 67502
620 665-7032

(G-6968)
GATEHOUSE MEDIA LLC
Also Called: McPherson Daily Sentinel
116 S Main St (67460-4852)
PHONE..................................620 241-2422
Amy Simmons, *Advt Staff*
Randy Mitchell, *Branch Mgr*
Gary Mehl, *Manager*
Linda Born, *Art Dir*
Linda-Born Smith, *Art Dir*
EMP: 15
SALES (corp-wide): 1.5B **Publicly Held**
WEB: www.wellingtondailynews.com
SIC: 2711 Newspapers, publishing & printing
HQ: Gatehouse Media, Llc
175 Sullys Trl Fl 3
Pittsford NY 14534
585 598-0030

(G-6969)
GIBSON INDUSTRIAL CONTROLS INC (PA)
Also Called: Gibson Electric Motor Shop
525 N Baer St (67460-3812)
PHONE..................................620 241-3551
Fax: 620 241-3587
EMP: 5
SQ FT: 14,500
SALES (est): 3MM **Privately Held**
SIC: 5063 5084 7694 7699 Whol Electrical Equip Whol Industrial Equip Armature Rewinding Repair Services

(G-6970)
GRAIN CRAFT INC
416 N Main St (67460-3404)
PHONE..................................620 241-2410
Brent Wall, *President*
EMP: 34
SALES (corp-wide): 288.5MM **Privately Held**
WEB: www.cerealfood.com
SIC: 2041 Flour & other grain mill products
PA: Grain Craft, Inc.
201 W Main St Ste 203
Chattanooga TN 37408
423 265-2313

(G-6971)
GREAT PLAINS FEDERAL CR UN
720 N Main St (67460-3410)
P.O. Box 786 (67460-0786)
PHONE..................................620 241-4181
David Myers, *Manager*
EMP: 10
SALES (corp-wide): 7.1MM **Privately Held**
WEB: www.greatplainsfcu.com
SIC: 6061 Federal credit unions
PA: Great Plains Federal Credit Union (Inc)
2306 S Range Line Rd
Joplin MO 64804
417 626-8500

(G-6972)
HEDLUND ELECTRIC INC
1201 S Main St (67460-5739)
P.O. Box 528 (67460-0528)
PHONE..................................620 241-3757
Terry Hedlund, *President*
Lilly Hedlund, *Office Mgr*
▲ **EMP:** 25
SQ FT: 4,000
SALES (est): 4.6MM **Privately Held**
WEB: www.hedlundelectric.com
SIC: 1731 5719 General electrical contractor; lighting, lamps & accessories

(G-6973)
HESS OIL COMPANY (PA)
2080 E Kansas Ave (67460)
P.O. Box 1009 (67460-1009)
PHONE..................................620 241-4640
Bryan Hess, *President*
James H Hess, *Treasurer*
EMP: 27 **EST:** 1980
SQ FT: 2,100
SALES (est): 1.7MM **Privately Held**
SIC: 1311 Crude petroleum production; natural gas production

(G-6974)
HOME STATE BANK & TRUST CO (PA)
223 N Main St (67460-4339)
P.O. Box 1266 (67460-1266)
PHONE..................................620 241-3732
Chad Odle, *President*
Ted Odle, *Senior VP*
Fred Bohmenblust, *Vice Pres*
Joe Harkins, *Vice Pres*
Loreen Smith, *Vice Pres*
EMP: 50 **EST:** 1903
SQ FT: 7,300
SALES: 6.5MM **Privately Held**
WEB: www.hsbt.com
SIC: 6022 State trust companies accepting deposits, commercial

(G-6975)
HOSPICE CARE OF KANSAS (PA)
117 E Euclid St (67460-4301)
PHONE..................................316 283-2116
Michelle Mosiman, *Director*
EMP: 20
SALES (est): 1.2MM **Privately Held**
WEB: www.hospicecareofkansas.com
SIC: 8051 Skilled nursing care facilities

(G-6976)
HOSPIRA INC
1776 Centennial Dr (67460-9301)
P.O. Box 1247 (67460-1247)
PHONE..................................620 241-6200
Robin Morgan, *Project Mgr*
Karen Spinden, *Project Mgr*
Brent Wine, *Sales Staff*
Russell Gall, *Manager*
Jerry Kremeier, *Technician*
EMP: 460
SALES (corp-wide): 53.6B **Publicly Held**
WEB: www.abbotthpd.com
SIC: 2834 Pharmaceutical preparations
HQ: Hospira, Inc.
275 N Field Dr
Lake Forest IL 60045
224 212-2000

(G-6977)
ICS INC
210 N Elder St (67460-4115)
PHONE..................................620 654-3020
Larry Rickner, *President*
EMP: 27
SQ FT: 15,000
SALES (est): 3.4MM **Privately Held**
SIC: 3471 3568 Chromium plating of metals or formed products; power transmission equipment

(G-6978)
JAYHAWK PIPELINE LLC (DH)
Also Called: N C R A
2000 S Main St (67460-9402)
PHONE..................................620 241-9270
Rick Petersen, *General Mgr*
Katie Young, *Manager*
Craig Harms, *Supervisor*
EMP: 10
SQ FT: 2,100
SALES: 40.7MM
SALES (corp-wide): 31.9B **Publicly Held**
WEB: www.jayhawkpl.com
SIC: 4612 Crude petroleum pipelines
HQ: Chs Mcpherson Refinery Inc.
2000 S Main St
Mcpherson KS 67460
620 241-2340

(G-6979)
JOHNS MANVILLE CORPORATION
1465 17th Ave (67460)
P.O. Box 1287 (67460-1287)
PHONE..................................620 241-6260
Benjamin Campbell, *Safety Mgr*
Mickey Reinhart, *Safety Mgr*
Dawaye Stos, *Safety Mgr*
Ted Hammarlund, *Buyer*
Glen Pettit, *QC Mgr*
EMP: 288
SALES (corp-wide): 225.3B **Publicly Held**
WEB: www.jm.com
SIC: 3296 Fiberglass insulation
HQ: Johns Manville Corporation
717 17th St Ste 800
Denver CO 80202
303 978-2000

(G-6980)
KANSAS AMERICAN TOOLING INC
1101 W 1st St (67460-3257)
PHONE..................................620 241-4200
Harlan Doering, *President*
EMP: 14
SQ FT: 10,000
SALES (est): 1.9MM **Privately Held**
SIC: 3544 Forms (molds), for foundry & plastics working machinery

(G-6981)
KANSAS DEPT FOR CHLDREN FMLIES
115 E Euclid St Ste 1 (67460-4301)
P.O. Box 305 (67460-0305)
PHONE....................................620 241-3802
Sandra Russell, *Manager*
EMP: 12 **Privately Held**
SIC: 8322 9441 Rehabilitation services; administration of social & manpower programs;
HQ: Kansas Department For Children And Families
555 S Kansas Ave
Topeka KS 66603
785 368-6358

(G-6982)
KANSAS FAST LUBE INC
Also Called: Pennzoil 10 Minute Lube Center
201 W Kansas Ave (67460-4738)
P.O. Box 347 (67460-0347)
PHONE....................................620 241-5656
Jon Jantz, *President*
EMP: 11
SALES: 500K **Privately Held**
SIC: 7549 Lubrication service, automotive

Mcpherson
Mcpherson County

(G-6983)
KIDS KAMPUS
1381 S Main St (67460-5750)
PHONE....................................620 241-8499
Wanda Williams, *Director*
EMP: 20
SALES: 1.1MM **Privately Held**
SIC: 8351 Group day care center

McPherson
Mcpherson County

(G-6984)
KOCH INDUSTRIES INC
Also Called: One Oak
462 Hwy 56 (67460-6129)
PHONE....................................620 834-2204
Jon Sauer, *Branch Mgr*
EMP: 6
SALES (corp-wide): 40.6B **Privately Held**
WEB: www.kochind.com
SIC: 2869 Industrial organic chemicals
PA: Koch Industries, Inc.
4111 E 37th St N
Wichita KS 67220
316 828-5500

(G-6985)
KREHBIELS SPECIALTY MEATS INC
1636 Mohawk Rd (67460-8001)
PHONE....................................620 241-0103
Sarah Krehbiel, *President*
Jeff Krehbiel, *Shareholder*
EMP: 37
SALES (est): 7.8MM **Privately Held**
SIC: 5147 5421 0751 Meats, fresh; meat markets, including freezer provisioners; slaughtering: custom livestock services

(G-6986)
LACY RV RANCH INC
2475 E Kansas Ave (67460-4011)
P.O. Box 708 (67460-0708)
PHONE....................................620 245-9608
Michael Lacy, *President*
Dance Lacy, *Admin Sec*
EMP: 7
SALES (est): 831K **Privately Held**
SIC: 3792 Travel trailers & campers

(G-6987)
MAGELLAN MIDSTREAM PARTNERS LP
Also Called: Koch Hydrcrbon LPG Stge Fac
1299 8th Ave (67460-6049)
PHONE....................................620 834-2205
Jon Sauer, *Manager*
EMP: 10
SALES (corp-wide): 2.8B **Publicly Held**
WEB: www.twc.com
SIC: 4226 Liquid storage
PA: Magellan Midstream Partners, Lp
1 Williams Ctr Bsmt 2
Tulsa OK 74172
918 574-7000

(G-6988)
MC PHERSON AREA SOLID WAST
1431 17th Ave (67460-2200)
PHONE....................................620 585-2321
John Hawk, *General Mgr*
EMP: 44
SALES (est): 7.8MM **Privately Held**
WEB: www.maswu.org
SIC: 4953 Garbage: collecting, destroying & processing; sanitary landfill operation

(G-6989)
MC PHERSON COUNTY FOOD BANK
707 S Main St (67460-5429)
PHONE....................................620 241-8050
Rev Ben Hellmer, *President*
EMP: 11
SALES: 217.4K **Privately Held**
SIC: 8322 Disaster service

(G-6990)
MC PHERSON EYE CARE LLP
1323 E 1st St (67460-3601)
P.O. Box 1314 (67460-1314)
PHONE....................................620 241-2262
Tammy Goering, *Partner*
Jan Hageman, *Partner*
EMP: 11
SALES (est): 1.1MM **Privately Held**
WEB: www.mcphersoneyecare.com
SIC: 8042 Specialized optometrists

(G-6991)
MCDS CLUBHOUSE 5
935 Clubhouse Dr (67460-5267)
PHONE....................................620 504-6044
Melani Gumm, *Principal*
EMP: 10
SALES (est): 264.6K **Privately Held**
SIC: 7997 Membership sports & recreation clubs

(G-6992)
MCPHERSON BD OF PUB UTILITIES
401 W Kansas Ave (67460-4740)
P.O. Box 1008 (67460-1008)
PHONE....................................620 245-2515
Rick N Anderson, *General Mgr*
Tim Maier, *General Mgr*
Chad Hitt, *Comptroller*
Lee Burgess, *Info Tech Mgr*
EMP: 73
SQ FT: 8,500
SALES: 69.5MM **Privately Held**
WEB: www.mcphcity-bpu.com
SIC: 4941 Water supply

(G-6993)
MCPHERSON CARE CENTER LLC
1601 N Main St (67460-1601)
PHONE....................................620 241-5360
Glenda Parsons, *Administration*
EMP: 50
SALES (est): 2.8MM **Privately Held**
SIC: 8051 Skilled nursing care facilities
PA: Deseret Health Group, Llc.
190 S Main St
Bountiful UT 84010

(G-6994)
MCPHERSON CON STOR SYSTEMS INC (PA)
116 N Augustus St (67460-4138)
P.O. Box 369 (67460-0369)
PHONE....................................620 241-4362
Wade Wentling, *President*
Jerry Linn, *Vice Pres*
Dustin Heckroth, *Project Mgr*
Dub Johnson, *Sales Mgr*
Nathan Rowson, *Manager*
EMP: 13
SQ FT: 1,500
SALES (est): 17.9MM **Privately Held**
SIC: 1542 Farm building construction; silo construction, agricultural

(G-6995)
MCPHERSON CONCRETE PDTS INC
116 N Augustus St (67460-4138)
P.O. Box 369 (67460-0369)
PHONE....................................620 241-1678
Chris Anderson, *President*
Rex Stephenson, *Corp Secy*
Clif McIrvin, *QC Mgr*
EMP: 72 **EST:** 1945
SQ FT: 3,000
SALES: 9.2MM **Privately Held**
SIC: 3272 3273 Pipe, concrete or lined with concrete; manhole covers or frames, concrete; ready-mixed concrete

Mcpherson
Mcpherson County

(G-6996)
MCPHERSON COUNTRY CLUB INC
1396 Pioneer Rd (67460-8043)
P.O. Box 1041 (67460-1041)
PHONE....................................620 241-3541
Dr Troy Fox, *President*
Jeff Cunningham, *President*
Margareta Haidon, *Admin Sec*
EMP: 13
SALES: 472.2K **Privately Held**
SIC: 7997 Country club, membership; golf club, membership; swimming club, membership

McPherson
Mcpherson County

(G-6997)
MCPHERSON DENTAL CARE LLC (PA)
700 N Maple St (67460-3325)
PHONE....................................620 241-5000
Brian Kynaston, *Owner*
Mary Mc Nally, *Principal*
EMP: 12 **EST:** 2009
SALES (est): 906.8K **Privately Held**
SIC: 8021 Dental clinic

(G-6998)
MCPHERSON FAMILY CLINIC
322 N Main St Ste 101 (67460-4316)
PHONE....................................785 861-8800
EMP: 22
SALES (est): 61.3K
SALES (corp-wide): 26.2MM **Privately Held**
SIC: 8093 Specialty outpatient clinics
PA: Gracemed Health Clinic, Inc.
1122 N Topeka St
Wichita KS 67214
316 866-2001

(G-6999)
MCPHERSON FAMILY YMCA INC
220 N Walnut St (67460-4223)
P.O. Box 1066 (67460-1066)
PHONE....................................620 241-0363
Gwyn Muto, *CEO*
Pamala Axelson, *Principal*
Keith Janzen, *Treasurer*
Todd Stephenson, *Manager*
Kyle Roberts, *Director*
EMP: 100
SQ FT: 100,000
SALES: 1.1MM **Privately Held**
SIC: 7997 8641 Swimming club, membership; civic social & fraternal associations

(G-7000)
MCPHERSON HOSPITAL INC
Also Called: McPherson Ems
1000 Hospital Dr (67460-2326)
PHONE....................................620 241-0917
Rob Monical, *CEO*
Terri Goering, *Vice Pres*
George Halama, *CFO*
Bret Heskett, *Obstetrician*
Clinton Terry, *IT/INT Sup*
EMP: 270
SQ FT: 160,000
SALES: 24.4MM **Privately Held**
SIC: 8062 Hospital, affiliated with AMA residency

(G-7001)
MCPHERSON OPERA HOUSE COMPANY
219 S Main St (67460-4843)
P.O. Box 333 (67460-0333)
PHONE....................................620 241-1952
Troy Wiens, *President*
Evelyn Nelson, *Vice Pres*
Jordan Bandy, *Opers Staff*
John Holecek, *Exec Dir*
EMP: 17
SALES: 437.5K **Privately Held**
SIC: 7922 Performing arts center production

(G-7002)
MICHAEL YOWELL DDS PA
1540 N Main St (67460-1904)
PHONE....................................620 241-0842
Michael Yowell, *Owner*
EMP: 15
SALES (est): 616.4K **Privately Held**
SIC: 8021 Orthodontist

(G-7003)
MID KANSAS MACHINE INC
801 N Us Highway 81 Byp (67460-6020)
P.O. Box 560 (67460-0560)
PHONE....................................620 241-2959
Doug Schulz, *President*
Kathy Weigel, *Controller*
Corey Flood, *Manager*
EMP: 30 **EST:** 1977
SQ FT: 16,000
SALES (est): 5.6MM **Privately Held**
SIC: 3599 7692 Machine shop, jobbing & repair; welding repair

(G-7004)
MID-KANSAS CYLINDER HEAD INC
1308 1/2 N Us Hwy 81 Byp (67460-6005)
P.O. Box 312 (67460-0312)
PHONE....................................620 241-6800
Vernon L Dossett, *President*
Brynel Dossett, *Vice Pres*
Michael Dossett, *Vice Pres*
EMP: 11
SALES: 600K **Privately Held**
SIC: 7699 Industrial machinery & equipment repair; industrial truck repair

(G-7005)
MIDWAY MOTORS INC
2045 E Kansas Ave (67460-4005)
P.O. Box 966 (67460-0966)
PHONE....................................620 241-7737
Jason Hoover, *President*
Glenn Hoover, *President*
Billy Frary, *General Mgr*
Jeanette James, *Corp Secy*
Bob Ruxlow, *Sales Mgr*
EMP: 100 **EST:** 1960
SQ FT: 11,000
SALES (est): 32.7MM **Privately Held**
SIC: 5511 7538 5531 5521 Automobiles, new & used; trucks, tractors & trailers: new & used; general automotive repair shops; automotive parts; used car dealers

(G-7006)
MIDWEST ELECTRIC SERVICE INC
621 N Hickory St (67460-3229)
PHONE....................................620 241-8655
James Vangoethem, *President*
EMP: 17
SALES (est): 1.8MM **Privately Held**
SIC: 1731 General electrical contractor

(G-7007)
MIDWEST INDUSTRIES & DEV LTD
1125 W 1st St (67460-3203)
P.O. Box 824 (67460-0824)
PHONE....................................620 241-5996
Jeffrey W Bremyer, *President*

Jill Bremyer Archer, *Admin Sec*
EMP: 71
SQ FT: 47,000
SALES (est): 11.8MM **Privately Held**
SIC: 3599 Custom machinery

(G-7008)
MILACRON MARKETING COMPANY LLC
Wear Technology
2085 E 1st St (67460-3963)
P.O. Box 1123 (67460-1123)
PHONE..................................620 241-1624
Ryan Reitsma, *Purchasing*
Craig Rump, *Manager*
Jim Reynolds,
EMP: 93 **Publicly Held**
SIC: 3452 Screws, metal
HQ: Milacron Marketing Company Llc
4165 Half Acre Rd
Batavia OH 45103

(G-7009)
MULTI COMMUNITY DIVERSFD SVCS (PA)
2107 Industrial Dr (67460-8128)
PHONE..................................620 241-6693
Colin McKenney, *President*
Jan Meliza, *General Mgr*
Chris Rocker, *Principal*
Todd Case, *COO*
Doug Wisby, *CFO*
EMP: 14 **EST:** 1974
SQ FT: 8,000
SALES: 6.5MM **Privately Held**
WEB: www.cartridgekingks.com
SIC: 8361 8331 Residential care for the handicapped; vocational training agency

(G-7010)
NORTH AMRCN SPECIALTY PDTS LLC
500 W 1st St (67460-3218)
PHONE..................................620 241-5511
Joseph Bondi,
EMP: 11 **Publicly Held**
SIC: 2821 Plastics materials & resins
HQ: North American Specialty Products Llc
993 Old Eagle School Rd
Wayne PA 19087
484 253-4545

(G-7011)
ONEOK INC
1644 W Kansas Ave (67460-6054)
PHONE..................................620 241-0837
Gary Peterson, *Branch Mgr*
EMP: 12
SALES (corp-wide): 12.5B **Publicly Held**
WEB: www.oneok.com
SIC: 4922 Pipelines, natural gas
PA: Oneok, Inc.
100 W 5th St Ste Ll
Tulsa OK 74103
918 588-7000

(G-7012)
ORSCHELN FARM AND HOME LLC
Also Called: Orschelin Farm and Home 60
2204 E Kansas Ave (67460-4010)
PHONE..................................620 241-0707
Leland Cillberg, *Manager*
EMP: 10
SALES (corp-wide): 822.7MM **Privately Held**
WEB: www.orschelnfarmhome.com
SIC: 5191 5251 5699 Feed; hardware; work clothing
PA: Orscheln Farm And Home Llc
1800 Overcenter Dr
Moberly MO 65270
800 577-2580

(G-7013)
PEOPLES BANK & TRUST CO (PA)
101 S Main St (67460-4842)
P.O. Box 1226 (67460-1226)
PHONE..................................620 241-2100
Tom Pruitt, *President*
Dale Ladd, *Assistant VP*
Bryce Brewer, *Vice Pres*
Cy Rolfs, *Vice Pres*
Chad Alexander, *Broker*
EMP: 50 **EST:** 1960
SQ FT: 15,000
SALES: 22.1MM **Privately Held**
WEB: www.peoplesbankonline.com
SIC: 6022 State trust companies accepting deposits, commercial

(G-7014)
PEOPLES BANK & TRUST CO
1320 1/2 N Main St (67460-2506)
PHONE..................................620 241-6908
Paula Dearhart, *Branch Mgr*
EMP: 38
SALES (corp-wide): 22.1MM **Privately Held**
WEB: www.peoplesbankonline.com
SIC: 6022 State commercial banks
PA: Peoples Bank & Trust Co (Inc)
101 S Main St
Mcpherson KS 67460
620 241-2100

(G-7015)
PEOPLES BANK & TRUST CO
719 N Main St (67460-3409)
PHONE..................................620 241-7664
Judy Anderson, *Manager*
EMP: 38
SALES (corp-wide): 22.1MM **Privately Held**
WEB: www.peoplesbankonline.com
SIC: 6022 State commercial banks
PA: Peoples Bank & Trust Co (Inc)
101 S Main St
Mcpherson KS 67460
620 241-2100

(G-7016)
PIPING TECHNOLOGY CO
1331 N Us Highway 81 Byp (67460-6006)
P.O. Box 404 (67460-0404)
PHONE..................................620 241-3592
Doug Unruh, *President*
EMP: 82 **EST:** 1990
SQ FT: 2,000
SALES (est): 17.3MM **Privately Held**
SIC: 1711 Process piping contractor

Mcpherson
Mcpherson County

(G-7017)
PRAIRIE LANDWORKS INC
905 N Vngard St Mcpherson (67460)
P.O. Box 431, McPherson (67460-0431)
PHONE..................................620 504-5049
Tom Saffel, *President*
Tyler Greer, *Project Mgr*
EMP: 15
SALES (est): 3.3MM **Privately Held**
SIC: 1794 1542 1522 1623 Excavation & grading, building construction; nonresidential construction; commercial & office building, new construction; multi-family dwellings, new construction; oil & gas line & compressor station construction; parking lot construction

McPherson
Mcpherson County

(G-7018)
PRAIRIE VIEW INC
1102 Hospital Dr (67460-2318)
PHONE..................................620 245-5000
Jeannie Hett, *Manager*
EMP: 18
SALES (est): 814.8K
SALES (corp-wide): 21.2MM **Privately Held**
WEB: www.pvi.org
SIC: 8093 Mental health clinic, outpatient
PA: Prairie View, Inc.
1901 E 1st St
Newton KS 67114
316 284-6400

(G-7019)
PRECISION INDUSTRIES INC (PA)
533 N Baer St (67460-3812)
P.O. Box 1088 (67460-1088)
PHONE..................................620 241-5010
Larry D Catton, *President*
Debbie Gray, *Human Res Dir*
Kevin Johnson, *Sales Executive*
EMP: 50 **EST:** 1968
SQ FT: 15,000
SALES (est): 9.3MM **Privately Held**
SIC: 3471 Chromium plating of metals or formed products

(G-7020)
PREMIER CASTING & MACHINE SVC
2118 Industrial Dr (67460-8126)
P.O. Box 1183 (67460-1183)
PHONE..................................620 241-2040
Jeffrey S Johnson, *President*
Monty Koehn, *Vice Pres*
Delbert Hunt, *Treasurer*
EMP: 10
SALES (est): 1.2MM **Privately Held**
WEB: www.premier-casting.com
SIC: 7699 Industrial machinery & equipment repair

(G-7021)
R & K HORN LLC
Also Called: McPherson Dairy Queen
1514 Sunflower Dr (67460-2207)
PHONE..................................620 241-5083
EMP: 30
SALES (est): 1.7MM **Privately Held**
SIC: 0241 Dairy Farm

(G-7022)
SAGAR INC
Also Called: Best Western
2302 E Kansas Ave (67460-4002)
PHONE..................................620 241-5566
Larry Patel, *President*
EMP: 56
SALES (est): 2.9MM **Privately Held**
SIC: 7011 Hotels & motels

(G-7023)
SAGAR INC (PA)
Also Called: Holiday Manor Motel
2211 E Kansas Ave (67460-4009)
PHONE..................................620 241-5343
Gale Premer, *President*
Premer Le Wayne, *Vice Pres*
EMP: 34
SQ FT: 4,800
SALES (est): 826.5K **Privately Held**
SIC: 7011 Hotels & motels

(G-7024)
SAGAR INC
Also Called: Best Western
2211 E Kansas Ave (67460-4009)
P.O. Box 923 (67460-0923)
PHONE..................................620 241-5343
Kevin Bingman, *Manager*
EMP: 28
SALES (est): 721.3K
SALES (corp-wide): 826.5K **Privately Held**
SIC: 7011 7991 6512 5813 Hotels & motels; physical fitness facilities; nonresidential building operators; drinking places; eating places
PA: Sagar, Inc.
2211 E Kansas Ave
Mcpherson KS 67460
620 241-5343

(G-7025)
SECURITY NATIONAL FINCL CORP
822 N Main St (67460-2840)
PHONE..................................620 241-3400
Don Pennington, *Manager*
Linda Dahle, *Manager*
EMP: 363
SALES (corp-wide): 279.6MM **Publicly Held**
SIC: 6162 Mortgage bankers
PA: Security National Financial Corporation
5300 S 360 W Ste 250
Salt Lake City UT 84123
801 264-1060

(G-7026)
SHEETS ADAMS REALTORS INC
1605 N Main St (67460-1513)
PHONE..................................620 241-3648
Myron Barrow, *President*
Pauline Jones, *Agent*
EMP: 13
SALES (est): 981.5K **Privately Held**
WEB: www.sheets-adams.com
SIC: 6531 6552 Selling agent, real estate; subdividers & developers

(G-7027)
SPECIALTY TECHNOLOGY INC
Also Called: STI
618 N Mulberry St (67460-3251)
P.O. Box 221 (67460-0221)
PHONE..................................620 241-6307
Rick Schulz, *President*
Stan Schulz, *Vice Pres*
EMP: 11
SQ FT: 10,000
SALES (est): 1.3MM **Privately Held**
SIC: 3471 3554 Chromium plating of metals or formed products; paper industries machinery

(G-7028)
STEWARTS SPORTS & AWARDS
117 N Main St (67460-4303)
P.O. Box 1331 (67460-1331)
PHONE..................................620 241-5990
Bruce Stewart, *Owner*
EMP: 7
SQ FT: 2,600
SALES (est): 712.9K **Privately Held**
SIC: 2261 5699 5941 3914 Screen printing of cotton broadwoven fabrics; sports apparel; sporting goods & bicycle shops; trophies; screen printing; embroidery products, except schiffli machine

(G-7029)
SUNFLOWER HOLDINGS INC
Also Called: Sunflower Bank NA
120 W Kansas Ave Ste A (67460-4756)
PHONE..................................620 241-1220
Karl Klingenberg, *Vice Pres*
Chat Lang, *Manager*
EMP: 13
SALES (corp-wide): 52.4MM **Privately Held**
SIC: 6021 National trust companies with deposits, commercial
PA: Sunflower Holdings, Inc.
2090 S Ohio St
Salina KS 67401
785 827-5564

(G-7030)
SWINDOLL JANZEN HAWK LLOYD LLC (PA)
123 S Main St (67460-4842)
P.O. Box 1337 (67460-1337)
PHONE..................................620 241-1826
Kyle Hawk, *Managing Prtnr*
Chet Buchman, *Partner*
Keith Janzen, *Treasurer*
Colton Castelli, *Accountant*
Josh Menard, *Accountant*
EMP: 22
SALES (est): 3.5MM **Privately Held**
WEB: www.sjhl.com
SIC: 8721 Accounting services, except auditing

(G-7031)
TESSENDERLO KERLEY INC
Kerley AG Products
1360 Iron Horse Rd (67460-6013)
P.O. Box 883 (67460-0883)
PHONE..................................620 241-1727
EMP: 15
SALES (corp-wide): 668.8MM **Privately Held**
SIC: 2873 Mfg Nitrogenous Fertilizers
HQ: Tessenderlo Kerley, Inc.
2255 N 44th St Ste 300
Phoenix AZ 85008
602 889-8300

(G-7032)
TURKEY CREEK GOLF COURSE
Also Called: Turkey Creek Golf Course & Dev
1000 Fox Run Rd (67460-9768)
PHONE..................................620 241-8530
Chester W Anderson, *President*
Rex Stephenson, *Corp Secy*
Chris Anderson, *Vice Pres*
EMP: 10
SQ FT: 3,500
SALES (est): 342.5K **Privately Held**
SIC: 7997 6552 Golf club, membership; subdividers & developers

(G-7033)
ULTRAFAB INC
811 W 1st St (67460-3266)
PHONE..................................620 245-0781
Tom Kendrick, *Branch Mgr*
EMP: 20
SALES (corp-wide): 31.7MM **Privately Held**
SIC: 7539 Machine shop, automotive
PA: Ultrafab, Inc.
1050 Hook Rd
Farmington NY 14425
585 924-2186

(G-7034)
UNION PACIFIC RAILROAD COMPANY
1399 Oakmont St (67460-2540)
PHONE..................................316 250-0260
EMP: 82
SALES (corp-wide): 22.8B **Publicly Held**
SIC: 4011 Railroads, line-haul operating
HQ: Union Pacific Railroad Company Inc
1400 Douglas St
Omaha NE 68179
402 544-5000

(G-7035)
UNITED RENTALS NORTH AMER INC
1101 W Woodside St (67460-3267)
PHONE..................................620 245-0550
EMP: 31
SALES (corp-wide): 8B **Publicly Held**
SIC: 7359 Equipment rental & leasing
HQ: United Rentals (North America), Inc.
100 Frederick St 700
Stamford CT 06902
203 622-3131

(G-7036)
UNITED WAY OF MCPHERSON COUNTY
306 N Main St (67460-4351)
P.O. Box 55 (67460-0055)
PHONE..................................620 241-5152
Steve Burghart, *President*
Brenda Sales, *Director*
EMP: 20
SALES: 250.5K **Privately Held**
SIC: 8322 Individual & family services

(G-7037)
VANGUARD INDUSTRIES INC (PA)
831 N Vanguard St (67460-3118)
PHONE..................................620 241-6369
W Keith Swinehart Sr, *Ch of Bd*
W Keith Swinehart II, *Vice Ch Bd*
John Fraser, *President*
Nathan Spearman, *Treasurer*
Dinah Swinehart, *Admin Sec*
EMP: 5
SQ FT: 73,200
SALES (est): 24.2MM **Privately Held**
SIC: 3084 3432 3088 Plastics pipe; plumbing fixture fittings & trim; plastics plumbing fixtures

(G-7038)
VANGUARD PIPING SYSTEMS INC (HQ)
2211 Viega Ave (67460-8139)
PHONE..................................620 241-6369
John Frafer, *President*
Nathan Spearman, *Treasurer*
▲ **EMP:** 148
SQ FT: 120,000
SALES (est): 7.2MM **Privately Held**
SIC: 3084 5074 Plastics pipe; pipes & fittings, plastic

(G-7039)
VANGUARD PLASTICS INC
901 N Vanguard St (67460-3112)
PHONE..................................620 241-6369
Keith Swineheart, *CEO*
John Frasier, *President*
John Fraser, *Chairman*
Nathan Spearman, *Treasurer*
Dinah Swinehart, *Admin Sec*
EMP: 150
SQ FT: 73,200
SALES (est): 16.3MM **Privately Held**
SIC: 3084 Plastics pipe
PA: Vanguard Industries, Inc.
831 N Vanguard St
Mcpherson KS 67460

(G-7040)
VIEGA LLC
2211 Viega Ave (67460-8139)
PHONE..................................678 447-1882
David Perciful, *Branch Mgr*
EMP: 10
SALES (corp-wide): 769.8K **Privately Held**
SIC: 5074 Plumbing fittings & supplies
HQ: Viega Llc
585 Interlocken Blvd
Broomfield CO 80021

(G-7041)
WELCO SERVICES INC
1426 13th Ave (67460-8137)
PHONE..................................620 241-3000
Robert Cullen, *CEO*
Rick Parrack, *Superintendent*
Eric Sweet, *Purch Mgr*
Bob Cullen, *Finance Mgr*
Michele Cullen, *Office Mgr*
EMP: 40
SQ FT: 17,400
SALES (est): 7.6MM **Privately Held**
SIC: 7692 1791 1796 7389 Welding repair; structural steel erection; millwright; pipeline & power line inspection service; electrical services

(G-7042)
WINCE FAMILY DENTAL
1325 E 1st St (67460-3601)
P.O. Box 964 (67460-0964)
PHONE..................................620 241-0266
Stacy Wince, *Principal*
EMP: 17 **EST:** 2013
SALES (est): 1.1MM **Privately Held**
SIC: 8021 Dentists' office

(G-7043)
WINGATE INNS INTERNATIONAL INC
Also Called: Holiday Inn
2302 E Kansas Ave (67460-4002)
PHONE..................................620 241-5566
Sam Patel, *Owner*
EMP: 24 **Publicly Held**
WEB: www.wingateatlanta.com
SIC: 7011 Hotels & motels
HQ: Wingate Inns International, Inc.
339 Jefferson Rd
Parsippany NJ 07054
973 753-8000

(G-7044)
WISE & BREYMER
120 W Kansas Ave Ste B (67460-4756)
PHONE..................................620 241-0554
Robert Wise,
Archer J Bremyer,
Casey R Law,
Brett A Reber,
EMP: 18
SQ FT: 4,000
SALES (est): 1.2MM **Privately Held**
WEB: www.bwisecounsel.com
SIC: 8111 General practice attorney, lawyer

(G-7045)
ZEITLOW DISTRIBUTING CO INC (PA)
2060 E South Front St (67460-7087)
P.O. Box 424 (67460-0424)
PHONE..................................620 241-4279
Doug Zeitlow, *President*
▲ **EMP:** 10 **EST:** 1960
SQ FT: 19,000
SALES: 4.2MM **Privately Held**
WEB: www.zeitlow.com
SIC: 5083 5999 Livestock equipment; farm equipment & supplies

Meade
Meade County

(G-7046)
BACK ROOM PRINTING LLC
102 N Fowler St (67864-6769)
P.O. Box 700 (67864-0700)
PHONE..................................620 873-2900
Craig Unrush, *Mng Member*
EMP: 5
SQ FT: 2,900
SALES (est): 716.1K **Privately Held**
WEB: www.backroomprinting.com
SIC: 2752 5943 Commercial printing, offset; office forms & supplies

(G-7047)
COOPERATIVE ELEVATOR & SUP CO (PA)
801 N Fowler St (67864-6797)
P.O. Box 220 (67864-0220)
PHONE..................................620 873-2161
Randy Ackerman, *Manager*
EMP: 29 **EST:** 1913
SQ FT: 12,800
SALES: 25.2MM **Privately Held**
SIC: 5153 5191 5984 Grain elevators; feed; seeds: field, garden & flower; fertilizer & fertilizer materials; chemicals, agricultural; liquefied petroleum gas dealers

(G-7048)
COOPERATIVE ELEVATOR & SUP CO
Also Called: Car Care
917 W Carthage St (67864-6406)
PHONE..................................620 873-2376
Randy Ackerman, *General Mgr*
EMP: 12
SALES (corp-wide): 25.2MM **Privately Held**
SIC: 7538 General automotive repair shops
PA: Cooperative Elevator & Supply Co Inc
801 N Fowler St
Meade KS 67864
620 873-2161

(G-7049)
GREAT PLAINS CHRISTIAN RADIO
Also Called: KJIL
909 W Carthage St (67864-6406)
P.O. Box 991 (67864-0991)
PHONE..................................620 873-2991
Michael Luskey, *President*
Craig McDonald, *Prdtn Dir*
Blake Carter, *Director*
Darren Kinser, *Director*
Stella Harder, *Traffic Dir*
EMP: 10
SALES: 1.8MM **Privately Held**
SIC: 4832 7313 Radio broadcasting stations, music format; radio advertising representative

(G-7050)
MAX PAPAY LLC
14010 17th Rd (67864)
P.O. Box 1060 (67864-1060)
PHONE..................................620 873-5350
Max Papay,
Cecelia Papay,
EMP: 14
SALES: 3MM **Privately Held**
SIC: 3561 Pumps, oil well & field

(G-7051)
MBC WELL LOGGING & LEASING
21156 22 Rd (67864-9531)
P.O. Box 956 (67864-0956)
PHONE..................................620 873-2953
Marla Garner, *Owner*
EMP: 5
SALES: 300K **Privately Held**
SIC: 1389 Oil field services

(G-7052)
MEADE HOSPITAL DISTRICT
Also Called: Lone Tree Retirement Center
801 E Grant St (67864-9557)
P.O. Box 340 (67864-0340)
PHONE..................................620 873-2146
Lori Smith, *CFO*
EMP: 159
SALES (corp-wide): 12.6MM **Privately Held**
SIC: 8361 8059 8051 Rest home, with health care incidental; nursing home, except skilled & intermediate care facility; skilled nursing care facilities
PA: Meade Hospital District
510 E Carthage St
Meade KS 67864
620 873-2141

(G-7053)
MEADE RURAL HEALTH CLINIC (PA)
119 N Hart St (67864-6402)
P.O. Box 820 (67864-0820)
PHONE..................................620 873-2112
Seeley T Feldmyer MD, *Owner*
EMP: 15
SALES (est): 718.4K **Privately Held**
SIC: 8011 Clinic, operated by physicians

(G-7054)
STOCKGROWERS STATE BANK
203 N Fowler St (67864-6405)
P.O. Box 250 (67864-0250)
PHONE..................................620 873-2123
Darrin Golliher, *Vice Pres*
EMP: 15
SALES (est): 2.2MM **Privately Held**
SIC: 6022 State trust companies accepting deposits, commercial
HQ: Stockgrowers State Bank Of Ashland, Kansas
622 Main St
Ashland KS 67831
800 772-2265

(G-7055)
VERIPRIME INC
806 E Washington St (67864-6438)
P.O. Box 1089 (67864-1089)
PHONE..................................620 873-7175
Scott L Crain, *President*
Arnie Sumner, *COO*
EMP: 22
SQ FT: 10,000
SALES (est): 1MM **Privately Held**
WEB: www.veriprime.com
SIC: 8734 Food testing service

Medicine Lodge
Barber County

(G-7056)
ARROWHEAD WEST INC
Hwys 281 & 160 (67104)
P.O. Box 327 (67104-0327)
PHONE..................................620 886-3711
Andrea Pols, *Manager*
EMP: 50
SALES (corp-wide): 13.9MM **Privately Held**
SIC: 8331 Vocational rehabilitation agency
PA: Arrowhead West, Inc.
1100 E Wyatt Earp Blvd
Dodge City KS 67801
620 227-8803

▲ = Import ▼=Export ◆ =Import/Export

(G-7057)
BARBER COUNTY HOME HEALTH AGCY
118 E Washington Ave (67104-1452)
P.O. Box 194 (67104-0194)
PHONE..................................620 886-3775
Paul Harber, *Mayor*
Sheri Weeks, *Treasurer*
EMP: 12
SALES: 329.8K **Privately Held**
SIC: 8082 Home health care services

(G-7058)
CITIZENS BANK OF KANSAS NA
120 E Kansas Ave (67104-1405)
PHONE..................................620 886-5686
George Cook, *Branch Mgr*
Leesa Beam, *Manager*
EMP: 19 **Privately Held**
SIC: 6021 6022 6162 6163 National commercial banks; state commercial banks; mortgage bankers & correspondents; loan agents
HQ: Citizens Bank Of Kansas
300 N Main St
Kingman KS 67068
620 532-5162

(G-7059)
COUNTY OF BARBER
1027 Ne Isabel Rd (67104-8309)
PHONE..................................620 886-5087
Donald Lunsford, *Manager*
EMP: 20 **Privately Held**
SIC: 0721 Weed control services after planting
PA: County Of Barber
120 E Washington Ave
Medicine Lodge KS 67104
620 886-3961

(G-7060)
FINCHERS FINDINGS INC
900 W Central (67104)
P.O. Box 289 (67104-0289)
PHONE..................................620 886-5952
Brett Fincher, *President*
Ron Fincher, *President*
EMP: 7
SQ FT: 5,000
SALES (est): 807.9K **Privately Held**
SIC: 2396 5136 5199 Screen printing on fabric articles; caps, men's & boys'; shirts, men's & boys'; advertising specialties

(G-7061)
G & S ROUSTABOUT SERVICE LLC
902 N Walnut St (67104-1053)
P.O. Box 151 (67104-0151)
PHONE..................................620 213-0172
Robert Gabriel, *Mng Member*
EMP: 5
SALES: 600K **Privately Held**
SIC: 1389 Roustabout service

(G-7062)
GYP HILLS ROUSTABOUT LLC
318 W Kansas Ave (67104-1439)
PHONE..................................620 886-0931
Zachary Oldham, *Principal*
EMP: 5
SALES (est): 261.7K **Privately Held**
SIC: 1389 Roustabout service

(G-7063)
H-40 DRILLING INC
5735 Sw Walstead (67104-8095)
PHONE..................................316 773-3640
Norman Johnson, *President*
EMP: 12
SALES (est): 1.5MM **Privately Held**
SIC: 1381 Drilling oil & gas wells

(G-7064)
HUMMON CORPORATION
101 N Main St (67104-1316)
P.O. Box 365 (67104-0365)
PHONE..................................620 930-2645
Byron E Hummon Jr, *President*
Bryant Theis, *Office Mgr*
EMP: 8 **EST:** 1966
SALES (est): 1.3MM **Privately Held**
SIC: 1311 Crude petroleum production; natural gas production

(G-7065)
LARRISON-FORSYTH FNRL HM LLC
120 E Lincoln Ave (67104-1557)
PHONE..................................620 886-5641
Eric Larrison, *CEO*
Larrison Van Pratt, *Owner*
EMP: 10
SALES (est): 294.7K **Privately Held**
SIC: 7261 Funeral home

(G-7066)
MEDICINE LODGE INDIAN & PEACE
103 E Washington Ave (67104-1420)
P.O. Box 128 (67104-0128)
PHONE..................................620 886-9815
Rick Swaden, *President*
Sara Whalen, *President*
EMP: 10
SALES: 75.1K **Privately Held**
WEB: www.peacetreaty.org
SIC: 8412 Museum

(G-7067)
MEDICINE LODGE MEMORIAL HOSP
710 N Walnut St (67104-1019)
P.O. Box C (67104-0803)
PHONE..................................620 886-3771
Danny Dutton, *Facilities Mgr*
Beth Hardin, *Purch Dir*
Steve Walton, *Purch Mgr*
Tom Lee, *CFO*
Sara Harmon, *Credit Staff*
EMP: 125 **EST:** 1950
SQ FT: 36,000
SALES: 9.2MM **Privately Held**
WEB: www.mlmh.net
SIC: 8062 General medical & surgical hospitals

(G-7068)
MID-WEST OILFIELD SERVICE
1990 Se Us Highway 160 (67104-8300)
P.O. Box 150 (67104-0150)
PHONE..................................620 930-2051
David L Brown Jr, *President*
James McLemore, *Vice Pres*
EMP: 7 **EST:** 2008
SALES (est): 816.7K **Privately Held**
SIC: 1389 Oil field services

(G-7069)
NEW NGC INC
Also Called: National Gibson Company
1218 Sw Mill Rd (67104-8001)
PHONE..................................620 886-5613
Linda Bonewell, *Safety Mgr*
Jason Gibson, *Engineer*
Greg Whelan, *Branch Mgr*
Jo Boor, *Admin Sec*
EMP: 131
SALES (corp-wide): 723.5MM **Privately Held**
WEB: www.natgyp.com
SIC: 1499 3275 Gypsum mining; building board, gypsum
HQ: New Ngc, Inc.
2001 Rexford Rd
Charlotte NC 28211

(G-7070)
NICHOLAS WATER SERVICE LLC
1201 Sw Mill Rd (67104-8001)
P.O. Box 170 (67104-0170)
PHONE..................................620 930-7511
Kevin Nicholas, *Mng Member*
Jerry Cushenbery,
Staci Cushenbery,
EMP: 15
SALES (est): 1.4MM **Privately Held**
SIC: 1389 4731 Haulage, oil field; oil field services; freight forwarding

(G-7071)
ORSCHELN FARM AND HOME LLC
Also Called: Orscheln Farm & Home
300 S Iliff St (67104-1900)
PHONE..................................620 930-3276
Kathie Powell, *President*
EMP: 10
SALES (corp-wide): 822.7MM **Privately Held**
SIC: 5999 5251 5191 5083 Feed & farm supply; tools; farm supplies; farm & garden machinery
PA: Orscheln Farm And Home Llc
1800 Overcenter Dr
Moberly MO 65270
800 577-2580

(G-7072)
SOURDOUGH EXPRESS INCORPORATED
219 S Main St (67104-1410)
PHONE..................................907 452-1181
Sandy Small, *Branch Mgr*
EMP: 15
SALES (corp-wide): 21.8MM **Privately Held**
SIC: 4213 Trucking, except local
PA: Sourdough Express, Incorporated
600 Driveway St
Fairbanks AK 99701
907 452-1181

(G-7073)
SOUTH CENTL COMMUNICATIONS INC
Also Called: South Central Telephone Assn
215 S Iliff St (67104-1901)
P.O. Box B (67104-0802)
PHONE..................................620 930-1000
Paul Harbaugh, *President*
EMP: 35
SQ FT: 4,046
SALES: 12MM
SALES (corp-wide): 3MM **Privately Held**
WEB: www.sctelcom.com
SIC: 5065 Telephone & telegraphic equipment
PA: South Central Telephone Association, Inc.
215 S Iliff St
Medicine Lodge KS 67104
620 930-1000

(G-7074)
SOUTH CENTRAL TELE ASSN INC (PA)
Also Called: Sctelcom
215 S Iliff St (67104-1901)
P.O. Box B (67104-0802)
PHONE..................................620 930-1000
Mike Vancampen, *President*
Brent Garvie, *Vice Pres*
EMP: 28 **EST:** 1953
SALES: 3MM **Privately Held**
WEB: www.sctelcom.com
SIC: 7389 8699 Telephone services; charitable organization

(G-7075)
SOUTH CENTRAL WIRELESS INC
Also Called: Sctelcom
215 S Iliff St (67104-1901)
P.O. Box B (67104-0802)
PHONE..................................620 930-1000
Mike Vancampen, *President*
Sam Hartley, *Vice Pres*
Ramon Parker, *Admin Sec*
EMP: 35 **EST:** 1998
SALES (est): 3MM
SALES (corp-wide): 3MM **Privately Held**
WEB: www.sctelcom.net
SIC: 7389 Telephone services
PA: South Central Telephone Association, Inc.
215 S Iliff St
Medicine Lodge KS 67104
620 930-1000

(G-7076)
WOOLSEY PETROLEUM CORPORATION
1966 Se Rodeo Dr (67104-8114)
PHONE..................................620 886-5606
Carl Durr, *Branch Mgr*
EMP: 6
SALES (est): 593.5K
SALES (corp-wide): 9.8MM **Privately Held**
WEB: www.woolseyco.com
SIC: 1382 Oil & gas exploration services
PA: Woolsey Petroleum Corporation
125 N Market St Ste 1000
Wichita KS 67202
316 267-4379

Melvern
Osage County

(G-7077)
VALLEY VIEW GREENHOUSE LLC
31272 S Croco Rd (66510-9290)
PHONE..................................785 549-3621
John Starch, *Partner*
EMP: 13
SALES: 300K **Privately Held**
SIC: 0181 0782 Flowers: grown under cover (e.g. greenhouse production); landscape contractors

Meriden
Jefferson County

(G-7078)
ATM CONCRETE INC
111 Water St (66512-9581)
P.O. Box 323 (66512-0323)
PHONE..................................785 484-2013
Lee Tuck, *President*
Adam Tuck, *General Mgr*
EMP: 17
SQ FT: 1,800
SALES (est): 2.2MM **Privately Held**
SIC: 1771 1741 Foundation & footing contractor; foundation building

(G-7079)
CRECHE ACADEMY LLC
7043 Wells Rd (66512-9000)
PHONE..................................785 484-3100
Kysa Sarrient, *Director*
EMP: 18 **EST:** 2013
SALES (est): 303.1K **Privately Held**
SIC: 8351 Preschool center

(G-7080)
ERNEST-SPENCER INC (PA)
3323 82nd St (66512-8701)
P.O. Box 550 (66512-0550)
PHONE..................................785 484-3165
Neal Spencer, *President*
Jared Thomann, *Purch Mgr*
Cindy Umscheid, *Admin Sec*
▼ **EMP:** 40
SQ FT: 2,000,000
SALES (est): 43.7MM **Privately Held**
WEB: www.esmetals.com
SIC: 1541 Grain elevator construction

(G-7081)
FIVE STAR MASONRY LLC
7529 Lakeview Rd (66512-9011)
PHONE..................................785 484-9737
Jeff White, *Project Mgr*
Barry White,
EMP: 45
SALES: 8MM **Privately Held**
SIC: 1741 Tuckpointing or restoration

(G-7082)
TDI GLOBAL SOLUTIONS INC
6736 Grace Edmond Dr (66512-8805)
PHONE..................................877 834-6750
▲ **EMP:** 10
SQ FT: 3,000
SALES: 20MM **Privately Held**
SIC: 5199 3565 Whol Nondurable Goods Mfg Packaging Machinery

(G-7083)
VAN PETTEN ANIMAL HEALTH INC
Also Called: Meriden Animal Hospital
7146 K4 Hwy (66512-9219)
PHONE..................................785 484-3358
Jeffrey F Van Petten, *President*
Jackie Van Petten, *Corp Secy*
EMP: 10
SQ FT: 2,500

SALES (est): 1MM **Privately Held**
SIC: 0742 Veterinarian, animal specialties

(G-7084)
W F LEONARD CO INC
111 W Main St (66512-9595)
P.O. Box 385 (66512-0385)
PHONE..................................785 484-3342
Frank Hachinski, *President*
EMP: 6
SQ FT: 4,800
SALES (est): 1MM **Privately Held**
WEB: www.shurfoot.net
SIC: 2842 Degreasing solvent; cleaning or polishing preparations

Merriam
Johnson County

(G-7085)
A GLASS & TINT SHOP KC INC (PA)
Also Called: Kc Window Film
9928 W 62nd Ter (66203-3200)
PHONE..................................913 491-8468
Beatrice Baldi, *CEO*
Nickolas Baldi, *Vice Pres*
Kay Baldi, *Marketing Staff*
EMP: 15 **EST:** 1997
SQ FT: 3,000
SALES: 1.2MM **Privately Held**
SIC: 7536 7549 1793 Automotive glass replacement shops; glass tinting, automotive; glass & glazing work

(G-7086)
BARR-THORP ELECTRIC COMPANY (PA)
9245 W 53rd St (66203-2111)
P.O. Box 2709, Shawnee Mission (66201-2709)
PHONE..................................913 789-8840
Todd Thorp, *President*
Sheila Thorp, *Corp Secy*
Nicholas Cole, *Opers Mgr*
Kurtis Kisker, *Purch Mgr*
Natalie Baar, *Purchasing*
EMP: 24
SQ FT: 28,000
SALES (est): 36.4MM **Privately Held**
WEB: www.barr-thorp.com
SIC: 5063 Motor controls, starters & relays: electric

(G-7087)
BUILDING CONTROL SOLUTIONS LLC
5138 Merriam Dr (66203-2158)
PHONE..................................816 439-6046
Bill Morton, *Project Engr*
Andrea Knutter, *Accounting Mgr*
Cheryl Morton,
Rhonda Stamper, *Admin Asst*
EMP: 9
SQ FT: 2,000
SALES: 2MM **Privately Held**
WEB: www.bcs-kc.com
SIC: 3822 1711 Auto controls regulating residntl & coml environmt & applncs; heating & air conditioning contractors

(G-7088)
CHARTER FUNERALS KANSAS LLC (PA)
10250 Shwnee Mission Pkwy (66203-3645)
PHONE..................................913 671-7222
Mary Franklin, *Accountant*
Dusan Radoeich,
EMP: 10
SALES (est): 577.3K **Privately Held**
SIC: 7261 Funeral home

(G-7089)
CREATIVE PRINTING COMPANY INC
9014 W 51st Ter (66203-2193)
PHONE..................................913 262-5000
Sheryl Leavey, *President*
David Leavey, *Vice Pres*
Michael Leavey, *Vice Pres*
Bret Holloway, *Purchasing*
Kristy Brady, *CFO*
EMP: 40 **EST:** 1966
SQ FT: 44,000
SALES: 13MM **Privately Held**
WEB: www.creativeprintingcompany.com
SIC: 2752 Commercial printing, offset

(G-7090)
DDSPORTS INC
Also Called: Dd Sports
7220 W Frontage Rd (66203-4638)
PHONE..................................913 636-0432
Bruce Ianni, *CEO*
Davyeon Ross, *COO*
Joe Ianni, *Finance*
Lori Gery, *Chief Mktg Ofcr*
Haley Jeffrey, *Marketing Staff*
EMP: 9
SQ FT: 2,500
SALES (est): 1.2MM **Privately Held**
SIC: 7372 7371 Application computer software; computer software development & applications

(G-7091)
ENT ASSCTES GREATER KANS CY PC
Also Called: Merriam Office
6815 Frontage Rd (66204-1398)
PHONE..................................816 478-4200
Antionette Guadagnano, *Manager*
EMP: 40
SALES (corp-wide): 6.7MM **Privately Held**
SIC: 8011 Offices & clinics of medical doctors
PA: Ent Associates Of Greater Kansas City, Pc
4880 Ne Goodview Cir
Lees Summit MO 64064
816 478-3008

(G-7092)
ESA P PRTFOLIO OPER LESSEE LLC
Also Called: Extended Stay America, Inc.
6451 Frontage Rd (66202-4717)
PHONE..................................913 236-6006
Michael Cryan, *Branch Mgr*
EMP: 15
SALES (corp-wide): 1.2B **Publicly Held**
WEB: www.homesteadgs.com
SIC: 7011 Hotels & motels
HQ: Esa P Portfolio Operating Lessee, Llc
11525 N Community House R
Charlotte NC 28277
980 345-1600

(G-7093)
GREAT PLAINS SPCA
5428 Antioch Dr (66202-1020)
PHONE..................................913 831-7722
Courtney Thomas, *Principal*
Hannah Rinehart, *Technician*
Jacqueline Morino,
EMP: 29 **EST:** 2011
SALES: 6MM **Privately Held**
SIC: 8699 Animal humane society

(G-7094)
HANGER INC
9301 W 74th St (66204-2207)
PHONE..................................913 677-1488
EMP: 13
SALES (corp-wide): 1B **Publicly Held**
SIC: 3842 Surgical appliances & supplies
PA: Hanger, Inc.
10910 Domain Dr Ste 300
Austin TX 78758
512 777-3800

(G-7095)
HOME DEPOT USA INC
Also Called: Home Depot, The
5700 Antioch Rd (66202-2015)
PHONE..................................913 789-8899
Kenton Tuttle, *Manager*
EMP: 135
SALES (corp-wide): 108.2B **Publicly Held**
WEB: www.homerentalsdepot.com
SIC: 5211 7359 Home centers; tool rental
HQ: Home Depot U.S.A., Inc.
2455 Paces Ferry Ave
Atlanta GA 30339

(G-7096)
INDUSTRIAL BATTERY PDTS INC
5360 Merriam Dr (66203-2122)
PHONE..................................913 236-6500
Nate Reitz, *Branch Mgr*
EMP: 12
SALES (corp-wide): 45.7MM **Privately Held**
WEB: www.ibpstl.com
SIC: 5063 1731 Batteries; computer installation
PA: Industrial Battery Products, Inc.
1250 Ambassador Blvd
Saint Louis MO 63132
314 473-2200

(G-7097)
JOHNSON COUNTY PEDIATRICS
8800 W 75th St Ste 220 (66204-4001)
PHONE..................................913 384-5500
Gerald D Wigginton MD, *President*
Bryan Nelson, *Partner*
Allison H Anderson, *Director*
Richard Decker, *Shareholder*
Kathleen Shaffer, *Shareholder*
EMP: 65
SQ FT: 7,000
SALES (est): 6.6MM **Privately Held**
SIC: 8011 Pediatrician

(G-7098)
KANSAS GLOBAL HOTEL LLC
Also Called: Hampton Inn
7400 W Frontage Rd (66203-4670)
PHONE..................................913 722-0800
Monica Magee, *General Mgr*
Michael Callan, *COO*
EMP: 24
SALES (est): 1MM **Privately Held**
SIC: 7011 Hotels & motels

(G-7099)
LEE JEANS COMPANY INC (HQ)
9001 W 67th St (66202-3699)
P.O. Box 21488, Greensboro NC (27420-1488)
PHONE..................................913 384-4000
Mike Lettera, *President*
Kent Pech, *Vice Pres*
EMP: 39
SALES (est): 471.2K
SALES (corp-wide): 13.8B **Publicly Held**
WEB: www.leejeans.com
SIC: 2325 2339 2369 Jeans: men's, youths' & boys'; jeans: women's, misses' & juniors'; jeans: girls', children's & infants'
PA: V.F. Corporation
105 Corporate Center Blvd
Greensboro NC 27408
336 424-6000

(G-7100)
MID AMERICA PRINTED
5401 Hayes St (66203-2160)
PHONE..................................913 432-2700
Donald Eikel, *Owner*
EMP: 11
SALES (est): 310.2K **Privately Held**
SIC: 7822 Motion picture & tape distribution

(G-7101)
QUALITY INVENTORY SERVICES (PA)
6231 Ikea Way (66202-2804)
PHONE..................................913 888-7700
John Boullear, *President*
Michael Jones, *General Mgr*
Christie Boullear, *Sales Staff*
EMP: 18
SQ FT: 2,800
SALES (est): 3.8MM **Privately Held**
SIC: 7389 Inventory computing service

(G-7102)
REESE GROUP INC
6200 Mastin St (66203-3254)
PHONE..................................913 383-8260
Phil Otto, *Branch Mgr*
EMP: 10
SALES (corp-wide): 12.4MM **Privately Held**
SIC: 5141 Food brokers
PA: The Reese Group Inc
2820 Bransford Ave
Nashville TN 37204
615 269-3456

(G-7103)
SEABOARD CORPORATION (HQ)
9000 W 67th St (66202-3638)
PHONE..................................913 676-8800
Steven J Bresky, *Ch of Bd*
James Sullivan, *General Mgr*
Bruce Brecheisen, *Exec VP*
David M Becker, *Senior VP*
David Rankin, *Senior VP*
EMP: 175
SALES: 6.5B **Publicly Held**
WEB: www.prairiefresh.com
SIC: 2011 0133 4412 6221 Pork products from pork slaughtered on site; sugarcane farm; deep sea foreign transportation of freight; commodity traders, contracts; flour milling custom services; hogs
PA: Seaboard Flour Llc
6 Liberty Sq
Boston MA 02109
917 928-6040

(G-7104)
SIGNATURE MANUFACTURING
9825 W 67th St (66203-3619)
PHONE..................................913 766-0680
EMP: 12
SALES (est): 1.9MM **Privately Held**
SIC: 3999 Barber & beauty shop equipment

(G-7105)
SPRINT SPECTRUM LP
5640 Antioch Rd (66202-2013)
PHONE..................................913 671-7007
Geoff Overfeld, *Executive*
EMP: 13 **Publicly Held**
WEB: www.sprintpcs.com
SIC: 5999 4812 Mobile telephones & equipment; radio telephone communication
HQ: Sprint Spectrum L.P.
6800 Sprint Pkwy
Overland Park KS 66251

(G-7106)
STEM 2 LLC
Also Called: Stem Hair & Body Salon
5660 Antioch Rd (66202-2013)
PHONE..................................913 236-9368
Angela Janssen,
Suzanne Phelps,
EMP: 22
SALES (est): 110.1K **Privately Held**
SIC: 7231 Unisex hair salons

(G-7107)
STRAWBERRY HILL POVITICA INC
Also Called: Strawberry Hill Povitica Co
7226 W Frontage Rd (66203-4638)
PHONE..................................800 631-1002
Dennis O Leary, *President*
Steve Trenholm, *Director*
EMP: 8
SQ FT: 7,818
SALES (est): 1.6MM **Privately Held**
WEB: www.povitica.com
SIC: 2051 Breads, rolls & buns

(G-7108)
US BANK NATIONAL ASSOCIATION
Also Called: US Bank
8600 Shwn Mssn Pkwy A (66202)
PHONE..................................913 671-2723
Sharon Brown, *Manager*
EMP: 12
SALES (corp-wide): 25.7B **Publicly Held**
WEB: www.firstar.com
SIC: 6021 National commercial banks
HQ: U.S. Bank National Association
425 Walnut St Fl 14
Cincinnati OH 45202
513 632-4234

(G-7109)
WALGREEN CO
Also Called: Walgreens
8701 Johnson Dr (66202-2150)
PHONE....913 789-9275
Jessica Bowers, *Branch Mgr*
EMP: 30
SALES (corp-wide): 136.8B **Publicly Held**
WEB: www.walgreens.com
SIC: 5912 7384 Drug stores; photofinishing laboratory
HQ: Walgreen Co.
200 Wilmot Rd
Deerfield IL 60015
800 925-4733

(G-7110)
WC CONSTRUCTION LLC
5410 Antioch Rd (66202-1026)
P.O. Box 29009, Kansas City MO (64152-0309)
PHONE....816 741-4810
William Carter,
▲ **EMP:** 20
SQ FT: 3,500
SALES (est): 4.1MM **Privately Held**
WEB: www.wc-construction.com
SIC: 1542 Commercial & office building, new construction; commercial & office buildings, renovation & repair

Milford
Geary County

(G-7111)
CITY OF JUNCTION CITY
Also Called: Rolling Meadows Golf Club
6514 Old Milford Rd (66514-9324)
PHONE....785 238-4303
Jhon Bernstein, *Principal*
John Bernstein, *Manager*
Darrel Penland, *Manager*
EMP: 15 **Privately Held**
WEB: www.jcks.com
SIC: 7992 Public golf courses
PA: City Of Junction City
700 N Jefferson St Ste B
Junction City KS 66441
785 238-7142

Miltonvale
Cloud County

(G-7112)
TWIN VALLEY TELEPHONE INC (PA)
Also Called: Twin Valley Communications
22 W Spruce Ave (67466-5026)
P.O. Box 1937, Salina (67402-1937)
PHONE....785 427-2211
Benjamin Foster, *President*
John Gisselbeck, *Vice Pres*
Jackie Foster, *Shareholder*
Peggy S Foster, *Shareholder*
Penny Gisselbeck, *Shareholder*
EMP: 45 **EST:** 1957
SALES (est): 14.6MM **Privately Held**
WEB: www.twinvalley.net
SIC: 4813 Local & long distance telephone communications

Minneapolis
Ottawa County

(G-7113)
BENNINGTON OIL CO INC
Also Called: D & G Oil Company
107 E 2nd St (67467-2401)
PHONE....785 392-3031
Wayne Reed, *President*
EMP: 16
SALES: 548K **Privately Held**
SIC: 5171 5541 Petroleum bulk stations; filling stations, gasoline

(G-7114)
BENNINGTON STATE BANK
320 W 2nd St Ste 1 (67467-2314)
P.O. Box 225 (67467-0225)
PHONE....785 392-2136
Kent Mike Berkley, *President*
EMP: 13
SQ FT: 5,000
SALES (corp-wide): 33.3MM **Privately Held**
SIC: 6022 State trust companies accepting deposits, commercial
PA: Bennington State Bank
2130 S Ohio St
Salina KS 67401
785 827-5522

(G-7115)
C & R PLATING INC
1120 E 10th St (67467-9164)
PHONE....785 392-2626
Kevin Cline, *President*
Sandy Cline, *Vice Pres*
EMP: 10
SQ FT: 11,500
SALES (est): 1.7MM **Privately Held**
WEB: www.crplating.com
SIC: 3471 Plating of metals or formed products

(G-7116)
CLASSIC WOOD INTERIOR INC
705 Laurel St (67467-3005)
PHONE....785 392-9937
Norm Mick, *President*
Betty Mick, *Corp Secy*
EMP: 7
SQ FT: 8,000
SALES (est): 510K **Privately Held**
SIC: 2541 Cabinets, lockers & shelving

(G-7117)
FLINTHILLS TRADING COMPANY (PA)
Also Called: G L Huyett
G L Huyett Expy Exit 49 (67467)
P.O. Box 232 (67467-0232)
PHONE....785 392-3017
Timothy O'Keeffe, *CEO*
Scott Longfe, *Vice Pres*
Paul Sellers, *Vice Pres*
Greg Tabor, *Vice Pres*
Kelley Kerr, *Regl Sales Mgr*
▲ **EMP:** 110
SQ FT: 50,000
SALES (est): 72.7MM **Privately Held**
WEB: www.huyett.com
SIC: 5085 Fasteners, industrial: nuts, bolts, screws, etc.

(G-7118)
MINNEAPOLIS MESSENGER PUBG CO
401 W 2nd St (67467-2397)
PHONE....785 392-2129
John W Wilson, *President*
Mary Wilson, *Treasurer*
EMP: 6
SALES (est): 354.6K **Privately Held**
WEB: www.minneapolismessenger.net
SIC: 2711 2752 Newspapers: publishing only, not printed on site; lithographing on metal

(G-7119)
OTTAWA COUNTY HEALTH CENTER
Also Called: Ottawa County Health Plg Comm
215 E 8th St (67467-1907)
PHONE....785 392-2044
Joy Reed, *Principal*
Chris Robins, *Maintenance Dir*
Cheryl Lanoue, *CFO*
Judette Fields, *Director*
Jeanette Roberg, *Director*
EMP: 113
SALES (est): 14.6MM **Privately Held**
WEB: www.ochc.net
SIC: 8062 General medical & surgical hospitals

(G-7120)
P A COMCARE
311 N Mill St Ste 1 (67467-2145)
P.O. Box 260 (67467-0260)
PHONE....785 392-2144
Nancy McIntosh, *Executive*
Daryl Ehrlich, *Administration*
EMP: 30
SALES (est): 1.3MM
SALES (corp-wide): 14.9MM **Privately Held**
SIC: 8011 General & family practice, physician/surgeon
PA: P A Comcare
2090 S Ohio St
Salina KS 67401
785 825-8221

(G-7121)
PROFAB
1110 Limestone Rd Bldg C (67467-8756)
P.O. Box 102 (67467-0102)
PHONE....785 392-3442
Bill Little, *Owner*
EMP: 22
SALES (est): 1.2MM **Privately Held**
SIC: 7542 Carwashes

(G-7122)
PROFESSIONAL ROOFING SYSTEMS
615 N Rothsay Ave (67467-1929)
PHONE....785 392-0603
Chad Leisey, *Owner*
EMP: 40
SALES (est): 244K **Privately Held**
SIC: 1761 Roofing contractor

(G-7123)
SCOULAR COMPANY
524 W 2nd St (67467-2318)
PHONE....785 392-9024
Ray M Gavran, *Branch Mgr*
EMP: 10
SALES (corp-wide): 4.2B **Privately Held**
SIC: 5153 Grains
PA: The Scoular Company
2027 Dodge St Ste 200
Omaha NE 68102
402 342-3500

Minneola
Clark County

(G-7124)
EMERGENT GREEN ENERGY INC
Also Called: E G E
450 County Rd Cll C (67865)
P.O. Box 538 (67865-0538)
PHONE....620 450-4320
Matt Jaeger, *President*
EMP: 15 **EST:** 2007
SQ FT: 1,500
SALES (est): 1.8MM **Privately Held**
SIC: 2869 Fuels

(G-7125)
MINNEOLA CO-OP INC
500 W Front St (67865-4545)
P.O. Box 376 (67865-0376)
PHONE....620 885-4361
Alan Hornback, *President*
EMP: 12
SQ FT: 4,500
SALES (est): 3.7MM **Privately Held**
SIC: 5153 5191 Grain elevators; feed; fertilizer & fertilizer materials; seeds: field, garden & flower; chemicals, agricultural

(G-7126)
MINNEOLA HOSPITAL DISTRICT 2
Also Called: Minneola Long Term Unit
207 S Chestnut St (67865-8567)
PHONE....620 885-4238
Curt Thomas, *Manager*
EMP: 52
SALES (corp-wide): 8.9MM **Privately Held**
SIC: 8062 8051 General medical & surgical hospitals; skilled nursing care facilities
PA: Minneola Hospital District 2
212 Main St
Bloom KS 67865

(G-7127)
NATURAL GAS PIPELINE AMER LLC
Also Called: Colorado Interstate Gas Co
12653 114 Rd (67865-8528)
PHONE....620 885-4505
Ben Lawson, *Branch Mgr*
EMP: 5 **Publicly Held**
SIC: 1311 4922 8741 Natural gas production; pipelines, natural gas; storage, natural gas; management services
HQ: Natural Gas Pipeline Company Of America Llc
1001 Louisiana St
Houston TX 77002
713 369-9000

Mission
Johnson County

(G-7128)
CASA JHNSON WYNDTTE CNTIES INC
6950 Squibb Rd Ste 300 (66202-3260)
PHONE....913 715-4040
Allison Richter, *Supervisor*
Amy Boydston, *Exec Dir*
Alyssa Perbeck, *Director*
Amorita Johnson, *Program Dir*
Christy McCulloch, *Admin Asst*
EMP: 13
SQ FT: 2,624
SALES: 832K **Privately Held**
SIC: 8322 Child related social services

(G-7129)
CHILDRENS THERAPY GROUP
Also Called: Childrens Threrapy
6223 Slater St (66202-2848)
PHONE....913 383-9014
Sarah Banker, *Director*
EMP: 15
SQ FT: 3,500
SALES (est): 783K **Privately Held**
WEB: www.childrenstherapygroup.com
SIC: 8322 8093 Child guidance agency; rehabilitation center, outpatient treatment

(G-7130)
DION A DANIEL INC
5400 Johnson Dr Ste 214 (66205-2911)
PHONE....816 287-1452
Dion A Daniel, *CEO*
EMP: 10
SALES: 450K **Privately Held**
SIC: 7389 Business services

(G-7131)
ITALK TELECONTRACTING INC
6950 Squibb Rd Ste 200 (66202-3260)
PHONE....816 436-8080
Angel Harbison, *President*
Ken Harbison, *Vice Pres*
EMP: 12
SQ FT: 4,000
SALES: 1.2MM **Privately Held**
WEB: www.italktelcom.com
SIC: 1731 Telephone & telephone equipment installation

(G-7132)
KEITH AND ASSOC DENTISTRY LLC
6299 Nall Ave Ste 300 (66202-3551)
PHONE....913 384-0044
William Keith,
EMP: 25
SALES (est): 162.8K **Privately Held**
SIC: 8021 Offices & clinics of dentists

(G-7133)
NOTES TO SELF LLC
5442 Martway St (66205-2915)
PHONE....913 730-0037
Laura Schmidt, *Founder*
EMP: 8 **EST:** 2011
SQ FT: 4,800
SALES (est): 850.1K **Privately Held**
SIC: 2252 Socks

(G-7134)
ORANGE INDUSTRIES LLC
5806 Walmer St (66202-2603)
PHONE..................................816 694-1919
James Dustin Denham, *Administration*
EMP: 5
SALES (est): 541.6K **Privately Held**
SIC: 3999 Manufacturing industries

(G-7135)
QUANTUM HEALTH PROFESSIONALS
6901 Shawnee Mission Pkwy # 207 (66202-4082)
PHONE..................................913 894-1910
Troy Roberts, *President*
EMP: 70
SALES (est): 584.6K **Privately Held**
SIC: 7361 Executive placement

(G-7136)
RBA ASSOCIATES INC
Also Called: Ruth Burke & Associates
6299 Nall Ave Ste 300 (66202-3551)
PHONE..................................816 444-4270
Sara Malone, *President*
Sally O'Neill, *Vice Pres*
Linda Norfleet, *Treasurer*
EMP: 12
SQ FT: 1,400
SALES (est): 2.3MM **Privately Held**
WEB: www.rburke.com
SIC: 7311 Advertising agencies

(G-7137)
REDWOOD GROUP LLC (HQ)
5920 Nall Ave Ste 400 (66202-3429)
PHONE..................................816 979-1786
Michael Kincaid II, *President*
Andrew Koplin, *COO*
Roger Obrist, *CFO*
EMP: 60
SQ FT: 2,500
SALES (est): 324.5MM **Privately Held**
SIC: 5153 5172 5159 Grain & field beans; petroleum products; farm animals
PA: Redwood Trading, Llc
5920 Nall Ave Ste 308
Mission KS 66202
816 979-1786

(G-7138)
SPIDEROAK INC
5920 Nall Ave Ste 200 (66202-3456)
PHONE..................................847 564-8900
Ethan Oberman, *CEO*
Christina Trakas, *Human Res Mgr*
Alan Fairless, *CTO*
EMP: 10
SALES (est): 570.8K **Privately Held**
SIC: 8999 Artists & artists' studios

(G-7139)
TWENTY-FIRST CENTURY
Also Called: Ideolity
5800 Foxridge Dr Ste 102 (66202-2338)
PHONE..................................913 713-2121
Thomas O'Brian, *President*
EMP: 10
SALES (est): 797.2K **Privately Held**
SIC: 7379 Computer related consulting services

(G-7140)
WALZ TETRICK ADVERTISING INC (PA)
5201 Johnson Dr Ste 500 (66205-2930)
PHONE..................................913 789-8778
Charles Tetrick, *President*
Debbie Harris, *Accounts Mgr*
Chris Weir, *Office Mgr*
Dawn Thibodeau, *Supervisor*
Sarah Malone, *Director*
EMP: 26
SQ FT: 4,000
SALES (est): 7.4MM **Privately Held**
SIC: 7311 8732 8743 Advertising consultant; market analysis or research; public relations & publicity

Mission Hills
Johnson County

(G-7141)
CLARO FINANCIERO LLC
6612 Willow Ln (66208-1973)
PHONE..................................913 608-5444
EMP: 10
SALES (est): 774.9K **Privately Held**
SIC: 6141 Personal Credit Institution

(G-7142)
GLOBAL PRAIRIE MARKETING LLC
5527 E Mission Dr (66208-1141)
PHONE..................................913 722-7244
Anne S Peter, *CEO*
EMP: 50
SALES (est): 104.6K **Privately Held**
SIC: 8611 Growers' marketing advisory service

(G-7143)
HEARTLAND GOLF DEV II LLC
6431 Sagamore Rd (66208-1944)
PHONE..................................913 856-7235
EMP: 14
SALES (est): 1.3MM **Privately Held**
SIC: 8741 Management services

(G-7144)
INDIAN HILLS COUNTRY CLUB
6847 Tomahawk Rd (66208-2199)
PHONE..................................913 362-6200
Michael Stacks, *General Mgr*
Michae Stacks, *General Mgr*
Raelene Zollman, *Director*
EMP: 100
SQ FT: 75,000
SALES: 10MM **Privately Held**
SIC: 7997 Country club, membership

(G-7145)
KANSAS CITY COUNTRY CLUB
6200 Indian Ln (66208-1299)
PHONE..................................913 236-2100
Nathan Stewart, *General Mgr*
David Buenger, *Principal*
Nathan M Stewart, *COO*
Robert Tibbetts, *Opers Mgr*
Kristen Lenz, *Asst Mgr*
EMP: 140
SQ FT: 10,000
SALES: 8.4MM **Privately Held**
SIC: 7997 Golf club, membership

(G-7146)
MISSION HILLS COUNTRY CLUB INC
5400 Mission Dr (66208-1199)
PHONE..................................913 722-5400
Cory Conklin, *COO*
Joyce Hess, *Controller*
Jill Hough, *Manager*
Shaun Hall, *Manager*
John Baumgartner, *Director*
EMP: 100
SQ FT: 8,000
SALES: 8.6MM **Privately Held**
WEB: www.missionhillscc.com
SIC: 7997 Country club, membership

(G-7147)
PHARMACY DIST PARTNERS LLC
6416 Ensley Ln (66208-1932)
P.O. Box 12231, Overland Park (66282-2231)
PHONE..................................903 357-3391
John M Blosser,
Shawn Paul Andersen,
EMP: 12
SALES (est): 909.4K **Privately Held**
SIC: 5047 7389 Medical & hospital equipment;

(G-7148)
RONCO INC
Also Called: Prairie Village Phillips 66
2201 W 70th St (66208-2721)
PHONE..................................913 362-7200
EMP: 14
SQ FT: 5,000
SALES (est): 2MM **Privately Held**
SIC: 5541 7542 7538 Gasoline Service Station Carwash General Auto Repair

(G-7149)
TECH INVESTMENTS III LLC
5900 Overhill Rd (66208-1211)
PHONE..................................816 674-9993
Charles M Newell, *CEO*
Tracy Christian, *CFO*
Henry Newell, *Mng Member*
EMP: 68 **Privately Held**
SIC: 6719 Investment holding companies, except banks

Mission Woods
Johnson County

(G-7150)
COLLATERAL RE CAPITL LLC
Also Called: Charter American Mortgage Co
2001 Shawnee Mission Pkwy (66205-2007)
PHONE..................................913 677-2001
Michael Dunn, *Principal*
EMP: 14
SALES (corp-wide): 13B **Publicly Held**
WEB: www.charteramerican.com
SIC: 6162 Mortgage bankers
HQ: Collateral Real Estate Capital, Llc
3000 Riverchse Gall
Hoover AL 35244
205 978-1840

(G-7151)
MIDLAND PROPERTIES INC (PA)
2001 Shawnee Mission Pkwy (66205-2099)
PHONE..................................913 677-5300
A K Weber, *Ch of Bd*
Alan L Atterbury, *President*
David Woods, *Treasurer*
Tom Kimmerly, *Controller*
Melanie Radosevich, *Assistant*
EMP: 12
SQ FT: 7,000
SALES (est): 4.9MM **Privately Held**
WEB: www.midland2001.com
SIC: 6531 6552 6799 8742 Real estate managers; subdividers & developers; investors; real estate consultant; hotels

(G-7152)
MIDLAND PROPERTY MANAGEMENT (HQ)
2001 Shawnee Mission Pkwy (66205-2099)
PHONE..................................913 677-5300
A Keith Weber, *Ch of Bd*
Greg Bates, *President*
Tom Kimmerly, *Vice Pres*
Dave Woods, *Treasurer*
EMP: 12 **EST:** 1976
SALES (est): 2.2MM
SALES (corp-wide): 4.9MM **Privately Held**
SIC: 6531 Real estate managers
PA: Midland Properties, Inc.
2001 Shawnee Mission Pkwy
Mission Woods KS 66205
913 677-5300

Modoc
Wichita County

(G-7153)
HEARTLAND MILL INC
904 E Highway 96 (67863-6375)
PHONE..................................620 379-4472
Larry Decker, *President*
Karlan Koehne, *Corp Secy*
Mark Nightengale, *Vice Pres*
Cindy Baker, *Controller*
EMP: 35
SQ FT: 14,000
SALES (est): 5.4MM **Privately Held**
WEB: www.heartlandmill.com
SIC: 2041 Flour

Montezuma
Gray County

(G-7154)
ARCHER-DANIELS-MIDLAND COMPANY
Also Called: ADM
28605 12 Rd (67867-9155)
P.O. Box 318 (67867-0318)
PHONE..................................620 846-2218
John Wall, *Branch Mgr*
EMP: 14
SALES (corp-wide): 64.3B **Publicly Held**
WEB: www.admworld.com
SIC: 5153 Grains; grain elevators
PA: Archer-Daniels-Midland Company
77 W Wacker Dr Ste 4600
Chicago IL 60601
312 634-8100

(G-7155)
BANK 7
209 N Aztec St (67867-8881)
PHONE..................................620 846-2221
William B Haines, *Branch Mgr*
EMP: 15 **Publicly Held**
SIC: 6022 State commercial banks
HQ: Bank7
1039 Nw 63rd St
Oklahoma City OK 73116
580 395-2321

(G-7156)
HY PLAINS FEEDYARD LLC
Hwy 56 (67867)
P.O. Box 356 (67867-0356)
PHONE..................................620 846-2226
Tom Jones,
Jerald Riemann,
EMP: 41
SQ FT: 2,000
SALES (est): 5.8MM **Privately Held**
SIC: 0211 Beef cattle feedlots

(G-7157)
KOEHN CUSTOMS
107 W Texcoco St (67867-2100)
PHONE..................................316 304-7979
EMP: 8
SALES (est): 88.7K **Privately Held**
SIC: 7692 Welding repair

(G-7158)
MAX JANTZ EXCAVATING INC
26503 11 Rd (67867-9065)
PHONE..................................620 846-2634
Dean Chesnut, *Principal*
John Minick, *Principal*
Justin Hendrickson, *Project Mgr*
Ben Loewen, *Project Mgr*
Jill Wahl, *Accountant*
EMP: 160
SQ FT: 4,000
SALES (est): 40MM **Privately Held**
WEB: www.maxjantzexcavating.com
SIC: 1794 Excavation & grading, building construction

(G-7159)
MENNONITE UNION AID
102 E Parks Ave (67867-8818)
P.O. Box 336 (67867-0336)
PHONE..................................620 846-2286
Gary Jentz, *President*
Kevin Ensz, *Manager*
EMP: 11
SALES (est): 3.2MM **Privately Held**
SIC: 6321 Accident & health insurance

(G-7160)
PAYROLL PLUS
Also Called: Terry Koehn
8505 Dd Rd (67867-8849)
P.O. Box 418 (67867-0418)
PHONE..................................620 846-2658
Terry Koehn, *Owner*
EMP: 20 **EST:** 1997
SALES (est): 1.3MM **Privately Held**
SIC: 8721 Payroll accounting service

▲ = Import ▼=Export
◆ =Import/Export

(G-7161)
UNRUH-FOSTER INC (PA)
501 E Texcoco St (67867-9168)
P.O. Box 278 (67867-0278)
PHONE..................................620 846-2215
Bill Wall, *President*
Dan Cammack, *Shareholder*
Mike Wall, *Shareholder*
EMP: 29 **EST:** 1945
SQ FT: 15,000
SALES: 45MM **Privately Held**
WEB: www.unruhfoster.com
SIC: 5083 7699 Agricultural machinery; farm implements; farm machinery repair

Moran
Allen County

(G-7162)
MFA ENTERPRISES INC
Agchoice Division
203 N Locust St (66755)
P.O. Box 128 (66755-0128)
PHONE..................................620 237-4668
Jim Stoud, *Manager*
EMP: 10
SALES (corp-wide): 1.3B **Privately Held**
SIC: 5191 5261 Fertilizer & fertilizer materials; fertilizer
HQ: Mfa Enterprises, Inc.
201 Ray Young Dr
Columbia MO 65201
573 874-5111

(G-7163)
MORAN MEAT LOCKER
209 S Cedar St (66755-4601)
P.O. Box 28 (66755-0028)
PHONE..................................620 237-4331
Mitch Bollimg, *Owner*
Sharon Bollimg, *Owner*
Mitch Bolling, *Partner*
EMP: 5
SQ FT: 3,000
SALES (est): 332.9K **Privately Held**
SIC: 2011 Meat packing plants

(G-7164)
RH MONTGOMERY PROPERTIES INC
Also Called: Moran Manor Nursing Center
3940 Us Highway 54 (66755-3921)
PHONE..................................620 237-4300
Mary Lucas, *Administration*
EMP: 50
SALES (corp-wide): 31.9MM **Privately Held**
SIC: 8051 Convalescent home with continuous nursing care
PA: Rh Montgomery Properties, Inc.
214 N Scott St
Sikeston MO 63801
573 471-1113

Morganville
Clay County

(G-7165)
MELLIES PRODUCTS INC
Also Called: Mpi
307 Allen Ave (67468-9141)
P.O. Box 137, Whiting (66552-0137)
PHONE..................................785 926-4331
Jim L Mellies, *President*
EMP: 7
SQ FT: 20,000
SALES (est): 1.2MM **Privately Held**
SIC: 3441 Fabricated structural metal

Morland
Graham County

(G-7166)
APPLIED CONTENT RES TECH LLC
Also Called: Logicsafari
205 E Main St (67650)
P.O. Box 62 (67650-0062)
PHONE..................................785 422-4980
EMP: 12 **EST:** 2014
SQ FT: 20,000
SALES: 4MM **Privately Held**
SIC: 7371 Custom Computer Programing

Moscow
Stevens County

(G-7167)
DC OILFIELD SERVICES
W Hwy 56 (67952)
PHONE..................................620 598-2643
Mike Colantonio, *Owner*
Darla Colantonio, *Co-Owner*
EMP: 5
SALES (est): 306.9K **Privately Held**
SIC: 1389 Oil field services

(G-7168)
NORTHWEST COT GROWERS COOP INC
3 And A Half Mile Sw (67952)
P.O. Box 300 (67952-0300)
PHONE..................................620 598-2008
Kent Dunn, *President*
Jerry Stuckey, *General Mgr*
Tom Lahey, *Vice Pres*
EMP: 36
SALES (est): 3.1MM **Privately Held**
SIC: 0724 Cotton ginning

Mound City
Linn County

(G-7169)
CROWN REALTY OF KANSAS INC
501 Main St (66056-4001)
P.O. Box 194 (66056-0194)
PHONE..................................913 795-4555
Gary Hoseck, *Manager*
Larry Holt, *Manager*
EMP: 20
SALES (corp-wide): 10MM **Privately Held**
WEB: www.crownrealty.com
SIC: 0191 General farms, primarily crop
PA: Crown Realty Of Kansas Inc
102 S Silver St
Paola KS
913 557-4333

(G-7170)
CUNNINGHAM AGENCY INC (PA)
103 S 5th St (66056-5400)
P.O. Box A (66056-0600)
PHONE..................................913 795-2212
Jeff Dawson, *President*
EMP: 10
SQ FT: 4,000
SALES (est): 2.4MM **Privately Held**
WEB: www.cunninghamagency.com
SIC: 6712 Bank holding companies

(G-7171)
DOUBLE K CNSTR OF MOUND CY
5624 Knapp Rd (66056-5396)
P.O. Box 303 (66056-0303)
PHONE..................................913 795-3147
Duane Kellstadt, *Owner*
Robert Kellstadt, *Vice Pres*
Diane Bland, *Admin Sec*
EMP: 13
SALES: 250K **Privately Held**
SIC: 1521 Single-family housing construction

(G-7172)
LINN COUNTY NUTRITION PROJECT (PA)
Also Called: Linn County Congregate Meals
306 Main St (66056-2500)
PHONE..................................913 795-2279
Melinda Bolling, *Director*
EMP: 15
SALES: 330K **Privately Held**
SIC: 8322 Meal delivery program

(G-7173)
MOUND CITY VAULT CO INC
Also Called: Stockton Burial Vault Company
414 S 4th St (66056-5264)
PHONE..................................913 795-2529
David Simons, *President*
EMP: 5 **EST:** 1962
SQ FT: 1,408
SALES (est): 635.9K **Privately Held**
SIC: 3272 Burial vaults, concrete or precast terrazzo

(G-7174)
PUBLIC WHL WTR SUP DST NO 13
318 Montgomery Ct (66056-5231)
PHONE..................................913 795-2503
Edwin Andersen, *Chairman*
Virgil Ray, *Vice Pres*
Gary Gobel, *Admin Sec*
EMP: 12
SALES: 800K **Privately Held**
SIC: 4941 Water supply

(G-7175)
SUGAR VALLEY LAKES HOMES ASSN
Also Called: Hidden Valley Homeowners Assn
53 Fairway Dr (66056-5410)
P.O. Box 247 (66056-0247)
PHONE..................................913 795-2120
Ray Sunk, *President*
Paul Filla, *Manager*
EMP: 20
SALES (est): 894.3K **Privately Held**
SIC: 8641 Homeowners' association

(G-7176)
TRIBE CONSTRUCTION LLC
13358 Leasure Rd (66056-9153)
PHONE..................................913 850-0211
Tonya Ball,
EMP: 10 **EST:** 2017
SALES (est): 337.6K **Privately Held**
SIC: 1521 Single-family housing construction

Mound Valley
Labette County

(G-7177)
MERIDIAN ANALYTICAL LABS LLC
111 E 5th St (67354-9349)
PHONE..................................620 328-3222
Duane P Koszalka,
EMP: 12
SALES (est): 282.5K **Privately Held**
SIC: 8734 Testing laboratories

Moundridge
Mcpherson County

(G-7178)
BRADBURY CO INC (PA)
Also Called: Bradbury Group, The
1200 E Cole St (67107-8803)
P.O. Box 667 (67107-0667)
PHONE..................................620 345-6394
David Cox, *President*
David Bradbury, *Chairman*
Jamie Bradbury, *Manager*
William Maurer, *Technician*
◆ **EMP:** 300 **EST:** 1959
SQ FT: 215,000
SALES (est): 141.4MM **Privately Held**
SIC: 3547 3549 Rolling mill machinery; coiling machinery

(G-7179)
CARPENTER CONSTRUCTION COMPANY
320 S Avenue A (67107-8895)
PHONE..................................620 386-4155
Michael Carpenter, *President*
Rachel Carpenter, *Corp Secy*
EMP: 10
SQ FT: 5,000
SALES: 2.2MM **Privately Held**
SIC: 1771 Foundation & footing contractor

(G-7180)
COMPANION INDUSTRIES INC
500 S Drucilla Ave (67107-7163)
P.O. Box 494 (67107-0494)
PHONE..................................620 345-3277
Anna Storer, *President*
Patricia Gray, *Vice Pres*
EMP: 30
SQ FT: 9,000
SALES (est): 4MM **Privately Held**
SIC: 2448 Wood pallets & skids

(G-7181)
CRADLE TO CRYONS CHILDCARE CTR
311 E Thornton St (67107-8825)
P.O. Box 703 (67107-0703)
PHONE..................................620 345-2390
Christina Graber, *Director*
EMP: 18
SALES (est): 282.1K **Privately Held**
SIC: 8351 Group day care center

(G-7182)
CUSTOM ROLLFORMING CORP
201 S Avenue C (67107-8855)
P.O. Box 698 (67107-0698)
PHONE..................................800 457-8837
David Bradbury, *President*
David Cox, *COO*
▼ **EMP:** 25
SQ FT: 53,000
SALES (est): 6.9MM
SALES (corp-wide): 141.4MM **Privately Held**
WEB: www.customrollformingcorp.com
SIC: 3449 Miscellaneous metalwork
PA: The Bradbury Co Inc
1200 E Cole St
Moundridge KS 67107
620 345-6394

(G-7183)
GOSPEL PUBLISHERS
Also Called: Gospel Publishers Book Store
100 S Avenue C (67107-7193)
P.O. Box 230 (67107-0230)
PHONE..................................620 345-2532
Dale Koehn, *Manager*
EMP: 6
SQ FT: 1,200
SALES: 962.6K **Privately Held**
SIC: 2741 5942 Miscellaneous publishing; books, religious

(G-7184)
HARVEST AG FABRICATING LLC
11528 Nw 96th St (67107-8016)
PHONE..................................620 345-8205
Daniel Wangler, *Principal*
EMP: 6
SQ FT: 200
SALES: 2MM **Privately Held**
SIC: 7692 Welding repair

(G-7185)
HAVEN COMMODITIES INC (HQ)
Also Called: Mid-Kansas Cooperative Assn
307 W Cole St (67107-7533)
P.O. Box D (67107-0582)
PHONE..................................620 345-6328
Ted Schultz, *Exec VP*
Brent Heizelman, *Credit Mgr*
Larry Brake, *Manager*
Chuck Knight, *Manager*
EMP: 28
SALES: 960.7K
SALES (corp-wide): 371.5MM **Privately Held**
WEB: www.mkcoop.com
SIC: 5153 Grains

PA: Mid-Kansas Cooperative Association
307 W Cole St
Moundridge KS 67107
620 345-6328

(G-7186)
JANTZ INC
Also Called: Jantz Trucking
2175 Cheyenne Rd (67107-7426)
PHONE..................................620 345-2783
Robert Jantz, *President*
Connie Jantz, *Vice Pres*
EMP: 15
SALES (est): 1.4MM **Privately Held**
SIC: 4212 4213 Farm to market haulage, local; trucking, except local

(G-7187)
KOEHN CONSTRUCTION
720 S Christian Ave (67107-7186)
P.O. Box 6 (67107-0006)
PHONE..................................620 345-6457
Starla Unruh, *Owner*
EMP: 16 **EST:** 1959
SQ FT: 3,200
SALES: 3MM **Privately Held**
WEB: www.koehnconstruction.net
SIC: 1521 New construction, single-family houses

(G-7188)
MERCY HOSPITAL INC
Also Called: MERCY HOSPITAL & SKILLED NURSI
218 E Pack St (67107-8815)
P.O. Box 180 (67107-0180)
PHONE..................................620 345-6391
Aaron Herbel, *CEO*
EMP: 42 **EST:** 1945
SQ FT: 19,000
SALES: 3MM **Privately Held**
SIC: 8062 Hospital, affiliated with AMA residency

(G-7189)
MID KANSAS CABLE SERVICES INC
109 N Christian Ave (67107-8801)
P.O. Box 960 (67107-0960)
PHONE..................................620 345-2832
Carl Krehbiel, *President*
Delonna Barnett, *Vice Pres*
Harry Weelborg, *Vice Pres*
Cathryn Krehbiel, *Admin Sec*
EMP: 14
SQ FT: 1,000
SALES (est): 861K **Privately Held**
SIC: 1731 Cable television installation

(G-7190)
MID-KANSAS COOPERATIVE ASSN (PA)
Also Called: Mkc
307 W Cole St (67107-7533)
PHONE..................................620 345-6328
Dave Christiansen, *President*
Lawson Hemberger, *Opers Staff*
Danny Posch, *CFO*
David Spears, *Chief Mktg Ofcr*
James Bettenbrock, *Manager*
EMP: 40
SQ FT: 9,000
SALES (est): 371.5MM **Privately Held**
WEB: www.mkcoop.com
SIC: 5153 5191 Grain elevators; farm supplies

(G-7191)
MID-KANSAS COOPERATIVE ASSN
117 N Edwards Ave (67107-8826)
P.O. Box D (67107-0582)
PHONE..................................620 345-6361
David Christianson, *Manager*
EMP: 16
SALES (corp-wide): 371.5MM **Privately Held**
WEB: www.mkcoop.com
SIC: 5153 Grain elevators
PA: Mid-Kansas Cooperative Association
307 W Cole St
Moundridge KS 67107
620 345-6328

(G-7192)
MID-KANSAS CREDIT UNION (PA)
104 S Avenue B (67107-8901)
P.O. Box 608 (67107-0608)
PHONE..................................620 543-2662
Rick Krehbiel, *President*
Cameron Voth, *Loan Officer*
Susan Johnson, *Loan*
Naomi Poloniecki,
EMP: 18
SALES: 1.6MM **Privately Held**
SIC: 6061 Federal credit unions

(G-7193)
MORIDGE MANUFACTURING INC
Also Called: Grass Hopper Company
105 Old Us Highway 81 (67107-7110)
P.O. Box 810 (67107-0810)
PHONE..................................620 345-6301
E Guyer, *President*
Ryan Hefley, *Purch Mgr*
Eric Bussen, *Draft/Design*
Blaine Hageman, *Engineer*
Michael Garner, *Electrical Engi*
◆ **EMP:** 290 **EST:** 1958
SQ FT: 350,000
SALES (est): 126.7MM **Privately Held**
SIC: 3524 3523 Lawnmowers, residential: hand or power; driers (farm): grain, hay & seed

(G-7194)
MOUNDRIDGE TELEPHONE COMPANY
Also Called: Moundridge Telcom
109 N Christian Ave (67107-8801)
P.O. Box 960 (67107-0960)
PHONE..................................620 345-2831
Carl Krehbiel, *President*
Kathryn Krehbiel, *Corp Secy*
Delonna Barnett, *Vice Pres*
Harry Weelborg, *Vice Pres*
EMP: 12
SQ FT: 12,000
SALES (est): 1.8MM **Privately Held**
WEB: www.mtelco.net
SIC: 4813 Local telephone communications
PA: Emmental Inc
109 S Christian Ave
Moundridge KS

(G-7195)
PARTNERS FAMILY PRACTICE LLC (PA)
Also Called: Partners In Family Care
200 E Pack St (67107-8854)
P.O. Box 640 (67107-0640)
PHONE..................................620 345-6322
Lori Begnoche, *Office Mgr*
Marla Ullom-Minnich, *Med Doctor*
Paul Ninnich, *Mng Member*
James Ratzlaff, *Family Practiti*
Paul Ullom-Minnich, *Family Practiti*
EMP: 21 **EST:** 1957
SALES (est): 3MM **Privately Held**
WEB: www.partnersinfamilycare.com
SIC: 8011 General & family practice, physician/surgeon

(G-7196)
PINE VILLAGE
86 22nd Ave (67107-7003)
PHONE..................................620 345-2901
Tim Nikkel, *CFO*
Jason Stucky, *CFO*
Jeannie Chestnut, *Director*
Jenna Lehrman, *Nursing Dir*
James N Huxman, *Administration*
EMP: 120
SALES: 6.8MM **Privately Held**
WEB: www.memorialhome.org
SIC: 8052 8661 8051 Intermediate care facilities; religious organizations; skilled nursing care facilities

(G-7197)
SMART START OF KANSAS LLC
141 S Christian Ave (67107-8899)
P.O. Box 697 (67107-0697)
PHONE..................................620 345-6000
Matt Strausz, *Principal*
EMP: 14
SALES (est): 404.9K **Privately Held**
SIC: 8351 Child day care services

(G-7198)
TEAM MARKETING ALLIANCE LLC (PA)
307 W Cole St (67107-7533)
P.O. Box 380 (67107-0380)
PHONE..................................620 345-3560
Toll Free:..877 -
Ted Schultz, *Principal*
Tricia Jantz, *Controller*
Mike Corbus, *Marketing Staff*
Cory Dieball, *Marketing Staff*
Jacob Gatz, *Marketing Staff*
EMP: 15
SQ FT: 1,500
SALES: 314.2MM **Privately Held**
WEB: www.tmagrain.com
SIC: 5153 Grain elevators

(G-7199)
TORTILLA KING INC
Also Called: Mama Lupe's Tortilla Products
249 23rd Ave (67107-7417)
P.O. Box 763 (67107-0763)
PHONE..................................620 345-2674
Juan Guardiola, *President*
Jerry Tucker, *Maint Mgr*
Dev Gautam, *QC Mgr*
Jeremy Bowen, *Controller*
Beth Nolan, *Human Res Dir*
EMP: 140
SQ FT: 45,000
SALES (est): 32.7MM **Privately Held**
WEB: www.mamalupes.com
SIC: 2099 Tortillas, fresh or refrigerated

(G-7200)
UNRUH EXCAVATING LLC
10028 N Hertzler Rd (67107-8069)
PHONE..................................620 345-3344
Mike Unruh,
EMP: 10
SALES: 2.9MM **Privately Held**
SIC: 1794 Excavation & grading, building construction

(G-7201)
USA MISSIONS CHURCH OF GOD
100 S Avenue C (67107-7193)
P.O. Box 230 (67107-0230)
PHONE..................................620 345-2532
Todd Becker, *Director*
EMP: 20
SALES (est): 600K **Privately Held**
SIC: 8661 7389 Religious organizations;

Mount Hope
Sedgwick County

(G-7202)
96 AGRI SALES INC
10400 N 247th St W (67108-9779)
PHONE..................................316 661-2281
Jack Kountz, *President*
Nancy Kountz, *Treasurer*
EMP: 11
SQ FT: 3,900
SALES (est): 4.4MM **Privately Held**
SIC: 5083 1542 Irrigation equipment; agricultural machinery; farm building construction

(G-7203)
AMERICAN EXTERIORS LLC
9730 N 215th St W (67108-9490)
PHONE..................................913 712-9668
EMP: 16 **Privately Held**
SIC: 1521 Single-family home remodeling, additions & repairs
PA: American Exteriors, Llc
7100 E Belleview Ave # 210
Greenwood Village CO 80111

(G-7204)
FIRST NATIONAL BANK OF HUTCHIN
Also Called: THE FIRST NATIONAL BANK OF HUTCHINSON INVESTMENT COMPANY, INC
100 N Ohio St (67108-1001)
PHONE..................................316 661-2471
R A Edwards, *President*
EMP: 26
SALES (corp-wide): 26.4MM **Privately Held**
SIC: 6021 National commercial banks
HQ: The First National Bank Of Hutchinson
1 N Main St Ste 320
Hutchinson KS 67501
620 663-1521

(G-7205)
JOHN SCHMIDT & SONS INC (PA)
12903 E Silver Lake Rd (67108-9617)
PHONE..................................316 445-2103
Leroy D Schmidt, *Owner*
John H Schmidt, *Vice Pres*
Barry Schmidt, *Treasurer*
Marlene Schmidt, *Admin Sec*
EMP: 30 **EST:** 1936
SQ FT: 18,000
SALES (est): 12.5MM **Privately Held**
WEB: www.schmidtinc.com
SIC: 5083 5511 Farm implements; automobiles, new & used

(G-7206)
MID-AMERICA DIABETES ASSOC PA
Also Called: Guthrie, Richard A MD
22015 W 101st St N (67108-9710)
PHONE..................................316 687-3100
EMP: 22
SQ FT: 10,000
SALES (est): 2.2MM **Privately Held**
SIC: 8011 Medical Doctor's Office

(G-7207)
MT HOPE COMMUNITY DEVELOPMENT (PA)
Also Called: MT HOPE NURSING CENTER
704 E Main St (67108-9408)
PHONE..................................316 667-2431
Gina Terry, *Director*
EMP: 75
SALES: 3.1MM **Privately Held**
SIC: 8051 6513 Convalescent home with continuous nursing care; apartment building operators

Mulberry
Crawford County

(G-7208)
MULBERRY LIMESTONE QUARRY CO
325 N 260th St (66756-4298)
PHONE..................................620 764-3337
Matt Blessant, *President*
Elizabeth Blessant, *Treasurer*
EMP: 14
SALES (est): 1.3MM **Privately Held**
SIC: 1411 Limestone, dimension-quarrying

Mullinville
Kiowa County

(G-7209)
HAYSE MANAGEMENT SERVICES
107 Northern Rd (67109)
P.O. Box 107 (67109-0107)
PHONE..................................620 548-2369
Monica Hayse, *Owner*
Dale Hayse, *Co-Owner*
EMP: 10
SALES: 500K **Privately Held**
SIC: 8742 Management consulting services

(G-7210)
NORTHERN NATURAL GAS COMPANY
14049 17th Ave (67109-7186)
PHONE..................................620 723-2151
Guy Bruner, *Branch Mgr*
EMP: 33
SQ FT: 4,000
SALES (corp-wide): 225.3B **Publicly Held**
SIC: 4226 4922 Special warehousing & storage; natural gas transmission
HQ: Northern Natural Gas Company
1111 S 103rd St
Omaha NE 68124

Mulvane
Sedgwick County

(G-7211)
BUFFCO ENGINEERING INC
Also Called: Buffco Engineering Office
200 Industrial Dr (67110-9203)
PHONE..................................316 558-5390
Karl Jones, *President*
Leeschelle Simon, *Marketing Staff*
EMP: 25
SQ FT: 2,400
SALES: 6.7MM **Privately Held**
SIC: 3324 Steel investment foundries

(G-7212)
CHRIS CARLSON HOT RODS LLC
Also Called: Chaotic Customs, LLC
246 Industrial Dr (67110-9203)
PHONE..................................316 777-4774
Christopher D Carlson,
Chris Carlson,
EMP: 15
SALES (est): 748.9K **Privately Held**
SIC: 7549 Automotive customizing services, non-factory basis

(G-7213)
CITY OF MULVANE
Also Called: Dept of Utilities
410 W Bridge St (67110-1900)
PHONE..................................316 777-0191
Kent Hixso, *Administration*
EMP: 60 **Privately Held**
WEB: www.mulvanekansas.com
SIC: 1731 Electrical work
PA: City Of Mulvane
211 N 2nd Ave
Mulvane KS 67110
316 777-4262

(G-7214)
CMJ MANUFACTURING INC
242 Industrial Dr (67110-9203)
PHONE..................................316 777-9692
Rodney Bruntz, *President*
Kent Bruntz, *General Mgr*
Maygan Doll, *Business Mgr*
EMP: 10 **EST:** 2010
SQ FT: 12,500
SALES: 1.3MM **Privately Held**
SIC: 3728 Aircraft parts & equipment

(G-7215)
DELTA HOMES INC
1555 E 120th Ave N (67110-8337)
PHONE..................................316 777-0009
Perry Caldwell, *President*
EMP: 26
SALES (est): 1.9MM **Privately Held**
SIC: 1752 Carpet laying

(G-7216)
HAZEN CONSTRUCTION SERVICES
10809 S Greenwich Rd (67110-9006)
PHONE..................................316 777-0206
Randy Hazen, *President*
Britt Hazen, *Vice Pres*
Heath Hazen, *Vice Pres*
Virginia Hazen, *Treasurer*
EMP: 15
SALES: 960K **Privately Held**
WEB: www.hazenconstruction.com
SIC: 1611 Concrete construction: roads, highways, sidewalks, etc.

(G-7217)
KMI INC
Also Called: Wolfe Machine
101 Industrial Dr (67110-9237)
PHONE..................................316 777-0146
Don Keimig, *CEO*
Michael Keimig, *COO*
Deanna Keimig, *CFO*
EMP: 35
SQ FT: 13,000
SALES (est): 7.2MM **Privately Held**
WEB: www.wolfemachine.com
SIC: 3728 3429 Aircraft parts & equipment; manufactured hardware (general)

(G-7218)
LAURIES KITCHEN INC
113 W Main St (67110-1764)
PHONE..................................316 777-9198
Laurie Waller, *President*
Dale Waller, *Treasurer*
EMP: 10
SALES (est): 795.1K **Privately Held**
WEB: www.laurieskitchen.com
SIC: 7389 Personal service agents, brokers & bureaus

(G-7219)
LEARN & GROW CHILDCARE CENTER
Also Called: LEARN & GROW CHILDCARE CTR
1020 N 2nd Ave (67110-1334)
P.O. Box 69 (67110-0069)
PHONE..................................316 777-0355
Betty A Smith, *Director*
EMP: 18
SALES: 294.4K **Privately Held**
SIC: 8351 Group day care center

(G-7220)
MARIA VILLA INC (PA)
116 S Central Ave (67110-1718)
PHONE..................................316 777-1129
Charlene Mathis, *CEO*
EMP: 65
SQ FT: 28,243
SALES: 5.8MM **Privately Held**
WEB: www.mariavilla.com
SIC: 8052 Intermediate care facilities

(G-7221)
MARIA VILLA INC
Also Called: Maria Court
633 E Main St (67110-1781)
PHONE..................................316 777-9917
Rebecca Murray, *Administration*
EMP: 20
SALES (est): 855.3K
SALES (corp-wide): 5.8MM **Privately Held**
WEB: www.mariavilla.com
SIC: 8052 Personal care facility
PA: Maria Villa Inc
116 S Central Ave
Mulvane KS 67110
316 777-1129

(G-7222)
MID-KANSAS MACHINE & TOOL
1057 E 147th Ave N (67110-8314)
PHONE..................................316 777-1189
Don Gilliam, *President*
Christine Gilliam, *Corp Secy*
EMP: 6
SQ FT: 9,000
SALES (est): 787.9K **Privately Held**
SIC: 3599 Machine shop, jobbing & repair

(G-7223)
MULVANE COOPERATIVE UNION INC (PA)
220 Poplar St (67110-1795)
PHONE..................................316 777-1121
Martin Paris, *Manager*
Spencer Branine, *Manager*
Mel Schanz, *Clerk*
EMP: 17
SQ FT: 3,000
SALES (est): 9.1MM **Privately Held**
SIC: 5153 5191 5171 Grains; feed; seeds: field, garden & flower; fertilizer & fertilizer materials; chemicals, agricultural; petroleum bulk stations

(G-7224)
MULVANE FAMILY MEDCENTER
1004 Se Louis Dr (67110-1109)
PHONE..................................316 777-0176
Antonio Carro MD, *Owner*
EMP: 10
SALES (est): 707.7K **Privately Held**
SIC: 8011 General & family practice, physician/surgeon

(G-7225)
MULVANE NEWS AND BANDWAGON
204 W Main St (67110-1765)
P.O. Box 157 (67110-0157)
PHONE..................................316 777-4233
Mike Robinson, *Owner*
Mike Robibson, *Partner*
Lynda Robinson, *Partner*
EMP: 5
SQ FT: 2,300
SALES (est): 374K **Privately Held**
SIC: 2711 Newspapers: publishing only, not printed on site

(G-7226)
PAC MIG INC
1002 Se Louis Dr (67110-1109)
PHONE..................................316 269-3040
Joseph Cusick, *CEO*
Brian Cusick, *President*
EMP: 8
SQ FT: 9,600
SALES (est): 760K **Privately Held**
WEB: www.pacmig.com
SIC: 3548 5084 Welding & cutting apparatus & accessories; welding machinery & equipment

(G-7227)
STROOT LOCKER INC
115 N 1st Ave (67110-1771)
PHONE..................................316 777-4421
Fred Stroot, *President*
EMP: 9
SALES (corp-wide): 1.4MM **Privately Held**
SIC: 2011 5421 Meat packing plants; meat markets, including freezer provisioners
PA: Stroot Locker Inc
111 N Main St
Goddard KS 67052
316 794-8762

(G-7228)
TODAYS TOMORROWS LRNG CTR LLC
Also Called: Cynthia's Playhouse
1639 N Timbers Edge Ct (67110-1123)
PHONE..................................888 602-1815
Jerome Christmon, *Mng Member*
Cynthia Christmon, *Mng Member*
EMP: 10
SALES: 500K **Privately Held**
SIC: 8351 Group day care center

Munden
Republic County

(G-7229)
PROHOE MFG LLC
204 Munden Ave (66959-5002)
P.O. Box 87 (66959-0087)
PHONE..................................785 987-5450
Loren G Kisby, *Mng Member*
EMP: 12
SQ FT: 6,000
SALES (est): 442.8K **Privately Held**
WEB: www.prohoe.com
SIC: 3524 Lawn & garden equipment

Nashville
Kingman County

(G-7230)
S & G WATER SERVICE INC
10286 Sw 170 Ave (67112-8336)
P.O. Box 40, Spivey (67142-0040)
PHONE..................................620 246-5212
Scott Adelhardt, *President*
Joan Adelhardt, *Corp Secy*
Gary Adelhart, *Vice Pres*
EMP: 5
SALES: 400K **Privately Held**
SIC: 1389 Oil field services

Natoma
Osborne County

(G-7231)
MACCONNELL ENTERPRISES LLC
Also Called: Pioneer Toy Company
102 N Main St (67651-9731)
PHONE..................................785 885-8081
Matthew Macconnell, *Mng Member*
EMP: 34
SALES (est): 319K **Privately Held**
SIC: 4212 7538 5531 Mail carriers, contract; diesel engine repair: automotive; automotive tires

(G-7232)
NALCO COMPANY LLC
419 6th St (67651-9714)
PHONE..................................785 885-4161
EMP: 10
SALES (corp-wide): 14.6B **Publicly Held**
SIC: 2992 Lubricating oils
HQ: Nalco Company Llc
1601 W Diehl Rd
Naperville IL 60563
630 305-1000

(G-7233)
TASLER INC
Also Called: Schneider Pallets
2716 W 210th Dr (67651-9326)
PHONE..................................785 885-4533
Donald Schneider, *Branch Mgr*
EMP: 8
SALES (corp-wide): 16.6MM **Privately Held**
SIC: 3086 Packaging & shipping materials, foamed plastic
PA: Tasler, Inc.
1804 Tasler Dr
Webster City IA 50595
515 832-5200

Neodesha
Wilson County

(G-7234)
AIROSOL CO INC
1101 Illinois St (66757-1475)
P.O. Box 120 (66757-0120)
PHONE..................................620 325-2666
Carl G Stratemeier, *President*
▲ **EMP:** 30 **EST:** 1949
SQ FT: 112,000
SALES (est): 12MM **Privately Held**
WEB: www.airosol.com
SIC: 5169 Aerosols

(G-7235)
CITY OF NEODESHA
Also Called: Neodesha Fire Department
112 S 4th St (66757-1706)
PHONE..................................620 325-2642
Duane Bandet, *Branch Mgr*
EMP: 11 **Privately Held**
WEB: www.neodesha.com
SIC: 9224 8322 ; fire department, not including volunteer; emergency social services

GEOGRAPHIC

PA: City Of Neodesha
1407 N 8th St
Neodesha KS 66757
620 325-2828

(G-7236)
COBALT BOATS LLC (PA)
1715 N 8th St (66757-1283)
PHONE....620 325-2653
Sean Callan, *CEO*
Gary Schultz, *Senior VP*
Garry Lambert, *Vice Pres*
Mindy Buoy, *Purch Agent*
Cody Smith, *Purchasing*
▼ **EMP:** 480
SQ FT: 350,000
SALES: 132.4MM **Privately Held**
WEB: www.cobaltboats.com
SIC: 3732 Boats, fiberglass: building & repairing

(G-7237)
COMMUNITY NATIONAL BANK
Also Called: First National Bank
102 N 4th St (66757-1508)
P.O. Box 300 (66757-0300)
PHONE....620 325-2900
Rod Frobe, *Manager*
EMP: 11 **Privately Held**
SIC: 6022 State commercial banks
HQ: Community National Bank & Trust
14 N Lincoln Ave
Chanute KS 66720

(G-7238)
CONTRACTORS ENGINEER INC
7563 Quinter Dr (66757-1495)
PHONE....620 568-2391
Dave Kramer, *President*
David Kramer, *Treasurer*
EMP: 15
SQ FT: 16,000
SALES (est): 3.9MM **Privately Held**
SIC: 3444 Concrete forms, sheet metal

(G-7239)
ELK COUNTY DEVELOPMENT CORP
Also Called: NEW BEGINING ENTERPRISES
1001 Wilson St (66757-1981)
P.O. Box 344 (66757-0344)
PHONE....620 325-3333
Joe O'Rourke, *President*
Kirbie Hutchinson, *Property Mgr*
EMP: 40
SALES: 45.8K **Privately Held**
SIC: 8699 Charitable organization

(G-7240)
FIRST NEODESHA BANK (HQ)
Also Called: SOUTHEAST CHECK PRINTING
524 Main St (66757-1739)
P.O. Box 538, Chanute (66720-0538)
PHONE....620 325-2632
Casey Lair, *President*
Nancy Loflin, *Vice Pres*
D Lee Steanson, *Vice Pres*
EMP: 14 **EST:** 1872
SQ FT: 5,000
SALES: 4.7MM **Privately Held**
SIC: 6022 State trust companies accepting deposits, commercial

(G-7241)
FOCALPOINT IMAGING LLC
3347 County Road 6400 (66757-9101)
PHONE....620 325-2298
Joni Scott, *Principal*
EMP: 5 **EST:** 2014
SALES (est): 424.7K **Privately Held**
SIC: 3823 8713 Digital displays of process variables;

(G-7242)
FOUR CNTY MENTAL HLTH CTR INC
101 S 8th St (66757-1611)
P.O. Box 688, Independence (67301-0688)
PHONE....620 325-2141
Greg Hennen, *Exec Dir*
Jodi Hayse, *Director*
EMP: 11
SALES (corp-wide): 15.9MM **Privately Held**
SIC: 8093 Mental health clinic, outpatient
PA: Four County Mental Health Center, Inc.
3751 W Main St
Independence KS 67301
620 331-1748

(G-7243)
GBW RAILCAR SERVICES LLC
701 Klayder Dr (66757-1983)
PHONE....620 325-3001
Dion Wilkins, *Branch Mgr*
EMP: 70
SALES (corp-wide): 3B **Publicly Held**
SIC: 4789 Railroad car repair
HQ: Gbw Railcar Services, L.L.C.
4350 Nw Front Ave
Portland OR 97210

(G-7244)
MEDICAL LODGES INC
Also Called: Grand Villas
400 Fir St (66757-1298)
PHONE....620 325-2244
Terri Greaves, *Manager*
EMP: 25
SALES (est): 454.8K **Privately Held**
WEB: www.grandvillas.com
SIC: 8361 Home for the aged

(G-7245)
NEODESHA PLASTICS INC (PA)
1206 Worley Dr Twin Twin Rivers (66757)
P.O. Box 539 (66757-0539)
PHONE....620 325-3096
Theodore K Peitz, *President*
Sophie Peitz, *Vice Pres*
Chris Tinsley, *Vice Pres*
Wanda Fink, *Administration*
▼ **EMP:** 50
SQ FT: 105,000
SALES (est): 13.5MM **Privately Held**
WEB: www.neodeshaplasticsinc.com
SIC: 3089 Injection molding of plastics; plastic processing

(G-7246)
NEODESHA PLASTICS INC
1000 Reece St (66757)
PHONE....620 325-3096
Wanda Fink, *Office Mgr*
EMP: 40
SALES (corp-wide): 13.5MM **Privately Held**
SIC: 3089 Plastic processing
PA: Neodesha Plastics, Inc.
1206 Worley Dr Twin Twin Rivers
Neodesha KS 66757
620 325-3096

(G-7247)
R & S CONSTRUCTION INC
221 S 11th St (66757-1630)
PHONE....620 325-2130
Rodney Schlegel, *President*
Darlene Schlegel, *Admin Sec*
EMP: 10
SQ FT: 960
SALES: 2MM **Privately Held**
SIC: 1771 Concrete pumping

(G-7248)
SANDS LEVEL AND TOOL COMPANY
Also Called: Sands Level & Tool Div
1250 Tank Ave (66757)
P.O. Box 370 (66757-0370)
PHONE....620 325-2687
Ron Meiur, *CEO*
David Harmon, *General Mgr*
▲ **EMP:** 65
SQ FT: 60,000
SALES (est): 9.2MM **Privately Held**
WEB: www.harmon.com
SIC: 3423 3829 Carpenters' hand tools, except saws: levels, chisels, etc.; measuring & controlling devices

(G-7249)
SOUTHEAST BANCSHARES INC
Also Called: First Neodesha Bank
524 Main St (66757-1739)
P.O. Box 150 (66757-0150)
PHONE....620 325-2632
Casey Lair, *President*
EMP: 19 **Privately Held**
SIC: 6022 State commercial banks
PA: Southeast Bancshares Inc
101 W Main St
Chanute KS 66720

(G-7250)
WILSON COUNTY HOSPITAL (PA)
Also Called: WILSON MEDICAL CENTER
2600 Ottawa Rd (66757-1897)
P.O. Box 360 (66757-0360)
PHONE....620 325-2611
Dennis Shelby, *CEO*
John Gutshenritter, *CFO*
EMP: 110 **EST:** 1913
SQ FT: 28,400
SALES: 18.5MM **Privately Held**
WEB: www.wilsoncountyhospital.org
SIC: 8062 General medical & surgical hospitals

Ness City
Ness County

(G-7251)
ALLIANCE AG AND GRAIN LLC
918 W Sycamore St (67560-1402)
PHONE....785 798-3775
Tom Redman, *General Mgr*
EMP: 10
SALES (corp-wide): 55.1MM **Privately Held**
SIC: 5153 4221 Grains; grain elevator, storage only
PA: Alliance Ag And Grain, Llc
313 N Main St
Spearville KS 67876
620 385-2898

(G-7252)
BOJACK ROUSTABOUT LLC
11457 R Rd (67560-6142)
PHONE....785 798-3504
Wendy Hoss, *Owner*
EMP: 5
SALES (est): 732.3K **Privately Held**
SIC: 1389 Roustabout service

(G-7253)
BTI NESS CITY
Also Called: John Deere Authorized Dealer
118 S 7th St (67560-1700)
P.O. Box 440 (67560-0440)
PHONE....785 798-2251
Kelly Estes, *Owner*
EMP: 20
SALES (est): 1.9MM
SALES (corp-wide): 44.7MM **Privately Held**
WEB: www.gti-bti.com
SIC: 5261 5082 Lawnmowers & tractors; construction & mining machinery
PA: The Bucklin Tractor & Implement Company Inc
115 W Railroad St
Bucklin KS 67834
620 826-3271

(G-7254)
CHC MCPHERSON REFINERY INC
2000 S Kansas (67560)
P.O. Box 398 (67560-0398)
PHONE....785 798-3684
Bob Wyatt, *Manager*
EMP: 9
SALES (corp-wide): 31.9B **Publicly Held**
SIC: 4213 2911 Contract haulers; petroleum refining
HQ: Chs Mcpherson Refinery Inc.
2000 S Main St
Mcpherson KS 67460
620 241-2340

(G-7255)
CHEYENNE OIL SERVICES INC
118 N Pennsylvania Ave (67560-1634)
P.O. Box 384 (67560-0384)
PHONE....785 798-2282
Paul Cambron, *President*
Marilyn Cambron, *Treasurer*
EMP: 45 **EST:** 1957
SALES (est): 2.5MM **Privately Held**
SIC: 1389 Oil field services

(G-7256)
CHEYENNE WELL SERVICE INC (PA)
118 N Pennsylvania Ave (67560-1634)
P.O. Box 384 (67560-0384)
PHONE....785 798-2282
Paul Cambron, *President*
Marilyn Cambron, *Treasurer*
EMP: 17
SQ FT: 4,000
SALES (est): 5.4MM **Privately Held**
SIC: 1381 1389 Service well drilling; servicing oil & gas wells

(G-7257)
COBANK ACB
Also Called: Farm Credit Ness City F L C A
101 Eagle Dr (67560-1001)
PHONE....785 798-2278
Scott Stockwell, *Manager*
EMP: 13
SALES (corp-wide): 4.3B **Privately Held**
WEB: www.usagbank.com
SIC: 6159 Agricultural credit institutions
PA: Cobank, Acb
6340 S Fiddlers Green Cir
Greenwood Village CO 80111
303 740-6527

(G-7258)
CRAIG HOMECARE
103 S Iowa Ave (67560-1901)
P.O. Box 443 (67560-0443)
PHONE....785 798-4821
Richard Giblin, *President*
EMP: 35 **EST:** 1993
SALES (est): 540.7K **Privately Held**
SIC: 8082 Home health care services

(G-7259)
D & S MACHINE AND WELDING INC
N Hwy 283 (67560)
P.O. Box 461 (67560-0461)
PHONE....785 798-3359
Andy Fellhoelter, *President*
Pat Fellhoelter, *Vice Pres*
EMP: 8
SQ FT: 14,000
SALES: 1.1MM **Privately Held**
SIC: 3599 7699 Machine shop, jobbing & repair; farm machinery repair

(G-7260)
D E BONDURANT GRAIN CO INC
Also Called: Ness City Farm and Feed
223 S Iowa Ave (67560-1903)
P.O. Box 280 (67560-0280)
PHONE....785 798-3322
Gary Gantz, *President*
Colby Gatz, *Vice Pres*
Debbie Foos, *Admin Sec*
EMP: 20 **EST:** 1888
SALES (est): 1.3MM **Privately Held**
SIC: 4221 5153 Grain elevator, storage only; grains

(G-7261)
DERRICK INN
409 E Sycamore St (67560-1925)
P.O. Box 454 (67560-0454)
PHONE....785 798-3617
Men Nguyen, *Owner*
Shelley Clemens, *Manager*
EMP: 25
SALES (est): 422.8K **Privately Held**
SIC: 7011 Hotel, franchised

(G-7262)
FIRST STATE BANK
206 N Pennsylvania Ave (67560-1636)
P.O. Box 397 (67560-0397)
PHONE....785 798-2212
Boyd Beutler, *Ch of Bd*
Kevin Beutler, *President*
Ron Stoecklein, *Vice Pres*
EMP: 11 **EST:** 1906
SQ FT: 5,000
SALES: 2.2MM **Privately Held**
SIC: 6022 State trust companies accepting deposits, commercial

▲ = Import ▼=Export
◆ =Import/Export

(G-7263)
GABEL LEASE SERVICE INC
319 W Sycamore St (67560-1830)
P.O. Box 405 (67560-0405)
PHONE..................................785 798-3122
Brian Gabel, *President*
▲ **EMP:** 7 **EST:** 1996
SALES (est): 793.5K **Privately Held**
SIC: 1389 Oil field services

(G-7264)
NESS COUNTY ENGINEERS OFFICE
12330 Us Highway 283 (67560-6149)
PHONE..................................785 798-3350
Fred Flax, *Chairman*
EMP: 25
SALES (est): 1.5MM **Privately Held**
SIC: 1611 Highway & street maintenance

(G-7265)
NESS COUNTY HOSPITAL DST NO 2
312 Custer St (67560-1654)
PHONE..................................785 798-2107
Mary Schwindt, *Manager*
Krina Filbert, *Director*
Katie Luetters, *Director*
Marlena Koerner, *Nursing Dir*
Lisa Flax, *Business Dir*
EMP: 125
SQ FT: 37,000
SALES: 8.6MM **Privately Held**
WEB: www.nchospital.org
SIC: 8062 Hospital, affiliated with AMA residency

(G-7266)
RICHS ROUSTABOUT SERVICE INC
1020 N Pennsylvania (67560)
P.O. Box 400 (67560-0400)
PHONE..................................785 798-3323
Lanny Unruh, *President*
Vicki Unruh, *Corp Secy*
EMP: 5
SQ FT: 2,500
SALES (est): 678.5K **Privately Held**
SIC: 1389 Roustabout service

(G-7267)
SWIFT SERVICES INC
100 S Pennsylvania Ave (67560-1938)
P.O. Box 466 (67560-0466)
PHONE..................................785 798-2380
Ted Fuchs, *President*
EMP: 20
SQ FT: 4,800
SALES (est): 7.6MM **Privately Held**
WEB: www.gbea.net
SIC: 1389 Oil field services

(G-7268)
WELL WATCH LLC
804 E Cedar St (67560-1737)
PHONE..................................785 798-0020
Brad Seib,
EMP: 6
SQ FT: 1,600
SALES (est): 1.3MM **Privately Held**
SIC: 3561 Pumps, oil well & field

New Cambria
Saline County

(G-7269)
ARCHER-DANIELS-MIDLAND COMPANY
Also Called: ADM
1884a E Old Highway 40 (67470-8609)
PHONE..................................785 820-8831
Mark Wegner, *Principal*
EMP: 6
SALES (corp-wide): 64.3B **Publicly Held**
WEB: www.collingwoodgrain.com
SIC: 2041 Flour & other grain mill products
PA: Archer-Daniels-Midland Company
77 W Wacker Dr Ste 4600
Chicago IL 60601
312 634-8100

(G-7270)
FARMER DIRECT FOODS INC
5641 E Mariposa Rd (67470-8535)
PHONE..................................785 823-8787
Mark Fowler, *CEO*
Ian Goding, *Manager*
Arissa Moyer, *Office Admin*
Charles Ayers, *Director*
Maurice Bleumer, *Director*
EMP: 13
SQ FT: 22,000
SALES: 3.2MM **Privately Held**
WEB: www.farmerdirectfoods.com
SIC: 0723 2041 Cash grain crops market preparation services; wheat flour

New Century
Johnson County

(G-7271)
BUTLER AVIONICS INC
Also Called: King's Avionics Inc
280 Gardner Dr Ste 3 (66031-1104)
PHONE..................................913 829-4606
David B Hayden, *President*
Gary L Morris, *Treasurer*
EMP: 18
SQ FT: 5,000
SALES (est): 4.7MM
SALES (corp-wide): 58.7MM **Publicly Held**
WEB: www.kingsavionics.net
SIC: 5599 7699 Aircraft instruments, equipment or parts; aircraft flight instrument repair
PA: Butler National Corporation
19920 W 161st St
Olathe KS 66062
913 780-9595

(G-7272)
CAV ICE PROTECTION INC
30 Leawood Dr (66031-1152)
PHONE..................................913 738-5391
David Owen McSarlane, *President*
Ian Jackson, *VP Opers*
EMP: 21
SALES: 5.4MM **Privately Held**
WEB: www.weepingwings.com
SIC: 5088 4581 Aircraft equipment & supplies; aircraft servicing & repairing

(G-7273)
CENTURYLINK INC
600 New Century Pkwy (66031-1101)
PHONE..................................913 791-4971
Douglas Cea, *Project Mgr*
Mark Crowley, *Senior Engr*
Phillip Burks, *Branch Mgr*
Kim Bruce, *Manager*
Richard Crossen, *Technology*
EMP: 23
SALES (corp-wide): 23.4B **Publicly Held**
SIC: 4813 Local & long distance telephone communications
PA: Centurylink, Inc.
100 Centurylink Dr
Monroe LA 71203
318 388-9000

(G-7274)
CONOPCO INC
Unilever Bestfoods
27080 W 159th St (66031-1129)
PHONE..................................913 782-7171
Ian Ricketts, *Branch Mgr*
EMP: 126
SALES (corp-wide): 56.5B **Privately Held**
SIC: 2844 Toilet preparations
HQ: Conopco, Inc.
700 Sylvan Ave
Englewood Cliffs NJ 07632
201 894-7760

(G-7275)
DANISCO INGREDIENTS USA INC
4 New Century Pkwy (66031-1144)
PHONE..................................913 764-8100
▼ **EMP:** 15 **EST:** 2011
SALES (est): 3.5MM **Privately Held**
SIC: 2099 Food preparations

(G-7276)
DANISCO USA INC (DH)
4 New Century Pkwy (66031-1144)
PHONE..................................913 764-8100
Germain Despres, *President*
Corinne Renaudie, *VP Finance*
Bill Swanson, *Finance Other*
Steve St Arnold, *Finance*
Renee Brown, *Accounts Mgr*
◆ **EMP:** 250
SALES (est): 147.3MM
SALES (corp-wide): 30.6B **Publicly Held**
SIC: 2099 Emulsifiers, food
HQ: E. I. Du Pont De Nemours And Company
974 Centre Rd Bldg 735
Wilmington DE 19805
302 485-3000

(G-7277)
DANISCO USA INC
201 Century Pkwy (66031)
PHONE..................................913 764-8100
Germain Despres, *Branch Mgr*
EMP: 200
SALES (corp-wide): 30.6B **Publicly Held**
SIC: 5169 5963 Food additives & preservatives; manmade fibers; swimming pool & spa chemicals; food services, direct sales
HQ: Danisco Usa Inc.
4 New Century Pkwy
New Century KS 66031
913 764-8100

(G-7278)
DEELLIOTTE COMPANY INC
201 Prairie Village Dr (66031-1115)
PHONE..................................913 764-0606
H Dwane Smith, *Ch of Bd*
James R Erhart, *President*
John Krayca, *Opers Mgr*
Paul Hayman, *Sales Executive*
Debbie Moeder, *Manager*
▲ **EMP:** 80
SQ FT: 45,000
SALES: 18.3MM **Privately Held**
WEB: www.deelliotte.com
SIC: 2673 Plastic bags: made from purchased materials

(G-7279)
DILIGENCE INC
Also Called: Russell-Hampton Co
110 Leawood Dr (66031-1136)
PHONE..................................913 254-0500
Robert C Lowe, *President*
Joe Beveridge, *Vice Pres*
Bradley J Lowe, *Vice Pres*
Kathrin Ditlevson, *Purch Mgr*
Tom Hansen, *Treasurer*
▲ **EMP:** 25 **EST:** 1920
SQ FT: 23,700
SALES (est): 8.7MM **Privately Held**
SIC: 5199 5961 Advertising specialties; mail order house

(G-7280)
DOMESTIC FASTENER & FORGE INC
150 New Century Pkwy B (66031-1150)
P.O. Box 14642, Shawnee Mission (66285-4642)
PHONE..................................913 888-9447
William G Mullin, *President*
Brian Brooks, *Vice Pres*
EMP: 15
SQ FT: 12,000
SALES (est): 2.6MM **Privately Held**
WEB: www.domesticfastener.com
SIC: 3965 5085 Fasteners; fasteners, industrial: nuts, bolts, screws, etc.

(G-7281)
DUKE REALTY CORPORATION
27200 W 157th St (66031-1114)
PHONE..................................913 829-1453
EMP: 61
SALES (corp-wide): 902.2MM **Privately Held**
SIC: 6531 Real Estate Agent/Manager
PA: Duke Realty Corporation
600 E 96th St Ste 100
Indianapolis IN 46240
317 808-6000

(G-7282)
E I DU PONT DE NEMOURS & CO
Also Called: Dupont Denisco Plant
4 New Century Pkwy (66031-1144)
PHONE..................................302 774-1000
Byron Harper, *Human Res Mgr*
Wendy Curry, *Accounts Mgr*
Joseph Barber, *Branch Mgr*
Jerry Stumpf, *Manager*
Eric Tovey, *Analyst*
EMP: 16
SALES (corp-wide): 30.6B **Publicly Held**
SIC: 2834 2899 Pharmaceutical preparations; chemical preparations
HQ: E. I. Du Pont De Nemours And Company
974 Centre Rd Bldg 735
Wilmington DE 19805
302 485-3000

(G-7283)
E I DU PONT DE NEMOURS & CO
Also Called: Danisco
4 New Century Pkwy (66031-1144)
PHONE..................................913 764-8100
David Estell, *President*
Pamela Beach, *Vice Pres*
Philip Johnson, *Vice Pres*
Carol Rethemeyer, *Vice Pres*
Verna Howell, *Purchasing*
EMP: 200
SALES (corp-wide): 30.6B **Publicly Held**
SIC: 5169 Food additives & preservatives
HQ: E. I. Du Pont De Nemours And Company
974 Centre Rd Bldg 735
Wilmington DE 19805
302 485-3000

(G-7284)
EXECUTIVE BEECHCRAFT INC
280 Gardner Dr (66031-1134)
PHONE..................................913 782-9003
Sean Hutman, *Manager*
EMP: 20
SALES (corp-wide): 2.3B **Privately Held**
WEB: www.executivebeechcraft.com
SIC: 5172 7699 5599 4581 Aircraft fueling services; aircraft & heavy equipment repair services; aircraft, self-propelled; aircraft storage at airports
HQ: Executive Beechcraft, Inc.
10 Nw Richards Rd
Kansas City MO 64116
816 842-8484

(G-7285)
GARMIN INTERNATIONAL INC
151 New Century Pkwy (66031-1139)
PHONE..................................913 440-8462
EMP: 7
SALES (corp-wide): 261.7K **Privately Held**
SIC: 3812 Search & navigation equipment
HQ: Garmin International, Inc.
1200 E 151st St
Olathe KS 66062

(G-7286)
HEARTLAND PRECISION FAS INC
301 Prairie Village Dr (66031-1121)
PHONE..................................913 829-4447
Dave Rose, *President*
Teddie Clark, *Vice Pres*
Kyle Dye, *Production*
Mark Mueller, *Purch Mgr*
Bart Cohen, *Shareholder*
EMP: 76
SQ FT: 30,000
SALES (est): 13.5MM **Privately Held**
WEB: www.heartlandfasteners.com
SIC: 3452 Bolts, nuts, rivets & washers

(G-7287)
HIPERFORMANCE LLC
Also Called: Aerocharger
402 New Century Pkwy (66031-1153)
PHONE..................................913 829-3400
Nathan Haring, *Opers Staff*
Brad Riley,
EMP: 8
SQ FT: 2,500
SALES: 2.6MM **Privately Held**
SIC: 3724 Turbo-superchargers, aircraft

(G-7288)
HONEYWELL INTERNATIONAL INC
101 New Century Pkwy (66031-1117)
PHONE....................................913 712-6017
Greg Triplett, *Principal*
EMP: 35
SALES (corp-wide): 41.8B **Publicly Held**
WEB: www.honeywell.com
SIC: 3724 Aircraft engines & engine parts
PA: Honeywell International Inc.
300 S Tryon St
Charlotte NC 28202
973 455-2000

(G-7289)
HOWELL MOULDINGS LC
201 Overland Park Pl (66031-1103)
PHONE....................................913 782-0500
Matt Murray, *Plant Mgr*
Thomas Howell,
Sandy Howell,
Johnetta Hume,
Mat Murray,
EMP: 40
SQ FT: 185,000
SALES (est): 6.7MM **Privately Held**
SIC: 2899 2499 Plastic wood; picture & mirror frames, wood

(G-7290)
KERRY INC
Kerry Ingredients
400 Prairie Village Dr (66031-1123)
PHONE....................................913 780-1212
Scott Scharinger, *Manager*
EMP: 240 **Privately Held**
WEB: www.kerryingredients.com
SIC: 2066 2099 2023 2079 Baking chocolate; food preparations; dry, condensed, evaporated dairy products; edible fats & oils; fluid milk; chocolate
HQ: Kerry Inc.
3400 Millington Rd
Beloit WI 53511
608 363-1200

(G-7291)
KGP PRODUCTS INC
Also Called: Premier
600 New Century Pkwy (66031-1101)
PHONE....................................800 755-1950
Kathleen G Putrah, *CEO*
▲ **EMP:** 179
SQ FT: 472,000
SALES (est): 94.2MM
SALES (corp-wide): 1.4B **Privately Held**
SIC: 3661 Telephones & telephone apparatus; facsimile equipment
PA: Kgp Telecommunications, Llc
3305 Highway 60 W
Faribault MN 55021
507 334-2268

(G-7292)
KGP TELECOMMUNICATIONS INC
600 New Century Pkwy (66031-1101)
PHONE....................................800 755-1950
Dale G Putrah, *Principal*
EMP: 52
SALES (corp-wide): 1.4B **Privately Held**
SIC: 5065 Telephone equipment
PA: Kgp Telecommunications, Llc
3305 Highway 60 W
Faribault MN 55021
507 334-2268

(G-7293)
METALWEST LLC
201 Leawood Dr (66031-1124)
PHONE....................................913 829-8585
Richard Williams, *Marketing Mgr*
Mike Severin, *Branch Mgr*
John Lawless, *Branch Mgr*
EMP: 60
SALES (corp-wide): 213MM **Privately Held**
WEB: www.metalwest.com
SIC: 5051 Steel
HQ: Metalwest, L.L.C.
1229 Fulton St
Brighton CO 80601
303 654-0300

(G-7294)
NEW CENTURY AIR
2 Aero Plz (66031-1110)
P.O. Box 19, Rantoul (66079-0019)
PHONE....................................913 768-9400
Brandy Nichols, *Opers Mgr*
Tom Stellwag, *Manager*
Robert Dodson Jr, *Info Tech Mgr*
EMP: 10
SALES (est): 1MM **Privately Held**
SIC: 4581 Airports, flying fields & services

(G-7295)
PCDISPOSALCOM LLC
400 New Century Pkwy (66031-1111)
PHONE....................................913 980-4750
Germain Despres, *Principal*
Chris McConnell, *Vice Pres*
Paul Sackett, *Human Res Dir*
John Breeden, *Sales Mgr*
Kevin Paul, *Technical Staff*
EMP: 50
SALES (est): 2.6MM **Privately Held**
SIC: 4953 Non-hazardous waste disposal sites

(G-7296)
ROYAL TRACTOR COMPANY INC
109 Overland Park Pl (66031-1125)
P.O. Box 480215, Kansas City MO (64148-0215)
PHONE....................................913 782-2598
Thomas Hardwick, *President*
Jack Garfinkle, *Vice Pres*
▼ **EMP:** 28 **EST:** 1970
SQ FT: 85,000
SALES (est): 9.3MM **Privately Held**
SIC: 3537 3532 5084 Forklift trucks; mining machinery; lift trucks & parts

(G-7297)
SAUER BRANDS INC
101 Prairie Village Dr (66031-1112)
PHONE....................................913 324-3700
William W Lovette, *CEO*
EMP: 174
SALES (corp-wide): 74.9MM **Privately Held**
SIC: 2079 Margarine, including imitation
PA: Sauer Brands, Inc.
2000 W Broad St
Richmond VA 23220
804 359-5786

(G-7298)
STAR INNOVATIONS II LLC
Also Called: Ballstars
100 Mission Woods Dr (66031-1151)
PHONE....................................913 764-7738
Scott K Weidler, *Prdtn Mgr*
Marshall Widman,
EMP: 20
SQ FT: 30,000
SALES (est): 2.3MM **Privately Held**
WEB: www.starinnovations.com
SIC: 3949 3555 Baseball, softball & cricket sports equipment; printing trades machinery

(G-7299)
STEEL AND PIPE SUPPLY CO INC
401 New Century Pkwy (66031-1127)
P.O. Box 31 (66031)
PHONE....................................913 768-4333
Ed Bare, *Branch Mgr*
EMP: 56
SALES (corp-wide): 409.8MM **Privately Held**
SIC: 5051 Steel
HQ: Steel And Pipe Supply Company, Inc.
555 Poyntz Ave Ste 122
Manhattan KS 66502
785 587-5100

(G-7300)
STENNER SALES COMPANY
401 Prairie Village Dr (66031-1116)
PHONE....................................913 768-4114
Perla Garcia, *Branch Mgr*
EMP: 8
SALES (corp-wide): 13.3MM **Privately Held**
SIC: 3561 5251 Pump jacks & other pumping equipment; pumps & pumping equipment
PA: Stenner Pump Company, Inc.
3174 Desalvo Rd
Jacksonville FL 32246
904 641-1666

(G-7301)
STOUSE LLC (PA)
300 New Century Pkwy (66031-1128)
P.O. Box 3, Gardner (66030-0003)
PHONE....................................913 764-5757
Clay Davis, *President*
Bary Marquardt, *President*
William J Lewis, *Vice Pres*
Carol Byard, *Accounts Mgr*
Crissy Martinez, *Accounts Exec*
◆ **EMP:** 107 **EST:** 1977
SQ FT: 180,000
SALES (est): 56MM **Privately Held**
WEB: www.stouse.com
SIC: 2752 3993 2396 Poster & decal printing, lithographic; signs & advertising specialties; automotive & apparel trimmings

(G-7302)
UNITED MANUFACTURING INC
301 Overland Park Pl (66031-1105)
PHONE....................................913 780-0056
Thomas Howell, *President*
Frank V George, *Vice Pres*
Sandra Howell, *Treasurer*
Beverly Sheridan, *Director*
EMP: 30
SQ FT: 95,000
SALES (est): 5MM **Privately Held**
SIC: 3699 2449 3412 2441 Electrical equipment & supplies; rectangular boxes & crates, wood; metal barrels, drums & pails; nailed wood boxes & shook

New Strawn
Coffey County

(G-7303)
B & H APPLIANCE
330 N 3rd St (66839-9002)
PHONE....................................620 364-8700
Mark Harris, *Owner*
EMP: 12
SALES (est): 280K **Privately Held**
SIC: 7629 Electrical repair shops

(G-7304)
ROCK CREEK TECHNOLOGIES LLC
117 Osage St (66839-9119)
PHONE....................................620 364-1400
Gregg Clarkson, *Partner*
Denise McNabb, *Partner*
EMP: 24
SALES (est): 1.1MM **Privately Held**
SIC: 8711 Consulting engineer

(G-7305)
SKILLMAN CONSTRUCTION LLC
345 N Main St (66839-8933)
PHONE....................................620 364-2505
Mike Skillman, *Mng Member*
Jo Skillman, *Mng Member*
EMP: 80
SQ FT: 16,000
SALES: 14.4MM **Privately Held**
SIC: 1611 Gravel or dirt road construction

Newton
Harvey County

(G-7306)
ADRIAN & PANKRATZ PA
301 N Main St Ste 400 (67114-3464)
P.O. Box 825 (67114-0825)
PHONE....................................316 283-8746
Thomas A Adrian, *Partner*
Randall Pankratz, *Partner*
Marilyn M Wilder, *Partner*
Debbie Murry, *Admin Sec*
EMP: 16
SQ FT: 2,600
SALES (est): 1.2MM **Privately Held**
SIC: 8111 General practice attorney, lawyer

(G-7307)
ADRIAN MANUFACTURING INC
191 120th (67114-7916)
PHONE....................................507 381-9746
Duane Adrian, *President*
Sharon Adrian, *Corp Secy*
EMP: 6
SALES: 75K **Privately Held**
SIC: 3523 Farm machinery & equipment

(G-7308)
AIR CAPITAL STUCCO L L C
124 W 8th St (67114-1938)
PHONE....................................316 650-2450
Leslie Graves,
EMP: 24
SQ FT: 2,000
SALES (est): 3MM **Privately Held**
SIC: 5032 Stucco

(G-7309)
ANESTHESIA BILLING INC
1715 Medical Pkwy Ste 200 (67114-9042)
PHONE....................................316 281-3700
Phillip Blann, *President*
EMP: 30 **EST:** 2001
SALES (est): 2.6MM **Privately Held**
SIC: 8721 Billing & bookkeeping service

(G-7310)
APRIA HEALTHCARE LLC
2305 S Kansas Rd (67114-9009)
PHONE....................................316 283-1936
EMP: 23
SALES (corp-wide): 2.4B **Privately Held**
SIC: 8082 Home Health Care Services
HQ: Apria Healthcare Llc
26220 Enterprise Ct
Lake Forest CA 92630
949 616-2606

(G-7311)
ASBURY PARK INC
200 Sw 14th St (67114-4701)
PHONE....................................316 283-4770
Tom Williams, *CEO*
EMP: 240
SQ FT: 90,000
SALES: 10.1MM **Privately Held**
WEB: www.asbury-park.org
SIC: 8052 Personal care facility

(G-7312)
ASSOCIATES IN WOMENS HEALTH PA
700 Medical Center Dr # 120 (67114-9016)
PHONE....................................316 283-4153
Jennifer Streier, *Branch Mgr*
EMP: 12
SALES (corp-wide): 5.5MM **Privately Held**
SIC: 8011 Gynecologist
PA: Associates In Women's Health, Pa
3232 E Murdock St
Wichita KS 67208
316 219-6777

(G-7313)
AVCON INDUSTRIES INC
714 N Oliver Rd (67114-9444)
P.O. Box 748 (67114-0748)
PHONE....................................913 780-9595
Clark D Stewart, *CEO*
Larry W Franke, *President*
Marcus Abendroth, *Vice Pres*
John Solonynka, *QC Mgr*
David Lanning, *Engineer*
EMP: 40 **EST:** 1994
SALES (est): 7.6MM
SALES (corp-wide): 58.7MM **Publicly Held**
WEB: www.butlernationalcorp.com
SIC: 3728 3721 Aircraft parts & equipment; aircraft
PA: Butler National Corporation
19920 W 161st St
Olathe KS 66062
913 780-9595

(G-7314)
AXTELL CLINIC P A
700 Medical Center Dr # 210 (67114-4446)
PHONE....................................316 283-2800
Brooke Dunlavy, *Med Doctor*
Robyn Hartvickson, *Med Doctor*

▲ = Import ▼=Export
◆ =Import/Export

Mandy Hiner, *Office Admin*
Elisha Malo, *Administration*
Troy Holdeman, *Family Practiti*
EMP: 70 **EST:** 1986
SALES (est): 7.5MM **Privately Held**
SIC: 8011 General & family practice, physician/surgeon

(G-7315)
B & C SPECIALTY PRODUCTS INC
123 E 4th St (67114-2240)
P.O. Box B (67114-0894)
PHONE..................................316 283-8000
Bill Bainbridge, *President*
Celesta Bainbridge, *Corp Secy*
EMP: 10
SALES (est): 1.9MM **Privately Held**
WEB: www.bandcspecialty.com
SIC: 3679 Electronic circuits

(G-7316)
B N S F INC
301 W 4th St (67114-3626)
PHONE..................................316 284-3260
Matt Rose, *President*
EMP: 1000
SALES (est): 29.7MM
SALES (corp-wide): 225.3B **Publicly Held**
WEB: www.bnsf.com
SIC: 4011 Railroads, line-haul operating
HQ: Burlington Northern Santa Fe, Llc
2650 Lou Menk Dr
Fort Worth TX 76131

(G-7317)
BANK OF WEST
100 W 12th St (67114-1954)
PHONE..................................316 283-7310
Brian Domley, *Manager*
EMP: 11
SALES (corp-wide): 2.7B **Privately Held**
SIC: 6022 State commercial banks
HQ: Bank Of The West
180 Montgomery St # 1400
San Francisco CA 94104
415 765-4800

(G-7318)
BECKER CABINET SHOP
Also Called: Becker Cabinet & Furniture
9113 N Meridian Rd (67114-9710)
P.O. Box 699, Hesston (67062-0699)
PHONE..................................620 327-4448
Brad Koehn, *Owner*
Dale Koehn, *Co-Owner*
EMP: 8
SALES: 600K **Privately Held**
WEB: www.coffestaindesign.com
SIC: 5712 2511 Cabinet work, custom; wood household furniture

(G-7319)
BEST WESTERN RED COACH INN
1301 E 1st St (67114-4003)
PHONE..................................316 283-9120
Andy Gupita, *Manager*
EMP: 10
SQ FT: 1,800
SALES (est): 642.7K **Privately Held**
SIC: 7011 Hotels & motels

(G-7320)
BNSF RAILWAY COMPANY
Also Called: Burlington Northern
620 S Boyd Ave (67114-5227)
PHONE..................................316 284-3224
Jim Watts, *Manager*
EMP: 150
SALES (corp-wide): 225.3B **Publicly Held**
WEB: www.billpurdy.com
SIC: 4011 Railroads, line-haul operating
HQ: Bnsf Railway Company
2650 Lou Menk Dr
Fort Worth TX 76131
800 795-2673

(G-7321)
BRENNEMAN & BREMMEMAN INC (PA)
Also Called: B & B Wrecker
812 W 1st St (67114-3325)
PHONE..................................316 282-8834
Robert H Brenneman, *President*
EMP: 18
SQ FT: 6,500
SALES (est): 1MM **Privately Held**
SIC: 7532 5521 7549 Paint shop, automotive; body shop, automotive; used car dealers; towing services

(G-7322)
BRIDGES INC
911 Sw 14th St (67114-4731)
P.O. Box 823 (67114-0823)
PHONE..................................316 283-9350
Stan Scudder, *President*
Rosalind Scudder, *Vice Pres*
EMP: 25
SQ FT: 6,900
SALES (est): 5.9MM **Privately Held**
SIC: 1622 Bridge construction

(G-7323)
BUDGET EQUIPMENT INC
1521 Nw 36th St (67117-8805)
P.O. Box 420, North Newton (67117-0420)
PHONE..................................316 284-9994
Kevin Wray, *President*
EMP: 20 **EST:** 2001
SALES (est): 1MM **Privately Held**
SIC: 4953 Non-hazardous waste disposal sites

(G-7324)
BUILDERS CONCRETE & SUPPLY (PA)
505 W 1st St (67114-3301)
P.O. Box 225 (67114-0225)
PHONE..................................316 283-4540
Richard Allen, *President*
EMP: 19 **EST:** 1956
SQ FT: 3,200
SALES (est): 2.2MM **Privately Held**
WEB: www.bcconcrete.com
SIC: 3273 Ready-mixed concrete

(G-7325)
BUNTING GROUP INC (PA)
500 S Spencer Rd (67114-4109)
P.O. Box 468 (67114-0468)
PHONE..................................316 284-2020
Robert J Bunting Sr, *President*
Kevin Miller, *General Mgr*
Jackie McManus, *Buyer*
Joshua Barden, *Engineer*
Josh Martinson, *Engineer*
◆ **EMP:** 125 **EST:** 1959
SQ FT: 60,000
SALES (est): 30.6MM **Privately Held**
WEB: www.bunting-magnetics.com
SIC: 3264 Magnets, permanent: ceramic or ferrite

(G-7326)
CARING HANDS HUMANE SOCIETY
1400 Se 3rd St (67114-4100)
PHONE..................................316 284-0487
Kevin Stubbs, *Exec Dir*
Angela Base, *Director*
EMP: 17
SALES: 668.7K **Privately Held**
WEB: www.caringhandshs.com
SIC: 8322 8699 Adoption services; animal humane society

(G-7327)
CD CUSTOM ENTERPRISES LLC
1800 Se 9th St (67114-4134)
PHONE..................................316 804-4520
Renee Poschen, *Human Resources*
Robert Dreiling, *Sales Staff*
Alan Carsten,
EMP: 18
SALES (est): 3.4MM **Privately Held**
SIC: 3443 1761 Metal parts; sheet metalwork

(G-7328)
CHISHOLM TRAIL COUNTRY STR LLC
507 Se 36th St (67114-8730)
PHONE..................................316 283-3276
Mike Weber, *Partner*
EMP: 15
SALES (est): 4.1MM **Privately Held**
WEB: www.chisholmtrailcountrystore.com
SIC: 5191 5999 5941 5699 Animal feeds; pet food; saddlery & equestrian equipment; western apparel; nurseries & garden centers

(G-7329)
CITY OF NEWTON
Also Called: Newton City Parks Dept
304 Grandview Ave (67114)
P.O. Box 426 (67114-0426)
PHONE..................................316 284-6083
Hondo Collins, *Superintendent*
Debra Perbeck, *Human Res Dir*
Burk Lewis, *Manager*
Jeri Yoder, *Manager*
EMP: 10
SALES (est): 274.7K **Privately Held**
WEB: www.newtonkansas.com
SIC: 7521 Automobile parking
PA: Newton, City Of (Inc)
201 E 6th St
Newton KS 67114
316 284-6002

(G-7330)
CITY OF NEWTON
Also Called: Warkentin House Museum
211 E 1st St (67114-3702)
PHONE..................................316 283-3113
Patricia Randall, *Principal*
EMP: 20 **Privately Held**
WEB: www.newtonkansas.com
SIC: 8412 Museum
PA: Newton, City Of (Inc)
201 E 6th St
Newton KS 67114
316 284-6002

(G-7331)
COMFORT INN AND SUITES
1205 E 1st St (67114-4002)
PHONE..................................316 804-4866
EMP: 20
SALES (est): 696.1K **Privately Held**
SIC: 7011 Hotels & motels

(G-7332)
COMMUNITY NATIONAL BANK & TR
Also Called: El Dorado Banking Center
127 N Main St (67114-3440)
P.O. Box 223, El Dorado (67042-0223)
PHONE..................................316 283-0059
Colin Rowell, *Branch Mgr*
EMP: 15 **Privately Held**
SIC: 6021 National commercial banks
HQ: Community National Bank & Trust
14 N Lincoln Ave
Chanute KS 66720

(G-7333)
CONCRETE VAULTS INC (PA)
Also Called: Doric Vaults
901 Sharps Dr (67114-5225)
PHONE..................................316 283-3790
James R Wiens, *President*
▲ **EMP:** 12
SQ FT: 10,000
SALES (est): 5.3MM **Privately Held**
WEB: www.concrete-vaults.com
SIC: 3272 Burial vaults, concrete or precast terrazzo

(G-7334)
CONTINENTAL-AGRA EQUIP INC
Also Called: Continental Agra Grain Eqp
1400 S Spencer Rd (67114-4127)
PHONE..................................316 283-9602
Dan Hirschler, *President*
Rosemary Hirschler, *Corp Secy*
Daniel Hirschler, *Vice Pres*
Jill Hirschler, *Treasurer*
◆ **EMP:** 13
SQ FT: 32,000
SALES (est): 9.4MM **Privately Held**
WEB: www.continentalagra.com
SIC: 5084 Industrial machinery & equipment

(G-7335)
COTTONWOOD PEDIATRICS
700 Medical Center Dr # 150 (67114-9015)
PHONE..................................316 283-7100
Jonathan Jantz, *Owner*
Angela Gatz, *Pediatrics*
EMP: 13
SALES (est): 1.2MM **Privately Held**
WEB: www.cottonwoodpeds.com
SIC: 8011 Pediatrician

(G-7336)
COUNTRY FRESH FOODS
1515 N Main St (67114-1919)
P.O. Box 423 (67114-0423)
PHONE..................................316 283-4414
Randy D Durr, *Owner*
EMP: 24
SQ FT: 2,500
SALES (est): 2.1MM **Privately Held**
SIC: 5149 2099 Specialty food items; food preparations

(G-7337)
COUNTY OF HARVEY
Also Called: Harvey County Health Dept
215 S Pine St (67114-3745)
PHONE..................................316 283-1637
Rita Flickinger, *Manager*
EMP: 13 **Privately Held**
WEB: www.harveycounty.com
SIC: 8011 9111 Clinic, operated by physicians; county supervisors' & executives' offices
PA: County Of Harvey
800 N Main St
Newton KS 67114
316 284-6800

(G-7338)
DRUBERS DONUT SHOP
116 W 6th St (67114-2118)
PHONE..................................316 283-1206
Martin Norris, *Owner*
▲ **EMP:** 6
SALES (est): 212.3K **Privately Held**
SIC: 5461 2051 Doughnuts; doughnuts, except frozen

(G-7339)
EMBERHOPE INC (PA)
Also Called: YOUTHVILLE
900 W Broadway St (67114-2004)
P.O. Box 210 (67114-0210)
PHONE..................................316 529-9100
Shelley Duncan, *President*
Nancy Compton, *Vice Pres*
Lori Gonzales, *VP Business*
Toyia Bulla, *CFO*
Brian Voth, *Info Tech Mgr*
EMP: 150
SQ FT: 10,000
SALES: 8MM **Privately Held**
SIC: 8361 Residential care for children

(G-7340)
EMERGENCY SERVICES OF KANSAS
301 N Main St Ste 300 (67114-3461)
P.O. Box 507 (67114-0507)
PHONE..................................866 815-9776
Ron Morford, *President*
Nancy Morford, *Human Res Dir*
EMP: 25
SALES (est): 863.7K **Privately Held**
WEB: www.emerphys.com
SIC: 8011 Freestanding emergency medical center

(G-7341)
ENSERV LLC
1021 S Spencer Rd (67114-4118)
PHONE..................................316 283-5943
Tim Reed, *Manager*
EMP: 15
SALES (corp-wide): 3.4B **Publicly Held**
SIC: 4953 Medical waste disposal
HQ: Enserv, Llc
2355 Waukegan Rd Ste 300
Bannockburn IL

(G-7342)
EVERGY KANSAS CENTRAL INC
300 W 1st St (67114-3606)
PHONE..................................316 283-5521
EMP: 52
SALES (corp-wide): 4.2B **Publicly Held**
SIC: 4925 4911 Gas production and/or distribution; electric services
HQ: Evergy Kansas Central, Inc.
818 S Kansas Ave
Topeka KS 66612
785 575-6300

(G-7343)
FAMILY FIRST CHILD CARE LLC
215 N Meridian Rd (67114-5102)
PHONE..................................316 333-1481
Courtney Cantrell,
Steven Cantrell,
EMP: 18
SALES (est): 160.5K **Privately Held**
SIC: 8351 Child day care services

(G-7344)
FASTENAL COMPANY
1605 W 1st St (67114-3200)
PHONE..................................316 283-2266
Jesse Mendoza, *Branch Mgr*
EMP: 10
SALES (corp-wide): 4.9B **Publicly Held**
WEB: www.fastenal.com
SIC: 5085 Fasteners, industrial: nuts, bolts, screws, etc.
PA: Fastenal Company
2001 Theurer Blvd
Winona MN 55987
507 454-5374

(G-7345)
FIRST BANK OF NEWTON (PA)
128 E Broadway St (67114-2222)
P.O. Box 587 (67114-0587)
PHONE..................................316 283-2600
Ray Tenner, *President*
Melvin Schadler, *Exec VP*
Don Sauerwein, *Assistant VP*
Rick Toews, *Assistant VP*
Laura Moore, *Vice Pres*
EMP: 50 **EST:** 1873
SALES: 9.1MM **Privately Held**
SIC: 6022 6021 State trust companies accepting deposits, commercial; national commercial banks

(G-7346)
FLORENCE ROCK COMPANY LLC
13707 Nw Diamond Rd (67114-8064)
PHONE..................................620 878-4544
Jerrold Unruh,
Warren Harshman,
EMP: 7
SALES (est): 870K **Privately Held**
SIC: 5032 3274 Stone, crushed or broken; lime

(G-7347)
FP SUPPLY LLC
701 S Spencer Rd (67114-4112)
PHONE..................................316 284-6700
Richard Millman, *Branch Mgr*
EMP: 15
SALES (corp-wide): 61MM **Privately Held**
SIC: 5099 Firearms & ammunition, except sporting
PA: F.P. Supply, Llc
9264 Manchester Rd
Saint Louis MO 63144
314 968-1700

(G-7348)
FRIENDS KANSAS CHRISTN HM INC
1035 Se 3rd St (67114-3904)
PHONE..................................316 283-6600
Jim Nachtigal, *CEO*
EMP: 117
SQ FT: 51,000
SALES: 6.8MM **Privately Held**
SIC: 8051 8052 Skilled nursing care facilities; intermediate care facilities

(G-7349)
FULL VISION INC
3017 Full Vision Dr (67114-9750)
PHONE..................................316 283-3344
Peter Benson, *President*
Doug Scheible, *General Mgr*
Patty Benson, *Corp Secy*
Mike Luquette, *Vice Pres*
◆ **EMP:** 60
SQ FT: 105,000
SALES (est): 28.2MM **Privately Held**
WEB: www.full-vision.com
SIC: 3537 3531 3713 3312 Cabs, for industrial trucks & tractors; backhoes; truck & bus bodies; blast furnaces & steel mills

(G-7350)
FUTURE FOAM INC
520 S Payton Ave (67114-4135)
PHONE..................................316 283-8600
Joe Eickman, *Plant Mgr*
Susie Entz, *Purch Mgr*
West Puttman, *Manager*
EMP: 62
SQ FT: 125,000
SALES (corp-wide): 376.3MM **Privately Held**
SIC: 3086 Insulation or cushioning material, foamed plastic
PA: Future Foam, Inc.
1610 Avenue N
Council Bluffs IA 51501
712 323-9122

(G-7351)
GRANNIES HOMEMADE MUSTARD
410 W 7th St (67114-2622)
PHONE..................................620 947-3259
Lydia Hein, *Owner*
Eugene Hein, *Partner*
EMP: 7
SALES: 350K **Privately Held**
WEB: www.grannieshomemademustard.com
SIC: 2035 Mustard, prepared (wet)

(G-7352)
GRAPHIC IMAGES INC
407 W 10th St (67114-1756)
PHONE..................................316 283-3776
Dwight Deckert, *President*
Jo Hoskins, *Administration*
EMP: 10
SQ FT: 7,000
SALES (est): 1.2MM **Privately Held**
SIC: 2752 7338 2791 2789 Commercial printing, offset; secretarial & court reporting; typesetting; bookbinding & related work

(G-7353)
GUERRILLA MARKETING INC
1027 Washington Rd Ste D (67114-4400)
PHONE..................................800 946-9150
Andrew Hansen, *Administration*
EMP: 5
SALES (est): 177.7K **Privately Held**
SIC: 8742 2396 2261 2752 Marketing consulting services; screen printing on fabric articles; screen printing of cotton broadwoven fabrics; commercial printing, lithographic; screen printing

(G-7354)
GUST ORTHODONTICS
504 N Main St (67114-2229)
PHONE..................................316 283-1090
Jeffrey Gust, *Principal*
EMP: 11 **EST:** 2007
SALES (est): 299.6K **Privately Held**
SIC: 8021 Orthodontist

(G-7355)
H&R BLOCK INC
Also Called: H & R Block
105 E Broadway St (67114-2221)
PHONE..................................316 283-1495
Rebecca Kasper, *Manager*
EMP: 20
SALES (corp-wide): 3B **Publicly Held**
WEB: www.hrblock.com
SIC: 7291 Tax return preparation services
PA: H&R Block, Inc.
1 H&R Block Way
Kansas City MO 64105
816 854-3000

(G-7356)
HAIR CUTTING COMPANY
526 N Main St (67114-2229)
PHONE..................................316 283-0532
Wayne Reif, *Owner*
EMP: 11
SALES (est): 253K **Privately Held**
SIC: 7231 Unisex hair salons

(G-7357)
HARVEY COUNTY DV/SA TASK FORCE
800 N Main St Ste 104 (67114-1807)
P.O. Box 942 (67114-0942)
PHONE..................................316 284-6920
Jan Jones, *Exec Dir*
EMP: 10
SALES: 1MM **Privately Held**
SIC: 8399 Advocacy group

(G-7358)
HEALTH MINISTRIES CLINIC INC
720 Medical Center Dr (67114-8778)
PHONE..................................316 283-6103
Dan Evans, *Finance*
Matthew Schmidt, *Exec Dir*
EMP: 100
SALES: 5.5MM **Privately Held**
SIC: 8011 General & family practice, physician/surgeon

(G-7359)
HEALTH MINISTRIES CLINIC INC
209 S Pine St Ste 200 (67114-3745)
PHONE..................................620 727-1183
Jerre Forbes, *Exec Dir*
EMP: 15
SALES: 1.8MM **Privately Held**
SIC: 8011 Clinic, operated by physicians

(G-7360)
HERITAGE HOME WORKS LLC
5734 W Us Highway 50 (67114-8982)
PHONE..................................316 288-9033
Dan Harder, *Principal*
EMP: 11
SALES (est): 1.6MM **Privately Held**
SIC: 1521 Single-family housing construction

(G-7361)
HERTZ CORPORATION
810 N Oliver Newton (67114)
PHONE..................................316 284-6084
EMP: 23
SALES (corp-wide): 9.5B **Publicly Held**
SIC: 7514 Rent-a-car service
HQ: The Hertz Corporation
8501 Williams Rd
Estero FL 33928
239 301-7000

(G-7362)
HOLIDAY INN EXPRESS & SUITES
1430 E Broadway Ct (67114-2519)
PHONE..................................316 804-7040
Malisa Silver, *General Mgr*
EMP: 16 **EST:** 2011
SALES (est): 774.6K **Privately Held**
SIC: 7011 Hotels & motels

(G-7363)
HOSPICE INCORPORATED
Also Called: Harry Hynes Memorial Hospice
606 N Main St Ste 202 (67114-2219)
PHONE..................................316 283-1103
EMP: 40
SALES (corp-wide): 18.1MM **Privately Held**
SIC: 7011 Inns
PA: Hospice, Incorporated
313 S Market St
Wichita KS 67202
316 265-9441

(G-7364)
HWA DAVIS CNSTR & SUP INC
414 N Main St Ste 150 (67114-2225)
P.O. Box 51 (67114-0051)
PHONE..................................316 283-0330
Linda Hwa Davis, *President*
Michael Davis, *Vice Pres*
EMP: 15
SQ FT: 120
SALES: 2.5MM **Privately Held**
SIC: 1611 General contractor, highway & street construction

(G-7365)
HYBRID TURKEYS LLC
1418 Cow Palace Rd (67114-8677)
P.O. Box 250 (67114-0250)
PHONE..................................620 951-4705
EMP: 8 **EST:** 2015
SALES (est): 1.1MM
SALES (corp-wide): 590.4MM **Privately Held**
SIC: 2015 Turkey processing & slaughtering
HQ: Hendrix Genetics Limited
650 Riverbend Dr Unit C
Kitchener ON N2K 3
519 578-2740

(G-7366)
INDUSTRIAL MTAL FBRICATION INC
1401 S Spencer Rd (67114-4126)
PHONE..................................316 283-3303
Renee Dalrymple, *President*
Carl Dalrymple, *Vice Pres*
Jimmy Dalrymple, *Opers Staff*
EMP: 65
SQ FT: 66,500
SALES (est): 17.3MM **Privately Held**
SIC: 3441 Fabricated structural metal

(G-7367)
J P WEIGAND AND SONS INC
400 S Main St Ste 101 (67114-3772)
PHONE..................................316 283-1330
Arlyn Newell, *Principal*
EMP: 25
SALES (corp-wide): 22.7MM **Privately Held**
SIC: 6531 Real estate agent, residential
PA: J. P. Weigand And Sons, Inc.
150 N Market St
Wichita KS 67202
316 292-3991

(G-7368)
K5 PAINTING INC
204 W 6th St (67114-2131)
PHONE..................................316 283-9612
Laura Waterson, *President*
EMP: 10
SALES (est): 273.9K **Privately Held**
SIC: 1721 Painting & paper hanging

(G-7369)
KANSAS ELECTRIC INC
1420 Nw 36th St (67114-9035)
PHONE..................................316 283-4750
Tim Sweigart, *President*
Shane Jeffery, *Project Mgr*
Christy Rossiter, *Accountant*
EMP: 70
SQ FT: 3,000
SALES (est): 12.1MM **Privately Held**
WEB: www.kansas-electric.com
SIC: 1731 General electrical contractor

(G-7370)
KHAOS APPAREL LLC
601 Se 36th St Ste 121 (67114-8769)
PHONE..................................316 804-4900
Victor Garcia, *Sales Staff*
Justin Friesen, *Mng Member*
EMP: 12
SALES (est): 972.8K **Privately Held**
SIC: 2759 7389 7336 Screen printing; embroidering of advertising on shirts, etc.; silk screen design

(G-7371)
KNUDSEN MONROE & COMPANY LLC
512 N Main St (67114-2229)
PHONE..................................316 283-5366

Douh Widow, *Partner*
Robert Sjogren,
EMP: 18
SALES (est): 1.3MM **Privately Held**
SIC: 8721 Certified public accountant

(G-7372)
KOEHN MACHINE INC
315 W 16th St (67114-1321)
PHONE..................................316 282-2298
Lee Ann Koehn, *President*
Robert E Koehn, *Vice Pres*
EMP: 5
SQ FT: 2,400
SALES (est): 597.6K **Privately Held**
SIC: 3429 Aircraft hardware

(G-7373)
KOEHN PAINTING CO LLC
204 W 6th St (67114-2131)
PHONE..................................316 283-9612
Leroy Koehn,
Susan Koehn,
EMP: 40
SQ FT: 7,200
SALES (est): 2.6MM **Privately Held**
SIC: 1771 1799 1721 Concrete work; sandblasting of building exteriors; commercial painting

(G-7374)
KUSTOM KARRIERS LLC
Also Called: Kustom Warehousing
1450 S Spencer Rd (67114-4127)
P.O. Box 75076, Wichita (67275-0076)
PHONE..................................316 283-1060
Mark Breese, *General Mgr*
Scott Hewitt,
John Henry,
Mitch Paradis,
▲ **EMP:** 55
SQ FT: 1,300
SALES (est): 6MM **Privately Held**
WEB: www.kustomkarriers.com
SIC: 4213 4225 Trucking, except local; general warehousing

(G-7375)
MANUFACTURING SOLUTIONS INC
Also Called: Mfg Solutions
2320 N Oliver Rd (67114-9552)
PHONE..................................316 282-0556
Paul Vermilyea, *President*
Bill Stahl, *Vice Pres*
EMP: 33
SQ FT: 50,000
SALES (est): 3.1MM **Privately Held**
SIC: 3599 Machine shop, jobbing & repair

(G-7376)
MARILYN M WILDER
301 N Main St Ste 400 (67114-3464)
PHONE..................................316 283-8746
Marilyn M Wilder, *Partner*
EMP: 13
SALES (est): 478K **Privately Held**
SIC: 8111 General practice attorney, lawyer

(G-7377)
MASTER PNT INDUS COATING CORP
Also Called: Master Paint Indus Coating
1701 Se 9th St (67114-4133)
P.O. Box 1242 (67114-8242)
PHONE..................................316 283-3999
Forouhar Vahdat, *President*
John Fathi, *Vice Pres*
Richard Vore, *Treasurer*
EMP: 19
SQ FT: 20,000
SALES (est): 1.2MM **Privately Held**
SIC: 2851 5198 Paints & paint additives; paints

(G-7378)
MENNONITE CHURCH USA (PA)
Also Called: Mennonite Gen Cnfrnce Cntl Off
718 N Main St (67114-1703)
PHONE..................................316 283-5100
Ervin Stutzman, *Principal*
Glen Guyton, *COO*
Sue Park-Hur, *Minister*
Shana Peachey, *Minister*
Alex Woodring, *Manager*
EMP: 6
SQ FT: 31,500
SALES: 2MM **Privately Held**
SIC: 8661 2752 Mennonite Church; commercial printing, lithographic

(G-7379)
MENNONITE MISSION NETWORK
Also Called: Mennonite Media
718 N Main St (67114-1703)
PHONE..................................540 434-6701
Burton Buller, *Branch Mgr*
Rose Mtoka, *Personnel Assit*
Karla Minter, *Associate*
EMP: 12
SALES (corp-wide): 12.1MM **Privately Held**
WEB: www.mennonitemission.net
SIC: 8661 5192 8743 Churches, temples & shrines; books, periodicals & newspapers; public relations services
PA: Mennonite Mission Network
3145 Benham Ave Ste 3
Elkhart IN 46517
574 523-3014

(G-7380)
MENNONITE PRESS INC
532 N Oliver Rd (67114-9403)
P.O. Box 867 (67114-0867)
PHONE..................................316 283-3060
Steven Rudiger, *Director*
EMP: 30 **EST:** 1949
SQ FT: 24,000
SALES (est): 2MM **Privately Held**
SIC: 2752 2789 2759 2791 Commercial printing, offset; bookbinding & related work; magazines: printing; typesetting
PA: Mennonite Church Usa
718 N Main St
Newton KS 67114
316 283-5100

(G-7381)
MENNONITE WEEKLY REVIEW INC
129 W 6th St (67114-2117)
P.O. Box 568 (67114-0568)
PHONE..................................316 283-3670
Robert Schrag, *CEO*
Robert Shcrag, *CEO*
EMP: 6
SQ FT: 15,000
SALES: 437.3K **Privately Held**
WEB: www.mennoweekly.org
SIC: 2721 5942 Periodicals: publishing & printing; books, religious

(G-7382)
MID WEST ELC TRANSFORMERS INC
1324 N Oliver Rd (67114-8400)
PHONE..................................316 283-7500
David W Miller, *President*
Mark Hopkins, *Corp Secy*
EMP: 10
SQ FT: 6,000
SALES: 900K **Privately Held**
SIC: 7629 3825 Electrical equipment repair, high voltage; instruments to measure electricity

(G-7383)
MID-AMRICA YUTH BASKETBALL INC
2309 S Kansas Rd (67114-9032)
P.O. Box 466 (67114-0466)
PHONE..................................316 284-0354
Greg Raleigh, *President*
Layne Frick, *Mktg Dir*
Hujing Ryan, *Office Mgr*
Matt Flaming, *Exec Dir*
Matt Fleming, *Director*
EMP: 12
SALES: 270K **Privately Held**
SIC: 8322 Youth center

(G-7384)
MID-CONTINENT INDUSTRIES INC
1801 Se 9th St (67114-4134)
P.O. Box 563 (67114-0563)
PHONE..................................316 283-9648
Steve Wells, *President*
Darren Wells, *Vice Pres*
Lloyd Wolf, *VP Opers*
Donna Wells, *Admin Sec*
EMP: 12
SALES (est): 2.4MM **Privately Held**
SIC: 3523 3599 5083 Farm machinery & equipment; machine & other job shop work; grain elevators equipment & supplies

(G-7385)
MIDLAND NATIONAL BANK
Also Called: Washington Road Branch
1212 Washington Rd (67114-4856)
PHONE..................................316 283-1700
John Suderman, *Branch Mgr*
EMP: 25 **Privately Held**
SIC: 6022 State commercial banks
PA: Midland National Bank
527 N Main St
Newton KS 67114

(G-7386)
MIDLAND NATIONAL BANK (PA)
527 N Main St (67114-2256)
P.O. Box 427 (67114-0427)
PHONE..................................316 283-1700
Ronald Lang, *President*
Joy Bestgen, *Senior VP*
EMP: 15
SALES: 6.1MM **Privately Held**
WEB: www.midlandnb.com
SIC: 6021 6163 National commercial banks; loan brokers

(G-7387)
MILLENNIUM MACHINE & TOOL INC
900 W 1st St (67114-3326)
PHONE..................................316 282-0884
Kris D Wondra, *President*
Eric Calbert, *Vice Pres*
Brian Franz, *Vice Pres*
▲ **EMP:** 45
SQ FT: 23,000
SALES (est): 8MM **Privately Held**
SIC: 3599 Machine shop, jobbing & repair

(G-7388)
MIRROR INC
1309 N Duncan St (67114-5704)
PHONE..................................316 283-7829
EMP: 10
SALES (corp-wide): 11.2MM **Privately Held**
SIC: 8093 Substance abuse clinics (outpatient)
PA: The Mirror Inc
130 E 5th St
Newton KS 67114
316 283-6743

(G-7389)
MIRROR INC (PA)
130 E 5th St (67114-2206)
P.O. Box 711 (67114-0711)
PHONE..................................316 283-6743
Barth Hague, *CEO*
Beverly Metcalf, *President*
John Gilbert, *President*
Charles Applegate, *Vice Pres*
Donald Denney, *Vice Pres*
EMP: 20
SALES: 11.2MM **Privately Held**
SIC: 8093 8361 8069 Drug clinic, outpatient; residential care; alcoholism rehabilitation hospital

(G-7390)
MORRIS COMMUNICATIONS CO LLC
Also Called: Newton Kansan
121 W 6th St (67114-2117)
P.O. Box 268 (67114-0268)
PHONE..................................316 283-1500
Dave Phillips, *Principal*
Kurt Oswald, *Advt Staff*
Paul Nelson, *Instructor*
EMP: 31 **Privately Held**
WEB: www.morris.com
SIC: 2711 7313 Newspapers; newspaper advertising representative
HQ: Morris Communications Company Llc
725 Broad St
Augusta GA 30901
706 724-0851

(G-7391)
MOTIVATIONAL TUBING LLC
2610 Nw 12th St (67114-8601)
PHONE..................................316 283-7301
Arlen Wiens, *President*
Carol Wiens, *Vice Pres*
EMP: 6
SQ FT: 5,000
SALES (est): 787.8K **Privately Held**
WEB: www.motivationaltubing.com
SIC: 3799 5531 Off-road automobiles, except recreational vehicles; automotive & home supply stores

(G-7392)
NEWTON CMNTY CHILD CARE CTR
207 Se 9th St (67114-4323)
PHONE..................................316 284-6525
Heidi Collins, *Exec Dir*
EMP: 24
SALES: 282.5K **Privately Held**
SIC: 8351 Child day care services

(G-7393)
NEWTON HEALTHCARE CORPORATION
Also Called: Newton Medical Center
600 Medical Center Dr (67114-8780)
P.O. Box 308 (67114-0308)
PHONE..................................316 283-2700
Steven G Kelly, *CEO*
Nancy Craig, *Chairman*
Jeff Barton, *Vice Pres*
Melanie Graber, *Maintenance Dir*
Shari Sattler, *Project Mgr*
EMP: 539
SQ FT: 110,000
SALES (est): 69.9MM **Privately Held**
WEB: www.newtonmed.com
SIC: 8062 8011 2411 General medical & surgical hospitals; offices & clinics of medical doctors; wooden logs

(G-7394)
NEWTON MEDICAL CTR CHILD CARE
805 Medical Center Dr (67114-7807)
PHONE..................................316 804-6094
Susan Graber, *Owner*
EMP: 18
SALES: 409.1K **Privately Held**
SIC: 8351 Child day care services

(G-7395)
NEWTON RECREATION COMMISSION
Also Called: Newton Wellness Center
415 N Poplar St (67114-2124)
PHONE..................................316 283-7330
Brian Bascue, *Superintendent*
Lori Hien, *Manager*
EMP: 50
SQ FT: 48,000
SALES: 2MM **Privately Held**
WEB: www.newtonrec.org
SIC: 7999 Recreation center

(G-7396)
NEWTON SURGERY CTR
800 Medical Center Dr # 240 (67114-7808)
PHONE..................................316 283-9977
Melanie Graber, *Manager*
Janie Hofflinger, *Manager*
Sandra Leatherman, *Director*
Allen Graber, *Pharmacy Dir*
EMP: 10
SALES (est): 535.4K **Privately Held**
SIC: 8011 Orthopedic physician

(G-7397)
NORCRAFT COMPANIES LP
Also Called: Mid Continent Cabinetry
810 S Columbus Ave (67114-5223)
PHONE..................................316 283-8804
Mark Harpenau, *Branch Mgr*
EMP: 11
SALES (corp-wide): 5.4B **Publicly Held**
SIC: 2434 Wood kitchen cabinets
HQ: Norcraft Companies, L.P.
950 Blue Gentian Rd # 200
Saint Paul MN 55121
651 234-3300

(G-7398)
NORCRAFT COMPANIES LP
Mid Continent Cabinetry
900 S Meridian Rd (67114-5217)
PHONE..................................316 283-2859
Joe Freud, *Branch Mgr*
Mike Ingalls, *Manager*
Karen Junkans, *Manager*
Chuck Schilling, *Manager*
Kevin Wilfong, *Manager*
EMP: 500
SALES (corp-wide): 5.4B **Publicly Held**
WEB: www.norcraftcabinetry.com
SIC: 2434 1751 Wood kitchen cabinets; cabinet & finish carpentry
HQ: Norcraft Companies, L.P.
950 Blue Gentian Rd # 200
Saint Paul MN 55121
651 234-3300

(G-7399)
NORTHVIEW DEVELOPMENT SERVICES
300 S Spencer Rd (67114-4105)
PHONE..................................316 281-3213
Robin Stewart, *Manager*
EMP: 200
SALES (est): 19.2MM **Privately Held**
SIC: 5113 8331 Industrial & personal service paper; job training & vocational rehabilitation services

(G-7400)
NORTHVIEW DEVELOPMENTAL SVCS (PA)
700 E 14th St (67114-5702)
P.O. Box 646 (67114-0646)
PHONE..................................316 283-5170
Stan Zienkewicz, *President*
Virginia Gaede, *Vice Pres*
EMP: 16 **EST:** 1974
SQ FT: 7,000
SALES: 100.9K **Privately Held**
WEB: www.northviewdsi.com
SIC: 8331 8361 Vocational rehabilitation agency; home for the mentally handicapped

(G-7401)
ORSCHELN FARM AND HOME LLC
321 Windward Dr (67114-5422)
PHONE..................................316 283-2969
Beth Wonders, *Manager*
EMP: 15
SALES (corp-wide): 822.7MM **Privately Held**
SIC: 5191 Farm supplies
PA: Orscheln Farm And Home Llc
1800 Overcenter Dr
Moberly MO 65270
800 577-2580

(G-7402)
P & B TRUCKING INC
1307 Cow Palace Rd (67114-8963)
P.O. Box 432 (67114-0432)
PHONE..................................316 283-6868
Ronald Nicholson, *President*
Kathleen Wiens, *Corp Secy*
EMP: 15
SALES: 1.8MM **Privately Held**
WEB: www.pbtrucking.com
SIC: 4213 Trucking, except local

(G-7403)
PARK AEROSPACE TECH CORP
Also Called: Patc's
486 N Oliver Rd Bldg Z (67114-9495)
PHONE..................................316 283-6500
Brian E Shore, *CEO*
Mark Esquivel, *President*
Anand Kathula, *Vice Pres*
◆ **EMP:** 78
SQ FT: 80,000
SALES (est): 18.7MM
SALES (corp-wide): 51.1MM **Publicly Held**
WEB: www.parkelectro.com
SIC: 3728 Aircraft parts & equipment
PA: Park Aerospace Corp.
1400 Old Country Rd # 409
Westbury NY 11590
631 465-3662

(G-7404)
PFALTZGRAFF CO
601 Se 36th St (67114-8767)
PHONE..................................316 283-7754
EMP: 10
SALES (corp-wide): 502.7MM **Publicly Held**
SIC: 3269 Cookware Stoneware Coarse Earthenware And Pottery
HQ: Pfaltzgraff Factory Stores, Inc.
140 E Market St
York PA 17401
717 848-5500

(G-7405)
PHANTOM ENTERPRISES INC
Also Called: Knork Flatware
101 S Evans St (67114-9212)
P.O. Box 420, North Newton (67117-0420)
PHONE..................................316 264-7070
Tom Carson, *President*
Lacy Simon, *Vice Pres*
Mike Miller, *Shareholder*
◆ **EMP:** 10
SQ FT: 40,000
SALES (est): 907.5K **Privately Held**
WEB: www.knork.net
SIC: 5023 5719 Stainless steel flatware; cutlery

(G-7406)
PRAIRIE INN INC
Also Called: Days Inn
105 Manchester Ave (67114-5023)
PHONE..................................316 283-3330
Sangib Mitra, *President*
Kerry Newell, *Vice Pres*
EMP: 20
SALES (est): 871.7K **Privately Held**
SIC: 7011 Hotels & motels

(G-7407)
PRAIRIE VIEW INC (PA)
1901 E 1st St (67114-5010)
P.O. Box 467 (67114-0467)
PHONE..................................316 284-6400
Jessie Kaye, *CEO*
Mel Goering, *CEO*
Diana Waddell-Gilbert, *Vice Pres*
Dan Evans, *CFO*
Jessica Kerzner, *Psychologist*
EMP: 410
SQ FT: 80,000
SALES: 21.2MM **Privately Held**
WEB: www.pvi.org
SIC: 8063 8361 8093 Psychiatric hospitals; residential care; specialty outpatient clinics

(G-7408)
PRESBYTERIAN MANORS INC
Also Called: Newton Presbyterian Manor
1200 E 7th St (67114-2820)
PHONE..................................316 283-5400
Shawn Sulivan, *Director*
EMP: 55
SALES (corp-wide): 8.6MM **Privately Held**
SIC: 8051 Convalescent home with continuous nursing care
HQ: Presbyterian Manors, Inc.
2414 N Woodlawn Blvd
Wichita KS 67220
316 685-1100

(G-7409)
PWD INC
1214 Cow Palace Rd (67114-8913)
P.O. Box 603 (67114-0603)
PHONE..................................316 283-0335
Russell Rucker, *President*
▲ **EMP:** 20
SQ FT: 48,000
SALES (est): 12.3MM **Privately Held**
SIC: 5031 Lumber, plywood & millwork

(G-7410)
RES-CARE INC
700 E 14th St (67114-5702)
PHONE..................................316 283-5170
Darrek Hopkins, *Owner*
EMP: 48
SALES (corp-wide): 2B **Privately Held**
WEB: www.rescare.com
SIC: 8082 Home health care services
HQ: Res-Care, Inc.
805 N Whittington Pkwy
Louisville KY 40222
502 394-2100

(G-7411)
ROOFING SERVICES UNLIMITED
202 E 4th St (67114-2243)
PHONE..................................316 284-9900
Brent Koffman, *President*
Paul Partridge, *Admin Sec*
EMP: 19 **EST:** 1990
SQ FT: 3,000
SALES (est): 2.3MM **Privately Held**
SIC: 1761 Roofing contractor

(G-7412)
SAINT FRANCIS ACADEMY NEWTON
516 N Main St (67114-2229)
PHONE..................................316 284-2477
Michell Schauf, *Manager*
EMP: 22
SALES (est): 367.2K **Privately Held**
SIC: 8361 Residential care

(G-7413)
SALVATION ARMY
Also Called: Salvation Army The
208 W 6th St (67114-2131)
PHONE..................................316 283-3190
Marcia Brazil, *Manager*
EMP: 10
SALES (corp-wide): 2.2B **Privately Held**
WEB: www.salarmychicago.org
SIC: 8661 8699 Religious organizations; charitable organization
HQ: The Salvation Army
5550 Prairie Stone Pkwy # 130
Hoffman Estates IL 60192
847 294-2000

(G-7414)
SAND CREEK STATION GOLF COURSE
920 Meadowbrook Dr (67114-5502)
PHONE..................................316 284-6161
Laurie Kimerer, *Controller*
Chris Touhey, *Manager*
EMP: 22
SALES (est): 847.8K **Privately Held**
SIC: 7992 Public golf courses

(G-7415)
SCHABEN INDUSTRIES INC
7000 Schaben Ct (67114-9313)
PHONE..................................316 283-4444
Darren Zerr, *Branch Mgr*
EMP: 25
SALES (corp-wide): 151.6MM **Privately Held**
SIC: 3523 Sprayers & spraying machines, agricultural
HQ: Schaben Industries, Inc.
5834 E 23rd St
Columbus NE 68601
402 564-4544

(G-7416)
SERVICEMASTER CONSUMER SERVICE
2216 N Anderson Ave (67114-1207)
PHONE..................................316 283-5404
Daryl Skibee, *Branch Mgr*
EMP: 11
SALES (corp-wide): 1.9B **Publicly Held**
WEB: www.ahswarranty.com
SIC: 7349 Building maintenance services
HQ: Servicemaster Consumer Services Limited Partnership
889 Ridge Lake Blvd Fl 2
Memphis TN 38120

(G-7417)
SHANE PAUL INC
Also Called: Newton Animal Hospital
3700 S Kansas Rd (67114-9031)
PHONE..................................316 283-1650
Shane Tonn, *President*
Paul Frieesen, *Vice Pres*
Denise Jasso, *Office Mgr*
EMP: 16
SQ FT: 5,000
SALES (est): 799.8K **Privately Held**
SIC: 0742 Animal hospital services, pets & other animal specialties

(G-7418)
SHANE PAUL LLC
Also Called: Newton Animal Hospital
3700 S Kansas Rd (67114-9031)
PHONE..................................316 283-1650
Paul Friesen,
Shane Tonn,
EMP: 15
SALES (est): 702.2K **Privately Held**
WEB: www.shanepaul.com
SIC: 0742 Animal hospital services, pets & other animal specialties

(G-7419)
STANDRIDGE COLOR CORPORATION
1011 Industrial Dr (67114-4137)
PHONE..................................316 283-5061
Harry Rosenboom, *Branch Mgr*
Summer Wiebke, *Manager*
EMP: 13
SALES (corp-wide): 146.1MM **Privately Held**
WEB: www.standridgecolor.com
SIC: 2865 2816 Color pigments, organic; color pigments
PA: Standridge Color Corporation
1196 E Hightower Trl
Social Circle GA 30025
770 464-3362

(G-7420)
TOWN & COUNTRY ANIMAL CLINIC (PA)
504 N Meridian Rd (67114-5112)
PHONE..................................316 283-1650
Shane A Tonn, *Owner*
Dr Cyril M Brown, *Owner*
EMP: 15 **EST:** 1961
SQ FT: 3,680
SALES (est): 1MM **Privately Held**
SIC: 0742 Veterinary services, specialties

(G-7421)
TRIBINE HARVESTER LLC
1010 Industrial Dr (67114-4106)
PHONE..................................316 282-8011
Ben N Dillon, *President*
EMP: 6 **EST:** 2014
SALES (est): 815.8K **Privately Held**
SIC: 3523 Grain stackers

(G-7422)
TWISTED COW LLC
1400 S Kansas Ave # 1400 (67114-5305)
PHONE..................................316 804-4949
EMP: 5
SALES (est): 336.5K **Privately Held**
SIC: 2024 Mfg Ice Cream/Frozen Desert

(G-7423)
VELLO KASS MD
Also Called: Whitichata Clinic
720 Medical Center Dr (67114-8778)
PHONE..................................316 283-3600
Vello Kass, *Principal*
EMP: 27
SALES (est): 327.6K **Privately Held**
SIC: 8011 Internal medicine, physician/surgeon

(G-7424)
VOESTALPINE NORTRAK INC
405 W 1st St (67114-3356)
P.O. Box 571 (67114-0571)
PHONE..................................316 284-0088
Bob McKercher, *Branch Mgr*
EMP: 51
SALES (corp-wide): 103.1MM **Privately Held**
SIC: 3462 5084 3743 Railroad wheels, axles, frogs or other equipment: forged; industrial machinery & equipment; railroad equipment
HQ: Voestalpine Nortrak Inc.
1740 Pacific Ave
Cheyenne WY 82007
307 778-8700

(G-7425)
VOGTS-PARGA CONSTRUCTION LLC
717 N Main St (67114-1805)
PHONE..................................316 284-2801
Alan Vogts,
EMP: 16
SQ FT: 1,200
SALES (est): 3.4MM **Privately Held**
SIC: **3272** Building materials, except block or brick: concrete

(G-7426)
WEBCO AIR CRAFT
Also Called: Webco Aircraft & Engine Svc
1134 N Oliver Rd (67114-9446)
PHONE..................................316 283-7929
Bob Weber, *Owner*
EMP: 7
SQ FT: 9,000
SALES (est): 1.4MM **Privately Held**
WEB: www.webcoaircraft.com
SIC: **3728** 4581 Aircraft parts & equipment; aircraft maintenance & repair services

(G-7427)
WENGER OIL INC (PA)
Also Called: Total/One Stop
2701 N Anderson Ave (67114-1203)
PHONE..................................316 283-8795
Marvin Wenger, *President*
Naomi M Wenger, *Corp Secy*
EMP: 13 **EST**: 1959
SQ FT: 15,000
SALES (est): 6.1MM **Privately Held**
SIC: **5171** Petroleum bulk stations

(G-7428)
WEYERHAEUSER COMPANY
701 S Spencer Rd (67114-4112)
PHONE..................................316 284-6700
Jeff Miller, *Sales/Mktg Mgr*
EMP: 20
SALES (corp-wide): 7.4B **Publicly Held**
SIC: **5031** Lumber: rough, dressed & finished
PA: Weyerhaeuser Company
220 Occidental Ave S
Seattle WA 98104
206 539-3000

(G-7429)
WIEBE TIRE & AUTOMOTIVE
1107 Washington Rd (67114-4853)
PHONE..................................316 283-4242
Kristy Wiebe Cox, *Owner*
EMP: 10
SQ FT: 6,000
SALES: 500K **Privately Held**
SIC: **5531** 7538 5014 Automotive tires; general automotive repair shops; tires & tubes

(G-7430)
WRAY ROOFING INC
1521 Nw 36th St (67117-8805)
P.O. Box 420, North Newton (67117-0420)
PHONE..................................316 283-6840
Kevin Wray, *President*
Jeff Schultz, *Warehouse Mgr*
Rick Wray, *Treasurer*
Craig Helser, *Sales Staff*
Jim Hollinger, *Sales Staff*
EMP: 75 **EST**: 1977
SALES (est): 11.4MM **Privately Held**
WEB: www.wrayroofing.com
SIC: **1761** 1742 Roofing contractor; insulation, buildings

Nickerson
Reno County

(G-7431)
CENTRAL PRAIRIE CO-OP
Also Called: Farmers Co-Op Crop Consulting
404 S Nickerson St (67561-9022)
P.O. Box 6 (67561-0006)
PHONE..................................620 422-3221
Jay Brack, *Branch Mgr*
EMP: 10
SALES (corp-wide): 42.5MM **Privately Held**
WEB: www.nickcoop.com
SIC: **8748** Agricultural consultant
PA: Central Prairie Co-Op
225 S Broadway Ave
Sterling KS 67579
620 278-2141

(G-7432)
GRAVEL & CONCRETE INC
7010 N Nickerson Rd (67561-9061)
PHONE..................................620 422-3249
John R Paulson, *CEO*
Kay Paulson, *President*
Laruan R Paulson, *Vice Pres*
Liyle S Paulson, *Vice Pres*
EMP: 5 **EST**: 1962
SQ FT: 1,000
SALES (est): 541.8K **Privately Held**
SIC: **1442** 3273 Construction sand & gravel; ready-mixed concrete

(G-7433)
HEDRICK EXOTIC ANIMAL FARM
Also Called: Bed Breakfast Inn
7910 N Roy L Smith Rd (67561-9049)
PHONE..................................620 422-3245
Joe Hedrick, *President*
Sondra Hedrick, *Corp Secy*
EMP: 20
SALES (est): 1MM **Privately Held**
SIC: **0291** 7011 7999 Animal specialty farm, general; hotels & motels; zoological garden, commercial

(G-7434)
HEDRICKS PROMOTIONS INC
7910 N Roy L Smith Rd (67561-9049)
PHONE..................................620 422-3296
Joe D Hedrick, *President*
Sondra Hedrick, *Vice Pres*
EMP: 20
SALES (est): 787.7K **Privately Held**
WEB: www.hedricks.com
SIC: **8422** 7299 Animal & reptile exhibit; banquet hall facilities

North Newton
Harvey County

(G-7435)
DENNYS HEATING & COOLING
506 W 22nd St (67117-2801)
PHONE..................................316 283-1598
Dennis Franz, *President*
Rita Franz, *Treasurer*
Mike Swartz, *Manager*
EMP: 10
SQ FT: 4,500
SALES: 730K **Privately Held**
SIC: **1711** Warm air heating & air conditioning contractor

(G-7436)
KAUFFMAN MUSEUM ASSOCIATION
2801 N Main St (67117-1700)
PHONE..................................316 283-1612
Cindy Beth, *Vice Pres*
Greg Dick, *Controller*
Marilyn Flaming, *Manager*
Rachel Pannabecker, *Director*
Karen Buerge, *Clerk*
EMP: 10
SALES (est): 267.3K **Privately Held**
SIC: **8412** Museum

(G-7437)
LIPPERT COMPONENTS MFG INC
600 W 24th St (67117-9201)
PHONE..................................323 663-1261
Clayton Penner, *Manager*
EMP: 130
SALES (corp-wide): 2.4B **Publicly Held**
WEB: www.hehrintl.com
SIC: **3444** 3442 Sheet metalwork; metal doors, sash & trim
HQ: Lippert Components Manufacturing, Inc.
3501 County Road 6 E
Elkhart IN 46514
574 535-1125

(G-7438)
LIPPERT COMPONENTS MFG INC
600 W 24th St (67117-9201)
P.O. Box 846, Newton (67114-0846)
PHONE..................................316 283-0627
EMP: 75
SALES (corp-wide): 2.4B **Publicly Held**
WEB: www.hehrintl.com
SIC: **3211** 5039 3231 Tempered glass; glass construction materials; products of purchased glass
HQ: Lippert Components Manufacturing, Inc.
3501 County Road 6 E
Elkhart IN 46514
574 535-1125

(G-7439)
SUPER SPEED PRINTING INC
3200 Witmarsum Dr (67117-8041)
PHONE..................................316 283-5828
Sterling M Shelly, *President*
Dean Eric Shelly, *Vice Pres*
EMP: 15
SALES (est): 960.7K **Privately Held**
SIC: **2752** 5699 Commercial printing, offset; T-shirts, custom printed

Norton
Norton County

(G-7440)
AG VALLEY COOP NON-STOCK
314 W North St (67654-1722)
PHONE..................................785 877-5131
Delbert Harvey, *Branch Mgr*
EMP: 14
SALES (corp-wide): 194MM **Privately Held**
WEB: www.agvalley.com
SIC: **5153** 5261 Grain elevators; fertilizer
PA: Ag Valley Cooperative Non-Stock
72133 State Hwy 136
Edison NE 68936
308 927-3681

(G-7441)
ANDBE HOME INC
201 W Crane St (67654-1117)
PHONE..................................785 877-2601
Jerry Hawks, *CEO*
Nancy McGinnis, *Administration*
EMP: 100
SQ FT: 20,000
SALES: 4.8MM **Privately Held**
SIC: **8052** 8051 8049 Intermediate care facilities; skilled nursing care facilities; physical therapist

(G-7442)
COUNTY OF NORTON
Also Called: Norton County Ems/Ambulance
11822 Road W1 (67654-5703)
PHONE..................................785 877-5784
Kathleen Conrad, *Director*
EMP: 33 **Privately Held**
SIC: **4119** 9111 Ambulance service; county supervisors' & executives' offices
PA: County Of Norton
105 S Kansas Ave
Norton KS 67654
785 877-5710

(G-7443)
DEVELOPMENTAL SVCS NW KANS INC
Also Called: Frontier Developemental Center
1104 N State St (67654-1134)
P.O. Box 9 (67654-0009)
PHONE..................................785 877-5154
Lisa Shearer, *Manager*
EMP: 14
SALES (corp-wide): 14.4MM **Privately Held**
SIC: **8059** 8093 Home for the mentally retarded, exc. skilled or intermediate; rehabilitation center, outpatient treatment
PA: Developmental Services Of Northwest Kansas, Inc.
2703 Hall St Ste B10
Hays KS 67601
785 625-5678

(G-7444)
ENGELS SALES & SERVICE CENTER (PA)
209 W Lincoln St (67654-1990)
PHONE..................................785 877-3391
Gregory L Engel, *President*
Darla D Engel, *Treasurer*
EMP: 10
SQ FT: 9,000
SALES (est): 1.3MM **Privately Held**
SIC: **7538** 5531 5261 General automotive repair shops; automotive & home supply stores; lawnmowers & tractors

(G-7445)
F & F IRON & METAL CO
514 W Washington St (67654-1965)
P.O. Box 53 (67654-0053)
PHONE..................................785 877-3830
Von Fahrenbruch, *President*
EMP: 21
SALES (est): 3.9MM **Privately Held**
SIC: **4953** 5093 Recycling, waste materials; metal scrap & waste materials

(G-7446)
FIRST SECURITY BANK & TRUST CO (PA)
201 E Main St (67654-2044)
P.O. Box 383 (67654-0383)
PHONE..................................785 877-3313
Carl Aohseod, *President*
Mike Watkins, *Vice Pres*
EMP: 20 **EST**: 1887
SALES (est): 5.6MM **Privately Held**
SIC: **6022** 6021 State trust companies accepting deposits, commercial; national commercial banks

(G-7447)
FIRST STATE BANK (PA)
105 W Main St (67654-1947)
P.O. Box 560 (67654-0560)
PHONE..................................785 877-3341
Norman Nelson, *President*
Lindsay Wilson, *Manager*
EMP: 26
SALES: 20.1MM **Privately Held**
SIC: **6411** 6022 Insurance agents, brokers & service; state commercial banks

(G-7448)
MAPES & MILLER CPA
418 E Holme St (67654-1413)
PHONE..................................785 877-5833
John Mapes, *Partner*
Denis Miller, *Partner*
EMP: 10
SALES (est): 571.9K **Privately Held**
SIC: **8721** Certified public accountant

(G-7449)
MIDWEST CONTRACTORS INC
912 N State St (67654-1150)
P.O. Box 243 (67654-0243)
PHONE..................................785 877-3565
Franklin Cooper, *President*
EMP: 30
SQ FT: 7,500
SALES (est): 4.8MM **Privately Held**
SIC: **1623** Telephone & communication line construction

(G-7450)
MILTECH MACHINE CORPORATION
Also Called: Microline Products
15277 Washington Rd (67654-5586)
P.O. Box 422 (67654-0422)
PHONE..................................785 877-5381
John Milnes, *President*
EMP: 25
SQ FT: 600

GEOGRAPHIC

SALES (est): 1.7MM **Privately Held**
WEB: www.miltechmachine.com
SIC: 3599 Machine shop, jobbing & repair

(G-7451)
NATOMA CORPORATION
16596 Us Highway 36 (67654-5440)
P.O. Box 88 (67654-0088)
PHONE..................................785 877-3529
Gail Boller, *President*
Darin Campbell, *COO*
Josh Stalder, *Foreman/Supr*
Todd Boller, *CFO*
EMP: 70
SQ FT: 46,000
SALES (est): 13.6MM **Privately Held**
WEB: www.natomacorp.com
SIC: 3599 Machine shop, jobbing & repair

(G-7452)
NATOMA LEASING LLC
16596 Us Highway 36 (67654-5440)
P.O. Box 88 (67654-0088)
PHONE..................................785 877-3529
Darin Campbell,
Mark Griffey,
EMP: 70
SALES (est): 1.9MM **Privately Held**
SIC: 3599 Machine & other job shop work

(G-7453)
NATOMA MANUFACTURING CORP
16596 Us Highway 36 (67654-5440)
P.O. Box 88 (67654-0088)
PHONE..................................785 877-3529
Darin Campbell,
Mark Griffey,
EMP: 70
SALES (est): 2MM **Privately Held**
SIC: 3599 Machine shop, jobbing & repair

(G-7454)
NATOMA REALTY LLC
16596 Us Highway 36 (67654-5440)
P.O. Box 88 (67654-0088)
PHONE..................................785 877-3529
Darin Campbell,
Mark Griffey,
EMP: 70 **EST:** 2017
SALES (est): 1.9MM **Privately Held**
SIC: 3599 Machine & other job shop work

(G-7455)
NEW AGE INDUSTRIAL CORP INC
16788 Us Highway 36 (67654-5488)
P.O. Box 520 (67654-0520)
PHONE..................................785 877-5121
Larry Nelson, *President*
Thomas Sharp, *Vice Pres*
James H Sharp, *Admin Sec*
▲ **EMP:** 155
SQ FT: 200,000
SALES (est): 48.1MM **Privately Held**
SIC: 3441 3444 3556 2542 Fabricated structural metal; sheet metalwork; food products machinery; partitions & fixtures, except wood

(G-7456)
NORTON COUNTY CO-OP ASSN INC (PA)
Also Called: Norton County Cooperative Assn
314 W North St (67654-1722)
PHONE..................................785 877-5900
Robert Smith, *CEO*
EMP: 10 **EST:** 1955
SQ FT: 3,600
SALES (est): 8.8MM **Privately Held**
SIC: 5153 5191 5172 Grains; grain elevators; feed; seeds: field, garden & flower; fertilizer & fertilizer materials; petroleum products

(G-7457)
NORTON COUNTY HOSPITAL (PA)
102 E Holme St (67654-1406)
P.O. Box 250 (67654-0250)
PHONE..................................785 877-3351
Von Fahrenbruch, *President*
Jenny Braun, *Principal*
Ron Fisher, *Principal*
Peggy Pratt, *Principal*
Steve Berry, *Vice Pres*
EMP: 11
SQ FT: 57,000
SALES: 11.4MM **Privately Held**
WEB: www.ntcohosp.com
SIC: 8062 General medical & surgical hospitals

(G-7458)
NORTON COUNTY HOSPITAL
Also Called: Hartley, Roy W MD
711 N Norton Ave (67654-1449)
PHONE..................................785 877-3305
Pam Copper, *Manager*
EMP: 12
SALES (corp-wide): 11.4MM **Privately Held**
WEB: www.ntcohosp.com
SIC: 8062 8011 General medical & surgical hospitals; offices & clinics of medical doctors
PA: Norton County Hospital
102 E Holme St
Norton KS 67654
785 877-3351

(G-7459)
NORTON COUNTY HOSPITAL
Also Called: Norton County Health Dept
801 N Norton Ave (67654-1432)
P.O. Box 403 (67654-0403)
PHONE..................................785 877-5745
Gina Frack, *Administration*
EMP: 10
SALES (corp-wide): 11.4MM **Privately Held**
WEB: www.ntcohosp.com
SIC: 8062 9111 8082 General medical & surgical hospitals; county supervisors' & executives' offices; home health care services
PA: Norton County Hospital
102 E Holme St
Norton KS 67654
785 877-3351

(G-7460)
NORTON RETIREMENT AND ASSISTED
Also Called: Whispering Pines Retirement HM
200 Whispering Pines St (67654-1260)
PHONE..................................785 874-4314
Robert Stephenson,
Theodore Sanco,
EMP: 22
SALES (est): 805.4K **Privately Held**
SIC: 8059 Nursing home, except skilled & intermediate care facility

(G-7461)
PRAIRIE LAND ELECTRIC COOP INC
14935 Us Highway 36 (67654-5615)
P.O. Box 360 (67654-0360)
PHONE..................................785 877-3323
Allan Miller, *CEO*
EMP: 86
SQ FT: 13,578
SALES: 69.6MM **Privately Held**
WEB: www.prairielandelectric.com
SIC: 4911 Distribution, electric power

(G-7462)
ROBIN WHITE HILLS INC
Also Called: Prairie Dog Golf Club
P.O. Box 159 (67654-0159)
PHONE..................................785 877-3399
Ron Fisher, *President*
Roger Hartman, *Vice Pres*
Joe Herman, *Treasurer*
Charles Vsetecka, *Manager*
Michael Vincent, *Manager*
EMP: 13
SQ FT: 20,000
SALES: 211.7K **Privately Held**
SIC: 5812 7992 Eating places; public golf courses

(G-7463)
VALLEY HOPE ASSOCIATION (PA)
Also Called: Valley Hope Treatment Center
103 S Wabash Ave (67654-2117)
P.O. Box 510 (67654-0510)
PHONE..................................785 877-2421
Daniel McCormick, *President*
John Leipold, *COO*
Thomas Baumann, *CFO*
Faith Wanja, *Program Dir*
Dawn Johnson, *Gnrl Med Prac*
EMP: 50
SQ FT: 20,000
SALES: 46.7MM **Privately Held**
WEB: www.valleyhope.com
SIC: 8069 8093 Alcoholism rehabilitation hospital; drug addiction rehabilitation hospital; alcohol clinic, outpatient

(G-7464)
VALLEY HOPE ASSOCIATION
Also Called: Valley Hope Treatment Center
709 W Holme St (67654-1251)
P.O. Box 366 (67654-0366)
PHONE..................................785 877-5101
Dan Lara, *Comms Mgr*
Ashley Barcum, *Manager*
Ray Calligan Larry Black, *Director*
Renee Hawks, *Director*
EMP: 45
SALES (corp-wide): 46.7MM **Privately Held**
WEB: www.valleyhope.com
SIC: 8093 Alcohol clinic, outpatient; drug clinic, outpatient
PA: Valley Hope Association
103 S Wabash Ave
Norton KS 67654
785 877-2421

Nortonville
Jefferson County

(G-7465)
VILLAGE VILLA INC
412 E Walnut St (66060-4008)
P.O. Box 346 (66060-0346)
PHONE..................................913 886-6400
Suzanne Misenhelter, *Principal*
Christy Bogner, *CFO*
Gerald Fowler, *Administration*
EMP: 45
SALES: 3.5MM **Privately Held**
WEB: www.villagevilla.com
SIC: 8051 Convalescent home with continuous nursing care

Norwich
Kingman County

(G-7466)
FARRAR CORPORATION (PA)
142 W Burns Ave (67118-9354)
PHONE..................................785 537-7733
Joe E Farrar, *President*
Todd Farrar, *COO*
Kari Adams, *Purchasing*
Kraig Vondran, *CFO*
Fred McClaren, *Controller*
EMP: 299 **EST:** 1925
SQ FT: 110,000
SALES: 25.9MM **Privately Held**
WEB: www.farrarusa.com
SIC: 3599 3321 3322 Machine shop, jobbing & repair; gray & ductile iron foundries; malleable iron foundries

(G-7467)
FARRAR CORPORATION
142 W Burns Ave (67118-9354)
PHONE..................................620 478-2212
Kelly Poe, *Manager*
EMP: 20
SALES (est): 3.3MM
SALES (corp-wide): 25.9MM **Privately Held**
WEB: www.farrarusa.com
SIC: 3599 Machine shop, jobbing & repair
PA: Farrar Corporation
142 W Burns Ave
Norwich KS 67118
785 537-7733

(G-7468)
FARRAR CORPORATION
129 S Somerset St (67118)
PHONE..................................620 478-2212
Joe Farrar, *Branch Mgr*
EMP: 45
SALES (est): 6.2MM
SALES (corp-wide): 25.9MM **Privately Held**
WEB: www.farrarusa.com
SIC: 3321 Gray & ductile iron foundries
PA: Farrar Corporation
142 W Burns Ave
Norwich KS 67118
785 537-7733

(G-7469)
FARRAR CORPORATION
218 Main (67118)
PHONE..................................620 478-2212
Dave Dohrmann, *Manager*
EMP: 120
SALES (est): 9MM
SALES (corp-wide): 25.9MM **Privately Held**
WEB: www.farrarusa.com
SIC: 3599 Machine shop, jobbing & repair
PA: Farrar Corporation
142 W Burns Ave
Norwich KS 67118
785 537-7733

(G-7470)
INLAND CORPORATION
15243 Se 150 St (67118-9101)
PHONE..................................620 478-2450
Nancy Hubble, *President*
Thomas L Steele, *Treasurer*
Mandy Butler, *Manager*
EMP: 10
SALES: 600K **Privately Held**
SIC: 1611 Highway & street paving contractor

Oakley
Logan County

(G-7471)
ARCHER-DANIELS-MIDLAND COMPANY
Also Called: ADM
104 S Freeman Ave (67748-8900)
PHONE..................................785 671-3171
Steve Badger, *Branch Mgr*
EMP: 12
SALES (corp-wide): 64.3B **Publicly Held**
WEB: www.collingwoodgrain.com
SIC: 2041 5191 5261 Flour & other grain mill products; fertilizer & fertilizer materials; fertilizer
PA: Archer-Daniels-Midland Company
77 W Wacker Dr Ste 4600
Chicago IL 60601
312 634-8100

(G-7472)
BEVERLY ENTERPRISES-KANSAS LLC
Also Called: Oakley Manor
615 Price Ave (67748-2048)
PHONE..................................785 672-3115
Ronald Farnsworth, *Branch Mgr*
EMP: 26
SALES (corp-wide): 393.8MM **Privately Held**
SIC: 8051 Extended care facility
HQ: Beverly Enterprises-Kansas, Llc
1 1000 Beverly Way
Fort Smith AR 72919
479 201-2000

(G-7473)
BLUE BEACON USA LP II
Also Called: Blue Beacon Truck Wash
1003 Highway 40 (67748-6061)
PHONE..................................785 672-3328
Andy Lee, *Manager*
EMP: 20

SALES (corp-wide): 108.6MM **Privately Held**
WEB: www.bluebeacon.com
SIC: 7542 Truck wash
PA: Blue Beacon U.S.A., L.P. Ii
500 Graves Blvd
Salina KS 67401
785 825-2221

(G-7474)
FARMERS STATE BANK OF OAKLEY
100 Center Ave (67748-1712)
P.O. Box 170, Scott City (67871-0170)
PHONE.................................785 672-3251
Matthew Engle, *CEO*
Susan Glassman, *Vice Pres*
EMP: 16 **EST:** 1907
SALES: 6.4MM **Privately Held**
WEB: www.fsboakley.com
SIC: 6022 State trust companies accepting deposits, commercial
PA: Security Bancshares, Inc
506 S Main St
Scott City KS

(G-7475)
FRONTIER AG INC (PA)
415 W 2nd St (67748-1545)
P.O. Box 248 (67748-0248)
PHONE.................................785 462-2063
Brad Cowan, *CEO*
Brian Linin, *CFO*
Lynette Ball, *Accountant*
Aaron Racette, *Sales Staff*
Rachel Gilliland, *Office Mgr*
EMP: 25
SQ FT: 10,000
SALES (est): 89.9MM **Privately Held**
SIC: 5531 5191 Automotive parts; farm supplies

(G-7476)
HOSPITALITY OAKLEY GROUP LLC
Also Called: Oakley Sleep Inn and Suites
3768 E Hwy 40 (67748)
PHONE.................................785 671-1111
Matt Mildenberger,
EMP: 18
SALES: 950K **Privately Held**
SIC: 7011 Hotels

(G-7477)
JIM MITTEN TRUCKING INC
3660 Us 40 (67748-6002)
PHONE.................................785 672-3279
Larry Dinkel, *President*
Dina Dinkel, *Admin Sec*
EMP: 10
SQ FT: 7,000
SALES (est): 784.5K **Privately Held**
SIC: 4212 4213 Delivery service, vehicular; contract haulers

(G-7478)
KANSAS DEPARTMENT TRNSP
3501 Highway 40 (67748-6001)
P.O. Box 130 (67748-0130)
PHONE.................................785 672-3113
Robert Weiss, *Principal*
EMP: 58 **Privately Held**
WEB: www.nwwichitabypass.com
SIC: 1611 9621 Highway & street maintenance; regulation, administration of transportation;
HQ: Kansas Department Of Transportation
700 Sw Harrison St # 500
Topeka KS 66603
785 296-3501

(G-7479)
LOGAN COUNTY HOSPITAL
211 Cherry Ave (67748-1218)
PHONE.................................785 672-3211
Mel Snow, *CEO*
Bonnie Hagel, *CFO*
EMP: 120 **EST:** 1951
SQ FT: 32,000
SALES: 11.9MM **Privately Held**
WEB: www.logancountyhospital.org
SIC: 8062 Hospital, affiliated with AMA residency

(G-7480)
LOGAN COUNTY MANOR
Also Called: Logan County Health Services
615 Price Ave (67748-2048)
PHONE.................................785 672-8109
Diana Dible, *Manager*
EMP: 10
SALES (est): 461K **Privately Held**
SIC: 8051 8011 Skilled nursing care facilities; primary care medical clinic

(G-7481)
MITTEN INC
Also Called: Mitten Truck Stop
1001 Highway 40 (67748-6061)
PHONE.................................785 672-3062
Patricia Brinks, *Manager*
EMP: 30
SALES (est): 2.3MM
SALES (corp-wide): 20.1MM **Privately Held**
SIC: 5541 5171 7538 5511 Truck stops; petroleum bulk stations & terminals; general automotive repair shops; trucks, tractors & trailers: new & used
PA: Mitten, Inc.
1001 Highway 40
Oakley KS 67748
785 672-3062

(G-7482)
NEW FRONTIERS
Also Called: New Frontiers Health Services
212 Maple Ave (67748-1220)
PHONE.................................785 672-3261
Rodney Bates, *Principal*
Crystal Faulkenter, *Manager*
EMP: 10
SALES (est): 520K **Privately Held**
SIC: 8011 General & family practice, physician/surgeon

(G-7483)
OAKLEY AREA CHAMBER COMMERCE
222 Center Ave 1 (67748-1714)
PHONE.................................785 672-4862
Dave Nelson, *President*
EMP: 10
SALES (est): 360K **Privately Held**
SIC: 8611 Chamber of Commerce

(G-7484)
OAKLEY MOTORS INC (PA)
611 S Freeman Ave (67748-8934)
PHONE.................................785 672-3238
James L Robben, *President*
Daniel Robben, *Corp Secy*
Gerald Robben, *Vice Pres*
Larry Robben, *Vice Pres*
EMP: 30
SALES (est): 8.4MM **Privately Held**
WEB: www.oakleymotors.com
SIC: 5511 5083 5571 7538 Automobiles, new & used; pickups, new & used; vans, new & used; farm & garden machinery; motorcycle dealers; general automotive repair shops; passenger car leasing; used car dealers

(G-7485)
PIONEER FEEDYARD LLC
1021 County Road Cc (67748-6093)
PHONE.................................785 672-3257
James L Keller, *President*
Scott Foote,
EMP: 35
SALES: 350MM **Privately Held**
SIC: 0111 0211 0115 0212 Wheat; beef cattle feedlots; corn; beef cattle except feedlots

(G-7486)
QES PRESSURE PUMPING LLC
226 Prospect Ave (67748-8818)
PHONE.................................785 672-8822
Walt Dinkel, *Branch Mgr*
EMP: 14
SALES (corp-wide): 1.1B **Privately Held**
SIC: 1389 Oil field services; cementing oil & gas well casings; acidizing wells
HQ: Qes Pressure Pumping Llc
1322 S Grant Ave
Chanute KS 66720
620 431-9210

(G-7487)
SPORER LAND DEVELOPMENT INC
431 Us Highway 83 (67748-8901)
P.O. Box 246 (67748-0246)
PHONE.................................785 672-4319
Jay Sporer, *Vice Pres*
Troy Sporer, *Vice Pres*
Mark Hubert, *Project Mgr*
EMP: 45 **EST:** 1961
SQ FT: 2,200
SALES: 14.4MM **Privately Held**
SIC: 1629 1611 Dam construction; general contractor, highway & street construction

(G-7488)
WESTERN PLAINS ENERGY LLC (PA)
3022 County Road 18 (67748-6064)
PHONE.................................785 672-8810
Derek Peine, *CEO*
Jeff Torluemke, *President*
Rick Holaday, *Plant Mgr*
Curt V Sheldon, *CFO*
Curt Sheldon, *CFO*
EMP: 48
SQ FT: 1,120
SALES: 120MM **Privately Held**
WEB: www.westernplainsenergy.com
SIC: 2869 Ethyl alcohol, ethanol

Oberlin
Decatur County

(G-7489)
COUNTY OF DECATUR
Also Called: Northwest Kansas Juvenile Svcs
120 E Hall St (67749-2327)
P.O. Box 89 (67749-0089)
PHONE.................................785 475-8113
Peggy Pratt, *Director*
EMP: 11 **Privately Held**
WEB: www.ajcf.ksjja.org
SIC: 8322 Individual & family services
PA: County Of Decatur
120 E Hall St Ste 9
Oberlin KS 67749
785 475-8102

(G-7490)
DECATUR COOPERATIVE ASSN (PA)
Also Called: Decatur Coop Assoc
305 S York Ave (67749-2256)
P.O. Box 68 (67749-0068)
PHONE.................................785 475-2234
Chris Bailey, *President*
Brenda Fought, *Admin Asst*
EMP: 11 **EST:** 1953
SQ FT: 7,500
SALES (est): 52.7MM **Privately Held**
WEB: www.decaturcoop.net
SIC: 5153 5191 5171 Grain elevators; farm supplies; feed; fertilizer & fertilizer materials; chemicals, agricultural; petroleum bulk stations

(G-7491)
DECATUR COUNTY FEED YARD INC
2361 Highway 83 (67749-5136)
PHONE.................................785 475-2212
S Warren Weibert, *President*
Carol Weibert, *Corp Secy*
EMP: 35 **EST:** 1971
SQ FT: 2,500
SALES (est): 5.3MM **Privately Held**
WEB: www.decaturfeedyard.com
SIC: 0211 Beef cattle feedlots

(G-7492)
DECATUR HEALTH SYSTEMS INC
Also Called: Decatur County Hospital
810 W Columbia St (67749-2450)
P.O. Box 268 (67749-0268)
PHONE.................................785 475-2208
Kris Matthews, *COO*
Kris Mathews, *COO*
Ashley Ploussard, *Purch Dir*
Lindsey Osterhaus, *Human Res Dir*
Lauren Bird, *Records Dir*
EMP: 95
SALES: 6MM **Privately Held**
SIC: 8062 General medical & surgical hospitals

(G-7493)
EVANGELICAL LUTHERAN
Also Called: Good Smrtan Soc - Decatur Cnty
108 E Ash St (67749-1908)
P.O. Box 5038, Sioux Falls SD (57117-5038)
PHONE.................................785 475-2245
Morgan Burton, *Branch Mgr*
EMP: 93 **Privately Held**
WEB: www.good-sam.com
SIC: 8059 Nursing home, except skilled & intermediate care facility
HQ: The Evangelical Lutheran Good Samaritan Society
4800 W 57th St
Sioux Falls SD 57108
866 928-1635

(G-7494)
FOWLERS LLC
Also Called: Ron's Tire Service
201 E Frontier Pkwy (67749-1530)
PHONE.................................785 475-3451
Ronald Fowler,
Ron Fowler,
Sondra Fowler,
EMP: 15
SQ FT: 1,500
SALES: 750K **Privately Held**
SIC: 5531 7539 Automotive tires; batteries, automotive & truck; brake repair, automotive; wheel alignment, automotive

(G-7495)
GARY DEAN ANDERSON
Also Called: Landmark Inn Hstrc Bnk Oberlin
189 S Penn Ave (67749-2242)
P.O. Box 162 (67749-0162)
PHONE.................................785 475-2340
Gary D Anderson, *Owner*
Gary Anderson, *Owner*
EMP: 25
SQ FT: 8,000
SALES: 125K **Privately Held**
SIC: 7011 5947 5812 Bed & breakfast inn; gifts & novelties; eating places

(G-7496)
HAYNES PUBLISHING CO
Also Called: Oberlin Harrold News
204 Penn Ave (67749)
PHONE.................................785 475-2206
Pat Kozak, *Manager*
EMP: 9
SALES (corp-wide): 3.3MM **Privately Held**
SIC: 2711 2741 Newspapers, publishing & printing; miscellaneous publishing
PA: Haynes Publishing Co
170 S Penn Ave
Oberlin KS 67749
785 475-2206

(G-7497)
HAYNES PUBLISHING CO (PA)
Also Called: Oberlin Herald
170 S Penn Ave (67749-2243)
PHONE.................................785 475-2206
Steve Haynes, *President*
Cynthia Haynes, *Corp Secy*
Evan Barnum, *Opers Staff*
EMP: 8
SALES (est): 3.3MM **Privately Held**
SIC: 2711 Commercial printing & newspaper publishing combined; newspapers, publishing & printing

(G-7498)
OBERLIN LIVESTOCK AUCTION INC
Hwy 83 (67749)
P.O. Box 14 (67749-0014)
PHONE.................................785 475-2323
Jerry Fortin, *President*
Jolene Fortin, *Admin Sec*
EMP: 10 **EST:** 1962
SQ FT: 3,500
SALES (est): 1.4MM **Privately Held**
SIC: 5154 Auctioning livestock

(G-7499)
POE WELL SERVICE INC (PA)
215 S York Ave (67749-2321)
P.O. Box 115 (67749-0115)
PHONE..................................785 475-3422
Marvin Poe, *President*
Ruby Poe, *Corp Secy*
EMP: 13
SALES: 1MM **Privately Held**
SIC: 1389 Oil field services

Offerle
Edwards County

(G-7500)
OFFERLE COOP GRN & SUP CO (PA)
222 E Santa Fe (67563-6431)
PHONE..................................620 659-2165
Duane Boyd, *President*
EMP: 11 **EST:** 1910
SQ FT: 5,000
SALES (est): 32.2MM **Privately Held**
WEB: www.offerle.coop
SIC: 5153 5191 5541 Grains; fertilizer & fertilizer materials; feed; gasoline service stations

Olathe
Johnson County

(G-7501)
24 HOUR FITNESS USA INC
13370 S Blackfoot Dr (66062-4527)
PHONE..................................913 829-4503
EMP: 20
SALES (corp-wide): 480.7MM **Privately Held**
SIC: 7991 Health club
HQ: 24 Hour Fitness Usa, Inc.
12647 Alcosta Blvd # 500
San Ramon CA 94583
925 543-3100

(G-7502)
4TH GNERATION PROMOTIONAL PDTS
Also Called: Www.4thgenerationinc.com
14470 W 122nd St (66062-6053)
PHONE..................................913 393-0837
EMP: 6
SQ FT: 2,600
SALES (est): 537.1K **Privately Held**
SIC: 5199 2759 2395 Whol Nondurable Goods Commercial Printing Pleating/Stitching Services

(G-7503)
A ARNOLD OF KANSAS CITY LLC
15761 S Keeler St (66062-3513)
PHONE..................................913 829-8267
Gary Brann,
Sherry Brann,
EMP: 35
SQ FT: 40,000
SALES: 2.5MM **Privately Held**
WEB: www.brann-tech.com
SIC: 4213 4214 Household goods transport; household goods moving & storage, local

(G-7504)
A C PRINTING CO INC
1475 N Winchester St (66061-5881)
PHONE..................................913 780-3377
Graig Russel, *President*
Greg Russell, *President*
Aleta Russell, *Vice Pres*
Jim Gilroy, *Accounts Exec*
Loretta Russell, *Office Mgr*
EMP: 9
SALES (est): 1.4MM **Privately Held**
WEB: www.acprints.com
SIC: 2752 Commercial printing, offset

(G-7505)
A CARING DOCTOR MINNESOTA PA
Also Called: Banfield Pet Hospital 241
15255 W 119th St (66062-5605)
PHONE..................................913 393-4654
Aubrey Wilson, *Branch Mgr*
EMP: 20
SALES (corp-wide): 37.6B **Privately Held**
WEB: www.banfield.net
SIC: 0742 Animal hospital services, pets & other animal specialties
HQ: A Caring Doctor Minnesota Pa
8000 Ne Tillamook St
Portland OR 97213
503 922-5000

(G-7506)
ABAXIS INC
14830 W 117th St (66062-9304)
PHONE..................................913 787-7400
Mark Harrison, *Division Mgr*
EMP: 45
SALES (est): 5.1MM
SALES (corp-wide): 5.8B **Publicly Held**
SIC: 2835 In vitro & in vivo diagnostic substances
HQ: Abaxis, Inc.
3240 Whipple Rd
Union City CA 94587
510 675-6500

(G-7507)
ABERDEEN VILLAGE INC
17500 W 119th St (66061-9524)
PHONE..................................913 599-6100
Robert Kotsull, *Exec Dir*
EMP: 29
SALES (est): 11.7MM **Privately Held**
SIC: 8082 Home health care services

(G-7508)
AC PROFESSIONAL LLC
1499 E 151st St (66062-2854)
PHONE..................................816 668-4760
Mannette Carter, *Mng Member*
EMP: 20
SALES (est): 971.4K **Privately Held**
SIC: 1711 7291 8721 Warm air heating & air conditioning contractor; tax return preparation services; accounting, auditing & bookkeeping

(G-7509)
ADKI GROUP LLC
18730 S Ridgeview Rd (66062-9506)
PHONE..................................913 208-7899
Chad Fulk, *CEO*
EMP: 10 **EST:** 2008
SALES (est): 1MM **Privately Held**
SIC: 0781 0782 Landscape services; landscape architects; landscape contractors

(G-7510)
ADOBE TRUCK & EQUIPMENT LLC
11510 S Strang Line Rd (66062-4900)
PHONE..................................913 498-9888
EMP: 7
SALES (est): 1MM **Privately Held**
SIC: 3537 Industrial trucks & tractors

(G-7511)
ADVANCE AUTO PARTS INC
13794 S Blackbob Rd (66062-1932)
PHONE..................................913 782-0076
Mark General, *Manager*
EMP: 10
SALES (corp-wide): 9.5B **Publicly Held**
SIC: 7538 General automotive repair shops
PA: Advance Auto Parts, Inc.
2635 E Millbrook Rd Ste A
Raleigh NC 27604
540 362-4911

(G-7512)
AEGIS BUSINESS SOLUTIONS LLC (PA)
14453 Shady Bend Rd (66061-9219)
P.O. Box 14326, Kansas City MO (64152-7326)
PHONE..................................913 307-9922
Randall W Crawford, *President*
Garold Sokolenko, *Vice Pres*
EMP: 5
SALES: 8MM **Privately Held**
WEB: www.aegisbusinesssolutions.com
SIC: 2522 3571 7373 5021 Office furniture, except wood; electronic computers; computer integrated systems design; furniture; floor laying & floor work; roofing, siding & sheet metal work

(G-7513)
AGAPE MONTESSORI SCHOOL
16550 W 129th St (66062-1378)
PHONE..................................913 768-0812
Deborah Pulliam,
Cecil Pulliam,
EMP: 23
SALES (est): 390.1K **Privately Held**
SIC: 8351 Montessori child development center

(G-7514)
AIR POWER CONSULTANTS INC
18903 W 157th Ter (66062-6805)
PHONE..................................913 894-0044
Martin Bosch, *President*
Barbara Bosch, *Corp Secy*
Braxton Stowers, *Sales Staff*
EMP: 10
SQ FT: 7,000
SALES (est): 2.7MM **Privately Held**
WEB: www.airpowerconsultants.com
SIC: 7623 7373 Air conditioning repair; computer system selling services

(G-7515)
AIRFIELD TECHNOLOGY INC
12897 W 151st St Ste A (66062-7220)
PHONE..................................913 780-9800
Larry Brady, *President*
Jim Sitton, *President*
Debbie Cummer, *Vice Pres*
Nicholas Fehner, *Engineer*
Tom Tietze, *Engineer*
EMP: 8
SQ FT: 2,500
SALES (est): 1.1MM **Privately Held**
WEB: www.airfield.com
SIC: 3812 Navigational systems & instruments

(G-7516)
ALDERSGATE UNTD METH PRE SCHL
15315 W 151st St (66062-3066)
PHONE..................................913 764-2407
Cyndi Mawhiney, *Director*
Kayla Houck, *Director*
Shelly Lawrence, *Director*
EMP: 30
SQ FT: 2,200
SALES (est): 883.3K **Privately Held**
SIC: 8661 8351 Methodist Church; child day care services

(G-7517)
ALDI INC
Also Called: Aldi Foods Divisional Office
10505 S K 7 Hwy (66061-9735)
PHONE..................................913 768-1119
Mark Boersted, *President*
Anna Nastasi, *Opers Mgr*
Jeff Engle, *Warehouse Mgr*
Amy Peters, *Opers Staff*
Amy Watson, *Opers Staff*
EMP: 300
SALES (corp-wide): 355.8K **Privately Held**
WEB: www.aldi.com
SIC: 4225 General warehousing & storage
HQ: Aldi Inc.
1200 N Kirk Rd
Batavia IL 60510
630 879-8100

(G-7518)
ALLEGION S&S US HOLDING CO
2119 E Kansas City Rd (66061-7050)
PHONE..................................913 393-8629
J Riggs, *Opers Staff*
Bob Ryder, *Branch Mgr*
EMP: 33 **Privately Held**
SIC: 3561 Pumps & pumping equipment
HQ: Allegion S&S Holding Company Inc.
11819 N Penn St
Carmel IN 46032
317 810-3700

(G-7519)
ALLENBRAND-DREWS AND ASSOC (PA)
122 N Water St (66061-3415)
PHONE..................................913 764-1076
Kenneth Nellor, *President*
Dick Allenbrand, *Vice Pres*
Roger Norris, *Vice Pres*
Jim Long, *Research*
EMP: 23
SQ FT: 3,400
SALES (est): 3.1MM **Privately Held**
WEB: www.allenbrand-drews.com
SIC: 8711 Civil engineering

(G-7520)
ALLIANCE JANTR ADVISORS INC
119 N Parker St Ste 120 (66061-3139)
PHONE..................................913 815-8807
Mel Quillen, *President*
James White, *Director*
EMP: 10
SALES (est): 517.7K **Privately Held**
SIC: 4581 7349 7217 4741 Aircraft cleaning & janitorial service; building & office cleaning services; carpet & furniture cleaning on location; railroad car cleaning, icing, ventilating & heating

(G-7521)
ALLSTATE ROOFING INC
523 N Mur Len Rd (66062-1267)
PHONE..................................913 782-2000
Bernie Belcher, *President*
EMP: 10
SQ FT: 2,000
SALES: 4MM **Privately Held**
WEB: www.allstateroofing.net
SIC: 1761 Roofing contractor

(G-7522)
ALTERNACARE INFUSION PHRM INC
15065 W 116th St (66062-1098)
PHONE..................................913 906-9260
Darold F Jackson, *President*
Charles M Hayden, *President*
Charles Lane, *Vice Pres*
EMP: 14
SQ FT: 16,500
SALES (est): 958.8K
SALES (corp-wide): 2B **Privately Held**
SIC: 8082 Visiting nurse service
HQ: Amerita, Inc.
7307 S Revere Pkwy # 200
Centennial CO 80112

(G-7523)
ALTERNATIVE CLAIMS SERVICES
15665 S Mahaffie St (66062-4039)
PHONE..................................816 298-7506
Gary Hoffman, *President*
EMP: 11
SQ FT: 4,000
SALES (est): 1.9MM **Privately Held**
SIC: 6411 Insurance claim adjusters, not employed by insurance company; insurance adjusters

(G-7524)
AMANDA BLU & CO LLC
883 N Jan Mar Ct (66061-3693)
PHONE..................................913 381-9494
Mark Ferrel, *Mng Member*
Jeffrey Vanhara,
Michele Ferrel,
◆ **EMP:** 15
SQ FT: 10,000
SALES (est): 2.2MM **Privately Held**
SIC: 5112 Albums, scrapbooks & binders

(G-7525)
AMBROSE PACKAGING INC
1654 S Lone Elm Rd (66061-6837)
PHONE..................................913 780-5666
Matt Ambrose, *President*
Debbie Ambrose, *Owner*
Norman Ambrose, *Founder*
Michael Ambrose, *COO*
Karl Lavender, *Vice Pres*
▲ **EMP:** 40
SQ FT: 36,000

▲ = Import ▼=Export
◆ =Import/Export

SALES (est): 17.7MM Privately Held
SIC: 5199 Packaging materials

(G-7526)
AMBROSE SALES INC
1654 S Lone Elm Rd (66061-6837)
PHONE..................................913 780-5666
Matt Ambrose, *President*
Michael Ambrose, *COO*
David Sloan, *CFO*
Shana Spradling, *Accounting Mgr*
Mike Laffere, *VP Sales*
EMP: 25
SALES (est): 8.6MM Privately Held
WEB: www.ambrosepackaging.com
SIC: 5199 5074 Packaging materials; plumbing & hydronic heating supplies

(G-7527)
AMERICAN REFRIGERATED EX INC
505 N Mur Len Rd (66062-1237)
PHONE..................................913 406-8562
Art Shoener, *CEO*
Thomas Campbell, *Vice Pres*
David Lundgren, *Treasurer*
Chris Doll, *Admin Sec*
EMP: 10
SALES (est): 666.3K Privately Held
SIC: 4011 Steam railroads

(G-7528)
AMERICAN SUPERCLEAN
2011 E Crossroads Ln # 301 (66062-1657)
PHONE..................................913 815-3257
Dyanna McCann, *Principal*
EMP: 10
SALES (est): 261.6K Privately Held
SIC: 7349 Building & office cleaning services

(G-7529)
AMZ CONSTRUCTION INC
14561 Greentree Ln (66061-8804)
PHONE..................................913 915-7867
Aaron M Zemencik, *President*
EMP: 19
SALES: 370K Privately Held
SIC: 1521 Single-family housing construction

(G-7530)
ANTES CONCRETE INC
30914 W 119th St (66061-9014)
PHONE..................................913 856-4535
Leo Antes, *President*
Robert Grant, *Vice Pres*
EMP: 13
SALES: 2.3MM Privately Held
SIC: 1521 Single-family housing construction

(G-7531)
APEX INNOVATIONS INC
19951 W 162nd St (66062-2787)
PHONE..................................913 254-0250
Joe Abrams, *President*
Caroline Chong, *Manager*
EMP: 10
SALES (est): 958.4K Privately Held
SIC: 7371 Software programming applications

(G-7532)
ARCHER-DANIELS-MIDLAND COMPANY
Also Called: ADM
100 S Paniplus Dr (66061-9406)
PHONE..................................913 782-8800
Gerry Degnan, *President*
EMP: 120
SALES (corp-wide): 64.3B Publicly Held
WEB: www.admworld.com
SIC: 2075 Soybean oil mills
PA: Archer-Daniels-Midland Company
77 W Wacker Dr Ste 4600
Chicago IL 60601
312 634-8100

(G-7533)
ARR ROOFING LLC
Also Called: Boone Brothers Roofing
1060 W Santa Fe St (66061-3156)
PHONE..................................913 829-0447
Ron Boone, *Manager*
EMP: 60
SALES (corp-wide): 16.6MM Privately Held
WEB: www.boonebrothers.com
SIC: 1761 Roofing contractor
PA: Arr Roofing, Llc
8909 Washington Cir
Omaha NE 68127
712 277-2103

(G-7534)
ARROW RENOVATION & CNSTR LLC
305 E Dennis Ave (66061-4519)
PHONE..................................913 703-3000
Danny Davis, *CEO*
Candace Davis, *President*
James Bohon, *Advt Staff*
EMP: 32
SQ FT: 3,200
SALES: 2MM Privately Held
SIC: 1522 5033 1761 1521 Remodeling, multi-family dwellings; roofing, asphalt & sheet metal; roofing, siding & sheet metal work; roofing & gutter work; siding contractor; single-family home remodeling, additions & repairs

(G-7535)
ASPEN LAWN LANDSCAPING INC
Also Called: Midwest Holiday Creations
1265 N Winchester St (66061-5879)
PHONE..................................913 829-6135
Kent Girton, *President*
Stan Lopeman, *Manager*
Tarah Elston, *Admin Asst*
EMP: 30
SQ FT: 4,000
SALES (est): 2.3MM Privately Held
SIC: 0782 Lawn care services

(G-7536)
ASPHALT SALES COMPANY (PA)
23200 W 159th St (66061-9421)
P.O. Box 6263, Kansas City (66106-0263)
PHONE..................................913 788-8806
Thomas K Frye, *President*
Pat McAnany, *Corp Secy*
Elaine Treese, *Controller*
EMP: 22 EST: 1951
SQ FT: 1,500
SALES (est): 3.4MM Privately Held
SIC: 2951 Asphalt & asphaltic paving mixtures (not from refineries)

(G-7537)
ASSOCIATES IN INTERNAL MEDPED
20375 W 151st St Ste 251 (66061-7253)
PHONE..................................913 393-4888
Scott A Nitzel, *Principal*
EMP: 18 EST: 2001
SALES (est): 600K Privately Held
SIC: 8011 Internal medicine, physician/surgeon

(G-7538)
AT&T CORP
11971 S Blackbob Rd (66062-1014)
PHONE..................................913 254-0303
EMP: 14
SALES (corp-wide): 170.7B Publicly Held
SIC: 4812 Cellular telephone services
HQ: At&T Corp.
1 At&T Way
Bedminster NJ 07921
800 403-3302

(G-7539)
AT&T MOBILITY LLC
20163 W 153rd St (66062-9132)
PHONE..................................913 254-0303
Scott Dye, *Branch Mgr*
EMP: 26
SALES (corp-wide): 170.7B Publicly Held
WEB: www.cingular.com
SIC: 4812 4813 5999 Cellular telephone services; telephone communication, except radio; telephone & communication equipment
HQ: At&T Mobility Llc
1025 Lenox Park Blvd Ne
Brookhaven GA 30319
800 331-0500

(G-7540)
ATMOS ENERGY CORPORATION
Also Called: Colorado-Kansas Division
25090 W 110th Ter (66061-8464)
PHONE..................................913 254-6300
Mike Dearmond, *Manager*
EMP: 77
SALES (corp-wide): 2.9B Publicly Held
WEB: www.atmosenergy.com
SIC: 4924 Natural gas distribution
PA: Atmos Energy Corporation
5430 Lyndon B Johnson Fwy
Dallas TX 75240
972 934-9227

(G-7541)
ATTIC MANAGEMENT GROUP LLC
Also Called: Strickland Properties
720 S Rogers Rd (66062-1874)
P.O. Box 3807 (66063-3807)
PHONE..................................913 269-4583
Claudia Britz, *Vice Pres*
Bryan Brubeck, *Financial Analy*
Kasey B Vigen, *Mng Member*
EMP: 15
SALES (est): 1MM Privately Held
SIC: 4225 General warehousing & storage

(G-7542)
AUSTIN TILE INC (PA)
704 E Dennis Ave (66061-4609)
PHONE..................................913 829-6607
Don Austin, *President*
Erin Austin, *Corp Secy*
EMP: 13
SALES (est): 1.2MM Privately Held
SIC: 1743 1752 Tile installation, ceramic; carpet laying

(G-7543)
AUTOMOTIVE EQUIPMENT SERVICES
Also Called: AES Lawnparts
1651 E Kansas City Rd (66061-5847)
PHONE..................................913 254-2600
Thomas L Zschoche, *President*
John Musgrove, *Vice Pres*
Garret Barber, *Opers Mgr*
Randy Peterson, *Warehouse Mgr*
Randy Carter, *Sales Mgr*
EMP: 30
SQ FT: 60,000
SALES (est): 11.1MM Privately Held
WEB: www.lawnparts.com
SIC: 5013 5999 Automotive engines & engine parts; engine & motor equipment & supplies

(G-7544)
B A BARNES ELECTRIC INC
2014 E Spruce Cir (66062-5404)
P.O. Box 10148 (66051-1448)
PHONE..................................913 764-4455
Brent A Barnes, *President*
EMP: 33
SQ FT: 3,700
SALES (est): 2.6MM Privately Held
SIC: 1731 7349 General electrical contractor; building maintenance, except repairs

(G-7545)
B W FOUNDATIONS COMPANY INC
19125 W 151st Ter Ste C (66062-2724)
PHONE..................................913 764-8222
Robert Williams, *President*
EMP: 10
SALES (est): 660K Privately Held
SIC: 1741 Foundation building

(G-7546)
BANK AMERICA NATIONAL ASSN
15025 W 119th St (66062-9628)
PHONE..................................913 768-1340
EMP: 19
SALES (corp-wide): 110.5B Publicly Held
SIC: 6021 National commercial banks
HQ: Bank Of America, National Association
100 S Tryon St
Charlotte NC 28202
704 386-5681

(G-7547)
BANK AMERICA NATIONAL ASSN
175 N Clairborne (66062)
PHONE..................................816 979-8561
Kevin Roberts, *Manager*
EMP: 15
SALES (corp-wide): 110.5B Publicly Held
WEB: www.bofa.com
SIC: 6021 National commercial banks
HQ: Bank Of America, National Association
100 S Tryon St
Charlotte NC 28202
704 386-5681

(G-7548)
BANK OF PRAIRIE (HQ)
Also Called: MARSHALL COUNTY BANK OF BEATTIE
18675 W 151st St (66062-2738)
P.O. Box 49, Beattie (66406-0049)
PHONE..................................785 353-2298
Chris Donnelly, *President*
James Thomas, *Senior VP*
Thomas Galbrecht, *Vice Pres*
Debbie Harrison, *Vice Pres*
Shawn Turner, *Vice Pres*
EMP: 18
SQ FT: 4,000
SALES: 7.5MM Privately Held
WEB: www.bankoftheprairie.com
SIC: 6022 State commercial banks

(G-7549)
BEAUTY BRANDS LLC
Also Called: Beauty Brnds Slon Spa Sprstore
15225 W 119th St (66062-5605)
PHONE..................................913 393-4800
Steve Nickelson, *Manager*
EMP: 25 Privately Held
SIC: 5999 7231 Toiletries, cosmetics & perfumes; beauty shops
PA: Beauty Brands Llc
15507 W 99th St
Lenexa KS 66219

(G-7550)
BERNICES FOODS INC
15447 W 164th Ter (66062-9024)
PHONE..................................913 334-8283
William J Mulich, *President*
Sherry L Mulich, *Vice Pres*
EMP: 9 EST: 1973
SQ FT: 8,000
SALES (est): 1MM Privately Held
SIC: 2051 Bread, cake & related products

(G-7551)
BETHESDA LTHRAN CMMUNITIES INC
14150 W 113th St (66215-4819)
PHONE..................................913 906-5000
Mark Wester, *Manager*
EMP: 150
SALES (corp-wide): 126.8MM Privately Held
WEB: www.sdccpa.com
SIC: 8361 Residential care
PA: Bethesda Lutheran Communities, Inc.
600 Hoffmann Dr
Watertown WI 53094
920 261-3050

(G-7552)
BETTER CONCRETE CONSTRUCTION
21935 W 122nd St (66061-6393)
PHONE..................................913 390-8500
Michael Backman, *Owner*
EMP: 10
SQ FT: 17,500
SALES: 1MM Privately Held
WEB: www.betterconcreteconstr.com
SIC: 1771 Concrete work

GEOGRAPHIC

(G-7553)
BI BROOKS & SONS INC (PA)
15625 S Keeler Ter (66062-3509)
PHONE..................................913 829-5494
Thomas A Brooks, *President*
Carol Brooks, *CFO*
EMP: 5
SQ FT: 13,750
SALES (est): 1.2MM **Privately Held**
WEB: www.bibrooks.com
SIC: 5084 1796 3535 Conveyor systems; installing building equipment; conveyors & conveying equipment

(G-7554)
BILL DAVIS ROOFING
26359 W 110th St (66061-7492)
PHONE..................................913 764-4449
Bill Davis, *Owner*
EMP: 12
SALES (est): 198.1K **Privately Held**
SIC: 1761 Roofing contractor

(G-7555)
BILLS PLUMBING SERVICE LLC
308 E Park St (66061-5408)
PHONE..................................913 829-8213
William Pflumm,
EMP: 10
SALES (est): 1MM **Privately Held**
WEB: www.billsplumbingservice.com
SIC: 1711 5999 Plumbing contractors; plumbing & heating supplies

(G-7556)
BLACKBOB PET HOSPITAL
15200 S Blackbob Rd (66062-3316)
PHONE..................................913 829-7387
Carita Meyer, *Owner*
EMP: 20
SALES (est): 713.3K **Privately Held**
SIC: 0742 0752 Animal hospital services, pets & other animal specialties; grooming services, pet & animal specialties

(G-7557)
BLOOM LIVING SENIOR APARTMENTS
14001 W 133rd St (66062-4699)
PHONE..................................913 738-4335
EMP: 62
SALES (est): 169.2K
SALES (corp-wide): 32.7MM **Privately Held**
SIC: 6513 Retirement hotel operation
PA: Midwest Health, Inc
3024 Sw Wanamaker Rd # 300
Topeka KS 66614
785 272-1535

(G-7558)
BOYD & BOYD INC
Also Called: Olathe Lanes East
303 N Lindenwood Dr (66062-1238)
PHONE..................................913 764-4568
Charles Boyd, *President*
EMP: 67 **EST:** 1955
SQ FT: 20,000
SALES (est): 1.7MM **Privately Held**
SIC: 7933 Ten pin center

(G-7559)
BRETS AUTOWORKS CORP (PA)
128 N Mahaffie St (66061-3738)
PHONE..................................913 764-8677
Bret Tredway, *President*
Sheri Tredway, *Admin Sec*
EMP: 11
SQ FT: 4,080
SALES (est): 996.7K **Privately Held**
WEB: www.bretsautoworks.com
SIC: 7538 General automotive repair shops

(G-7560)
BRIDGESTONE RET OPERATIONS LLC
Also Called: Tires Plus Total Car Care
13512 S Alden St (66062-5840)
PHONE..................................913 393-2212
Travis Webb, *Manager*
EMP: 11 **Privately Held**
WEB: www.tiresplus.com
SIC: 7534 7539 5014 Tire retreading & repair shops; automotive repair shops; automobile tires & tubes; truck tires & tubes
HQ: Bridgestone Retail Operations, Llc
333 E Lake St Ste 300
Bloomingdale IL 60108
630 259-9000

(G-7561)
BRIDGESTONE RET OPERATIONS LLC
Also Called: Firestone
15050 W 135th St (66062-1599)
PHONE..................................913 782-1833
Richard Marlow, *Manager*
EMP: 12 **Privately Held**
WEB: www.bfis.com
SIC: 5531 7539 Automotive tires; brake services
HQ: Bridgestone Retail Operations, Llc
333 E Lake St Ste 300
Bloomingdale IL 60108
630 259-9000

(G-7562)
BRULEZ FOUNDATION INC
10363 S Highland Cir (66061-8441)
PHONE..................................913 422-3355
John Brulez, *President*
Justin Teddy, *Representative*
EMP: 30
SALES: 1.5MM **Privately Held**
SIC: 1771 Concrete work

(G-7563)
BS FAMILY DEVELOPMENT LLC
15350 S Constance St (66062-3732)
PHONE..................................913 961-6579
Oua Baccam,
EMP: 22 **EST:** 2014
SALES (est): 423.9K **Privately Held**
SIC: 8351 Child day care services

(G-7564)
BUD BROWN AUTOMOTIVE INC (PA)
925 N Rawhide Dr (66061-6900)
PHONE..................................913 393-8100
Phillip J Brown, *CEO*
Bernard Brown, *Chairman*
Larry Swanson, *Vice Pres*
David Kugler, *CFO*
EMP: 54
SQ FT: 35,000
SALES (est): 11.7MM **Privately Held**
SIC: 5511 7515 7513 Automobiles, new & used; passenger car leasing; truck leasing, without drivers

(G-7565)
BUGS EARLY LEARNING CTR I
1330 W Dennis Ave (66061-5234)
PHONE..................................913 254-0088
Priscilla Armstrong, *President*
EMP: 18
SALES (est): 375.4K **Privately Held**
WEB: www.bugselc.com
SIC: 8351 Group day care center

(G-7566)
BUILDER DESIGNS INC
125 S Kansas Ave (66061-4434)
PHONE..................................913 393-3367
William Johnson, *President*
Jennifer Bradshaw, *Accounts Mgr*
Scott Smith, *Art Dir*
EMP: 15
SALES (est): 2.5MM **Privately Held**
WEB: www.builderdesigns.com
SIC: 7371 Custom computer programming services

(G-7567)
BUILDERS STONE & MASONRY INC
Also Called: Bsm Wall Systems
616 N Rogers Rd (66062-1210)
PHONE..................................913 764-4446
T Dietz, *General Mgr*
Brandon Becker, *Principal*
Tj Dietz, *Principal*
Stephen Jasper, *Principal*
Doug Walker, *Manager*
EMP: 99 **EST:** 2016
SALES (est): 4.3MM **Privately Held**
SIC: 1741 Masonry & other stonework

(G-7568)
BUILDING ERECTION SVCS CO INC (PA)
15585 S Keeler St (66062-3517)
P.O. Box 970 (66051-0970)
PHONE..................................913 764-5560
Tim Olah, *President*
Chris Olah, *Vice Pres*
EMP: 35 **EST:** 1977
SQ FT: 10,500
SALES (est): 4.9MM **Privately Held**
WEB: www.builderec.com
SIC: 1542 7353 1541 7359 Commercial & office building, new construction; commercial & office buildings, renovation & repair; cranes & aerial lift equipment, rental or leasing; industrial buildings, new construction; renovation, remodeling & repairs: industrial buildings; equipment rental & leasing; structural steel erection

(G-7569)
BURNS PUBLISHING COMPANY INC
Also Called: Burns Printing Company
14465 W 140th Ter (66062-5187)
P.O. Box 995 (66051-0995)
PHONE..................................913 782-0321
Alan Redinger, *President*
Tom Ford, *President*
John Burnell, *Exec VP*
Tom Rust,
EMP: 23 **EST:** 1924
SQ FT: 16,500
SALES (est): 3.8MM **Privately Held**
WEB: www.burnsprinting.com
SIC: 2752 Commercial printing, offset

(G-7570)
BUSHNELL HOLDINGS INC
Also Called: Vista Outdoor Sales
22101 W 167th St (66062-9629)
PHONE..................................913 981-1929
Rodrigo Felipe, *Branch Mgr*
EMP: 9
SALES (corp-wide): 2B **Publicly Held**
SIC: 3851 Ophthalmic goods
HQ: Bushnell Holdings, Inc.
9200 Cody St
Overland Park KS 66214
913 752-3400

(G-7571)
BUTLER NATIONAL CORPORATION (PA)
Also Called: BNC
19920 W 161st St (66062-2700)
PHONE..................................913 780-9595
R Warren Wagoner, *Ch of Bd*
Clark D Stewart, *President*
Christopher J Reedy, *Vice Pres*
Christopher Reedy, *Vice Pres*
Craig D Stewart, *Vice Pres*
EMP: 49 **EST:** 1960
SQ FT: 9,000
SALES: 58.7MM **Publicly Held**
WEB: www.butlernationalcorp.com
SIC: 3721 3728 7389 8741 Aircraft; aircraft parts & equipment; inspection & testing services; management services

(G-7572)
C & T ENTERPRISES INC (PA)
Also Called: Nationwide
14812 W 117th St (66062-9304)
PHONE..................................913 782-1404
Terri Gravley, *President*
Dan Murray, *COO*
Allison Swaim, *Accounting Mgr*
Candy Bowen, *Accounts Mgr*
Sharon Dibella, *Accounts Mgr*
EMP: 20
SQ FT: 2,000
SALES (est): 3.5MM **Privately Held**
WEB: www.insurancesourceagency.com
SIC: 6411 Insurance agents

(G-7573)
CALIBER ELECTRONICS INC
1105 S Ridgeview Rd (66062-2238)
PHONE..................................913 782-7787
Randall A Scheckler, *President*
Bernard Hittner, *Admin Sec*
EMP: 35
SQ FT: 4,000
SALES (est): 2.9MM **Privately Held**
WEB: www.caliberelectronics.com
SIC: 3679 5065 Oscillators; electronic crystals; electronic parts & equipment

(G-7574)
CANDLEWOOD SUITES HOTEL
15490 S Rogers Rd (66062-3497)
PHONE..................................913 768-8888
Jaime Dozark, *Principal*
EMP: 14
SALES (est): 705.8K **Privately Held**
SIC: 7011 Hotels

(G-7575)
CANYON STONE INC (PA)
550 E Old Highway 56 B (66061-4604)
PHONE..................................913 254-9300
Jason Cohorst, *President*
John Folker, *Division Mgr*
Wiley Salsbury, *Vice Pres*
Wylie Saulsbury, *Vice Pres*
Brian Templeton, *Sales Mgr*
EMP: 25
SQ FT: 30,000
SALES (est): 5.9MM **Privately Held**
WEB: www.canyon-stone.com
SIC: 3272 Concrete products

(G-7576)
CAPITOL LLC
Also Called: Capitol Discovery Services
17795 W 106th St Ste 201 (66061-3155)
PHONE..................................602 462-5888
Jack Hughlette, *Manager*
EMP: 37
SALES (corp-wide): 17.9MM **Privately Held**
WEB: www.capitolusa.com
SIC: 7334 Photocopying & duplicating services
PA: Capitol, Llc
615 Las Tunas Dr Ste L
Arcadia CA 91007
626 445-0402

(G-7577)
CAPITOL FEDERAL SAVINGS BANK
1408 E Santa Fe St (66061-3697)
PHONE..................................913 782-5100
Bernie Holley, *Manager*
EMP: 13
SALES (corp-wide): 351.9MM **Publicly Held**
WEB: www.capfed.com
SIC: 6035 Federal savings & loan associations
HQ: Capitol Federal Savings Bank
700 S Kansas Ave Fl 1
Topeka KS 66603
785 235-1341

(G-7578)
CAREFORE MEDICAL INC
11605 S Alden St (66062-6924)
PHONE..................................913 327-5445
Pamela Squire, *President*
Pamela J Squire, *President*
Linda Mogue, *Corp Secy*
Sean Squire, *Vice Pres*
EMP: 24
SQ FT: 10,000
SALES (est): 3.5MM **Privately Held**
SIC: 5047 Medical laboratory equipment

(G-7579)
CARRIER LOGISTICS LLC (PA)
15641 S Mahaffie St (66062-4039)
P.O. Box 23009, Shawnee Mission (66283-0009)
PHONE..................................913 681-2780
Michael Copp, *Mng Member*
Kenneth Latto,
EMP: 22
SALES (est): 10.5MM **Privately Held**
SIC: 4789 Cargo loading & unloading services

(G-7580)
CASTLE CREATIONS INC
540 N Rogers Rd (66062-1211)
PHONE..................................913 390-6939

Patrick Delcastillo, *CEO*
Kate O'Neil, *General Mgr*
Ashley Penland, *Purch Mgr*
Robert Harrold, *Engineer*
Kate O Neil, *Treasurer*
▲ **EMP:** 80
SQ FT: 10,000
SALES (est): 38.1MM **Privately Held**
WEB: www.castlecreations.net
SIC: 3625 Motor controls & accessories

(G-7581)
CECO CONCRETE CNSTR DEL LLC
1290 W 151st St (66061-6833)
PHONE..................................913 362-1855
Kevin Timken, *Manager*
EMP: 11 **Privately Held**
WEB: www.cecoconcrete.com
SIC: 1799 1771 Erection & dismantling of forms for poured concrete; concrete work
HQ: Ceco Concrete Construction, L.L.C.
10100 N Ambassador Dr # 400
Kansas City MO 64153

(G-7582)
CELLINT USA INC
14670 S Kaw Dr (66062-4867)
PHONE..................................913 871-6500
Joe Heikes, *President*
Arthur Frank, *Software Dev*
EMP: 10
SALES (est): 541K **Privately Held**
SIC: 8748 Traffic consultant

(G-7583)
CENTAUR INC
1351 W Old Highway 56 F (66061-5219)
PHONE..................................913 390-6184
Mark J Metrokotsas, *President*
Russel B Clark, *Chairman*
Skip Metrokotsas, *Vice Pres*
Howard Jones, *Marketing Staff*
Debra Nickelson, *Technical Staff*
EMP: 6
SALES (est): 890K **Privately Held**
SIC: 2834 5047 Pharmaceutical preparations; veterinarians' equipment & supplies

(G-7584)
CENTENNIAL HEALTHCARE CORP
Also Called: Royal Ter Nrsing Rhbltion Ctr
201 E Flaming Rd (66061-5343)
PHONE..................................913 829-2273
Stephanie Green, *Principal*
EMP: 150 **Privately Held**
WEB: www.centennialhc.com
SIC: 8741 8069 8051 Nursing & personal care facility management; specialty hospitals, except psychiatric; skilled nursing care facilities
HQ: Centennial Healthcare Corporation
400 Perimeter Ctr Ter Ne
Atlanta GA 30346
770 698-9040

(G-7585)
CENTURY CONCRETE INC
1340 W 149th St (66061-6814)
P.O. Box 13401 (66061)
PHONE..................................913 764-4264
Jay Ratula, *President*
EMP: 10
SALES (corp-wide): 29.7B **Privately Held**
SIC: 3273 Ready-mixed concrete
HQ: Century Concrete, Inc.
11011 Cody St Ste 300
Shawnee Mission KS 66210
913 451-8900

(G-7586)
CENTURY PARTNERS LLC
Also Called: Smittys Lawn & Grdn Equiptment
2300 N Rogers Rd (66062-4993)
PHONE..................................913 642-2489
David D Wood, *President*
Christie Wood, *Vice Pres*
Richard Seabaugh, *Manager*
EMP: 10
SALES (est): 1.6MM **Privately Held**
SIC: 3524 7699 5083 Lawn & garden equipment; lawn mower repair shop; lawn & garden machinery & equipment

(G-7587)
CENTURY WOOD PRODUCTS INC
15435 S Keeler St (66062-2711)
PHONE..................................913 839-8725
Arthur Zebley, *Ch of Bd*
David Zebley, *President*
Chris Zebley, *Corp Secy*
Michael Zebley, *Vice Pres*
EMP: 7 **EST:** 1950
SQ FT: 10,000
SALES (est): 52.4K **Privately Held**
WEB: www.centurywood.com
SIC: 2434 5031 Wood kitchen cabinets; vanities, bathroom: wood; kitchen cabinets

(G-7588)
CERTIFIED WATER & MOLD RESTRTN
P.O. Box 880 (66051-0880)
PHONE..................................816 835-4959
EMP: 5
SALES (est): 445K **Privately Held**
SIC: 3544 Industrial molds

(G-7589)
CHAD EQUIPMENT LLC
19950 W 161st St Ste A (66062-2717)
PHONE..................................913 764-0321
Mike Gangel, *President*
Elis Owens, *Technical Staff*
Chris Duffin, *Director*
Drew Mohnen, *Director*
Bob Ogren, *Director*
EMP: 13 **EST:** 1971
SQ FT: 20,000
SALES (est): 3.5MM
SALES (corp-wide): 19.6MM **Privately Held**
SIC: 3556 Meat processing machinery
PA: Birko Corporation
9152 Yosemite St
Henderson CO 80640
303 287-9604

(G-7590)
CHAUDHRYS INVESTMENT GROUP INC
Also Called: Hampton Inn
12081 S Strang Line Rd (66062-5207)
PHONE 913 393-1111
Ali Chaudhry, *President*
Jay Chaudhry, *Manager*
Pete Preezner, *Manager*
Thomas Ramirez, *Manager*
EMP: 20
SALES (est): 1.8MM **Privately Held**
SIC: 7011 Hotels & motels

(G-7591)
CHELSOFT SOLUTIONS CO
527 N Mur Len Rd Ste B (66062-1218)
PHONE..................................913 579-1399
Kiran Chellur, *President*
EMP: 70
SALES (est): 234K **Privately Held**
SIC: 7371 Custom computer programming services

(G-7592)
CHICAGO TITLE INSURANCE CO
110 S Cherry St Ste 202 (66061-3441)
PHONE..................................913 782-0041
Ann Macane, *Manager*
EMP: 13
SALES (corp-wide): 7.5B **Publicly Held**
SIC: 6361 6541 Real estate title insurance; title & trust companies
HQ: Chicago Title Insurance Company
601 Riverside Ave
Jacksonville FL 32204

(G-7593)
CHILDRENS MERCY HOSPITAL
14943 S Summit St (66062-3336)
PHONE..................................913 234-8683
Julie Musick, *Principal*
EMP: 265
SALES (corp-wide): 826.4MM **Privately Held**
SIC: 8069 Children's hospital
PA: Mercy Children's Hospital
2401 Gillham Rd
Kansas City MO 64108
816 234-3000

(G-7594)
CHIROSERVE INC
Also Called: Fulk's Chiropractic
2110 E Santa Fe St (66062-1607)
PHONE..................................913 764-6237
Anthony Pizzuti, *President*
Becky Ahlenstorf, *Vice Pres*
EMP: 40
SALES (est): 2.4MM **Privately Held**
WEB: www.chiroserve.com
SIC: 8041 Offices & clinics of chiropractors

(G-7595)
CINTAS CORPORATION
Also Called: Cintas-The Uniform People
2050 E Kansas City Rd (66061-5859)
PHONE..................................913 782-8333
Ken Marks, *Manager*
EMP: 200
SALES (corp-wide): 6.8B **Publicly Held**
WEB: www.cintas-corp.com
SIC: 7213 Uniform supply
PA: Cintas Corporation
6800 Cintas Blvd
Cincinnati OH 45262
513 459-1200

(G-7596)
CINTAS CORPORATION NO 2
2050 E Kansas City Rd (66061-5859)
PHONE..................................913 782-8333
Ryan Williams, *Manager*
EMP: 150
SQ FT: 1,200
SALES (corp-wide): 6.8B **Publicly Held**
WEB: www.cintas-corp.com
SIC: 7211 Power laundries, family & commercial
HQ: Cintas Corporation No. 2
6800 Cintas Blvd
Mason OH 45040

(G-7597)
COLEMAN COMPANY INC
17150 Mercury St (66061-6058)
PHONE..................................316 832-3015
Coleman Toubia, *Branch Mgr*
Chris Hunter, *Analyst*
EMP: 100
SALES (corp-wide): 8.6B **Publicly Held**
SIC: 3086 Ice chests or coolers (portable), foamed plastic
HQ: The Coleman Company Inc
180 N Lasalle St Ste 700
Chicago IL 60601

(G-7598)
COLLEGE PARK FMLY CARE CTR INC
Also Called: Collage Pk Fmly Care Ctr Olthe
1803 S Ridgeview Rd # 100 (66062-2377)
PHONE..................................913 829-0505
Leah Sidney, *Manager*
EMP: 30
SALES (corp-wide): 25.8MM **Privately Held**
SIC: 8011 Physicians' office, including specialists
PA: College Park Family Care Center Inc.
11725 W 112th St
Shawnee Mission KS 66210
913 469-5579

(G-7599)
COLLIS CRANEWORKS INC
100 S Paniplus Dr (66061-9406)
PHONE..................................913 764-1315
Jim Mendenhall, *President*
David Collis, *Mng Member*
EMP: 21
SALES (est): 8.1MM **Privately Held**
SIC: 3536 Hoists, cranes & monorails

(G-7600)
COLT TECH LLC
14830 W 117th St (66062-9304)
P.O. Box 4710 (66063-4710)
PHONE..................................913 839-8198
Robert L Lynn, *CEO*
Shawn Rooney, *Prdtn Mgr*
EMP: 7
SQ FT: 30,000
SALES (est): 1MM **Privately Held**
WEB: www.colttech.com
SIC: 7389 3672 8734 8711 Brokers' services; printed circuit boards; testing laboratories; engineering services; electrical equipment & supplies

(G-7601)
COLUMBIA CONSTRUCTION INC
19965 W 162nd St (66062-2787)
P.O. Box 445, Spring Hill (66083-0445)
PHONE..................................913 247-3114
Joseph John Grossman, *CEO*
Ashley Grossman, *Admin Sec*
EMP: 35
SALES (est): 2.2MM **Privately Held**
SIC: 1721 Painting & paper hanging

(G-7602)
COMCAST CORPORATION
772 N Ridgeview Rd (66061-2900)
PHONE..................................800 934-6489
Chris Fry, *Sales Staff*
Deon Clarke, *Technician*
EMP: 199
SALES (corp-wide): 94.5B **Publicly Held**
SIC: 4841 Cable television services
PA: Comcast Corporation
1701 Jfk Blvd
Philadelphia PA 19103
215 286-1700

(G-7603)
COMMERCE BANK
15910 S Mur Len Rd (66062-8301)
PHONE..................................816 234-2000
Mark McGavran, *Manager*
EMP: 13
SALES (corp-wide): 1.3B **Publicly Held**
SIC: 6021 National commercial banks
HQ: Commerce Bank
1000 Walnut St Fl 700
Kansas City MO 64106
816 234-2000

(G-7604)
COMMERCE BANK
11900 S Strang Line Rd (66062-5267)
PHONE..................................816 234-2000
Kevin Barth, *President*
EMP: 13
SALES (corp-wide): 1.3B **Publicly Held**
SIC: 6022 State commercial banks
HQ: Commerce Bank
1000 Walnut St Fl 700
Kansas City MO 64106
816 234-2000

(G-7605)
COMMUNITYAMERICA CREDIT UNION
Also Called: Community America Credit Union
13590 S Blackbob Rd (66062-1936)
PHONE..................................913 397-6600
Rachelle Jackson, *Manager*
EMP: 15
SALES (corp-wide): 81.9MM **Privately Held**
WEB: www.cacu.com
SIC: 6062 State credit unions, not federally chartered
PA: Communityamerica Credit Union
9777 Ridge Dr
Lenexa KS 66219
913 905-7000

(G-7606)
COMPANY BUSINESS INTL SARL
988 N Findley St (66061-7570)
PHONE..................................913 286-9771
Ahmed Tidiane Kaba, *Principal*
Houleymatou Aminah Kaba, *Principal*
Mohamed Lamine Kaba, *Principal*
Sekou Kaba, *Principal*
Issiaga Kaba, *Vice Pres*
EMP: 8
SALES (est): 270.4K **Privately Held**
SIC: 5063 3952 Panelboards; paints, gold or bronze: artists'

GEOGRAPHIC

(G-7607)
COMPASS FINCL RESOURCES LLC
13095 S Mur Len Rd # 100 (66062-1425)
PHONE....................................913 747-2000
Russell Lane, *President*
Robert Lane, *Sales Staff*
EMP: 12
SALES (est): 1.7MM **Privately Held**
SIC: 6282 Investment advice

(G-7608)
COMPLETE DENTAL CARE
Also Called: Bikson, Bruce
11150 S Pflumm Rd (66215-4810)
PHONE....................................913 469-5646
Bruce Bikson, *Owner*
Michael Kahn, *Co-Owner*
EMP: 14
SALES (est): 698.6K **Privately Held**
SIC: 8021 Dentists' office

(G-7609)
COMPUTERWISE INC
302 N Winchester St (66062-1299)
PHONE....................................408 389-8241
William W Brown, *President*
EMP: 10
SQ FT: 12,000
SALES (est): 3.8MM **Privately Held**
WEB: www.computerwise.com
SIC: 3575 7371 3661 3577 Computer terminals; custom computer programming services; telephone & telegraph apparatus; computer peripheral equipment

(G-7610)
CONCRETE EXPRESS INC
11137 S Crestone St (66061-6621)
PHONE....................................805 643-2992
Robert F Biorkman, *President*
EMP: 10
SALES (est): 30.1K **Privately Held**
SIC: 3273 Ready-mixed concrete

(G-7611)
CONRAD FIRE EQUIPMENT INC
887 N Jan Mar Ct (66061-3693)
PHONE....................................913 780-5521
Paul Schultz, *President*
Dennis Myers, *Vice Pres*
Adam Payne, *Sales Staff*
James Conrad, *Shareholder*
Sara Schultz, *Shareholder*
EMP: 15
SQ FT: 8,800
SALES (est): 4.3MM **Privately Held**
SIC: 5099 Safety equipment & supplies

(G-7612)
CONSTRUCTION MGT SVCS INC
18901 W 158th St (66062-8014)
PHONE....................................913 231-5736
Carla Brock, *Office Mgr*
Michael Brock, *Director*
EMP: 21
SALES (est): 3MM **Privately Held**
SIC: 8741 Construction management

(G-7613)
CONVERG MEDIA LLC
804 N Meadowbrook Dr (66062-5428)
PHONE....................................913 871-0453
Shane Kinsch,
EMP: 5
SALES (est): 215K **Privately Held**
SIC: 2741

(G-7614)
CONVERGYS CORPORATION
400 N Rogers Rd (66062-1212)
PHONE....................................913 782-3333
Doug Jones, *Branch Mgr*
EMP: 21
SALES (corp-wide): 20B **Publicly Held**
WEB: www.convergys.com
SIC: 7374 7389 Data processing service; telemarketing services
HQ: Concentrix Cvg Corporation
201 E 4th St
Cincinnati OH 45202
513 723-7000

(G-7615)
COOPER ELECTRONICS INC
310 N Marion St (66061-3107)
P.O. Box 1130 (66051-1130)
PHONE....................................913 782-0012
Jack O Cooper III, *President*
Karen Cooper, *Admin Sec*
Brenda Bowers, *Administration*
EMP: 43 **EST:** 1959
SQ FT: 19,000
SALES: 3.9MM **Privately Held**
WEB: www.hisonic.com
SIC: 3677 3812 5065 Filtration devices, electronic; electronic transformers; inductors, electronic; search & navigation equipment; electronic parts & equipment

(G-7616)
CORNERSTONE CNSTR SVCS LLC
106 S Janell Dr (66061-3850)
PHONE....................................913 207-1751
Mitchall Hazen, *Mng Member*
EMP: 10
SALES (est): 82.7K **Privately Held**
SIC: 1521 Single-family housing construction

(G-7617)
CORNWELL & SCHERIFF
201 E Loula St Ste 101 (66061-3459)
PHONE....................................913 254-7600
Carl Cornwell, *Owner*
EMP: 10
SALES (est): 692.4K **Privately Held**
SIC: 8111 Specialized law offices, attorneys

(G-7618)
COTTONWOOD SPRINGS LLC
13351 S Arapaho Dr (66062-1520)
PHONE....................................913 353-3000
Lisa Siskey, *Human Res Dir*
W Earl Reed III, *Mng Member*
EMP: 12 **EST:** 2015
SALES: 18.5MM **Privately Held**
SIC: 8069 Drug addiction rehabilitation hospital

(G-7619)
COUNTY OF JOHNSON
Also Called: Public Works Dept
1800 W Old Highway 56 (66061-5178)
PHONE....................................913 782-2640
Larry McClain, *Safety Mgr*
Mac Andrew, *Director*
EMP: 100 **Privately Held**
WEB: www.jocoks.com
SIC: 8711 9511 Engineering services; air, water & solid waste management;
PA: County Of Johnson
111 S Cherry St Ste 1200
Olathe KS 66061
913 715-0435

(G-7620)
COUNTY OF JOHNSON
Also Called: Transit Services
1701 W 56 Hwy (66061)
PHONE....................................913 782-2210
Alice Amrein, *Director*
EMP: 11 **Privately Held**
WEB: www.jocoks.com
SIC: 4111 9621 Local & suburban transit; regulation, administration of transportation;
PA: County Of Johnson
111 S Cherry St Ste 1200
Olathe KS 66061
913 715-0435

(G-7621)
COUNTY OF JOHNSON
Also Called: Evergreen Community
11875 S Sunset Dr Ste 100 (66061-2794)
PHONE....................................913 894-8383
Yvonne Love, *Director*
Charles Nigro, *Administration*
Victoria Hanley,
EMP: 110 **Privately Held**
WEB: www.jocoks.com
SIC: 8051 9431 Skilled nursing care facilities; administration of public health programs;
PA: County Of Johnson
111 S Cherry St Ste 1200
Olathe KS 66061
913 715-0435

(G-7622)
COUNTY OF JOHNSON
Also Called: Kansas 10th Judicial District
100 N Kansas Ave (66061-3278)
PHONE....................................913 715-3300
Katherine Stocks, *Administration*
EMP: 180 **Privately Held**
SIC: 8111 Administrative & government law
PA: County Of Johnson
111 S Cherry St Ste 1200
Olathe KS 66061
913 715-0435

(G-7623)
COUNTY OF JOHNSON
Also Called: Parks & Recreation Department
16445 Lackman St (66062)
PHONE....................................913 829-4653
W Montgomery, *General Mgr*
EMP: 25 **Privately Held**
WEB: www.jocoks.com
SIC: 7992 9512 5091 Public golf courses; recreational program administration, government; ; golf equipment
PA: County Of Johnson
111 S Cherry St Ste 1200
Olathe KS 66061
913 715-0435

(G-7624)
COURTYARD KANSAS CITY OLATHE
12151 S Strang Line Ct (66062-5209)
PHONE....................................913 839-4500
Sanjay Koshiya, *Principal*
Jay Koshiya, *Principal*
Jandee Rohr, *Principal*
EMP: 20
SALES (est): 108K **Privately Held**
SIC: 7011 Hotels & motels

(G-7625)
COWAN SYSTEMS LLC
19943 W 162nd St (66062-2787)
PHONE....................................913 393-0110
EMP: 129 **Privately Held**
SIC: 4213 Automobiles, transport & delivery
PA: Cowan Systems, Llc
4555 Hollins Ferry Rd
Baltimore MD 21227

(G-7626)
CRETEN BASEMENT CONTRACTORS
Also Called: Creten J G Basement Contractor
10212 S Shadow Cir (66061-8401)
PHONE....................................913 441-3333
John Gary, *President*
EMP: 14
SALES: 1MM **Privately Held**
SIC: 1771 Foundation & footing contractor

(G-7627)
CRETEN JOHN G BASEMENT CONTR
10212 S Shadow Cir (66061-8401)
PHONE....................................913 441-3333
John G Creten, *President*
EMP: 12
SALES (est): 1.2MM **Privately Held**
SIC: 1771 Foundation & footing contractor

(G-7628)
CROWN REALTY OF KANSAS INC
2099 E 151st St (66062-2935)
PHONE....................................913 782-1155
Claude Madison, *Project Mgr*
Marvin Zimmerman, *CFO*
Barbara Hoffman, *Manager*
Kay Lowrie, *Real Est Agnt*
EMP: 35
SALES (corp-wide): 10MM **Privately Held**
WEB: www.crownrealty.com
SIC: 6531 Broker of manufactured homes, on site; real estate brokers & agents
PA: Crown Realty Of Kansas Inc
102 S Silver St
Paola KS
913 557-4333

(G-7629)
CULTURE HOUSE INC
14808 W 117th St (66062-9304)
PHONE....................................913 393-3141
Jeremiah Enna, *Exec Dir*
Nancy Kaiser-Caplan, *Exec Dir*
EMP: 26
SALES: 1.1MM **Privately Held**
SIC: 8412 Museums & art galleries

(G-7630)
CUSTOM DESIGN INC
14131 S Mur Len Rd (66062-1873)
PHONE....................................913 764-6511
Steve Cutler, *President*
Chris Geisler, *Vice Pres*
EMP: 10
SQ FT: 700
SALES (est): 830K **Privately Held**
WEB: www.perczek.com
SIC: 7336 Commercial art & graphic design

(G-7631)
CUSTOM LAWN & LANDSCAPE INC
15204 S Keeler St (66062-2715)
PHONE....................................913 782-8315
Reg Robertson, *President*
Denise Brown, *Sales Mgr*
EMP: 29
SQ FT: 8,000
SALES: 2.6MM **Privately Held**
WEB: www.customlawn.com
SIC: 0782 Lawn care services; landscape contractors

(G-7632)
CW CONCRETE INC
605 S Kansas Ave (66061-4524)
PHONE....................................913 780-2316
Charles Viscek, *President*
Ward Vanlerberg, *Vice Pres*
EMP: 48
SALES: 8MM **Privately Held**
SIC: 1771 Concrete work

(G-7633)
CYPRESS RECOVERY INC
1009 E Highway 56 (66061-4969)
PHONE....................................913 764-7555
Jeremy Frantze, *President*
Michael Scott, *Corp Secy*
Mario Washington, *Vice Pres*
James Sanford, *Treasurer*
Thomas Culala, *Exec Dir*
EMP: 12
SALES: 376.7K **Privately Held**
SIC: 8069 Substance abuse hospitals; alcoholism rehabilitation hospital; drug addiction rehabilitation hospital

(G-7634)
D & B PRINT SHOP INC
1175 W Dennis Ave (66061-5229)
PHONE....................................913 782-6688
Robert Sheldon, *CEO*
EMP: 7
SALES (est): 1.2MM **Privately Held**
SIC: 2752 Commercial printing, lithographic

(G-7635)
D B INVESTMENTS INC (DH)
Also Called: Target Felker Brilliant Truco
17400 W 119th St (66061-7740)
PHONE....................................913 928-1000
Bernard Goblet, *President*
Louis Lipari, *Corp Secy*
Lyle S Stone, *Exec VP*
Ronald R Hubbard, *Vice Pres*
Roger L Lewis, *Vice Pres*
EMP: 5
SALES (est): 21.8MM
SALES (corp-wide): 4.3B **Privately Held**
WEB: www.dbstone.com
SIC: 3545 Diamond cutting tools for turning, boring, burnishing, etc.

HQ: Husqvarna Construction Products
North America, Inc.
17400 W 119th St
Olathe KS 66061
913 928-1000

(G-7636)
D H PACE COMPANY INC
Also Called: Overhead Door Company Kans Cy
1901 E 119th St (66061-9502)
PHONE..................................816 221-0072
Stephen B Klein, *CEO*
Steve Pascuzzi, *Engr R&D*
EMP: 136
SALES (corp-wide): 433.8MM **Privately Held**
WEB: www.dhpace.com
SIC: 5031 7699 5063 Doors; door & window repair; burglar alarm systems
HQ: D. H. Pace Company, Inc.
1901 E 119th St
Olathe KS 66061
816 221-0543

(G-7637)
D H PACE COMPANY INC (HQ)
Also Called: D H Pace Door Services
1901 E 119th St (66061-9502)
PHONE..................................816 221-0543
Rex E Newcomer, *CEO*
Steve Pascuzzi, *President*
Van Rowe, *Regional Mgr*
Gary Lombard, *Business Mgr*
Emily J Bailey, *Exec VP*
▲ **EMP:** 610 **EST:** 1972
SQ FT: 25,000
SALES: 433.8MM **Privately Held**
WEB: www.dhpace.com
SIC: 1751 7699 Garage door, installation or erection; door & window repair
PA: E.E. Newcomer Enterprises, Inc.
1901 E 119th St
Olathe KS 66061
816 221-0543

(G-7638)
D H PACE COMPANY INC
Also Called: Overhead Door Co Kansas City
1901 E 119th St (66061-9502)
PHONE..................................816 480-2600
Rex Newcomer, *CEO*
Jake Coleman, *Purch Mgr*
Darlene Hanson, *Admin Asst*
EMP: 300
SALES (corp-wide): 433.8MM **Privately Held**
WEB: www.dhpace.com
SIC: 5031 7699 5063 Doors; door & window repair; burglar alarm systems
HQ: D. H. Pace Company, Inc.
1901 E 119th St
Olathe KS 66061
816 221-0543

(G-7639)
DA PAINTING INC
13724 W 158th St (66062-4688)
PHONE..................................913 829-2075
Courtney Bratkiv, *President*
Walter Bratkiv, *CFO*
EMP: 20
SQ FT: 1,000
SALES: 1.3MM **Privately Held**
WEB: www.dapainting.com
SIC: 1721 Painting & paper hanging

(G-7640)
DALES TOW SERVICE INC
15345 S Keeler St (66062-2712)
PHONE..................................913 782-2289
Troy Allenbrand, *President*
EMP: 12
SALES (est): 104.2K **Privately Held**
SIC: 7549 Towing services

(G-7641)
DANIEL TODD INDUSTRIES INC
Also Called: Dti Machining
230 N Monroe St Ste A (66061-3180)
PHONE..................................913 780-0382
Daniel E Todd, *President*
Donald Cress, *Controller*
EMP: 6 **EST:** 2009
SALES: 480K **Privately Held**
SIC: 3444 Sheet metalwork

(G-7642)
DAYS INN OLATHE MEDICAL CENTER
20662 W 151st St (66061-7239)
PHONE..................................913 390-9500
Shawn Saruqi, *Principal*
EMP: 20
SALES (est): 512.6K **Privately Held**
SIC: 8011 Medical centers

(G-7643)
DEAF CULTURAL CTR FOUNDATION
455 E Park St (66061-5436)
PHONE..................................913 782-5808
Terry Hostin, *President*
Mark Tausher, *Vice Pres*
David Wilcox, *Treasurer*
Sandra Kelly, *Exec Dir*
Vickie Baska, *Admin Sec*
EMP: 12
SALES: 191.2K **Privately Held**
SIC: 8412 8641 Museum; educator's association

(G-7644)
DEERE & COMPANY
10789 S Ridgeview Rd (66061-6448)
PHONE..................................309 765-4826
Roch Dold, *Business Mgr*
Luke Gakstatter, *Vice Pres*
Deb Denavs, *Project Mgr*
Ann Snider, *Project Mgr*
Bryan Dorsey, *Research*
EMP: 37
SALES (corp-wide): 39.2B **Publicly Held**
SIC: 5083 Farm & garden machinery
PA: Deere & Company
1 John Deere Pl
Moline IL 61265
309 765-8000

(G-7645)
DEERE & COMPANY
Also Called: John Deere AG Center
10789 S Ridgeview Rd (66061-6448)
PHONE..................................913 310-8100
Dominic Ruccolo, *Vice Pres*
Denise Leinen, *Sales Staff*
Terry Porter, *Marketing Mgr*
Dean Acheson, *Manager*
EMP: 25
SALES (corp-wide): 39.2B **Publicly Held**
WEB: www.deere.com
SIC: 8742 8732 Management consulting services; commercial nonphysical research
PA: Deere & Company
1 John Deere Pl
Moline IL 61265
309 765-8000

(G-7646)
DEERE & COMPANY
Also Called: John Deere
10789 S Ridgeview Rd (66061-6448)
PHONE..................................913 310-8344
Rick Haun, *President*
John Lagemann, *Vice Pres*
Pravin Bhat, *Project Mgr*
Deb Denavs, *Project Mgr*
Maureen O'Connor, *Human Resources*
EMP: 19
SALES (corp-wide): 39.2B **Publicly Held**
WEB: www.deere.com
SIC: 5083 Farm & garden machinery
PA: Deere & Company
1 John Deere Pl
Moline IL 61265
309 765-8000

(G-7647)
DEFFENBAUGH INDUSTRIES INC
Also Called: Shawnee Rock Company
1600 E 151st Ter (66062-2845)
PHONE..................................913 208-1000
Ronald D Deffenbaugh, *Owner*
EMP: 25
SALES (corp-wide): 14.9B **Publicly Held**
WEB: www.deffenbaughindustries.com
SIC: 5032 Stone, crushed or broken
HQ: Deffenbaugh Industries, Inc.
2601 Midwest Dr
Kansas City KS 66111
913 631-3300

(G-7648)
DENTAL CONCEPTS INC
13849 S Mur Len Rd Ste H (66062-1664)
P.O. Box 2785 (66063-0785)
PHONE..................................913 829-0242
Larry Freeman, *President*
Don Edmundson, *Vice Pres*
EMP: 15
SALES (est): 800K **Privately Held**
SIC: 8072 Dental laboratories

(G-7649)
DEPARTMENT CORRECTIONS KANSAS
Also Called: Olathe Parole Office
804 N Meadowbrook Dr # 100 (66062-5428)
PHONE..................................913 829-6207
Jennifer Keating, *Manager*
EMP: 12 **Privately Held**
WEB: www.kdoc.dc.state.ks.us
SIC: 8322 9223 Parole office; correctional institutions;
HQ: Kansas Department Of Corrections
714 Sw Jackson St Fl 3
Topeka KS 66603
785 296-3317

(G-7650)
DESCO COATINGS LLC (PA)
19890 W 156th St (66062-3500)
P.O. Box 2658 (66063-0658)
PHONE..................................913 782-3330
Richard M Crouch, *President*
Walter Hutsell, *Vice Pres*
Sue Shelton, *Controller*
Sheryl Watkins, *Officer*
EMP: 89 **EST:** 1959
SALES (est): 13.1MM **Privately Held**
WEB: www.descocoatings.com
SIC: 1799 Coating, caulking & weather, water & fireproofing

(G-7651)
DESIGN CONCEPTS INC
Also Called: DCI
886 N Jan Mar Ct (66061-3692)
P.O. Box 2877 (66063-0877)
PHONE..................................913 782-5672
Larry Shelton, *President*
Larry Klusman, *President*
Chris Hammond, *Vice Pres*
Mary Owens, *Manager*
Mike Pressgrove, *Manager*
EMP: 15
SQ FT: 5,000
SALES (est): 3.8MM **Privately Held**
WEB: www.dcimeters.com
SIC: 3825 5074 Digital panel meters, electricity measuring; heating equipment & panels, solar

(G-7652)
DIAGNOSTIC IMAGING CENTER
13795 S Mur Len Rd # 105 (66062-1675)
PHONE..................................913 344-9989
Jenny Ingraham, *Manager*
EMP: 16
SALES (corp-wide): 18.1MM **Privately Held**
WEB: www.dic-kc.com
SIC: 8011 Radiologist
PA: Diagnostic Imaging Center
6724 Troost Ave Ste 800
Kansas City MO 64131
816 455-5959

(G-7653)
DIAMOND PARTNERS INC
Also Called: Keller Williams Realtors
13671 S Mur Len Rd (66062-1648)
PHONE..................................913 322-7500
Wayne Janner, *President*
Chris Lengquist, *Broker*
Sara Henry, *Agent*
Jay Darst, *Asst Broker*
Rollene Croucher, *Real Est Agnt*
EMP: 20
SALES (est): 1.5MM **Privately Held**
SIC: 6531 Real estate agent, residential

(G-7654)
DILLARDS INC
Also Called: Dillard's Distribution Center
700 E 151st St (66062-3428)
PHONE..................................913 791-6400
John Paul, *Manager*
EMP: 300
SALES (corp-wide): 6.5B **Publicly Held**
WEB: www.dillards.com
SIC: 4225 General warehousing & storage
PA: Dillard's Inc.
1600 Cantrell Rd
Little Rock AR 72201
501 376-5200

(G-7655)
DIMENSION X DESIGN LLC
18001 W 106th St Ste 150 (66061-6445)
PHONE..................................913 908-3824
Sean Hopkins,
Gary Baker,
EMP: 19
SQ FT: 5,000
SALES (est): 1.6MM **Privately Held**
WEB: www.d-x-d.com
SIC: 7374 Data processing & preparation

(G-7656)
DINOSAUR DEN CHILD DEV CTR
Also Called: Feal Invesments
14299 S Darnell St (66062-6560)
PHONE..................................913 780-2626
Rene Burford, *Owner*
Lindsey Norman, *Director*
EMP: 18
SQ FT: 6,240
SALES: 425K **Privately Held**
SIC: 8351 Preschool center; group day care center

(G-7657)
DITCH WITCH SALES INC
Also Called: Ditch Witch Sales Kansas City
1325 S Enterprise St (66061-5358)
PHONE..................................913 782-5223
Butch Fuzzell, *Manager*
EMP: 12
SALES (corp-wide): 19.1MM **Privately Held**
WEB: www.ditchwitchsales.com
SIC: 5082 General construction machinery & equipment
PA: Ditch Witch Sales, Inc.
1617 S Service Rd
Sullivan MO 63080
573 468-8012

(G-7658)
DOLAN TECHNOLOGIES CORPORATION (HQ)
Also Called: Compdata Surveys & Consulting
1713 E 123rd St (66061-5983)
P.O. Box 25627, Overland Park (66225-5627)
PHONE..................................913 390-5156
Kent Plunkett, *CEO*
Shawna Simon, *General Mgr*
Mark Robertson, *Accounting Mgr*
Kevin Steutermann, *Info Svcs Mgr*
Sarah Wheaton, *Director*
EMP: 30
SQ FT: 10,000
SALES (est): 6.3MM
SALES (corp-wide): 163.4MM **Privately Held**
WEB: www.compdatasurvey.com
SIC: 8713 Surveying services
PA: Salary.Com, Llc
610 Lincoln St Ste 200
Waltham MA 02451
781 989-9488

(G-7659)
DON COFFEY COMPANY INC (PA)
Also Called: Coffey, Dan Co
15375 S Us 169 Hwy (66062-3403)
PHONE..................................913 764-2108
Don Coffey, *President*
Steve Stelter, *Mfg Staff*
Beverly Basso, *Sales Staff*
Cindy Herron, *Office Mgr*
Shelby Spaur, *Admin Sec*
EMP: 10
SQ FT: 2,000

SALES (est): 10.2MM Privately Held
SIC: 5091 Sporting & recreation goods

(G-7660)
DONS BODY SHOP INC
Also Called: Don's Tow Service
207 W Cedar St (66061-4422)
PHONE..................................913 782-9255
Tony N Barton, *President*
EMP: 12
SALES (est): 1.8MM Privately Held
SIC: 7538 7532 General automotive repair shops; body shop, automotive

(G-7661)
DURANOTIC DOOR INC
14901 W 117th St (66062-9307)
PHONE..................................913 764-3408
Mark Thomas, *President*
Denise Thomas, *Treasurer*
EMP: 15
SQ FT: 20,000
SALES (est): 7.9MM Privately Held
WEB: www.duranoticdoor.com
SIC: 5031 5211 Doors; door frames, all materials; door & window products

(G-7662)
DW INDUSTRIES LLC
310 N Winchester St Ste A (66062-1249)
PHONE..................................913 782-7575
Dan Milford, *Principal*
EMP: 8
SALES (est): 723K Privately Held
SIC: 3999 Manufacturing industries

(G-7663)
E T C INSTITUTE INC
725 W Frontier Ln (66061-7203)
PHONE..................................913 747-0646
Elaine Tatham, *President*
Andrew Kolcz, *Vice Pres*
Chris Thasem, *Vice Pres*
Ryan Murray, *Project Mgr*
Val Donham, *Opers Staff*
EMP: 30
SQ FT: 6,000
SALES (est): 5.8MM Privately Held
WEB: www.etcresearch.com
SIC: 8742 8732 Management consulting services; market analysis or research

(G-7664)
E3 ROOFING GROUP INC
Also Called: Infinity Roofing
310 N Winchester St Ste C (66062-1249)
PHONE..................................913 782-3332
Jason Berry, *President*
Carl Aubrey, *CFO*
EMP: 10
SALES (est): 946.9K Privately Held
WEB: www.e3roofinggroup.com
SIC: 1761 Roof repair

(G-7665)
EARTH CONTACT PRODUCTS LLC
Also Called: E C P
15612 S Keeler Ter (66062-3510)
PHONE..................................913 393-0007
Jeff Tully, *General Mgr*
Jon-Michael Mitchell, *Accountant*
Aaron Grayham, *Sales Staff*
Russell Rima, *Manager*
Brad Mitchell,
▼ EMP: 17
SQ FT: 100,000
SALES (est): 7.7MM Privately Held
WEB: www.earthcontactproducts.com
SIC: 3312 Structural shapes & pilings, steel

(G-7666)
EB GROUP
Also Called: Bickford House
13795 S Mur Len Rd (66062-1675)
PHONE..................................217 787-9000
Don EBY, *CEO*
EMP: 40
SALES (est): 1MM Privately Held
SIC: 8361 Home for the aged

(G-7667)
EBCO CONSTRUCTION GROUP LLC (PA)
13795 S Mur Len Rd # 301 (66062-1675)
PHONE..................................866 297-2185
Don EBY,
Ray Cook MD,
Mike EBY,
EMP: 15
SQ FT: 7,200
SALES (est): 18.1MM Privately Held
WEB: www.eby.com
SIC: 6531 1542 1522 Real estate agents & managers; nonresidential construction; residential construction

(G-7668)
EBY GROUP INC
Also Called: EBY Holdings
13795 S Mur Len Rd # 301 (66062-1675)
PHONE..................................913 782-3200
Joe EBY, *President*
Andy EBY, *President*
Alan Fairbanks, *Senior VP*
Mike EBY, *CFO*
Christy Dienstbier, *Human Res Dir*
EMP: 1300 Privately Held
SIC: 6719 Personal holding companies, except banks

(G-7669)
EBY REALTY GROUP LLC (HQ)
13795 S Mur Len Rd # 301 (66062-1675)
PHONE..................................913 782-3200
Brian Clegg, *Controller*
Beth Fleming, *Manager*
Mike EBY,
EMP: 28 EST: 1999
SALES (est): 14.3MM Privately Held
SIC: 6531 Real estate agent, commercial

(G-7670)
EDUCATION MARKET RESOURCES INC
Also Called: Kidsay
804 N Meadowbrook Dr # 116 (66062-5428)
PHONE..................................913 390-8110
Robert Reynolds, *President*
Terence Burke, *Vice Pres*
Leslie Franks, *Manager*
EMP: 20
SQ FT: 1,000
SALES (est): 1.6MM Privately Held
WEB: www.kidsay.com
SIC: 8732 Market analysis or research

(G-7671)
EE NEWCOMER ENTERPRISES INC (PA)
1901 E 119th St (66061-9502)
PHONE..................................816 221-0543
Eric Hanson, *Ch of Bd*
Rex E Newcomer, *President*
Brian C Gillespie, *Exec VP*
N Nelson Newcomer, *Exec VP*
Rick Martin, *Vice Pres*
EMP: 287
SQ FT: 110,000
SALES (est): 433.8MM Privately Held
WEB: www.eenewcomer.com
SIC: 1751 5211 7699 Garage door, installation or erection; garage doors, sale & installation; doors, wood or metal, except storm; door & window repair; garage door repair

(G-7672)
ELECSYS CORPORATION (HQ)
846 N Martway Ct (66061-7065)
PHONE..................................913 647-0158
Karl B Gemperli, *President*
Mike Morgan, *COO*
Monica Sumner, *COO*
Matthew Andrews, *Vice Pres*
James Beaver, *Vice Pres*
EMP: 120
SQ FT: 60,000
SALES: 30.4MM
SALES (corp-wide): 444MM Publicly Held
WEB: www.elecsyscorp.com
SIC: 3672 3648 3679 Printed circuit boards; lighting equipment; electronic circuits
PA: Lindsay Corporation
18135 Burke St Ste 100
Elkhorn NE 68022
402 829-6800

(G-7673)
ELECSYS INTERNATIONAL CORP
846 N Martway Ct (66061-7065)
PHONE..................................913 647-0158
Karl B Gemperli, *CEO*
Mike Morgan, *COO*
Dan Hughes, *Vice Pres*
Mike Pressgrove, *Vice Pres*
Chris Thomas, *Vice Pres*
EMP: 125 EST: 1976
SQ FT: 85,000
SALES (est): 28MM
SALES (corp-wide): 444MM Publicly Held
WEB: www.dciincorporated.com
SIC: 3625 3679 3571 7629 Electric controls & control accessories, industrial; liquid crystal displays (LCD); electronic computers; electrical equipment repair services; personal service agents, brokers & bureaus
HQ: Elecsys Corporation
846 N Martway Ct
Olathe KS 66061
913 647-0158

(G-7674)
ELECTRICAL ASSOCIATES LLC
308 W Elm St (66061-4024)
PHONE..................................913 825-2537
Robert D Brown, *Mng Member*
EMP: 45 EST: 2007
SQ FT: 5,000
SALES (est): 2.6MM Privately Held
SIC: 1731 General electrical contractor

(G-7675)
ELECTRONIC CONTRLS ASSEMBLY CO
886 N Jan Mar Ct (66061-3692)
PHONE..................................913 780-0036
Bonnie Sue Armstrong, *President*
EMP: 8
SQ FT: 7,500
SALES (est): 720K Privately Held
SIC: 3672 3679 Printed circuit boards; harness assemblies for electronic use: wire or cable

(G-7676)
ELIAS ANIMAL HEALTH LLC
10900 S Clay Blair Blvd (66061-1301)
PHONE..................................913 492-2221
Tammie Wahaus, *CEO*
Charles Burton, *Principal*
Larry Maddox, *Principal*
Mark Patterson, *Principal*
Chuck Stephens, *Principal*
EMP: 7 EST: 2014
SALES (est): 349.6K Privately Held
SIC: 2834 Pharmaceutical preparations

(G-7677)
EMBASSY SUITES OLATHE
10401 S Ridgeview Rd (66061-6451)
PHONE..................................913 353-9280
EMP: 13 EST: 2015
SALES (est): 777.8K Privately Held
SIC: 7011 Hotels & motels

(G-7678)
EMERGENCY ASSISTANCE SITES
Also Called: Salvation Army
420 E Santa Fe St (66061-3446)
PHONE..................................913 782-3640
Maj Mark Marsolf, *Pastor*
Mark Marsolf, *Pastor*
EMP: 12
SALES (est): 363K Privately Held
SIC: 8322 Individual & family services

(G-7679)
EMERGENCY MEDICAL CARE
20333 W 151st St (66061-5350)
PHONE..................................913 791-4357
Kevin Gould, *Principal*
EMP: 13 EST: 2010
SALES (est): 487.1K Privately Held
SIC: 8099 Blood related health services

(G-7680)
EN ENGINEERING LLC
17775 W 106th St Ste 200 (66061-3198)
PHONE..................................913 901-4400
Sam Thiessen, *Project Mgr*
EMP: 90 Privately Held
SIC: 8711 Consulting engineer
HQ: En Engineering Llc
28100 Torch Pkwy Ste 400
Warrenville IL 60555
630 353-4000

(G-7681)
ENDLESS IDEAS INC
Also Called: Red Tail Mfg
15845 S Mahaffie St (66062-4037)
PHONE..................................913 766-0680
Mike Everhart, *President*
EMP: 14
SALES (est): 641.5K Privately Held
SIC: 3484 3483 Guns (firearms) or gun parts, 30 mm. & below; ammunition, except for small arms

(G-7682)
ENTERPRISE BANK & TRUST
Also Called: Black Bob Banking Center BR
15084 S Blackbob Rd (66062-2663)
PHONE..................................913 791-9950
Tina Gray, *Branch Mgr*
EMP: 18 Publicly Held
SIC: 6021 National commercial banks
HQ: Enterprise Bank & Trust
150 N Meramec Ave Ste 300
Saint Louis MO 63105
314 725-5500

(G-7683)
ENTERPRISE BANK & TRUST
110 N Clairborne Rd (66062-1639)
P.O. Box 1500 (66051-1500)
PHONE..................................913 782-3211
Dennis Cheney, *Manager*
EMP: 20 Publicly Held
SIC: 6022 State commercial banks
HQ: Enterprise Bank & Trust
150 N Meramec Ave Ste 300
Saint Louis MO 63105
314 725-5500

(G-7684)
ENTERPRISE BANK & TRUST
14670 S Harrison St (66061-7224)
P.O. Box 1500 (66051-1500)
PHONE..................................913 791-9300
Dan Long, *Manager*
EMP: 16 Publicly Held
SIC: 6022 State commercial banks
HQ: Enterprise Bank & Trust
150 N Meramec Ave Ste 300
Saint Louis MO 63105
314 725-5500

(G-7685)
ENTERPRISE BANK & TRUST
444 E Santa Fe St (66061-3446)
PHONE..................................913 791-9100
Peter Benoist, *CEO*
EMP: 18 Publicly Held
SIC: 6022 State commercial banks
HQ: Enterprise Bank & Trust
150 N Meramec Ave Ste 300
Saint Louis MO 63105
314 725-5500

(G-7686)
ENTERPRISE LEASING CO KS LLC
Also Called: Enterprise Rent-A-Car
1610 E Santa Fe St (66061-3645)
PHONE..................................913 254-0012
EMP: 26
SALES (corp-wide): 4.5B Privately Held
SIC: 7514 Rent-a-car service
HQ: Enterprise Leasing Company Of Ks Llc
5359 Merriam Dr
Shawnee Mission KS 66203
913 383-1515

(G-7687)
ENTERPRISE LEASING CO KS LLC
Also Called: Enterprise Rent-A-Car
15500 W 117th St (66062-1048)
PHONE....913 782-6381
EMP: 26
SALES (corp-wide): 4.5B **Privately Held**
SIC: 7514 Passenger car rental
HQ: Enterprise Leasing Company Of Ks Llc
5359 Merriam Dr
Shawnee Mission KS 66203
913 383-1515

(G-7688)
ENVIRONMENTAL MECH CONTRS INC
14872 W 117th St (66062-9304)
PHONE....913 829-0100
Thomas J Loscalzo, *President*
Andy Tiemann, *Superintendent*
David Debiasse, *Exec VP*
Paul Bloemer, *Vice Pres*
Gene Darby, *Vice Pres*
EMP: 60
SQ FT: 15,000
SALES (est): 11MM **Privately Held**
WEB: www.environmentalmech.com
SIC: 1711 Mechanical contractor

(G-7689)
EP RESORTS INC
Also Called: Marys Lake Lodge
15954 S Mur Len Rd (66062-8300)
PHONE....970 586-5958
Morgan Mulch, *CEO*
EMP: 25 **EST:** 2012
SALES (est): 1.6MM **Privately Held**
SIC: 7011 Resort hotel; vacation lodges

(G-7690)
EPIC IRRIGATION INC
Also Called: Epic Landscape
15460 S Keeler St (66062-2710)
PHONE....913 764-0178
Carey B Jagels, *President*
Mike Flynn, *Sales Mgr*
Lucas Fulton, *Cust Mgr*
Maria Axmann, *Admin Asst*
Lonny Ryburn, *Maintence Staff*
EMP: 150
SALES (est): 8.2MM **Privately Held**
WEB: www.epiclandscaping.com
SIC: 1711 0782 Irrigation sprinkler system installation; lawn & garden services

(G-7691)
ERMATOR INC
Also Called: Heilind Electronics
17400 W 119th St (66061-7740)
PHONE....813 684-7091
▲ **EMP:** 15
SQ FT: 100,000
SALES: 5MM
SALES (corp-wide): 4.6B **Privately Held**
SIC: 5064 Whol Appliances/Tv/Radio
HQ: Pullman - Ermator Ab
Husqvarna Construction Produ
Partille 433 8
365 706-030

(G-7692)
ESCOUTE LLC
Also Called: Escoute Consulting
18401 W 114th St (66061-9362)
PHONE....816 678-8398
Mark Thomas,
EMP: 10
SALES: 200K **Privately Held**
WEB: www.escoute.com
SIC: 7379 Computer related consulting services

(G-7693)
ESKRIDGE INC
1900 E Kansas City Rd (66061-3005)
P.O. Box 875 (66051-0875)
PHONE....913 782-1238
Craig Patterson, *Ch of Bd*
Lloyd German, *President*
▲ **EMP:** 66
SQ FT: 78,000
SALES (est): 28MM
SALES (corp-wide): 306.4MM **Privately Held**
WEB: www.eskridgeinc.com
SIC: 3568 Drives, chains & sprockets
HQ: Ramsey Industries Inc
4707 N Mingo Rd
Tulsa OK 74117
918 438-2760

(G-7694)
EVANGELICAL LUTHERAN
Also Called: Good Samaritan Soc - Olathe
20705 W 151st St (66061-7222)
P.O. Box 5038, Sioux Falls SD (57117-5038)
PHONE....913 782-1372
Samantha Bowlin, *Nursing Dir*
Robert Williams, *Food Svc Dir*
EMP: 284 **Privately Held**
WEB: www.good-sam.com
SIC: 8059 Nursing home, except skilled & intermediate care facility
HQ: The Evangelical Lutheran Good Samaritan Society
4800 W 57th St
Sioux Falls SD 57108
866 928-1635

(G-7695)
EVERGREEN LVING INNVATIONS INC
11875 S Sunset Dr Ste 100 (66061-2794)
PHONE....913 477-8227
Jamie Paredes, *Exec Dir*
Justine Ogdon, *Director*
Jaime Paredes, *Administration*
Eddie Campbell, *Maintence Staff*
EMP: 100
SALES: 9.7MM **Privately Held**
SIC: 8059 Nursing home, except skilled & intermediate care facility

(G-7696)
EVOLVE GRAN NATURAL STONE INC
1140 S Enterprise St (66061-5324)
PHONE....913 254-1800
Jason Cohorst, *President*
Wylie Sausbury, *Vice Pres*
EMP: 12
SALES: 3MM **Privately Held**
SIC: 3281 Table tops, marble; bathroom fixtures, cut stone; granite, cut & shaped; limestone, cut & shaped

(G-7697)
EXCELLART SIGN PRODUCTS LLC (PA)
1654 S Lone Elm Rd (66061-6837)
PHONE....913 764-2364
Greg Ambrose,
EMP: 14
SALES (est): 1.5MM **Privately Held**
WEB: www.excellart.com
SIC: 3993 Neon signs

(G-7698)
EXPRESSIONS EMBROIDERY LLC
1794 E Kansas City Rd (66061-3004)
PHONE....913 764-7070
Shirley Mason,
EMP: 11
SQ FT: 5,000
SALES: 500K **Privately Held**
SIC: 2395 Embroidery products, except schiffli machine; embroidery & art needle-work

(G-7699)
EXTREME DETAIL KC LLC
1356 E 155th St (66062-6713)
PHONE....913 568-4045
John Weves, *Mng Member*
EMP: 10
SALES (est): 280.4K **Privately Held**
SIC: 7542 Carwash, self-service

(G-7700)
FAIRFIELD INN BY MARRIOTT
12245 S Strang Line Rd (66062-5224)
PHONE....913 768-7000
Richard H Wiens, *President*
Monte Jenkins, *General Mgr*
Pat Hale, *Opers Staff*
EMP: 25
SALES (est): 1.3MM **Privately Held**
SIC: 7011 Hotels & motels
PA: Rhw Hotel Holdings Company, Llc
6704 W 121st St
Shawnee Mission KS 66209

(G-7701)
FAITH VILLAGE INC (HQ)
14150 W 113th St (66215-4819)
PHONE....913 906-5000
David Geske, *President*
Teresa Hook, *Manager*
Linda Ayers, *Administration*
EMP: 95
SQ FT: 5,000
SALES (est): 2.6MM
SALES (corp-wide): 126.8MM **Privately Held**
SIC: 8361 8059 Home for the mentally handicapped; home for the mentally retarded; home for the mentally retarded, exc. skilled or intermediate
PA: Bethesda Lutheran Communities, Inc.
600 Hoffmann Dr
Watertown WI 53094
920 261-3050

(G-7702)
FAMILY VIDEO MOVIE CLUB INC
12708 S Blackbob Rd (66062-1409)
PHONE....913 254-7219
EMP: 11
SALES (corp-wide): 189.9MM **Privately Held**
SIC: 7841 7359 5735 Video disk/tape rental to the general public; video cassette recorder & accessory rental; video discs & tapes, prerecorded
HQ: Family Video Movie Club Inc.
2500 Lehigh Mt Ave
Glenview IL 60026
847 904-9000

(G-7703)
FARMERS GROUP INC
Also Called: Farmers Insurance
10551 S Ridgeview Rd (66061-6401)
PHONE....913 227-2000
Frank Gregory, *Branch Mgr*
Steve Schrader, *Manager*
Tony Melchionne, *Director*
Jon Johnson, *Planning*
EMP: 25
SALES (corp-wide): 48.2B **Privately Held**
WEB: www.farmers.com
SIC: 6411 Insurance agents, brokers & service
HQ: Farmers Group, Inc.
6301 Owensmouth Ave
Woodland Hills CA 91367
323 932-3200

(G-7704)
FARMERS GROUP INC
Also Called: Farmers Insurance
17000 W 119th St (66061-7064)
PHONE....913 227-3200
Donna Wren, *Branch Mgr*
John Johnson, *Analyst*
EMP: 25
SALES (corp-wide): 48.2B **Privately Held**
WEB: www.farmers.com
SIC: 6411 6399 Insurance agents, brokers & service; deposit insurance
HQ: Farmers Group, Inc.
6301 Owensmouth Ave
Woodland Hills CA 91367
323 932-3200

(G-7705)
FEDEX CORPORATION
15014 S Blackbob Rd (66062-2663)
PHONE....913 393-0953
EMP: 11
SALES (corp-wide): 47.4B **Publicly Held**
SIC: 7389 Business Services
PA: Fedex Corporation
942 Shady Grove Rd S
Memphis TN 38120
901 818-7500

(G-7706)
FEDEX GROUND PACKAGE SYS INC
22161 W 167th St (66062-9629)
PHONE....800 463-3339
EMP: 146
SALES (corp-wide): 69.6B **Publicly Held**
SIC: 4213 Contract haulers
HQ: Fedex Ground Package System, Inc.
1000 Fed Ex Dr
Coraopolis PA 15108
800 463-3339

(G-7707)
FEDEX OFFICE & PRINT SVCS INC
15014 S Blackbob Rd (66062-2663)
PHONE....913 393-0953
EMP: 10
SALES (corp-wide): 69.6B **Publicly Held**
WEB: www.kinkos.com
SIC: 7334 Photocopying & duplicating services
HQ: Fedex Office And Print Services, Inc.
7900 Legacy Dr
Plano TX 75024
800 463-3339

(G-7708)
FEDEX OFFICE & PRINT SVCS INC
2099 E Santa Fe St (66062-1669)
PHONE....913 780-6010
EMP: 15
SALES (corp-wide): 69.6B **Publicly Held**
WEB: www.kinkos.com
SIC: 7334 Photocopying & duplicating services
HQ: Fedex Office And Print Services, Inc.
7900 Legacy Dr
Plano TX 75024
800 463-3339

(G-7709)
FINISHPRO TOOLS LLC
15785 S Keeler Ter (66062-3519)
PHONE....913 631-0804
Scott Murray,
Lionel Jiang,
▲ **EMP:** 22
SQ FT: 65,000
SALES: 15MM **Privately Held**
SIC: 3423 Masons' hand tools

(G-7710)
FIREBOARD LABS LLC
24260 W 112th Ter (66061-7372)
PHONE....816 945-2232
Ted Conrad, *Mng Member*
EMP: 8 **EST:** 2015
SALES (est): 20K **Privately Held**
SIC: 3829 7373 Thermometers & temperature sensors; systems software development services

(G-7711)
FIRST BAPTIST CHURCH OLATHE
Also Called: Noah's Ark
2024 E 151st St (66062-2944)
PHONE....913 764-7088
Roger Robertson, *Pastor*
Derek Varney, *Pastor*
EMP: 19
SALES (est): 1MM **Privately Held**
SIC: 8661 8351 Baptist Church; preschool center

(G-7712)
FIRST NATIONAL BANK OF OMAHA
13518 S Alden St (66062-5840)
PHONE....913 768-1120
Rick Godsil, *Branch Mgr*
EMP: 89
SALES (corp-wide): 1.2B **Privately Held**
SIC: 6021 National commercial banks
HQ: First National Bank Of Omaha Inc
1620 Dodge St
Omaha NE 68197
402 341-0500

GEOGRAPHIC

(G-7713)
FIRST STUDENT INC
18950 W 157th Ter (66062-6805)
PHONE..................................913 782-1050
Bob Osburn, *Manager*
EMP: 144
SALES (corp-wide): 9.1B **Privately Held**
WEB: www.leag.com
SIC: 4151 School buses
HQ: First Student, Inc.
600 Vine St Ste 1400
Cincinnati OH 45202

(G-7714)
FLEXCON COMPANY INC
Also Called: Midwest Distribution Center
1305 S Fountain Dr (66061-7204)
PHONE..................................913 768-8669
Ron Vieux, *Branch Mgr*
EMP: 13
SALES (corp-wide): 333.1MM **Privately Held**
WEB: www.flexcon.com
SIC: 4225 General warehousing
PA: Flexcon Company, Inc.
1 Flexcon Industrial Park
Spencer MA 01562
508 885-8200

(G-7715)
FLORIDA INFORMATION CONSORTIUM
25501 W Valley Pkwy # 300 (66061-8453)
PHONE..................................913 498-3468
EMP: 10
SALES (est): 681.2K
SALES (corp-wide): 292.3MM **Publicly Held**
SIC: 7374 Data Processing/Preparation
HQ: Nicusa, Inc.
25501 W Valley Pkwy # 300
Olathe KS 66061
913 498-3468

(G-7716)
FOLEY EQUIPMENT COMPANY
15854 S Us 169 Hwy (66062-3502)
PHONE..................................913 393-0303
Mike Jenkins, *Branch Mgr*
EMP: 70
SALES (corp-wide): 124.2MM **Privately Held**
SIC: 5082 Construction & mining machinery
HQ: Foley Equipment Company
1550 S West St
Wichita KS 67213
316 943-4211

(G-7717)
FOODBRANDS SUP CHAIN SVCS INC
20701 W 159th St (66062-9040)
PHONE..................................913 393-7000
R Randolph Devening, *President*
Bryant Bynum, *Senior VP*
William L Brady, *Vice Pres*
EMP: 140
SQ FT: 130,000
SALES (est): 22.7MM
SALES (corp-wide): 42.4B **Publicly Held**
SIC: 5142 Packaged frozen goods
PA: Tyson Foods, Inc.
2200 W Don Tyson Pkwy
Springdale AR 72762
479 290-4000

(G-7718)
FREMONT INDUSTRIES INC
1358 S Enterprise St (66061-5357)
PHONE..................................913 962-7676
Gary Keefer, *Branch Mgr*
EMP: 6 **Privately Held**
SIC: 3999 Barber & beauty shop equipment
HQ: Fremont Industries, Llc
4400 Valley Indus Blvd N
Shakopee MN 55379
952 445-4121

(G-7719)
FRONTR-RRWHEAD JOINT VENTR LLC
14635 S Rene St (66062-8860)
PHONE..................................913 461-3804
Scott F Siegwald,
EMP: 50
SALES (est): 2MM **Privately Held**
SIC: 1542 4959 Nonresidential construction; sanitary services

(G-7720)
FULLER FOUNDATION COMPANY INC
19125 W 151st Ter Ste A (66062-2724)
PHONE..................................913 764-8222
Rex W Fuller, *President*
EMP: 25
SQ FT: 3,000
SALES (est): 1.8MM **Privately Held**
SIC: 1741 Foundation building

(G-7721)
GARMIN INTERNATIONAL INC
1200 E 151st St (66062-3426)
PHONE..................................312 787-3221
Joel Apostol, *Branch Mgr*
EMP: 25
SALES (corp-wide): 261.7K **Privately Held**
WEB: www.navtalk.com
SIC: 3812 Search & navigation equipment
HQ: Garmin International, Inc.
1200 E 151st St
Olathe KS 66062

(G-7722)
GARMIN INTERNATIONAL INC (DH)
1200 E 151st St (66062-3426)
PHONE..................................913 397-8200
Clifton Pemble, *CEO*
Dr Min KAO, *Chairman*
David Ayres, *Counsel*
Andrew Etkind, *Vice Pres*
Alfredo Gunara, *Project Mgr*
◆ **EMP:** 950
SQ FT: 995,950
SALES (est): 2.2B
SALES (corp-wide): 261.7K **Privately Held**
WEB: www.navtalk.com
SIC: 3812 3669 8713 Navigational systems & instruments; visual communication systems; surveying services
HQ: Garmin Switzerland Gmbh
Muhlentalstrasse 2
Schaffhausen SH 8200
526 301-600

(G-7723)
GARRISON PLUMBING INC
1375 N Winchester St (66061-5880)
PHONE..................................913 768-1311
Garrison Pslumm, *President*
EMP: 10
SALES (est): 1.6MM **Privately Held**
SIC: 1711 Plumbing contractors

(G-7724)
GARWIN ELECTRIC LLC
432 S Kansas Ave (66061-4441)
PHONE..................................913 780-1200
Steve Winegar, *Mng Member*
EMP: 14
SQ FT: 3,550
SALES (est): 1.7MM **Privately Held**
SIC: 1731 General electrical contractor

(G-7725)
GECKO PAINTING INC
700 E Dennis Ave (66061-4609)
PHONE..................................913 782-7000
C Scott Johnson, *President*
Daniel J Higgins, *Vice Pres*
EMP: 30
SQ FT: 1,800
SALES (est): 2.3MM **Privately Held**
WEB: www.geckopainting.com
SIC: 1721 Residential painting

(G-7726)
GEMTECH LLC
15665 S Keeler St (66062-3515)
PHONE..................................913 782-3080
Mike Miller, *Sales Staff*
Michael Miller, *Mng Member*
▲ **EMP:** 37 **EST:** 2012
SALES (est): 6MM **Privately Held**
SIC: 3089 Plastic processing

(G-7727)
GENERAL TECH A SVCS & PDTS CO
2016 E Spruce Cir (66062-5404)
PHONE..................................913 766-5566
Feiyu MA, *President*
▲ **EMP:** 5
SQ FT: 3,000
SALES (est): 1.1MM **Privately Held**
SIC: 5169 3589 5083 5191 Resins, synthetic rubber; sewage & water treatment equipment; tractors, agricultural; chemicals, agricultural

(G-7728)
GEO FORM INTERNATIONAL INC
Also Called: Geo Form Int'l
519 E Kansas City Rd (66061-3300)
PHONE..................................913 782-1166
Sam Minnich, *President*
Richard Wickoren, *President*
Daniel Wickoren, *Vice Pres*
EMP: 6
SALES (est): 1.1MM **Privately Held**
SIC: 3312 Blast furnaces & steel mills

(G-7729)
GLEN SHADOW GOLF CLUB (PA)
26000 Shadow Glen Dr (66061-7456)
PHONE..................................913 764-2299
Richard Landon, *President*
Scott Johnson, *Superintendent*
Heath Fisher, *Asst Supt*
Fred Shaw, *Vice Pres*
Joseph Ledin, *Treasurer*
EMP: 80
SALES: 5.2MM **Privately Held**
WEB: www.shadowglen.org
SIC: 7997 Golf club, membership

(G-7730)
GLEN SHADOW GOLF CLUB
Also Called: Cedar Lnscape Maintence Fcilty
26577 College Blvd (66061-9368)
PHONE..................................913 764-6572
Scott Johnson, *Superintendent*
EMP: 25
SALES (corp-wide): 5.2MM **Privately Held**
WEB: www.shadowglen.org
SIC: 7997 Golf club, membership
PA: Glen Shadow Golf Club
26000 Shadow Glen Dr
Olathe KS 66061
913 764-2299

(G-7731)
GLOBAL AVIATION SERVICES LLC (PA)
540 E Old Highway 56 (66061-4640)
PHONE..................................913 780-0300
Walter Clark, *Ch of Bd*
Nick Swensen, *Ch of Bd*
EMP: 70
SALES (est): 10.9MM **Privately Held**
SIC: 7699 Aircraft & heavy equipment repair services

(G-7732)
GLOBAL GROUND SUPPORT LLC
540 E Old Highway 56 (66061-4640)
PHONE..................................913 780-0300
Charles Preston, *Prdtn Mgr*
Greg Todd, *Purch Agent*
Marshall Keith, *Buyer*
Conner Richenburg, *Buyer*
Air T Inc, *Mng Member*
◆ **EMP:** 70
SQ FT: 112,000
SALES (est): 25.2MM
SALES (corp-wide): 249.8MM **Publicly Held**
WEB: www.global-llc.com
SIC: 3728 5088 Deicing equipment, aircraft; aircraft & parts
PA: T Air Inc
5930 Balsom Ridge Rd
Denver NC 28037
828 464-8741

(G-7733)
GLOBAL STONE LLC (PA)
421 N Rawhide Dr (66061-3636)
PHONE..................................913 310-9500
Jason Larsen, *Partner*
David Jennejahn, *Partner*
EMP: 6
SQ FT: 20,000
SALES: 2.5MM **Privately Held**
SIC: 3281 5211 5032 Curbing, granite or stone; counter tops; granite building stone

(G-7734)
GLOBAL SYSTEMS INCORPORATED
Also Called: Gsi-Flo
13470 S Arapaho Dr # 130 (66062-1615)
PHONE..................................913 829-5900
Mike Killion, *Sales/Mktg Mgr*
EMP: 13 **Privately Held**
SIC: 5084 Pneumatic tools & equipment
PA: Global Systems Incorporated
7208 Weil Ave Ste A
Saint Louis MO 63119

(G-7735)
GLOVER INC
878 N Jan Mar Ct (66061-3692)
PHONE..................................800 654-1511
Jim Glover, *President*
Anissa Mick, *Buyer*
Kim Glover, *Treasurer*
Joyce Bubniak, *Data Proc Staff*
Maria Marsh, *Graphic Designe*
EMP: 38
SQ FT: 12,000
SALES (est): 11.2MM **Privately Held**
WEB: www.palmermarketing.com
SIC: 5199 2741 8742 8732 Gifts & novelties; catalogs: publishing only, not printed on site; management consulting services; commercial nonphysical research; noncommercial research organizations

(G-7736)
GODDARD SCHOOL
15040 W 138th St (66062-4554)
PHONE..................................913 764-1331
Betsy Allen, *Owner*
Marci Richter, *Principal*
Christie Haase, *Director*
EMP: 30
SALES (est): 576K **Privately Held**
SIC: 8351 Preschool center

(G-7737)
GOODWILL WSTN MO & EASTRN KANS
Also Called: Goodwill Store 12
16630 W 135th St (66062-1543)
PHONE..................................913 768-9540
Gary Raines, *Branch Mgr*
EMP: 30
SALES (corp-wide): 21.3MM **Privately Held**
WEB: www.mokangoodwill.org
SIC: 5932 7349 8331 3444 Clothing, secondhand; furniture, secondhand; janitorial service, contract basis; job training services; sheet metalwork; fabricated structural metal
PA: Goodwill Of Western Missouri & Eastern Kansas
800 E 18th St
Kansas City MO 64108
816 220-1779

(G-7738)
GRACE UNITED METHODIST CHURCH
11485 S Ridgeview Rd (66061-6459)
PHONE..................................913 859-0111
Nanette Roberts, *Relg Ldr*
EMP: 20
SALES (est): 288.7K **Privately Held**
SIC: 8661 8351 Methodist Church; group day care center

(G-7739)
GRASS PAD INC (PA)
425 N Rawhide Dr (66061-3695)
PHONE..................................913 764-4100
Michael J Mc Dermott, *President*
Don Bain, *Officer*
EMP: 60

SQ FT: 10,000
SALES (est): 40.8MM **Privately Held**
WEB: www.grasspad.com
SIC: 5191 5193 5261 Seeds: field, garden & flower; fertilizer & fertilizer materials; nursery stock; sod; nursery stock, seeds & bulbs; fertilizer

(G-7740)
GRASSLAND HERITAGE FOUNDATION
26062 W 150th St (66061-8510)
PHONE..................................913 856-4784
Steven Holcomb, *Treasurer*
EMP: 11
SALES (est): 74.3K **Privately Held**
SIC: 8999 Natural resource preservation service

(G-7741)
GROUPSOURCE GPO LLC (PA)
1570 S Mahaffie Cir (66062-3432)
PHONE..................................913 888-9191
Judd Conner, *Principal*
EMP: 18
SALES (est): 4.1MM **Privately Held**
SIC: 8748 Business consulting

(G-7742)
GUNTER PEST MANAGEMENT INC
13505 S Mur Len Rd (66062-1600)
PHONE..................................913 397-0220
Jay Besheer, *Branch Mgr*
EMP: 20
SALES (corp-wide): 3.5MM **Privately Held**
SIC: 7342 Pest control in structures; pest control services
PA: Gunter Pest Management, Inc.
220 W 72nd St
Kansas City MO 64114
816 523-0777

(G-7743)
GUNZE PLAS & ENGRG CORP AMER
1400 S Hamilton Cir (66061-5375)
PHONE..................................913 829-5577
Tomohisa Okuda, *President*
Nodoka Kodama, *Principal*
◆ **EMP:** 78
SQ FT: 35,000
SALES (est): 21.3MM **Privately Held**
WEB: www.zb4.so-net.ne.jp
SIC: 2671 Packaging paper & plastics film, coated & laminated
PA: Gunze Limited
2-5-25, Umeda, Kita-Ku
Osaka OSK 530-0

(G-7744)
H & R BLOCK TAX SERVICES LLC
15254 W 119th St (66062-5604)
PHONE..................................913 648-1040
EMP: 12
SALES (corp-wide): 3B **Publicly Held**
SIC: 7291 Tax return preparation services
HQ: H & R Block Tax Services Llc
1 H And R Block Way
Kansas City MO 64105

(G-7745)
HAIR SHOP & RETAILING CENTER
16140 W 135th St (66062-1517)
PHONE..................................913 397-9888
Orn Odel, *Owner*
EMP: 20
SALES (est): 349.5K **Privately Held**
SIC: 7231 7299 5999 Hairdressers; personal appearance services; hair care products

(G-7746)
HAIR SHOP WEST INC
Also Called: Hair Shop & Retailing Center
131 N Parker St (66061-3139)
PHONE..................................913 829-4868
Oren O Dell, *President*
EMP: 20
SALES (est): 497.3K **Privately Held**
SIC: 7231 7299 5999 Hairdressers; tanning salon; hair care products

(G-7747)
HAIREM OF OLATHE LLC
Also Called: The Hairem
12805 S Mur Len Rd Ste C5 (66062-5441)
PHONE..................................913 829-1260
Sheryl Bjorgo, *Owner*
EMP: 13
SALES (est): 376.6K **Privately Held**
SIC: 7231 Unisex hair salons

(G-7748)
HALF PRICE BKS REC MGZINES INC
15309 W 119th St (66062-1074)
PHONE..................................913 829-9959
Starr Rockhill, *Site Mgr*
EMP: 17
SALES (corp-wide): 208MM **Privately Held**
SIC: 2721 5735 5932 Magazines: publishing & printing; records; book stores, secondhand
PA: Half Price Books, Records, Magazines, Incorporated
5803 E Northwest Hwy
Dallas TX 75231
214 360-0833

(G-7749)
HANNAH & OLTJEN (PA)
1441 E 151st St (66062-2803)
PHONE..................................913 829-2244
Joseph Hannah, *President*
EMP: 11
SALES (est): 1.9MM **Privately Held**
SIC: 8021 Orthodontist

(G-7750)
HAPPY HOUSE DAY CARE (PA)
825 E Sheridan St (66061-4936)
PHONE..................................913 782-1115
Linda Torres, *Owner*
Linda Torrez, *Co-Owner*
EMP: 10
SALES (est): 564.8K **Privately Held**
SIC: 8351 Child day care services

(G-7751)
HAPPY HOUSE DAY CARE
Also Called: Happy House Child Care Ctr 2
825 E Sheridan St (66061-4936)
PHONE..................................913 782-1115
Linda Torrez, *Director*
EMP: 12
SALES (corp-wide): 564.8K **Privately Held**
SIC: 8351 8211 Group day care center; kindergarten
PA: Happy House Day Care
825 E Sheridan St
Olathe KS 66061
913 782-1115

(G-7752)
HARLAN C PARKER INSURANCE AGCY
13095 S Mur Len Rd # 180 (66062-1298)
PHONE..................................913 782-3310
Harlan C Parker, *President*
EMP: 10
SQ FT: 2,500
SALES (est): 1.4MM **Privately Held**
SIC: 6411 Insurance agents & brokers

(G-7753)
HARMON CONSTRUCTION INC
18989 W 158th St (66062-8014)
PHONE..................................913 962-5888
Tim J Harmon, *President*
Janet Harmon, *Vice Pres*
David Clark, *Treasurer*
EMP: 20
SQ FT: 4,125
SALES: 18MM **Privately Held**
WEB: www.harmonconst.com
SIC: 1542 Commercial & office building, new construction

(G-7754)
HARRIS BMO BANK NATIONAL ASSN
Also Called: Bmo Harris Bank
15203 W 119th St (66062-5605)
PHONE..................................913 254-6600
Melanie Glassman, *Site Mgr*
Nonie Glassman, *Branch Mgr*
EMP: 10
SALES (corp-wide): 17.7B **Privately Held**
WEB: www.uhb-fl.com
SIC: 6022 State trust companies accepting deposits, commercial
HQ: Harris Bmo Bank National Association
111 W Monroe St Ste 1200
Chicago IL 60603
312 461-2323

(G-7755)
HARRIS QUALITY INC
11623 S Iowa St (66061-6452)
PHONE..................................402 332-5857
William Harris, *President*
Roxanne Harris, *Manager*
EMP: 70
SALES (est): 13.9MM **Privately Held**
WEB: www.harrisquality.com
SIC: 4212 Local trucking, without storage

(G-7756)
HARRISON MACHINE SHOP & WLDG
806 S Kansas Ave (66061-4529)
PHONE..................................913 764-0730
Claud Harrison, *President*
EMP: 9
SQ FT: 2,000
SALES (est): 920K **Privately Held**
WEB: www.foleycompany.com
SIC: 7692 3599 Welding repair; machine shop, jobbing & repair

(G-7757)
HAYES TOOLING & PLASTICS INC
640 S Rogers Rd (66062-1738)
PHONE..................................913 782-0046
James W Hayes, *President*
Irene Hayes, *Vice Pres*
Mario Zarlengo, *Vice Pres*
EMP: 10 **EST:** 1954
SQ FT: 12,500
SALES (est): 1.2MM **Privately Held**
SIC: 3089 3544 Injection molding of plastics; blow molded finished plastic products; dies, plastics forming

(G-7758)
HAYWARD BAKER INC
114 N Water St (66061-3415)
PHONE..................................913 390-0085
Shirley Jay, *Admin Sec*
EMP: 65
SALES (corp-wide): 2.9B **Privately Held**
SIC: 1799 Building site preparation
HQ: Hayward Baker Inc
7550 Teague Rd Ste 300
Hanover MD 21076
410 551-8200

(G-7759)
HAZ-MAT RESPONSE INC (PA)
1203 S Parker St Ste C (66061-4291)
PHONE..................................913 782-5151
Luke Stockdale, *President*
Jack Stockdale, *President*
Jo Wilhite, *Corp Secy*
Robert McRae, *Vice Pres*
John Negrete, *Vice Pres*
EMP: 48
SQ FT: 15,000
SALES (est): 56.5MM **Privately Held**
WEB: www.haz-matresponse.com
SIC: 4959 Environmental cleanup services

(G-7760)
HEALTH PARTNERSHIP CLINIC INC (PA)
407 S Clairborne Rd # 104 (66062-1744)
PHONE..................................913 433-7583
Amy Falk, *CEO*
Brenda McLaughlin, *CFO*
Cindy Daugherty, *Hlthcr Dir*
EMP: 40
SALES: 7MM **Privately Held**
SIC: 8099 8399 8011 Health screening service; health & welfare council; clinic, operated by physicians

(G-7761)
HEALTHRIDGE FITNESS CENTER LLC
23990 W 121st St (66061-6220)
P.O. Box 902 (66051-0902)
PHONE..................................913 888-0656
Jeff Rowe, *Director*
Joe Sharbaugh,
Paul Sharbaugh,
EMP: 160
SQ FT: 106,000
SALES (est): 5.2MM **Privately Held**
WEB: www.healthridgefitnesscenter.com
SIC: 7991 Health club

(G-7762)
HEART AMERICA MANAGEMENT LLC
Also Called: Comfort Inn
12070 S Strang Line Rd (66062-5255)
PHONE..................................913 397-0100
Chris Bernat, *Manager*
EMP: 27
SALES (corp-wide): 75.3MM **Privately Held**
WEB: www.nifast.com
SIC: 7011 7299 Hotels & motels; banquet hall facilities
PA: Heart Of America Management Llc
1501 River Dr
Moline IL 61265
309 797-9300

(G-7763)
HEARTLAND MIDWEST LLC
15795 S Mahaffie St # 100 (66062-4002)
PHONE..................................913 397-9911
Don Guthrie, *General Mgr*
Travis Clark, *Safety Mgr*
Raymond L Chapman, *Mng Member*
Ken Kearney, *Manager*
EMP: 185
SQ FT: 7,500
SALES (est): 27MM **Privately Held**
SIC: 4939 Combination utilities

(G-7764)
HELPERS INC
15540 S Pflumm Rd (66062-8511)
PHONE..................................913 322-7212
Stacy W Jones, *Principal*
EMP: 19
SALES (est): 699K **Privately Held**
SIC: 8351 Child day care services

(G-7765)
HERITAGE ELECTRIC LLC
841 N Martway Dr (66061-7053)
PHONE..................................913 747-0528
Jeremy Hansen, *Vice Pres*
Andrew Poecker, *Project Mgr*
Jane Conner, *Mng Member*
David Conner, *Mng Member*
EMP: 22
SQ FT: 5,000
SALES (est): 4.2MM **Privately Held**
SIC: 1731 General electrical contractor

(G-7766)
HERITAGE TRACTOR INC
Also Called: John Deere Authorized Dealer
19905 W 157th St (66062-3824)
PHONE..................................913 529-2376
Keith Classen, *Branch Mgr*
EMP: 20
SALES (corp-wide): 66.3MM **Privately Held**
SIC: 5083 Farm & garden machinery
PA: Heritage Tractor, Inc.
915 Industrial Park Rd
Baldwin City KS 66006
785 594-6486

(G-7767)
HI-LINE PLASTICS INC
801 E Old Highway 56 (66061-4914)
PHONE..................................913 782-3535
Jim Stawarz, *CEO*
Joyce D Stawarz, *Ch of Bd*
Galen T Soule, *President*
Adrian Page, *Vice Pres*
EMP: 53 **EST:** 1959
SQ FT: 44,000
SALES (est): 9.8MM **Privately Held**
SIC: 3089 Injection molding of plastics

GEOGRAPHIC

(G-7768)
HIMOINSA POWER SYSTEMS INC
Also Called: Himoinsa USA
16600 Theden St (66062-9607)
PHONE....................................913 495-5557
Rafael R Acosta, *President*
Pam Sill, *General Mgr*
Samuel Silva, *COO*
Rino Sbriglia, *Opers Mgr*
Estefania Soriano, *Production*
▲ **EMP:** 50
SALES (est): 33.2MM **Privately Held**
WEB: www.himoinsausa.com
SIC: 5063 Generators
HQ: Himoinsa Sl
Calle Edison (Pg Ind Las Mezquitas) 57
Getafe 28906
916 842-106

(G-7769)
HISONIC LLC
310 N Marion St (66061-3107)
PHONE....................................913 782-0012
Don McElheny,
Brian Miller,
EMP: 48
SALES (est): 1.5MM
SALES (corp-wide): 18.7MM **Privately Held**
SIC: 3728 Aircraft assemblies, subassemblies & parts
PA: Gowanda Holdings, Llc
1 Magnetic Pkwy
Gowanda NY 14070
716 532-2234

(G-7770)
HITCHIN POST STEAK CO
808 N Meadowbrook Dr (66062-5442)
PHONE....................................913 647-0543
Kim Cunningham, *President*
Jason Cunningham, *Vice Pres*
EMP: 100 **EST:** 1999
SQ FT: 40,000
SALES (est): 27.4MM **Privately Held**
SIC: 2015 Chicken slaughtering & processing

(G-7771)
HOMESTEAD OF OLATHE NORTH
791 N Somerset Ter (66062-5450)
PHONE....................................913 829-1403
Jeri Willson, *Principal*
EMP: 165
SALES (est): 203.9K
SALES (corp-wide): 32.7MM **Privately Held**
SIC: 8361 Geriatric residential care
PA: Midwest Health, Inc
3024 Sw Wanamaker Rd # 300
Topeka KS 66614
785 272-1535

(G-7772)
HONEYWELL INTERNATIONAL INC
23500 W 105th St (66061-8425)
PHONE....................................913 782-0400
Marvin Black, *Branch Mgr*
EMP: 120
SQ FT: 3,000
SALES (corp-wide): 41.8B **Publicly Held**
WEB: www.honeywell.com
SIC: 5065 7629 Electronic parts; electronic equipment repair
PA: Honeywell International Inc.
300 S Tryon St
Charlotte NC 28202
973 455-2000

(G-7773)
HONEYWELL INTERNATIONAL INC
23500 W 105th St Md300 (66061-8425)
PHONE....................................816 997-7149
Christopher Gentile, *President*
EMP: 2500
SALES (corp-wide): 41.8B **Publicly Held**
SIC: 3724 Aircraft engines & engine parts
PA: Honeywell International Inc.
300 S Tryon St
Charlotte NC 28202
973 455-2000

(G-7774)
HONEYWELL INTERNATIONAL INC
23500 W 105th St (66061-8425)
PHONE....................................913 712-3000
Stefan Komarek, *Branch Mgr*
EMP: 80
SALES (corp-wide): 41.8B **Publicly Held**
WEB: www.honeywell.com
SIC: 3724 Aircraft engines & engine parts
PA: Honeywell International Inc.
300 S Tryon St
Charlotte NC 28202
973 455-2000

(G-7775)
HONEYWELL INTERNATIONAL INC
23500 W 105th St (66061-8425)
PHONE....................................402 597-2279
Dan Pistulka, *Manager*
EMP: 20
SALES (corp-wide): 41.8B **Publicly Held**
WEB: www.honeywell.com
SIC: 3822 3669 1711 Air conditioning & refrigeration controls; burglar alarm apparatus, electric; plumbing, heating, air-conditioning contractors
PA: Honeywell International Inc.
300 S Tryon St
Charlotte NC 28202
973 455-2000

(G-7776)
HONEYWELL INTERNATIONAL INC
23500 W 105th St (66061-8425)
PHONE....................................913 712-0400
Mike Boyd, *Branch Mgr*
EMP: 44
SALES (corp-wide): 41.8B **Publicly Held**
WEB: www.honeywell.com
SIC: 4581 5088 Aircraft maintenance & repair services; aircraft equipment & supplies
PA: Honeywell International Inc.
300 S Tryon St
Charlotte NC 28202
973 455-2000

(G-7777)
HOOPER HOLMES INC (DH)
Also Called: Provant Health
560 N Rogers Rd (66062-1211)
PHONE....................................913 764-1045
Ronald V Aprahamian, *Ch of Bd*
Mark Clermont, *President*
Daniel Porazzo, *Counsel*
Albert Tavarez, *Supervisor*
Judy Butler, *Director*
EMP: 80
SALES: 56.1MM
SALES (corp-wide): 7.5B **Publicly Held**
WEB: www.hooperholmes.com
SIC: 8099 6411 7375 Physical examination service, insurance; information bureaus, insurance; information retrieval services
HQ: Summit Health, Inc.
27175 Haggerty Rd
Novi MI 48377
248 799-8303

(G-7778)
HOUSE OF DANCE
18833 W 158th St (66062-8022)
PHONE....................................913 839-1962
Gaby Lucas, *Owner*
EMP: 10 **EST:** 2016
SALES (est): 50.5K **Privately Held**
SIC: 7911 Dance studio & school

(G-7779)
HTC INC
17400 W 119th St (66061-7740)
P.O. Box 5077, Knoxville TN (37928-0077)
PHONE....................................865 689-2311
Henrik Rosencrantz, *CEO*
Patrik Knudsen, *CFO*
◆ **EMP:** 28
SQ FT: 25,000
SALES: 19.4MM
SALES (corp-wide): 4.3B **Privately Held**
WEB: www.htc-floorsystems.com
SIC: 5082 Construction & mining machinery
HQ: Husqvarna Construction Products North America, Inc.
17400 W 119th St
Olathe KS 66061
913 928-1000

(G-7780)
HUSQVARNA US HOLDING INC
17400 W 119th St (66061-7740)
PHONE....................................913 928-1000
Darin Morse, *Facilities Mgr*
Kevin Eichhorst, *Production*
Matthew Mosko, *Engineer*
Robert Wallace, *Engineer*
Patricia Crabtree, *Credit Staff*
EMP: 18
SALES (corp-wide): 4.3B **Privately Held**
SIC: 3582 Dryers, laundry: commercial, including coin-operated
HQ: Husqvarna U.S. Holding, Inc.
20445 Emerald Pkwy Ste 2
Cleveland OH 44135
216 898-1800

(G-7781)
HUSQVRNA CNSTR PDTS N AMER INC (DH)
Also Called: Dimas Division
17400 W 119th St (66061-7740)
PHONE....................................913 928-1000
Steve Chamberlin, *President*
Cheryl Bishop, *Business Mgr*
Jay Lockhart, *Opers Staff*
Chris Noeth, *CFO*
Lura O'Neal, *Auditor*
◆ **EMP:** 570
SALES (est): 166.1MM
SALES (corp-wide): 4.3B **Privately Held**
WEB: www.felkersaws.com
SIC: 3541 3291 5085 5082 Saws & sawing machines; abrasive products; abrasives; contractors' materials; saw blades & handsaws; asphalt paving mixtures & blocks
HQ: Husqvarna Holding Ab
Drottninggatan 2
Huskvarna 561 3
873 880-77

(G-7782)
HUSTON CONTRACTING INC
614 S Kansas Ave (66061-4525)
PHONE....................................913 782-1333
Doug Huston, *President*
EMP: 12
SALES (est): 1.3MM **Privately Held**
SIC: 1623 Underground utilities contractor

(G-7783)
HYLAND LLC (DH)
18103 W 106th St Ste 200 (66061-2884)
PHONE....................................440 788-5045
Bill Premier, *CEO*
Teresa Carter, *President*
Christopher Hyland, *CFO*
EMP: 320
SQ FT: 95,655
SALES (est): 81MM
SALES (corp-wide): 461.8MM **Privately Held**
WEB: www.imagenow.com
SIC: 7372 Business oriented computer software
HQ: Hyland Holdings Llc
8900 Renner Blvd
Lenexa KS 66219
913 227-7000

(G-7784)
ILLINOIS TOOL WORKS INC
Also Called: ITW Pro Brands
805 E Old Highway 56 (66061-4914)
PHONE....................................913 397-9889
Paul Taylor, *Vice Pres*
Deb Fullington, *Purchasing*
Robert Martin, *Research*
Lee Rieth, *Research*
Jim Hamilton, *Sales Staff*
EMP: 100
SALES (corp-wide): 14.7B **Publicly Held**
WEB: www.dymon.com
SIC: 2842 Cleaning or polishing preparations
PA: Illinois Tool Works Inc.
155 Harlem Ave
Glenview IL 60025
847 724-7500

(G-7785)
ILS NATIONAL LLC (PA)
Also Called: Ilsn
1570 S Mahaffie Cir (66062-3432)
PHONE....................................913 888-9191
Judd Conner,
Ross Conner,
EMP: 18
SQ FT: 2,000
SALES: 40MM **Privately Held**
WEB: www.ilsnational.com
SIC: 7389 Purchasing service

(G-7786)
IM OLATHE LP
Also Called: Residence Inn By Marriott
12215 S Strang Line Rd (66062-5224)
PHONE....................................913 829-6700
Ruby Huang, *Senior VP*
EMP: 25
SALES (est): 932.4K **Privately Held**
SIC: 7011 Hotels & motels

(G-7787)
INDUSTRIAL SALES COMPANY INC (PA)
1150 W Marley Rd (66061-7208)
PHONE....................................913 829-3500
Jake J Cooper III, *President*
Brett Fulmer, *Sales Staff*
EMP: 33 **EST:** 1973
SQ FT: 28,000
SALES (est): 19.8MM **Privately Held**
SIC: 5074 5083 Pipes & fittings, plastic; irrigation equipment

(G-7788)
INDUSTRIAL SLING LBRCATION INC
Also Called: I S L
15430 S Keeler St (66062-2710)
PHONE....................................913 294-3001
Dave Consiglio, *President*
Gayla Consiglio, *Vice Pres*
EMP: 10
SQ FT: 2,000
SALES (est): 8.5MM **Privately Held**
SIC: 5172 Lubricating oils & greases

(G-7789)
INFORMA BUSINESS MEDIA INC
17300 W 119th St (66061-7759)
PHONE....................................913 341-1300
EMP: 99
SALES (corp-wide): 3.1B **Privately Held**
SIC: 2721 Periodicals
HQ: Informa Business Media, Inc.
605 3rd Ave
New York NY 10158
212 204-4200

(G-7790)
INFUTOR DATA SOLUTIONS LLC
Also Called: Ruf Strategic Solution
1533 E Spruce St (66061-3646)
PHONE....................................913 782-8544
Don Buck, *Marketing Staff*
EMP: 18
SALES (corp-wide): 8MM **Privately Held**
SIC: 7374 7375 Computer time-sharing; data processing service; data base information retrieval
PA: Infutor Data Solutions Llc
18w140 Bttrfeld Rd Ste 10
Oakbrook Terrace IL 60181
312 348-7900

(G-7791)
INLAND ASSOCIATES INC (PA)
18965 W 158th St (66062-8014)
PHONE....................................913 764-7977
Peggy Meader, *President*
Chuck Floyd, *CFO*
Craig Meader, *Admin Sec*
EMP: 11
SQ FT: 12,000

▲ = Import ▼=Export
◆ =Import/Export

SALES (est): 10.2MM **Privately Held**
WEB: www.inlandassoc.com
SIC: 5045 Computer peripheral equipment

(G-7792)
INLAND TRUCK PARTS COMPANY
1370 S Hamilton Cir (66061-7241)
PHONE..................................913 492-7559
Rey Post, *Branch Mgr*
EMP: 15
SALES (corp-wide): 167.3MM **Privately Held**
WEB: www.inlandtruck.com
SIC: 5013 Truck parts & accessories; automotive supplies & parts
PA: Inland Truck Parts Company Inc
7015 College Blvd Ste 650
Overland Park KS 66211
913 345-9664

(G-7793)
INNARA HEALTH INC
10900 S Clay Blair Blvd # 900
(66061-1301)
PHONE..................................913 742-7770
Michael Litscher, *CEO*
Bruce Richardson, *CFO*
EMP: 5
SALES (est): 681.5K **Privately Held**
SIC: 3841 Surgical & medical instruments

(G-7794)
INNOVATIVE FLUID POWER
Also Called: If
19000 W 158th St Ste A (66062-8012)
P.O. Box 10107, Cedar Rapids IA (52410-0107)
PHONE..................................913 768-7008
James A Kaaf, *President*
Don Kaaf, *CFO*
EMP: 10
SALES (est): 3.4MM **Privately Held**
SIC: 5084 Hydraulic systems equipment & supplies; pneumatic tools & equipment

(G-7795)
INSULITE GLASS CO INC (PA)
780 W Frontier Ln (66061-7202)
P.O. Box 2803 (66063-0803)
PHONE..................................800 452-7721
Beau Guyette, *President*
▲ **EMP:** 80
SQ FT: 60,000
SALES (est): 37MM **Privately Held**
SIC: 5039 3211 Glass construction materials; insulating glass, sealed units

(G-7796)
INTEGRATED CONTROLS INC
15707 S Mahaffie St (66062-4038)
PHONE..................................913 782-9600
David K Nance, *President*
Roger Hansen, *Vice Pres*
Mark Martin, *Manager*
EMP: 10
SQ FT: 6,000
SALES (est): 1.8MM **Privately Held**
WEB: www.icicontrols.com
SIC: 3613 Control panels, electric

(G-7797)
INTEGRITY LOCATING SVCS LLC
18993 W 158th St Olathe (66062)
P.O. Box 27195, Shawnee Mission (66225-7195)
PHONE..................................913 530-6315
EMP: 31
SQ FT: 2,000
SALES: 3.2MM **Privately Held**
SIC: 1623 Underground utilities contractor

(G-7798)
INTERACTIVE TECHNOLOGIES INC
15655 S Mahaffie St (66062-4039)
PHONE..................................913 254-0887
Rob Dorrell, *President*
Jeremy Smith, *Principal*
Scott Finnell, *Vice Pres*
John Adzema, *Purchasing*
EMP: 15
SALES (est): 2.6MM **Privately Held**
SIC: 8711 Engineering services

(G-7799)
INTERIOR SURFACE ENTPS LLC
19940 W 161st St (66062-2700)
PHONE..................................913 397-8100
Tim Poter, *President*
Larry Burt, *Vice Pres*
Janell Porter, *Opers Staff*
Jerry Musil, *Mng Member*
Don Planinshek, *Mng Member*
EMP: 10
SQ FT: 9,750
SALES: 6MM **Privately Held**
WEB: www.interiorsurface.com
SIC: 1752 1743 Carpet laying; vinyl floor tile & sheet installation; terrazzo, tile, marble, mosaic work

(G-7800)
INTERNTNAL SCLPTURE FOUNDATION
14246 W 124th Ter (66062-5989)
PHONE..................................785 864-2599
Minghsiang Kuo, *Exec Dir*
EMP: 10
SALES (est): 101.9K **Privately Held**
SIC: 8412 Museums & art galleries

(G-7801)
INTERSTATE CLEANING CORP
20700 W 151st St (66061-5352)
PHONE..................................314 428-0566
EMP: 187
SALES (corp-wide): 57MM **Privately Held**
SIC: 7699 Cleaning services
PA: Interstate Cleaning Corporation
1566 N Warson Rd
Saint Louis MO 63132
314 428-0566

(G-7802)
INTRUST BANK NATIONAL ASSN
Also Called: Olathe Branch
18225 W 106th St (66061-2898)
PHONE..................................913 385-8330
Connie Thomas, *Manager*
EMP: 16
SALES (corp-wide): 134.2MM **Privately Held**
SIC: 6022 State commercial banks
HQ: Intrust Bank National Association
105 N Main St
Wichita KS 67202
316 383-1111

(G-7803)
ITW DYMON
805 E Old 56 Hwy (66061)
PHONE..................................913 397-9889
Kristen Foth, *Manager*
Sarah Tharp, *Supervisor*
EMP: 19
SALES (est): 4.4MM **Privately Held**
SIC: 2842 Specialty cleaning, polishes & sanitation goods

(G-7804)
J & M CONTRACTING INC
1712 E 123rd St (66061-5882)
PHONE..................................913 397-0272
J Jones, *President*
Craig Jones, *President*
Rudy Manes, *Vice Pres*
EMP: 10
SQ FT: 4,000
SALES: 6.8MM **Privately Held**
WEB: www.jmcontracting.net
SIC: 1542 Commercial & office building, new construction

(G-7805)
JAAFAR INC
15968 S Clairborne St (66062-7025)
PHONE..................................913 269-5113
Nasir Jaafar, *President*
Jennifer Jaafar, *Vice Pres*
EMP: 10
SQ FT: 1,000
SALES: 350K **Privately Held**
SIC: 6111 7299 Export/Import Bank; tanning salon

(G-7806)
JAMES L RUHLEN MD PA
Also Called: Schermoly, Martin J
20805 W 151st St 224 (66061-7249)
PHONE..................................913 829-4001
James L Ruhlen MD, *Owner*
James Sebghati, *Internal Med*
EMP: 22 **EST:** 1970
SALES (est): 2.3MM **Privately Held**
SIC: 8011 Internal medicine, physician/surgeon; physicians' office, including specialists

(G-7807)
JARDEN BRANDED CONSUMABLE
17150 Mercury St (66061-6058)
PHONE..................................913 856-1177
EMP: 6
SALES (est): 711.8K **Privately Held**
SIC: 3221 Glass containers

(G-7808)
JAY HENGES ENTERPRISES INC
Also Called: Henges Insulation Company
15640 S Keeler St (66062-3516)
PHONE..................................913 764-4600
Greg Kudrna, *Branch Mgr*
EMP: 30
SALES (corp-wide): 62.4MM **Privately Held**
WEB: www.portaking.com
SIC: 1742 8748 5719 2434 Insulation, buildings; energy conservation consultant; fireplace equipment & accessories; wood kitchen cabinets; kitchens, complete (sinks, cabinets, etc.)
PA: Jay Henges Enterprises Inc.
4133 Shoreline Dr
Earth City MO 63045
314 291-6600

(G-7809)
JAYHAWK FIRE SPRINKLER CO INC
12030 S Hedge Lane Ter (66061-9705)
PHONE..................................913 422-3770
Zach Parrington, *Engineer*
Bradford Seaman, *Controller*
Daniel Ochs, *Sales Mgr*
Keith Alexander, *Sales Staff*
Dan Ochs, *Manager*
EMP: 20
SALES (corp-wide): 23.9MM **Privately Held**
WEB: www.jayhawkfire.com
SIC: 1711 5087 Fire sprinkler system installation; firefighting equipment
PA: Jayhawk Fire Sprinkler Co., Inc.
110 Ne Gordon St
Topeka KS 66608
785 232-0975

(G-7810)
JDAMC INC
10789 S Ridgeview Rd (66061-6448)
PHONE..................................913 310-8100
John Lageman, *Vice Pres*
John Mockaman, *Vice Pres*
Anne East, *Project Mgr*
EMP: 695 **EST:** 1998
SALES (est): 65.7MM
SALES (corp-wide): 39.2B **Publicly Held**
WEB: www.deere.com
SIC: 5083 Farm & garden machinery
PA: Deere & Company
1 John Deere Pl
Moline IL 61265
309 765-8000

(G-7811)
JOHN FALES DR
Also Called: Children's Dental Specialists
13496 S Arapaho Dr (66062-1553)
PHONE..................................913 782-2207
John Fales, *Owner*
EMP: 13
SALES (est): 474.6K **Privately Held**
SIC: 8021 Dentists' office

(G-7812)
JOHNSON & WHITE SALES COMPANY
1710 E 123rd Ter (66061-5874)
PHONE..................................913 390-9808
Rusty Johnson, *President*
Dan White, *Vice Pres*
Dustin Johnson, *Sales Staff*
John Langle, *Sales Staff*
Rick Rehorn, *Admin Sec*
EMP: 10
SQ FT: 4,108
SALES (est): 3.3MM **Privately Held**
SIC: 5074 Plumbing fittings & supplies

(G-7813)
JOHNSON CNTY DEPT HLTH & ENVMT
11875 S Sunset Dr Ste 300 (66061-2794)
PHONE..................................913 826-1200
Richard Brewington, *Director*
EMP: 99
SALES (est): 2.4MM **Privately Held**
SIC: 8099 Health & allied services

(G-7814)
JOHNSON COUNTY AGGREGATES
Also Called: Johnson County Aggregiates
23555 W 151st St (66061-9418)
PHONE..................................913 764-2127
Joe Horne, *Manager*
EMP: 27
SQ FT: 900
SALES (est): 3.8MM
SALES (corp-wide): 29.7B **Privately Held**
WEB: www.ashgrove.com
SIC: 1422 Crushed & broken limestone
HQ: Ash Grove Cement Company
11011 Cody St Ste 300
Overland Park KS 66210
913 451-8900

(G-7815)
JOHNSON COUNTY COMMUNICATIONS
Also Called: Johnson County Answering Svc
407 S Clairborne Rd # 208 (66062-1857)
PHONE..................................913 764-2876
Russell Mann, *President*
EMP: 30
SQ FT: 2,000
SALES (est): 1.7MM **Privately Held**
SIC: 7389 Telephone answering service

(G-7816)
JOHNSON COUNTY DERMATOLOGY
Also Called: Proffitt, John
153 W 151st St Ste 100 (66061-5300)
PHONE..................................913 764-1125
John L Proffitt, *President*
Glenn Van Stavern, *Office Mgr*
EMP: 13
SALES (est): 1.4MM **Privately Held**
SIC: 8011 Dermatologist

(G-7817)
JOHNSON COUNTY KANSAS HERITAGE
1200 E Kansas City Rd (66061-3002)
PHONE..................................913 481-3137
Sandra Kelly, *President*
EMP: 30
SALES (est): 107.4K **Privately Held**
SIC: 8699 Charitable organization

(G-7818)
JOHNSON COUNTY MED-ACT
11811 S Sunset Dr # 1100 (66061-2793)
PHONE..................................913 715-1950
Ted McFarlane, *Chief*
EMP: 15
SQ FT: 2,000
SALES: 79K **Privately Held**
SIC: 8099 Blood related health services

(G-7819)
JOHNSON COUNTY UNIFIED WSTWTR (PA)
11811 S Sunset Dr # 2500 (66061-2793)
PHONE..................................913 715-8500
Nathan Strawder, *Engineer*
John O'Neal, *Administration*
Kim Wasko, *Executive Asst*
Troy Young, *Technician*
EMP: 60 **EST:** 1947
SQ FT: 20,000

GEOGRAPHIC

SALES (est): 66.9MM **Privately Held**
WEB: www.jcw.org
SIC: 4952 Sewerage systems

(G-7820)
JURYSYNC LLC
25255 W 102nd Ter Ste A (66061-8417)
PHONE..................................913 338-4301
Jeanine Tettenborn, *Principal*
Paulette Robinette, *Mng Member*
Scott Robinette, *Mng Member*
EMP: 13
SQ FT: 2,760
SALES: 1.2MM **Privately Held**
WEB: www.jurysync.com
SIC: 8748 Communications consulting

(G-7821)
K & W UNDERGROUND INCORPORATED
15608 S Keeler Ter (66062-3510)
PHONE..................................913 782-7387
Rex Schick President, *CEO*
Greg Pate, *Supervisor*
Patty Schick, *Admin Sec*
EMP: 60
SQ FT: 9,000
SALES (est): 16.3MM **Privately Held**
SIC: 1623 Cable television line construction

(G-7822)
K B MACHINE SHOP INC
15325 S Keeler St (66062-2712)
P.O. Box 250 (66051-0250)
PHONE..................................913 829-3100
Donald Kauffman, *President*
Dennis Kauffman, *Vice Pres*
EMP: 10
SQ FT: 5,000
SALES: 1MM **Privately Held**
SIC: 3599 1799 Machine shop, jobbing & repair; welding on site

(G-7823)
KANSAS CITY AVIATION CTR INC
15325 S Pflumm Rd (66062-8505)
P.O. Box 1850 (66063-1850)
PHONE..................................913 782-0530
David S Armacost, *President*
Angelo Fiataruolo, *General Mgr*
O Nelson Auer, *Corp Secy*
Don Armacost Jr, *Vice Pres*
Bill Lento, *QC Mgr*
EMP: 75
SQ FT: 60,000
SALES (est): 6.6MM
SALES (corp-wide): 585.4MM **Privately Held**
WEB: www.kcac.com
SIC: 8299 4522 4581 5599 Flying instruction; flying charter service; aircraft maintenance & repair services; aircraft dealers
PA: Peterson Manufacturing Company
4200 E 135th St
Grandview MO 64030
816 765-2000

(G-7824)
KANSAS CITY BLUES SOCIETY INC
13624 S Sycamore St (66062-5357)
P.O. Box 32396, Kansas City MO (64171-5396)
PHONE..................................913 660-4692
Bruce Hibbs, *President*
Paul Grahovac,
EMP: 11
SALES (est): 35.8K **Privately Held**
SIC: 7999 7922 8621 Festival operation; concert management service; professional membership organizations

(G-7825)
KANSAS CITY MILLWORK COMPANY
1120 W 149th St (66061-5354)
PHONE..................................913 768-0068
EMP: 40
SALES (est): 3.5MM
SALES (corp-wide): 147.7MM **Privately Held**
WEB: www.moehlmillwork.com
SIC: 5211 5031 Lumber & other building materials; lumber, plywood & millwork
PA: Building Material Distributors, Inc.
225 Elm Ave
Galt CA 95632
209 745-3001

(G-7826)
KANSAS CITY MILLWORK COMPANY
1120 W 149th St (66061-5354)
PHONE..................................913 768-0068
EMP: 40
SALES (est): 1MM
SALES (corp-wide): 147.7MM **Privately Held**
SIC: 5211 5031 Lumber & other building materials; lumber, plywood & millwork
PA: Building Material Distributors, Inc.
225 Elm Ave
Galt CA 95632
209 745-3001

(G-7827)
KANSAS CITY SC LLC
Also Called: Kcsc
15009 W 150th Ter (66062-4607)
PHONE..................................913 575-1278
John Duker,
EMP: 10
SALES: 50K **Privately Held**
SIC: 7997 Soccer club, except professional & semi-professional

(G-7828)
KANSAS CY FREIGHTLINER SLS INC
15580 S Highway 169 (66062-3508)
PHONE..................................913 780-6606
Wally Bauer, *Manager*
EMP: 20
SALES (corp-wide): 63.9MM **Privately Held**
WEB: www.kcfreightliner.com
SIC: 7538 5511 5012 General automotive repair shops; trucks, tractors & trailers: new & used; automobiles & other motor vehicles
PA: Kansas City Freightliner Sales, Inc.
7800 Ne 38th St
Kansas City MO 64161
816 453-4400

(G-7829)
KANSAS GYMNASTICS & DANCE CTR
Also Called: Kansas Gymnastics Dance Cheer
1702 E 123rd Ter (66061-5874)
PHONE..................................913 764-8282
James Sampel, *President*
Billie Pinkham, *Treasurer*
Kristen Butcher, *Bd of Directors*
EMP: 30
SALES (est): 1.6MM **Privately Held**
WEB: www.kansasgymandcheer.com
SIC: 7999 Gymnastic instruction, non-membership

(G-7830)
KANSYS INC (PA)
910 W Frontier Ln (66061-7201)
PHONE..................................913 780-5291
Joseph Simmons, *President*
Arthur Koenig, *Vice Pres*
Ashley Ogren, *Accounts Mgr*
John Dillon, *Consultant*
EMP: 35
SQ FT: 10,000
SALES (est): 7MM **Privately Held**
WEB: www.kansys.com
SIC: 7371 8748 Computer software development; telecommunications consultant

(G-7831)
KAW VALLEY RABBIT CLUB
32320 W 363 (66061)
PHONE..................................913 764-1531
Shaun Penston, *President*
Bruce Chase, *President*
Star Chase, *President*
Janice Lindsay, *Vice Pres*
EMP: 10
SALES (est): 141.2K **Privately Held**
SIC: 8699 Personal interest organization

(G-7832)
KC RESTORATION LLC
1465 N Winchester St (66061-5881)
P.O. Box 23147, Overland Park (66283-0147)
PHONE..................................913 766-2200
Bill Luemmen, *Principal*
Steve Lehne, *Vice Pres*
Greg Bringaze, *Opers Mgr*
EMP: 13 **EST:** 2012
SALES (est): 398K **Privately Held**
SIC: 1743 3471 Terrazzo work; cleaning, polishing & finishing

(G-7833)
KC TOOL LLC
1280 N Winchester St (66061-5878)
PHONE..................................913 440-9766
Kyle John Baccus,
EMP: 10
SALES (est): 1.1MM **Privately Held**
SIC: 5072 5049 5085 Hand tools; precision tools; electric tools; industrial tools

(G-7834)
KC WINE CO
13875 S Gardner Rd (66061-9600)
PHONE..................................913 908-3039
Kirk Berggren, *Principal*
EMP: 7
SALES (est): 231.5K **Privately Held**
SIC: 2084 Wines

(G-7835)
KEY IMPACT SALES & SYSTEMS INC
831 N Martway Dr (66061-7053)
PHONE..................................913 648-6611
Roger Eilts, *Branch Mgr*
EMP: 44
SALES (corp-wide): 56.6MM **Privately Held**
SIC: 5141 Food brokers
PA: Key Impact Sales & Systems, Inc.
1701 Crossroads Dr
Odenton MD 21113
410 381-1239

(G-7836)
KIDDI KOLLEGE INC (PA)
340 N Lindenwood Dr (66062-1261)
PHONE..................................913 764-4423
Jonathan Kopek, *President*
Geraldine Dolinar, *President*
Patricia Kopek, *Exec Dir*
EMP: 25
SALES (est): 2.5MM **Privately Held**
SIC: 8351 Group day care center

(G-7837)
KIDDI KOLLEGE INC
1000 E Harold St (66061-2724)
PHONE..................................913 780-0246
Jody Ally, *Branch Mgr*
EMP: 15
SALES (corp-wide): 2.5MM **Privately Held**
SIC: 8351 Group day care center
PA: Kiddi Kollege Inc
340 N Lindenwood Dr
Olathe KS 66062
913 764-4423

(G-7838)
KIDS R KIDS
Also Called: Kids R Kids 1 Kansas
1585 S Mahaffie Cir (66062-3433)
PHONE..................................913 390-0234
Beth Robinson, *Owner*
Russ Robinson, *Principal*
EMP: 40
SALES (est): 1.5MM **Privately Held**
SIC: 8351 Preschool center

(G-7839)
KIDSTLC INC
480 S Rogers Rd (66062-1706)
PHONE..................................913 764-2887
Charles Warren, *Ch of Bd*
Robert K Drummond, *President*
Mark Siegman, *COO*
Rob Boyer, *Treasurer*
Erin Dugan, *Admin Sec*
EMP: 246
SALES: 16.8MM **Privately Held**
WEB: www.kidstlc.org
SIC: 8361 Children's home

(G-7840)
KINGS COURT INVESTORS
Also Called: King's Court Association
2300 E Willow Dr (66062-1601)
PHONE..................................913 764-7500
Fred N Colson III, *Partner*
Alson R Martin, *Partner*
Kevin Nunnick, *Partner*
EMP: 10
SALES (est): 379.4K **Privately Held**
SIC: 8641 Dwelling-related associations

(G-7841)
KINNEY PLUMBING CO INC
Also Called: Kinney's Plumbing Co
15755 S Keeler Ter (66062-3519)
PHONE..................................913 782-2840
Richard Moore, *President*
Mary Moore, *Treasurer*
EMP: 50
SQ FT: 1,800
SALES (est): 6.3MM **Privately Held**
SIC: 1711 Plumbing contractors

(G-7842)
KNK TELECOM LLC
1010 W Santa Fe St (66061-3116)
PHONE..................................913 768-8000
Karl Bettencourt,
EMP: 28
SQ FT: 5,000
SALES (est): 3.5MM **Privately Held**
WEB: www.knktelecom.com
SIC: 8748 Telecommunications consultant

(G-7843)
KONRADYS LAWN & LDSCPG INC
15705 S Pflumm Rd (66062-9724)
PHONE..................................913 722-1163
Duane J Konrady, *President*
EMP: 25
SALES (est): 1.7MM **Privately Held**
WEB: www.konradyslawnandsnow.com
SIC: 0781 1741 Landscape architects; retaining wall construction

(G-7844)
KVC BEHAVIORAL HEALTHCARE INC (HQ)
Also Called: KAW VALLEY CENTER
21350 W 153rd St (66061-5413)
PHONE..................................913 322-4900
Chad Anderson, *President*
Alex Mendez, *Superintendent*
Jodie Austin, *Vice Pres*
Danielle Bartelli, *Vice Pres*
Michelle Lawrence, *Vice Pres*
EMP: 60
SQ FT: 50,000
SALES: 85.6MM **Privately Held**
SIC: 8361 Residential care for children

(G-7845)
KVC HEALTH SYSTEMS INC (PA)
21350 W 153rd St (66061-5413)
PHONE..................................913 322-4900
Jason Hooper, *CEO*
Erin Stuckey, *COO*
Renny Arensberg, *Exec VP*
Marilyn Jacobson, *CFO*
Afsoun Moradi, *Manager*
EMP: 60
SALES (est): 123.8MM **Privately Held**
SIC: 8361 Residential care for children

(G-7846)
KVC HOSPITALS INC (HQ)
21350 W 153rd St (66061-5413)
PHONE..................................913 322-4900
Diana J Kurtz, *CFO*
Paul Klayder, *CFO*
Shannan Drake, *Accounting Mgr*
Kelly Young, *Director*
Kimberly Knapp, *Admin Asst*
EMP: 21

SALES: 24.3MM **Privately Held**
SIC: 8093 Mental health clinic, outpatient

(G-7847)
L & W SUPPLY CORPORATION
Also Called: Arrowhead Drywall Supply
15660 S Keeler Ter (66062-3510)
PHONE..................................913 782-1777
John Twarek, *Branch Mgr*
EMP: 20
SALES (corp-wide): 3.5B **Privately Held**
WEB: www.lwsupply.com
SIC: 5032 Drywall materials
HQ: L & W Supply Corporation
300 S Riverside Plz # 200
Chicago IL 60606
312 606-4000

(G-7848)
LA PETITE ACADEMY INC
1810 S Scarborough St (66062-5504)
PHONE..................................913 764-2345
Melinda Henderson, *Director*
EMP: 10
SALES (corp-wide): 164MM **Privately Held**
WEB: www.lapetite.com
SIC: 8351 Preschool center
HQ: La Petite Academy, Inc.
21333 Haggerty Rd Ste 300
Novi MI 48375
877 861-5078

(G-7849)
LA PETITE ACADEMY INC
1825 N Ridgeview Rd (66061-7101)
PHONE..................................913 780-2318
Brandy Peterson, *Branch Mgr*
Brandi Addadi, *Director*
EMP: 17
SALES (corp-wide): 164MM **Privately Held**
WEB: www.lapetite.com
SIC: 8351 Preschool center
HQ: La Petite Academy, Inc.
21333 Haggerty Rd Ste 300
Novi MI 48375
877 861-5078

(G-7850)
LABOR SOURCE LLC (PA)
Also Called: One Source Staffing
235 S Kansas Ave (66061-4436)
PHONE..................................913 764-5333
Alfred Munoz, *General Mgr*
Derrick Triscornia, *Project Mgr*
Brenda Lyden, *Sales Mgr*
Kelly Mages, *Sales Staff*
Noe Marquez, *Asst Mgr*
EMP: 16
SQ FT: 25,000
SALES (est): 1.9MM **Privately Held**
SIC: 7361 Employment agencies

(G-7851)
LAD GLOBAL ENTERPRISES INC
25000 College Blvd (66061-7348)
PHONE..................................913 768-0888
Chris J Davis, *President*
◆ **EMP:** 10
SALES: 2.1MM **Privately Held**
SIC: 5013 5015 5131 5047 Automotive servicing equipment; hardware, used: automotive; fiberglass fabrics; medical & hospital equipment; grills, barbecue

(G-7852)
LAFARGE NORTH AMERICA INC
1245 W 149th St (66061-6813)
PHONE..................................913 780-6809
Dennis Martens, *Principal*
EMP: 500
SALES (corp-wide): 4.5B **Privately Held**
SIC: 3531 4111 4121 Concrete plants; airport transportation; taxicabs
HQ: Lafarge North America Inc.
8700 W Bryn Mawr Ave
Chicago IL 60631
773 372-1000

(G-7853)
LAKEMARY CENTER INC
15145 S Keeler St Ste A (66062-2758)
PHONE..................................913 768-6831
Tammy Carpenter, *Director*
EMP: 20
SALES (corp-wide): 26.7MM **Privately Held**
WEB: www.lakemaryctr.org
SIC: 8211 8361 8322 8741 School for the retarded; home for the mentally retarded; adult day care center; management services
PA: Lakemary Center, Inc.
100 Lakemary Dr
Paola KS
913 557-4000

(G-7854)
LANDMASTERS LANDSCAPE
718 W Wabash St (66061-4235)
P.O. Box 860293, Shawnee (66286-0293)
PHONE..................................913 667-3382
Jesus Rico, *President*
Renee Rico, *Corp Secy*
EMP: 13
SALES (est): 896.3K **Privately Held**
SIC: 0781 Landscape services

(G-7855)
LARRY D SHELDON DDS
125 E Park St (66061-3428)
PHONE..................................913 782-7580
Larry D Sheldon DDS, *Owner*
Danielle Sheldon DDS, *Owner*
EMP: 12
SALES (est): 743.9K **Privately Held**
SIC: 8021 Dentists' office

(G-7856)
LASER SPECIALISTS INC (PA)
19879 W 156th St (66062-3521)
PHONE..................................913 780-9990
Larry Phipps, *President*
Brian Phipps, *Vice Pres*
Richard Johnson, *Technology*
Shirley Phipps, *Shareholder*
EMP: 21
SQ FT: 5,000
SALES (est): 5.1MM **Privately Held**
SIC: 5082 7699 7359 Construction & mining machinery; construction equipment repair; equipment rental & leasing

(G-7857)
LAZER SPOT INC
815 S Clairborne Rd 275c (66062-1790)
PHONE..................................913 839-2654
EMP: 73
SALES (corp-wide): 386.5MM **Privately Held**
SIC: 0762 Farm management services
PA: Lazer Spot, Inc.
6525 Shiloh Rd Ste 900
Alpharetta GA 30005
770 886-6851

(G-7858)
LEO J DEBRABANDER FOUNDATION
21035 College Blvd (66061-8756)
PHONE..................................913 780-1600
Leo J Debrabander, *Owner*
EMP: 16
SALES (est): 1MM **Privately Held**
SIC: 1771 Foundation & footing contractor

(G-7859)
LESLIE COMPANY INC
15290 S Keeler St (66062-2715)
P.O. Box 610 (66051-0610)
PHONE..................................913 764-6660
Jerald Byrd, *President*
Dana Pieschl, *Sales Staff*
Karin Windsor, *Sales Staff*
Jerry Byrd, *Executive*
EMP: 80
SQ FT: 34,000
SALES (est): 13.8MM **Privately Held**
WEB: www.leslieco.com
SIC: 2782 2675 Looseleaf binders & devices; index cards, die-cut: made from purchased materials

(G-7860)
LEWIS LEGAL NEWS INC
1701 E Cedar St Ste 111 (66062-1775)
PHONE..................................913 780-5790
Kate Umphray, *Principal*
EMP: 6 **EST:** 2009
SALES (est): 319.9K **Privately Held**
SIC: 2711 Job printing & newspaper publishing combined; newspapers, publishing & printing

(G-7861)
LITTLE LEARNERS EARLY CHILDHO
26121 W Valley Pkwy (66061-7482)
PHONE..................................913 254-1818
Christine Eaton, *Exec Dir*
Kim Maples, *Exec Dir*
EMP: 15
SALES (est): 622.9K **Privately Held**
SIC: 8351 8211 Preschool center; kindergarten

(G-7862)
LITTLE WNDERS CHRISTN DAY CARE
Also Called: What A Wonder Christian Daycre
651 N Somerset Ter Ste C (66062-1399)
PHONE..................................913 393-3035
Laurie Rundberg, *President*
Beverly Smith, *Vice Pres*
EMP: 32
SALES: 240K **Privately Held**
SIC: 8351 Preschool center

(G-7863)
LOCAL GVERNMENT ONLINE IND LLC
Also Called: Logo Indiana
25501 W Valley Pkwy # 300 (66061-8453)
P.O. Box 7109, Indianapolis IN (46207-7109)
PHONE..................................913 498-3468
EMP: 20
SALES (est): 959.9K
SALES (corp-wide): 344.9MM **Publicly Held**
SIC: 7379
HQ: Nicusa, Inc.
25501 W Valley Pkwy # 300
Olathe KS 66061

(G-7864)
LOCKE EQUIPMENT SALES CO
15705 S Us 169 Hwy (66062-3591)
P.O. Box 243, Shawnee Mission (66201-0243)
PHONE..................................913 782-8500
Timothy R Locke, *President*
Glaisle Allen, *Accounting Mgr*
EMP: 27
SQ FT: 2,500
SALES (est): 7.2MM **Privately Held**
WEB: www.lockeequipment.com
SIC: 5084 5074 8711 1711 Power plant machinery; chemical process equipment; boilers, power (industrial); mechanical engineering; boiler maintenance contractor; mechanical contractor; process piping contractor

(G-7865)
LOGAN CONTRACTORS SUPPLY INC
1325 S Enterprise St (66061-5358)
PHONE..................................913 768-1551
Jerry Logan, *Owner*
Scott Dybad, *Director*
EMP: 25
SALES (corp-wide): 96.9MM **Privately Held**
WEB: www.logancontractors.com
SIC: 5082 General construction machinery & equipment
PA: Logan Contractors Supply, Inc.
4101 106th St
Urbandale IA 50322
515 253-9048

(G-7866)
LOWES HOME CENTERS LLC
13750 S Blackbob Rd (66062-1932)
PHONE..................................913 397-7070
Amby Schweizer, *Branch Mgr*
EMP: 150
SALES (corp-wide): 71.3B **Publicly Held**
SIC: 5211 5031 5722 5064 Home centers; building materials, exterior; building materials, interior; household appliance stores; electrical appliances, television & radio
HQ: Lowe's Home Centers, Llc
1605 Curtis Bridge Rd
Wilkesboro NC 28697
336 658-4000

(G-7867)
LUMINOUS NEON INC
Also Called: Sign Systems
1255 N Winchester St (66061-5879)
PHONE..................................913 780-3330
Don Williams, *Manager*
EMP: 20
SALES (corp-wide): 11.6MM **Privately Held**
SIC: 3993 1761 1799 Signs & advertising specialties; roofing contractor; sign installation & maintenance
PA: Luminous Neon, Inc.
1429 W 4th Ave
Hutchinson KS 67501
620 662-2363

(G-7868)
LYNNS HEAVY HAULING LLC
22780 College Blvd (66061-8766)
PHONE..................................913 393-3863
Teresa Lynn, *Mng Member*
EMP: 12 **EST:** 1995
SALES (est): 562.8K **Privately Held**
SIC: 4213 3531 Heavy hauling; construction machinery

(G-7869)
M-C FABRICATION INC
15612 S Keeler Ter (66062-3510)
PHONE..................................913 764-5454
Don L Mitchell, *President*
Janice Mitchell, *Corp Secy*
Mitchell Jon-Michael, *Vice Pres*
Brad Mitchell, *Vice Pres*
Doug Hunt, *Purch Agent*
EMP: 79
SQ FT: 80,000
SALES (est): 26.5MM **Privately Held**
WEB: www.m-cfabrication.com
SIC: 3441 3599 Fabricated structural metal; machine shop, jobbing & repair

(G-7870)
MACCALLUM CHAR RE GROUP
1819 S Ridgeview Rd (66062-2288)
PHONE..................................913 782-8857
Char Maccallum, *Owner*
Stephanie Maccallum, *Buyer*
Julia Adams, *Manager*
EMP: 10
SALES (est): 502.2K **Privately Held**
WEB: www.char4homes.com
SIC: 6531 Real estate brokers & agents

(G-7871)
MACK MCCLAIN & ASSOCIATES INC (PA)
15090 W 116th St (66062-1000)
PHONE..................................913 339-6677
Mike Mc Clain, *President*
Tamara Finley, *Sales Mgr*
Forrest Cook, *Sales Staff*
Mary Mc Clain, *Admin Sec*
EMP: 17 **EST:** 1964
SQ FT: 16,000
SALES (est): 7.7MM **Privately Held**
WEB: www.mackmcclain.com
SIC: 5074 5084 Plumbing fittings & supplies; heating equipment (hydronic); industrial machinery & equipment

(G-7872)
MANN FENCE COMPANY INC
15415 S Us 169 Hwy (66062-3401)
PHONE..................................913 782-2332
Scott R Mann, *President*
EMP: 14 **EST:** 1954
SQ FT: 8,000
SALES (est): 1.4MM **Privately Held**
SIC: 1799 Fence construction

(G-7873)
MANNING CONSTRUCTION CO INC
1708 E 123rd St (66061-5882)
PHONE..................................913 390-1007
Thomas Manning, *President*
EMP: 35
SQ FT: 4,200

GEOGRAPHIC

SALES (est): 6.7MM Privately Held
SIC: 1542 1541 8742 8741 Commercial & office building, new construction; industrial buildings & warehouses; construction project management consultant; construction management

(G-7874)
MARK DEBRABANDER FOUNDATION CO
31715 W 115th St (66061-8605)
PHONE....913 856-4044
Mark Debrabander, *Owner*
EMP: 10
SALES (est): 554.7K Privately Held
SIC: 1771 Foundation & footing contractor

(G-7875)
MARTIN MARIETTA MATERIALS INC
14670 S Harrison St (66061-7224)
PHONE....913 390-8396
Doug Gale, *Manager*
EMP: 9 Publicly Held
SIC: 1422 Crushed & broken limestone
PA: Martin Marietta Materials Inc
2710 Wycliff Rd
Raleigh NC 27607

(G-7876)
MARVINS TOW SERVICE INC (PA)
15607 S Keeler St (66062-3515)
P.O. Box 184, Gardner (66030-0184)
PHONE....913 764-7630
Marvin Vail, *President*
EMP: 11 EST: 2009
SQ FT: 3,000
SALES (est): 1.6MM Privately Held
SIC: 7549 Towing service, automotive

(G-7877)
MASTERPIECE ENGINEERING LLC
17400 W 119th St (66061-7740)
PHONE....928 771-2040
Morley Williams, *President*
Carolyn Williams, *Vice Pres*
EMP: 28
SQ FT: 13,000
SALES (est): 2.4MM Privately Held
WEB: www.mecosaws.com
SIC: 3546 Saws, portable & handheld: power driven

(G-7878)
MBS INC
601 N Mur Len Rd Ste 16 (66062-5417)
PHONE....913 393-2525
Michael Postlewait, *President*
Steve Postlewait, *Vice Pres*
Sharon Postlewait, *Admin Sec*
▼ EMP: 11 EST: 1979
SQ FT: 3,600
SALES: 1MM Privately Held
WEB: www.strengths.com
SIC: 8742 Business consultant

(G-7879)
MC JANITORIAL LLC
118 N Emma St (66061-3732)
PHONE....913 780-0731
Michael Cox, *Mng Member*
Martha Cox, *Mng Member*
EMP: 11 EST: 1992
SALES: 1.2MM Privately Held
SIC: 7349 1799 Janitorial service, contract basis; construction site cleanup

(G-7880)
MCAFEE ENTERPRISES LLC
Also Called: Magic Distributors/Rms
902 N Canyon Dr (66061-9270)
P.O. Box 24084, Shawnee Mission (66283-4084)
PHONE....913 839-3328
Shanita McAfee, *Partner*
Mark McAfee, *Partner*
EMP: 10
SALES (est): 635.6K Privately Held
SIC: 5087 Service establishment equipment

(G-7881)
MCCARTHY COLLISION CENTER
Also Called: McCarthy Auto Grp
1610 E Prairie St (66061-3648)
PHONE....913 324-7300
Jim Finn, *General Mgr*
Dane Griffin, *Director*
EMP: 37
SALES: 1,000K Privately Held
SIC: 7549 Automotive services

(G-7882)
MCCRAY LUMBER COMPANY
Also Called: McCray Lumber & Millwork
15295 S Highway 169 (66062-3405)
PHONE....913 780-0060
Keith Bricker, *Sales Dir*
Tony Burks, *Sales Staff*
Shawn Copeland, *Sales Staff*
Steve Haynes, *Manager*
EMP: 35
SALES (corp-wide): 71.1MM Privately Held
WEB: www.mccraylumber.com
SIC: 5211 5031 2426 2421 Planing mill products & lumber; siding; lumber: rough, dressed & finished; hardwood dimension & flooring mills; sawmills & planing mills, general
PA: Mccray Lumber Company
10741 El Monte St
Shawnee Mission KS 66211
913 341-6900

(G-7883)
MERIT GENERAL CONTRACTORS
16400 W 118th Ter (66061-6644)
PHONE....913 747-7400
Donald Crabtree, *CEO*
Stan Bachman, *President*
Randy Smith, *Sr Project Mgr*
Kyle Kemp, *Officer*
EMP: 14
SALES (est): 5.9MM Privately Held
WEB: www.meritkc.com
SIC: 1542 1541 1799 Commercial & office building, new construction; industrial buildings & warehouses; swimming pool construction

(G-7884)
METAL CUT TO LENGTH
700 S Rogers Rd Ste B (66062-1713)
PHONE....913 829-8600
Bill Enochs, *Owner*
EMP: 13
SALES (est): 1MM Privately Held
SIC: 7389 Metal cutting services

(G-7885)
METCALF BANK
13446 S Blackbob Rd (66062-1503)
P.O. Box 4249, Shawnee Mission (66204-0249)
PHONE....913 782-6522
Adrian Shands, *Manager*
EMP: 15
SALES (corp-wide): 62.6MM Privately Held
SIC: 6022 6163 State commercial banks; loan brokers
HQ: Metcalf Bank
7840 Metcalf Ave
Shawnee Mission KS 66204
913 648-4540

(G-7886)
METRO COLLISION REPAIR INC
2202 N Rogers Rd (66062-4934)
PHONE....913 839-1044
Mike Gerrity, *President*
Judy Gerrity, *Vice Pres*
EMP: 17
SQ FT: 21,000
SALES (est): 2MM Privately Held
WEB: www.metrocollisionrepair.com
SIC: 7532 7538 Body shop, automotive; general automotive repair shops

(G-7887)
MEYER TRUCK CENTER INC
19930 W 159th St (66062-8987)
PHONE....913 764-2000
Randy Meyer, *President*
Mary Meyer, *Vice Pres*
EMP: 13
SQ FT: 7,418
SALES (est): 11MM Privately Held
WEB: www.meyertruckcenter.com
SIC: 5012 7538 Trucks, commercial; truck engine repair, except industrial

(G-7888)
MGM MARKETING INC
12732 S Pflumm Rd (66062-3664)
PHONE....913 451-0023
Robb Murphy, *President*
Chuck Ritter, *Accounting Mgr*
Jason Murphy, *Marketing Staff*
Kim Hightower, *Manager*
Mike Bear, *Business Dir*
EMP: 15
SALES (est): 3.8MM Privately Held
SIC: 8742 Marketing consulting services

(G-7889)
MIAMI COUNTY MEDICAL CENTER
Also Called: Pharmacy Express
20375 W 151st St Ste 351 (66061-7242)
PHONE....913 791-4940
Frank H Devocelle, *CEO*
EMP: 11
SALES: 20.8MM Privately Held
SIC: 8099 Blood related health services

(G-7890)
MIAS BRIDAL & TAILORING LLC
2235 E Kansas City Rd (66061-3083)
PHONE....913 764-9114
Tonya Ricard, *Manager*
Mia Dohrman,
EMP: 12
SQ FT: 1,000
SALES: 1MM Privately Held
WEB: www.miasbridal.com
SIC: 5621 5611 7219 Bridal shops; suits, men's; garment making, alteration & repair

(G-7891)
MICHAEL S KLEIN DDS
975 N Mur Len Rd Ste C (66062-1803)
PHONE....913 829-4466
Michael S Klein DDS, *Owner*
EMP: 15
SALES (est): 514.8K Privately Held
SIC: 8021 Orthodontist

(G-7892)
MID-STATE AEROSPACE INC (PA)
710 N Lindenwood Dr (66062-1877)
PHONE....913 764-3600
Cleo Brager, *CEO*
Robert Rogers, *President*
EMP: 15
SQ FT: 6,500
SALES (est): 8MM Privately Held
SIC: 5088 Aircraft & parts

(G-7893)
MIDCONTINENTAL CHEMICAL CO INC
Also Called: McC
1802 E 123rd Ter (66061-5876)
PHONE....913 390-5556
Jim Elder, *President*
Rankin Hobbs, *Treasurer*
Kimberly Augustine, *Controller*
Mike Hiatt, *Sales Staff*
Bill Hanson, *Admin Sec*
▲ EMP: 40
SQ FT: 15,000
SALES (est): 30.4MM Privately Held
WEB: www.mcchemical.com
SIC: 5169 2911 8742 Chemical additives; fuel additives; management consulting services

(G-7894)
MIDWEST CRANE AND RIGGING LLC
15520 S Mahaffie St (66062-4040)
PHONE....913 747-5100
Larry Gilliam, *Branch Mgr*
Bill Miller, *Mng Member*
EMP: 25 EST: 2008
SALES (est): 2.6MM Privately Held
SIC: 7353 Cranes & aerial lift equipment, rental or leasing

(G-7895)
MIDWEST EAR NOSE THROAT PA
Also Called: Gaughan Rebecca N M.D.
20375 W 151st St Ste 106 (66061-5353)
PHONE....913 764-2737
Brian A Metz MD, *Partner*
Bruce E Zimmerman MD, *Partner*
Bruce Zimmerman MD, *Principal*
Brian Metz MD, *Principal*
EMP: 13
SALES (est): 2MM Privately Held
WEB: www.mwent.com
SIC: 8011 Eyes, ears, nose & throat specialist: physician/surgeon; ears, nose & throat specialist: physician/surgeon

(G-7896)
MIDWEST HEALTH SERVICES INC
751 N Somerset Ter (66062-5450)
PHONE....913 829-4663
EMP: 269
SALES (corp-wide): 32.7MM Privately Held
SIC: 8051 Skilled nursing care facilities
PA: Midwest Health, Inc
3024 Sw Wanamaker Rd # 300
Topeka KS 66614
785 272-1535

(G-7897)
MIDWEST REPRODUCTIVE CENTER PA
20375 W 151st St Ste 403 (66061-7209)
PHONE....913 780-4300
Dan Lee Gehlbach, *Principal*
EMP: 17
SALES (est): 2.2MM Privately Held
WEB: www.midwestreproductive.com
SIC: 8011 Fertility specialist, physician

(G-7898)
MIDWEST TITLE CO INC
124 E Park St (66061-3429)
PHONE....913 393-2511
Brent J Curry, *President*
Brent Curry, *President*
Leah Curry, *Vice Pres*
EMP: 15
SALES (est): 1.5MM Privately Held
SIC: 6541 Title & trust companies

(G-7899)
MIKES HEATING & COOLING LLC
1711 E 123rd Ter (66061-5875)
P.O. Box 2002 (66051-2002)
PHONE....913 441-7807
Mike Bryant,
EMP: 30
SALES (est): 3MM Privately Held
SIC: 1711 Warm air heating & air conditioning contractor

(G-7900)
MILL VALLEY CONSTRUCTION INC
16510 W 119th St (66061-5892)
P.O. Box 14186, Shawnee Mission (66285-4186)
PHONE....913 764-6539
Randall L Fruits, *President*
Leland Wilkerson, *Corp Secy*
George Hornung, *Director*
EMP: 15 EST: 1981
SQ FT: 1,800
SALES (est): 2MM Privately Held
SIC: 1521 1522 General remodeling, single-family houses; remodeling, multi-family dwellings

(G-7901)
MILTON B GRIN MD PA
Also Called: Grin Eye Care
21020 W 151st St (66061-7200)
PHONE....913 829-5511
Milton B Grin MD, *Owner*
Milton Grin, *Owner*
EMP: 50

▲ = Import ▼=Export
◆ =Import/Export

SALES: 4MM Privately Held
WEB: www.grineyecare.com
SIC: 8011 8042 Ophthalmologist; offices & clinics of optometrists

(G-7902)
MINICK GAMBRELL CONTRS LLC
Also Called: Mgc
405 S Clairborne Rd Ste 6 (66062-1774)
PHONE.................................913 538-5391
Peyton Gambrell, *Manager*
EMP: 16 EST: 2013
SQ FT: 2,500
SALES (est): 2.7MM Privately Held
SIC: 1542 Commercial & office building contractors

(G-7903)
MINUTEMAN PRESS
924 E Park St (66061-3773)
PHONE.................................913 829-0300
Clayton Lamberd, *Owner*
EMP: 6
SALES (est): 487.1K Privately Held
SIC: 2752 Commercial printing, lithographic

(G-7904)
MISS MRIAS ACRBAT DANCE STUDIO
10370 S Ridgeview Rd (66061-6436)
PHONE.................................913 888-0060
Maria Imm, *Owner*
EMP: 20
SALES (est): 394.3K Privately Held
SIC: 7911 Dance instructor & school services

(G-7905)
MISSION BOWL N OLATHE
1020 S Weaver St (66061-4348)
PHONE.................................913 782-0279
Beverly O Donnell, *President*
EMP: 24
SALES (est): 607.4K Privately Held
SIC: 7933 Bowling centers

(G-7906)
MISSION RECREATION INC
Also Called: Mission Bowl
1020 S Weaver St (66061-4348)
PHONE.................................913 782-0279
Beverly A O'Donnell, *President*
Beverly O'Donnell, *President*
Beverly Odonnell, *President*
Micheal J O'Donnell, *Vice Pres*
Micheal J Odonnell, *Vice Pres*
EMP: 28 EST: 1957
SQ FT: 22,000
SALES (est): 1.1MM Privately Held
WEB: www.missionbowl.com
SIC: 7933 5812 Ten pin center; eating places

(G-7907)
MOKAN HOSPITALITY LLC
10360 S Ridgeview Rd (66061-6436)
PHONE.................................913 541-9999
Grace Hara, *Principal*
Tom Koenigsfeld, *Mng Member*
EMP: 20
SALES (est): 173.2K Privately Held
SIC: 7011 Hotels

(G-7908)
MW LAWN & LANDSCAPE
19003 W 157th Ter (66062-4041)
PHONE.................................913 829-4949
Matt Winter, *Owner*
Steve Patrick, *Manager*
EMP: 50
SALES (est): 4.2MM Privately Held
SIC: 0782 Lawn care services

(G-7909)
MY CHILD ADVOCATE PA
201 E Loula St Ste 109 (66061-3459)
PHONE.................................913 829-8838
Trina A Nudson, *President*
Amanda King, *Admin Asst*
EMP: 16
SALES (est): 672.6K Privately Held
SIC: 8351 Child day care services

(G-7910)
MY CONTRACTING LLC
2013 E Prairie Cir Ste A (66062-1339)
PHONE.................................913 747-9015
Kevin York, *Mng Member*
EMP: 10
SALES (est): 208.4K Privately Held
SIC: 1521 General remodeling, single-family houses

(G-7911)
NATHAN WEINER & ASSOCIATES (PA)
Also Called: Sterling
1450 S Lone Elm Rd (66061-7256)
PHONE.................................913 390-0508
Lawrence Weiner, *President*
Stanford Weiner, *Vice Pres*
▲ EMP: 10
SQ FT: 13,500
SALES (est): 3.8MM Privately Held
SIC: 5199 Christmas novelties

(G-7912)
NATIONAL VETERINARY ASSOCIATES
457 N K 7 Hwy (66061-8906)
PHONE.................................913 782-0173
EMP: 17
SALES (corp-wide): 876MM Privately Held
SIC: 0742 Animal hospital services, pets & other animal specialties
PA: National Veterinary Associates, Inc.
29229 Canwood St Ste 100
Agoura Hills CA 91301
805 777-7722

(G-7913)
NATURAL CREATIONS INC
995 N Marion St (66061-6380)
PHONE.................................913 390-8058
Troy Gormally, *President*
EMP: 10
SALES (est): 991.4K Privately Held
SIC: 0781 Landscape planning services

(G-7914)
NBH BANK
Also Called: Bank Midwest
2002 E Santa Fe St (66062-1690)
P.O. Box 428 (66051-0428)
PHONE.................................913 782-5400
Matt Devine, *Loan Officer*
Yna Delgado, *Manager*
Kendra Lafferty, *Manager*
Carol Sevy, *Officer*
EMP: 10 Publicly Held
SIC: 6022 State commercial banks
HQ: Nbh Bank
7800 E Orchard Rd
Greenwood Village CO 80111
720 554-6680

(G-7915)
NEPHROLOGY ASSOCIATES INC
1295 E 151st St Ste 7 (66062-3429)
PHONE.................................913 381-0622
Andrew J Stingo, *Principal*
Melinda White, *Manager*
EMP: 10
SALES (est): 1MM Privately Held
SIC: 8011 Nephrologist

(G-7916)
NEVIN K WATERS DDS PA
Also Called: Waters, Nevin K
751 N Mur Len Rd Ste B (66062-5555)
PHONE.................................913 782-1330
Nevin K Waters DDS, *President*
EMP: 13
SQ FT: 2,500
SALES (est): 1.3MM Privately Held
SIC: 8021 Dentists' office

(G-7917)
NEW DAY EDUCARE
Also Called: Grace United Methodist Church
520 S Harrison St (66061-4611)
PHONE.................................913 764-1353
Linda Noyes, *Director*
EMP: 13
SALES (est): 280.2K Privately Held
SIC: 8351 Group day care center

(G-7918)
NEWELL & ASSOCIATES
17935 W 183rd St (66062-9267)
PHONE.................................913 592-4421
EMP: 10 EST: 1992
SALES: 800K Privately Held
SIC: 1741 Masonry/Stone Contractor

(G-7919)
NEXT TO NATURE LANDSCAPE LLC
11785 S Conley St (66061-9501)
PHONE.................................913 963-8180
Wayne Barber,
David Ward,
EMP: 27
SALES (est): 2.9MM Privately Held
SIC: 0781 Landscape services

(G-7920)
NIC INC (PA)
25501 W Valley Pkwy # 300 (66061-8474)
PHONE.................................877 234-3468
Harry H Herington, *Ch of Bd*
Aaron Boyd, *General Mgr*
Brian Stevenson, *General Mgr*
Andy Ford, *Chief*
Robert Chandler, *Vice Pres*
EMP: 270 EST: 1991
SQ FT: 42,000
SALES: 344.9MM Publicly Held
WEB: www.nicusa.com
SIC: 7371 Custom computer programming services; computer software development & applications

(G-7921)
NIC SOLUTIONS LLC
25501 W Valley Pkwy # 300 (66061-8474)
PHONE.................................913 498-3468
EMP: 10
SALES (est): 286.6K
SALES (corp-wide): 344.9MM Publicly Held
SIC: 7374 Computer graphics service
HQ: Nicusa, Inc.
25501 W Valley Pkwy # 300
Olathe KS 66061

(G-7922)
NICUSA INC (HQ)
25501 W Valley Pkwy # 300 (66061-8453)
PHONE.................................913 498-3468
Harry H Herington, *President*
Ron Thornburgh, *Vice Pres*
Robert Swartz, *Opers Staff*
Christopher Varn, *Opers Staff*
Stephen M Kovzan, *Treasurer*
EMP: 210
SQ FT: 50,000
SALES (est): 267.3MM
SALES (corp-wide): 344.9MM Publicly Held
WEB: www.nicusa.com
SIC: 7371 Computer software development & applications
PA: Nic Inc.
25501 W Valley Pkwy # 300
Olathe KS 66061
877 234-3468

(G-7923)
NL WILSON MOVING INC
15360 S Mahaffie St (66062-2751)
PHONE.................................913 652-9488
Mark Drier, *President*
Theresa Turner, *Principal*
EMP: 20
SALES (est): 2.6MM Privately Held
SIC: 4212 Moving services

(G-7924)
NPS SALES INC
Also Called: Topeka Metro News, The
1701 E Cedar St Ste 111 (66062-1775)
PHONE.................................913 406-1454
EMP: 5
SALES (est): 210K Privately Held
SIC: 2711 Newspapers-Publishing/Printing

(G-7925)
NULOOK CUSTOM FINISHES
16406 W 156th Ter (66062-3860)
PHONE.................................913 385-2574
Dan Allan, *Owner*
EMP: 5
SALES (est): 439.5K Privately Held
SIC: 2541 Counter & sink tops

(G-7926)
NURSING BY NUMBERS LLC
2364 W Elizabeth St (66061-5036)
PHONE.................................913 788-0566
Melissa M Herlein, *Administration*
EMP: 10
SALES (est): 161.9K Privately Held
SIC: 8051 Skilled nursing care facilities

(G-7927)
OLATHE ANIMAL HOSPITAL INC
Also Called: Mark G Romain
13800 W 135th St (66062-6253)
PHONE.................................913 764-1415
Mark G Romain, *CEO*
Nancy Potter, *Practice Mgr*
EMP: 12
SALES (est): 493.8K Privately Held
WEB: www.olatheanimalhospital.com
SIC: 0742 Veterinarian, animal specialties; animal hospital services, pets & other animal specialties

(G-7928)
OLATHE BILLIARDS INC (PA)
Also Called: Shooters
810 W Old Highway 56 (66061-4210)
PHONE.................................913 780-5740
Jeff Sorrell, *President*
Dan Tull, *Chairman*
EMP: 18
SQ FT: 17,000
SALES: 1.5MM Privately Held
SIC: 7999 5812 5813 5091 Billiard parlor; grills (eating places); bar (drinking places); billiard equipment & supplies

(G-7929)
OLATHE CHAMBER OF COMMERCE
18103 W 106th St 100 (66061-2884)
PHONE.................................913 764-1050
Tim McKee, *CEO*
Laura Baldwin, *Vice Pres*
Allison Calvin, *Manager*
Shannon Latham, *Asst Director*
EMP: 16
SALES: 2.4MM Privately Held
WEB: www.olathe.org
SIC: 8611 Chamber of Commerce

(G-7930)
OLATHE DENTAL CARE CENTER
234 S Cherry St (66061-4425)
PHONE.................................913 782-1420
Charles Leins, *Owner*
EMP: 12
SALES (est): 691.1K Privately Held
SIC: 8021 Dentists' office

(G-7931)
OLATHE ENDODONTICS
16093 W 135th St Ste A (66062-1507)
PHONE.................................913 829-0060
Beth Saveston, *Manager*
Bart W Putnam DDS, *Fmly & Gen Dent*
Bart Putnam, *Fmly & Gen Dent*
EMP: 11 EST: 2008
SALES (est): 712.3K Privately Held
SIC: 8021 Endodontist

(G-7932)
OLATHE FAMILY DENTISTRY PA
450 S Parker St (66061-4231)
PHONE.................................913 829-1438
Jon G Bevan, *Managing Prtnr*
Craig M Alexander, *Partner*
Jon Bevan, *Fmly & Gen Dent*
EMP: 10
SALES (est): 1MM Privately Held
SIC: 8021 Dentists' office

(G-7933)
OLATHE FAMILY PRACTICE PA
1750 S Mahaffie Pl (66062-3431)
PHONE.................................913 782-3322
William Mathews, *Partner*
Dr Cedric B Fortune, *Partner*
Dr James Soeldner, *Partner*
Dr George Watkins, *Partner*
Patrick Yao, *Family Practiti*
EMP: 20

GEOGRAPHIC

SQ FT: 1,200
SALES (est): 1.1MM **Privately Held**
WEB: www.inoventions.com
SIC: 8011 General & family practice, physician/surgeon

(G-7934)
OLATHE FAMILY VISION (PA)
13839 S Mur Len Rd Ste A (66062-1661)
PHONE..................................913 782-5993
Wayne R Hemphill, *Owner*
EMP: 11 **EST:** 2015
SALES (est): 876.6K **Privately Held**
SIC: 8042 Specialized optometrists

(G-7935)
OLATHE FAMILY VISION
740 W Cedar St (66061-4004)
PHONE..................................913 254-0200
Melissa Hahn, *Branch Mgr*
EMP: 11
SALES (est): 840.8K
SALES (corp-wide): 876.6K **Privately Held**
SIC: 8042 Specialized optometrists
PA: Olathe Family Vision
13839 S Mur Len Rd Ste A
Olathe KS 66062
913 782-5993

(G-7936)
OLATHE FORD SALES INC (PA)
Also Called: Olathe Ford Lincoln
1845 E Santa Fe St (66062-1695)
PHONE..................................913 782-0881
D F Bradley, *President*
Sam Mansker, *General Mgr*
Don W Maddux, *Vice Pres*
Brian Dowlen, *Parts Mgr*
Casey Calhoun, *Sales Staff*
EMP: 26 **EST:** 1965
SQ FT: 35,000
SALES (est): 99MM **Privately Held**
SIC: 5511 5561 5012 Automobiles, new & used; recreational vehicle dealers; trucks, commercial

(G-7937)
OLATHE FORD SALES INC
Also Called: Olathe Ford Outlet
205 S Fir St (66061-3626)
PHONE..................................913 829-1957
Jason Beers, *Sales Staff*
Dennis Casey, *Sales Staff*
Stephanie Lessard, *Sales Staff*
Brian Rector, *Sales Staff*
Rob Miller, *Manager*
EMP: 30
SALES (corp-wide): 99MM **Privately Held**
SIC: 5511 7532 5521 Automobiles, new & used; body shop, automotive; automobiles, used cars only
PA: Ford Olathe Sales Inc
1845 E Santa Fe St
Olathe KS 66062
913 782-0881

(G-7938)
OLATHE GLASS COMPANY INC
Also Called: Olathe Glass & Framed Prints
510 E Santa Fe St (66061-3448)
PHONE..................................913 782-7444
Trey Schroeder, *President*
▲ **EMP:** 20
SQ FT: 7,000
SALES (est): 5.7MM **Privately Held**
WEB: www.olatheglass.com
SIC: 5039 5023 5031 5719 Glass construction materials; mirrors & pictures, framed & unframed; doors; mirrors

(G-7939)
OLATHE HOTELS LLC
Also Called: Residence Inn Olathe
12215 S Strang Line Rd (66062-5224)
PHONE..................................913 829-6700
Cindy Kaunley, *Branch Mgr*
EMP: 11
SALES (corp-wide): 1.4MM **Privately Held**
WEB: www.olathehotels.com
SIC: 7011 Hotels & motels
PA: Olathe Hotels, L.L.C.
2390 Tower Dr
Monroe LA 71201
318 325-5561

(G-7940)
OLATHE MEDICAL CENTER INC (HQ)
20333 W 151st St (66061-7211)
PHONE..................................913 791-4200
Stan Holm, *President*
Brian Roby, *Trustee*
Dorothy Carey, *Senior VP*
John Staton, *Senior VP*
Mike Jensen, *Vice Pres*
EMP: 25
SQ FT: 187,431
SALES: 252MM
SALES (corp-wide): 5.1MM **Privately Held**
WEB: www.olathehealthsystem.com
SIC: 8082 8062 Home health care services; general medical & surgical hospitals
PA: Olathe Health System, Inc.
20333 W 151st St
Olathe KS 66061
913 791-4200

(G-7941)
OLATHE MEDICAL CENTER INC
Also Called: Hospice HM Hlth Olathe Med Ctr
20333 W 151st St St301 (66061-7211)
PHONE..................................913 791-4315
Char Shibel, *Director*
EMP: 45
SALES (corp-wide): 5.1MM **Privately Held**
WEB: www.olathehealthsystem.com
SIC: 8082 Home health care services
HQ: Olathe Medical Center, Inc.
20333 W 151st St
Olathe KS 66061
913 791-4200

(G-7942)
OLATHE MEDICAL SERVICES INC
Also Called: Cardiology Service
20805 W 51st 400dtrs (66061)
PHONE..................................913 780-4900
Carol Powell, *Administration*
Rangarao V Tummala, *Cardiology*
EMP: 80 **Privately Held**
SIC: 8011 Cardiologist & cardio-vascular specialist
PA: Olathe Medical Services, Inc
15435 W 134th Pl
Olathe KS 66062

(G-7943)
OLATHE MEDICAL SERVICES INC (PA)
Also Called: Associates In Family Care
15435 W 134th Pl (66062-6135)
PHONE..................................913 782-7515
Pat Katzer, *Director*
EMP: 85
SQ FT: 36,000
SALES (est): 16MM **Privately Held**
SIC: 8011 General & family practice, physician/surgeon

(G-7944)
OLATHE MEDICAL SERVICES INC
Also Called: Olathe Family Physicians
20375 W 151st St Ste 105 (66061-5353)
PHONE..................................913 782-8487
David E Graham, *Med Doctor*
Lynne Sosna, *Manager*
EMP: 16 **Privately Held**
SIC: 8011 Physicians' office, including specialists
PA: Olathe Medical Services, Inc
15435 W 134th Pl
Olathe KS 66062

(G-7945)
OLATHE MEDICAL SERVICES INC
Also Called: Family Medical Care of Olathe
1701 E Cedar St Ste 111 (66062-1775)
PHONE..................................913 764-0036
Karen Yokish, *Principal*
EMP: 14 **Privately Held**
SIC: 8011 Offices & clinics of medical doctors
PA: Olathe Medical Services, Inc
15435 W 134th Pl
Olathe KS 66062

(G-7946)
OLATHE MEDICAL SERVICES INC
Also Called: Delphia Family Practice
18695 W 151st St (66062-2738)
PHONE..................................913 782-1610
Robert Nottingham, *Med Doctor*
Karen Voigts, *Manager*
Curtis Moore, *Family Practiti*
EMP: 20 **Privately Held**
SIC: 8011 Offices & clinics of medical doctors
PA: Olathe Medical Services, Inc
15435 W 134th Pl
Olathe KS 66062

(G-7947)
OLATHE MILLWORK LLC
15785 S Keeler Ter # 100 (66062-3642)
PHONE..................................913 738-8074
Brian North, *General Mgr*
▲ **EMP:** 8 **EST:** 2012
SALES (est): 3.1MM
SALES (corp-wide): 859.8MM **Privately Held**
SIC: 5031 2431 Metal doors, sash & trim; millwork
HQ: Pacific Mutual Door Company Inc
1525 W 31st St
Kansas City MO 64108
816 531-0161

(G-7948)
OLATHE REGIONAL ONCOLOGY CTR
20375 W 151st St Ste 180 (66061-4575)
PHONE..................................913 768-7200
Stephen R Smalley, *Partner*
Brad Koffman, *Partner*
EMP: 10 **EST:** 1996
SALES (est): 739.3K **Privately Held**
SIC: 8011 Oncologist

(G-7949)
OLATHE SOCCER CLUB
Also Called: KANSAS RUSH SOCCER CLUB
1570 S Mahaffie Cir (66062-3432)
PHONE..................................913 764-4111
Kimball Leavitt, *CEO*
EMP: 10
SALES: 1.2MM **Privately Held**
SIC: 7941 7997 Soccer club; membership sports & recreation clubs

(G-7950)
OLATHE UNIFIED SCHOOL DST 233
Also Called: North Lindenwood Support Ctr
315 N Lindenwood Dr (66062-1238)
PHONE..................................913 780-7002
Cindy Galemore, *Principal*
EMP: 50
SALES (corp-wide): 442.3MM **Privately Held**
SIC: 8322 Multi-service center
PA: Olathe Unified School District 233
14160 S Blackbob Rd
Olathe KS 66062
913 780-7000

(G-7951)
OLATHE UNIFIED SCHOOL DST 233
Also Called: Olathe Service Center
1500 W 56th Hwy (66061)
P.O. Box 2000 (66063-2000)
PHONE..................................913 780-7011
Jim Houghton, *Manager*
EMP: 75
SALES (corp-wide): 442.3MM **Privately Held**
WEB: www.olathe.k12.ks.us
SIC: 7349 8299 Building maintenance services; educational services
PA: Olathe Unified School District 233
14160 S Blackbob Rd
Olathe KS 66062
913 780-7000

(G-7952)
OLATHE UNIFIED SCHOOL DST 233
Retired Employees Association
311 E Park St (66061)
PHONE..................................913 780-7880
Amanda York, *Manager*
EMP: 120
SALES (corp-wide): 442.3MM **Privately Held**
SIC: 8621 Education & teacher association
PA: Olathe Unified School District 233
14160 S Blackbob Rd
Olathe KS 66062
913 780-7000

(G-7953)
OLATHE UNIFIED SCHOOL DST 233
Also Called: Heartland Early Childhood Ctr
1700 W Sheridan St (66061-4135)
PHONE..................................913 780-7410
Carol Affholder, *Principal*
EMP: 75
SALES (corp-wide): 442.3MM **Privately Held**
WEB: www.olathe.k12.ks.us
SIC: 8351 Preschool center
PA: Olathe Unified School District 233
14160 S Blackbob Rd
Olathe KS 66062
913 780-7000

(G-7954)
OLATHE WOMENS CENTER INC
20375 W 151st St Ste 250 (66061-4576)
PHONE..................................913 780-3388
Bruce B Snider MD, *President*
Luina Estrada, *Principal*
EMP: 15
SALES (est): 2.4MM **Privately Held**
SIC: 8011 Gynecologist

(G-7955)
OLATHE YOUTH BASEBALL INC
885 S Parker St (66061-4260)
PHONE..................................913 393-9891
Mick Murphy, *General Mgr*
Bob Davis, *Manager*
EMP: 12 **EST:** 1998
SALES: 389.2K **Privately Held**
SIC: 7997 Baseball club, except professional & semi-professional

(G-7956)
OLSSON INC
1700 E 123rd St (66061-5882)
PHONE..................................913 829-0078
Sterling Cramer, *Branch Mgr*
Dylan Sileo, *Manager*
EMP: 21
SALES (corp-wide): 198MM **Privately Held**
WEB: www.oaconsulting.com
SIC: 8711 Consulting engineer
PA: Olsson, Inc.
601 P St Ste 200
Lincoln NE 68508
417 781-0643

(G-7957)
OMC DISTRIBUTION CENTER
1660 S Lone Elm Rd (66061-6837)
PHONE..................................913 791-3592
EMP: 10
SALES (est): 999.8K **Privately Held**
SIC: 5199 Nondurable goods

(G-7958)
OPEN MINDS CHILD DEV CTR LLC
1778 E Harold St (66061-2700)
PHONE..................................913 703-6736
Abdulrasak Yahaya,
Alicia Yahaya,
EMP: 15
SALES (est): 89.5K **Privately Held**
SIC: 8351 Preschool center; nursery school

(G-7959)
OPPLIGER BANKING SYSTEMS INC
1355 N Winchester St (66061-5880)
P.O. Box 14575, Lenexa (66285-4575)
PHONE..................................913 829-6300
Donna Oppliger, *Principal*
EMP: 25
SQ FT: 7,000
SALES (est): 6MM **Privately Held**
SIC: 5049 Bank equipment & supplies

(G-7960)
OPTIC FUEL CLEAN INC
15503 W 147th Dr (66062-5007)
PHONE..................................913 712-8373
Shelly Sundeng, *President*
EMP: 6
SALES (est): 696K **Privately Held**
SIC: 2899 Fuel tank or engine cleaning chemicals

(G-7961)
ORAL & FACIAL SURGERY ASSOC
1441 E 151st St Ste 4 (66062-2861)
PHONE..................................913 782-1529
Kirk C Collier, *Branch Mgr*
EMP: 20
SALES (corp-wide): 3.5MM **Privately Held**
SIC: 8021 Dental surgeon
PA: Oral & Facial Surgery Associates
3700 W 83rd St Ste 103
Prairie Village KS 66208
913 381-5194

(G-7962)
OREILLY AUTOMOTIVE STORES INC
Also Called: O'Reilly Auto Parts
913 E Santa Fe St (66061-3759)
PHONE..................................913 764-8685
Chadd Toddler, *Manager*
EMP: 29 **Publicly Held**
WEB: www.oreillyauto.com
SIC: 5531 5013 Automotive parts; motor vehicle supplies & new parts
HQ: O'reilly Automotive Stores, Inc.
233 S Patterson Ave
Springfield MO 65802
417 862-2674

(G-7963)
OREILLY AUTOMOTIVE STORES INC
Also Called: O'Reilly Auto Parts 196
1115 W Dennis Ave (66061-5229)
PHONE..................................913 829-6188
Adam Clark, *Manager*
EMP: 12 **Publicly Held**
WEB: www.oreillyauto.com
SIC: 5013 5531 Automotive supplies & parts; automotive parts
HQ: O'reilly Automotive Stores, Inc.
233 S Patterson Ave
Springfield MO 65802
417 862-2674

(G-7964)
ORIZON AROSTRUCTURES - NKC LLC (HQ)
801 W Old Highway 56 (66061-4902)
PHONE..................................816 788-7800
Charlie Newell, *CEO*
EMP: 11
SALES (est): 24.9MM
SALES (corp-wide): 74.6MM **Privately Held**
SIC: 3728 Aircraft assemblies, subassemblies & parts
PA: Orizon Aerostructures, Llc
1200 Main St Ste 4000
Kansas City MO 64105
816 788-7800

(G-7965)
ORTHOSYNETICS INC
Also Called: Lovinggood, Thomas A
1295 E 151st St Ste 1 (66062-3429)
PHONE..................................913 782-1663
Thomas A Lovinggood, *Principal*
Roy Burnett, *Branch Mgr*
EMP: 26 **Privately Held**
SIC: 8021 Orthodontist
PA: Orthosynetics, Inc.
3850 N Causeway Blvd # 800
Metairie LA 70002

(G-7966)
OTTAWA BUS SERVICE INC
Also Called: Crossroad Tours
1320 W 149th St (66061-6814)
PHONE..................................913 829-6644
Dan Newby, *President*
Jeanne Bell, *Info Tech Mgr*
EMP: 40
SQ FT: 3,000
SALES (est): 2.9MM **Privately Held**
WEB: www.crossroadtours.com
SIC: 4142 Bus charter service, except local

(G-7967)
OVERBUDGET PRODUCTIONS
Also Called: Pastimes Catering
1528 W Forest Dr (66061-6801)
PHONE..................................913 254-1186
C Wayne Owens, *Owner*
Pamela Owens, *Co-Owner*
EMP: 28
SALES: 150K **Privately Held**
SIC: 7922 Theatrical producers

(G-7968)
OVERLAND CONCRETE CNSTR INC
1401 W Ott St (66061-5236)
P.O. Box 325 (66051-0325)
PHONE..................................913 393-4200
Carol Brown, *President*
Pat Brown, *Vice Pres*
EMP: 15 **EST:** 1994
SALES (est): 1.6MM **Privately Held**
WEB: www.overlandconcrete.com
SIC: 1771 Foundation & footing contractor

(G-7969)
P & D INC (PA)
Also Called: Dale's Body Shop
300 W Park St (66061-3219)
PHONE..................................913 782-2247
Troy Allenbrand, *President*
EMP: 10 **EST:** 1957
SQ FT: 4,000
SALES (est): 2.1MM **Privately Held**
WEB: www.dalesbodyshop.com
SIC: 7532 Body shop, automotive

(G-7970)
P-AMERICAS LLC
Pepsico
1775 E Kansas City Rd (66061-5856)
PHONE..................................913 791-3000
Todd Roberts, *General Mgr*
Joshua Elliott, *Manager*
EMP: 350
SALES (corp-wide): 64.6B **Publicly Held**
SIC: 2086 5149 Carbonated soft drinks, bottled & canned; groceries & related products
HQ: P-Americas Llc
1 Pepsi Way
Somers NY 10589
336 896-5740

(G-7971)
PACCAR LEASING CORPORATION
Also Called: PacLease
1301 S Hamilton Cir (66061-5374)
PHONE..................................913 829-1444
Steve Mayhew, *Manager*
EMP: 30
SALES (corp-wide): 23.5B **Publicly Held**
WEB: www.glsayre.com
SIC: 7513 Truck leasing, without drivers
HQ: Paccar Leasing Corporation
777 106th Ave Ne
Bellevue WA 98004
425 468-7400

(G-7972)
PALMER JOHNSON PWR SYSTEMS LLC
Also Called: John Deere Authorized Dealer
15360 S Mahaffie St (66062-2751)
PHONE..................................913 268-2941
Steve Sorg, *Branch Mgr*
EMP: 10
SALES (corp-wide): 103.9MM **Privately Held**
WEB: www.pjpower.com
SIC: 5084 Industrial machinery & equipment
HQ: Palmer Johnson Power Systems, Llc
1835 Haynes Dr
Sun Prairie WI 53590

(G-7973)
PARTNERS IN PRIMARY CARE
16575 W 119th St (66061-7770)
PHONE..................................913 815-5508
Tell Copening, *Manager*
EMP: 29 **Privately Held**
SIC: 8011 Offices & clinics of medical doctors
PA: Partners In Primary Care, P.C.
401 Route 73 N Ste 201
Marlton NJ 08053

(G-7974)
PARTNERS N PROMOTION INC (PA)
Also Called: Partners In Promotion
1465 N Winchester St (66061-5881)
PHONE..................................913 397-9500
Vicki Clayman, *President*
Debbie Hawley, *Accounts Exec*
Kelly Skinner, *Accounts Exec*
Anita Daniels, *Marketing Staff*
EMP: 11
SALES (est): 3.3MM **Privately Held**
SIC: 7312 7319 Outdoor advertising services; shopping news, advertising & distributing service

(G-7975)
PATRIOT ABATEMENT SERVICES LLC
19021 W 160th Ct (66062-9620)
P.O. Box 2226 (66051-2226)
PHONE..................................913 397-6181
Teresa R Frey, *Manager*
Roger Gibson,
Glenn Daly,
EMP: 10
SALES: 519K **Privately Held**
SIC: 3292 7389 Asbestos products;

(G-7976)
PAYNE & BROCKWAY P A
426 S Kansas Ave (66061-4441)
PHONE..................................913 782-4800
John Ray, *President*
Mark Huggins, *Vice Pres*
Linda Gerber, *Admin Asst*
Danielle Mora, *Admin Asst*
EMP: 20
SQ FT: 3,600
SALES (est): 2.3MM **Privately Held**
WEB: www.payne-brockway.com
SIC: 8713 Surveying services

(G-7977)
PCS INCORPORATED
1948 E Santa Fe St (66062-1611)
PHONE..................................913 981-1100
Tamer Christo, *CEO*
EMP: 17
SQ FT: 12,000
SALES: 4.2MM **Privately Held**
SIC: 4813 ; telephone/video communications

(G-7978)
PEDIATRIC DENTAL SPECIALIST PA
Also Called: Parrish, David L
975 N Mur Len Rd Ste A (66062-1803)
PHONE..................................913 829-0981
David J Cobb, *Owner*
EMP: 10
SQ FT: 1,800
SALES (est): 503.1K **Privately Held**
SIC: 8021 Dentists' office

(G-7979)
PERNOD RICARD USA LLC
14235 W 124th St (66062-5988)
PHONE..................................913 393-2015
EMP: 52
SALES (corp-wide): 182.4MM **Privately Held**
WEB: www.pernod-ricard-usa.com
SIC: 2085 Distilled & blended liquors
HQ: Pernod Ricard Usa, Llc
250 Park Ave Ste 17a
New York NY 10177
212 372-5400

(G-7980)
PETSMART INC
15255 W 119th St (66062-5605)
PHONE..................................913 393-4111
David Haesele, *Manager*
Sean Luethmers, *Director*
EMP: 30
SALES (corp-wide): 9.4B **Publicly Held**
WEB: www.petsmart.com
SIC: 5999 0752 Pet food; animal specialty services
HQ: Petsmart, Inc.
19601 N 27th Ave
Phoenix AZ 85027
623 580-6100

(G-7981)
PETTY PRODUCTS INC
224 N Monroe St (66061-3109)
PHONE..................................913 782-0028
Robert E Peterson, *President*
Diana Peterson, *Vice Pres*
EMP: 8 **EST:** 1966
SQ FT: 6,300
SALES (est): 590K **Privately Held**
SIC: 3231 5023 Products of purchased glass; mirrors & pictures, framed & unframed

(G-7982)
PFEFFERKORN ENGRG & ENVMTL LLC
19957 W 162nd St (66062-2787)
PHONE..................................913 490-3967
Katherine Manske, *Principal*
Gabriel Pfefferkorn,
EMP: 10 **EST:** 2016
SALES (est): 712.5K **Privately Held**
SIC: 1771 8711 Concrete work; civil engineering; construction & civil engineering

(G-7983)
PHELPS ENGINEERING INC
1270 N Winchester St (66061-5878)
PHONE..................................913 393-1155
Harold A Phelps, *President*
Wendall D Ubben, *Vice Pres*
Jeffery Zimmerman, *Project Engr*
Thomas D Phelps, *Asst Sec*
EMP: 36
SALES (est): 3.6MM **Privately Held**
WEB: www.phelpsengineering.com
SIC: 8711 8713 Civil engineering; surveying services

(G-7984)
PHENIX LABEL COMPANY INC
11610 S Alden St (66062-6923)
PHONE..................................913 327-7000
Hans Peter, *President*
Arthur C McCrum, *President*
Gregory Ellis, *QC Mgr*
Charles Casteel, *CFO*
Sharon Donahoo, *CFO*
◆ **EMP:** 90 **EST:** 1896
SQ FT: 70,000
SALES (est): 33.9MM **Privately Held**
WEB: www.phenixlabel.com
SIC: 2679 Labels, paper: made from purchased material

(G-7985)
PHYSICIANS OPTICAL
21020 W 151st St (66061-7200)
PHONE..................................913 829-5511
Milton Grin, *Owner*
EMP: 15
SALES (est): 437.8K **Privately Held**
SIC: 8042 Offices & clinics of optometrists

(G-7986)
PIAT INC
Also Called: SERVPRO
15365 S Keeler St (66062-2712)
PHONE..................................913 782-4693
Clo A Whitaker, *President*
Jack H Whitaker, *Vice Pres*

Maura Donnell, *Sales Staff*
EMP: 15
SALES (est): 1.1MM **Privately Held**
SIC: 7349 Building maintenance services

(G-7987)
PINKERTON PAIN THERAPY LLC
10680 S Cedar Niles Blvd (66061-7414)
PHONE..................................417 649-6406
Mark C Pinkerton, *Branch Mgr*
EMP: 16
SALES (corp-wide): 834.1K **Privately Held**
SIC: 8093 Rehabilitation center, outpatient treatment
PA: Pinkerton Pain Therapy, Llc
10940 Parallel Pkwy Ste K
Kansas City KS 66109
913 981-0830

(G-7988)
PLATFORM ADVERTISING
500 N Rogers Rd (66062-1436)
PHONE..................................913 254-6000
Michael Platt, *Principal*
Jeremy Schoen, *Vice Pres*
Jai Shankar, *Vice Pres*
Mallory Curry, *Buyer*
Dory Reasoner, *Human Res Dir*
EMP: 20
SALES (est): 2.6MM **Privately Held**
SIC: 7311 Advertising agencies

(G-7989)
POINT INC
16900 W 118th Ter (66061-6590)
PHONE..................................913 928-2720
Shigeyuki Sawaguchi, *President*
Lena Smith, *Controller*
▲ **EMP:** 15
SQ FT: 19,000
SALES (est): 1.5MM **Privately Held**
WEB: www.point.net
SIC: 3829 Surveying & drafting equipment
HQ: Sokkia Topcon Co., Ltd.
75-1, Hasunumacho
Itabashi-Ku TKY 174-0

(G-7990)
POLARIS ELECTRONICS CORP
630 S Rogers Rd (66062-1797)
PHONE..................................913 764-5210
Jack R Kay, *Ch of Bd*
Jim Kay, *President*
Brian Dicker, *Vice Pres*
EMP: 26
SQ FT: 8,000
SALES (est): 4.6MM **Privately Held**
WEB: www.polariselectronics.com
SIC: 3548 Resistance welders, electric

(G-7991)
POLESTAR AC & PLBG HTG
1900 E 123rd St (66061-5886)
PHONE..................................913 432-3342
Mark Snell, *Owner*
Nathan Burns, *Manager*
EMP: 13
SALES (est): 1.6MM **Privately Held**
SIC: 1711 Plumbing contractors; warm air heating & air conditioning contractor

(G-7992)
PONZERYOUNGQUIST PA
Also Called: Consulting Engineers
227 E Dennis Ave (66061-4517)
PHONE..................................913 782-0541
John Brann, *President*
Jim Challis, *Admin Sec*
EMP: 13 **EST:** 1973
SQ FT: 3,200
SALES (est): 1.5MM **Privately Held**
WEB: www.pyengineers.com
SIC: 8711 8713 Civil engineering; sanitary engineers; surveying services

(G-7993)
POOLE FIRE PROTECTION INC
19910 W 161st St (66062-2700)
PHONE..................................913 747-2044
Laura Poole, *President*
John W Poole III, *Vice Pres*
Brian Love, *Project Mgr*
Jack Poole, *Engineer*
Nancy Arlesic, *Administration*
EMP: 15
SQ FT: 15,800
SALES: 4.9MM **Privately Held**
WEB: www.poolefire.com
SIC: 8711 Fire protection engineering

(G-7994)
POWER ADMIN LLC
12710 S Pflumm Rd Ste 206 (66062-3884)
PHONE..................................800 401-2339
Doug Nebeker, *Mng Member*
EMP: 6
SALES (est): 941.8K **Privately Held**
WEB: www.poweradmin.com
SIC: 3823 Programmers, process type

(G-7995)
POWER CONTROL DEVICES INC
Also Called: American Time Products
821 N Martway Dr (66061-7053)
PHONE..................................913 829-1900
Patrick E Antonucci, *President*
Mike Allmayer, *Vice Pres*
Karen Snider, *Personnel*
EMP: 20
SQ FT: 14,000
SALES (est): 3.5MM **Privately Held**
WEB: www.powercontroldevices.com
SIC: 3679 Power supplies, all types: static; electronic circuits

(G-7996)
PPS INC
Also Called: Pine Decals
14824 W 117th St (66062-9304)
PHONE..................................913 791-0164
Janice Green, *Ch of Bd*
Mike Farmer, *President*
Dave Raya, *Prdtn Mgr*
Janet Green, *Human Res Mgr*
Matt Wilson, *Sales Executive*
EMP: 64
SQ FT: 50,000
SALES (est): 11MM **Privately Held**
WEB: www.ppsinc.com
SIC: 2752 Transfers, decalcomania or dry: lithographed

(G-7997)
PRAIRIE CTR CHRISTN CHILDCARE
105 S Montclaire Dr (66061-3858)
PHONE..................................913 390-0230
John Newson, *Chairman*
EMP: 20
SALES (est): 432K **Privately Held**
SIC: 8351 Child day care services

(G-7998)
PRAIRIE LF CTR OF OVERLAND PK
13655 S Alden St (66062-5830)
PHONE..................................913 764-5444
Neal Huston, *Owner*
Reginald Golson, *Sales Staff*
Connie Roll, *Executive*
EMP: 11 **Privately Held**
SIC: 7991 Health club
PA: Prairie Life Center Of Overland Park, Ltd
10351 Barkley St
Overland Park KS 66212

(G-7999)
PRECISION BORING TECH INC
14713 S Saint Andrews Ave (66061-6873)
P.O. Box 3570 (66063-3570)
PHONE..................................913 735-4728
Daniel Smith, *President*
Melissa Coleman, *Vice Pres*
EMP: 14
SALES (est): 1.9MM **Privately Held**
SIC: 1623 Underground utilities contractor

(G-8000)
PRECISION CRAFT INC
19919 W 162nd St (66062-2787)
PHONE..................................913 780-9077
Roger B Hays, *President*
EMP: 15
SALES: 3.5MM **Privately Held**
SIC: 2499 2521 Decorative wood & woodwork; cabinets, office: wood

(G-8001)
PRECISION MANIFOLD SYSTEMS INC
700 W Frontier Ln (66061-7202)
PHONE..................................913 829-1221
Garold L McPeak, *President*
Mary McPeak, *Vice Pres*
EMP: 35
SQ FT: 10,000
SALES (est): 7MM **Privately Held**
WEB: www.precisionmanifold.com
SIC: 3714 5084 Manifolds, motor vehicle; hydraulic systems equipment & supplies

(G-8002)
PREFERRED PEDIATRICS PA
824 W Frontier Ln (66061-7216)
PHONE..................................913 764-7060
Stuart Shanker, *Partner*
F Lance Miller, *Pediatrics*
EMP: 15
SQ FT: 2,272
SALES (est): 2MM **Privately Held**
SIC: 8011 Pediatrician

(G-8003)
PREMIER PLASTIC SURGERY
Also Called: Moore, John B IV
20375 W 151st St Ste 370 (66061-7207)
PHONE..................................913 782-0707
John Moore, *Principal*
Cathy Smith, *Manager*
Federico Gonzalez, *Plastic Surgeon*
Brad Storm, *Plastic Surgeon*
Cathi Czyzewsk, *Administration*
EMP: 15
SALES (est): 2.2MM **Privately Held**
WEB: www.ppskc.com
SIC: 8011 Surgeon; plastic surgeon

(G-8004)
PREMIUM HEATING & COOLING INC
11860 S Conley St (66061-9510)
P.O. Box 3543 (66063-3543)
PHONE..................................913 780-5639
Dave Sibert, *President*
Melissa Sibert, *Admin Sec*
EMP: 12
SQ FT: 3,200
SALES: 933.8K **Privately Held**
SIC: 1711 Heating & air conditioning contractors

(G-8005)
PRICE & YOUNG & ODLE
15311 W 119th St (66062-1074)
PHONE..................................913 780-3200
Sam W Odle Od, *Branch Mgr*
Nathan Kluttz,
EMP: 17
SALES (corp-wide): 4.3MM **Privately Held**
SIC: 8042 Contact lense specialist optometrist
PA: Price & Young & Odle
3012 Anderson Ave
Manhattan KS 66503
785 537-1118

(G-8006)
PRIMARY CARE LANDSCAPE INC
15739 W 150th St (66062-4779)
P.O. Box 3164 (66063-1164)
PHONE..................................913 768-8880
Melvin N Schartz Jr, *President*
EMP: 12
SALES (est): 963.7K **Privately Held**
SIC: 0782 7389 Landscape contractors;

(G-8007)
PRINT TECH INC
11696 W 177th Ter (66062)
PHONE..................................913 894-6644
William L Carrington, *President*
Leasa Carrington, *Admin Sec*
EMP: 6
SALES (est): 698.8K **Privately Held**
SIC: 2759 Labels & seals: printing

(G-8008)
PRINTING DYNAMICS INC
12645 S Parker Ter (66061-5629)
PHONE..................................816 524-0444
Roy Acklin, *President*
EMP: 5
SQ FT: 3,000
SALES (est): 693.7K **Privately Held**
SIC: 2752 Commercial printing, offset

(G-8009)
PRIOR PRODUCTIONS INCORPORATED
15513 W 152nd St (66062-3088)
PHONE..................................816 654-5473
Wyatt Maxwell, *Exec Dir*
EMP: 25
SALES (est): 112.4K **Privately Held**
SIC: 7922 Legitimate live theater producers

(G-8010)
PSI SERVICES INC
Also Called: Logic Extension Resources
18000 W 105th St (66061-7543)
PHONE..................................843 520-2992
J Tindall, *President*
Robert Smith, *President*
Rhett Tindall, *Branch Mgr*
EMP: 10
SALES (corp-wide): 200.7MM **Privately Held**
WEB: www.lxr.com
SIC: 8748 7372 Testing services; prepackaged software
HQ: Psi Services Inc.
18000 W 105th St
Olathe KS 66061
913 895-4600

(G-8011)
PSI SERVICES INC (HQ)
Also Called: A M P
18000 W 105th St (66061-7543)
PHONE..................................913 895-4600
Steve Tapp, *President*
Brett Greenwood, *COO*
Lori Tinkler, *COO*
Gregg Becker, *Exec VP*
Tadas Dabsys, *Exec VP*
EMP: 130
SQ FT: 70,000
SALES (est): 26.4MM
SALES (corp-wide): 200.7MM **Privately Held**
WEB: www.lxr.com
SIC: 7372 2759 8741 8748 Prepackaged software; commercial printing; management services; testing services; business associations
PA: Psi Services Llc
611 N Brand Blvd Ste 10
Glendale CA 91203
818 847-6180

(G-8012)
PYRAMID CONTRACTORS INC
795 W Ironwood St (66061-7220)
PHONE..................................913 764-6225
Gavin Barmby, *President*
Walter Bauer, *General Mgr*
Ryan Bilovesky, *Project Mgr*
Jeff Shoemaker, *Project Mgr*
Connie Lewis, *Controller*
EMP: 50
SQ FT: 250
SALES (est): 10.3MM **Privately Held**
SIC: 1611 1622 General contractor, highway & street construction; bridge, tunnel & elevated highway

(G-8013)
QTI INC
15880 S Cherry Ct (66062-9039)
PHONE..................................913 579-3131
Jason Lofton, *CEO*
Natalia Cerna, *Office Mgr*
Sondra Little, *Office Mgr*
Steve Kucharski, *Director*
EMP: 15
SQ FT: 3,000
SALES (est): 3MM **Privately Held**
WEB: www.qti5.com
SIC: 1541 1731 Prefabricated building erection, industrial; warehouse construction; fiber optic cable installation

(G-8014)
QUARK STUDIOS LLC
12595 S Race St (66061-7810)
PHONE..................................913 871-5154
Kunjan Shah, *President*
Bhadrik Patel, *CTO*
EMP: 12
SALES: 500K **Privately Held**
SIC: 7379 7373 Computer related consulting services; systems software development services

(G-8015)
QUEST DIAGNOSTICS INCORPORATED
20920 W 151st St (66061-7247)
PHONE..................................913 768-1959
Casey Fox, *Branch Mgr*
Carolyn Hazzard, *Supervisor*
EMP: 17
SALES (corp-wide): 7.5B **Publicly Held**
SIC: 8071 Medical laboratories
HQ: Quest Diagnostics Incorporated
4100 Pier North Blvd D
Flint MI 48504
248 364-1324

(G-8016)
R B MANUFACTURING COMPANY
1301 W Dennis Ave (66061-5233)
PHONE..................................913 829-3233
Allan Jackson, *President*
Patrick Hughey, *Manager*
Edith Jackson, *Admin Sec*
EMP: 6
SQ FT: 8,000
SALES (est): 1MM **Privately Held**
SIC: 3713 3715 Truck beds; truck trailers

(G-8017)
R K BLACK MISSOURI LLC (PA)
Also Called: Ebe
15080 W 116th St Ste 100 (66062-1000)
PHONE..................................913 577-8100
Larhesa Burk, *Sales Staff*
Chris Black, *Mng Member*
EMP: 17
SQ FT: 9,280
SALES (est): 5.7MM **Privately Held**
WEB: www.ebe-usa.com
SIC: 5044 Copying equipment

(G-8018)
R O TEREX CORPORATION
Also Called: Terex Cranes
550 E Old Highway 56 (66061-4640)
PHONE..................................913 782-1200
Fil Filipov, *President*
Rodney Hyeng, *General Mgr*
Norman Noblat, *CFO*
EMP: 80
SQ FT: 80,000
SALES: 4.5MM
SALES (corp-wide): 5.1B **Publicly Held**
SIC: 3728 3537 3536 3531 Deicing equipment, aircraft; industrial trucks & tractors; hoists, cranes & monorails; aerial work platforms: hydraulic/elec. truck/carrier mounted
PA: Terex Corporation
200 Nyala Farms Rd Ste 2
Westport CT 06880
203 222-7170

(G-8019)
RAY LINDSEY CO
17221 Bel Ray Pl (66062)
PHONE..................................913 339-6666
Jo Maris, *President*
EMP: 10
SALES (est): 106.8K **Privately Held**
SIC: 4952 Sewerage systems

(G-8020)
REDDY ELECTRIC SYSTEMS INC
15385 S Us 169 Hwy Ste 4 (66062-3430)
P.O. Box 968 (66051-0968)
PHONE..................................913 764-0840
Edgar Davey, *President*
Arleta E Davey, *Treasurer*
EMP: 10
SQ FT: 7,000
SALES (est): 1.4MM **Privately Held**
SIC: 1731 General electrical contractor

(G-8021)
REDIVUS HEALTH
22201 W Innovation Dr (66061-1304)
PHONE..................................816 582-5428
Jeff Dunn, *CEO*
Achal Desai,
Tony Fangman,
Heath Latham,
EMP: 5 **EST:** 2012
SALES: 1MM **Privately Held**
SIC: 7372 Application computer software

(G-8022)
REECE & NICHOLS ALLIANCE INC (DH)
2140 E Santa Fe St (66062-1607)
PHONE..................................913 782-8822
Sandy Green, *Director*
Nan Gerike, *Real Est Agnt*
Lisa Moore, *Real Est Agnt*
Kristi Pinnick, *Real Est Agnt*
EMP: 80
SQ FT: 6,000
SALES (est): 4.4MM
SALES (corp-wide): 225.3B **Publicly Held**
SIC: 6531 Real estate agent, residential
HQ: Homeservices Of America, Inc.
333 S 7th St Fl 27
Minneapolis MN 55402
612 336-5900

(G-8023)
REGARDING KITCHENS INC
Also Called: Overland Park Appliance
1736 E Harold St (66061-2700)
PHONE..................................913 642-6184
Bev Gilbert, *President*
Bruce Gilbert, *CFO*
EMP: 18
SQ FT: 15,000
SALES (est): 3.7MM **Privately Held**
WEB: www.regardingkitchens.com
SIC: 1542 Commercial & office buildings, renovation & repair

(G-8024)
RELIABLE CAPS LLC
1001 W Old Highway 56 (66061-5257)
PHONE..................................913 764-2277
Gail Staples, *Cust Mgr*
Mahlon Laible, *Mng Member*
Phil Feist, *Manager*
Ken Sonnevik,
EMP: 35
SQ FT: 90,000
SALES (est): 8MM **Privately Held**
WEB: www.reliablecap.com
SIC: 3089 Bottle caps, molded plastic

(G-8025)
RELIABLE CONSTRUCTION SVCS INC (PA)
13505 S Mur Len Rd (66062-1600)
PHONE..................................913 764-7274
Cliff Coleman, *President*
Jeff Wernes, *Controller*
Jennifer Kearns, *Mktg Dir*
EMP: 19
SALES: 4.2MM **Privately Held**
WEB: www.reliablecs.net
SIC: 1521 Single-family housing construction

(G-8026)
RENEW
Also Called: Renew Counseling Center
11695 S Blackbob Rd Ste B (66062-1058)
PHONE..................................913 768-6606
Kori Hintz-Bohn, *Exec Dir*
EMP: 12 **EST:** 2007
SALES (est): 602.3K **Privately Held**
SIC: 8093 Rehabilitation center, outpatient treatment

(G-8027)
RESQ SYSTEMS LLC
Also Called: Iresq
15346 S Keeler St (66062-2713)
PHONE..................................913 390-1030
Brian Buffington, *General Mgr*
James C Harris,
Sarah Foster,
James Harris,
EMP: 15
SQ FT: 8,000
SALES (est): 1.4MM **Privately Held**
SIC: 7378 Computer maintenance & repair

(G-8028)
RETURN PRODUCTS MANAGEMENT INC (PA)
2111 E Crossroads Ln # 201 (66062-1658)
P.O. Box 3658 (66063-3658)
PHONE..................................913 768-1747
Michael Champion, *President*
Paula Champion, *Corp Secy*
▲ **EMP:** 12
SQ FT: 1,400
SALES (est): 5.8MM **Privately Held**
WEB: www.rpmrlm.com
SIC: 7389 4731 8742 Cotton sampling & inspection service; freight transportation arrangement; transportation consultant

(G-8029)
REYNOLDS CONSTRUCTION INC
11793 S Clare Rd (66061-8780)
PHONE..................................913 780-6624
Randy Reynolds, *President*
Amy Stark, *Accountant*
EMP: 38
SQ FT: 3,600
SALES (est): 3.2MM **Privately Held**
SIC: 1742 Stucco work, interior

(G-8030)
RGI PUBLICATIONS INC
14258 W 131st St (66062-6234)
PHONE..................................913 829-8723
Phillip Wacker, *President*
EMP: 22
SQ FT: 14,000
SALES (est): 2.2MM **Privately Held**
WEB: www.rgipublications.com
SIC: 2741 2789 2752 2672 Telephone & other directory publishing; bookbinding & related work; commercial printing, lithographic; coated & laminated paper

(G-8031)
RGS INDUSTRIES INC
Also Called: Custom Metal & Fabrication
15612 S Keeler St (66062-3516)
PHONE..................................913 780-9033
Loren Briggs, *President*
Barry Briggs, *Vice Pres*
EMP: 5
SQ FT: 7,500
SALES (est): 660K **Privately Held**
SIC: 3531 5051 3441 Construction machinery; metals service centers & offices; fabricated structural metal

(G-8032)
RHULEN & MORGAN PROF ASSN
Also Called: Morgan, David L
20805 W 151st St (66061-7249)
PHONE..................................913 782-8300
EMP: 17
SALES (est): 1MM **Privately Held**
SIC: 8011 Medical Doctor's Office

(G-8033)
RHW MANAGEMENT INC
Also Called: Fairfield Inn
12245 S Strang Line Rd (66062-5224)
PHONE..................................913 768-7000
Kevin Bundy, *General Mgr*
Lou Dean Marks, *Manager*
EMP: 27
SALES (corp-wide): 16MM **Privately Held**
WEB: www.rhwhotels.com
SIC: 7011 Hotels & motels
PA: Rhw Management, Inc.
6704 W 121st St
Shawnee Mission KS 66209
913 451-1222

(G-8034)
RHW MANAGEMENT INC
Also Called: Motel 6
1501 S Hamilton Cir (66061-5378)
PHONE..................................913 397-9455
Chris Patel, *Branch Mgr*
EMP: 12
SALES (corp-wide): 16MM **Privately Held**
WEB: www.rhwhotels.com
SIC: 7011 Hotels & motels
PA: Rhw Management, Inc.
6704 W 121st St
Shawnee Mission KS 66209
913 451-1222

(G-8035)
RIDGEVIEW ANIMAL HOSPITAL
816 N Ridgeview Rd (66061-2985)
PHONE..................................913 780-0078
Barbara Stuart, *Owner*
Karn Burton, *Finance*
EMP: 10
SALES (est): 462.2K **Privately Held**
WEB: www.ridgeviewanimalhospital.com
SIC: 0742 0752 Animal hospital services, pets & other animal specialties; grooming services, pet & animal specialties

(G-8036)
RIMPULL CORPORATION (PA)
15600 S Us 169 Hwy (66062-3506)
P.O. Box 748 (66051-0748)
PHONE..................................913 782-4000
Richard Davis, *President*
Daniel Vaughan, *Branch Mgr*
▼ **EMP:** 192
SQ FT: 6,000
SALES (est): 49.9MM **Privately Held**
WEB: www.rimpull.com
SIC: 3532 3537 Mining machinery; industrial trucks & tractors

(G-8037)
RITA OPLOTNIK DO
801 N Mur Len Rd (66062-1794)
PHONE..................................913 764-0036
Rita Oplotnik, *Principal*
Rita Oplontik, *Principal*
Christine Eliason, *Med Doctor*
EMP: 17
SALES (est): 219.7K **Privately Held**
SIC: 8031 Offices & clinics of osteopathic physicians

(G-8038)
ROBERT BROGDEN BUICK GMC INC
Also Called: Robert Brogden Auto Plaza
1500 E Santa Fe St (66061-3643)
PHONE..................................913 782-1500
Robert Brogden, *President*
Dave Yoakum, *General Mgr*
Nancy Brainard, *Comptroller*
John Greenquist, *Sales Staff*
EMP: 40
SQ FT: 35,000
SALES (est): 17.5MM **Privately Held**
WEB: www.brogdenauto.com
SIC: 5511 7538 Automobiles, new & used; general automotive repair shops

(G-8039)
ROBERTS PRODUCTS INC
10415 S Millbrook Ln (66061-9100)
PHONE..................................913 780-1702
Bob Baumgartner, *President*
EMP: 17
SQ FT: 24,000
SALES: 4.6MM **Privately Held**
SIC: 5031 Windows; doors

(G-8040)
ROGERS MANUFACTURING INC (PA)
Also Called: R M I Golf Carts
19882 W 156th St (66062-3500)
PHONE..................................843 423-4680
Steven Rogers, *President*
EMP: 30
SQ FT: 40,000
SALES (est): 3.6MM **Privately Held**
WEB: www.rogersmfginc.com
SIC: 3479 Painting, coating & hot dipping

(G-8041)
RONALD J BURGMEIER DDS PA
Also Called: Burgmeier, Ronald J
13025 S Mur Len Rd # 250 (66062-5452)
PHONE..................................913 764-1169
Ronald J Burgmeier DDS, *Owner*
EMP: 10

SALES (est): 637K **Privately Held**
SIC: 8021 Dentists' office

(G-8042)
ROSE COMPANIES INC (PA)
Also Called: Rose Construction
863 N Martway Dr (66061-7053)
P.O. Box 100 (66051-0100)
PHONE..................................913 782-0777
Chris Herre, *President*
Morgan Rose, *Vice Pres*
Christopher Herre, *Project Mgr*
Mike Massey, *Foreman/Supr*
Marcia Herre, *Manager*
EMP: 10
SQ FT: 6,000
SALES (est): 6.4MM **Privately Held**
WEB: www.rose-const.com
SIC: 1541 1542 Industrial buildings, new construction; renovation, remodeling & repairs: industrial buildings; commercial & office buildings, renovation & repair

(G-8043)
ROSE CONSTRUCTION CO INC
863 N Martway Dr (66061-7053)
P.O. Box 100 (66051-0100)
PHONE..................................913 782-0777
Christopher L Herre, *President*
Mary Ring, *Principal*
Morgan D Rose, *CFO*
EMP: 18 **EST:** 1924
SQ FT: 6,000
SALES (est): 2.1MM
SALES (corp-wide): 6.4MM **Privately Held**
WEB: www.buildwithrose.com
SIC: 1541 1542 Industrial buildings, new construction; commercial & office building, new construction
PA: Rose Companies, Inc.
863 N Martway Dr
Olathe KS 66061
913 782-0777

(G-8044)
ROYAL METAL INDUSTRIES INC (PA)
1000 W Ironwood St (66061-5385)
PHONE..................................913 829-3000
Mike Jacobs, *President*
Richard Jacobson, *Vice Pres*
Denise Martin, *Sales Staff*
EMP: 44
SQ FT: 30,000
SALES (est): 20MM **Privately Held**
WEB: www.royalmetal.com
SIC: 5051 Steel

(G-8045)
ROYAL TERRACE HEALTHCARE LLC
201 E Flaming Rd (66061-5343)
PHONE..................................913 829-2273
Kimptom Hopkins, *Mng Member*
EMP: 99
SALES (est): 3MM **Privately Held**
SIC: 8051 Skilled nursing care facilities
HQ: Consulate Health Care, Llc
800 Concourse Pkwy S
Maitland FL 32751

(G-8046)
RT PAINTING INC
1330 S Hamilton Cir (66061-7241)
PHONE..................................913 390-6650
Randy Tucker, *President*
EMP: 17
SALES (est): 300K **Privately Held**
SIC: 1721 Painting & paper hanging

(G-8047)
RUSH TRUCK CENTERS KANSAS INC
Also Called: Rush Truck Center, Kansas City
11525 S Rogers Rd (66062-1083)
PHONE..................................913 764-6000
Nick Hunt, *General Mgr*
Jib Felter, *Principal*
EMP: 23
SALES (est): 5.6MM
SALES (corp-wide): 5.5B **Publicly Held**
SIC: 5012 Trucks, commercial
PA: Rush Enterprises, Inc.
555 S Ih 35 Ste 500
New Braunfels TX 78130
830 302-5200

(G-8048)
RUTH GRIMSLEY
Also Called: Great Clips
13538 S Alden St (66062-5840)
PHONE..................................913 393-1711
Ruth Grimsley, *Owner*
Tracy Hein, *Partner*
EMP: 10
SALES (est): 161.5K **Privately Held**
SIC: 7231 Unisex hair salons

(G-8049)
RUTLAND INC
Also Called: Icon Poker
15610 S Keeler St (66062-3516)
PHONE..................................913 782-8862
Jay Rutler, *President*
Spencer Hawerlander, *Vice Pres*
▲ **EMP:** 11 **EST:** 2000
SQ FT: 2,000
SALES (est): 1.2MM **Privately Held**
SIC: 3089 Injection molding of plastics; organizers for closets, drawers, etc.: plastic

(G-8050)
SAFETY-KLEEN SYSTEMS INC
19930 W 157th St (66062-3823)
PHONE..................................913 829-6677
EMP: 20
SALES (corp-wide): 2.1B **Publicly Held**
SIC: 7389 Solvent Recovery
HQ: Safety-Kleen Systems, Inc.
2600 N Central Expy # 400
Richardson TX 75080
972 265-2000

(G-8051)
SALON AVANTI
115 S Clairborne Rd Ste B (66062-6105)
PHONE..................................913 829-2424
James Burrus, *Owner*
EMP: 10
SALES (est): 136.5K **Privately Held**
SIC: 7231 Hairdressers; facial salons

(G-8052)
SALVATION ARMY
420 E Santa Fe St (66061-3446)
PHONE..................................913 782-3640
Beth Erickson, *Director*
EMP: 14
SALES (est): 488.9K **Privately Held**
SIC: 8351 Preschool center

(G-8053)
SALVATION ARMY
420 E Santa Fe St (66061-3446)
PHONE..................................913 782-3640
Beth Erickson, *Director*
EMP: 12
SALES (corp-wide): 2.2B **Privately Held**
WEB: www.salarmychicago.org
SIC: 8351 Preschool center
HQ: The Salvation Army
5550 Prairie Stone Pkwy # 130
Hoffman Estates IL 60192
847 294-2000

(G-8054)
SANTA MARTA RETIREMENT CMNTY
13800 W 116th St (66062-7809)
PHONE..................................913 906-0990
David Gentile, *Principal*
Shannon Shoop, *Purch Dir*
Chet Surnmaczewicz, *Exec Dir*
Kristina Berkovich, *Director*
EMP: 17
SALES (est): 1.5MM **Privately Held**
SIC: 6513 Retirement hotel operation

(G-8055)
SARA SOFTWARE SYSTEMS LLC
804 N Meadowbrook Dr # 114 (66062-5501)
PHONE..................................913 370-4197
Maninder Kaur, *CEO*
Arvinder Singh, *President*
Gurinder Singh, *Vice Pres*
EMP: 22
SALES (est): 434.5K **Privately Held**
SIC: 7371 7373 7376 Computer software development; systems software development services; computer facilities management

(G-8056)
SCHENDEL SERVICES INC
Also Called: Schendel Pest Control
215 S Kansas Ave (66061-4436)
PHONE..................................913 498-1811
Roger Dahn, *Manager*
EMP: 10
SALES (corp-wide): 1.9B **Publicly Held**
WEB: www.schendelpest.com
SIC: 7342 5191 Pest control in structures; pesticides
HQ: Schendel Services, Inc.
1035 Se Quincy St
Topeka KS
785 232-9344

(G-8057)
SCHLAGE LOCK COMPANY LLC
2119 E Kansas City Rd (66061-7050)
PHONE..................................888 805-9837
Sue Craft, *Manager*
EMP: 150 **Privately Held**
SIC: 3429 Locks or lock sets
HQ: Schlage Lock Company Llc
11819 N Penn St
Carmel IN 46032
317 810-3700

(G-8058)
SCHLAGEL KINZER LLC
100 E Park St Ste 8 (66061-3463)
PHONE..................................913 782-5885
George Schlagel, *Mng Member*
EMP: 12
SALES (est): 1.4MM **Privately Held**
WEB: www.sdg-law.com
SIC: 8111 General practice attorney, lawyer

(G-8059)
SERVICE CORP INTERNATIONAL
Also Called: SCI
105 E Loula St (66061-3424)
PHONE..................................913 782-0582
Mark McGuilley, *President*
EMP: 11
SALES (corp-wide): 3.1B **Publicly Held**
SIC: 7261 Crematory
PA: Service Corporation International
1929 Allen Pkwy
Houston TX 77019
713 522-5141

(G-8060)
SHAHROKHI INC
Also Called: Advance Printing and Copy Ctr
525 N Lindenwood Dr Ste A (66062-1340)
PHONE..................................913 764-5775
Kay Shahrokhi, *President*
Shirley Shahrokhi, *President*
Frank Shahrokhi, *Treasurer*
EMP: 8
SALES: 450K **Privately Held**
WEB: www.shahrokhi.com
SIC: 2752 7334 2759 Commercial printing, offset; photocopying & duplicating services; thermography

(G-8061)
SHEET METAL CONTRACTORS INC
15655 S Keeler Ter (66062-3509)
P.O. Box 3742 (66063-3742)
PHONE..................................913 397-9130
Andrew Seibolt, *President*
Steve Seibolt, *Principal*
EMP: 35
SQ FT: 10,000
SALES (est): 7.1MM **Privately Held**
SIC: 3444 1761 Ducts, sheet metal; sheet metalwork

(G-8062)
SHERWIN-WILLIAMS COMPANY
1209 E Santa Fe St (66061-3765)
PHONE..................................913 782-0126
Renee Johnson, *Branch Mgr*
EMP: 13
SALES (corp-wide): 17.5B **Publicly Held**
WEB: www.sherwin.com
SIC: 5231 5713 5198 Paint; wallcoverings; wallpaper; floor covering stores; paints
PA: The Sherwin-Williams Company
101 W Prospect Ave # 1020
Cleveland OH 44115
216 566-2000

(G-8063)
SHINING STARS DAYCARE CENTER
16310 W 159th Ter (66062-4025)
PHONE..................................913 829-5000
Robert Mora, *President*
Lisa Mora, *Vice Pres*
Bob Mora, *Sales Executive*
EMP: 20
SALES (est): 450.5K **Privately Held**
SIC: 8351 Group day care center

(G-8064)
SHIRCONN INVESTMENTS INC
Also Called: Sleep Inn
20662 W 151st St (66061-7239)
PHONE..................................913 390-9500
Shirley Curley, *President*
Jerry Curley, *Vice Pres*
EMP: 15
SALES (est): 872.1K **Privately Held**
SIC: 7011 Hotels & motels

(G-8065)
SHREE RAM INVESTMENTS OF PLTTE
Also Called: Comfort Inn Olathe
15475 S Rogers Rd (66062-3497)
PHONE..................................913 948-9000
Sanjay Patel, *President*
EMP: 11
SALES: 900K **Privately Held**
SIC: 7011 Hotels & motels

(G-8066)
SIGNATURE LANDSCAPE LLC
15705 S Pflumm Rd (66062-9724)
PHONE..................................913 829-8181
William Gordon, *President*
Jeff Foulds, *Opers Staff*
William Smith, *Treasurer*
Joe Bond, *Accounts Mgr*
Cox Brian, *Accounts Mgr*
EMP: 240
SALES: 20MM **Privately Held**
SIC: 0781 4959 1711 0782 Landscape services; snowplowing; irrigation sprinkler system installation; landscape contractors

(G-8067)
SKYTON LAWN & LANDSCAPE LLC
11202 W 163rd Ter (66062)
PHONE..................................913 302-9056
William S Fuester, *Principal*
Scott Fuester, *Mng Member*
EMP: 11 **EST:** 2003
SALES (est): 740.6K **Privately Held**
SIC: 0782 Lawn care services

(G-8068)
SMART BEVERAGE INC (PA)
Also Called: Www.frozendrinkrus.biz
16113 W 130th Ter (66062-1383)
PHONE..................................785 656-2166
Luke N Einsel, *President*
Garth Einsel, *Opers Mgr*
EMP: 12
SQ FT: 5,000
SALES: 280K **Privately Held**
SIC: 2033 Fruit juices: concentrated, hot pack

(G-8069)
SMART WAY
Also Called: Bud Smart Janitorial
540 E 126th Ter (66061-2732)
PHONE..................................913 764-3071
Bud Smart, *Owner*
EMP: 15
SALES (est): 144.6K **Privately Held**
SIC: 7349 Janitorial service, contract basis

(G-8070)
SMITH & BOUCHER INC (PA)
25501 W Valley Pkwy # 200 (66061-8469)
PHONE..................................913 345-2127
Phil Ptacek, *President*
Adam Tryon, *Technician*
EMP: 22
SQ FT: 15,000
SALES (est): 4.8MM **Privately Held**
WEB: www.smithboucher.com
SIC: 8711 Consulting engineer

(G-8071)
SOKKIA CORPORATION (DH)
Also Called: Topcon Positioning Systems
16900 W 118th Ter (66061-6590)
PHONE..................................816 322-0939
Toll Free:..................................888 -
Eitoku Yamanaka, *President*
▲ **EMP:** 32
SQ FT: 62,000
SALES (est): 12.5MM **Privately Held**
WEB: www.sokkia.com
SIC: 5049 Surveyors' instruments

(G-8072)
SOMETHING DIFFERENT MEDIA PROD
13401 S Mur Len Rd # 100 (66062-1213)
P.O. Box 10372, Kansas City MO (64171-0372)
PHONE..................................913 764-9500
David Miller, *Owner*
EMP: 12
SALES (est): 811.4K **Privately Held**
SIC: 8748 7812 Business consulting; video production

(G-8073)
SOUND PRODUCTS INC
1365 N Winchester St (66061-5880)
PHONE..................................913 599-3666
Robbin Reynolds, *President*
Mark Rau, *General Mgr*
Cindy Owen, *Shareholder*
Fritz Reynolds, *Shareholder*
Jeanne Reynolds, *Shareholder*
EMP: 16
SQ FT: 7,500
SALES (est): 3.8MM **Privately Held**
WEB: www.soundproductsinc.com
SIC: 5065 Security control equipment & systems; video equipment, electronic

(G-8074)
SOUTHSIDE PET HOSPITAL
457 N K 7 Hwy (66061-8906)
PHONE..................................913 782-0173
Rod J Schieffer, *Partner*
EMP: 10
SQ FT: 2,700
SALES (est): 411.5K **Privately Held**
SIC: 0742 Animal hospital services, pets & other animal specialties; veterinarian, animal specialties

(G-8075)
SPECIAL BEGINNINGS INC
14169 S Mur Len Rd (66062-1873)
PHONE..................................913 393-2223
Mary Hornbeck, *Branch Mgr*
Jean Katt, *Exec Dir*
Shannon Trowbridge, *Director*
EMP: 54 **Privately Held**
SIC: 8351 Preschool center
PA: Special Beginnings, Inc.
10216 Pflumm Rd
Shawnee Mission KS 66215

(G-8076)
SPECTRUM ELITE CORP
Also Called: Spectrum Elite Wireless
16644 W 147th St (66062-2540)
PHONE..................................913 579-7037
Rhonda Burdick, *Business Mgr*
Benjamin Burdick, *Shareholder*
EMP: 8
SALES (est): 213.1K **Privately Held**
SIC: 8748 3661 5063 9631 Telecommunications consultant; telephone sets, all types except cellular radio; telephone & telegraph wire & cable; communications commission, government; telecommunication equipment repair (except telephones)

(G-8077)
SPEEDWAY SERVICE CORPORATION
15217 W 121st Ter (66062-4927)
PHONE..................................913 488-6695
Steve Dolittle, *President*
EMP: 14
SQ FT: 6,000
SALES (est): 1.1MM **Privately Held**
SIC: 4212 Moving services

(G-8078)
SPOON CREEK HOLDINGS LLC
12700 S Spoon Creek Rd (66061-9108)
PHONE..................................913 375-2275
Richard Rees,
EMP: 10 **Privately Held**
SIC: 6719 Holding companies

(G-8079)
SPX COOLING TECHNOLOGIES INC
1200 W Marley Rd (66061-7215)
PHONE..................................913 782-1600
Howard Rinne, *Opers-Prdtn-Mfg*
EMP: 220
SALES (corp-wide): 1.5B **Publicly Held**
WEB: www.cts.spx.com
SIC: 3559 3443 Sewing machines & hat & zipper making machinery; fabricated plate work (boiler shop)
HQ: Spx Cooling Technologies, Inc.
7401 W 129th St
Overland Park KS 66213
913 664-7400

(G-8080)
STANDARD ELECTRIC CO INC
2006 E Prairie Cir (66062-1268)
PHONE..................................913 782-5409
Doug Hulse, *President*
David Rogers, *Vice Pres*
Jack Suess, *Treasurer*
EMP: 15
SQ FT: 6,500
SALES: 3MM **Privately Held**
SIC: 5063 Electrical apparatus & equipment

(G-8081)
STANION WHOLESALE ELC CO INC
1370 N Winchester St (66061-7024)
PHONE..................................913 829-8111
Ed Stremel, *Branch Mgr*
EMP: 16
SALES (corp-wide): 97.6MM **Privately Held**
WEB: www.stanion.com
SIC: 5063 Electrical supplies
PA: Stanion Wholesale Electric Co., Inc.
812 S Main St
Pratt KS 67124
620 672-5678

(G-8082)
STEALTH TECHNOLOGIES LLC
Also Called: Bumper Bling Shop
15752 S Mahaffie St (66062-4038)
PHONE..................................913 228-2214
Lisa Rader, *Mng Member*
Douglas Evans,
Michael Miller,
Dennis Rader,
EMP: 13 **EST:** 2015
SQ FT: 3,000
SALES: 167.4K **Privately Held**
SIC: 3089 5961 Engraving of plastic; novelties, plastic; novelty merchandise, mail order

(G-8083)
STILL BUILDERS INC
Also Called: Valley Property
15740 S Mahaffie St (66062-4038)
PHONE..................................913 780-0702
Billy Still, *President*
EMP: 12
SQ FT: 1,200
SALES (est): 1.4MM
SALES (corp-wide): 1.7MM **Privately Held**
WEB: www.stillbuilders.com
SIC: 1521 New construction, single-family houses
PA: Still Contractors, Llc
15740 S Mahaffie St
Olathe KS 66062
913 768-4440

(G-8084)
STONE LOCK GLOBAL INC
101 N Church St Ste A (66061-3749)
PHONE..................................800 970-6168
Colleen Dunlap, *CEO*
Carter Stewart, *Vice Pres*
Jeff Sebek, *VP Bus Dvlpt*
Katrina Yao, *CFO*
EMP: 49
SQ FT: 3,580
SALES: 1.2MM **Privately Held**
SIC: 5045 Computers, peripherals & software

(G-8085)
STRICKLAND CONSTRUCTION CO
720 S Rogers Rd Ste B (66062-1779)
PHONE..................................913 764-7000
Rogers Strickland, *CEO*
Glen E Richardson, *President*
Rick Ulrich, *Principal*
Tracie Wilson, *Project Mgr*
Derrick Sullentrup, *Sales Staff*
EMP: 50
SALES (est): 15.9MM **Privately Held**
WEB: www.stricklandconstruction.com
SIC: 1541 1542 Industrial buildings & warehouses; commercial & office building, new construction

(G-8086)
STRUCTURA
19922 W 162nd St (66062-2787)
PHONE..................................913 390-8787
Dan Conan, *President*
Derek Seitz, *COO*
McKenzie Smith, *Project Mgr*
Shannon Yust, *Natl Sales Mgr*
Brandon Rohr, *Associate*
EMP: 19
SALES (est): 3.9MM **Privately Held**
SIC: 3449 Bars, concrete reinforcing: fabricated steel

(G-8087)
SUGAR RUSH INC
13778 S Blackbob Rd (66062-1932)
P.O. Box 4723 (66063-4723)
PHONE..................................913 839-2158
Linda Lynch, *President*
EMP: 5
SALES (est): 250K **Privately Held**
SIC: 2053 Cakes, bakery: frozen

(G-8088)
SUPERIOR SIGNALS INC
16355 S Lone Elm Rd (66062-9238)
P.O. Box 1246 (66051-1246)
PHONE..................................913 780-1440
Robert F Gawlik, *CEO*
Dirk Von Holt, *Principal*
George Brown, *Engineer*
Nathan Taylor, *Engineer*
Nathan Leseberg, *Human Res Mgr*
▲ **EMP:** 50
SQ FT: 67,500
SALES (est): 13.5MM
SALES (corp-wide): 178.9MM **Privately Held**
WEB: www.superiorsignals.com
SIC: 5099 5063 Safety equipment & supplies; signaling equipment, electrical
PA: Tvh Parts Co.
16355 S Lone Elm Rd
Olathe KS 66062
913 829-1000

(G-8089)
SURGERY CENTER OLATHE LLC
20375 W 151st St Ste 351 (66061-7242)
PHONE..................................913 829-4001
James K Bradley, *Director*
Mark Williamson,
EMP: 15
SQ FT: 10,000
SALES (est): 860K **Privately Held**
SIC: 8011 Surgeon

(G-8090)
SWAN CORPORATION
Also Called: Kidspark
15296 W 119th St (66062-5604)
PHONE..................................913 390-1411
Elizabeth Sileo, *President*
EMP: 10
SALES (est): 377.6K **Privately Held**
WEB: www.theswancorp.com
SIC: 8351 Child day care services

(G-8091)
SYSCO CORPORATION
1915 E Kansas City Rd (66061-5858)
P.O. Box 1300 (66051-1300)
PHONE..................................913 829-5555
EMP: 20
SALES (corp-wide): 60.1B **Publicly Held**
SIC: 5141 Groceries, general line
PA: Sysco Corporation
1390 Enclave Pkwy
Houston TX 77077
281 584-1390

(G-8092)
SYSCO KANSAS CITY INC (HQ)
1915 E Kansas City Rd (66061-5858)
P.O. Box 820 (66051-0820)
PHONE..................................913 829-5555
Bill Delaney, *President*
Manny Fernandez, *Chairman*
Troy Vesp, *Exec VP*
Terri Couture, *Vice Pres*
Doug Kramer, *Vice Pres*
EMP: 563 **EST:** 1924
SQ FT: 435,000
SALES (est): 295MM
SALES (corp-wide): 60.1B **Publicly Held**
SIC: 5149 5141 Canned goods: fruit, vegetables, seafood, meats, etc.; groceries, general line
PA: Sysco Corporation
1390 Enclave Pkwy
Houston TX 77077
281 584-1390

(G-8093)
SYSTRONICS INC
14902 W 117th St (66062-9306)
PHONE..................................913 829-9229
Edward Mc Loud, *President*
Dennis Mann, *CFO*
Dennis McCloud, *Manager*
Carmen Hollerich, *CIO*
EMP: 11
SQ FT: 4,985
SALES (est): 1MM **Privately Held**
WEB: www.systronics.com
SIC: 7374 Data processing service

(G-8094)
T & M CONTRACTING INC
17498 W 158th Pl (66062-6766)
PHONE..................................913 393-1087
Mike Wethered, *President*
Tammy Wethered, *Vice Pres*
EMP: 11
SALES (est): 1MM **Privately Held**
SIC: 4213 Heavy hauling

(G-8095)
T AND C AVIATION ENTERPRISES (PA)
Also Called: Air Associates of Kansas
12901 W 151st St Ste B (66062-7219)
PHONE..................................913 764-4800
Tom Cargin, *President*
Lisa Lynch, *General Mgr*
David Miller, *Opers Staff*
Mike Logan, *CFO*
Lois Thompson, *Finance*
EMP: 21
SALES (est): 1.8MM **Privately Held**
SIC: 7699 5599 8299 4581 Aircraft & heavy equipment repair services; aircraft dealers; flying instruction; aircraft servicing & repairing

(G-8096)
T D C LTD
11860 S Conley St (66061-9510)
PHONE..................................913 780-9631
Susan Devaney, *President*
Edward Devaney, *Treasurer*
Megan Devaney, *Manager*
Megan Fritz, *Senior Mgr*

GEOGRAPHIC

Dexter Devaney, *Supervisor*
EMP: 40
SALES (est): 3.9MM **Privately Held**
SIC: 5087 7349 Cleaning & maintenance equipment & supplies; janitorial service, contract basis

(G-8097)
T T COMPANIES INC
10841 S Ridgeview Rd (66061-6456)
PHONE..................................913 599-6886
David Gaboury, *CEO*
Wayne Schweizer, *Analyst*
EMP: 4000
SALES (est): 86.2MM **Privately Held**
SIC: 8742 8711 8748 8741 Industry specialist consultants; engineering services; testing services; administrative management; inspection & testing services

(G-8098)
T-MOBILE USA INC
Also Called: T Mobile 8631
14953 W 119th St (66062-9656)
PHONE..................................913 254-1674
Tami Meenahan, *Manager*
EMP: 12
SALES (corp-wide): 83.9B **Publicly Held**
WEB: www.voicestream.com
SIC: 4812 Cellular telephone services
HQ: T-Mobile Usa, Inc.
12920 Se 38th St
Bellevue WA 98006
425 378-4000

(G-8099)
TAFS INC
15910 S Us 169 Hwy (66062-3800)
P.O. Box 872632, Kansas City MO (64187-2632)
PHONE..................................877 898-9797
Katherine Mahnken, *Sales Staff*
Josh Goode, *Director*
EMP: 30
SALES (est): 8.9MM
SALES (corp-wide): 131.3MM **Privately Held**
SIC: 6153 Factoring services
PA: Transam Trucking, Inc.
15910 S Us 169 Hwy
Olathe KS 66062
913 782-5300

(G-8100)
TALLEY INC
19935 W 157th St (66062-3824)
PHONE..................................913 390-8484
Peter Brake, *Manager*
EMP: 15
SALES (corp-wide): 113.9MM **Privately Held**
WEB: www.talleycom.com
SIC: 5065 Communication equipment
PA: Talley Inc.
12976 Sandoval St
Santa Fe Springs CA 90670
562 906-8000

(G-8101)
TANDEM TRUCK SERVICE INC
19944 W 157th St (66062-3823)
P.O. Box 51 (66051-0051)
PHONE..................................913 782-5454
Billy G Garton, *President*
EMP: 17 **EST:** 1960
SQ FT: 4,800
SALES (est): 2.1MM **Privately Held**
SIC: 4212 Local trucking, without storage

(G-8102)
TAX 911COM INCORPORATED
Also Called: Provident Payroll
501 N Mur Len Rd Ste B (66062-1258)
PHONE..................................913 712-8539
Bret Willoughby, *President*
EMP: 14
SALES: 220K **Privately Held**
WEB: www.willcpa.com
SIC: 8721 7291 Payroll accounting service; tax return preparation services

(G-8103)
TEAM DRIVE-AWAY INC
401 W Frontier Ln Ste 100 (66061-7250)
PHONE..................................913 825-4776
Steve Wambold, *CEO*
Micah Redman, *COO*
Al Heitman, *CFO*
Chris Pesce, *VP Finance*
Josh Allison, *VP Sales*
EMP: 150
SALES (est): 25.1MM **Privately Held**
SIC: 4731 Truck transportation brokers

(G-8104)
TECHNICAL MFG CONCEPTS INC
19000 W 158th St Ste B (66062-8012)
PHONE..................................913 764-1011
Carl Hayward, *President*
Dan Bolz, *Purchasing*
EMP: 25
SQ FT: 5,500
SALES (est): 4.7MM **Privately Held**
SIC: 3825 Test equipment for electronic & electric measurement

(G-8105)
TEE & BEE ELECTRIC COMPANY
1401 N Woodland St (66061-2723)
P.O. Box 12412, Shawnee Mission (66282-2412)
PHONE..................................913 782-8161
Jim Belcher, *Owner*
EMP: 12
SQ FT: 4,000
SALES (est): 940.1K **Privately Held**
SIC: 1731 General electrical contractor

(G-8106)
TEMP-CON INC
Also Called: Temp Con
15670 S Keeler St (66062-3516)
PHONE..................................913 768-4888
Jerry D Bain, *President*
Kent Myers, *Supervisor*
Heather Smith, *Executive Asst*
EMP: 96
SQ FT: 15,000
SALES: 20MM **Privately Held**
WEB: www.temp-con.net
SIC: 1796 7623 Installing building equipment; refrigeration repair service

(G-8107)
TENNESSEE INFO CONSORTIUM LLC
25501 W Valley Pkwy # 300 (66061-8453)
PHONE..................................913 498-3468
Craig Shinn, *Mng Member*
EMP: 30
SQ FT: 11,000
SALES (est): 1.4MM
SALES (corp-wide): 344.9MM **Publicly Held**
SIC: 7371 Computer software development
HQ: Nicusa, Inc.
25501 W Valley Pkwy # 300
Olathe KS 66061

(G-8108)
THATS A WRAP LLC
665 N Lindenwood Dr (66062-1276)
PHONE..................................913 390-0035
Roger Hammer, *President*
EMP: 30 **EST:** 2015
SALES (est): 1.6MM **Privately Held**
SIC: 8742 Business consultant

(G-8109)
TIME INC
Also Called: Tim Razumovsky
15585 S Keeler St (66062-3517)
PHONE..................................816 288-5394
Timophey V Razumovsky, *President*
EMP: 14
SALES (est): 1.4MM **Privately Held**
SIC: 4213 Trucking, except local

(G-8110)
TITAN CNSTR ORGANIZATION INC
11865 S Conley St (66061-9510)
PHONE..................................913 782-6700
Tom L Saul, *President*
John Holloway, *Vice Pres*
Michael Strenth, *Project Mgr*
EMP: 19
SQ FT: 8,000
SALES (est): 2MM **Privately Held**
WEB: www.titanbuilt.com
SIC: 1541 1542 Industrial buildings, new construction; renovation, remodeling & repairs: industrial buildings; commercial & office building, new construction; institutional building construction; commercial & office buildings, renovation & repair

(G-8111)
TITAN CONSTRUCTION INC
11865 S Conley St (66061-9510)
PHONE..................................913 782-6700
Tom Saul, *President*
George Rebeck, *CFO*
Craig Buller, *Treasurer*
Scott Gordon, *Admin Sec*
▲ **EMP:** 157
SALES (est): 17.2MM **Privately Held**
SIC: 1542 1522 Commercial & office building, new construction; apartment building construction

(G-8112)
TLC LAWN CARE INC
19600 W 159th St (66062-8989)
PHONE..................................913 780-5296
Daniel J Becker, *President*
Candice Becker, *Vice Pres*
EMP: 55
SQ FT: 10,000
SALES (est): 4.7MM **Privately Held**
WEB: www.tlclawncareinc.com
SIC: 0782 5083 0781 Lawn care services; lawn & garden machinery & equipment; landscape planning services

(G-8113)
TOMPKINS INDUSTRIES INC (PA)
Also Called: Tompkins Manufacturing
1912 E 123rd St (66061-5886)
P.O. Box 2110 (66051-2110)
PHONE..................................913 764-8088
Dave Dunlap, *President*
Benjamin Blades, *CFO*
◆ **EMP:** 40 **EST:** 1967
SQ FT: 35,000
SALES (est): 51.4MM **Privately Held**
WEB: www.tompkinsind.com
SIC: 5085 Pistons & valves

(G-8114)
TOP FLIGHT KIDS LEARNING CTR
300 S Rogers Rd (66062-1707)
PHONE..................................913 768-4661
John Rickless, *Owner*
Nicki England, *Director*
EMP: 24
SALES: 300K **Privately Held**
SIC: 8351 Preschool center

(G-8115)
TOROTEL INC (PA)
520 N Rogers Rd (66062-1211)
PHONE..................................913 747-6111
Dale H Sizemore Jr, *Ch of Bd*
Lisa Tang, *Business Mgr*
H James Serrone, *Vice Pres*
Heath C Hancock, *CFO*
Dale Sizemore, *Director*
EMP: 50 **EST:** 1956
SQ FT: 72,000
SALES: 20.5MM **Publicly Held**
WEB: www.torotelprod.com
SIC: 3677 3823 Inductors, electronic; magnetic flow meters, industrial process type

(G-8116)
TOROTEL PRODUCTS INC
550 N Rogers Rd (66062)
PHONE..................................913 747-6111
Dale H Sizemore Jr, *President*
Larry Morin, *Vice Pres*
Lindsay Chikes, *Purchasing*
Paul Stanton, *Engineer*
David Stanton, *Design Engr*
EMP: 151
SQ FT: 72,000
SALES (est): 20MM
SALES (corp-wide): 20.5MM **Publicly Held**
WEB: www.torotelproducts.com
SIC: 3769 3612 3728 3677 Guided missile & space vehicle parts & aux eqpt, rsch & dev; transformers, except electric; aircraft parts & equipment; electronic transformers
PA: Torotel, Inc.
520 N Rogers Rd
Olathe KS 66062
913 747-6111

(G-8117)
TOUCH ENTERPRISES LLC (PA)
117 N Cooper St (66061-3434)
PHONE..................................913 638-2130
Mark Gregory, *Exec Dir*
EMP: 20
SALES: 20MM **Privately Held**
SIC: 5199 5331 Variety store merchandise; variety stores

(G-8118)
TR SALES & DISTRIBUTION INC
Also Called: Catalog Dog
15352 S Keeler St Ste A (66062-2721)
P.O. Box 3267 (66063-1267)
PHONE..................................800 478-5468
Thomas Rine, *CEO*
EMP: 12
SALES: 2.9MM **Privately Held**
SIC: 3999 Pet supplies

(G-8119)
TRANSAM TRUCKING INC (PA)
15910 S Us 169 Hwy (66062-3800)
PHONE..................................913 782-5300
Russ McElliott, *President*
Sara Long, *Asst Controller*
Emily Eagan, *Human Res Dir*
Savannah Ernewein, *HR Admin*
Kari Fry, *Sales Mgr*
EMP: 699
SQ FT: 13,000
SALES (est): 131.3MM **Privately Held**
WEB: www.transamfinancial.com
SIC: 4213 Contract haulers

(G-8120)
TRI CITY ASSISTED LIVING LLC (PA)
Also Called: Bickford Senior Living
13795 S Mur Len Rd # 301 (66062-1675)
PHONE..................................913 782-3200
Michael D EBY, *President*
Judy Swartzell, *Senior VP*
Donna Moss, *Finance*
Natalie Janes, *Marketing Mgr*
Shawna Milatovich, *Exec Dir*
EMP: 75
SALES (est): 6.1MM **Privately Held**
SIC: 8361 Home for the aged

(G-8121)
TRI-COUNTY CONCRETE INC
15520 S Us 169 Hwy (66062-3508)
PHONE..................................913 764-7700
Jim McCourt, *President*
EMP: 25
SQ FT: 2,500
SALES (est): 2.4MM **Privately Held**
SIC: 3273 Ready-mixed concrete

(G-8122)
TRUDI R GRIN
Also Called: Pediatric Eye Care
11735 W 144th Ter (66062-8425)
PHONE..................................913 888-1888
Trudi R Grin, *Partner*
Melrilo Stass-Isern, *Partner*
Rebecca Jones, *Manager*
EMP: 10
SALES (est): 1.2MM **Privately Held**
SIC: 8011 Eyes, ears, nose & throat specialist: physician/surgeon

(G-8123)
TSUNAMI SURF RIDERS LLC
25501 W Valley Pkwy # 300 (66061-8453)
PHONE..................................913 498-3468
Harry H Herington, *Principal*
EMP: 10

▲ = Import ▼=Export
◆ =Import/Export

SALES (est): 124.8K
SALES (corp-wide): 344.9MM **Publicly Held**
SIC: 7374 Computer graphics service
HQ: Nicusa, Inc.
25501 W Valley Pkwy # 300
Olathe KS 66061

(G-8124)
TSVC INC (PA)
10841 S Ridgeview Rd (66061-6456)
PHONE..................................913 599-6886
EMP: 190
SALES: 751.7MM **Privately Held**
SIC: 8741 Business management

(G-8125)
TVH PARTS CO (PA)
16355 S Lone Elm Rd (66062-9238)
P.O. Box 1245 (66051-1245)
PHONE..................................913 829-1000
Patrick McLaughlin, *President*
Els Thermote, *Principal*
Dirk Von Holt, *Principal*
Karen Sprenger, *Editor*
Kevin Caggiano, *Regional Mgr*
◆ **EMP:** 300 **EST:** 1972
SQ FT: 67,500
SALES (est): 178.9MM **Privately Held**
SIC: 5084 Lift trucks & parts

(G-8126)
TWO GUYS & A GRILL
109 N Chester St (66061-3612)
PHONE..................................913 393-4745
Troy Tedder, *President*
EMP: 18
SALES (est): 449.7K **Privately Held**
SIC: 5812 7299 Grills (eating places); party planning service

(G-8127)
TYSON FOODS INC
20701 W 159th St (66062-9040)
PHONE..................................913 393-7000
Ginger Wehner, *Vice Pres*
John Tyson, *Branch Mgr*
Chris Ford, *Manager*
Susan Hobbs, *Executive*
▲ **EMP:** 11
SALES (corp-wide): 42.4B **Publicly Held**
SIC: 5078 Cold storage machinery
PA: Tyson Foods, Inc.
2200 W Don Tyson Pkwy
Springdale AR 72762
479 290-4000

(G-8128)
U BATHE PETS
100 S Parker St (66061-4044)
PHONE..................................913 829-3275
Hadley Warwick, *Owner*
EMP: 12
SALES (est): 144.7K **Privately Held**
SIC: 0752 Grooming services, pet & animal specialties

(G-8129)
U P S STORES
13505 S Mur Len Rd # 105 (66062-1600)
PHONE..................................913 829-3750
Stuart Ellers, *Owner*
EMP: 10
SQ FT: 1,200
SALES (est): 728.4K **Privately Held**
SIC: 7389 4731 7331 5943 Mailbox rental & related service; agents, shipping; mailing service; office forms & supplies

(G-8130)
U-HAUL CO OF OREGON
12540 S Rogers Rd (66062-1206)
PHONE..................................913 780-4494
Douglas Carrithers, *Manager*
EMP: 11
SALES (corp-wide): 3.7B **Publicly Held**
WEB: www.shouldersmotors.com
SIC: 7513 Truck rental & leasing, no drivers
HQ: U-Haul Co. Of Oregon
7100 Sw Mcewan Rd
Lake Oswego OR 97035
503 774-3203

(G-8131)
UMB BANK NATIONAL ASSOCIATION
Also Called: Olathe Branch
18261 W 119th St (66061-9507)
P.O. Box 419226, Kansas City MO (64141-6226)
PHONE..................................913 791-6600
Julie Hughes, *Branch Mgr*
EMP: 12
SALES (corp-wide): 1.1B **Publicly Held**
SIC: 6021 National commercial banks
HQ: Umb Bank, National Association
1010 Grand Blvd Fl 3
Kansas City MO 64106
816 842-2222

(G-8132)
UNITED OFFICE PRODUCTS INC
601 W Dennis Ave (66061-4307)
P.O. Box 845 (66051-0845)
PHONE..................................913 782-4441
James R Hutchinson, *President*
Margaret A Hutchinson, *Corp Secy*
Theresa Haney, *Vice Pres*
Shawn Hutchinson, *Vice Pres*
Kimberley Mitchell, *Vice Pres*
EMP: 23 **EST:** 1971
SQ FT: 6,000
SALES (est): 4.9MM **Privately Held**
SIC: 5943 5112 5021 Office forms & supplies; office supplies; office furniture

(G-8133)
UNITED RENTALS NORTH AMER INC
11615 S Rogers Rd (66062-1084)
PHONE..................................913 696-5628
Cary Barrows, *Manager*
EMP: 13
SALES (corp-wide): 8B **Publicly Held**
SIC: 7359 5082 Equipment rental & leasing; general construction machinery & equipment
HQ: United Rentals (North America), Inc.
100 Frederick St 700
Stamford CT 06902
203 622-3131

(G-8134)
UNIVERSAL CABLE SERVICES INC
18900 W 158th St Ste F (66062-8016)
PHONE..................................913 481-7839
John Howell, *President*
EMP: 15
SQ FT: 2,000
SALES (est): 1.2MM **Privately Held**
SIC: 4841 Cable television services; subscription television services

(G-8135)
UNIVERSAL COMMUNICATIONS LLC
19915 W 161st St Ste E (66062-2762)
PHONE..................................913 839-1634
John Howell, *President*
Stephanie Hrabe, *Office Mgr*
EMP: 30
SALES: 5MM **Privately Held**
SIC: 1731 Fiber optic cable installation

(G-8136)
UNIVERSAL ELECTRIC INC
19947 W 162nd St Ste 103 (66062-3577)
PHONE..................................913 238-3024
EMP: 20
SALES: 2.5MM **Privately Held**
SIC: 1731 Electrical Contractor

(G-8137)
V G ELECTRACON INC
1812 E 123rd St (66061-5884)
PHONE..................................913 780-9995
Gregory Breedlove, *President*
Debbie Breedlove, *CFO*
EMP: 15
SQ FT: 4,000
SALES (est): 922.6K **Privately Held**
WEB: www.breedloveandassociates.com
SIC: 7291 Tax return preparation services

(G-8138)
VAN-WALL EQUIPMENT INC
Also Called: John Deere Authorized Dealer
1362 S Enterprise St (66061-5357)
PHONE..................................913 397-6009
Angela Gibson, *Vice Pres*
Kathy Johnson, *Human Res Mgr*
Mike Van Houweling, *Manager*
Bryan Gentner, *Manager*
Dusty Kostman, *Manager*
EMP: 30
SALES (corp-wide): 41.7MM **Privately Held**
SIC: 5083 7699 Farm implements; farm machinery repair
PA: Van-Wall Equipment, Inc.
22728 141st Dr
Perry IA 50220
515 465-5681

(G-8139)
VERMEER GREAT PLAINS INC (PA)
Also Called: Vermeer Equipment
15505 S Us 169 Hwy (66062-3507)
PHONE..................................913 782-3655
Art Swank, *President*
Virginia Swank, *Corp Secy*
Mark Sonnenberg, *VP Sales*
EMP: 23 **EST:** 1964
SQ FT: 13,000
SALES (est): 43.5MM **Privately Held**
WEB: www.vermeeroklahoma.com
SIC: 5082 Contractors' materials

(G-8140)
VILLA ST FRANCIS INC
16600 W 126th St (66062-1184)
PHONE..................................913 254-3264
John May, *CEO*
Debbie Fallon, *Director*
Jeff Kyle, *Director*
Sarah McEnerney, *Director*
Priscilla Salinas, *Director*
EMP: 225 **EST:** 1945
SQ FT: 225,871
SALES: 12.9MM **Privately Held**
SIC: 8051 8052 Skilled nursing care facilities; intermediate care facilities

(G-8141)
VINCENT PENNIPEDE OD (PA)
Also Called: Eye Associates
15257 W 135th St (66062-1534)
PHONE..................................913 780-9696
Vincent Pennipede Od, *Owner*
Brian Lojka Od, *Associate*
Mark L Siefkes Od, *Associate*
Mark L Siefkes, *Associate*
EMP: 24
SALES (est): 724.6K **Privately Held**
SIC: 8042 Specialized optometrists

(G-8142)
VISION TODAY INC
12120 S Strang Line Rd (66062-5219)
PHONE..................................913 397-9111
Matthew Philip Laurie, *Owner*
EMP: 14
SALES (est): 1.6MM **Privately Held**
SIC: 8011 5995 Physical medicine, physician/surgeon; opticians

(G-8143)
VOLUNTEERS WITH HEART INC
Also Called: Docs Whole Care
800 W Frontier Ln (66061-7216)
PHONE..................................913 563-5100
Gary Morsch, *President*
EMP: 14
SALES (est): 203.7K **Privately Held**
SIC: 8011 Physical medicine, physician/surgeon

(G-8144)
W R GRACE & CO - CONN
Also Called: W R Grace Construction Pdts
701 S Kansas Ave (66061-4526)
PHONE..................................913 764-8040
Allan Bandyk, *Manager*
EMP: 5
SALES (corp-wide): 1.9B **Publicly Held**
WEB: www.grace.com
SIC: 2899 Concrete curing & hardening compounds
HQ: W. R. Grace & Co.-Conn.
7500 Grace Dr
Columbia MD 21044
410 531-4000

(G-8145)
WAGONER BANKRUPTCY GROUP PC
Also Called: Wm Law
15095 W 116th St (66062-1098)
PHONE..................................913 422-0909
Jeffrey Wagoner, *President*
EMP: 14
SALES: 1.1MM **Privately Held**
SIC: 8111 Bankruptcy law

(G-8146)
WALGREEN CO
Also Called: Walgreens
545 E Santa Fe St (66061-3462)
PHONE..................................913 393-2757
Pat Starr, *Manager*
EMP: 25
SALES (corp-wide): 136.8B **Publicly Held**
WEB: www.walgreens.com
SIC: 5912 7384 7299 Drug stores; photofinishing laboratory; personal document & information services
HQ: Walgreen Co.
200 Wilmot Rd
Deerfield IL 60015
800 925-4733

(G-8147)
WALGREEN CO
Also Called: Walgreens
13450 S Blackbob Rd (66062-1503)
PHONE..................................913 829-3176
Karim Schuaib, *Manager*
EMP: 30
SALES (corp-wide): 136.8B **Publicly Held**
WEB: www.walgreens.com
SIC: 5912 7384 Drug stores; photofinishing laboratory
HQ: Walgreen Co.
200 Wilmot Rd
Deerfield IL 60015
800 925-4733

(G-8148)
WATER DEPOT INC
15605 S Keeler Ter Ste B (66062-3588)
PHONE..................................913 782-7277
Weldel J Vice, *President*
EMP: 6
SALES: 600K **Privately Held**
WEB: www.thewaterdepot.com
SIC: 2086 Water, pasteurized: packaged in cans, bottles, etc.

(G-8149)
WEBCO MANUFACTURING INC
20570 W 162nd St (66062-2750)
PHONE..................................913 764-7111
Peter Badami, *President*
Matt Briegel, *Vice Pres*
Gary Rettman, *Vice Pres*
Kara Barlett, *Purchasing*
Clayton Rockers, *Engineer*
EMP: 100
SALES (est): 28.3MM **Privately Held**
WEB: www.webcomfg.com
SIC: 3444 7692 Sheet metalwork; welding repair

(G-8150)
WELLS FARGO & COMPANY
2137 E Santa Fe St Ste A (66062-1667)
PHONE..................................913 782-9603
EMP: 12
SALES (corp-wide): 101B **Publicly Held**
SIC: 6021 National commercial banks
PA: Wells Fargo & Company
420 Montgomery St Fmt
San Francisco CA 94104
866 249-3302

(G-8151)
WEST SIDE KIDS DAY OUT PROGRAM
1700 W Santa Fe St (66061-5055)
PHONE..................................913 764-0813
Cindy Potter, *Director*
EMP: 13

GEOGRAPHIC

SALES (est): 245.7K **Privately Held**
SIC: 8351 Preschool center

(G-8152)
WESTERN CHEMICAL PUMPS INC
603 S Kansas Ave (66061-4524)
PHONE..................................913 829-1888
Thomas J Seitz Jr, *President*
EMP: 22 **EST:** 1971
SQ FT: 5,000
SALES (est): 3.9MM **Privately Held**
SIC: 3599 Machine shop, jobbing & repair

(G-8153)
WHEATLAND WATERS INC
Also Called: Culligan
19625 W Old 56th Hwy (66061)
P.O. Box 2170 (66051-2170)
PHONE..................................785 267-0512
Connie Rishworth, *Chairman*
Dave Brewer, *COO*
William Rishworth, *Vice Pres*
EMP: 55 **EST:** 1951
SQ FT: 35,000
SALES (est): 6.2MM **Privately Held**
WEB: www.culligankc.com
SIC: 5999 5074 5149 7359 Water purification equipment; fire extinguishers; water softeners; mineral or spring water bottling; equipment rental & leasing
PA: Enrec Enterprises, Inc
19625 W Old Highway 56
Olathe KS 66061

(G-8154)
WILBUR INC
Also Called: Community Gates SEC Solutions
12285 S Nelson Rd (66061-5532)
PHONE..................................913 207-6535
Larry Wilbur, *President*
Patricia Wilbur, *Vice Pres*
Randy Carlson, *Treasurer*
Donna Carlson, *Admin Sec*
EMP: 11
SALES (est): 1.4MM **Privately Held**
SIC: 3699 4225 Security devices; warehousing, self-storage

(G-8155)
WINCHESTER PLACE PET CARE CTR
15070 W 116th St (66062-1000)
PHONE..................................913 451-2827
B Vinson Rucker, *Owner*
EMP: 10
SALES (est): 320K **Privately Held**
WEB: www.winchesterpetcare.com
SIC: 0742 0752 Animal hospital services, pets & other animal specialties; boarding services, kennels; grooming services, pet & animal specialties

(G-8156)
WITZKES SCREEN PRINTING
1165 W Dennis Ave (66061-5229)
PHONE..................................913 839-8270
Sheldon Witzke, *Owner*
EMP: 6
SALES: 270K **Privately Held**
SIC: 2759 Commercial printing

(G-8157)
WOLF CREEK GOLF LINKS INC
18695 S Lackman Rd (66062-9589)
PHONE..................................913 592-3329
Rodney Wray, *General Mgr*
Bill Irving, *Superintendent*
Marla Burvee, *Technology*
EMP: 50
SQ FT: 7,500
SALES (est): 3.2MM **Privately Held**
SIC: 7997 Golf club, membership

(G-8158)
WOLFERT LANDSCAPE CO LLC
17140 S Us 169 Hwy (66062-3540)
PHONE..................................913 592-4189
Tim Smith, *Opers Mgr*
Hank Wolfert,
Susan Wolfert,
EMP: 18 **EST:** 1978
SQ FT: 2,000
SALES (est): 1.5MM **Privately Held**
SIC: 0782 Landscape contractors; lawn care services

(G-8159)
WOOD RE NEW JOCO INC
11507 S Strang Line Rd A (66062-4902)
PHONE..................................913 661-9663
Wayne Howe, *President*
Patricia Howe, *Principal*
EMP: 5
SALES: 200K **Privately Held**
WEB: www.woodrenew.com
SIC: 1521 2491 1751 1542 Patio & deck construction & repair; wood preserving; carpentry work; commercial & office buildings, renovation & repair

(G-8160)
WOOD ROT PRO
15126 W 157th Ter (66062-3674)
PHONE..................................913 638-5732
Ben Romano, *Owner*
EMP: 6
SALES (est): 418.9K **Privately Held**
SIC: 2491 Wood preserving

(G-8161)
WOOFS PLAY & STAY INC
585 N Central St (66061-4868)
PHONE..................................913 768-9663
Chad Wade, *President*
EMP: 15
SALES (est): 261.9K **Privately Held**
SIC: 0752 Grooming services, pet & animal specialties

(G-8162)
WYNCROFT HILL APARTMENTS
Also Called: Homestead
12235 S Blackbob Rd (66062-1008)
PHONE..................................913 829-1404
Jessica Harns, *Office Mgr*
EMP: 15 **EST:** 2007
SALES (est): 1.1MM **Privately Held**
SIC: 6513 6531 Apartment hotel operation; rental agent, real estate

(G-8163)
YOUNG MENS CHRISTIAN GR KANSAS
Also Called: Hastings Books Music & Video
21400 W 153rd St (66061-5449)
PHONE..................................913 393-9622
Erica Ritter, *Director*
EMP: 150
SALES (corp-wide): 48.1MM **Privately Held**
WEB: www.ymca-kc.org
SIC: 8641 7991 8351 7032 Youth organizations; physical fitness facilities; child day care services; youth camps; individual & family services
PA: Young Men's Christian Association Of Greater Kansas City
3100 Broadway Blvd # 1020
Kansas City MO 64111
816 561-9622

(G-8164)
YOUNG MENS CHRISTIAN GR KANSAS
Also Called: Olathe Family YMCA
1700 E Pawnee Dr (66062-3200)
PHONE..................................913 782-7707
AMI Henry, *Branch Mgr*
EMP: 73
SALES (corp-wide): 48.1MM **Privately Held**
WEB: www.ymca-kc.org
SIC: 8641 7991 8351 7032 Youth organizations; physical fitness facilities; child day care services; youth camps; individual & family services
PA: Young Men's Christian Association Of Greater Kansas City
3100 Broadway Blvd # 1020
Kansas City MO 64111
816 561-9622

(G-8165)
YUSEN LOGISTICS AMERICAS INC
16500 Indian Creek Pkwy # 108
(66062-1429)
PHONE..................................913 768-4484
Fax: 913 815-5047
EMP: 20
SALES (corp-wide): 20.2B **Privately Held**
SIC: 4731 Freight Transportation Arrangement
HQ: Yusen Logistics (Americas) Inc.
300 Lighting Way Ste 600
Secaucus NJ 07094
201 553-3800

Olpe
Lyon County

(G-8166)
OLPE STATE BANK INC
202 Westphalia St (66865-9802)
P.O. Box 207 (66865-0207)
PHONE..................................620 475-3213
Joseph J Wendling, *President*
Beth Skalsky, *Loan Officer*
EMP: 12 **EST:** 1905
SQ FT: 5,000
SALES: 1.6MM **Privately Held**
WEB: www.olpestatebank.com
SIC: 6022 State trust companies accepting deposits, commercial

(G-8167)
PANHANDLE EASTRN PIPE LINE LP
985 Road 90 (66865-9367)
PHONE..................................620 475-3226
Gary Trear, *Branch Mgr*
EMP: 18
SALES (corp-wide): 54B **Publicly Held**
SIC: 4922 Natural gas transmission
HQ: Panhandle Eastern Pipe Line Company, Lp
8111 Westchester Dr # 600
Dallas TX 75225
214 981-0700

Olsburg
Pottawatomie County

(G-8168)
ASSOCIATION OF KANSAS NEBRASKA
Also Called: Broken Arrow Ranch
1950 Sagebrush Rd (66520-9715)
P.O. Box 65 (66520-0065)
PHONE..................................785 468-3638
Darin Gottfried, *Vice Pres*
John Sweigart, *Vice Pres*
John Clark, *Manager*
EMP: 10
SALES (corp-wide): 10.5MM **Privately Held**
WEB: www.ks-ne.org
SIC: 7032 Bible camp
HQ: Kansas-Nebraska Association Of Seventh-Day Adventists
3440 Sw Urish Rd
Topeka KS 66614
785 478-4726

(G-8169)
UNION STATE BANK INC (PA)
204 E Highway 16 (66520-9766)
P.O. Box 67 (66520-0067)
PHONE..................................785 468-3341
Dan A Holt, *President*
EMP: 26 **EST:** 1910
SALES: 1.3MM **Privately Held**
SIC: 6022 State trust companies accepting deposits, commercial

(G-8170)
V & V ELECTRIC INC
7860 Greene Rd (66520-9718)
PHONE..................................785 468-3364
Victor S Olson II, *President*
Todd Olson, *Vice Pres*
Victor Olson III, *Treasurer*
Patricia Olson, *Admin Sec*
EMP: 10
SALES (est): 774.1K **Privately Held**
SIC: 1731 Electrical work

Onaga
Pottawatomie County

(G-8171)
BANK OF BLUE VALLEY
301 Leonard St (66521-9485)
P.O. Box 180 (66521-0180)
PHONE..................................785 889-4211
Michael D Major, *Vice Pres*
Nick Hrencher, *Branch Mgr*
Jolene Wiltz, *Officer*
EMP: 30 **Publicly Held**
SIC: 6022 State trust companies accepting deposits, commercial
HQ: Bank Of Blue Valley
11935 Riley St
Overland Park KS 66213
913 338-1000

(G-8172)
COMMUNITY HEALTHCARE SYS INC
Also Called: Community Health System
120 W 8th St (66521-9574)
P.O. Box 460 (66521-0460)
PHONE..................................785 889-4241
Marcia Walsh, *Director*
EMP: 10
SALES (corp-wide): 28.4MM **Privately Held**
SIC: 8062 8011 Hospital, affiliated with AMA residency; clinic, operated by physicians
PA: Community Healthcare System, Inc.
120 W 8th St
Onaga KS 66521
785 889-4274

(G-8173)
COMMUNITY HEALTHCARE SYS INC (PA)
120 W 8th St (66521-9574)
P.O. Box 460 (66521-0460)
PHONE..................................785 889-4274
Greg Unruh, *President*
Jeremy Brandt, *Med Doctor*
Marlene Wolfe, *Executive Asst*
Cindy Flentie, *Recruiter*
Manda Thompson,
EMP: 202
SQ FT: 95,000
SALES: 28.4MM **Privately Held**
SIC: 8062 8082 Hospital, affiliated with AMA residency; home health care services

(G-8174)
DESERET HLTH RHAB AT ONAGA LLC
Also Called: Golden Acres Nursing Center
500 Western St (66521-9424)
P.O. Box 179 (66521-0179)
PHONE..................................785 889-4227
John Robertson, *President*
Scott Stingham, *Vice Pres*
EMP: 45
SALES (est): 2.8MM **Privately Held**
SIC: 8051 Skilled nursing care facilities
PA: Deseret Health Group, Llc.
190 S Main St
Bountiful UT 84010

(G-8175)
DOT GREEN BIOPLASTICS LLC
Also Called: Green DOT
210 S Leonard St (66521-9796)
PHONE..................................785 889-4600
Harbaugh Sarah, *Sales Staff*
Mark Remmert, *Branch Mgr*
EMP: 7
SALES (est): 885.4K
SALES (corp-wide): 3MM **Privately Held**
SIC: 2821 Plastics materials & resins
PA: Dot Green Bioplastics Inc
527 Commercial St Ste 310
Emporia KS 66801
620 273-8919

(G-8176)
FARMERS STATE BNK OF WSTMRLAND
301 Leonard St (66521-9485)
P.O. Box 180 (66521-0180)
PHONE..................................785 889-4211
EMP: 15
SALES (est): 3.7MM
SALES (corp-wide): 6.9MM **Privately Held**
SIC: 6022 State trust companies accepting deposits, commercial
PA: The Farmers State Bank Of Westmoreland
307 Main St
Westmoreland KS 66549
785 457-3316

(G-8177)
KANSAS ASSN FOR CONSERV & ENVR
22900 Independence Rd (66521-9724)
PHONE..................................785 889-4384
Laura Downey, *Branch Mgr*
EMP: 6
SALES (corp-wide): 233.6K **Privately Held**
SIC: 3944 Kites
PA: The Kansas Association For Conservation & Environmental Education
2610 Claflin Rd
Manhattan KS 66502
785 532-3322

(G-8178)
ONAGA HISTORICAL SOCIETY
310 E 2nd St (66521)
P.O. Box 443 (66521-0443)
PHONE..................................785 889-7104
Linda Tessendorf, *President*
Debbie Berges,
EMP: 20
SALES (est): 777.6K **Privately Held**
SIC: 8699 Historical club

(G-8179)
OTTAWAY AMUSEMENT CO INC
19650 Straight Creek Rd (66521-9511)
PHONE..................................316 529-0086
Laney Flattery, *Principal*
EMP: 8
SALES (est): 611.9K **Privately Held**
SIC: 2711 Newspapers

Opolis
Crawford County

(G-8180)
COUNTRY CRAFTS
306 S Walnut St (66760)
P.O. Box 86 (66760-0086)
PHONE..................................620 232-1818
Charles Mertz, *Owner*
Debbie Hertz, *Co-Owner*
EMP: 5
SQ FT: 3,600
SALES: 190K **Privately Held**
SIC: 2499 Decorative wood & woodwork

Osage City
Osage County

(G-8181)
BROWN MANAGEMENT INC
Also Called: Marilynn's Place
Hwy 31 E (66523)
PHONE..................................785 528-3769
John Brown, *President*
Naomi Brown, *Treasurer*
EMP: 12
SQ FT: 9,000
SALES (est): 428.7K **Privately Held**
WEB: www.marilynnsplace.com
SIC: 5812 7299 Fast-food restaurant, chain; banquet hall facilities

(G-8182)
CONKLIN PLUMBING LLC
512 Main St (66523-1365)
PHONE..................................785 806-5827
Shawn Conklin, *Principal*
EMP: 11
SALES (est): 521.5K **Privately Held**
SIC: 1711 Plumbing contractors

(G-8183)
COTTON ONEIL OSAGE CITY
131 W Market St Ste B (66523-1099)
PHONE..................................785 528-3161
Carrie Hagemann, *Principal*
James Seeman, *Executive*
EMP: 13 **EST:** 2007
SALES (est): 482.4K **Privately Held**
SIC: 8011 General & family practice, physician/surgeon

(G-8184)
GRAN VILLAS
1403 Laing St (66523-9203)
PHONE..................................785 528-5095
Susan Korphanke, *Administration*
EMP: 14
SALES (est): 305.9K **Privately Held**
SIC: 8051 Convalescent home with continuous nursing care

(G-8185)
ORBIS CORPORATION
515 S 4th St (66523-1501)
PHONE..................................785 528-4875
Heath Oho, *Branch Mgr*
EMP: 120
SALES (corp-wide): 1.8B **Privately Held**
WEB: www.orbiscorporation.com
SIC: 3089 Synthetic resin finished products
HQ: Orbis Corporation
1055 Corporate Center Dr
Oconomowoc WI 53066
262 560-5000

(G-8186)
OSAGE COUNTY HERALD
527 Market St (66523-1157)
P.O. Box 266 (66523-0266)
PHONE..................................785 528-3511
Jodie Karns, *Principal*
EMP: 7
SALES (est): 322.9K **Privately Held**
SIC: 2711 Commercial printing & newspaper publishing combined; newspapers: publishing only, not printed on site

(G-8187)
RESOURCE CENTER FOR IND LIVING (PA)
1137 Laing St (66523-1635)
P.O. Box 257 (66523-0257)
PHONE..................................785 528-3105
Chad Wilkins, *Director*
Margaret Gallaway, *Director*
EMP: 70
SALES: 18.7MM **Privately Held**
WEB: www.rcilinc.org
SIC: 8322 Social services for the handicapped

(G-8188)
RH MONTGOMERY PROPERTIES INC
Also Called: Osage Nursing Center
1017 Main St (66523-1249)
PHONE..................................785 528-3138
Chris Anderson, *Administration*
EMP: 50
SALES (corp-wide): 31.9MM **Privately Held**
SIC: 8051 Skilled nursing care facilities
PA: Rh Montgomery Properties, Inc.
214 N Scott St
Sikeston MO 63801
573 471-1113

(G-8189)
RURAL WATER DST 7 OSAGE CNTY
104 N 9th St (66523-1187)
P.O. Box 31 (66523-0031)
PHONE..................................785 528-5090
Loren Bryan, *Owner*
EMP: 11 **EST:** 1973
SALES (est): 650K **Privately Held**
SIC: 4941 Water supply

(G-8190)
SALTCREEK FITNESS & REHAB
104 W Market St Ste B&C (66523-1277)
PHONE..................................785 528-1123
Kevin A Swindale, *Owner*
EMP: 11
SALES (est): 312.1K **Privately Held**
SIC: 8049 Physical therapist

Osawatomie
Miami County

(G-8191)
ABB INSTALLATION PRODUCTS INC
820 6th St (66064-1231)
PHONE..................................913 755-3181
Robert Davidson, *Opers Mgr*
EMP: 67
SALES (corp-wide): 36.7B **Privately Held**
WEB: www.tnb.com
SIC: 3585 Heating & air conditioning combination units
HQ: Abb Installation Products Inc.
860 Ridge Lake Blvd
Memphis TN 38120
901 252-5000

(G-8192)
DURHAM SCHOOL SERVICES L P
Also Called: Apple Butte Company
611 1/2 Parker Ave (66064-1407)
PHONE..................................913 755-3593
Doris Stephens, *Manager*
EMP: 22 **Privately Held**
SIC: 4151 School buses
HQ: Durham School Services, L. P.
2601 Navistar Dr
Lisle IL 60532
630 836-0292

(G-8193)
FIRST OPTION BANK AND TRUST (HQ)
601 Main St (66064-1420)
PHONE..................................913 294-3811
Blake Heid, *President*
Gregg P Lewis, *Exec VP*
Gerry Bates, *Vice Pres*
Keri Peterson, *Trust Officer*
Thelma Whiteford, *Shareholder*
EMP: 10 **EST:** 1923
SQ FT: 10,000
SALES: 11.6MM
SALES (corp-wide): 15MM **Privately Held**
WEB: www.firstoptionbank.com
SIC: 6021 National trust companies with deposits, commercial
PA: The Osawatomie Agency Inc
601 Main St
Osawatomie KS 66064
913 755-3811

(G-8194)
GUNDERSON RAIL SERVICES LLC
Also Called: Greenbrier Rail Services
610 Kelly Ave (66064-1200)
P.O. Box 265 (66064-0265)
PHONE..................................913 827-3536
David Shieles, *Branch Mgr*
EMP: 17
SALES (corp-wide): 3B **Publicly Held**
SIC: 4789 Railroad car repair
HQ: Gunderson Rail Services Llc
1 Centerpointe Dr Ste 200
Lake Oswego OR 97035
503 684-7000

(G-8195)
KANSAS DEPT FOR AGING & DISABI
Also Called: Osawatomie State Hospital
500 State Hospital Dr (66064-1813)
P.O. Box 500 (66064-0500)
PHONE..................................913 755-7000
Jerry REA, *Principal*
Venkata RAO, *Human Res Dir*
Jon Welsh, *Family Practiti*
Syed Akhter, *Internal Med*
EMP: 99 **Privately Held**
SIC: 8063 9441 Hospital for the mentally ill; administration of social & manpower programs;
HQ: Kansas Department For Aging And Disability Services
503 S Kansas Ave
Topeka KS 66603

(G-8196)
KANSAS DEPT FOR CHLDREN FMLIES
500 State Hospital Dr (66064-1813)
PHONE..................................913 755-7000
Martha Town, *Branch Mgr*
EMP: 125 **Privately Held**
SIC: 8093 9431 Mental health clinic, outpatient; administration of public health programs;
HQ: Kansas Department For Children And Families
555 S Kansas Ave
Topeka KS 66603
785 368-6358

(G-8197)
KANSAS DEPT FOR CHLDREN FMLIES
616 Brown Ave (66064-1415)
PHONE..................................913 755-2162
Connie Payne, *Branch Mgr*
EMP: 20 **Privately Held**
SIC: 8322 9441 Rehabilitation services; administration of social & manpower programs;
HQ: Kansas Department For Children And Families
555 S Kansas Ave
Topeka KS 66603
785 368-6358

(G-8198)
LIFE CARE CENTERS AMERICA INC
Also Called: Life Care Center of Osawatomie
1615 Parker Ave (66064-1703)
P.O. Box 159 (66064-0159)
PHONE..................................913 755-4165
Andy Buckholtz, *Branch Mgr*
EMP: 130
SALES (corp-wide): 144MM **Privately Held**
SIC: 8051 Convalescent home with continuous nursing care
PA: Life Care Centers Of America, Inc.
3570 Keith St Nw
Cleveland TN 37312
423 472-9585

(G-8199)
MIDWEST SURVEYS INC
35750 Plum Creek Rd (66064-4217)
P.O. Box 68 (66064-0068)
PHONE..................................913 755-2128
Steven W Windisch, *President*
Jackie L Windisch, *Corp Secy*
EMP: 5
SALES (est): 580.7K **Privately Held**
SIC: 1389 Well logging; oil field services

(G-8200)
OLATHE MEDICAL SERVICES INC
Also Called: Associates In Family Care
100 E Main St (66064-1126)
PHONE..................................913 755-3044
Joyce Stoughton, *Manager*
EMP: 18 **Privately Held**
SIC: 8011 General & family practice, physician/surgeon
PA: Olathe Medical Services, Inc
15435 W 134th Pl
Olathe KS 66062

(G-8201)
OSAWATOMIE AGENCY INC (PA)
Also Called: FIRST OPTION BANK
601 Main St (66064-1420)
P.O. Box 277 (66064-0277)
PHONE..................................913 755-3811
Gregg Lewis, *President*
Shelli Barnes, *Assistant VP*
Russell Pope, *Assistant VP*
Angela Kline, *Vice Pres*
Judy Miller, *Vice Pres*

EMP: 61
SQ FT: 10,000
SALES: 15MM **Privately Held**
SIC: 6022 State commercial banks

(G-8202)
OVER CAT PRODUCTS LLC
607 Kelly Ave (66064-1274)
PHONE..................................913 256-2126
EMP: 13 **EST:** 2016
SALES (est): 162.6K **Privately Held**
SIC: 7822 Motion picture & tape distribution

(G-8203)
RURAL WATER DISTRIBUTION 3
35680 Plum Creek Rd (66064-4218)
PHONE..................................913 755-4503
Lorna McCrea, *Ch of Bd*
EMP: 11
SALES (est): 1.1MM **Privately Held**
SIC: 4941 Water supply

(G-8204)
TECH-AIR INC
E Mill St (66064)
P.O. Box 337 (66064-0337)
PHONE..................................913 677-5777
Troy Troutman, *Manager*
EMP: 10
SALES (est): 1.5MM
SALES (corp-wide): 2.6MM **Privately Held**
WEB: www.techairinc.com
SIC: 3564 Air purification equipment
PA: Tech-Air, Inc.
10200 W 75th St Ste 102
Shawnee Mission KS 66204
913 677-5777

(G-8205)
TRI-KO INC (PA)
301 1st St (66064-1810)
PHONE..................................913 755-3025
Kris Straighter, *Director*
EMP: 38
SQ FT: 7,250
SALES: 6.7MM **Privately Held**
WEB: www.tri-ko.com
SIC: 8331 Sheltered workshop

(G-8206)
VINTAGE PARK AT OSAWATOMIE LLC
1520 Parker Ave (66064-1702)
PHONE..................................913 755-2167
Eddie Parades, *Principal*
EMP: 11
SALES (est): 402K **Privately Held**
SIC: 8059 Rest home, with health care

Osborne
Osborne County

(G-8207)
COUNTY OF OSBORNE
Also Called: Osborne County Ambulance
117 N 1st St (67473-2001)
PHONE..................................785 346-2379
Janice Boland, *Director*
EMP: 12 **Privately Held**
SIC: 4119 Ambulance service
PA: County Of Osborne
423 W Main St
Osborne KS 67473
785 346-2431

(G-8208)
FARMERS NAT BNK OF CANFIELD
102 W Main St (67473-2403)
PHONE..................................785 346-2000
Randall Wyatt, *Principal*
EMP: 16
SALES (corp-wide): 117.2MM **Publicly Held**
SIC: 6022 State commercial banks
HQ: The Farmers National Bank Of Canfield
20 S Broad St
Canfield OH 44406
330 533-3341

(G-8209)
HARDMAN WHOLESALE LLC
404 N 1st St (67473-1820)
P.O. Box 10 (67473-0010)
PHONE..................................785 346-2131
Jon Lambert, *President*
Randy G Caldwell, *General Mgr*
Sandy Lambert Jr, *Chairman*
Ted Lambert, *Vice Pres*
Sandy Lambert III, *Treasurer*
EMP: 34
SALES (est): 3.2MM
SALES (corp-wide): 859.8MM **Privately Held**
SIC: 5031 Building materials, exterior; building materials, interior; doors & windows; lumber: rough, dressed & finished
HQ: Pacific Mutual Door Company Inc
1525 W 31st St
Kansas City MO 64108
816 531-0161

(G-8210)
KW TRUCKING INC
1123 W Us Highway 24 (67473-1731)
P.O. Box 268 (67473-0268)
PHONE..................................785 346-5881
Lucy William, *President*
Barbara Mc Cammon, *Corp Secy*
Dan William, *Vice Pres*
EMP: 30
SALES (est): 4.5MM **Privately Held**
SIC: 4213 Trucking, except local

(G-8211)
MIDWAY CO-OP ASSOCIATION
411 N 1st St (67473-1821)
PHONE..................................785 346-5401
Dean Oliver, *Manager*
EMP: 19
SALES (corp-wide): 130.2MM **Privately Held**
SIC: 8611 Merchants' association
PA: Midway Co-Op Association
210 W Harrison St
Osborne KS
785 346-5451

(G-8212)
MIDWAY CO-OP ASSOCIATION
403 N 1st St (67473-1821)
PHONE..................................785 346-5451
Dell Princ, *General Mgr*
EMP: 10
SALES (corp-wide): 130.2MM **Privately Held**
WEB: www.midwaycoop.com
SIC: 8611 Merchants' association
PA: Midway Co-Op Association
210 W Harrison St
Osborne KS
785 346-5451

(G-8213)
MOORE BUICK CHEVROLET PONTIAC
Also Called: Swank-Standley Motors
120 S 2nd St (67473-2413)
P.O. Box 3676, Salina (67402-3676)
PHONE..................................785 346-5972
Kim Oore, *President*
EMP: 13
SALES (corp-wide): 3.5MM **Privately Held**
SIC: 7532 Body shop, automotive
PA: Moore Buick Chevrolet Pontiac
1114 W Us Highway 24
Osborne KS 67473
785 346-5417

(G-8214)
OSBORNE COUNTY MEMORIAL HOSP
424 W New Hampshire St (67473-2314)
P.O. Box 70 (67473-0070)
PHONE..................................785 346-2121
Michelle Watkins, *Vice Pres*
Linda Murphy, *Office Mgr*
Monica Mullender, *Nursing Mgr*
Mandy Simon, *Manager*
Tammy Spears, *Radiology Dir*
EMP: 62
SALES (est): 5.2MM **Privately Held**
WEB: www.ocmh.org
SIC: 8062 Hospital, affiliated with AMA residency

(G-8215)
OSBORNE DEVELOPMENT COMPANY
Also Called: PARKVIEW CARE CENTER
811 N 1st St (67473-1512)
P.O. Box 247 (67473-0247)
PHONE..................................785 346-2114
Robert Bloomer, *President*
Weldon Quenzer, *Treasurer*
T Robert Acre, *Admin Sec*
EMP: 75
SQ FT: 5,000
SALES: 3.4MM **Privately Held**
SIC: 8052 Personal care facility

(G-8216)
OSBORNE INDUSTRIES INC
120 N Industrial Ave (67473-1633)
P.O. Box 388 (67473-0388)
PHONE..................................785 346-2192
George Eakin, *President*
Vicki Corbett, *Vice Pres*
Brent Brown, *Engineer*
Richard Murphy, *Engineer*
Jason Rash, *Project Engr*
▼ **EMP:** 90 **EST:** 1973
SQ FT: 250,000
SALES: 13.3MM **Privately Held**
WEB: www.osborneindustries.com
SIC: 3089 Plastic processing

(G-8217)
OSBORNE INVESTMENT INC
102 W Main St (67473-2403)
P.O. Box 189 (67473-0189)
PHONE..................................785 346-2147
Steve Bihlmaire, *President*
Don Kopps, *Senior VP*
EMP: 10
SQ FT: 3,000
SALES: 2.3MM **Privately Held**
SIC: 7389 Personal service agents, brokers & bureaus

(G-8218)
SIMS FERTILIZER AND CHEM CO
1006 Industrial Ave (67473-1634)
P.O. Box 330 (67473-0330)
PHONE..................................785 346-5681
Kathy Sims, *President*
Joe Sims, *Vice Pres*
Katie Lix, *Treasurer*
EMP: 15
SQ FT: 12,800
SALES (est): 7.7MM **Privately Held**
SIC: 5191 Farm supplies

(G-8219)
STAR SEED INC (PA)
101 N Industrial Ave (67473-1633)
P.O. Box 228 (67473-0228)
PHONE..................................800 782-7311
Toll Free:..................................877 -
Thomas L Lutgen, *President*
Dennis Lutgen, *Corp Secy*
Schoen Denise, *Admin Asst*
EMP: 13
SQ FT: 30,000
SALES (est): 9.6MM **Privately Held**
WEB: www.gostarseed.com
SIC: 5191 5261 Seeds: field, garden & flower; nursery stock, seeds & bulbs

Oskaloosa
Jefferson County

(G-8220)
A CHILDS WORLD DAY CARE CTR
302 Madison St (66066-5342)
Rural Route 27 (66066)
PHONE..................................785 863-2161
Debbie Hunt, *Director*
EMP: 10
SALES: 244.6K **Privately Held**
SIC: 8351 Preschool center

(G-8221)
COUNTY OF JEFFERSON
Also Called: Weed Department
15049 94th St (66066-4158)
PHONE..................................785 863-2581
Mark Richard, *Director*
EMP: 10 **Privately Held**
WEB: www.theatreinthepark.org
SIC: 0721 9111 Weed control services after planting; county supervisors' & executives' offices
PA: County Of Jefferson
300 Jefferson St
Oskaloosa KS 66066

(G-8222)
COUNTY OF JEFFERSON
Also Called: Jefferson County Health Dept
1212 Walnut St (66066-4200)
PHONE..................................785 863-2447
Eileen Filbert, *Manager*
James Tweed, *Director*
EMP: 30 **Privately Held**
WEB: www.theatreinthepark.org
SIC: 8399 9111 Health systems agency; county supervisors' & executives' offices
PA: County Of Jefferson
300 Jefferson St
Oskaloosa KS 66066

(G-8223)
CRETEX
5150 Us 59 Hwy (66066-5099)
PHONE..................................785 863-3300
Ed Sxe, *Principal*
EMP: 20
SQ FT: 120,000
SALES: 2.1MM **Privately Held**
SIC: 5049 Engineers' equipment & supplies

(G-8224)
CRETEX CONCRETE PRODUCTS INC
5150 Us Hwy 59 (66066)
PHONE..................................785 863-3300
EMP: 19
SALES (corp-wide): 119.1MM **Privately Held**
SIC: 3272 Mfg Concrete Products
HQ: Cretex Concrete Products, Inc.
6655 Wedgwood Rd N # 130
Maple Grove MN 55311
763 545-7473

(G-8225)
EVEREST BANCSHARES INC
Also Called: State Bank
518 Liberty St (66066)
PHONE..................................785 863-2267
Larry C Bowser, *Branch Mgr*
EMP: 14 **Privately Held**
SIC: 6022 State trust companies accepting deposits, commercial
PA: Everest Bancshares, Inc.
545 Main St
Everest KS 66424

(G-8226)
HICKORY POINTE
Also Called: Hickory Pointe Care Rehab Ctr
700 Cherokee St (66066-5054)
P.O. Box 307 (66066-0307)
PHONE..................................785 863-2108
Roxanne Urban, *Corp Comm Staff*
Joyce Gonzales, *Office Mgr*
Lori Conway, *Director*
Linda Hubbard, *Director*
Debbie Hull, *Director*
EMP: 10
SALES: 2.8MM **Privately Held**
SIC: 8051 Convalescent home with continuous nursing care

(G-8227)
JEFFERSON CNTY SVC ORGNIZATION
Also Called: JEFFERSON CO SERV ORGANIZATION
610 Delaware St (66066-5431)
P.O. Box 212 (66066-0212)
PHONE..................................785 863-2637
Lynn Luck, *Director*
EMP: 23

▲ = Import ▼=Export
◆ =Import/Export

SALES: 235K **Privately Held**
SIC: 8322 Senior citizens' center or association

(G-8228)
KINGS CONSTRUCTION CO INC
205 Walnut St (66066-4000)
P.O. Box 188 (66066-0188)
PHONE..................................785 863-2534
Kent King, *President*
Dan C King, *Vice Pres*
EMP: 65
SQ FT: 2,000
SALES: 16.4MM **Privately Held**
SIC: 1629 Earthmoving contractor

(G-8229)
MCLAUGHLIN ROOFING LLC
3514 Elton Pkwy Ste 426a (66066)
PHONE..................................785 764-9582
David McLaughlin,
EMP: 12
SALES (est): 613.9K **Privately Held**
SIC: 1761 Roofing contractor

(G-8230)
STORMONT-VAIL HEALTHCARE INC
Also Called: Cotton-Oneil Clinicoskaloosa
209 W Jefferson St (66066-5359)
PHONE..................................785 863-3417
EMP: 383
SALES (corp-wide): 719MM **Privately Held**
SIC: 8062 General medical & surgical hospitals
PA: Stormont-Vail Healthcare, Inc.
1500 Sw 10th Ave
Topeka KS 66604
785 354-6000

Oswego
Labette County

(G-8231)
BOSS INDUSTRIES LLC
Also Called: Boss Tank
12057 Us Highway 59 (67356-8781)
PHONE..................................620 795-2143
William Neighbors,
EMP: 50
SQ FT: 5,000
SALES (est): 10.3MM **Privately Held**
WEB: www.bosstank.com
SIC: 3443 Industrial vessels, tanks & containers

(G-8232)
DIAMOND ACQUISITION LLC
2300 4th St (67356-2520)
P.O. Box 489 (67356-0489)
PHONE..................................620 795-2191
Michael Wedel, *Ch of Bd*
EMP: 43 **EST:** 2015
SALES (est): 1.8MM **Privately Held**
SIC: 3713 Truck & bus bodies

(G-8233)
DIAMOND COACH CORPORATION
2300 4th St (67356-2520)
P.O. Box 489 (67356-0489)
PHONE..................................620 795-2191
Richard Seybolt, *President*
Brady Bates, *Purch Agent*
Levi Gott, *Project Engr*
Pam Blackburn, *Treasurer*
Caleb Strickland, *Sales Engr*
EMP: 55
SALES (est): 10.1MM **Privately Held**
WEB: www.diamondcoach.com
SIC: 3711 5015 Bus & other large specialty vehicle assembly; buses, all types, assembly of; automotive parts & supplies, used

(G-8234)
LABETTE AVENUE
711 4th St (67356-1601)
P.O. Box 269 (67356-0269)
PHONE..................................620 795-2550
Rudy Taylor, *Owner*
Rena Russell, *Editor*
EMP: 10 **EST:** 2010
SALES (est): 383.1K **Privately Held**
SIC: 2711 Newspapers: publishing only, not printed on site

(G-8235)
OSWEGO MEDICAL CENTER LLC
800 Barker Dr Ste A (67356-9022)
PHONE..................................620 795-2386
Tom Pryor, *Director*
Bruce Bird,
EMP: 22
SALES (est): 1.1MM **Privately Held**
WEB: www.oswegomedical.com
SIC: 8011 Offices & clinics of medical doctors

(G-8236)
SOUTHEAST KANSAS COMMUNITY
Also Called: SE Kansas
207 Commercial St (67356-1616)
P.O. Box 183 (67356-0183)
PHONE..................................620 795-2102
Jennifer Hall, *Branch Mgr*
EMP: 10
SALES (corp-wide): 13.8MM **Privately Held**
WEB: www.sek-cap.com
SIC: 8351 Head start center, except in conjunction with school
PA: Southeast Kansas Community Action Program, Incorporated
401 N Sinnett St
Girard KS 66743
620 724-8204

(G-8237)
SPRIGGS CONCRETE INC
611 Kansas St (67356-2427)
PHONE..................................620 795-4841
Joe Spriggs, *President*
EMP: 30
SALES: 1.2MM **Privately Held**
SIC: 1771 Concrete work

(G-8238)
VIKING INDUSTRIES INC (PA)
12057 Us Highway 59 (67356-8781)
PHONE..................................620 795-2143
Dennis Banning, *President*
EMP: 16
SQ FT: 18,000
SALES: 2MM **Privately Held**
SIC: 3441 Building components, structural steel

(G-8239)
WESTIRLAND INDUSTRIES INC
1108 6th St (67356-1916)
P.O. Box 261 (67356-0261)
PHONE..................................620 795-4421
Ben Coppock, *President*
John Westall, *Vice Pres*
Mary Westall, *Admin Sec*
EMP: 6
SQ FT: 45,000
SALES (est): 62.4K **Privately Held**
SIC: 3089 Bearings, plastic

Otis
Rush County

(G-8240)
LINDE GAS NORTH AMERICA LLC
W Hwy 4 (67565)
PHONE..................................785 387-2281
Tim Pivonka, *Branch Mgr*
EMP: 8 **Privately Held**
SIC: 2813 Helium
HQ: Linde Gas North America Llc
200 Smrst Corp Blvd # 7000
Bridgewater NJ 08807

(G-8241)
MESSER LLC
3805 Highway 4 (67565-6519)
PHONE..................................785 387-2281
Tim Pivonka, *Manager*
EMP: 22
SALES (corp-wide): 1.4B **Privately Held**
SIC: 2813 Oxygen, compressed or liquefied; nitrogen; argon; hydrogen
HQ: Messer Llc
200 Somerset Corp Blvd # 7000
Bridgewater NJ 08807
908 464-8100

(G-8242)
WEST WIND ENERGY LLC
405 N Main St (67565-9504)
PHONE..................................785 387-2623
Scott Brantley, *Mng Member*
EMP: 12
SALES: 947K **Privately Held**
SIC: 3621 Windmills, electric generating

Ottawa
Franklin County

(G-8243)
ADAMSON BROTHERS SHEET METAL
Also Called: Adamson Bros Sheetmetal
102 S Walnut St (66067-2210)
PHONE..................................785 242-9273
Charles Adamson, *President*
Missy Adamson, *Vice Pres*
EMP: 10
SALES: 1.4MM **Privately Held**
SIC: 1711 Ventilation & duct work contractor; warm air heating & air conditioning contractor

(G-8244)
AMERICAN EAGLE OUTFITTERS INC
1301 N Davis Ave (66067-9778)
PHONE..................................724 779-5209
Michael Sostyk, *Manager*
Phil Miller, *Supervisor*
EMP: 300 **Publicly Held**
WEB: www.ae.com
SIC: 5621 4225 Ready-to-wear apparel, women's; general warehousing & storage
PA: American Eagle Outfitters, Inc.
77 Hot Metal St
Pittsburgh PA 15203

(G-8245)
ARVEST BANK
119 E 3rd St (66067-2313)
P.O. Box 57 (66067-0057)
PHONE..................................785 229-3950
Edward York, *Branch Mgr*
EMP: 17
SALES (corp-wide): 2.3B **Privately Held**
SIC: 6022 State commercial banks
HQ: Arvest Bank
103 S Bloomington St
Fayetteville AR 72745
479 575-1000

(G-8246)
ASTRO TRUCK COVERS INC
Also Called: Atc Truck Covers
801 E North St (66067-9680)
PHONE..................................785 448-5577
Robert B Combs, *President*
Philbert John, *Human Res Mgr*
EMP: 65
SALES: 6MM **Privately Held**
SIC: 3792 Travel trailers & campers

(G-8247)
B & B CINEMAS
Also Called: Plaza Theatre
209 S Main St (66067-2329)
PHONE..................................785 242-0777
Steve Bagby, *Owner*
Peggy Armstrong, *Manager*
EMP: 10
SQ FT: 6,250
SALES (est): 127.9K **Privately Held**
SIC: 7832 7841 Exhibitors, itinerant: motion picture; video disk/tape rental to the general public

(G-8248)
BANK OF WEST
700 S Main St (66067-2804)
PHONE..................................785 242-2804
Dennis Chanay, *Manager*
EMP: 11
SALES (corp-wide): 2.7B **Privately Held**
SIC: 6022 State trust companies accepting deposits, commercial
HQ: Bank Of The West
180 Montgomery St # 1400
San Francisco CA 94104
415 765-4800

(G-8249)
BISHOP BREW
120 E Dundee St (66067-1505)
PHONE..................................785 242-8920
Sheri Bishop, *Owner*
EMP: 6 **EST:** 1999
SALES (est): 456.6K **Privately Held**
SIC: 2082 Malt beverages

(G-8250)
BONES CO INC
3557 Highway 59 (66067-8223)
P.O. Box 41 (66067-0041)
PHONE..................................785 242-3070
David Bones, *President*
Mark Bones, *Vice Pres*
Cindy Bones, *Treasurer*
EMP: 5 **EST:** 1996
SQ FT: 3,750
SALES (est): 5MM **Privately Held**
SIC: 3537 Trucks: freight, baggage, etc.: industrial, except mining

(G-8251)
CARGOTEC HOLDING INC (HQ)
415 E Dundee St (66067-1543)
PHONE..................................785 242-2200
Lennart Brelin, *President*
Greg Hewitt, *President*
Mike Manning, *President*
Tom Spizzirri, *Regional Mgr*
Robert Inchausti, *Vice Pres*
EMP: 340
SALES (est): 192.1MM
SALES (corp-wide): 3.6B **Privately Held**
SIC: 3593 3537 Fluid power cylinders, hydraulic or pneumatic; industrial trucks & tractors
PA: Cargotec Oyj
Porkkalankatu 5
Helsinki 00180
207 774-000

(G-8252)
CARGOTEC USA INC
1230 N Mulberry St (66067)
PHONE..................................785 229-7111
EMP: 5 **EST:** 1962
SALES (est): 638.7K
SALES (corp-wide): 3.6B **Privately Held**
SIC: 3535 Unit handling conveying systems
HQ: Cargotec Finland Oy
Ruskontie 55
Tampere 33710
207 775-000

(G-8253)
CARRIAGE SERVICES INC
Also Called: Lamb-Roberts-Heise Funeral HM
325 S Hickory St (66067-2310)
P.O. Box 14 (66067-0014)
PHONE..................................785 242-3550
EMP: 11 **Publicly Held**
SIC: 7261 Funeral home
PA: Carriage Services, Inc.
3040 Post Oak Blvd # 300
Houston TX 77056

(G-8254)
CITY OF OTTAWA
Also Called: City of Ottawa Power Plant
1000 W 2nd St (66067)
PHONE..................................785 229-3750
David Hunsaker, *Superintendent*
EMP: 11 **EST:** 1867
SALES (est): 1.1MM **Privately Held**
SIC: 4939 Combination utilities

(G-8255)
CITY OF OTTAWA
Also Called: City of Ottawa Utility Center
324 S Beech St (66067-2657)
P.O. Box 358 (66067-0358)
PHONE..................................785 229-3710
Dana Stevenson, *Manager*
EMP: 25 **Privately Held**

GEOGRAPHIC

WEB: www.cityofottawa.org
SIC: 4939 Combination utilities
PA: City Of Ottawa
101 S Hickory St
Ottawa KS 66067
785 242-2190

(G-8256)
CLARCOR AIR FILTRATION PDTS
Also Called: Parker ATI
1612 N Davis Ave (66067-9783)
PHONE..................................785 242-1811
Kevin Bush, *President*
EMP: 35
SALES (corp-wide): 14.3B **Publicly Held**
WEB: www.ati-filters.com
SIC: 3564 3569 Filters, air: furnaces, air conditioning equipment, etc.; filters
HQ: Clarcor Air Filtration Products, Inc
100 River Ridge Cir
Jeffersonville IN 47130
502 969-2304

(G-8257)
COF RESIDENTIAL AUTHORITY INC
1516 N Davis Ave (66067-9781)
P.O. Box 459 (66067-0459)
PHONE..................................785 242-5035
Dan L Andrews, *Exec Dir*
Dan Andrews, *Exec Dir*
EMP: 11 **EST:** 2001
SALES: 124.7K **Privately Held**
SIC: 6514 Dwelling operators, except apartments

(G-8258)
COF TRAINING SERVICES INC (PA)
1516 N Davis Ave (66067-9781)
PHONE..................................785 242-5035
Benita Howard, *Manager*
Connie Larios, *Manager*
David C Patton, *Director*
EMP: 100
SQ FT: 43,000
SALES: 8.3MM **Privately Held**
SIC: 8331 8361 Sheltered workshop; residential care for the handicapped

(G-8259)
COF TRAINING SERVICES INC
707 N Cherry St (66067-1615)
PHONE..................................785 242-6064
Dan Andrews, *Branch Mgr*
EMP: 65
SALES (corp-wide): 8.3MM **Privately Held**
SIC: 8331 Sheltered workshop
PA: Cof Training Services, Inc.
1516 N Davis Ave
Ottawa KS 66067
785 242-5035

(G-8260)
COUNTY OF FRANKLIN
Also Called: Franklin County Ambulance Svc
219 E 14th St (66067-3542)
PHONE..................................785 229-7300
Brian Ferguson, *Sheriff*
Nick Robbins, *Chief*
James Haag, *Director*
EMP: 16
SALES (est): 569.8K **Privately Held**
WEB: www.fcmhc.com
SIC: 4119 Ambulance service
PA: County Of Franklin
315 S Main St Rm 106
Ottawa KS 66067
785 229-3410

(G-8261)
COUNTY OF FRANKLIN
Also Called: Old Depot Museum
135 W Tecumseh St (66067-1902)
P.O. Box 145 (66067-0145)
PHONE..................................785 242-1250
Deborah Barker, *Director*
EMP: 20
SALES (est): 138.6K **Privately Held**
WEB: www.fcmhc.com
SIC: 8412 Museum
PA: County Of Franklin
315 S Main St Rm 106
Ottawa KS 66067
785 229-3410

(G-8262)
CROOKS FLOOR COVERING
636 N Main St (66067-1925)
PHONE..................................785 242-4153
Dick Crooks, *Owner*
Wanda Crooks, *Co-Owner*
EMP: 6
SQ FT: 6,000
SALES (est): 940.5K **Privately Held**
SIC: 5713 2434 Floor covering stores; wood kitchen cabinets; vanities, bathroom: wood

(G-8263)
CROWN REALTY OF KANSAS INC
336 S Main St (66067-2332)
PHONE..................................785 242-7700
Randall L Renoud, *Broker*
Don Burroughs, *Manager*
EMP: 12
SALES (corp-wide): 10MM **Privately Held**
WEB: www.crownrealty.com
SIC: 6531 Real estate brokers & agents
PA: Crown Realty Of Kansas Inc
102 S Silver St
Paola KS
913 557-4333

(G-8264)
DEACONESS LONG TERM CARE OF MI
Also Called: Ottawa Rtirement Vlg Vlg Manor
1100 W 15th St Ofc (66067-3956)
PHONE..................................785 242-5399
Sue Fergson, *Administration*
EMP: 140 **Privately Held**
WEB: www.deaconessltc.org
SIC: 8059 Nursing home, except skilled & intermediate care facility
PA: Deaconess Long Term Care Of Missouri, Inc.
330 Straight St Ste 310
Cincinnati OH 45219

(G-8265)
DEACONESS LONG TERM CARE OF MI
Also Called: Ottawa Rtrment Vlg Vlg Med Svc
1527 S Twyman St (66067-3478)
PHONE..................................785 242-9378
Sue Ferguson, *Manager*
EMP: 17 **Privately Held**
WEB: www.deaconessltc.org
SIC: 8059 Nursing home, except skilled & intermediate care facility
PA: Deaconess Long Term Care Of Missouri, Inc.
330 Straight St Ste 310
Cincinnati OH 45219

(G-8266)
EAST CENTRAL KANSAS ECONOMIC (PA)
Also Called: ECKAN
1320 S Ash St (66067-3419)
P.O. Box 40 (66067-0040)
PHONE..................................785 242-6413
Richard Jackson, *CEO*
Aaron Heckman, *COO*
Renessa Mehrtens, *COO*
Thor Brown, *Human Res Dir*
Lynnette Fields, *Director*
EMP: 30
SQ FT: 19,000
SALES: 10.1MM **Privately Held**
SIC: 8322 Social service center

(G-8267)
EAST CNTL KANS AREA AGCY ON AG
117 S Main St (66067-2327)
PHONE..................................785 242-7200
Elizabeth Maxwell, *Director*
EMP: 20
SQ FT: 2,400
SALES: 2.8MM **Privately Held**
WEB: www.eckaaa.state.ks.us
SIC: 8322 Senior citizens' center or association

(G-8268)
ECONO LODGE
2331 S Cedar St (66067-9534)
PHONE..................................785 242-3400
Ranchor Shanker, *President*
Andy Patel, *General Mgr*
Govind Patel, *Admin Sec*
EMP: 20
SALES (est): 786.1K **Privately Held**
SIC: 7011 Hotels & motels

(G-8269)
ELECTRICAL ENTERPRISES INC
414 W Wilson St (66067)
PHONE..................................785 242-7971
Lori Hoy, *President*
EMP: 27
SQ FT: 4,000
SALES (est): 2.6MM **Privately Held**
SIC: 1731 General electrical contractor

(G-8270)
ELIZABETH LAYTON CENTER INC
2537 Eisenhower Rd (66067-9482)
P.O. Box 677 (66067-0677)
PHONE..................................785 242-3780
Reg Ayres, *Principal*
John Peimann, *CFO*
Diane Drake, *Exec Dir*
EMP: 90
SALES: 7.6MM **Privately Held**
SIC: 8093 Mental health clinic, outpatient

(G-8271)
ERNEST-SPENCER METALS INC
Also Called: Ernest Spencer Custom Coatings
1510 N Davis Ave (66067-9781)
PHONE..................................785 242-8538
John Smith, *Branch Mgr*
EMP: 50 **Privately Held**
SIC: 3441 Fabricated structural metal
PA: Ernest-Spencer Metals, Inc.
3323 82nd St
Meriden KS 66512

(G-8272)
FASHION INC
Also Called: Steeltec
1019 E North St (66067-9684)
P.O. Box 1050 (66067-1050)
PHONE..................................785 242-8111
Lonnie King, *CEO*
Dwayne Kibbe, *Vice Pres*
EMP: 50
SQ FT: 116,000
SALES (est): 20.8MM **Privately Held**
WEB: www.fashioninc.com
SIC: 3444 Canopies, sheet metal; awnings, sheet metal; roof deck, sheet metal

(G-8273)
FOURTH JUDICIAL DIST COMNITY C
1418 S Main St Ste 3 (66067-3544)
PHONE..................................785 229-3510
Keith Clark, *Director*
EMP: 12
SALES (est): 311K **Privately Held**
SIC: 8322 Probation office

(G-8274)
FRANKLIN CNTY CNCER FOUNDATION
215 S Main St (66067-2329)
PHONE..................................785 242-6703
Darlene Armstrong, *President*
EMP: 15
SALES: 72.6K **Privately Held**
SIC: 8322 Individual & family services

(G-8275)
GENERAL ELECTRIC COMPANY
324 S Beech St (66067-2657)
PHONE..................................785 229-3710
Dana Stevenson, *Manager*
EMP: 24
SALES (corp-wide): 121.6B **Publicly Held**
SIC: 1731 Electrical work
PA: General Electric Company
5 Necco St
Boston MA 02210
617 443-3000

(G-8276)
H&R BLOCK INC
Also Called: H & R Block
2334 S Princeton St (66067-4028)
PHONE..................................913 837-5418
James Cameron, *Branch Mgr*
EMP: 12
SALES (corp-wide): 3B **Publicly Held**
SIC: 7291 Tax return preparation services
PA: H&R Block, Inc.
1 H&R Block Way
Kansas City MO 64105
816 854-3000

(G-8277)
HAMM INC
745 N Locust St (66067-1952)
P.O. Box 4449, Topeka (66604-0449)
PHONE..................................785 242-1045
Craig Hinderliter, *Branch Mgr*
EMP: 10
SALES (corp-wide): 2.1B **Publicly Held**
SIC: 1771 Concrete work
HQ: Hamm, Inc.
609 Perry Pl
Perry KS 66073
785 597-5111

(G-8278)
HASTY AWARDS INC
1015 Enterprise St (66067-4101)
PHONE..................................785 242-5297
Steve Hasty, *Owner*
Anne Hasty, *Vice Pres*
Jason Crist, *Sales Staff*
◆ **EMP:** 60
SALES (est): 15MM **Privately Held**
WEB: www.hastyawards.com
SIC: 3499 3993 2396 Trophies, metal, except silver; novelties & specialties, metal; signs & advertising specialties; automotive & apparel trimmings

(G-8279)
KALMAR SOLUTIONS LLC (DH)
415 E Dundee St (66067-1543)
PHONE..................................785 242-2200
Ton Case, *President*
Jorma Tirkkonen, *President*
Tomas Blomberg, *Prdtn Mgr*
Alan Wilson, *Opers Staff*
Tim Bunch, *Engineer*
◆ **EMP:** 340
SQ FT: 130,000
SALES (est): 144.6MM
SALES (corp-wide): 3.6B **Privately Held**
SIC: 3537 3714 3713 3643 Forklift trucks; fifth wheel, motor vehicle; truck & bus bodies; current-carrying wiring devices

(G-8280)
KANSAS STATE BANK (PA)
236 N Main St (66067-1919)
P.O. Box 720 (66067-0720)
PHONE..................................785 242-1011
Jeff Mourning, *President*
Robert Player, *Senior VP*
Roger Maxwell, *Assistant VP*
Reid Hillmer, *Vice Pres*
Toni Mietchen, *Loan Officer*
EMP: 26 **EST:** 1917
SQ FT: 5,000
SALES: 5.2MM **Privately Held**
SIC: 6022 State trust companies accepting deposits, commercial

(G-8281)
KILLOUGH CONSTRUCTION INC
3633 Highway 59 (66067-8224)
P.O. Box 810 (66067-0810)
PHONE..................................785 242-1500
John Killough, *President*
Mark Smith, *Vice Pres*
Brian Killough, *Engineer*
Dee Killough, *Treasurer*
Amy Sink, *Sales Mgr*
EMP: 15

SQ FT: 10,000
SALES: 8MM Privately Held
WEB: www.killoughconstruction.com
SIC: 1611 1794 Highway & street paving contractor; excavation work

(G-8282)
LAKE REGION RESOURCE CONSERVAT
Also Called: Lake Region RC&d
113 N Oak St (66067-2062)
P.O. Box 220 (66067-0220)
PHONE....785 242-2073
Donald Stottelmire, *President*
EMP: 21
SALES: 25K Privately Held
SIC: 8699 8641 Charitable organization; environmental protection organization

(G-8283)
LIL SPROUTS PLAYCARE LLC
1250 E Commercial Rd (66067-9675)
PHONE....785 343-7529
Brandi Randel, *Principal*
EMP: 17
SALES (est): 274.3K Privately Held
SIC: 7389 Business services

(G-8284)
LOMA VISTA GARDEN CENTER INC
1107 E 23rd St (66067-8659)
PHONE....913 897-7010
Mark Clear, *President*
Fernando Fernandez, *Opers Mgr*
Torrae Kolbeck, *Manager*
EMP: 50
SALES (est): 8.7MM Privately Held
WEB: www.lomavistanursery.com
SIC: 5193 5261 0181 Nursery stock; nursery stock, seeds & bulbs; fertilizer; ornamental nursery products

(G-8285)
LOUIS DENGEL & SON MORTUARY
235 S Hickory St (66067-2308)
PHONE....785 242-2323
Craig Dengel, *President*
EMP: 11 EST: 1949
SQ FT: 8,000
SALES (est): 679.1K Privately Held
SIC: 7261 5999 Funeral home; monuments, finished to custom order

(G-8286)
LOYD BUILDERS INC
2126 S Elm St (66067-4043)
P.O. Box 266 (66067-0266)
PHONE....785 242-1213
Joshua Walker, *President*
EMP: 16 EST: 1964
SQ FT: 2,100
SALES (est): 4.9MM Privately Held
WEB: www.loydbuilders.com
SIC: 1542 1541 Commercial & office building, new construction; commercial & office buildings, renovation & repair; industrial buildings, new construction; renovation, remodeling & repairs: industrial buildings

(G-8287)
MAC FASTENERS INC
1110 Enterprise St (66067-4138)
PHONE....785 242-2538
Bob Macdonald, *President*
Brian Macdonald, *VP Opers*
EMP: 32
SQ FT: 27,000
SALES (est): 8.3MM
SALES (corp-wide): 877.1MM Publicly Held
SIC: 3429 Aircraft hardware
PA: Trimas Corporation
38505 Woodward Ave # 200
Bloomfield Hills MI 48304
248 631-5450

(G-8288)
MACKIE CLEMENS FUEL COMPANY (PA)
2526 Hwy 59 (66067)
PHONE....785 242-2177
Dennis G Woolman, *President*
James D Worley, *Corp Secy*
Andrew Mackie, *Vice Pres*
Michael R Puffinbarger, *Vice Pres*
EMP: 10 EST: 1911
SQ FT: 3,200
SALES: 11.6MM Privately Held
SIC: 5172 Fuel oil

(G-8289)
MARTIN MARIETTA MATERIALS INC
Also Called: Martin Marietta Aggregates
2807 Sand Creek Rd (66067-8487)
PHONE....785 242-3232
J R Downs, *Manager*
EMP: 39 Publicly Held
WEB: www.martinmarietta.com
SIC: 1422 Crushed & broken limestone
PA: Martin Marietta Materials Inc
2710 Wycliff Rd
Raleigh NC 27607

(G-8290)
MARTIN PECK BEA ANMAL SHLTER I
Also Called: Prairie Paws Animal Shelter
3173 Highway K 68 (66067-8802)
PHONE....785 248-3454
Craig Evans, *President*
Vondie O'Conner, *Treasurer*
Michielle Cooper, *Exec Dir*
Larry Mages, *Director*
Tim Yeaglin, *Director*
EMP: 21
SALES: 806.5K Privately Held
SIC: 0752 Shelters, animal

(G-8291)
MID-AMERICA NUTRITION PROGRAM (PA)
Also Called: Radish Patch Catering
117 S Main St (66067-2327)
PHONE....785 242-8341
Sharon Geiss, *Exec Dir*
Pam Parkin, *Food Svc Dir*
EMP: 20
SALES: 1.4MM Privately Held
SIC: 8322 Meal delivery program

(G-8292)
MONOFLO INTERNATIONAL INC
1550 N Davis Ave (66067-9781)
PHONE....785 242-2928
EMP: 9
SALES (est): 1.3MM Privately Held
SIC: 3089 Injection molding of plastics

(G-8293)
NATIONAL SIGN COMPANY INC
1415 N Industrial Ave (66067-9762)
P.O. Box 25 (66067-0025)
PHONE....785 242-4111
Edward Jukes, *President*
Christine Lawton, *Human Res Mgr*
Heather Willard, *Office Mgr*
EMP: 11 EST: 1915
SQ FT: 28,000
SALES (est): 2.1MM
SALES (corp-wide): 2.3MM Privately Held
WEB: www.barcomunicipalproducts.com
SIC: 3993 Signs, not made in custom sign painting shops
PA: Barco Municipal Products, Inc.
11811 I St
Omaha NE 68137
402 334-8000

(G-8294)
NBH BANK
Also Called: Bank Midwest
434 S Main St (66067-2334)
PHONE....785 242-2900
Brendan Zahl, *Exec VP*
EMP: 30 Publicly Held
SIC: 6022 State commercial banks
HQ: Nbh Bank
7800 E Orchard Rd
Greenwood Village CO 80111
720 554-6680

(G-8295)
ONEOK INC
1300 E Logan St (66067-2048)
PHONE....913 599-8936
Ken Rogel, *Superintendent*
EMP: 19
SALES (corp-wide): 12.5B Publicly Held
WEB: www.oneok.com
SIC: 4922 Pipelines, natural gas
PA: Oneok, Inc.
100 W 5th St Ste Ll
Tulsa OK 74103
918 588-7000

(G-8296)
ORSCHELN FARM AND HOME LLC
Also Called: Orschelin Farm and Home 52
2008 Princeton Rd (66067)
P.O. Box 697 (66067-0697)
PHONE....785 242-3133
Norm Roberts, *Manager*
EMP: 25
SALES (corp-wide): 822.7MM Privately Held
WEB: www.orschelnfarmhome.com
SIC: 5191 5251 5699 Farm supplies; hardware; work clothing
PA: Orscheln Farm And Home Llc
1800 Overcenter Dr
Moberly MO 65270
800 577-2580

(G-8297)
OTTAWA FMLY PHYSCANS CHARTERED
1418 S Main St Ste 5 (66067-3544)
PHONE....785 242-1620
Dennis Pratt, *President*
Wb Ransom, *Vice Pres*
Dr John Gollier, *Treasurer*
Lance A Reynoso, *Director*
EMP: 45
SQ FT: 10,000
SALES (est): 6.9MM Privately Held
WEB: www.ottawamuslim.net
SIC: 8011 Physicians' office, including specialists

(G-8298)
OTTAWA HERALD INC
214 S Hickory St (66067-2392)
PHONE....785 242-4700
Jeanny Sharp, *President*
Tom Love, *Treasurer*
Jeff Gulley, *Manager*
EMP: 40 EST: 1907
SQ FT: 5,000
SALES (est): 2.5MM
SALES (corp-wide): 1.5B Publicly Held
WEB: www.hgbc.com
SIC: 2711 Newspapers, publishing & printing
HQ: Harris Enterprises, Inc.
1 N Main St Ste 616
Hutchinson KS
620 694-5830

(G-8299)
OTTAWA RECREATION COMMISSION
705 W 15th St (66067-3807)
PHONE....785 242-1939
Therron Dieckmann, *Exec Dir*
EMP: 157
SQ FT: 3,600
SALES: 915K Privately Held
SIC: 7999 Recreation services

(G-8300)
OTTAWA RETIREMENT PLAZA INC
Also Called: Ottawa Retirement Vlg Complex
1042 W 15th St Ofc (66067-3900)
PHONE....785 242-1127
Toni Nutt, *Director*
EMP: 20
SALES (est): 677.7K Privately Held
SIC: 8361 Rest home, with health care incidental

(G-8301)
OTTAWA SANITATION SERVICE
211 W Wilson St (66067-1941)
P.O. Box 487 (66067-0487)
PHONE....785 242-3227
John Taylor, *President*
Leo Ferguson, *Principal*
Claude Ferguson, *Vice Pres*
EMP: 11
SQ FT: 6,000
SALES (est): 1.7MM Privately Held
SIC: 4953 Garbage: collecting, destroying & processing

(G-8302)
OTTAWA TRUCK INC
415 E Dundee St (66067-1543)
PHONE....785 242-2200
Frank Tubbert, *President*
Miika Aintila, *Sales Mgr*
Marques Askins, *Sales Staff*
Ed Bloomer, *Manager*
Mike Piccora, *Manager*
▲ EMP: 300
SQ FT: 130,000
SALES (est): 41.7MM Privately Held
SIC: 3537 Tractors, used in plants, docks, terminals, etc.: industrial

(G-8303)
PELTON PAINTING INC
109 S Main St (66067-2327)
PHONE....785 242-7363
Barry Pelton, *President*
Jacob Tullis, *Maintence Staff*
EMP: 10
SALES (est): 427.1K Privately Held
SIC: 1721 Painting & paper hanging

(G-8304)
PENNYS CONCRETE & RDYMX LLC
745 N Locust St (66067-1952)
P.O. Box 106 (66067-0106)
PHONE....785 242-1045
Larry Marney, *Owner*
Jerry Marney, *Opers Mgr*
Craig Hinderliter, *Manager*
EMP: 11
SALES (est): 1.2MM Privately Held
SIC: 3273 Ready-mixed concrete

(G-8305)
PERFORMANCE ELECTRIC LLC
206 N Oak St (66067-2000)
P.O. Box 212 (66067-0212)
PHONE....785 242-5748
Dave Rossman, *Partner*
Greg Colbern, *Partner*
EMP: 12
SQ FT: 8,500
SALES (est): 1.1MM Privately Held
SIC: 1731 General electrical contractor

(G-8306)
PRESTIGE REAL ESTATE
406 S Main St (66067-2334)
PHONE....785 242-1167
Laura Ansley, *Owner*
Robert Miner, *Real Est Agnt*
EMP: 10
SALES (est): 517.3K Privately Held
SIC: 6531 Real estate agent, residential

(G-8307)
QES PRESSURE PUMPING LLC
Also Called: Consolidated Industrial Svcs
2631 S Eisenhower Ave (66067-9381)
PHONE....785 242-4044
James Green, *Branch Mgr*
EMP: 10
SQ FT: 1,400
SALES (corp-wide): 1.1B Privately Held
SIC: 1389 Oil field services
HQ: Qes Pressure Pumping Llc
1322 S Grant Ave
Chanute KS 66720
620 431-9210

(G-8308)
RANSOM MEMORIAL HOSPITAL CHARI
901 S Main St (66067-3315)
PHONE....785 229-8200
Larry Felix, *Principal*
EMP: 174
SALES (corp-wide): 47.9MM Privately Held
SIC: 8062 General medical & surgical hospitals

GEOGRAPHIC

PA: Ransom Memorial Hospital Charitable Association, Inc.
1301 S Main St
Ottawa KS 66067
785 229-8200

(G-8309)
RANSOM MEMORIAL HOSPITAL CHARI (PA)
Also Called: RANSOM MEMORIAL HOME HEALTH AG
1301 S Main St (66067-3598)
PHONE..................................785 229-8200
Stephanie Townsend, *Principal*
Julie Jansen, *Director*
Bill Pfizenmaier, *Director*
Doug Rich, *Director*
Pam Harris, *Nursing Dir*
EMP: 275
SQ FT: 48,000
SALES: 47.9MM **Privately Held**
WEB: www.ransom.org
SIC: 8062 8099 General medical & surgical hospitals; blood related health services

(G-8310)
RICHESON ANDERSON BYRD
216 S Hickory St (66067-2309)
P.O. Box 17 (66067-0017)
PHONE..................................785 242-1234
John Richeson, *Partner*
Richard C Byrd, *Partner*
James G Flaherty, *Partner*
Dee A Henricks, *Partner*
EMP: 13
SALES (est): 1.4MM **Privately Held**
SIC: 8111 General practice law office; general practice attorney, lawyer

(G-8311)
SHELDON C CLAYTON
3685 Reno Rd (66067-8477)
PHONE..................................913 927-9248
Sheldon Clayton, *Owner*
EMP: 54 **EST:** 1999
SALES (est): 1.5MM **Privately Held**
SIC: 0781 Landscape services

(G-8312)
SHRIJI INC
Also Called: Comfort Inn
2335 S Oak St (66067-8413)
PHONE..................................785 242-9898
Sunny Patel, *President*
EMP: 18
SALES (est): 1.8MM **Privately Held**
SIC: 7011 Hotels & motels

(G-8313)
SOUTH STAR CHRYSLER INC
440 E 11th St (66067-3602)
PHONE..................................785 242-5600
William Pedersen, *President*
Kay Pedersen, *Vice Pres*
EMP: 18
SQ FT: 14,000
SALES (est): 5.8MM **Privately Held**
SIC: 5511 7538 7515 5521 Automobiles, new & used; general automotive repair shops; passenger car leasing; used car dealers

(G-8314)
STERLING CENTRECORP INC
Also Called: Days Inn
2209 S Princeton St (66067-4005)
PHONE..................................785 242-7000
Ken Patel, *Manager*
EMP: 16
SALES (corp-wide): 15.8MM **Privately Held**
WEB: www.villagerlodgeflorence.com
SIC: 7011 Hotels & motels
HQ: Sterling Centrecorp Inc
1 N Clematis St Ste 305
West Palm Beach FL 33401

(G-8315)
SYLVESTER RANCH INC
Also Called: Midland Genetics
1906 Kingman Rd (66067-8954)
PHONE..................................785 242-3598
Ronald Sylvester, *President*
Russell Sylvester, *Vice Pres*
Angela Sylvester, *Treasurer*
Clyde Sylvester, *Treasurer*
Sandra Sylvester, *Admin Sec*
EMP: 24
SQ FT: 18,000
SALES: 1.6MM **Privately Held**
SIC: 0119 0212 Cowpea farm; beef cattle except feedlots

(G-8316)
TRANSPORTATION INC
2643 Kingman Rd (66067-8961)
PHONE..................................785 242-3660
Dolores French, *President*
EMP: 31
SQ FT: 720
SALES (est): 8MM **Privately Held**
SIC: 4731 Truck transportation brokers

(G-8317)
UNIVERSAL SIGN & DISPLAY LLC
1535 N Industrial Ave (66067-9763)
P.O. Box 888 (66067-0888)
PHONE..................................785 242-8111
Telly Fowler, *Principal*
EMP: 11
SALES (est): 1.3MM **Privately Held**
SIC: 2499 Signboards, wood

(G-8318)
US PIPE FABRICATION LLC
1534 N Industrial Ave (66067-9763)
PHONE..................................785 242-6284
John Williamson, *Branch Mgr*
EMP: 18
SALES (corp-wide): 1.4B **Publicly Held**
SIC: 3312 3498 3441 Pipes, iron & steel; fabricated pipe & fittings; fabricated structural metal
HQ: Us Pipe Fabrication, Llc
2 Chase Corporate Dr # 200
Hoover AL 35244

(G-8319)
VETERINARY CLINIC
3633 Highway 59 (66067-8224)
PHONE..................................785 242-4780
Larry Mages, *Owner*
EMP: 20
SALES (est): 286.7K **Privately Held**
SIC: 0742 Veterinarian, animal specialties

(G-8320)
VINTAGE PARK AT OTTAWA LLC
2250 S Elm St (66067-4003)
PHONE..................................785 242-3715
Betsy Elkinton, *Principal*
EMP: 15 **EST:** 2008
SALES (est): 489.1K **Privately Held**
SIC: 8361 Home for the aged

(G-8321)
WATER SYSTEMS ENGINEERING INC
3201 Labette Ter (66067-8817)
P.O. Box 700 (66067-0700)
PHONE..................................785 242-5853
Michael Schneider, *President*
Michelle Vink, *Manager*
Karin Ybarra, *Manager*
EMP: 12
SALES (est): 1.4MM
SALES (corp-wide): 1.3MM **Privately Held**
WEB: www.h2osystems.com
SIC: 8742 Business consultant
PA: Schnieders, Inc
3201 Labette Ter
Ottawa KS
785 242-6166

Overbrook
Osage County

(G-8322)
ALEGRIA LIVING & HEALTHCARE
Also Called: BROOKSIDE RETIREMENT COMMUNITY
700 W 7th St (66524-9496)
PHONE..................................785 665-7124
Scott G Averill, *President*
Levi J Davis, *Exec Dir*
EMP: 90
SALES: 5.5MM **Privately Held**
SIC: 8082 8051 Home health care services; mental retardation hospital

(G-8323)
CHLOROFIELDS LLC
6901 E 149th St (66524-9234)
P.O. Box 12 (66524-0012)
PHONE..................................785 304-3226
Aaron Chase,
EMP: 15
SALES (est): 2.9MM **Privately Held**
SIC: 5148 Vegetables, fresh

(G-8324)
FIRST SECURITY BANK (PA)
312 Maple St (66524-9747)
P.O. Box 306 (66524-0306)
PHONE..................................785 665-7155
Kent Needhim, *President*
Jamie Inglett, *Vice Pres*
EMP: 10
SALES: 2.7MM **Privately Held**
SIC: 6022 State commercial banks

(G-8325)
KANSAS STATE BANK (PA)
400 Maple St (66524-9303)
P.O. Box 325 (66524-0325)
PHONE..................................785 665-7121
Derrick Dahl, *President*
Wendy Debacker, *Vice Pres*
Carla Hazen, *Vice Pres*
Lynn Schoonover, *Vice Pres*
Brad Shaffer, *Technology*
EMP: 13 **EST:** 1889
SALES: 2.9MM **Privately Held**
WEB: www.theksb.com
SIC: 6022 State trust companies accepting deposits, commercial

(G-8326)
MIDWEST HEALTH SERVICES INC
Also Called: Brookside Manor
700 W 7th St (66524-9496)
PHONE..................................785 665-7124
Kathy Lantz, *Manager*
EMP: 150
SALES (corp-wide): 32.7MM **Privately Held**
WEB: www.halsteadhealthrehab.com
SIC: 8051 Skilled nursing care facilities
PA: Midwest Health, Inc
3024 Sw Wanamaker Rd # 300
Topeka KS 66614
785 272-1535

(G-8327)
OVERBROOK LIVESTOCK COMM CO
507 Sunset Ln (66524-9395)
P.O. Box 252 (66524-0252)
PHONE..................................785 665-7181
John Dillon, *President*
Joyce Dillon, *Owner*
EMP: 20
SALES: 2MM **Privately Held**
SIC: 5154 Auctioning livestock

Overland Park
Johnson County

(G-8328)
1138 INC
Also Called: Validity Screening Solutions
8717 W 110th St Ste 750 (66210-2129)
P.O. Box 25406 (66225-5406)
PHONE..................................913 322-5900
Darren Dupriest, *President*
Kelly Brannan, *Vice Pres*
Caroline Drisko, *Accounts Mgr*
Jessica Troncoso, *Comp Spec*
Erika Ricketts, *Executive*
EMP: 34
SQ FT: 7,300
SALES (est): 1MM **Privately Held**
WEB: www.validityscreening.com
SIC: 7381 7323 Detective services; credit bureau & agency

(G-8329)
24 HOUR FITNESS USA INC
Also Called: Overland Park Super-Sport Club
12075 Metcalf Ave (66213-1121)
PHONE..................................913 338-2442
Anne Wilkins, *Manager*
EMP: 30
SALES (corp-wide): 480.7MM **Privately Held**
SIC: 7991 Health club
HQ: 24 Hour Fitness Usa, Inc.
12647 Alcosta Blvd # 500
San Ramon CA 94583
925 543-3100

(G-8330)
435 MAGAZINE LLC
11775 W 112th St Ste 200 (66210-2756)
PHONE..................................913 469-6700
Martin Cizmar, *Chief*
Madison Jennings, *Accounts Exec*
Stacy Arey, *Office Mgr*
Shelayne Lawyer, *Executive*
Kathy Boos,
EMP: 15
SALES (est): 238.6K **Privately Held**
SIC: 5192 2721 Magazines; magazines: publishing only, not printed on site

(G-8331)
7240 SHAWNEE MISSION HOSPITALI
Also Called: Ramada Inn
7240 Shawnee Mission Pkwy (66202)
PHONE..................................913 217-7283
Shazia Memon, *Principal*
EMP: 35
SALES (est): 1.3MM **Privately Held**
SIC: 7011 Hotels & motels

(G-8332)
7600 COLLEGE PARTNR TED GREENE
6750 W 93rd St Ste 250 (66212-1465)
PHONE..................................913 341-1000
Linda Summers, *Co-Owner*
Ted Greene, *Manager*
EMP: 10
SQ FT: 2,800
SALES: 67K **Privately Held**
SIC: 6512 Nonresidential building operators

(G-8333)
911 DATAMASTER INC
7500 College Blvd Ste 500 (66210-4043)
PHONE..................................913 469-6401
Lyle Krehbiel, *Ch of Bd*
Scott Krehbiel, *President*
Babu Cherian, *Exec VP*
Eric Regnier, *Exec VP*
Richard Kelly, *Vice Pres*
EMP: 37 **EST:** 1993
SALES: 4MM **Privately Held**
WEB: www.911datamaster.com
SIC: 7371 Computer software development

(G-8334)
A DIVIS OF P MIDLA LOAN SERVI (HQ)
10851 Mastin St Ste 300 (66210-1690)
P.O. Box 25965 (66225-5965)
PHONE..................................913 253-9000
Steven W Smith, *President*
Matt Atwood, *President*
Susan Deegear, *President*
EMP: 350
SQ FT: 80,000
SALES (est): 120.3MM
SALES (corp-wide): 19.9B **Publicly Held**
WEB: www.midlandls.com
SIC: 6035 6162 Federal savings banks; mortgage bankers & correspondents
PA: The Pnc Financial Services Group Inc
300 5th Ave
Pittsburgh PA 15222
888 762-2265

(G-8335)
A G SPANOS DEVELOPMENT INC
Also Called: Spanos, The
8300 College Blvd Ste 350 (66210-2603)
PHONE..................................913 663-2400

Jennifer Mahurin, *Manager*
EMP: 10 **Privately Held**
SIC: 6513 1542 1531 Apartment building operators; commercial & office building, new construction; shopping center construction; condominium developers; speculative builder, multi-family dwellings
HQ: A. G. Spanos Development, Inc.
10100 Trinity Pkwy Fl 5
Stockton CA 95219
209 478-7954

(G-8336)
A1 STAFFING (PA)
7050 W 107th St Ste 120 (66212-1829)
PHONE..................................913 652-0005
Bruce Puttman, *President*
EMP: 10
SALES (est): 1MM **Privately Held**
WEB: www.a-1staffing.com
SIC: 7361 Executive placement

(G-8337)
ABB ENTERPRISE SOFTWARE INC
Also Called: Power Technologies
12980 Metcalf Ave Ste 400 (66213-2646)
PHONE..................................913 317-1310
Mike Austell, *Branch Mgr*
EMP: 76
SALES (corp-wide): 36.7B **Privately Held**
WEB: www.elsterelectricity.com
SIC: 3612 Transformers, except electric
HQ: Abb Inc.
305 Gregson Dr
Cary NC 27511

(G-8338)
ABWA MANAGEMENT LLC (PA)
9820 Metcalf Ave Ste 110 (66212-6188)
PHONE..................................913 732-5100
Rene Street, *Exec Dir*
Carolyn B Elman, *Exec Dir*
EMP: 23
SQ FT: 15,000
SALES (est): 3.2MM **Privately Held**
WEB: www.abwa.org
SIC: 8611 8322 8299 Business associations; individual & family services; educational services

(G-8339)
ACCELIGENT INC (PA)
9415 W 163rd Ter (66085-7854)
PHONE..................................972 504-6660
Neelima Potula, *President*
EMP: 14
SALES (est): 1MM **Privately Held**
SIC: 7379 Computer related consulting services

(G-8340)
ACCENTURE LLP
7300 W 110th St Ste 850 (66210-2318)
PHONE..................................913 319-1000
Shawn Roman, *Managing Dir*
Jeriad Zoghby, *Managing Dir*
Mary Schmalz, *Opers Staff*
Paul Keane, *Manager*
Sue Lapointe, *Manager*
EMP: 250 **Privately Held**
WEB: www.wavesecurities.com
SIC: 8742 7374 Business consultant; data processing & preparation
HQ: Accenture Llp
161 N Clark St Ste 1100
Chicago IL 60601
312 693-0161

(G-8341)
ACCOUNTABLE FINANCE INC
7733a Metcalf Ave (66204-2935)
PHONE..................................913 381-4077
Don Collins, *Manager*
EMP: 11
SALES (est): 950K **Privately Held**
SIC: 8742 Financial consultant

(G-8342)
ACCREDITATION COUNCIL FOR BUSI
Also Called: ACBSP
11520 W 119th St (66213-2002)
PHONE..................................913 339-9356
Jeffrey Alderman, *President*
Nathan Eberline, *VP Opers*
EMP: 13
SALES: 2.5MM **Privately Held**
WEB: www.acbsp.com
SIC: 8621 Education & teacher association

(G-8343)
ACCURATE TITLE COMPANY LLC
7171 W 95th St Ste 200 (66212-2249)
PHONE..................................913 338-0100
Ronald L Kraft,
EMP: 12
SALES (est): 928.1K **Privately Held**
WEB: www.stewart.com
SIC: 6541 Title abstract offices

(G-8344)
ACTION CUSTOM SPORTSWEAR LLC
Also Called: ACS Apparel
9401 Indian Creek Pkwy (66210-2007)
PHONE..................................913 433-9900
EMP: 5
SALES (est): 390K **Privately Held**
SIC: 2329 Mfg Men's/Boy's Clothing

(G-8345)
ACTUARIAL RESOURCES CORP KANS
6720 W 121st St Ste 200 (66209-2035)
PHONE..................................913 451-0044
James Lamson, *President*
Pamela R Lamson, *Principal*
Bill Wilton, *Exec VP*
Linden Willis, *Investment Ofcr*
Bryan Miller, *Consultant*
EMP: 40
SQ FT: 3,200
SALES (est): 3.1MM **Privately Held**
SIC: 8999 7371 Actuarial consultant; computer software development & applications; computer software writing services

(G-8346)
ADAMS-GABBERT & ASSOCIATES LLC (PA)
9200 Indian Creek Pkwy # 205 (66210-2036)
PHONE..................................913 735-4390
Lexi Alexander, *Human Resources*
Denise Kruse, *Mng Member*
Mark Grieman,
EMP: 18 **EST:** 1999
SQ FT: 1,000
SALES (est): 3.1MM **Privately Held**
WEB: www.adamsgabbert.com
SIC: 8621 8742 8721 8748 Professional membership organizations; management consulting services; accounting, auditing & bookkeeping; business consulting

(G-8347)
ADAMSON AND ASSOCIATES INC (PA)
7800 College Blvd Ste 200 (66210-1870)
PHONE..................................913 722-5432
Henry Adamson IV, *President*
Bradley Eldridge, *Vice Pres*
Henry Adamson III, *Treasurer*
Joye Adamson, *Admin Sec*
EMP: 26
SQ FT: 9,900
SALES (est): 2.8MM **Privately Held**
WEB: www.admsoninc.com
SIC: 6531 Appraiser, real estate

(G-8348)
ADM MILLING CO (HQ)
8000 W 110th St Ste 300 (66210-2315)
P.O. Box 7007, Shawnee Mission (66207-0007)
PHONE..................................913 491-9400
Mark Kolkhorst, *President*
Juan R Luciano, *Principal*
Mike Marsh, *Vice Pres*
Loren Urquhart, *Vice Pres*
Nick Weigel, *Vice Pres*
EMP: 60
SQ FT: 27,000
SALES (est): 325.3MM
SALES (corp-wide): 64.3B **Publicly Held**
WEB: www.admmilling.com
SIC: 2041 Flour mills, cereal (except rice); grain mills (except rice)
PA: Archer-Daniels-Midland Company
77 W Wacker Dr Ste 4600
Chicago IL 60601
312 634-8100

(G-8349)
ADVANCED HEALTH CARE CORP
4700 Indian Creek Pkwy (66207-4068)
PHONE..................................913 890-8400
EMP: 247
SALES (corp-wide): 9.1MM **Privately Held**
SIC: 8621 Health association
PA: Advanced Health Care Corporation
215 N Whitley Dr Ste 1
Fruitland ID 83619
208 452-6392

(G-8350)
ADVANCED TECHNOLOGY GROUP INC (PA)
9401 Indian Creek Pkwy # 670 (66210-2114)
PHONE..................................913 239-0050
Michael Walsh, *President*
Steve Raye, *Vice Pres*
Carey Davis, *Opers Staff*
Kate Gamel, *Accountant*
Brad Anderson, *Accounts Exec*
EMP: 25
SQ FT: 3,500
SALES: 12.6MM **Privately Held**
WEB: www.atginfo.com
SIC: 7372 Business oriented computer software

(G-8351)
ADVANTAGE SALES & MKTG LLC
8001 College Blvd Ste 100 (66210-1800)
PHONE..................................913 696-1700
Brian Stanley, *Business Mgr*
EMP: 10
SALES (corp-wide): 11.7B **Privately Held**
SIC: 5141 Food brokers
HQ: Advantage Sales & Marketing Llc
2201 E 6th St
Austin TX 78702
949 797-2900

(G-8352)
ADVANTAGE TECH INC
4400 W 107th St (66207-4003)
PHONE..................................913 888-5050
Andrew Marquardt, *CEO*
Madysyn Daniel, *Vice Pres*
Drew Ritter, *Vice Pres*
Tyke Sapp, *Technical Mgr*
Kevin Buehler, *Accounts Mgr*
EMP: 80 **EST:** 1997
SQ FT: 4,700
SALES (est): 7.5MM **Privately Held**
WEB: www.advantagetech.net
SIC: 7361 8748 7363 Employment agencies; business consulting; help supply services

(G-8353)
ADVATECH LLC (DH)
8300 College Blvd Ste 200 (66210-2603)
P.O. Box 73, Boise ID (83729-0073)
PHONE..................................913 344-1000
Gerg Brown,
EMP: 70
SQ FT: 8,000
SALES (est): 10.9MM
SALES (corp-wide): 20.1B **Publicly Held**
SIC: 8711 Construction & civil engineering
HQ: Aecom Global Ii, Llc
1999 Avenue Of The Stars
Los Angeles CA 90067
213 593-8100

(G-8354)
ADVENTURETECH GROUP INC
7450 W 130th St Ste 320 (66213-2685)
P.O. Box 4647, Olathe (66063-4647)
PHONE..................................913 402-9600
Douglas McDaniel, *President*
Kevin Conner, *Vice Pres*
Brett Gibson, *Vice Pres*
Timothy King, *CFO*
Kim Morrow, *Sr Consultant*
EMP: 15 **EST:** 2001
SALES: 2.3MM **Privately Held**
SIC: 7371 Computer software systems analysis & design, custom; computer software development

(G-8355)
AEROTEK INC
Also Called: Aerotek 410
7900 College Blvd Ste 200 (66210-2194)
PHONE..................................913 905-3000
Kyle Ferrell, *Accounts Mgr*
EMP: 18
SALES (corp-wide): 13.4B **Privately Held**
WEB: www.searchhomesmn.com
SIC: 7363 Temporary help service
HQ: Aerotek, Inc.
7301 Parkway Dr
Hanover MD 21076
410 694-5100

(G-8356)
AFFINIS CORP
8900 Indian Creek Pkwy # 450 (66210-1513)
PHONE..................................913 239-1100
Rick Worrel, *President*
John Thomas, *Principal*
Brad Schleeter, *Engineer*
Kristen Leathers, *Sales Staff*
EMP: 31
SALES (est): 5.2MM **Privately Held**
WEB: www.affinis.us
SIC: 8711 Consulting engineer

(G-8357)
AGELIX CONSULTING LLC
8101 College Blvd Ste 100 (66210-2671)
PHONE..................................913 708-8145
Rajit Garg, *COO*
Abinash Parida,
EMP: 32
SALES (est): 1.3MM **Privately Held**
SIC: 7379 8711 8742 8741 Computer related consulting services; consulting engineer; management consulting services; management engineering; management services; software programming applications

(G-8358)
AGREX INC (HQ)
8205 W 108th Ter Ste 200 (66210-1685)
PHONE..................................913 851-6300
Naoki Yoshizumi, *CEO*
Robert Obrock, *Senior VP*
Amy Ashlock, *Vice Pres*
Robert Barr, *Vice Pres*
David Christofore Sr, *Vice Pres*
◆ **EMP:** 34
SALES (est): 2.9B **Privately Held**
WEB: www.agrex.com
SIC: 5153 Grains

(G-8359)
AGRILOGIC INSURANCE SVCS LLC
4551 W 107th St Ste 250 (66207-4012)
PHONE..................................913 982-2450
Stephen L Stephano, *CEO*
Joey K Davis, *President*
Jeff Smith, *Principal*
EMP: 16
SALES (est): 3.1MM **Publicly Held**
SIC: 6411 Insurance agents & brokers
HQ: Aspen Insurance Holdings Limited
141 Front Street
Hamilton HM 19

(G-8360)
AHC OF OVERLAND PARK LLC
4700 Indian Creek Pkwy (66207-4068)
PHONE..................................913 232-2413
Cindy M Stice, *Principal*
EMP: 14
SALES (est): 440.3K **Privately Held**
SIC: 8051 Skilled nursing care facilities

(G-8361)
AIG
P.O. Box 25588 (66225-5588)
PHONE..................................503 323-2500
Stacey Decker, *Principal*
EMP: 107
SALES (est): 15.8MM **Privately Held**
SIC: 8742 Financial consultant

(G-8362)
AIR & WASTE MANAGEMENT ASSN
8717 W 110th St Ste 650 (66210-2113)
PHONE..................................913 940-0081
Brian Symons, *Treasurer*
EMP: 15
SALES (est): 515.2K **Privately Held**
SIC: 8748 Environmental consultant

(G-8363)
AIRTECH ENGINEERING INC
Also Called: Qxt
11936 W 119th St (66213-2216)
PHONE..................................913 888-5900
Mark Swade, *President*
Ty Johnson, *President*
EMP: 12
SALES: 3MM **Privately Held**
SIC: 1711 Warm air heating & air conditioning contractor

(G-8364)
AL STEVENS CONSTRUCTION LLC (PA)
6800 W 152nd Ter (66223-3127)
PHONE..................................913 897-0688
Alan W Stevens, *Mng Member*
EMP: 10
SQ FT: 7,500
SALES (est): 2.3MM **Privately Held**
SIC: 5051 Steel

(G-8365)
ALASKAN FUR COMPANY INC
9029 Metcalf Ave (66212-1479)
PHONE..................................913 649-4000
Myron Wang, *CEO*
Melisa Love, *President*
Gary Zimmerman, *Vice Pres*
Myrtis Scott, *Admin Sec*
EMP: 30 **EST:** 1926
SQ FT: 16,000
SALES (est): 2.7MM **Privately Held**
SIC: 5632 7219 Furriers; fur garment cleaning, repairing & storage

(G-8366)
ALL STATES WINDOWS SIDING LLC
6414 College Blvd (66211-1507)
PHONE..................................913 800-5211
EMP: 22 **Privately Held**
SIC: 1761 Siding contractor
PA: All States Windows & Siding, Llc
776 N West St
Wichita KS 67203

(G-8367)
ALL WTHER WIN DOORS SIDING INC (PA)
7710 Shawnee Mission Pkwy
(66202-3061)
PHONE..................................913 262-4380
Douglas Bennett, *President*
Jolene Bennett, *Admin Sec*
EMP: 15
SALES (est): 2MM **Privately Held**
SIC: 1751 Window & door (prefabricated) installation

(G-8368)
ALLERGY & ASTHMA CARE PA
10787 Nall Ave Ste 200 (66211-1371)
PHONE..................................913 491-3300
James Neiburger, *President*
H Terry Levine, *Admin Sec*
EMP: 20
SALES (est): 2.8MM **Privately Held**
SIC: 8011 Allergist

(G-8369)
ALLERGY RHMTLOGY CLNICS KC LLC
Also Called: Arckc
8401 W 125th St (66213-1449)
PHONE..................................913 338-3222
Kim Weaver, *Principal*
EMP: 15
SALES (est): 749K **Privately Held**
SIC: 8011 Allergist

(G-8370)
ALLIANCE EQUITIES CORPORATION
7227 Metcalf Ave Ste 201 (66204-1979)
PHONE..................................913 428-8278
David Dyer, *Principal*
Heather Gatewood, *Executive*
EMP: 11 **EST:** 2010
SALES (est): 501.5K **Privately Held**
SIC: 8322 Community center

(G-8371)
ALLIANCE TECHNOLOGIES INC
Also Called: Absolute Computer Solutions
10881 Lowell Ave Ste 110 (66210-2481)
PHONE..................................913 262-7977
Dennis Strumberger, *Branch Mgr*
EMP: 15 **Privately Held**
SIC: 7378 1731 Computer maintenance & repair; computer installation
PA: Alliance Technologies, Inc.
7760 Office Plaza Dr S
West Des Moines IA 50266

(G-8372)
ALMIGHTY TOW SERVICE LLC
8787 Lenexa Dr (66214-3236)
PHONE..................................913 362-8697
David L Griffiths, *Mng Member*
EMP: 15
SQ FT: 10,000
SALES: 1.5MM **Privately Held**
WEB: www.almightytow.com
SIC: 7549 Towing services

(G-8373)
ALTASCIENCES CLINICAL KANS INC (DH)
Also Called: Vince & Assoc Clinical RES
10103 Metcalf Ave (66212-1758)
PHONE..................................913 696-1601
Shawnna Blitz, *Project Mgr*
Tiffany Chennault, *Project Mgr*
Adaluz Torres, *Research*
Joni Glandon, *Controller*
Dana Munaco, *Human Res Mgr*
EMP: 69
SALES (est): 17.4MM
SALES (corp-wide): 1.7MM **Privately Held**
WEB: www.vinceandassociates.com
SIC: 8731 Medical research, commercial
HQ: Altasciences Us Intermediate, Llc
302 W Fayette St
Baltimore MD 21201
765 463-4527

(G-8374)
AMERICAN ADOPTIONS INC (PA)
7500 W 110th St Ste 500 (66210-2407)
PHONE..................................913 492-2229
Ronald N Anderson, *Exec VP*
Theodore Mars, *Vice Pres*
Desiree Koudele, *Corp Comm Staff*
Shawn Kane, *Exec Dir*
Scott Mars, *Director*
EMP: 25 **EST:** 1991
SQ FT: 3,500
SALES (est): 2.7MM **Privately Held**
WEB: www.americanadoptions.com
SIC: 8322 Adoption services

(G-8375)
AMERICAN BRIDGE COMPANY
7301 W 129th St Ste 130 (66213-2635)
PHONE..................................913 948-5800
Pamela A Bena, *Branch Mgr*
EMP: 10
SALES (corp-wide): 180MM **Privately Held**
SIC: 1622 Bridge construction
HQ: American Bridge Company
1000 American Bridge Way
Coraopolis PA 15108
412 631-1000

(G-8376)
AMERICAN FENCE COMPANY LLC
Amerifence
7616 Wedd St (66204-2227)
PHONE..................................913 307-0306
Calvin Bender, *Branch Mgr*
EMP: 29
SALES (corp-wide): 297.6K **Privately Held**
SIC: 1799 Fence construction
PA: American Fence Company, Llc
12330 Cary Cir
La Vista NE 68128
402 896-6722

(G-8377)
AMERICAN GEN LF INSUR CO DEL
Also Called: AIG
13220 Metcalf Ave Ste 360 (66213-2813)
PHONE..................................913 402-5000
Michael Bauer, *Sales Executive*
Erica Atchity, *Underwriter*
EMP: 28
SALES (corp-wide): 47.3B **Publicly Held**
WEB: www.aiglifeinsurancecompany.com
SIC: 6411 8742 Insurance agents, brokers & service; financial consultant
HQ: American General Life Insurance Company Of Delaware
2727 Allen Pkwy Ste A
Houston TX 77019
713 522-1111

(G-8378)
AMERICAN INCOME LIFE INSURANCE
11235 Mastin St Ste 201 (66210-2929)
PHONE..................................402 699-3366
EMP: 23
SALES (corp-wide): 4.3B **Publicly Held**
SIC: 6311 Life insurance
HQ: American Income Life Insurance Hernandez Agency
3333 N Mayfair Rd Ste 302
Wauwatosa WI 53222
254 741-5701

(G-8379)
AMERICAN MIDWEST DISTRS LLC
12009 Stearns St (66213-1965)
PHONE..................................816 842-1905
Thomas J Elafros, *Mng Member*
EMP: 18
SALES (est): 14MM **Privately Held**
SIC: 5191 Animal feeds

(G-8380)
AMERICAN TRUST ADMINISTRATORS (PA)
7223 W 95th St Ste 301 (66212-6177)
PHONE..................................913 378-9860
Tj McNerney, *CEO*
Tj Mc Nerney, *CEO*
EMP: 90
SQ FT: 25,000
SALES (est): 8.5MM **Privately Held**
WEB: www.ataamerica.com
SIC: 6411 Insurance agents

(G-8381)
AMERITRUST GROUP INC
11880 College Blvd # 500 (66210-2766)
PHONE..................................913 339-5000
Joe Mattingly, *Branch Mgr*
Nancy Clay, *Asst Mgr*
EMP: 11 **Privately Held**
SIC: 6399 6411 Deposit insurance; insurance agents, brokers & service
HQ: Ameritrust Group, Inc.
26255 American Dr
Southfield MI 48034

(G-8382)
AMF BOWLING CENTERS INC
10201 College Blvd (66210-1407)
PHONE..................................913 451-6400
Robert Blackwell, *Manager*
EMP: 50
SQ FT: 35,000
SALES (corp-wide): 342.2MM **Privately Held**
WEB: www.kidsports.org
SIC: 7933 7999 Ten pin center; tourist attractions, amusement park concessions & rides
HQ: Amf Bowling Centers, Inc.
7313 Bell Creek Rd
Mechanicsville VA 23111

(G-8383)
AMLI MANAGEMENT COMPANY
Also Called: Lexington Farms
8500 W 131st Ter (66213-5142)
PHONE..................................913 851-3200
Jennifer Ashborg, *Branch Mgr*
EMP: 10
SALES (corp-wide): 50.1B **Publicly Held**
SIC: 6531 Real estate managers
HQ: Amli Management Company
141 W Jackson Blvd # 300
Chicago IL 60604
312 283-4700

(G-8384)
AMSTED RAIL COMPANY INC (PA)
Also Called: Amsted RPS
8101 College Blvd Ste 200 (66210-2777)
PHONE..................................913 956-2400
▲ **EMP:** 60
SALES (est): 34.2MM **Privately Held**
SIC: 3743 Mfg Railroad Equipment

(G-8385)
ANESTHESIA ASSOC KANS CY PC (PA)
Also Called: Kc Pain Centers
8717 W 110th St Ste 600 (66210-2126)
PHONE..................................913 428-2900
James A Glenski, *President*
Mark Meisel,, *COO*
Lisa Bernard, *MIS Dir*
EMP: 150 **EST:** 1965
SQ FT: 10,000
SALES (est): 13.7MM **Privately Held**
WEB: www.aakc.com
SIC: 8011 8721 Anesthesiologist; accounting, auditing & bookkeeping

(G-8386)
ANIXTER INC
10457 W 84th Ter (66214-1641)
PHONE..................................913 492-2622
Dan Martin, *Manager*
EMP: 17
SALES (corp-wide): 8.4B **Publicly Held**
SIC: 5063 Electronic wire & cable
HQ: Anixter Inc.
2301 Patriot Blvd
Glenview IL 60026
800 323-8167

(G-8387)
ANNAN MARKETING SERVICES INC
Also Called: Telesales Group
12603 Hemlock St Ste B (66213-1484)
PHONE..................................913 254-0050
Rodney E Annan, *President*
EMP: 21
SALES (est): 1.4MM **Privately Held**
SIC: 8742 Marketing consulting services

(G-8388)
ANTECH DIAGNOSTICS INC
11950 W 110th St (66210-3904)
PHONE..................................913 529-4392
Tomas Fuller, *CFO*
Rachelle Kelly, *Manager*
EMP: 23
SALES (corp-wide): 37.6B **Privately Held**
SIC: 8734 Veterinary testing
HQ: Antech Diagnostics, Inc.
17620 Mount Herrmann St
Fountain Valley CA 92708
800 745-4725

(G-8389)
APPLE EGHT HOSPITALITY MGT INC
Also Called: Fairfield Inn
12440 Blue Valley Pkwy (66213-2626)
PHONE..................................913 338-3600
Jeanette Clarke, *Vice Pres*
Rachel Labrecque, *Vice Pres*
Cindy Kaunley, *Manager*
EMP: 43 **Privately Held**
SIC: 7011 Hotels & motels
HQ: Apple Eight Hospitality Management, Inc.
814 E Main St
Richmond VA 23219

(G-8390)
APPLE EGHT SVCS OVRLAND PK INC
Also Called: Residence Inn Overland Park
12010 Blue Valley Pkwy (66213-2647)
PHONE..................................913 327-7484
Joe Andrick, *General Mgr*
EMP: 20 **EST:** 2011
SALES (est): 995.6K **Privately Held**
WEB: www.truenorthhotels.com
SIC: 7011 Hotels & motels

(G-8391)
APS STAFFING SERVICES INC
7015 College Blvd Ste 150 (66211-1579)
PHONE..................................913 327-7605
Robert Meiling, *Administration*
EMP: 12
SALES (est): 180K **Privately Held**
SIC: 7363 8082 Help supply services; home health care services

(G-8392)
ARCH DESIGN BUILDERS LLC
Also Called: Arch Roofing
11100 W 91st St Ste 200 (66214-1709)
PHONE..................................913 599-5565
Diana Jones, *Manager*
William Meza,
Robert Morrissey,
EMP: 23 **EST:** 1999
SQ FT: 10,000
SALES: 2.2MM **Privately Held**
SIC: 1761 7389 Roofing contractor; interior design services

(G-8393)
ARCHER-DANIELS-MIDLAND COMPANY
Also Called: ADM
8000 W 110th St (66210-2338)
PHONE..................................913 491-9400
James Brainard, *Vice Pres*
Garrett Wrecke, *Planning*
EMP: 106
SALES (corp-wide): 64.3B **Publicly Held**
SIC: 5153 Grains
PA: Archer-Daniels-Midland Company
77 W Wacker Dr Ste 4600
Chicago IL 60601
312 634-8100

(G-8394)
ARCHER-DANIELS-MIDLAND COMPANY
Also Called: ADM
8000 W 110th St Ste 300 (66210-2315)
PHONE..................................913 491-9400
EMP: 42
SALES (corp-wide): 67.7B **Publicly Held**
SIC: 2041 Mfg Flour/Grain Mill Prooducts
PA: Archer-Daniels-Midland Company
77 W Wacker Dr Ste 4600
Chicago IL 60601
312 634-8100

(G-8395)
ARGUS CONSULTING INC (PA)
6363 College Blvd Ste 600 (66211-1882)
PHONE..................................816 228-7500
Kent F Bredehoeft, *Principal*
Steve Waag, *Vice Pres*
Paul Johnke, *Opers Staff*
Karl Angerer, *Engineer*
Martin Hook, *Engineer*
EMP: 23
SALES (est): 5.9MM **Privately Held**
SIC: 8711 Consulting engineer

(G-8396)
ARROW ELECTRONICS INC
Also Called: Arrow Zeus Electronics
7500 College Blvd Ste 500 (66210-4043)
PHONE..................................913 242-3012
R Misconish, *Branch Mgr*
EMP: 30
SALES (corp-wide): 29.6B **Publicly Held**
WEB: www.arrow.com
SIC: 5065 5045 Electronic parts; semiconductor devices; computer peripheral equipment
PA: Arrow Electronics, Inc.
9201 E Dry Creek Rd
Centennial CO 80112
303 824-4000

(G-8397)
ARVEST BANK
7401 W 135th St (66223-1203)
PHONE..................................913 953-4000
Susanne Hammond, *Branch Mgr*
EMP: 17
SALES (corp-wide): 2.3B **Privately Held**
SIC: 6022 State trust companies accepting deposits, commercial
HQ: Arvest Bank
103 S Bloomington St
Fayetteville AR 72745
479 575-1000

(G-8398)
ARY INC (HQ)
Also Called: Ary Professional Cutlery Div
5200 W 110th St Ste 200 (66211-1203)
P.O. Box 412888, Kansas City MO (64141-2888)
PHONE..................................913 214-4813
Bernard Huff, *CEO*
▲ **EMP:** 15
SQ FT: 5,000
SALES (est): 3.4MM
SALES (corp-wide): 161.3MM **Privately Held**
WEB: www.ary.com
SIC: 3421 5072 Cutlery; cutlery
PA: Hantover, Inc.
5200 W 110th St Ste 200
Overland Park KS 66211
913 214-4800

(G-8399)
ASCEND MDIA MED HEALTHCARE LLC
171 W 95th Ste 300 (66212)
PHONE..................................913 469-1110
Barbara Kay, *Principal*
EMP: 10
SALES (est): 234K **Privately Held**
SIC: 8082 Home health care services

(G-8400)
ASCENSION INSUR HOLDINGS LLC
9225 Indian Creek Pkwy # 700 (66210-2010)
PHONE..................................800 955-1991
EMP: 447 **EST:** 2007
SQ FT: 1,500
SALES: 67MM **Privately Held**
SIC: 6411 Insurance Agent/Broker

(G-8401)
ASGN INCORPORATED
7171 W 95th St (66212-2283)
PHONE..................................913 341-9100
Nciholas Abinos, *Branch Mgr*
EMP: 11
SALES (corp-wide): 3.4B **Publicly Held**
SIC: 7363 Temporary help service
PA: Asgn Incorporated
26745 Malibu Hills Rd
Calabasas CA 91301
818 878-7900

(G-8402)
ASH GROVE AGGREGATES INC (DH)
11011 Cody St Ste 300 (66210-1430)
PHONE..................................660 679-4128
Mike Lutz, *President*
EMP: 68
SALES (est): 20.2MM
SALES (corp-wide): 29.7B **Privately Held**
WEB: www.ashgroveagg.com
SIC: 1422 Limestones, ground
HQ: Ash Grove Materials Corporation
11011 Cody St Ste 300
Overland Park KS 66210
913 345-2030

(G-8403)
ASH GROVE CEMENT COMPANY (HQ)
11011 Cody St Ste 300 (66210-1430)
P.O. Box 25900 (66225-5900)
PHONE..................................913 451-8900
J Randall Vance, *President*
Rob Henning, *Principal*
James P Sunderland, *Chairman*
Michael Koch, *Business Mgr*
Eileen Flink, *Vice Pres*
◆ **EMP:** 130 **EST:** 1949
SQ FT: 90,000
SALES (est): 784.7MM
SALES (corp-wide): 29.7B **Privately Held**
WEB: www.ashgrove.com
SIC: 3241 3273 1422 3271 Portland cement; ready-mixed concrete; crushed & broken limestone; concrete block & brick
PA: Crh Public Limited Company
Stonemasons Way
Dublin D16 K
140 410-00

(G-8404)
ASH GROVE MATERIALS CORP (DH)
Also Called: Central Region
11011 Cody St Ste 300 (66210-1430)
P.O. Box 25900 (66225-5900)
PHONE..................................913 345-2030
J Randall Vance, *President*
Dick Johnson, *General Mgr*
Quentin Vandal, *Superintendent*
Robert B Henning, *Vice Pres*
Edwin S Pierce, *Vice Pres*
EMP: 65
SALES (est): 99.3MM
SALES (corp-wide): 29.7B **Privately Held**
SIC: 3273 3272 1411 7389 Ready-mixed concrete; concrete products; trap rock, dimension-quarrying; volcanic rock, dimension-quarrying; packaging & labeling services; local trucking, without storage
HQ: Ash Grove Cement Company
11011 Cody St Ste 300
Overland Park KS 66210
913 451-8900

(G-8405)
ASSET SERVICES INC
6750 Antioch Rd Ste 300 (66204-1519)
PHONE..................................913 383-2738
Scott T Wyckoff, *President*
Kathleen Murray, *Marketing Staff*
EMP: 10
SALES (est): 920.5K **Privately Held**
WEB: www.enterpriseassetservices.com
SIC: 8742 Management consulting services

(G-8406)
ASSOCIATED PURCH SVCS CORP
7015 College Blvd Ste 150 (66211-1579)
PHONE..................................913 327-8730
Tom Bell, *President*
Bob Meling, *COO*
Steve Poage, *CFO*
Bruce Frerking, *Director*
Linda Bailey, *Executive Asst*
EMP: 10
SQ FT: 7,000
SALES: 2.3MM **Privately Held**
SIC: 7389 Purchasing service

(G-8407)
AT&T CORP
9444 Nall Ave (66207-2516)
PHONE..................................913 383-4943
Jim Limer, *Branch Mgr*
EMP: 68
SALES (corp-wide): 170.7B **Publicly Held**
SIC: 4812 Cellular telephone services
HQ: At&T Corp.
1 At&T Way
Bedminster NJ 07921
800 403-3302

(G-8408)
AT&T CORP
9761 Quivira Rd (66215-1665)
PHONE..................................913 894-0800
EMP: 12
SALES (corp-wide): 170.7B **Publicly Held**
SIC: 4812 Cellular telephone services
HQ: At&T Corp.
1 At&T Way
Bedminster NJ 07921
800 403-3302

(G-8409)
ATHENA COMMUNICATIONS LTD
4905 Antioch Rd (66203-1312)
PHONE..................................913 599-3444
Noelle P Scaramucci, *President*
Robert Phillips, *Vice Pres*
Sharon Phillips, *Vice Pres*
EMP: 10
SQ FT: 1,652
SALES (est): 868.7K **Privately Held**
WEB: www.athenacomm.com
SIC: 7629 Telecommunication equipment repair (except telephones)

(G-8410)
ATLAS RECOVERY SYSTEMS LLC
7932 Foster St Ste B (66204-3642)
PHONE..................................913 281-7000
David Griffiths, *Mng Member*
EMP: 18
SALES: 902.1K **Privately Held**
WEB: www.repopeople.net
SIC: 7389 Repossession service

(G-8411)
ATONIX DIGITAL LLC
11401 Lamar Ave (66211-1508)
PHONE..................................913 458-2000
Paul McRoberts, *President*
Timothy W Triplett, *Exec VP*
Kenneth L Williams, *CFO*
Michael Williams, *Treasurer*
Jacqueline Hansen, *Chief Mktg Ofcr*
EMP: 42
SQ FT: 600,000
SALES (est): 1MM
SALES (corp-wide): 2.8B **Privately Held**
SIC: 7371 Computer software development
HQ: Black & Veatch Holding Company
11401 Lamar Ave
Overland Park KS 66211

(G-8412)
ATTERRO INC
Also Called: Pro Staff
10740 Nall Ave Ste 110 (66211-1223)
PHONE..................................913 338-3020
Justin McCollum, *Accounts Exec*
Brian Hoffbauer, *Branch Mgr*
EMP: 15 **Privately Held**
WEB: www.prostaff.com
SIC: 7363 7361 Temporary help service; placement agencies
HQ: Atterro, Inc.
201 E 4th St Ste 800
Cincinnati OH 45202
800 938-9675

(G-8413)
AUGUSTINE EXTERMINATORS INC
Also Called: Augustine Carpenting HM Imprv
9280 Flint St (66214-1738)
PHONE..................................913 362-4399
Margaret L Augustine, *CEO*
Christopher S Augustine, *President*
Robert E Croom Jr, *Vice Pres*
Jared Ingalls, *Director*
Margaret Augustine, *Executive*
EMP: 39 **EST:** 1970
SQ FT: 8,700
SALES (est): 4.2MM **Privately Held**
WEB: www.augustineexterminators.com
SIC: 7342 Pest control services; exterminating & fumigating

(G-8414)
AVAZPOUR NETWORKING SVCS INC
12980 Metcalf Ave Ste 400 (66213-2646)
PHONE..................................913 323-1411
EMP: 22
SQ FT: 8,100
SALES (est): 2.3MM **Privately Held**
SIC: 7379 Computer Related Services

(G-8415)
AVCORP BUSINESS SYSTEMS LLC (HQ)
Also Called: Lineage
8200 Nieman Rd (66214-1507)
PHONE....913 888-0333
Tony Ambrosia, *General Mgr*
Alison Hall, *General Mgr*
Jody Keene, *General Mgr*
Chris Owens, *General Mgr*
Little Rock, *General Mgr*
EMP: 24
SQ FT: 11,000
SALES: 3.9MM
SALES (corp-wide): 381K **Privately Held**
SIC: 5044 5045 5021 Mailing machines; computers, peripherals & software; office furniture
PA: Williams Holdings, Llc
150 Lawrence Bell Dr
Williamsville NY 14221
716 631-3345

(G-8416)
AVERY CAPITAL LLC
7803 W 61st Ter (66202-3035)
PHONE....913 742-3002
Frederick Avery,
EMP: 15 **EST:** 2017
SALES (est): 249.3K **Privately Held**
SIC: 6531 Real estate agents & managers

(G-8417)
AWAD NICOLA (PA)
Also Called: Classy Kids
11477 W 95th St (66214-1827)
PHONE....913 381-6969
Nicola Awad, *Owner*
EMP: 22
SQ FT: 2,000
SALES (est): 1.8MM **Privately Held**
SIC: 5995 1541 Opticians; renovation, remodeling & repairs: industrial buildings

(G-8418)
AWARD DECALS INC
12507 Hemlock St (66213-1453)
P.O. Box 396, Spring Hill (66083-0396)
PHONE....913 677-6681
Donald C Hirner, *President*
Mallory Hirner, *Vice Pres*
Max Watson, *Art Dir*
Caleb Berciunas, *Graphic Designe*
EMP: 14
SQ FT: 3,700
SALES (est): 1.1MM **Privately Held**
SIC: 2752 Decals, lithographed

(G-8419)
AXA FINANCIAL INC
7400 W 110th St Ste 700 (66210-2374)
PHONE....913 345-2800
Douglas Propeck, *Branch Mgr*
EMP: 30
SALES (corp-wide): 12B **Publicly Held**
SIC: 8742 Financial consultant
HQ: Axa Financial, Inc.
1290 Ave Of The Am Fl Con
New York NY 10104

(G-8420)
AXCET HR SOLUTIONS INC
10975 Grandview Dr # 200 (66210-1522)
PHONE....913 383-2999
Gerald Diddle Jr, *President*
Eric Kesselring, *Vice Pres*
Anne Thacker, *Manager*
EMP: 35
SALES (est): 2.4MM **Privately Held**
WEB: www.midweststaff.com
SIC: 8742 8721 Compensation & benefits planning consultant; payroll accounting service

(G-8421)
B AND L MOTELS (PA)
10874 Nieman Rd (66210-3207)
PHONE....913 451-5874
Bruce Weilert, *President*
EMP: 20
SALES (est): 1.5MM **Privately Held**
SIC: 7011 Motels

(G-8422)
B&G GROUP LLC
9930 W 116th Pl Apt 7 (66210-3138)
PHONE....816 616-4034
Steven Deshazer,
EMP: 10
SALES (est): 189.7K **Privately Held**
SIC: 6531 Real estate agents & managers

(G-8423)
B&V E&E JV
6800 W 115th St Ste 2200 (66211-2413)
PHONE....913 458-4300
Matthew Webber, *Senior VP*
Timothy Grady,
EMP: 99 **EST:** 2014
SQ FT: 10,000
SALES (est): 3.1MM **Privately Held**
SIC: 8711 Engineering services

(G-8424)
B&V-BAKER GUAM JV
6601 College Blvd (66211-1504)
PHONE....913 458-4300
Robert S Kulash, *Partner*
Black Veatch Corp, *Partner*
David M Martin, *Partner*
Mike Lefholz, *Technology*
EMP: 4500
SALES (est): 98.4MM **Privately Held**
SIC: 8711 Consulting engineer

(G-8425)
BANK AMERICA NATIONAL ASSN
8695 College Blvd Ste 100 (66210-1871)
PHONE....816 979-4592
Jenny Rucker, *Branch Mgr*
EMP: 25
SALES (corp-wide): 110.5B **Publicly Held**
WEB: www.bofa.com
SIC: 6021 National commercial banks
HQ: Bank Of America, National Association
100 S Tryon St
Charlotte NC 28202
704 386-5681

(G-8426)
BANK AMERICA NATIONAL ASSN
8440 W 135th St (66223-1158)
PHONE....816 979-8200
Thomas Gingrich, *Branch Mgr*
EMP: 15
SALES (corp-wide): 110.5B **Publicly Held**
WEB: www.bofa.com
SIC: 6021 National commercial banks
HQ: Bank Of America, National Association
100 S Tryon St
Charlotte NC 28202
704 386-5681

(G-8427)
BANK AMERICA NATIONAL ASSN
15811 Metcalf Ave (66223-3001)
PHONE....913 897-1470
Shelli Mason, *Branch Mgr*
EMP: 19
SALES (corp-wide): 110.5B **Publicly Held**
WEB: www.bofa.com
SIC: 6021 National commercial banks
HQ: Bank Of America, National Association
100 S Tryon St
Charlotte NC 28202
704 386-5681

(G-8428)
BANK OF BLUE VALLEY (HQ)
Also Called: HEARTLAND
11935 Riley St (66213-1127)
P.O. Box 778, Dubuque IA (52004-0778)
PHONE....913 338-1000
Robert D Regnier, *CEO*
Wendy Reynolds, *President*
Alex Gordillo, *Vice Pres*
Nick Harling, *Vice Pres*
Janetta Kendrick, *Vice Pres*
EMP: 30
SALES: 26.5MM **Publicly Held**
WEB: www.mjbtrc.com
SIC: 6022 State trust companies accepting deposits, commercial

(G-8429)
BANK OF LABOR
Also Called: Brotherhood Bank & Trust
11810 W 75th St (66214-1366)
PHONE....913 321-4242
Sharon Hollingsworth, *Vice Pres*
EMP: 13
SALES (corp-wide): 26.3MM **Privately Held**
SIC: 6022 State commercial banks
HQ: Bank Of Labor
756 Minnesota Ave
Kansas City KS 66101
913 321-6800

(G-8430)
BANKERS LIFE & CASUALTY CO
8207 Melrose Dr Ste 150 (66214-1696)
PHONE....913 894-6553
Lawrence Martin, *Manager*
EMP: 16
SALES (corp-wide): 4.3B **Publicly Held**
SIC: 6099 Check clearing services
HQ: Bankers Life & Casualty Co
111 E Wacker Dr Ste 2100
Chicago IL 60601
312 396-6000

(G-8431)
BANKS SWIMMING POOL COMPANY (PA)
Also Called: Banks Pool & Spa Designs
8026 W 151st St (66223-2116)
PHONE....913 897-9290
Roger Banks, *President*
Lynn Banks, *Treasurer*
EMP: 25
SQ FT: 3,600
SALES (est): 3.7MM **Privately Held**
SIC: 1799 7389 5999 Swimming pool construction; spa or hot tub installation or construction; swimming pool & hot tub service & maintenance; swimming pools, hot tubs & sauna equipment & supplies

(G-8432)
BARBERA & WATKINS LLC
6701 W 64th St Ste 315 (66202-4091)
PHONE....913 677-3800
Joanne M Barbera, *Partner*
Natalie Stice, *Legal Staff*
Melissa L Blair, *Associate*
Shannon Sinn, *Associate*
EMP: 10
SALES (est): 1.2MM **Privately Held**
SIC: 8111 General practice attorney, lawyer

(G-8433)
BARDAVON HLTH INNOVATIONS LLC
6803 W 64th St (66202-4128)
PHONE....913 236-1020
Dorothy Riviere, *CFO*
Brian Gillespie, *CTO*
EMP: 41
SALES (est): 7.6MM **Privately Held**
SIC: 7371 Computer software development & applications

(G-8434)
BARRIER COMPLIANCE SVCS LLC
8245 Nieman Rd (66214-1508)
PHONE....913 905-2695
Mike Haverty,
EMP: 10
SQ FT: 2,000
SALES (est): 490.9K **Privately Held**
SIC: 7389 Building inspection service

(G-8435)
BARTUNEK GROUP INC
14137 Nicklaus Dr (66223-3349)
PHONE....913 327-8800
Jeri W Kling, *CEO*
Rick Nash, *Director*
Sean Goodale,
EMP: 24
SALES: 1.5MM **Privately Held**
WEB: www.bartunekgroup.com
SIC: 7361 7373 Executive placement; computer integrated systems design

(G-8436)
BEAM-WARD KRUSE WILSON
8645 College Blvd Ste 250 (66210-1801)
PHONE....913 339-6888
Mark Beam-Ward, *Managing Prtnr*
Kevin J Kruse, *Partner*
Christopher Wilson, *Partner*
Gregory Wright, *Partner*
Christophe T Wilson,
EMP: 15
SALES (est): 2MM **Privately Held**
WEB: www.hbwkwlaw.com
SIC: 8111 General practice attorney, lawyer

(G-8437)
BEAUTY ESCNTUALS SALON DAY SPA
12675 Metcalf Ave (66213-1317)
P.O. Box 24411 (66283-4411)
PHONE....913 851-4644
Dawn Kallftrom, *Owner*
EMP: 20
SALES (est): 333.5K **Privately Held**
SIC: 7231 Cosmetologist

(G-8438)
BEEBE HEATING & AC INC
9104 Cody St (66214-1732)
PHONE....913 541-1222
Chris Haag, *CEO*
Paul Willhite, *Director*
EMP: 12
SALES (est): 1.9MM **Privately Held**
WEB: www.beebehvac.com
SIC: 1711 Warm air heating & air conditioning contractor; heating & air conditioning contractors

(G-8439)
BELLER DANCE STUDIO INC
Also Called: Beller, Pattie Dance Studio
7820 Foster St (66204-2955)
PHONE....913 648-2626
Patricia Beller, *President*
Diane Fesler, *Vice Pres*
EMP: 20
SQ FT: 12,500
SALES (est): 507.4K **Privately Held**
WEB: www.bellerdance.com
SIC: 7911 Dance studio & school

(G-8440)
BERKLEY RISK ADM CO LLC
10851 Mastin St Ste 200 (66210-1689)
PHONE....913 385-4960
Gary Oricher, *Manager*
EMP: 12
SALES (corp-wide): 7.6B **Publicly Held**
SIC: 6411 Insurance agents & brokers
HQ: Berkley Risk Administration Company, Llc
222 S 9th St Ste 2700
Minneapolis MN 55402
612 766-3000

(G-8441)
BERKSHIRE RISK SERVICES LLC
Also Called: Lrs Financial
7400 W 132nd St Ste 200 (66213-1153)
P.O. Box 410679, Kansas City MO (64141-0679)
PHONE....913 433-7000
Bob Henderson, *Opers Mgr*
Scott Frayer, *Manager*
Kimberly Lopez, *Manager*
Christopher J Kirwan,
Aura Obando, *Representative*
EMP: 22 **EST:** 2007
SQ FT: 3,500
SALES (est): 4.1MM **Privately Held**
SIC: 6411 Insurance agents

(G-8442)
BERMAN & RABIN PA
15280 Metcalf Ave # 200 (66223-2811)
P.O. Box 24327 (66283-4327)
PHONE....913 649-1555
Michael Berman, *CEO*
Daniel S Rabin, *President*

EMP: 19
SALES (est): 3.4MM **Privately Held**
WEB: www.bermanrabin.com
SIC: 8111 Debt collection law; specialized law offices, attorneys

(G-8443)
BEUMER KANSAS CITY LLC
7300 W 110th St Ste 530 (66210-2332)
PHONE..................................816 245-7260
Dr Thomas Dalstein,
Marcia Casas,
▲ **EMP:** 25 **EST:** 2011
SALES (est): 13.4MM **Privately Held**
SIC: 5084 Materials handling machinery

(G-8444)
BGR CONSULTING ENGINEERS INC
8908 W 106th St (66212-5533)
PHONE..................................816 842-2800
Katrina Gerber, *President*
Jim Basquette, *Vice Pres*
Dominick Rucereto, *Vice Pres*
EMP: 12
SALES (est): 1.2MM **Privately Held**
WEB: www.bgrengineers.com
SIC: 8711 Consulting engineer

(G-8445)
BHA ALTAIR LLC (DH)
Also Called: Clarcor Industrial Air
11501 Outlook St Ste 100 (66211-1810)
PHONE..................................816 356-8400
Kieth White, *President*
Christopher Conway, *Vice Pres*
Adam Matfil, *CFO*
Pam Kile, *VP Human Res*
Timothy Stark, *Sales Staff*
▲ **EMP:** 150
SALES (est): 266.4MM
SALES (corp-wide): 14.3B **Publicly Held**
SIC: 3564 Air purification equipment
HQ: Clarcor Inc.
840 Crescent Centre Dr # 600
Franklin TN 37067
615 771-3100

(G-8446)
BHR INC
Also Called: Billing Healthcare Resources
7939 Floyd St (66204-3724)
PHONE..................................913 469-1599
Richard Beamon, *President*
Mark Holcomb, *Principal*
Richard Rosenthal, *Principal*
Mark Scarborough, *Principal*
Barbara Smith, *Principal*
EMP: 13
SALES (est): 841.5K **Privately Held**
SIC: 8721 Billing & bookkeeping service

(G-8447)
BICKNELL FAMILY HOLDING CO LLC
7400 College Blvd Ste 205 (66210-4028)
PHONE..................................913 387-2743
Martin C Bicknell,
EMP: 40 **Privately Held**
SIC: 6719 Personal holding companies, except banks

(G-8448)
BILL BARR & COMPANY (PA)
8800 Grant Ave (66212-3741)
PHONE..................................913 599-6668
William Barr, *President*
Eric Arnold, *General Mgr*
Kevin Burns, *Vice Pres*
Howard Bodine, *Accounts Mgr*
Tory Smith, *Sales Staff*
▲ **EMP:** 14
SQ FT: 3,000
SALES (est): 21.1MM **Privately Held**
SIC: 5122 Animal medicines; vitamins & minerals

(G-8449)
BIO-MDCAL APPLCATIONS KANS INC
Also Called: BMA Leawood
6751 W 119th St (66209-2013)
PHONE..................................913 498-1780
Kerri Spurling, *Manager*
EMP: 10
SALES (corp-wide): 18.3B **Privately Held**
SIC: 8092 Kidney dialysis centers
HQ: Bio-Medical Applications Of Kansas, Inc.
920 Winter St
Waltham MA 02451

(G-8450)
BIOSTAR RENEWABLES LLC
Also Called: Biostar Lighting
9400 Reeds Rd Ste 150 (66207-2523)
PHONE..................................913 369-4100
Nancy Hellige, *Accountant*
EMP: 26
SALES (corp-wide): 904.1K **Privately Held**
SIC: 4931
PA: Biostar Renewables Llc
9400 Reeds Rd Ste 150
Overland Park KS 66207
913 369-4100

(G-8451)
BIOSTAR SYSTEMS LLC
9400 Reeds Rd Ste 150 (66207-2523)
PHONE..................................913 438-3002
William Love, *CEO*
Missy Love, *Managing Dir*
John Martin, *COO*
Steve Graham, *Exec VP*
Mark O'Ffill, *Controller*
EMP: 5
SQ FT: 2,300
SALES (est): 877.2K **Privately Held**
SIC: 2873 Fertilizers: natural (organic), except compost

(G-8452)
BIRCH CONTRACTING GROUP LLC
16220 Birch St (66085-7825)
P.O. Box 26143 (66225-6143)
PHONE..................................913 400-3975
Thomas E Riggs, *Principal*
Martha Cromwell, *Principal*
EMP: 10
SALES (est): 419.3K **Privately Held**
SIC: 1721 1522 1521 Commercial painting; hotel/motel & multi-family home construction; hotel/motel & multi-family home renovation & remodeling; remodeling, multi-family dwellings; repairing fire damage, single-family houses

(G-8453)
BLACK & VEATCH - ER JV
6800 W 115th St Ste 2200 (66211-2413)
PHONE..................................913 458-6650
Randy Castro, *Principal*
EMP: 800
SALES (est): 5.6MM **Privately Held**
SIC: 7389

(G-8454)
BLACK & VEATCH CNSTR INC
11880 College Blvd # 410 (66210-2766)
P.O. Box 11450 (66207-1450)
PHONE..................................913 458-2000
R Neil Riddle Jr, *President*
Peter D Loftspring, *Senior VP*
Shelby B Barbier, *Vice Pres*
Kevin T Hinkle, *Treasurer*
Andrea C Bernica, *Asst Sec*
EMP: 44
SALES (est): 14.7MM
SALES (corp-wide): 2.8B **Privately Held**
SIC: 1629 Power plant construction
HQ: Black & Veatch Corporation
11401 Lamar Ave
Overland Park KS 66211
913 458-2000

(G-8455)
BLACK & VEATCH CORPORATION (DH)
11401 Lamar Ave (66211-1598)
P.O. Box 11450 (66207-1450)
PHONE..................................913 458-2000
Steven L Edwards, *CEO*
Lynn Bertuglia, *President*
Randy Castro, *President*
Timothy W Triplett, *President*
Cindy Wallis-Lage, *President*
▲ **EMP:** 2552 **EST:** 1998
SALES (est): 1.2B
SALES (corp-wide): 2.8B **Privately Held**
WEB: www.bv.com
SIC: 8711 Consulting engineer

(G-8456)
BLACK & VEATCH CORPORATION
6800 W 115th St Ste 600 (66211-9838)
PHONE..................................913 458-2000
Samuel Hegarty, *Engineer*
G White, *Branch Mgr*
Tracy Swalley, *Manager*
EMP: 30
SALES (corp-wide): 2.8B **Privately Held**
WEB: www.bv.com
SIC: 8711 Consulting engineer
HQ: Black & Veatch Corporation
11401 Lamar Ave
Overland Park KS 66211
913 458-2000

(G-8457)
BLACK & VEATCH HOLDING COMPANY (HQ)
11401 Lamar Ave (66211-1598)
P.O. Box 8405, Kansas City MO (64114-0405)
PHONE..................................913 458-2000
Steven L Edwards, *Ch of Bd*
Steve Mizerany, *General Mgr*
Edward Zhu, *Business Mgr*
Timothy W Triplett, *Exec VP*
Tonya Anton, *Engineer*
◆ **EMP:** 74
SQ FT: 600,000
SALES (est): 2.8B **Privately Held**
SIC: 8711 8741 Consulting engineer; sanitary engineers; construction management
PA: Bvh, Inc.
11401 Lamar Ave
Overland Park KS 66211
913 458-2000

(G-8458)
BLACK & VEATCH-GEC JOINT VENTR
6800 W 115th St Ste 2200 (66211-2413)
PHONE..................................913 458-4300
William Van Dyke, *President*
EMP: 450
SALES (est): 11.3MM **Privately Held**
SIC: 8711 Engineering services

(G-8459)
BLACK & VEATCH-OLSSON JV
6800 W 115th St Ste 2200 (66211-2413)
PHONE..................................913 458-6650
EMP: 21 **EST:** 2015
SALES (est): 1.7MM **Privately Held**
SIC: 8711 Consulting engineer

(G-8460)
BLACK VATCH MGT CONSULTING LLC
11401 Lamar Ave (66211-1508)
P.O. Box 11450 (66207-1450)
PHONE..................................913 458-2000
John M Chevrette, *President*
Timothy W Triplett, *Exec VP*
Kenneth L Williams, *CFO*
Kimberly K Demel, *Admin Sec*
Andrea C Bernica, *Asst Sec*
EMP: 252
SALES (est): 6.4MM
SALES (corp-wide): 2.8B **Privately Held**
SIC: 8742 Management consulting services
HQ: Black & Veatch Holding Company
11401 Lamar Ave
Overland Park KS 66211

(G-8461)
BLACK VEATCH-ALTAN JOINT VENTR
6800 W 115th St Ste 2200 (66211-2413)
PHONE..................................913 458-4300
William Van Dyke, *President*
EMP: 400
SQ FT: 10,000
SALES: 1MM **Privately Held**
SIC: 8711 8712 Consulting engineer; architectural services

(G-8462)
BLACK VTCH - GSYNTEC JINT VNTR
6800 W 115th St Ste 2200 (66211-2413)
PHONE..................................913 458-4300
Thomas Peel, *Partner*
W Todd Dudley, *Partner*
Eric Nesbit, *Partner*
Thomas A Peel, *Partner*
EMP: 99
SALES (est): 1.5MM **Privately Held**
SIC: 8711 Engineering services

(G-8463)
BLACK VTCH SPCIAL PRJECTS CORP (DH)
6800 W 115th St Ste 2200 (66211-2413)
PHONE..................................913 458-2000
Randal Castro, *President*
Timothy W Triplett, *Exec VP*
William T Dudley, *Vice Pres*
Peter D Loftspring, *Vice Pres*
Steven L Scott, *Vice Pres*
EMP: 295
SQ FT: 101,241
SALES (est): 39MM
SALES (corp-wide): 2.8B **Privately Held**
SIC: 8711 Consulting engineer

(G-8464)
BLOCK REAL ESTATE SERVICES LLC
7101 College Blvd Ste 735 (66210-2028)
PHONE..................................816 412-8457
Eric Mann, *Principal*
EMP: 16 **Privately Held**
SIC: 8742 Real estate consultant
PA: Block Real Estate Services, Llc
700 W 47th St Ste 200
Kansas City MO 64112

(G-8465)
BLOCK REAL ESTATE SERVICES LLC
8349 Melrose Dr (66214-1629)
PHONE..................................816 746-9922
Rebecca Denault, *Branch Mgr*
EMP: 21 **Privately Held**
SIC: 6531 Real estate agents & managers
PA: Block Real Estate Services, Llc
700 W 47th St Ste 200
Kansas City MO 64112

(G-8466)
BLUE EAGLE PRODUCTIONS INC
13805 Fontana St (66224-3007)
PHONE..................................816 225-2980
Michael Herbel, *Owner*
EMP: 10
SALES (corp-wide): 2.4MM **Privately Held**
WEB: www.blueeagleproductions.com
SIC: 2759 Commercial printing
PA: Blue Eagle Productions Inc
346 N Lindenwood Dr Ste C
Olathe KS
913 780-0100

(G-8467)
BLUE RIVER ELEMENTARY PTO INC
5101 W 163rd Ter (66085-9383)
PHONE..................................913 239-6000
EMP: 37
SALES: 78.4K **Privately Held**
SIC: 8641 Parent-teachers' association

(G-8468)
BLUE VALLEY ANIMAL HOSPITAL (PA)
16200 Metcalf Ave (66085-9147)
PHONE..................................913 681-2818
Brad Payne, *President*
EMP: 10
SQ FT: 4,000
SALES (est): 1.4MM **Privately Held**
SIC: 0742 Animal hospital services, pets & other animal specialties

GEOGRAPHIC

(G-8469)
BLUE VALLEY CHEMICAL LLC
Also Called: Blue Valley Tan
5423 W 131st Ter (66209-2907)
PHONE.....816 984-2125
Lisa Buchanan, *Mng Member*
Elham Michael,
EMP: 10
SALES (est): 1.3MM **Privately Held**
SIC: 5169 Chemicals & allied products

(G-8470)
BLUETOOTH SIG INC
7300 College Blvd Ste 200 (66210-1879)
PHONE.....913 317-4700
Michael McCamon, *Branch Mgr*
EMP: 12
SALES (corp-wide): 11.3MM **Privately Held**
SIC: 8611 Trade associations
PA: Bluetooth Sig Inc
5209 Lake Wash Blvd Ne
Kirkland WA 98033
425 691-3524

(G-8471)
BNC NATIONAL BANK
7007 College Blvd Ste 330 (66211-2447)
PHONE.....913 647-7000
Scott Spillman, *President*
Michael Zerr, *Marketing Staff*
Patricia Spilker, *Underwriter*
EMP: 21
SALES (est): 6MM **Privately Held**
SIC: 6162 Mortgage bankers & correspondents

(G-8472)
BOAN CONNEALY & HOULEHAN LLC
Also Called: Boan & Connealy
13220 Metcalf Ave Ste 100 (66213-2813)
PHONE.....913 491-9178
Tracy L Boan, *Principal*
Kevin Connealy, *Sales Staff*
Scott Boan,
EMP: 10
SALES (est): 880.5K **Privately Held**
SIC: 8721 Certified public accountant

(G-8473)
BOB ALLEN FORD INC
Also Called: City Rent-A-Truck
9239 Metcalf Ave (66212-1405)
PHONE.....913 381-3000
Robert T Hewlett, *President*
John K Wiegers, *Vice Pres*
Brad Hewlett, *Treasurer*
EMP: 94
SQ FT: 72,000
SALES: 3.4MM **Privately Held**
WEB: www.boballenford.com
SIC: 5511 7515 7514 7538 Automobiles, new & used; trucks, tractors & trailers: new & used; passenger car leasing; passenger car rental; general automotive repair shops

(G-8474)
BOK FINANCIAL CORPORATION
7500 College Blvd Ste 100 (66210-4035)
PHONE.....913 234-6632
Bryan S Klimek, *Principal*
Brent Varzaly, *Vice Pres*
EMP: 55 **Publicly Held**
SIC: 6162 Mortgage bankers & correspondents
PA: Bok Financial Corporation
320 S Boston Ave
Tulsa OK 74103

(G-8475)
BOTT RADIO NETWORK INC (PA)
10550 Barkley St Ste 100 (66212-1824)
PHONE.....913 642-7770
Richard P Bott II, *President*
Paul Sublett, *General Mgr*
Angela Buckley, *Production*
Tom Holdeman, *CFO*
Sue Stoltz, *Manager*
EMP: 59
SQ FT: 3,000
SALES: 15MM **Privately Held**
SIC: 4832 Religious

(G-8476)
BOULEVARD INSURANCE LLC
Also Called: Nationwide
7501 College Blvd Ste 115 (66210-2758)
PHONE.....785 865-0077
Tom Arensberg, *Owner*
David Mathys, *Accounts Mgr*
EMP: 12
SALES (est): 1MM **Privately Held**
SIC: 6411 Insurance agents, brokers & service

(G-8477)
BOWMAN SOFTWARE SYSTEMS LLC
11300 Switzer St (66210-3665)
PHONE.....318 213-8780
Robert P Bowman,
Robert Bowman,
EMP: 64
SALES (est): 2.7MM **Privately Held**
SIC: 7372 Business oriented computer software

(G-8478)
BOWMAN SYSTEMS LLC
11300 Switzer St (66210-3665)
PHONE.....318 213-8780
Robert Bowman, *President*
Peter Rokitski, *QC Mgr*
Lisa Allen, *Manager*
Levin Corbin, *Manager*
Steven Millard, *Manager*
EMP: 65
SALES (est): 7.4MM
SALES (corp-wide): 118.3MM **Privately Held**
WEB: www.bowmansystems.com
SIC: 7371 Computer software development
PA: Wellsky Corporation
11300 Switzer St
Overland Park KS 66210
913 307-1000

(G-8479)
BRADLEY R LEWIS
Also Called: Creativenergy Options
13900 Nicklaus Dr (66223-2999)
PHONE.....816 453-7198
Bradley R Lewis, *Owner*
Gary Clemens, *Sales Staff*
Brad Lewis, *Manager*
EMP: 11
SALES (est): 896.3K **Privately Held**
SIC: 4911 Generation, electric power

(G-8480)
BRANCHPATTERN INC
Also Called: M.E. Group
7400 College Blvd Ste 150 (66210-4028)
PHONE.....913 951-8311
Ravi Maniktala, *President*
Debora Swanson, *Principal*
Rick Maniktala, *Manager*
EMP: 18 **Privately Held**
SIC: 8711 Consulting engineer
PA: Branchpattern, Inc.
2820 N 48th St
Lincoln NE 68504

(G-8481)
BRANDED CUSTOM SPORTSWEAR INC
Also Called: Bcs Apparel
7007 College Blvd Ste 700 (66211-2425)
PHONE.....913 663-6800
David L Reid, *President*
EMP: 50
SALES (est): 15.3MM **Privately Held**
SIC: 5136 5137 Men's & boys' sportswear & work clothing; women's & children's sportswear & swimsuits

(G-8482)
BREDSON AND ASSOCIATES INC
Also Called: Bredson & Assoc Consulting Eng
9225 Indian Creek Pkwy # 300 (66210-2009)
PHONE.....913 663-0100
Barbara Hoppas, *President*
Dan Koehly, *Vice Pres*
David Hartzler, *Treasurer*
EMP: 21
SALES (est): 2.1MM **Privately Held**
SIC: 8711 Professional engineer

(G-8483)
BRENTON FINANCIAL GROUP INC
13232 Craig St (66213-1401)
PHONE.....913 451-9072
Robert O Brenton, *President*
EMP: 14
SQ FT: 5,000
SALES (est): 550K **Privately Held**
SIC: 8111 Legal services

(G-8484)
BREW LAB
8004 Foster St (66204-3613)
PHONE.....913 400-2343
Kevin Combs, *CEO*
EMP: 6 **EST:** 2013
SALES (est): 556.7K **Privately Held**
SIC: 2082 Malt beverages

(G-8485)
BRIDGESTONE RET OPERATIONS LLC
Also Called: Tires Plus Total Car Care
7425 Metcalf Ave Ste B (66204-1975)
PHONE.....913 831-9955
Shane Nagayama, *Manager*
EMP: 10 **Privately Held**
SIC: 7534 Tire retreading & repair shops
HQ: Bridgestone Retail Operations, Llc
333 E Lake St Ste 300
Bloomingdale IL 60108
630 259-9000

(G-8486)
BRITISH SALT HOLDINGS LLC
10955 Lowell Ave Ste 600 (66210-2363)
PHONE.....913 253-2203
Mark C Demetree, *Principal*
Barry Wall, *VP Finance*
EMP: 133
SALES (est): 4.6MM
SALES (corp-wide): 5MM **Privately Held**
SIC: 2899 Chemical preparations
HQ: Us Salt, Llc
3580 Salt Point Rd
Watkins Glen NY 14891

(G-8487)
BROOKDALE OVERLAND PK GLENWOOD
9201 Foster St (66212-2295)
PHONE.....913 385-2052
ARC Overland, *Principal*
EMP: 12
SALES (est): 425.1K **Privately Held**
SIC: 8051 Skilled nursing care facilities

(G-8488)
BROOKDALE SENIOR LIVING INC
Also Called: Grand Court of Overland Park
6101 W 119th St (66209-2728)
PHONE.....913 345-9339
David Thompson, *Director*
EMP: 50
SALES (corp-wide): 4.5B **Publicly Held**
WEB: www.grandcourtlifestyles.com
SIC: 6513 Retirement hotel operation
PA: Brookdale Senior Living
111 Westwood Pl Ste 400
Brentwood TN 37027
615 221-2250

(G-8489)
BRR ARCHITECTURE INC (PA)
8131 Metcalf Ave Ste 300 (66204-3846)
PHONE.....913 262-9095
James Hailey, *CEO*
Chris M Rhea, *Ch of Bd*
Rich Majors, *COO*
Brian Roggy, *Vice Pres*
Rachel Taylor, *Vice Pres*
EMP: 104
SQ FT: 36,000
SALES (est): 27.3MM **Privately Held**
SIC: 8712 Architectural engineering

(G-8490)
BRUNGARDT HONOMICHL & CO PA (PA)
Also Called: Bhc Rhodes
7101 College Blvd Ste 400 (66210-2081)
PHONE.....913 663-1900
Kevin Honomichl, *President*
Steven Bachenbery, *Vice Pres*
Balthasar A Brungardt, *Vice Pres*
Matt Brungardt, *Vice Pres*
Yves Lang, *Vice Pres*
EMP: 100
SQ FT: 20,000
SALES (est): 17.9MM **Privately Held**
WEB: www.ibhc.com
SIC: 8711 Civil engineering

(G-8491)
BUNGII LLC
11011 King St Ste 280 (66210-1208)
PHONE.....913 353-6683
Harrison Proffitt, *Mng Member*
Ben Jackson,
EMP: 20
SALES: 2MM **Privately Held**
SIC: 7371 Computer software development & applications

(G-8492)
BURDISS LETTERSHOP SERVICES CO
3439 Merriam Dr (66203-1375)
PHONE.....913 492-0545
Robert Burdiss, *President*
Bobby Ross, *Vice Pres*
Noni Burdiss, *Admin Sec*
EMP: 12
SQ FT: 25,000
SALES (est): 2.4MM **Privately Held**
WEB: www.burdiss.com
SIC: 7331 Mailing service

(G-8493)
BURLINGAME VISION ASSOCIATES
11500 W 119th St (66213-2002)
PHONE.....913 338-1948
Cynthia Burlingame Od, *Owner*
Jay Burlingame Od, *Co-Owner*
EMP: 10
SQ FT: 3,000
SALES (est): 1MM **Privately Held**
SIC: 8042 Specialized optometrists

(G-8494)
BURNETT AUTOMOTIVE INC
8210 W 135th St (66223-1208)
PHONE.....913 681-8824
Andrew Kaebel, *Manager*
EMP: 14
SALES (corp-wide): 37.4MM **Privately Held**
SIC: 5531 5014 5013 5541 Automotive tires; automotive parts; tires & tubes; automotive supplies & parts; gasoline service stations
PA: Burnett Automotive, Inc.
400 Mccall Rd
Manhattan KS 66502
785 539-8970

(G-8495)
BUSEY BANK
4550 W 109th St Ste 100 (66211-1308)
PHONE.....913 338-4300
Brian Cross, *Manager*
EMP: 50
SALES (corp-wide): 376MM **Publicly Held**
SIC: 6022 State commercial banks
HQ: Busey Bank
100 W University Ave # 100
Champaign IL 61820
217 365-4500

(G-8496)
BUSHNELL GROUP HOLDINGS INC
Also Called: Bushnell Outdoor Products
9200 Cody St (66214-1734)
PHONE.....913 894-4224
Robert Caulk, *CEO*
Michael Callahan, *Principal*
Rob Sharp, *Principal*
Edward Virtue, *Principal*

EMP: 316
SALES (est): 13.6MM
SALES (corp-wide): 2B **Publicly Held**
SIC: **3851** Eyeglasses, lenses & frames
PA: Vista Outdoor Inc.
1 Vista Way
Anoka MN 55303
801 447-3000

(G-8497)
BUSHNELL HOLDINGS INC (HQ)
Also Called: Bushnell Outdoor Products
9200 Cody St (66214-1734)
PHONE..................................913 752-3400
Scott D Chaplin, *Senior VP*
Stephen M Nolan, *CFO*
◆ **EMP**: 250
SALES (est): 149.7MM
SALES (corp-wide): 2B **Publicly Held**
SIC: **3851** 5049 5091 Ophthalmic goods; optical goods; sporting & recreation goods
PA: Vista Outdoor Inc.
1 Vista Way
Anoka MN 55303
801 447-3000

(G-8498)
BUSHNELL INC
9200 Cody St (66214-1734)
PHONE..................................913 752-6178
Kim Schank, *Branch Mgr*
EMP: 200
SALES (corp-wide): 2B **Publicly Held**
WEB: www.bushnellreports.com
SIC: **3827** Optical instruments & lenses
HQ: Bushnell Inc.
9200 Cody St
Overland Park KS 66214
913 752-3400

(G-8499)
BUSHNELL INC (HQ)
Also Called: Bushnell Outdoor Products
9200 Cody St (66214-1734)
PHONE..................................913 752-3400
Scott D Chaplin, *Senior VP*
Jacob Werthman, *Senior Buyer*
Scott Nyhart, *Engineer*
Stephen M Nolan, *CFO*
Deedee Gaston, *Credit Staff*
◆ **EMP**: 135
SQ FT: 6,000
SALES (est): 159.3MM
SALES (corp-wide): 2B **Publicly Held**
WEB: www.bushnellreports.com
SIC: **3827** Binoculars
PA: Vista Outdoor Inc.
1 Vista Way
Anoka MN 55303
801 447-3000

(G-8500)
BUYROLLSCOM INC
11150 W 163rd Pl (66221-3524)
PHONE..................................913 851-7100
James Jones, *Manager*
EMP: 13
SALES (est): 2.1MM **Privately Held**
SIC: **3554** Paper industries machinery

(G-8501)
BVSPC - ENVIROCON JV
6800 W 115th St Ste 2200 (66211-2413)
PHONE..................................913 458-6665
W Todd Dudley, *Partner*
Connie Nikravan, *Partner*
EMP: 99 **EST**: 2016
SQ FT: 60,000
SALES (est): 1.5MM **Privately Held**
SIC: **8711** Engineering services

(G-8502)
C & B EQUIPMENT MIDWEST INC
Also Called: Douglas Pump Service, Inc.
4719 Merriam Dr (66203-1345)
PHONE..................................913 236-8222
Dennis Noyes, *President*
EMP: 18
SALES (corp-wide): 8MM **Privately Held**
SIC: **7699** Pumps & pumping equipment repair
PA: C & B Equipment Midwest, Inc.
3717 N Ridgewood St
Wichita KS 67220
316 262-5156

(G-8503)
C & S MAINTENANCE INC
5705 W 153rd Ter (66223-3647)
PHONE..................................913 227-9609
Lynette Morris, *President*
Juan Martinez, *Manager*
EMP: 20
SALES: 500K **Privately Held**
SIC: **7349** Janitorial service, contract basis

(G-8504)
C&L MANAGEMENT LLC
Also Called: Senior Helpers of East Kansas
7400 W 130th St (66213-2715)
PHONE..................................913 851-4800
Lou Warren,
Carol Warren,
EMP: 45
SALES (est): 764.4K **Privately Held**
SIC: **8082** Home health care services

(G-8505)
C3I
10955 Granada Ln (66211-1440)
PHONE..................................913 327-2255
Jamie Phillips, *CFO*
EMP: 10
SALES (est): 1MM **Privately Held**
SIC: **7389** Design services

(G-8506)
CACTUS SOFTWARE LLC
10950 Grandview Dr # 200 (66210-1514)
PHONE..................................913 677-0092
Wayne Auer, *President*
John Wandless, *Chairman*
Scott Stillman, *Exec VP*
Branson Reynolds, *Project Mgr*
Paul Yeoman, *Sales Mgr*
EMP: 80
SQ FT: 17,000
SALES (est): 13.8MM **Privately Held**
SIC: **7371** Computer software development
PA: Vendor Credentialing Service, Llc
315 Capitol St Ste 100
Houston TX 77002

(G-8507)
CAMBRIDGEN INC
Also Called: Peterson Companies
10000 W 75th St Ste 100 (66204-2241)
PHONE..................................913 384-3800
Gordon J Peterson, *Ch of Bd*
Kenneth Reidemann, *President*
Roger Siegrist, *Admin Sec*
EMP: 27
SALES (est): 2MM **Privately Held**
SIC: **6799** Real estate investors, except property operators

(G-8508)
CANON SOLUTIONS AMERICA INC
7300 W 110th St Ste 100 (66210-2447)
PHONE..................................913 323-5010
EMP: 5 **Privately Held**
SIC: **5044** 7699 3861 Copying equipment; photocopy machine repair; photographic equipment & supplies
HQ: Canon Solutions America, Inc.
1 Canon Park
Melville NY 11747
631 330-5000

(G-8509)
CAPITAL FRSGHT GOLF FITNES LLC
Also Called: Brookridge Golf & Fitness
8223 W 103rd St (66212-4359)
PHONE..................................913 648-1600
Robert Usher, *Owner*
Denise White, *Accountant*
Troy Mueller, *Director*
Bob Usher, *Director*
EMP: 30
SALES (est): 2.7MM
SALES (corp-wide): 2.7MM **Privately Held**
SIC: **7992** 7991 Public golf courses; physical fitness clubs with training equipment
PA: Brookridge Golf & Country Club
8223 W 103rd St
Shawnee Mission KS 66212
913 648-1600

(G-8510)
CAPITAL REALTY LLC
7500 College Blvd Ste 920 (66210-4035)
PHONE..................................913 469-4600
Phillip Algrim, *Senior VP*
Andrew C Cooper, *Vice Pres*
Jeff Kembel, *Vice Pres*
Patrick Meraz, *Vice Pres*
Jason Green, *Property Mgr*
EMP: 20
SALES (est): 1.6MM **Privately Held**
SIC: **6531** Real estate agent, commercial

(G-8511)
CAPITAL RESOURCES LLC
7960 W 135th St Ste 200 (66223-1240)
PHONE..................................913 469-1630
Miriam Henry, *Senior VP*
Dean Crouch, *Mng Member*
Dean Trouch, *Mng Member*
EMP: 10
SALES (est): 2.2MM **Privately Held**
SIC: **6141** 6153 Consumer finance companies; working capital financing

(G-8512)
CAR STAR SPC
8400 W 110th St Ste 200 (66210-2307)
PHONE..................................201 444-0601
Carstar Metcalf, *Principal*
EMP: 22 **EST**: 2013
SALES (est): 1.7MM **Privately Held**
SIC: **7532** 7539 7542 Body shop, automotive; automotive repair shops; washing & polishing, automotive

(G-8513)
CARDINAL HEALTH 127 INC
Also Called: Speciality Services
7400 W 110th St (66210-2358)
PHONE..................................913 451-3955
Meghan Fitzgerald, *President*
Boyd Lund, *Director*
Brenda Schlenk, *Director*
Melanie Weaver, *Director*
Rebecca Wharton, *Director*
EMP: 60
SQ FT: 20,000
SALES (est): 5.7MM
SALES (corp-wide): 145.5B **Publicly Held**
WEB: www.beckloff.com
SIC: **8748** Business consulting
PA: Cardinal Health, Inc.
7000 Cardinal Pl
Dublin OH 43017
614 757-5000

(G-8514)
CARDIOTABS INC
6701 W 91st St (66212-1458)
PHONE..................................816 753-4298
Joan Okeefe, *General Mgr*
Joan O'Keefe, *General Mgr*
James O Keefe Jr, *Med Doctor*
EMP: 7
SQ FT: 2,296
SALES (est): 975.7K
SALES (corp-wide): 21MM **Privately Held**
WEB: www.cc-pc.com
SIC: **2023** Dietary supplements, dairy & non-dairy based
PA: Cardiovascular Consultants, Inc.
4330 Wornall Rd Ste 2000
Kansas City MO 64111
816 303-3292

(G-8515)
CARECENTRIX INC
6130 Sprint Pkwy Ste 200 (66211-1149)
PHONE..................................913 749-5600
Tracy Lewandowski, *Vice Pres*
Suzanne Blackburn, *Vice Pres*
Scott Quade, *Analyst*
EMP: 51 **Privately Held**
SIC: **8082** Home health care services
PA: Carecentrix, Inc.
20 Church St Ste 900
Hartford CT 06103

(G-8516)
CARESTAF INC
8001 College Blvd Ste 250 (66210-2470)
PHONE..................................913 498-2888
Dennis Brown, *President*
Margaret Brown, *Corp Secy*
Tiffany Davis, *Supervisor*
Mary Fernau, *Director*
EMP: 400
SQ FT: 3,300
SALES (est): 6.3MM **Privately Held**
WEB: www.carestaf.com
SIC: **8082** 7363 Visiting nurse service; medical help service

(G-8517)
CARGILL INCORPORATED
5200 Metcalf Ave Ste 150 (66202-1200)
PHONE..................................913 236-0346
EMP: 44
SALES (corp-wide): 113.4B **Privately Held**
SIC: **5153** Grain & field beans
PA: Cargill, Incorporated
15407 Mcginty Rd W
Wayzata MN 55391
952 742-7575

(G-8518)
CARLTON-BATES COMPANY
Also Called: Rs Electronics
10814 W 78th St (66214-1262)
PHONE..................................913 375-1160
Michelle Pagette, *Branch Mgr*
EMP: 13 **Publicly Held**
WEB: www.ectronics.com
SIC: **5065** Electronic parts
HQ: Carlton-Bates Company
3600 W 69th St
Little Rock AR 72209
501 562-9100

(G-8519)
CAROL J FELTHEIM
11725 W 112th St (66210-2761)
PHONE..................................913 469-5579
Carol J Feltheim, *Principal*
Robert Pierron, *Surgeon*
EMP: 80
SALES (est): 194.2K **Privately Held**
SIC: **8011** General & family practice, physician/surgeon

(G-8520)
CARONDELET HEALTH
Also Called: Villa St Joseph
11901 Rosewood St (66209-3533)
PHONE..................................913 345-1745
Kathy Ensign, *Administration*
EMP: 70
SALES (corp-wide): 59.6MM **Privately Held**
SIC: **8059** Nursing home, except skilled & intermediate care facility
PA: Carondelet Health
4600 Edmundson Rd
Saint Louis MO 63134
816 942-4400

(G-8521)
CARONDELET ORTHPDC SRGNS SPRTS
10777 Nall Ave Ste 300 (66211-1330)
PHONE..................................913 642-0200
Brian E Healy, *Principal*
EMP: 25
SALES (est): 3.7MM **Privately Held**
SIC: **8011** Clinic, operated by physicians; orthopedic physician

(G-8522)
CARSON DEVELOPMENT INC
7248 W 121st St (66213-1201)
PHONE..................................913 499-1926
Mike Schlup, *President*
EMP: 19
SALES (est): 2.6MM **Privately Held**
SIC: **8741** Management services

(G-8523)
CARTER-WATERS LLC
6803 W 64th St (66202-4128)
PHONE..................................913 671-1870
EMP: 21

SALES (corp-wide): 482.9MM **Privately Held**
SIC: 5031 Lumber, plywood & millwork
HQ: Carter-Waters Llc
2435 Jefferson St
Kansas City MO 64108
816 471-2570

(G-8524)
CARTESIAN INC (HQ)
6405 Metcalf Ave Ste 417 (66202-3930)
PHONE..................................913 345-9315
Jim Serafin, *CEO*
William Hill, *President*
EMP: 43
SQ FT: 10,400
SALES: 50.7MM **Publicly Held**
SIC: 8742 Business consultant

(G-8525)
CASSIAN ENERGY LLC
9300 W 110th St Ste 235 (66210-1405)
PHONE..................................913 948-1107
Adam Herrman,
EMP: 13
SALES (est): 358.1K **Privately Held**
SIC: 6799 Commodity contract trading companies

(G-8526)
CATHOLIC CHARITIES OF NORTHEAS
Also Called: Catholic Community Hospice
9740 W 87th St (66212-4563)
PHONE..................................913 621-5090
Tiffany C James, *Branch Mgr*
EMP: 38 **Privately Held**
SIC: 8052 8322 Personal care facility; individual & family services
PA: Catholic Charities Of Northeast Kansas, Inc.
2220 Central Ave
Kansas City KS 66102

(G-8527)
CAVANAUGH EYE CENTER PA
6200 W 135th St Ste 300 (66223-4847)
PHONE..................................913 897-9200
Timothy Cavanaugh, *President*
Vicki L Honack, *Manager*
EMP: 11
SALES (est): 1.6MM **Privately Held**
SIC: 8011 Ophthalmologist

(G-8528)
CBIZ INC
Also Called: Cottonwood Group The
6900 College Blvd Ste 300 (66211-1596)
PHONE..................................913 345-0500
John R John R Dykes, *Managing Dir*
Janet Thompson,
Barbara Hofstetter, *Analyst*
EMP: 15 **Publicly Held**
SIC: 8748 Business consulting
PA: Cbiz, Inc.
6050 Oak Tree Blvd # 500
Cleveland OH 44131

(G-8529)
CC SERVICES INC
10561 Barkley St (66212-1860)
PHONE..................................913 381-1995
Mike Kleen, *Branch Mgr*
EMP: 15
SALES (corp-wide): 49.9MM **Privately Held**
SIC: 6411 Insurance agents, brokers & service
HQ: Cc Services, Inc.
1711 General Electric Rd
Bloomington IL 61704
309 821-3372

(G-8530)
CCL CONSTRUCTION CONSULTANTS (PA)
4600 College Blvd Ste 104 (66211-1606)
PHONE..................................913 491-0807
Harry Callahan, *Ch of Bd*
Michael T Callahan, *President*
EMP: 20
SQ FT: 3,200
SALES (est): 2.1MM **Privately Held**
WEB: www.cclcc.com
SIC: 8742 Construction project management consultant

(G-8531)
CD MCCORMICK & COMPANY INC
Also Called: Cleaning Authority, The
12020 W 87th Street Pkwy (66215-2808)
PHONE..................................913 541-0106
Darrell McCormick, *Principal*
EMP: 30
SQ FT: 1,800
SALES: 1MM **Privately Held**
SIC: 7349 Maid services, contract or fee basis

(G-8532)
CDS INC
Also Called: Corporate Document Service
9095 Bond St (66214-1724)
PHONE..................................913 541-1166
Joel McGinnis, *President*
Mark Wolfe, *Vice Pres*
EMP: 19
SQ FT: 20,000
SALES (est): 3MM **Privately Held**
WEB: www.cdskc.com
SIC: 2752 Commercial printing, offset

(G-8533)
CEC ENTERTAINMENT INC
Also Called: Chuck E. Cheese's
10510 Metcalf Ave (66212-1814)
PHONE..................................913 648-4920
Eric Becker, *General Mgr*
EMP: 45
SQ FT: 9,900
SALES (corp-wide): 886.7MM **Privately Held**
WEB: www.chuckecheese.com
SIC: 5812 7299 Pizzeria, chain; party planning service
HQ: Cec Entertainment, Inc.
1707 Market Pl Ste 200
Irving TX 75063
972 258-8507

(G-8534)
CELGENE CORPORATION
9225 Indian Creek Pkwy # 900 (66210-2015)
PHONE..................................913 266-0300
Stephen Matthews, *Principal*
Scott McFarland, *Sales Staff*
Mary Vandekauter, *Manager*
John Morrill, *Senior Mgr*
EMP: 13
SALES (corp-wide): 22.5B **Publicly Held**
SIC: 2834 Pharmaceutical preparations
HQ: Celgene Corporation
86 Morris Ave
Summit NJ 07901
908 673-9000

(G-8535)
CELLCO PARTNERSHIP
Also Called: Verizon Wireless
6925 W 135th St (66223-4803)
PHONE..................................913 897-5022
EMP: 14
SALES (corp-wide): 130.8B **Publicly Held**
SIC: 5065 4812 Telephone & telegraphic equipment; cellular telephone services
HQ: Cellco Partnership
1 Verizon Way
Basking Ridge NJ 07920

(G-8536)
CELLCO PARTNERSHIP
Also Called: Verizon Wireless
11868 W 95th St (66214-1831)
PHONE..................................913 631-0677
EMP: 76
SALES (corp-wide): 130.8B **Publicly Held**
SIC: 4812 Cellular telephone services
HQ: Cellco Partnership
1 Verizon Way
Basking Ridge NJ 07920

(G-8537)
CENTRAL BANK OF MIDWEST
Also Called: 69 Highway Branch
7960 W 135th St (66223-1231)
PHONE..................................913 791-9988
Julie King, *Branch Mgr*
EMP: 82
SALES (corp-wide): 4.1MM **Privately Held**
SIC: 6022 State commercial banks
PA: Central Bank Of The Midwest
609 Ne State Route 291
Lees Summit MO 64086
816 525-5754

(G-8538)
CENTRALIZED SHOWING SVC INC (PA)
11225 College Blvd # 450 (66210-2748)
PHONE..................................913 851-8405
Robert Faherty, *President*
Ron Fuller, *Accounts Exec*
Ann Lowe, *Accounts Exec*
Susan Meyerowich, *Sales Staff*
Nicholas Knight, *Chief Mktg Ofcr*
EMP: 64
SALES (est): 40MM **Privately Held**
WEB: www.showings.com
SIC: 7371 Computer software development

(G-8539)
CENTRINEX LLC
Also Called: Novasource
11933 W 95th St Ste 147 (66215)
PHONE..................................913 744-3410
Bart Miller, *Mng Member*
Angie Lee, *Manager*
EMP: 300
SALES (est): 13.7MM **Privately Held**
SIC: 8748 Telecommunications consultant

(G-8540)
CERAMIC CAFE
9510 Nall Ave (66207-2950)
PHONE..................................913 383-0222
Sara Thompson, *Owner*
EMP: 10
SALES (est): 742.6K **Privately Held**
SIC: 5023 Pottery

(G-8541)
CHARLES I DAVIS MD PA
Also Called: Hartland Geriatric
8312 W 102nd St (66212-3420)
PHONE..................................913 648-8880
Charles I Davis, *Owner*
EMP: 10
SALES (est): 914.7K **Privately Held**
SIC: 8011 Geriatric specialist, physician/surgeon

(G-8542)
CHARLES RITZ INC
Also Called: Ritz, Charles O P
5833 W 145th St (66223-1152)
PHONE..................................913 685-2600
Bill Frye, *Vice Pres*
EMP: 12
SALES (est): 1.5MM
SALES (corp-wide): 4.1MM **Privately Held**
WEB: www.ritzcharles.com
SIC: 8111 7299 Bankruptcy law; banquet hall facilities
PA: Charles Ritz Inc
12156 N Meridian St
Carmel IN 46032
317 843-9529

(G-8543)
CHASE GROUP INC
10975 Grandview Dr # 100 (66210-1521)
PHONE..................................913 696-6300
Karen Allison, *President*
Ken Allison, *Corp Secy*
Moira Newbanks, *Vice Pres*
Lindsay Roesler, *Project Mgr*
EMP: 10
SQ FT: 4,500
SALES (est): 1.2MM **Privately Held**
SIC: 7361 Executive placement

(G-8544)
CHELEPIS & ASSOCIATES INC
8695 College Blvd Ste 200 (66210-1871)
PHONE..................................913 912-7113
Tracy Chelepis, *President*
Jon Petree, *Research*
Benjamin Reker, *Research*
David Ainsworth, *Senior Engr*
Michelle Edson, *Accountant*
EMP: 32
SALES (est): 4.4MM **Privately Held**
WEB: www.chelepis.com
SIC: 8742 Real estate consultant

(G-8545)
CHEROKEE ANIMAL CLINIC PA
9630 Antioch Rd (66212-4060)
PHONE..................................913 649-0440
James Klntras, *President*
EMP: 20 **EST:** 1973
SALES (est): 2.2MM **Privately Held**
WEB: www.cherokeeac.com
SIC: 0742 Animal hospital services, pets & other animal specialties

(G-8546)
CHICAGO TITLE INSURANCE CO
11005 Metcalf Ave (66210-1815)
PHONE..................................913 451-1200
Lorenna Patterson, *Manager*
EMP: 12
SALES (corp-wide): 7.5B **Publicly Held**
WEB: www.goldleaf-tech.com
SIC: 6361 Real estate title insurance
HQ: Chicago Title Insurance Company
601 Riverside Ave
Jacksonville FL 32204

(G-8547)
CHILDRENS HOSPITAL ASSOCIATION
6803 W 64th St (66202-4128)
PHONE..................................913 262-1436
EMP: 23
SALES (est): 2.9MM **Privately Held**
SIC: 8069 8099 Children's hospital; blood related health services

(G-8548)
CHILDRENS MERCY HOSPITAL
Also Called: Children's Mercy South
5808 W 110th St (66211-2504)
PHONE..................................913 696-8000
Melonie Clifton, *Opers Staff*
Debra Shepherd, *Branch Mgr*
Jenifer L Butler, *Med Doctor*
Gerry Gey, *Med Doctor*
Lance Shipman, *Med Doctor*
EMP: 302
SALES (corp-wide): 826.4MM **Privately Held**
SIC: 8062 General medical & surgical hospitals
PA: Mercy Children's Hospital
2401 Gillham Rd
Kansas City MO 64108
816 234-3000

(G-8549)
CHILDRENS MERCY SPECIALTY CTR
5808 W 110th St (66211-2504)
PHONE..................................816 234-3000
Tamara Peterson, *Principal*
Trudi Grin, *Med Doctor*
EMP: 85 **EST:** 2010
SALES (est): 11.9MM **Privately Held**
SIC: 8069 Children's hospital

(G-8550)
CHOICE SOLUTIONS LLC (PA)
7015 College Blvd Ste 300 (66211-1574)
PHONE..................................913 338-4950
James F Steinlage, *CEO*
Nick Rosa, *Business Mgr*
Shane M Steinlage, *COO*
Lindsay Clayton, *Opers Staff*
Lacretia Bates, *Engineer*
EMP: 50
SALES: 36.6MM **Privately Held**
SIC: 8748 Systems engineering consultant, ex. computer or professional

(G-8551)
CIGNA DENTAL HEALTH KANSAS INC
7400 W 110th St Ste 400 (66210-2395)
PHONE..................................913 339-4700
Tom Julien, *Manager*
Charles Meade, *Director*
EMP: 11
SALES (corp-wide): 141.6B **Publicly Held**
SIC: 6324 Dental insurance

HQ: Cigna Dental Health Of Kansas, Inc.
300 Nw 82nd Ave Ste 700
Plantation FL

(G-8552)
CIMARRON UNDERGROUND INC (PA)
7900 College Blvd Ste 106 (66210-2194)
PHONE..................................913 438-2981
Michelle Lowe, *CEO*
Kurt Gowdy, *President*
Fred Harrah, *Vice Pres*
Ray Linden, *CFO*
Dewayne Powell, *Manager*
EMP: 25 **EST:** 1977
SQ FT: 25,000
SALES (est): 77.6MM **Privately Held**
WEB: www.alunderground.com
SIC: 1623 1731 Underground utilities contractor; fiber optic cable installation

(G-8553)
CITIZENS BANK NA
8101 W 135th St (66223-1111)
PHONE..................................913 239-2700
Allan Sarris, *Manager*
EMP: 10 **Privately Held**
SIC: 6021 National commercial banks
HQ: Citizens Bank, Na
200 S Main St
Fort Scott KS 66701
620 223-1200

(G-8554)
CITY OF OVERLAND PARK
Also Called: Law Department
8500 Santa Fe Dr (66212-2866)
PHONE..................................913 895-6080
Carol Gerlach, *Mayor*
Joe Stapp, *Officer*
EMP: 300 **Privately Held**
SIC: 8111 General practice law office
PA: City Of Overland Park
8500 Santa Fe Dr
Overland Park KS 66212
913 895-6000

(G-8555)
CITY OF OVERLAND PARK
Also Called: Overland Park Convention Ctr
6000 College Blvd (66211-2401)
PHONE..................................913 339-3000
Brett Mitchell, *General Mgr*
Devin Carver, *Sales Mgr*
Dan Veglahn, *Manager*
EMP: 33 **Privately Held**
SIC: 7389 Convention & show services
PA: City Of Overland Park
8500 Santa Fe Dr
Overland Park KS 66212
913 895-6000

(G-8556)
CITY OF OVERLAND PARK
Also Called: Overland Park Public Works
11300 W 91st St (66214-1714)
PHONE..................................913 895-6040
Dave Bergner, *Branch Mgr*
EMP: 40 **Privately Held**
SIC: 7389 1611 9199 Flagging service (traffic control); highway & street maintenance;
PA: City Of Overland Park
8500 Santa Fe Dr
Overland Park KS 66212
913 895-6000

(G-8557)
CITY OF OVERLAND PARK
Also Called: Overand Park Turf Care Center
12698 Nieman Rd (66213)
PHONE..................................913 897-3805
Doug Malchior, *Branch Mgr*
Shawna Irwin, *Technical Staff*
Tony Roberts, *Director*
Tim Rains, *Officer*
EMP: 14 **Privately Held**
SIC: 7992 Public golf courses
PA: City Of Overland Park
8500 Santa Fe Dr
Overland Park KS 66212
913 895-6000

(G-8558)
CITYWIDE MORTGAGE ASSOCIATES
10800 Farley St Ste 300 (66210-1693)
PHONE..................................913 498-8822
Jeb Both, *President*
Johnnell Jones, *Vice Pres*
EMP: 13
SALES (est): 1MM **Privately Held**
SIC: 6162 Mortgage bankers & correspondents

(G-8559)
CLANCEY CO (PA)
8081 Flint St (66214-3335)
PHONE..................................913 894-4444
James G Clancey, *President*
Rick Glover, *Opers Mgr*
Robert J Clancey Jr, *Treasurer*
Richard W Clancey, *Admin Sec*
Shaun Aelmore, *Associate*
▲ **EMP:** 12
SQ FT: 14,000
SALES (est): 3.4MM **Privately Held**
WEB: www.clancey.com
SIC: 5072 5013 Miscellaneous fasteners; seat belts

(G-8560)
CLARUS GROUP LLC
9401 Indian Creek Pkwy # 500 (66210-2019)
PHONE..................................913 599-5255
Brian Crews, *Vice Pres*
Brian Dryer, *Vice Pres*
Nikki Smith, *Human Res Dir*
Sean Crews,
EMP: 50
SALES (est): 6.7MM **Privately Held**
SIC: 7371 7373 7379 Custom computer programming services; computer systems analysis & design; computer related consulting services;

(G-8561)
CLASSIC FLOORS & DESIGN CENTER (PA)
15425 Metcalf Ave (66223-2801)
PHONE..................................913 780-2171
Des D Harms, *President*
Haldor Harms, *Vice Pres*
EMP: 50
SQ FT: 8,000
SALES (est): 5.6MM **Privately Held**
WEB: www.integrityinteriors.com
SIC: 1752 5023 5032 Floor laying & floor work; wood flooring; tile & clay products

(G-8562)
CLASSIC SHOWER DOOR INC
8841 Lenexa Dr (66214-3240)
PHONE..................................913 492-9670
Tammy Graham, *President*
Keith Brown, *President*
EMP: 7
SQ FT: 3,000
SALES (est): 548.3K **Privately Held**
SIC: 3089 Doors, folding: plastic or plastic coated fabric

(G-8563)
CLEARWIRE CORPORATION (DH)
6200 Sprint Pkwy (66251-6117)
PHONE..................................425 216-7600
John W Stanton, *Ch of Bd*
Teresa Elder, *President*
Erik E Prusch, *President*
Broady R Hodder, *Senior VP*
John C B Saw, *Senior VP*
◆ **EMP:** 25
SQ FT: 105,000
SALES (est): 118.9MM **Publicly Held**
SIC: 4813
HQ: Sprint Communications, Inc.
6200 Sprint Pkwy
Overland Park KS 66251
855 848-3280

(G-8564)
CLEARWIRE LLC
6391 Sprint Pkwy (66251-6100)
PHONE..................................202 628-3544
EMP: 16 **EST:** 2010
SALES (est): 907.5K **Privately Held**
SIC: 4812 Radiotelephone Communication

(G-8565)
CLEVELAND UNIVERSITY - KANS CY (PA)
10850 Lowell Ave (66210-1613)
PHONE..................................913 234-0600
Carl Cleveland III DC, *President*
Jeff Karp, *COO*
Clark Beckley, *Vice Pres*
Dale Marrant, *Vice Pres*
Lexa Watroba, *Advisor*
EMP: 90
SQ FT: 60,000
SALES (est): 15.4MM **Privately Held**
WEB: www.clevelandchiropractic.edu
SIC: 8221 8041 Professional schools; offices & clinics of chiropractors

(G-8566)
CLIFF TOZIER INSURANCE AGENCY
5750 W 95th St Ste 105 (66207-2974)
PHONE..................................913 385-5000
Dave Tozier, *President*
EMP: 12
SALES (est): 1.4MM **Privately Held**
SIC: 6411 Insurance agents

(G-8567)
CLIFTONLARSONALLEN LLP
12721 Metcalf Ave Ste 201 (66213-2619)
PHONE..................................913 491-6655
Jerry Gottlieb, *Branch Mgr*
EMP: 13
SALES (corp-wide): 755.1MM **Privately Held**
SIC: 8721 Certified public accountant
PA: Cliftonlarsonallen Llp
220 S 6th St Ste 300
Minneapolis MN 55402
612 376-4500

(G-8568)
CLOROX COMPANY
7101 College Blvd Ste 320 (66210-2079)
PHONE..................................913 664-9000
Sarah Kerske, *Manager*
EMP: 19
SALES (corp-wide): 6.2B **Publicly Held**
SIC: 2842 2812 Laundry cleaning preparations; chlorine, compressed or liquefied
PA: The Clorox Company
1221 Broadway Ste 1300
Oakland CA 94612
510 271-7000

(G-8569)
CLOROX PRODUCTS MFG CO
7101 College Blvd Ste 320 (66210-2079)
PHONE..................................913 620-1777
Fred Porterfield, *Manager*
EMP: 8
SALES (corp-wide): 6.2B **Publicly Held**
SIC: 2842 Disinfectants, household or industrial plant
HQ: Clorox Manufacturing Company
1221 Broadway
Oakland CA 94612

(G-8570)
CNA FINANCIAL CORPORATION
Also Called: CNA Insurance
7400 W 110th St Ste 650 (66210-2303)
PHONE..................................913 661-2700
Matt Hartigan, *Manager*
EMP: 58
SALES (corp-wide): 14B **Publicly Held**
SIC: 6411 6351 Insurance agents, brokers & service; surety insurance
HQ: Cna Financial Corporation
151 N Franklin St Ste 700
Chicago IL 60606
312 822-5000

(G-8571)
COBBS ALLEN & HALL INC
Also Called: Nationwide
7300 College Blvd Ste 300 (66210-1879)
PHONE..................................913 267-5600
EMP: 20
SALES (corp-wide): 31.3MM **Privately Held**
SIC: 6411 Insurance agents
PA: Cobbs, Allen & Hall, Incorporated
115 Office Park Dr # 200
Mountain Brk AL 35223
205 414-8100

(G-8572)
COCHRAN HEAD VICK & CO PA
7255 W 98th Ter Ste 100 (66212-2200)
PHONE..................................913 378-1100
Bud Vick, *Branch Mgr*
EMP: 12 **Privately Held**
SIC: 8721 Certified public accountant
PA: Cochran Head Vick & Co., P.A.
1251 Nw Briarcliff Pkwy # 125
Kansas City MO 64116

(G-8573)
COHEN-ESREY LLC (PA)
Also Called: Cohen Esrey
6800 W 64th St Ste 101 (66202-4179)
PHONE..................................913 671-3300
Robert E Esrey, *Ch of Bd*
R Lee Harris, *President*
Jackie Klacik, *District Mgr*
Jeanette Jayne, *Exec VP*
Ryan Huffman, *Senior VP*
EMP: 40
SQ FT: 6,000
SALES (est): 27.2MM **Privately Held**
WEB: www.cohenesrey.com
SIC: 6531 Real estate managers

(G-8574)
COHEN-ESREY COMMUNITIES LLC
6800 W 64th St Ste 101 (66202-4179)
PHONE..................................913 671-3300
Robert Esrey, *Ch of Bd*
R Lee Harris, *President*
Jeanette Jayne, *Vice Pres*
EMP: 99
SQ FT: 16,000
SALES (est): 1.5MM **Privately Held**
SIC: 6531 Real estate managers

(G-8575)
COLDWELL BANKER ADVANTAGE
10865 Grandview Dr # 2050 (66210-1580)
PHONE..................................913 345-9999
Karen Bergin, *Owner*
Ann Taylor, *Asst Broker*
EMP: 63
SQ FT: 12,000
SALES (est): 3.8MM **Privately Held**
SIC: 6531 Real estate agent, residential

(G-8576)
COLISEUM IMGING VENTURES I LLC
8000 College Blvd (66210-1822)
PHONE..................................913 338-3344
Joshua Linn, *Office Mgr*
EMP: 15 **EST:** 2012
SALES (est): 363.3K **Privately Held**
SIC: 8099 Health screening service

(G-8577)
COLLEGE PARK ENDOSCOPY CTR LLC
10787 Nall Ave (66211-1375)
PHONE..................................913 385-4400
EMP: 644
SALES (est): 4.4MM **Publicly Held**
SIC: 8062 General medical & surgical hospitals
HQ: Midamerica Division, Inc.
903 E 104th St Ste 500
Kansas City MO 64131
816 508-4000

(G-8578)
COMMERCE BANK
9501 Antioch Rd (66212-4059)
PHONE..................................913 381-2386
EMP: 21
SALES (corp-wide): 1.3B **Publicly Held**
SIC: 6022 State commercial banks
HQ: Commerce Bank
1000 Walnut St Fl 700
Kansas City MO 64106
816 234-2000

GEOGRAPHIC

(G-8579)
COMMERCE BANK
12280 W 135th St (66221-9391)
PHONE..................................816 234-2000
Cindy Ford, *Manager*
EMP: 13
SALES (corp-wide): 1.3B **Publicly Held**
SIC: 6022 State commercial banks
HQ: Commerce Bank
1000 Walnut St Fl 700
Kansas City MO 64106
816 234-2000

(G-8580)
COMMERCIAL REAL ESTATE NEWS
10870 Benson Dr Ste 2160 (66210-1509)
PHONE..................................913 345-2378
Kenneth Flaspohr, *President*
EMP: 25
SALES (est): 686.2K **Privately Held**
SIC: 6531 Real estate brokers & agents

(G-8581)
COMMUNITY BROADCASTING INC
10550 Barkley St (66212-1824)
PHONE..................................913 642-7770
Richard P Bott, *Principal*
EMP: 10
SALES (est): 64.5K **Privately Held**
SIC: 4832 Radio broadcasting stations

(G-8582)
COMMUNITY LIVING OPPORTUNITIES
6900 W 80th St (66204-3837)
PHONE..................................913 341-9316
Jennifer Wagner, *Director*
Yolanda Hargett, *Administration*
EMP: 10 **EST:** 2010
SALES (est): 385.9K **Privately Held**
SIC: 8361 Home for the mentally handicapped

(G-8583)
COMMUNITY LVING OPPRTNTIES INC
7725 W 87th St (66212-1905)
PHONE..................................913 499-8894
EMP: 37
SALES (corp-wide): 22.5MM **Privately Held**
SIC: 8361 Home for the mentally handicapped
PA: Community Living Opportunities, Inc.
11627 W 79th St
Lenexa KS 66214
913 341-9316

(G-8584)
COMMUNITYWORKS INC
7819 Conser Pl (66204-2820)
PHONE..................................913 789-9900
Janet Williams, *CEO*
Laura Boswell, *COO*
EMP: 99
SALES (est): 2.8MM **Privately Held**
SIC: 8742 Hospital & health services consultant

(G-8585)
COMPASS MINERALS
9900 W 109th St Ste 600 (66210-1436)
P.O. Box 1190, Ogden UT (84402-1190)
PHONE..................................913 344-9200
Robert Boyle, *Principal*
Logan Bateman, *Vice Pres*
Bashar Sader, *Plant Supt*
Gordon Hyde, *Facilities Mgr*
Deone Judkins, *Sales Staff*
EMP: 499
SALES (est): 419.1K **Privately Held**
SIC: 1474 Potash mining

(G-8586)
COMPASS MINERALS AMERICA INC
Big Quill Resources
9900 W 109th St Ste 100 (66210-1436)
PHONE..................................913 344-9100
EMP: 200
SALES (corp-wide): 1.4B **Publicly Held**
SIC: 2899 Salt
HQ: Compass Minerals America Inc
9900 W 109th St Ste 600
Overland Park KS 66210
913 344-9100

(G-8587)
COMPASS MINERALS AMERICA INC (HQ)
9900 W 109th St Ste 600 (66210-1436)
PHONE..................................913 344-9100
Angelo C Brisimitzakis, *CEO*
Keith Clark, *Vice Pres*
▲ **EMP:** 168
SQ FT: 28,686
SALES (est): 413.5MM
SALES (corp-wide): 1.4B **Publicly Held**
SIC: 2899 1479 Salt; rock salt mining
PA: Compass Minerals International, Inc.
9900 W 109th St Ste 100
Overland Park KS 66210
913 344-9200

(G-8588)
COMPASS MINERALS GROUP INC
9900 W 109th St Ste 600 (66210-1436)
PHONE..................................913 344-9100
Angelo C Brisimitzakis, *President*
Steve Berger, *Vice Pres*
Michael Birger, *Vice Pres*
Jeffrey Curtis, *Vice Pres*
Victoria Heider, *Vice Pres*
◆ **EMP:** 180
SQ FT: 35,000
SALES: 857.3MM
SALES (corp-wide): 1.4B **Publicly Held**
SIC: 2819 2899 Sodium compounds or salts, inorg., ex. refined sod. chloride; salt
PA: Compass Minerals International, Inc.
9900 W 109th St Ste 100
Overland Park KS 66210
913 344-9200

(G-8589)
COMPASS MINERALS INTL INC (PA)
9900 W 109th St Ste 100 (66210-1436)
PHONE..................................913 344-9200
Richard S Grant, *Ch of Bd*
George J Schuller Jr, *COO*
S Bradley Griffith, *Senior VP*
Angela Y Jones, *Senior VP*
David Goadby, *Vice Pres*
◆ **EMP:** 169
SALES: 1.4B **Publicly Held**
SIC: 1479 1474 2899 2819 Salt (common) mining; potash, soda & borate minerals; salt; potassium compounds or salts, except hydroxide or carbonate; sodium compounds or salts, inorg., ex. refined sod. chloride; sodium sulfate, glauber's salt, salt cake

(G-8590)
COMPLETE LLC
8666 W 96th St (66212-3315)
PHONE..................................913 238-0206
Austin H Chamberlin, *Principal*
Sherry Sullivan, *Office Mgr*
EMP: 10 **EST:** 2011
SALES (est): 1.3MM **Privately Held**
SIC: 8711 Building construction consultant

(G-8591)
COMPLEX PROPERTY ADVISERS CORP
Also Called: Property Valuation Services
14400 Metcalf Ave (66223-2989)
PHONE..................................913 498-0790
Dave Dlugopolski, *Partner*
Robert Hileman, *Partner*
Pam Carley, *Managing Dir*
Tyler Rognlie, *Personnel*
James Lee, *Consultant*
EMP: 18
SALES (est): 2.1MM **Privately Held**
SIC: 8742 8721 Real estate consultant; accounting, auditing & bookkeeping

(G-8592)
COMPTECH GROUP LLC
Also Called: Comptech Group The
3853 W 95th St (66206-2038)
PHONE..................................913 341-7600
Mike Geanes, *Manager*
Jay Rohrs,
EMP: 10
SALES (est): 1.3MM **Privately Held**
SIC: 6411 8011 Insurance agents; medical insurance associations

(G-8593)
COMPUTER SCIENCES CORPORATION
7701 College Blvd Ste 200 (66210-1866)
PHONE..................................913 469-8700
Lori Barrett, *Branch Mgr*
EMP: 145
SALES (corp-wide): 20.7B **Publicly Held**
SIC: 7376 7374 7379 7373 Computer facilities management; data processing & preparation; computer processing services; computer related consulting services; systems integration services; credit reporting services
HQ: Computer Sciences Corporation
1775 Tysons Blvd Ste 1000
Tysons VA 22102
703 245-9675

(G-8594)
CONCEPT MACHINERY INC
6319 W 110th St (66211-1509)
PHONE..................................317 845-5588
Jeff Tucker, *Vice Pres*
EMP: 5 **EST:** 2015
SALES (est): 187.6K **Privately Held**
SIC: 3549 Metalworking machinery

(G-8595)
CONSTRUCTIVE ENGRG DESIGN
Also Called: C E D
9400 Reeds Rd Ste 200 (66207-2531)
PHONE..................................913 341-3300
Michael Farrahi, *President*
Bob Fezio, *Vice Pres*
EMP: 16
SQ FT: 4,000
SALES (est): 1.7MM **Privately Held**
WEB: www.cedweb.com
SIC: 8711 Structural engineering

(G-8596)
CONTEMPORARY WOMENS CENTRE
8675 College Blvd Ste 100 (66210-1863)
PHONE..................................913 345-2322
Dennis Katz, *Partner*
Mark Curry, *Vice Pres*
EMP: 10
SALES (est): 620K **Privately Held**
SIC: 8011 Obstetrician; gynecologist

(G-8597)
CONVERGEONE INC
12980 Foster St Ste 300 (66213-2692)
PHONE..................................913 307-2300
EMP: 103
SALES (corp-wide): 96.1MM **Privately Held**
SIC: 5045 7373 8748 7376 Computer peripheral equipment; systems software development services; local area network (LAN) systems integrator; business consulting; computer facilities management; computer peripheral equipment; electrical work
HQ: Convergeone, Inc.
10900 Nesbitt Ave S
Minneapolis MN 55437

(G-8598)
COOKBOOK PUBLISHERS INC (PA)
Also Called: CPI Printing and Bindery Svcs
11633 W 83rd Ter (66214-1538)
P.O. Box 15920, Shawnee Mission (66285-5920)
PHONE..................................913 689-3038
Kevin Derry, *President*
Dennis E Evans, *Chairman*
Valerie Van Hoecke, *Opers Mgr*
EMP: 35
SQ FT: 16,000
SALES (est): 5.9MM **Privately Held**
WEB: www.cookbookpublishers.com
SIC: 2731 2791 2789 2752 Books: publishing & printing; typesetting; bookbinding & related work; commercial printing, lithographic

(G-8599)
CORNERSTONE BANK
9120 W 135th St Ste 200 (66221-2047)
PHONE..................................913 239-8100
John Doull, *President*
Vickie Fastnacht, *Assistant VP*
Michelle Guthrie, *Vice Pres*
Matthew Brown, *Officer*
EMP: 52
SALES: 8.9MM **Privately Held**
WEB: www.cornerstonebk.com
SIC: 6022 State commercial banks

(G-8600)
CORNERSTONE HOME LENDING INC
9393 W 110th St Ste 250 (66210-1440)
PHONE..................................913 317-5626
Mark Rome, *Branch Mgr*
EMP: 15
SALES (corp-wide): 296.1MM **Privately Held**
SIC: 6162 Mortgage bankers & correspondents
PA: Cornerstone Home Lending, Inc.
1177 West Loop S Ste 700
Houston TX 77027
713 621-4663

(G-8601)
CORT BUSINESS SERVICES CORP
Also Called: Cort Furniture Rental
9111 Quivira Rd (66215-3903)
PHONE..................................913 888-0100
Ray Randall, *CEO*
Melissa Arciga, *Manager*
Christine Dunkin, *Consultant*
EMP: 20
SQ FT: 5,000
SALES (corp-wide): 225.3B **Publicly Held**
SIC: 7359 5932 5712 Furniture rental; office furniture, secondhand; office furniture
HQ: Cort Business Services Corporation
15000 Conference
Chantilly VA 20151
703 968-8500

(G-8602)
CORVEL CORPORATION
9401 Indian Creek Pkwy # 400
(66210-2096)
PHONE..................................913 253-7200
Cathy Casil, *COO*
Wanda Horne, *Branch Mgr*
Debra Dampaucher, *Manager*
EMP: 25
SALES (corp-wide): 595.7MM **Publicly Held**
WEB: www.corvel.com
SIC: 8741 Management services
PA: Corvel Corporation
2010 Main St Ste 600
Irvine CA 92614
949 851-1473

(G-8603)
COTTAGECARE INC (PA)
6323 W 110th St (66211-1509)
PHONE..................................913 469-8778
Thomas Schrader, *President*
Michael Christ, *Supervisor*
EMP: 13
SQ FT: 3,500
SALES (est): 1.6MM **Privately Held**
SIC: 7699 7349 Cleaning services; maid services, contract or fee basis

(G-8604)
COUCH PIERCE KING & HOFFMEISTE
10975 Benson Dr Ste 370 (66210-2135)
PHONE..................................913 451-8430
Harold Pierce, *President*
Mark Hoffmeister, *Principal*
William King, *Principal*
Michael Wharton,

▲ = Import ▼=Export
◆ =Import/Export

EMP: 15
SALES (est): 1.5MM **Privately Held**
SIC: 8111 Specialized law offices, attorneys

(G-8605)
COUNTY OF JOHNSON
Museums
8788 Metcalf Ave (66212-2041)
PHONE..................................913 715-2550
Mindi Love, *Director*
EMP: 12 **Privately Held**
WEB: www.jocoks.com
SIC: 8412 9199 Museum; general government administration;
PA: County Of Johnson
111 S Cherry St Ste 1200
Olathe KS 66061
913 715-0435

(G-8606)
COVENTRY HEALTH CARE KANS INC (DH)
Also Called: Chc Kansas
9401 Indian Creek Pkwy # 1300
(66210-2007)
P.O. Box 7109, London KY (40742-7109)
PHONE..................................800 969-3343
Allan Wise, *President*
Stephanie Mellor, *Manager*
George Wheeler, *Exec Dir*
EMP: 150
SQ FT: 3,625
SALES (est): 617.9MM
SALES (corp-wide): 194.5B **Publicly Held**
WEB: www.chckansas.com
SIC: 6324 8011 Health maintenance organization (HMO), insurance only; pediatrician
HQ: Coventry Health Care, Inc.
6720 Rockledge Dr 700b
Bethesda MD 20817
301 581-0600

(G-8607)
COX ENTERPRISES INC
Also Called: Autotrader Com
6405 Metcalf Ave (66202-3931)
PHONE..................................913 825-6124
EMP: 40
SALES (corp-wide): 29.2B **Privately Held**
SIC: 4841 Cable & other pay television services
PA: Cox Enterprises, Inc.
6205 Pachtree Dunwoody Rd
Atlanta GA 30328
678 645-0000

(G-8608)
CREATIVE CAPSULE LLC
10875 Benson Dr Ste 275 (66210-1568)
PHONE..................................816 421-1714
Julia Talauliker,
EMP: 80 **EST:** 2012
SALES (est): 261.9K **Privately Held**
SIC: 8742 7371 Management consulting services; custom computer programming services

(G-8609)
CREATIVE CARNIVALS EVENTS LLC (PA)
11121 W 87th Ter (66214-3218)
PHONE..................................913 642-0900
Kevin Wilson, *Principal*
Sandra Wilson, *Mng Member*
EMP: 10
SALES (est): 618.3K **Privately Held**
SIC: 7999 Carnival operation

(G-8610)
CREATIVE CONSUMER CONCEPTS INC (PA)
Also Called: C3
10955 Granada Ln Ste 200 (66211-1440)
PHONE..................................913 491-6444
Robert S Cutler, *President*
Randy Jordan, *President*
Jamie Phillips, *COO*
Barb Smith, *Production*
Ginny Harris, *Controller*
▲ **EMP:** 44
SQ FT: 14,000
SALES (est): 32.8MM **Privately Held**
WEB: www.c3mail.com
SIC: 5199 Advertising specialties

(G-8611)
CREATIVE MKTG UNLIMITED INC
9548 Buena Vista St (66207-3531)
PHONE..................................913 894-0077
William J Zirger, *President*
Elizabeth Hochsceid, *Vice Pres*
EMP: 5
SQ FT: 1,400
SALES (est): 490K **Privately Held**
WEB: www.creativemarketingunlimited.com
SIC: 8743 5113 2679 Promotion service; bags, paper & disposable plastic; labels, paper: made from purchased material

(G-8612)
CREATIVE PLANNING INC (PA)
5454 W 110th St (66211-1204)
PHONE..................................913 341-0900
Peter A Mallouk, *President*
Mike Roberts, *Managing Prtnr*
Carleen Acosta, *Opers Mgr*
Lacey Cowan, *Opers Mgr*
Joe Walrod, *Broker*
EMP: 30
SALES (est): 11.2MM **Privately Held**
SIC: 6282 Investment advisory service

(G-8613)
CRESTLINE HOTELS & RESORTS LLC
6801 W 112th St (66211-1577)
PHONE..................................913 451-2553
Pete Fortunev, *Manager*
EMP: 38
SALES (corp-wide): 52.2MM **Privately Held**
SIC: 8741 Hotel or motel management
PA: Crestline Hotels & Resorts, Llc
3950 University Dr # 301
Fairfax VA 22030
571 529-6100

(G-8614)
CRICKET COMMUNICATIONS INC
7620 Metcalf Ave (66204-2907)
PHONE..................................913 341-2799
EMP: 11
SALES (corp-wide): 3.1B **Publicly Held**
SIC: 4812 Radiotelephone Communication
HQ: Cricket Communications, Inc.
5887 Copley Dr
San Diego CA 92121
858 882-6000

(G-8615)
CROP USA HUTSON INSUR GROUP
7300 W 110th St Ste 400 (66210-2332)
PHONE..................................913 345-1515
Randy Rhodes, *President*
EMP: 40
SALES (est): 4.5MM **Privately Held**
SIC: 6411 Insurance agents

(G-8616)
CROSS MANUFACTURING INC (PA)
11011 King St Ste 210 (66210-1230)
PHONE..................................913 451-1233
John Cross, *President*
Patrice Cross, *Corp Secy*
Larry Boos, *Vice Pres*
Andy Mizzi, *Facilities Mgr*
▲ **EMP:** 6
SQ FT: 3,000
SALES (est): 21.3MM **Privately Held**
WEB: www.crossmfg.com
SIC: 3593 Fluid power actuators, hydraulic or pneumatic

(G-8617)
CROSSFIRST BANK (PA)
4707 W 135th St (66224-7613)
PHONE..................................913 327-1212
Terry Blain, *Partner*
Tom McGrath, *Partner*
Eric R Schroeder, *Exec VP*
Stacy Cook, *Vice Pres*
Glenda Deflon, *Vice Pres*
EMP: 51
SALES: 162.4MM **Privately Held**
SIC: 6022 State commercial banks

(G-8618)
CROSSFIRST BANKSHARES INC
4707 W 135th St (66224-7613)
PHONE..................................913 754-9700
Melanie Galassnan, *Manager*
EMP: 151
SALES (corp-wide): 162.9MM **Publicly Held**
SIC: 6512 Bank building operation
PA: Crossfirst Bankshares, Inc.
11440 Tomahawk Creek Pkwy
Leawood KS 66211
913 312-6822

(G-8619)
CROWN RECOVERY SERVICES LLC
12811 W 131st St (66213-5019)
PHONE..................................816 777-2366
John Hedrick, *Partner*
Nancy Hedrick, *Partner*
EMP: 12
SALES (est): 870K **Privately Held**
WEB: www.crown-recovery.com
SIC: 7389 Repossession service

(G-8620)
CSM-CSI JOINT VENTURE
6920 W 154th St Ste B (66223)
PHONE..................................913 227-9609
Juan Martinez, *Partner*
EMP: 99
SALES: 500K **Privately Held**
SIC: 6531 Real estate agents & managers

(G-8621)
CSTK INC (PA)
Also Called: CENTRAL STATES THERMO KING
7200 W 132nd St Ste 270 (66213-1135)
PHONE..................................913 233-7220
Michael Kahn, *President*
Allen Lane, *COO*
Don Soetaert, *CFO*
Ronald A Kahn, *Shareholder*
▲ **EMP:** 20 **EST:** 1955
SQ FT: 14,000
SALES: 34.4MM **Privately Held**
WEB: www.cstk.com
SIC: 5078 7623 5084 Refrigeration units, motor vehicles; refrigeration repair service; engines & transportation equipment

(G-8622)
CU CAPITAL MKT SOLUTIONS LLC
Also Called: Cnbs
7200 W 132nd St Ste 240 (66213-1135)
PHONE..................................913 402-2627
Matt Johnson, *President*
Ryan Enright, *VP Bus Dvlpt*
Brent Hippert, *CFO*
Ashley Reece, *Mktg Coord*
Lewis Lester, *Manager*
EMP: 15
SALES (corp-wide): 2.5MM **Privately Held**
SIC: 6211 Security brokers & dealers
PA: Cu Capital Market Solutions, Llc
6120 Windward Pkwy # 200
Alpharetta GA 30005
678 960-2900

(G-8623)
CULVERS FROZEN CUSTARD
8600 W 135th St (66223-1214)
PHONE..................................913 402-9777
John Clark, *Owner*
EMP: 50
SALES (est): 749.9K **Privately Held**
SIC: 5812 2024 Ice cream stands or dairy bars; custard, frozen

(G-8624)
CUSHMAN & WAKEFIELD ILL INC
7304 W 130th St Ste 150 (66213-2654)
PHONE..................................913 440-0420
Sidney Womack, *Principal*
Benjamin D Lutz, *Associate*
EMP: 16
SALES (corp-wide): 8.2B **Privately Held**
SIC: 6531 Appraiser, real estate
HQ: Cushman & Wakefield Of Illinois, Inc.
200 S Wacker Dr Ste 2800
Chicago IL 60606
312 470-1800

(G-8625)
CUSTOM BRANDED SPORTSWEAR INC
Also Called: Ping Apparel
7007 College Blvd (66211-1558)
PHONE..................................866 441-7464
David Reid, *President*
EMP: 15
SALES (est): 1.3MM **Privately Held**
SIC: 5699 2329 Sports apparel; athletic (warmup, sweat & jogging) suits: men's & boys'

(G-8626)
D & L TRANSPORT LLC (PA)
8101 College Blvd 110 (66210-1978)
P.O. Box 7690 (66207-0690)
PHONE..................................913 402-4514
Jenelle Jackson, *Broker*
Eric Defrain, *Mng Member*
Katie Flood, *Agent*
Brian Defrain,
Jim Langenbach,
EMP: 51
SQ FT: 2,000
SALES: 48MM **Privately Held**
SIC: 4731 Truck transportation brokers

(G-8627)
D D I REALTY SERVICES INC
Also Called: Southcreek Viii Associates
7200 W 132nd St Ste 300 (66213-1136)
PHONE..................................913 685-4100
Marshall H Dean Jr, *President*
Vincent W Dean, *Vice Pres*
Janice Haley, *Accountant*
Westy Carpenter, *Sales Staff*
Matthew Carson, *Sales Staff*
EMP: 11
SALES (est): 1.8MM **Privately Held**
SIC: 6531 Real estate agent, commercial

(G-8628)
D L P SERVICES INC
8181 W 123rd Ter (66213-1460)
PHONE..................................913 685-1477
Dan Pickens, *Executive Asst*
EMP: 12
SALES (est): 755.8K **Privately Held**
SIC: 4959 Sweeping service: road, airport, parking lot, etc.

(G-8629)
D W NEWCOMERS SONS INC
Johnson County Memorial Grdns
11200 Metcalf Ave (66210-1803)
PHONE..................................913 451-1860
Gina Lanzrath, *Branch Mgr*
EMP: 13
SALES (corp-wide): 3.1B **Publicly Held**
WEB: www.dwnewcomers.com
SIC: 7261 Funeral home
HQ: D W Newcomer's Sons Inc
7000 Blue Ridge Blvd
Raytown MO 64133
816 353-1218

(G-8630)
DAHMER CONTRACTING GROUP LLC
Also Called: Dusty Dahmer Construction
8375 Nieman Rd (66214-1511)
PHONE..................................816 795-3332
Dusty Dahmer, *CEO*
Teresa Dahmer, *President*
EMP: 90
SALES (est): 2.3MM **Privately Held**
SIC: 5231 5031 1751 Paint & painting supplies; wallboard; carpentry work

(G-8631)
DALAN INC
Also Called: Home Cleaning Centers America
8220 Travis St Ste 200 (66204-3966)
PHONE..................................913 384-5662
Alan Hierseman, *President*
David Calhoon, *Vice Pres*
EMP: 40

GEOGRAPHIC

SALES (est): 1.9MM **Privately Held**
WEB: www.dalan.com
SIC: 7217 7349 Carpet & upholstery cleaning on customer premises; carpet & furniture cleaning on location; building maintenance services; window cleaning

(G-8632)
DANA F COLE & COMPANY LLP
9300 W 110th St Ste 145 (66210-1432)
PHONE..................................913 341-8200
Susan Sherry, *Manager*
EMP: 10
SALES (corp-wide): 19.2MM **Privately Held**
WEB: www.danacole.com
SIC: 8721 Certified public accountant
PA: Dana F. Cole & Company, Llp
1248 O St Ste 500
Lincoln NE 68508
402 479-9312

(G-8633)
DANIEL S DURRIE COKINGTIN LLC
Also Called: Durrie Vsion Cokingtin Eye Ctr
8300 College Blvd Ste 201 (66210-2812)
PHONE..................................913 491-3330
Daniel S Durrie, *Partner*
Courtney Moilanen, *Marketing Staff*
Shari Clark, *Surgeon*
Tammy Crane, *Exec Dir*
Kristi Daugherty, *Director*
EMP: 50 **EST:** 2002
SALES (est): 3.4MM **Privately Held**
WEB: www.durrievision.com
SIC: 8042 Offices & clinics of optometrists

(G-8634)
DANIEL ZIMMERMAN
Also Called: Number 7 Software
12009 W 163rd St (66221-8544)
PHONE..................................303 378-2511
Daniel Zimmerman, *Owner*
EMP: 5
SALES (est): 310K **Privately Held**
SIC: 7372 Application computer software

(G-8635)
DARROW COMPANY
9310 W 85th St (66212-3560)
PHONE..................................800 525-6084
Matthew Darrow, *Owner*
EMP: 7
SALES: 115K **Privately Held**
SIC: 3669 Smoke detectors

(G-8636)
DATA LOCKER INC
Also Called: Datalocker
7300 College Blvd Ste 600 (66210-1895)
PHONE..................................913 310-9088
Jay Kim, *President*
Andy Cordial, *Vice Pres*
Bob Gronski, *Vice Pres*
Yong Duk Lee, *Research*
Ross Buhr, *Engineer*
EMP: 9 **EST:** 2008
SALES: 3MM **Privately Held**
SIC: 5065 3572 3695 7372 Electronic parts & equipment; computer storage devices; magnetic & optical recording media; application computer software

(G-8637)
DATA SYSTEMS INC
Also Called: Kansas City Cash Register
11505 W 79th St (66214-1410)
PHONE..................................913 281-1333
Veronica Lister, *Sales Staff*
EMP: 15
SALES (corp-wide): 1.6MM **Privately Held**
SIC: 5044 Cash registers
HQ: Data Systems, Inc.
6515 S 118th St Ste 100
Omaha NE 68137
402 597-6477

(G-8638)
DATASYSTEM SOLUTIONS INC
6901 Shawnee Mission Pkwy # 207 (66202-4082)
PHONE..................................913 362-6969
Gay H Manning, *President*
Lorna Fenimore, *Sales Staff*
Nancy Spear, *CTO*
EMP: 21 **EST:** 1978
SQ FT: 4,500
SALES (est): 2.9MM **Privately Held**
SIC: 7373 Systems software development services

(G-8639)
DAUGHTERS & COMPANY INC
10560 Barkley St Ste 320 (66212-1822)
PHONE..................................913 341-2500
Gary Hammilton, *President*
EMP: 20
SALES (est): 956.1K **Privately Held**
SIC: 8322 Senior citizens' center or association

(G-8640)
DAVID B LAHA MD BPM
7230 W 129th St (66213-2624)
PHONE..................................913 338-4440
David Laha, *Owner*
EMP: 10
SALES (est): 462.4K **Privately Held**
WEB: www.kcfoot.com
SIC: 8043 Offices & clinics of podiatrists

(G-8641)
DAVID CAMP INC
Also Called: Branded Emblem
7920 Foster St (66204-3642)
PHONE..................................913 648-0573
David Willson, *President*
Mark Willson, *Vice Pres*
Kim Mitchell, *CFO*
Pam Bowron, *Sales Dir*
Laura Reaka, *Marketing Mgr*
▲ **EMP:** 110 **EST:** 1993
SQ FT: 42,000
SALES (est): 10.7MM **Privately Held**
SIC: 2395 2759 Emblems, embroidered; screen printing

(G-8642)
DAVID W HEAD
Also Called: Re/Max
12721 W 138th Pl (66221-4141)
PHONE..................................913 402-0057
EMP: 75
SALES (est): 1.6MM **Privately Held**
SIC: 6531 Rl Este Agntresidntl

(G-8643)
DAVIDSON ARCH ENGRG LLC
4301 Indian Creek Pkwy (66207-4109)
PHONE..................................913 451-9390
John Davidson, *Principal*
Paul Miller, *Engineer*
Hilary Zerr, *Engineer*
Chad Howerton, *Manager*
EMP: 16
SALES (est): 1.8MM **Privately Held**
SIC: 8711 Engineering services

(G-8644)
DEARBORN MID WEST CONVEYOR CO
8245 Nieman Rd Ste 123 (66214-1509)
PHONE..................................913 261-2428
Katarina Katsavrias, *Vice Pres*
EMP: 9
SALES (est): 2.6MM **Privately Held**
SIC: 3535 Conveyors & conveying equipment

(G-8645)
DECHRA VETERINARY PRODUCTS LLC (HQ)
7015 College Blvd Ste 525 (66211-1551)
PHONE..................................913 327-0015
Mike Eldred, *President*
Paul Ray, *General Mgr*
John Bardsley, *Vice Pres*
Victor Gonzalez, *Mfg Spvr*
Cathy Gaudio, *Opers Staff*
▲ **EMP:** 15
SALES (est): 18.4MM
SALES (corp-wide): 610.1MM **Privately Held**
WEB: www.dechra.com
SIC: 0742 Animal hospital services, pets & other animal specialties
PA: Dechra Pharmaceuticals Plc
24 Cheshire Business Park
Northwich CW9 7
160 681-4730

(G-8646)
DEER CREEK SURGERY CENTER LLC
7220 W 129th St (66213-2624)
PHONE..................................913 897-0022
Kerri Ragsdale, *Nursing Dir*
Robin Smith, *Nursing Dir*
Timothy Cavanaugh,
Michelle M Sullivan, *Administration*
EMP: 13
SALES (est): 1.7MM **Privately Held**
SIC: 8011 Surgeon

(G-8647)
DEFY MEDICAL GROUP LLC
14105 Kessler St (66221-2123)
PHONE..................................913 396-2888
Patrick Howell,
EMP: 10 **EST:** 2017
SALES (est): 67.1K **Privately Held**
SIC: 8099 Health & allied services

(G-8648)
DEMARCHE ASSOCIATES INC
6700 Antioch Rd Ste 420 (66204-1541)
P.O. Box 7027, Kansas City MO (64113-0027)
PHONE..................................913 384-4994
Thimothy Marchesi, *Ch of Bd*
Christina R Danner, *Senior VP*
Debra Vanderwerf, *Human Res Mgr*
Mark Andes, *Manager*
James Dykstal, *Consultant*
EMP: 65
SALES (est): 18.2MM **Privately Held**
WEB: www.demarche.com
SIC: 6411 6282 Pension & retirement plan consultants; investment advice

(G-8649)
DEMARS PNSION CNSLTING SVCS IN
8700 Indian Creek Pkwy (66210-1563)
PHONE..................................913 469-6111
Jimmy A Demars, *President*
John Finn, *Vice Pres*
Cyndi Johnson, *Vice Pres*
Joanne Trompeter, *Vice Pres*
Nancy Love, *Accounting Mgr*
EMP: 42
SQ FT: 9,000
SALES (est): 7.5MM **Privately Held**
WEB: www.demarspension.com
SIC: 6411 Pension & retirement plan consultants

(G-8650)
DERMATOLOGY CONS MIDWEST
10777 Nall Ave Ste 220 (66211-1359)
PHONE..................................913 469-0110
Nancy R Waxman, *Partner*
David Oconnell, *Partner*
Braden Rance, *Partner*
EMP: 10
SALES (est): 867.1K **Privately Held**
SIC: 8011 Dermatologist

(G-8651)
DESIGN RESOURCES INC
Also Called: Caps Direct
7007 College Blvd Ste 700 (66211-2425)
PHONE..................................913 652-6522
David Reid, *President*
Mary Reid, *Vice Pres*
Linda Sinnett, *CFO*
▲ **EMP:** 63
SQ FT: 16,700
SALES (est): 23.7MM **Privately Held**
WEB: www.dridesign.com
SIC: 5136 Caps, men's & boys'

(G-8652)
DESTINATION PROPERTIES INC
7715 Shawnee Mission Pkwy (66202-3068)
PHONE..................................913 583-1515
JD Asbell, *President*
EMP: 10
SALES (est): 908K **Privately Held**
SIC: 6531 Real estate brokers & agents; buying agent, real estate

(G-8653)
DIABETES & ENDOCRINOLOGY ASSOC
8901 W 74th St Ste 372 (66204-2203)
PHONE..................................913 676-7585
Joseph Simonem, *Principal*
EMP: 17
SALES (est): 1.1MM **Privately Held**
SIC: 8011 General & family practice, physician/surgeon

(G-8654)
DICKINSON THEATRES
6801 W 107th St (66212-1825)
P.O. Box 179, Liberty MO (64069-0179)
PHONE..................................913 383-6114
Brett Mill, *Opers Mgr*
Bruce Wittman, *CFO*
EMP: 26 **EST:** 2010
SALES (est): 1.3MM **Privately Held**
SIC: 7832 Motion picture theaters, except drive-in

(G-8655)
DIGITAL EVOLUTION GROUP LLC
6601 College Blvd 6 (66211-1504)
PHONE..................................913 498-9988
Neal Sharma, *CEO*
Greg Bustamante, *Engineer*
Dale Hazlett, *CFO*
Bethany Kemper, *Manager*
Dawn Kernen, *Director*
EMP: 102
SQ FT: 60,000
SALES (est): 13.7MM **Privately Held**
WEB: www.digitalev.com
SIC: 7374 7371 Computer graphics service; custom computer programming services
HQ: Aegis Media Americas, Llc
150 E 42nd St New York
New York NY 10017
212 591-9122

(G-8656)
DIGITAL LAGOON INC
9121 Bond St (66214-1726)
PHONE..................................913 648-6900
Jordan Gershon, *President*
▲ **EMP:** 18
SQ FT: 6,000
SALES: 2MM **Privately Held**
WEB: www.digitallagoon.com
SIC: 2759 7374 Commercial printing; computer graphics service

(G-8657)
DIRECT COMMUNICATIONS INC
11817 Gillette St (66210-3508)
PHONE..................................913 599-5577
Tom Scrivner, *President*
EMP: 12
SQ FT: 5,200
SALES: 1.9MM **Privately Held**
WEB: www.dci-kc.com
SIC: 5065 5045 4813 Telephone equipment; computers; voice telephone communications

(G-8658)
DIRECT SOURCE GRAN & STONE IMP
8675 College Blvd Ste 150 (66210-1890)
PHONE..................................913 766-9200
Tracy Chelepis,
▲ **EMP:** 17
SALES (est): 910K **Privately Held**
SIC: 5032 Granite building stone

(G-8659)
DLR GROUP INC (HQ)
7290 W 133rd St (66213-4748)
PHONE..................................913 897-7811
James D French, *President*
James C Anderson Jr, *Vice Pres*
Donald L Barnum, *Vice Pres*
O H Martin Berglund, *Vice Pres*
David P Boehm, *Vice Pres*
EMP: 65
SQ FT: 25,000

▲ = Import ▼=Export
◆ =Import/Export

SALES (est): 8.5MM
SALES (corp-wide): 109.7MM Privately Held
SIC: 8712 8711 0781 Architectural engineering; engineering services; landscape architects
PA: Dlr Holding Company
6457 Frances St Ste 200
Omaha NE
402 393-4100

(G-8660)
DOUGLAS A FIREBAUGH CNSTR
9393 W 110th St Ste 120 (66210-1464)
PHONE....913 451-8599
Doug Firebaugh, *President*
Kevin Whited, *Vice Pres*
Jeff Dimon, *Treasurer*
EMP: 200
SQ FT: 1,687
SALES (est): 8MM Privately Held
SIC: 1742 1751 Drywall; acoustical & ceiling work; insulation, buildings; carpentry work

(G-8661)
DRI DUCK TRADERS INC (PA)
7007 College Blvd Ste 700 (66211-2425)
PHONE....913 648-8222
David Reid, *CEO*
Jason Krakow, *President*
Scott Tubbs, *President*
Mary Reid, *Vice Pres*
Linda Sinnett, *CFO*
EMP: 14
SALES (est): 3.7MM Privately Held
SIC: 5136 5137 Men's & boys' clothing; women's & children's clothing

(G-8662)
DRURY HOTELS COMPANY LLC
Also Called: Drury Inn & Suites Overland Pk
10963 Metcalf Ave (66210-2301)
PHONE....913 345-1500
Curt Cerise, *Branch Mgr*
EMP: 28
SALES (corp-wide): 389.3MM Privately Held
WEB: www.druryhotels.com
SIC: 7011 Hotels
PA: Drury Hotels Company, Llc
721 Emerson Rd Ste 400
Saint Louis MO 63141
314 429-2255

(G-8663)
DUFFENS OPTICALS
Also Called: Essilor Labs of America
8140 Marshall Dr (66214-1536)
PHONE....785 234-3481
Gary Duffens, *Principal*
Brian Duffens, *Manager*
Butch Fralix, *Manager*
EMP: 70
SALES (est): 5.5MM Privately Held
SIC: 3851 Ophthalmic goods

(G-8664)
DUGGAN SHADWICK DOERR KURLBAUM
9101 W 110th St Ste 200 (66210-1449)
PHONE....913 498-3536
John Duggan, *President*
Scuyler Kurlbaum, *Principal*
Jay T Shadwick, *Vice Pres*
Brian D Doerr, *Treasurer*
EMP: 17
SALES (est): 2.1MM Privately Held
WEB: www.skylaw.com
SIC: 8111 General practice attorney, lawyer

(G-8665)
DUNAMI INC
7500 College Blvd Ste 450 (66210-4036)
PHONE....303 981-3303
Pat Butler, *CEO*
Andrew Woglom, *CFO*
Tony Marshall, *CTO*
EMP: 27 EST: 2015
SALES (est): 501.2K Privately Held
SIC: 7371 7379 Computer software development & applications; computer related consulting services

(G-8666)
DUPONT
6363 College Blvd Ste 300 (66211-1882)
PHONE....913 327-3518
Phil Birk, *Engineer*
Jay Ledou, *Engineer*
John Lusan, *Technical Staff*
EMP: 11
SALES (est): 2MM Privately Held
SIC: 2879 Agricultural chemicals

(G-8667)
DVT LLC
7325 W 161st St (66085-8807)
PHONE....913 636-3056
Michael Hankins, *Engineer*
Rodney Steve Dickey,
EMP: 34
SALES (est): 641.1K Privately Held
SIC: 8734 Product testing laboratories

(G-8668)
DYNAMIC LOGISTIX LLC (PA)
7220 W 98th Ter Bldg 9 (66212-2255)
P.O. Box 26353 (66225-6353)
PHONE....913 274-3800
Huw Jones, *General Mgr*
Alex Wray, *Opers Staff*
Amy Clardy, *VP Finance*
Jeff Auslander, *Mng Member*
Jason Yeager,
EMP: 36
SQ FT: 7,500
SALES: 54.4MM Privately Held
SIC: 4731 Truck transportation brokers

(G-8669)
EATHERLY CONSTRUCTORS INC
4831 W 136th St (66224-5924)
PHONE....913 685-9026
Robert Eatherly, *President*
EMP: 18
SALES (corp-wide): 10.7MM Privately Held
SIC: 1389 Cementing oil & gas well casings
PA: Eatherly Constructors, Inc.
1810 Boots Rd
Garden City KS 67846
620 276-6611

(G-8670)
ECOLOGY AND ENVIRONMENT INC
9300 W 110th St Ste 460 (66210-1450)
PHONE....913 339-9519
Dennis Lawlor, *Sales/Mktg Mgr*
EMP: 10
SQ FT: 4,000
SALES (corp-wide): 88.5MM Privately Held
SIC: 8748 8711 Environmental consultant; professional engineer
PA: Ecology And Environment Inc.
368 Pleasant View Dr
Lancaster NY 14086
716 684-8060

(G-8671)
EFREIGHTSHIP LLC
6900 College Blvd Ste 470 (66211-1596)
P.O. Box 26641 (66225-6641)
PHONE....913 871-9309
Brian Michel, *Mng Member*
EMP: 10
SQ FT: 5,000
SALES (est): 3MM Privately Held
SIC: 4731 Freight transportation arrangement

(G-8672)
ELAVON INC
9400 Antioch Rd (66212-3952)
PHONE....913 648-6444
EMP: 400
SALES (corp-wide): 25.7B Publicly Held
SIC: 7375 Information retrieval services
HQ: Elavon, Inc.
2 Concourse Pkwy Ste 800
Atlanta GA 30328
678 731-5000

(G-8673)
ELDER & DISABILITY LAW FIRM PA (PA)
Also Called: Elder & Disability Law Firm PA
9225 Indian Creek Pkwy # 1100
(66210-2029)
PHONE....913 338-5713
William G Hammond, *President*
EMP: 15
SALES (est): 2.1MM Privately Held
SIC: 8111 General practice attorney, lawyer; general practice law office

(G-8674)
ELM SERVICES LLC
9393 W 110th St Ste 500 (66210-1464)
P.O. Box 11422 (66207-1422)
PHONE....913 954-4414
Erika Larson, *CEO*
Greg Bergman, *Senior VP*
Lauren Carter, *Senior VP*
Paula Larson, *Exec Sec*
EMP: 68
SALES: 700K Privately Held
SIC: 8748 Business consulting

(G-8675)
ELRAC LLC
Also Called: Enterprise Rent-A-Car
10661 Metcalf Ave (66212-1817)
PHONE....913 642-9669
Cris Antrobus, *Manager*
EMP: 10
SALES (corp-wide): 4.5B Privately Held
WEB: www.elrac.com
SIC: 7514 Passenger car rental
HQ: Elrac Llc
1550 Route 23
Wayne NJ 07470
973 709-2499

(G-8676)
EMB STATISTICAL SOLUTIONS LLC
9300 W 110th St Ste 550 (66210-1427)
PHONE....913 322-6555
Ruth Johnson, *Prgrmr*
Rick Moore, *Prgrmr*
Lisa Spielman, *Director*
Edward Brown,
Brenda Bishop,
EMP: 19 EST: 2000
SALES (est): 1.3MM Privately Held
WEB: www.embstats.com
SIC: 8748 Business consulting

(G-8677)
EMC CORPORATION
11225 College Blvd # 200 (66210-2772)
PHONE....913 530-0433
Tony Matteoni, *Accounts Exec*
Sam Elias, *Manager*
Mark Gardner, *Technical Staff*
EMP: 65
SALES (corp-wide): 90.6B Publicly Held
WEB: www.emc.com
SIC: 3572 Computer storage devices
HQ: Emc Corporation
176 South St
Hopkinton MA 01748
508 435-1000

(G-8678)
EMERALD CITY GYMNASTICS INC
9063 Bond St (66214-1724)
PHONE....913 438-4444
Steve Glickley, *President*
EMP: 25
SALES (est): 916.8K Privately Held
WEB: www.emeraldcitygym.com
SIC: 7999 Gymnastic instruction, non-membership

(G-8679)
EMPLOYERS MUTUAL CASUALTY CO
Also Called: EMC Insurance Companies
7300 W 110th St Ste 300 (66210-2300)
PHONE....913 663-0119
Ben Dehart, *Branch Mgr*
Mary E Kramer, *Underwriter*
Dan Pence, *Supervisor*
EMP: 50
SALES (corp-wide): 1.1B Privately Held
SIC: 6411 6321 6311 6519 Insurance agents; reinsurance carriers, accident & health; life insurance carriers; real property lessors
PA: Employers Mutual Casualty Company
717 Mulberry St
Des Moines IA 50309
515 280-2511

(G-8680)
ENDOSCOPIC ASSOCIATES LLC
Also Called: Endoscopic Imaging Center
10200 W 105th St Ste 100 (66212-5750)
PHONE....913 492-0800
Christopher A Holden, *President*
Kari Lorenzen, *Manager*
Jennifer Richmond, *Administration*
EMP: 30
SALES (est): 2.4MM
SALES (corp-wide): 643.1MM Privately Held
WEB: www.amsurg.com
SIC: 8011 Gastronomist
HQ: Envision Healthcare Corporation
1a Burton Hills Blvd
Nashville TN 37215
615 665-1283

(G-8681)
ENGIE SERVICES US INC
12980 Foster St Ste 400 (66213-2601)
PHONE....913 225-7081
EMP: 23
SALES (corp-wide): 30.8B Privately Held
SIC: 8711 Energy conservation engineering
HQ: Engie Services U.S. Inc.
500 12th St Ste 300
Oakland CA 94607
844 678-3772

(G-8682)
ENHANCED HOME CARE LLC
10600 W 87th St (66214-1651)
PHONE....913 327-0000
Randy Block,
EMP: 14
SALES (est): 586.7K Privately Held
SIC: 8082 Home health care services

(G-8683)
ENJET AERO LLC (PA)
9401 Indian Creek Pkwy (66210-2007)
PHONE....913 717-7396
Bruce Breckenridge, *CEO*
Lacy Adams, *Business Mgr*
Kayla Walker, *Business Mgr*
Christopher Ferraro, *CFO*
EMP: 18
SALES: 42.7MM Privately Held
SIC: 3728 Aircraft parts & equipment

(G-8684)
ENTERPRISE LEASING CO KS LLC
Also Called: Enterprise Rent-A-Car
14873 Metcalf Ave (66223-2205)
PHONE....913 402-1322
EMP: 26
SALES (corp-wide): 4.5B Privately Held
SIC: 7514 Passenger car rental
HQ: Enterprise Leasing Company Of Ks Llc
5359 Merriam Dr
Shawnee Mission KS 66203
913 383-1515

(G-8685)
ENVISION TECHNOLOGY GROUP LLC
6985 W 153rd St (66223-3116)
PHONE....913 390-5141
David Borth, *President*
Todd Sattman,
EMP: 32 EST: 2010
SALES: 961K Privately Held
SIC: 4899 Data communication services

(G-8686)
ERISE IP
7015 College Blvd Ste 700 (66211-1524)
PHONE....913 777-5600
Adam Seitz, *President*
Mark McGrory, *Counsel*

Patricia Atchison, *Office Mgr*
Adam Sandwell, *Technical Staff*
Jason Mudd, *Shareholder*
EMP: 17 **EST:** 2012
SALES (est): 1.8MM **Privately Held**
SIC: 8111 Patent, trademark & copyright law

(G-8687)
ERM-WEST INC
9225 Indian Creek Pkwy # 1050 (66210-2003)
PHONE..................................913 661-0770
EMP: 16
SALES (corp-wide): 358.4MM **Privately Held**
WEB: www.ermrm.com
SIC: 8711 8748 Consulting engineer; environmental consultant
HQ: Erm-West, Inc.
1277 Treat Blvd Ste 500
Walnut Creek CA 94597
925 946-0455

(G-8688)
ERMC II LP
11149 W 95th St (66214-1824)
PHONE..................................913 859-9621
EMP: 34 **Privately Held**
SIC: 7349 Janitorial service, contract basis
PA: Ermc Ii, L.P.
1 Park Pl 6148
Chattanooga TN 37421

(G-8689)
ESA P PRTFOLIO OPER LESSEE LLC
Also Called: Extended Stay America
10750 Quivira Rd (66210-1217)
PHONE..................................913 661-9299
Joe Diehl, *Manager*
EMP: 16
SALES (corp-wide): 1.2B **Publicly Held**
WEB: www.extendedstayhotels.com
SIC: 7011 Hotels & motels
HQ: Esa P Portfolio Operating Lessee, Llc
11525 N Community House R
Charlotte NC 28277
980 345-1600

(G-8690)
ESOLUTIONS INC (PA)
8215 W 108th Ter (66210-1661)
PHONE..................................866 633-4726
Gerry McCarthy, *CEO*
Bill Creach, *President*
Derek Smith, *Exec VP*
Gene Creach, *Vice Pres*
Dan Feimster, *Vice Pres*
EMP: 63
SALES (est): 25MM **Privately Held**
WEB: www.esolutions.no
SIC: 7371 Computer software systems analysis & design, custom

(G-8691)
ESSILOR LABORATORIES AMER INC
Also Called: Duffens Optical
8140 Marshall Dr (66214-1536)
PHONE..................................800 397-2020
Gene Thomas, *Principal*
EMP: 60
SALES (corp-wide): 1.4MM **Privately Held**
WEB: www.crizal.com
SIC: 5048 3851 Frames, ophthalmic; lenses, ophthalmic; ophthalmic goods
HQ: Essilor Laboratories Of America, Inc.
13515 N Stemmons Fwy
Dallas TX 75234
972 241-4141

(G-8692)
ETC ENDURE ENERGY LLC
7400 W 129th St Ste 250 (66213-2669)
PHONE..................................913 956-4500
Kelcy Warren, *CEO*
Marshall McCrea III, *President*
Martin Salinas Jr, *CFO*
EMP: 20
SQ FT: 7,000
SALES (est): 6MM
SALES (corp-wide): 54B **Publicly Held**
SIC: 4911 Generation, electric power
HQ: Etp Legacy Lp
8111 Westchester Dr # 600
Dallas TX 75225
214 981-0700

(G-8693)
EUROTECH INC
12721 Metcalf Ave Ste 102 (66213-2619)
PHONE..................................913 549-1000
EMP: 25
SALES (corp-wide): 11.3MM **Privately Held**
SIC: 3823 Mfg Process Control Instruments
HQ: Eurotech, Inc.
10260 Old Columbia Rd G
Columbia MD 21046
301 490-4007

(G-8694)
EVEANS BASH KLEIN INC
Also Called: Meritage Portfolio Management
7500 College Blvd # 1212 (66210-4035)
PHONE..................................913 345-7000
Mark Eveans, *President*
James Klein, *Principal*
Lisa Davis, *Portfolio Mgr*
John Wallis, *Director*
EMP: 15
SQ FT: 5,000
SALES (est): 3.4MM **Privately Held**
WEB: www.meritageportfolio.com
SIC: 6282 8742 Investment advisory service; manager of mutual funds, contract or fee basis; financial consultant

(G-8695)
EVERGREEN APARTMENTS
7913 Grant St (66204-3345)
PHONE..................................913 341-5572
Allen Quigley, *President*
EMP: 10
SALES (est): 470.2K **Privately Held**
SIC: 6513 Apartment building operators

(G-8696)
EVERHANCE LLC
9800 Metcalf Ave Ste 5 (66212-2216)
PHONE..................................785 218-1406
Ramsey Mohsen, *CEO*
Eric Hazen,
EMP: 14
SQ FT: 90,000
SALES (est): 115.6K **Privately Held**
SIC: 8732 5192 Commercial sociological & educational research; books, periodicals & newspapers

(G-8697)
EVOQUA WATER TECHNOLOGIES LLC
Also Called: US Filter
7019 Mackey St (66204-1243)
PHONE..................................913 422-7600
Ed Jordan, *Manager*
EMP: 50
SALES (corp-wide): 1.4B **Publicly Held**
SIC: 3589 Water treatment equipment, industrial
HQ: Evoqua Water Technologies Llc
210 6th Ave Ste 3300
Pittsburgh PA 15222
724 772-0044

(G-8698)
EXAMINETICS INC (PA)
10561 Barkley St Ste 400 (66212-1836)
PHONE..................................913 748-2000
Jeffrey S Kerns, *President*
Simon P D Barker, *Chairman*
Melinda Tiffany, *Vice Pres*
Troy R Heppner, *CFO*
Jeana Ensley, *Accounts Exec*
EMP: 168
SQ FT: 18,522
SALES (est): 27.2MM **Privately Held**
WEB: www.examinetics.com
SIC: 8099 Health screening service

(G-8699)
EXCEL CONSTRUCTORS INC
8041 W 47th St (66203-1301)
PHONE..................................913 261-1000
Michael E Johnson, *President*
Andy Gill, *Superintendent*
Konnee Cook, *Vice Pres*
John Hess, *Vice Pres*
Jerry Katlin, *CFO*
EMP: 60
SQ FT: 11,000
SALES: 46.1MM **Privately Held**
WEB: www.excelconstructors.com
SIC: 1542 1541 Commercial & office building, new construction; design & erection, combined: non-residential; specialized public building contractors; industrial buildings, new construction

(G-8700)
EXPERIS US INC
7300 W 110th St (66210-2332)
PHONE..................................913 800-3027
Mike Copp, *Branch Mgr*
EMP: 10 **Publicly Held**
SIC: 7361 Executive placement
HQ: Experis Us, Inc.
100 W Manpower Pl
Milwaukee WI 53212

(G-8701)
EYE ASSOCIATION OVERLAND PARK (PA)
Also Called: Eye Associates of Olathe
10120 W 119th St (66213-1600)
PHONE..................................913 339-9090
Vincent Pennipede, *President*
John Davis, *Shareholder*
EMP: 18
SQ FT: 5,000
SALES (est): 1.3MM **Privately Held**
WEB: www.eyeassociatesop.com
SIC: 8042 8011 5995 Low vision specialist optometrist; offices & clinics of medical doctors; contact lenses, prescription

(G-8702)
FAITHLINK LLC
7180 W 107th St Ste 24 (66212-2523)
PHONE..................................913 904-1070
Randolph Hiser,
EMP: 16
SALES (est): 314.9K **Privately Held**
SIC: 7371 Computer software development & applications

(G-8703)
FAMILY MEDIA GROUP INC
Also Called: Kc Parent
11936 W 119th St 335 (66213-2216)
PHONE..................................913 815-6600
Michael C Gimotty Jr, *Administration*
EMP: 21 **EST:** 2002
SALES (est): 3.2MM **Privately Held**
SIC: 2721 Magazines: publishing & printing

(G-8704)
FANNECT LLC
16132 Birch St (66085-7813)
PHONE..................................913 271-2346
Hunter Browning, *CEO*
EMP: 10 **EST:** 2012
SALES (est): 515.5K **Privately Held**
SIC: 7371 Computer software development

(G-8705)
FARMERS BANK & TRUST
14231 Metcalf Ave Ste 100 (66223-3339)
PHONE..................................913 402-7257
Jacinda Zerr, *Manager*
EMP: 12
SALES (corp-wide): 34.9MM **Privately Held**
WEB: www.farmersbankna.com
SIC: 6021 6029 National commercial banks; commercial banks
HQ: Farmers Bank & Trust
1017 Harrison St
Great Bend KS 67530
620 792-2411

(G-8706)
FASTFITTINGSCOM
10561 Barkley St Ste 62 (66212-1860)
PHONE..................................913 709-4467
Mark Koetting, *Owner*
◆ **EMP:** 5
SALES (est): 300K **Privately Held**
SIC: 3321 Cast iron pipe & fittings

(G-8707)
FASTSIGNS INC
8844 W 95th St (66212-4051)
PHONE..................................913 649-3600
Jerry Goldstein, *President*
EMP: 7
SQ FT: 1,500
SALES (est): 500K **Privately Held**
SIC: 3993 7532 7389 5999 Signs & advertising specialties; truck painting & lettering; engraving service; banners

(G-8708)
FAVORITE HLTHCARE STAFFING INC (PA)
7255 W 98th Ter Ste 150 (66212-2215)
PHONE..................................913 383-9733
Gerhard J Kuti, *CEO*
Stephanie Render, *Vice Pres*
Cathy Vollmer, *Vice Pres*
Christopher Brink, *CFO*
Sue Labonte, *Human Res Mgr*
EMP: 150 **EST:** 1981
SQ FT: 18,000
SALES (est): 447.6MM **Privately Held**
WEB: www.favoritestaffing.com
SIC: 7363 Temporary help service

(G-8709)
FBD CONSULTING INC (HQ)
12017 Bluejacket St (66213-2038)
PHONE..................................913 319-8850
Michael R Juffa, *CEO*
Julie Riggle McKee, *President*
EMP: 15 **EST:** 1972
SQ FT: 26,000
SALES (est): 4.5MM
SALES (corp-wide): 9.2MM **Privately Held**
WEB: www.fbdconsult.com
SIC: 8742 Planning consultant
PA: Robert E Miller Insurance Agency Inc
6363 College Blvd Ste 400
Leawood KS 66211
816 333-3000

(G-8710)
FEDEX OFFICE & PRINT SVCS INC
7340 W 135th St (66223-1205)
PHONE..................................913 239-9399
EMP: 11
SALES (corp-wide): 69.6B **Publicly Held**
WEB: www.fedex.com
SIC: 7334 Photocopying & duplicating services
HQ: Fedex Office And Print Services, Inc.
7900 Legacy Dr
Plano TX 75024
800 463-3339

(G-8711)
FEDEX OFFICE & PRINT SVCS INC
8829 Metcalf Ave (66212-2074)
PHONE..................................913 383-2178
EMP: 18
SALES (corp-wide): 69.6B **Publicly Held**
WEB: www.kinkos.com
SIC: 7334 Photocopying & duplicating services
HQ: Fedex Office And Print Services, Inc.
7900 Legacy Dr
Plano TX 75024
800 463-3339

(G-8712)
FERRELL COMPANIES INC (PA)
7500 College Blvd # 1000 (66210-4035)
PHONE..................................913 661-1500
Kenneth A Heinz, *Senior VP*
George Koloroutis, *Vice Pres*
Patrick J Walsh, *Vice Pres*
Gordy Thomas, *Opers Staff*
Joni Barrows, *Asst Controller*
▲ **EMP:** 100
SQ FT: 20,000
SALES (est): 540.6MM **Privately Held**
WEB: www.ferrellgas.com
SIC: 1311 5984 Crude petroleum & natural gas production; liquefied petroleum gas dealers

▲ = Import ▼=Export
◆ =Import/Export

(G-8713)
FERRELLGAS INC (HQ)
7500 College Blvd # 1000 (66210-4035)
PHONE..................................913 661-1500
James E Ferrell, *Ch of Bd*
Stephen L Wambold, *President*
Chad Burns, *District Mgr*
Josh Allison, *Vice Pres*
Jessica Ashe, *Vice Pres*
EMP: 12 **EST:** 1986
SQ FT: 73,988
SALES (est): 240MM
SALES (corp-wide): 540.6MM **Privately Held**
SIC: 5084 5172 Propane conversion equipment; gases, liquefied petroleum (propane)
PA: Ferrell Companies, Inc.
7500 College Blvd # 1000
Overland Park KS 66210
913 661-1500

(G-8714)
FERRELLGAS PARTNERS LP (PA)
7500 College Blvd # 1000 (66210-4035)
PHONE..................................913 661-1500
James E Ferrell, *CEO*
Terry McGuire, *General Mgr*
Josh Allison, *Vice Pres*
Eric Kruger, *Vice Pres*
Alfonso Ortiz, *Opers Mgr*
EMP: 94
SQ FT: 73,988
SALES: 1.6B **Privately Held**
SIC: 5084 5172 Propane conversion equipment; petroleum products; gases, liquefied petroleum (propane)

(G-8715)
FINANCIAL DESIGNS INC
11225 College Blvd # 420 (66210-2771)
PHONE..................................913 451-4747
Terry Westlund, *President*
Gary Eickhurst, *Vice Pres*
Jada Casey, *Research*
Brandon Dye, *Client Mgr*
Nancy Carl, *Sales Associate*
EMP: 11
SALES (est): 2.9MM **Privately Held**
SIC: 6311 Life insurance

(G-8716)
FINANCIAL INSURANCE CORP
8600 Farley St Ste 200 (66212-4677)
PHONE..................................913 631-7441
Ken Schweitzer, *President*
Linda Schweitzer, *Corp Secy*
Lou Wilson, *COO*
Mike Watts, *CFO*
EMP: 11
SQ FT: 3,200
SALES (est): 1.4MM
SALES (corp-wide): 316.9MM **Privately Held**
WEB: www.ficor.com
SIC: 6411 Insurance agents, brokers & service
PA: Southwest Business Corporation
9311 San Pedro Ave # 600
San Antonio TX 78216
210 525-1241

(G-8717)
FIREMON LLC (PA)
8400 W 110th St Ste 500 (66210-2388)
PHONE..................................913 948-9570
Satin H Mirchandani, *President*
Gary Fish, *Chairman*
Jeff Barker, *Vice Pres*
F Ward Holloway III, *Vice Pres*
Bruce Jennings, *Vice Pres*
EMP: 20
SALES (est): 9MM **Privately Held**
WEB: www.securepassage.com
SIC: 7371 3825 Software programming applications; network analyzers

(G-8718)
FIRST CHOICE CHIROPRACTIC PA
11960 Quivira Rd Ste 200 (66213-2579)
PHONE..................................913 402-7444
Alyssa Rae Zonarich, *President*
EMP: 11 **EST:** 2005
SALES (est): 661.1K **Privately Held**
SIC: 8041 Offices & clinics of chiropractors

(G-8719)
FIRST HORIZON BANK
7400 W 110th St Ste 520 (66210-2371)
P.O. Box 26106, Shawnee Mission (66225-6106)
PHONE..................................913 317-2000
E Craig Keohan, *Branch Mgr*
EMP: 40
SALES (corp-wide): 2.2B **Publicly Held**
WEB: www.firsttennessee.com
SIC: 6021 6162 7389 National commercial banks; mortgage bankers; financial services
HQ: First Horizon Bank
165 Madison Ave
Memphis TN 38103
901 523-4444

(G-8720)
FIRST HORIZON NATIONAL CORP
7500 College Blvd # 1170 (66210-4035)
PHONE..................................913 339-5400
Rod Turner, *Business Mgr*
EMP: 97
SALES (corp-wide): 2.2B **Publicly Held**
SIC: 6282 Investment advisory service
PA: First Horizon National Corporation
165 Madison Ave
Memphis TN 38103
901 523-4444

(G-8721)
FIRST NATIONAL BANK OF OMAHA
4650 College Blvd (66211-1605)
PHONE..................................913 451-5824
Lathem Scott, *Vice Pres*
EMP: 89
SALES (corp-wide): 1.2B **Privately Held**
SIC: 6021 National commercial banks
HQ: First National Bank Of Omaha Inc
1620 Dodge St
Omaha NE 68197
402 341-0500

(G-8722)
FIRST SEACOAST BANK
10551 Barkley St Ste 308 (66212-1813)
PHONE..................................913 766-2500
Camilo R Escalante, *Vice Pres*
Tammy K Hajjar, *Vice Pres*
Gregory Janicki, *Vice Pres*
Dino Schulatz, *Vice Pres*
Andres Prieto, *Opers Spvr*
EMP: 11
SALES (corp-wide): 60.2MM **Privately Held**
SIC: 6035 6162 Federal savings banks; mortgage bankers & correspondents
PA: The Federal Savings Bank
300 N Elizabeth St Ste 3e
Chicago IL 60607
312 738-6000

(G-8723)
FIRST-CITIZENS BANK & TRUST CO
Also Called: Atlantic States Bank
7950 College Blvd Ste A (66210-1869)
PHONE..................................913 312-5108
Linda Childress, *Manager*
EMP: 10
SALES (corp-wide): 1.6B **Publicly Held**
WEB: www.atlanticstatesbank.com
SIC: 6022 State commercial banks
HQ: First-Citizens Bank & Trust Company
239 Fayetteville St
Raleigh NC 27601
919 716-7000

(G-8724)
FISHMAN AND CO REALTORS INC
Also Called: Coldwell Bnkr Coml Fishman Co
7939 Floyd St (66204-3724)
PHONE..................................913 782-9000
Michael H Fishman, *President*
Michele Hart, *Admin Sec*
EMP: 11
SQ FT: 5,000
SALES: 1.8MM **Privately Held**
WEB: www.fishmanandcompany.com
SIC: 6531 Real estate agent, residential

(G-8725)
FITNESS PLUS MORE LLC
4500 W 107th St (66207-4025)
PHONE..................................913 383-2636
Fax: 913 383-8418
EMP: 15 **EST:** 2004
SALES: 900K **Privately Held**
SIC: 7991 Health Club

(G-8726)
FIVE CLOTHES LLC (PA)
Also Called: Helen Jon
8251 Melrose Dr (66214-1625)
PHONE..................................913 713-6216
Barbara Stubbenek, *CEO*
Gwyn Prentice, *Mng Member*
EMP: 12 **EST:** 2013
SALES (est): 2.9MM **Privately Held**
SIC: 5137 Swimsuits: women's, children's & infants'

(G-8727)
FLEET AUTO RENT INC
Also Called: One Fleet Source
9831 Outlook Dr (66207-2848)
P.O. Box 7183 (66207-0183)
PHONE..................................913 901-9900
Chris Brock, *President*
Steve Giarraputo, *Vice Pres*
EMP: 12
SALES (est): 640K **Privately Held**
WEB: www.onefleetsource.com
SIC: 7515 Passenger car leasing

(G-8728)
FLEET EARLY LEARNING STN LLC
13304 W 172nd St (66221-6934)
PHONE..................................913 638-7178
Rob Wilkin, *Mng Member*
EMP: 34
SALES: 480K **Privately Held**
SIC: 8351 Child day care services

(G-8729)
FLI INC (PA)
Also Called: F L I
12980 Metcalf Ave Ste 240 (66213-2646)
PHONE..................................913 851-2247
John Hartmann, *President*
Stephen Nodolf, *Opers Mgr*
Bob Laporte, *Sales Staff*
Eric Winner, *Sales Staff*
Brigitte Calahan, *Manager*
EMP: 38
SQ FT: 4,000
SALES (est): 22.1MM **Privately Held**
WEB: www.fli.com
SIC: 4731 Brokers, shipping

(G-8730)
FLINT TELECOM GROUP INC (PA)
7500 College Blvd Ste 500 (66210-4043)
PHONE..................................913 815-1570
Vincent Browne, *Ch of Bd*
Bernard Fried, *President*
▲ **EMP:** 16
SALES (est): 4.7MM **Publicly Held**
WEB: www.flinttelecomgroup.com
SIC: 4812 4813 Cellular telephone services; telephone communication, except radio; telephone communications broker

(G-8731)
FMH BENEFIT SERVICES INC
Also Called: Fmh Bnfit Svcs A Div Cresource
13160 Foster St Ste 190 (66213-2689)
P.O. Box 25946, Shawnee Mission (66225-5946)
PHONE..................................913 685-4740
George McDonnell, *President*
Joel Frisch, *Principal*
Scott Holland, *Exec VP*
EMP: 180
SQ FT: 30,000
SALES (est): 42MM **Privately Held**
SIC: 6411 Insurance agents, brokers & service

(G-8732)
FOOD TRENDS INC
5600 W 95th St Ste 212 (66207-2968)
PHONE..................................913 383-3600
Richard Adler, *President*
Ron Martin, *Vice Pres*
Doug Youngblood, *Admin Sec*
EMP: 5
SQ FT: 1,700
SALES (est): 1MM **Privately Held**
SIC: 5141 5112 2752 Food brokers; envelopes; lithographing on metal

(G-8733)
FOOT SPECIALIST KANSAS CITY (PA)
8550 Marshall Dr Ste 120 (66214-9836)
PHONE..................................913 677-3600
Steven Geduldig, *Owner*
EMP: 12
SALES (est): 1.2MM **Privately Held**
SIC: 8043 Offices & clinics of podiatrists

(G-8734)
FORESITE MSP LLC
7311 W 132nd St Ste 305 (66213-1118)
PHONE..................................800 940-4699
Marc Brungardt, *President*
Jason Humphreys, *Vice Pres*
Jason Leduc, *Vice Pres*
Jana Pinkerton, *VP Sales*
EMP: 35
SALES (est): 309.1K
SALES (corp-wide): 7.4MM **Privately Held**
SIC: 7382 7373 Security systems services; systems engineering, computer related
PA: Moneo Technology Solutions, Llc
50 Inwood Rd Ste 1
Rocky Hill CT

(G-8735)
FOULSTON SIEFKIN LLP
9225 Indian Creek Pkwy # 600 (66210-2000)
PHONE..................................913 498-2100
R Douglas Reagan, *Branch Mgr*
EMP: 24
SALES (corp-wide): 19MM **Privately Held**
WEB: www.foulston.com
SIC: 8111 General practice attorney, lawyer
PA: Foulston Siefkin Llp
1551 N Waterfront Pkwy # 100
Wichita KS 67206
316 267-6371

(G-8736)
FRANK AGENCY INC
10561 Barkley St Ste 200 (66212-1835)
PHONE..................................913 648-8333
Tony Ali, *CEO*
Nick Barkman, *President*
Sarah Cline, *President*
Susan Reiter, *COO*
Kelly Bohlken, *Vice Pres*
EMP: 75
SALES: 18MM **Privately Held**
SIC: 7311 8743 Advertising consultant; public relations & publicity

(G-8737)
FRANKLIN COVEY CO
11006 Metcalf Ave (66210-1834)
PHONE..................................800 819-1812
Kim Humbert, *Manager*
EMP: 8
SALES (corp-wide): 225.3MM **Publicly Held**
WEB: www.franklincovey.com
SIC: 2741 8299 8742 Miscellaneous publishing; educational service, nondegree granting: continuing educ.; training & development consultant
PA: Franklin Covey Co.
2200 W Parkway Blvd
Salt Lake City UT 84119
801 817-1776

(G-8738)
FRANKLIN L TAYLOR PA
7450 W 130th St Ste 140 (66213-2665)
P.O. Box 550, Olathe (66051-0550)
PHONE..................................913 782-2350

GEOGRAPHIC

L Franklin Taylor, *President*
EMP: 19 **EST:** 1996
SALES (est): 980.8K **Privately Held**
SIC: 8111 General practice law office

(G-8739)
FRECHIN PEST CONTROL LLC
6501 W 156th St (66223-3601)
PHONE..................................816 358-5776
Edward Hutchison, *President*
Debbie Hutchison, *Vice Pres*
EMP: 11 **EST:** 1953
SALES: 650K **Privately Held**
SIC: 7342 Exterminating & fumigating; pest control services

(G-8740)
FREIGHT BROKERS AMERICA LLC
10460 Mastin St Ste 120 (66212-5701)
PHONE..................................913 438-4300
Chris Kruse, *Principal*
EMP: 1422
SALES (est): 8MM **Privately Held**
SIC: 4213 Trucking, except local
PA: Super Service Holdings, Llc
6000 Clay Ave Sw
Grand Rapids MI 49548

(G-8741)
FRESENIUS MED CARE W WLLOW LLC
6751 W 119th St (66209-2013)
PHONE..................................913 491-6341
Ella Ladd, *Branch Mgr*
EMP: 12
SALES (corp-wide): 18.3B **Privately Held**
SIC: 8099 Blood related health services
HQ: Fresenius Medical Care West Willow, Llc
2201 W Plano Pkwy Ste 200
Plano TX 75075

(G-8742)
FRIEDMAN GROUP
11065 Hauser St (66210-3708)
PHONE..................................310 590-1248
Harry Friedman, *President*
Thomas Post, *Sr Consultant*
Wendi Swanson, *Sr Consultant*
EMP: 20
SALES (est): 1.6MM **Privately Held**
WEB: www.thefriedmangroup.com
SIC: 8748 Business consulting

(G-8743)
FUSION GLOBAL SOLUTIONS LLC
7300 W 110th St Ste 743 (66210-2332)
PHONE..................................913 707-2866
Venkat Vanka, *Principal*
EMP: 50
SQ FT: 1,000
SALES (est): 3.2MM **Privately Held**
SIC: 7371 Computer software development

(G-8744)
FYRS CAR CARE
9535 Nall Ave (66207-2949)
PHONE..................................913 385-3600
Kim Fry, *Owner*
EMP: 10
SALES (est): 226.6K **Privately Held**
SIC: 7538 General automotive repair shops

(G-8745)
GARVER LLC
7301 W 129th St Ste 330 (66213-2635)
PHONE..................................913 696-9755
Derek Butler, *Project Mgr*
Andrea Odegard-Begay, *Project Mgr*
Mark Williams, *Branch Mgr*
Steve Haynes, *Real Est Agnt*
EMP: 27
SALES (corp-wide): 84MM **Privately Held**
WEB: www.garverengineers.com
SIC: 8711 Consulting engineer
PA: Garver, Llc
4701 Northshore Dr
North Little Rock AR 72118
501 376-3633

(G-8746)
GASTROINTESTINAL ASSOCIATES PA
10116 W 105th St (66212-5746)
PHONE..................................913 495-9600
James Mavec, *President*
William Buser, *Principal*
William Hartong, *Principal*
EMP: 17
SQ FT: 1,850
SALES (est): 2.2MM **Privately Held**
SIC: 8011 Gastronomist

(G-8747)
GATES SHIELDS FERGUSON SWALL H
10990 Quivira Rd Ste 200 (66210-1284)
PHONE..................................913 661-0222
Jane Irish, *Office Mgr*
EMP: 15
SALES (est): 526.4K **Privately Held**
SIC: 8111 General practice law office

(G-8748)
GATEWAY SOLUTIONS INC (PA)
12980 Metcalf Ave Ste 330 (66213-2646)
PHONE..................................913 851-1055
Sandra Gettha, *President*
Sunil Kumar, *Manager*
Vinod Kumar, *Technology*
Tom Taylor, *Technical Staff*
Kiranmai Peddi, *Recruiter*
EMP: 14
SQ FT: 1,000
SALES: 2MM **Privately Held**
WEB: www.gatewaysi.com
SIC: 5045 7379 Computer software; data processing consultant

(G-8749)
GBW RAILCAR SERVICES LLC
10895 Grandview Dr # 350 (66210-1536)
P.O. Box 713, Golden CO (80402-0713)
PHONE..................................888 968-4364
Brent Benham, *Manager*
EMP: 35
SALES (corp-wide): 3B **Publicly Held**
WEB: www.gundersonrailservices.com
SIC: 4789 Railroad car repair
HQ: Gbw Railcar Services, L.L.C.
4350 Nw Front Ave
Portland OR 97210

(G-8750)
GENERAL AUTOMATIC SPRINKLER FI
10324 W 79th St (66214-1561)
PHONE..................................913 390-1105
Sue Ferris, *President*
Tom Ferris, *Vice Pres*
Lisa Snider, *Admin Sec*
EMP: 23
SQ FT: 22,000
SALES (est): 3MM **Privately Held**
WEB: www.gasfpc.com
SIC: 1711 3569 Fire sprinkler system installation; sprinkler systems, fire: automatic

(G-8751)
GENERAL ELECTRIC COMPANY
7101 College Blvd Ste 800 (66210-2082)
PHONE..................................816 244-9672
Gary Matocha, *Branch Mgr*
EMP: 20
SALES (corp-wide): 121.6B **Publicly Held**
SIC: 7699 Industrial machinery & equipment repair
PA: General Electric Company
5 Necco St
Boston MA 02210
617 443-3000

(G-8752)
GENERATIONS BANK
7900 College Blvd (66210-2194)
PHONE..................................913 928-6181
Roger Messner, *President*
William Morton, *CFO*
EMP: 10 **EST:** 2000
SALES: 76.3MM **Privately Held**
WEB: www.bankwithgenbank.com
SIC: 6021 National commercial banks

PA: Chicago Bancorp
300 N Elizabeth St Ste 3e
Chicago IL 60607

(G-8753)
GENTIVA HEALTH SERVICES INC
12900 Foster St Ste 400 (66213-2696)
PHONE..................................913 814-2800
Lafonda Morris, *President*
Michele Tierney, *Vice Pres*
Jeff Copeland, *CFO*
Gina Edgar, *Sales Staff*
EMP: 1527
SALES (corp-wide): 1.4B **Privately Held**
SIC: 8082 Home health care services
PA: Gentiva Health Services, Inc.
3350 Riverwood Pkwy Se # 1
Atlanta GA 30339
770 951-6450

(G-8754)
GENTIVA HEALTH SERVICES INC
11880 Quivira Rd Ste 4a (66210)
PHONE..................................913 906-0522
Cindy Fahlgren, *Branch Mgr*
EMP: 20
SALES (corp-wide): 1.4B **Privately Held**
WEB: www.gentiva.com
SIC: 8082 Visiting nurse service
PA: Gentiva Health Services, Inc.
3350 Riverwood Pkwy Se # 1
Atlanta GA 30339
770 951-6450

(G-8755)
GILLILAND & HAYES PA
9225 Indian Creek Pkwy # 1070 (66210-2029)
PHONE..................................913 317-5100
Keith Whitten, *Managing Prtnr*
EMP: 10
SALES (est): 527.2K
SALES (corp-wide): 6MM **Privately Held**
WEB: www.gillilandandhayes.com
SIC: 8111 General practice attorney, lawyer
PA: Gilliland & Hayes Pa
20 W 2nd Ave Ste 200
Hutchinson KS 67501
620 662-0537

(G-8756)
GLENWOOD ARTS THEATER (PA)
3859 W 95th St (66206-2038)
PHONE..................................913 642-1132
Brian Mossman, *Owner*
Ben Mossman, *Co-Owner*
EMP: 10
SALES (est): 750K **Privately Held**
SIC: 7832 Motion picture theaters, except drive-in

(G-8757)
GLI LLC (PA)
Also Called: Comforn Inn and Suites
7200 W 107th St (66212-2564)
PHONE..................................913 648-7858
Doug Gamble, *Owner*
Mike Lawsky, *Owner*
Donald Ray, *Director*
EMP: 19
SALES: 6.5MM **Privately Held**
SIC: 7011 Hostels

(G-8758)
GLOBAL INDUSTRIES INC
11617 W 81st St (66214-3302)
PHONE..................................913 310-9963
John Banta, *Manager*
EMP: 10
SALES (corp-wide): 116MM **Privately Held**
WEB: www.evolvefurnituregroup.com
SIC: 5021 Office furniture
PA: Global Industries, Inc.
17 W Stow Rd
Marlton NJ 08053
856 596-3390

(G-8759)
GLOBAL PROCUREMENT CORPORATION
11401 Lamar Ave (66211-1508)
P.O. Box 11450 (66207-1450)
PHONE..................................913 458-2000
Timothy W Triplett, *Exec VP*
Peter D Loftspring, *Senior VP*
G Cheng, *Vice Pres*
M E Gammill, *Vice Pres*
W J James, *Vice Pres*
EMP: 13 **EST:** 2000
SALES (est): 9MM
SALES (corp-wide): 2.8B **Privately Held**
SIC: 8711 Consulting engineer
HQ: Black & Veatch Holding Company
11401 Lamar Ave
Overland Park KS 66211

(G-8760)
GLOBAL SOFT SYSTEMS INC
10801 Mastin St Ste 510 (66210-1776)
PHONE..................................913 338-1400
Vishal Adma, *Chairman*
EMP: 38
SALES (est): 2.8MM **Privately Held**
SIC: 7371 Computer software development

(G-8761)
GO LOCAL LLC
10975 Benson Dr Ste 250 (66210-2133)
PHONE..................................913 231-3083
Chriss Thompson, *Vice Pres*
Dan Quinlivan, *Controller*
Wendy McCune, *Marketing Mgr*
Taylor Cain, *Mktg Coord*
Shari Valdez, *Mktg Coord*
EMP: 21
SALES (est): 1.7MM **Privately Held**
SIC: 8631 Labor unions & similar labor organizations

(G-8762)
GOLD STAR TRANSPORTATION INC (PA)
9424 Reeds Rd Ste 201 (66207-2518)
P.O. Box 11350, Shawnee Mission (66207-1050)
PHONE..................................913 341-0081
Rayla A Erding, *President*
Jerome P Erding, *Admin Sec*
EMP: 27 **EST:** 1982
SQ FT: 3,600
SALES (est): 18.1MM **Privately Held**
WEB: www.goldstartransportation.com
SIC: 4731 Transportation agents & brokers

(G-8763)
GOLDEN BOY PIES INC
4945 Hadley St (66203-5392)
PHONE..................................913 384-6460
Terry D Hunt, *President*
Nancy Williams, *Exec VP*
Jim Patrzykont, *CFO*
Connie Campbell, *Sales Mgr*
Bradley Hunt, *Manager*
EMP: 31
SQ FT: 15,200
SALES: 49K **Privately Held**
WEB: www.goldenboypies.com
SIC: 2051 Pies, bakery: except frozen

(G-8764)
GOLF OPERATIONS MANAGEMENT LLC
12501 Quivira Rd (66213-2403)
PHONE..................................913 897-3809
Tim Eleeson, *Partner*
Steve Jablonowski, *Partner*
EMP: 50 **EST:** 1988
SQ FT: 4,500
SALES (est): 2.9MM **Privately Held**
SIC: 5941 7999 7992 5812 Golf goods & equipment; golf services & professionals; golf driving range; public golf courses; eating places

(G-8765)
GONZALES CMMUNICATIONS INC GCI
15145 Metcalf Ave (66223-2807)
PHONE..................................913 685-4866
Alfred Gonzales Jr, *President*
Paul May, *CFO*

EMP: 45
SQ FT: 17,900
SALES (est): 3.1MM **Privately Held**
SIC: 1731 Sound equipment specialization

(G-8766)
GORHAM GOLD GREENWICH & ASSOC
Also Called: Ggga Management Consultants
9150 Glenwood St (66212-1364)
PHONE..................................913 981-4442
Gregory Mann, *President*
Mann Jeanne Fisher, *Director*
EMP: 10
SALES: 1.4MM **Privately Held**
SIC: 8742 Business consultant

(G-8767)
GRACE DENTAL
12611 Antioch Rd (66213-1701)
PHONE..................................913 685-9111
Gloria Roberts, *Owner*
EMP: 15
SALES (est): 1.1MM **Privately Held**
SIC: 8021 Dentists' office

(G-8768)
GRAFTON INC (PA)
Also Called: Grafton Staffing Companies
6801 W 121st St Ste 100 (66209-2005)
PHONE..................................913 498-0701
Carol Carroll, *CEO*
Greg Dabbs, *Business Mgr*
Richard Carroll, *Senior VP*
Dick Carroll, *Engineer*
Jeffrey Hagen, *CFO*
EMP: 855
SQ FT: 6,100
SALES: 8.4MM **Privately Held**
WEB: www.graftoninc.com
SIC: 7363 7361 8742 Temporary help service; executive placement; human resource consulting services

(G-8769)
GRAYLING INC
10258 W 87th St (66212-4674)
PHONE..................................913 341-5444
David Bertuglia, *President*
Craig Singleton, *Manager*
EMP: 12 **EST**: 1962
SQ FT: 1,200
SALES (est): 3.7MM **Privately Held**
WEB: www.graylinginc.com
SIC: 1542 Commercial & office building, new construction; commercial & office buildings, renovation & repair

(G-8770)
GREAT CLIPS FOR HAIR (PA)
11540 W 95th St (66214-1865)
PHONE..................................913 888-3400
Rick Patton, *President*
EMP: 29
SALES (est): 969.2K **Privately Held**
SIC: 7231 Unisex hair salons

(G-8771)
GREAT CLIPS FOR HAIR
10154 W 119th St (66213-1462)
PHONE..................................913 338-2580
Ruth Grimsley, *Owner*
EMP: 16
SALES (est): 187.9K **Privately Held**
SIC: 7231 Unisex hair salons

(G-8772)
GREAT PLAINS ANNUITY MARKETING
10901 W 84th Ter Ste 125 (66214-1601)
PHONE..................................913 888-0488
Rich Hellerich, *Owner*
Mike Lair, *Senior VP*
Cindy Nelson, *Vice Pres*
EMP: 15
SALES (est): 2.5MM **Privately Held**
SIC: 6311 Life insurance

(G-8773)
GREAT PLAINS INVESTMENTS LTD
Also Called: W D Mavchinery
11300 W 80th St (66214-3307)
PHONE..................................913 492-9880
Winkler Dunnevier, *General Ptnr*
Shawn Dade, *Technical Mgr*
Mary Jo Ernst, *Bookkeeper*
Dr Doderer Winkler, *Manager*
EMP: 90
SQ FT: 50,000
SALES (est): 4MM **Privately Held**
SIC: 6512 Commercial & industrial building operation

(G-8774)
GREAT PLAINS LABORATORY INC
11813 W 77th St (66214-1457)
PHONE..................................913 341-8949
William Shaw, *President*
Chad D Christopher, *Info Tech Dir*
Wilberto Castillo, *Relations*
EMP: 63
SQ FT: 14,000
SALES (est): 10.4MM **Privately Held**
WEB: www.greatplainslaboratory.com
SIC: 8071 Testing laboratories

(G-8775)
GREAT PLAINS TRUST COMPANY
7700 Shawnee Miksion Pkwy (66202)
PHONE..................................913 831-7999
Willard R Lynch, *President*
Selene Werkowitch, *Controller*
Shauna Rice, *Mktg Coord*
Blake Burton, *Executive*
Daniel Johnson, *Executive*
EMP: 16
SALES (est): 3.5MM **Privately Held**
WEB: www.greatplainstrust.com
SIC: 6282 6733 Investment advisory service; trusts

(G-8776)
GREAT-WEST FINANCIAL RETIREMEN
11500 Outlook St (66211-1804)
PHONE..................................847 857-3000
EMP: 2900
SQ FT: 217,000
SALES (est): 329.7MM
SALES (corp-wide): 36.3B **Privately Held**
WEB: www.jpmorganchase.com
SIC: 6411 Pension & retirement plan consultants
HQ: Gwl&A Financial Inc.
8515 E Orchard Rd
Greenwood Village CO 80111
303 737-3000

(G-8777)
GREEN CLEAN KC LLC
8220 Travis St Ste 210 (66204-3966)
PHONE..................................913 499-7106
Jud Coester,
Richard Phelps,
Anthony Treccariche,
Meredith Wynn,
EMP: 10
SQ FT: 100
SALES: 80K **Privately Held**
SIC: 7699 Cleaning services

(G-8778)
GREEN PRODUCT SOLUTIONS LLC
8310 Reeds Rd (66207-1663)
PHONE..................................913 633-1274
James Goode, *Mng Member*
EMP: 6
SALES: 150K **Privately Held**
SIC: 8711 3589 Engineering services; water filters & softeners, household type

(G-8779)
GREGGPIERCY INC
12400 Blue Valley Pkwy (66213-2626)
PHONE..................................913 469-9274
Spencer Gregg, *President*
Brain Piercy, *Vice Pres*
EMP: 15 **EST**: 2000
SQ FT: 750
SALES (est): 945.8K **Privately Held**
SIC: 7542 Carwashes

(G-8780)
GROWING FUTURES EARLY EDUC
8155 Santa Fe Dr (66204-3607)
PHONE..................................913 649-6057
Terrie Vanzandt-Travis, *Exec Dir*
Terrie Travis, *Exec Dir*
Elizabeth Nichols, *Director*
EMP: 50
SALES: 3.2MM **Privately Held**
SIC: 8351 Head start center, except in conjunction with school

(G-8781)
GRUNDFOS CBS INC
11936 W 119th St Ste 232 (66213-2216)
PHONE..................................281 994-2830
EMP: 9
SALES (est): 506.2K **Privately Held**
SIC: 3561 Pumps & pumping equipment

(G-8782)
GUPTA GANESH
Also Called: Pediatric Assoc of Kansan City
10730 Nall Ave (66211-1366)
PHONE..................................913 451-0000
Ganesh Gupta, *Owner*
EMP: 10 **EST**: 2001
SALES (est): 301.5K **Privately Held**
SIC: 8011 General & family practice, physician/surgeon

(G-8783)
HAIR CLUB FOR MEN LTD INC
Also Called: Hcm
7500 College Blvd Ste 600 (66210-4035)
PHONE..................................888 888-8986
Steve Stickney, *Manager*
EMP: 12 **Privately Held**
WEB: www.hcfm.com
SIC: 7299 Hair weaving or replacement
HQ: Hc (Usa), Inc.
1499 W Palmetto
Boca Raton FL 33486
888 534-0239

(G-8784)
HAIR DESIGN COMPANY
Also Called: Corbys Hair Salon
7936 W 151st St (66223-2118)
PHONE..................................913 897-4776
EMP: 12
SALES (est): 173.3K **Privately Held**
SIC: 7231 Beauty Shop

(G-8785)
HALEY & ALDRICH INC
11020 King St Ste 450 (66210-1233)
PHONE..................................913 693-1900
Haley Aldrich, *Principal*
Wayne Hardison, *Vice Pres*
Paul Ozarwoski, *Vice Pres*
Steve Phillips, *Project Mgr*
Laura Spann, *Project Mgr*
EMP: 13
SALES (corp-wide): 155.1MM **Privately Held**
SIC: 8748 Environmental consultant
PA: Haley & Aldrich, Inc.
70 Blanchard Rd Ste 204
Burlington MA 01803
617 886-7400

(G-8786)
HALL CHIROPRACTIC CENTER
10216 W 87th St (66212-4674)
PHONE..................................785 242-6444
Rory E Hall, *Branch Mgr*
EMP: 17 **Privately Held**
SIC: 8041 Offices & clinics of chiropractors
PA: Hall Chiropractic Center
137 S Main St
Ottawa KS 66067

(G-8787)
HALSTONTINE CORP
15425 Metcalf Ave (66223-2801)
PHONE..................................913 780-2171
Haldor Harms, *President*
EMP: 15
SALES (est): 1MM **Privately Held**
SIC: 1751 1752 Cabinet building & installation; floor laying & floor work

(G-8788)
HAMMERSMITH MFG & SALES INC
10801 Mastin St Ste 1050 (66210-1776)
PHONE..................................913 338-0754
EMP: 6
SALES (corp-wide): 21.5MM **Privately Held**
SIC: 3443 Fabricated plate work (boiler shop)
PA: Hammersmith Mfg. & Sales, Inc.
401 Central Ave
Horton KS 66439
785 486-2121

(G-8789)
HAMS POOL SERVICE LLC
4400 W 97th St (66207-3527)
PHONE..................................913 927-0882
Lee Ham Terry, *Administration*
EMP: 6
SALES (est): 616.5K **Privately Held**
SIC: 2013 Prepared pork products from purchased pork

(G-8790)
HANGER PROSTHETICS &
10777 Nall Ave Ste 300 (66211-1330)
PHONE..................................913 341-8897
Sam Liang, *President*
Caroline Oliver, *Business Anlyst*
Brian Kerl, *Branch Mgr*
Kevin King, *Associate*
EMP: 5
SALES (corp-wide): 1B **Publicly Held**
SIC: 5999 3842 Orthopedic & prosthesis applications; limbs, artificial
HQ: Hanger Prosthetics & Orthotics East, Inc.
33 North Ave Ste 101
Tallmadge OH 44278

(G-8791)
HANOVER RS LIMITED PARTNERSHIP
Also Called: Weston Point Apartment
13340 Outlook St (66209-4006)
PHONE..................................913 851-4200
John Striker, *Partner*
EMP: 10 **Privately Held**
SIC: 6513 Apartment building operators
PA: Hanover R.S. Limited Partnership
1780 S Post Oak Ln
Houston TX 77056

(G-8792)
HANTOVER INC (PA)
5200 W 110th St Ste 200 (66211-1203)
P.O. Box 410646, Kansas City MO (64141-0646)
PHONE..................................913 214-4800
Bernard Huff, *Ch of Bd*
Karon Huff, *Corp Secy*
Cory Hutson, *Warehouse Mgr*
Charley Willsie, *Warehouse Mgr*
Victor Gomez, *Sales Staff*
◆ **EMP**: 109
SQ FT: 22,000
SALES (est): 161.3MM **Privately Held**
WEB: www.hantover.com
SIC: 5099 5084 Safety equipment & supplies; food industry machinery

(G-8793)
HAPPY FOOD CO LLC
11878 W 91st St (66214-1716)
PHONE..................................816 835-3600
EMP: 19
SALES (corp-wide): 200K **Privately Held**
SIC: 5145 Snack foods
PA: Happy Food Co Llc
11880 W 91st St
Overland Park KS 66214
816 835-3600

(G-8794)
HAREN LAUGHLIN RESTORATION INC
Also Called: HARENLAUGHLIN RESTORATION
7700 Wedd St Ste 500 (66204-2250)
PHONE..................................913 495-9558
Charles Penner, *President*
Carl Mannino, *Vice Pres*
Donna Lollman, *Treasurer*

GEOGRAPHIC

Wells Haren III, *Admin Sec*
EMP: 27
SALES: 7.6MM **Privately Held**
SIC: 1542 Commercial & office building, new construction

(G-8795)
HARRAHS NORTH KANSAS CITY LLC
9401 Reeds Rd (66207-2519)
PHONE..................................816 472-7777
Gary W Loveman,
EMP: 1200
SALES (est): 18.8MM
SALES (corp-wide): 8.3B **Publicly Held**
SIC: 7999 Gambling establishment
PA: Caesars Entertainment Corporation
1 Caesars Palace Dr
Las Vegas NV 89109
702 407-6000

(G-8796)
HARRIS BMO BANK NATIONAL ASSN
6860 W 115th St (66211-2457)
PHONE..................................913 307-0707
Stephanie Goodnight, *Principal*
EMP: 35
SALES (corp-wide): 17.7B **Privately Held**
WEB: www.uhb-fl.com
SIC: 6022 State commercial banks
HQ: Harris Bmo Bank National Association
111 W Monroe St Ste 1200
Chicago IL 60603
312 461-2323

(G-8797)
HARTFIEL AUTOMATION INC
8017 Flint St (66214-3335)
PHONE..................................913 894-6545
Eric Ferguson, *Design Engr*
Todd Thomas, *Branch Mgr*
EMP: 17
SALES (corp-wide): 1MM **Privately Held**
WEB: www.hartfiel.com
SIC: 5084 Hydraulic systems equipment & supplies
PA: Hartfiel Automation, Inc.
6533 Flying Cloud Dr # 100
Eden Prairie MN 55344
952 974-2500

(G-8798)
HARVEST AMERICA CORPORATION (PA)
10000 W 75th St Ste 247 (66204-9812)
PHONE..................................913 342-2121
Terri Bookless, *CEO*
Steve Sandoval, *Vice Chairman*
Alfred Kayhil, *Exec Dir*
EMP: 29
SALES: 1MM **Privately Held**
SIC: 8631 Employees' association

(G-8799)
HAWTHORN SUITES
11400 College Blvd (66210-4103)
PHONE..................................913 344-8100
Ron Raney, *Principal*
EMP: 11
SALES (est): 599.1K **Privately Held**
SIC: 7011 Hotels & motels

(G-8800)
HCA INC
Also Called: Menorah Medical Ctr Cancer Ctr
12140 Nall Ave Ste 200 (66209-2507)
PHONE..................................913 498-7409
Richard M Bracken, *Ch of Bd*
Jennifer Dix, *Office Mgr*
Ujjaval Patel, *Med Doctor*
Mark Hoban, *Manager*
EMP: 49 **Publicly Held**
SIC: 8011 Medical centers
HQ: Hca Inc.
1 Park Plz
Nashville TN 37203
615 344-9551

(G-8801)
HEADACHE & PAIN CENTER PA
8101 W 135th St (66223-1111)
PHONE..................................913 491-3999
Mauricio Garcia, *President*
Greg Webster, *COO*
EMP: 75
SALES (est): 9.4MM **Privately Held**
SIC: 8011 Neurologist

(G-8802)
HEADHAULCOM LLC
8500 W 110th St Ste 300 (66210-1804)
PHONE..................................913 905-5189
JB Britton,
EMP: 20
SALES (est): 4.7MM **Privately Held**
WEB: www.Headhaul.com
SIC: 4731 Brokers, shipping

(G-8803)
HEALTHCARE ADMINISTRATIVE SVCS
8717 W 110th St Ste 600 (66210-2126)
PHONE..................................816 763-5446
Mark Meisel, *COO*
EMP: 30 **EST:** 1990
SALES (est): 1.7MM
SALES (corp-wide): 13.7MM **Privately Held**
WEB: www.aakc.com
SIC: 8011 Offices & clinics of medical doctors
PA: Anesthesia Associates Of Kansas City Pc
8717 W 110th St Ste 600
Overland Park KS 66210
913 428-2900

(G-8804)
HEART AMERICA EYE CARE PA
Also Called: Christianson, Timothy H
10985 Cody St Ste 120 (66210-1243)
PHONE..................................913 492-0021
Joseph Sione, *President*
EMP: 10
SALES (est): 766.4K **Privately Held**
WEB: www.heartofamericaeyecare.com
SIC: 8011 Ophthalmologist
PA: Heart Of America Eye Care, P.A.
8800 W 75th St Ste 140
Overland Park KS 66204

(G-8805)
HEART AMERICA EYE CARE PA (PA)
8800 W 75th St Ste 140 (66204-4001)
PHONE..................................913 362-3210
Joseph Simone MD, *President*
Louis J Badeen, *Exec VP*
Bradley R Kwapiszeski, *Vice Pres*
Bradley Kwapiszeski, *Med Doctor*
EMP: 38
SQ FT: 6,000
SALES (est): 2.3MM **Privately Held**
WEB: www.heartofamericaeyecare.com
SIC: 8043 Offices & clinics of podiatrists

(G-8806)
HEART CTR AT OVRLAND PK RGONAL
10500 Quivira Rd (66215-2306)
PHONE..................................913 541-5374
Cindy Asher, *Director*
EMP: 23
SALES (est): 1.3MM **Privately Held**
SIC: 8011 Cardiologist & cardio-vascular specialist

(G-8807)
HEARTLAND CREDIT UNION ASSN (PA)
6800 College Blvd Ste 300 (66211-1595)
PHONE..................................913 297-2480
Brad Douglas, *CEO*
Stephanie Greenwood, *Vice Pres*
Brooke Callahan, *Consultant*
Tim Loveless, *Director*
EMP: 10
SQ FT: 1,000
SALES (est): 1.4MM **Privately Held**
SIC: 8611 Trade associations

(G-8808)
HEARTLAND SURGICAL CARE
Also Called: Surgical Weight Loss Center
7201 W 110th St Ste 120 (66210-2373)
PHONE..................................913 647-3999
Dr Jesse Lopez Jr, *Owner*
EMP: 11 **EST:** 2008
SALES (est): 499.1K **Privately Held**
SIC: 8093 Weight loss clinic, with medical staff

(G-8809)
HEARTTRAINING LLC
7300 W 110th St Ste 700 (66210-2332)
PHONE..................................913 402-6012
EMP: 5 **EST:** 2008
SALES (est): 520.9K **Privately Held**
SIC: 3845 Pacemaker, cardiac

(G-8810)
HENDERSON ENGINEERS INC
8345 Lenexa Dr Ste 300 (66214-1777)
PHONE..................................913 742-5000
Joe Brauchle, *Vice Pres*
Marc Feyh, *Vice Pres*
Shane Lutz, *Vice Pres*
Tom Simmons, *Vice Pres*
Michael Branson, *Project Mgr*
EMP: 76 **Privately Held**
SIC: 8711 Civil engineering
PA: Henderson Engineers, Inc.
8345 Lenexa Dr Ste 300
Lenexa KS 66214

(G-8811)
HERALD AND BANNER PRESS
7407 Metcalf Ave (66204-1975)
P.O. Box 4060, Shawnee Mission (66204-0060)
PHONE..................................913 432-0331
Steve Kelso, *General Mgr*
EMP: 11 **EST:** 1938
SQ FT: 8,400
SALES: 622.1K **Privately Held**
WEB: www.heraldandbanner.com
SIC: 2721 Periodicals

(G-8812)
HERITAGE CMPT CONSULTING INC
10104 W 105th St (66212-5746)
PHONE..................................913 529-4227
Arlene Watkins, *President*
Jim Watkins, *Vice Pres*
EMP: 16
SALES (est): 107.5K **Privately Held**
SIC: 7371 7378 5199 Computer software systems analysis & design, custom; computer maintenance & repair; badges

(G-8813)
HERTZ CORPORATION
8130 Metcalf Ave (66204-3849)
PHONE..................................913 341-1782
Jeremy Elliot, *Branch Mgr*
EMP: 23
SALES (corp-wide): 9.5B **Publicly Held**
SIC: 7514 Rent-a-car service
HQ: The Hertz Corporation
8501 Williams Rd
Estero FL 33928
239 301-7000

(G-8814)
HIGHLANDS HIGHPOINT VILLAGE
Also Called: Highlands North and South, The
10020 W 80th St (66204-1197)
PHONE..................................913 381-0335
Sue Scofield, *Manager*
Kellie Bennett, *Manager*
Stephanie Shaffer, *Manager*
EMP: 12
SALES (est): 631.7K **Privately Held**
WEB: www.highpointvillage.com
SIC: 6513 Apartment building operators

(G-8815)
HINRICHSZENK + PESAVENTO
7285 W 132nd St Ste 140 (66213-1164)
PHONE..................................785 691-5407
Justin Pothoven, *Sr Associate*
EMP: 10 **EST:** 2017
SALES (est): 881.2K **Privately Held**
SIC: 8721 Certified public accountant

(G-8816)
HIT PORTFOLIO I HIL TRS LLC
Also Called: Hampton Inn Kansas City Arprt
10591 Metcalf Frontage Rd (66212-1884)
PHONE..................................816 464-5454
Kim Fears, *General Mgr*
Betty Burgman, *Vice Pres*
EMP: 35
SALES (corp-wide): 606MM **Privately Held**
SIC: 7011 Hotels & motels
HQ: Hit Portfolio I Hil Trs, Llc
3950 University Dr # 301
Fairfax VA 22030
212 415-6500

(G-8817)
HIT PORTFOLIO I TRS LLC
Also Called: Hyatt Place Kansas
6801 W 112th St (66211-1577)
PHONE..................................913 451-2553
Pete Fortune, *CEO*
EMP: 16
SALES (corp-wide): 52.2MM **Privately Held**
SIC: 7011 Hotels & motels
HQ: Hit Portfolio I Trs, Llc
106 York Rd
Jenkintown PA 19046
571 529-6390

(G-8818)
HMN ARCHITECTS INC (PA)
7400 W 110th St Ste 200 (66210-2346)
PHONE..................................913 451-9075
Larry Ralph, *President*
Rick L Gannon, *Principal*
Patricia Kistler, *Principal*
Teri Doty, *CFO*
EMP: 100
SQ FT: 4,800
SALES (est): 14.6MM **Privately Held**
WEB: www.hmnarchitects.com
SIC: 8712 Architectural engineering

(G-8819)
HNRY LOGISTICS INC (DH)
5200 W 110th St (66211-1203)
PHONE..................................833 810-4679
Sonny Catlett, *CEO*
EMP: 15
SALES (est): 4.2MM
SALES (corp-wide): 5B **Publicly Held**
WEB: www.roadwayreverselogistics.com
SIC: 4213 Trucking, except local
HQ: Yrc Inc.
10990 Roe Ave
Overland Park KS 66211
913 696-6100

(G-8820)
HNTB CORPORATION
7400 W 129th St Ste 100 (66213-2668)
PHONE..................................913 491-9333
Max Comstock, *Partner*
Levi Borntreger, *Engineer*
Ryan Gillespie, *Engineer*
Andy Nelson, *Engineer*
Lisa Ely, *Human Resources*
EMP: 98
SALES (corp-wide): 85.3MM **Privately Held**
WEB: www.hntb.com
SIC: 8711 Consulting engineer
HQ: Hntb Corporation
715 Kirk Dr
Kansas City MO 64105
816 472-1201

(G-8821)
HODES & NAUSER MDS PA
4840 College Blvd (66211-1601)
PHONE..................................913 491-6878
Traci L Nauser, *Partner*
Herbert Hodes, *Partner*
EMP: 11
SALES (est): 789.7K **Privately Held**
SIC: 8011 8049 Gynecologist; dietician

(G-8822)
HOLIDAY CLEANERS
Also Called: Holiday Cleaning Center
7945 Frontage Rd (66204-2352)
PHONE..................................913 631-6181
Robert Johnson, *Owner*
EMP: 11
SQ FT: 5,600
SALES (est): 277.3K **Privately Held**
SIC: 7216 Drycleaning collecting & distributing agency

(G-8823)
HOME DEPOT USA INC
Also Called: Home Depot, The
8805 Lenexa Dr (66214-3240)
PHONE....................913 310-0204
EMP: 20
SALES (corp-wide): 108.2B **Publicly Held**
SIC: 5074 Plumbing fittings & supplies
HQ: Home Depot U.S.A., Inc.
2455 Paces Ferry Ave
Atlanta GA 30339

(G-8824)
HOME DEPOT USA INC
Also Called: Home Depot, The
11940 Metcalf Ave (66213-1124)
PHONE....................913 871-1221
EMP: 299
SALES (corp-wide): 108.2B **Publicly Held**
SIC: 5023 Decorative home furnishings & supplies
HQ: Home Depot U.S.A., Inc.
2455 Paces Ferry Ave
Atlanta GA 30339

(G-8825)
HOME RENTAL SERVICES INC
6900 College Blvd Ste 990 (66211-1844)
PHONE....................913 469-6633
Kandy Meehan, *President*
Caitlin Meehan-Coover, *Director*
EMP: 10
SQ FT: 2,500
SALES (est): 1MM **Privately Held**
SIC: 6531 Real estate managers

(G-8826)
HOSPICE ADVANTAGE LLC
10101 W 87th St Ste 200 (66212-4606)
PHONE....................913 859-9582
Kaye Mysberge, *Branch Mgr*
EMP: 12 **Privately Held**
SIC: 8052 Personal care facility
HQ: Hospice Advantage Llc
401 Center Ave Ste 130
Bay City MI 48708
989 891-2200

(G-8827)
HOSPITAL MANAGEMENT CORP
12920 Metcalf Ave (66213-2699)
PHONE....................913 492-0159
Douglas Galgar, *President*
EMP: 17
SALES (est): 1MM **Privately Held**
SIC: 8051 Extended care facility

(G-8828)
HOSPITALITY MANAGEMENT SYSTEMS (PA)
Also Called: Micros of Kansas City
8064 Reeder St (66214-1554)
PHONE....................913 438-5040
Mark Carroll, *President*
Tony Baldassarre, *Vice Pres*
Joel Priest, *Accounts Mgr*
Hannah Arnold, *Sales Executive*
Jason Bradley, *Sales Executive*
EMP: 15
SALES (est): 3.5MM **Privately Held**
SIC: 5045 Computers, peripherals & software

(G-8829)
HOTEL CLUBS CORP WOODS INC
Also Called: Doubletree By
10100 College Blvd (66210-1416)
PHONE....................913 451-6100
Ken Gordhamer, *Principal*
EMP: 100
SALES (est): 3.8MM **Privately Held**
SIC: 7011 5812 Hotels & motels; eating places
PA: The Ecclestone Organization Inc
1555 Palm Beach Lks
West Palm Beach FL 33401

(G-8830)
HOTEL MGT & CONSULTING INC
7200 W 132nd St Ste 220 (66213-1144)
PHONE....................913 602-8470
EMP: 12
SALES (est): 1.6MM **Privately Held**
SIC: 8748 Business Consulting Services

(G-8831)
HOVEY WILLIAMS LLP
10801 Mastin St Ste 1000 (66210-1697)
PHONE....................913 647-9050
Thomas B Luebbering, *Partner*
EMP: 50
SQ FT: 7,200
SALES (est): 6.5MM **Privately Held**
WEB: www.hoveywilliams.com
SIC: 8111 General practice law office

(G-8832)
HSS IT MANAGEMENT INC (PA)
Also Called: Deg
6601 College Blvd Fl 6 (66211-1504)
PHONE....................913 498-9988
Neal Sharma, *President*
Jeff Vonseldeneck, *Business Mgr*
Maureen Dempsey, *Project Mgr*
Ashley Dvorak, *Project Mgr*
Chad Elliott, *Project Mgr*
EMP: 120
SALES (est): 15.5MM **Privately Held**
SIC: 8742 7311 Marketing consulting services; advertising agencies

(G-8833)
HUDSON CROP INSURANCE SVCS INC
7300 W 110th St Ste 400 (66210-2332)
PHONE....................866 450-1446
Dan Gasser, *President*
Barry Coday, *Executive*
EMP: 137 **EST:** 2008
SALES (est): 5.4MM **Privately Held**
SIC: 6331 Federal crop insurance corporation

(G-8834)
HUMANA INC
7311 W 132nd St Ste 200 (66213-1157)
PHONE....................913 217-3300
Michelle Edgington, *Accounts Exec*
David Miller, *Branch Mgr*
Jackie Sewing, *Case Mgr*
EMP: 40
SALES (corp-wide): 56.9B **Publicly Held**
WEB: www.humana.com
SIC: 6324 Health maintenance organization (HMO), insurance only
PA: Humana Inc.
500 W Main St Ste 300
Louisville KY 40202
502 580-1000

(G-8835)
HYR GLOBAL SOURCE INC
7304 W 130th St Ste 220 (66213-2638)
PHONE....................913 815-2597
Pranita Kishore Yampati, *President*
Rajani Kant Yampati, *Vice Pres*
EMP: 12
SALES (est): 239.8K **Privately Held**
SIC: 7379 8742 7389 Computer related consulting services; human resource consulting services; business services

(G-8836)
ICLEAN PROF CLG SVCS LLC
12022 Blue Valley Pkwy # 1 (66213-2647)
PHONE....................913 521-5995
EMP: 11
SALES (corp-wide): 478.5K **Privately Held**
SIC: 7699 Cleaning services
PA: Iclean Professional Cleaning Services Llc
11944 W 95th St 216
Lenexa KS

(G-8837)
ICON INTEGRATION & DESIGN INC
9393 W 110th St Ste 500 (66210-1464)
PHONE....................913 221-8801
Michael Thibault, *President*
Leon Schwartz, *Vice Pres*
EMP: 15
SALES (est): 935.4K **Privately Held**
SIC: 7389 Design services

(G-8838)
IFFT & CO PA
11030 Granada Ln Ste 100 (66211-1417)
PHONE....................913 345-1120
Wayne Ifft, *President*
Diane Gottsch, *Vice Pres*
Meredith Dickinson, *Accountant*
Alex Penhallow, *CPA*
Ashlee Swearingen, *Auditor*
EMP: 17
SALES (est): 1.8MM **Privately Held**
WEB: www.ifftcpa.com
SIC: 8721 Certified public accountant; accounting services, except auditing; auditing services; billing & bookkeeping service

(G-8839)
IMAGINTIVE CNSULTING GROUP INC
7111 W 151st St Ste 154 (66223-2231)
PHONE....................913 481-1936
Nadia Nazir, *President*
EMP: 19
SALES: 500K **Privately Held**
SIC: 7379 Computer related consulting services

(G-8840)
INCISIVE CONSULTANTS LLC
13725 Metcalf Ave Ste 296 (66223-7899)
PHONE....................800 973-1743
Kyle Adams, *Principal*
John Freeman, *Mng Member*
Chris Blackerby, *Mng Member*
EMP: 11
SALES: 1.2MM **Privately Held**
SIC: 8742 Management information systems consultant

(G-8841)
INCRED-A-BOWL LLC
16332 Larsen St (66221-8520)
PHONE....................913 851-1700
Dannie Jackson, *Mng Member*
Danny L Jackson,
Danny Jackson,
Jodi Jackson,
EMP: 70
SALES (est): 2.2MM **Privately Held**
WEB: www.incredabowl.com
SIC: 7933 7999 5813 5812 Ten pin center; tourist attractions, amusement park concessions & rides; drinking places; eating places

(G-8842)
INFICON EDC INC
9075 Cody St (66214-1731)
PHONE....................913 888-1750
Tim Abbott, *President*
Gabe Heredia, *Plant Mgr*
Adam Gadway, *Opers Staff*
Gina Cox, *Sales Mgr*
Russell Foster, *Manager*
▲ **EMP:** 54
SQ FT: 30,000
SALES: 10.8K
SALES (corp-wide): 410.4MM **Privately Held**
WEB: www.electrodynamics.com
SIC: 3679 Quartz crystals, for electronic application
HQ: Inficon, Inc.
2 Technology Pl
East Syracuse NY 13057
315 434-1100

(G-8843)
INFINITE FITNESS
3617 W 133rd St (66209-3345)
PHONE....................913 469-8850
Kathy Holmes, *Owner*
EMP: 10
SALES (est): 241.9K **Privately Held**
SIC: 7991 Athletic club & gymnasiums, membership

(G-8844)
INGENIUM SOLUTIONS INC
10801 Mastin St Ste 550 (66210-1670)
PHONE....................913 239-0050
Christopher J Herbig, *CEO*
Christopher Herbig, *General Mgr*
EMP: 25
SALES (est): 531K **Privately Held**
SIC: 7361 Executive placement

(G-8845)
INNOVA CONSULTING LLC
13220 Metcalf Ave Ste 310 (66213-2842)
PHONE....................913 210-2002
Bruce Scott, *Vice Pres*
Michael Corbin, *Director*
Sandeep Khandelwal,
EMP: 15
SALES (est): 734K **Privately Held**
SIC: 8748 7371 7373 Business consulting; custom computer programming services; computer systems analysis & design

(G-8846)
INNOVATIVE SERVICE SOLUTIONS
16021 King St (66221-6905)
PHONE....................913 851-7745
Matthew Freeman, *President*
EMP: 10
SALES: 1.4MM **Privately Held**
WEB: www.innovativeserv.com
SIC: 8748 Telecommunications consultant

(G-8847)
INNOVISION CORPORATION
12022 Blue Valley Pkwy (66213-2647)
PHONE....................913 438-3200
Bill Cary, *President*
Ed Scherer, *Engineer*
EMP: 20
SALES (est): 1.3MM **Privately Held**
WEB: www.innovision.com
SIC: 7371 Computer software development

(G-8848)
INSCYT LLC
Also Called: Riskanalytics
7285 W 132nd St Ste 100 (66213-1164)
PHONE....................913 579-7335
Jeff Stull, *Mng Member*
Brian Branner,
EMP: 800
SALES: 10MM **Privately Held**
SIC: 7371 Computer software development & applications

(G-8849)
INSIDE SPORTS AND FITNESS LLC (PA)
11301 W 88th St (66214-1701)
PHONE....................913 888-9247
Reginald Lyerla, *Principal*
EMP: 16
SALES (est): 749.5K **Privately Held**
SIC: 7991 Physical fitness facilities

(G-8850)
INSIDE SPORTS AND FITNESS LLC
9111 Flint St (66214-1737)
PHONE....................913 894-4752
Duane Zee, *Branch Mgr*
EMP: 15
SALES (est): 394.5K
SALES (corp-wide): 749.5K **Privately Held**
SIC: 7991 Physical fitness facilities
PA: Inside Sports And Fitness, Llc
11301 W 88th St
Overland Park KS 66214
913 888-9247

(G-8851)
INSIDERESPONSE LLC
9800 Metcalf Ave (66212-2216)
PHONE....................855 969-0812
Trevor Nohe, *President*
Blaine Kauk, *COO*
Michael Weber, *CFO*
Jeffrey Huggins, *Sales Staff*
Ryan Wasinger, *Chief Mktg Ofcr*
EMP: 50
SQ FT: 5,000
SALES (est): 2.5MM **Privately Held**
SIC: 7311 Advertising agencies

(G-8852)
INSIGHT 2 DESIGN LLC
8681 W 137th St (66223-1286)
PHONE....................913 937-9386

GEOGRAPHIC

Kevin Tarter, *President*
Nick Vaughn, *Director*
▲ **EMP:** 10 **EST:** 2012
SALES: 5.6MM **Privately Held**
SIC: 7389 Design services

(G-8853)
INSIGHT FINANCIAL SERVICES LLC
7101 College Blvd # 1501 (66210-2079)
PHONE..................................913 402-2020
Tete Martinez,
EMP: 15
SALES (est): 1.9MM **Privately Held**
SIC: 6282 Investment advisory service

(G-8854)
INSPIRE HOSPICE LLC
11827 W 112th St Ste 100 (66210-2726)
PHONE..................................913 521-2727
Luke Adams,
EMP: 10
SALES (est): 69.5K **Privately Held**
SIC: 8082 Home health care services

(G-8855)
INTEGRITY HOME CARE INC
8826 Santa Fe Dr Ste 209 (66212-3626)
PHONE..................................913 685-1616
Greg Horton, *CEO*
EMP: 14
SALES (corp-wide): 950K **Privately Held**
SIC: 8082 Home health care services
PA: Integrity Home Care, Inc.
2960 N Eastgate Ave
Springfield MO 65803
417 889-9773

(G-8856)
INTERNATIONAL ASSN PLAS DIST (PA)
6734 W 121st St (66209-2002)
PHONE..................................913 345-1005
Susan Avery, *Exec Dir*
Darla Hall, *Executive*
EMP: 11 **EST:** 1991
SQ FT: 4,500
SALES: 1.4MM **Privately Held**
WEB: www.iapd.org
SIC: 8611 Trade associations

(G-8857)
INTERNATIONAL FOREST PDTS LLC
9393 W 110th St Ste 500 (66210-1464)
PHONE..................................913 451-6945
Robert Wilde, *Officer*
Robert Stephen Wilde,
Michael Kincaid,
◆ **EMP:** 96
SALES (est): 8.1MM **Privately Held**
SIC: 2411 2439 Logging; timbers, structural: laminated lumber

(G-8858)
INTERNATIONAL INST CHRISTIAN S
Also Called: IICS
10100 W 87th St Ste 303 (66212-4628)
P.O. Box 12147, Shawnee Mission (66282-2147)
PHONE..................................913 962-4422
Daryl McCarthy, *CEO*
EMP: 28
SQ FT: 2,559
SALES: 2MM **Privately Held**
SIC: 8299 8661 8641 Educational services; religious organizations; educator's association

(G-8859)
INTERNTIONAL WHEAT GLUTEN ASSN
9300 Metcalf Ave (66212-1463)
PHONE..................................913 381-8180
Tim Newkirk, *Principal*
EMP: 15
SALES: 72.2K **Privately Held**
SIC: 8699 Membership organizations

(G-8860)
INTOUCH GROUP LLC (PA)
7045 College Blvd Ste 300 (66211-1529)
PHONE..................................913 317-9700
Faruk Capan, *CEO*
Wendy Blackburn, *Exec VP*
Angela Tenuta, *Exec VP*
David Windhausen, *Exec VP*
Ann Cave, *Senior VP*
EMP: 124
SQ FT: 18,006
SALES (est): 62.3MM **Privately Held**
WEB: www.intouchsol.com
SIC: 8742 Marketing consulting services

(G-8861)
IQVIA PHASE ONE SERVICES LLC
6700 W 115th St (66211-1553)
PHONE..................................913 708-6000
Joesph Lacz, *President*
Sandy James, *Manager*
EMP: 99
SALES (est): 12.5MM **Publicly Held**
SIC: 1522 Residential construction
PA: Iqvia Holdings Inc.
4820 Emperor Blvd
Durham NC 27703

(G-8862)
IQVUA RDS INC
6700 W 115th St (66211-1553)
PHONE..................................913 708-6000
Melissa Leedom, *Project Mgr*
Noy Follett, *Opers Staff*
Janie Bush, *Research*
Maulsary Dhillon, *Research*
Paul Guo, *Research*
EMP: 79 **Publicly Held**
SIC: 8731 Commercial physical research
HQ: Iqvia Rds Inc
4820 Emperor Blvd
Durham NC 27703
919 998-2000

(G-8863)
ISIGMA CONSULTING LLC
4745 W 136th St Ste 48 (66224-5923)
PHONE..................................620 757-6363
Amir Ali Mofid, *Mng Member*
EMP: 12
SQ FT: 300
SALES (est): 1.1MM **Privately Held**
SIC: 7379 7373 7378 Computer related consulting services; computer integrated systems design; computer maintenance & repair

(G-8864)
IT21 INC
11955 W 153rd St (66221-2317)
PHONE..................................913 393-4821
Michael Bohning, *President*
EMP: 13
SALES (est): 1.3MM
SALES (corp-wide): 3.6MM **Privately Held**
WEB: www.it21.com
SIC: 4813 7379 8748 ; ; business consulting
PA: Hsmc Orizon Llc
16924 Frances St Ste 210
Omaha NE 68130
402 330-7008

(G-8865)
ITEDIUM INC
6717 Shawnee Mission Pkwy C (66202-4022)
P.O. Box 39, Shawnee Mission (66201-0039)
PHONE..................................913 499-4850
Robert Meyers, *President*
Chris Ballard, *COO*
Debra Mootz, *Opers Staff*
Christopher Ballard, *Info Tech Mgr*
John Turpin, *Analyst*
EMP: 40
SQ FT: 10,000
SALES (est): 4.9MM **Privately Held**
SIC: 7371 Computer software development & applications

(G-8866)
IVY FUNDS VIP SMALL CAP GROWTH
6300 Lamar Ave (66202-4247)
PHONE..................................800 777-6472
EMP: 13
SALES (est): 119.3K **Publicly Held**
SIC: 6722 Money market mutual funds
HQ: Ivy Funds Distributor, Inc.
6300 Lamar Ave
Shawnee Mission KS 66202
913 261-2800

(G-8867)
IVY LEAGUE LEARNING CENTER
Also Called: Ivy League Learning Ctr & Nurs
7260 W 121st St (66213-1201)
PHONE..................................913 338-4060
Diane King, *Principal*
EMP: 25
SALES: 164.9K **Privately Held**
SIC: 8351 Preschool center

(G-8868)
J&J DRIVEAWAY SYSTEMS LLC
7270 W 162nd St (66085-9139)
PHONE..................................913 387-0158
Rodney Ruth, *CEO*
EMP: 23
SALES (est): 564.5K
SALES (corp-wide): 30MM **Privately Held**
SIC: 4213 4731 Automobiles, transport & delivery; truck transportation brokers
PA: Auto Driveaway Franchise Systems, Llc
1 E 22nd St Ste 107
Lombard IL 60148
312 341-1900

(G-8869)
JACKSON LEWIS PC
7101 College Blvd # 1150 (66210-1845)
PHONE..................................913 982-5747
Lewis Jackson, *Branch Mgr*
EMP: 37
SALES (corp-wide): 250.5MM **Privately Held**
SIC: 8111 General practice law office
PA: Jackson Lewis Pc
1133 Weschester Ave
West Harrison NY 10604
914 872-8060

(G-8870)
JAHNKE & SONS CONSTRUCTION INC
Also Called: Whp Training Towers
9130 Flint St (66214-1736)
PHONE..................................800 351-2525
William M Jahnke, *CEO*
Marilyn K Jahnke, *President*
Alan Henderson, *Sales Associate*
Maggie Scaletty, *Manager*
EMP: 19
SQ FT: 1,600
SALES (est): 7.5MM **Privately Held**
WEB: www.trainingtowers.com
SIC: 1542 3448 Nonresidential construction; prefabricated metal buildings

(G-8871)
JAMES AVERY CRAFTSMAN INC
11149 W 95th St (66214-1824)
PHONE..................................913 307-0419
EMP: 18
SALES (corp-wide): 375.6MM **Privately Held**
SIC: 3911 Manufacturing Precious Metal Jewelry
PA: James Avery Craftsman, Inc.
145 Avery Rd
Kerrville TX 78028
830 895-6800

(G-8872)
JAMES MIRABILE
Also Called: Mirabile MD Hlth Buty Wellness
4550 W 109th St Ste 130 (66211-1354)
PHONE..................................913 888-7546
James Mirabile, *Owner*
Clt C Le, *Cust Mgr*
EMP: 25
SALES (est): 483.4K **Privately Held**
SIC: 7991 Spas

(G-8873)
JCOR INC
10510 W 142nd Ter (66221-8500)
P.O. Box 26864 (66225-6864)
PHONE..................................913 461-8804
Judy Mayfield, *President*
Michael Whitchurch, *Vice Pres*
Jennifer Konzem, *Office Mgr*
EMP: 18
SALES (est): 2.5MM **Privately Held**
SIC: 1611 General contractor, highway & street construction

(G-8874)
JEWISH FAMILY SERVICES
5801 W 115th St Ste 103 (66211-1800)
PHONE..................................913 327-8250
Don Goldman, *CEO*
Sarah Albin, *Manager*
Todd Stettner, *Exec Dir*
Taly Friedman, *Director*
EMP: 50 **Privately Held**
SIC: 8322 Social service center
PA: Jewish Family Services
425 E 63rd St Ste 120
Kansas City MO

(G-8875)
JOB BOARD NETWORK LLC
5211 W 156th St (66224-3524)
PHONE..................................913 238-1181
Cory Jackson, *Founder*
Gary Upah, *Sales Staff*
EMP: 14
SALES (est): 1MM **Privately Held**
SIC: 8621 Professional membership organizations

(G-8876)
JOCO BARKING CLUB
15109 Rosewood Dr (66224-3503)
P.O. Box 4193 (66204-0193)
PHONE..................................913 558-2625
Shawn Moses, *Owner*
EMP: 20
SALES (est): 894.8K **Privately Held**
SIC: 5999 7299 Pets & pet supplies; pet sitting,in-home

(G-8877)
JODY PHILLIPS DANCE COMPANY
14840 Metcalf Ave (66223-2206)
PHONE..................................913 897-9888
Jody Phillips, *Owner*
EMP: 20
SALES (est): 271K **Privately Held**
SIC: 7911 Dance instructor & school services

(G-8878)
JOHNSON COUNTY IMAGING CTR PA
11717 W 112th St (66210-2761)
PHONE..................................913 469-8998
Charles Karlin, *President*
Michael Brun MD, *Principal*
EMP: 50
SQ FT: 2,000
SALES (est): 7.7MM **Privately Held**
SIC: 8011 8071 Physicians' office, including specialists; radiologist; X-ray laboratory, including dental

(G-8879)
JONES LANG LASALLE INC
7500 College Blvd Ste 920 (66210-4035)
PHONE..................................816 531-2323
Todd Pike, *General Mgr*
Kevin Wilkerson, *Managing Dir*
Patrick Meraz, *Vice Pres*
Lawrence Glaze, *Branch Mgr*
Meaghan Kelly,
EMP: 16
SALES (corp-wide): 16.3B **Publicly Held**
WEB: www.joneslanglasalle.com
SIC: 6531 Real estate managers
PA: Jones Lang Lasalle Incorporated
200 E Randolph St # 4300
Chicago IL 60601
312 782-5800

(G-8880)
JP MURRAY COMPANY INC
7400 College Blvd Ste 210 (66210-4038)
PHONE..................................913 451-1279
Philip Schultze, *Principal*
EMP: 10
SALES (est): 2.5MM **Privately Held**
SIC: 1542 Commercial & office building, new construction

PA: J.P. Murray Company, Inc.
1215 Fern Ridge Pkwy # 213
Saint Louis MO 63141

(G-8881)
JT MAINTENANCE INC
5750 W 95th St Ste 200 (66207-2976)
PHONE....................................913 642-5656
Ron Jury, *President*
EMP: 14
SALES (est): 406K **Privately Held**
WEB: www.rdjury.com
SIC: 7349 Building maintenance services

(G-8882)
JT2 INC
9393 W 110th St Ste 533 (66210-1442)
PHONE....................................913 323-4915
Larry Odonnell, *Branch Mgr*
EMP: 15 **Privately Held**
SIC: 7361 Employment agencies
PA: Jt2, Inc.

Blue Ash OH

(G-8883)
JUSTIS LAW FIRM LLC
10955 Lowell Ave Ste 520 (66210-2336)
PHONE....................................913 955-3710
Gary D Justis,
EMP: 10
SALES (est): 458.9K **Privately Held**
SIC: 8111 General practice law office

(G-8884)
KAESER COMPRESSORS INC
8334 Melrose Dr (66214-1630)
PHONE....................................913 599-5100
Drew Johnson, *Branch Mgr*
EMP: 11
SALES (corp-wide): 1.6MM **Privately Held**
WEB: www.kaeser.com
SIC: 5084 Compressors, except air conditioning
HQ: Kaeser Compressors, Inc.
511 Sigma Dr
Fredericksburg VA 22408
540 898-5500

(G-8885)
KALIAPERUMAL MAMALAY
Also Called: Hippalus Technologies
10901 W 144th St (66221-8170)
PHONE....................................816 210-1248
Mamalay Kaliaperumal, *Owner*
EMP: 5
SALES (est): 327.1K **Privately Held**
SIC: 7371 7373 7372 7389 Custom computer programming services; computer software systems analysis & design, custom; software programming applications; computer integrated systems design; business oriented computer software;

(G-8886)
KANA SOFTWARE INC
7400 W 129th St Ste 200 (66213-2667)
PHONE....................................913 802-6756
Chad Wolf, *Principal*
EMP: 135 **Publicly Held**
SIC: 7372 Prepackaged software
HQ: Kana Software, Inc.
2550 Walsh Ave Ste 120
Santa Clara CA 95051
650 614-8300

(G-8887)
KANBREWS LLC (PA)
9100 Bond St (66214-1725)
PHONE....................................913 499-6495
Kirk S Williams, *Administration*
EMP: 11
SALES (est): 1.5MM **Privately Held**
SIC: 8641 Bars & restaurants, members only

(G-8888)
KANSAS BUILDING SUPPLY CO INC
7600 Wedd St (66204-2227)
PHONE....................................913 962-5227
Dennis Donelly, *President*
Jay Waldenmeyer, *Division Mgr*
Steve Tolbert, *General Mgr*
Jim Loftin, *Sales Staff*
Cheri Morgan, *Manager*
EMP: 80
SALES (est): 44.8MM **Privately Held**
SIC: 5031 Building materials, exterior; building materials, interior

(G-8889)
KANSAS CITY BONE & JOINT CLINI
10701 Nall Ave Ste 200 (66211-1358)
PHONE....................................913 381-5225
Atul Patel, *Med Doctor*
Robert Bruce, *Surgeon*
Suzanne Elton, *Surgeon*
Jeffrey Salin, *Surgeon*
Mike A Stephenson, *Administration*
EMP: 29
SALES (est): 3.3MM **Privately Held**
SIC: 8011 Clinic, operated by physicians; orthopedic physician

(G-8890)
KANSAS CITY BROKERAGE INC
Also Called: Kc Brokerage
6700 Antioch Rd Ste 420 (66204-1541)
P.O. Box 7027, Kansas City MO (64113-0027)
PHONE....................................913 384-4994
Mark Donaldson, *President*
Doug Ebert, *COO*
Bill Miskell, *Exec VP*
Emily Jewett, *Production*
Michael Marsh, *Research*
EMP: 30
SALES (est): 5.3MM **Privately Held**
SIC: 6211 Security brokers & dealers

(G-8891)
KANSAS CITY CANCER CENTER LLC (PA)
9200 Indian Creek Pkwy # 300 (66210-2036)
PHONE....................................913 541-4600
Stephanie Bycraft, *Principal*
EMP: 25
SALES (est): 7.5MM **Privately Held**
SIC: 8011 Oncologist

(G-8892)
KANSAS CITY COMPENSATION & BEN
Also Called: KCCBA
8826 Santa Fe Dr Ste 208 (66212-3672)
PHONE....................................913 381-4458
Sandra Sabanske, *Administration*
EMP: 16
SALES: 36.9K **Privately Held**
SIC: 8699 Professional golf association

(G-8893)
KANSAS CITY CTR FOR ANXTY TRMT
10555 Marty St Ste 100 (66212-2555)
PHONE....................................913 649-8820
Lisa Hale, *Principal*
Becky Ohalloran, *Manager*
EMP: 11
SALES (est): 625.1K **Privately Held**
SIC: 8093 Mental health clinic, outpatient

(G-8894)
KANSAS CITY DEAERATOR INC
Also Called: Kansas City Heater Company
6731 W 121st St (66209-2003)
PHONE....................................913 312-5800
Michael G Koontz, *President*
Carolyn Domanico, *Purch Mgr*
Dave Stewart, *Engineer*
Matt Hickman, *Project Engr*
Deirdre Patterson, *Project Engr*
▼ **EMP:** 13
SQ FT: 8,000
SALES (est): 2.9MM **Privately Held**
WEB: www.kansascitydeaerator.com
SIC: 3433 Heating equipment, except electric

(G-8895)
KANSAS CITY FINANCIAL GROUP
4801 W 110th St Ste 200 (66211-1239)
P.O. Box 7190, Shawnee Mission (66207-0190)
PHONE....................................913 649-7447
R David Wentz Sr, *President*
EMP: 35
SALES (est): 3.3MM **Privately Held**
SIC: 6411 8742 Insurance agents, brokers & service; financial consultant

(G-8896)
KANSAS CITY HOSPICE INC
10100 W 87th St Ste 100 (66212-4628)
PHONE....................................816 363-2600
Bill Dichiser, *CFO*
Lori Schellenberg, *Branch Mgr*
EMP: 30
SALES (corp-wide): 21.1MM **Privately Held**
SIC: 8052 Personal care facility
PA: Kansas City Hospice, Inc.
1500 Meadow Lake Pkwy # 200
Kansas City MO 64114
816 276-2657

(G-8897)
KANSAS CITY UROLOGY CARE
10701 Nall Ave Ste 100 (66211-1244)
PHONE....................................913 338-5585
Gary Leifer, *Owner*
Elaine Richman,
EMP: 23
SALES (est): 2.9MM **Privately Held**
SIC: 8011 Urologist

(G-8898)
KANSAS CITY UROLOGY CARE PA
10701 Nall Ave Ste 100 (66211-1244)
P.O. Box 802259, Kansas City MO (64180-2259)
PHONE....................................913 341-7985
Keith Potter, *CEO*
Gary Leifer, *Principal*
Judy Searcy, *Research*
Jill Smith, *Office Mgr*
Sherri Taylor, *Office Mgr*
EMP: 127
SQ FT: 20,000
SALES (est): 18.3MM **Privately Held**
SIC: 8011 Urologist

(G-8899)
KANSAS CY GEN VSCULAR SURGEONS
10730 Nall Ave Ste 101 (66211-1242)
PHONE....................................913 754-2800
Joe A Cates, *President*
Jeffrey W Cameron MD, *Principal*
Edward F Higgins Jr, *Principal*
Brian L McCroskey MD, *Principal*
EMP: 30
SALES (est): 3.1MM **Privately Held**
WEB: www.kcgvs.com
SIC: 8011 Surgeon

(G-8900)
KANSAS CY INTERNAL MEDICINE PA
12140 Nall Ave Ste 100 (66209-2504)
PHONE....................................913 451-8500
David Wilt, *President*
Lori A Mallory, *President*
EMP: 21
SALES (est): 4.5MM **Privately Held**
SIC: 8011 Internal medicine, physician/surgeon

(G-8901)
KANSAS CY OB GYN PYSICIANS PC
10339 Alhambra St (66207-4017)
PHONE....................................913 648-1840
William J Huse III, *President*
Paula L Eaton, *Vice Pres*
EMP: 19
SQ FT: 3,500
SALES (est): 604.6K **Privately Held**
SIC: 8011 Obstetrician; gynecologist

(G-8902)
KANSAS GAS SERVICE
11401 W 89th St (66214-1705)
PHONE....................................800 794-4780
Bradley Dixon, *President*
Dennis Okenfuss, *VP Admin*
EMP: 17
SALES (est): 5.4MM **Privately Held**
SIC: 4911 Electric services

(G-8903)
KANSAS LTD LIABILITY COMPANY
7240 W 98th Ter (66212-2255)
PHONE....................................888 222-6359
Brian Cleary,
EMP: 15
SALES (est): 205.9K **Privately Held**
SIC: 7361 Labor contractors (employment agency)

(G-8904)
KANSAS MUNICIPAL ENERGY AGENCY
6300 W 95th St (66212-1431)
PHONE....................................913 677-2884
Jim Widener, *Principal*
EMP: 15
SQ FT: 2,570
SALES (est): 6MM **Privately Held**
WEB: www.kmea.com
SIC: 4911 Generation, electric power

(G-8905)
KC CLEANING SOLUTIONS
9290 Bond St Ste 112 (66214-1729)
P.O. Box 7234 (66207-0234)
PHONE....................................913 236-0040
Tim Roccia, *President*
Ron Vincent, *Vice Pres*
EMP: 143
SALES (est): 3MM **Privately Held**
SIC: 7349 Janitorial service, contract basis

(G-8906)
KC HOPPS LTD (PA)
9401 Reeds Rd Ste 101 (66207-2532)
PHONE....................................913 322-2440
EMP: 33
SALES (est): 7.1MM **Privately Held**
SIC: 8742 Management Consulting Services

(G-8907)
KC HOUSE OF HOPE
7044 Antioch Rd (66204-1246)
PHONE....................................913 262-8885
Jeff Anderson, *Principal*
EMP: 13
SALES (est): 324.4K **Privately Held**
SIC: 8361 Residential care

(G-8908)
KC SMILE PA
12850 Metcalf Ave 200 (66213-2622)
PHONE....................................913 491-6874
Ross Headley, *President*
Kennedy Rogers, *Principal*
Debbie Brown, *Dental Hygenist*
EMP: 13
SALES (est): 1.1MM **Privately Held**
WEB: www.kcsmile.com
SIC: 8021 Dentists' office

(G-8909)
KC SOLAR LLC
8101 College Blvd Ste 100 (66210-2671)
PHONE....................................913 444-9593
Scott Briley,
Hunter Hoss,
EMP: 10
SALES (est): 886.5K **Privately Held**
SIC: 1711 Solar energy contractor

(G-8910)
KEIL VTRNARY OPHTHALMOLOGY LLC
11519 W 83rd Ter (66214-1532)
PHONE....................................785 331-4600
Susan Keil,
EMP: 12
SALES (est): 1.1MM **Privately Held**
SIC: 8011 Ophthalmologist

(G-8911)
KELLER & OWENS LLC
Also Called: Payroll Partners Plus
10955 Lowell Ave Ste 800 (66210-2354)
PHONE....................................913 338-3500
Greg Owens,
Richard Bili,
EMP: 34

GEOGRAPHIC

SALES (est): 5.9K **Privately Held**
WEB: www.kellerowens.com
SIC: 8721 7291 Certified public accountant; tax return preparation services

(G-8912)
KELLY ENTERPRISE INC (PA)
13224 Craig St (66213-1401)
PHONE....913 685-1800
EMP: 12
SALES (est): 2.1MM **Privately Held**
SIC: 6531 Real estate managers

(G-8913)
KELLY SERVICES INC
9200 Indian Creek Pkwy (66210-2036)
PHONE....913 451-1400
Michelle Bradford, *Branch Mgr*
Donna Robinson, *Branch Mgr*
EMP: 2000
SALES (corp-wide): 5.5B **Publicly Held**
SIC: 7363 Temporary help service
PA: Kelly Services, Inc.
999 W Big Beaver Rd
Troy MI 48084
248 362-4444

(G-8914)
KENAI DIALYSIS LLC
Also Called: Nall Dialysis
10787 Nall Ave Ste 130 (66211-1375)
PHONE....913 649-2671
EMP: 31 **EST:** 2012
SALES (est): 447.2K **Publicly Held**
SIC: 8092 Kidney dialysis centers
PA: Davita Inc.
2000 16th St
Denver CO 80202

(G-8915)
KENNEL CREEK
10750 El Monte St (66211-1406)
PHONE....913 498-9900
Chris Taylor, *Principal*
EMP: 20
SALES (est): 580K **Privately Held**
SIC: 0752 Boarding services, kennels

(G-8916)
KFORCE INC
7101 College Blvd Ste 750 (66210-2173)
PHONE....913 890-5000
Jeff Berger, *Branch Mgr*
EMP: 33
SALES (corp-wide): 1.4B **Publicly Held**
WEB: www.kforce.com
SIC: 7361 Executive placement
PA: Kforce Inc.
1001 E Palm Ave
Tampa FL 33605
813 552-5000

(G-8917)
KIDDI KOLLEGE INC
15020 Antioch Rd (66221-8502)
PHONE....913 814-7770
Robyn Fall, *Teacher Per Dir*
EMP: 16
SALES (corp-wide): 2.5MM **Privately Held**
SIC: 8351 Group day care center
PA: Kiddi Kollege Inc
340 N Lindenwood Dr
Olathe KS 66062
913 764-4423

(G-8918)
KIDS AT HEART INC
Also Called: Kids At Heart Childcare
7401 W 97th St (66212-2211)
PHONE....913 648-8577
Tammy Siegrist, *President*
EMP: 24
SALES (est): 863.5K **Privately Held**
SIC: 8351 Preschool center

(G-8919)
KINDRED HEALTHCARE OPER LLC
11880 College Blvd Ste 4a (66210-2778)
PHONE....913 906-0522
Alyssa Hellebusch, *Branch Mgr*
EMP: 41
SALES (corp-wide): 6B **Privately Held**
SIC: 9431 8082 Administration of public health programs; home health care services
HQ: Kindred Healthcare Operating, Llc
680 S 4th St
Louisville KY 40202
502 596-7300

(G-8920)
KISSNER GROUP HOLDINGS LP (PA)
10955 Lowell Ave Ste 500 (66210-2363)
PHONE....913 713-0600
John Cox, *Officer*
EMP: 5
SALES (est): 3.5MM **Privately Held**
SIC: 2899 Heat treating salts

(G-8921)
KJWW CORP
7381 W 133rd St Ste 201 (66213-4834)
PHONE....913 952-6636
EMP: 34
SALES (corp-wide): 90.6MM **Privately Held**
SIC: 8711 Engineering services
PA: Kjww Corp.
623 26th Ave
Rock Island IL 61201
309 788-0673

(G-8922)
KLEEB SERVICES INC (PA)
Also Called: Excel Temporary Services
10901 W 84th Ter Ste 100 (66214-1631)
PHONE....913 253-7000
Nancy Kleeb, *President*
Marvin Kleeb, *Corp Secy*
EMP: 11
SQ FT: 3,500
SALES (est): 1.9MM **Privately Held**
SIC: 7363 Help supply services

(G-8923)
KLEINFELDER INC
11529 W 79th St (66214-1410)
PHONE....913 962-0909
Forrest Erickson, *Manager*
EMP: 20
SALES (corp-wide): 249.4MM **Privately Held**
SIC: 8711 Consulting engineer
HQ: Kleinfelder, Inc.
550 W C St Ste 1200
San Diego CA 92101
619 831-4600

(G-8924)
KNIGHTON BUS SOLUTIONS LLC
9120 Nieman Rd (66214-1801)
PHONE....913 747-2818
Nancy Fielder, *Opers Mgr*
Chad Duckers, *Accounts Exec*
Matt Peters, *Accounts Exec*
Pam Webster, *Sales Executive*
Robert Knighton, *Mng Member*
EMP: 30
SALES (est): 6MM **Privately Held**
SIC: 5044 Photocopy machines

(G-8925)
KNOX PRESBT CH CHILD DEV CTR
9595 W 95th St (66212-5063)
PHONE....913 888-0089
Lindsey Roeder, *Director*
EMP: 17
SALES (est): 638.1K **Privately Held**
WEB: www.knoxchurch.org
SIC: 8351 Preschool center

(G-8926)
KOPPERS RECOVERY RESOURCES LLC
Also Called: M.A. Energy Resources, LLC
9401 Indian Creek Pkwy (66210-2007)
PHONE....913 213-6127
Mike Sorcher,
EMP: 21
SALES (est): 4.8MM
SALES (corp-wide): 1.7B **Publicly Held**
SIC: 8741 Management services
HQ: Koppers Inc.
436 7th Ave
Pittsburgh PA 15219
412 227-2001

(G-8927)
KREAMER KINCAID TAYLOR
7450 W 130th St Ste 140 (66213-2665)
PHONE....913 782-2350
Frank Lipsman, *Mng Member*
James Hubbard, *Manager*
Franklin Taylor, *Manager*
Todd Arney,
Greg Kincaid,
EMP: 10
SQ FT: 2,000
SALES (est): 2.2MM **Privately Held**
WEB: www.nhrk.com
SIC: 8111 General practice attorney, lawyer

(G-8928)
KRUCIAL STAFFING LLC
7240 W 98th Ter (66212-2255)
PHONE....913 802-2560
Brian Cleary,
EMP: 15
SALES (est): 232.7K **Privately Held**
SIC: 7361 Employment agencies

(G-8929)
KRUGER TECHNOLOGIES INC (PA)
Also Called: K T I
8271 Melrose Dr (66214-1625)
PHONE....913 498-1114
O Gene Bicknell, *Ch of Bd*
Otto J Kruger Jr, *President*
Susan Evans, *Corp Secy*
EMP: 30
SQ FT: 16,750
SALES (est): 5.4MM **Privately Held**
WEB: www.ktionline.com
SIC: 8734 8711 Forensic laboratory; civil engineering

(G-8930)
KS CITY MARRIOTT OVERLAND PARK
10800 Metcalf Ave (66210-2320)
PHONE....913 338-8627
Regina Peruggi, *Principal*
EMP: 23
SALES (est): 1.2MM **Privately Held**
SIC: 7011 Hotel, franchised

(G-8931)
KS TRANSIT INC
3716 W 154th St (66224-3861)
PHONE....281 841-6078
Lance Kilgore, *President*
EMP: 15
SALES (est): 249.2K **Privately Held**
SIC: 4789 Transportation services

(G-8932)
KUHN AND WITTENBORN INC
Also Called: Kuhn & Wittenborn Advertising
9325 Linden Reserve Dr (66207-3419)
PHONE....816 471-7888
Richard Kuhn, *President*
Dale Whittenborn, *Chairman*
EMP: 25
SALES (est): 5.2MM **Privately Held**
WEB: www.kuhnwitt.com
SIC: 7311 Advertising agencies

(G-8933)
KWMG LLC
Also Called: Keen Wealth Advisors
6201 Cllege Pk Blvd 325 (66211)
PHONE....913 624-1841
Bill Keen, *CEO*
Matt Wilson, *Managing Dir*
Carol Dawson, *Executive Asst*
Heather Collins, *Associate*
Cassandra Miller, *Associate*
EMP: 10
SALES (est): 763.6K **Privately Held**
SIC: 6282 Investment advisory service

(G-8934)
L C EPOCH GROUP
Also Called: Cobalt Medplans
10740 Nall Ave Ste 100 (66211-1223)
PHONE....855 753-7624
Chris Huber, *Interim Pres*
Jeff L Rudell, *CFO*
EMP: 160 **EST:** 1978
SALES (est): 22.1MM **Privately Held**
WEB: www.epochgrp.com
SIC: 8741 Management services

(G-8935)
L J GLIEM & ASSOCIATES LLC
Also Called: Gliem & Giddings
9120 W 135th St Ste 203 (66221-2006)
PHONE....913 557-9402
EMP: 20
SQ FT: 5,880
SALES (est): 3.7MM **Privately Held**
SIC: 6411 Insurance Agency

(G-8936)
LA PETITE ACADEMY INC
8621 W 96th St (66212-3316)
PHONE....913 649-5773
Lainie Dauster, *Director*
Dana Tatum, *Director*
EMP: 12
SALES (corp-wide): 164MM **Privately Held**
WEB: www.lapetite.com
SIC: 8351 Preschool center
HQ: La Petite Academy, Inc.
21333 Haggerty Rd Ste 300
Novi MI 48375
877 861-5078

(G-8937)
LA PETITE ACADEMY INC
11114 Antioch Rd (66210-2420)
PHONE....913 469-1006
Sandy Ballard, *Director*
EMP: 15
SALES (corp-wide): 164MM **Privately Held**
WEB: www.lapetite.com
SIC: 8351 Preschool center
HQ: La Petite Academy, Inc.
21333 Haggerty Rd Ste 300
Novi MI 48375
877 861-5078

(G-8938)
LABORATORY CORPORATION AMERICA
7800 W 110th St (66210-2304)
PHONE....913 338-4070
Kimberly Williams, *Owner*
EMP: 400 **Publicly Held**
SIC: 8071 Pathological laboratory
HQ: Laboratory Corporation Of America
358 S Main St Ste 458
Burlington NC 27215
336 229-1127

(G-8939)
LAKEWOOD MIDDLE SCHOOL PTO
6601 Edgewater Dr (66223-2465)
PHONE....913 239-5800
Scott Currier, *Principal*
Kim White, *Teacher*
EMP: 83
SALES: 42.8K **Privately Held**
SIC: 8641 Parent-teachers' association

(G-8940)
LAMAR ADVERTISING COMPANY
9088 Bond St (66214-1723)
PHONE....913 438-4048
Fax: 913 438-7636
EMP: 17
SALES (corp-wide): 1.1B **Publicly Held**
SIC: 7312 Outdoor Advertising Services
PA: Lamar Advertising Company
5321 Corporate Blvd
Baton Rouge LA 70808
225 926-1000

(G-8941)
LAMAR COURT
11909 Lamar Ave (66209-2706)
PHONE....913 906-9696

Amiee Seck, *Administration*
Miles Nease, *Administration*
EMP: 100
SALES (est): 6.9MM
SALES (corp-wide): 4.5B **Publicly Held**
WEB: www.lamarcourtalf.com
SIC: 8741 Nursing & personal care facility management
HQ: Brookdale Living Communities, Inc.
515 N State St Ste 1750
Chicago IL 60654

(G-8942)
LANDMARK NATIONAL BANK
8101 W 135th St (66223-1111)
PHONE..................................913 239-2719
Alan Farris, *President*
EMP: 11
SALES (corp-wide): 48.7MM **Publicly Held**
SIC: 6021 National commercial banks
HQ: Landmark National Bank
701 Poyntz Ave
Manhattan KS 66502
620 225-1745

(G-8943)
LANSING ETHANOL SERVICES LLC
10975 Benson Dr Ste 400 (66210-2137)
PHONE..................................913 748-3000
Bill Krueger, *President*
Gary Smith, *Chairman*
Tom Carew, *Exec VP*
Mike Lemke, *Exec VP*
Scott Mills, *Exec VP*
EMP: 20
SALES (est): 7.7MM
SALES (corp-wide): 3B **Publicly Held**
WEB: www.lansingethanolservices.com
SIC: 6221 Commodity contracts brokers, dealers
HQ: Lansing Trade Group, Llc
10975 Benson Dr Ste 400
Overland Park KS 66210
913 748-3000

(G-8944)
LANSING GRAIN COMPANY LLC
10975 Benson Dr Ste 400 (66210-2137)
PHONE..................................913 748-4320
Bruce E Dawson,
EMP: 11
SALES (est): 5.5MM **Privately Held**
SIC: 5153 Grains

(G-8945)
LANSING TRADE GROUP LLC (HQ)
10975 Benson Dr Ste 400 (66210-2137)
P.O. Box 27267 (66225-7267)
PHONE..................................913 748-3000
William E Krueger, *CEO*
Shannon Himango, *Exec VP*
Scott Mills, *Exec VP*
Weston Heide, *Vice Pres*
Eric Watts, *Vice Pres*
◆ **EMP:** 150
SQ FT: 22,000
SALES (est): 915.5MM
SALES (corp-wide): 3B **Publicly Held**
WEB: www.lansingtradegroup.com
SIC: 5153 2085 2869 Wheat; distillers' dried grains & solubles & alcohol; ethyl alcohol, ethanol
PA: The Andersons Inc
1947 Briarfield Blvd
Maumee OH 43537
419 893-5050

(G-8946)
LAQUINTA INN AND SUITES
10610 Marty St (66212-2595)
PHONE..................................913 648-5555
Joe Gates, *Manager*
EMP: 17
SALES (est): 903.3K **Privately Held**
SIC: 7011 Hotels & motels

(G-8947)
LAURIE D FISHER MD
5701 W 119th St Ste 410 (66209-3721)
PHONE..................................913 345-3650
Laurie Fisher, *Principal*
EMP: 30 **EST:** 2008
SALES (est): 249.6K **Privately Held**
SIC: 8011 General & family practice, physician/surgeon

(G-8948)
LAWING FINANCIAL GROUP INC (PA)
6201 College Blvd Fl 7 (66211-2427)
PHONE..................................913 491-6226
Kerry L Lawing, *President*
EMP: 60
SALES (est): 10.4MM **Privately Held**
SIC: 8742 6282 Real estate consultant; financial consultant; investment advice

(G-8949)
LE JOHN MINH DDS
Also Called: Friendly Dentistry
10616 W 87th St (66214-1651)
PHONE..................................913 888-9399
John Minh Le DDS, *Owner*
Thanh Ngyen, *Manager*
EMP: 10 **EST:** 1999
SALES (est): 665.5K **Privately Held**
SIC: 8021 Dentists' office

(G-8950)
LEADER ONE FINANCIAL CORP (PA)
7500 College Blvd # 1150 (66210-4022)
PHONE..................................913 747-4000
A W Pickel, *President*
Scott Evans, *Vice Pres*
EMP: 20
SALES (est): 6.4MM **Privately Held**
SIC: 6162 Mortgage brokers, using own money

(G-8951)
LEAVENWRTH-KNSAS CY IMAGING PA
10800 Farley St Ste 265 (66210-1693)
PHONE..................................913 651-6066
Caprice Olomon MD, *President*
Robert Thompson, *Top Exec*
John Bramble MD, *Vice Pres*
Jeffrey Borders MD, *Admin Sec*
EMP: 24
SQ FT: 1,200
SALES (est): 2.7MM **Privately Held**
SIC: 8011 Radiologist

(G-8952)
LEISURE OPERATIONS LLC
Also Called: Serenty Rehab Nrsng Ovrlnd Prk
5211 W 103rd St (66207-3154)
PHONE..................................718 327-5762
Mordechai Hellman,
Howard Neuman,
EMP: 85 **EST:** 2017
SALES (est): 300.8K **Privately Held**
SIC: 8051 Skilled nursing care facilities

(G-8953)
LEISURETERRACE LLC
5211 W 103rd St (66207-3154)
PHONE..................................773 945-1000
Kevin Chankin, *CFO*
Scott Weisberg, *Controller*
EMP: 99
SQ FT: 106,001
SALES: 10.5MM **Privately Held**
SIC: 8051 Mental retardation hospital

(G-8954)
LEWER AGENCY INC
9900 W 109th St Ste 200 (66210-1409)
PHONE..................................816 753-4390
Mike Lewer, *President*
Mike Dlugolecki, *Senior VP*
Joe Vitti, *Vice Pres*
Eric Edwards, *Marketing Staff*
Robert V Stompoly, *General Counsel*
EMP: 100
SALES (est): 29.1MM **Privately Held**
SIC: 6411 Insurance brokers

(G-8955)
LEWIS & ELLIS INC
11225 College Blvd # 320 (66210-2770)
PHONE..................................913 491-3388
Gary Rose, *President*
Michael Brown, *Vice Pres*
Cabe Chadick, *Vice Pres*
EMP: 27
SALES (est): 1.4MM
SALES (corp-wide): 20MM **Privately Held**
WEB: www.lewisellis.com
SIC: 8999 6411 Actuarial consultant; insurance information & consulting services
PA: Lewis & Ellis, Inc.
700 Central Expy S # 550
Allen TX 75013
972 850-0850

(G-8956)
LIBERTY TERRACE CARE CENTER
10540 Barkley St Ste 280 (66212-1823)
PHONE..................................816 792-2211
Terence Reardon, *President*
M Sue Reardon, *Corp Secy*
Suzie Briscoe, *Director*
EMP: 126
SQ FT: 49,500
SALES (est): 4.2MM **Privately Held**
SIC: 8051 Skilled nursing care facilities

(G-8957)
LIFE CARE CENTERS AMERICA INC
7541 Switzer St (66214-1170)
PHONE..................................423 472-9585
Michelle Camp, *Office Mgr*
Debbie Biehl, *Branch Mgr*
EMP: 10
SALES (corp-wide): 144MM **Privately Held**
SIC: 8051 Skilled nursing care facilities
PA: Life Care Centers Of America, Inc.
3570 Keith St Nw
Cleveland TN 37312
423 472-9585

(G-8958)
LIFE TIME FITNESS INC
6800 W 138th St (66223-4851)
PHONE..................................913 239-9000
Jeremy Ludovissie, *Principal*
EMP: 132
SALES (corp-wide): 773.5MM **Privately Held**
SIC: 7991 Health club
HQ: Life Time, Inc.
2902 Corporate Pl
Chanhassen MN 55317

(G-8959)
LIGHTWILD INC
7320 W 162nd St (66085-9140)
PHONE..................................913 851-3000
Jeannine Sargent, *CEO*
Tom Stafford, *General Mgr*
Chris Stratus, *Vice Pres*
Fergus McKay, *CFO*
Jennifer Nekuda, *Sales Engr*
EMP: 45
SQ FT: 12,000
SALES (est): 5MM **Privately Held**
SIC: 3646 Commercial indusl & institutional electric lighting fixtures

(G-8960)
LION NATHAN USA INC
Also Called: Argyle Winery
8717 W 110th St Ste 430 (66210-2150)
PHONE..................................913 338-4433
Steve Myers, *President*
EMP: 38
SALES (corp-wide): 4.2MM **Privately Held**
SIC: 5182 Wine
PA: Lion Nathan Usa, Inc.
691 N Highway 99w
Dundee OR 97115
503 538-8520

(G-8961)
LIONSGATE PET HOSPITAL
14327 Metcalf Ave (66223-2988)
PHONE..................................913 402-8300
Ann McHugh, *Owner*
EMP: 11
SALES (est): 425.2K **Privately Held**
SIC: 0742 Animal hospital services, pets & other animal specialties

(G-8962)
LITIGATION INSIGHTS INC (PA)
9393 W 110th St Ste 400 (66210-1419)
PHONE..................................913 339-9885
Merrie Jo Pitera, *CEO*
Robert Featherly, *President*
Adam Bloomberg, *Corp Secy*
Adam Wirtzfeld, *Corp Comm Staff*
Carey Hand, *Manager*
EMP: 24
SQ FT: 4,000
SALES (est): 3.9MM **Privately Held**
SIC: 8748 Business consulting

(G-8963)
LIVESTOCK NUTRITION CENTER LLC
11225 College Blvd # 220 (66210-2748)
PHONE..................................913 725-0300
EMP: 13
SALES (corp-wide): 250MM **Privately Held**
SIC: 5154 Livestock
PA: Livestock Nutrition Center, Llc
6263 Poplar Ave Ste 1100
Memphis TN 38119
901 763-7055

(G-8964)
LIZ GONZALEZ EXAMINETICS INC
8900 Indian Creek Pkwy # 500 (66210-1554)
PHONE..................................913 748-2042
Liz Gonzalez, *Principal*
Jordan Bunce, *Accounts Exec*
EMP: 22
SALES (est): 842.3K **Privately Held**
SIC: 8059 Personal care home, with health care

(G-8965)
LLP MOSS ADAMS
7285 W 132nd St Ste 220 (66213-1164)
PHONE..................................913 599-3236
Jarret REA, *Partner*
EMP: 15
SALES (corp-wide): 340.5MM **Privately Held**
SIC: 8721 Certified public accountant
PA: Moss Adams Llp
999 3rd Ave Ste 2800
Seattle WA 98104
206 302-6800

(G-8966)
LOCKPATH INC
6240 Sprint Pkwy Ste 100 (66211-1193)
PHONE..................................913 601-4800
Chris Caldwell, *CEO*
Tony Rock, *COO*
Brian Dillbeck, *CFO*
Dennis Keglovits, *Ch Credit Ofcr*
Chris Geisert, *Chief Mktg Ofcr*
EMP: 80
SQ FT: 15,000
SALES (est): 13.9MM
SALES (corp-wide): 189MM **Privately Held**
SIC: 7371 7372 Computer software development; business oriented computer software
PA: Navex Global, Inc.
5500 Meadows Rd Ste 500
Lake Oswego OR 97035
971 250-4100

(G-8967)
LOCKS & PULLS INC
10333 Metcalf Ave (66212-1805)
PHONE..................................913 381-1335
Tom O'Malley, *President*
Thomas Orrick, *Opers Staff*
Brittney Lawrence, *Buyer*
EMP: 16
SQ FT: 6,200
SALES (est): 2.1MM **Privately Held**
SIC: 5251 5072 Builders' hardware; builders' hardware

(G-8968)
LOCKTON AFFINITY LLC
Also Called: Nationwide
10895 Lowell Ave Ste 300 (66210-1679)
PHONE..................................913 652-7500

Steven Eginoire, *CEO*
Rob Blankers, *President*
Joseph Ziegler, *COO*
Marianne K Sears, *Exec VP*
Jeff Hewitt, *Senior VP*
EMP: 180
SALES (est): 61.1MM
SALES (corp-wide): 1.8B **Privately Held**
WEB: www.lockton.com
SIC: 6411 Insurance brokers
PA: Lockton, Inc.
444 W 47th St Ste 900
Kansas City MO 64112
816 960-9000

(G-8969)
LODGE OF OVERLAND PARK LLC
7575 W 106th St (66212-5920)
PHONE....913 648-8000
Erin Poblade,
Kelly Tagg,
EMP: 20
SALES (est): 1.6MM **Privately Held**
WEB: www.lodgeofoverlandpark.com
SIC: 6513 Apartment building operators

(G-8970)
LOUISBERG SQUARE APARTMENTS
9301 Santa Fe Ln (66212-3762)
PHONE....913 381-4997
Shelly Elliot, *Principal*
EMP: 10
SALES (est): 384.7K **Privately Held**
SIC: 6513 Apartment hotel operation

(G-8971)
LOYALTY PROPERTIES LLC
9393 W 110th St Ste 500 (66210-1464)
PHONE....913 323-6850
Quashena Wallace, *CEO*
Samantha Johnson, *President*
EMP: 12
SALES (est): 619.7K **Privately Held**
SIC: 6512 Nonresidential building operators

(G-8972)
LPI INFORMATION SYSTEMS
10020 Fontana Ln (66207-3640)
PHONE....913 381-9118
David A Land, *President*
Camille Land, *CFO*
Matthew Lewis, *Sales Staff*
EMP: 5
SALES (est): 502.3K **Privately Held**
WEB: www.datasmithpayroll.com
SIC: 7372 7371 Business oriented computer software; computer software systems analysis & design, custom

(G-8973)
LUCITY INC
10561 Barkley St Ste 100 (66212-1836)
PHONE....800 492-2468
Donald E Pinkston, *President*
James C Graham, *COO*
Rob Kraft, *Project Mgr*
Victoria Gibson, *QC Mgr*
Sarah Casey, *Controller*
EMP: 22 **EST:** 2000
SQ FT: 12,000
SALES (est): 3.2MM
SALES (corp-wide): 227.8MM **Privately Held**
WEB: www.gbamasterseries.com
SIC: 7371 Computer software systems analysis & design, custom
PA: Centralsquare Technologies, Llc
1000 Business Center Dr
Lake Mary FL 32746
800 727-8088

(G-8974)
LUDWIKOSKI & ASSOCIATES INC
1920 143rd St Ste 140 (66224-7813)
PHONE....913 879-2224
John H Ludwikoski, *President*
Chad Bisinger, *Vice Pres*
Frank Flack, *Sales Staff*
Michael Egan, *Representative*
Dave Wickert, *Representative*
EMP: 10
SALES (est): 1.6MM **Privately Held**
WEB: www.ludreps.com
SIC: 5091 Fishing equipment & supplies; hunting equipment & supplies

(G-8975)
LW HOLDING LC
Also Called: Flextronics Lighting Solution
7320 W 162nd St (66085-9140)
PHONE....913 851-3000
Tom Stafford, *President*
Wade Johnson, *Regl Sales Mgr*
▲ **EMP:** 40
SQ FT: 24,000
SALES (est): 6.7MM **Privately Held**
SIC: 3646 Commercial indusl & institutional electric lighting fixtures

(G-8976)
LYLE LAW LLC (PA)
7270 W 98th Ter Ste 100 (66212-6166)
PHONE....913 225-6463
Kristopher Lyle, *Administration*
EMP: 13
SALES (est): 1.7MM **Privately Held**
SIC: 8111 General practice law office

(G-8977)
LYNN CARE LLC
Also Called: Zack Group
6335 W 110th St (66211-1509)
PHONE....913 707-4639
EMP: 50
SALES (est): 1.7MM **Privately Held**
SIC: 7361 Employment Agencies, Nsk

(G-8978)
LYNN CARE LLC
Also Called: Zack Group
6600 College Blvd Ste 300 (66211-1869)
PHONE....913 491-3562
Tony Pontier, *Mng Member*
Blake Saffels, *Manager*
Ronald Zack,
EMP: 150
SALES (est): 2.9MM **Privately Held**
SIC: 7361 Employment agencies

(G-8979)
MAGNA INFOTECH LTD
9300 W 110th St Ste 650 (66210-1487)
PHONE....203 748-7680
Pradeep Mittal, *President*
Syed Ahmed, *Admin Mgr*
Niraj Mital, *Admin Sec*
EMP: 80
SQ FT: 2,800
SALES (est): 8MM **Privately Held**
WEB: www.magnai.com
SIC: 7379 Computer related consulting services

(G-8980)
MAJOR VIDEO OF KANSAS INC
Also Called: Blockbuster
6979 W 75th St (66204-3028)
PHONE....913 649-7137
Fax: 913 649-7714
EMP: 11
SALES (corp-wide): 15.4MM **Privately Held**
SIC: 7841 Video Disk/Tape Rent
PA: Major Video Of Kansas Inc
208 S Maize Rd
Wichita KS
316 722-5670

(G-8981)
MALONE FINKLE ECHARDT & CLNS
7780 W 119th St (66213-1104)
PHONE....913 322-1400
Mike Thome, *Vice Pres*
Chase Bretches, *Project Engr*
EMP: 20
SALES (est): 1.9MM
SALES (corp-wide): 5.4MM **Privately Held**
WEB: www.mfec.com
SIC: 8711 Electrical or electronic engineering
PA: Malone Finkle Eckhardt & Collins, Inc.
3333 E Battlefield St
Springfield MO 65804
417 881-0020

(G-8982)
MAMA SOCORROS
8879 Lenexa Dr (66214-3240)
PHONE....913 541-1074
Don Johnson, *CEO*
EMP: 5
SALES (est): 372.1K **Privately Held**
SIC: 2032 Mexican foods: packaged in cans, jars, etc.

(G-8983)
MANCHESTER INC
10573 Riley St (66212-2428)
PHONE....913 262-0440
Doug Steele, *Principal*
EMP: 18 **Publicly Held**
SIC: 7363 Help supply services
HQ: Manchester Inc
1 Independent Dr Ste 206
Jacksonville FL 32202
904 360-2200

(G-8984)
MANOR CARE OF KANSAS INC
Also Called: Manorcare Hlth Svcs Ovrland Pk
5211 W 103rd St (66207-3154)
PHONE....913 383-2569
Shani Jones, *Manager*
EMP: 200
SALES (corp-wide): 8.2B **Privately Held**
SIC: 8051 Convalescent home with continuous nursing care
HQ: Manor Care Of Kansas, Inc.
333 N Summit St Ste 100
Toledo OH 43604
419 252-5500

(G-8985)
MAPLE HILLS HEALTHCARE INC
7600 Antioch Rd (66204-2622)
PHONE....913 383-2001
Soon Burnam, *Treasurer*
EMP: 20 **EST:** 2015
SALES: 8.7MM
SALES (corp-wide): 2B **Publicly Held**
SIC: 8099 Health & allied services
PA: The Ensign Group Inc
29222 Rncho Vejo Rd Ste 1
San Juan Capistrano CA 92675
949 487-9500

(G-8986)
MARC A ASHER MD COMPREHENSI
Also Called: Indian Creek
10730 Nall Ave Ste 200 (66211-1285)
PHONE....913 945-9800
Bob Page, *CEO*
EMP: 50
SALES (est): 26.8K **Privately Held**
SIC: 8099 Health screening service

(G-8987)
MARCH INC
101 S Kansas Ave (66223)
PHONE....913 449-7640
Gretchen Hembree, *Vice Pres*
EMP: 20
SALES (est): 1.5MM **Privately Held**
SIC: 6512 Nonresidential building operators

(G-8988)
MARCH OF DIMES INC
Also Called: Greater Kansas Chapter
4400 College Blvd Ste 180 (66211-2326)
P.O. Box 673667, Marietta GA (30006-0062)
PHONE....913 469-3611
Ken Jackson, *Manager*
EMP: 12
SALES (corp-wide): 111MM **Privately Held**
SIC: 8399 Fund raising organization, non-fee basis
PA: March Of Dimes Inc.
1550 Crystal Dr Ste 1300
Arlington VA 22202
571 257-2324

(G-8989)
MARCUS MLLCHAP RE INV SVCS INC
7400 College Blvd Ste 105 (66210-4028)
PHONE....816 410-1010
Marcus Millichap, *Branch Mgr*
EMP: 20
SALES (corp-wide): 814.8MM **Publicly Held**
SIC: 6531 Real estate agent, commercial
HQ: Marcus & Millichap Real Estate Investment Services, Inc.
23975 Park Sorrento # 400
Calabasas CA 91302

(G-8990)
MARILLAC CENTER INC (PA)
8000 W 127th St (66213-2714)
PHONE....816 508-3300
Mark S Richards, *President*
Brian D Barash, *Director*
EMP: 38
SQ FT: 74,000
SALES: 12.7MM **Privately Held**
WEB: www.marillac.org
SIC: 8011 Psychiatrists & psychoanalysts

(G-8991)
MARINER WEALTH ADVISORS LLC (PA)
5700 W 112th St Ste 500 (66211-1746)
PHONE....913 904-5700
Martin C Bicknell, *CEO*
Scott Voss, *Managing Prtnr*
Timothy M Connealy, *COO*
Bethanie Glawson, *Counsel*
Megan Jennings, *Counsel*
EMP: 30
SALES: 1.7MM **Privately Held**
SIC: 6719 Investment holding companies, except banks

(G-8992)
MARKETSPHERE CONSULTING LLC
Also Called: Marketsphere Unclmed Prprty Sp
9393 W 110th St Ste 430 (66210-1406)
PHONE....913 608-3648
Steve Sestak, *Mng Member*
Alvin Roberts, *Manager*
EMP: 80
SALES (est): 4.8MM
SALES (corp-wide): 18.1MM **Privately Held**
SIC: 8748 Business consulting
PA: Marketsphere Consulting, L.L.C.
14301 Fnb Pkwy Ste 201
Omaha NE 68154
402 392-4000

(G-8993)
MARLEY COOLING TOWER CO INC
P.O. Box 25948 (66225-5948)
PHONE....913 664-7400
Roland Wright, *Principal*
EMP: 8
SALES (est): 951.8K **Privately Held**
SIC: 3443 Fabricated plate work (boiler shop)

(G-8994)
MASSACHUSETTS MUTL LF INSUR CO
Also Called: Massmutual
10975 Benson Dr Ste 350 (66210-2130)
PHONE....913 234-0300
K W Carpenter, *Principal*
Salvotor Labely, *Manager*
Kimberly Cole, *Director*
Stan Omarra, *Officer*
John L Brown, *Analyst*
EMP: 50
SALES (corp-wide): 254.5B **Privately Held**
WEB: www.massmutual.com
SIC: 6311 Life insurance
PA: Massachusetts Mutual Life Insurance Company
1295 State St
Springfield MA 01111
413 788-8411

(G-8995)
MAVICOR LLC
4425 Indian Creek Pkwy (66207-4013)
PHONE..................................888 387-1620
Jesse Mayhew, *Principal*
Michael Meyers, *Chief*
Jill Henry, *Finance Mgr*
EMP: 24 **EST:** 2008
SALES (est): 3.9MM **Privately Held**
SIC: 4813 ;

(G-8996)
MAX SHARE FUND INC
4400 College Blvd Ste 250 (66211-2339)
PHONE..................................913 338-1100
Karen Morrone, *Marketing Staff*
EMP: 20
SALES: 55.5K **Privately Held**
SIC: 6411 Insurance agents, brokers & service

(G-8997)
MAXIM HEALTHCARE SERVICES INC
10881 Lowell Ave Ste 100 (66210-1666)
PHONE..................................913 381-8233
Brian Wynne, *Branch Mgr*
EMP: 150
SALES (corp-wide): 1.5B **Privately Held**
WEB: www.maximstaffing.com
SIC: 8082 Home health care services
PA: Maxim Healthcare Services, Inc.
7227 Lee Deforest Dr
Columbia MD 21046
410 910-1500

(G-8998)
MAXIM HEALTHCARE SERVICES INC
Also Called: Kansas City Staffing
10881 Lowell Ave Ste 100 (66210-1666)
PHONE..................................913 383-2220
EMP: 15
SALES (corp-wide): 1.2B **Privately Held**
SIC: 7363 Help Supply Services
PA: Maxim Healthcare Services, Inc.
7227 Lee Deforest Dr
Columbia MD 21046
410 910-1500

(G-8999)
MAZUMA CREDIT UNION (PA)
7260 W 135th St (66223-1258)
PHONE..................................913 574-5000
Russ Petry, *CFO*
Craig Caskey, *Loan Officer*
Jay Broz, *Manager*
Carson Ford, *IT/INT Sup*
Mike Schreck, *Risk Mgmt Dir*
EMP: 111 **EST:** 1948
SQ FT: 38,500
SALES: 29.2MM **Privately Held**
SIC: 6061 Federal credit unions

(G-9000)
MCCARTHY BLDG COMPANIES INC
Also Called: Kansas City Office
7930 Santa Fe Dr Ste 200 (66204-3670)
PHONE..................................913 202-7002
Jason Pavia, *Asst Supt*
Joseph Bedros, *Project Engr*
Greg Lee, *Project Engr*
Richard McCarthy, *Branch Mgr*
EMP: 29
SALES (corp-wide): 3.9B **Privately Held**
SIC: 1542 Institutional building construction
HQ: Mccarthy Building Companies, Inc.
1341 N Rock Hill Rd
Saint Louis MO 63124
314 968-3300

(G-9001)
MCDONALDS PLAZA LLC
6310 Lamar Ave Ste 220 (66202-4265)
PHONE..................................913 362-1999
EMP: 43
SALES (est): 1MM **Privately Held**
SIC: 7389 Personal service agents, brokers & bureaus

(G-9002)
MCICV COURTYARD BY MARRIOTT
11001 Woodson Ave (66211-1656)
PHONE..................................913 317-8500
Marcy Drake, *General Mgr*
Shannon Waters, *Director*
EMP: 15
SALES (est): 879K **Privately Held**
SIC: 7011 Hotels & motels

(G-9003)
MCMC LLC
9300 W 110th St Ste 520 (66210-1421)
PHONE..................................913 341-8811
Crista Lane, *Vice Pres*
EMP: 39 **Privately Held**
SIC: 8742 Hospital & health services consultant
PA: Mcmc Llc
300 Crown Colony Dr # 203
Quincy MA 02169

(G-9004)
MCQUEENY GROUP INC
8820 Bond St (66214-1706)
PHONE..................................913 396-4700
Quentin McArthur, *President*
Rod Slump, *Vice Pres*
Chris Lunvquist, *CFO*
EMP: 14
SQ FT: 6,000
SALES (est): 7.8MM **Privately Held**
WEB: www.mcqueenygroup.com
SIC: 5075 Air conditioning & ventilation equipment & supplies

(G-9005)
MED JAMES INC (PA)
8595 College Blvd Ste 200 (66210-2617)
P.O. Box 2014, Shawnee Mission (66201-1014)
PHONE..................................913 663-5500
Med James, *President*
Ellen Black, *Superintendent*
Bill Murray, *Vice Pres*
Dave Schuhler, *Vice Pres*
Dave Karpowich, *Controller*
EMP: 100 **EST:** 1976
SQ FT: 20,000
SALES (est): 65.2MM **Privately Held**
WEB: www.medjames.com
SIC: 6411 Insurance agents

(G-9006)
MEDIACORP LLC
Also Called: Mediacorp Marketing & Dist
8712 W 151st St (66221-8705)
PHONE..................................913 317-8900
Mark Mansheim, *Mng Member*
Earl Pardo,
Ed Waldberg,
▲ **EMP:** 20
SALES (est): 3.6MM **Privately Held**
SIC: 5199 5961 General merchandise, non-durable; general merchandise, mail order

(G-9007)
MEDICAL PLAZA CONSULTANTS P C
10787 Nall Ave Ste 310 (66211-1301)
PHONE..................................913 945-6900
David Hof MD, *President*
Joseph Allan MD, *Vice Pres*
Paul Diederich MD, *Treasurer*
Bruce Salvaggio MD, *Admin Sec*
Elbie Loeb MD, *Asst Sec*
EMP: 31
SQ FT: 2,500
SALES (est): 2.7MM **Privately Held**
SIC: 8011 Internal medicine, physician/surgeon

(G-9008)
MEDTRAK SERVICES LLC
7101 College Blvd # 1000 (66210-2075)
PHONE..................................913 262-2187
C Larkin O'Keefe, *CEO*
Mark Fendler, *COO*
Marc Albers, *Vice Pres*
Tom Golding, *Vice Pres*
Matt Jennings, *Vice Pres*
EMP: 90
SALES (est): 8.4MM
SALES (corp-wide): 40.1MM **Privately Held**
WEB: www.medtrakservices.com
SIC: 8741 Administrative management
PA: Envision Pharmaceutical Holdings Llc
2181 E Aurora Rd Ste 201
Twinsburg OH 44087
800 361-4542

(G-9009)
MEMORY AND MUSIC INC
11936 W 119th St (66213-2216)
PHONE..................................913 449-4473
Charles Andrew Ross, *President*
EMP: 10 **EST:** 2017
SALES (est): 283.1K **Privately Held**
SIC: 3999 Manufacturing industries

(G-9010)
MERCER-ZIMMERMAN INC (PA)
8981 Bond St (66214-1745)
PHONE..................................913 438-4546
Shon Yust, *President*
Kate Wimer, *VP Sales*
Kim Crum, *Sales Staff*
EMP: 15
SALES (est): 5.1MM **Privately Held**
WEB: www.mzltg.com
SIC: 5063 Lighting fixtures, commercial & industrial; lighting fixtures

(G-9011)
MERIDIAN CHEMICALS LLC (HQ)
10955 Lowell Ave Ste 600 (66210-2363)
PHONE..................................913 253-2220
Mark Demetree, *CEO*
Frank Brady, *President*
Tim Dolan, *CFO*
EMP: 7
SALES (est): 5.8MM
SALES (corp-wide): 9.3MM **Privately Held**
SIC: 5169 2819 2899 4953 Acids; sulfuric acid, oleum; water treating compounds; acid waste, collection & disposal
PA: Demetree Meridian, Llc
10955 Lowell Ave Ste 600
Overland Park KS 66210
913 253-2220

(G-9012)
MERRY MAIDS LTD PARTNERSHIP
7959 Frontage Rd (66204-2352)
PHONE..................................913 403-0813
Rotimi Williams, *Branch Mgr*
EMP: 20
SALES (corp-wide): 1.9B **Publicly Held**
WEB: www.merrymaids.com
SIC: 7349 Maid services, contract or fee basis
HQ: Merry Maids Limited Partnership
150 Peabody Pl Ste 100
Memphis TN 38103
901 597-8100

(G-9013)
MERRY X-RAY CHEMICAL CORP
11621 W 83rd Ter (66214-1538)
PHONE..................................858 565-4472
Tod Danner, *Manager*
EMP: 25
SALES (corp-wide): 98.8MM **Privately Held**
SIC: 7699 5047 Medical equipment repair, non-electric; X-ray equipment repair; X-ray machines & tubes
PA: Merry X-Ray Chemical Corporation
4909 Murphy Canyon Rd # 120
San Diego CA 92123
858 565-4472

(G-9014)
METCALF 107 ANIMAL CLINIC INC
6881 W 107th St (66212-1825)
PHONE..................................913 642-1077
Marc Hardin, *President*
EMP: 10
SQ FT: 2,664
SALES (est): 575.7K **Privately Held**
SIC: 0742 Animal hospital services, pets & other animal specialties

(G-9015)
METROPOLITAN COURT REPORTERS
1880 College Blvd Ste 405 (66210)
PHONE..................................913 317-8800
Carol Dorothy, *President*
Janene Thibault, *Managing Prtnr*
Kim Kramer, *Marketing Staff*
Jeremy Martin, *Department Mgr*
Linda Edgington, *Clerk*
EMP: 31
SALES: 1.6MM **Privately Held**
SIC: 7338 Court reporting service

(G-9016)
METROPOLITAN LIFE INSUR CO
Also Called: MetLife
10801 Mastin St Ste 550 (66210-1670)
PHONE..................................913 234-4800
Anthony Corporon, *Counsel*
Robin Slapper, *Accounts Exec*
Chris Jaco, *Underwriter*
Greg Seaboldt, *Underwriter*
Jahn Harris, *Manager*
EMP: 30
SALES (corp-wide): 67.9B **Publicly Held**
SIC: 6411 Insurance agents & brokers
HQ: Metropolitan Life Insurance Company (Inc)
1095 Ave Of The Americas
New York NY 10036
908 253-1000

(G-9017)
METROPOLITAN MORTGAGE CORP
7381 W 133rd St Ste 200 (66213-4771)
PHONE..................................913 642-8300
Rick Woodruff, *President*
Lisa Woodruff, *Treasurer*
EMP: 13
SALES: 700K **Privately Held**
WEB: www.e-metropolitan.com
SIC: 6162 Mortgage bankers & correspondents

(G-9018)
METROPOLITAN SPINE REHAB PA
10777 Nall Ave (66211-1362)
PHONE..................................913 387-2800
Joseph F Galate MD, *Principal*
Amy Stehli, *Administration*
Chandra Walters, *Administration*
EMP: 16 **EST:** 2007
SALES (est): 1MM **Privately Held**
SIC: 8011 Orthopedic physician

(G-9019)
MHS HOME HEALTH LLC
8600 W 110th St Ste 210 (66210-1805)
PHONE..................................913 663-9930
Sia Shadfar, *Principal*
Michelle Shadfar, *Administration*
EMP: 20 **EST:** 2013
SALES (est): 115.6K **Privately Held**
SIC: 8082 Home health care services

(G-9020)
MICROSOFT CORPORATION
10801 Mastin St Ste 620 (66210-1658)
PHONE..................................913 323-1200
Kent Nicholls, *Partner*
Becky Longfellow, *Accounts Mgr*
Michael Levin, *Manager*
Jim Ryan, *Technical Staff*
Carrie Viser, *Technical Staff*
EMP: 566
SALES (corp-wide): 125.8B **Publicly Held**
SIC: 7372 Application computer software
PA: Microsoft Corporation
1 Microsoft Way
Redmond WA 98052
425 882-8080

(G-9021)
MID AMERICA CRDIOLGY ASSOC PC
10787 Nall Ave Ste 300 (66211-1372)
PHONE..................................913 588-9400
Carol Skidgel, *Office Mgr*
James J Harbrecht, *Med Doctor*
EMP: 30

GEOGRAPHIC

SALES (corp-wide): 13.5MM **Privately Held**
WEB: www.mac.md
SIC: 8011 Offices & clinics of medical doctors
PA: Mid America Cardiology Associates Pc Inc
3901 Rainbow Blvd G600
Kansas City KS 66160
913 588-9600

(G-9022)
MID AMERICA PATHOLOGY LAB LLC
7301 College Blvd Ste 110 (66210-1856)
PHONE..................................913 341-6275
Margie Valemti, *Principal*
Russell L Benson, *Med Doctor*
EMP: 22
SALES (est): 2MM **Privately Held**
SIC: 8071 Testing laboratories

(G-9023)
MID AMERICA POLYCLINIC PA
7100 College Blvd (66210-1862)
PHONE..................................913 599-2440
Steven Simon, *President*
EMP: 20
SALES (est): 2MM **Privately Held**
SIC: 8011 Offices & clinics of medical doctors

(G-9024)
MID-AMERICA FITTINGS LLC
Also Called: Mas Manufacturing
7604 Wedd St (66204-2227)
PHONE..................................913 962-7277
Scott Shane, *CEO*
Phil Crawley, *President*
Beverly Shane, *Corp Secy*
Richard B Cheney, *Vice Pres*
▲ **EMP:** 30
SQ FT: 75,000
SALES (est): 7.9MM **Privately Held**
WEB: www.midamericafittings.com
SIC: 3494 5074 3432 Valves & pipe fittings; plumbing fittings & supplies; plumbing fixture fittings & trim

(G-9025)
MID-AMERICA MFG TECH CTR INC
Also Called: KANSAS MANUFACTURING SOLUTIONS
10550 Barkley St Ste 116 (66212-1824)
PHONE..................................913 649-4333
Mark Chalfant, *CEO*
Scott Wedel, *COO*
Danica Rome, *VP Opers*
Jesse West, *Project Mgr*
Steve Cowan, *CFO*
EMP: 10
SQ FT: 3,000
SALES: 2.4MM **Privately Held**
WEB: www.mamtc.com
SIC: 8711 Consulting engineer

(G-9026)
MID-AMERICA SURGERY INSTITUTE
5525 W 119th St Ste 100 (66209-3723)
PHONE..................................913 906-0855
Jeff Taylor, *Administration*
EMP: 25
SALES (est): 2.2MM **Publicly Held**
SIC: 8011 Ambulatory surgical center
HQ: Midamerica Division, Inc.
903 E 104th St Ste 500
Kansas City MO 64131
816 508-4000

(G-9027)
MID-AMRICA RHUMATOLOGY CONS PA (PA)
5701 W 119th St Ste 209 (66209-3749)
PHONE..................................913 661-9980
Perri A Ginder, *President*
Carrie A Mihordin, *Vice Pres*
Kathryn E Welch, *Treasurer*
Matthew J Svoboda, *Physician Asst*
EMP: 30
SALES (est): 4.3MM **Privately Held**
SIC: 8011 General & family practice, physician/surgeon

(G-9028)
MID-STATES MILLWORK INC
9111 Cody St (66214-1733)
PHONE..................................913 492-6300
Anthony V Kostusik Jr, *President*
Jean M Brower, *Vice Pres*
EMP: 12
SQ FT: 42,000
SALES (est): 5MM **Privately Held**
WEB: www.heartland-windows.com
SIC: 5031 Windows; millwork

(G-9029)
MIDAMERICAN SALES GROUP
2645 W 139th Ter (66224-3925)
PHONE..................................913 689-8505
Rob Davis, *Principal*
EMP: 5
SALES (est): 317.1K **Privately Held**
SIC: 2097 Manufactured ice

(G-9030)
MIDWEST A TRAFFIC CTRL SVC INC
7300 W 129th St (66213-2631)
PHONE..................................913 782-7082
Shane Cordes, *President*
Greg Schoofs, *CFO*
EMP: 12
SQ FT: 9,100
SALES (est): 80.3MM **Privately Held**
WEB: www.atctower.com
SIC: 4581 Airport control tower operation, except government

(G-9031)
MIDWEST CONSULTING GROUP INC (PA)
11880 College Blvd # 400 (66210-1318)
PHONE..................................913 693-8200
David A Ward, *President*
Victor Isaacs, *Vice Pres*
Doug Martin, *Vice Pres*
Bruce Schrotberger, *Vice Pres*
Erin Clark, *Technical Staff*
EMP: 199
SQ FT: 8,700
SALES (est): 17.7MM **Privately Held**
WEB: www.mcginfo.com
SIC: 8748 7361 Systems analysis & engineering consulting services; employment agencies

(G-9032)
MIDWEST DAIRY ASSOCIATION
Also Called: Midwest Dairy Council
8645 College Blvd Ste 250 (66210-1801)
PHONE..................................913 345-2225
Stan Erwine, *Vice Pres*
Mary Thorsell, *Director*
EMP: 12
SALES (est): 650K **Privately Held**
SIC: 0241 Milk production

(G-9033)
MIDWEST MERCHANDISING INC
3701 W 95th St (66206-2036)
PHONE..................................913 428-8430
EMP: 104
SALES (corp-wide): 23.3MM **Privately Held**
SIC: 7699 5941 Professional instrument repair services; sporting goods & bicycle shops
PA: Midwest Merchandising Inc.
2690 E County Line Rd
Highlands Ranch CO 80126
303 221-4840

(G-9034)
MIDWEST OFFICE TECHNOLOGY
11316 W 80th St (66214-3307)
PHONE..................................913 894-9600
Dennis Fehn, *Manager*
Rick Hoffman, *Producer*
EMP: 20
SALES (corp-wide): 9MM **Privately Held**
SIC: 5044 7629 7359 5112 Office equipment; business machine repair, electric; office machine rental, except computers; office supplies
PA: Sta-Mot-Ks, Llc
11316 W 80th St
Overland Park KS 66214
913 894-9600

(G-9035)
MIDWEST PATHOLOGY ASSOC LLC
7301 College Blvd (66210-1937)
PHONE..................................913 341-6275
Russell Lee Benson, *Principal*
EMP: 14
SALES (est): 2.2MM **Privately Held**
SIC: 8011 Pathologist

(G-9036)
MIDWEST TINTING INC (PA)
7755 Shawnee Mission Pkwy (66202-3062)
PHONE..................................913 384-2665
Brian Arnett, *President*
Ron Talley, *General Mgr*
EMP: 12 **EST:** 1976
SALES (est): 1.6MM **Privately Held**
WEB: www.midwesttinting.com
SIC: 1799 7549 1731 Glass tinting, architectural or automotive; glass tinting, automotive; safety & security specialization

(G-9037)
MILLER & NEWBERG INC
8717 W 110th St Ste 530 (66210-2151)
PHONE..................................913 393-2522
John Miller, *President*
Trevor Huseman, *Managing Dir*
Eric Newberg, *Vice Pres*
Nancy Wunderlich, *QC Dir*
Kristen Carlson, *Corp Comm Staff*
EMP: 11
SALES (est): 543.8K **Privately Held**
WEB: www.miller-newberg.com
SIC: 8999 Actuarial consultant

(G-9038)
MILLETT INDUSTRIES (PA)
Also Called: Millett Sights
9200 Cody St (66214-1734)
PHONE..................................913 752-3572
▲ **EMP:** 9
SQ FT: 25,000
SALES (est): 3.3MM **Privately Held**
SIC: 3484 3444 Mfg Small Arms Mfg Sheet Metalwork

(G-9039)
MILLION PACKAGING INC
14508 Ballentine St (66221-8198)
PHONE..................................913 402-0055
Robert W Million, *President*
EMP: 23 **EST:** 2002
SQ FT: 2,000
SALES (est): 5.4MM **Privately Held**
SIC: 5112 2621 Stationery & office supplies; wrapping & packaging papers

(G-9040)
MINDS MATTER LLC
7819 Conser Pl (66204-2820)
PHONE..................................866 429-6757
Janet Williams, *President*
Erica Bates, *Director*
EMP: 10
SALES (est): 276K **Privately Held**
SIC: 8082 Home health care services

(G-9041)
MIQ LOGISTICS LLC (DH)
11501 Outlook St Ste 500 (66211-1808)
P.O. Box 7930 (66207-0930)
PHONE..................................913 696-7100
John E Carr, *President*
Thomas Gronen, *General Mgr*
Somchai Thaitaechawat, *General Mgr*
Marco Gaeta, *Managing Dir*
Shesh Kulkarni, *Managing Dir*
◆ **EMP:** 201
SQ FT: 51,000
SALES (est): 340.2MM **Privately Held**
WEB: www.miq.com
SIC: 4731 8741 Freight forwarding; management services

(G-9042)
MISSION MORTGAGE LLC
40 Corporate Woods 9401 (66210)
PHONE..................................913 469-1999
EMP: 13
SALES (est): 940K **Privately Held**
SIC: 6163 Loan Broker

(G-9043)
MISSOURI VLY TENNIS FOUNDATION
6400 W 95th St Ste 102 (66212-1432)
PHONE..................................913 322-4800
Mary Buschmann, *Director*
EMP: 17
SALES: 1.3K **Privately Held**
SIC: 7997 Tennis club, membership

(G-9044)
MITTELMANS FURNITURE CO INC
3704 W 141st St (66224-1122)
PHONE..................................913 897-5505
Philip A Koffman, *President*
Marie Koffman, *Vice Pres*
David Kuluva, *Vice Pres*
▲ **EMP:** 25 **EST:** 1956
SQ FT: 130,000
SALES (est): 5.8MM **Privately Held**
SIC: 5021 Household furniture

(G-9045)
MKEC ENGINEERING CONS INC
11827 W 112th St Ste 200 (66210-2718)
PHONE..................................913 317-9390
Ken Bengtson, *Branch Mgr*
EMP: 46
SALES (corp-wide): 26.1MM **Privately Held**
SIC: 8711 Professional engineer
PA: Mkec Engineering , Inc.
411 N Webb Rd
Wichita KS 67206
316 684-9600

(G-9046)
MMC CORP (PA)
10955 Lowell Ave Ste 350 (66210-2408)
PHONE..................................913 469-0101
Tim Chadwick, *President*
R Jason Evelyn, *COO*
Erica Jones, *Vice Pres*
David Lauck, *Vice Pres*
Craig Woodson, *Vice Pres*
EMP: 30
SALES (est): 440.7MM **Privately Held**
SIC: 1542 1711 Commercial & office building contractors; mechanical contractor

(G-9047)
MNVC FINANCIAL SERVICES LLC
7701 College Blvd (66210-1991)
PHONE..................................816 589-4336
Rob Metcalf, *Principal*
Larry Vohland, *COO*
John Stolte, *Manager*
EMP: 28
SALES (est): 2.2MM **Privately Held**
SIC: 7389 Financial services

(G-9048)
MOBILECARE 2U LLC
8500 W 110th St Ste 450 (66210-4029)
PHONE..................................913 362-1112
Tim Grasser, *CFO*
EMP: 20
SALES (est): 2.6MM **Privately Held**
WEB: www.hallmarkdentalcare.com
SIC: 8021 Dental surgeon

(G-9049)
MONARCH PLASTIC SURGERY
Also Called: Bene, Richard J
4801 W 135th St (66224-8901)
PHONE..................................913 663-3838
Daniel P Bortnick, *Managing Prtnr*
Richard Bene, *Partner*
Jeffrey Dillow, *Partner*
Regina Nauhan, *Partner*
Rich Bene, *Med Doctor*
EMP: 20
SALES (est): 3.9MM **Privately Held**
WEB: www.monarchps.com
SIC: 8011 8712 Plastic surgeon; architectural services

▲ = Import ▼=Export
◆ =Import/Export

(G-9050)
MOON ABSTRACT COMPANY
7300 W 110th St Ste 700 (66210-2332)
PHONE..................................620 342-1917
Barbara Moyer, *President*
Larry Putnam, *Corp Secy*
EMP: 10
SQ FT: 2,400
SALES (est): 542.2K **Privately Held**
SIC: **6541** Title & trust companies

(G-9051)
MOONSHOT INNOVATIONS LLC
7220 W 98th Ter Ste 150 (66212-2255)
PHONE..................................913 815-6611
Bill Marshall, *President*
John McCreight,
EMP: 20
SALES: 4MM **Privately Held**
SIC: **7371** Custom computer programming services

(G-9052)
MOORE ENTERPRISES INC
8000 W 110th St Ste 115 (66210-2315)
PHONE..................................913 451-5900
Pat Moore, *President*
EMP: 237
SQ FT: 1,500
SALES: 7.4MM **Privately Held**
SIC: **8082** 8049 Home health care services; nurses, registered & practical

(G-9053)
MORGAN HUNTER CORPORATION
7600 W 110th St Ste 100 (66210-2391)
PHONE..................................913 491-3434
Jerry Hellebusch, *President*
Carol Schmidt, *Division Mgr*
Tamara Miller, *Regional Mgr*
JD Huxman, *CFO*
Joseph Guckin, *Regl Sales Mgr*
EMP: 50
SQ FT: 20,000
SALES (est): 5.3MM **Privately Held**
WEB: www.morganhunter.com
SIC: **7361** Executive placement

(G-9054)
MORNINGSTAR COMMUNICATIONS CO
12307 Flint St (66213-2121)
PHONE..................................913 660-9630
Shanny Morgenstern, *COO*
Sheri Johnson, *Senior VP*
Hannah Babcock, *Accounts Exec*
EMP: 10 **EST**: 1997
SALES (est): 1.4MM **Privately Held**
WEB: www.morningstarcomm.com
SIC: **8743** 8742 Public relations & publicity; marketing consulting services

(G-9055)
MORNINGSTAR FAMILY DENTAL PA
7000 W 121st St Ste 200 (66209-2010)
PHONE..................................913 344-9990
James P Lucero, *Principal*
EMP: 15
SALES (est): 896.7K **Privately Held**
SIC: **8021** Dental clinic

(G-9056)
MOTIVTION THRUGH INCNTIVES INC
Also Called: MTI Events
10400 W 103rd St Ste 10 (66214-2664)
PHONE..................................913 438-2600
Melissa Deleon, *President*
Dennis Krupp, *CFO*
John Deleon, *VP Sales*
Melinda Jurczak, *Marketing Staff*
Dan Holk, *Director*
EMP: 34
SQ FT: 2,400
SALES: 5.5MM **Privately Held**
WEB: www.miinc.com
SIC: **8742** Marketing consulting services; incentive or award program consultant

(G-9057)
MOTOROLA SOLUTIONS INC
7500 College Blvd Ste 500 (66210-4043)
PHONE..................................913 317-3020
Cindie Noe, *Manager*
EMP: 30
SALES (corp-wide): 7.3B **Publicly Held**
WEB: www.motorola.com
SIC: **4813** Telephone communication, except radio
PA: Motorola Solutions, Inc.
500 W Monroe St Ste 4400
Chicago IL 60661
847 576-5000

(G-9058)
MOVING KINGS LLC
9393 W 110th St (66210-1442)
PHONE..................................913 882-2121
Jesse King, *Principal*
EMP: 20
SALES (est): 73.5K **Privately Held**
SIC: **4212** Moving services

(G-9059)
MSAVER RESOURCES LLC
7400 W 110th St Ste 520 (66210-2371)
PHONE..................................913 663-4672
EMP: 24
SALES (est): 2.1MM **Privately Held**
SIC: **6411** Insurance Agents,Brokers,And Service,Nsk

(G-9060)
MTC HOLDING CORPORATION
5901 College Blvd Ste 100 (66211-1834)
PHONE..................................913 319-0300
Brad Bergman, *President*
Stacey Perry, *Officer*
EMP: 13 **EST**: 2008
SALES: 50MM **Privately Held**
SIC: **6719** Investment holding companies, except banks

(G-9061)
MTS QUANTA LLC
10551 Barkley St Ste 200 (66212-1813)
PHONE..................................913 383-0800
Mark Anderson, *President*
Mike Scrivener, *Business Mgr*
Derek Klinkenborg, *Vice Pres*
EMP: 30 **EST**: 2015
SQ FT: 8,000
SALES (est): 1MM
SALES (corp-wide): 11.1B **Publicly Held**
SIC: **8713** 8711 4932 1389 Surveying services; engineering services; gas & other services combined; construction, repair & dismantling services
PA: Quanta Services, Inc.
2800 Post Oak Blvd # 2600
Houston TX 77056
713 629-7600

(G-9062)
MUELLER-YURGAE ASSOCIATES INC
10500 Barkley St Ste 102 (66212-1859)
PHONE..................................913 362-7777
Phillip Yurgae, *President*
EMP: 15
SALES (corp-wide): 49.5MM **Privately Held**
SIC: **5141** Food brokers
PA: Mueller-Yurgae Associates, Inc.
1055 Se 28th St
Grimes IA 50111
515 986-0491

(G-9063)
MULTI SVC TECH SOLUTIONS INC (HQ)
Also Called: Red Wing Bus Advantage Account
8650 College Blvd (66210-1886)
P.O. Box 844329, Dallas TX (75284-4329)
PHONE..................................800 239-1064
Martha Salinas, *President*
Inez Berkhof, *Managing Dir*
Tara Martinez, *Regional Mgr*
Daniel Miller, *Business Mgr*
Kauleen Adiutori, *COO*
EMP: 400 **EST**: 2012
SALES (est): 70.6MM
SALES (corp-wide): 39.7B **Publicly Held**
SIC: **7389** Credit card service
PA: World Fuel Services Corp
9800 Nw 41st St Ste 400
Doral FL 33178
305 428-8000

(G-9064)
MUTUAL FUND STORE LLC (DH)
10950 Grandview Dr # 500 (66210-1585)
PHONE..................................913 319-8181
John Bunch, *President*
Chris Bouffard, *CIO*
EMP: 16
SALES (est): 10.1MM
SALES (corp-wide): 389.2MM **Privately Held**
SIC: **6282** Investment counselors
HQ: Edelman Financial Engines, Llc
1050 Entp Way Fl 3 Flr 3
Sunnyvale CA 94089
408 498-6000

(G-9065)
MUTUALAID EXCHANGE (PA)
Also Called: M I I Managing Group
4400 College Blvd Ste 250 (66211-2339)
PHONE..................................913 338-1100
David Wine, *Chairman*
Sheryl Jantzi, *Opers Mgr*
Bill Williams, *CFO*
Dawn Huff, *Accountant*
Brad Shrum, *Agent*
EMP: 22
SALES (est): 10.4MM **Privately Held**
WEB: www.mutualaidexchange.com
SIC: **6411** Insurance agents, brokers & service

(G-9066)
MYFREIGHTWORLD CARRIER MGT INC
7007 College Blvd Ste 150 (66211-2415)
PHONE..................................877 549-9438
Kevin C Childress, *President*
Michael E Chalfant, *Corp Secy*
EMP: 25
SALES (est): 4MM **Privately Held**
SIC: **4212** 7371 Local trucking, without storage; computer software development & applications

(G-9067)
NAILERY
11655 W 95th St Ste 120 (66214-1829)
PHONE..................................913 599-2225
Tan Nguyen, *Owner*
EMP: 15
SALES (est): 211.4K **Privately Held**
SIC: **7231** Manicurist, pedicurist

(G-9068)
NATIONAL ADVISORS HOLDINGS INC
8717 W 110th St Ste 700 (66210-2127)
PHONE..................................913 234-8200
James Combs, *CEO*
David Roberts, *President*
Tom Linhoff, *Senior VP*
Roger Dunham, *Vice Pres*
Kevin Hobbs, *Vice Pres*
EMP: 49
SQ FT: 6,900
SALES (est): 2.5MM **Privately Held**
WEB: www.nationaladvisorstrust.com
SIC: **6733** Private estate, personal investment & vacation fund trusts

(G-9069)
NATIONAL BD FOR RSPRATORY CARE
Also Called: Nbrc
10801 Mastin St Ste 300 (66210-1658)
PHONE..................................913 895-4900
Laurie Tinkler, *Editor*
AMI Bishop, *Corp Comm Staff*
Melanie Thomas, *Manager*
Steven K Bryant, *Exec Dir*
Robert Shaw, *Asst Director*
EMP: 13 **EST**: 1960
SQ FT: 32,000
SALES: 34MM **Privately Held**
SIC: **8621** 8748 8741 2759 Medical field-related associations; testing services; management services; commercial printing

(G-9070)
NATIONAL CROP INSUR SVCS INC
8900 Indian Creek Pkwy (66210-1554)
PHONE..................................913 685-2767
Thomas P Zacharias, *President*
Jim Crist, *CFO*
EMP: 50
SQ FT: 13,500
SALES: 12.6MM **Privately Held**
SIC: **6411** Research services, insurance

(G-9071)
NATIONAL CTSTRPHE RSTRTION INC
8065 Flint St (66214-3335)
PHONE..................................913 663-4111
Carl Maxson, *Branch Mgr*
EMP: 10
SALES (corp-wide): 39.2MM **Privately Held**
WEB: www.ncricat.com
SIC: **7389** Salvaging of damaged merchandise, service only
PA: National Catastrophe Restoration, Inc.
8447 E 35th St N
Wichita KS 67226
316 636-5700

(G-9072)
NATIONAL RGSTRED AGENTS INC NJ
11600 College Blvd # 210 (66210-2786)
PHONE..................................913 754-0637
Kent Rockwell, *Branch Mgr*
EMP: 10
SALES (corp-wide): 4.7B **Privately Held**
SIC: **7389** Artists' agents & brokers
HQ: National Registered Agents Inc. Of Nj
820 Bear Tavern Rd # 305
Ewing NJ 08628
888 579-0286

(G-9073)
NETAPP INC
9393 W 110th St Ste 200 (66210-1422)
PHONE..................................913 451-6718
Dick Burton, *Principal*
Storry Seifert, *Sales Staff*
EMP: 215 **Publicly Held**
SIC: **7373** Computer integrated systems design
PA: Netapp, Inc.
1395 Crossman Ave
Sunnyvale CA 94089

(G-9074)
NETCHEMIA LLC (DH)
7801 Nieman Rd Ste 200 (66214-1204)
PHONE..................................913 789-0996
Eric Diebold, *Vice Pres*
Jennifer Irving, *Manager*
Johnna River, *Manager*
Joanna Sullivan, *Manager*
Ken Halford, *Director*
EMP: 25
SALES (est): 4.7MM
SALES (corp-wide): 5.1B **Privately Held**
WEB: www.netchemia.com
SIC: **8731** 7373 Computer (hardware) development; systems software development services
HQ: Peopleadmin, Inc.
805 Las Cimas Pkwy # 400
Austin TX 78746
877 637-5800

(G-9075)
NETSMART LLC (PA)
4950 College Blvd (66211-1612)
PHONE..................................913 327-7444
Michael Valentine, *CEO*
Hythem El-Nazer, *Managing Dir*
Howard Park, *Managing Dir*
Tom Herzog, *COO*
Paul Anderson, *Exec VP*
EMP: 32
SQ FT: 32,600
SALES (est): 222.5MM **Privately Held**
SIC: **7371** Computer software development

(G-9076)
NETSMART TECHNOLOGIES INC (HQ)
4950 College Blvd (66211-1612)
PHONE..................................913 327-7444
Michael Valentine, *CEO*
David Gordon, *General Mgr*
Kevin Scalia, *Exec VP*

GEOGRAPHIC

Alan B Tillinghast, *Exec VP*
Deb Bickford, *Vice Pres*
EMP: 160
SQ FT: 32,600
SALES (est): 204.1MM
SALES (corp-wide): 222.5MM **Privately Held**
SIC: 7371 7372 Custom computer programming services; prepackaged software
PA: Netsmart Llc
4950 College Blvd
Overland Park KS 66211
913 327-7444

(G-9077)
NETSTANDARD INC (PA)
10300 W 103rd St Ste 100 (66214-2629)
PHONE..................................913 428-4200
Jeff Melcher, *CEO*
Walt Lane, *President*
Kenneth Kortas, *Partner*
David Baxter, *Senior VP*
Maddy Dychtwald, *Senior VP*
EMP: 56
SALES (est): 15MM **Privately Held**
WEB: www.netstandard.com
SIC: 7373 8748 Computer integrated systems design; systems engineering consultant, ex. computer or professional

(G-9078)
NETWORKS INTERNATIONAL CORP
15237 Broadmoor St (66223-3199)
PHONE..................................913 685-3400
Alok Bisarya, *President*
Abhay Bisarya, *Chairman*
Lawrence Davis, *QC Mgr*
Mitul Bisarya, *Director*
EMP: 46
SQ FT: 15,000
SALES (est): 8.4MM **Privately Held**
WEB: www.nickc.com
SIC: 3679 3829 3677 3663 Electronic crystals; measuring & controlling devices; electronic coils, transformers & other inductors; radio & TV communications equipment

(G-9079)
NEUFINANCIAL INC
Also Called: Neu Consulting Group
8417 Santa Fe Dr Ste 200 (66212-2727)
PHONE..................................913 825-0000
Ryan Neuweg, *CEO*
Amy Klassen, *Business Anlyst*
Justin Roberts, *Software Dev*
EMP: 40 **Privately Held**
SIC: 7374 Data processing & preparation
PA: Neufinancial, Inc.
4741 Central St Ste 415
Kansas City MO 64112

(G-9080)
NEW DRCTONS BHAVIORAL HLTH LLC (HQ)
6100 Sprint Pkwy Ste 200 (66211-1196)
P.O. Box 6729, Shawnee Mission (66206-0729)
PHONE..................................816 237-2300
Lee Tuveson, *President*
Amanda Koukol, *Accountant*
Rose Pacheco, *Case Mgr*
Dawn Broun, *Manager*
Diane F Lee, *Manager*
EMP: 122 **EST:** 1994
SQ FT: 130,000
SALES: 325MM **Privately Held**
WEB: www.ndbh.com
SIC: 6324 6321 Hospital & medical service plans; accident & health insurance
PA: Ndbh Holding Company, L.L.C.
8140 Ward Pkwy Ste 500
Kansas City MO 64114
816 237-2300

(G-9081)
NEW YORK LIFE INSURANCE CO
7500 College Blvd Ste 800 (66210-4035)
PHONE..................................913 451-9100
Troy Braswell, *Manager*
Rick Austin, *Agent*
David R Colflesh, *Agent*
Brooks Schaar, *Agent*
Tami Duvall, *Advisor*
EMP: 45
SALES (corp-wide): 10.8B **Privately Held**
WEB: www.newyorklife.com
SIC: 6311 Life insurance
PA: New York Life Insurance Company
51 Madison Ave Bsmt 1b
New York NY 10010
212 576-7000

(G-9082)
NEXTAFF LLC (PA)
11225 College Blvd # 250 (66210-2748)
PHONE..................................913 562-5620
James Windmiller, *Principal*
Jon Elscott, *Mktg Dir*
EMP: 34
SALES (est): 9.4MM **Privately Held**
SIC: 7361 Employment agencies

(G-9083)
NEXTEL OF CALIFORNIA INC (DH)
Also Called: Sprint
6200 Sprint Pkwy (66251-6117)
PHONE..................................866 505-2385
EMP: 50
SALES (est): 517.3MM **Publicly Held**
SIC: 4812 Cellular telephone services
HQ: Sprint Corporation
6200 Sprint Pkwy
Overland Park KS 66251
877 564-3166

(G-9084)
NEXTEL PARTNERS OPERATING CORP (DH)
6200 Sprint Pkwy (66251-6117)
PHONE..................................800 829-0965
John Chapple, *CEO*
John D Thompson, *Treasurer*
EMP: 170
SALES (est): 1.7B **Publicly Held**
WEB: www.nymobilellc.com
SIC: 4812 Cellular telephone services
HQ: Sprint Communications, Inc.
6200 Sprint Pkwy
Overland Park KS 66251
855 848-3280

(G-9085)
NEXUS IT GROUP INC
7512 W 80th St (66204-3411)
PHONE..................................913 815-1750
Nick Gamis, *Accounts Mgr*
Travis Lindemoen, *Director*
EMP: 16
SALES (est): 918.9K **Privately Held**
WEB: www.nexusitgroup.com
SIC: 7363 Temporary help service

(G-9086)
NICKLAUS GOLF CLUB LP
Also Called: Nicklaus Golf CLB At Lionsgate
14225 Dearborn St (66223-2594)
PHONE..................................913 402-1000
Chris Hanns, *General Mgr*
Jess Schauer, *General Mgr*
EMP: 51 **EST:** 1998
SQ FT: 4,200
SALES (est): 2.6MM
SALES (corp-wide): 841.1MM **Privately Held**
WEB: www.remington-gc.com
SIC: 7997 Country club, membership
HQ: Clubcorp Usa, Inc.
3030 Lyndon B Johnson Fwy
Dallas TX 75234
972 243-6191

(G-9087)
NILL BROS SPORTING GOODS INC (PA)
Also Called: Nill Bros Sports
2814 S 44th St (66213)
PHONE..................................913 345-8655
Wyatt Nill, *President*
Sarah Alexander, *Sales Mgr*
EMP: 15 **EST:** 1960
SQ FT: 15,000
SALES: 9.5MM **Privately Held**
WEB: www.nillbros.com
SIC: 5941 5091 Specialty sport supplies; sporting & recreation goods

(G-9088)
NN8 LLC
9300 W 110th St Ste 235 (66210-1405)
PHONE..................................913 948-1107
Adam Herrman,
EMP: 14 **EST:** 2017
SALES (est): 235.4K **Privately Held**
SIC: 7389 Business services

(G-9089)
NOATUM LOGISTICS USA LLC (HQ)
11501 Outlook St Ste 500 (66211-1808)
PHONE..................................913 696-7100
John E Carr, *President*
Clint Dvorak, *Senior VP*
Tina Jansen, *Vice Pres*
Peter Gimblette, *Export Mgr*
Brenda Stasiulis, *CFO*
▲ **EMP:** 20
SALES (est): 340.2MM **Privately Held**
SIC: 4731 4513 Freight transportation arrangement; air courier services

(G-9090)
NOBLE HOUSE JEWELRY LTD (PA)
11620 Metcalf Ave (66210-2233)
PHONE..................................913 491-4861
Zoe Herrington, *President*
Doug Brooks, *VP Sales*
Zoe Brooks, *Director*
EMP: 10
SQ FT: 2,500
SALES (est): 916.6K **Privately Held**
WEB: www.noblehousejewelry.com
SIC: 7631 5944 Jewelry repair services; jewelry, precious stones & precious metals

(G-9091)
NOLAN COMPANY
8900 Indian Creek Pkwy # 200 (66210-1554)
PHONE..................................913 888-3500
James R Nolan, *President*
Nancy Lustig, *QC Dir*
EMP: 28
SQ FT: 35,000
SALES: 3MM **Privately Held**
WEB: www.thenolancompanyonline.com
SIC: 6411 Pension & retirement plan consultants

(G-9092)
NOONSHINE WINDOW CLEANING SVC
8100 Marty St Ste 105 (66204-3737)
PHONE..................................913 381-3780
William Noon, *Principal*
EMP: 10 **EST:** 2008
SALES: 400K **Privately Held**
SIC: 7699 7349 1799 Cleaning services; window cleaning; construction site cleanup

(G-9093)
NORBROOK INC
9401 Indian Creek Pkwy # 80 (66210-2007)
PHONE..................................913 802-5050
EMP: 9
SALES (est): 1.3MM **Privately Held**
SIC: 2834 Pharmaceutical preparations

(G-9094)
NPC QUALITY BURGERS INC (DH)
7300 W 129th St (66213-2631)
PHONE..................................913 327-5555
Troy D Cook, *CFO*
EMP: 15
SALES (est): 10.8MM
SALES (corp-wide): 1.2B **Privately Held**
SIC: 6794 5812 Franchises, selling or licensing; hamburger stand
HQ: Npc International, Inc.
7300 W 129th St
Overland Park KS 66213
913 327-5555

(G-9095)
O H GERRY OPTICAL COMPANY (PA)
8857 W 75th St (66204-2206)
PHONE..................................913 362-8822
Matthew A Murphy, *President*
Matthew A Murphy III, *Exec VP*
EMP: 44
SQ FT: 12,000
SALES (est): 6.8MM **Privately Held**
WEB: www.gerryopt.com
SIC: 5995 5049 Opticians; optical goods

(G-9096)
OAK PARK MALL
Also Called: Oak Park Merchants
11149 W 95th St (66214-1824)
PHONE..................................913 888-4400
Paul Copaken, *Principal*
Wayne Cash, *Manager*
EMP: 25
SALES (est): 2MM **Privately Held**
SIC: 6512 Shopping center, property operation only

(G-9097)
OLD WORLD BALLOONERY LLC
12600 W 142nd St (66221-8072)
PHONE..................................913 338-2628
Jason Jones, *Mng Member*
EMP: 10
SALES (est): 39.9K **Privately Held**
WEB: www.oldworldballoonery.com
SIC: 7999 5599 7319 Hot air balloon rides; hot air balloons & equipment; aerial advertising services

(G-9098)
OLD WORLD SPICES SEASONING INC
Also Called: Laurie's Kitchen
5320 College Blvd (66211-1621)
PHONE..................................816 861-0400
John Jungk, *President*
Amy Jungk, *Vice Pres*
Elizabeth Betteman, *Treasurer*
Amy Polson, *Sales Mgr*
Christopher Marks, *Sales Staff*
▲ **EMP:** 25
SQ FT: 22,000
SALES (est): 11.2MM **Privately Held**
WEB: www.oldworldspices.com
SIC: 5149 2099 2035 Seasonings, sauces & extracts; food preparations; pickles, sauces & salad dressings

(G-9099)
OLIVER INSURANCE AGENCY INC
10955 Lowell Ave Ste 1010 (66210-2337)
PHONE..................................913 341-1900
Keith C Oliver, *President*
Lisa Oliver, *Corp Secy*
Oliver Agency, *E-Business*
Linda Morgan, *Admin Asst*
EMP: 16
SQ FT: 5,000
SALES (est): 2.5MM **Privately Held**
SIC: 6411 Insurance agents

(G-9100)
OLSSON INC
7301 W 133rd St Ste 200 (66213-4774)
PHONE..................................913 381-1170
Brad Strittmatter, *Manager*
Andy Ohlman, *Manager*
George Laliberte, *Consultant*
Joanna Longsdon, *Deputy Dir*
Kathy Fulton, *Technician*
EMP: 114
SALES (corp-wide): 198MM **Privately Held**
WEB: www.oaconsulting.com
SIC: 8711 8713 Consulting engineer; surveying services
PA: Olsson, Inc.
601 P St Ste 200
Lincoln NE 68508
417 781-0643

▲ = Import ▼=Export
◆ =Import/Export

(G-9101)
OMNI EMPLOYMENT MGT SVC LLC
8700 Indian Creek Pkwy # 250 (66210-1563)
PHONE....................913 341-2119
Sherry Marko, *HR Admin*
Michael Tracy, *Mng Member*
Julie Anderson, *Consultant*
Brianna Steinke, *Consultant*
Sonja Ambur, *Director*
EMP: 20
SALES (est): 1.3MM **Privately Held**
WEB: www.omniemployment.com
SIC: 8742 Human resource consulting services

(G-9102)
ON DEMAND TECHNOLOGIES LLC (PA)
Also Called: O D T
9291 Cody St (66214-1735)
PHONE....................913 438-1800
Dave Kentch, *Prdtn Mgr*
Wynne Jennings, *CFO*
Tami Lansford, *Controller*
Phillip Allen, *Chief Mktg Ofcr*
Dave Jolicoeur, *Consultant*
▲ **EMP:** 14
SALES (est): 2.2MM **Privately Held**
WEB: www.odtinc.com
SIC: 2752 5045 8731 7371 Commercial printing, offset; computers; computer software; computer (hardware) development; computer software development; bookbinding & related work; commercial printing

(G-9103)
ONE GAS INC
Kansas Gas Service
7421 W 129th St (66213-2713)
PHONE....................913 319-8617
Dennis Okenfuss, *VP Opers*
EMP: 130
SALES (corp-wide): 1.6B **Publicly Held**
WEB: www.oneok.com
SIC: 1311 Natural gas production
PA: One Gas, Inc.
15 E 5th St
Tulsa OK 74103
918 947-7000

(G-9104)
ONEOK INC
Kansas Gas Service
7421 W 129th St Ste 100 (66213-2645)
P.O. Box 25957, Shawnee Mission (66225-5957)
PHONE....................913 319-8600
Brad Dixon, *President*
Dennis Okenfuss, *VP Admin*
Margaret Steele, *Pub Rel Mgr*
Don Whitlock, *Accounting Mgr*
Ron Ragan, *Marketing Staff*
EMP: 50
SALES (corp-wide): 12.5B **Publicly Held**
WEB: www.oneok.com
SIC: 4924 Natural gas distribution
PA: Oneok, Inc.
100 W 5th St Ste Ll
Tulsa OK 74103
918 588-7000

(G-9105)
ONSPRING TECHNOLOGIES LLC
10801 Mastin St Ste 400 (66210-1697)
PHONE....................913 601-4900
Chris Pantaenius, *CEO*
Matt Pugh, *Vice Pres*
Chris Mandernach, *Sales Staff*
Sarah Nord, *Mktg Dir*
Chad Kreimendahl, *CTO*
EMP: 15 **EST:** 2010
SALES (est): 1.3MM **Privately Held**
SIC: 7371 Computer software development

(G-9106)
ONYX MEETINGS INC
Also Called: Onyx Meetings and Events
7200 W 75th St (66204-2949)
PHONE....................913 381-1123
Steve Hines, *President*
Douglas Fager, *Manager*
Mandie Bannwarth, *Exec Dir*
Amie Brock, *Meeting Planner*
Elton Ching, *Meeting Planner*
EMP: 19
SALES: 11MM **Privately Held**
WEB: www.meetingsbyonyx.com
SIC: 8742 Business planning & organizing services

(G-9107)
OPHTHALMIC SERVICES PA
9950 W 151st St (66221-9324)
PHONE....................913 498-2015
D W Bell, *Principal*
EMP: 11
SALES (est): 675.9K **Privately Held**
SIC: 8011 Ophthalmologist

(G-9108)
OPRC INC
Also Called: Overland Park Racquet Club
6800 W 91st St (66212-1453)
PHONE....................913 642-6880
Eugene Ellis, *President*
Liza Arl, *Manager*
Jason Kane, *Director*
EMP: 25 **EST:** 1978
SQ FT: 120,000
SALES (est): 1.5MM **Privately Held**
WEB: www.opracquetclub.com
SIC: 7997 7991 Tennis club, membership; physical fitness facilities

(G-9109)
OPTION CARE ENTERPRISES INC
8940 Nieman Rd (66214-1747)
PHONE....................913 599-3745
Patrick Moloney, *Manager*
EMP: 20 **Publicly Held**
SIC: 8082 Home health care services
HQ: Option Care Enterprises, Inc.
3000 Lakeside Dr Ste 300n
Bannockburn IL 60015

(G-9110)
OPTIV SECURITY INC
6130 Sprint Pkwy Ste 400 (66211-1155)
PHONE....................816 421-6611
Bryan Wiese, *Vice Pres*
Ben Barnhart, *Manager*
Jack Coleman, *Manager*
Summer Ziggas, *Director*
Gavin Reynolds, *Technician*
EMP: 12
SALES (corp-wide): 4.8B **Privately Held**
SIC: 5045 7379 7382 5065 Accounting machines using machine readable programs; ; burglar alarm maintenance & monitoring; diskettes, computer
HQ: Optiv Security Inc.
1144 15th St Ste 2900
Denver CO 80202
303 298-0600

(G-9111)
OREILLY AUTOMOTIVE STORES INC
Also Called: O'Reilly Auto Parts
6725 W 75th St (66204-3021)
PHONE....................913 381-0451
Curtiss White, *Manager*
EMP: 14 **Publicly Held**
WEB: www.oreillyauto.com
SIC: 5531 5013 Automotive parts; motor vehicle supplies & new parts
HQ: O'reilly Automotive Stores, Inc.
233 S Patterson Ave
Springfield MO 65802
417 862-2674

(G-9112)
ORION COMMUNICATIONS INC
10650 Roe Ave (66207-3907)
PHONE....................913 538-7110
Ryan Herrman, *President*
EMP: 5
SALES (est): 600K **Privately Held**
SIC: 7372 Business oriented computer software

(G-9113)
ORION INFORMATION SYSTEMS LLC
12302 W 129th Ter (66213-3570)
PHONE....................913 825-3272
Iva Salmon, *Partner*
Jesse Salmon,
EMP: 15
SQ FT: 450
SALES (est): 519.4K **Privately Held**
SIC: 7371 7373 Computer software development; computer system selling services

(G-9114)
ORION SECURITY INC
5600 W 95th St Ste 315 (66207-2968)
PHONE....................913 385-5657
Charles P Stephenson, *President*
EMP: 70
SQ FT: 2,090
SALES (est): 1.6MM **Privately Held**
SIC: 7381 Security guard service

(G-9115)
ORTHO INNOVATIONS LLC
13401 W 125th St (66213-5036)
PHONE....................913 449-8376
EMP: 10 **EST:** 2012
SALES (est): 84.9K **Privately Held**
SIC: 7363 Medical help service

(G-9116)
OUTDOOR CUSTOM SPORTSWEAR LLC
Also Called: Columbia Sportswear
7007 College Blvd Ste 200 (66211-2452)
PHONE....................866 288-5070
Lindsay Ehemann, *Accounts Mgr*
Michael Gary,
▲ **EMP:** 32 **EST:** 2013
SALES (est): 3.2MM **Privately Held**
SIC: 2329 2339 Men's & boys' sportswear & athletic clothing; women's & misses' athletic clothing & sportswear

(G-9117)
OVERLAND PARK DEVELOPMENT CORP (PA)
Also Called: Sheraton Overland Park Hotel
6100 College Blvd (66211-2403)
PHONE....................913 234-2100
Thomas Healy, *President*
Patrick McMonigle, *Human Res Dir*
EMP: 75
SALES: 17.7MM **Privately Held**
WEB: www.opconventioncenter.com
SIC: 7011 Hotels & motels

(G-9118)
OVERLAND PARK FMLY HLTH PRTNR
5405 W 151st St (66224-8700)
PHONE....................913 894-6500
Carmen Dawn Zirjacks, *Principal*
EMP: 15
SALES (est): 1.3MM **Privately Held**
SIC: 8011 General & family practice, physician/surgeon

(G-9119)
OVERLAND PARK HEATING & COOLG
Also Called: Honeywell Authorized Dealer
16172 Metcalf Ave (66085-9100)
PHONE....................913 649-0303
Doug Crews, *President*
Vince Holzer, *Principal*
EMP: 30
SQ FT: 4,032
SALES (est): 5.8MM **Privately Held**
SIC: 1541 1711 Renovation, remodeling & repairs: industrial buildings; warm air heating & air conditioning contractor

(G-9120)
OVERLAND PARK HOTEL ASSOC LC
Also Called: Holiday Inn
8787 Reeder St (66214-1921)
PHONE....................913 888-8440
David Brown, *Manager*
Bruce Kinseth,
EMP: 130
SALES (est): 5MM **Privately Held**
WEB: www.holidayinnkansascity.com
SIC: 7011 7299 Hotels & motels; banquet hall facilities

(G-9121)
OVERLAND PARK REGIONAL HOSP
10500 Quivira Rd (66215-2306)
PHONE....................913 541-5406
Sheila Jones, *Principal*
EMP: 37 **EST:** 2010
SALES (est): 4.3MM **Privately Held**
SIC: 8062 General medical & surgical hospitals

(G-9122)
OVERLAND PARK SENIOR LIVING
10101 W 127th St (66213-3201)
PHONE....................913 912-7800
Kip Pammenter, *President*
David Thompson, *Vice Pres*
Alixandria Ruoff, *Exec Dir*
Alix Knight, *Director*
EMP: 21
SALES (est): 1.1MM **Privately Held**
SIC: 8059 Personal care home, with health care

(G-9123)
OVERLAND PARK SURGERY CTR LLC
10601 Quivira Rd Ste 100 (66215-2320)
PHONE....................913 894-7260
Brad Irvin,
Warren Sylvester, *Administration*
Denise Trobon,
EMP: 100
SALES (est): 7.5MM **Publicly Held**
SIC: 8011 Surgeon
HQ: Midamerica Division, Inc.
903 E 104th St Ste 500
Kansas City MO 64131
816 508-4000

(G-9124)
OVERLAND PARK VETERINARY CTR
8120 Santa Fe Dr (66204-3608)
PHONE....................913 642-9371
Bruce Freeman, *Owner*
EMP: 15
SALES (est): 493.5K **Privately Held**
SIC: 0742 Animal hospital services, pets & other animal specialties

(G-9125)
OVERLAND PK NURSING REHAB CTR
6501 W 75th St (66204-3017)
PHONE....................913 383-9866
Kelsie Tryon, *Director*
Mike Phillips, *Director*
Lindsay Gorman, *Social Dir*
Jodie Kleinowski, *Records Dir*
EMP: 12
SALES: 6.9MM **Privately Held**
SIC: 8059 Nursing home, except skilled & intermediate care facility

(G-9126)
OVERLAND PK RGONAL MED CTR INC
10500 Quivira Rd (66215-2306)
PHONE....................913 541-0000
Kevin Hicks, *President*
EMP: 1125 **EST:** 2014
SALES (est): 43.3MM **Privately Held**
SIC: 8062 General medical & surgical hospitals

(G-9127)
OVERLAND SOLUTIONS INC (HQ)
10975 Grandview Dr # 400 (66210-1523)
PHONE....................913 451-3222
Mike Ferguson, *President*
Pat O Glesby, *General Mgr*
Eric Schlueter, *Regional Mgr*
Gilbert Bourk, *Senior VP*
David Greene, *Senior VP*
EMP: 140
SQ FT: 20,000

GEOGRAPHIC

SALES (est): 378.9MM
SALES (corp-wide): 883.1MM **Publicly Held**
WEB: www.overlandsolutions.com
SIC: 6411 Loss prevention services, insurance
PA: Exlservice Holdings, Inc.
320 Park Ave Fl 29
New York NY 10022
212 277-7100

(G-9128)
OVERLAND TOW SERVICE INC (PA)
3505 Merriam Dr (66203-1377)
P.O. Box 4262, Shawnee Mission (66204-0262)
PHONE..................................913 722-3505
Joe L Meyer, *President*
EMP: 10
SQ FT: 800
SALES (est): 1.1MM **Privately Held**
SIC: 7549 Towing service, automotive

(G-9129)
OVERLND PRK CNVNTN & VSTRS BRE
9001 W 110th St Ste 100 (66210-2116)
PHONE..................................913 491-0123
Gerald Cook, *President*
EMP: 12
SALES: 2.9MM **Privately Held**
SIC: 7389 Convention & show services; tourist information bureau

(G-9130)
OXFORD ANIMAL HOSPITAL P A
13433 Switzer Rd (66213-3301)
PHONE..................................913 681-2600
Ross Burd, *Owner*
EMP: 15
SQ FT: 9,800
SALES (est): 1.1MM **Privately Held**
SIC: 0742 Animal hospital services, pets & other animal specialties

(G-9131)
OZ ACCOMMODATIONS INC
7925 Bond St (66214-1557)
PHONE..................................913 894-8400
Marlene Abbey, *President*
EMP: 15
SQ FT: 3,960
SALES (est): 1MM **Privately Held**
WEB: www.aplacelikehome.com
SIC: 7011 Hotels & motels

(G-9132)
P C SOUTHLAW (PA)
13160 Foster St Ste 100 (66213-2848)
P.O. Box 10900 (66225-9000)
PHONE..................................913 663-7600
Alan E South, *Partner*
Michael Zevitz, *Partner*
Josh Chamberlain, *Administration*
EMP: 110
SQ FT: 30,000
SALES (est): 16.3MM **Privately Held**
WEB: www.southlaw.com
SIC: 8111 Real estate law

(G-9133)
P K C REALTY COMPANY LLC
Also Called: Prudential
8300 College Blvd Ste 100 (66210-2600)
PHONE..................................913 491-1550
Kristi Ferrara, *Broker*
Debra Chambers, *Sales Staff*
Emma Young, *Sales Staff*
Francine Winn, *Consultant*
James Burrows,
EMP: 200
SQ FT: 21,000
SALES (est): 6.7MM **Privately Held**
WEB: www.summerson.com
SIC: 6531 Real estate agent, residential

(G-9134)
P1 TRANSPORTATION LLC
7360 W 162nd St Ste 108 (66085-9367)
PHONE..................................913 249-1505
Jonathan Payne, *Mng Member*
Tim Payne,
Mike Purmort,
EMP: 14
SALES (est): 1.4MM
SALES (corp-wide): 6.9MM **Privately Held**
SIC: 4731 Transportation agents & brokers
PA: Brier, Payne, Meade Insurance, Inc.
10540 Marty St Ste 160
Overland Park KS 66212
913 402-9576

(G-9135)
PAIGE TECHNOLOGIES LLC
Also Called: Pt Solutions Group
7171 W 95th St Ste 500 (66212-2254)
PHONE..................................913 381-0600
Chris Wood, *Managing Prtnr*
Bill Groff, *Recruiter*
Andrew Alldredge,
EMP: 50
SALES (est): 5.2MM **Privately Held**
WEB: www.paigetech.com
SIC: 7371 Computer software systems analysis & design, custom

(G-9136)
PAINCARE PA
10501 Metcalf Ave (66212-1815)
PHONE..................................913 901-8880
Daniel Bruning, *President*
Kelly Travis, *Office Mgr*
Erich Helfer,
EMP: 20
SALES (est): 2.4MM **Privately Held**
WEB: www.kcpaincare.com
SIC: 8011 Orthopedic physician

(G-9137)
PAINT GLAZE & FIRE
Also Called: Paint Glaze and Fire Ceramics
12683 Metcalf Ave (66213-1317)
PHONE..................................913 661-2529
Debbie Wright, *President*
EMP: 6 **EST:** 1997
SALES (est): 517.5K **Privately Held**
WEB: www.paintglazeandfire.com
SIC: 3251 5947 Ceramic glazed brick, clay; gift shop

(G-9138)
PAINT PRO INC
6930 W 152nd Ter (66223-3125)
PHONE..................................913 685-4089
Bill Ruisinger, *President*
Brian Ruisinger, *Vice Pres*
EMP: 14
SQ FT: 8,500
SALES (est): 1.4MM **Privately Held**
WEB: www.paintproinc.net
SIC: 1721 1521 1761 Residential painting; general remodeling, single-family houses; siding contractor

(G-9139)
PANHANDLE EASTRN PIPE LINE LP
Also Called: Panhandle Energy
7500 College Blvd Ste 300 (66210-4020)
PHONE..................................913 906-1500
Lisa Haloey, *Superintendent*
Lisa Halsey, *Director*
EMP: 30
SALES (corp-wide): 54B **Publicly Held**
SIC: 4612 Crude petroleum pipelines
HQ: Panhandle Eastern Pipe Line Company, Lp
8111 Westchester Dr # 600
Dallas TX 75225
214 981-0700

(G-9140)
PAPA MURPHYS TAKE N BAKE
13473 Switzer Rd Unit G (66213-3301)
PHONE..................................913 897-0008
Kevin Fonte, *President*
EMP: 12
SALES (est): 288.1K **Privately Held**
SIC: 5812 4813 Pizzeria, chain;

(G-9141)
PARK MEADOWS SENIOR LIVING LLC
Also Called: Spectrum Retirement
5901 W 107th St (66207-3882)
PHONE..................................913 901-8200
David Thompson,
EMP: 90
SALES (est): 4MM **Privately Held**
SIC: 8361 Home for the aged

(G-9142)
PARK-RN OVERLAND PARK LLC
Also Called: Holiday Inn
7580 W 135th St (66223-1202)
PHONE..................................913 850-5400
EMP: 18
SALES (est): 1MM **Privately Held**
SIC: 7011 Hotels & motels

(G-9143)
PARTNERS INC (PA)
11005 Metcalf Ave (66210-1815)
PHONE..................................913 906-5400
Judy Johns, *President*
Ken Johns, *Vice Pres*
Dave Johns, *Treasurer*
Steve Johns, *Admin Sec*
EMP: 10
SQ FT: 11,500
SALES: 82.3K **Privately Held**
WEB: www.olathehomes4sale.com
SIC: 6531 Real estate agent, residential

(G-9144)
PASTORSERVE INC
6804 W 107th St Ste 100 (66212-1831)
P.O. Box 27123, Shawnee Mission (66225-7123)
PHONE..................................877 918-4746
Jim Fenlason, *CEO*
James Dodd, *President*
Roy Bilyeu, *Director*
EMP: 12
SALES (est): 63.4K **Privately Held**
SIC: 8699 Charitable organization

(G-9145)
PATIENT RESOURCE PUBG LLC
8455 Lenexa Dr (66214-1550)
PHONE..................................913 725-1000
Linette Atwood, *CEO*
Laurie Johnson, *Vice Pres*
Yared Tekle, *Project Mgr*
Elaina Smith, *Prdtn Mgr*
EMP: 10
SALES (est): 981.5K **Privately Held**
SIC: 2721 Magazines: publishing only, not printed on site

(G-9146)
PATRICK PROPERTIES SERVICES
11755 W 86th Ter (66214-1534)
PHONE..................................913 262-6824
Robert Patrick, *President*
EMP: 15
SALES (est): 1.2MM **Privately Held**
WEB: www.patrickpainting.org
SIC: 6512 Nonresidential building operators

(G-9147)
PAYNE AND JONES CHARTERED
100 King (66225)
PHONE..................................913 469-4100
Tim Chadwick, *CEO*
Jason Evelyn, *President*
Thomas Griswold, *Manager*
Beth Lowe, *Executive*
Roger Templin, *Administration*
EMP: 139 **EST:** 2011
SALES (est): 6.4MM **Privately Held**
SIC: 1711 Plumbing, heating, air-conditioning contractors

(G-9148)
PB&J
10220 W 87th St (66212-4674)
PHONE..................................913 648-6033
EMP: 6
SALES (est): 478.9K **Privately Held**
SIC: 3421 Table & food cutlery, including butchers'

(G-9149)
PDA OF KANSAS CITY INC
Also Called: Property Damage Appraisers
6400 Glenwood St Ste 313 (66202-4025)
PHONE..................................913 631-0711
Dan Wright, *President*
EMP: 10
SALES: 2.5MM **Privately Held**
SIC: 7389 Appraisers, except real estate

(G-9150)
PEANUT CO LLC
Also Called: Kids R Kids International
7489 W 161st St (66085-8854)
PHONE..................................913 647-2240
Eric R Kallevig, *Mng Member*
EMP: 30
SQ FT: 15,000
SALES (est): 1MM **Privately Held**
SIC: 8351 Preschool center

(G-9151)
PEDIATRIC CARE SPECIALIST PA
12541 Foster St Ste 260 (66213-2301)
PHONE..................................913 906-0900
Harvey Grossman, *President*
Anne E Bray, *Med Doctor*
Robert Schloegel, *Med Doctor*
Tammy Cornell, *Administration*
Claire White, *Pediatrics*
EMP: 32 **EST:** 2000
SALES (est): 4.1MM **Privately Held**
SIC: 8011 Pediatrician

(G-9152)
PEDIATRIC PARTNERS
7301 W 133rd St Ste 102 (66213-4773)
PHONE..................................913 888-4567
Michael A Blum, *Owner*
Christine Stuppy, *Co-Owner*
EMP: 30
SALES (est): 2.6MM **Privately Held**
SIC: 8011 Pediatrician

(G-9153)
PEGASUS COMMUNICATION SOLUTION
12181 Craig St (66213-1474)
PHONE..................................913 937-8552
Sheena Simon, *CEO*
EMP: 10
SALES (est): 263.2K **Privately Held**
SIC: 7371 Computer software systems analysis & design, custom

(G-9154)
PERFECT OUTPUT LLC (PA)
Also Called: Laserequipment
9200 Indian Creek Pkwy (66210-2036)
PHONE..................................913 317-8400
John Walker, *CEO*
Ken Landau, *President*
Farrah Walker, *Vice Pres*
Wendy Hladky, *CFO*
Cynthia Mitchell, *Human Res Mgr*
EMP: 79
SQ FT: 10,000
SALES (est): 23.5MM **Privately Held**
WEB: www.perfectoutput.com
SIC: 7334 2759 5112 3955 Photocopying & duplicating services; commercial printing; laserjet supplies; print cartridges for laser & other computer printers; ink, printers'; photocopy machine repair

(G-9155)
PERFORMANCE REHAB LLC
11408 W 135th St (66221-9398)
PHONE..................................913 681-9909
Kerry Clemetson, *Supervisor*
Mark Buckingham,
Brian Boerner,
Paul Craig,
EMP: 20
SALES (est): 345.5K **Privately Held**
SIC: 8093 Rehabilitation center, outpatient treatment

(G-9156)
PERIODONTIST PA
10870 Benson Dr Ste 2100 (66210-1509)
PHONE..................................913 451-6158
Stanley Wint DDS, *President*
EMP: 13
SALES (est): 775.1K **Privately Held**
SIC: 8021 Periodontist

(G-9157)
PERMANENT PAVING INC
11011 Cody St Ste 300 (66210-1430)
P.O. Box 25348, Shawnee Mission (66225-5348)
PHONE..................................913 451-7834
Steve Bird, *President*
EMP: 10
SALES (est): 1.8MM
SALES (corp-wide): 29.7B **Privately Held**
WEB: www.permanentpaving.com
SIC: 3272 Concrete products
HQ: Ash Grove Materials Corporation
11011 Cody St Ste 300
Overland Park KS 66210
913 345-2030

(G-9158)
PERSERVE AT OVERLAND PARK
12401 W 120th St (66213-4838)
PHONE..................................913 685-3700
Mark Fogelman, *President*
Renee Mustard, *General Mgr*
Don Williams, *Business Mgr*
Gina Hope, *Manager*
EMP: 10
SALES (est): 765.1K **Privately Held**
WEB: www.thepreserveop.com
SIC: 6513 Apartment hotel operation

(G-9159)
PERSONAL MARKETING COMPANY INC
11511 W 83rd Ter (66214-1532)
P.O. Box 656, Shawnee Mission (66201-0656)
PHONE..................................913 492-0377
John J Wendorff, *Ch of Bd*
Elizabeth Wendorff, *Editor*
Robert P Jonas, *COO*
Susan Carter, *Cust Svc Dir*
Bob Kakareka, *CTO*
EMP: 25
SQ FT: 30,000
SALES (est): 6.2MM **Privately Held**
WEB: www.tpmco.com
SIC: 7331 Direct mail advertising services

(G-9160)
PETNET SOLUTIONS INC
9012 Cody St (66214-1730)
PHONE..................................913 310-9270
Jeff Schultz, *Manager*
EMP: 5
SALES (corp-wide): 96.9B **Privately Held**
SIC: 2835 Radioactive diagnostic substances
HQ: Petnet Solutions, Inc.
810 Innovation Dr
Knoxville TN 37932
865 218-2000

(G-9161)
PHARMION CORPORATION
9900 W 109th St Ste 300 (66210-1436)
PHONE..................................913 266-0300
Richard Lev, *Counsel*
Stefano Ferrara, *Research*
Judy Hemberger, *Branch Mgr*
Komal Deb, *Manager*
Dana Kanarvogel, *Manager*
EMP: 50
SALES (corp-wide): 22.5B **Publicly Held**
WEB: www.pharmion.com
SIC: 2834 Pharmaceutical preparations
HQ: Pharmion Corporation
86 Morris Ave
Summit NJ 07901
908 673-9000

(G-9162)
PHONE TECH COMMUNICATIONS INC
6004 W 146th St (66223-2683)
PHONE..................................913 859-9150
Vivek Dayal, *Principal*
EMP: 14
SALES (est): 1.5MM **Privately Held**
SIC: 8748 Telecommunications consultant

(G-9163)
PHYSICIAN OFFICE PARTNERS LLC
6050 Sprint Pkwy Ste 300 (66211-1195)
PHONE..................................913 754-0467
Rob Davey, *COO*
Rebecca Franklin, *Executive Asst*
Carl Slater,
EMP: 30
SALES (est): 3MM **Privately Held**
WEB: www.physicianofficepartners.com
SIC: 8011 General & family practice, physician/surgeon

(G-9164)
PHYSICIANS BUSINESS NETWRK LLC (HQ)
Also Called: Physicians Business Netwrk Inc
8900 Indian Creek Pkwy # 500 (66210-1556)
PHONE..................................913 381-5200
Neal Judson, *President*
Kurt Krueger, *Treasurer*
Heather Butterfield, *Manager*
Edward Robertson, *Admin Sec*
EMP: 24
SQ FT: 15,000
SALES (est): 9.5MM **Privately Held**
WEB: www.pbnmed.com
SIC: 7374 8721 Data processing service; accounting, auditing & bookkeeping
PA: Silvercreek Rcm, Llc
8900 Indian Creek Pkwy St
Pittsburg KS 66762
877 211-3001

(G-9165)
PI ARM
8717 W 110th St Ste 300 (66210-2103)
PHONE..................................913 661-1662
Jeff Hargroves, *President*
EMP: 210
SALES (est): 71K
SALES (corp-wide): 98.7MM **Privately Held**
SIC: 8748 Business consulting
HQ: Propharma Group, Llc
8717 W 110th St Ste 300
Overland Park KS 66210
888 242-0559

(G-9166)
PI TIMBERLINE LLC
8826 Santa Fe Dr Ste 300 (66212-3672)
PHONE..................................913 674-0438
Michelle Laughlin, *Principal*
Paul Himmelstein,
EMP: 10 **EST:** 2013
SALES (est): 605.4K **Privately Held**
SIC: 0811 Timber tracts

(G-9167)
PICTURE PERFECT INTERIORS LLC
11922 College Blvd (66210-3943)
PHONE..................................913 829-3365
Brenda Freebern,
Rick Freebern,
EMP: 11 **EST:** 1999
SALES (est): 1.1MM **Privately Held**
SIC: 7389 Interior designer; interior design services

(G-9168)
PINNACLE CONSULTING GROUP LLC
Also Called: Pinnacle Plus Financial
11225 College Blvd # 150 (66210-2771)
PHONE..................................913 254-3030
Kait Fox, *Vice Pres*
Allie Copeland, *Human Res Dir*
Matthew Walker, *Mng Member*
Travis Horn, *Agent*
Nicole Maneth, *Software Engr*
EMP: 31
SQ FT: 6,962
SALES: 2.5MM **Privately Held**
SIC: 6311 Life insurance

(G-9169)
PINNACLE REGIONAL HOSPITAL INC
12850 Metcalf Ave (66213-2622)
PHONE..................................913 541-0230
Doug Palzer, *CEO*
Douglas Palzer, *CEO*
Thomas Bembynista, *Med Doctor*
Christopher Hecker, *Director*
Scott Barnes, *Nurse*
EMP: 23 **EST:** 2009
SALES (est): 7.5MM **Privately Held**
SIC: 8062 General medical & surgical hospitals

(G-9170)
PIVOT COMPANIES LLC
Also Called: Employment Edge
11225 College Blvd (66210-2748)
PHONE..................................800 581-6398
Cary T Daniel, *CEO*
James Windmiller, *COO*
EMP: 13
SALES (est): 649.4K
SALES (corp-wide): 151.6MM **Publicly Held**
SIC: 7363 7361 Temporary help service; employment agencies
PA: Gee Group Inc.
7751 Belfort Pkwy Ste 150
Jacksonville FL 32256
630 954-0400

(G-9171)
PLANNED PRENTHOOD GREAT PLAINS (PA)
4401 W 109th St Ste 200 (66211-1303)
PHONE..................................913 312-5100
Laura McQuade, *CEO*
EMP: 45
SQ FT: 10,000
SALES: 4.6MM **Privately Held**
SIC: 8093 Birth control clinic

(G-9172)
PNC BANK NATIONAL ASSOCIATION
10851 Mastin St Ste 300 (66210-1690)
PHONE..................................913 253-9490
Phillip Frost, *Vice Pres*
Bill Stock, *Branch Mgr*
Chris Notestein, *Officer*
EMP: 15
SALES (corp-wide): 19.9B **Publicly Held**
SIC: 6022 State commercial banks
HQ: Pnc Bank, National Association
222 Delaware Ave
Wilmington DE 19801
877 762-2000

(G-9173)
POWER TECH ELECTRIC MOTORS LLC
9054 Cody St (66214-1730)
PHONE..................................913 888-4488
Lee Cochran, *Mng Member*
▲ **EMP:** 7
SQ FT: 12,500
SALES (est): 1MM **Privately Held**
WEB: www.powertechelectricmotors.com
SIC: 3621 Motors, electric

(G-9174)
PPG INDUSTRIES INC
Also Called: PPG 4622
7960 W 151st St (66223-2100)
PHONE..................................913 681-5573
Chris Tinsley, *Manager*
EMP: 24
SALES (corp-wide): 15.3B **Publicly Held**
WEB: www.ppg.com
SIC: 2851 Paints & allied products
PA: Ppg Industries, Inc.
1 Ppg Pl
Pittsburgh PA 15272
412 434-3131

(G-9175)
PPM SERVICES INC
11880 College Blvd # 300 (66210-2766)
PHONE..................................913 262-2585
Steve Sanford, *President*
Deanna Olson, *CFO*
EMP: 26
SQ FT: 9,700
SALES: 36MM
SALES (corp-wide): 336.4MM **Privately Held**
SIC: 6411 Insurance agents, brokers & service
PA: Norcal Mutual Insurance Co Inc
575 Market St Fl 10
San Francisco CA 94105
415 397-9703

(G-9176)
PRAIRIE ELDER HOMES LLC
Also Called: Prairie Elder Care
15354 Quivira Rd (66221-2452)
P.O. Box 26201 (66225-6201)
PHONE..................................913 257-5425
Mary Shoemaker,
EMP: 10
SQ FT: 3,500
SALES (est): 272.9K **Privately Held**
SIC: 8361 Home for the aged

(G-9177)
PRAIRIE LF CTR OF OVERLAND PK (PA)
10351 Barkley St (66212-1876)
PHONE..................................913 648-8077
David Putensen, *General Ptnr*
Dean Rasmussen, *General Ptnr*
EMP: 50
SQ FT: 68,000
SALES (est): 5.8MM **Privately Held**
SIC: 7991 Health club

(G-9178)
PRAIRIEBROOKE ARTS INC
7900 Santa Fe Dr (66204-3643)
PHONE..................................913 341-0333
Brooke Morehead, *President*
Megan Hoban, *Vice Pres*
Mike Morehead, *Vice Pres*
Rachel Prentiss, *Sales Staff*
EMP: 11
SALES (est): 1.3MM **Privately Held**
WEB: www.pbarts.com
SIC: 5999 7699 Art dealers; picture framing, custom

(G-9179)
PREFERRED PHYSICIANS MDCL RRG
Also Called: Ppm Information Solutions
11880 College Blvd # 300 (66210-2766)
PHONE..................................913 262-2585
Steve Sanford, *President*
Wade Willard, *Vice Pres*
Brad Anderson, *Opers Staff*
Deanna Olson, *CFO*
Linda McCumber, *Human Res Dir*
EMP: 26
SQ FT: 9,700
SALES: 25.2MM **Privately Held**
WEB: www.ppminfo.com
SIC: 6411 Insurance agents

(G-9180)
PREMIER DERMATOLOGIC
14404 Outlook St (66223-1226)
PHONE..................................913 327-1117
Tom Spenceri, *Manager*
EMP: 13
SALES (est): 1.2MM **Privately Held**
WEB: www.premierdermsurgery.com
SIC: 8011 Dermatologist

(G-9181)
PREMIER PAINTING CO LLC
8109 W 129th St (66213-3716)
PHONE..................................913 897-7000
Dean Denis,
Debra Dennis,
EMP: 18
SALES (est): 1.1MM **Privately Held**
SIC: 1721 Residential painting

(G-9182)
PREMIER PEDIATRICS PA
8675 College Blvd Ste 100 (66210-1863)
PHONE..................................913 384-5500
Deborah Winburn, *Principal*
Ashley Ahring, *Volunteer Dir*
EMP: 11
SALES (est): 1.1MM **Privately Held**
SIC: 8011 Pediatrician

(G-9183)
PREMIERE MARKETING GROUP INC (PA)
10561 Barkley St (66212-1860)
PHONE..................................913 362-9100
Lee Cries, *President*
Jeff Taubin, *President*
EMP: 9

SALES (est): 1.7MM **Privately Held**
WEB: www.premieremarketinggroup.com
SIC: 2731 Pamphlets: publishing only, not printed on site

(G-9184)
PRESIG HOLDINGS LLC
12318 Beverly St (66209-2760)
PHONE..................................913 706-1315
John Bertrand, *Partner*
EMP: 10
SALES (est): 217.5K **Privately Held**
SIC: 7371 7389 Computer software development;

(G-9185)
PRIAS PRAIRIE VIEW LLC
11415 W 87th Ter (66214-3212)
PHONE..................................816 437-9636
Scott Asner,
EMP: 10
SALES (est): 381.6K **Privately Held**
SIC: 6799 Venture capital companies

(G-9186)
PRIORITY LOGISTICS INC
6900 College Blvd Ste 470 (66211-1596)
P.O. Box 26682 (66225-6682)
PHONE..................................913 991-7281
Stephen Wilson, *President*
Gene Edwards, *COO*
David Burdick, *Vice Pres*
EMP: 20
SQ FT: 5,000
SALES: 83.8K **Privately Held**
WEB: www.prioritylogistics.com
SIC: 4731 8741 Freight forwarding; business management

(G-9187)
PRISM REAL ESTATE SERVICES LLC
8826 Santa Fe Dr Ste 300 (66212-3672)
PHONE..................................913 674-0438
Cathy Munoz, *Regional Mgr*
January Barr, *Accountant*
Barbara Bernstein, *Human Res Dir*
Jeremy Antes,
Heidi Merricks, *Administration*
EMP: 17
SALES (est): 819.6K **Privately Held**
SIC: 6531 Real estate agent, commercial

(G-9188)
PROFESSIONALS BUSINESS MGT INC
6703 W 91st St (66212-1458)
PHONE..................................913 888-1444
Robert L Anderson, *President*
EMP: 14
SQ FT: 4,600
SALES (est): 1.5MM **Privately Held**
SIC: 8742 8721 General management consultant; billing & bookkeeping service

(G-9189)
PROFESSNAL TOXICOLOGY SVCS INC
7917 Bond St (66214-1557)
PHONE..................................913 599-3535
Stanley Kammerer, *President*
Barbara Kammerer, *Info Tech Mgr*
EMP: 12
SALES (est): 1.2MM **Privately Held**
SIC: 8734 Testing laboratories

(G-9190)
PROFORMA MARKETING
8220 Nieman Rd (66214-1507)
PHONE..................................913 685-9098
Keith Steiniger, *Principal*
EMP: 10 **EST:** 2010
SALES (est): 1.4MM **Privately Held**
SIC: 7319 Advertising

(G-9191)
PROGRESS RAIL SERVICES CORP
8400 W 110th St Ste 300 (66210-2432)
PHONE..................................913 345-4807
West Hodges, *Vice Pres*
EMP: 20
SALES (corp-wide): 54.7B **Publicly Held**
SIC: 5088 8711 Railroad equipment & supplies; engineering services
HQ: Progress Rail Services Corporation
1600 Progress Dr
Albertville AL 35950
256 505-6421

(G-9192)
PROGRSSIVE TECH INTGRATORS LLC
Also Called: Pt Integrators
5901 College Blvd Ste 200 (66211-1937)
PHONE..................................913 663-0870
Darell Irby, *CFO*
Spencer Hibler, *Sr Ntwrk Engine*
EMP: 15
SALES (est): 1.4MM **Privately Held**
SIC: 7379

(G-9193)
PROMISE HOSP OVERLAND PK INC
6509 W 103rd St (66212-1728)
PHONE..................................913 275-5092
Richard Gold, *President*
Jim Hopwood, *Treasurer*
Peter Baranoff, *Director*
April Abbott, *Director*
Sarah Karvelas, *Director*
EMP: 71
SALES (est): 132.5K
SALES (corp-wide): 611.1MM **Privately Held**
SIC: 8062 General medical & surgical hospitals
PA: Promise Healthcare, Inc.
900 N Federal Hwy Ste 350
Boca Raton FL 33432
561 869-3100

(G-9194)
PROPERTY TAX ADVISORY GROUP
11300 Tomahawk Creek Pkwy (66211-2610)
PHONE..................................913 897-4744
Stephen Katz, *CEO*
Jeff Katz, *President*
Kevin Kombrink, *President*
Emily Porten, *Personnel*
EMP: 10
SALES (est): 803.1K **Privately Held**
WEB: www.ptag.com
SIC: 8721 Certified public accountant

(G-9195)
PROPHARMA GROUP LLC (HQ)
Also Called: Acadeus
8717 W 110th St Ste 300 (66210-2103)
PHONE..................................888 242-0559
Dawn Sherman, *President*
Jeff Hargroves, *Founder*
Rachel Bias, *Senior VP*
Joe Biehl, *Senior VP*
Steve Swantek, *Senior VP*
EMP: 60 **EST:** 2001
SALES: 91.4MM
SALES (corp-wide): 98.7MM **Privately Held**
WEB: www.propharmagroup.com
SIC: 8748 Business consulting
PA: Linden, Llc
111 S Wacker Dr Ste 3350
Chicago IL 60606
312 506-5657

(G-9196)
PROPIO LS LLC
Also Called: Propio Language Services
11020 King St Ste 420 (66210-1214)
P.O. Box 12204, Shawnee Mission (66282-2204)
PHONE..................................913 381-3143
Joseph Frackell, *Mng Member*
Rob Campbell,
Douglas Judd,
Bryan Simkims,
EMP: 12
SALES (est): 1.2MM **Privately Held**
WEB: www.propiospanish.com
SIC: 7389 Translation services

(G-9197)
PROSPERITY NETWRK ADVISORS LLC (PA)
100955 Lowell Ste 900 (66210)
PHONE..................................913 451-4501
Paul Ewing, *Mng Member*
EMP: 30
SALES (est): 1.1MM **Privately Held**
SIC: 6211 Investment firm, general brokerage

(G-9198)
PROTIVITI INC
9401 Indian Creek Pkwy # 730 (66210-2007)
PHONE..................................913 685-6200
Gordon Braun, *Managing Dir*
Claudia Stilwell, *Executive Asst*
EMP: 16
SALES (corp-wide): 5.8B **Publicly Held**
SIC: 8721 8742 Auditing services; industry specialist consultants
HQ: Protiviti Inc.
2884 Sand Hill Rd Ste 200
Menlo Park CA 94025
650 234-6000

(G-9199)
PRS INC
Also Called: Casemax
13160 Foster St Ste 100 (66213-2848)
PHONE..................................844 679-2273
Alan South, *CEO*
Kevin Tonovitz, *CFO*
EMP: 12
SALES: 550K **Privately Held**
SIC: 7371 Computer software development & applications

(G-9200)
PRUDENTIAL KANSAS CITY REALTY
8101 College Blvd Ste 210 (66210-2671)
PHONE..................................913 491-1550
David Cooper, *President*
Marilyn Worley, *Principal*
Mike Belzer, *CFO*
Karen Howell, *Accounting Mgr*
Joanna Williams, *Broker*
EMP: 100
SALES (est): 3.5MM **Privately Held**
SIC: 6531 Real estate agent, residential; real estate brokers & agents

(G-9201)
PS HOLDINGS LLC
Also Called: Apu Solutions
10881 Lowell Ave Ste 250 (66210-2162)
PHONE..................................913 599-1600
John Leach, *Ch of Bd*
Charles Lukens, *President*
Jeff Fears, *Senior Engr*
Evie Royse, *CFO*
Anthony Guerriero, *Accounts Mgr*
EMP: 30
SQ FT: 7,000
SALES (est): 3.1MM **Privately Held**
WEB: www.planetsalvage.com
SIC: 7371 Computer software development & applications

(G-9202)
PSC GROUP LLC
10561 Barkley St (66212-1860)
PHONE..................................847 517-7200
Jeff Ney, *Manager*
Kathy Brown, *Sr Consultant*
EMP: 20
SALES (corp-wide): 20.3MM **Privately Held**
SIC: 7371 7379 Computer software systems analysis & design, custom; computer related consulting services
PA: Psc Group, Llc
1051 Perimeter Dr Ste 500
Schaumburg IL 60173
847 517-7200

(G-9203)
PTA KANSAS CONGRESS OXFORD
12500 Switzer Rd (66213-1804)
PHONE..................................913 897-1719
Susan Swift, *Principal*
EMP: 11
SALES (est): 373.8K **Privately Held**
SIC: 8641 Parent-teachers' association

(G-9204)
PURDUM INC
Also Called: Purdum Construction
7301 W 133rd St Ste 100 (66213-4773)
PHONE..................................913 766-0835
Don Payne, *President*
Shea Groom, *Superintendent*
Mitchell Welty, *Superintendent*
Brad Stabenow, *Project Mgr*
Steve Purdum, *Associate*
EMP: 22
SQ FT: 6,000
SALES (est): 5.2MM **Privately Held**
WEB: www.purdco.com
SIC: 1542 Commercial & office building, new construction

(G-9205)
Q4 INDUSTRIES LLC
8261 Melrose Dr (66214-1625)
PHONE..................................913 894-6240
Alan Jacobs, *CEO*
Jason Kisor, *Accounts Mgr*
EMP: 12
SQ FT: 3,000
SALES (est): 6.5MM **Privately Held**
WEB: www.q4industries.com
SIC: 5113 5169 Industrial & personal service paper; specialty cleaning & sanitation preparations

(G-9206)
QAE ACQUISITION COMPANY LLC
12851 Foster St (66213-2705)
PHONE..................................913 814-9988
Chad Williams, *Principal*
EMP: 15
SALES (est): 505.8K
SALES (corp-wide): 450.5MM **Privately Held**
SIC: 6519 Real property lessors
HQ: Qualitytech, Lp
12851 Foster St
Overland Park KS 66213

(G-9207)
QSPEC SOLUTIONS INC
7949 Bond St (66214-1557)
PHONE..................................877 467-7732
Tim Alsin, *President*
Kenneth Richcreek, *General Mgr*
Chris Craig, *Technical Mgr*
Paige Brewer, *Project Engr*
James Curtice, *Treasurer*
EMP: 10 **EST:** 1999
SQ FT: 2,800
SALES: 821K **Privately Held**
WEB: www.qspec.com
SIC: 8748 Business consulting

(G-9208)
QTS FINANCE CORPORATION
12851 Foster St (66213-2705)
PHONE..................................913 814-9988
Chad Williams, *CEO*
EMP: 15
SALES (est): 1.2MM
SALES (corp-wide): 450.5MM **Privately Held**
SIC: 6211 Note brokers
HQ: Qualitytech, Lp
12851 Foster St
Overland Park KS 66213

(G-9209)
QTS INVSTMNT PROPS CARPATHIA
12851 Foster St (66213-2705)
PHONE..................................913 814-9988
Chad Williams, *CEO*
EMP: 21
SALES (est): 1.3MM
SALES (corp-wide): 450.5MM **Privately Held**
SIC: 6798 Real estate investment trusts
HQ: Qualitytech, Lp
12851 Foster St
Overland Park KS 66213

(G-9210)
QTS REALTY TRUST INC (PA)
12851 Foster St (66213-2705)
PHONE..................................913 814-9988
Chad L Williams, *CEO*

Matt Tyndall, *Owner*
Jan Daan Luycks, *Managing Dir*
Daniel T Bennewitz, *COO*
David S Robey, *COO*
EMP: 49 **EST:** 2013
SALES: 450.5MM **Privately Held**
SIC: 7374 6798 7375 Data processing service; real estate investment trusts; data base information retrieval

(G-9211)
QUALITY GROUP COMPANIES LLC (PA)
12851 Foster St Ste 205 (66213-2612)
PHONE..................................913 814-9988
Chad Williams, *CEO*
Christina Lamb, *COO*
Scott Burns, *Opers Staff*
Ronald Aviles, *Engineer*
William Matthews, *Engineer*
EMP: 22
SALES (est): 89MM **Privately Held**
SIC: 6531 Real estate agent, commercial

(G-9212)
QUALITY INV PRPTS LAND CO LLC
12851 Foster St Ste 100 (66213-2611)
PHONE..................................913 312-5500
Chad Williams,
EMP: 10
SALES (est): 485.5K **Privately Held**
SIC: 6552 Land subdividers & developers, commercial

(G-9213)
QUALITY INVESTMENT PROPERTIES
12851 Foster St Ste 205 (66213-2612)
PHONE..................................913 814-9988
EMP: 13
SALES (est): 1.9MM **Privately Held**
SIC: 6798 Real estate investment trusts

(G-9214)
QUALITY TECH SVCS FRT WORTH II
12851 Foster St (66213-2705)
PHONE..................................913 814-9988
Chad Williams, *CEO*
Daniel T Bennewitz, *COO*
James H Reinheart, *COO*
William H Schafer, *Exec VP*
Jeffrey H Berson, *CFO*
EMP: 17
SALES (est): 585.2K
SALES (corp-wide): 450.5MM **Privately Held**
SIC: 7376 Computer facilities management
HQ: Qualitytech, Lp
12851 Foster St
Overland Park KS 66213

(G-9215)
QUALITY TECH SVCS LENEXA LLC
12851 Foster St (66213-2705)
PHONE..................................913 814-9988
Chad Williams, *CEO*
EMP: 20
SALES (est): 1MM
SALES (corp-wide): 450.5MM **Privately Held**
SIC: 6512 Nonresidential building operators
HQ: Qualitytech, Lp
12851 Foster St
Overland Park KS 66213

(G-9216)
QUALITY TECH SVCS NRTHEAST LLC
12851 Foster St (66213-2705)
PHONE..................................913 814-9988
Chad Williams, *Principal*
EMP: 15
SALES (est): 505.4K
SALES (corp-wide): 450.5MM **Privately Held**
SIC: 7376 Computer facilities management
HQ: Qualitytech, Lp
12851 Foster St
Overland Park KS 66213

(G-9217)
QUALITY TECHNOLOGY SVCS LLC (DH)
12851 Foster St (66213-2705)
PHONE..................................913 814-9988
Chad Williams, *CEO*
Frank Eagle, *Partner*
Shelagh Montgomery, *Exec VP*
William H Schafer, *Exec VP*
Alan French, *Vice Pres*
EMP: 80
SQ FT: 36,000
SALES (est): 192.4MM
SALES (corp-wide): 450.5MM **Privately Held**
SIC: 7376 8741 Computer facilities management; management services

(G-9218)
QUALITY TECHNOLOGY SVCS NJ LLC
12851 Foster St (66213-2705)
PHONE..................................913 814-9988
Chad Williams, *CEO*
EMP: 15
SALES (est): 527.9K
SALES (corp-wide): 450.5MM **Privately Held**
SIC: 6519 Real property lessors
HQ: Qualitytech, Lp
12851 Foster St
Overland Park KS 66213

(G-9219)
QUALITYTECH LP (HQ)
12851 Foster St (66213-2705)
PHONE..................................877 787-3282
Chad Williams, *CEO*
Mark Waddington, *President*
Jay Ketterling, *Vice Pres*
William H Schafer, *CFO*
Tina Trimble, *Manager*
EMP: 23
SALES (est): 109.4MM
SALES (corp-wide): 450.5MM **Privately Held**
SIC: 7374 Data processing & preparation
PA: Qts Realty Trust, Inc.
12851 Foster St
Overland Park KS 66213
913 814-9988

(G-9220)
QWEST CORPORATION
15440 Long St (66221-2376)
PHONE..................................913 851-9024
EMP: 60
SALES (corp-wide): 17.4B **Publicly Held**
SIC: 4813 Telephone Communications
HQ: Qwest Corporation
100 Centurylink Dr
Monroe LA 71203
318 388-9000

(G-9221)
RALPH S PASSMAN & ASSOCIATES
Also Called: Acorn Underwriters
12218 Ash St (66209-3508)
PHONE..................................913 642-5432
Ralph S Passman, *President*
Shirley Passman, *Treasurer*
Stanford Zeldin, *Admin Sec*
EMP: 10
SALES (est): 1.1MM **Privately Held**
SIC: 6411 Insurance agents, brokers & service

(G-9222)
RAMBOLL ENVIRON US CORPORATION
7500 College Blvd Ste 920 (66210-4035)
PHONE..................................816 891-8228
EMP: 38
SALES (corp-wide): 314.9MM **Privately Held**
SIC: 8748 Environmental consultant
HQ: Ramboll Us Corporation
4350 Fairfax Dr Ste 300
Arlington VA 22203
703 516-2300

(G-9223)
RANCH MART INC
3705 W 95th St (66206-2036)
PHONE..................................913 649-0123
Robert D Regnier, *President*
EMP: 15
SQ FT: 210,000
SALES (est): 1.3MM
SALES (corp-wide): 2.9MM **Privately Held**
SIC: 6512 Commercial & industrial building operation
PA: Vic Regnier Builders Inc
3705 W 95th St
Overland Park KS 66206
913 649-0123

(G-9224)
RANDEL SOLUTIONS LLC
7300 W 110th St Ste 700 (66210-2332)
PHONE..................................703 459-7672
Roushan Kumar,
EMP: 12 **EST:** 2011
SALES (est): 514.1K **Privately Held**
SIC: 7379 Computer related consulting services

(G-9225)
RANDSTAD TECHNOLOGIES LLC
Also Called: Technisource
9200 Indian Creek Pkwy # 670 (66210-2008)
PHONE..................................913 696-0808
Michelle Ventress, *Director*
Jason Hight, *Tech Recruiter*
EMP: 10
SALES (corp-wide): 26.4B **Privately Held**
SIC: 7361 Employment agencies
HQ: Randstad Technologies, Llc
150 Presidential Way # 300
Woburn MA 01801
781 938-1910

(G-9226)
RARE MOON MEDIA
4551 W 107th St Ste 250 (66207-4012)
P.O. Box 14065, Lenexa (66285-4065)
PHONE..................................913 951-8360
Jeremy Shaffer, *CEO*
EMP: 11 **EST:** 2011
SALES (est): 604.7K **Privately Held**
SIC: 4899 Communication services

(G-9227)
RAU CONSTRUCTION COMPANY
9101 W 110th St Ste 150 (66210-1449)
PHONE..................................913 642-6000
Gus R Meyer, *President*
H Stanley Meyer, *Chairman*
Dan R Meyer, *Senior VP*
Ronald B Anderson, *Vice Pres*
Jason Meyer, *Project Mgr*
EMP: 44
SQ FT: 4,400
SALES (est): 16.2MM **Privately Held**
WEB: www.rauconstruction.com
SIC: 1542 Commercial & office building, new construction; commercial & office buildings, renovation & repair

(G-9228)
REAL MEDIA LLC
9101 Barton St (66214-1720)
PHONE..................................913 894-8989
Brad Burrow,
Tracie Burrow,
EMP: 12
SQ FT: 8,000
SALES (est): 1.9MM **Privately Held**
WEB: www.realme.com
SIC: 7819 Video tape or disk reproduction

(G-9229)
REDMON HOUSING LLC
Also Called: Rebuild Homes
10200 W 75th St Ste 100 (66204-2242)
PHONE..................................913 432-4945
Robert Redmon, *Mng Member*
EMP: 12 **EST:** 1955
SALES (est): 1.3MM **Privately Held**
SIC: 1542 Commercial & office buildings, renovation & repair

(G-9230)
REDSTONE LOGISTICS LLC (PA)
8500 W 110th St Ste 260 (66210-1892)
PHONE..................................913 998-7905
James Ritchie, *CEO*
Eric Hissong, *Accounts Mgr*
Duncan Hopwood,
Chris Kovacs,
EMP: 20
SALES (est): 13MM **Privately Held**
SIC: 4731 Freight transportation arrangement

(G-9231)
REECE & NICHOLS REALTORS INC
8410 W 128th St (66213-3718)
PHONE..................................913 620-3419
Joanna Mispagel, *Principal*
Kate Johnson, *Agent*
Camilla Jones, *Real Est Agnt*
EMP: 34
SALES (corp-wide): 225.3B **Publicly Held**
SIC: 6531 Real estate agent, residential; real estate brokers & agents
HQ: Reece & Nichols Realtors, Inc.
11601 Granada St
Leawood KS 66211
913 491-1001

(G-9232)
REFRESH MEDICAL SPA LLC
13453 Switzer Rd (66213-3301)
PHONE..................................913 681-6200
Angela Garner MD, *Principal*
EMP: 14
SALES (est): 427.8K **Privately Held**
SIC: 7991 Spas

(G-9233)
RELATION INSURANCE SERVICES
9225 Indian Creek Pkwy (66210-2009)
PHONE..................................800 955-1991
Edward Nathan Page, *President*
Angela King, *Vice Pres*
EMP: 40
SALES (est): 8.4MM
SALES (corp-wide): 146MM **Privately Held**
SIC: 6411 Insurance agents
PA: Relation Insurance, Inc.
1277 Treat Blvd Ste 400
Walnut Creek CA 94597
800 404-4969

(G-9234)
RELATION INSURANCE SERVICES
9225 Indian Creek Pkwy # 700 (66210-2009)
P.O. Box 25936 (66225-5936)
PHONE..................................800 955-1991
EMP: 10
SALES (corp-wide): 178.5MM **Privately Held**
SIC: 6411 Insurance Agent/Broker
HQ: Relation Insurance Services - Specialty Risk, Inc.
7400 College Blvd
Overland Park KS 66210
913 327-0200

(G-9235)
REPORTING SERVICES COMPANY
Also Called: AAA Court Reporting Company
8001 Conser St Ste 200 (66204-3409)
PHONE..................................913 385-2699
Timothy Stein, *President*
Kelly Smith, *Corp Secy*
EMP: 20
SALES (est): 1MM **Privately Held**
WEB: www.aaacourtreporters.com
SIC: 7338 Court reporting service

(G-9236)
RESONATE RELATIONSHIP CLINIC
7381 W 133rd St (66213-4750)
PHONE..................................913 647-8092
Grant Wood, *Principal*

EMP: 10 **EST:** 2010
SALES (est): 191.9K **Privately Held**
SIC: 8322 Family (marriage) counseling

(G-9237)
RESTAURANT PURCHASING SVCS LLC
Also Called: Restaurantlink
12101 W 110th St Ste 300 (66210-3935)
PHONE..................................800 548-2292
Richard King, *President*
Misty Winter, *Vice Pres*
EMP: 10 **EST:** 2015
SALES (est): 1.2MM **Privately Held**
SIC: 8742 Restaurant & food services consultants

(G-9238)
RESULTS TECHNOLOGY INC (PA)
10333 W 84th Ter (66214-1639)
PHONE..................................913 928-8300
John E French, *CEO*
Patrick Murphy, *Exec VP*
Evonne Johanson, *Vice Pres*
Toni Morris, *Vice Pres*
Patrick A Murphy, *Vice Pres*
EMP: 27
SQ FT: 15,000
SALES (est): 8.8MM **Privately Held**
WEB: www.csourcekc.com
SIC: 5045 7373 Computers, peripherals & software; systems integration services

(G-9239)
RETIREMENT PLANNING GROUP INC
4811 W 136th St (66224-5924)
PHONE..................................913 498-8898
Kevin Conard, *CEO*
Suzanne McDonald, *COO*
David Dreher, *Vice Pres*
Dwight Twillman, *Vice Pres*
EMP: 15 **EST:** 2003
SALES (est): 273.4K **Privately Held**
SIC: 7389 Financial services

(G-9240)
RHYCOM ADVERTISING
10975 Grandview Dr (66210-1564)
PHONE..................................913 451-9102
Rick Rhyner, *President*
EMP: 10
SALES (est): 1.2MM **Privately Held**
WEB: www.rhycom.com
SIC: 7311 Advertising consultant

(G-9241)
RIDEN SERVICE COMPANY INC
Also Called: Riden Plumbing
11306 W 89th St (66214-1702)
PHONE..................................913 432-8495
Dan Riden, *President*
EMP: 11
SALES: 1.5MM **Privately Held**
SIC: 1711 Plumbing contractors

(G-9242)
RIGDON INC
Also Called: 360 Commercial Cleaning
13827 Mackey St (66223-1122)
PHONE..................................913 322-9274
Kerri Rigdon, *President*
EMP: 11 **EST:** 1992
SALES (est): 458K **Privately Held**
WEB: www.rigdoninc.com
SIC: 7349 1799 Exhaust hood or fan cleaning; window cleaning; cleaning building exteriors; cleaning new buildings after construction

(G-9243)
RISKANALYTICS LLC
6700 Antioch Rd Ste 100 (66204-1392)
PHONE..................................913 685-6526
Jeff Sull, *CEO*
Richard Detrick, *Managing Prtnr*
Kurt Lee, *COO*
Thomas Currie, *Vice Pres*
Bill Parish, *Sales Associate*
EMP: 30 **EST:** 2013
SALES: 4MM **Privately Held**
SIC: 7382 Security systems services

(G-9244)
RIVER OAK MECHANICAL
7800 Nieman Rd (66214-1491)
PHONE..................................573 338-7203
Landon Cummins, *Principal*
EMP: 11
SALES (est): 1.3MM **Privately Held**
SIC: 8711 Mechanical engineering

(G-9245)
RIVERPOINT GROUP ILLINOIS LLC
8700 Indian Creek Pkwy (66210-1563)
PHONE..................................913 663-2002
Dominic Schilt, *Branch Mgr*
EMP: 15
SALES (corp-wide): 7MM **Privately Held**
SIC: 7379
PA: Riverpoint Group Of Illinois, Llc
6400 Shafer Ct Ste 275
Rosemont IL 60018
847 233-9600

(G-9246)
RNN ENTERPRISES LLC
Also Called: Soft Armor
15520 Windsor St (66224-5904)
PHONE..................................913 499-1230
Patrick Dierks, *Mng Member*
EMP: 17
SALES: 800K **Privately Held**
SIC: 3949 Shooting equipment & supplies, general

(G-9247)
ROBERT HALF INTERNATIONAL INC
7400 College Blvd Ste 200 (66210-4028)
PHONE..................................913 451-7600
Melanie Franklin, *Branch Mgr*
EMP: 92
SALES (corp-wide): 5.8B **Publicly Held**
SIC: 7361 Placement agencies
PA: Robert Half International Inc.
2884 Sand Hill Rd Ste 200
Menlo Park CA 94025
650 234-6000

(G-9248)
ROBERT HALF INTERNATIONAL INC
10851 Mastin St (66210-1769)
PHONE..................................816 421-6623
Jill Reyes, *Branch Mgr*
EMP: 92
SALES (corp-wide): 5.8B **Publicly Held**
SIC: 7361 Placement agencies
PA: Robert Half International Inc.
2884 Sand Hill Rd Ste 200
Menlo Park CA 94025
650 234-6000

(G-9249)
ROBERT HALF INTERNATIONAL INC
7400 College Blvd Ste 200 (66210-4028)
PHONE..................................913 451-1014
EMP: 15
SALES (corp-wide): 4.2B **Publicly Held**
SIC: 7361 Employment Agency
PA: Robert Half International Inc.
2884 Sand Hill Rd Ste 200
Menlo Park CA 94025
650 234-6000

(G-9250)
ROBERT J HAMILTON INC
Also Called: Hamilton Bob Plumbing Htg & AC
7899 Frontage Rd (66204-2311)
PHONE..................................913 888-4262
Bob Hamilton, *CEO*
EMP: 30
SQ FT: 3,500
SALES (est): 3.7MM **Privately Held**
WEB: www.bobhamiltonplumbing.com
SIC: 1711 Plumbing contractors

(G-9251)
ROBERT WILSON CO INC
Also Called: R Wilson Co
10530 Marty St (66212-2551)
PHONE..................................913 642-1500
Robert Wilson III, *President*
◆ **EMP:** 50 **EST:** 1975
SQ FT: 21,000
SALES (est): 10.6MM **Privately Held**
SIC: 5722 5719 5064 5063 Fans, electric; lighting fixtures; lamps & lamp shades; fans, household: electric; lighting fixtures; lamps: floor, boudoir, desk

(G-9252)
ROBERTS GROUP INC (PA)
10076 Hemlock Dr (66212-3426)
PHONE..................................913 381-3930
Robert S Kirkendall, *Director*
EMP: 5
SALES (est): 818.2K **Privately Held**
SIC: 5084 3089 7389 Industrial machinery & equipment; injection molding of plastics;

(G-9253)
ROCKGATE MANAGEMENT COMPANY
Also Called: Hawthorn Suites
10990 Quivira Rd Ste 200 (66210-1284)
PHONE..................................402 331-0101
Kevin Oats, *Manager*
EMP: 27
SALES (corp-wide): 17.5MM **Privately Held**
SIC: 7011 Hotels & motels
PA: Rockgate Management Company
10990 Quivira Rd Ste 210
Overland Park KS 66210
913 428-1940

(G-9254)
RODROCK & ASSOCIATES INC
Also Called: Rodrock Development
12643 Hemlock St (66213-1455)
P.O. Box 25390, Shawnee Mission (66225-5390)
PHONE..................................913 533-9980
Darol Rodrock, *President*
Neil Mackay, *Supervisor*
Karen Rodrock, *Admin Sec*
EMP: 30
SALES: 30MM **Privately Held**
WEB: www.rodrock.com
SIC: 6531 Real estate agent, residential

(G-9255)
ROESER HOMES LLC
P.O. Box 24165 (66283-4165)
PHONE..................................913 220-7477
Austin Roeser, *Principal*
Thad Snider, *Vice Pres*
EMP: 10
SALES (corp-wide): 1.7MM **Privately Held**
SIC: 1521 New construction, single-family houses
PA: Roeser Homes, Llc
26143 W 108th Pl
Olathe KS

(G-9256)
ROOFING SOLUTIONS INC
6728 W 153rd St (66223-3158)
PHONE..................................913 897-1840
Jim Williams, *President*
EMP: 10
SQ FT: 2,500
SALES (est): 844.4K **Privately Held**
WEB: www.roofingsolutionsinc.com
SIC: 1761 Roofing contractor

(G-9257)
ROONEY ENTERPRISES CORPORATION
Also Called: Griswold Home Care
3861 W 95th St (66206-2038)
PHONE..................................913 325-4770
Brian Rooney, *President*
EMP: 35 **EST:** 2016
SALES (est): 152.6K **Privately Held**
SIC: 8082 Home health care services

(G-9258)
ROSS CONSULTANTS INC
6230 W 137th St Apt 104 (66223-3438)
PHONE..................................213 926-2090
Rick B Ross, *President*
EMP: 20
SQ FT: 3,500
SALES: 250K **Privately Held**
SIC: 8742 Restaurant & food services consultants

(G-9259)
ROUSE FRETS WHITE GOSS GENTILE
Also Called: Douthit Frets Rouse Gentile
5250 W 116th Pl Ste 400 (66211-7827)
PHONE..................................913 387-1600
Evan Douthit, *Principal*
Tim Frest, *Principal*
Doug Gentile, *Principal*
Randy Rhodes, *Principal*
Chuck Rouse, *Principal*
EMP: 40
SALES (est): 4.9MM **Privately Held**
WEB: www.dfrglaw.com
SIC: 8111 General practice law office

(G-9260)
ROYAL MECHANICAL SERVICES INC
19175 Metcalf Ave (66085-8523)
P.O. Box 23116 (66283-0116)
PHONE..................................913 897-3436
Bradley Shyver, *CEO*
D Timothy Shyver, *Vice Pres*
Chris Willis, *Project Mgr*
Nathan Shyver, *CFO*
Robert Smith, *Sales Staff*
EMP: 20
SQ FT: 7,000
SALES: 8.7MM **Privately Held**
WEB: www.royalsvcs.com
SIC: 8742 Construction project management consultant

(G-9261)
RPMS LLC
Also Called: Rep Profit Management Systems
11771 W 112th St Ste 200 (66210-2782)
P.O. Box 15298, Lenexa (66285-5298)
PHONE..................................800 776-7435
Angela Scott, *Engineer*
Brent Charles,
James Adam,
EMP: 11
SQ FT: 2,000
SALES (est): 797.8K **Privately Held**
SIC: 7372 Prepackaged software

(G-9262)
RSVP MEDSPA LLC
13300 Metcalf Ave (66213-2804)
PHONE..................................913 387-1104
Brenda Roberts,
EMP: 12
SQ FT: 2,600
SALES (est): 702.3K **Privately Held**
SIC: 7991 Spas

(G-9263)
RTS FINANCIAL SERVICE INC
9300 Metcalf Ave (66212-1463)
PHONE..................................877 642-8553
William Ryan, *President*
Joshua Hanson, *Business Mgr*
Ryan Steigleder, *Business Mgr*
Ken Bowman, *CFO*
Martin Ryan, *VP Sales*
EMP: 150
SALES (est): 37.8MM
SALES (corp-wide): 105.7MM **Privately Held**
WEB: www.rtsfinancial.com
SIC: 6153 Short-term business credit
PA: Shamrock Trading Corporation
9300 Metcalf Ave
Overland Park KS 66212
877 642-8553

(G-9264)
RX SAVINGS LLC
Also Called: Rx Savings Solutions
11225 College Blvd # 400 (66210-2771)
PHONE..................................913 815-3139
Michael REA, *CEO*
Ashley Moyer, *Sales Executive*
Emily Schuster, *Marketing Staff*
David Bledsoe, *Analyst*
Michael REA,
EMP: 12
SALES (est): 1.5MM **Privately Held**
SIC: 7379 Computer related consulting services

(G-9265)
RYAN LAWN & TREE INC (PA)
9120 Barton St (66214-1719)
PHONE..................................913 381-1505
Larry Ryan, *President*
Daryl Nutt, *CFO*
Kathy Ryan, *Treasurer*
Ann Germain, *Controller*
Pamela Costanzo, *Accounting Mgr*
EMP: 63
SQ FT: 20,000
SALES: 28.6MM **Privately Held**
WEB: www.ryanlawn.com
SIC: 0783 0782 Ornamental shrub & tree services; lawn services

(G-9266)
RYAN TRANSPORTATION SVC INC (HQ)
9350 Metcalf Ave (66212-1463)
PHONE..................................800 860-7926
William Ryan, *Chairman*
Dustin Bolton, *Business Mgr*
Chris Ensley, *Business Mgr*
Ryan Terry, *Business Mgr*
Matt Emison, *Senior VP*
EMP: 150
SQ FT: 30,000
SALES (est): 63.3MM
SALES (corp-wide): 105.7MM **Privately Held**
WEB: www.ryantrans.com
SIC: 4731 Transportation agents & brokers
PA: Shamrock Trading Corporation
9300 Metcalf Ave
Overland Park KS 66212
877 642-8553

(G-9267)
S C F INC
Also Called: Fire Sprinkler Consultant
9225 Indian Creek Pkwy (66210-2009)
PHONE..................................913 722-3473
Hasu Doshi, *President*
Subhi Doshi, *Treasurer*
Lorraine Adcock, *Marketing Staff*
Madhavi Vora, *Office Mgr*
Chris Woker, *Manager*
EMP: 38
SQ FT: 10,416
SALES: 980K **Privately Held**
SIC: 8711 8748 7389 Fire protection engineering; business consulting; fire protection service other than forestry or public

(G-9268)
S&K
13030 W 105th St (66215-2177)
PHONE..................................913 634-2234
Sam Santora, *Partner*
EMP: 25
SALES: 500K **Privately Held**
SIC: 1741 Masonry & other stonework

(G-9269)
SAFE HOME INC
P.O. Box 4563 (66204-0563)
PHONE..................................913 432-9300
Sheri Bird, *Principal*
Janee Hanzlick, *Principal*
Sharon Katz, *Exec Dir*
EMP: 32
SALES (est): 2.9MM **Privately Held**
WEB: www.safehome-ks.org
SIC: 8322 Emergency shelters

(G-9270)
SAFELY DELICIOUS LLC
13029 Flint St (66213-4460)
PHONE..................................913 963-5140
Lisa Ragan, *Principal*
EMP: 11
SALES (est): 1.6MM **Privately Held**
SIC: 2099 Food preparations

(G-9271)
SAGE RESTORATION LLC
6520 W 110th St Ste 201b (66211-1898)
PHONE..................................913 905-0500
Stephanie Sage, *Owner*
EMP: 11 **EST:** 2013
SALES (est): 513.9K **Privately Held**
SIC: 7349 Building maintenance services

(G-9272)
SAICON CONSULTANTS INC (PA)
9300 W 110th St Ste 650 (66210-1487)
PHONE..................................913 451-1178
Ramesh Lokre, *CEO*
Swati Yelmar, *President*
Dan Valia, *Vice Pres*
Shirish Shah, *Controller*
Dinesh Wagalgave, *Finance*
EMP: 14
SQ FT: 5,700
SALES: 46MM **Privately Held**
WEB: www.saiconinc.com
SIC: 7373 7379 Computer systems analysis & design; computer related consulting services

(G-9273)
SAINT LKES S SRGERY CENTRE LLC
12541 Foster St Ste 120 (66213-2307)
PHONE..................................913 317-3200
Mary Lee Fortin, *Principal*
Nueterra Holdings, *Mng Member*
Ronald Nichol, *Family Practiti*
EMP: 18
SALES (est): 3.1MM **Privately Held**
SIC: 8011 Ambulatory surgical center

(G-9274)
SAINT LUKES PRIMARY CARE AT
4061 Indian Creek Pkwy # 200 (66207-4030)
PHONE..................................913 317-7990
Dr Bradly Palmer, *Principal*
Carol Wood, *Purch Agent*
Gary Christian, *Engineer*
Amy Nachtegal, *CFO*
Christopher E Bowser, *Med Doctor*
EMP: 72
SALES (est): 7.8MM **Privately Held**
SIC: 8093 8011 Specialty outpatient clinics; offices & clinics of medical doctors; primary care medical clinic

(G-9275)
SAINT LUKES SOUTH HOSPITAL INC
12541 Foster St Ste 300 (66213-2304)
PHONE..................................913 317-7990
Nancy E Ogden, *Manager*
EMP: 11
SALES (est): 327.3K
SALES (corp-wide): 138MM **Privately Held**
SIC: 8041 Offices & clinics of chiropractors
PA: Saint Luke's South Hospital, Inc.
12300 Metcalf Ave
Shawnee Mission KS 66213
913 317-7000

(G-9276)
SALON 103
10344 Metcalf Ave (66212-1866)
PHONE..................................913 383-9040
Lorna Olsen, *Owner*
EMP: 12
SALES (est): 142.5K **Privately Held**
SIC: 7231 7241 Beauty shops; barber shops

(G-9277)
SALON MISSION INC
Also Called: Salon Mission & Day Spa
3791 W 95th St (66206-2036)
PHONE..................................913 642-8333
Ed Kelly, *President*
Misty Kelly, *Vice Pres*
EMP: 25
SALES (est): 519.4K **Privately Held**
SIC: 7231 Unisex hair salons

(G-9278)
SANDERS WARREN & RUSSELL LLP
40 Corporate Woods Ste (66210)
PHONE..................................913 234-6100
William Sanders Jr, *Partner*
Marcia Toplikar, *Office Mgr*
Angela Shores, *Legal Staff*
Joe McGreevy, *Associate*
EMP: 50
SALES (est): 3MM **Privately Held**
SIC: 8111 General practice attorney, lawyer

(G-9279)
SANTA FE PRODUCTS LLC
4307 Merriam Dr (66203-1337)
PHONE..................................913 362-6611
EMP: 16
SALES (est): 301.7K **Privately Held**
SIC: 7822 Motion picture & tape distribution

(G-9280)
SARA IT SOLUTIONS INC
9393 W 110th St (66210-1442)
PHONE..................................913 269-6980
Gurinder Singh, *CEO*
EMP: 10
SALES (est): 217.5K **Privately Held**
SIC: 7371 Software programming applications

(G-9281)
SARIN ENERGY INC
Also Called: Sarin Energy Solutions
9209 Quivira Rd (66215-3905)
PHONE..................................913 912-3235
Inayat Noormohmad, *President*
Rebeccah Stanley, *Manager*
Stephen Downing, *Director*
EMP: 12
SALES (est): 1.2MM **Privately Held**
SIC: 1751 Lightweight steel framing (metal stud) installation

(G-9282)
SATELLITE ENGRG GROUP INC
10814 W 78th St (66214-1262)
PHONE..................................913 324-6000
Arthur Liebenthal, *President*
Bruce Riesman, *Vice Pres*
Scott Widney, *Engineer*
Chris Childs, *Sales Staff*
John Strandell, *Sales Staff*
EMP: 20
SQ FT: 12,000
SALES (est): 21.4MM **Privately Held**
SIC: 7629 5065 5063 Telecommunication equipment repair (except telephones); electronic parts; antennas, receiving, satellite dishes

(G-9283)
SCHRAAD & ASSOCIATES
10100 W 119th St Ste 102 (66213-4100)
P.O. Box 481517, Kansas City MO (64148-1517)
PHONE..................................913 661-2404
Fax: 913 661-2481
EMP: 15
SALES (est): 2.8MM **Privately Held**
SIC: 5141 Whol General Groceries

(G-9284)
SCHUFF STEEL COMPANY
Also Called: Schuff Steel Midwest
6701 W 64th St (66202-4123)
PHONE..................................913 677-2485
Dennis Randall, *Manager*
Earl Horton, *Manager*
EMP: 18 **Publicly Held**
SIC: 1791 3441 Structural steel erection; building components, structural steel
HQ: Schuff Steel Company
3003 N Central Ave # 700
Phoenix AZ 85012
602 252-7787

(G-9285)
SCOTWOOD INDUSTRIES INC
12980 Metcalf Ave Ste 240 (66213-2646)
PHONE..................................913 851-3500
Chase Wilson, *CEO*
Mary Helen Wilson, *Ch of Bd*
Jim Wilson, *General Mgr*
Rick Belzer, *VP Mktg*
Sharon Chartier, *Manager*
▲ **EMP:** 50
SQ FT: 4,300
SALES (est): 65.8MM **Privately Held**
SIC: 5169 5191 Industrial chemicals; antifreeze compounds; fertilizers & agricultural chemicals

(G-9286)
SEARLES VALLEY MINERALS INC (DH)
9401 Indian Creek Pkwy # 1000 (66210-2091)
PHONE..................................913 344-9500
Avinash Puri, *President*
Don Pemberton, *Principal*
John F Tancredi, *Principal*
Burnell Blanchard, *Vice Pres*
Stephen W Cole, *Vice Pres*
◆ **EMP:** 26
SQ FT: 14,872
SALES (est): 792.4MM
SALES (corp-wide): 873MM **Privately Held**
WEB: www.svminerals.com
SIC: 1479 Salt & sulfur mining
HQ: Svm Minerals Holdings Inc
9401 Indian Creek Pkwy
Overland Park KS 66210
913 344-9500

(G-9287)
SEASONAL SOLUTIONS LLC
6920 W 153rd St Ste A (66223-3117)
PHONE..................................913 685-4222
Paula Wolff, *CFO*
Barry M Wolff, *Mng Member*
Paula J Wolff,
EMP: 14
SQ FT: 1,800
SALES: 700K **Privately Held**
SIC: 0781 Landscape services

(G-9288)
SEBRING & CO
9261 Cody St (66214-1735)
PHONE..................................913 888-8141
David C Edwards, *President*
Anne S Edwards, *Corp Secy*
EMP: 10
SQ FT: 22,000
SALES (est): 1.5MM **Privately Held**
SIC: 5023 5131 Window shades; venetian blinds; window covering parts & accessories; drapery material, woven; piece goods & other fabrics

(G-9289)
SELECT HOTELS GROUP LLC
Also Called: Hyatt Place KS Cty/Overlnd Pk
5001 W 110th St (66211-1225)
PHONE..................................913 491-9002
John McEntee, *Branch Mgr*
EMP: 35
SALES (corp-wide): 4.4B **Publicly Held**
WEB: www.amerisuites.com
SIC: 7011 Hotels & motels
HQ: Select Hotels Group, L.L.C.
71 S Wacker Dr Ste 2500
Chicago IL 60606
312 750-1234

(G-9290)
SELECT MEDICAL CORPORATION
11330 W 135th St (66221-8100)
PHONE..................................913 239-9539
Randy Russell, *Branch Mgr*
EMP: 13
SALES (corp-wide): 5B **Publicly Held**
WEB: www.selectmedicalcorp.com
SIC: 8049 Physical therapist
HQ: Select Medical Corporation
4714 Gettysburg Rd
Mechanicsburg PA 17055
717 972-1100

(G-9291)
SELECT MEDICAL CORPORATION
Also Called: Select Physical Therapy
10730 Nall Ave Ste 204 (66211-1202)
PHONE..................................913 385-0075
Kim Salanski, *Manager*
EMP: 11
SALES (corp-wide): 5B **Publicly Held**
WEB: www.selectmedicalcorp.com
SIC: 8322 8049 Rehabilitation services; physical therapist
HQ: Select Medical Corporation
4714 Gettysburg Rd
Mechanicsburg PA 17055
717 972-1100

GEOGRAPHIC

(G-9292)
SELECTIVE SITE CONSULTANTS INC (PA)
7171 W 95th St Ste 600 (66212-2300)
PHONE..................................913 438-7700
James Steele, *President*
Larry Louk, *Vice Pres*
Terry Super, *Vice Pres*
Daniel Christie, *Project Mgr*
EMP: 45
SQ FT: 20,000
SALES: 17MM **Privately Held**
WEB: www.selectivesite.com
SIC: 8742 8748 8711 Quality assurance consultant; communications consulting; professional engineer

(G-9293)
SELEX ES INC (DH)
11300 W 89th St (66214-1702)
PHONE..................................913 945-2600
Michael Warner, *CEO*
Randy Harper, *VP Mfg*
Roger Cook, *Engineer*
Robert King, *Engineer*
David Orr, *Controller*
▼ **EMP:** 100
SALES (est): 21MM
SALES (corp-wide): 8.9B **Privately Held**
WEB: www.selex-si-us.com
SIC: 3812 3993 Instrument landing systems (ILS), airborne or ground; signs & advertising specialties

(G-9294)
SENIO LIVIN RETIR COMMU LLC
13800 Metcalf Ave (66223-1200)
PHONE..................................913 534-8872
Eric Donley, *Info Tech Mgr*
EMP: 116
SALES (corp-wide): 92.2MM **Privately Held**
SIC: 6411 Pension & retirement plan consultants
PA: Senior Living Retirement Communities, Llc
701 Maiden Choice Ln
Baltimore MD 21228
410 242-2880

(G-9295)
SENTINEL REAL ESTATE CORP
Also Called: Skyler Ridge Apartments
7171 W 115th St (66210-1889)
PHONE..................................913 451-8976
Molly Heinlein, *Manager*
EMP: 11
SALES (corp-wide): 2MM **Privately Held**
WEB: www.andoverplaceapartments.com
SIC: 6513 Apartment building operators
HQ: Sentinel Real Estate Corporation
1251 Ave Of The Americas
New York NY 10020
212 408-2900

(G-9296)
SERVANT CHRSTN CMNTY FUNDATION
Also Called: Christian Cmnty Fundation Kans
7171 W 95th St Ste 501 (66212-2254)
PHONE..................................913 310-0279
William High, *Principal*
Kathy Hoeck, *Director*
Julliane Stark, *Administration*
EMP: 30 **EST:** 2000
SALES: 1.8MM **Privately Held**
SIC: 8699 Charitable organization

(G-9297)
SERVANT FOUNDATION
Also Called: National Christian Charita
7171 W 95th St Ste 501 (66212-2254)
PHONE..................................913 310-0279
Bill High, *CEO*
Ken Bowers, *COO*
EMP: 25
SALES: 1.4MM **Privately Held**
SIC: 8641 Civic social & fraternal associations

(G-9298)
SERVERVAULT LLC
12851 Foster St (66213-2705)
PHONE..................................913 814-9988
Chad Williams, *CEO*
Bill Ranney, *CFO*
Brent Bensten, *CTO*
Peter Weber,
EMP: 14
SALES (est): 150.8K
SALES (corp-wide): 450.5MM **Privately Held**
WEB: www.servervault.com
SIC: 7374 Data processing & preparation
HQ: Carpathia Acquisition, Llc
12851 Foster St
Overland Park KS 66213
913 312-5514

(G-9299)
SERVICE TECHNOLOGIES MIDWEST
6800 W 64th St Ste 101 (66202-4179)
PHONE..................................913 671-3340
Debra Van Dyne, *Office Mgr*
EMP: 50
SALES (est): 2.9MM **Privately Held**
SIC: 1542 Bank building construction

(G-9300)
SETTLE INN
Also Called: Crown Group
4401 W 107th St (66207-4002)
PHONE..................................913 381-5700
EMP: 13
SALES (est): 520K **Privately Held**
SIC: 7011 Hotel/Motel Operation

(G-9301)
SEW EASY SEWING CENTER INC
9840 W 87th St (66212-4564)
PHONE..................................913 341-1122
J C Mapel, *President*
Dutch Mapel, *Vice Pres*
EMP: 13
SQ FT: 1,840
SALES (est): 1.2MM **Privately Held**
SIC: 7699 5722 Sewing machine repair shop; sewing machines

(G-9302)
SHAMROCK TRADING CORPORATION (PA)
9300 Metcalf Ave (66212-1463)
PHONE..................................877 642-8553
William Ryan, *President*
JP McNeely, *Business Mgr*
Patrick Kellerman, *Vice Pres*
Ken Bowman, *CFO*
Alex Boyd, *Sales Staff*
EMP: 400
SALES (est): 105.7MM **Privately Held**
SIC: 4731 6153 8742 7323 Freight transportation arrangement; short-term business credit; management consulting services; credit reporting services

(G-9303)
SHANER APPRAISALS INC
10990 Quivira Rd Ste 100 (66210-2016)
PHONE..................................913 451-1451
Laird Goldsborough, *President*
Bernie Shaner, *Chairman*
EMP: 19
SQ FT: 3,000
SALES (est): 2.2MM **Privately Held**
WEB: www.shanerappraisals.com
SIC: 6531 Appraiser, real estate

(G-9304)
SHARON SIGMA REALTORS LLC
5267 W 95th St (66207-3201)
PHONE..................................913 381-6794
Sharon Sigman,
EMP: 23
SQ FT: 2,500
SALES: 1.5MM **Privately Held**
WEB: www.sharonsigman.net
SIC: 6531 Real estate agent, residential

(G-9305)
SHAWNEE MISSION PEDIATRICS PA
7450 Kessler Ln Ste 105 (66204-2357)
PHONE..................................913 362-1660
Robert V Jackson MD, *President*
Robert Maxwell MD, *Vice Pres*
Sherri D Martin, *Med Doctor*
Thomas H Olsen MD, *Admin Sec*
Deborah McCurnin, *Pediatrics*
EMP: 22
SALES (est): 2.7MM **Privately Held**
SIC: 8011 Pediatrician

(G-9306)
SHC SERVICES INC
6700 Antioch Rd Ste 120 (66204-1200)
PHONE..................................913 652-9229
EMP: 238
SALES (corp-wide): 241MM **Privately Held**
SIC: 8049 7361 Nutrition specialist; employment agencies
PA: Shc Services, Inc.
1640 Redstone Center Dr # 200
Park City UT 84098
435 645-0788

(G-9307)
SHI INTERNATIONAL CORP
12980 Foster St (66213-2703)
PHONE..................................512 226-3984
Mike Schelbert, *Branch Mgr*
EMP: 12
SALES (corp-wide): 9.7B **Privately Held**
SIC: 5045 Computer peripheral equipment; computer software
PA: Shi International Corp.
290 Davidson Ave
Somerset NJ 08873
732 764-8888

(G-9308)
SHORTS TRAVEL MANAGEMENT INC (PA)
Also Called: Passport Incentives Meetings
7815 Floyd St (66204-2917)
PHONE..................................319 234-5577
David Lecompte, *President*
Michael Phenix, *Principal*
Susan Rice, *VP Admin*
Megan Howard, *Sales Mgr*
Valerie Oren, *Consultant*
EMP: 45
SQ FT: 19,000
SALES (est): 13.3MM **Privately Held**
SIC: 4724 Travel agencies

(G-9309)
SHOSTAK IRON AND METAL CO INC
6517 W 106th St (66212-1883)
PHONE..................................913 321-9210
EMP: 20
SQ FT: 30,000
SALES: 3MM **Privately Held**
SIC: 5093 3341 3312 Wholesales Scrap/Waste Material Secondary Nonferrous Metal Producer Blast Furnace-Steel Works

(G-9310)
SI OVERLAND PARK LP
Also Called: Hilton
5800 College Blvd (66211-1660)
PHONE..................................913 345-2661
Heide Wilcox, *CEO*
Debbie Bliss, *Accounting Mgr*
Joshua Wilson, *Asst Mgr*
EMP: 60 **EST:** 2002
SALES (est): 3.4MM **Privately Held**
SIC: 7011 Hotels & motels

(G-9311)
SIMON & SIMON INC
Also Called: Classic Awards
7806 W 100th Ter (66212-2447)
PHONE..................................913 888-9889
Theodore Simon, *President*
EMP: 5 **EST:** 1949
SALES: 260K **Privately Held**
SIC: 2759 5999 3993 5094 Screen printing; trophies & plaques; signs & advertising specialties; coins, medals & trophies; novelties & giftware, including trophies

(G-9312)
SIMPLY FUEL LLC
14330 Juniper St (66224-3747)
PHONE..................................913 269-1889
Mitzi Dulan, *Administration*
EMP: 5 **EST:** 2015
SALES (est): 187.5K **Privately Held**
SIC: 2869 Fuels

(G-9313)
SIMPSON LGBACK LYNCH NORRIS PA (PA)
7400 W 110th St Ste 600 (66210-2360)
PHONE..................................913 342-2500
Dona Riley, *President*
Reid F Holbrook, *President*
Jeffrey Bullins, *Manager*
Timothy P Orrick, *Shareholder*
Thomas M Sutherland, *Shareholder*
EMP: 39
SQ FT: 11,000
SALES (est): 5.9MM **Privately Held**
SIC: 8111 Divorce & family law; real estate law; corporate, partnership & business law

(G-9314)
SIRIUS COMPUTER SOLUTIONS INC
10801 Mastin St Ste 900 (66210-1677)
PHONE..................................913 469-7900
Jim Simpson, *President*
Lewis Thomas, *Project Mgr*
Kevin Kavanaugh, *Opers Staff*
Damon Barnett, *Sales Staff*
Shane Kalil, *Sales Staff*
EMP: 10
SALES (corp-wide): 3.1B **Privately Held**
SIC: 7373 Computer integrated systems design
PA: Sirius Computer Solutions, Inc.
10100 Reunion Pl Ste 500
San Antonio TX 78216
800 460-1237

(G-9315)
SKIN RENEWAL
8490 College Blvd (66210-2123)
PHONE..................................913 722-5551
Eric Christensen, *Principal*
Chris Welch, *Med Doctor*
EMP: 20 **EST:** 2001
SALES (est): 418.7K **Privately Held**
SIC: 8011 Dermatologist

(G-9316)
SKYLINE CONSTRUCTION COMPANY
9120 Flint St (66214-1736)
PHONE..................................913 642-7100
Robin Sawyer, *President*
John Pierce, *Vice Pres*
EMP: 70
SQ FT: 7,500
SALES: 3MM **Privately Held**
SIC: 1542 Commercial & office building, new construction

(G-9317)
SLEEP ONE INC (PA)
5737 W 146th St (66223-1223)
PHONE..................................913 859-0001
Stephen D McGiffert, *Administration*
EMP: 12 **EST:** 2007
SALES (est): 6.1MM **Privately Held**
SIC: 5021 Mattresses

(G-9318)
SMART MONEY CONCEPTS INC
7300 W 110th St Fl 7 (66210-2332)
P.O. Box 15553, Lenexa (66285-5553)
PHONE..................................913 962-9806
David J Crouch, *Owner*
EMP: 10
SQ FT: 400
SALES: 5MM **Privately Held**
SIC: 6411 Insurance agents, brokers & service

(G-9319)
SMART SECURITY SOLUTIONS INC
11539 Hadley St (66210-2430)
PHONE..................................913 568-2573
Steven Conner, *President*
EMP: 25
SALES (est): 444K **Privately Held**
SIC: 7379

(G-9320)
SMARTWAY TRANSPORTATION INC
10901 Granada Ln (66211-1470)
P.O. Box 24387 (66283-4387)
PHONE..................................877 537-2681
Chris Rice, *Vice Pres*
Chad Jegen, *Officer*
Justin Boehm, *Officer*
EMP: 16
SQ FT: 3,000
SALES: 14MM **Privately Held**
SIC: 4731 Freight transportation arrangement

(G-9321)
SOFTEK ILLUMINATE INC
7299 W 98th Ter Ste 130 (66212-6183)
PHONE..................................913 981-5300
Matthew McLenon, *CEO*
EMP: 13
SQ FT: 2,500
SALES (est): 303.8K **Privately Held**
SIC: 7371 Computer software development & applications

(G-9322)
SOGETI USA LLC
7101 College Blvd # 1150 (66210-1845)
PHONE..................................913 451-9600
Jay Accurso, *Branch Mgr*
Dan Luciano, *Manager*
EMP: 50
SALES (corp-wide): 343.9MM **Privately Held**
WEB: www.sogeti-usa.com
SIC: 7379
HQ: Sogeti Usa Llc
10100 Innovation Dr # 200
Miamisburg OH 45342
937 291-8100

(G-9323)
SOHUM SYSTEMS LLC
7900 College Blvd Ste 135 (66210-2194)
PHONE..................................913 221-7204
Srinivas Moshugu, *CEO*
EMP: 50 **EST:** 2013
SALES (est): 91.8K **Privately Held**
SIC: 7371 Custom computer programming services

(G-9324)
SOLERAN INC
Also Called: Emeditrack
7400 W 132nd St Ste 140 (66213-1142)
PHONE..................................913 647-5900
Grady Hawley, *President*
Greg Truitt, *COO*
Amanda Haviland, *Project Mgr*
Jonathan Holiday, *Project Mgr*
Will Walburn, *VP Bus Dvlpt*
EMP: 8
SALES (est): 801.1K **Privately Held**
SIC: 7372 Application computer software

(G-9325)
SOLUTIONS NOW INC
6400 Glenwood St Ste 314 (66202-4014)
PHONE..................................913 327-5805
Lori Kurovski, *Principal*
EMP: 24
SALES (corp-wide): 2.5MM **Privately Held**
SIC: 7371 Custom computer programming services
PA: Solutions Now Inc
8695 College Blvd Ste 220
Overland Park KS 66210
913 677-1954

(G-9326)
SOMNICARE INC
10590 Barkley St (66212-1811)
PHONE..................................913 498-1331
Fax: 913 341-2023
EMP: 40
SQ FT: 1,000
SALES (est): 3.8MM
SALES (corp-wide): 126.1MM **Publicly Held**
SIC: 5999 5047 Ret Misc Merchandise Whol Medical/Hospital Equipment
PA: Foundation Healthcare, Inc.
14000 N Portland Ave
Oklahoma City OK 73134
405 608-1700

(G-9327)
SOMNITECH INC (HQ)
10590 Barkley St (66212-1811)
PHONE..................................913 498-8120
Pamela Gillis, *CEO*
Steven Hull, *President*
EMP: 50
SQ FT: 10,013
SALES (est): 4.8MM
SALES (corp-wide): 126.1MM **Publicly Held**
SIC: 8011 8071 Offices & clinics of medical doctors; testing laboratories
PA: Foundation Healthcare, Inc.
13900 N Portland Ave # 200
Oklahoma City OK 73134
800 783-0404

(G-9328)
SOUNDTUBE ENTERTAINMENT INC (PA)
8005 W 110th St Ste 208 (66210-2619)
PHONE..................................435 647-9555
Chris Combest, *President*
Laura Waldon, *President*
James McManus, *Manager*
▲ **EMP:** 25
SALES (est): 4.2MM **Privately Held**
WEB: www.soundtube.com
SIC: 3651 Speaker systems

(G-9329)
SOURCE BUILDING SERVICES INC
7211 W 98th Ter Ste 100 (66212-2257)
PHONE..................................913 341-7500
Mohamed Omer, *President*
Annie Hamblin, *Accounts Mgr*
Kim Kelly, *Director*
EMP: 14 **EST:** 2005
SALES (est): 719.8K **Privately Held**
SIC: 7349 Janitorial service, contract basis

(G-9330)
SOUTH KANS CY SURGICAL CTR LC
10730 Nall Ave Ste 100 (66211-1242)
PHONE..................................913 901-9000
Joyce Swenson, *Administration*
EMP: 22
SALES (est): 4.7MM **Privately Held**
SIC: 8011 Surgeon

(G-9331)
SOUTHERN GLAZERS WINE AND SP
5200 Metcalf Ave (66202-1265)
PHONE..................................913 396-4900
EMP: 53
SALES (corp-wide): 12.3B **Privately Held**
SIC: 5182 Liquor
HQ: Southern Glazer's Wine And Spirits Of Texas, Llc
2001 Diplomat Dr
Farmers Branch TX 75234
972 277-2000

(G-9332)
SPANGLER GRAPHICS LLC
8345 Lenexa Dr Ste 275 (66214-1765)
PHONE..................................913 722-4500
Brian Yokley, *President*
Patti Summers, *HR Admin*
Cliff Benedict, *Accounts Exec*
Emily O'Shea, *Accounts Exec*
Chris Coharh,
▲ **EMP:** 100 **EST:** 2000
SALES: 10MM
SALES (corp-wide): 6.8B **Publicly Held**
WEB: www.spanglergraphics.com
SIC: 2752 2759 Commercial printing, offset; letterpress printing
HQ: Consolidated Graphics, Inc.
5858 Westheimer Rd # 200
Houston TX 77057
713 787-0977

(G-9333)
SPEC PERSONNEL LLC
6750 Antioch Rd Ste 201 (66204-1299)
PHONE..................................913 534-8430
Lee Jorgenson, *Branch Mgr*
EMP: 100
SALES (corp-wide): 41.9MM **Privately Held**
SIC: 7361 Employment agencies
PA: Spec Personnel, Llc
4625 Creekstone Dr # 130
Durham NC 27703
203 254-9935

(G-9334)
SPENCER FANE BRITT BROWNE LLP
9401 Indian Creek Pkwy # 700 (66210-2038)
PHONE..................................913 345-8100
James Badgerow, *Managing Prtnr*
Barry L Pickens,
Dale K Ramsey,
EMP: 34
SALES (corp-wide): 46.5MM **Privately Held**
SIC: 8111 General practice law office
PA: Spencer Fane Llp
1000 Walnut St Ste 1400
Kansas City MO 64106
816 474-8100

(G-9335)
SPORTS REHAB/PHYSL THRPY ASSOC (PA)
Also Called: Sports Rhblttion Physcl Thrapy
10701 Nall Ave (66211-1363)
PHONE..................................913 663-2555
Paul T McGannon, *President*
Craig Klos, *Vice Pres*
Mary Sauder, *Manager*
Doug Wiesner, *Executive*
Mary E Sauder, *Admin Sec*
EMP: 23
SALES: 1.9MM **Privately Held**
WEB: www.kcsportsrehab.com
SIC: 8049 Physiotherapist

(G-9336)
SPRINT
6391 Sprint Pkwy (66251-6100)
PHONE..................................703 433-4000
EMP: 44 **EST:** 2011
SALES (est): 3.8MM **Privately Held**
SIC: 4813 Telephone Communications

(G-9337)
SPRINT COMMUNICATIONS INC (DH)
6200 Sprint Pkwy (66251-6117)
PHONE..................................855 848-3280
Brian S Miller, *President*
Matt Carter, *President*
Keith Cowan, *President*
Steven L Elfman, *President*
Nestor Cano, *COO*
▲ **EMP:** 950
SQ FT: 3,853,000
SALES (est): 17.5B **Publicly Held**
WEB: www.sprint.com
SIC: 4813 4812 5999 Local & long distance telephone communications; long distance telephone communications; voice telephone communications; data telephone communications; radio telephone communication; cellular telephone services; telephone & communication equipment; telephone equipment & systems
HQ: Sprint Corporation
6200 Sprint Pkwy
Overland Park KS 66251
877 564-3166

(G-9338)
SPRINT COMMUNICATIONS CO LP (DH)
6391 Sprint Pkwy (66251-6100)
PHONE..................................800 829-0965
Michel Combes, *President*
Timothy Kelly, *Managing Prtnr*
Daniel R Hesse, *Partner*
Christie A Hill, *Partner*
Nestor Cano, *COO*
EMP: 800
SQ FT: 216,000
SALES (est): 5.5B **Publicly Held**
SIC: 4813 Long distance telephone communications; voice telephone communications; data telephone communications
HQ: Sprint Communications, Inc.
6200 Sprint Pkwy
Overland Park KS 66251
855 848-3280

(G-9339)
SPRINT COMMUNICATIONS NH INC (DH)
6200 Sprint Pkwy (66251-6117)
PHONE..................................800 829-0965
William Esrey, *Ch of Bd*
Ronald T Lemay, *President*
EMP: 23
SQ FT: 216,000
SALES (est): 3.1MM **Publicly Held**
SIC: 4812 Cellular telephone services
HQ: Sprint Communications Company L.P.
6391 Sprint Pkwy
Overland Park KS 66251
800 829-0965

(G-9340)
SPRINT CORPORATION (HQ)
6200 Sprint Pkwy (66251-6117)
PHONE..................................877 564-3166
Masayoshi Son, *Ch of Bd*
Michel Combes, *President*
Mohamad Nasser, *General Mgr*
Marcelo Claure, *Chairman*
Nestor Cano, *COO*
EMP: 170
SQ FT: 3,790,000
SALES: 33.6B **Publicly Held**
SIC: 4813 4812 Long distance telephone communications; data telephone communications; ; ; cellular telephone services

(G-9341)
SPRINT SOLUTIONS INC
Ksopht0101-Z4300 6391 (66251-0001)
PHONE..................................800 829-0965
Charles Wunsch, *President*
Mark V Beshears, *Vice Pres*
Timothy O'Grady, *Admin Sec*
EMP: 96
SALES (est): 37MM **Publicly Held**
SIC: 4813 Telephone communication, except radio
HQ: Sprint Communications, Inc.
6200 Sprint Pkwy
Overland Park KS 66251
855 848-3280

(G-9342)
SPRINT SPECTRUM LP
11788 W 95th St (66214-1867)
PHONE..................................913 894-1375
Bob Napierala, *Branch Mgr*
EMP: 13 **Publicly Held**
WEB: www.sprintpcs.com
SIC: 4813 Local & long distance telephone communications
HQ: Sprint Spectrum L.P.
6800 Sprint Pkwy
Overland Park KS 66251

(G-9343)
SPRINT SPECTRUM LP (DH)
6800 Sprint Pkwy (66251-0001)
PHONE..................................703 433-4000
Timothy Kelly, *Managing Prtnr*
William Arendt, *Partner*
Christie A Hill, *Partner*
Samuel Mayson, *Partner*
▲ **EMP:** 170
SQ FT: 156,000
SALES (est): 11B **Publicly Held**
WEB: www.sprintpcs.com
SIC: 4813 Local & long distance telephone communications
HQ: Sprint Corporation
6200 Sprint Pkwy
Overland Park KS 66251
877 564-3166

GEOGRAPHIC

(G-9344)
SPX COOLING TECHNOLOGIES INC (HQ)
7401 W 129th St (66213-2694)
P.O. Box 25948, Shawnee Mission (66225-5948)
PHONE.....913 664-7400
Gene Lowe, *President*
Scott Sproule, *CFO*
Pat Kellerman, *Treasurer*
◆ **EMP**: 325 **EST**: 1981
SQ FT: 100,000
SALES (est): 571.8MM
SALES (corp-wide): 1.5B **Publicly Held**
WEB: www.cts.spx.com
SIC: **3585** Refrigeration & heating equipment
PA: Spx Corporation
13320a Balntyn Corp Pl
Charlotte NC 28277
980 474-3700

(G-9345)
SPX COOLING TECHNOLOGIES INC
Also Called: Hamon Cooling Towers Division
7401 W 129th St (66213-2694)
PHONE.....913 722-3600
Doug Jones, *Manager*
EMP: 8
SALES (corp-wide): 1.5B **Publicly Held**
WEB: www.cts.spx.com
SIC: **3443** Cooling towers, metal plate
HQ: Spx Cooling Technologies, Inc.
7401 W 129th St
Overland Park KS 66213
913 664-7400

(G-9346)
SPX DRY COOLING USA LLC
7450 W 130th St Ste 310 (66213-2684)
PHONE.....913 685-0009
Dorothy Sakele, *Principal*
EMP: 5 **EST**: 2016
SALES (est): 166.4K **Privately Held**
SIC: **3443** Finned tubes, for heat transfer

(G-9347)
SQUARETWO FINANCIAL COMMERCIAL
10865 Grandview Dr (66210-1503)
PHONE.....913 888-8300
EMP: 10
SALES (est): 2MM **Privately Held**
SIC: **6153** Short-Term Business Credit Institution

(G-9348)
SRG III LLC
5700 W 112th St Ste 100 (66211-1747)
PHONE.....913 663-4400
William Solon, *CEO*
EMP: 17
SQ FT: 4,000
SALES (est): 227.2K **Privately Held**
SIC: **7361** Executive placement

(G-9349)
STA-MOT-KS LLC (PA)
Also Called: Midwest Office Technology
11316 W 80th St (66214-3307)
PHONE.....913 894-9600
Susan Illig-Brame, *President*
Susan Illig Brame, *President*
Michael Hobbs, *Exec VP*
Paul Ficken, *Human Res Mgr*
Sean Cihacek, *Accounts Exec*
EMP: 45
SQ FT: 22,000
SALES (est): 9MM **Privately Held**
SIC: **5044** 7629 7359 5112 Office equipment; business machine repair, electric; office machine rental, except computers; office supplies

(G-9350)
STAFFBRIDGE LLC
7240 W 98th Ter Bldg 8 (66212-2255)
PHONE.....913 381-4044
Kathy Perry, *President*
Gerhard Kuti, *Chairman*
Len Bates, *VP Sales*
EMP: 10
SALES: 2.6MM **Privately Held**
SIC: **7371** Computer software development & applications

(G-9351)
STALLARD TECHNOLOGIES INC
Also Called: STI
16041 Marty Cir (66085-9541)
PHONE.....913 851-2260
Whitney Elliott, *CEO*
Simon Elliott, *President*
Rob Waits, *Vice Pres*
Chris Grindinger, *Accounts Exec*
Brent Ivey, *Accounts Exec*
◆ **EMP**: 30
SALES (est): 11.4MM **Privately Held**
WEB: www.stikc.com
SIC: **5734** 3571 5093 5961 Modems, monitors, terminals & disk drives: computers; electronic computers; scrap & waste materials; computer equipment & electronics, mail order; computers, peripherals & software; computer integrated systems design

(G-9352)
STANDARD INSURANCE COMPANY
Also Called: Standard Emplyee Bnefits Insur
7500 College Blvd Ste 750 (66210-4000)
PHONE.....913 661-9241
Thomas Trussell, *Manager*
EMP: 15 **Privately Held**
WEB: www.standard.com
SIC: **6311** Life insurance carriers
HQ: Standard Insurance Company
920 Sw 6th Ave Ste 1100
Portland OR 97204
971 321-7000

(G-9353)
STANLEY BANK (PA)
Also Called: STANLEY BANK COLUMBUS
7835 W 151st St (66223-2217)
P.O. Box 23069, Shawnee Mission (66283-3069)
PHONE.....913 681-8800
Joe Jackson, *President*
Debbie Mitts, *General Mgr*
Ron Holmes, *Vice Pres*
Jerry Hulvey, *Vice Pres*
Angela Stuhr, *Manager*
EMP: 12 **EST**: 1995
SALES: 5.8MM **Privately Held**
WEB: www.stanleybank.com
SIC: **6021** National commercial banks

(G-9354)
STANTEC CONSULTING SVCS INC
6800 College Blvd Ste 750 (66211-1855)
PHONE.....913 202-6867
Lori Van Dermark, *Marketing Staff*
EMP: 23
SALES (corp-wide): 3.2B **Privately Held**
SIC: **8748** Environmental consultant
HQ: Stantec Consulting Services Inc.
475 5th Ave Fl 12
New York NY 10017
212 352-5160

(G-9355)
STAR TRANSPORT LLC
Also Called: Star Fuel Center
7415 W 130th St Ste 100 (66213-2658)
PHONE.....913 396-5070
Deidra Atchley, *General Mgr*
James Dtraylor, *Vice Pres*
Chuck Knight, *Terminal Mgr*
Dan Engle, *CFO*
James Koop, *VP Sales*
EMP: 40
SALES (est): 10.5MM **Privately Held**
SIC: **4923** Gas transmission & distribution

(G-9356)
STEARNS CONRAD AND SCHMIDT
Also Called: Scs Aquaterra
7311 W 130th St Ste 100 (66213-2686)
PHONE.....913 681-0030
Jack Pryor, *Owner*
EMP: 57
SALES (corp-wide): 191.6MM **Privately Held**
SIC: **8711** Consulting engineer
PA: Stearns, Conrad And Schmidt, Consulting Engineers, Inc.
3900 Kilroy Arprt Way # 100
Long Beach CA 90806
562 426-9544

(G-9357)
STEP TWO INVESTMENTS LLC
Also Called: Lineage
11551 W 83rd Ter (66214-1532)
PHONE.....913 888-9000
Drew Peterson, *General Mgr*
Sharon Siuda, *Vice Pres*
Richard Williams,
EMP: 40
SALES: 1.3MM **Privately Held**
WEB: www.stamp-ede.com
SIC: **7331** 4215 Mailing service; courier services, except by air

(G-9358)
STEPHENS & ASSOCIATES ADVG INC
14720 Metcalf Ave (66223-2204)
PHONE.....913 661-0910
Chuck Stephens, *CEO*
Patrick Sweet, *Corp Secy*
Charlotte Stephens, *Vice Pres*
EMP: 25
SQ FT: 6,000
SALES (est): 5MM **Privately Held**
WEB: www.stephensad.com
SIC: **7311** Advertising consultant

(G-9359)
STEPP AND ROTHWELL
7300 College Blvd Ste 100 (66210-1847)
PHONE.....913 345-4800
Kathy Stepp, *Managing Prtnr*
Ken Eaton, *Partner*
Howard Rothwell, *Partner*
Howarda Rothwell, *Info Tech Dir*
Blake Setzer, *Planning*
EMP: 13
SALES (est): 1.6MM **Privately Held**
WEB: www.steppandrothwell.com
SIC: **8742** Business planning & organizing services; financial consultant

(G-9360)
STERLING ENERGY RESOURCES INC
10551 Barkley St Ste 108 (66212-1813)
PHONE.....913 469-9072
Reid Scofield, *Principal*
EMP: 13
SALES (est): 503.9K **Privately Held**
SIC: **4924** Natural gas distribution

(G-9361)
STEVEN L HECHLER DDS MS
Also Called: Hechler, Steven L
12800 Metcalf Ave Ste 2 (66213-2607)
PHONE.....913 345-0541
Steven L Hechler DDS, *Owner*
EMP: 13
SALES (est): 903.5K **Privately Held**
WEB: www.hechler.com
SIC: **8021** Orthodontist

(G-9362)
STIFEL NICOLAUS & COMPANY INC
9401 Indian Creek Pkwy # 1100 (66210-1439)
PHONE.....913 345-4200
Arthur Kennedy, *Branch Mgr*
EMP: 12
SALES (corp-wide): 3.2B **Publicly Held**
SIC: **6211** Stock brokers & dealers
HQ: Stifel, Nicolaus & Company Incorporated
501 N Broadway
Saint Louis MO 63102
314 342-2000

(G-9363)
STILES GLAUCOMA CONS P A
7200 W 129th St (66213-2624)
PHONE.....913 897-9299
Ann Stechschulte, *Managing Dir*
Michael C Stiles, *Principal*
EMP: 13
SALES (est): 904.7K **Privately Held**
SIC: **8042** Specialized optometrists

(G-9364)
STOLTZ REALTY DELAWARE INC
Also Called: Stoltz Management Company
8717 W 110th St Ste 240 (66210-2103)
PHONE.....913 451-4466
Wes Johnson, *Branch Mgr*
Matthew Miller, *Property Mgr*
EMP: 22
SALES (corp-wide): 17.3MM **Privately Held**
SIC: **6531** Real estate leasing & rentals
PA: Stoltz Realty Of Delaware, Inc.
725 Conshohocken State Rd
Bala Cynwyd PA 19004
610 667-5800

(G-9365)
STONE CROFT MINISTRIES INC
10561 Barkley St Ste 500 (66212-1834)
PHONE.....816 763-7800
Geneva Vollrath, *CEO*
Jim Baker, *CFO*
Rachel Fou, *Director*
Autumn Katz, *Director*
Sarah Leblanc, *Director*
EMP: 92
SQ FT: 1,500
SALES: 5.6MM **Privately Held**
SIC: **8641** 8661 Business persons club; religious organizations

(G-9366)
STONELOCK GLOBAL
12635 Hemlock St Ste A (66213-1487)
PHONE.....800 970-6168
Colleen Dunlap, *CEO*
Katrina Yao, *CFO*
EMP: 10 **EST**: 2017
SALES (est): 238.2K **Privately Held**
SIC: **7371** Computer software development & applications

(G-9367)
STRATEGIC VALUE MEDIA
8700 Indian Creek Pkwy # 300 (66210-1563)
PHONE.....913 214-5203
Daniel Sylvester, *Vice Pres*
Kassie Fennewald, *Natl Sales Mgr*
Adam Daher, *Advt Staff*
Catherine Roby, *Advt Staff*
Jonathan Schwartzbard, *Manager*
EMP: 50
SALES (est): 2.1MM **Privately Held**
SIC: **7389** Advertising, promotional & trade show services

(G-9368)
STUDIO 13 INC
6731 W 121st St (66209-2003)
PHONE.....913 948-1284
Xiii Ing, *Exec Dir*
EMP: 12
SALES (est): 360K **Privately Held**
SIC: **8748** Telecommunications consultant

(G-9369)
STYERS EQUIPMENT COMPANY
8301 W 125th St Ste 100 (66213-1415)
PHONE.....913 681-5225
Paul H Styers, *President*
Diana Styers, *Treasurer*
Reva Brown, *Admin Asst*
▲ **EMP**: 16
SQ FT: 10,000
SALES (est): 10.3MM **Privately Held**
WEB: www.styersequipment.com
SIC: **5084** 3555 7359 7699 Printing trades machinery, equipment & supplies; printing trades machinery; business machine & electronic equipment rental services; printing trades machinery & equipment repair

(G-9370)
SUGAR SCHOLL MAGEE CARRIKER (PA)
Also Called: Womens Care
9301 W 74th St Ste 325 (66204-2217)
P.O. Box 2705, Shawnee Mission (66201-2705)
PHONE..................................913 384-4990
John Schroll, *President*
Christine Carriker, *Principal*
Michael Magee, *Principal*
Brandan Mitchell, *Principal*
Brendan B Mitchell, *Principal*
EMP: 30
SALES (est): 2.9MM **Privately Held**
SIC: 8011 Gynecologist; obstetrician; physicians' office, including specialists

(G-9371)
SUHOR INDUSTRIES INC
Also Called: Si Funeral Services
10965 Granada Ln Ste 300 (66211-1412)
PHONE..................................620 421-4434
Joseph U Suhor III, *CEO*
Marvin G Smith, *Senior VP*
Mike Anderson, *Plant Mgr*
Herb Roop, *Plant Mgr*
Barry Rosenberg, *Engineer*
▲ **EMP:** 670 **EST:** 1934
SQ FT: 4,500
SALES (est): 92.8K **Privately Held**
WEB: www.suhor.com
SIC: 3272 1799 5099 7261 Burial vaults, concrete or precast terrazzo; grave excavation; monuments & grave markers; crematory

(G-9372)
SUN MICROSYSTEMS INC
9200 Indian Creek Pkwy # 560 (66210-2036)
PHONE..................................913 327-7820
Sally Gordon, *Principal*
EMP: 10
SALES (est): 624K **Privately Held**
SIC: 7379 Computer related services

(G-9373)
SUNBELT BUSINESS BROKERS
7101 College Blvd # 1600 (66210-1845)
PHONE..................................913 383-2671
Dan Pedersen, *President*
Anita Lieser, *Broker*
EMP: 13
SALES: 5MM **Privately Held**
SIC: 7389 6163 Brokers' services; mortgage brokers arranging for loans, using money of others

(G-9374)
SUNFLOWER STATE HLTH PLAN INC
8325 Lenexa Dr (66214-1654)
PHONE..................................877 644-4623
Michael F Neidorff, *President*
Andrea Hathaway, *Manager*
Lynn Schmidt, *Manager*
EMP: 192
SALES (est): 31.3MM **Publicly Held**
SIC: 6324 Health maintenance organization (HMO), insurance only
PA: Centene Corporation
7700 Forsyth Blvd Ste 800
Saint Louis MO 63105

(G-9375)
SUNRISE POINT ELEMENTARY PTO
15800 Roe Blvd (66224-3908)
PHONE..................................913 239-7500
Karen Dunlap, *Principal*
Susan Sibenaller, *Teacher*
EMP: 11
SALES: 61.1K **Privately Held**
SIC: 8641 Parent-teachers' association

(G-9376)
SUNRISE SENIOR LIVING LLC
Also Called: Sunrise of Overland Park
12500 W 135th St (66221-9323)
PHONE..................................913 685-3340
Barley Mayyahi, *Director*
Steve Lackner, *Nursing Dir*
James Linzie, *Food Svc Dir*
EMP: 58
SALES (corp-wide): 4.7B **Publicly Held**
WEB: www.sunrise.com
SIC: 8051 8361 Skilled nursing care facilities; home for the aged
HQ: Sunrise Senior Living, Llc
7902 Westpark Dr
Mc Lean VA 22102

(G-9377)
SUPERIOR CRT REPORTING SVC LLC
Also Called: Hostetler & Associates
8001 Conser St Ste 200 (66204-3409)
PHONE..................................913 262-0100
Myles Megee,
Kelly Smith,
Timothy Stein,
EMP: 14
SQ FT: 2,400
SALES (est): 850K **Privately Held**
SIC: 7338 Court reporting service

(G-9378)
SURFACE SOLUTIONS INTL INC
14400 Maple St (66223-1256)
PHONE..................................913 742-7744
Chris Hobbs, *President*
Robin Sawyer, *Vice Pres*
EMP: 22
SQ FT: 24,000
SALES (est): 1.1MM **Privately Held**
SIC: 1799 Counter top installation

(G-9379)
SURVEYING AND MAPPING LLC
9393 W 110th St (66210-1442)
PHONE..................................913 344-9933
Scott Perkins, *Office Mgr*
EMP: 125 **Privately Held**
SIC: 8713 Surveying services
PA: Surveying And Mapping, Llc
4801 Sw Pkwy Bldg 2
Austin TX 78735

(G-9380)
SUTURE EXPRESS INC
11020 King St Ste 400 (66210-1201)
PHONE..................................913 384-2220
Ron Labrum, *Ch of Bd*
Ed Kuklenski, *President*
Charlie Galvin, *Business Mgr*
Steve Boyer, *Vice Pres*
Kerry McDonald, *Opers Mgr*
EMP: 40
SQ FT: 20,000
SALES (est): 33.3MM **Privately Held**
WEB: www.sutureexpress.com
SIC: 5047 Medical equipment & supplies
PA: Diamond Castle Holdings, Llc
280 Pk Ave Fl 25 E Tower Flr 25
New York NY 10017
212 300-1900

(G-9381)
SWAROVSKI NORTH AMERICA LTD
11559 W 95th St (66214-1828)
PHONE..................................913 599-3791
Catherine Lynch, *Branch Mgr*
Jennifer Zino, *Manager*
EMP: 5
SALES (corp-wide): 4.7B **Privately Held**
SIC: 3961 Costume jewelry
HQ: Swarovski North America Limited
1 Kenney Dr
Cranston RI 02920
401 463-6400

(G-9382)
SWEET LIFE AT ROSEHILL
Also Called: Allen Park III
12605 W 132nd St (66213-4015)
PHONE..................................913 962-7600
Mark Perkinson, *Principal*
Stacey Perkinson, *Principal*
Kyle Kar, *Opers Staff*
Maureen Armstrong, *Treasurer*
Gail McFarland, *Office Mgr*
EMP: 148
SALES (est): 4.4MM **Privately Held**
SIC: 8051 Skilled nursing care facilities

(G-9383)
SWISS MADE INC
7251 W 97th St (66212-2209)
PHONE..................................913 341-6400
Myron A Schwery, *President*
Chris Schwery, *Vice Pres*
EMP: 14
SQ FT: 3,000
SALES (est): 1.6MM **Privately Held**
SIC: 3639 Sewing equipment

(G-9384)
SWISS RE AMERICA HOLDING CORP (DH)
5200 Metcalf Ave (66202-1265)
P.O. Box 2991, Shawnee Mission (66201-1391)
PHONE..................................913 676-5200
Michel M Lis, *CEO*
Walter B Kielholz, *Ch of Bd*
Fernando Orellana, *President*
Ronald R Pressman, *President*
Thomas Wellauer, *COO*
EMP: 1000
SQ FT: 315,000
SALES (est): 2.4B
SALES (corp-wide): 37B **Privately Held**
WEB: www.swissre.com
SIC: 6331 6311 Property damage insurance; fire, marine & casualty insurance: stock; life reinsurance
HQ: Schweizerische Ruckversicherungs-Gesellschaft Ag
Mythenquai 60
ZUrich ZH 8002
432 852-121

(G-9385)
SWISS RE MANAGEMENT US CORP
5200 Metcalf Ave (66202-1265)
P.O. Box 2991, Mission (66201-1391)
PHONE..................................913 676-5200
EMP: 14
SALES (est): 2.7MM
SALES (corp-wide): 37B **Privately Held**
SIC: 6411 Insurance agents, brokers & service
PA: Swiss Re Ag
Mythenquai 50-60
ZUrich ZH 8002
432 852-121

(G-9386)
SWISS RE SOLUTIONS HOLDG CORP (DH)
5200 Metcalf Ave (66202-1265)
P.O. Box 2991, Mission (66201-1391)
PHONE..................................913 676-5200
Walter B Kielholz, *President*
Dan Eudy, *President*
Renato Fassbind, *Vice Chairman*
Hoyt H Wood Jr, *Exec VP*
John M Connelly, *Senior VP*
▲ **EMP:** 1000 **EST:** 1914
SQ FT: 315,000
SALES (est): 520.5MM
SALES (corp-wide): 37B **Privately Held**
SIC: 6331 Fire, marine & casualty insurance & carriers
HQ: Schweizerische Ruckversicherungs-Gesellschaft Ag
Mythenquai 60
ZUrich ZH 8002
432 852-121

(G-9387)
SWISS REINSURANCE AMERICA CORP
5200 Metcalf Ave (66202-1265)
P.O. Box 2991 (66201-1391)
PHONE..................................913 676-5200
Patrick Mailloux, *President*
Christopher R Ritter, *Vice Pres*
Kim Wulf, *Senior Engr*
EMP: 1410 **EST:** 2014
SALES (est): 286.1MM
SALES (corp-wide): 37B **Privately Held**
SIC: 6311 Life reinsurance
HQ: Swiss Re America Holding Corporation
5200 Metcalf Ave
Overland Park KS 66202

(G-9388)
SYNEXIS LLC (PA)
8905 Lenexa Dr (66214-3228)
PHONE..................................816 399-0895
James D Lee,
EMP: 11
SALES (est): 1.3MM **Privately Held**
SIC: 8071 Testing laboratories

(G-9389)
T & C TANK RENTAL & ANCHOR SVC
Also Called: T & C Tank Rentals Anchr Serv
7400 W 130th St Ste 270 (66213-2682)
PHONE..................................806 592-3286
Mark Spolton, *President*
Brenda Bailey, *Corp Secy*
EMP: 29
SALES (est): 3.7MM **Privately Held**
SIC: 7353 Oil equipment rental services

(G-9390)
T-143 INC
Also Called: Tanners
14337 Metcalf Ave (66223-2988)
PHONE..................................913 681-8313
Matt Brentano, *Regional Mgr*
Jim Fager, *Manager*
EMP: 50
SQ FT: 6,700
SALES (est): 1.3MM **Privately Held**
SIC: 5813 8741 5812 Bar (drinking places); restaurant management; food bars

(G-9391)
TARGET INSURANCE SERVICES LLC
11020 Oakmont St (66210-1100)
PHONE..................................913 384-6300
Matthew Mc Avoy, *President*
Louis J Mc Avoy, *Treasurer*
Alison Campbell, *Sales Staff*
Diane Kramer, *Sales Associate*
Helen Aaron, *Manager*
EMP: 30
SQ FT: 2,600
SALES (est): 5.2MM
SALES (corp-wide): 108.7MM **Privately Held**
SIC: 6411 Insurance agents
PA: Ash Brokerage, Llc
888 S Harrison St
Fort Wayne IN 46802
260 459-0823

(G-9392)
TAX FAVORED BENEFITS INC
4801 W 110th St Ste 200 (66211-1239)
P.O. Box 7190, Shawnee Mission (66207-0190)
PHONE..................................913 648-5526
R David Wentz, *President*
Dee W James, *Regional Mgr*
David B Wentz, *Exec VP*
Adam Bettis, *Vice Pres*
Audrey Chinnock, *Vice Pres*
EMP: 35
SQ FT: 10,000
SALES (est): 8.1MM **Privately Held**
WEB: www.taxfavoredbenefits.com
SIC: 6411 Pension & retirement plan consultants

(G-9393)
TD ELECTRIC SERVICES LLC
8843 Bond St (66214-1774)
PHONE..................................913 722-5560
Trent Daniels,
EMP: 11
SQ FT: 5,000
SALES: 750K **Privately Held**
WEB: www.tdelectricllc.com
SIC: 1731 Lighting contractor; general electrical contractor

(G-9394)
TDC FILTER MANUFACTURING INC
11501 Outlook St Ste 100 (66211-1810)
P.O. Box 99989, Chicago IL (60696-7789)
PHONE..................................630 410-6200
Stephen McLeod, *President*
John Mark Foster, *President*
Michael D Bennett, *Admin Sec*
Frank Lau, *Admin Sec*
◆ **EMP:** 125
SQ FT: 100,000

GEOGRAPHIC

SALES (est): 14.9MM
SALES (corp-wide): 14.3B **Publicly Held**
WEB: www.tdcfilter.com
SIC: 2393 2674 Textile bags; bags: uncoated paper & multiwall
HQ: Bha Altair, Llc
11501 Outlook St Ste 100
Overland Park KS 66211
816 356-8400

(G-9395)
TEAKWOOD INVESTMENTS LLC
Also Called: Firstlight HM Care Overland Pk
8101 College Blvd Ste 100 (66210-2671)
PHONE..................................913 203-7444
Michael Brainerd,
Andrew Brainerd,
EMP: 60
SQ FT: 2,000
SALES (est): 90.3K **Privately Held**
SIC: 8082 Home health care services

(G-9396)
TEAM CONSTRUCTION LLC
6920 W 82nd St (66204-3945)
PHONE..................................913 469-9990
Vivian Love, *President*
Rob Koons, *Project Mgr*
Jeff White, *Sr Project Mgr*
Scott Love,
Vivan Love,
EMP: 10
SALES (est): 1.9MM **Privately Held**
SIC: 1541 Industrial buildings & warehouses

(G-9397)
TEAM INTERNATIONAL INC
3906 W 141st Dr (66224-9713)
P.O. Box 23566 (66283-0566)
PHONE..................................913 681-0740
EMP: 12
SALES (est): 607.1K **Privately Held**
SIC: 7363 Help Supply Services

(G-9398)
TEAM KO LLC
12066 W 135th St (66221-8136)
PHONE..................................913 897-1300
Seth Wilson,
EMP: 10
SALES (est): 86.7K **Privately Held**
SIC: 7999 Martial arts school; physical fitness instruction

(G-9399)
TECHNCAL TRNING PRFSSONALS LLC
9401 Indian Creek Pkwy (66210-2007)
PHONE..................................865 312-4189
Fred Foster, *President*
Kelsey Foster, *Vice Pres*
Ruben Garcia, *Vice Pres*
Kristen Clements, *Engineer*
EMP: 18
SQ FT: 10,000
SALES (est): 598.6K **Privately Held**
SIC: 8748 Business consulting

(G-9400)
TELCON ASSOCIATES INC
10500 Barkley St Ste 100 (66212-1838)
P.O. Box 7973 (66207-0973)
PHONE..................................855 864-1571
Karen S Thatcher, *President*
Robert G Potter, *Vice Pres*
Elizabeth Subica, *Vice Pres*
Crystal Musil, *Project Mgr*
Shon Thatcher, *Broker*
EMP: 14 **EST:** 1971
SQ FT: 3,500
SALES (est): 1MM **Privately Held**
WEB: www.telconassociates.com
SIC: 8742 Business consultant

(G-9401)
TELECOMMUNICATION SYSTEMS INC
7300 W 110th St Fl 7 (66210-2332)
PHONE..................................913 593-9489
EMP: 47
SALES (corp-wide): 671.8MM **Publicly Held**
SIC: 3674 3812 8711 Semiconductors & related devices; search & navigation equipment; electrical or electronic engineering
HQ: Telecommunication Systems, Inc.
275 West St
Annapolis MD 21401
410 263-7616

(G-9402)
TERMINIX INTL CO LTD PARTNR
9214 Bond St (66214-1727)
PHONE..................................913 696-0351
Chuck Dockery, *Manager*
EMP: 35
SALES (corp-wide): 1.9B **Publicly Held**
SIC: 7342 Pest control services
HQ: The Terminix International Company Limited Partnership
150 Peabody Pl
Memphis TN 38103
901 766-1400

(G-9403)
TERRADATUM
14221 Metcalf Ave Ste 150 (66223-3580)
P.O. Box 387, Glen Ellen CA (95442-0387)
PHONE..................................888 212-4793
Mark Spraetz, *CEO*
Peter Krause, *Vice Pres*
Eric Biggs, *Info Tech Dir*
Patrick Brannigan, *Sr Software Eng*
Courtney Pipes, *Software Dev*
EMP: 52
SALES (est): 2.5MM **Privately Held**
SIC: 7371 Computer software development & applications

(G-9404)
TFI FAMILY SERVICES INC
8300 College Blvd Ste 301 (66210-2603)
PHONE..................................913 894-2985
EMP: 10
SALES (corp-wide): 55.2MM **Privately Held**
SIC: 8361 8322 Residential Care Services Individual/Family Services
PA: Tfi Family Services, Inc.
618 Commercial St Ste C
Emporia KS 66801
620 342-2239

(G-9405)
THI OF KANS AT SPCLTY HOSP LLC
6509 W 103rd St (66212-1728)
PHONE..................................913 649-3701
Karen Leverich, *President*
Bill Scott, *CFO*
EMP: 125
SALES (est): 3.9MM **Privately Held**
SIC: 8062 General medical & surgical hospitals

(G-9406)
THI OF KANSAS INDIAN MEADOWS
6505 W 103rd St (66212-1728)
PHONE..................................913 649-5110
Karen Leverich, *Principal*
EMP: 33 **EST:** 2007
SALES (est): 1.9MM **Privately Held**
SIC: 8059 8051 Convalescent home; skilled nursing care facilities

(G-9407)
THREE CLICK VENTRES INC DBA AV
10975 Grandview Dr (66210-1564)
PHONE..................................913 955-3700
Nathan Roberts, *CEO*
Michael Stults, *Vice Pres*
Keith Pendleton, *Marketing Staff*
EMP: 16
SALES (est): 2MM **Privately Held**
SIC: 8742 Marketing consulting services

(G-9408)
THYSSENKRUPP ELEVATOR CORP
11314 W 80th St (66214-3307)
PHONE..................................913 888-8046
Aaron Westwick, *Sales/Mktg Mgr*
EMP: 14
SALES (corp-wide): 46.8B **Privately Held**
WEB: www.tyssenkrupp.com
SIC: 5084 7699 1796 Elevators; elevators: inspection, service & repair; elevator installation & conversion
HQ: Thyssenkrupp Elevator Corporation
11605 Haynes Bridge Rd # 650
Alpharetta GA 30009
678 319-3240

(G-9409)
TIC INTERNATIONAL CORPORATION
6405 Metcalf Ave Ste 200 (66202-4084)
PHONE..................................913 236-5490
Michael Gauthier, *Branch Mgr*
EMP: 30
SALES (corp-wide): 28.5MM **Privately Held**
SIC: 6411 Pension & retirement plan consultants
PA: Tic International Corporation
11590 N Meridian St # 600
Carmel IN 46032
317 580-8686

(G-9410)
TIDY UP ANGELS LLC
6600 W 95th St Ste 103 (66212-1436)
PHONE..................................913 642-2006
Ely Nascimento, *Manager*
EMP: 10 **EST:** 2016
SQ FT: 700
SALES: 385K **Privately Held**
SIC: 7349 Janitorial service, contract basis
PA: Principium, Llc
6400 W 95th St Ste 100
Overland Park KS 66212
816 898-3432

(G-9411)
TIGER COOL EXPRESS LLC (PA)
5750 W 95th St Ste 250 (66207-2969)
PHONE..................................913 305-3510
Steve Van Kirk, *CEO*
Thomas Shurstad, *Principal*
Theodore Prince, *COO*
Cortney Keenan, *Vice Pres*
Bill Welker, *Vice Pres*
EMP: 10
SALES (est): 4.1MM **Privately Held**
SIC: 4731 Truck transportation brokers

(G-9412)
TIRUPATI BALAJI LLC
Also Called: Econo Lodge
7508 Shawnee Mission Pkwy (66202-3058)
PHONE..................................913 262-9600
Ramesh Patel, *General Mgr*
EMP: 12
SALES (est): 237.2K **Privately Held**
SIC: 7011 Hotels & motels

(G-9413)
TITAN BUILT LLC
8207 Melrose Dr Ste 200 (66214-1662)
PHONE..................................913 782-6700
Mike Burson, *Project Mgr*
Carrie Buttron, *Accountant*
Tracey Vaeth, *Mktg Coord*
John Holloway,
EMP: 22
SALES (est): 7.2MM **Privately Held**
SIC: 1542 Commercial & office building, new construction

(G-9414)
TITAN MONITORING INC
9350 Metcalf Ave Ste 110 (66212-1463)
PHONE..................................913 441-0911
Ryan Smith, *Administration*
EMP: 25 **EST:** 2015
SALES (est): 625.8K **Privately Held**
SIC: 7382 Confinement surveillance systems maintenance & monitoring

(G-9415)
TITLE BOXING CLUB LLC
5360 College Blvd Ste 120 (66211-1641)
PHONE..................................913 991-8285
Danny Azzo, *General Mgr*
Fred Cabrera, *General Mgr*
Christine N Seaton, *Principal*
Benton Alleman, *Regional Mgr*
Ryan McGee, *Manager*
EMP: 22 **EST:** 2010
SALES (est): 1MM **Privately Held**
SIC: 7997 6794 Membership sports & recreation clubs; franchises, selling or licensing

(G-9416)
TIVOL PLAZA INC
4721 W 119th St (66209-1558)
PHONE..................................913 345-0200
Steffon Carlson, *Sales Staff*
Laura Craft, *Sales Associate*
Hunter T McGrath, *Sales Associate*
David Behnke, *Branch Mgr*
Annie Powell, *Asst Mgr*
EMP: 25
SALES (est): 1.6MM
SALES (corp-wide): 6.8MM **Privately Held**
SIC: 5944 7631 Jewelry, precious stones & precious metals; watch repair
PA: Tivol Plaza, Inc.
220 Nichols Rd
Kansas City MO 64112
816 531-5800

(G-9417)
TMFS MANAGEMENT LLC
10950 Grandview Dr # 500 (66210-1585)
PHONE..................................913 319-8100
EMP: 111
SALES (est): 1.6MM
SALES (corp-wide): 389.2MM **Privately Held**
SIC: 8741 Management services
HQ: Edelman Financial Engines, Llc
1050 Entp Way Fl 3 Flr 3
Sunnyvale CA 94089
408 498-6000

(G-9418)
TODDS CLOTHIERS & TAILOR SHOP
7052 W 135th St (66223-4843)
PHONE..................................913 681-8633
David Garcia, *Buyer*
EMP: 7 **EST:** 2015
SALES (est): 107.9K **Privately Held**
SIC: 2311 Tailored suits & formal jackets

(G-9419)
TOW ALL OF KANSAS CITY LLC
4839 Merriam Dr (66203-5300)
PHONE..................................913 208-0327
Cody Kidd, *General Mgr*
Michael Kidd,
Mike Kidd,
EMP: 50
SALES (est): 2.1MM **Privately Held**
SIC: 7549 Towing service, automotive; towing services

(G-9420)
TOWN & COUNTRY LANDSCAPING (PA)
12741 Grandview St (66213-3042)
PHONE..................................816 358-4511
James S Johnson, *President*
EMP: 15
SALES (est): 1.4MM **Privately Held**
SIC: 0782 0783 Lawn services; ornamental shrub & tree services

(G-9421)
TPP ACQUISITION INC
12055 Metcalf Ave (66213-1121)
PHONE..................................913 317-5591
Rory McCrave, *Branch Mgr*
EMP: 12
SALES (corp-wide): 168.6MM **Privately Held**
SIC: 7221 Photographer, still or video
PA: Tpp Acquisition Inc
1155 Kas Dr Ste 180
Richardson TX 75081

(G-9422)
TPP CRTFIED PUB ACCNTANTS LLC
Also Called: Tpp Rtirement Plan Specialists
7300 College Blvd Ste 400 (66210-1883)
PHONE..................................913 498-2200
Julie Miller, *Accountant*
Brent R Blacklock, *Manager*

Justin Park, *Supervisor*
Dave Perky,
Karla Anderson, *Admin Asst*
EMP: 26
SALES (est): 2.4MM **Privately Held**
WEB: www.tppkc.com
SIC: 8721 Certified public accountant

(G-9423)
TRAINING & EDUCATIONAL SERVICE
7007 College Blvd Ste 385 (66211-2440)
PHONE..................................913 498-1914
Nancy Graham, *Principal*
EMP: 50
SALES (est): 1.3MM **Privately Held**
SIC: 4832 Educational

(G-9424)
TRANSATLANTIC REINSURANCE CO
7500 College Blvd # 1100 (66210-4035)
PHONE..................................913 319-2510
Sharon Iseman, *Branch Mgr*
EMP: 29
SALES (corp-wide): 6.8B **Publicly Held**
SIC: 6331 Reciprocal interinsurance exchanges: fire, marine, casualty
HQ: Transatlantic Reinsurance Co
1 Liberty Plz
New York NY 10006
212 365-2200

(G-9425)
TRANSPORT FUNDING LLC
8717 W 110th St Ste 700 (66210-2127)
PHONE..................................913 319-7400
Scott Carr, *Mng Member*
Jason Miller, *Manager*
Theresa Zink, *Producer*
EMP: 30
SALES (est): 2.9MM **Privately Held**
WEB: www.transportfunding.com
SIC: 6153 Working capital financing

(G-9426)
TRAQ-IT INC
Also Called: Traq-It Software
7300 W 110th St Ste 920 (66210-2310)
PHONE..................................913 498-1221
Dr Robin F Potter, *President*
Jackie Pruitt, *Vice Pres*
John Yount, *Vice Pres*
EMP: 15
SALES (est): 1.3MM **Privately Held**
WEB: www.traqit.com
SIC: 7371 Computer software development

(G-9427)
TRIA HEALTH LLC
7101 College Blvd Ste 600 (66210-2083)
PHONE..................................888 799-8742
Jessica W Lea, *President*
Tracey Hopper, *COO*
Matthew Baki, *Vice Pres*
EMP: 20
SALES (est): 650K **Privately Held**
SIC: 8099 Medical services organization

(G-9428)
TRINITY ANIMATION INC
9200 Indian Creek Pkwy # 650 (66210-2022)
PHONE..................................816 525-0103
Jim Lammers, *President*
Gail Lammers, *Vice Pres*
EMP: 17
SALES (est): 739.9K **Privately Held**
WEB: www.trinityanimation.com
SIC: 7374 7819 Computer graphics service; video tape or disk reproduction

(G-9429)
TRIPLE B INVESTMENTS INC
Also Called: Briggs Turf Farm
3401 W 159th St (66224-9748)
PHONE..................................913 681-2500
Bryan Briggs, *President*
Brad McBee, *Treasurer*
Brent McBee, *Admin Sec*
EMP: 12
SALES (est): 558.4K **Privately Held**
SIC: 3423 Hooks: bush, grass, baling, husking, etc.

(G-9430)
TRISTAR PUBLISHING INC
7285 W 132nd St Ste 300 (66213-1102)
PHONE..................................913 491-4200
Eric Reynolds, *CEO*
Dora Grote, *Editor*
Cody Holt, *Vice Pres*
Michelle Klein, *Vice Pres*
Michele Staus, *Vice Pres*
EMP: 9
SALES (est): 1MM **Privately Held**
SIC: 2741 Miscellaneous publishing

(G-9431)
TRITATS LLC
10819 W 157th Ter (66221-7104)
P.O. Box 26222 (66225-6222)
PHONE..................................913 219-5949
Sean Jackson, *President*
EMP: 5
SALES: 1.8MM **Privately Held**
SIC: 2759 Commercial printing

(G-9432)
TRUENORTH COMPANIES LC
9290 Bond St Ste 205 (66214-1742)
P.O. Box 1863, Cedar Rapids IA (52406-1863)
PHONE..................................913 307-0838
Megan Miller, *Accounts Mgr*
Dean Allen, *Branch Mgr*
EMP: 55
SALES (corp-wide): 100.1MM **Privately Held**
SIC: 6411 Insurance agents
PA: Truenorth Companies, Lc
500 1st St Se
Cedar Rapids IA 52401
319 364-5193

(G-9433)
TRUMOVE PHYSICAL THERAPY PA
7279 W 105th St (66212-2515)
PHONE..................................913 642-7746
Drew Dischinger, *CEO*
Salvatore Sesti, *Exec Dir*
Kim Erisman, *Director*
Megan Dischinger, *Admin Dir*
Amy Mahnken, *Administration*
EMP: 12
SQ FT: 7,500
SALES (est): 871K **Privately Held**
SIC: 8049 Physical therapist

(G-9434)
TRUMPET BEHAVIORAL HEALTH LLC
7001 W 79th St (66204-3179)
PHONE..................................816 802-6969
EMP: 13
SALES (corp-wide): 24.5MM **Privately Held**
SIC: 8099 Childbirth preparation clinic
PA: Trumpet Behavioral Health, Llc
390 Union Blvd Ste 300
Lakewood CO 80228
303 989-8169

(G-9435)
TYR ENERGY INC (HQ)
7500 College Blvd Ste 400 (66210-4016)
PHONE..................................913 754-5800
Tomoo Yokobori, *CEO*
Bradford Nordholm, *CEO*
Karl Usami, *CEO*
Thomas Wertz, *President*
Sean Missey, *Controller*
EMP: 16
SALES (est): 5.7MM **Privately Held**
WEB: www.tyrenergy.com
SIC: 8741 Business management

(G-9436)
U INC
9200 Glenwood St Ste 102 (66212-1300)
PHONE..................................913 814-7708
Lirel Holt, *CEO*
Bryce Holt, *Author*
EMP: 16 **EST:** 1999
SALES (est): 2.3MM **Privately Held**
WEB: www.jobconfidence.com
SIC: 7372 8742 Prepackaged software; management consulting services

(G-9437)
UBIQUITEL INC (DH)
6391 Sprint Pkwy (66251-6100)
PHONE..................................913 315-5800
Donald A Harris, *Ch of Bd*
Dean E Russell, *COO*
Patricia E Knese, *Senior VP*
James J Volk, *CFO*
David L Zylka, *CTO*
EMP: 60
SQ FT: 21,500
SALES (est): 57.4MM **Publicly Held**
SIC: 4812 Cellular telephone services
HQ: Sprint Communications, Inc.
6200 Sprint Pkwy
Overland Park KS 66251
855 848-3280

(G-9438)
ULTIMATE ESCAPE DAY SPA LLC
11674 W 135th St (66221-2837)
PHONE..................................913 851-3385
Steve Humbert, *Mng Member*
Nancy Humbert, *Mng Member*
EMP: 24
SALES (est): 762.5K **Privately Held**
WEB: www.ultimateescapedayspa.com
SIC: 7991 7231 Spas; facial salons

(G-9439)
UNI FLOOR INC
6711 W 157th Ter (66223-3579)
PHONE..................................913 238-4633
Diana P Aragonez, *President*
John D McCullum Jr, *Manager*
EMP: 12
SALES: 2.8MM **Privately Held**
SIC: 5713 1752 Floor covering stores; floor laying & floor work

(G-9440)
UNIFORMED SERVICES BENEFT ASSN
7301 W 129th St Ste 200 (66213-2671)
P.O. Box 25956, Shawnee Mission (66225-5956)
PHONE..................................913 327-5500
Col Robin A Snyder, *President*
Connie Markovich, *Exec VP*
Matt Anderson, *Vice Pres*
Pam Oyler, *Marketing Staff*
Pam Reichard, *Marketing Staff*
EMP: 13
SALES: 45.7MM **Privately Held**
SIC: 6399 Deposit insurance

(G-9441)
UNITAS GLOBAL LLC
Also Called: Aoscloud
9900 W 109th St Ste 400 (66210-1451)
PHONE..................................913 339-2300
Jaime Simpson, *Branch Mgr*
EMP: 95
SALES (corp-wide): 80MM **Privately Held**
SIC: 7372 Prepackaged software
PA: Unitas Global Llc
453 S Spring St Ste 201
Los Angeles CA 90013
213 785-6200

(G-9442)
UNITED BIOSOURCE LLC
12900 Foster St (66213-2704)
PHONE..................................913 339-7000
Jim Blondin, *Branch Mgr*
Heather Walsh, *Analyst*
EMP: 100
SALES (corp-wide): 106.9MM **Privately Held**
SIC: 8731 Biotechnical research, commercial
PA: United Biosource Llc
920 Harvest Dr Ste 200
Blue Bell PA 19422
215 591-2880

(G-9443)
UNITED HEALTHCARE SERVICES INC
10895 Grandview Dr # 200 (66210-1532)
PHONE..................................888 340-9716
Leslie Jamar, *Manager*
Bill Tracy, *Exec Dir*
EMP: 80
SALES (corp-wide): 226.2B **Publicly Held**
WEB: www.firstlinepharmacy.com
SIC: 6324 Health maintenance organization (HMO), insurance only
HQ: United Healthcare Services Inc.
9900 Bren Rd E Ste 300w
Minnetonka MN 55343
952 936-1300

(G-9444)
UNITED STATES TENNIS
Also Called: USTA
6400 W 95th St Ste 102 (66212-1432)
PHONE..................................913 322-4823
Gordon Smith, *Exec Dir*
EMP: 17
SQ FT: 2,960
SALES: 3MM
SALES (corp-wide): 176.9MM **Privately Held**
SIC: 7999 Tennis services & professionals
PA: United States Tennis Association Incorporated
70 W Red Oak Ln Fl 1
White Plains NY 10604
914 696-7000

(G-9445)
UNITEDHEALTH GROUP INC
6860 W 115th St (66211-2457)
PHONE..................................952 936-1300
Scott Winkler, *Branch Mgr*
Denise Trabon, *Manager*
EMP: 38
SALES (corp-wide): 226.2B **Publicly Held**
WEB: www.unitedhealthgroup.com
SIC: 6324 Health maintenance organization (HMO), insurance only
PA: Unitedhealth Group Incorporated
9900 Bren Rd E Ste 300w
Minnetonka MN 55343
952 936-1300

(G-9446)
UNITEDLEX CORPORATION (PA)
6130 Sprint Pkwy Ste 300 (66211-1115)
PHONE..................................913 685-8900
Daniel Reed, *CEO*
Rodney Rogers, *Ch of Bd*
Dave Deppe, *President*
Doug Goodall, *President*
Lauren Leonard, *President*
EMP: 129
SALES (est): 116.8MM **Privately Held**
SIC: 7389 Legal & tax services

(G-9447)
UNIVERSAL ENGRAVING INC (PA)
9090 Nieman Rd (66214-1799)
P.O. Box 15090, Lenexa (66285-5090)
PHONE..................................913 599-0600
Larry Hutchison, *President*
Glenn Hutchison, *Chairman*
Jim Hutchison, *Senior VP*
Andy Tuck, *CFO*
Robert Janes, *Treasurer*
▲ **EMP:** 152
SQ FT: 26,000
SALES: 30MM **Privately Held**
WEB: www.ueigroup.com
SIC: 2796 Engraving on copper, steel, wood or rubber: printing plates

(G-9448)
UPPER LAKE PROCESSING SERVICES
7201 W 110th St Ste 225 (66210-2365)
PHONE..................................855 418-9500
Sherry Treppa, *President*
EMP: 12 **EST:** 2013
SALES (est): 1.1MM **Privately Held**
SIC: 7389 Financial services

(G-9449)
UPS SRVICE PARTS LOGISTICS INC
10881 Lowell Ave Ste 220 (66210-1666)
PHONE..................................800 451-4550
Dan Dimaggio, *CEO*
Doug Anderson, *CEO*
John Sutthoff, *COO*

GEOGRAPHIC

James Thompson, *Senior VP*
Jay Walsh, *CIO*
EMP: 536
SQ FT: 17,000
SALES (est): 38.9MM
SALES (corp-wide): 71.8B **Publicly Held**
SIC: 4513 4225 Air courier services; general warehousing
PA: United Parcel Service, Inc.
55 Glenlake Pkwy
Atlanta GA 30328
404 828-6000

(G-9450)
UPS SUPPLY CHAIN SOLUTIONS INC
Also Called: UPS Express Critical
10881 Lowell Ave (66210-1768)
PHONE....................................800 714-8779
Wayne Hall, *Branch Mgr*
EMP: 300
SALES (corp-wide): 71.8B **Publicly Held**
SIC: 4731 Freight transportation arrangement
HQ: Ups Supply Chain Solutions, Inc.
12380 Morris Rd
Alpharetta GA 30005
800 742-5727

(G-9451)
US BANK NATIONAL ASSOCIATION
Also Called: US Bank
7000 W 75th St (66204-3029)
PHONE....................................913 432-9633
Pete Morse, *Branch Mgr*
Randi Dinges, *Branch Mgr*
Wayne Hayton, *Manager*
EMP: 12
SALES (corp-wide): 25.7B **Publicly Held**
WEB: www.firstar.com
SIC: 6021 National commercial banks
HQ: U.S. Bank National Association
425 Walnut St Fl 14
Cincinnati OH 45202
513 632-4234

(G-9452)
US BANK NATIONAL ASSOCIATION
Also Called: US Bank
10100 W 119th St (66213-1604)
PHONE....................................913 323-5314
Tony Caloroso, *Vice Pres*
EMP: 10
SALES (corp-wide): 25.7B **Publicly Held**
WEB: www.firstar.com
SIC: 6021 National commercial banks
HQ: U.S. Bank National Association
425 Walnut St Fl 14
Cincinnati OH 45202
513 632-4234

(G-9453)
US BANK NATIONAL ASSOCIATION
Also Called: US Bank
6450 Sprint Pkwy (66251-6105)
PHONE....................................913 338-0646
EMP: 12
SALES (corp-wide): 25.7B **Publicly Held**
SIC: 6021 National commercial banks
HQ: U.S. Bank National Association
425 Walnut St Fl 14
Cincinnati OH 45202
513 632-4234

(G-9454)
US BANK NATIONAL ASSOCIATION
Also Called: US Bank
12800 Foster St (66213-2623)
PHONE....................................913 725-7000
Sharon Angotti, *Branch Mgr*
EMP: 12
SALES (corp-wide): 25.7B **Publicly Held**
SIC: 6021 National commercial banks
HQ: U.S. Bank National Association
425 Walnut St Fl 14
Cincinnati OH 45202
513 632-4234

(G-9455)
US BANK NATIONAL ASSOCIATION
Also Called: US Bank
6900 W 135th St (66223-4800)
PHONE....................................913 402-6919
EMP: 12
SALES (corp-wide): 25.7B **Publicly Held**
SIC: 6021 National commercial banks
HQ: U.S. Bank National Association
425 Walnut St Fl 14
Cincinnati OH 45202
513 632-4234

(G-9456)
US BANK NATIONAL ASSOCIATION
Also Called: US Bank
8401 W 135th St (66223-1199)
PHONE....................................913 239-8204
Marla Frazier, *Principal*
EMP: 12
SALES (corp-wide): 25.7B **Publicly Held**
WEB: www.firstar.com
SIC: 6021 National commercial banks
HQ: U.S. Bank National Association
425 Walnut St Fl 14
Cincinnati OH 45202
513 632-4234

(G-9457)
V WEALTH ADVISORS LLC
Also Called: V Wealth Management
6800 College Blvd Ste 630 (66211-1564)
PHONE....................................913 827-4600
Dj Balzer, *Owner*
Christopher Wade, *Vice Pres*
Brett Lange, *Manager*
Max Mason, *Advisor*
Richard H Meyer, *Advisor*
EMP: 20
SALES (est): 2.2MM **Privately Held**
SIC: 8742 Financial consultant

(G-9458)
VALLEY VIEW STATE BANK
10300 Mastin St (66212-5451)
PHONE....................................913 381-3311
Britney Connett, *Branch Mgr*
EMP: 10
SALES (corp-wide): 100MM **Privately Held**
SIC: 6022 State commercial banks
HQ: Valley View State Bank
7500 W 95th St
Shawnee Mission KS 66212
913 381-3311

(G-9459)
VALUE PLACE TOPEKA
7200 W 132nd St Ste 220 (66213-1144)
P.O. Box 250, Mission (66201-0250)
PHONE....................................785 271-8862
Jetaime Parker, *Manager*
EMP: 11 **EST:** 2010
SALES (est): 573.7K **Privately Held**
SIC: 7011 Hotels & motels

(G-9460)
VELOCITY STAFF INC
5251 W 116th Pl Ste 200 (66211-2011)
PHONE....................................913 693-4626
Robert Zavala, *Principal*
EMP: 25
SALES (est): 669.4K **Privately Held**
WEB: www.velocitystaff.com
SIC: 7361 Executive placement

(G-9461)
VENTURE CONSTRUCTION COMPANY
7010 W 107th St Ste 220 (66212-1837)
PHONE....................................913 642-2972
EMP: 34
SALES (corp-wide): 324.6MM **Privately Held**
SIC: 1542 Commercial & office building, new construction
PA: Venture Construction Company Inc
5660 Peachtree Indus Blvd
Norcross GA 30071
770 441-6555

(G-9462)
VERACITY CONSULTING INC
8100 Newton St (66204-3623)
PHONE....................................913 945-1912
Angela Hurt, *President*
Shawn McCarrick, *COO*
Chris Barr, *Vice Pres*
Hillary Stamper, *Accounts Exec*
Amanda Ebberts, *Director*
EMP: 52
SALES (est): 6.9MM **Privately Held**
WEB: www.veracity-solutions.com
SIC: 8742 7371 7379 8748 Management consulting services; custom computer programming services; computer related maintenance services; computer related consulting services; business consulting; systems analysis or design

(G-9463)
VIC REGNIER BUILDERS INC (PA)
Also Called: Regnier Properties
3705 W 95th St (66206-2036)
PHONE....................................913 649-0123
Robert Regnier, *President*
Kerrie Moore, *Office Mgr*
EMP: 25
SQ FT: 225,000
SALES (est): 2.9MM **Privately Held**
SIC: 6531 Real estate leasing & rentals

(G-9464)
VINCENT PENNIPEDE OD
10120 W 119th St (66213-1600)
PHONE....................................913 825-2600
Vincent A Pennipede, *Owner*
EMP: 20
SALES (est): 950.2K **Privately Held**
SIC: 8042 Specialized optometrists
PA: Vincent Pennipede Od
15257 W 135th St
Olathe KS 66062

(G-9465)
VIRALNOVA LLC
12722 Flint Ln (66213-4443)
PHONE....................................913 706-9710
Sean Beckner, *CEO*
Scott Delong, *Founder*
Shaun Tilford, *CTO*
EMP: 25
SALES (est): 1.4MM
SALES (corp-wide): 6MM **Privately Held**
SIC: 4813 7313 2741 ; electronic media advertising representatives; miscellaneous publishing
PA: Zealot Networks, Inc.
2114 Narcissus Ct
Venice CA 90291
310 821-3737

(G-9466)
VIRTUS LLC
Also Called: Virtus Insurance
9800 Metcalf Ave Ste 500 (66212-2216)
PHONE....................................816 919-2323
Andrew Gray, *CEO*
Charlie Stenger, *COO*
Tom Pollock, *Senior VP*
Collin Chlebak, *Vice Pres*
Jon Corbin, *Controller*
EMP: 47
SALES (est): 218.2K **Privately Held**
SIC: 6411 Insurance brokers

(G-9467)
VISTA OUTDOOR INC
9200 Cody St (66214-1734)
PHONE....................................913 752-3400
Brett Nelson, *Surgery Dir*
EMP: 142
SALES (corp-wide): 2B **Publicly Held**
SIC: 3483 Ammunition, except for small arms
PA: Vista Outdoor Inc.
1 Vista Way
Anoka MN 55303
801 447-3000

(G-9468)
VITAS HEALTHCARE CORP MIDWEST (DH)
8527 Bluejacket St (66214-1656)
PHONE....................................913 722-1631
David A Wester, *President*
EMP: 31
SALES (est): 3.7MM
SALES (corp-wide): 1.7B **Publicly Held**
SIC: 8082 8051 Home health care services; skilled nursing care facilities
HQ: Vitas Healthcare Corporation
201 S Biscayne Blvd # 400
Miami FL 33131
305 374-4143

(G-9469)
VIZION INTERACTIVE
7500 W 151 St (66213)
P.O. Box 24262 (66283-4262)
PHONE....................................888 484-9466
Mark Jackson, *President*
EMP: 10
SALES: 1.5MM **Privately Held**
SIC: 7379

(G-9470)
VOLD & MORRIS LLC
9225 Indian Creek Pkwy # 1100 (66210-2009)
PHONE....................................913 696-0001
E Denver Vold, *Partner*
EMP: 10
SALES (est): 770.8K **Privately Held**
SIC: 8111 General practice law office

(G-9471)
VOLT MANAGEMENT CORP
Also Called: Volt Workforce Solutions
7300 W 110th St Ste 140 (66210-2308)
PHONE....................................913 906-9568
Rhona Driggs, *Branch Mgr*
EMP: 56
SALES (corp-wide): 997MM **Publicly Held**
SIC: 7363 Help supply services
HQ: Volt Management Corp.
50 Charles Lindbergh Blvd # 206
Uniondale NY 11553

(G-9472)
W & R CORPORATE LLC
6300 Lamar Ave (66202-4247)
PHONE....................................913 236-2000
Michael Strohm, *President*
James Hughes, *Admin Sec*
EMP: 40
SALES (est): 8.3MM **Publicly Held**
SIC: 6211 Security brokers & dealers
PA: Waddell & Reed Financial, Inc.
6300 Lamar Ave
Overland Park KS 66202

(G-9473)
W + D MACHINERY CO INC
11300 W 80th St (66214-3307)
PHONE....................................913 492-9880
Shaun Kilsoyle, *President*
Randall Gossage, *Train & Dev Mgr*
EMP: 36
SALES: 40MM
SALES (corp-wide): 453.1K **Privately Held**
SIC: 3554 Bag & envelope making machinery, paper
PA: Wd&P Consulting Gmbh
Unterdornen 101
Wuppertal
173 862-7000

(G-9474)
W + D NORTH AMERICA INC
11300 W 80th St (66214-3307)
PHONE....................................913 492-9880
Shaun Kilfoyle, *President*
▲ **EMP:** 35 **EST:** 1973
SQ FT: 24,000
SALES (est): 11.9MM
SALES (corp-wide): 3B **Privately Held**
WEB: www.koerber.de
SIC: 5084 Industrial machinery & equipment
HQ: Barry-Wehmiller Companies, Inc.
8020 Forsyth Blvd
Saint Louis MO 63105
314 862-8000

(G-9475)
W ROSS GREENLAW DMD
Also Called: Blue Hill Peninsula Dental
8001 Conser St Ste 200 (66204-3409)
PHONE..................................207 374-5538
W Ross Greenlaw DMD, *Owner*
EMP: 10
SALES (est): 368.7K **Privately Held**
SIC: 8021 Dentists' office

(G-9476)
W S GRIFFITH INC
Also Called: Midwestern Financial Group
9401 Indian Creek Pkwy # 475
(66210-2007)
PHONE..................................913 451-1855
Richard R Jenkins, *President*
John Ellis, *Partner*
Daniel Hughes, *Manager*
EMP: 25
SALES (est): 2.5MM **Privately Held**
WEB: www.midwesternfinancialgroup.com
SIC: 8742 Financial consultant

(G-9477)
WADDELL & REED FINANCIAL INC (PA)
6300 Lamar Ave (66202-4200)
P.O. Box 29217, Shawnee Mission (66201-9217)
PHONE..................................913 236-2000
Philip J Sanders, *CEO*
Thomas C Godlasky, *Ch of Bd*
Leslie Dobyns, *President*
Brent K Bloss, *COO*
Bradley Hofmeister, *Exec VP*
EMP: 53
SQ FT: 298,000
SALES: 1.1B **Publicly Held**
SIC: 6211 6282 6411 Security brokers & dealers; investment advice; insurance agents, brokers & service

(G-9478)
WADDELL & REED FINCL SVCS INC (HQ)
6300 Lamar Ave (66202-4200)
P.O. Box 29217, Shawnee Mission (66201-9217)
PHONE..................................913 236-2000
Henry Herrmann, *President*
Yvonne Devine, *President*
Jim Turner, *President*
Kurt Triebold, *General Mgr*
Richard Forte, *District Mgr*
EMP: 370
SQ FT: 487,000
SALES (est): 133.7MM **Publicly Held**
SIC: 6722 6311 6211 6531 Money market mutual funds; life insurance; security brokers & dealers; real estate managers

(G-9479)
WALDECK MATTEUZZI & SLOAN
10111 W 105th St (66212-5747)
PHONE..................................913 253-2500
Lori Kandow, *President*
Michael Waldeck, *Partner*
Mike Matteuzzi, *Partner*
Tina Schoenfelder, *Receptionist*
EMP: 25
SALES (est): 1.8MM **Privately Held**
SIC: 8111 General practice attorney, lawyer

(G-9480)
WALGREEN CO
Also Called: Walgreens
8450 W 151st St (66223-2108)
PHONE..................................913 814-7977
Tom Keeling, *Manager*
EMP: 30
SALES (corp-wide): 136.8B **Publicly Held**
WEB: www.walgreens.com
SIC: 5912 7384 Drug stores; photofinishing laboratory
HQ: Walgreen Co.
200 Wilmot Rd
Deerfield IL 60015
800 925-4733

(G-9481)
WALGREEN CO
Also Called: Walgreens
7500 Metcalf Ave (66204-2926)
PHONE..................................913 341-1725
Damon Brower, *Branch Mgr*
EMP: 30
SALES (corp-wide): 136.8B **Publicly Held**
WEB: www.walgreens.com
SIC: 5912 7384 Drug stores; photofinishing laboratory
HQ: Walgreen Co.
200 Wilmot Rd
Deerfield IL 60015
800 925-4733

(G-9482)
WALLACE SAUNDERS CHARTERED (PA)
10111 W 87th St (66212-4673)
P.O. Box 12290, Shawnee Mission (66282-2290)
PHONE..................................913 888-1000
Mark McKinzie, *Managing Prtnr*
Richard Merker, *Managing Prtnr*
James Butler Jr, *Corp Secy*
Leo Logan, *Counsel*
Kevin Weakley, *Counsel*
EMP: 90
SQ FT: 28,000
SALES (est): 17.4MM **Privately Held**
SIC: 8111 General practice law office

(G-9483)
WALSWORTH PUBLISHING CO INC
7300 W 110th St Ste 600 (66210-2392)
PHONE..................................800 265-6795
Veronika Levine, *Marketing Staff*
Jim Penney, *Branch Mgr*
EMP: 32
SALES (corp-wide): 296.6MM **Privately Held**
WEB: www.walsworth.com
SIC: 2741 Yearbooks: publishing & printing
PA: Walsworth Publishing Company, Inc.
306 N Kansas Ave
Marceline MO 64658
660 376-3543

(G-9484)
WATERMAN GROUP INC
7415 W 130th St (66213-2717)
P.O. Box 25682, Shawnee Mission (66225-5682)
PHONE..................................913 685-4900
George O Waterman, *President*
EMP: 15
SQ FT: 4,000
SALES: 2MM **Privately Held**
SIC: 7361 Employment agencies

(G-9485)
WATERWAY GAS & WASH COMPANY
8110 W 135th St (66223-1112)
PHONE..................................913 897-3111
Dave Maryas, *Branch Mgr*
EMP: 47
SALES (corp-wide): 381.2MM **Privately Held**
WEB: www.waterway.com
SIC: 7542 Washing & polishing, automotive
PA: Waterway Gas & Wash Company
727 Goddard Ave
Chesterfield MO 63005
636 537-1111

(G-9486)
WEATHER METRICS INC
Also Called: Alpha Security Midwest
11100 W 91st St (66214-1713)
P.O. Box 7071 (66207-0071)
PHONE..................................913 438-7666
Peter A Levy, *President*
Leigh Geither, *Accounting Mgr*
Julie Ross, *Sales Dir*
Tom Bell, *Manager*
Andrew Boyce, *IT/INT Sup*
EMP: 9
SQ FT: 4,160
SALES: 2MM **Privately Held**
WEB: www.weathermetrics.com
SIC: 3829 Weather tracking equipment

(G-9487)
WELKER HEATING AND COOLING
Also Called: Crystal Company
St 6830 152 Ter (66223)
PHONE..................................913 669-7555
Welker Walker, *CEO*
EMP: 10
SALES: 150K **Privately Held**
SIC: 1711 Warm air heating & air conditioning contractor

(G-9488)
WELLS FARGO BANK NATIONAL ASSN
7500 College Blvd Ste 250 (66210-4095)
PHONE..................................816 234-2929
Lynn Steve, *Manager*
EMP: 15
SALES (corp-wide): 101B **Publicly Held**
WEB: www.wellsfargo.com
SIC: 6021 6029 National commercial banks; commercial banks
HQ: Wells Fargo Bank, National Association
101 N Phillips Ave
Sioux Falls SD 57104
605 575-6900

(G-9489)
WELLS FARGO CLEARING SVCS LLC
Also Called: Wells Fargo Advisors
7400 W 130th St Ste 200 (66213-2659)
PHONE..................................913 402-5100
James McEnerney, *Branch Mgr*
Tammy Lawrence, *Associate*
EMP: 57
SALES (corp-wide): 101B **Publicly Held**
WEB: www.wachoviasec.com
SIC: 6211 Stock brokers & dealers
HQ: Wells Fargo Clearing Services, Llc
1 N Jefferson Ave Fl 7
Saint Louis MO 63103
314 955-3000

(G-9490)
WELLSKY CORPORATION (PA)
11300 Switzer St (66210-3665)
PHONE..................................913 307-1000
Bill Miller, *CEO*
Thomas Kelly Mann, *President*
Robert Tysall-Blay, *President*
Robert C Weber, *Exec VP*
Cynthia Hammersley, *Vice Pres*
EMP: 120
SALES (est): 118.3MM **Privately Held**
WEB: www.mediware.com
SIC: 7372 Prepackaged software

(G-9491)
WESTERN CHANDELIER COMPANY
14975 Metcalf Ave (66223-2203)
PHONE..................................913 685-2000
Wayne Burton, *President*
EMP: 13
SQ FT: 20,000
SALES (est): 3.3MM **Privately Held**
WEB: www.westernchandelier.com
SIC: 5063 5719 Lighting fixtures; lighting fixtures

(G-9492)
WESTPORT INSURANCE CORPORATION (DH)
5200 Metcalf Ave (66202-1265)
PHONE..................................913 676-5270
Steven O'Hern, *Vice Pres*
William Noellen, *Director*
EMP: 225
SALES (est): 128.6MM
SALES (corp-wide): 37B **Privately Held**
SIC: 6331 Property damage insurance
HQ: Swiss Re Solutions Holding Corporation
5200 Metcalf Ave
Overland Park KS 66202
913 676-5200

(G-9493)
WHALE VENTURES LLC
12851 Foster St (66213-2705)
PHONE..................................913 814-9988
EMP: 107
SALES (est): 323.9K
SALES (corp-wide): 450.5MM **Privately Held**
SIC: 7374 Data processing & preparation
HQ: Qts Investment Properties Piscataway, Llc
101 Possumtown Rd
Piscataway NJ

(G-9494)
WILBERT FUNERAL SERVICES INC (PA)
Also Called: Wilbert Manufacturers Assn
10965 Granada Ln Ste 300 (66211-1412)
PHONE..................................913 345-2120
Joseph Suhor, *CEO*
Dennis Welzenbach, *President*
▲ **EMP:** 277
SQ FT: 85,300
SALES (est): 244.6MM **Privately Held**
SIC: 3272 Burial vaults, concrete or precast terrazzo

(G-9495)
WILLIS NORTH AMERICA INC
Also Called: Nationwide
12980 Metcalf Ave Ste 500 (66213-2652)
PHONE..................................913 339-0800
Dwane Albert, *Branch Mgr*
Brenae L Tapp, *Agent*
EMP: 60 **Privately Held**
SIC: 6411 Insurance agents, brokers & service
HQ: Willis North America Inc.
200 Liberty St Lbby 3
New York NY 10281
212 915-8888

(G-9496)
WILSON INC ENGINEERS ARCHITECTS
Also Called: Western Air Maps
9401 Reeds Rd (66207-2519)
PHONE..................................913 652-9911
Eric Cenovich, *Principal*
EMP: 50 **EST:** 1960
SALES: 6.3MM
SALES (corp-wide): 62.4MM **Privately Held**
WEB: www.westernair.com
SIC: 7389 Mapmaking services
PA: Wilson & Company, Inc. Engineers & Architects
4401 Masthead St Ne # 15
Albuquerque NM 87109
505 348-4000

(G-9497)
WILSON TRANSPORTATION INC
16226 Foster St (66085-8418)
PHONE..................................913 851-7900
Mark Wilson, *President*
Ann Symmonds, *Accounts Mgr*
EMP: 11
SQ FT: 1,200
SALES (est): 4.9MM **Privately Held**
SIC: 4213 Trucking, except local

(G-9498)
WINDJAMMER COMMUNICATIONS LLC
Also Called: Windjammer Cables
8500 W 110th St Ste 600 (66210-1860)
PHONE..................................913 563-5450
Cecelia Moreno, *CFO*
EMP: 175
SQ FT: 5,600
SALES (est): 542.6K **Publicly Held**
SIC: 4841 Cable & other pay television services
HQ: Windjammer Holdings, Inc.
401 Main St Ste 205
Salem NH 03079
603 589-7600

(G-9499)
WIRELESS LIFESTYLE LLC (PA)
11200 W 93rd St (66214-1717)
PHONE..................................913 962-0002
Paul Kushnir, *CEO*

Mike Kushnir, *President*
Cory Griffin, *District Mgr*
Eric Mikle, *District Mgr*
Matthew Clark, *Store Mgr*
◆ **EMP:** 54
SALES (est): 59.9MM **Privately Held**
WEB: www.pashadistribution.com
SIC: 5999 5065 Mobile telephones & equipment; mobile telephone equipment

(G-9500)
WISE CONNECT
7501 College Blvd Ste 100 (66210-2670)
PHONE..................................913 276-4100
Michael Oyster, *CEO*
Bob Newell, *CFO*
Tracie Ferchek, *Admin Sec*
EMP: 200
SQ FT: 2,500
SALES (est): 25.8MM **Privately Held**
SIC: 4822 Telegraph & other communications

(G-9501)
WOMENS CARE (PA)
9301 W 74th St Ste 325 (66204-2281)
PHONE..................................913 384-4990
Dr Robert L Sugar, *Partner*
Cristine Carriker, *Partner*
Dr Michael R Magee, *Partner*
Breand Mitchell, *Partner*
Angel Piquard, *Partner*
EMP: 30
SQ FT: 6,000
SALES (est): 7.1MM **Privately Held**
SIC: 8011 Gynecologist; obstetrician; physicians' office, including specialists

(G-9502)
WOMENS CLINIC JOHNSON COUNTY
9119 W 74th St Ste 268 (66204-2268)
PHONE..................................913 491-4020
Dr Laura Kenny, *President*
Cheryl Rips, *Obstetrician*
EMP: 10 **Privately Held**
WEB: www.wcjcobgyn.com
SIC: 8011 Clinic, operated by physicians
PA: Women's Clinic Of Johnson County
5525 W 119th St
Leawood KS 66209

(G-9503)
WOOD RIBBLE & TWYMAN INC
Also Called: Adaptive Solutions Group
7301 W 129th St Ste 110 (66213-2635)
PHONE..................................913 396-4400
Bradley Wood, *Branch Mgr*
EMP: 52
SALES (corp-wide): 15.8MM **Privately Held**
SIC: 7379
PA: Wood, Ribble & Twyman Inc.
725 Old Ballas Rd
Saint Louis MO 63141
314 236-3850

(G-9504)
WOODS OF CHERRY CREEK INC
Also Called: Marriott
12321 Metcalf Ave (66213-1323)
PHONE..................................913 491-3030
Rachael Miller, *Manager*
EMP: 10
SALES (est): 625.3K **Privately Held**
WEB: www.thewoodsofcherrycreek.com
SIC: 7011 Hotels & motels

(G-9505)
WORLD FUEL SERVICES INC
Also Called: Carter Energy
6000 Metcalf Ave Ste 200 (66202-2306)
P.O. Box 29106, Shawnee Mission (66201-1406)
PHONE..................................913 643-2300
Dave Milligan, *Vice Chairman*
Dave Achten, *Area Mgr*
Susie Coleman, *Area Mgr*
Akash Singh, *Area Mgr*
Jim Prosser, *Vice Pres*
EMP: 125
SALES (corp-wide): 39.7B **Publicly Held**
SIC: 5171 Petroleum bulk stations
HQ: World Fuel Services, Inc.
9800 Nw 41st St Ste 400
Doral FL 33178
305 428-8000

(G-9506)
WORLD FUEL SERVICES CORP
8650 College Blvd (66210-1886)
PHONE..................................913 451-2400
EMP: 300
SALES (corp-wide): 39.7B **Publicly Held**
SIC: 7389 Credit card service
PA: World Fuel Services Corp
9800 Nw 41st St Ste 400
Doral FL 33178
305 428-8000

(G-9507)
WW NORTH AMERICA HOLDINGS INC
Also Called: Weight Watchers
11752 W 95th St (66214-1867)
PHONE..................................913 227-0152
EMP: 25
SALES (corp-wide): 1.5B **Publicly Held**
SIC: 7299 Diet center, without medical staff
HQ: Ww North America Holdings, Inc.
999 Stewart Ave Ste 215
Bethpage NY 11714
516 390-1400

(G-9508)
WW NORTH AMERICA HOLDINGS INC
Also Called: Weight Watchers
7171 W 95th St Ste 400 (66212-2300)
PHONE..................................913 495-1400
Susan Weiner, *Branch Mgr*
EMP: 40
SALES (corp-wide): 1.5B **Publicly Held**
WEB: www.wwadirondacks.com
SIC: 7299 Diet center, without medical staff
HQ: Ww North America Holdings, Inc.
999 Stewart Ave Ste 215
Bethpage NY 11714
516 390-1400

(G-9509)
WYNDHAM INTERNATIONAL INC
7000 W 108th St (66211-1103)
PHONE..................................913 383-2550
EMP: 50
SALES (corp-wide): 86.8MM **Privately Held**
SIC: 7011 Hotel/Motel Operation
HQ: Wyndham International, Inc
22 Sylvan Way
Parsippany NJ 07054
973 753-6000

(G-9510)
XCEL ERECTORS INC (DH)
7401 W 129th St (66213-2694)
PHONE..................................913 664-7400
Patrick Oleary, *President*
G A Eisenberg, *Vice Pres*
R L Magee, *Vice Pres*
T J Snyder, *Treasurer*
R P McKinney, *Admin Sec*
EMP: 12
SALES (est): 17MM
SALES (corp-wide): 1.5B **Publicly Held**
SIC: 1791 Structural steel erection
HQ: Spx Cooling Technologies, Inc.
7401 W 129th St
Overland Park KS 66213
913 664-7400

(G-9511)
XEC INC
11200 W 79th St (66214-1492)
PHONE..................................913 563-4260
Michael Gossman, *President*
Sterling Tyler, *Vice Pres*
Charlie Martel, *Project Engr*
EMP: 35
SQ FT: 3,700
SALES (est): 13MM **Privately Held**
SIC: 1542 6531 Commercial & office building contractors; real estate agents & managers

(G-9512)
XELOCITY INC
9300 W 110th St Ste 620 (66210-1411)
PHONE..................................913 647-8660
William T Polese, *President*
Mike Stobbs, *Partner*
Chris Wilson, *Consultant*
Jigs Jamnadas, *Admin Sec*
EMP: 18
SQ FT: 2,500
SALES (est): 1.8MM **Privately Held**
SIC: 8742 Management consulting services

(G-9513)
XK SOLUTIONS INC
6709 W 119th St Ste 242 (66209-2013)
PHONE..................................877 954-9656
EMP: 37
SQ FT: 3,000
SALES: 652K **Privately Held**
SIC: 8742 General Management Srvcs

(G-9514)
XTREME CLEAN 88 LLC
11872 W 91st St (66214-1716)
PHONE..................................913 451-9274
Dennis Allen, *Mng Member*
EMP: 14
SALES (est): 281K **Privately Held**
SIC: 7349 Janitorial service, contract basis

(G-9515)
YAEGER-ACUITY SOLUTIONS
7780 W 119th St (66213-1104)
PHONE..................................913 742-8000
Carl Yaeger,
Jeffrey Kennard,
David Haley,
EMP: 20
SALES (est): 611.3K **Privately Held**
SIC: 8712 Architectural engineering

(G-9516)
YELLOW FRT SYS EMPLOYEES CLB
10990 Roe Ave (66211-1213)
PHONE..................................913 344-3000
EMP: 19
SALES: 67.9K **Privately Held**
SIC: 4213 Trucking, except local

(G-9517)
YELLOW ROADWAY RECEIVABLES FUN
10990 Roe Ave (66211-1213)
PHONE..................................913 491-6363
EMP: 13
SALES (est): 1.5MM
SALES (corp-wide): 5B **Publicly Held**
SIC: 7322 Collection agency, except real estate
PA: Yrc Worldwide Inc.
10990 Roe Ave
Overland Park KS 66211
913 696-6100

(G-9518)
YOH SERVICES LLC
10740 Nall Ave Ste 330 (66211-1297)
PHONE..................................913 648-4004
Cynthia Mason, *Manager*
EMP: 14
SALES (corp-wide): 2.2B **Privately Held**
SIC: 7363 Help supply services
HQ: Yoh Services Llc
1500 Spring Garden St
Philadelphia PA 19130
215 656-2650

(G-9519)
YOUNG MANAGEMENT CORPORATION
8580 Farley St (66212-4621)
PHONE..................................913 341-3113
EMP: 62
SALES (corp-wide): 5.8MM **Privately Held**
SIC: 8741 Management services
PA: Young Management Corporation
22602 State Line Rd
Bucyrus KS 66013
913 947-3134

(G-9520)
YOUNG MANAGEMENT GROUP INC
10660 Barkley St Ste 300 (66212-1861)
PHONE..................................913 213-3827
John Young, *President*
Linda Kemp, *Supervisor*
EMP: 12
SALES (est): 351K **Privately Held**
SIC: 8741 Business management

(G-9521)
YRC ENTERPRISE SERVICES INC
10990 Roe Ave (66211-1213)
PHONE..................................913 696-6100
Justin M Hall, *President*
Phil J Gaines, *Senior VP*
Leah K Dawson, *Admin Sec*
EMP: 16
SALES (est): 2.6MM
SALES (corp-wide): 5B **Publicly Held**
WEB: www.yellowcorp.com
SIC: 4213 Contract haulers; less-than-truckload (LTL) transport
PA: Yrc Worldwide Inc.
10990 Roe Ave
Overland Park KS 66211
913 696-6100

(G-9522)
YRC GLOBAL
10990 Roe Ave (66211-1213)
PHONE..................................913 696-6100
Mike Smid, *Principal*
Michael J Smid, *Principal*
EMP: 11
SALES (est): 897.8K **Privately Held**
SIC: 4213 Trucking, except local

(G-9523)
YRC INC (DH)
Also Called: Yrc Freight
10990 Roe Ave (66211-1213)
P.O. Box 7903 (66207-0903)
PHONE..................................913 696-6100
Thomas J O'Connor, *President*
Ivan Sierra, *Business Mgr*
Duncan C F Walters, *Vice Pres*
Rickey Davis, *Opers Mgr*
Michael Gines, *Opers Mgr*
▼ **EMP:** 500 **EST:** 1954
SALES (est): 3.7B
SALES (corp-wide): 5B **Publicly Held**
WEB: www.roadway.com
SIC: 4213 Contract haulers; less-than-truckload (LTL) transport
HQ: Roadway Llc
10990 Roe Ave
Overland Park KS 66211
913 344-3000

(G-9524)
YRC WORLDWIDE INC (PA)
10990 Roe Ave (66211-1213)
PHONE..................................913 696-6100
Darren D Hawkins, *CEO*
James E Hoffman, *Ch of Bd*
Howard C Moshier, *President*
Loren R Stone, *President*
Thomas J O'Connor III, *COO*
EMP: 400
SALES: 5B **Publicly Held**
WEB: www.yellowcorp.com
SIC: 4213 Trucking, except local; contract haulers; less-than-truckload (LTL) transport

(G-9525)
Z3 GRAPHIX INC (PA)
Also Called: Stationery Now
8455 Lenexa Dr (66214-1550)
PHONE..................................913 599-3355
Kelly Schoen, *President*
EMP: 40
SQ FT: 42,000
SALES (est): 4.6MM **Privately Held**
WEB: www.z3graphix.com
SIC: 2752 Commercial printing, offset

(G-9526)
ZEROBURN LLC
Also Called: Zeroburn Fire Prevention Sys
7700 Wedd St Ste 200 (66204-2237)
PHONE..................................877 207-7100

Mitch Kerns, *CEO*
Patrick Cheek, *CFO*
EMP: 5 **EST:** 2012
SQ FT: 1,100
SALES (est): 456.5K **Privately Held**
SIC: 3569 Sprinkler systems, fire: automatic

(G-9527)
ZILLOW HOME LOANS LLC
Also Called: Gibraltar Mortgage
10975 El Monte St (66211-1407)
PHONE....................................913 491-4299
Rich Barton, *CEO*
Jeremy Wacksman, *President*
Kristin Acker, *Senior VP*
Jun Choo, *Senior VP*
Tim Correia, *Senior VP*
EMP: 42
SQ FT: 9,000
SALES (est): 8.5MM
SALES (corp-wide): 1.3B **Publicly Held**
WEB: www.mortgagelendersofamerica.com
SIC: 6163 Mortgage brokers arranging for loans, using money of others
PA: Zillow Group, Inc.
1301 2nd Ave Fl 31
Seattle WA 98101
206 470-7000

(G-9528)
ZIMMERMAN CONSTRUCTION COMPANY
12509 Hemlock St (66213-1453)
PHONE....................................913 685-2255
Jack Zimmerman, *President*
Nancy Zimmerman, *Treasurer*
EMP: 15
SQ FT: 1,500
SALES (est): 4.2MM **Privately Held**
SIC: 1542 Commercial & office building contractors

(G-9529)
ZIWI USA INCORPORATED
Also Called: Ziwipeak USA Inc.
10985 Cody St Ste 110 (66210-1219)
PHONE....................................913 291-0189
Mary Helen Horn, *President*
EMP: 11
SALES (est): 132K
SALES (corp-wide): 2MM **Privately Held**
SIC: 2047 5149 Dog & cat food; pet foods
HQ: Ziwi Limited
27 Bath Street, Level 2
Auckland 1052
757 524-26

(G-9530)
ZURICH AGENCY SERVICES INC (DH)
Also Called: Zurich Direct Markets
7045 College Blvd (66211-1523)
PHONE....................................913 339-1000
Michael Foley, *CEO*
Linda Hodo, *President*
Kathleen Savio, *President*
Steve R Smith, *President*
Robert Burne, *Treasurer*
EMP: 452
SQ FT: 236,435
SALES (est): 228.8MM
SALES (corp-wide): 48.2B **Privately Held**
WEB: www.uug.com
SIC: 6311 6331 Life insurance; property damage insurance
HQ: Zurich Holding Company Of America, Inc.
1299 Zurich Way
Schaumburg IL 60196
847 605-6000

(G-9531)
ZURICH AMERICAN INSURANCE CO
7045 College Blvd (66211-1523)
PHONE....................................913 339-1000
Arlene Layne, *Vice Pres*
Larry Sederstrom, *Branch Mgr*
Vicki Evans, *Manager*
Tim Jacobson, *Manager*
Dick Hodes, *Director*
EMP: 70
SALES (corp-wide): 48.2B **Privately Held**
WEB: www.zurichna.com
SIC: 6331 Fire, marine & casualty insurance
HQ: Zurich American Insurance Company
1299 Zurich Way
Schaumburg IL 60196
800 987-3373

Oxford
Sumner County

(G-9532)
CORNEJO & SONS LLC
1438 122nd Rd (67119-9011)
PHONE....................................620 455-3720
Tim McGuire, *Branch Mgr*
EMP: 8
SALES (corp-wide): 2.1B **Publicly Held**
SIC: 1442 Construction sand & gravel
HQ: Cornejo & Sons, L.L.C.
2060 E Tulsa St
Wichita KS 67216
316 522-5100

(G-9533)
LAFARGE NORTH AMERICA INC
1438 122nd Rd (67119-9011)
P.O. Box 398 (67119-0398)
PHONE....................................620 455-3720
Tim McGuire, *Manager*
EMP: 27
SALES (corp-wide): 4.5B **Privately Held**
SIC: 3241 Cement, hydraulic
HQ: Lafarge North America Inc.
8700 W Bryn Mawr Ave
Chicago IL 60631
773 372-1000

(G-9534)
PROFESSIONAL BANK FORMS
605 W Main St (67119-3006)
P.O. Box 759 (67119-0759)
PHONE....................................620 455-2205
Kevin A Price, *President*
EMP: 5
SQ FT: 6,000
SALES (est): 660K **Privately Held**
WEB: www.probankforms.com
SIC: 5112 2759 Business forms; business forms: printing

(G-9535)
RIVERVIEW MANOR INC
Also Called: Riverview Manor & Village
200 S Ohio (67119-8080)
P.O. Box 458 (67119-0458)
PHONE....................................620 455-2214
Amanda Harris, *Director*
EMP: 48 **EST:** 1965
SQ FT: 11,700
SALES: 1.4MM **Privately Held**
SIC: 8051 Convalescent home with continuous nursing care

Ozawkie
Jefferson County

(G-9536)
NORTHEAST KANS EDUCATN SVC CTR
Also Called: Keystone Learning Services
500 Sunflower Blvd (66070-9511)
PHONE....................................913 538-7250
Tim Marshall, *General Mgr*
Paul Crawford, *Opers Staff*
Lisa Morando, *Purch Dir*
Melody Tubby, *Pub Rel Dir*
Amy Conklin, *Psychologist*
EMP: 250
SALES (est): 11.9MM **Privately Held**
SIC: 8211 7622 Specialty education; radio & television repair

Palco
Rooks County

(G-9537)
ARCHER-DANIELS-MIDLAND COMPANY
Also Called: ADM
104 S Main St (67657)
P.O. Box G (67657-0178)
PHONE....................................785 737-4135
Scott Kortan, *Manager*
EMP: 5
SALES (corp-wide): 64.3B **Publicly Held**
WEB: www.collingwoodgrain.com
SIC: 2041 5153 Flour & other grain mill products; grain elevators
PA: Archer-Daniels-Midland Company
77 W Wacker Dr Ste 4600
Chicago IL 60601
312 634-8100

Palmer
Washington County

(G-9538)
PALMER GRAIN INC
Also Called: Palmer Grain Fert & Chem Plant
208 N Nadeau Ave (66962-8759)
P.O. Box 10 (66962-0010)
PHONE....................................785 692-4212
Reynold Schaas, *President*
Rich Arpin, *Corp Secy*
Larry Reith, *Vice Pres*
EMP: 10 **EST:** 1973
SALES (est): 3MM **Privately Held**
WEB: www.palmergrain.com
SIC: 5153 5191 Grain elevators; farm supplies; feed

Paola
Miami County

(G-9539)
AMERICAN LEGION POST 156
5 Delaware St (66071-1901)
P.O. Box 126 (66071-0126)
PHONE....................................913 294-4676
Carl Greg, *Manager*
EMP: 25
SALES: 35.5K **Privately Held**
SIC: 8641 Veterans' organization

(G-9540)
B J F INC
Also Called: Master Maintance Services
31030 Spring Valley Rd (66071)
PHONE....................................913 837-2726
Robert G Ford, *President*
Joyce Ford, *Vice Pres*
EMP: 14
SALES (est): 653.3K **Privately Held**
SIC: 0782 Lawn care services

(G-9541)
B&C MECHANICAL SERVICES LLC (PA)
19403 W 335th St (66071-8280)
PHONE....................................913 681-0088
Kimberly Brown, *Administration*
EMP: 14
SALES (est): 4.1MM **Privately Held**
SIC: 1711 Mechanical contractor

(G-9542)
BLUE EAGLE INVESTIGATIONS INC
18890 W 252nd St (66071-5691)
Rural Route 6709 W 119th 125, Overland Park (66209)
PHONE....................................913 685-2583
Cathrine Macfarlane, *Principal*
Stuart Ford, *Vice Pres*
Cathy Macfarlane, *Sales Dir*
EMP: 19
SALES: 300K **Privately Held**
WEB: www.blueeagleinvestigations.com
SIC: 7381 Private investigator

(G-9543)
BRYAN-OHLMEIER CONSTRUCTION
911 N Pearl St (66071-1139)
PHONE....................................913 557-9972
John W Bryan, *President*
Wilbur Ohlmeier, *Vice Pres*
EMP: 25
SALES (est): 3.7MM **Privately Held**
SIC: 1622 Bridge construction

(G-9544)
CARROTHERS CONSTRUCTION CO INC
401 W Wea St (66071-1451)
P.O. Box 269 (66071-0269)
PHONE....................................913 294-2361
Michael J Morrand, *Principal*
Dennis Kurtenbach, *Principal*
Michael Morrand, *Principal*
Lacie Burgoon, *Admin Asst*
EMP: 50
SALES (est): 10.6MM **Privately Held**
WEB: www.carrothersconstruction.com
SIC: 1542 Commercial & office building, new construction

(G-9545)
CARROTHERS CONSTRUCTION CO LLC
401 W Wea St (66071-1451)
PHONE....................................913 294-8120
Robert A Caffarelli,
Deb Stifter,
EMP: 30
SALES (est): 924.1K **Privately Held**
SIC: 1623 Water, sewer & utility lines

(G-9546)
CHARGE IT LLC
Also Called: Capital Business Service
14 E Peoria St (66071-1707)
PHONE....................................913 341-8772
John Cobine,
EMP: 20
SALES: 840K **Privately Held**
SIC: 7389 Charge account service

(G-9547)
CITY OF PAOLA
Also Called: Paola Fire Department
19 E Peoria St (66071-1706)
P.O. Box 409 (66071-0409)
PHONE....................................913 259-3600
Bob Harris, *Chief*
EMP: 55 **Privately Held**
SIC: 7389 Personal service agents, brokers & bureaus
PA: City Of Paola
19 E Peoria St
Paola KS 66071
913 259-3600

(G-9548)
CMG CONSTRUCTION INC
1601 E Peoria St (66071-1893)
PHONE....................................913 384-2883
Fax: 913 384-2885
EMP: 24
SQ FT: 2,200
SALES (est): 5.2MM **Privately Held**
SIC: 1542 Nonresidential Construction

(G-9549)
CONTECH ENGNERED SOLUTIONS LLC
Also Called: Kahn Culvert
702 N Pearl St (66071-1136)
PHONE....................................913 294-2131
EMP: 35 **Privately Held**
SIC: 3317 Mfg Steel Pipe/Tubes
HQ: Contech Engineered Solutions Llc
9025 Ctr Pinte Dr Ste 400
West Chester OH 45069
513 645-7000

(G-9550)
CUSTOM STUCCO LLC
1106 Jeff Cir (66071-9156)
P.O. Box 297 (66071-0297)
PHONE....................................913 294-3100
Don Morris, *President*
Leo R Johnson, *Vice Pres*
EMP: 10 **EST:** 1998

GEOGRAPHIC

SALES (est): 563.6K **Privately Held**
SIC: 1742 Stucco work, interior; plaster & drywall work

(G-9551)
DEBRICK TRUCK LINE COMPANY (PA)
33130 Lone Star Rd (66071-4840)
P.O. Box 421 (66071-0421)
PHONE..................................913 294-5020
Kevin E Debrick, *President*
Ken A Debrick, *Vice Pres*
Karen S Windler, *Treasurer*
Kathy L Haley, *Admin Sec*
EMP: 19 **EST:** 1958
SQ FT: 1,200
SALES: 9.4MM **Privately Held**
WEB: www.debrick.net
SIC: 4213 Contract haulers

(G-9552)
DL MACHINE LLC
210 N Silver St (66071-1441)
PHONE..................................913 557-2000
David Trieve, *Mng Member*
EMP: 5 **EST:** 2012
SALES (est): 200K **Privately Held**
SIC: 3499 Fire- or burglary-resistive products

(G-9553)
DOHERTY STEEL INC
21110 W 311th St (66071-7447)
P.O. Box 428 (66071-0428)
PHONE..................................913 557-9200
Dennis Doherty, *President*
Pete Stephen, *Vice Pres*
EMP: 105
SQ FT: 30,000
SALES: 38.8MM **Privately Held**
SIC: 3441 Building components, structural steel

(G-9554)
EAST CENTRAL KANSAS ECONOMIC
Also Called: Eckan
22795 W 255th St (66071-5521)
P.O. Box 40, Ottawa (66067-0040)
PHONE..................................913 294-4880
EMP: 39
SALES (corp-wide): 10.1MM **Privately Held**
SIC: 8351 Head start center, except in conjunction with school
PA: East Central Kansas Economic Opportunity Corporation
1320 S Ash St
Ottawa KS 66067
785 242-6413

(G-9555)
EC MANUFACTURING LLC
27508 Lone Star Rd (66071-5446)
PHONE..................................913 825-3077
Norman Beal, *Principal*
Mike Keenan, *Principal*
EMP: 180
SQ FT: 15,000
SALES (est): 33.7MM **Privately Held**
SIC: 3599 3679 Tubing, flexible metallic; electronic loads & power supplies

(G-9556)
EROSION CONTROL INC
31306 W 268th Ter (66071-4071)
PHONE..................................913 397-7324
Margie Sobczynski, *CEO*
EMP: 17
SALES (est): 1.6MM **Privately Held**
SIC: 5039 Soil erosion control fabrics

(G-9557)
EUREKA TECHNOLOGY LLC
2 S Gold St (66071-1403)
PHONE..................................913 557-9639
Fred Green, *Mng Member*
EMP: 5
SALES (est): 685.2K **Privately Held**
SIC: 3341 Recovery & refining of nonferrous metals

(G-9558)
EVERGY METRO INC
Also Called: Paola Commercial Office
101 W Ottawa St (66071-1632)
P.O. Box 299 (66071-0299)
PHONE..................................913 294-6200
Dale Warman, *Manager*
EMP: 50
SALES (corp-wide): 4.2B **Publicly Held**
WEB: www.kcpl.com
SIC: 4911 Generation, electric power
HQ: Evergy Metro, Inc.
1200 Main St
Kansas City MO 64105
816 556-2200

(G-9559)
FIRST RESPONSE
Also Called: First Response Emergency Train
21495 W 303rd St (66071-9514)
PHONE..................................913 557-2187
Debra Wright, *President*
EMP: 18
SALES (est): 752.4K **Privately Held**
SIC: 8621 7217 7699 Education & teacher association; carpet & rug cleaning & repairing plant; rug repair shop, not combined with cleaning

(G-9560)
G K SMITH & SONS INC
1700 Industrial Park Dr (66071-9504)
PHONE..................................913 294-5379
Kenneth L Smith, *President*
Janet Straley, *General Mgr*
Les Smith, *Corp Secy*
EMP: 16 **EST:** 1955
SQ FT: 15,000
SALES (est): 3MM **Privately Held**
SIC: 1711 1731 Warm air heating & air conditioning contractor; electrical work

(G-9561)
GERKEN RENT-ALL INC (PA)
31600 Old Kc Rd (66071-4844)
PHONE..................................913 294-3783
Rusty Gerken, *Owner*
EMP: 12
SQ FT: 6,000
SALES (est): 5.1MM **Privately Held**
SIC: 7359 Rental store, general

(G-9562)
GOODART CONSRTUCTION INC
Also Called: Goodart Construction
26685 Waverly Rd (66071-4135)
PHONE..................................913 557-0044
Brad Goodart, *Superintendent*
EMP: 10
SALES (est): 1.2MM **Privately Held**
SIC: 1611 Highway & street construction

(G-9563)
GREAT SOUTHERN BANK
1 S Pearl St (66071-1461)
P.O. Box 369 (66071-0369)
PHONE..................................913 557-4311
Sandra Moll, *Branch Mgr*
EMP: 231
SALES (corp-wide): 242.1MM **Publicly Held**
SIC: 6022 State commercial banks
HQ: Great Southern Bank
1451 E Battlefield St
Springfield MO 65804
417 887-4400

(G-9564)
HAUER TURF FARMS INC
15355 W 263rd St (66071-8513)
P.O. Box 104, Louisburg (66053-0104)
PHONE..................................913 837-2400
Gary L Hauer, *President*
Cindy L Hauer, *Treasurer*
EMP: 14 **EST:** 1975
SALES: 400K **Privately Held**
SIC: 0782 Sodding contractor

(G-9565)
HEALTH CONNECTION INC
Also Called: Family Fitness Center
708 Baptiste Dr (66071-1337)
PHONE..................................913 294-1000
Larry Fulk, *Owner*
Penny Fulk, *Co-Owner*
EMP: 15
SALES (est): 427.2K **Privately Held**
SIC: 7991 Aerobic dance & exercise classes; health club

(G-9566)
HERRON INC
1601 E Peoria St (66071-1893)
PHONE..................................913 731-2507
Terry Herron, *CEO*
Amy Herron, *President*
EMP: 5
SALES: 225K **Privately Held**
SIC: 3949 5941 Hunting equipment; hunting equipment

(G-9567)
HOLDERMAN PRINTING LLC
11 W Wea St (66071-1462)
PHONE..................................913 557-6848
Lynn Holderman, *Branch Mgr*
EMP: 5
SALES (corp-wide): 555K **Privately Held**
SIC: 2759 Commercial printing
PA: Holderman Printing, Llc
110 W 4th Ave
Garnett KS 66032
913 557-6848

(G-9568)
KANZOU EXPLORATIONS INC
16205 W 287th St (66071-8482)
PHONE..................................913 294-2125
Lester Town, *President*
Winton Town, *Vice Pres*
Michael Town, *Admin Sec*
EMP: 26
SQ FT: 2,950
SALES (est): 1MM **Privately Held**
SIC: 1311 1382 Crude petroleum production; oil & gas exploration services

(G-9569)
LAKEMARY CENTER HOMES INC
100 Lakemary Dr (66071-1855)
PHONE..................................913 557-4000
Harold Mitts, *Ch of Bd*
Paul Sokoloff, *Vice Ch Bd*
William Craig, *President*
Shawn Kelsey, *CFO*
Patricia Lynch, *Admin Sec*
EMP: 10
SALES: 159.8K **Privately Held**
SIC: 8059 Home for the mentally retarded, exc. skilled or intermediate

(G-9570)
LOUISBURG HERALD
Also Called: Miami County Publishing Co
121 S Pearl St (66071-1754)
P.O. Box 389 (66071-0389)
PHONE..................................913 837-4321
Phil Mc Laughlin, *President*
EMP: 5 **EST:** 1876
SALES (est): 247.1K **Privately Held**
WEB: www.herald-online.com
SIC: 2711 2752 Newspapers: publishing only, not printed on site; commercial printing, offset

(G-9571)
MIAMI COUNTY EMERGENCY MED SVC
Also Called: Miami County Ambulance
32765 Clover Dr (66071-4781)
P.O. Box 536 (66071-0536)
PHONE..................................913 294-5010
Jason Jenkins, *Director*
Shane Krull, *Administration*
EMP: 35
SALES (est): 1.1MM **Privately Held**
SIC: 4119 Ambulance service

(G-9572)
MIAMI COUNTY MEDICAL CTR INC
Also Called: OLATHE MEDICAL CENTER
2100 Baptiste Dr (66071-1314)
P.O. Box 365 (66071-0365)
PHONE..................................913 294-2327
Frank H Devocelle, *President*
Meredith Drummond, *Vice Pres*
Heather McMurphey, *Vice Pres*
Nancy Schnegelberger, *Vice Pres*
Larry Crawford, *Technology*
EMP: 130
SQ FT: 22,875
SALES: 26.3MM
SALES (corp-wide): 5.1MM **Privately Held**
SIC: 8062 General medical & surgical hospitals
PA: Olathe Health System, Inc.
20333 W 151st St
Olathe KS 66061
913 791-4200

(G-9573)
MIAMI COUNTY PUBLISHING CO
Also Called: Miami County Republic, The
121 S Pearl St (66071-1754)
P.O. Box 389 (66071-0389)
PHONE..................................913 294-2311
Greg Branson, *President*
Phil Mc Laughlin, *President*
Brian McCauley, *Editor*
Gene Morris, *Editor*
Dave Bradley, *Vice Pres*
EMP: 40
SQ FT: 1,750
SALES (est): 1.8MM **Privately Held**
WEB: www.republic-online.com
SIC: 2711 Newspapers: publishing only, not printed on site

(G-9574)
MIAMI LUMBER INC
1014 N Pearl St (66071-1142)
P.O. Box 362 (66071-0362)
PHONE..................................913 294-2041
Pete Peterson, *President*
Gerald J Peterson Jr, *President*
Kenna Peterson, *Vice Pres*
Dave Eidson, *Sales Staff*
EMP: 15 **EST:** 1960
SQ FT: 10,000
SALES (est): 3.4MM **Privately Held**
WEB: www.miamilumber.com
SIC: 5211 5031 Door & window products; lumber: rough, dressed & finished; building materials, interior; building materials, exterior

(G-9575)
MIDWEST ENGRAVING INC
9 E Piankishaw St (66071-1716)
PHONE..................................913 294-5348
Bill Johns, *President*
EMP: 11
SQ FT: 6,000
SALES (est): 632.8K **Privately Held**
WEB: www.midwestengraving.com
SIC: 7389 Engraving service

(G-9576)
MORRILL HAY COMPANY INC
24021 Eagle Ct (66071-5708)
PHONE..................................620 285-6941
George Morrill, *President*
Joshua Morrill, *Opers Mgr*
Rick Hagerty, *Administration*
EMP: 11
SQ FT: 10,000
SALES (est): 2.2MM **Privately Held**
WEB: www.morrillhay.com
SIC: 0722 5191 2041 Hay, machine harvesting services; hay; flour & other grain mill products

(G-9577)
OSAWATOMIE AGENCY INC
Also Called: First Option Bank
702 Baptiste Dr (66071-1337)
P.O. Box B (66071-0702)
PHONE..................................913 294-3811
Casey Jones, *Vice Pres*
Mark Slauson, *Branch Mgr*
Chad Lewis, *Bd of Directors*
EMP: 14
SALES (est): 2.2MM
SALES (corp-wide): 15MM **Privately Held**
SIC: 6029 6022 Commercial banks; state trust companies accepting deposits, commercial
PA: The Osawatomie Agency Inc
601 Main St
Osawatomie KS 66064
913 755-3811

(G-9578)
PAOLA ASSEMBLY OF GOD INC
Also Called: Paola Christian Academy
1016 N Pearl St (66071-1142)
PHONE..................................913 294-5198
Victoria Railey, *Director*
Susan Watterson, *Director*
EMP: 19
SALES (est): 613.2K **Privately Held**
SIC: 8661 8351 8211 Miscellaneous denomination church; child day care services; private combined elementary & secondary school

(G-9579)
PAOLA COUNTRY CLUB INC
29651 Old Kansas City Rd (66071)
P.O. Box 467 (66071-0467)
PHONE..................................913 294-2910
Bob Blachly, *President*
Bob Lachley, *President*
Ernie Pratt, *Vice Pres*
EMP: 18
SALES: 591.8K **Privately Held**
SIC: 7997 Country club, membership

(G-9580)
PAOLA INN AND SUITES
1600 E Hedge Lane Ct (66071-9508)
PHONE..................................913 294-3700
Alen Hire, *President*
Brenda Reeder, *General Mgr*
EMP: 12
SALES (est): 527.5K **Privately Held**
SIC: 7011 Hotel, franchised

(G-9581)
PAOLA LIFESTOCK AUCTION INC
Also Called: McLa
26701 Eagle Dr (66071-4950)
P.O. Box 251 (66071-0251)
PHONE..................................913 294-3335
Moore Brooklyn, *President*
EMP: 25
SALES (est): 1.3MM **Privately Held**
SIC: 7389 Auctioneers, fee basis

(G-9582)
PEMCO INC (PA)
401 W Wea St (66071-1451)
P.O. Box 269 (66071-0269)
PHONE..................................913 294-2361
Denis A Kurtenbach, *President*
Tayfun Ozbaki, *Technical Staff*
EMP: 15
SQ FT: 3,000
SALES (est): 9MM **Privately Held**
WEB: www.pemcoinc.com
SIC: 1542 School building construction

(G-9583)
PENNYS CONCRETE INC
30078 Lone Star Rd (66071-4489)
PHONE..................................913 441-8781
David Hoover, *President*
EMP: 11
SALES (corp-wide): 43.9MM **Privately Held**
WEB: www.pennysconcrete.com
SIC: 3273 Ready-mixed concrete
PA: Penny's Concrete, Inc.
23400 W 82nd St
Shawnee Mission KS 66227
913 441-8781

(G-9584)
PRODUCT DEV & DESIGNERS
21565 W 255th St (66071-5507)
PHONE..................................913 783-4364
Ross Key, *President*
EMP: 11
SALES (est): 936K **Privately Held**
SIC: 2842 2844 2841 Deodorants, nonpersonal; cleaning or polishing preparations; perfumes, natural or synthetic; soap: granulated, liquid, cake, flaked or chip

(G-9585)
RELIANCE LABEL SOLUTIONS INC
205 N Gold St (66071-1272)
P.O. Box 25250, Overland Park (66225-5250)
PHONE..................................913 294-1600
Jay Frankenberg, *President*
Bill Sargent, *Business Mgr*
Rich Earnshaw, *Vice Pres*
Pat Flaherty, *Vice Pres*
Jim Warren, *Vice Pres*
EMP: 39
SQ FT: 40,000
SALES (est): 11.1MM **Privately Held**
WEB: www.reliancelabel.com
SIC: 2672 Labels (unprinted), gummed: made from purchased materials

(G-9586)
RH MONTGOMERY PROPERTIES INC
Also Called: Country Haven Nursing Center
908 N Pearl St (66071-1140)
PHONE..................................913 294-4308
Barbara Faust, *Manager*
EMP: 61
SALES (corp-wide): 31.9MM **Privately Held**
SIC: 8051 Extended care facility
PA: Rh Montgomery Properties, Inc.
214 N Scott St
Sikeston MO 63801
573 471-1113

(G-9587)
SOMMERSET RIDGE VINEYARD
29725 Somerset Rd (66071-8428)
PHONE..................................913 491-0038
Dennis Reynolds, *Owner*
EMP: 10
SALES (est): 853K **Privately Held**
SIC: 2084 Wines

(G-9588)
SOUTHWEST SALT COMPANY LLC
4 S Silver St (66071-1469)
P.O. Box 445 (66071-0445)
PHONE..................................913 755-1955
Charles Dixon,
EMP: 7
SALES (est): 1.5MM **Privately Held**
SIC: 2899 Salt

(G-9589)
SPLASHTACULAR LLC
102 W Kaskaskia St # 201 (66071-1206)
PHONE..................................800 844-5334
Alex Weidman, *President*
Brian Faulkner, *Vice Pres*
Randy Flint, *Vice Pres*
Kodi Theilgaard, *Vice Pres*
Anita Burdge, *CFO*
EMP: 17
SALES (est): 2.1MM **Privately Held**
SIC: 8711 Engineering services

(G-9590)
SPLASHTACULAR INC
Also Called: Splashtacular Entertainment
102 W Kaskaskia St # 201 (66071-1206)
PHONE..................................800 844-5334
Steve Levine, *CEO*
Jim Mohr, *Sales Staff*
EMP: 15
SALES (corp-wide): 3.5MM **Privately Held**
SIC: 7996 Theme park, amusement
PA: Splashtacular Inc
78670 Highway 111
La Quinta CA 92253
800 844-5334

(G-9591)
STEPHANIE WILSON
Also Called: Corporate Solutions
209 N Silver St (66071-1247)
PHONE..................................913 563-1240
Stephanie Wilson, *Owner*
EMP: 6
SQ FT: 3,500
SALES (est): 669.8K **Privately Held**
SIC: 2679 5131 Tags & labels, paper; labels

(G-9592)
TAYLOR FORGE ENGINEERED (PA)
208 N Iron St (66071-1299)
PHONE..................................785 867-2590
R G Kilkenny, *Ch of Bd*
Michael Kilkenny, *President*
Thomas J Walsh, *Exec VP*
Scott Brandt, *Vice Pres*
John Nelson, *Project Mgr*
◆ **EMP:** 190
SQ FT: 250,000
SALES (est): 49.3MM **Privately Held**
WEB: www.tfes.com
SIC: 3443 Separators, industrial process: metal plate

(G-9593)
TOWN OIL COMPANY
Also Called: Town Drilling & Production
16205 W 287th St (66071-8482)
PHONE..................................913 294-2125
Lester M Town Jr, *Partner*
Michael L Town, *Partner*
Winton Town, *Partner*
EMP: 15
SQ FT: 2,950
SALES (est): 1.4MM **Privately Held**
SIC: 1311 1381 Crude petroleum production; drilling oil & gas wells

(G-9594)
VINTAGE PARK OF PAOLA
601 N East St (66071-1183)
PHONE..................................913 557-0202
Tina Rhodes, *Director*
EMP: 25
SALES (est): 676.1K **Privately Held**
SIC: 8052 Intermediate care facilities

(G-9595)
W H DEBRICK CO INC
610 W Shawnee St (66071-1649)
PHONE..................................913 294-3281
EMP: 12
SQ FT: 4,000
SALES (est): 1.1MM **Privately Held**
SIC: 1711 3272 1794 Plumbing Contractor Mfg Concrete Septic Tanks & Backhoe Contractor

(G-9596)
WINDCREEK DIALYSIS LLC
Also Called: Paola Dialysis
1605 E Peoria St (66071-1893)
PHONE..................................913 294-8417
James K Hilger,
EMP: 31 **EST:** 2012
SALES (est): 358.7K **Publicly Held**
SIC: 8092 Kidney dialysis centers
PA: Davita Inc.
2000 16th St
Denver CO 80202

Park
Gove County

(G-9597)
KRISTIE WINTERS
Also Called: Twin Fitness
201 W 4th St (67751-5130)
PHONE..................................913 648-8946
Kristie Winter, *Mng Member*
Michelle Hutton,
EMP: 15
SALES: 55K **Privately Held**
SIC: 7991 Physical fitness clubs with training equipment

Park City
Sedgwick County

(G-9598)
A-PLUS LOGISTICS LLC
Also Called: A Plus Mini Market
6015 N Broadway Ave (67219-2013)
P.O. Box 12238, Wichita (67277-2238)
PHONE..................................316 945-5757
John Jacobson, *President*
EMP: 43
SQ FT: 11,000
SALES (est): 5.7MM **Privately Held**
WEB: www.a-plus.com
SIC: 4212 7538 7539 4213 Dump truck haulage; general automotive repair shops; wheel alignment, automotive; heavy hauling

(G-9599)
AIR CAPITOL DLVRY & WHSE LLC
5841 N Prospect Rd (67204-2000)
PHONE..................................316 303-9005
Justin Robelli, *General Mgr*
Lewis Robelli, *Mng Member*
Deborah Robelli,
EMP: 60
SQ FT: 343,000
SALES (est): 16MM **Privately Held**
WEB: www.aircapitol.com
SIC: 4214 Local trucking with storage

(G-9600)
AMERICAN FUN FOOD COMPANY INC
6010 N Broadway Ave (67219-2014)
PHONE..................................316 838-9329
Laurie D Jones, *President*
Bryan S Kristenson, *Vice Pres*
Britt Samuelson, *Sales Staff*
Tricia Weber, *Marketing Mgr*
EMP: 16
SQ FT: 7,200
SALES (est): 8.9MM **Privately Held**
WEB: www.americanfunfood.com
SIC: 5046 5141 Restaurant equipment & supplies; groceries, general line

(G-9601)
APEX TRUCKING INC (PA)
6031 N Prospect Rd (67204-2022)
PHONE..................................316 943-0774
Travis Littlejohn, *President*
EMP: 24
SALES (est): 2.6MM **Privately Held**
SIC: 4212 1794 Dump truck haulage; excavation work

(G-9602)
ATWOOD DISTRIBUTING LP
6235 N Broadway Ave (67219-1101)
PHONE..................................316 744-8888
Casey Borger, *Branch Mgr*
EMP: 19
SALES (corp-wide): 266.6MM **Privately Held**
SIC: 5191 Farm supplies
PA: Atwood Distributing, L.P.
500 S Garland Rd
Enid OK 73703
580 233-3702

(G-9603)
BECKER CONSTRUCTION INC
100 W 61st St N Ste F (67204-1552)
PHONE..................................316 744-6800
Mark K Becker, *President*
Christine Becker, *Treasurer*
EMP: 10
SQ FT: 2,000
SALES (est): 250K **Privately Held**
SIC: 1623 Water, sewer & utility lines

(G-9604)
BELFOR USA GROUP INC
100 W 61st St N (67204-1532)
PHONE..................................316 260-4087
EMP: 45
SALES (corp-wide): 1.5B **Privately Held**
SIC: 1799 Post-disaster renovations
HQ: Belfor Usa Group Inc.
185 Oakland Ave Ste 150
Birmingham MI 48009

(G-9605)
BRUENGER TRUCKING COMPANY (HQ)
6250 N Broadway Ave (67219-1102)
PHONE..................................316 744-0494
Butch Bruenger, *President*
Maurice W Bruenger, *President*
Chris Calvert, *Vice Pres*
Joe Diekemper, *Vice Pres*
EMP: 50
SQ FT: 35,000

GEOGRAPHIC

SALES (est): 22.8MM
SALES (corp-wide): 2.2B Publicly Held
SIC: 4731 Transportation agents & brokers
PA: Roadrunner Transportation Systems, Inc.
1431 Opus Pl Ste 530
Downers Grove IL 60515
414 615-1500

(G-9606)
BUCKLEY INDUSTRIES INC (DH)
Also Called: Polyplastics
1850 E 53rd St N (67219-2630)
PHONE..................................316 744-7587
Travis Thomas, *President*
Chris Hart, *CFO*
▲ EMP: 100
SQ FT: 130,000
SALES (est): 42.2MM
SALES (corp-wide): 2.5B Privately Held
WEB: www.buckleyind.com
SIC: 5033 5169 3086 Insulation, thermal; polyurethane products; plastics foam products
HQ: Psc Industries, Inc.
1100 W Market St
Louisville KY 40203
502 625-7700

(G-9607)
C & I LLC
Also Called: Motel 6
990 N Connolly Ct (67219-1300)
PHONE..................................316 214-7308
Neil Bhula, *General Mgr*
EMP: 15
SQ FT: 35,000
SALES: 650K Privately Held
SIC: 7011 Hotels & motels

(G-9608)
CARLSON COMPANY INC
6045 N Broadway Ave (67219-2085)
PHONE..................................316 744-0481
Maynard N Wood, *President*
Maynard Wood, *President*
EMP: 35 EST: 1948
SQ FT: 32,300
SALES (est): 9.3MM Privately Held
WEB: www.carlsoncompany.com
SIC: 3568 Power transmission equipment

(G-9609)
CHISHOLM TRAIL ANIMAL CARE CTR
Also Called: Chisholm Trail Animal Hospital
1726 E 61st St N (67219-1918)
PHONE..................................316 744-0501
Daniel Thompson Dvm, *President*
EMP: 15
SALES (est): 1.1MM Privately Held
WEB: www.ctah.kscoxmail.com
SIC: 0742 Animal hospital services, pets & other animal specialties

(G-9610)
CHISHOLM TRAIL STATE BANK (PA)
6160 N Broadway Ave (67219-2016)
P.O. Box 4658, Wichita (67204-0658)
PHONE..................................316 744-1293
Cuy Mauck, *President*
Elmer Peters Jr, *Vice Pres*
Robert J Sabolik, *Vice Pres*
EMP: 28
SQ FT: 15,000
SALES: 2.6MM Privately Held
WEB: www.chisholmbank.com
SIC: 6036 6022 State savings banks, not federally chartered; state commercial banks

(G-9611)
COMFORT INN
990 N Connolly Ct (67219-1300)
PHONE..................................316 744-7711
Neal Bahula, *Manager*
EMP: 19 EST: 1995
SALES (est): 423.4K Privately Held
SIC: 7011 Hotels & motels

(G-9612)
CONSPEC INC
Also Called: Kansas Paving
4880 N Old Lawrence Rd (67219-2711)
P.O. Box 4204, Wichita (67204-0204)
PHONE..................................316 832-0828
Larry Hacker, *Owner*
Chris Wolken, *Safety Mgr*
Curtis Cody, *Opers Staff*
EMP: 70
SQ FT: 8,000
SALES (est): 16.3MM Privately Held
SIC: 1611 Highway & street paving contractor

(G-9613)
CREASON CORRUGATING MCHY INC (PA)
5844 N Broadway Ave 44 (67219-2010)
PHONE..................................423 629-5532
Howard Creason, *Ch of Bd*
Arthur Henry, *President*
Sandra Henry, *Admin Sec*
▲ EMP: 17 EST: 1959
SQ FT: 5,000
SALES (est): 3.7MM Privately Held
SIC: 3599 3999 Machine shop, jobbing & repair; custom pulverizing & grinding of plastic materials

(G-9614)
CSTK INC
7915 N Hartman Arena Dr (67147-8341)
PHONE..................................316 744-2061
Mike Caylor, *Branch Mgr*
EMP: 15
SQ FT: 8,000
SALES (corp-wide): 34.4MM Privately Held
WEB: www.cstk.com
SIC: 5012 7538 Trucks, commercial; general automotive repair shops
PA: Cstk Inc.
7200 W 132nd St Ste 270
Overland Park KS 66213
913 233-7220

(G-9615)
CUMMINS CENTRAL POWER LLC
5101 N Broadway Ave (67219-2727)
PHONE..................................316 838-0875
David Eaton, *Branch Mgr*
EMP: 25
SQ FT: 5,000
SALES (corp-wide): 23.7B Publicly Held
SIC: 5084 Engines & parts, diesel
HQ: Cummins Central Power, Llc
10088 S 136th St
Omaha NE 68138
402 551-7678

(G-9616)
DANIKSCO OFFICE INTERIORS LLC (PA)
Also Called: Office Plus of Kansas
6010 N Broadway Ave (67219-2014)
PHONE..................................316 491-2607
Laurie Jones, *CEO*
Jim Heimerman, *Sales Associate*
Jeannie Meeker, *Marketing Staff*
EMP: 17
SALES (est): 43.9MM Privately Held
WEB: www.officeplusks.com
SIC: 5044 Office equipment

(G-9617)
EVERGREEN PALLET LLC
302 W 53rd St N (67204-2235)
PHONE..................................316 821-9991
Jeff Ralls,
EMP: 30
SALES (est): 5.6MM Privately Held
SIC: 4953 Recycling, waste materials

(G-9618)
FIREFIGHTERS BNFIT ASN-SEDGWIC
7750 N Wild West Dr (67147-7929)
PHONE..................................316 660-3473
Brad Broyles, *President*
Brad Burdick, *Admin Sec*
EMP: 40
SALES (est): 134.5K Privately Held
SIC: 8631 Labor unions & similar labor organizations

(G-9619)
FOLEY EQUIPMENT COMPANY
1601 E 77th St N (67147-8685)
PHONE..................................316 943-4211
Scott Koehn, *Manager*
EMP: 11
SALES (est): 1MM Privately Held
SIC: 5082 Construction & mining machinery

(G-9620)
IAA INC
Also Called: Iaa 533
270 W 53rd St N (67204-2233)
PHONE..................................316 832-1101
Charles E Gerety, *Manager*
EMP: 13 Publicly Held
SIC: 5012 Automobile auction
HQ: Insurance Auto Auctions, Inc.
2 Westbrook Corporate Ctr # 1000
Westchester IL 60154
708 492-7000

(G-9621)
KANSAS COLISEUM INC
1229 E 85th St N (67147-8701)
PHONE..................................316 440-0888
Marvin Bastian, *President*
EMP: 15
SALES (est): 543.7K Privately Held
SIC: 7941 Stadium event operator services

(G-9622)
KANSAS GOLF AND TURF INC
Also Called: E-Z-Go Golf Cars
5701 N Chuzy Dr (67219-2308)
PHONE..................................316 267-9111
Pauline Mc Greevy, *President*
Corey McGreevy, *Owner*
Brian Mc Greevy, *Vice Pres*
William Mc Greevy, *Treasurer*
Jeff McDonough, *Sales Associate*
EMP: 15 EST: 1978
SQ FT: 20,000
SALES (est): 6.2MM Privately Held
WEB: www.kansasgolfandturf.com
SIC: 5599 5088 Golf cart, powered; golf carts

(G-9623)
KANSAS READY MIX LLC
4850 N Broadway Ave (67219)
P.O. Box 4204, Wichita (67204-0204)
PHONE..................................316 832-0828
Larry Hacker,
EMP: 30
SALES (est): 4.1MM Privately Held
SIC: 3273 Ready-mixed concrete

(G-9624)
KANSASLAND TIRE INC
Also Called: Kansasland Tr/Cmmrical Svc Ctr
5941 N Air Cap Dr (67219-2106)
PHONE..................................316 744-0401
Ray Orr, *Branch Mgr*
EMP: 15
SALES (corp-wide): 94.3MM Privately Held
WEB: www.nktiregroup.com
SIC: 5531 7538 Automotive tires; general automotive repair shops
HQ: Kansasland Tire, Inc.
2904 S Spruce St
Wichita KS 67216
316 522-5434

(G-9625)
KICE INDUSTRIES INC (PA)
5500 N Mill Heights Dr (67219-2358)
PHONE..................................316 744-7148
Edward M Kice, *Ch of Bd*
Robert Williams, *Regional Mgr*
Ed Kice, *Vice Pres*
James D Kice, *Vice Pres*
Robert G Kice, *Vice Pres*
◆ EMP: 150
SQ FT: 70,000
SALES (est): 36.1MM Privately Held
WEB: www.kice.com
SIC: 3444 3564 3494 3556 Sheet metal specialties, not stamped; air cleaning systems; valves & pipe fittings; food products machinery; gray & ductile iron foundries; fabricated structural metal

(G-9626)
KLEIN CONSTRUCTION INC
919 E 53rd St N (67219-2611)
PHONE..................................316 262-3313
Arnold Klein, *President*
Jan Fish, *Office Mgr*
EMP: 15
SALES: 2.5MM Privately Held
WEB: www.kleinconstruction.com
SIC: 1521 1542 General remodeling, single-family houses; commercial & office buildings, renovation & repair

(G-9627)
LEISURE HOTEL CORPORATION
Also Called: Best Western Wichita North
915 E 53rd St N (67219-2611)
PHONE..................................316 832-9387
John Zavada, *Branch Mgr*
EMP: 65
SALES (corp-wide): 6.9MM Privately Held
SIC: 7011 Hotels & motels
PA: Leisure Hotel Corporation
8725 Rosehill Rd Ste 300
Lenexa KS 66215
913 905-1460

(G-9628)
LIGHTNING AEROSPACE LLC
6650 N Broadway Ave (67219-1100)
PHONE..................................316 295-4670
Craig Bakel, *Mng Member*
Connie Bakel, *Mng Member*
EMP: 5
SQ FT: 9,000
SALES (est): 918.1K Privately Held
SIC: 3599 Machine shop, jobbing & repair

(G-9629)
M I F INC (PA)
5615 N Broadway Ave (67219-2005)
PHONE..................................316 838-3970
Rick Nutt, *President*
Rt Williams, *Manager*
EMP: 84
SQ FT: 50,000
SALES: 46.8MM Privately Held
WEB: www.fmi-incorporated.com
SIC: 3728 Aircraft assemblies, subassemblies & parts

(G-9630)
MID-CONTINENT HARLEY-DAVIDSON
5427 N Chuzy Dr (67219-2340)
PHONE..................................316 440-5700
Michael Bahnmaier, *President*
EMP: 14
SQ FT: 12,000
SALES (est): 2.6MM Privately Held
SIC: 5571 7699 Motorcycle dealers; motorcycle repair service

(G-9631)
MIDWEST LEGACY LLC
Also Called: Midwest Services
1411 E Ashford St (67219-2202)
PHONE..................................316 518-9350
William Henderson, *Manager*
William E Henderson,
EMP: 10
SQ FT: 1,000
SALES (est): 205.1K Privately Held
SIC: 0782 0783 6799 Mowing services, lawn; tree trimming services for public utility lines; removal services, bush & tree; real estate investors, except property operators

(G-9632)
MIDWEST TRAILER SUPPLY INC
5929 N Broadway Ave (67219-2011)
PHONE..................................316 744-1515
Roy Ebarb, *President*
Sandy Ebarb, *Treasurer*
EMP: 20
SQ FT: 18,000

SALES (est): 1.1MM **Privately Held**
SIC: 7534 Rebuilding & retreading tires

(G-9633)
MIDWEST TRUCK EQUIPMENT INC
200 W 61st St N (67204-1530)
PHONE..................................316 744-2889
Michael Hahnfeld, *President*
Alice Schulte, *Corp Secy*
Bryan Wilson, *Vice Pres*
EMP: 17
SQ FT: 23,000
SALES (est): 5.2MM **Privately Held**
WEB: www.mwte.com
SIC: 5012 5082 5531 3713 Automobiles & other motor vehicles; blades for graders, scrapers, dozers & snow plows; truck equipment & parts; truck bodies & parts

(G-9634)
MILL-TEL INC (PA)
5550 N Hydraulic St (67219-2404)
P.O. Box 1580, Wichita (67201-1580)
PHONE..................................316 262-7171
Michael J Miller, *President*
Tim Myler, *Technician*
EMP: 50
SQ FT: 30,000
SALES (est): 13.7MM **Privately Held**
WEB: www.milltel.com
SIC: 1731 Cable television installation

(G-9635)
MJ TRANSPORTATION INC
601 E 49th St N (67219-2802)
P.O. Box 4446, Wichita (67204-0446)
PHONE..................................316 832-1321
James M Mies, *President*
James Mies, *President*
Mary Capps, *Treasurer*
EMP: 25
SQ FT: 8,000
SALES: 3MM **Privately Held**
SIC: 4213 Trucking, except local

(G-9636)
MOBILE MINI INC
250 W 53rd St N (67204-2233)
PHONE..................................316 838-2663
Gayle Pollard, *Sales Staff*
Chris Thornton, *Manager*
EMP: 10
SALES (corp-wide): 593.2MM **Publicly Held**
WEB: www.mobilemini.com
SIC: 3448 3441 3412 7359 Buildings, portable: prefabricated metal; fabricated structural metal; drums, shipping: metal; shipping container leasing
PA: Mobile Mini, Inc.
4646 E Van Buren St # 400
Phoenix AZ 85008
480 894-6311

(G-9637)
MOORES LNNY COLLISION REPR LLC
201 W 61st St N (67204-1531)
PHONE..................................316 744-1151
Lonny Moore, *Mng Member*
EMP: 12 **EST:** 1994
SQ FT: 12,000
SALES (est): 705.9K **Privately Held**
SIC: 7532 Body shop, automotive

(G-9638)
MURPHY TRACTOR & EQP CO INC (HQ)
Also Called: John Deere Authorized Dealer
5375 N Deere Rd (67219-3307)
PHONE..................................855 246-9124
Bill Buckles, *President*
Robert D Young, *Corp Secy*
Joe Blanke, *Parts Mgr*
Jase Breece, *Parts Mgr*
Jana Cornish, *Parts Mgr*
◆ **EMP:** 45
SQ FT: 16,000
SALES (est): 91.7MM **Privately Held**
WEB: www.murphytractor.com
SIC: 5082 Contractors' materials; general construction machinery & equipment

(G-9639)
NORTH AMERICAN AVIATION INC
7330 N Broadway Ave (67219-1124)
PHONE..................................316 744-6450
Dan Robertson, *President*
Rodney Gerlach, *Vice Pres*
Rebecca Robertson, *Admin Sec*
EMP: 35
SQ FT: 22,000
SALES (est): 7.2MM **Privately Held**
WEB: www.naavinc.com
SIC: 3089 3429 Molding primary plastic; aircraft & marine hardware, inc. pulleys & similar items

(G-9640)
ROBERTS TRUCK CTR HOLDG CO LLC
5549 N Chuzy Dr (67219-2317)
PHONE..................................316 262-8413
Blaire Roberts, *Owner*
EMP: 60 **Privately Held**
SIC: 5012 7513 Trucks, commercial; truck rental & leasing, no drivers
PA: Roberts Truck Center Holding Company, Llc
4354 Canyon Dr
Amarillo TX 79109

(G-9641)
SCRAP MANAGEMENT KANSAS INC
850 E 45th St N (67219-3204)
PHONE..................................316 832-1198
Brian McChristian, *Principal*
EMP: 15
SALES (est): 2.6MM **Privately Held**
SIC: 4953 Recycling, waste materials

(G-9642)
SD & S TRUCKING LLC
300 W 61st St N (67204-1528)
PHONE..................................316 744-2318
Samuel Delarosa,
EMP: 25
SALES: 2.5MM **Privately Held**
SIC: 4212 Dump truck haulage

(G-9643)
SHIRE SIGNS LLC
Also Called: Shire Graphics
225 W 59th St N Ste A (67204-2106)
PHONE..................................316 838-1362
Brice Simon, *Mng Member*
EMP: 5
SALES: 500K **Privately Held**
SIC: 2759 Commercial printing

(G-9644)
SIDS CORRUGATING & MACHINERY
5844 N Broadway Ave (67219-2010)
PHONE..................................316 744-0061
Sid Sadowske, *President*
Cindy Lee, *Manager*
▲ **EMP:** 5
SALES: 750K **Privately Held**
SIC: 3599 Machine shop, jobbing & repair

(G-9645)
SIGNS BY SHIRE INC
225 W 59th St N Ste A (67204-2106)
PHONE..................................316 838-1362
Gail Shire, *President*
Jan Shire, *Manager*
EMP: 8
SQ FT: 2,250
SALES (est): 300K **Privately Held**
SIC: 3993 Signs & advertising specialties

(G-9646)
TA MILLWORK LLC
6024 N Broadway Ave (67219-2014)
PHONE..................................316 744-3440
Tracy Algrim, *Mng Member*
Judith Algrim,
EMP: 9
SQ FT: 25,000
SALES (est): 1.1MM **Privately Held**
WEB: www.tamillwork.com
SIC: 2431 Awnings, blinds & shutters, wood

(G-9647)
TECT HYPERVELOCITY INC
5545 N Mill Heights Dr (67219-2311)
PHONE..................................316 529-5000
Bob Sanford, *Prgrmr*
EMP: 65
SALES (corp-wide): 39.5MM **Privately Held**
SIC: 3728 Aircraft parts & equipment
HQ: Tect Hypervelocity, Inc.
5545 N Mill Heights Dr
Park City KS 67219

(G-9648)
TECT HYPERVELOCITY INC (HQ)
5545 N Mill Heights Dr (67219-2311)
PHONE..................................316 529-5000
Glenn Warren, *Opers Mgr*
Ray Carroll, *Facilities Mgr*
Bev Anderson, *Buyer*
Daren Krier, *Buyer*
Tully Smith, *Buyer*
▲ **EMP:** 65
SALES (est): 11.8MM
SALES (corp-wide): 39.5MM **Privately Held**
SIC: 3728 Aircraft parts & equipment
PA: Tect Aerospace Kansas Holdings, Llc
300 W Douglas Ave Ste 100
Wichita KS 67202
620 395-5000

(G-9649)
TELL INDUSTRIES LLC
6255 N Hydraulic St (67219-1401)
PHONE..................................316 260-3297
Tell Wood, *Mng Member*
Krisyn Wood,
EMP: 11
SALES: 14MM **Privately Held**
SIC: 5131 Synthetic fabrics

(G-9650)
TW METALS INC
1200 E Blake Dr (67219-2309)
PHONE..................................316 744-5000
Larry Cosby, *Accounts Mgr*
Sam Peters, *Branch Mgr*
Ellie Drake, *Clerk*
EMP: 46
SALES (corp-wide): 1.8B **Privately Held**
WEB: www.twmetals.com
SIC: 5051 Steel
HQ: Tw Metals, Llc
760 Constitution Dr # 204
Exton PA 19341
610 458-1300

(G-9651)
UNITED PETRO TRANSPORTS INC
Also Called: OK Tank Line
6021 N Broadway Ave (67219-2013)
PHONE..................................316 263-6868
Russ Shinart, *Manager*
EMP: 40
SALES (corp-wide): 70.8MM **Privately Held**
SIC: 4212 4213 Petroleum haulage, local; trucking, except local
HQ: United Petroleum Transports, Inc.
4312 S Georgia Pl
Oklahoma City OK 73129
316 263-6868

(G-9652)
UNITED WAREHOUSE COMPANY (PA)
901 E 45th St N (67219-3113)
PHONE..................................316 712-1000
Brett Schaefer, *President*
Brent Blackmon, *Business Mgr*
Jamie Bright, *QC Mgr*
▲ **EMP:** 60 **EST:** 1915
SQ FT: 300,000
SALES (est): 11.9MM **Privately Held**
WEB: www.unitedwarehouse.com
SIC: 4225 General warehousing

(G-9653)
UTAH MACHINE & MILL SUPPLY
5844 N Broadway Ave (67219-2010)
PHONE..................................801 364-2812
Fax: 801 363-6056
EMP: 8 **EST:** 1950
SQ FT: 10,000
SALES (est): 750K **Privately Held**
SIC: 3547 Repairs Rolling Mill Machinery

(G-9654)
WICHITA FENCE CO INC
4901 N Broadway Ave (67219-2723)
PHONE..................................316 838-1342
Debbie Bowman, *Vice Pres*
EMP: 15
SQ FT: 4,000
SALES (est): 2MM **Privately Held**
SIC: 1799 5031 5211 Fence construction; fencing, wood; fencing

(G-9655)
WICHITA KENWORTH INC (PA)
Also Called: Dodge City Kenworth
5115 N Broadway Ave (67219-2727)
P.O. Box 4226, Wichita (67204-0226)
PHONE..................................316 838-0867
Cliff Adams, *President*
Ronnie Eilerts, *Foreman/Supr*
Nate Lane, *Parts Mgr*
Misty Long, *Manager*
Ian Sneeringer, *Technology*
EMP: 59 **EST:** 1971
SQ FT: 12,000
SALES (est): 53.4MM **Privately Held**
WEB: www.wichitakenworth.com
SIC: 5511 7538 Automobiles, new & used; general truck repair

Parker
Linn County

(G-9656)
1-STOP LLC
423 E Woodward St (66072-4114)
P.O. Box 226 (66072-0226)
PHONE..................................913 898-6211
Coleen Stahl, *Manager*
EMP: 5
SALES (est): 671.1K **Privately Held**
SIC: 3578 Automatic teller machines (ATM)

(G-9657)
DIVERSIFIED CONTRACTING LLC
21368 Earnest Rd (66072-9191)
PHONE..................................913 898-4722
Michael Page,
Sue Page,
EMP: 12
SQ FT: 1,000
SALES: 2MM **Privately Held**
SIC: 1731 1794 1611 General electrical contractor; excavation work; general contractor, highway & street construction

(G-9658)
MARAIS DES CYGNES CHAPTER DAUG
5630 W 2200 Rd (66072-5080)
PHONE..................................913 898-3088
Renee Slinkard, *President*
EMP: 45
SALES (est): 123K **Privately Held**
SIC: 8641 Civic social & fraternal associations

(G-9659)
PAGE ENTERPRISE LLC
21368 Earnest Rd (66072-9191)
PHONE..................................913 898-4722
Chad Page, *CEO*
Evan Sternberg, *Manager*
Nancy Howell, *Consultant*
Kristina Vitullo, *Director*
Michael C Page,
EMP: 15
SALES (est): 661.7K **Privately Held**
SIC: 1611 General contractor, highway & street construction

(G-9660)
PARKER TRUSS & STUFF
19825 County Road 1077 (66072-5033)
P.O. Box 286 (66072-0286)
PHONE..................................913 898-2775
Rod Clinton, *Owner*
Pam Clinton, *Co-Owner*

EMP: 5
SALES (est): 558.9K **Privately Held**
SIC: 2439 Trusses, wooden roof

Parsons
Labette County

(G-9661)
A & R CSTM FRMS FBRCATIONS LLC
2601 Flynn Dr (67357-7448)
PHONE..................................620 423-0401
Allan Baker, *Mng Member*
EMP: 33
SALES (est): 2.3MM **Privately Held**
SIC: 3499 Fabricated metal products

(G-9662)
A&R CUSTOM FORM & FABRICATIO
24080 Scott Rd (67357-8443)
PHONE..................................620 423-0170
Baker Joseph, *Principal*
EMP: 5
SALES (est): 798.5K **Privately Held**
SIC: 7692 Welding repair

(G-9663)
ACME CINEMA INC
Also Called: Parsons Theatre
210 N 17th (67357)
P.O. Box 281 (67357-0281)
PHONE..................................620 421-4404
Lee Salyers, *President*
Pat Haley, *Vice Pres*
Paula Haley, *Treasurer*
P Diane Salyers, *Admin Sec*
EMP: 26
SALES: 600K **Privately Held**
WEB: www.parsonstheatre.com
SIC: 7832 Motion picture theaters, except drive-in

(G-9664)
ALEXANDER MANUFACTURING CO INC
1407 Corporate Dr (67357-4964)
P.O. Box 568 (67357-0568)
PHONE..................................620 421-5010
Michael D Alexander, *President*
Don M Alexander, *President*
Joey Alexander, *Plant Supt*
Joe Stringer, *Marketing Staff*
◆ **EMP:** 14
SQ FT: 55,000
SALES (est): 2.2MM **Privately Held**
SIC: 3599 3317 Machine shop, jobbing & repair; steel pipe & tubes

(G-9665)
ALLEN VETERINARY CENTER
Also Called: Center Feed Co
1425 Us Highway 59 (67357-2800)
PHONE..................................620 421-1341
James Allen, *Owner*
EMP: 10
SQ FT: 2,600
SALES (est): 480K **Privately Held**
SIC: 0741 0742 Veterinary services for livestock; veterinary services, specialties

(G-9666)
ANATOMICAL PATHOLOGY SERVICES
Also Called: Cyto Check Labor
1902 S Us Highway 59 D (67357-4948)
PHONE..................................620 421-2424
James Welch, *Owner*
Ronald Leonard,
EMP: 35
SALES (est): 414K **Privately Held**
SIC: 8071 Pathological laboratory

(G-9667)
ASSISTIVE TECHNOLOGY FOR KANS
2601 Gabriel Ave (67357-2341)
PHONE..................................620 421-8367
Sara Sack, *Director*
EMP: 30
SALES (est): 1.7MM **Privately Held**
SIC: 3842 Technical aids for the handicapped

(G-9668)
AT&T CORP
5015 Main St (67357-8823)
PHONE..................................620 421-7612
EMP: 10
SALES (corp-wide): 170.7B **Publicly Held**
WEB: www.swbell.com
SIC: 4812 Cellular telephone services
HQ: At&T Corp.
1 At&T Way
Bedminster NJ 07921
800 403-3302

(G-9669)
BEACHNER GRAIN INC (PA)
2600 Flynn Dr (67357-7448)
PHONE..................................620 820-8600
Gary Beachner, *CEO*
Eugene Beachner, *President*
EMP: 46
SQ FT: 10,000
SALES (est): 112.2MM **Privately Held**
WEB: www.beachner.com
SIC: 5153 Grains; grain elevators

(G-9670)
CANCER CENTER OF KANSAS PA
1902 S Us Highway 59 (67357-4948)
PHONE..................................620 421-2855
Bradley Deutsch, *Branch Mgr*
EMP: 17
SALES (corp-wide): 24.4MM **Privately Held**
SIC: 8011 Oncologist
PA: Cancer Center Of Kansas, P.A.
818 N Emporia St Ste 403
Wichita KS 67214
316 262-4467

(G-9671)
CITY OF PARSONS
Also Called: Public Works Department
1000 N 21st St (67357-2918)
P.O. Box 1037 (67357-1037)
PHONE..................................620 421-7025
Mark Lynn, *Manager*
EMP: 36 **Privately Held**
WEB: www.mlbair.com
SIC: 9199 1611 General government administration; ; highway & street construction
PA: City Of Parsons
112 S 17th St
Parsons KS 67357
620 421-7000

(G-9672)
CLASS LTD
Also Called: Quality Industries
1207 Partridge Ave (67357-5055)
PHONE..................................620 421-2800
Jan Bolin, *President*
EMP: 70
SALES (corp-wide): 9.8MM **Privately Held**
SIC: 8331 Job training & vocational rehabilitation services
PA: Class Ltd
1200 E Merle Evans Dr
Columbus KS 66725
620 429-1212

(G-9673)
CNHI LLC
Also Called: Farm Talk
1801 S 59 Hwy (67357-4958)
P.O. Box 601 (67357-0601)
PHONE..................................620 421-9450
Mark Parker, *President*
EMP: 33 **Privately Held**
SIC: 2711 Newspapers: publishing only, not printed on site
HQ: Cnhi, Llc
445 Dexter Ave Ste 7000
Montgomery AL 36104

(G-9674)
COMMERCIAL BANK (HQ)
1901 Main St (67357-3336)
P.O. Box 280, Ithaca MI (48847-0280)
PHONE..................................620 423-0770
Phillip R Eaton, *President*
Ray Jacquinot, *Exec VP*
Bill Mead, *Senior VP*
Joseph A Mc Liney, *Vice Pres*
Kanak Patel, *Vice Pres*
EMP: 30 **EST:** 1874
SQ FT: 10,000
SALES: 14.1MM
SALES (corp-wide): 30.2MM **Publicly Held**
WEB: www.commercialbank.net
SIC: 6022 8721 State trust companies accepting deposits, commercial; accounting, auditing & bookkeeping
PA: Commercial National Financial Corporation
101 N Pine River St
Ithaca MI 48847
989 875-4144

(G-9675)
COMMERCIAL BANK
1830 Parsons Plz (67357)
PHONE..................................620 423-0770
Shirley Cholker, *Vice Pres*
EMP: 24
SALES (corp-wide): 30.2MM **Publicly Held**
WEB: www.commercialbank.net
SIC: 6022 State commercial banks
HQ: Commercial Bank
1901 Main St
Parsons KS 67357
620 423-0770

(G-9676)
COMMUNITY CHILD CARE CENTER
Also Called: Parsons State Child Care Ctr
2601 Gabriel Ave (67357-2341)
PHONE..................................620 421-6550
Charlotte Hopper, *Director*
EMP: 25
SALES (est): 638.7K **Privately Held**
SIC: 8351 Head start center, except in conjunction with school

(G-9677)
COMMUNITY NATIONAL BANK
Also Called: Parsons Banking Center
330 N 16th St (67357-3229)
P.O. Box 799 (67357-0799)
PHONE..................................620 423-0314
Pete Hutley, *Manager*
EMP: 10 **Privately Held**
SIC: 6021 National commercial banks
HQ: Community National Bank & Trust
14 N Lincoln Ave
Chanute KS 66720

(G-9678)
CYTOCHECK LABORATORY LLC
1201 Corporate Dr (67357-4934)
PHONE..................................620 421-2424
Jamie Vinson, *Opers Staff*
Jason Dantic, *Mktg Dir*
Talya Couch, *Marketing Staff*
Anne Reid, *Office Mgr*
James R Welch MD, *Mng Member*
EMP: 29
SALES (est): 2.4MM **Privately Held**
SIC: 8071 Pathological laboratory

(G-9679)
DAY & ZIMMERMANN KANSAS LLC
23102 Rush Rd (67357-8497)
PHONE..................................620 421-7400
William Holmes, *Principal*
Daniel Weilert, *Engineer*
EMP: 200
SALES (est): 2MM **Privately Held**
SIC: 7381 Security guard service

(G-9680)
DAY AND ZIMMERMANN INC
Also Called: Kansas Div
23102 Rush Rd (67357-8497)
PHONE..................................620 421-7400
Lisa Miller, *Program Mgr*
EMP: 200
SALES (corp-wide): 2.2B **Privately Held**
WEB: www.dayzim.com
SIC: 3483 Ammunition, except for small arms
HQ: Day And Zimmermann, Incorporated
1500 Spring Garden St
Philadelphia PA 19130
215 299-8000

(G-9681)
DAYTON SUPERIOR CORPORATION
Also Called: American Highway Technology
1900 Wilson Ave (67357-4944)
P.O. Box 768 (67357-0768)
PHONE..................................937 866-0711
Terry Weidert, *Plant Mgr*
Michael A Barnett, *Branch Mgr*
EMP: 130
SALES (corp-wide): 42.9B **Publicly Held**
WEB: www.daytonsuperior.com
SIC: 3496 3444 Concrete reinforcing mesh & wire; sheet metalwork
HQ: Dayton Superior Corporation
1125 Byers Rd
Miamisburg OH 45342
937 866-0711

(G-9682)
DUCOMMUN AEROSTRUCTURES INC
3333 Main St (67357-3632)
PHONE..................................620 421-3401
Tony Reardon, *Branch Mgr*
EMP: 24
SALES (corp-wide): 629.3MM **Publicly Held**
SIC: 3728 Aircraft parts & equipment
HQ: Ducommun Aerostructures, Inc.
268 E Gardena Blvd
Gardena CA 90248
310 380-5390

(G-9683)
EJREX INC
1818 Broadway Ave (67357-3314)
PHONE..................................620 421-6200
C Eugene Rexwinkle, *President*
Larry Reed, *Vice Pres*
EMP: 60 **EST:** 1944
SQ FT: 66,200
SALES (est): 6.1MM **Privately Held**
WEB: www.sun-graphics.com
SIC: 2752 2796 2791 2789 Commercial printing, lithographic; lithographic plates, positives or negatives; typesetting; bookbinding & related work; commercial printing

(G-9684)
EVANGELICAL LUTHERAN
Also Called: Good Samaritan Soc - Parsons
709 Leawood Dr (67357-3436)
P.O. Box 5038, Sioux Falls SD (57117-5038)
PHONE..................................620 421-1110
Debbie Lansdowne, *Education*
EMP: 75 **Privately Held**
WEB: www.good-sam.com
SIC: 8059 Nursing home, except skilled & intermediate care facility
HQ: The Evangelical Lutheran Good Samaritan Society
4800 W 57th St
Sioux Falls SD 57108
866 928-1635

(G-9685)
EVERGY KANSAS CENTRAL INC
2605 Flynn Dr (67357-7448)
PHONE..................................620 820-8205
Debbie Nelson, *Manager*
EMP: 17
SALES (corp-wide): 4.2B **Publicly Held**
SIC: 4911 Generation, electric power
HQ: Evergy Kansas Central, Inc.
818 S Kansas Ave
Topeka KS 66612
785 575-6300

(G-9686)
FLESH COMPANY
2407 Jothi Ave (67357-8471)
P.O. Box 207 (67357-0207)
PHONE..................................620 421-6120
Philip Sparks, *Engineer*
Tracy Long, *Accounts Mgr*
Amy Reliford, *Regl Sales Mgr*
Karen Meyer, *Sales Staff*
Tracy Pohl, *Sales Staff*
EMP: 83
SALES (corp-wide): 30MM **Privately Held**
WEB: www.impressions-direct.net
SIC: 2761 Continuous forms, office & business
PA: The Flesh Company
915 Horan Dr
Fenton MO 63026
314 781-4400

(G-9687)
FRONTIER FARM CREDIT
2005 Harding Dr (67357-8110)
PHONE..................................620 421-4030
Jeff Van Horn, *Branch Mgr*
Jordan Anderson, *Officer*
EMP: 19
SALES (corp-wide): 12.1MM **Privately Held**
SIC: 0191 General farms, primarily crop
PA: Frontier Farm Credit
9370 E Us Highway 24
Manhattan KS
785 776-6931

(G-9688)
GRANDVIEW PRODUCTS CO INC (HQ)
1601 Superior Dr (67357-1003)
P.O. Box 874 (67357-0874)
PHONE..................................620 421-6950
Stanley Tidwell, *President*
Teresa Hays, *Exec VP*
EMP: 250 **EST:** 1946
SQ FT: 212,500
SALES: 34MM **Privately Held**
WEB: www.grandviewcabinets.com
SIC: 2434 2541 Wood kitchen cabinets; table or counter tops, plastic laminated
PA: Western Cabinets, Inc.
3444 Morse Dr
Dallas TX 75236
469 916-5350

(G-9689)
GREAT SOUTHERN BANK
1900 Main St (67357-3337)
P.O. Box 877 (67357-0877)
PHONE..................................620 421-5700
Montie Taylor, *Manager*
EMP: 20
SALES (corp-wide): 242.1MM **Publicly Held**
WEB: www.teambank-na.com
SIC: 6022 State commercial banks
HQ: Great Southern Bank
1451 E Battlefield St
Springfield MO 65804
417 887-4400

(G-9690)
H & R BLOCK
1705 Parsons Plz (67357)
PHONE..................................620 421-2850
Viva Price, *Owner*
Tom Duran, *Corp Comm Staff*
EMP: 15
SALES (est): 380K **Privately Held**
SIC: 7291 Tax return preparation services

(G-9691)
H&H DESIGN & MANUFACTURING LLC
304 S 53rd St (67357-8839)
PHONE..................................620 421-9800
Jonathan Norris, *Prdtn Mgr*
Andre Kellogg, *Engineer*
Tonya Phillips, *Controller*
Josh Hoppes, *Mng Member*
Glen Hoppes,
EMP: 10
SQ FT: 10,000
SALES: 2MM **Privately Held**
SIC: 3565 Packing & wrapping machinery

(G-9692)
HOME STORE (PA)
1725 Main St (67357-3338)
PHONE..................................620 421-4272
Richard Babcock,
Sandy Babcock,
EMP: 10
SALES (est): 1.3MM **Privately Held**
SIC: 2541 Counter & sink tops

(G-9693)
INTERSTATE ELEC CNSTR INC
1715 Us Highway 59 (67357-7403)
P.O. Box 676 (67357-0676)
PHONE..................................620 421-5510
EMP: 40
SQ FT: 5,000
SALES: 5MM **Privately Held**
SIC: 1731 1711 Electrical Contractor Plumbing/Heating/Air Cond Contractor

(G-9694)
JOSEPH WOMMACK DDS
1701 Washington Ave (67357-3204)
PHONE..................................620 421-0980
Toll Free:..888 -
Joseph Wommack DDS, *Owner*
Joe Wommack, *Med Doctor*
EMP: 18 **EST:** 1996
SALES (est): 383.4K **Privately Held**
SIC: 8021 Dentists' office

(G-9695)
KANSAS BIG BROS BIG SSTERS INC
120 N 22nd St (67357-2751)
PHONE..................................620 421-0472
Nancy Bailey, *Director*
EMP: 11
SALES (corp-wide): 4.1MM **Privately Held**
SIC: 8322 Helping hand service (Big Brother, etc.)
PA: Kansas Big Brothers Big Sisters, Inc.
310 E 2nd St N
Wichita KS 67202
316 263-3300

(G-9696)
KANSAS DEPT FOR CHLDREN FMLIES
Also Called: Parsons Area SRS
300 N 17th St (67357-3232)
PHONE..................................620 421-4500
Steve Fincher, *Branch Mgr*
EMP: 55 **Privately Held**
SIC: 8322 9441 Individual & family services;
HQ: Kansas Department For Children And Families
555 S Kansas Ave
Topeka KS 66603
785 368-6358

(G-9697)
KANSAS STATE UNIVERSITY
Also Called: Southeast Kans Experiment Stn
N 32nd And Pefley (67357)
P.O. Box 316 (67357-0316)
PHONE..................................620 421-4826
Lyle W Lomas, *Systems Mgr*
EMP: 21
SALES (corp-wide): 637.6MM **Privately Held**
WEB: www.ksu.edu
SIC: 8731 0741 0711 8734 Agricultural research; veterinary services for livestock; soil testing services; hydrostatic testing laboratory
PA: Kansas State University
Anderson Hall 110 1301 Mi St Anderson Ha
Manhattan KS 66506
785 532-6011

(G-9698)
KANSAS TIRE & WHEEL CO LLC
1530 Flynn Dr (67357-7454)
PHONE..................................620 421-0005
Sean O'Bryan, *Mng Member*
EMP: 10
SQ FT: 3,200
SALES (est): 1.3MM **Privately Held**
SIC: 7538 General automotive repair shops

(G-9699)
KEVIN MOSIER MD
S Hwy 59 Bldg D (67357)
PHONE..................................620 421-0881
Kevin M Mosier, *Med Doctor*
Doris Yeolman MD, *Manager*
EMP: 12 **EST:** 2001
SALES (est): 209K **Privately Held**
SIC: 8011 Orthopedic physician

(G-9700)
KNIGHTS OF COLUMBUS
1723 Main St (67357-3338)
P.O. Box 175, Coffeyville (67337-0175)
PHONE..................................620 251-2891
James B Scott, *Branch Mgr*
EMP: 13
SALES (corp-wide): 2.3B **Privately Held**
SIC: 8641 Fraternal associations
PA: Knights Of Columbus
1 Columbus Plz Ste 1700
New Haven CT 06510
203 752-4000

(G-9701)
KVC BEHAVIORAL HEALTHCARE INC
2410 Main St (67357-2726)
PHONE..................................620 820-7680
EMP: 57 **Privately Held**
SIC: 9431 8011 Administration of public health programs; offices & clinics of medical doctors
HQ: Kvc Behavioral Healthcare, Inc.
21350 W 153rd St
Olathe KS 66061
913 322-4900

(G-9702)
LABETTE CENTER FOR MENTAL INC
Also Called: Community Support Program
906 S 13th St (67357-5042)
PHONE..................................620 421-9402
Matt Atteberry, *Exec Dir*
Clark Grimes, *Director*
EMP: 10
SALES (est): 281.6K **Privately Held**
SIC: 8093 Mental health clinic, outpatient

(G-9703)
LABETTE COUNTY MEDICAL CENTER
1902 S Us Highway 59 D (67357-4948)
PHONE..................................620 421-4880
William Mahoney, *CEO*
Brock Sutherland, *Facilities Mgr*
Thomas Macaronas, *CFO*
Chris Sykes, *Human Res Dir*
Don Dixon, *Pharmacist*
EMP: 29
SALES: 63.7MM **Privately Held**
SIC: 8011 Clinic, operated by physicians

(G-9704)
LABETTE CTR FOR MNTAL HLTH SVC
1730 Belmont Ave (67357-4229)
P.O. Box 258 (67357-0258)
PHONE..................................620 421-3770
Matthew Hatteberry, *Exec Dir*
Shereen Ellis, *Director*
EMP: 55
SALES: 3.5MM **Privately Held**
WEB: www.lcmhs.com
SIC: 8093 Mental health clinic, outpatient

(G-9705)
LABETTE HEALTH FOUNDATION INC (PA)
1902 S Us Highway 59 (67357-4948)
PHONE..................................620 421-4881
William Mahoney, *CEO*
Vincent Schibi, *President*
Wl Dillon, *Vice Pres*
Perry Sorrell, *Vice Pres*
Ashley Alloway, *Opers Staff*
EMP: 459 **EST:** 1961
SQ FT: 140,000
SALES: 1.2MM **Privately Held**
WEB: www.lcmc.com
SIC: 8062 General medical & surgical hospitals

(G-9706)
LAFORGE AND BUDD CNSTR CO INC
Also Called: Laforge & Budd
2020 N 21st St (67357-8090)
P.O. Box 833 (67357-0833)
PHONE..................................620 421-4470
Patrick Laforge, *President*
Paul F Laforge, *Chairman*
Bernard Dougherty, *Vice Pres*
Jane Rae, *Project Mgr*
Brian REA, *Project Mgr*
EMP: 100 **EST:** 1960
SQ FT: 15,000
SALES (est): 24.1MM **Privately Held**
WEB: www.laforgebudd.com
SIC: 1542 1611 1541 Commercial & office building, new construction; highway & street construction; industrial buildings & warehouses

(G-9707)
MAGNUM SYSTEMS INC (PA)
Also Called: Taylor Products & Smoot Co
2205 Jothi Ave (67357-8477)
PHONE..................................620 421-5550
Travis Wallace, *CEO*
Debra Weidert, *CFO*
▲ **EMP:** 45
SALES (est): 22.8MM **Privately Held**
WEB: www.magnumsystems.com
SIC: 3565 Packaging machinery

(G-9708)
MCCARTY OFFICE MACHINES INC (PA)
1715 Main St (67357-3338)
P.O. Box 917 (67357-0917)
PHONE..................................620 421-5530
Jim Mc Carty, *President*
Sheryl Mc Carty, *Corp Secy*
EMP: 17 **EST:** 1959
SQ FT: 12,000
SALES (est): 2.4MM **Privately Held**
WEB: www.mccartysoffice.com
SIC: 5943 7629 Office forms & supplies; business machine repair, electric

(G-9709)
MERIDIANPRO INC
3207 Grand Ave (67357)
P.O. Box 124 (67357-0124)
PHONE..................................620 421-1107
Grant Steinle, *Principal*
EMP: 25
SALES (est): 2.6MM **Privately Held**
SIC: 5043 Photographic equipment & supplies

(G-9710)
NEIGHBORS & ASSOCIATES INC
1801 S 21st St (67357-4907)
P.O. Box 579 (67357-0579)
PHONE..................................620 423-3010
William E Neighbors, *President*
Shane Nash, *Vice Pres*
Bransie Qualls, *Sales Dir*
Vince Horton, *Accounts Mgr*
EMP: 12
SQ FT: 5,000
SALES (est): 3.7MM
SALES (corp-wide): 42.2MM **Privately Held**
SIC: 5084 Materials handling machinery
PA: Tank Connection, L.L.C.
3609 N 16th St
Parsons KS 67357
620 423-0251

(G-9711)
OBRIEN ROCK COMPANY INC
Also Called: O'Brien Ready Mix
N Blvd (67357)
PHONE..................................620 421-5127
Gene O'Brien, *Principal*
EMP: 9
SALES (corp-wide): 9.6MM **Privately Held**
SIC: 5032 3273 Cement; ready-mixed concrete
PA: O'brien Rock Company Inc
712 Central St
Saint Paul KS 66771
620 449-2257

GEOGRAPHIC

(G-9712)
OLD DOMINION FREIGHT LINE INC
2600 Flynn Dr (67357-7448)
PHONE..................................620 421-4121
Kerry AST, *Branch Mgr*
EMP: 48
SALES (corp-wide): 4B **Publicly Held**
WEB: www.odfl.com
SIC: 4213 Less-than-truckload (LTL) transport
PA: Old Dominion Freight Line Inc
500 Old Dominion Way
Thomasville NC 27360
336 889-5000

(G-9713)
OLD PPP INC (DH)
3333 Main St (67357-3632)
PHONE..................................620 421-3400
Tony Reardon, *President*
John Kelley, *Vice Pres*
EMP: 80
SQ FT: 120,000
SALES (est): 7.5MM
SALES (corp-wide): 629.3MM **Publicly Held**
SIC: 3728 Aircraft assemblies, subassemblies & parts
HQ: Ahf-Ducommun Incorporated
268 E Gardena Blvd
Gardena CA 90248
310 380-5390

(G-9714)
OREILLY AUTOMOTIVE STORES INC
Also Called: O'Reilly Auto Parts
2424 Main St (67357-2726)
PHONE..................................620 421-6070
Geramy Collans, *Manager*
EMP: 10 **Publicly Held**
WEB: www.oreillyauto.com
SIC: 5013 Automotive supplies; truck parts & accessories
HQ: O'reilly Automotive Stores, Inc.
233 S Patterson Ave
Springfield MO 65802
417 862-2674

(G-9715)
ORSCHELN FARM AND HOME LLC
Also Called: Orschelin Farm and Home 21
211 Main St (67357-3546)
P.O. Box 614 (67357-0614)
PHONE..................................620 421-0555
Michael Gonzales, *Manager*
EMP: 22
SALES (corp-wide): 822.7MM **Privately Held**
WEB: www.orschelnfarmhome.com
SIC: 5191 5251 5699 Farm supplies; hardware; work clothing
PA: Orscheln Farm And Home Llc
1800 Overcenter Dr
Moberly MO 65270
800 577-2580

(G-9716)
PAR FORMS CORPORATION
Also Called: Par Forms Printing
1716 Corning Ave (67357-4237)
P.O. Box 372 (67357-0372)
PHONE..................................620 421-0970
Dan L Nelson, *President*
Brenda Nelson, *Co-Owner*
Tim Nelson, *Treasurer*
Kermit A Nelson, *Shareholder*
EMP: 14
SQ FT: 10,000
SALES: 800K **Privately Held**
WEB: www.parforms.com
SIC: 2752 2791 Commercial printing, offset; typesetting; typographic composition, for the printing trade

(G-9717)
PARSONS EYE CLINIC PA
220 N 32nd St (67357-2226)
P.O. Box B (67357-0080)
PHONE..................................620 421-5900
Terry Rothstein MD, *President*
Beverly Anderson, *Admin Sec*
EMP: 16
SQ FT: 4,000
SALES (est): 1.2MM **Privately Held**
SIC: 8011 Ophthalmologist

(G-9718)
PARSONS GOLF CLUB RESTAURANT
Also Called: Sterlingmeadow
1808 24000 Rd (67357-8401)
PHONE..................................620 421-5290
Bob Rizza, *President*
Michelle Wallace, *Corp Secy*
EMP: 18
SQ FT: 3,000
SALES (est): 790K **Privately Held**
SIC: 7997 Country club, membership; golf club, membership

(G-9719)
PARSONS LIVESTOCK AUCTION LLC
25012 Us Highway 59 (67357)
Rural Route 6525 Scott, Saint Paul (66771)
PHONE..................................620 421-2900
Wade Dillinger, *Mng Member*
Kristin Dillinger, *Mng Member*
EMP: 25
SALES (est): 371.6K **Privately Held**
SIC: 7389 Auction, appraisal & exchange services

(G-9720)
PARSONS LIVESTOCK MARKET INC
N Hwy 59 (67357)
P.O. Box 216, Edna (67342-0216)
PHONE..................................620 421-2900
Russell McKee, *President*
Mark McKee, *Corp Secy*
EMP: 35
SALES (est): 5.3MM **Privately Held**
SIC: 5154 Livestock

(G-9721)
PARSONS PUBLISHING COMPANY LLC
Also Called: Parsons Sun
220 S 18th St (67357-4218)
P.O. Box 836 (67357-0836)
PHONE..................................620 421-2000
Ann Charles, *President*
Jamie Willey, *Editor*
James Jensen, *Prdtn Mgr*
Jan Strait, *Treasurer*
Peter Cook, *Adv Mgr*
EMP: 20
SQ FT: 8,000
SALES (est): 1.3MM
SALES (corp-wide): 1.5B **Publicly Held**
WEB: www.parsonssun.com
SIC: 2711 Job printing & newspaper publishing combined; newspapers, publishing & printing
HQ: Harris Enterprises, Inc.
1 N Main St Ste 616
Hutchinson KS
620 694-5830

(G-9722)
PARSONS STATE HOSP TRINING CTR
2601 Gabriel Ave (67357-2341)
PHONE..................................620 421-6550
Jerry REA, *Superintendent*
EMP: 475
SALES (est): 25MM **Privately Held**
SIC: 8069 Specialty hospitals, except psychiatric

(G-9723)
PERFORMANCE ENHANCEMENT CENTER
2100 Commerce Dr (67357-4951)
P.O. Box 1042 (67357-1042)
PHONE..................................620 421-2125
Mike Giager, *Partner*
Kevin Mosier, *Partner*
EMP: 10
SALES (est): 380K **Privately Held**
SIC: 7991 Aerobic dance & exercise classes

(G-9724)
POWER FLAME INCORPORATED
2001 S 21st St (67357-4911)
P.O. Box 974 (67357-0974)
PHONE..................................620 421-0480
Brenda Dunlap, *Materials Mgr*
Jaime Pemberton, *Buyer*
Jerry Cruz, *Purchasing*
Joe Purdon, *Research*
Keith Akkerman, *Engineer*
◆ **EMP:** 190
SQ FT: 85,000
SALES (est): 37.2MM
SALES (corp-wide): 1.1B **Publicly Held**
WEB: www.powerflame.com
SIC: 3433 3822 3586 Gas-oil burners, combination; controls, combination oil & hydronic; oil pumps, measuring or dispensing
PA: Astec Industries, Inc.
1725 Shepherd Rd
Chattanooga TN 37421
423 899-5898

(G-9725)
PRESBYTERIAN MANORS INC
3501 Dirr Ave (67357-2298)
PHONE..................................620 421-1450
Wade Gushee, *Director*
EMP: 50
SALES (corp-wide): 8.6MM **Privately Held**
SIC: 8059 Nursing home, except skilled & intermediate care facility
HQ: Presbyterian Manors, Inc.
2414 N Woodlawn Blvd
Wichita KS 67220
316 685-1100

(G-9726)
PROUD ANMAL LOVERS SHELTER INC
P.O. Box 48 (67357-0048)
PHONE..................................620 421-0445
Joanne Tongier, *President*
Linda Samrad, *Chairman*
EMP: 12
SALES (est): 72.8K **Privately Held**
SIC: 0752 8699 Shelters, animal; charitable organization

(G-9727)
QUALITY PRINTING INC
124 Ricewick Rd (67357-8100)
P.O. Box 274 (67357-0274)
PHONE..................................620 421-0630
Richard Marlow, *President*
EMP: 5
SALES (est): 552K **Privately Held**
SIC: 2752 2791 2789 2759 Commercial printing, offset; typesetting; bookbinding & related work; commercial printing

(G-9728)
RAY PRODUCTS INC
1212 Corporate Dr (67357-4962)
PHONE..................................620 421-1510
John Joseph Ray, *Principal*
David Ray, *Vice Pres*
Stephanie Carter, *Cust Mgr*
EMP: 45 **EST:** 1966
SQ FT: 55,000
SALES (est): 9.4MM **Privately Held**
WEB: www.rayproducts.com
SIC: 2652 Setup paperboard boxes

(G-9729)
RAYMOND BAUGHER
20100 Kiowa Rd (67357-8219)
PHONE..................................620 421-1253
Raymond Baugher, *Owner*
EMP: 15
SALES (est): 985K **Privately Held**
SIC: 0115 0116 0111 0119 Corn; soybeans; wheat; milo farm

(G-9730)
RENAL TRTMNT CENTERS-WEST INC
Also Called: Parsons Dialysis Center
1902 S Us Highway 59 B (67357-4948)
PHONE..................................620 421-1081
Lisa Wenger, *Manager*
EMP: 14 **Publicly Held**
WEB: www.davita.com
SIC: 8092 Kidney dialysis centers
HQ: Renal Treatment Centers-West, Inc.
2000 16th St
Denver CO 80202

(G-9731)
RES-CARE INC
1772 24000 Rd (67357-8400)
P.O. Box 766 (67357-0766)
PHONE..................................620 421-2454
Andrea Meyas, *Branch Mgr*
EMP: 28
SALES (corp-wide): 2B **Privately Held**
SIC: 8082 Home health care services
HQ: Res-Care, Inc.
805 N Whittington Pkwy
Louisville KY 40222
502 394-2100

(G-9732)
RESIDENTIAL TREATMENT SERVICE
1407 Broadway Ave (67357-3306)
P.O. Box 1174 (67357-1174)
PHONE..................................620 421-1155
Jamie King, *Director*
EMP: 50
SALES (est): 4.1MM **Privately Held**
SIC: 6099 8399 Automated teller machine (ATM) network; community development groups

(G-9733)
RUSKIN COMPANY
1700 N 21st St (67357-8088)
P.O. Box 767 (67357-0767)
PHONE..................................620 421-6090
Delmer Fisher, *Branch Mgr*
EMP: 26 **Privately Held**
SIC: 3569 3823 3564 Firefighting apparatus; industrial instrmnts msrmnt display/control process variable; blowers & fans
HQ: Ruskin Company
3900 Doctor Greaves Rd
Grandview MO 64030
816 761-7476

(G-9734)
SA IMPRINTS INC
1730 Main St (67357-3339)
P.O. Box 289 (67357-0289)
PHONE..................................620 421-6380
Phil Russell, *Mng Member*
EMP: 10
SALES: 800K **Privately Held**
SIC: 2395 Embroidery & art needlework

(G-9735)
SAINT VINCENT DEPAUL SOCIETY
1122 Main St (67357-3325)
PHONE..................................620 421-8004
Francis Polz, *President*
Charlene Stotman, *Treasurer*
EMP: 60
SALES (est): 662.8K **Privately Held**
SIC: 8322 Individual & family services

(G-9736)
SE KANSAS ORTHOPEDIC CLINIC
1902 S Us Highway 59 (67357-4948)
P.O. Box 678 (67357-0678)
PHONE..................................620 421-0881
Kevin M Mosier, *Partner*
EMP: 14 **EST:** 1980
SALES (est): 699.2K **Privately Held**
SIC: 8011 Clinic, operated by physicians; orthopedic physician

(G-9737)
SGL LLC (HQ)
Also Called: Donlevy Lithograph
1818 Broadway Ave (67357-3314)
PHONE..................................800 835-0588
David Martin, *President*
John Hohenshell, *Vice Pres*
Michael Diskin, *Finance*
John Hammett, *Sales Mgr*
David Nesbitt, *Mng Member*
EMP: 41
SQ FT: 2,000

SALES (est): 8.6MM
SALES (corp-wide): 11.5MM Privately Held
SIC: 7336 Commercial art & graphic design
PA: Brush Art Corporation
343 W Highway 24
Downs KS 67437
785 454-3415

(G-9738)
SLEEP INN & SUITES PARSONS
1807 Harding Dr (67357-8101)
PHONE.................................620 421-6126
Richard Nichols, Manager
EMP: 16
SALES (est): 415.9K Privately Held
SIC: 7011 Hotels & motels

(G-9739)
SOUTHAST KANS IND LVING RSRCE (PA)
1801 Main St (67357-3367)
P.O. Box 957 (67357-0957)
PHONE.................................620 421-5502
Shari Coatney, President
Rebecca Bernd, Director
Greg Jones, Director
David Sorrick, Director
Sorrick Dave, Telecom Exec
EMP: 40 EST: 1992
SALES: 24.1MM Privately Held
SIC: 8322 Association for the handicapped

(G-9740)
SOUTHEAST KANSAS ORTHPD CLINIC
1902 S Us Highway 59 (67357-4948)
PHONE.................................620 421-0881
William Dillon MD, Partner
Kevin Mosier MD, Partner
EMP: 15
SALES (est): 1MM Privately Held
SIC: 8011 Orthopedic physician; surgeon

(G-9741)
STEINLE INC
Also Called: Dwayne's Photo Service
415 S 32nd St (67357-3903)
P.O. Box 274 (67357-0274)
PHONE.................................620 421-3940
Dwayne J Steinle, President
Betty Steinle, Corp Secy
Grant Steinle, Vice Pres
Melissa Alloway, Info Tech Mgr
EMP: 200
SQ FT: 40,000
SALES (est): 11.4MM Privately Held
SIC: 7384 Photofinishing laboratory

(G-9742)
SUPER 8 MOTEL
229 Main St (67357-3546)
PHONE.................................620 421-8000
EMP: 13
SALES (est): 624.7K Privately Held
SIC: 7011 Hotels & motels

(G-9743)
SUPERIOR SCHOOL SUPPLIES INC
1410 Corporate Dr (67357-4947)
PHONE.................................620 421-3190
Fax: 620 421-8788
EMP: 16
SALES (corp-wide): 7.5MM Privately Held
SIC: 5049 2759 2671 Whol Professional Equipment Commercial Printing Mfg Packaging Paper/Film
PA: Superior School Supplies, Inc
1818 W 2nd St N
Wichita KS 67203
316 265-7683

(G-9744)
TANK CONNECTION LLC (PA)
3609 N 16th St (67357-3401)
P.O. Box 579 (67357-0579)
PHONE.................................620 423-0251
Glenda Reynolds, General Mgr
Kent Schenker, Vice Pres
Terry McMunn, Project Mgr
Jesse Merritt, Project Mgr
Tom Nading, Maint Spvr
◆ EMP: 13
SQ FT: 120,000
SALES (est): 42.2MM Privately Held
WEB: www.tankconnection.com
SIC: 3443 5084 Industrial vessels, tanks & containers; tanks, storage

(G-9745)
TANK WIND-DOWN CORP
Also Called: Columbian Tech Tank
2101 S 21st St (67357-4961)
P.O. Box 996 (67357-0996)
PHONE.................................620 421-0200
Steve McRoberts, Project Mgr
Craig Yantis, Branch Mgr
EMP: 170
SALES (corp-wide): 353.7MM Privately Held
WEB: www.tanks.com
SIC: 3443 3824 Tanks, standard or custom fabricated: metal plate; fluid meters & counting devices
PA: Tank Wind-Down Corp.
903 E 104th St Ste 900
Kansas City MO 64131

(G-9746)
TAYLOR PRODUCTS CO INC (HQ)
2205 Jothi Ave (67357-8477)
PHONE.................................620 421-5550
Lewis Ribich, CEO
Russell Brachman, Engineer
Tommy Williamson, Manager
EMP: 50
SQ FT: 60,000
SALES (est): 9.2MM
SALES (corp-wide): 22.8MM Privately Held
WEB: www.taylorproducts.com
SIC: 3565 Packaging machinery
PA: Magnum Systems, Inc.
2205 Jothi Ave
Parsons KS 67357
620 421-5550

(G-9747)
UNITED PARCEL SERVICE INC
Also Called: UPS
1901 S 21st St (67357-4909)
PHONE.................................620 421-1346
Roger Ridell, Manager
EMP: 70
SALES (corp-wide): 71.8B Publicly Held
WEB: www.upsscs.com
SIC: 4215 Parcel delivery, vehicular
HQ: United Parcel Service, Inc.
55 Glenlake Pkwy
Atlanta GA 30328
404 828-6000

(G-9748)
VETERANS HEALTH ADMINISTRATION
Also Called: Parsons Clinic
1401 Main St (67357-3330)
PHONE.................................620 423-3858
EMP: 264 Publicly Held
WEB: www.veterans-ru.org
SIC: 8011 9451 Clinic, operated by physicians;
HQ: Veterans Health Administration
810 Vermont Ave Nw
Washington DC 20420

(G-9749)
WASTE CORPORATION KANSAS LLC
Also Called: Parsons Transfer Station
21075 Us Highway 59 (67357-8459)
PHONE.................................713 292-2400
William Caeser,
Dianna Cervantes,
Jeannette Clark,
Matthew Graham,
Scott Lukach,
EMP: 99
SALES (est): 634.2K Privately Held
SIC: 4953 Hazardous waste collection & disposal

(G-9750)
WICHITA SOUTHEAST KANSAS TRNST
Also Called: Wskt
2600 Flynn Dr (67357-7448)
PHONE.................................620 421-2272
Kelly B Rector, President
Charles Williams, Vice Pres
Lester Rhodes, Admin Sec
EMP: 230
SQ FT: 30,000
SALES: 66.1MM Privately Held
SIC: 4213 Less-than-truckload (LTL) transport

(G-9751)
WOODRIDGE ESTATES LLC
329 Kay Ln (67357-3501)
PHONE.................................620 421-2431
Brad Woodworth, General Mgr
Donald Woodworth,
EMP: 15 EST: 1997
SALES (est): 450.5K Privately Held
WEB: www.woodridgeestates.com
SIC: 8052 Intermediate care facilities

(G-9752)
YOUTH CRISIS SHELTER INC
1915 Crawford Ave (67357-3212)
PHONE.................................620 421-6941
Ernest Moreland, Director
EMP: 23
SALES: 380.8K Privately Held
SIC: 8361 8322 Residential care for children; emergency social services

Pawnee Rock
Barton County

(G-9753)
MULL FAMILY FARMS OPER PARTNR
553 R Rd (67567-6708)
PHONE.................................620 982-4336
Glenn A Mull, Partner
EMP: 10
SALES: 950K Privately Held
SIC: 0722 Crop harvesting

(G-9754)
MULL INVESTMENTS LP
553 R Rd (67567-6708)
PHONE.................................620 982-4336
Glenn A Mull, Partner
EMP: 10
SALES: 950K Privately Held
SIC: 0722 Crop harvesting

(G-9755)
TRI RESOURCES INC
Also Called: Dynegy
Great Bend At Patton 10th (67567)
PHONE.................................620 982-4568
EMP: 5
SALES (corp-wide): 5.8B Publicly Held
SIC: 1321 Gas Transmission/Distribution
HQ: Tri Resources, Inc.
1000 Louisiana St # 4300
Houston TX 77002
713 584-1000

Paxico
Wabaunsee County

(G-9756)
KNIGHTS OF COLUMBUS
22800 Newbury Rd (66526)
PHONE.................................785 636-5453
Joe Hund, Exec Dir
EMP: 37
SALES (corp-wide): 2.3B Privately Held
WEB: www.kofc.org
SIC: 8641 Fraternal associations
PA: Knights Of Columbus
1 Columbus Plz Ste 1700
New Haven CT 06510
203 752-4000

(G-9757)
PRAIRIE FIRE WINERY LLC
20250 Hudson Ranch Rd (66526)
PHONE.................................785 636-5533
Robert Desruisseaux,
EMP: 7
SALES (est): 471.1K Privately Held
SIC: 2084 Wines

Peabody
Marion County

(G-9758)
AMERICAN LEGION POST 95 INC
108 N Walnut St (66866-1060)
PHONE.................................620 983-2048
Lance Koslowsky, President
EMP: 13
SALES (est): 370K Privately Held
SIC: 8641 Veterans' organization

(G-9759)
GMLS INDUSTRIES INC (PA)
Also Called: Golden Fox Buildings
1658 Us Highway 50 (66866-9842)
PHONE.................................620 983-2136
Alice Kay Liefer, President
EMP: 8
SQ FT: 44,614
SALES (est): 1.6MM Privately Held
WEB: www.gmlsindustries.com
SIC: 3444 3448 Bins, prefabricated sheet metal; prefabricated metal buildings

(G-9760)
HECKENDORN EQP CO OF KANS
122 W 2nd St (66866-1015)
P.O. Box 134 (66866-0134)
PHONE.................................620 983-2186
Terry Rhodes, President
EMP: 7 EST: 1973
SQ FT: 26,000
SALES (est): 927.2K Privately Held
SIC: 3523 3441 Turf & grounds equipment; fabricated structural metal

(G-9761)
PEABODY STATE BANCORP INC (PA)
589 Quail Crk (66866-9832)
P.O. Box 50 (66866-0050)
PHONE.................................620 983-2810
Robert S Avery, President
Charles E Good, Vice Pres
Maranda Avery, Treasurer
Catherine Debrect, Admin Sec
EMP: 13 EST: 1995 Privately Held
SIC: 6712 Bank holding companies

(G-9762)
PEABODY STATE BANK (HQ)
201 N Walnut St (66866-1063)
P.O. Box 131 (66866-0131)
PHONE.................................620 983-2181
Charles Good, President
Cathy Debbrecht, Vice Pres
EMP: 11 EST: 1899
SQ FT: 5,000
SALES: 1.6MM Privately Held
WEB: www.peabodystatebank.com
SIC: 6022 State trust companies accepting deposits, commercial
PA: Peabody State Bancorp Inc
589 Quail Crk
Peabody KS 66866
620 983-2810

Peck
Sumner County

(G-9763)
GRESSEL OIL FIELD SERVICE LLC (PA)
9801 S Meridian St (67120-9750)
P.O. Box 438, Haysville (67060-0438)
PHONE.................................316 524-1225
R A Schremmer, President

Ed Gressel, *President*
EMP: 6
SQ FT: 2,000
SALES (est): 10.7MM **Privately Held**
SIC: 5084 1389 Oil well machinery, equipment & supplies; servicing oil & gas wells

(G-9764)
WYLDEWOOD CELLARS INC (PA)
951 E 119th St S (67120-8714)
P.O. Box 45, Mulvane (67110-0045)
PHONE..................................316 554-9463
John A Brewer, *President*
Merry Bauman, *Vice Pres*
Beth Brewer, *Vice Pres*
Pearl Humble, *Human Res Dir*
Sara L Cash, *VP Mktg*
EMP: 16
SQ FT: 36,000
SALES (est): 2.4MM **Privately Held**
WEB: www.wyldewoodcellars.com
SIC: 5921 2084 2033 2099 Wine; wines; jams, jellies & preserves: packaged in cans, jars, etc.; syrups

Perry
Jefferson County

(G-9765)
ALPHA MINISTRIES
15017 27th St (66073-8110)
P.O. Box 727 (66073-0727)
PHONE..................................785 597-5235
Michelle Kincaid, *Director*
EMP: 10
SALES: 160K **Privately Held**
SIC: 8699 Charitable organization

(G-9766)
BREASON EXCAVATING & TRUCKING
Also Called: Breason Excavating Service
5353 Marion Rd (66073-4182)
PHONE..................................785 597-5596
Terry Breason, *President*
Denise Breason, *Vice Pres*
EMP: 11
SALES: 430K **Privately Held**
SIC: 1794 Excavation work

(G-9767)
FIRST STATE BANK & TRUST
402 Plaza Dr (66073-4158)
P.O. Box 7 (66073-0007)
PHONE..................................785 597-5151
Anna Glynn, *Manager*
EMP: 20 **Privately Held**
SIC: 6022 State trust companies accepting deposits, commercial
HQ: First State Bank & Trust
400 S Bury St
Tonganoxie KS 66086
913 845-2500

(G-9768)
HAMM INC (DH)
Also Called: Hamm Asphalt
609 Perry Pl (66073-4201)
P.O. Box 17 (66073-0017)
PHONE..................................785 597-5111
Gary Hamm, *President*
C Scott Anderson, *CFO*
EMP: 20 **EST:** 2001
SQ FT: 12,000
SALES: 21MM
SALES (corp-wide): 2.1B **Publicly Held**
SIC: 1422 4953 Crushed & broken limestone; sanitary landfill operation
HQ: Hamm, Inc.
609 Perry Pl
Perry KS 66073
785 597-5111

(G-9769)
HAMM INC (DH)
609 Perry Pl (66073-4201)
P.O. Box 17 (66073-0017)
PHONE..................................785 597-5111
Gary Hamm, *President*
Ryan Blosser, *General Mgr*
Tom Boxberger, *Plant Mgr*
Kent Miller, *Safety Mgr*
Justin Sanders, *Sales Mgr*
EMP: 6
SQ FT: 12,000
SALES (est): 152MM
SALES (corp-wide): 2.1B **Publicly Held**
WEB: www.hamm.com
SIC: 1411 1771 1611 Limestone, dimension-quarrying; blacktop (asphalt) work; highway & street construction
HQ: Summit Materials Corporations I, Inc
1550 Wynkoop St Fl 3
Denver CO 80202
303 893-0012

(G-9770)
HAMM ASPHALT INC
Also Called: Hamm Maintenance Shop
Hwy 24 & 59 Jct (66073)
P.O. Box 17 (66073-0017)
PHONE..................................785 597-5421
Gary E Hamma, *Vice Pres*
EMP: 15
SALES (corp-wide): 2.1B **Publicly Held**
SIC: 1611 Highway & street paving contractor
HQ: Hamm Asphalt, Inc
609 Perry Pl
Perry KS 66073
785 597-5111

(G-9771)
LAKE PERRY YACHT & MARINA LLC
10770 Perry Park Dr (66073-5059)
PHONE..................................785 783-4927
Peter Anzo, *President*
Bryan Best, *General Mgr*
EMP: 17
SQ FT: 20,000
SALES (est): 578.5K **Privately Held**
SIC: 7011 4493 Motels; boat yards, storage & incidental repair

(G-9772)
MT 3 CORPORATION
Also Called: Diamond-Everley Roofing Contrs
1556 Lecompton Rd (66073-5119)
P.O. Box 3509, Lawrence (66046-0509)
PHONE..................................785 843-3433
Mark Gwaltney, *President*
Tamara Gwaltney, *Corp Secy*
Deanna Othmer, *Office Mgr*
Kyle Gwaltney, *Manager*
EMP: 30
SQ FT: 3,000
SALES (est): 2.7MM **Privately Held**
SIC: 1761 Roofing contractor

(G-9773)
N R HAMM CONTRACTOR INC
609 Perry Pl (66073-4201)
P.O. Box 17 (66073-0017)
PHONE..................................785 597-5111
Rodney Hamm, *President*
Jeff Hamm, *General Mgr*
Marvin Zielsdorf, *General Mgr*
Bradley T Hamm, *Vice Pres*
Gary Hamm, *Vice Pres*
EMP: 65 **EST:** 1940
SQ FT: 12,000
SALES (est): 4.4MM
SALES (corp-wide): 2.1B **Publicly Held**
WEB: www.hamm.com
SIC: 1611 General contractor, highway & street construction
HQ: Hamm, Inc.
609 Perry Pl
Perry KS 66073
785 597-5111

(G-9774)
U S ARMY CORPS OF ENGINEERS
Also Called: Terry Lake Project Office
10419 Perry Park Dr (66073-5058)
PHONE..................................785 597-5144
Kenneth Wate, *Branch Mgr*
EMP: 10 **Publicly Held**
WEB: www.sac.usace.army.mil
SIC: 9711 8711 Army; ; building construction consultant
HQ: U.S. Army Corps Of Engineers
441 G St Nw
Washington DC 20314
202 761-0001

(G-9775)
WOOD HAVEN INC
Also Called: Midwest Cypress Siding
401 W Bridge St (66073-5132)
P.O. Box 165 (66073-0165)
PHONE..................................785 597-5618
Jim Guffey, *President*
Mary Guffey, *CFO*
EMP: 9
SQ FT: 35,000
SALES: 1.5MM **Privately Held**
SIC: 2499 1761 2431 Decorative wood & woodwork; furniture inlays (veneers); novelties, wood fiber; siding contractor; millwork

Phillipsburg
Phillips County

(G-9776)
B & B REDIMIX INC
1873 1st St (67661-8701)
P.O. Box 2 (67661-0002)
PHONE..................................785 543-5133
Albert Mongeau, *Branch Mgr*
EMP: 5
SQ FT: 1,200
SALES (corp-wide): 2.5MM **Privately Held**
SIC: 3273 Ready-mixed concrete
PA: B & B Redimix, Inc
1873 1st St
Phillipsburg KS 67661
785 543-5133

(G-9777)
B & B REDIMIX INC (PA)
1873 1st St (67661-8701)
P.O. Box 513, Stockton (67669-0513)
PHONE..................................785 543-5133
Albert Mongeau, *President*
Dolores Mongeau, *Corp Secy*
Shane Mongeau, *Vice Pres*
Crystal Kearns, *Treasurer*
EMP: 17 **EST:** 1972
SQ FT: 750
SALES: 2.5MM **Privately Held**
SIC: 3273 7538 4213 1771 Ready-mixed concrete; general automotive repair shops; trucking, except local; concrete work

(G-9778)
B&B REDI MIX
1873 1st St (67661-8701)
PHONE..................................785 543-5133
Robert Mongeau, *Owner*
EMP: 10 **EST:** 2010
SALES: 1.5MM **Privately Held**
SIC: 3273 5082 Ready-mixed concrete; construction & mining machinery

(G-9779)
CHC MCPHERSON REFINERY INC
Also Called: N C R A
N H Way 183 (67661)
P.O. Box 608 (67661-0608)
PHONE..................................785 543-5246
Terry Redinger, *Manager*
EMP: 17
SALES (corp-wide): 31.9B **Publicly Held**
SIC: 2911 4213 Petroleum refining; contract haulers
HQ: Chs Mcpherson Refinery Inc.
2000 S Main St
Mcpherson KS 67460
620 241-2340

(G-9780)
CLIFFS WELDING SHOP INC
Also Called: Cliff's Welding Service
45 W Ridge Rd (67661-7003)
PHONE..................................785 543-5895
Clifford Van Kooten, *President*
EMP: 5
SQ FT: 3,600
SALES (est): 851.2K **Privately Held**
WEB: www.cliffsweldinginc.com
SIC: 3523 7692 1799 Farm machinery & equipment; welding repair; welding on site

(G-9781)
COOMES INC
1697 E 250 Ln (67661-9477)
PHONE..................................785 543-2759
Rick Coomes, *President*
Steve Coomes, *Vice Pres*
Ilene Lebeda, *Treasurer*
EMP: 83
SQ FT: 4,780
SALES (est): 16MM **Privately Held**
SIC: 4213 4212 Contract haulers; local trucking, without storage

(G-9782)
COOMES BROTHERS LTD
1697 E 250 Ln (67661-9477)
PHONE..................................785 543-5896
Jeff Coomes, *President*
Steve Coomes, *Vice Pres*
EMP: 45
SALES (est): 1.7MM **Privately Held**
WEB: www.coomesinc.com
SIC: 4213 Building materials transport

(G-9783)
COTTONWOOD INN
1200 State St (67661-8759)
PHONE..................................785 543-2125
Dave Dreiling, *Owner*
Debra Dreiling, *Co-Owner*
EMP: 22
SALES (est): 489.4K **Privately Held**
WEB: www.cottonwoodinn.net
SIC: 7011 Motels

(G-9784)
D & K INSURANCE SERVICES INC
466 State St (67661-1932)
P.O. Box 329 (67661-0329)
PHONE..................................785 540-4133
Darin McDowell, *Branch Mgr*
EMP: 15
SALES (corp-wide): 1.1MM **Privately Held**
SIC: 6411 Insurance agents
PA: D & K Insurance Services, Inc.
70690 Highway 8
Fairbury NE 68352
402 587-1159

(G-9785)
FARMERS NATIONAL BANK (PA)
759 State St (67661-1715)
P.O. Box 546 (67661-0546)
PHONE..................................785 543-6541
Lavern Holle, *President*
Monte Abell, *Loan Officer*
EMP: 12
SALES: 5.9MM **Privately Held**
SIC: 6411 6021 Insurance agents, brokers & service; national commercial banks

(G-9786)
FIRST NATIONAL BANK & TRUST (PA)
225 State St (67661-1927)
P.O. Box 627 (67661-0627)
PHONE..................................785 543-6511
Lloyd K Culbertson, *President*
Russell Bowman, *Vice Pres*
Debra Kennedy, *Vice Pres*
EMP: 29 **EST:** 1884
SALES: 11.6MM **Privately Held**
WEB: www.agbank.com
SIC: 6021 National commercial banks

(G-9787)
GREAT PLAINS HLTH ALIANCE INC (PA)
Also Called: Gpha
625 3rd St (67661-2138)
P.O. Box 366 (67661-0366)
PHONE..................................785 543-2111
Dave Dellasega, *President*
Roger S John, *President*
Rex Walk, *President*
Steve Carlson, *Chairman*
Robert E Hamilton, *Corp Secy*
EMP: 13
SQ FT: 4,000
SALES (est): 112.9MM **Privately Held**
WEB: www.gpha.com
SIC: 8742 Productivity improvement consultant

(G-9788)
HIGH PLAINS MENTAL HEALTH CTR
783 7th St (67661-2141)
PHONE..................................785 543-5284
Rex Harmen, *Manager*
EMP: 12
SALES (corp-wide): 9.5MM **Privately Held**
SIC: 8052 8322 8093 Home for the mentally retarded, with health care; family counseling services; mental health clinic, outpatient
PA: High Plains Mental Health Center
208 E 7th St
Hays KS 67601
785 628-2871

(G-9789)
HOSPICE SERVICES INC
424 8th St (67661-2513)
P.O. Box 116 (67661-0116)
PHONE..................................785 543-2900
Sandy Kuhlman, *Exec Dir*
EMP: 12
SALES: 1.6MM **Privately Held**
WEB: www.hospiceservices.com
SIC: 8052 Personal care facility

(G-9790)
KINDER MRGAN ENRGY PARTNERS LP
105 E Quail Rd (67661-8756)
PHONE..................................785 543-6602
EMP: 14 **Publicly Held**
WEB: www.kindermorgan.com
SIC: 4613 Refined petroleum pipelines
HQ: Kinder Morgan Energy Partners, L.P.
1001 La St Ste 1000
Houston TX 77002
713 369-9000

(G-9791)
MINERAL-RIGHT INC
10 W Quail Rd (67661)
P.O. Box 427 (67661-0427)
PHONE..................................785 543-6571
Janet L Gruett, *President*
Glen H Gruett, *Admin Sec*
EMP: 12
SQ FT: 15,750
SALES (est): 3.4MM
SALES (corp-wide): 3.1B **Publicly Held**
SIC: 2899 2819 Water treating compounds; industrial inorganic chemicals
PA: A. O. Smith Corporation
11270 W Park Pl Ste 1200
Milwaukee WI 53224
414 359-4000

(G-9792)
PHILLIPS COUNTY HOSPITAL
Also Called: Phillips County Health Systems
1150 State St (67661-1743)
P.O. Box 607 (67661-0607)
PHONE..................................785 543-5226
David Engel, *CEO*
Rhonda Kellerman, *General Mgr*
Arthur Henrickson, *Chairman*
Jennifer Brumbaugh, *Opers Staff*
Jan Johnson, *Purch Dir*
EMP: 80
SALES: 11.4MM **Privately Held**
SIC: 8062 General medical & surgical hospitals

(G-9793)
PHILLIPS COUNTY RETIREMENT CTR
1300 State St (67661-8758)
P.O. Box 628 (67661-0628)
PHONE..................................785 543-2131
Chris Kuck, *Director*
EMP: 60 **EST:** 1976
SALES (est): 2.4MM **Privately Held**
SIC: 8051 Convalescent home with continuous nursing care

(G-9794)
PRAIRIE HORZN AGRI-ENERGY LLC
1664 E 100 Rd (67661-8757)
P.O. Box 368 (67661-0368)
PHONE..................................785 543-6719
Mike Erhart, *CEO*
Monte Abell, *President*
Leonard Robinson, *CFO*
Daniel Heinze, *Treasurer*
Denise Miller, *Admin Sec*
EMP: 35
SQ FT: 12,000
SALES: 75.3MM **Privately Held**
WEB: www.phaellc.com
SIC: 2869 Ethanolamines

(G-9795)
PRAIRIE WIND VILLA ASSSTANT
1302 State St (67661-8758)
P.O. Box 628 (67661-0628)
PHONE..................................785 543-6180
Chris Kuck, *Principal*
EMP: 10
SALES (est): 192.3K **Privately Held**
SIC: 8361 Home for the aged

(G-9796)
RAILAMERICA INC
Also Called: Kyle Railroad Company
38 Railroad Ave (67661-8700)
PHONE..................................785 543-6527
Shane Dwald, *General Mgr*
Deb Alexander, *Marketing Staff*
Sonja Kinter, *Office Mgr*
Marc Syring, *Manager*
EMP: 65
SALES (corp-wide): 2.3B **Privately Held**
SIC: 4011 Interurban railways
HQ: Railamerica, Inc.
20 West Ave
Darien CT 06820

(G-9797)
RANGELAND COOPERATIVES INC (PA)
250 W F St (67661-1809)
P.O. Box 624 (67661-0624)
PHONE..................................785 543-2114
Ryan Frakes, *Division Mgr*
Bruce William, *General Mgr*
Jared Grauerholz, *Sales Staff*
Renee Miles, *Office Mgr*
EMP: 34
SQ FT: 3,200
SALES: 27.5MM **Privately Held**
SIC: 5153 5191 Grain elevators; feed

(G-9798)
REBEL STAFFING LLC
205 F St Ste 230 (67661-1943)
P.O. Box 57 (67661-0057)
PHONE..................................888 372-3302
Christina Shrader,
EMP: 99
SQ FT: 1,334
SALES (est): 482.8K **Privately Held**
SIC: 7363 Temporary help service

(G-9799)
SOLIDA JOHN & SONS TREE SVC
95 E Santa Fe Rd (67661-2555)
P.O. Box 421 (67661-0421)
PHONE..................................785 543-2810
Rick Solida, *President*
Janice Solida, *Treasurer*
EMP: 19
SALES (est): 608.3K **Privately Held**
SIC: 0783 Ornamental shrub & tree services

(G-9800)
TAMKO BUILDING PRODUCTS INC
1598 Highway 183 (67661-7005)
PHONE..................................785 543-2144
Deb Leblanc, *Human Res Mgr*
Jerry Meyer, *Manager*
Doug Keesee, *Manager*
Randy Stegmaier, *Supervisor*
EMP: 220
SQ FT: 60,000
SALES (corp-wide): 510.4MM **Privately Held**
WEB: www.tamko.com
SIC: 2952 Roof cement: asphalt, fibrous or plastic; roofing felts, cements or coatings
PA: Tamko Building Products, Inc.
198 Four States Dr
Galena KS 66739
800 641-4691

Piqua
Woodson County

(G-9801)
PIQUA FARMERS COOP ASSN INCTHE
201 S Washington St (66761-1673)
PHONE..................................620 468-2535
Marvin Lanch, *President*
Curt Miller, *Chairman*
EMP: 12
SQ FT: 3,000
SALES (est): 13.6MM **Privately Held**
SIC: 4221 5999 5251 Grain elevator, storage only; feed & farm supply; hardware

(G-9802)
PIQUA PETRO INC
1331 Xylan Rd (66761-1667)
PHONE..................................620 468-2681
Gregory Lair, *President*
Judith Lair, *Corp Secy*
EMP: 6
SALES (est): 519.1K **Privately Held**
SIC: 1389 Oil field services

Pittsburg
Crawford County

(G-9803)
A+ DECOR LLC
1146 S 220th St (66762-6851)
PHONE..................................816 699-6817
Christopher King, *CEO*
Marlin Carson, *Manager*
John Randall, *Manager*
EMP: 11
SALES (est): 194.7K **Privately Held**
SIC: 7389

(G-9804)
ACCENT DENTAL LLC
2002 S Rouse St (66762-6629)
PHONE..................................620 231-2871
Dan Minnis, *Owner*
EMP: 10
SALES (est): 673.2K **Privately Held**
SIC: 8021 Dental clinic

(G-9805)
ACE FORMS OF KANSAS INC
2900 N Rotary Ter (66762-2795)
PHONE..................................620 232-9290
Leon Bogner, *President*
Don V Becelaere, *Vice Pres*
Darrell Westhoff, *Sales Mgr*
EMP: 57
SQ FT: 52,500
SALES (est): 9.6MM **Privately Held**
WEB: www.aceforms.com
SIC: 2752 2754 2761 Commercial printing, offset; business forms, lithographed; promotional printing, gravure; manifold business forms

(G-9806)
ALABAMA SOUTHERN RAILROAD LLC
315 W 3rd St (66762-4706)
PHONE..................................620 231-2230
Terry Towner,
Gina Williams, *Admin Asst*
EMP: 34
SALES (est): 2.5MM **Privately Held**
SIC: 4011 Railroads, line-haul operating

(G-9807)
AMERICAN CONCRETE CO INC
504 N Smelter St (66762-4298)
PHONE..................................620 231-1520
Dennis Crain, *President*
Jane Crain, *Vice Pres*
EMP: 5
SQ FT: 820
SALES: 1.4MM **Privately Held**
WEB: www.americanconcreteco.net
SIC: 3273 Ready-mixed concrete

(G-9808)
AMERICAN MEDIA INVESTMENTS INC
Also Called: K K O W AM FM
1162 E Highway 126 (66762-8712)
PHONE..................................620 231-7200
Gene Bicknell, *President*
EMP: 35
SALES (est): 2.5MM **Privately Held**
WEB: www.kkowam.com
SIC: 4832 Radio broadcasting stations

(G-9809)
ANN ARBOR RAILROAD INC
315 W 3rd St (66762-4706)
PHONE..................................620 231-2230
Richard Webb, *CEO*
EMP: 60 **EST:** 2012
SALES (est): 2.8MM
SALES (corp-wide): 997.9MM **Privately Held**
SIC: 4011 Railroads, line-haul operating
PA: Watco Companies, L.L.C.
315 W 3rd St
Pittsburg KS 66762
575 745-2329

(G-9810)
ARVEST BANK
2313 S Rouse St (66762-6636)
PHONE..................................417 627-8000
EMP: 17
SALES (corp-wide): 2.3B **Privately Held**
SIC: 6022 State trust companies accepting deposits, commercial
HQ: Arvest Bank
103 S Bloomington St
Lowell AR 72745
479 575-1000

(G-9811)
ASCENSION VIA CHRISTI (PA)
1 Mt Carmel Way (66762-7587)
PHONE..................................620 231-6100
Mike Mullins, *CEO*
Bill Aquino, *President*
Todd Conklin, *COO*
Ann Buess, *CFO*
Samer Antonios, *Chief Mktg Ofcr*
EMP: 620
SQ FT: 190,000
SALES: 84.9MM **Privately Held**
WEB: www.mtcarmel.org
SIC: 8062 General medical & surgical hospitals

(G-9812)
ASCENSION VIA CHRISTI
Also Called: Mount Carmel Home Health Svcs
3 Medical Ctr Cir Ste B (66762)
P.O. Box 746 (66762-0746)
PHONE..................................620 231-3088
Pam Ireland, *Manager*
EMP: 16
SALES (corp-wide): 84.9MM **Privately Held**
WEB: www.mtcarmel.org
SIC: 8082 Home health care services
PA: Ascension Via Christi Hospital Pittsburg, Inc
1 Mt Carmel Way
Pittsburg KS 66762
620 231-6100

(G-9813)
ASCENSION VIA CHRISTI
411 E 12th St (66762-3200)
PHONE..................................620 231-6788
Nancy Evans, *Branch Mgr*
EMP: 52
SALES (corp-wide): 84.9MM **Privately Held**
WEB: www.mtcarmel.org
SIC: 8011 Clinic, operated by physicians
PA: Ascension Via Christi Hospital Pittsburg, Inc
1 Mt Carmel Way
Pittsburg KS 66762
620 231-6100

(G-9814)
ASCENSION VIA CHRISTI
Also Called: Mount Crmel Rhabilitation Svcs
1 Med Center Cir Ste B (66762-6711)
PHONE..................................620 232-0178

GEOGRAPHIC

Joe Dubois, *Director*
EMP: 25
SALES (corp-wide): 84.9MM **Privately Held**
WEB: www.mtcarmel.org
SIC: 8093 Rehabilitation center, outpatient treatment
PA: Ascension Via Christi Hospital Pittsburg, Inc
1 Mt Carmel Way
Pittsburg KS 66762
620 231-6100

(G-9815)
AT&T CORP
611 N Locust St (66762-4016)
PHONE..................................620 231-9941
Mark Thompson, *Manager*
EMP: 18
SALES (corp-wide): 170.7B **Publicly Held**
WEB: www.swbell.com
SIC: 4813 Telephone communication, except radio
HQ: At&T Corp.
1 At&T Way
Bedminster NJ 07921
800 403-3302

(G-9816)
ATKINSON INDUSTRIES INC
1801 E 27th Ter (66762-2754)
P.O. Box 268 (66762-0268)
PHONE..................................620 231-6900
Dana Perry, *Corp Secy*
Jared Holt, *Info Tech Mgr*
▲ **EMP:** 75 **EST:** 1919
SQ FT: 88,000
SALES (est): 24.2MM
SALES (corp-wide): 927MM **Publicly Held**
WEB: www.aztecgalvanizing.com
SIC: 3532 7694 Mining machinery; armature rewinding shops; electric motor repair
PA: Azz Inc.
3100 W 7th St Ste 500
Fort Worth TX 76107
817 810-0095

(G-9817)
AUSTIN WESTERN RAILROAD
315 W 3rd St (66762-4706)
PHONE..................................620 231-2230
EMP: 28
SALES (est): 3MM **Privately Held**
SIC: 4011 Railroad Line-Haul Operator

(G-9818)
AUTOMOTIVE ASSOCIATES
103 S Elm St (66762-5221)
P.O. Box 208 (66762-0208)
PHONE..................................620 231-6350
Randy Vilela, *Owner*
John Vilela, *Co-Owner*
EMP: 20
SQ FT: 9,000
SALES (est): 1.5MM **Privately Held**
SIC: 4212 1795 7538 5013 Baggage transfer; concrete breaking for streets & highways; diesel engine repair: automotive; alternators

(G-9819)
AZZ INC
1801 E 27th St Ter (66762)
PHONE..................................620 231-6900
Keith Ritchey, *Marketing Mgr*
Richard Butler, *Branch Mgr*
Tony Simon, *Maintence Staff*
EMP: 37
SALES (corp-wide): 927MM **Publicly Held**
SIC: 3699 Electrical equipment & supplies
PA: Azz Inc.
3100 W 7th St Ste 500
Fort Worth TX 76107
817 810-0095

(G-9820)
B & H CONSTRUCTION COMPANY
2601 E 20th St (66762-8430)
P.O. Box 361 (66762-0361)
PHONE..................................620 231-0326
Leo Hudiburg, *President*
George Hudiburg, *Vice Pres*
EMP: 12
SALES (est): 960K **Privately Held**
SIC: 1771 Foundation & footing contractor

(G-9821)
BACKYARD ADVENTURES LLC
3305 Airport Cir (66762-8547)
PHONE..................................620 308-6863
David Thornhill, *CEO*
Chris Connors, *Vice Pres*
David Reece, *Vice Pres*
Scott Moser, *Engineer*
Thalia Ortega, *Technical Staff*
▲ **EMP:** 30
SALES (est): 209.9K **Privately Held**
SIC: 3949 Playground equipment

(G-9822)
BARNES MILLWORKS INC
2920 N Rotary Ter (66762-2795)
PHONE..................................620 232-8746
David Barnes, *President*
Clara Barnes, *Vice Pres*
Brian Hart, *Vice Pres*
EMP: 10
SQ FT: 14,000
SALES: 2.7MM **Privately Held**
SIC: 1751 Cabinet & finish carpentry

(G-9823)
BATH-NAYLOR INC
Also Called: Bath Naylor Funeral Home
522 S Broadway St (66762-5302)
PHONE..................................620 231-4700
Joe E Naylor, *President*
Ashley Long, *Business Mgr*
EMP: 12
SQ FT: 12,500
SALES (est): 1.2MM **Privately Held**
SIC: 7261 Funeral home

(G-9824)
BEAVER DAM HEALTH CARE CENTER
1005 E Centennial Dr (66762-6603)
PHONE..................................620 231-1120
Angela King, *Branch Mgr*
EMP: 21
SALES (corp-wide): 393.8MM **Privately Held**
SIC: 8051 Skilled nursing care facilities
PA: Beaver Dam Health Care Center
5220 Tennyson Pkwy # 400
Plano TX 75024
972 372-6300

(G-9825)
BEVERLY ENTERPRISES-KANSAS LLC
Also Called: Beverly Rehabilitation Center
1005 E Centennial Dr (66762-6603)
PHONE..................................620 231-1120
Faith Sanders, *Exec Dir*
EMP: 80
SALES (corp-wide): 393.8MM **Privately Held**
SIC: 8051 Convalescent home with continuous nursing care
HQ: Beverly Enterprises-Kansas, Llc
1 1000 Beverly Way
Fort Smith AR 72919
479 201-2000

(G-9826)
BUDGET PLUMBING & HEATING
3706 E 20th St (66762-8478)
PHONE..................................620 231-5232
Richard A Rhuems, *Owner*
EMP: 12
SALES: 790K **Privately Held**
SIC: 1711 Heating systems repair & maintenance; plumbing contractors

(G-9827)
BUSINESS & TECHNOLOGY INST
Also Called: Center For Design Dev & Prod
1501 S Joplin St (66762-5945)
PHONE..................................620 235-4920
Nathaniel Lee, *Producer*
Steve Ropb, *Exec Dir*
EMP: 30 **EST:** 1987
SALES (est): 1MM **Privately Held**
WEB: www.btikansas.com
SIC: 8732 Market analysis or research

(G-9828)
CANCER CENTER
Also Called: Mount Crmel Rgional Cancer Ctr
1 Mt Carmel Way (66762-7587)
PHONE..................................620 235-7900
Debrah Davidson, *Director*
EMP: 30
SALES (est): 1.6MM **Privately Held**
WEB: www.cancercenter.com
SIC: 8069 Cancer hospital

(G-9829)
CDL ELECTRIC COMPANY INC
1308 N Walnut St (66762-3034)
PHONE..................................620 232-1242
Larry Seward, *President*
EMP: 134
SQ FT: 6,060
SALES (est): 67.4MM **Privately Held**
WEB: www.cdl-electric.com
SIC: 1731 General electrical contractor

(G-9830)
CENTRAL PLAINS CONTRACTING CO
Also Called: Holliday Sand & Gravel
733 E 520th Ave (66762-6261)
P.O. Box 171 (66762-0171)
PHONE..................................620 231-2660
Don Walrod, *Manager*
EMP: 16
SALES (corp-wide): 205.5MM **Privately Held**
SIC: 7699 Construction equipment repair
HQ: Central Plains Contracting Company
9660 Legler Rd
Shawnee Mission KS
913 894-6692

(G-9831)
CHRIS O D JACQUINOT
Also Called: Eye Care
2521 N Broadway St (66762-2620)
PHONE..................................620 235-1737
EMP: 11
SALES (est): 370K **Privately Held**
SIC: 8042 Optometrist's Office

(G-9832)
CITY OF PITTSBURG
Also Called: Four Oaks Golf Course
910 Memorial Dr (66762)
P.O. Box 688 (66762-0688)
PHONE..................................620 231-8070
Lee Farmer, *Manager*
EMP: 10 **Privately Held**
WEB: www.pittks.org
SIC: 7992 Public golf courses
PA: City Of Pittsburg
201 W 4th St
Pittsburg KS 66762
620 231-4170

(G-9833)
CITY OF PITTSBURG
Also Called: Memorial Adtrium Cnvention Ctr
503 N Pine St (66762-3818)
PHONE..................................620 231-7827
Mark Turnbull, *Manager*
EMP: 12 **Privately Held**
WEB: www.pittks.org
SIC: 7922 Community theater production
PA: City Of Pittsburg
201 W 4th St
Pittsburg KS 66762
620 231-4170

(G-9834)
CITY OF PITTSBURG
Also Called: Pittsburg Police Dept
201 N Pine St (66762-4725)
P.O. Box 611 (66762-0111)
PHONE..................................620 308-6916
Mendy Hulvey, *Chief*
Haley Drenick, *Accountant*
EMP: 65 **Privately Held**
WEB: www.pittks.org
SIC: 9221 8611 ; business associations
PA: City Of Pittsburg
201 W 4th St
Pittsburg KS 66762
620 231-4170

(G-9835)
CLASS LTD
2928 N Rouse St (66762-2480)
P.O. Box 297 (66762-0297)
PHONE..................................620 231-3131
Debbie Leahan, *Case Mgr*
Ellen Baker, *Manager*
EMP: 70
SALES (corp-wide): 9.8MM **Privately Held**
SIC: 8331 8361 Job training & vocational rehabilitation services; rehabilitation center, residential: health care incidental
PA: Class Ltd
1200 E Merle Evans Dr
Columbus KS 66725
620 429-1212

(G-9836)
CLIFF HIX ENGINEERING INC
3411 Airport Rd (66762-8556)
P.O. Box 21 (66762-0021)
PHONE..................................620 232-3000
Cliff Hix, *President*
Judith Hix, *Corp Secy*
EMP: 20
SQ FT: 8,500
SALES (est): 3.6MM **Privately Held**
SIC: 3552 2752 Printing machinery, textile; commercial printing, lithographic

(G-9837)
CLP HEALTHCARE SERVICES INC
200 E Centennial Dr Ste 9 (66762-6507)
PHONE..................................620 232-9898
Melissa Gulick, *Branch Mgr*
EMP: 89 **Privately Held**
SIC: 8052 Personal care facility
PA: Clp Healthcare Services, Inc.
10 Cadillac Dr Ste 400
Brentwood TN 37027

(G-9838)
COMFORT INN & SUITES
4009 Parkview Dr (66762-2305)
PHONE..................................620 231-8800
Portell Ratzlass, *Owner*
Jill Alexander, *Director*
EMP: 22
SALES (est): 747.8K **Privately Held**
SIC: 7011 Hotels & motels

(G-9839)
COMMERCE BANK
100 S Broadway St (66762-5202)
P.O. Box 326 (66762-0326)
PHONE..................................620 231-8400
Toll Free:..877 -
Kim Pakitsos, *Manager*
EMP: 13
SALES (corp-wide): 1.3B **Publicly Held**
SIC: 6022 State commercial banks
HQ: Commerce Bank
1000 Walnut St Fl 700
Kansas City MO 64106
816 234-2000

(G-9840)
COMMUNITY HEALTH CENTER OF SOU
Also Called: Dental Clinic
924 N Broadway St (66762-3910)
PHONE..................................620 231-6788
Holley Forrest, *Opers Staff*
Lisa Wells, *Pharmacist*
Jason Wesco, *Manager*
Jamie Shaffer, *Manager*
EMP: 20
SALES (corp-wide): 25MM **Privately Held**
SIC: 8011 Clinic, operated by physicians
PA: Community Health Center Of Southeast Kansas, Inc.
3011 N Michigan St
Pittsburg KS 66762
620 231-9873

(G-9841)
COMMUNITY HLTH CTR STHAST KANS (PA)
Also Called: Apothecare
3011 N Michigan St (66762-2546)
P.O. Box 1832 (66762-1832)
PHONE..................................620 231-9873

▲ = Import ▼=Export
◆ =Import/Export

Dawn McNay, *Opers Staff*
Douglas Stuckey, *CFO*
Ken Wood, *Pharmacist*
Darwin Anderson, *Psychologist*
Susan L Pence, *Med Doctor*
EMP: 75
SQ FT: 15,000
SALES: 25MM **Privately Held**
WEB: www.chcsek.org
SIC: 8011 Clinic, operated by physicians

(G-9842)
COMMUNITY NATIONAL BANK
401 E Centennial Dr (66762-6505)
P.O. Box 1186 (66762-1186)
PHONE..................................620 235-1345
Paul Christman, *Manager*
EMP: 20 **Privately Held**
SIC: 6141 6021 Personal credit institutions; national commercial banks
HQ: Community National Bank & Trust
14 N Lincoln Ave
Chanute KS 66720

(G-9843)
CONDOR HOSPITALITY TRUST INC
Also Called: Super 8 Motel
3108 N Broadway St (66762-2633)
PHONE..................................620 232-1881
Scott McVey, *Manager*
EMP: 15 **Privately Held**
WEB: www.southernrailleasing.com
SIC: 7011 Hotels & motels
PA: Condor Hospitality Trust, Inc.
4800 Montgomery Ln # 220
Bethesda MD 20814

(G-9844)
CONRAD MACHINE INC
1627 E 27th Ter (66762-2760)
PHONE..................................620 231-9458
Jim Conrad, *President*
Mrs Kelly Conrad, *Corp Secy*
EMP: 22
SQ FT: 10,000
SALES (est): 6.3MM **Privately Held**
SIC: 3533 Oil & gas drilling rigs & equipment

(G-9845)
CONTROL VISION CORPORATION
Also Called: Controlvision.com
1902 E 27th Ter (66762-2765)
P.O. Box 596 (66762-0596)
PHONE..................................620 231-5816
Jay Humbard, *President*
Tom Reed, *Vice Pres*
Greg Yotz, *Vice Pres*
EMP: 26
SQ FT: 3,600
SALES (est): 4.9MM **Privately Held**
WEB: www.controlvision.com
SIC: 3679 7372 7371 5045 Electronic circuits; prepackaged software; custom computer programming services; computers, peripherals & software

(G-9846)
CORNEJO & SONS LLC
709 N Locust St (66762-4038)
PHONE..................................620 231-8120
EMP: 95
SALES (corp-wide): 2.1B **Publicly Held**
SIC: 1422 Limestones, ground
HQ: Cornejo & Sons, L.L.C.
2060 E Tulsa St
Wichita KS 67216
316 522-5100

(G-9847)
COUNTRY TRADITIONS INC
1227 E 540th Ave (66762-8724)
PHONE..................................620 231-5382
Robert Hosier, *President*
Lois Hosier, *Admin Sec*
EMP: 5
SQ FT: 3,200
SALES (est): 394.9K **Privately Held**
WEB: www.countrytraditionsinc.com
SIC: 2511 Wood household furniture

(G-9848)
COUNTY OF CRAWFORD
Also Called: Crawford Cnty Mental Hlth Ctr
911 E Centennial Dr (66762-6601)
PHONE..................................620 231-5130
Richard Pfeiffer, *Exec Dir*
EMP: 30 **Privately Held**
WEB: www.crawfordcohd.org
SIC: 8322 8093 Family counseling services; drug clinic, outpatient
PA: County Of Crawford
100 E Forest Ave
Girard KS 66743
620 724-6390

(G-9849)
COUNTY OF CRAWFORD
Also Called: Crawford Cnty Mental Hlth Ctr
911 E Cennetial Ave (66762)
PHONE..................................620 231-5141
Richard Pfeiffer, *Manager*
EMP: 110 **Privately Held**
WEB: www.crawfordcohd.org
SIC: 8322 8093 Family counseling services; drug clinic, outpatient
PA: County Of Crawford
100 E Forest Ave
Girard KS 66743
620 724-6390

(G-9850)
CRESTWOOD COUNTRY CLUB INC
304 W Crestview Ave (66762-6288)
PHONE..................................620 231-9697
Todd Casey, *Manager*
EMP: 50
SQ FT: 4,000
SALES: 1.5MM **Privately Held**
SIC: 7997 Country club, membership

(G-9851)
DCCCA INC
1102 S Rouse St (66762-6048)
PHONE..................................620 670-2803
Deidra Johnson, *Branch Mgr*
EMP: 16 **Privately Held**
SIC: 8093 Alcohol clinic, outpatient; drug clinic, outpatient
PA: Dccca, Inc.
3312 Clinton Pkwy
Lawrence KS

(G-9852)
DEPCO LLC
264 N Industrial Dr (66762-4552)
P.O. Box 178 (66762-0178)
PHONE..................................620 231-0019
Ron Sripsick, *Owner*
Mike Onelio, *Controller*
Rich Hahn, *Sales Staff*
Ernie Wake, *Sales Staff*
Nathan Cook, *Manager*
EMP: 22 **EST:** 2004
SALES: 7MM **Privately Held**
SIC: 7373 Computer-aided engineering (CAE) systems service

(G-9853)
DIRECTV GROUP INC
115 E 23rd St (66762-2944)
PHONE..................................620 235-0743
EMP: 128
SALES (corp-wide): 170.7B **Publicly Held**
SIC: 4841 Direct broadcast satellite services (DBS)
HQ: The Directv Group Inc
2260 E Imperial Hwy
El Segundo CA 90245
310 964-5000

(G-9854)
EAGLEPICHER TECHNOLOGIES LLC
2919 N Rotary Ter (66762-2796)
PHONE..................................620 232-3631
Jeff Daniel, *Branch Mgr*
Steve Kroeker, *Manager*
Jay Sherfy, *Manager*
Patrick Funke, *Administration*
EMP: 11 **Privately Held**
SIC: 8731 Commercial physical research
PA: Eaglepicher Technologies, Llc
C & Porter St
Joplin MO 64801

(G-9855)
ELM ACRES YOUTH & FAMILY SVCS (PA)
Also Called: Elm Acres Youth Home
1102 S Rouse St (66762-6048)
P.O. Box 1135 (66762-1135)
PHONE..................................620 231-9840
Ann Ciambo, *Exec Dir*
EMP: 130 **EST:** 1957
SQ FT: 800
SALES: 2.7MM **Privately Held**
WEB: www.dccca.org
SIC: 8361 8093 Children's home; biofeedback center

(G-9856)
ELM ACRES YOUTH & FAMILY SVCS
Also Called: D C C A
503 N Walnut St (66762-3823)
PHONE..................................620 231-6129
Janet Snider, *Manager*
EMP: 25
SALES (est): 469.5K
SALES (corp-wide): 2.7MM **Privately Held**
WEB: www.dccca.org
SIC: 8361 Children's home
PA: Elm Acres Youth & Family Services Inc
1102 S Rouse St
Pittsburg KS 66762
620 231-9840

(G-9857)
ELNICKI INC
Also Called: Circle E Feeds
3078 N Free King Hwy (66762)
PHONE..................................620 232-5800
Rick Elnicki, *President*
EMP: 12
SALES (est): 1.3MM **Privately Held**
SIC: 2048 Livestock feeds

(G-9858)
EVENING TELEGRAM COMPANY
Also Called: Koam-TV
2950 Ne Hwy 69 (66762)
PHONE..................................417 624-0233
Danny Thomas, *Manager*
EMP: 90
SALES (corp-wide): 142.6MM **Privately Held**
WEB: www.rock102.com
SIC: 4833 Television broadcasting stations
PA: Evening Telegram Company
7025 Raymond Rd
Madison WI 53719
608 271-4321

(G-9859)
EXTRA INN INC
4023 Parkview Dr (66762-2305)
PHONE..................................620 232-2800
Yvonne Robertson, *President*
Brad Mattivi, *Vice Pres*
August Rua, *Treasurer*
EMP: 20
SQ FT: 30,000
SALES (est): 498.4K **Privately Held**
SIC: 7011 Motels

(G-9860)
FAMILY RESOURCE CENTER INC
1600 N Walnut St (66762-3036)
PHONE..................................620 235-3150
Sue Taylor, *General Mgr*
Monica Murnan, *Director*
EMP: 65
SALES: 2.8MM **Privately Held**
WEB: www.center.net
SIC: 8351 Child day care services

(G-9861)
FIRST EDITION INC
3411 Airport Rd (66762-8556)
P.O. Box 21 (66762-0021)
PHONE..................................620 232-6002
Judith A Hix, *President*
EMP: 7
SALES (est): 852K **Privately Held**
SIC: 2396 Screen printing on fabric articles

(G-9862)
FRED SPIGARELLI PA (PA)
100 S Broadway St Ste 200 (66762-5202)
P.O. Box 1449 (66762-1449)
PHONE..................................620 231-1290
Fred Spigarelli, *President*
Carlton W Kennard,
EMP: 18
SALES (est): 1.7MM **Privately Held**
SIC: 8111 General practice attorney, lawyer

(G-9863)
FREDDY VAN INC
2513 E 4th St (66762-8704)
PHONE..................................620 231-1127
Fred Van Becelaere, *President*
Barbra Van Becelaere, *Vice Pres*
Travis Van Becelaere, *Opers-Prdtn-Mfg*
EMP: 7
SALES (est): 1.4MM **Privately Held**
SIC: 1629 1381 1794 Blasting contractor, except building demolition; drilling water intake wells; directional drilling oil & gas wells; excavation work

(G-9864)
FREEMAN SRGCL CTR PTTSBRG LLC
100 N Pine St (66762-4756)
P.O. Box 2625, Joplin MO (64803-2625)
PHONE..................................620 231-9072
Paula Baker, *CEO*
Steven Graddy, *CFO*
Donald Ward, *Director*
EMP: 12
SQ FT: 18,488
SALES (est): 112K **Privately Held**
SIC: 8093 Specialty outpatient clinics

(G-9865)
GENERAL MACHINERY & SUP CO INC
510 N Elm St Ste 12 (66762-4010)
P.O. Box 1124 (66762-1124)
PHONE..................................620 231-1550
Kevin Mitchelson, *CEO*
Fred Mitchelson, *President*
EMP: 10 **EST:** 1914
SQ FT: 7,500
SALES (est): 4MM **Privately Held**
SIC: 5084 Industrial machinery & equipment

(G-9866)
GINA B PINAMONTI DDS
2602 S Rouse St (66762-6632)
PHONE..................................620 231-6910
Gina B Pinamonti DDS, *Owner*
EMP: 10 **EST:** 2001
SALES (est): 701.5K **Privately Held**
WEB: www.smileoutloud.com
SIC: 8021 Orthodontist

(G-9867)
GOODRICH QUALITY THEATERS INC
Also Called: Pittsburg 8 Theater
202 E Centennial Dr (66762-6572)
P.O. Box 571 (66762-0571)
PHONE..................................620 232-2256
Brad Yantzi, *Branch Mgr*
EMP: 15
SALES (corp-wide): 43.1MM **Privately Held**
WEB: www.goodrichmovies.com
SIC: 7832 Motion picture theaters, except drive-in
PA: Goodrich Quality Theaters Inc
4417 Broadmoor Ave Se
Grand Rapids MI 49512
616 698-7733

(G-9868)
GREAT NORTHWEST RAILROAD
315 W 3rd St (66762-4706)
PHONE..................................620 231-2230
Terry Towner, *Principal*
Gina Williams, *Admin Asst*
EMP: 19
SALES (est): 762K **Privately Held**
SIC: 4011 Railroads, line-haul operating

(G-9869)
GUEST HOME ESTATES (PA)
1910 E Centennial Dr (66762-8734)
PHONE....................................620 431-7115
Shelley Rae Gromer, *Principal*
EMP: 13 **EST:** 2007
SALES (est): 1.6MM **Privately Held**
SIC: 8059 8361 Nursing & personal care; home for the aged

(G-9870)
H & R BLOCK TAX SERVICES LLC
101 W 29th St Ste H (66762-2664)
PHONE....................................620 231-5563
Rob Dickerson, *Manager*
EMP: 12
SALES (corp-wide): 3B **Publicly Held**
SIC: 7291 Tax return preparation services
HQ: H & R Block Tax Services Llc
1 H And R Block Way
Kansas City MO 64105

(G-9871)
HARRIS BMO BANK NATIONAL ASSN
Also Called: Bmo Harris Bank
417 N Broadway St (66762-3913)
P.O. Box 709 (66762-0709)
PHONE....................................620 231-2000
Plennis Peck, *Principal*
EMP: 10
SALES (corp-wide): 17.7B **Privately Held**
WEB: www.uhb-fl.com
SIC: 6022 State trust companies accepting deposits, commercial
HQ: Harris Bmo Bank National Association
111 W Monroe St Ste 1200
Chicago IL 60603
312 461-2323

(G-9872)
HARRIS BMO BANK NATIONAL ASSN
Also Called: Bmo Harris Bank
402 N Walnut St (66762)
PHONE....................................620 235-7250
Tad Dumham, *Manager*
EMP: 19
SALES (corp-wide): 17.7B **Privately Held**
WEB: www.uhb-fl.com
SIC: 6022 State trust companies accepting deposits, commercial
HQ: Harris Bmo Bank National Association
111 W Monroe St Ste 1200
Chicago IL 60603
312 461-2323

(G-9873)
HARVEST BRANDS STOCKADE
1057 S Highway 69 (66762-6267)
PHONE....................................620 231-6700
Paul Lamert, *Director*
EMP: 50 **EST:** 1946
SALES (est): 2.5MM **Privately Held**
SIC: 0751 Livestock services, except veterinary

(G-9874)
HECKERT CONSTRUCTION CO INC
746 E 520th Ave (66762-6261)
PHONE....................................620 231-6090
Charles Heckert, *President*
Janice Heckert, *Vice Pres*
EMP: 10
SQ FT: 3,000
SALES (est): 2.3MM **Privately Held**
WEB: www.heckertconstruction.com
SIC: 1611 General contractor, highway & street construction; highway & street maintenance

(G-9875)
HERITAGE TRACTOR INC
Also Called: John Deere Tractors
1076 S Highway 69 (66762-6267)
PHONE....................................620 231-0950
Jack Dent, *Branch Mgr*
EMP: 35
SALES (corp-wide): 66.3MM **Privately Held**
SIC: 5083 Farm & garden machinery
PA: Heritage Tractor, Inc.
915 Industrial Park Rd
Baldwin City KS 66006
785 594-6486

(G-9876)
HIX CORPORATION
Also Called: Doughxpress
1201 E 27th Ter (66762-2752)
PHONE....................................620 231-8568
Jack Deboer, *Ch of Bd*
Bruce Huelat, *President*
John Morse, *Senior VP*
Arnold Marshall, *Plant Mgr*
Kay Dunbar, *CFO*
◆ **EMP:** 60
SQ FT: 111,000
SALES (est): 15.9MM **Privately Held**
WEB: www.hixcorp.com
SIC: 3567 2299 3443 3555 Industrial furnaces & ovens; flock (recovered textile fibers); fabricated plate work (boiler shop); printing trades machinery; textile machinery

(G-9877)
HOME CENTER CONSTRUCTION INC
420 W Atkinson Rd (66762-8634)
PHONE....................................620 231-5607
William W Warlop, *President*
Bonnie L Warlop, *Corp Secy*
Louis L Casaletto, *Vice Pres*
EMP: 20 **EST:** 1970
SQ FT: 3,000
SALES: 2.1MM **Privately Held**
SIC: 1542 1521 1531 Commercial & office building, new construction; general remodeling, single-family houses; speculative builder, single-family houses

(G-9878)
HONEYWELL INTERNATIONAL INC
U.S Route 69a (66762)
PHONE....................................620 783-1343
David R Nance, *Branch Mgr*
EMP: 92
SALES (corp-wide): 41.8B **Publicly Held**
WEB: www.honeywell.com
SIC: 3724 Aircraft engines & engine parts
PA: Honeywell International Inc.
300 S Tryon St
Charlotte NC 28202
973 455-2000

(G-9879)
HUDSON INC
450 E 540th Ave (66762-5293)
P.O. Box 1141 (66762-1141)
PHONE....................................620 232-1145
Stanley Hudson, *President*
Phillip Hudson, *Vice Pres*
Gerald Hudson, *Treasurer*
Mark Hudson, *Shareholder*
Jeff Lee, *Admin Sec*
EMP: 35
SALES (est): 2.2MM **Privately Held**
SIC: 1541 1542 1741 1521 Renovation, remodeling & repairs: industrial buildings; commercial & office buildings, renovation & repair; masonry & other stonework; repairing fire damage, single-family houses

(G-9880)
INNOVATIVE BROADCASTING CORP
Also Called: Kwxd
412 N Locust St (66762-4014)
P.O. Box 383 (66762-0383)
PHONE....................................620 232-5993
Toll Free:....................................888 -
Lance Sayoer, *President*
Robert Strand, *President*
EMP: 14
SQ FT: 1,500
SALES: 150K **Privately Held**
SIC: 4832 7313 Radio broadcasting stations; radio advertising representative

(G-9881)
JAKES FIREWORKS INC (PA)
1500 E 27th Ter (66762-2757)
PHONE....................................620 231-2264
Michael Marietta, *President*
Jacob A Marietta, *Corp Secy*
Eric W Clawson, *Counsel*
Eric Easter, *Project Mgr*
Jim Ramsey, *Human Res Mgr*
▲ **EMP:** 10
SQ FT: 10,000
SALES (est): 7.4MM **Privately Held**
WEB: www.jakesfireworks.net
SIC: 5999 5092 Fireworks; fireworks

(G-9882)
JIM BISHOP & ASSOCIATES
Also Called: Coldwell Banker
904 S Broadway St (66762-5412)
PHONE....................................620 231-4370
Jim Bishop, *Owner*
EMP: 15
SALES (est): 911.4K **Privately Held**
WEB: www.jimbishop.com
SIC: 6531 Real estate agent, residential

(G-9883)
JOE SMITH COMPANY
902 E Jefferson St (66762-6013)
P.O. Box 4 (66762-0004)
PHONE....................................620 231-3610
Kelly M Kays, *President*
EMP: 50
SQ FT: 50,000
SALES (est): 24.1MM **Privately Held**
WEB: www.jsc.kscoxmail.com
SIC: 5194 5145 5113 Tobacco & tobacco products; candy; industrial & personal service paper

(G-9884)
K W BROCK DIRECTORIES INC (PA)
Also Called: Names and Numbers
1225 E Centennial Dr (66762-6623)
P.O. Box 1479 (66762-1479)
PHONE....................................620 231-4000
Ken W Brock, *President*
Debra Brock, *Vice Pres*
Chris Harrison, *Facilities Mgr*
Amy Ross, *Accounts Exec*
Teresa Coulter, *Sales Staff*
EMP: 133
SQ FT: 37,000
SALES (est): 29.6MM **Privately Held**
WEB: www.namesandnumbers.com
SIC: 2741 Telephone & other directory publishing

(G-9885)
KANAWHA RIVER RAILROAD LLC
Also Called: Knwa
315 W 3rd St (66762-4706)
PHONE....................................620 231-2030
Richard Webb, *Mng Member*
EMP: 25 **EST:** 2016
SALES (est): 685.8K
SALES (corp-wide): 997.9MM **Privately Held**
SIC: 4011 Railroads, line-haul operating
PA: Watco Companies, L.L.C.
315 W 3rd St
Pittsburg KS 66762
575 745-2329

(G-9886)
KANNARR EYE CARE LLC
2521 N Broadway St (66762-2620)
PHONE....................................620 235-1737
Shane R Kannarr,
Katie Painter,
EMP: 10
SALES (est): 947.5K **Privately Held**
SIC: 8042 Specialized optometrists

(G-9887)
KANSAS & OKLAHOMA RAILROAD LLC (HQ)
315 W 3rd St (66762-4706)
PHONE....................................620 231-2230
Richard Webb, *CEO*
EMP: 12
SQ FT: 45,000
SALES (est): 3.3MM
SALES (corp-wide): 997.9MM **Privately Held**
WEB: www.watcocompanies.com
SIC: 4011 Railroads, line-haul operating
PA: Watco Companies, L.L.C.
315 W 3rd St
Pittsburg KS 66762
575 745-2329

(G-9888)
KANSAS BIG BROS BIG SSTERS INC
310 N Pine St Ste B (66762-4752)
PHONE....................................620 231-1145
Gail Dubray, *Branch Mgr*
EMP: 18
SALES (corp-wide): 4.1MM **Privately Held**
SIC: 8322 Youth center
PA: Kansas Big Brothers Big Sisters, Inc.
310 E 2nd St N
Wichita KS 67202
316 263-3300

(G-9889)
KANSAS TEACHERS CMNTY CR UN (PA)
416 N Broadway St (66762-3919)
P.O. Box 1296 (66762-1296)
PHONE....................................620 231-5719
Mark Kolarik, *President*
Becky Franklin, *Vice Pres*
EMP: 28
SALES: 3.2MM **Privately Held**
SIC: 6141 Personal credit institutions

(G-9890)
KANSASLAND TIRE INC
901 N Broadway St (66762-3907)
PHONE....................................620 231-7210
Travis Berger, *Manager*
EMP: 10
SALES (corp-wide): 94.3MM **Privately Held**
WEB: www.nktiregroup.com
SIC: 5531 7538 Automotive tires; general automotive repair shops
HQ: Kansasland Tire, Inc.
2904 S Spruce St
Wichita KS 67216
316 522-5434

(G-9891)
KENDALL PACKAGING CORPORATION
1901 E 27th Ter (66762-2766)
PHONE....................................620 231-9804
Bobbie Kellogg, *Accountant*
Randy Mjelde, *Sales Staff*
Robert Bean, *Branch Mgr*
Howard Darmer, *Executive*
EMP: 45
SALES (corp-wide): 26.2MM **Privately Held**
WEB: www.kendallpkg.com
SIC: 2671 2759 2673 Packaging paper & plastics film, coated & laminated; commercial printing; garment & wardrobe bags, (plastic film)
PA: Kendall Packaging Corporation
10335 N Port Washington R
Mequon WI 53092
262 404-1200

(G-9892)
KEY REHABILITATION INC
2614 N Joplin St (66762-2643)
PHONE....................................620 231-3887
Melissa Kester, *Manager*
EMP: 10
SALES (est): 231.3K **Privately Held**
SIC: 8093 Rehabilitation center, outpatient treatment

(G-9893)
KUNSHEK CHAT & COAL INC
304 Memorial Dr (66762-3026)
PHONE....................................620 231-8270
Robert Kunshek, *President*
Julia Kunshek, *Treasurer*
EMP: 23 **EST:** 1945
SQ FT: 500
SALES: 4.3MM **Privately Held**
SIC: 4213 5032 Trucking, except local; sand, construction

(G-9894)
LEISURE TIME PRODUCTS
3305 Airport Dr (66762-8567)
PHONE..................................620 308-5224
EMP: 14
SALES (est): 728K **Privately Held**
SIC: 7822 Motion picture & tape distribution

(G-9895)
LOUISIANA SOUTHERN RAILROAD
4746 Quitman Hwy (66762)
PHONE..................................620 235-7360
Pat Lacaze, *General Mgr*
EMP: 16
SALES (est): 509.5K **Privately Held**
SIC: 4011 Railroads, line-haul operating

(G-9896)
LYNCO REC INC
Also Called: Holiday Lanes
2406 N Broadway St (66762-2619)
PHONE..................................620 231-2222
Kenneth G Lynch Jr, *President*
Kimberly R Lynch, *Corp Secy*
EMP: 18
SQ FT: 15,000
SALES (est): 981.4K **Privately Held**
SIC: 7933 5941 5812 Ten pin center; bowling equipment & supplies; snack bar

(G-9897)
MARRONES INC
800 E 14th St (66762-3466)
P.O. Box 600 (66762-0600)
PHONE..................................620 231-6610
Albert J Marrone Jr, *President*
Ronald L Marrone, *Corp Secy*
Kenneth Marrone, *COO*
Dale Wayne Marrone, *Vice Pres*
EMP: 49 **EST:** 1945
SQ FT: 48,000
SALES (est): 27.9MM **Privately Held**
WEB: www.marronesinc.com
SIC: 5141 Food brokers

(G-9898)
MARTINOUS PRODUCE COMPANY INC
3510 Lone Star (66762)
P.O. Box 568 (66762-0568)
PHONE..................................620 231-5840
Farris Martinous, *President*
Paul Martinous, *Vice Pres*
Raymond Martinous, *Manager*
EMP: 32 **EST:** 1989
SQ FT: 7,000
SALES: 17.8MM **Privately Held**
WEB: www.martinousproduceco.com
SIC: 5148 Fruits, fresh; vegetables, fresh

(G-9899)
MASONITE INTERNATIONAL CORP
Masonite Entry Systems-Pittsbu
911 E Jefferson St (66762-6012)
P.O. Box 76 (66762-0076)
PHONE..................................620 231-8200
Vicki Moody, *Mktg Dir*
Steve Cox, *Manager*
Jerred Bennett, *Supervisor*
Debbie Redfern, *Supervisor*
James Stevens, *Info Tech Mgr*
EMP: 30
SALES (corp-wide): 2.1B **Publicly Held**
WEB: www.masoniteinternational.com
SIC: 3442 3089 Metal doors, sash & trim; fiberglass doors
PA: Masonite International Corporation
201 N Franklin St Ste 300
Tampa FL 33602
800 895-2723

(G-9900)
MASTERCRAFT PATTERN INC
765 E 520th Ave (66762-6261)
PHONE..................................620 231-3530
Paul Bishop, *CEO*
Jonah Bishop, *President*
EMP: 6
SQ FT: 11,500
SALES (est): 1.2MM **Privately Held**
SIC: 3543 3544 Industrial patterns; forms (molds), for foundry & plastics working machinery

(G-9901)
MCPU POLYMER ENGINEERING LLC
826 E 4th St (66762-4249)
P.O. Box 6 (66762-0006)
PHONE..................................620 231-4239
Thomas M Garrett, *Mng Member*
EMP: 8
SQ FT: 25,000
SALES: 5MM
SALES (corp-wide): 126.4MM **Privately Held**
SIC: 2821 8711 Polyurethane resins; engineering services
PA: Mcp Industries, Inc.
708 S Temescal St Ste 101
Corona CA 92879
951 736-1881

(G-9902)
MEDICALODGES INC
Also Called: Medicalodge South
2520 S Rouse St (66762-6605)
PHONE..................................620 231-0300
Blair Wagner, *Manager*
EMP: 60
SALES (corp-wide): 100.2MM **Privately Held**
WEB: www.medicalodges.com
SIC: 8052 8051 Intermediate care facilities; skilled nursing care facilities
PA: Medicalodges, Inc.
201 W 8th St
Coffeyville KS 67337
620 251-6700

(G-9903)
MID CENTRAL CONTRACT SVCS INC
450 E 540th Ave (66762-5293)
P.O. Box 1161 (66762-1161)
PHONE..................................620 231-1166
Jason Scheumann, *President*
Sylvia Scheumann, *Admin Sec*
EMP: 30
SQ FT: 7,500
SALES: 2MM **Privately Held**
WEB: www.midcentralcontractservices.com
SIC: 7349 Building maintenance services

(G-9904)
MIDAMERICA APPRAISALS INC
1800 E 4th St (66762-8573)
P.O. Box 18 (66762-0018)
PHONE..................................620 231-0939
Ronald Fraizer, *President*
EMP: 10
SALES (est): 513.6K **Privately Held**
SIC: 6531 Appraiser, real estate

(G-9905)
MILLENNIUM RAIL INC (HQ)
315 W 3rd St (66762-4706)
PHONE..................................620 231-2230
William J Groos, *CEO*
David R Turner, *President*
Rich Goldstein, *Principal*
Mike Herman, *Principal*
Steve Kaplan, *Principal*
EMP: 15 **EST:** 1996
SALES (est): 42.1MM
SALES (corp-wide): 997.9MM **Privately Held**
SIC: 4789 3743 7699 Railroad car repair; railroad car rebuilding; railroad car customizing
PA: Watco Companies, L.L.C.
315 W 3rd St
Pittsburg KS 66762
575 745-2329

(G-9906)
MILLERS INC (PA)
610 E Jefferson St (66762-5913)
P.O. Box 777 (66762-0777)
PHONE..................................620 231-8050
Richard G Miller, *Ch of Bd*
Todd R Coleman, *President*
Todd Coleman, *COO*
H Richard Coleman, *Vice Pres*
John Martin, *Production*
EMP: 280 **EST:** 1939
SQ FT: 135,000
SALES (est): 141.8MM **Privately Held**
WEB: www.millerslab.com
SIC: 7384 Film developing & printing; photofinishing laboratory

(G-9907)
MKL ACQUISITIONS LLC
1014 E 580th Ave (66762-8417)
PHONE..................................620 704-5228
Michael Loy, *Principal*
EMP: 10
SALES (est): 343.9K **Privately Held**
SIC: 6799 Investors

(G-9908)
MORRIS COMMUNICATIONS CO LLC
Also Called: Pittsburg Morning Sun
701 N Locust St (66762-4038)
P.O. Box H (66762-0570)
PHONE..................................620 231-2600
Steven Wade, *Manager*
Leann Pipkin, *Administration*
EMP: 65 **Privately Held**
WEB: www.morris.com
SIC: 2711 2752 Newspapers, publishing & printing; commercial printing, lithographic
HQ: Morris Communications Company Llc
725 Broad St
Augusta GA 30901
706 724-0851

(G-9909)
MOSAIC
2807 N Broadway St (66762-2626)
PHONE..................................620 231-5590
Stephen Graham, *Branch Mgr*
EMP: 101
SALES (corp-wide): 257.7MM **Privately Held**
SIC: 8322 Social services for the handicapped
PA: Mosaic
4980 S 118th St
Omaha NE 68137
402 896-3884

(G-9910)
NATIONL SOC DAUGHT AMR REV
1074 S 160th St (66762-6840)
PHONE..................................620 457-8747
Jackie Casey, *President*
Elouise Height, *Treasurer*
EMP: 25
SALES (est): 157K **Privately Held**
SIC: 8699 Personal interest organization

(G-9911)
NEW HOPE SERVICES
2614 N Joplin St (66762-2643)
PHONE..................................620 231-9895
Suzi Johnson, *Principal*
EMP: 14
SALES (est): 633.8K **Privately Held**
SIC: 8051 8361 Skilled nursing care facilities; residential care

(G-9912)
PEPSI-COLA BTLG OF PITTSBURG
1211 N Broadway St (66762-3099)
P.O. Box 1924 (66762-1924)
PHONE..................................620 231-3800
Charles L Farabi, *President*
EMP: 23
SQ FT: 15,000
SALES (est): 4.3MM **Privately Held**
SIC: 2086 3085 Soft drinks: packaged in cans, bottles, etc.; plastics bottles

(G-9913)
PH ENTERPRISES INC
200 E Centennial Dr 10a (66762-6571)
PHONE..................................620 232-1900
Gary Peterson, *President*
Jeannie Peterson, *Treasurer*
EMP: 11
SALES: 1.3MM **Privately Held**
SIC: 8071 Medical laboratories

(G-9914)
PITSCO INC (PA)
Also Called: Technological Literacy Group
915 E Jefferson St (66762-6012)
P.O. Box 1708 (66762-1708)
PHONE..................................620 231-0000
Harvey Dean, *President*
Carla Book, *Prdtn Mgr*
Virginia Herford, *Purch Mgr*
Eric Hopkins, *Human Resources*
Mendi Brazil, *Sales Staff*
▲ **EMP:** 185
SQ FT: 12,000
SALES (est): 63.8MM **Privately Held**
WEB: www.pitsco.com
SIC: 5049 School supplies

(G-9915)
PITSCO INC
1003 E Adams St (66762-6051)
PHONE..................................800 835-0686
Harvey Dean, *Branch Mgr*
Carter Terry, *Comp Spec*
Randy Yocum, *Administration*
▲ **EMP:** 13
SALES (corp-wide): 63.8MM **Privately Held**
SIC: 5049 School supplies
PA: Pitsco, Inc.
915 E Jefferson St
Pittsburg KS 66762
620 231-0000

(G-9916)
PITSCO INC
Also Called: Printed Media Center
1002 E Adams St (66762-6050)
PHONE..................................620 231-2424
Shela Hensley, *Principal*
EMP: 10
SALES (corp-wide): 63.8MM **Privately Held**
WEB: www.pitsco.com
SIC: 7389 Printed circuitry graphic layout
PA: Pitsco, Inc.
915 E Jefferson St
Pittsburg KS 66762
620 231-0000

(G-9917)
PITSCO INC
Catalog Division
1002 E Adams St (66762-6050)
P.O. Box 1708 (66762-1708)
PHONE..................................620 231-0010
Harvey Dean, *Owner*
Duwana Hines, *Warehouse Mgr*
Melissa Karsten, *Marketing Staff*
Daniel Eckelberry, *Info Tech Mgr*
EMP: 15
SALES (corp-wide): 63.8MM **Privately Held**
WEB: www.pitsco.com
SIC: 5046 Commercial equipment
PA: Pitsco, Inc.
915 E Jefferson St
Pittsburg KS 66762
620 231-0000

(G-9918)
PITT PLASTICS INC (HQ)
1400 E Atkinson Ave (66762-8564)
P.O. Box 356 (66762-0356)
PHONE..................................620 231-4030
Jeff Poe, *President*
Joey Caskey, *Principal*
Jody Flora, *Principal*
Michelle Green, *Principal*
Andrea Stiles, *Principal*
▲ **EMP:** 400
SQ FT: 275,000
SALES (est): 162MM **Privately Held**
WEB: www.pittplastics.com
SIC: 2673 Plastic bags: made from purchased materials

(G-9919)
PITT STEEL LLC (PA)
748 E 520th Ave (66762-6261)
PHONE..................................620 231-8100
Cody Elnicki, *President*
EMP: 5
SALES: 1MM **Privately Held**
SIC: 3312 Structural shapes & pilings, steel

GEOGRAPHIC

(G-9920)
PITTCRAFT PRINTING INC (PA)
112 E Rose St (66762-5252)
P.O. Box 718 (66762-0718)
PHONE....................................620 231-6200
Tim Collar, *President*
Tom Dayton, *Treasurer*
Neil Bond, *Accounts Mgr*
Dan Dayton, *Shareholder*
Gene Dayton, *Shareholder*
EMP: 29
SQ FT: 83,000
SALES (est): 3.5MM **Privately Held**
WEB: www.pittcraft.com
SIC: 2752 2789 2759 Color lithography; bookbinding & related work; commercial printing

(G-9921)
PITTSBURG INTERNAL MEDCINE PA
Also Called: Carlson, Mark MD
2401 S Tucker Ave Ste 1 (66762-6619)
PHONE....................................620 231-1650
EMP: 10
SALES (est): 1MM **Privately Held**
SIC: 8011 Internal medicine, physician/surgeon; physicians' office, including specialists

(G-9922)
PITTSBURG STATE UNIV FOUNDATIO
401 E Ford St (66762-6369)
PHONE....................................620 235-4764
Donna J Geisler, *Ch of Bd*
Kathleen Flannery, *President*
Vicki S Dennett, *Treasurer*
EMP: 30
SALES: 14.4MM **Privately Held**
SIC: 7389 Fund raising organizations

(G-9923)
PRO X PROPERTY SOLUTIONS LLC
107 E Rose St (66762-5267)
PHONE....................................620 249-5767
Tyler Casey, *Mng Member*
EMP: 12
SALES (est): 146.4K **Privately Held**
SIC: 6531 Real estate managers

(G-9924)
PROFESSIONAL ENGRG CONS PA
Also Called: PEC
104 S Pine St (66762-5115)
PHONE....................................620 235-0195
Bruce Remsberg, *Manager*
EMP: 10
SALES (corp-wide): 66.5MM **Privately Held**
WEB: www.pec.org
SIC: 8711 Consulting engineer
PA: Professional Engineering Consultants P.A.
303 S Topeka Ave
Wichita KS 67202
316 262-2691

(G-9925)
PROGRESSIVE PRODUCTS INC
3305 Airport Cir (66762-8547)
PHONE....................................620 235-1712
Todd Allison, *President*
Rod Herring, *Purch Agent*
Justin Brown, *Design Engr*
Stephen Hinton, *Design Engr*
Beth Perry, *Human Resources*
EMP: 30
SQ FT: 120,000
SALES (est): 8.8MM **Privately Held**
WEB: www.progressiveproductsinc.com
SIC: 3444 3494 3317 Elbows, for air ducts, stovepipes, etc.: sheet metal; valves & pipe fittings; steel pipe & tubes

(G-9926)
RELOAD EXPRESS INC (HQ)
315 W 3rd St (66762-4706)
PHONE....................................620 231-2230
Rick Baden, *President*
EMP: 12 **EST:** 2012
SALES (est): 5MM
SALES (corp-wide): 997.9MM **Privately Held**
SIC: 4173 Bus terminal & service facilities
PA: Watco Companies, L.L.C.
315 W 3rd St
Pittsburg KS 66762
575 745-2329

(G-9927)
RESTORATIVE JUSTICE AUTHORITY
665 S Highway 69 (66762-8600)
PHONE....................................620 235-7118
Angie Hadley, *Manager*
Kristin S Thomas, *Manager*
Angie K Hadley, *Director*
EMP: 10
SALES (est): 232.7K **Privately Held**
SIC: 8322 Individual & family services

(G-9928)
RFB CONSTRUCTION CO INC
565 E 520th Ave (66762-6829)
PHONE....................................620 232-2900
Deborah Beachner, *President*
EMP: 25
SQ FT: 8,000
SALES (est): 5.1MM **Privately Held**
SIC: 1611 General contractor, highway & street construction

(G-9929)
RIDLEY USA INC
Also Called: Ridley Block Operations
1057 S Highway 69 (66762-6267)
PHONE....................................620 231-6700
Tim Murphy, *Plant Mgr*
Timothy Murphy, *Branch Mgr*
EMP: 25
SALES (corp-wide): 1.6B **Privately Held**
SIC: 2048 Livestock feeds
HQ: Ridley Usa Inc.
111 W Cherry St Ste 500
Mankato MN 56001
507 388-9400

(G-9930)
RYAN D&M INC
Also Called: Comet Cleaners
1005 Canterbury Rd (66762-3547)
PHONE....................................620 231-4559
Dennis Ryan, *CEO*
EMP: 18
SALES (est): 1.4MM **Privately Held**
SIC: 5087 Laundry & dry cleaning equipment & supplies

(G-9931)
RYANS COMET CLEANER
1005 Canterbury Rd (66762-3547)
PHONE....................................620 231-4559
Dennis Ryan, *President*
EMP: 12
SALES (est): 217.7K **Privately Held**
SIC: 7699 Cleaning services

(G-9932)
S & S UNDERGROUND LLC
1623 E 20th St (66762-3468)
PHONE....................................620 704-1397
Stephen Smithson, *Mng Member*
EMP: 10
SQ FT: 100
SALES: 400K **Privately Held**
SIC: 3661 Fiber optics communications equipment

(G-9933)
S E K OTOLARYNGOLOGY PA
Also Called: Baker Clinic The
107 N Pine St Ste B (66762-4757)
P.O. Box 1628 (66762-1628)
PHONE....................................620 232-7500
Michael P Baker, *President*
EMP: 10
SALES: 1MM **Privately Held**
SIC: 8011 Ears, nose & throat specialist: physician/surgeon

(G-9934)
SAFEHOUSE CRISIS CENTER INC
Also Called: SAFEHOUSE FOR BATTERED SPOUSES
409 N Walnut St Ste 1 (66762-3869)
PHONE....................................620 231-8692
Rebecca L Brubaker, *Exec Dir*
EMP: 23
SQ FT: 1,800
SALES: 952.1K **Privately Held**
SIC: 8322 Crisis intervention center

(G-9935)
SARAGENES SHORT STOP
Also Called: Whistle Stop Carwash
4002 N Broadway St (66762)
PHONE....................................620 235-1141
Saragene Rhuems, *Owner*
EMP: 13
SQ FT: 2,400
SALES: 557.7K **Privately Held**
SIC: 5411 7542 Convenience stores; carwash, automatic; carwash, self-service

(G-9936)
SENIOR SVCS OF SOUTHEAST KANS
Also Called: Homer Cove
3003 N Joplin St (66762-2540)
PHONE....................................620 232-7443
Fax: 620 232-7443
EMP: 12
SALES (corp-wide): 1.3MM **Privately Held**
SIC: 8322 Individual/Family Services
PA: Senior Services Of Southeast Kansas Inc
618 Union St
Coffeyville KS 67337
620 251-7313

(G-9937)
SEWARD AND WILSON ELECTRIC
Also Called: Seward & Wilson Rentals
1202 E 4th St (66762-4406)
PHONE....................................620 232-1696
Bill Wilson, *President*
James Seward, *Vice Pres*
William K Wilson, *Vice Pres*
EMP: 11 **EST:** 1977
SALES: 811.7K **Privately Held**
SIC: 1731 General electrical contractor

(G-9938)
SHARPS AUTO BDY COLLISION INC
202 N Elm St (66762-4822)
PHONE....................................620 231-6011
Richard E Smith Jr, *President*
Richard Smith, *President*
Beth Smith, *CFO*
Brandie Nading, *Administration*
EMP: 11
SQ FT: 10,200
SALES (est): 1.2MM **Privately Held**
WEB: www.sharpsautobodycollision.com
SIC: 7532 Body shop, automotive

(G-9939)
SOUTH KANSAS AND OKLA RR INC (HQ)
315 W 3rd St (66762-4706)
PHONE....................................620 231-2230
Richard Webb, *President*
EMP: 30
SQ FT: 30,000
SALES (est): 4.9MM
SALES (corp-wide): 997.9MM **Privately Held**
SIC: 4011 Railroads, line-haul operating
PA: Watco Companies, L.L.C.
315 W 3rd St
Pittsburg KS 66762
575 745-2329

(G-9940)
STEP2 DISCOVERY LLC (PA)
Also Called: Backyard Discovery
3001 N Rouse St (66762-2404)
PHONE....................................620 232-2400
Ron Scripsick, *CEO*
Rich Adams, *COO*
Charlie Sammann, *Exec VP*
Richard Snow, *CFO*
▲ **EMP:** 36
SALES (est): 439.6MM **Privately Held**
WEB: www.politron.com
SIC: 3944 Games, toys & children's vehicles

(G-9941)
STOCKADE BRANDS INCORPORATED
1057 S Highway 69 (66762-6267)
PHONE....................................620 231-6700
Lester Cashmere, *President*
David Verner, *Shareholder*
Mike Verner, *Shareholder*
EMP: 43 **EST:** 2006
SALES (est): 5MM **Privately Held**
SIC: 2048 Livestock feeds

(G-9942)
STUDENT HEALTH CENTER PSU
1701 S Broadway St (66762-5856)
PHONE....................................620 235-4452
Gary Grimaldi, *Director*
EMP: 10 **EST:** 1970
SALES (est): 627.6K **Privately Held**
SIC: 8011 Group health association

(G-9943)
STUDENT IN FREE ENTERPRIS
1701 S Broadway St (66762-5856)
PHONE....................................620 235-4574
June Fraund, *Owner*
EMP: 35
SALES (est): 1.2MM **Privately Held**
SIC: 8748 Testing service, educational or personnel

(G-9944)
T H ROGERS LUMBER COMPANY
1701 N Broadway St (66762-3023)
PHONE....................................620 231-0900
Bill Atkinson, *Manager*
EMP: 14
SALES (corp-wide): 69.8MM **Privately Held**
WEB: www.throgers.com
SIC: 5211 5031 Lumber & other building materials; lumber: rough, dressed & finished
PA: The T H Rogers Lumber Company
1717 S State St
Edmond OK 73013
405 330-2181

(G-9945)
TFI FAMILY SERVICES INC
105 W 7th St (66762-3807)
P.O. Box 1953 (66762-1953)
PHONE....................................620 231-0443
Peggy Martin, *Manager*
EMP: 15
SALES (corp-wide): 20.7MM **Privately Held**
SIC: 8322 Individual & family services
PA: Tfi Family Services, Inc.
618 Commercial St Ste C
Emporia KS 66801
620 342-2239

(G-9946)
TOUCHTON ELECTRIC INC
Also Called: Touchton Alarms
111 N Broadway St (66762-4889)
PHONE....................................620 232-9294
Doris Touchton, *Corp Secy*
David Touchton, *Exec VP*
Elijah E Touchton, *Manager*
EMP: 28
SQ FT: 2,400
SALES: 1.1MM **Privately Held**
WEB: www.touchtonalarms.com
SIC: 1731 Fire detection & burglar alarm systems specialization

(G-9947)
TRANSERVE INC
Also Called: Watco Companies
315 W 3rd St (66762-4706)
PHONE....................................620 231-2230
Kirk Hawley, *President*
Andy Laurent, *President*
Penny Wood, *CFO*
EMP: 85

SALES (est): 7.9MM
SALES (corp-wide): 997.9MM **Privately Held**
WEB: www.transerve.com
SIC: 8742 7361 Management consulting services; labor contractors (employment agency)
PA: Watco Companies, L.L.C.
315 W 3rd St
Pittsburg KS 66762
575 745-2329

(G-9948)
TRI STATE CONSTRUCTION INC
816 E Jefferson St (66762-6011)
P.O. Box 1416 (66762-1416)
PHONE..................................620 231-5260
John Jemison, *President*
EMP: 20
SALES (est): 1.2MM **Privately Held**
SIC: 1611 General contractor, highway & street construction

(G-9949)
UNIQUE METAL FABRICATION INC
2888 N Rotary Ter (66762-2753)
P.O. Box 201 (66762-0201)
PHONE..................................620 232-3060
Adam C Endicott, *President*
EMP: 35
SQ FT: 100,000
SALES (est): 12MM **Privately Held**
WEB: www.umfi.com
SIC: 3441 3446 Building components, structural steel; architectural metalwork

(G-9950)
UNITED PARCEL SERVICE INC
Also Called: UPS
2106 W 4th St (66762-8622)
PHONE..................................620 235-1220
Travis Peter, *Business Mgr*
Roger Riddle, *Manager*
EMP: 37
SALES (corp-wide): 71.8B **Publicly Held**
WEB: www.upsscs.com
SIC: 4215 Parcel delivery, vehicular
HQ: United Parcel Service, Inc.
55 Glenlake Pkwy
Atlanta GA 30328
404 828-6000

(G-9951)
UNITED STATES AWARDS INC
603 E Washington St (66762-5346)
P.O. Box 1537 (66762-1537)
PHONE..................................620 231-8470
Doug Dellasega, *President*
Alex Yager, *Admin Asst*
EMP: 20 **EST**: 1987
SALES: 1.8MM **Privately Held**
WEB: www.usawards.com
SIC: 5199 2399 2395 Advertising specialties; emblems, badges & insignia: from purchased materials; pleating & stitching

(G-9952)
UNITED STATES CELLULAR CORP
2597 S Broadway St (66762-6396)
PHONE..................................620 231-2444
Chuck Parsons, *Manager*
EMP: 18
SALES (corp-wide): 5.1B **Publicly Held**
SIC: 4812 Cellular telephone services
HQ: United States Cellular Corporation
8410 W Bryn Mawr Ave # 700
Chicago IL 60631
773 399-8900

(G-9953)
US BANK NATIONAL ASSOCIATION
Also Called: US Bank
306 N Broadway St Ste 100 (66762-4816)
PHONE..................................620 231-4040
Birdger Robinson, *Manager*
EMP: 10
SALES (corp-wide): 25.7B **Publicly Held**
WEB: www.firstar.com
SIC: 6021 National commercial banks
HQ: U.S. Bank National Association
425 Walnut St Fl 14
Cincinnati OH 45202
513 632-4234

(G-9954)
VENTURE HOTELS LLC
Also Called: Holiday Inn
4011 Parkview Dr (66762-2305)
PHONE..................................620 231-1177
EMP: 35
SALES (corp-wide): 5.1MM **Privately Held**
SIC: 7011 Hotels & motels
PA: Venture Hotels, Llc
31321 Brooks St
Laguna Beach CA 92651
949 433-9190

(G-9955)
VERITIV OPERATING COMPANY
Also Called: Rollsource
3004 N Rotary Ter (66762-2902)
PHONE..................................620 231-2508
Steve Robinson, *Manager*
EMP: 10
SALES (corp-wide): 8.7B **Publicly Held**
WEB: www.unisourcelink.com
SIC: 5113 Industrial & personal service paper
HQ: Veritiv Operating Company
1000 Abernathy Rd Bldg 4
Atlanta GA 30328
770 391-8200

(G-9956)
VIA CHRISTI VLG PITTSBURG INC
Also Called: VIA CHRISTI HEALTH
1502 E Centennial Dr (66762-6718)
PHONE..................................620 235-0020
Jeff Korsmo, *CEO*
David R Hadley, *CFO*
Mindi Garner, *Director*
Sr Marie Janousek, *Director*
Helen Kriegsman, *Director*
EMP: 50
SQ FT: 91,198
SALES: 8.4MM
SALES (corp-wide): 25.3B **Privately Held**
SIC: 8051 Skilled nursing care facilities
HQ: Via Christi Villages, Inc
2622 W Central Ave # 100
Wichita KS 67203
316 946-5200

(G-9957)
VILELA RNDY AUTO BDY REPR PNTG
Also Called: Vilela, Randy Auto Salvage
103 S Elm St (66762-5221)
P.O. Box 208 (66762-0208)
PHONE..................................620 231-6350
Randy Vilela, *Owner*
EMP: 16
SALES (est): 723.9K **Privately Held**
SIC: 7532 5015 1795 1794 Body shop, automotive; automotive parts & supplies, used; wrecking & demolition work; excavation work

(G-9958)
VINTAGE PLACE OF PITTSBURG
Also Called: Vintage Place Assisted Living
1004 E Centennial Dr (66762-6565)
PHONE..................................620 231-4554
Thomas Reddy, *President*
Brian Warren, *Vice Pres*
Paul Wurth, *Treasurer*
Shanna Taylor, *Executive*
EMP: 20
SQ FT: 3,000
SALES (est): 603.2K **Privately Held**
SIC: 7363 Domestic help service

(G-9959)
VINYLPLEX INC
1800 E Atkinson Ave (66762-2781)
PHONE..................................620 231-8290
G R Baker, *CEO*
William Coleman, *President*
EMP: 43
SQ FT: 70,000
SALES (est): 8.9MM **Privately Held**
WEB: www.vinylplex.com
SIC: 3084 Plastics pipe

(G-9960)
WALMART INC
2710 N Broadway St (66762-2625)
PHONE..................................620 232-1593
Marlon Westen, *General Mgr*
EMP: 400
SQ FT: 175,499
SALES (corp-wide): 514.4B **Publicly Held**
WEB: www.walmartstores.com
SIC: 5311 5411 5912 7384 Department stores, discount; supermarkets, hypermarket; drug stores & proprietary stores; photofinishing laboratory; offices & clinics of chiropractors
PA: Walmart Inc.
702 Sw 8th St
Bentonville AR 72716
479 273-4000

(G-9961)
WALNUT RIDGE GROUP INC
304 W 11th St (66762-3000)
P.O. Box 668 (66762-0668)
PHONE..................................620 232-3359
Dean Spears, *President*
David Spears, *Treasurer*
EMP: 10
SALES (est): 1MM **Privately Held**
WEB: www.absupplies.com
SIC: 5712 6519 Furniture stores; real property lessors

(G-9962)
WATCO INC (HQ)
315 W 3rd St (66762-4706)
PHONE..................................208 734-4644
Richard Webb, *CEO*
Charles R Webb, *Ch of Bd*
Rick Baden, *President*
Ed McKechnie, *Exec VP*
Craig Richey, *Exec VP*
EMP: 75
SQ FT: 10,800
SALES (est): 96.7MM
SALES (corp-wide): 997.9MM **Privately Held**
SIC: 4013 4741 4789 Railroad switching; rental of railroad cars; railroad car repair
PA: Watco Companies, L.L.C.
315 W 3rd St
Pittsburg KS 66762
575 745-2329

(G-9963)
WATCO COMPANIES LLC (PA)
Also Called: Baton Rouge Southern Railroad
315 W 3rd St (66762-4706)
PHONE..................................575 745-2329
Gary Lundy, *Chairman*
Terry Towner, *COO*
Nick Coomes, *Exec VP*
Arthure McKechnie III, *Exec VP*
Jared Radke, *Senior VP*
EMP: 200
SQ FT: 45,000
SALES: 997.9MM **Privately Held**
WEB: www.watcocompanies.com
SIC: 4011 7538 Railroads, line-haul operating; general automotive repair shops

(G-9964)
WATCO RAILROAD CO HOLDINGS (PA)
315 W 3rd St (66762-4706)
PHONE..................................620 231-2230
Rick Webb, *CEO*
Terry Towner, *President*
Gary Lundy, *Exec VP*
Craig Richey, *Exec VP*
Ed McKechnie, *Chief Mktg Ofcr*
EMP: 17 **EST**: 2010
SALES (est): 4.9MM **Privately Held**
SIC: 4011 Railroads, line-haul operating

(G-9965)
WATCO SWITCHING INC
Also Called: Watco Sek Railroad
315 W 3rd St (66762-4706)
PHONE..................................620 231-2230
Richard B Webb, *President*
Susan K Lundy, *Vice Pres*
EMP: 100
SQ FT: 2,500
SALES (est): 6MM **Privately Held**
SIC: 4789 4741 Railroad car repair; rental of railroad cars

(G-9966)
WATCO TRANSLOADING LLC (HQ)
315 W 3rd St (66762-4706)
PHONE..................................620 231-2230
Richard Webb, *CEO*
Rick Baden, *President*
Dan Smith, *COO*
Arthur McKechnie, *Exec VP*
Jared Radke, *Senior VP*
EMP: 94
SALES (est): 173.3MM
SALES (corp-wide): 997.9MM **Privately Held**
SIC: 4013 Railroad terminals
PA: Watco Companies, L.L.C.
315 W 3rd St
Pittsburg KS 66762
575 745-2329

(G-9967)
WATCO TRANSPORTATION SVCS LLC (HQ)
315 W 3rd St (66762-4706)
PHONE..................................620 231-2230
Rick Baden, *President*
David Bader, *General Mgr*
Mark Blazer, *Senior VP*
EMP: 26
SALES (est): 5MM
SALES (corp-wide): 997.9MM **Privately Held**
SIC: 4225 General warehousing & storage
PA: Watco Companies, L.L.C.
315 W 3rd St
Pittsburg KS 66762
575 745-2329

(G-9968)
WHEELER & MITCHELSON CHARTERED
319 N Broadway St (66762-4806)
P.O. Box 610 (66762-0610)
PHONE..................................620 231-4650
John H Mitchelson, *President*
Kevin Mitchelson, *Corp Secy*
Mary Goedeke, *Manager*
EMP: 11
SQ FT: 2,000
SALES (est): 813.5K **Privately Held**
WEB: www.wm-law.com
SIC: 8111 General practice attorney, lawyer

(G-9969)
WILBERT & TOWNER PA (PA)
Also Called: Wachter, Bill
506 N Pine St (66762-3857)
PHONE..................................620 231-5620
Bill Wachter, *President*
Craig R Richey, *President*
A J Wachter,
EMP: 10
SALES (est): 1.4MM **Privately Held**
WEB: www.wilbertonline.com
SIC: 8111 Legal services

(G-9970)
WILBERT SCREEN PRINTING INC
1012 N Broadway St (66762-3994)
PHONE..................................620 231-1730
Bill Wilbert, *President*
Vicki Wilbert, *Corp Secy*
EMP: 5 **EST**: 1972
SALES (est): 408.5K **Privately Held**
SIC: 7336 2752 Silk screen design; commercial printing, lithographic

(G-9971)
WOMENS CHLDREN SHELTER LINWOOD
Also Called: Salvation Army
307 E 5th St (66762-4002)
PHONE..................................620 231-0415
David Womack, *Manager*
EMP: 74
SALES (corp-wide): 1.8MM **Privately Held**
SIC: 8361 8322 Home for the aged; individual & family services

PA: Womens Children Shelter Of Linwood
101 W Linwood Blvd
Kansas City MO 64111
816 756-1455

(G-9972)
YOUNG MNS CHRSTN ASSN PTTSBURG
Also Called: YMCA
1100 N Miles St (66762-6901)
PHONE..................................620 231-1100
Jack Dache, *Director*
Kim Amos, *Director*
Gloria Henrie, *Admin Sec*
EMP: 60
SQ FT: 50,000
SALES: 1.2MM **Privately Held**
SIC: 8641 7991 8351 7032 Youth organizations; physical fitness facilities; child day care services; youth camps; individual & family services

Plains
Meade County

(G-9973)
212 LOGISTICS LLC
2063 O Rd (67869-9177)
PHONE..................................620 563-7656
Amy Turner,
EMP: 35
SALES (est): 3.6MM **Privately Held**
SIC: 4731 Foreign freight forwarding

(G-9974)
ELITE ENDEAVORS LLC
Also Called: Masterhand Milling
2063 O Rd (67869-9177)
P.O. Box 770, Sublette (67877-0770)
PHONE..................................620 391-1577
Don D Turner, *Principal*
EMP: 13
SALES (est): 858.2K **Privately Held**
SIC: 2048 Livestock feeds
PA: Flying 4t Ranch
2063 O Rd
Plains KS 67869

(G-9975)
HIGH PLAINS DAIRY LLC
2042 V Rd (67869-9190)
PHONE..................................620 563-9441
David Clawsen,
EMP: 40
SALES (est): 4.3MM **Privately Held**
SIC: 0241 Milk production

(G-9976)
KANSAS-SMITH FARMS LLC
23179 5 Rd (67869-9162)
P.O. Box 741, Garland NC (28441-0741)
PHONE..................................620 417-6765
Lorenzo Olvera, *Manager*
Alfred Button, *Manager*
Mark Verhoff, *Manager*
EMP: 85
SALES: 34.7MM **Privately Held**
SIC: 0213 Hogs

(G-9977)
PLAINS EQUITY EXCH & COOP UN (PA)
206 E Indiana St (67869-7026)
P.O. Box 157 (67869-0157)
PHONE..................................620 563-9566
Michael Schlochtermeier, *General Mgr*
Mike Schlochtermeier, *General Mgr*
Terry Shinogle, *Safety Dir*
EMP: 30 **EST:** 1913
SQ FT: 1,000
SALES: 71.4MM **Privately Held**
SIC: 5153 5191 Grain elevators; feed; seeds: field, garden & flower; fertilizer & fertilizer materials; chemicals, agricultural

(G-9978)
WEST PLAINS TRANSPORT INC
1402 Superior St (67869-6920)
P.O. Box 544 (67869-0544)
PHONE..................................620 563-7665
Gary Dunn, *President*
Derek Dunn, *Opers Mgr*
Dirk Dunn, *Payroll Mgr*
EMP: 48
SQ FT: 4,800
SALES: 7MM **Privately Held**
SIC: 4213 Contract haulers

Plainville
Rooks County

(G-9979)
CHITOS WELL SERVICE LLC
111 1/2 N Jefferson St (67663-1907)
P.O. Box 181 (67663-0181)
PHONE..................................785 434-4942
Chito Mendez,
EMP: 15
SALES (est): 699.6K **Privately Held**
SIC: 1389 Oil field services

(G-9980)
CLASSIC CLOTH INC
308 W Mill St (67663-2229)
PHONE..................................785 434-7200
Charles G Comeau, *President*
Charles Comeau, *President*
EMP: 10
SQ FT: 1,500
SALES (est): 1.1MM **Privately Held**
SIC: 2211 5131 Broadwoven fabric mills, cotton; piece goods & other fabrics

(G-9981)
CLAYTON HOMES INC
Also Called: Schult Homes
507 N Industrial Park Rd (67663)
P.O. Box 409 (67663-0409)
PHONE..................................785 434-4617
Rod Cellmer, *Manager*
EMP: 210
SQ FT: 100,000
SALES (corp-wide): 225.3B **Publicly Held**
WEB: www.clayton.net
SIC: 5271 5039 2452 2451 Mobile homes; mobile homes; prefabricated wood buildings; mobile homes
HQ: Clayton Homes, Inc.
5000 Clayton Rd
Maryville TN 37804
865 380-3000

(G-9982)
COFFEYVILLE RESOURCES LLC
606 S Cemetery Rd (67663)
P.O. Box C (67663-0090)
PHONE..................................785 434-4832
Susan Ball, *Branch Mgr*
EMP: 7 **Publicly Held**
SIC: 2911 Petroleum refining
HQ: Coffeyville Resources, Llc
2277 Plaza Dr Ste 500
Sugar Land TX 77479
281 207-3200

(G-9983)
COFFEYVILLE RESOURCES LLC
606 S Cemetary Rd (67663)
PHONE..................................785 434-4832
Pat Quinn, *Branch Mgr*
Patrick Brown, *Representative*
EMP: 15 **Publicly Held**
WEB: www.coffeyvillegroup.com
SIC: 2911 Petroleum refining
HQ: Coffeyville Resources, Llc
2277 Plaza Dr Ste 500
Sugar Land TX 77479
281 207-3200

(G-9984)
CRAWFORD SUPPLY CO (PA)
Also Called: Treger Texas
604 Nw 3rd St (67663-1709)
P.O. Box 363 (67663-0363)
PHONE..................................785 434-4631
Scott Crawford, *President*
John Crawford, *Senior VP*
Dan Crawford, *Vice Pres*
Jim Sexton, *Opers Mgr*
Don Hageman, *Store Mgr*
EMP: 11
SQ FT: 8,000
SALES (est): 21.6MM **Privately Held**
WEB: www.crawfordsupplyco.com
SIC: 5082 5023 Construction & mining machinery; home furnishings

(G-9985)
DESSIN FOURNIR INC (HQ)
Also Called: Dessin Fournir Companies
308 W Mill St (67663-2229)
PHONE..................................785 434-2777
Charles G Comeau, *President*
Charles Comeau, *President*
Len Larson, *President*
Chris Marz, *Vice Pres*
Ashley Dopita, *General Counsel*
▲ **EMP:** 44
SQ FT: 6,000
SALES (est): 10.2MM **Privately Held**
WEB: www.dessinfournir.com
SIC: 2512 Upholstered household furniture
PA: Dfc Holdings, Inc.
308 W Mill St
Plainville KS 67663
785 434-2777

(G-9986)
DFC HOLDINGS INC (PA)
Also Called: Dessin Fournir Companies
308 W Mill St (67663-2229)
PHONE..................................785 434-2777
Charles G Comeau, *President*
Charles Comeau, *President*
EMP: 11
SALES (est): 10.2MM **Privately Held**
SIC: 2512 Upholstered household furniture

(G-9987)
EMPIRE ENERGY E&P LLC
904 W Mill St (67663-2132)
PHONE..................................785 434-4900
Randy Weigel, *Principal*
EMP: 7
SALES (corp-wide): 13.2MM **Privately Held**
SIC: 1381 Drilling oil & gas wells
PA: Empire Energy E&P, Llc
380 Sthpinte Blvd Ste 130
Canonsburg PA 15317
724 483-2070

(G-9988)
KEMIRA CHEMICALS INC
1733 W Rd (67663-7072)
P.O. Box 1387, Hays (67601-8387)
PHONE..................................785 434-2474
EMP: 5
SALES (corp-wide): 2.8B **Privately Held**
SIC: 2869 2819 Industrial organic chemicals; industrial inorganic chemicals
HQ: Kemira Chemicals, Inc.
1000 Parkwood Cir Se # 500
Atlanta GA 30339
770 436-1542

(G-9989)
PLAINVILLE AMBULANCE SERVICE
1111 Sw 8th St (67663-3105)
PHONE..................................785 434-2530
Diane Becker, *Director*
EMP: 15
SALES (est): 350.2K **Privately Held**
SIC: 4119 Ambulance service

(G-9990)
PLAINVILLE RURAL HOSPITAL
Also Called: ROOKS COUNTY HEALTH CENTER
1210 N Washington St (67663-1632)
P.O. Box 389 (67663-0389)
PHONE..................................785 434-2622
Michael Sinclair, *CEO*
Steve Law, *General Mgr*
Aimee Gardanier, *Opers Staff*
Frank Rajewski, *CFO*
Lynn Fisher, *Med Doctor*
EMP: 150
SQ FT: 22,800
SALES: 15.8MM **Privately Held**
WEB: www.rookscountyhealthcenter.com
SIC: 8062 General medical & surgical hospitals

(G-9991)
R & O PARTNERSHIP
Also Called: Mister K'S Food Town
109 S Jefferson St (67663-2204)
PHONE..................................785 434-4534
Mogens Kndesen, *President*
Rich Miller, *President*
EMP: 25 **EST:** 1947
SQ FT: 7,200
SALES (est): 3MM **Privately Held**
SIC: 5411 7371 Grocery stores, independent; computer software development & applications

(G-9992)
STEVES ELECTRIC ROUSTABOUT CO
1695 Y Rd (67663-9000)
PHONE..................................785 434-7590
Steve Fellhoelter, *President*
Tracy Fellhoelter, *Vice Pres*
EMP: 19
SALES (est): 3.1MM **Privately Held**
SIC: 1389 Oil field services; roustabout service

(G-9993)
THERIEN & COMPANY INC (PA)
Also Called: Therien Studios
308 W Mill St (67663-2229)
PHONE..................................415 956-8850
Robert Garcia, *President*
Bruce Tremayne, *Vice Pres*
▲ **EMP:** 16
SQ FT: 5,000
SALES (est): 10MM **Privately Held**
WEB: www.therien.com
SIC: 5099 7389 5932 Antiques; interior designer; antiques

(G-9994)
TOMS MACHINE & WELDING SVC
510 S Washington St (67663-2915)
P.O. Box 157 (67663-0157)
PHONE..................................785 434-2800
Thomas C Noone, *President*
Normadine Noone, *Corp Secy*
EMP: 8 **EST:** 1968
SQ FT: 9,000
SALES: 1.2MM **Privately Held**
SIC: 3599 7692 Machine shop, jobbing & repair; welding repair

Pleasanton
Linn County

(G-9995)
FRANKENSTEIN TRIKES LLC
9453 Trump Ter (66075-8327)
PHONE..................................913 352-6788
Frank Pederesen,
Steinar Bergby,
EMP: 9
SQ FT: 9,000
SALES (est): 560K **Privately Held**
SIC: 3714 5571 Motor vehicle parts & accessories; motorcycle parts & accessories

(G-9996)
HEARTLAND MIDWEST LLC
8270 Wood Rd (66075-8131)
PHONE..................................913 471-4840
Raymond Lee Chapman,
EMP: 20
SALES: 950K **Privately Held**
SIC: 1521 Single-family housing construction

(G-9997)
LINN COUNTY PUBLISHING INC
Also Called: Linn County News
808 Main St (66075-4077)
PHONE..................................913 352-6235
Larry Brownlee, *President*
Patsey Brownlee, *Vice Pres*
EMP: 12
SQ FT: 4,400
SALES (est): 332.7K **Privately Held**
SIC: 2711 2752 2759 Commercial printing & newspaper publishing combined; commercial printing, offset; commercial printing

(G-9998)
MEEMAWS COUNTRY KITCHEN
602 Main St (66075-4085)
PHONE.................................913 352-6297
Douglas Dirent, *President*
EMP: 12
SALES (est): 98.5K **Privately Held**
SIC: 5812 4212 Caterers; delivery service, vehicular

(G-9999)
MERCY KANSAS COMMUNITIES INC
Also Called: Mercy Clinic Glenn County
11155 Tucker Rd (66075-8401)
PHONE.................................913 352-8379
Nancy Shadden, *Manager*
EMP: 15
SALES (corp-wide): 6.5B **Privately Held**
WEB: www.mercykansas.com
SIC: 8062 8011 General medical & surgical hospitals; clinic, operated by physicians
HQ: Mercy Kansas Communities, Inc
401 Woodland Hills Blvd
Fort Scott KS 66701
620 223-7075

(G-10000)
PROGRESS RAIL SERVICES CORP
1710 Laurel St (66075-9110)
PHONE.................................913 352-6613
John Stout, *President*
Jim Smith, *Branch Mgr*
EMP: 110
SALES (corp-wide): 54.7B **Publicly Held**
SIC: 5088 Railroad equipment & supplies
HQ: Progress Rail Services Corporation
1600 Progress Dr
Albertville AL 35950
256 505-6421

(G-10001)
R L C INC
1511 Ash St (66075-4064)
P.O. Box 642 (66075-0642)
PHONE.................................913 352-8744
Richard Carpenter, *President*
Chad Carpenter, *Vice Pres*
Sandy Carpenter, *Admin Sec*
EMP: 17
SQ FT: 800
SALES (est): 3.1MM **Privately Held**
WEB: www.rlcinc.net
SIC: 1799 Welding on site

(G-10002)
SOUTHEAST KANS MENTAL HLTH CTR
505 W 15th St (66075-4095)
PHONE.................................913 352-8214
Robert Chase, *Branch Mgr*
EMP: 10
SALES (corp-wide): 8.3MM **Privately Held**
SIC: 8093 8322 Mental health clinic, outpatient; social service center
PA: Southeast Kansas Mental Health Center
1106 S 9th St
Humboldt KS 66748
620 473-2241

(G-10003)
WALKER PUBLISHING INC
Also Called: Linn County Printing
808 Main St (66075-4077)
P.O. Box 478 (66075-0478)
PHONE.................................913 352-6700
Jacqueline I Walker, *President*
EMP: 7
SALES (est): 442.9K **Privately Held**
SIC: 2711 Newspapers, publishing & printing

Pomona
Franklin County

(G-10004)
HEALTH DATA SPECIALISTS LLC
1720 Sand Creek Rd (66076-8707)
P.O. Box 125, Luling LA (70070-0125)
PHONE.................................785 242-3419
Bob Hayden, *CEO*
Paul Triche, *President*
Brent Budke, *Vice Pres*
Troy Hendrixson, *Vice Pres*
Krista Osborn, *Human Resources*
EMP: 27
SALES: 5.4MM **Privately Held**
WEB: www.hds-llc.com
SIC: 8742 7379 Hospital & health services consultant; computer related consulting services

(G-10005)
JERRY WRAY
Also Called: Wray's Woodworking
1183 Stafford Rd (66076-8981)
PHONE.................................785 255-4644
Jerry Wray, *Owner*
EMP: 6
SALES: 600K **Privately Held**
SIC: 0115 2434 Corn; wood kitchen cabinets

Portis
Osborne County

(G-10006)
RUN-R-WAY EXPRESS CO INC
20031 300 Rd (67474-5319)
P.O. Box 205 (67474-0205)
PHONE.................................785 346-2900
Russell Hendrich, *President*
Penny Henrich, *Corp Secy*
EMP: 12
SALES (est): 1.7MM **Privately Held**
SIC: 4213 Trucking, except local

Potwin
Butler County

(G-10007)
HAW RANCH FEEDLOT 2 LLC
Also Called: Livestock Exchange
7800 Nw Piwakoni Rd (67123)
P.O. Box 248 (67123-0248)
PHONE.................................620 752-3221
David Lowe, *Principal*
EMP: 16
SALES (est): 842.7K **Privately Held**
SIC: 0211 Beef cattle feedlots

(G-10008)
POTWIN LIONS CLUB
7400 Nw Ayr Rd (67123-9669)
PHONE.................................620 752-3644
Cindy Ricker, *President*
Pat Kasper, *President*
Shari Neidhrdt, *President*
EMP: 12
SALES (est): 126.6K **Privately Held**
SIC: 8641 Civic associations

Powhattan
Brown County

(G-10009)
SAC & FOX GAMING COMMISSION
1324 Us Highway 75 (66527-9624)
PHONE.................................785 467-8070
Dawn Walker, *Office Mgr*
Kelly Galietti, *Manager*
Rachel Price, *Manager*
Michael Doughterty, *Director*
EMP: 13
SALES: 550K **Privately Held**
SIC: 8611 Regulatory associations

(G-10010)
SAC & FOX NTION MO IN KANS NEB
Also Called: Sac & Fox Casino
1322 Us Highway 75 (66527-9624)
PHONE.................................785 467-8000
James Stewart, *Branch Mgr*
EMP: 400 **Privately Held**
WEB: www.sacandfoxcasino.com
SIC: 7999 5813 5812 Gambling establishment; drinking places; eating places
PA: Sac & Fox Nation Of Missouri In Kansas And Nebraska
305 N Main St
Reserve KS 66434
785 742-7471

Prairie View
Phillips County

(G-10011)
J AND S TRUCKING INC
1276 W Mohawk Rd (67664-6445)
P.O. Box 405 (67664-0405)
PHONE.................................785 973-2768
Jim Kats, *President*
Donna Kats, *Corp Secy*
Stanley Kats, *Vice Pres*
EMP: 15
SALES (est): 1.1MM **Privately Held**
SIC: 4213 Contract haulers

Prairie Village
Johnson County

(G-10012)
B FOUR CORP
Also Called: Hen House Supermarket 22
4050 W 83rd St (66208-5301)
PHONE.................................913 648-1441
Lee Snavly, *Manager*
EMP: 200
SALES (corp-wide): 578.2MM **Privately Held**
WEB: www.ballsfoods.com
SIC: 5411 2051 Supermarkets; bread, cake & related products
PA: B Four Corp
5300 Speaker Rd
Kansas City KS 66106
913 321-4223

(G-10013)
BANK AMERICA NATIONAL ASSN
7624 State Line Rd (66208-3705)
PHONE.................................816 979-8482
Lauri Steffens, *Branch Mgr*
EMP: 19
SALES (corp-wide): 110.5B **Publicly Held**
SIC: 6021 National commercial banks
HQ: Bank Of America, National Association
100 S Tryon St
Charlotte NC 28202
704 386-5681

(G-10014)
BANK OF PRAIRIE VILLAGE
3515 W 75th St Ste 115 (66208-4100)
PHONE.................................913 713-0300
Daniel Bolen, *CEO*
Tom Oltjen, *President*
Paul Clendening, *Vice Chairman*
Patrick Bolen, *Vice Pres*
Marilyn Hillix, *Vice Pres*
EMP: 12
SQ FT: 5,063
SALES: 4.3MM **Privately Held**
WEB: www.bankofprairievillage.com
SIC: 6022 State commercial banks

(G-10015)
BEL-AIR DENTAL CARE CHARTERED
5000 W 95th St Ste 300 (66207-3300)
PHONE.................................913 649-0310
Ronald Gier DMD, *President*
EMP: 20
SALES (est): 2MM **Privately Held**
WEB: www.bel-airdental.com
SIC: 8021 Dentists' office

(G-10016)
BLUE VALLEY PARTNERS LP
8008 Granada Rd (66208-5061)
PHONE.................................913 963-5534
EMP: 20
SALES (est): 288.9K **Privately Held**
SIC: 7021 Rooming/Boarding House

(G-10017)
BULK INDUSTRIAL GROUP LLC (PA)
3500 W 75th St Ste 360 (66208-4102)
PHONE.................................913 362-6000
Fred Coulson,
EMP: 16
SALES (est): 2.2MM **Privately Held**
SIC: 6531 Real estate agent, commercial

(G-10018)
CAPFUSION LLC
2310 W 75th St (66208-3507)
PHONE.................................816 888-5302
Ryan C Sullivan, *President*
EMP: 20 **EST:** 2016
SALES (est): 3MM **Privately Held**
SIC: 6141 Licensed loan companies, small

(G-10019)
CENTRAL STATES CAPITAL MARKETS
4200 W 83rd St (66208-5304)
PHONE.................................913 766-6565
Dan Stepp, *CEO*
Stephen Friedell, *Partner*
Michael Horton, *Partner*
Jim Brownfield, *Senior VP*
Dale Pfeifer, *Vice Pres*
EMP: 10
SALES (est): 964.1K **Privately Held**
SIC: 6799 Venture capital companies

(G-10020)
COLT INVESTMENTS INC
Also Called: Colt, Mack V
4121 W 83rd St Ste 120 (66208-5316)
PHONE.................................913 385-5010
Mack V Colt, *President*
EMP: 20
SQ FT: 800
SALES (est): 2.9MM **Privately Held**
WEB: www.thecoltgroup.com
SIC: 6411 6022 Insurance agents; state commercial banks

(G-10021)
COMFORT CARE HOMES KANS CY LLC
3848 W 75th St (66208-4126)
PHONE.................................913 643-0111
Neil Barnett, *Owner*
EMP: 19
SALES (est): 823.2K **Privately Held**
SIC: 8361 Residential care

(G-10022)
COSENTINO GROUP INC
Also Called: Cosentino's Food Stores
3901 W 83rd St (66208-5308)
PHONE.................................913 749-1500
Victo Cosentino, *President*
Dennis Reilly, *CFO*
EMP: 41
SALES (est): 45.2MM **Privately Held**
SIC: 5141 Groceries, general line

(G-10023)
CRYO MANAGEMENT INC
Also Called: North East Medical Home Health
2209 W 72nd Ter (66208-3346)
PHONE.................................913 362-9005
Denis Viscek, *President*
Jon Sisk,
EMP: 20
SALES: 2MM **Privately Held**
SIC: 8741 Management services

(G-10024)
D & B LEGAL SERVICES INC
5350 W 94th Ter Ste 206 (66207-2520)
P.O. Box 7471, Shawnee Mission (66207-0471)
PHONE..................................913 362-8110
William J Powell, *CEO*
Deeann Powell, *President*
Janice Phillips, *Accounts Mgr*
Jackie Honomichl, *Accounts Exec*
Lisa Summers, *Executive*
EMP: 54
SQ FT: 3,000
SALES: 1MM **Privately Held**
SIC: 7381 Private investigator

(G-10025)
DAKA INC (PA)
Also Called: Cottage Care
8841 Roe Ave (66207-2201)
PHONE..................................913 768-1803
Harold B Smith, *President*
EMP: 22 **EST:** 1994
SALES (est): 1.5MM **Privately Held**
WEB: www.daka.com
SIC: 7699 Cleaning services

(G-10026)
DCI STUDIOS
Also Called: Redtreestudios.com
8010 State Line Rd # 200 (66208-3702)
PHONE..................................913 385-9550
Tom Drake, *Owner*
EMP: 10 **EST:** 2001
SALES (est): 831.6K **Privately Held**
SIC: 5112 Greeting cards

(G-10027)
ENGLEWOOD BEACH HOUSE LLC
5100 W 95th St (66207-3305)
P.O. Box 11611, Overland Park (66207-4311)
PHONE..................................913 385-5400
Lee J Hollis, *Principal*
EMP: 12 **EST:** 2011
SALES (est): 739.7K **Privately Held**
SIC: 7011 Bed & breakfast inn

(G-10028)
FAGAN CONSTRUCTION CO
4511 W 82nd Ter (66208-5044)
PHONE..................................913 238-5903
Pat Fagan, *President*
EMP: 10
SALES (est): 956.5K **Privately Held**
SIC: 1542 Commercial & office building, new construction

(G-10029)
FRIENDS OF MONTESSORI ASSN
Also Called: Highlawn Montessori School
3531 Somerset Dr (66208-5150)
PHONE..................................913 649-6160
Katherine Morrison, *Director*
Patty Wright, *Executive*
Wilma Rubenstein, *Admin Asst*
Nancy Doolittle, *Assistant*
EMP: 19
SQ FT: 3,300
SALES (est): 750K **Privately Held**
SIC: 8351 8211 Preschool center; Montessori child development center; private elementary school

(G-10030)
FRY ORTHODONTICS PRAIRIE VLG
4026 W 83rd St (66208-5301)
PHONE..................................913 387-2500
Jeremy Fry, *Owner*
EMP: 40
SALES (est): 686.1K **Privately Held**
SIC: 8021 Orthodontist

(G-10031)
GERBER INSURANCE GROUP
Also Called: Kemper Insurance
5200 W 94th Ter Ste 110 (66207-2521)
PHONE..................................913 649-7800
Spencer J Gerber, *President*
Chris Rex, *Admin Sec*
EMP: 10
SQ FT: 3,066
SALES (est): 1.7MM **Privately Held**
SIC: 6411 Insurance agents, brokers & service

(G-10032)
GLOBAL MONTESSORI ACADEMY
7457 Cherokee Dr (66208-3232)
PHONE..................................816 561-4533
Brian Gordon, *Exec Dir*
Jodie Nolen, *Director*
EMP: 10
SALES: 1.1MM **Privately Held**
SIC: 8351 Montessori child development center

(G-10033)
GRAHAM SHIP BY TRUCK CO
7916 Fontana St (66208-5053)
P.O. Box 2121, Kansas City (66110-0121)
PHONE..................................913 621-7500
Richard Arnold, *Owner*
Ric Arnorld, *Co-Owner*
EMP: 62
SALES (est): 5.3MM **Privately Held**
SIC: 4213 Trucking, except local

(G-10034)
GRAHAM SHIP BY TRUCK COMPANY (PA)
7916 Fontana St (66208-5053)
P.O. Box 2121, Kansas City (66110-0121)
PHONE..................................913 621-7575
Richard Arnold, *President*
EMP: 40 **EST:** 1921
SQ FT: 20,000
SALES: 5.7MM **Privately Held**
SIC: 4213 Contract haulers

(G-10035)
HOMESTEAD COUNTRY CLUB
Also Called: HOMESTEAD, THE
4100 Homestead Ct (66208-1798)
PHONE..................................913 262-4100
Cydney S Nelson, *President*
Brian Collins, *General Mgr*
Kris Tucker, *Director*
Rod Zerni, *Director*
EMP: 60
SQ FT: 5,000
SALES: 1.1MM **Privately Held**
WEB: www.homesteadcc.com
SIC: 7997 Country club, membership; tennis club, membership

(G-10036)
INTERSTATE PUBLISHERS INC
8014 State Line Rd # 208 (66208-3723)
PHONE..................................913 341-4445
Jim Bates, *President*
EMP: 13
SQ FT: 1,400
SALES (est): 1.2MM **Privately Held**
WEB: www.interstatetravelbuddy.com
SIC: 2721 2741 Magazines: publishing only, not printed on site; telephone & other directory publishing

(G-10037)
J & M INDUSTRIES INC
8800 Rosewood Dr (66207-2226)
PHONE..................................913 362-8994
Michael F McHugh, *President*
EMP: 22
SALES (est): 5.7MM **Privately Held**
WEB: www.jmiinc.com
SIC: 5045 7372 7371 Computer software; word processing equipment; prepackaged software; custom computer programming services

(G-10038)
JENKINS & LEBLANC PA (PA)
8226 Mission Rd (66208-5211)
PHONE..................................913 378-9610
Michael Leblanc, *Principal*
EMP: 20
SALES (est): 3.1MM **Privately Held**
SIC: 8021 Orthodontist

(G-10039)
K CRAIG PLACE MD
9009 Roe Ave (66207-2202)
PHONE..................................913 385-9009
K C Place MD, *Owner*
EMP: 15
SALES (est): 473.6K **Privately Held**
SIC: 8011 Ophthalmologist

(G-10040)
KANSAS CITY CHRISTIAN SCHOOL
4801 W 79th St (66208-4471)
PHONE..................................913 648-5227
Allan Schugg, *Superintendent*
EMP: 63 **EST:** 1951
SQ FT: 60,000
SALES: 4.1MM **Privately Held**
SIC: 8211 8351 Private combined elementary & secondary school; child day care services

(G-10041)
KC COMMERCIAL REALTY GROUP
5000 W 95th St Ste 200 (66207-3300)
PHONE..................................913 232-5100
David Bayer, *President*
EMP: 12 **EST:** 2007
SALES: 159.2K **Privately Held**
SIC: 6531 Real estate agent, commercial

(G-10042)
KEN OKELLY
Also Called: Paper Supply
1912 W 74th St (66208-3422)
PHONE..................................816 868-6028
Ken O'Kelly, *Owner*
EMP: 6
SALES (est): 450.7K **Privately Held**
SIC: 2679 5113 Paperboard products, converted; paperboard & products

(G-10043)
KRIZMANS BEAUTY SALONS INC
Also Called: Krizman Hairdressing Salon
5215 W 94th Ter (66207-2501)
PHONE..................................913 648-6080
Richard Krizman, *President*
Donald Krizman, *Vice Pres*
Arlene Krizman, *Treasurer*
Sue Krizman, *Admin Sec*
EMP: 13 **EST:** 1958
SALES (est): 164.9K **Privately Held**
SIC: 7231 Hairdressers

(G-10044)
LCRC
8101 Mission Rd (66208-5245)
PHONE..................................913 383-2085
Bernadette Weber, *Principal*
EMP: 11
SALES (est): 152.6K **Privately Held**
SIC: 8051 Skilled nursing care facilities

(G-10045)
M SQUARED FINANCIAL LLC
Also Called: Fountain Mortgage
8340 Mission Rd Ste 240 (66206-1339)
PHONE..................................913 745-7000
Mike Miles, *COO*
Katie Grimes, *Loan Officer*
Suzanne Parker, *Loan Officer*
Kellie Waters, *Loan Officer*
Lance Herring, *Consultant*
EMP: 13
SALES (est): 396.3K **Privately Held**
SIC: 6162 Mortgage bankers

(G-10046)
MCLINEY LUMBER AND SUPPLY LLC
4200 W 83rd St Ste 200 (66208-5309)
PHONE..................................913 766-7102
Joe McLiney Jr, *Mng Member*
▲ **EMP:** 18
SALES (est): 6MM **Privately Held**
SIC: 3559 Kilns, lumber

(G-10047)
MEDALLION DENTAL LAB INC
4650 W 90th Ter (66207-2308)
PHONE..................................913 642-0039
Jon M Finley Jr, *President*
Jodie Linsin, *Info Tech Mgr*
EMP: 11
SQ FT: 1,800
SALES (est): 932.9K **Privately Held**
SIC: 8072 8021 Crown & bridge production; offices & clinics of dentists

(G-10048)
MID AMERICA EYE CENTER INC (PA)
3830 W 75th St (66208-4128)
PHONE..................................913 384-1441
Joseph Parelman, *President*
Sue Kalwei, *Administration*
EMP: 20
SALES (est): 2.4MM **Privately Held**
WEB: www.midamericaeye.com
SIC: 8011 Ophthalmologist

(G-10049)
NALL AVE BAPTIST CHURCH
Also Called: Nall Avenue Child Dev Center
6701 Nall Ave (66208-1429)
PHONE..................................913 432-4141
James Reynolds, *Pastor*
Bob Clark, *Administration*
EMP: 41
SQ FT: 4,500
SALES (est): 1MM **Privately Held**
WEB: www.nallave.org
SIC: 8661 8351 Baptist Church; child day care services

(G-10050)
NATIONS HOLDING COMPANY (PA)
5370 W 95th St (66207-3204)
PHONE..................................913 383-8185
Chris Likens, *President*
Howard Easley, *Business Mgr*
Charles Burton, *COO*
Kurt McLey, *Counsel*
David Link, *Vice Pres*
EMP: 43
SQ FT: 6,000
SALES (est): 50.2MM **Privately Held**
SIC: 6719 Investment holding companies, except banks

(G-10051)
NATIONS TITLE AGENCY (HQ)
Also Called: Nations Lending Services
5370 W 95th St (66207-3204)
PHONE..................................913 341-2705
Steve Likens, *President*
Kelly Kern, *President*
Chris Likens, *Corp Secy*
Larry Likens, *Vice Pres*
Catherine Mayerle, *Accounts Exec*
EMP: 50
SALES (est): 33.6MM
SALES (corp-wide): 50.2MM **Privately Held**
SIC: 6411 6541 6531 ; title & trust companies; appraiser, real estate
PA: Nations Holding Company
5370 W 95th St
Prairie Village KS 66207
913 383-8185

(G-10052)
NEARING STAATS PRELOGAR
3515 W 75th St Ste 201 (66208-4100)
PHONE..................................913 831-1415
William Preloagar, *President*
Richard Jones, *President*
George Higgins, *Vice Pres*
Mark Wendlindt, *Vice Pres*
Todd Hicks, *Project Mgr*
EMP: 25 **EST:** 1961
SQ FT: 4,100
SALES (est): 3.5MM **Privately Held**
WEB: www.nspjarch.com
SIC: 8712 Architectural engineering

(G-10053)
ODONNELL-WAY CNSTR CO INC
7321 High Dr (66208-3363)
P.O. Box 8043, Shawnee Mission (66208-0043)
PHONE..................................913 498-3355
John O'Donnell, *President*
EMP: 10
SALES (est): 1.4MM **Privately Held**
SIC: 1611 Surfacing & paving

▲ = Import ▼=Export
◆ =Import/Export

(G-10054)
ORAL & FACIAL SURGERY ASSOC (PA)
Also Called: Michael Barber
3700 W 83rd St Ste 103 (66208-5120)
PHONE....................913 381-5194
Thomas J Schugel, *President*
Dr Kirk Collier, *Vice Pres*
Dr Douglas Fain, *Treasurer*
EMP: 45
SALES (est): 3.5MM **Privately Held**
SIC: 8021 8011 Dental surgeon; dentists' office; offices & clinics of medical doctors

(G-10055)
ORAL AND FACIAL ASSOCIATE
Also Called: Fain, Douglas W
3700 W 83rd St Ste 103 (66208-5120)
PHONE....................913 381-5194
Marla Sellers, *Manager*
EMP: 22
SALES (est): 1.1MM **Privately Held**
SIC: 8021 Dental surgeon

(G-10056)
PAUL HENSON FAMILY YMCA INC
4200 W 79th St (66208-4201)
PHONE....................913 642-6800
Erik Holme, *Director*
Alex Clark, *Director*
EMP: 20
SALES (est): 484.6K **Privately Held**
SIC: 8641 Youth organizations

(G-10057)
PEDIATRIC ORTHOPEDIC SURGERY
5250 W 94th Ter (66207-2502)
PHONE....................913 451-0000
Tom Smit, *Partner*
Ganesh Gupta, *Partner*
Dale Jarka, *Partner*
Kevin Latz, *Partner*
Nigel Price, *Partner*
EMP: 10
SALES (est): 1.2MM **Privately Held**
WEB: www.pedorthokc.com
SIC: 8011 Group health association; orthopedic physician; pediatrician

(G-10058)
PENDELLO SOLUTIONS
7301 Mission Rd Ste 100 (66208-3036)
PHONE....................913 677-6744
Mike Jackson, *President*
Bryan Zouiden, *Vice Pres*
EMP: 15 **EST:** 2012
SALES (est): 1.5MM **Privately Held**
SIC: 8748 Business consulting

(G-10059)
PHILLIPS AND ASSOCIATES INC
8001 Granada Rd (66208-5062)
PHONE....................913 706-7625
Jim Phillips, *President*
EMP: 60
SALES: 3MM **Privately Held**
SIC: 8742 Management consulting services

(G-10060)
PHOENIX MEDICAL RESEARCH INC
7301 Mission Rd Ste 135 (66208-3005)
PHONE....................913 381-7180
Hayden Thomas, *President*
Hayden Mikel Thomas, *President*
EMP: 10
SALES (est): 874.5K **Privately Held**
SIC: 8733 Medical research

(G-10061)
PRAIRIE VILLAGE ANIMAL HOSP PA
4045 Somerset Dr (66208-5216)
PHONE....................913 642-7060
George Gates, *President*
George A Gates, *Principal*
Dr Mark Daly, *Treasurer*
EMP: 10
SALES (est): 516K **Privately Held**
SIC: 0742 Animal hospital services, pets & other animal specialties

(G-10062)
REAL ESTATE CORPORATION INC
8014 State Line Rd # 210 (66208-3723)
PHONE....................913 642-5134
Rolf B Snyder, *President*
Nick Diaz, *General Mgr*
Williard B Snyder, *Corp Secy*
Eugene Barrett Jr, *Vice Pres*
George Breidenthal Jr, *Vice Pres*
EMP: 10
SALES: 549.8K **Privately Held**
SIC: 6512 6513 Commercial & industrial building operation; apartment building operators

(G-10063)
REECE & NICHOLS ALLIANCE INC
7455 Mission Rd (66208-3009)
PHONE....................913 262-7755
Bob Ludwig, *Broker*
Sharon Orr, *Sales Staff*
Scott Lane, *Manager*
EMP: 60
SALES (corp-wide): 225.3B **Publicly Held**
SIC: 6531 Real estate agent, residential
HQ: Reece & Nichols Alliance Inc
2140 E Santa Fe St
Olathe KS 66062
913 782-8822

(G-10064)
RIGHT STUFF CO
7105 Mission Rd Apt 313 (66208-3091)
PHONE....................913 722-4002
Glenn Haynes, *Owner*
EMP: 5
SALES (est): 360K **Privately Held**
SIC: 3471 Plating & polishing

(G-10065)
SANI WAX INC
4500 W 90th Ter Ste 206 (66207-2339)
PHONE....................913 383-9703
James Flynn, *President*
EMP: 5
SALES (est): 511.7K **Privately Held**
WEB: www.saniwax.com
SIC: 2842 Cleaning or polishing preparations

(G-10066)
SENIORCARE HOMES LLC
5200 W 94th Ter (66207-2522)
PHONE....................913 236-0036
Jerald Pullins, *Principal*
Jerald Leslie Pullins, *Mng Member*
EMP: 12 **EST:** 2008
SALES (est): 513.6K **Privately Held**
SIC: 8322 Senior citizens' center or association

(G-10067)
SOFTEK SOLUTIONS INC (PA)
4500 W 89th St Ste 100 (66207-2295)
PHONE....................913 649-1024
Matt Mc Lenon, *CEO*
Christine R Rorie, *Vice Pres*
Jesse Hodes, *Director*
Ken Westphal, *Art Dir*
EMP: 26
SALES: 4.7MM **Privately Held**
SIC: 7371 Computer software systems analysis & design, custom

(G-10068)
SOFTWARFARE LLC
7301 Mission Rd Ste 141 (66208-3014)
PHONE....................202 854-9268
Wyatt Cobb,
EMP: 10
SALES: 250K **Privately Held**
SIC: 7379 7373 ; systems software development services

(G-10069)
STANDEES PV LLC
Also Called: Standees-Entertaining Eatery
3935 W 69th Ter (66208-2602)
PHONE....................913 601-5250
Frank Rash, *President*
Doug Stone, *Exec VP*
Brian Hagenhoff, *CFO*
EMP: 65
SALES (est): 3.8MM **Privately Held**
SIC: 7389 Reservation services
PA: Dineplex International, Llc
801 E 47th St Ste 400
Kansas City MO

(G-10070)
SUNRISE SENIOR LIVING INC
Also Called: Brighton Gardens Prairie Vlg
7105 Mission Rd (66208-3000)
PHONE....................913 262-1611
Troy Florian, *Manager*
EMP: 60
SALES (corp-wide): 4.7B **Publicly Held**
WEB: www.sunrise.com
SIC: 8051 8361 Skilled nursing care facilities; home for the aged
HQ: Sunrise Senior Living, Llc
7902 Westpark Dr
Mc Lean VA 22102

(G-10071)
SUNRISE SENIOR LIVING SVCS INC
Also Called: BRIGHTON GARDENS OF PRAIRIE VI
7105 Mission Rd (66208-3000)
PHONE....................913 262-1611
EMP: 25
SALES: 9.2MM **Privately Held**
SIC: 8051 8361 Skilled nursing care facilities; home for the aged

(G-10072)
T S A INC
Also Called: Nationwide
7400 State Line Rd Ste 20 (66208-3444)
P.O. Box 8318 (66208-0318)
PHONE....................913 322-2800
Richard M Sloan, *President*
Mandy Bronaugh, *Vice Pres*
Sheri Harding, *Personnel*
Kelsey Rehrer, *Personnel*
Kari Callahan, *Accounts Mgr*
EMP: 11
SALES: 1.1MM **Privately Held**
WEB: www.thesloanagency.com
SIC: 6411 Insurance agents

(G-10073)
T W LACY & ASSOCIATES INC (PA)
Also Called: P D Q Sales and Service
8001 Granada Rd (66208-5062)
PHONE....................913 706-7625
Kimberly Lacy Philips, *President*
EMP: 18
SQ FT: 6,000
SALES (est): 2.5MM **Privately Held**
SIC: 8741 7699 5072 7349 Management services; tool repair services; hardware; lighting maintenance service; telemarketing services

(G-10074)
THOMAS G GEHA & ASSOCIATES
8012 State Line Rd # 200 (66208-3722)
PHONE....................913 563-6707
Thomas G Geha, *President*
Kenneth Geha, *Vice Pres*
Susan C Geha, *Treasurer*
EMP: 10
SQ FT: 1,400
SALES (est): 856.8K **Privately Held**
WEB: www.tgeha.com
SIC: 8742 Financial consultant

(G-10075)
THOUGHTFUL CARE INC
8340 Mission Rd Ste 118b (66206-1362)
PHONE....................816 256-8200
Tim Tholen, *Principal*
EMP: 12 **EST:** 2011
SALES (est): 454.6K **Privately Held**
SIC: 8082 Home health care services

(G-10076)
TRAMMELL CROW COMPANY
6810 Roe Ave (66208-1666)
PHONE....................913 722-1155
EMP: 19
SALES (corp-wide): 9B **Publicly Held**
SIC: 6531 Real Estate Agent/Manager
HQ: Trammell Crow Company
2100 Mckinney Ave Ste 900
Dallas TX 75201

(G-10077)
ULTIMATE GROUP LLP
8014 State Line Rd # 206 (66208-3712)
PHONE....................816 813-8182
George Brophy, *Director*
EMP: 11 **EST:** 2017
SALES (est): 854.9K **Privately Held**
SIC: 7361 Employment agencies

(G-10078)
UMB BANK NATIONAL ASSOCIATION
6900 Mission Rd (66208-2609)
PHONE....................913 236-0300
EMP: 12
SALES (corp-wide): 1.1B **Publicly Held**
SIC: 6021 National commercial banks
HQ: Umb Bank, National Association
1010 Grand Blvd Fl 3
Kansas City MO 64106
816 842-2222

(G-10079)
US BANK NATIONAL ASSOCIATION
Also Called: US Bank
6940 Mission Rd (66208-2609)
PHONE....................913 261-5663
Brian Peter, *Manager*
EMP: 22
SALES (corp-wide): 25.7B **Publicly Held**
WEB: www.firstar.com
SIC: 6021 National commercial banks
HQ: U.S. Bank National Association
425 Walnut St Fl 14
Cincinnati OH 45202
513 632-4234

(G-10080)
VILLAGE PEDIATRICS LLC
8340 Mission Rd Ste 100 (66206-1367)
PHONE....................913 642-2100
Lance Slaymaker, *Owner*
EMP: 25
SALES (est): 4.4MM **Privately Held**
WEB: www.village-pediatrics.com
SIC: 8011 Pediatrician

(G-10081)
WARDEN TRIPLETT GRIER LLP
3515 W 75th St Ste 102 (66208-4100)
PHONE....................816 877-8100
James Warden, *Partner*
J Michael Grier, *Partner*
Michael Kuckekman, *Partner*
Christopher Kuehn, *Partner*
Timothy Triplett, *Partner*
EMP: 17
SQ FT: 11,790
SALES (est): 2.3MM **Privately Held**
WEB: www.wtglaw.com
SIC: 8111 Corporate, partnership & business law

(G-10082)
WHITE PALADIN GROUP INC
5500 W 69th St (66208-2025)
PHONE....................913 722-4688
Anthony Pontier, *President*
Suzanne Perrault, *Vice Pres*
EMP: 30
SQ FT: 1,000
SALES: 4.2MM **Privately Held**
WEB: www.whitepaladin.com
SIC: 7379 Computer related consulting services

(G-10083)
WINCO FIREWORKS INTL LLC (PA)
5200 W 94th Ter Ste 114 (66207-2521)
PHONE....................913 649-2071
David Collar, *Ch of Bd*
Gene Nelson, *Opers Staff*
Regie Rhoads, *Sales Staff*
John Collar,
Mike Collar,
◆ **EMP:** 30
SALES: 6.7MM **Privately Held**
SIC: 5092 5999 Fireworks; fireworks

GEOGRAPHIC

(G-10084)
WIRECO WORLDGROUP INC
2400 W 75th St (66208-3509)
PHONE..................................816 270-4700
Dane Trantham, *Manager*
EMP: 21 **Privately Held**
WEB: www.wrca.com
SIC: 3496 Miscellaneous fabricated wire products
HQ: Wireco Worldgroup Inc.
2400 75th
Prairie Village KS 66208
816 270-4700

(G-10085)
WIRECO WORLDGROUP INC (HQ)
2400 75th (66208)
PHONE..................................816 270-4700
Jim O'Leary, *CEO*
Brian G Block, *President*
Jos Gramaxo, *President*
W Wynne Wister III, *Senior VP*
Miguel Gomez, *Vice Pres*
◆ **EMP:** 425
SALES (est): 910.3MM **Privately Held**
WEB: www.wrca.com
SIC: 3496 Cable, uninsulated wire: made from purchased wire

(G-10086)
WIRECO WRLDGROUP US HLDNGS INC (PA)
2400 W 75th St (66208-3509)
PHONE..................................816 270-4700
Christopher L Ayers, *CEO*
Jos Gramaxo, *Senior VP*
Dan Gustafson, *Mfg Staff*
Melinda Luthye, *Manager*
Todd Rumsey, *CIO*
▲ **EMP:** 12
SALES (est): 827.5MM **Privately Held**
SIC: 3496 Woven wire products

(G-10087)
WSC SERVICES INC
7534 Windsor St (66208-4020)
PHONE..................................913 660-0454
Timothy Welsh, *CEO*
EMP: 12
SALES: 628K **Privately Held**
WEB: www.wscservices.com
SIC: 7381 Burglary protection service; private investigator

(G-10088)
YOUNG MENS CHRISTIAN GR KANSAS
Also Called: YMCA Child Care Sites
7230 Belinder Ave (66208-3302)
PHONE..................................913 362-3489
Sally Andrade, *Manager*
EMP: 73
SALES (corp-wide): 48.1MM **Privately Held**
WEB: www.ymca-kc.org
SIC: 8641 7991 8351 7032 Youth organizations; physical fitness facilities; child day care services; youth camps; individual & family services
PA: Young Men's Christian Association Of Greater Kansas City
3100 Broadway Blvd # 1020
Kansas City MO 64111
816 561-9622

(G-10089)
ZIEGENHORN & LINNEMAN DDS
Also Called: Prairie Dental Care
7515 Nall Ave (66208-4762)
PHONE..................................913 649-7500
Terry C Linneman DDS, *Partner*
Dallas Ziegenhorn, *Fmly & Gen Dent*
EMP: 13
SALES (est): 1MM **Privately Held**
WEB: www.prairiedentalcare.com
SIC: 8021 Dentists' office

Pratt
Pratt County

(G-10090)
A/R ROOFING LLC (PA)
40100 N Us Highway 281 (67124-7913)
P.O. Box 8712 (67124-8712)
PHONE..................................620 672-2999
Aaron Walker, *Owner*
Luke George, *CFO*
Griselda Castillo, *Office Mgr*
Kathie Walker, *Manager*
Andrew Walker,
EMP: 16
SALES: 8.7MM **Privately Held**
SIC: 1761 Roofing contractor

(G-10091)
ABC PHONES NORTH CAROLINA INC
Also Called: Verizon Wreless Authorized Ret
103 S Parke St (67124-3032)
PHONE..................................620 508-6167
EMP: 24
SALES (corp-wide): 149.7MM **Privately Held**
SIC: 4812 Cellular telephone services
PA: Abc Phones Of North Carolina, Inc.
8510 Colonnade Center Dr
Raleigh NC 27615
252 317-0388

(G-10092)
ADAMS ELECTRIC & PLUMBING LLC (PA)
606 N Main St (67124-1660)
P.O. Box 914 (67124-0914)
PHONE..................................620 672-7279
Robert A Blasi,
Teresa Blasi,
EMP: 33
SQ FT: 6,000
SALES (est): 5.5MM **Privately Held**
WEB: www.adamsep.com
SIC: 5731 1731 Radio, television & electronic stores; electrical work

(G-10093)
ADELHARDT ENTERPRISES INC
210 S Jackson St (67124-2647)
PHONE..................................620 672-6463
Roger Adelhardt, *President*
EMP: 10 **EST:** 1939
SQ FT: 15,000
SALES: 650K **Privately Held**
SIC: 5231 5039 Paint; glass, leaded or stained; glass construction materials

(G-10094)
ADT 24 7 ALARM AND SECURITY
516 E 1st St (67124-2003)
PHONE..................................620 860-0229
EMP: 57 **Privately Held**
SIC: 9229 9224 9221 7382 Public order & safety; fire protection; police protection; security systems services

(G-10095)
ALLIANCE WELL SERVICE INC
271 Lake Rd (67124-8114)
PHONE..................................620 672-1065
Kelly Richardson, *Principal*
EMP: 5
SALES (est): 554.2K **Privately Held**
SIC: 1389 Oil field services

(G-10096)
AMERICAN WELL SERVICE LLC
10213 Bluestem Blvd (67124-8476)
P.O. Box 464 (67124-0464)
PHONE..................................620 672-5625
EMP: 7
SALES (est): 519.6K **Privately Held**
SIC: 1389 Oil/Gas Field Services

(G-10097)
APOLLO ENERGIES INC
40134 N Us Highway 281 (67124-7913)
PHONE..................................620 672-5071
James L Byers, *President*
Sue Byers, *Vice Pres*
Gordon Stull,
EMP: 18
SQ FT: 5,000
SALES (est): 2.6MM **Privately Held**
WEB: www.apolloenergies.com
SIC: 1311 Crude petroleum production

(G-10098)
AR COMMERCIAL ROOFING LLC
40100 N Us Highway 281 (67124-7913)
PHONE..................................620 672-3332
Andrew Walker,
Wl Walker,
EMP: 10
SALES: 4MM **Privately Held**
SIC: 1761 Roofing contractor

(G-10099)
B-29 MUSEUM INC
82 Curran Rd (67124)
P.O. Box 29 (67124-0029)
PHONE..................................620 282-1123
Phillip Schulz, *President*
Curtis Nightingale, *Principal*
EMP: 10
SALES (est): 154.6K **Privately Held**
SIC: 8412 Museum

(G-10100)
BOLEN OFFICE SUPPLY INC (PA)
114 S Main St (67124-2711)
P.O. Box 886 (67124-0886)
PHONE..................................620 672-7535
Dale Bolen, *President*
Bob Bolen, *Vice Pres*
EMP: 10 **EST:** 1977
SQ FT: 8,000
SALES (est): 2.7MM **Privately Held**
WEB: www.bolenofficesupply.net
SIC: 5044 5112 5021 2759 Office equipment; office supplies; office furniture; commercial printing; typewriters & business machines

(G-10101)
CITY OF PRATT
Also Called: Pratt Cy Municpl Pwr Plant 1
321 W 10th St (67124-2566)
P.O. Box 807 (67124-0807)
PHONE..................................620 672-3831
Evan Hance, *Opers Spvr*
Kelly Hemphill, *Director*
EMP: 14 **Privately Held**
WEB: www.prattrecreation.com
SIC: 4911 Electric services
PA: City Of Pratt
619 S Main St
Pratt KS 67124
620 672-5571

(G-10102)
COMFORT SUITES
704 Allison Ln (67124-8472)
PHONE..................................620 672-9999
Yogesh Pate, *Executive*
EMP: 12
SALES (est): 501.1K **Privately Held**
SIC: 7011 Hotel, franchised

(G-10103)
COUNTY OF PRATT
Also Called: Pratt County Ems
1001 E 1st St (67124-2055)
PHONE..................................620 672-4130
Mark Mc Manaman, *Director*
EMP: 27 **Privately Held**
WEB: www.prattcountyextension.com
SIC: 4119 Ambulance service
PA: County Of Pratt
300 S Ninnescah St
Pratt KS 67124
620 672-4110

(G-10104)
COXMONTGOMERY INC
75 Nw 40th Ave (67124-7761)
PHONE..................................620 508-6260
Bobby Cox, *Principal*
Anel Cox, *Treasurer*
EMP: 17 **EST:** 2007
SALES (est): 1.5MM **Privately Held**
SIC: 1623 Electric power line construction

(G-10105)
COXPOWERLINE INC
75 Nw 40th Ave (67124-7761)
PHONE..................................620 508-6260
Bobby Darrell Cox, *Principal*
EMP: 20
SALES (est): 2.4MM **Privately Held**
SIC: 3643 Power line cable

(G-10106)
D & R TRUCKING CO
201 Simpson St (67124-9067)
P.O. Box J (67124-1109)
PHONE..................................620 672-7713
Daniel Gamblin, *Owner*
EMP: 43
SQ FT: 6,000
SALES (est): 4MM **Privately Held**
SIC: 4213 Trucking, except local

(G-10107)
DCCCA INC
501 S Ninnescah St (67124-2838)
PHONE..................................620 672-7546
Rahcal Harper, *Branch Mgr*
EMP: 15 **Privately Held**
SIC: 8093 Alcohol clinic, outpatient; drug clinic, outpatient
PA: Dccca, Inc.
3312 Clinton Pkwy
Lawrence KS

(G-10108)
DIRECT VOLTAGE
323 Illinois Ave (67124-3408)
PHONE..................................713 485-9999
Bright Ibeawuchi, *President*
▲ **EMP:** 12
SALES (est): 1MM **Privately Held**
SIC: 3699 Household electrical equipment

(G-10109)
DOUG REH CHEVROLET INC
1501 E 1st St (67124-2069)
PHONE..................................620 672-5633
Doug Reh, *President*
Dave Hanchu, *Vice Pres*
Donnie Goertzen, *Sales Mgr*
Julie McCall, *Sales Staff*
Susan Mayberry, *Admin Sec*
EMP: 29 **EST:** 1951
SQ FT: 15,000
SALES (est): 9.7MM **Privately Held**
WEB: www.dougrehchevrolet.com
SIC: 5511 7538 Automobiles, new & used; general automotive repair shops

(G-10110)
ELKS LODGE INC
Also Called: B P O Elks Lodge 1451
1103 W 5th St (67124-2214)
PHONE..................................620 672-2011
Bill Dorman, *President*
EMP: 22
SALES: 103.3K **Privately Held**
SIC: 8641 5813 Fraternal associations; bars & lounges

(G-10111)
EVERGY KANSAS CENTRAL INC
Also Called: Kpl Gas Service
Rr 3 (67124)
P.O. Box 65a
PHONE..................................800 794-6101
Jim Koch, *Branch Mgr*
EMP: 18
SALES (corp-wide): 4.2B **Publicly Held**
SIC: 4911 Electric services
HQ: Evergy Kansas Central, Inc.
818 S Kansas Ave
Topeka KS 66612
785 575-6300

(G-10112)
EXCEL WIRELINE LLC
457 Yucca Ln (67124-8457)
PHONE..................................785 764-9557
John D Beverlin II, *Administration*
EMP: 5
SALES (est): 309.7K **Privately Held**
SIC: 1389 Removal of condensate gasoline from field (gathering) lines

(G-10113)
FIRST NATIONAL BANK IN PRATT
223 S Main St (67124-2714)
P.O. Box N (67124-1113)
PHONE..................................620 672-6421
Kelly Mason, *President*
David T Chandler, *Chairman*
Don Peters, *Exec VP*
Dan Meyers, *Senior VP*
Mike Koler, *Vice Pres*
EMP: 33 **EST:** 1891
SQ FT: 17,500
SALES: 3.4MM
SALES (corp-wide): 5.7MM **Privately Held**
WEB: www.fnbpratt.com
SIC: 6021 National trust companies with deposits, commercial
PA: First Pratt Bankshares Inc
223 S Main St
Pratt KS 67124
620 672-6421

(G-10114)
FIRST PRATT BANKSHARES INC (PA)
Also Called: First National Bank
223 S Main St (67124-2714)
PHONE..................................620 672-6421
George T Chandler, *President*
Jaon Scarbrough, *Corp Secy*
Diana Barnard, *Loan*
EMP: 33
SQ FT: 3,000
SALES (est): 5.7MM **Privately Held**
SIC: 6021 National commercial banks

(G-10115)
FOSSIL DRILLING INC
10213 Bluestem Blvd (67124-8476)
P.O. Box 464 (67124-0464)
PHONE..................................620 672-5625
Brian Siroky, *President*
EMP: 12
SALES (est): 1.7MM **Privately Held**
SIC: 1381 Drilling oil & gas wells

(G-10116)
FRYSLIE INC
Also Called: Hillcrest Best Western Motel
1336 E 1st St (67124-2064)
PHONE..................................620 672-6407
Don Fryslie, *President*
Elizabeth Fryslie, *Admin Sec*
EMP: 10 **EST:** 1970
SQ FT: 9,000
SALES: 204K **Privately Held**
SIC: 7011 Motel, franchised

(G-10117)
GATEHOUSE MEDIA LLC
Pratt Tribune
320 S Main St (67124-2706)
P.O. Box 909 (67124-0909)
PHONE..................................620 672-5512
Kim Smith, *Advt Staff*
Randy Mitchell, *Manager*
Shannon Briles, *Manager*
EMP: 32
SQ FT: 5,600
SALES (corp-wide): 1.5B **Publicly Held**
WEB: www.gatehousemedia.com
SIC: 2711 Commercial printing & newspaper publishing combined; newspapers, publishing & printing
HQ: Gatehouse Media, Llc
175 Sullys Trl Fl 3
Pittsford NY 14534
585 598-0030

(G-10118)
GATEWAY ETHANOL LLC
10333 Ne 30th St (67124-8428)
PHONE..................................620 933-2288
Lane Hann,
EMP: 30
SALES (est): 3.2MM **Privately Held**
SIC: 2869 Ethyl alcohol, ethanol

(G-10119)
GREAT PLAINS ALFALFA INC
70036 Nw 30th St (67124-7795)
PHONE..................................620 672-9431
Steve Maechtlen, *President*
Kenneth Maechtlen, *Corp Secy*
EMP: 12
SALES: 3.8MM **Privately Held**
SIC: 0139 Alfalfa farm

(G-10120)
HOLIDAY INN & SUITES
1903 Pauline Pl (67124-3503)
PHONE..................................620 508-6350
Grace Palmar, *Principal*
EMP: 15
SALES (est): 737K **Privately Held**
SIC: 7011 Hotels & motels

(G-10121)
IAN S KOVACH MD PHD
Also Called: Health Centl Bone & Joint Ctr
203 Watson St Ste 300 (67124-3092)
PHONE..................................620 672-1002
Ian S Kovach MD, *Principal*
Ian Kovach, *Med Doctor*
EMP: 20 **EST:** 2001
SALES (est): 1MM **Privately Held**
SIC: 8011 Orthopedic physician

(G-10122)
KANZA COOPERATIVE ASSOCIATION
916 S Main St (67124-2635)
PHONE..................................620 672-6761
Jo Heronema, *Manager*
EMP: 12
SALES (corp-wide): 300MM **Privately Held**
SIC: 5153 Grain elevators
PA: Kanza Cooperative Association
102 N Main St
Iuka KS 67066
620 546-2231

(G-10123)
KINCHELOE INC
10517 N Us Highway 281 (67124-7917)
PHONE..................................620 672-6401
David Borho, *President*
EMP: 10
SALES (est): 3.3MM **Privately Held**
WEB: www.kincheloe.com
SIC: 5083 Farm implements

(G-10124)
KIWANIS INTERNATIONAL INC
106 S Oak St (67124-2719)
PHONE..................................620 672-6257
Glen Cunningham, *Branch Mgr*
EMP: 14
SALES (corp-wide): 23.6MM **Privately Held**
WEB: www.kfne.org
SIC: 8641 Civic associations
PA: Kiwanis International, Inc.
3636 Woodview Trce
Indianapolis IN 46268
317 875-8755

(G-10125)
MEAD RENTAL CENTER
Also Called: Mead Lumber
1502 E 1st St (67124-2068)
PHONE..................................620 672-7718
Eric Wilson, *Manager*
EMP: 15
SALES (est): 122.7K **Privately Held**
SIC: 7513 Truck rental & leasing, no drivers

(G-10126)
MUD-CO/SERVICE MUD INC
279 Ne 70th Ave Ste 3 (67124-8465)
PHONE..................................620 672-2957
Kevin Freeman, *Manager*
EMP: 10
SALES (corp-wide): 3.8MM **Privately Held**
SIC: 4225 5082 5169 General warehousing; oil field equipment; drilling mud
PA: Mud-Co/Service Mud Inc
100 S Main St Ste 405
Wichita KS
316 264-2814

(G-10127)
ONEOK INC
Also Called: Kansas Gas Service
40135 N Us Highway 281 (67124-7913)
PHONE..................................620 672-6706
Michael Day, *Manager*
EMP: 30
SALES (corp-wide): 12.5B **Publicly Held**
WEB: www.oneok.com
SIC: 4922 Natural gas transmission
PA: Oneok, Inc.
100 W 5th St Ste Ll
Tulsa OK 74103
918 588-7000

(G-10128)
ONEOK FIELD SERVICES CO LLC
30317 N Us Highway 281 (67124-7931)
PHONE..................................620 248-3258
Blaine Bender, *Branch Mgr*
EMP: 12
SALES (corp-wide): 12.5B **Publicly Held**
SIC: 1321 Natural gas liquids
HQ: Oneok Field Services Company, L.L.C.
100 W 5th St Ste Ll
Tulsa OK 74103

(G-10129)
PARK HILLS GOLF & SUPPER CLUB
Also Called: Park Hills Country Club
337 Lake Rd (67124-8118)
P.O. Box 803 (67124-0803)
PHONE..................................620 672-7541
Eddie Eastes, *President*
Steven K Eastes, *Principal*
Susan Lynch, *Vice Pres*
EMP: 10
SQ FT: 4,000
SALES: 500K **Privately Held**
SIC: 7997 Golf club, membership

(G-10130)
PARKWOOD VILLAGE
Also Called: Parkwood Village Pratt
401 Rochester St Apt 102 (67124-2985)
PHONE..................................620 672-5541
Kelly Thomas, *Manager*
Kelli Denny, *Nursing Dir*
EMP: 26
SQ FT: 38,500
SALES (est): 1.2MM **Privately Held**
WEB: www.parkwoodvillage.com
SIC: 6513 Retirement hotel operation

(G-10131)
PATTON CRAMER & LAPROD CHARTER
Also Called: Cramer, Dona H CPA
113 E 3rd St (67124-2703)
P.O. Box H (67124-1108)
PHONE..................................620 672-5533
Shelly Patton, *President*
Donna Cramer, *Treasurer*
EMP: 13
SQ FT: 1,500
SALES: 379.9K **Privately Held**
SIC: 8721 Accounting services, except auditing; auditing services; billing & bookkeeping service; certified public accountant

(G-10132)
PEOPLES BANK (PA)
222 S Main St (67124-2713)
P.O. Box B (67124-1102)
PHONE..................................620 672-5611
J Porter Loomis, *President*
Billy B Morgan, *Vice Chairman*
Emonte Hostetler, *Vice Pres*
Mike Anderson, *Loan Officer*
Wayne Dublerstadt, *CIO*
EMP: 50 **EST:** 1887
SQ FT: 10,500
SALES: 20.8MM **Privately Held**
WEB: www.thepeoplesbank.net
SIC: 6022 State trust companies accepting deposits, commercial

(G-10133)
PIONEER TANK & STEEL INC
40190 Runway Blvd (67124-7927)
P.O. Box 866 (67124-0866)
PHONE..................................620 672-2153
Michael Pina, *President*
Connie Meyers, *Corp Secy*
EMP: 5
SQ FT: 3,200
SALES (est): 550.9K **Privately Held**
SIC: 3443 5051 Tanks, standard or custom fabricated: metal plate; steel

(G-10134)
PRATER OIL GAS OPERATIONS INC
10356 Bluestem Blvd (67124-8431)
PHONE..................................620 672-7600
Joan Prater, *President*
EMP: 5
SALES (est): 514K **Privately Held**
SIC: 1311 Crude petroleum production

(G-10135)
PRATT COUNTY ACHIEVEMENT PLACE
104 N Oak St (67124-1845)
PHONE..................................620 672-6610
Tonie Perez, *Administration*
EMP: 10
SALES: 438.1K **Privately Held**
SIC: 8361 Residential care for children

(G-10136)
PRATT ENERGY LLC
10333 Ne 30th St (67124-8428)
P.O. Box 410 (67124-0410)
PHONE..................................620 933-2288
Lyle Schyler, *President*
Jerry Schroeder, *Plant Mgr*
Jen Slater, *Controller*
Jennifer Slater, *Controller*
Sue Hemphill, *Accountant*
EMP: 35 **EST:** 2010
SALES: 31MM **Privately Held**
SIC: 2869 Ethyl alcohol, ethanol

(G-10137)
PRATT FAMILY PRACTICE
203 Watson St Ste 200 (67124-3092)
P.O. Box 308 (67124-0308)
PHONE..................................620 672-7422
Gene Canata, *Principal*
David L Bohlender,
Wakon Fowler,
EMP: 25
SALES (est): 2.7MM **Privately Held**
SIC: 8011 General & family practice, physician/surgeon

(G-10138)
PRATT FEEDERS LLC (PA)
40010 Nw 20th Ave (67124-7801)
P.O. Box 945 (67124-0945)
PHONE..................................620 672-3401
Megan Ludwig, *Office Mgr*
Jerry Bohn, *Mng Member*
Kenny Montgomery, *Manager*
Robert Cather,
Lester Goyen,
EMP: 35
SQ FT: 3,000
SALES (est): 5.8MM **Privately Held**
WEB: www.prattfeeders.com
SIC: 0211 Beef cattle feedlots

(G-10139)
PRATT GLASS INC
210 S Jackson St (67124-2688)
PHONE..................................620 672-6463
Roger Adelhardt, *President*
EMP: 10
SALES (est): 1.1MM **Privately Held**
SIC: 1793 5999 5719 5231 Glass & glazing work; picture frames, ready made; window shades; glass; doors & windows; window & door (prefabricated) installation

(G-10140)
PRATT HEALTH AND REHAB
1221 Larimer St (67124-1241)
PHONE..................................620 672-6541
Linda Watson, *Administration*
EMP: 60
SALES (est): 859.9K **Privately Held**
SIC: 8051 Skilled nursing care facilities

(G-10141)
PRATT INTRNAL MDICINE GROUP PA
420 Country Club Rd # 100 (67124-3125)
PHONE..................................620 672-7417
Daniel J Suiter, *President*
EMP: 24

SALES (est): 2.7MM **Privately Held**
SIC: 8011 Internal medicine, physician/surgeon; gastronomist

(G-10142)
PRATT LIVESTOCK INC
30274 E Us Highway 54 (67124-8310)
PHONE..................................620 672-5961
Michael Lewis, *Branch Mgr*
EMP: 20
SALES (corp-wide): 3.8MM **Privately Held**
SIC: 5154 Auctioning livestock
PA: Pratt Livestock, Inc.
111 S Broadway Ave
Sterling KS 67579
620 672-5961

(G-10143)
PRATT REGIONAL MED CTR CORP
Pratt Rhbltation Residence Ctr
227 S Howard St (67124-3044)
PHONE..................................620 672-3424
Susan Page, *CEO*
Renae Kersenbrock, *Administration*
EMP: 50
SALES (corp-wide): 47.5MM **Privately Held**
SIC: 8051 Convalescent home with continuous nursing care
PA: Pratt Regional Medical Center Corporation
200 Commodore St
Pratt KS 67124
620 672-7451

(G-10144)
PRATT REGIONAL MED CTR CORP (PA)
200 Commodore St (67124-3099)
PHONE..................................620 672-7451
Susan Page, *President*
J Gordon Stofer, *CFO*
Alan Waites, *CFO*
Mark Green, *Psychologist*
Gene Cannata, *Med Doctor*
EMP: 391
SQ FT: 108,000
SALES: 47.5MM **Privately Held**
WEB: www.prmc.org
SIC: 8062 Hospital, affiliated with AMA residency

(G-10145)
PRATT UNIFIED 12TH DIST TRANSP
1007 W 5th St (67124-2212)
PHONE..................................620 672-4590
Mike Tuint, *General Mgr*
EMP: 12
SALES (est): 110K **Privately Held**
SIC: 4151 School buses

(G-10146)
R & R INDUSTRIES INC
Also Called: R & R Manufacturing
30340 Runway Blvd (67124-7923)
PHONE..................................620 672-7463
Paul Goertz, *President*
Brenda Richardson, *Treasurer*
EMP: 15 **EST:** 1956
SQ FT: 44,000
SALES (est): 2.6MM **Privately Held**
SIC: 3535 3523 Bucket type conveyor systems; fertilizing machinery, farm

(G-10147)
R & R MANUFACTURING INC
30340 Runway Blvd (67124-7923)
PHONE..................................620 672-7461
Paul Goertz, *President*
Brenda Richardson, *Corp Secy*
EMP: 10 **EST:** 1998
SQ FT: 3,500
SALES (est): 2MM **Privately Held**
WEB: www.rrmanufacturing.com
SIC: 2875 Fertilizers, mixing only

(G-10148)
SKAGGS INC
Also Called: Ace Hardware
107 S Main St (67124-2712)
PHONE..................................620 672-5312
Bill Skaggs, *President*
Gary C Skaggs, *Vice Pres*
Diane Mc Intosh, *Manager*
EMP: 25 **EST:** 1946
SALES (est): 3.2MM **Privately Held**
WEB: www.skaggsinc.com
SIC: 5261 5722 5251 7629 Lawn & garden supplies; electric household appliances; hardware; electrical household appliance repair

(G-10149)
SOUTH CENTRAL TELE ASSN INC
214 S Main St (67124-2713)
P.O. Box B (67124-1102)
PHONE..................................620 933-1000
Suzette Fetterman, *Manager*
EMP: 32
SALES (est): 949.6K
SALES (corp-wide): 3MM **Privately Held**
WEB: www.sctelcom.com
SIC: 4813 Voice telephone communications
PA: South Central Telephone Association, Inc.
215 S Iliff St
Medicine Lodge KS 67104
620 930-1000

(G-10150)
SOUTH CNTL KANS BONE JOINT CTR
203 Watson St Ste 300 (67124-3092)
PHONE..................................620 672-1002
Ian Kovach, *Principal*
Gina Hoffman, *Bd of Directors*
Connie Schaef, *Teacher*
Tara Woolfolk, *Teacher*
EMP: 15
SALES (est): 570K **Privately Held**
SIC: 8011 Orthopedic physician

(G-10151)
SOUTHWEST TRUCK PARTS INC (PA)
1630 E 1st St (67124-2070)
PHONE..................................620 672-5686
Dale Withers, *President*
Tim Elder, *Store Mgr*
▲ **EMP:** 60 **EST:** 1976
SQ FT: 134,000
SALES: 14MM **Privately Held**
SIC: 5531 5521 7538 Truck equipment & parts; trucks, tractors & trailers: used; truck engine repair, except industrial

(G-10152)
SOUTHWIND HOSPICE INC (PA)
496 Yucca Ln (67124-8457)
PHONE..................................620 672-7553
Toll Free:..888 -
Georgene Wade, *Vice Pres*
Diane L Johnson, *Director*
Alanna Harrison, *Admin Sec*
EMP: 19
SALES: 1.7MM **Privately Held**
SIC: 8399 8082 Health systems agency; home health care services

(G-10153)
STANION WHOLESALE ELC CO INC (PA)
812 S Main St (67124-2600)
P.O. Box F (67124-1106)
PHONE..................................620 672-5678
Bill Keller, *President*
Monty Matthews, *Exec VP*
Dennis Guey, *Vice Pres*
Cynthia Keller, *Vice Pres*
Monty Mathews, *Vice Pres*
EMP: 42 **EST:** 1993
SQ FT: 15,000
SALES (est): 97.6MM **Privately Held**
WEB: www.stanion.com
SIC: 5063 Electrical supplies

(G-10154)
STERLING DRILLING COMPANY
573 Yucca Ln (67124)
PHONE..................................620 672-9508
Steve E McClain, *President*
Nancy McClain, *Corp Secy*
Gary Talbott, *Vice Pres*
EMP: 60
SALES (est): 10.9MM **Privately Held**
WEB: www.sterlingdrilling.com
SIC: 1381 1311 Drilling oil & gas wells; crude petroleum production

(G-10155)
STEVEN DONNENWERTH
203 Watson St Ste 200 (67124-3092)
P.O. Box 308 (67124-0308)
PHONE..................................620 672-7422
Steven Donnenwerth, *Principal*
Steven Donnenweth, *Principal*
EMP: 25 **EST:** 2010
SALES (est): 365.1K **Privately Held**
SIC: 8011 Internal medicine, physician/surgeon

(G-10156)
STRAUB INTERNATIONAL INC
10134 Ne State Road 61 (67124-8316)
PHONE..................................620 672-2998
Larry Straub, *President*
EMP: 11
SALES (corp-wide): 93MM **Privately Held**
WEB: www.straubint.com
SIC: 5083 5571 Agricultural machinery & equipment; all terrain vehicle parts and accessories
PA: Straub International, Inc.
200 S Patton Rd
Great Bend KS 67530
620 792-5256

(G-10157)
SUPER 8 MOTEL OF PRATT INC
1906 E 1st St (67124-9763)
PHONE..................................620 672-5945
Miran No, *President*
EMP: 15
SALES (est): 737.1K **Privately Held**
SIC: 7011 Hotels & motels

(G-10158)
T R SERVICE & RENTAL
470 Yucca Ln (67124-8457)
PHONE..................................620 672-9100
Terry Richardson, *President*
EMP: 10
SALES (est): 1.3MM **Privately Held**
SIC: 1389 Oil field services

(G-10159)
TAYLOR PRINTING INC
405 S Main St (67124-2626)
P.O. Box 922 (67124-0922)
PHONE..................................620 672-3656
Jeff Taylor, *President*
Brian Taylor, *Treasurer*
Mary L Taylor, *Admin Sec*
EMP: 8
SQ FT: 2,125
SALES (est): 1.2MM **Privately Held**
SIC: 2752 2759 2791 2789 Commercial printing, offset; letterpress printing; typesetting; bookbinding & related work

(G-10160)
TR SERVICES INC
271 Lake Rd (67124-8114)
PHONE..................................785 623-1066
Terry Richardson, *President*
EMP: 5 **EST:** 2001
SALES (est): 320K **Privately Held**
SIC: 1389 Oil consultants

(G-10161)
TRACTOR SUPPLY COMPANY
1727 E 1st St (67124-2073)
PHONE..................................620 672-1102
EMP: 10
SALES (corp-wide): 7.9B **Publicly Held**
SIC: 5191 Farm supplies
PA: Tractor Supply Company
5401 Virginia Way
Brentwood TN 37027
615 440-4000

(G-10162)
TRI RESOURCES INC
Also Called: Dynegy
30317 N Us Highway 281 (67124-7931)
PHONE..................................620 672-9425
Blaine Bender, *Manager*
EMP: 15 **Publicly Held**
SIC: 1311 Crude petroleum & natural gas
HQ: Tri Resources Inc.
811 Louisiana St Ste 2100
Houston TX 77002
713 584-1000

(G-10163)
UNION PACIFIC RAILROAD COMPANY
727 N Main St (67124-1663)
PHONE..................................209 642-1032
Tom Sader, *Branch Mgr*
EMP: 140
SALES (corp-wide): 22.8B **Publicly Held**
WEB: www.uprr.com
SIC: 4011 Railroads, line-haul operating
HQ: Union Pacific Railroad Company Inc
1400 Douglas St
Omaha NE 68179
402 544-5000

(G-10164)
X F ENTERPRISES INC
Xtra Factors
211 Pedigo Dr (67124-3624)
PHONE..................................620 672-5616
Kent Smith, *Division Mgr*
Keith R Hansen Ms, *Vice Pres*
Jim Gatz, *Plant Mgr*
David Foster, *Mill Mgr*
Janie Bishop, *Office Mgr*
EMP: 15
SALES (corp-wide): 45.8MM **Privately Held**
WEB: www.anipro.net
SIC: 2048 Mineral feed supplements; feed premixes
PA: X F Enterprises, Inc.
500 S Taylor St Unit 301
Amarillo TX 79101
806 367-5810

(G-10165)
YOUNIE LAWNSCAPES
10093 Ne 10th St (67124-8366)
PHONE..................................620 672-3301
Kevin Younie, *Owner*
EMP: 10
SALES (est): 361.8K **Privately Held**
SIC: 0781 Landscape architects

Prescott
Linn County

(G-10166)
CUSTOM ALLOY SALES 34P LLC
4008 Vernon Rd (66767-8132)
PHONE..................................913 471-4800
Rhett King, *General Mgr*
Kenneth Cox, *Mng Member*
EMP: 52
SALES (est): 10.9MM
SALES (corp-wide): 150MM **Privately Held**
SIC: 3341 5051 Aluminum smelting & refining (secondary); ferroalloys
PA: Custom Alloy Sales, Inc.
13191 Crssrds Pkwy N
City Of Industry CA 91746
626 369-3641

(G-10167)
PRESCOTT STATE BNK HOLDG INC
283 Main St (66767)
P.O. Box 98 (66767-0098)
PHONE..................................913 471-4321
Frank Dunnick, *President*
EMP: 12 **EST:** 1981
SALES: 618K **Privately Held**
SIC: 6022 State commercial banks

Pretty Prairie
Reno County

(G-10168)
PRAIRIE SUNSET HOME INC
Also Called: MINANITE SUNSET MANOR
601 E Main St (67570-9202)
PHONE..................................620 459-6822

Rew Maris, *Principal*
Shiley E Smith, *Principal*
Rex Maris, *Director*
EMP: 50
SQ FT: 12,000
SALES: 3.5MM **Privately Held**
SIC: 8052 Intermediate care facilities

(G-10169)
RANE MANAGEMENT
21007 S Whiteside Rd (67570-8704)
PHONE.................................620 663-3341
Ray E Siebert, *Owner*
EMP: 12
SALES (est): 703.9K **Privately Held**
WEB: www.ranemanagement.com
SIC: 6513 Apartment building operators

Princeton
Franklin County

(G-10170)
RVC ENTERPRISES INC
202 Main St (66078-9159)
PHONE.................................785 937-4386
EMP: 10
SQ FT: 5,000
SALES (est): 1.6MM **Privately Held**
SIC: 3523 Mfg Farm Products

(G-10171)
WILDCAT CONNECTORS INC
Also Called: Sensor-1
202 Main St (66078-9159)
PHONE.................................785 937-4385
Ralph Cassone, *President*
EMP: 5
SQ FT: 5,000
SALES (est): 786.8K **Privately Held**
WEB: www.sensor-one.com
SIC: 3678 Electronic connectors

Protection
Comanche County

(G-10172)
ALLIANCE AG AND GRAIN LLC
108 W Chestnut St (67127-2720)
P.O. Box 338 (67127-0338)
PHONE.................................620 622-4511
Jay Sherman, *Branch Mgr*
EMP: 10
SALES (est): 1MM
SALES (corp-wide): 55.1MM **Privately Held**
SIC: 5153 Grains
PA: Alliance Ag And Grain, Llc
313 N Main St
Spearville KS 67876
620 385-2898

(G-10173)
BANK OF PROTECTION INC
302 N Broadway (67127-8833)
P.O. Box 98 (67127-0098)
PHONE.................................620 622-4224
Candice Murphy, *President*
Joe Murphy, *Vice Pres*
Tylor Woolfolk, *Vice Pres*
EMP: 11
SALES: 3MM **Privately Held**
SIC: 6022 State trust companies accepting deposits, commercial

(G-10174)
BAR SIX MANUFATURING INC
E Hwy 160 (67127)
P.O. Box 455 (67127-0455)
PHONE.................................620 622-4456
Randy Bayne, *President*
EMP: 7 **EST:** 1965
SQ FT: 5,000
SALES: 600K **Privately Held**
SIC: 3523 Cattle feeding, handling & watering equipment

(G-10175)
LANE MYERS COMPANY INC
415 N Broadway (67127-8831)
P.O. Box 538 (67127-0538)
PHONE.................................620 622-4310
Tom Murphy, *President*
Tyler Myers, *Superintendent*
Larry Smith, *Vice Pres*
EMP: 20 **EST:** 1963
SQ FT: 4,500
SALES (est): 1.8MM **Privately Held**
SIC: 3496 3449 3315 Miscellaneous fabricated wire products; miscellaneous metalwork; steel wire & related products

(G-10176)
PROTECTION VALLEY MANOR INC
600 S Broadway (67127-8801)
P.O. Box 448 (67127-0448)
PHONE.................................620 622-4261
Bobbie Chase, *Admin Dir*
Ruth A Jellison, *Administration*
EMP: 53 **EST:** 1972
SQ FT: 15,000
SALES: 2.2MM **Privately Held**
SIC: 8052 Intermediate care facilities

(G-10177)
WORSHIP WOODWORKS INC
Also Called: Worship Woodworks.com
207 W Walnut St (67127-2716)
P.O. Box 132 (67127-0132)
PHONE.................................620 622-4568
Sally R Selzer, *Owner*
EMP: 9
SALES (est): 783.8K **Privately Held**
WEB: www.worshipwoodworks.com
SIC: 2499 8661 5999 Decorative wood & woodwork; religious organizations; religious goods

Quenemo
Osage County

(G-10178)
NORTH SHORE MARINA MGT LLC
200 N Shore Marina Dr (66528-8015)
PHONE.................................785 453-2240
EMP: 5
SALES: 100K **Privately Held**
SIC: 4493 7033 3731 Marina Operation Trailer Park/Campsites Shipbuilding/Repairing

Quinter
Gove County

(G-10179)
BLUESTEM MEDICAL LLP
501 Garfield St (67752-9795)
P.O. Box 510 (67752-0510)
PHONE.................................785 754-2458
Michael Machen, *Partner*
Victor Nemechek, *Partner*
Douglas Gruenbacher, *Family Practiti*
Shelly Gruenbacher, *Family Practiti*
Jill Stewart, *Family Practiti*
EMP: 16 **EST:** 1986
SALES (est): 1.8MM **Privately Held**
SIC: 8011 Physicians' office, including specialists

(G-10180)
CHS INC
7085 Highway 40 (67752-2703)
PHONE.................................785 754-3318
Rich Meier, *Branch Mgr*
EMP: 10
SALES (corp-wide): 31.9B **Publicly Held**
SIC: 5191 Farm supplies
PA: Chs Inc.
5500 Cenex Dr
Inver Grove Heights MN 55077
651 355-6000

(G-10181)
COUNTY OF GOVE
Also Called: Gove County Medical Center
520 W 5th St (67752-9705)
P.O. Box 129 (67752-0129)
PHONE.................................785 754-3335
Connie Breese, *Chf Purch Ofc*
Dee Foster, *Director*
Paul Davis, *Administration*
EMP: 175 **Privately Held**
SIC: 8062 General medical & surgical hospitals
PA: County Of Gove
520 W 5th St
Quinter KS 67752
785 938-2300

(G-10182)
KANSASLAND BANK (PA)
314 Main St (67752-9526)
P.O. Box 10 (67752-0010)
PHONE.................................785 754-2500
Scott Bird, *President*
EMP: 10
SALES: 2.1MM **Privately Held**
SIC: 6022 State commercial banks

(G-10183)
ORTHMAN MFG
2550 County Road 74 (67752-6116)
PHONE.................................785 754-9985
John McCoy, *Owner*
EMP: 20
SALES (est): 784.1K **Privately Held**
SIC: 3999 Furs, dressed: bleached, curried, scraped, tanned or dyed

(G-10184)
PREMIER TILLAGE INC (PA)
301 Park St (67752)
P.O. Box 207 (67752-0207)
PHONE.................................785 754-2381
Dan Chupp, *President*
EMP: 25
SQ FT: 5,500
SALES (est): 2.9MM **Privately Held**
SIC: 7692 1799 Welding repair; welding on site

(G-10185)
QUINTER AMBULANCE SERVICE INC
412 Main St (67752-5205)
P.O. Box 310 (67752-0310)
PHONE.................................785 754-3734
David Burgess, *Admin Sec*
EMP: 22
SALES: 246.4K **Privately Held**
SIC: 4119 Ambulance service

(G-10186)
QUINTER MFG & CNSTR INC
Also Called: Qmc
2520 Castle Rock Rd (67752-6100)
P.O. Box 100 (67752-0100)
PHONE.................................785 754-3310
Jeff Bawman, *President*
Jesse Bauman, *Vice Pres*
Ray Hawbaker, *Vice Pres*
EMP: 12 **EST:** 1962
SQ FT: 16,848
SALES (est): 2.6MM **Privately Held**
SIC: 1542 Commercial & office building, new construction; commercial & office buildings, renovation & repair; agricultural building contractors

(G-10187)
SWIFT BULLET CO
201 Main St (67752-9517)
P.O. Box 27 (67752-0027)
PHONE.................................785 754-2374
William Hober, *CEO*
EMP: 15
SQ FT: 4,556
SALES (est): 2.8MM **Privately Held**
WEB: www.swiftbullet.com
SIC: 3482 Small arms ammunition

(G-10188)
TENDER HEARTS CHILD CARE CTR
504 Castle Rock St (67752-9514)
P.O. Box 129 (67752-0129)
PHONE.................................785 754-3937
Rayann Mattke, *Director*
Paul Davis, *Administration*
EMP: 10
SALES (est): 83.3K **Privately Held**
SIC: 8351 Child day care services

Ramona
Marion County

(G-10189)
TATGE MANUFACTURING INC (PA)
607 N D St (67475-9014)
PHONE.................................785 965-7213
Warren H Gfeller, *President*
C E Miller, *Corp Secy*
EMP: 5
SQ FT: 8,500
SALES (est): 584.6K **Privately Held**
SIC: 3523 Sprayers & spraying machines, agricultural

Randall
Jewell County

(G-10190)
RANDALL FARMERS COOP UN INC (PA)
101 Walnut St (66963-4003)
P.O. Box 95 (66963-0095)
PHONE.................................785 739-2312
Greg Mc Millan, *President*
Jerry Dune, *Vice Pres*
Steve McKintyre, *Admin Sec*
EMP: 15 **EST:** 1926
SQ FT: 3,280
SALES (est): 5.5MM **Privately Held**
SIC: 5153 4221 5191 Grains; grain elevator, storage only; feed; seeds: field, garden & flower; fertilizer & fertilizer materials; chemicals, agricultural

Randolph
Riley County

(G-10191)
UNION STATE BANK INC
201 S Front St (66554-9211)
P.O. Box 175 (66554-0175)
PHONE.................................785 293-5516
Dan Holt, *Branch Mgr*
EMP: 17
SALES (corp-wide): 1.3MM **Privately Held**
SIC: 6022 State commercial banks
PA: Union State Bank Inc
204 E Highway 16
Olsburg KS 66520
785 468-3341

Ransom
Ness County

(G-10192)
GEMS INC
410 S Vermont Ave (67572-9500)
P.O. Box 267 (67572-0267)
PHONE.................................785 731-2849
Gregory Lutters, *President*
Moma Lutters, *Admin Sec*
EMP: 6
SQ FT: 7,400
SALES: 400K **Privately Held**
SIC: 7694 5999 Electric motor repair; engine & motor equipment & supplies

(G-10193)
GRISELL MEMORIAL HOSPITAL ASSN (PA)
210 S Vermont Ave (67572-9525)
P.O. Box 268 (67572-0268)
PHONE.................................785 731-2231
Jay Jecha, *Lab Dir*
Chris Oaks, *Administration*
EMP: 86
SQ FT: 33,105
SALES: 3.8MM **Privately Held**
WEB: www.grisell.org
SIC: 8062 General medical & surgical hospitals

GEOGRAPHIC

(G-10194)
GRISELL MEMORIAL HOSPITAL ASSN
Also Called: McClain Medical Clinic
210 S Vermont Ave (67572-9525)
PHONE..................................785 731-2231
Chris Oaks, *Manager*
EMP: 100
SALES (corp-wide): 3.8MM **Privately Held**
WEB: www.grisell.org
SIC: 8011 General & family practice, physician/surgeon
PA: Grisell Memorial Hospital Association
210 S Vermont Ave
Ransom KS 67572
785 731-2231

(G-10195)
SIMPSON FARM ENTERPRISES INC (PA)
20333 N Ness Cnty Line Rd (67572-7334)
P.O. Box 70 (67572-0070)
PHONE..................................785 731-2700
Jed Simpson, *President*
Gregory Simpson, *Vice Pres*
Jay Simpson, *Treasurer*
Jason Pavlu, *Sales Associate*
EMP: 14 **EST:** 1981
SQ FT: 20,000
SALES (est): 8MM **Privately Held**
WEB: www.simpsonfarm.com
SIC: 5191 3523 0191 5083 Farm supplies; sprayers & spraying machines, agricultural; general farms, primarily crop; farm equipment parts & supplies

Rantoul
Franklin County

(G-10196)
DODSON INTERNATIONAL PARTS INC (HQ)
2155 Vermont Rd (66079-9014)
P.O. Box 19 (66079-0019)
PHONE..................................785 878-8000
Robert Lee Dodson Jr, *President*
Jonathan Harnden, *General Mgr*
Michael Schrick, *Research*
Butch Holtgrive, *VP Sales*
Kathy Feighner, *Sales Staff*
◆ **EMP:** 84
SQ FT: 45,000
SALES (est): 35.2MM
SALES (corp-wide): 20.6MM **Privately Held**
SIC: 5088 Aircraft & parts
PA: Dodson Investments Inc
2155 Vermont Rd
Rantoul KS 66079
785 878-4000

(G-10197)
DODSON INVESTMENTS INC (PA)
2155 Vermont Rd (66079-9014)
P.O. Box 19 (66079-0019)
PHONE..................................785 878-4000
Robert Lee Dodson Sr, *President*
Jacob Savage, *Sales Staff*
Robert Lee Dodson Jr, *Admin Sec*
◆ **EMP:** 97
SALES: 20.6MM **Privately Held**
SIC: 5088 Aircraft & parts; aircraft equipment & supplies

Reading
Lyon County

(G-10198)
BRIGGS TRUCKING INC
2594 Road X (66868-9273)
PHONE..................................620 699-3448
John Briggs, *President*
Scott Briggs, *Treasurer*
EMP: 21
SALES: 2.2MM **Privately Held**
SIC: 4212 4213 Local trucking, without storage; trucking, except local

(G-10199)
K AND C TECHNICAL SERVICE LLC
11341 W 325th St (66868-9056)
PHONE..................................316 650-4464
Christopher Marquez, *CEO*
Kassandra Hall, *CFO*
EMP: 10
SALES (est): 301.8K
SALES (corp-wide): 1.6MM **Privately Held**
SIC: 5065 Electronic parts & equipment
PA: Cable Pros Llc
11341 W 325th St
Reading KS
316 650-4464

Republic
Republic County

(G-10200)
JESSE LATHAM & SONS INC
417 Main St (66964-9501)
P.O. Box 39 (66964-0039)
PHONE..................................785 361-4281
Jesse E Latham, *President*
Phyllis Latham, *Treasurer*
Joni Latham, *Admin Sec*
EMP: 13
SQ FT: 800
SALES (est): 1.3MM **Privately Held**
SIC: 4213 Trucking, except local

Rexford
Thomas County

(G-10201)
MCCARTY DAIRY LLC (PA)
2231 County Road 31 (67753-9437)
P.O. Box 968, Colby (67701-0968)
PHONE..................................785 465-9002
Courtney Goodman, *Executive*
Tom McCarty,
Clayton McCarty,
Kenneth McCarty,
Michael McCarty,
EMP: 25
SALES: 15.4MM **Privately Held**
SIC: 0241 Milk production

(G-10202)
MCCARTY FAMILY FARMS LLC
2231 County Road 31 (67753-9437)
PHONE..................................785 465-9006
Antonio Balbuena, *Prdtn Mgr*
Garland Faircloth, *Prdtn Mgr*
Clay McCarty, *Mng Member*
Justin Spresser, *Maintence Staff*
Ken McCarty,
EMP: 15
SALES (est): 2MM **Privately Held**
SIC: 0241 Milk production

Richmond
Franklin County

(G-10203)
QUALITY STRUCTURES INC (PA)
167 Highway 59 (66080-9184)
PHONE..................................785 835-6100
Robert Pearce, *President*
Kevin Pietro, *Branch Mgr*
EMP: 42
SALES: 12.4MM **Privately Held**
WEB: www.qualitystructures.com
SIC: 1522 1542 Residential construction; nonresidential construction

(G-10204)
RICHMOND HEALTHCARE
340 E South St (66080-4021)
PHONE..................................785 835-6135
Melanie Bowman, *Administration*
EMP: 60
SALES: 3.7MM **Publicly Held**
SIC: 8051 Skilled nursing care facilities
HQ: Genesis Healthcare Llc
101 E State St
Kennett Square PA 19348

Riley
Riley County

(G-10205)
BPW MASONRY INC
7714 Jenkins Rd (66531-9651)
PHONE..................................785 485-2840
Richard Pride Sr, *President*
Richard Pride Jr, *Treasurer*
Scott Brown, *Admin Sec*
EMP: 37
SQ FT: 900
SALES: 2.5MM **Privately Held**
SIC: 1741 Masonry & other stonework

(G-10206)
HOWE LANDSCAPE INC (PA)
12780 Madison Rd Ste A (66531-9521)
PHONE..................................785 485-2857
Scott Howe, *President*
EMP: 17
SALES: 3MM **Privately Held**
WEB: www.howelandscape.com
SIC: 0781 Landscape planning services; landscape services

(G-10207)
RICHARD L PRIDE
7714 Jenkins Rd (66531-9651)
PHONE..................................785 485-2900
Richard Pride, *Owner*
Richard L Pride, *Owner*
Randy Wood, *Owner*
EMP: 15
SALES (est): 463.5K **Privately Held**
SIC: 1741 Stone masonry

(G-10208)
RILEY STATE BANK OF RILEY KANS (PA)
201 S Broadway St (66531-9559)
P.O. Box 218 (66531-0218)
PHONE..................................785 485-2811
Edgar Copeland, *Ch of Bd*
Mike Hagenmaier, *President*
Kent Doyn, *Senior VP*
Gary Hanna, *Vice Pres*
Quinton Pultz, *Vice Pres*
EMP: 10 **EST:** 1943
SALES: 4MM **Privately Held**
WEB: www.rileystatebank.com
SIC: 6022 State trust companies accepting deposits, commercial

(G-10209)
SCHURLE SIGNS INC (PA)
7555 Falcon Rd (66531-9808)
P.O. Box 186 (66531-0186)
PHONE..................................785 485-2885
Janet Schurle, *President*
Jeanne Evers, *Sales Staff*
Scott Kulp, *Manager*
EMP: 16
SQ FT: 14,000
SALES (est): 2.3MM **Privately Held**
WEB: www.schurlesigns.com
SIC: 3993 Neon signs

Riverton
Cherokee County

(G-10210)
BAILEY MACHINE INC
1 Mile N On Hwy 69 A (66770)
P.O. Box 207 (66770-0207)
PHONE..................................620 848-3116
Tony Bailey, *President*
Anthony Bailey, *Vice Pres*
Tracy Sigg, *CFO*
Tracy Williams, *CFO*
Margaret Bailey, *Treasurer*
EMP: 10
SALES: 820K **Privately Held**
WEB: www.baileymachine.com
SIC: 3599 Machine shop, jobbing & repair

(G-10211)
CUNNINGHAM SNDBLST PNTG CO INC
5960 Se Beasley Rd (66770-4160)
PHONE..................................620 848-3030
James Brookshire, *President*
Tom Walters, *Vice Pres*
Ned Walters, *Treasurer*
EMP: 10
SQ FT: 1,500
SALES (est): 1.2MM **Privately Held**
SIC: 1799 Sandblasting of building exteriors

(G-10212)
EMPIRE DISTRICT ELECTRIC CO
Empire Dst Riverton Pwr Plant
7240 Se Highway 66 (66770-4133)
P.O. Box 300 (66770-0300)
PHONE..................................620 848-3456
Duane Zerr, *Manager*
EMP: 55
SALES (corp-wide): 1.6B **Privately Held**
WEB: www.empiredistrict.com
SIC: 4911 ; generation, electric power
HQ: The Empire District Electric Company
602 S Joplin Ave
Joplin MO 64801
417 625-5100

(G-10213)
SPRING RVER MNTAL HLTH WLLNESS (PA)
6610 Se Quakervale Rd (66770-4185)
P.O. Box 550 (66770-0550)
PHONE..................................620 848-2300
Scott Jackson, *Exec Dir*
EMP: 65
SQ FT: 48,400
SALES: 3MM **Privately Held**
SIC: 8093 Mental health clinic, outpatient

(G-10214)
WIMASE INTERNATIONAL INC
8500 Se Jayhawk Dr (66770)
P.O. Box 320 (66770-0320)
PHONE..................................620 783-1361
EMP: 8
SALES (est): 1MM **Privately Held**
SIC: 2892 Explosives
PA: Wimase International, Inc.
222 E Eufaula St Ste 120
Norman OK 73069
405 928-7061

Robinson
Brown County

(G-10215)
STATE ASSN OF KANS WATERSHEDS
Also Called: SAKW
121 Parsons St (66532-9775)
P.O. Box 216 (66532-0216)
PHONE..................................785 544-6686
Barb Oltjen, *President*
EMP: 11
SALES: 78.7K **Privately Held**
SIC: 8611 Business associations

Roeland Park
Johnson County

(G-10216)
ALLIED CONSTRUCTION SVCS INC
4700 Roe Pkwy (66205-1114)
PHONE..................................913 321-3170
Chris Edwards, *Branch Mgr*
EMP: 10
SALES (corp-wide): 129.5MM **Privately Held**
SIC: 1742 Drywall; acoustical & ceiling work; plastering, plain or ornamental
PA: Allied Construction Services, Inc.
2122 Fleur Dr
Des Moines IA 50321
515 288-4855

(G-10217)
BANK NEWS PUBLICATIONS INC
Also Called: Financial Placements
5115 Roe Blvd Ste 200 (66205-2393)
P.O. Box 29156, Shawnee Mission (66201-9156)
PHONE..................................913 261-7000
Pamela Baker, *President*
Bill Poquette, *Principal*
Rich Galloway, *Vice Pres*
Laura Baldwin, *Mktg Dir*
Pam Green,
EMP: 15
SQ FT: 3,000
SALES (est): 1.6MM **Privately Held**
WEB: www.banknews.com
SIC: 2721 Magazines: publishing only, not printed on site

(G-10218)
BILLS FRIENDS AA GROUP
Also Called: Aa World Services
4700 Mission Rd (66205-1625)
PHONE..................................913 722-9801
Bill Wilson, *President*
EMP: 12
SALES (est): 279.9K **Privately Held**
SIC: 8069 Alcoholism rehabilitation hospital

(G-10219)
BOULEVARD APPRTMENTS TOWNHOMES
5405 Skyline Dr (66205-1170)
PHONE..................................913 722-3171
Ron Nolan, *President*
EMP: 10
SALES (est): 890K **Privately Held**
SIC: 6513 Apartment building operators

(G-10220)
CHILDRENS CENTER LLC
5023 Granada St (66205-1322)
PHONE..................................913 432-5114
Amelia Reyes, *Mng Member*
Marsha Wiard, *Director*
EMP: 15 **EST:** 1998
SALES (est): 438.7K **Privately Held**
SIC: 8351 Group day care center

(G-10221)
CORINTH SCOUTS INC
5011 Neosho Ln (66205-1431)
PHONE..................................913 236-8920
Terry Walls, *President*
EMP: 30
SALES (est): 1.1MM **Privately Held**
SIC: 8641 Youth organizations

(G-10222)
CRICKET COMMUNICATIONS LLC
4980 Roe Blvd (66205-1110)
PHONE..................................913 999-0163
Jess Smith, *Branch Mgr*
EMP: 18
SALES (corp-wide): 170.7B **Publicly Held**
WEB: www.cricketcommunications.com
SIC: 4812 Cellular telephone services
HQ: Cricket Communications, Llc
7337 Trade St
San Diego CA 92121
858 882-6000

(G-10223)
GSM SALES LLC
4110 W 47th Ter (66205-1334)
PHONE..................................816 674-1066
Michael Schuette,
Adrian Garza,
Dean Mitchell,
Jason Mitchell,
EMP: 10
SALES (est): 828.8K **Privately Held**
SIC: 7373 Computer integrated systems design

(G-10224)
HEARTLAND REG ALCHL & DRUG
Also Called: HEARTLAND RADAC
5500 Buena Vista St # 202 (66205-2704)
P.O. Box 1063, Shawnee Mission (66222-0063)
PHONE..................................913 789-0951
Kris Carnahan, *Opers Staff*
Dana Osborne, *Opers Staff*
Dalyn Schmidt, *Exec Dir*
Jason Hess, *Exec Dir*
EMP: 31
SALES: 6.7MM **Privately Held**
SIC: 8093 Alcohol clinic, outpatient

(G-10225)
HSBC FINANCE CORPORATION
5115 Roe Blvd (66205-2394)
PHONE..................................913 362-1400
Robert Welgos, *Principal*
EMP: 10
SALES (corp-wide): 87.7B **Privately Held**
WEB: www.household.com
SIC: 6141 Consumer finance companies
HQ: Hsbc Finance Corporation
1421 W Shure Dr Ste 100
Arlington Heights IL 60004
224 880-7000

(G-10226)
LIBERTY TAX
4994 Roe Blvd (66205-1110)
PHONE..................................913 384-1040
Andrew Banker, *Owner*
EMP: 10
SALES: 160K **Privately Held**
SIC: 7291 Tax return preparation services

(G-10227)
LOWES HOME CENTERS LLC
4960 Roe Blvd (66205-1110)
PHONE..................................913 261-1040
Lee Alejos, *Manager*
EMP: 150
SALES (corp-wide): 71.3B **Publicly Held**
SIC: 5211 5031 5722 5064 Home centers; building materials, exterior; building materials, interior; household appliance stores; electrical appliances, television & radio
HQ: Lowe's Home Centers, Llc
1605 Curtis Bridge Rd
Wilkesboro NC 28697
336 658-4000

(G-10228)
NAIL PERFECTION LLC
5110 Johnson Dr (66205-2905)
PHONE..................................913 722-0799
Tong Bui, *Mng Member*
EMP: 14
SALES (est): 308.4K **Privately Held**
SIC: 7231 Manicurist, pedicurist

(G-10229)
ROELAND PARK COMMUNITY CENTER
Also Called: Roeland Park Multi Service Ctr
4850 Rosewood Dr (66205-1106)
PHONE..................................913 722-0310
Jane Hurst, *Manager*
EMP: 10
SALES (est): 340K **Privately Held**
SIC: 8641 Community membership club

(G-10230)
US BANK NATIONAL ASSOCIATION
Also Called: US Bank
4970 Roe Blvd (66205-1110)
PHONE..................................913 261-5401
Shannon McDowel, *Branch Mgr*
EMP: 12
SALES (corp-wide): 25.7B **Publicly Held**
WEB: www.firstar.com
SIC: 6021 National commercial banks
HQ: U.S. Bank National Association
425 Walnut St Fl 14
Cincinnati OH 45202
513 632-4234

(G-10231)
WILLIAM H GRIFFIN
Also Called: William H Griffin Trustee
5115 Roe Blvd Ste 200 (66205-2393)
PHONE..................................913 677-1311
William H Griffin, *Owner*
Andrea Cozadd, *Human Res Mgr*
Tiffany Sigler, *Admin Asst*
EMP: 10
SALES (est): 833K **Privately Held**
SIC: 8111 Bankruptcy law

Rolla
Morton County

(G-10232)
DOUBLE T IND INC
980 Hwy 51 N (67954)
P.O. Box 401 (67954-0401)
PHONE..................................620 593-4357
Johnnie A Denton, *President*
Paula Cowser, *Corp Secy*
EMP: 30
SQ FT: 1,200
SALES (est): 8MM **Privately Held**
SIC: 3443 4213 4212 Tanks, standard or custom fabricated: metal plate; heavy hauling; heavy machinery transport, local

(G-10233)
SEABOARD FOODS LLC
Dermont Rd (67954)
PHONE..................................620 593-4353
Abe Easton, *Manager*
EMP: 5
SALES (corp-wide): 6.5B **Publicly Held**
WEB: www.seaboardpork.com
SIC: 2011 0191 Pork products from pork slaughtered on site; general farms, primarily crop
HQ: Seaboard Foods Llc
9000 W 67th St Ste 200
Shawnee Mission KS 66202
913 261-2600

Rosalia
Butler County

(G-10234)
J AND J PLASTICS
P.O. Box 6 (67132-0006)
PHONE..................................620 660-9048
Jody Coffey, *Owner*
EMP: 10
SALES: 50K **Privately Held**
SIC: 3087 Custom compound purchased resins

Rose Hill
Butler County

(G-10235)
AMERICAN CTRL & ENGRG SVC INC
14433 Sw 150th St (67133-8078)
PHONE..................................316 776-7500
Ross Lumbert, *President*
Butch Duren, *Engineer*
Diane Nichols, *Admin Sec*
EMP: 14
SALES (est): 3MM **Privately Held**
SIC: 7373 Systems integration services

(G-10236)
BANZET CONCRETE INC
19664 Sw Butler Rd (67133-9606)
P.O. Box 219 (67133-0219)
PHONE..................................316 776-9961
Craig Banzet, *President*
Amy Banzet, *Corp Secy*
EMP: 11
SALES: 400K **Privately Held**
SIC: 1771 1611 Concrete work; highway & street construction

(G-10237)
DYNAMIC N/C LLC
16531 Sw 190th St (67133-8596)
PHONE..................................316 712-5028
James Gibbs, *President*
EMP: 65 **EST:** 2006
SALES: 34.5MM **Privately Held**
SIC: 3728 Wing assemblies & parts, aircraft

(G-10238)
EMPRISE BANK
1402 N Rose Hill Rd (67133-9400)
P.O. Box 2970, Wichita (67201-2970)
PHONE..................................316 776-9584
Sheryl Harris, *Site Mgr*
Tiffany Newman, *Branch Mgr*
EMP: 11
SALES (corp-wide): 80MM **Privately Held**
SIC: 6022 State trust companies accepting deposits, commercial
HQ: Emprise Bank
257 N Broadway Ave
Wichita KS 67202
316 383-4400

(G-10239)
FOUNTAINVIEW NURSING &
601 N Rose Hill Rd (67133-9336)
PHONE..................................316 776-2194
EMP: 16
SALES: 4.1MM **Privately Held**
SIC: 8051 Skilled nursing care facilities

(G-10240)
INDUSTRIAL VENTURES INC (PA)
Also Called: Viking Peterson
731 S Industrial Ct (67133-8541)
PHONE..................................316 634-6699
Deron J Lock, *President*
EMP: 77
SALES (est): 8.6MM **Privately Held**
SIC: 3559 Foundry machinery & equipment

(G-10241)
LAKEPINT NRSING RHBLTATION CTR
601 N Rose Hill Rd (67133-9336)
PHONE..................................316 776-2194
Larry Wilkerson, *Administration*
▲ **EMP:** 50
SALES (est): 1.6MM **Privately Held**
WEB: www.lakepointnc.com
SIC: 8051 Convalescent home with continuous nursing care

(G-10242)
MARK TROILO DDS PA
106 E Yeager St (67133-9107)
P.O. Box 98 (67133-0098)
PHONE..................................316 776-2144
Mark Troilo DDS, *President*
EMP: 12 **EST:** 1978
SALES (est): 409.2K **Privately Held**
SIC: 8021 Dentists' office

(G-10243)
PAULS VALLEY THIRD ADDITON
14752 Sw Anemone Rd (67133-8387)
PHONE..................................316 733-1648
Robert Gibbins, *President*
EMP: 15
SALES (est): 150.5K **Privately Held**
SIC: 8641 Homeowners' association

(G-10244)
PEACE OF MIND
400 E School St (67133-9794)
P.O. Box 173, Derby (67037-0173)
PHONE..................................316 260-7046
Chandra K Bilhimer, *Principal*
EMP: 10 **EST:** 2011
SALES (est): 375.5K **Privately Held**
SIC: 8082 Home health care services

(G-10245)
PETERSON MCH TL ACQISITION INC
731 S Industrial Ct (67133-8541)
PHONE..................................316 634-6699
Deron Lock, *President*
Robert Balding, *CFO*

GEOGRAPHIC

◆ **EMP:** 15
SQ FT: 30,000
SALES: 7MM **Privately Held**
SIC: 3589 Commercial cleaning equipment

(G-10246)
RHUM WEE ROCKETS PRE SCHOOL
Also Called: Rose Hill United Youth Center
109 S Main St (67133-9701)
PHONE..................................316 776-9330
Fax: 316 776-0273
EMP: 15
SALES (est): 420K **Privately Held**
SIC: 8351 Child Day Care Services

(G-10247)
ROSE HILL BANK (HQ)
107 N Rose Hill Rd (67133-9785)
P.O. Box 68 (67133-0068)
PHONE..................................316 776-2131
Roger Kepley, *President*
George H Waitt III, *President*
Larry Britegam, *Exec VP*
Garth Kellenbarger, *Exec VP*
Larry Cohoon, *Senior VP*
EMP: 30 **EST:** 1906
SALES: 13.3MM **Privately Held**
WEB: www.rosehillbank.com
SIC: 6022 State trust companies accepting deposits, commercial
PA: Rose Hill Bancorp
107 N Rose Hill Rd
Rose Hill KS 67133
316 776-2131

(G-10248)
ROSE HILL UNIFIED SCHOOL DST
Also Called: Rose Hl Prmry Schl/Kndergarten
104 N Rose Hill Rd (67133-9785)
PHONE..................................316 776-3340
Terri Reilly, *Principal*
Marcia Helmke, *Teacher*
Cynthia Shavlik, *Teacher*
EMP: 43
SALES (corp-wide): 14.8MM **Privately Held**
SIC: 8351 8211 Child day care services; public elementary school
PA: Rose Hill Unified School District
104 N Rose Hill Rd
Rose Hill KS 67133
316 776-3300

(G-10249)
STEEL BUILDING SALES LLC
13323 Sw Butler Rd (67133-8442)
PHONE..................................316 733-5380
Kim Hocker, *Co-Owner*
Cody Schwope, *Vice Pres*
Jacob E Hocker, *Administration*
EMP: 13
SALES (est): 4.8MM **Privately Held**
SIC: 5051 Steel

(G-10250)
VIKING CORPORATION
Also Called: Viking Blast and Wash Systems
731 S Industrial Ct (67133-8541)
PHONE..................................316 634-6699
Deron Lock, *President*
Jake Reimer, *Engineer*
Patty Wray, *Admin Asst*
▼ **EMP:** 46
SQ FT: 37,500
SALES: 7MM
SALES (corp-wide): 8.6MM **Privately Held**
WEB: www.vikingcorporation.com
SIC: 3559 Foundry machinery & equipment
PA: Industrial Ventures Inc
731 S Industrial Ct
Rose Hill KS 67133
316 634-6699

Rossville
Shawnee County

(G-10251)
DUNNS CUSTOM KNIVES INC
Also Called: Dunn Knives
5830 Nw Carlson Rd (66533-9615)
PHONE..................................785 584-6856
EMP: 5
SQ FT: 864
SALES (est): 287.5K **Privately Held**
SIC: 5719 3421 Ret Misc Homefurnishings Mfg Cutlery

(G-10252)
FOUNDATION FOR A CHRISTIAN CIV
426 Main St (66533-9001)
P.O. Box 787 (66533-0787)
PHONE..................................785 584-6251
Charles P Noell III, *Director*
EMP: 14
SALES (corp-wide): 14.5MM **Privately Held**
SIC: 8699 Charitable organization
PA: The Foundation For A Christian Civilization Inc
1358 Jefferson Rd
Spring Grove PA 17362
717 225-7197

(G-10253)
L C MCCLAIN INC (PA)
Also Called: Carquest Auto Parts
203 Perry St (66533-9761)
P.O. Box 218 (66533-0218)
PHONE..................................785 584-6151
Luther C McClain, *President*
Roger Braden, *Vice Pres*
Edith McClain, *Treasurer*
Rosella Feltner, *Admin Sec*
EMP: 10 **EST:** 1954
SQ FT: 2,600
SALES: 2.5MM **Privately Held**
SIC: 5531 5171 5541 5172 Automotive parts; petroleum bulk stations; gasoline service stations; gases, liquefied petroleum (propane); propane gas, bottled

(G-10254)
MODUS GROUP LLC
555 Nishnabe Trl (66533-9681)
PHONE..................................785 584-6057
Thomas Hoffman, *Mng Member*
Tom Hoffman, *Manager*
EMP: 20 **EST:** 2011
SALES (est): 2.2MM **Privately Held**
SIC: 1731 Electronic controls installation

(G-10255)
ROSSVILLE HEALTHCARE
600 Perry St (66533-9784)
PHONE..................................785 584-6104
George V Hager Jr,
EMP: 66
SALES: 5.8MM **Publicly Held**
WEB: www.rossville.net
SIC: 8051 Convalescent home with continuous nursing care
HQ: Genesis Healthcare Llc
101 E State St
Kennett Square PA 19348

(G-10256)
STORMONT-VAIL HEALTHCARE INC
Also Called: Cotton-O'neil Clinicrossville
423 Main St (66533-9803)
P.O. Box 86 (66533-0086)
PHONE..................................785 584-6705
EMP: 383
SALES (corp-wide): 719MM **Privately Held**
SIC: 8062 General medical & surgical hospitals
PA: Stormont-Vail Healthcare, Inc.
1500 Sw 10th Ave
Topeka KS 66604
785 354-6000

Roxbury
Mcpherson County

(G-10257)
SCOTTS WELL SERVICE INC
110 N Memory Ln (67476-7601)
P.O. Box 136 (67476-0136)
PHONE..................................785 254-7828
Jeff Scott, *President*
Jay Scott, *Vice Pres*
EMP: 7
SQ FT: 1,000
SALES (est): 765.5K **Privately Held**
SIC: 1389 Servicing oil & gas wells

Rozel
Pawnee County

(G-10258)
GOLDEN VALLEY INC (PA)
102 S Main (67574)
P.O. Box 68 (67574-0068)
PHONE..................................620 527-4216
Lee Olsen, *President*
EMP: 22
SQ FT: 3,500
SALES (est): 4.5MM **Privately Held**
SIC: 4221 5191 5541 Grain elevator, storage only; farm supplies; filling stations, gasoline

Rush Center
Rush County

(G-10259)
GOLDEN BELT TELEPHONE ASSN INC (PA)
103 Lincoln St (67575-3000)
P.O. Box 229 (67575-0229)
PHONE..................................785 372-4236
Beau Rebel, *General Mgr*
EMP: 33 **EST:** 1953
SQ FT: 2,078
SALES (est): 8.3MM **Privately Held**
WEB: www.gbta.net
SIC: 4813 Local telephone communications

(G-10260)
KBK INDUSTRIES LLC (PA)
1914 Highway 183 (67575-7714)
P.O. Box 216 (67575-0216)
PHONE..................................785 372-4331
William G Baalman, *President*
Bill Baalmann, *Chairman*
Scott Case, *Vice Pres*
Jay Muller, *Mfg Staff*
James Clements, *CFO*
▲ **EMP:** 125
SALES (est): 42.1MM **Privately Held**
SIC: 3443 7699 3088 Tanks, lined: metal plate; tank repair; plastics plumbing fixtures

(G-10261)
MID-STATE FARMERS CO-OP INC (PA)
819 W Un (67575)
P.O. Box 195 (67575-0195)
PHONE..................................785 372-4239
Craig Jecha, *President*
EMP: 14
SALES: 28MM **Privately Held**
WEB: www.midstatefarmerscoop.net
SIC: 0161 Vegetables & melons

(G-10262)
MR PS TRUCKN INC
102 E Florence (67575-7626)
PHONE..................................785 372-4371
Chad Folkerts, *President*
EMP: 20 **EST:** 2000
SALES (est): 1.4MM **Privately Held**
SIC: 4212 Local trucking, without storage

Russell
Russell County

(G-10263)
AGCO INC (PA)
913 N Fossil St (67665-3232)
P.O. Box 668 (67665-0668)
PHONE..................................785 483-2128
Dan Bernard, *General Mgr*
Dusty McGuire, *Buyer*
EMP: 12
SQ FT: 3,200
SALES (est): 25.3MM **Privately Held**
SIC: 5191 5153 4221 5541 Feed; fertilizer & fertilizer materials; grains; grain elevator, storage only; filling stations, gasoline; feed & farm supply

(G-10264)
ALLIANCE INC
255 S Vanhouten (67665)
P.O. Box 473 (67665-0473)
PHONE..................................785 445-3701
Mark Davis, *President*
Michelle Davis, *Corp Secy*
EMP: 6
SALES (est): 1.2MM **Privately Held**
SIC: 1389 Haulage, oil field

(G-10265)
ALLIED OF KANSAS INC (PA)
24 S Lincoln St (67665-2906)
P.O. Box 133366, Spring TX (77393-3366)
PHONE..................................785 483-2627
Steve Dreiling, *President*
Sylvia Newton, *Corp Secy*
Ronald Davis, *Vice Pres*
EMP: 11
SQ FT: 8,000
SALES (est): 8.1MM **Privately Held**
SIC: 1389 Cementing oil & gas well casings

(G-10266)
ALLIED OFS LLC
24 S Lincoln St (67665-2906)
PHONE..................................785 483-2627
Steve Orlando, *Branch Mgr*
EMP: 12
SALES (corp-wide): 13.5MM **Privately Held**
SIC: 1389 1382 Cementing oil & gas well casings; oil & gas exploration services
PA: Allied Ofs, Llc
11211 Fm 2920 Rd
Tomball TX 77375
832 482-3730

(G-10267)
BUCKEYE CORPORATION
Also Called: Buckeye Supply
1021 E Wichita Ave (67665)
P.O. Box 667 (67665-0667)
PHONE..................................785 483-3111
Rick Cross, *Manager*
EMP: 5
SALES (est): 408K
SALES (corp-wide): 8.9MM **Privately Held**
SIC: 5084 1311 5082 Oil well machinery, equipment & supplies; crude petroleum production; oil field equipment
PA: Buckeye Corporation
625 S Main St
El Dorado KS 67042
316 321-1060

(G-10268)
BURLINGAME WIRE PRODUCTS INC (PA)
Also Called: Abco Wire & Metal Products
535 S Front St (67665-3602)
P.O. Box 313 (67665-0313)
PHONE..................................785 483-3138
Dale J Silva, *President*
Diane Risher, *Human Res Mgr*
EMP: 15
SALES (est): 2.6MM **Privately Held**
SIC: 3496 Miscellaneous fabricated wire products

(G-10269)
COUNTY OF RUSSELL
Also Called: Russel County Ems
311 S Fossil St (67665-3031)
PHONE..................................785 445-3720
Alan Kuntzsch, *Commissioner*
EMP: 27 **Privately Held**
SIC: 4119 Ambulance service
PA: County Of Russell
401 N Main St
Russell KS 67665
785 483-4641

(G-10270)
COUNTY OF RUSSELL
Also Called: Highway Dept
4288 Us Highway 40 (67665-9019)
PHONE..................................785 483-4032
Kelly Branum, *Superintendent*
EMP: 25 **Privately Held**
SIC: 1611 9111 Highway & street maintenance; county supervisors' & executives' offices
PA: County Of Russell
401 N Main St
Russell KS 67665
785 483-4641

(G-10271)
DEVELOPMENTAL SVCS NW KANS INC
Also Called: Developmental Services NW KS
15 N Maple St (67665-2734)
PHONE..................................785 483-6686
Paula Donley, *Principal*
EMP: 17
SALES (corp-wide): 14.4MM **Privately Held**
SIC: 8322 8093 Rehabilitation services; rehabilitation center, outpatient treatment
PA: Developmental Services Of Northwest Kansas, Inc.
2703 Hall St Ste B10
Hays KS 67601
785 625-5678

(G-10272)
DEVELOPMENTAL SVCS NW KANS INC
1212 N Krug St (67665-1809)
PHONE..................................785 483-3020
Jamey Roth, *Manager*
EMP: 10
SALES (corp-wide): 14.4MM **Privately Held**
SIC: 8059 Home for the mentally retarded, exc. skilled or intermediate
PA: Developmental Services Of Northwest Kansas, Inc.
2703 Hall St Ste B10
Hays KS 67601
785 625-5678

(G-10273)
EAGLE COMMUNICATIONS INC
Also Called: Russell Cable TV
336 E Wichita Ave (67665-2133)
P.O. Box 871, Hays (67601-0871)
PHONE..................................785 483-3244
Pam Freund, *Manager*
EMP: 25
SALES (corp-wide): 71.7MM **Privately Held**
WEB: www.eaglecom.net
SIC: 4832 7313 4813 4841 Radio broadcasting stations; television & radio time sales; ; cable & other pay television services
PA: Eagle Communications, Inc.
2703 Hall St 15
Hays KS 67601
785 625-5910

(G-10274)
FOSSIL CREEK HOTEL & SUITES
1430 S Fossil St (67665-3611)
PHONE..................................785 483-4200
Heather Ross, *General Mgr*
EMP: 20 **EST:** 2011
SALES (est): 257.5K **Privately Held**
SIC: 7011 Hotels

(G-10275)
GLOBAL OILFIELD SERVICES LLC
Also Called: Oilfield Cementing
24 S Lincoln St (67665-2906)
PHONE..................................785 445-3525
Terry Wong, *Mng Member*
Heath Wong, *Mng Member*
EMP: 10
SQ FT: 15,000
SALES: 3MM **Privately Held**
SIC: 1389 Cementing oil & gas well casings

(G-10276)
GOODENCOFF & MALONE INC
Also Called: Gudenkauf, Pam CPA
639 N Main St (67665-1901)
P.O. Box 631 (67665-0631)
PHONE..................................785 483-6220
James Malone, *President*
Pam Goodencoff, *Vice Pres*
EMP: 11
SALES (est): 770.7K **Privately Held**
SIC: 8721 Accounting services, except auditing; certified public accountant

(G-10277)
JOHN O FARMER INC
370 W Wichita Ave (67665-2635)
P.O. Box 352 (67665-0352)
PHONE..................................785 483-3144
John O Farmer III, *President*
Ron G Feller, *Corp Secy*
John Farmer IV, *Vice Pres*
Rosemary Farmer, *Vice Pres*
Mary K Lyczak, *Vice Pres*
EMP: 16 **EST:** 1946
SQ FT: 3,000
SALES (est): 1.7MM **Privately Held**
WEB: www.johnofarmer.com
SIC: 1311 Crude petroleum production

(G-10278)
LAND OLAKES INC
1068 E 15th St (67665-2255)
PHONE..................................785 445-4030
James Colombo, *Manager*
EMP: 20
SALES (corp-wide): 6.8B **Privately Held**
WEB: www.landolakes.com
SIC: 5191 Feed
PA: Land O'lakes, Inc.
4001 Lexington Ave N
Arden Hills MN 55126
651 375-2222

(G-10279)
LO-MAR BOWLING SUPPLY INC
Also Called: Lo Mar Bowling Supply
341 S Fossil St (67665-3031)
P.O. Box 708 (67665-0708)
PHONE..................................785 483-2222
Joleen Lawson, *Vice Pres*
Loa J Boxberger, *Treasurer*
EMP: 17 **EST:** 1965
SQ FT: 15,000
SALES (est): 4.2MM **Privately Held**
WEB: www.lomarbowling.com
SIC: 5091 Bowling equipment

(G-10280)
MAI EXCAVATING INC
906 W Witt Ave (67665-8770)
PHONE..................................785 483-3387
Mike Mark MAI, *President*
Michael D MAI, *President*
Mark W MAI, *Vice Pres*
EMP: 9
SQ FT: 8,000
SALES (est): 999.5K **Privately Held**
SIC: 1389 4213 1623 Oil field services; trucking, except local; oil & gas pipeline construction

(G-10281)
MAIN STREET MEDIA INC
Also Called: Russell County News
958 E Wichita Ave (67665)
P.O. Box 513 (67665-0513)
PHONE..................................785 483-2116
Jack Krier, *President*
Kathy Krier, *Vice Pres*
EMP: 16
SQ FT: 5,000
SALES (est): 3.3MM **Privately Held**
SIC: 5192 Newspapers

(G-10282)
MURFIN DRILLING COMPANY INC
400 S Van Houten St (67665-9635)
P.O. Box 288 (67665-0288)
PHONE..................................785 483-5371
Stanley Froetschner, *Manager*
EMP: 20 **Privately Held**
SIC: 1381 1311 Drilling oil & gas wells; crude petroleum production
HQ: Murfin Drilling Company, Inc.
250 N Water St Ste 300
Wichita KS 67202
316 267-3241

(G-10283)
ONEOK INC
450 S Front St (67665-3036)
PHONE..................................785 483-2501
Andy Brown, *Branch Mgr*
EMP: 23
SALES (corp-wide): 12.5B **Publicly Held**
SIC: 4922 Natural gas transmission
PA: Oneok, Inc.
100 W 5th St Ste Ll
Tulsa OK 74103
918 588-7000

(G-10284)
PLAINS MARKETING LP
2559 Hwy 40 (67665)
P.O. Box 706 (67665-0706)
PHONE..................................785 483-3171
Jim Small, *Principal*
EMP: 19 **Publicly Held**
SIC: 4612 Crude petroleum pipelines
HQ: Plains Marketing, L.P.
333 Clay St Ste 1600
Houston TX 77002
713 646-4100

(G-10285)
QUALITY OILWELL CEMENTING INC
740 W Wichita Ave (67665-3327)
P.O. Box 32 (67665-0032)
PHONE..................................785 483-1071
David Funk, *President*
Richard McYintire, *Principal*
Jim Schoemberger, *Vice Pres*
David Brady, *Admin Sec*
EMP: 12
SALES (est): 1.3MM **Privately Held**
SIC: 1389 Cementing oil & gas well casings

(G-10286)
RADKE IMPLEMENT INC (PA)
Also Called: Kubota Authorized Dealer
3099 182nd St (67665-8819)
PHONE..................................620 935-4310
Harlan Radke, *President*
Marty Radke, *Vice Pres*
Monty MAI, *Parts Mgr*
Alane Radke, *Treasurer*
Cole Dinges, *Manager*
EMP: 11 **EST:** 1931
SQ FT: 12,200
SALES: 15.7MM **Privately Held**
WEB: www.radkeimplement.com
SIC: 5999 5083 Farm equipment & supplies; farm & garden machinery

(G-10287)
REINHARDT SERVICES INC
14th E Laray & S 281 Hwy (67665)
P.O. Box 601 (67665-0601)
PHONE..................................785 483-2556
Richard Pasek, *President*
Glenda Pasek, *Corp Secy*
EMP: 5
SALES (est): 810.3K **Privately Held**
SIC: 7353 5084 1389 Oil field equipment, rental or leasing; oil well machinery, equipment & supplies; oil field services

(G-10288)
REPUBLIC BANCSHARES INC (PA)
436 N Main St (67665-2732)
PHONE..................................785 483-2300
Vance Ruggels, *President*
Thurleen Ruggels, *President*
EMP: 10
SALES (est): 3.6MM **Privately Held**
WEB: www.united-national.net
SIC: 6712 Bank holding companies

(G-10289)
RESURRECTION HOSPITAL PHYSN CL
222 S Kansas St Ste E (67665-3029)
PHONE..................................785 483-3333
Michelle Peeland, *Manager*
Shelley Boden, *Director*
EMP: 30
SALES (est): 585.4K **Privately Held**
SIC: 8062 General medical & surgical hospitals

(G-10290)
RH MONTGOMERY PROPERTIES INC
Also Called: Wheatland Nursing Center
320 S Lincoln St (67665-2910)
PHONE..................................785 445-3732
Dianne Cohen, *Manager*
EMP: 48
SALES (corp-wide): 31.9MM **Privately Held**
SIC: 8051 Skilled nursing care facilities
PA: Rh Montgomery Properties, Inc.
214 N Scott St
Sikeston MO 63801
573 471-1113

(G-10291)
RONS WELDING & PIPELINE SVCS
18542 I 70 Rd (67665-8856)
PHONE..................................620 935-4275
Ron Wehling, *Owner*
EMP: 5
SALES (est): 602.3K **Privately Held**
SIC: 7692 Welding repair

(G-10292)
ROYAL DRILLING INC
719 W Witt Ave (67665-8703)
P.O. Box 342 (67665-0342)
PHONE..................................785 483-6446
Mitch Driscoll, *President*
Sherry Tayne, *Corp Secy*
John Driscoll, *Vice Pres*
EMP: 35
SALES (est): 2.9MM **Privately Held**
SIC: 1781 Water well drilling

(G-10293)
RURAL TELEPHONE SERVICE CO INC
Also Called: Telephone Cooperative
238 E Wichita Ave (67665-2040)
PHONE..................................785 483-5555
Larry Sevier, *CEO*
Jeffrey Wick, *COO*
EMP: 18
SALES (est): 964.4K
SALES (corp-wide): 174.9MM **Privately Held**
SIC: 4813 Local telephone communications
HQ: Nex-Tech, Llc
2418 Vine St
Hays KS 67601

(G-10294)
RUSSELL BLOCK COMPANY INC
Also Called: Puddle Jumpers Dive Shop
2123 Us Highway 40 (67665-9037)
P.O. Box 1000, Humboldt (66748-0900)
PHONE..................................785 483-6271
Fax: 785 483-6263
EMP: 11
SQ FT: 12,000
SALES (est): 1.3MM **Privately Held**
SIC: 3272 Mfg Concrete Products

(G-10295)
RUSSELL LIVESTOCK COMMISSION
51 S Fossil St (67665-3007)
PHONE..................................785 483-2961
Jay Sweeney, *President*
Margaret M Sweeney, *Treasurer*
EMP: 20
SQ FT: 60,000

SALES (est): 2.2MM Privately Held
WEB: www.russellks.org
SIC: 5154 Auctioning livestock

(G-10296)
RUSSELL LIVESTOCK LLC
720 S Fossil St (67665-3522)
PHONE..................................785 483-2961
Greg Crey, *Mng Member*
EMP: 30
SALES (est): 185.8K Privately Held
SIC: 5154 Auctioning livestock

(G-10297)
RUSSELL PUBLISHING CO (PA)
802 N Maple St (67665-1937)
P.O. Box 513 (67665-0513)
PHONE..................................785 483-2116
Jack Krier, *President*
Kathy Krier, *President*
EMP: 8
SALES (est): 999.5K Privately Held
WEB: www.russellpublishing.com
SIC: 2711 Newspapers, publishing & printing; commercial printing & newspaper publishing combined; job printing & newspaper publishing combined

(G-10298)
RUSSELLS AMERICA INN LLC
1430 S Fossil St (67665-3611)
PHONE..................................785 483-4200
Marylynn Meitler, *General Mgr*
EMP: 13
SALES (est): 559.7K Privately Held
SIC: 7011 Motel, franchised

(G-10299)
SHIELDS OIL PRODUCERS INC
326 N Main St (67665-2754)
P.O. Box 709 (67665-0709)
PHONE..................................785 483-3141
Richard L Shields, *President*
Bert Berry, *Superintendent*
Jack Beeman, *Corp Secy*
EMP: 41 EST: 1950
SQ FT: 6,000
SALES (est): 2.8MM Privately Held
SIC: 1311 1381 Crude petroleum production; drilling oil & gas wells

(G-10300)
UMB BANK NATIONAL ASSOCIATION
507 N Main St (67665-2703)
P.O. Box 713 (67665-0713)
PHONE..................................785 483-6800
John O Olarry, *Branch Mgr*
EMP: 10
SALES (corp-wide): 1.1B Publicly Held
WEB: www.umbwebsolutions.com
SIC: 6021 6282 National commercial banks; investment advice
HQ: Umb Bank, National Association
1010 Grand Blvd Fl 3
Kansas City MO 64106
816 842-2222

(G-10301)
UNITED NATIONAL BANK
436 N Main St (67665-2732)
P.O. Box 433 (67665-0433)
PHONE..................................785 483-2146
Vance Ruggels, *Manager*
EMP: 10
SALES (corp-wide): 3.6MM Privately Held
SIC: 6021 National commercial banks
HQ: United National Bank
702 N 2nd St
Natoma KS 67651
785 483-3006

(G-10302)
VINTAGE GROUP INC
Also Called: Vintage Place Assistant Living
1070 E Wichita Ave (67665-2409)
PHONE..................................785 483-5882
Jerri Willson, *Manager*
EMP: 20
SALES (corp-wide): 2MM Privately Held
SIC: 8051 Skilled nursing care facilities
PA: Vintage Group Inc
550 N 159th St E Ste 101
Wichita KS 67230
316 733-0690

(G-10303)
WEST CENTRAL KANSAS ASSN INC (PA)
Also Called: Russell Regional Hospital
200 S Main St (67665-2920)
PHONE..................................785 483-3131
Shelley Boden, *CEO*
Morris Krug, *Ch of Bd*
David Harrison, *Safety Dir*
Duane Fields, *CFO*
Alexander Chung, *Med Doctor*
EMP: 107
SQ FT: 88,000
SALES: 16.3MM Privately Held
WEB: www.russellhospital.org
SIC: 8062 8011 Hospital, professional nursing school; offices & clinics of medical doctors

Sabetha
Nemaha County

(G-10304)
ANCIENT FREE & ACCEPTED M
708 Jefferson St (66534-1726)
PHONE..................................785 284-3169
Edward Garber, *President*
EMP: 40
SALES (est): 334.4K Privately Held
SIC: 8641 Fraternal associations

(G-10305)
APOSTOLIC CHRISTIAN HOME
511 Paramount St (66534-2199)
P.O. Box 97 (66534-0097)
PHONE..................................785 284-3471
Donna Edelman, *Human Res Dir*
Ramona Strahn, *Human Res Dir*
Julie Welch, *Office Mgr*
John E Lehman, *Director*
Chris Grote, *Nursing Dir*
EMP: 150
SQ FT: 140,000
SALES: 9.1MM Privately Held
WEB: www.apostolicsabetha.com
SIC: 8059 8052 8051 Rest home, with health care; home for the mentally retarded, with health care; skilled nursing care facilities

(G-10306)
BANK OF BLUE VALLEY
21 Main St (66534-2322)
P.O. Box 209 (66534-0209)
PHONE..................................785 284-3433
Joni Tangeman, *Sales Executive*
Kurt Saylor, *Manager*
EMP: 16 Publicly Held
WEB: www.mjbtrc.com
SIC: 6022 State trust companies accepting deposits, commercial
HQ: Bank Of Blue Valley
11935 Riley St
Overland Park KS 66213
913 338-1000

(G-10307)
BERWICK COOPERATIVE OIL CO (PA)
Also Called: Berwick Oil
1111 S Us Old Highway 75 (66534-9401)
PHONE..................................785 284-2227
Mike Sadler, *General Mgr*
EMP: 10
SQ FT: 1,500
SALES (est): 6.4MM Privately Held
WEB: www.berwickoil.com
SIC: 5171 5984 Petroleum bulk stations; liquefied petroleum gas dealers

(G-10308)
C W MILL EQUIPMENT CO INC
Also Called: Hogzilla Grinders
14 Commerce Dr (66534-9413)
P.O. Box 246 (66534-0246)
PHONE..................................785 284-3454
Tim Wenger, *President*
John Wenger, *Vice Pres*
Amy Bergman, *Manager*
Brian Bergman, *Executive*
EMP: 30
SQ FT: 24,000
SALES (est): 17.8MM Privately Held
WEB: www.hogzilla.com
SIC: 5084 Industrial machinery & equipment

(G-10309)
EXTRU-TECH INC
100 Airport Rd (66534-9418)
P.O. Box 8 (66534-0008)
PHONE..................................785 284-2153
La Von Wenger, *President*
Scott Krebs, *Exec VP*
Paul Tedman, *Exec VP*
R Scott Krebs, *Vice Pres*
R Krebs, *Vice Pres*
▲ EMP: 80
SQ FT: 56,000
SALES: 40MM
SALES (corp-wide): 50.6MM Privately Held
WEB: www.extru-techinc.com
SIC: 3523 3556 Feed grinders, crushers & mixers; food products machinery
PA: Wenger Manufacturing Inc.
15 Commerce Dr
Sabetha KS 66534
785 284-2133

(G-10310)
FARMERS COOPERATIVE ELEV INC (PA)
204 N 9th St (66534-1700)
PHONE..................................785 284-2185
Dan Brubeck, *General Mgr*
EMP: 12 EST: 1919
SQ FT: 4,000
SALES: 18.5MM Privately Held
SIC: 5153 5191 5411 Grains; feed; fertilizer & fertilizer materials; seeds: field, garden & flower; convenience stores

(G-10311)
GREAT PLAINS HLTH ALIANCE INC
14th & Oregon St (66534)
PHONE..................................785 284-2121
Lora Key, *Branch Mgr*
EMP: 55
SALES (corp-wide): 112.9MM Privately Held
WEB: www.gpha.com
SIC: 8062 General medical & surgical hospitals
PA: Great Plains Health Alliance, Inc.
625 3rd St
Phillipsburg KS 67661
785 543-2111

(G-10312)
GREAT PLAINS OF SABETHA INC
Also Called: Sabetha Community Hospital
14th And Oregon Sts (66534)
P.O. Box 229 (66534-0229)
PHONE..................................785 284-2121
Lora Key, *CEO*
Jianna Zahner, *COO*
Keith Lackey, *Facilities Dir*
Lori A Lakey, *CFO*
Julie Holthaus, *Human Res Mgr*
EMP: 120
SALES: 10.7MM
SALES (corp-wide): 112.9MM Privately Held
SIC: 8062 General medical & surgical hospitals
PA: Great Plains Health Alliance, Inc.
625 3rd St
Phillipsburg KS 67661
785 543-2111

(G-10313)
HERALD SABETHA INC
1024 Main St (66534-1831)
P.O. Box 208 (66534-0208)
PHONE..................................785 284-3300
Brian McDaniel, *President*
Ralph D Tennal, *President*
Tim Kellenberger, *Publisher*
Ruth I Tennal, *Admin Sec*
EMP: 7
SQ FT: 2,000
SALES (est): 506.6K Privately Held
SIC: 2711 Commercial printing & newspaper publishing combined; newspapers, publishing & printing

(G-10314)
KSI CONVEYOR INC (PA)
2345 U Rd (66534-2591)
PHONE..................................785 284-0600
Paul Kaeb, *President*
Harvey Kaeb, *COO*
Hartzell Kaeb, *Vice Pres*
Neal Kellenberger, *CFO*
Doug Wertenberger, *Sales Staff*
EMP: 52
SQ FT: 50,000
SALES: 34MM Privately Held
WEB: www.ksiconveyors.com
SIC: 3523 Farm machinery & equipment

(G-10315)
LAKESIDE TERRACE
1100 Harrison St (66534-1633)
PHONE..................................785 284-0005
Sheila Mosher, *Manager*
EMP: 23
SALES: 818.8K Privately Held
WEB: www.lakesideterrace.net
SIC: 8361 Home for the mentally handicapped

(G-10316)
LANG DIESEL INC
15 N Old 75 Hwy (66534)
PHONE..................................785 284-3401
Clinton Lambotte, *Manager*
EMP: 10
SALES (corp-wide): 7.8MM Privately Held
SIC: 5083 Agricultural machinery & equipment
PA: Lang Diesel, Inc.
2818 Plaza Ave
Hays KS 67601
785 301-2426

(G-10317)
MAC EQUIPMENT INC
Also Called: Mac Process
810 S Old 75 Hwy (66534)
P.O. Box 205 (66534-0205)
PHONE..................................785 284-2191
Gary Cavey, *CEO*
Joel Luzmoor, *Safety Mgr*
Nathan Hemman, *Engineer*
David Rieschick, *Engineer*
Diane Ward, *Accountant*
EMP: 12
SALES (est): 2.4MM Privately Held
SIC: 5075 3535 3564 Air filters; conveyors & conveying equipment; purification & dust collection equipment

(G-10318)
MEL RICK INC
P.O. Box 33 (66534-0033)
PHONE..................................785 284-3577
Richard Bestwick, *Principal*
EMP: 12
SALES (est): 1.2MM Privately Held
SIC: 4213 Trucking, except local

(G-10319)
MID WEST READY MIX & BLDG SUPS (PA)
Also Called: Midwest Ready Mix & Bldg Sup
926 Grant St (66534-1819)
PHONE..................................785 284-2911
Dennis Meyer, *President*
Ryan Meyer, *Treasurer*
Gary Meyer, *Admin Sec*
EMP: 9 EST: 1958
SQ FT: 5,500
SALES (est): 1.3MM Privately Held
SIC: 3273 Ready-mixed concrete

(G-10320)
NEMAHA COUNTY COMMUNITY HLTH
1004 Main St (66534-1831)
P.O. Box 146 (66534-0146)
PHONE..................................785 284-2152
Jane Sunderland, *Director*
EMP: 17
SALES: 586.3K Privately Held
SIC: 8011 General & family practice, physician/surgeon

▲ = Import ▼=Export
◆ =Import/Export

(G-10321)
NEMAHA COUNTY TRAINING CENTER
Also Called: Nctc
329 N 11th St (66534-1711)
PHONE..................................785 300-1306
Susan Futcher, *Manager*
EMP: 12
SALES (est): 284.2K
SALES (corp-wide): 2MM **Privately Held**
SIC: 8331 Job training services
PA: Nemaha County Training Center Inc
12 S 11th St
Seneca KS 66538
785 336-6116

(G-10322)
NORTHRIDGE FAMILY DEV CTR
316 Lincoln St (66534)
PHONE..................................785 284-2401
Jocelyn Dunmire, *Partner*
EMP: 20
SALES: 269.1K **Privately Held**
SIC: 8351 Child day care services

(G-10323)
NORTHWIND TECHNICAL SVCS LLC
2751 Antelope Rd (66534-9635)
PHONE..................................785 284-0080
Michael A Bosworth, *President*
Marlene Bosworth, *Vice Pres*
Marlene K Bosworth, *Admin Sec*
Jason Steiner, *Technician*
EMP: 16
SQ FT: 7,500
SALES: 650K **Privately Held**
WEB: www.northwindts.com
SIC: 8711 Consulting engineer

(G-10324)
RH MONTGOMERY PROPERTIES INC
Also Called: Sabetha Manor Nursing Rehabili
1441 Oregon St (66534-2134)
PHONE..................................785 284-3411
Laurie Riger, *Administration*
EMP: 50
SALES (corp-wide): 31.9MM **Privately Held**
SIC: 8051 Skilled nursing care facilities
PA: Rh Montgomery Properties, Inc.
214 N Scott St
Sikeston MO 63801
573 471-1113

(G-10325)
RH MONTGOMERY PROPERTIES INC
Also Called: Sabetha Residential Care Ctr
913 Dakota St (66534-2008)
PHONE..................................785 284-3418
Laurie Rieger, *Administration*
EMP: 12
SALES (corp-wide): 31.9MM **Privately Held**
SIC: 8361 Residential care
PA: Rh Montgomery Properties, Inc.
214 N Scott St
Sikeston MO 63801
573 471-1113

(G-10326)
RNW TRANSIT LLC
2436 168th Rd (66534-2232)
PHONE..................................785 285-0083
Rixey Wertenberger, *Principal*
EMP: 12
SALES (est): 514.2K **Privately Held**
SIC: 4111 Local & suburban transit

(G-10327)
SABETHA COUNTRY INN INC
1473 S 75 Hwy (66534)
PHONE..................................785 284-2300
Mary Kay Winger, *Admin Sec*
EMP: 25
SALES (est): 448K **Privately Held**
SIC: 7011 Motels

(G-10328)
SABETHA GOLF CLUB INC
2551 X Rd (66534-9481)
P.O. Box 27 (66534-0027)
PHONE..................................785 284-2023
John Pierson, *President*
EMP: 10 **EST:** 1923
SQ FT: 3,750
SALES (est): 270.3K **Privately Held**
SIC: 7997 Golf club, membership

(G-10329)
SABETHA MANOR INCORPORATED
Also Called: SABETHA NURSING & REHAB CENTER
1441 Oregon St (66534-2198)
PHONE..................................785 284-3411
Lori Reiger, *Director*
EMP: 43
SALES: 2.4MM **Privately Held**
SIC: 8052 Intermediate care facilities

(G-10330)
SCHENCK ACCURATE INC
P.O. Box 205 (66534-0205)
PHONE..................................262 473-2441
EMP: 6
SALES (est): 1.3MM **Privately Held**
SIC: 3535 Conveyors & conveying equipment

(G-10331)
SCHENCK PROCESS LLC
810 S Us Old 75 Hwy (66534)
P.O. Box 205 (66534-0205)
PHONE..................................785 284-2191
Dwight Edelman, *Plant Mgr*
Linda Montgomery, *Engineer*
Holly Snyder, *Accountant*
Charlotte McElroy, *Human Res Mgr*
Fred Beckers, *Manager*
EMP: 200
SALES (corp-wide): 177.9K **Privately Held**
SIC: 3535 3564 5084 Pneumatic tube conveyor systems; dust or fume collecting equipment, industrial; pneumatic tools & equipment
HQ: Schenck Process Llc
7901 Nw 107th Ter
Kansas City MO 64153
816 891-9300

(G-10332)
SCOOTERS LLC
1008 Main St (66534-1831)
PHONE..................................785 284-2978
Scott McGuire, *Owner*
EMP: 15
SALES (est): 203.5K **Privately Held**
SIC: 8641 Civic social & fraternal associations

(G-10333)
T S KEIM INC (PA)
Also Called: Keim T S
1249 N Ninth St (66534)
P.O. Box 226 (66534-0226)
PHONE..................................785 284-2147
Stan Keim, *President*
Randy Hoffman, *General Mgr*
Sam Keim, *Vice Pres*
Peggy Moore, *Safety Dir*
Paul Herl, *CFO*
EMP: 202 **EST:** 1955
SQ FT: 15,000
SALES (est): 50.8MM **Privately Held**
SIC: 4213 Building materials transport

(G-10334)
TRIPLE C MANUFACTURING INC
902 Hwy K 246 (66534)
P.O. Box 248 (66534-0248)
PHONE..................................785 284-3674
Don Bickel, *President*
Brian Nelson, *President*
Mark Jackman, *Purchasing*
EMP: 25
SQ FT: 25,000
SALES: 7MM **Privately Held**
SIC: 3523 Farm machinery & equipment

(G-10335)
UNITED BANK & TRUST
511 Paramount St (66534-2120)
P.O. Box E (66534-0136)
PHONE..................................785 284-2187
Tale Cook, *President*
Holly Wisdom, *Manager*
EMP: 10 **Privately Held**
SIC: 6022 State commercial banks
PA: United Bank & Trust
2333 Broadway
Marysville KS 66508

(G-10336)
USC LLC
Also Called: Universal Consulting & Svcs
2320 124th Rd (66534-9459)
PHONE..................................785 431-7900
Jim Renyer, *Mng Member*
Andy Renyer,
Eric Sevatson,
EMP: 15 **EST:** 1998
SQ FT: 1,400
SALES (est): 8.2MM **Privately Held**
WEB: www.uscllc.com
SIC: 3523 Farm machinery & equipment

(G-10337)
WENGER MANUFACTURING INC (PA)
15 Commerce Dr (66534-8400)
P.O. Box 130 (66534-0130)
PHONE..................................785 284-2133
Lavon G Wenger, *Ch of Bd*
Donald L Wenger, *Exec VP*
Mike Strahm, *Vice Pres*
John Pierson, *CFO*
Scott Angell, *Planning*
◆ **EMP:** 200 **EST:** 1943
SQ FT: 253,000
SALES (est): 50.6MM **Privately Held**
WEB: www.wenger.com
SIC: 3556 Food products machinery

Saint Francis
Cheyenne County

(G-10338)
CALLICRATE CATTLE CO LLC
Also Called: Callicrate Feed Yard
940 Road 12 (67756-5784)
P.O. Box 748 (67756-0748)
PHONE..................................785 332-3344
Mike Callicrate,
EMP: 17
SALES (est): 1.5MM **Privately Held**
WEB: www.bornandraisedintheusa.com
SIC: 0212 Beef cattle except feedlots

(G-10339)
CHEYENNE COUNTY HOSPITAL (PA)
210 W 1st St (67756-3540)
P.O. Box 547 (67756-0547)
PHONE..................................785 332-2104
Scott Jenkins, *CEO*
Heidi Tice, *CFO*
Brooke Lohr, *Lab Dir*
Emily Loyd, *Radiology Dir*
EMP: 72
SALES: 7.6MM **Privately Held**
WEB: www.cheyennecountyhospital.com
SIC: 8062 General medical & surgical hospitals

(G-10340)
CHEYENNE COUNTY HOSPITAL
221 W 1st St (67756-3540)
P.O. Box 1075 (67756-1075)
PHONE..................................785 332-2682
Leslie Lacy, *Branch Mgr*
EMP: 20
SALES (corp-wide): 7.6MM **Privately Held**
SIC: 8011 Clinic, operated by physicians
PA: Cheyenne County Hospital
210 W 1st St
Saint Francis KS 67756
785 332-2104

(G-10341)
EVANGELICAL LUTHERAN
Also Called: Good Samaritan NW KS Home
217 Us Highway 36 (67756-5934)
PHONE..................................785 332-3588
Celeste Hays, *Branch Mgr*
EMP: 116 **Privately Held**
SIC: 8051 8052 Convalescent home with continuous nursing care; intermediate care facilities
HQ: The Evangelical Lutheran Good Samaritan Society
4800 W 57th St
Sioux Falls SD 57108
866 928-1635

(G-10342)
GREAT PLAINS HLTH ALIANCE INC
210 W 1st St (67756-3540)
P.O. Box 547 (67756-0547)
PHONE..................................785 332-2104
Les Lacy, *Administration*
EMP: 72
SALES (corp-wide): 112.9MM **Privately Held**
WEB: www.gpha.com
SIC: 8062 General medical & surgical hospitals
PA: Great Plains Health Alliance, Inc.
625 3rd St
Phillipsburg KS 67661
785 543-2111

(G-10343)
NOR WEST NEWSPAPER INC
Also Called: St Francis Herald
310 W Washington St (67756-9606)
P.O. Box 1050 (67756-1050)
PHONE..................................785 332-3162
Steve Haynes, *President*
Karen Krien, *Principal*
EMP: 5 **EST:** 1974
SALES (est): 279K **Privately Held**
SIC: 2711 Newspapers

(G-10344)
RIVERSIDE RECREATION ASSN
W Hwy 36 (67756)
P.O. Box 872 (67756-0872)
PHONE..................................785 332-3401
Troy Hilt, *President*
Richard Grace, *Vice Pres*
EMP: 18
SQ FT: 8,000
SALES: 168K **Privately Held**
SIC: 7997 5812 Country club, membership; restaurant, family: independent

(G-10345)
ROSS MANUFACTURING INC
301 W Washington St (67756-5686)
P.O. Box 1191 (67756-1191)
PHONE..................................785 332-3012
Gordon Ross, *President*
Carol Ross, *Vice Pres*
EMP: 5
SALES (est): 1.7MM **Privately Held**
WEB: www.rossmanufacturing.com
SIC: 3841 Veterinarians' instruments & apparatus

Saint George
Pottawatomie County

(G-10346)
DUKE AERIAL INC
11080 Legion Dr (66535-9467)
PHONE..................................785 494-8001
Kevin Embrey, *Branch Mgr*
Sally Thelen, *Manager*
EMP: 13 **Privately Held**
SIC: 7353 Cranes & aerial lift equipment, rental or leasing
PA: Duke Aerial, Inc.
65037 Boston Rd
Atlantic IA 50022

(G-10347)
FRUGAL INC
Also Called: Network Computer Solutions
3625 Legion Ln (66535-9630)
P.O. Box 852, Manhattan (66505-0852)
PHONE..................................785 776-9088
Aaron Adams, *President*
Jennifer Boos, *Manager*
Sandra Adams, *Admin Sec*
EMP: 9
SQ FT: 5,000
SALES (est): 2.4MM **Privately Held**
WEB: www.ncs-online.com
SIC: 3825 Network analyzers

(G-10348)
VANNAHMEN CONSTRUCTION INC
3541 Vineyard Rd (66535-9482)
P.O. Box 1081, Manhattan (66505-1081)
PHONE....................785 494-2354
Landon Vannahmen, *President*
Marlena Vannahmen, *Admin Sec*
EMP: 20
SALES (est): 950K **Privately Held**
SIC: 1771 Concrete work

Saint John
Stafford County

(G-10349)
AMERICAN STATE BANK & TRUST CO
216 N Main St (67576-1938)
P.O. Box 158 (67576-0158)
PHONE....................620 549-3244
Don Hildabrand, *Manager*
EMP: 14
SALES (corp-wide): 28.4MM **Privately Held**
WEB: www.americanstatebankna.com
SIC: 6022 State commercial banks
PA: American State Bank & Trust Company
1321 Main St Ste A
Great Bend KS 67530
620 793-5900

(G-10350)
DUDREY CATTLE CO INC
802 E 1st Ave (67576-2245)
P.O. Box 65 (67576-0065)
PHONE....................620 549-3234
Carl Dudrey, *President*
EMP: 10 **EST:** 1975
SALES (est): 804.8K **Privately Held**
SIC: 0211 Beef cattle feedlots

(G-10351)
GOLDEN BELT FEEDERS INC (PA)
1149 Nw 10th Ave (67576-8704)
P.O. Box 307 (67576-0307)
PHONE....................620 549-3241
Merlin D Grimes, *President*
Chuck White, *President*
Stan Kaiser, *COO*
Nelva D Grimes, *Vice Pres*
Tessa Lickiss, *Finance Mgr*
EMP: 53 **EST:** 1968
SQ FT: 2,000
SALES (est): 8.7MM **Privately Held**
WEB: www.goldenbeltfeeders.com
SIC: 0211 0115 0111 Beef cattle feedlots; corn; wheat

(G-10352)
HUTCHINSON CLINIC PA
Also Called: St John Clinic
609 E 1st Ave (67576-2223)
PHONE....................620 486-2985
Fax: 620 549-3853
EMP: 13
SALES (corp-wide): 43.9MM **Privately Held**
SIC: 8011 Medical Doctor's Office
PA: Hutchinson Clinic, P.A.
2101 N Waldron St
Hutchinson KS 67502
620 669-2500

(G-10353)
JOE ROSENBERG DDS
Also Called: Rosenberg, Joe O
205 N Santa Fe St (67576-2029)
PHONE....................620 285-3886
Joe Rosenberg, *Owner*
EMP: 11
SALES (est): 656K **Privately Held**
SIC: 8021 Dentists' office

(G-10354)
KENWOOD PLAZA INC
Also Called: Vintage Companies
607 E 1st Ave (67576-2223)
PHONE....................620 549-6133
Angela Heape, *Administration*
EMP: 18
SALES (est): 761.4K **Privately Held**
SIC: 8361 Home for the aged

(G-10355)
LEISURE HOMESTEAD AT ST JOHN
Also Called: LEISURE HOMESTEAD AT STAFFORD
402 N Santa Fe St (67576-1800)
PHONE....................620 549-3541
Jennifer Gillespee, *Director*
EMP: 30 **EST:** 2000
SALES: 1.7MM **Privately Held**
SIC: 8051 Skilled nursing care facilities

(G-10356)
SJN BANC CO
116 E 3rd Ave (67576-2032)
P.O. Box 68 (67576-0068)
PHONE....................620 549-3225
Chad D Fisher, *Principal*
EMP: 17 **EST:** 2011
SALES (est): 5MM **Privately Held**
SIC: 6022 State commercial banks

(G-10357)
SJN BANK OF KANSAS (PA)
116 E 3rd Ave (67576-2032)
P.O. Box 68 (67576-0068)
PHONE....................620 549-3225
Brenda Reno, *Exec VP*
J D Hager, *Vice Pres*
Kristin Burgan, *Vice Pres*
Lisa Minnis, *Officer*
EMP: 10 **EST:** 1905
SALES: 4.6MM **Privately Held**
WEB: www.sjnbsj.com
SIC: 6022 State commercial banks

Saint Marys
Pottawatomie County

(G-10358)
ANDAX INDUSTRIES LLC
613 W Palmer St (66536-1629)
PHONE....................785 437-0604
Jim Bunn, *Sales Mgr*
Chad Bordelon, *Sales Staff*
Robin Sullivan, *Sales Associate*
Brenda Meairs, *Mktg Dir*
Patrick McAtarian, *Mng Member*
EMP: 40
SALES (est): 39.3MM **Privately Held**
WEB: www.andax.com
SIC: 5172 4959 Petroleum products; oil spill cleanup

(G-10359)
COIL SPRINGS SPECIALTIES LLC
632 W Bertrand Ave (66536-1654)
PHONE....................785 437-2025
Matthew Rioux, *Production*
Gregory Pflum, *Mng Member*
Kevin Crane, *Manager*
EMP: 9
SQ FT: 3,200
SALES (est): 1.7MM **Privately Held**
WEB: www.coilsprings.com
SIC: 3495 Wire springs

(G-10360)
COMMUNITY HEALTHCARE SYS INC
Also Called: Community Hospital Onaga
206 S Grand Ave (66536-1637)
PHONE....................785 437-3407
Tonya Bush, *Office Mgr*
EMP: 300
SALES (corp-wide): 28.4MM **Privately Held**
SIC: 8062 Hospital, affiliated with AMA residency
PA: Community Healthcare System, Inc.
120 W 8th St
Onaga KS 66521
785 889-4274

(G-10361)
COMMUNITY HEALTHCARE SYS INC
Also Called: Saint Marys Manor
206 S Grand Ave (66536-1637)
PHONE....................785 437-3734
Annette Engell, *Office Mgr*
Michael Bonderger, *Manager*
Roger McAsey, *Director*
Kim Wild, *Director*
Carol Wells, *Food Svc Dir*
EMP: 100
SALES (corp-wide): 28.4MM **Privately Held**
SIC: 8051 Skilled nursing care facilities
PA: Community Healthcare System, Inc.
120 W 8th St
Onaga KS 66521
785 889-4274

(G-10362)
EMOTORPRO (PA)
Also Called: Line Central
27010 Highway 24 (66536-9803)
PHONE....................785 437-2046
Robert Wiemann, *Director*
Ken Moats,
Tom Hoffman,
Christopher Johnson,
▲ **EMP:** 15
SALES (est): 3.3MM **Privately Held**
WEB: www.linecentral.com
SIC: 5063 5032 Motors, electric; granite building stone

(G-10363)
EVERGY KANSAS CENTRAL INC
Also Called: Kpl Gas Service
25905 Jeffrey Rd (66536-9609)
PHONE....................785 456-6125
Geoffrey Greene, *Opers Staff*
Dave Nuefeld, *Manager*
EMP: 325
SALES (corp-wide): 4.2B **Publicly Held**
SIC: 4911 Generation, electric power
HQ: Evergy Kansas Central, Inc.
818 S Kansas Ave
Topeka KS 66612
785 575-6300

(G-10364)
FIRST NATIONAL BANK CLIFTON
414 W Bertrand Ave (66536-1617)
P.O. Box C (66536-0076)
PHONE....................785 437-6585
Ed Martin, *Branch Mgr*
EMP: 15
SALES (corp-wide): 2.3MM **Privately Held**
SIC: 6021 National commercial banks
PA: First National Bank Of Clifton
103 E Parallel St
Clifton KS
785 437-6585

(G-10365)
FOX CERAMIC TILE INC
916 E Jesuit Ln (66536-9624)
P.O. Box 97 (66536-0097)
PHONE....................785 437-2792
Kevin Fox, *President*
Janie Quiett, *Admin Sec*
▲ **EMP:** 35
SQ FT: 4,650
SALES: 3MM **Privately Held**
SIC: 1771 1743 1542 Flooring contractor; terrazzo, tile, marble, mosaic work; commercial & office building contractors

(G-10366)
J B PEARL SALES & SVC INC (PA)
27425 Highway 24 (66536-9700)
P.O. Box 128 (66536-0128)
PHONE....................785 437-2772
Toll Free:....................877 -
Doyle Pearl, *General Mgr*
Don Pearl, *Vice Pres*
Laura Pearl, *Treasurer*
Patty Pearl, *Admin Sec*
EMP: 22 **EST:** 1961
SQ FT: 1,800
SALES: 10MM **Privately Held**
WEB: www.jbpearl.com
SIC: 5191 Chemicals, agricultural; fertilizer & fertilizer materials

(G-10367)
JEFFREY ENERGY
25905 Jeffrey Rd (66536-9609)
PHONE....................785 456-2035
Chuck Hodson, *Principal*
▲ **EMP:** 13 **EST:** 2008
SALES (est): 1.3MM **Privately Held**
SIC: 4911 Distribution, electric power

(G-10368)
K G MOATS & SONS LLC
27010 Highway 24 (66536-9803)
PHONE....................785 437-2021
Tom Hoffman, *Engineer*
Ken Moats, *Mng Member*
Isaac A Moats,
Mary A Moats,
Nicholas Moats,
EMP: 22
SQ FT: 12,500
SALES: 4MM **Privately Held**
WEB: www.kgmoats.com
SIC: 3625 3613 7373 3577 Motor control accessories, including overload relays; control panels, electric; computer integrated systems design; computer peripheral equipment

(G-10369)
KAW VALLEY STATE BANK & TR CO
414 W Bertrand Ave (66536-1617)
PHONE....................785 437-6585
Edward Martin, *Branch Mgr*
EMP: 18
SALES (corp-wide): 8.4MM **Privately Held**
SIC: 6022 State commercial banks
PA: Kaw Valley State Bank & Trust Co
1015 Kaw Valley Park Cir
Wamego KS 66547
785 456-2025

(G-10370)
KOLDE CONSTRUCTION INC
28630 Highway 24 (66536-9708)
PHONE....................785 437-3730
Joseph Kolde, *President*
Michael Kolde, *Vice Pres*
Jeremy Garrett, *Project Mgr*
Johnny Ingram, *Project Engr*
Mark Hall, *Manager*
EMP: 45
SALES: 7MM **Privately Held**
SIC: 1771 Concrete work

(G-10371)
LENERE LLC
1213 N Pawnee Dr (66536-9774)
PHONE....................785 320-0208
Shardy Diamantia,
EMP: 13
SALES (est): 75.6K **Privately Held**
SIC: 8082 7349 Home health care services; building & office cleaning services

(G-10372)
LIVEWATCH SECURITY LLC
522 W Bertrand Ave (66536-1695)
P.O. Box 219 (66536-0219)
PHONE....................785 844-2130
Chris Johnson, *Branch Mgr*
Matthew Castle, *Consultant*
Maria Dvorak, *Consultant*
Syed Hussaini, *Consultant*
Robert Murphy, *Consultant*
EMP: 12 **Publicly Held**
SIC: 7381 Security guard service
HQ: Livewatch Security, Llc
620 Davis St 2f
Evanston IL 60201
855 548-3928

(G-10373)
REZAC SALES BARN
27425 W Drew Rd (66536-9735)
P.O. Box 6 (66536-0006)
PHONE....................785 437-2785
Dennis L Rezac, *President*
Kenneth Rezac, *Vice Pres*
Howard Rezac, *Treasurer*

▲ = Import ▼=Export
◆ =Import/Export

Nancy Rezac, *Admin Sec*
EMP: 25
SQ FT: 4,000
SALES (est): 4.4MM **Privately Held**
SIC: 5154 Auctioning livestock

(G-10374)
ROLL PRODUCTS INC
Also Called: Label Express/Excel Brand
511 W Palmer St (66536-1627)
P.O. Box 10 (66536-0010)
PHONE..................................785 437-6000
Dudley E Latham III, *President*
Andrew Latham, *Exec VP*
Del Latham, *Vice Pres*
Kathleen B Latham, *Vice Pres*
EMP: 16 **EST:** 1976
SALES (est): 3.4MM **Privately Held**
WEB: www.rpikansas.com
SIC: 2672 2679 Labels (unprinted), gummed: made from purchased materials; tape, pressure sensitive: made from purchased materials; paper products, converted

(G-10375)
SARTO COUNTERTOPS
930 E Jesuit Ln (66536-9624)
PHONE..................................785 437-3344
Robert Weimann, *Co-Owner*
EMP: 50
SALES (est): 46.1K **Privately Held**
SIC: 0782 Lawn & garden services

(G-10376)
ST MARYS LITERARY CLUB
101 E Lasley St (66536-1753)
PHONE..................................785 437-6418
Laura Pearl, *Principal*
Barbara Denton, *Principal*
Claire Pearl, *Principal*
Cindy Sweany, *Principal*
EMP: 30
SALES (est): 540K **Privately Held**
SIC: 8641 Social club, membership

(G-10377)
ST MARYS STATE BANK (HQ)
Also Called: ROSSVILLE STATE BANK
905 E Bertrand Ave (66536-1655)
P.O. Box 188 (66536-0188)
PHONE..................................785 437-2271
Brian Vaubel, *President*
James Mees, *Vice Pres*
Stephen M Mees, *Vice Pres*
Mark Metzler, *Vice Pres*
Lora Wehrly, *Director*
EMP: 29 **EST:** 1927
SALES: 4.5MM **Privately Held**
WEB: www.smsb.org
SIC: 6022 State commercial banks

Saint Paul
Neosho County

(G-10378)
A PLUS CONSTRUCTION LLC
107 Saint Joseph St (66771-4093)
P.O. Box 278 (66771-0278)
PHONE..................................620 212-4029
Charles R Brown,
Derek Nally,
EMP: 26
SALES (est): 383.2K **Privately Held**
SIC: 7389

(G-10379)
B & B BRIDGES COMPANY LLC
411 6th St (66771-4111)
P.O. Box 38 (66771-0038)
PHONE..................................620 449-2286
EMP: 14
SALES (est): 1.9MM **Privately Held**
SIC: 1611 General contractor, highway & street construction

(G-10380)
BEACHNER BROS (KANSAS) INC (PA)
6th & Central (66771)
P.O. Box 128 (66771-0128)
PHONE..................................620 449-2286
Eugene Beachner, *President*
Robert F Beachner, *Corp Secy*
Jerry Beachner, *Vice Pres*
William Beachner, *Vice Pres*
EMP: 10
SQ FT: 5,000
SALES (est): 1MM **Privately Held**
SIC: 0191 0291 General farms, primarily crop; livestock farm, general

(G-10381)
INDUSTRIAL CRATING INC
413 N Front St (66771)
P.O. Box 248 (66771-0248)
PHONE..................................620 449-2003
Christopher Carter, *President*
Mac Clasen, *Sales Mgr*
EMP: 35
SQ FT: 80,000
SALES (est): 5MM **Privately Held**
SIC: 2448 2441 Pallets, wood; nailed wood boxes & shook

(G-10382)
OBRIEN ROCK COMPANY INC (PA)
712 Central St (66771-4040)
P.O. Box 217 (66771-0217)
PHONE..................................620 449-2257
Louis O'Brien, *President*
Felix O'Brien, *Vice Pres*
Joseph Jay O'Brien, *Treasurer*
EMP: 55 **EST:** 1946
SQ FT: 1,950
SALES (est): 9.6MM **Privately Held**
SIC: 3273 1442 Ready-mixed concrete; construction sand & gravel

(G-10383)
OSAGE HILLS INC
8520 Wallace Rd (66771)
P.O. Box 284 (66771-0284)
PHONE..................................620 449-2713
Wade Laforte, *President*
EMP: 13
SALES: 63.4K **Privately Held**
SIC: 7997 5812 Golf club, membership; American restaurant

(G-10384)
PRAIRIE MISSION RETIREMENT VLG
Also Called: Prairie Mission Retirement Vlg
242 Carroll St (66771-4044)
PHONE..................................620 449-2400
Eugene Beachner, *President*
Mike Carter, *Vice Pres*
Linda Sartin, *Manager*
Melinda Ewaen, *Director*
Jed Hetlinger, *Director*
EMP: 60
SALES: 3.2MM **Privately Held**
WEB: www.pmrv.com
SIC: 8051 Skilled nursing care facilities

(G-10385)
WESTERN CONTRACTING CORP
6th And Central (66771)
PHONE..................................620 449-2286
Jerry Beachner, *President*
Robert Beachner, *Corp Secy*
Eugene Beachner, *Vice Pres*
Dan Plake, *Controller*
EMP: 100
SQ FT: 5,000
SALES (est): 3.8MM **Privately Held**
SIC: 1611 General contractor, highway & street construction

(G-10386)
WESTHOFF INTERIORS INC
14006 Wast 107th St (66771)
PHONE..................................620 449-2900
Joseph Westhoff, *President*
Connie Westhoff, *Corp Secy*
Ashley Dent, *Accountant*
EMP: 37
SALES: 5MM **Privately Held**
SIC: 2431 Interior & ornamental woodwork & trim

Salina
Saline County

(G-10387)
A & B MACHINE INC
2259b Centennial Rd (67401-1707)
PHONE..................................785 827-5171
Mark Brighthill, *President*
Karen Brighthill, *Vice Pres*
EMP: 14 **EST:** 1971
SQ FT: 15,000
SALES (est): 2.2MM **Privately Held**
WEB: www.abmachineinc.com
SIC: 3599 3523 3549 Machine shop, jobbing & repair; farm machinery & equipment; metalworking machinery

(G-10388)
A PLUS GALVANIZING
1100 N Ohio St (67401-2403)
P.O. Box 2266 (67402-2266)
PHONE..................................785 820-9823
Charles Blankenship, *President*
Frieda MAI, *Treasurer*
EMP: 40
SQ FT: 172,000
SALES (est): 3.9MM **Privately Held**
WEB: www.aplusgalv.com
SIC: 3479 Galvanizing of iron, steel or end-formed products

(G-10389)
ABILENE UNIFIED SCHL DST 435
Also Called: Dickinson County Learning Exch
605 E Crawford St (67401-5101)
PHONE..................................785 825-9185
Brian Roth, *Principal*
EMP: 10
SALES (corp-wide): 15.3MM **Privately Held**
SIC: 8211 8351 Public elementary & secondary schools; child day care services
PA: Abilene Unified School District 435
213 N Broadway St
Abilene KS 67410
785 263-2630

(G-10390)
ACCESSIBLE HOME CARE
1300 E Iron Ave Ste 121 (67401-3239)
P.O. Box 942 (67402-0942)
PHONE..................................785 493-0340
Debra Blomquist, *Principal*
EMP: 14
SALES (est): 414.2K **Privately Held**
SIC: 8082 Home health care services

(G-10391)
ACCURATE ELECTRIC INC
510 N Santa Fe Ave (67401-1950)
PHONE..................................785 825-4010
Ron A Stratman, *President*
Julie Trapman, *Treasurer*
EMP: 7
SALES (est): 1MM **Privately Held**
WEB: www.accurateelectric.kscoxmail.com
SIC: 1731 7629 5719 3625 General electrical contractor; electrical equipment repair services; lighting fixtures; motor controls, electric

(G-10392)
ACOUSTIC SOUNDS INC
518 N 10th St (67401-2002)
PHONE..................................785 825-8609
Chad Kassem, *Branch Mgr*
EMP: 30
SALES (corp-wide): 7.7MM **Privately Held**
SIC: 5735 3652 Records, audio discs & tapes; pre-recorded records & tapes
PA: Acoustic Sounds, Inc.
605 W North St
Salina KS 67401
785 825-8609

(G-10393)
ACUSTEP LLC (PA)
2850 Caywood (67401-9368)
PHONE..................................785 826-2500
Jeryl Fullen, *CEO*
Matt Fullen, *Vice Pres*
EMP: 5
SQ FT: 400
SALES (est): 50K **Privately Held**
WEB: www.acustep.com
SIC: 3842 Orthopedic appliances

(G-10394)
ADI SYSTEMS INC
628 N Broadway Blvd (67401-2079)
PHONE..................................785 825-5975
Robert R Frisbie, *President*
Brenda Armijo, *President*
Jon Moyer, *Representative*
EMP: 14
SALES (est): 1.2MM **Privately Held**
WEB: www.adisystems.net
SIC: 7378 Computer peripheral equipment repair & maintenance

(G-10395)
ADM MILLING CO
850 E Pacific Ave (67401)
P.O. Box 1400 (67402-1400)
PHONE..................................785 825-1541
Steve Storniolo, *Branch Mgr*
EMP: 100
SALES (corp-wide): 64.3B **Publicly Held**
WEB: www.admmilling.com
SIC: 2041 5149 5153 3541 Grain mills (except rice); flour; grain elevators; machine tools, metal cutting type; food products machinery
HQ: Adm Milling Co.
8000 W 110th St Ste 300
Overland Park KS 66210
913 491-9400

(G-10396)
ADVANCE STORES COMPANY INC
Also Called: Advance Auto Parts
3633 S 9th St (67401-7806)
PHONE..................................785 826-2400
Steve Johnson, *Branch Mgr*
EMP: 187
SQ FT: 431,000
SALES (corp-wide): 9.5B **Publicly Held**
SIC: 4225 5531 5013 General warehousing & storage; automotive parts; motor vehicle supplies & new parts
HQ: Advance Stores Company Incorporated
5008 Airport Rd Nw
Roanoke VA 24012
540 362-4911

(G-10397)
ADVANCED ENGINE MACHINE INC
1206 N 9th St (67401-8721)
PHONE..................................785 825-6684
Marc Brown, *President*
EMP: 7
SQ FT: 16,000
SALES (est): 1MM **Privately Held**
SIC: 3944 5999 Engines, miniature; engine & motor equipment & supplies

(G-10398)
AIRGAS USA LLC
300 N Santa Fe Ave (67401-2329)
PHONE..................................785 823-8100
Lyle Tinkler, *Principal*
EMP: 26
SALES (corp-wide): 121.9MM **Privately Held**
SIC: 5085 5084 5099 5169 Welding supplies; welding machinery & equipment; safety equipment & supplies; chemicals & allied products
HQ: Airgas Usa, Llc
259 N Radnor Chester Rd
Radnor PA 19087
610 687-5253

(G-10399)
AKA WIRELESS INC
Also Called: Z Wireless
2401 S 9th St (67401-7624)
PHONE..................................785 823-6605
Brian Burner, *Branch Mgr*
EMP: 71 **Privately Held**
SIC: 4812 Cellular telephone services

GEOGRAPHIC

HQ: Aka Wireless, Inc.
7505 S Louise Ave
Sioux Falls SD 57108
605 275-3733

(G-10400)
ALPHA MEDIA LLC
Also Called: Ksal-FM
131 N Santa Fe Ave (67401-2642)
PHONE.................................785 823-1111
Robert Protzman, *General Mgr*
Bob Protzman, *Sales Mgr*
EMP: 13 **Privately Held**
SIC: 4832 Radio broadcasting stations
PA: Alpha Media Llc
1211 Sw 5th Ave Ste 600
Portland OR 97204

(G-10401)
AMERICAN NATIONAL RED CROSS
Also Called: American Red Cross
120 W Prescott Ave (67401-4138)
PHONE.................................785 309-0263
EMP: 39
SALES (corp-wide): 2.6B **Privately Held**
SIC: 8322 Emergency social services
PA: The American National Red Cross
430 17th St Nw
Washington DC 20006
202 737-8300

(G-10402)
ANDREA INVESTMENTS LLC
Also Called: Salina Ambassador Hotel
1616 W Crawford St (67401-4581)
PHONE.................................785 823-1739
Joshua Joseph, *President*
Bregg Wahlers, *District Mgr*
EMP: 35 **EST:** 2009
SALES (est): 233K **Privately Held**
SIC: 7011 Hotels

(G-10403)
ANESTHIA ASSN CENTL KANS PA
200 S 5th St Ste A (67401-3906)
PHONE.................................785 827-2238
Bruce Sternke Do, *Principal*
EMP: 20
SALES (est): 898.7K **Privately Held**
SIC: 8031 Offices & clinics of osteopathic physicians

(G-10404)
ANGELS LITTLE PLAYGRND DAYCARE
200 W Key Ave (67401-7689)
PHONE.................................785 823-1448
Glynis Jennings, *President*
EMP: 15
SQ FT: 1,700
SALES (est): 517.6K **Privately Held**
SIC: 8351 Child day care services

(G-10405)
APAC-KANSAS INC
Rr 3 (67401)
PHONE.................................785 823-8944
Ron Befort, *Manager*
EMP: 13
SALES (corp-wide): 29.7B **Privately Held**
SIC: 1771 Blacktop (asphalt) work
HQ: Apac-Kansas, Inc.
9660 Legler Rd
Lenexa KS 66219

(G-10406)
APAC-KANSAS INC
1622 Sunflower Rd (67401)
P.O. Box 1095 (67402-1095)
PHONE.................................785 823-5537
Vern Hopkins, *Manager*
EMP: 35
SALES (corp-wide): 29.7B **Privately Held**
SIC: 1611 Highway & street paving contractor
HQ: Apac-Kansas, Inc.
9660 Legler Rd
Lenexa KS 66219

(G-10407)
ARCHER-DANIELS-MIDLAND COMPANY
Also Called: ADM
850 E Pacific Ave (67401-2948)
P.O. Box 1400 (67402-1400)
PHONE.................................785 825-1541
Steve Storniolo, *Manager*
EMP: 55
SALES (corp-wide): 64.3B **Publicly Held**
WEB: www.admworld.com
SIC: 2041 8741 8711 3556 Flour & other grain mill products; management services; engineering services; food products machinery
PA: Archer-Daniels-Midland Company
77 W Wacker Dr Ste 4600
Chicago IL 60601
312 634-8100

(G-10408)
ARCHER-DANIELS-MIDLAND COMPANY
ADM
124 S 4th St (67401)
PHONE.................................785 820-8019
Steve Storniolo, *Branch Mgr*
EMP: 35
SALES (corp-wide): 64.3B **Publicly Held**
WEB: www.admworld.com
SIC: 2041 Flour & other grain mill products
PA: Archer-Daniels-Midland Company
77 W Wacker Dr Ste 4600
Chicago IL 60601
312 634-8100

(G-10409)
ARROW PRINTING COMPANY INC
115 W Woodland Ave (67401-2935)
P.O. Box 2898 (67402-2898)
PHONE.................................785 825-8124
Robert K Fellers, *President*
Jason Fellers, *Vice Pres*
Mike Hartung, *Mfg Staff*
Terry Fellers, *Treasurer*
EMP: 9
SQ FT: 10,000
SALES: 1.7MM **Privately Held**
WEB: www.arrowprintco.com
SIC: 2752 2759 7389 Commercial printing, offset; commercial printing; printers' services: folding, collating

(G-10410)
ASHBY HOUSE LTD
150 S 8th St (67401-2808)
P.O. Box 3482 (67402-3482)
PHONE.................................785 826-4935
Bryan Andersaon, *President*
Kathy Allen, *Program Dir*
Bryan Anderson, *Administration*
EMP: 15
SALES: 1.3MM **Privately Held**
SIC: 8322 Emergency shelters

(G-10411)
ASSURANCE PARTNERS LLC
Also Called: Nationwide
201 E Iron Ave (67401-2665)
P.O. Box 1213 (67402-1213)
PHONE.................................785 825-0286
Jim Wilson, *President*
Phil Krug, *Vice Pres*
Phillip Krug, *Vice Pres*
Jessica Goubeaux, *Prdtn Mgr*
April Torske, *QC Mgr*
EMP: 43
SQ FT: 9,000
SALES (est): 10.1MM **Privately Held**
SIC: 6411 Insurance information & consulting services

(G-10412)
AUDIOLOGY CONSULTANTS INC
520 S Santa Fe Ave # 400 (67401-4190)
PHONE.................................785 823-3761
Connie Karber, *Manager*
EMP: 16
SALES (est): 1MM **Privately Held**
SIC: 5999 8049 7629 Hearing aids; audiologist; hearing aid repair

(G-10413)
AUTO HOUSE INC
565 Westport Blvd (67401-4359)
PHONE.................................785 825-6644
EMP: 11
SQ FT: 9,600
SALES (corp-wide): 1.1MM **Privately Held**
SIC: 7549 Towing service, automotive
PA: Auto House, Inc.
245 W Highway 56
Galva KS 67443
620 654-3210

(G-10414)
AUTOZONE INC
1916 S 9th St (67401-5634)
PHONE.................................785 452-9790
Ken Gawith, *Manager*
EMP: 10
SALES (corp-wide): 11.8B **Publicly Held**
WEB: www.autozone.com
SIC: 5531 5063 Automotive parts; storage batteries, industrial
PA: Autozone, Inc.
123 S Front St
Memphis TN 38103
901 495-6500

(G-10415)
AVFLIGHT SALINA CORPORATION
2035 Beechcraft Rd (67401-5008)
PHONE.................................734 663-6466
Chuck Greene, *Asst Controller*
EMP: 15
SALES (est): 1.6MM
SALES (corp-wide): 329.1MM **Privately Held**
SIC: 4581 Airports, flying fields & services
HQ: Avflight Corporation
47 W Ellsworth Rd
Ann Arbor MI 48108
734 663-6466

(G-10416)
BALLOU PAVEMENT SOLUTIONS INC
1100 W Grand Ave (67401-1863)
P.O. Box 2000 (67402-2000)
PHONE.................................785 827-4439
Rex Eberly, *President*
Robert Northcutt, *Plant Mgr*
EMP: 120
SALES (est): 8.1MM
SALES (corp-wide): 80.9MM **Privately Held**
SIC: 1629 1622 1611 Land reclamation; bridge, tunnel & elevated highway; surfacing & paving; highway & street paving contractor
HQ: Delta Companies Inc.
114 S Silver Springs Rd
Cape Girardeau MO 63703

(G-10417)
BAMFORD FIRE SPRINKLER CO INC (HQ)
1383 W North St (67401-9301)
PHONE.................................785 825-7710
Joe Heinrich, *President*
Doug Roeder, *Supervisor*
EMP: 37
SALES (est): 4.8MM
SALES (corp-wide): 4.9MM **Privately Held**
SIC: 1711 Fire sprinkler system installation
PA: Bamford, Inc.
2815 W 24th St
Kearney NE 68845
308 237-2157

(G-10418)
BANK OF TESCOTT
600 S Santa Fe Ave (67401-4148)
P.O. Box 2537 (67402-2537)
PHONE.................................785 825-1621
Steve Kraus, *Vice Pres*
Mitchell Obermueller, *Vice Pres*
Larry Fief, *Manager*
EMP: 25
SALES (corp-wide): 18.7MM **Privately Held**
SIC: 6022 6141 6021 State trust companies accepting deposits, commercial; personal credit institutions; national commercial banks
PA: The Bank Of Tescott
104 S Main St
Tescott KS 67484
785 283-4217

(G-10419)
BANK VI (PA)
1900 S Ohio St (67401-6643)
P.O. Box 77 (67402-0077)
PHONE.................................785 825-4321
Tom Wilbur, *President*
EMP: 16
SALES: 4.9MM **Privately Held**
WEB: www.banksix.com
SIC: 6022 State trust companies accepting deposits, commercial

(G-10420)
BANKERS LIFE & CASUALTY CO
328 N Ohio St (67401-2400)
PHONE.................................785 820-8815
Bob Reynolds, *Branch Mgr*
Lawrence Martin, *Manager*
EMP: 14
SALES (corp-wide): 4.3B **Publicly Held**
SIC: 6411 Insurance agents, brokers & service
HQ: Bankers Life & Casualty Co
111 E Wacker Dr Ste 2100
Chicago IL 60601
312 396-6000

(G-10421)
BARKS N BOWS DOG GROOMING
314 S Broadway Blvd Ste B (67401-3860)
PHONE.................................785 823-1627
Kim Base, *Owner*
EMP: 5
SALES (est): 106.4K **Privately Held**
SIC: 0752 5999 3999 Grooming services, pet & animal specialties; pets & pet supplies; pet supplies

(G-10422)
BELMONT HOTELS LLC
Also Called: Candlewood Suites
2650 Planet Ave (67401-7604)
PHONE.................................785 823-6939
Michael Brumgardt, *General Mgr*
Tricia Weems, *Manager*
EMP: 13
SALES (est): 1.2MM **Privately Held**
WEB: www.cws.kscoxmail.com
SIC: 7011 Hotels

(G-10423)
BENNINGTON STATE BANK (PA)
2130 S Ohio St (67401-6852)
P.O. Box 1280 (67402-1280)
PHONE.................................785 827-5522
Mike Berkley, *CEO*
Dennis Lull, *President*
Burk Matthews, *Vice Pres*
Ron Weis, *Vice Pres*
Zachary Weis, *Loan Officer*
EMP: 37
SQ FT: 20,000
SALES: 33.3MM **Privately Held**
SIC: 6022 State trust companies accepting deposits, commercial

(G-10424)
BIO-MDCAL APPLCATIONS KANS INC
Also Called: Fresenius Medical Care Saline
700 E Iron Ave (67401-3038)
PHONE.................................785 823-6460
Bobbie Sullivan, *Manager*
EMP: 24
SALES (corp-wide): 18.3B **Privately Held**
SIC: 8092 Kidney dialysis centers
HQ: Bio-Medical Applications Of Kansas, Inc.
920 Winter St
Waltham MA 02451

(G-10425)
BJ KOETTING INC
321 Pine Ridge Dr (67401-3865)
PHONE..................................785 823-8580
Richard Koetting, *President*
EMP: 10
SALES (est): 685.5K **Privately Held**
SIC: 1541 Steel building construction

(G-10426)
BLIND PIG
2501 Market Pl Ste A (67401-7666)
PHONE..................................785 827-7449
Denise Ward, *Principal*
EMP: 10
SALES (est): 275.3K **Privately Held**
SIC: 5812 5813 8641 Grills (eating places); bar (drinking places); civic social & fraternal associations

(G-10427)
BLUE BEACON LP II
500 Graves Blvd (67401-4306)
PHONE..................................785 825-2221
Trace Walker, *Partner*
Charles Walker, *Principal*
EMP: 300 **EST:** 1978
SQ FT: 4,000
SALES (est): 3.7MM
SALES (corp-wide): 14.8MM **Privately Held**
SIC: 7542 Truck wash
PA: Blue Beacon International Inc
500 Graves Blvd
Salina KS 67401
785 825-2221

(G-10428)
BLUE BEACON USA LP (PA)
500 Graves Blvd (67401-4306)
P.O. Box 856 (67402-0856)
PHONE..................................785 825-2221
Trace Walker, *President*
EMP: 2500 **EST:** 1989
SQ FT: 20,000
SALES (est): 22.4K **Privately Held**
SIC: 7542 Truck wash

(G-10429)
BOHM FARM & RANCH INC
Also Called: Bfr Metals
1504 W State St (67401-9570)
PHONE..................................785 823-0303
Peter Bohm, *President*
Glen Soldan, *Manager*
EMP: 20
SALES (est): 1.6MM **Privately Held**
SIC: 5093 Scrap & waste materials

(G-10430)
BORDER STATES INDUSTRIES INC
Also Called: Kriz-Daviz Whlesle Electl Sups
232 N 3rd St (67401-2322)
PHONE..................................785 827-4497
John Jacobs, *Branch Mgr*
EMP: 17
SALES (corp-wide): 2B **Privately Held**
WEB: www.krizdavis.com
SIC: 5063 Electrical supplies
PA: Border States Industries, Inc.
2400 38th St S
Fargo ND 58104
701 293-5834

(G-10431)
BRISTOL HOTEL & RESORTS INC
1616 W Crawford St (67401-4581)
PHONE..................................785 823-1739
Shannon Jones, *Manager*
EMP: 70 **Privately Held**
WEB: www.bristolhotels.com
SIC: 8741 7011 Hotel or motel management; hotels
HQ: Bristol Hotel & Resorts Inc.
3 Ravinia Dr Ste 100
Atlanta GA 30346

(G-10432)
BROOKDALE SENIOR LIVING COMMUN
Also Called: Sterling House Salina
1200 E Kirwin Ave (67401-6333)
PHONE..................................785 820-2991
J Backhus, *Exec Dir*
EMP: 23
SALES (corp-wide): 4.5B **Publicly Held**
WEB: www.assisted.com
SIC: 8051 Skilled nursing care facilities
HQ: Brookdale Senior Living Communities, Inc.
6737 W Wa St Ste 2300
Milwaukee WI 53214
414 918-5000

(G-10433)
BRUNDAGE-BONE CON PMPG INC
1265 W Diamond Dr (67401-9357)
PHONE..................................785 823-7706
Rip Ringle, *Manager*
EMP: 26
SALES (corp-wide): 154.2MM **Privately Held**
SIC: 1771 Concrete pumping
PA: Brundage-Bone Concrete Pumping, Inc.
6461 Downing St
Denver CO 80229
303 289-4444

(G-10434)
BUSBOOM & RAUH CONSTRUCTION CO
145 1/2 S Santa Fe Ave (67401-2809)
P.O. Box 1037 (67402-1037)
PHONE..................................785 825-4664
EMP: 25 **EST:** 1920
SQ FT: 1,000
SALES (est): 6MM **Privately Held**
WEB: www.busboom.kscoxmail.com
SIC: 1542 1541 Commercial & office building contractors; industrial buildings, new construction

(G-10435)
CALLABRESI HEATING & COOLG INC
Also Called: Honeywell Authorized Dealer
1311 Armory Rd (67401-4067)
PHONE..................................785 825-2599
Jerry Callabresi, *President*
Sharon Callabresi, *Corp Secy*
Scott Krous, *Vice Pres*
EMP: 20
SQ FT: 7,500
SALES (est): 4.2MM **Privately Held**
SIC: 1711 Warm air heating & air conditioning contractor

(G-10436)
CARGILL INCORPORATED
1112 N Halstead Rd (67401-9314)
PHONE..................................785 825-8128
David Givens, *Manager*
EMP: 30
SALES (corp-wide): 113.4B **Privately Held**
WEB: www.cargill.com
SIC: 4221 5153 Grain elevator, storage only; grain elevators
PA: Cargill, Incorporated
15407 Mcginty Rd W
Wayzata MN 55391
952 742-7575

(G-10437)
CATHOLIC CHARITIES OF SALINA (PA)
1500 S 9th St (67401-5627)
P.O. Box 1366 (67402-1366)
PHONE..................................785 825-0208
Toll Free:..................................888 -
Jeanie Warner, *Marketing Staff*
Karen Hauser, *Director*
EMP: 15
SALES: 1.7MM **Privately Held**
WEB: www.catholiccharitiessalina.org
SIC: 8322 8661 Social service center; religious organizations

(G-10438)
CELLCO PARTNERSHIP
621 Westport Blvd (67401-4373)
PHONE..................................785 820-6311
Karen Vidricksen, *Principal*
Harry Kaszycki, *Engineer*
EMP: 71
SALES (corp-wide): 130.8B **Publicly Held**
SIC: 4812 Cellular telephone services
HQ: Cellco Partnership
1 Verizon Way
Basking Ridge NJ 07920

(G-10439)
CENTRAL KANSAS AUTO RENTAL (PA)
Also Called: Hertz
3230 Arnold Ave (67401-8107)
PHONE..................................785 827-7237
Gerry Harris, *President*
EMP: 12
SALES (est): 1MM **Privately Held**
SIC: 7514 7513 Rent-a-car service; truck rental, without drivers

(G-10440)
CENTRAL KANSAS ENT ASSOC PA
Also Called: Audiometric Aides
520 S Santa Fe Ave # 200 (67401-4190)
PHONE..................................785 823-7225
Jerrold Cossette MD, *President*
Connie Hofmier, *General Mgr*
EMP: 20
SQ FT: 1,000
SALES (est): 2.3MM **Privately Held**
SIC: 8011 5999 Eyes, ears, nose & throat specialist: physician/surgeon; hearing aids

(G-10441)
CENTRAL KANSAS MENTAL HLTH CTR (PA)
Also Called: CROSSROADS CLUB
809 Elmhurst Blvd (67401-7428)
PHONE..................................785 823-6322
Chris Scherberger,
EMP: 100
SQ FT: 7,500
SALES: 9MM **Privately Held**
WEB: www.ckmhc.org
SIC: 8093 Mental health clinic, outpatient

(G-10442)
CENTRAL KNSS CNCIL OF GRL SCT
3115 Enterprise Dr (67401-8461)
PHONE..................................785 827-3679
Karin Bigler, *CEO*
EMP: 11
SALES (est): 380K **Privately Held**
SIC: 8641 8661 8322 Girl Scout organization; religious organizations; youth center

(G-10443)
CENTRAL MALL REALTY HOLDG LLC
2259 S 9th St (67401-7313)
PHONE..................................785 825-7733
Mike Kohan, *Principal*
EMP: 29
SALES (est): 1.4MM **Privately Held**
SIC: 6512 Shopping center, regional (300,000 - 1,000,000 sq ft); shopping center, property operation only

(G-10444)
CENTRAL PWR SYSTEMS & SVCS LLC
1944b N 9th St (67401-8617)
PHONE..................................785 825-8291
Zach Brown, *Branch Mgr*
EMP: 17
SALES (corp-wide): 80MM **Privately Held**
SIC: 7538 Diesel engine repair: automotive
PA: Central Power Systems & Services, Llc
9200 Liberty Dr
Pleasant Valley MO 64068
816 781-8070

(G-10445)
CENTRAL STATES ENTERPRISES LLC
Also Called: Central States Fumigation
1908 W Old Highway 40 (67401-9798)
P.O. Box 1692 (67402-1692)
PHONE..................................785 827-8215
Roger Sandborne, *President*
Richard Thadd Bigler, *Vice Pres*
Richard Bigler, *Vice Pres*
Chris Mack, *Manager*
Mike Wasserman, *Manager*
EMP: 27
SALES (est): 3.2MM **Privately Held**
WEB: www.centralstatesenterprises.com
SIC: 7342 Pest control in structures

(G-10446)
CERTIFIED ENVIRONMENTAL MGT
3115 Enterprise Dr Ste C (67401-8462)
P.O. Box 504 (67402-0504)
PHONE..................................785 823-0492
Brenda Tolson, *President*
John Markas, *Treasurer*
Bruce T Fast, *Manager*
Bruce Fast, *Lab Dir*
EMP: 27
SALES (est): 2.3MM **Privately Held**
SIC: 8742 8734 Industrial hygiene consultant; testing laboratories

(G-10447)
CHOICES NETWORK INC
2151 Centennial Rd (67401-1700)
P.O. Box 2657 (67402-2657)
PHONE..................................785 820-8018
Donald R Merriman, *President*
Kenna Boyce, *Vice Pres*
Brenda Cook, *Vice Pres*
Janny Vance, *Vice Pres*
Velyn Fagan, *Manager*
EMP: 263
SQ FT: 6,000
SALES (est): 4.9MM **Privately Held**
WEB: www.choicesnetwork.net
SIC: 8322 8361 8721 Public welfare center; social service center; residential care for the handicapped; payroll accounting service

(G-10448)
CITY OF SALINA
Salina Water Treatment Plant
401 S 5th St Rm 200 (67401-4110)
PHONE..................................785 826-7305
James Wendel, *Director*
EMP: 33 **Privately Held**
WEB: www.saline.org
SIC: 4941 9111 Water supply; mayors' offices
PA: City Of Salina
300 W Ash St 202
Salina KS 67401
785 309-5700

(G-10449)
CITY OF SALINA
Salina Bi Centennial Center
800 The Midway (67401-7442)
PHONE..................................785 826-7200
Sheri Chase Jones, *Finance*
Keith Rawling, *Manager*
EMP: 20 **Privately Held**
WEB: www.saline.org
SIC: 7389 9111 7299 6512 Convention & show services; mayors' offices; banquet hall facilities; auditorium & hall operation
PA: City Of Salina
300 W Ash St 202
Salina KS 67401
785 309-5700

(G-10450)
CITY OF SALINA
Also Called: Smoky Hill Museum
211 W Iron Ave (67401-2613)
PHONE..................................785 309-5775
Susan Hawksworth, *Director*
EMP: 10 **Privately Held**
WEB: www.saline.org
SIC: 8412 9111 Museum; mayors' offices
PA: City Of Salina
300 W Ash St 202
Salina KS 67401
785 309-5700

(G-10451)
CITY OF SALINA
Also Called: Salina Fire Department
222 W Elm St (67401-2351)
P.O. Box 736 (67402-0736)
PHONE..................................785 826-7340
Darrell Eastin, *Chief*
EMP: 86 **Privately Held**

GEOGRAPHIC

WEB: www.saline.org
SIC: 9224 4119 Fire department, not including volunteer; ambulance service
PA: City Of Salina
300 W Ash St 202
Salina KS 67401
785 309-5700

(G-10452)
CITY OF SALINA
Also Called: City of Salina Central Garage
418 E Ash St (67401-2324)
P.O. Box 736 (67402-0736)
PHONE.................................785 309-5752
Bob Peck, *Manager*
EMP: 10 Privately Held
WEB: www.saline.org
SIC: 7538 9111 General automotive repair shops; executive offices
PA: City Of Salina
300 W Ash St 202
Salina KS 67401
785 309-5700

(G-10453)
CLARE GENERATOR SERVICE INC
801 N 10th St (67401-2944)
P.O. Box 543 (67402-0543)
PHONE.................................785 827-3321
Paul Hemmy, *President*
Sharon Hemmy, *Corp Secy*
EMP: 10 EST: 1975
SQ FT: 10,000
SALES (est): 1.2MM Privately Held
SIC: 5013 3694 3621 Automotive supplies & parts; alternators, automotive; generators, automotive & aircraft; motors & generators; starters, for motors

(G-10454)
CLARIOS
Also Called: Johnson Controls
2001 W Grand Ave Bldg 2-5 (67401-1870)
PHONE.................................785 827-6829
John West, *Branch Mgr*
EMP: 22 Privately Held
SIC: 2531 1711 5074 Seats, automobile; boiler maintenance contractor; boilers, power (industrial)
HQ: Johnson Controls Inc
5757 N Green Bay Ave
Milwaukee WI 53209
414 524-1200

(G-10455)
CLARK ENTERPRISES 2000 INC
3603 S Knoll Ln (67401-9459)
PHONE.................................785 825-7172
Clifford S Clark, *CEO*
Amanda Clark, *President*
Deanna Clark, *Co-Owner*
Mary Ann Base, *Office Mgr*
▲ EMP: 48 EST: 1959
SQ FT: 25,000
SALES (est): 8MM Privately Held
WEB: www.clarkenterprises2000.com
SIC: 5064 7622 5731 Electrical appliances, television & radio; radios; radio repair shop; radios, two-way, citizens' band, weather, short-wave, etc.

(G-10456)
CLARK MIZE LINVILLE CHARTERED
Also Called: Mize, John W
129 S 8th St (67401-2807)
P.O. Box 380 (67402-0380)
PHONE.................................785 823-6325
Eric N Anderson, *President*
Lawton M Nuss, *President*
Robert M Adrian, *Vice Pres*
Greg A Bengtson, *Vice Pres*
L O Bengtson, *Vice Pres*
EMP: 23
SALES (est): 2.4MM Privately Held
WEB: www.cml-law.com
SIC: 8111 General practice law office

(G-10457)
COLE & COOPER PA
1000 E Cloud St (67401-6416)
PHONE.................................785 823-6391
David Cooper, *Managing Prtnr*
Christopher Banninger, *Partner*
EMP: 13
SALES (est): 711.9K Privately Held
WEB: www.drscoleandcooper.com
SIC: 8042 8011 Offices & clinics of optometrists; offices & clinics of medical doctors

(G-10458)
COMPCARE
Also Called: Petrakis, Patricia M
520 S Santa Fe Ave # 300 (67401-4190)
PHONE.................................785 823-7470
Alan Wedel MD, *President*
EMP: 45
SALES (est): 1.4MM Privately Held
SIC: 8011 Clinic, operated by physicians

(G-10459)
CONSOLIDATED ELEC DISTRS INC
Also Called: American Electric Company
1103 W South St (67401-4014)
P.O. Box 1097 (67402-1097)
PHONE.................................785 823-7161
Brad Haynes, *Manager*
Sharon Root, *Manager*
EMP: 12
SALES (corp-wide): 4.1B Privately Held
SIC: 5063 Electrical supplies
PA: Consolidated Electrical Distributors, Inc.
1920 Westridge Dr
Irving TX 75038
972 582-5300

(G-10460)
CONSOLIDATED PRTG & STY CO INC (PA)
319 S 5th St (67401-3907)
P.O. Box 1217 (67402-1217)
PHONE.................................785 825-5426
Fred P Vandegrift, *Ch of Bd*
Donald P Vandegrift, *President*
Don Commerford, *Corp Secy*
Caroline Nachtrab, *Sales Dir*
EMP: 47 EST: 1916
SQ FT: 24,000
SALES: 4.7MM Privately Held
SIC: 2752 5044 2791 5112 Commercial printing, offset; office equipment; typesetting; stationery; office supplies; office & public building furniture

(G-10461)
CONTINENTAL ANALYTICAL SVCS
525 N 8th St (67401-1937)
P.O. Box 3737 (67402-3737)
PHONE.................................785 827-1273
Clifford Baker, *President*
Gregory Groene, *Vice Pres*
Kathy Mitchell, *Vice Pres*
Denise Stclair, *Accounts Mgr*
EMP: 35
SQ FT: 16,500
SALES: 3.6MM Privately Held
WEB: www.cas-lab.com
SIC: 8734 Water testing laboratory

(G-10462)
COPERION K-TRON SALINA INC
606 N Front St (67401-1926)
P.O. Box 17 (67402-0017)
PHONE.................................785 825-1611
Matt Burt, *General Mgr*
Thomas Kehl, *Principal*
Todd W Smith, *Vice Pres*
Laurie Davis, *Buyer*
Layne Parry, *Engineer*
▲ EMP: 110
SQ FT: 120,000
SALES (est): 35.7MM Publicly Held
WEB: www.premierpneumatics.com
SIC: 3535 Pneumatic tube conveyor systems
HQ: K-Tron Investment Co.
300 Delaware Ave Ste 900
Wilmington DE 19801

(G-10463)
COPY CO CORPORATION (PA)
2346 Planet Ave (67401-7514)
PHONE.................................785 823-2679
Hossein Gerami, *President*
Ali Pakravan, *Corp Secy*
EMP: 36
SQ FT: 4,400
SALES (est): 3.6MM Privately Held
WEB: www.wwwebservice.net
SIC: 7336 2759 7334 Graphic arts & related design; invitations: printing; blueprinting service

(G-10464)
CORONADO AREA COUNCIL BSA (PA)
644 S Ohio St (67401-3346)
PHONE.................................785 827-4461
Matt Devore, *President*
EMP: 12
SALES: 1.3MM Privately Held
WEB: www.coronadoscout.org
SIC: 8641 Boy Scout organization

(G-10465)
COUNTY OF SALINE
Also Called: Saline County Health
125 W Elm St (67401-2315)
PHONE.................................785 826-6606
Director Tiller, *Director*
EMP: 10 Privately Held
SIC: 8082 9111 8049 Home health care services; county supervisors' & executives' offices; speech pathologist
PA: County Of Saline
300 W Ash St
Salina KS 67401
785 309-5810

(G-10466)
COURTYARD BY MARRIOTT
3020 Riffel Dr (67401-8971)
PHONE.................................785 309-1300
Michelle Jensen, *General Mgr*
Stan Weilaert, *Principal*
EMP: 19
SALES (est): 874.9K Privately Held
SIC: 7011 Hotels & motels

(G-10467)
CRESTWOOD INC (PA)
601 E Water Well Rd (67401-8990)
PHONE.................................785 823-1532
Paul Junk, *CEO*
Mike Junk, *President*
Sharon Burt, *Vice Pres*
Richard Greene, *Vice Pres*
Greg Holeman, *Vice Pres*
EMP: 150
SQ FT: 160,000
SALES (est): 17.7MM Privately Held
WEB: www.crestwood-inc.com
SIC: 2434 Wood kitchen cabinets

(G-10468)
CRESTWOOD INC
353 E Avenue A (67401-9144)
PHONE.................................785 827-0317
Mike Junk, *Manager*
EMP: 8
SALES (corp-wide): 17.7MM Privately Held
WEB: www.crestwood-inc.com
SIC: 2434 Wood kitchen cabinets
PA: Crestwood, Inc
601 E Water Well Rd
Salina KS 67401
785 823-1532

(G-10469)
CS CLEANERS INC
Also Called: Merry Maids
1123 Holiday St (67401-4011)
PHONE.................................785 825-8636
Candy Siko, *Owner*
EMP: 15 EST: 1998
SALES (est): 406.4K Privately Held
WEB: www.merrymaids.kscoxmail.com
SIC: 7349 Maid services, contract or fee basis

(G-10470)
DAUER IMPLEMENT COMPANY INC
1101 E Iron Ave (67401-3009)
PHONE.................................785 825-2141
Steven R Dauer, *President*
EMP: 16
SQ FT: 19,000
SALES (est): 3.1MM Privately Held
WEB: www.dauerimplement.com
SIC: 5083 7699 Agricultural machinery & equipment; agricultural equipment repair services

(G-10471)
DAYS INN
407 W Diamond Dr (67401-8603)
PHONE.................................785 823-9791
Jill Fink, *Manager*
EMP: 16
SALES (corp-wide): 1.8MM Privately Held
SIC: 7011 Hotels & motels
PA: Days Inn
3032 W Us Highway 50
Emporia KS

(G-10472)
DELBERT CHOPP CO INC
Also Called: Mod-Co Garage Door and Sup Div
448 N Front St (67401-2057)
P.O. Box 167 (67402-0167)
PHONE.................................785 825-8530
Tom Chopp, *President*
Marion Chopp, *Corp Secy*
Kathleen Yeager, *Vice Pres*
EMP: 13
SQ FT: 6,000
SALES: 1.3MM Privately Held
WEB: www.delbertchopp.com
SIC: 1742 5211 7699 1751 Acoustical & ceiling work; drywall; garage doors, sale & installation; garage door repair; framing contractor

(G-10473)
DELS ALTERNATOR & STARTER SVC
901 N 8th St (67401-2910)
P.O. Box 2306 (67402-2306)
PHONE.................................785 825-4466
Del Herbel, *President*
Clara Herbel, *Corp Secy*
EMP: 5
SQ FT: 5,000
SALES (est): 764.2K Privately Held
SIC: 3694 3621 Alternators, automotive; starters, for motors

(G-10474)
DESIGN CENTRAL INC
152 S 5th St (67401-2891)
PHONE.................................785 825-4131
Suzanne Hokett, *President*
Angela Campbell, *Corp Secy*
EMP: 11
SQ FT: 7,500
SALES (est): 6.3MM Privately Held
WEB: www.designcentral.com
SIC: 5021 5712 7389 7641 Office furniture; office furniture; interior designer; upholstery work

(G-10475)
DESIGNPLAST INC
431 N 13th St (67401-2007)
PHONE.................................785 825-7714
Michael Fabrizius, *President*
David Griffith, *Treasurer*
Tom Nowak, *Admin Sec*
EMP: 23
SQ FT: 3,500
SALES (est): 6.2MM Privately Held
WEB: www.designplast.net
SIC: 1799 Plastic wall tile installation

(G-10476)
DIAMOND TRANSFER & DIST CO
Also Called: Wholesale Feed Co
1012 W North St (67401-2030)
P.O. Box 1725 (67402-1725)
PHONE.................................785 825-1531
Gary Gorrell, *President*
EMP: 12
SQ FT: 57,000
SALES (est): 1.4MM Privately Held
SIC: 4214 Local trucking with storage

(G-10477)
DIGNITY CARE HOME INC
745 Faith Dr (67401-5269)
PHONE.................................785 823-3434
Joan Myers, *President*

Kathy Duphorne, *Director*
Paul Myers, *Director*
EMP: 14
SQ FT: 5,150
SALES: 500K **Privately Held**
SIC: 8052 Personal care facility

(G-10478)
DILLON COMPANIES INC
Also Called: Dillon's 00074
2350 Planet Ave (67401-7514)
PHONE....................................785 823-9403
Jerry Taylor, *Manager*
EMP: 100
SALES (corp-wide): 121.1B **Publicly Held**
WEB: www.dillons.com
SIC: 5411 5992 5912 5421 Supermarkets, chain; florists; drug stores & proprietary stores; meat & fish markets; bread, cake & related products
HQ: Dillon Companies, Inc.
2700 E 4th Ave
Hutchinson KS 67501
620 665-5511

(G-10479)
DISABLED AMERICAN VETERENS STR
Also Called: D A V
901 W Crawford St (67401-4707)
PHONE....................................785 827-6477
Dixie Weefei, *Principal*
EMP: 12
SALES: 525.6K **Privately Held**
SIC: 7389 5932 Flea market; clothing, secondhand

(G-10480)
DOMESTIC VLNCE ASSN OF CNTL KA
Also Called: Dvack
148 N Oakdale Ave (67401-3043)
P.O. Box 1854 (67402-1854)
PHONE....................................785 827-5862
Andrea Quill, *Director*
EMP: 13
SALES: 1.4MM **Privately Held**
WEB: www.dvack.org
SIC: 8621 Professional membership organizations

(G-10481)
DOUG BRADLEY TRUCKING INC (PA)
680 E Water Well Rd (67401-8990)
PHONE....................................785 826-9681
Doug Bradley, *President*
Jamie Bradley, *Vice Pres*
Kathy Bradley, *Treasurer*
Jake Bradley, *Manager*
EMP: 69
SQ FT: 8,500
SALES: 22.8MM **Privately Held**
SIC: 4213 Contract haulers

(G-10482)
EAGLE COMMUNICATIONS INC
Also Called: Kina
1825 S Ohio St (67401-6601)
PHONE....................................785 825-4631
Jerry Hinrikus, *Manager*
EMP: 12
SALES (corp-wide): 71.7MM **Privately Held**
WEB: www.eaglecom.net
SIC: 4832 7313 Radio broadcasting stations; radio advertising representative
PA: Eagle Communications, Inc.
2703 Hall St 15
Hays KS 67601
785 625-5910

(G-10483)
EAGLE SOFTWARE INC
Also Called: Eagle Technologies
124 Indiana Ave (67401-3214)
PHONE....................................785 823-7257
David Hiechel, *President*
Brian Anderson, *Engineer*
Casey Knudson, *Engineer*
Patrick Mann, *Engineer*
Milton Larson, *CFO*
EMP: 22
SQ FT: 6,000
SALES (est): 20.6MM **Privately Held**
WEB: www.eaglesoft.com
SIC: 5734 7379 Computer peripheral equipment; computer related maintenance services

(G-10484)
EAGLECREST RETIREMENT CMNTY
1501 E Magnolia Rd # 239 (67401-9112)
PHONE....................................785 309-1501
Brenda O'Gorman, *Principal*
EMP: 39
SALES (est): 1.2MM
SALES (corp-wide): 32.7MM **Privately Held**
WEB: www.eaglecrestseniorliving.com
SIC: 6513 Retirement hotel operation
PA: Midwest Health, Inc
3024 Sw Wanamaker Rd # 300
Topeka KS 66614
785 272-1535

(G-10485)
EDWARD FRENCH LOY
Also Called: All Radio Cab Co
1100 Louise Ln (67401-8317)
PHONE....................................785 825-4646
Edward Loy French, *Owner*
EMP: 10
SALES (est): 344.9K **Privately Held**
SIC: 4121 Taxicabs

(G-10486)
ELDORADO NATIONAL KANSAS INC (HQ)
1655 Wall St (67401-1759)
P.O. Box 3260 (67402-3260)
PHONE....................................785 827-1033
Andrew Imanse, *President*
Sheldon Walle, *General Mgr*
Walter L Bennett, *Vice Pres*
Peter B Orthwein, *Treasurer*
▼ **EMP:** 118
SQ FT: 92,000
SALES (est): 50.2MM **Publicly Held**
WEB: www.thorindustries.com
SIC: 3711 Buses, all types, assembly of

(G-10487)
EWY ANIMAL HOSP INC
Also Called: Ewy, Kenneth L Dvm
545 E North St (67401-1956)
PHONE....................................785 823-8428
Kenneth Ewy, *President*
EMP: 5
SALES (est): 436.3K **Privately Held**
SIC: 0742 3999 Animal hospital services, pets & other animal specialties; pet supplies

(G-10488)
EXIDE TECHNOLOGIES
413 E Berg Rd (67401-8907)
PHONE....................................785 825-6276
Billy Broadhead, *Safety Mgr*
David Hutchinson, *Manager*
EMP: 78
SALES (corp-wide): 2.3B **Privately Held**
WEB: www.exideworld.com
SIC: 3691 5063 3629 Storage batteries; storage batteries, industrial; battery chargers, rectifying or nonrotating
PA: Exide Technologies
13000 Drfeld Pkwy Bldg 20
Milton GA 30004
678 566-9000

(G-10489)
EXLINE INC (PA)
Also Called: Exline Services
3256 E Country Club Rd (67401-9528)
P.O. Box 1487 (67402-1487)
PHONE....................................785 825-4683
Robert William Exline Jr, *President*
Jon Ramsey, *Exec VP*
Kevin Koolchell, *Vice Pres*
Jim Preston, *Project Mgr*
Lloyd Arensman, *Engineer*
▲ **EMP:** 120
SQ FT: 11,000
SALES: 36.5MM **Privately Held**
WEB: www.exline-inc.com
SIC: 7699 3599 3563 Industrial machinery & equipment repair; machine & other job shop work; air & gas compressors

(G-10490)
EXLINE LEASING INC
3256 E Country Club Rd (67401-9528)
P.O. Box 1487 (67402-1487)
PHONE....................................785 825-4683
Robert Exline, *President*
Jo Gile, *Office Mgr*
EMP: 150 **EST:** 1959
SQ FT: 7,000
SALES (est): 15.8MM **Privately Held**
SIC: 5084 Compressors, except air conditioning

(G-10491)
EXPRESS PRINT AND SIGNS LLC
248 S Santa Fe Ave (67401-3932)
PHONE....................................785 825-8434
Andy Hansen, *Mng Member*
EMP: 20
SALES (est): 2.9MM **Privately Held**
SIC: 2752 3993 2261 Promotional printing, lithographic; advertising posters, lithographed; signs & advertising specialties; screen printing of cotton broadwoven fabrics

(G-10492)
EXPRESS SERVICES INC
Also Called: Express Personnel Services
2326 Planet Ave (67401-7514)
PHONE....................................785 825-4545
Lisa Heath, *Co-Owner*
Phillip Heath, *Manager*
EMP: 60
SALES (est): 1.5MM **Privately Held**
SIC: 7361 Employment agencies

(G-10493)
EXSALONCE LLC
2115 E Crawford St (67401-1326)
PHONE....................................785 823-1724
Marlene Oxandale, *Owner*
EMP: 14
SALES (est): 329.3K **Privately Held**
SIC: 7231 Beauty shops

(G-10494)
EYE CARE ASSOCIATES
Also Called: Murphey, Robert L
900 Westchester Dr (67401-7447)
PHONE....................................785 823-7403
John Welsh, *Partner*
David C Lewerenz, *Partner*
Robert L Murphey, *Partner*
John M Welsh, *Partner*
EMP: 13
SALES (est): 1.3MM **Privately Held**
SIC: 8042 Offices & clinics of optometrists

(G-10495)
FARM AND FAMILY INSUR ASSOC
2105 E Crawford Pl (67401-3719)
P.O. Box 646 (67402-0646)
PHONE....................................785 823-5071
Sherry Myers, *Principal*
Scott Gilpin, *Administration*
EMP: 20 **EST:** 1976
SALES (est): 3.3MM **Privately Held**
SIC: 6411 Insurance agents, brokers & service

(G-10496)
FARMERS RNCHERS LIVSTOCK CMNTY
1500 W Old Highway 40 (67401-2084)
P.O. Box 2595 (67402-2595)
PHONE....................................785 825-0211
Christian C Hoffman III, *President*
William C Hoffman, *Corp Secy*
Michael T Samples, *Vice Pres*
EMP: 57
SQ FT: 6,400
SALES: 135MM **Privately Held**
SIC: 5154 Auctioning livestock

(G-10497)
FEDERAL EXPRESS CORPORATION
Also Called: Fedex
3450 Centennial Rd (67401-8186)
PHONE....................................800 463-3339
EMP: 150
SALES (corp-wide): 69.6B **Publicly Held**
WEB: www.federalexpress.com
SIC: 4513 Letter delivery, private air; package delivery, private air; parcel delivery, private air
HQ: Federal Express Corporation
3610 Hacks Cross Rd
Memphis TN 38125
901 369-3600

(G-10498)
FEDEX FREIGHT CORPORATION
505 Graves Blvd Ste 4 (67401-4370)
PHONE....................................800 541-2032
EMP: 14
SALES (corp-wide): 69.6B **Publicly Held**
SIC: 4213 Trucking, except local
HQ: Fedex Freight Corporation
1715 Aaron Brenner Dr
Memphis TN 38120

(G-10499)
FEDEX GROUND PACKAGE SYS INC
3660 Scanlan Ave (67401-1716)
PHONE....................................800 463-3339
Kevin Champion, *Branch Mgr*
EMP: 20
SALES (corp-wide): 69.6B **Publicly Held**
SIC: 4215 Package delivery, vehicular
HQ: Fedex Ground Package System, Inc.
1000 Fed Ex Dr
Coraopolis PA 15108
800 463-3339

(G-10500)
FERCO INC
Also Called: Ferco Rental
264 S Broadway Blvd (67401-2798)
PHONE....................................785 825-6380
Ronald Frank, *President*
Joseph Frank, *Vice Pres*
EMP: 45
SQ FT: 3,500
SALES (est): 6.7MM **Privately Held**
SIC: 1794 7353 4212 5082 Excavation work; heavy construction equipment rental; heavy machinery transport, local; construction & mining machinery

(G-10501)
FIRST BANK KANSAS (HQ)
235 S Santa Fe Ave (67401-3931)
P.O. Box 1337 (67402-1337)
PHONE....................................785 825-2211
Lloyd Davidson, *President*
Steve Michel, *CFO*
Malinda Cunningham, *Cust Mgr*
Christina Moore, *Loan*
EMP: 75 **EST:** 1961
SQ FT: 5,000
SALES: 25.4MM
SALES (corp-wide): 22.4MM **Privately Held**
WEB: www.firstbankkansas.com
SIC: 6022 State commercial banks

(G-10502)
FIRST CHOICE SUPPORT SERVICES
Also Called: CHILD ADULT CARE FOOD PROGRAM
115 N 7th St (67401-2603)
PHONE....................................785 823-3555
Beverly David, *President*
Kingsford David, *Vice Pres*
Dusty Stuart, *Vice Pres*
Mindi David, *Director*
Brad Henne, *Admin Sec*
EMP: 11
SALES: 2.1MM **Privately Held**
SIC: 8322 Individual & family services

(G-10503)
FOLEY EQUIPMENT COMPANY
Also Called: Foley Equiptment
2225 N Ohio St (67401-9208)
PHONE....................................785 825-4661
Rick Sulsar, *Branch Mgr*
EMP: 25
SALES (corp-wide): 124.2MM **Privately Held**
SIC: 5082 General construction machinery & equipment

HQ: Foley Equipment Company
1550 S West St
Wichita KS 67213
316 943-4211

(G-10504)
FOR CENTRAL KANSAS FOUNDATION (PA)
617 E Elm St (67401-8537)
P.O. Box 2117 (67402-2117)
PHONE.................................785 825-6224
Les Sperling, *CEO*
Cindy Markel, *COO*
Richard Gargis, *CFO*
EMP: 60
SALES: 6.2MM **Privately Held**
SIC: 8322 8069 Self-help organization; drug addiction rehabilitation hospital

(G-10505)
FRANK CONSTRUCTION COMPANY
Also Called: Ferco
262 S Broadway Blvd (67401-2796)
PHONE.................................785 825-4213
Joseph S Frank, *President*
Ronald T Frank, *Treasurer*
EMP: 35
SQ FT: 5,000
SALES (est): 2.7MM **Privately Held**
SIC: 1791 1794 Structural steel erection; excavation & grading, building construction

(G-10506)
FRAZIER BROTHERS PLBG & CONTG
1408 Prospect Ave (67401-2414)
P.O. Box 2145 (67402-2145)
PHONE.................................785 452-9707
Mike Frazier, *President*
Mark Frazier, *Admin Sec*
EMP: 15
SALES (est): 2.9MM **Privately Held**
SIC: 1542 Nonresidential construction

(G-10507)
GARRISON TRANSPORTATION LLC
1630 Copper Ct (67401-4688)
PHONE.................................785 404-6744
Richard Garrison,
EMP: 5
SALES: 100K **Privately Held**
SIC: 3537 Trucks, tractors, loaders, carriers & similar equipment

(G-10508)
GE OIL & GAS COMPRESSION
Turbine Specialties
1648 W Magnolia Rd (67401-8148)
PHONE.................................785 823-9211
Roger Rochel, *Manager*
EMP: 90
SALES (corp-wide): 127.4MM **Privately Held**
SIC: 3511 Turbines & turbine generator set units, complete
PA: Ge Oil & Gas Compression Systems, Llc
16250 Port Nw
Houston TX 77041
713 354-1900

(G-10509)
GEOCORE LLC
2775 Arnold Ave Ste D (67401-8290)
P.O. Box 386 (67402-0386)
PHONE.................................785 826-1616
Dale Robl, *President*
Judy Robl, *Vice Pres*
Dave Corl, *Project Mgr*
Jon W Mills, *Admin Sec*
EMP: 24
SQ FT: 5,000
SALES: 1.9MM **Privately Held**
WEB: www.geocore.net
SIC: 8748 1781 4959 Environmental consultant; water well drilling; environmental cleanup services

(G-10510)
GIBSON PRODUCTS CO SALINA INC
Also Called: Ace Hardware
321 S Broadway Blvd (67401-3803)
PHONE.................................785 827-4474
Mark S Jones, *President*
Scott Jones, *Corp Secy*
Thomas F Jones, *Vice Pres*
EMP: 37 **EST:** 1961
SQ FT: 44,000
SALES: 7MM **Privately Held**
SIC: 5251 5199 Hardware; variety store merchandise

(G-10511)
GLASS SERVICES INC
161 S Broadway Blvd (67401-2767)
PHONE.................................785 823-5444
Steve R Eshleman, *President*
Carla D Eshleman, *Admin Sec*
Carla Eshleman, *Admin Sec*
EMP: 11
SQ FT: 9,000
SALES (est): 1.5MM **Privately Held**
SIC: 1751 7699 Window & door installation & erection; door & window repair

(G-10512)
GLEASON & SON SIGNS INC
2440 N 9th St (67401-8622)
PHONE.................................785 823-8615
Gary Gleason, *President*
Mary Gleason, *Bookkeeper*
EMP: 7
SALES (est): 410K **Privately Held**
SIC: 3993 1799 Signs & advertising specialties; sign installation & maintenance

(G-10513)
GLOBALINK INC
2725 Arnold Ave Ste 528 (67401)
P.O. Box 2582 (67402-2582)
PHONE.................................785 823-8284
Chris Chelvan, *President*
Brenda Chelvan, *Marketing Staff*
EMP: 51
SALES: 480K **Privately Held**
SIC: 7379 5045 Data processing consultant; computers, peripherals & software

(G-10514)
GRAIN BELT SUPPLY COMPANY INC
217 E Diamond Dr (67401-8624)
P.O. Box 615 (67402-0615)
PHONE.................................785 827-4491
Dl Sampson, *CEO*
Marc Wingo, *President*
Greg Myers, *Engineer*
Ben Hansen, *Sales Associate*
Steve Trumbo, *Info Tech Dir*
EMP: 134 **EST:** 1949
SQ FT: 300,000
SALES (est): 36.4MM **Privately Held**
WEB: www.grainbeltsupply.com
SIC: 3441 3523 3444 3535 Fabricated structural metal; farm machinery & equipment; sheet metalwork; conveyors & conveying equipment

(G-10515)
GREAT PLAINS FEDERAL CR UN
605 S Ohio St (67401-3362)
PHONE.................................785 823-9226
Dave Neuman, *Manager*
EMP: 10
SALES (corp-wide): 7.1MM **Privately Held**
WEB: www.greatplainsfcu.com
SIC: 6061 Federal credit unions
PA: Great Plains Federal Credit Union (Inc)
2306 S Range Line Rd
Joplin MO 64804
417 626-8500

(G-10516)
GREAT PLAINS INTERNATIONAL LLC (DH)
1525 E North St (67401-8562)
PHONE.................................785 823-3276
Roy Applequist, *President*
Jesse Smith, *Business Mgr*
Greg Arnett, *Engineer*
Jeff Carolan, *Elder*
▲ **EMP:** 13
SALES (est): 5.9MM **Privately Held**
SIC: 3523 Farm machinery & equipment
HQ: Great Plains Manufacturing Incorporated
1525 E North St
Salina KS 67401
785 823-3276

(G-10517)
GREAT PLAINS LOGISTICS INC
Also Called: A C I Brokerage
1935 E North St (67401-8588)
P.O. Box 166 (67402-0166)
PHONE.................................785 823-2261
Sherwin Fast, *CEO*
Roy Applequist, *President*
Sheldon Muninger, *Corp Secy*
EMP: 70
SALES (est): 10.1MM **Privately Held**
WEB: www.greatplainsmfg.com
SIC: 4731 Brokers, shipping
HQ: Great Plains Manufacturing Incorporated
1525 E North St
Salina KS 67401
785 823-3276

(G-10518)
GREAT PLAINS MANUFACTURING INC (DH)
Also Called: Land Pride
1525 E North St (67401-8562)
P.O. Box 5060 (67402-5060)
PHONE.................................785 823-3276
Linda Salem, *President*
Masato Yoshikawa, *Chairman*
Rye Degarmo, *Vice Pres*
Mark Demoss, *Opers Mgr*
Derek Urbanek, *Facilities Mgr*
◆ **EMP:** 153
SQ FT: 23,000
SALES (est): 559.4MM **Privately Held**
WEB: www.greatplainsmfg.com
SIC: 5083 3523 Farm & garden machinery; planting, haying, harvesting & processing machinery

(G-10519)
GREAT PLAINS MANUFACTURING INC
1733 Dewey St (67401-8503)
PHONE.................................785 825-1509
James C Johnson, *Human Resources*
Darrell Deneault, *Manager*
EMP: 450 **Privately Held**
WEB: www.greatplainsmfg.com
SIC: 3523 Farm machinery & equipment
HQ: Great Plains Manufacturing Incorporated
1525 E North St
Salina KS 67401
785 823-3276

(G-10520)
GREAT PLAINS MANUFACTURING INC
Also Called: Great Plains Trucking
1935 E North St (67401-8588)
PHONE.................................785 823-2255
Fred Morgan, *Principal*
EMP: 7 **Privately Held**
WEB: www.greatplainsmfg.com
SIC: 3523 Farm machinery & equipment
HQ: Great Plains Manufacturing Incorporated
1525 E North St
Salina KS 67401
785 823-3276

(G-10521)
GREAT PLAINS MUTUAL INSUR CO
Also Called: Columbia Insurance Group
124 Iowa Ave (67401-3228)
P.O. Box 2180 (67402-2180)
PHONE.................................785 825-5531
Bob Wagner, *President*
Roger Ballard, *Treasurer*
Becky Good, *Underwriter*
Jim Cunningham, *Admin Sec*
EMP: 35
SQ FT: 10,000
SALES (est): 9.2MM
SALES (corp-wide): 178.6MM **Privately Held**
SIC: 6331 Fire, marine & casualty insurance & carriers
HQ: Columbia Insurance Group, Inc.
2102 Whitegate Dr
Columbia MO 65202
573 474-6193

(G-10522)
GREAT PLAINS TRUCKING INC
1621 Dewey St (67401-8508)
P.O. Box 5060 (67402-5060)
PHONE.................................785 823-2261
Sherwin Fast, *President*
EMP: 65
SQ FT: 1,400
SALES (est): 9.8MM **Privately Held**
WEB: www.greatplainsmfg.com
SIC: 4213 Trucking, except local
HQ: Great Plains Manufacturing Incorporated
1525 E North St
Salina KS 67401
785 823-3276

(G-10523)
GREYHOUND LINES INC
671 Westport Blvd (67401-4304)
PHONE.................................785 827-9754
EMP: 25
SALES (corp-wide): 8.9B **Privately Held**
SIC: 4111 Local/Suburban Transportation
HQ: Greyhound Lines, Inc.
350 N Saint Paul St # 300
Dallas TX 75201
214 849-8000

(G-10524)
GUARDIAN BUSINESS SERVICES
141 S 4th St (67401-2801)
P.O. Box 1906 (67402-1906)
PHONE.................................785 823-1635
Terry Holovach, *Owner*
EMP: 10
SALES (est): 380K **Privately Held**
SIC: 7389 5049 Repossession service; bank equipment & supplies

(G-10525)
H K W OIL COMPANY INC
Graves Blvd (67401)
P.O. Box 1851 (67402-1851)
PHONE.................................785 483-6185
Le Roy Waymaster, *President*
Carol Herber, *Corp Secy*
EMP: 7
SALES (est): 400.9K **Privately Held**
SIC: 1311 Crude petroleum production

(G-10526)
H W LOCHNER INC
1823 S Ohio St (67401-6601)
PHONE.................................785 827-3603
James Bishop, *President*
EMP: 40
SALES (corp-wide): 91.2MM **Privately Held**
WEB: www.bwrcorp.com
SIC: 8711 Consulting engineer
PA: H. W. Lochner, Inc.
225 W Washington St # 1200
Chicago IL 60606
312 372-7346

(G-10527)
H&R BLOCK INC
Also Called: H & R Block
1219 W Crawford St Ste A (67401-4686)
PHONE.................................785 827-4253
Chris Tempe, *Manager*
EMP: 12
SALES (corp-wide): 3B **Publicly Held**
WEB: www.hrblock.com
SIC: 7291 Tax return preparation services
PA: H&R Block, Inc.
1 H&R Block Way
Kansas City MO 64105
816 854-3000

(G-10528)
HABCO INC
248 E Berg Rd (67401-8907)
PHONE.................................785 823-0440

Joe Hodges, *President*
Tim Buyse, *Vice Pres*
Andy Fuller, *Project Mgr*
Klint Woods, *Sales Staff*
Mike Byers, *Marketing Staff*
EMP: 45
SQ FT: 13,500
SALES (est): 9.2MM **Privately Held**
WEB: www.habcoinc.com
SIC: 1796 Millwright

(G-10529)
HAIR AFFAIRE
Also Called: Hair Affair'e Beauty Salon
808 E Crawford St (67401-5106)
PHONE..................................785 827-0445
Dixie Jones, *Owner*
EMP: 12
SQ FT: 1,200
SALES (est): 170.7K **Privately Held**
WEB: www.hairaffaire.com
SIC: 7231 Hairdressers

(G-10530)
HAIR LOFT
Also Called: Hair Loft Salon
1330 W Crawford St (67401-4572)
PHONE..................................785 827-2306
Shirley Jargenson, *Partner*
Tina Lanoue, *Partner*
EMP: 16 **EST:** 1975
SALES (est): 480K **Privately Held**
SIC: 7231 Facial salons

(G-10531)
HAJOCA CORPORATION
333 N Front St (67401-2037)
PHONE..................................785 825-1333
Lynn Kelso, *Manager*
EMP: 11
SALES (corp-wide): 2.3B **Privately Held**
WEB: www.hajoca.com
SIC: 5074 5999 5084 5075 Plumbing fittings & supplies; heating equipment (hydronic); plumbing & heating supplies; pumps & pumping equipment; air conditioning & ventilation equipment & supplies; water heaters, electric; pipe & tubing, steel
PA: Hajoca Corporation
2001 Joshua Rd
Lafayette Hill PA 19444
610 649-1430

(G-10532)
HAMPTON & ROYCE LC
119 W Iron Ave Ste 1000 (67401-2629)
P.O. Box 1247 (67402-1247)
PHONE..................................785 827-7251
David Mosher, *Principal*
Terry E Crisp,
Deborah E James,
Jeffery E King,
Tish S Morrical,
EMP: 32
SALES (est): 3.5MM **Privately Held**
WEB: www.hamptonlaw.com
SIC: 8111 General practice attorney, lawyer

(G-10533)
HAMPTON INNS LLC
401 W Schilling Rd (67401-8902)
PHONE..................................785 823-9800
Teryl McGaha, *Branch Mgr*
EMP: 25
SALES (corp-wide): 8.9B **Publicly Held**
WEB: www.premierhotels.us
SIC: 7011 Hotels & motels
HQ: Hampton Inns, Llc
755 Crossover Ln
Memphis TN 38117
901 374-5000

(G-10534)
HANNEBAUM GRAIN CO INC (PA)
2130 S Ohio St Ste A (67401-6852)
P.O. Box 1157 (67402-1157)
PHONE..................................785 825-8205
Leon Hannebaum, *President*
Judy Hannebaum, *Vice Pres*
EMP: 14 **EST:** 1979
SQ FT: 3,600
SALES: 200K **Privately Held**
WEB: www.hannebaumgrain.com
SIC: 5153 4731 Grains; truck transportation brokers

(G-10535)
HARBIN CONSTRUCTION LLC
2200 Centennial Rd (67401-8119)
P.O. Box 534 (67402-0534)
PHONE..................................785 825-1651
Ross Hoffhines,
Melva Hoffhines,
EMP: 30
SQ FT: 1,600
SALES (est): 8.2MM **Privately Held**
WEB: www.harbinconstruction.com
SIC: 1542 1541 Commercial & office building, new construction; commercial & office buildings, renovation & repair; industrial buildings, new construction; renovation, remodeling & repairs: industrial buildings

(G-10536)
HARRIS ENTERPRISES GROUP
Also Called: Buyers Guide
1118 W Cloud St (67401-7063)
P.O. Box 740 (67402-0740)
PHONE..................................785 827-6035
Olaf Frandsen, *President*
Michelle Burton, *Office Mgr*
EMP: 15
SALES (est): 801.2K **Privately Held**
SIC: 2711 Newspapers, publishing & printing

(G-10537)
HEART LIVING CENTERS COLO LLC
2035 E Iron Ave Ste 224 (67401-3433)
PHONE..................................817 739-8529
Dave Reed, *Ch of Bd*
Kurt Ravenstein, *President*
EMP: 99
SALES (est): 1.1MM **Privately Held**
SIC: 8051 Skilled nursing care facilities

(G-10538)
HEART OF AMERICA INN INC
Also Called: Best Western
632 Westport Blvd Ste 1 (67401-4360)
PHONE..................................785 827-9315
Thomas Weis, *President*
Jan Weis, *Corp Secy*
EMP: 30 **EST:** 1972
SQ FT: 35,000
SALES (est): 876.8K **Privately Held**
SIC: 7011 Hotels & motels

(G-10539)
HEARTLAND ADJUSTMENTS INC
801 E Prescott Rd (67401-7412)
P.O. Box 2666 (67402-2666)
PHONE..................................785 823-5100
Sam Vigare, *President*
EMP: 10
SALES: 800K **Privately Held**
SIC: 6411 Insurance claim adjusters, not employed by insurance company

(G-10540)
HEDGES NEON SALES INC
616 Reynolds St (67401-1932)
P.O. Box 765 (67402-0765)
PHONE..................................785 827-9341
Nancy J Hedges, *President*
EMP: 5
SQ FT: 19,500
SALES: 300K **Privately Held**
SIC: 3993 7359 Neon signs; sign rental

(G-10541)
HEINEKEN ELECTRIC COMPANY INC
1627 Sunflower Rd (67401-1758)
PHONE..................................785 404-3157
Jenny Heineken, *President*
EMP: 17
SALES (corp-wide): 3.8MM **Privately Held**
SIC: 1731 General electrical contractor
PA: Heineken Electric Co., Inc.
3121b Us 24 Hwy
Beloit KS 67420
785 738-3831

(G-10542)
HOFFS MACHINE & WELDING INC
925 E North St (67401-2407)
PHONE..................................785 823-6215
Henry Lee Hoff, *President*
Mark Hoff, *General Mgr*
Carol Hoff, *Bookkeeper*
Donald E Hoff, *Admin Sec*
EMP: 10
SQ FT: 15,000
SALES (est): 1.9MM **Privately Held**
SIC: 3599 Machine shop, jobbing & repair

(G-10543)
HOLIDAY HEALTHCARE LLC
Also Called: Holiday Rsort Adult Care Rehab
2825 Resort Dr (67401-9535)
PHONE..................................785 825-2201
Randy Jost, *Manager*
EMP: 55
SALES (corp-wide): 6.9MM **Privately Held**
SIC: 8051 Convalescent home with continuous nursing care
PA: Holiday Healthcare Llc
2700 W 30th Ave
Emporia KS 66801
620 343-9285

(G-10544)
HOLIDAY INN EXPRESS & SUITES
755 W Diamond Dr (67401-9544)
PHONE..................................785 404-3300
Darren Nearhood, *General Mgr*
EMP: 25
SALES (est): 165.2K **Privately Held**
SIC: 7011 Hotels & motels

(G-10545)
HOLMES BASEMENT CONSTRUCTION
Also Called: Wayne Holmes Basements
1950 Ridgelea Dr (67401-3652)
PHONE..................................785 823-6770
Colleen Holmes, *Owner*
EMP: 10
SALES (est): 690K **Privately Held**
WEB: www.basements.org
SIC: 1771 Concrete work

(G-10546)
HOME HEALTH AGENCY
125 W Elm St (67401-2315)
PHONE..................................785 826-6600
Bronson Farmer, *Director*
EMP: 10
SALES (est): 174.3K **Privately Held**
SIC: 8099 Health & allied services

(G-10547)
HOSPICE OF SALINA INC
730 Holly Ln (67401-8452)
P.O. Box 2238 (67402-2238)
PHONE..................................785 825-1717
Kim Fair, *President*
EMP: 15
SALES: 1.5MM **Privately Held**
SIC: 8052 Personal care facility

(G-10548)
HRE—COLORADO SPRINGS LLC
2035 E Iron Ave Ste 224 (67401-3433)
PHONE..................................817 739-8529
Dave Reed, *Ch of Bd*
Kurt Ravenstein, *President*
EMP: 99
SQ FT: 103,428
SALES (est): 604.9K **Privately Held**
SIC: 8051 Skilled nursing care facilities

(G-10549)
IMAGES (PA)
Also Called: Images Recycling
132 S 4th St (67401-2802)
P.O. Box 773 (67402-0773)
PHONE..................................785 827-0824
Ken M Reitz, *Owner*
EMP: 6 **EST:** 1976
SQ FT: 8,000
SALES (est): 450K **Privately Held**
SIC: 5943 5734 5112 2752 Office forms & supplies; computer software & accessories; photocopying supplies; data processing supplies; computer paper; carbon paper; commercial printing, lithographic; refuse systems

(G-10550)
ISG TECHNOLOGY LLC (PA)
3030 Cortland Cir 300 (67401-7874)
PHONE..................................785 823-1555
Ben Foster, *President*
Julie Greiner, *General Mgr*
Walter Hirsekorn, *General Mgr*
Larry Pankratz, *COO*
Kipp Adkins, *Vice Pres*
EMP: 148
SQ FT: 5,000
SALES: 75MM **Privately Held**
WEB: www.isgtech.com
SIC: 7379 Computer related maintenance services

(G-10551)
JACK M SCHWARTZ (PA)
Also Called: Linsco Priovate Ledger
111 S 5th St (67401-2858)
PHONE..................................785 823-3035
Jack Schwartz, *Owner*
Rick Roberts, *CTO*
EMP: 13
SALES (est): 1.8MM **Privately Held**
WEB: www.jmsfin.com
SIC: 6211 Brokers, security

(G-10552)
JAYHAWK ROOFING & SUPPLY CO
917 W North St (67401-2060)
P.O. Box 391 (67402-0391)
PHONE..................................785 825-5466
Fax: 785 825-4532
EMP: 23 **EST:** 1925
SQ FT: 3,500
SALES (est): 1.2MM **Privately Held**
SIC: 1761 Roofing Contractor

(G-10553)
JEFFREY A HARRIS
Also Called: Precision Machine & Welding
2231d Centennial Rd Ste 1 (67401-1765)
PHONE..................................785 823-8760
Jeffrey A Harris, *Owner*
EMP: 20
SQ FT: 12,000
SALES (est): 1.5MM **Privately Held**
WEB: www.pmw-wheeltracker.com
SIC: 3821 1799 Laboratory equipment: fume hoods, distillation racks, etc.; welding on site

(G-10554)
JERRY R LUNDGRIN DDS
Also Called: Lungrin Dntl Assctes Chartered
909 E Wayne Ave (67401-2201)
P.O. Box 1424 (67402-1424)
PHONE..................................785 825-5473
Jerry R Lundgrin DDS, *Owner*
EMP: 10
SALES (est): 618.1K **Privately Held**
WEB: www.lundgrindds.com
SIC: 8021 Dentists' office

(G-10555)
JIMS FORMAL WEAR LLC
Also Called: Mr Penguin
2118 Planet Ave (67401-7391)
PHONE..................................785 825-1529
David Fazel, *Manager*
EMP: 25
SALES (corp-wide): 28.7MM **Privately Held**
WEB: www.jimsfw.com
SIC: 7299 Tuxedo rental
PA: Jim's Formal Wear Llc
804 E Broadway
Trenton IL 62293
618 224-9211

(G-10556)
JMH CLEANING SERVICE
P.O. Box 2985 (67402-2985)
PHONE..................................785 819-0725

Jamy Hurren, *Principal*
EMP: 15
SALES (est): 634.6K **Privately Held**
SIC: 7699 Cleaning services

(G-10557)
JRM ENTERPRISES INC
Also Called: America Jet
2010 Rogers Ct (67401-1750)
PHONE..................................785 404-1328
Fax: 785 825-6264
EMP: 20
SALES (est): 1.6MM **Privately Held**
SIC: 4581 7359 5172 Aviation Maintenance Fueling Instruction

(G-10558)
K C D INC
808 E Crawford St (67401-5106)
PHONE..................................785 827-0445
Dixie Jones, *President*
EMP: 14
SALES (est): 99.8K **Privately Held**
SIC: 7231 Beauty shops

(G-10559)
K S A J OLDIES
Also Called: Ebc
131 N Santa Fe Ave Fl 3 (67401-2670)
PHONE 785 823-1111
Larry Riggins, *President*
EMP: 65
SALES (est): 1.7MM **Privately Held**
WEB: www.ebclink.com
SIC: 4832 7313 Radio broadcasting stations; radio advertising representative

(G-10560)
KA-COMM INC (PA)
326 S Clark St (67401-3838)
PHONE..................................785 827-8555
Roland L Fischer, *President*
Craig Fischer, *Vice Pres*
Scott Fischer, *Vice Pres*
Nancy Fischer, *Treasurer*
Rj Meierhoff, *Sales Staff*
EMP: 11 **EST:** 1960
SQ FT: 3,000
SALES (est): 7.1MM **Privately Held**
SIC: 5065 7622 Communication equipment; radio repair shop

(G-10561)
KAN TEX HOSPITALITY INC
Also Called: Hammer Realty Group
222 E Diamond Dr (67401-8624)
P.O. Box 891, Addison TX (75001-0891)
PHONE..................................785 404-1870
Lynn Hammer, *Owner*
EMP: 15
SALES (est): 385.8K **Privately Held**
SIC: 7011 Motels

(G-10562)
KANSAS ASSOCIATION OF CHILD
Also Called: CHILD CARE AWARE OF KANSAS
1508 E Iron Ave (67401-3236)
P.O. Box 2294 (67402-2294)
PHONE..................................785 823-3343
George Lewis, *Vice Pres*
Kara Revell, *Finance*
Leadell Ediger, *Exec Dir*
EMP: 22 **EST:** 1991
SQ FT: 3,400
SALES: 2.4MM **Privately Held**
WEB: www.kaccrra.org
SIC: 8351 Group day care center

(G-10563)
KANSAS BROADBAND INTERNET
Charles W Jameson Ste 601 (67401)
P.O. Box 2221 (67402-2221)
PHONE..................................785 825-0199
Scott Rosebrook, *President*
EMP: 10
SALES (est): 1.2MM **Privately Held**
SIC: 4813

(G-10564)
KANSAS DEPARTMENT TRNSP
1006 N 3rd St (67401-8239)
P.O. Box 857 (67402-0857)
PHONE..................................785 823-3754
Don Drickey, *District Mgr*
Damian Hancock, *Technician*
EMP: 350 **Privately Held**
WEB: www.nwwichitabypass.com
SIC: 1611 9621 Highway & street maintenance; regulation, administration of transportation;
HQ: Kansas Department Of Transportation
700 Sw Harrison St # 500
Topeka KS 66603
785 296-3501

(G-10565)
KANSAS GRAIN INSPECTION SVC
1700 E Iron Ave Ste A (67401-3403)
PHONE..................................785 827-3671
Kevin Peoples, *Manager*
EMP: 10
SALES (corp-wide): 7.2MM **Privately Held**
WEB: www.kansasgrain.com
SIC: 7389 0723 Inspection & testing services; cash grain crops market preparation services
PA: Kansas Grain Inspection Service Inc
3800 Nw 14th St
Topeka KS 66618
785 233-7063

(G-10566)
KANSAS KENWORTH INC
Also Called: Midwest Kenworth
2301 N Ohio St (67401-2467)
P.O. Box 1907 (67402-1907)
PHONE..................................785 823-9700
David Rohleter, *Manager*
EMP: 22
SALES (corp-wide): 1B **Privately Held**
SIC: 5012 7699 Truck tractors; tractor repair
HQ: Kansas Kenworth, Inc.
1524 N Corrington Ave
Kansas City MO 64120

(G-10567)
KANSAS STATE UNIVERSITY
Also Called: Engineering Technology Dept
2310 Centennial Rd Tc100a (67401-8196)
PHONE..................................785 826-2646
Dennis Kuhlman, *Principal*
EMP: 65
SALES (corp-wide): 637.6MM **Privately Held**
WEB: www.ksu.edu
SIC: 8221 7231 University; beauty shops
PA: Kansas State University
Anderson Hall 110 1301 Mi St Anderson Ha
Manhattan KS 66506
785 532-6011

(G-10568)
KARCHER INVESTMENTS INC
Also Called: Landscape Management Services
4820 N Dorman Dr (67401-9220)
PHONE..................................785 452-2850
Paul Karcher, *President*
Lynette Karcher, *Vice Pres*
EMP: 10
SALES (est): 453.8K **Privately Held**
SIC: 4959 1711 0782 Snowplowing; sprinkler contractors; sodding contractor

(G-10569)
KASA COMPANIES INC
Also Called: Kasa Fabrication
304 E Avenue B (67401-8923)
PHONE..................................785 825-5612
Mike Haug, *Branch Mgr*
EMP: 60
SALES (corp-wide): 31.8MM **Privately Held**
WEB: www.kasacontrols.com
SIC: 3613 3444 3441 3714 Control panels, electric; sheet metalwork; fabricated structural metal; motor vehicle parts & accessories
PA: Kasa Companies, Inc.
418 E Avenue B
Salina KS 67401
785 825-7181

(G-10570)
KASA COMPANIES INC (PA)
Also Called: Kasa Fab
418 E Avenue B (67401-8960)
PHONE..................................785 825-7181
Mike Haug, *CEO*
Dan Stutterheim, *President*
Steve Pistora, *VP Opers*
Brad Affolter, *Project Mgr*
Mike Nelson, *Buyer*
▼ **EMP:** 115
SQ FT: 55,000
SALES: 31.8MM **Privately Held**
WEB: www.kasacontrols.com
SIC: 3613 3714 3625 Control panels, electric; panel & distribution boards & other related apparatus; motor vehicle parts & accessories; relays & industrial controls

(G-10571)
KASA COMPANIES INC
Also Called: Kasa Fab
41 E Ave B (67401)
PHONE..................................785 825-5612
Peter Charowhas, *Branch Mgr*
EMP: 88
SALES (corp-wide): 31.8MM **Privately Held**
WEB: www.kasacontrols.com
SIC: 3613 3714 3625 Control panels, electric; panel & distribution boards & other related apparatus; motor vehicle parts & accessories; relays & industrial controls
PA: Kasa Companies, Inc.
418 E Avenue B
Salina KS 67401
785 825-7181

(G-10572)
KCOE ISOM LLP
3030 Cortland Cir (67401-7874)
P.O. Box 1100 (67402-1100)
PHONE..................................785 825-1561
Chris Bonacorsi, *CPA*
Julie E Kauffman, *CPA*
Lisa Baalman, *Manager*
James Blade, *Manager*
Emily Clark, *Manager*
EMP: 46
SALES (corp-wide): 52.8MM **Privately Held**
SIC: 8741 Management services
PA: Kcoe Isom, Llp
3030 Courtland Cir
Salina KS
785 825-1561

(G-10573)
KEJR INC (PA)
Also Called: Geoprobe Systems
1835 Wall St (67401-1736)
PHONE..................................785 825-1842
Melvin Kejr, *President*
Tom Christy, *Vice Pres*
▲ **EMP:** 118
SQ FT: 28,500
SALES (est): 46.5MM **Privately Held**
WEB: www.geoprobe-di.com
SIC: 3523 Soil sampling machines

(G-10574)
KENNEDY BRKLEY YRNVICH WLLMSON (PA)
119 W Iron Ave Ste 710 (67401-2600)
P.O. Box 2567 (67402-2567)
PHONE..................................785 825-4674
George Yarnevich, *President*
Lynn Herbic, *Business Mgr*
James Angell, *Shareholder*
EMP: 15 **EST:** 1961
SALES (est): 1.4MM **Privately Held**
SIC: 8111 General practice law office

(G-10575)
KING INDUSTRIES INC
Also Called: King's Window Coverings
1368 W Grand Ave (67401-1857)
P.O. Box 3378 (67402-3378)
PHONE..................................785 823-1785
Craig King, *President*
Brenda King, *Vice Pres*
Paul Stusalitus, *Production*
David Moretti, *Engineer*
Ashley Zuraitis, *Engineer*
▲ **EMP:** 23
SQ FT: 22,500
SALES (est): 2.4MM **Privately Held**
SIC: 2591 5023 Window blinds; vertical blinds

(G-10576)
KLA ENVIRONMENTAL SERVICES
1700 E Iron Ave (67401-3401)
PHONE..................................785 823-0097
Richard McKee, *President*
Cindy Roush, *Corp Secy*
EMP: 11
SALES: 1.6MM **Privately Held**
WEB: www.klaenviro.com
SIC: 8748 8711 Environmental consultant; consulting engineer

(G-10577)
L & S SCOTT INC
511 N Santa Fe Ave (67401-1949)
P.O. Box P.O 1575 (67402)
PHONE..................................785 643-1488
Lucas Scott, *President*
EMP: 15
SALES (est): 1MM **Privately Held**
SIC: 4212 Local trucking, without storage

(G-10578)
LAND INSTITUTE
2440 E Water Well Rd (67401-9051)
PHONE..................................785 823-5376
Conn Nugent, *Ch of Bd*
Wes Jackson, *President*
Tim Crews, *Research*
John M Simpson, *Treasurer*
EMP: 20 **EST:** 1976
SQ FT: 2,200
SALES: 4.2MM **Privately Held**
WEB: www.landinstitute.org
SIC: 8731 Natural resource research

(G-10579)
LAND TITLE SERVICES INC
136 N 7th St (67401-2604)
PHONE..................................785 823-7223
Charles Griffin, *President*
Michael Hoppock, *Senior VP*
Linda Griffin, *Treasurer*
EMP: 11
SALES (est): 662.1K **Privately Held**
SIC: 6541 Title & trust companies

(G-10580)
LEE HAWORTH CONSTRUCTION CO
348 E Avenue A (67401-9144)
PHONE..................................785 823-7168
Bob Haworth, *President*
Lee Haworth, *Vice Pres*
Carol Brown, *Admin Sec*
EMP: 10 **EST:** 1957
SALES (est): 945.8K **Privately Held**
SIC: 1521 1542 New construction, single-family houses; commercial & office building, new construction

(G-10581)
LIBERTY HEALTHCARE OF OKLAHOMA
Also Called: Smoky Hill Rehabilitation Ctr
1007 Johnstown Ave (67401-3021)
PHONE..................................785 823-7107
Joe Beneer, *Administration*
EMP: 100 **Privately Held**
SIC: 8051 8059 Skilled nursing care facilities; nursing home, except skilled & intermediate care facility
PA: Liberty Healthcare Of Oklahoma Inc
3073 Horseshoe Dr S # 100
Naples FL 34104

(G-10582)
LIFE TOUCH EMS INC
901 E Crawford St Ste 300 (67401-5124)
PHONE..................................785 825-5115
Karyn Fields, *President*
EMP: 15

▲ = Import ▼=Export
◆ =Import/Export

SALES (est): 497.6K Privately Held
SIC: 4119 Ambulance service

(G-10583)
LIGHTHOUSE PROPERTIES LLC (PA)
500 Graves Blvd (67401-4306)
PHONE....785 825-2221
Trace E Walker,
EMP: 50
SALES (est): 4.5MM Privately Held
SIC: 7011 Hotels & motels

(G-10584)
LONG SHOT ENTERPRISES LLC
824 N 8th & 9th St # 9 (67401)
PHONE....785 493-0171
Toll Free:....877 -
Douglas Long, *Mng Member*
Cynthia Long,
EMP: 12 EST: 2000
SALES (est): 1.6MM Privately Held
SIC: 5199 2391 Tarpaulins; curtains & draperies

(G-10585)
LOWES HOME CENTERS LLC
3035 S 9th St (67401-7869)
PHONE....785 452-9303
Mark Scruton, *Branch Mgr*
EMP: 150
SALES (corp-wide): 71.3B Publicly Held
SIC: 5211 5031 5722 5064 Home centers; building materials, exterior; building materials, interior; household appliance stores; electrical appliances, television & radio
HQ: Lowe's Home Centers, Llc
1605 Curtis Bridge Rd
Wilkesboro NC 28697
336 658-4000

(G-10586)
LUMINOUS NEON INC
Also Called: Luminous Neon Art Sign Systems
1500 W Schilling Rd (67401-1734)
PHONE....785 823-1789
Don Schnider, *Sales/Mktg Mgr*
EMP: 6
SALES (corp-wide): 11.6MM Privately Held
SIC: 3993 1799 Electric signs; sign installation & maintenance
PA: Luminous Neon, Inc.
1429 W 4th Ave
Hutchinson KS 67501
620 662-2363

(G-10587)
M L K CHILD DEVELOPMENT CENTER
1215 N Santa Fe Ave (67401-8737)
PHONE....785 827-3841
Karen Henderson, *Director*
EMP: 20
SALES: 409.1K Privately Held
SIC: 8351 Child day care services

(G-10588)
MAI SKY SYSTEMS INC
Also Called: Material Management Solutions
234 E Avenue A (67401-9143)
P.O. Box 920 (67402-0920)
PHONE....785 825-9151
Paul K MAI, *President*
Marilyn MAI, *Director*
Frieda J MAI, *Admin Sec*
Frieda MAI, *Admin Sec*
EMP: 5
SALES (est): 484K Privately Held
SIC: 3441 Building components, structural steel

(G-10589)
MALLERY CLINIC LLC
655 S Santa Fe Ave (67401-4147)
PHONE....785 825-9024
EMP: 14 EST: 1994
SALES (est): 710K Privately Held
SIC: 8011 Medical Doctor's Office

(G-10590)
MANE EVENT
1529 W Crawford St (67401-4571)
PHONE....785 827-1999
Cleo Francisco, *Owner*
EMP: 12
SALES: 120K Privately Held
SIC: 7231 5699 5122 Hairdressers; wigs, toupees & wiglets; cosmetics, perfumes & hair products

(G-10591)
MANKO CORPORATION
410 N Front St (67401-2057)
P.O. Box 1965 (67402-1965)
PHONE....785 825-1301
Robert R Konzem, *President*
Beverly J Konzem, *Treasurer*
EMP: 10
SQ FT: 6,000
SALES (est): 1.8MM Privately Held
SIC: 5085 3562 Bearings; ball bearings & parts

(G-10592)
MARIETTA KELLOGG & PRICE
148 S 7th St (67401-2892)
P.O. Box 2478 (67402-2478)
PHONE....785 825-5403
Robert Marietta, *Partner*
Wendell Kellogg, *Partner*
Elizabeth Marietta, *Partner*
Scott Price, *Partner*
EMP: 10
SALES (est): 1MM Privately Held
SIC: 8111 General practice law office

(G-10593)
MARTIN LUTHER KING JR CHILD DE
1215 N Santa Fe Ave (67401-8737)
PHONE....785 827-3841
Karen Hendersen, *Exec Dir*
EMP: 23
SALES: 536K Privately Held
SIC: 8351 Child day care services

(G-10594)
MATHESON TRI-GAS INC
Also Called: Linweld
100b E Avenue A (67401-8920)
PHONE....785 493-8200
Rusty Booth, *Branch Mgr*
EMP: 12 Privately Held
WEB: www.linweld.net
SIC: 5084 Welding machinery & equipment
HQ: Matheson Tri-Gas, Inc.
150 Allen Rd Ste 302
Basking Ridge NJ 07920
908 991-9200

(G-10595)
MC INTIRE WELDING INC
Also Called: McIntire Welding Service
1630 Copper Ct (67401-4688)
PHONE....785 823-5454
Richard Garrison, *President*
Karen Garrison, *Treasurer*
EMP: 23
SQ FT: 15,582
SALES: 1.5MM Privately Held
WEB: www.mw.kscoxmail.com
SIC: 7692 Welding repair

(G-10596)
MCGINLEYS CRPT PRO JANTR SVCS
2141 Centennial Rd (67401-1763)
P.O. Box 2983 (67402-2983)
PHONE....785 825-2627
Marylea McGinley, *Owner*
Mary L McGinley, *Owner*
EMP: 30
SALES (est): 748.3K Privately Held
SIC: 7217 Carpet & upholstery cleaning

(G-10597)
MCSHARES INC (PA)
Also Called: Viobin U.S.A.
1835 E North St (67401-8587)
P.O. Box 1460 (67402-1460)
PHONE....785 825-2181
Monte White, *President*
William L Edison, *Chairman*
Dan Lee, *CFO*
◆ EMP: 46
SQ FT: 75,000
SALES (est): 27.5MM Privately Held
WEB: www.mcshares.com
SIC: 2041 Flour; wheat germ

(G-10598)
MCSHARES INC
Repco
1835 E North St (67401-8587)
PHONE....785 825-2181
Monte White, *President*
Stacy Gonzales, *Director*
EMP: 35
SALES (corp-wide): 27.5MM Privately Held
WEB: www.mcshares.com
SIC: 2834 3295 Vitamin, nutrient & hematinic preparations for human use; minerals, ground or treated
PA: Mcshares, Inc.
1835 E North St
Salina KS 67401
785 825-2181

(G-10599)
MDF INDUSTRIES INC
1012 N Marymount Rd (67401)
P.O. Box 2302 (67402-2302)
PHONE....785 827-4450
Mike Forristal, *President*
Joan Forristal, *Corp Secy*
EMP: 10
SQ FT: 37,000
SALES (est): 2.2MM Privately Held
SIC: 3441 5039 Building components, structural steel; joists; metal guardrails

(G-10600)
MID KANSAS TOOL & ELECTRIC INC (PA)
Also Called: Mid Kansas Tool and Electric
314 W Cloud St (67401-5613)
P.O. Box 251 (67402-0251)
PHONE....785 825-9521
Steve Albrecht, *President*
Rhonda Albrecht, *Principal*
EMP: 12
SQ FT: 3,200
SALES (est): 1.4MM Privately Held
WEB: www.midkansastool.com
SIC: 7629 7699 0191 5072 Tool repair, electric; compressor repair; general farms, primarily crop; hand tools; motors, electric; saws & sawing equipment

(G-10601)
MID-STATES ENERGY WORKS INC
618 N Santa Fe Ave (67401-1952)
P.O. Box 1098 (67402-1098)
PHONE....785 827-3631
Mike Schmaderer, *President*
J Derek Shockley, *Corp Secy*
Carol Cameron, *Manager*
Sharon Schmaderer, *Admin Sec*
EMP: 11
SQ FT: 5,000
SALES (est): 1.6MM Privately Held
WEB: www.msew.biz
SIC: 8748 8711 1731 Energy conservation consultant; energy conservation engineering; energy management controls

(G-10602)
MIDWEST SIDING INCORPORATED (PA)
Also Called: A B C Midwest Siding
1550 S Broadway Blvd (67401-7048)
PHONE....785 825-5576
Grant Warhurst, *Treasurer*
Mary Warhurst, *Treasurer*
EMP: 25
SALES (est): 2.4MM Privately Held
SIC: 1761 1751 7353 Siding contractor; window & door (prefabricated) installation; heavy construction equipment rental

(G-10603)
MIDWEST SIDING INC
1504 W State St (67401-9570)
PHONE....785 825-0606
EMP: 24
SALES (corp-wide): 2.7MM Privately Held
SIC: 1761 5031 2394 1751 Roofing/Siding Contr Whol Lumber/Plywd/Millwk Mfg Canvas/Related Prdts Carpentry Contractor Masonry/Stone Contractor
PA: Midwest Siding Inc
4240 W State St
Salina KS 67401
785 825-0606

(G-10604)
MORRIS COMMUNICATIONS CO LLC
131 N Santa Fe Ave Fl 3 (67401-2670)
P.O. Box 80 (67402-0080)
PHONE....785 823-1111
Jerry Hinrikus, *Vice Pres*
Andreya Sooby, *Marketing Staff*
EMP: 35 Privately Held
WEB: www.morris.com
SIC: 4832 2711 Radio broadcasting stations; newspapers
HQ: Morris Communications Company Llc
725 Broad St
Augusta GA 30901
706 724-0851

(G-10605)
MORTGAGE COMPANY
155 N 7th St (67401-2603)
P.O. Box 3527 (67402-3527)
PHONE....785 825-8100
Randy Graham, *President*
Larry S Curran, *Vice Pres*
Larry Curran, *CTO*
EMP: 15
SQ FT: 1,800
SALES (est): 1.8MM Privately Held
SIC: 6162 Mortgage brokers, using own money

(G-10606)
MORTON BUILDINGS INC
711 W Diamond Dr (67401-9544)
P.O. Box 588 (67402-0588)
PHONE....785 823-6359
Phil Shneider, *Manager*
Phil Schneider, *Manager*
EMP: 15
SALES (corp-wide): 463.7MM Privately Held
WEB: www.mortonbuildings.com
SIC: 5039 Prefabricated structures
PA: Morton Buildings, Inc.
252 W Adams St
Morton IL 61550
800 447-7436

(G-10607)
MOTEL 6 OPERATING LP
635 W Diamond Dr (67401-9357)
PHONE....785 827-8397
Carol Piland, *Manager*
EMP: 15
SQ FT: 20,000
SALES (corp-wide): 579.1MM Privately Held
WEB: www.motel6.com
SIC: 7011 Hotels & motels
HQ: Motel 6 Operating L.P.
4001 Intl Pkwy Ste 500
Carrollton TX 75007
972 360-9000

(G-10608)
MOWERY CLINIC LLC
737 E Crawford St (67401-5103)
P.O. Box 260 (67402-0260)
PHONE....785 827-7261
Bob Gaekwad MD, *President*
Chris A Rupe, *Med Doctor*
Julie Asch, *Manager*
Randy Paden, *Technology*
Terry Mar, *IT/INT Sup*
EMP: 150
SQ FT: 50,000
SALES (est): 20.3MM Privately Held
SIC: 8011 Gynecologist

(G-10609)
MSS TRANSPORT INC
200 E Avenue B (67401-8959)
P.O. Box 3345 (67402-3345)
PHONE....785 825-7291
Paul MAI, *President*

GEOGRAPHIC

Marge Reed, *Office Mgr*
EMP: 30
SQ FT: 6,000
SALES (est): 7.3MM **Privately Held**
WEB: www.msstrans.com
SIC: 4213 Contract haulers

(G-10610)
NEBCO INC (PA)
Also Called: Budget Host Inn
723 Osage Ave (67401-4501)
PHONE..................................785 462-3943
Miles Baldwin, *President*
Irene Baldwin, *Corp Secy*
EMP: 12
SQ FT: 7,500
SALES (est): 656K **Privately Held**
SIC: 7011 Hotels & motels

(G-10611)
NETWORKS PLUS
753 N 12th St (67401-1865)
PHONE..................................785 825-0400
Tony Gagnon, *Branch Mgr*
EMP: 50
SALES (est): 1.6MM **Privately Held**
SIC: 1731 7629 7373 Computer installation; telephone set repair; local area network (LAN) systems integrator
PA: Networks Plus
2627 Kfb Plz Ste 206w
Manhattan KS 66503

(G-10612)
NEW HORIZONS DENTAL CARE (PA)
1920 S Ohio St (67401-6643)
PHONE..................................785 376-0250
Guy Gross, *President*
Laura Mordica, *Dental Hygenist*
EMP: 16
SALES (est): 2.4MM **Privately Held**
WEB: www.newhorizonsdentalcare.com
SIC: 8021 Dentists' office

(G-10613)
NICKELL BARRACKS TRAINING CTR
Also Called: Kansas Training Center
2930 Scanlan Ave (67401-8129)
PHONE..................................785 822-1198
George A Lowe, *Principal*
EMP: 25
SALES (est): 965.5K **Privately Held**
SIC: 8331 Skill training center

(G-10614)
NORTON WSSRMAN JONES KELLY LLC
213 S Santa Fe Ave (67401-3931)
P.O. Box 2388 (67402-2388)
PHONE..................................785 827-3646
Norman Kelly, *Managing Prtnr*
Kenneth Wasserman, *Mng Member*
Robert S Jones, *Mng Member*
Norman R Kelly, *Mng Member*
Robert A Martin, *Mng Member*
EMP: 20
SQ FT: 1,500
SALES (est): 2.6MM **Privately Held**
SIC: 8111 General practice attorney, lawyer

(G-10615)
NORVELL COMPANY INC
468 Upper Mill Heights Dr (67401-3357)
PHONE..................................785 825-6663
Mack A Hale, *President*
EMP: 20 **EST:** 1995
SALES (est): 1.5MM **Privately Held**
SIC: 3556 5083 5046 Flour mill machinery; farm & garden machinery; commercial equipment

(G-10616)
OARDS AUTO & TRUCK REPR SVCS
Also Called: Oard's Auto & Truck Repair Svc
2259 Centennial Rd Ste A (67401-1707)
PHONE..................................785 823-9732
Terry Oard, *CEO*
EMP: 10
SQ FT: 4,000
SALES (est): 1MM **Privately Held**
WEB: www.oards.com
SIC: 7538 Engine repair, except diesel: automotive

(G-10617)
OCCK INC (PA)
1710 W Schilling Rd (67401-8131)
P.O. Box 1160 (67402-1160)
PHONE..................................785 827-9383
Patrick Wallerius, *CEO*
Carolee Miner, *President*
Jan Pfannenstiel, *Superintendent*
Shelia Nelson-Stout, *Vice Pres*
Jacque Skieff, *Personnel*
EMP: 138 **EST:** 1966
SQ FT: 35,000
SALES: 14.7MM **Privately Held**
WEB: www.occk.net
SIC: 8331 8361 3699 3641 Job training services; job counseling; residential care for the handicapped; children's home; electrical equipment & supplies; electric lamps

(G-10618)
OCCUPATIONAL HLTH PARTNERS LLC
Also Called: Comcare
1101 E Republic Ave (67401-5282)
PHONE..................................785 823-8381
Larry Muff, *Director*
EMP: 22
SALES (est): 1MM **Privately Held**
SIC: 8049 8011 8093 Physical therapist; medical centers; drug clinic, outpatient

(G-10619)
OMAHA TRUCK CENTER INC
Also Called: Freightliner Trucks
2552 N 9th St (67401-8623)
PHONE..................................785 823-2204
Trey Mytty, *President*
Aaron Hummel, *General Mgr*
Brady Ray, *Sales Staff*
Ann Lagersterom, *Admin Sec*
EMP: 35
SQ FT: 13,500
SALES (est): 4MM
SALES (corp-wide): 231.8MM **Privately Held**
WEB: www.truckershop.com
SIC: 5012 5013 7538 Truck tractors; truck parts & accessories; general automotive repair shops
PA: Omaha Truck Center Inc.
14321 Cornhusker Rd
Omaha NE 68138
402 592-2440

(G-10620)
OMAHA TRUCK CENTER INC
Also Called: Kansas Truck Center
2552 N 9th St (67401-8623)
PHONE..................................785 823-2204
Don Kind, *General Mgr*
EMP: 46
SALES (corp-wide): 231.8MM **Privately Held**
WEB: www.norfolktruck.com
SIC: 5511 5531 7538 Trucks, tractors & trailers: new & used; automobile & truck equipment & parts; general truck repair
PA: Omaha Truck Center Inc.
14321 Cornhusker Rd
Omaha NE 68138
402 592-2440

(G-10621)
ONE HOPE UNITED - NORTHERN REG
2026 Starlight Dr (67401-3664)
PHONE..................................785 827-1756
Gene Davis, *Pastor*
EMP: 21
SALES (corp-wide): 52.8MM **Privately Held**
SIC: 8361 8661 Children's home; Baptist Church
PA: One Hope United
215 N Milwaukee Ave
Lake Villa IL 60046
847 245-6500

(G-10622)
ONEOK INC
1001 Edison Pl (67401-7419)
PHONE..................................785 822-3522
Teryl Rose, *Branch Mgr*
EMP: 30
SALES (corp-wide): 12.5B **Publicly Held**
WEB: www.oneok.com
SIC: 4922 Natural gas transmission
PA: Oneok, Inc.
100 W 5th St Ste Ll
Tulsa OK 74103
918 588-7000

(G-10623)
ORKIN LLC
Also Called: Orkin Pest Control 792
1207 Holiday St (67401-4072)
P.O. Box 1431 (67402-1431)
PHONE..................................785 827-0314
Ed Earmon, *Systems Mgr*
EMP: 16
SALES (corp-wide): 1.8B **Publicly Held**
WEB: www.orkin.com
SIC: 7342 Pest control services
HQ: Orkin, Llc
2170 Piedmont Rd Ne
Atlanta GA 30324
404 888-2000

(G-10624)
ORSCHELN FARM AND HOME LLC
Also Called: Orschelin Farm and Home 57
360 N Ohio St (67401-2434)
PHONE..................................785 825-1681
Lynn Clark, *Branch Mgr*
EMP: 12
SALES (corp-wide): 822.7MM **Privately Held**
WEB: www.orschelnfarmhome.com
SIC: 5191 5251 5699 5084 Farm supplies; hardware; work clothing; engines, gasoline
PA: Orscheln Farm And Home Llc
1800 Overcenter Dr
Moberly MO 65270
800 577-2580

(G-10625)
OVATION CABINETRY INC
1750 Wall St (67401-1760)
PHONE..................................785 452-9000
Dan Gooden, *President*
Jonathan Lorentz, *Finance*
Lisa Hays,
EMP: 52
SQ FT: 13,700
SALES (est): 9.9MM **Privately Held**
WEB: www.ovationcabinetry.com
SIC: 2521 1751 2434 Filing cabinets (boxes), office: wood; cabinet & finish carpentry; wood kitchen cabinets

(G-10626)
OVERHEAD DOOR N CENTL KANS INC
425 E Avenue A (67401-8918)
PHONE..................................785 823-3786
Christine T Lindley, *President*
Mark Lindley, *Admin Sec*
EMP: 16
SQ FT: 2,500
SALES (est): 2.5MM **Privately Held**
SIC: 1751 Garage door, installation or erection

(G-10627)
P A COMCARE (PA)
2090 S Ohio St (67401-6702)
P.O. Box 2120 (67402-2120)
PHONE..................................785 825-8221
Alan Wedel, *President*
Dr Charles H Bossermeyer II, *Vice Pres*
W Reese Baxter, *Treasurer*
Gary Williams, *Med Doctor*
Mark Krehbiel, *Gnrl Med Prac*
EMP: 50 **EST:** 1997
SQ FT: 14,500
SALES (est): 14.9MM **Privately Held**
SIC: 8011 Clinic, operated by physicians

(G-10628)
P A COMCARE
Also Called: Statcare Family Medical Clinic
1001 S Ohio St (67401-5364)
PHONE..................................785 827-6453
Duane Wedel, *Manager*
EMP: 30
SALES (corp-wide): 14.9MM **Privately Held**
SIC: 8011 8093 Clinic, operated by physicians; specialty outpatient clinics
PA: P A Comcare
2090 S Ohio St
Salina KS 67401
785 825-8221

(G-10629)
P K M STEEL SERVICE INC
228 E Avenue A (67401-9143)
P.O. Box 920 (67402-0920)
PHONE..................................785 827-3638
Frieda MAI Weis, *Ch of Bd*
Mark Hamade, *COO*
Jason Torrey, *Safety Dir*
Richard Roland, *Purch Mgr*
Richard Glavin, *Manager*
EMP: 95
SQ FT: 290,000
SALES (est): 60.2MM **Privately Held**
WEB: www.pkmsteel.com
SIC: 5051 Steel

(G-10630)
PACIFIC INVESTMENT INC
2760 S 9th St (67401-7601)
PHONE..................................785 827-1271
Murali Chowdarapu, *Principal*
EMP: 10
SALES (est): 981.8K **Privately Held**
SIC: 6282 Investment advice

(G-10631)
PALMER WEBBER MACY
338 N Front St (67401-2038)
P.O. Box 2027 (67402-2027)
PHONE..................................785 823-7201
Shelly Gaskill, *Mktg Dir*
Farah Erickson, *Consultant*
James Cooper, *Pathologist*
EMP: 25
SALES (est): 2.1MM **Privately Held**
SIC: 8071 Medical laboratories

(G-10632)
PAVERS INC
505 Francis Ave (67401-2451)
P.O. Box 1967 (67402-1967)
PHONE..................................785 825-6771
Jeffrey Wilson, *President*
Neal Saskowski, *Engineer*
EMP: 20
SQ FT: 3,000
SALES: 6MM **Privately Held**
SIC: 1611 Surfacing & paving

(G-10633)
PEPSI COLA BTLG CO OF SALINA (HQ)
Also Called: Pepsi-Cola
604 N 9th St (67401-1944)
P.O. Box 1243 (67402-1243)
PHONE..................................785 827-7297
Bradley G Muhl, *President*
Jim Frush, *General Mgr*
EMP: 60 **EST:** 1969
SQ FT: 12,000
SALES (est): 21.4MM
SALES (corp-wide): 51.4MM **Privately Held**
SIC: 5149 2097 Soft drinks; manufactured ice
PA: Mahaska Bottling Company
1407 17th Ave E
Oskaloosa IA 52577
641 673-3481

(G-10634)
PESTINGER HEATING & AC INC (PA)
Also Called: Honeywell Authorized Dealer
125 E Avenue A (67401-8920)
PHONE..................................785 827-6361
Thomas R Pestinger, *President*
Nancy S Pestinger, *Treasurer*
EMP: 33 **EST:** 1964

SQ FT: 18,000
SALES (est): 7.9MM **Privately Held**
WEB: www.pestingerheating.com
SIC: 1711 1731 1761 Warm air heating & air conditioning contractor; electrical work; sheet metalwork

(G-10635)
PONTON CONSTRUCTION INC
Also Called: Pontons Construction
1325 Armory Rd (67401-4067)
PHONE..................................785 823-9584
Archie Ponton, *President*
EMP: 12
SQ FT: 5,600
SALES: 900K **Privately Held**
SIC: 1761 1521 1542 Roofing contractor; general remodeling, single-family houses; commercial & office buildings, renovation & repair

(G-10636)
POOLS PLUS
2501 Market Pl Ste I (67401-7666)
PHONE..................................785 823-7665
George Henry Plante, *Owner*
Gina Plante, *Co-Owner*
EMP: 12
SQ FT: 1,200
SALES (est): 1MM **Privately Held**
WEB: www.poolsplusofsalina.com
SIC: 7389 1799 5999 5091 Swimming pool & hot tub service & maintenance; swimming pool construction; swimming pools, hot tubs & sauna equipment & supplies; billiard equipment & supplies; grills, barbecue; patio & deck construction & repair

(G-10637)
POP-A-SHOT ENTERPRISE LLC
200 N 3rd St (67401-2322)
PHONE..................................785 827-6229
Christina Lau, *Cust Mgr*
Tony Stucker, *Mng Member*
▲ **EMP:** 6
SQ FT: 10,000
SALES (est): 400K **Privately Held**
WEB: www.pop-a-shot.com
SIC: 3999 5099 Coin-operated amusement machines; game machines, coin-operated

(G-10638)
POWER AD COMPANY INC
3344 Scanlan Ave (67401-1746)
PHONE..................................785 823-9483
Roger Naylor Jr, *President*
Debra Marseline, *Vice Pres*
EMP: 32
SQ FT: 30,400
SALES (est): 3.1MM **Privately Held**
WEB: www.power-ad.com
SIC: 3993 Scoreboards, electric

(G-10639)
POWER VAC INC
508 Graves Blvd (67401-4306)
PHONE..................................785 826-8220
Charles W Walker, *CEO*
Trace Walker, *President*
Morrie Soderberg, *Corp Secy*
Greg Soldan, *Vice Pres*
EMP: 28 **EST:** 1964
SQ FT: 50,000
SALES (est): 15MM **Privately Held**
WEB: www.powervac.com
SIC: 5169 3589 Detergents & soaps, except specialty cleaning; car washing machinery

(G-10640)
PRECISION ELEC CONTRS LLC
668 N Ohio Ct (67401-2449)
P.O. Box 1153 (67402-1153)
PHONE..................................785 309-0094
Trever Hillegeist, *Manager*
Tom Perez,
Royce Hillegeist,
EMP: 45
SQ FT: 3,600
SALES (est): 5.5MM **Privately Held**
WEB: www.precisionelectricllc.com
SIC: 1731 Electrical work

(G-10641)
PRESBYTERIAN MANORS INC
Also Called: Salina Presbytarian Manor
2601 E Crawford St Ofc (67401-3898)
PHONE..................................785 825-1366
Fran Paxton, *Director*
EMP: 62
SALES (corp-wide): 8.6MM **Privately Held**
SIC: 8059 8052 8051 Rest home, with health care; intermediate care facilities; skilled nursing care facilities
HQ: Presbyterian Manors, Inc.
2414 N Woodlawn Blvd
Wichita KS 67220
316 685-1100

(G-10642)
PRO PAY LLC
1217 Shoreline Dr W (67401-6429)
PHONE..................................913 826-6300
EMP: 21
SQ FT: 8,000
SALES (est): 1.6MM **Privately Held**
SIC: 8721 Accounting Auditing & Bookkeeping

(G-10643)
PROBUILD COMPANY LLC
707 N Broadway Blvd (67401-1818)
PHONE..................................785 827-2644
EMP: 12
SALES (corp-wide): 1.6B **Publicly Held**
SIC: 5031 Whol Lumber/Plywood/Millwork
HQ: Probuild Company Llc
7595 E Technology Way # 500
Denver CO 80237
303 262-8500

(G-10644)
PRONTO PRINT
627 E Crawford St (67401-5101)
PHONE..................................785 823-2285
Mark Neubrand, *General Mgr*
EMP: 5
SALES (est): 492.7K **Privately Held**
SIC: 2752 Commercial printing, offset

(G-10645)
QUALITY RECORD PRESSINGS
543 N 10th St (67401-2001)
PHONE..................................785 820-2931
Chad Kassem, *President*
Gary Salstrom, *Plant Mgr*
Michael Steinbruck, *Manager*
Kristy Sanger, *Administration*
EMP: 50
SALES (est): 387.7K **Privately Held**
SIC: 3542 Pressing machines

(G-10646)
QUALITY REMODELER
2501 Market Pl Ste I (67401-7666)
PHONE..................................785 823-7665
George Plante, *Owner*
EMP: 12
SALES (est): 743.7K **Privately Held**
SIC: 1521 General remodeling, single-family houses

(G-10647)
QUALITY WATER INC
Also Called: Culligan
658 E North St (67401-2454)
P.O. Box 282 (67402-0282)
PHONE..................................785 825-4912
Tina Zimmer, *President*
EMP: 10
SQ FT: 10,000
SALES (est): 1.1MM **Privately Held**
SIC: 5149 5499 5999 Water, distilled; water: distilled mineral or spring; water purification equipment

(G-10648)
QUENTIN MC KEE & SON LDSCPG
Also Called: Quentin, McKee & Son
21 Red Fox Ln (67401-6619)
PHONE..................................785 827-5155
Quentin R Mc Kee, *President*
Weston Mc Kee, *Vice Pres*
Sherry Mc Kee, *Treasurer*
Mary Mc Kee, *Admin Sec*
EMP: 18
SALES (est): 809.5K **Privately Held**
SIC: 0781 Landscape architects

(G-10649)
R & J SALINA TAX SERVICE INC
318 W Cloud St (67401-5613)
PHONE..................................785 827-1304
Rodney Sommer, *Owner*
EMP: 25
SALES (est): 744.4K **Privately Held**
SIC: 7291 8721 Tax return preparation services; auditing services

(G-10650)
RAMADA CONFERENCE CENTER SALIN
1616 W Crawford St (67401-1523)
PHONE..................................785 823-1739
Cody Harris, *Manager*
EMP: 12
SALES (est): 489.3K **Privately Held**
SIC: 7011 Inns

(G-10651)
REALTY ASSOCIATES INC
Also Called: Kansas General Appraisal Svc
2103 S Ohio St (67401-6809)
PHONE..................................785 827-0331
Ellie Ritter, *President*
EMP: 16 **EST:** 1976
SQ FT: 900
SALES (est): 1.3MM **Privately Held**
WEB: www.realtyassociateskansas.com
SIC: 6531 Real estate agent, residential

(G-10652)
ROLLING HILLS ZOO FOUNDATION
625 N Hedville Rd (67401-9764)
PHONE..................................785 827-9488
Sandy Walker, *President*
Morrie Soderberg, *Corp Secy*
Robert Jenkins, *Exec Dir*
Vickee Spicer, *Exec Dir*
EMP: 29
SALES: 3.7MM **Privately Held**
SIC: 8412 Museum

(G-10653)
RONNIE DIEHL CONSTRUCTION INC
521 Bishop St (67401-2040)
PHONE..................................785 823-7800
Ronnie Diehl, *President*
EMP: 20 **EST:** 2000
SALES: 700K **Privately Held**
WEB: www.ronniediehlconstruction.com
SIC: 1629 Railroad & railway roadbed construction

(G-10654)
RUSSELL & RUSSELL LLC
1100 W Grand Ave Ste H (67401-1863)
P.O. Box 1635 (67402-1635)
PHONE..................................785 827-4878
Derek Forsberg, *Sales Staff*
Dennis Russell, *Mng Member*
EMP: 15
SQ FT: 4,300
SALES (est): 5MM **Privately Held**
WEB: www.russellrussell.com
SIC: 7353 Cranes & aerial lift equipment, rental or leasing

(G-10655)
RYAN MORTUARY INC
Also Called: Ryan Mortuary & Crematory
137 N 8th St (67401-2686)
PHONE..................................785 825-4242
Steve C Ryan, *President*
Marc R Ryan, *Corp Secy*
Jerry J Ryan, *Vice Pres*
Marc Yan, *Human Res Mgr*
Kara Heier, *Director*
EMP: 18 **EST:** 1874
SALES (est): 1MM **Privately Held**
WEB: www.ryanmortuary.com
SIC: 7261 Funeral home; crematory

(G-10656)
S & B MOTELS INC
Also Called: Super 8 Motel
120 E Diamond Dr (67401-8601)
PHONE..................................785 823-8808
Stanley Weilert, *President*
EMP: 15
SALES (est): 1MM
SALES (corp-wide): 12MM **Privately Held**
SIC: 7011 Hotels & motels
PA: S & B Motels, Inc.
400 N Woodlawn St Ste 205
Wichita KS 67208
316 522-3864

(G-10657)
S S OF KANSAS INC
Also Called: Sirloin Stockade
2351 S 9th St Fl 1 (67401-7556)
PHONE..................................785 823-2787
Dave Breivy, *Manager*
EMP: 60
SALES (corp-wide): 18.9MM **Privately Held**
SIC: 5812 7299 Restaurant, family: chain; banquet hall facilities
PA: S. S. Of Kansas Inc
335 N Washington St # 120
Hutchinson KS 67501
620 669-1194

(G-10658)
SAINT FRANCIS CMNTY SVCS INC
1646b N 9th St (67401-8763)
PHONE..................................785 825-0541
Trish Bryant, *Vice Pres*
Neal Zouvas, *Branch Mgr*
EMP: 25
SALES (corp-wide): 108.2MM **Privately Held**
SIC: 8741 8211 Hospital management; academy
PA: Saint Francis Community Services, Inc.
509 E Elm St
Salina KS 67401
785 825-0541

(G-10659)
SAINT FRANCIS CMNTY SVCS INC (PA)
509 E Elm St (67401-2353)
P.O. Box 1340 (67402-1340)
PHONE..................................785 825-0541
Fr Edward Fellhauer, *CEO*
Trish Bryant, *Vice Pres*
Cory Rathbun, *Vice Pres*
John Cambridge, *QC Mgr*
Melanie Owens, *CFO*
EMP: 37
SQ FT: 5,400
SALES: 108.2MM **Privately Held**
SIC: 8741 8361 Hospital management; residential care

(G-10660)
SAINT FRANCIS CMNTY SVCS INC
Also Called: Able Program
509 E Elm St (67401-2353)
PHONE..................................785 452-9653
Shirley Andria, *Manager*
EMP: 50
SALES (corp-wide): 108.2MM **Privately Held**
SIC: 8741 8361 Hospital management; residential care
PA: Saint Francis Community Services, Inc.
509 E Elm St
Salina KS 67401
785 825-0541

(G-10661)
SAINT FRANCIS COMMUNITY
509 E Elm St (67401-2353)
PHONE..................................785 825-0541
Edward W Fellhauer, *President*
Janet Atteberry, *Treasurer*
EMP: 99
SALES: 94.1MM **Privately Held**
SIC: 8399 Social services

(G-10662)
SAINT FRANCIS COMMUNITY AND RE
509 E Elm St (67401-2353)
PHONE..................................785 825-0541
Melanie Owens, *CEO*
Gayl Lee, *Transportation*
Tammie Patterson, *Supervisor*

GEOGRAPHIC

EMP: 99
SALES: 8.9MM **Privately Held**
SIC: 8322 Child related social services

(G-10663)
SAINT FRNCIS CMNTY SVCS IN ILL
509 E Elm St (67401-2353)
PHONE..................................785 825-0541
Robert N Smith, *CEO*
EMP: 50
SALES (est): 310.1K **Privately Held**
SIC: 8322 Child related social services

(G-10664)
SALINA AIRPORT AUTHORITY
3237 Arnold Ave (67401-8163)
PHONE..................................785 827-3914
Michelle Swanson, *CFO*
Timothy F Rogers, *Exec Dir*
Kaycie Taylor, *Admin Asst*
EMP: 12
SQ FT: 9,000
SALES: 2.5MM **Privately Held**
WEB: www.salair.org
SIC: 4581 Airport

(G-10665)
SALINA AREA CHMBER CMMERCE INC
120 W Ash St (67401-2308)
P.O. Box 586 (67402-0586)
PHONE..................................785 827-9301
Dennis Lauver, *President*
Sylvia Rice, *Vice Pres*
Don Weiser, *Vice Pres*
M Maureen, *Director*
EMP: 13
SALES: 2.9MM **Privately Held**
WEB: www.salinakansas.org
SIC: 8611 Chamber of Commerce

(G-10666)
SALINA BUILDING SYSTEMS INC
4329 E Cntry Estates Cir (67401-9662)
PHONE..................................785 823-6812
E Andrew England, *President*
Reginald E Leiker, *Corp Secy*
EMP: 22 **EST:** 1969
SQ FT: 2,000
SALES (est): 4.3MM **Privately Held**
SIC: 5211 1541 Prefabricated buildings; prefabricated building erection, industrial

(G-10667)
SALINA CHILD CARE ASSOCIATION
155 N Oakdale Ave Ste 100 (67401-3001)
PHONE..................................785 827-6431
Elaine Edwards, *Director*
EMP: 21
SALES: 800.1K **Privately Held**
SIC: 8621 Professional membership organizations

(G-10668)
SALINA CONCRETE PRODUCTS INC (HQ)
Also Called: Kansas Building Products
1100 W Ash St (67401-2559)
P.O. Box 136 (67402-0136)
PHONE..................................785 827-7281
Steven L Morgan, *President*
Peter Browning, *General Mgr*
Jorge Varela, *Sales Mgr*
EMP: 29 **EST:** 1913
SQ FT: 12,000
SALES (est): 5MM
SALES (corp-wide): 147MM **Publicly Held**
WEB: www.salinaconcreteproducts.com
SIC: 3273 5032 5211 3271 Ready-mixed concrete; brick, stone & related material; lumber & other building materials; masonry materials & supplies; concrete block & brick; precast terrazo or concrete products
PA: The Monarch Cement Company
449 1200th St
Humboldt KS 66748
620 473-2222

(G-10669)
SALINA COUNTRY CLUB
2101 E Country Club Rd (67401-1626)
P.O. Box 2056 (67402-2056)
PHONE..................................785 827-0388
Max Holthaus, *General Mgr*
Brad McMillan, *General Mgr*
Jessica Davis, *Accountant*
Steven Fowler, *Manager*
Melissa Ivey, *Director*
EMP: 70
SQ FT: 44,000
SALES (est): 3.2MM **Privately Held**
WEB: www.salinacountryclub.com
SIC: 7997 Country club, membership; swimming club, membership; tennis club, membership; golf club, membership

(G-10670)
SALINA COUNTY MEDICAL SUPPLY (PA)
Also Called: Salina County Dialysis
700 E Iron Ave. (67401-3038)
PHONE..................................785 823-6416
Brad Stuewe, *President*
EMP: 17
SALES (est): 3.2MM **Privately Held**
SIC: 8092 Kidney dialysis centers

(G-10671)
SALINA DENTAL ARTS
1829 S Ohio St (67401-6601)
PHONE..................................785 823-2472
Jason Barth, *Owner*
EMP: 14
SALES (est): 845.4K **Privately Held**
SIC: 8021 Dentists' office

(G-10672)
SALINA DENTAL ASSOCIATES PA
950 Elmhurst Blvd (67401-7429)
PHONE..................................785 827-4401
Thomas Jett, *President*
Jeffrey Koksal, *Principal*
EMP: 12 **EST:** 1965
SALES (est): 910.4K **Privately Held**
SIC: 8021 Dentists' office

(G-10673)
SALINA ECONOMIC DEV CORP
120 W Ash St (67401-2308)
P.O. Box 586 (67402-0586)
PHONE..................................785 827-9301
Dennis Lauver, *President*
EMP: 14
SALES: 7.9K **Privately Held**
SIC: 8611 Chamber of Commerce

(G-10674)
SALINA HLTH EDUCATN FOUNDATION
Also Called: SALINA FAMILY HEALTHCARE AND D
651 E Prescott Rd (67401-7408)
PHONE..................................785 825-7251
Mary Jo Stedry, *CEO*
Robert Freelove, *Med Doctor*
EMP: 70
SALES: 14.4MM **Privately Held**
SIC: 8099 8011 Medical services organization; offices & clinics of medical doctors

(G-10675)
SALINA HOMES
300 S 9th St Ste 101 (67401-3894)
PHONE..................................785 820-5900
Todd Welsh, *Owner*
Jerry Short, *Consultant*
Gina Wilson, *Real Est Agnt*
EMP: 15
SALES (est): 1MM **Privately Held**
WEB: www.salinahomes.com
SIC: 6531 Real estate brokers & agents

(G-10676)
SALINA HOUSING AUTHORITY
469 S 5th St (67401-4110)
P.O. Box 1202 (67402-1202)
PHONE..................................785 827-0441
Karlene Lawson, *Office Mgr*
Tina Bartlett, *Exec Dir*
Nan Rollins, *Director*
EMP: 11
SQ FT: 2,800
SALES (est): 831K **Privately Held**
SIC: 6531 Housing authority operator

(G-10677)
SALINA IRON & METAL COMPANY
312 N 5th St (67401-2048)
P.O. Box 1155 (67402-1155)
PHONE..................................785 826-9838
Robert Butts, *President*
EMP: 39
SQ FT: 5,000
SALES (est): 7.8MM **Privately Held**
SIC: 5093 4953 Metal scrap & waste materials; refuse collection & disposal services

(G-10678)
SALINA JOURNAL INC
Also Called: Salina Journal, The
333 S 4th St (67401-3903)
P.O. Box 740 (67402-0740)
PHONE..................................785 823-6363
Tom Bell, *President*
Amanda Abrams, *Manager*
EMP: 130 **EST:** 1871
SQ FT: 126,000
SALES (est): 7.6MM
SALES (corp-wide): 1.5B **Publicly Held**
WEB: www.saljournal.com
SIC: 2711 2741 Newspapers, publishing & printing; shopping news: publishing only, not printed on site
HQ: Harris Enterprises, Inc.
1 N Main St Ste 616
Hutchinson KS
620 694-5830

(G-10679)
SALINA KS LODGING LLC
Also Called: Country Inn Suites By Carlson
2760 S 9th St (67401-7601)
PHONE..................................785 827-1271
Gerard Smith, *Manager*
Leo M Sand,
Daniel Krahn,
Charlie Walker,
EMP: 30
SALES (est): 1.3MM **Privately Held**
SIC: 7011 Hotels & motels

(G-10680)
SALINA MICROFILM
Also Called: Salina Blueprint
212 S 5th St (67401-3906)
PHONE..................................785 827-6648
Gary Stansberry, *Owner*
EMP: 12
SALES (est): 664.9K **Privately Held**
SIC: 7389 4226 3861 Microfilm recording & developing service; document & office records storage; microfilm equipment: cameras, projectors, readers, etc.

(G-10681)
SALINA PEDIATRIC CARE
501 S Santa Fe Ave # 100 (67401-4189)
PHONE..................................785 825-2273
Harvey Brian Do, *Principal*
EMP: 10
SALES (est): 1MM **Privately Held**
SIC: 8011 Pediatrician

(G-10682)
SALINA PHYSICAL THERAPY CLINIC
1101 E Republic Ave (67401-5282)
PHONE..................................785 825-1361
Leslie Durst, *Principal*
EMP: 17
SALES (est): 1.1MM **Privately Held**
SIC: 8093 8049 Specialty outpatient clinics; physical therapist

(G-10683)
SALINA PLANING MILL INC
1100 W Crawford St (67401-4674)
P.O. Box 1576 (67402-1576)
PHONE..................................785 825-0588
Steven Dunning, *President*
EMP: 30
SQ FT: 28,000
SALES (est): 6.1MM **Privately Held**
WEB: www.salinaplaningmill.com
SIC: 2431 Planing mill, millwork

(G-10684)
SALINA RED COACH INN
2110 W Crawford St (67401-4591)
P.O. Box 526, El Dorado (67042-0526)
PHONE..................................785 825-2111
John Pyle, *Owner*
Bill Pyle, *Partner*
Patty Pyle, *Partner*
Tom Pyle, *Partner*
EMP: 18
SALES (est): 703.9K **Privately Held**
WEB: www.rcisal.com
SIC: 7011 5812 7389 7299 Motels; eating places; convention & show services; banquet hall facilities

(G-10685)
SALINA REGIONAL HEALTH CTR INC
501 S Santa Fe Ave # 300 (67401-4189)
PHONE..................................785 823-1032
Kay Hawthorne, *Principal*
EMP: 95
SALES (corp-wide): 215.1MM **Privately Held**
SIC: 8071 Neurological laboratory
PA: Salina Regional Health Center, Inc.
400 S Santa Fe Ave
Salina KS 67401
785 452-7000

(G-10686)
SALINA REGIONAL HEALTH CTR INC (PA)
400 S Santa Fe Ave (67401-4144)
P.O. Box 5080 (67402-5080)
PHONE..................................785 452-7000
Randy Peterson, *President*
Heather Fuller, *Vice Pres*
Cheryl Mason, *Vice Pres*
Ashley Flax, *Pharmacist*
Lisa Hoffman, *Manager*
EMP: 800
SQ FT: 245,000
SALES: 215.1MM **Privately Held**
WEB: www.srhc.com
SIC: 8062 General medical & surgical hospitals

(G-10687)
SALINA REGIONAL HEALTH CTR INC
511 S Santa Fe Ave (67401-4145)
PHONE..................................785 452-4850
Claudia Perez, *Branch Mgr*
Levi Kinderknecht,
EMP: 63
SALES (corp-wide): 215.1MM **Privately Held**
SIC: 8011 8049 8062 Oncologist; nutrition specialist; general medical & surgical hospitals
PA: Salina Regional Health Center, Inc.
400 S Santa Fe Ave
Salina KS 67401
785 452-7000

(G-10688)
SALINA REGIONAL HEALTH CTR INC
Also Called: Saint Johns Regional Hlth Ctr
139 N Penn Ave (67401-3044)
PHONE..................................785 452-7000
Randy Peterson, *Manager*
Ron McWilliams, *Analyst*
EMP: 483
SALES (corp-wide): 215.1MM **Privately Held**
WEB: www.srhc.com
SIC: 8082 8062 8093 Home health care services; general medical & surgical hospitals; rehabilitation center, outpatient treatment
PA: Salina Regional Health Center, Inc.
400 S Santa Fe Ave
Salina KS 67401
785 452-7000

(G-10689)
SALINA RESCUE MISSION INC
1716 Summers Rd (67401-8134)
P.O. Box 1667 (67402-1667)
PHONE..................................785 823-3317
Fax: 785 542-9121
EMP: 12

SALES: 1MM **Privately Held**
SIC: 8322 Individual/Family Services

(G-10690)
SALINA SCALE SALES & SERVICE (PA)
415 N 9th St (67401-2074)
P.O. Box 3261 (67402-3261)
PHONE..................................785 827-4441
Ray Wierman, *President*
Gary Wagner, *Corp Secy*
William Hoffman, *Vice Pres*
EMP: 11 **EST:** 1964
SQ FT: 12,000
SALES (est): 5.5MM **Privately Held**
SIC: 7699 5046 Scale repair service; scales, except laboratory

(G-10691)
SALINA SPORTS MED &ORTH CLINIC
Also Called: Gary L Harbin, Md, PA
523 S Santa Fe Ave (67401-4145)
PHONE..................................785 823-7213
Gary L Harbin, *President*
EMP: 13
SQ FT: 2,000
SALES (est): 1.5MM **Privately Held**
SIC: 8011 Orthopedic physician

(G-10692)
SALINA STEEL SUPPLY INC
234 E Avenue A (67401-9143)
P.O. Box 2897 (67402-2897)
PHONE..................................785 825-2138
Paul MAI, *President*
Frieda MAI, *President*
Tammy Black, *CFO*
Rosella Bremenkamp, *Financial Exec*
Cris Chamberlain, *Manager*
EMP: 39
SQ FT: 60,000
SALES (est): 42.9MM **Privately Held**
WEB: www.salinasteel.com
SIC: 5051 Steel

(G-10693)
SALINA SUPPLY COMPANY
302 N Santa Fe Ave (67401-2345)
P.O. Box 5100 (67402-5100)
PHONE..................................785 823-2221
John Zimmerman, *Ch of Bd*
Marty Opat, *Warehouse Mgr*
Kelcey Smith, *Credit Mgr*
Sandy Farrell, *Office Mgr*
Anne Zimmerman, *Admin Sec*
EMP: 31
SQ FT: 143,000
SALES: 9MM **Privately Held**
WEB: www.salinasupply.com
SIC: 5075 5074 Furnaces, warm air; plumbing fittings & supplies

(G-10694)
SALINA SURGICAL CENTER LLC
Also Called: SALINA SURGICAL HOSPITAL
401 S Santa Fe Ave (67401-4143)
PHONE..................................785 827-0610
Lisa Hoss, *Vice Pres*
Troy Nickel, *Plant Mgr*
Rex Harrell, *Info Tech Dir*
Luann Puvogel, *Director*
Serena Helvey, *Risk Mgmt Dir*
EMP: 99
SQ FT: 33,462
SALES: 27MM **Privately Held**
WEB: www.salinasurgical.com
SIC: 8062 General medical & surgical hospitals

(G-10695)
SALINA UROLOGY ASSOCIATES PA
Also Called: Dr William Mauch
501 S Santa Fe Ave # 380 (67401-4189)
PHONE..................................785 827-9635
William Mauch, *Principal*
Ryan Dayne, *Principal*
Randy Hassler, *Principal*
Micheal Matteucci, *Principal*
Brian Smith, *Principal*
EMP: 19
SALES: 4MM **Privately Held**
WEB: www.salinaurology.com
SIC: 8011 Urologist

(G-10696)
SALINA VORTEX CORP
Also Called: Vortex Valves
1725 Vortex Ave (67401-1768)
PHONE..................................785 825-7177
Lee Young, *Ch of Bd*
Brian Burmaster, *President*
Jeff Thompson, *President*
John Peterson, *Vice Pres*
Monty Leach, *Mfg Staff*
▲ **EMP:** 120 **EST:** 1977
SQ FT: 120,000
SALES (est): 34.9MM **Privately Held**
SIC: 3491 5084 3494 Industrial valves; industrial machinery & equipment; valves & pipe fittings

(G-10697)
SALINE COUNTY COMM ON AGING
Also Called: Sunflower Adult Day Services
245 N 9th St (67401-2111)
PHONE..................................785 823-6666
Thomas Mulhern, *Director*
EMP: 24
SALES (est): 735.9K **Privately Held**
SIC: 8322 Senior citizens' center or association; geriatric social service

(G-10698)
SCIENTIFIC ENGINEERING INC
2782 Arnold Ave (67401-8102)
PHONE..................................785 827-7071
Jim Pratt, *President*
William Warner, *Vice Pres*
Phyllis Johnson, *Treasurer*
Morgan Pearl, *Admin Sec*
EMP: 10 **EST:** 1965
SQ FT: 20,000
SALES: 924.6K **Privately Held**
SIC: 3599 3559 8712 Machine shop, jobbing & repair; ammunition & explosives, loading machinery; architectural engineering

(G-10699)
SCOULAR COMPANY
Also Called: Scoular Elevator
2880 E Country Club Rd (67401-9513)
P.O. Box 1275 (67402-1275)
PHONE..................................785 823-6301
Curt Engold, *Manager*
Kevin Heiman, *Manager*
EMP: 20
SALES (corp-wide): 4.2B **Privately Held**
WEB: www.scoular.com
SIC: 5153 3523 Grains; farm machinery & equipment
PA: The Scoular Company
2027 Dodge St Ste 200
Omaha NE 68102
402 342-3500

(G-10700)
SCROMMEL RESOURCE MANAGEMENT
2775 Arnold Ave Ste E (67401-8290)
P.O. Box 2838 (67402-2838)
PHONE..................................785 825-7771
Brad Byquist, *President*
Mick Wodke, *Mng Member*
EMP: 7
SALES: 2MM **Privately Held**
SIC: 3537 Stackers, power (industrial truck stackers)

(G-10701)
SEARS ROEBUCK AND CO
2259 S 9th St Ste 7200 (67401-7368)
PHONE..................................785 826-4378
EMP: 140
SALES (corp-wide): 16.7B **Publicly Held**
SIC: 5311 7221 5995 5531 Department Store Photo Portrait Studio Ret Optical Goods Ret Auto/Home Supplies
HQ: Sears, Roebuck And Co.
3333 Beverly Rd
Hoffman Estates IL 60179
847 286-2500

(G-10702)
SELLERS COMPANIES INC (PA)
400 N Chicago St (67401-2020)
P.O. Box 1940 (67402-1940)
PHONE..................................785 823-6378
David P Sellers, *President*
Helen V Sellers, *Corp Secy*
Dan Sellers, *Vice Pres*
EMP: 20
SQ FT: 17,150
SALES: 17MM **Privately Held**
WEB: www.sellerstractor.com
SIC: 5082 5084 Road construction & maintenance machinery; industrial machinery & equipment

(G-10703)
SELLERS EQUIPMENT INC (HQ)
Also Called: Kubota Authorized Dealer
400 N Chicago St (67401-2020)
P.O. Box 1940 (67402-1940)
PHONE..................................785 823-6378
David P Sellers, *President*
Ron Mitchell, *Senior VP*
Dan Seller, *Vice Pres*
Connie Gragg, *Manager*
▲ **EMP:** 22
SQ FT: 17,150
SALES (est): 17MM **Privately Held**
WEB: www.sellersequipment.com
SIC: 5082 5084 Road construction & maintenance machinery; industrial machinery & equipment
PA: Sellers Companies Inc
400 N Chicago St
Salina KS 67401
785 823-6378

(G-10704)
SEMMATERIALS LP
1100 W Grand Ave Ste M (67401-1863)
P.O. Box 440 (67402-0440)
PHONE..................................785 825-1535
Robert Northcutt, *Manager*
EMP: 7
SALES (corp-wide): 54B **Publicly Held**
WEB: www.semgroup.com
SIC: 2951 Asphalt paving mixtures & blocks
HQ: Semmaterials, L.P.
6520 S Yale Ave Ste 700
Tulsa OK 74136
918 524-8100

(G-10705)
SFC GLOBAL SUPPLY CHAIN INC
Also Called: Schwan's Food Manufacturing
3019 Scanlan Ave (67401-1702)
PHONE..................................785 825-1671
Alfred Schwan, *Chairman*
David Burnett, *Manager*
Edith Hopson, *Manager*
Bonnie Jones, *Admin Asst*
EMP: 251
SALES (corp-wide): 5B **Privately Held**
SIC: 2038 2099 Pizza, frozen; food preparations
HQ: Sfc Global Supply Chain, Inc.
115 W College Dr
Marshall MN 56258
507 532-3274

(G-10706)
SHEARS SHOP
1329 W North St (67401-9301)
PHONE..................................785 823-6201
Jason Heis, *Principal*
EMP: 12 **EST:** 2001
SALES (est): 737.4K **Privately Held**
SIC: 5082 Road construction & maintenance machinery

(G-10707)
SIGN HOUSE INC
3110 Enterprise Dr (67401-8442)
PHONE..................................785 827-2729
Robert Harper, *Owner*
Brian Eliot, *Sales Dir*
EMP: 27
SALES (est): 4.1MM **Privately Held**
WEB: www.signhouseusa.com
SIC: 3993 Neon signs

(G-10708)
SIGNIFY NORTH AMERICA CORP
Philips Lighting
3861 S 9th St (67401-8911)
PHONE..................................785 826-5218
Gary Newbrey, *Electrical Engi*
Chris Denicx, *Branch Mgr*
EMP: 75
SALES (corp-wide): 7B **Privately Held**
WEB: www.usa.philips.com
SIC: 3641 Lamps, fluorescent, electric
HQ: Signify North America Corporation
200 Franklin Square Dr
Somerset NJ 08873
732 563-3000

(G-10709)
SIX CONTINENTS HOTELS INC
Also Called: Holiday Inn
201 E Diamond Dr (67401-8624)
PHONE..................................785 827-9000
Jessica Robison, *Manager*
EMP: 75 **Privately Held**
WEB: www.sixcontinenthotels.com
SIC: 7011 Hotels & motels
HQ: Six Continents Hotels, Inc.
3 Ravinia Dr Ste 100
Dunwoody GA 30346
770 604-2000

(G-10710)
SMOKY HILL LLC
645 E Crawford St Unit E8 (67401-5117)
PHONE..................................785 825-0810
Steve Bartholomew, *Vice Pres*
Michael Chart, *Project Mgr*
Richard E Brown,
Kim E Brown,
Scott Erickson,
EMP: 95
SQ FT: 2,500
SALES: 17.4MM **Privately Held**
SIC: 1771 1623 Concrete work; water & sewer line construction

(G-10711)
SMOKY VALLEY CONCRETE INC
1700 W State St (67401-9571)
P.O. Box 1884 (67402-1884)
PHONE..................................785 820-8113
Nick Gent, *Principal*
Stan Byquist, *Principal*
Terry Ray, *Principal*
EMP: 6
SALES (est): 1.2MM **Privately Held**
SIC: 3273 Ready-mixed concrete

(G-10712)
SOIL CONSERVATION SERVICE USDA
760 S Broadway Blvd (67401-4642)
PHONE..................................785 823-4500
Grace McGrath, *Principal*
Kelly Klausmeyer, *Engineer*
Connie S Allen, *Technician*
Carolyn Andres, *Technician*
Pamala J Bain, *Technician*
EMP: 35
SALES (est): 1.3MM **Privately Held**
SIC: 8641 Environmental protection organization

(G-10713)
SS&C WEALTH MGT GROUP LLC
218 S Santa Fe Ave (67401-3932)
PHONE..................................785 825-5479
Brenda Flannagan, *President*
EMP: 22
SALES (corp-wide): 2.1MM **Privately Held**
SIC: 8721 Accounting services, except auditing
PA: Ss&C Wealth Management Group, Llc
5825 Sw 29th St Ste 200
Topeka KS 66614
785 272-4484

(G-10714)
ST FRANCIS ACADEMY INC
Also Called: Saint Francis At Salina
5097 W Cloud St (67401-9743)
PHONE..................................785 825-0563
Kerstin Lang, *Director*
EMP: 50

SALES: 2.8MM **Privately Held**
WEB: www.stfrancisacademy.com
SIC: 8059 Convalescent home

(G-10715)
STANION WHOLESALE ELC CO INC

1061 E North St (67401-8548)
P.O. Box 1755 (67402-1755)
PHONE..................................785 823-2323
Willie Perez, *Manager*
EMP: 16
SALES (corp-wide): 97.6MM **Privately Held**
WEB: www.stanion.com
SIC: 5063 5719 Electrical supplies; lighting, lamps & accessories
PA: Stanion Wholesale Electric Co., Inc.
812 S Main St
Pratt KS 67124
620 672-5678

(G-10716)
STEWART TRUCK LEASING INC

1944a N 9th St (67401-8617)
P.O. Box 165 (67402-0165)
PHONE..................................785 827-0336
Robert S Stewart, *President*
EMP: 30
SALES (est): 1.7MM **Privately Held**
SIC: 7513 Truck rental & leasing, no drivers

(G-10717)
STRAUB INTERNATIONAL INC

3637 S 9th St (67401-7806)
PHONE..................................785 825-1300
Larry Straub, *Manager*
Mike Kolman, *Technology*
EMP: 10
SALES (corp-wide): 93MM **Privately Held**
WEB: www.straubint.com
SIC: 5083 Agricultural machinery & equipment
PA: Straub International, Inc.
200 S Patton Rd
Great Bend KS 67530
620 792-5256

(G-10718)
SUMMIT GROUP OF SALINA KS LP

Also Called: Comfort Inn
1820 W Crawford St (67401-4585)
PHONE..................................785 826-1711
Debby Lynch, *Manager*
EMP: 14
SALES (est): 920K **Privately Held**
SIC: 7011 6552 Hotels & motels; land subdividers & developers, commercial

(G-10719)
SUMMIT HOSPITALITY LLC

2760 S 9th St (67401-7601)
PHONE..................................970 765-5690
Mohammed Islam, *Managing Prtnr*
EMP: 20
SQ FT: 5,880
SALES (est): 132.1K **Privately Held**
SIC: 7011 Motels

(G-10720)
SUMMIT HOTEL PROPERTIES INC

Also Called: AmericInn Hotel
1820 W Crawford St (67401-4585)
PHONE..................................785 826-1711
Deb Isaacson, *Branch Mgr*
EMP: 20 **Publicly Held**
WEB: www.summitgroupco.com
SIC: 7011 Hotels
PA: Summit Hotel Properties, Inc.
13215 Bee Cave Pkwy B300
Austin TX 78738

(G-10721)
SUMMIT PRODUCERS COMPANY INC

1700 E Iron Ave Ste A (67401-3403)
P.O. Box 737 (67402-0737)
PHONE..................................785 827-9331
Ren Ingemanson, *President*
EMP: 13
SQ FT: 2,000
SALES (est): 661.9K **Privately Held**
SIC: 0213 Hogs

(G-10722)
SUNFLOWER ADULT DAY SERVICES

401 W Iron Ave (67401-2563)
PHONE..................................785 823-6666
Sue Banninger, *Principal*
Deena Horst, *Principal*
Michelle Martin, *Principal*
Carolyn Peterson, *Principal*
Fr Keith Weber, *Principal*
EMP: 14
SQ FT: 3,454
SALES: 335.6K **Privately Held**
SIC: 8322 Adult day care center

(G-10723)
SUNFLOWER BANK

3025 Cortland Cir (67401-7874)
PHONE..................................785 827-5564
Mollie Carter, *CEO*
Nick Malone, *President*
Jeris Romeo, *President*
Christopher Chlumsky, *Assistant VP*
Eric Clemenson, *Vice Pres*
EMP: 535 **EST:** 1994
SQ FT: 80,000
SALES: 62.2MM **Privately Held**
SIC: 6029 Commercial banks

(G-10724)
SUNFLOWER BANK NATIONAL ASSN

Also Called: First National Bank
2450 S 9th St (67401-7663)
P.O. Box 800 (67402-0800)
PHONE..................................785 827-5564
Brandon Baker, *Branch Mgr*
Rob Cafera, *Clerk*
EMP: 11
SALES (corp-wide): 52.4MM **Privately Held**
WEB: www.sunflowerbank.com
SIC: 6021 6029 National trust companies with deposits, commercial; commercial banks
HQ: Sunflower Bank, National Association
1400 16th St Ste 250
Denver CO 80202
888 827-5564

(G-10725)
SUNFLOWER BANK NATIONAL ASSN

Also Called: First National Bank
176 N Santa Fe Ave (67401-2616)
PHONE..................................785 825-6900
Brian Rorie, *Vice Pres*
Sandy Vinson, *Branch Mgr*
EMP: 10
SALES (corp-wide): 52.4MM **Privately Held**
WEB: www.sunflowerbank.com
SIC: 6021 National trust companies with deposits, commercial
HQ: Sunflower Bank, National Association
1400 16th St Ste 250
Denver CO 80202
888 827-5564

(G-10726)
SUNFLOWER RESTAURANT SUP INC (PA)

1647 Sunflower Rd (67401-1758)
P.O. Box 1277 (67402-1277)
PHONE..................................785 823-6394
Norman Eilert, *President*
Kelly Piersee, *Office Mgr*
EMP: 14
SQ FT: 36,000
SALES: 8MM **Privately Held**
WEB: www.sunflowersrs.com
SIC: 5046 Restaurant equipment & supplies

(G-10727)
SUNFLOWER TAXI COURIER SVC LLC

752 Duvall Ave (67401-4543)
P.O. Box 224 (67402-0224)
PHONE..................................785 826-1881
Bryan Serocki,
Edwin Piersee,
EMP: 11
SALES: 250K **Privately Held**
WEB: www.sunflowercourierservice.com
SIC: 4212 4121 Delivery service, vehicular; taxicabs

(G-10728)
SUPERIOR PLUMBING & HEATING CO

1645 Copper Ct (67401-4687)
PHONE..................................785 827-5611
Chris Harapat, *President*
Christopher Harapat, *President*
EMP: 25 **EST:** 1978
SQ FT: 1,000
SALES: 7MM **Privately Held**
WEB: www.sph.kscoxmail.com
SIC: 1711 Plumbing contractors; heating & air conditioning contractors

(G-10729)
SURE CHECK BROKERAGE INC (PA)

141 S 4th St (67401-2801)
P.O. Box 1906 (67402-1906)
PHONE..................................785 823-1334
Terry Holovach, *Owner*
EMP: 15
SQ FT: 6,600
SALES (est): 1.6MM **Privately Held**
WEB: www.surecheckbrokerage.com
SIC: 7322 Collection agency, except real estate

(G-10730)
SYSTEMS 4 INC

430 N Santa Fe Ave (67401-2054)
P.O. Box 1425 (67402-1425)
PHONE..................................785 823-9119
Fax: 785 823-1125
EMP: 25
SQ FT: 10,100
SALES (est): 4.1MM **Privately Held**
SIC: 1711 1761 Plumbing/Heating/Air Cond Contractor Roofing/Siding Contractor

(G-10731)
T L C PROFESSIONAL LLC

747 Manchester Rd (67401-5209)
P.O. Box 1144 (67402-1144)
PHONE..................................785 823-7444
Sonya Vanamburg, *Managing Prtnr*
Diane Nunemaker, *Partner*
EMP: 23
SALES (est): 539.3K **Privately Held**
SIC: 7299 Babysitting bureau

(G-10732)
TECHNICAL SERVICES LLC

Also Called: Cabinet Connection
3125 Enterprise Dr (67401-8460)
PHONE..................................785 825-1250
Mike Mick, *Mng Member*
EMP: 6
SQ FT: 1,500
SALES: 1MM **Privately Held**
SIC: 2434 Wood kitchen cabinets

(G-10733)
TEXTRON AVIATION INC

2656 Scanlan Ave (67401-8126)
PHONE..................................316 676-7111
Rob Scholl, *President*
Charlene Oropesa, *Buyer*
Bill Williams, *Technical Mgr*
Ronda Downs, *Controller*
Brian Rohloff, *VP Sales*
EMP: 2000
SALES (corp-wide): 13.9B **Publicly Held**
SIC: 3721 3728 7359 Airplanes, fixed or rotary wing; aircraft parts & equipment; aircraft rental
HQ: Textron Aviation Inc.
1 Cessna Blvd
Wichita KS 67215
316 517-6000

(G-10734)
TISCHLEREI-FINE WDWKG LLC

2656 Scanlan Ave (67401-8126)
PHONE..................................785 404-3322
Olaf Gerhardt, *Mng Member*
EMP: 14
SALES (est): 1.7MM **Privately Held**
SIC: 2431 Millwork

(G-10735)
TOTAL TURFCARE INC

827 York Ave (67401-2416)
PHONE..................................785 827-6983
Gary Arpin, *President*
EMP: 13
SALES (est): 1MM **Privately Held**
WEB: www.totalturfcareinc.com
SIC: 0782 0781 5261 Landscape contractors; landscape architects; hydroponic equipment & supplies

(G-10736)
TOWN & COUNTRY ANIMAL HOSPITAL

1001 Schippel Dr (67401-6682)
PHONE..................................785 823-2217
Karen Young, *Owner*
Kelly Culbertson, *Med Doctor*
Pam Neiser, *Med Doctor*
Jennifer Rhodes, *Manager*
EMP: 10
SALES (est): 416.5K **Privately Held**
SIC: 0742 0752 Veterinary services, specialties; grooming services, pet & animal specialties

(G-10737)
TOX-EOL PEST MANAGEMENT INC

417 S Clark St (67401-4006)
PHONE..................................785 825-5143
Shonda Meitler, *President*
Brian Meitler, *Vice Pres*
EMP: 12
SALES (est): 332.7K **Privately Held**
SIC: 7342 Exterminating & fumigating

(G-10738)
TRACTOR SUPPLY COMPANY

3120 Riffel Dr (67401-8969)
PHONE..................................785 827-3300
John Delair, *Manager*
EMP: 14
SALES (corp-wide): 7.9B **Publicly Held**
WEB: www.tractorsupplyco.com
SIC: 5999 5261 5531 5251 Farm equipment & supplies; lawn & garden equipment; lawn & garden supplies; truck equipment & parts; tools; work clothing; processing & packaging equipment
PA: Tractor Supply Company
5401 Virginia Way
Brentwood TN 37027
615 440-4000

(G-10739)
TRANSERVICE LOGISTICS INC

413 E Berg Rd (67401-8907)
PHONE..................................785 493-4295
Bob Grothoff, *Manager*
EMP: 75 **Privately Held**
SIC: 4212 Truck rental with drivers
PA: Transervice Logistics Inc.
5 Dakota Dr Ste 209
New Hyde Park NY 11042

(G-10740)
TRIAD MANUFACTURING INC

1100 W Grand Ave Ste K (67401-1863)
P.O. Box 1211 (67402-1211)
PHONE..................................785 825-6050
Barbara Young, *President*
William G Mc Whorter, *Vice Pres*
EMP: 20 **EST:** 1977
SQ FT: 18,000
SALES (est): 2.2MM **Privately Held**
WEB: www.triadmfginc.com
SIC: 2531 2522 2512 2511 Public building & related furniture; office furniture, except wood; upholstered household furniture; wood household furniture; chairs, office: padded, upholstered or plain: wood

(G-10741)
TRIANGLE TRUCKING INC

2250 Hein Ave (67401-8114)
PHONE..................................785 827-5500
Patty Counts, *President*
EMP: 65
SQ FT: 6,000
SALES (est): 7.3MM **Privately Held**
SIC: 4213 Trucking, except local

(G-10742)
TRIPLETT INC (PA)
Also Called: 24/7 Store
429 N Ohio St (67401-2435)
P.O. Box 647 (67402-0647)
PHONE..................................785 823-7839
Mark Augustine, *CEO*
Carolyn Kohlmeier, *Corp Secy*
Butch Stucky, *Vice Pres*
Jamie Tucker, *Office Mgr*
EMP: 15
SQ FT: 2,400
SALES (est): 38.7MM **Privately Held**
WEB: www.triplettinc.com
SIC: 5541 5171 Truck stops; petroleum bulk stations

(G-10743)
TWIN OAKS INDUSTRIES INC
2001 W Grand Ave (67401-1870)
P.O. Box 1723 (67402-1723)
PHONE..................................785 827-4839
Timothy Ochs, *President*
James Henry, *QC Mgr*
Connie Fry, *Shareholder*
EMP: 40
SQ FT: 45,000
SALES (est): 9.8MM **Privately Held**
WEB: www.twino.com
SIC: 3443 3444 3441 Metal parts; sheet metalwork; fabricated structural metal

(G-10744)
UMB FINANCIAL CORPORATION
2375 S 9th St (67401-7502)
P.O. Box 560 (67402-0560)
PHONE..................................785 826-4000
EMP: 16
SALES (corp-wide): 1.1B **Publicly Held**
SIC: 6021 National commercial banks
PA: Umb Financial Corporation
1010 Grand Blvd
Kansas City MO 64106
816 860-7000

(G-10745)
UNIFIRST CORPORATION
1924 Jumper Rd (67401-8138)
PHONE..................................785 825-8766
Jeremy Dinneen, *Branch Mgr*
EMP: 12
SALES (corp-wide): 1.8B **Publicly Held**
SIC: 7218 7213 Industrial uniform supply; linen supply, non-clothing; uniform supply
PA: Unifirst Corporation
68 Jonspin Rd
Wilmington MA 01887
978 658-8888

(G-10746)
UNITED PARCEL SERVICE INC
Also Called: UPS
1502 W North St (67401-9301)
PHONE..................................800 742-5877
EMP: 11
SALES (corp-wide): 71.8B **Publicly Held**
SIC: 4512 Air cargo carrier, scheduled
HQ: United Parcel Service, Inc.
55 Glenlake Pkwy
Atlanta GA 30328
404 828-6000

(G-10747)
UNITED RDLGY GROUP CHARTERED
Also Called: United Rdlgy Group Chartered
148 S Santa Fe Ave (67401-2810)
P.O. Box 2327 (67402-2327)
PHONE..................................785 827-9526
James Peterson, *President*
Debbie Bostleman, *Business Mgr*
EMP: 15 **EST:** 1965
SQ FT: 1,600
SALES (est): 2.9MM **Privately Held**
SIC: 8011 Radiologist

(G-10748)
USA INC (PA)
Also Called: United Sports of America
122 S Santa Fe Ave (67401-2810)
P.O. Box 704 (67402-0704)
PHONE..................................785 825-6247
Mike Shane, *President*
Cecil Lane, *Treasurer*
▲ **EMP:** 15
SALES: 2.3MM **Privately Held**
SIC: 5091 5941 2396 Sporting & recreation goods; sporting goods & bicycle shops; screen printing on fabric articles

(G-10749)
VALMONT INDUSTRIES INC
Also Called: Valmont Ctngs Slina Glvanizing
1100 N Ohio St (67401-2403)
PHONE..................................785 452-9630
Richard Cornish, *Vice Pres*
Mike Burns, *Manager*
EMP: 69
SALES (corp-wide): 2.7B **Publicly Held**
SIC: 3441 Fabricated structural metal
PA: Valmont Industries, Inc.
1 Valmont Plz Ste 500
Omaha NE 68154
402 963-1000

(G-10750)
VERIDIAN BEHAVORIAL HEALTH
501 S Santa Fe Ave # 300 (67401-4189)
P.O. Box 5080 (67402-5080)
PHONE..................................785 452-4930
Sally Schneider, *Director*
EMP: 20
SALES (est): 907.5K **Privately Held**
SIC: 8093 Mental health clinic, outpatient

(G-10751)
VERNON JEWELERS OF SALINA INC
123 N Santa Fe Ave (67401-2615)
PHONE..................................785 825-0531
Pat Anderson, *President*
Gary Anderson, *Vice Pres*
EMP: 11
SQ FT: 2,000
SALES (est): 1.2MM **Privately Held**
WEB: www.vernonjewelers.com
SIC: 5944 7631 Jewelry, precious stones & precious metals; jewelry repair services

(G-10752)
VETERANS HEALTH ADMINISTRATION
Also Called: Salina Clinic
1410 E Iron Ave Ste 1 (67401-3285)
PHONE..................................785 826-1580
Terry McLaughlin, *Manager*
EMP: 264 **Publicly Held**
WEB: www.veterans-ru.org
SIC: 8011 9451 Clinic, operated by physicians; psychiatric clinic;
HQ: Veterans Health Administration
810 Vermont Ave Nw
Washington DC 20420

(G-10753)
VIDRICKSEN DISTRIBUTING CO
1825 Bailey Rd (67401-1719)
PHONE..................................785 827-2386
Norman Vidricksen, *President*
Mary Ann Vidricksen, *Corp Secy*
Dan Vidricksen, *Vice Pres*
EMP: 17
SQ FT: 11,000
SALES (est): 2.1MM **Privately Held**
SIC: 5181 Beer & other fermented malt liquors

(G-10754)
WADDELL & REED INC
Waddell & Reed Office 1606-00
2036 S Ohio St (67401-6708)
P.O. Box 285 (67402-0285)
PHONE..................................785 827-3606
Ken Ebert, *Executive*
Lance Billings, *Administration*
EMP: 35 **Publicly Held**
SIC: 6282 Investment advice
HQ: Waddell & Reed, Inc.
6300 Lamar Ave
Shawnee Mission KS 66202
913 236-2000

(G-10755)
WADDLES HEATING & COOLING
346 N 9th St (67401-2198)
PHONE..................................785 827-2621
Charles Waddle, *President*
Elaine Waddle, *Corp Secy*
Bruce Waddle, *Vice Pres*
EMP: 22
SQ FT: 10,000
SALES (est): 3.8MM **Privately Held**
SIC: 1711 1761 Boiler & furnace contractors; heating & air conditioning contractors; sheet metalwork

(G-10756)
WADDLES MANUFACTURING & MCH CO
2816 Centennial Rd (67401-8112)
PHONE..................................785 825-6166
Brad Waddle, *President*
Elizabeth Waddle, *Corp Secy*
EMP: 7
SQ FT: 12,500
SALES (est): 1.2MM **Privately Held**
SIC: 3491 3599 Industrial valves; machine shop, jobbing & repair

(G-10757)
WALKER CENTRIFUGE SERVICES LLC
516 Graves Blvd Apt B (67401-4371)
PHONE..................................785 826-8265
Dennis Berndt, *CFO*
Morries Soderberg, *Treasurer*
Charles W Walker,
EMP: 15
SQ FT: 60,000
SALES (est): 1.3MM **Privately Held**
SIC: 7389 Water softener service

(G-10758)
WARMACK AND COMPANY LLC
Also Called: Central Mall
2259 S 9th St (67401-7313)
PHONE..................................785 825-0122
Lisa McDowell, *Manager*
EMP: 20
SALES (corp-wide): 5.5MM **Privately Held**
WEB: www.indianmalljonesboro.com
SIC: 6512 Shopping center, community (100,000 - 300,000 sq ft)
PA: Warmack And Company, L.L.C.
30 Morris Ln
Texarkana TX 75503
903 838-4000

(G-10759)
WASTE CONNECTIONS KANSAS INC
Also Called: Salina Waste Systems
1848 Summers Rd (67401-8135)
PHONE..................................785 827-3939
Eric Bergin, *Branch Mgr*
EMP: 20
SALES (corp-wide): 4.6B **Privately Held**
WEB: www.wcnx.org
SIC: 4953 Refuse collection & disposal services
HQ: Waste Connections Of Kansas, Inc.
2745 N Ohio St
Wichita KS 67219

(G-10760)
WATERS INC
Also Called: Earthcare Services Landscape
3213 Arnold Ave (67401-8163)
PHONE..................................785 822-6540
Paul Griffith, *General Mgr*
Mike Terry, *Branch Mgr*
EMP: 22
SALES (corp-wide): 49.8MM **Privately Held**
SIC: 5251 0781 0181 0811 Hardware; landscape services; nursery stock, growing of; tree farm
PA: Waters, Inc.
3213 Arnold Ave
Salina KS 67401
785 825-7309

(G-10761)
WATSON ELECTRIC INC
318 N 8th St (67401-2312)
PHONE..................................785 827-2924
Richard M Watson, *President*
Ernestine Watson, *Corp Secy*
Robert Watson, *Vice Pres*
Robert D Watson Jr, *Vice Pres*
EMP: 10
SQ FT: 2,300
SALES: 1.3MM **Privately Held**
SIC: 1731 General electrical contractor

(G-10762)
WEB CREATIONS & CONSULTING LLC
Also Called: Slappy's Electric Paradise
119 W Iron Ave Fl 3 (67401-2600)
PHONE..................................785 823-7630
Sharon Sadler, *CEO*
Shawn Williams, *Web Dvlpr*
Michael Sadler,
EMP: 6
SQ FT: 5,760
SALES (est): 880.3K **Privately Held**
WEB: www.slappys.net
SIC: 7374 4931 7372 Computer graphics service; electric & other services combined; prepackaged software

(G-10763)
WEBER PALMER & MACY CHARTERED (PA)
Also Called: Wpm
338 N Front St (67401-2038)
P.O. Box 2027 (67402-2027)
PHONE..................................785 823-7201
Chris Raines, *President*
EMP: 39 **EST:** 1969
SQ FT: 5,500
SALES (est): 1.9MM **Privately Held**
SIC: 8071 Pathological laboratory

(G-10764)
WEBSTER CONFERENCE CENTER INC
2601 N Ohio St (67401-9238)
PHONE..................................785 827-6565
Ron Emery, *Supervisor*
Bill Cooke, *Director*
Terry McIlavin, *Administration*
EMP: 25 **EST:** 1981
SALES (est): 1.4MM **Privately Held**
WEB: www.websterconferencecenter.com
SIC: 8322 Community center

(G-10765)
WEIS FIRE SAFETY EQUIP CO INC
Also Called: W F E
111 E Pacific Ave (67401-8282)
P.O. Box 3467 (67402-3467)
PHONE..................................785 825-9527
Toll Free:..888 -
Gary L Weis, *Ch of Bd*
Mike Weis, *President*
Charlotte Weis, *Senior VP*
Dave Smith, *Sales Staff*
Jennifer Ames, *Administration*
▼ **EMP:** 17
SQ FT: 13,500
SALES (est): 3MM **Privately Held**
WEB: www.weisfiresafety.com
SIC: 3999 5511 5999 3444 Fire extinguishers, portable; trucks, tractors & trailers: new & used; fire extinguishers; alarm & safety equipment stores; hoods, range: sheet metal; air pollution control equipment & supplies; firefighting apparatus & related equipment

(G-10766)
WELBORN SALES INC
3288 S Avenue C (67401-8921)
P.O. Box 1666 (67402-1666)
PHONE..................................785 823-2394
Stephen K Welborn, *President*
Montre L Garry, *Director*
EMP: 10
SQ FT: 4,000
SALES (est): 5.5MM **Privately Held**
WEB: www.welbornsales.com
SIC: 5082 5051 Blades for graders, scrapers, dozers & snow plows; pipe & tubing, steel

(G-10767)
WELLS FARGO CLEARING SVCS LLC
Also Called: Wells Fargo Advisors
118 W Iron Ave (67401-2612)
P.O. Box 1035 (67402-1035)
PHONE..................................785 825-4636
Robert Justus, *Vice Pres*
Mark Wedel, *Branch Mgr*
Stuart Hieger, *Branch Mgr*
Kimberly Fink, *Agent*
Douglas W Stein, *Agent*

GEOGRAPHIC

EMP: 10
SALES (corp-wide): 101B **Publicly Held**
SIC: 6211 8742 6411 Brokers, security; financial consultant; pension & retirement plan consultants
HQ: Wells Fargo Clearing Services, Llc
1 N Jefferson Ave Fl 7
Saint Louis MO 63103
314 955-3000

(G-10768)
WILD WILD WEST INC
1035 N 3rd St (67401-8240)
PHONE..................................785 827-8938
Kirk Roberts, *President*
EMP: 10 **EST:** 2000
SALES (est): 147.5K **Privately Held**
SIC: 7929 Entertainment service

(G-10769)
WILSON INC ENGINEERS ARCHITECTS
1700 E Iron Ave (67401-3401)
P.O. Box 1640 (67402-1640)
PHONE..................................785 827-0433
Ryan Branfort, *Vice Pres*
Mark Wentzel, *Engineer*
Ryan R Branfort, *Branch Mgr*
EMP: 70
SALES (corp-wide): 62.4MM **Privately Held**
WEB: www.wilsonco.com
SIC: 8711 8712 Consulting engineer; architectural services
PA: Wilson & Company, Inc. Engineers & Architects
4401 Masthead St Ne # 15
Albuquerque NM 87109
505 348-4000

(G-10770)
WINDSOR ESTATES INC
Also Called: McCall Manor
626 S 3rd St (67401-4105)
PHONE..................................785 825-8183
Jack Ferguson, *President*
Doris Ann McCall, *Corp Secy*
EMP: 15
SALES: 1.1MM **Privately Held**
WEB: www.mccall-windsor.com
SIC: 6513 Retirement hotel operation

(G-10771)
WINDSOR NURSING HOME ASSOC
Also Called: Windsor Estates
623 S 3rd St (67401-4104)
PHONE..................................785 825-6757
Kara Fiske, *Administration*
EMP: 85 **EST:** 1984
SQ FT: 15,000
SALES (est): 2.8MM **Privately Held**
SIC: 8051 8052 Convalescent home with continuous nursing care; intermediate care facilities

(G-10772)
WOODS & DURHAM LLC (PA)
Also Called: Woods and Durham Chartered
1619 E Iron Ave (67401-3237)
PHONE..................................785 825-5494
Jim Trower, *President*
James Trower, *CPA*
Bridget Brown, *Meeting Planner*
EMP: 40 **EST:** 1957
SALES (est): 4.1MM **Privately Held**
SIC: 8721 Accounting services, except auditing; certified public accountant

(G-10773)
WORLDWIDE WINDOWS
736 N 9th St (67401-1841)
P.O. Box 824 (67402-0824)
PHONE..................................785 826-1701
Kathleen Schwegmann, *President*
Donald Schwegmann, *Vice Pres*
EMP: 12
SQ FT: 12,000
SALES (est): 1.9MM **Privately Held**
WEB: www.worldwindowsmusic.com
SIC: 3083 5211 1751 Window sheeting, plastic; door & window products; window & door (prefabricated) installation

(G-10774)
XPO LOGISTICS FREIGHT INC
Also Called: Con-Way
358 E Berg Rd (67401-8907)
PHONE..................................785 823-3926
Tim Rakes, *Manager*
EMP: 62
SALES (corp-wide): 17.2B **Publicly Held**
WEB: www.con-way.com
SIC: 4213 Contract haulers
HQ: Xpo Logistics Freight, Inc.
2211 Old Earhart Rd # 100
Ann Arbor MI 48105
800 755-2728

(G-10775)
YOUNG MNS CHRSTN ASSN SLINA KA (PA)
Also Called: YMCA of Salina Kansas, The
570 Ymca Dr (67401-7433)
PHONE..................................785 825-2151
Dewayne Donaldson, *Exec Dir*
EMP: 100
SQ FT: 75,000
SALES: 2.7MM **Privately Held**
WEB: www.salinaymca.com
SIC: 8641 8322 7991 7997 Youth organizations; youth center; aerobic dance & exercise classes; membership sports & recreation clubs

Satanta
Haskell County

(G-10776)
ARCHER-DANIELS-MIDLAND COMPANY
Also Called: ADM
6500 S Road X (67870-9426)
PHONE..................................620 657-3411
Jeff Mayfield, *Opers-Prdtn-Mfg*
EMP: 12
SALES (corp-wide): 64.3B **Publicly Held**
WEB: www.collingwoodgrain.com
SIC: 2041 5261 Flour & other grain mill products; fertilizer
PA: Archer-Daniels-Midland Company
77 W Wacker Dr Ste 4600
Chicago IL 60601
312 634-8100

(G-10777)
BP AMERICA PRODUCTION COMPANY
Also Called: Hugoton Jay Hawk Gas Plant
13201 E Hwy 160 (67870-8772)
PHONE..................................620 657-4300
Richard Rose, *Manager*
EMP: 25
SALES (corp-wide): 298.7B **Privately Held**
WEB: www.firstchurchtulsa.org
SIC: 3824 Production counters
HQ: Bp America Production Company
501 Westlake Park Blvd
Houston TX 77079
281 366-2000

(G-10778)
CASILLAS PETROLEUM CORP
348 Road Dd (67870-8775)
PHONE..................................620 276-3693
EMP: 50
SALES (corp-wide): 8.8MM **Privately Held**
SIC: 5172 Petroleum products
PA: Casillas Petroleum Corp
401 S Boston Ave Ste 2400
Tulsa OK 74103
918 582-5310

(G-10779)
CATTLE EMPIRE LLC
2425 Road Dd (67870-9432)
PHONE..................................620 649-2235
Roy Brown,
EMP: 40
SALES (est): 1.2MM **Privately Held**
SIC: 0211 Beef cattle feedlots

(G-10780)
CENTERA BANK
218 Sequoyah St (67870-2579)
P.O. Box 39 (67870-0039)
PHONE..................................620 649-2220
Bill Anton, *Manager*
EMP: 15
SALES (corp-wide): 11.1MM **Privately Held**
WEB: www.centerabank.com
SIC: 6022 State commercial banks
PA: Centera Bank
119 S Inman St
Sublette KS 67877
620 675-8611

(G-10781)
CIRCLE BAR CATTLE COMPANY INC
842 Road 60 (67870-7010)
PHONE..................................620 275-1182
Darcy Kells, *President*
EMP: 15
SQ FT: 3,000
SALES (est): 2.3MM **Privately Held**
SIC: 0211 Beef cattle feedlots

(G-10782)
CROPLAND CO-OP INC
506 W Hwy 56 (67870)
P.O. Box 99 (67870-0099)
PHONE..................................620 649-2230
Brad Lane, *Manager*
EMP: 13
SALES (corp-wide): 16.9MM **Privately Held**
WEB: www.croplandco-op.com
SIC: 5153 5191 4221 2875 Grain elevators; fertilizer & fertilizer materials; farm product warehousing & storage; fertilizers, mixing only
PA: Cropland Co-Op, Inc.
1125 W Oklahoma Ave
Ulysses KS 67880
620 356-1241

(G-10783)
DESERET CATTLE FEEDERS LLC
521 Road 50 (67870-8702)
PHONE..................................620 275-6181
Michael Archibald, *Principal*
Brian Debban, *Sales Mgr*
EMP: 10
SALES (est): 940K **Privately Held**
SIC: 0211 Beef cattle feedlots

(G-10784)
ELDREDGE WELL SERVICE LLC
509 N Shoshone Ct (67870)
P.O. Box 549 (67870-0549)
PHONE..................................620 649-2841
David Thacker,
Penny Thacker,
EMP: 20
SALES: 880K **Privately Held**
SIC: 1389 Oil & gas wells: building, repairing & dismantling

(G-10785)
FRIONA INDUSTRIES LP (HQ)
Also Called: Friona Cattle Feeders N 1 2
1174 Empire Cir (67870-9600)
PHONE..................................620 649-3700
Don Gales, *CEO*
Jeffrey Jorgenson, *CFO*
Roy Brown,
EMP: 75
SALES (est): 3MM
SALES (corp-wide): 90.4MM **Privately Held**
WEB: www.cattle-empire.net
SIC: 0211 Beef cattle feedlots
PA: Friona Industries, L.P.
500 S Taylor St Unit 253
Amarillo TX 79101
806 374-1811

(G-10786)
HIGH PLAINS RANCH LLC
12225 E Hwy 160 (67870-8725)
PHONE..................................559 805-5636
Bernard Te Velde, *Branch Mgr*
EMP: 30
SALES (corp-wide): 15.6MM **Privately Held**
SIC: 0241 Dairy farms
PA: High Plains Ranch, Llc
2911 Hanford Armona Rd
Hanford CA 93230
559 583-1277

(G-10787)
KEY ENERGY SERVICES INC
P.O. Box 747 (67870-0747)
PHONE..................................620 649-2368
John Warren, *Manager*
EMP: 7
SALES (corp-wide): 521.7MM **Publicly Held**
WEB: www.keyenergy.com
SIC: 1389 Fishing for tools, oil & gas field
PA: Key Energy Services, Inc.
1301 Mckinney St Ste 1800
Houston TX 77010
713 651-4300

(G-10788)
MSIP-SSCC HOLDINGS LLC
12725 E Us Highway 160 (67870-8770)
PHONE..................................620 657-4166
Brian Sullivan, *Branch Mgr*
EMP: 19
SALES (corp-wide): 216.1MM **Privately Held**
SIC: 4932 Gas & other services combined
PA: Msip-Sscc Holdings, Llc
1585 Broadway
New York NY 10036
270 852-5000

(G-10789)
PRAXAIR INC
Ste Dd Rr 1 Box 14 (67870)
PHONE..................................620 657-2711
Bobby Sura, *Manager*
EMP: 23 **Privately Held**
SIC: 5084 Welding machinery & equipment
HQ: Praxair, Inc.
10 Riverview Dr
Danbury CT 06810
203 837-2000

(G-10790)
SATANTA DISTRICT HOSP & LONG T
401 Cheyenne Ste 401 # 401
(67870-8748)
P.O. Box 159 (67870-0159)
PHONE..................................620 649-2761
Jeremy Clingenpeel, *President*
John Brown, *Director*
Peggy Parker, *Nurse Practr*
Kari Brown,
EMP: 148 **EST:** 1953
SQ FT: 64,000
SALES: 9.6MM **Privately Held**
SIC: 8062 General medical & surgical hospitals

(G-10791)
SOUTHERN STAR CENTRAL GAS PIPE
13 Mils Nw Stnt Hwy 160 (67870)
PHONE..................................620 657-2130
Don Tory, *Manager*
EMP: 36
SALES (corp-wide): 216.1MM **Privately Held**
WEB: www.sscgp.com
SIC: 4923 1321 Gas transmission & distribution; natural gasoline production
HQ: Southern Star Central Gas Pipeline, Inc.
4700 Highway 56
Owensboro KY 42301
270 852-5000

(G-10792)
SUNFLOWER ELECTRIC POWER CORP
14255 E Hwy 160 (67870-8790)
PHONE..................................620 657-4400
Joe Humpries, *Manager*
EMP: 10 **Privately Held**
SIC: 4911 Generation, electric power

HQ: Sunflower Electric Power Corporation
301 W 13th St
Hays KS 67601
785 628-2845

Savonburg
Allen County

(G-10793)
VERDE OIL COMPANY
3345 Arizona Rd (66772-4062)
PHONE..................................620 754-3800
Stephen Ballantyne, *President*
Jeff Dale, *Principal*
EMP: 5
SALES (corp-wide): 1.2MM **Privately Held**
SIC: 1311 Crude petroleum production
PA: Verde Oil Company
8700 Crownhill Blvd
San Antonio TX 78209
210 828-7852

Sawyer
Pratt County

(G-10794)
AMERICAN TRUCKING INC
204 S Main St (67134-9580)
P.O. Box 54 (67134-0054)
PHONE..................................620 594-2481
Mike Van Ranken, *President*
Nancy Van Ranken, *Treasurer*
EMP: 11
SALES (est): 1.3MM **Privately Held**
SIC: 4212 Local trucking, without storage

Scammon
Cherokee County

(G-10795)
CREATIVE HARDWOODS
2542 Nw Highway 102 (66773-2221)
PHONE..................................620 249-4160
EMP: 6
SALES: 500K **Privately Held**
SIC: 2434 Mfg Wood Kitchen Cabinets

(G-10796)
MID AMERICA PIPE FABG SUP LLC
2674 Nw Highway 102 (66773-2222)
PHONE..................................620 827-6121
Dean Gravett, *Project Mgr*
John W Parsons, *Mng Member*
David Cox, *Manager*
John L Parsons, *Executive*
Teresa Parsons,
▲ **EMP:** 140
SQ FT: 110,000
SALES (est): 47MM **Privately Held**
WEB: www.midamericapipe.com
SIC: 3498 3443 Fabricated pipe & fittings; industrial vessels, tanks & containers

(G-10797)
RIPPELS INC
6694 Ne Belleview Rd (66773-7100)
PHONE..................................620 674-1944
Ronnie D Rippel, *President*
EMP: 12
SQ FT: 500
SALES: 1.5MM **Privately Held**
SIC: 1794 Excavation work

Scandia
Republic County

(G-10798)
ASTRA BANK (HQ)
323 4th St (66966-9600)
P.O. Box 200 (66966-0200)
PHONE..................................785 335-2243
Kyle Campbell, *President*
Jane Coutrure, *Senior VP*
T J Couture, *Senior VP*
Paul Kallman, *Senior VP*
Bryan Armendariz, *Assistant VP*
EMP: 28 **EST:** 1887
SQ FT: 2,000
SALES: 14.4MM **Privately Held**
SIC: 6022 State commercial banks

(G-10799)
GRANDVIEW WATER DISPOSAL INC
1390 70 Rd (66966-8020)
PHONE..................................785 335-2649
Delton Robison, *President*
EMP: 8
SALES: 460K **Privately Held**
SIC: 1389 Impounding & storing salt water, oil & gas field

(G-10800)
NESIKA ENERGY LLC
1020 70 Rd (66966-8032)
P.O. Box 169 (66966-0169)
PHONE..................................785 335-2054
David Wood, *COO*
Dave Wood, *Mng Member*
EMP: 9
SQ FT: 2,500
SALES (est): 4MM **Privately Held**
SIC: 2869 Ethyl alcohol, ethanol
PA: Butamax Advanced Biofuels, Llc
Henry Clay Rr 141
Wilmington DE 19880

(G-10801)
PREMIUM FEEDERS INC
705 Hwy 36 (66966)
PHONE..................................785 335-2221
Jeff Strnad, *President*
EMP: 25
SQ FT: 1,000
SALES (est): 5.3MM **Privately Held**
WEB: www.premiumfeeders.com
SIC: 0211 Beef cattle feedlots

Schoenchen
Ellis County

(G-10802)
CASTLE RESOURCES INC
114 Oak St (67667-2403)
PHONE..................................785 625-5155
Jerry Green, *President*
Susan Green, *Treasurer*
EMP: 20
SALES (est): 2.1MM **Privately Held**
SIC: 1382 6792 1311 Oil & gas exploration services; oil leases, buying & selling on own account; crude petroleum & natural gas production

Scott City
Scott County

(G-10803)
AMERICAN IMPLEMENT INC
Also Called: John Deere Authorized Dealer
807 N Main St (67871-4160)
P.O. Box 20 (67871-0020)
PHONE..................................620 872-7244
Rod Eitel, *Manager*
Tyler Kough, *Manager*
EMP: 22
SALES (corp-wide): 79.4MM **Privately Held**
WEB: www.americanimplement.com
SIC: 5083 5261 Agricultural machinery & equipment; lawnmowers & tractors
PA: American Implement, Inc.
2611 W Jones Ave
Garden City KS 67846
620 275-4114

(G-10804)
ARCHER-DANIELS-MIDLAND COMPANY
Also Called: ADM
181 N Front St (67871-5023)
PHONE..................................620 872-2174
Chad Befeda, *Sales & Mktg St*
Tod Depperschmidt, *Sales Staff*
EMP: 11
SALES (corp-wide): 64.3B **Publicly Held**
WEB: www.admworld.com
SIC: 2041 5191 5261 Flour & other grain mill products; chemicals, agricultural; feed; fertilizer & fertilizer materials; fertilizer
PA: Archer-Daniels-Midland Company
77 W Wacker Dr Ste 4600
Chicago IL 60601
312 634-8100

(G-10805)
B & H PAVING INC
711 E 7th St (67871-1624)
P.O. Box 524 (67871-0524)
PHONE..................................620 872-3146
EMP: 12
SALES: 1.2MM **Privately Held**
WEB: www.bhpaving.com
SIC: 1611 Highway & street paving contractor

(G-10806)
BEEF BELT LLC
1350 E Road 70 (67871-5044)
PHONE..................................620 872-3059
Charles Duff, *President*
Dominic Stephens, *Manager*
EMP: 14 **EST:** 2013
SALES (est): 410.9K **Privately Held**
SIC: 0211 Beef cattle feedlots

(G-10807)
CHAMBLESS ROOFING INC (PA)
1005 W 5th St (67871-6000)
PHONE..................................620 275-8410
Curtis Chambless, *President*
Tracy Chambless, *Treasurer*
EMP: 10
SALES: 1MM **Privately Held**
SIC: 1761 1542 Roof repair; commercial & office buildings, renovation & repair

(G-10808)
COMPASS BEHAVIORAL HEALTH
204 S College St (67871-1253)
PHONE..................................620 872-5338
Angela Wolke, *Director*
EMP: 12
SALES (corp-wide): 10MM **Privately Held**
SIC: 8093 Mental health clinic, outpatient
PA: Compass Behavioral Health
531 Campus View St
Garden City KS 67846
620 276-6470

(G-10809)
FAIRLEIGH CORPORATION
207 E Bellevue Ave (67871-1031)
P.O. Box 560 (67871-0560)
PHONE..................................620 872-1111
John Fairlegh, *CEO*
John Fairleigh, *CEO*
EMP: 94 **EST:** 1970
SALES (est): 4.2MM **Privately Held**
SIC: 0212 Beef cattle except feedlots

(G-10810)
FAIRLEIGH RANCH CORPORATION
Also Called: Fairleigh Feed Yard
7400 S Falcon Rd (67871-5107)
P.O. Box 560 (67871-0560)
PHONE..................................620 872-2111
John Fairleigh, *Principal*
EMP: 14
SALES (corp-wide): 3.6MM **Privately Held**
WEB: www.fairleigh.com
SIC: 6519 2048 5541 Real property lessors; livestock feeds; filling stations, gasoline
PA: Fairleigh Ranch Corporation
207 E Bellevue Ave
Scott City KS 67871
620 872-1111

(G-10811)
FIRST NAT BNKSHRES OF SCOTT CY
Also Called: First Natl Bank
501 S Main St (67871-1516)
P.O. Box 290 (67871-0290)
PHONE..................................620 872-2143
Skip Numrich, *President*
Sharon Powers, *CFO*
EMP: 24
SALES: 4.8MM **Privately Held**
WEB: www.fnbscott.com
SIC: 6021 National commercial banks

(G-10812)
FIRST NATIONAL BNK OF SCOTT CY
501 S Main St (67871-1516)
P.O. Box 290 (67871-0290)
PHONE..................................620 872-2143
Skip Numrich, *President*
Trudy Eikenberry, *Vice Pres*
EMP: 20 **EST:** 1902
SALES: 5MM **Privately Held**
SIC: 6021 National commercial banks
PA: Hoeme Family Partnership
501 S Main St
Scott City KS

(G-10813)
GRAIN SORGHUM HOGS INC
1014 S Washington St (67871-1750)
PHONE..................................620 872-3866
L D Parkinson, *President*
Bill Winters, *Vice Pres*
Louise V Parkinson, *Treasurer*
EMP: 10
SALES (est): 417.8K **Privately Held**
SIC: 0213 Hog feedlot

(G-10814)
HEARTLAND FEEDERS INC
Also Called: Stampede Feeders
5503 E Road 210 (67871-4055)
PHONE..................................620 872-0800
James Prickett, *President*
Jeffrey Craig, *Vice Pres*
Charles Mc Cauley, *Treasurer*
Matthew Mc Cauley, *Admin Sec*
EMP: 15
SALES (est): 1.2MM **Privately Held**
WEB: www.stampedefeeders.com
SIC: 0751 Livestock services, except veterinary

(G-10815)
HIGH CHOICE FEEDERS LLC (PA)
553 W Road 40 (67871-5038)
PHONE..................................620 872-7271
Bradley Scott, *President*
Nancy Templeton, *Treasurer*
EMP: 20
SQ FT: 5,500
SALES (est): 4.2MM **Privately Held**
WEB: www.cristfeedyard.com
SIC: 0211 0111 0115 0119 Beef cattle feedlots; wheat; corn; sorghum farm

(G-10816)
HIGH CHOICE FEEDERS LLC
Also Called: K C Feeders
553 W Road 40 (67871-5038)
PHONE..................................620 872-5376
Ty Rumford, *Manager*
EMP: 15
SALES (est): 1.1MM
SALES (corp-wide): 4.2MM **Privately Held**
WEB: www.cristfeedyard.com
SIC: 0211 Beef cattle feedlots
PA: High Choice Feeders, Llc
553 W Road 40
Scott City KS 67871
620 872-7271

(G-10817)
IRSIK & DOLL FEED SERVICES INC
Also Called: Royal Beef
11060 N Falcon Rd (67871-6037)
PHONE..................................620 872-5371
Rick Weber, *Branch Mgr*
EMP: 33

GEOGRAPHIC

SALES (corp-wide): 62.5MM **Privately Held**
WEB: www.irsikanddoll.com
SIC: 0211 Beef cattle feedlots
PA: Irsik & Doll Feed Services, Inc.
104 W Ave A
Cimarron KS 67835
620 855-3747

(G-10818)
JOSEPH F BEAVER
Also Called: J F Beaver Advertising
514 S Main St (67871-1515)
PHONE..................................620 872-2395
Joseph F Beaver, *Owner*
Michael Jay Beaver, *Manager*
▲ **EMP:** 10
SQ FT: 10,500
SALES (est): 1.3MM **Privately Held**
WEB: www.jfbeaveradvertising.com
SIC: 5199 Advertising specialties

(G-10819)
LAKESIDE CAMP OF THE UNITED
Also Called: Camp Lakeside
300 E Scott Lake Dr (67871-4034)
PHONE..................................620 872-2021
Kay Schmitt, *President*
Keith Schadel, *Director*
EMP: 15
SALES: 424K **Privately Held**
SIC: 7032 Bible camp

(G-10820)
LOVES TRAVEL STOPS
1720 S Main St (67871-1951)
PHONE..................................620 872-5727
EMP: 15
SALES (corp-wide): 4.6B **Privately Held**
SIC: 4724 Travel agencies
PA: Love's Travel Stops & Country Stores, Inc.
10601 N Pennsylvania Ave
Oklahoma City OK 73120
405 302-6500

(G-10821)
MCCARTY FARMS SCOTT CITY LLC
6650 N Highway 83 (67871-4147)
PHONE..................................620 872-5661
Ken McCarty,
EMP: 23
SALES (est): 1.2MM **Privately Held**
SIC: 0241 Dairy farms

(G-10822)
MIDWEST ENERGY INC
1301 S Main St (67871-1860)
P.O. Box 437 (67871-0437)
PHONE..................................620 872-2179
Jerry Schoenseld, *Branch Mgr*
EMP: 12
SALES (corp-wide): 219.6MM **Privately Held**
WEB: www.mwenergy.com
SIC: 4924 Natural gas distribution
PA: Midwest Energy, Inc.
1330 Canterbury Dr
Hays KS 67601
785 625-3437

(G-10823)
MIDWEST MIXER SERVICE LLC
40 E Road 160 (67871-4157)
P.O. Box 572 (67871-0572)
PHONE..................................620 872-7251
Aaron Goodman,
EMP: 23
SALES (est): 2.4MM **Privately Held**
SIC: 7389 5083 Authors' agents & brokers; agricultural machinery & equipment

(G-10824)
MIDWEST PMS LLC
Also Called: Scott-Pro
810 E 1st St (67871-2201)
P.O. Box 587 (67871-0587)
PHONE..................................620 872-2189
Lance Huck, *Manager*
EMP: 20 **Privately Held**
WEB: www.fairleigh.com
SIC: 2048 Stock feeds, dry
PA: Midwest Pms Llc
11347 Business Park Cir
Firestone CO 80504

(G-10825)
NORDER SUPPLY INC
250 N Pawnee Rd (67871-4145)
PHONE..................................620 872-3058
Bill John, *Branch Mgr*
EMP: 24
SALES (corp-wide): 23.3MM **Privately Held**
SIC: 5191 Farm supplies
PA: Norder Supply, Inc.
136 E Main St
Bruning NE 68322
402 353-6175

(G-10826)
NUTRIEN AG SOLUTIONS INC
181 N Front St (67871-5023)
PHONE..................................620 872-2174
EMP: 13 **Privately Held**
SIC: 5191 Farm supplies
HQ: Nutrien Ag Solutions, Inc.
3005 Rocky Mountain Ave
Loveland CO 80538
970 685-3300

(G-10827)
PLAINJANS FEEDLOT SERVICE
Also Called: Plain Jan's
511 Monroe St (67871-1664)
PHONE..................................620 872-5777
Jan Huck, *President*
Richard Huck, *Corp Secy*
EMP: 12 **EST:** 1975
SQ FT: 3,500
SALES (est): 1.1MM **Privately Held**
WEB: www.plainjans.com
SIC: 7342 0721 2395 7336 Pest control services; weed control services after planting; embroidery products, except schiffli machine; silk screen design

(G-10828)
POKY FEEDERS INC
Also Called: Poky Pig
600 E Road 30 (67871-5043)
PHONE..................................620 872-7046
Wayne Anderson, *President*
Joe Morgan, *Corp Secy*
Barry Bramstadt, *Vice Pres*
EMP: 60
SQ FT: 800
SALES (est): 13.7MM **Privately Held**
SIC: 0211 0213 Beef cattle feedlots; hog feedlot

(G-10829)
PREMIERE PORK INC
440 N Eagle Rd (67871-6082)
PHONE..................................620 872-7073
Duane Ramsey, *President*
Dennis Kingston, *Manager*
EMP: 12
SALES (est): 960K **Privately Held**
SIC: 5154 Livestock

(G-10830)
ROTO-MIX LLC
1451 S Highway 83 (67871-5004)
PHONE..................................620 872-1100
Mark Cooksey, *Manager*
EMP: 5
SALES (corp-wide): 21.5MM **Privately Held**
WEB: www.rotomix.com
SIC: 3523 5083 Cattle feeding, handling & watering equipment; livestock equipment
PA: Roto-Mix, Llc
2205 E Wyatt Earp Blvd
Dodge City KS 67801
620 225-1142

(G-10831)
SCOTT COOPERATIVE ASSOCIATION
4993 N Venison Rd (67871-4086)
PHONE..................................620 872-5823
Tony Wienter, *President*
EMP: 27
SALES (corp-wide): 76.5MM **Privately Held**
SIC: 5153 Grains
PA: Scott Cooperative Association Inc
410 E 1st St
Scott City KS 67871
620 872-5823

(G-10832)
SCOTT COUNTY HOSPITAL
204 S College St (67871-1253)
PHONE..................................620 872-2187
Gayla Nickel, *Executive*
EMP: 161
SALES (corp-wide): 19.1MM **Privately Held**
SIC: 8011 Clinic, operated by physicians
PA: Scott County Hospital, Inc.
201 Albert Ave
Scott City KS 67871
620 872-5811

(G-10833)
SCOTT COUNTY HOSPITAL INC (PA)
201 Albert Ave (67871-6117)
PHONE..................................620 872-5811
Mark Burnett, *CEO*
Philip Karnaze, *Materials Mgr*
Gloria Fulton, *Sales Staff*
Patty Hughes, *Office Mgr*
Janie Griswold, *Manager*
EMP: 59
SALES (est): 19.1MM **Privately Held**
SIC: 8062 General medical & surgical hospitals

(G-10834)
SECURITY STATE BANK (HQ)
506 S Main St (67871-1515)
P.O. Box 170 (67871-0170)
PHONE..................................620 872-7224
Duane K Ramsey, *President*
Randal Loder, *Exec VP*
David Summers, *CFO*
Matt Dickman, *Controller*
EMP: 64 **EST:** 1961
SQ FT: 6,000
SALES: 13.2MM **Privately Held**
WEB: www.ssbscott.com
SIC: 6022 State trust companies accepting deposits, commercial

(G-10835)
WESTERN KANSAS CHILD ADVOCACY
212 E 5th St (67871-1601)
PHONE..................................620 872-3706
Wade Dixon, *President*
Callie Dyer, *Vice Pres*
Betty Greer, *Treasurer*
Jenny Newberry, *Office Mgr*
Kelly Robbins, *Exec Dir*
EMP: 17
SALES: 1.5MM **Privately Held**
SIC: 8322 Children's aid society

(G-10836)
WHEATLAND BROADBAND SERVICES
101 N Main St (67871-1029)
PHONE..................................620 872-0006
Lynn Epler, *General Mgr*
Jevin Kasselman, *Director*
EMP: 10
SALES (est): 567.9K **Privately Held**
SIC: 4813

(G-10837)
Z BOTTLING CORP
907 W 5th St (67871-1262)
PHONE..................................620 872-0100
Phil Steffens, *President*
EMP: 5
SALES (est): 380K **Privately Held**
SIC: 5963 2086 Bottled water delivery; bottled & canned soft drinks

Scottsville
Mitchell County

(G-10838)
FARMWAY COOPERATIVE INC
2332 Commercial Ave (67420-2664)
PHONE..................................785 439-6457
Collin Collins, *Principal*
EMP: 36
SALES (est): 3.8MM **Privately Held**
SIC: 5153 Grains

Scranton
Osage County

(G-10839)
MID-STATES MATERIALS LLC
18486 S Berryton Rd (66537-9183)
P.O. Box 236, Topeka (66601-0236)
PHONE..................................785 887-6038
Michelle Miller, *Accountant*
Eric Bettis,
EMP: 8
SALES (est): 3.2MM **Privately Held**
WEB: www.midstatematerials.com
SIC: 1422 Crushed & broken limestone

Sedan
Chautauqua County

(G-10840)
CITY OF SEDAN (PA)
111 E Cherokee St (67361-1399)
PHONE..................................620 725-3193
Jack Warren, *Mayor*
EMP: 20 **Privately Held**
SIC: 9111 4941 City & town managers' offices; ; water supply

(G-10841)
COUNTY OF CHAUTAUQUA
Also Called: Road & Bridge
215 N Chautauqua St # 10 (67361-1326)
PHONE..................................620 725-5860
Cathy Rink, *Manager*
EMP: 18 **Privately Held**
SIC: 1611 Concrete construction: roads, highways, sidewalks, etc.
PA: County Of Chautauqua
215 N Chautauqua St Ste 6
Sedan KS 67361
620 725-5800

(G-10842)
ECONOMY MFG CO INC
Also Called: Economy Store
833 State Highway 99 (67361-8501)
PHONE..................................620 725-3520
Jene Dewey, *President*
Darrell Bish, *Corp Secy*
Grady Kelley, *Vice Pres*
EMP: 24
SQ FT: 8,000
SALES (est): 8.1MM **Privately Held**
WEB: www.economymfg.com
SIC: 5084 3713 5531 Oil well machinery, equipment & supplies; truck beds; automotive tires

(G-10843)
FIRST NATIONAL BNK OF SEDAN KS
101 W Main St (67361-1511)
P.O. Box E (67361-0429)
PHONE..................................620 725-3106
Bradley E Lloyd, *President*
Timothy A Hills, *President*
Bradley Loyd, *Exec VP*
Rolan Leniton, *Vice Pres*
Linda Martin, *Vice Pres*
EMP: 15 **EST:** 1874
SQ FT: 4,000
SALES: 2.3MM **Privately Held**
SIC: 6021 National commercial banks

(G-10844)
JONES & BUCK DEVELOPMENT OIL
Also Called: J B D
7777 Hwy 99 (67361)
P.O. Box 68 (67361-0068)
PHONE..................................620 725-3636
Mike Jones, *Partner*
Pj Buck, *Partner*
Matt Jones, *Partner*
EMP: 14
SALES (est): 1.2MM **Privately Held**
SIC: 1381 Drilling oil & gas wells

(G-10845)
PLEASANT VALLEY NURSING LLC
613 E Elm St (67361-1406)
P.O. Box 40 (67361-0040)
PHONE..................................620 725-3154
V Manor, *Principal*
EMP: 12
SALES (est): 511.8K **Privately Held**
SIC: 8051 Skilled nursing care facilities

(G-10846)
RH MONTGOMERY PROPERTIES INC
Also Called: Pleasant Vly Nursing Rehab Ctr
613 E Elm St (67361-1406)
PHONE..................................620 725-3154
Iris Turner, *Administration*
EMP: 82
SALES (corp-wide): 31.9MM **Privately Held**
SIC: 8051 Skilled nursing care facilities
PA: Rh Montgomery Properties, Inc.
214 N Scott St
Sikeston MO 63801
573 471-1113

(G-10847)
SEDAN AR EGY MDL SV DT 2 INC
120 S Chautauqua St (67361-1603)
PHONE..................................620 725-5670
Margaret Hadley, *Director*
EMP: 20
SALES: 406.1K **Privately Held**
SIC: 4119 Ambulance service

(G-10848)
SEDAN CITY HOSPITAL
300 W North St (67361-1051)
PHONE..................................620 725-3115
Odel McCoy, *Engineer*
Cindy Lovelace, *Lab Dir*
Michelle Williams, *Administration*
Sam Guird, *Administration*
EMP: 51
SQ FT: 19,000
SALES: 4.1MM **Privately Held**
SIC: 8062 Hospital, affiliated with AMA residency

Sedgwick
Harvey County

(G-10849)
ADVANTAGE COMMERCIAL LENDING
1410 N Washington Ave (67135-9378)
PHONE..................................316 215-0115
Roy Wilkinson, *President*
EMP: 13
SALES (est): 621.4K **Privately Held**
SIC: 6163 Mortgage brokers arranging for loans, using money of others

(G-10850)
GREEN ENERGY PRODUCTS LLC
250 E Industrial Dr (67135-3501)
PHONE..................................316 416-4106
Ronald Beemiller, *Partner*
Benjamin Healy, *Partner*
Richard Belt,
EMP: 8
SQ FT: 12,000
SALES (est): 2.4MM **Privately Held**
SIC: 2911 Oils, fuel

(G-10851)
NATIONAL HEALTHCARE CORP
Also Called: Sedgwick Healthcare Center
712 N Monroe Ave (67135-9492)
P.O. Box 49 (67135-0049)
PHONE..................................316 772-5185
Keith McCord, *Manager*
EMP: 75
SALES (corp-wide): 980.3MM **Publicly Held**
WEB: www.healthcarebenefits.com
SIC: 8051 Convalescent home with continuous nursing care
PA: National Healthcare Corporation
100 E Vine St
Murfreesboro TN 37130
615 890-2020

(G-10852)
TIM R SCHWAB INC
Also Called: Trs Logistics
101 E Industrial Dr (67135-3500)
PHONE..................................316 772-9055
Fax: 316 772-0280
EMP: 20
SQ FT: 28,000
SALES: 2MM **Privately Held**
SIC: 4213 Trucking Operator-Nonlocal

(G-10853)
UNRUH FAB INC (PA)
100 Indl Dr (67135)
PHONE..................................316 772-5400
Charles Brown, *President*
Steve Brown, *President*
Amy Wiggins, *Controller*
Pat Prouse, *Sales Staff*
Wes Schamle, *Consultant*
▲ **EMP:** 48 **EST:** 1977
SQ FT: 50,000
SALES (est): 6.5MM **Privately Held**
WEB: www.unruhfab.com
SIC: 3713 3715 5021 Truck bodies (motor vehicles); trailer bodies; racks

(G-10854)
UNRUH FIRE INC (HQ)
100 E Industrial Dr (67135-9704)
PHONE..................................316 772-5400
Thomas McDonald, *Ch of Bd*
Charles Brown, *President*
Alex McDonald, *Marketing Mgr*
Todd Newlin, *Consultant*
EMP: 8
SQ FT: 48,000
SALES (est): 1.1MM
SALES (corp-wide): 6.5MM **Privately Held**
WEB: www.unruhfire.com
SIC: 3711 Fire department vehicles (motor vehicles), assembly of
PA: Unruh Fab, Inc.
100 Indl Dr
Sedgwick KS 67135
316 772-5400

Selden
Sheridan County

(G-10855)
CHS INC
7756 W Us Highway 83 (67757-5912)
PHONE..................................785 386-4546
Dan Juenemann, *Branch Mgr*
EMP: 11
SALES (corp-wide): 31.9B **Publicly Held**
SIC: 5153 Grains
PA: Chs Inc.
5500 Cenex Dr
Inver Grove Heights MN 55077
651 355-6000

Seneca
Nemaha County

(G-10856)
AG CONNECTION SALES INC
Also Called: Sure Crop Liquid Fertilizers
877 Us Highway 36 (66538-2093)
PHONE..................................785 336-2121
Shirley Schurman, *President*
EMP: 15
SQ FT: 1,800
SALES: 3.5MM **Privately Held**
WEB: www.assurecrop.com
SIC: 5191 5261 Fertilizer & fertilizer materials; fertilizer

(G-10857)
AGSYNERGY LLC
1183 120th Rd (66538-2590)
PHONE..................................785 336-6333
Ryan Hammes,
Andy Renyer,
Jim Renyer,
▲ **EMP:** 7
SALES (est): 650K **Privately Held**
SIC: 3523 Tractors, farm

(G-10858)
BRUNA BROTHERS IMPLEMENT LLC
12 E North St (66538-2522)
PHONE..................................785 336-2111
Joseph A Henry Jr, *Branch Mgr*
EMP: 18
SALES (corp-wide): 26.5MM **Privately Held**
WEB: www.brunaimplementco.com
SIC: 5083 7699 Agricultural machinery & equipment; agricultural equipment repair services
PA: Bruna Brothers Implement, Llc
1128 Pony Express Hwy
Marysville KS 66508
785 562-5304

(G-10859)
COMMUNITY NATIONAL BANK (PA)
210 Main St (66538-1922)
P.O. Box 210 (66538-0210)
PHONE..................................785 336-6143
Ronald C Johnson, *President*
Billy Hatfield, *Technology*
EMP: 30
SALES: 21.4MM **Privately Held**
WEB: www.communitynationalbank.net
SIC: 6022 State commercial banks

(G-10860)
COUNTRY PLACE SENIOR LIVING
Also Called: Nemaha County Assisted Living
1700 Community Dr (66538-9810)
PHONE..................................785 336-6868
Debra Rethman,
EMP: 14
SALES (est): 400.7K **Privately Held**
SIC: 8051 8361 Skilled nursing care facilities; geriatric residential care

(G-10861)
COUNTRYSIDE FEED LLC
1972 State Highway 187 (66538-2186)
PHONE..................................785 336-6777
Luke Lindsey, *Mng Member*
EMP: 15
SALES (corp-wide): 21MM **Privately Held**
SIC: 5191 5999 Feed; feed & farm supply
PA: Countryside Feed, L.L.C.
101 Santa Fe St
Hillsboro KS 67063
620 947-3111

(G-10862)
CRESTVIEW OPERATION INC
808 N 8th St (66538-1419)
PHONE..................................785 336-2156
Sara Sourk, *President*
EMP: 55
SALES: 2.2MM **Privately Held**
SIC: 8051 Convalescent home with continuous nursing care

(G-10863)
DAN DIEHL
Also Called: Courier Tribune
512 Main St (66538-1928)
P.O. Box 100 (66538-0100)
PHONE..................................785 336-2175
Dan Diehl, *Owner*
EMP: 6 **EST:** 1971
SALES: 250K **Privately Held**
SIC: 2711 Newspapers: publishing only, not printed on site

(G-10864)
DARLING INGREDIENTS INC
1188 144th Rd (66538-2611)
P.O. Box 151 (66538-0151)
PHONE..................................785 336-2535
Lester Fangman, *Manager*
John Enneking, *Supervisor*
EMP: 19
SALES (corp-wide): 3.3B **Publicly Held**
WEB: www.darlingii.com
SIC: 4213 2077 Contract haulers; animal & marine fats & oils
PA: Darling Ingredients Inc.
5601 N Macarthur Blvd
Irving TX 75038
972 717-0300

(G-10865)
EISENBARTH PLUMBING INC
13 N 2nd St (66538-1801)
PHONE..................................785 336-2361
Phill Boeding, *President*
Barbara Boeding, *Corp Secy*
EMP: 15 **EST:** 1947
SQ FT: 3,000
SALES: 1.5MM **Privately Held**
SIC: 1711 Plumbing contractors; warm air heating & air conditioning contractor

(G-10866)
FAIRVIEW MILLS LLC (HQ)
604 Nemaha St (66538-1735)
P.O. Box 170 (66538-0170)
PHONE..................................785 336-2148
Nick Bunck, *Opers Mgr*
Darrin Hermesch, *Site Mgr*
Joseph Kramer, *CFO*
Colleen Terpening, *CFO*
Wade Willming, *Sales Staff*
EMP: 29
SALES (est): 107.6MM
SALES (corp-wide): 108.6MM **Privately Held**
SIC: 3999 Pet supplies
PA: J-Six Enterprises, L.L.C.
604 Nemaha St
Seneca KS 66538
785 336-2149

(G-10867)
FEXP INC
Also Called: Fairview Express
604 Nemaha St (66538-1735)
P.O. Box 170 (66538-0170)
PHONE..................................785 336-2148
Joseph A Kramer, *Vice Pres*
Mike Bulk, *Director*
EMP: 29 **EST:** 2008
SALES (est): 1MM
SALES (corp-wide): 108.6MM **Privately Held**
SIC: 4212 Local trucking, without storage
PA: J-Six Enterprises, L.L.C.
604 Nemaha St
Seneca KS 66538
785 336-2149

(G-10868)
J-SIX ENTERPRISES LLC (PA)
604 Nemaha St (66538-1735)
PHONE..................................785 336-2149
John Kramer, *Owner*
Bob Kramer, *Director*
EMP: 16
SALES (est): 108.6MM **Privately Held**
SIC: 7389 Automobile recovery service

(G-10869)
J-SIX FARMS LLC
604 Nemaha St (66538-1735)
PHONE..................................785 336-2148
John Kramer, *President*
EMP: 15
SALES (est): 3.8MM **Privately Held**
SIC: 0213 0191 7389 Hogs; general farms, primarily crop;

(G-10870)
JAK 3 INC (PA)
604 Nemaha St (66538-1735)
P.O. Box 170 (66538-0170)
PHONE..................................785 336-2148
John Kramer, *President*
Joe Kramer, *Project Mgr*
Tom Scott, *Prdtn Mgr*
Colleen Terpening, *Treasurer*
EMP: 6
SALES (est): 4.3MM **Privately Held**
SIC: 2048 Dry pet food (except dog & cat)

GEOGRAPHIC

(G-10871)
KOCH & CO INC (PA)
Also Called: KOCH CABINETS
1809 North St (66538-2415)
PHONE..................................785 336-6022
Jim Koch, *President*
Dan Koch, *Principal*
Jeffrey R Connor, *CFO*
Dan Carlson, *Sales Mgr*
William Brannan, *Admin Sec*
EMP: 450
SQ FT: 450,000
SALES: 84MM **Privately Held**
WEB: www.kochandco.com
SIC: 2434 3442 2431 Wood kitchen cabinets; metal doors; doors, wood

(G-10872)
LIFE CARE CENTERS AMERICA INC
Also Called: Life Care Center of Seneca
512 Community Dr (66538-9781)
PHONE..................................785 336-3528
Connie Winkler, *Office Mgr*
Tracie Wagner, *Director*
Sandy Koch, *Social Dir*
Travis Hecht, *Administration*
EMP: 60
SALES (corp-wide): 144MM **Privately Held**
SIC: 8052 8051 Intermediate care facilities; skilled nursing care facilities
PA: Life Care Centers Of America, Inc.
3570 Keith St Nw
Cleveland TN 37312
423 472-9585

(G-10873)
MICHAEL BENNETT TRUCKING INC
Hwy 36 W (66538)
P.O. Box 26 (66538-0026)
PHONE..................................785 336-2942
Mike Bennett, *President*
Debbie Bennett, *Corp Secy*
Paul Bennett, *Vice Pres*
Steve Bennett, *Manager*
EMP: 13
SQ FT: 600
SALES (est): 1.8MM **Privately Held**
SIC: 4212 4213 Local trucking, without storage; trucking, except local

(G-10874)
NEMAHA COUNTY COOPERATIVE ASSN (PA)
223 E Main St (66538)
P.O. Box 204 (66538-0204)
PHONE..................................785 336-6153
Bobby Martin, *CEO*
Kent Heinen, *Vice Ch Bd*
EMP: 88
SQ FT: 3,000
SALES: 108.6MM **Privately Held**
WEB: www.ncca.net
SIC: 5153 5191 5541 Grains; grain elevators; feed; fertilizer & fertilizer materials; chemicals, agricultural; filling stations, gasoline

(G-10875)
NEMAHA COUNTY TRAINING CENTER (PA)
12 S 11th St (66538-1900)
PHONE..................................785 336-6116
Cindy Krotzinger, *COO*
Alice Lackey, *Director*
EMP: 40
SQ FT: 6,200
SALES: 2MM **Privately Held**
SIC: 8331 Vocational training agency

(G-10876)
NEMAHA VALLEY COMMUNITY HOSP (PA)
1600 Community Dr (66538-9739)
PHONE..................................785 336-6181
Stan Regehr, *CEO*
Linda Edelman, *QA Dir*
Lori Huerter, *Manager*
Tony Bartkoski, *Director*
Lynda Cross, *Director*
EMP: 135
SQ FT: 35,500
SALES: 17.2MM **Privately Held**
SIC: 8062 Hospital, affiliated with AMA residency

(G-10877)
NEMAHA VALLEY COMMUNITY HOSP
Also Called: Seneca Family Practice
1600 Community Dr (66538-9739)
PHONE..................................785 336-6107
Connie Steinlage, *Manager*
EMP: 20
SALES (corp-wide): 17.2MM **Privately Held**
SIC: 8011 Clinic, operated by physicians
PA: Nemaha Valley Community Hospital
1600 Community Dr
Seneca KS 66538
785 336-6181

(G-10878)
OHLSEN RIGHT OF WAY AND MAINT
892 Us Highway 36 (66538-2093)
PHONE..................................785 336-6112
Brett Ohlsen, *President*
EMP: 10
SQ FT: 1,500
SALES (est): 428K **Privately Held**
SIC: 1623 Water & sewer line construction

(G-10879)
RANIERI CAMERA & VIDEO INC
Also Called: Ranieri Prof One Hr Photo
413 Main St (66538-1925)
PHONE..................................785 336-3719
Robin Ranieri, *President*
EMP: 12
SQ FT: 1,000
SALES (est): 1.2MM **Privately Held**
SIC: 5946 7384 7335 Cameras; photographic supplies; photofinishing laboratory; commercial photography

(G-10880)
SBS INSURANCE
Also Called: Gold Insurance Agency
305 Main St (66538-1923)
P.O. Box 148 (66538-0148)
PHONE..................................785 336-2821
Jim Runnepaum, *President*
Bryce Burdiek, *Producer*
Jeff Kidd, *Producer*
Ralph Snyder, *Producer*
EMP: 11
SALES (est): 1.7MM **Privately Held**
SIC: 6411 Insurance agents

(G-10881)
SENECA READY MIX CONCRETE INC
1201 Baltimore St (66538-2113)
PHONE..................................785 336-3511
Dean Luckeroth, *President*
Terry Luckeroth, *Vice Pres*
EMP: 15
SQ FT: 600
SALES (est): 2.3MM **Privately Held**
SIC: 3273 Ready-mixed concrete

(G-10882)
SENECA WHOLESALE COMPANY INC
Also Called: Seneca Wholesale Dr Pepper
36 S 8th St (66538-1998)
PHONE..................................785 336-2118
Richard Strathman, *President*
Donald Strathman, *Treasurer*
Phil Strathman, *Director*
Andrew Strathman, *Admin Sec*
EMP: 15
SQ FT: 15,000
SALES: 4.5MM **Privately Held**
SIC: 2086 5149 5145 5181 Soft drinks: packaged in cans, bottles, etc.; soft drinks; candy; beer & ale

(G-10883)
SUTHER BUILDING SUPPLY INC
Also Called: Do It Best
103 N 1st St (66538-1701)
PHONE..................................785 336-2255
Rod Suther, *President*
Sonya Suther, *Corp Secy*
Jay Suther, *Vice Pres*
EMP: 15 **EST:** 1971
SQ FT: 5,000
SALES: 3MM **Privately Held**
SIC: 5211 1521 5251 1531 Lumber & other building materials; single-family housing construction; hardware; speculative builder, single-family houses

(G-10884)
TODD TRACTOR CO INC
Also Called: John Deere Authorized Dealer
2004 State Highway 63 (66538-9636)
PHONE..................................785 336-2138
Douglas J Todd, *President*
Warren Todd, *Vice Pres*
Roger Todd, *Sales Mgr*
EMP: 12 **EST:** 1950
SQ FT: 12,660
SALES (est): 2.4MM **Privately Held**
SIC: 5083 7699 0191 0291 Agricultural machinery & equipment; farm machinery repair; general farms, primarily crop; livestock farm, general

(G-10885)
UNITED BANK & TRUST
Also Called: Drive-In Facility
602 North St (66538-1401)
P.O. Box 208 (66538-0208)
PHONE..................................785 336-2123
Tracy Dockter, *COO*
Larry Kuckelman, *Branch Mgr*
EMP: 13 **Privately Held**
SIC: 6022 State commercial banks
PA: United Bank & Trust
2333 Broadway
Marysville KS 66508

(G-10886)
VALLEY VIEW MILLING
2875 State Highway 63 (66538-2145)
PHONE..................................785 858-4777
EMP: 14
SALES (est): 2.4MM **Privately Held**
SIC: 3541 Mfg Machine Tools-Cutting

(G-10887)
VALLEY VIEW MILLING LLC
2875 State Highway 63 (66538-2145)
PHONE..................................785 858-4777
Mark Haverkamp, *Mng Member*
EMP: 10
SALES: 25MM **Privately Held**
SIC: 0723 Feed milling custom services

(G-10888)
WINDMILL INN INC
603 N 4th St (66538-1515)
PHONE..................................785 336-3696
Steven Rothers, *President*
Morris Rettele, *Vice Pres*
Jamie Rettele, *Admin Sec*
EMP: 10
SQ FT: 54,000
SALES (est): 388.1K **Privately Held**
SIC: 5812 7299 American restaurant; banquet hall facilities

Severy
Greenwood County

(G-10889)
BILLS FRANK TRUCKING INC
Old Hwy 99 (67137)
P.O. Box 211 (67137-0211)
PHONE..................................620 736-2875
Frank Bills, *President*
EMP: 50
SQ FT: 8,000
SALES (est): 7.6MM **Privately Held**
SIC: 4213 Trucking, except local

(G-10890)
FRANK BILLS
Also Called: Bills, Frank Ranch
Hwy 99 (67137)
P.O. Box 211 (67137-0211)
PHONE..................................620 736-2875
Frank Bills, *Owner*
EMP: 20
SALES (est): 505.9K **Privately Held**
SIC: 0212 Beef cattle except feedlots

(G-10891)
MARIETTA MARTIN MATERIALS INC
Also Called: Martin Marietta Aggregates
1900 Us Highway 400 St (67137-3700)
P.O. Box 188 (67137)
PHONE..................................620 736-2962
Todd Beckmann, *Branch Mgr*
EMP: 20 **Publicly Held**
WEB: www.martinmarietta.com
SIC: 1422 Crushed & broken limestone
PA: Martin Marietta Materials Inc
2710 Wycliff Rd
Raleigh NC 27607

(G-10892)
SAMCO DRYWALL COMPANY
Also Called: Sampson Homes
273 M Rd (67137-4001)
PHONE..................................620 864-2289
Ronnie Samson, *President*
EMP: 10
SALES (est): 767.1K **Privately Held**
SIC: 1742 Drywall

(G-10893)
SEVERY COOPERATIVE ASSOCIATION
210 N Kansas Ave (67137-8806)
P.O. Box 127 (67137-0127)
PHONE..................................620 736-2211
John Griesel, *President*
Terry Evans, *Vice Pres*
EMP: 15 **EST:** 1953
SQ FT: 3,200
SALES (est): 9.1MM **Privately Held**
SIC: 5153 5191 5171 Grain elevators; feed; petroleum bulk stations

Sharon Springs
Wallace County

(G-10894)
AG POWER EQUIPMENT CO (PA)
1385 Kansas 27 (67758-6028)
P.O. Box 249 (67758-0249)
PHONE..................................785 852-4235
Kenneth Kuhlman, *President*
Norb Badding, *Sales Associate*
EMP: 18 **EST:** 1958
SQ FT: 11,000
SALES (est): 7.8MM **Privately Held**
WEB: www.caseihcombines.com
SIC: 5083 Farm implements

(G-10895)
CHS INC
102 N Front St (67758)
PHONE..................................785 852-4241
Patt Peterson, *Branch Mgr*
EMP: 24
SALES (corp-wide): 31.9B **Publicly Held**
WEB: www.cenexharveststates.com
SIC: 5153 5191 Grain elevators; feed; fertilizer & fertilizer materials; chemicals, agricultural
PA: Chs Inc.
5500 Cenex Dr
Inver Grove Heights MN 55077
651 355-6000

(G-10896)
COUNTY OF WALLACE (PA)
313 N Main St (67758-9752)
P.O. Box 70 (67758-0070)
PHONE..................................785 852-4282
Jacalyn MAI, *Accounting Mgr*
Bruce Buck, *Commissioner*
EMP: 32
SQ FT: 2,400
SALES (est): 5.2MM **Privately Held**
SIC: 8721 Payroll accounting service

(G-10897)
FIRST NATIONAL BANK
133 N Main St (67758-9703)
P.O. Box 129 (67758-0129)
PHONE..................................785 852-2000
Joanne Charles, *Branch Mgr*
EMP: 10 **Privately Held**
WEB: www.fnb.com
SIC: 6021 National commercial banks

HQ: First National Bank
202 E 11th St
Goodland KS 67735
785 890-2000

(G-10898)
GREELEY CNTY HOSP & LONG TRM C
Also Called: Wallace County Family Practice
104 E 4th (67758-9715)
P.O. Box 310 (67758-0310)
PHONE..................................785 852-4230
Bonnie Mote, *Manager*
EMP: 11 **Privately Held**
SIC: 8011 Offices & clinics of medical doctors
PA: Greeley County Hospital & Long Term Care Inc
302 E Greeley Ave
Tribune KS 67879

(G-10899)
JULIE K SAMUELSON
Also Called: Western Times, The
126 N Main St (67758-9703)
P.O. Box 279 (67758-0279)
PHONE..................................785 852-4900
Julie Samuelson, *Owner*
EMP: 5 **EST:** 1998
SALES (est): 301.2K **Privately Held**
SIC: 2711 Commercial printing & newspaper publishing combined

(G-10900)
LODGING ENTERPRISES LLC
109 E Commerce St (67758-9708)
PHONE..................................785 852-4664
Carla Kitch, *Manager*
EMP: 10
SALES (corp-wide): 52.1MM **Privately Held**
SIC: 7011 Inns
HQ: Lodging Enterprises, Llc
8080 E Central Ave # 180
Wichita KS 67206
316 630-6300

(G-10901)
UNITED PLAINS AG (PA)
102 N Front St (67758)
P.O. Box 280 (67758-0280)
PHONE..................................785 852-4241
Bryan Pearce, *President*
David MAI, *Admin Sec*
EMP: 24 **EST:** 1948
SQ FT: 3,200
SALES: 36MM **Privately Held**
WEB: www.wallacecountycoop.com
SIC: 5153 5191 Grain elevators; feed; fertilizer & fertilizer materials; chemicals, agricultural

(G-10902)
WESTERN KANSAS VALLEY INC
W Hwy 40 (67758)
P.O. Box 399 (67758-0399)
PHONE..................................785 852-4606
Verlynn Wagoner, *President*
EMP: 10
SQ FT: 7,000
SALES (est): 1.6MM **Privately Held**
SIC: 1711 5083 1629 Irrigation sprinkler system installation; irrigation equipment; trenching contractor

Shawnee
Johnson County

(G-10903)
2POINT CONSTRUCTION CO LLC
7252 W Frontage Rd (66203-4638)
PHONE..................................913 749-1855
Brandon Bezner, *CEO*
Tony Penny, *President*
Greg Watt, *Superintendent*
Gary Tumberger, *Opers Staff*
EMP: 32
SALES (est): 8.1MM **Privately Held**
SIC: 1542 Commercial & office building, new construction

(G-10904)
A CARING DOCTOR MINNESOTA PA
Also Called: Banfield Pet Hospital 242
15200 Shawnee Msn (66217-9315)
PHONE..................................913 962-2901
Wieicher Shannon, *Branch Mgr*
EMP: 20
SALES (corp-wide): 37.6B **Privately Held**
SIC: 0742 Animal hospital services, pets & other animal specialties
HQ: A Caring Doctor Minnesota Pa
8000 Ne Tillamook St
Portland OR 97213
503 922-5000

(G-10905)
AAPC INC
Also Called: Autism Asperger Publishing Co
6448 Vista Dr (66218-9239)
P.O. Box 861116 (66286-1116)
PHONE..................................877 277-8254
Keith Myles, *President*
▲ **EMP:** 8
SQ FT: 3,000
SALES (est): 1.1MM **Privately Held**
WEB: www.asperger.net
SIC: 2731 2741 Books: publishing only; miscellaneous publishing

(G-10906)
ADAMSON AND ASSOCIATES
Also Called: Axiom Rligious Fcilty Advisors
7451 Switzer St Ste 100 (66203-4551)
PHONE..................................913 722-5432
Henry Adamson III, *President*
Catherine Adamson, *Vice Pres*
Joye Adamson, *Vice Pres*
Matt Angelo, *Vice Pres*
EMP: 13
SALES (est): 1.3MM
SALES (corp-wide): 2.8MM **Privately Held**
WEB: www.adamsoninc.com
SIC: 6531 Appraiser, real estate
PA: Adamson And Associates, Inc.
7800 College Blvd Ste 200
Overland Park KS 66210
913 722-5432

(G-10907)
ALL AMERICAN PET BRANDS INC
8310 Hedge Lane Ter (66227-3543)
PHONE..................................913 951-4999
Barry Schwartz, *President*
Lisa Bershan, *Treasurer*
EMP: 8 **EST:** 2009
SALES (est): 665.5K **Privately Held**
SIC: 3999 Pet supplies

(G-10908)
ALLIED RETAIL CONCEPTS LLC
Also Called: A.R.c General Contracting
6205 Goddard St (66203-2933)
PHONE..................................913 492-8008
Gerry Crawley, *Mng Member*
EMP: 11
SQ FT: 2,400
SALES (est): 14.4MM **Privately Held**
SIC: 1542 Commercial & office building, new construction

(G-10909)
AMERICAN BOX & TAPE CO
23128 W 43rd St (66226-2202)
PHONE..................................913 384-0992
Richard H Hayden, *President*
Dolores Goetz, *Corp Secy*
Diane Pryor, *Sales Staff*
Sean Bulva, *Manager*
EMP: 25
SQ FT: 4,500
SALES (est): 8.8MM **Privately Held**
SIC: 2653 Boxes, corrugated: made from purchased materials

(G-10910)
AMERICAN INDIAN HEALTH RESEARC
Also Called: Aihrea
6819 Woodstock Ct (66218-7806)
PHONE..................................913 422-7523
Michell Bointy, *Bd of Directors*
Christine Daley, *Bd of Directors*
Jordyn Gunville, *Bd of Directors*
Jason Hale, *Bd of Directors*
Charley Lewis, *Bd of Directors*
EMP: 10 **EST:** 2010
SALES (est): 294.5K **Privately Held**
SIC: 8732 Educational research

(G-10911)
ARS REPORTING LLC
22052 W 66th St Ste 314 (66226-3500)
PHONE..................................913 422-5198
Jennifer Molinaro, *Principal*
EMP: 25
SQ FT: 700
SALES (est): 1.4MM **Privately Held**
SIC: 7338 Court reporting service

(G-10912)
AUTO SERVICE CTR SHAWNEE LLC
6590 Vista Dr (66218-9240)
PHONE..................................913 422-5388
Ron Broyles, *Mng Member*
EMP: 10
SALES (est): 541.3K **Privately Held**
SIC: 7538 General automotive repair shops

(G-10913)
BANK AMERICA NATIONAL ASSN
22425 W 66th St (66226-3501)
PHONE..................................913 441-1067
EMP: 19
SALES (corp-wide): 110.5B **Publicly Held**
SIC: 6021 National commercial banks
HQ: Bank Of America, National Association
100 S Tryon St
Charlotte NC 28202
704 386-5681

(G-10914)
BANK OF LABOR
12500 W 63rd St (66216-1843)
PHONE..................................913 321-4242
Marty Cansler, *Manager*
EMP: 25
SALES (corp-wide): 26.3MM **Privately Held**
SIC: 6022 State trust companies accepting deposits, commercial
HQ: Bank Of Labor
756 Minnesota Ave
Kansas City KS 66101
913 321-6800

(G-10915)
BAYER HLTHCARE ANIMAL HLTH INC
12809 Shwnee Mission Pkwy (66216-1848)
PHONE..................................913 268-2731
Fintan Molloy, *Manager*
EMP: 30
SALES (corp-wide): 43.9B **Privately Held**
SIC: 2834 Veterinary pharmaceutical preparations
HQ: Bayer Healthcare Animal Health Inc.
3915 S 48th St Ter
Saint Joseph MO 64503
816 364-3777

(G-10916)
BEYOND 21ST CENTURY INC
7306 Reeder St (66203-4436)
PHONE..................................913 631-4790
Hemant Thakur, *President*
EMP: 8
SALES (est): 460.3K **Privately Held**
SIC: 3843 Dental equipment

(G-10917)
BIRD ENGINEERING COMPANY PA
6100 Nieman Rd Ste 200 (66203-2903)
P.O. Box 3558, Shawnee Mission (66203-0558)
PHONE..................................913 631-2222
Bruce Bird, *President*
Rebbeda Bird, *Admin Sec*
EMP: 10
SQ FT: 1,200
SALES (est): 483.2K **Privately Held**
WEB: www.birdengineering.com
SIC: 8711 Civil engineering

(G-10918)
BISHOP RINK HOLDINGS LLC
5225 Renner Rd (66217-9757)
PHONE..................................913 268-2625
Dennis Langley,
EMP: 50
SALES (est): 916.1K **Privately Held**
WEB: www.icemidwest.com
SIC: 7999 Tennis courts, outdoor/indoor: non-membership

(G-10919)
BLOT ENGINEERING INC (PA)
5420 Martindale Rd (66218-9680)
PHONE..................................913 441-1636
Edward Michael Blot, *President*
Alan Gore, *Engineer*
Lotte Blot, *Admin Sec*
EMP: 12
SALES (est): 1.6MM **Privately Held**
SIC: 8711 Consulting engineer

(G-10920)
BRATTON BROS CONTRACTING INC
6091 Woodland Dr (66218-9079)
PHONE..................................913 422-7771
Ronald D Bratton, *President*
EMP: 12 **EST:** 1978
SQ FT: 9,000
SALES: 3MM **Privately Held**
SIC: 1542 1794 Commercial & office building, new construction; commercial & office buildings, renovation & repair; excavation work

(G-10921)
BULLEIGH ORTHODONTICS
6804 Silver Hls (66226)
PHONE..................................913 962-7223
Chad Bulleigh, *Principal*
EMP: 25 **EST:** 2012
SALES (est): 373.3K **Privately Held**
SIC: 8021 Orthodontist

(G-10922)
CAENEN CASTLE
12401 Johnson Dr (66216-1949)
PHONE..................................913 631-4100
Nancy Neighbors, *General Mgr*
Ann Neighbors, *Principal*
EMP: 12
SALES (est): 767.6K **Privately Held**
SIC: 8742 Restaurant & food services consultants

(G-10923)
CALKINS ELECTRIC SUPPLY CO INC
Also Called: Cesco
5707 Nieman Rd (66203-2899)
P.O. Box 3498 (66203-0498)
PHONE..................................913 631-6363
Wendi Levitt, *President*
Jeffrey E Calkins, *Vice Pres*
Chris Calkins, *CFO*
EMP: 11 **EST:** 1929
SQ FT: 6,500
SALES (est): 5.6MM **Privately Held**
SIC: 5063 Electrical supplies

(G-10924)
CARONDELET HOME CARE SERVICES
Also Called: Ascension Health
7255 Renner Rd (66217-3043)
PHONE..................................913 529-4800
Bruce Vanclede MD, *CEO*
EMP: 40
SALES: 7.2MM **Privately Held**
WEB: www.ascensionhealth.com
SIC: 8082 8011 Home health care services; offices & clinics of medical doctors

(G-10925)
CENTRAL BANK OF MIDWEST
15100 W 67th St (66217-9328)
PHONE..................................913 268-3202
Nick Pflumm, *Branch Mgr*
EMP: 15

GEOGRAPHIC

SALES (corp-wide): 4.1MM **Privately Held**
SIC: 6022 State commercial banks
PA: Central Bank Of The Midwest
609 Ne State Route 291
Lees Summit MO 64086
816 525-5754

(G-10926)
CHAVEY VENTURES INC
Also Called: Red Wheel Fundraising
6640 Wedd St (66203-3903)
PHONE..................................913 888-5108
Mark Chavey, *President*
Julie Chavey, *Admin Sec*
EMP: 15 **EST:** 1987
SQ FT: 3,500
SALES (est): 1.4MM **Privately Held**
SIC: 7389 Fund raising organizations

(G-10927)
CHEMSYSTEMS KANSAS INC
Also Called: Decorative Concrete Supply
8329 Monticello Rd Ste E (66227-3120)
PHONE..................................913 422-4443
Jessica Davis, *President*
Bruce Meikle, *Vice Pres*
Donna Murray, *Vice Pres*
Chris Sullivan, *Vice Pres*
Denise Valdepena, *Vice Pres*
EMP: 7
SQ FT: 5,000
SALES (est): 2.9MM **Privately Held**
SIC: 3272 Concrete products

(G-10928)
CHERUB MEDICAL SUPPLY LLC
11217 Johnson Dr (66203-2751)
PHONE..................................913 227-0440
Nita S Cress, *President*
EMP: 13
SALES (est): 1.6MM **Privately Held**
WEB: www.cherubmedical.com
SIC: 5047 Medical equipment & supplies

(G-10929)
CLARENCE M KELLEY & ASSOC OF K
Also Called: Cmka
6840 Silverheel St (66226-5300)
PHONE..................................913 647-7700
C Thomas Dupriest, *President*
Todd Dupriest, *President*
Todd M Dupriest, *COO*
EMP: 80
SQ FT: 10,000
SALES (est): 1.3MM **Privately Held**
SIC: 7381 8748 Private investigator; business consulting
PA: Clarence M. Kelley Enterprises
3217 Broadway Blvd # 400
Kansas City MO 64111

(G-10930)
COLEMAN AMERICAN MVG SVCS INC
12905 W 63rd St (66216-1850)
PHONE..................................913 248-1766
Michael Jones, *Branch Mgr*
EMP: 20 **Privately Held**
SIC: 4214 Household goods moving & storage, local
HQ: Coleman American Moving Services, Inc.
1 Covan Dr
Midland City AL 36350
334 983-6500

(G-10931)
COMMERCE BANK
11000 Shwnee Mission Pkwy (66203-3516)
PHONE..................................816 234-2000
Cindy Watts, *Manager*
John Hart, *Director*
EMP: 13
SALES (corp-wide): 1.3B **Publicly Held**
SIC: 6022 State commercial banks
HQ: Commerce Bank
1000 Walnut St Fl 700
Kansas City MO 64106
816 234-2000

(G-10932)
COMMERCE BANK
21800 Midland Dr (66218-9186)
P.O. Box 860224 (66286-0224)
PHONE..................................816 234-2000
Zachary Allen, *Accounts Exec*
EMP: 20
SALES (corp-wide): 1.3B **Publicly Held**
SIC: 6022 State commercial banks
HQ: Commerce Bank
1000 Walnut St Fl 700
Kansas City MO 64106
816 234-2000

(G-10933)
CONTINENTAL CAST STONE LLC
22001 W 83rd St (66227-3131)
PHONE..................................800 989-7866
Bryan Hinkle, *Mng Member*
John Tully, *Sr Project Mgr*
EMP: 50
SALES (est): 1.5MM **Privately Held**
SIC: 3281 Cut stone & stone products

(G-10934)
COREFIRST BANK & TRUST
7430 Switzer St (66203-4550)
PHONE..................................913 248-7000
Sandy Falcn, *Vicc Pres*
Lissa Trujillo, *Manager*
EMP: 18
SALES (corp-wide): 48MM **Privately Held**
SIC: 6021 National commercial banks
HQ: Corefirst Bank & Trust
3035 Sw Topeka Blvd
Topeka KS 66611
785 267-8900

(G-10935)
COSENTINO GROUP II INC
22210 W 66th St (66226-3521)
PHONE..................................913 422-2130
Jaysen Pauley, *Branch Mgr*
Terri Johnson, *Director*
EMP: 7 **Privately Held**
SIC: 3751 Motorcycles & related parts
PA: Cosentino Group Ii, Inc
8700 E 63rd St
Kansas City MO 64133

(G-10936)
COUNTRY CLUB BANK
21911 W 66th St Ste 100 (66226-3549)
PHONE..................................913 441-2444
Schaun Colin, *Owner*
John G Houlehan, *Exec VP*
Michelle Bishop, *Advisor*
EMP: 17
SALES (corp-wide): 38MM **Privately Held**
SIC: 6029 Commercial banks
HQ: Country Club Bank
1 Ward Pkwy
Kansas City MO 64112

(G-10937)
CRYSTAL TRENCHING INC
4622 Merriam Dr (66203-1344)
PHONE..................................913 677-1233
Richard S Crystal, *President*
EMP: 16 **EST:** 1979
SQ FT: 7,500
SALES (est): 2.2MM **Privately Held**
SIC: 1629 Trenching contractor

(G-10938)
D DOUBLED INC
Also Called: Dale Brothers
66210 (66203)
P.O. Box 12541, Kansas City (66112-0541)
PHONE..................................913 334-1075
Clifford Dale, *President*
Travis Dale, *Vice Pres*
Amy Kuplic, *Info Tech Mgr*
EMP: 10
SALES (est): 1.3MM **Privately Held**
SIC: 4212 Local trucking, without storage

(G-10939)
DANCO SYSTEMS INC (PA)
11101 Johnson Dr (66203-2749)
PHONE..................................913 962-0600
Daniel Pflumm, *President*
Julie Pflumm, *Treasurer*
Jill Barrier, *Sales Staff*
Mary Ann Kuestersteffen, *Administration*
EMP: 12
SQ FT: 3,600
SALES: 2.7MM **Privately Held**
WEB: www.dancosystems.com
SIC: 7373 5045 Systems integration services; computers, peripherals & software

(G-10940)
DANDELION & MUDD PUDDLES CDC
13811 W 63rd St (66216-3800)
PHONE..................................913 825-0399
Carrie Sckar, *CEO*
EMP: 50 **EST:** 2010
SALES (est): 2MM **Privately Held**
SIC: 8322 8351 Social service center; preschool center

(G-10941)
DONE WITH CARE AUTO REPAIR LLC
5810 Merriam Dr (66203-2526)
PHONE..................................913 722-3466
EMP: 12
SALES (corp-wide): 530.7K **Privately Held**
SIC: 7538 General automotive repair shops
PA: Done With Care Auto Repair Llc
11708 W 102nd Ter
Overland Park KS 66214
217 690-0263

(G-10942)
E C MANUFACTURING
23501 W 84th St (66227-3296)
PHONE..................................913 825-3077
EMP: 95 **EST:** 2013
SALES (est): 4.7MM **Privately Held**
SIC: 3999 Mfg Misc Products

(G-10943)
EDGE PEST CONTROL KANS CY LLC
6230 Merriam Dr (66203-3258)
PHONE..................................913 262-3343
Blaine Richardson, *Owner*
EMP: 13 **EST:** 2010
SALES (est): 942.8K **Privately Held**
SIC: 7342 Pest control services

(G-10944)
EIKO GLOBAL LLC
8420 Hedge Ln (66227)
PHONE..................................913 441-8500
Gary Withers, *Branch Mgr*
EMP: 15 **Privately Held**
SIC: 5063 Light bulbs & related supplies
PA: Eiko Global, Llc
23220 W 84th St
Shawnee KS 66227

(G-10945)
EIKO GLOBAL LLC (PA)
23220 W 84th St (66227-3293)
PHONE..................................800 852-2217
Rick Laird, *President*
Rick Roberts, *Exec VP*
Kevin Harney, *CFO*
Anita Nolan, *Controller*
Bruce Taylor, *Marketing Staff*
▲ **EMP:** 40
SQ FT: 31,300
SALES (est): 28.5MM **Privately Held**
WEB: www.eiko-ltd.com
SIC: 5063 Light bulbs & related supplies

(G-10946)
EKA CONSULTING LLC
Also Called: Emily Kaemmer and Associates
5626 Brownridge Dr (66218-8904)
PHONE..................................913 244-2980
Emily Kaemmer, *President*
EMP: 10 **EST:** 2015
SALES (est): 170K **Privately Held**
SIC: 8999 7389 Scientific consulting; technical manual preparation;

(G-10947)
EMPYRE CONSTRUCTION LLC
6902 Martindale Rd (66218-9330)
P.O. Box 860985 (66286-0985)
PHONE..................................316 558-8186
Matthew Hurd,
EMP: 20
SALES: 950K **Privately Held**
SIC: 1742 Plastering, drywall & insulation

(G-10948)
ENPOWER OPERATIONS CORP
Also Called: E I F K C Landfill Gas
15941 W 65th St (66217-9342)
PHONE..................................913 441-3633
Doug Lloyd, *Principal*
EMP: 10
SALES (est): 1.2MM **Privately Held**
SIC: 1629 Power plant construction

(G-10949)
EQUITY BANK NA
Also Called: Parkway Center
10314 Shawnee Msn 100 (66203-3500)
PHONE..................................731 989-2161
Lawrence G Barcus, *Branch Mgr*
EMP: 11 **Publicly Held**
SIC: 6021 National commercial banks
HQ: Equity Bank, N.A.
7701 E Kellogg Dr Stc 300
Wichita KS 67207
316 612-6000

(G-10950)
EVERGY KANSAS CENTRAL INC
Kpl Gas Service
23505 W 86th St (66227-3298)
PHONE..................................913 667-5134
Robert Ortiz Jr, *Manager*
EMP: 44
SALES (corp-wide): 4.2B **Publicly Held**
SIC: 4911 Generation, electric power
HQ: Evergy Kansas Central, Inc.
818 S Kansas Ave
Topeka KS 66612
785 575-6300

(G-10951)
EXTREME LIMOUSINE LLC
9916 W 67th St (66203-3622)
PHONE..................................913 831-2039
Mary Curry,
EMP: 10
SALES (est): 435.8K **Privately Held**
SIC: 4111 4119 Airport transportation; limousine rental, with driver

(G-10952)
FACILITY SOLUTIONS GROUP INC
6435 Vista Dr (66218-9239)
PHONE..................................913 422-8400
Randy Sounakhen, *Senior Buyer*
Jim Frank, *Branch Mgr*
EMP: 21
SALES (corp-wide): 1B **Privately Held**
WEB: www.americanlight.com
SIC: 5063 1731 Lighting fixtures, commercial & industrial; light bulbs & related supplies; electrical work; lighting contractor
PA: Facility Solutions Group, Inc.
4401 West Gate Blvd # 310
Austin TX 78745
512 440-7985

(G-10953)
FALCON DESIGN AND MFG
23825 W 40th St (66226-2284)
PHONE..................................913 441-1074
Terry Sherpherd, *CEO*
Terry Shepherd, *CEO*
Reine Shepherd, *President*
Brent Plager, *Vice Pres*
EMP: 20 **EST:** 1978
SQ FT: 15,000
SALES (est): 1.7MM **Privately Held**
WEB: www.falcondesignmfg.com
SIC: 2759 3643 2396 Screen printing; current-carrying wiring devices; automotive & apparel trimmings

(G-10954)
FEDERATED RURAL ELC INSUR EXCH (PA)
7725 Renner Rd (66217-9414)
P.O. Box 15147, Lenexa (66285-5147)
PHONE....................................913 541-0150
Brian Krambeer, *Chairman*
Richard Burns, *Vice Pres*
Carl Schroer, *Vice Pres*
EMP: 21
SALES (est): 112.5MM **Privately Held**
SIC: 6411 Insurance agents

(G-10955)
FEYERHERM CONSTRUCTION INC
7424 Constance St (66216-5506)
PHONE....................................913 962-5888
Roger Feyerherm, *President*
Sarah M Feyerherm, *Chairman*
EMP: 14
SQ FT: 3,000
SALES (est): 2.5MM **Privately Held**
SIC: 1541 1542 Industrial buildings, new construction; commercial & office building, new construction

(G-10956)
FIRST NATIONAL BANK OF OMAHA
6301 Pflumm Rd (66216-2401)
PHONE....................................913 631-0016
EMP: 89
SALES (corp-wide): 1.2B **Privately Held**
SIC: 6021 National commercial banks
HQ: First National Bank Of Omaha Inc
1620 Dodge St
Omaha NE 68197
402 341-0500

(G-10957)
FORTERRA CONCRETE PRODUCTS INC
23600 W 40th St (66226-2247)
PHONE....................................913 422-3634
Joe Marsh, *Branch Mgr*
EMP: 28
SALES (corp-wide): 1.4B **Publicly Held**
WEB: www.iowacp.com
SIC: 3272 Culvert pipe, concrete
HQ: Forterra Concrete Products, Inc.
6655 Wedgwood Rd N # 130
Maple Grove MN 55311
763 545-7473

(G-10958)
FRESH KC WATER INC
6917 Martindale Rd (66218-9331)
PHONE....................................913 745-0002
Al Lozier, *President*
EMP: 6
SQ FT: 15,000
SALES (est): 917.8K **Privately Held**
WEB: www.kcwater.com
SIC: 3589 Water treatment equipment, industrial

(G-10959)
FRIEND THAT COOKS LLC
6100 Nieman Rd Ste 150b (66203-2903)
PHONE....................................913 660-0790
Brandon O'Dell, *Mng Member*
Brandon Odell, *Manager*
Rebecca Nedrow, *Director*
EMP: 27
SALES: 900K **Privately Held**
SIC: 7299 Personal appearance services

(G-10960)
GENERAL FIRE SPRINKLER CO LLC
10324 W 79th St (66214-1561)
PHONE....................................913 390-1105
Kevin Eubanks,
EMP: 19
SALES: 2.8MM **Privately Held**
SIC: 1711 Fire sprinkler system installation

(G-10961)
GENIGRAPHICS LLC
5645 Lakecrest Dr (66218-8900)
P.O. Box 860111 (66286-0111)
PHONE....................................913 441-1410
Linda Larson,
Jay Larson,
EMP: 10
SALES: 950K **Privately Held**
SIC: 2759 Commercial printing

(G-10962)
GEOTECHNOLOGY INC
5055 Antioch Rd (66203-1314)
PHONE....................................913 438-1900
William C Jones, *Branch Mgr*
Dan Greenwood, *Sr Project Mgr*
EMP: 27
SALES (corp-wide): 30.2MM **Privately Held**
SIC: 8711 Consulting engineer
PA: Geotechnology, Inc.
11816 Lackland Rd Ste 150
Saint Louis MO 63146
314 997-7440

(G-10963)
GOLCONDA GROUP LLC
6878 Martindale Rd (66218-9353)
PHONE....................................913 579-4795
Benjamin E Ross, *Mng Member*
Jenny Ross, *Mng Member*
EMP: 13
SALES: 1.2MM **Privately Held**
SIC: 1542 Commercial & office building, new construction

(G-10964)
GRAPHICS FOUR INC
7838 Oakview Ln (66216-4245)
PHONE....................................913 268-0564
Donald E Ahnen, *President*
Dave Keller, *Treasurer*
EMP: 9
SALES (est): 665.2K **Privately Held**
WEB: www.gfour.com
SIC: 7335 2752 Color separation, photographic & movie film; commercial printing, lithographic

(G-10965)
GREEN LAWN INC
6906 Martindale Rd (66218-9330)
PHONE....................................913 393-2238
Craig Hawkins, *President*
Chris Hawkins, *General Mgr*
EMP: 20
SQ FT: 2,500
SALES (est): 2.9MM **Privately Held**
SIC: 0782 Landscape contractors; lawn care services

(G-10966)
HALFPRICEBANNERSCOM INC
8130 Monticello Ter (66227-2603)
PHONE....................................913 441-9299
Kelly R Doty, *President*
Jered Nussbaum, *President*
Lisa Meyer, *Opers Mgr*
EMP: 7
SALES (est): 1.1MM **Privately Held**
SIC: 3993 Signs & advertising specialties

(G-10967)
HANS RUDOLPH INC
8325 Cole Pkwy (66227-3128)
PHONE....................................913 422-7788
Kevin Rudolph, *CEO*
John H Rudolph, *Ch of Bd*
Kelly Rudolph, *President*
▲ **EMP:** 42 **EST:** 1960
SQ FT: 33,000
SALES: 6.3MM **Privately Held**
WEB: www.rudolphkc.com
SIC: 3841 Surgical & medical instruments

(G-10968)
HEARTLAND ASSISTED LIVING
16207 Midland Dr Apt 3 (66217-9496)
PHONE....................................913 248-6600
Noime Wilcox, *President*
Phillip Hornbaker, *Principal*
EMP: 20
SALES (est): 1MM **Privately Held**
SIC: 8052 Personal care facility

(G-10969)
HEARTLAND LEASING SERVICES INC (PA)
Also Called: Heartland Seating
11222 Johnson Dr (66203-2752)
PHONE....................................913 268-0069
Brad Peterson, *President*
Kathy Peterson, *Corp Secy*
Mark Clark, *Vice Pres*
Monty Kinman, *Sales Staff*
EMP: 10
SALES (est): 1.5MM **Privately Held**
SIC: 2531 Bleacher seating, portable; stadium seating

(G-10970)
HEARTLAND SEATING INC
11222 Johnson Dr (66203-2752)
PHONE....................................913 268-0069
Brad Peterson, *President*
Kathy Peterson, *Corp Secy*
Mark Clark, *Vice Pres*
EMP: 10
SALES (est): 1.5MM **Privately Held**
WEB: www.heartlandseating.com
SIC: 2531 Bleacher seating, portable; stadium seating
PA: Heartland Leasing Services, Inc.
11222 Johnson Dr
Shawnee KS 66203
913 268-0069

(G-10971)
HELENA CHEMICAL COMPANY
8215 Hedge Lane Ter (66227-3038)
PHONE....................................913 441-0676
Mark Person, *Branch Mgr*
Brian Ruder, *Representative*
EMP: 11 **Privately Held**
WEB: www.helenachemical.com
SIC: 5169 Chemicals & allied products
HQ: Helena Agri-Enterprises, Llc
255 Schilling Blvd # 300
Collierville TN 38017
901 761-0050

(G-10972)
I2 ASIA LLC
21983 W 83rd St (66227-3133)
PHONE....................................913 422-1600
James K Davis Jr, *Mng Member*
▲ **EMP:** 10
SALES: 110MM **Privately Held**
SIC: 5084 Industrial machinery & equipment

(G-10973)
INKCYCLE INC
Also Called: Tonercycle
10601 W 79th St (66214-3311)
PHONE....................................913 894-8387
Rick Krska, *President*
Brad Roderick, *Exec VP*
Cathy Lynch, *Vice Pres*
Keith Riley, *Vice Pres*
Mike Lutz, *CFO*
◆ **EMP:** 65
SQ FT: 16,000
SALES: 2MM **Privately Held**
SIC: 3861 2893 Toners, prepared photographic (not made in chemical plants); lithographic ink

(G-10974)
INSCO ENVIRONMENTAL INC
6902 Martindale Rd (66218-9330)
PHONE....................................912 422-8001
Matthew D Hurd, *President*
Marc Pasley, *Vice Pres*
Sharon Barber, *Accounting Mgr*
EMP: 10
SALES: 950K
SALES (corp-wide): 6.1MM **Privately Held**
SIC: 1799 Special trade contractors
PA: Insco Industries, Inc.
6902 Martindale Rd
Shawnee Mission KS 66218
913 422-8001

(G-10975)
INTELLECTUAL GROWTH ENGRG
19300 W 64th Ter (66218-9177)
PHONE....................................913 210-8570
Michael Bluhm,
EMP: 10
SQ FT: 3,500
SALES (est): 925.2K **Privately Held**
SIC: 8742 Business consultant

(G-10976)
JACKSON AGROBUILDERS LLC
26000 W 69th Ter (66226-3323)
PHONE....................................913 909-6391
Taylor Jackson,
EMP: 10 **EST:** 2016
SALES: 650K **Privately Held**
SIC: 1542 Greenhouse construction

(G-10977)
JANSSEN GLASS & MIRROR INC
Also Called: Janssen Glass & Door
4949 Hadley St (66203-1329)
PHONE....................................913 677-5727
Tom Janssen, *President*
Matt Janssen, *Vice Pres*
Pat Janssen, *Vice Pres*
Tim Janssen, *Treasurer*
Joyce Janssen, *Admin Sec*
EMP: 11
SQ FT: 4,800
SALES (est): 2.8MM **Privately Held**
SIC: 1793 5231 7699 1799 Glass & glazing work; glass; door & window repair; building board-up contractor

(G-10978)
JEM INTERNATIONAL INC (PA)
6873 Martindale Rd (66218-9354)
PHONE....................................913 441-4788
James Mattson, *President*
Brett Mattson, *Vice Pres*
Kendra Morrison, *Controller*
Lori Thomas, *Accountant*
Tony Mroz, *Sales Staff*
◆ **EMP:** 10
SALES (est): 4.1MM **Privately Held**
SIC: 5084 Industrial machinery & equipment

(G-10979)
JIM JAM INC
Also Called: Envirotech Heating & Cooling
11003 W 59th Ter (66203-2956)
PHONE....................................913 268-6700
James Gallet, *President*
Terri Gallet, *Admin Sec*
EMP: 11
SALES (est): 1.3MM **Privately Held**
SIC: 1711 Warm air heating & air conditioning contractor; refrigeration contractor

(G-10980)
KANSAS UNIV PHYSICIANS INC
7420 Switzer St (66203-4550)
PHONE....................................913 742-7611
EMP: 372 **Privately Held**
SIC: 8011 Offices & clinics of medical doctors
PA: Kansas University Physicians, Inc.
3901 Rainbow Blvd
Kansas City KS 66160

(G-10981)
KID STOP LLC
5542 Hedge Lane Ter (66226-2253)
PHONE....................................913 422-9999
Monica Jensen, *Mng Member*
EMP: 10
SQ FT: 3,600
SALES: 250K **Privately Held**
SIC: 8351 Group day care center

(G-10982)
KINDERCARE EDUCATION LLC
5416 Martindale Rd (66218-9680)
PHONE....................................913 441-9202
EMP: 17
SALES (corp-wide): 1B **Privately Held**
SIC: 8351 Child Day Care Services
PA: Kindercare Education Llc
650 Ne Holladay St # 1400
Portland OR 97232
503 872-1300

(G-10983)
KLS INDUSTRIES LLC
3439 Merriam Dr (66203-1375)
PHONE....................................877 952-2548
Scott Guest, *Principal*
Keith Fridlington, *Software Dev*
EMP: 5 **EST:** 2007
SALES (est): 306.2K **Privately Held**
SIC: 3999 Manufacturing industries

GEOGRAPHIC

(G-10984)
L L C FUN SERVICES OF K C
7803 Meadow View Dr (66227-3026)
PHONE..................................913 441-9200
Zack Wilson, *Mng Member*
EMP: 15
SQ FT: 12,750
SALES (est): 1.7MM **Privately Held**
WEB: www.funservicesmidwest.com
SIC: 7389 6531 Fund raising organizations; real estate leasing & rentals

(G-10985)
LEE DENTAL LABORATORY
24202 W 68th St (66226-3539)
PHONE..................................913 599-3888
EMP: 10
SALES (est): 747.7K **Privately Held**
SIC: 8734 Testing laboratories

(G-10986)
LEGACY TECHNOLOGIES INC
Also Called: L T I
6700 W 47th Ter (66203-1392)
PHONE..................................913 432-2487
Jack E Launtz, *President*
Mickey Finn, *CFO*
▲ **EMP:** 75
SQ FT: 7,000
SALES (est): 12MM **Privately Held**
WEB: www.legacytechnologies.com
SIC: 3679 Electronic crystals

(G-10987)
LENEXA SERVICES INC
7725 Renner Rd (66217-9414)
PHONE..................................913 541-0150
Philip Irwin, *President*
Susan Olander, *Admin Sec*
EMP: 54
SALES (est): 99.4K
SALES (corp-wide): 112.5MM **Privately Held**
SIC: 8999 Personal services
HQ: Federated Rural Electric Management Corp.
7725 Renner Rd
Lenexa KS 66217
913 541-0150

(G-10988)
LIFEWORKS CHIROPRACTIC
22742 Midland Dr (66226-3553)
PHONE..................................913 441-2293
Matthew T Gianforte, *Executive Asst*
EMP: 11 **EST:** 2007
SALES (est): 860.9K **Privately Held**
SIC: 8041 Offices & clinics of chiropractors

(G-10989)
LISA R GONZALES DDS P C
7503 Park St (66216-4270)
PHONE..................................913 299-3999
Lisa Gonzales, *Owner*
EMP: 12
SALES (est): 662.8K **Privately Held**
SIC: 8021 Dentists' office

(G-10990)
LUKA IRRIGATION SYSTEMS INC
7015 Martindale Rd (66218-9766)
P.O. Box 3921 (66203-0921)
PHONE..................................913 248-0400
Douglas S Luka, *President*
Douglas Luka, *President*
EMP: 20
SALES (est): 2.4MM **Privately Held**
SIC: 1629 5083 0782 0781 Irrigation system construction; irrigation equipment; landscape contractors; landscape planning services

(G-10991)
MAX RIEKE & BROTHERS INC (PA)
15400 Midland Dr (66217-9606)
P.O. Box 860227 (66286-0227)
PHONE..................................913 631-7111
Leon Rieke, *President*
Leona Young, *COO*
Derrick Rieke, *Vice Pres*
Steven Rieke, *Treasurer*
EMP: 63
SQ FT: 30,000
SALES: 8.3MM **Privately Held**
WEB: www.maxrieke.com
SIC: 1623 1611 1629 4212 Water & sewer line construction; highway & street construction; dams, waterways, docks & other marine construction; levee construction; earthmoving contractor; dump truck haulage; parking lot construction; excavation & grading, building construction

(G-10992)
MCN SHAWNEE LLC
Also Called: Carlyle Apartments
7530 Cody St (66214-1365)
PHONE..................................913 631-2100
Ron Taylor, *Principal*
Carole McNeal, *Principal*
EMP: 99
SALES: 950K **Privately Held**
SIC: 1522 Multi-family dwelling construction

(G-10993)
MEDI COACH LLC
Also Called: Non-Emergency Medical Trnspt
12510 W 62nd Ter Ste 103 (66216-1869)
PHONE..................................913 825-1945
Robert McTarsney,
Jeff Jolliffe,
Paul Jolliffe,
EMP: 30 **EST:** 2010
SQ FT: 1,500
SALES (est): 676.6K **Privately Held**
SIC: 4119 Local passenger transportation

(G-10994)
METAL ARTS ENGRAVERS INC
Also Called: Johnson Business Cards
22615 W 46th Ter (66226-2449)
P.O. Box 860115 (66286-0115)
PHONE..................................913 262-1979
Charles L Miller, *President*
Joe Waldon, *Vice Pres*
Melinda A Waldron, *Treasurer*
Linda Miller, *Admin Sec*
EMP: 12
SQ FT: 12,000
SALES (est): 1.4MM **Privately Held**
SIC: 3544 Special dies & tools

(G-10995)
MIDAMERICA METER
6922 Martindale Rd (66218-9330)
PHONE..................................913 441-0790
Cliff Jerome, *Branch Mgr*
EMP: 5
SALES (est): 615.9K **Privately Held**
SIC: 3825 Instruments to measure electricity
PA: Midamerica Meter
710 Hamel Rd
Medina MN 55340

(G-10996)
MILLER BUILDING SERVICES INC
10312 W 79th St (66214-1561)
PHONE..................................913 649-5599
David Miller, *President*
Deborah Mulcahy, *Project Mgr*
Cindy Markey, *Info Tech Mgr*
EMP: 30
SQ FT: 1,000
SALES (est): 7.5MM **Privately Held**
WEB: www.millerbuildingservices.com
SIC: 1521 Single-family housing construction

(G-10997)
MIXTURE LLC
9325 W 53rd St (66203-2113)
PHONE..................................913 944-2441
Daniel H Deleon, *Administration*
EMP: 14 **EST:** 2009
SALES (est): 2.3MM **Privately Held**
SIC: 4226 Household goods, warehousing

(G-10998)
MIZE ELEMENTARY PTO
7301 Mize Rd (66227-2402)
PHONE..................................913 441-0880
Kim Gracy, *Principal*
EMP: 10
SALES: 70.5K **Privately Held**
SIC: 8641 Parent-teachers' association

(G-10999)
MO-CAN FLOORING INC
Also Called: Mc Flooring
6800 W 47th Ter (66203-1398)
PHONE..................................913 362-0711
Robert Shaw, *President*
John Crider, *Accounts Mgr*
Christine Poplau, *Admin Sec*
Dale Vestal, *Master*
Rick Frazee, *Representative*
EMP: 25
SQ FT: 20,000
SALES (est): 4.3MM **Privately Held**
WEB: www.mcflooringkc.com
SIC: 5713 1752 Carpets; carpet laying

(G-11000)
MOOREKC ENTERPRISES LLC
Also Called: Commercial Concepts and Furn
13418 W 77th Ter (66216-3024)
PHONE..................................316 347-0121
Ted Moore,
EMP: 10
SALES (est): 555.8K **Privately Held**
SIC: 7389 Design services

(G-11001)
MVP ELECTRIC LLC
Also Called: Mvp Electric Heating & Cooling
21514 W 51st Ter (66226-9729)
PHONE..................................913 322-0868
Amy Gabbert, *Owner*
Karen Standish, *Admin Asst*
EMP: 15
SALES (est): 1.7MM **Privately Held**
SIC: 1731 Electrical work

(G-11002)
NATIONWIDE TRANSPORTATION AND
5940 Nieman Rd (66203-2954)
P.O. Box 3190 (66203-0190)
PHONE..................................913 888-1685
Kim Isenhower, *President*
Jerry Isenhower, *Vice Pres*
EMP: 18
SALES (est): 9.3MM **Privately Held**
WEB: www.nationwidetransportation.com
SIC: 4213 Trucking, except local

(G-11003)
NAZDAR COMPANY (HQ)
Also Called: Nazdar Source One
8501 Hedge Lane Ter (66227-3289)
PHONE..................................913 422-1888
J Jeffrey Thrall, *CEO*
Mike Fox, *President*
Robin Hoyle, *Editor*
Stanley D Christianson, *Chairman*
Richard Bowles, *Vice Pres*
◆ **EMP:** 170
SQ FT: 117,000
SALES (est): 177MM
SALES (corp-wide): 200.3MM **Privately Held**
WEB: www.nazdar.com
SIC: 2893 Screen process ink
PA: Thrall Enterprises, Inc.
180 N Stetson Ave # 4330
Chicago IL 60601
312 621-8200

(G-11004)
NAZDAR COMPANY
8420 Hedge Ln (66227)
PHONE..................................913 422-1888
Bill Geers, *Accounts Exec*
John Morgan, *Manager*
Tim Quinn, *Consultant*
EMP: 12
SALES (corp-wide): 200.3MM **Privately Held**
SIC: 5085 5199 5999 3555 Ink, printers'; artists' materials; artists' supplies & materials; printing trades machinery; printing ink
HQ: Nazdar Company
8501 Hedge Lane Ter
Shawnee KS 66227
913 422-1888

(G-11005)
NEW IMAGE CONCRETE DESIGN LLC
5300 Hedge Lane Ter (66226-2208)
PHONE..................................913 489-1699
Brett Lingo,
Anthony David,
Tony David,
EMP: 10
SALES: 200K **Privately Held**
SIC: 4212 1771 Local trucking, without storage; exterior concrete stucco contractor

(G-11006)
OUTDOOR LIGHTING SERVICES LP
Also Called: Design Electric
6435 Vista Dr (66218-9239)
PHONE..................................913 422-8400
Jim Frank, *Manager*
EMP: 15
SALES (corp-wide): 1B **Privately Held**
WEB: www.fsgconnect.com
SIC: 1731 General electrical contractor; lighting contractor
HQ: Outdoor Lighting Services Lp
4401 West Gate Blvd # 310
Austin TX 78745
512 440-7985

(G-11007)
OVERLAND TOOL & MACHINERY INC
Also Called: O T M
7431 Monrovia St (66216-3611)
PHONE..................................913 599-4044
Daniel W Bashaw, *President*
Lois Bashaw, *Corp Secy*
Troy D Bashaw, *Vice Pres*
EMP: 29
SQ FT: 20,000
SALES (est): 7MM **Privately Held**
WEB: www.overlandtool.com
SIC: 5072 7699 Power tools & accessories; knife, saw & tool sharpening & repair

(G-11008)
P B HOIDALE CO INC
6909 Martindale Rd (66218-9331)
P.O. Box 40395, Shawnee Mission (66204)
PHONE..................................913 438-1500
Stephen Dixon, *CEO*
Richard Dixon, *Principal*
Michael Keul, *Branch Mgr*
EMP: 10
SALES (corp-wide): 26.5MM **Privately Held**
WEB: www.hoidale.com
SIC: 5172 3569 5084 Service station supplies, petroleum; lubricating equipment; petroleum industry machinery
PA: P. B. Hoidale Co., Inc.
3801 W Harry St
Wichita KS 67213
316 942-1361

(G-11009)
PBI-GORDON CORPORATION (PA)
Also Called: Gordon Lawn & Garden Co
22701 W 68th Ter (66226-3567)
PHONE..................................816 421-4070
William E Mealman, *Ch of Bd*
Donald A Chew, *President*
Darlene Frudakis, *President*
Jim Armbruster, *Vice Pres*
William R Brocker, *Vice Pres*
◆ **EMP:** 70 **EST:** 1947
SALES (est): 31.9MM **Privately Held**
WEB: www.pbigordon.com
SIC: 2879 Pesticides, agricultural or household

(G-11010)
PERCISION MFG
5734 Barton Dr (66203-2205)
PHONE..................................913 362-9244
Robert Parker, *Principal*
EMP: 8
SALES (est): 948.2K **Privately Held**
SIC: 3999 Manufacturing industries

(G-11011)
PINNACLE PLOTTING AND SUP LC
9339 W 53rd St (66203-2113)
PHONE..................................913 766-1822
Alan Dunz, *President*
Angela Dunz, *Vice Pres*
EMP: 8 **EST:** 2010
SALES: 400K **Privately Held**
SIC: 2759 Commercial printing

(G-11012)
PIVOT-DIGITTRON INC
23875 W 83rd Ter (66227-3141)
PHONE..................................913 441-0221
Victor Turnbaugh, *General Mgr*
EMP: 16
SQ FT: 14,000
SALES (est): 1.8MM **Privately Held**
SIC: 3672 Printed circuit boards
PA: Pivot International, Inc.
11030 Strang Line Rd
Lenexa KS 66215

(G-11013)
PUNCH BOXING PLUS FITNESS
5421 Martindale Rd (66218-9681)
PHONE..................................816 589-2690
Brad Botes, *General Mgr*
EMP: 30
SALES (est): 500.2K **Privately Held**
SIC: 7991 Athletic club & gymnasiums, membership

(G-11014)
PURPLEFROGINTL
14407 W 65th Ter (66216-2122)
PHONE..................................816 510-0871
Lydia Istomina, *Owner*
Julia Oden, *Contractor*
EMP: 7
SALES: 50K **Privately Held**
SIC: 8399 2731 8748 Council for social agency; books: publishing & printing; test development & evaluation service

(G-11015)
REBUILDING TOGETHER SHAWNEE/JO
5802 Lackman Rd (66217-9701)
P.O. Box 3617 (66203-0617)
PHONE..................................913 558-5079
Jeff Bahnson David Morris, *Principal*
EMP: 13 **EST:** 2008
SALES: 60.7K **Privately Held**
SIC: 8641 8399 Neighborhood association; community development groups

(G-11016)
REECE & NICHOLS REALTORS INC
7070 Renner Rd (66217-3047)
PHONE..................................913 307-4000
Nancy Whalen, *Broker*
Darrel Quiring, *Sales Staff*
Lonnie Eichelberger, *Sales Executive*
Don Burns, *Branch Mgr*
Linda Maher, *Agent*
EMP: 34
SALES (corp-wide): 225.3B **Publicly Held**
WEB: www.reece-nichols.com
SIC: 6531 Real estate agent, residential
HQ: Reece & Nichols Realtors, Inc.
11601 Granada St
Leawood KS 66211
913 491-1001

(G-11017)
RESIDENTIALSOULTION LLC
12684 Shwnee Mission Pkwy
(66216-1800)
PHONE..................................913 268-2967
Brandon Walker, *Exec Dir*
EMP: 28
SALES (est): 506.3K **Privately Held**
SIC: 8361 Residential care

(G-11018)
RETROCHEM INC
4923 Lakecrest Dr (66218-8964)
PHONE..................................913 422-8810
Bryan W Painter, *President*
EMP: 11
SALES: 900K **Privately Held**
SIC: 1741 1542 Tuckpointing or restoration; commercial & office buildings, renovation & repair

(G-11019)
RHW MANAGEMENT INC
Also Called: Shawnee Courtyard
17250 Midland Dr (66217-8901)
PHONE..................................913 631-8800
Ryan Cipolla, *General Mgr*
Kenneth Hough, *Manager*
EMP: 27
SALES (corp-wide): 16MM **Privately Held**
WEB: www.rhwhotels.com
SIC: 7011 Hotels & motels
PA: Rhw Management, Inc.
6704 W 121st St
Shawnee Mission KS 66209
913 451-1222

(G-11020)
RICKS BARBR SP & NATURAL HAIR
6423 Quivira Rd (66216-2745)
PHONE..................................913 268-3944
Ricky Phillips, *Principal*
EMP: 15 **EST:** 2009
SALES (est): 245.8K **Privately Held**
SIC: 7241 Barber shops

(G-11021)
ROCKWELL SECURITY LLC
11201 W 59th Ter (66203-2723)
PHONE..................................913 362-3300
Jeff Taylor, *Principal*
Stuart Clark, *Regional Mgr*
Kelby Hopkins, *CFO*
Sarah Yoakum, *Sales Staff*
EMP: 18
SALES (est): 771.5K **Privately Held**
SIC: 7381 Security guard service

(G-11022)
S D M DIE CUTTING EQUIPMENT
9320 W 54th St (66203-2164)
PHONE..................................913 782-3737
David Nelson, *President*
Rebecca Nelson, *Treasurer*
EMP: 5
SQ FT: 5,000
SALES (est): 647.5K **Privately Held**
WEB: www.sdmicrosystems.com
SIC: 3542 7629 Electroforming machines; presses: hydraulic & pneumatic, mechanical & manual; electrical repair shops

(G-11023)
SAFELITE FULFILLMENT INC
Also Called: Safelite Autoglass 6270
10306 Shwnee Mission Pkwy
(66203-3502)
PHONE..................................913 236-5888
Terry Jackson, *Manager*
EMP: 10
SALES (corp-wide): 177.9K **Privately Held**
WEB: www.belronus.com
SIC: 7536 Automotive glass replacement shops
HQ: Safelite Fulfillment, Inc.
7400 Safelite Way
Columbus OH 43235
614 210-9000

(G-11024)
SAM CARLINI
Also Called: Maverick Floor Management
6936 Martindale Rd (66218-9330)
P.O. Box 860981 (66286-0981)
PHONE..................................913 416-1280
Sam Carlini, *Principal*
EMP: 18
SQ FT: 1,500
SALES (est): 894.1K **Privately Held**
SIC: 1752 Floor laying & floor work

(G-11025)
SCHMITZ KING & ASSOCIATES INC
10501 W 70th Ter Apt 101 (66203-4149)
PHONE..................................913 397-6080
EMP: 16
SALES: 1.5MM **Privately Held**
SIC: 8713 Surveying Services

(G-11026)
SEEN MERCHANDISING LLC
5024 Hadley St (66203-1366)
PHONE..................................913 233-1981
Michael Brooks, *Principal*
EMP: 18
SALES (est): 2.3MM **Privately Held**
SIC: 2396 Screen printing on fabric articles

(G-11027)
SHAWNEE GARDENS HEALTH
6416 Long Ave (66216-2579)
PHONE..................................913 631-2146
George V Hager Jr, *CEO*
Jan Edwards, *Treasurer*
EMP: 165
SQ FT: 53,000
SALES: 9.8MM **Privately Held**
SIC: 8093 8051 Rehabilitation center, outpatient treatment; skilled nursing care facilities

(G-11028)
SHAWNEE MISSION MED CTR INC
6815 Hilltop Rd (66226-3532)
PHONE..................................913 422-2020
Finny Stilley, *Branch Mgr*
Steven Rettinger, *Family Practiti*
Vicente Palmeri,
EMP: 38 **Privately Held**
SIC: 8011 Clinic, operated by physicians; general & family practice, physician/surgeon
HQ: Shawnee Mission Medical Center, Inc.
9100 W 74th St
Shawnee Mission KS 66204
913 676-2000

(G-11029)
SHAWNEE MISSION TREE SVC INC (PA)
Also Called: Arbor Msters/SMC Utility Cnstr
8250 Cole Pkwy (66227-2715)
PHONE..................................913 441-8888
Ron Keith, *CEO*
EMP: 80
SALES (est): 56MM **Privately Held**
WEB: www.smtree.com
SIC: 1623 0783 0782 Gas main construction; electric power line construction; tree trimming services for public utility lines; landscape contractors

(G-11030)
SOURCE INCORPORATED MISSOURI
Also Called: Source Inc.
6840 Silverheel St (66226-5300)
PHONE..................................913 663-2700
Ray F Medlock, *CEO*
John Schissel, *President*
Bill Boyle, *Business Mgr*
Debbie Gasparovich, *Vice Pres*
Brandon Reid, *Vice Pres*
EMP: 15
SQ FT: 1,400
SALES: 18MM **Privately Held**
SIC: 7373 Computer integrated systems design

(G-11031)
SPECIAL PRODUCT COMPANY (PA)
Also Called: Spc Telequip
8540 Hedge Lane Ter (66227-3200)
PHONE..................................913 491-8088
Jerry Garrett, *CEO*
James M Needham, *Ch of Bd*
R S Seraphim, *Vice Ch Bd*
Doug Mackenzie, *President*
Hans Marosfalvy, *Principal*
▲ **EMP:** 12
SQ FT: 30,000
SALES (est): 42.2MM **Privately Held**
WEB: www.spc.net
SIC: 3669 5065 3661 Intercommunication systems, electric; telephone equipment; telephone & telegraph apparatus

(G-11032)
SPECTRUM PRIVATE CARE SERVICES
7740 Hedge Lane Ter (66227-3017)
PHONE..................................913 299-7100
Marilyn Apple, *President*
EMP: 56
SALES: 5.9MM **Privately Held**
SIC: 8082 Home health care services

(G-11033)
STATE TRACTOR TRUCKING INC
4101 Powell Dr (66226-7810)
P.O. Box 12542, Kansas City (66112-0542)
PHONE..................................913 287-3322
Travis Dale, *President*
EMP: 15
SQ FT: 2,040
SALES (est): 4.7MM **Privately Held**
SIC: 4213 Trucking, except local

(G-11034)
STERLING SCREEN PRINTING INC
23825 W 40th St (66226-2284)
PHONE..................................913 441-4411
Chris Routh, *President*
Dan Hrencher, *Vice Pres*
EMP: 14
SQ FT: 10,500
SALES: 1.6MM **Privately Held**
SIC: 2759 Screen printing

(G-11035)
SUNBELT CHEMICALS INC
P.O. Box 860665 (66286-0665)
PHONE..................................972 296-3920
Caesar Ricci, *President*
Paula Ricci, *Corp Secy*
Michael Kaza, *Vice Pres*
▲ **EMP:** 13
SQ FT: 1,400
SALES (est): 5.2MM **Privately Held**
SIC: 5198 2821 Paints; plastics materials & resins

(G-11036)
SUR-TEC INC
6840 Silverheel St (66226-5300)
P.O. Box 860176 (66286-0176)
PHONE..................................913 647-7720
Todd Dupriest, *President*
C Thomas Dupriest, *Vice Pres*
Corey Smith, *Info Tech Dir*
Rick Kerns, *Software Engr*
EMP: 7 **EST:** 1985
SQ FT: 11,500
SALES (est): 1.2MM **Privately Held**
SIC: 3572 7371 Computer storage devices; computer software systems analysis & design, custom

(G-11037)
SURFACE CENTER INTERIORS LLC
Also Called: SCI
12800 Shwnee Mission Pkwy
(66216-1849)
PHONE..................................913 422-0500
Julia Saykally, *Sales Staff*
Paul Ghilino,
▲ **EMP:** 10
SALES (est): 1.6MM **Privately Held**
WEB: www.asigranite.com
SIC: 3281 Dimension stone for buildings

(G-11038)
T-MOBILE USA INC
15610 Shwnee Mission Pkwy
(66217-9324)
PHONE..................................913 268-4414
Stephanie McGranahan, *Branch Mgr*
EMP: 12
SALES (corp-wide): 83.9B **Publicly Held**
SIC: 4812 Cellular telephone services
HQ: T-Mobile Usa, Inc.
12920 Se 38th St
Bellevue WA 98006
425 378-4000

(G-11039)
TEVIS ARCHITECTURAL GROUP
10820 Shawnee Msn (66203-3512)
PHONE..................................913 599-3003

GEOGRAPHIC

Daniel Tevis, *President*
Mariah Scott, *Internal Med*
EMP: 13
SALES: 650K **Privately Held**
SIC: 8712 7389 Architectural engineering; personal service agents, brokers & bureaus

(G-11040)
TILE SHOP LLC
6400 Nieman Rd (66203-3326)
PHONE..................................913 631-8453
Dacy Corley, *Manager*
EMP: 15
SALES (corp-wide): 357.2MM **Publicly Held**
WEB: www.tileshop.com
SIC: 5713 5023 Floor tile; resilient floor coverings: tile or sheet
HQ: The Tile Shop Llc
14000 Carlson Pkwy
Plymouth MN 55441
763 541-1444

(G-11041)
TOWN & COUNTRY SHEETMETAL INC
6423 Vista Dr (66218-9239)
PHONE..................................913 441-1208
Vince Wohleptz, *President*
EMP: 13
SALES: 2.5MM **Privately Held**
SIC: 3446 Architectural metalwork

(G-11042)
TRANSCRIPTION UNLIMITED INC
11013 W 48th Ter (66203-1181)
PHONE..................................816 350-3800
Linda S Hill, *President*
Donald L Somers, *Treasurer*
EMP: 20
SALES (est): 1MM **Privately Held**
WEB: www.tuinc.net
SIC: 7338 Secretarial & typing service

(G-11043)
UNITED STTES BOWL CONGRESS INC
12210 Johnson Dr (66216-1910)
PHONE..................................913 631-7209
Leo Hickerson, *Branch Mgr*
EMP: 51
SALES (corp-wide): 32.9MM **Privately Held**
SIC: 8699 Athletic organizations
PA: United States Bowling Congress, Inc.
621 Six Flags Dr
Arlington TX 76011
817 385-8200

(G-11044)
UNIVERSAL MANUFACTURING CO
Also Called: Umcprint
5030 Mackey St (66203-1334)
PHONE..................................816 231-2771
Delbert Coleman, *Ch of Bd*
Mike Dehlic, *Vice Pres*
Herbert Minnus, *Vice Pres*
Paul Quinlan, *Vice Pres*
Joseph Wilner, *Vice Pres*
▲ **EMP:** 250 **EST:** 1946
SQ FT: 200,000
SALES (est): 50.1MM **Privately Held**
WEB: www.jarodo.com
SIC: 2759 Tickets: printing

(G-11045)
US BANK NATIONAL ASSOCIATION
Also Called: US Bank
12010 W 63rd St (66216-1867)
PHONE..................................913 248-1001
Randy Dinges, *Principal*
EMP: 12
SALES (corp-wide): 25.7B **Publicly Held**
SIC: 6021 National commercial banks
HQ: U.S. Bank National Association
425 Walnut St Fl 14
Cincinnati OH 45202
513 632-4234

(G-11046)
VASCULAR SURGERY ASSOCIATES PA (PA)
7420 Switzer St (66203-4550)
PHONE..................................913 262-9201
Michael Beezley, *President*
Daniel Connely, *Principal*
Richard Arnspiger, *Treasurer*
EMP: 12
SALES (est): 1.8MM **Privately Held**
SIC: 8011 Surgeon

(G-11047)
VIDTRONIX LLC
6607 Martindale Rd (66218-9622)
PHONE..................................913 441-9777
Josh Unger, *Engineer*
Ryan Mang, *General Counsel*
Stanley K Peterson,
EMP: 11
SQ FT: 10,000
SALES (est): 1.6MM **Privately Held**
SIC: 4729 Airline ticket offices

(G-11048)
VOLLEY BALL INC
4925 Widmer Rd (66216-1264)
PHONE..................................913 422-4070
Dave McKay, *President*
EMP: 20
SALES (est): 218.9K **Privately Held**
SIC: 7032 Sporting & recreational camps

(G-11049)
WALL-TIES & FORMS INC
4000 Bonner Industrial Dr (66226-2103)
PHONE..................................913 441-0073
Ross W Worley, *CEO*
Charles Engleken, *President*
Carl Engleken, *Vice Pres*
Janice Jolin, *Vice Pres*
Richard Orrison, *Vice Pres*
◆ **EMP:** 150
SALES (est): 109.7MM **Privately Held**
WEB: www.wallties.com
SIC: 5082 3444 3443 Contractors' materials; concrete forms, sheet metal; fabricated plate work (boiler shop)

(G-11050)
WEAVERS AUTO BODY INC
Also Called: Weaver's Auto Center
6502 Vista Dr (66218-9240)
PHONE..................................913 441-0001
John Weaver, *President*
Susan Weaver, *Corp Secy*
EMP: 18
SALES (est): 1.8MM **Privately Held**
SIC: 7532 7539 Body shop, automotive; wheel alignment, automotive

(G-11051)
WEIS FIRE & SAFETY EQP LLC
6720 Mccormick Dr (66226-3547)
PHONE..................................303 421-2001
David Hansen,
EMP: 30
SALES (est): 1.6MM **Privately Held**
SIC: 5084 Safety equipment

(G-11052)
WELLS FARGO BANK NA
11809 Shwnee Mission Pkwy (66203-3337)
PHONE..................................913 631-6600
Tim Hensel, *Manager*
EMP: 15
SALES (corp-wide): 101B **Publicly Held**
SIC: 6021 National commercial banks
HQ: Wells Fargo Bank, National Association
101 N Phillips Ave
Sioux Falls SD 57104
605 575-6900

(G-11053)
WILLLOWTREE SUPPORTS INC
23733 W 83rd Ter (66227-3142)
PHONE..................................913 353-1970
Patricia Long, *Co-Owner*
Connie Morris, *Co-Owner*
Michael Morris, *CFO*
EMP: 27
SQ FT: 7,000
SALES (est): 559K **Privately Held**
SIC: 8399 Advocacy group

(G-11054)
WINDOW FLAIR DRAPERIES
11810 W 62nd Pl (66203-2655)
PHONE..................................913 722-6070
John Cochran, *Owner*
EMP: 5
SALES (est): 412.1K **Privately Held**
SIC: 2391 5023 5719 Curtains & draperies; window furnishings; window furnishings

(G-11055)
WM F HURST CO LLC
21981 W 83rd St (66227-3133)
PHONE..................................800 741-0543
Whitney Gleason, *Bookkeeper*
EMP: 10
SALES (corp-wide): 35.9MM **Privately Held**
SIC: 5088 Aircraft equipment & supplies
PA: Wm. F. Hurst Co., Llc
2121 Southwest Blvd
Wichita KS 67213
316 942-7474

(G-11056)
XSIS ELECTRONICS INC
12620 Shawnee Mission Pkw (66216-1897)
PHONE..................................913 631-0448
Mohan L Gupta, *President*
EMP: 12 **EST:** 1978
SQ FT: 9,500
SALES (est): 2MM **Privately Held**
WEB: www.xsis.com
SIC: 3679 Oscillators

(G-11057)
YELLOWFIN TRANSPORTATION INC
5817 Constance St (66216-5607)
PHONE..................................913 645-4834
Dale Bohn, *President*
David Tinsley, *Vice Pres*
EMP: 15
SALES (est): 526.2K **Privately Held**
SIC: 4111 4131 4119 Bus transportation; intercity & rural bus transportation; local passenger transportation

Shawnee Mission
Johnson County

(G-11058)
24 HOUR FITNESS USA INC
Also Called: Shawnee Club
11311 Shwnee Mission Pkwy (66203-3335)
PHONE..................................913 248-0724
Mike Polich, *Branch Mgr*
EMP: 40
SALES (corp-wide): 480.7MM **Privately Held**
SIC: 7991 Health club
HQ: 24 Hour Fitness Usa, Inc.
12647 Alcosta Blvd # 500
San Ramon CA 94583
925 543-3100

(G-11059)
4T TOTAL LAWN INC
10960 Eicher Dr (66219-2600)
PHONE..................................913 888-0997
Joel Beaver, *President*
Patricia Beaver, *Corp Secy*
EMP: 25
SALES (est): 1.4MM **Privately Held**
WEB: www.4tlawn.com
SIC: 0782 4959 Lawn care services; snowplowing

(G-11060)
A & P CRUISES & TOURS
Also Called: AP Travel
11800 Shawnee Mission Pkw (66203-3367)
PHONE..................................913 248-9800
Charles Curtis Lenoir, *Partner*
Willie Jackson, *Partner*
EMP: 14
SALES (est): 1.8MM **Privately Held**
SIC: 4724 Tourist agency arranging transport, lodging & car rental

(G-11061)
A CARING DOCTOR MINNESOTA PA
Also Called: Banfield Pet Hospital 237
11501 Metcalf Ave (66210-2232)
PHONE..................................913 345-8383
EMP: 20
SALES (corp-wide): 37.6B **Privately Held**
WEB: www.banfield.net
SIC: 0742 Animal hospital services, pets & other animal specialties
HQ: A Caring Doctor Minnesota Pa
8000 Ne Tillamook St
Portland OR 97213
503 922-5000

(G-11062)
A D L M LLC
Also Called: Maaco Auto Painting
8787 Lenexa Dr (66214-3236)
PHONE..................................913 888-0770
David Griffiths, *Mng Member*
EMP: 10 **EST:** 1976
SQ FT: 10,000
SALES: 1MM **Privately Held**
SIC: 7532 5531 Paint shop, automotive; body shop, automotive; automotive parts

(G-11063)
A G I INC
8008 Floyd St Ste 300 (66204-3700)
PHONE..................................913 281-5533
Eric Amundson, *President*
EMP: 10
SALES (est): 810K **Privately Held**
SIC: 7336 Package design

(G-11064)
A L HUBER INC
10770 El Monte St (66211-1449)
PHONE..................................913 341-4880
August L Huber III, *CEO*
Phil Thomas, *President*
Bill Draney, *Superintendent*
Mark Goracke, *Superintendent*
Joseph Huber, *Vice Pres*
EMP: 35
SQ FT: 9,000
SALES: 33MM **Privately Held**
WEB: www.alhuber.com
SIC: 1542 Commercial & office building, new construction

(G-11065)
ACADEMY OF ARTS LLC
5413 Martindale Rd (66218-9681)
PHONE..................................913 441-7300
Tonya Ebner,
Paul Ebner,
EMP: 15 **EST:** 1998
SALES (est): 1MM **Privately Held**
WEB: www.academyarts.net
SIC: 8299 7911 Voice lessons; dance instructor & school services

(G-11066)
ACCU-TECH CORPORATION
15731 W 100th Ter Bldg 3 (66219-1285)
PHONE..................................913 894-0444
Kevin Weiss, *Manager*
EMP: 11
SQ FT: 15,000
SALES (corp-wide): 8.4B **Publicly Held**
WEB: www.accu-tech.com
SIC: 5065 Electronic parts & equipment
HQ: Accu-Tech Corporation
11350 Old Roswell Rd # 100
Alpharetta GA 30009
888 222-8832

(G-11067)
ACE PERSONNEL INC (PA)
5909 Woodson St (66202-3302)
PHONE..................................913 384-1100
Shane Jones, *CEO*
Jennifer Craig, *Vice Pres*
Carol Jones, *Treasurer*
Terry Jones, *Admin Sec*
EMP: 18
SQ FT: 6,000
SALES (est): 990.8K **Privately Held**
WEB: www.acepersonnel.com
SIC: 7361 Executive placement

(G-11068)
ACOSTA INC
Also Called: Acosta Sales & Marketing
8155 Lenexa Dr (66214-1653)
PHONE..................................913 227-1000
Dan Karst, *General Mgr*
Melinda Davis, *Business Mgr*
Alan Holmgren, *Manager*
EMP: 75
SALES (corp-wide): 84.4MM **Privately Held**
WEB: www.acosta.com
SIC: 5141 Food brokers
HQ: Acosta, Inc.
6600 Corporate Ctr Pkwy
Jacksonville FL 32216
904 281-9800

(G-11069)
ACOUSTICAL STRETCHED FABRIC
14014 W 107th St (66215-2005)
PHONE..................................913 345-1520
Diane Mather, *President*
Zachary Harris, *Vice Pres*
EMP: 6
SQ FT: 2,500
SALES (est): 798.2K **Privately Held**
SIC: 2211 1742 Stretch fabrics, cotton; acoustical & ceiling work

(G-11070)
ACS DATA SEARCH LLC (PA)
Also Called: Apartment Credit Service
6701 W 64th St Ste 108 (66202-4175)
P.O. Box 12587 (66282-2587)
PHONE..................................913 649-1771
Sean Brune,
EMP: 15
SALES (est): 1.7MM **Privately Held**
WEB: www.acsdatasearch.com
SIC: 7323 Credit investigation service

(G-11071)
ACTION PLUMBING INC
6405 Caenen Lake Rd (66216-2466)
PHONE..................................913 631-1188
David Roy, *President*
EMP: 10
SQ FT: 1,000
SALES (est): 1.3MM **Privately Held**
SIC: 1711 Plumbing contractors

(G-11072)
ACTION TIRE & SERVICE INC
Also Called: Shawnee Goodyear
10823 Shwnee Mission Pkwy (66203-3511)
PHONE..................................913 631-9600
Timothy H Potter, *President*
Joan Potter, *Treasurer*
EMP: 12 **EST:** 1973
SQ FT: 6,000
SALES (est): 1.9MM **Privately Held**
WEB: www.actiontireservice.com
SIC: 5531 7538 Automotive tires; general automotive repair shops

(G-11073)
AD ASTRA INFO SYSTEMS LLC
6900 W 80th St Ste 300 (66204-3837)
PHONE..................................913 652-4100
Bridget Shannon, *Regl Sales Mgr*
Elizabeth Hoffman, *Accounts Exec*
Rebecca Hougland, *Accounts Exec*
Brett Adams, *Consultant*
Nicholas Ehlers, *Consultant*
EMP: 42
SQ FT: 20,000
SALES: 5.3MM **Privately Held**
WEB: www.aais.com
SIC: 7371 Computer software development

(G-11074)
ADAM & MCDONALD PA
9300 W 110th St Ste 470 (66210-1421)
PHONE..................................913 647-0670
Scott Adam, *Partner*
Ted Mc Donald, *Ltd Ptnr*
EMP: 13
SALES (est): 1.1MM **Privately Held**
SIC: 8111 General practice law office

(G-11075)
ADELPHI CONSTRUCTION LC
4800 Lamar Ave Ste 104 (66202-1775)
PHONE..................................913 384-5511
Glenn A Smith Jr, *President*
EMP: 85
SALES (est): 8.6MM
SALES (corp-wide): 54.5MM **Privately Held**
SIC: 1796 7699 5084 Machinery installation; pollution control equipment installation; industrial equipment services; materials handling machinery
PA: Industrial Accessories Company
4800 Lamar Ave Ste 203
Shawnee Mission KS 66202
913 384-5511

(G-11076)
ADKINS SYSTEMS INC
Also Called: Val Pak of Kansas City
9714 Rosehill Rd (66215-1414)
PHONE..................................913 438-8440
Bobby Adkins, *President*
EMP: 16
SALES (est): 1.6MM **Privately Held**
SIC: 7331 Direct mail advertising services

(G-11077)
ADM MILLING CO
8000 W 110th St Ste 220 (66210-2315)
PHONE..................................913 266-6300
Gregory H Johnston, *Manager*
EMP: 10
SALES (corp-wide): 64.3B **Publicly Held**
WEB: www.admmilling.com
SIC: 0723 Grain milling, custom services
HQ: Adm Milling Co.
8000 W 110th St Ste 300
Overland Park KS 66210
913 491-9400

(G-11078)
ADVANCED DERMATOLOGIC SURGERY
6901 W 121st St (66209-2007)
PHONE..................................913 661-1755
Timothy L Parker, *President*
EMP: 12
SALES (est): 1.8MM **Privately Held**
SIC: 8011 Surgeon

(G-11079)
ADVANSTAR COMMUNICATIONS INC
8033 Flint St (66214-3335)
PHONE..................................913 871-3800
DOT Theisen, *Sales Mgr*
Rebecca Turner-Chapman, *Manager*
Mark Eisler, *MIS Mgr*
Brendan Howard, *Senior Editor*
EMP: 26
SALES (corp-wide): 1.3B **Privately Held**
WEB: www.advanstar.com
SIC: 2721 Magazines: publishing only, not printed on site
HQ: Advanstar Communications Inc.
2501 Colorado Ave Ste 280
Santa Monica CA 90404
310 857-7500

(G-11080)
ADVENTIST HEALTH MID-AMERICA (PA)
9100 W 74th St (66204-4004)
PHONE..................................913 676-2184
Samuel Turner, *President*
Megan Schlick, *Med Doctor*
Peggy Shelton, *Office Admin*
Linda Riggs, *Director*
EMP: 160
SQ FT: 2,960
SALES: 8K **Privately Held**
SIC: 8741 Hospital management; nursing & personal care facility management

(G-11081)
ADVENTIST HEALTH SYSTEM/SUNBEL
Also Called: Shawnee Mission Home Hlth Care
7312 Antioch Rd (66204-2739)
PHONE..................................913 676-2163
Jack Wagner, *Principal*
Mary Orr, *Exec Dir*
EMP: 979 **Privately Held**
WEB: www.adventisthealth.org
SIC: 8062 General medical & surgical hospitals
HQ: Adventist Health System/Sunbelt, Inc.
900 Hope Way
Altamonte Springs FL 32714
407 357-1000

(G-11082)
AEROMOTIVE INC
7805 Barton St (66214-3403)
PHONE..................................913 647-7300
Steve Matusek, *President*
Jack Hylton, *COO*
Amanda Matusek, *Sales Staff*
Jonathan Pestinger, *Sales Staff*
EMP: 10
SALES (est): 2.2MM **Privately Held**
WEB: www.aeromotiveinc.com
SIC: 3714 3599 Filters: oil, fuel & air, motor vehicle; machine & other job shop work

(G-11083)
AFFILIATED MANAGEMENT SVCS INC
5651 Broadmoor St (66202-2407)
PHONE..................................913 677-9470
Richard McCoy, *President*
Jason Beeding, *Vice Pres*
Robert Devins, *Sales Mgr*
EMP: 15
SQ FT: 1,200
SALES (est): 1.1MM **Privately Held**
SIC: 7322 Collection agency, except real estate

(G-11084)
AGENDA USA INC
5509 Foxridge Dr (66202-1556)
PHONE..................................913 268-4466
Alton Hagen, *President*
Sandi Harkins, *Vice Pres*
Adam Harkins, *Opers Mgr*
Jeff Hardeman, *Manager*
Lindsey Jones, *Manager*
EMP: 23
SQ FT: 5,000
SALES (est): 1.4MM **Privately Held**
WEB: www.agendakansascity.com
SIC: 4141 4119 8742 Local bus charter service; limousine rental, with driver; food & beverage consultant; planning consultant

(G-11085)
AGGREKO LLC
Also Called: Aggreko Rental
9601 Alden St (66215-1126)
PHONE..................................913 281-9782
Robert Petersohn, *Manager*
EMP: 10
SALES (corp-wide): 2.3B **Privately Held**
WEB: www.aggreko.com
SIC: 7359 5075 5063 Equipment rental & leasing; air conditioning & ventilation equipment & supplies; generators
HQ: Aggreko, Llc
4607 W Admiral Doyle Dr
New Iberia LA 70560
337 367-7884

(G-11086)
AIH RECEIVABLE MANAGEMENT SVCS
5800 Foxridge Dr Ste 105 (66202-2335)
P.O. Box 70 (66201-0070)
PHONE..................................800 666-4606
Charles Holtgraves, *President*
EMP: 15
SQ FT: 10,000
SALES (est): 1.3MM **Privately Held**
SIC: 7322 Collection agency, except real estate

(G-11087)
AIR CARE HEATING & COOLING CO
6235 Eby Ave (66202-2831)
PHONE..................................913 362-5274
EMP: 12
SQ FT: 4,200
SALES (est): 1.3MM **Privately Held**
SIC: 1711 Warm air heating & air conditioning contractor

(G-11088)
AIRCRAFT BLUEBOOK
9800 Metcalf Ave (66212-2286)
PHONE..................................913 967-1719
EMP: 200
SALES (est): 5.5MM **Privately Held**
SIC: 2731 Books-Publishing/Printing

(G-11089)
AIRSOURCE TECHNOLOGIES INC
20505 W 67th St (66218-9620)
PHONE..................................913 422-9001
George Cobb, *President*
Steven Fryberger, *Vice Pres*
EMP: 10
SQ FT: 6,000
SALES (est): 1.3MM **Privately Held**
WEB: www.airsourcetech.com
SIC: 8748 Environmental consultant

(G-11090)
AKROFIRE INC
Also Called: Akro Fireguard Products
9001 Rosehill Rd (66215-3515)
PHONE..................................913 888-7172
Tom Roudebush, *Principal*
Jonathan Green, *Vice Pres*
Chris Crouch, *Project Mgr*
Tom Haxton, *Manager*
John Robertson, *Admin Sec*
EMP: 24
SQ FT: 13,000
SALES (est): 7.6MM **Privately Held**
WEB: www.akrofire.com
SIC: 2899 Fire retardant chemicals

(G-11091)
AL HUBER CONSTRUCTION INC
10770 El Monte St Ste 100 (66211-1450)
PHONE..................................913 341-4880
August L Huber III, *CEO*
Phillip Thomas, *President*
Stuart Olinger, *Superintendent*
Joseph Huber, *Vice Pres*
Randy Huber, *Vice Pres*
EMP: 35
SQ FT: 9,000
SALES (est): 7.2MM **Privately Held**
SIC: 1542 Commercial & office building, new construction

(G-11092)
ALEXANDER C DAVIS
5701 W 119th St Ste 345 (66209-3750)
PHONE..................................913 888-5577
Alexander C Davis, *Principal*
EMP: 12
SALES (est): 464K **Privately Held**
SIC: 8011 Internal medicine, physician/surgeon

(G-11093)
ALL AMERICAN INDOOR SPORTS (PA)
8875 Rosehill Rd (66215-3532)
PHONE..................................913 888-5425
Ron Matsch, *Ch of Bd*
David Quinn, *President*
Mike Urban, *Sales Staff*
Julie Campbell, *Office Mgr*
Carol Matsch, *Asst Sec*
EMP: 59
SALES (est): 4MM **Privately Held**
WEB: www.allamericanindoorsports.com
SIC: 6512 7997 7941 Property operation, retail establishment; membership sports & recreation clubs; soccer club

(G-11094)
ALL AMERICAN INDOOR SPORTS
British Soccer
8045 Flint St (66214-3335)
PHONE..................................913 599-4884
Ron Match, *Manager*
MO Abarak, *Director*
Mike Rees, *Director*
Julian Steinman, *Director*
EMP: 15

GEOGRAPHIC

SALES (corp-wide): 4MM **Privately Held**
WEB: www.allamericanindoorsports.com
SIC: 7941 Soccer club
PA: All American Indoor Sports, Inc
8875 Rosehill Rd
Shawnee Mission KS 66215
913 888-5425

(G-11095)
ALLCARE ANIMAL HOSPITAL INC
7252 Renner Rd (66217-9901)
PHONE....913 268-5011
Verona Chaffin, *President*
EMP: 20
SALES (est): 780.4K **Privately Held**
SIC: 0742 Animal hospital services, pets & other animal specialties

(G-11096)
ALLEN PRESCHOOL LLC
11060 Oakmont St (66210-1100)
PHONE....913 451-1066
Betsy Allen, *Principal*
Jack Allen,
EMP: 30
SALES (est): 425.5K **Privately Held**
SIC: 8351 Preschool center

(G-11097)
ALLIANCE DATA SYSTEMS CORP
8035 Quivira Rd Ste 100 (66215-2746)
PHONE....214 494-3000
Kim Prange, *Sales Executive*
John Messall, *Branch Mgr*
EMP: 250 **Publicly Held**
SIC: 6153 Credit card services, central agency collection
PA: Alliance Data Systems Corporation
3075 Loyalty Cir
Columbus OH 43219

(G-11098)
ALLIANCE SHIPPERS INC
5700 Broadmoor St Ste 600 (66202-2494)
PHONE....913 262-7060
Ed Spore, *Manager*
EMP: 30
SALES (corp-wide): 226.3MM **Privately Held**
WEB: www.alliance.com
SIC: 4731 Freight forwarding
PA: Alliance Shippers, Inc.
516 Sylvan Ave
Englewood Cliffs NJ 07632
201 227-0400

(G-11099)
ALS ASSCTION MD-MERICA CHAPTER (PA)
6950 Squibb Rd Ste 210 (66202-3260)
PHONE....913 648-2062
Terry Belzelberger, *President*
Jin Lebow, *President*
John Chalfant, *Vice Pres*
Marilyn Senter, *Vice Pres*
Crain Mahurin, *Treasurer*
EMP: 16
SQ FT: 2,500
SALES: 2.5MM **Privately Held**
WEB: www.als-ny.org
SIC: 8399 Fund raising organization, non-fee basis

(G-11100)
ALZHEIMRS DSEASE RLTD DSORDRS (HQ)
Also Called: Alzheimer's Disease and Relate
3846 W 75th St (66208-4126)
PHONE....913 381-3888
Debra Brook, *Exec Dir*
EMP: 15
SALES (est): 493.6K
SALES (corp-wide): 2.1MM **Privately Held**
SIC: 8322 8399 Individual & family services; health & welfare council
PA: Alzheimer's Disease And Related Disorders Association, Inc.
225 N Michigan Ave Fl 17
Chicago IL 60601
312 335-8700

(G-11101)
AMERICAN ACADEMY FAMILY PHYSCN (PA)
Also Called: AAFP FOUNDATION
11400 Tomahawk Creek Pkwy (66211-2680)
P.O. Box 7388 (66207-0388)
PHONE....913 906-6000
David Massanari MD, *President*
Sandra Panther, *Vice Pres*
Brian Manning, *Research*
Mark Belfer MD, *Treasurer*
Phyllis Naragon, *Director*
EMP: 13 **EST:** 1958
SQ FT: 3,500
SALES: 4MM **Privately Held**
SIC: 8621 6411 Medical field-related associations; insurance agents

(G-11102)
AMERICAN BAPTIST CHURCH
Also Called: Prairie Early Childhood Center
7416 Roe Ave (66208-2848)
PHONE....913 236-7067
Heather Entrekin, *Pastor*
Kyle Gardner, *Pastor*
Lisa Holiday, *Pastor*
EMP: 13
SQ FT: 15,000
SALES: 600K **Privately Held**
SIC: 8661 8351 Baptist Church; child day care services

(G-11103)
AMERICAN GOLF CORPORATION
Also Called: Deer Creek Golf Club
7000 W 133rd St (66209-3932)
PHONE....913 681-3100
Marty Martinez, *General Mgr*
Rachel Caruthers, *Sales Staff*
David Price, *Branch Mgr*
Greg Sherf, *Food Svc Dir*
EMP: 30 **Publicly Held**
WEB: www.americangolf.com
SIC: 7997 7992 Golf club, membership; public golf courses
HQ: American Golf Corporation
909 N Pacific Coast Hwy
El Segundo CA 90245
310 664-4000

(G-11104)
AMERICAN HEART ASSOCIATION KA
Also Called: Greater Kansas City Division
6800 W 93rd St (66212-1461)
PHONE....913 652-1913
Emily Plank, *Manager*
EMP: 25
SALES (corp-wide): 16.9MM **Privately Held**
SIC: 8621 Professional membership organizations
PA: American Heart Association, Kansas Affiliate, Inc
5375 Sw 7th St Ste 300
Topeka KS 66606
785 272-7056

(G-11105)
AMERICAN MANAGEMENT ASSN INTL
Also Called: Padgett-Thompson Division
11221 Roe Ave (66211-1922)
PHONE....913 451-2700
Raelene Dietz, *Branch Mgr*
EMP: 150
SALES (corp-wide): 84.4MM **Privately Held**
WEB: www.amanet.org
SIC: 8249 8742 Business training services; training & development consultant
PA: American Management Association International
1601 Broadway Fl 7
New York NY 10019
212 586-8100

(G-11106)
AMERICAN NATIONAL INSURANCE CO
Also Called: Anico
6405 Metcalf Ave Ste 314 (66202-3930)
PHONE....913 722-2232
Greg Carter, *Manager*
EMP: 20
SALES (corp-wide): 3.3B **Publicly Held**
WEB: www.american-national.com
SIC: 6411 6321 Insurance agents, brokers & service; accident & health insurance
PA: American National Insurance Company Inc
1 Moody Plz Fl 18
Galveston TX 77550
409 763-4661

(G-11107)
AMERICAN PAPER PRODUCTS INC
12333 Wedd St (66213-1815)
PHONE....913 681-5777
Robert Hughes, *CEO*
Linda Hughes, *President*
Chris O'Dell, *Vice Pres*
Dan Faubion, *Director*
Bob Mealman, *Director*
EMP: 12
SALES (est): 1.2MM **Privately Held**
SIC: 5044 Check writing, signing & endorsing machines

(G-11108)
AMERICAN RETIREMENT CORP
Also Called: Sweet Life At Shawnee
11400 W 65th St (66203-5555)
PHONE....913 248-1500
Shirley Allanbrande, *Manager*
EMP: 50
SALES (corp-wide): 4.5B **Publicly Held**
WEB: www.arclp.com
SIC: 8051 Skilled nursing care facilities
HQ: American Retirement Corporation
111 Westwood Pl Ste 200
Brentwood TN 37027
615 221-2250

(G-11109)
AMERIPRISE FINANCIAL SVCS INC
6800 College Blvd Ste 500 (66211-1888)
PHONE....913 451-2811
Frances Mossett, *Vice Pres*
Jamie Rietzke, *Advisor*
Brandon Turner, *Advisor*
Catherine Wear, *Advisor*
EMP: 35
SALES (corp-wide): 12.8B **Publicly Held**
WEB: www.amps.com
SIC: 6282 8742 Investment advisory service; financial consultant
HQ: Ameriprise Financial Services Inc.
707 2nd Ave S
Minneapolis MN 55402
612 671-2733

(G-11110)
AMLI MANAGEMENT COMPANY
Also Called: Amli At Regents Crest
12401 W 120th St (66213-4838)
PHONE....913 685-3700
Debbie Wells, *Branch Mgr*
EMP: 10
SALES (corp-wide): 50.1B **Publicly Held**
SIC: 6531 Real estate managers
HQ: Amli Management Company
141 W Jackson Blvd # 300
Chicago IL 60604
312 283-4700

(G-11111)
AMOS FAMILY INC (PA)
Also Called: Amos Family Funeral Home
10901 Johnson Dr (66203-2829)
PHONE....913 631-7314
Eugene P Amos, *Ch of Bd*
Gregg E Amos, *President*
Margaret Z Amos, *Vice Pres*
Amy A Ruo, *Office Mgr*
James Hawkins, *Manager*
EMP: 20
SQ FT: 17,000
SALES (est): 1.8MM **Privately Held**
WEB: www.amosfamily.com
SIC: 7261 Funeral home; crematory

(G-11112)
ANCHOR PROPERTIES INC (PA)
6400 W 110th St Ste 201 (66211-1585)
PHONE....913 661-2250
Steve Sherwood, *President*
Mary Lynn Sherwood, *Treasurer*
EMP: 78 **EST:** 1980
SQ FT: 3,500
SALES (est): 2.3MM **Privately Held**
WEB: www.anchorproperties.us
SIC: 6513 Apartment building operators

(G-11113)
APPLE EGHT HOSPITALITY MGT INC
Also Called: Springhill Suites Overland Pk
12000 Blue Valley Pkwy (66213-2647)
PHONE....913 491-0010
Danny Lagore, *Manager*
EMP: 43 **Privately Held**
SIC: 7011 Hotel, franchised
HQ: Apple Eight Hospitality Management, Inc.
814 E Main St
Richmond VA 23219

(G-11114)
APPLE TREE KID DAY OUT/PRESCH
10551 Quivira Rd (66215-2301)
PHONE....913 888-3702
Don Huienk, *Principal*
Geen Carlson, *Director*
EMP: 30
SALES (est): 358.1K **Privately Held**
SIC: 8351 Preschool center

(G-11115)
AQUENT LLC
7450 W 130th St Ste 100 (66213-2685)
PHONE....913 345-9119
Anthony Dehart, *Branch Mgr*
EMP: 24
SALES (corp-wide): 331.4MM **Privately Held**
WEB: www.akwent.com
SIC: 7361 7371 Executive placement; computer software systems analysis & design, custom
HQ: Aquent Llc
501 Boylston St Ste 3
Boston MA 02116
617 535-5000

(G-11116)
ARC PHYSICA THERA PLUS LIMITE (PA)
6400 Glenwood St Ste 111 (66202-4014)
PHONE....913 831-2721
Rachel Chick, *Human Res Dir*
Matthew Condon, *Mng Member*
Leslie Borden, *Manager*
Julie Hughes, *Systems Dir*
EMP: 20
SQ FT: 10,000
SALES (est): 10.2MM **Privately Held**
SIC: 8049 Physical therapist

(G-11117)
ARCHDIOCESE KANSAS CY IN KANS
Also Called: Saint Joseph Early Educatn Ctr
11525 Johnson Dr (66203-2643)
PHONE....913 631-0004
Nancy Wacker, *Director*
EMP: 50
SALES (corp-wide): 77.1MM **Privately Held**
WEB: www.archkck.org
SIC: 8351 8211 Child day care services; kindergarten
PA: Archdiocese Of Kansas City In Kansas
12615 Parallel Pkwy
Kansas City KS 66109
913 721-1570

(G-11118)
ARCHON RESIDENTIAL MGT LP
Also Called: Arrowhead Apartments
7530 Cody St (66214-1365)
PHONE....913 631-2100
Debbie Hall, *Manager*
EMP: 11
SALES (corp-wide): 52.5B **Publicly Held**
SIC: 6531 6513 Real estate managers; apartment building operators
HQ: Archon Residential Management Lp
6011 Connection Dr
Irving TX 75039
972 368-2200

▲ = Import ▼=Export
◆ =Import/Export

(G-11119)
ARNOLD KATZ MD
Also Called: Artheritis Specs of Gtr Kns Cy
10550 Quivira Rd Ste 320 (66215-2308)
PHONE..................................913 888-3231
Arnold Katz MD, *Owner*
Stephen Ruhlman MD, *Partner*
EMP: 10
SALES (est): 628.4K **Privately Held**
SIC: 8011 General & family practice, physician/surgeon

(G-11120)
ARROWOOD INDEMNITY COMPANY
7500 College Blvd Ste 650 (66210-4096)
PHONE..................................913 345-1776
Jim Harms, *Manager*
EMP: 45
SALES (corp-wide): 188.4MM **Privately Held**
SIC: 6311 Life insurance
HQ: Arrowood Indemnity Company
3600 Arco Corporate Dr
Charlotte NC 28273
704 522-2000

(G-11121)
ARVEST BANK OPERATIONS INC
Also Called: First National Bank
6300 Nall Ave Ste 100 (66202-4300)
P.O. Box 1165 (66222-0165)
PHONE..................................913 261-2265
Linda Pardon, *Manager*
Dwane Russell, *Manager*
EMP: 20
SALES (corp-wide): 2.3B **Privately Held**
WEB: www.harringtonbank.com
SIC: 6021 6162 National commercial banks; mortgage bankers & correspondents
HQ: Arvest Bank Operations, Inc.
921 W Monroe Ave
Lowell AR 72745
479 750-5400

(G-11122)
ASD SPECIALTY HEALTHCARE LLC
9652 Loiret Blvd (66219-2406)
PHONE..................................913 492-5505
Kathee Kramm, *Branch Mgr*
EMP: 20
SALES (corp-wide): 179.5B **Publicly Held**
WEB: www.asdhealthcare.com
SIC: 5122 Drugs, proprietaries & sundries
HQ: Asd Specialty Healthcare, Llc
5025 Plano Pkwy
Carrollton TX 75010
469 365-8000

(G-11123)
ASHBURY CHURCH PRE SCHOOL
Also Called: Ashbury Children Center
5400 W 75th St (66208-4711)
PHONE..................................913 432-5573
Steve Langhofer, *Pastor*
EMP: 15
SALES (est): 156.3K **Privately Held**
WEB: www.asburyumcpv.org
SIC: 8351 8661 Preschool center; churches, temples & shrines

(G-11124)
ASIAN AMRCN CHMBER OF COMMERCE
8645 College Blvd Ste 110 (66210-1891)
PHONE..................................913 338-0774
Renee Stevenson, *President*
EMP: 15
SALES: 251.2K **Privately Held**
WEB: www.asianchamberkc.com
SIC: 8611 Chamber of Commerce

(G-11125)
ASSOCIATED AUDIOLOGISTS INC (PA)
8800 W 75th St Ste 101 (66204-4001)
P.O. Box 19087, Lenexa (66285-9087)
PHONE..................................913 403-0018
Timothy Steele, *President*
Julie Steele, *Opers Staff*
Brenda Michels, *Admin Asst*
Alisha Sisney, *Admin Asst*
EMP: 33
SALES (est): 1.1MM **Privately Held**
WEB: www.hearingyourbest.com
SIC: 8049 Audiologist

(G-11126)
ASSOCIATED PLASTIC SURGEONS PC (PA)
11501 Granada St (66211-1454)
PHONE..................................913 451-3722
Joseph Cannova, *President*
Dr Sheryl L Young, *Vice Pres*
Sheryl Young, *Vice Pres*
Dr E Phillip Gutek, *Treasurer*
Jon Rast, *Med Doctor*
EMP: 15 **EST:** 1977
SQ FT: 10,000
SALES (est): 3.4MM **Privately Held**
WEB: www.apskc.com
SIC: 8011 Plastic surgeon

(G-11127)
ASTRONOMICAL SOCIETY KANSAS CY
7311 Stearns St (66203-4541)
PHONE..................................913 631-8413
Joseph Wright, *President*
Kristine Fox, *Treasurer*
EMP: 15 **EST:** 1946
SALES (est): 372.2K **Privately Held**
WEB: www.askconline.org
SIC: 8621 7336 Professional membership organizations; commercial art & graphic design

(G-11128)
AT&T CORP
5400 Foxridge Dr Ste 240 (66202-1555)
PHONE..................................913 676-1261
Rich Guthrie, *Manager*
Steve Franklin, *Manager*
EMP: 447
SALES (corp-wide): 170.7B **Publicly Held**
WEB: www.swbell.com
SIC: 4812 Cellular telephone services
HQ: At&T Corp.
1 At&T Way
Bedminster NJ 07921
800 403-3302

(G-11129)
AT&T CORP
13201 W 103rd St (66215-2176)
PHONE..................................913 676-1000
EMP: 23
SALES (corp-wide): 170.7B **Publicly Held**
WEB: www.swbell.com
SIC: 4813 Local & long distance telephone communications
HQ: At&T Corp.
1 At&T Way
Bedminster NJ 07921
800 403-3302

(G-11130)
AT&T CORP
7400 Johnson Dr (66202-2325)
PHONE..................................913 676-1000
Ronald Powell, *Principal*
EMP: 102
SALES (corp-wide): 170.7B **Publicly Held**
WEB: www.swbell.com
SIC: 4813 Local & long distance telephone communications
HQ: At&T Corp.
1 At&T Way
Bedminster NJ 07921
800 403-3302

(G-11131)
ATHLETIC & REHABILITATION CTR
6405 Metcalf Ave Ste 504 (66202-3928)
PHONE..................................913 378-0778
John Beal, *President*
Jeff Weeks, *COO*
Dawn M Lovelace, *Manager*
EMP: 13
SALES (est): 700.5K **Privately Held**
SIC: 8322 8052 Rehabilitation services; personal care facility

(G-11132)
ATRIUMS RETIREMENT HOME
Also Called: Atriums, The
7300 W 107th St Apt 118 (66212-6600)
PHONE..................................913 381-9133
Joe Tutura, *President*
EMP: 80
SQ FT: 189,000
SALES (est): 5.4MM **Privately Held**
SIC: 6513 Retirement hotel operation

(G-11133)
AUDITING FOR CMPLIANCE EDUCATN
8900 State Line Rd # 350 (66206-1960)
PHONE..................................913 648-8572
Devona Slater, *CEO*
EMP: 10
SALES (est): 1.1MM **Privately Held**
SIC: 6411 8748 Inspection & investigation services, insurance; business consulting

(G-11134)
AUGUSTINE HOME IMPROVEMENT CO
Also Called: Augustine Exterminators
9280 Flint St (66214-1738)
PHONE..................................913 362-4707
James W Augustine, *President*
Margaret L Augustine, *Corp Secy*
Phil Augustine, *Vice Pres*
EMP: 45
SALES (est): 2.4MM **Privately Held**
SIC: 1521 General remodeling, single-family houses

(G-11135)
AUTOMOBILE CLUB OF MISSOURI
Also Called: A A A Insurance and Travel
15810b Shwnee Mssion Pkwy (66217-9326)
PHONE..................................913 248-1627
Tam Bollin, *Manager*
EMP: 17
SALES (corp-wide): 101.5MM **Privately Held**
SIC: 8699 Automobile owners' association
PA: Automobile Club Of Missouri
12901 N 40 Dr
Saint Louis MO 63141
314 523-7350

(G-11136)
AW SCHULTZ INC
6861 Martindale Rd (66218-9354)
PHONE..................................913 307-0399
Kenny Hartman, *President*
Steve McGhee, *Project Engr*
Donald Anderson, *Sales Mgr*
EMP: 15
SQ FT: 2,500
SALES (est): 9.3MM **Privately Held**
WEB: www.awschultz.com
SIC: 5084 Heat exchange equipment, industrial

(G-11137)
AXA ADVISORS LLC
7400 W 110th St Ste 700 (66210-2374)
PHONE..................................913 345-2800
Jake Bubenik, *Vice Pres*
Doug Propeck, *Sales/Mktg Mgr*
Kenneth Walton, *Consultant*
Wayne Town, *Advisor*
EMP: 50
SALES (corp-wide): 12B **Publicly Held**
WEB: www.axacs.com
SIC: 6411 Insurance agents
HQ: Axa Advisors, Llc
1290 Ave Of Amrcs Fl Cnc1
New York NY 10104
212 554-1234

(G-11138)
B & C RESTAURANT CORPORATION
Also Called: Hereford House, The
5001 Town Center Dr (66211-2058)
PHONE..................................913 327-0800
Don Jose, *Manager*
EMP: 112
SALES (corp-wide): 6.4MM **Privately Held**
WEB: www.herefordhouse.com
SIC: 5812 5813 7299 Steak restaurant; drinking places; banquet hall facilities
PA: B & C Restaurant Corporation
30 W Pershing Rd
Kansas City MO 64108
816 842-8718

(G-11139)
B & R INSULATION INC
15001 W 101st Ter (66215-1162)
PHONE..................................913 492-1346
Richard Hall, *President*
Rosemary Laird, *Manager*
EMP: 50
SQ FT: 3,000
SALES: 5MM
SALES (corp-wide): 7.7MM **Privately Held**
SIC: 1799 Asbestos removal & encapsulation
PA: D & D Services Inc
15001 W 101st Ter
Shawnee Mission KS 66215
913 492-1346

(G-11140)
B FOUR CORP
7000 W 75th St (66204-3029)
PHONE..................................913 432-1107
Bob Scott, *Director*
EMP: 125
SALES (corp-wide): 578.2MM **Privately Held**
WEB: www.ballsfoods.com
SIC: 5411 2051 Supermarkets, chain; bread, cake & related products
PA: B Four Corp
5300 Speaker Rd
Kansas City KS 66106
913 321-4223

(G-11141)
B L RIEKE & ASSOCIATES INC
14352 W 96th Ter (66215-4708)
P.O. Box 14693 (66285-4693)
PHONE..................................913 599-3393
Bruce Rieke, *President*
Antonia Rieke, *Corp Secy*
Karen Leftwich, *Accountant*
EMP: 10
SQ FT: 2,500
SALES (est): 2.2MM **Privately Held**
WEB: www.blrieke.com
SIC: 1531 1521 Speculative builder, single-family houses; new construction, single-family houses

(G-11142)
B/E AEROSPACE INC
10800 Pflumm Rd (66215-4061)
P.O. Box 25905 (66225-5905)
PHONE..................................913 338-7292
Larry Huser, *Vice Pres*
EMP: 200
SALES (corp-wide): 66.5B **Publicly Held**
WEB: www.beaerospace.com
SIC: 3842 3841 3812 3769 Surgical appliances & supplies; surgical & medical instruments; search & navigation equipment; guided missile & space vehicle parts & auxiliary equipment; electric housewares & fans; oxygen systems, aircraft
HQ: B/E Aerospace, Inc.
1400 Corporate Center Way
Wellington FL 33414
561 791-5000

(G-11143)
BA KARBANK & CO LLP (PA)
2000 Shawnee Mission Pkwy (66205-3605)
PHONE..................................816 221-4488
Jack L Allen, *President*
Barney A Karbank, *Partner*
Steven M Karbank, *Chairman*
Adam D Feldman, *Vice Pres*
Paul Fogel, *Vice Pres*
EMP: 10
SALES (est): 1.4MM **Privately Held**
SIC: 6531 Real estate agent, commercial

(G-11144)
BAILEY SHOWROOM 2 LLC
5301 Johnson Dr (66205-2910)
PHONE..................................913 432-9696
Jim Armour, *General Mgr*
Sonja Cain, *Business Mgr*
Jeff Bailey, *Mng Member*
EMP: 10
SQ FT: 10,000
SALES (est): 970K **Privately Held**
SIC: 7389 Interior designer

(G-11145)
BAMFORD FIRE SPRINKLER CO INC
5134 Merriam Dr (66203-2158)
PHONE..................................913 432-6688
Mark McKenzie, *Manager*
EMP: 20
SALES (corp-wide): 4.9MM **Privately Held**
SIC: 1711 5087 5085 Fire sprinkler system installation; firefighting equipment; valves & fittings
HQ: Bamford Fire Sprinkler Co Inc
1383 W North St
Salina KS 67401
785 825-7710

(G-11146)
BANK AMERICA NATIONAL ASSN
12345 W 95th St (66215-3853)
PHONE..................................816 979-8608
Greg Wallman, *Branch Mgr*
EMP: 19
SALES (corp-wide): 110.5B **Publicly Held**
WEB: www.bofa.com
SIC: 6021 National commercial banks
HQ: Bank Of America, National Association
100 S Tryon St
Charlotte NC 28202
704 386-5681

(G-11147)
BANK OF BLUE VALLEY
9500 Lackman Rd (66219-1204)
PHONE..................................913 888-7852
Lisa Tomlinson, *Manager*
EMP: 16 **Publicly Held**
WEB: www.bankbv.com
SIC: 6021 National commercial banks
HQ: Bank Of Blue Valley
11935 Riley St
Overland Park KS 66213
913 338-1000

(G-11148)
BANK OF WEST
6263 Nall Ave (66202-3546)
PHONE..................................913 362-8900
Herman Baptiste, *Manager*
EMP: 15
SALES (corp-wide): 2.7B **Privately Held**
SIC: 6022 State trust companies accepting deposits, commercial
HQ: Bank Of The West
180 Montgomery St # 1400
San Francisco CA 94104
415 765-4800

(G-11149)
BANK OF WEST
9400 Antioch Rd (66212-3999)
PHONE..................................913 642-5212
Martin Fries, *Manager*
EMP: 18
SALES (corp-wide): 2.7B **Privately Held**
SIC: 6022 State commercial banks
HQ: Bank Of The West
180 Montgomery St # 1400
San Francisco CA 94104
415 765-4800

(G-11150)
BAPTIST SENIOR MINISTRIES
Also Called: Manor At Grace Gardens, The
5201 W 143rd St (66224-9562)
PHONE..................................913 685-4800
Donnie Simpson, *Pastor*
Kathy Wilcox, *Director*
EMP: 50
SALES: 524.6K **Privately Held**
SIC: 8322 Old age assistance

(G-11151)
BAR CODE SYSTEMS
12230 Santa Fe Trail Dr (66215-3522)
P.O. Box 400, Olathe (66051-0400)
PHONE..................................913 894-6368
EMP: 15
SQ FT: 35,000
SALES (est): 1.5MM **Privately Held**
SIC: 5046 7389 Whol Commercial Equipment Business Services

(G-11152)
BARNDS BROTHERS INC
Also Called: Barnds Brothers Lawn & Garden
10000 W 135th St (66221-9737)
P.O. Box 26385 (66225-6385)
PHONE..................................913 897-2340
Ronald C Barnds, *President*
Doris G Barnds, *Treasurer*
EMP: 35 **EST:** 1978
SQ FT: 67,000
SALES (est): 3.3MM **Privately Held**
SIC: 6531 0782 0781 1711 Real estate managers; lawn services; landscape planning services; mechanical contractor

(G-11153)
BARRINGTON PARK TOWN HOMES
10963 Richards Ct (66210-3751)
PHONE..................................913 469-5449
Kate Hankins, *Manager*
EMP: 10
SALES (est): 915.6K **Privately Held**
SIC: 6513 Apartment building operators

(G-11154)
BAYER HEALTHCARE LLC
Also Called: Animal Health Division
12707 Shwnee Mission Pkwy
(66216-1846)
P.O. Box 390 (66201-0390)
PHONE..................................913 268-2000
Paul Moore, *Manager*
Mark Althoff, *Manager*
Marjaana Tapio, *Director*
EMP: 25
SALES (corp-wide): 43.9B **Privately Held**
SIC: 4225 3841 2834 General warehousing & storage; surgical & medical instruments; pharmaceutical preparations
HQ: Bayer Healthcare Llc
100 Bayer Blvd
Whippany NJ 07981
862 404-3000

(G-11155)
BEACON SALES ACQUISITION INC
6000 Merriam Dr (66203-3100)
PHONE..................................913 262-7663
James Carnes, *Manager*
EMP: 62
SALES (corp-wide): 7.1B **Publicly Held**
WEB: www.shelterdistribution.com
SIC: 5033 5211 5031 Roofing & siding materials; roofing material; lumber, plywood & millwork
HQ: Beacon Sales Acquisition, Inc.
50 Webster Ave
Somerville MA 02143
877 645-7663

(G-11156)
BEAUTY BRANDS LLC
15501 W 99th St (66219-1254)
PHONE..................................913 227-0797
Greg Vandergriff, *Manager*
EMP: 19 **Privately Held**
WEB: www.beautybrands.com
SIC: 7319 Distribution of advertising material or sample services
PA: Beauty Brands Llc
15507 W 99th St
Lenexa KS 66219

(G-11157)
BEAUTY BRANDS LLC
Also Called: Beauty Brnds Slon Spa Sprstres
7501 W 119th St (66213-1107)
PHONE..................................913 663-4848
Kathy Brosseau, *Branch Mgr*
EMP: 40 **Privately Held**
SIC: 5999 7231 Cosmetics; manicurist, pedicurist
PA: Beauty Brands Llc
15507 W 99th St
Lenexa KS 66219

(G-11158)
BELGER CARTAGE SERVICE INC
Also Called: Belger Cartage Co
9805 Alden St (66215-1130)
PHONE..................................913 541-9100
Sharon Morrison, *Manager*
EMP: 25
SALES (corp-wide): 49.5MM **Privately Held**
SIC: 1796 Installing building equipment
HQ: Belger Cartage Service, Inc.
2100 Walnut St
Kansas City MO 64108
816 474-3250

(G-11159)
BENCHMARK REHABILITATION PARTN
6640 Johnson Dr (66202-2617)
PHONE..................................913 384-5810
EMP: 69 **Privately Held**
SIC: 7389 Personal service agents, brokers & bureaus
PA: Benchmark Rehabilitation Partners, Llc
1200 Corporate Dr Ste 400
Birmingham AL 35242

(G-11160)
BENEDICTINE HEALTH SYSTEM
Also Called: Villa Saint Joseph
11901 Rosewood St (66209-3533)
PHONE..................................913 498-2700
Petrick Gates, *Branch Mgr*
EMP: 109
SALES (corp-wide): 272.2MM **Privately Held**
SIC: 8059 Personal care home, with health care
PA: Benedictine Health System
4560 Norway Pines Pl
Duluth MN 55811
218 786-2370

(G-11161)
BENEFICIAL KANSAS INC (DH)
14207 W 95th St (66215-5208)
PHONE..................................913 492-1383
Steve Hill, *General Mgr*
Rex E Rudy, *Vice Pres*
EMP: 22
SALES (est): 33.8MM
SALES (corp-wide): 87.7B **Privately Held**
SIC: 6141 Consumer finance companies
HQ: Hsbc Finance Corporation
1421 W Shure Dr Ste 100
Arlington Heights IL 60004
224 880-7000

(G-11162)
BICKFORD OVERLAND PARK LLC
10665 Barkley St (66212-1848)
PHONE..................................913 782-3200
Mike EBY, *Principal*
Cora Webster, *Director*
EMP: 50
SALES (est): 1.4MM **Privately Held**
SIC: 8361 Home for the aged

(G-11163)
BIG BOBS OUTLETS KANSAS CY INC (PA)
Also Called: Big Bobs U Crpt Shops Kans Cy
10001 W 75th St (66204-2220)
PHONE..................................913 362-2627
Adam Elyachar, *President*
David Elyachar, *Chairman*
Andrea Elyachar, *Vice Pres*
EMP: 18
SQ FT: 21,000
SALES (est): 3.5MM **Privately Held**
SIC: 5713 6794 Floor covering stores; franchises, selling or licensing

(G-11164)
BIG SKY DISTRIBUTORS KANS LLC
1900 W 142nd St (66224-4502)
PHONE..................................913 897-4488
Joe Montana,
Tim Pettit,
Robert Weingarten,
EMP: 105
SQ FT: 60,000
SALES (est): 8.7MM **Privately Held**
SIC: 5181 Beer & other fermented malt liquors

(G-11165)
BIJIN FOR HAIR
Also Called: Bijin Salon & Day Spa
6960 Mission Rd Ste 18 (66208-2609)
PHONE..................................913 671-7777
Connie Suss, *Partner*
Mary Jane Vandecassle, *Partner*
Alison Shelby, *Opers Staff*
Brent Thompson, *Opers Staff*
Cheyenne Rufer, *Manager*
EMP: 52
SALES (est): 1.8MM **Privately Held**
WEB: www.bijinsalonanddayspa.com
SIC: 7231 Hairdressers

(G-11166)
BILLS FLOOR COVERING INC
14316 W 99th St (66215-1102)
PHONE..................................913 492-1964
William J Ricci, *President*
Darla D Ricci, *Admin Sec*
EMP: 15 **EST:** 1971
SQ FT: 2,700
SALES (est): 1.6MM **Privately Held**
SIC: 1752 Carpet laying; linoleum installation; wood floor installation & refinishing; vinyl floor tile & sheet installation

(G-11167)
BITUMINOUS CASUALTY CORP
6718 Hauser Dr (66216-2425)
PHONE..................................913 268-9176
Richard Weekly, *Principal*
EMP: 27
SALES (corp-wide): 6B **Publicly Held**
SIC: 6331 Fire, marine & casualty insurance
HQ: Bituminous Casualty Corporation
3700 Market Square Cir
Davenport IA 52807
309 786-5401

(G-11168)
BLACKMORE AND GLUNT INC
13835 W 107th St (66215-2086)
PHONE..................................913 469-5715
Kent W Mowe, *Sales/Mktg Mgr*
EMP: 12
SQ FT: 12,000
SALES (corp-wide): 17.4MM **Privately Held**
SIC: 5084 3443 5064 Heat exchange equipment, industrial; heat exchangers, condensers & components; electrical appliances, television & radio
PA: Blackmore And Glunt, Inc.
12 Kimler Dr
Maryland Heights MO 63043
314 878-4313

(G-11169)
BLOCKBUSTER LLC
13630 W 87th Street Pkwy (66215-4509)
PHONE..................................913 438-3203
Fax: 913 438-3187
EMP: 10
SALES (corp-wide): 14.2B **Publicly Held**
SIC: 7841 Video Disk/Tape Rent
HQ: Blockbuster Llc
9601 S Meridian Blvd
Englewood CO 80112
866 692-2789

(G-11170)
BLUE VALLEY GOODYEAR SERVICE
6717 W 119th St (66209-2013)
PHONE..................................913 345-1380
William H Oades, *President*
William Oades, *Site Mgr*
EMP: 14
SQ FT: 10,000
SALES (est): 2MM **Privately Held**
SIC: 5531 7539 Automotive tires; automotive repair shops

▲ = Import ▼=Export
◆ =Import/Export

(G-11171)
BLUE VALLEY RECREATION COMM
9701 W 137th St (66221-2000)
PHONE..................................913 685-6030
Dawn Grosdidier, *Branch Mgr*
EMP: 40
SALES (corp-wide): 14.6MM **Privately Held**
SIC: 7999 Recreation services
PA: Blue Valley Recreation Commission
6545 W 151st St
Overland Park KS
913 685-6000

(G-11172)
BLUEPARL VTRINARY PARTNERS LLC
Also Called: Emergency Veterinary Clinic
11950 W 110th St Ste B (66210-4011)
PHONE..................................913 642-9563
Jeff Dennis, *Mng Member*
Betsy Reichenberg, *Practice Mgr*
Catherine A Popovitch, *Surgeon*
Jeffrey S Dennis,
EMP: 50
SQ FT: 48,000
SALES (est): 3.2MM **Privately Held**
SIC: 0742 Veterinarian, animal specialties; animal hospital services, pets & other animal specialties

(G-11173)
BNSF RAILWAY COMPANY
Also Called: Burlington Northern
13301 Santa Fe Trail Dr (66215-3687)
PHONE..................................913 888-5250
Greta Baker, *Manager*
EMP: 12
SALES (corp-wide): 225.3B **Publicly Held**
WEB: www.billpurdy.com
SIC: 4011 Railroads, line-haul operating
HQ: Bnsf Railway Company
2650 Lou Menk Dr
Fort Worth TX 76131
800 795-2673

(G-11174)
BNSF RAILWAY COMPANY
Also Called: Burlington Northern
12345 College Blvd (66210-1283)
PHONE..................................817 352-1000
Steve Weatherby, *Director*
EMP: 100
SALES (corp-wide): 225.3B **Publicly Held**
WEB: www.billpurdy.com
SIC: 4011 Railroads, line-haul operating
HQ: Bnsf Railway Company
2650 Lou Menk Dr
Fort Worth TX 76131
800 795-2673

(G-11175)
BOBEC INC
Also Called: Park Lanes Family Fun Center
7701 Renner Rd (66217-9414)
PHONE..................................913 248-1110
Robert Johannes, *President*
Becky Johannes, *Vice Pres*
EMP: 35
SALES (est): 1.8MM **Privately Held**
WEB: www.parklaneskc.com
SIC: 7933 Ten pin center

(G-11176)
BOTT COMMUNICATIONS INC (PA)
Also Called: Kccv
10550 Barkley St Ste 100 (66212-1824)
PHONE..................................913 642-7770
Richard Bott Sr, *President*
Sherley Bott, *Corp Secy*
Richard Bott II, *Exec VP*
EMP: 15 **EST:** 1947
SQ FT: 8,000
SALES: 14.2MM **Privately Held**
SIC: 4832 Radio broadcasting stations

(G-11177)
BRADFORD AND GALT INCORPORATED
Also Called: Bradford Galt Consulting Svcs
9200 Indian Creek Pkwy # 570
(66210-2017)
PHONE..................................913 663-1264
April Garlington, *Manager*
EMP: 30
SALES (corp-wide): 18.4MM **Privately Held**
WEB: www.bradfordandgalt.com
SIC: 7361 7374 Executive placement; data processing service
PA: Bradford And Galt, Incorporated
11457 Olde Cabin Rd # 200
Saint Louis MO 63141
314 997-4644

(G-11178)
BRADLEY KWAPISZESKI MD
8901 W 74th St Ste 285 (66204-2202)
PHONE..................................913 362-3210
Bradley R Kwapiszeski, *Principal*
EMP: 10 **EST:** 2001
SALES (est): 291.9K **Privately Held**
SIC: 8011 Ophthalmologist

(G-11179)
BRENNCO TRAVEL SERVICES INC
6600 College Blvd Ste 130 (66211-1610)
PHONE..................................913 660-0121
John C Brenneman, *President*
James C Brenneman, *President*
EMP: 15
SALES (est): 2.7MM **Privately Held**
WEB: www.brenncoagent.com
SIC: 4724 Travel agencies

(G-11180)
BRIDGESTONE RET OPERATIONS LLC
Also Called: Tires Plus Total Car Care
7601 W 119th St (66213-1105)
PHONE..................................913 498-0880
Danny Strother, *Manager*
EMP: 11 **Privately Held**
WEB: www.tiresplus.com
SIC: 7534 Tire retreading & repair shops
HQ: Bridgestone Retail Operations, Llc
333 E Lake St Ste 300
Bloomingdale IL 60108
630 259-9000

(G-11181)
BRIDGESTONE RET OPERATIONS LLC
Also Called: Firestone
12380 W 95th St (66215-3807)
PHONE..................................913 492-8160
Curtis Vestal, *Executive*
EMP: 17 **Privately Held**
WEB: www.bfis.com
SIC: 5531 7534 7539 Automotive tires; rebuilding & retreading tires; brake services
HQ: Bridgestone Retail Operations, Llc
333 E Lake St Ste 300
Bloomingdale IL 60108
630 259-9000

(G-11182)
BRILEYS DESIGNS & SIGNS
14842 Robinson St (66223-1246)
PHONE..................................913 579-7533
Scott Briley, *CEO*
EMP: 22
SALES (est): 1.2MM **Privately Held**
SIC: 2759 3993 Publication printing; signs & advertising specialties

(G-11183)
BROOKDALE SENIOR LIVING COMMUN
Also Called: Vintage Park
8710 Caenen Lake Rd (66215-2069)
PHONE..................................913 894-6979
D J Brown, *Manager*
EMP: 20
SALES (corp-wide): 4.5B **Publicly Held**
WEB: www.assisted.com
SIC: 8051 Skilled nursing care facilities
HQ: Brookdale Senior Living Communities, Inc.
6737 W Wa St Ste 2300
Milwaukee WI 53214
414 918-5000

(G-11184)
BROOKDALE SNIOR LVING CMMNTIES
Also Called: Clare Bridge of Overland Park
11000 Oakmont St (66210-1100)
PHONE..................................913 491-1144
Jennifer Cazers, *Director*
EMP: 60
SALES (corp-wide): 4.5B **Publicly Held**
WEB: www.assisted.com
SIC: 8059 8051 Rest home, with health care; extended care facility
HQ: Brookdale Senior Living Communities, Inc.
6737 W Wa St Ste 2300
Milwaukee WI 53214
414 918-5000

(G-11185)
BROOKRIDGE DAY SCHOOL (PA)
Also Called: Brookridge Day School
9555 Hadley Dr (66212-3392)
PHONE..................................913 649-2228
Richard Savage, *President*
Pandora Thacker, *Opers Staff*
Dr Carol J Savage, *Treasurer*
Kim Binder, *Teacher*
Donya Booth, *Teacher*
EMP: 35
SQ FT: 4,000
SALES (est): 3.7MM **Privately Held**
WEB: www.dayschools.com
SIC: 8211 8351 Private elementary school; child day care services

(G-11186)
BROOKRIDGE GOLF & COUNTRY CLUB (PA)
Also Called: Brookridge Swimming Pool
8223 W 103rd St (66212-4359)
PHONE..................................913 648-1600
Judi Renzi, *General Mgr*
EMP: 10
SQ FT: 21,500
SALES: 2.7MM **Privately Held**
SIC: 7997 Country club, membership

(G-11187)
BRUNNER ELECTRIC INC
5730 Reeder St (66203-2868)
P.O. Box 3293 (66203-0293)
PHONE..................................913 268-5463
James M Brunner, *President*
Christopher Lee Brunner, *Vice Pres*
Paula Brunner, *Admin Sec*
EMP: 11
SQ FT: 1,800
SALES: 730K **Privately Held**
SIC: 1731 General electrical contractor

(G-11188)
BUBBLE RM COIN LDRY DRY CLEAN
Also Called: Little Laundrymat
7735 Quivira Rd (66216-3405)
PHONE..................................913 962-4046
Katherine Haughney, *Owner*
EMP: 18
SALES (est): 321.5K **Privately Held**
SIC: 7215 Laundry, coin-operated

(G-11189)
BUFFALO BALANCED FUND INC
5420 W 61st Pl (66205-3001)
PHONE..................................913 677-7778
John C Kornitzer, *Principal*
John Kornitzer, *Principal*
EMP: 11
SALES (est): 1.5MM **Privately Held**
SIC: 6722 Money market mutual funds

(G-11190)
BUFFALO FUNDS
5420 W 61st Pl (66205-3001)
PHONE..................................913 677-7778
John Kornitzer, *President*
Denise Minet, *Opers Staff*
Barry Koster, *CFO*
Paul Dlugosch, *Portfolio Mgr*
Jeffrey Sitzmann, *Portfolio Mgr*
EMP: 41
SALES (est): 5MM **Privately Held**
WEB: www.buffalofunds.com
SIC: 6722 Money market mutual funds

(G-11191)
BUILDING BLOCKS CHILD DEV CTR
15215 College Blvd (66219-1357)
PHONE..................................913 888-7244
Khristi Kramer, *President*
EMP: 20 **EST:** 1997
SALES (est): 391.7K **Privately Held**
WEB: www.buildingblockscdc.com
SIC: 8351 Group day care center

(G-11192)
BUTLER ENTERPRISES INC
Also Called: Butler's C-D Collision/Repair
5747 Kessler Ln (66203-2517)
PHONE..................................913 262-9109
Ronald M Butler, *President*
▲ **EMP:** 11
SQ FT: 6,000
SALES (est): 1.6MM **Privately Held**
SIC: 7532 5521 Body shop, automotive; automobiles, used cars only

(G-11193)
C & H HEALTH LLC
Also Called: SHARON LANE NURSING HOME
10315 Johnson Dr (66203-3065)
PHONE..................................913 631-8200
Harry Braum, *President*
Angela Moore, *Admin Asst*
EMP: 75
SALES: 5.5MM **Privately Held**
SIC: 8051 Convalescent home with continuous nursing care

(G-11194)
C & O ELEC SALES CO INC
10201 W 105th St (66212-5751)
PHONE..................................913 981-0008
Douglas Carlson, *President*
Doug McGough, *Vice Pres*
Very Rev Kevin O O'Niell, *Vice Pres*
Jim Stanker, *Vice Pres*
Mark Bishop, *Sales Staff*
EMP: 14
SALES (est): 3.6MM **Privately Held**
WEB: www.candoelec.com
SIC: 5063 Electrical supplies

(G-11195)
C & R MFG INC
6790 Martindale Rd (66218-9640)
PHONE..................................913 441-4120
Ronald J Wosel, *President*
Cynthia Wosel, *Corp Secy*
Steve Messick, *Purchasing*
EMP: 18
SQ FT: 32,000
SALES: 4.6MM **Privately Held**
WEB: www.c-rmfg.com
SIC: 3599 Machine shop, jobbing & repair

(G-11196)
C & W OPERATIONS LTD (PA)
Also Called: Fantastic Sams
9108 Barton St (66214-1719)
PHONE..................................913 438-6400
James Copeland, *President*
EMP: 120
SQ FT: 5,700
SALES (est): 1.7MM **Privately Held**
WEB: www.fscw.com
SIC: 7231 5122 Unisex hair salons; hair preparations

(G-11197)
C & W OPERATIONS LTD
Also Called: Fantastic Sams
7407 Quivira Rd (66216-3525)
PHONE..................................913 268-1032
Joy Renolds, *Office Mgr*
EMP: 12
SALES (est): 215.1K
SALES (corp-wide): 1.7MM **Privately Held**
WEB: www.fscw.com
SIC: 7231 Unisex hair salons

PA: C & W Operations, Ltd.
9108 Barton St
Shawnee Mission KS 66214
913 438-6400

(G-11198)
C L NATIONWIDE INC
9290 Bond St Ste 203 (66214-1729)
PHONE..................................913 492-5200
Len Lamourie, *President*
Linda Lowe, *Opers Staff*
Chris McCune,
EMP: 13
SQ FT: 1,274
SALES (est): 5.5MM **Privately Held**
WEB: www.clnationwide.net
SIC: 4731 Truck transportation brokers

(G-11199)
CAHILL BUSINESS SERVICES LLC
Also Called: CBS
10003 W 120th St (66213-1648)
PHONE..................................913 515-8398
Dan Cahill, *Mng Member*
EMP: 10
SALES: 600K **Privately Held**
SIC: 7331 Direct mail advertising services

(G-11200)
CAMELOT COURT ANIMAL CLINIC
4320 W 119th St (66209-1549)
PHONE..................................913 469-9330
Donald Dinges, *Owner*
Paula Kowalski,
Megan Balcom, *Receptionist*
EMP: 15
SQ FT: 1,860
SALES (est): 571.9K **Privately Held**
WEB: www.camelotcourtac.com
SIC: 0742 0752 Animal hospital services, pets & other animal specialties; veterinarian, animal specialties; boarding services, kennels

(G-11201)
CAR WASH CENTER OF MISSION INC
5960 Barkley St (66202-3269)
P.O. Box 2512 (66201-2512)
PHONE..................................913 236-6886
Kelly Smith, *President*
Jim Pair, *Manager*
EMP: 19
SALES: 750K **Privately Held**
SIC: 7542 Washing & polishing, automotive

(G-11202)
CARDINAL HEALTH INC
Also Called: Enturia
11400 Tomahawk Crk Pkwy # 310 (66211-2724)
PHONE..................................800 523-0502
Jim Mitchum, *Manager*
EMP: 70
SALES (corp-wide): 145.5B **Publicly Held**
SIC: 3841 Surgical & medical instruments
PA: Cardinal Health, Inc.
7000 Cardinal Pl
Dublin OH 43017
614 757-5000

(G-11203)
CARDIOVASCULAR CONSULTANTS INC
12300 Metcalf Ave 280 (66213-1324)
PHONE..................................913 491-1000
Randall C Thompson, *Branch Mgr*
Timothy Bateman, *Med Doctor*
EMP: 25
SALES (corp-wide): 21MM **Privately Held**
WEB: www.cc-pc.com
SIC: 8011 Cardiologist & cardio-vascular specialist
PA: Cardiovascular Consultants, Inc.
4330 Wornall Rd Ste 2000
Kansas City MO 64111
816 303-3292

(G-11204)
CARGILL INCORPORATED
5200 Metcalf Ave Ste 250 (66202-1214)
PHONE..................................806 659-3554
Chuck Thorn, *Vice Pres*
Walt Deesley, *Manager*
EMP: 12
SALES (corp-wide): 113.4B **Privately Held**
WEB: www.cargill.com
SIC: 5153 Grain elevators
PA: Cargill, Incorporated
15407 Mcginty Rd W
Wayzata MN 55391
952 742-7575

(G-11205)
CAT CALLS
9621 W 87th St (66212-4570)
PHONE..................................913 642-2024
Bruce Freeman, *Owner*
EMP: 15
SALES (est): 214K **Privately Held**
SIC: 0742 Veterinarian, animal specialties

(G-11206)
CATHOLIC CHARITIES
Also Called: Catholic Community Services
9700 W 87th St (66212-4563)
PHONE..................................913 433-2061
EMP: 28
SALES (est): 969K **Privately Held**
SIC: 8322 Individual/Family Services

(G-11207)
CBIZ ACCOUNTING TAX & ADVISOR
11440 Tomahawk Creek Pkwy (66211-2672)
PHONE..................................913 234-1932
EMP: 13
SALES (est): 1MM **Publicly Held**
SIC: 8721 Accounting/Auditing/Bookkeeping
PA: Cbiz, Inc.
6050 Oak Tree Blvd # 500
Cleveland OH 44131

(G-11208)
CBIZ MED MGT PROFESSIONALS INC
10100 Santa Fe Ln Ste 100 (66212-4628)
PHONE..................................913 652-1899
Laura Olvera, *Principal*
EMP: 15
SALES (corp-wide): 144.1MM **Privately Held**
WEB: www.llms.net
SIC: 8721 Billing & bookkeeping service
HQ: Cbiz Medical Management Professionals, Inc.
5959 Shallowford Rd # 575
Chattanooga TN 37421

(G-11209)
CC SERVICES INC
14867 W 95th St (66215-5220)
PHONE..................................913 894-0700
Rick Lowe, *Branch Mgr*
EMP: 15
SALES (corp-wide): 49.9MM **Privately Held**
SIC: 6411 Insurance agents, brokers & service
HQ: Cc Services, Inc.
1711 General Electric Rd
Bloomington IL 61704
309 821-3372

(G-11210)
CENTER FOR WOMAN HEALTH
Also Called: Woman's Choice A
4840 College Blvd (66211-1601)
PHONE..................................913 491-6878
Andy Hodes, *Exec VP*
Cindy Brown, *Office Mgr*
EMP: 11
SALES (est): 1.5MM **Privately Held**
SIC: 8011 Obstetrician; gynecologist

(G-11211)
CENTRAL BANK OF MIDWEST
6114 Nieman Rd (66203-2940)
PHONE..................................913 791-9288
Jane Vallier, *Branch Mgr*
EMP: 82
SALES (corp-wide): 4.1MM **Privately Held**
SIC: 6022 State trust companies accepting deposits, commercial
PA: Central Bank Of The Midwest
609 Ne State Route 291
Lees Summit MO 64086
816 525-5754

(G-11212)
CENTRAL BIOMEDIA INC (PA)
9900 Pflumm Rd Ste 63 (66215-1231)
PHONE..................................913 541-0090
William G Skelly, *President*
Don Myers, *Vice Pres*
Ryan Anderson, *Purch Agent*
Mary Rix, *Controller*
EMP: 22
SALES (est): 3.4MM **Privately Held**
SIC: 2836 Veterinary biological products

(G-11213)
CENTURY CONCRETE INC (DH)
Also Called: Century Ready-Mix
11011 Cody St Ste 300 (66210-1430)
PHONE..................................913 451-8900
Allan Emby, *President*
Charles T Sunderland, *Vice Pres*
Robert Henning, *Treasurer*
Lanny Kern, *Sales Mgr*
Eileen Sollars, *Admin Sec*
EMP: 33
SQ FT: 4,000
SALES (est): 17.4MM
SALES (corp-wide): 29.7B **Privately Held**
SIC: 3273 Ready-mixed concrete
HQ: Ash Grove Materials Corporation
11011 Cody St Ste 300
Overland Park KS 66210
913 345-2030

(G-11214)
CEO ENTERPRISES INC (PA)
Also Called: Shawnee Storm Water Hardware
6124 Merriam Dr (66203-3256)
PHONE..................................913 432-8046
Carl E Orser, *President*
William Orser, *Shareholder*
EMP: 13
SQ FT: 20,000
SALES (est): 2.1MM **Privately Held**
SIC: 3441 1791 7692 Fabricated structural metal; structural steel erection; welding repair

(G-11215)
CHALLENGER FENCE CO INC
20201 W 55th St Ste B (66218-9307)
P.O. Box 482, Basehor (66007-0482)
PHONE..................................913 432-3535
Larry Schmidt, *President*
Ty Martin, *Manager*
EMP: 10
SALES: 1.5MM **Privately Held**
WEB: www.challengerfence.com
SIC: 1799 Fence construction

(G-11216)
CHANCE PURINTON AND MILLS LLC
6900 College Blvd Ste 350 (66211-1578)
PHONE..................................913 491-8200
Robert M Purinton,
Craig Chance,
EMP: 11
SALES (est): 767.6K **Privately Held**
WEB: www.pcmcpa.com
SIC: 8721 Certified public accountant

(G-11217)
CHARLES L BRROKS MD
6850 Hilltop Rd Ste 170 (66226-3562)
PHONE..................................913 248-8008
Charles L Brooks MD, *Owner*
EMP: 10
SQ FT: 6,900
SALES (est): 344.6K **Privately Held**
SIC: 8011 General & family practice, physician/surgeon

(G-11218)
CHEROKEE CAT CLINIC
9620 Antioch Rd (66212-4060)
PHONE..................................913 649-0446
Mike Stenstrom, *President*
James Kontras, *Owner*
EMP: 20 **EST:** 1995
SALES (est): 620K **Privately Held**
SIC: 0752 0742 Grooming services, pet & animal specialties; veterinarian, animal specialties

(G-11219)
CHICAGO TITLE INSURANCE CO
1900 W 75th St Lowr Ll20 (66208-3517)
PHONE..................................913 385-9307
Vicky Went, *Manager*
Naomi Shupp, *Officer*
EMP: 11
SALES (corp-wide): 7.5B **Publicly Held**
SIC: 6361 Title insurance
HQ: Chicago Title Insurance Company
601 Riverside Ave
Jacksonville FL 32204

(G-11220)
CHILDRENS MERCY HOSPITAL
Also Called: Childrens Mercy Specialty Ctr
5520 College Blvd Ste 415 (66211-1659)
PHONE..................................913 696-5767
EMP: 30
SALES (corp-wide): 826.4MM **Privately Held**
SIC: 8062 General medical & surgical hospitals
PA: Mercy Children's Hospital
2401 Gillham Rd
Kansas City MO 64108
816 234-3000

(G-11221)
CHILDRENS MERCY HOSPITAL
Also Called: Children's Home Care
1900 W 47th Pl Ste 250 (66205-1888)
PHONE..................................913 696-8000
Adam Zorn, *Engineer*
Pete Delripa, *Manager*
EMP: 100
SALES (corp-wide): 826.4MM **Privately Held**
SIC: 8082 8062 3663 8069 Home health care services; general medical & surgical hospitals; radio & TV communications equipment; specialty hospitals, except psychiatric
PA: Mercy Children's Hospital
2401 Gillham Rd
Kansas City MO 64108
816 234-3000

(G-11222)
CHRIS-LEEF GENERAL AGENCY INC
11503 W 75th St Ste 100 (66214-1359)
P.O. Box 3747 (66203-0747)
PHONE..................................913 631-1232
Gary Peterson, *President*
Glenda Dowell, *Vice Pres*
Chris Peterson, *Vice Pres*
Kelly Dale, *Treasurer*
Lyn Bower-Felber, *Broker*
EMP: 20
SQ FT: 1,600
SALES (est): 4.8MM **Privately Held**
WEB: www.chrisleef.com
SIC: 6411 Insurance brokers

(G-11223)
CHRISTOPHER B GEHA
Also Called: Word Park Services
8800 State Line Rd (66206-1553)
PHONE..................................913 383-9099
Christopher B Geha DDS, *Owner*
EMP: 20 **EST:** 2001
SALES (est): 472.8K **Privately Held**
SIC: 8011 Neurologist

(G-11224)
CHUBB US HOLDING INC
Also Called: Ace USA
7007 College Blvd Ste 600 (66211-2415)
P.O. Box 419310, Kansas City MO (64141)
PHONE..................................913 491-2000
Bret Spicer, *President*
Cindi Rollins, *Opers Mgr*
Brad Stark, *Branch Mgr*
EMP: 75
SALES (corp-wide): 32.7B **Privately Held**
WEB: www.ace.bm
SIC: 6411 Insurance agents, brokers & service

HQ: Chubb Us Holding Inc.
1601 Chestnut St
Philadelphia PA 19192

(G-11225)
CIENA CORPORATION
13220 Metcalf Ave Ste 200 (66213-2822)
PHONE..................................913 402-4800
Tony Tappan, *Manager*
EMP: 8 **Publicly Held**
WEB: www.ciena.com
SIC: 3661 Fiber optics communications equipment
PA: Ciena Corporation
7035 Ridge Rd
Hanover MD 21076

(G-11226)
CINEMARK USA INC
Also Called: Cinemark Cinema 20
5500 Antioch Rd (66202-2011)
PHONE..................................913 789-7038
Richard Hildebrand, *Manager*
EMP: 125 **Publicly Held**
SIC: 7832 Motion picture theaters, except drive-in
HQ: Cinemark Usa, Inc.
3900 Dallas Pkwy Ste 500
Plano TX 75093
972 665-1000

(G-11227)
CISCO SYSTEMS INC
7400 College Blvd Ste 400 (66210-4017)
PHONE..................................913 344-6100
Joseph A Lorino, *Principal*
Ambrose Mariachinnappan, *Engineer*
Lee Posz, *Engineer*
Jake Butterbaugh, *Manager*
EMP: 100
SALES (corp-wide): 51.9B **Publicly Held**
WEB: www.cisco.com
SIC: 3577 5045 Computer peripheral equipment; computers, peripherals & software
PA: Cisco Systems, Inc.
170 W Tasman Dr
San Jose CA 95134
408 526-4000

(G-11228)
CITY OF LEAWOOD
Also Called: Iron Horse Golf Club
15400 Mission Rd (66224-9526)
PHONE..................................913 685-4550
Amy Adent, *Sales Staff*
Dennis Coplen, *Branch Mgr*
Paul Dunn, *Supervisor*
EMP: 75 **Privately Held**
SIC: 7992 9111 7999 7299 Public golf courses; mayors' offices; golf services & professionals; banquet hall facilities
PA: Leawood, City Of (Inc)
4800 Town Center Dr
Leawood KS 66211
913 339-6700

(G-11229)
CITY OF MISSION
Also Called: Sylvester Powell Jr Cmnty Ctr
6200 Martway St (66202-3359)
PHONE..................................913 722-8200
Steve Corry, *Director*
EMP: 60 **Privately Held**
WEB: www.missionks.org
SIC: 8322 Community center
PA: City Of Mission
6090 Woodson St
Shawnee Mission KS 66202
913 676-8350

(G-11230)
CITY OF OVERLAND PARK
Also Called: Maintaince Shop
10515 W 135th St (66223)
PHONE..................................913 897-3806
Terry Rodenberg, *Branch Mgr*
EMP: 15 **Privately Held**
SIC: 7992 Public golf courses
PA: City Of Overland Park
8500 Santa Fe Dr
Overland Park KS 66212
913 895-6000

(G-11231)
CITY OF OVERLAND PARK
Also Called: Overland Park Police Dept
8500 Santa Fe Dr (66212-2866)
PHONE..................................913 895-6000
Larry Killer, *Engineer*
John Nachbar, *Branch Mgr*
Jack Messer, *Planning*
Amy Gross, *Analyst*
Robert J Watson,
EMP: 200 **Privately Held**
SIC: 9221 8611 ; business associations
PA: City Of Overland Park
8500 Santa Fe Dr
Overland Park KS 66212
913 895-6000

(G-11232)
CITY OF PRAIRIE VILLAGE
Also Called: Prairie Village Swimming Pool
7711 Delmar St (66208)
PHONE..................................913 642-6010
Joel Rios, *Manager*
EMP: 11 **Privately Held**
WEB: www.pvkansas.com
SIC: 7999 Swimming pool, non-membership
PA: City Of Prairie Village
7700 Mission Rd
Prairie Village KS 66208
913 381-6464

(G-11233)
CITY OF SHAWNEE
Also Called: Fire Station Headquarters
6501 Quivira Rd (66216-2746)
PHONE..................................913 631-1080
John Mattox, *Fire Chief*
Ryan Pyle, *Chief*
Jeff Hudson, *Manager*
EMP: 15 **Privately Held**
WEB: www.cityofshawnee.org
SIC: 3699 9111 Fire control or bombing equipment, electronic; executive offices
PA: City Of Shawnee
11110 Johnson Dr
Shawnee KS 66203
913 631-2500

(G-11234)
CITYWIDE ELECTRIC INC
5911 Barton Dr (66203-2739)
PHONE..................................913 631-1189
Jeff Stoneburner, *President*
Elizabeth Stoneburner, *Vice Pres*
Amy Stapp, *Executive Asst*
EMP: 20
SALES (est): 4MM **Privately Held**
WEB: www.cweinc.net
SIC: 1731 General electrical contractor

(G-11235)
CJD & ASSOCIATES LLC (PA)
Also Called: Davidson-Babcock
10875 Benson Dr Ste 110 (66210-1531)
PHONE..................................913 469-1188
Michael Hess, *President*
Colin Davidson, *Vice Pres*
EMP: 19
SALES (est): 8.2MM **Privately Held**
SIC: 6411 Insurance brokers

(G-11236)
CLAIM SOLUTION INC
8900 Indian Creek Pkwy # 450 (66210-1554)
PHONE..................................913 322-2300
Mark Snow, *President*
Troy Rader, *President*
Chris Snow, *Vice Pres*
Christine Snow, *Chief Mktg Ofcr*
EMP: 34 **EST:** 1995
SALES (est): 2MM **Privately Held**
WEB: www.claimsolution.com
SIC: 7389 6411 Appraisers, except real estate; insurance agents, brokers & service

(G-11237)
CLARIOS
Also Called: Johnson Controls
9850 Legler Rd (66219-1263)
PHONE..................................913 307-4200
Gunther Dziuzenis, *Manager*
EMP: 100 **Privately Held**
SIC: 5075 1731 Thermostats; electrical work
HQ: Johnson Controls Inc
5757 N Green Bay Ave
Milwaukee WI 53209
414 524-1200

(G-11238)
CLASSONE SOFTWARE
6316 Riley St (66202-3954)
PHONE..................................913 831-4976
Gregg M Haywood, *Principal*
EMP: 5
SALES (est): 483.6K **Privately Held**
SIC: 7372 Prepackaged software

(G-11239)
CLEVLUN ENTERPRISES INC
Also Called: Shawnee Cycle Plaza
13020 Shawnee Mission Pkwy (66216-1853)
PHONE..................................913 631-1111
Barry Bunner, *President*
EMP: 19
SQ FT: 14,000
SALES (est): 5.3MM **Privately Held**
WEB: www.shawneecycleplaza.com
SIC: 5571 7699 Motorcycles; motorcycle parts & accessories; motorcycle repair service

(G-11240)
CLOVERLEAF OFFICE PARK
Also Called: Cloverleaf Buildings
6811 Shwn Mssn Pkwy 104 (66202)
PHONE..................................913 831-3200
Tana Moore, *Partner*
EMP: 10 **EST:** 1944
SQ FT: 450,000
SALES (est): 1.7MM **Privately Held**
WEB: www.cloverleafofficepark.com
SIC: 6512 Commercial & industrial building operation

(G-11241)
CLUNE & COMPANY LC (PA)
5950 Roe Ave (66205-3050)
PHONE..................................913 498-3000
Kevin Clune, *CEO*
Mary K Clune,
EMP: 43
SQ FT: 3,200
SALES (est): 11.4MM **Privately Held**
WEB: www.clune.net
SIC: 6159 Equipment & vehicle finance leasing companies

(G-11242)
CLUNE & COMPANY LC
Clune Equipment Leasing
5950 Roe Ave (66205-3050)
PHONE..................................913 498-3000
Kevin Clune, *Branch Mgr*
EMP: 16 **Privately Held**
SIC: 7359 Equipment rental & leasing
PA: Clune & Company Lc
5950 Roe Ave
Shawnee Mission KS 66205

(G-11243)
COCA-COLA REFRESHMENTS USA INC
9000 Marshall Dr (66215-3842)
P.O. Box 500 (66201-0500)
PHONE..................................913 492-8100
Andrew Heenan, *Vice Pres*
EMP: 310
SALES (corp-wide): 31.8B **Publicly Held**
WEB: www.cokecce.com
SIC: 2086 5149 Bottled & canned soft drinks; soft drinks
HQ: Coca-Cola Refreshments Usa, Inc.
2500 Windy Ridge Pkwy Se
Atlanta GA 30339
770 989-3000

(G-11244)
COKINGTIN EYE CENTER PA (PA)
5520 College Blvd Ste 201 (66211-1658)
PHONE..................................913 491-3737
Clifton D Cokingtin, *Principal*
Chris Balestrieri, *Manager*
Clifton Cokingtin, *Director*
EMP: 65
SALES (est): 4.7MM **Privately Held**
SIC: 8011 5999 Ophthalmologist; medical apparatus & supplies

(G-11245)
COLDWELL BANKER REGAN REALTORS
11800 Shawnee Mission Pkw (66203-3367)
PHONE..................................913 631-2900
Patric Regan, *President*
Erin Cecil, *Sales Associate*
Patricia Regan, *Admin Sec*
EMP: 25
SQ FT: 1,200
SALES (est): 1.7MM **Privately Held**
WEB: www.coldwellbankerregan.com
SIC: 6531 Real estate agent, residential

(G-11246)
COLEMAN AMERICAN MVG SVCS INC (DH)
Also Called: Quality Movers Express of Kans
12905 Shawnee Mission Pkwy (66216-1850)
PHONE..................................913 631-1440
William Brakefield, *President*
Jeffrey Coleman, *Admin Sec*
EMP: 20 **EST:** 1964
SALES (est): 1.7MM **Privately Held**
SIC: 4214 Household goods moving & storage, local
HQ: Coleman American Companies, Inc
1 Eagle Ridge Dr
Midland City AL 36350
800 239-7700

(G-11247)
COLLEGE BLVD ANIMAL HOSP PA
Also Called: College Boulevard Animal Hosp
11733 College Blvd (66210-1398)
PHONE..................................913 469-5869
Gary Modrcin, *Partner*
Fred J Schroeder, *Partner*
EMP: 10
SALES (est): 362.9K **Privately Held**
SIC: 0742 0752 Animal hospital services, pets & other animal specialties; grooming services, pet & animal specialties

(G-11248)
COLLEGE PARK FMLY CARE CTR INC
Also Called: College Park Family Care Ctr
12210 W 87th Street Pkwy (66215-2812)
PHONE..................................913 438-6700
Richard Randolph, *Partner*
EMP: 30
SALES (corp-wide): 25.8MM **Privately Held**
SIC: 8011 Offices & clinics of medical doctors
PA: College Park Family Care Center Inc.
11725 W 112th St
Shawnee Mission KS 66210
913 469-5579

(G-11249)
COLLEGE PARK FMLY CARE CTR INC (PA)
11725 W 112th St (66210-2761)
PHONE..................................913 469-5579
Thomas Miller, *President*
Dr Mark Kahler, *Vice Pres*
David Dobratz, *Med Doctor*
Teri Grisham, *Med Doctor*
Kelly Henderson, *Med Doctor*
EMP: 115 **EST:** 1980
SQ FT: 21,000
SALES (est): 25.8MM **Privately Held**
SIC: 8011 Physicians' office, including specialists

(G-11250)
COLLEGE PARK FMLY CARE CTR INC
15101 Glenwood Ave (66223-3154)
PHONE..................................913 681-8866
Janean Gaa, *Branch Mgr*
Anne Kettler, *Dermatology*
EMP: 15

SALES (corp-wide): 25.8MM **Privately Held**
SIC: 8011 General & family practice, physician/surgeon
PA: College Park Family Care Center Inc.
11725 W 112th St
Shawnee Mission KS 66210
913 469-5579

(G-11251)
COLT ENERGY INC
6299 Nall Ave Ste 100 (66202-3547)
PHONE..................................913 236-0016
Nicolas Powell, *President*
EMP: 5
SALES (corp-wide): 9.6MM **Privately Held**
WEB: www.coltenergyinc.com
SIC: 1382 Oil & gas exploration services
PA: Colt Energy, Inc.
1112 Rhode Island Rd
Iola KS 66749
620 365-3111

(G-11252)
COMMERCE BANK
4050 W 83rd St (66208-5301)
PHONE..................................816 234-2000
David Schmidt, *General Mgr*
EMP: 13
SALES (corp-wide): 1.3B **Publicly Held**
SIC: 6022 State commercial banks
HQ: Commerce Bank
1000 Walnut St Fl 700
Kansas City MO 64106
816 234-2000

(G-11253)
COMMERCE BANK
4006 W 83rd St (66208-5301)
PHONE..................................816 234-2000
David Swinehart, *Manager*
EMP: 13
SALES (corp-wide): 1.3B **Publicly Held**
SIC: 6022 State commercial banks
HQ: Commerce Bank
1000 Walnut St Fl 700
Kansas City MO 64106
816 234-2000

(G-11254)
COMMUNITY WORKS INC
7819 Conser Pl (66204-2820)
PHONE..................................913 789-9900
Laura Boswell, *COO*
Madeline Giesler, *Program Mgr*
Janet Williams, *Director*
EMP: 150 **EST:** 1993
SALES (est): 3.4MM **Privately Held**
WEB: www.communityworksinc.com
SIC: 8082 Home health care services

(G-11255)
COMPANY KITCHEN LLC
8500 Shawnee Mission Pkwy
(66202-2967)
PHONE..................................913 384-4900
James Mitchell, *President*
June Staice, *Business Mgr*
Cory White, *Sales Staff*
Michael Kricsfeld, *Marketing Staff*
EMP: 24
SALES (est): 3.7MM **Privately Held**
SIC: 7375 Information retrieval services

(G-11256)
COMPLETE VIDEO PRODUCTION
12209 W 88th St (66215-4608)
PHONE..................................913 888-2383
Robert Fanning, *President*
Paula Fanning, *Vice Pres*
EMP: 10 **EST:** 1995
SQ FT: 2,000
SALES (est): 850.5K **Privately Held**
WEB: www.cvpproductions.com
SIC: 7812 Video tape production; video production

(G-11257)
COMPREHENSIVE WOMENS CARE
21624 Midland Dr (66218-9064)
PHONE..................................913 643-0075
Tracy Clark, *Principal*
Gordon Clark, *Med Doctor*
EMP: 14
SALES (est): 1MM **Privately Held**
SIC: 8011 Gynecologist

(G-11258)
CONCEPTS FOR BUSINESS LLC
8343 Melrose Dr (66214-1629)
PHONE..................................913 888-8686
Larry Morrissette, *Vice Pres*
John Archer,
EMP: 10 **EST:** 1998
SALES (est): 1.6MM **Privately Held**
WEB: www.conceptsforbusiness.com
SIC: 5046 Store equipment

(G-11259)
CONSOLIDATED CONTAINER CO LP
Also Called: Continental Plastic Container
11725 W 85th St (66214-1517)
PHONE..................................913 888-9494
Derek Hines, *Safety Mgr*
Greg Pedigo, *Opers-Prdtn-Mfg*
Cindy Waters, *Purch Agent*
EMP: 200
SALES (corp-wide): 14B **Publicly Held**
SIC: 3089 Plastic containers, except foam
HQ: Consolidated Container Company Lp
2500 Windy Ridge Pkwy Se # 1400
Atlanta GA 30339
678 742-4600

(G-11260)
CONSTRUCTION SYSTEMS INC
14611 W 62nd St (66216-1573)
PHONE..................................913 208-6401
Matt Hissong, *President*
EMP: 10
SALES: 500K **Privately Held**
SIC: 1521 Single-family housing construction

(G-11261)
CONSTRUCTION TECHNOLOGIES LLC
6800 W 64th St (66202-4100)
PHONE..................................913 671-3440
John Hinman, *Managing Dir*
Mark Fletcher, *CIO*
R Lee Harris,
David R Anderson,
Robert E Esrey,
EMP: 14
SQ FT: 15,000
SALES (est): 2.1MM **Privately Held**
WEB: www.constructiontechkc.com
SIC: 1521 Single-family housing construction

(G-11262)
CONSULTANTS IN NEUROLOGY PA
Also Called: Vernon D Rowe, MD
8550 Marshall Dr Ste 100 (66214-9836)
PHONE..................................913 894-1500
Vernon D Rowe MD, *President*
Elizabeth Rowe, *COO*
George Moreng MD, *Vice Pres*
Tammy Tubbs, *Manager*
Scott Hunter, *Info Tech Mgr*
EMP: 50
SALES (est): 3.5MM **Privately Held**
SIC: 8011 8071 8049 Neurologist; medical laboratories; physical therapist

(G-11263)
CONTINENTAL COAL INC
10801 Mastin St Ste 920 (66210-1673)
PHONE..................................913 491-1717
Philip E Tearney, *President*
William Moore III, *Admin Sec*
EMP: 26
SQ FT: 3,000
SALES (est): 5.5MM **Privately Held**
SIC: 1241 Coal mining exploration & test boring

(G-11264)
CONTROL SYSTEMS INTL INC (DH)
Also Called: Material Control Systems
8040 Nieman Rd (66214-1523)
PHONE..................................913 599-5010
Kevin McGlensy, *President*
James J Buri, *COO*
David P Fleming, *Vice Pres*
Robert W Lewis, *Vice Pres*
Therese Hinds, *Project Mgr*
EMP: 65 **EST:** 1968
SQ FT: 27,000
SALES (est): 28.5MM
SALES (corp-wide): 12.6B **Privately Held**
WEB: www.csiks.com
SIC: 7372 7373 5045 8711 Prepackaged software; computer integrated systems design; computer peripheral equipment; industrial engineers; management consulting services; relays & industrial controls
HQ: Fmc Technologies, Inc.
11740 Katy Fwy Enrgy Twr
Houston TX 77079
281 591-4000

(G-11265)
COOKBOOK PUBLISHERS INC
9900 Pflumm Rd Ste 17 (66215-1231)
PHONE..................................913 706-6069
Kevin L Derry, *Branch Mgr*
EMP: 65
SALES (corp-wide): 5.9MM **Privately Held**
WEB: www.cookbookpublishers.com
SIC: 4222 Cheese warehouse
PA: Cookbook Publishers, Inc.
11633 W 83rd Ter
Overland Park KS 66214
913 689-3038

(G-11266)
CORPORATE FLOORING INC
8018 Reeder St (66214-1554)
PHONE..................................913 859-9180
Michael Miller, *President*
Stacy Miller, *Vice Pres*
Blakeley Nauert, *Office Mgr*
EMP: 10
SALES (est): 1.3MM **Privately Held**
SIC: 1752 Floor laying & floor work

(G-11267)
CORRIDOR GROUP HOLDINGS LLC (PA)
6405 Metcalf Ave Ste 108 (66202-3928)
PHONE..................................913 362-0600
Des Varady, *CEO*
Robbin Boyatt, *Vice Pres*
Karl Dobrzelecki, *Vice Pres*
Leslie Niblock, *Marketing Staff*
Amanda Fletcher, *Manager*
EMP: 25 **EST:** 2007
SALES (est): 6.2MM **Privately Held**
SIC: 8742 Hospital & health services consultant

(G-11268)
COUNTRY CLUB BANK
9400 Mission Rd (66206-2042)
PHONE..................................816 931-4060
Byron Thompson, *Chairman*
Dan Teahan, *Vice Pres*
Kevin Clifford, *Invest Mgr*
Jan Wiedemann, *Advisor*
Mark Tranckino, *Representative*
EMP: 17
SALES (corp-wide): 38MM **Privately Held**
SIC: 6029 Commercial banks
HQ: Country Club Bank
1 Ward Pkwy
Kansas City MO 64112

(G-11269)
COUNTRY KIDS DAY CARE INC
8745 Bourgade St (66219-1441)
PHONE..................................913 888-9400
Linda Shay, *President*
L Inda Shay, *President*
EMP: 25
SALES (est): 1MM **Privately Held**
SIC: 8351 Group day care center

(G-11270)
COUNTY OF JOHNSON
Environmental Dept
4800 Nall Ave (66202-1710)
PHONE..................................913 432-3868
EMP: 11 **Privately Held**
SIC: 8734 9511 Environmental Laboratory
PA: County Of Johnson
111 S Cherry St Ste 1200
Olathe KS 66061
913 715-0435

(G-11271)
COUNTY OF JOHNSON
Also Called: Park & Recreation- Maint Sp
7700 Renner Rd (66217-9414)
PHONE..................................913 631-5208
Michael Meadors, *Director*
EMP: 10 **Privately Held**
WEB: www.jocoks.com
SIC: 7999 9512 Tourist attractions, amusement park concessions & rides; land, mineral & wildlife conservation;
PA: County Of Johnson
111 S Cherry St Ste 1200
Olathe KS 66061
913 715-0435

(G-11272)
COUNTY OF JOHNSON
Also Called: Parks & Recreation Dept
7900 Renner Rd (66219-9723)
PHONE..................................913 888-4713
Grant Evans, *Manager*
EMP: 150 **Privately Held**
WEB: www.jocoks.com
SIC: 7999 9512 Recreation services; recreational program administration, government;
PA: County Of Johnson
111 S Cherry St Ste 1200
Olathe KS 66061
913 715-0435

(G-11273)
COUNTY OF JOHNSON
Also Called: Parks & Recrection Dept
9301 W 73rd St (66204-1667)
PHONE..................................913 403-8069
Tom Richards, *Director*
EMP: 150 **Privately Held**
WEB: www.jocoks.com
SIC: 7999 9512 Gymnastic instruction, non-membership; recreational program administration, government;
PA: County Of Johnson
111 S Cherry St Ste 1200
Olathe KS 66061
913 715-0435

(G-11274)
COURTYARD BY MARRIOTT
11301 Metcalf Ave (66210-4013)
PHONE..................................913 339-9900
Jeff Miles, *Principal*
EMP: 17
SALES (est): 725.5K **Privately Held**
SIC: 7011 Hotels & motels

(G-11275)
COVANSYS CORPORATION
7701 College Blvd Fl 2 (66210-1991)
PHONE..................................913 469-8700
Larry Allen, *Info Tech Dir*
Pat Moidl, *Admin Asst*
EMP: 180
SALES (corp-wide): 20.7B **Publicly Held**
SIC: 7373 7374 Systems software development services; computer processing services
HQ: Csc Covansys Corporation
3170 Fairview Park Dr
Falls Church VA 22042
703 876-1000

(G-11276)
CPG COMMUNICATIONS GROUP LLC
Also Called: C P G
7300 W 110th St Ste 700 (66210-2332)
PHONE..................................913 317-2888
Georgia Clark, *President*
N M Paige, *Partner*
EMP: 6
SQ FT: 1,300
SALES (est): 477.6K **Privately Held**
SIC: 8743 2721 8742 Public relations services; magazines: publishing & printing; management consulting services

▲ = Import ▼=Export
◆ =Import/Export

(G-11277)
CRAWFORD & COMPANY
Also Called: Global Technical Services
12802 Pembrooke Cir (66209)
PHONE..................................913 909-4552
Dennis Rendina, *Branch Mgr*
EMP: 11
SALES (corp-wide): 1.1B **Publicly Held**
WEB: www.crawfordandcompany.com
SIC: 6411 Insurance adjusters
PA: Crawford & Company
5335 Triangle Pkwy Ofc C
Peachtree Corners GA 30092
404 300-1000

(G-11278)
CREDIT WORLD SERVICES INC
6000 Martway St (66202-3389)
PHONE..................................913 362-3950
Kelly Wilkinson, *President*
Shirley Chappel, *Vice Pres*
Kelli Lowe, *Manager*
EMP: 35
SQ FT: 4,500
SALES (est): 6MM **Privately Held**
WEB: www.creditworldservices.com
SIC: 7322 Collection agency, except real estate

(G-11279)
CREME DE LA CREME KANSAS INC
4600 W 115th St (66211-2676)
PHONE..................................913 451-0858
Bruce Karpas, *President*
EMP: 46
SQ FT: 20,000
SALES (est): 1.4MM
SALES (corp-wide): 15MM **Privately Held**
SIC: 8351 8211 Child day care services; elementary & secondary schools
PA: Creme De La Creme (Colorado), Inc.
8400 E Prentice Ave # 1320
Greenwood Village CO 80111
303 662-9150

(G-11280)
CRISP CUTS & STYLES ETCLLC
7625 Quivira Rd (66216-3503)
PHONE..................................816 916-1841
Robert Terry, *Mng Member*
EMP: 10 **EST:** 2007
SALES (est): 71.4K **Privately Held**
SIC: 7241 Barber shops

(G-11281)
CRITICAL CARE SYSTEMS INTL INC
Also Called: Shawnee Mission Wound Care Ctr
9100 W 74th St (66204-4004)
PHONE..................................913 789-5560
EMP: 30
SALES (corp-wide): 43.6MM **Privately Held**
SIC: 8093 Specialty outpatient clinics
PA: Critical Care Systems International, Inc.
61 Spit Brook Rd Ste 505
Nashua NH 03060
603 888-1500

(G-11282)
CROSSROADS SHOP CTR LLC
6310 Lamar Ave Ste 220 (66202-4265)
PHONE..................................913 362-1999
John Ruvenstein, *Mng Member*
John Rubenstein, *Mng Member*
Andy Epstein,
EMP: 15
SALES (est): 686.3K **Privately Held**
SIC: 6531 5999 Real estate agent, commercial; miscellaneous retail stores

(G-11283)
CROWN PACKAGING CORP
15301 W 110th St Ste 1 (66219-1243)
PHONE..................................913 888-1951
Rick Hunter, *Branch Mgr*
EMP: 20
SALES (corp-wide): 281.4MM **Privately Held**
WEB: www.crownpack.com
SIC: 5113 5169 5131 5084 Pressure sensitive tape; corrugated & solid fiber boxes; polyurethane products; labels; packaging machinery & equipment; industrial supplies
PA: Crown Packaging Corp.
17854 Chstrfld Aprt Rd
Chesterfield MO 63005
636 681-8000

(G-11284)
CSC GOLD INC
9300 W 110th St Ste 115 (66210-1405)
P.O. Box 2908 (66201-1308)
PHONE..................................913 664-8100
Roff Brainard, *Manager*
EMP: 17
SALES (corp-wide): 745.3MM **Privately Held**
WEB: www.csc-world.com
SIC: 5141 5191 Food brokers; animal feeds
HQ: Csc Gold, Inc.
920 2nd Ave S Ste 850
Minneapolis MN 55402

(G-11285)
CUMULUS MEDIA INC
5800 Foxridge Dr Ste 600 (66202-2335)
PHONE..................................913 514-3000
Bill Ryan, *Branch Mgr*
Matt Malone, *Director*
EMP: 50
SALES (corp-wide): 1.8B **Publicly Held**
SIC: 4832 Radio broadcasting stations
PA: Cm Wind Down Topco Inc.
3280 Peachtree Rd Ne Ne2300
Atlanta GA 30305
404 949-0700

(G-11286)
CUSTOM CONTROL MFR KANS INC
5601 Merriam Dr (66203-2521)
PHONE..................................913 722-0343
Raymond Myers, *President*
Ben Hilsabeck, *Project Engr*
Lewis Sanders, *Project Engr*
Adam Strough, *Project Engr*
Tyge Hess, *Sales Engr*
EMP: 21
SQ FT: 9,000
SALES (est): 6.3MM **Privately Held**
WEB: www.customcontrolmfr.com
SIC: 3613 Control panels, electric

(G-11287)
CVS PHARMACY INC
6300 Johnson Dr (66202-2611)
PHONE..................................913 722-3711
John Cooper, *Manager*
EMP: 13
SALES (corp-wide): 194.5B **Publicly Held**
WEB: www.cvsedi.com
SIC: 5912 7384 Drug stores; photofinishing laboratory
HQ: Cvs Pharmacy, Inc.
1 Cvs Dr
Woonsocket RI 02895
401 765-1500

(G-11288)
D & D SERVICES INC (PA)
Also Called: B and R Insulation
15001 W 101st Ter (66215-1162)
PHONE..................................913 492-1346
Richard Hall, *President*
David L Hall, *President*
Sheryl Cossey, *Supervisor*
EMP: 60
SQ FT: 3,000
SALES (est): 7.7MM **Privately Held**
SIC: 1799 Asbestos removal & encapsulation

(G-11289)
D AND D INSULATION INC
15001 W 101st Ter (66215-1162)
PHONE..................................913 492-1346
Richard Hall, *President*
EMP: 30
SQ FT: 3,000
SALES (est): 2MM **Privately Held**
SIC: 1742 Acoustical & insulation work

(G-11290)
DAIKIN APPLIED AMERICAS INC
10623 Rene St (66215-4052)
PHONE..................................913 492-8885
Ken Seaton, *Principal*
EMP: 10
SQ FT: 2,400 **Privately Held**
SIC: 5075 Warm air heating & air conditioning
HQ: Daikin Applied Americas Inc.
13600 Industrial Pk Blvd
Minneapolis MN 55441
763 553-5330

(G-11291)
DATA2LOGISTICS LLC
5427 Johnson Dr 265 (66205-2912)
PHONE..................................816 483-9000
EMP: 135 **Privately Held**
SIC: 4731 Freight rate information service
HQ: Data2logistics, Llc
12631 Westlinks Dr Ste 3
Fort Myers FL 33913
239 936-2800

(G-11292)
DAVIDSON ARCHITURE AND ENGR
4301 Indian Creek Pkwy (66207-4109)
PHONE..................................913 451-9390
John Davidson, *President*
Michael Brown,
EMP: 15
SQ FT: 8,000
SALES: 2MM **Privately Held**
WEB: www.davidson-brown.com
SIC: 8712 Architectural engineering

(G-11293)
DAVIS G SAM INSURANCE
6240 W 135th St Ste 100 (66223-4848)
PHONE..................................913 451-1800
G Sam Davis, *Owner*
EMP: 12
SALES (est): 1MM **Privately Held**
SIC: 6411 Insurance agents & brokers

(G-11294)
DAYMARK SOLUTIONS INC
7800 Shawnee Mission Pkwy # 14 (66202-4433)
PHONE..................................913 541-8980
Linda Livengood, *President*
Terry Livengood, *Corp Secy*
Ken Livengood, *Exec VP*
Richard Weast, *Exec VP*
EMP: 11
SQ FT: 4,800
SALES (est): 2.3MM **Privately Held**
WEB: www.daymarksolutions.com
SIC: 5043 2759 Photographic equipment & supplies; commercial printing

(G-11295)
DDDI COMMERCIAL INC
7200 W 132nd St Ste 300 (66213-1136)
PHONE..................................913 685-4100
Marshall H Dean Jr, *President*
Marshall Dean, *President*
EMP: 10
SALES (est): 455K **Privately Held**
WEB: www.ddicommercial.com
SIC: 6531 Real estate leasing & rentals

(G-11296)
DEAN DEVELOPMENT INC
7200 W 132nd St Ste 300 (66213-1136)
PHONE..................................913 685-4100
Marshall H Dean Jr, *CEO*
Vincent W Dean, *Vice Pres*
EMP: 10
SQ FT: 2,576
SALES (est): 534.8K **Privately Held**
SIC: 6799 Real estate investors, except property operators

(G-11297)
DEAN E SMALL
9425 W 75th St (66204-2213)
PHONE..................................913 642-2714
Dean Small, *Principal*
EMP: 10
SALES (est): 198.1K **Privately Held**
WEB: www.johnsoncountyanimalclinic.com
SIC: 0742 Veterinarian, animal specialties

(G-11298)
DEARBORN ANIMAL CLINIC PA
6100 Johnson Dr (66202-3333)
PHONE..................................913 722-2800
James R Guglielmino, *President*
EMP: 10
SQ FT: 1,700
SALES (est): 552.1K **Privately Held**
WEB: www.dearbornanimalclinic.com
SIC: 0742 Animal hospital services, pets & other animal specialties; veterinarian, animal specialties

(G-11299)
DELMAR GARDENS OF LENEXA INC
Also Called: Garden Villas Retirement Cmnty
9705 Monrovia St Ofc (66215-1500)
PHONE..................................913 492-8682
Jennifer Drozda, *Sales/Mktg Mgr*
EMP: 44
SALES (corp-wide): 12.9MM **Privately Held**
SIC: 6513 Retirement hotel operation
PA: Delmar Gardens Of Lenexa Inc
9701 Monrovia St
Lenexa KS 66215
913 492-1130

(G-11300)
DELMAR GARDENS OF OVERLAND PK
12100 W 109th St (66210-1200)
PHONE..................................913 469-4210
Gabe Grossberg, *President*
Harry Grossberg, *Chairman*
Christy Brooks, *Administration*
EMP: 135
SQ FT: 27,000
SALES: 7.3MM
SALES (corp-wide): 108.6MM **Privately Held**
SIC: 8741 Hospital management; nursing & personal care facility management
PA: Delmar Gardens Enterprises, Inc.
14805 North Outer 40 Rd # 300
Chesterfield MO 63017
636 733-7000

(G-11301)
DENTAL INNOVATION
11221 Shwnee Mission Pkwy (66203-3333)
PHONE..................................913 236-8899
Mark W Manroe, *Owner*
EMP: 19
SALES (est): 1.5MM **Privately Held**
WEB: www.markmanroedds.com
SIC: 8021 Dental clinic

(G-11302)
DERMATOLOGY & SKIN CANCER CTR (PA)
Also Called: Dermatology & Skin Cancer Ctr
11550 Granada St (66211-1453)
PHONE..................................913 451-7546
Mark Fleischman, *Med Doctor*
Glen Goldstein MD, *Director*
Shawn Sabin, *Dermatology*
EMP: 10
SALES (est): 1.7MM **Privately Held**
SIC: 8011 8049 7991 Dermatologist; speech pathologist; aerobic dance & exercise classes

(G-11303)
DESIGNERS LIBRARY INC
9102 Barton St (66214-1719)
PHONE..................................913 227-0010
Don Kopp Sr, *President*
Steve Goodman, *Admin Sec*
EMP: 12
SQ FT: 12,000
SALES (est): 3.7MM **Privately Held**
SIC: 5131 5198 5021 Piece goods & other fabrics; wallcoverings; furniture

(G-11304)
DIAGNOSTIC IMAGING CENTER
5500 College Blvd (66211-1600)
PHONE..................................913 491-9299
Nancy Hoppa, *Manager*

Neal Lurz, *Radiology*
EMP: 40
SALES (corp-wide): 18.1MM **Privately Held**
WEB: www.dic-kc.com
SIC: 8011 Radiologist
PA: Diagnostic Imaging Center
6724 Troost Ave Ste 800
Kansas City MO 64131
816 455-5959

(G-11305)
DIAGNOSTIC IMAGING CENTER
5520 College Blvd Ste 100 (66211-1690)
PHONE..................................913 491-9299
Nancy Hoppa, *Branch Mgr*
EMP: 45
SALES (est): 1.5MM
SALES (corp-wide): 18.1MM **Privately Held**
WEB: www.dic-kc.com
SIC: 8071 Medical laboratories
PA: Diagnostic Imaging Center
6724 Troost Ave Ste 800
Kansas City MO 64131
816 455-5959

(G-11306)
DICKSON-DIVELEY MIDWEST ORTHO
3651 College Blvd 100c (66211-1910)
PHONE..................................913 319-7600
Brian Divelbiss, *President*
Mark Bernhardt, *Vice Pres*
Stanley Bowling, *Vice Pres*
Lan Fotopoulos, *Vice Pres*
Robert Gardiner, *Vice Pres*
EMP: 85
SALES (est): 7.9MM **Privately Held**
SIC: 8011 Orthopedic physician

(G-11307)
DIMENSIONAL STONEWORK LLC
8301 W 125th St Ste 110 (66213-1415)
PHONE..................................913 851-9390
Gary Sowell, *President*
Tim McDonough, *Treasurer*
EMP: 14
SALES (est): 1.1MM **Privately Held**
SIC: 1799 Counter top installation

(G-11308)
DISCOVER DENTAL CARE
21620 Midland Dr Ste A (66218-9064)
PHONE..................................913 268-1337
Alberto Castaneda, *Owner*
EMP: 10
SALES (est): 1MM **Privately Held**
SIC: 8021 Dentists' office

(G-11309)
DISCOVERY CONCEPTS INC (PA)
Also Called: Trade Finders
5201 Johnson Dr Ste 301 (66205-2920)
PHONE..................................913 814-7100
Bill Fowler, *President*
Ed Irons, *President*
Ed Markley, *Vice Pres*
EMP: 6
SQ FT: 3,000
SALES (est): 745.1K **Privately Held**
WEB: www.discoveryconceptsinc.com
SIC: 8743 3269 Promotion service; china decorating

(G-11310)
DISPOSABLE INSTRUMENT CO INC
14248 Santa Fe Trail Dr (66215-1238)
P.O. Box 14248, Lenexa (66285-4248)
PHONE..................................913 492-6492
Brian Chansky, *President*
Ken Erich, *Engineer*
EMP: 10
SQ FT: 11,866
SALES: 2.3MM **Privately Held**
WEB: www.disposableinstrument.com
SIC: 3841 Surgical & medical instruments

(G-11311)
DOBSON-DAVIS CO
8521 Richards Rd (66215-2841)
PHONE..................................913 894-4922
Glenn L Dobson, *Partner*
Jerry Davis, *Partner*
EMP: 16
SALES (est): 1.1MM **Privately Held**
SIC: 1623 Electric power line construction

(G-11312)
DOCUMART INC
10316 W 79th St (66214-1561)
PHONE..................................913 649-3800
Greg Miller, *President*
Collette R Miller, *Corp Secy*
EMP: 11
SQ FT: 5,500
SALES (est): 1.6MM **Privately Held**
SIC: 2759 7334 2789 Commercial printing; photocopying & duplicating services; bookbinding & related work

(G-11313)
DOLL CRADLE
10910 Johnson Dr (66203-2830)
PHONE..................................913 631-1900
Connie Harrell, *Owner*
EMP: 12
SQ FT: 5,300
SALES (est): 685.2K **Privately Held**
SIC: 5945 5947 7699 Dolls & accessories; gift shop; doll & accessory repair

(G-11314)
DONEGAN OPTICAL COMPANY INC
Also Called: Optical Industries
15549 W 108th St (66219-1303)
P.O. Box 14308 (66285-4308)
PHONE..................................913 492-2500
Frank Donegan, *President*
Marianne Cummins, *Corp Secy*
▲ **EMP:** 23
SQ FT: 32,000
SALES (est): 4.3MM **Privately Held**
WEB: www.doneganoptical.com
SIC: 3851 Contact lenses

(G-11315)
DONMAR INC
Also Called: A W T
5401 Hayes St Ste A (66203-2119)
PHONE..................................913 432-2700
Don Eikel, *President*
Richard Armstrong, *General Mgr*
Marcia Eikel, *Vice Pres*
EMP: 15
SALES (est): 1.7MM **Privately Held**
WEB: www.awtkc.com
SIC: 2759 Thermography

(G-11316)
DONNELLEY FINANCIAL LLC
14702 W 105th St (66215-4414)
PHONE..................................913 541-4099
John Rhein, *Branch Mgr*
EMP: 13
SALES (corp-wide): 963MM **Publicly Held**
WEB: www.bowne.com
SIC: 2752 Commercial printing, offset
HQ: Donnelley Financial, Llc
35 W Wacker Dr
Chicago IL 60601
844 866-4337

(G-11317)
DOWELL & SYPHER LLC
10955 Lowell Ave Ste 630 (66210-2319)
PHONE..................................913 451-8833
Sarah Mitchell, *Principal*
EMP: 20
SALES (est): 1.5MM **Privately Held**
SIC: 8111 General practice law office

(G-11318)
DREWCO INC
14904 W 87th Pkwy 143 (66215)
PHONE..................................913 384-6226
Andrew K Anderson, *President*
Barbara Harkness, *Treasurer*
EMP: 20
SQ FT: 2,000
SALES (est): 1.9MM **Privately Held**
SIC: 1742 Drywall

(G-11319)
DRURY HOTELS COMPANY LLC
Also Called: Drury Inn Shawnee Mission
9009 Shawnee Mission Pkwy (66202-2865)
PHONE..................................913 236-9200
Jessica Arenholz, *General Mgr*
EMP: 28
SALES (corp-wide): 389.3MM **Privately Held**
WEB: www.druryhotels.com
SIC: 7011 Hotels
PA: Drury Hotels Company, Llc
721 Emerson Rd Ste 400
Saint Louis MO 63141
314 429-2255

(G-11320)
DUFFINS-LANGLEY OPTICAL CO
8140 Marshall Dr (66214-1536)
PHONE..................................913 492-5379
John Carrier, *President*
Jean Thomas, *General Mgr*
EMP: 69
SQ FT: 31,500
SALES (est): 5.3MM
SALES (corp-wide): 1.4MM **Privately Held**
WEB: www.crizal.com
SIC: 3851 5048 Ophthalmic goods; ophthalmic goods
HQ: Essilor Laboratories Of America, Inc.
13515 N Stemmons Fwy
Dallas TX 75234
972 241-4141

(G-11321)
DUFFY CONSTRUCTION COMPANY INC
7211 W 98th Ter Ste 110 (66212-2257)
PHONE..................................913 381-1668
John P Duffy, *President*
Sandra Duffy, *Corp Secy*
Kelly Duffy, *Vice Pres*
EMP: 13
SQ FT: 2,000
SALES: 2MM **Privately Held**
SIC: 1542 Commercial & office buildings, renovation & repair

(G-11322)
E F HADEL REALTY INC
13246 Long St (66213-5030)
PHONE..................................913 681-1600
Eugene F Hadel, *President*
EMP: 10
SALES: 75K **Privately Held**
SIC: 6531 Real estate agent, residential

(G-11323)
E M SPECIALIST PA
Also Called: David Vodonick MD
9100 W 74th St (66204-4004)
PHONE..................................913 676-2214
David Vodonick MD, *Principal*
EMP: 18 **EST:** 2000
SALES (est): 710.1K **Privately Held**
SIC: 8011 General & family practice, physician/surgeon

(G-11324)
E-Z SHELVING SYSTEMS INC
5538 Merriam Dr (66203-2548)
PHONE..................................913 384-1331
Ronald D Johnson, *Ch of Bd*
Ralph Larkin, *President*
Stephen Johnson, *General Mgr*
EMP: 14
SQ FT: 8,000
SALES (est): 2.2MM **Privately Held**
WEB: www.e-zshelving.com
SIC: 2542 Shelving, office & store: except wood

(G-11325)
EARTH DESIGNS INC
10101 W 156th St (66221-9710)
PHONE..................................913 791-2858
Brad Forbes, *President*
EMP: 6
SALES (est): 243.8K **Privately Held**
SIC: 0781 3569 Landscape architects; sprinkler systems, fire: automatic

(G-11326)
EAST ORLNDO HLTH REHAB CTR INC
Also Called: Overland Park Manor
6501 W 75th St (66204-3017)
PHONE..................................913 383-9866
Pamela Gray, *Manager*
EMP: 100 **Privately Held**
SIC: 8361 8051 Home for the aged; skilled nursing care facilities
HQ: East Orlando Health & Rehab Center, Inc.
250 S Chickasaw Trl
Orlando FL 32825
407 380-3466

(G-11327)
EDEN WEST INC
10000 W 75tj St Ste 100 Tj (66204)
PHONE..................................913 384-3800
Brian Hyatt, *E-Business*
Kennith Riedemann, *Director*
EMP: 20
SALES (est): 387.1K
SALES (corp-wide): 11.8MM **Privately Held**
WEB: www.edenwest.com
SIC: 6513 6531 Apartment building operators; real estate managers
PA: J A Peterson Enterprises, Inc
10000 W 75th St Ste 100
Shawnee Mission KS 66204
913 384-3800

(G-11328)
EDOC PRINTING
9401 Indian Creek Pkwy # 250 (66210-2007)
PHONE..................................913 469-0071
Ron Harland, *Partner*
EMP: 8
SALES (est): 608.8K **Privately Held**
SIC: 2759 Commercial printing

(G-11329)
EFI GLOBAL INC
10323 Maple Dr (66207-3819)
PHONE..................................913 648-5232
Melvin Kogan, *Principal*
EMP: 12
SALES (corp-wide): 14.9B **Publicly Held**
SIC: 8711 Consulting engineer
HQ: Efi Global, Inc.
3030 N Rocky Point Dr W # 530
Tampa FL 33607
281 358-4441

(G-11330)
ELECTRONIC TECHNOLOGY INC
5700 Merriam Dr (66203-2500)
PHONE..................................913 962-8083
Barbara Carr, *CEO*
Sara Carr, *Manager*
EMP: 15
SQ FT: 3,000
SALES (est): 2.5MM **Privately Held**
WEB: www.electronictechnology.com
SIC: 7379 1731 Computer related consulting services; electrical work

(G-11331)
ELEMENT FITNESS
Also Called: Quivira Sports Clubs
7880 Quivira Rd (66216-3322)
PHONE..................................913 268-3633
Susan Zinner, *General Mgr*
Hal Edwards, *Principal*
Lora Edwards,
EMP: 80
SQ FT: 45,000
SALES (est): 1.3MM **Privately Held**
SIC: 7991 Physical fitness facilities

(G-11332)
ELITE FIREPLACE FACINGS INC
6540 Pflumm Rd (66216-2406)
PHONE..................................913 631-5443
Joseph Petersen, *President*
EMP: 8
SALES (est): 861.8K **Privately Held**
SIC: 3429 Fireplace equipment, hardware: andirons, grates, screens

▲ = Import ▼=Export
◆ =Import/Export

(G-11333)
EMERGENCY DEPT PHYSICIANS
14400 College Blvd # 105 (66215-2063)
P.O. Box 716 (66201-0716)
PHONE....913 469-1411
Richard Beamon, *President*
Mark Holcomb, *Admin Sec*
EMP: 50 **EST:** 1978
SALES (est): 2.9MM **Privately Held**
SIC: 8011 Offices & clinics of medical doctors

(G-11334)
EMERSON ELECTRIC CO
10048 Industrial Blvd (66215-1219)
PHONE....913 752-6000
Grant Waldemer, *Project Engr*
Chris Abel, *Branch Mgr*
EMP: 145
SALES (corp-wide): 18.3B **Publicly Held**
WEB: www.gotoemerson.com
SIC: 3823 Industrial instrmnts msrmnt display/control process variable
PA: Emerson Electric Co.
8000 West Florissant Ave
Saint Louis MO 63136
314 553-2000

(G-11335)
EMPIRE CONSTRUCTION GROUP LLC
9128 W 91st Ter (66212-3901)
PHONE....913 375-8886
Sean Sediqzad, *Mng Member*
EMP: 10
SALES: 350K **Privately Held**
SIC: 1521 7389 Single-family housing construction;

(G-11336)
EMPLOYERS REASSURANCE CORP
5200 Metcalf Ave (66202-1265)
P.O. Box 2991 (66201-1391)
PHONE....913 676-5200
Ron Pressman, *President*
James Maughn, *Exec VP*
John Connelly, *Admin Sec*
EMP: 70
SALES (est): 11.5MM
SALES (corp-wide): 121.6B **Publicly Held**
SIC: 6411 Insurance agents, brokers & service
PA: General Electric Company
5 Necco St
Boston MA 02210
617 443-3000

(G-11337)
ENCOMPASS HEALTH CORPORATION
Also Called: HealthSouth
6509 W 103rd St (66212-1728)
PHONE....913 649-3701
Bill Scott, *Manager*
EMP: 70
SALES (corp-wide): 4.2B **Publicly Held**
WEB: www.healthsouth.com
SIC: 8069 Specialty hospitals, except psychiatric
PA: Encompass Health Corporation
9001 Liberty Pkwy
Birmingham AL 35242
205 967-7116

(G-11338)
ENTERCOM KANSAS CITY LLC
Also Called: Kyys-Knbc-Kudl-wdaf-kcmo
7000 Squibb Rd Ste 200 (66202-3253)
PHONE....913 744-3600
Dave Alpert, *General Mgr*
EMP: 200 **EST:** 2015
SALES (est): 38.4MM
SALES (corp-wide): 1.4B **Publicly Held**
SIC: 4832 Radio broadcasting stations
PA: Entercom Communications Corp.
2400 Market St Fl 4
Philadelphia PA 19103
610 660-5610

(G-11339)
ENTERPRISE BANK (HQ)
Also Called: Enterprise Banking N A
12695 Metcalf Ave (66213-1317)
P.O. Box 25250 (66225-5250)
PHONE....913 663-5525
Jack L Sutherland, *Regional Pres*
EMP: 30
SQ FT: 15,000
SALES: 805K **Publicly Held**
SIC: 6022 State commercial banks

(G-11340)
ENTERPRISE LEASING CO KS LLC (DH)
5359 Merriam Dr (66203-2100)
PHONE....913 383-1515
Emilie Rottinghaus, *Human Res Mgr*
Chris Peterson, *Train & Dev Mgr*
Maggie Root, *Manager*
EMP: 240 **EST:** 1972
SQ FT: 20,000
SALES (est): 20.6MM
SALES (corp-wide): 4.5B **Privately Held**
SIC: 7515 7514 5521 Passenger car leasing; rent-a-car service; automobiles, used cars only
HQ: Enterprise Holdings, Inc.
600 Corporate Park Dr
Saint Louis MO 63105
314 512-5000

(G-11341)
ENTERPRISE LEASING CO KS LLC
Also Called: Enterprise Rent-A-Car
6000 Nieman Rd (66203-2938)
PHONE....913 631-7663
Lewis Gilbert, *Manager*
EMP: 26
SALES (corp-wide): 4.5B **Privately Held**
SIC: 7514 Passenger car rental
HQ: Enterprise Leasing Company Of Ks Llc
5359 Merriam Dr
Shawnee Mission KS 66203
913 383-1515

(G-11342)
ENTERPRISE LEASING CO KS LLC
10000 Shwnee Mission Pkwy (66203-3641)
PHONE....913 262-8888
Christina Grahack, *Branch Mgr*
EMP: 11
SALES (corp-wide): 4.5B **Privately Held**
SIC: 7514 7515 Rent-a-car service; passenger car leasing
HQ: Enterprise Leasing Company Of Ks Llc
5359 Merriam Dr
Shawnee Mission KS 66203
913 383-1515

(G-11343)
ENTRACARE LLC
11315 Strang Line Rd (66215-4042)
PHONE....913 451-2234
W Cary Dikeman,
▲ **EMP:** 5
SALES: 800K **Privately Held**
WEB: www.entracare.com
SIC: 3841 Surgical & medical instruments

(G-11344)
ENVIRNMNTAL ADVISORS ENGINEERS
19211 W 64th Ter (66218-9176)
PHONE....913 599-4326
Jill Biesma, *President*
Robert Bens, *Vice Pres*
Deborah Gallegos, *Project Mgr*
Julie Finn, *Engineer*
Julia Rol, *Mktg Coord*
EMP: 31
SALES (est): 2.9MM **Privately Held**
WEB: www.eaei.com
SIC: 8748 8711 8744 Environmental consultant; engineering services; facilities support services

(G-11345)
EPLUS ENVRMENTAL SOLUTIONS LLC
4948 W 130th Ter (66209-1855)
PHONE....913 814-9860
James C Noe, *President*
EMP: 20
SALES (est): 483.1K **Privately Held**
SIC: 3564 Air purification equipment

(G-11346)
EQUILON ENTERPRISES LLC
Also Called: Shell Oil Products U S
9640 Nall Ave (66207-2952)
PHONE....913 648-0535
Wanda Taylor, *Manager*
EMP: 15
SALES (corp-wide): 388.3B **Privately Held**
WEB: www.shellus.com
SIC: 5541 2911 Filling stations, gasoline; petroleum refining
HQ: Equilon Enterprises Llc
910 Louisiana St Ste 2
Houston TX 77002
713 767-5337

(G-11347)
EURODENT DENTAL LAB INC
8303 W 126th St Ste D (66213-1483)
PHONE....913 685-9930
Max Ambro, *President*
EMP: 10
SALES (est): 843.9K **Privately Held**
SIC: 8072 Crown & bridge production

(G-11348)
EVANS & MULLINIX PA
7225 Renner Rd Ste 200 (66217-3046)
PHONE....913 962-8700
Richard Wallace, *President*
Timothy J Evans, *Partner*
Colin Gotham, *Vice Pres*
Thomas M Mullinix, *Vice Pres*
Joanne Butaud, *Treasurer*
EMP: 35
SQ FT: 3,300
SALES: 1.6MM **Privately Held**
WEB: www.evans-mullinix.com
SIC: 8111 General practice attorney, lawyer

(G-11349)
EVELAND BROTHERS BODY SHOP
Also Called: Eveland Bros Collision Repair
7200 W Frontage Rd (66203-4638)
PHONE....913 262-6050
Bill Eveland, *President*
John Pankau, *General Mgr*
Mark Eveland, *Corp Secy*
Dan Oelschlaeger, *Vice Pres*
James Button, *Prdtn Mgr*
EMP: 37
SALES (est): 4.2MM **Privately Held**
WEB: www.evelandbros.com
SIC: 7532 Body shop, automotive

(G-11350)
EVERGANCE PARTNERS LLC
6900 College Blvd Ste 470 (66211-1596)
PHONE....913 825-1000
Chad Wolf, *President*
Allen Bonde,
Stephen Raye,
EMP: 31
SALES (est): 2MM **Privately Held**
SIC: 7389 Personal service agents, brokers & bureaus

(G-11351)
EVERSEAL GASKET INC (PA)
8309 Cole Pkwy (66227-3128)
PHONE....913 441-9232
Ken Lane, *CEO*
Chuck Lane, *President*
Tim Vos, *Sales Mgr*
Mike Scarpelli, *Technology*
Joanne Acker, *Admin Sec*
▲ **EMP:** 44
SQ FT: 56,000
SALES (est): 4.7MM **Privately Held**
WEB: www.eversealgasket.com
SIC: 3053 3061 2822 Gaskets, all materials; mechanical rubber goods; synthetic rubber

(G-11352)
EVOLV SOLUTIONS LLC (PA)
9401 Indian Creek Pkwy # 250 (66210-1840)
PHONE....913 469-8900
Ronald Harland Sr, *President*
Eric W Harland, *Vice Pres*
Ron Harland Jr, *Vice Pres*
Aurelio Lopez, *Project Mgr*
EMP: 50
SQ FT: 2,500
SALES: 18.5MM **Privately Held**
SIC: 5044 7334 5112 7377 Copying equipment; photocopying & duplicating services; photocopying supplies; computer rental & leasing

(G-11353)
EXCEL PERSONNEL SERVICES INC (PA)
9401 Indian Creek Pkwy # 40 (66210-2007)
PHONE....913 341-1150
Marvin Kleeb, *President*
EMP: 40
SALES (est): 1.9MM **Privately Held**
SIC: 7363 7361 8742 Temporary help service; employment agencies; general management consultant

(G-11354)
EXECUTIVE HILLS FAMILY DENTAL
8605 College Blvd (66210-1835)
PHONE....913 451-1606
Gary Z Hatutian DDS, *Owner*
Gary Hatutian, *Fmly & Gen Dent*
EMP: 13
SALES (est): 781.6K **Privately Held**
SIC: 8021 Dental clinic

(G-11355)
EXECUTIVE HILLS STYLE SHOP
8660 College Blvd (66210-1820)
PHONE....913 451-1204
Kim Kapp, *President*
EMP: 15 **EST:** 1981
SALES: 107K **Privately Held**
SIC: 7231 Hairdressers

(G-11356)
EXPERITEC INC
7932 Nieman Rd (66214-1560)
PHONE....913 894-4044
Bill Thompson, *Branch Mgr*
EMP: 16
SALES (corp-wide): 115.3MM **Privately Held**
WEB: www.mungerpd.com
SIC: 5085 3612 3492 Valves & fittings; transformers, except electric; fluid power valves & hose fittings
PA: Experitec, Inc.
504 Trade Center Blvd
Chesterfield MO 63005
636 681-1500

(G-11357)
F/X TERMITE AND PEST CONTROL
13036 W 79th St (66215-2552)
PHONE....913 599-5990
Sondra Milberger, *President*
EMP: 12 **EST:** 1936
SQ FT: 3,000
SALES (est): 650K **Privately Held**
SIC: 7342 Exterminating & fumigating

(G-11358)
FAERBER SURGICAL ARTS
4601 W 109th St Ste 118 (66211-1314)
PHONE....913 469-8895
Thomas H Faerber MD, *Owner*
Thomas Faerber, *Med Doctor*
Ann Faerber, *Admin Sec*
EMP: 10
SQ FT: 2,700

GEOGRAPHIC

SALES (est): 1.1MM **Privately Held**
WEB: www.surgicalarts.com
SIC: 8011 8021 Plastic surgeon; maxillofacial specialist

(G-11359)
FALCON RIDGE GOLF CLUB
20200 Prairie Star Pkwy (66220-3645)
PHONE..................................913 393-4653
Dean Lytton, *General Mgr*
James West, *Director*
EMP: 15
SALES (est): 781.7K **Privately Held**
WEB: www.falconridgegolfclub.com
SIC: 7992 7999 7299 Public golf courses; golf services & professionals; banquet hall facilities

(G-11360)
FAMILY FTRES EDTORIAL SYND INC
5825 Dearborn St (66202-2745)
PHONE..................................913 722-0055
Brian Agnes, *President*
Cindy Long, *Manager*
Dianne Hogerty, *Shareholder*
EMP: 27
SQ FT: 5,500
SALES (est): 4.5MM **Privately Held**
WEB: www.culinary.net
SIC: 8743 Public relations services

(G-11361)
FARRIS BURNS CORP
6210 Merriam Dr (66203-3258)
P.O. Box 3187 (66203-0187)
PHONE..................................913 262-0555
Alan Johnson, *General Mgr*
▲ **EMP:** 9 **EST:** 1951
SQ FT: 18,000
SALES (est): 1.4MM **Privately Held**
SIC: 5063 3496 Electrical apparatus & equipment; clips & fasteners, made from purchased wire

(G-11362)
FEDEX CORPORATION
5700 Broadmoor St (66202-2426)
PHONE..................................913 677-5005
EMP: 11
SALES (corp-wide): 47.4B **Publicly Held**
SIC: 7389 Business Services
PA: Fedex Corporation
942 Shady Grove Rd S
Memphis TN 38120
901 818-7500

(G-11363)
FEDEX GROUND PACKAGE SYS INC
8000 Cole Pkwy (66227-2725)
PHONE..................................913 422-3161
EMP: 500
SALES (corp-wide): 47.4B **Publicly Held**
SIC: 4212 Local Trucking Operator
HQ: Fedex Ground Package System, Inc.
1000 Fed Ex Dr
Coraopolis PA 15108
412 269-1000

(G-11364)
FEDEX OFFICE & PRINT SVCS INC
11026 Metcalf Ave Ste 7a (66210-1834)
PHONE..................................913 661-0192
EMP: 20
SALES (corp-wide): 69.6B **Publicly Held**
WEB: www.kinkos.com
SIC: 7334 Photocopying & duplicating services
HQ: Fedex Office And Print Services, Inc.
7900 Legacy Dr
Plano TX 75024
800 463-3339

(G-11365)
FEDEX OFFICE & PRINT SVCS INC
5437 Johnson Dr (66205-2912)
PHONE..................................913 677-4488
EMP: 18
SALES (corp-wide): 69.6B **Publicly Held**
WEB: www.kinkos.com
SIC: 7334 2759 Photocopying & duplicating services; commercial printing
HQ: Fedex Office And Print Services, Inc.
7900 Legacy Dr
Plano TX 75024
800 463-3339

(G-11366)
FERREE BUNN OGRADY & RUNDBERG
9300 Metcalf Ave Ste 300 (66212-1463)
PHONE..................................913 381-8180
Lawrence L Ferree III, *President*
Carl Radom, *Partner*
Jerry Kelley, *Administration*
Kirk Ridgway,
Ronald Rundberg,
EMP: 15 **EST:** 1975
SQ FT: 4,400
SALES (est): 1.6MM **Privately Held**
WEB: www.fbolaw.com
SIC: 8111 General practice attorney, lawyer

(G-11367)
FINANCIAL ADVISORY SERVICE INC
Also Called: Fas
4747 W 135th St Ste 100 (66224-9745)
PHONE..................................913 239-2300
Max Greer Jr, *President*
John Meier, *Principal*
James Dussold, *Vice Pres*
Jerome McKenzie, *Manager*
Stan Biggs, *Director*
EMP: 19
SALES (est): 955.8K **Privately Held**
WEB: www.faskc.com
SIC: 8742 Financial consultant

(G-11368)
FIRST CALL HOSPITALITY LLC
5800 College Blvd (66211-1660)
PHONE..................................913 345-2661
Tripp Synder,
EMP: 50 **EST:** 2001
SALES: 3.8MM **Privately Held**
SIC: 7011 Hotels & motels

(G-11369)
FIRST EXCESS REINSURANCE CORP
Also Called: G E Reinsurance
6329 Glenwood St Ste 300 (66202-4291)
P.O. Box 29164 (66201-9164)
PHONE..................................913 676-5524
James R Miller, *President*
EMP: 1000
SALES: 389.6MM
SALES (corp-wide): 37B **Privately Held**
SIC: 6331 Fire, marine & casualty insurance
HQ: Swiss Re Solutions Holding Corporation
5200 Metcalf Ave
Overland Park KS 66202
913 676-5200

(G-11370)
FIRST FINANCIAL LEASING INC
6300 Nall Ave Ste 200 (66202-4334)
PHONE..................................913 236-8800
Dough S Moskowitz, *President*
EMP: 25 **EST:** 1999
SALES (est): 1.1MM **Privately Held**
WEB: www.sunbridgecapital.com
SIC: 7359 Equipment rental & leasing

(G-11371)
FIRST HORIZON BANK
7500 College Blvd Ste 850 (66210-4030)
PHONE..................................913 339-5400
Rod Turner, *Manager*
EMP: 15
SALES (corp-wide): 2.2B **Publicly Held**
WEB: www.firsttennessee.com
SIC: 6211 Bond dealers & brokers
HQ: First Horizon Bank
165 Madison Ave
Memphis TN 38103
901 523-4444

(G-11372)
FIRST LAYER COMMUNICATIONS (PA)
14906 Benson St (66221-9369)
PHONE..................................913 491-0062
James Knutson, *CEO*
David Menzel, *COO*
Bill Gault, *VP Opers*
Jeffrey Sauter, *CFO*
Roger Flint, *CTO*
EMP: 14 **EST:** 2000
SALES (est): 1.4MM **Privately Held**
SIC: 8711 Engineering services

(G-11373)
FIRST NATIONAL BANK LOUISBURG
4200 W 83rd St Ste 100 (66208-5314)
P.O. Box 219038, Kansas City MO (64121-9038)
PHONE..................................913 766-6701
Marshall Schenck, *Manager*
EMP: 15
SALES (corp-wide): 4.5MM **Privately Held**
WEB: www.bofa.com
SIC: 6021 National commercial banks
PA: First National Bank Of Louisburg
1201 W Amity St
Louisburg KS 66053
913 837-5191

(G-11374)
FLEX BUILD LLC
5410 Antioch Dr (66202-1020)
PHONE..................................913 890-2500
William Carter, *Mng Member*
EMP: 10
SALES (est): 1.1MM **Privately Held**
SIC: 1542 Commercial & office building contractors

(G-11375)
FOGELMAN MANAGEMENT GROUP LLC
Also Called: Pointe Royal Town Houses
8401 W 123rd St (66213-1405)
PHONE..................................913 345-2888
Michelle Burns, *Manager*
EMP: 12
SALES (corp-wide): 123.8MM **Privately Held**
SIC: 6513 6514 Apartment building operators; dwelling operators, except apartments
HQ: Fogelman Management Group, Llc
6060 Poplar Ave Ste 200
Memphis TN 38119

(G-11376)
FOOD SERVICE SPECIALISTS INC (PA)
9290 Glenwood St (66212-1365)
PHONE..................................913 648-6611
James Peine, *President*
EMP: 18 **EST:** 1970
SQ FT: 4,500
SALES (est): 4.1MM **Privately Held**
WEB: www.fsskc.com
SIC: 5141 Food brokers

(G-11377)
FORUM HEALTH CARE
3509 W 95th St (66206-2032)
PHONE..................................913 648-4980
Jennifer Evers, *Director*
EMP: 200
SALES (est): 3.5MM **Privately Held**
SIC: 8099 Blood related health services

(G-11378)
FRANK C ALLISON JR
8000 Foster St (66204-3613)
PHONE..................................913 648-2080
Frank C Allison Jr, *Owner*
EMP: 20
SALES (est): 896.4K **Privately Held**
SIC: 8111 General practice attorney, lawyer

(G-11379)
FRED PFLUMM PLUMBING INC
8329 Monticello Rd Ste E (66227-3120)
PHONE..................................913 441-6309
Tim Zarda, *President*
Lisa Zarda, *Admin Sec*
EMP: 20
SALES (est): 2MM **Privately Held**
SIC: 1711 Plumbing contractors

(G-11380)
FREE STATE SECURITY SVCS LLC
P.O. Box 746, Baldwin City (66006-0746)
PHONE..................................785 843-7073
Doug Cansler, *Principal*
Rusty Burton, *Mng Member*
EMP: 18
SALES (est): 94.1K **Privately Held**
SIC: 7381 Guard services

(G-11381)
FRESH APPRACH CLG PRFESSIONALS
16030 W 80th St (66219-2028)
PHONE..................................913 707-5500
Sharon Auck, *Owner*
EMP: 13
SALES (est): 1.2MM **Privately Held**
SIC: 7699 Cleaning services

(G-11382)
FRITO-LAY NORTH AMERICA INC
9600 Dice Ln (66215-1152)
PHONE..................................913 261-4700
Linda Coch, *Manager*
EMP: 70
SALES (corp-wide): 64.6B **Publicly Held**
WEB: www.fritolay.com
SIC: 5145 Snack foods
HQ: Frito-Lay North America, Inc.
7701 Legacy Dr
Plano TX 75024

(G-11383)
FRITZS MT SUPERIOR SAUSAGE LLC
Also Called: Fritz's Superior Meat Co
10326 State Line Rd (66206-2658)
PHONE..................................913 381-4618
Eric Beckner, *Mng Member*
EMP: 5 **EST:** 1927
SQ FT: 70,000
SALES (est): 630K **Privately Held**
WEB: www.fritzskcmeats.com
SIC: 2013 5421 Sausages from purchased meat; smoked meats from purchased meat; meat markets, including freezer provisioners

(G-11384)
FUJITSU AMERICA INC
6900 College Blvd Ste 700 (66211-1842)
PHONE..................................913 327-2800
Mike Osborne, *Manager*
EMP: 50 **Privately Held**
SIC: 8742 7371 Management consulting services; computer software systems analysis & design, custom
HQ: Fujitsu America Inc
1250 E Arques Ave
Sunnyvale CA 94085
408 746-6000

(G-11385)
FUN SERVICES OF KANSAS CITY (PA)
12119 Johnson Dr (66216-1907)
PHONE..................................913 631-3772
Thomas M Wilson, *President*
Elizabeth Wilson, *Vice Pres*
EMP: 20 **EST:** 1973
SQ FT: 19,000
SALES: 219.3K **Privately Held**
SIC: 5092 5947 Amusement goods; party favors

(G-11386)
FURST IN TILE INC
18320 W 66th Ter (66218-9527)
PHONE..................................913 962-4599
Joe N Furst, *President*
Karen Furst, *Admin Sec*
EMP: 15
SALES: 700K **Privately Held**
SIC: 1752 Ceramic floor tile installation

(G-11387)
FUSION TELECOM INTL INC
5700 Broadmoor St (66202-2426)
PHONE..................................913 262-4638
James Butler, *Director*
EMP: 10

SALES (corp-wide): 124.6MM **Publicly Held**
WEB: www.ionex.com
SIC: 7375 Information retrieval services
HQ: Fusion Telecommunications International, Inc.
210 Intrstate N Pkwy Se S
Atlanta GA 30339
888 772-4724

(G-11388)
FUTURE ELECTRONICS CORP
8700 Indian Creek Pkwy # 200
(66210-1563)
PHONE....913 498-1531
Barry Von Ada, *Manager*
EMP: 16
SALES (corp-wide): 3.1B **Privately Held**
WEB: www.futureelectronics.com
SIC: 5065 Electronic parts
HQ: Future Electronics Corp.
41 Main St
Bolton MA 01740
800 444-0050

(G-11389)
GABLERS NURSERY INC
8131 Metcalf Ave (66204-3846)
PHONE....913 642-4164
John Gabler, *President*
EMP: 15
SALES (est): 861.5K **Privately Held**
SIC: 0181 5261 Nursery stock, growing of; garden supplies & tools

(G-11390)
GAROZZOS ILL INC
Also Called: Cafe Garozzo
9950 College Blvd (66210-1756)
PHONE....913 491-8300
Micheal Garozzo, *President*
EMP: 70
SALES (est): 1.5MM **Privately Held**
SIC: 5812 7299 Cafe; banquet hall facilities

(G-11391)
GE CAPITAL MONTGOMERY WARD
9510 W 67th St (66203-3614)
PHONE....913 676-4100
Jan Doane, *Branch Mgr*
Robert Young, *Info Tech Mgr*
EMP: 1000
SALES (corp-wide): 121.6B **Publicly Held**
SIC: 6799 Investors
HQ: Monogram Retailer Credit Services Inc
3135 Easton Tpke
Fairfield CT
203 357-4000

(G-11392)
GEESU INC
Also Called: Supercuts
6939 W 75th St (66204-3028)
PHONE....913 648-0087
Kamran Dowlatshahi, *President*
EMP: 12
SQ FT: 1,300
SALES (est): 161.6K **Privately Held**
SIC: 7231 Unisex hair salons

(G-11393)
GENESIS CORP
Also Called: Genesis 10
6950 Squibb Rd Ste 430 (66202-3258)
PHONE....913 906-9991
Jason Elcher, *Manager*
EMP: 120
SALES (corp-wide): 197.7MM **Privately Held**
SIC: 7379 8742 Computer related consulting services; management consulting services
PA: Genesis Corp.
950 3rd Ave Ste 900
New York NY 10022
212 688-5522

(G-11394)
GENEVA-ROTH VENTURES INC
6950 W 56th St (66202-2590)
PHONE....913 825-1200
Mark Curry, *President*
EMP: 35
SALES (est): 3.5MM **Privately Held**
SIC: 8742 Business consultant

(G-11395)
GENUINE PARTS COMPANY
Also Called: NAPA Auto Parts
6550 Nieman Rd (66203-3328)
PHONE....913 631-4329
John Branski, *Manager*
EMP: 10
SALES (corp-wide): 18.7B **Publicly Held**
WEB: www.genpt.com
SIC: 5531 5013 Automobile & truck equipment & parts; automotive supplies & parts
PA: Genuine Parts Company
2999 Wildwood Pkwy
Atlanta GA 30339
678 934-5000

(G-11396)
GEORGE KING BIO-MEDICAL INC
11771 W 112th St Ste 100 (66210-2782)
PHONE....913 469-5464
Kathryn A Blasco, *President*
Edward Blasco, *COO*
Katie Wilkes, *Vice Pres*
Judith Gillissen, *Pub Rel Mgr*
Barbara Young, *Director*
EMP: 16
SQ FT: 9,000
SALES (est): 3.1MM **Privately Held**
WEB: www.kingbiomed.com
SIC: 2835 In vitro diagnostics

(G-11397)
GLENN V HEMBERGER DDS
8575 W 110th St Ste 310 (66210-2774)
PHONE....913 345-0331
Glenn V Hemberger, *Owner*
Glenn Hemberger, *Fmly & Gen Dent*
EMP: 12
SALES (est): 565.6K **Privately Held**
SIC: 8021 Pedodontist

(G-11398)
GODDARD SCHOOL
11060 Oakmont St (66210-1100)
PHONE....913 451-1066
Betsy Allen, *Owner*
EMP: 22
SALES (est): 114.4K **Privately Held**
SIC: 8351 Preschool center

(G-11399)
GOODWIN PRO TURF INC
Also Called: Goodwin Proturf
6945 W 152nd Ter (66223-3124)
PHONE....913 685-1000
Steve Goodwin, *President*
Mark Goodwin, *Vice Pres*
Lisa Davis, *Admin Sec*
EMP: 35
SQ FT: 2,000
SALES: 1MM **Privately Held**
SIC: 0782 Lawn care services; garden maintenance services

(G-11400)
GREAT PLAINS SUPPLY INC
13891 W 101st St (66215-1211)
PHONE....913 492-1520
Stephen Reiff, *President*
Susan Ahn, *Vice Pres*
EMP: 12
SQ FT: 25,000
SALES (est): 5.3MM **Privately Held**
SIC: 5091 Swimming pools, equipment & supplies; spa equipment & supplies

(G-11401)
GREAT WESTERN BANK
10610 Shawnee Mission Pkw
(66203-3501)
PHONE....913 248-3300
Rick Poccia, *Branch Mgr*
EMP: 11
SALES (corp-wide): 603.6MM **Publicly Held**
SIC: 6022 State commercial banks
HQ: Great Western Bank
225 S Main Ave
Sioux Falls SD 57104
605 782-0540

(G-11402)
GREENHOUSE EFFECT INC
7931 Darnell Ln (66215-6121)
PHONE....913 492-7407
John H Teeter, *President*
Bruce Freeman, *Vice Pres*
EMP: 14
SALES: 120K **Privately Held**
WEB: www.greenhouseeffect.net
SIC: 0181 Ornamental nursery products

(G-11403)
GREG BAIR TRACK HOE SVC INC
15300 Broadmoor St (66223-3141)
PHONE....913 897-1243
Greg Bair, *President*
Barbara Bair, *Vice Pres*
EMP: 18
SQ FT: 2,500
SALES (est): 3.1MM **Privately Held**
WEB: www.gregbair.com
SIC: 1794 1795 Excavation work; wrecking & demolition work

(G-11404)
GT KANSAS LLC
12321 Metcalf Ave (66213-1323)
PHONE....913 266-1106
Chris Curtin,
Rick Mann,
EMP: 25
SALES (est): 896.8K **Privately Held**
SIC: 6531 Real estate managers

(G-11405)
GUEST COMMUNICATIONS CORP
15009 W 101st Ter (66215-1162)
PHONE....913 888-1217
Richard Travers, *CEO*
James Shappell, *Vice Pres*
Phillis Travers, *Financial Exec*
Alison Sapikoski-Arnet, *Manager*
Debbie Zellner, *Technology*
EMP: 20
SQ FT: 14,500
SALES (est): 2.8MM **Privately Held**
WEB: www.gcckc.com
SIC: 2741 Directories: publishing & printing

(G-11406)
HALINGS FLORIST
Also Called: Haling's Greenhouse
6303 W 75th St (66204-3002)
PHONE....913 642-5034
J P Teeter,
Bruce Lisa Freeman,
EMP: 15
SQ FT: 1,850
SALES (est): 431.7K **Privately Held**
SIC: 0181 Flowers grown in field nurseries; nursery stock, growing of

(G-11407)
HANGER PROSTHETICS &
6600 College Blvd Ste 215 (66211-1522)
PHONE....913 498-1540
Sam Liang, *President*
Thomas Eis, *Branch Mgr*
EMP: 7
SALES (corp-wide): 1B **Publicly Held**
SIC: 3842 Limbs, artificial; prosthetic appliances
HQ: Hanger Prosthetics & Orthotics East, Inc.
33 North Ave Ste 101
Tallmadge OH 44278

(G-11408)
HANNAH & OLTJEN
Also Called: Oltjen, Jay M
7505 Quivira Rd (66216-3511)
PHONE....913 268-5559
Jay M Oltjen, *Principal*
EMP: 10
SALES (corp-wide): 1.9MM **Privately Held**
SIC: 8021 Orthodontist
PA: Hannah & Oltjen
1441 E 151st St
Olathe KS 66062
913 829-2244

(G-11409)
HARDAGE HOTELS I LLC
Also Called: Chase Suite Hotel By Woodfin
6300 W 110th St (66211-1527)
PHONE....913 491-3333
Cristina Baker, *Manager*
EMP: 15 **Privately Held**
WEB: www.woodfinsuitehotels.com
SIC: 7011 Hotels
PA: Hardage Hotels I, Llc
12555 High Bluff Dr # 330
San Diego CA 92130

(G-11410)
HARRINGTON BROS HTG & COOLG
Also Called: Honeywell Authorized Dealer
8147 Cole Pkwy (66227-2714)
PHONE....913 422-5444
Jerry Harrington, *Partner*
Robert Harrington, *Partner*
EMP: 15
SQ FT: 6,000
SALES: 1.3MM **Privately Held**
SIC: 1711 Warm air heating & air conditioning contractor

(G-11411)
HARRIS BMO BANK NATIONAL ASSN
Also Called: Bmo Harris Bank
21900 Shwnee Mission Pkwy
(66226-3528)
PHONE....913 441-7900
Mark Degenhardt, *President*
EMP: 19
SALES (corp-wide): 17.7B **Privately Held**
WEB: www.uhb-fl.com
SIC: 6022 State trust companies accepting deposits, commercial
HQ: Harris Bmo Bank National Association
111 W Monroe St Ste 1200
Chicago IL 60603
312 461-2323

(G-11412)
HARRIS BMO BANK NATIONAL ASSN
Also Called: Bmo Harris Bank
7225 Renner Rd (66217-3300)
PHONE....913 962-1400
Steve Nepote, *Manager*
EMP: 22
SALES (corp-wide): 17.7B **Privately Held**
WEB: www.uhb-fl.com
SIC: 6022 State commercial banks
HQ: Harris Bmo Bank National Association
111 W Monroe St Ste 1200
Chicago IL 60603
312 461-2323

(G-11413)
HARTE-HANKS INC
Also Called: Harte-Hankes Direct Marketing
7801 Nieman Rd (66214-1407)
PHONE....913 312-8100
Robert Mason, *Manager*
EMP: 300
SALES (corp-wide): 284.6MM **Publicly Held**
SIC: 8732 8742 Commercial nonphysical research; marketing consulting services
PA: Harte Hanks, Inc.
2800 Wells Branch Pkwy
Austin TX 78728
512 343-1100

(G-11414)
HARTFORD FIRE INSURANCE CO
7300 W 110th St Ste 300 (66210-2300)
PHONE....913 693-8500
Richard Hubbard, *Manager*
EMP: 100 **Publicly Held**
WEB: www.hartfordinvestmentscanada.com
SIC: 6411 Insurance agents, brokers & service
HQ: Hartford Fire Insurance Company
1 Hartford Plz
Hartford CT 06115
860 547-5000

GEOGRAPHIC

(G-11415)
HARVEST GRAPHICS LLC
14625 W 100th St (66215-1147)
PHONE..................................913 438-5556
John Cowan, *President*
Pat Kierl, *Principal*
Price Williams, *Vice Pres*
Greg Ranallo, *Sales Associate*
Liz Moore, *Office Mgr*
EMP: 45
SQ FT: 3,200
SALES: 12MM **Privately Held**
WEB: www.harvestgraphics.biz
SIC: 7336 2752 Graphic arts & related design; commercial printing, lithographic

(G-11416)
HAWKS BSLER RGERS OPTMTRIST PA
Also Called: Hawks Besler, Rogers & Gerson
5703 W 95th St (66207-2919)
PHONE..................................913 341-4508
Terry F Hawks, *President*
EMP: 18
SQ FT: 1,200
SALES (est): 708.7K **Privately Held**
SIC: 8042 Offices & clinics of optometrists

(G-11417)
HAWTHORNE ANIMAL HOSPITAL
11966 Roe Ave (66209-1566)
PHONE..................................913 345-8147
Susan Brundrett Dvm, *Partner*
Robert David Dvm, *Partner*
EMP: 11
SALES (est): 512.7K **Privately Held**
SIC: 0742 Animal hospital services, pets & other animal specialties

(G-11418)
HD ENGINEERING & DESIGN INC
11656 W 75th St (66214-1372)
P.O. Box 3884, Shawnee (66203-0884)
PHONE..................................913 631-2222
John F Hulse, *President*
EMP: 10
SALES (est): 1.3MM **Privately Held**
SIC: 8711 Civil engineering

(G-11419)
HEALTH ADMINISOURCE LLC
Also Called: Kansas Cy Physcl Therapy Group
6640 Johnson Dr (66202-2617)
PHONE..................................913 384-5600
Angela Duncan, *Administration*
Mary Jo Hegstrom,
Thomas Rorabaugh,
EMP: 12
SALES (est): 590K **Privately Held**
SIC: 8049 Physical therapist

(G-11420)
HEART OF AMERICA BONE MARROW D (PA)
8700 State Line Rd # 340 (66206-1572)
PHONE..................................913 901-3131
Kurt Hanlin, *Senior Engr*
Gayle Bass, *Director*
Anthony Barber, *Analyst*
EMP: 10
SQ FT: 2,000
SALES (est): 1.3MM **Privately Held**
SIC: 6324 Hospital & medical service plans

(G-11421)
HEARTLAND ANIMAL CLINIC PA
7821 Marty St (66204-2925)
PHONE..................................913 648-1662
Jill Sandler, *Owner*
Jamie A Wilson,
EMP: 11 **EST:** 1992
SALES (est): 510K **Privately Held**
SIC: 0742 0752 Animal hospital services, pets & other animal specialties; grooming services, pet & animal specialties

(G-11422)
HEARTLAND BUILDING MAINTENANCE
7127 Oakview St (66216-4037)
PHONE..................................913 268-7132
Steve Marsden, *Owner*
EMP: 64 **EST:** 1989
SALES: 1.2MM **Privately Held**
SIC: 7349 Janitorial service, contract basis

(G-11423)
HEARTLAND DEISEL REPAIR
2200 W 47th Pl Apt 216 (66205-1874)
PHONE..................................913 403-0208
Nate Ordo, *Owner*
EMP: 12 **EST:** 2007
SALES (est): 1.1MM **Privately Held**
SIC: 7699 Repair services

(G-11424)
HEARTLAND FOOD PRODUCTS INC
Also Called: Heartland Foods
1900 W 47th Pl (66205-1815)
PHONE..................................866 571-0222
William R Steeb, *President*
Tom Gray, *Vice Pres*
Dana Roos, *Vice Pres*
Mary Steeb, *Treasurer*
Dana Laird, *Accounting Mgr*
▼ **EMP:** 15
SALES (est): 3.3MM **Privately Held**
WEB: www.heartlandfoodproducts.com
SIC: 2099 5046 Food preparations; restaurant equipment & supplies

(G-11425)
HEARTSTRINGS CMNTY FOUNDATION (PA)
Also Called: ON MY OWN
7086 W 105th St (66212-1803)
PHONE..................................913 649-5700
Bunny Higgins, *Exec Dir*
Roseanne Thiry, *Director*
Jonathan Watkins, *Director*
EMP: 15
SALES: 1MM **Privately Held**
SIC: 8699 Charitable organization

(G-11426)
HENRY J KANAREK
4601 W 109th St Ste 350 (66211-1349)
PHONE..................................913 451-8555
Henry J Kanarek, *Owner*
EMP: 11 **EST:** 1998
SALES (est): 935.3K **Privately Held**
SIC: 8011 Allergist

(G-11427)
HENRY SCHEIN INC
Also Called: Sullivan Schein Dental
11135 W 79th St (66214-1482)
PHONE..................................913 894-8444
Tom McGraph, *Principal*
Dedra Montgomery, *Sales Staff*
EMP: 19
SALES (corp-wide): 13.2B **Publicly Held**
WEB: www.henryschein.com
SIC: 3843 5047 Dental equipment & supplies; dental equipment & supplies
PA: Henry Schein, Inc.
135 Duryea Rd
Melville NY 11747
631 843-5500

(G-11428)
HERMAN MILLER INC
10930 Lackman Rd (66219-1232)
PHONE..................................913 599-4700
Jeff Fregeres, *Manager*
EMP: 5
SALES (corp-wide): 2.5B **Publicly Held**
WEB: www.hermanmiller.com
SIC: 2521 Wood office furniture
PA: Herman Miller, Inc.
855 E Main Ave
Zeeland MI 49464
616 654-3000

(G-11429)
HERMES NURSERY INC
20000 W 47th St (66218-9416)
PHONE..................................913 441-2400
Niel Henriksen, *CEO*
EMP: 30
SALES (corp-wide): 17.6MM **Privately Held**
SIC: 5261 5193 Nurseries; nursery stock
HQ: Hermes Nursery Inc
12421 Santa Fe Trail Dr
Shawnee Mission KS
913 888-2400

(G-11430)
HERTZ CORPORATION
6001 Nieman Rd (66203-2937)
PHONE..................................913 962-1226
EMP: 23
SALES (corp-wide): 9.5B **Publicly Held**
SIC: 7514 Rent-a-car service
HQ: The Hertz Corporation
8501 Williams Rd
Estero FL 33928
239 301-7000

(G-11431)
HIGDON AND HALE CPAS P C
Also Called: Higdon & Hale
6310 Lamar Ave Ste 110 (66202-4284)
PHONE..................................913 831-7000
John Keech, *President*
D Bob Hale, *Vice Pres*
David B Higdon, *Vice Pres*
John P Martin, *Treasurer*
EMP: 11
SALES (est): 941.3K **Privately Held**
WEB: www.higdonhale.com
SIC: 8721 Certified public accountant

(G-11432)
HILLCREST CHRSTN CHILD DEV CTR
11411 Quivira Rd (66210-1345)
PHONE..................................913 663-1997
Shelly Truxall, *Exec Dir*
Anne Sammur, *Director*
EMP: 26
SALES (est): 301K **Privately Held**
WEB: www.hillcrestchristiankc.org
SIC: 8351 8661 Montessori child development center; Christian & Reformed Church

(G-11433)
HILLCREST COVENANT CHURCH
Also Called: Hillcrest Covenant Pre-School
8801 Nall Ave (66207-2199)
PHONE..................................913 901-2300
Mark Seversen, *Pastor*
Dan Mapes, *Exec Dir*
EMP: 46
SALES (est): 1.7MM **Privately Held**
SIC: 8661 8351 5942 Covenant & Evangelical Church; preschool center; group day care center; book stores

(G-11434)
HIMALAYA MORTGAGE INC
11881 W 112th St (66210-2717)
PHONE..................................913 649-9700
Maneesha Dang, *President*
Rajiv Dang, *Manager*
EMP: 12
SALES (est): 1.6MM **Privately Held**
SIC: 6163 Mortgage brokers arranging for loans, using money of others

(G-11435)
HMK CONCRETE
5713 Kessler Ln Ste 101 (66203-2517)
PHONE..................................913 262-1555
Harvey Kascht, *Owner*
EMP: 15
SALES (est): 672.2K **Privately Held**
SIC: 1771 Concrete work

(G-11436)
HOCKENBERGS RESTAURANT SUPPLY
14603 W 112th St (66215-4096)
PHONE..................................913 696-9773
Tom Schrack, *President*
Kirk Farmer, *Vice Pres*
▼ **EMP:** 13
SALES (est): 4.6MM **Privately Held**
SIC: 5046 Restaurant equipment & supplies

(G-11437)
HOME DEPOT USA INC
9900 Pflumm Rd Ste 64 (66215-1231)
PHONE..................................913 888-9090
EMP: 41
SALES (corp-wide): 108.2B **Publicly Held**
WEB: www.rmahomeservices.com
SIC: 8741 Construction management
HQ: Home Depot U.S.A., Inc.
2455 Paces Ferry Ave
Atlanta GA 30339

(G-11438)
HOME DEPOT USA INC
Also Called: Home Depot, The
9600 Metcalf Ave (66212-2213)
PHONE..................................913 648-7811
Jerry Simer, *Manager*
EMP: 150
SALES (corp-wide): 108.2B **Publicly Held**
WEB: www.homerentalsdepot.com
SIC: 5211 7359 Home centers; tool rental
HQ: Home Depot U.S.A., Inc.
2455 Paces Ferry Ave
Atlanta GA 30339

(G-11439)
HOPE LUTHERAN CHURCH SHAWNEE
Also Called: Hope Lutheran School
6308 Quivira Rd (66216-2744)
PHONE..................................913 631-6940
Diane Eichholz, *Principal*
Michael Penikis, *Pastor*
Leann Miller, *Teacher*
EMP: 30
SALES (corp-wide): 1.4MM **Privately Held**
WEB: www.hopelutheran.org
SIC: 8351 8661 Preschool center; Lutheran Church
PA: Hope Lutheran Church Of Shawnee
6308 Quivira Rd
Shawnee Mission KS 66216
913 631-6940

(G-11440)
HORMEL FOODS CORP SVCS LLC
8700 Monrovia St Ste 200 (66215-3500)
PHONE..................................913 888-8744
Nathan Zeit, *QC Mgr*
Gary Esbeck, *Sales/Mktg Mgr*
Mike Bell, *Sales Mgr*
EMP: 15
SALES (corp-wide): 9.5B **Publicly Held**
SIC: 5147 Meats & meat products
HQ: Hormel Foods Corporate Services, Llc
1 Hormel Pl
Austin MN 55912
507 437-5611

(G-11441)
HPB BIODIESEL INC
9000 W 67th St Ste 200 (66202-3656)
PHONE..................................800 262-7907
Harry R Fruehauf III, *Manager*
EMP: 10
SALES (est): 4.9MM
SALES (corp-wide): 6.5B **Publicly Held**
SIC: 2911 Diesel fuels
HQ: Seaboard Foods Llc
9000 W 67th St Ste 200
Shawnee Mission KS 66202
913 261-2600

(G-11442)
HPT TRS IHG-2 INC
Also Called: Candlewood Suites
11001 Oakmont St (66210-1187)
PHONE..................................913 469-5557
Chuck Sourbeer, *General Mgr*
EMP: 14 **Publicly Held**
SIC: 7011 Hotels
HQ: Hpt Trs Ihg-2, Inc.
255 Washington St Ste 300
Newton MA 02458
617 964-8389

(G-11443)
HUNKELER EYE INSTITUTE PA
7950 College Blvd Ste B (66210-1869)
PHONE..................................913 338-4733
John D Hunkeler, *Owner*
EMP: 17
SALES (est): 1.3MM **Privately Held**
SIC: 8011 Eyes, ears, nose & throat specialist: physician/surgeon

(G-11444)
HUTCHINS & ASSOCIATES
11900 College Blvd # 310 (66210-4048)
PHONE..................................913 338-4455

Daniel F Hutchins, *Owner*
Daniel Haake, *Owner*
Dan Haake, *Partner*
Susie Hutchins, *Admin Asst*
EMP: 14
SALES (est): 927.8K **Privately Held**
SIC: 8721 Certified public accountant

(G-11445)
HYDROGEOLOGIC INC
Also Called: Hydro Geologic
6340 Glenwood St Ste 200 (66202-4008)
PHONE..................................913 317-8860
John Borthwick, *Engineer*
Alan Rittgers, *Branch Mgr*
EMP: 29
SALES (corp-wide): 56.1MM **Privately Held**
WEB: www.hgl.com
SIC: 8744
PA: Hydrogeologic, Inc.
11107 Sunset Hills Rd # 400
Reston VA 20190
703 478-5186

(G-11446)
I M S OF KANSAS CITY INC
Also Called: Nations Mailing Systems
11555 W 83rd Ter (66214-1532)
PHONE..................................913 599-6007
John E Thomas, *President*
▲ **EMP:** 11
SQ FT: 5,000
SALES (est): 837.2K **Privately Held**
SIC: 5712 5044 Office furniture; mailing machines

(G-11447)
I SAMCO INVESTMENTS LTD (PA)
Also Called: Holiday Inn
10985 Cody St Ste 220 (66210-1224)
PHONE..................................913 345-2111
Donald E Culbertson, *Partner*
EMP: 75
SALES (est): 933K **Privately Held**
SIC: 7011 Hotels & motels

(G-11448)
I T POWER LLC
6811 Shawnee Mission Pkwy # 107 (66202-4031)
PHONE..................................913 384-5800
Christopher Wren, *Invest Mgr*
Liz Mitchell, *Accounts Mgr*
Mike Boatright, *Manager*
Joyce Olds, *Info Tech Dir*
Sid Singh, *Tech Recruiter*
EMP: 43
SALES (est): 3.7MM **Privately Held**
SIC: 7371 Custom computer programming services

(G-11449)
IAC SYSTEMS INC
4800 Lamar Ave Ste 203 (66202-1711)
PHONE..................................913 384-5511
Glenn Smith Jr, *President*
Robert M Frye, *Vice Pres*
Kae Huff, *Sales Staff*
EMP: 26
SQ FT: 15,170
SALES (est): 6.6MM **Privately Held**
SIC: 5075 5084 Air pollution control equipment & supplies; pneumatic tools & equipment

(G-11450)
IBT INC
5420 England (66203)
P.O. Box 2982 (66201-1382)
PHONE..................................913 677-3151
Steve Cloud, *President*
Joe Dix, *Sales Associate*
EMP: 150
SALES (corp-wide): 161.7MM **Privately Held**
WEB: www.ibtinc.com
SIC: 5085 Industrial supplies
PA: Ibt, Inc.
9400 W 55th St
Shawnee Mission KS 66203
913 677-3151

(G-11451)
ICE SPORTS KANSAS CITY LLC
Also Called: Ice Sports-Kansas City
19900 Johnson Dr (66218-9661)
PHONE..................................913 441-3033
Jim McCain, *Regional Mgr*
Dave Groulx, *Mng Member*
Kay Olive, *Director*
EMP: 20
SALES (est): 772.6K
SALES (corp-wide): 66.2MM **Privately Held**
WEB: www.icesportskc.com
SIC: 7999 7299 5941 Skating rink operation services; party planning service; skating equipment
PA: Canlan Ice Sports Corp
6501 Sprott St
Burnaby BC V5B 3
604 291-0626

(G-11452)
ICE-MASTERS INC (HQ)
6218 Melrose Ln (66203-3036)
PHONE..................................660 827-6900
Robert W Tramposh, *President*
Judy Tramposh, *Vice Pres*
Pam Meyer, *Technology*
EMP: 11
SQ FT: 11,000
SALES (est): 2MM
SALES (corp-wide): 7.7MM **Privately Held**
SIC: 7359 Equipment rental & leasing
PA: Tresko Inc
6218 Melrose Ln
Shawnee Mission KS 66203
913 631-6900

(G-11453)
ILLINOIS TOOL WORKS INC
Also Called: Seaboard Logistics
9000 W 67th St (66202-3638)
PHONE..................................800 262-7907
EMP: 8
SALES (corp-wide): 14.7B **Publicly Held**
SIC: 3089 Injection molded finished plastic products
PA: Illinois Tool Works Inc.
155 Harlem Ave
Glenview IL 60025
847 724-7500

(G-11454)
INDEVCO INC
Also Called: Mid America Truss
6911 W 66th Ter (66202-4150)
PHONE..................................913 236-7222
Randy Cassmeyer, *Manager*
EMP: 75
SALES (est): 5.1MM **Privately Held**
WEB: www.indevco.com
SIC: 2439 Trusses, wooden roof

(G-11455)
INDUSTRIAL ACCESSORIES COMPANY (PA)
4800 Lamar Ave Ste 203 (66202-1711)
PHONE..................................913 384-5511
Glenn A Smith Jr, *President*
Darrell L Childress, *General Mgr*
Ben Giefer, *General Mgr*
Brian Clements, *Superintendent*
Kassandra Dinwiddie, *Business Mgr*
EMP: 90
SQ FT: 15,170
SALES (est): 54.5MM **Privately Held**
WEB: www.iac-intl.com
SIC: 5075 5084 8711 Air pollution control equipment & supplies; pneumatic tools & equipment; industrial engineers

(G-11456)
INFANT TDDLER SVCS JHNSON CNTY
6400 Glenwood St Ste 205 (66202-4019)
PHONE..................................913 432-2900
Amy Owens, *Director*
Monica Ross, *Program Dir*
EMP: 12 **EST:** 1985
SALES: 3.7MM **Privately Held**
WEB: www.itsjc.org
SIC: 8322 Child related social services

(G-11457)
INLAND NEWSPAPER MCHY CORP
14500 W 105th St (66215-2014)
PHONE..................................913 492-9050
Clark O Murray, *Ch of Bd*
Beau Campbell, *President*
Jack D Burton, *Exec VP*
Brian D Murray, *Executive*
EMP: 31 **EST:** 1910
SQ FT: 28,000
SALES (est): 3.8MM
SALES (corp-wide): 20.8MM **Privately Held**
SIC: 5084 3555 Printing trades machinery, equipment & supplies; printing trades machinery
PA: Inland Industries, Inc.
19841 Benson St
Bucyrus KS 66013
913 492-9050

(G-11458)
INNCO HOSPITALITY INC (PA)
7300 W 110th St Ste 990 (66210-2392)
PHONE..................................913 451-1300
Roland Samples, *President*
Merkel Richard L, *Director*
EMP: 22 **EST:** 1974
SALES (est): 2.8MM **Privately Held**
SIC: 8741 Hotel or motel management; restaurant management

(G-11459)
INSCO INDUSTRIES INC (PA)
6902 Martindale Rd (66218-9330)
PHONE..................................913 422-8001
Matt Hurd, *President*
Thad Bartlett, *Vice Pres*
Jeremy Chambers, *Safety Dir*
Travis Hamilton, *Project Mgr*
Adam Perkins, *Project Mgr*
EMP: 40
SQ FT: 10,000
SALES (est): 6.1MM **Privately Held**
WEB: www.inscoind.com
SIC: 1742 Insulation, buildings

(G-11460)
INSTITUTE FOR PROFESSIONAL DEV
8001 College Blvd (66210-1980)
PHONE..................................913 491-4432
Jan Asnicar, *Manager*
EMP: 25
SALES (corp-wide): 1.1B **Privately Held**
SIC: 8742 8221 School, college, university consultant; merchandising consultant; colleges universities & professional schools
HQ: Institute For Professional Development, Inc
4615 E Elwood St
Phoenix AZ 85040
480 966-5394

(G-11461)
INSURANCE DESIGNER KANSAS CITY
Also Called: Insurance Designers
9401 Indian Creek Pkwy # 150 (66210-2007)
PHONE..................................913 451-3960
Dick White, *President*
Steven Burke, *Owner*
Jaye Ediger, *Mktg Dir*
Maury Loridon, *Manager*
Tom Moore, *Manager*
EMP: 15
SALES (est): 2.1MM **Privately Held**
WEB: www.idakc.com
SIC: 6411 Insurance agents

(G-11462)
INTEGRA REALTY RESOURCES (PA)
1901 W 47th Pl Ste 300 (66205-1834)
PHONE..................................913 236-4700
Joann Nunnink, *CEO*
Kevin K Nunnink, *President*
Tracy Nelson, *Info Tech Dir*
EMP: 30 **EST:** 1975
SQ FT: 10,000
SALES (est): 5.8MM **Privately Held**
SIC: 6531 8742 Real estate agent, commercial; real estate agent, residential; real estate managers; appraiser, real estate; real estate consultant

(G-11463)
INTEGRAL CARE PROVIDER INC
6811 Shawnee Mission Pkwy # 115 (66202-4031)
PHONE..................................913 384-2273
Jason Mateo, *President*
Gigi Mateo, *Admin Sec*
EMP: 150
SQ FT: 1,600
SALES (est): 2.5MM **Privately Held**
WEB: www.integralcare.com
SIC: 8082 8049 Home health care services; nurses, registered & practical

(G-11464)
INTERNATIONAL CODE COUNCIL INC
11711 W 85th St (66214-1517)
PHONE..................................913 888-0304
Cesar Monterio, *Manager*
EMP: 15
SALES (corp-wide): 36.6MM **Privately Held**
WEB: www.icccampus.com
SIC: 4225 Warehousing, self-storage
PA: International Code Council, Inc.
500 New Jersey Ave Nw # 6
Washington DC 20001
202 370-1800

(G-11465)
INTERNET SVC PRVDERS NTWRK INC
Also Called: Ispn
14303 W 95th St (66215-5210)
PHONE..................................913 859-9500
Bijan Moaveni, *President*
Charlie Brenneman, *Vice Pres*
EMP: 35
SALES (est): 3.9MM **Privately Held**
SIC: 4813

(G-11466)
INTRUST BANK NATIONAL ASSN
4000 Somerset Dr (66208-5294)
PHONE..................................913 385-8200
Kris Kirkes, *Manager*
EMP: 100
SALES (corp-wide): 134.2MM **Privately Held**
WEB: www.intrustbank.com
SIC: 6021 National commercial banks
HQ: Intrust Bank National Association
105 N Main St
Wichita KS 67202
316 383-1111

(G-11467)
IQVUA RDS INC
11250 Corporate Ave (66219-1392)
P.O. Box 14325, Durham NC (27709-4325)
PHONE..................................913 894-5533
Donovan Griffith, *Research*
Linda Owens, *Sls & Mktg Exec*
Jim Nixon, *Branch Mgr*
EMP: 79 **Publicly Held**
SIC: 8731 Commercial physical research
HQ: Iqvia Rds Inc
4820 Emperor Blvd
Durham NC 27703
919 998-2000

(G-11468)
IRONHORSE GOLF CLUB MAINT
15300 Mission Rd (66224-9527)
PHONE..................................913 897-8181
Chris Glaxton, *Manager*
EMP: 10
SALES (est): 170.1K **Privately Held**
SIC: 7997 Country club, membership

(G-11469)
IVY FUNDS DISTRIBUTOR INC (HQ)
6300 Lamar Ave (66202-4247)
PHONE..................................913 261-2800
Thomas W Butch, *Principal*
Terry L Lister, *Risk Mgmt Dir*

GEOGRAPHIC

EMP: 12
SALES (est): 1.8MM Publicly Held
SIC: 6722 Money market mutual funds

(G-11470)
J & B INC
11552 Carter St (66210-2924)
PHONE..................................816 590-1174
Bertha Lawson, *CEO*
EMP: 10
SALES (est): 763.2K Privately Held
SIC: 4212 Delivery service, vehicular

(G-11471)
J A PETERSON ENTERPRISES INC (PA)
Also Called: Peterson Companies, The
10000 W 75th St Ste 100 (66204-2241)
PHONE..................................913 384-3800
Gordon Peterson, *President*
Roger Siegrist, *Controller*
EMP: 34
SQ FT: 70,000
SALES (est): 11.8MM Privately Held
SIC: 5812 6552 6512 Pizzeria, chain; subdividers & developers; commercial & industrial building operation

(G-11472)
J A PETERSON ENTERPRISES INC
Also Called: Regents Walk
9130 Riggs Ln (66212-1312)
PHONE..................................913 642-9020
Dawn Mason, *Manager*
EMP: 10
SALES (corp-wide): 11.8MM Privately Held
SIC: 6513 Apartment building operators
PA: J A Peterson Enterprises, Inc
10000 W 75th St Ste 100
Shawnee Mission KS 66204
913 384-3800

(G-11473)
J A PETERSON REALTY CO INC (HQ)
Also Called: PETERSON COMPANIES, THE
10000 W 75th St Ste 100 (66204-2241)
PHONE..................................913 384-3800
Gordon J Peterson, *Ch of Bd*
Kenneth Riedemann, *President*
Ruth Peterson, *Principal*
Diane Schwirtz, *Personnel*
Roger Siegrist, *Admin Sec*
EMP: 17
SQ FT: 80,000
SALES: 1.5MM
SALES (corp-wide): 11.8MM Privately Held
WEB: www.petersoncompanies.com
SIC: 6513 6512 Apartment hotel operation; commercial & industrial building operation
PA: J A Peterson Enterprises, Inc
10000 W 75th St Ste 100
Shawnee Mission KS 66204
913 384-3800

(G-11474)
J A PETERSON REALTY CO INC
Also Called: Fox Run Apartments
7650 Goddard St (66214-1152)
PHONE..................................913 631-2332
Toni Pearson, *Manager*
EMP: 12
SALES (corp-wide): 11.8MM Privately Held
WEB: www.petersoncompanies.com
SIC: 6513 Apartment building operators
HQ: J. A. Peterson Realty Co. Inc.
10000 W 75th St Ste 100
Shawnee Mission KS 66204
913 384-3800

(G-11475)
J A PETERSON REALTY CO INC
Also Called: Kings Cove Apts
7350 Kings Cove Dr (66203-4660)
PHONE..................................913 432-5050
Carrie Short, *Manager*
EMP: 12
SALES (corp-wide): 11.8MM Privately Held
WEB: www.petersoncompanies.com
SIC: 6513 Apartment building operators
HQ: J. A. Peterson Realty Co. Inc.
10000 W 75th St Ste 100
Shawnee Mission KS 66204
913 384-3800

(G-11476)
J B HINZ
Also Called: Lawn Magic
9818 W 100th Ter (66212-5305)
PHONE..................................913 492-5566
J B Hinz, *Owner*
EMP: 10 EST: 1980
SALES (est): 290K Privately Held
SIC: 0782 Lawn care services

(G-11477)
J M OCONNOR INC
Also Called: O'Connor Company
14925 W 99th St (66215-1112)
PHONE..................................913 438-7867
Lynn Piller, *President*
Kim Adams, *General Mgr*
Kyle Leeser, *Sales Staff*
Terry Grimes, *Branch Mgr*
▲ EMP: 12
SALES (est): 2.3MM Privately Held
WEB: www.jmoconnor.net
SIC: 5075 Warm air heating & air conditioning

(G-11478)
J SCHMID & ASSOC INC
5800 Foxridge Dr Ste 200 (66202-2338)
PHONE..................................913 236-8988
John E Schmid, *Ch of Bd*
Lois Brayfield, *President*
Michele Drohan, *Exec VP*
Neal Schuler, *Vice Pres*
Cheryl Zatz, *Marketing Staff*
EMP: 18
SQ FT: 6,000
SALES (est): 1.5MM Privately Held
WEB: www.jschmid.com
SIC: 8742 Marketing consulting services

(G-11479)
JACK HENRY & ASSOCIATES INC
23001 W 81st St (66227-2619)
PHONE..................................913 422-3233
Michael E Henry, *Manager*
EMP: 128
SALES (corp-wide): 1.5B Publicly Held
WEB: www.jackhenry.com
SIC: 5045 7371 7378 Computers; computer software development; software programming applications; computer maintenance & repair
PA: Jack Henry & Associates, Inc.
663 W Highway 60
Monett MO 65708
417 235-6652

(G-11480)
JACK HENRY & ASSOCIATES INC
10910 W 87th St (66214-1603)
PHONE..................................913 341-3434
Jack Hoppers, *Manager*
Jeannine Dunlap, *Manager*
Rob Loethen, *Manager*
Curtis Rayburn, *Info Tech Mgr*
Kirk Searcey, *IT/INT Sup*
EMP: 30
SALES (corp-wide): 1.5B Publicly Held
WEB: www.jackhenry.com
SIC: 7374 Data processing service
PA: Jack Henry & Associates, Inc.
663 W Highway 60
Monett MO 65708
417 235-6652

(G-11481)
JADE DENTAL LAB INC
13720 W 108th St (66215-2026)
PHONE..................................913 469-9500
Jeff Green, *President*
EMP: 23
SQ FT: 3,400
SALES (est): 1.4MM Privately Held
WEB: www.jadedentallab.com
SIC: 8072 Crown & bridge production

(G-11482)
JAMES R KIENE JR DDS PA LLC
Also Called: Kiene, Pete
11005 W 60th St Ste 240 (66203-2789)
PHONE..................................913 825-9373
James R Kiene Jr DDS,
Rebecca Kiene,
EMP: 15
SALES (est): 1.3MM Privately Held
SIC: 8021 Dentists' office

(G-11483)
JEFFERSON POINTE APARTMENTS
11810 Farley St (66210-2803)
PHONE..................................913 906-9100
Frank Oddo, *CEO*
Rick Oddo, *President*
EMP: 10 EST: 2001
SALES (est): 871.5K Privately Held
SIC: 6513 Apartment hotel operation

(G-11484)
JERRY BORESOW
Also Called: Boresow's Lawn Enforcement
5695 Clare Rd (66226-2815)
PHONE..................................913 441-1111
Jerry Boresow, *Owner*
Jerry Boresaw, *Owner*
Beth Boresow,
EMP: 15
SALES (est): 883.7K Privately Held
SIC: 0782 Lawn services

(G-11485)
JET STREAM GUTTERING CORP
5023 Antioch Rd (66203-1314)
PHONE..................................913 262-2913
Rick Kuebelbeck, *President*
EMP: 12
SQ FT: 6,000
SALES: 1MM Privately Held
SIC: 1761 Gutter & downspout contractor

(G-11486)
JEWISH CMNTY CTR GRTER KANS CY
5801 W 115th St Ste 101 (66211-1800)
PHONE..................................913 327-8000
Samantha Hammontree, *COO*
Leanne Nash, *Accountant*
Krisandra Spell, *Accountant*
Jacob Shreiber, *Exec Dir*
Felice Azorsky, *Relations*
EMP: 300
SALES: 10.2MM Privately Held
SIC: 8641 8351 8322 7991 Social club, membership; child day care services; individual & family services; physical fitness facilities

(G-11487)
JEWISH COMMUNITY CAMPUS
5801 W 115th St Ste 100 (66211-1800)
PHONE..................................913 327-8200
Alan Bram, *Exec Dir*
Gayle Levin, *Director*
EMP: 20
SQ FT: 224,500
SALES: 2.1MM Privately Held
SIC: 8322 Community center

(G-11488)
JEWISH FAMILY AND CHLD SVC
Also Called: Alfred Benjamin Conseling Svc
5801 W 115th St Ste 103 (66211-1800)
PHONE..................................913 327-8250
Eddie Feinstein, *Exec Dir*
EMP: 13
SALES (corp-wide): 5.7MM Privately Held
SIC: 8322 Family service agency; general counseling services
PA: Jewish Family And Children's Service
10950 Schuetz Rd
Saint Louis MO 63146
314 993-1000

(G-11489)
JEWISH FDRTION GREATER KANS CY
5801 W 115th St Ste 201 (66211-1800)
PHONE..................................913 327-8100
Todd Steetner, *Exec Dir*
EMP: 20
SQ FT: 6,000
SALES: 8MM Privately Held
SIC: 8399 Fund raising organization, non-fee basis

(G-11490)
JHON-JOSEPHSONS SALON
Also Called: Hair Professionals
4324 W 119th St (66209-1549)
PHONE..................................913 338-4443
Jhon Josephson, *Partner*
EMP: 20
SALES (est): 429.1K Privately Held
SIC: 7231 Unisex hair salons

(G-11491)
JOHN H MOFFITT & CO INC (PA)
Also Called: Coldwell Banker
5300 College Blvd (66211-1621)
PHONE..................................913 491-6800
John H Moffitt Jr, *President*
EMP: 35
SQ FT: 15,000
SALES (est): 2.5MM Privately Held
WEB: www.robmullins.net
SIC: 6531 6552 Real estate agent, residential; land subdividers & developers, residential

(G-11492)
JOHN K BURCH COMPANY
Also Called: Burch Fabrics
5775 Foxridge Dr (66202-2496)
PHONE..................................800 365-1988
Joseph Gorman, *Branch Mgr*
EMP: 12
SQ FT: 16,250
SALES (corp-wide): 29.3MM Privately Held
WEB: www.burchfabric.com
SIC: 5131 Upholstery fabrics, woven
PA: John K. Burch Company
4200 Brockton Dr Se
Grand Rapids MI 49512
616 698-2800

(G-11493)
JOHNSON CNTY GRLS ATHC COMPLEX
20200 Johnson Dr (66218-9304)
PHONE..................................913 422-7837
Tom Turley, *Manager*
EMP: 60
SALES (est): 754.6K Privately Held
SIC: 8699 Athletic organizations

(G-11494)
JOHNSON CNTY OB-GYN CHARTERED
Also Called: Cederlind, Cranston J
7440 W Frontage Rd (66203-4670)
PHONE..................................913 236-6455
Dr Cranston J Cederlind, *Partner*
Christophe M Lynch MD, *Partner*
Randy Sheridan, *Partner*
Teresa Thompson, *Partner*
Dr Melanie Martin, *Med Doctor*
EMP: 24
SALES (est): 3.9MM Privately Held
WEB: www.joco-obgyn.com
SIC: 8011 Obstetrician; gynecologist

(G-11495)
JOHNSON CNTY PK RECREATION DST
7900 Renner Rd (66219-9723)
PHONE..................................913 438-7275
Jo Ann Courtney, *Human Res Mgr*
Michael D Meadors, *Director*
Daniel Goodman, *Director*
EMP: 29
SALES: 38.5MM Privately Held
SIC: 7997 Membership sports & recreation clubs

(G-11496)
JOHNSON COUNTY ANIMAL CLINIC
9425 W 75th St (66204-2213)
PHONE..................................913 642-2714
Dean Small, *Partner*
EMP: 15

SALES (est): 890.4K **Privately Held**
SIC: 0742 0752 Animal hospital services, pets & other animal specialties; boarding services, kennels

(G-11497)
JOHNSON COUNTY AUTOMOTIVE LLC
5829 Kessler Ln (66203-2519)
PHONE..................................913 432-1721
Alan Heriford, *Principal*
EMP: 14
SALES (est): 2MM **Privately Held**
WEB: www.jocoauto.com
SIC: 7539 Automotive repair shops

(G-11498)
JOHNSON COUNTY INVESTORS INC
11501 Shwnee Mission Pkwy (66203-3359)
P.O. Box 3179 (66203-0179)
PHONE..................................913 631-0000
Richard Shull, *President*
EMP: 154
SQ FT: 43,000
SALES (est): 63.9MM **Privately Held**
WEB: www.shawneemissionford.com
SIC: 5511 7538 Automobiles, new & used; pickups, new & used; vans, new & used; general automotive repair shops

(G-11499)
JOHNSON COUNTY LANDFILL
17955 Holiday Dr (66217-9700)
PHONE..................................913 631-8181
Beverly Taylor, *Manager*
EMP: 37
SALES (est): 202.1K **Privately Held**
SIC: 4953 Sanitary landfill operation

(G-11500)
JOHNSON WILSON EMBERS
Also Called: W J E Healthcare Architects
8207 Melrose Dr Ste 145 (66214-1624)
PHONE..................................913 438-9095
Richard Johnson, *Partner*
Don Wilson, *Partner*
Richard L Embers, *Principal*
EMP: 27
SALES (est): 1.9MM **Privately Held**
WEB: www.wje-architects.com
SIC: 8712 Architectural services

(G-11501)
JOHNSTON INSURANCE AGENCY
Also Called: G R Fiss and Company
5225 W 75th St Ste 200 (66208-4403)
PHONE..................................913 396-0800
Robert Fiss, *President*
Scott Fiss, *Vice Pres*
Bob Cox, *CFO*
EMP: 20
SQ FT: 3,400
SALES (est): 3.9MM **Privately Held**
WEB: www.johnstonfiss.com
SIC: 6411 Insurance agents

(G-11502)
JOSEPH STOWERS PAINTING INC
6839 Nall Ave (66208-1431)
PHONE..................................913 722-2534
Robert Nelson, *President*
Roy Merryfield, *Vice Pres*
EMP: 20
SALES (est): 955.4K **Privately Held**
SIC: 1721 Commercial painting; industrial painting; commercial wallcovering contractor

(G-11503)
JRKO LLC
Also Called: Comfort Inn
7200 W 107th St (66212-2564)
PHONE..................................913 648-7858
Emily Vogele, *Manager*
EMP: 25
SALES (est): 569.4K **Privately Held**
SIC: 7011 Hotels & motels

(G-11504)
JURY & ASSOCIATES INC
5750 W 95th St Ste 200 (66207-2976)
PHONE..................................913 642-5656
Ronald D Jury, *President*
EMP: 50
SALES (est): 4.9MM **Privately Held**
SIC: 6531 Real estate agent, residential

(G-11505)
JUST OUR LAUNDRY INC
Also Called: My Laundry
8730 Santa Fe Dr (66212-3654)
PHONE..................................913 649-8364
Chong Hoon Kim, *President*
EMP: 14
SQ FT: 3,000
SALES (est): 680K **Privately Held**
SIC: 7216 7211 7215 Drycleaning plants, except rugs; power laundries, family & commercial; laundry, coin-operated

(G-11506)
K C SIGN EXPRESS INC
5033 Mackey St (66203-1333)
PHONE..................................913 432-2500
Leslie Murray, *President*
Bill Brown, *Prdtn Mgr*
Pat Murray, *Sales Mgr*
Jeff Murray, *Associate*
▲ **EMP:** 5
SQ FT: 10,000
SALES (est): 1.2MM **Privately Held**
WEB: www.kcsignexpress.com
SIC: 5046 3993 Signs, electrical; signs & advertising specialties

(G-11507)
K2B INCORPORATED (PA)
7500 College Blvd # 1213 (66210-4035)
PHONE..................................913 663-3311
Neal Underberg, *President*
Ted Stock, *COO*
EMP: 20 **EST:** 2000
SQ FT: 5,000
SALES (est): 2MM **Privately Held**
WEB: www.k2b.net
SIC: 7371 Computer software development

(G-11508)
KANSAS BUILDERS SUPPLY CO INC
Also Called: K B S
5723 Kessler Ln (66203-2517)
PHONE..................................913 831-1511
Jeff Hembree, *President*
Bradley K Hembree, *Vice Pres*
W T Hembree, *Vice Pres*
Carrie Winshky, *Treasurer*
Carolyn S Hembree, *Admin Sec*
EMP: 13 **EST:** 1961
SQ FT: 12,000
SALES (est): 4.5MM **Privately Held**
SIC: 5031 5211 Doors; metal doors, sash & trim; door frames, all materials; doors, wood or metal, except storm

(G-11509)
KANSAS CITY EYE CLINIC PA
7504 Antioch Rd (66204-2622)
PHONE..................................913 341-3100
Carl Megliazzo MD, *President*
Dr Sara O'Connell, *Partner*
Fred Bodker MD, *Principal*
Michael E Hettinger MD, *Vice Pres*
David M Amos MD, *Treasurer*
EMP: 41
SQ FT: 12,000
SALES (est): 5.2MM **Privately Held**
WEB: www.kceyeclinic.com
SIC: 8011 Ophthalmologist

(G-11510)
KANSAS CITY RACQUET CLUB
6501 Frontage Rd (66202-3646)
PHONE..................................913 789-8000
Brian Clark, *General Mgr*
EMP: 15
SQ FT: 110,000
SALES: 400K **Privately Held**
WEB: www.thenextleaders.org
SIC: 7997 Membership sports & recreation clubs

(G-11511)
KANSAS CITY STRINGS VIOLIN SP
Also Called: Kc Strings
5842 Merriam Dr (66203-2526)
PHONE..................................913 677-0400
Anton Krutz, *Owner*
▲ **EMP:** 20
SALES (est): 873.9K **Privately Held**
WEB: www.kcstrings.com
SIC: 5736 7699 String instruments; musical instrument repair services

(G-11512)
KANSAS CITY TRANSCRIPTION INC
Also Called: 24 7 Transcription
4550 W 109th St Ste 303 (66211-1354)
P.O. Box 26013 (66225-6013)
PHONE..................................913 469-1000
Wendy Miller, *President*
EMP: 15
SALES (est): 359.2K **Privately Held**
SIC: 7363 Medical help service

(G-11513)
KANSAS CITY TREE CARE LLC
5217 Walmer St (66202-1611)
PHONE..................................913 722-4048
Zach Johnson,
Shelby Johnson,
EMP: 20
SALES (est): 952.7K **Privately Held**
SIC: 0783 Ornamental shrub & tree services

(G-11514)
KANSAS CITY WOMENS CLINIC PA (PA)
Also Called: Kcwc
10600 Quivira Rd Ste 320 (66215-2311)
PHONE..................................913 894-8500
J A Heit, *President*
Tony Heit MD, *Managing Prtnr*
Dr Richard Sinclair, *Corp Secy*
Chip Butrick MD, *Vice Pres*
Maggie Smith MD, *Vice Pres*
EMP: 65
SQ FT: 10,090
SALES: 6.6MM **Privately Held**
WEB: www.kansascitywomensclinic.com
SIC: 8011 Gynecologist; obstetrician; physicians' office, including specialists

(G-11515)
KANSAS COACHWORKS LTD
9116 Marshall Dr (66215-3843)
PHONE..................................913 888-0991
Catherine M Smith, *President*
David Irvin, *Corp Secy*
Beverly Denk, *Vice Pres*
EMP: 15
SQ FT: 13,000
SALES (est): 1.4MM **Privately Held**
WEB: www.kansascoachworks.com
SIC: 7532 Body shop, automotive

(G-11516)
KANSAS EAST CONFERENCE UNITED
Also Called: Shawnee United Methodist Ch
10700 Johnson Dr (66203-2846)
PHONE..................................913 631-2280
Fritz Clark, *Pastor*
EMP: 20
SALES (corp-wide): 3.9MM **Privately Held**
WEB: www.shawneeumc.org
SIC: 8661 8351 Methodist Church; child day care services
PA: Kansas East Conference Of The United Methodist Church, Inc
4201 Sw 15th St
Topeka KS 66604
785 272-9111

(G-11517)
KANSAS EAST CONFERENCE UNITED
Also Called: Valley View Mothers Day Out
8412 W 95th St (66212-3241)
PHONE..................................913 383-9146
Leona Murphy, *Director*
EMP: 12
SALES (corp-wide): 3.9MM **Privately Held**
WEB: www.shawneeumc.org
SIC: 8661 8351 Methodist Church; child day care services
PA: Kansas East Conference Of The United Methodist Church, Inc
4201 Sw 15th St
Topeka KS 66604
785 272-9111

(G-11518)
KANSAS NATIONAL EDUCATION ASSN
11015 W 75th Ter (66214-2908)
PHONE..................................913 268-4005
Marilyn Flannigan, *Systems Mgr*
EMP: 12
SALES (corp-wide): 7.7MM **Privately Held**
SIC: 8621 8641 8211 Education & teacher association; educator's association; public elementary & secondary schools
PA: Kansas National Education Association
715 Sw 10th Ave Ste B
Topeka KS 66612
785 232-8271

(G-11519)
KANSAS REGIONAL ASSN REALTORS
11150 Overbrook Rd # 100 (66211-2240)
PHONE..................................913 498-1100
Diane Ruggiero, *CEO*
Renee Ryan Edwards, *President*
Lee McClelland, *President*
Patti Dauer, *Manager*
Erin Wells, *Manager*
EMP: 20
SALES: 3.5MM **Privately Held**
SIC: 8611 Trade associations

(G-11520)
KAREN TOBIN
Also Called: Encounters In Hair
11156 Antioch Rd (66210-2420)
PHONE..................................913 341-1976
Karen Tobin, *Owner*
EMP: 14
SQ FT: 1,500
SALES (est): 246.3K **Privately Held**
WEB: www.encountersinhair.com
SIC: 7231 Hairdressers

(G-11521)
KAW VALLEY ENGINEERING INC
14700 W 114th Ter (66215-4881)
PHONE..................................913 894-5150
Mike Osbourn, *Branch Mgr*
EMP: 50
SALES (est): 6.6MM
SALES (corp-wide): 24.8MM **Privately Held**
WEB: www.kveng.com
SIC: 8711 Civil engineering
PA: Kaw Valley Engineering, Inc.
2319 N Jackson St
Junction City KS 66441
785 762-5040

(G-11522)
KB COMPLETE INC
5621 Foxridge Dr (66202-4522)
PHONE..................................913 722-6835
Lesa Garcia, *General Mgr*
Karlton Bohrn, *Principal*
Chris Koelling, *Office Mgr*
Jim McNeel, *Technician*
EMP: 19
SALES (est): 2.8MM **Privately Held**
SIC: 1711 Plumbing contractors

(G-11523)
KC COLORS AUTO BODY LTD
2007 W 103rd Ter (66206-2642)
PHONE..................................913 491-0696
Tim Schumacher, *President*
EMP: 14
SQ FT: 2,625
SALES (est): 1.8MM **Privately Held**
SIC: 7532 Paint shop, automotive

(G-11524)
KCAS LLC
Also Called: Kcas Bio Anlytcal Bmarker Svcs
12400 Shwnee Mission Pkwy
(66216-1841)
PHONE..................................913 248-3000
John Bucksath, *CEO*
Marsha Wood, *Technician*
EMP: 135
SQ FT: 33,000
SALES (est): 10.3MM
SALES (corp-wide): 47.1MM **Privately Held**
SIC: 8734 8731 Testing laboratories; biotechnical research, commercial
PA: Kansas Venture Capital, Inc.
9401 Indian Creek Pkwy # 200
Overland Park KS 66210
913 262-7117

(G-11525)
KCCV AM 760
Also Called: Bott Radio Network
10550 Barkley St Ste 100 (66212-1824)
PHONE..................................913 642-7600
Richard Bott, *President*
Eben Fowler, *Manager*
EMP: 40
SALES (est): 1.6MM **Privately Held**
SIC: 4832 Radio broadcasting stations

(G-11526)
KCI KANSAS COUNSELORS INC
8725 Rosehill Rd Ste 415 (66215-4611)
PHONE..................................913 541-9704
Scott Tacke, *Principal*
EMP: 30
SALES (est): 1.8MM **Privately Held**
SIC: 8742 Banking & finance consultant

(G-11527)
KDJM CONSULTING INC (PA)
Also Called: Corridor Group, The
6405 Metcalf Ave Ste 108 (66202-3928)
PHONE..................................913 362-0600
Kathleen Dodd, *President*
Lilly Fostvedt, *Partner*
Nick Dobrzelecki, *Vice Pres*
Marsha Lambert, *Vice Pres*
Bob Kearn, *CFO*
EMP: 11
SALES (est): 2MM **Privately Held**
WEB: www.corridorgroup.com
SIC: 8742 Hospital & health services consultant

(G-11528)
KELSEY CONSTRUCTION INC
14308 W 96th Ter (66215-4708)
PHONE..................................913 894-0330
Mark Ottaway, *President*
Pamela Ottaway, *Treasurer*
EMP: 6 **EST:** 1994
SQ FT: 2,000
SALES (est): 531.9K **Privately Held**
SIC: 2759 2791 2789 2752 Commercial printing; typesetting; bookbinding & related work; commercial printing, lithographic

(G-11529)
KESSINGER/HUNTER & COMPANY LC
Also Called: King Street III
11020 King St (66210-1214)
PHONE..................................816 842-2690
Joseph Accurso, *Principal*
Vicki Omali, *Manager*
EMP: 102
SALES (corp-wide): 15.4MM **Privately Held**
WEB: www.kessingerhunter.com
SIC: 6531 8742 6552 8741 Real estate agent, commercial; real estate leasing & rentals; real estate managers; appraiser, real estate; real estate consultant; subdividers & developers; construction management
PA: Kessinger/Hunter & Company, L.C.
2600 Grand Blvd Ste 700
Kansas City MO 64108
816 842-2690

(G-11530)
KIDDI KOLLEGE INC
Also Called: Kiddie Kollege 6
9921 W 86th St (66212-4654)
PHONE..................................913 649-4747
ERA Kole, *Director*
EMP: 20
SALES (corp-wide): 2.5MM **Privately Held**
SIC: 8351 Group day care center
PA: Kiddi Kollege Inc
340 N Lindenwood Dr
Olathe KS 66062
913 764-4423

(G-11531)
KINDERCARE EDUCATION LLC
Also Called: Kindercare Learning Center
6350 Long Ave (66216-2560)
PHONE..................................913 631-6910
Lisa Spoonmore, *Exec Dir*
EMP: 14
SALES (corp-wide): 963.9MM **Privately Held**
WEB: www.knowledgelearning.com
SIC: 8351 Group day care center
PA: Kindercare Education Llc
650 Ne Holladay St # 1400
Portland OR 97232
503 872-1300

(G-11532)
KINDERCARE LEARNING CTRS LLC
Also Called: Overland Park South Kindercare
7600 W 150th St (66223-2214)
PHONE..................................913 402-1024
Kristal Pate, *Branch Mgr*
EMP: 25
SALES (corp-wide): 963.9MM **Privately Held**
WEB: www.kindercare.com
SIC: 8351 Group day care center
HQ: Kindercare Learning Centers, Llc
650 Ne Holladay St # 1400
Portland OR 97232
503 872-1300

(G-11533)
KINDERCARE LEARNING CTRS LLC
Also Called: Kindercare Learning Ctr 760
10456 Mastin St (66212-5701)
PHONE..................................913 492-3221
Rose Eberly, *Branch Mgr*
EMP: 17
SALES (corp-wide): 963.9MM **Privately Held**
WEB: www.kindercare.com
SIC: 8351 Group day care center
HQ: Kindercare Learning Centers, Llc
650 Ne Holladay St # 1400
Portland OR 97232
503 872-1300

(G-11534)
KINDERCARE LEARNING CTRS LLC
Also Called: Kindercare Learning Ctr 1300
11842 W 112th St (66210-2779)
PHONE..................................913 451-6066
Annette Durgoon, *Director*
EMP: 23
SALES (corp-wide): 963.9MM **Privately Held**
WEB: www.kindercare.com
SIC: 8351 Group day care center
HQ: Kindercare Learning Centers, Llc
650 Ne Holladay St # 1400
Portland OR 97232
503 872-1300

(G-11535)
KING CABINETS INC
20201 W 55th St (66218-9372)
PHONE..................................913 422-7554
Greg King, *President*
Beth King, *Treasurer*
EMP: 13
SQ FT: 5,500
SALES (est): 1.4MM **Privately Held**
SIC: 2511 Wood household furniture

(G-11536)
KNICKERBOCKER PROPERTIES INC
8717 W 110th St Ste 240 (66210-2103)
PHONE..................................913 451-4466
Sara Queen, *President*
Charles Grossman, *Vice Pres*
Peter Zapulla, *Treasurer*
Mark Brody, *Admin Sec*
EMP: 40
SALES: 36MM **Privately Held**
WEB: www.corporatewoods.com
SIC: 6531 Real estate agents & managers

(G-11537)
KOESTEN HIRSCHMANN & CRABTREE
10000 College Blvd # 260 (66210-1435)
PHONE..................................913 345-1881
Stewart Koesten, *President*
Matt Starkey, *Vice Pres*
EMP: 13
SALES (est): 1MM **Privately Held**
WEB: www.makinglifecount.com
SIC: 8742 Financial consultant

(G-11538)
KRAFT TOOL COMPANY (PA)
8325 Hedge Lane Ter (66227-3544)
P.O. Box 860230 (66286-0230)
PHONE..................................913 422-4848
Ron Meyer, *President*
Steve Cook, *Engineer*
Lena Ziolo, *Controller*
Evan Theno, *Credit Mgr*
Marie Flaker, *Human Res Mgr*
◆ **EMP:** 180
SQ FT: 216,000
SALES (est): 43.5MM **Privately Held**
WEB: www.krafttool.com
SIC: 3423 Hand & edge tools

(G-11539)
KU MIDWEST AMBULATORY SVC CTR
Also Called: Ku Midwest Surgery Center
7405 Renner Rd (66217-9414)
PHONE..................................913 588-8452
David Granthun, *Administration*
EMP: 35
SALES (est): 4.6MM **Privately Held**
SIC: 8011 Surgeon

(G-11540)
L L L TRANSPORT INC
6950 Squibb Rd Ste 520 (66202-3261)
PHONE..................................913 777-5400
Gary Waller, *CEO*
David Briggs, *Controller*
Brett Carmical, *Human Res Dir*
EMP: 19
SALES (est): 2.6MM **Privately Held**
SIC: 4789 Car loading

(G-11541)
LA PETITE ACADEMY INC
15012 Newton Dr (66223-2210)
PHONE..................................913 685-2800
Lee Dublin, *Director*
EMP: 15
SALES (corp-wide): 164MM **Privately Held**
WEB: www.lapetite.com
SIC: 8351 Preschool center
HQ: La Petite Academy, Inc.
21333 Haggerty Rd Ste 300
Novi MI 48375
877 861-5078

(G-11542)
LA PETITE ACADEMY INC
22211 W 66th St (66226-3522)
PHONE..................................913 441-5100
Tara Van Fleet, *Director*
EMP: 25
SALES (corp-wide): 164MM **Privately Held**
WEB: www.lapetite.com
SIC: 8351 Preschool center
HQ: La Petite Academy, Inc.
21333 Haggerty Rd Ste 300
Novi MI 48375
877 861-5078

(G-11543)
LA PETITE ACADEMY INC
6410 Antioch Rd (66202-4714)
PHONE..................................913 432-5053
Jill Wilson, *Director*
EMP: 17
SALES (corp-wide): 164MM **Privately Held**
WEB: www.lapetite.com
SIC: 8351 Preschool center
HQ: La Petite Academy, Inc.
21333 Haggerty Rd Ste 300
Novi MI 48375
877 861-5078

(G-11544)
LA SUPERIOR FOOD PRODUCTS INC
4307 Merriam Dr (66203-1337)
PHONE..................................913 362-6611
George Young, *President*
EMP: 32
SQ FT: 20,000
SALES (est): 4.6MM **Privately Held**
WEB: www.lasuperiorfood.com
SIC: 2099 2096 2032 Tortillas, fresh or refrigerated; corn chips & other corn-based snacks; Mexican foods: packaged in cans, jars, etc.

(G-11545)
LABONE INC
11000 Renner Rd (66201)
PHONE..................................913 577-1643
Lana Newman, *Manager*
EMP: 5
SALES (corp-wide): 7.5B **Publicly Held**
SIC: 2869 Laboratory chemicals, organic
HQ: Labone, Inc.
10101 Renner Blvd
Lenexa KS 66219
913 888-1770

(G-11546)
LAKE POINTE HOTEL CO LLC
Also Called: Courtyard By Marriott
6704 W 121st St (66209-2002)
PHONE..................................913 451-1222
Richard Wiens, *Principal*
EMP: 11
SALES (est): 417.7K **Privately Held**
SIC: 7011 Hotels & motels

(G-11547)
LAND OF PAWS LLC (PA)
4021 Somerset Dr (66208-5216)
PHONE..................................913 341-1011
Dr Mark Daly,
Patty Daly,
Pam Gates,
Dr Garett Schmidt,
EMP: 15
SQ FT: 6,000
SALES (est): 1.7MM **Privately Held**
SIC: 5999 5947 0752 Pets; pet supplies; gift shop; grooming services, pet & animal specialties

(G-11548)
LATHROP & GAGE LLP
10851 Mastin St Ste 1000 (66210-1687)
PHONE..................................913 451-5100
William Beck,
William Fford,
Thomas Jmcmahon,
EMP: 90
SALES (corp-wide): 90.3MM **Privately Held**
SIC: 8111 General practice attorney, lawyer
PA: Lathrop & Gage Llp
2345 Grand Blvd Ste 2200
Kansas City MO 64108
816 292-2000

(G-11549)
LAWNS BY BECK INC
Also Called: Beck's Lawn and Landscaping
14404 W 74th St (66216-5530)
PHONE..................................913 631-8873
Michael Beck, *President*
Mitch Beck, *Vice Pres*
EMP: 10

SALES: 1MM Privately Held
WEB: www.byronbeck.com
SIC: 0782 1629 Landscape contractors; irrigation system construction

(G-11550)
LAWRENCE GLASS & MIRROR CO
12215 Johnson Dr (66216-1909)
PHONE 913 631-5533
Jeff La Combe, *President*
Tom Walker, *Manager*
EMP: 10
SQ FT: 10,000
SALES (est): 2.1MM Privately Held
WEB: www.lawrenceglassco.com
SIC: 1793 Glass & glazing work

(G-11551)
LBA AIR CNDTONING HTG PLBG INC
6850 W 47th Ter (66203-1398)
PHONE 816 454-5515
Bill Anderson, *President*
Brad McGhee, *General Mgr*
J D McGhee, *Vice Pres*
Liz Martinez,
EMP: 40
SQ FT: 12,000
SALES (est): 9.7MM Privately Held
SIC: 1711 7699 7623 5075 Warm air heating & air conditioning contractor; plumbing contractors; boiler repair shop; air conditioning repair; air conditioning & ventilation equipment & supplies

(G-11552)
LEARNING CARE GROUP INC
Also Called: Montessori Unlimited
11100 W 135th St (66221-9731)
PHONE 913 851-7800
Dena Rutter, *Principal*
EMP: 23
SALES (corp-wide): 164MM Privately Held
WEB: www.childrenscourtyard.com
SIC: 8351 Preschool center
HQ: Learning Care Group, Inc.
21333 Haggerty Rd Ste 300
Novi MI 48375

(G-11553)
LEAWOOD CTR FOR DNTL EXCLLENCE
11201 Nall Ave Ste 120 (66211-1832)
PHONE 913 491-4466
Craig W Herre, *President*
Van Tran, *Administration*
EMP: 19
SALES (est): 1MM Privately Held
SIC: 8021 Dentists' office

(G-11554)
LEAWOOD FAMILY PHYSICIANS
7020 W 121st St (66209-2008)
PHONE 913 451-4443
John Saxer MD, *Partner*
Sara Hicks MD, *Partner*
Sara A Hicks, *Med Doctor*
EMP: 15
SALES (est): 1.6MM Privately Held
SIC: 8011 General & family practice, physician/surgeon

(G-11555)
LEAWOOD SOUTH COUNTRY CLUB
12700 Overbrook Rd (66209-1622)
PHONE 913 491-1313
Nick Casale, *Manager*
Marty Sullivan, *Food Svc Dir*
EMP: 45
SQ FT: 12,000
SALES: 2.8MM Privately Held
SIC: 7997 Country club, membership

(G-11556)
LEE ANN BRITIAN INFANT DEV CTR
Also Called: Britain Center, The
9100 W 74th St (66204-4004)
PHONE 913 676-2253
Amy Milroy, *Exec Dir*
Connie Schmitt, *Admin Sec*
EMP: 29
SALES (est): 1.1MM Privately Held
SIC: 8069 Specialty hospitals, except psychiatric

(G-11557)
LEE APPAREL COMPANY INC (HQ)
1 Lee Dr (66202-3620)
PHONE 913 789-0330
Terry Lay, *President*
Claudia Broddus, *President*
Chris Waldeck, *President*
R Ray Trowbridge, *Admin Sec*
EMP: 450
SQ FT: 147,000
SALES (est): 552.6MM
SALES (corp-wide): 13.8B Publicly Held
SIC: 2325 2339 Jeans: men's, youths' & boys'; jeans: women's, misses' & juniors'
PA: V.F. Corporation
105 Corporate Center Blvd
Greensboro NC 27408
336 424-6000

(G-11558)
LEE APPAREL COMPANY INC
Also Called: Lee Jeans Co
9001 W 67th St (66202-3632)
P.O. Box 21488, Greensboro NC (27420-1488)
PHONE 913 384-4000
Joe Dzialo, *Manager*
EMP: 150
SALES (corp-wide): 13.8B Publicly Held
SIC: 2325 2339 2369 2329 Jeans: men's, youths' & boys'; women's & misses' outerwear; girls' & children's outerwear; men's & boys' sportswear & athletic clothing
HQ: The Lee Apparel Company Inc
1 Lee Dr
Shawnee Mission KS 66202
913 789-0330

(G-11559)
LEGACY TECHNOLOGIES LLC
6700 W 47th Ter (66203-1392)
PHONE 913 432-2020
Bruce Digget, *CEO*
Ann Marie Clark, *CFO*
◆ EMP: 38
SQ FT: 27,500
SALES (est): 3.8MM Privately Held
SIC: 1623 3825 3711 Transmitting tower (telecommunication) construction; radio frequency measuring equipment; military motor vehicle assembly

(G-11560)
LEIDOS INC
7015 College Blvd (66211-1862)
PHONE 913 317-5120
John Male, *Manager*
EMP: 6
SALES (corp-wide): 10.1B Publicly Held
WEB: www.saic.com
SIC: 8731 7371 7373 8742 Commercial physical research; energy research; environmental research; medical research, commercial; computer software development; systems engineering, computer related; training & development consultant; recording & playback apparatus, including phonograph; integrated circuits, semiconductor networks, etc.
HQ: Leidos, Inc.
11951 Freedom Dr Ste 500
Reston VA 20190
571 526-6000

(G-11561)
LENEXA AUTOMOTIVE INC
13311 Walnut St (66215-3660)
PHONE 913 492-8250
Mike Fromholtz, *President*
EMP: 10
SALES (est): 949.3K Privately Held
SIC: 7538 5531 General automotive repair shops; automobile air conditioning equipment, sale, installation

(G-11562)
LENEXA CHAMBER OF COMMERCE
11180 Lackman Rd (66219-1236)
PHONE 913 888-1414
Blake Schreck, *President*
Ashley Sherard, *Vice Pres*
Jeff Carlson, *Supervisor*
EMP: 12
SALES: 913.1K Privately Held
WEB: www.lenexa.org
SIC: 8611 Chamber of Commerce

(G-11563)
LENEXA DENTAL GROUP CHARTERED
9430 Gillette St Ste 100 (66215-3788)
PHONE 913 888-8008
EMP: 10
SALES (est): 424K Privately Held
SIC: 8021 Dentist's Office

(G-11564)
LENNOX INDUSTRIES INC
11350 Strang Line Rd (66215-4041)
PHONE 913 339-9993
Rick Bastmeyer, *District Mgr*
Cynthia Green, *Manager*
EMP: 28
SALES (corp-wide): 3.8B Publicly Held
WEB: www.davelennox.com
SIC: 5075 Warm air heating & air conditioning
HQ: Lennox Industries Inc.
2100 Lake Park Blvd
Richardson TX 75080
972 497-5000

(G-11565)
LETS GROW PRESCHOOL
Also Called: Mothers Day Out
8718 W 62nd Ter (66202-2810)
PHONE 913 262-2261
Beth Bremenkamp, *Owner*
EMP: 16
SALES (est): 374.4K Privately Held
SIC: 8351 Preschool center

(G-11566)
LEUKEMIA & LYMPHOMA SOC INC
Also Called: Leukemia Soc of Amrca, MD Amrc
6811 W 63rd St Ste 202 (66202)
PHONE 913 262-1515
Jana Lacock, *Exec Dir*
EMP: 12
SALES (corp-wide): 281.6MM Privately Held
WEB: www.bachelorbidauction.com
SIC: 8699 Charitable organization
PA: The Leukemia & Lymphoma Society Inc
3 International Dr # 200
Rye Brook NY 10573
914 949-5213

(G-11567)
LIBERTY MUTUAL INSURANCE CO
10561 Barkley St Ste 400 (66212-1836)
PHONE 913 648-5900
Tom England, *Opers Mgr*
A Washington, *Branch Mgr*
EMP: 100
SALES (corp-wide): 38.3B Privately Held
WEB: www.libertymutual.com
SIC: 6331 Fire, marine & casualty insurance
HQ: Liberty Mutual Insurance Company
175 Berkeley St
Boston MA 02116
617 357-9500

(G-11568)
LICAUSI-STYERS COMPANY
8301 W 125th St Ste 210 (66213-1416)
PHONE 913 681-5888
Paul Licausi, *President*
Paul Styers, *Vice Pres*
EMP: 20
SQ FT: 2,000
SALES (est): 743.9K Privately Held
SIC: 6531 6552 6799 Real estate agent, commercial; real estate managers; land subdividers & developers, commercial; real estate investors, except property operators

(G-11569)
LIFE CARE CENTERS AMERICA INC
Also Called: Life Care Ctr Shawnee Mission
7541 Switzer St (66214-1170)
PHONE 913 631-2273
Deborah Biehl, *Manager*
Megan Foland, *Director*
EMP: 160
SALES (corp-wide): 144MM Privately Held
SIC: 8051 Skilled nursing care facilities
PA: Life Care Centers Of America, Inc.
3570 Keith St Nw
Cleveland TN 37312
423 472-9585

(G-11570)
LIFESPACE COMMUNITIES INC
Also Called: Claridge Court
8101 Mission Rd Apt 322 (66208-5247)
PHONE 913 383-2085
Andrew Fisher, *Director*
Derrick Jackson, *Director*
Jeanette Strickling, *Hlthcr Dir*
EMP: 170
SALES (corp-wide): 245.8MM Privately Held
WEB: www.lcrc.net
SIC: 6513 8082 8051 Retirement hotel operation; home health care services; skilled nursing care facilities
PA: Lifespace Communities, Inc.
4201 Corporate Dr
West Des Moines IA 50266
515 288-5805

(G-11571)
LIGHT BULBS ETC INC
14821 W 99th St (66215-1110)
PHONE 913 894-9030
Colleen Black, *President*
Larry Fuqua, *General Mgr*
Dean H Becker, *Dean*
Robert Allen, *Sales Staff*
Craig Leonard, *Sales Staff*
▼ EMP: 16
SQ FT: 5,000
SALES (est): 5.9MM Privately Held
SIC: 5063 Light bulbs & related supplies

(G-11572)
LIGHTNING GROUNDS SERVICES INC (PA)
Also Called: Lightning Ldscp & Irrigation
8315 Monticello Rd (66227-3120)
P.O. Box 860032, Shawnee (66286-0032)
PHONE 913 441-3900
Chris Edin, *President*
EMP: 25
SQ FT: 5,000
SALES (est): 3.2MM Privately Held
WEB: www.lightning-landscape.com
SIC: 0782 5083 1629 Landscape contractors; lawn & garden machinery & equipment; drainage system construction

(G-11573)
LINCOLN FINCL ADVISORS CORP
10851 Mastin St Ste 950 (66210-1687)
PHONE 913 451-1505
Edwin Kerley, *Branch Mgr*
Kevin P Connor, *Agent*
Charlotte A Gist, *Agent*
Tim Helfer, *Agent*
Jeffrey A Nelson, *Agent*
EMP: 28
SALES (corp-wide): 16.4B Publicly Held
WEB: www.lfaonline.com
SIC: 6282 Investment advice
HQ: Lincoln Financial Advisors Corporation
1300 S Clinton St
Fort Wayne IN 46802
800 237-3813

(G-11574)
LINDAN AUTO MECHANICAL & BODY
9200 W 57th St (66203-2504)
PHONE 913 722-4243
Danny Sosebee, *President*
Juan Garcia, *Co-Owner*
EMP: 26

SALES (est): 2MM **Privately Held**
SIC: 7532 Body shop, automotive

(G-11575)
LINE CONSTRUCTION COMPANY
9119 Barton St (66214-1720)
PHONE..................................913 341-1212
D Lee Shipley, *President*
Wade Shipley, *Vice Pres*
EMP: 14
SQ FT: 7,400
SALES (est): 1.9MM **Privately Held**
SIC: 1521 1542 General remodeling, single-family houses; commercial & office buildings, renovation & repair

(G-11576)
LMS COMPANY LLC
Also Called: L M S
10005 Howe Dr (66206-2414)
PHONE..................................913 648-4123
Lloyd J Griffith, *President*
Mike Griffith, *Vice Pres*
Steve Griffith, *Vice Pres*
EMP: 10
SALES (est): 425.5K **Privately Held**
SIC: 7349 Building maintenance, except repairs

(G-11577)
LOQUIENT INC
Also Called: Loqvient Technology Services
2016 W 72nd Ter (66208-3341)
PHONE..................................913 221-0430
Craig Armstrong, *President*
EMP: 15
SALES (est): 1MM **Privately Held**
SIC: 7378 7379 Computer maintenance & repair; computer related consulting services

(G-11578)
LOWE FRYLDNHOVEN MDS CHARTERED
8901 W 74th St Ste 356 (66204-2203)
PHONE..................................913 677-2508
C T Hitchcock MD, *Principal*
Bettina Lowe, *Med Doctor*
EMP: 15
SQ FT: 1,500
SALES (est): 1.1MM **Privately Held**
SIC: 8011 General & family practice, physician/surgeon

(G-11579)
LOWES HOME CENTERS LLC
16300 W 65th St (66217-9799)
PHONE..................................913 631-3003
Scott Mathews, *Manager*
EMP: 150
SALES (corp-wide): 71.3B **Publicly Held**
SIC: 5211 5031 5722 5064 Home centers; building materials, exterior; building materials, interior; household appliance stores; electrical appliances, television & radio
HQ: Lowe's Home Centers, Llc
1605 Curtis Bridge Rd
Wilkesboro NC 28697
336 658-4000

(G-11580)
LS CONSTRUCTION SERVICES INC (PA)
Also Called: Licausi-Styers Company
8301 W 125th St Ste 210 (66213-1416)
PHONE..................................913 681-5888
Paul Licausi, *President*
Debbie Hoover, *Controller*
Andrea Rice, *Accountant*
Amie Styers, *Accountant*
Leonard Licausi, *Sales Staff*
EMP: 37
SQ FT: 2,000
SALES (est): 12.9MM **Privately Held**
SIC: 1542 6531 Commercial & office building, new construction; commercial & office buildings, renovation & repair; real estate managers

(G-11581)
LUKE KUSHS PAINTING
9218 Metcalf Ave Ste 396 (66212-1476)
PHONE..................................913 888-0230
Luke Kush, *President*
EMP: 14 **EST:** 2002
SALES: 2MM **Privately Held**
SIC: 1721 Residential painting

(G-11582)
LULU MIMI HSCLNERS EXTRRDNAIRE
Also Called: Contemerary Cleaning Services
7620 Metcalf Ave Ste P (66204-2996)
PHONE..................................913 649-6022
Dennise ALC, *Owner*
Nancy ALC, *Co-Owner*
EMP: 16
SALES (est): 1.2MM **Privately Held**
SIC: 7363 7349 Domestic help service; building maintenance services

(G-11583)
LULU SALON & SPA
4480 W 107th St (66207-4003)
PHONE..................................913 648-3658
Leslie Kubas, *Owner*
EMP: 12
SALES (est): 222.8K **Privately Held**
WEB: www.lulusalonandspa.com
SIC: 7231 Hairdressers

(G-11584)
LUTZ DAILY & BRAIN LLC
6400 Glenwood St Ste 200 (66202-4074)
PHONE..................................913 831-0833
Joe Arello, *Engineer*
Tom Dey, *Engineer*
Tom Lutz, *Sales Executive*
Fred J Lutz, *Mng Member*
Daniel Bauerkemper, *Director*
EMP: 35 **EST:** 1948
SQ FT: 20,000
SALES (est): 4.4MM **Privately Held**
WEB: www.ldbeng.com
SIC: 8711 Consulting engineer

(G-11585)
LYERLA ASSOCIATES
Also Called: Dale's Athletic Club
11301 W 88th St (66214-1701)
PHONE..................................913 888-9247
Reginald Lyerla, *Partner*
Jeff Wiard, *Ltd Ptnr*
EMP: 30
SQ FT: 65,000
SALES (est): 970K **Privately Held**
SIC: 7991 Athletic club & gymnasiums, membership

(G-11586)
LYNK INC
8241 Melrose Dr 43 (66214-3623)
PHONE..................................913 492-9202
Rich Klein, *President*
Lynn Klein, *Treasurer*
Bill Markey, *VP Sales*
▲ **EMP:** 15
SQ FT: 15,000
SALES (est): 3MM **Privately Held**
WEB: www.lynk.net
SIC: 3496 Shelving, made from purchased wire

(G-11587)
LYNTEC INC
8401 Melrose Dr (66214-1647)
PHONE..................................913 529-2233
Lynn J Potter, *President*
Alan Tschirner, *General Mgr*
Leah Bigley, *Sales Mgr*
Jody Mayer, *Marketing Staff*
Martin Dornfeld, *Director*
EMP: 6
SALES (est): 1.1MM **Privately Held**
SIC: 3651 Audio electronic systems

(G-11588)
M & K DAYLIGHT DONUTS
8736 Lackman Rd (66219-1197)
PHONE..................................913 495-2529
Jeff Miller, *Owner*
Sarah Miller, *Co-Owner*
EMP: 6
SQ FT: 1,000
SALES (est): 200K **Privately Held**
SIC: 2051 5461 Doughnuts, except frozen; doughnuts

(G-11589)
MACFARLANE GROUP LLC
6950 W 56th St (66202-2590)
PHONE..................................913 825-1200
Don Prince, *President*
Stephen Drees, *Chief Mktg Ofcr*
Dave Windhorst, *CIO*
Travis Kelso, *Admin Dir*
EMP: 44 **EST:** 2010
SALES (est): 8.5MM **Privately Held**
SIC: 8741 8742 7361 Management services; marketing consulting services; employment agencies

(G-11590)
MAGELLAN PIPELINE COMPANY LP
13424 W 98th St (66215-1362)
PHONE..................................913 310-7710
Rick Olson, *Branch Mgr*
EMP: 10
SALES (corp-wide): 2.8B **Publicly Held**
SIC: 4613 Refined petroleum pipelines
HQ: Magellan Pipeline Company, L.P.
1 Williams Ctr
Tulsa OK 74172
918 574-7000

(G-11591)
MAINSTREET FEDERAL CREDIT UN
6025 Lamar Ave (66202-3235)
PHONE..................................913 754-3926
Marty Peterson, *Manager*
Mark Schlueter, *Technology*
EMP: 23
SALES (corp-wide): 14.7MM **Privately Held**
WEB: www.cujc.com
SIC: 6061 Federal credit unions
PA: Mainstreet Federal Credit Union
13001 W 95th St
Lenexa KS 66215
913 599-1010

(G-11592)
MAKING THE MARK INC
Also Called: Adventures In Advertising
12120 State Line Rd 376 (66209-1254)
PHONE..................................913 402-8000
Michael Keith, *President*
EMP: 5
SALES (est): 822.3K **Privately Held**
WEB: www.makingthemark.com
SIC: 7311 7372 Advertising agencies; prepackaged software

(G-11593)
MALKIN PROPERTIES LLC
Also Called: Georgetown Apartments
7200 Eby Ave (66204-1659)
PHONE..................................913 262-2666
Paula Bunse, *Manager*
EMP: 15
SALES (corp-wide): 20.9MM **Privately Held**
SIC: 6513 Apartment hotel operation
PA: Malkin Properties, L.L.C.
1 Grand Central Terminal
New York NY 10017
212 953-0888

(G-11594)
MARK A MCCUNE
10600 Quivira Rd 430450 (66215-2309)
PHONE..................................913 541-3230
Mark McCure, *Owner*
EMP: 30
SALES (est): 530.5K **Privately Held**
SIC: 8011 Dermatologist

(G-11595)
MARK IV ASSOCIATES LLC
10965 Granada Ln Ste 300 (66211-1412)
PHONE..................................913 345-2120
Dennis Welzenbach,
EMP: 25
SALES (est): 2.5MM **Privately Held**
SIC: 6552 Land subdividers & developers, commercial

(G-11596)
MARK MOLOS
Also Called: West Glenn Gstrintestinal Cons
7230 Renner Rd (66217-9901)
PHONE..................................913 962-2122
Mark Molos MD, *Owner*
Dee Richardson, *Opers Staff*
Janet Morffi, *Office Mgr*
EMP: 15
SALES (est): 1.7MM **Privately Held**
SIC: 8011 Gastronomist

(G-11597)
MARK S HUMPHREY MD
10600 Quivira Rd Ste 130 (66215-2311)
PHONE..................................913 541-8897
Mark S Humphrey MD, *Owner*
EMP: 10
SALES (est): 264.1K **Privately Held**
SIC: 8011 Orthopedic physician

(G-11598)
MARK S JENSEN DDS PA
Also Called: Jensen, Mark S DDS PA
8901 W 74th St Ste 245 (66204-2202)
PHONE..................................913 384-0600
Mark S Jensen DDS, *Partner*
Kenneth Laney DDS, *Partner*
EMP: 12
SALES (est): 905.6K **Privately Held**
SIC: 8021 Dentists' office

(G-11599)
MARKETING SERVICES OF KANSAS (PA)
9903 Pflumm Rd (66215-1222)
PHONE..................................913 888-4555
Sam Bazdarich, *President*
EMP: 7
SQ FT: 4,500
SALES (est): 689.5K **Privately Held**
SIC: 3651 Household audio & video equipment

(G-11600)
MARRIOTT INTERNATIONAL INC
10800 Metcalf Ave (66210-2320)
PHONE..................................913 451-8000
George Camalier, *Manager*
Scott Casey, *Manager*
Romunda Gillespie, *Analyst*
EMP: 300
SALES (corp-wide): 20.7B **Publicly Held**
SIC: 7011 Hotels & motels
PA: Marriott International, Inc.
10400 Fernwood Rd
Bethesda MD 20817
301 380-3000

(G-11601)
MASONRY & GLASS SYSTEMS INC
9024 Cody St (66214-1730)
PHONE..................................913 748-6142
Paul Ehrnman, *Manager*
EMP: 5
SALES (corp-wide): 2.5MM **Privately Held**
SIC: 3231 1793 5039 Products of purchased glass; glass & glazing work; glass construction materials
PA: Masonry & Glass Systems, Inc.
1503 S Kingshighway Blvd
Saint Louis MO 63110
314 535-6515

(G-11602)
MATERIALS TRANSPORT COMPANY
11011 Cody St (66210-1313)
P.O. Box 25900 (66225-5900)
PHONE..................................913 345-2030
Chuck Wietenhoft, *President*
Joe Rieger, *Treasurer*
Allan Enby, *Manager*
John Ross, *Admin Sec*
EMP: 300
SQ FT: 7,500
SALES (est): 13.4MM
SALES (corp-wide): 29.7B **Privately Held**
SIC: 4212 Local trucking, without storage

HQ: Ash Grove Materials Corporation
11011 Cody St Ste 300
Overland Park KS 66210
913 345-2030

(G-11603)
MB HEALTH SPECIALIST INC
12345 W 95th St Ste 215 (66215-3837)
PHONE....................................913 438-6337
David Minich, *President*
Steve Beaumont, *Vice Pres*
EMP: 11 **EST:** 1994
SQ FT: 1,000
SALES (est): 789.3K **Privately Held**
WEB: www.healthspecialists.com
SIC: 7363 Medical help service

(G-11604)
MC DOWELL RICE SMITH BUCHANAN
7101 College Blvd Ste 200 (66210-2076)
PHONE....................................913 338-5400
EMP: 14
SALES (corp-wide): 7.2MM **Privately Held**
SIC: 8111 Law Firm
PA: Mc Dowell, Rice, Smith & Buchanan
605 W 47th St Ste 350
Kansas City MO
816 753-5400

(G-11605)
MC REAL ESTATE SERVICE INC
Also Called: C W Associates
8717 W 110th St Ste 240 (66210-2103)
PHONE....................................913 451-4466
Denise Stewart, *President*
EMP: 19
SALES (est): 503K **Privately Held**
SIC: 6531 Real estate agents & managers

(G-11606)
MCANANY CONSTRUCTION INC
15320 Midland Dr (66217-9605)
P.O. Box 860009 (66286-0009)
PHONE....................................913 631-5440
Eric Vossman, *President*
Roger Vossman, *Vice Pres*
Phil J McAnany, *Treasurer*
EMP: 60 **EST:** 1954
SQ FT: 4,000
SALES: 40.7MM **Privately Held**
SIC: 1611 Highway & street paving contractor; grading

(G-11607)
MCCARTY MECHANICAL INC
Also Called: Honeywell Authorized Dealer
5100 Merriam Dr Ste B (66203-2114)
PHONE....................................913 432-5100
Edward McCarty, *President*
Timothy E McCarty, *Corp Secy*
EMP: 10 **EST:** 1949
SQ FT: 6,000
SALES (est): 1.7MM **Privately Held**
WEB: www.mccartymechanical.com
SIC: 1711 Warm air heating & air conditioning contractor

(G-11608)
MCCLATCHY NEWSPAPERS INC
8455 College Blvd (66210-1838)
PHONE....................................816 234-4636
O J Nelson, *Manager*
EMP: 100
SALES (corp-wide): 807.2MM **Publicly Held**
WEB: www.sacbee.com
SIC: 2711 Newspapers, publishing & printing
HQ: Mcclatchy Newspapers, Inc.
2100 Q St
Sacramento CA 95816
916 321-1855

(G-11609)
MCLANE COMPANY INC
16945 W 116th St (66219-9604)
PHONE....................................913 492-7090
Jim Christiansen, *Branch Mgr*
EMP: 30
SALES (corp-wide): 225.3B **Publicly Held**
WEB: www.mclaneco.com
SIC: 5311 5113 Department stores, discount; industrial & personal service paper; cups, disposable plastic & paper; towels, paper; dishes, disposable plastic & paper
HQ: Mclane Company, Inc.
4747 Mclane Pkwy
Temple TX 76504
254 771-7500

(G-11610)
MCQUAID BROTHERS RMDLG CO INC
7927 Bond St (66214-1557)
PHONE....................................913 894-9128
Timothy J McQuaid, *President*
Mike McQuaid, *Treasurer*
EMP: 50 **EST:** 1979
SQ FT: 5,000
SALES (est): 7.5MM **Privately Held**
SIC: 1521 General remodeling, single-family houses

(G-11611)
MD ASSOCIATES 3 INC
Also Called: MD Management
5201 Johnson Dr Ste 450 (66205-2930)
P.O. Box 129 (66201-0129)
PHONE....................................913 831-2996
Sherman Dreiseszen, *Principal*
David Feingold, *Principal*
EMP: 10
SALES (est): 1MM **Privately Held**
SIC: 6513 Apartment building operators

(G-11612)
MD ASSOCIATES 4 INC
Also Called: MD Management
5201 Johnson Dr Ste 411 (66205-2920)
PHONE....................................913 831-2996
Thomas Morgan, *President*
EMP: 12
SALES (est): 798.1K **Privately Held**
WEB: www.mdmgt.com
SIC: 6512 Nonresidential building operators

(G-11613)
MEDICAL EQUIPMENT EXCHANGE
14170 W 107th St (66215-4035)
PHONE....................................913 451-2888
Charles Johnson, *President*
Patricia Johnson, *Treasurer*
EMP: 14
SQ FT: 5,000
SALES (est): 3MM **Privately Held**
WEB: www.medeqex.com
SIC: 5047 Medical equipment & supplies

(G-11614)
MEDNAX INC
Also Called: Midwest Perinatal Associates
12200 W 106th St Ste 110 (66215-2305)
PHONE....................................913 599-1396
Tracy A Cowles, *Med Doctor*
Brent Finley, *Director*
EMP: 16 **Publicly Held**
SIC: 8011 Specialized medical practitioners, except internal
PA: Mednax, Inc.
1301 Concord Ter
Sunrise FL 33323

(G-11615)
MEDPLANS PARTNERS INC
3601 W 133rd St (66209-3345)
PHONE....................................620 223-8200
Tony Pino, *CEO*
EMP: 99
SALES (est): 7.7MM **Privately Held**
SIC: 6411 Medical insurance claim processing, contract or fee basis
PA: Business Process Management, Inc
4500 Campbell Dr
Fort Scott KS 66701
620 223-8200

(G-11616)
MEICO LAMP PARTS COMPANY
13840 W 108th St (66215-2027)
P.O. Box 12064 (66282-2064)
PHONE....................................913 469-5888
Mark E Isenberg, *President*
Rose Isenberg, *Admin Sec*
▲ **EMP:** 12
SQ FT: 20,000
SALES (est): 2.6MM **Privately Held**
WEB: www.meilamp.com
SIC: 5094 5063 Clocks, watches & parts; movements, clock or watch; lighting fittings & accessories

(G-11617)
MERITEX ENTERPRISES INC
Also Called: Lenexa-Records Management
17501 W 98th St Spc 2632 (66219-1736)
PHONE....................................913 888-0601
William Seymore, *Manager*
EMP: 15
SALES (corp-wide): 10.4MM **Privately Held**
WEB: www.meritexlogistics.com
SIC: 4225 General warehousing & storage
PA: Meritex Enterprises, Inc.
24 University Ave Ne # 200
Minneapolis MN 55413
651 855-9700

(G-11618)
METCALF BANK (HQ)
7840 Metcalf Ave (66204-2932)
P.O. Box 4249 (66204-0249)
PHONE....................................913 648-4540
Jon Stewart, *President*
Jeanne Clayton, *Senior VP*
Vicki Fisher, *Senior VP*
Cris Smith, *Senior VP*
Laura Nally, *Vice Pres*
EMP: 30 **EST:** 1962
SQ FT: 4,000
SALES (est): 16.2MM
SALES (corp-wide): 62.6MM **Privately Held**
SIC: 6022 State commercial banks
PA: Metcalf Bank
609 Ne State Route 291
Lees Summit MO 64086
816 525-5300

(G-11619)
METCALF BANK
15100 Metcalf St (66204)
P.O. Box 4249 (66204-0249)
PHONE....................................913 685-3801
Emily Redding, *Branch Mgr*
EMP: 12
SALES (corp-wide): 62.6MM **Privately Held**
SIC: 6022 6163 State commercial banks; loan brokers
HQ: Metcalf Bank
7840 Metcalf Ave
Shawnee Mission KS 66204
913 648-4540

(G-11620)
METCALF BANK
7800 College Blvd (66210-1992)
PHONE....................................913 451-1199
Matt Lunetta, *Manager*
EMP: 15
SALES (corp-wide): 62.6MM **Privately Held**
SIC: 6022 State commercial banks
PA: Metcalf Bank
609 Ne State Route 291
Lees Summit MO 64086
816 525-5300

(G-11621)
METROPOLITAN LIFE INSUR CO
Also Called: MetLife
8717 W 110th St Ste 700 (66210-2127)
PHONE....................................913 451-8282
Darrell J Smith, *Vice Pres*
EMP: 22
SALES (corp-wide): 67.9B **Publicly Held**
SIC: 6411 Insurance agents & brokers
HQ: Metropolitan Life Insurance Company (Inc)
1095 Ave Of The Americas
New York NY 10036
908 253-1000

(G-11622)
MICHAEL E FROMHOLTZ
13311 Walnut St (66215-3660)
PHONE....................................913 492-8290
Michael E Fromholtz, *Owner*
EMP: 12 **EST:** 2001
SALES (est): 280.3K **Privately Held**
SIC: 7539 Automotive repair shops

(G-11623)
MICHAEL R MAGEE
123 Metcalf Ste 320 (66209)
PHONE....................................913 339-6551
Robert Sugar MD, *Partner*
Michael R Magee, *Principal*
EMP: 40 **EST:** 2001
SALES (est): 453.8K **Privately Held**
SIC: 8049 Offices of health practitioner

(G-11624)
MICRO ELECTRONICS INC
Also Called: Micro Center
9294 Metcalf Ave (66212-1478)
PHONE....................................913 341-4297
Susan Hall, *Manager*
EMP: 50
SALES (corp-wide): 191.5MM **Privately Held**
WEB: www.microcenter.com
SIC: 5045 Computers, peripherals & software
PA: Micro Electronics, Inc.
4119 Leap Rd
Hilliard OH 43026
614 850-3000

(G-11625)
MICROTOOL INC
14430 W 100th St (66215-1100)
P.O. Box 15433 (66285-5433)
PHONE....................................913 492-1588
Paul Rink, *CEO*
EMP: 17
SQ FT: 6,000
SALES: 1.6MM **Privately Held**
SIC: 3599 Machine shop, jobbing & repair

(G-11626)
MID AMERICA CRDIOLGY ASSOC PC
5799 Broadmoor St (66202-2427)
PHONE....................................913 588-9554
Carol Skidgel, *Manager*
EMP: 20
SALES (corp-wide): 13.5MM **Privately Held**
WEB: www.mac.md
SIC: 8011 Offices & clinics of medical doctors
PA: Mid America Cardiology Associates Pc Inc
3901 Rainbow Blvd G600
Kansas City KS 66160
913 588-9600

(G-11627)
MID AMERICA PHYSICIANS CHARTER
6815 Hilltop Rd Ste 100 (66226-3551)
PHONE....................................913 422-2020
Phillip Martin, *President*
Steven Reddinger, *Vice Pres*
Kathleen Mc Innis, *VP Mktg*
Clifford Johnson, *Admin Sec*
EMP: 25
SALES (est): 1.5MM **Privately Held**
SIC: 8011 Surgeon

(G-11628)
MID WEST PNSION ADMINISTRATORS
15641 S Mahafie St (66215)
PHONE....................................913 663-2777
Sandy Ohlhausen, *President*
EMP: 11 **EST:** 1997
SALES (est): 1MM **Privately Held**
SIC: 6411 Pension & retirement plan consultants

(G-11629)
MIDAMERICA REHABILITATION CTR
5701 W 110th St (66211-2503)
PHONE....................................913 491-2432
Kristen Dehart, *CEO*
EMP: 17
SALES (est): 1.3MM **Privately Held**
SIC: 8093 Rehabilitation center, outpatient treatment

(G-11630)
MIDLAND CLIPPERS
Also Called: Great Clips
11906 Shwnee Mission Pkwy (66216-1865)
PHONE.................................913 962-7070
Larry Lady, *Owner*
EMP: 12
SALES (est): 161.5K **Privately Held**
SIC: 7231 Unisex hair salons

(G-11631)
MIDWEST CARDIOLOGY ASSOCIATES (PA)
5701 W 119th St Ste 430 (66209-3721)
PHONE.................................913 253-3045
Daniel Scharf, *President*
Stephen Bloom, *Med Doctor*
Bernard Levi, *Admin Sec*
EMP: 58
SALES (est): 5.2MM **Privately Held**
WEB: www.midwestcardiology.com
SIC: 8011 Cardiologist & cardio-vascular specialist

(G-11632)
MIDWEST DIVISION - OPRMC LLC
Also Called: Overland Park Regional Med Ctr
10500 Quivira Rd (66215-2306)
PHONE.................................913 541-5000
Shari Collier, *Principal*
Kathy Denesia, *Human Res Dir*
Mary Goeke, *Manager*
Luanne Growe, *Director*
Christine Meyer, *Executive Asst*
EMP: 703
SALES (est): 741.7K **Publicly Held**
SIC: 8052 8742 8062 Intermediate care facilities; hospital & health services consultant; general medical & surgical hospitals
HQ: Midamerica Division, Inc.
903 E 104th St Ste 500
Kansas City MO 64131
816 508-4000

(G-11633)
MIDWEST DUCT CLEANING SERVICES
9111 W 51st Ter (66203-2129)
PHONE.................................913 648-5300
Bradley Kuhlmann, *Owner*
Christine Kuhlmann, *Owner*
EMP: 12
SQ FT: 7,500
SALES (est): 1.7MM **Privately Held**
WEB: www.midwestductcleaning.com
SIC: 7699 Cleaning services

(G-11634)
MIDWEST LENS INC
14304 W 100th St (66215-1236)
PHONE.................................913 894-1030
Edward Gibson, *President*
Lana Gibson, *Principal*
EMP: 12
SQ FT: 4,500
SALES (est): 1.6MM **Privately Held**
WEB: www.midwestlens.com
SIC: 3851 5049 Eyeglasses, lenses & frames; optical goods

(G-11635)
MIDWEST MERCHANDISING INC
11500 W 135th St (66221-2892)
PHONE.................................913 451-1515
Mark Neace, *Manager*
EMP: 15
SALES (corp-wide): 23.3MM **Privately Held**
WEB: www.midwestmerch.com
SIC: 5941 7699 Bicycle & bicycle parts; bicycle repair shop
PA: Midwest Merchandising Inc.
2690 E County Line Rd
Highlands Ranch CO 80126
303 221-4840

(G-11636)
MIDWEST ORTHOPEDICS PA
8800 W 75th St Ste 350 (66204-4029)
PHONE.................................913 362-8317
Carol Jones, *Controller*
Shannyn Tinberg, *Manager*
Leslie Riley, *Supervisor*
Burrel C Gaddy Jr, *Surgeon*
Barb Sack, *Exec Dir*
EMP: 21 **EST:** 1961
SALES (est): 4.4MM **Privately Held**
WEB: www.midwest-orthopaedics.com
SIC: 8011 Orthopedic physician

(G-11637)
MIDWEST TRANSPLANT NETWORK INC (PA)
1900 W 47th Pl Ste 400 (66205-1801)
PHONE.................................913 262-1668
Jim Boyd, *CFO*
Jan Finn, *Exec Dir*
Tina Kirsch, *Director*
Mark Reintjes, *Director*
Christopher Bryan, *Lab Dir*
EMP: 95
SQ FT: 80,000
SALES (est): 12.2MM **Privately Held**
WEB: www.mwtn.org
SIC: 8099 Medical services organization

(G-11638)
MIDWEST TRUST COMPANY (PA)
5901 College Blvd Ste 100 (66211-1834)
PHONE.................................913 319-0300
Bradley A Bergman, *President*
David Groe, *Managing Dir*
Monique Noah, *Trust Officer*
EMP: 15
SALES (est): 7.2MM **Privately Held**
WEB: www.midwesttrust.com
SIC: 6733 6282 Trusts; investment advice

(G-11639)
MILBURN GOLF AND COUNTRY CLUB
Also Called: Milburn Country Club
7501 W 69th St (66204-1333)
PHONE.................................913 432-0490
Charles Bab, *President*
Warren C Hill, *Corp Secy*
Max Pehl, *Vice Pres*
EMP: 50 **EST:** 1917
SQ FT: 16,000
SALES: 5.8MM **Privately Held**
SIC: 7997 Country club, membership

(G-11640)
MILL CREEK ANIMAL CLINIC PA
13428 W 62nd Ter (66216-1784)
PHONE.................................913 268-0900
Dr Mark Mears, *President*
EMP: 17
SALES (est): 1MM **Privately Held**
SIC: 0742 Animal hospital services, pets & other animal specialties

(G-11641)
MILLER SULLIVAN & ASSOC DDS PA
12136 W 87th Street Pkwy (66215-2810)
PHONE.................................913 492-5052
Richard E Miller DDS, *Partner*
Michael Sullivan, *Partner*
EMP: 10 **EST:** 1988
SQ FT: 2,200
SALES: 1MM **Privately Held**
SIC: 8021 Dentists' office

(G-11642)
MIRROR INC
6221 Richards Dr (66216-1724)
PHONE.................................913 248-1943
Doug Johnson, *Manager*
EMP: 14
SALES (corp-wide): 11.2MM **Privately Held**
SIC: 8361 Rehabilitation center, residential: health care incidental
PA: The Mirror Inc
130 E 5th St
Newton KS 67114
316 283-6743

(G-11643)
MISSION ANIMAL CLINIC PA
Also Called: Brown, Heath
5915 Broadmoor St (66202-3241)
PHONE.................................913 432-3341
Russ Ericson, *President*
Dr Todd Goodman, *Partner*
EMP: 12 **EST:** 1930
SALES (est): 816.9K **Privately Held**
WEB: www.missionvetsrx.com
SIC: 0742 Animal hospital services, pets & other animal specialties

(G-11644)
MISSION CAR WASH LLC
Also Called: Diamond Finish Car Wash
5960 Barkley St (66202-3269)
PHONE.................................913 236-6886
Richard Kochuyt,
EMP: 40 **EST:** 2010
SALES (est): 220.4K **Privately Held**
SIC: 7542 Washing & polishing, automotive

(G-11645)
MISSION HEATING AND AC
11012 W 58th St (66203-2811)
PHONE.................................913 631-6506
Doug Duvall, *President*
Sandra Duvall, *Vice Pres*
EMP: 15
SALES (est): 1.3MM **Privately Held**
WEB: www.missionheatingandairconditioning.com
SIC: 1711 Warm air heating & air conditioning contractor

(G-11646)
MISSION MEDVET
5914 Johnson Dr (66202-3329)
PHONE.................................913 722-5566
David Allen, *President*
Kelly Ann Perry, *Data Proc Staff*
EMP: 16
SALES (est): 761.9K **Privately Held**
WEB: www.medvetrehab.com
SIC: 0742 Veterinarian, animal specialties

(G-11647)
MISSION PROJECT INC
5960 Dearborn St Ste 201 (66202-9804)
PHONE.................................913 777-6722
Avner Stern, *President*
Charlie Jennings, *Exec Dir*
Sarah MAI, *Exec Dir*
Rachel Harada, *Director*
EMP: 12
SALES: 281.4K **Privately Held**
SIC: 8322 Social services for the handicapped

(G-11648)
MIXON-HILL INC
12980 Metcalf Ave Ste 470 (66213-2646)
PHONE.................................913 239-8400
Lee T Mixon, *President*
Jacqueline Mixon, *Principal*
Christopher Hill, *Vice Pres*
EMP: 11
SALES: 1,000K **Privately Held**
WEB: www.mixonhill.com
SIC: 8742 Transportation consultant

(G-11649)
MIZE HOUSER & COMPANY PA
7101 College Blvd Ste 900 (66210-1984)
PHONE.................................913 451-1882
Tom Farrell, *Manager*
Diane Nge, *Manager*
Stacy Smith, *Shareholder*
EMP: 30
SALES (corp-wide): 23.3MM **Privately Held**
SIC: 8699 Athletic organizations
PA: Mize Houser & Company P.A.
534 S Kansas Ave Ste 700
Topeka KS 66603
785 233-0536

(G-11650)
MJV HOLDINGS LLC
Also Called: Pride Cleaners 31081
5924 Broadmoor St (66202-3226)
PHONE.................................913 432-5348
Joe Brancato, *Branch Mgr*
EMP: 16
SALES (corp-wide): 1.5MM **Privately Held**
WEB: www.pridecleaners.com
SIC: 7216 Cleaning & dyeing, except rugs
PA: Mjv Holdings, Llc
13613 S Us Highway 71
Grandview MO 64030
816 442-8555

(G-11651)
MODERN MAINTENANCE INC
14400 W 96th Ter (66215-4710)
PHONE.................................913 345-9777
Nasi Zarinkia, *President*
Michael Zarinkia, *Vice Pres*
EMP: 400
SQ FT: 7,000
SALES (est): 11.7MM **Privately Held**
SIC: 7349 Janitorial service, contract basis

(G-11652)
MODERN PAVING SYSTEMS INC
14001 W 56th Ter (66216-5005)
PHONE.................................913 962-7208
John Cook, *President*
EMP: 10 **EST:** 1996
SQ FT: 100,000
SALES (est): 960K **Privately Held**
SIC: 1771 Blacktop (asphalt) work

(G-11653)
MONARCH SKIN CARE
Also Called: Monarch Skin Rejuvenation Ctr
5401 College Blvd # 203204 (66211-1923)
PHONE.................................913 317-9386
EMP: 25
SALES (est): 230.2K **Privately Held**
SIC: 7231 Facial salons

(G-11654)
MOORE RUBBER CO INC
20151 W 55th St (66218-9725)
P.O. Box 860050 (66286-0050)
PHONE.................................913 422-5679
Tom Moore, *President*
EMP: 13 **EST:** 1962
SQ FT: 12,500
SALES (est): 2.1MM **Privately Held**
SIC: 3061 Mechanical rubber goods

(G-11655)
MOTEL 6 OPERATING LP
9725 Lenexa Dr (66215-1345)
PHONE.................................913 541-8558
Richard Alvared, *Manager*
EMP: 16
SALES (corp-wide): 579.1MM **Privately Held**
WEB: www.motel6.com
SIC: 7011 Hotels & motels
HQ: Motel 6 Operating L.P.
4001 Intl Pkwy Ste 500
Carrollton TX 75007
972 360-9000

(G-11656)
MPP CO INC
8500 Shawnee Mission Pkwy # 200 (66202-2960)
P.O. Box 795 (66201-0795)
PHONE.................................913 895-0269
Cecil V Tuyl, *President*
Robert J Holcomb, *Corp Secy*
Gerald Lamb, *Manager*
Matt Lickteig, *Manager*
EMP: 15
SQ FT: 2,000
SALES (est): 2.4MM
SALES (corp-wide): 27.5MM **Privately Held**
WEB: www.mppco.com
SIC: 8741 Administrative management
PA: Van Enterprises, Inc. Of Kansas
8500 Shawnee Mission Pkwy # 200
Shawnee Mission KS 66202
913 432-6400

(G-11657)
MT PLEASANT NEWS INC (HQ)
Also Called: Mt Pleasant News, The
14500 W 105th St (66215-2014)
PHONE.................................913 492-9050
Darwin K Sherman, *President*
Emory Styron, *General Mgr*
Brian D Murray, *Sr Exec VP*
Jack D Burton, *Vice Pres*
EMP: 14 **EST:** 1971
SQ FT: 64,000
SALES (est): 1.3MM
SALES (corp-wide): 20.8MM **Privately Held**
SIC: 2711 Newspapers, publishing & printing

PA: Inland Industries, Inc.
19841 Benson St
Bucyrus KS 66013
913 492-9050

(G-11658)
MULTI SYSTEMS INSTALLATION INC (PA)
Also Called: MSI
20101 W 55th St (66218-9725)
PHONE....................913 422-8282
Richard Kelly, *President*
Robert D Hall, *Vice Pres*
Allen Harvey, *Admin Sec*
EMP: 70
SQ FT: 25,000
SALES (est): 7.3MM **Privately Held**
SIC: 1799 Office furniture installation

(G-11659)
MULTI-MEDIA INTERNATIONAL LLC (PA)
13915 W 107th St (66215-2043)
PHONE....................913 469-6800
Rick Teng, *Principal*
EMP: 6
SALES (est): 2.1MM **Privately Held**
SIC: 2721 Magazines: publishing & printing

(G-11660)
MUTUAL FUND STORE INC
11095 Metcalf Ave (66210-1815)
PHONE....................913 338-2323
David Byers, *CEO*
Adam Bold, *Ch of Bd*
Chris Basch, *Senior VP*
Clark Gay, *Senior VP*
Jack Mannino, *Senior VP*
EMP: 20
SQ FT: 7,000
SALES (est): 3.3MM **Privately Held**
SIC: 6282 Investment advisory service

(G-11661)
MVP ELECTRIC LLC
21514 W 51st Ter (66226-9729)
PHONE....................913 322-0868
EMP: 22
SALES (est): 2.1MM **Privately Held**
SIC: 1731 Electrical Contractor

(G-11662)
MWM GROUP INC
11100 Ash St Ste 100 (66211-1700)
PHONE....................913 469-0101
Michael W Gossman, *Ch of Bd*
EMP: 180
SALES (est): 6.1MM
SALES (corp-wide): 440.7MM **Privately Held**
WEB: www.mwbuildersks.com
SIC: 1711 Plumbing, heating, air-conditioning contractors
PA: Mmc Corp
10955 Lowell Ave Ste 350
Overland Park KS 66210
913 469-0101

(G-11663)
N A C M CREDIT SERVICES INC
10670 Barkley St (66212-1861)
P.O. Box 12370 (66282-2370)
PHONE....................913 383-9300
Patrick Tolle, *President*
Kurt Borneman, *Vice Pres*
Kathy Tolle, *Treasurer*
Donna Rogers, *Admin Sec*
EMP: 20
SQ FT: 5,000
SALES (est): 2.3MM **Privately Held**
WEB: www.nacmkc.org
SIC: 7323 Credit bureau & agency

(G-11664)
N2 KIDS ENTERPRISES INC
9215 Slater St (66212-3826)
PHONE....................913 648-5457
EMP: 45
SQ FT: 15,000
SALES (est): 1.6MM **Privately Held**
SIC: 8351 Early Childhood Services

(G-11665)
NAIL PRO
12086 W 135th St (66221-8136)
PHONE....................913 402-0882
Trinh Vu, *Owner*
Michael Vu, *Owner*
EMP: 10
SALES (est): 188.3K **Privately Held**
SIC: 7231 Manicurist, pedicurist

(G-11666)
NAILERY TOO
11373 W 95th St Ste 37 (66214-1826)
PHONE....................913 599-3331
Tan Nguyen, *Owner*
EMP: 10
SALES (est): 181.4K **Privately Held**
WEB: www.thenailery.com
SIC: 7231 Manicurist, pedicurist

(G-11667)
NALL HILLS ANIMAL HOSPITAL
9610 Nall Ave (66207-2952)
PHONE....................913 341-8836
John Teeter, *Partner*
Robin Goodyear, *Partner*
EMP: 10
SQ FT: 1,370
SALES (est): 527.9K **Privately Held**
SIC: 0742 Animal hospital services, pets & other animal specialties

(G-11668)
NALLWOOD HEIGHTS CORPORATION
10770 El Monte St (66211-1449)
PHONE....................913 341-4880
August Huber III, *President*
EMP: 18
SALES: 960K **Privately Held**
SIC: 6512 Commercial & industrial building operation

(G-11669)
NAMSCO INC
8300 College Blvd Ste 300 (66210-2813)
PHONE....................913 344-9100
Robert F Clark, *President*
Michael Ducey, *President*
Rodney Underdown, *President*
Keith Clark, *Vice Pres*
Steven Wolf, *Vice Pres*
EMP: 76
SALES (est): 3.7MM
SALES (corp-wide): 1.4B **Publicly Held**
SIC: 1479 Salt (common) mining; rock salt mining
PA: Compass Minerals International, Inc.
9900 W 109th St Ste 100
Overland Park KS 66210
913 344-9200

(G-11670)
NATIO ASSOC FOR THE ADVAN OF
6505 Frontage Rd Ste 3 (66202-3712)
PHONE....................913 362-2272
Fred Jones, *President*
EMP: 12
SALES (corp-wide): 26.6MM **Privately Held**
WEB: www.detroitnaacp.org
SIC: 8641 Social associations
PA: National Association For The Advancement Of Colored People
4805 Mount Hope Dr
Baltimore MD 21215
410 580-5777

(G-11671)
NATIONAL AUCTIONEERS ASSN
8880 Ballentine St (66214-1900)
PHONE....................913 541-8084
Bob Shivley, *CEO*
Curtis Kitchen, *CTO*
Cynthia Malone, *Executive Asst*
Aaron Ensminger, *Education*
EMP: 12
SQ FT: 8,200
SALES: 2.6MM **Privately Held**
SIC: 8611 Trade associations

(G-11672)
NATIONAL CENTER FOR COMPETENCY
Also Called: Ncct
7007 College Blvd Ste 250 (66211-2437)
PHONE....................913 498-1000
Nancy Graham, *President*
Stan Adams, *Vice Pres*
Vince Brackett, *Vice Pres*
Lantz Brackett, *VP Opers*
Bruce Brackett, *Human Res Dir*
EMP: 40
SALES (est): 3.5MM **Privately Held**
SIC: 7389 Personal service agents, brokers & bureaus

(G-11673)
NATIONAL CTSTRPHE RSTRTION INC
8065 Flint St (66214-3335)
PHONE....................913 663-4111
Sam Shaffer, *Manager*
EMP: 10
SALES (corp-wide): 39.2MM **Privately Held**
WEB: www.ncricat.com
SIC: 1521 Repairing fire damage, single-family houses
PA: National Catastrophe Restoration, Inc.
8447 E 35th St N
Wichita KS 67226
316 636-5700

(G-11674)
NATURAL WAY CHIROPRACTIC
9150 Glenwood St (66212-1364)
PHONE....................913 385-1999
Brian Schnitta, *President*
EMP: 10
SALES (est): 886.9K **Privately Held**
SIC: 8041 Offices & clinics of chiropractors

(G-11675)
NEIGHBORHOOD GROUP INC
8826 Santa Fe Dr Ste 190 (66212-3672)
PHONE....................913 362-0000
Bill P Charcut, *President*
EMP: 50
SQ FT: 7,000
SALES (est): 3.9MM **Privately Held**
WEB: www.neighborhoodgroup.com
SIC: 6531 Real estate managers

(G-11676)
NETZER SALES INC (PA)
Also Called: State Beauty Supply
12625 W 92nd St (66215-3783)
PHONE....................913 599-6464
Jeffrey A Netzer, *President*
EMP: 15
SALES (est): 5.5MM **Privately Held**
SIC: 5087 Beauty parlor equipment & supplies

(G-11677)
NEURAL TECHNOLOGIES INC
6340 Glenwood St Ste 110 (66202-4008)
PHONE....................913 831-0273
Ian Gebbett, *CEO*
EMP: 116
SALES (est): 8.6MM **Privately Held**
SIC: 7371 Computer software development

(G-11678)
NEUROLOGY CONS CHARTERED
8800 W 75th St Ste 100 (66204-4001)
PHONE....................913 632-9810
Michael E Ryan, *President*
EMP: 10
SALES (est): 851.5K **Privately Held**
SIC: 8011 Neurologist

(G-11679)
NEW CINGULAR WIRELESS SVCS INC
Also Called: AT&T Wireless
10895 Lowell Ave Ste 100 (66210-1678)
PHONE....................913 344-2845
Jeffrey Harkman, *Principal*
EMP: 300
SALES (corp-wide): 170.7B **Publicly Held**
WEB: www.attws.com
SIC: 4812 Cellular telephone services
HQ: New Cingular Wireless Services, Inc.
7277 164th Ave Ne
Redmond WA 98052

(G-11680)
NEW MOUNTAIN CAPITAL I LLC
Also Called: Choicepoint
10975 Grandview Dr # 400 (66210-1564)
P.O. Box 419215, Kansas City MO (64141-6215)
PHONE....................913 451-3222
Jack Qian, *Vice Pres*
Jeffrey Haniewich, *Branch Mgr*
EMP: 84
SALES (corp-wide): 108.1MM **Privately Held**
WEB: www.newmountaincapital.com
SIC: 6411 Information bureaus, insurance
PA: New Mountain Capital I, L.L.C.
787 7th Ave Fl 49
New York NY 10019
212 720-0300

(G-11681)
NEW THEATRE COMPANY
Also Called: New Theatre Restaurant
9229 Foster St (66212-2273)
PHONE....................913 649-7469
Dennis Hennessy, *CEO*
Richard Carrothers, *President*
Jennifer Taylor, *Payroll Mgr*
EMP: 250
SALES (est): 5.5MM **Privately Held**
WEB: www.newtheatre.com
SIC: 5812 7922 5813 Dinner theater; theatrical producers & services; drinking places

(G-11682)
NEXUS MEDICAL LLC
11315 Strang Line Rd (66215-4042)
PHONE....................913 451-2234
Cary Dikeman, *Ch of Bd*
Heather Turner, *Manager*
▲ **EMP:** 60
SALES (est): 8.8MM **Privately Held**
SIC: 3841 Surgical & medical instruments

(G-11683)
NFI MANAGEMENT CO INC (PA)
7031 W 97th Ter (66212-1505)
P.O. Box 4190 (66204-0190)
PHONE....................913 341-4411
Stephen Jagoda, *President*
Nathan Jagoda, *Vice Pres*
EMP: 12
SQ FT: 1,000
SALES (est): 3.4MM **Privately Held**
SIC: 6513 Apartment building operators

(G-11684)
NFI MANAGEMENT CO INC
Also Called: Meadowlark Hill Apts
9152 Foster St (66212-2240)
PHONE....................913 642-3700
Donna McCloud, *Manager*
EMP: 10
SALES (corp-wide): 3.4MM **Privately Held**
SIC: 1522 Apartment building construction
PA: Nfi Management Co Inc
7031 W 97th Ter
Shawnee Mission KS 66212
913 341-4411

(G-11685)
NICKLAUS GOLF CLUB MAINTENANCE
14220 Nall Ave (66223-2983)
PHONE....................913 897-1624
Coub Corp, *Owner*
Gary Sailer, *Principal*
EMP: 14
SALES (est): 228.2K **Privately Held**
SIC: 7997 Golf club, membership

(G-11686)
NOLAN REAL ESTATE SERVICES INC
Also Called: Falls Apartments
6565 Foxridge Dr Ofc (66202-1370)
PHONE....................913 362-1920

GEOGRAPHIC

Daniel Allen, *Manager*
Jenny Hess, *Manager*
EMP: 15
SALES (corp-wide): 24.8MM **Privately Held**
SIC: 6513 Apartment building operators
PA: Nolan Real Estate Services, Inc.
2020 W 89th St Ste 320
Leawood KS 66206

(G-11687)
NOONSHINE WINDOW CLEANING SVC
9180 W 92nd St (66212-3909)
P.O. Box 860450, Shawnee (66286-0450)
PHONE..................................913 381-9666
William Thomas Noon, *President*
Cindy Weintraub, *Vice Pres*
EMP: 15
SALES (est): 500K **Privately Held**
WEB: www.noonshine.com
SIC: 1799 7349 Glass tinting, architectural or automotive; window cleaning

(G-11688)
NORTONLIFELOCK INC
Also Called: Symantec
9393 W 110th St Ste 500 (66210-1464)
PHONE..................................913 451-6710
Jim Kimberling, *Branch Mgr*
EMP: 45
SALES (corp-wide): 4.7B **Publicly Held**
WEB: www.symantec.com
SIC: 7372 Prepackaged software
PA: Nortonlifelock Inc.
60 E Rio Salado Pkwy # 1
Tempe AZ 85281
650 527-8000

(G-11689)
NPI PROPERTY MANAGEMENT CORP
8000 Perry St (66204-4743)
PHONE..................................913 648-4339
Roxane Tevis, *Manager*
EMP: 15 **Publicly Held**
WEB: www.npi.org
SIC: 6513 Apartment building operators
HQ: Npi Property Management Corporation
55 Beattie Pl
Greenville SC 29601
864 239-1000

(G-11690)
NUMERICAL CONTROL SUPPORT INC
Also Called: Ncs Precision Manufacturing
21945 W 83rd St (66227-3133)
PHONE..................................913 441-3500
Mary Dobbins, *CEO*
Gary Dobbins, *President*
Mark Douglas, *Production*
Amanda Dobbins, *Purch Mgr*
James Patterson, *Engineer*
EMP: 45
SQ FT: 60,000
SALES (est): 8.4MM **Privately Held**
WEB: www.ncsmanufacturing.com
SIC: 3599 7692 3812 3769 Machine shop, jobbing & repair; welding repair; search & navigation equipment; guided missile & space vehicle parts & auxiliary equipment; food products machinery

(G-11691)
NUNIK ENGINEERING
9301 W 53rd St (66203-2113)
PHONE..................................913 384-0010
Rod Mayfield, *President*
EMP: 10
SALES (est): 721.6K **Privately Held**
WEB: www.nuink.net
SIC: 2899 8711 Ink or writing fluids; engineering services

(G-11692)
OAK PARK CLEANERS INC
12230 W 95th St (66215-3806)
PHONE..................................913 599-3040
Jake Kim, *President*
EMP: 10
SQ FT: 3,750
SALES (est): 389K **Privately Held**
SIC: 7216 Drycleaning plants, except rugs

(G-11693)
OBRIEN PHARMACY
Also Called: Obrian Pharmacy
5453 W 61st Pl (66205-3002)
PHONE..................................913 322-0001
Harry M Everett, *Owner*
EMP: 10
SALES (est): 1.9MM **Privately Held**
WEB: www.obrienrx.com
SIC: 2834 Pharmaceutical preparations

(G-11694)
OCH REGIONAL OFFICE
8235 Melrose Dr (66214-1625)
PHONE..................................913 599-6137
Randy Roelofsv, *Principal*
EMP: 20
SALES (est): 532.8K **Privately Held**
SIC: 6531 Housing authority operator

(G-11695)
OLD UNITED CASUALTY COMPANY
8500 Shwnee Mksn Pkwy 2 (66202)
P.O. Box 795 (66201-0795)
PHONE..................................913 432-6400
Cecil Van Tuyl, *President*
Dan Mattox, *Vice Pres*
John A Morford, *Vice Pres*
Robert J Holcomb, *Treasurer*
EMP: 50
SQ FT: 8,000
SALES (est): 17MM
SALES (corp-wide): 27.5MM **Privately Held**
WEB: www.oldunited.com
SIC: 6331 Fire, marine & casualty insurance
PA: Van Enterprises, Inc. Of Kansas
8500 Shawnee Mission Pkwy # 200
Shawnee Mission KS 66202
913 432-6400

(G-11696)
OLIVER P STEINNAGEL INC
Also Called: Oliver's Salon
7512 W 119th St (66213-1108)
PHONE..................................913 338-2266
Oliver P Steinnagel, *President*
EMP: 32
SALES (est): 774.5K **Privately Held**
WEB: www.oliverssalon.com
SIC: 7231 Hairdressers

(G-11697)
ONE POWER LLC
9770 Legler Rd (66219-1282)
PHONE..................................913 219-5061
Scott Wright, *Partner*
Robert Hunt, *Mng Member*
EMP: 24
SALES (est): 2.6MM **Privately Held**
SIC: 7389 Telephone services

(G-11698)
ONSITE SOLUTIONS LLC
6950 Squibb Rd Ste 320 (66202-3260)
PHONE..................................913 912-7384
Heath Mayor, *President*
Dennis Angrisani,
EMP: 250
SQ FT: 1,400
SALES (est): 8MM **Privately Held**
SIC: 7361 Labor contractors (employment agency)

(G-11699)
ORACLE SYSTEMS CORPORATION
9200 Indian Creek Pkwy # 560 (66210-2036)
PHONE..................................913 663-3400
David White, *Branch Mgr*
Kathy Morris, *Recruiter*
EMP: 56
SALES (corp-wide): 39.5B **Publicly Held**
WEB: www.forcecapital.com
SIC: 7372 Prepackaged software
HQ: Oracle Systems Corporation
500 Oracle Pkwy
Redwood City CA 94065
650 506-7000

(G-11700)
ORAL & FACIAL SURGERY ASSOC
12208 W 87th Street Pkwy # 150 (66215-2812)
PHONE..................................913 541-1888
Kirk Collier, *Branch Mgr*
EMP: 23
SALES (est): 546.1K
SALES (corp-wide): 3.5MM **Privately Held**
SIC: 8021 Dental surgeon
PA: Oral & Facial Surgery Associates
3700 W 83rd St Ste 103
Prairie Village KS 66208
913 381-5194

(G-11701)
ORAL MXILO OFCIAL SRGERY ASSOC
Also Called: Burke, Evans, Allen, Pannell
11005 W 60th St Ste 150 (66203-2789)
PHONE..................................913 268-9500
Dr Gregory Allen, *Partner*
Taylor L Markle, *Fmly & Gen Dent*
EMP: 25
SALES (est): 638.1K **Privately Held**
SIC: 8021 Oral pathologist; dental surgeon

(G-11702)
OREILLY AUTOMOTIVE STORES INC
Also Called: O Reilly Auto Parts 133
6136 Nieman Rd (66203-2940)
PHONE..................................913 268-6001
Chuck Kaiser, *Branch Mgr*
EMP: 15 **Publicly Held**
WEB: www.oreillyauto.com
SIC: 5013 5531 Automotive supplies & parts; automotive parts
HQ: O'reilly Automotive Stores, Inc.
233 S Patterson Ave
Springfield MO 65802
417 862-2674

(G-11703)
ORTHOPAEDIC MGT SVCS LLC
3651 College Blvd 100a (66211-1910)
PHONE..................................913 319-7500
Tim Badwey,
Cris Barnthouse,
Mark Bernhardt,
Stan Bowling,
Jon Browne,
EMP: 70
SALES: 4.5MM **Privately Held**
SIC: 8011 Orthopedic physician

(G-11704)
OUTLAWS GROUP LLC
Also Called: Chet's Lock & Key
4587 Indian Creek Pkwy (66207-4004)
PHONE..................................913 381-5565
Richard Adams, *General Mgr*
Kevin King, *Manager*
Sandi Outlaw,
EMP: 12
SQ FT: 20,000
SALES (est): 1.9MM **Privately Held**
WEB: www.chetslock.com
SIC: 7699 Locksmith shop

(G-11705)
OVERLAND PARK CHAMBER COMMERCE
9001 W 110th St Ste 150 (66210-2118)
PHONE..................................913 491-3600
Tracy Osborne, *President*
Andrea Bruening, *President*
EMP: 11
SQ FT: 3,800
SALES: 1.7MM **Privately Held**
WEB: www.opks.org
SIC: 8611 Chamber of Commerce

(G-11706)
OVERLAND PARK DENTAL
Also Called: Douglas J Knop DDS
9601 Antioch Rd (66212-4061)
PHONE..................................913 383-2343
Douglas J Knop, *Partner*
David Mitchell, *Partner*
EMP: 12
SQ FT: 950
SALES (est): 550K **Privately Held**
SIC: 8021 Dentists' office

(G-11707)
OVERLAND PARK DENTISTRY PA
8700 W 151st St (66221-8705)
PHONE..................................913 647-8700
Charles Kimes, *Principal*
EMP: 13
SALES (est): 726.7K **Privately Held**
SIC: 8021 Dentists' office

(G-11708)
OVERLAND PARK HOSPITALITY LLC
Also Called: Holiday Inn
10920 Nall Ave (66211-1207)
PHONE..................................913 312-0900
Joe Behrman, *General Mgr*
Don Boos,
EMP: 45
SALES (est): 1.4MM **Privately Held**
SIC: 7011 Hotels & motels

(G-11709)
OVERLAND PARK REG MED STAFF DF
10500 Quivira Rd Ste 40 (66215-2306)
PHONE..................................913 541-5000
EMP: 10
SALES: 214.3K **Privately Held**
SIC: 8062 General medical & surgical hospitals

(G-11710)
OVERLAND PARK SENIORCARE LLC
Also Called: Cypress Court At Overland Park
11000 Oakmont St (66210-1100)
PHONE..................................913 491-1144
Tom Gangler, *Manager*
EMP: 50
SALES (est): 1.5MM **Privately Held**
SIC: 8361 Rehabilitation center, residential: health care incidental

(G-11711)
OVERLAND TV INC
Also Called: Factory Authorized Video Svc
7135 W 80th St (66204-3716)
PHONE..................................913 648-2222
John J Ganapini, *President*
EMP: 10
SQ FT: 2,000
SALES (est): 728.6K **Privately Held**
SIC: 7622 Television repair shop

(G-11712)
PA ACQUISITION CORP
Also Called: Party City
11635 Metcalf Ave (66210-2234)
PHONE..................................913 498-3700
Cindy Jordan, *Manager*
EMP: 13
SALES (corp-wide): 2.4B **Publicly Held**
WEB: www.partyamerica.com
SIC: 5947 7389 Party favors; balloons, novelty & toy
HQ: Pa Acquisition Corp.
25 Green Pond Rd Ste 1
Rockaway NJ 07866
973 453-8600

(G-11713)
PACO DESIGNS INC
14306 W 99th St (66215-1102)
PHONE..................................913 541-1708
Paul N Cohen, *President*
EMP: 6
SQ FT: 4,000
SALES (est): 861.3K **Privately Held**
WEB: www.pacodesigns.com
SIC: 3911 5944 Jewelry, precious metal; jewelry stores

(G-11714)
PALMER SQUARE CAPITAL MGT LLC
2000 Shawnee Mission Pkwy # 300 (66205-3601)
PHONE..................................816 994-3201
Christopher D Long, *President*
Christopher Long, *Principal*
Scott Betz, *COO*

Michael Daniel, *Vice Pres*
Kyra Floyd, *Vice Pres*
EMP: 25
SALES (est): 2.2MM **Privately Held**
SIC: 6722 Money market mutual funds

(G-11715)
PAR EXSALONCE (PA)
11849 College Blvd (66210-1314)
PHONE..................................913 469-9532
Suzanne Doehring, *President*
Kevin Doehring, *Vice Pres*
EMP: 22
SQ FT: 3,300
SALES (est): 995.4K **Privately Held**
SIC: 7231 7991 Cosmetology & personal hygiene salons; spas

(G-11716)
PARK HOTELS & RESORTS INC
Also Called: Embassy Suites
10601 Metcalf Ave (66212-1817)
PHONE..................................913 649-7060
Jack Curtis, *Branch Mgr*
EMP: 75
SALES (corp-wide): 2.7B **Publicly Held**
WEB: www.esirvine.com
SIC: 7011 5813 5812 Hotels & motels; drinking places; eating places
PA: Park Hotels & Resorts Inc.
1775 Tysons Blvd Fl 7
Tysons VA 22102
571 302-5757

(G-11717)
PARKING SYSTEMS INC
Also Called: Rubin, Robert
12452 Granada Dr (66209-2271)
PHONE..................................913 345-9272
Robert D Rubin, *President*
Jack P Gibbons, *Vice Pres*
Brian T Meyers, *Admin Sec*
EMP: 13
SALES (est): 541.2K **Privately Held**
SIC: 7521 Parking lots

(G-11718)
PARKWAY INSURANCE AGENCY INC
5750 W 95th St Ste 105 (66207-2974)
PHONE..................................913 385-5000
Vance Logan, *President*
EMP: 12
SALES (est): 1MM **Privately Held**
SIC: 6411 Insurance agents

(G-11719)
PAYCOR INC
8050 Marshall Dr Ste 100 (66214-1570)
PHONE..................................913 262-9484
Susan Hotzel, *Manager*
EMP: 55
SALES (corp-wide): 92.8MM **Privately Held**
SIC: 8721 7291 Payroll accounting service; tax return preparation services
PA: Paycor, Inc.
4811 Montgomery Rd
Cincinnati OH 45212
513 381-0505

(G-11720)
PAYNE AND JONES CHARTERED (PA)
11000 King St Ste 200 (66210-1286)
P.O. Box 25625 (66225-5625)
PHONE..................................816 960-3600
Jodde Olanning, *President*
Elizabeth Small, *Admin Sec*
Sue Leach, *Legal Staff*
April Sage, *Legal Staff*
EMP: 55
SALES (est): 6.1MM **Privately Held**
WEB: www.paynejones.com
SIC: 8111 General practice attorney, lawyer

(G-11721)
PDQ TOOLS AND EQUIPMENT INC
Also Called: PDQ Auto Reconditioning
9018 Rosehill Rd (66215-3516)
PHONE..................................913 492-5800
Johnette Martin, *President*
EMP: 5
SQ FT: 45,000
SALES (est): 347.4K **Privately Held**
WEB: www.pdqtools.com
SIC: 7532 3312 5013 Body shop, automotive; tool & die steel; automotive servicing equipment

(G-11722)
PECKHAM GYTON ALBERS VIETS INC
1900 W 47th Pl Ste 300 (66205-1871)
PHONE..................................913 362-6500
Steve Troester, *Vice Pres*
Mark Viets, *Treasurer*
EMP: 45
SALES (corp-wide): 11.8MM **Privately Held**
WEB: www.pgav.com
SIC: 8712 Architectural engineering
PA: Peckham Guyton Albers & Viets, Inc.
200 N Broadway Ste 1000
Saint Louis MO 63102
314 231-7318

(G-11723)
PEDIATRIC PROFESSIONAL ASSN
10600 Quivira Rd Ste 210 (66215-2311)
PHONE..................................913 541-3300
Russell Etzenhouser, *President*
Edward Belzer, *Vice Pres*
Donald Vannaman, *Admin Sec*
EMP: 35
SALES (est): 4.6MM **Privately Held**
WEB: www.ppadocs.com
SIC: 8011 Pediatrician

(G-11724)
PENNYS CONCRETE INC (PA)
Also Called: Green Ready Mix of Missouri
23400 W 82nd St (66227-2705)
PHONE..................................913 441-8781
William J Penny, *President*
Marlene Penny, *Corp Secy*
David Keller, *Opers Mgr*
Cory Claxton, *Director*
Melanie Lorenzo, *Director*
EMP: 30
SQ FT: 30,000
SALES (est): 43.9MM **Privately Held**
WEB: www.pennysconcrete.com
SIC: 3273 Ready-mixed concrete

(G-11725)
PEPPERMINT PTTYS MNTSSORI SCHL
11010 W 56th Ter (66203-2314)
PHONE..................................913 631-9376
Brandon Vore, *President*
Jim Vore, *Owner*
Patty Vore, *Co-Owner*
Audra Darner, *Director*
EMP: 10
SQ FT: 1,100
SALES (est): 395.8K **Privately Held**
SIC: 8351 Preschool center

(G-11726)
PERFORMANCE CONTG INTL INC
16400 College Blvd (66219-1389)
PHONE..................................913 888-8600
William P Massey, *President*
Bill Massey, *President*
Ross Malikowski, *Project Mgr*
Tony Settles, *Project Mgr*
EMP: 98
SALES (est): 5.6MM
SALES (corp-wide): 1.1B **Privately Held**
SIC: 1796 Machinery installation
PA: Performance Contracting Group, Inc.
11145 Thompson Ave
Lenexa KS 66219
800 255-6886

(G-11727)
PERFORMANCE PACKG GROUP LLC
17501 W 98th St 32 (66219-1704)
PHONE..................................913 438-2012
Bruce Young, *Managing Prtnr*
Thomas Lott, *Partner*
▲ **EMP:** 30
SALES (est): 2.4MM **Privately Held**
SIC: 3565 Packaging machinery

(G-11728)
PETSMART INC
11501 Metcalf Ave (66210-2232)
PHONE..................................913 338-5544
Kerry Mills, *Branch Mgr*
EMP: 30
SALES (corp-wide): 9.4B **Publicly Held**
WEB: www.petsmart.com
SIC: 5999 0752 Pet food; animal specialty services
HQ: Petsmart, Inc.
19601 N 27th Ave
Phoenix AZ 85027
623 580-6100

(G-11729)
PETSMART INC
5810 Antioch Rd (66202-2017)
PHONE..................................913 384-4445
Les Pelsrey, *Manager*
EMP: 30
SALES (corp-wide): 9.4B **Publicly Held**
WEB: www.petsmart.com
SIC: 5999 0752 Pet food; animal specialty services
HQ: Petsmart, Inc.
19601 N 27th Ave
Phoenix AZ 85027
623 580-6100

(G-11730)
PETWORKS INC
Also Called: Petworks Vtrnary Hosp Pet Sups
9232 Metcalf Ave (66212-1476)
PHONE..................................913 381-3131
Kent Callicott, *President*
EMP: 10
SALES (est): 648K **Privately Held**
WEB: www.petworkskc.com
SIC: 0742 0752 Animal hospital services, pets & other animal specialties; grooming services, pet & animal specialties

(G-11731)
PHILIP MORRIS USA INC
4000 W 114th St Ste 110 (66211-2622)
PHONE..................................913 339-9317
Mary Ellen Johnson, *Manager*
EMP: 18
SALES (corp-wide): 25.3B **Publicly Held**
WEB: www.philipmorrisusa.com
SIC: 5194 Tobacco & tobacco products
HQ: Philip Morris Usa Inc.
6601 W Brd St
Richmond VA 23230
804 274-2000

(G-11732)
PHILLIPS RESOURCE NETWORK INC
8041 W 47th St (66203-1301)
PHONE..................................913 236-7777
Jerry T Katlin, *President*
EMP: 22
SQ FT: 2,500
SALES (est): 2MM **Privately Held**
WEB: www.phillipsresource.com
SIC: 8742 Construction project management consultant; financial consultant

(G-11733)
PHYSICIANS SURGERY CENTER
3840 W 75th St (66208-4126)
PHONE..................................913 384-9600
Nicole De Tar, *Manager*
Lucy Lara, *Manager*
EMP: 21
SALES (est): 3.2MM **Privately Held**
SIC: 8011 Surgeon

(G-11734)
PINNACLE LAWN CARE INC
15315 Kenneth Rd (66224-9645)
PHONE..................................913 851-0423
Benjamin Wiese, *President*
Haley Wiese, *Human Resources*
EMP: 20
SQ FT: 2,500
SALES: 1.5MM **Privately Held**
WEB: www.pinnaclelawncare.com
SIC: 0782 Lawn care services

(G-11735)
PIONEER PRE SCHOOL LLC
11100 College Blvd (66210-2796)
P.O. Box 14594 (66285-4594)
PHONE..................................913 338-4282
Geri Allcorn,
Barry Allcorn,
Michelle Brenan,
EMP: 22
SQ FT: 2,859
SALES: 280K **Privately Held**
SIC: 8351 Preschool center

(G-11736)
PITNEY BOWES INC
7908 W 140th St (66223-1301)
PHONE..................................913 681-5579
Joseph Moses, *Owner*
Joseph Davison, *Manager*
Romel Bumanlag, *Software Engr*
EMP: 60
SALES (corp-wide): 3.5B **Publicly Held**
SIC: 3579 7359 Postage meters; business machine & electronic equipment rental services
PA: Pitney Bowes Inc.
3001 Summer St Ste 3
Stamford CT 06905
203 356-5000

(G-11737)
PLATINUM CONTRACTING LLC
4800 Lamar Ave 101 (66202-1775)
PHONE..................................913 210-2003
Marty Crews, *President*
EMP: 11 **EST:** 2014
SALES (est): 399.8K **Privately Held**
SIC: 1799 Special trade contractors

(G-11738)
PLAZA BELMONT MGT GROUP II LLC (PA)
8016 State Line Rd (66208-3721)
PHONE..................................913 381-7177
John T Stout Jr,
Jim Olson,
Robert Parnow,
EMP: 257 **EST:** 1999
SQ FT: 3,000
SALES (est): 19.3MM **Privately Held**
WEB: www.plazabelmont.com
SIC: 8741 Business management

(G-11739)
PLAZA MORTGAGE
2000 Shawnee Mission Pkwy # 225 (66205-3605)
PHONE..................................913 671-1865
Leland Gerhart, *Corp Secy*
Ester Mays, *VP Opers*
Rick Powell, *Manager*
EMP: 10
SALES (est): 721.3K
SALES (corp-wide): 225.3B **Publicly Held**
WEB: www.plazamtg.com
SIC: 6163 Mortgage brokers arranging for loans, using money of others
HQ: Reece & Nichols Realtors, Inc.
11601 Granada St
Leawood KS 66211
913 491-1001

(G-11740)
PMTI INC
5425 Antioch Dr (66202-1021)
PHONE..................................913 432-7500
Fred V Dellett Jr, *President*
EMP: 46 **EST:** 1997
SALES (est): 4.3MM **Privately Held**
WEB: www.petersonmachine.com
SIC: 3548 5084 Welding & cutting apparatus & accessories; industrial machinery & equipment

(G-11741)
PODIATRY ASSOCIATES PA
Also Called: Nachlas, Michael J
8901 W 74th St Ste 200 (66204-2200)
PHONE..................................913 432-5052
Michael Nachlas, *President*
Jessica Troester, *Office Admin*
Mitchell Dorris, *Officer*
Todd Van Wyngarden, *Officer*
EMP: 15

SALES (est): 1.6MM **Privately Held**
SIC: 8043 Offices & clinics of podiatrists

(G-11742)
POLSINELLI PC
6201 College Blvd Ste 500 (66211-2435)
PHONE..................................913 451-8788
John Peterson, *Principal*
Luke Hagedorn, *Associate*
Mark L Sprecker, *Associate*
EMP: 40
SALES (corp-wide): 227.6MM **Privately Held**
WEB: www.pswlaw.com
SIC: 8111 General practice law office
PA: Polsinelli Pc
900 W 48th Pl Ste 900 # 900
Kansas City MO 64112
816 753-1000

(G-11743)
POOL & PATIO INC (PA)
Also Called: Courtyard and Patio
11409 W 89th St (66214-1705)
PHONE..................................913 888-2226
Louis D Ferlo, *President*
Beverly Ferlo, *Vice Pres*
Natalie Gibbs, *Vice Pres*
EMP: 12
SQ FT: 15,800
SALES (est): 2.1MM **Privately Held**
WEB: www.poolandpatiokc.com
SIC: 7389 5712 5999 Swimming pool & hot tub service & maintenance; outdoor & garden furniture; swimming pool chemicals, equipment & supplies

(G-11744)
POOL & PATIO SUPPLY INC
Also Called: Courtyard & Patio
11409 W 89th St (66214-1797)
PHONE..................................913 888-2226
Louis D Ferlo, *President*
Beverly A Ferlo, *Vice Pres*
Natalie Gibbs, *Vice Pres*
EMP: 10
SQ FT: 15,800
SALES: 2MM
SALES (corp-wide): 2.1MM **Privately Held**
WEB: www.poolandpatiokc.com
SIC: 7389 5712 5999 1799 Swimming pool & hot tub service & maintenance; outdoor & garden furniture; swimming pool chemicals, equipment & supplies; spas & hot tubs; swimming pool construction
PA: Pool & Patio Inc
11409 W 89th St
Shawnee Mission KS 66214
913 888-2226

(G-11745)
POTTS LAW FIRM LLP
1901 W 47th Pl Ste 210 (66205-1834)
PHONE..................................816 931-2230
Timothy Sifers, *Branch Mgr*
EMP: 10
SALES (corp-wide): 6.5MM **Privately Held**
SIC: 8111 General practice law office
PA: The Potts Law Firm Llp
3737 Buffalo Speedway # 100
Houston TX 77098
713 963-8881

(G-11746)
PRA INTRNTIONAL OPERATIONS INC
9755 Ridge Dr (66219-9746)
PHONE..................................913 410-2000
Edie Burns, *Office Mgr*
EMP: 300
SALES (corp-wide): 2.8B **Publicly Held**
SIC: 8731 Commercial physical research
HQ: Pra International, Llc
4130 Parklake Ave Ste 400
Raleigh NC 27612
919 786-8200

(G-11747)
PRECISION CUT INC
23410 W 79th St (66227-3040)
PHONE..................................913 422-0777
Scott Ellis, *President*
Elizabeth Ellis, *Vice Pres*
▲ **EMP:** 40
SALES (est): 3.4MM **Privately Held**
SIC: 2299 Apparel filling: cotton waste, kapok & related material

(G-11748)
PREMIER BANK (HQ)
15301 W 87th Street Pkwy # 100
(66219-1402)
P.O. Box 15956 (66285-5956)
PHONE..................................913 888-8490
David W Caffrey, *President*
Donald L Sturm, *Principal*
Martin W Cole Jr, *Exec VP*
Markus J Miller, *Exec VP*
EMP: 40 **EST:** 1979
SQ FT: 30,000
SALES: 15.4MM
SALES (corp-wide): 221.2MM **Privately Held**
WEB: www.premierbank.net
SIC: 6022 State commercial banks
PA: Sturm Financial Group, Inc.
3033 E 1st Ave Ste 300
Denver CO 80206
303 394-5023

(G-11749)
PREMIER BANK
11830 W 135th St (66221-9399)
PHONE..................................913 541-6180
Scott Miller, *Branch Mgr*
EMP: 10
SALES (corp-wide): 221.2MM **Privately Held**
WEB: www.premierbank.net
SIC: 6022 State commercial banks
HQ: Premier Bank
15301 W 87th Street Pkwy # 100
Shawnee Mission KS 66219
913 888-8490

(G-11750)
PREMIUM NUTRITIONAL PDTS INC
Also Called: Zu Preem
10504 W 79th St (66214-3346)
P.O. Box 2094 (66201-1094)
PHONE..................................913 962-8887
David R Morris, *President*
Mark Zander, *COO*
Vanna Hendrix, *Opers Staff*
Brian Sharbaugh, *CFO*
Guy Oudejans, *VP Sales*
▼ **EMP:** 15
SQ FT: 18,000
SALES (est): 9.1MM **Privately Held**
WEB: www.zupreem.com
SIC: 5199 Pet supplies

(G-11751)
PRICE BROTHERS REALTY INC (PA)
Also Called: Louisburg Square Apartments
12721 Metcalf Ave Ste 200 (66213-2619)
PHONE..................................913 381-2280
Douglas M Price, *President*
Steve Price, *Principal*
Tracy J McHugh, *Vice Pres*
Kent Price, *Vice Pres*
Mark Rockloge, *Project Mgr*
EMP: 125
SQ FT: 10,000
SALES (est): 9MM **Privately Held**
SIC: 6513 6531 6512 Apartment hotel operation; real estate agents & managers; commercial & industrial building operation

(G-11752)
PRO-TOW LLC
11410 W 89th St (66214-1704)
PHONE..................................913 262-3300
Kevin Schorgl, *General Mgr*
Joe Richard,
EMP: 14
SALES (est): 1.1MM **Privately Held**
WEB: www.protowllc.com
SIC: 7549 4213 Towing service, automotive; automobiles, transport & delivery

(G-11753)
PROACTIVE SOLUTIONS INC (PA)
5625 Foxridge Dr (66202-4522)
PHONE..................................913 948-8000
Vicki Dean, *President*
Dean Thiede, *Vice Pres*
Brian Norman, *Technical Mgr*
Rick J Randazzo, *Accounts Exec*
Patricia Kovach, *Marketing Staff*
EMP: 25
SQ FT: 15,000
SALES: 45.6MM **Privately Held**
WEB: www.proactivesolutions.com
SIC: 8742 Industry specialist consultants

(G-11754)
PROFESSIONAL BENEFIT CONS
11014 W 50th Ter (66203-1608)
PHONE..................................913 268-0515
Arthur Schlaikjer, *Owner*
EMP: 19
SALES (est): 1.8MM **Privately Held**
SIC: 6411 Insurance information & consulting services

(G-11755)
PROFESSIONAL GRAPHICS INC
Also Called: Precision Printing
15025 W 114th Ter (66215-3634)
PHONE..................................913 663-3330
Brian G Diddle, *President*
Matthew Thompson, *Business Mgr*
Gerald F Diddle Jr, *Vice Pres*
EMP: 10
SQ FT: 4,000
SALES (est): 1.9MM **Privately Held**
WEB: www.precisionprintkc.com
SIC: 2752 Commercial printing, offset

(G-11756)
PROPANE RESOURCES LLC (PA)
6950 Squibb Rd Ste 306 (66202-3258)
P.O. Box 2308 (66201-2308)
PHONE..................................913 262-8345
Tammy Day, *Office Mgr*
Laraine Bias, *Manager*
Martin Lerum,
Reid Simonett, *Training Spec*
Bonnie Walker,
EMP: 25
SQ FT: 5,000
SALES: 6.9MM **Privately Held**
WEB: www.propaneprice.com
SIC: 2741 8742 Business service newsletters: publishing & printing; management consulting services

(G-11757)
PROPANE RESOURCES TRNSP INC
6950 Squibb Rd Ste 306 (66202-3258)
P.O. Box 2308 (66201-2308)
PHONE..................................913 262-8345
Martin Lerum, *President*
Mark Bailey, *Admin Sec*
EMP: 26
SQ FT: 5,000
SALES: 2.5MM **Privately Held**
WEB: www.propaneresources.com
SIC: 4213 Trucking, except local

(G-11758)
PRUDENTIAL HENRY & BURROWS
11150 Overbrook Rd # 150 (66211-2238)
PHONE..................................913 345-3000
Steve Moyer, *General Mgr*
EMP: 50
SALES (est): 987.8K **Privately Held**
SIC: 6531 Real estate agent, residential

(G-11759)
PRUDENTIAL INSUR CO OF AMER
10801 Mastin St Ste 200 (66210-1658)
PHONE..................................913 327-1060
Ken Cunningham, *Manager*
EMP: 39
SALES (corp-wide): 62.9B **Publicly Held**
SIC: 6411 Insurance agents, brokers & service
HQ: The Prudential Insurance Company Of America
751 Broad St
Newark NJ 07102
973 802-6000

(G-11760)
PRYOR LEARNING SOLUTIONS INC (PA)
Also Called: Fred Pryor Seminars
5700 Broadmoor St Ste 300 (66202-2415)
PHONE..................................913 967-8300
Michael B Hayes, *CEO*
Michael Droge, *President*
Roger W Hershey, *Vice Pres*
Paul Rounds, *Vice Pres*
Jim Anderson, *CFO*
EMP: 37
SALES: 69.8MM **Privately Held**
WEB: www.readingdynamics.com
SIC: 8331 Job training services; vocational rehabilitation agency

(G-11761)
PSYCHIATRIC ASSOCIATES
Also Called: Psychiatric Associates Billing
4601 W 109th St Ste 208 (66211-1314)
PHONE..................................913 438-8221
William R Murphy, *Owner*
Marla Brown, *Manager*
EMP: 20
SALES (est): 860K **Privately Held**
WEB: www.psychiatric-associates.net
SIC: 8063 Psychiatric hospitals

(G-11762)
PSYCHIATRY ASSOC KANS CY PC
Also Called: Psychiatry Associates Kans Cy
8900 State Line Rd # 380 (66206-1960)
PHONE..................................913 385-7252
Sherman Cole MD, *President*
EMP: 20
SALES (est): 4.3MM **Privately Held**
SIC: 8011 Psychiatrist

(G-11763)
QC FINANCIAL SERVICES INC (HQ)
Also Called: Quik Cash
9401 Indian Creek Pkwy # 1500
(66210-2020)
PHONE..................................913 439-1100
Don Early, *Ch of Bd*
Darrin Andersen, *President*
Jevan Taylor, *Marketing Staff*
Lovell Johnson, *Manager*
◆ **EMP:** 100
SQ FT: 10,000
SALES (est): 186.3MM
SALES (corp-wide): 194.2MM **Publicly Held**
WEB: www.qcholdings.com
SIC: 6099 6141 Check cashing agencies; consumer finance companies
PA: Qc Holdings, Inc.
8208 Melrose Dr
Lenexa KS 66214
866 660-2243

(G-11764)
QUAIL RIDGE HOMES ASSOC INC
10764 Walmer St (66211-1113)
PHONE..................................913 381-2042
Allan Weil, *Representative*
EMP: 46
SALES (est): 1.6MM **Privately Held**
SIC: 8641 Homeowners' association

(G-11765)
QUEEN-MORRIS VENTURES LLC
Also Called: Queens Price Shopper
8686 Antioch Rd (66212-3648)
PHONE..................................913 383-2563
Jerry Masterson, *Manager*
EMP: 140 **Privately Held**
SIC: 5411 5992 5912 5421 Grocery stores; florists; drug stores & proprietary stores; meat & fish markets; bread, cake & related products
PA: Queen-Morris Ventures, L.L.C.
8 W Peoria St
Paola KS 66071

(G-11766)
QUEST CAPITAL MANAGEMENT INC (PA)
Also Called: National Home Buyers Alliance
15482 College Blvd (66219-1352)
PHONE....................................913 599-6422
Jeffery D Lyon, *President*
Lynette Lyon, *Office Mgr*
EMP: 17
SQ FT: 3,000
SALES: 2.1MM **Privately Held**
SIC: 6411 Insurance agents, brokers & service

(G-11767)
QUEST DIAGNOSTICS INCORPORATED
10101 Renner Blvd (66219-9752)
PHONE....................................913 982-2900
Alan Henderson, *Manager*
EMP: 17
SALES (corp-wide): 7.5B **Publicly Held**
WEB: www.questdiagnostics.com
SIC: 8071 Testing laboratories
PA: Quest Diagnostics Incorporated
500 Plaza Dr Ste G
Secaucus NJ 07094
973 520-2700

(G-11768)
QUIVIRA FALLS COMMUNITY ASSN
10990 Westgate Rd (66210-1165)
PHONE....................................913 469-5463
Ryan Rader, *President*
Martel Jordanson, *Vice Pres*
Katherine Stone, *Treasurer*
Linda Rohde, *Manager*
Gene Beaman, *Admin Sec*
EMP: 24
SQ FT: 5,200
SALES (est): 620.2K **Privately Held**
SIC: 8641 Homeowners' association

(G-11769)
QUIVIRA INTERNAL MEDICINE
10601 Quivira Rd Ste 200 (66215-2320)
PHONE....................................913 541-3340
Liz Prezant, *General Mgr*
EMP: 50
SQ FT: 21,000
SALES (est): 3.9MM **Privately Held**
SIC: 8011 Internal medicine, physician/surgeon

(G-11770)
R & D FITNESS INC
Also Called: Golds Gym
6501 Frontage Rd (66202-3646)
PHONE....................................913 722-2001
Anna Marie Russo, *President*
EMP: 30
SALES (est): 1.1MM **Privately Held**
SIC: 7991 Physical fitness facilities

(G-11771)
R D C INC
Also Called: Lyntec
8385 Melrose Dr (66214-1629)
PHONE....................................913 529-2233
Mark Bishop, *President*
Dan Nguyen, *Design Engr*
EMP: 5
SALES: 2MM **Privately Held**
WEB: www.lyntec.com
SIC: 3651 Audio electronic systems

(G-11772)
R MILLER SALES CO INC
9215 Cherokee Ln Ste 230 (66206-1701)
PHONE....................................913 341-3727
Russell Miller, *President*
EMP: 50
SALES (est): 3.3MM **Privately Held**
SIC: 2791 2759 5099 3499 Hand composition typesetting; decals: printing; firearms & ammunition, except sporting; fire- or burglary-resistive products; etching & engraving; furniture stock & parts, hardwood

(G-11773)
R P PRODUCTS INC
Also Called: Royal Prestige
13611 W 109th St (66215-4185)
P.O. Box 14070 (66285-4070)
PHONE....................................913 492-6380
Garry Fowler, *President*
Doug Rinas, *Treasurer*
EMP: 30
SQ FT: 10,000
SALES (est): 3.3MM **Privately Held**
WEB: www.celebritychina.com
SIC: 5719 5023 Kitchenware; cookware, except aluminum; china; kitchenware; china; stainless steel flatware

(G-11774)
R S BICKFORD & CO INC
8600 W 110th St Ste 110 (66210-1805)
PHONE....................................913 451-1480
Robert Scott Bickford, *President*
Scott Bickford, *President*
Kerry McMillan, *Principal*
Julie Hathman-Wint, *Corp Secy*
Julie Hathman, *Accounting Mgr*
EMP: 12
SALES (est): 1.3MM **Privately Held**
WEB: www.bick.com
SIC: 8712 House designer

(G-11775)
RAAB SALES INC
14521 W 96th Ter (66215-1165)
PHONE....................................913 227-0814
Mark Raab, *President*
Steve Raab, *Vice Pres*
EMP: 17
SQ FT: 10,800
SALES (est): 6.1MM **Privately Held**
WEB: www.raabsales.com
SIC: 5084 Packaging machinery & equipment; printing trades machinery, equipment & supplies

(G-11776)
RAINTREE INC
10700 State Line Rd (66211-2101)
P.O. Box 11547 (66207-4247)
PHONE....................................913 262-7013
David Stolberg, *President*
Lori Stolberg, *Admin Sec*
EMP: 20
SALES (est): 3.1MM **Privately Held**
SIC: 5087 Sprinkler systems

(G-11777)
RAL CONTRACTORS
8305 Rosehill Rd (66215-2651)
PHONE....................................913 888-8128
Ralph Light, *President*
EMP: 10
SALES (est): 620K **Privately Held**
SIC: 1721 Exterior commercial painting contractor; interior commercial painting contractor

(G-11778)
RAYMARR INC
11615 W 108th Ct (66210-1297)
PHONE....................................913 648-3480
Raymond M Feitl, *President*
Michelle Collins, *Admin Sec*
EMP: 12
SQ FT: 5,000
SALES: 600K **Privately Held**
SIC: 5099 8743 Signs, except electric; promotion service

(G-11779)
RAYNOR GAR DOOR CO INC KANS CY
8235 Mccoy St (66227-2609)
PHONE....................................913 422-0441
Larry Bain, *President*
David Guthrie, *Vice Pres*
Sheila Guthrie, *Admin Sec*
EMP: 16
SQ FT: 10,000
SALES (est): 3.4MM
SALES (corp-wide): 14MM **Privately Held**
WEB: www.raynorkc.com
SIC: 5211 3699 Garage doors, sale & installation; doors, wood or metal, except storm; door opening & closing devices, electrical
PA: Adams Door Co., Inc. Of Des Moines
69 Washington Ave
Des Moines IA 50314
515 289-2070

(G-11780)
RD THOMANN CONTRACTING
12810 W 70th St (66216-2623)
PHONE....................................913 268-5580
Mike Dubbert, *Partner*
EMP: 10
SALES (est): 683.8K **Privately Held**
SIC: 1522 Residential construction

(G-11781)
RE PEDROTTI COMPANY INC (PA)
5855 Beverly Ave Ste A (66202-2609)
PHONE....................................913 677-7754
Richard E Pedrotti, *President*
Maureen T Pedrotti, *Corp Secy*
Nick Jackson, *Engineer*
Tana Clement, *Sales Staff*
Dallas Massie, *Sales Staff*
EMP: 13
SQ FT: 7,500
SALES (est): 7.5MM **Privately Held**
SIC: 5063 5084 Motor controls, starters & relays: electric; instruments & control equipment

(G-11782)
RECALL SECURE DESTRUCTION SERV
Also Called: Recall S D S Lenexa Fcilty 23
8059 Flint St (66214-3335)
PHONE....................................913 310-0811
EMP: 12
SALES (corp-wide): 16.7MM **Privately Held**
SIC: 4953 Refuse System
PA: Recall Secure Destruction Services, Inc.
6111 Live Oak Pkwy
Norcross GA 30093
770 246-0345

(G-11783)
REDDI SERVICES INC (PA)
Also Called: Able Plumbing
4011 Bonner Industrial Dr (66226-2104)
PHONE....................................913 287-5005
Jay Gravatt, *President*
Phyllis Gangloff, *Info Tech Mgr*
Carolyn Adkinson, *Admin Asst*
EMP: 90 **EST:** 1957
SQ FT: 14,000
SALES (est): 21.3MM **Privately Held**
WEB: www.reddiservices.com
SIC: 1711 Plumbing contractors

(G-11784)
REECE & NICHOLS ALLIANCE INC
11100 Antioch Rd (66210-2420)
PHONE....................................913 451-4415
Darrel Stiles, *Manager*
EMP: 53
SALES (corp-wide): 225.3B **Publicly Held**
SIC: 6531 Real estate brokers & agents
HQ: Reece & Nichols Alliance Inc
2140 E Santa Fe St
Olathe KS 66062
913 782-8822

(G-11785)
REECE & NICHOLS REALTORS INC
11901 W 119th St (66213-2215)
PHONE....................................913 339-6800
Lynette Arrasmith, *General Mgr*
Karen Laube, *Sales Staff*
Cynthia Hayward, *Real Est Agnt*
Debra Weaver, *Real Est Agnt*
EMP: 50
SALES (corp-wide): 225.3B **Publicly Held**
WEB: www.reece-nichols.com
SIC: 6531 Real estate agent, residential
HQ: Reece & Nichols Realtors, Inc.
11601 Granada St
Leawood KS 66211
913 491-1001

(G-11786)
REES CONTRACT SERVICE INC (PA)
10111 W 105th St (66212-5747)
P.O. Box 24287, Overland Park (66283-4287)
PHONE....................................913 888-0590
B M Foster, *President*
EMP: 400
SALES: 39.3MM **Privately Held**
SIC: 7381 Security guard service

(G-11787)
REES MSILIONIS TURLEY ARCH LLC
2000 Shawnee Mission Pkwy (66205-3605)
PHONE....................................816 842-1292
Janelle Matlosz, *Engineer*
Camilla Keech, *Finance Mgr*
Matt Masilionis, *Mng Member*
Kim Vincent, *Office Admin*
Skip Hymer,
EMP: 35
SQ FT: 9,500
SALES (est): 4.6MM **Privately Held**
WEB: www.rees-studio.com
SIC: 8712 Architectural engineering

(G-11788)
REPRODUCTIVE RSRCE CTR OF GRTR
12200 W 106th St Ste 120 (66215-2305)
PHONE....................................913 894-2323
Celeste Brabeck, *Director*
Michael Wilson PH, *Director*
Marge Vogt, *Nurse Practr*
EMP: 20
SALES (est): 2MM **Privately Held**
SIC: 8011 Fertility specialist, physician

(G-11789)
RESIDENTIAL APPRAISAL SERVICES
13830 Santa Fe Trail Dr # 100 (66215-3310)
PHONE....................................913 492-0226
Gib Wood, *President*
Greg Werick, *Principal*
Brad Henry, *Administration*
EMP: 14
SALES (est): 1MM **Privately Held**
WEB: www.winchestermeadows.com
SIC: 7389 Auction, appraisal & exchange services

(G-11790)
RESNICK ASSOCIATES
8500 W 110th St (66210-1874)
PHONE....................................913 681-5454
Leon Resnick, *President*
EMP: 10 **EST:** 1966
SALES (est): 832.1K **Privately Held**
SIC: 6411 Insurance agents, brokers & service

(G-11791)
RETAIL SERVICES WIS CORP
10200 W 75th St Ste 115 (66204-2260)
PHONE....................................913 831-6400
Rocky Butler, *Manager*
EMP: 50
SALES (corp-wide): 69.5MM **Privately Held**
WEB: www.wisusa.com
SIC: 7389 Inventory computing service
HQ: Retail Services Wis Corporation
9265 Sky Park Ct Ste 100
San Diego CA 92123
858 565-8111

(G-11792)
RETREAT OF SHAWNEE APARTMENTS
11128 W 76th Ter (66214-1295)
PHONE....................................913 624-1326
Jim Lippert, *President*
Teresa Lippert, *President*
EMP: 10
SALES (est): 575.5K **Privately Held**
SIC: 6513 Apartment building operators

GEOGRAPHIC

(G-11793)
REVOLUTIONARY BUS CONCEPTS INC (PA)
Also Called: Rbc Medical Innovations
13715 W 109th St Ste 100 (66215-4276)
PHONE....913 385-5700
Carl Mayer, *CEO*
Ron Macklin, *President*
Koni Macklin, *Purch Mgr*
Anne Ahonen, *Engineer*
Emily Collins, *Engineer*
EMP: 60
SQ FT: 10,000
SALES (est): 12.2MM **Privately Held**
WEB: www.rbccorp.com
SIC: 3845 8731 Electromedical equipment; medical research, commercial

(G-11794)
RFC LOGO INC
7500 W 110th St (66210-2372)
PHONE....913 319-3100
Roger Henry, *CEO*
Richard Witaszak, *CFO*
EMP: 850 **EST:** 1946
SQ FT: 75,000
SALES (est): 243.1K **Privately Held**
SIC: 5199 2321 Advertising specialties; men's & boys' furnishings

(G-11795)
RHEUARK FSI SALES INC (PA)
5809 Reeds Rd (66202-2741)
PHONE....913 432-9500
Michael Rheuark, *President*
EMP: 15
SQ FT: 4,200
SALES (est): 2.9MM **Privately Held**
SIC: 5141 Food brokers

(G-11796)
RHEUMATOLOGY CONS CHARTERED
12330 Metcalf Ave Ste 570 (66213-1308)
PHONE....913 661-9990
David Cooley, *Partner*
EMP: 20
SALES (est): 1.7MM **Privately Held**
SIC: 8011 Internal medicine, physician/surgeon

(G-11797)
RHW CONSTRUCTION INC
6704 W 100 121st St (66209)
PHONE....913 451-1222
Richard Wiens, *President*
Thomas Deutsch, *Vice Pres*
EMP: 10
SALES (est): 847K **Privately Held**
SIC: 1542 Commercial & office building, new construction; commercial & office buildings, renovation & repair

(G-11798)
RHW HOTEL HOLDINGS COMPANY LLC (PA)
6704 W 121st St (66209-2002)
PHONE....913 451-1222
Richard H Wiens, *President*
David Montero, *Exec VP*
Brad Eckenroth, *Vice Pres*
Patrick Hale, *Vice Pres*
Tom Deutsch, *Property Mgr*
EMP: 12
SALES (est): 3.1MM **Privately Held**
SIC: 7011 8741 Hotels & motels; hotel or motel management

(G-11799)
RHW MANAGEMENT INC (PA)
6704 W 121st St (66209-2002)
PHONE....913 451-1222
Richard Wiens, *President*
Chandler Thayer, *COO*
Tom Deutsch, *Vice Pres*
Brad Eckenroth, *Vice Pres*
Patrick Hale, *Vice Pres*
EMP: 12
SQ FT: 6,000
SALES (est): 16MM **Privately Held**
WEB: www.rhwhotels.com
SIC: 7011 Hotels & motels

(G-11800)
RHW MANAGEMENT INC
Also Called: Hampton Inn
7400 W Frontage Rd (66203-4670)
PHONE....913 722-0800
Dana Webb, *Manager*
EMP: 25
SALES (corp-wide): 16MM **Privately Held**
WEB: www.rhwhotels.com
SIC: 7011 Hotels & motels
PA: Rhw Management, Inc.
6704 W 121st St
Shawnee Mission KS 66209
913 451-1222

(G-11801)
RICHARD WINBURN
Also Called: Winburn, Richard L
10351 Mastin St (66212-5452)
PHONE....913 492-5180
Richard Winburn, *Owner*
EMP: 15
SALES (est): 900.8K **Privately Held**
SIC: 8021 Offices & clinics of dentists

(G-11802)
RICOH USA INC
8050 Marshall Dr Ste 150 (66214-1572)
PHONE....913 890-5100
Jeff Galovic, *General Mgr*
Corey Backues, *Sales Executive*
Mary Hassler, *Manager*
Shelley Rodriguez, *Manager*
EMP: 200 **Privately Held**
WEB: www.ikon.com
SIC: 5044 5065 5712 7378 Photocopy machines; typewriters; facsimile equipment; office furniture; computer maintenance & repair
HQ: Ricoh Usa, Inc.
300 Eagleview Blvd # 200
Exton PA 19341
610 296-8000

(G-11803)
RIEKE CONCRETE SYSTEMS INC
9014 Parkhill St (66215-3536)
PHONE....913 492-0270
Frederick L Rieke, *President*
EMP: 10 **EST:** 1978
SQ FT: 2,900
SALES: 1.4MM **Privately Held**
SIC: 1771 Concrete pumping

(G-11804)
RIEKE GRADING INC
8200 Hedge Lane Ter (66227-3037)
PHONE....913 441-2669
John J Rieke Jr, *President*
John P Lynch, *Vice Pres*
Susan Rieke, *Treasurer*
EMP: 17
SQ FT: 5,000
SALES (est): 3.9MM **Privately Held**
SIC: 1794 Excavation & grading, building construction

(G-11805)
RIGHT MANAGEMENT INC
7300 W 110th St Ste 800 (66210-2387)
PHONE....913 451-1100
Steven Carter, *Manager*
EMP: 30 **Publicly Held**
WEB: www.right.com
SIC: 8742 Human resource consulting services
HQ: Right Management Inc.
100 W Manpower Pl
Milwaukee WI 53212
414 961-1000

(G-11806)
ROBERT A KUMIN PC
6901 Shawnee Mission Pkwy # 250 (66202-4005)
P.O. Box 8867, Kansas City MO (64114-8867)
PHONE....913 432-1826
Robert A Kumin, *President*
Craig S Laird, *Vice Pres*
Craig Laird, *Vice Pres*
Carole L Kumin, *Admin Sec*
Carole Kumin, *Admin Sec*
EMP: 18
SALES (est): 1.9MM **Privately Held**
WEB: www.kuminlaw.com
SIC: 8111 General practice law office

(G-11807)
ROBERT G SMITH DDS CHARTERED
Also Called: Robert Smith Dental Clinic
3700 W 83rd St Ste 103 (66208-5120)
PHONE....913 649-5600
Robert G Smith DDS, *President*
EMP: 15
SQ FT: 2,200
SALES (est): 1.3MM **Privately Held**
SIC: 8021 Dentists' office

(G-11808)
ROBERT HALF INTERNATIONAL INC
7400 College Blvd Ste 200 (66210-4028)
PHONE....913 339-9849
Mert Hersh, *Branch Mgr*
EMP: 20
SALES (corp-wide): 5.8B **Publicly Held**
WEB: www.rhii.com
SIC: 7361 Employment agencies
PA: Robert Half International Inc.
2884 Sand Hill Rd Ste 200
Menlo Park CA 94025
650 234-6000

(G-11809)
ROBERT VANLERBERG FOUNDATIONS
Also Called: Van Lerberg Robert Foundations
24630 W 79th St (66227-2805)
PHONE....913 441-6823
Robert Vanlerberg, *President*
Sheryl Vanlerberg, *Vice Pres*
EMP: 20
SALES (est): 2.2MM **Privately Held**
SIC: 1771 1741 Foundation & footing contractor; foundation building

(G-11810)
ROBIN CHIROPRACTIC & ACUPNCTUR
Also Called: Dr Michelle Robin
7410 Switzer St (66203-4550)
PHONE....913 962-7408
Michelle Robin, *Owner*
EMP: 15
SALES (est): 377.6K **Privately Held**
WEB: www.yourwellnessconnection.com
SIC: 8041 Offices & clinics of chiropractors

(G-11811)
ROBINSON JS CONSTRUCTION INC
8325 Monticello Rd Ste D (66227-3120)
PHONE....913 441-2988
Jeff S Robinson, *President*
Lisa D Brauch, *Treasurer*
Nancy P Robinson, *Admin Sec*
EMP: 22
SALES (est): 4MM **Privately Held**
WEB: www.jsrobinsonhomes.com
SIC: 1521 New construction, single-family houses

(G-11812)
ROCKHURST UNIVERSITY CONTINUIN
National Press Publications
6901 W 63rd St Fl 3 Flr 3 (66202)
P.O. Box 419107, Kansas City MO (64141-6107)
PHONE....913 432-7755
Gary Weinberg, *Manager*
EMP: 100
SALES (corp-wide): 55.4MM **Privately Held**
SIC: 2741 8221 Miscellaneous publishing; colleges universities & professional schools
HQ: Rockhurst University Continuing Education Center, Inc.
6901 W 63rd St
Shawnee Mission KS 66202

(G-11813)
RODNEY LYLES MD
12200 W 106th St Ste 120 (66215-2305)
PHONE....913 894-2323
Rodney Lyles, *Owner*
Toni Clark, *Business Mgr*
EMP: 21
SALES (est): 619.6K **Privately Held**
SIC: 8011 Fertility specialist, physician

(G-11814)
ROUND HILL BATH &TENNIS CLUB
8932 Maple Cir (66207-2142)
P.O. Box 11610, Overland Park (66207-4310)
PHONE....913 381-2603
EMP: 12
SALES: 278.2K **Privately Held**
SIC: 7997 7299 Swimming club, membership; facility rental & party planning services

(G-11815)
RUBENSTEIN REAL ESTATE CO LLC
6310 Lamar Ave Ste 220 (66202-4265)
PHONE....913 362-1999
Sherilyn Eversole, *Sales Mgr*
Diane Dominick, *Property Mgr*
Kim Norris, *Property Mgr*
Jill Ulrich, *Property Mgr*
John Rubenstein,
EMP: 10
SQ FT: 2,500
SALES (est): 880K **Privately Held**
WEB: www.rubensteinre.com
SIC: 6512 6531 Shopping center, property operation only; real estate agent, commercial

(G-11816)
RUTHER & ASSOCIATES LLC
8877 Bourgade St Ste B (66219-1471)
PHONE....913 894-8877
Scott Ruther, *Mng Member*
EMP: 12 **EST:** 1997
SALES (est): 1.1MM **Privately Held**
SIC: 8721 Accounting, auditing & bookkeeping

(G-11817)
RX POWER
Also Called: Power Group
10800 Farley St (66210-1414)
PHONE....913 696-0691
Paul Power, *Owner*
Mark Avery, *Co-Owner*
EMP: 20
SALES (est): 3.9MM **Privately Held**
WEB: www.rxpower.com
SIC: 6321 Health insurance carriers

(G-11818)
RYDER TRUCK RENTAL INC
10000 Darnell St (66215-1151)
PHONE....913 888-5040
Claude Hough, *General Mgr*
EMP: 25
SALES (corp-wide): 8.4B **Publicly Held**
SIC: 7513 7519 Truck rental, without drivers; truck leasing, without drivers; utility trailer rental
HQ: Ryder Truck Rental, Inc.
11690 Nw 105th St
Medley FL 33178
305 500-3726

(G-11819)
S K DESIGN GROUP INC
4600 College Blvd Ste 100 (66211-1606)
PHONE....913 451-1818
Sasson Mahboubian, *President*
Katereh Mahboubian, *Vice Pres*
EMP: 20
SALES (est): 2.4MM **Privately Held**
WEB: www.skdesigngroup.net
SIC: 8711 Civil engineering

(G-11820)
S P D TRANSFER SERVICE LC
7015 Richards Dr (66216-2666)
PHONE....913 321-0333
Todd Fruehling, *Mng Member*
Allan S Fruehling,
EMP: 10
SALES (est): 1.1MM **Privately Held**
SIC: 4212 Local trucking, without storage

(G-11821)
S T CARTER INC (PA)
Also Called: Right Management Consultants
7300 W 110th St Ste 800 (66210-2387)
PHONE....................................913 451-1100
Stephen T Carter, *CEO*
EMP: 28
SQ FT: 23,430
SALES (est): 5.5MM **Privately Held**
SIC: 8742 Human resource consulting services

(G-11822)
SABATES EYE CENTERS PC (PA)
11261 Nall Ave Ste 100 (66211-1669)
PHONE....................................913 261-2020
Felix N Sabates MD, *President*
Michael Cassell, *Managing Dir*
King Lee MD, *Vice Pres*
Sharon Fagan, *CFO*
Nelson R Sabates, *Admin Sec*
EMP: 16
SALES (est): 4.3MM **Privately Held**
SIC: 8011 Ophthalmologist

(G-11823)
SABATES EYE CENTERS PC
11213 Nall Ave Ste 100 (66211-1833)
PHONE....................................913 469-8806
Felix Sabates, *Branch Mgr*
EMP: 20
SALES (corp-wide): 4.3MM **Privately Held**
SIC: 5995 8011 Optical goods stores; ophthalmologist
PA: Sabates Eye Centers P.C.
11261 Nall Ave Ste 100
Shawnee Mission KS 66211
913 261-2020

(G-11824)
SAINT ANN CHILD CARE CENTER
7225 Mission Rd (66208-3004)
PHONE....................................913 362-4660
Toddy Nidleman, *Director*
EMP: 17
SALES (est): 297.8K **Privately Held**
SIC: 8351 Child day care services

(G-11825)
SAINT LUKES SOUTH HOSPITAL INC (PA)
12300 Metcalf Ave (66213-1324)
PHONE....................................913 317-7000
Charles Horner, *President*
Marie Griffin, *Vice Pres*
Kathy Gover, *Opers Mgr*
Amy Nachtegal, *CFO*
Shelby Frigon, *Controller*
EMP: 310
SALES: 138MM **Privately Held**
SIC: 8062 General medical & surgical hospitals

(G-11826)
SANDEN NORTH AMERICA INC
Also Called: Miner Technologies
9900 Pflumm Rd Ste 22 (66215-1231)
PHONE....................................913 888-6667
EMP: 1098
SALES (est): 98.7MM **Privately Held**
SIC: 5084 Industrial machinery & equipment
HQ: Sanden Of America Inc
601 Sanden Blvd
Wylie TX 75098
972 442-8400

(G-11827)
SANDSTONE INC
Also Called: Stoneworth Building Products
4025 Bonner Industrial Dr (66226-2104)
PHONE....................................913 422-0794
Andrew Alingh, *President*
▲ **EMP:** 18
SALES (est): 2.4MM **Privately Held**
WEB: www.stoneworthcompany.com
SIC: 3281 Cut stone & stone products

(G-11828)
SANDSTONE CREEK APARTMENTS
7450 W 139th Ter (66223-4207)
PHONE....................................913 402-8282
Tom Foluny, *Owner*
EMP: 15
SALES (est): 1MM **Privately Held**
WEB: www.sandstonecreek.net
SIC: 6531 Real estate agents & managers

(G-11829)
SANIBEL INVESTMENTS INC
Also Called: Crown Cleaning
6447 Vista Dr (66218-9239)
P.O. Box 860488 (66286-0488)
PHONE....................................913 422-7949
Ron Ratkey, *President*
Ivy Zumwalt, *Manager*
EMP: 20
SALES (est): 162.1K **Privately Held**
WEB: www.gandkservicecompany.com
SIC: 7349 Exhaust hood or fan cleaning

(G-11830)
SANTA FE BODY INC
8717 Lenexa Dr (66214-3236)
PHONE....................................913 894-6090
Christopher Kupchin, *President*
Betsy Kupchin, *Vice Pres*
EMP: 10
SQ FT: 5,000
SALES: 1MM **Privately Held**
SIC: 7532 Body shop, automotive

(G-11831)
SANTA FE DISTRIBUTING INC
9640 Legler Rd (66219-1291)
PHONE....................................913 492-8288
Gary T Henshaw, *President*
Jeff Henshaw, *Vice Pres*
Ellen Henshaw, *Treasurer*
Cory Kay, *Sales Staff*
Steve Abbott, *Marketing Staff*
▲ **EMP:** 20
SQ FT: 40,000
SALES (est): 8.1MM **Privately Held**
WEB: www.s-f-d.com
SIC: 5065 Citizens band radios; radio & television equipment & parts; amateur radio communications equipment; telephone equipment

(G-11832)
SANTA FE LAW BUILDING
Also Called: Santa Fe Law Office
8000 Foster St (66204-3613)
PHONE....................................913 648-3220
James Shetlar, *Owner*
James R Shetler, *Owner*
John C Donham,
Steven R Jarrett,
Gary R Mathews,
EMP: 19
SQ FT: 5,000
SALES (est): 1MM **Privately Held**
WEB: www.powerlawgroup.com
SIC: 6512 Nonresidential building operators

(G-11833)
SANTA FE TOW SERVICE INC (PA)
9125 Rosehill Rd (66215-3768)
PHONE....................................417 553-3676
Stanley J Kupchin, *Ch of Bd*
John Kupchin, *President*
Kaleigh Kupchin, *Office Mgr*
Misty Degonia, *Manager*
EMP: 52
SALES (est): 6.2MM **Privately Held**
WEB: www.santafetowservice.com
SIC: 7532 7549 Body shop, automotive; towing services

(G-11834)
SANTA FE TRAILS PLUMBING INC
8325 Monticello Rd Ste E (66227-3120)
PHONE....................................913 441-1441
Debbie Adams, *President*
EMP: 15
SQ FT: 5,000
SALES (est): 1.7MM **Privately Held**
SIC: 1711 Plumbing contractors

(G-11835)
SCHLAGEL & ASSOCIATES PA
14920 W 107th St (66215-4018)
PHONE....................................913 492-5158
Ed Schlagel, *Owner*
Aaron Reuter, *Chief*
Daniel Foster, *Vice Pres*
Gary Loumaster, *Vice Pres*
David Rinney, *Vice Pres*
EMP: 25
SQ FT: 3,500
SALES (est): 2.6MM **Privately Held**
SIC: 8711 Consulting engineer; civil engineering

(G-11836)
SCHOLASTIC BOOK FAIRS INC
14710 W 105th St (66215-4414)
PHONE....................................913 599-5700
John Jones, *Manager*
EMP: 10
SALES (corp-wide): 1.6B **Publicly Held**
WEB: www.scholasticbookfairs.com
SIC: 5192 2732 Books; books: printing only
HQ: Scholastic Book Fairs, Inc.
1080 Greenwood Blvd
Lake Mary FL 32746
407 829-7300

(G-11837)
SCHOLASTIC PHOTOGRAPHY INC
5808 Maple St (66202-2725)
PHONE....................................913 384-9126
Bill Caster, *President*
Nancy Feldman, *Principal*
David Pearson, *Principal*
EMP: 19
SQ FT: 3,000
SALES (est): 1.2MM **Privately Held**
SIC: 7221 Photographer, still or video

(G-11838)
SCHROFF DEVELOPMENT CORP
Also Called: SDC Publications
6800 Squibb Rd (66202-3224)
P.O. Box 1334 (66222-0334)
PHONE....................................913 262-2664
Roger Schroff, *President*
Stephen Schroff, *Vice Pres*
Moe Dubreuil, *Prgrmr*
EMP: 11
SQ FT: 650
SALES (est): 1.2MM **Privately Held**
WEB: www.silverscreen.com
SIC: 2731 Book clubs: publishing & printing

(G-11839)
SCRIPTPRO LLC (PA)
5828 Reeds Rd (66202-2740)
PHONE....................................913 384-1008
Renee Dye, *General Mgr*
Mike Coughlin, *Principal*
Tracy Thomas, *VP Opers*
Stephen Brown, *Project Mgr*
Carl Gumina, *Project Mgr*
▲ **EMP:** 100
SQ FT: 150,000
SALES (est): 88.5MM **Privately Held**
WEB: www.pharmacyrobotics.com
SIC: 3559 3586 Pharmaceutical machinery; measuring & dispensing pumps

(G-11840)
SCRIPTPRO USA INC
5828 Reeds Rd (66202-2740)
PHONE....................................913 384-1008
Michael E Coughlin, *Ch of Bd*
Sharon Coughlin, *Vice Pres*
Joseph N McCormack, *Vice Pres*
Tracy Thomas, *Vice Pres*
Doug Maughan, *CFO*
EMP: 415 **EST:** 1997
SQ FT: 150,000
SALES (est): 87.3MM **Privately Held**
WEB: www.scriptpro.com
SIC: 5087 Vending machines & supplies
PA: Scriptpro Llc
5828 Reeds Rd
Shawnee Mission KS 66202

(G-11841)
SEABOARD ENERGY OKLAHOMA LLC (DH)
9000 W 67th St Ste 200 (66202-3656)
PHONE....................................913 261-2620
Kevin K Henn,
Steve J Bresky,
Gary F Louis,
Robert L Steer,
EMP: 23
SALES (est): 5.9MM
SALES (corp-wide): 6.5B **Publicly Held**
SIC: 2869 Glycerin
HQ: Seaboard Foods Llc
9000 W 67th St Ste 200
Shawnee Mission KS 66202
913 261-2600

(G-11842)
SEABOARD FOODS LLC (DH)
9000 W 67th St Ste 200 (66202-3656)
PHONE....................................913 261-2600
Darwin Sand, *President*
Brian Bybee, *President*
Jeffrey Ruby, *Superintendent*
Joe Locke, *Regional Mgr*
Gary Louis, *Exec VP*
◆ **EMP:** 57
SQ FT: 15,000
SALES (est): 315.8MM
SALES (corp-wide): 6.5B **Publicly Held**
WEB: www.seaboardpork.com
SIC: 0213 5147 2011 Hogs; meats & meat products; meat packing plants
HQ: Seaboard Corporation
9000 W 67th St
Merriam KS 66202
913 676-8800

(G-11843)
SEABOARD TRANSPORT LLC
9000 W 67th St Ste 200 (66202-3656)
PHONE....................................913 676-8800
Steve Bresky, *President*
EMP: 17
SQ FT: 1,800
SALES (est): 5MM
SALES (corp-wide): 6.5B **Publicly Held**
WEB: www.seaboardtransport.com
SIC: 4213 Refrigerated products transport
HQ: Seaboard Corporation
9000 W 67th St
Merriam KS 66202
913 676-8800

(G-11844)
SEALS INC
9900 Pflumm Rd Ste 67 (66215-1231)
PHONE....................................913 438-1212
Jeffrey B Winkel, *President*
Deborah Winkel, *Admin Sec*
▲ **EMP:** 8 **EST:** 1977
SQ FT: 6,000
SALES (est): 1.5MM **Privately Held**
WEB: www.sealsinc.com
SIC: 5084 7699 3561 Pumps & pumping equipment; pumps & pumping equipment repair; pumps & pumping equipment

(G-11845)
SEARS HOME IMPRV PDTS INC
8246 Nieman Rd (66214-1507)
PHONE....................................913 438-5911
Brian Tenove, *Manager*
EMP: 22
SALES (corp-wide): 26.9B **Publicly Held**
WEB: www.searshomepro.com
SIC: 1521 General remodeling, single-family houses
HQ: Sears Home Improvement Products, Inc.
1024 Florida Central Pkwy
Longwood FL 32750
407 767-0990

(G-11846)
SECURITY BANK OF KANSAS CITY
5800 Foxridge Dr Ste 400 (66202-2348)
PHONE....................................913 621-8430
Karen Mayberry, *Branch Mgr*
EMP: 18

GEOGRAPHIC

SALES (corp-wide): 100MM **Privately Held**
SIC: 6022 State trust companies accepting deposits, commercial
HQ: Security Bank Of Kansas City
701 Minnesota Ave
Kansas City KS 66101
913 281-3165

(G-11847)
SELFS INC
5340 Merriam Dr (66203-2122)
PHONE..................................913 962-7353
Bem Nickum, *Manager*
Adam Rodenberger, *Manager*
EMP: 26
SQ FT: 9,000
SALES (corp-wide): 348.7MM **Privately Held**
WEB: www.selfs.com
SIC: 2273 Carpets & rugs
HQ: Self's Inc.
721 E Mount Vernon St
Wichita KS 67211
316 267-1295

(G-11848)
SERA INC
9900 Pflumm Rd Ste 61 (66215-1231)
P.O. Box 15866 (66285-5866)
PHONE..................................913 541-1307
William Skelly, *President*
Cathy Wright, *Vice Pres*
EMP: 10
SALES (est): 1.4MM **Privately Held**
WEB: www.seramune.com
SIC: 5122 Animal medicines; biologicals & allied products

(G-11849)
SHANK & HAMILTON PC
1968 Shawnee Mission Pkwy # 100 (66205-2065)
PHONE..................................816 471-0909
Christopher S Shank, *President*
Brenda Hamilton, *Admin Sec*
EMP: 11 **EST:** 1997
SALES (est): 1.4MM **Privately Held**
WEB: www.shankhamilton.com
SIC: 8111 General practice attorney, lawyer

(G-11850)
SHAWNEE CHURCH OF NAZARENE
5539 Quivira Rd (66216-1969)
PHONE..................................913 631-5555
Jeren Rowell, *Pastor*
EMP: 13
SALES (est): 637.5K **Privately Held**
WEB: www.shawneenaz.org
SIC: 8661 8351 Church of the Nazarene; child day care services

(G-11851)
SHAWNEE COPY CENTER INC
12211 Shwnee Mission Pkwy (66216-1831)
P.O. Box 860730, Shawnee (66286-0730)
PHONE..................................913 268-4343
William D Shippee, *President*
Bill Shippee, *Sales Staff*
Jon Shippee, *Admin Sec*
EMP: 11
SQ FT: 30,000
SALES (est): 1.7MM **Privately Held**
WEB: www.sccink.com
SIC: 2752 5112 5943 Commercial printing, offset; stationery & office supplies; stationery stores

(G-11852)
SHAWNEE INN INC
Also Called: Hampton Inn
16555 Midland Dr (66217-9533)
PHONE..................................913 248-1900
Randy Bull, *General Mgr*
Tessa McCarthy, *Opers Staff*
Terry Reiss, *Manager*
Josh Sandell, *Director*
EMP: 30 **EST:** 1989
SALES (est): 2.4MM
SALES (corp-wide): 16MM **Privately Held**
WEB: www.rhwhotels.com
SIC: 7011 Hotels & motels
PA: Rhw Management, Inc.
6704 W 121st St
Shawnee Mission KS 66209
913 451-1222

(G-11853)
SHAWNEE MISSION BCH VOLLEYBALL
Also Called: Beach Bar and Grill, The
19800 Johnson Dr (66218-9659)
PHONE..................................913 422-4070
Dave McKay, *Owner*
Scott Harold, *Co-Owner*
Chris Busenhart, *Manager*
EMP: 25
SALES (est): 911K **Privately Held**
WEB: www.smbv.com
SIC: 7997 Golf club, membership

(G-11854)
SHAWNEE MISSION BUILDERS LLC
10662 Widmer Rd (66215-2073)
PHONE..................................913 631-7020
Donald K Pflumm,
EMP: 9 **EST:** 1962
SQ FT: 3,200
SALES (est): 1MM **Privately Held**
SIC: 1521 3949 General remodeling, single-family houses; cases, gun & rod (sporting equipment)

(G-11855)
SHAWNEE MISSION CORP CARE LLC
11140 Thompson Ave (66219-2301)
PHONE..................................913 492-9675
Scott Woods,
Roger Thomas, *Gnrl Med Prac*
Megan Armbruster, *Social Worker*
EMP: 20 **EST:** 2001
SALES (est): 548.7K **Privately Held**
SIC: 8011 Clinic, operated by physicians

(G-11856)
SHAWNEE MISSION HEALTH CARE
Also Called: Overland Park Manor
9100 W 74th St (66204-4004)
PHONE..................................913 676-2000
Sam Turner, *President*
Robin Harold, *Vice Pres*
Joyce Portela, *Vice Pres*
G Keith Richardson, *Treasurer*
Lynn Stolz, *Director*
EMP: 100
SALES (est): 5.7MM
SALES (corp-wide): 8K **Privately Held**
SIC: 8051 Convalescent home with continuous nursing care
PA: Adventist Health Mid-America, Inc
9100 W 74th St
Shawnee Mission KS 66204
913 676-2184

(G-11857)
SHAWNEE MISSION MED CTR INC
Also Called: Santa Fe Medical Building
9301 W 74th St Ste 300 (66204-2239)
PHONE..................................913 632-9800
Sang Pak, *Branch Mgr*
Ronald B Hartman, *Med Doctor*
Marsha Weaver, *Med Doctor*
EMP: 17 **Privately Held**
SIC: 8062 General medical & surgical hospitals
HQ: Shawnee Mission Medical Center, Inc.
9100 W 74th St
Shawnee Mission KS 66204
913 676-2000

(G-11858)
SHAWNEE MISSION MED CTR INC (DH)
Also Called: Adventhealth Shawnee Mission
9100 W 74th St (66204-4004)
PHONE..................................913 676-2000
Ken Bacon, *CEO*
Sam Turner, *President*
Robin Harrold, *Senior VP*
Maxine Grassinger, *Vice Pres*
Peggy Todd, *Vice Pres*
EMP: 1783
SQ FT: 605,000
SALES: 491.1MM **Privately Held**
WEB: www.shawneemissionmedicalcenter.com
SIC: 8062 General medical & surgical hospitals
HQ: Adventist Health System/Sunbelt, Inc.
900 Hope Way
Altamonte Springs FL 32714
407 357-1000

(G-11859)
SHAWNEE MISSION MED CTR INC
Also Called: Shawnee Mission Fmly Practice
9119 W 74th St Ste 150 (66204-2229)
PHONE..................................913 789-1980
Ralph Mingle, *Vice Pres*
Marandapalli Jayaram, *Med Doctor*
David B Yu, *Med Doctor*
Gary N Thomsen, *Nurse*
EMP: 40 **Privately Held**
SIC: 8011 Internal medicine, physician/surgeon
HQ: Shawnee Mission Medical Center, Inc.
9100 W 74th St
Shawnee Mission KS 66204
913 676-2000

(G-11860)
SHAWNEE MISSION MED CTR INC
Also Called: Lenexa Family Practice
8700 Bourgade St Ste 2 (66219-1440)
PHONE..................................913 676-8400
Bob Burell, *Manager*
EMP: 12 **Privately Held**
WEB: www.shawneemissionmedicalcenter.com
SIC: 8011 General & family practice, physician/surgeon
HQ: Shawnee Mission Medical Center, Inc.
9100 W 74th St
Shawnee Mission KS 66204
913 676-2000

(G-11861)
SHAWNEE MSSION PLMNARY CONS PA
Also Called: Shawnee Mssion Plmonary Conslt
8901 W 74th St Ste 390 (66204-2203)
PHONE..................................913 362-0300
Fax: 913 362-0269
EMP: 10 **EST:** 1978
SQ FT: 800
SALES (est): 890K **Privately Held**
SIC: 8011 Medical Doctor's Office

(G-11862)
SHAWNEE PRESBYTERIAN CHURCH
Also Called: Shawnee Presby Preschool
6837 Nieman Rd (66203-3899)
PHONE..................................913 631-6689
C Randall Odam, *Relg Ldr*
EMP: 20
SALES (est): 659.3K **Privately Held**
SIC: 8661 8351 Presbyterian Church; child day care services

(G-11863)
SHAWNEE STEEL & WELDING INC (PA)
6124 Merriam Dr (66203-3297)
PHONE..................................913 432-8046
Craig Pardue, *President*
Edward Bartak, *CFO*
William R Ose, *Director*
EMP: 28
SALES (est): 11.2MM **Privately Held**
SIC: 3441 Fabricated structural metal

(G-11864)
SHIMADZU SCIENTIFIC INSTRS INC
8052 Reeder St (66214-1554)
PHONE..................................913 888-9449
Christina Peomio, *Manager*
Greg Feldman, *Technical Staff*
EMP: 11 **Privately Held**
SIC: 5049 Analytical instruments
HQ: Shimadzu Scientific Instruments Incorporated
7102 Riverwood Dr
Columbia MD 21046
800 477-1227

(G-11865)
SHIRLEY MARLEY ENTERPRISES
Also Called: Miller-Marley Schl Dance Voice
10443 Mastin St (66212-5701)
PHONE..................................913 492-0004
Shirley Marley, *President*
Shawn Marley, *Vice Pres*
Joan Walsh, *Treasurer*
Brian McGuinness, *Admin Sec*
Pam Arnott, *Assistant*
EMP: 13
SALES (est): 498K **Privately Held**
WEB: www.millermarley.com
SIC: 7911 8211 Children's dancing school; elementary & secondary schools

(G-11866)
SHORMAN & ASSOCIATES INC
7299 W 98th Ter Ste 100 (66212-6183)
PHONE..................................913 341-8811
Judy Shorman, *President*
J Roberts, *Medical Dir*
EMP: 25
SALES (est): 971K **Privately Held**
WEB: www.dolphinshopplus.com
SIC: 8093 Rehabilitation center, outpatient treatment

(G-11867)
SIDE POCKETS INC
13320 W 87th Street Pkwy (66215-4536)
PHONE..................................913 888-7665
Travis Wheeler, *President*
Matthew Urkavich, *General Mgr*
EMP: 17
SALES (est): 594.8K **Privately Held**
SIC: 7999 5812 5813 Billiard parlor; American restaurant; bar (drinking places)

(G-11868)
SIGNATURE LOGO EMBROIDERY INC
5855 Beverly Ave Ste C (66202-2609)
PHONE..................................913 671-8548
Eric Deakan, *President*
Sarah Kohake, *Accounts Mgr*
Steve Taylor, *Manager*
EMP: 9
SQ FT: 3,750
SALES (est): 661.4K **Privately Held**
SIC: 2395 Embroidery products, except schiffli machine; embroidery & art needlework

(G-11869)
SILVER CREST AT DEERCREEK
13060 Metcalf Ave (66213-2709)
PHONE..................................913 681-1101
Sarah Penn, *Office Mgr*
Phyllis J Prusia, *Administration*
EMP: 18
SALES (est): 1.4MM **Privately Held**
WEB: www.silvercrestdeercreek.com
SIC: 8361 Residential care

(G-11870)
SKC COMMUNICATION PRODUCTS LLC (PA)
8320 Hedge Lane Ter (66227-3543)
P.O. Box 874843, Kansas City MO (64187-4843)
PHONE..................................913 422-4222
Tray Vedock, *President*
Chris Laing, *Vice Pres*
Mitch Truesdale, *Vice Pres*
Kelli Herr, *VP Opers*
Ben Patke, *Project Mgr*
▲ **EMP:** 150
SQ FT: 20,000
SALES (est): 135.5MM **Privately Held**
WEB: www.skccom.com
SIC: 5065 5999 Communication equipment; communication equipment

(G-11871)
SKC CORPORATION
8320 Hedge Lane Ter (66227-3543)
PHONE..................................800 882-7779

Tray Bedock, *CEO*
CTS-I Venner, *Project Mgr*
Chris Wright, *Engineer*
Tom Lewis, *Project Engr*
Paul Lively, *Design Engr*
EMP: 24
SALES (est): 2.7MM **Privately Held**
SIC: 8748 Telecommunications consultant

(G-11872)
SKILLPATH SEMINARS INC (HQ)
6900 Squibb Rd (66202-3247)
PHONE....................913 362-3900
Jack Cabe, *President*
Steve Newbold, *Vice Pres*
Jeff Gibbs, *Corp Comm Staff*
Denise Loeb, *Director*
EMP: 165
SQ FT: 98,000
SALES (est): 13.1MM **Privately Held**
SIC: 7389 Promoters of shows & exhibitions

(G-11873)
SKY PRINTING AND PUBG INC
Also Called: Moss Printing
5406 Johnson Dr (66205-2911)
PHONE....................913 362-9292
Jose Ramirez, *President*
EMP: 6
SALES (est): 669.3K **Privately Held**
SIC: 2752 Commercial printing, lithographic

(G-11874)
SMALL BEGINNINGS
15801 Metcalf Ave (66223-3001)
PHONE....................913 851-2223
Patricia Vore, *President*
James Vore, *Corp Secy*
EMP: 42
SQ FT: 21,000
SALES (est): 2MM **Privately Held**
SIC: 8351 Child day care services

(G-11875)
SMITH AND LOVELESS INC (PA)
14040 Santa Fe Trail Dr (66215-1284)
PHONE....................913 888-5201
Frank Rebori, *President*
Chuck Miller, *Exec VP*
William Flores, *Vice Pres*
Mason Donald G, *Vice Pres*
Stuart Marschall, *Vice Pres*
◆ **EMP:** 230
SQ FT: 100,000
SALES (est): 133.6MM **Privately Held**
WEB: www.smithandloveless.com
SIC: 3589 5074 Water treatment equipment, industrial; plumbing & hydronic heating supplies

(G-11876)
SMITHYMAN & ZAKOURA CHARTERED
7400 W 110th St Ste 750 (66210-2362)
PHONE....................913 661-9800
James P Zakoura, *Owner*
Lee M Smithyman, *Director*
EMP: 10
SALES (est): 1.4MM **Privately Held**
WEB: www.smizak-law.com
SIC: 8111 General practice attorney, lawyer

(G-11877)
SOCIETY OF TCHERS FMLY MDICINE
11400 Thawk Ck Pkwy 540 (66211)
PHONE....................913 906-6000
Stacy Brungardt, *Exec Dir*
EMP: 17 **EST:** 1967
SQ FT: 3,907
SALES: 4.2MM **Privately Held**
WEB: www.stfm.org
SIC: 8621 Education & teacher association

(G-11878)
SOCIETY OF TEACHERS OF FAMILY
11400 Tomahawk Creek Pkwy (66211-2680)
PHONE....................913 906-6000
Stacy Brungardt, *Exec Dir*
EMP: 18
SALES: 330.7K **Privately Held**
SIC: 8621 Medical field-related associations

(G-11879)
SOKOLOV DENTAL LABORATORY INC
8056 Reeder St (66214-1554)
PHONE....................913 262-5444
Alexander Sokolovsky, *President*
Alex Sokolov, *Partner*
Michael Sokolov, *Partner*
EMP: 40
SQ FT: 3,000
SALES (est): 2.7MM **Privately Held**
SIC: 8072 Dental laboratories

(G-11880)
SPECIAL BEGINNINGS INC (PA)
10216 Pflumm Rd (66215-1245)
PHONE....................913 894-0131
Mary Hornbeck, *President*
Carol Reed, *Principal*
Treva Summers, *Director*
EMP: 55
SQ FT: 6,600
SALES (est): 3.6MM **Privately Held**
SIC: 8351 Preschool center

(G-11881)
SPECIAL OLYMPICS KANSAS INC (PA)
5280 Foxridge Dr (66202-1567)
PHONE....................913 236-9290
John Lair, *CEO*
Glen Grunwald, *Ch of Bd*
Allan Henderson, *Ch of Bd*
Rick Jones, *Ch of Bd*
Chris Burt, *COO*
EMP: 12
SQ FT: 10,000
SALES: 2.3MM **Privately Held**
WEB: www.ksso.org
SIC: 8322 Association for the handicapped

(G-11882)
SPECTRUM RETIREMENT SHAWNEE KS
Also Called: Shawnee Hills Sr Living
6335 Maurer Rd (66217-8345)
PHONE....................913 631-0058
Shawnee Hills, *Principal*
EMP: 21 **EST:** 2009
SALES (est): 1.2MM **Privately Held**
SIC: 8361 8322 Home for the aged; senior citizens' center or association

(G-11883)
SPEEDY FALCON LLC (PA)
Also Called: Speedy Falcon Carwash
11401 Strang Line Rd (66215-4047)
PHONE....................913 451-2100
Roland Thomas, *Director*
EMP: 10
SALES (est): 957.8K **Privately Held**
SIC: 7542 Washing & polishing, automotive

(G-11884)
SPENCER REED GROUP LLC
Also Called: Mechanical Engineering Tech
5800 Foxridge Dr Ste 100 (66202-2338)
PHONE....................913 722-7860
Doug Letsch, *Branch Mgr*
EMP: 50 **Privately Held**
WEB: www.spencerreed.com
SIC: 7361 8711 Placement agencies; professional engineer
PA: Spencer Reed Group, Llc
5700 W 112th St Ste 100
Leawood KS 66211

(G-11885)
SPRINT SPECTRUM HOLDING CO LP
6160 Sprint Pkwy (66251-6115)
PHONE....................800 829-0965
Comcast Telephony Services, *Partner*
TCI Telephony Services, *Partner*
Charles Levine, *Principal*
EMP: 8529
SALES (est): 2.5B **Publicly Held**
SIC: 4813 Telephone communication, except radio
HQ: Sprint Communications, Inc.
6200 Sprint Pkwy
Overland Park KS 66251
855 848-3280

(G-11886)
SPRINT SPECTRUM LP
15150 Shawnee Mission Pkw (66217-9314)
PHONE....................913 962-7777
Debbie Mercer, *Manager*
EMP: 23 **Publicly Held**
WEB: www.sprintpcs.com
SIC: 4813 Local & long distance telephone communications
HQ: Sprint Spectrum L.P.
6800 Sprint Pkwy
Overland Park KS 66251

(G-11887)
SPRINT SPECTRUM LP
4901 Town Center Dr (66211-2057)
PHONE....................913 323-5000
Jeremy Gulley, *Manager*
EMP: 20 **Publicly Held**
WEB: www.sprintpcs.com
SIC: 4813 Local & long distance telephone communications
HQ: Sprint Spectrum L.P.
6800 Sprint Pkwy
Overland Park KS 66251

(G-11888)
SRA BENEFITS
5201 Johnson Dr Ste 500 (66205-2930)
PHONE....................913 236-3090
David Wetzler, *President*
Cory Fischbach, *Accounts Mgr*
Grant Burnside, *Mktg Coord*
EMP: 15
SALES (est): 6.2MM **Privately Held**
SIC: 6371 Union welfare, benefit & health funds

(G-11889)
SSB MANUFACTURING COMPANY
Also Called: Simmons Manufacturing
7910 Hedge Lane Ter (66227-3000)
PHONE....................913 422-8000
Joel Davial, *Plant Mgr*
Roger Eagle, *Maint Spvr*
Michele Moron, *Human Res Mgr*
Joel Davila, *Branch Mgr*
EMP: 120 **Privately Held**
WEB: www.simmonscompany.com
SIC: 2515 5021 Box springs, assembled; mattresses, containing felt, foam rubber, urethane, etc.; sofa beds (convertible sofas); mattresses
HQ: Ssb Manufacturing Company
1 Concourse Pkwy Ste 800
Atlanta GA 30328
770 512-7700

(G-11890)
ST MICHAELS DAY SCHOOL INC
6630 Nall Ave (66202-4325)
PHONE....................913 432-1174
Charlene Andrews, *Admin Dir*
Susan Thayer, *Administration*
EMP: 23
SQ FT: 4,000
SALES: 540.7K **Privately Held**
SIC: 8351 Group day care center; preschool center

(G-11891)
ST PAUL FIRE AND MAR INSUR CO
15829 Maple St (66223-3559)
PHONE....................913 469-2720
Dave Loritz, *Manager*
EMP: 375
SALES (corp-wide): 30.2B **Publicly Held**
SIC: 6411 Insurance agents, brokers & service
HQ: St. Paul Fire And Marine Insurance Company
385 Washington St
Saint Paul MN 55102
651 221-7911

(G-11892)
STANLEY DAIRY QUEEN
7580 W 151st St (66223-2224)
PHONE....................913 851-1850
Greg Miller, *Owner*
EMP: 20
SALES (est): 527.1K **Privately Held**
SIC: 5812 6794 Ice cream stands or dairy bars; franchises, selling or licensing

(G-11893)
STANLEY WOOD PRODUCTS INC
15248 Broadmoor St (66223-3137)
PHONE....................913 681-2804
David A Davis, *President*
Pamela K Davis, *Admin Sec*
EMP: 30
SQ FT: 8,000
SALES (est): 3.1MM **Privately Held**
WEB: www.stanleywoodproducts.com
SIC: 2434 2517 Wood kitchen cabinets; wood television & radio cabinets

(G-11894)
STANNLEY VETERINARY CLINIC
Also Called: Stanley Veterinary Clinic
8695 W 151st St (66223-2329)
PHONE....................913 897-2080
Pel Frey, *Owner*
EMP: 21
SALES (est): 1.2MM **Privately Held**
SIC: 0742 3841 Animal hospital services, pets & other animal specialties; veterinarians' instruments & apparatus

(G-11895)
STAR MOTORS LTD
5400 Antioch Dr (66202-1067)
PHONE....................913 432-7800
Emery Zanagal, *President*
EMP: 21
SALES (est): 5.7MM **Privately Held**
SIC: 5511 7539 Automobiles, new & used; automotive repair shops

(G-11896)
STARSTRUCK PRFRMG ARTS CTR LLC
11650 W 85th St (66214-1541)
PHONE....................913 492-3186
Terri Novak, *Mng Member*
Erin Novak,
Richard Novak,
EMP: 15
SALES: 400K **Privately Held**
SIC: 7911 Dance studio & school

(G-11897)
STATLAND CLINIC LTD PA
5701 W 119th St Ste 240 (66209-3749)
PHONE....................913 345-8500
John M Goldberg, *President*
Stephanie Snyder, *Med Doctor*
EMP: 40 **EST:** 1980
SALES (est): 2.3MM **Privately Held**
SIC: 8011 Internal medicine, physician/surgeon

(G-11898)
STEVE HNSENS PRCISION DNTL LAB (PA)
5755 Foxridge Dr (66202-2401)
P.O. Box 2731, Mission (66201-2731)
PHONE....................913 432-6951
Steve Hansen, *President*
John Hansen, *Vice Pres*
Kristin Hansen, *Executive*
EMP: 40
SQ FT: 2,000
SALES (est): 2.9MM **Privately Held**
SIC: 8072 Crown & bridge production

(G-11899)
STEVEN J PIERCE DDS PA
Also Called: Babock, Julie E DDS
8615 Rosehill Rd Ste 101 (66215-2897)
PHONE....................913 888-2882
Steven Pierce, *Partner*
EMP: 11
SALES (est): 644.6K **Privately Held**
SIC: 8021 Dentists' office

(G-11900)
STEVEN L THOMAS DDS
12800 Metcalf Ave Ste 2 (66213-2607)
PHONE..................................913 451-7680
Steven Thomas, *Owner*
EMP: 10
SQ FT: 1,000
SALES (est): 515.2K **Privately Held**
SIC: 8021 Dental surgeon

(G-11901)
STINSON LEONARD STREET LLP
9200 Indian Creek Pkwy (66210-2036)
PHONE..................................913 451-8600
Mark Hendricks, *Manager*
EMP: 35
SALES (corp-wide): 120.9MM **Privately Held**
SIC: 8111 General practice attorney, lawyer
PA: Stinson Llp
1201 Walnut St Ste 2900
Kansas City MO 64106
816 842-8600

(G-11902)
STRASBURG-JARVIS INC
Also Called: Strasburg-Children
9810 Industrial Blvd (66215-1218)
PHONE..................................913 888-1115
Terrance Jarvis, *President*
Aggie Cooper, *Vice Pres*
Harry Leffler, *Vice Pres*
▲ **EMP:** 380
SALES (est): 36.8MM **Privately Held**
SIC: 5137 Women's & children's clothing

(G-11903)
STRETCH IT LIMOUSINE SERVICE
11800 Shwnee Mission Pkwy (66203-3305)
PHONE..................................913 269-1955
Gary Mortell, *President*
EMP: 10
SALES (est): 242.9K **Privately Held**
SIC: 4119 Limousine rental, with driver

(G-11904)
STYLING STUDIOS
12661 Antioch Rd (66213-1701)
PHONE..................................913 685-8800
Michelle Mc Nair, *Owner*
EMP: 20
SALES (est): 304.5K **Privately Held**
SIC: 7231 Hairdressers

(G-11905)
SUBSCRIPTION INK CO
Also Called: Millennium Marketing
10406 Shwnee Mission Pkwy
(66203-3504)
PHONE..................................913 248-1800
Russell J Rahm, *President*
EMP: 55
SQ FT: 2,000
SALES (est): 5.9MM **Privately Held**
SIC: 5192 Magazines

(G-11906)
SUBURBAN LAWN & GARDEN INC
10501 Roe Ave (66207-3999)
PHONE..................................913 649-8700
Matt Stueck, *Manager*
EMP: 25
SALES (corp-wide): 61.3MM **Privately Held**
SIC: 0181 0782 Nursery stock, growing of; lawn & garden services
PA: Suburban Lawn & Garden, Inc.
13635 Wyandotte St
Kansas City MO 64145
816 941-4700

(G-11907)
SUNBRDGE ASSSTED LVING RSDNCES
Also Called: Epoch Asssted Lving Ovrland Pk
9201 Foster St (66212-2295)
PHONE..................................913 385-2052
B J Reed, *Exec Dir*
EMP: 85 **EST:** 1999
SQ FT: 2,731
SALES (est): 958K **Privately Held**
SIC: 8051 Skilled nursing care facilities

(G-11908)
SUNFLOWER HOUSE
15440 W 65th St (66217-9306)
PHONE..................................913 631-5800
Michelle Herman, *CEO*
Shannon Moriarty, *Manager*
Virginia Lewis-Brunk, *Director*
Pamela Brown, *Admin Asst*
Bev Turner, *Administration*
EMP: 23
SALES: 1.5MM **Privately Held**
WEB: www.sunflowerhouse.org
SIC: 8322 Child related social services

(G-11909)
SUNFLOWER MEDICAL GROUP
5555 W 58th St (66202-1999)
PHONE..................................913 432-2080
Yvette Crabtree, *President*
Firmin Snodell, *Vice Pres*
Paul Kurth, *Treasurer*
Janel Chilson, *Administration*
EMP: 30 **EST:** 1955
SALES (est): 4.7MM **Privately Held**
SIC: 8011 Physicians' office, including specialists

(G-11910)
SUNFLOWER MEDICAL GROUP PA
8800 W 75th St Ste 300 (66204-4001)
PHONE..................................913 261-5800
Charles Ratland MD, *Principal*
EMP: 80
SALES (est): 4.8MM **Privately Held**
SIC: 8011 Physicians' office, including specialists; internal medicine, physician/surgeon

(G-11911)
SUNFLOWER MEDICAL GROUP PA
5555 W 58th St (66202-1999)
PHONE..................................913 722-4240
Charles Ragland, *President*
EMP: 20
SALES (est): 1.7MM **Privately Held**
SIC: 8011 Physicians' office, including specialists

(G-11912)
SUPERIOR PRODUCTS INTL II INC
10835 W 78th St (66214-1265)
P.O. Box 12790, Overland Park (66282-2790)
PHONE..................................913 962-4848
Joseph E Pritchett, *CEO*
Tim Cappel, *General Mgr*
Juli Pritchett, *Exec VP*
Boris Minasov, *Engineer*
Benjamin Ray, *Technical Staff*
▲ **EMP:** 7
SQ FT: 17,000
SALES: 4.6MM **Privately Held**
SIC: 2851 Paints & paint additives

(G-11913)
SURGERY CENTER OF LEAWOOD LLC
11413 Ash St Ste 100 (66211-1692)
PHONE..................................913 661-9977
Thomas Boldry, *Mng Member*
EMP: 25
SQ FT: 9,600
SALES (est): 2.5MM **Privately Held**
SIC: 8011 Plastic surgeon

(G-11914)
SURGICENTER JOHNSON COUNTY LTD
Also Called: Johnson County Surgery Center
8800 Ballentine St (66214-1900)
PHONE..................................913 894-4050
Donald E Steen, *Ch of Bd*
Robert Gibbins, *Principal*
Emmett E Moore, *Exec VP*
William H Wilcox, *Exec VP*
Robert Gibbons, *Exec Dir*
EMP: 35
SQ FT: 14,000
SALES (est): 3.6MM **Publicly Held**
SIC: 8011 Ambulatory surgical center
HQ: Midamerica Division, Inc.
903 E 104th St Ste 500
Kansas City MO 64131
816 508-4000

(G-11915)
SWANSONS STREAMWAY DOG P
6241 Woodland Rd (66218)
PHONE..................................913 422-8242
Lisa Swanson, *Owner*
EMP: 10
SALES (est): 233.1K **Privately Held**
SIC: 8351 Group day care center

(G-11916)
T-MOBILE USA INC
12980 Foster St Ste 200 (66213-2691)
PHONE..................................913 402-6500
Nick Drake, *Manager*
EMP: 100
SALES (corp-wide): 83.9B **Publicly Held**
WEB: www.voicestream.com
SIC: 4812 Cellular telephone services
HQ: T-Mobile Usa, Inc.
12920 Se 38th St
Bellevue WA 98006
425 378-4000

(G-11917)
T-MOBILE USA INC
5303 Johnson Dr (66205-2910)
PHONE..................................913 262-2789
Nick Drake, *President*
EMP: 12
SALES (corp-wide): 83.9B **Publicly Held**
WEB: www.voicestream.com
SIC: 4812 Cellular telephone services
HQ: T-Mobile Usa, Inc.
12920 Se 38th St
Bellevue WA 98006
425 378-4000

(G-11918)
TABEN GROUP LLC
10875 Benson Dr Ste 130 (66210-1526)
P.O. Box 7330 (66207-0330)
PHONE..................................913 649-0468
Charles R Tantillo Jr, *President*
C R Tantillo Jr, *Mng Member*
EMP: 15
SQ FT: 4,800
SALES (est): 4.4MM **Privately Held**
SIC: 6371 Pension, health & welfare funds

(G-11919)
TANTILLO FINANCIAL GROUP LLC
10777 Barkley St Ste 200 (66211-1162)
P.O. Box 7330 (66207-0330)
PHONE..................................913 649-3200
Curt Tantillo, *President*
EMP: 15
SALES (est): 475.5K **Privately Held**
SIC: 7389 8742 Financial services; financial consultant

(G-11920)
TAPCO PRODUCTS CO
Also Called: Tapco Mat Rental
15553 W 110th St (66219-1394)
PHONE..................................913 492-2777
Thomas Pepin, *President*
Carol Pepin, *Corp Secy*
EMP: 25
SALES (est): 7.7MM **Privately Held**
WEB: www.tapcoproducts.com
SIC: 5023 7342 Floor coverings; rest room cleaning service

(G-11921)
TD AUTO FINANCE LLC
6800 College Blvd Ste 700 (66211-1557)
P.O. Box 25952 (66225-5952)
PHONE..................................913 663-6300
Joe Greeson, *Manager*
EMP: 40
SALES (corp-wide): 22.8B **Privately Held**
SIC: 6153 Financing of dealers by motor vehicle manufacturers organ.
HQ: Td Auto Finance Llc
27777 Inkster Rd
Farmington Hills MI 48334
248 427-6800

(G-11922)
TEAM CAR CARE LLC
Also Called: Jiffy Lube
5850 Broadmoor St (66202-2332)
PHONE..................................913 362-3349
Steve Isom, *Vice Pres*
EMP: 10 **Privately Held**
SIC: 7549 Lubrication service, automotive
PA: Team Car Care, Llc
105 Decker Ct Ste 900
Irving TX 75062

(G-11923)
TECH-AIR INC (PA)
10200 W 75th St Ste 102 (66204-2242)
PHONE..................................913 677-5777
Jerry Collins, *President*
Mike Gabbert, *Corp Secy*
Mark Gabbert, *Vice Pres*
EMP: 5 **EST:** 1977
SQ FT: 1,300
SALES (est): 2.6MM **Privately Held**
WEB: www.techairinc.com
SIC: 3564 3535 Air purification equipment; conveyors & conveying equipment

(G-11924)
TED MFG CORPORATION
11415 Johnson Dr (66203-2641)
P.O. Box 3099 (66203-0099)
PHONE..................................913 631-6211
Ted McGrade, *Ch of Bd*
Connor McGrade, *General Mgr*
EMP: 26 **EST:** 1956
SQ FT: 15,000
SALES (est): 5.2MM **Privately Held**
SIC: 3643 Connectors & terminals for electrical devices

(G-11925)
TENDER HEARTS INC
Also Called: Tender Hrts Preschool Day Care
11740 W 77th St (66214-1454)
PHONE..................................913 962-2200
Christina Strub, *Director*
EMP: 12
SALES (est): 574.9K **Privately Held**
SIC: 8351 Group day care center

(G-11926)
TENNIS CORPORATION OF AMERICA
Also Called: Indian Creek Racquet Club
6700 W 110th St (66211-1502)
PHONE..................................913 491-4116
Aj Pant, *General Mgr*
EMP: 35
SQ FT: 60,000
SALES (corp-wide): 131.5MM **Privately Held**
SIC: 7999 Tennis services & professionals
PA: Tennis Corporation Of America
3611 N Kedzie Ave Fl 2
Chicago IL 60618
773 463-1234

(G-11927)
TFWILSON LLC (PA)
7400 College Blvd Ste 100 (66210-4012)
PHONE..................................913 327-0200
Thomas F Wilson Jr, *CEO*
Janice M Briggs, *Senior VP*
Angela King, *Senior VP*
Krista Stanek, *Senior VP*
Caroline Florez, *Vice Pres*
EMP: 40 **EST:** 2005
SQ FT: 7,000
SALES (est): 5.3MM **Privately Held**
WEB: www.summitamerica-ins.com
SIC: 6411 Insurance agents, brokers & service

(G-11928)
THERMAL KING WINDOWS INC
14368 W 96th Ter (66215-4708)
PHONE..................................913 451-2300
Steve Sage, *President*
EMP: 20
SALES (est): 1MM **Privately Held**
SIC: 7299 Home improvement & renovation contractor agency

▲ = Import ▼=Export
◆ =Import/Export

(G-11929)
THOMAS P EYEN
5520 College Blvd (66211-1630)
PHONE....................................913 663-5100
Thomas Eyen, *Owner*
EMP: 12 **EST**: 2001
SALES (est): 303K **Privately Held**
SIC: **8011** Ears, nose & throat specialist: physician/surgeon

(G-11930)
THOMSPON R WAYNE DDS INC (PA)
11005 W 60th St Ste 180 (66203-2789)
PHONE....................................913 631-0110
Wayne Thompson DDS, *President*
Robert Thompson Sr,
EMP: 12
SALES (est): 691.2K **Privately Held**
SIC: **8021** Orthodontist

(G-11931)
THRIFT MARKETING INC
5960 Dearborn St Ste 204 (66202-3393)
P.O. Box 2529 (66201-2529)
PHONE....................................913 236-7474
John Braden, *President*
Elmer Haupt, *Corp Secy*
Judy Braden, *Director*
EMP: 5
SALES (est): 440K **Privately Held**
WEB: www.thriftmarketing.com
SIC: **2842** Drain pipe solvents or cleaners

(G-11932)
TICKET SOLUTIONS LLC (PA)
10000 College Blvd # 130 (66210-1400)
PHONE....................................913 384-4751
Terry Hillman, *COO*
Elaine Haverty, *CFO*
Jake Lindmark, *Sales Staff*
Emily Berry, *Manager*
Jake Dubin, *CTO*
EMP: 42
SQ FT: 3,500
SALES (est): 2.1MM **Privately Held**
SIC: **7999** 7922 Ticket sales office for sporting events, contract; theatrical producers & services

(G-11933)
TOM BURGE FENCE & IRON INC
6770 W 152nd Ter (66223-3172)
PHONE....................................913 681-7600
Christopher V Burge, *President*
Roxanna V Burge, *Corp Secy*
EMP: 34 **EST**: 1975
SALES (est): 5.4MM **Privately Held**
WEB: www.burgefence.com
SIC: **1799** Fence construction

(G-11934)
TOM JONES REAL ESTATE COMPANY
Also Called: Tom Jones Realtors
9036 W 95th St Ste 5 (66212-4000)
PHONE....................................913 341-7777
Tom Jones, *President*
EMP: 10
SQ FT: 900
SALES (est): 730K **Privately Held**
SIC: **6531** Real estate brokers & agents

(G-11935)
TOWN & COUNTRY GUTTERING INC
6423 Vista Dr (66218-9239)
PHONE....................................913 441-0003
Vince Wohletz, *President*
EMP: 12
SALES: 2MM **Privately Held**
SIC: **3444** 1761 Sheet metalwork; gutter & downspout contractor

(G-11936)
TOWN VILLAGE LEAWOOD LLC
4400 W 115th St Apt 145 (66211-2687)
PHONE....................................913 491-3681
EMP: 30 **EST**: 1999
SALES (est): 1.2MM **Privately Held**
SIC: **8361** Residential care

(G-11937)
TOYOTA MOTOR CREDIT CORP
10851 Mastin St Ste 220 (66210-1687)
PHONE....................................913 661-6800
Jim Owens, *Branch Mgr*
EMP: 16 **Privately Held**
WEB: www.toyota.com
SIC: **6141** Financing: automobiles, furniture, etc., not a deposit bank; automobile loans, including insurance
HQ: Toyota Motor Credit Corporation
6565 Headquarters Dr
Plano TX 75024
469 486-9300

(G-11938)
TPI PETROLEUM INC
Also Called: Total 4164
6501 Johnson Dr (66202-2616)
PHONE....................................913 831-3145
EMP: 70
SALES (corp-wide): 130.8B **Publicly Held**
SIC: **2911** Petroleum Refiner
HQ: Tpi Petroleum, Inc
6000 N Loop 1604 W
San Antonio TX 78249
210 592-2000

(G-11939)
TRAC STAFFING SERVICE INC (PA)
10901 W 84th Ter (66214-1649)
PHONE....................................913 341-1150
Ron Trachsel, *President*
EMP: 18
SQ FT: 4,500
SALES (est): 2.3MM **Privately Held**
SIC: **7363** Temporary help service

(G-11940)
TREAT AMERICA LIMITED (PA)
8500 Shawnee Mission Pkwy # 100 (66202-2960)
PHONE....................................913 384-4900
John Mitchell, *CEO*
EMP: 400 **EST**: 1991
SALES (est): 274.3MM **Privately Held**
SIC: **5087** Vending machines & supplies

(G-11941)
TRESKO INC (PA)
6218 Melrose Ln (66203-3036)
PHONE....................................913 631-6900
Robert W Tramposh, *President*
Judy Tramposh, *Vice Pres*
Linda Shriver, *CFO*
EMP: 20
SQ FT: 11,000
SALES (est): 7.7MM **Privately Held**
SIC: **7359** 7623 5078 Equipment rental & leasing; refrigeration service & repair; ice making machines

(G-11942)
TRIANGLE SALES INC (PA)
15300 W 110th St (66219-1244)
P.O. Box 14628 (66285-4600)
PHONE....................................913 541-1800
Glenn Zumbehl, *President*
Dan Edmonds, *Vice Pres*
John Stone, *Vice Pres*
Cathy Zumbehl, *Treasurer*
EMP: 22
SQ FT: 32,000
SALES (est): 8.1MM **Privately Held**
WEB: www.trianglesales.com
SIC: **5075** Warm air heating equipment & supplies

(G-11943)
TRINITY NURSING & REHAB CENTER
9700 W 62nd St (66203-3220)
PHONE....................................913 671-7376
Michelle Fetters, *President*
EMP: 27
SALES: 7.6MM **Privately Held**
SIC: **8051** Convalescent home with continuous nursing care

(G-11944)
TRUE NORTH HOTEL GROUP INC
Also Called: Super 8 Motel
10750 Barkley St (66211-1151)
PHONE....................................913 341-4440
Brad Weins, *Manager*
EMP: 10 **Privately Held**
WEB: www.truenorthhotels.com
SIC: **7011** Hotels & motels
PA: True North Hotel Group, Inc.
7300 W 110th St Ste 990
Overland Park KS 66210

(G-11945)
TRUE NORTH SERVICES LLC (PA)
5400 Johnson Dr (66205-2911)
PHONE....................................888 478-9470
Michael D Jones, *CEO*
Timothy Fritz, *Sales Staff*
EMP: 20
SALES (est): 3.2MM **Privately Held**
SIC: **4959** Snowplowing

(G-11946)
TRUST SOURCING SOLUTIONS LLC
5901 College Blvd Ste 100 (66211-1834)
PHONE....................................913 319-0300
Shalia McPherson, *President*
Brad Bergaman, *Partner*
EMP: 28
SALES (est): 1.6MM **Privately Held**
SIC: **6733** Trusts

(G-11947)
TUFF SHED INC
8811 Lenexa Dr (66214-3240)
PHONE....................................913 541-8833
Eric J Peterson, *General Mgr*
Eric Peterson, *Manager*
Matthew Toll, *Asst Mgr*
EMP: 18
SALES (corp-wide): 292.4MM **Privately Held**
SIC: **2452** 5211 5039 1751 Prefabricated wood buildings; prefabricated buildings; prefabricated structures; garage door, installation or erection
PA: Tuff Shed, Inc.
1777 S Harrison St # 600
Denver CO 80210
303 753-8833

(G-11948)
TUFF TURF INC
5948 Merriam Dr (66203-3162)
PHONE....................................913 362-4545
Alan Schroeder, *President*
Prudence Schroeder, *Treasurer*
EMP: 10
SQ FT: 5,000
SALES: 900K **Privately Held**
SIC: **0781** 4959 0782 Landscape services; snowplowing; lawn services

(G-11949)
TURNTINE OCLAR PROSTHETICS INC
6342 Long Ave Ste H (66216-2578)
PHONE....................................913 962-6299
Harold W Turntine, *Principal*
EMP: 50
SALES (est): 4.5MM **Privately Held**
SIC: **3842** Prosthetic appliances

(G-11950)
TURTLE WAX INC
Also Called: Turtle Wax Auto Appearance Ctr
5960 Barkley St (66202-3269)
PHONE....................................913 236-6886
Bob Formosa, *Manager*
EMP: 25
SALES (corp-wide): 96.4MM **Privately Held**
WEB: www.turtlewax.com
SIC: **7542** Carwashes
PA: Turtle Wax, Inc
2250 W Pinehurst Blvd # 150
Addison IL 60101
630 455-3700

(G-11951)
TUTERA GROUP INC
Also Called: Stratford Commons
12340 Quivira Rd (66213-2408)
PHONE....................................913 851-0215
Vicky Anderson, *Manager*
EMP: 25
SALES (corp-wide): 12.7MM **Privately Held**
WEB: www.tutera.com
SIC: **6531** 6552 8051 1542 Real estate managers; real estate brokers & agents; subdividers & developers; skilled nursing care facilities; hospital construction
PA: Tutera Group Inc.
7611 State Line Rd # 301
Kansas City MO 64114
816 444-0900

(G-11952)
TUTERA GROUP INC
Atream Retirement Home
7300 W 107th St Ofc (66212-6600)
PHONE....................................913 381-6000
Dolly Latorre, *Director*
EMP: 80
SALES (corp-wide): 12.7MM **Privately Held**
WEB: www.tutera.com
SIC: **8051** Skilled nursing care facilities
PA: Tutera Group Inc.
7611 State Line Rd # 301
Kansas City MO 64114
816 444-0900

(G-11953)
U S AUTOMATION INC
8803 Long St (66215-3585)
P.O. Box 14874 (66285-4874)
PHONE....................................913 894-2410
Dan Roethler, *President*
Chester Godsy, *Treasurer*
EMP: 9
SQ FT: 1,500
SALES (est): 1MM **Privately Held**
SIC: **7389** 8742 5084 3613 Design, commercial & industrial; industry specialist consultants; conveyor systems; control panels, electric

(G-11954)
UBS FINANCIAL SERVICES INC
11150 Overbrook Rd # 300 (66211-2240)
PHONE....................................913 345-3200
Kerry Wilson, *Manager*
John Brown, *Agent*
EMP: 50
SALES (corp-wide): 29.9B **Privately Held**
SIC: **6211** Security brokers & dealers
HQ: Ubs Financial Services Inc.
1285 Ave Of The Americas
New York NY 10019
212 713-2000

(G-11955)
ULTRA-CHEM INC (PA)
8043 Flint St (66214-3335)
P.O. Box 14608, Lenexa (66285-4608)
PHONE....................................913 492-2929
John P Crane Sr, *President*
Linda Beecham, *Corp Secy*
Patricia Crane, *Vice Pres*
Justin Barnard, *Manager*
EMP: 164
SALES (est): 26.8MM **Privately Held**
SIC: **5169** 5087 2842 Industrial chemicals; laundry soap chips & powder; detergents; janitors' supplies; specialty cleaning preparations

(G-11956)
UMB BANK NATIONAL ASSOCIATION
7109 W 80th St (66204-3716)
PHONE....................................913 234-2070
Linda McLean, *Vice Pres*
EMP: 24
SALES (corp-wide): 1.1B **Publicly Held**
SIC: **6021** 6282 National commercial banks; investment advice
HQ: Umb Bank, National Association
1010 Grand Blvd Fl 3
Kansas City MO 64106
816 842-2222

(G-11957)
UMB BANK NATIONAL ASSOCIATION
6960 W 135th St (66223-4800)
PHONE..................................913 402-3600
Tammy Canida, *Branch Mgr*
EMP: 12
SALES (corp-wide): 1.1B **Publicly Held**
SIC: 6021 National commercial banks
HQ: Umb Bank, National Association
1010 Grand Blvd Fl 3
Kansas City MO 64106
816 842-2222

(G-11958)
UMB BANK NATIONAL ASSOCIATION
22320 W 66th St (66226-3560)
PHONE..................................913 667-5400
Pat Michaelis, *Branch Mgr*
EMP: 12
SALES (corp-wide): 1.1B **Publicly Held**
SIC: 6021 National commercial banks
HQ: Umb Bank, National Association
1010 Grand Blvd Fl 3
Kansas City MO 64106
816 842-2222

(G-11959)
UMB BANK NATIONAL ASSOCIATION
11101 W 87th St (66214-1503)
PHONE..................................913 894-4088
Nathan Stassord, *Manager*
EMP: 14
SALES (corp-wide): 1.1B **Publicly Held**
SIC: 6021 National commercial banks
HQ: Umb Bank, National Association
1010 Grand Blvd Fl 3
Kansas City MO 64106
816 842-2222

(G-11960)
UNIFIED LIFE INSUR CO TEXAS
7201 W 129th St Ste 300 (66213-2693)
P.O. Box 25326 (66225-5326)
PHONE..................................913 685-2233
Bill Buchanan, *President*
Suzi Kovac, *Business Mgr*
Robert Eshleman, *Vice Pres*
Jill Leadbetter, *Vice Pres*
Larry Wiltse, *Vice Pres*
EMP: 35
SALES (est): 8.9MM **Privately Held**
WEB: www.unifiedlife.com
SIC: 6311 Life insurance

(G-11961)
UNION BROADCASTING INC
Also Called: Sports Radio 1510
6721 W 121st St Ste 200 (66209-2031)
PHONE..................................913 344-1500
Chad Boeger, *President*
Sandy Cohen, *Officer*
Kevin Kietzman, *Officer*
Brian Mc Rae, *Officer*
Jeff Montgomery, *Officer*
EMP: 35
SALES (est): 4MM **Privately Held**
WEB: www.810whb.com
SIC: 4832 Radio broadcasting stations, music format

(G-11962)
UNITED DISASTER RESPONSE LLC
5217 Walmer St (66202-1611)
PHONE..................................913 963-8403
Shelby Johnson,
EMP: 35
SALES (est): 2MM **Privately Held**
SIC: 8322 Disaster service

(G-11963)
UNITED OMAHA LIFE INSURANCE CO
7200 W 132nd St Ste 270 (66213-1135)
PHONE..................................913 402-1191
Jim Amundson, *Business Mgr*
Joseph Miller, *Manager*
EMP: 25
SALES (corp-wide): 8.7B **Privately Held**
SIC: 6311 6321 6324 Life insurance carriers; health insurance carriers; group hospitalization plans
HQ: United Of Omaha Life Insurance Company
Mutual Of Omaha Plaza
Omaha NE 68175
402 342-7600

(G-11964)
UNITED PARCEL SERVICE INC
Also Called: UPS
11944 W 95th St (66215-3801)
PHONE..................................913 599-0899
EMP: 152
SALES (corp-wide): 71.8B **Publicly Held**
WEB: www.upsscs.com
SIC: 4215 Parcel delivery, vehicular
HQ: United Parcel Service, Inc.
55 Glenlake Pkwy
Atlanta GA 30328
404 828-6000

(G-11965)
UNITED SERVICES AUTO ASSN
Also Called: USAA
10100 College Blvd (66210-1416)
PHONE..................................913 451-6100
Joann Smucker, *Vice Pres*
Link Kittrell, *Opers-Prdtn-Mfg*
Steph Flores, *Engineer*
Yvonne Krzywonski, *Executive*
EMP: 265
SQ FT: 17,000
SALES (corp-wide): 24.3B **Privately Held**
WEB: www.usaa.com
SIC: 6331 6311 Property damage insurance; life insurance
PA: United Services Automobile Association
9800 Fredericksburg Rd
San Antonio TX 78288
210 531-8722

(G-11966)
UNITY CHURCH OF OVERLAND PARK
10300 Antioch Rd (66212-4331)
PHONE..................................913 649-1750
Mary Omwake, *Principal*
Greg Barette, *Pastor*
EMP: 25
SALES (est): 930K **Privately Held**
WEB: www.ucop.org
SIC: 8661 7299 Miscellaneous denomination church; wedding chapel, privately operated

(G-11967)
UNIVERSITY OF KANSAS
Also Called: Ku Medcal Cntr/Dept Opthmology
3901 Rainbow Blvd (66213)
PHONE..................................913 588-5238
Polly L Sheridan, *Vice Pres*
Sara Sack, *Project Dir*
Cynthia Lane, *Research*
Barry Swanson, *Comptroller*
Betsy Ostrander, *Marketing Staff*
EMP: 126
SALES (corp-wide): 1.2B **Privately Held**
WEB: www.ukans.edu
SIC: 8062 8249 Hospital, medical school affiliated with residency; medical & dental assistant school
PA: University Of Kansas
1450 Jayhawk Blvd Rm 225
Lawrence KS 66045
785 864-4868

(G-11968)
UNIVERSITY OF KANSAS HOSPITAL
Also Called: Ku Medwest Primary Care
7405 Renner Rd (66217-9414)
PHONE..................................913 588-8400
Chris Hanson, *Principal*
Kendall Tomes, *Manager*
Katie Rowland, *Nurse*
Maggie Hudson, *Associate*
Sara Kush, *Associate*
EMP: 110
SALES (corp-wide): 708.6MM **Privately Held**
SIC: 8062 General medical & surgical hospitals
PA: The University Of Kansas Hospital Authority
4000 Cambridge St
Kansas City KS 66160
913 588-5000

(G-11969)
UROLOGIC SURGERY ASSOCIATES PA (PA)
10550 Quivira Rd Ste 105 (66215-2302)
PHONE..................................913 438-3833
Bradley E Davis MD, *President*
Robert S Smith, *Associate*
EMP: 11
SALES (est): 1.5MM **Privately Held**
SIC: 8011 Urologist

(G-11970)
US TEXTILES LLC (PA)
9540 W 62nd St (66203-3216)
PHONE..................................913 660-0995
Charles Skillman, *Principal*
Donald Denning, *Principal*
Charles V Skillman, *Manager*
EMP: 13
SALES (est): 2.6MM **Privately Held**
SIC: 7389 Textile & apparel services

(G-11971)
V MACH INC
10936 Eicher Dr (66219-2600)
PHONE..................................913 894-2001
Don Sebesta, *President*
EMP: 20
SQ FT: 7,500
SALES: 1MM **Privately Held**
SIC: 3491 5085 3492 Industrial valves; valves & fittings; fluid power valves & hose fittings

(G-11972)
VALENT ARSTRCTRES - LENEXA LLC
Also Called: LMI Aerospace - Lenexa
11064 Strang Line Rd (66215-2113)
PHONE..................................913 469-6400
Bruce Breckenridge,
EMP: 35
SQ FT; 10,000
SALES (est): 6.2MM **Privately Held**
WEB: www.ctsystems.com
SIC: 3315 Wire & fabricated wire products
HQ: Lmi Aerospace, Inc.
411 Fountain Lakes Blvd
Saint Charles MO 63301
636 946-6525

(G-11973)
VALLEY VIEW STATE BANK (HQ)
7500 W 95th St (66212-2202)
P.O. Box 2924 (66201-1324)
PHONE..................................913 381-3311
Larry G McLenon, *President*
Timothy Kelley, *Exec VP*
Glen Wellman, *Senior VP*
Mark Dean, *Vice Pres*
Dick Mathews, *Vice Pres*
EMP: 120 **EST:** 1966
SQ FT: 24,000
SALES: 24.4MM
SALES (corp-wide): 100MM **Privately Held**
WEB: www.valleystatebank.net
SIC: 6022 State trust companies accepting deposits, commercial
PA: Valley View Bancshares, Inc
7500 W 95th St
Shawnee Mission KS 66212
913 381-3311

(G-11974)
VALLEY VIEW STATE BANK
11813 Roe Ave (66211-2607)
PHONE..................................913 381-3311
Edi Hepner, *Manager*
EMP: 12
SALES (corp-wide): 100MM **Privately Held**
WEB: www.valleystatebank.net
SIC: 6022 State trust companies accepting deposits, commercial
HQ: Valley View State Bank
7500 W 95th St
Shawnee Mission KS 66212
913 381-3311

(G-11975)
VALUE PLACE HOTEL
6950 Foxridge Dr (66202-4600)
PHONE..................................913 831-1417
EMP: 10
SALES (est): 379.3K **Privately Held**
SIC: 7011 Hotels & motels; hotels

(G-11976)
VF OUTDOOR INC
Also Called: North Face Logistics
16910 W 116th St (66219-9604)
PHONE..................................913 384-4000
Brian Masewicz, *Sales Staff*
Nathan Baker, *Sales Associate*
Micheal Miller, *Manager*
EMP: 80
SALES (corp-wide): 13.8B **Publicly Held**
WEB: www.thenorthface.com
SIC: 5611 4225 Men's & boys' clothing stores; general warehousing
HQ: Vf Outdoor, Llc
2701 Harbor Bay Pkwy
Alameda CA 94502
855 500-8639

(G-11977)
VIA EXPRESS DELIVERY SYSTEMS
11235 Mastin St Ste 103 (66210-2900)
P.O. Box 12207 (66282-2207)
PHONE..................................913 341-8101
John F Hale, *President*
Colette Hale, *Admin Sec*
EMP: 12
SALES: 980K **Privately Held**
SIC: 7389 Courier or messenger service

(G-11978)
VIELHAUER PLUMBING INC
12107 Johnson Dr (66216-1907)
PHONE..................................913 268-9385
Michael T Vielhauer, *President*
Linda Vielhauer, *Corp Secy*
EMP: 19 **EST:** 1973
SQ FT: 5,200
SALES (est): 2.3MM **Privately Held**
SIC: 1711 Plumbing contractors

(G-11979)
VILLAGE SHALOM INC
5500 W 123rd St (66209-3193)
PHONE..................................913 317-2600
Matthew Lewis, *CEO*
Karin McCrary, *COO*
Paul Herder, *Vice Pres*
Paige Wheeler, *Vice Pres*
Nikol Terrill, *Manager*
EMP: 205
SQ FT: 170,000
SALES: 18.8MM **Privately Held**
WEB: www.villageshalom.org
SIC: 8361 Geriatric residential care; home for the aged

(G-11980)
VINSOLUTIONS (DH)
5700 Broadmoor St Ste 901 (66202-2405)
PHONE..................................913 825-6124
Mike Dullea, *CEO*
Lori Wittman, *Senior VP*
Jim Nelson, *Vice Pres*
Keith Polsinelli, *Vice Pres*
Brian Skutta, *Vice Pres*
EMP: 161
SQ FT: 16,861
SALES (est): 30.8MM
SALES (corp-wide): 29.2B **Privately Held**
WEB: www.vinsolutions.com
SIC: 7371 Computer software development
HQ: Autotrader.Com, Inc.
3003 Summit Blvd Fl 200
Brookhaven GA 30319
404 568-8000

(G-11981)
VINTAGE PARK OF LENEXA LLC
8710 Caenen Lake Rd (66215-2069)
PHONE..................................913 894-6979
Thomas J Reddy, *Mng Member*
Richard Carlson,
EMP: 16
SQ FT: 15,000
SALES: 1.2MM **Privately Held**
SIC: 8059 Rest home, with health care

(G-11982)
VITA CRAFT CORPORATION
11100 W 58th St (66203-2299)
P.O. Box 3129 (66203-0129)
PHONE..................................913 631-6265
Gary Martin, *President*
Mike Zahner, *Purch Agent*
Vita Craft, *Natl Sales Mgr*
Kevin Ashcraft, *Supervisor*
◆ **EMP:** 100
SQ FT: 60,000
SALES (est): 16.3MM **Privately Held**
WEB: www.vitacraft.com
SIC: **3914** 3469 Stainless steel ware; metal stampings

(G-11983)
VIVA INTERNATIONAL
8357 Melrose Dr (66214-1629)
PHONE..................................913 859-0438
EMP: 5
SALES (est): 600K **Privately Held**
SIC: **1382** Oil/Gas Exploration Services

(G-11984)
VOS WINDOW & DOOR INC
Also Called: Kansas Building Supply
7600 Wedd St (66204-2227)
PHONE..................................913 962-5227
Jay Waldenmeyer, *Division Mgr*
Jay Vosburgh, *Manager*
EMP: 67
SALES (corp-wide): 13.6MM **Privately Held**
SIC: **5031** 5714 Lumber, plywood & millwork; drapery & upholstery stores
PA: Vos Window & Door, Inc.
13018 E Pinehurst Dr
Wichita KS 67230
316 733-1237

(G-11985)
W R KING CONTRACTING INC
7915 W 51st St (66202-1113)
PHONE..................................913 238-7496
Willard R King, *President*
EMP: 40
SALES: 1.2MM **Privately Held**
SIC: **4959** 1611 Environmental cleanup services; surfacing & paving

(G-11986)
W RALPH WILKERSON JR INC
Also Called: Haas & Wilkerson Ins Agency
4300 Shwn Miksn Pkwy 10 (66205)
P.O. Box 2946 (66201-1346)
PHONE..................................913 432-4400
W R Wilkerson III, *President*
Mike Soukup, *Corp Secy*
EMP: 208
SQ FT: 36,000
SALES (est): 41.6MM **Privately Held**
SIC: **6411** 6331 Insurance agents; fire, marine & casualty insurance

(G-11987)
WADDELL & REED INC (HQ)
6300 Lamar Ave (66202-4200)
P.O. Box 29217 (66201-9217)
PHONE..................................913 236-2000
Henry J Herrmann, *CEO*
Keith A Tucker, *Ch of Bd*
Michael L Avery, *President*
Derek D Burke, *President*
Robert L Hechler, *President*
EMP: 509 **EST:** 1937
SQ FT: 110,000
SALES (est): 446.5MM **Publicly Held**
SIC: **6282** 6211 6289 6411 Investment counselors; underwriters, security; distributors, security; security transfer agents; life insurance agents

(G-11988)
WADDELL & REED INV MGT CO (DH)
6300 Lamar Ave (66202-4200)
P.O. Box 29217 (66201-9217)
PHONE..................................913 236-2000
Henry J Herrmann, *President*
Robert Hechler, *General Mgr*
Daniel P Connealy, *CFO*
Philip J Sanders, *Ch Invest Ofcr*
David Ginther, *Portfolio Mgr*
EMP: 50
SALES (est): 170.6MM **Publicly Held**
SIC: **6282** Investment counselors
HQ: Waddell & Reed, Inc.
6300 Lamar Ave
Shawnee Mission KS 66202
913 236-2000

(G-11989)
WAISNER INC (PA)
Also Called: UPS Store, The
11184 Antioch Rd (66210-2420)
PHONE..................................913 345-2663
Kory Waisner, *President*
EMP: 10
SQ FT: 2,300
SALES (est): 869.7K **Privately Held**
SIC: **7389** Mailbox rental & related service

(G-11990)
WALLACE SAUNDERS CHARTERED
10111 W 87th St (66212-4673)
PHONE..................................913 888-1000
Jim Butler, *Branch Mgr*
EMP: 125
SALES (corp-wide): 17.4MM **Privately Held**
SIC: **6519** 8111 Landholding office; general practice attorney, lawyer
PA: Wallace Saunders, Chartered
10111 W 87th St
Overland Park KS 66212
913 888-1000

(G-11991)
WALLBOARD SPECIALTIES INC
23759 W 81st Ter (66227-2702)
PHONE..................................913 422-5023
Dennis Hillhouse, *President*
Sherry Sunderland, *Admin Sec*
EMP: 34
SALES (est): 3.4MM **Privately Held**
SIC: **1742** Drywall

(G-11992)
WARD PARKWAY MEDICAL GROUP
Also Called: Ward Parkway Health Services
8800 State Line Rd (66206-1553)
PHONE..................................913 383-9099
Braham J Geha, *President*
Christopher Geha, *Corp Secy*
David Peters, *Med Doctor*
EMP: 13
SALES (est): 1.6MM **Privately Held**
WEB: www.wardparkwayhealthservices.com
SIC: **8011** Offices & clinics of medical doctors

(G-11993)
WARREN MOORE PAINTING LLC
9600 W 104th St (66212-5605)
P.O. Box 12582, Overland Park (66282-2582)
PHONE..................................913 558-8549
Warren Moore,
EMP: 10 **EST:** 2007
SALES: 1.5MM **Privately Held**
SIC: **1721** Commercial painting

(G-11994)
WATERS EDGE AQUATIC DESIGN LLC
Also Called: Water's Edge Aquatic Design
11205 W 79th St (66214-1493)
PHONE..................................913 438-4338
Craig Roy,
EMP: 12 **EST:** 2000
SALES: 2MM **Privately Held**
WEB: www.watersedgeaquaticdesign.com
SIC: **8711** Civil engineering

(G-11995)
WATERWAY GAS & WASH COMPANY
12100 College Blvd (66210-3947)
PHONE..................................913 339-9542
Chris Hodges, *Branch Mgr*
EMP: 47
SALES (corp-wide): 381.2MM **Privately Held**
SIC: **7542** Washing & polishing, automotive
PA: Waterway Gas & Wash Company
727 Goddard Ave
Chesterfield MO 63005
636 537-1111

(G-11996)
WATERWAY GAS & WASH COMPANY
Also Called: Waterway Gas & Wash 32
4200 W 119th St Ste 32 (66209-1547)
PHONE..................................913 339-9964
Chris Nill, *General Mgr*
Brent Lamaster, *Branch Mgr*
EMP: 70
SALES (corp-wide): 381.2MM **Privately Held**
SIC: **7542** 5541 Washing & polishing, automotive; filling stations, gasoline
PA: Waterway Gas & Wash Company
727 Goddard Ave
Chesterfield MO 63005
636 537-1111

(G-11997)
WAVE REVIEW SALON
12010 College Blvd (66210-3945)
PHONE..................................913 345-9252
James Dyer, *Owner*
EMP: 11
SALES (est): 127.8K **Privately Held**
SIC: **7231** Unisex hair salons

(G-11998)
WELCH SIGN CO INC
9410 W 61st St (66203-3259)
P.O. Box 1209, Louisburg (66053-1209)
PHONE..................................913 831-4499
Mike E Welch, *President*
Mark Welch, *Vice Pres*
EMP: 9
SQ FT: 4,000
SALES: 600K **Privately Held**
SIC: **3993** Electric signs

(G-11999)
WELLINGTON EXPERIENCE INC (PA)
Also Called: Wellington Promotions
7304 W 130th St Ste 370 (66213-2672)
PHONE..................................913 897-9229
Joan Wells, *CEO*
Jada Hill, *President*
Nicole Reed, *Accounts Mgr*
Erin Splittorff, *Accounts Exec*
David Frazier, *Sales Staff*
EMP: 10
SQ FT: 5,800
SALES (est): 3.8MM **Privately Held**
WEB: www.twgproposal.com
SIC: **7389** Advertising, promotional & trade show services; convention & show services; trade show arrangement

(G-12000)
WELLNESS SERVICES INC
Also Called: Business and Indust Hlth Group
9724 Legler Rd (66219-1282)
PHONE..................................913 438-8779
Gretchen Mason, *Manager*
EMP: 18
SQ FT: 2,500 **Publicly Held**
SIC: **8011** Clinic, operated by physicians
HQ: Wellness Services, Inc.
9724 Legler Rd
Lenexa KS 66219
913 894-6600

(G-12001)
WELLS FARGO BANK NATIONAL ASSN
7500 College Blvd (66210-4035)
PHONE..................................913 663-6040
Lynn Steve, *Branch Mgr*
EMP: 26
SALES (corp-wide): 101B **Publicly Held**
WEB: www.wellsfargo.com
SIC: **6021** National commercial banks
HQ: Wells Fargo Bank, National Association
101 N Phillips Ave
Sioux Falls SD 57104
605 575-6900

(G-12002)
WELLS FARGO CLEARING SVCS LLC
Also Called: Wells Fargo Advisors
1900 Shawnee Mission Pkwy # 210 (66205-2001)
PHONE..................................913 267-7200
Frank Kirk, *Manager*
EMP: 60
SQ FT: 10,000
SALES (corp-wide): 101B **Publicly Held**
WEB: www.wachoviasec.com
SIC: **6211** Stock brokers & dealers
HQ: Wells Fargo Clearing Services, Llc
1 N Jefferson Ave Fl 7
Saint Louis MO 63103
314 955-3000

(G-12003)
WELLS FARGO HOME MORTGAGE INC
7127 W 110th St (66210-2348)
PHONE..................................913 319-7900
Peter Wissinger, *Manager*
EMP: 20
SALES (corp-wide): 101B **Publicly Held**
WEB: www.wfhm.com
SIC: **6162** Bond & mortgage companies
HQ: Wells Fargo Home Mortgage Inc
1 Home Campus
Des Moines IA 50328
515 324-3707

(G-12004)
WELSTONE
6050 Broadmoor St (66202-3256)
PHONE..................................913 788-6045
EMP: 12
SALES (est): 609.6K **Privately Held**
SIC: **8361** Residential care

(G-12005)
WESTERN EXTRALITE COMPANY
14903 W 99th St (66215-1112)
PHONE..................................913 438-1777
Steve Bland, *Manager*
EMP: 10
SALES (corp-wide): 2B **Privately Held**
WEB: www.westernextralite.com
SIC: **5063** Electrical supplies
HQ: Western Extralite Company
1470 Liberty St
Kansas City MO 64102
816 421-8404

(G-12006)
WESTGLEN ENDOSCOPY CENTER LLC
16663 Midland Dr Ste 200 (66217-3042)
PHONE..................................913 248-8800
Evelyn Cheshire, *CEO*
EMP: 20 **EST:** 1998
SALES (est): 2.2MM
SALES (corp-wide): 643.1MM **Privately Held**
WEB: www.amsurg.com
SIC: **8011** Gastronomist
HQ: Envision Healthcare Corporation
1a Burton Hills Blvd
Nashville TN 37215
615 665-1283

(G-12007)
WILLIAM E HOFFMAN DDS
Also Called: Hoffman Orthodontics
11213 Nall Ave Ste 130 (66211-1833)
PHONE..................................913 663-2992
William E Hoffman DDS, *Owner*
Kurt W Hoffman, *Fmly & Gen Dent*
EMP: 12
SALES (est): 690K **Privately Held**
WEB: www.hoffmanorthodontics.com
SIC: **8021** Orthodontist

(G-12008)
WILLIAM F FREY INC
11184 Antioch Rd (66210-2420)
PHONE..................................913 541-1000
William F Frey, *President*
EMP: 30
SQ FT: 800
SALES (est): 665.6K **Privately Held**
SIC: **0782** Lawn care services

GEOGRAPHIC

(G-12009)
WILLIAM HOFFMAN
3700 W 83rd St Ste 206 (66208-5120)
PHONE..................................913 649-8890
EMP: 12
SALES (est): 139.9K **Privately Held**
SIC: 8021 Dentist's Office

(G-12010)
WILLIAM R HARRIS TRUCKING
20501 W 67th St Ste A (66218-9615)
PHONE..................................913 422-5551
William R Harris, *President*
EMP: 10
SALES (est): 910K **Privately Held**
SIC: 3715 4212 Truck trailers; local trucking, without storage

(G-12011)
WILLIAMS NATURAL GAS COMPANY
8195 Cole Pkwy (66227-2714)
PHONE..................................913 422-4496
Fax: 913 422-4838
EMP: 12
SALES (est): 2.5MM **Privately Held**
SIC: 4924 Natural Gas Distribution

(G-12012)
WINDSTREAM NUVOX KANSAS LLC
7957 Bond St (66214-1557)
PHONE..................................913 747-7000
Greg Truitt, *Manager*
EMP: 25
SALES (corp-wide): 5.7B **Publicly Held**
SIC: 4813 Telephone communication, except radio
HQ: Windstream Nuvox Kansas, Llc
8200 E 34th Cir N Ste 10
Wichita KS 67226

(G-12013)
WINDTRAX INC
6800 Foxridge Dr (66202-4621)
PHONE..................................913 789-9100
Brad Daniels, *CEO*
Margaret Wilhelm, *President*
Brian Harves, *General Mgr*
Marvin Wilhelm, *Chairman*
Patricia Daniels, *Vice Pres*
▼ **EMP:** 27
SQ FT: 23,000
SALES: 8.5MM **Privately Held**
WEB: www.windtrax.com
SIC: 5087 3589 Carwash equipment & supplies; car washing machinery

(G-12014)
WISTON PROPERTY MANAGEMENT (PA)
8826 Santa Fe Dr Ste 310 (66212-3676)
PHONE..................................913 383-8100
Robert Thompson, *Partner*
Jenny Thompson, *Exec VP*
EMP: 11 **EST:** 1980
SALES (est): 994K **Privately Held**
SIC: 6513 Apartment hotel operation

(G-12015)
WOMENS HEALTH ASSOCIATES INC (PA)
Also Called: Women's Health Associates PA
9119 W 74th St Ste 300 (66204-2229)
PHONE..................................913 677-3113
Leah Ridgway, *President*
Lisa Howard, *Office Mgr*
Sylvia M Haverty, *Office Admin*
Lisa Sarmiento, *Nurse*
EMP: 25
SALES (est): 3.7MM **Privately Held**
SIC: 8011 Gynecologist

(G-12016)
WOODCRAFT SUPPLY LLC
8645 Bluejacket St (66214-1604)
PHONE..................................913 599-2800
Charlie Wilson, *Manager*
EMP: 8
SALES (corp-wide): 205.3MM **Privately Held**
WEB: www.woodcraft.com
SIC: 5251 5084 2499 Tools; woodworking machinery; carved & turned wood
PA: Woodcraft Supply, Llc
1177 Rosemar Rd
Parkersburg WV 26105
304 422-5412

(G-12017)
WOODSIDE TENNIS & HEALTH CLUB
2000 W 47th Pl (66205-1803)
PHONE..................................913 831-0034
David Freeland, *President*
Blair Tanner, *Principal*
Karen Schotanus, *Comms Dir*
Christopher Bell, *Manager*
Devon Carter, *Manager*
EMP: 125
SQ FT: 106,000
SALES (est): 6MM **Privately Held**
WEB: www.clubwoodside.com
SIC: 5812 7991 7997 Eating places; physical fitness facilities; tennis club, membership

(G-12018)
WOODSTONE INC
Also Called: Woodstone Homes
14300 Kenneth Rd (66224-4598)
PHONE..................................913 685-2282
Paul Robben, *President*
EMP: 12
SQ FT: 10,000
SALES (est): 1.2MM **Privately Held**
SIC: 1531 6552 6531 Speculative builder, single-family houses; subdividers & developers; real estate brokers & agents

(G-12019)
WORD-TECH INC
Also Called: Word-Tech Business Systems
5625 Foxridge Dr Ste 110 (66202-1599)
PHONE..................................913 722-3334
Bruce L Karlson, *President*
Jean Elledge, *CFO*
Lee Shearer, *Assistant*
EMP: 20
SQ FT: 15,000
SALES (est): 2.3MM **Privately Held**
WEB: www.wordtech.com
SIC: 7378 5045 7379 Computer & data processing equipment repair/maintenance; computers; computer related consulting services

(G-12020)
WRIGHT INTL STUDNT SVCS
6405 Metcalf Ave Ste 504 (66202-3928)
PHONE..................................913 677-1142
John Beal, *Director*
EMP: 65
SALES (est): 1.5MM **Privately Held**
WEB: www.wisservices.com
SIC: 8322 General counseling services

(G-12021)
XCELLENCE INC (PA)
Also Called: Xact
5800 Foxridge Dr Ste 406 (66202-2338)
PHONE..................................913 362-8662
Robert Polus, *CEO*
Tim Kilgallen, *Managing Prtnr*
Bill Anderson, *Vice Pres*
Chris Chapman, *Vice Pres*
Nick Reizen, *Vice Pres*
EMP: 91
SQ FT: 5,000
SALES (est): 67.4MM **Privately Held**
WEB: www.xactduplicating.com
SIC: 7374 Data processing service

(G-12022)
YELLOW CUSTOMER SOLUTIONS INC
10990 Roe Ave (66211-1213)
PHONE..................................913 696-6100
Bill Martin, *President*
EMP: 18
SALES (est): 1.4MM
SALES (corp-wide): 5B **Publicly Held**
SIC: 8742 Management consulting services
PA: Yrc Worldwide Inc.
10990 Roe Ave
Overland Park KS 66211
913 696-6100

(G-12023)
YERETSKY & MAHER LLC
Also Called: Yeretsky & Maher Law Firm
7200 W 132nd St Ste 330 (66213-1152)
P.O. Box 70007, Overland Park (66207-1307)
PHONE..................................913 897-5813
Greg Maher,
Kristen Funk, *Legal Staff*
James Yeretsky,
EMP: 11
SQ FT: 4,612
SALES (est): 1.3MM **Privately Held**
WEB: www.yeretskymaher.com
SIC: 8111 Legal services

(G-12024)
YOUNG MENS CHRISTIAN GR KANSAS
Also Called: Y M C A Fitness Center
4200 W 79th St (66208-4201)
PHONE..................................913 642-6800
Alex Clark, *Manager*
EMP: 73
SALES (corp-wide): 48.1MM **Privately Held**
WEB: www.ymca-kc.org
SIC: 8641 7991 Youth organizations; aerobic dance & exercise classes
PA: Young Men's Christian Association Of Greater Kansas City
3100 Broadway Blvd # 1020
Kansas City MO 64111
816 561-9622

(G-12025)
YRC WORLDWIDE TECHNOLOGIES INC
10990 Roe Ave (66211-1213)
PHONE..................................913 344-3000
Gary S Loveday, *President*
John Ward, *General Mgr*
Walley N Blodgett, *Business Mgr*
Jackie Carter, *Business Mgr*
Mark Sidden, *Business Mgr*
EMP: 94
SALES (est): 15.1MM
SALES (corp-wide): 5B **Publicly Held**
WEB: www.yellowcorp.com
SIC: 4213 Less-than-truckload (LTL) transport
PA: Yrc Worldwide Inc.
10990 Roe Ave
Overland Park KS 66211
913 696-6100

(G-12026)
ZAMANI DAVIS AND ASSOCIATE
Also Called: Zda
12912 Lucille St (66213-4465)
PHONE..................................913 851-0092
Rudy Davis, *CEO*
Bruce Zamani, *CFO*
EMP: 50
SALES (est): 2.1MM **Privately Held**
SIC: 8742 Marketing consulting services

(G-12027)
ZMC INC
8725 Rosehill Rd Ste 209 (66215-4611)
PHONE..................................913 599-3230
EMP: 35
SALES (est): 3MM **Privately Held**
SIC: 7311 Advertising Agency

Silver Lake
Shawnee County

(G-12028)
SKILLED SAWS INC
8617 Nw 66th St (66539-9555)
PHONE..................................785 249-5084
Chris Schaefer, *Principal*
EMP: 14
SALES (est): 683.5K **Privately Held**
SIC: 7299 Home improvement & renovation contractor agency

(G-12029)
WILBUR-ELLIS COMPANY LLC
2620 Nw Huxman Rd (66539-9236)
PHONE..................................785 582-4052
Wilbur Ellis, *Branch Mgr*
EMP: 10
SALES (corp-wide): 2.6B **Privately Held**
SIC: 5999 5191 5169 Feed & farm supply; chemicals, agricultural; fertilizer & fertilizer materials; animal feeds; industrial chemicals
HQ: Wilbur-Ellis Company Llc
345 California St Fl 27
San Francisco CA 94104
415 772-4000

(G-12030)
WINDOW DESIGN COMPANY
Also Called: Home Remodeling Specialist
9939 Nw Us Highway 24 # 1 (66539-9559)
PHONE..................................785 582-2888
Rodney Roberson, *President*
Bill Wheatley, *Sales Mgr*
EMP: 8
SQ FT: 9,200
SALES (est): 1.6MM **Privately Held**
WEB: www.windowdesignco.com
SIC: 5211 1799 5031 2431 Door & window products; siding; kitchen & bathroom remodeling; doors & windows; porch work, wood; patio & deck construction & repair; interior commercial painting contractor

Smith Center
Smith County

(G-12031)
ARLWIN MFG CO INC
720 E Highway 36 (66967-9584)
P.O. Box 92 (66967-0092)
PHONE..................................785 282-6487
Wendell Peterson, *President*
Joe Wilson, *Vice Pres*
Arlie Peterson, *Treasurer*
Charles J Wilson, *Technical Staff*
Coleen Peterson, *Admin Sec*
EMP: 13
SQ FT: 20,000
SALES (est): 2MM **Privately Held**
SIC: 3088 Shower stalls, fiberglass & plastic

(G-12032)
CENTRAL PLAINS COOP (PA)
318 S Madison St (66967-2716)
P.O. Box A (66967-0901)
PHONE..................................785 282-6813
Gerald Ratliff, *President*
EMP: 8 **EST:** 1909
SQ FT: 2,200
SALES (est): 16.2MM **Privately Held**
SIC: 3523 Elevators, farm

(G-12033)
COUNTY OF SMITH
Also Called: Smith County Ems
914 E Highway 36 (66967-9582)
PHONE..................................785 282-6924
Patrick Eastes, *Director*
EMP: 20 **Privately Held**
SIC: 8011 9111 Freestanding emergency medical center; county supervisors' & executives' offices
PA: County Of Smith
218 S Grant St Ste 5
Smith Center KS 66967
785 282-5110

(G-12034)
GREAT PLAINS SMITH CO INC
Also Called: Smith County Memorial Hospital
921 E Highway 36 (66967-9582)
P.O. Box 349 (66967-0349)
PHONE..................................785 282-6845
Allen Van Driel, *CEO*
Randy Archer, *Facilities Mgr*
Julie Williams, *CFO*
Becky Meyer, *Marketing Staff*
Kate Garman, *Manager*
EMP: 150
SALES: 11MM **Privately Held**
WEB: www.smithcohosp.org
SIC: 8062 General medical & surgical hospitals

(G-12035)
KIWANIS INTERNATIONAL INC
Also Called: Kiwanis Club
205 S Main St (66967-2607)
PHONE..................................785 282-6680
James Fetters, *Branch Mgr*
EMP: 14
SALES (corp-wide): 23.6MM **Privately Held**
WEB: www.kfne.org
SIC: 8641 Civic associations
PA: Kiwanis International, Inc.
3636 Woodview Trce
Indianapolis IN 46268
317 875-8755

(G-12036)
LANDMARK IMPLEMENT INC
910 W Highway 36 (66967-9595)
PHONE..................................785 282-6601
Rick Fischer, *Sales Associate*
Chris Cole, *Branch Mgr*
EMP: 30
SALES (corp-wide): 17.5MM **Privately Held**
SIC: 5083 Farm & garden machinery
PA: Landmark Implement, Inc.
915 Brewster Rd
Holdrege NE 68949
308 995-2194

(G-12037)
LIPPERT COMPONENTS INC
20090 Highway 281 (66967-6511)
PHONE..................................785 282-6366
Todd Haven, *Manager*
EMP: 5
SALES (corp-wide): 2.4B **Publicly Held**
WEB: www.lci1.com
SIC: 3441 3524 Building components, structural steel; rollers, lawn
HQ: Lippert Components, Inc.
3501 County Road 6 E
Elkhart IN 46514
574 312-7480

(G-12038)
ORSCHELN FARM AND HOME LLC
Also Called: Orschelin Farm and Home 97
122 W Highway 36 (66967-9588)
P.O. Box 266 (66967-0266)
PHONE..................................785 282-3272
Eric Dexter, *Branch Mgr*
EMP: 10
SALES (corp-wide): 822.7MM **Privately Held**
WEB: www.orschelnfarmhome.com
SIC: 5191 Farm supplies
PA: Orscheln Farm And Home Llc
1800 Overcenter Dr
Moberly MO 65270
800 577-2580

(G-12039)
PEOPLES BANK
136 S Main St (66967-2606)
P.O. Box 307 (66967-0307)
PHONE..................................785 282-6682
Jill McGuire, *Owner*
EMP: 18
SALES (corp-wide): 20.8MM **Privately Held**
SIC: 6022 State trust companies accepting deposits, commercial
PA: The Peoples Bank
222 S Main St
Pratt KS 67124
620 672-5611

(G-12040)
PRAIRIE HAVEN
117 W 1st St (66967-2005)
PHONE..................................785 476-2623
Shelly Threlkel, *Principal*
EMP: 10
SALES (est): 227.8K **Privately Held**
SIC: 8051 Convalescent home with continuous nursing care

(G-12041)
SMITH CENTER CHAMBER COMMERCE
219 S Main St (66967-2607)
PHONE..................................785 282-3895
Diane Peterson, *President*
EMP: 10
SALES: 20K **Privately Held**
SIC: 8611 Chamber of Commerce

(G-12042)
SMITH COUNTY FAMILY PRACTICE
Also Called: Ferrill Conant MD
119 E Parliament St (66967-3015)
P.O. Box 285 (66967-0285)
PHONE..................................785 282-6834
Joe Barnes, *Partner*
Ferrill Conant, *Partner*
Terri Jones, *Treasurer*
EMP: 12
SALES: 480K **Privately Held**
SIC: 8011 General & family practice, physician/surgeon

(G-12043)
SMITH COUNTY PIONEER
Also Called: Smith Cnty Pionr Newsppr Agcy
201 S Main St (66967-2607)
P.O. Box 266 (66967-0266)
PHONE..................................785 282-3371
Jack Krier, *Owner*
EMP: 6 **EST:** 1943
SQ FT: 4,000
SALES (est): 371.7K **Privately Held**
WEB: www.smithcountypioneer.com
SIC: 2711 Newspapers, publishing & printing

(G-12044)
SUNPORCH OF SMITH CENTER
614 S Main St (66967-3001)
PHONE..................................785 506-6003
John Grace, *Principal*
EMP: 12 **EST:** 2017
SALES (est): 1.1MM **Privately Held**
SIC: 8322 Individual & family services

Smolan
Mcpherson County

(G-12045)
ANDERSON MACHINE & SUPPLY INC
111 Main St (67456-8069)
PHONE..................................785 668-2233
Kricket Anderson, *President*
EMP: 5 **EST:** 1924
SQ FT: 10,000
SALES (est): 480K **Privately Held**
WEB: www.andersonmachine.net
SIC: 3599 Machine shop, jobbing & repair

Solomon
Dickinson County

(G-12046)
ABILENE MACHINE LLC (PA)
407 Old Highway 40 (67480-8829)
P.O. Box 129, Abilene (67410-0129)
PHONE..................................785 655-9455
Mike Aufdenberg, *CEO*
Randy Roelofsen, *President*
Todd Roelofsen, *Vice Pres*
Rick Ardis, *Warehouse Mgr*
Colin Taylor, *Export Mgr*
▲ **EMP:** 150
SQ FT: 100,000
SALES (est): 48.9MM **Privately Held**
WEB: www.abilenemachine.com
SIC: 5083 7629 3714 Agricultural machinery; farm equipment parts & supplies; electrical repair shops; motor vehicle parts & accessories

(G-12047)
B J BEST BUY PALLETS
661 N 240th Rd (67480-8617)
PHONE..................................785 488-2923
June Schoenhofer, *Principal*
Bernard G Schoenhofer, *Principal*
EMP: 8
SALES (est): 795K **Privately Held**
SIC: 2448 Pallets, wood & wood with metal

(G-12048)
BAKER ABILENE MACHINE INC
2150 Daisy Rd (67480-8828)
PHONE..................................785 565-9455
▲ **EMP:** 20
SALES (est): 4.9MM **Privately Held**
SIC: 5083 Wholesales Farm Equipment

(G-12049)
CHUCK HENRY SALES INC
525 N Poplar St Ste A (67480-8236)
PHONE..................................785 655-9430
Charles Henry, *President*
Janine Henry, *Admin Sec*
EMP: 11
SQ FT: 20,000
SALES (est): 7.2MM **Privately Held**
WEB: www.chuckhenry.com
SIC: 5012 5511 Trucks, commercial; trucks, tractors & trailers: new & used

(G-12050)
DS&O ELECTRIC COOPERATIVE
201 Dakota (67480-5500)
P.O. Box 286 (67480-0286)
PHONE..................................785 655-2011
Timothy Power, *CEO*
Ron Seyfert, *President*
EMP: 30 **EST:** 1937
SQ FT: 1,680
SALES: 21.1MM **Privately Held**
WEB: www.dsoelectric.com
SIC: 4911 Distribution, electric power

(G-12051)
GEORGE GORACKE BASEMENT
Also Called: Basement and Stem Wall Cnstr
120 3200 Ave (67480-8652)
PHONE..................................785 388-9542
George Goracke, *Owner*
EMP: 11
SALES: 390K **Privately Held**
SIC: 1771 Foundation & footing contractor

(G-12052)
QUALITY POWER PRODUCTS INC
427 Old 40 Hwy (67480)
P.O. Box 307 (67480-0307)
PHONE..................................785 263-0060
Randy Roelofsen, *President*
Randy Madden, *Corp Secy*
Todd Roelofsen, *Vice Pres*
Julie Swanson, *Controller*
▲ **EMP:** 6
SQ FT: 7,800
SALES (est): 950.2K **Privately Held**
WEB: www.q-power.com
SIC: 3599 5083 Crankshafts & camshafts, machining; harvesting machinery & equipment

(G-12053)
SOLOMON STATE BANK (PA)
126 W Main St (67480-9760)
P.O. Box 305 (67480-0305)
PHONE..................................785 655-2941
Kirk Berneking, *Vice Pres*
Dennis Riordan, *Exec Dir*
EMP: 19 **EST:** 1905
SALES: 9.2MM **Privately Held**
WEB: www.solomonstate.com
SIC: 6022 State commercial banks

(G-12054)
SOLOMON TRANSFORMERS LLC (PA)
Also Called: Solomon Electric Company
103 W Main St (67480-9760)
P.O. Box 245 (67480-0245)
PHONE..................................785 655-2191
Thomas M Hemmer, *CEO*
Phillip E Hemmer, *COO*
Jerry Newton, *COO*
Katherine M Platten, *Vice Pres*
Katie Platten, *Vice Pres*
◆ **EMP:** 350 **EST:** 1971
SQ FT: 213,000
SALES (est): 144MM **Privately Held**
WEB: www.solomoncorp.com
SIC: 3612 5093 Voltage regulating transformers, electric power; scrap & waste materials

South Hutchinson
Reno County

(G-12055)
ARK VALLEY ELECTRIC COOP ASSN
10 E 10th Ave (67505-1030)
P.O. Box 1246, Hutchinson (67504-1246)
PHONE..................................620 662-6661
Jackie Holmberg, *CEO*
EMP: 15 **EST:** 1939
SQ FT: 3,200
SALES: 14.3MM **Privately Held**
WEB: www.arkvalley.com
SIC: 4911 Distribution, electric power

(G-12056)
BORTON CORPORATION
21 Des Moines Ave (67505-2143)
P.O. Box 2108, Hutchinson (67504-2108)
PHONE..................................620 669-8211
Billy Joe Socha Jr, *Principal*
Andy Bergstrom, *Foreman/Supr*
EMP: 56
SALES (est): 10.3MM **Privately Held**
SIC: 1521 General remodeling, single-family houses

(G-12057)
BORTON LC (PA)
21 Des Moines Ave (67505-2143)
P.O. Box 2108, Hutchinson (67504-2108)
PHONE..................................620 669-8211
John Kretzer, *President*
Ron Covalcine, *Site Mgr*
Bill Socha, *Engineer*
Brian Augustine,
Aaron T Snook,
EMP: 40
SQ FT: 20,000
SALES: 46.1MM **Privately Held**
WEB: www.bortonlc.com
SIC: 1542 1796 Silo construction, agricultural; millwright

(G-12058)
COUNTY OF RENO
600 Scott Blvd (67505-8714)
PHONE..................................620 694-2976
David R McComb, *Branch Mgr*
EMP: 65 **Privately Held**
SIC: 1611 Highway & street construction
PA: County Of Reno
206 W 1st Ave
Hutchinson KS 67501
620 694-2911

(G-12059)
HOEFER ENTERPRISES INC
Also Called: Hoefer Custom Stained Glass
910 S Main St (67505-2130)
PHONE..................................620 663-1778
Scott Hoefer, *President*
EMP: 7
SQ FT: 15,000
SALES: 500K **Privately Held**
SIC: 3231 Stained glass: made from purchased glass

(G-12060)
MACHINE DESIGN SERVICES INC
225 N Main St (67505-1129)
PHONE..................................620 663-4949
Mark Kidd, *President*
Kristy Kidd, *Manager*
EMP: 7
SQ FT: 9,900
SALES: 1.2MM **Privately Held**
SIC: 3599 7699 Machine shop, jobbing & repair; industrial equipment services; machinery cleaning; agricultural equipment repair services

(G-12061)
MCKENZIE PAINT & BODY INC
45 Kansas Ave (67505-1025)
PHONE..................................620 662-3721
Danny J Coonce, *President*
Dan Coonce, *Owner*
David Coonce, *Corp Secy*
EMP: 10 **EST:** 1948

GEOGRAPHIC

SALES: 980K **Privately Held**
SIC: 7532 7538 Body shop, automotive; bump shops, automotive repair; paint shop, automotive; general automotive repair shops; general truck repair

(G-12062)
MENNONITE FRNDSHIP COMMUNITIES (PA)
600 W Blanchard Ave (67505-1526)
PHONE..................................620 663-7175
Lowell Peachey, *CEO*
Leigh Peck, *Vice Pres*
James Henderson, *Transportation*
Naomi Wagler, *Finance*
Pamela Brack, *Manager*
EMP: 200
SQ FT: 125,000
SALES: 11.3MM **Privately Held**
WEB: www.mennonitemanor.org
SIC: 8051 8361 Skilled nursing care facilities; rest home, with health care incidental

(G-12063)
MORTON SALT INC
1000 Morton Dr (67505-1302)
P.O. Box 1547, Hutchinson (67504-1547)
PHONE..................................620 669-0401
Dana Bauer, *Human Res Dir*
Steve Borchardt, *Branch Mgr*
Pamela Berry, *Clerk*
Kellie Hilliard, *Clerk*
EMP: 17
SALES (corp-wide): 4.4B **Privately Held**
SIC: 2899 Salt
HQ: Morton Salt, Inc.
444 W Lake St Ste 3000
Chicago IL 60606

(G-12064)
QUALITY INN
11 Des Moines Ave (67505-2143)
PHONE..................................620 663-4444
EMP: 56
SQ FT: 54,000
SALES (est): 1.2MM **Privately Held**
SIC: 7011 5812 5813 Hotels & motels; restaurant, family: independent; drinking places

(G-12065)
RED ROCK AUTO CENTER INC
200 N Main St (67505-1130)
PHONE..................................620 663-9822
Ervin Miller, *President*
Steve Miller, *Vice Pres*
EMP: 10
SALES: 1.7MM **Privately Held**
SIC: 5541 7538 Gasoline service stations; general automotive repair shops

(G-12066)
STAINLESS SYSTEMS INC
300 E 4th Ave (67505-1228)
PHONE..................................620 663-4346
Gregory Roepka, *President*
Sue Roepka, *Vice Pres*
EMP: 21
SQ FT: 4,000
SALES (est): 2.9MM **Privately Held**
WEB: www.sssystems.com
SIC: 3556 Food products machinery

(G-12067)
TYSON FOODS INC
9 N Washington St (67505-1111)
P.O. Box 1570, Hutchinson (67504-1570)
PHONE..................................620 663-6141
Lori Decou-Bryan, *QC Mgr*
John Elam, *Plant Engr*
Susan Redd, *Controller*
Bill Woodward, *Manager*
Bill Ritzdorf, *Manager*
EMP: 375
SALES (corp-wide): 42.4B **Publicly Held**
SIC: 2013 Sausages & other prepared meats
PA: Tyson Foods, Inc.
2200 W Don Tyson Pkwy
Springdale AR 72762
479 290-4000

(G-12068)
YODER BUILDERS INC
1718 W Blanchard Ave (67505-1543)
PHONE..................................620 669-8542
Leon Yoder, *President*
Clayton Yoder, *Principal*
Barb Yoder, *Treasurer*
John Yoder, *Office Mgr*
EMP: 28 **EST:** 1996
SALES: 950K **Privately Held**
SIC: 1521 New construction, single-family houses

Spearville
Ford County

(G-12069)
ALLIANCE AG AND GRAIN LLC (PA)
313 N Main St (67876-9500)
P.O. Box 98 (67876-0098)
PHONE..................................620 385-2898
Stan Stark, *CEO*
Jason Murray, *CFO*
EMP: 160 **EST:** 2015
SALES (est): 55.1MM **Privately Held**
SIC: 5153 Grains

(G-12070)
BUSTER CRUST INC
Main St (67876)
P.O. Box 1438, Dodge City (67801-1438)
PHONE..................................620 385-2651
Donald Hornung, *President*
Ken Stracker, *Branch Mgr*
EMP: 25
SALES (est): 2.5MM
SALES (corp-wide): 14.6MM **Privately Held**
SIC: 3523 Farm machinery & equipment
PA: Buster Crust Inc
2300 E Trail St
Dodge City KS 67801
620 227-7106

(G-12071)
SPEARVILLE DISTRICT HOSPITAL
Also Called: Parkview Villa
202 Park St (67876-8544)
PHONE..................................620 385-2632
Gretta Myric, *Manager*
EMP: 10 **EST:** 1985
SALES: 300K **Privately Held**
SIC: 6513 Retirement hotel operation

Spivey
Kingman County

(G-12072)
ABES OILFIELD SERVICE LLC
220 W Stanley St (67142-4203)
P.O. Box 43 (67142-0043)
PHONE..................................620 532-5551
Abe Erdman,
EMP: 21 **EST:** 1996
SALES (est): 3MM **Privately Held**
SIC: 1389 Oil field services

(G-12073)
SPIVEY OIL FIELD SERVICE LLC
115 S Main St (67142-4202)
P.O. Box 35 (67142-0035)
PHONE..................................620 532-5178
Mark Kanngiesser, *Partner*
Robert Howlett,
EMP: 25 **EST:** 1996
SQ FT: 2,200
SALES (est): 2.7MM **Privately Held**
SIC: 1389 Oil field services

Spring Hill
Johnson County

(G-12074)
A&M PRODUCTS MANUFACTURING CO
705 N Lincoln St (66083-8840)
PHONE..................................913 592-4344
Rich Mowrer, *Branch Mgr*
EMP: 25
SALES (corp-wide): 6.2B **Publicly Held**
SIC: 3295 Minerals, ground or treated
HQ: A&M Products Manufacturing Company
1221 Broadway Ste 51
Oakland CA 94612
510 271-7000

(G-12075)
ADVANTAGE FRAMING SYSTEMS INC
701 N Lincoln St (66083-8840)
P.O. Box 420, Gardner (66030-0420)
PHONE..................................913 592-4150
Kim Humbert, *President*
James Humbert, *Vice Pres*
EMP: 20
SQ FT: 5,000
SALES (est): 5.2MM **Privately Held**
SIC: 2421 1751 Building & structural materials, wood; framing contractor

(G-12076)
AGC FLAT GLASS NORTH AMER INC
Also Called: Afg Spring Hill Plant
20400 Webster St (66083-9602)
PHONE..................................913 592-6100
Jamie Colbertson, *Branch Mgr*
EMP: 300 **Privately Held**
WEB: www.afg.com
SIC: 3211 Flat glass
HQ: Agc Flat Glass North America, Inc.
11175 Cicero Dr Ste 400
Alpharetta GA 30022
404 446-4200

(G-12077)
APPLE BUS COMPANY
802 S A Line Dr (66083-8817)
PHONE..................................913 592-5121
Liane Penichet, *Manager*
EMP: 77
SALES (corp-wide): 44.1MM **Privately Held**
SIC: 4151 School buses
PA: Apple Bus Company
230 E Main St
Cleveland MO 64734
816 618-3310

(G-12078)
BEACHNER SEED CO INC
Also Called: Tri-Star Seed
20300 W 191st St (66083-8982)
PHONE..................................913 686-2090
Carrie Beachner, *Branch Mgr*
EMP: 11
SALES (corp-wide): 11.6MM **Privately Held**
SIC: 5191 Seeds: field, garden & flower
PA: Beachner Seed Co., Inc.
616 7th St
Saint Paul KS
620 449-2286

(G-12079)
BEAVER DAM HEALTH CARE CENTER
Also Called: Beverly
251 E Wilson St (66083-8713)
P.O. Box 388 (66083-0388)
PHONE..................................913 592-3100
Randy Sutterfield, *Manager*
EMP: 45
SALES (corp-wide): 393.8MM **Privately Held**
SIC: 8051 Extended care facility
PA: Beaver Dam Health Care Center
5220 Tennyson Pkwy # 400
Plano TX 75024
972 372-6300

(G-12080)
BOAN MASONRY COMPANY INC
19155 S Hedge Ln (66083-8856)
PHONE..................................913 592-5369
Phil Boan, *President*
EMP: 18
SALES (est): 1.3MM **Privately Held**
SIC: 1741 Masonry & other stonework

(G-12081)
CENTRAL GC CONSTRUCTION INC
22599 Columbia Rd (66083-4030)
P.O. Box 467 (66083-0467)
PHONE..................................913 484-2400
Brock Stinemetz, *President*
EMP: 12 **EST:** 2012
SALES: 5MM **Privately Held**
SIC: 1522 Co-op construction

(G-12082)
CITY OF SPRING HILL
22400 W 207th St (66083-8869)
PHONE..................................913 592-3781
EMP: 18 **Privately Held**
SIC: 9199 2086 ; water, pasteurized: packaged in cans, bottles, etc.
PA: City Of Spring Hill
401 N Madison St
Spring Hill KS 66083
913 592-3274

(G-12083)
D B EXCAVATING INC
802 S A Line Dr (66083-8817)
P.O. Box 284, La Cygne (66040-0284)
PHONE..................................913 208-7100
Don Benthusen, *President*
EMP: 30 **EST:** 1997
SQ FT: 7,200
SALES: 2.5MM **Privately Held**
WEB: www.dbexcavating.com
SIC: 1794 Excavation work

(G-12084)
GGNSC SPRING HILL LLC
251 E Wilson St (66083-8713)
PHONE..................................913 592-3100
Randy Sutterfield, *President*
Tom Inderhees, *Exec Dir*
Holly A Rasmussen Jones, *Admin Sec*
EMP: 46
SALES (est): 833.8K
SALES (corp-wide): 2.6B **Privately Held**
SIC: 8059 Nursing home, except skilled & intermediate care facility
HQ: Ggnsc Holdings Llc
1000 Fianna Way
Fort Smith AR 72919

(G-12085)
HAUPT CONSTRUCTION COMPANY
19951 W 207th St (66083-8826)
P.O. Box 428 (66083-0428)
PHONE..................................913 686-4411
Mark Haupt, *President*
Jason Haupt, *Superintendent*
Bradley Haupt, *Vice Pres*
Michelle McCool, *Administration*
EMP: 10 **EST:** 1965
SQ FT: 6,000
SALES: 18.3MM **Privately Held**
SIC: 1611 Grading

(G-12086)
HEALTHCARE PRFMCE GROUP INC
23419 W 215th St (66083-2519)
P.O. Box 588 (66083-0588)
PHONE..................................316 796-0337
Matthew Terstriep, *CEO*
Mathew Terstriep, *CEO*
Nancy Ward, *President*
James Flynn, *Principal*
Chad Terstriep, *Principal*
EMP: 96
SALES (est): 8.8MM **Privately Held**
WEB:
www.healthcareperformancegroup.com
SIC: 8742 7371 Hospital & health services consultant; computer software systems analysis & design, custom

(G-12087)
LOWE-NORTH CONSTRUCTION INC
800 S A Line Dr (66083-8817)
PHONE..................................913 592-4025
Lawrence J North, *President*
David Lowe, *Vice Pres*
Ryan Gaskill, *Foreman/Supr*
▲ **EMP:** 40
SQ FT: 6,000

SALES (est): 14.9MM Privately Held
WEB: www.lowe-north.com
SIC: 1623 Transmitting tower (telecommunication) construction

(G-12088)
MAINE FLAME LLC
20775 W 227th St (66083-7901)
PHONE..................................913 208-9484
Allan Jackson, *Mng Member*
EMP: 5 EST: 1996
SQ FT: 200
SALES: 102.7K Privately Held
SIC: 2493 Reconstituted wood products

(G-12089)
MID-AM BUILDING SUPPLY INC
20301 W 207th St (66083-8961)
PHONE..................................913 592-4313
Mark Mattox, *Buyer*
Scott Oatman, *Buyer*
Mike Ferhat, *Controller*
Brian Benge, *Sales Staff*
Brian Bergman, *Sales Staff*
EMP: 67
SQ FT: 51,000
SALES (corp-wide): 260.3MM Privately Held
WEB: www.midambuilding.com
SIC: 5031 5033 1751 Building materials, exterior; building materials, interior; millwork; roofing & siding materials; window & door (prefabricated) installation
PA: Mid-Am Building Supply, Inc.
1615 Omar Bradley Rd
Moberly MO 65270
660 263-2140

(G-12090)
MILLER VETERINARY SERVICES PA
Also Called: Spring Hill Veterinary Clinic
602 N Webster St (66083-9410)
P.O. Box 410 (66083-0410)
PHONE..................................913 592-2770
Ryan Miller, *President*
Erin Miller, *Vice Pres*
EMP: 18
SALES: 2.5MM Privately Held
SIC: 0742 Veterinary services, specialties

(G-12091)
NIFFIE PRINTING INC
111 W Johnson St (66083-6700)
PHONE..................................913 592-3040
Laurie Smith, *President*
Rick Smith, *Treasurer*
EMP: 10
SALES (est): 620K Privately Held
SIC: 2759 7378 Commercial printing; computer maintenance & repair

(G-12092)
NIPS LLC
20150 W 191st St (66083-9020)
P.O. Box 644, Louisburg (66053-0644)
PHONE..................................913 592-2365
Diane Boyd, *Mng Member*
Robert A Boyd,
EMP: 9
SALES (est): 1.4MM Privately Held
SIC: 3272 Precast terrazo or concrete products

(G-12093)
NORTH ENTERPRISES LLC
800 S A Line Dr (66083-8817)
PHONE..................................913 592-4025
Larry North, *Mng Member*
EMP: 15
SALES (est): 1MM Privately Held
SIC: 1541 Industrial buildings, new construction

(G-12094)
ORTHODONTICS P A YOUNG
22438 S Harrison St (66083-3151)
PHONE..................................913 592-2900
Andrew Young, *Owner*
EMP: 16
SALES (est): 405.6K Privately Held
SIC: 8021 Orthodontist

(G-12095)
OSAWATOMIE AGENCY INC
21101 W 223rd St (66083-3042)
PHONE..................................913 592-3811
Chad Lewis, *Branch Mgr*
EMP: 21
SALES (est): 3MM
SALES (corp-wide): 15MM Privately Held
SIC: 6029 Commercial banks
PA: The Osawatomie Agency Inc
601 Main St
Osawatomie KS 66064
913 755-3811

(G-12096)
PERFECT DETAILS INC
516 N Webster St (66083-9169)
PHONE..................................913 592-5022
Carol Keenison, *President*
Rachel Howard, *Consultant*
EMP: 10
SALES (est): 318.9K Privately Held
SIC: 7231 Unisex hair salons

(G-12097)
REECE & NICHOLS REALTORS INC
104 E Cedar St (66083-8889)
PHONE..................................913 247-3064
Bruce Harlan, *Partner*
Steve Wehner, *Branch Mgr*
EMP: 12
SALES (corp-wide): 225.3B Publicly Held
WEB: www.reece-nichols.com
SIC: 6519 6531 Real property lessors; real estate agents & managers
HQ: Reece & Nichols Realtors, Inc.
11601 Granada St
Leawood KS 66211
913 491-1001

(G-12098)
SEATS INCORPORATED
701 N Lincoln St (66083-8840)
PHONE..................................913 686-3137
EMP: 5
SALES (corp-wide): 320MM Privately Held
SIC: 2531 Seats, miscellaneous public conveyances; vehicle furniture
HQ: Seats, Incorporated
1515 Industrial St
Reedsburg WI 53959
608 524-8261

(G-12099)
SPRING HILL CHAMBER COMMERCE
613 S Race St (66083-8895)
P.O. Box 15 (66083-0015)
PHONE..................................913 592-3893
Sharon Mitchell, *E-Commerce*
Ann Jensen, *Exec Dir*
EMP: 15
SALES: 104.8K Privately Held
SIC: 8611 Chamber of Commerce

(G-12100)
STATE BANK OF SPRING HILL
201 S Webster St (66083-8928)
P.O. Box 387 (66083-0387)
PHONE..................................913 592-3326
Fred A Dunmire, *President*
David B Dunmire, *President*
Nick Stroda, *Officer*
EMP: 12 EST: 1927
SALES: 1.6MM Privately Held
WEB: www.sbsh-ks.com
SIC: 6022 State trust companies accepting deposits, commercial

(G-12101)
TRAFFIC TECH INC
22418 S Harrison St (66083-3151)
PHONE..................................888 592-2009
Rick Cordova, *General Mgr*
EMP: 155
SALES (corp-wide): 214MM Privately Held
SIC: 4731 Brokers, shipping; domestic freight forwarding; foreign freight forwarding
HQ: Traffic Tech, Inc.
180 N Michigan Ave # 700
Chicago IL 60601
877 383-1167

(G-12102)
TRANS SERVICES INC
Also Called: Tsi
702 N Lincoln St (66083-8840)
P.O. Box 13223, Shawnee Mission (66282-3223)
PHONE..................................913 592-3878
David Nickell, *President*
Scott Hanna, *Opers Mgr*
Fran Fatool, *Opers-Prdtn-Mfg*
Brenda Smith, *Asst Mgr*
EMP: 25
SQ FT: 6,500
SALES (est): 2.8MM Privately Held
SIC: 4212 Local trucking, without storage

(G-12103)
WEIGEL CONSTRUCTION INC
19015 Madison St Ste A (66083-7573)
PHONE..................................913 780-1274
Jim Weigel, *President*
Kenette Weigel, *Admin Sec*
EMP: 10
SALES: 2MM Privately Held
SIC: 1541 5039 Prefabricated building erection, industrial; metal buildings

Stafford
Stafford County

(G-12104)
KANZA COOPERATIVE ASSOCIATION
700 S Main St (67578-2000)
PHONE..................................620 234-5252
Donny Pound, *Manager*
EMP: 15
SALES (corp-wide): 300MM Privately Held
SIC: 5153 Grain elevators
PA: Kanza Cooperative Association
102 N Main St
Iuka KS 67066
620 546-2231

(G-12105)
KANZA COOPERATIVE ASSOCIATION
611 S Buckeye St (67578-2001)
PHONE..................................620 234-5252
Donnie Pound, *Branch Mgr*
EMP: 12
SALES (corp-wide): 300MM Privately Held
SIC: 5153 Grain elevators
PA: Kanza Cooperative Association
102 N Main St
Iuka KS 67066
620 546-2231

(G-12106)
LEISURE HOMESTEAD ASSOCIATION
Also Called: Intermediate Adult Care Fcilty
405 Grand Ave (67578-2009)
PHONE..................................620 234-5208
Jennifer Gilespie, *CEO*
EMP: 50
SALES: 4MM Privately Held
SIC: 8051 Skilled nursing care facilities

(G-12107)
PRAIRIE BANK OF KANSAS (PA)
Also Called: FARMERS NATIONAL BANK OF STAFF
200 S Main St (67578-1432)
P.O. Box 130 (67578-0130)
PHONE..................................620 234-5226
James Richardson, *CEO*
Rick Smith, *President*
Glenda D Hernandez, *Vice Pres*
EMP: 26 EST: 1886
SQ FT: 5,000
SALES: 4.2MM Privately Held
SIC: 6022 State commercial banks

(G-12108)
RAMA OPERATING CO INC
Also Called: Austin, Robert L
101 S Main St (67578-1429)
P.O. Box 159 (67578-0159)
PHONE..................................620 234-6034
Robert L Austin, *President*
Robin Austin, *Corp Secy*
EMP: 6
SQ FT: 2,160
SALES (est): 537.9K Privately Held
SIC: 1311 Crude petroleum production; natural gas production

(G-12109)
SEMCRUDE LP
598 Arthur Ave (67578-1105)
P.O. Box 250 (67578-0250)
PHONE..................................620 234-5532
Kenny King, *Branch Mgr*
EMP: 15
SALES (corp-wide): 54B Publicly Held
WEB: www.semcrude.com
SIC: 4612 5171 2951 Crude petroleum pipelines; petroleum bulk stations & terminals; asphalt paving mixtures & blocks
HQ: Semcrude, L.P.
6120 S Yale Ave Ste 700
Tulsa OK 74136

(G-12110)
STAFFORD COUNTY HISTORICAL
100 N Main St (67578-1343)
PHONE..................................620 234-5664
Marion Hearn, *President*
Silva Schols, *Vice Pres*
Jean Fanshier, *Treasurer*
Michael Hathaway, *Admin Sec*
Zelema Lee Wendelburg, *Admin Sec*
EMP: 10
SALES: 45.9K Privately Held
SIC: 8412 Museum

(G-12111)
STAFFORD DISTRICT HOSPITAL 4
Also Called: STAFFORD DISTRICT HOSPITAL HOM
502 S Buckeye St (67578-2035)
P.O. Box 190 (67578-0190)
PHONE..................................620 234-5221
Todd Taylor, *President*
EMP: 45
SQ FT: 24,000
SALES: 6.3MM Privately Held
WEB: www.sdh4.org
SIC: 8062 Hospital, affiliated with AMA residency

Stark
Neosho County

(G-12112)
SMITH BROTHERS INC
21585 Victory Rd (66775)
P.O. Box 68 (66775-0068)
PHONE..................................620 754-3958
Patrick Smith, *President*
EMP: 10 EST: 1932
SQ FT: 1,500
SALES (est): 1.3MM Privately Held
SIC: 4213 Trucking, except local

Sterling
Rice County

(G-12113)
CENTRAL PRAIRIE CO-OP
Also Called: Hub Chemical Storage
1775 State Rd 14 Hwy (67579)
P.O. Box 159 (67579-0159)
PHONE..................................620 278-2470
Dion Yost, *Manager*
EMP: 13
SALES (corp-wide): 42.5MM Privately Held
SIC: 5153 5191 4221 0721 Grains; farm supplies; farm product warehousing & storage; crop spraying services

PA: Central Prairie Co-Op
225 S Broadway Ave
Sterling KS 67579
620 278-2141

(G-12114)
CHILD CARE SERVICES STRLNG INC
Also Called: LIL CUB CHILDCARE
309 N Broadway Ave (67579-1918)
P.O. Box 292 (67579-0292)
PHONE..................................620 904-4231
Leanna Hook, *Director*
EMP: 10 **EST:** 2015
SQ FT: 15,000
SALES: 93.1K **Privately Held**
SIC: 8351 Child day care services

(G-12115)
CORONADO INC (PA)
Also Called: First Bank of Sterling
128 S Broadway Ave (67579-2133)
P.O. Box 67 (67579-0067)
PHONE..................................620 278-2161
Jeff Laudermilk, *President*
EMP: 17
SALES: 4.5MM **Privately Held**
WEB: www.first-bank.net
SIC: 6712 Bank holding companies

(G-12116)
FARMERS CO-OPERATIVE UNION
225 S Broadway Ave (67579-2339)
P.O. Box 159 (67579-0159)
PHONE..................................620 278-2141
EMP: 70 **EST:** 1917
SQ FT: 6,000
SALES (est): 952.2K **Privately Held**
SIC: 5153 5191 4221 5541 Grains; farm supplies; grain elevator, storage only; filling stations, gasoline

(G-12117)
FIRST BANK (HQ)
Also Called: FIRST BANK OF STERLING
128 S Broadway Ave (67579-2133)
P.O. Box 67 (67579-0067)
PHONE..................................620 278-2161
Jeff Laudermilk, *President*
Sam Lewis, *COO*
Marcia Diasio, *Vice Pres*
EMP: 19 **EST:** 1907
SALES: 5.7MM **Privately Held**
WEB: www.first-bank.net
SIC: 6022 State trust companies accepting deposits, commercial

(G-12118)
G & L WELL SERVICE INC
Also Called: Well Servicing & Completions
612 E Washington Ave (67579-1731)
P.O. Box 183 (67579-0183)
PHONE..................................620 278-3105
Karen Gillespie, *President*
Dan Gillespie, *Vice Pres*
John W Gillespie, *Vice Pres*
EMP: 7
SALES (est): 985K **Privately Held**
SIC: 1389 Servicing oil & gas wells

(G-12119)
GENZADA PHARMACEUTICALS LLC (PA)
119 W Main St (67579-2017)
P.O. Box 303 (67579-0303)
PHONE..................................620 204-7150
Gene Zaid, *CEO*
Cameron West, *COO*
Jason West, *Exec VP*
Jack Mull, *Vice Pres*
Bill Schneider, *Finance*
EMP: 9 **EST:** 2010
SQ FT: 6,000
SALES (est): 1.6MM **Privately Held**
SIC: 2834 Druggists' preparations (pharmaceuticals)

(G-12120)
GENZADA PHARMACEUTICALS USA
101 S Broadway Ave (67579-2132)
P.O. Box 303 (67579-0303)
PHONE..................................620 204-7150
Gene H Zaid, *CEO*
EMP: 17
SALES (est): 472.2K **Privately Held**
SIC: 5122 Pharmaceuticals

(G-12121)
HOSPITAL DST 1 OF RICE CNTY
Also Called: Sterling Medical Center
239 N Broadway Ave (67579-1916)
P.O. Box 7 (67579-0007)
PHONE..................................620 278-2123
Treva Kintigh, *Manager*
EMP: 18
SALES (corp-wide): 13.6MM **Privately Held**
SIC: 8099 8011 Medical services organization; general & family practice, physician/surgeon
PA: Hospital District 1 Of Rice County (Inc)
619 S Clark Ave
Lyons KS 67554
620 257-5173

(G-12122)
JACAM CARRIERS 2013 LLC
205 S Broadway Ave (67579-2339)
PHONE..................................620 278-3355
Jason West, *President*
Gary Zorn, *Technical Staff*
EMP: 12
SALES (est): 1MM
SALES (corp-wide): 54.1MM **Privately Held**
SIC: 4213 Trucking, except local
PA: Jacam Chemicals 2013, Llc
205 S Broadway Ave
Sterling KS 67579
620 278-3355

(G-12123)
JACAM CHEMICALS 2013 LLC (PA)
205 S Broadway Ave (67579-2339)
P.O. Box 96 (67579-0096)
PHONE..................................620 278-3355
Jason West, *President*
Glenn Woods, *Info Tech Mgr*
EMP: 250
SALES (est): 54.1MM **Privately Held**
SIC: 2869 Laboratory chemicals, organic

(G-12124)
KMW LTD (PA)
535 W Garfield Ave (67579-2370)
P.O. Box 327 (67579-0327)
PHONE..................................620 278-3641
Michael Bender, *President*
Dave Schneider, *Vice Pres*
Jeremy Bennett, *Opers Staff*
Katie Harrington, *Production*
Nicolas Taylor, *Engineer*
▲ **EMP:** 140
SQ FT: 40,000
SALES (est): 31.4MM **Privately Held**
WEB: www.kmwloaders.com
SIC: 3523 3537 Loaders, farm type: manure, general utility; industrial trucks & tractors

(G-12125)
MARSHALL PUBLISHING INC
Also Called: Sterling Bulletin
107 N Broadway Ave (67579-2130)
P.O. Box 97 (67579-0097)
PHONE..................................620 278-2114
Ben Marshall, *President*
EMP: 5
SALES (est): 49.9K **Privately Held**
WEB: www.sterlingbulletin.com
SIC: 2711 Newspapers: publishing only, not printed on site

(G-12126)
MIKE KEIMIG HARVESTING
7317 N Andre Rd (67579-9322)
PHONE..................................620 278-2334
Mike Keimig, *Owner*
EMP: 16
SALES (est): 1.2MM **Privately Held**
SIC: 0722 Crop harvesting

(G-12127)
PRATT LIVESTOCK INC (PA)
111 S Broadway Ave (67579-2132)
PHONE..................................620 672-5961
Mike Lewis, *President*
Robert Cundith, *Corp Secy*
Robert Wilkey, *Vice Pres*
Karen Cundith, *Treasurer*
EMP: 25
SQ FT: 2,400
SALES (est): 3.8MM **Privately Held**
SIC: 5154 Auctioning livestock

(G-12128)
PRESBYTERIAN MANORS INC
204 W Washington Ave (67579-1614)
PHONE..................................620 278-3651
Michael Rajewski, *Director*
EMP: 55
SALES (corp-wide): 8.6MM **Privately Held**
SIC: 8051 Convalescent home with continuous nursing care
HQ: Presbyterian Manors, Inc.
2414 N Woodlawn Blvd
Wichita KS 67220
316 685-1100

(G-12129)
PROFITT BUILDERS AND SUPPLY
2470 18th Rd (67579-9064)
PHONE..................................620 278-3667
Gary Profitt, *Owner*
EMP: 13
SALES (est): 850K **Privately Held**
SIC: 1542 Farm building construction

(G-12130)
STERLING COUNTRY CLUB INC
2225 13th Rd (67579)
P.O. Box 173 (67579-0173)
PHONE..................................620 278-9956
Bob Cundith, *Corp Secy*
EMP: 13
SALES: 104.3K **Privately Held**
SIC: 7997 Golf club, membership

(G-12131)
UNITED INDUSTRIES INC
Also Called: Swimtime
202 E Cleveland Ave (67579-1732)
P.O. Box 58 (67579-0058)
PHONE..................................620 278-3160
Mac Stromberg, *President*
Jack Walton, *Vice Pres*
EMP: 16
SQ FT: 36,000
SALES: 6MM **Privately Held**
WEB: www.towerflo.com
SIC: 5091 3589 Swimming pools, equipment & supplies; swimming pool filter & water conditioning systems

(G-12132)
WALTON PLUMBING & HEATING INC
112 N Broadway Ave (67579-2131)
P.O. Box 187 (67579-0187)
PHONE..................................620 278-3462
Scott Walton, *President*
Stephanie Walton, *Treasurer*
EMP: 15
SQ FT: 8,000
SALES (est): 2MM **Privately Held**
SIC: 1711 Plumbing contractors

Stilwell
Johnson County

(G-12133)
AGRI-RISK SERVICES INC
7540 W 160th St Ste 100 (66085-8114)
PHONE..................................913 897-1699
Lance Allen, *President*
Barbara Kirby, *Vice Pres*
Edna Gaylord, *Technician*
EMP: 13
SQ FT: 10,000
SALES: 4MM **Privately Held**
WEB: www.agririsk.com
SIC: 6411 6331 Property & casualty insurance agent; fire, marine & casualty insurance & carriers

(G-12134)
ALLIED COURIER SYSTEMS INC
7540 W 160th St Ste 180 (66085-8114)
P.O. Box 23082, Overland Park (66283-0017)
PHONE..................................913 383-8666
Craig Demeo, *President*
EMP: 10
SALES (est): 671.1K **Privately Held**
WEB: www.alliedcourierkc.com
SIC: 4212 Delivery service, vehicular

(G-12135)
BANKONIP
17745 Metcalf Ave (66085-9464)
PHONE..................................913 928-6297
Mark Petheram, *Vice Pres*
EMP: 15
SALES (est): 864.4K **Privately Held**
SIC: 8742 Marketing consulting services

(G-12136)
BLACKSTONE ENVIRONMENTAL INC (PA)
16200 Foster St (66085-8418)
PHONE..................................913 495-9990
Michael Kukuk, *President*
Rowley Tedlock, *Engineer*
Ed Guernsey, *Project Engr*
Austin Quick, *Project Engr*
Melanie Rehor, *Accountant*
EMP: 10 **EST:** 2010
SALES (est): 1.5MM **Privately Held**
SIC: 8744

(G-12137)
CAMBRIDGE CABINETRY
6800 W 180th St (66085-9148)
PHONE..................................816 795-5082
Brian Tally, *Partner*
EMP: 7
SALES: 750K **Privately Held**
SIC: 2434 Wood kitchen cabinets

(G-12138)
CANARY RESOURCES INC (PA)
7230 W 162nd St Ste A (66085-9143)
PHONE..................................913 239-8960
William Chandler, *President*
Steve Allee, *Vice Pres*
Rex Ashllck, *Vice Pres*
James H Steinheider, *Vice Pres*
EMP: 8
SALES (est): 3.1MM **Privately Held**
SIC: 1381 Drilling oil & gas wells

(G-12139)
CARSTAR INC
7235 W 162nd St (66085-9139)
PHONE..................................913 685-2886
Josh Burke, *Branch Mgr*
EMP: 18
SALES (corp-wide): 136.9MM **Privately Held**
WEB: www.carstar.com
SIC: 7532 Body shop, automotive
HQ: Carstar, Inc.
440 S Church St Ste 700
Charlotte NC 28202

(G-12140)
CHOCOLATE SPECIALTY CORP
18009 Broadmoor St (66085-9437)
P.O. Box 7264, Shawnee Mission (66207-0264)
PHONE..................................816 941-3088
Bramwell A Nelson, *President*
Kerri Nelson, *Vice Pres*
EMP: 100
SQ FT: 200,000
SALES: 7MM **Privately Held**
SIC: 2066 Chocolate

(G-12141)
CITOXLAB USA LLC
Also Called: Xenometrics
17745 Metcalf Ave (66085-9464)
P.O. Box 401 (66085-0401)
PHONE..................................913 850-5000
Alfred Botchway, *President*
Deven Dandekar, *Director*
Thomas Haymaker, *Director*
EMP: 82
SQ FT: 10,000

▲ = Import ▼=Export
◆ =Import/Export

SALES (est): 13.6MM
SALES (corp-wide): 1.5MM **Privately Held**
SIC: 8731 Commercial research laboratory
HQ: Crl Group France
Rue De Pacy
Miserey 27930
232 292-626

(G-12142)
COGEN CLEANING TECHNOLOGY INC
Also Called: CCT
16014 Foster St (66085-8876)
PHONE..................................281 339-5751
Allan G Alper, *President*
Brian Cumming, *Vice Pres*
Lisa Murphy, *Administration*
◆ **EMP:** 30
SALES (est): 2MM **Privately Held**
WEB: www.cogencleaning.com
SIC: 7349 8711 Cleaning service, industrial or commercial; engineering services

(G-12143)
CU - ONCE JOINT VENTURE LLC
7215 W 162nd Ter (66085-8238)
PHONE..................................913 707-2165
David J Wenkel,
EMP: 10
SALES: 950K **Privately Held**
SIC: 1522 Residential construction

(G-12144)
DIAMOND GYMNSTICS DNCE ACADEMY
7270 W 161st St (66085-8879)
PHONE..................................913 851-7500
Kim Lauderdale, *Partner*
EMP: 32
SQ FT: 23,400
SALES (est): 963.2K **Privately Held**
SIC: 7999 Gymnastic instruction, non-membership

(G-12145)
DOCTORS INC (PA)
7425 W 161st St (66085-8854)
PHONE..................................913 681-8041
Carol Wingate, *Administration*
EMP: 23
SALES (est): 2.5MM **Privately Held**
SIC: 0782 0781 1711 1629 Lawn services; landscape planning services; irrigation sprinkler system installation; land clearing contractor

(G-12146)
EDUCATIONAL RESOURCES INC
7500 W 160th St (66085-8100)
PHONE..................................913 262-0448
Michael Frost, *President*
Robert C Treas, *President*
Karen Harrison, *Vice Pres*
EMP: 55
SQ FT: 12,000
SALES (est): 3.6MM **Privately Held**
WEB: www.eriworld.com
SIC: 8748 Educational consultant; testing service, educational or personnel

(G-12147)
FIRST IMPRSSONS CRBSCAPING LLC
18220 Windsor Dr (66085-9047)
PHONE..................................913 620-5164
Marcus McCullough, *Principal*
EMP: 5 **EST:** 2011
SALES (est): 310K **Privately Held**
SIC: 3272 Well curbing, concrete

(G-12148)
GC LABELS INC
6870 W 206th St (66085)
P.O. Box 196 (66085-0196)
PHONE..................................913 897-6966
Mary Ann Gerber, *President*
EMP: 15
SQ FT: 9,500
SALES: 3.6MM **Privately Held**
WEB: www.gc-labels.com
SIC: 2679 2759 Labels, paper: made from purchased material; labels & seals: printing

(G-12149)
GHOST LAKE CORPORATION
6500 W 194th St (66085-9401)
PHONE..................................816 809-9411
Nelson Shirley, *President*
EMP: 10
SALES: 3.7MM **Privately Held**
SIC: 0291 Livestock farm, general

(G-12150)
HAIL SIGNATURE TECH LLC
2720 W 161st Ter (66085-7818)
PHONE..................................913 620-4928
Robert Lynch,
EMP: 5 **EST:** 2012
SALES (est): 302K **Privately Held**
SIC: 3829 Measuring & controlling devices

(G-12151)
HEALTHCARE REVENUE GROUP LLC
19800 Metcalf Ave # 414 (66085-2600)
PHONE..................................913 717-4000
EMP: 17
SALES (est): 887.3K **Privately Held**
SIC: 8742 Hospital & health services consultant

(G-12152)
HEATING AND COOLING DISTRS INC
5150 W 175th St (66085-8936)
PHONE..................................913 262-5848
G Robert Lang, *President*
Lawrence Lang, *Vice Pres*
James Lang, *Treasurer*
Amy Lang, *Admin Sec*
EMP: 11
SQ FT: 8,000
SALES: 3.5MM **Privately Held**
WEB: www.radiantkc.com
SIC: 5074 5075 Heating equipment (hydronic); warm air heating equipment & supplies

(G-12153)
HOWELL CONSTRUCTION CO INC
16687 Lamar Ave (66085-8766)
PHONE..................................816 474-7766
Carol Howell, *President*
EMP: 20
SQ FT: 5,000
SALES (est): 2.4MM **Privately Held**
SIC: 1542 Commercial & office buildings, renovation & repair

(G-12154)
HUME MUSIC INC
16010 Metcalf Ave Ste 200 (66085-8975)
PHONE..................................816 474-1960
Ralph Weber, *Manager*
EMP: 15
SALES (corp-wide): 3.5MM **Privately Held**
SIC: 5736 7699 7359 5932 Musical instrument stores; musical instrument repair services; musical instrument rental services; musical instruments, secondhand
PA: Hume Music, Inc.
2010 Broadway Blvd
Kansas City MO
816 474-1960

(G-12155)
INTEGRATED HEALTH SYSTEMS LLC
7520 W 160th St Ste 101 (66085-8137)
P.O. Box 23072, Overland Park (66283-0015)
PHONE..................................913 647-9020
Shawna Freeman, *Project Mgr*
Kevin Green, *CFO*
Karen Staley, *Human Res Dir*
Bob Gault, *Sales Staff*
Gary Trabant, *Manager*
EMP: 17
SQ FT: 2,500
SALES (est): 5.8MM **Privately Held**
SIC: 5045 Computers & accessories, personal & home entertainment

(G-12156)
JEFF HOGE CONCRETE LLC
6884 W 183rd St (66085-9422)
PHONE..................................913 239-0903
Jeff Hoge,
Jeffrey Hoge,
EMP: 27
SALES (est): 1.7MM **Privately Held**
SIC: 1771 Concrete work

(G-12157)
JIM HAAS BUILDERS INC
7230 W 162nd St Ste C (66085-9143)
P.O. Box 25366, Shawnee Mission (66225-5366)
PHONE..................................913 897-9721
James R Haas Jr, *President*
Pam Haas, *Admin Sec*
EMP: 16
SALES (est): 1.6MM **Privately Held**
SIC: 1521 New construction, single-family houses

(G-12158)
JOE THOELE FOUNDATION
16012 Metcalf Ave (66085-9249)
PHONE..................................913 685-2282
Joe Thoele, *Owner*
EMP: 6
SALES (est): 290K **Privately Held**
SIC: 2515 Foundations & platforms

(G-12159)
JOHNSON CMMUNICATIONS SVCS INC
Also Called: Jcs
16144 Foster St (66085-8417)
PHONE..................................913 681-5505
Louis M Johnson, *President*
Linda B Johnson, *Vice Pres*
Pat Ryan, *Accounts Mgr*
Hary Baldwin, *Manager*
EMP: 13
SQ FT: 2,700
SALES (est): 1.9MM **Privately Held**
WEB: www.johnson-comm.com
SIC: 1731 8748 Telephone & telephone equipment installation; telecommunications consultant

(G-12160)
KCA INTERNET
5580 W 201st St (66085-9222)
PHONE..................................913 735-7206
Ruth E Moore, *Owner*
Aaron Connelly, *Software Dev*
EMP: 10
SALES (est): 489.2K **Privately Held**
WEB: www.kcainternet.com
SIC: 4813 7336 ; commercial art & graphic design

(G-12161)
KD CHRISTIAN CONSTRUCTION CO
7387 W 162nd St (66085-9160)
PHONE..................................913 451-0466
Kevin D Christian, *President*
Steve Vehige, *Superintendent*
Frank Christian, *Vice Pres*
Bret Buckmaster, *Foreman/Supr*
EMP: 35
SQ FT: 4,800
SALES (est): 5.2MM **Privately Held**
SIC: 1742 Plastering, plain or ornamental; drywall

(G-12162)
KEITH CONNELL INC (PA)
7500 W 151st St (66085)
PHONE..................................913 681-5585
Keith Connell, *President*
Bonnie Connell, *Corp Secy*
Jimmy Connell, *Vice Pres*
Joe Baer, *Broker*
Danny Connell, *Sales Staff*
EMP: 10
SQ FT: 2,000
SALES (est): 20MM **Privately Held**
SIC: 5148 Fruits, fresh

(G-12163)
LEVEL FIVE SOLUTIONS INC
7525 W 160th St (66085-8101)
PHONE..................................913 400-2014
David V Berck, *President*
EMP: 14
SALES (est): 1.6MM **Privately Held**
SIC: 8742 Business planning & organizing services

(G-12164)
LINDERS WELDING INC
19490 Metcalf Ave (66085-8520)
P.O. Box 420 (66085-0420)
PHONE..................................913 681-2394
Jeff Linder, *President*
Kelly Craft, *Manager*
EMP: 7 **EST:** 1966
SQ FT: 8,000
SALES (est): 750K **Privately Held**
SIC: 3446 7692 Stairs, staircases, stair treads: prefabricated metal; welding repair

(G-12165)
MARTENS ENTERPRISES INC
2111 E Santa Fe St (66085)
PHONE..................................913 851-2772
Philip W Martens, *President*
EMP: 10
SALES (est): 1.4MM **Privately Held**
SIC: 1521 New construction, single-family houses

(G-12166)
MESSENGER LAWN AND LDSCPG LLC (PA)
19160 Metcalf Ave (66085-8523)
P.O. Box 24203, Shawnee Mission (66283-4203)
PHONE..................................913 681-6165
Gail Messenger, *Mng Member*
EMP: 20 **EST:** 2003
SALES: 5MM **Privately Held**
SIC: 0781 Landscape services

(G-12167)
MESSENGER LAWN AND LDSCPG LLC
7360 W 162nd St (66085-9364)
PHONE..................................913 681-6165
Gail Messenger, *Branch Mgr*
EMP: 60
SALES (corp-wide): 5MM **Privately Held**
SIC: 0782 Lawn care services
PA: Messenger Lawn And Landscaping Llc
19160 Metcalf Ave
Stilwell KS 66085
913 681-6165

(G-12168)
MEYERS BROTHERS CNSTR CO
19055 Metcalf Ave (66085-8533)
P.O. Box 69 (66085-0069)
PHONE..................................913 681-2667
William H Meyers, *President*
Tom Meyers, *Vice Pres*
EMP: 10
SQ FT: 4,000
SALES (est): 773.7K **Privately Held**
SIC: 0782 0191 Sodding contractor; seeding services, lawn; mulching services, lawn; mowing services, lawn; general farms, primarily crop

(G-12169)
MPRESSIONS
16230 Metcalf Ave (66085-9147)
PHONE..................................913 897-4401
Mary Linda Boling, *Owner*
EMP: 5
SALES (est): 341.1K **Privately Held**
SIC: 3442 Window & door frames

(G-12170)
NATION-WIDE REPR HOLDG CO INC
16151 Foster St (66085-8417)
PHONE..................................913 248-1722
Christopher Pasco, *President*
EMP: 34
SQ FT: 44,000
SALES (est): 3.5MM **Privately Held**
WEB: www.nwrsinc.com
SIC: 7629 Circuit board repair

(G-12171)
PHOENIX RNVTION RSTORATION INC
16250 Foster St (66085-8418)
PHONE..................................913 599-0055
Mark Heinze, *President*
Pat Murphy, *Vice Pres*
Jackie Murphy, *Treasurer*
Stephney Heinze, *Admin Sec*
EMP: 29 **EST:** 1999
SQ FT: 1,200
SALES (est): 4.9MM **Privately Held**
WEB: www.kcphoenix.com
SIC: 1799 Post-disaster renovations

(G-12172)
REGISTERED GRAPHICS INC
8070 W 172nd Ter (66085-8859)
PHONE..................................913 681-4907
Lance Hodges, *President*
EMP: 10
SQ FT: 3,000
SALES (est): 1.1MM **Privately Held**
SIC: 3625 Industrial controls: push button, selector switches, pilot

(G-12173)
STILWELL VENTURING CREW
19950 Broadmoor Ln (66085-8901)
PHONE..................................913 306-2419
Izabella Borowiak-Miller, *Principal*
Lawrence Guenther, *Principal*
Paul Van Dyne, *Principal*
EMP: 10 **EST:** 2016
SALES (est): 64.6K **Privately Held**
SIC: 8641 Youth organizations

(G-12174)
SUNBURST PROPERTIES INC
16120 Foster St (66085-8417)
PHONE..................................913 393-4747
Roger Rector, *President*
Forrest Bruce, *Vice Pres*
EMP: 17
SALES (est): 2MM **Privately Held**
WEB: www.sunburstproperties.com
SIC: 6531 6411 Real estate managers; real estate brokers & agents; insurance agents & brokers

(G-12175)
SYNTECH RESEARCH LAB SVCS LLC
17745 Metcalf Ave (66085-9464)
PHONE..................................913 378-0998
Khosro Khodayari, *CEO*
Ashley Smith, *Research*
Eric Lorenz,
EMP: 33 **EST:** 2012
SALES (est): 6.3MM **Privately Held**
SIC: 8734 Testing laboratories

(G-12176)
TED ROW INC
7745 W 183rd St (66085-8746)
P.O. Box 385 (66085-0385)
PHONE..................................816 223-9666
Ted Herzog, *President*
EMP: 15
SQ FT: 1,400
SALES (est): 2.4MM **Privately Held**
SIC: 1794 1771 1795 Excavation work; concrete work; wrecking & demolition work

(G-12177)
UNIMED II INC (PA)
6785 W 193rd St (66085-8706)
PHONE..................................913 533-2202
Brennen Gary, *President*
Mike Reynolds, *General Mgr*
Donald Thomas, *Shareholder*
▲ **EMP:** 150
SALES (est): 11.7MM **Privately Held**
WEB: www.unimed2.com
SIC: 5047 Medical equipment & supplies

(G-12178)
UNLIMITED LOGISTICS LLC
7500 W 161st St (66085-9387)
PHONE..................................913 851-4900
Cynthia Smith, *Sales Mgr*
Jeff Knox, *Accounts Mgr*
Brian Banach, *Sales Staff*
Drew Wright, *Manager*
James Connell,
EMP: 13
SALES: 3MM **Privately Held**
SIC: 4212 Local trucking, without storage

(G-12179)
WEE WORKSHOP INC
7305 W 162nd St (66085-9140)
PHONE..................................913 681-2191
S T Foundopoulos, *President*
Maryln Foundopoulos, *Treasurer*
Anna Marie Wix, *Admin Sec*
EMP: 50
SQ FT: 8,000
SALES: 1.5MM **Privately Held**
SIC: 8351 Preschool center

(G-12180)
WOODS PAINTING CO INC
3505 W 194th St (66085-8412)
PHONE..................................913 897-3741
William A Woods, *President*
EMP: 11
SALES (est): 704.4K **Privately Held**
SIC: 1721 Painting & paper hanging

Stockton
Rooks County

(G-12181)
CITY OF STOCKTON
Also Called: Solomon Valley Manor
315 S Ash St (67669-2136)
PHONE..................................785 425-6754
Nancy Conyac, *Administration*
EMP: 30 **Privately Held**
WEB: www.stocktonkansas.net
SIC: 8059 8051 Nursing home, except skilled & intermediate care facility; skilled nursing care facilities
PA: City Of Stockton
115 S Walnut St
Stockton KS 67669
785 425-6703

(G-12182)
JOHN E JONES OIL CO INC
1016 S Cedar St (67669-2306)
P.O. Box 546 (67669-0546)
PHONE..................................785 425-6746
Eugene Westhusing, *President*
Patricia Westhusing, *Vice Pres*
Patrick Lingg, *Admin Sec*
EMP: 15 **EST:** 1941
SQ FT: 4,000
SALES: 52.7MM **Privately Held**
SIC: 4213 5172 Contract haulers; gases, liquefied petroleum (propane); gasoline; diesel fuel

(G-12183)
PETERS-HOWELL LUJEANA
Also Called: Rooks County Trailer Sales
1116 Main St (67669-2030)
PHONE..................................785 415-2125
Lujeana Peters-Howell, *Owner*
EMP: 5
SALES (est): 349.1K **Privately Held**
SIC: 3523 Trailers & wagons, farm

(G-12184)
REDBUD VILLAGE
Also Called: Rooks County Sheriff S Dept
115 N Walnut St (67669-1663)
P.O. Box 193 (67669-0193)
PHONE..................................785 425-6312
Roger Mongeau, *Sheriff*
EMP: 11 **Privately Held**
WEB: www.rookscounty.net
SIC: 9221 8611 Sheriffs' offices; business associations
PA: Redbud Village
1000 S Washington St
Plainville KS 67663
785 434-4536

(G-12185)
ROOKS COUNTY HISTORICAL MUSEUM
Also Called: Frank Walker Museum
Hwy S 183 (67669)
P.O. Box 43 (67669-0043)
PHONE..................................785 425-7217
Sandy Rogers, *President*
Viloet Riffe, *Vice Pres*
Jeane Linsdey, *Admin Sec*
EMP: 10
SALES (est): 180.4K **Privately Held**
SIC: 8412 Museum

(G-12186)
ROOKS COUNTY HOLDINGS LLC
Also Called: M Motel, The
1401 Main St (67669-2035)
PHONE..................................785 261-0455
Steven Mongeau,
EMP: 10
SALES (est): 362.3K **Privately Held**
SIC: 1531 Cooperative apartment developers

(G-12187)
SMITH MONUMENTS INC
110 S Cedar St (67669-1969)
PHONE..................................785 425-6762
Ron W Gallaway, *President*
Addie Foster, *Admin Sec*
Gail Gallaway, *Admin Sec*
EMP: 6
SALES: 400K **Privately Held**
SIC: 5999 5099 3366 Monuments, finished to custom order; monuments & grave markers; bronze foundry

(G-12188)
SOLUTIONS NORTH BANK (PA)
123 N Cedar St (67669-1635)
P.O. Box 511 (67669-0511)
PHONE..................................785 425-6721
Dale Winkelcleck, *President*
EMP: 20 **EST:** 1951
SALES: 10.9MM **Privately Held**
WEB: www.wakeeney.org
SIC: 6022 7371 State commercial banks; computer software development & applications

(G-12189)
STOCKTON NATIONAL BANK (PA)
123 N Cedar St (67669-1635)
P.O. Box 511 (67669-0511)
PHONE..................................785 425-6721
Dale Winklepleck, *President*
James E Berkley, *Chairman*
EMP: 20 **EST:** 1900
SQ FT: 3,500
SALES: 6.9MM **Privately Held**
WEB: www.snbks.com
SIC: 6021 National commercial banks

(G-12190)
WILKENS MANUFACTURING INC (PA)
Also Called: Tarps Unlimited/Wilkens Mfg
1480 Highway 183 (67669-8868)
PHONE..................................785 425-7070
Art Wilkens, *President*
E Mae Wilkens, *Corp Secy*
Robert Fiola, *CFO*
James Owens, *CFO*
Amanda Handschuh, *Manager*
EMP: 80
SQ FT: 113,000
SALES (est): 18MM **Privately Held**
WEB: www.tarpsunlimited.com
SIC: 3523 5012 7539 Trailers & wagons, farm; trailers for trucks, new & used; automotive repair shops

Strong City
Chase County

(G-12191)
BESTMARK EXPRESS INC
2286 Rd U (66869)
P.O. Box 269 (66869-0269)
PHONE..................................620 273-7018
Mark E Miller, *President*
EMP: 30
SQ FT: 10,000
SALES (est): 5.6MM **Privately Held**
WEB: www.bestmarkexpress.com
SIC: 4213 Contract haulers

(G-12192)
CHASE CHILDRENS SERVICES INC
410 Palmer St (66869-9700)
PHONE..................................620 273-6650
Dana Gass, *Director*
EMP: 11
SALES: 10.4K **Privately Held**
SIC: 8351 Preschool center

(G-12193)
LUCO MANUFACTURING CO INC
705 N Cottonwood St (66869-9602)
P.O. Box 385 (66869-0385)
PHONE..................................620 273-6723
Bill Luder, *President*
Jim Luder, *Treasurer*
EMP: 11
SQ FT: 8,000
SALES (est): 2.2MM **Privately Held**
WEB: www.lucoinc.com
SIC: 3523 Cattle feeding, handling & watering equipment; hog feeding, handling & watering equipment

(G-12194)
PALENSKE RANCH INC
2274a Old Highway 50 (66869-9808)
PHONE..................................620 279-4467
Hal J Palenske, *President*
Charlene Palenske, *Corp Secy*
Jason Palenske, *Vice Pres*
EMP: 10
SALES (est): 2.8MM **Privately Held**
SIC: 0211 0191 0722 Beef cattle feedlots; general farms, primarily crop; cash grains, machine harvesting services

(G-12195)
STRONG CITY ELEVATOR
P.O. Box 210 (66869-0210)
PHONE..................................620 273-6483
Dennis Murphy, *Principal*
EMP: 10
SALES (est): 1.2MM **Privately Held**
SIC: 4221 Grain elevator, storage only

Sublette
Haskell County

(G-12196)
ALFALFA INC
1242 Road 180 (67877-8026)
PHONE..................................620 675-8686
Don Norman, *Manager*
EMP: 7
SALES (corp-wide): 4.5MM **Privately Held**
SIC: 2048 5191 Alfalfa or alfalfa meal, prepared as animal feed; alfalfa
PA: Alfalfa Inc
122 N Main St
Lakin KS

(G-12197)
APC INC
Also Called: Apc-Sublette
Hwy 83 N Hc 1 (67877)
PHONE..................................620 675-8691
Nixon Lauridsen, *Ch of Bd*
Keith Barnes, *President*
EMP: 27
SQ FT: 5,000
SALES (est): 3.9MM
SALES (corp-wide): 67.5K **Privately Held**
WEB: www.apccompany.com
SIC: 2011 2048 Meat by-products from meat slaughtered on site; prepared feeds
HQ: Apc Company, Inc.
2425 Se Oak Tree Ct
Ankeny IA 50021
515 289-7600

(G-12198)
ARCHER-DANIELS-MIDLAND COMPANY
Also Called: ADM
1892 Hwy 83 (67877-8108)
P.O. Box 220 (67877-0220)
PHONE..................................620 675-2226
Darrel Henderson, *Manager*
EMP: 5

SALES (corp-wide): 64.3B **Publicly Held**
WEB: www.admworld.com
SIC: 2041 2875 Flour & other grain mill products; fertilizers, mixing only
PA: Archer-Daniels-Midland Company
77 W Wacker Dr Ste 4600
Chicago IL 60601
312 634-8100

(G-12199)
BARTLETT CATTLE COMPANY LP
Hc 1 Box 14 (67877)
P.O. Box 14 (67877-0014)
PHONE..................................620 675-2244
Mike Gesling, *Branch Mgr*
EMP: 25
SALES (corp-wide): 1B **Privately Held**
SIC: 0211 5999 Beef cattle feedlots; feed & farm supply
HQ: Bartlett Cattle Company, L.P.
4900 Main St Ste 1200
Kansas City MO 64112
816 753-6300

(G-12200)
CENTERA BANK (PA)
119 S Inman St (67877-7700)
P.O. Box 400 (67877-0400)
PHONE..................................620 675-8611
Micheal Cearley, *President*
Charles Meyers, *President*
Michael Cearley, *Exec VP*
Jay Meyer, *Exec VP*
Rhesa Dohrmann, *Assistant VP*
EMP: 16 **EST:** 1937
SALES: 11.1MM **Privately Held**
WEB: www.centerabank.com
SIC: 6022 State trust companies accepting deposits, commercial

(G-12201)
FRIONA INDUSTRIES LP
Also Called: Friona Cattle Feeders North 1
922 Road 90 2 (67877-8010)
PHONE..................................620 649-2235
EMP: 30
SALES (corp-wide): 90.4MM **Privately Held**
SIC: 0211 Beef cattle feedlots
HQ: Friona Industries, L.P.
1174 Empire Cir
Satanta KS 67870

(G-12202)
GOLDEN PRAIRIE HUNTING SERVICE
607 W Gwinn Ct (67877-6728)
P.O. Box 119 (67877-0119)
PHONE..................................620 675-8490
Jeffrey White, *Owner*
Debra White, *Owner*
EMP: 12
SALES (est): 189.7K **Privately Held**
WEB: www.goldenprairiehunting.com
SIC: 7999 Hunting guides

(G-12203)
HERITAGE FEEDERS LP
Also Called: Heritage Sublette
1506 Road 30 (67877-8020)
P.O. Box 41 (67877-0041)
PHONE..................................620 275-4195
Galen Wright, *Manager*
EMP: 30
SALES (corp-wide): 2.5MM **Privately Held**
WEB: www.heritagebeef.com
SIC: 0211 Beef cattle feedlots
PA: Heritage Feeders, L.P.
13913 Tech Dr Ste A2
Oklahoma City OK 73134
405 286-4100

(G-12204)
K & K WATER WELLS LLC
806 W La Lande Ave (67877-8124)
P.O. Box 428 (67877-0428)
PHONE..................................620 675-2222
Andre Dominguez, *CEO*
Cecelia Mahara, *Admin Sec*
EMP: 10
SALES (est): 566.3K **Privately Held**
SIC: 1781 Water well drilling

(G-12205)
MERIT ENERGY COMPANY LLC
703 W La Lande Ave (67877)
PHONE..................................620 675-8372
EMP: 5
SALES (corp-wide): 533.8MM **Privately Held**
SIC: 1311 Crude Petroleum And Natural Gas, Nsk
PA: Merit Energy Company, Llc
13737 Noel Rd Ste 1200
Dallas TX 75240
972 701-8377

(G-12206)
PENNER TRUCKING INC
1808 Road Pp (67877)
P.O. Box 39 (67877-0039)
PHONE..................................620 353-8475
John P Penner, *President*
John Penner, *Principal*
EMP: 10
SALES: 130K **Privately Held**
SIC: 4212 4213 Local trucking, without storage; trucking, except local

(G-12207)
SOUTHWEST PLINS RGONAL SVC CTR
W Hwy 56 Lark Ave (67877)
P.O. Box 1010 (67877-1010)
PHONE..................................620 675-2241
Bill Biermann, *Principal*
Susan Jenkins, *Research*
Volora Hanzlicek, *Consultant*
Jason Johnson, *Consultant*
Kelly Gillespie, *Director*
EMP: 75
SQ FT: 4,000
SALES (est): 2.3MM **Privately Held**
WEB: www.swprsc.org
SIC: 8299 8748 8211 Educational services; business consulting; elementary & secondary schools

(G-12208)
STOPPEL DIRT INC
910 W Edelle Ave (67877-7851)
P.O. Box 866 (67877-0866)
PHONE..................................620 675-2653
Greg Stoppel, *President*
Tina Stoppel, *Corp Secy*
EMP: 20
SQ FT: 1,400
SALES (est): 4.1MM **Privately Held**
SIC: 1794 Excavation & grading, building construction

(G-12209)
SUBLETTE COOPERATIVE INC (PA)
500 W Lalande Ave (67877)
P.O. Box 340 (67877-0340)
PHONE..................................620 675-2297
Kendall Poland, *President*
Dawn Freeman, *Office Mgr*
Terry Presley, *Manager*
Joyce Rice, *Clerk*
EMP: 37
SQ FT: 12,000
SALES (est): 9.5MM **Privately Held**
SIC: 5153 5191 Grain elevators; fertilizer & fertilizer materials; feed; seeds: field, garden & flower; chemicals, agricultural

(G-12210)
SUBLETTE ENTERPRISES INC
Also Called: Sublette Feeders
6 Mi E 1 Mi N On Hwy 56 (67877)
P.O. Box 917 (67877-0917)
PHONE..................................620 668-5501
Lewis Trentman, *President*
EMP: 55
SALES (est): 4.9MM **Privately Held**
SIC: 0211 5153 Beef cattle feedlots; grain elevators

(G-12211)
SUBLETTE RECREATION COMMISSION
Also Called: Sublette Recreational Center
406 Wallace St (67877)
P.O. Box 914 (67877-0914)
PHONE..................................620 675-8211
Shandi Lopez, *Principal*
Robert Lamborn, *Director*
EMP: 12
SALES: 500K **Privately Held**
SIC: 7997 Membership sports & recreation clubs

(G-12212)
T-L IRRIGATION CO
1893 Us Highway 83 (67877-8108)
P.O. Box 429 (67877-0429)
PHONE..................................620 675-2253
Michael Brown, *Branch Mgr*
EMP: 12
SALES (corp-wide): 70.4MM **Privately Held**
SIC: 4971 Irrigation systems
PA: T-L Irrigation Co.
151 E Highway 6
Hastings NE 68901
402 462-4128

(G-12213)
WE LAND & CATTLE CO INC
2108 Us Highway 83 (67877-8040)
P.O. Box 864 (67877-0864)
PHONE..................................620 675-2747
Eugene Wright, *President*
EMP: 11
SALES (est): 990K **Privately Held**
SIC: 0211 Beef cattle feedlots

Summerfield
Marshall County

(G-12214)
GOOD SHEPHERD VILLAGES INC
613 3rd St (66541-8619)
PHONE..................................785 244-6418
Rosalie Maybrunn, *President*
Ladonna Thomas, *Admin Sec*
EMP: 27
SALES (est): 970K **Privately Held**
SIC: 8322 8051 Old age assistance; skilled nursing care facilities

(G-12215)
PRECISION TRUSS INC
Also Called: Home Resource
2537 Eagle Rd (66541-8633)
PHONE..................................785 244-6456
Kent Buessing, *President*
Loren Sehmelvle, *Corp Secy*
Barry Broxterman, *Vice Pres*
Brad Broxterman, *Vice Pres*
EMP: 12
SQ FT: 16,800
SALES (est): 1.5MM **Privately Held**
SIC: 2439 Trusses, wooden roof

(G-12216)
QUALITY HOMES INC
Also Called: Do It Best
N State Line (66541)
P.O. Box 8 (66541-0008)
PHONE..................................402 248-6218
Bruce Fahfholtz, *President*
Lori Hardin, *Treasurer*
EMP: 20
SQ FT: 10,496
SALES (est): 2.3MM **Privately Held**
WEB: www.qualityhomesinc.com
SIC: 5251 5211 1521 Hardware; lumber & other building materials; single-family housing construction

Sun City
Barber County

(G-12217)
NATIONAL GYMPSON
20672 Nw White Sands Rd (67143-9003)
PHONE..................................620 248-3247
Mark Long, *General Mgr*
Jesse Rickmon, *Principal*
EMP: 13 **EST:** 1999
SALES (est): 633.9K **Privately Held**
SIC: 1499 Gypsum mining

(G-12218)
NGC INDUSTRIES LLC
20672 Nw White Sands Rd (67143-9003)
PHONE..................................620 248-3248
Mark Long, *Branch Mgr*
EMP: 11
SALES (corp-wide): 723.5MM **Privately Held**
SIC: 1429 Igneous rock, crushed & broken-quarrying
HQ: Ngc Industries, Llc
2001 Rexford Rd
Charlotte NC 28211

Sylvan Grove
Lincoln County

(G-12219)
BATS INC
Also Called: World Pest Control
206 N Main St (67481-8104)
PHONE..................................785 526-7185
Brian Meitler, *President*
Shonda Meitler, *Partner*
Shannon Meitler, *Vice Pres*
Janet Weseloh, *Admin Sec*
EMP: 12
SQ FT: 1,500
SALES (est): 1MM **Privately Held**
SIC: 7342 Exterminating & fumigating; pest control in structures

(G-12220)
SYLVAN SALES COMMISSION LLC
400 E 1st St (67481-8844)
PHONE..................................785 526-7123
Toby Meyer,
EMP: 20
SALES (est): 3.2MM **Privately Held**
SIC: 5154 Auctioning livestock

Sylvia
Reno County

(G-12221)
STAFFORD COUNTY FLOUR MILLS CO
118 N Main St (67581-9703)
P.O. Box 214 (67581-0214)
PHONE..................................620 486-2493
Reuel Foote, *President*
EMP: 12
SALES (corp-wide): 9.9MM **Privately Held**
SIC: 2041 Flour
PA: Stafford County Flour Mills Co Inc
108 S Church St
Hudson KS 67545
620 458-4121

Syracuse
Hamilton County

(G-12222)
CACTUS FEEDERS INC
Also Called: Syracuse Feed Yard
Hwy 50 E (67878)
P.O. Box 1226 (67878-1226)
PHONE..................................620 384-7431
Herman Plunkett, *Manager*
EMP: 33
SALES (corp-wide): 136.5MM **Privately Held**
WEB: www.cactusfeeders.com
SIC: 0211 Beef cattle feedlots
PA: Cactus Feeders, Inc
600 S Tyler St Ste 2800
Amarillo TX 79101
806 373-2333

(G-12223)
COUNTY OF HAMILTON
Also Called: Hamilton Cnty Hospital Extnded
E G St (67878)
PHONE..................................620 384-7780
Ed Hurysz, *Administration*

EMP: 40 **Privately Held**
SIC: 8062 8051 General medical & surgical hospitals; skilled nursing care facilities
PA: County Of Hamilton
219 N Main St
Syracuse KS 67878
620 384-5451

(G-12224)
FIRST NAT BNK SYRACUSE INC (PA)
11 N Main St (67878-7881)
P.O. Box 928 (67878-0928)
PHONE..................................620 384-7441
Terryl Spiker, *President*
Bernard Hugo, *Senior VP*
Christopher Floyd, *Vice Pres*
Daliz Oquendo, *Vice Pres*
Vance Keller, *CIO*
EMP: 18 **EST:** 2014
SALES: 19MM **Privately Held**
WEB: www.fnb-windmill.com
SIC: 6021 National commercial banks

(G-12225)
FRONTIER DAIRY LLC
11501 Sw Cr 31 (67878-7847)
PHONE..................................620 372-2156
Eric Goedhart,
Amos De Groot,
EMP: 50
SALES (est): 9.3MM **Privately Held**
SIC: 0241 Dairy farms

(G-12226)
FULLMER CATTLE CO KS LLC
3200 S Hwy 27 (67878)
P.O. Box 986 (67878-0986)
PHONE..................................620 384-7499
Que Fullmer,
Zed Fullmer,
EMP: 50
SALES (est): 1.8MM **Privately Held**
SIC: 0291 Animal specialty farm, general

(G-12227)
HAMILTON COUNTY HOSPITAL
700 N Huser St (67878-7700)
PHONE..................................620 384-7461
Patrick Geschwind, *CEO*
Phyllis Horning, *CFO*
EMP: 99
SALES: 5.6MM **Privately Held**
SIC: 8062 General medical & surgical hospitals

(G-12228)
KINDER MORGAN KANSAS INC
Hc Box 83 (67878)
PHONE..................................620 384-7830
Tab Bailor, *Manager*
EMP: 5 **Publicly Held**
WEB: www.kne.com
SIC: 4924 5172 1311 4922 Natural gas distribution; gases; crude petroleum production; natural gas production; pipelines, natural gas
HQ: Kinder Morgan Kansas, Inc.
1001 La St Ste 1000
Houston TX 77002
713 369-9000

(G-12229)
PREMIER CATTLE CO LLC (PA)
State Lake Rd (67878)
P.O. Box 847 (67878-0847)
PHONE..................................620 384-5711
Charles Whitaker,
EMP: 20
SALES (est): 2.6MM **Privately Held**
SIC: 0211 Beef cattle feedlots

(G-12230)
R & H IMPLEMENT COMPANY INC
Also Called: Lrw Partnership
1100 W Hwy 50 (67878)
PHONE..................................620 384-7421
Eldon D Reed, *President*
Robert H Gale Jr, *Corp Secy*
EMP: 12
SQ FT: 22,000
SALES (est): 2MM **Privately Held**
WEB: www.randhimplement.com
SIC: 5083 5261 Farm implements; nurseries & garden centers

(G-12231)
RC GEVEN FARMS LLC
12701 Sw Counrty Rd 32 (67878)
PHONE..................................620 372-2021
Richard Geven,
EMP: 52
SALES: 950K **Privately Held**
SIC: 0241 Dairy farms

(G-12232)
SOUTHWEST DAIRY QUALITY SVC
200 E Hwy 50 (67878-7068)
P.O. Box 1026 (67878-1026)
PHONE..................................620 384-6953
William Kissell, *President*
EMP: 12
SALES (est): 992.9K **Privately Held**
SIC: 5143 Dairy products, except dried or canned

(G-12233)
SOUTHWEST PLAINS DAIRY LLC
12701 Sw Cr 32 (67878-7816)
P.O. Box 831 (67878-0831)
PHONE..................................620 384-6813
Carla Geven,
Richard Geven,
EMP: 47
SALES (est): 25MM **Privately Held**
SIC: 0241 Dairy farms

(G-12234)
SYRACUSE DAIRY II LLC
Also Called: West Side Dairy
751 S Suuny Rd 36 (67878)
PHONE..................................620 492-2525
Dan Senestraro, *Partner*
A James Streelman, *Partner*
Jay Houtsma, *General Mgr*
EMP: 25
SQ FT: 12,000
SALES (est): 2.1MM **Privately Held**
SIC: 0241 Dairy farms

(G-12235)
TIME LINE DAIRY LLC
2000 E Rd 2 (67878)
PHONE..................................620 492-3232
Jay Houtsna, *Partner*
Dan Senestraro, *Partner*
James Streelman, *Partner*
EMP: 25
SALES (est): 1.1MM **Privately Held**
SIC: 0241 Milk production

(G-12236)
VALLEY STATE BANK (HQ)
110 W Ave B (67878)
P.O. Box 1277 (67878-1277)
PHONE..................................620 384-7451
Timothy C Kohart, *President*
Steve J Schell, *Senior VP*
Tasha Dupree, *Vice Pres*
Jim Randall, *Vice Pres*
Brent Parks, *Bd of Directors*
EMP: 12 **EST:** 1905
SALES: 7.8MM **Privately Held**
SIC: 6022 State commercial banks

Talmage
Dickinson County

(G-12237)
DICKINSON COUNTY RUR WTR DST 1
2979 Main St (67482-9700)
P.O. Box 777 (67482-0777)
PHONE..................................785 388-2290
Austin Britt, *Ch of Bd*
John Daudel, *Vice Pres*
Dennis Marston, *Admin Sec*
EMP: 10
SQ FT: 15,000
SALES (est): 397.1K **Privately Held**
SIC: 4941 Water supply

Tecumseh
Shawnee County

(G-12238)
CLAY JARS CHILDRENS CENTER INC
2930 Se Tecumseh Rd (66542-9754)
PHONE..................................785 379-9098
Michelle Garlock, *Director*
Michelle Steflik, *Executive Asst*
EMP: 12
SALES: 339.5K **Privately Held**
SIC: 8351 Preschool center

(G-12239)
FLINTHILLS CONSTRUCTION INC
5221 Se Stanley Rd (66542-9533)
PHONE..................................785 379-5499
Dave Barkes, *President*
EMP: 10
SQ FT: 2,400
SALES (est): 1.8MM **Privately Held**
SIC: 1542 Commercial & office buildings, renovation & repair

(G-12240)
PREFERRED LAWN SERVICE
4000 Se Shawnee Hts Rd (66542-9534)
P.O. Box 3909, Lawrence (66046-0909)
PHONE..................................785 379-8873
Chad Price, *Owner*
Scott Aisner, *General Mgr*
EMP: 10
SALES (est): 370.5K **Privately Held**
SIC: 0782 Lawn services

(G-12241)
SHAMBURG UNLIMITED LLC
3244 Se Stanley Rd (66542-9631)
PHONE..................................785 379-0760
John Shamburg,
Margi Shamburg,
EMP: 10
SALES (est): 1.4MM **Privately Held**
SIC: 1542 Commercial & office buildings, renovation & repair

(G-12242)
SHAWNEE HTS BOOSTER CLB PTO
4201 Se Shawnee Hts Rd (66542-9535)
PHONE..................................785 379-5880
Diana Zimmerman, *Principal*
EMP: 15
SALES (est): 165K **Privately Held**
SIC: 8641 Parent-teachers' association

(G-12243)
SHAWNEE HTS UNTD METHDST CH
Also Called: Heights of Learning Preschool
6020 Se 44th St (66542-9741)
PHONE..................................785 379-5492
Sandy Vogel, *Pastor*
Judy O'Neil, *Pastor*
EMP: 25
SALES (est): 643.4K **Privately Held**
WEB: www.heightsoflearning.kscoxmail.com
SIC: 8351 8661 Preschool center; religious organizations

Tescott
Ottawa County

(G-12244)
BANK OF TESCOTT (PA)
104 S Main St (67484-4701)
P.O. Box 195 (67484-0195)
PHONE..................................785 283-4217
Larry Fief, *President*
Curt Marshall, *Vice Pres*
EMP: 15 **EST:** 1887
SALES: 18.7MM **Privately Held**
SIC: 6022 State trust companies accepting deposits, commercial

(G-12245)
INTERNATIONAL ASSOCIATION OF
Also Called: Tescott Lions CLB 1055007136
148 N 90th Rd (67484-9124)
PHONE..................................785 283-4746
Harold Horting, *Admin Sec*
EMP: 10
SALES (corp-wide): 63.7MM **Privately Held**
WEB: www.iaopc.com
SIC: 8641 Civic associations
PA: The International Association Of Lions Clubs Incorporated
300 W 22nd St
Oak Brook IL 60523
630 571-5466

Thayer
Neosho County

(G-12246)
WELL REFINED DRILLING CO INC
4270 Gray Rd (66776-5049)
PHONE..................................620 763-2619
Jeff Kephart, *President*
Charlotte Kephart, *Admin Sec*
EMP: 14
SALES: 2MM **Privately Held**
SIC: 1381 Drilling oil & gas wells

Tipton
Mitchell County

(G-12247)
BLUE HL GAMEBIRDS & HTCHY LLC
517 Grasshopper (67485-1010)
P.O. Box 174 (67485-0174)
PHONE..................................785 373-4965
Don Montgomery,
EMP: 10 **EST:** 2009
SALES: 75K **Privately Held**
SIC: 0971 Game propagation

(G-12248)
GREAT PLAINS MANUFACTURING INC
607 Main (67485-9363)
P.O. Box 147 (67485-0147)
PHONE..................................785 373-4145
Kent Hake, *General Mgr*
Mark Eilert, *Engineer*
EMP: 40 **Privately Held**
WEB: www.greatplainsmfg.com
SIC: 3523 Farm machinery & equipment
HQ: Great Plains Manufacturing Incorporated
1525 E North St
Salina KS 67401
785 823-3276

(G-12249)
RINGNECK RANCH INCORPORATED
655 Solomon Ln (67485-9348)
PHONE..................................785 373-4835
Keith Houghton, *President*
Debra Houghton, *Treasurer*
EMP: 50
SQ FT: 15,000
SALES (est): 1.4MM **Privately Held**
WEB: www.ringneckranch.net
SIC: 0291 General farms, primarily animals

(G-12250)
TREB CONSTRUCTION INC
609 Iowa (67485-9374)
P.O. Box 98 (67485-0098)
PHONE..................................785 373-4935
Robert M Ellenz, *President*
Edward Adam, *Vice Pres*
Debbie McKain, *Admin Sec*
EMP: 10
SQ FT: 15,000
SALES: 1.3MM **Privately Held**
SIC: 1541 1542 Steel building construction; farm building construction

Tonganoxie
Leavenworth County

(G-12251)
ALONGE STONE MASONRY
23604 Cantrell Rd (66086-3315)
PHONE..................................785 832-1438
Joseph A Alonge, *President*
EMP: 10
SALES: 860K **Privately Held**
SIC: 1741 Masonry & other stonework

(G-12252)
BARTEC CONSTRUCTION LLC
16834 182nd St (66086-5134)
PHONE..................................913 208-0015
Tony Simanowitz,
EMP: 23
SALES (est): 1.6MM **Privately Held**
SIC: 1521 Single-family housing construction

(G-12253)
BEVERLY ENTERPRISES-KANSAS LLC
1010 East St (66086-9557)
PHONE..................................620 273-6369
Lisa Bowlin, *Principal*
EMP: 52
SALES (corp-wide): 393.8MM **Privately Held**
SIC: 8051 Convalescent home with continuous nursing care
HQ: Beverly Enterprises-Kansas, Llc
1 1000 Beverly Way
Fort Smith AR 72919
479 201-2000

(G-12254)
BIOMEDICAL DEVICES OF KS LLC
1205 E Highway 24-40 (66086-9507)
P.O. Box 971 (66086-0971)
PHONE..................................913 845-3851
William Graveman, *Principal*
EMP: 9 **EST:** 2007
SALES (est): 1MM **Privately Held**
SIC: 3841 Surgical & medical instruments

(G-12255)
CABINET SHOPOF BASEHOR INC
Also Called: Cabinet Shop of Basehor
21522 203rd St (66086-4203)
P.O. Box 451, Basehor (66007-0451)
PHONE..................................913 845-2182
Donald Dyster, *President*
Joanne Lindsley, *President*
Ken Lindsley, *President*
EMP: 20
SQ FT: 5,000
SALES (est): 1.8MM **Privately Held**
SIC: 2434 2514 2541 1751 Wood kitchen cabinets; kitchen cabinets: metal; table or counter tops, plastic laminated; cabinet & finish carpentry; wood television & radio cabinets

(G-12256)
COMMUNITY NATIONAL BANK
Also Called: Community National Mortgage Co
231 N Main St (66086-9658)
P.O. Box 986 (66086-0986)
PHONE..................................913 369-0100
Jeff Fisher, *COO*
Bryan Skitt, *Chief Mktg Ofcr*
Jamie Smith, *Manager*
EMP: 12
SALES (corp-wide): 21.4MM **Privately Held**
WEB: www.communitynationalbank.net
SIC: 6021 National commercial banks
PA: Community National Bank
210 Main St
Seneca KS 66538
785 336-6143

(G-12257)
CONSOLIDATED MAILING CORP (PA)
16740 259th St (66086-3238)
PHONE..................................913 262-4400
Lewis S Buz Prosser, *President*
Susan Orr Prosser, *Exec VP*
Carol Magness, *Treasurer*
Carol Lee Prosser, *Admin Sec*
EMP: 37
SQ FT: 17,000
SALES (est): 5.4MM **Privately Held**
WEB: www.consolidatedmailing.com
SIC: 7331 Mailing service; mailing list brokers

(G-12258)
CONTINENTAL EQUIPMENT COMPANY (PA)
315 N Village St (66086-5361)
P.O. Box 488 (66086-0488)
PHONE..................................913 845-2148
James E Bell, *President*
EMP: 12
SQ FT: 12,000
SALES (est): 2.5MM **Privately Held**
SIC: 5049 5999 Laboratory equipment, except medical or dental; medical apparatus & supplies

(G-12259)
CROOKHAM CONSTRUCTION LLC
325 E Highway 24-40 (66086-9506)
P.O. Box 339 (66086-0339)
PHONE..................................913 369-3341
Katy Crookham,
EMP: 30 **EST:** 2007
SQ FT: 6,500
SALES: 3.3MM **Privately Held**
SIC: 1542 Commercial & office building, new construction

(G-12260)
ENERGY AND ENVMTL SYSTEMS INC
Also Called: Magnatec Engineer
1204 Tonganoxie Rd (66086-4101)
PHONE..................................913 845-3553
William F Graveman, *President*
Kathleen M Graveman, *Treasurer*
Donald F Graveman, *Director*
Agnes M Graveman, *Admin Sec*
EMP: 20
SALES (est): 1.4MM **Privately Held**
SIC: 1791 Structural steel erection

(G-12261)
FIRST STATE BANK & TRUST (HQ)
Also Called: 1ST STATE BANK INTEREST
400 S Bury St (66086-9607)
P.O. Box 219 (66086-0219)
PHONE..................................913 845-2500
Bill E New, *Ch of Bd*
William D Grant Jr, *President*
Neil Rutter, *Exec VP*
Jilinda White, *Exec VP*
Brent Lathrom, *Senior VP*
EMP: 52 **EST:** 1987
SQ FT: 8,000
SALES: 14.7MM **Privately Held**
WEB: www.firststateks.com
SIC: 6022 State trust companies accepting deposits, commercial

(G-12262)
GENESIS SCHOOL INC
Also Called: Genesis Children Pre-School
204 E Washington St (66086-9663)
P.O. Box 994 (66086-0994)
PHONE..................................913 845-9498
Mendy Lietzen, *Director*
EMP: 20
SALES (est): 566.3K **Privately Held**
SIC: 8351 8211 Preschool center; elementary & secondary schools

(G-12263)
HOBBY MONSTER CUSTOMS LLC
Also Called: HMC Performance Coatings
1625 Tonganoxie Rd Ste B (66086-4185)
PHONE..................................913 417-7088
Shawn Bristol,
EMP: 8
SQ FT: 8,400
SALES: 175K **Privately Held**
SIC: 3479 Coating of metals & formed products; painting, coating & hot dipping

(G-12264)
KANSAS HEAVY CONSTRUCTION LLC
19425 State Ave (66086-5239)
P.O. Box 860603, Shawnee Mission (66286-0603)
PHONE..................................913 845-2121
Matt Gripka, *Project Mgr*
Alicia Segura, *Office Admin*
Tom Giefer,
Chris Gratton,
EMP: 23
SQ FT: 6,000
SALES (est): 4.5MM **Privately Held**
SIC: 1521 Single-family housing construction

(G-12265)
MAGNATECH ENGINEERING INC
1204 Tonganoxie Rd (66086-4101)
P.O. Box 971 (66086-0971)
PHONE..................................913 845-3553
William E Graveman, *President*
Don Graveman, *Vice Pres*
Kathleen M Graveman, *Treasurer*
Suewanna Lucero, *Admin Sec*
EMP: 9
SQ FT: 8,600
SALES (est): 1.9MM **Privately Held**
SIC: 3535 5084 Conveyors & conveying equipment; industrial machinery & equipment

(G-12266)
MEADOWS CONST CO INC
1014 Front St (66086-9706)
P.O. Box 500 (66086-0500)
PHONE..................................913 369-3335
Fax: 913 369-1106
EMP: 25
SQ FT: 2,000
SALES (est): 2.6MM **Privately Held**
SIC: 1623 1771 1794 Water/Sewer/Utility Cnst Concrete Contractor Excavation Contractor

(G-12267)
MEITLER CONSULTING INC
16979 Chieftain Rd (66086-3352)
P.O. Box 444 (66086-0444)
PHONE..................................913 422-9339
Brian S Meitler, *President*
EMP: 11
SALES (est): 1.2MM **Privately Held**
SIC: 8748 Environmental consultant

(G-12268)
MID STAR LAB INC (PA)
1701 Commerce Rd (66086-5369)
PHONE..................................913 369-8734
Kari Wagner, *President*
Ron Wagner, *Vice Pres*
EMP: 12
SALES (est): 1.8MM **Privately Held**
SIC: 8071 Medical laboratories

(G-12269)
SAFELINK SECURITY SYSTEMS INC
103 W 4th St (66086-9770)
PHONE..................................913 338-3888
Gary Graham, *President*
Kelly Smith, *Vice Pres*
Joseph Kaub, *Wholesale*
James Graham, *Admin Sec*
EMP: 22
SQ FT: 2,400
SALES (est): 1.2MM **Privately Held**
WEB: www.safelinksecurity.com
SIC: 7382 Burglar alarm maintenance & monitoring

(G-12270)
TEC FAB PARTS INC
1015 E 1st St (66086-8925)
PHONE..................................913 369-0882
Georgiana L Banks, *President*
EMP: 10
SALES (est): 1.8MM **Privately Held**
SIC: 3441 Fabricated structural metal

(G-12271)
THORNES TREE SERVICE INC
15170 234th St (66086-3322)
PHONE..................................913 845-2387
Delores J Thorne, *President*
EMP: 16
SQ FT: 8,000
SALES (est): 1.3MM **Privately Held**
SIC: 0783 Tree trimming services for public utility lines

(G-12272)
VINTAGE PARK AT TONGANOXIE LLC
120 W 8th St (66086-8810)
PHONE..................................913 845-2204
Julie Hansan, *Administration*
EMP: 20
SALES (est): 515.3K **Privately Held**
SIC: 8082 Home health care services

(G-12273)
WES MATERIAL HANDLING INC (PA)
23659 Parallel Rd (66086-3146)
PHONE..................................913 369-9375
Valerie Francis, *President*
Dean Francis, *Vice Pres*
EMP: 10
SQ FT: 1,300
SALES (est): 1.3MM **Privately Held**
SIC: 5084 7699 Industrial machinery & equipment; industrial equipment services

Topeka
Shawnee County

(G-12274)
190TH MEDICAL GROUP
5920 Se Coyote Dr (66619-1429)
PHONE..................................785 861-4663
Msgt John Willey, *Principal*
EMP: 99
SALES (est): 5.2MM **Privately Held**
SIC: 8733 Noncommercial research organizations

(G-12275)
94 5 COUNTRY INC
1210 Sw Executive Dr (66615-3850)
P.O. Box 1818 (66601-1818)
PHONE..................................785 272-3456
William Morris, *President*
Larry Riggians, *General Mgr*
Jim Daniels, *Engineer*
EMP: 65
SALES (est): 1.3MM **Privately Held**
SIC: 4832 8661 Radio broadcasting stations; religious organizations

(G-12276)
A & A AUTO SALVAGE
Also Called: A & A Auto and Truck Parts
1440 Se Jefferson St (66607-1242)
PHONE..................................785 286-2728
Curt Lewis, *Owner*
EMP: 11
SQ FT: 10,000
SALES (est): 970K **Privately Held**
SIC: 5015 5531 Automotive parts & supplies, used; automotive parts

(G-12277)
A & A MEDICAL TRNSP INC
Also Called: A & A Services
135 Nw Harrison St (66603-3013)
PHONE..................................785 233-8212
Richard Meier, *President*
Molly Meier, *Administration*
EMP: 10
SQ FT: 3,000
SALES (est): 520.1K **Privately Held**
SIC: 4119 Local passenger transportation

GEOGRAPHIC

(G-12278)
A CARING DOCTOR MINNESOTA PA
Also Called: Banfield Pet Hospital 244
2020 Sw Westport Dr (66604-3735)
PHONE..................................785 272-1541
EMP: 20
SALES (corp-wide): 37.6B **Privately Held**
SIC: 0742 Animal hospital services, pets & other animal specialties
HQ: A Caring Doctor Minnesota Pa
8000 Ne Tillamook St
Portland OR 97213
503 922-5000

(G-12279)
A TOTAL IMAGE
4005 Sw 21st St (66604-3413)
PHONE..................................785 272-2855
Delmar Tucking, *Owner*
EMP: 11
SQ FT: 3,000
SALES (est): 285.8K **Privately Held**
SIC: 7231 7299 Unisex hair salons; tanning salon

(G-12280)
A&ATRUCK RENTAL/3 MEN WITH
200 Sw Jackson St Ste B (66603-3305)
PHONE..................................785 236-0003
Curt Cochran, *Principal*
Kent Lindemuth,
EMP: 16
SALES: 650K **Privately Held**
SIC: 4212 Moving services

(G-12281)
AAA ALLIED GROUP INC
1223 Sw Wanamaker Rd (66604-3864)
PHONE..................................785 233-0222
Katie Lord, *Branch Mgr*
EMP: 13
SALES (corp-wide): 128.2MM **Privately Held**
SIC: 8699 4724 Automobile owners' association; travel agencies
PA: Aaa Allied Group, Inc.
15 W Central Pkwy
Cincinnati OH 45202
513 762-3301

(G-12282)
ABC LEASING CO INC
401 Sw 30th St (66611-2204)
P.O. Box 2459 (66601-2459)
PHONE..................................785 267-4555
Mel Woods, *President*
Marshall Hanson, *Corp Secy*
EMP: 50
SQ FT: 10,500
SALES (est): 2.2MM
SALES (corp-wide): 57.9MM **Privately Held**
SIC: 7359 Office machine rental, except computers
PA: Century Business Technologies, Inc
401 Sw 30th St
Topeka KS 66611
785 267-4555

(G-12283)
ACCU-FAB INC
235 Se 53rd St (66609-1006)
PHONE..................................785 862-0100
Calvin Lutz, *President*
Kathy Lutz, *Corp Secy*
Barry Metcalf, *Data Proc Staff*
EMP: 12
SQ FT: 250,000
SALES (est): 2.8MM **Privately Held**
WEB: www.accufab-topeka.com
SIC: 3444 Sheet metal specialties, not stamped

(G-12284)
ACE ELECTRIC-JONES COMPANY INC
223 Se 53rd St (66609-1006)
PHONE..................................785 862-8200
Steven Jones, *President*
EMP: 21
SQ FT: 9,000
SALES (est): 3.4MM **Privately Held**
SIC: 1731 General electrical contractor

(G-12285)
ACTIVE PRIME TIMERS INC
2219 Sw Fairlawn Rd Apt 2 (66614-1514)
PHONE..................................785 272-0237
Marianne Hinen, *President*
Edith Hund, *President*
Sue Smith, *Vice Pres*
Evelyn Erhsam, *Treasurer*
Robert May, *Director*
EMP: 12
SALES (est): 422K **Privately Held**
SIC: 6513 8699 Retirement hotel operation; membership organizations

(G-12286)
ADAPA INCORPORATED
Also Called: Shop Carts
5525 Sw Randolph Ave (66609-1100)
PHONE..................................785 862-2060
K Scott Halsey, *President*
Marilyn Halsey, *Corp Secy*
Robin Ortiz, *Office Mgr*
EMP: 12 **EST:** 1964
SQ FT: 40,000
SALES (est): 3.6MM **Privately Held**
WEB: www.adapausa.com
SIC: 3535 3537 3444 Conveyors & conveying equipment; industrial trucks & tractors; sheet metalwork

(G-12287)
ADDICTION AND PREVENTION SVCS
915 Sw Harrison St Fl 9 (66612-1505)
PHONE..................................785 296-6807
David Dickinson, *Director*
Stacy Chamberlain, *Administration*
EMP: 10
SALES (est): 710K **Privately Held**
SIC: 7363 Medical help service

(G-12288)
ADJUTANT GENERALS DEPT KANS
Also Called: Museum of Kansas Nat Guard
125 Se Airport Dr (66619-1373)
PHONE..................................785 862-1020
Roger Wilson, *President*
EMP: 12 **Privately Held**
SIC: 8412 9711 Museum; National Guard;
HQ: Adjutant General's Department, Kansas
2800 Sw Topeka Blvd
Topeka KS 66611
785 274-1000

(G-12289)
ADMINISTRATION KANSAS DEPT
Division of Printing
201 Nw Macvicar Ave (66606-2428)
PHONE..................................785 296-3631
Sheryl Boxton, *Director*
EMP: 51 **Privately Held**
SIC: 2759 9111 2791 2789 Commercial printing; executive offices; ; typesetting; bookbinding & related work; commercial printing, lithographic
HQ: Kansas Department Of Administration
1000 Sw Jackson St # 500
Topeka KS 66612

(G-12290)
ADMINISTRATION KANSAS DEPT
Central Duplicating
201 Nw Macvicar Ave (66606-2428)
PHONE..................................785 296-3001
EMP: 121 **Privately Held**
SIC: 7334 9111 Photocopying Services Lithographic Commercial Printing Executive Office
HQ: Kansas Department Of Administration
1000 Sw Jackson St # 500
Topeka KS 66612
785 296-3011

(G-12291)
ADMINISTRATION KANSAS DEPT
Also Called: Office of Long-Term Care
900 Sw Jackson St Rm 1041 (66612-1220)
PHONE..................................785 296-3017
Belinda Vierthaler, *Director*
EMP: 11 **Privately Held**
SIC: 8111 9431 Legal services; administration of public health programs;
HQ: Kansas Department Of Administration
1000 Sw Jackson St # 500
Topeka KS 66612

(G-12292)
ADVANCE BUSINESS SUPPLY
631 Nw Tyler Ct Ste 303 (66608-1794)
P.O. Box 750413 (66675-0413)
PHONE..................................785 440-7826
Mark Miamble, *Partner*
Jerry Dyche, *Partner*
Susan Maendele, *Partner*
EMP: 5
SALES: 175K **Privately Held**
SIC: 3953 2499 Postmark stamps, hand: rubber or metal; engraved wood products

(G-12293)
ADVANCE INSURANCE COMPANY KANS (HQ)
1133 Sw Topeka Blvd (66629-0001)
PHONE..................................785 273-9804
Michael Mattox, *President*
Darrald Levan, *Vice Pres*
Steve Morris, *Finance Mgr*
Lori Christy, *CTO*
EMP: 19
SQ FT: 10,000
SALES: 10.5MM
SALES (corp-wide): 636.3MM **Privately Held**
WEB: www.advanceinsurance.com
SIC: 6411 Insurance agents, brokers & service
PA: Blue Cross And Blue Shield Of Kansas, Inc.
1133 Sw Topeka Blvd
Topeka KS 66629
785 291-7000

(G-12294)
ADVANCE REHABILITATION LLC
6001 Sw 6th Ave Ste 230 (66615-1004)
PHONE..................................785 232-9805
Tracey Hatcher,
EMP: 11
SQ FT: 600
SALES (est): 477.3K **Privately Held**
SIC: 8049 Physical therapist

(G-12295)
ADVANCED ENVIRONMENTAL SVCS
3825 Sw Dukeries Rd (66610-1506)
PHONE..................................785 231-9324
Hali Dahlby, *President*
Roger Behlby, *Vice Pres*
EMP: 11
SALES: 300K **Privately Held**
SIC: 8711 Engineering services

(G-12296)
ADVANTAGE BUILDING SYSTEMS LLC
2027 Nw Brickyard Rd (66618-2812)
PHONE..................................785 233-1393
EMP: 12
SQ FT: 12,500
SALES (est): 71.1K **Privately Held**
SIC: 3441 Mfg Steel Buildings

(G-12297)
ADVANTAGE METALS RECYCLING LLC
1628 Nw Gordon St (66608-1606)
PHONE..................................785 232-5152
William Massey, *President*
EMP: 11
SALES (corp-wide): 25B **Publicly Held**
SIC: 5093 Ferrous metal scrap & waste; metal scrap & waste materials
HQ: Advantage Metals Recycling Llc
510 Walnut St Ste 300
Kansas City MO 64106
816 861-2700

(G-12298)
ADVANTAGED HOME CARE
1940 Sw Gage Blvd Ste C (66604-3390)
PHONE..................................785 267-4433
Renea Bulmer, *President*
EMP: 45
SALES (est): 778.5K **Privately Held**
SIC: 8082 Visiting nurse service

(G-12299)
ADVISORS TECH LLC
6001 Sw 6th Ave Ste 101 (66615-1004)
PHONE..................................844 671-6071
David J Callanan, *Mng Member*
EMP: 14
SALES: 500K **Privately Held**
SIC: 7379 Computer related consulting services

(G-12300)
AEGIS PROCESSING SOLUTIONS INC
240 Se Madison St (66607-1147)
P.O. Box 8538 (66608-0538)
PHONE..................................785 232-0061
David Ohse, *CEO*
Thomas Bender, *President*
Kenneth Romine, *COO*
Paul Spurgeon, *Prdtn Mgr*
EMP: 90
SQ FT: 22,000
SALES: 3.6MM
SALES (corp-wide): 34.5MM **Privately Held**
WEB: www.swcaging.com
SIC: 7374 7331 Data processing & preparation; mailing service
PA: Southwest Holding Corporation
4000 Se Adams St
Topeka KS 66609
785 233-5662

(G-12301)
AGENCY SERVICES CORP KANSAS
Also Called: Nationwide
815 Sw Topeka Blvd Ste 2b (66612-1672)
PHONE..................................785 232-0561
Dan Deener, *President*
Larry McGill, *Exec VP*
EMP: 12
SALES (est): 1MM **Privately Held**
SIC: 6411 Insurance agents, brokers & service

(G-12302)
AHP H6 TOPEKA
Also Called: Hyatt Place
6021 Sw 6th Ave (66615-1006)
PHONE..................................785 273-0066
EMP: 40
SALES (est): 3.1MM **Privately Held**
SIC: 7011 Hotels & motels

(G-12303)
ALDERSON ALDERSON WEILER CO
2101 Sw 21st St (66604-3174)
PHONE..................................785 232-0753
Gayle Alejos, *CFO*
W R Alderson Jr,
Mark A Burghart,
Darrin M Conklin,
Dan W Crow,
EMP: 25
SALES (est): 2.3MM **Privately Held**
WEB: www.aldersonlaw.com
SIC: 8111 General practice law office

(G-12304)
ALERT ENTERPRISES INC
Also Called: ServiceMaster AAA
4900 Sw Topeka Blvd Ste 1 (66609-1123)
PHONE..................................785 862-9800
Tim Howell, *President*
EMP: 12
SQ FT: 2,500
SALES (est): 472K **Privately Held**
WEB: www.servicemasteraaa.com
SIC: 7349 Building maintenance services

(G-12305)
ALL POINT TRANSPORTATION LLC
6342 Sw 21st St Ste 100 (66615-1156)
PHONE..................................785 273-4730
Christopher Hane, *Administration*
EMP: 18 **EST:** 2012
SALES (est): 395.9K **Privately Held**
SIC: 4151 School buses

(G-12306)
ALL-STEEL BUILDING SYSTEMS LLC
1300 Nw Us Highway 24 (66608-2026)
P.O. Box 4921 (66604-0921)
PHONE....................................785 271-5559
Jeanne M Hanks, *Principal*
Jeanne Hanks, *Mng Member*
Kirk Hanks,
EMP: 12
SQ FT: 6,000
SALES (est): 1.5MM **Privately Held**
SIC: 1541 Steel building construction

(G-12307)
ALLIANCE BANK (HQ)
3001 Sw Wanamaker Rd (66614-4430)
PHONE....................................785 271-1800
Jeff Berkley, *President*
Mark Ault, *Exec VP*
Steve Herron, *Vice Pres*
EMP: 20
SQ FT: 4,800
SALES: 4.9MM **Privately Held**
SIC: 6022 State trust companies accepting deposits, commercial

(G-12308)
ALLSIGNS LLC
414 Se Jefferson St (66607-1134)
PHONE....................................785 232-5512
Kent A Brennan, *Marketing Staff*
Greg Brennan, *Mng Member*
Kent Brennan,
Bob Hannon,
EMP: 5
SALES (est): 400K **Privately Held**
SIC: 3993 7389 Signs & advertising specialties; lettering & sign painting services

(G-12309)
ALLTECH COMMUNICATIONS INC
430 W 1st Ave (66603-3002)
PHONE....................................785 267-0316
Michael Rothfuss, *President*
Scott Wheat, *Vice Pres*
Mark Taylor, *Manager*
Angela Rothfuss, *Director*
EMP: 16
SALES (est): 2MM **Privately Held**
SIC: 4899 Data communication services

(G-12310)
ALPHA MEDIA LLC
Also Called: Ktpk-FM
1210 Sw Executive Dr (66615-3850)
PHONE....................................785 272-3456
William Morris, *Principal*
Roy Baum, *Chief Engr*
Cissy Long, *Sales Staff*
EMP: 18 **Privately Held**
SIC: 4832 Radio broadcasting stations
PA: Alpha Media Llc
1211 Sw 5th Ave Ste 600
Portland OR 97204

(G-12311)
ALTMAR INC
Also Called: Altmar Inc General Contractors
3860 Nw 16th St (66618-2846)
PHONE....................................785 233-0053
John G Ostermann, *President*
Robert Johnson, *Treasurer*
EMP: 20
SQ FT: 5,000
SALES (est): 6.1MM **Privately Held**
WEB: www.altmar.com
SIC: 1542 Commercial & office building, new construction; commercial & office buildings, renovation & repair; school building construction; specialized public building contractors

(G-12312)
AMEC FSTER WHELER E C SVCS INC
100 Se 9th St Ste 400 (66612-1213)
PHONE....................................785 272-6830
Bradley Johnson, *Office Mgr*
EMP: 50
SALES (corp-wide): 10B **Privately Held**
SIC: 8711 Engineering services
HQ: Amec Foster Wheeler E&C Services, Inc.
1979 Lkeside Pkwy Ste 400
Tucker GA 30084

(G-12313)
AMERICAN BLDRS CONTRS SUP INC
Also Called: ABC Supply 326
2031 Nw Us Highway 24 (66618-1445)
PHONE....................................785 354-7398
Darren Brennan, *Branch Mgr*
EMP: 17
SALES (corp-wide): 3.5B **Privately Held**
SIC: 5033 5031 Roofing & siding materials; windows
HQ: American Builders & Contractors Supply Co., Inc.
1 Abc Pkwy
Beloit WI 53511
608 362-7777

(G-12314)
AMERICAN BOTTLING COMPANY
3526 Se 21st St (66607-2371)
PHONE....................................785 233-7471
Michael Ingmire, *Sales Staff*
EMP: 30 **Publicly Held**
WEB: www.cs-americas.com
SIC: 2086 Bottled & canned soft drinks
HQ: The American Bottling Company
5301 Legacy Dr
Plano TX 75024

(G-12315)
AMERICAN FEDERATION
Also Called: Kansas AFL
2131 Sw 36th St (66611-2553)
PHONE....................................785 267-0100
Mark Love, *President*
EMP: 18
SALES (corp-wide): 154.8MM **Privately Held**
SIC: 8631 Labor unions & similar labor organizations
PA: American Federation Of Labor & Congress Of Industrial Organzation
815 16th St Nw
Washington DC 20006
202 637-5000

(G-12316)
AMERICAN FIDELITY ASSURANCE CO
3100 Sw Huntoon St # 102 (66604-6154)
PHONE....................................785 232-8100
Joe Patterson, *Principal*
Rod Spangler, *Manager*
EMP: 99 **Privately Held**
SIC: 6411 Insurance agents
HQ: American Fidelity Assurance Company
9000 Cameron Pkwy
Oklahoma City OK 73114
405 523-2000

(G-12317)
AMERICAN HEART ASSOCIATION KA (PA)
5375 Sw 7th St Ste 300 (66606-2552)
PHONE....................................785 272-7056
Jeff Willett, *Senior VP*
Glenn Horn, *Exec Dir*
EMP: 37
SQ FT: 18,000
SALES (est): 16.9MM **Privately Held**
SIC: 8621 Professional membership organizations

(G-12318)
AMERICAN HOME LIFE INSUR CO
400 S Kansas Ave Ste 100 (66603-3413)
P.O. Box 1497 (66601-1497)
PHONE....................................785 235-6276
Steve Lobell, *President*
Les Diehl, *Vice Pres*
Mike Donnelly, *Vice Pres*
Molly McEntee, *Vice Pres*
Roger Prather, *Vice Pres*
EMP: 30
SQ FT: 36,000
SALES (est): 12.9MM **Privately Held**
SIC: 6411 Insurance agents, brokers & service

(G-12319)
AMERICAN LEGION POST 400
3029 Nw Us Highway 24 (66618-2710)
PHONE....................................785 296-9400
John Feretti, *Manager*
EMP: 10
SALES (est): 310K **Privately Held**
SIC: 8641 Veterans' organization

(G-12320)
AMERICAN PHOENIX INC
7215 Sw Topeka Blvd (66619-1456)
P.O. Box 19294 (66619-0294)
PHONE....................................785 862-7722
EMP: 30 **Privately Held**
SIC: 3069 2819 Custom compounding of rubber materials; industrial inorganic chemicals
PA: American Phoenix, Inc.
5500 Wayzata Blvd # 1010
Golden Valley MN 55416

(G-12321)
AMERICAN PRE SORT INC
540 Nw Tyler Ct Ste 101 (66608-1695)
PHONE....................................785 232-2633
Pamela Wold, *President*
Ila Jolly, *Admin Sec*
EMP: 12
SQ FT: 6,000
SALES (est): 1.3MM **Privately Held**
SIC: 7389 Presorted mail service; labeling bottles, cans, cartons, etc.

(G-12322)
AMERICAN SENIOR BENEFITS
Also Called: Bankers Life
3745 Sw Wanamaker Rd A (66610-1369)
PHONE....................................785 273-8200
Lawrence Martin, *General Mgr*
EMP: 35 **Privately Held**
SIC: 6411 Insurance agents, brokers & service
PA: American Senior Benefits
19208 Sw Missouri Rd
Welda KS 66091

(G-12323)
AMERICAN SENTRY SECURITY SYS
Also Called: AAA Night Watchman Service
120 Se 6th Ave Ste 265 (66603-3514)
P.O. Box 4104 (66604-0104)
PHONE....................................785 232-1525
Thomas B Deatrick, *President*
Thomas West Jones, *Vice Pres*
EMP: 42
SALES (est): 613K **Privately Held**
WEB: www.americansentrysecurity.com
SIC: 7381 5063 Guard services; alarm systems

(G-12324)
AMERIPRIDE SERVICES INC
Also Called: Ameripride Linen
400 Se 1st Ave (66607-1101)
P.O. Box 8157 (66608-0157)
PHONE....................................785 234-3475
Gary Newberry, *General Mgr*
Garry Newberry, *Manager*
EMP: 55 **Publicly Held**
WEB: www.ameripride.com
SIC: 7218 7213 Industrial launderers; uniform supply
HQ: Ameripride Services, Inc.
10801 Wayzata Blvd # 100
Minnetonka MN 55305
800 750-4628

(G-12325)
AMERITAS LIFE INSURANCE CORP
6540 Sw 10th Ave (66615-3811)
PHONE....................................785 273-3504
Don Schwart, *Manager*
EMP: 13
SALES (corp-wide): 2.3B **Privately Held**
WEB: www.uclfinancial.com
SIC: 6311 Mutual association life insurance
HQ: Ameritas Life Insurance Corp.
5900 O St
Lincoln NE 68510
402 467-1122

(G-12326)
ANDREWS ASPHALT & CNSTR INC
2327 Nw 39th St (66618-1618)
P.O. Box 750015 (66675-0015)
PHONE....................................785 232-0188
Jim D Andrews, *CEO*
Dean R Andrews, *President*
Debbie Huff, *Treasurer*
EMP: 9
SALES: 6MM **Privately Held**
WEB: www.andrewsasphalt.com
SIC: 1611 1771 3531 7389 Concrete construction: roads, highways, sidewalks, etc.; blacktop (asphalt) work; asphalt plant, including gravel-mix type;

(G-12327)
ANESTHESIA ASSOCIATES TOPEKA
823 Sw Mulvane St Ste 210 (66606-1679)
PHONE....................................785 235-3451
Song Dow Lee, *President*
Kelly A Liby, *Office Mgr*
EMP: 25
SALES (est): 2.4MM **Privately Held**
WEB: www.aaot.kscoxmail.com
SIC: 8011 Anesthesiologist

(G-12328)
ANGELS AT HOME CARE
112 Sw 6th Ave Ste 403 (66603-3845)
PHONE....................................785 271-4376
EMP: 11
SALES (est): 358.6K **Privately Held**
SIC: 8082 Visiting nurse service

(G-12329)
ANIMAL CARE CENTER OF TOP
2061 Se California Ave (66607-1443)
PHONE....................................785 232-2205
Kelly Hamerski, *Office Mgr*
EMP: 12 **EST:** 2009
SALES (est): 209K **Privately Held**
SIC: 8099 0752 0742 Blood related health services; animal boarding services; grooming services, pet & animal specialties; veterinarian, animal specialties

(G-12330)
ANIMAL CLINIC NORTH TOPEKA PA
625 Nw Us Highway 24 (66608-1905)
PHONE....................................785 357-5188
Tom Mah, *Owner*
Bryan Stancliffe, *Principal*
Allison Crow,
EMP: 10
SQ FT: 2,000
SALES (est): 677.2K **Privately Held**
SIC: 0742 Animal hospital services, pets & other animal specialties

(G-12331)
ANSWER TOPEKA INC
1717 Sw Gage Blvd (66604-3333)
PHONE....................................785 234-4444
Craig Woodbury, *President*
Kimberly Jones, *General Mgr*
Linda Woodbury, *Corp Secy*
EMP: 20
SQ FT: 1,500
SALES: 1.7MM **Privately Held**
WEB: www.answertopeka.com
SIC: 4812 7389 Cellular telephone services; paging services; telephone answering service

(G-12332)
ANTIOCH CHURCH
Also Called: ANTIOCH FAMILY LIFE CENTER
1921 Se Indiana Ave (66607-1425)
PHONE....................................785 232-1937
Tracy D Hicks, *Pastor*
EMP: 10
SALES: 72.1K **Privately Held**
WEB: www.antiochfamilylifecenter.com
SIC: 8661 8322 Community church; family service agency

GEOGRAPHIC

(G-12333)
APPINO BIGGS REPORTING SVC INC (PA)
5111 Sw 21st St (66604-4419)
PHONE..................................785 273-3063
Lora Appino Barnett, *President*
Sandy Biggs, *Owner*
EMP: 13
SALES: 1.9MM **Privately Held**
WEB: www.appinobiggs.com
SIC: 7338 Court reporting service

(G-12334)
APPLIED INDUSTRIAL TECH INC
Also Called: Applied Industrial Tech 0471
115 Nw Jackson St (66603-3309)
PHONE..................................785 232-5508
Jeff Watson, *Branch Mgr*
EMP: 10
SALES (corp-wide): 3.4B **Publicly Held**
WEB: www.appliedindustrial.com
SIC: 5085 Bearings; power transmission equipment & apparatus
PA: Applied Industrial Technologies, Inc.
1 Applied Plz
Cleveland OH 44115
216 426-4000

(G-12335)
APRIA HEALTHCARE LLC
6261 Sw 9th St Ste B (66615-3856)
PHONE..................................785 272-8411
Theresa Peterson, *Branch Mgr*
EMP: 12 **Privately Held**
WEB: www.apria.com
SIC: 7352 5999 Medical equipment rental; medical apparatus & supplies
HQ: Apria Healthcare Llc
26220 Enterprise Ct
Lake Forest CA 92630
949 639-2000

(G-12336)
ARCHDIOCESE OF MIAMI INC
Also Called: Catholic Charities
234 S Kansas Ave (66603-3617)
PHONE..................................785 233-6300
Cathy Lyon, *Director*
EMP: 20
SALES (corp-wide): 210.5MM **Privately Held**
WEB: www.svdp.edu
SIC: 8322 Family counseling services
PA: Archdiocese Of Miami, Inc
9401 Biscayne Blvd
Miami Shores FL 33138
305 757-6241

(G-12337)
ARCHITECTURAL CAST METALS INC
5600 Sw Topeka Blvd Ste D (66609-1011)
PHONE..................................785 221-6901
Michael Davis, *President*
EMP: 9
SALES (est): 864.1K **Privately Held**
SIC: 3446 Architectural metalwork

(G-12338)
ARLA JEAN GENSTLER MD PA (PA)
Also Called: Genstler Eye Center
3630 Sw Fairlawn Rd (66614-3966)
PHONE..................................785 273-8080
Arla Genstler, *President*
Anthony Barelli, *Med Doctor*
EMP: 21 **EST:** 1996
SQ FT: 15,000
SALES (est): 1.7MM **Privately Held**
SIC: 8011 Ophthalmologist

(G-12339)
ASH GROVE CEMENT COMPANY
1520 Sw 41st St (66609-1209)
PHONE..................................785 267-1996
Brady Pryor, *Branch Mgr*
EMP: 36
SALES (corp-wide): 29.7B **Privately Held**
WEB: www.ashgrove.com
SIC: 3241 Masonry cement
HQ: Ash Grove Cement Company
11011 Cody St Ste 300
Overland Park KS 66210
913 451-8900

(G-12340)
ASH GROVE RESOURCES LLC
5375 Sw 7th St Ste 400 (66606-2552)
PHONE..................................785 267-1996
Chris Williams, *Sales Staff*
Kyle Seevers, *Officer*
Brady Pryor,
EMP: 15
SALES (est): 860K **Privately Held**
SIC: 4789 7389 Freight car loading & unloading; advertising, promotional & trade show services

(G-12341)
ASSET LIFECYCLE LLC (PA)
7215 Sw Topeka Blvd # 1 (66619-1456)
P.O. Box 19286 (66619-0286)
PHONE..................................785 861-3100
Shawn Vanfossen, *COO*
Donnie Hanson, *Sales Mgr*
Beverly Drew, *Mng Member*
Martha Harding, *Manager*
Rick Markley, *Manager*
▼ **EMP:** 16
SQ FT: 110,000
SALES (est): 15.6MM **Privately Held**
WEB: www.assetlc.com
SIC: 5065 4953 5084 2448 Electronic parts & equipment; recycling, waste materials; hazardous waste collection & disposal; industrial machinery & equipment; pallets, wood; wood containers

(G-12342)
ASSISTED TRANSPORTATION SVCS (PA)
6342 Sw 21st St Ste 100 (66615-1156)
PHONE..................................785 291-2900
Gary March, *President*
EMP: 10
SALES (est): 1.3MM **Privately Held**
SIC: 8082 Home health care services

(G-12343)
ASSOCIATED COMMERCIAL BRKS CO (PA)
1111 Sw Gage Blvd Ste 100 (66604-2283)
PHONE..................................785 228-9494
Thomas R Petersen, *Owner*
Steve Ballou, *Broker*
Richard Laird, *Broker*
EMP: 20
SQ FT: 2,100
SALES (est): 1.2MM **Privately Held**
WEB: www.acbcomp.com
SIC: 6531 Real estate brokers & agents

(G-12344)
ASSOCIATED MANAGEMENT SERVICES
1111 Sw Gage Blvd Ste 100 (66604-2283)
PHONE..................................785 228-9494
Thomas Peterson, *President*
James Creviston, *Assistant VP*
Steven Sofro, *Vice Pres*
EMP: 12
SQ FT: 2,100
SALES (est): 934.3K
SALES (corp-wide): 1.2MM **Privately Held**
WEB: www.acbcomp.com
SIC: 6531 Real estate managers
PA: Associated Commercial Brokers Co.
1111 Sw Gage Blvd Ste 100
Topeka KS 66604
785 228-9494

(G-12345)
ASSOCIATION OF KANSAS NEBRASKA (HQ)
3440 Sw Urish Rd (66614-4601)
PHONE..................................785 478-4726
Jim Hoehn, *President*
Ron Carlson, *President*
Don Stricker, *Treasurer*
Jodi Diede, *Accountant*
EMP: 20
SQ FT: 10,000
SALES (est): 4.1MM
SALES (corp-wide): 10.5MM **Privately Held**
WEB: www.ks-ne.org
SIC: 8661 8211 7033 Seventh Day Adventist Church; private elementary & secondary schools; Catholic elementary & secondary schools; campgrounds
PA: Mid-America Union Conference Association Of Seventh-Day Adventists
8307 Pine Lake Rd
Lincoln NE
402 484-3000

(G-12346)
ASSOCIATION OF NATIONAL
3107 Sw 21st St (66604-3245)
PHONE..................................785 296-5474
Denise Nelsen, *Treasurer*
Connie Stewart, *Director*
EMP: 12
SALES: 12.2K **Privately Held**
SIC: 8621 Professional membership organizations

(G-12347)
ASSOCTION CHRISTN SCHOOLS INTL
Also Called: Cair Paravel Latin School
635 Sw Clay St (66606-1431)
PHONE..................................785 232-3878
Michael Johnson, *Principal*
EMP: 56
SALES (corp-wide): 17.7MM **Privately Held**
WEB: www.maranathaacademy.net
SIC: 8351 Child day care services
PA: Association Of Christian Schools International
731 Chapel Hills Dr
Colorado Springs CO 80920
719 528-6906

(G-12348)
AT&T CORP
4112 Nw 16th (66603)
PHONE..................................785 276-8201
Shawn McKenzie, *President*
EMP: 362
SALES (corp-wide): 170.7B **Publicly Held**
WEB: www.swbell.com
SIC: 4813 Local telephone communications
HQ: At&T Corp.
1 At&T Way
Bedminster NJ 07921
800 403-3302

(G-12349)
AT&T CORP
2201 Sw Wanamaker Rd # 101 (66614-4963)
PHONE..................................785 272-4002
Erik Keats, *Branch Mgr*
EMP: 49
SALES (corp-wide): 170.7B **Publicly Held**
SIC: 4812 Cellular telephone services
HQ: At&T Corp.
1 At&T Way
Bedminster NJ 07921
800 403-3302

(G-12350)
AT&T CORP
220 Se 6th Ave Rm 505 (66603-3507)
PHONE..................................785 276-8514
David Kerr, *President*
Michael Lewis, *Manager*
William Miller, *Technical Staff*
EMP: 69
SALES (corp-wide): 170.7B **Publicly Held**
WEB: www.swbell.com
SIC: 4813 Telephone communication, except radio
HQ: At&T Corp.
1 At&T Way
Bedminster NJ 07921
800 403-3302

(G-12351)
AT&T CORP
1622 Nw Saline St (66618-2832)
PHONE..................................785 276-5553
Ken Powell, *Manager*
EMP: 50
SALES (corp-wide): 170.7B **Publicly Held**
WEB: www.swbell.com
SIC: 7371 Custom computer programming services
HQ: At&T Corp.
1 At&T Way
Bedminster NJ 07921
800 403-3302

(G-12352)
AT&T CORP
714 1/2 Sw Fairlawn Rd (66606-2337)
PHONE..................................800 403-3022
David Strait, *Principal*
EMP: 13
SALES (corp-wide): 170.7B **Publicly Held**
WEB: www.swbell.com
SIC: 4813 Local telephone communications
HQ: At&T Corp.
1 At&T Way
Bedminster NJ 07921
800 403-3302

(G-12353)
ATRIA SENIOR LIVING INC
3415 Sw 6th Ave (66606-0001)
PHONE..................................785 234-6225
Donita Payne, *Office Mgr*
Michael Daigler, *Director*
Christen North, *Director*
Brett Eakes, *Food Svc Dir*
EMP: 22
SALES (corp-wide): 3.7B **Publicly Held**
SIC: 8361 Home for the aged
HQ: Atria Senior Living Inc.
300 E Market St Ste 100
Louisville KY 40202

(G-12354)
AZURA CREDIT UNION (PA)
610 Sw 10th Ave Fl 1 (66612-1674)
P.O. Box 1128 (66601-1128)
PHONE..................................785 233-5556
Greg Winkler, *President*
Jennifer Kirmse, *VP Bus Dvlpt*
Jeff Stack, *Loan Officer*
Ray White, *Loan Officer*
Daylene Wittman, *Loan Officer*
EMP: 21
SQ FT: 24,000
SALES: 17.8MM **Privately Held**
SIC: 6061 Federal credit unions

(G-12355)
B & B BACKYARD
2134 N Kansas Ave (66608-1817)
PHONE..................................785 246-6348
Bill Brading, *President*
Lee Browning, *Principal*
EMP: 10
SALES (est): 121.5K **Privately Held**
SIC: 7929 5813 Musical entertainers; tavern (drinking places)

(G-12356)
B A DESIGNS LLC
Also Called: Superior Installation Services
117 Se 10th Ave Apt 100 (66612-1173)
PHONE..................................785 267-8110
Russ Branden, *Vice Pres*
William Prohaska, *Vice Pres*
Dennis Gifford, *Manager*
Ryan Baxter, *Executive*
Elizabeth C Branden,
EMP: 28
SALES: 5.9MM **Privately Held**
SIC: 7389 Design, commercial & industrial; design services

(G-12357)
BAILEY MOVING & STORAGE CO LLC
235 Sw Gage Blvd (66606-2025)
PHONE..................................785 232-0521
Carla Bailey,
Curt Cochran,
Kent D Lindemuth,
EMP: 30
SALES (est): 648.2K **Privately Held**
SIC: 4214 Household goods moving & storage, local

(G-12358)
BAISCH & SKINNER INC
1720 Sw 42nd St (66609-1254)
PHONE..................................785 267-6931
Bob Oliva, *Manager*
EMP: 10
SALES (corp-wide): 38MM **Privately Held**
SIC: 5193 Florists' supplies
PA: Baisch & Skinner, Inc.
2721 Lasalle St
Saint Louis MO 63104
314 664-1212

(G-12359)
BAJILLION AGENCY
100 S Kansas Ave (66603-3615)
PHONE..................................785 408-5927
Andrea Engstrom, *Owner*
EMP: 20
SALES (est): 900.9K **Privately Held**
SIC: 8742 Marketing consulting services

(G-12360)
BALLET MIDWEST INC
4300 Sw Huntoon St (66604-1955)
PHONE..................................785 272-5991
Melanie Whitmore, *Principal*
Barbara Ebert, *Director*
EMP: 15
SALES: 99.8K **Privately Held**
SIC: 7911 Dance studio & school; dance instructor & school services

(G-12361)
BAND BOX CORPORATION (PA)
Also Called: Village Cleaners
2033 Sw Seabrook Ave (66604-3447)
PHONE..................................785 272-6646
Clark Deshazer, *President*
EMP: 22
SQ FT: 1,500
SALES (est): 1MM **Privately Held**
SIC: 7216 7212 Cleaning & dyeing, except rugs; pickup station, laundry & drycleaning

(G-12362)
BANK AMERICA NATIONAL ASSN
700 Sw Topeka Blvd (66603-3412)
PHONE..................................785 235-1532
Fax: 785 232-3426
EMP: 15
SALES (corp-wide): 93B **Publicly Held**
SIC: 6021 Natl Commercial Banks
HQ: Bank Of America, National Association
101 S Tryon St
Charlotte NC 28202
704 386-5681

(G-12363)
BANK COMMSSNR KANSAS OFFCE (DH)
Also Called: Executive Office of The St KS
700 Sw Jackson St Ste 300 (66603-3782)
PHONE..................................785 296-2266
Dale Kirmer, *Manager*
Clancey W Norris, *Commissioner*
Kristin Schartz, *Commissioner*
Matt Jones, *IT/INT Sup*
Dana Branam, *Director*
EMP: 75 **Privately Held**
WEB: www.osbckansas.org
SIC: 9651 6163 Banking regulatory agency, government; ; loan brokers
HQ: Executive Office Of The State Of Kansas
300 Sw 10th Ave
Topeka KS 66612
785 296-6240

(G-12364)
BARBARAS CONSERVATORY DANCE
4300 Sw Huntoon St (66604-1955)
PHONE..................................785 272-5991
Barbara Ebert, *Owner*
EMP: 10
SALES (est): 327.8K **Privately Held**
SIC: 7911 Dance instructor

(G-12365)
BARKER PRINTING AND COPY SVCS
925 S Kansas Ave (66612)
PHONE..................................785 233-5533
Jerome Barker, *President*
EMP: 9
SQ FT: 3,000
SALES (est): 1.3MM **Privately Held**
WEB: www.bpctheprinter.com
SIC: 2752 7334 7389 Commercial printing, offset; business form & card printing, lithographic; photocopying & duplicating services; printing broker

(G-12366)
BARTLETT & WEST INC (PA)
1200 Sw Executive Dr A (66615-3854)
PHONE..................................785 272-2252
Keith Warta, *President*
Steven Briman, *Corp Secy*
Bill Naeger, *Vice Pres*
Mark Salvatore, *Finance Dir*
Hallie Zacharczuk, *Mktg Coord*
EMP: 140 **EST:** 1951
SQ FT: 33,000
SALES (est): 85.5MM **Privately Held**
WEB: www.bartwest.com
SIC: 8711 Civil engineering

(G-12367)
BCBSKS
1133 Sw Topeka Blvd (66629-0001)
PHONE..................................785 291-7498
Tommy Olsen, *Principal*
EMP: 20
SALES (est): 5.8MM **Privately Held**
SIC: 6321 Health insurance carriers

(G-12368)
BEACON SALES ACQUISITION INC
4008 Nw 14th St (66618-2828)
PHONE..................................785 234-8406
Reid Ayres, *Manager*
Nathan Wedermyer, *Manager*
EMP: 14
SALES (corp-wide): 7.1B **Publicly Held**
WEB: www.shelterdistribution.com
SIC: 5033 Roofing & siding materials
HQ: Beacon Sales Acquisition, Inc.
50 Webster Ave
Somerville MA 02143
877 645-7663

(G-12369)
BEAUTY BRANDS LLC
5820 Sw 21st St (66604-4007)
PHONE..................................785 228-9778
Bobby Ortega, *Branch Mgr*
John Miller, *Manager*
EMP: 38 **Privately Held**
SIC: 5999 7231 Cosmetics; beauty shops
PA: Beauty Brands Llc
15507 W 99th St
Lenexa KS 66219

(G-12370)
BERBERICH TRAHAN & CO PA (PA)
4301 Sw Huntoon St (66604-1659)
PHONE..................................785 234-3427
Ginger Powell, *President*
Karen Linn, *Corp Secy*
Brad Koehn, *Vice Pres*
Terry Young, *Vice Pres*
Theresa Young CPA, *Vice Pres*
EMP: 30
SQ FT: 10,500
SALES (est): 38.6MM **Privately Held**
WEB: www.cpakansas.com
SIC: 8721 Billing & bookkeeping service

(G-12371)
BERKSHIRE HTHWAY FRST REALTORS
Also Called: Kansas Assoc
2858 Sw Vlla W Dr Ste 200 (66614)
PHONE..................................785 271-2888
Doug Bassett, *President*
Lindsey Carroll, *Broker*
Jerry Brosius, *Sales Associate*
Cory Clutter, *Real Est Agnt*
Laine Hash, *Real Est Agnt*
EMP: 10
SQ FT: 3,500
SALES (est): 675.1K **Privately Held**
WEB: www.prudentialfirstrealtors.com
SIC: 6531 Real estate agent, residential

(G-12372)
BERLIN-WHEELER INC
2942 Sw Wanamaker Rd (66614)
P.O. Box 479 (66601-0479)
PHONE..................................785 271-1000
Mary Ann Wheeler, *CEO*
Steve Wheeler, *Assistant VP*
Matthew Wheeler, *Vice Pres*
Mark Wheeler, *CFO*
Shanna Leonard, *Manager*
EMP: 135
SQ FT: 11,947
SALES: 10.1MM **Privately Held**
WEB: www.berlinwheeler.com
SIC: 7322 Collection agency, except real estate

(G-12373)
BERRY COMPANIES INC
Also Called: Berry Tractor & Equipment Co
1750 Sw 41st St (66609-1251)
PHONE..................................785 266-9509
Ken Wassinger, *Branch Mgr*
Harry Craig, *Manager*
Mike Stevens, *Manager*
EMP: 12
SALES (corp-wide): 181.7MM **Privately Held**
WEB: www.berrycompaniesinc.com
SIC: 5082 General construction machinery & equipment
PA: Berry Companies, Inc.
3223 N Hydraulic St
Wichita KS 67219
316 838-3321

(G-12374)
BERRY COMPANIES INC
Also Called: Berry Material Handling
1300 Nw Us Highway 24 (66608-2026)
PHONE..................................785 228-2225
Joe Wilson, *President*
Gene Ogle, *Sales Associate*
EMP: 15
SALES (corp-wide): 181.7MM **Privately Held**
WEB: www.berrycompaniesinc.com
SIC: 5082 5084 General construction machinery & equipment; materials handling machinery
PA: Berry Companies, Inc.
3223 N Hydraulic St
Wichita KS 67219
316 838-3321

(G-12375)
BERRY COMPANIES INC
Also Called: White Star Machinery & Sup Co
835 Ne Us Highway 24 (66608-1756)
PHONE..................................785 232-7731
Eric Wooderson, *Site Mgr*
Greg Dedonder, *Sales Staff*
Laura McGonigle, *Sales Staff*
John Cunningham, *Branch Mgr*
EMP: 25
SALES (corp-wide): 181.7MM **Privately Held**
WEB: www.berrycompaniesinc.com
SIC: 5082 7353 General construction machinery & equipment; heavy construction equipment rental
PA: Berry Companies, Inc.
3223 N Hydraulic St
Wichita KS 67219
316 838-3321

(G-12376)
BERRYS ARCTIC ICE LLC
200 N Kansas Ave (66603-3623)
PHONE..................................785 357-4466
Walter Berry, *Mng Member*
Lourdes Cardoso, *Admin Mgr*
Phil Perkins,
EMP: 15 **EST:** 1997
SQ FT: 110,000
SALES (est): 2.7MM **Privately Held**
SIC: 2097 4222 Manufactured ice; refrigerated warehousing & storage

(G-12377)
BETTIS ASPHALT & CNSTR INC
1800 Nw Brickyard Rd (66618-2807)
P.O. Box 1694 (66601-1694)
PHONE..................................785 235-8444
Eric Bettis, *President*
Sean Washatka, *Project Mgr*
Suzanne Johnston, *Controller*
Macy Noland, *Manager*
Ryan Randall, *Manager*
EMP: 42 **EST:** 1979
SQ FT: 2,000
SALES (est): 18.5MM **Privately Held**
WEB: www.bettisasphalt.com
SIC: 1611 Highway & street paving contractor

(G-12378)
BETTIS CONTRACTORS INC
1800 Nw Brickyard Rd (66618-2807)
P.O. Box 1515 (66601-1515)
PHONE..................................785 783-8353
Eric Bettis, *President*
Justin Collins, *Project Mgr*
Kyle Collins, *Project Mgr*
EMP: 50
SALES (est): 136.8K **Privately Held**
SIC: 8741 8611 Construction management; contractors' association

(G-12379)
BHJLLC INC
1145 Sw Wanamaker Rd (66604-3808)
PHONE..................................785 272-8800
Mary Martens, *Manager*
EMP: 32
SALES (est): 974K
SALES (corp-wide): 22.3MM **Privately Held**
WEB: www.kcfda.com
SIC: 5722 1751 5087 5063 Electric household appliances, major; cabinet building & installation; vacuum cleaning systems; electric alarms & signaling equipment
PA: Bhjllc, Inc.
14105 Marshall Dr
Lenexa KS 66215
913 888-8028

(G-12380)
BIG HEART PET BRANDS
Also Called: Star-Kist
2200 Nw Brickyard Rd (66618-2814)
PHONE..................................785 338-9240
Susie Barlow, *Purch Mgr*
Jill Hutcherson, *Purch Mgr*
Randall Cotton, *Project Engr*
Tom Ferriter, *Manager*
Andy Heston, *Manager*
EMP: 150
SALES (corp-wide): 7.8B **Publicly Held**
SIC: 2047 Dog food
HQ: Big Heart Pet Brands, Inc.
1 Maritime Plz Fl 2
San Francisco CA 94111
415 247-3000

(G-12381)
BIG TWIN INC
Also Called: Historic Harley Davidson
2047 Sw Topeka Blvd Frnt (66612-1461)
PHONE..................................785 234-6174
Michael A Patterson, *President*
Sherry Burgen, *Manager*
EMP: 50 **EST:** 1940
SQ FT: 28,000
SALES: 12MM **Privately Held**
WEB: www.topekaharley.com
SIC: 5571 7699 Motorcycle dealers; motorcycle repair service

(G-12382)
BINSWANGER ENTERPRISES LLC
Also Called: Binswanger Glass
211 Sw 37th St (66611-2352)
PHONE..................................785 267-4090
Jason Spreer, *Branch Mgr*
EMP: 15
SQ FT: 15,000 **Privately Held**
WEB: www.vvpamerica.com
SIC: 5039 5231 Glass construction materials; glass

GEOGRAPHIC

PA: Binswanger Enterprises, Llc
965 Ridge Lake Blvd # 305
Memphis TN 38120

(G-12383)
BIO-MDCAL APPLCATIONS KANS INC
Also Called: Fresenius Kidney Care Topeka E
3408 Se 29th St (66605-1812)
PHONE..................................785 266-3087
Mary Garber, *Principal*
William Valle, *Principal*
EMP: 25
SALES (est): 248.3K **Privately Held**
SIC: 8011 Offices & clinics of medical doctors

(G-12384)
BIOMAT USA INC
2120 Sw 6th Ave (66606-1603)
PHONE..................................785 233-0079
Greg Frankum, *Manager*
EMP: 14
SALES (corp-wide): 717.8MM **Privately Held**
SIC: 8099 Plasmapherous center; blood bank
HQ: Biomat Usa, Inc.
2410 Lillyvale Ave
Los Angeles CA 90032
323 225-2221

(G-12385)
BIRTH & WOMEN CENTER INC
1109 Sw Topeka Blvd (66612-1602)
PHONE..................................785 232-6950
Josie Norris MD, *President*
Kelly Green, *Systems Mgr*
EMP: 10
SALES (est): 1MM **Privately Held**
SIC: 8011 Offices & clinics of medical doctors

(G-12386)
BLACK GOLD INC
Also Called: Black Gold Installation
2404 Ne Grantville Rd (66608-1723)
PHONE..................................785 354-4000
Timothy Mulroy, *President*
EMP: 22
SALES (est): 2.9MM **Privately Held**
SIC: 1742 Insulation, buildings

(G-12387)
BLACKBURN NURSERY INC
Also Called: Topeka Sprinkler Supply
5645 Sw 33rd St (66614-4518)
PHONE..................................785 272-2707
Brett Blackburn, *President*
Susan E Blackburn, *Corp Secy*
EMP: 30
SALES (est): 3MM **Privately Held**
WEB: www.blackburnnursery.com
SIC: 1711 0781 5261 5087 Irrigation sprinkler system installation; landscape counseling & planning; nurseries & garden centers; sprinkler systems

(G-12388)
BLOOM & ASSOCIATES THERAPY (PA)
2300 Se Sagis Ct (66605-3542)
PHONE..................................785 273-7700
Carolyn Bloom, *President*
EMP: 15
SALES (est): 848.3K **Privately Held**
SIC: 8049 Physiotherapist

(G-12389)
BLUE CROSS AND BLUE SHIELD OF
1133 Sw Topeka Blvd (66629-0002)
PHONE..................................785 291-4180
Andrew C Corbin, *President*
EMP: 41
SALES: 775K **Privately Held**
SIC: 6324 Hospital & medical service plans

(G-12390)
BLUE CROSS BLUE SHELD KANS INC (PA)
1133 Sw Topeka Blvd (66629-0001)
PHONE..................................785 291-7000
Andrew C Corbin, *CEO*
Michael Mattox, *President*
Marlou Wegener, *COO*
Treena Mason, *Vice Pres*
Sunee Mickle, *Vice Pres*
EMP: 950
SQ FT: 80,000
SALES (est): 636.3MM **Privately Held**
WEB: www.bcbsks.com
SIC: 6321 6324 Health insurance carriers; hospital & medical service plans

(G-12391)
BME INC
Also Called: Briggs Dodge
3001 S Kansas Ave (66611-2218)
PHONE..................................785 274-5116
Russell Briggs, *President*
Dwayne Miller, *Vice Pres*
EMP: 45 **EST:** 1947
SQ FT: 24,000
SALES (est): 14.3MM **Privately Held**
WEB: www.bmelabstore.com
SIC: 5511 5012 7538 5521 Automobiles, new & used; pickups, new & used; vans, new & used; trucks, commercial; general automotive repair shops; used car dealers

(G-12392)
BNSF RAILWAY COMPANY
Also Called: Burlington Northern
920 Se Quincy St (66612-1116)
PHONE..................................785 435-7021
Mike Lawrence, *Finance Other*
Mark Weber, *Technology*
EMP: 100
SALES (corp-wide): 225.3B **Publicly Held**
WEB: www.billpurdy.com
SIC: 4011 Railroads, line-haul operating
HQ: Bnsf Railway Company
2650 Lou Menk Dr
Fort Worth TX 76131
800 795-2673

(G-12393)
BNSF RAILWAY COMPANY
Also Called: Burlington Northern
1001 Ne Atchison Ave (66616-1116)
PHONE..................................785 435-2000
M B Johnson, *Branch Mgr*
EMP: 400
SALES (corp-wide): 225.3B **Publicly Held**
WEB: www.billpurdy.com
SIC: 4011 Railroads, line-haul operating
HQ: Bnsf Railway Company
2650 Lou Menk Dr
Fort Worth TX 76131
800 795-2673

(G-12394)
BOB DURBIN DDS
5310 Sw 37th St (66614-4540)
PHONE..................................785 267-5010
Bob Durbin DDS, *Owner*
EMP: 17
SALES (est): 698.6K **Privately Held**
SIC: 8021 Dentists' office

(G-12395)
BOBS JANITORIAL SERVICE & SUP (HQ)
725 Ne Us Highway 24 A (66608-1787)
PHONE..................................785 271-6600
Alan Bibler, *CEO*
Vermel Bibler, *Corp Secy*
Debbie Basel, *Manager*
EMP: 145
SQ FT: 3,200
SALES (est): 3.1MM **Privately Held**
SIC: 7349 5169 Janitorial service, contract basis; chemicals & allied products
PA: Consolidated Capital Investments Group, Inc
1901 Sw Arrowhead Rd
Topeka KS
785 267-0660

(G-12396)
BOK FINANCIAL CORPORATION
Also Called: Bok Financial The Private Bank
900 S Kansas Ave (66612-1218)
PHONE..................................785 273-9993
EMP: 44 **Publicly Held**
SIC: 8742 6021 Financial consultant; national commercial banks
PA: Bok Financial Corporation
320 S Boston Ave
Tulsa OK 74103

(G-12397)
BOOKS & BLOCKS ACADEMY INC
Also Called: Kennedy Academy
206 Se Lakewood Ct (66609-1418)
PHONE..................................785 266-5150
Karla Meggison, *President*
Steve Meggison, *Assistant VP*
Kandice Hamner, *Director*
EMP: 13
SALES (est): 552K **Privately Held**
WEB: www.kennedyacademy.com
SIC: 8351 Preschool center

(G-12398)
BORDER STATES INDUSTRIES INC
1516 Nw Saline St (66618-2837)
PHONE..................................785 354-9532
David Brown, *Branch Mgr*
EMP: 24
SALES (corp-wide): 2B **Privately Held**
WEB: www.krizdavis.com
SIC: 5063 5065 Electrical supplies; electronic parts & equipment
PA: Border States Industries, Inc.
2400 38th St S
Fargo ND 58104
701 293-5834

(G-12399)
BOYLES PORTABLE SIGN RENT
3652 Se Indiana Ave (66605-3281)
PHONE..................................785 266-5401
Jerry Boyles, *Owner*
EMP: 12
SALES (est): 1MM **Privately Held**
SIC: 7312 Outdoor advertising services

(G-12400)
BOYS AND GIRLS CLUB OF TOPEKA
550 Se 27th St (66605-1106)
PHONE..................................785 234-5601
Ahjah Alexander, *Vice Pres*
Jennifer Leclair, *Vice Pres*
Amy Mullins, *Vice Pres*
Simone Patterson, *Human Res Dir*
Amy Erickson, *Director*
EMP: 45
SQ FT: 28,000
SALES: 2.3MM **Privately Held**
WEB: www.bgctopeka.com
SIC: 8641 Boy Scout organization; youth organizations

(G-12401)
BRACK/ASSCTS CNSLTNG ENGNRS PA
3501 Sw Gage Blvd (66614-3824)
PHONE..................................785 271-6644
Les Brack, *President*
D Jeff Dikeman, *Vice Pres*
D Dikeman, *Vice Pres*
Dave Krug, *Vice Pres*
Bruce Brown, *Engineer*
EMP: 18
SALES (est): 2.1MM **Privately Held**
SIC: 8711 Consulting engineer

(G-12402)
BRACKETT INC
7115 Se Forbes Ave (66619-1443)
P.O. Box 19306 (66619-0306)
PHONE..................................785 862-2205
Michael Murray, *President*
Laura Haynes, *Buyer*
◆ **EMP:** 7 **EST:** 1910
SQ FT: 38,000
SALES: 2MM **Privately Held**
WEB: www.brackett-inc.com
SIC: 3555 Bookbinding machinery

(G-12403)
BRB CONTRACTORS INC (PA)
3805 Nw 25th St (66618-3744)
P.O. Box 750940 (66675-0940)
PHONE..................................785 232-1245
Michael Laird, *President*
Richard Johnson, *Division Mgr*
Gregory Hoglund, *Vice Pres*
Charles Landwehr, *Vice Pres*
David Van Dyne, *Vice Pres*
EMP: 175 **EST:** 1959
SQ FT: 36,000
SALES: 23.5MM **Privately Held**
WEB: www.brbcontractors.com
SIC: 1629 1623 1622 Waste water & sewage treatment plant construction; sewer line construction; water main construction; bridge construction

(G-12404)
BREAKTHROUGH HOUSE INC
1195 Sw Buchanan St # 202 (66604-1172)
PHONE..................................785 232-6807
Lynn Davis, *Exec Dir*
Theresa Douthart, *Director*
Lee Jones,
EMP: 23
SALES: 697.7K **Privately Held**
SIC: 8322 Social service center

(G-12405)
BRIDGESTONE AMERICAS
GCR Tires & Service 526
1400 Sw 41st St (66609-1208)
PHONE..................................785 267-0074
Brent Schneider, *Manager*
EMP: 12 **Privately Held**
WEB: www.bfis.com
SIC: 5531 5014 Automotive tires; truck tires & tubes
HQ: Bridgestone Americas Tire Operations, Llc
200 4th Ave S Ste 100
Nashville TN 37201
615 937-1000

(G-12406)
BRIGHT CIRCLE MONTESORRI SCHL
401 Sw Oakley Ave (66606-1915)
PHONE..................................785 235-1033
Betsy Fletcher, *Director*
EMP: 10
SALES: 263.1K **Privately Held**
SIC: 8351 Preschool center

(G-12407)
BRIGHTON PLACE W OPER CO LLC
331 Sw Oakley Ave (66606-1914)
PHONE..................................785 232-1212
Wayne Sanner, *President*
EMP: 31 **EST:** 2013
SALES: 2.9MM **Privately Held**
SIC: 8051 Skilled nursing care facilities

(G-12408)
BRIMANS LEADING JEWELERS INC (PA)
734 S Kansas Ave (66603-3808)
PHONE..................................785 357-4438
Debbie Briman Latta, *President*
Rob Briman, *Vice Pres*
EMP: 14
SQ FT: 3,750
SALES: 800K **Privately Held**
SIC: 5944 7631 Jewelry, precious stones & precious metals; jewelry repair services

(G-12409)
BROWNS SUPER SERVICE INC
3812 Sw South Park Ave (66609-1422)
PHONE..................................785 267-1080
Keith Brown, *President*
Doreen Brown, *Vice Pres*
EMP: 12
SQ FT: 700
SALES (est): 1.5MM **Privately Held**
SIC: 7538 7549 4213 General automotive repair shops; towing service, automotive; heavy hauling

(G-12410)
BROWNS TREE SERVICE LLC
1801 Se Madison St (66607-1244)
PHONE..................................785 379-9212
EMP: 10 **EST:** 2000
SALES (est): 660K **Privately Held**
SIC: 7342 0783 Pest control services; planting, pruning & trimming services

(G-12411)
BRUCE SPEAK
2887 Sw Macvicar Ave # 3 (66611-1782)
PHONE..................................785 267-6301
Bruce Speak, *Owner*
EMP: 10
SALES (est): 524.8K **Privately Held**
SIC: **8021** 8011 Dentists' office; offices & clinics of medical doctors

(G-12412)
BRYAN LYKINS HJTMNEK FNCHER PA
222 Sw 7th St (66603-3717)
P.O. Box 797 (66601-0797)
PHONE..................................785 428-4566
John Bryan, *President*
Roger D Fincher, *Principal*
Danton Hejtmanek, *Corp Secy*
Daniel Lykins, *Vice Pres*
EMP: 17
SQ FT: 8,000
SALES (est): 1.2MM **Privately Held**
SIC: **8111** General practice law office

(G-12413)
BUILDING BLOCKS OF TOPEKA INC
620 Sw Lane St (66606-1537)
PHONE..................................785 232-0441
Vernon Long, *President*
EMP: 50
SALES: 915.6K **Privately Held**
SIC: **8351** Child day care services

(G-12414)
BURLINGAME ROAD ANIMAL HOSP
3715 Sw Burlingame Rd (66609-1216)
PHONE..................................785 267-1012
Donald E Hrenchir Dvm, *Owner*
Kim Moorcroft, *Practice Mgr*
Heidi Bradford,
EMP: 20
SALES (est): 807.4K **Privately Held**
SIC: **0742** Veterinarian, animal specialties; animal hospital services, pets & other animal specialties

(G-12415)
BURLINGTON NTHRN SANTA FE LLC
Also Called: Topeka Mechanical Shops
100 Ne Jefferson Trwy (66607-1182)
PHONE..................................785 435-5065
Curt Myers, *Superintendent*
EMP: 10
SALES (corp-wide): 225.3B **Publicly Held**
SIC: **4731** Freight transportation arrangement
HQ: Burlington Northern Santa Fe, Llc
2650 Lou Menk Dr
Fort Worth TX 76131

(G-12416)
BUTLER & ASSOCIATES PA
3706 Sw Topeka Blvd # 300 (66609-1291)
PHONE..................................785 267-6444
Kathleen Butler, *Principal*
Todd Butler, *Chief Mktg Ofcr*
Ann Eakin, *Office Mgr*
Shannon Eastman, *Manager*
Danielle Moravec, *Assistant*
EMP: 28
SALES (est): 3.1MM **Privately Held**
SIC: **8111** Criminal law

(G-12417)
CABINETRY & MLLWK CONCEPTS INC
3433 Nw 18th St (66618-2823)
PHONE..................................785 232-1234
Raul Gutierrez Jr, *President*
Jim Ziegler, *Vice Pres*
Larry Ziegler, *Treasurer*
Jacob Ziegler, *Web Dvlpr*
John Campbell, *Admin Sec*
EMP: 18
SQ FT: 11,000
SALES (est): 3.1MM **Privately Held**
WEB: www.cabinetryandmillworkconceptsinc.com
SIC: **2521** 2431 Cabinets, office: wood; millwork

(G-12418)
CAL SOUTHERN TRANSPORT CO
3728 Se 6th St (66607-2368)
P.O. Box 1652 (66601-1652)
PHONE..................................785 232-4202
Randy Burkhardt, *Branch Mgr*
EMP: 38
SALES (corp-wide): 6.3MM **Privately Held**
SIC: **4213** Trucking, except local
PA: Cal Southern Transport Co
15570 Sw Jenkins Rd
Beaverton OR 97006
503 643-6431

(G-12419)
CALVIN INVESTMENTS LLC
Also Called: Dock, The
2838 Se 29th St (66605-2229)
PHONE..................................785 266-8755
Sue Calvin,
EMP: 12
SALES: 200K **Privately Held**
SIC: **6512** 8631 Property operation, retail establishment; labor unions & similar labor organizations

(G-12420)
CAMPUS ELECTRIC POWER COMPANY
Also Called: Cepco
600 Sw Corporate Vw (66615-1233)
P.O. Box 4877 (66604-0877)
PHONE..................................785 271-4824
Ken Maginley, *President*
EMP: 24
SALES (est): 498.2K **Privately Held**
SIC: **4939** Combination utilities

(G-12421)
CANON SOLUTIONS AMERICA INC
1131 Sw Winding Rd Ste A (66615-3805)
PHONE..................................785 232-8222
Mike Poplier, *Branch Mgr*
Dena Obrien, *Admin Mgr*
EMP: 16 **Privately Held**
WEB: www.imagistics.com
SIC: **5044** Copying equipment
HQ: Canon Solutions America, Inc.
1 Canon Park
Melville NY 11747
631 330-5000

(G-12422)
CAP CARPET INC
Also Called: Carpet One Topeka
5131 Sw 29th St (66614-2350)
PHONE..................................785 273-1402
Lee A Schwartz, *Branch Mgr*
EMP: 10
SALES (corp-wide): 38.8MM **Privately Held**
WEB: www.capcarpetinc.com
SIC: **5713** 5023 Carpets; carpets
PA: Cap Carpet, Inc.
535 S Emerson St
Wichita KS 67209
316 262-3496

(G-12423)
CAPELLI HAIR & NAIL SALON
2824 Sw Arrowhead Rd (66614-2447)
PHONE..................................785 271-6811
Carmella Siegel, *Owner*
EMP: 13
SQ FT: 1,500
SALES (est): 160.6K **Privately Held**
SIC: **7231** Unisex hair salons

(G-12424)
CAPITAL AREA GYMNSTICS EMPRIUM
3740 Sw South Park Ave (66609-1420)
PHONE..................................785 266-4151
Trini Beckman, *Director*
EMP: 10
SALES (est): 458.3K **Privately Held**
WEB: www.cagegymnastics.com
SIC: **7999** Gymnastic instruction, non-membership

(G-12425)
CAPITAL CITY CORRAL INC
Also Called: Gloden Corral
1601 Sw Wanamaker Rd (66604-3814)
PHONE..................................785 273-5354
Darryl Dammann, *President*
EMP: 80
SALES (est): 8.1MM **Privately Held**
SIC: **6794** 5812 Franchises, selling or licensing; restaurant, family: chain

(G-12426)
CAPITAL CITY GUN CLUB INC
Nw 4th St (66601)
P.O. Box 332 (66601-0332)
PHONE..................................785 478-4682
Tom Rork, *Treasurer*
EMP: 11
SALES: 105.7K **Privately Held**
WEB: www.capitalcitygunclub.com
SIC: **7999** Shooting range operation

(G-12427)
CAPITAL CITY INVESTMENTS INC
3710 Sw Topeka Blvd (66609-1230)
P.O. Box 1433 (66601-1433)
PHONE..................................785 274-5600
Bob Kobbman, *CEO*
Bruce Krueger, *CFO*
EMP: 30
SALES (est): 1.3MM
SALES (corp-wide): 351.9MM **Publicly Held**
SIC: **6799** Real estate investors, except property operators
HQ: Capitol Federal Savings Bank
700 S Kansas Ave Fl 1
Topeka KS 66603
785 235-1341

(G-12428)
CAPITAL CITY OIL INC (PA)
911 Se Adams St (66607-1127)
P.O. Box 618 (66601-0618)
PHONE..................................785 233-8008
Marvin Spees, *President*
Tom Ney, *Transportation*
Jennifer Vogts, *Sales Staff*
Barbara Koelling, *Office Mgr*
EMP: 28
SQ FT: 22,000
SALES: 69.5MM **Privately Held**
WEB: www.capitalcityoil.com
SIC: **5171** 2911 Petroleum bulk stations; greases, lubricating

(G-12429)
CAPITAL CITY PALLET INC
804 Ne Us Highway 24 (66608-1757)
P.O. Box 1572 (66601-1572)
PHONE..................................785 379-5099
James Inman, *President*
Linda Inman, *Office Mgr*
EMP: 14
SQ FT: 1,800
SALES: 1.3MM **Privately Held**
SIC: **7359** 7699 2499 Equipment rental & leasing; pallet repair; mulch, wood & bark

(G-12430)
CAPITAL FINANCIAL GROUP
2820 Sw Mission Woods Dr # 150 (66614-9962)
PHONE..................................785 228-1234
Jeffrey Vogel, *Owner*
EMP: 12
SALES: 750K **Privately Held**
SIC: **8742** Financial consultant

(G-12431)
CAPITAL GRAPHICS INC
305 Se 17th St Ste C (66607-1266)
PHONE..................................785 233-6677
Vicky Walters, *Ch of Bd*
Don Walters, *President*
James J Walters, *Vice Pres*
Kathryn Walters, *Treasurer*
EMP: 26
SQ FT: 2,500
SALES (est): 2.1MM **Privately Held**
SIC: **7374** Computer graphics service

(G-12432)
CAPITAL INSULATION INC
2714 Nw Topeka Blvd # 106 (66617-1148)
PHONE..................................785 246-1775
Travis McKinly, *President*
Dan Darby, *Principal*
EMP: 20
SALES (est): 1.2MM **Privately Held**
WEB: www.capitalinsulation.com
SIC: **1742** Insulation, buildings

(G-12433)
CAPITAL LABEL LLC
305 Se 17th St Ste C (66607-1266)
PHONE..................................785 291-9702
Aimee Haebsprom, *General Mgr*
Amy Arnold, *Exec Dir*
Randall Arnold,
EMP: 6
SALES: 640K **Privately Held**
WEB: www.copycentertopeka.com
SIC: **2759** Labels & seals: printing

(G-12434)
CAPITAL TITLE INSURANCE CO LC
2655 Sw Wanamaker Rd C (66614-4491)
PHONE..................................785 272-2900
Jeff Amrein, *President*
EMP: 15
SALES (est): 720.8K **Privately Held**
WEB: www.capitaltitlecompany.com
SIC: **6541** Title abstract offices

(G-12435)
CAPITOL CITY TAXI INC
2050 Se 30th St (66605-2476)
PHONE..................................785 267-3777
Albert O Roy, *President*
Karen E Roy, *Admin Sec*
EMP: 10
SALES: 297K **Privately Held**
SIC: **4121** Taxicabs

(G-12436)
CAPITOL CONCRETE PDTS CO INC (PA)
627 Nw Tyler St (66608-1591)
P.O. Box 8159 (66608-0159)
PHONE..................................785 233-3271
James S Browning, *President*
Terry Spriggs, *President*
EMP: 18
SQ FT: 10,000
SALES (est): 7MM **Privately Held**
WEB: www.capitolconcreteproducts.com
SIC: **5032** 3271 Brick, except refractory; blocks, concrete or cinder: standard

(G-12437)
CAPITOL FEDERAL FINANCIAL INC (PA)
700 S Kansas Ave Fl 1 (66603-3809)
PHONE..................................785 235-1341
John B Dicus, *Ch of Bd*
Anthony Barry, *Exec VP*
Natalie G Haag, *Exec VP*
Kevin Brittain, *Vice Pres*
Travis Buchanan, *Vice Pres*
EMP: 66
SALES: 351.9MM **Publicly Held**
SIC: **6035** Federal savings banks

(G-12438)
CAPITOL FEDERAL SAVINGS BANK
2100 Sw Fairlawn Rd (66614-1502)
PHONE..................................785 235-1341
Nancy Muller, *Vice Pres*
EMP: 32
SALES (corp-wide): 351.9MM **Publicly Held**
SIC: **6035** Federal savings & loan associations
HQ: Capitol Federal Savings Bank
700 S Kansas Ave Fl 1
Topeka KS 66603
785 235-1341

GEOGRAPHIC

(G-12439)
CAPITOL FEDERAL SAVINGS BANK (HQ)
700 S Kansas Ave Fl 1 (66603-3894)
PHONE..................................785 235-1341
John B Dicus, *Ch of Bd*
R Joe Aleshire, *Exec VP*
Larry K Brubaker, *Exec VP*
Rick Jackson, *Exec VP*
Sharon Dodd, *Assistant VP*
EMP: 200 **EST:** 2015
SQ FT: 79,275
SALES: 346.7MM
SALES (corp-wide): 351.9MM **Publicly Held**
WEB: www.capfed.com
SIC: 6035 Federal savings & loan associations; federal savings banks
PA: Capitol Federal Financial, Inc.
700 S Kansas Ave Fl 1
Topeka KS 66603
785 235-1341

(G-12440)
CAPPER FOUNDATION
3500 Sw 10th Ave (66604-1995)
PHONE..................................785 272-4060
Jim Leiker, *President*
James L Leiker, *President*
Sandy Warren, *Exec VP*
Debbi O'Neil, *Vice Pres*
Pam Walstrom, *Vice Pres*
EMP: 38
SQ FT: 37,681
SALES: 13.5MM **Privately Held**
WEB: www.capper.org
SIC: 8049 Physical therapist

(G-12441)
CAPPERS INSURANCE SERVICE INC
1503 Sw 42nd St (66609-1265)
PHONE..................................785 274-4300
Bryan Welch, *President*
EMP: 40
SQ FT: 24,000
SALES (est): 6.1MM **Privately Held**
WEB: www.cappersinsurance.com
SIC: 6411 Insurance agents
HQ: The Ogden Newspapers Inc
1500 Main St
Wheeling WV 26003
304 233-0100

(G-12442)
CAPSTAN AG SYSTEMS INC (HQ)
Also Called: Re/Max
4225 Sw Kirklawn Ave (66609-1284)
PHONE..................................785 232-4477
Graeme W Henderson, *Ch of Bd*
Pam Reynolds, *CFO*
Andre Anderson, *Marketing Staff*
Chuck Frost, *Executive*
EMP: 5
SALES (est): 1.6MM **Privately Held**
WEB: www.capstanag.com
SIC: 3625 Industrial controls: push button, selector switches, pilot
PA: Capstan, Inc.
16100 S Figueroa St
Gardena CA 90248
310 366-5999

(G-12443)
CAR STAR INC
Also Called: Carstar
313 Sw Jackson St (66603-3325)
PHONE..................................785 232-2084
Kory Rupp, *Site Mgr*
Becky Hemphill, *Manager*
EMP: 15 **EST:** 1959
SQ FT: 7,500
SALES (est): 910K **Privately Held**
SIC: 7532 Body shop, automotive

(G-12444)
CARDIOLOGY CONS TOPEKA PA
600 Sw College Ave (66606-1684)
PHONE..................................785 233-9643
Allen L Gutovitz, *President*
O W Meyer MD, *Admin Sec*
EMP: 25
SQ FT: 10,000
SALES (est): 1MM **Privately Held**
SIC: 8011 Cardiologist & cardio-vascular specialist

(G-12445)
CARDIVSCLAR THRCIC SURGEONS PA
Also Called: Lutes, David W
830 Sw Mulvane St (66606-1654)
PHONE..................................785 270-8625
Norman Thoms MD, *President*
EMP: 12
SQ FT: 1,400
SALES (est): 680K **Privately Held**
SIC: 8011 Cardiologist & cardio-vascular specialist; thoracic physician; surgeon

(G-12446)
CARDONA COFFEE LLP
6540 Se Johnston St (66619-1366)
PHONE..................................785 554-6060
Kevin Conrad, *Partner*
EMP: 5
SALES: 750K **Privately Held**
SIC: 5149 2095 Coffee, green or roasted; instant coffee

(G-12447)
CAREGIVERS OF KS INC
3715 Sw 29th St (66614-2107)
PHONE..................................785 354-0767
Edward J Schulte, *Principal*
EMP: 10 **EST:** 2007
SALES (est): 336.9K **Privately Held**
SIC: 8082 Home health care services

(G-12448)
CARGILL INCORPORATED
1845 Nw Gordon St (66608-1612)
PHONE..................................785 357-1989
Andrea Koch, *Manager*
EMP: 43
SALES (corp-wide): 113.4B **Privately Held**
SIC: 5153 Grain elevators
PA: Cargill, Incorporated
15407 Mcginty Rd W
Wayzata MN 55391
952 742-7575

(G-12449)
CARGILL INCORPORATED
5135 Nw Us Highway 24 (66618-3814)
PHONE..................................785 235-3003
Brent Emch, *Manager*
EMP: 14
SALES (corp-wide): 113.4B **Privately Held**
WEB: www.cargill.com
SIC: 5153 Grain elevators; grains
PA: Cargill, Incorporated
15407 Mcginty Rd W
Wayzata MN 55391
952 742-7575

(G-12450)
CARING COMPASSIONATE CARE LLC
220 Sw 33rd St Ste 101 (66611-2230)
PHONE..................................785 215-8127
Shawna D Link, *Principal*
EMP: 10 **EST:** 2010
SALES (est): 244.3K **Privately Held**
SIC: 8082 Home health care services

(G-12451)
CARLSON AUCTION SERVICE INC
Also Called: I-70 Auto Auction
11048 Sw Us Highway 40 (66615-9253)
PHONE..................................785 478-4250
Daniel Carlson, *President*
David Carlson, *Vice Pres*
Beverly Carlson, *Admin Sec*
EMP: 50
SQ FT: 10,000
SALES: 3MM **Privately Held**
WEB: www.i70autoauction.com
SIC: 7389 Auctioneers, fee basis; auction, appraisal & exchange services

(G-12452)
CAVANAUGH BIGGS AND LEMON PA
2942 Sw Wnamaker Dr Ste A (66614)
PHONE..................................785 440-4000
Thomas Lemon, *President*
EMP: 10
SALES (est): 910K **Privately Held**
WEB: www.csl-law.com
SIC: 8111 General practice law office

(G-12453)
CBIZ ACCOUNTING TAX & A
990 Sw Fairlawn Rd (66606-2340)
PHONE..................................785 272-3176
Denise Peterson, *President*
David Allison, *Admin Sec*
EMP: 36 **EST:** 1976
SQ FT: 9,000
SALES (est): 1.7MM **Publicly Held**
WEB: www.cbizinc.com
SIC: 8721 Accounting, auditing & bookkeeping
PA: Cbiz, Inc.
6050 Oak Tree Blvd # 500
Cleveland OH 44131

(G-12454)
CBIZ M&S CONSULTING SVCS LLC (HQ)
4123 Sw Gage Center Dr # 200
(66604-1655)
PHONE..................................785 228-6700
Tim Hannon, *President*
Keenan Buoy, *Vice Pres*
Kevin Londeen, *Vice Pres*
Kathryn Wade, *Vice Pres*
EMP: 50
SQ FT: 5,000
SALES (est): 7.9MM **Publicly Held**
SIC: 7363 Employee leasing service

(G-12455)
CBRE INC
920 Se Quincy St (66612-1116)
PHONE..................................785 435-2399
Randy Ridgway, *Manager*
EMP: 13
SALES (corp-wide): 21.3B **Publicly Held**
SIC: 6531 Real estate agent, commercial
HQ: Cbre, Inc.
400 S Hope St Ste 25
Los Angeles CA 90071
213 613-3333

(G-12456)
CENTRAL NATIONAL BANK
800 Se Quincy St (66612-1114)
PHONE..................................785 234-2265
Joan Wagnon, *President*
Jason Schmitt, *President*
David Brant, *Vice Pres*
EMP: 15
SALES (corp-wide): 55.4MM **Privately Held**
WEB: www.centralnational.com
SIC: 6021 National commercial banks
HQ: Central National Bank (Inc)
802 N Washington St
Junction City KS 66441
785 238-4114

(G-12457)
CENTRAL STATES MACHINING WLDG
300 W 1st Ave (66603-3003)
PHONE..................................785 233-1376
Melissa Hanley, *President*
Scottie Hanley, *Vice Pres*
EMP: 5 **EST:** 1974
SQ FT: 7,500
SALES (est): 602.8K **Privately Held**
SIC: 3599 7692 Machine shop, jobbing & repair; welding repair

(G-12458)
CENTURY BUSINESS TECHNOLOGIES (PA)
401 Sw 30th St (66611-2204)
P.O. Box 2459 (66601-2459)
PHONE..................................785 267-4555
Dawna McCabe, *CEO*
Susie Weick, *Vice Pres*
Judy Titus, *Warehouse Mgr*
Kevin Umscheid, *Parts Mgr*
Michael Scott, *Research*
EMP: 50
SQ FT: 10,500
SALES (est): 57.9MM **Privately Held**
SIC: 5044 7359 7374 Photocopy machines; office machine rental, except computers; optical scanning data service

(G-12459)
CENTURY HEALTH SOLUTIONS INC
2951 Sw Woodside Dr (66614-4181)
P.O. Box 1676 (66601-1676)
PHONE..................................785 233-1816
Gina Ochsner, *President*
EMP: 14
SQ FT: 5,000
SALES: 505.5K **Privately Held**
WEB: www.century-health.com
SIC: 8748 6411 8742 Employee programs administration; insurance agents, brokers & service; management consulting services

(G-12460)
CENTURY OFFICE PDTS INC TOPEKA (HQ)
401 Sw 30th St (66611-2204)
P.O. Box 2459 (66601-2459)
PHONE..................................785 267-4555
Melvin D Woods, *President*
Marshall Hanson, *Corp Secy*
Phil Howard, *Vice Pres*
Susie Weick, *Vice Pres*
EMP: 36
SQ FT: 10,500
SALES: 5MM
SALES (corp-wide): 57.9MM **Privately Held**
WEB: www.centuryunited.com
SIC: 5044 7699 Photocopy machines; cash registers; mailing machines; photocopy machine repair
PA: Century Business Technologies, Inc
401 Sw 30th St
Topeka KS 66611
785 267-4555

(G-12461)
CFCC & ASSOCIATES
Also Called: CHRIST FIRST COUNSELING CENTER
2000 Sw Gage Blvd (66604-3340)
PHONE..................................785 272-0778
Corey Schliep, *Director*
EMP: 20
SALES: 1.1MM **Privately Held**
SIC: 8322 General counseling services

(G-12462)
CGB DIVERSIFIED SERVICES INC
Also Called: Diversified Crop Insur Svcs
120 Se 6th Ave Ste 210 (66603-3515)
PHONE..................................785 235-5566
EMP: 11 **Privately Held**
SIC: 5153 Grains
HQ: Cgb Diversified Services, Inc.
1608b W Lafayette Ave
Jacksonville IL 62650
217 245-4599

(G-12463)
CHAVEZ RESTORATION & CLEANING (PA)
2400 S Kansas Ave (66611-1144)
PHONE..................................785 232-3779
Dan Chavez, *President*
Richard Chavez, *President*
Trinidad Chavez, *Treasurer*
EMP: 18
SALES (est): 2MM **Privately Held**
WEB: www.chavezrestoration.com
SIC: 7349 Building maintenance services

(G-12464)
CHILDREN & FAMILY SERVICES
Also Called: Children & Family Policy
915 Sw Harrison St Fl 5 (66612-1505)
PHONE..................................785 296-4653
Sandra Hazlett, *Director*
EMP: 75
SALES (est): 657.1K **Privately Held**
SIC: 8399 Health & welfare council

(G-12465)
CHOCOLATEY SOFTWARE INC (PA)
3620 Sw Fairlawn Rd # 220 (66614-3967)
PHONE....................................785 783-4720
Mukesh Sharma, *Principal*
Rob Reynolds, *Founder*
EMP: 10
SQ FT: 2,100
SALES (est): 336.1K **Privately Held**
SIC: 7371 Computer software development & applications

(G-12466)
CHRIST KING EARLY EDUCATN CTR
5973 Sw 25th St (66614-1972)
PHONE....................................785 272-2999
Dalon Brown, *Director*
Dawn Brown, *Director*
EMP: 34
SALES (est): 472.2K **Privately Held**
SIC: 8351 Child day care services

(G-12467)
CITY GLASS AND MIRROR INC
2017 Sw 6th Ave (66606-1602)
PHONE....................................785 233-5650
Greg Frederick, *President*
Bob Escalante, *Vice Pres*
Dennis Jones, *Vice Pres*
Larry Frederick, *Admin Sec*
EMP: 11
SQ FT: 7,500
SALES (est): 2MM **Privately Held**
SIC: 1793 5039 Glass & glazing work; glass construction materials

(G-12468)
CITY OF TOPEKA
Also Called: Topeka Zoological Park
635 Sw Gage Blvd (66606-2066)
PHONE....................................785 368-9180
Mike Colcur, *Exec Dir*
Brendan Wiley, *Director*
EMP: 40 **Privately Held**
SIC: 8422 9111 Zoological garden, noncommercial; mayors' offices
PA: City Of Topeka
215 Se 7th St Ste 352
Topeka KS 66603
785 368-3111

(G-12469)
CITY OF TOPEKA
Also Called: Pro Shop
2533 Sw Urish Rd (66614-4335)
PHONE....................................785 291-2670
Scott Weller, *Sales/Mktg Mgr*
EMP: 10 **Privately Held**
SIC: 7992 9111 Public golf courses; mayors' offices
PA: City Of Topeka
215 Se 7th St Ste 352
Topeka KS 66603
785 368-3111

(G-12470)
CITY OF TOPEKA
Also Called: Topeka Water Pollution Control
1115 Ne Poplar St (66616-1327)
PHONE....................................785 368-3851
Mark Green, *Superintendent*
Linda Scott, *Info Tech Mgr*
EMP: 85 **Privately Held**
SIC: 3634 9111 1711 Water pulsating devices, electric; mayors' offices; plumbing, heating, air-conditioning contractors
PA: City Of Topeka
215 Se 7th St Ste 352
Topeka KS 66603
785 368-3111

(G-12471)
CITY OF TOPEKA
Also Called: Topeka Engineering Division
515 S Kansas Ave Ste 301 (66603-3428)
PHONE....................................785 295-3842
Thomas Flanagan, *Manager*
EMP: 45 **Privately Held**
SIC: 8711 9111 Civil engineering; mayors' offices
PA: City Of Topeka
215 Se 7th St Ste 352
Topeka KS 66603
785 368-3111

(G-12472)
CITY OF TOPEKA
Also Called: Water Treatment Plant
3245 Nw Water Works Dr (66606-1984)
PHONE....................................785 368-3860
Larry Shannon, *Manager*
EMP: 40 **Privately Held**
SIC: 4952 9111 Sewerage systems; mayors' offices
PA: City Of Topeka
215 Se 7th St Ste 352
Topeka KS 66603
785 368-3111

(G-12473)
CITY OF TOPEKA
Also Called: Cypress Ridge Golf Course
6921 Sw 21st St (66615-1313)
PHONE....................................785 273-0811
Andrew Huffman, *Manager*
Mike Hren, *Officer*
EMP: 12 **Privately Held**
SIC: 7699 Golf club & equipment repair
PA: City Of Topeka
215 Se 7th St Ste 352
Topeka KS 66603
785 368-3111

(G-12474)
CITY OF TOPEKA
Also Called: Street Maintenance Division
201 Nw Topeka Blvd Ste B (66603-3019)
PHONE....................................785 295-3803
Tom Watson, *Manager*
EMP: 52 **Privately Held**
SIC: 1611 9111 Highway & street maintenance; mayors' offices
PA: City Of Topeka
215 Se 7th St Ste 352
Topeka KS 66603
785 368-3111

(G-12475)
CITY OF TOPEKA EMPLOYEES
620 Se Madison St (66607-1299)
PHONE....................................785 368-3749
Larry Wolgast, *Mayor*
Jay Oyler, *Manager*
John Sanders, *Supervisor*
Stacy Trahoon, *Software Dev*
Bill Fiander, *Director*
EMP: 1500
SALES (est): 83.8MM **Privately Held**
SIC: 8399 Fund raising organization, non-fee basis

(G-12476)
CITY OF TOPEKA EMPLOYEES
Also Called: Crestview Community Center
4801 Sw Shunga Dr (66614-1366)
PHONE....................................785 272-5503
EMP: 12 **Privately Held**
SIC: 7999 9111 Amusement/Recreation Services Executive Office
PA: City Of Topeka Employees Friendship Fund
620 Se Madison St Ste 203
Topeka KS 66607
785 368-3749

(G-12477)
CITY TRAFFIC OPERATION
927 Nw Harrison St (66608-1434)
PHONE....................................785 368-3913
Carlos Salazar, *Manager*
EMP: 14
SALES (est): 1.1MM **Privately Held**
SIC: 3669 Traffic signals, electric

(G-12478)
CLARIOS
Also Called: Johnson Controls
4024 Sw Topeka Blvd (66609-1236)
PHONE....................................785 267-0801
Tim Swope, *Manager*
EMP: 16 **Privately Held**
SIC: 5075 Thermostats
HQ: Johnson Controls Inc
5757 N Green Bay Ave
Milwaukee WI 53209
414 524-1200

(G-12479)
CLARK DARGAL BUILDERS INC
Also Called: Custom 1 Construction
1324 Sw Auburn Rd (66615-1540)
PHONE....................................785 478-4811
Dargal L Clark, *President*
Dargal Clark, *President*
Brenda Clark, *Treasurer*
EMP: 18
SALES (est): 2.1MM **Privately Held**
SIC: 1521 New construction, single-family houses

(G-12480)
CLEAR VIEW INC
5709 Sw 21st St Ste 102 (66604-3719)
PHONE....................................785 286-2070
Stephen Stoll, *Owner*
David Stoll, *Opers Mgr*
EMP: 20
SALES (est): 221.6K **Privately Held**
SIC: 7349 Window cleaning

(G-12481)
CM WIND DOWN TOPCO INC
Also Called: Kmaj
825 S Kansas Ave Fl 1 (66612-1253)
PHONE....................................785 272-2122
Nancy Lawrence, *Manager*
EMP: 60
SALES (corp-wide): 1.8B **Publicly Held**
WEB: www.cumulusmedia.com
SIC: 4832 Radio broadcasting stations
PA: Cm Wind Down Topco Inc.
3280 Peachtree Rd Ne Ne2300
Atlanta GA 30305
404 949-0700

(G-12482)
CNI THL PROPCO FE LLC
Also Called: Courtyard Topeka
2033 Sw Wanamaker Rd (66604-3830)
PHONE....................................785 271-6165
Keon Marvasti,
EMP: 30
SALES (est): 299.1K **Privately Held**
SIC: 7011 Hotels & motels

(G-12483)
COCA COLA BOTTLING CO MID AMER (DH)
Also Called: Coca-Cola
435 Se 70th St (66619-1367)
PHONE....................................785 243-1071
Mike Barry, *President*
EMP: 20
SALES (est): 2.8MM
SALES (corp-wide): 31.8B **Publicly Held**
WEB: www.phillycoke.com
SIC: 2086 Bottled & canned soft drinks
HQ: Coca-Cola Refreshments Usa, Inc.
2500 Windy Ridge Pkwy Se
Atlanta GA 30339
770 989-3000

(G-12484)
COFFMAN DEFRIES & NOTHERN
534 S Kansas Ave Ste 925 (66603-3407)
PHONE....................................785 234-3461
Austin Nothern, *President*
Janice Wilch, *Manager*
Susan J Krehbiel,
EMP: 16
SALES (est): 1.7MM **Privately Held**
WEB: www.cdnlaw.com
SIC: 8111 Real estate law

(G-12485)
COHAKE DEUTSCHER AND HEFNER
4848 Sw 21st St Ste 101 (66604-4415)
PHONE....................................785 271-8181
Cecil Cohake, *Partner*
Chris Deutscher, *Partner*
William Heffner, *Partner*
Cecil B Kohake, *Partner*
EMP: 25
SALES (est): 952.1K **Privately Held**
SIC: 5995 8042 Contact lenses, prescription; contact lense specialist optometrist

(G-12486)
COLLECTION BUREAU KANSAS INC
3615 Sw 29th St Bsmt 101 (66614-2055)
PHONE....................................785 228-3636
Kent Hollins, *President*
EMP: 25 **EST:** 2008
SALES: 100K **Privately Held**
SIC: 7322 Collection agency, except real estate

(G-12487)
COLLEGE BODY SHOP
1134 Sw Kent Pl (66604-2047)
PHONE....................................785 235-5628
Michael F O'Connor, *Owner*
Mark Bell, *Partner*
Michael Oconnor, *General Mgr*
EMP: 13 **EST:** 1974
SALES (est): 1.1MM **Privately Held**
WEB: www.collegebodyshop.com
SIC: 7532 Body shop, automotive

(G-12488)
COMFORT KEEPERS
2611 Sw 17th St Ste 7 (66604-2696)
PHONE....................................785 215-8330
Randy Cox, *Owner*
Sarah Cox, *Co-Owner*
EMP: 25
SALES (est): 795.7K **Privately Held**
SIC: 8082 Home health care services

(G-12489)
COMMERCIAL MANAGEMENT COMPANY (PA)
6220 Sw 29th St Ste 200 (66614-5028)
PHONE....................................785 234-2882
J D Lakhani, *President*
Subhi Doshi, *Shareholder*
EMP: 14
SQ FT: 2,500
SALES (est): 1.8MM **Privately Held**
WEB: www.hmrproperties.com
SIC: 6531 Real estate managers

(G-12490)
COMMUNITY ACTION INC
1000 Se Hancock St (66607-1578)
P.O. Box 5256 (66605-0256)
PHONE....................................785 235-9561
Susan Wheatley, *Exec Dir*
EMP: 50
SQ FT: 4,000
SALES: 5.2MM **Privately Held**
SIC: 8322 Individual & family services

(G-12491)
COMMUNITY BANK (PA)
5431 Sw 29th St Ste 100 (66614-4484)
P.O. Box 4876 (66604-0876)
PHONE....................................785 440-4400
Carl Koupal, *CEO*
Barbara Barnard, *Vice Pres*
Jeannine Bethke, *Vice Pres*
Thomas Pfannenstiel, *Vice Pres*
Nick Armstrong, *Officer*
EMP: 25
SALES: 4.6MM **Privately Held**
WEB: www.cnbtopeka.com
SIC: 6022 State commercial banks

(G-12492)
COMMUNITY CARE NETWRK KANS INC
700 Sw Jackson St Ste 600 (66603-3786)
PHONE....................................785 233-8483
Kendra Poole, *CFO*
Trish Harkness, *Technology*
Denise Cyzman, *Exec Dir*
Susan Temaat, *Admin Asst*
EMP: 22
SQ FT: 7,000
SALES: 3.9MM **Privately Held**
SIC: 8621 Medical field-related associations

(G-12493)
COMMUNITYAMERICA CREDIT UNION
1129 S Kansas Ave Ste B (66612-1184)
PHONE....................................785 232-6900
Lisa Warner, *Branch Mgr*
EMP: 15

GEOGRAPHIC

SALES (corp-wide): 81.9MM **Privately Held**
WEB: www.cacu.com
SIC: 6062 State credit unions, not federally chartered
PA: Communityamerica Credit Union
9777 Ridge Dr
Lenexa KS 66219
913 905-7000

(G-12494)
COMPANION ANIMAL CLINIC
3335 Sw Fairlawn Rd (66614-3968)
PHONE..................................785 271-7387
Michael A Esau, *Owner*
EMP: 10
SALES (est): 352.7K **Privately Held**
SIC: 0742 Animal hospital services, pets & other animal specialties

(G-12495)
COMPASSIONATE CARE COMMUNITY
6118 Sw 38th St (66610-1308)
PHONE..................................785 783-8785
Gina Allen, *Owner*
Jonathan Allen, *Co-Owner*
Troy Russell, *Supervisor*
EMP: 35
SALES: 1MM **Privately Held**
SIC: 8082 Home health care services

(G-12496)
COMPONE SERVICES LTD
2348 Sw Topeka Blvd # 200 (66611-1283)
PHONE..................................785 267-9196
EMP: 10 **Privately Held**
SIC: 8721 Physician Billing Service
PA: Compone Services, Ltd.
4400 Will Rogers Pkwy # 105
Oklahoma City OK
405 947-5557

(G-12497)
COMPUTECH SERVICE OF KANSAS
Also Called: Integrated Solutions Group
3301 S Kansas Ave Ste B (66611-2488)
PHONE..................................785 266-2585
John Gunn, *President*
Kelly Lipprand, *COO*
Michael Larson, *Senior Engr*
F H Goforth, *Manager*
Kevin Helt, *Network Enginr*
EMP: 20
SALES (est): 1.2MM **Privately Held**
SIC: 7378 5045 Computer maintenance & repair; computers, peripherals & software; computer software

(G-12498)
COMPUTER DISTRIBUTION CORP
Also Called: Digitech Systems
524 Ne Gordon St (66608-1110)
PHONE..................................785 354-1086
◆ **EMP:** 24 **EST:** 1999
SQ FT: 9,600
SALES: 1.2MM **Privately Held**
SIC: 5734 5045 5199 5999 Computer Manufacturer & Sales Oem Distributor & Isp

(G-12499)
CONCRETE UNLIMITED CNSTR INC
3160 Se 21st St (66607-2515)
PHONE..................................785 232-8636
Donna J Marney, *President*
Perry L Marney, *Corp Secy*
EMP: 40
SQ FT: 2,400
SALES (est): 5.7MM **Privately Held**
SIC: 1771 Foundation & footing contractor; flooring contractor

(G-12500)
CONCRETE UNLIMITED INC
3160 Se 21st St (66607-2515)
PHONE..................................785 232-8636
Donna Marney, *President*
Perry Marney, *Corp Secy*
EMP: 60
SQ FT: 1,000
SALES (est): 6.3MM **Privately Held**
SIC: 1771 Concrete work

(G-12501)
CONGREGATIONAL HOME
Also Called: BREWSTER PLACE RETIREMENT COM
1205 Sw 29th St (66611-1203)
PHONE..................................785 274-3350
Lea Chaffee, *Vice Pres*
Jeremy Hall, *Vice Pres*
Larry Riggins, *CFO*
Melissa Reynolds, *Finance*
Manuel Martinez, *Manager*
EMP: 215
SQ FT: 356,000
SALES: 20.4MM **Privately Held**
SIC: 8361 8051 Home for the aged; skilled nursing care facilities

(G-12502)
CONSOLDATED RUR WTR DISTIRCT 4
1741 Ne 46th St (66617-2522)
P.O. Box 750777 (66675-0777)
PHONE..................................785 286-1729
Mike Weisehaar, *Principal*
Mike Weishaar, *Principal*
EMP: 13
SQ FT: 1,500
SALES: 2.8MM **Privately Held**
SIC: 4941 Water supply

(G-12503)
CONSORTIUM INC
Also Called: Tmhc
2121 Sw Chelsea Dr (66614-1756)
PHONE..................................785 232-1196
Diane E Bergman, *President*
EMP: 53
SQ FT: 11,000
SALES (est): 3MM **Privately Held**
WEB: www.tmhc-ks.org
SIC: 7389 Personal service agents, brokers & bureaus

(G-12504)
CONTECH ENGNERED SOLUTIONS LLC
2707 Ne Seward Ave (66616-1463)
PHONE..................................785 234-1000
Roland Holiday, *Director*
EMP: 30 **Privately Held**
SIC: 3443 3444 3312 Fabricated plate work (boiler shop); sheet metalwork; blast furnaces & steel mills
HQ: Contech Engineered Solutions Llc
9025 Centre Pointe Dr # 400
West Chester OH 45069
513 645-7000

(G-12505)
CONTEMPRARY HSING ALTRNTVES OF (HQ)
Also Called: Kelly House II
1800 Sw Fairmont Rd (66604-3699)
PHONE..................................785 271-9594
Brenda Saldoni, *President*
EMP: 30
SALES (est): 1.2MM
SALES (corp-wide): 32.7MM **Privately Held**
SIC: 6513 Retirement hotel operation
PA: Midwest Health, Inc
3024 Sw Wanamaker Rd # 300
Topeka KS 66614
785 272-1535

(G-12506)
COPE PLASTICS INC
1751 Sw 41st St (66609-1287)
PHONE..................................785 267-0552
James Carroll, *Branch Mgr*
EMP: 10
SALES (corp-wide): 246.9MM **Privately Held**
WEB: www.copeplastics.com
SIC: 3089 Plastic processing
PA: Cope Plastics, Inc.
4441 Indl Dr
Alton IL 62002
618 466-0221

(G-12507)
COPY CENTER OF TOPEKA INC
305 Se 17th St Ste C (66607-1266)
PHONE..................................785 233-6677
Matt Pivarnik, *Principal*
David Hupp, *Treasurer*
EMP: 21
SQ FT: 5,000
SALES (est): 4.4MM **Privately Held**
SIC: 2752 7334 2796 2791 Commercial printing, offset; photocopying & duplicating services; blueprinting service; platemaking services; typesetting; bookbinding & related work; secretarial & court reporting

(G-12508)
COPY SHOPPE
Also Called: Kaw Valley Printing
715 Se 8th Ave (66607-1805)
PHONE..................................785 232-0403
Al Lei, *Owner*
EMP: 5
SQ FT: 4,000
SALES: 400K **Privately Held**
SIC: 2752 7334 Lithographing on metal; photocopying & duplicating services

(G-12509)
COREFIRST BANK & TRUST (HQ)
3035 Sw Topeka Blvd (66611-2122)
P.O. Box 5049 (66605-0049)
PHONE..................................785 267-8900
Emery E Fager, *Ch of Bd*
Duane L Fager, *President*
Brian Verman, *President*
John F Fager, *Exec VP*
David Fricke, *Exec VP*
EMP: 25 **EST:** 1959
SQ FT: 30,000
SALES: 48MM **Privately Held**
WEB: www.cbtks.com
SIC: 6022 State trust companies accepting deposits, commercial
PA: Commerce Financial Corporation
3035 Sw Topeka Blvd
Topeka KS 66611
785 267-0123

(G-12510)
COREFIRST BANK & TRUST
Also Called: Hunters Ridge Branch
2841 Se Croco Rd Ste 2 (66605-1814)
PHONE..................................785 286-5100
Qiana Anthony, *Branch Mgr*
EMP: 12
SALES (corp-wide): 48MM **Privately Held**
SIC: 6022 State commercial banks
HQ: Corefirst Bank & Trust
3035 Sw Topeka Blvd
Topeka KS 66611
785 267-8900

(G-12511)
COREFIRST BANK & TRUST
1205 Sw 29th St Unit 2 (66611-1270)
P.O. Box 5049 (66605-0049)
PHONE..................................785 267-8900
Gene Wheeler, *Manager*
EMP: 10
SALES (corp-wide): 48MM **Privately Held**
WEB: www.cbtks.com
SIC: 6022 State trust companies accepting deposits, commercial
HQ: Corefirst Bank & Trust
3035 Sw Topeka Blvd
Topeka KS 66611
785 267-8900

(G-12512)
COTTON ONEIL CLINIC ENDOSCOPY
Also Called: Digestive Health Center
720 Sw Lane St (66606-1539)
PHONE..................................785 270-4850
Debra Yocum, *Principal*
EMP: 40
SALES (est): 1.6MM **Privately Held**
SIC: 8011 Clinic, operated by physicians

(G-12513)
COTTON-NEIL CLNIC REVOCABLE TR
Also Called: Stormont-Vail Healthcare, Inc.
1500 Sw 10th Ave (66604-1301)
PHONE..................................785 354-9591
Kenneth Stone, *Principal*
Curtis Baum, *Med Doctor*
Priti Duggal, *Family Practiti*
Ashley Hisel, *Family Practiti*
Hartej Sethi, *Neurology*
EMP: 99
SALES (est): 1.2MM
SALES (corp-wide): 719MM **Privately Held**
SIC: 8011 Primary care medical clinic
PA: Stormont-Vail Healthcare, Inc.
1500 Sw 10th Ave
Topeka KS 66604
785 354-6000

(G-12514)
COUNSLMAN WADE CHRPRCTIC CLNIC
Also Called: Chiropratic Clinic
1408 Sw Topeka Blvd (66612-1987)
PHONE..................................785 234-0521
Gary Counselman, *President*
Dennis D Wade, *Corp Secy*
Brett Counselman,
EMP: 10 **EST:** 1974
SQ FT: 3,000
SALES (est): 899K **Privately Held**
SIC: 8041 Offices & clinics of chiropractors

(G-12515)
COUNTRYSIDE HEALTH CENTER
440 Se Woodland Ave (66607-2172)
PHONE..................................785 234-6147
Dennis Bahr, *Principal*
EMP: 43
SALES (est): 808.7K **Privately Held**
SIC: 8051 Skilled nursing care facilities

(G-12516)
COUNTRYSIDE UNITED METHDST CH
Also Called: UNITED METHODIST PRE SCHOOL
3221 Sw Burlingame Rd (66611-2006)
PHONE..................................785 266-7541
Heather Hoffmans, *Facilities Mgr*
Eddie Kidd, *Director*
EMP: 18
SALES: 237.4K **Privately Held**
SIC: 8351 8661 Preschool center; Methodist Church

(G-12517)
COUNTY OF SHAWNEE
Also Called: Shawnee County Solid Waste
1515 Nw Saline St Ste 150 (66618-2868)
PHONE..................................785 233-4774
Brandy Biltoft, *Division Mgr*
Deanna Starkebaum, *Corp Comm Staff*
Ed Kalas, *Manager*
Steve Bolton, *Director*
Angela McHardie, *Deputy Dir*
EMP: 70 **Privately Held**
WEB: www.co.shawnee.ks.us
SIC: 4953 9111 Refuse collection & disposal services; county supervisors' & executives' offices
PA: County Of Shawnee
200 Se 7th St
Topeka KS 66603
785 233-8200

(G-12518)
COUNTY OF SHAWNEE
712 S Kansas Ave Ste 3e (66603-3821)
PHONE..................................785 233-8856
Dina Hales, *Director*
EMP: 23 **Privately Held**
WEB: www.co.shawnee.ks.us
SIC: 8322 Probation office
PA: County Of Shawnee
200 Se 7th St
Topeka KS 66603
785 233-8200

(G-12519)
COUNTY OF SHAWNEE
1515 Nw Saline St (66618-2866)
PHONE..................................785 233-2882
Mark Hixon, *Branch Mgr*
EMP: 38 **Privately Held**
WEB: www.co.shawnee.ks.us
SIC: 6531 Appraiser, real estate
PA: County Of Shawnee
200 Se 7th St
Topeka KS 66603
785 233-8200

(G-12520)
COUNTY OF SHAWNEE
1515 Nw Saline St Ste 200 (66618-2867)
PHONE..................................785 862-2071
Dean Porter, *Branch Mgr*
EMP: 70 **Privately Held**
WEB: www.co.shawnee.ks.us
SIC: 1611 9111 Highway & street construction; county supervisors' & executives' offices
PA: County Of Shawnee
200 Se 7th St
Topeka KS 66603
785 233-8200

(G-12521)
COUNTY OF SHAWNEE
Also Called: Shawnee County Public Works
1515 Nw Saline St Ste 200 (66618-2867)
PHONE..................................785 233-7702
Lynn Couch, *Deputy Dir*
EMP: 70 **Privately Held**
WEB: www.co.shawnee.ks.us
SIC: 1611 9111 Highway & street construction; county supervisors' & executives' offices
PA: County Of Shawnee
200 Se 7th St
Topeka KS 66603
785 233-8200

(G-12522)
COUNTY OF SHAWNEE
Also Called: Shawnee County Health Agency
1615 Nw 8th St (66608-1961)
P.O. Box 118 (66601-0118)
PHONE..................................785 368-2000
Nancy Mitchell, *Accountant*
Katharine Rathbun, *Branch Mgr*
Deanna Miles, *Case Mgr*
EMP: 200 **Privately Held**
SIC: 8011 9111 Clinic, operated by physicians; county supervisors' & executives' offices
PA: County Of Shawnee
200 Se 7th St
Topeka KS 66603
785 233-8200

(G-12523)
COX COMMUNICATIONS INC
1615 Sw Washburn Ave (66604-2859)
PHONE..................................785 233-3383
Scott Terry, *Manager*
EMP: 100
SALES (corp-wide): 29.2B **Privately Held**
SIC: 4813 Telephone communication, except radio
HQ: Cox Communications, Inc.
6205 B Pchtree Dnwdy Rd
Atlanta GA 30328

(G-12524)
COX COMMUNICATIONS INC
931 Sw Henderson Rd (66615-3848)
PHONE..................................785 368-1000
Drew Fleming, *Manager*
EMP: 29
SALES (corp-wide): 29.2B **Privately Held**
SIC: 4841 Cable television services
HQ: Cox Communications, Inc.
6205 B Pchtree Dnwdy Rd
Atlanta GA 30328

(G-12525)
COX MEDIA LLC
931 Sw Henderson Rd (66615-3847)
PHONE..................................785 215-8880
Deann Waldron, *Branch Mgr*
EMP: 508
SALES (corp-wide): 29.2B **Privately Held**
SIC: 4899 Data communication services
HQ: Cox Media, L.L.C.
1400 Lake Hearn Dr Ne
Brookhaven GA 30319

(G-12526)
CP ENGNERS LAND SRVEYORS INC (PA)
2710 Oak Ridge Rd (66617-9222)
PHONE..................................785 267-5071
Jim Stickler, *President*
Vivian Fuchs, *Corp Secy*
Martin Long, *Vice Pres*
EMP: 13
SQ FT: 2,000
SALES (est): 1.8MM **Privately Held**
WEB: www.cpels.kscoxmail.com
SIC: 8711 8713 7389 Engineering services; surveying services; inspection & testing services

(G-12527)
CREATIVE LANDSCAPING INC
Also Called: Schendel Lawn & Landscape
4100 Sw 40th St (66610-2341)
P.O. Box 750654 (66675-0654)
PHONE..................................785 286-0015
Brandon Moore, *President*
Amanda Hartshorn, *CFO*
EMP: 10 **EST:** 1980
SALES (est): 565K **Privately Held**
SIC: 0781 Landscape services

(G-12528)
CREATIVE SIGNS & DESIGN INC
2910 S Kansas Ave (66611-2217)
PHONE..................................785 233-8000
Michael P Weinbrecht, *President*
EMP: 6
SQ FT: 6,500
SALES (est): 630.7K **Privately Held**
SIC: 2759 3993 7389 Screen printing; signs & advertising specialties; sign painting & lettering shop

(G-12529)
CREDITORS SERVICE BUREAU INC
3410 Sw Van Buren St # 101 (66611-2258)
P.O. Box 5009 (66605-0009)
PHONE..................................785 266-3223
Pete Huston, *CEO*
EMP: 10
SQ FT: 1,500
SALES (est): 843.6K **Privately Held**
SIC: 7322 Collection agency, except real estate

(G-12530)
CRESCENT LIMOUSINES
Also Called: Leo Nia's Crescent Limousines
4216 Ne Seward Ave (66616-9516)
PHONE..................................785 232-2236
Leo Rrapaj, *President*
EMP: 12
SALES: 495K **Privately Held**
SIC: 4119 Limousine rental, with driver

(G-12531)
CRONISTER & COMPANY INC
5612 Sw Fairlawn Rd (66610-9442)
PHONE..................................785 862-5003
Richard Cronister, *President*
Judy Cronister, *Chairman*
Tim Cronister, *Vice Pres*
Kevin Cronister, *Treasurer*
Joyce Douglas, *Admin Sec*
EMP: 20
SQ FT: 6,000
SALES (est): 2.4MM **Privately Held**
WEB: www.cronister.com
SIC: 1623 Telephone & communication line construction

(G-12532)
CROSSWIND INDUSTRIES INC
2127 Se Lakewood Blvd (66605-1188)
PHONE..................................785 380-8668
EMP: 7
SALES (corp-wide): 64.3B **Publicly Held**
SIC: 3999 Atomizers, toiletry
HQ: Crosswind Industries, Inc.
6300 Nw Kelly Dr
Kansas City MO 64152
816 891-7979

(G-12533)
CRPENTER CHARTED
Also Called: Carpenter Chartered
1525 Sw Topeka Blvd Ste A (66612-1838)
P.O. Box 2099 (66601-2099)
PHONE..................................785 357-5251
Glenda Herl, *CEO*
Ken Carpenter, *Owner*
Richard Showalter,
EMP: 15
SALES (est): 1.5MM **Privately Held**
SIC: 8111 General practice law office

(G-12534)
CUMMINS COFFMAN &
3706 Sw Topeka Blvd # 302 (66609-1239)
PHONE..................................785 267-2030
Terry Cummins, *President*
Diane Coffman, *Vice Pres*
Greg Schmidtein, *Vice Pres*
Joe Anderson, *Accountant*
EMP: 17
SALES (est): 1.5MM **Privately Held**
WEB: www.cumminscoffmancpa.com
SIC: 8721 Certified public accountant

(G-12535)
CURRENT ELECTRICAL CO INC
3811 Sw South Park Ave (66609-1482)
PHONE..................................785 267-2108
Craig Cooper, *President*
Cindy Cooper, *Vice Pres*
EMP: 48 **EST:** 1978
SQ FT: 7,500
SALES: 5.7MM **Privately Held**
WEB: www.currentelectrical.net
SIC: 1731 General electrical contractor

(G-12536)
CURVES AHEAD LLC
109 Nw Woodlawn Ave (66606)
PHONE..................................785 221-9652
Timothy A Kelly, *Principal*
EMP: 14
SALES (est): 382.2K **Privately Held**
SIC: 7991 Exercise salon

(G-12537)
CUSTOM CABINET & RACK INC
Also Called: C C R
5600 Sw Topeka Blvd Ste E (66609-1011)
PHONE..................................785 862-2271
H Gerdes, *President*
Heinrich Gerdes, *President*
Leonard Kuenstler, *Vice Pres*
Betty Kuenstler, *Treasurer*
Louise Gerdes, *Director*
EMP: 20
SQ FT: 180,000
SALES (est): 4.7MM **Privately Held**
WEB: www.ccr5600.com
SIC: 5046 5021 Shelving, commercial & industrial; racks

(G-12538)
CUSTOM NEON & VINYL GRAPHICS
530 Nw Broad St (66608-1819)
PHONE..................................785 233-3218
Todd Schaefer, *Owner*
Rod Hart, *Sales Associate*
Todd Schaffer, *Manager*
Kevin Dickerson, *Admin Sec*
EMP: 7
SALES (est): 1MM **Privately Held**
SIC: 3993 Electric signs

(G-12539)
CUSTOM SHEET METAL & ROOFG INC
828 Nw Buchanan St (66608-1501)
PHONE..................................785 357-6200
Jack E Craver Jr, *President*
EMP: 32
SQ FT: 13,500
SALES (est): 6.3MM **Privately Held**
SIC: 1761 1711 Sheet metalwork; roofing contractor; siding contractor; plumbing contractors; warm air heating & air conditioning contractor; mechanical contractor

(G-12540)
CUSTOM TREE CARE INC
3431 Se 21st St Topeka (66607)
P.O. Box 67593 (66667-0593)
PHONE..................................785 478-9805
Greg Gathers, *President*
Maura Gathers, *Vice Pres*
EMP: 25
SQ FT: 2,400
SALES: 3.2MM **Privately Held**
SIC: 0783 Planting, pruning & trimming services

(G-12541)
CUT-N-EDGE INC
Also Called: Greentouch Lawn Service
3530 Se 21st St (66607-2371)
PHONE..................................785 232-9800
Jesson Ross, *President*
EMP: 10
SQ FT: 9,000
SALES: 1.3MM **Privately Held**
WEB: www.greentouchservice.com
SIC: 0781 Landscape services

(G-12542)
CYTEK MEDIA SYSTEMS INC (PA)
126 Nw Jackson St (66603-3310)
PHONE..................................785 295-4200
Bill Jones, *President*
Chris Rigdon, *Accounts Exec*
Steve Patton, *Sales Staff*
EMP: 31
SQ FT: 15,000
SALES: 10.2MM **Privately Held**
WEB: www.cytekmedia.com
SIC: 5099 5045 5065 Video & audio equipment; computers, peripherals & software; video equipment, electronic

(G-12543)
D L SMITH ELECTRICAL CNSTR
1405 Sw 41st St (66609-1295)
PHONE..................................785 267-4920
Shawn Smith, *President*
Douglas Tucker, *General Mgr*
Chase Ebert, *Project Mgr*
Maria O Smith, *Treasurer*
Janice Griffiths, *Office Mgr*
EMP: 110
SQ FT: 3,000
SALES: 20MM **Privately Held**
WEB: www.dlsmith.com
SIC: 1731 1623 General electrical contractor; communication line & transmission tower construction

(G-12544)
DALLAS CASTER DDS
8370 Sw Auburn Rd (66699-0001)
PHONE..................................785 256-2476
Dallas Caster, *Principal*
EMP: 15 **EST:** 2001
SALES (est): 222.5K **Privately Held**
SIC: 0742 Veterinarian, animal specialties

(G-12545)
DANCE FACTORY INC
5331 Sw 22nd Pl Ste 42 (66614-1550)
PHONE..................................785 272-4548
Tarah Jehlik, *Director*
EMP: 11
SALES (est): 434.1K **Privately Held**
WEB: www.dancefactorynews.com
SIC: 7911 Dance studio & school

(G-12546)
DAVE MCDERMOTT
Also Called: Premier One Data Systems
1130 Sw Winding Rd (66615-3821)
PHONE..................................785 354-8233
Dave McDermott, *Owner*
Julie Falk, *Network Enginr*
Adam Thieschafer, *Administration*
EMP: 10
SALES (est): 1.2MM **Privately Held**
SIC: 7379 Computer related consulting services

(G-12547)
DAVID COBLER
Also Called: Ace Plumbing & Sewer Service
908 N Kansas Ave (66608-1213)
PHONE..................................785 234-3384

David Cobler, *Owner*
EMP: 14
SQ FT: 2,500
SALES (est): 1.7MM **Privately Held**
SIC: 1711 7699 Plumbing contractors; sewer cleaning & rodding

(G-12548)
DAVIN ELECTRIC INC
2131 Ne Grantville Rd (66608-1717)
PHONE..................................785 234-2350
Randy Davin, *President*
Diane Davin, *Corp Secy*
EMP: 38 **EST:** 1967
SQ FT: 5,000
SALES (est): 6.8MM **Privately Held**
SIC: 1731 General electrical contractor

(G-12549)
DAVIS UNREIN HUMMER MCCALISTER
100 Se 9th St Fl 2 (66612-1213)
PHONE..................................785 354-1100
Fax: 785 354-1113
EMP: 12
SALES (est): 690K **Privately Held**
SIC: 8111 Legal Services Office

(G-12550)
DEBACKERS INC
1520 Se 10th Ave (66607-1500)
PHONE..................................785 232-6999
John D Debacker, *President*
Flora Debacker, *Corp Secy*
Greg Debacker, *Vice Pres*
EMP: 22
SQ FT: 6,800
SALES (est): 3.2MM **Privately Held**
SIC: 1711 1761 3444 Warm air heating & air conditioning contractor; sheet metalwork; sheet metalwork

(G-12551)
DENNIS M COOLEY MD
3500 Sw 6th Ave (66606-2814)
PHONE..................................785 235-0335
Dennis M Cooley, *Partner*
EMP: 30
SALES (est): 432K **Privately Held**
SIC: 8011 Pediatrician

(G-12552)
DENNIS R SUMNER CONSTRUCTION
915 Nw Valencia Rd (66615-9263)
PHONE..................................785 478-1701
Dennis R Sumner, *Owner*
EMP: 12
SALES (est): 936K **Privately Held**
SIC: 1521 Single-family housing construction

(G-12553)
DESIGNED BUS INTRORS TPEKA INC
107 Sw 6th Ave (66603-3874)
PHONE..................................785 233-2078
Kevin Sutcliffe, *President*
Lana Miller, *Facilities Mgr*
Angela Sutcliffe, *Admin Sec*
Jeanne Keller, *Admin Asst*
EMP: 10
SQ FT: 10,000
SALES (est): 5.1MM **Privately Held**
WEB: www.dbi-topeka.com
SIC: 5021 5023 5198 7389 Office furniture; carpets; draperies; wallcoverings; interior designer

(G-12554)
DF OSBORNE CONSTRUCTION INC
3310 Sw Harrison St Ste 1 (66611-2252)
PHONE..................................785 862-0333
David F Osborne, *President*
Suzanne Osborne, *Principal*
Suzanne E Osborne, *Corp Secy*
Kurt Bossert, *CFO*
EMP: 10
SQ FT: 2,500
SALES (est): 3.1MM **Privately Held**
WEB: www.theosbornecompany.com
SIC: 1542 1522 Religious building construction; commercial & office building contractors; multi-family dwelling construction; multi-family dwellings, new construction

(G-12555)
DIAMOND INTL TRCKS INC
Also Called: KCR International
500 E Tenth St (66607)
PHONE..................................785 235-8711
Dave Spinner, *Branch Mgr*
EMP: 26
SALES (corp-wide): 78.2MM **Privately Held**
WEB: www.diamondtrk.com
SIC: 5511 7538 Trucks, tractors & trailers: new & used; general truck repair
PA: Diamond International Trucks, Inc.
11401 Diamond Dr
North Little Rock AR 72117
501 945-8400

(G-12556)
DIANE LONDENE
2926 Sw 10th Ave (66604-1595)
PHONE..................................785 233-1991
Diane Londene, *Owner*
EMP: 11
SALES (est): 129.1K **Privately Held**
SIC: 7231 Beauty shops

(G-12557)
DILLON COMPANIES INC
Also Called: Dillons 47
2815 Sw 29th St (66614-2050)
PHONE..................................785 272-0661
Lynette Hall, *Manager*
EMP: 160
SALES (corp-wide): 121.1B **Publicly Held**
WEB: www.dillons.com
SIC: 5411 5992 5421 2051 Supermarkets, chain; florists; meat & fish markets; bread, cake & related products; drug stores
HQ: Dillon Companies, Inc.
2700 E 4th Ave
Hutchinson KS 67501
620 665-5511

(G-12558)
DINKEL CONSTRUCTION INC
3311 Se 21st St (66607-2520)
PHONE..................................785 232-3377
William J Dinkel, *President*
Charles E Cool, *Corp Secy*
EMP: 15
SQ FT: 1,000
SALES (est): 1.2MM **Privately Held**
SIC: 1771 Concrete work

(G-12559)
DISABILITY RIGHTS CTR OF KANS
Also Called: DRC
214 Sw 6th Ave Ste 100 (66603-3719)
PHONE..................................785 273-9661
Stephanie West, *Corp Comm Staff*
Nick Cobos, *Office Admin*
Rocky Nichols, *Exec Dir*
Debby White, *Director*
EMP: 15
SALES: 1.6MM **Privately Held**
WEB: www.drckansas.org
SIC: 8322 Social service center

(G-12560)
DORMAKABA USA INC
2300 Se Lakewood Blvd (66605-1184)
PHONE..................................717 335-4334
Vicky Wallace, *Branch Mgr*
EMP: 10
SQ FT: 10,000
SALES (corp-wide): 2.8B **Privately Held**
SIC: 5031 Doors
HQ: Dormakaba Usa Inc.
100 Dorma Dr
Reamstown PA 17567
717 336-3881

(G-12561)
DREDGE TRANSPORT SERVICE INC
1105-C Nw Lowr (66608)
P.O. Box 8207 (66608-0207)
PHONE..................................785 506-8285
Charles H Jones, *President*
John Jones, *Corp Secy*
Ryan Hedman, *Opers Mgr*
EMP: 12
SALES (est): 1.4MM **Privately Held**
SIC: 4213 Trucking, except local

(G-12562)
DUNCANS MOVIE MAGIC INC
108 Se 29th St (66605-1124)
PHONE..................................785 266-3010
Josette Duncan, *President*
Gary Duncan, *Corp Secy*
EMP: 26
SQ FT: 6,000
SALES: 637.5K **Privately Held**
SIC: 7841 Film or tape rental, motion picture

(G-12563)
DYNAMIC CMPT SLTONS TOPEKA INC
2214 Sw 10th Ave (66604-3904)
PHONE..................................785 354-7000
Frances G Miller, *CEO*
Mitchell Miller, *President*
Brad Hollingsworth, *Project Mgr*
Mark Bohnenkemper, *Senior Engr*
Irene Haws, *Sales Staff*
EMP: 19
SQ FT: 6,000
SALES: 2MM **Privately Held**
WEB: www.dcstopeka.com
SIC: 7373 Systems integration services

(G-12564)
E ARCHITECTS PA
1250 Sw Oakley Ave # 200 (66604-1618)
PHONE..................................785 234-6664
Peter Gierer, *President*
Robert D Fincham, *Vice Pres*
Robert Fincham, *Vice Pres*
EMP: 13
SQ FT: 2,100
SALES (est): 897.6K **Privately Held**
WEB: www.e-arch.info
SIC: 8712 Architectural services

(G-12565)
EAGLE AUTO SALON INC
Also Called: Eagle Auto Wash Dtailing Salon
2110 Sw Chelsea Dr (66614-1748)
PHONE..................................785 272-2886
Thomas L Enstrom, *President*
Cynthia Enstrom, *Vice Pres*
Steve Clatterbuck, *Manager*
EMP: 35
SQ FT: 8,500
SALES (est): 1.3MM **Privately Held**
SIC: 7542 Washing & polishing, automotive

(G-12566)
EAGLECREST OPERATIONS LLC
3715 Sw 29th St (66614-2107)
PHONE..................................785 272-1535
EMP: 10
SALES (est): 85.7K **Privately Held**
SIC: 8051 Skilled nursing care facilities

(G-12567)
EARLY HEADSTART CMNTY ACTION
2400 Se Highland Ave (66605-1765)
PHONE..................................785 266-3152
Phyllis Marmon, *Director*
Amy Blosstr, *Director*
Sue Wheatley, *Director*
Sylvia Selara, *Administration*
EMP: 60 **EST:** 2001
SALES (est): 930.8K **Privately Held**
SIC: 8351 Head start center, except in conjunction with school

(G-12568)
EAST KANSAS QUARTLY CNFRCE FRE
5864 Sw 26th St (66614-2404)
PHONE..................................785 272-1843
James Brewer, *Administration*
EMP: 8
SALES (est): 635.7K **Privately Held**
SIC: 2721 8661 Periodicals; religious organizations

(G-12569)
EASTSIDE BARBERSHOP & SALON
2410 Se 6th Ave (66607-2022)
PHONE..................................800 857-2906
Ronnie Brooks, *CEO*
EMP: 21 **EST:** 2016
SALES (est): 74.6K **Privately Held**
SIC: 7231 Unisex hair salons; cosmetology & personal hygiene salons

(G-12570)
ECONOMIC & EMPOLYMENT SUPPORT
915 Sw Harrison St 681w (66612-1505)
PHONE..................................785 296-4276
Bobbi Mariani, *Director*
EMP: 65
SALES (est): 1.1MM **Privately Held**
SIC: 8399 Health & welfare council

(G-12571)
EDUCATIONAL CREDIT UNION (PA)
2808 Sw Arrowhead Rd (66614-2447)
PHONE..................................785 271-6900
Gavin Wittman, *President*
Stan Seidel, *Chairman*
Lisa Marshall, *Exec VP*
Jennifer Kirmse, *VP Bus Dvlpt*
Michael Griffin, *Branch Mgr*
EMP: 27
SQ FT: 7,000
SALES: 7.5MM **Privately Held**
SIC: 6061 Federal credit unions

(G-12572)
EDUCATIONAL CREDIT UNION
Also Called: Quest Credit Union
3623 Se 29th St (66605-2072)
PHONE..................................785 267-4900
Jackie Anderson, *Branch Mgr*
Sheryl Crawford,
EMP: 13
SALES (est): 1.5MM
SALES (corp-wide): 7.5MM **Privately Held**
SIC: 6062 State credit unions, not federally chartered
PA: Educational Credit Union
2808 Sw Arrowhead Rd
Topeka KS 66614
785 271-6900

(G-12573)
EGOS SALON & DAY SPA INC
2120 Sw Brandywine Ln # 130
(66614-5448)
PHONE..................................785 272-1181
Mark Sowders, *President*
EMP: 16 **EST:** 2000
SALES (est): 332.4K **Privately Held**
WEB: www.egossalon.com
SIC: 7991 Spas

(G-12574)
EMERSON CONSTRUCTION INC (PA)
4149 Nw 25th St (66618-3713)
P.O. Box 4067 (66604-0067)
PHONE..................................785 235-0555
V Harley Emerson, *Ch of Bd*
Stan Emerson, *President*
Todd Emerson, *Corp Secy*
EMP: 18
SQ FT: 3,000
SALES: 4.2MM **Privately Held**
WEB: www.emersonconst.com
SIC: 1623 1794 1771 Sewer line construction; water main construction; excavation work; concrete work

(G-12575)
EMPORIA FREIGHT AND DLVRY SVC
Also Called: Crosstown Couriers
4631 Se Adams St (66609-9421)
P.O. Box 19051 (66619-0051)
PHONE....785 862-1611
James Stallbaumer, *President*
Joyce Stallbaumer, *Corp Secy*
EMP: 16
SQ FT: 10,600
SALES (est): 1.9MM **Privately Held**
SIC: 4213 Contract haulers

(G-12576)
ENCHANTED SMILES EASTHETIC
2949 Sw Wanamaker Dr # 1 (66614-5325)
PHONE....785 246-6300
Stefania A Caracioni, *Owner*
EMP: 34
SALES (est): 304.2K **Privately Held**
SIC: 8021 Dentists' office

(G-12577)
ENDOSCOPY & SURGERY CTR TOPEKA
Also Called: Amsurg
2200 Sw 6th Ave Ste 103 (66606-1707)
PHONE....785 354-1254
Skekhar K Challa, *Treasurer*
Jerry Feagan, *Director*
EMP: 10
SALES (est): 1.3MM **Privately Held**
SIC: 8011 Surgeon

(G-12578)
ENERGY MANAGEMENT & CTRL CORP
6600 Sw 10th Ave Ste B (66615-3858)
PHONE....785 233-0289
William Bruce Corbin, *President*
Darrin R Godfrey, *Vice Pres*
Darrin Godfrey, *Vice Pres*
Bruce Corbin, *Supervisor*
EMP: 14 **EST:** 1977
SALES: 1.2MM **Privately Held**
WEB: www.lsapa.com
SIC: 8711 Engineering services

(G-12579)
ENVIRO-HEALTH CORP
1608 Sw Macvicar Ave (66604-2744)
PHONE....785 235-8300
Glenn Freeman, *President*
EMP: 12
SQ FT: 3,200
SALES (est): 2MM **Privately Held**
WEB: www.ehcdirect.com
SIC: 2899 Water treating compounds

(G-12580)
ERC/RESOURCE & REFERRAL INC
1100 Sw Wanamaker Rd # 101 (66604-2678)
PHONE....785 357-5171
Reva Wywadis, *Exec Dir*
EMP: 15
SALES: 1.7MM **Privately Held**
WEB: www.ercrefer.org
SIC: 8399 8322 Social service information exchange; referral service for personal & social problems

(G-12581)
ERIC K JOHNSON
Also Called: Hamilton Laughlin
3649 Sw Burlingame Rd # 102 (66611-2051)
PHONE....785 267-2410
Eric Johnson, *Partner*
John Hamilton, *Partner*
Jeff Jones, *Counsel*
EMP: 10 **EST:** 2000
SALES (est): 855.6K **Privately Held**
WEB: www.hamiltonlaughlin.com
SIC: 8111 General practice attorney, lawyer

(G-12582)
EVENTIDE CONVALESCENT CENTER
2015 Se 10th Ave (66607-1615)
PHONE....785 233-8918
Mac Austin, *President*
Jodi Hicks, *Admin Sec*
EMP: 65
SQ FT: 22,000
SALES (est): 3.2MM **Privately Held**
WEB: www.eventidecc.com
SIC: 8051 8052 Skilled nursing care facilities; intermediate care facilities

(G-12583)
EVERGY KANSAS CENTRAL INC (HQ)
818 S Kansas Ave (66612-1203)
P.O. Box 889 (66601-0889)
PHONE....785 575-6300
Terry Bassham, *President*
Kevin E Bryant, *COO*
Gregory A Greenwood, *Exec VP*
Heather A Humphrey, *Senior VP*
Karolyn Bergman, *Vice Pres*
EMP: 600
SALES: 2.6B
SALES (corp-wide): 4.2B **Publicly Held**
WEB: www.westarenergy.com
SIC: 4911 Generation, electric power
PA: Evergy, Inc.
1200 Main St
Kansas City MO 64105
816 556-2200

(G-12584)
EVERGY KANSAS CENTRAL INC
4001 Nw 14th St (66618-2829)
PHONE....785 575-1352
Martin Jones, *Branch Mgr*
Carlene Barkley, *Executive Asst*
EMP: 53
SALES (corp-wide): 4.2B **Publicly Held**
SIC: 4911 4923 Distribution, electric power; gas transmission & distribution
HQ: Evergy Kansas Central, Inc.
818 S Kansas Ave
Topeka KS 66612
785 575-6300

(G-12585)
EWELL CONSTRUCTION INC
5324 Sw 53rd St (66610-9411)
PHONE....913 499-7331
Gale Ewell, *President*
Delome Ewell, *Vice Pres*
EMP: 15
SALES (est): 2.6MM **Privately Held**
SIC: 1541 Steel building construction

(G-12586)
EXECUTIVE MNOR LEAVENWORTH INC (PA)
Also Called: Ramada Inn Downtown Hotel Conv
420 Se 6th Ave Ste A (66607-1181)
PHONE....785 234-5400
Jim Parrish, *President*
EMP: 10 **EST:** 1974
SQ FT: 40,000
SALES (est): 2.4MM **Privately Held**
SIC: 7011 5812 7991 7999 Hotels & motels; diner; physical fitness facilities; game parlor; bars & lounges

(G-12587)
EXECUTIVE OFFICE OF KANSAS
Also Called: Pawnee Rock State Hstoric Site
6425 Sw 6th Ave (66615-1099)
PHONE....785 272-8681
Susan Forbes, *Librarian*
Bob Knecht, *Librarian*
Darrell Garwood, *Manager*
Christine Desmuke, *Prgrmr*
Jennie Chinn, *Exec Dir*
EMP: 15 **Privately Held**
SIC: 8412 9199 Historical society;
HQ: Executive Office Of The State Of Kansas
300 Sw 10th Ave
Topeka KS 66612
785 296-6240

(G-12588)
EXPERT ROOFING LLC
2730 Ne Spring Creek Dr (66617-3717)
PHONE....785 286-1999
Dan Bratcher, *Owner*
EMP: 10
SALES (est): 664.5K **Privately Held**
WEB: www.expertroofing.com
SIC: 1761 Roofing contractor

(G-12589)
EXPRESS CARD AND LABEL CO INC
2012 Ne Meriden Rd (66608-1737)
P.O. Box 4247 (66604-0247)
PHONE....785 233-0369
Mark W Stillings, *Ch of Bd*
John W George, *President*
Pam Whitfield, *Executive*
EMP: 40 **EST:** 1977
SQ FT: 20,000
SALES (est): 5.6MM **Privately Held**
WEB: www.exflexo.com
SIC: 2759 Flexographic printing

(G-12590)
F & L ENTERPRISES INC
4431 Se California Ave (66609-1567)
PHONE....785 266-4933
Kristina Leifried, *Principal*
EMP: 11
SALES (est): 1.1MM **Privately Held**
SIC: 8748 Business consulting

(G-12591)
F&F PRODUCTIONS INC
1608 Sw Macvicar Ave (66604-2744)
PHONE....785 235-8300
Glenn Freeman, *Principal*
EMP: 12
SALES (est): 130.8K **Privately Held**
SIC: 7822 Motion picture & tape distribution

(G-12592)
FACTORY DIRECT APPLIANCE
1040 Sw Wanamaker Rd (66604-3807)
PHONE....785 272-8800
Mary Mehrtens, *President*
Randy Korte, *Manager*
EMP: 19
SQ FT: 17,000
SALES (est): 2.6MM **Privately Held**
WEB: www.appliancefactorydirect.com
SIC: 5722 7629 Electric household appliances, major; electrical household appliance repair

(G-12593)
FAMILY SVC GDNCE CTR TPEKA INC (PA)
325 Sw Frazier Ave (66606-1963)
PHONE....785 232-5005
Brenda Mills, *CEO*
Ed Cullumber, *COO*
Chris Hartman, *CFO*
Gaylene Cook, *Manager*
Erin Landreth, *Data Proc Staff*
EMP: 171
SQ FT: 17,500
SALES: 15.6MM **Privately Held**
WEB: www.fsgctopeka.com
SIC: 8093 Mental health clinic, outpatient

(G-12594)
FAMILY VIDEO MOVIE CLUB INC
6749 Sw 29th St Ste A (66614-5657)
PHONE....785 478-0606
Tyler Johnson, *Branch Mgr*
EMP: 26
SALES (corp-wide): 189.9MM **Privately Held**
SIC: 7841 Video disk/tape rental to the general public
HQ: Family Video Movie Club Inc.
2500 Lehigh Mt Ave
Glenview IL 60026
847 904-9000

(G-12595)
FARMERS GROUP INC
Also Called: Farmers Insurance
5654 Sw 29th St (66614-2443)
PHONE....785 271-8088
Bob Newton, *Manager*
EMP: 25
SALES (corp-wide): 48.2B **Privately Held**
WEB: www.farmers.com
SIC: 6411 Insurance agents, brokers & service
HQ: Farmers Group, Inc.
6301 Owensmouth Ave
Woodland Hills CA 91367
323 932-3200

(G-12596)
FARMERS GROUP INC
Farmers Insurance
3646 Sw Plass Ave (66611-2578)
P.O. Box 268994, Oklahoma City OK (73126-8994)
PHONE....785 267-4653
James W Rempe, *Manager*
Brian Gross, *Agent*
EMP: 20
SALES (corp-wide): 48.2B **Privately Held**
WEB: www.farmers.com
SIC: 6411 Insurance agents, brokers & service
HQ: Farmers Group, Inc.
6301 Owensmouth Ave
Woodland Hills CA 91367
323 932-3200

(G-12597)
FARVIEW FARMS MEAT CO
6325 Nw Topeka Blvd (66617-1813)
PHONE....785 246-1154
Drew Forster, *Owner*
EMP: 6
SALES (est): 290K **Privately Held**
SIC: 2011 Meat packing plants

(G-12598)
FAST SIGNS INC
Also Called: Fastsigns
5999 Sw 22nd Park Ste C (66614-1910)
PHONE....785 271-8899
Steve Gee, *President*
Terri Gee, *Vice Pres*
EMP: 6 **EST:** 1997
SALES (est): 922.5K **Privately Held**
SIC: 3993 Signs & advertising specialties

(G-12599)
FEDERAL EXPRESS CORPORATION
Also Called: Fedex
1850 Sw 42nd St (66609-1234)
PHONE....800 463-3339
EMP: 11
SALES (corp-wide): 69.6B **Publicly Held**
SIC: 4513 Package delivery, private air
HQ: Federal Express Corporation
3610 Hacks Cross Rd
Memphis TN 38125
901 369-3600

(G-12600)
FEDERAL HOME LOAN BANK TOPEKA (PA)
Also Called: FHLBANK TOPEKA
500 Sw Wanamaker Rd (66606-2448)
P.O. Box 176 (66601-0176)
PHONE....785 233-0507
Mark E Yardley, *President*
Kelly Malone, *Business Mgr*
Patrick C Doran, *Exec VP*
Donald Cushing, *Assistant VP*
Gant Welborn, *Assistant VP*
EMP: 100
SQ FT: 32,000
SALES: 1.2B **Privately Held**
WEB: www.fhlbtopeka.com
SIC: 6111 Federal & federally sponsored credit agencies

(G-12601)
FEDEX FREIGHT CORPORATION
2115 Ne Meriden Rd (66608-1738)
PHONE....800 752-0047
EMP: 20
SALES (corp-wide): 69.6B **Publicly Held**
SIC: 4213 Trucking, except local
HQ: Fedex Freight Corporation
1715 Aaron Brenner Dr
Memphis TN 38120

GEOGRAPHIC

(G-12602)
FEDEX GROUND PACKAGE SYS INC
6700 Sw Topeka Blvd 820 (66620-1441)
P.O. Box 19231 (66619-0231)
PHONE....................................800 463-3339
EMP: 30
SALES (corp-wide): 69.6B **Publicly Held**
SIC: 4212 Delivery service, vehicular
HQ: Fedex Ground Package System, Inc.
1000 Fed Ex Dr
Coraopolis PA 15108
800 463-3339

(G-12603)
FEDEX OFFICE & PRINT SVCS INC
2201 Sw Wanamaker Rd # 102
(66614-4964)
PHONE....................................785 272-2500
EMP: 20
SALES (corp-wide): 69.6B **Publicly Held**
WEB: www.kinkos.com
SIC: 7334 2759 2752 Photocopying & duplicating services; commercial printing; commercial printing, lithographic
HQ: Fedex Office And Print Services, Inc.
7900 Legacy Dr
Plano TX 75024
800 463-3339

(G-12604)
FERGUSON ENTERPRISES LLC
2220 Se Lakewood Blvd (66605-1170)
PHONE....................................785 354-4305
James Rid, *Principal*
Josh Wiggins, *Branch Mgr*
James Reid, *Manager*
EMP: 15
SALES (corp-wide): 20.7B **Privately Held**
WEB: www.ferguson.com
SIC: 5074 5999 Heating equipment (hydronic); plumbing & heating supplies
HQ: Ferguson Enterprises, Llc
12500 Jefferson Ave
Newport News VA 23602
757 874-7795

(G-12605)
FIDELITY KANSAS BANKSHARES
Also Called: Fidelity State Bank & Trust
600 S Kansas Ave (66603-3804)
P.O. Box 1737 (66601-1737)
PHONE....................................785 295-2100
Anderson Chandler, *President*
Allan Pawle, *Exec VP*
Beverly Anderson, *Vice Pres*
EMP: 45
SALES (est): 2.3MM **Privately Held**
SIC: 6022 State commercial banks

(G-12606)
FIDELITY MANAGEMENT CORP
Also Called: Misty Glenn Apts
3201 Sw Randolph Ave Ofc (66611-1774)
PHONE....................................785 266-8010
Rhonda Mercer, *Manager*
EMP: 10
SALES (corp-wide): 100.1MM **Privately Held**
WEB: www.fidelitymgmt.com
SIC: 6513 Apartment hotel operation
HQ: Fidelity Management Corporation
100 E English St Ste 500
Wichita KS 67202
316 291-5950

(G-12607)
FIDELITY STATE BANK AND TR CO (PA)
600 S Kansas Ave (66603-3804)
P.O. Box 1737 (66601-1737)
PHONE....................................785 295-2100
Anderson Chandler, *President*
Allan Towle, *Exec VP*
Beverly Anderson, *Vice Pres*
Mark Kossler, *Vice Pres*
David Trask, *Treasurer*
EMP: 25 **EST:** 1922
SQ FT: 12,000
SALES: 5MM **Privately Held**
WEB: www.fidelitytopeka.com
SIC: 6022 State trust companies accepting deposits, commercial

(G-12608)
FIELD & STREAM CLUB INC
1901 Sw Collins Ave (66604-3222)
PHONE....................................785 233-4793
Russel Green, *President*
EMP: 19
SALES (est): 182K **Privately Held**
SIC: 8641 Social club, membership

(G-12609)
FINANCIAL INSTITUTION TECH INC
6301 Sw 9th St (66615-3859)
PHONE....................................785 273-5578
Duane Lankard, *CEO*
Ronnie Wooten, *President*
EMP: 17
SALES (est): 1.2MM **Privately Held**
SIC: 6282 Investment advice

(G-12610)
FINANCIAL INSTITUTION TECH INC
Also Called: Suntell
6206 Sw 9th Ter B (66615-3822)
PHONE....................................888 848-7349
Duane Lankard, *CEO*
Scott Wickham, *Software Dev*
Jack Brier, *Director*
Duane Fager, *Director*
Michael Hatesohl, *Director*
EMP: 21
SQ FT: 1,200
SALES (est): 3.1MM **Privately Held**
SIC: 7373 7372 Computer integrated systems design; application computer software

(G-12611)
FINNEY & TRNP SD TRNSPRTTN
603 Sw Topeka Blvd # 401 (66603-3361)
PHONE....................................785 235-2393
Robert B Thorn, *Managing Prtnr*
Craig Mattox, *Partner*
EMP: 14
SALES (est): 1.4MM **Privately Held**
WEB: www.ftstructures.com
SIC: 8711 Civil engineering

(G-12612)
FIRST CALL
1137 Sw Gage Blvd (66604-1760)
PHONE....................................785 234-2881
Robert Freeman, *President*
EMP: 10
SALES: 300K **Privately Held**
SIC: 7261 Funeral service & crematories

(G-12613)
FIRST CLASS TRANSPORTATION
2300 Sw 29th St Ste 125 (66611-1739)
PHONE....................................785 266-1331
R Steinbock, *Principal*
EMP: 10
SALES (est): 502.2K **Privately Held**
SIC: 4789 Transportation services

(G-12614)
FIRST MANAGEMENT INC
1425 Sw Lane St Apt 205 (66604-3475)
PHONE....................................785 232-5555
Ashley Rudolph, *Branch Mgr*
EMP: 10 **Privately Held**
SIC: 6513 Apartment building operators
PA: First Management, Inc.
901 New Hampshire St # 201
Lawrence KS 66044

(G-12615)
FISHER PTTRSON SYLER SMITH LLP (PA)
3550 Sw 5th St (66606-1910)
P.O. Box 949 (66601-0949)
PHONE....................................785 232-7761
Justice King, *Partner*
Steve Fabert, *Partner*
Steve Johnson, *Partner*
JB King, *Partner*
Chris Larscheid, *Partner*
EMP: 32
SALES (est): 5MM **Privately Held**
WEB: www.fisherpatterson.com
SIC: 8111 General practice attorney, lawyer

(G-12616)
FLEET SERVICES TOPEKA
210 Se 4th St (66603-3509)
PHONE....................................785 368-3735
Ron Raines, *Manager*
EMP: 20
SALES (est): 772.3K **Privately Held**
SIC: 4173 Maintenance facilities for motor vehicle passenger transport

(G-12617)
FLEETPRIDE INC
4812 Sw Topeka Blvd (66609-1135)
PHONE....................................785 862-1540
Edward Newlin, *Manager*
EMP: 10 **Privately Held**
WEB: www.tpe-pdi.com
SIC: 5013 5012 5531 Truck parts & accessories; automobiles & other motor vehicles; automotive & home supply stores
HQ: Fleetpride, Inc.
600 Las Colinas Blvd E # 400
Irving TX 75039
469 249-7500

(G-12618)
FLORENCE BOB CONTRACTOR INC
1934 S Kansas Ave (66612-1437)
P.O. Box 5258 (66605-0258)
PHONE....................................785 357-0341
Bob Florence Jr, *Ch of Bd*
Stacy Florence, *President*
Adam Florence, *Corp Secy*
Diane Fox, *Controller*
EMP: 60 **EST:** 1900
SQ FT: 6,000
SALES (est): 7.4MM **Privately Held**
WEB: www.florencecontractor.com
SIC: 1742 Plastering, plain or ornamental; drywall; acoustical & ceiling work

(G-12619)
FLORENCE CRITTENTON SERVICES
2649 Sw Arrowhead Rd (66614-2458)
PHONE....................................785 233-0516
Dana Schoffelman, *CEO*
Jolana Pinon, *CFO*
Charlotte Munoz, *Asst Director*
Deborah Agnew, *Nurse*
EMP: 50
SALES: 2.1MM **Privately Held**
WEB: www.flocritkansas.org
SIC: 8322 Individual & family services

(G-12620)
FLORISTS REVIEW ENTPS INC
Also Called: Super Floral Retailing Magazin
3300 Sw Van Buren St (66611-2226)
P.O. Box 4368 (66604-0368)
PHONE....................................785 266-0888
Frances Dudley, *President*
▲ **EMP:** 25
SQ FT: 5,000
SALES (est): 11.9MM **Privately Held**
WEB: www.floristsreview.com
SIC: 5192 Magazines

(G-12621)
FOIL STAMPING & EMBOSSING ASSN
2150 Sw Westport Dr # 101 (66614-1918)
PHONE....................................785 271-5816
Jeff Peterson, *Exec Dir*
EMP: 6
SALES: 332.7K **Privately Held**
WEB: www.fsea.com
SIC: 2721 Magazines: publishing only, not printed on site

(G-12622)
FOLEY EQUIPMENT COMPANY
Caterpillar Authorized Dealer
1637 Sw 42nd St (66609-1253)
P.O. Box 1698 (66601-1698)
PHONE....................................785 266-5784
Jeff Fouraker, *Vice Pres*
EMP: 70
SALES (corp-wide): 124.2MM **Privately Held**
WEB: www.martintractor.com
SIC: 5082 Construction & mining machinery
HQ: Foley Equipment Company
1550 S West St
Wichita KS 67213
316 943-4211

(G-12623)
FOLEY EQUIPMENT COMPANY
Also Called: Caterpillar Authorized Dealer
1737 Sw 42nd St (66609-1215)
P.O. Box 1698 (66601-1698)
PHONE....................................785 266-5770
George Mullinix, *Finance*
Bob Johnson, *Sales Mgr*
Brock Schwartz, *Sales Staff*
Felicia Marlar, *Mktg Coord*
Louis Ericson, *Branch Mgr*
EMP: 180
SALES (corp-wide): 124.2MM **Privately Held**
SIC: 5082 7538 5083 5084 Road construction & maintenance machinery; diesel engine repair: automotive; agricultural machinery; engines & parts, diesel
HQ: Foley Equipment Company
1550 S West St
Wichita KS 67213
316 943-4211

(G-12624)
FOSTER CALLANAN FINANCIAL SVC
Also Called: Advisor's Excel
2950 Sw Mcclure Rd (66614-4109)
PHONE....................................866 363-9595
Brad Johnson, *Vice Pres*
Shannon Kruger, *Vice Pres*
Matt Neuman, *Vice Pres*
Jason Ross, *Vice Pres*
Damon Thompson, *Vice Pres*
EMP: 40 **EST:** 2007
SALES (est): 72.2K **Privately Held**
SIC: 6311 Life insurance

(G-12625)
FOULSTON SIEFKIN LLP
534 S Kansas Ave Ste 1400 (66603-3436)
PHONE....................................785 233-3600
Charles R Hay, *Counsel*
Kyle J Steadman, *Counsel*
Jim Rankin, *Branch Mgr*
EMP: 13
SALES (corp-wide): 19MM **Privately Held**
WEB: www.foulston.com
SIC: 8111 General practice attorney, lawyer
PA: Foulston Siefkin Llp
1551 N Waterfront Pkwy # 100
Wichita KS 67206
316 267-6371

(G-12626)
FOX RIDGE COOP TOWNHOUSES INC
1209 Sw Glendale Dr (66604-2110)
PHONE....................................785 273-0640
Lee Anne Skinner, *Manager*
Rosie Oderamtt, *Manager*
EMP: 14 **EST:** 1971
SALES (est): 879.8K **Privately Held**
SIC: 6513 Apartment building operators

(G-12627)
FREEMAN HOLDINGS LLC
Also Called: Million Air Topeka
740 Se Airport Dr Ste 10 (66619-1385)
PHONE....................................785 862-0950
Gary Richard, *Manager*
EMP: 11
SALES (est): 752.3K
SALES (corp-wide): 2.6MM **Privately Held**
WEB: www.free-man.net
SIC: 4581 Airports, flying fields & services
PA: Freeman Holdings, L.L.C.
740 Se Airport Dr Ste 10
Topeka KS 66619
913 951-5600

(G-12628)
FREEMAN HOLDINGS LLC (PA)
Also Called: Million Air
740 Se Airport Dr Ste 10 (66619-1385)
PHONE....................................913 951-5600
Chris Freeman, *Principal*
EMP: 19

▲ = Import ▼=Export
◆ =Import/Export

SALES (est): 2.6MM **Privately Held**
WEB: www.free-man.net
SIC: 4581 Aircraft maintenance & repair services

(G-12629)
FRITO-LAY NORTH AMERICA INC
4236 Sw Kirklawn Ave (66609-1266)
PHONE..................................785 267-2600
Danny Sheern, *Safety Mgr*
Judy Reid, *Buyer*
Allen Moore, *Technical Mgr*
Marla Isaac, *Accounting Mgr*
Susan Pleasant, *Branch Mgr*
EMP: 580
SALES (corp-wide): 64.6B **Publicly Held**
WEB: www.fritolay.com
SIC: 2096 2099 Cheese curls & puffs; food preparations
HQ: Frito-Lay North America, Inc.
7701 Legacy Dr
Plano TX 75024

(G-12630)
G COOPERS INC
Also Called: Coopers
401 Sw 32nd Ter (66611-2205)
PHONE..................................785 267-4100
Greg Cooper, *President*
EMP: 11
SQ FT: 7,200
SALES (est): 820.6K **Privately Held**
SIC: 1711 1731 Plumbing contractors; electrical work

(G-12631)
GAGE CENTER DENTAL GROUP PA
Also Called: Burkett, Jeffrey L DDS
1271 Suthwest Woodhull St (66604)
PHONE..................................785 273-4770
Brenda Vink Wilson, *Mng Officer*
Darren Lowen, *Admin Sec*
EMP: 59
SQ FT: 10,000
SALES (est): 4.2MM **Privately Held**
SIC: 8021 Dentists' office

(G-12632)
GARDNER FLOOR COVERING INC (PA)
Also Called: Gardeners Flooring America
3401 S Kansas Ave (66611-2222)
P.O. Box 5003 (66605-0003)
PHONE..................................785 266-6220
Fax: 785 266-8534
EMP: 29
SQ FT: 13,000
SALES (est): 5.1MM **Privately Held**
SIC: 5713 5023 Ret Floor Covering

(G-12633)
GARY J NEWMAN DDS PA
Also Called: Mark Hall DDS
5225 Sw 7th St Ste 1 (66606-2480)
PHONE..................................785 273-1544
Mark J Hall DDS, *President*
Gary J Newman DDS, *President*
EMP: 14
SALES (est): 1MM **Privately Held**
SIC: 8021 Orthodontist

(G-12634)
GENOA HEALTHCARE KANSAS LLC
330 Sw Oakley Ave (66606-1995)
PHONE..................................785 783-0209
Kelly Bowers, *Principal*
EMP: 10
SALES (est): 409K **Privately Held**
SIC: 8082 Home health care services

(G-12635)
GEOSOURCE LLC
1605 Sw 41st St (66609-1250)
PHONE..................................785 272-7200
John J Zey,
Tracie O'Brate, *Admin Sec*
Axel S Novion,
EMP: 11 **EST**: 2007
SALES (est): 1.5MM **Privately Held**
WEB: www.geosourceeng.com
SIC: 8711 Professional engineer

(G-12636)
GHD SERVICES INC
1502 Sw 41st St (66609-1200)
PHONE..................................785 783-8982
Michael Staffileno, *President*
EMP: 21
SALES (corp-wide): 386.9MM **Privately Held**
SIC: 8742 Management consulting services
PA: Ghd Services Inc.
2055 Niagara Falls Blvd # 3
Niagara Falls NY 14304
716 297-6150

(G-12637)
GIRL SCTS OF NE KANSAS & NW MO (PA)
2919 Sw Wanamaker Rd L (66614-4972)
PHONE..................................816 358-8750
Joy Wheeler, *CEO*
EMP: 18
SQ FT: 24,000
SALES (est): 3.8MM **Privately Held**
WEB: www.girlscoutsmcc.org
SIC: 8641 Girl Scout organization

(G-12638)
GLEN THURBER
Also Called: Arrow Dynamics
2041 Sw Western Ave (66604-3077)
PHONE..................................785 233-9541
Glen Thurber, *Owner*
EMP: 20
SALES (est): 2.9MM **Privately Held**
SIC: 5091 Fishing tackle

(G-12639)
GO-MODERN LLC
2950 Sw Mcclure Rd (66614-4109)
PHONE..................................785 271-1445
EMP: 6 **EST**: 2015
SALES (est): 776.6K **Privately Held**
SIC: 2752 Commercial printing, lithographic

(G-12640)
GOLD STAR CONCRETE CNSTR
6021 Sw 29th St (66614-6200)
PHONE..................................785 478-4495
Ralph A Steinlage, *President*
Larry S Law, *Corp Secy*
Damian F Steinlage, *Vice Pres*
EMP: 20
SQ FT: 500
SALES: 1.4MM **Privately Held**
SIC: 1771 Concrete work

(G-12641)
GOODELL STRATTON EDMONDS & P
Also Called: Goodell, Gerald L
515 S Kansas Ave Ste 100 (66603-3415)
PHONE..................................785 233-0593
Belinda Crocker, *President*
H Philip Elwood, *Managing Prtnr*
N Larry Bork, *Partner*
David E Bruns, *Partner*
Les E Diehl, *Partner*
EMP: 40
SQ FT: 25,000
SALES (est): 5.6MM **Privately Held**
WEB: www.goodellstrattonlaw.com
SIC: 8111 General practice law office

(G-12642)
GOODWILL WSTN MO & EASTRN KANS
Also Called: Goodwill Store 11
5515 Sw 21st St Ste C (66604-3745)
PHONE..................................785 228-9774
EMP: 23
SALES (corp-wide): 21.3MM **Privately Held**
WEB: www.mokangoodwill.org
SIC: 5932 8331 3444 Clothing, secondhand; furniture, secondhand; job training services; sheet metalwork
PA: Goodwill Of Western Missouri & Eastern Kansas
800 E 18th St
Kansas City MO 64108
816 220-1779

(G-12643)
GOODYEAR TIRE & RUBBER COMPANY
420 Sw Croix St (66611-2212)
PHONE..................................785 266-3862
Mike Krallman, *Manager*
EMP: 16
SALES (corp-wide): 15.4B **Publicly Held**
WEB: www.goodyear.com
SIC: 5531 7534 Automotive tires; tire repair shop
PA: The Goodyear Tire & Rubber Company
200 E Innovation Way
Akron OH 44316
330 796-2121

(G-12644)
GRAY & COMPANY INC
625 Se Hancock St (66607-1818)
PHONE..................................785 232-0913
Walker Gray, *President*
Phil Gray, *Treasurer*
Paul Gray, *Admin Sec*
EMP: 29
SQ FT: 4,400
SALES (est): 3.8MM **Privately Held**
SIC: 1721 1771 Commercial painting; industrial painting; commercial wallcovering contractor; flooring contractor

(G-12645)
GRAY TELEVISION GROUP INC
Also Called: Wibw TV 13
631 Sw Commerce Pl (66615-1234)
PHONE..................................785 272-6397
Michael Turner, *Opers Mgr*
Jim Ogle, *Opers-Prdtn-Mfg*
EMP: 46
SALES (corp-wide): 1B **Publicly Held**
WEB: www.graycommunication.com
SIC: 4833 Television broadcasting stations
HQ: Gray Television Group, Inc.
4370 Peachtree Rd Ne # 500
Brookhaven GA 30319
404 266-8333

(G-12646)
GREATER TOPEKA COMMERCE
719 S Kansas Ave 100 (66603-3807)
PHONE..................................785 234-2644
Doug Kinsinger, *President*
Christy Caldwell, *Vice Pres*
Kathy Muhlenberg, *Vice Pres*
EMP: 21
SALES: 1.6MM **Privately Held**
SIC: 8611 Chamber of Commerce

(G-12647)
GREENBRIER COMPANIES INC
Also Called: Greenbrier Repair & Services
100 Ne Woodruff Ave (66616-1174)
PHONE..................................866 722-7068
Aaron Welton, *Branch Mgr*
EMP: 20
SALES (corp-wide): 3B **Publicly Held**
SIC: 4789 Railroad car repair
PA: The Greenbrier Companies Inc
1 Centerpointe Dr Ste 200
Lake Oswego OR 97035
503 684-7000

(G-12648)
GREENPOINT CNSTR DEM PROC CTR
1405 Se Madison St (66607-1213)
PHONE..................................785 234-6000
David Bahm, *Owner*
EMP: 10 **EST**: 2008
SALES (est): 272.6K **Privately Held**
SIC: 4953 Recycling, waste materials

(G-12649)
GREG COHEN DDS
1125 Sw Gage Blvd Ste A (66604-2281)
PHONE..................................785 273-2350
Greg Cohen DDS, *Owner*
EMP: 10
SQ FT: 2,200
SALES: 600K **Privately Held**
SIC: 8021 Dentists' office

(G-12650)
GREG E ROSS DRYWALL
7934 Sw 10th Ave (66615-1218)
PHONE..................................785 478-9557
Greg E Ross, *Owner*
Becky Ross, *Manager*
EMP: 12
SALES (est): 576.8K **Privately Held**
SIC: 1742 Drywall

(G-12651)
GREGG TIRE CO INC (PA)
300 Sw 6th Ave (66603-3196)
PHONE..................................785 233-4156
John R Gregg, *President*
Rob Gregg, *Vice Pres*
Robert Brown, *Treasurer*
EMP: 10
SQ FT: 14,000
SALES: 5.9MM **Privately Held**
WEB: www.greggtire.com
SIC: 5531 7538 5014 Automotive tires; general automotive repair shops; automobile tires & tubes

(G-12652)
GREGG TIRE CO INC
300 Sw 6th Ave (66603-3196)
PHONE..................................785 233-4156
Tony Doll, *Branch Mgr*
EMP: 11
SALES (corp-wide): 5.9MM **Privately Held**
WEB: www.greggtire.com
SIC: 7533 5531 Auto exhaust system repair shops; automotive tires
PA: Gregg Tire Co Inc
300 Sw 6th Ave
Topeka KS 66603
785 233-4156

(G-12653)
GUILFOYLE ROOFING
3432 Nw Lwer Silver Lk Rd (66618)
PHONE..................................785 233-9315
Kenneth Guilfoyle, *Owner*
EMP: 10
SQ FT: 1,200
SALES: 700K **Privately Held**
SIC: 1761 Roofing contractor; sheet metalwork

(G-12654)
H & R BLOCK INC
2900 Sw Oakley Ave Ste I (66614-2600)
PHONE..................................785 271-0706
EMP: 16
SALES (corp-wide): 3B **Publicly Held**
SIC: 7291 Tax Return Preparation Services
PA: H & R Block, Inc.
1 H&R Block Way
Kansas City MO 64105
816 854-3000

(G-12655)
H & R PLUMBING INC
1300 Se Monroe St (66612-1140)
PHONE..................................785 233-4427
Harry Thornton, *President*
Ruby Thornton, *Corp Secy*
EMP: 14
SALES: 48K **Privately Held**
SIC: 1711 Plumbing contractors

(G-12656)
HAAG OIL CO LLC
Also Called: Haag & Decker Oil
326 Se 15th St (66607-1204)
PHONE..................................785 357-0270
Thomas J Haag, *Mng Member*
EMP: 100
SQ FT: 7,800
SALES (est): 21.7MM **Privately Held**
SIC: 5171 Petroleum bulk stations

(G-12657)
HAAG OIL COMPANY LLC
Also Called: Haag Decker Oil Company
326 Se 15th St (66607-1204)
PHONE..................................785 357-0270
Harry Coker, *Branch Mgr*
EMP: 14
SALES (corp-wide): 3.6MM **Privately Held**
SIC: 4212 Petroleum haulage, local
PA: Haag Oil Company, Llc
326 Se 15th St
Topeka KS 66607
785 357-0270

GEOGRAPHIC

(G-12658)
HAIR PRODUCTIONS INC
4002 Sw Huntoon St (66604-1837)
PHONE....................................785 273-2881
Jeanie Custer, *President*
William Custer, *Vice Pres*
EMP: 10
SQ FT: 2,100
SALES (est): 274.9K **Privately Held**
SIC: 7231 Hairdressers

(G-12659)
HALL PUBLICATIONS INC
Also Called: Topeka Home Buyers Guide
630 S Kansas Ave Lowr (66603-3479)
PHONE....................................785 232-8600
EMP: 9
SQ FT: 3,600
SALES (est): 420K **Privately Held**
WEB: www.topekametro.com
SIC: 2711 2741 2721 Job printing & newspaper publishing combined; telephone & other directory publishing; periodicals: publishing only

(G-12660)
HAMILTON & WILSON DDS (PA)
2235 Sw Westport Dr (66614-1945)
PHONE....................................785 272-3722
Scott Hamilton DDS, *Partner*
Don Wilson, *Partner*
EMP: 13
SQ FT: 1,800
SALES (est): 1.2MM **Privately Held**
WEB: www.hwortho.com
SIC: 8021 Orthodontist

(G-12661)
HAMM INC
2450 Nw Water Works Dr (66606)
PHONE....................................785 235-6568
Joe Marney, *Branch Mgr*
EMP: 20
SALES (corp-wide): 2.1B **Publicly Held**
SIC: 3273 Ready-mixed concrete
HQ: Hamm, Inc.
609 Perry Pl
Perry KS 66073
785 597-5111

(G-12662)
HAMM INC
Also Called: Builders Choice Aggregates
6721 Nw 17th St (66618-5500)
PHONE....................................785 233-7263
Steve Lutz, *Branch Mgr*
EMP: 6
SALES (corp-wide): 2.1B **Publicly Held**
SIC: 3273 Ready-mixed concrete
HQ: Hamm, Inc.
609 Perry Pl
Perry KS 66073
785 597-5111

(G-12663)
HAMPTON INN
1515 Sw Arrowhead Rd (66604-4051)
PHONE 785 228-0111
Aris Chaudhary, *Principal*
EMP: 19
SALES (est): 963.3K **Privately Held**
SIC: 7011 Hotels & motels

(G-12664)
HANGER PROSTHETICS &
Also Called: Hanger Clinic
830 Sw Lane St Ste B (66606-2488)
PHONE....................................785 232-5382
Sam Liang, *President*
Larry Hanson, *Manager*
EMP: 5
SALES (corp-wide): 1B **Publicly Held**
SIC: 5999 3842 Orthopedic & prosthesis applications; limbs, artificial
HQ: Hanger Prosthetics & Orthotics East, Inc.
33 North Ave Ste 101
Tallmadge OH 44278

(G-12665)
HARVEST FACILITY HOLDINGS LP
Also Called: Thornton Place
2901 Sw Armstrong Ave # 215 (66614-5640)
PHONE....................................785 228-0555
Joe Rowlette, *Manager*
EMP: 30 **Publicly Held**
WEB: www.holidaytouch.com
SIC: 6513 Retirement hotel operation
HQ: Harvest Facility Holdings Lp
5885 Meadows Rd Ste 500
Lake Oswego OR 97035
503 370-7070

(G-12666)
HASTCO INC
2801 Nw Button Rd (66618-1457)
PHONE....................................785 235-8718
Art Kuehler, *President*
Nancy Kuehler, *President*
Brian Griffith, *Superintendent*
Brian Springer, *Superintendent*
Jerry Walter, *Superintendent*
EMP: 27
SQ FT: 4,800
SALES (est): 7.6MM **Privately Held**
WEB: www.hastco.com
SIC: 1541 1542 Industrial buildings, new construction; commercial & office building, new construction

(G-12667)
HATCHER CONSULTANTS INC (PA)
2955 Sw Wanamaker Dr C (66614-5340)
PHONE....................................785 271-5557
David Hatcher, *President*
Curtis Hatcher, *Vice Pres*
Mike Scott, *Project Mgr*
Jan Hatcher, *Admin Sec*
EMP: 13
SQ FT: 2,500
SALES (est): 1.1MM **Privately Held**
WEB: www.hatcherconsultants.com
SIC: 8742 Business consultant

(G-12668)
HAYDEN TOWER SERVICE INC
2836 Nw Us Highway 24 (66618-2700)
PHONE....................................785 232-1840
Kevin Hayden, *President*
Kevin J Hayden, *President*
Robert Prellwitz, *General Mgr*
Dan McCabe, *Vice Pres*
Tommy Lewis, *Project Mgr*
EMP: 55
SQ FT: 6,000
SALES: 8MM **Privately Held**
WEB: www.haydentower.com
SIC: 1799 1623 Antenna installation; transmitting tower (telecommunication) construction

(G-12669)
HDB CONSTRUCTION INC
2040 Ne Meriden Rd (66608-1737)
PHONE....................................785 232-5444
Walter Harrison Sr, *Branch Mgr*
EMP: 20
SALES (corp-wide): 4.6MM **Privately Held**
WEB: www.hdbconstruction.com
SIC: 4212 Local trucking, without storage
PA: Hdb Construction, Inc.
729 Se Wear Ave
Topeka KS 66607
785 232-5444

(G-12670)
HDB CONSTRUCTION INC
729 Se Wear Ave Ste A (66607-1769)
PHONE....................................785 232-5444
Alonzo Harrison, *President*
EMP: 25
SQ FT: 900
SALES (est): 1.1MM **Privately Held**
SIC: 1629 Earthmoving contractor

(G-12671)
HEALTH CARE STABILIZATION FUND
Also Called: Kansas Healthcare
300 Sw 8th Ave Ste 200 (66603-3952)
PHONE....................................785 291-3777
Bob Hayes, *Exec Dir*
EMP: 16
SQ FT: 5,000
SALES (est): 1.4MM **Privately Held**
WEB: www.hcsf.org
SIC: 8099 Blood related health services

(G-12672)
HEALTH DPKNSAS ASSN LCAL DEPTS
Also Called: Kalhd
300 Sw 8th Ave Fl 3 (66603-3940)
PHONE....................................785 271-8391
Sara Spinks, *Principal*
Edie Snethen, *Exec Dir*
Michelle Ponce, *Exec Dir*
EMP: 12
SALES (est): 478.3K **Privately Held**
SIC: 8621 Professional membership organizations

(G-12673)
HEALTH MANAGEMENT STRATEGIES
107 Sw 6th Ave (66603-3874)
PHONE....................................785 233-1165
David Magill, *Director*
EMP: 16
SALES (est): 228.3K **Privately Held**
SIC: 8322 Individual & family services

(G-12674)
HEART AMERICA HOSPICE KANS LLC
3715 Sw 29th St Ste 100 (66614-2111)
PHONE....................................785 228-0400
Steve Parkey,
EMP: 40
SQ FT: 2,600
SALES: 4.3MM **Privately Held**
WEB: www.heartofamericahospice.com
SIC: 8052 Personal care facility

(G-12675)
HEARTLAND COCA-COLA BTLG LLC
435 Se 70th St (66619-1367)
PHONE....................................785 232-9372
EMP: 3433
SALES (corp-wide): 23.9B **Privately Held**
SIC: 5149 2086 Beverages, except coffee & tea; carbonated beverages, nonalcoholic: bottled & canned
PA: Heartland Coca-Cola Bottling Company Llc
9000 Marshall Dr
Lenexa KS

(G-12676)
HEARTLAND COFFEE & PACKG CORP
719 Se Hancock St (66607-1820)
PHONE....................................785 232-0383
John Harter, *President*
EMP: 6
SALES: 425K **Privately Held**
SIC: 2095 Coffee roasting (except by wholesale grocers)

(G-12677)
HEARTLAND ELECTRIC INC
1721 Sw Van Buren St (66612-1440)
PHONE....................................785 233-9546
Dave Gigous, *President*
Don Gigous, *Corp Secy*
EMP: 25
SQ FT: 5,000
SALES: 3MM **Privately Held**
SIC: 1731 General electrical contractor

(G-12678)
HEARTLAND EYE CARE LLC
619 Sw Corporate Vw (66615-1233)
PHONE....................................785 235-3322
Dr John Marsh, *President*
Trent Vande Garde,
Rita Tablante,
EMP: 20
SQ FT: 2,400
SALES: 5MM **Privately Held**
SIC: 8042 Offices & clinics of optometrists

(G-12679)
HEARTLAND HOSPICE SERVICES LLC
Also Called: Heartland HM Hlth Care Hospice
2231 Sw Wanamaker Rd # 202 (66614-4275)
PHONE....................................785 271-6500
Lisa Walder, *Director*
EMP: 25
SALES (corp-wide): 8.2B **Privately Held**
SIC: 8082 Home health care services
HQ: Heartland Hospice Services, Llc
333 N Summit St
Toledo OH 43604

(G-12680)
HEARTLAND MANAGEMENT COMPANY
Also Called: Newcomer Funeral Home-Casper
520 Sw 27th St (66611-1228)
P.O. Box 5516 (66605-0516)
PHONE....................................785 233-6655
Warren J Newcomer, *President*
Russ Burlew, *Accounting Mgr*
Bailee Howard, *Marketing Staff*
Cole Lanum, *IT/INT Sup*
EMP: 13
SALES (est): 1.2MM **Privately Held**
SIC: 8741 Management services

(G-12681)
HEARTLAND WORKS INC
5020 Sw 28th St Ste 100 (66614-2348)
PHONE....................................785 234-0500
David Brennan, *Exec Dir*
Theresa Figge, *Director*
Jerry Long,
EMP: 22
SALES: 2.8MM **Privately Held**
WEB: www.odjcc.com
SIC: 8331 Job training & vocational rehabilitation services

(G-12682)
HEATH FAMILY DENTISTRY
2714 Nw Topeka Blvd # 101 (66617-1147)
PHONE....................................785 234-5410
Michael Mead DDS, *President*
Paul Heath, *President*
EMP: 10
SALES (est): 730.5K **Privately Held**
SIC: 8021 Dentists' office

(G-12683)
HELPING HANDS HUMANE SOCIETY
5720 Sw 21st St (66604-3720)
PHONE....................................785 233-7325
Carol Stubbs, *Exec Dir*
EMP: 20
SALES: 1.7MM **Privately Held**
SIC: 8699 Animal humane society

(G-12684)
HENSON HUTTON MUDRICK GRAGSON
100 Se 9th St Fl 2 (66612-1213)
PHONE....................................785 232-2200
John Hutton, *Partner*
Chuck Henson, *Partner*
Amanda S Vogelsberg, *Associate*
EMP: 10
SALES: 58K **Privately Held**
SIC: 8621 Bar association

(G-12685)
HERITAGE MANAGEMENT CORP (PA)
5629 Sw Barrington Ct S (66614-2565)
PHONE....................................785 273-2995
Richard Plush Jr, *President*
Marsha Plush, *Executive*
EMP: 10 **EST:** 1978
SQ FT: 2,400
SALES (est): 2.7MM **Privately Held**
SIC: 6531 Real estate managers

(G-12686)
HERITAGE TRACTOR INC
Also Called: John Deere Authorized Dealer
2701 Nw Us Highway 24 (66618-1468)
PHONE....................................785 235-5100
Ken Wagner, *President*
EMP: 25
SALES (corp-wide): 66.3MM **Privately Held**
SIC: 3524 5261 7699 5082 Lawn & garden tractors & equipment; lawn & garden supplies; lawn mower repair shop; construction & mining machinery
PA: Heritage Tractor, Inc.
915 Industrial Park Rd
Baldwin City KS 66006
785 594-6486

(G-12687)
HERRMANS EXCAVATING INC
1459 Se Jefferson St (66607-1297)
PHONE....................................785 233-4146
David A Herrman, *President*
Jack D Herrman, *Vice Pres*
Mary Herrman, *Admin Sec*
EMP: 40 **EST:** 1949
SQ FT: 3,000
SALES (est): 4.2MM **Privately Held**
SIC: 1794 1623 4212 Excavation & grading, building construction; underground utilities contractor; water main construction; sewer line construction; dump truck haulage

(G-12688)
HF RUBBER MACHINERY INC (DH)
1701 Nw Topeka Blvd (66608-1822)
P.O. Box 8250 (66608-0250)
PHONE....................................785 235-2336
Andreas Limper, *President*
Jon Hanft, *Sales Dir*
Vida Belic, *Manager*
▲ **EMP:** 45 **EST:** 1960
SQ FT: 56,000
SALES (est): 14.7MM
SALES (corp-wide): 360.4K **Privately Held**
WEB: www.hfrmusa.com
SIC: 3542 Extruding machines (machine tools), metal
HQ: Harburg-Freudenberger Maschinenbau Gmbh
Seevestr. 1
Hamburg 21079
407 717-90

(G-12689)
HILL & COMPANY INC (PA)
1424 Se Monroe St (66612-1199)
PHONE....................................785 235-5374
Larry Hill, *President*
Craig Hill, *Vice Pres*
Daryl Hill, *Admin Sec*
EMP: 14
SQ FT: 36,500
SALES: 5.4MM **Privately Held**
WEB: www.hillcoinc.com
SIC: 5063 Electrical supplies

(G-12690)
HILLS PET NUTRITION INC (HQ)
400 Sw 8th Ave Ste 101 (66603-3925)
P.O. Box 148 (66601-0148)
PHONE....................................800 255-0449
Neil Thompson, *CEO*
Joe Giles, *General Mgr*
Jeni Sloan, *General Mgr*
Jesper Nordengaard, *Vice Pres*
Bob Howard, *Plant Mgr*
◆ **EMP:** 500 **EST:** 1969
SALES (est): 1.1B
SALES (corp-wide): 15.5B **Publicly Held**
SIC: 5149 2048 2047 Pet foods; prepared feeds; dog & cat food
PA: Colgate-Palmolive Company
300 Park Ave Fl 3
New York NY 10022
212 310-2000

(G-12691)
HILLS PET NUTRITION INC
Also Called: Hill's Pet Products
320 Ne Crane St (66603-3613)
PHONE....................................785 231-2812
Aaron Pursley, *General Mgr*
Todd Watson, *QC Mgr*
EMP: 150
SALES (corp-wide): 15.5B **Publicly Held**
SIC: 2047 2048 Dog & cat food; prepared feeds
HQ: Hill's Pet Nutrition, Inc.
400 Sw 8th Ave Ste 101
Topeka KS 66603
800 255-0449

(G-12692)
HILLS PET NUTRITION INC
Also Called: Hill's Tech Center
1035 Ne 43rd St (66617-1587)
P.O. Box 1658 (66601-1658)
PHONE....................................785 286-1451
Deborah Nicholes, *Vice Pres*
Amber Artzer, *Technician*
EMP: 150
SALES (corp-wide): 15.5B **Publicly Held**
SIC: 5199 2048 Gifts & novelties; prepared feeds
HQ: Hill's Pet Nutrition, Inc.
400 Sw 8th Ave Ste 101
Topeka KS 66603
800 255-0449

(G-12693)
HILLS PET NUTRITION SALES INC (DH)
400 Sw 8th Ave Ste 101 (66603-3925)
PHONE....................................785 354-8523
Robert Wheeler, *CEO*
Neil Thomson, *CEO*
Justin Skala, *President*
Andrew Hendry, *Admin Sec*
▼ **EMP:** 47 **EST:** 1998
SALES (est): 262.7MM
SALES (corp-wide): 15.5B **Publicly Held**
SIC: 5149 Pet foods
HQ: Hill's Pet Nutrition, Inc.
400 Sw 8th Ave Ste 101
Topeka KS 66603
800 255-0449

(G-12694)
HIS AND HER HAIRSTYLING INC
3311 Sw 6th Ave (66606-1905)
PHONE....................................785 232-9724
Cynthia S Martin, *President*
EMP: 10
SALES (est): 299.3K **Privately Held**
SIC: 7231 Cosmetology & personal hygiene salons

(G-12695)
HMS HOLDINGS CORP
2348 Sw Topeka Blvd # 101 (66611-1286)
PHONE....................................785 271-9300
EMP: 36
SALES (corp-wide): 598.2MM **Publicly Held**
SIC: 8742 Business consultant
PA: Hms Holdings Corp.
5615 High Point Dr # 100
Irving TX 75038
214 453-3000

(G-12696)
HOBART TRANSPORTATION CO INC (PA)
Also Called: Hertz
313 S Kansas Ave (66603-3618)
PHONE....................................785 267-4468
EMP: 15
SQ FT: 1,500
SALES (est): 1.6MM **Privately Held**
SIC: 7514 Rent-A-Car Service

(G-12697)
HOLIDAY INN EX SUITES TOPEKA N
601 Nw Us Highway 24 (66608-1985)
P.O. Box 8189 (66608-0189)
PHONE....................................785 861-7200
Madan Rattan,
EMP: 15
SALES (est): 831.4K **Privately Held**
SIC: 7011 Hotels & motels

(G-12698)
HOLY NAME CATHOLIC CHURCH (PA)
Also Called: Holy Name Church
911 Sw Clay St (66606-1437)
PHONE....................................785 232-7744
Jon Hullinger, *Owner*
EMP: 110
SALES (est): 2MM **Privately Held**
SIC: 8661 8211 8351 Catholic Church; Catholic elementary & secondary schools; preschool center

(G-12699)
HOLY NAME CHURCH
Also Called: Materdei Childhood Center
911 Sw Clay St (66606-1437)
PHONE....................................785 232-1603
Sharon Long, *Treasurer*
Judy Wohletz, *Director*
Sarah Sthmidtlein, *Director*
EMP: 23
SALES (est): 270.6K **Privately Held**
SIC: 8351 Preschool center

(G-12700)
HOME DEPOT USA INC
Also Called: Home Depot, The
5200 Sw Wenger Dr (66609-1183)
PHONE....................................785 217-2260
Aaron Dewitt, *Supervisor*
EMP: 13
SALES (corp-wide): 108.2B **Publicly Held**
SIC: 5211 7359 Home centers; tool rental
HQ: Home Depot U.S.A., Inc.
2455 Paces Ferry Ave
Atlanta GA 30339

(G-12701)
HOME DEPOT USA INC
Also Called: Home Depot, The
5900 Sw Huntoon St Frnt (66604-2290)
PHONE....................................785 272-5949
Shelly Crossland, *Manager*
EMP: 150
SALES (corp-wide): 108.2B **Publicly Held**
WEB: www.homerentalsdepot.com
SIC: 5211 7359 Home centers; tool rental
HQ: Home Depot U.S.A., Inc.
2455 Paces Ferry Ave
Atlanta GA 30339

(G-12702)
HOME INSTEAD SENIOR CARE
2900 Sw Wanamaker Dr # 103
(66614-4167)
PHONE....................................785 272-6101
Gail Shaheed, *Owner*
Peter Shaheed, *Co-Owner*
EMP: 40
SALES (est): 562.1K **Privately Held**
SIC: 8082 Home health care services

(G-12703)
HOMESTEAD ASSISTED LIVING
5820 Sw Drury Ln (66604-2262)
PHONE....................................785 272-2200
Susan Bullock, *Exec Dir*
EMP: 25
SALES (est): 68.1K **Privately Held**
SIC: 8322 Old age assistance

(G-12704)
HORST TRRILL KRST ARCHITECTS PA (PA)
Also Called: Htk Architects
900 S Kansas Ave Ste 200 (66612-1245)
PHONE....................................785 266-5373
Mark Franzen, *President*
Donald Pruitt, *Vice Pres*
Russ Arfmann, *Project Mgr*
Zach Snethen, *Project Mgr*
Charles Smith, *Treasurer*
EMP: 23 **EST:** 1959
SQ FT: 10,000
SALES (est): 3.2MM **Privately Held**
WEB: www.htkarchitects.net
SIC: 8712 Architectural engineering

(G-12705)
HOUSING AND CREDIT COUNSELING (PA)
Also Called: Cccs of Topeka/Lawrence
1195 Sw Buchanan St # 101 (66604-1172)
PHONE....................................785 234-0217
Marilyn Stanley, *CEO*
Terry Leatherman, *President*
Karen Hiller, *Exec Dir*
EMP: 25
SQ FT: 4,000
SALES: 856.1K **Privately Held**
WEB: www.hcci-ks.org
SIC: 8399 8748 Neighborhood development group; advocacy group; business consulting

(G-12706)
HUMBERT ENVELOPE MACHINERY
3742 Ne Kincaid Rd (66617-3625)
PHONE....................................785 845-6085
Rodney Humbert, *Owner*
EMP: 12
SALES (est): 1.1MM **Privately Held**
WEB:
www.humbertenvelopemachinery.com
SIC: 7389 Brokers, business: buying & selling business enterprises

(G-12707)
HUMMERT INTERNATIONAL INC
1415 Nw Moundview Dr (66618-2891)
PHONE....................................785 234-5652
Brian Broughton, *Engineer*
Dennis Whitedon, *Manager*
EMP: 14
SALES (corp-wide): 39.5MM **Privately Held**
WEB: www.hummert.com
SIC: 4225 General warehousing & storage
PA: Hummert International, Inc.
4500 Earth City Expy
Earth City MO 63045
314 506-4500

(G-12708)
HUNTINGDON PARK STANDARD SVC
Also Called: BP
3120 Sw Gage Blvd (66614-2900)
PHONE....................................785 272-4499
Gary Haage, *Owner*
EMP: 10
SALES (est): 742.1K **Privately Held**
SIC: 5541 7538 Filling stations, gasoline; general automotive repair shops

(G-12709)
HUYETT JONES PARTNERS
Also Called: Jones-Seel-Huyett
3200 Sw Huntoon St (66604-1606)
P.O. Box 4512 (66604-0512)
PHONE....................................785 228-0900
Gary Jones, *President*
Rod Seel, *Vice Pres*
Kurt Eskilson, *CFO*
Linda Eisenhut, *Web Dvlpr*
Sherri Wilson, *Director*
EMP: 13
SQ FT: 3,200
SALES (est): 2.8MM **Privately Held**
WEB: www.jshadv.com
SIC: 7311 Advertising consultant

(G-12710)
HYGIENIC DRY CLEANERS INC (PA)
2930 Sw Mcclure Rd (66614-4120)
PHONE....................................785 478-0066
Grady Golden, *President*
Brenda Golden, *Treasurer*
Grady M Golden, *Sales Executive*
EMP: 23
SQ FT: 4,000
SALES (est): 697.7K **Privately Held**
WEB: www.hygienicdryclean.com
SIC: 7216 Cleaning & dyeing, except rugs

(G-12711)
I T G CONSULTING INC
2207 Sw Alameda Ct (66614-4218)
PHONE....................................785 228-1585
Jared Arnold, *President*
EMP: 15

GEOGRAPHIC

SQ FT: 5,000
SALES (est): 1.4MM **Privately Held**
WEB: www.itgconsulting.com
SIC: 7379 Computer related consulting services

(G-12712)
IDEALEASE OF MO-KAN INC
Also Called: K C R International Trucking
500 E Tenth St (66607)
PHONE..................................785 235-8711
Greg Johnson, *Manager*
EMP: 25
SALES (corp-wide): 78.2MM **Privately Held**
SIC: 7513 Truck leasing, without drivers; truck rental, without drivers
HQ: Idealease Of Mo-Kan, Inc.
7700 Ne 38th St
Kansas City MO 64161

(G-12713)
IGT GLOBAL SOLUTIONS CORP
128 N Kansas Ave Fl 1 (66603-3536)
PHONE..................................785 861-7300
Bob Heptig, *General Mgr*
Marc Collette, *Technology*
EMP: 30
SALES (corp-wide): 4.8B **Privately Held**
WEB: www.gtech.com
SIC: 7999 3575 7372 Lottery operation; computer terminals; prepackaged software
HQ: Igt Global Solutions Corporation
10 Memorial Blvd
Providence RI 02903
401 392-1000

(G-12714)
IMA FINANCIAL GROUP INC
2820 Sw Mission Woods Dr # 150 (66614-9962)
PHONE..................................785 232-2202
Mark Wilkerson, *Principal*
EMP: 42
SALES (corp-wide): 53.4MM **Privately Held**
SIC: 6399 Warranty insurance, product; except automobile
PA: The Ima Financial Group Inc
8200 E 32nd St N
Wichita KS 67226
316 267-9221

(G-12715)
INDEL CORPORATION
2257 Sw Romar Rd (66614-6067)
PHONE..................................785 478-9719
Dean Wineinger, *President*
Wayne Reiners, *Treasurer*
William Brown, *Admin Sec*
EMP: 11
SALES (est): 1.2MM **Privately Held**
SIC: 1521 New construction, single-family houses

(G-12716)
INDEPENDENT ELECTRIC MCHY CO
2221 Nw Vail Ave (66608-1906)
PHONE..................................785 233-4282
Robert Mount, *Branch Mgr*
EMP: 7
SALES (corp-wide): 9MM **Privately Held**
WEB: www.iemco.com
SIC: 7694 Electric motor repair
PA: Independent Electric Machinery Company
4425 Oliver St
Kansas City KS 66106
913 362-1155

(G-12717)
INDIGENTS DEFENSE SVCS KANS BD
701 Sw Jackson St (66603-3700)
PHONE..................................785 296-1833
Albert Bandy, *Branch Mgr*
EMP: 19 **Privately Held**
SIC: 8111 9222 Legal services; legal counsel & prosecution;
HQ: Kansas Board Of Indigents' Defense Services
700 Sw Jackson St
Topeka KS 66603
785 296-6631

(G-12718)
INDIGENTS DEFENSE SVCS KANS BD (DH)
700 Sw Jackson St (66603-3743)
PHONE..................................785 296-6631
Patricia Scalia, *Exec Dir*
EMP: 13
SALES (est): 14.8MM **Privately Held**
SIC: 8111 Legal services
HQ: Executive Office Of The State Of Kansas
300 Sw 10th Ave
Topeka KS 66612
785 296-6240

(G-12719)
INDIGENTS DEFENSE SVCS KANS BD
Also Called: Appellate Defender Office
700 Sw Jackson St Ste 900 (66603-3733)
PHONE..................................785 296-5484
Patrick Lawless, *Chief*
EMP: 25 **Privately Held**
SIC: 8111 9222 Legal services; legal counsel & prosecution;
HQ: Kansas Board Of Indigents' Defense Services
700 Sw Jackson St
Topeka KS 66603
785 296-6631

(G-12720)
INDIVIDUAL SUPPORT SYSTEMS INC
3500 Sw 10th Ave (66604-1904)
PHONE..................................785 228-9443
Kathy Stiffler, *President*
Dale Stiffler, *Vice Pres*
EMP: 100
SQ FT: 1,200
SALES: 2.9MM **Privately Held**
WEB: www.isskansas.org
SIC: 8082 Home health care services

(G-12721)
INDUSTRIAL CHROME INC (PA)
Also Called: ICI Manufacturing
834 Ne Madison St (66608-1128)
PHONE..................................785 235-3463
Ellis Needham, *CEO*
Naomi Needham, *Corp Secy*
Chris Needham, *Vice Pres*
Jessica Meadors, *Accountant*
◆ **EMP:** 72 **EST:** 1955
SQ FT: 75,000
SALES (est): 18.9MM **Privately Held**
WEB: www.industrial-chrome.com
SIC: 3714 3471 Motor vehicle parts & accessories; chromium plating of metals or formed products

(G-12722)
INDUSTRIAL CLEANING AND MAINT
Also Called: ICM
4330 Nw Westgate Rd (66618-3419)
P.O. Box 750581 (66675-0581)
PHONE..................................785 246-9262
Stephen Edwards, *President*
Bonnie Edwards, *Corp Secy*
EMP: 25
SALES (est): 645K **Privately Held**
WEB: www.icmgo.net
SIC: 7699 1771 Machinery cleaning; concrete work

(G-12723)
INDUSTRIAL MAINT TOPEKA INC
Also Called: IMI
4501 Nw Us Highway 24 (66618-3809)
P.O. Box 754, Perry (66073-0754)
PHONE..................................785 842-6252
Todd Harrington, *President*
EMP: 42
SQ FT: 3,000
SALES (est): 15.1MM **Privately Held**
SIC: 3441 Fabricated structural metal

(G-12724)
INNOVATIVE TECHNOLOGY SERVICES
5924 Sw Cherokee Ct (66614-4563)
PHONE..................................785 271-2070
Barclay Mead, *CEO*
EMP: 20
SALES (est): 966.1K **Privately Held**
WEB: www.itstopeka.com
SIC: 7371 Custom computer programming services

(G-12725)
INSULATION DRYWALL CONTRS INC
510 Sw 49th St (66609-1151)
PHONE..................................785 862-0554
Stuart Kemble, *President*
Denise Kemble, *Treasurer*
Patricia Kemble, *Shareholder*
EMP: 36
SQ FT: 5,600
SALES: 2.3MM **Privately Held**
SIC: 1742 Insulation, buildings; drywall

(G-12726)
INTERIM HEALTHCARE INC
Also Called: Interim Healthcare of Topeka
1251 Sw Arrowhead Rd (66604-4061)
PHONE..................................785 272-1616
Jay M Stehley, *Principal*
EMP: 181
SALES (corp-wide): 69.2MM **Privately Held**
SIC: 7363 Temporary help service
PA: Interim Healthcare Inc.
1601 Swgrs Corp Pkwy # 200
Sunrise FL 33323
800 338-7786

(G-12727)
INTERSTATE ELEVATOR INC
2406 Nw Clay St (66618-1467)
PHONE..................................785 234-2817
Bryan Ball, *President*
Jake Poteete, *Treasurer*
Brenda Simpson, *Manager*
EMP: 10
SQ FT: 6,000
SALES: 2.8MM **Privately Held**
WEB: www.interstateelevator.com
SIC: 3534 7699 Elevators & equipment; elevators: inspection, service & repair

(G-12728)
ISG TECHNOLOGY LLC
Also Called: Integrated Solutions Group
3301 S Kansas Ave Ste B (66611-2488)
PHONE..................................785 266-2585
Kelly Lipprand, *Senior Engr*
Mike Reece, *Sales Associate*
Kevin Brunton, *Branch Mgr*
EMP: 15
SALES (corp-wide): 75MM **Privately Held**
WEB: www.isgtech.com
SIC: 7379 Computer related consulting services
PA: Isg Technology, Llc
3030 Cortland Cir 300
Salina KS 67401
785 823-1555

(G-12729)
ITC GREAT PLAINS LLC
3500 Sw Fairlawn Rd # 101 (66614-3979)
PHONE..................................785 783-2226
Matthew Dills, *Vice Pres*
Joe Welch, *Mng Member*
▲ **EMP:** 13
SALES: 93.2MM **Privately Held**
WEB: www.itcgreatplains.com
SIC: 4911 Distribution, electric power

(G-12730)
J A LYDEN CONSTRUCTION CO
3825 Nw Button Rd (66618-1542)
PHONE..................................785 286-1427
Joann Lyden, *President*
Bill Lyden, *Officer*
EMP: 14
SQ FT: 1,000
SALES: 2.1MM **Privately Held**
SIC: 1542 Commercial & office building, new construction; commercial & office buildings, renovation & repair

(G-12731)
J F MCGIVERN INC
3333 Se 21st St (66607-2520)
PHONE..................................785 354-1787
John A McGivern, *President*
Stephen Beier, *Vice Pres*
EMP: 25
SQ FT: 4,200
SALES (est): 2.8MM **Privately Held**
SIC: 1721 Commercial painting; industrial painting

(G-12732)
J T LARDNER CUT STONE INC
128 Nw Van Buren St (66603-3316)
PHONE..................................785 234-8634
George Newton, *President*
Michelle Hoferer, *Corp Secy*
James C Lardner, *Vice Pres*
EMP: 11 **EST:** 1920
SQ FT: 22,500
SALES: 1MM **Privately Held**
SIC: 3281 5032 Cut stone & stone products; brick, stone & related material

(G-12733)
J&M TOOLS LLC
5241 Nw Arroyo Ct (66618-3151)
PHONE..................................785 608-3343
Jason Cook, *Principal*
EMP: 7
SALES (est): 667.6K **Privately Held**
SIC: 3423 Hand & edge tools

(G-12734)
J-DOT INC
Also Called: Blue DOT Services Company Kans
3365 Sw Gage Blvd (66614-3814)
PHONE..................................785 272-1633
Terry McCart, *President*
D Von Kopfman, *COO*
Susan Flynn, *Human Res Mgr*
Janice Davis, *Manager*
Garrett McCart, *Manager*
EMP: 44
SQ FT: 11,280
SALES: 5.8MM **Privately Held**
SIC: 1711 Plumbing, heating, air-conditioning contractors

(G-12735)
JACKSONS GREENHOUSE & GRDN CTR
1933 Nw Lwer Silver Lk Rd (66608)
PHONE..................................785 232-3416
David Jackson, *President*
EMP: 12 **EST:** 1968
SQ FT: 40,000
SALES (est): 1.5MM **Privately Held**
SIC: 5261 0782 Nurseries; lawn & garden supplies; landscape contractors

(G-12736)
JADE TRAVEL CENTER INC (PA)
2655 Sw Wanamaker Rd E (66614-4477)
PHONE..................................785 273-1226
Janet Nelson, *President*
Kimbra Henry, *Vice Pres*
Pat Gowan, *Consultant*
EMP: 10
SALES (est): 1.6MM **Privately Held**
SIC: 4724 4729 Travel agencies; airline ticket offices

(G-12737)
JAMES S WILLARD
Also Called: Scott Quilan & Heck Partnr
3301 Sw Van Buren St B (66611-2483)
PHONE..................................785 267-0040
James S Willard, *Partner*
EMP: 13
SALES (est): 553K **Privately Held**
SIC: 8111 Legal services

(G-12738)
JAY HAWK AREA AGENCY ON AGING
2910 Sw Topeka Blvd (66611-2121)
PHONE..................................785 235-1367
Jocelyn Lyons, *Principal*
Susan Arnold, *Case Mgr*
Nyree Green-Brooks, *Case Mgr*
EMP: 33
SALES: 3MM **Privately Held**
SIC: 8322 Senior citizens' center or association

▲ = Import ▼=Export
◆ =Import/Export

(G-12739)
JAYHAWK AREA CNCL BSA CNCL (PA)
1020 Se Monroe St (66612-1110)
P.O. Box 851 (66601-0851)
PHONE..................................785 354-0291
Wayne Pancoast, *Accountant*
EMP: 14
SQ FT: 2,000
SALES: 1.4MM **Privately Held**
SIC: 8641 Boy Scout organization

(G-12740)
JAYHAWK AUTO INCORPORATED
Also Called: Jayhawk Body
910 Sw 6th Ave (66606-1402)
PHONE..................................785 354-1758
Kevin Dunford, *President*
Debbie Ingenthron, *Vice Pres*
EMP: 12
SALES (est): 1MM **Privately Held**
SIC: 7532 Body shop, automotive

(G-12741)
JAYHAWK BEVERAGE INC
4435 Nw Us Highway 24 (66618-3809)
PHONE..................................785 234-8611
Paul Debauge, *President*
Janice Debauge, *Corp Secy*
EMP: 24
SQ FT: 30,000
SALES (est): 4.2MM **Privately Held**
SIC: 5181 Beer & other fermented malt liquors

(G-12742)
JEFFERSON ST HT PARTNERS LLC
Also Called: Ramada Inn
420 Se 6th Ave Ste A (66607-1181)
PHONE..................................785 234-5400
James W Parrish,
Lisa Wingert,
EMP: 60
SQ FT: 111,000
SALES (est): 3.9MM **Privately Held**
SIC: 7011 Hotels & motels

(G-12743)
JENS HOUSE & COML CLG LLC
4149 Ne State Road K4 (66617-3749)
PHONE..................................785 286-2463
Jennifer Reed,
Donald Reed,
EMP: 10
SALES (est): 695.5K **Privately Held**
SIC: 7699 Cleaning services

(G-12744)
JETZ SERVICE CO INC (PA)
901 Ne River Rd Ste 3 (66616-1142)
PHONE..................................785 354-7588
Timothy Etzel, *President*
Carole J Etzel, *Treasurer*
Pam Pierce, *Human Res Dir*
Jim Urban, *Sales Staff*
Buddy Johnson, *Manager*
EMP: 18 **EST:** 1966
SQ FT: 3,000
SALES (est): 15.7MM **Privately Held**
WEB: www.jetzservice.com
SIC: 7359 5064 Laundry equipment leasing; electrical appliances, television & radio; clothes dryers, electric & gas

(G-12745)
JOHN D EBELING MD
Also Called: Yorke, Craig H MD
634 Sw Mulvane St Ste 202 (66606-1678)
PHONE..................................785 232-3555
John D Ebeling MD, *Owner*
Craig H Yorke, *Med Doctor*
EMP: 10
SALES (est): 220.2K **Privately Held**
SIC: 8011 Neurologist

(G-12746)
JOHN G LEVIN (PA)
Also Called: Lindyspring Systems,
115 Nw Van Buren St (66603-3315)
PHONE..................................785 234-5551
John G Levin, *Owner*
EMP: 50
SQ FT: 10,000
SALES (est): 15MM **Privately Held**
WEB: www.lindyspring.com
SIC: 5074 5149 5199 5999 Water softeners; beverages, except coffee & tea; ice, manufactured or natural; water purification equipment; bottled water delivery

(G-12747)
JOHNSON BOWSER FUNERAL CHAPEL
723 Sw 6th Ave (66603-3128)
P.O. Box 396 (66601-0396)
PHONE..................................785 233-3039
Larry D Johnson, *President*
Larry Johnson Jr, *Vice Pres*
Harriett Johnson, *Treasurer*
EMP: 10
SQ FT: 15,000
SALES: 720K **Privately Held**
WEB: www.bowserjohnsonfuneralchapel.com
SIC: 7261 Funeral home

(G-12748)
JOHNSON CONTROLS FIRE
4024 Sw Topeka Blvd (66609-1236)
PHONE..................................785 267-9675
Eric Mikessell, *President*
EMP: 5 **Privately Held**
WEB: www.simplexgrinnell.com
SIC: 3669 1731 Emergency alarms; fire detection & burglar alarm systems specialization
HQ: Johnson Controls Fire Protection Lp
6600 Congress Ave
Boca Raton FL 33487
561 988-7200

(G-12749)
JOSIE NORRIS MD
Also Called: First Birth Women Center
1109 Sw Topeka Blvd (66612-1602)
PHONE..................................785 232-6950
Josie Norris MD, *President*
EMP: 10
SALES (est): 302.3K **Privately Held**
SIC: 8011 General & family practice, physician/surgeon; gynecologist

(G-12750)
JUDICIARY COURT OF THE STATE
Also Called: Court of Appeals
220 Se 6th Ave (66603-3507)
PHONE..................................785 296-6290
Mary Reyer, *Branch Mgr*
EMP: 39 **Privately Held**
SIC: 8322 9199 Rehabilitation services;
HQ: Judiciary Courts Of The State Of Kansas
301 Sw 10th Ave
Topeka KS 66612
785 296-4873

(G-12751)
JUDICIARY COURT OF THE STATE
Also Called: Clerk District Crt Ltd Actions
200 Se 7th St Ste 209 (66603-3933)
PHONE..................................785 233-8200
Angie Callahan, *Manager*
EMP: 59 **Privately Held**
SIC: 9211 8111 State courts; ; legal services
HQ: Judiciary Courts Of The State Of Kansas
301 Sw 10th Ave
Topeka KS 66612
785 296-4873

(G-12752)
KALOS INC
3518 Se 21st St Ste B (66607-2399)
PHONE..................................785 232-3606
James Springer, *President*
Cindy Miller, *Project Mgr*
Randy Larson, *Cust Mgr*
Davis Holden, *Business Anlyst*
Richard Bloom, *Manager*
EMP: 26
SQ FT: 8,000
SALES: 5MM **Privately Held**
WEB: www.kalos-inc.com
SIC: 5112 7371 Business forms; computer software development

(G-12753)
KAMMCO HEALTH SOLUTIONS INC
623 Sw 10th Ave (66612-1615)
PHONE..................................800 435-2104
Mark Synovec, *Chairman*
EMP: 10
SALES (est): 321.9K **Privately Held**
SIC: 6321 Health insurance carriers
PA: Kansas Medical Mutual Insurance Co Inc
623 Sw 10th Ave Fl 2
Topeka KS 66612

(G-12754)
KANEQUIP INC
2901 Nw Us Highway 24 (66618-2700)
P.O. Box 8569 (66608-0569)
PHONE..................................785 267-9200
Fax: 785 267-3139
EMP: 10
SALES (corp-wide): 117MM **Privately Held**
SIC: 5261 5083 Ret Nursery/Garden Supplies Whol Farm/Garden Machinery
PA: Kanequip, Inc.
18035 E Us Highway 24
Wamego KS 66547
785 456-2041

(G-12755)
KANS DEPT HEALTH AND ENVMT
1000 Sw Jackson St # 200 (66612-1300)
PHONE..................................785 296-0461
Roderick Bremby, *Branch Mgr*
EMP: 900 **Privately Held**
WEB: www.healthbookcorner.com
SIC: 4959 9431 Environmental cleanup services;
HQ: Kansas Department Of Health And Environment
1000 Sw Jackson St
Topeka KS 66612
785 296-1500

(G-12756)
KANSAS AFRICAN AMERICAN AFF
900 Sw Jackson St Rm 100 (66612-1246)
PHONE..................................785 296-4874
Mildred Edwards MD, *Director*
EMP: 10
SALES (est): 1MM **Privately Held**
SIC: 7375 On-line data base information retrieval

(G-12757)
KANSAS AIR CENTER TOPEKA INC
3600 Ne Sardou Ave Ste 4a (66616-1678)
PHONE..................................785 234-2602
EMP: 20 **EST:** 1998
SALES (est): 970K **Privately Held**
SIC: 7363 Help Supply Services

(G-12758)
KANSAS ASSC HOME FOR AGED INC
217 Se 8th Ave (66603-3906)
PHONE..................................785 233-7443
John Grace, *President*
Kevin McFarland, *Vice Pres*
Debra Zehr, *Vice Pres*
EMP: 15
SQ FT: 1,900
SALES: 2MM **Privately Held**
SIC: 8641 8741 Veterans' organization; management services

(G-12759)
KANSAS ASSN OF INSUR AGENTS
815 Sw Topeka Blvd Ste 1 (66612-1672)
PHONE..................................785 232-0561
Sandy Broadstreet, *President*
William Buckles, *President*
Thomas Murry, *President*
Larry McGill, *Exec VP*
Don Morris, *Treasurer*
EMP: 12
SALES: 1.1MM **Privately Held**
WEB: www.kaia.com
SIC: 8621 8611 Professional membership organizations; business associations

(G-12760)
KANSAS ASSN OF PUB EMPLOYEES
Also Called: KAPE
1300 Sw Topeka Blvd (66612-1817)
PHONE..................................785 233-1956
Brian Thompson, *President*
EMP: 10
SALES: 459.9K **Privately Held**
WEB: www.kape.org
SIC: 8631 Employees' association

(G-12761)
KANSAS ASSN OF SCHL BOARDS
Also Called: KASB
1420 Sw Arrowhead Rd (66604-4023)
PHONE..................................785 273-3600
Vicki Keller, *Manager*
John W Koepke, *Exec Dir*
Rod Spangler, *Director*
Melissa Holder, *Executive Asst*
David Cunningham,
EMP: 38
SQ FT: 41,000
SALES: 5.4MM **Privately Held**
WEB: www.kasb.org
SIC: 8621 Education & teacher association

(G-12762)
KANSAS BANKERS ASSOCIATION
Also Called: Kansas Bankers Services
610 Sw Corporate Vw (66615-1233)
P.O. Box 4407 (66604-0407)
PHONE..................................785 232-3444
Chuck Stones, *President*
Kurt Knutson, *Chairman*
Doug Wareham, *COO*
Alex Orel, *Senior VP*
EMP: 28
SALES: 3.2MM **Privately Held**
SIC: 8611 Trade associations

(G-12763)
KANSAS BAR ASSOCIATION
1200 Sw Harrison St (66612-1806)
PHONE..................................785 234-5696
Jordan Ylchim, *Exec Dir*
Jordan Yochim, *Exec Dir*
EMP: 20
SQ FT: 9,000
SALES: 2MM **Privately Held**
WEB: www.ksbar.org
SIC: 8621 Bar association

(G-12764)
KANSAS CHILDRENS SERVICE LEAG
Also Called: Prevention Services
3545 Sw 5th St (66606-1904)
P.O. Box B (66606)
PHONE..................................785 274-3100
Trudy Racine, *Manager*
Gail Cozadd, *Director*
EMP: 40
SALES (corp-wide): 15MM **Privately Held**
WEB: www.kcsl.org+kansas+childrens+service+garde
SIC: 8322 Child related social services; offender self-help agency
PA: Kansas Children's Service League
1365 N Custer St
Wichita KS 67203
316 942-4261

(G-12765)
KANSAS CHILDRENS SERVICE LEAG
3545 Sw 5th St (66606-1904)
PHONE..................................785 274-3800
Janet Schalansky, *Manager*
EMP: 14

GEOGRAPHIC

SALES (corp-wide): 15MM **Privately Held**
WEB: www.kcsl.org+kansas+childrens+service+garde
SIC: 8322 8351 Adoption services; head start center, except in conjunction with school
PA: Kansas Children's Service League
1365 N Custer St
Wichita KS 67203
316 942-4261

(G-12766)
KANSAS COALITTION AGAINST
Also Called: KCSDV
634 Sw Harrison St (66603-3706)
PHONE..................................785 232-9784
Lucca Wang, *Corp Comm Staff*
Joyce Grover, *Exec Dir*
Joyce Groover, *Director*
EMP: 30
SALES: 2.6MM **Privately Held**
WEB: www.kcsdv.org
SIC: 8322 Crisis center

(G-12767)
KANSAS CONSULTING ENGINEERS
Also Called: Grathes and Draden
825 S Kansas Ave Ste 500 (66612-1253)
PHONE..................................785 357-1824
Scott Heidner, *Director*
EMP: 10
SALES (est): 263.9K **Privately Held**
WEB: www.gbbaks.com
SIC: 8611 Trade associations

(G-12768)
KANSAS DEPARTMENT COMMERCE
Busines Development Division
1000 Sw Jackson St # 100 (66612-1354)
PHONE..................................785 296-5298
Becky Kester, *Opers Mgr*
Steve Kelly, *Director*
EMP: 25 **Privately Held**
WEB: www.kdoch.state.ks.us
SIC: 9611 8748 ; systems engineering consultant, ex. computer or professional
HQ: Department Of Commerce Kansas
1020 S Kansas Ave Fl 2
Topeka KS 66612
785 296-3481

(G-12769)
KANSAS DEPT FOR AGING & DISABI
Also Called: Kansas Neurological Institute
3107 Sw 21st St (66604-3245)
PHONE..................................785 296-5389
Brent Widick, *Superintendent*
EMP: 420 **Privately Held**
SIC: 8361 Home for the mentally retarded
HQ: Kansas Department For Aging And Disability Services
503 S Kansas Ave
Topeka KS 66603

(G-12770)
KANSAS DEPT FOR AGING & DISABI (DH)
Also Called: Kdads
503 S Kansas Ave (66603-3461)
PHONE..................................785 296-2917
Rita Logan, *Consultant*
Shawn Sullivan, *Admin Sec*
EMP: 90
SALES (est): 16.8MM **Privately Held**
WEB: www.agingkansas.org
SIC: 8322 9441 Geriatric social service;
HQ: Executive Office Of The State Of Kansas
300 Sw 10th Ave
Topeka KS 66612
785 296-6240

(G-12771)
KANSAS DEPT FOR CHLDREN FMLIES
Also Called: Regional Legal Counsel
500 Sw Van Buren St (66603-3335)
P.O. Box 1424 (66601-1424)
PHONE..................................785 296-1368
Jason Walker, *Pub Rel Dir*
Heather Lansdowne, *Comms Dir*
Betsy Thompson, *Director*
EMP: 200 **Privately Held**
SIC: 8111 9441 Legal services; administration of social & manpower programs;
HQ: Kansas Department For Children And Families
555 S Kansas Ave
Topeka KS 66603
785 368-6358

(G-12772)
KANSAS DEPT FOR CHLDREN FMLIES
Also Called: Child Support Enforcement
915 Sw Harrison St Fl 8 (66612-1505)
PHONE..................................785 296-3237
Tricia Thomas, *Administration*
EMP: 29 **Privately Held**
SIC: 8322 9441 Child related social services; administration of social & manpower programs;
HQ: Kansas Department For Children And Families
555 S Kansas Ave
Topeka KS 66603
785 368-6358

(G-12773)
KANSAS DEVELOPMENT FIN AUTH
534 S Kansas Ave Ste 800 (66603-3430)
PHONE..................................785 357-4445
Steve Weatherford, *President*
Rebecca Ford, *Vice Pres*
Jim Macmurray, *VP Finance*
EMP: 11
SALES (est): 2.2MM **Privately Held**
WEB: www.kdfa.org
SIC: 6211 Bond dealers & brokers

(G-12774)
KANSAS DIALYSIS SERVICES LLC
634 Sw Mulvane St Ste 300 (66606-1678)
PHONE..................................785 234-2277
Stan Langhofer, *Administration*
EMP: 55
SALES (est): 1.8MM **Privately Held**
SIC: 8071 Blood analysis laboratory

(G-12775)
KANSAS ELECTRIC COOPERATIVES
7332 Sw 21st St (66615-1318)
P.O. Box 4267 (66604-0267)
PHONE..................................785 478-4554
Bruce Gram, *President*
Vicki Estes, *Editor*
Stuart Lowry, *Exec VP*
Dough Sheperd, *Vice Pres*
Doug Shepherd, *Vice Pres*
EMP: 25
SQ FT: 10,000
SALES (est): 2.7MM **Privately Held**
SIC: 8611 2721 Better Business Bureau; periodicals

(G-12776)
KANSAS ELECTRIC POWER COOP INC
Also Called: KEPCO
600 Sw Corporate Vw (66615-1233)
P.O. Box 4877 (66604-0877)
PHONE..................................785 273-7010
Thuck Terrill, *CEO*
Paul Stone, *Opers Staff*
Mark Doljac, *Director*
Shawn Geil, *Director*
Phil Wages,
EMP: 24
SQ FT: 14,000
SALES: 164.6MM **Privately Held**
SIC: 4911 Distribution, electric power

(G-12777)
KANSAS FNDTION FOR MED CARE IN
Also Called: KFMC
800 Sw Jackson St Ste 700 (66612-1265)
PHONE..................................785 273-2552
Lynne Ruhlman-Valdivia, *President*
Sarah Irsik-Good, *Principal*
Beth Nech, *Project Mgr*
Betty Murrell, *CFO*
Brenda Davis, *Manager*
EMP: 35
SQ FT: 8,880
SALES: 3.9MM **Privately Held**
WEB: www.kfmc.org
SIC: 8621 Health association

(G-12778)
KANSAS GRAIN INSPECTION SVC (PA)
3800 Nw 14th St (66618-2854)
P.O. Box 750077 (66675-0077)
PHONE..................................785 233-7063
Thomas E Meyer, *President*
Randy McCormick, *Vice Pres*
Rebecca A Fleming, *Treasurer*
Thomas Meyer, *Manager*
Becky Arce, *Info Tech Mgr*
EMP: 80
SALES (est): 7.2MM **Privately Held**
WEB: www.kansasgrain.com
SIC: 7389 Commodity inspection

(G-12779)
KANSAS HEALTH INSTITUTE
212 Sw 8th Ave Ste 300 (66603-3938)
PHONE..................................785 233-5443
Robert St Peter MD, *CEO*
Andy Buckholtz, *Vice Pres*
Sharon Homan, *Vice Pres*
Gina Maree, *Vice Pres*
Jim McLean, *Vice Pres*
EMP: 26
SQ FT: 7,303
SALES: 5.9MM **Privately Held**
SIC: 8732 Business research service

(G-12780)
KANSAS HEALTH SOLUTIONS INC
2121 Sw Chelsea Dr (66614-1756)
PHONE..................................785 575-9393
Patrick Yancey, *CEO*
Matt Atteberry, *Principal*
Keith Rickard, *Principal*
EMP: 99
SALES: 6.8MM **Privately Held**
SIC: 6411 Insurance agents, brokers & service

(G-12781)
KANSAS HOSPITAL ASSOCIATION (PA)
215 Se 8th Ave (66603-3906)
PHONE..................................785 233-7436
Tom Bell, *President*
Melissa Hungerford, *Exec VP*
EMP: 35
SQ FT: 6,000
SALES: 4.9MM **Privately Held**
SIC: 8621 6411 Medical field-related associations; insurance agents, brokers & service

(G-12782)
KANSAS HOUSING RESOURCES CORP
611 S Kansas Ave Fl 3 (66603-3869)
PHONE..................................785 217-2001
Jeanette Spurgin, *Supervisor*
Dennis Mesa, *Exec Dir*
EMP: 41
SALES: 2.6MM **Privately Held**
SIC: 8748 Economic consultant

(G-12783)
KANSAS INFO CONSORTIUM LLC
Also Called: Access Kansas
534 S Kansas Ave Ste 1210 (66603-3434)
PHONE..................................785 296-5059
Robert Knapp, *President*
Eric Bur, *Treasurer*
Brad Bradley, *Admin Sec*
EMP: 18
SQ FT: 5,000
SALES (est): 3MM
SALES (corp-wide): 344.9MM **Publicly Held**
WEB: www.nicusa.com
SIC: 7373 7375 Systems software development services; information retrieval services
HQ: Nicusa, Inc.
25501 W Valley Pkwy # 300
Olathe KS 66061

(G-12784)
KANSAS LEGAL SERVICES INC (PA)
712 S Kansas Ave Ste 200 (66603-3873)
PHONE..................................785 354-8531
Theresa Shively, *General Mgr*
Mary Jo Lowe, *Vice Pres*
Eric Rosenblad, *Project Dir*
Heather File, *Hum Res Coord*
Jim Murphy, *Hum Res Coord*
EMP: 25
SALES: 7MM **Privately Held**
WEB: www.kansaslegalservices.org
SIC: 8111 Legal aid service

(G-12785)
KANSAS LIVESTOCK ASSOCIATION
Also Called: KANSAS BEEF COUNCIL
6031 Sw 37th St (66614-5129)
PHONE..................................785 273-5115
Matt Teagarden, *CEO*
Dee Likes, *CEO*
Aaron Popelka, *Vice Pres*
Todd Domer, *VP Corp Comm*
Scott Stebner, *Comms Dir*
EMP: 20
SQ FT: 13,760
SALES: 11.4MM **Privately Held**
WEB: www.kla.org
SIC: 8611 Trade associations

(G-12786)
KANSAS MEDICAL CLINIC PA
2860 Sw Mission Woods Dr C (66614-5604)
PHONE..................................785 233-3553
Gina Hopkins, *Branch Mgr*
EMP: 10 **Privately Held**
SIC: 8011 Gastronomist
PA: Kansas Medical Clinic, Pa
2200 Sw 6th Ave Ste 104
Topeka KS 66606

(G-12787)
KANSAS MEDICAL CLINIC PA
2200 Sw 6th Ave Ste 105 (66606-1707)
PHONE..................................785 233-3555
Jerry H Feagan, *Partner*
EMP: 13 **Privately Held**
SIC: 8011 Gastronomist
PA: Kansas Medical Clinic, Pa
2200 Sw 6th Ave Ste 104
Topeka KS 66606

(G-12788)
KANSAS MEDICAL CLINIC PA (PA)
2200 Sw 6th Ave Ste 104 (66606-1707)
PHONE..................................785 233-3555
Shekhar K Challa, *President*
Jerry Feagan, *Vice Pres*
Carol M Torrence, *Pathologist*
Mary Baumgartner, *Executive*
Candace Smith, *Executive Asst*
EMP: 10
SALES (est): 4.6MM **Privately Held**
SIC: 8011 Clinic, operated by physicians

(G-12789)
KANSAS MEDICAL INSUR SVCS CORP
Also Called: Kmis
W 10th Ave Ste 200 (66612)
PHONE..................................785 232-2224
David Ross, *President*
Kurt Scott, *Corp Secy*
Jerry Slaughter, *Exec VP*
Randy Shidvler, *CFO*
EMP: 10
SQ FT: 8,200
SALES: 1.9MM **Privately Held**
SIC: 8741 Hospital management; nursing & personal care facility management

(G-12790)
KANSAS MEDICAL MUTUAL INSUR CO (PA)
Also Called: Kammco
623 Sw 10th Ave Fl 2 (66612-1679)
P.O. Box 2307 (66601-2307)
PHONE..................................785 232-2224
Jimmy Gleason MD, *President*
Laura McCrary, *Vice Pres*

Jerry Slaughter, *Vice Pres*
Kurt Scott, *Treasurer*
Teresa Hadley, *Finance*
EMP: 30
SQ FT: 10,000
SALES (est): 42.2MM **Privately Held**
SIC: 6321 8111 Health insurance carriers; legal services

(G-12791)
KANSAS MEDICAL SOCIETY
623 Sw 10th Ave (66612-1627)
PHONE..................................785 235-2383
Jerry Slaughter, *Exec Dir*
EMP: 13
SQ FT: 2,000
SALES: 1.9MM **Privately Held**
SIC: 8621 8742 Medical field-related associations; scientific membership association; health association; management consulting services

(G-12792)
KANSAS MUTUAL INSURANCE CO
1435 Sw Topeka Blvd (66612-1818)
P.O. Box 1247 (66601-1247)
PHONE..................................785 354-1076
R Dan Scott, *President*
Brent Doane, *Chairman*
Paul Shields, *Vice Pres*
Raney Gilliland, *Treasurer*
Arnold Johnson, *Treasurer*
EMP: 13
SQ FT: 10,000
SALES (est): 1.2MM
SALES (corp-wide): 3.7MM **Privately Held**
WEB: www.kansasmutual.net
SIC: 6331 6411 Property damage insurance; reciprocal interinsurance exchanges: fire, marine, casualty; fire, marine & casualty insurance: mutual; insurance agents, brokers & service
PA: New York Farm Bureau Inc
159 Wolf Rd
Albany NY 12205
518 436-8495

(G-12793)
KANSAS NATIONAL EDUCATION ASSN (PA)
715 Sw 10th Ave Ste B (66612-1686)
PHONE..................................785 232-8271
John Metzger, *Business Mgr*
Claudette Johns, *Exec Dir*
EMP: 35 **EST:** 1863
SQ FT: 40,000
SALES: 7.7MM **Privately Held**
SIC: 8621 Education & teacher association

(G-12794)
KANSAS NEWSPAPER FOUNDATION
5423 Sw 7th St (66606-2330)
PHONE..................................785 271-5304
Dena Sattler, *President*
EMP: 23
SALES: 134.2K **Privately Held**
SIC: 2711 Newspapers, publishing & printing

(G-12795)
KANSAS OPERATION LIFESAVER
Also Called: KS OL
800 Sw Jackson St Ste 808 (66612-1292)
P.O. Box 474, Abilene (67410-0474)
PHONE..................................785 806-8801
Matt Vogt, *President*
Tara Mays, *Exec Dir*
EMP: 10
SALES: 69.9K **Privately Held**
SIC: 8748 Safety training service

(G-12796)
KANSAS PERSONNEL SERVICES INC
Also Called: Key Staffing
5840 Sw Huntoon St Ste C (66604-2523)
PHONE..................................785 272-9999
Patti Bossert, *CEO*
Paul Bossert, *Opers Staff*
Richard Kelly, *Recruiter*
EMP: 170
SQ FT: 5,330
SALES (est): 7.1MM **Privately Held**
WEB: www.keystaffing.com
SIC: 7361 7363 Placement agencies; temporary help service

(G-12797)
KANSAS POWERTRAIN & EQP LLC
1534 Nw Tyler St (66608-1549)
PHONE..................................785 861-7034
Chuck Stover, *Principal*
EMP: 13 **EST:** 2010
SALES (est): 2.6MM **Privately Held**
SIC: 5046 Commercial equipment

(G-12798)
KANSAS PUB EMPLYEE RTRMENT SYS
Also Called: Kpers
611 S Kansas Ave Fl 2 (66603-3868)
PHONE..................................785 296-1019
Robert V Smith, *Financial Exec*
Robert Smith, *Financial Exec*
Alan Conroy, *Exec Dir*
EMP: 100 **EST:** 1962
SALES (est): 6.4MM **Privately Held**
WEB: www.kpers.org
SIC: 8631 Employees' association

(G-12799)
KANSAS REAL ESTATE COMMISSION
3 Townsite Plz Ste 200 (66603-3511)
PHONE..................................785 296-3411
Sherry Diel, *Director*
EMP: 12
SALES (est): 555.4K **Privately Held**
WEB: www.krec.state.ks.us
SIC: 8611 9651 Real Estate Board;
HQ: Executive Office Of The State Of Kansas
300 Sw 10th Ave
Topeka KS 66612
785 296-6240

(G-12800)
KANSAS REHABILITATION HOSPITAL
Also Called: ENCOMPASS HEALTH
1504 Sw 8th Ave (66606-2714)
PHONE..................................785 235-6600
Bob Porter, *Corp Secy*
Clare Manganiello, *QA Dir*
Randy Carrier, *Engineer*
Barry Muninger, *Mktg Dir*
Paul Livingston, *Director*
EMP: 150
SALES: 17.8MM
SALES (corp-wide): 4.2B **Publicly Held**
WEB: www.healthsouth.com
SIC: 8069 Specialty hospitals, except psychiatric
PA: Encompass Health Corporation
9001 Liberty Pkwy
Birmingham AL 35242
205 967-7116

(G-12801)
KANSAS RENTAL INC
5966 Sw 29th St (66614-2524)
PHONE..................................785 272-1232
Bruce Wanamaker, *Manager*
EMP: 10
SALES (corp-wide): 1.2MM **Privately Held**
WEB: www.kansasrental.com
SIC: 7359 Party supplies rental services
PA: Kansas Rental, Inc.
926 Nw Topeka Blvd
Topeka KS 66608
785 233-2222

(G-12802)
KANSAS RURAL HOUSING SERVICE
7204 Sw Timberway Dr (66619-1114)
P.O. Box 19084 (66619-0084)
PHONE..................................785 862-4877
Diane Mannville, *Director*
EMP: 25
SALES: 1MM **Privately Held**
SIC: 8742 Maintenance management consultant

(G-12803)
KANSAS SAND AND CONCRETE INC
531 Nw Tyler St (66608-1586)
P.O. Box 656 (66601-0656)
PHONE..................................785 235-6284
Walter H Wulf Jr, *President*
Dan Woodward, *Vice Pres*
EMP: 50
SQ FT: 3,000
SALES (est): 8.4MM
SALES (corp-wide): 147MM **Publicly Held**
WEB: www.kansassand.com
SIC: 3273 5032 Ready-mixed concrete; sand, construction; gravel
PA: The Monarch Cement Company
449 1200th St
Humboldt KS 66748
620 473-2222

(G-12804)
KANSAS SECURED TTLE INC
3497 Sw Fairlawn Rd (66614-3983)
PHONE..................................785 232-9349
John Schuster, *President*
Mary Rogge, *Exec VP*
Melinda Huball, *Receptionist*
EMP: 18 **EST:** 1966
SALES (est): 2.4MM
SALES (corp-wide): 22MM **Privately Held**
WEB: www.kstshawnee.com
SIC: 6541 Title abstract offices
HQ: Title Midwest, Inc.
4400 Shawnee Mission Pkwy # 208
Fairway KS 66205
785 232-9110

(G-12805)
KANSAS STARBASE INC
5920 Sw Coyote Dr (66619)
PHONE..................................785 861-4709
Gary Cushinberry, *President*
Jeff Akin, *Business Mgr*
Dennis Hanson, *Vice Pres*
Jason Johnston, *Office Mgr*
Becky Catlin, *Director*
EMP: 10
SALES: 1.4MM **Privately Held**
WEB: www.kansasstarbase.org
SIC: 7999 Instruction schools, camps & services

(G-12806)
KANSAS STATE HIGH SCHL ACTVTIE
Also Called: KSHSAA
601 Sw Commerce Pl (66615-1234)
P.O. Box 495 (66601-0495)
PHONE..................................785 273-5329
Viola Straley, *Bookkeeper*
Brent Unruh, *Office Mgr*
Craig Manteuffel, *Manager*
Mindy Nichol, *Exec Dir*
Gary Musselman, *Director*
EMP: 19 **EST:** 1910
SALES: 4MM **Privately Held**
WEB: www.kshsaa.com
SIC: 8641 Civic associations

(G-12807)
KANSAS STATE HISTORICAL SOC (PA)
6425 Sw 6th Ave (66615-1099)
PHONE..................................785 272-8681
Elizabeth Page, *Opers Staff*
Vicky Henley, *Exec Dir*
EMP: 11
SALES: 1.1MM **Privately Held**
SIC: 8412 Historical society

(G-12808)
KANSAS TURNPIKE AUTHORITY
3939 Sw Topeka Blvd (66609-1240)
PHONE..................................785 266-9414
Michael Johnston, *CEO*
EMP: 10
SALES (corp-wide): 124.8MM **Privately Held**
WEB: www.ksturnpike.com
SIC: 4785 Toll road operation
PA: Kansas Turnpike Authority
9401 E Kellogg Dr
Wichita KS 67207
316 682-4537

(G-12809)
KANSAS VAN & STOR CRIQUI CORP
1650 Sw 41st St (66609-1249)
P.O. Box 5164 (66605-0164)
PHONE..................................785 266-6992
Larry Criqui, *President*
Teri Criqui, *Admin Sec*
EMP: 25 **EST:** 1947
SQ FT: 4,000
SALES: 3.1MM **Privately Held**
SIC: 4214 Local trucking with storage

(G-12810)
KAW VALLEY BANK (HQ)
1110 N Kansas Ave (66608-1244)
P.O. Box 8009 (66608-0009)
PHONE..................................785 232-2700
Glenn Swogger Jr, *Ch of Bd*
Gerald W Lauber, *President*
Dean Phillips, *Vice Chairman*
Grant Ryan, *Ch Credit Ofcr*
Richard Montano, *Officer*
EMP: 39
SQ FT: 15,000
SALES: 17.7MM **Privately Held**
WEB: www.kawvalleybank.com
SIC: 6022 State trust companies accepting deposits, commercial

(G-12811)
KAW VALLEY BANK
4848 Sw 21st St Ste 102 (66604-4415)
PHONE..................................785 272-8100
Lennie K Buck, *Site Mgr*
Lennie Buck, *Manager*
EMP: 10 **Privately Held**
WEB: www.kawvalleybank.com
SIC: 6022 State trust companies accepting deposits, commercial
HQ: Kaw Valley Bank
1110 N Kansas Ave
Topeka KS 66608
785 232-2700

(G-12812)
KAW VALLEY HARDWOOD INC
Also Called: Floors To Go
1131 Sw Winding Rd (66615-3805)
PHONE..................................785 925-0142
Robert D Russell, *President*
Mark Hewitt, *Vice Pres*
EMP: 22
SQ FT: 12,000
SALES (est): 1.7MM **Privately Held**
SIC: 1752 Floor laying & floor work

(G-12813)
KBS CONSTRUCTORS INC (PA)
1701 Sw 41st St (66609-1252)
PHONE..................................785 266-4222
Dan Foltz, *President*
Scott Bayless, *Superintendent*
Clyde Bricker, *Superintendent*
Matt Griffin, *Superintendent*
Jason Phillips, *Superintendent*
EMP: 34
SQ FT: 11,200
SALES (est): 14.1MM **Privately Held**
WEB: www.kbsinc.net
SIC: 1542 Nonresidential construction

(G-12814)
KDHE BER ATTN R AVILA
1000 Sw Jackson St # 410 (66612-1300)
PHONE..................................785 291-3121
Susan Mosier, *Principal*
EMP: 20
SALES (est): 1.5MM **Privately Held**
SIC: 8099 Health & allied services

(G-12815)
KELLEY CONSTRUCTION CO INC
2548 Nw Button Rd (66618-1480)
P.O. Box 750256 (66675-0256)
PHONE..................................785 235-6040
Jeff Griffith, *President*
Morrod Voughrimaji, *Vice Pres*
EMP: 20
SQ FT: 6,000

SALES: 5MM **Privately Held**
SIC: 1542 Commercial & office building, new construction; commercial & office buildings, renovation & repair

(G-12816)
KELLY B DEETER DDS CHARTERED
2300 Sw 29th St Ste 223 (66611-1739)
PHONE..................................785 267-6120
Kelly B Deeter DDS, *President*
EMP: 10
SQ FT: 600
SALES (est): 642.9K **Privately Held**
SIC: 8021 Dentists' office

(G-12817)
KENDALL CONSTRUCTION INC
2551 Nw Button Rd (66618-1411)
PHONE..................................785 246-1207
Richard M Kendall, *President*
David Cooper, *General Mgr*
Sheri Kendall, *Corp Secy*
Sheri L Kendall, *Manager*
EMP: 22 **EST:** 1994
SQ FT: 6,000
SALES: 3.5MM **Privately Held**
SIC: 1542 Commercial & office buildings, renovation & repair

(G-12818)
KENT W HAVERKAMP MD
2909 Se Walnut Dr (66605-2189)
PHONE..................................785 267-0744
Kent Haverkamp, *Principal*
EMP: 20
SALES (est): 366.1K **Privately Held**
SIC: 8011 Internal medicine, physician/surgeon

(G-12819)
KEYS FOR NETWORKING INC
900 S Kansas Ave Ste 301 (66612-1245)
PHONE..................................785 233-8732
Lori Christensen, *Principal*
Meaghan Girard, *Principal*
Janette Keil, *Principal*
Cherie Reynolds, *Principal*
Jane Adams, *Exec Dir*
EMP: 25
SQ FT: 1,000
SALES: 367.4K **Privately Held**
WEB: www.keys.org
SIC: 8322 Family service agency

(G-12820)
KEYSTONE AUTOMOTIVE INDS INC
5725 Sw Topeka Blvd (66619-1409)
PHONE..................................785 235-1920
Brian Henry, *General Mgr*
Alex Metcalf, *Sales Staff*
Buck Henery, *Manager*
Chris Clark, *Manager*
Andrew Hill, *Manager*
EMP: 19
SALES (corp-wide): 11.8B **Publicly Held**
WEB: www.kool-vue.com
SIC: 5013 Automotive supplies & parts
HQ: Keystone Automotive Industries, Inc.
5846 Crossings Blvd
Antioch TN 37013
615 781-5200

(G-12821)
KID STUFF MARKETING INC
1401 Nw Moundview Dr C (66618-2886)
PHONE..................................785 862-3707
John Woodward, *President*
Darrel Savage, *Opers Staff*
◆ **EMP:** 40
SALES (est): 15.1MM **Privately Held**
SIC: 5199 Advertising specialties

(G-12822)
KIDDICAT CHILD CARE CENTER
4640 Sw 35th St (66614-3802)
PHONE..................................785 272-2001
Cecilia Crummey, *Director*
EMP: 12
SALES (est): 255K **Privately Held**
SIC: 8351 Child day care services

(G-12823)
KIRK & COBB REALTY
2810 Sw Gage Blvd Ste 1 (66614-2119)
PHONE..................................785 272-5555
Steve Kirk, *Owner*
Helen R Crow, *Real Est Agnt*
EMP: 30
SALES (est): 1.4MM **Privately Held**
WEB: www.kirkandcobb.com
SIC: 6531 Real estate agent, residential

(G-12824)
KS COMMERCIAL RE SVCS INC
435 S Kansas Ave Ste 200 (66603-3441)
PHONE..................................785 272-2525
Steve Wieser, *CEO*
Mark Rezac, *President*
Curtis Fisher, *Principal*
Ed Eller, *Vice Pres*
Mike Morse, *Admin Sec*
EMP: 10
SALES (est): 520K **Privately Held**
WEB: www.kscommercial.com
SIC: 6519 6531 Real property lessors; real estate brokers & agents

(G-12825)
KWIK STAFF LLC
2600 Sw 17th St (66604-2670)
PHONE..................................785 430-5806
Todd Holmes, *Principal*
EMP: 10
SALES (est): 66.3K **Privately Held**
SIC: 7363 Help supply services

(G-12826)
L T HUXTABLE SERVICE INC
2150a S Kansas Ave (66611-1140)
PHONE..................................785 235-5331
Smitty Belcher, *President*
EMP: 35
SQ FT: 6,000
SALES (est): 2.3MM **Privately Held**
WEB: www.huxtop.com
SIC: 1711 1731 Mechanical contractor; general electrical contractor

(G-12827)
LA PETITE ACADEMY INC
3325 Sw Gage Blvd (66614-3814)
PHONE..................................785 273-9393
Veronica Davis, *Manager*
EMP: 16
SALES (corp-wide): 164MM **Privately Held**
WEB: www.lapetite.com
SIC: 8351 Preschool center
HQ: La Petite Academy, Inc.
21333 Haggerty Rd Ste 300
Novi MI 48375
877 861-5078

(G-12828)
LAIRD NOLLER FORD INC (PA)
2245 Sw Topeka Blvd (66611-1284)
P.O. Box 946 (66601-0946)
PHONE..................................785 235-9211
Laird Noller, *President*
Joshua Hoke, *Consultant*
Morgan Brown, *Administration*
Reaona Hemmingway, *Clerk*
EMP: 102
SQ FT: 45,000
SALES (est): 49.6MM **Privately Held**
WEB: www.stevenoller.com
SIC: 5511 5531 7538 Automobiles, new & used; pickups, new & used; automotive parts; general automotive repair shops

(G-12829)
LAIRD NOLLER FORD INC
Also Called: Laird Noller Tlmh
2946 S Kansas Ave (66611-2217)
PHONE..................................785 264-2800
Aaron Rowe, *General Mgr*
EMP: 25
SALES (corp-wide): 49.6MM **Privately Held**
SIC: 5511 5531 7538 Automobiles, new & used; automotive parts; general automotive repair shops
PA: Laird Noller Ford, Inc.
2245 Sw Topeka Blvd
Topeka KS 66611
785 235-9211

(G-12830)
LAIRD NOLLER FORD INC
Also Called: Laird Noler Ford Body Shop
2310 S Kansas Ave (66611-1142)
PHONE..................................785 232-8347
Larry Dolifka, *Manager*
EMP: 20
SALES (corp-wide): 49.6MM **Privately Held**
WEB: www.stevenoller.com
SIC: 7532 Top & body repair & paint shops
PA: Laird Noller Ford, Inc.
2245 Sw Topeka Blvd
Topeka KS 66611
785 235-9211

(G-12831)
LAKESHORE LEARNING CENTER SVCS
5525 Sw 17th St (66604-2432)
PHONE..................................785 271-9146
Roberta Sekavec, *Director*
EMP: 30
SALES: 736.5K **Privately Held**
SIC: 8351 Child day care services

(G-12832)
LAMAR ADVERTISING COMPANY
2501 Ne Meriden Rd (66617-2338)
P.O. Box 8537 (66608-0537)
PHONE..................................785 234-0501
Matt Zilsdors, *Branch Mgr*
EMP: 15 **Publicly Held**
SIC: 7312 Billboard advertising
PA: Lamar Advertising Company
5321 Corporate Blvd
Baton Rouge LA 70808

(G-12833)
LANDMARK LANDSCAPE LLC
1330 Nw 86th St (66618-2136)
PHONE..................................785 608-6907
Chad Wendee, *President*
EMP: 25
SALES (est): 1MM **Privately Held**
SIC: 0781 Landscape services

(G-12834)
LATIMER SOMMERS AND ASSOC PA
Also Called: Latimer Sommers & Associates
3639 Sw Smmrfeld Dr Ste A (66614)
PHONE..................................785 233-3232
Richard Beardmore, *CEO*
William R Bassette, *Principal*
Kyle Wilk, *Engineer*
Dorothy Meyer, *Treasurer*
Aimee Lane, *Office Mgr*
EMP: 25
SQ FT: 6,500
SALES: 1.5MM **Privately Held**
WEB: www.lsapa.com
SIC: 8711 Consulting engineer

(G-12835)
LAWYERS TITLE OF KANSAS INC (PA)
Also Called: Ltkansas
5715 Sw 21st St (66604-3719)
P.O. Box 4046 (66604-0046)
PHONE..................................785 271-9500
Christopher St John, *President*
Chris St John, *Vice Pres*
Linda Dain, *Office Mgr*
EMP: 16
SQ FT: 11,000
SALES (est): 3.1MM **Privately Held**
WEB: www.lttopeka.com
SIC: 6541 6361 Title & trust companies; title insurance

(G-12836)
LB STEEL LLC
Also Called: Topeka Metal Specialties
5600 Sw Topeka Blvd (66609-1016)
PHONE..................................785 862-1071
EMP: 350
SALES (corp-wide): 151.2MM **Privately Held**
SIC: 3499 3444 Mfg Misc Fabricated Metal Products Mfg Sheet Metalwork
PA: Lb Steel, Llc
15700 Lathrop Ave
Harvey IL 60426
708 331-2600

(G-12837)
LEAGUE KANSAS MUNICIPALITIES
300 Sw 8th Ave Ste 100 (66603-3941)
PHONE..................................785 354-9565
Rynae Plue, *Finance*
Andrey Ukrazhenko, *Corp Comm Staff*
Don Moler, *Exec Dir*
Anna Debusk, *Exec Dir*
Erik Sartorius, *Exec Dir*
EMP: 13
SQ FT: 10,000
SALES (est): 1.2MM **Privately Held**
WEB: www.kmit.net
SIC: 8611 Trade associations

(G-12838)
LEGACY ON 10TH OPCO LLC
Also Called: LEGACY ON 10TH AVENUE, THE
2015 Se 10th Ave (66607-1615)
PHONE..................................785 233-8918
William M Novotny,
Michelle D Novotny,
EMP: 60
SALES: 3.9MM **Privately Held**
SIC: 8051 Convalescent home with continuous nursing care

(G-12839)
LETS HELP INC
200 S Kansas Ave (66603-3617)
P.O. Box 2492 (66601-2492)
PHONE..................................785 234-6208
Shelly Lowery, *Exec Dir*
EMP: 35
SQ FT: 10,000
SALES: 1MM **Privately Held**
SIC: 8322 Social service center

(G-12840)
LEWIS AUTO PLAZA INC
Also Called: Lewis Collision Center
3206 Sw Topeka Blvd (66611-2394)
PHONE..................................785 266-8850
Sherry Prato, *Info Tech Mgr*
Rod Lewis,
Jerry Franz,
EMP: 17
SALES (est): 960K **Privately Held**
WEB: www.lewiscollisioncenter.com
SIC: 7532 Body shop, automotive

(G-12841)
LEWIS AUTO SALVAGE LLC
Also Called: Lewis Auto & Truck Parts
229 Ne Burgess St (66608-1705)
PHONE..................................785 233-0561
Karen S Lewis,
EMP: 16 **EST:** 1977
SQ FT: 7,800
SALES (est): 1.8MM **Privately Held**
WEB: www.lewisautoparts.com
SIC: 5531 5013 Automotive parts; automotive supplies & parts

(G-12842)
LIBERTY ASSISTED LIVING CENTER
Also Called: Westwood Manor
5015 Sw 28th St (66614-2319)
PHONE..................................785 273-0886
Carla Royer, *Manager*
EMP: 50 **Privately Held**
SIC: 6513 8051 Retirement hotel operation; skilled nursing care facilities
PA: Liberty Assisted Living Centers Of Florida Lp
3073 Horseshoe Dr S # 100
Naples FL 34104

(G-12843)
LIBERTY ASSISTED LIVING CENTER
Also Called: Drury Place Apartments
4200 Sw Drury Ln Ofc (66604-4341)
PHONE..................................785 273-6847
Andrea Graham, *Manager*
EMP: 10 **Privately Held**
SIC: 6513 Retirement hotel operation

▲ = Import ▼=Export
◆ =Import/Export

PA: Liberty Assisted Living Centers Of Florida Lp
3073 Horseshoe Dr S # 100
Naples FL 34104

(G-12844)
LIFELINE
1500 Sw 10th Ave (66604-1301)
PHONE..................................800 635-6156
Kent Palmberg, *President*
EMP: 8
SALES (est): 558.3K **Privately Held**
WEB: www.svrhc.com
SIC: 3669 Emergency alarms

(G-12845)
LINCOLN CTR OBSTRCS/GYNCLGY PA (PA)
Also Called: Lincoln Center Ob/Gyn
800 Sw Lincoln St (66606-1515)
PHONE..................................785 273-4010
Todd E Trobough MD, *President*
Douglas Gleason MD, *Corp Secy*
Michele Kychik, *Office Mgr*
Mariah Carlgren, *Nursing Mgr*
Heather Morrison, *Med Doctor*
EMP: 45
SQ FT: 2,500
SALES (est): 5.6MM **Privately Held**
WEB: www.lincolncenterobgyn.com
SIC: 8011 Obstetrician; gynecologist

(G-12846)
LINCOLN CTR OBSTRCS/GYNCLGY PA
2830 Sw Urish Rd (66614-5614)
PHONE..................................785 273-4010
Sonya Herbers, *Manager*
EMP: 15
SALES (est): 576.6K
SALES (corp-wide): 5.6MM **Privately Held**
WEB: www.lincolncenterobgyn.com
SIC: 8011 Gynecologist
PA: Lincoln Center Obstetrics & Gynecology, Pa
800 Sw Lincoln St
Topeka KS 66606
785 273-4010

(G-12847)
LKQ CORPORATION
Also Called: Lkq Mid-America Auto Parts
5725 Sw Topeka Blvd (66619-1409)
PHONE..................................785 862-0000
Mark Fitzgibbons, *Manager*
EMP: 34
SALES (corp-wide): 11.8B **Publicly Held**
WEB: www.lkqcorp.com
SIC: 5015 Automotive parts & supplies, used
PA: Lkq Corporation
500 W Madison St Ste 2800
Chicago IL 60661
312 621-1950

(G-12848)
LOGAN BUSINESS MACHINES INC (PA)
417b Ne Us Highway 24 (66608-1764)
PHONE..................................785 233-1102
Hal Wayne Logan, *President*
Erin Wallace, *Manager*
EMP: 21
SQ FT: 5,000
SALES (est): 3.2MM **Privately Held**
WEB: www.lbm-sharp.com
SIC: 5044 7699 Photocopy machines; photocopy machine repair

(G-12849)
LOVES ENTERPRISE INC
916 Se 4th St (66607-1828)
PHONE..................................785 235-0479
John Love, *President*
EMP: 10
SQ FT: 2,000
SALES (est): 1.2MM **Privately Held**
SIC: 8711 Construction & civil engineering

(G-12850)
LOVING HEART
4300 Sw Drury Ln (66604-2419)
PHONE..................................785 783-7200
Robert R Heitman, *Principal*
EMP: 78
SALES (est): 2MM **Privately Held**
SIC: 8322 Adult day care center

(G-12851)
LOWER HEATING & AC INC
Also Called: Honeywell Authorized Dealer
501 Se 17th St (66607-1298)
P.O. Box 1693 (66601-1693)
PHONE..................................785 357-5123
Charles A Lower, *President*
EMP: 44
SQ FT: 13,000
SALES (est): 6.6MM **Privately Held**
WEB: www.lowermech.com
SIC: 1711 Heating & air conditioning contractors; plumbing contractors

(G-12852)
LOWES HOME CENTERS LLC
1621 Sw Arvonia Pl (66615-1127)
PHONE..................................785 273-0888
Chris Dhoce, *Manager*
EMP: 150
SALES (corp-wide): 71.3B **Publicly Held**
SIC: 5211 5031 5722 5064 Home centers; building materials, exterior; building materials, interior; household appliance stores; electrical appliances, television & radio
HQ: Lowe's Home Centers, Llc
1605 Curtis Bridge Rd
Wilkesboro NC 28697
336 658-4000

(G-12853)
LUCE PRESS CLIPPINGS INC
Also Called: Burrellesluce Information Svcs
715 Sw Harrison St (66603-3711)
PHONE..................................785 232-0201
Alan Fries, *Vice Pres*
EMP: 77
SALES (corp-wide): 121.2MM **Privately Held**
WEB: www.burrellesluce.com
SIC: 7389 Press clipping service
HQ: Luce Press Clippings, Inc
44 W 1st Ave
Mesa AZ 85210
480 649-3070

(G-12854)
LUXURY LAWN & LANDSCAPE INC
2015 Nw Brickyard Rd (66618-2812)
PHONE..................................785 233-5296
John C Moser, *President*
Lori Moser, *Treasurer*
EMP: 10
SALES: 1.6MM **Privately Held**
SIC: 0782 0781 1629 Lawn services; landscape services; irrigation system construction

(G-12855)
M E H INC
Also Called: Haas Metal Engineering
2828 Nw Button Rd (66618-1456)
PHONE..................................785 235-1524
Jonny Haas, *President*
Anthony Peete, *Project Mgr*
Nathan Walker, *Project Mgr*
Ryan Payne, *Prdtn Mgr*
Preston Kilgore, *Safety Mgr*
EMP: 92
SQ FT: 50,080
SALES: 62.6MM **Privately Held**
SIC: 3441 Fabricated structural metal

(G-12856)
MAINLINE PRINTING INC
Also Called: Mainline Hollowgraphic
3500 Sw Topeka Blvd (66611-2374)
PHONE..................................785 233-2338
John Parker, *President*
▲ **EMP:** 90 **EST:** 1958
SQ FT: 90,000
SALES (est): 28.3MM **Privately Held**
WEB: www.mainlineholographics.com
SIC: 2752 2759 Commercial printing, offset; embossing on paper

(G-12857)
MANNING MUSIC INC
3400 Sw 6th Ave (66606-1907)
PHONE..................................785 272-1740
Todd Manning, *President*
Deborah Manning, *Vice Pres*
Ed Bartley, *Technician*
EMP: 11 **EST:** 1952
SQ FT: 2,665
SALES: 1MM **Privately Held**
WEB: www.manningmusic.net
SIC: 7359 5736 5932 7699 Musical instrument rental services; musical instrument stores; musical instruments, secondhand; musical instrument repair services

(G-12858)
MANOR CARE OF KANSAS INC
Also Called: Manorcare Health Svcs Topeka
2515 Sw Wanamaker Rd (66614-5269)
PHONE..................................785 271-6808
Jami Colson, *Branch Mgr*
EMP: 100
SALES (corp-wide): 8.2B **Privately Held**
SIC: 8051 Convalescent home with continuous nursing care
HQ: Manor Care Of Kansas, Inc.
333 N Summit St Ste 100
Toledo OH 43604
419 252-5500

(G-12859)
MARIAN CLINIC INC
Also Called: MARIAN DENTAL CLINIC
3164 Se 6th Ave (66607-2204)
PHONE..................................785 233-2800
Marylyn Page, *Exec Dir*
EMP: 23
SALES: 3.4MM **Privately Held**
WEB: www.marianclinic.org
SIC: 8011 Internal medicine, physician/surgeon

(G-12860)
MARK BOOSE
Also Called: David's Jewelers
623 S Kansas Ave (66603-3803)
PHONE..................................785 234-4808
Mark Boose, *Owner*
EMP: 5 **EST:** 1968
SQ FT: 3,200
SALES: 500K **Privately Held**
SIC: 5944 7631 3911 Jewelry, precious stones & precious metals; jewelry repair services; jewel settings & mountings, precious metal

(G-12861)
MARS CHOCOLATE NORTH AMER LLC
100 Mars Blvd (66619-1277)
PHONE..................................785 861-1800
EMP: 5
SALES (corp-wide): 37.6B **Privately Held**
SIC: 2064 2066 Candy & other confectionery products; chocolate & cocoa products
HQ: Mars Chocolate North America, Llc
800 High St
Hackettstown NJ 07840
908 852-1000

(G-12862)
MARTINEK & FLYNN WHOLESALE INC
118 Sw Roby Pl (66612-1444)
PHONE..................................785 233-6666
Darrell Martinek, *President*
Rick Flynn, *Admin Sec*
Brenda Martinek, *Admin Sec*
EMP: 20
SQ FT: 5,000
SALES (est): 1.9MM **Privately Held**
SIC: 1761 5211 5999 Siding contractor; roofing & gutter work; door & window products; awnings

(G-12863)
MATHER FLARE RENTAL INC (PA)
Also Called: Topeka Trailer Storage
7537 Sw Robinhood Ct (66614-4657)
PHONE..................................785 478-9696
Larry Mather, *President*
Cheryl Mather, *Corp Secy*
EMP: 12
SALES (est): 1.5MM **Privately Held**
WEB: www.matherrental.com
SIC: 7359 5082 7519 Sign rental; portable toilet rental; construction & mining machinery; trailer rental

(G-12864)
MATHESON TRI-GAS INC
Also Called: Lindweld
100 Se Madison St (66607-1146)
PHONE..................................785 234-3424
John Farkas, *Sales Staff*
Earl Goracke, *Manager*
EMP: 20 **Privately Held**
WEB: www.linweld.net
SIC: 5085 5084 Welding supplies; welding machinery & equipment
HQ: Matheson Tri-Gas, Inc.
150 Allen Rd Ste 302
Basking Ridge NJ 07920
908 991-9200

(G-12865)
MAXIMUS FITNESS AND WELLNESS
Also Called: Maximus Fitness Wellness
2061 Se 29th St (66605-2457)
PHONE..................................785 267-2132
Scott Huston, *Branch Mgr*
EMP: 13
SALES (corp-wide): 1.2MM **Privately Held**
SIC: 7991 Physical fitness facilities
PA: Maximus Fitness And Wellness
2909 Sw 37th St
Topeka KS 66614
785 266-8000

(G-12866)
MAXIMUS FITNESS AND WELLNESS (PA)
2909 Sw 37th St (66614-3569)
PHONE..................................785 266-8000
Scott Huston, *President*
Scott Houston, *President*
EMP: 17
SALES (est): 1.2MM **Privately Held**
WEB: www.maximusfitnessandwellness.com
SIC: 7991 Aerobic dance & exercise classes

(G-12867)
MAXIMUS FITNESS AND WELLNESS
2020 Nw Topeka Blvd # 200 (66608-2082)
PHONE..................................785 232-3133
Cade Sharples, *Manager*
EMP: 10
SALES (est): 195.5K
SALES (corp-wide): 1.2MM **Privately Held**
WEB: www.maximusfitnessandwellness.com
SIC: 7991 Health club
PA: Maximus Fitness And Wellness
2909 Sw 37th St
Topeka KS 66614
785 266-8000

(G-12868)
MCCRITE RETIREMENT ASSOCIATION
Also Called: MCCRITE PLAZA RETIREMENT CENTE
1608 Sw 37th St 1610 (66611-2589)
PHONE..................................785 267-2960
Patrick I McCrite, *President*
Melanie Butler, *Principal*
James Rider, *Director*
Alana Wilson, *Director*
Crystal Lee, *Social Dir*
EMP: 125
SALES: 6.6MM **Privately Held**
SIC: 8052 6513 8051 Intermediate care facilities; retirement hotel operation; skilled nursing care facilities

(G-12869)
MCCULLOUGH WAREHEIM & LABUNKER
1507 Sw Topeka Blvd (66612-1838)
P.O. Box 1453 (66601-1453)
PHONE..................................785 233-2323
John Ostrowski, *President*

GEOGRAPHIC

Pam Brown, *Corp Counsel*
David Alegria, *Shareholder*
EMP: 11
SALES (est): 1MM **Privately Held**
WEB: www.mcwala.com
SIC: 8111 General practice attorney, lawyer

(G-12870)
MCELROY ELECTRIC INC
3300 Sw Topeka Blvd Ste 1 (66611-2275)
PHONE..................................785 266-7111
Jerry D Mc Elroy, *Ch of Bd*
Chris Faulk, *President*
Wade Jueneman, *Vice Pres*
Alisa Murray, *Info Tech Mgr*
Dan Beal, *Admin Sec*
EMP: 40
SQ FT: 1,200
SALES (est): 6.1MM **Privately Held**
SIC: 1731 General electrical contractor

(G-12871)
MCELROYS INC
3310 Sw Topeka Blvd (66611-2292)
P.O. Box 5188 (66605-0188)
PHONE..................................785 266-4870
Dan Beal, *President*
Jerry Hansen, *General Mgr*
Wade Jueneman, *Vice Pres*
Lance Berry, *Info Tech Mgr*
Janet Mc Elroy, *Admin Sec*
EMP: 175 **EST:** 1956
SQ FT: 36,000
SALES (est): 64.3MM **Privately Held**
WEB: www.mcelroys.com
SIC: 1711 Mechanical contractor

(G-12872)
MCM MANUFACTURING INC (PA)
2001 Nw Us Highway 24 (66618-1445)
PHONE..................................785 235-1015
Debby Witthar, *Administration*
EMP: 5
SALES (est): 469.6K **Privately Held**
SIC: 3423 Knives, agricultural or industrial

(G-12873)
MCPHERSON CONTRACTORS INC
3501 Sw Fairlawn Rd # 100 (66614-3976)
PHONE..................................785 273-3880
Michael McPherson, *CEO*
Bruce McPherson, *President*
Jim Heath, *Superintendent*
Jane Gunn, *Corp Secy*
Bill Sims, *Vice Pres*
▲ **EMP:** 75
SQ FT: 1,317
SALES (est): 67.9MM **Privately Held**
WEB: www.mcphersongc.com
SIC: 1542 Commercial & office building, new construction

(G-12874)
MCPHERSON DEVELOPMENT CO INC
3501 Sw Fairlawn Rd # 100 (66614-3976)
PHONE..................................785 272-9521
Bruce McPherson, *CEO*
Michael McPherson, *President*
Jane Gunn, *Corp Secy*
Patricia McPherson, *Senior VP*
Belinda McPherson, *Vice Pres*
EMP: 10
SQ FT: 1,500
SALES (est): 6.2MM **Privately Held**
WEB: www.mrvinc.com
SIC: 1522 1542 1521 Multi-family dwellings, new construction; commercial & office building, new construction; single-family housing construction

(G-12875)
MEALS ON WHLS OF SHWNEE & JEFF
2701 Sw East Circle Dr S # 2 (66606-2436)
PHONE..................................785 354-5420
Jane Metzger, *CEO*
EMP: 30
SALES (est): 1.2MM **Privately Held**
SIC: 8322 Meal delivery program

(G-12876)
MED CARE OF KANSAS INC
1505 Sw 6th Ave (66606-1624)
PHONE..................................785 295-8548
EMP: 12
SALES (corp-wide): 2.7B **Privately Held**
SIC: 2834 Pharmaceutical preparations
HQ: Med Care Of Kansas, Inc.
1700 Sw 7th St
Topeka KS 66606
785 295-8548

(G-12877)
MED CARE OF KANSAS INC (DH)
Also Called: Integrated Nuclear Enterprises
1700 Sw 7th St (66606-2489)
PHONE..................................785 295-8548
David Setchel, *CEO*
Betty Williamson, *Manager*
EMP: 9
SQ FT: 1,200
SALES (est): 1.6MM
SALES (corp-wide): 2.7B **Privately Held**
SIC: 2834 Pharmaceutical preparations
HQ: Caritas Inc
4200 S 4th St
Leavenworth KS 66048
913 682-5151

(G-12878)
MEDEVAC MIDAMERICA INC
Also Called: AMR
401 Sw Jackson St (66603-3327)
PHONE..................................785 233-2400
Ted Van Horn, *CEO*
Todd Zimmerman, *Exec VP*
Tim Dorn, *Vice Pres*
Randel Owen, *CFO*
Ken Keller, *Manager*
EMP: 144
SALES (est): 2.3MM **Privately Held**
WEB: www.amr-inc.com
SIC: 4119 8299 Ambulance service; educational services
HQ: American Medical Response, Inc.
6363 S Fiddlers Green Cir # 1400
Greenwood Village CO 80111

(G-12879)
MEDFORCE TECHNOLOGIES INC
2348 Sw Topeka Blvd # 103 (66611-1286)
PHONE..................................845 426-0459
Esther Apter, *CEO*
Ellen Sluder, *Mktg Dir*
Benjamin Llamzon, *Business Anlyst*
An Pham, *Software Engr*
Adam Bronner, *Technical Staff*
EMP: 13
SALES: 120K
SALES (corp-wide): 61.5MM **Privately Held**
SIC: 7372 Prepackaged software
PA: Ideagen Plc
Ergo House
Nottingham NOTTS NG11
162 969-9100

(G-12880)
MEDINA LOGISTICS LLC
3831 Sw Munson Ave (66604-1721)
PHONE..................................785 506-4002
Nelson Medina,
EMP: 68
SALES (est): 1.4MM **Privately Held**
SIC: 5113 Shipping supplies

(G-12881)
MEDVENTURES INTERNATIONAL INC
929 Sw University Blvd E2 (66619-1432)
P.O. Box 4284 (66604-0284)
PHONE..................................785 862-2300
Hunter Munns, *President*
Lawrence D Munns, *Corp Secy*
EMP: 10 **EST:** 1965
SQ FT: 20,000
SALES (est): 1.3MM **Privately Held**
SIC: 5047 Medical equipment & supplies

(G-12882)
MEIERS READY MIX INC (PA)
2013 Nw Lwer Silver Lk Rd (66618)
P.O. Box 8477 (66608-0477)
PHONE..................................785 233-9900
Gene Meier, *President*
Vince Meier, *Corp Secy*
Jack Meier, *Vice Pres*
EMP: 20
SQ FT: 4,000
SALES (est): 2.8MM **Privately Held**
SIC: 3273 Ready-mixed concrete

(G-12883)
MERCURY WIRELESS KANSAS LLC
3301 S Kansas Ave Ste B (66611-2488)
PHONE..................................800 354-4915
Blake Wiseman, *Vice Pres*
EMP: 14 **EST:** 2015
SQ FT: 11,000
SALES (est): 208.1K
SALES (corp-wide): 2.5MM **Privately Held**
SIC: 4813
PA: Mercury Wireless, Inc.
1111 Main St Ste 600
Kansas City MO 46804

(G-12884)
MERRY MAIDS 391
211 Sw 33rd St (66611-2245)
PHONE..................................785 273-3422
Kim Hinkley, *Owner*
EMP: 15
SQ FT: 800
SALES (est): 250K **Privately Held**
SIC: 7349 Maid services, contract or fee basis

(G-12885)
METROPOLITAN TOPEKA ARPRT AUTH
Also Called: M T A A
6510 Se Forbes Ave (66619-1446)
PHONE..................................785 862-2362
Eric M Johnson, *President*
Jane Young, *Manager*
Juanita States, *Personnel Assit*
EMP: 45
SQ FT: 9,000
SALES: 5.9MM **Privately Held**
SIC: 4581 Airport

(G-12886)
MFL INC
Also Called: Memory Foam Liquidators
7215 Sw Topeka Blvd 5a (66619-1456)
P.O. Box 19161 (66619-0161)
PHONE..................................785 862-2767
Amy Farmer, *President*
Chris D Farmer, *Treasurer*
EMP: 20
SQ FT: 20,000
SALES (est): 3.5MM **Privately Held**
WEB: www.memoryfoamliquidators.com
SIC: 5199 5021 Foams & rubber; mattresses

(G-12887)
MICHAEL F CASSIDY DDS
Also Called: Cassidy Orthodontic
600 Sw Governor Vw (66606-2339)
PHONE..................................785 233-0582
Kevin F Cassidy, *Owner*
Michael F Cassidy DDS, *Owner*
EMP: 10
SALES (est): 764.2K **Privately Held**
SIC: 8021 Orthodontist

(G-12888)
MICHAEL J UNREIN ATTY
Also Called: Unrein, Eric I
100 Se 9th St Ofc (66612-1262)
PHONE..................................785 354-1100
Michael J Unrein, *Partner*
EMP: 12
SALES (est): 907.1K **Privately Held**
SIC: 8111 General practice attorney, lawyer

(G-12889)
MID AMERICA ASSC COMPUTER ED
1301 Sw Ward Pkwy (66604-1942)
PHONE..................................785 273-3680
Eldon Chlumsky, *President*
Karla Murray, *President*
Steve Schuler, *President*
Craig Haugsness, *Director*
EMP: 15
SALES: 73.4K **Privately Held**
SIC: 8641 Educator's association

(G-12890)
MID-LAND MANAGEMENT INC (PA)
3501 Sw Fairlawn Rd (66614-3976)
PHONE..................................785 272-1398
Michael E McPherson, *Ch of Bd*
Susan M Ismert, *President*
Bruce McPherson, *Corp Secy*
EMP: 100 **EST:** 1973
SQ FT: 2,960
SALES (est): 10MM **Privately Held**
SIC: 6531 Real estate managers

(G-12891)
MIDLAND CARE
200 Sw Frazier Cir (66606-2800)
PHONE..................................785 232-2044
Karren Weichert, *CEO*
Jeannie Herrin, *Vice Pres*
Chad Wilkins, *CFO*
EMP: 13 **EST:** 2008
SALES (est): 1.2MM **Privately Held**
SIC: 8082 Home health care services

(G-12892)
MIDLAND CARE CONNECTION INC (PA)
200 Sw Frazier Cir (66606-2800)
PHONE..................................785 232-2044
Karren Weichert, *President*
Margo Collins, *President*
Harmony Hines, *General Mgr*
Marsha Kent, *Vice Pres*
Heidi Pickerell, *Vice Pres*
EMP: 139
SALES: 32.7MM **Privately Held**
SIC: 8082 8051 8322 Home health care services; skilled nursing care facilities; adult day care center

(G-12893)
MIDWAY SALES & DISTRG INC (PA)
Also Called: Midway Wholesale
218 Se Branner St (66607-1886)
P.O. Box 1246 (66601-1246)
PHONE..................................785 233-7406
Bruce H Myers, *CEO*
John Ossello, *Vice Pres*
Clay Toomey, *Purchasing*
Kara Linser, *Asst Controller*
Shane Hunter, *Sales Staff*
EMP: 55
SQ FT: 22,000
SALES (est): 78.3MM **Privately Held**
WEB: www.midwaywholesale.com
SIC: 5033 5031 Roofing & siding materials; building materials, interior; building materials, exterior

(G-12894)
MIDWEST B R D INC
11731 Sw 49th St (66610-9604)
PHONE..................................785 256-6240
Duane E Corkill, *President*
Lucy Corkill, *Admin Sec*
EMP: 17
SQ FT: 17,000
SALES (est): 3.2MM **Privately Held**
WEB: www.midwestbrd.com
SIC: 3556 3599 Poultry processing machinery; custom machinery

(G-12895)
MIDWEST COATING INC
3830 Nw 16th St (66618-2846)
PHONE..................................785 232-4276
Randy Morris, *President*
Jeanette Cockerham, *Business Mgr*
Adam Schultz, *Sales Staff*
EMP: 30
SQ FT: 7,600

▲ = Import ▼=Export
◆ =Import/Export

SALES (est): 4.2MM Privately Held
SIC: 1761 Roofing contractor

(G-12896)
MIDWEST ELECTRICAL CNSTR INC
4601 Se Adams St (66609-9421)
PHONE....785 215-8902
Dean Lackey, *President*
Lisa Scott, *Treasurer*
EMP: 10
SQ FT: 4,000
SALES: 3.5MM Privately Held
SIC: 1731 General electrical contractor

(G-12897)
MIDWEST HEALTH SERVICES INC
1021 Sw Fleming Ct (66604-1851)
PHONE....785 440-0399
EMP: 207
SALES (corp-wide): 32.7MM Privately Held
SIC: 8051 Skilled nursing care facilities
PA: Midwest Health, Inc
3024 Sw Wanamaker Rd # 300
Topeka KS 66614
785 272-1535

(G-12898)
MIDWEST HEALTH SERVICES INC
Also Called: Midwest Homestead of Topeka
5820 Sw Drury Ln (66604-2262)
PHONE....785 272-2200
Susan Bullock, *Manager*
EMP: 15
SALES (corp-wide): 32.7MM Privately Held
WEB: www.halsteadhealthrehab.com
SIC: 8051 8059 Extended care facility; rest home, with health care
PA: Midwest Health, Inc
3024 Sw Wanamaker Rd # 300
Topeka KS 66614
785 272-1535

(G-12899)
MIDWEST HEALTH SERVICES INC
Also Called: Lexington Prk Nrsng Ctr
1031 Sw Fleming Ct (66604-1851)
PHONE....785 440-0500
Brandon Smith-Ziph, *Principal*
EMP: 120
SALES (corp-wide): 32.7MM Privately Held
WEB: www.halsteadhealthrehab.com
SIC: 8051 8052 Extended care facility; personal care facility
PA: Midwest Health, Inc
3024 Sw Wanamaker Rd # 300
Topeka KS 66614
785 272-1535

(G-12900)
MIDWEST HEALTH SERVICES INC
Also Called: Woodland Health Care Center
440 Se Woodland Ave (66607-2172)
PHONE....785 233-0544
Jefferey North, *Manager*
EMP: 100
SALES (corp-wide): 32.7MM Privately Held
WEB: www.halsteadhealthrehab.com
SIC: 8051 Skilled nursing care facilities
PA: Midwest Health, Inc
3024 Sw Wanamaker Rd # 300
Topeka KS 66614
785 272-1535

(G-12901)
MIDWEST HERITAGE INN
Also Called: Topeka Fairfield Inn
1530 Sw Westport Dr (66604-4030)
PHONE....785 273-6800
Lauris Moldert, *CEO*
Maletta Meyer, *Accountant*
EMP: 12 EST: 2014
SALES: 260K Privately Held
SIC: 7011 Hotels & motels
PA: Starwood Capital Group, L.L.C.
591 W Putnam Ave
Greenwich CT 06830

(G-12902)
MIDWEST MASONRY CONSTRUCTION
5606 Sw Topekablvd Ste C (66609)
PHONE....785 861-7500
Grant Caffrey, *President*
Steven Graham, *Project Mgr*
EMP: 45 EST: 2014
SALES (est): 401.9K Privately Held
SIC: 1542 Commercial & office building, new construction

(G-12903)
MIDWEST OFFICE TECHNOLOGIES (PA)
Also Called: Modern Office
1502 Sw 41st St (66609-1200)
PHONE....785 272-7704
Susan Brame, *Principal*
Kevin Gunn, *Technology*
EMP: 24
SQ FT: 7,500
SALES (est): 2.7MM Privately Held
SIC: 5044 7629 Office equipment; business machine repair, electric

(G-12904)
MIDWESTERN METALS INC (PA)
1105 Nw Lower Silver (66608)
P.O. Box 8207 (66608-0207)
PHONE....785 232-1582
Charles H Jones, *President*
John Jones, *Treasurer*
Lisa Glassel, *Office Mgr*
EMP: 45
SQ FT: 65,000
SALES (est): 13.7MM Privately Held
WEB: www.midwesternmetals.com
SIC: 3441 3532 Fabricated structural metal; mining machinery

(G-12905)
MINI MASTERS LRNG ACADEMY LLC
3909b Sw Burlingame Rd (66609-1219)
PHONE....785 862-0772
Jessica Romesburg,
EMP: 17
SALES (est): 513.1K Privately Held
SIC: 8351 Preschool center

(G-12906)
MINI WAREHOUSE LIMITED II
4101 Sw Twilight Dr (66614-3403)
PHONE....785 273-4004
EMP: 10
SALES (est): 265.9K Privately Held
SIC: 4226 Special Warehouse/Storage

(G-12907)
MINI-TRAIN GAGE PARK
Gage Park (66604)
PHONE....785 273-6108
Rex Haney, *General Mgr*
Amanda Hernadez, *Manager*
Cori Thellers, *Manager*
EMP: 10
SALES (est): 134.1K Privately Held
SIC: 7999 Recreation center

(G-12908)
MIZE HOUSER & COMPANY PA (PA)
534 S Kansas Ave Ste 700 (66603-3465)
PHONE....785 233-0536
Duane Bond, *President*
Tim Goodger, *Vice Pres*
Brad Owen, *Treasurer*
Wanda Armfield, *Accountant*
Jessica Soper, *Accountant*
EMP: 70
SQ FT: 16,000
SALES (est): 23.3MM Privately Held
SIC: 7374 7379 8721 7291 Data processing & preparation; computer related consulting services; accounting, auditing & bookkeeping; tax return preparation services

(G-12909)
MOHAN CONSTRUCTION INC
125 S Kansas Ave (66603-3614)
PHONE....785 233-1615
Steven J Mohan, *President*
Heather Crable, *General Mgr*
Duane Morford, *Superintendent*
EMP: 20
SQ FT: 11,250
SALES: 3.1MM Privately Held
WEB: www.mohanconstruction.com
SIC: 1542 1541 Commercial & office buildings, renovation & repair; industrial buildings, new construction

(G-12910)
MONACO & ASSOCIATES INC
1243 Sw Topeka Blvd Ste B (66612-1907)
PHONE....785 272-5501
Gregory Monaco, *President*
Jeanne Tomisser, *Vice Pres*
EMP: 6
SALES (est): 594.4K Privately Held
WEB: www.monacoassociates.com
SIC: 2731 Book publishing

(G-12911)
MONTARA LLC
7105 Sw Montara Pkwy (66619-1121)
PHONE....785 862-1030
Globe Resources, *Principal*
EMP: 15
SALES: 1,000K Privately Held
SIC: 6531 Real estate leasing & rentals

(G-12912)
MORRIS LAING EVANS BROCK
Also Called: Hayse, Richard F
800 Sw Jackson St # 1310 (66612-1216)
PHONE....785 232-2662
Roger Walter, *Partner*
EMP: 10
SALES (corp-wide): 8.6MM Privately Held
SIC: 8111 General practice law office
PA: Morris, Laing, Evans, Brock & Kennedy, Chartered
300 N Mead St Ste 200
Wichita KS 67202
316 838-1084

(G-12913)
MORRIS COMMUNICATIONS CO LLC
1210 Sw Executive Dr (66615-3850)
P.O. Box 1818 (66601-1818)
PHONE....785 272-3456
Greg Akagi, *Editor*
Dan Lindquist, *Sales Mgr*
Larry Riggins, *Manager*
EMP: 55 Privately Held
WEB: www.morris.com
SIC: 4832 Radio broadcasting stations
HQ: Morris Communications Company Llc
725 Broad St
Augusta GA 30901
706 724-0851

(G-12914)
MORRIS COMMUNICATIONS CO LLC
616 Se Jefferson St (66607-1137)
PHONE....785 295-1111
John Fish, *CEO*
Mike Scardina, *Superintendent*
Heather Johanning, *Director*
Sidney Louie, *Director*
EMP: 80 Privately Held
WEB: www.morris.com
SIC: 2721 Periodicals
HQ: Morris Communications Company Llc
725 Broad St
Augusta GA 30901
706 724-0851

(G-12915)
MOTEL 6 OPERATING LP
1224 Sw Wanamaker Rd (66604-3811)
PHONE....785 273-2896
Alex Rodriguez, *Branch Mgr*
EMP: 14
SALES (corp-wide): 579.1MM Privately Held
WEB: www.motel6.com
SIC: 7011 Hotels & motels
HQ: Motel 6 Operating L.P.
4001 Intl Pkwy Ste 500
Carrollton TX 75007
972 360-9000

(G-12916)
MOTEL 6 OPERATING LP
709 Sw Fairlawn Rd (66606-2393)
PHONE....785 272-8283
Shiva Krishnamoorthy, *Manager*
EMP: 13
SALES (corp-wide): 579.1MM Privately Held
WEB: www.motel6.com
SIC: 7011 Hotels & motels
HQ: Motel 6 Operating L.P.
4001 Intl Pkwy Ste 500
Carrollton TX 75007
972 360-9000

(G-12917)
MOUNT HOPE CEMETERY COMPANY
4700 Sw 17th St (66604-2454)
PHONE....785 272-1122
Carl A Seufert Jr, *Director*
EMP: 12 EST: 1906
SQ FT: 2,000
SALES (est): 793.5K Privately Held
SIC: 6553 Cemeteries, real estate operation; mausoleum operation

(G-12918)
MRV HOLDING COMPANY
3501 Sw Fairlawn Rd # 200 (66614-3976)
PHONE....785 272-1398
Bruce Christianson, *Partner*
EMP: 15 Privately Held
SIC: 6719 Personal holding companies, except banks

(G-12919)
MURPHY TRACTOR & EQP CO INC
Also Called: John Deere Authorized Dealer
1621 Nw Gage Blvd (66618-2831)
PHONE....785 233-0556
Matthew Willis, *Foreman/Supr*
Mike Curry, *Manager*
EMP: 12 Privately Held
WEB: www.murphytractor.com
SIC: 5084 5083 Industrial machinery & equipment; farm & garden machinery
HQ: Murphy Tractor & Equipment Co., Inc.
5375 N Deere Rd
Park City KS 67219
855 246-9124

(G-12920)
MURRAY AND SONS CNSTR CO INC
3641 Sw Plass Ave Ste C (66611-2588)
PHONE....785 267-1961
Eugene Murray, *President*
Viola Murray, *Admin Sec*
EMP: 20
SQ FT: 2,000
SALES (est): 4.4MM Privately Held
WEB: www.murrayandsonsconstruction.com
SIC: 1542 Nonresidential construction

(G-12921)
MURRAY CLARY ANITA C DDS
6231 Sw 29th St Ste 100 (66614-4549)
PHONE....785 272-6060
Anita C Murray-Clary DDS, *Owner*
EMP: 11
SALES (est): 828.8K Privately Held
WEB: www.asmileisforever.com
SIC: 8021 Dentists' office

(G-12922)
MYERS AND STAUFFER LC
1131 Sw Winding Rd Ste C (66615-3805)
PHONE....785 228-6700
Steve Alonzo, *Accountant*
Kevin Londeen, *Branch Mgr*
Barbara Goelz, *Manager*
Annette Guilford, *Manager*
Tonya Jones, *Manager*
EMP: 32
SALES (corp-wide): 148.6MM Privately Held
WEB: www.mslc.com
SIC: 8721 Accounting, auditing & bookkeeping

GEOGRAPHIC

PA: Myers And Stauffer Lc
700 W 47th St Ste 1100
Kansas City MO 64112
800 374-6858

(G-12923)
NATIONAL ASSN LTR CARRIERS
1949 Nw Topeka Blvd (66608-1826)
P.O. Box 24 (66601-0024)
PHONE..................................785 232-6835
Thomas Mock, *Manager*
EMP: 10
SALES (corp-wide): 1B **Privately Held**
WEB: www.nalc.org
SIC: 8631 Labor union
PA: National Association Of Letter Carriers
100 Indana Ave Nw Ste 709
Washington DC 20001
202 393-4695

(G-12924)
NATIONAL WEATHER SERVICE
1116 Ne Strait Ave (66616-1698)
PHONE..................................785 234-2592
Curtis S Holderbach, *Principal*
EMP: 33 **Publicly Held**
SIC: 8999 9611 Weather forecasting; administration of general economic programs;
HQ: National Weather Service
1325 E West Hwy
Silver Spring MD 20910

(G-12925)
NATIONWIDE LEARNING LLC
Also Called: Studentreasures Publishing
1345 Sw 42nd St (66609-1213)
PHONE..................................785 862-2292
Chad Zimmerman, *President*
Anita Dougherty, *Vice Pres*
Corrine Collins, *Mktg Coord*
Michelle Colley, *Supervisor*
Gladys Gigous, *Admin Sec*
EMP: 110
SQ FT: 52,000
SALES (est): 18.2MM **Privately Held**
WEB: www.nationwide-learning.com
SIC: 2741 Miscellaneous publishing

(G-12926)
NEW YORK BLOOD CENTER INC
6220 Sw 29th St Ste 100 (66614-5028)
PHONE..................................785 233-0195
Kathy Boldt, *Manager*
EMP: 39
SALES (corp-wide): 466.7MM **Privately Held**
SIC: 8099 8071 Blood bank; medical laboratories
PA: New York Blood Center, Inc.
310 E 67th St
New York NY 10065
212 570-3010

(G-12927)
NEWBERRY UNGERER & HECKERT LLP
2231 Sw Wanamaker Rd # 101
(66614-4275)
PHONE..................................785 273-5250
C David Newbery, *Partner*
B J Hickert, *Partner*
Sandra K Deitering,
Douglas C Fincher,
Gayle P Meierhoff,
EMP: 15
SALES (est): 1.4MM **Privately Held**
WEB: www.newberyungerer.com
SIC: 8111 Real estate law

(G-12928)
NEWCOMER FUNERAL SVC GROUP INC (PA)
Also Called: Web & Rodrick Funeral Home
520 Sw 27th St (66611-1228)
PHONE..................................785 233-6655
Warren J Newcomer Jr, *President*
David Campanella, *Area Mgr*
Mike Land, *Corp Secy*
Perry Hasselbeck, *Exec VP*
Edward Tuggle, *Exec VP*
EMP: 10
SQ FT: 3,300
SALES (est): 22.8MM **Privately Held**
WEB: www.penwellgabel.com
SIC: 7261 6531 6351 Funeral home; cemetery management service; surety insurance

(G-12929)
NEWCOMER FUNERAL SVC GROUP INC
Also Called: Penwell Gabel Midtwn Funrl Hme
1321 Sw 10th Ave (66604-1205)
PHONE..................................785 354-8558
Ren Newcomer, *Owner*
Paul Broyles, *Info Tech Dir*
EMP: 15
SALES (corp-wide): 22.8MM **Privately Held**
WEB: www.penwellgabel.com
SIC: 7261 Funeral home
PA: Newcomer Funeral Service Group, Inc.
520 Sw 27th St
Topeka KS 66611
785 233-6655

(G-12930)
NEXLYNX
123 Sw 6th Ave 100 (66603-3854)
PHONE..................................785 232-5969
Lee Ryan, *Owner*
EMP: 12
SALES (est): 786.4K **Privately Held**
WEB: www.nexlynx.com
SIC: 4813

(G-12931)
NEXSTAR BROADCASTING INC
Also Called: Ksnt
6835 Nw Us Highway 24 (66618-5507)
PHONE..................................785 582-4000
Robert Raff, *General Mgr*
Kim Stolle, *Accounts Exec*
Carrie Bramlett, *Sales Staff*
Kim Fellows, *Manager*
EMP: 15
SALES (corp-wide): 2.7B **Publicly Held**
SIC: 4833 Television broadcasting stations
HQ: Nexstar Broadcasting, Inc.
545 E John Carpenter Fwy # 700
Irving TX 75062
972 373-8800

(G-12932)
NOLLER LINCOLN-MERCURY INC
2946 S Kansas Ave (66611-2272)
PHONE..................................785 267-2800
Steven Noller, *CEO*
Bill Norton, *Business Mgr*
Jolene Basgall, *CFO*
EMP: 25
SQ FT: 12,000
SALES (est): 9.3MM **Privately Held**
SIC: 5511 5531 7538 7515 Automobiles, new & used; pickups, new & used; vans, new & used; automotive parts; general automotive repair shops; passenger car leasing

(G-12933)
NORTH SHAWNEE COMMUNITY CENTER
300 Ne 43rd St (66617-1507)
PHONE..................................785 286-0676
Susan Fowle-Hentzler, *Manager*
Susan Hentzler, *Exec Dir*
EMP: 15
SALES (est): 709.1K **Privately Held**
SIC: 8322 Community center

(G-12934)
NORTH TOPEKA FABRICATION LLC
3801 Nw 14th St (66618-2854)
PHONE..................................785 233-4430
James S Lee,
EMP: 21 **EST:** 2010
SALES: 4.7MM **Privately Held**
SIC: 3441 Fabricated structural metal

(G-12935)
NORTHAST KANS CHPTER 13 TRSTEE
509 Sw Jackson St (66603-3333)
PHONE..................................785 234-1551
Jan Hamilton, *Principal*
EMP: 15
SALES (est): 1.4MM **Privately Held**
SIC: 8111 Bankruptcy referee

(G-12936)
NORTHEAST KANSAS HYDRAULICS
1531 Nw Eugene St (66608-1408)
P.O. Box 8208 (66608-0208)
PHONE..................................785 235-0405
Randall McGinnis, *President*
EMP: 5
SQ FT: 7,100
SALES (est): 719.6K **Privately Held**
SIC: 7699 5084 3596 Hydraulic equipment repair; hydraulic systems equipment & supplies; scales & balances, except laboratory

(G-12937)
NORTHERN PIPELINE CONSTRUCTION
1120 Nw Us Highway 24 (66608-1993)
PHONE..................................785 232-0034
EMP: 12 **EST:** 2007
SALES (est): 1.2MM **Privately Held**
SIC: 1623 Pipeline construction

(G-12938)
NORTHROP GRUMMAN SYSTEMS CORP
Forbes Indus Pk Bldg 8 (66624-0001)
PHONE..................................785 861-3375
Robert L Carver, *Opers-Prdtn-Mfg*
EMP: 160 **Publicly Held**
SIC: 8711 7374 Engineering services; data processing service
HQ: Northrop Grumman Systems Corporation
2980 Fairview Park Dr
Falls Church VA 22042
703 280-2900

(G-12939)
NORTHROP GRUMMAN SYSTEMS CORP
Also Called: Advanced Information Systems
7215 Sw Topeka Blvd (66619-1456)
PHONE..................................785 861-3398
Gary Brown, *Manager*
EMP: 23 **Publicly Held**
WEB: www.logicon.com
SIC: 7373 Computer integrated systems design
HQ: Northrop Grumman Systems Corporation
2980 Fairview Park Dr
Falls Church VA 22042
703 280-2900

(G-12940)
NPL CONSTRUCTION CO
Also Called: N P L
1120 Nw Us Highway 24 (66608-1993)
PHONE..................................785 232-0034
Wade Criqui, *Superintendent*
EMP: 80
SALES (corp-wide): 2.8B **Publicly Held**
SIC: 1623 Oil & gas pipeline construction
HQ: Npl Construction Co.
19820 N 7th Ave Ste 120
Phoenix AZ 85027
623 582-1235

(G-12941)
OFG FINANCIAL SERVICES INC (PA)
120 Se 6th Ave Ste 105 (66603-3515)
PHONE..................................785 233-4071
J Kenneth Ogdon, *President*
Dick Jacobs, *Corp Secy*
Robert D Beal, *Vice Pres*
Lou Allen, *Manager*
Todd Payne, *Officer*
EMP: 11
SQ FT: 148,000
SALES: 8.2MM **Privately Held**
WEB: www.ofgfinancial.com
SIC: 6211 Security brokers & dealers; bond dealers & brokers; mutual funds, selling by independent salesperson

(G-12942)
OGDEN CHECK APPROVAL NETWORK
3615 Sw 29th St Bsmt 101 (66614-2055)
PHONE..................................785 228-5600
Fax: 785 271-6211
EMP: 30
SQ FT: 4,000
SALES: 3.6MM **Privately Held**
SIC: 7389 Check Approval Services

(G-12943)
OGDEN PUBLICATIONS INC
Also Called: Mother Earth News
1503 Sw 42nd St (66609-1214)
PHONE..................................785 274-4300
Robert M Nutting, *President*
Heidi Hunt, *Editor*
Hank Will, *Editor*
Duane Wittman, *Corp Secy*
William O Nutting, *Vice Pres*
EMP: 150
SQ FT: 24,000
SALES (est): 15.6MM **Privately Held**
WEB: www.ogdenpubs.com
SIC: 2741 Miscellaneous publishing
HQ: The Ogden Newspapers Inc
1500 Main St
Wheeling WV 26003
304 233-0100

(G-12944)
OLD CASTLE PRECAST INC
5230 Nw 17th St (66618-3803)
PHONE..................................785 232-2982
Mark Schack, *President*
Jean Eakin, *Accountant*
EMP: 44
SQ FT: 10,600
SALES (est): 9.4MM
SALES (corp-wide): 29.7B **Privately Held**
SIC: 3272 Concrete products, precast; manhole covers or frames, concrete
HQ: Oldcastle Infrastructure, Inc.
7000 Cntl Prkaway Ste 800
Atlanta GA 30328
470 602-2000

(G-12945)
OLD CREEK SENIOR LIVING
Also Called: Briarcliff Care Center
3224 Sw 29th St (66614-2009)
PHONE..................................785 272-2601
Michael Wilcox, *CEO*
EMP: 20
SQ FT: 13,000
SALES (est): 1MM **Privately Held**
WEB: www.briarcliffmanor.com
SIC: 8052 Intermediate care facilities

(G-12946)
OLD DOMINION FREIGHT LINE INC
3508 Se 21st St (66607-2371)
PHONE..................................785 354-7336
Joe Campos, *Manager*
EMP: 13
SALES (corp-wide): 4B **Publicly Held**
WEB: www.odfl.com
SIC: 4213 Less-than-truckload (LTL) transport
PA: Old Dominion Freight Line Inc
500 Old Dominion Way
Thomasville NC 27360
336 889-5000

(G-12947)
ONEOK INC
Also Called: Kansas Gas Service
200 E 1st Ave (66603-3603)
PHONE..................................785 431-4201
Robert Green, *Branch Mgr*
EMP: 51
SALES (corp-wide): 12.5B **Publicly Held**
WEB: www.oneok.com
SIC: 4922 4924 Natural gas transmission; natural gas distribution
PA: Oneok, Inc.
100 W 5th St Ste Ll
Tulsa OK 74103
918 588-7000

(G-12948)
ONEOK INC
Also Called: Kansas Gas Service
501 Sw Gage Blvd (66606-2001)
P.O. Box 3535 (66601-3535)
PHONE....................................785 575-8554
Bell Eliason, *Branch Mgr*
EMP: 50
SALES (corp-wide): 12.5B **Publicly Held**
WEB: www.oneok.com
SIC: 4922 Natural gas transmission
PA: Oneok, Inc.
100 W 5th St Ste Ll
Tulsa OK 74103
918 588-7000

(G-12949)
ONEOK ENERGY SERVICES CO II (HQ)
Also Called: Oneok Energy Marketing
3706 Sw Topeka Blvd # 100 (66609-1239)
PHONE....................................785 274-4900
Greg Ingenthron, *CEO*
Doug Morphis, *Exec Dir*
EMP: 20
SALES (est): 13.9MM
SALES (corp-wide): 12.5B **Publicly Held**
SIC: 4924 Natural gas distribution
PA: Oneok, Inc.
100 W 5th St Ste Ll
Tulsa OK 74103
918 588-7000

(G-12950)
OPTIMATION HOLOGRAPHICS INC
3500 Sw Topeka Blvd (66611-2374)
PHONE....................................785 233-6000
John Parker, *President*
EMP: 30
SALES (est): 2MM **Privately Held**
SIC: 7334 Photocopying & duplicating services

(G-12951)
OREILLY AUTOMOTIVE STORES INC
Also Called: O'Reilly Auto Parts
1701 S Kansas Ave (66612-1433)
PHONE....................................785 235-9241
Cory Laird, *General Mgr*
EMP: 19 **Publicly Held**
SIC: 5013 5531 Automotive supplies & parts; automotive parts
HQ: O'reilly Automotive Stores, Inc.
233 S Patterson Ave
Springfield MO 65802
417 862-2674

(G-12952)
OREILLY AUTOMOTIVE STORES INC
Also Called: O'Reilly Auto Parts
1726 Nw Topeka Blvd (66608-1823)
PHONE....................................785 235-5658
Dan Neely, *Manager*
EMP: 15 **Publicly Held**
WEB: www.oreillyauto.com
SIC: 5013 5531 Automotive supplies & parts; automotive parts
HQ: O'reilly Automotive Stores, Inc.
233 S Patterson Ave
Springfield MO 65802
417 862-2674

(G-12953)
OREILLY AUTOMOTIVE STORES INC
Also Called: O'Reilly Auto Parts
4710 Sw Topeka Blvd (66609-1133)
PHONE....................................785 862-4749
Charlie Blocher, *Manager*
EMP: 15 **Publicly Held**
WEB: www.oreillyauto.com
SIC: 5013 5531 Automotive supplies & parts; automotive parts
HQ: O'reilly Automotive Stores, Inc.
233 S Patterson Ave
Springfield MO 65802
417 862-2674

(G-12954)
OREILLY AUTOMOTIVE STORES INC
Also Called: O'Reilly Auto Parts
2950 Se California Ave (66605-2467)
PHONE....................................785 266-3688
EMP: 15 **Publicly Held**
WEB: www.oreillyauto.com
SIC: 5013 5531 Automotive supplies & parts; automotive parts
HQ: O'reilly Automotive Stores, Inc.
233 S Patterson Ave
Springfield MO 65802
417 862-2674

(G-12955)
ORSCHELN FARM AND HOME LLC
Also Called: Orschelin Farm and Home 37
1133 Sw Wanamaker Rd # 100 (66604-3848)
PHONE....................................785 228-9688
Joe Morris, *Manager*
EMP: 12
SALES (corp-wide): 822.7MM **Privately Held**
WEB: www.orschelnfarmhome.com
SIC: 5191 5251 5699 5941 Farm supplies; hardware; work clothing; sporting goods & bicycle shops; feed & farm supply
PA: Orscheln Farm And Home Llc
1800 Overcenter Dr
Moberly MO 65270
800 577-2580

(G-12956)
P A MED ASSIST
4011 Sw 29th St (66614-2218)
PHONE....................................785 272-2161
Jeff Martin PHD, *President*
EMP: 15
SALES (est): 2.4MM **Privately Held**
SIC: 8011 Freestanding emergency medical center

(G-12957)
P A TREANORHL
719 Sw Van Buren St Ste 2 (66603-3740)
PHONE....................................785 235-0012
Dan Rowe, *Branch Mgr*
EMP: 14
SALES (corp-wide): 14.6MM **Privately Held**
WEB: www.treanorarchitects.com
SIC: 8712 Architectural engineering
PA: Treanorhl, Inc.
1040 Vermont St
Lawrence KS 66044
785 842-4858

(G-12958)
P1 GROUP INC
2150a S Kansas Ave (66611-1140)
PHONE....................................785 235-5331
Mike Belcher, *Branch Mgr*
EMP: 12
SALES (corp-wide): 243.8MM **Privately Held**
WEB: www.p1group.com
SIC: 1711 1731 Mechanical contractor; electrical work
PA: P1 Group, Inc.
13605 W 96th Ter
Lenexa KS 66215
913 529-5000

(G-12959)
PALMER LEATHERMAN & WHITE LLP
2348 Sw Topeka Blvd # 100 (66611-1283)
PHONE....................................785 233-1836
Lj Leatherman, *Senior Partner*
Jerry R Palmer, *Senior Partner*
Dustin Bandike, *Partner*
Megan Gerald, *Partner*
Gary White, *Partner*
EMP: 10
SQ FT: 5,000
SALES (est): 1.3MM **Privately Held**
WEB: www.jpalmerlaw.com
SIC: 8111 General practice attorney, lawyer

(G-12960)
PARKDALE PRE-SCHOOL CENTER
2331 Sw Topeka Blvd (66611-1257)
PHONE....................................785 235-7240
Shara Meyer, *Principal*
Shara Kinzel, *Principal*
EMP: 35
SALES (est): 490.1K **Privately Held**
SIC: 8351 8211 Preschool center; elementary school

(G-12961)
PARKER & HAY LLP
2887 Sw Macvicar Ave # 4 (66611-1786)
PHONE....................................785 266-3044
Fax: 785 228-5741
EMP: 13
SALES (est): 1.3MM **Privately Held**
SIC: 8111 Legal Services Office

(G-12962)
PARKVIEW JOINT VENTURE
Also Called: Parkview Partnership
2887 Sw Macvicar Ave (66611-1782)
PHONE....................................785 267-3410
Larry Hendricks, *Partner*
Gary Hanson, *Partner*
EMP: 12
SQ FT: 6,600
SALES (est): 508.7K **Privately Held**
SIC: 6512 8111 Commercial & industrial building operation; general practice attorney, lawyer

(G-12963)
PARTNERS IN PEDIATRICS PA
631 Sw Horne St Ste 340 (66606-1663)
PHONE....................................785 234-4624
Camille Heeb, *President*
EMP: 15
SALES (est): 1.6MM **Privately Held**
SIC: 8011 Pediatrician

(G-12964)
PATTERSON ADVERTISING AGENCY
Also Called: First Impressions
305 Se 17th St Ste C (66607-1266)
PHONE....................................785 232-0533
Jim Walker, *President*
Mario Montecinos, *Vice Pres*
Steve Patterson, *Vice Pres*
EMP: 8 **EST:** 1954
SQ FT: 5,400
SALES (est): 908.7K **Privately Held**
SIC: 7311 2752 Advertising agencies; commercial printing, lithographic

(G-12965)
PAULINE FOOD CENTER
Also Called: John's Market
5812 S Topeka St (66619)
PHONE....................................785 862-2774
John Benson, *Owner*
EMP: 11
SQ FT: 15,114
SALES (est): 924.3K **Privately Held**
SIC: 5411 5812 5541 6512 Grocery stores, independent; cafe; gasoline service stations; shopping center, property operation only

(G-12966)
PDQ CONSTRUCTION INC
531 Nw Tyler Ct Ste A (66608-2007)
PHONE....................................785 842-6844
Mike Pressgrove, *President*
Rick Hudkins, *Vice Pres*
Cheryl Merrill, *Admin Sec*
EMP: 17
SALES: 2.3MM **Privately Held**
SIC: 1542 1521 Commercial & office buildings, renovation & repair; single-family home remodeling, additions & repairs

(G-12967)
PEDIATRICS ASSOCIATES
3500 Sw 6th Ave Ste 200 (66606-2801)
PHONE....................................785 235-0335
Monica Denise Wood, *Principal*
Dr Ed Saylor, *Admin Sec*
Greggory Vansickle, *Pediatrics*
EMP: 30
SQ FT: 4,500
SALES (est): 3.5MM **Privately Held**
SIC: 8011 Pediatrician

(G-12968)
PEOPLES/COMMERCIAL INSUR LLC
Also Called: Nationwide
1414 Sw Ashworth Pl # 10 (66604-3741)
PHONE....................................785 271-8097
Michael Lesser, *President*
Greg Fankhauser, *Vice Pres*
Nancy Gleason, *Vice Pres*
Don Lafferty, *Sales Mgr*
Parkhurst Lisa, *Accounts Mgr*
EMP: 11
SALES: 8MM **Privately Held**
SIC: 6411 Insurance agents

(G-12969)
PEPSI-COLA BTLG CO TOPEKA INC
Also Called: Pepsico
2625 Nw Topeka Blvd (66617-1198)
PHONE....................................785 232-9389
Steven Ford, *President*
David Woll, *Vice Pres*
EMP: 55 **EST:** 1950
SQ FT: 65,000
SALES (est): 8.2MM **Privately Held**
SIC: 2086 Carbonated soft drinks, bottled & canned
HQ: Linpepco Corporation
1901 Windhoek Dr
Lincoln NE 68512
402 423-7330

(G-12970)
PERSPECTA ENTP SOLUTIONS LLC
Also Called: EDS
6511 Se Forbes Ave (66619-1448)
PHONE....................................785 274-4200
Sonya Ames, *Branch Mgr*
EMP: 10
SALES (corp-wide): 11.1B **Publicly Held**
SIC: 7374 Data processing service
HQ: Perspecta Enterprise Solutions Llc
13600 Eds Dr A3s
Herndon VA 20171
703 245-9675

(G-12971)
PETERSEN DEVELOPMENT CORP
1111 Sw Gage Blvd Ste 100 (66604-2283)
P.O. Box 4507 (66604-0507)
PHONE....................................785 228-9494
Thomas Petersen, *President*
EMP: 12
SALES (est): 991.1K **Privately Held**
SIC: 6552 Land subdividers & developers, commercial

(G-12972)
PETERSON PUBLICATIONS INC
2150 Sw Westport Dr # 101 (66614-1918)
PHONE....................................785 271-5801
Jeff Peterson, *President*
Kelly Adams, *Editor*
Nancy Cates, *Editor*
Katy Ibsen, *Editor*
Liz Stevens, *Editor*
EMP: 9
SQ FT: 2,000
SALES (est): 1.3MM **Privately Held**
WEB: www.petersonpublications.com
SIC: 2721 Magazines: publishing only, not printed on site

(G-12973)
PETSMART INC
2020 Sw Westport Dr # 200 (66604-3739)
PHONE....................................785 272-3323
Ashley Hawkins, *Principal*
EMP: 30
SALES (corp-wide): 9.4B **Publicly Held**
WEB: www.petsmart.com
SIC: 5999 0752 Pet food; animal specialty services
HQ: Petsmart, Inc.
19601 N 27th Ave
Phoenix AZ 85027
623 580-6100

GEOGRAPHIC

(G-12974)
PILLAR HOTELS AND RESORTS LLC
2033 Sw Wanamaker Rd (66604-3830)
PHONE.................................785 271-6165
Coleen Lynch, *Manager*
EMP: 35 **Privately Held**
SIC: 7011 Hotels
HQ: Pillar Hotels And Resorts, Llc
5851 Legacy Cir Ste 400
Plano TX 75024
972 830-3100

(G-12975)
PIONEER JANITORIAL LLC
103 Sw 32nd Ter (66611-2231)
P.O. Box 5622 (66605-0622)
PHONE.................................785 379-5101
James H Grossenkemper,
EMP: 30
SALES: 300K **Privately Held**
SIC: 7349 Janitorial service, contract basis

(G-12976)
PIPING CONTRACTORS KANSAS INC
4141 Nw 25th St (66618-3747)
PHONE.................................785 233-4321
Mark Law, *Branch Mgr*
EMP: 17
SALES (corp-wide): 7.9MM **Privately Held**
WEB: www.pci.kscoxmail.com
SIC: 5075 1711 Warm air heating equipment & supplies; septic system construction
PA: Piping Contractors Of Kansas, Inc.
115 Sw Jackson St
Topeka KS 66603
785 233-2010

(G-12977)
PIPING CONTRACTORS KANSAS INC (PA)
Also Called: P C I
115 Sw Jackson St (66603-3311)
PHONE.................................785 233-2010
James Brown, *President*
Steve Brown, *Owner*
Mark Law, *General Mgr*
Connie Brown, *Corp Secy*
Kim Stallbaumer, *Info Tech Mgr*
EMP: 30
SQ FT: 18,000
SALES (est): 7.9MM **Privately Held**
WEB: www.pci.kscoxmail.com
SIC: 1711 Mechanical contractor

(G-12978)
PITNEY BOWES INC
3320 Sw Harrison St Ste 8 (66611-2253)
PHONE.................................785 266-6750
Jim Torres, *Branch Mgr*
EMP: 7
SALES (corp-wide): 3.5B **Publicly Held**
SIC: 3579 7359 Postage meters; business machine & electronic equipment rental services
PA: Pitney Bowes Inc.
3001 Summer St Ste 3
Stamford CT 06905
203 356-5000

(G-12979)
PLANS PROFESSIONAL INC
112 Sw 6th Ave Ste 400 (66603-3845)
P.O. Box 8642 (66608-0642)
PHONE.................................785 357-7777
Mark A Schneider, *President*
EMP: 10
SQ FT: 30,000
SALES (est): 900K **Privately Held**
WEB: www.planinc.org
SIC: 7389 Financial services

(G-12980)
PLAZA WEST CARE CENTER INC
Also Called: PLAZA WEST REGIONAL HEALTH CEN
1570 Sw Westport Dr (66604-4030)
PHONE.................................785 271-6700
Douglas Adams, *President*
Brenda Adams, *Vice Pres*
Bruce Harkins, *Asst Treas*
Shawn Douglas, *Director*
Julie Embrey, *Director*
EMP: 170
SALES: 11.1MM **Privately Held**
SIC: 8051 Convalescent home with continuous nursing care

(G-12981)
PLUMBING BY CARLSON INC
Also Called: Carlson Plumbing
1820 Sw Van Buren St (66612-1422)
PHONE.................................785 232-0515
R Neil Carlson, *President*
Diana Mercer, *Corp Secy*
Chris Carlson, *Vice Pres*
EMP: 21 **EST:** 1957
SQ FT: 3,800
SALES (est): 2.1MM **Privately Held**
SIC: 1711 Plumbing contractors

(G-12982)
PRECISION PIPE COVER INC
2700 Nw Button Rd Ste C (66618-1462)
PHONE.................................785 233-2000
W B Haughton III, *President*
EMP: 20
SQ FT: 12,000
SALES (est): 2.2MM **Privately Held**
SIC: 3292 Pipe covering (heat insulating material), except felt

(G-12983)
PREMIER PERSONNEL INC
Also Called: Premier Employment Solutions
2813 Sw Wanamaker Rd (66614-4267)
PHONE.................................785 273-9944
Patricia Bossert, *Owner*
Kurt Bossert, *Corp Secy*
Paul Bossert, *Vice Pres*
Gavin Garman, *Branch Mgr*
Premier Administration, *Admin Asst*
EMP: 51
SQ FT: 2,300
SALES (est): 2.1MM **Privately Held**
WEB: www.premierks.com
SIC: 7361 7363 Executive placement; temporary help service

(G-12984)
PRESBYTERIAN MANORS INC
Also Called: Topeka Presbyterian Manor
4712 Sw 6th Ave (66606-2299)
PHONE.................................785 272-6510
Bill Sample, *Manager*
Garold Fowler, *Exec Dir*
EMP: 80
SALES (corp-wide): 8.6MM **Privately Held**
SIC: 8051 Convalescent home with continuous nursing care
HQ: Presbyterian Manors, Inc.
2414 N Woodlawn Blvd
Wichita KS 67220
316 685-1100

(G-12985)
PRESTIGE MASONRY LLC
2510 Sw Valley Glen Ct (66614-4350)
PHONE.................................785 925-3090
Tod Schumacher, *Partner*
EMP: 15 **EST:** 2000
SALES (est): 1.3MM **Privately Held**
SIC: 1741 Masonry & other stonework

(G-12986)
PRESTIGE PROPERTY CO
2410 Se 6th Ave (66607-2022)
PHONE.................................800 730-1249
Ronnie Brooks, *CEO*
EMP: 32
SQ FT: 2,500
SALES (est): 666.8K **Privately Held**
SIC: 6531 Real estate leasing & rentals

(G-12987)
PRICE & YOUNG & ODLE
Also Called: Eye Doctors, The
2800 Sw Wanamaker Rd # 192 (66614-4293)
PHONE.................................785 272-0707
Lisa Long, *Manager*
EMP: 11
SALES (corp-wide): 4.3MM **Privately Held**
SIC: 8042 Contact lense specialist optometrist
PA: Price & Young & Odle
3012 Anderson Ave
Manhattan KS 66503
785 537-1118

(G-12988)
PRICE TRUCK LINE INC
2000 Se Rice Rd (66607-2375)
PHONE.................................785 232-1183
Donna Mason, *Manager*
EMP: 12
SALES (est): 780.6K
SALES (corp-wide): 27MM **Privately Held**
SIC: 4213 Contract haulers
PA: Price Truck Line, Inc.
4931 S Victoria St
Wichita KS 67216
316 945-6915

(G-12989)
PROFESSIONAL ENGRG CONS PA
1161 Sw Mulvane St (66604-1456)
PHONE.................................785 290-0550
Julie Lyle, *President*
EMP: 32
SALES (corp-wide): 66.5MM **Privately Held**
WEB: www.pec.org
SIC: 8711 Consulting engineer
PA: Professional Engineering Consultants P.A.
303 S Topeka Ave
Wichita KS 67202
316 262-2691

(G-12990)
PROFESSIONAL ENGRG CONS PA
Also Called: PEC
400 S Kansas Ave Ste 200 (66603-3438)
PHONE.................................785 233-8300
Jason Fundis, *Project Engr*
Michael Stewart, *Project Engr*
Samantha Dillon, *Design Engr*
Mike Berry, *Branch Mgr*
Rob Johnson, *Technician*
EMP: 30
SALES (corp-wide): 66.5MM **Privately Held**
WEB: www.pec.org
SIC: 8711 Consulting engineer
PA: Professional Engineering Consultants P.A.
303 S Topeka Ave
Wichita KS 67202
316 262-2691

(G-12991)
PROGRESSIVE CONTRACTORS INC
3333 Se 21st St (66607-2520)
PHONE.................................785 235-3032
Mike McKay, *President*
EMP: 60
SALES (est): 1.5MM **Privately Held**
SIC: 1799 Special trade contractors

(G-12992)
PROPRINT INCORPORATED (PA)
1033 Sw Gage Blvd Ste 200 (66604-2596)
PHONE.................................785 272-0070
Shirley Grantham, *President*
EMP: 6
SQ FT: 2,200
SALES (est): 2.4MM **Privately Held**
WEB: www.proprintks.com
SIC: 2752 7334 Commercial printing, offset; photocopying & duplicating services

(G-12993)
PROVIDENCE LIVING CENTER INC
1112 Se Republican Ave (66607-1614)
PHONE.................................785 233-0588
Virgil Goracke, *President*
Doug Goracke, *Shareholder*
Vick Munson, *Shareholder*
Jack Vetter, *Shareholder*
Tonya Tostado, *Administration*
EMP: 55
SQ FT: 24,000
SALES: 4.5MM **Privately Held**
SIC: 8063 Hospital for the mentally ill

(G-12994)
PTMW INC
5040 Nw Us Highway 24 (66618-3815)
PHONE.................................785 232-7792
Patti Jon Goff, *President*
John Butterfield, *COO*
Bryan Christensen, *Vice Pres*
Fred Gantz, *Vice Pres*
William Goff, *Vice Pres*
EMP: 200
SQ FT: 800,000
SALES: 43.8MM **Privately Held**
WEB: www.ptmw.com
SIC: 3441 Building components, structural steel

(G-12995)
QUALITY CARE
Also Called: Auto Care Center
1136 Sw Wanamaker Rd (66604-3809)
PHONE.................................785 228-1118
Laird Noller, *President*
EMP: 12
SALES (est): 774.2K **Privately Held**
SIC: 7538 General automotive repair shops

(G-12996)
R O K K CONCRETE INC
5139 Nw Rochester Rd (66617-1392)
PHONE.................................785 286-0662
Susan Kramer, *President*
Helen Kramer, *Treasurer*
Duane Kramer, *Admin Sec*
EMP: 15
SALES (est): 1MM **Privately Held**
SIC: 1771 Concrete pumping

(G-12997)
RADIOLOGY NUCLEAR MEDICINE LLC (PA)
Also Called: Radiologix
2200 Sw 10th Ave (66604-3904)
PHONE.................................785 234-3454
Kyle Miller,
Ralph D Reymond MD,
EMP: 20
SALES (est): 3MM **Privately Held**
SIC: 8011 Radiologist

(G-12998)
RAPID RUBBLE REMOVAL
2730 Sw 57th St Ste W1 (66609-9416)
PHONE.................................785 862-8875
EMP: 7
SALES (est): 374.8K **Privately Held**
SIC: 1411 Dimension Stone Quarry

(G-12999)
RAVENWOOD HUNTING PRESERVE INC
Also Called: Ravenwood Lodge
10147 Sw 61st St (66610-9655)
PHONE.................................785 256-6444
Ken Corbet, *President*
EMP: 15
SQ FT: 3,500
SALES (est): 459.3K **Privately Held**
WEB: www.ravenwoodoutdoors.com
SIC: 7997 Hunting club, membership

(G-13000)
RAY ANDERSON CO INC (PA)
Also Called: Overhead Door Co of Topeka
2322 Sw 6th Ave (66606-1760)
PHONE.................................785 233-7454
Ron Willis, *President*
Terry Wilson, *CFO*
EMP: 35 **EST:** 1926
SQ FT: 10,752
SALES (est): 4MM **Privately Held**
WEB: www.pellaks.com
SIC: 1751 5211 Garage door, installation or erection; garage doors, sale & installation; windows, storm: wood or metal

(G-13001)
RDR EXCAVATING INC
2222 Nw Huxman Rd (66618-5618)
P.O. Box 750652 (66675-0652)
PHONE.................................785 582-4645
Debbie Rees, *President*
Riley Rees, *Vice Pres*
EMP: 15

SALES (est): 1.1MM **Privately Held**
SIC: 1794 1629 1799 Excavation & grading, building construction; trenching contractor; boring for building construction

(G-13002)
REALTY PROFESSIONALS LLC
2900 Sw Wanamaker Dr # 200
(66614-4167)
PHONE....................785 271-8400
Stuart Elliott, *President*
Vicki Cunningham, *Executive*
EMP: 10
SALES (est): 155.8K **Privately Held**
SIC: 6531 Real estate agent, residential

(G-13003)
REBOUND PHYSICAL THERAPY
5220 Sw 17th St Ste 130 (66604-2514)
PHONE....................785 271-5533
Paul Silovsky, *Owner*
EMP: 30
SALES (est): 1MM **Privately Held**
WEB: www.reboundphysicaltherapy.com
SIC: 8049 Physiotherapist; physical therapist

(G-13004)
REGENCY MIDWEST VENTURES LIMIT
Also Called: Clubhouse Inn & Suites
924 Sw Henderson Rd (66615-3841)
PHONE....................785 273-8888
Lindsay Halderman, *General Mgr*
EMP: 30 **Privately Held**
SIC: 7011 Hotels
PA: Regency Midwest Ventures Limited Partnership
3211 W Sencore Dr
Sioux Falls SD 57107

(G-13005)
REGIS CORPORATION
1490 E Wanamaker Rd (66604)
PHONE....................785 273-2992
Nancy Jonak, *Branch Mgr*
EMP: 17
SALES (corp-wide): 1B **Publicly Held**
WEB: www.regiscorp.com
SIC: 7231 Beauty shops
PA: Regis Corporation
7201 Metro Blvd
Minneapolis MN 55439
952 947-7777

(G-13006)
REGIS SALON CORP
1801 Sw Wanamaker Rd (66604-3804)
P.O. Box 224 (66601-0224)
PHONE....................785 273-2992
Nancy Cooper, *Manager*
EMP: 20 **EST**: 2000
SALES (est): 184.8K **Privately Held**
SIC: 7231 Unisex hair salons

(G-13007)
REKAT RECREATION INC
Also Called: Gage Bowls
4200 Sw Huntoon St Ste A (66604-2299)
PHONE....................785 272-1881
Joe Mazur, *Partner*
EMP: 30 **Privately Held**
WEB: www.gagebowl.net
SIC: 5941 7299 7999 5812 Bowling equipment & supplies; party planning service; billiard parlor; eating places
PA: Rekat Recreation Inc
4200 Sw Huntoon St Ste A
Topeka KS 66604

(G-13008)
REKAT RECREATION INC (PA)
Also Called: Gage Center Bowl
4200 Sw Huntoon St Ste A (66604-2299)
PHONE....................785 272-1881
Rex Haney, *President*
Katherine L Haney, *Corp Secy*
EMP: 60
SALES: 2MM **Privately Held**
WEB: www.gagebowl.net
SIC: 7933 Ten pin center

(G-13009)
RESERS FINE FOODS INC
Also Called: La Siesta Foods
3728 Se 6th St (66607-2368)
PHONE....................785 233-6431
Michael Harding, *Opers Mgr*
John Hodder, *Opers-Prdtn-Mfg*
Allen Prato, *Engineer*
EMP: 500
SALES (corp-wide): 1.6B **Privately Held**
SIC: 2032 2099 2035 2098 Tortillas: packaged in cans, jars etc.; food preparations; pickles, sauces & salad dressings; macaroni & spaghetti
PA: Reser's Fine Foods, Inc.
15570 Sw Jenkins Rd
Beaverton OR 97006
503 643-6431

(G-13010)
RESOURCE CENTER FOR IND LIVING
1507 Sw 21st St Ste 203 (66604-3268)
PHONE....................785 267-1717
Mary Halloway, *Manager*
EMP: 12
SALES (est): 330.7K
SALES (corp-wide): 18.7MM **Privately Held**
WEB: www.rcilinc.org
SIC: 8322 Social service center
PA: Resource Center For Independent Living Inc
1137 Laing St
Osage City KS 66523
785 528-3105

(G-13011)
RESTORTION WTRPRFING CNTRS INC
1416 Sw Auburn Rd (66615-1503)
PHONE....................785 478-9538
Edd Parr, *Branch Mgr*
EMP: 12
SALES (corp-wide): 8.5MM **Privately Held**
WEB: www.restoration-waterproof.com
SIC: 1771 1799 Concrete work; waterproofing
PA: Restoration & Waterproofing Contractors, Inc.
2222 S Hoover Rd
Wichita KS 67209
316 942-6602

(G-13012)
REVISOR OF STATUTES
Capitol Federal Bldg Sw10th (66603-3818)
PHONE....................785 296-2321
Norman Furse, *Principal*
Bruce Kinzie, *Editor*
EMP: 30
SALES (est): 706.3K **Privately Held**
SIC: 8621 Professional membership organizations

(G-13013)
REW MATERIALS INC
730 Ne Us Highway 24 (66608-1770)
PHONE....................785 233-3651
Jim Bedsworth, *President*
EMP: 10
SALES (est): 880K **Privately Held**
SIC: 1742 Drywall

(G-13014)
RICHMAN HELSTROM TRUCKING INC
6017 Sw 46th St (66610-1319)
PHONE....................785 478-3186
Norman Richman, *President*
EMP: 10
SALES: 148K **Privately Held**
SIC: 4212 7389 Local trucking, without storage;

(G-13015)
RICK R TAGUE MD MPH
Also Called: Optimum Health Family Practice
2840 Sw Urish Rd (66614-5614)
PHONE....................785 228-2277
Rick R Tague, *Owner*
Nancy Burge, *Med Doctor*
Crystal Knott, *Physician Asst*
EMP: 18
SALES (est): 1.3MM **Privately Held**
SIC: 8011 General & family practice, physician/surgeon

(G-13016)
RICKS CONCRETE SAWING INC
4739 Se Adams St (66609-9421)
P.O. Box 5634 (66605-0634)
PHONE....................785 862-5400
James R Mann, *President*
Lori Mann, *Corp Secy*
Bobby J Mann, *Vice Pres*
EMP: 14 **EST**: 1978
SALES (est): 2.2MM **Privately Held**
SIC: 1795 Concrete breaking for streets & highways

(G-13017)
RICOH USA INC
2655 Sw Wanamaker Rd (66614-4491)
PHONE....................785 272-0248
EMP: 41
SALES (corp-wide): 18.7B **Privately Held**
SIC: 5044 Whol Office Equipment
HQ: Ricoh Usa, Inc.
70 Valley Stream Pkwy
Malvern PA 19341
610 296-8000

(G-13018)
RIDGE AUTO CENTER
Also Called: Market, The
4431 Nw Green Hills Rd (66618-5812)
PHONE....................785 286-1498
Terry Hummer, *Owner*
EMP: 10 **EST**: 1999
SALES (est): 196K **Privately Held**
SIC: 7549 Automotive services

(G-13019)
RITCHEY MOTORS LLC
Also Called: Big Phils Auto Plaza
1818 Sw Topeka Blvd (66612-1412)
PHONE....................785 380-0222
Mark Fitzgibbons, *Mng Member*
EMP: 18
SALES: 950K **Privately Held**
SIC: 5521 7549 Automobiles, used cars only; automotive maintenance services

(G-13020)
RJS DISCOUNT SALES INC
Also Called: Rj's Auction Service
3737 Sw South Park Ave (66609-1419)
PHONE....................785 267-7476
Phyllis Garvin, *CEO*
Bob Steele, *Vice Pres*
EMP: 14
SQ FT: 14,500
SALES (est): 2.5MM **Privately Held**
WEB: www.rjsks.com
SIC: 5199 General merchandise, non-durable

(G-13021)
ROACH BUILDING CO INC
Also Called: Roach Hardware
1321 Sw 21st St (66604-3066)
PHONE....................785 233-9606
Gary Chittenden, *President*
Robert Corbin, *Owner*
Ellen Roach, *Admin Sec*
EMP: 13
SQ FT: 14,000
SALES (est): 625.7K **Privately Held**
SIC: 6512 Commercial & industrial building operation

(G-13022)
ROBERTS DAIRY COMPANY LLC
Also Called: Hiland Dairy
7215 Sw Topeka Blvd (66619-1456)
P.O. Box 19066 (66619-0066)
PHONE....................785 232-1274
Paul Wildermuth, *Manager*
EMP: 15
SALES (corp-wide): 1.7B **Privately Held**
SIC: 5143 Dairy products, except dried or canned
HQ: Roberts Dairy Company, Llc
2901 Cuming St
Omaha NE 68131
402 344-4321

(G-13023)
ROCK PRE-K CENTER
3819 Sw Burlingame Rd (66609-1218)
PHONE....................785 266-2285
Linda Shipley, *Manager*
EMP: 16
SALES (est): 158.2K **Privately Held**
SIC: 8351 Preschool center

(G-13024)
ROGER FINCHER
Also Called: Fincher Office
1263 Sw Topeka Blvd (66612-1852)
PHONE....................785 430-5770
Roger Fincher, *Principal*
EMP: 10
SALES (est): 687.5K **Privately Held**
SIC: 8111 General practice attorney, lawyer

(G-13025)
ROGER L JOHNSON
534 S Kansas Ave Ste 1500 (66603-3437)
PHONE....................785 233-4226
Roger L Johnson, *Partner*
Darryl Lloyd, *Partner*
Erick Otting, *Partner*
John Wendling, *Partner*
EMP: 30
SALES (est): 1.1MM **Privately Held**
SIC: 8721 Certified public accountant

(G-13026)
ROLLING HILLS HEALTH CENTER (PA)
2400 Sw Urish Rd (66614-4347)
PHONE....................785 273-5001
James Klausman, *President*
Floyd Eaton, *Vice Pres*
Kim Brown, *Hlthcr Dir*
Fernando Lefort, *Administration*
EMP: 125
SQ FT: 40,000
SALES: 7.6MM **Privately Held**
SIC: 8051 Convalescent home with continuous nursing care

(G-13027)
ROLLING HILLS HEALTH CENTER
2410 Sw Urish Rd (66614-4347)
PHONE....................785 273-2202
Tammy Blake, *Manager*
EMP: 20
SALES (est): 510.7K
SALES (corp-wide): 7.6MM **Privately Held**
SIC: 8051 Skilled nursing care facilities
PA: Rolling Hills Health Center Inc
2400 Sw Urish Rd
Topeka KS 66614
785 273-5001

(G-13028)
RONALD MCDNALD HSE CHRTIES NRT
825 Sw Buchanan St (66606-1427)
PHONE....................785 235-6852
Martha Hagedorn-Krass, *CEO*
Patty Oliver, *Director*
EMP: 11
SQ FT: 10,000
SALES: 415.6K **Privately Held**
SIC: 8322 Individual & family services

(G-13029)
ROSE VILLA INC (PA)
2075 Sw Fillmore St (66604-3075)
PHONE....................785 232-0671
Lynn Nichols, *President*
Jay Nichols, *Vice Pres*
EMP: 27
SQ FT: 20,000
SALES (est): 1.7MM **Privately Held**
SIC: 8361 Residential care

(G-13030)
RUAN TRNSP MGT SYSTEMS INC
1100 Sw 57th St (66609-1261)
PHONE....................785 274-6672
Bryan Beets, *General Mgr*
EMP: 34

SALES (corp-wide): 1.7B **Privately Held**
WEB: www.ruan.com
SIC: 4213 Contract haulers
PA: Ruan Transportation Management Systems, Inc.
666 Grand Ave Ste 3100
Des Moines IA 50309
515 245-2500

(G-13031)
RYDEX FUND SERVICES INC
Also Called: Rydex Funds
1 Sw Security Benefit Pl (66636-1000)
PHONE..................................301 296-5100
Albert Viragh, *President*
Kimberly Christopher, *Marketing Staff*
Angela Goodrich, *Marketing Staff*
EMP: 220
SQ FT: 50,000
SALES (est): 13.1MM
SALES (corp-wide): 2B **Privately Held**
WEB: www.rydexfs.com
SIC: 6722 Mutual fund sales, on own account; money market mutual funds
HQ: Security Benefit Life Insurance Company,
1 Sw Security Benefit Pl
Topeka KS 66636
785 438-3000

(G-13032)
S J INVESTMENTS INC OF TOPEKA
3637 Se 6th St Lh (66607-2309)
PHONE..................................785 233-1568
Nancy Ketter, *Principal*
EMP: 10
SALES (est): 1.1MM **Privately Held**
SIC: 6799 Investors

(G-13033)
SALVATION ARMY
1320 Se 6th Ave (66607-1934)
PHONE..................................785 233-9648
Brian Burkett, *Principal*
EMP: 12
SALES (corp-wide): 2.2B **Privately Held**
WEB: www.salarmychicago.org
SIC: 8661 8699 Christian & Reformed Church; charitable organization
HQ: The Salvation Army
5550 Prairie Stone Pkwy # 130
Hoffman Estates IL 60192
847 294-2000

(G-13034)
SALVATION ARMY
1320 Se 6th Ave (66607-1934)
P.O. Box 599 (66601-0599)
PHONE..................................785 233-9648
Charles Yockey, *CEO*
EMP: 23
SALES (corp-wide): 2.2MM **Privately Held**
SIC: 8322 Multi-service center
PA: The Salvation Army
5469 Sunbird Dr
Loves Park IL

(G-13035)
SAMCO INC
3840 Nw 14th St Ste C (66618-2882)
PHONE..................................785 234-4000
Dale Warren, *President*
Larry McDaniel, *Admin Sec*
EMP: 40
SQ FT: 12,000
SALES: 5MM **Privately Held**
WEB: www.mcelroys.com
SIC: 1711 Mechanical contractor

(G-13036)
SARIK LLC
1517 Sw Medford Ave (66604-2637)
PHONE..................................785 379-1235
Abby Smith, *Office Mgr*
EMP: 18
SALES (est): 1.5MM **Privately Held**
SIC: 4789 Transportation services

(G-13037)
SBC FUNDING LLC
1 Sw Security Benefit Pl (66636-1000)
PHONE..................................785 438-3000
EMP: 2081
SALES (est): 299.2K
SALES (corp-wide): 2B **Privately Held**
SIC: 6722 Management investment, open-end
HQ: Security Benefit Corporation
1 Sw Security Benefit Pl
Topeka KS 66636

(G-13038)
SCHMIDT VENDING INC
1911 Nw Lower Silver Lk (66608-1631)
PHONE..................................785 354-7397
Lee Schmidt, *President*
Charles Schmidt, *Vice Pres*
Rose Marie Schmidt, *Treasurer*
EMP: 12
SQ FT: 8,400
SALES (est): 1.1MM **Privately Held**
SIC: 5962 5145 Merchandising machine operators; candy; nuts, salted or roasted

(G-13039)
SCHMIDTLEIN ELECTRIC INC
305 Ne Croco Rd (66616-1683)
PHONE..................................785 357-4572
Debbie K Schmidtlein, *President*
Tom Schmidtlein, *Vice Pres*
EMP: 22
SQ FT: 5,450
SALES (est): 2.6MM **Privately Held**
SIC: 1731 General electrical contractor

(G-13040)
SCHREINER M & SONS CNSTR
7731 Ne Indian Creek Rd (66617-2215)
PHONE..................................785 246-1130
Marvin Schreiner, *President*
Chris Schreiner, *Vice Pres*
Joe Schreiner, *Vice Pres*
Judy Schreiner, *Admin Sec*
EMP: 11
SALES: 800K **Privately Held**
SIC: 1771 Concrete work

(G-13041)
SCHWERDT DESIGN GROUP INC (PA)
2231 Sw Wanamaker Rd # 303 (66614-4275)
PHONE..................................785 273-7540
Greg Schwerdt, *President*
Gregory Allen, *Architect*
Ryman Kinney, *Nephrology*
EMP: 21
SALES: 8.9MM **Privately Held**
WEB: www.sdgarch.com
SIC: 8712 Architectural engineering

(G-13042)
SCOTCH INDUSTRIES INC
134 Se Quincy St (66603-3537)
P.O. Box 1557 (66601-1557)
PHONE..................................785 235-3401
Scott Shmalberg, *Manager*
EMP: 35
SALES (corp-wide): 4.7MM **Privately Held**
SIC: 7216 Drycleaning collecting & distributing agency
PA: Scotch Industries Inc
1029 Nh St Apt B
Lawrence KS 66044
785 843-0037

(G-13043)
SCOTT MASONRY INC
6001 Nw 35th St (66618-4634)
PHONE..................................785 286-3513
David Scott, *President*
Jackie Scott, *Admin Sec*
EMP: 15
SALES: 3.5MM **Privately Held**
SIC: 1741 Masonry & other stonework

(G-13044)
SCOTT QINLAN WILLARD BARNS LLC
1613 Sw 37th St (66611-2627)
PHONE..................................785 267-0040
Jim Willard,
EMP: 12
SALES (est): 920.7K **Privately Held**
WEB: www.sqwblaw.com
SIC: 8111 General practice law office

(G-13045)
SCS TECH LLC
Also Called: Dynamarine Performance Boats
2529 Nw Topeka Blvd (66617-1156)
PHONE..................................785 424-4478
Shane Lavalette,
EMP: 7
SALES (est): 1MM **Privately Held**
SIC: 3732 Boat building & repairing

(G-13046)
SD ENGINEERING LLC
3649 Nw 25th St (66618-2707)
PHONE..................................785 233-8880
Steve Duncan, *Principal*
EMP: 10
SALES (est): 1.3MM **Privately Held**
SIC: 8711 Engineering services

(G-13047)
SE2 LLC
5801 Sw 6th Ave (66636-1001)
PHONE..................................800 747-3940
Chirag Buch, *Vice Pres*
Heather Shaffer, *QC Mgr*
Errol Williams, *Human Resources*
Jody Clark, *Accounts Exec*
Ashish Jha, *Chief Mktg Ofcr*
EMP: 350
SALES (est): 103MM
SALES (corp-wide): 2B **Privately Held**
SIC: 6411 Insurance information & consulting services
HQ: Security Benefit Corporation
1 Sw Security Benefit Pl
Topeka KS 66636

(G-13048)
SEAMAN UNIFIED SCHOOL DST 345
Also Called: Mathes Early Learning Center
2032 N Kansas Ave (66608-1814)
PHONE..................................785 286-7103
Dedra Raines, *Supervisor*
EMP: 30
SALES (corp-wide): 29.9MM **Privately Held**
SIC: 8351 Preschool center
PA: Seaman Unified School District 345
901 Nw Lyman Rd
Topeka KS 66608
785 575-8600

(G-13049)
SEARS ROEBUCK AND CO
Also Called: Sears Auto Center
1781 Sw Wanamater Rd (66609)
PHONE..................................785 271-4200
EMP: 15
SALES (corp-wide): 16.7B **Publicly Held**
SIC: 7549 Automotive Services
HQ: Sears, Roebuck And Co.
3333 Beverly Rd
Hoffman Estates IL 60179
847 286-2500

(G-13050)
SECURITIES COMMISSIONER KANSAS (DH)
109 Sw 9th St Ste 600 (66612-1215)
PHONE..................................785 296-3307
Allison Conklin, *Human Res Mgr*
Brian Herder, *Librarian*
Jeff Jones, *Program Mgr*
Aaron Jack, *Commissioner*
Ora Mayes, *Network Enginr*
EMP: 22
SALES (est): 4.8MM **Privately Held**
WEB: www.securities.state.ks.us
SIC: 6211 9111 9199 Security brokers & dealers; executive offices; ;
HQ: Executive Office Of The State Of Kansas
300 Sw 10th Ave
Topeka KS 66612
785 296-6240

(G-13051)
SECURITY BENEFIT ACADEMY INC
1 Sw Security Benefit Pl (66636-1000)
PHONE..................................785 438-3000
Kris Robbins, *President*
Venette David, *Senior VP*
Malcolm E Robinson, *Senior VP*
EMP: 27
SQ FT: 13,380
SALES: 760K **Privately Held**
SIC: 8351 Child day care services

(G-13052)
SECURITY BENEFIT CORPORATION (DH)
1 Sw Security Benefit Pl (66636-1000)
PHONE..................................785 438-3000
Howard Fricke, *CEO*
Richard Wells, *President*
David J Keith, *Principal*
Michael Reidy, *Chairman*
Rui Guo, *Assistant VP*
EMP: 107
SALES (est): 1.8B
SALES (corp-wide): 2B **Privately Held**
SIC: 6311 Life insurance
HQ: Eldridge Sbc Holdings Llc
135 E 57th St
New York NY 10022
212 739-0700

(G-13053)
SECURITY BENEFIT GROUP INC
Also Called: Security Bneft Group Companies
1 Sw Security Benefit Pl (66636-1000)
PHONE..................................785 438-3000
Kris A Robbins, *President*
James F Mullery, *President*
Howard R Fricke, *Chairman*
John F Guyot, *Senior VP*
John F Frye, *CFO*
EMP: 500
SQ FT: 128,000
SALES (est): 232.3MM
SALES (corp-wide): 2B **Privately Held**
SIC: 6211 7311 6411 Security brokers & dealers; advertising agencies; insurance agents, brokers & service
HQ: Security Benefit Life Insurance Company,
1 Sw Security Benefit Pl
Topeka KS 66636
785 438-3000

(G-13054)
SECURITY BENEFIT LIFE INSUR CO (DH)
1 Sw Security Benefit Pl (66636-1000)
PHONE..................................785 438-3000
Howard R Fricke, *Ch of Bd*
Kris Robbins, *President*
Eric REA, *President*
Malcolm E Robinson, *Senior VP*
Jim Kiley, *Vice Pres*
EMP: 313 **EST:** 1892
SQ FT: 306,985
SALES (est): 792.3MM
SALES (corp-wide): 2B **Privately Held**
SIC: 6311 6722 6091 6211 Life insurance; management investment, open-end; nondeposit trust facilities; brokers, security; business consulting

(G-13055)
SECURITY MANAGEMENT CO LLC
1 Sw Security Benefit Pl (66636-1000)
PHONE..................................785 438-3000
Kris Robbins,
Howard Fricke,
EMP: 40
SALES (est): 1.7MM
SALES (corp-wide): 2B **Privately Held**
SIC: 8748 Business consulting
HQ: Security Benefit Corporation
1 Sw Security Benefit Pl
Topeka KS 66636

(G-13056)
SECURITY TRANSPORT SERVICE
1643 Sw 41st St (66609-1250)
PHONE..................................785 267-3030
Thomas L Baumann, *President*
EMP: 45
SALES (est): 1.9MM **Privately Held**
SIC: 4119 Local rental transportation; limousine rental, with driver

(G-13057)
SENATE LUXURY SUITES INC
Also Called: Senate Management
900 Sw Tyler St (66612-1624)
PHONE....................785 233-5050
Beckie Weichert, *Exec Dir*
EMP: 13
SQ FT: 45,000
SALES (est): 897.3K **Privately Held**
WEB: www.senatesuites.com
SIC: 7011 Hotels

(G-13058)
SENNE AND COMPANY INC
2001 Nw Us Highway 24 (66618-1445)
PHONE....................785 235-1015
Bruce Senne, *CEO*
Mike McGivern, *President*
Scott De Tar, *Sales Staff*
EMP: 40 **EST:** 1914
SQ FT: 14,500
SALES (est): 11.7MM **Privately Held**
WEB: www.sennecompany.com
SIC: 1542 1796 Commercial & office building, new construction; commercial & office buildings, renovation & repair; millwright

(G-13059)
SENTAGE CORPORATION
Also Called: Dental Services Group
2820 Sw Fairlawn Rd # 200 (66614-1509)
P.O. Box 33 (66601-0033)
PHONE....................785 235-9293
Dave Dittmer, *Branch Mgr*
EMP: 55
SALES (corp-wide): 59MM **Privately Held**
WEB: www.dentalservices.net
SIC: 8072 Artificial teeth production
PA: Sentage Corporation
146 2nd St N Ste 207
Saint Petersburg FL 33701
727 502-2069

(G-13060)
SERVICE CORPS RETIRED EXECS
Also Called: S C O R E
120 Se 6th Ave Ste 110 (66603-3515)
PHONE....................785 234-3049
Doug Kinsinger, *Branch Mgr*
EMP: 11
SALES (corp-wide): 13.1MM **Privately Held**
WEB: www.score199.mv.com
SIC: 8611 Business associations
PA: Service Corps Of Retired Executives Association
1175 Herndon Pkwy Ste 900
Herndon VA 20170
703 487-3612

(G-13061)
SEWING WORKSHOP
Also Called: Threadwear
301 S Kansas Ave Apt A (66603-3643)
PHONE....................785 357-6231
Linda Lee, *President*
Kathy Davis, *Production*
Craig Woodberry, *Treasurer*
EMP: 15
SALES (est): 1.2MM **Privately Held**
WEB: www.sewingworkshop.com
SIC: 5231 5714 5712 5713 Wallcoverings; draperies; furniture stores; floor covering stores; interior decorating

(G-13062)
SHAMIR CORP
Also Called: Plaza Inn
3802 Sw Topeka Blvd (66609-1232)
PHONE....................785 266-8880
Nick Bhakhta, *President*
EMP: 35
SALES (est): 819.8K **Privately Held**
SIC: 7011 5813 5812 Motels; drinking places; eating places

(G-13063)
SHAWNEE COUNTRY CLUB
913 Se 29th St (66605-1399)
PHONE....................785 233-2373
Ramona Halbouni, *Director*
EMP: 45
SQ FT: 12,000
SALES (est): 1.6MM **Privately Held**
SIC: 7997 7992 Country club, membership; public golf courses

(G-13064)
SHAWNEE REGL PREVENTION AN
Also Called: NCADD
2209 Sw 29th St (66611-1908)
PHONE....................785 266-8666
John Calbeck, *Exec Dir*
EMP: 12 **EST:** 1965
SALES: 465.7K
SALES (corp-wide): 533.6K **Privately Held**
WEB: www.ncadd.org
SIC: 8399 Community action agency
PA: National Council On Alcoholism And Drug Dependence Inc.
217 Broadway Rm 712
New York NY 10007
212 269-7797

(G-13065)
SHAWNEE WOODWORK INC
112 Sw Harrison St (66603-3015)
P.O. Box 633 (66601-0633)
PHONE....................785 354-1163
Jim Kuhn, *President*
EMP: 20
SQ FT: 22,000
SALES (est): 3.2MM **Privately Held**
SIC: 2431 Millwork

(G-13066)
SHELLEY ELECTRIC INC
5331 Sw Randolph Ave (66609-1114)
PHONE....................785 862-0507
Jim Fowler, *Branch Mgr*
EMP: 30
SALES (corp-wide): 26.6MM **Privately Held**
SIC: 1731 General electrical contractor
PA: Shelley Electric, Inc.
3619 W 29th St S
Wichita KS 67217
316 945-8311

(G-13067)
SHELTER INSURANCE
2701 Sw Wanamaker Rd (66614-4265)
PHONE....................785 272-7181
Greg Kueck, *Principal*
EMP: 25
SALES (est): 1.4MM **Privately Held**
SIC: 6411 Insurance agents & brokers

(G-13068)
SHELTERED LIVING INC (PA)
3401 Sw Harrison St (66611-2214)
PHONE....................785 233-2566
Lisa Jackson, *CEO*
Mike Gudenkauf, *President*
Kathy Brayton, *CFO*
Gary Knoll, *Treasurer*
Lisa Gates, *Exec Dir*
EMP: 24
SQ FT: 4,800
SALES: 6.9MM **Privately Held**
SIC: 8059 Home for the mentally retarded, exc. skilled or intermediate

(G-13069)
SHELTERED LIVING INC
2126 Sw 36th St (66611-2554)
PHONE....................785 266-8686
Traci Vincent, *Branch Mgr*
EMP: 10
SALES (corp-wide): 6.9MM **Privately Held**
SIC: 8059 Home for the mentally retarded, exc. skilled or intermediate
PA: Sheltered Living Inc
3401 Sw Harrison St
Topeka KS 66611
785 233-2566

(G-13070)
SHERWOOD LAKE CLUB INC
6910 Sw Fountaindale Rd (66614-4621)
PHONE....................785 478-3305
Gerald Block, *President*
Warren Schmidgall, *President*
Steve Brewster, *Manager*
EMP: 11
SALES: 342.6K **Privately Held**
SIC: 7997 Membership sports & recreation clubs

(G-13071)
SHREE-GURU INVESTMENTS INC
Also Called: Hampton Inn
1401 Sw Ashworth Pl (66604-3737)
PHONE....................785 273-0003
Wes Halsey, *Manager*
EMP: 13 **Privately Held**
SIC: 7011 Hotels & motels
PA: Shree-Guru Investments Inc
1716 Jefferson St
Jefferson City MO 65109

(G-13072)
SILVER LAKE BANK (PA)
201 Nw Us Highway 24 # 201 (66608-1898)
P.O. Box 8330 (66608-0330)
PHONE....................785 232-0102
Patrick Gideon, *President*
Kerry J Munsey, *Exec VP*
Don Hamilton, *Senior VP*
EMP: 20 **EST:** 1909
SQ FT: 8,000
SALES: 12.1MM **Privately Held**
WEB: www.silverlakebank.com
SIC: 6036 6022 State savings banks, not federally chartered; state commercial banks

(G-13073)
SISTERS OF CHARITY OF LEAVENWO
Also Called: Cancer Medicine & Hemotology
1700 Sw 7th St (66606-2489)
PHONE....................785 295-7800
Kathy Devlin, *Manager*
Don Abdallah, *Director*
EMP: 14
SALES (corp-wide): 2.7B **Privately Held**
WEB: www.sclhsc.org
SIC: 8062 General medical & surgical hospitals
PA: Sisters Of Charity Of Leavenworth Health System, Inc.
500 Eldorado Blvd # 6300
Broomfield CO 80021
303 813-5000

(G-13074)
SISTERS OF CHARITY OF LEAVENWO
Also Called: St Francis Medical Practice
600 Sw Jewell Ave (66606-1607)
PHONE....................785 295-5310
Becky Wessel, *President*
Mary Franz, *Family Practiti*
EMP: 35
SALES (corp-wide): 2.7B **Privately Held**
WEB: www.sclhsc.org
SIC: 8062 General medical & surgical hospitals
PA: Sisters Of Charity Of Leavenworth Health System, Inc.
500 Eldorado Blvd # 6300
Broomfield CO 80021
303 813-5000

(G-13075)
SK8AWAY INC
815 Sw Fairlawn Rd (66606-2338)
PHONE....................785 272-0303
Tina Robertson, *Owner*
Debbie Ray, *Manager*
EMP: 20
SQ FT: 18,000
SALES (est): 688.5K **Privately Held**
WEB: www.sk8away.com
SIC: 7999 5941 Roller skating rink operation; skating equipment

(G-13076)
SKYCOM INC
1020 Sw Wanamaker Rd (66604-4148)
PHONE....................785 273-1000
Tom Price, *President*
Parrish Burns, *Sales Staff*
Ed Cape, *Sales Staff*
EMP: 10
SALES (est): 650K **Privately Held**
WEB: www.skykansas.com
SIC: 4841 Direct broadcast satellite services (DBS)

(G-13077)
SLOAN EISENBARTH GLASSMAN (PA)
534 S Kansas Ave Ste 1000 (66603-3456)
PHONE....................785 357-6311
Vernon L Jarboe, *Mng Member*
Cynthia Phillips, *Office Admin*
Arthur A Glassman, *Director*
Sloan Eldon,
Allison Hibler, *Legal Staff*
EMP: 28
SQ FT: 10,000
SALES (est): 6MM **Privately Held**
WEB: www.sloanlawfirm.com
SIC: 8111 General practice law office

(G-13078)
SMG HOLDINGS INC
Also Called: Kansas Expocentre
1 Expocentre Dr (66612-1442)
PHONE....................785 235-1986
Hr Cook, *Manager*
Justin Gregory, *Director*
EMP: 28
SALES (corp-wide): 23.7B **Privately Held**
WEB: www.smgworld.com
SIC: 7941 9111 Stadium event operator services; county supervisors' & executives' offices
HQ: Smg Holdings, Llc
300 Cnshohckn State Rd # 450
Conshohocken PA 19428

(G-13079)
SMITH AUDIO VISUAL INC
5233 Sw 25th St (66614-1618)
PHONE....................785 235-3481
Larry Heilman, *President*
Susie Heilman, *Corp Secy*
EMP: 30
SQ FT: 7,500
SALES (est): 11.7MM **Privately Held**
WEB: www.smithav.com
SIC: 5065 Video equipment, electronic

(G-13080)
SOLID STATE SONICS & ELEC
4137 Nw Lwer Silver Lk Rd (66618)
PHONE....................785 232-0497
Ivan L Joy, *Ch of Bd*
Steve Carriger, *Principal*
Cable W Wilson, *Corp Secy*
EMP: 8 **EST:** 1954
SQ FT: 3,300
SALES (est): 968.9K **Privately Held**
SIC: 8731 3829 3845 Electronic research; measuring & controlling devices; medical cleaning equipment, ultrasonic

(G-13081)
SOUTHERN CARE INC
Also Called: Southerncare Lawrence
5375 Sw 7th St Ste 500 (66606-2553)
PHONE....................913 906-9497
Bronwyn Ruffalo, *Branch Mgr*
EMP: 50 **Privately Held**
SIC: 8082 Home health care services
PA: Southern Care, Inc
1000 Urban Center Dr # 115
Vestavia AL 35242

(G-13082)
SOUTHWEST BOWL
5265 Sw 28th Ct Ste A (66614)
PHONE....................785 272-1324
Steven Hohman, *Owner*
EMP: 14
SQ FT: 30,000
SALES (est): 173.1K **Privately Held**
SIC: 7933 6512 Ten pin center; commercial & industrial building operation

(G-13083)
SOUTHWEST HOLDING CORPORATION (PA)
Also Called: Southwest Publishing
4000 Se Adams St (66609-1481)
PHONE....................785 233-5662
David Ohse, *President*
EMP: 40
SQ FT: 40,000

GEOGRAPHIC

SALES (est): 34.5MM **Privately Held**
SIC: 7331 2752 2759 Direct mail advertising services; commercial printing, offset; laser printing

(G-13084)
SOUTHWEST PUBG & MAILING CORP (HQ)
4000 Se Adams St Ste 1 (66609-1466)
PHONE..................................785 233-5662
Shane Hillmer, *President*
Eric Bohn, *Vice Pres*
Angie McAtee, *Vice Pres*
Kevin Beam, *Plant Mgr*
John Wood, *CFO*
EMP: 237 **EST:** 1971
SQ FT: 80,000
SALES (est): 30.8MM
SALES (corp-wide): 34.5MM **Privately Held**
WEB: www.swpks.com
SIC: 7331 Mailing service
PA: Southwest Holding Corporation
4000 Se Adams St
Topeka KS 66609
785 233-5662

(G-13085)
SOUTHWESTERN BELL TELEPHONE CO
Also Called: AT&T
823 Se Quincy St Ste 1043 (66612-1189)
PHONE..................................785 862-5538
Caroline Joseph, *Manager*
Jolie Lagrange-Johnson, *Manager*
EMP: 32
SALES (corp-wide): 170.7B **Publicly Held**
WEB: www.swbell.com
SIC: 4813 Local telephone communications
HQ: Southwestern Bell Telephone Company
200 Rosemary Rd
North Little Rock AR

(G-13086)
SOWARDS GLASS INC
2600 Nw Topeka Blvd C (66617-1160)
PHONE..................................785 233-4466
Keith Sowards, *President*
Linda Sowards, *Treasurer*
Jessica Sowards, *Manager*
Tim Townsend, *Manager*
EMP: 12
SALES: 4.9MM **Privately Held**
WEB: www.sowardsglassinc.com
SIC: 1793 Glass & glazing work

(G-13087)
SPEARVILLE SENIOR LIVING INC
6025 Sw 39th Ct (66610-1372)
PHONE..................................785 506-6003
John Grace, *President*
EMP: 35
SALES (est): 210.9K **Privately Held**
SIC: 8361 Geriatric residential care

(G-13088)
SPECTRUM CONSTRUCTION CO
2400 Nw Water Works Dr (66606-2431)
P.O. Box 37, Berryton (66409-0037)
PHONE..................................785 232-3407
Fax: 785 232-5404
EMP: 10
SALES: 100K **Privately Held**
SIC: 1799 Decorative Concrete Contractor

(G-13089)
SPECULATIVE FUNDING LLC
Also Called: SF Trucking
5375 Sw 7th St Ste 400 (66606-2552)
PHONE..................................785 267-1996
Billy Pryor, *President*
EMP: 10
SQ FT: 500
SALES (est): 1.1MM **Privately Held**
SIC: 6153 Working capital financing

(G-13090)
SPENCER & COMPANY
Also Called: Hoyt's Truck Center
4425 Nw Us Highway 24 (66618-3809)
PHONE..................................785 235-3131
G Hoyt Moore, *President*
Mark Reeder, *General Mgr*
Laurie Moore, *Vice Pres*
EMP: 14
SQ FT: 2,000
SALES: 1.5MM **Privately Held**
SIC: 7538 7513 Diesel engine repair: automotive; truck leasing, without drivers

(G-13091)
SPORTS CAR CLUB AMERICA INC (PA)
Also Called: SCCA
6620 Se Dwight St (66619-1451)
P.O. Box 19400 (66619-0400)
PHONE..................................785 357-7222
Lisa Noble, *CEO*
Jeffrey S Dahnert, *President*
Scott Schmidt, *Chief*
Eric Prill, *COO*
Rick Ehret, *Vice Pres*
EMP: 34 **EST:** 1944
SQ FT: 16,000
SALES: 10.3MM **Privately Held**
WEB: www.scca-enterprises.com
SIC: 8699 Amateur sports promotion

(G-13092)
SPORTS CENTER INC
6545 Sw 10th Ave (66615-3810)
PHONE..................................785 272-5522
Stan Swanson, *President*
Sharyl Swanson, *Corp Secy*
Duane Dale, *Manager*
EMP: 35
SQ FT: 1,500
SALES (est): 1MM **Privately Held**
WEB: www.sportscenterinc.com
SIC: 7999 Golf driving range; miniature golf course operation; baseball batting cage; go-cart raceway operation & rentals

(G-13093)
SPT DISTRIBUTION CENTER
Also Called: Cec Entertainment
7215 Sw Topeka Blvd (66624-8700)
P.O. Box 19081 (66619-0081)
PHONE..................................785 862-5226
Gene Fincher, *Manager*
Gary Dale, *Manager*
James Dorsey, *Manager*
▲ **EMP:** 30
SALES (est): 4.2MM **Privately Held**
WEB: www.cecentertainment.com
SIC: 7389 Convention & show services

(G-13094)
SRS STRATEGIC DEVELOPMENT
555 S Kansas Ave Ste 100 (66603-3423)
PHONE..................................785 296-4327
Kelly Peak, *Director*
EMP: 17 **EST:** 2009
SALES (est): 880K **Privately Held**
SIC: 8748 Safety training service

(G-13095)
ST FRANCIS MEDICAL CLINIC
Also Called: Warrick, David A MD
6001 Sw 6th Ave Ste 320 (66615-1004)
PHONE..................................785 232-4248
Camille Anderson, *Manager*
EMP: 28
SALES (est): 2.1MM **Privately Held**
SIC: 8011 Medical centers

(G-13096)
STARLITE SKATE CENTER SOUTH
Also Called: Starlite Skate Center West
301 Se 45th St (66609-1852)
PHONE..................................785 862-2241
Loretta Long, *Owner*
EMP: 15
SQ FT: 17,280
SALES (est): 420K **Privately Held**
SIC: 7999 5941 Roller skating rink operation; skating equipment

(G-13097)
STEVENSON COMPANY INC
818 Nw Jackson St (66608-1331)
PHONE..................................785 233-0691
Jerry Pennington, *President*
EMP: 12
SALES (corp-wide): 4MM **Privately Held**
WEB: www.stevensoncompanyinc.com
SIC: 1761 Sheet metalwork
PA: Stevenson Company, Inc.
116 Nw Norris St
Topeka KS 66608
785 233-1303

(G-13098)
STEVENSON COMPANY INC (PA)
116 Nw Norris St (66608-1354)
P.O. Box 8310 (66608-0310)
PHONE..................................785 233-1303
Jerry Pennington, *President*
Howard Brooks, *Principal*
Brent Henry, *Principal*
Joe Pennington, *Principal*
EMP: 18
SQ FT: 10,000
SALES (est): 4MM **Privately Held**
WEB: www.stevensoncompanyinc.com
SIC: 1761 5046 Sheet metalwork; commercial cooking & food service equipment

(G-13099)
STIFEL NICOLAUS & COMPANY INC
2445 Sw Wanamaker Rd # 100
(66614-5470)
PHONE..................................785 271-1300
Dennis Nelson, *Manager*
Terry Jacquinot, *Manager*
EMP: 11
SALES (corp-wide): 3.2B **Publicly Held**
SIC: 6211 Security brokers & dealers
HQ: Stifel, Nicolaus & Company Incorporated
501 N Broadway
Saint Louis MO 63102
314 342-2000

(G-13100)
STONE HOUSE ANIMAL HOSPITAL
1010 Sw Fairlawn Rd (66604-2019)
PHONE..................................785 228-9411
Darrell Carter, *Partner*
EMP: 20
SALES (est): 1.3MM **Privately Held**
WEB: www.stonehousevet.com
SIC: 0742 Veterinarian, animal specialties; animal hospital services, pets & other animal specialties

(G-13101)
STONER DOOR & DOCK CORPORATION
1410 Sw Auburn Rd (66615-1503)
PHONE..................................785 478-3074
Seth Stoner, *President*
EMP: 10
SALES (est): 2.2MM **Privately Held**
SIC: 5211 1799 Garage doors, sale & installation; dock equipment installation, industrial

(G-13102)
STORMONT VALE HOSPITAL (PA)
Also Called: Pediatric Care
4100 Sw 15th St (66604-4333)
PHONE..................................785 273-8224
Naynard Oliverius, *CEO*
EMP: 30 **EST:** 1960
SALES (est): 3.2MM **Privately Held**
SIC: 8011 Pediatrician

(G-13103)
STORMONT-VAIL HEALTHCARE INC
Also Called: Stormont Vail West
3707 Sw 6th Ave (66606-2084)
PHONE..................................785 270-4600
Taylor Porter, *Med Doctor*
Julie Dejean, *Director*
Mary Ellen McBride, *Nurse Practr*
EMP: 120
SALES (corp-wide): 719MM **Privately Held**
SIC: 8062 8093 8011 8063 General medical & surgical hospitals; mental health clinic, outpatient; psychiatrist; psychiatric hospitals
PA: Stormont-Vail Healthcare, Inc.
1500 Sw 10th Ave
Topeka KS 66604
785 354-6000

(G-13104)
STORMONT-VAIL HEALTHCARE INC (PA)
Also Called: Stormont Vail Health
1500 Sw 10th Ave (66604-1301)
PHONE..................................785 354-6000
Randall Peterson, *CEO*
Randy Peterson, *CEO*
Kent P D, *Senior VP*
Kevin Steck, *Senior VP*
Bernard Becker, *Vice Pres*
▲ **EMP:** 2871
SQ FT: 660,000
SALES: 719MM **Privately Held**
SIC: 8062 General medical & surgical hospitals

(G-13105)
STORMONT-VAIL HEALTHCARE INC
Also Called: Cotton-Neil Digestive Hlth Ctr
720 Sw Lane St (66606-1539)
PHONE..................................785 270-4820
EMP: 383
SALES (corp-wide): 719MM **Privately Held**
SIC: 8062 General medical & surgical hospitals
PA: Stormont-Vail Healthcare, Inc.
1500 Sw 10th Ave
Topeka KS 66604
785 354-6000

(G-13106)
STORMONT-VAIL HEALTHCARE INC
Also Called: Cotton-Oneil Cardiot and Vascu
830 Sw Mulvane St (66606-1654)
PHONE..................................785 270-8625
EMP: 383
SALES (corp-wide): 719MM **Privately Held**
SIC: 8062 General medical & surgical hospitals
PA: Stormont-Vail Healthcare, Inc.
1500 Sw 10th Ave
Topeka KS 66604
785 354-6000

(G-13107)
STORMONT-VAIL HEALTHCARE INC
Also Called: Diabetes and Endocrinology Ctr
3520 Sw 6th Ave (66606-2806)
PHONE..................................785 354-9591
Katie Barger, *Endocrinology*
EMP: 383
SALES (corp-wide): 719MM **Privately Held**
SIC: 8062 General medical & surgical hospitals
PA: Stormont-Vail Healthcare, Inc.
1500 Sw 10th Ave
Topeka KS 66604
785 354-6000

(G-13108)
STORMONT-VAIL HEALTHCARE INC
Also Called: Excellent Surgery Center
920 Sw Lane St (66606-2549)
PHONE..................................785 231-1800
Barry J McCaskey, *Manager*
EMP: 383
SALES (corp-wide): 719MM **Privately Held**
SIC: 8062 General medical & surgical hospitals
PA: Stormont-Vail Healthcare, Inc.
1500 Sw 10th Ave
Topeka KS 66604
785 354-6000

(G-13109)
STORMONT-VAIL HEALTHCARE INC
Also Called: Pediatriccare
4100 Sw 15th St (66604-4333)
PHONE..................................785 273-8224
EMP: 383

SALES (corp-wide): 719MM **Privately Held**
SIC: 8062 General medical & surgical hospitals
PA: Stormont-Vail Healthcare, Inc.
1500 Sw 10th Ave
Topeka KS 66604
785 354-6000

(G-13110)
STORMONT-VAIL HEALTHCARE INC
Also Called: Rehabilitation Services
4019 Sw 10th Ave (66604-1916)
PHONE..................................785 354-6116
EMP: 383
SALES (corp-wide): 582.2MM **Privately Held**
SIC: 8062 General Hospital
PA: Stormont-Vail Healthcare, Inc.
1500 Sw 10th Ave
Topeka KS 66604
785 354-6000

(G-13111)
STORMONT-VAIL HEALTHCARE INC
Also Called: Stormont-Vail Mri Center Kans
731 Sw Mulvane St (66606-1665)
PHONE..................................785 354-5545
EMP: 383
SALES (corp-wide): 719MM **Privately Held**
SIC: 8062 General medical & surgical hospitals
PA: Stormont-Vail Healthcare, Inc.
1500 Sw 10th Ave
Topeka KS 66604
785 354-6000

(G-13112)
STORMONT-VAIL HEALTHCARE INC
Also Called: Stormont-Vail Workcare
1504 Sw 8th Ave (66606-1632)
PHONE..................................785 270-8605
Carolyn Kennedy, *Branch Mgr*
EMP: 383
SALES (corp-wide): 719MM **Privately Held**
SIC: 8062 General medical & surgical hospitals
PA: Stormont-Vail Healthcare, Inc.
1500 Sw 10th Ave
Topeka KS 66604
785 354-6000

(G-13113)
STORMONT-VAIL HEALTHCARE INC
Also Called: Cotton-Neil Clinic At Urish Rd
6725 Sw 29th St (66614-5625)
PHONE..................................785 354-5225
George Evans, *Branch Mgr*
EMP: 22
SALES (corp-wide): 719MM **Privately Held**
SIC: 8062 8011 General medical & surgical hospitals; clinic, operated by physicians
PA: Stormont-Vail Healthcare, Inc.
1500 Sw 10th Ave
Topeka KS 66604
785 354-6000

(G-13114)
STRATHMAN SALES COMPANY INC
2127 Se Lakewood Blvd (66605-3402)
PHONE..................................785 354-8537
Arthur C Strathman, *CEO*
Matthew H Strathman, *President*
Brad Broadbent, *Opers Mgr*
Jeff Jones, *Manager*
Colton Strathman, *Supervisor*
EMP: 35 **EST:** 1940
SQ FT: 35,000
SALES (est): 11.1MM **Privately Held**
WEB: www.strathmansales.com
SIC: 5181 Beer & other fermented malt liquors

(G-13115)
STRYKER SERVICES INC
Also Called: Latta Whitlow By Stryker
1440 Sw 41st St (66609-1208)
PHONE..................................785 357-1281
Gailia Stryker, *President*
Ronald Stryker, *President*
EMP: 20
SQ FT: 17,233
SALES (est): 2.2MM **Privately Held**
SIC: 1711 Heating & air conditioning contractors; boiler & furnace contractors; warm air heating & air conditioning contractor

(G-13116)
SUMMERS & SPENCER COMPANY (PA)
Also Called: SS&c Business & Tax Services
5825 Sw 29th St Ste 101 (66614-2483)
PHONE..................................785 272-4484
Brenda Flannagan, *President*
Gloria Horn, *President*
Michael Callison, *Vice Pres*
Brian Lang, *Advisor*
EMP: 30
SALES (est): 4MM **Privately Held**
WEB: www.ssccpas.com
SIC: 8721 8711 Accounting services, except auditing; certified public accountant; consulting engineer

(G-13117)
SUNFLOWER AUTO AUCTION LLC
545 Se Engle St Bldg 131 (66619-1375)
PHONE..................................785 862-2900
William Watkins, *Mng Member*
Christopher Watkins,
EMP: 25
SALES (est): 1.2MM **Privately Held**
SIC: 5012 Automobile auction

(G-13118)
SUNFLOWER DENTAL STUDIO INC
1527 Nw Tyler St (66608-1548)
P.O. Box 8032 (66608-0032)
PHONE..................................785 354-1981
Ron Hoffman, *President*
Eric Gooden, *Vice Pres*
Aaron Hoffman, *Treasurer*
Troy Gooden, *Admin Sec*
EMP: 10 **EST:** 1980
SQ FT: 1,000
SALES (est): 831.8K **Privately Held**
WEB: www.sunflowerdentalstudio.com
SIC: 8072 Dental laboratories

(G-13119)
SUNFLOWER PROMPT CARE
3405 Nw Hunters Ridge Ter # 100 (66618-2509)
PHONE..................................785 246-3733
Josie A Norris, *Owner*
EMP: 15
SALES (est): 1.3MM **Privately Held**
SIC: 8011 Clinic, operated by physicians

(G-13120)
SUNFLOWER RENTS INC (PA)
Also Called: Sunflower Rental
221 Sw Hampton St (66612-1498)
PHONE..................................785 233-9489
Nancy Kay Wendland, *President*
Richard Wendland, *Vice Pres*
Stacey Wendland, *Vice Pres*
Nicole Selvidge, *Treasurer*
Ted Versluys, *Manager*
EMP: 15 **EST:** 1951
SQ FT: 3,200
SALES: 4MM **Privately Held**
WEB: www.sunflowerrental.com
SIC: 7359 Tool rental

(G-13121)
SUNFLOWER SOCCER ASSN
4829 Nw 17th St (66618-3812)
P.O. Box 750194 (66675-0194)
PHONE..................................785 233-9700
Carrie Ogonowski, *Exec Dir*
Steven Schwartz, *Exec Dir*
EMP: 14
SALES: 423.3K **Privately Held**
SIC: 7941 7997 Soccer club; membership sports & recreation clubs

(G-13122)
SUNFLOWER SUPPORTS COMPANY
2521 Sw 37th St (66611-2036)
PHONE..................................785 267-3093
Maryann E Hughes, *President*
EMP: 110
SQ FT: 1,920
SALES (est): 3.5MM **Privately Held**
SIC: 8059 Home for the mentally retarded, exc. skilled or intermediate

(G-13123)
SUPER 8 FORBES LANDING
5922 Sw Topeka Blvd (66619-1404)
PHONE..................................785 862-2222
Kurt Young, *Owner*
EMP: 15
SALES (est): 1.2MM **Privately Held**
WEB: www.forbeslandingsuper8.com
SIC: 7389 Reservation services

(G-13124)
SUPER CHIEF INC
2120 Sw Belle Ave (66614-1746)
PHONE..................................785 272-7277
Fax: 785 272-1757
EMP: 15 **EST:** 1994
SALES (est): 670K **Privately Held**
SIC: 7389 Business Services

(G-13125)
SUPER OIL CO INC (PA)
Also Called: Performance Tire & Wheel Group
1735 N Kansas Ave (66608-1254)
PHONE..................................785 354-1410
Jerry Glasgow, *President*
Linda Glasgow, *Admin Sec*
EMP: 10
SQ FT: 10,000
SALES (est): 2.1MM **Privately Held**
WEB: www.performancetiregroup.com
SIC: 5531 7539 5014 Automotive tires; wheel alignment, automotive; brake repair, automotive; tires & tubes

(G-13126)
SUPREME COURT UNITED STATES
Also Called: US Probation & Parole Office
444 Se Quincy St Ste 375 (66683-3503)
PHONE..................................785 295-2790
Trey Burton, *Branch Mgr*
EMP: 27 **Publicly Held**
SIC: 8322 9211 Parole office; courts;
HQ: Supreme Court, United States
1 1st St Ne
Washington DC 20543
202 479-3000

(G-13127)
SUZANNA WESLEY CHILD CARE
7433 Sw 29th St (66614-4700)
PHONE..................................785 478-3703
Patty Jolley, *Director*
Patty Jolly, *Director*
Jaime Maddern, *Director*
Jaymie Genovese, *Admin Sec*
EMP: 15
SALES (est): 148.1K **Privately Held**
SIC: 8351 Preschool center

(G-13128)
SWAMI INC
Also Called: Sleep Inn
1024 Sw Wanamaker Rd (66604-3807)
PHONE..................................785 228-2500
Dennis Patel, *Principal*
EMP: 11 **EST:** 2000
SALES (est): 679.1K **Privately Held**
SIC: 7011 Hotels & motels

(G-13129)
T & M FINANCIAL INC
Also Called: T and M Financials
3706 Sw Topeka Blvd # 400 (66609-1292)
PHONE..................................785 266-8333
Richard Miller, *President*
Lori May, *Director*
EMP: 10 **EST:** 1962
SQ FT: 8,400
SALES (est): 1.1MM **Privately Held**
SIC: 8742 6411 Financial consultant; advisory services, insurance

(G-13130)
T R MANAGEMENT INC
Also Called: J B Turner Son Roofg & Shtmtl
6840 Se Johnston St (66619)
P.O. Box 19525 (66619-0525)
PHONE..................................785 233-9603
John Turner, *President*
Lori Turner, *Vice Pres*
EMP: 45
SQ FT: 2,000
SALES: 7MM **Privately Held**
WEB: www.jbturnerandsons.com
SIC: 1761 Roofing contractor

(G-13131)
T-MOBILE USA INC
Also Called: T-Mobile 8618
2040 Sw Wanamaker Rd # 102 (66604-3872)
PHONE..................................785 273-5021
Shanna Murry, *Branch Mgr*
EMP: 12
SALES (corp-wide): 83.9B **Publicly Held**
WEB: www.voicestream.com
SIC: 4812 Cellular telephone services
HQ: T-Mobile Usa, Inc.
12920 Se 38th St
Bellevue WA 98006
425 378-4000

(G-13132)
TALL GRASS PRARIE SURG SPCLSTS
Also Called: Orthopedic Sports Med Clinic O
631 Sw Horne St Ste 200 (66606-1663)
PHONE..................................785 233-7491
Kenneth Gimple, *President*
Kurt R Knappenberger, *Corp Secy*
Dr Kenneth Teter, *Vice Pres*
EMP: 28
SALES (est): 2.2MM **Privately Held**
SIC: 8011 Physicians' office, including specialists; orthopedic physician; surgeon

(G-13133)
TALLGRASS IMMEDIATE CARE LLC
601 Sw Corp Vw Ste 200 (66615)
PHONE..................................785 234-0880
Betsy Johns,
James Hamilton, *Admin Sec*
Nancy Henry, *Administration*
EMP: 55
SALES (est): 8.2MM **Privately Held**
SIC: 8011 Ears, nose & throat specialist: physician/surgeon

(G-13134)
TALLGRASS ORTHPDICS SPT MDCINE
6730 Sw Mission View Dr (66614-5652)
PHONE..................................785 228-9999
Doug Bowen, *Branch Mgr*
EMP: 13
SALES (est): 1MM **Privately Held**
SIC: 8011 Orthopedic physician
PA: Tallgrass Orthopedics And Sports Medicine
6001 Sw 6th Ave Ste 200
Topeka KS 66615

(G-13135)
TALLGRASS ORTHPDICS SPT MDCINE (PA)
6001 Sw 6th Ave Ste 200 (66615-1004)
PHONE..................................785 228-4700
Brad REA, *Principal*
EMP: 45
SALES (est): 3.8MM **Privately Held**
SIC: 8011 Orthopedic physician

(G-13136)
TALLGRASS PRAIRIE SURGICAL (PA)
Also Called: Orthopedics & Sports Medicine
6001 Sw 6th Ave Ste 220 (66615-1004)
PHONE..................................785 234-9830
Robert McElroy, *President*
James Hamilton Jr, *Admin Sec*
EMP: 21

GEOGRAPHIC

SQ FT: 98,000
SALES (est): 2.7MM **Privately Held**
SIC: 8011 Surgeon

(G-13137)
TALLGRASS PRAIRIE SURGICAL
601 Sw Corp Vw Ste 200 (66615)
PHONE..................................785 295-4500
EMP: 10
SALES (est): 848K
SALES (corp-wide): 2.7MM **Privately Held**
SIC: 8011 Physicians' office, including specialists
PA: Tallgrass Prairie Surgical Specialist, Pa
6001 Sw 6th Ave Ste 220
Topeka KS 66615
785 234-9830

(G-13138)
TALLGRASS SURGICAL CENTER LLC
6001 Sw 6th Ave Ste 100 (66615-1011)
PHONE..................................785 272-8807
Nancy Henry,
EMP: 30
SQ FT: 14,000
SALES (est): 3.4MM **Privately Held**
WEB: www.tallgrasstopeka.com
SIC: 8011 Ambulatory surgical center; surgeon

(G-13139)
TANGLEWOOD HLTH REHABILITATION
5015 Sw 28th St (66614-2319)
PHONE..................................785 273-0886
Melissa Ralston, *Director*
EMP: 45
SALES (est): 74.4K **Privately Held**
SIC: 8099 Health & allied services

(G-13140)
TARC INC
Also Called: Tarc Industries
1800 Sw 42nd St (66609-1234)
PHONE..................................785 266-2323
Brandon Hossain, *Prdtn Mgr*
Ginger Oroke, *Office Mgr*
Shelby Fry, *Manager*
Betsy Gerhardt, *Manager*
Geoffrey Hobin, *Manager*
EMP: 75
SALES (corp-wide): 12.1MM **Privately Held**
SIC: 7361 Placement agencies
PA: Tarc, Inc
2701 Sw Randolph Ave
Topeka KS 66611
785 232-0597

(G-13141)
TARGET CORPORATION
Also Called: Target DC 3803
5400 Wenger St (66609)
PHONE..................................785 274-6500
Hans Carttar, *Manager*
EMP: 181
SALES (corp-wide): 75.3B **Publicly Held**
SIC: 4226 Special warehousing & storage
PA: Target Corporation
1000 Nicollet Mall
Minneapolis MN 55403
612 304-6073

(G-13142)
TARRANT ENTERPRISES INC
Also Called: Quik Print
6300 Sw 9th Ter (66615-3824)
PHONE..................................785 273-8503
Johnny Tarrant, *President*
Jay Abney, *General Mgr*
EMP: 11
SQ FT: 4,400
SALES (est): 1.5MM **Privately Held**
SIC: 2752 Commercial printing, offset

(G-13143)
TARWATERS INC (PA)
Also Called: Tarwater Farm Supply
4107 Nw Topeka Blvd (66617-1767)
PHONE..................................785 286-2390
Richard Tarwater Jr, *President*
Lisa Tarwater, *Admin Sec*
EMP: 23
SQ FT: 170,000
SALES: 11.9MM **Privately Held**
WEB: www.tarwaters.com
SIC: 5191 5261 Farm supplies; lawn & garden supplies

(G-13144)
TBCSOFT INC
Also Called: Tbc Software
3410 Sw Van Buren St # 202 (66611-2258)
PHONE..................................785 272-5993
James Boatright, *President*
Gayle Simpson, *Corp Secy*
Lori Higgins, *Assistant*
EMP: 5
SALES (est): 350K **Privately Held**
WEB: www.tbcsoftware.com
SIC: 7372 Prepackaged software

(G-13145)
TDC LEARNING CENTERS INC
Also Called: Adventures In Early Lrng Ctr
817 Sw Harrison St (66612-1607)
PHONE..................................785 234-2273
Cheryl Rockhold, *Director*
EMP: 14 **EST:** 2007
SALES (est): 1.3MM **Privately Held**
SIC: 8351 Child day care services

(G-13146)
TDS ALLOCATION CO
2410 Se 6th Ave Ste D (66607-2022)
PHONE..................................800 857-2906
Ronnie Brooks, *CEO*
EMP: 36 **EST:** 2016
SALES (est): 2.1MM **Privately Held**
SIC: 5087 Beauty parlor equipment & supplies

(G-13147)
TEAM CAR CARE LLC
Also Called: Jiffy Lube
3301 Sw Topeka Blvd (66611-2236)
PHONE..................................785 266-7696
J Webb, *Branch Mgr*
EMP: 11 **Privately Held**
SIC: 7549 Lubrication service, automotive
PA: Team Car Care, Llc
105 Decker Ct Ste 900
Irving TX 75062

(G-13148)
TEAM CAR CARE LLC
Also Called: Jiffy Lube
1830 Sw Wanamaker Rd (66604-3825)
PHONE..................................785 228-1824
Cliss Sanders, *Manager*
EMP: 10 **Privately Held**
SIC: 7549 Lubrication service, automotive
PA: Team Car Care, Llc
105 Decker Ct Ste 900
Irving TX 75062

(G-13149)
TECH ELECTRONICS KANSAS LLC
6431 Se Bleckley St (66619-1374)
PHONE..................................785 379-0300
Kurt Canova, *President*
EMP: 25
SALES (est): 3.8MM
SALES (corp-wide): 77.7MM **Privately Held**
SIC: 5063 7382 Fire alarm systems; protective devices, security
HQ: Tech Electronics, Inc.
6437 Manchester Ave
Saint Louis MO 63139
314 951-1760

(G-13150)
TENTH STREET HT PARTNERS LLC (PA)
700 Sw Jackson St (66603-3743)
PHONE..................................785 233-5411
James W Parrish,
Lisa Wingert,
EMP: 16
SALES (est): 1.3MM **Privately Held**
SIC: 7011 Hotels & motels

(G-13151)
TENTH STREET HT PARTNERS LLC
Also Called: Holiday Inn
901 Sw Robinson Ave (66606-2610)
PHONE..................................785 228-9500
Mindy Stock, *General Mgr*
EMP: 20
SALES (corp-wide): 1.3MM **Privately Held**
WEB: www.topekaexpress.com
SIC: 7011 Hotels & motels
PA: Tenth Street Hotel Partners, Llc
700 Sw Jackson St
Topeka KS 66603
785 233-5411

(G-13152)
TERMINIX INTL CO LTD PARTNR
5604 Sw Topeka Blvd Ste A (66609-1009)
PHONE..................................785 266-2600
Peter Lake, *Manager*
EMP: 15
SALES (corp-wide): 1.9B **Publicly Held**
SIC: 7342 Pest control services
HQ: The Terminix International Company Limited Partnership
150 Peabody Pl
Memphis TN 38103
901 766-1400

(G-13153)
TERRACON CONSULTANTS INC
Also Called: Terracon Consultants 14
3113 Sw Van Buren St # 131 (66611-2467)
PHONE..................................785 267-3310
Stephen Pretsch, *Branch Mgr*
EMP: 17
SALES (corp-wide): 751.7MM **Privately Held**
SIC: 8742 8748 Industry specialist consultants; environmental consultant
HQ: Terracon Consultants, Inc.
10841 S Ridgeview Rd
Olathe KS 66061
913 599-6886

(G-13154)
TFI LLC
300 Sw Jackson St (66603-3326)
PHONE..................................785 235-1524
EMP: 10
SALES (est): 635K **Privately Held**
SIC: 8361 Residential care

(G-13155)
TFI FAMILY SERVICES INC
217 Se 4th St Fl 2 (66603-3504)
PHONE..................................785 232-1019
Mike Patrick, *Branch Mgr*
EMP: 83
SALES (corp-wide): 20.7MM **Privately Held**
WEB: www.the-farm.org
SIC: 8361 Residential care for children; juvenile correctional home; group foster home; self-help group home
PA: Tfi Family Services, Inc.
618 Commercial St Ste C
Emporia KS 66801
620 342-2239

(G-13156)
TFMCOMM INC (PA)
125 Sw Jackson St (66603-3311)
PHONE..................................785 233-2343
Douglas L Flair, *CEO*
Troy Flair, *President*
Richard Gibbs, *Senior VP*
Scott Rowland, *Vice Pres*
Marilyn Rowland, *Treasurer*
EMP: 20 **EST:** 1948
SQ FT: 7,000
SALES (est): 2.1MM **Privately Held**
WEB: www.tfmcomm.com
SIC: 7622 5065 Communication equipment repair; electronic parts & equipment; communication equipment; telephone & telegraphic equipment

(G-13157)
THE EYE DOCTORS
Also Called: Eye Doctors, The
2800 Sw Wanamaker Rd # 192 (66614-4293)
PHONE..................................785 272-3322
Alicia Skinner, *Sales Executive*
Lisa Long, *Manager*
Brett Keller,
Anthony Luongo,
EMP: 16
SALES (est): 1.1MM **Privately Held**
SIC: 8042 Offices & clinics of optometrists

(G-13158)
THE NATURE CONSERVANCY
Also Called: Kansas Chapter
2420 Nw Button Rd (66618-1410)
PHONE..................................785 233-4400
Alan Pollom, *Director*
EMP: 13
SALES (corp-wide): 992.1MM **Privately Held**
WEB: www.nature.org
SIC: 8641 Environmental protection organization
PA: The Nature Conservancy
4245 Fairfax Dr Ste 100
Arlington VA 22203
703 841-5300

(G-13159)
THOMAS E MOSKOW MD
Also Called: Stormont-Vail Cotton O'Nei
4100 Sw 15th St (66604-4333)
PHONE..................................785 273-8224
Thomas E Moskow, *Principal*
EMP: 30 **EST:** 2011
SALES (est): 141.3K **Privately Held**
SIC: 8011 Pediatrician

(G-13160)
THOMPSON DEHYDRATING CO INC
Also Called: Thompson Dryers
2953 Sw Wanamaker Dr (66614-5319)
PHONE..................................785 272-7722
Ted Thompson, *CEO*
Stanley Thompson, *President*
Julie Thompson, *Treasurer*
EMP: 18
SALES (est): 2.4MM **Privately Held**
SIC: 8711 7699 Heating & ventilation engineering; industrial machinery & equipment repair

(G-13161)
TMI CORP
Also Called: Print-Docs
127 Se 29th St (66605-1123)
PHONE..................................785 232-8705
Matthew J McManis, *President*
EMP: 11
SQ FT: 16,000
SALES (est): 1.5MM **Privately Held**
WEB: www.worldclasslocks.com
SIC: 2759 Promotional printing

(G-13162)
TODAYS DENTISTRY
5310 Sw 37th St (66614-4540)
PHONE..................................785 267-5010
Robert H Durbin, *Owner*
EMP: 19
SALES (est): 1MM **Privately Held**
SIC: 8021 Dentists' office

(G-13163)
TOP CITY HEALTHCARE INC
Also Called: Healthcare Resort of Topeka
6300 Sw 6th Ave (66615-1013)
PHONE..................................785 272-2124
Benjamin Leiker, *President*
EMP: 90
SALES (est): 1.1MM
SALES (corp-wide): 2B **Publicly Held**
SIC: 8059 Convalescent home
PA: The Ensign Group Inc
29222 Rncho Vejo Rd Ste 1
San Juan Capistrano CA 92675
949 487-9500

(G-13164)
TOPEKA ADULT CARE CENTER
3314 Sw Front St (66606-1952)
PHONE..................................785 233-7397
Mandy Coleman, *Owner*
EMP: 10
SALES (est): 185.6K **Privately Held**
WEB: www.deerparkmeriden.com
SIC: 8322 8051 Adult day care center; skilled nursing care facilities

(G-13165)
TOPEKA AIR AMBULANCE INC
Also Called: Life Star
1500 Sw 10th Ave (66604-1301)
P.O. Box 19224 (66619-0224)
PHONE..................................785 862-5433
Greg Hildenbrand, *Exec Dir*
EMP: 50
SALES: 6.6MM **Privately Held**
SIC: 4522 Ambulance services, air

(G-13166)
TOPEKA ALLRGY ASTHMA CLINIC PA
Also Called: Voica, Roxana I MD
1123 Sw Gage Blvd (66604-1774)
PHONE..................................785 273-9999
Roxana Voica, *President*
EMP: 10
SQ FT: 4,000
SALES (est): 1.1MM **Privately Held**
WEB: www.topekaallergy.kscoxmail.com
SIC: 8011 Allergist

(G-13167)
TOPEKA ANSTHSIA PAIN TRTMNT PA
1700 Sw 7th St (66606-2489)
PHONE..................................785 295-8000
Dale Askins, *Director*
EMP: 30 **EST:** 2012
SALES: 5MM **Privately Held**
SIC: 8011 Anesthesiologist

(G-13168)
TOPEKA ATTORNEYS
3649 Sw Burlingame Rd (66611-2051)
PHONE..................................785 267-2410
EMP: 10
SALES (est): 510K **Privately Held**
SIC: 8111 Legal Services Office

(G-13169)
TOPEKA BLUE PRINT & SUP CO INC
Also Called: Topeka Blueprint
608 Sw Jackson St (66603-3702)
PHONE..................................785 232-7209
Craig L Trapp, *President*
Galen Murphy, *Vice Pres*
EMP: 9 **EST:** 1927
SQ FT: 7,500
SALES (est): 940K **Privately Held**
WEB: www.topekablue.com
SIC: 7334 2752 5112 Blueprinting service; commercial printing, offset; office supplies

(G-13170)
TOPEKA CAPITAL JOURNAL
100 Se 9th St Ste 200 (66612-1213)
PHONE..................................785 295-1111
John Fish, *CEO*
Matt Galloway, *Editor*
Hal Lockard, *District Mgr*
Jacob Woodland, *Sales Staff*
Staci Fisher, *Art Dir*
EMP: 24
SALES (est): 2.3MM **Privately Held**
SIC: 2711 Commercial printing & newspaper publishing combined

(G-13171)
TOPEKA CEMETERY ASSOCIATION
1601 Se 10th Ave Ste 1 (66607-1697)
PHONE..................................785 233-4132
Lisa Sandmeyer, *Superintendent*
Chris Hutton, *Principal*
Neil Firestone, *Vice Pres*
EMP: 10 **EST:** 1859
SALES: 545.6K **Privately Held**
WEB: www.vpcharlescurtis.net
SIC: 6553 Cemetery association

(G-13172)
TOPEKA CIVIC THEATRE & ACADEMY
3028 Sw 8th Ave (66606-1867)
PHONE..................................785 357-5211
Mary Orr, *Ch of Bd*
Vicki Brokke, *President*
Scott Nellis, *Vice Pres*
Cassie Hermes, *Maint Spvr*
Kevin Burton, *Manager*
EMP: 14 **EST:** 1936
SQ FT: 50,000
SALES: 1.9MM **Privately Held**
WEB: www.topekacivictheatre.com
SIC: 7922 Legitimate live theater producers

(G-13173)
TOPEKA COUNTRY CLUB
2700 Sw Buchanan St (66611-1399)
PHONE..................................785 232-2090
Jennifer Howell, *Controller*
EMP: 100
SQ FT: 20,000
SALES: 3.9MM **Privately Held**
SIC: 7997 7991 5941 5812 Country club, membership; physical fitness facilities; sporting goods & bicycle shops; eating places

(G-13174)
TOPEKA DAY CARE INC
2200 Sw Gage Blvd (66622-0001)
PHONE..................................785 272-5051
Dixie Link, *Manager*
EMP: 12
SALES (corp-wide): 1.3MM **Privately Held**
WEB: www.topekadaycare.com
SIC: 8351 Child day care services
PA: Topeka Day Care Inc
1195 Sw Buchanan St # 204
Topeka KS 66604
785 232-1650

(G-13175)
TOPEKA EAR NOSE & THROAT (PA)
Also Called: Topeka Ent
920 Sw Lane St Ste 200 (66606-2550)
PHONE..................................620 340-0168
Michael Franklin, *Owner*
Douglas Barnes, *Co-Owner*
Matthew Glynn, *Co-Owner*
Tyler Grindal, *Co-Owner*
Scot Hirschi, *Co-Owner*
EMP: 19
SALES (est): 3MM **Privately Held**
SIC: 8011 Ears, nose & throat specialist: physician/surgeon

(G-13176)
TOPEKA FOUNDRY AND IR WORKS CO
300 Sw Jackson St (66603-3326)
PHONE..................................785 232-8212
Jack Lee Bybee, *President*
Thomas Dolsky, *Vice Pres*
Kenneth J Martin, *Treasurer*
EMP: 70 **EST:** 1878
SALES: 12.5MM **Privately Held**
WEB: www.topekafoundry.com
SIC: 5039 7699 Architectural metalwork; locksmith shop

(G-13177)
TOPEKA HOSPITAL LLC (DH)
1700 Sw 7th St Ste 840 (66606-2490)
PHONE..................................785 295-8000
David Vandewater, *CEO*
EMP: 10
SALES (est): 832.4K
SALES (corp-wide): 3.7B **Publicly Held**
SIC: 8069 Specialty hospitals, except psychiatric
HQ: Topeka Health System, Llc
1700 Sw 7th St
Topeka KS 66606
785 295-8000

(G-13178)
TOPEKA INCOME TAX SERVICE INC
213 Sw 6th Ave (66603-3703)
PHONE..................................785 478-2833
Gerald Block, *President*
Larry Stuewe, *President*
Brenda Block, *Admin Sec*
EMP: 10
SALES (est): 499.9K **Privately Held**
SIC: 7291 Tax return preparation services

(G-13179)
TOPEKA IND LVING RSRCE CTR INC
Also Called: TILRC
501 Sw Jackson St Ste 100 (66603-3300)
PHONE..................................785 233-4572
Regina Oxford, *Finance Mgr*
Karen Jones, *Manager*
Michael Oxford, *Exec Dir*
AMI Hyten, *Director*
EMP: 46
SALES: 1.1MM **Privately Held**
WEB: www.tilrc.org
SIC: 8322 Social service center

(G-13180)
TOPEKA LANDSCAPE INC
3220 Sw Auburn Rd (66614-4917)
PHONE..................................785 232-8873
Blain Bertrand, *President*
Frank Male, *Corp Secy*
Glen Westervelt, *Vice Pres*
Bita Givechi, *Mktg Dir*
Scott Cole, *Technology*
EMP: 32
SALES: 2.5MM **Privately Held**
WEB: www.topekalandscape.com
SIC: 0782 0781 Landscape contractors; landscape planning services

(G-13181)
TOPEKA METAL SPECIALTIES
02 Div Of Lb Steel Llc (66609)
PHONE..................................785 862-1071
Fax: 785 862-1138
EMP: 47
SALES (est): 10.1MM **Privately Held**
SIC: 3599 Mfg Industrial Machinery

(G-13182)
TOPEKA METROPOLITAN TRNST AUTH (PA)
Also Called: Topeka Transit
201 N Kansas Ave (66603-3622)
PHONE..................................785 233-2011
Janlyn Nesbett-Tucker, *General Mgr*
Chip Falldine, *General Mgr*
Denise Ensley, *COO*
Al Bradley, *Opers Staff*
Mary Burk, *CFO*
EMP: 78
SQ FT: 36,000
SALES (est): 5.9MM **Privately Held**
WEB: www.topekatransit.com
SIC: 4111 Commuter bus operation

(G-13183)
TOPEKA PATHOLOGY GROUP PA
1500 Se 10th Ave (66604)
PHONE..................................785 354-6031
William Schaetvel, *Partner*
Mark Synovec, *Principal*
EMP: 10
SALES (est): 828.9K **Privately Held**
SIC: 8011 Offices & clinics of medical doctors

(G-13184)
TOPEKA PERFORMING ARTS CENTER
Also Called: Tpac
214 Se 8th Ave Frnt Ste (66603-3970)
PHONE..................................785 234-2787
Barbara Wiggins, *Director*
EMP: 12
SALES: 710.5K **Privately Held**
WEB: www.tpactix.org
SIC: 7922 7929 Theatrical companies; entertainers & entertainment groups

(G-13185)
TOPEKA ROUND UP CLUB INC
7843 Sw 37th St (66614-4935)
PHONE..................................785 478-4431
Patty Brown, *President*
Betty Kirchner, *President*
Gwendolyn Kay Schram, *Treasurer*
Anita Fry, *Admin Sec*
EMP: 18
SALES: 189.1K **Privately Held**
WEB: www.topekaroundupclub.com
SIC: 7997 Membership sports & recreation clubs

(G-13186)
TOPEKA SURGERY CENTER INC
Also Called: Genstler Eye Center
3630 Sw Fairlawn Rd (66614-3966)
PHONE..................................785 273-8282
Arla Genstler MD, *President*
EMP: 30
SALES (est): 3.9MM **Privately Held**
SIC: 8011 Surgeon; ophthalmologist

(G-13187)
TOPEKA TRAILER REPAIR INC
929 Sw University Blvd (66619-1432)
P.O. Box 19052 (66619-0052)
PHONE..................................785 862-6010
Marge Chism, *President*
Kristin Milligan, *Principal*
Granville Chism, *Admin Sec*
EMP: 11
SALES (est): 610K **Privately Held**
SIC: 7539 Trailer repair

(G-13188)
TOPEKA TRANSMISSION SERVICE
1824 Sw Harrison St (66612-1419)
PHONE..................................785 234-2597
Bob Johnson, *CEO*
EMP: 12
SQ FT: 9,000
SALES (est): 1.1MM **Privately Held**
SIC: 7537 Automotive transmission repair shops

(G-13189)
TOPEKA UNIFIED SCHOOL DST 501
Also Called: Topeka Swim Association
2751 Sw East Circle Dr S # 1 (66606)
PHONE..................................785 295-3750
Jim Gilchrist, *Principal*
Aaron Becker, *Maint Spvr*
Annette Wiles, *Director*
Debbie Ashmore, *Admin Asst*
EMP: 55
SALES (corp-wide): 179.5MM **Privately Held**
SIC: 8621 Professional membership organizations
PA: Topeka Unified School District 501
624 Sw 24th St
Topeka KS 66611
785 295-3000

(G-13190)
TOPEKA UNIFIED SCHOOL DST 501
Also Called: Information Technical Dept
1900 Sw Hope St (66604-3984)
PHONE..................................785 438-4750
Bill Bridges, *Director*
Eileen Caspers, *Director*
Jennifer Barnhart, *Admin Sec*
Laura Maike, *Clerk*
EMP: 37
SALES (corp-wide): 179.5MM **Privately Held**
WEB: www.topeka.k12.ks.us
SIC: 8211 7376 7375 Public elementary & secondary schools; computer facilities management; information retrieval services
PA: Topeka Unified School District 501
624 Sw 24th St
Topeka KS 66611
785 295-3000

(G-13191)
TOPEKA UROLOGY CLINIC PA
Also Called: Hsu, C H
1516 Sw 6th Ave Ste 1 (66606-1696)
PHONE..................................785 232-1005
Cheng H Hsu, *President*
Cathy Mc Devitt, *VP Mktg*
Cathy Rhoten, *Clerk*
EMP: 15
SALES (est): 1.8MM **Privately Held**
SIC: 8011 Physicians' office, including specialists; urologist

GEOGRAPHIC

(G-13192)
TORGESON ELECTRIC COMPANY
3545 Sw 6th Ave Ste 2 (66606-1938)
PHONE..................................785 233-3060
Matthew Torgeson, *President*
Alan Kirmse, *Project Mgr*
EMP: 200
SQ FT: 1,800
SALES: 40MM **Privately Held**
SIC: 1731 General electrical contractor; safety & security specialization; electric power systems contractors; lighting contractor

(G-13193)
TORGESON TRENCHING INC
Also Called: Torgeson Trenching Service
3545 Sw 6th Ave (66606-1937)
PHONE..................................785 233-3060
Matthew Torgeson, *President*
Todd Pease, *Vice Pres*
Teresa Roberts, *Admin Sec*
Teresa Hageberg Roberts, *Admin Sec*
EMP: 35
SALES (est): 4MM **Privately Held**
SIC: 1629 Trenching contractor

(G-13194)
TOTAL RENAL CARE INC
Also Called: Topeka Dialysis
634 Sw Mulvane St Ste 300 (66606-1678)
PHONE..................................785 235-1094
James K Hilger,
EMP: 24 **Publicly Held**
SIC: 8092 Kidney dialysis centers
HQ: Total Renal Care, Inc.
2000 16th St
Denver CO 80202
303 405-2100

(G-13195)
TOTAL RENAL CARE INC
Also Called: Wanamaker Dialysis
3711 Sw Wanamaker Rd (66610-1368)
PHONE..................................785 273-1824
James K Hilger,
EMP: 22 **Publicly Held**
SIC: 8092 Kidney dialysis centers
HQ: Total Renal Care, Inc.
2000 16th St
Denver CO 80202
303 405-2100

(G-13196)
TRANE US INC
2200 Sw Gage Blvd (66622-0001)
PHONE..................................785 272-3224
Trey Fruge, *Branch Mgr*
EMP: 85 **Privately Held**
SIC: 3585 Refrigeration & heating equipment
HQ: Trane U.S. Inc.
3600 Pammel Creek Rd
La Crosse WI 54601
608 787-2000

(G-13197)
TRASH MOUNTAIN PROJECT INC
1555 Nw Gage Blvd (66618-2827)
PHONE..................................785 246-6845
Marianne Baumchen, *Finance*
Carol Mammoliti, *Office Mgr*
Joshua Bechard, *Info Tech Dir*
Brett Durbin, *Exec Dir*
EMP: 11
SALES: 1.3MM **Privately Held**
SIC: 8699 8399 Charitable organization; community development groups

(G-13198)
TREASURER KANSAS STATE (DH)
900 Sw Jackson St Rm 201 (66612-1221)
PHONE..................................785 296-3171
Ron Estes, *Treasurer*
Lynn Jenkins CPA, *Treasurer*
EMP: 40
SALES (est): 7.8MM **Privately Held**
WEB: www.kssos.org
SIC: 8611 9311 Business associations;
HQ: Executive Office Of The State Of Kansas
300 Sw 10th Ave
Topeka KS 66612
785 296-6240

(G-13199)
TRUSTEES OF THE BAKER UNIV
Also Called: School of Nursing
1500 Sw 10th Ave Fl 2 (66604-1301)
PHONE..................................785 354-5850
Kathleen Harr, *Principal*
EMP: 20
SALES (corp-wide): 50.3MM **Privately Held**
WEB: www.bakeru.edu
SIC: 8059 8221 Convalescent home; university
PA: The Trustees Of The Baker University
618 8th St
Baldwin City KS 66006
785 594-6451

(G-13200)
TUCKERS BAR & GRILL
3435 Se 39th Ter (66609-9430)
PHONE..................................785 235-3172
Jeff Ingroff, *Owner*
EMP: 12
SALES (est): 112.9K **Privately Held**
SIC: 7997 Membership sports & recreation clubs

(G-13201)
TUCSON HOTELS LP
Also Called: Capitol Plaza Hotel
1717 Sw Topeka Blvd (66612-1410)
P.O. Box 6190, Orlando FL (32802-6190)
PHONE..................................785 431-7200
Kevin Smith, *General Mgr*
EMP: 103 **Privately Held**
WEB: www.embassysuitesoutdoorworld.com
SIC: 7011 Hotels
PA: Tucson Hotels Lp
2711 Centerville Rd # 400
Wilmington DE 19808

(G-13202)
UI BENEFIT OVERPAYMENTS
Also Called: Kansas Dept Humn Resources
401 Sw Topeka Blvd (66603-3102)
PHONE..................................785 296-5000
Vickie Skinner, *Director*
EMP: 10
SALES (est): 896.7K **Privately Held**
SIC: 7322 Adjustment & collection services

(G-13203)
UNIFIRST CORPORATION
1309 Nw Western Ave (66608-2102)
PHONE..................................785 233-1550
Ted Boone, *CEO*
EMP: 10
SALES (corp-wide): 1.8B **Publicly Held**
SIC: 7218 7213 Industrial uniform supply; uniform supply
PA: Unifirst Corporation
68 Jonspin Rd
Wilmington MA 01887
978 658-8888

(G-13204)
UNION PACIFIC RAILROAD COMPANY
901 Nw Norris St (66608-1480)
PHONE..................................785 232-7814
Denny Cullan, *Branch Mgr*
EMP: 100
SALES (corp-wide): 22.8B **Publicly Held**
WEB: www.uprr.com
SIC: 4011 Railroads, line-haul operating
HQ: Union Pacific Railroad Company Inc
1400 Douglas St
Omaha NE 68179
402 544-5000

(G-13205)
UNIQUE DESIGN INC
1920 Sw Westport Dr # 100 (66604-4049)
PHONE..................................785 272-6044
Anthony Zemek, *President*
EMP: 11
SQ FT: 7,600
SALES (est): 1.5MM **Privately Held**
SIC: 5713 5231 1799 Floor covering stores; wallpaper; window treatment installation

(G-13206)
UNITED METHODIST HOMES INC
Also Called: ALDERSGATE VILLAGE
7220 Sw Asbury Dr (66614-4706)
PHONE..................................785 478-9440
Jerry Ney, *President*
Renae Wright, *Business Mgr*
Carol George, *Vice Pres*
Edna Marn, *Vice Pres*
Marcia Stecklein, *Vice Pres*
EMP: 280 **EST:** 1904
SQ FT: 425,000
SALES: 24MM **Privately Held**
WEB: www.umhomes.org
SIC: 8051 8059 Skilled nursing care facilities; personal care home, with health care

(G-13207)
UNITED PARCEL SERVICE INC
Also Called: UPS
126 Ne Madison St (66607-1144)
PHONE..................................785 354-1111
Wordelle Hooks, *Branch Mgr*
EMP: 158
SALES (corp-wide): 71.8B **Publicly Held**
SIC: 4215 Parcel delivery, vehicular
HQ: United Parcel Service, Inc.
55 Glenlake Pkwy
Atlanta GA 30328
404 828-6000

(G-13208)
UNITED PIPE & SUPPLY
5111 Nw Us Highway 24 (66618-3814)
PHONE..................................785 357-0612
Jeff Stighen, *Branch Mgr*
EMP: 10
SALES (est): 894.9K **Privately Held**
SIC: 5074 Pipes & fittings, plastic

(G-13209)
UNITED RENTALS NORTH AMER INC
5830 Sw 19th Ter (66604-4014)
PHONE..................................785 272-6006
Shannon Farr, *Manager*
EMP: 10
SALES (corp-wide): 8B **Publicly Held**
WEB: www.ur.com
SIC: 7359 Equipment rental & leasing
HQ: United Rentals (North America), Inc.
100 Frederick St 700
Stamford CT 06902
203 622-3131

(G-13210)
UNITED STEEL WRKRS OF AMERICA
1603 Nw Taylor St (66608-1556)
PHONE..................................785 234-5688
Robert Trip, *President*
Glen Griffinth, *Vice Pres*
Scott Tummons, *Treasurer*
Nelson Van Dyke, *Treasurer*
EMP: 10
SQ FT: 1,000
SALES (est): 970K **Privately Held**
WEB: www.uswalocal307.com
SIC: 8631 Labor union

(G-13211)
UNITED WAY OF GREATER TOPEKA
1315 Sw Arrowhead Rd B (66604-4057)
PHONE..................................785 228-5110
Brian Gallagher, *President*
Evelyn Amador, *Vice Pres*
Greg Berzonsky, *Vice Pres*
Robert Berdelle, *CFO*
Donna Swaffar, *Comms Mgr*
EMP: 14
SALES: 5.1MM **Privately Held**
WEB: www.unitedwaytopeka.org
SIC: 8399 Fund raising organization, non-fee basis

(G-13212)
UPSILON CHAPTER ALPHA PHI INTL
1839 Sw Jewell Ave (66621-1103)
PHONE..................................785 233-7466
Macie Thompson, *President*
EMP: 30
SALES: 213.5K **Privately Held**
SIC: 8641 University club

(G-13213)
UROLOGY ASSOCIATES TOPEKA PA
823 Sw Mulvane St Ste 275 (66606-1687)
PHONE..................................785 233-4256
Richard Isaacson MD, *President*
Mark Brandsted MD, *Principal*
EMP: 15
SALES (est): 1.1MM **Privately Held**
SIC: 8011 Urologist

(G-13214)
US BANK NATIONAL ASSOCIATION
Also Called: US Bank
719 S Kansas Ave (66603-3807)
PHONE..................................785 276-6300
EMP: 12
SALES (corp-wide): 25.7B **Publicly Held**
SIC: 6021 National commercial banks
HQ: U.S. Bank National Association
425 Walnut St Fl 14
Cincinnati OH 45202
513 632-4234

(G-13215)
VALEO BEHAVIORAL HEALTH CARE
Also Called: Substance Abuse Recovery Prog
330 Sw Oakley Ave (66606-1995)
PHONE..................................785 233-1730
Gary Lee, *Director*
EMP: 50
SALES (corp-wide): 18.4MM **Privately Held**
SIC: 8322 8361 8093 Individual & family services; residential care; specialty outpatient clinics
PA: Valeo Behavioral Health Care, Inc.
5401 Sw 7th St
Topeka KS 66606
785 273-2252

(G-13216)
VALEO BEHAVIORAL HLTH CARE INC (PA)
5401 Sw 7th St (66606-2330)
PHONE..................................785 273-2252
Joseph Scranton, *Ch of Bd*
Eunice Ruttinger, *Exec Dir*
EMP: 25
SALES: 18.4MM **Privately Held**
SIC: 8093 8069 Substance abuse clinics (outpatient); rehabilitation center, outpatient treatment; drug addiction rehabilitation hospital; alcoholism rehabilitation hospital

(G-13217)
VALEO BEHAVIORAL HLTH CARE INC
400 Sw Oakley Ave (66606-2039)
PHONE..................................785 233-1730
Joseph Scranton, *Ch of Bd*
EMP: 33
SALES (corp-wide): 18.4MM **Privately Held**
SIC: 8322 Crisis center
PA: Valeo Behavioral Health Care, Inc.
5401 Sw 7th St
Topeka KS 66606
785 273-2252

(G-13218)
VALLEY REALTORS INC (PA)
600 Sw Van Buren St (66603-3718)
PHONE..................................785 233-4222
John C Valley, *President*
EMP: 11 **EST:** 1962
SQ FT: 5,000
SALES (est): 1.2MM **Privately Held**
SIC: 6531 Real estate agent, residential

(G-13219)
VERITIV OPERATING COMPANY
Also Called: International Paper
3721 Sw South Park Ave (66609-1419)
PHONE....................................785 862-2233
Roy Vandeginste, *Branch Mgr*
EMP: 15
SALES (corp-wide): 8.7B **Publicly Held**
WEB: www.internationalpaper.com
SIC: 5113 Industrial & personal service paper
HQ: Veritiv Operating Company
1000 Abernathy Rd Bldg 4
Atlanta GA 30328
770 391-8200

(G-13220)
VET MEDICAL SURGERY
1515 Sw 29th St (66611-1901)
PHONE....................................785 267-6060
Joseph P Kamer, *Owner*
EMP: 10 **EST:** 2001
SALES (est): 395.3K **Privately Held**
SIC: 0742 Veterinarian, animal specialties; animal hospital services, pets & other animal specialties

(G-13221)
VETERANS AFFAIRS KANS COMM ON
2200 Sw Gage Blvd (66622-0001)
PHONE....................................785 350-4489
Tracy Crisp, *Administration*
EMP: 10 **Privately Held**
SIC: 8641 9199 Veterans' organization;
HQ: Veterans' Affairs, Kansas Commission On
700 Sw Jackson St # 1004
Topeka KS 66603
785 296-3976

(G-13222)
VETERANS HEALTH ADMINISTRATION
Also Called: VA Hospital
2200 Sw Gage Blvd (66622-0001)
PHONE....................................785 350-3111
Samuel Bradshaw, *Principal*
Tanya Stovall, *Administration*
EMP: 1500 **Publicly Held**
SIC: 8062 9451 General medical & surgical hospitals;
HQ: Veterans Health Administration
810 Vermont Ave Nw
Washington DC 20420

(G-13223)
VICTOR L PHILLIPS COMPANY
1305 Sw 42nd St (66609-1268)
PHONE....................................785 380-0678
Tim Carnagey, *Branch Mgr*
EMP: 14
SQ FT: 13,200
SALES (est): 1.2MM
SALES (corp-wide): 56MM **Privately Held**
WEB: www.vlpco.com
SIC: 5082 General construction machinery & equipment
HQ: The Victor L Phillips Company
4100 Gardner Ave
Kansas City MO 64120
816 241-9290

(G-13224)
VILLAGES INC (PA)
7240 Sw 10th Ave (66615-1209)
PHONE....................................785 267-5900
Gerald Letourneau, *President*
Jenny Jesseph, *Manager*
Judette Padilla, *Manager*
Sylvia Crawford, *Exec Dir*
EMP: 15
SQ FT: 20,000
SALES: 4.1MM **Privately Held**
WEB: www.thevillagesinc.org
SIC: 8361 8322 Children's home; individual & family services

(G-13225)
VINCENT ROOFING INC
340 Se 15th St (66607-1275)
P.O. Box 19525 (66619-0525)
PHONE....................................785 233-9603
Douglas Hutchinson, *President*
Steve Buchman, *CFO*
EMP: 20
SQ FT: 22,000
SALES: 12.8MM **Privately Held**
SIC: 1761 Roofing contractor; sheet metalwork

(G-13226)
VISION BANK (HQ)
3031 Sw Wanamaker Rd (66614-4430)
PHONE....................................785 357-4669
Gary Yager, *President*
EMP: 15 **EST:** 1999
SALES: 8.7MM
SALES (corp-wide): 1.9MM **Privately Held**
SIC: 6022 State commercial banks
PA: Bots Inc
3031 Sw Wanamaker Rd
Topeka KS 66614
785 357-4669

(G-13227)
VITALCORE HLTH STRATEGIES LLC
719 Sw Van Buren St # 100 (66603-3740)
PHONE....................................785 246-6840
Viola Riggin, *CEO*
Craig Hanson, *Marketing Staff*
EMP: 12
SALES (est): 192.3K **Privately Held**
SIC: 8082 Home health care services

(G-13228)
W2005/FARGO HOTELS (POOL C)
Also Called: Courtyard Topeka
2033 Sw Wanamaker Rd (66604-3830)
PHONE....................................785 271-6165
Brandon Cook, *Manager*
EMP: 22
SALES (corp-wide): 798MM **Privately Held**
WEB: www.daytonraiders.com
SIC: 7011 Hotels & motels
HQ: W2005/Fargo Hotels (Pool C) Realty, L.P.
5851 Legacy Cir Ste 400
Plano TX 75024

(G-13229)
WADDELL & REED INC (PA)
534 S Kansas Ave Ste 1300 (66603-3435)
PHONE....................................785 233-6400
Hatrrmann Corman, *CEO*
John Martin, *Manager*
David Stoll, *Administration*
Aric Harrington, *Advisor*
EMP: 15
SALES (est): 1.4MM **Privately Held**
SIC: 8742 6513 Financial consultant; apartment building operators

(G-13230)
WALT CARSTAR AUTO INC
5926 Sw 19th Ter (66604-4003)
PHONE....................................785 273-7701
Dean Koelzer, *President*
EMP: 20
SQ FT: 18,000
SALES (est): 1.1MM **Privately Held**
SIC: 7532 Body shop, automotive

(G-13231)
WASHBURN ENDOWMENT ASSOCIATION
1729 Sw Macvicar Ave (66604-3128)
PHONE....................................785 670-4483
Marshall Meek, *President*
Jeremy Wangler, *Corp Comm Staff*
Randall Scott, *Director*
Jim Stogsdill, *Director*
Sarah Towle, *Asst Director*
EMP: 25 **EST:** 2015
SALES (est): 380.2K **Privately Held**
SIC: 8641 Dwelling-related associations

(G-13232)
WASHBURN UNIVERSITY FOUNDATION
1729 Sw Macvicar Ave (66604-3128)
PHONE....................................785 670-4483
Juliann Mazachek, *President*
Randy Van Foeken, *IT/INT Sup*
Randall Scott, *Director*
EMP: 32 **EST:** 1865
SALES: 22MM **Privately Held**
WEB: www.wea.org
SIC: 6732 Educational trust management

(G-13233)
WASHBURN UNIVERSITY OF TOPEKA
Also Called: Ktwu Channel 11 Pbs
1700 Sw College Ave (66621-1101)
PHONE....................................785 670-1111
Eugene Williams, *General Mgr*
Ginger Spivey, *Manager*
Jay Hurst, *Producer*
EMP: 28
SALES (corp-wide): 49.7MM **Privately Held**
WEB: www.wuacc.edu
SIC: 4833 8221 Television broadcasting stations; university
PA: Washburn University Of Topeka
1700 Sw College Ave
Topeka KS 66621
785 670-1010

(G-13234)
WASTE MANAGEMENT OF KANSAS (DH)
3611 Nw 16th St (66618-2872)
P.O. Box 55558, Boston MA (02205-5558)
PHONE....................................785 233-3541
Troy Sanner, *Site Mgr*
EMP: 58
SQ FT: 9,700
SALES (est): 50MM
SALES (corp-wide): 14.9B **Publicly Held**
SIC: 4953 Refuse systems
HQ: Waste Management Holdings Inc
1001 Fannin St Ste 4000
Houston TX 77002
713 512-6200

(G-13235)
WASTE MANAGEMENT OF KANSAS
7351 Nw Us Highway 75 (66618-3016)
PHONE....................................785 246-0413
Randy Boehmke, *Opers-Prdtn-Mfg*
EMP: 11
SALES (corp-wide): 14.9B **Publicly Held**
WEB: www.wm.com
SIC: 4953 Sanitary landfill operation
HQ: Waste Management Of Kansas, Inc
3611 Nw 16th St
Topeka KS 66618
785 233-3541

(G-13236)
WEBBER WEBBER & EXON
Also Called: Exon, Robert A
1919 Sw 10th Ave Ste 102 (66604-1411)
PHONE....................................785 232-7707
C Edward Webber, *President*
Robert A Exon DDS, *Vice Pres*
EMP: 11
SQ FT: 1,700
SALES (est): 1MM **Privately Held**
SIC: 8021 Dentists' office

(G-13237)
WELLS FARGO BANK NATIONAL ASSN
6342 Sw 21st St (66615-1155)
PHONE....................................785 271-2492
Nega Geffus, *Manager*
EMP: 25
SALES (corp-wide): 101B **Publicly Held**
SIC: 6021 National commercial banks
HQ: Wells Fargo Bank, National Association
101 N Phillips Ave
Sioux Falls SD 57104
605 575-6900

(G-13238)
WELLS FARGO CLEARING SVCS LLC
Also Called: Wells Fargo Advisors
6342 Sw 21st St (66615-1155)
PHONE....................................785 271-2492
Rodd Miller, *Principal*
Neta Jeffus, *Vice Pres*
Dee Kirkpatrick, *Vice Pres*
EMP: 23
SALES (corp-wide): 101B **Publicly Held**
SIC: 6211 Security brokers & dealers
HQ: Wells Fargo Clearing Services, Llc
1 N Jefferson Ave Fl 7
Saint Louis MO 63103
314 955-3000

(G-13239)
WEST RIDGE LANES FMLY FUN CTR
1935 Sw Westport Dr (66604-4025)
PHONE....................................785 273-3333
Ron Hopper, *President*
EMP: 35
SALES (est): 740.1K **Privately Held**
SIC: 7933 Ten pin center

(G-13240)
WESTAR INDUSTRIES INC (DH)
818 S Kansas Ave (66612-1203)
PHONE....................................785 575-6507
Jim Haynes, *President*
Craig Greenwood, *Admin Sec*
EMP: 114
SALES (est): 5.4MM
SALES (corp-wide): 4.2B **Publicly Held**
SIC: 7382 1731 Security systems services; safety & security specialization
HQ: Evergy Kansas Central, Inc.
818 S Kansas Ave
Topeka KS 66612
785 575-6300

(G-13241)
WESTERN HILLS GOLF CLUB INC
Also Called: Right Golf At Western Hills
8533 Sw 21st St Ste A (66615-9266)
PHONE....................................785 478-4000
Jennifer Head, *President*
Rick Sarren, *President*
EMP: 30
SQ FT: 17,000
SALES (est): 1.2MM **Privately Held**
SIC: 7992 Public golf courses

(G-13242)
WHITE CLOUD GRAIN COMPANY INC
Also Called: Shawnee Terminal Elevator
2300 Nw Menoken Rd (66618-4715)
PHONE....................................785 235-5381
EMP: 10
SALES (corp-wide): 28MM **Privately Held**
SIC: 5153 Whol Grain/Field Beans
PA: The White Cloud Grain Company Inc
3245 Nw Button Rd
Topeka KS

(G-13243)
WHITELEYS INC
Also Called: Whiteley's Pallet & Blocking
310 Nw Norris St (66608-1466)
P.O. Box 8066 (66608-0066)
PHONE....................................785 233-3801
Brady Pryor, *President*
Steve Rothrock, *Vice Pres*
▼ **EMP:** 10 **EST:** 1958
SQ FT: 1,200
SALES: 500K **Privately Held**
WEB: www.whiteleys.com
SIC: 2448 Pallets, wood

(G-13244)
WILDCAT CONCRETE SERVICES INC
2244 Nw Brickyard Rd (66618-2814)
P.O. Box 750075 (66675-0075)
PHONE....................................785 478-9000
Stuart R Johnson, *President*
Tom Costello, *Superintendent*
Dick Poole, *Superintendent*
Lanny Gridley, *Vice Pres*
Raymond May, *Vice Pres*
EMP: 20
SQ FT: 3,000
SALES (est): 4.6MM
SALES (corp-wide): 69.5MM **Privately Held**
SIC: 1771 Concrete work
PA: Wildcat Construction Co., Inc.
3219 W May St
Wichita KS 67213
316 945-9408

GEOGRAPHIC

(G-13245)
WILDCAT CONSTRUCTION
2244 Nw Brickyard Rd (66618-2814)
P.O. Box 750075 (66675-0075)
PHONE..................................316 945-9408
Jim Tadtman, *President*
EMP: 45
SALES (est): 4.4MM
SALES (corp-wide): 69.5MM **Privately Held**
WEB: www.wildcatcompanies.com
SIC: 1623 Underground utilities contractor
PA: Wildcat Construction Co., Inc.
3219 W May St
Wichita KS 67213
316 945-9408

(G-13246)
WINSTON-BROWN CONSTRUCTION CO (PA)
Also Called: Handyman Services
5600 Sw 29th St Ste A (66614-2549)
PHONE..................................785 271-1661
Gary W Brown, *President*
Jake Brown, *President*
EMP: 20
SQ FT: 2,440
SALES (est): 6.1MM **Privately Held**
SIC: 1521 1542 General remodeling, single-family houses; commercial & office buildings, renovation & repair

(G-13247)
WOLF CONSTRUCTION INC (PA)
5630 Sw Randolph Ave (66609-1158)
PHONE..................................785 862-2474
Wolf Blaser Sr, *CEO*
David Gary, *President*
Adam Figgs, *Superintendent*
Wolf Blaser Jr, *Vice Pres*
Dusty Gary, *Vice Pres*
EMP: 90
SALES (est): 28MM **Privately Held**
SIC: 1541 Industrial buildings, new construction

(G-13248)
WOLFES CAMERA SHOPS INC
Also Called: Wolfes Cmras Cmcrders Cmputers
635 S Kansas Ave (66603-3886)
P.O. Box 1437 (66601-1437)
PHONE..................................785 235-1386
Michael Worswick, *CEO*
Dewitt Harkness, *President*
EMP: 32
SQ FT: 20,000
SALES (est): 6.1MM **Privately Held**
WEB: www.wolfes.com
SIC: 5734 5946 5043 7384 Computer & software stores; camera & photographic supply stores; photographic equipment & supplies; photofinish laboratories; video cameras, recorders & accessories; computer maintenance & repair

(G-13249)
WONER GLENN REDER GRANT RIORDN (PA)
5611 Sw Berrington (66614)
P.O. Box 1033 (66601-1033)
PHONE..................................785 235-5371
Bruce Woner, *President*
Grant Glenn, *Vice Pres*
Glenn Grant, *Vice Pres*
EMP: 15
SALES (est): 1.2MM **Privately Held**
SIC: 8111 General practice attorney, lawyer

(G-13250)
WOOD VALLEY RACQUET CLUB INC
Also Called: Wood Vly Rcquet CLB Fitnes Ctr
2909 Sw 37th St (66614-3569)
PHONE..................................785 506-8928
Kent Lammers, *President*
Thomas McBride, *President*
B Kent Garlinghouse, *Principal*
Robert Jones, *Principal*
Lisa Beam, *Finance Dir*
EMP: 30
SQ FT: 93,000
SALES (est): 932.2K **Privately Held**
WEB: www.wvstayfit.com
SIC: 7991 Health club

(G-13251)
WOODLAND HLTH CTR OPRTIONS LLC
440 Se Woodland Ave (66607-2172)
PHONE..................................785 234-6147
Dennis Bahr, *Principal*
EMP: 63
SALES (est): 493.4K **Privately Held**
SIC: 8059 Nursing & personal care

(G-13252)
WORLD PUBLISHING INC
Also Called: Olu
1622 Sw Knollwood Dr (66611-1620)
PHONE..................................785 221-8174
Olu Otudeka, *President*
EMP: 20
SQ FT: 600
SALES: 168K **Privately Held**
WEB: www.olu.com
SIC: 2771 3944 Greeting cards; board games, children's & adults'

(G-13253)
WRIGHT HENSON CLARK & BAKR LLP
Also Called: Wachter, John H
100 Se 9th St Fl 2 (66612-1213)
PHONE..................................785 232-2200
Tom Wright, *Partner*
Ann Baker, *Partner*
Bruce Clark, *Partner*
Charles Henson, *Partner*
Dale Somers, *Partner*
EMP: 20
SALES (est): 1.2MM **Privately Held**
WEB: www.wrighthenson.com
SIC: 8111 General practice attorney, lawyer

(G-13254)
YELLOW CAB TAXI TPEKA KANS LLC
1012 Sw 17th St (66604-2916)
PHONE..................................785 357-4444
Janis H Schinze, *Mng Member*
W Chris Avey,
EMP: 25
SQ FT: 700
SALES: 750K **Privately Held**
SIC: 4121 Taxicabs

(G-13255)
YINGLING AUTO ELECTRIC INC
2525 Nw Topeka Blvd (66617-1151)
PHONE..................................785 232-0484
Larry J Yingling, *President*
Pete Fail, *Manager*
EMP: 12 **EST:** 1965
SQ FT: 12,000
SALES (est): 1.7MM **Privately Held**
SIC: 7538 General automotive repair shops

(G-13256)
YMCA TOPEAKA DOWNTOWN BRANCH
Also Called: YMCA Topeaka Downtown Branch
3635 Sw Chelsea Dr (66614-3971)
PHONE..................................785 354-8591
Pete Doll, *Director*
EMP: 40
SALES (est): 283.9K **Privately Held**
SIC: 8641 7991 8351 7032 Youth organizations; physical fitness facilities; child day care services; youth camps; individual & family services

(G-13257)
YOUNG KANSAS CHRISTIAN
Also Called: YWCA OF TOPEKA
225 Sw 12th St (66612-1310)
PHONE..................................785 233-1750
Joyce Martin, *CEO*
EMP: 110
SQ FT: 65,000
SALES: 2.1MM **Privately Held**
SIC: 8399 8322 Community development groups; individual & family services

(G-13258)
YOUNG MENS CHRISTIAN
Also Called: YMCA of Topeka
1936 Nw Tyler St Fl 1 (66608-1664)
PHONE..................................785 233-9815
Bruce Holt, *Exec Dir*
EMP: 16
SALES (corp-wide): 3.4MM **Privately Held**
SIC: 8641 7991 8351 7032 Youth organizations; physical fitness facilities; child day care services; youth camps; individual & family services
PA: The Young Men's Christian Association Of Topeka Kansas
3635 Sw Chelsea Dr
Topeka KS 66614
785 354-8591

(G-13259)
YOUNG MNS CHRSTN ASSN OF TPEKA (PA)
Also Called: YMCA OF TOPEKA
3635 Sw Chelsea Dr (66614-3971)
PHONE..................................785 354-8591
John Mugeler, *CEO*
Bruce Holt, *COO*
Sharon Dela Cruz, *Personnel Exec*
Terry Jones, *Director*
Lorie Lahman, *Executive*
EMP: 150
SALES: 3.4MM **Privately Held**
SIC: 8641 7991 8351 7032 Youth organizations; physical fitness facilities; child day care services; youth camps; individual & family services

(G-13260)
ZACK TAYLOR CONTRACTING INC
711 Se Adams St (66607-1124)
PHONE..................................785 235-8704
Rocky Taylor, *President*
EMP: 10
SQ FT: 7,200
SALES (est): 1.6MM **Privately Held**
SIC: 1721 1752 Commercial painting; floor laying & floor work

(G-13261)
ZIESON CONSTRUCTION CO LLC (PA)
5853 Se 29th St (66614)
P.O. Box 7374, Kansas City MO (64116-0074)
PHONE..................................785 783-8335
Stephon A Ziegler, *President*
EMP: 10
SALES (est): 3MM **Privately Held**
SIC: 1542 Commercial & office building, new construction

Towanda
Butler County

(G-13262)
ACE CONSTRUCTION CORPORATION (PA)
301 Main St (67144-8832)
P.O. Box 297 (67144-0297)
PHONE..................................316 536-2202
Charles Warden, *President*
EMP: 32
SQ FT: 6,000
SALES (est): 8.6MM **Privately Held**
SIC: 1623 Pipeline construction

(G-13263)
DCM WICHITA INC (PA)
Also Called: Tux Shop, The
1233 Willowbrook Ln (67144-9393)
PHONE..................................800 662-9573
David C Martin, *President*
EMP: 15
SQ FT: 22,600
SALES (est): 454K **Privately Held**
SIC: 7299 5136 Tuxedo rental; men's & boys' suits & trousers

(G-13264)
DUSTROL INC (HQ)
1201 E Main (67144)
P.O. Box 309 (67144-0309)
PHONE..................................316 536-2262
Tim Murphy, *CEO*
Brian Hansen, *President*
Ron Wilson, *Vice Pres*
Dan Edwards, *Foreman/Supr*
Andrea Bullok, *CFO*
EMP: 100 **EST:** 1973
SQ FT: 27,000
SALES: 56.3MM **Privately Held**
WEB: www.dustrol.com
SIC: 1611 Highway & street maintenance; highway & street paving contractor

(G-13265)
MWM OIL CO INC
821 High St (67144-9047)
PHONE..................................316 265-1992
Charlene A Giles, *President*
Benjamin Giles, *President*
Charlene Giles, *Treasurer*
EMP: 6
SALES (est): 735.5K **Privately Held**
SIC: 1382 Oil & gas exploration services

(G-13266)
RECYCLING ENTERPRISES INC (PA)
1200 Main St (67144-8865)
P.O. Box 309 (67144-0309)
PHONE..................................316 536-2262
T D Dankert, *Ch of Bd*
Barbara Dankert, *Corp Secy*
Tim Murphy, *Exec VP*
Brian Hansen, *Vice Pres*
David E Wilson, *Director*
EMP: 13
SALES (est): 56.3MM **Privately Held**
SIC: 1611 Highway & street maintenance

Treece
Cherokee County

(G-13267)
BINGHAM TRANSPORTATION INC
Hwy 69 (66778)
P.O. Box 660, Baxter Springs (66713-0660)
PHONE..................................620 679-9810
Larry Bingham, *President*
Lucille Bingham, *Corp Secy*
EMP: 90
SQ FT: 20,000
SALES (est): 4.8MM **Privately Held**
SIC: 4212 Dump truck haulage

Tribune
Greeley County

(G-13268)
GREELEY CNTY HOSP & LONG TRM C (PA)
Also Called: Helmwood Long Term Care
302 E Greeley Ave (67879)
PHONE..................................620 376-4225
Cindy Schneider, *Principal*
EMP: 100
SALES (est): 3.1MM **Privately Held**
SIC: 8051 Skilled nursing care facilities

(G-13269)
GREELEY COUNTY FAMILY PRACTICE
321 E Harper St (67879-7708)
P.O. Box 640 (67879-0640)
PHONE..................................620 376-4251
Robert P Moser MD, *CEO*
EMP: 14
SALES (est): 775.5K **Privately Held**
SIC: 8011 General & family practice, physician/surgeon
PA: Greeley County Hospital & Long Term Care Inc
302 E Greeley Ave
Tribune KS 67879

(G-13270)
GREELEY COUNTY HEALTH SVCS INC
Also Called: GREELEY COUNTY FAMILY PRACTICE
506 3rd St (67879-9684)
P.O. Box 338 (67879-0338)
PHONE..........620 376-4221
Todd Burch, *CEO*
Janie Schmidt, *COO*
Kim Dansel, *Med Doctor*
Geni Wilcox, *Manager*
Drew Zerr, *Manager*
EMP: 140
SALES: 9.3MM **Privately Held**
SIC: 8062 General medical & surgical hospitals

(G-13271)
GREELEY COUNTY REPUBLICAN
507 Broadway Ave (67879-7702)
P.O. Box 610 (67879-0610)
PHONE..........620 376-4264
Dan Epp, *Owner*
Jan Epp, *Co-Owner*
EMP: 5
SQ FT: 2,000
SALES (est): 259.6K **Privately Held**
SIC: 2711 2752 2759 Newspapers: publishing only, not printed on site; commercial printing, offset; letterpress printing

(G-13272)
WOODS ALFALFA
1705 Road F (67879-7928)
PHONE..........620 376-4999
Koreen Woods, *Principal*
EMP: 5
SALES (est): 290.3K **Privately Held**
SIC: 2048 Cereal-, grain-, & seed-based feeds

Troy
Doniphan County

(G-13273)
COUNTY OF DONIPHAN
Also Called: Doniphan Cnty Council On Aging
Doniphan Cnty Courthouse (66087)
P.O. Box 247 (66087-0247)
PHONE..........785 985-2380
Connie Potter, *Director*
EMP: 11 **Privately Held**
SIC: 8322 Individual & family services
PA: County Of Doniphan
120 E Chestnut St
Troy KS 66087
785 985-3513

(G-13274)
HEARTLAND HEALTH
207 S Main St (66087-4017)
P.O. Box 547 (66087-0547)
PHONE..........785 985-2211
Shiela Gal, *Branch Mgr*
EMP: 660
SALES (corp-wide): 688.1MM **Privately Held**
SIC: 8062 General medical & surgical hospitals
PA: Heartland Health
5325 Faraon St
Saint Joseph MO 64506
816 271-6000

Turon
Reno County

(G-13275)
TURON WELDING AND FABRICATION
308 E Chicago St (67583-8338)
P.O. Box 382 (67583-0382)
PHONE..........620 388-4458
Jon Herrmann, *Owner*
EMP: 5
SALES: 100K **Privately Held**
SIC: 7692 Welding repair

Tyro
Montgomery County

(G-13276)
FALCON INDUSTRIES INC
100 W Main St (67364-4800)
PHONE..........620 289-4290
Steve Melander, *President*
EMP: 11
SALES (est): 790K **Privately Held**
SIC: 7699 Railroad car customizing

Udall
Cowley County

(G-13277)
GOLDEN WHEAT INC (PA)
Also Called: Wheat State
106 W 1st St (67146-4601)
P.O. Box 320 (67146-0320)
PHONE..........620 782-3341
Greg Reed, *President*
EMP: 20
SQ FT: 1,500
SALES (est): 1.9MM **Privately Held**
WEB: www.goldenwheat.com
SIC: 4813 5999 4841 Local & long distance telephone communications; communication equipment; cable television services

(G-13278)
KISTLER SERVICE INC (PA)
301 Highway K15 (67146-8813)
PHONE..........620 782-3611
Jeanie Kistler, *President*
Frank Kistler, *President*
Jack Kistler, *Principal*
Teresa Kistler, *Vice Pres*
EMP: 22
SALES (est): 4MM **Privately Held**
SIC: 5541 7534 7538 Filling stations, gasoline; tire retreading & repair shops; general automotive repair shops

(G-13279)
WHEAT STATE TELEPHONE INC (HQ)
Also Called: Wheat State Technologies
106 W 1st St (67146-4601)
P.O. Box 320 (67146-0320)
PHONE..........620 782-3341
Greg Reed, *President*
Randy Hoffman, *General Mgr*
EMP: 18 **EST:** 1949
SQ FT: 15,000
SALES (est): 3.2MM
SALES (corp-wide): 1.9MM **Privately Held**
WEB: www.wheatstate.com
SIC: 4813 Local telephone communications
PA: Golden Wheat Inc
106 W 1st St
Udall KS 67146
620 782-3341

(G-13280)
WICHITA CABINET COMPANY
6859 31st Rd (67146-7261)
PHONE..........316 617-0176
Tim Dreiling, *Principal*
EMP: 5
SALES (est): 465.2K **Privately Held**
SIC: 2434 Wood kitchen cabinets

Ulysses
Grant County

(G-13281)
ALAN BITTER
Also Called: Alltech Electrical Service
202 E Oklahoma Ave (67880-2541)
PHONE..........620 353-7407
Alan Bitter, *Owner*
EMP: 16
SALES (est): 1.1MM **Privately Held**
SIC: 1731 General electrical contractor

(G-13282)
AMERICAN IMPLEMENT MAIN OFFICE
Also Called: John Deere Authorized Dealer
2718 W Oklahoma Ave (67880-8467)
P.O. Box 40 (67880-0040)
PHONE..........620 356-3460
Aron Floyd, *Principal*
Nick Ortner, *Manager*
EMP: 14
SALES (est): 1.7MM **Privately Held**
SIC: 5083 Agricultural machinery & equipment

(G-13283)
BIRLA CARBON USA INC
3500 S Road S (67880-8103)
PHONE..........620 356-3151
Keith Steele, *Manager*
EMP: 48 **Privately Held**
WEB: www.columbianchemicals.com
SIC: 2895 3624 Carbon black; carbon & graphite products
HQ: Birla Carbon U.S.A., Inc.
1800 W Oak Commons Ct
Marietta GA 30062
770 792-9400

(G-13284)
BOB WILSON MEM GRANT CNTY HOSP
415 N Main St (67880-2133)
PHONE..........620 356-1266
Art Frable, *CEO*
Jon Loewen, *Ch Radiology*
Dan Enderson, *Vice Pres*
Amy King, *Vice Pres*
Janell M Moerer, *Vice Pres*
EMP: 143
SQ FT: 73,000
SALES: 11.8MM **Privately Held**
WEB: www.bwmgch.com
SIC: 8062 General medical & surgical hospitals
PA: County Of Grant
108 S Glenn St Ste 2
Ulysses KS 67880
620 356-1335

(G-13285)
BROWN - DUPREE OIL CO INC (PA)
111 E Kansas Ave (67880-2125)
P.O. Box 837 (67880-0837)
PHONE..........620 353-1874
Jerry Brown, *President*
Susanne Brown, *Corp Secy*
EMP: 13 **EST:** 1975
SQ FT: 4,000
SALES: 17.8MM **Privately Held**
SIC: 5171 Petroleum bulk stations

(G-13286)
CACTUS FEEDERS INC
Also Called: Ulysis Feed Yard
1765 E Road 21 (67880-8268)
PHONE..........620 356-1750
Martin Daharsh, *Branch Mgr*
EMP: 50
SALES (corp-wide): 136.5MM **Privately Held**
WEB: www.cactusfeeders.com
SIC: 0211 Beef cattle feedlots
PA: Cactus Feeders, Inc
600 S Tyler St Ste 2800
Amarillo TX 79101
806 373-2333

(G-13287)
CENTRAL STATES MECHANICAL INC
108 S Main St (67880-2518)
PHONE..........620 353-1797
Robert E Myers, *President*
Sara L Myers, *Admin Sec*
EMP: 10
SALES (est): 961.2K **Privately Held**
WEB: www.censtatesmech.com
SIC: 1711 Mechanical contractor

(G-13288)
CHAOSLAND SERVICES LLC
1020 W Road 19 (67880-8356)
P.O. Box 545 (67880-0545)
PHONE..........620 356-1259
Grant Florence,
EMP: 6
SALES (est): 593.3K **Privately Held**
SIC: 1389 Acidizing wells

(G-13289)
CHASE TUBING TESTING
1809 N Easy St (67880-9200)
PHONE..........620 356-4314
Toll Free:..........888 -
Jaye Chase, *Owner*
EMP: 6 **EST:** 1996
SALES (est): 750K **Privately Held**
SIC: 1389 Oil field services

(G-13290)
CORPORATE EAST LLC
1110 E Oklahoma St (67880)
P.O. Box 1085 (67880-1085)
PHONE..........620 356-5010
Martin Long, *Mng Member*
Debra Long,
EMP: 12
SQ FT: 23,500
SALES: 850K **Privately Held**
SIC: 7011 Hotels

(G-13291)
COUNTY OF GRANT
Also Called: County Engineer
1550 N Rd I (67880)
P.O. Box 506 (67880-0506)
PHONE..........620 356-4837
Frank Goldsby, *Manager*
EMP: 30 **Privately Held**
WEB: www.grantrec.com
SIC: 8711 9111 Engineering services; county supervisors' & executives' offices
PA: County Of Grant
108 S Glenn St Ste 2
Ulysses KS 67880
620 356-1335

(G-13292)
COUNTY OF GRANT
Also Called: Grant County Recreation Comm
815 E Oklahoma Ave (67880-2844)
P.O. Box 934 (67880-0934)
PHONE..........620 356-4233
Bobbie Lewis, *Branch Mgr*
Scott Nichols, *Exec Dir*
EMP: 15 **Privately Held**
WEB: www.grantrec.com
SIC: 7999 9111 Recreation center; county supervisors' & executives' offices
PA: County Of Grant
108 S Glenn St Ste 2
Ulysses KS 67880
620 356-1335

(G-13293)
CRITICAL CARE TRANSFER INC
930 N Joyce Dr (67880)
P.O. Box 1063 (67880-1063)
PHONE..........620 353-4145
Debra Barbo, *President*
EMP: 17
SALES (est): 642K **Privately Held**
SIC: 4119 Ambulance service

(G-13294)
CROPLAND CO-OP INC (PA)
1125 W Oklahoma Ave (67880-2362)
P.O. Box 947 (67880-0947)
PHONE..........620 356-1241
Scott Day, *General Mgr*
EMP: 14
SQ FT: 8,000
SALES (est): 16.9MM **Privately Held**
WEB: www.croplandco-op.com
SIC: 5153 4221 0723 5191 Grains; grain elevator, storage only; feed milling custom services; farm supplies; feed; seeds: field, garden & flower; chemicals, agricultural; filling stations, gasoline

(G-13295)
FAULKNER REAL ESTATE
112 S Main St (67880-2518)
P.O. Box 629 (67880-0629)
PHONE..........620 356-5808
Mark Faulkner, *Owner*
EMP: 12
SALES (est): 694.8K **Privately Held**
SIC: 6531 Real estate agent, residential; real estate brokers & agents

GEOGRAPHIC

(G-13296)
FIVE RIVERS CATTLE FEEDING LLC
Also Called: Grant County Feeders
7597 W Rd 17 (67880)
P.O. Box 1087 (67880-1087)
PHONE..................................620 356-4466
Cindy Burton, *Principal*
Lynda Riverman, *Safety Dir*
EMP: 90
SALES (corp-wide): 189.1MM **Privately Held**
SIC: 0211 Beef cattle feedlots
HQ: Five Rivers Cattle Feeding, Llc
4848 Thompson Pkwy # 410
Johnstown CO 80534
970 506-8363

(G-13297)
G & R TRUCKING INC
921 N Stubbs Rd (67880-8179)
P.O. Box 567 (67880-0567)
PHONE..................................620 356-4500
Guadalupe Rodriguez, *President*
EMP: 11
SALES (est): 1.8MM **Privately Held**
SIC: 4213 Trucking, except local

(G-13298)
GARDEN CITY CO-OP INC (PA)
501 S Colorado St (67880-2610)
P.O. Box 703 (67880-0703)
PHONE..................................620 356-1219
Joseph M Sullivan, *President*
Keric J Sullivan, *Vice Pres*
R Lynn Teeter, *Treasurer*
Juan Barron, *Manager*
M Kathy Olson-Wilson, *Director*
EMP: 15 **EST:** 1922
SQ FT: 2,048
SALES (est): 15.3MM **Privately Held**
WEB: www.sullivangift.com
SIC: 5153 5191 Grain elevators; farm supplies

(G-13299)
GERSTBERGER MEDICAL CLINIC
Also Called: Ramchandani Medical Clinic
301 E Grant Ave (67880-2515)
PHONE..................................620 356-2432
Mark Gerstberger, *Owner*
Laura Dykstra, *Office Mgr*
Mark A Gerstberger, *Gnrl Med Prac*
Charles H Zerr, *Gnrl Med Prac*
Martin J Kline, *Physician Asst*
EMP: 11
SALES (est): 1MM **Privately Held**
SIC: 8011 General & family practice, physician/surgeon

(G-13300)
GRANT COUNTY BANK
201 S Main St (67880-2521)
P.O. Box 389 (67880-0389)
PHONE..................................620 356-4142
Thomas Pinnick, *President*
Anita Lane, *Opers Staff*
Kim Flores, *Manager*
EMP: 50
SQ FT: 15,000
SALES: 11.2MM **Privately Held**
SIC: 6022 State commercial banks
PA: Resource One, Inc.
201 S Main St
Ulysses KS 67880

(G-13301)
J & L SMITH FARMS INC
Also Called: Tri-Rotor Spray & Chemical
9170 E Road 2 (67880-8151)
PHONE..................................620 356-1070
Larry Smith, *President*
EMP: 16
SQ FT: 5,600
SALES (est): 100K **Privately Held**
SIC: 0115 Corn

(G-13302)
KEY ENERGY SERVICES INC
2444 W Oklahoma Ave (67880-8417)
P.O. Box 73 (67880-0073)
PHONE..................................620 353-1002
Jerry Burgeman, *Manager*
EMP: 30
SALES (corp-wide): 521.7MM **Publicly Held**
WEB: www.keyenergy.com
SIC: 1389 Servicing oil & gas wells
PA: Key Energy Services, Inc.
1301 Mckinney St Ste 1800
Houston TX 77010
713 651-4300

(G-13303)
KEY ENERGY SERVICES INC
713 S Simpson St (67880-2655)
PHONE..................................620 353-1002
Gerry Burkman, *Manager*
EMP: 93
SALES (corp-wide): 521.7MM **Publicly Held**
WEB: www.keyenergy.com
SIC: 1389 Servicing oil & gas wells
PA: Key Energy Services, Inc.
1301 Mckinney St Ste 1800
Houston TX 77010
713 651-4300

(G-13304)
KUGLER OIL COMPANY
795 S Road H (67880-8488)
PHONE..................................620 356-4347
Jon Velacich, *Branch Mgr*
EMP: 6
SALES (corp-wide): 66.9MM **Privately Held**
WEB: www.k-lawn.com
SIC: 2875 5191 Fertilizers, mixing only; fertilizer & fertilizer materials
PA: Kugler Oil Company
209 W 3rd St
Mc Cook NE 69001
308 345-2280

(G-13305)
LINN ENERGY INC
Also Called: Satanta Gas Plant
10565 E Road 20 (67880-8377)
PHONE..................................620 657-8310
Terry Ochs, *Manager*
EMP: 30
SALES (corp-wide): 1.9MM **Privately Held**
SIC: 1311 Crude petroleum production
HQ: Linn Energy, Inc.
600 Travis St
Houston TX 77002
281 840-4000

(G-13306)
MERIT ENERGY COMPANY LLC
446 S Road M (67880-8347)
PHONE..................................620 356-3032
Corey Brown, *Branch Mgr*
EMP: 20
SALES (est): 1.3MM
SALES (corp-wide): 3.9B **Privately Held**
SIC: 1389 Construction, repair & dismantling services
PA: Merit Energy Company, Llc
13737 Noel Rd Ste 1200
Dallas TX 75240
972 701-8377

(G-13307)
NATIONAL SOCTY OF THE DAUGHTRS
1675 W Patterson Ave (67880-8423)
PHONE..................................620 356-2570
Linda Fort, *Branch Mgr*
EMP: 18
SALES (corp-wide): 25MM **Privately Held**
SIC: 8699 Historical club
PA: The National Society Of The Daughters Of The American Revolution
1776 D St Nw
Washington DC
202 628-1776

(G-13308)
NURSING HOME LEGACY AT PK VIEW
510 E San Jacinto Ave (67880-2241)
PHONE..................................620 356-3331
Kimberle Doty, *Principal*
EMP: 27 **EST:** 2009
SALES (est): 1.3MM **Privately Held**
SIC: 8059 Nursing home, except skilled & intermediate care facility

(G-13309)
ONEOK FIELD SERVICES CO LLC
1407 E Oklahoma Ave (67880-2923)
PHONE..................................620 356-2231
Daniel Sattler, *Principal*
EMP: 65
SALES (corp-wide): 12.5B **Publicly Held**
SIC: 1321 Natural gas liquids
HQ: Oneok Field Services Company, L.L.C.
100 W 5th St Ste Ll
Tulsa OK 74103

(G-13310)
PARK VIEW
750 N Missouri St (67880-1868)
PHONE..................................620 424-2000
Marcy Stingham, *Principal*
EMP: 20
SALES (est): 444.7K **Privately Held**
WEB: www.cix.co.uk
SIC: 8059 Rest home, with health care

(G-13311)
PIONEER ELECTRIC COOP INC (PA)
1850 W Oklahoma Ave (67880-8569)
P.O. Box 368 (67880-0368)
PHONE..................................620 356-1211
Steve Epperson, *CEO*
David L Jesse, *President*
Jim Bell, *Trustee*
Michael Brewer, *Trustee*
Fred Claassen, *Trustee*
EMP: 68 **EST:** 1944
SQ FT: 70,000
SALES: 77.4MM **Privately Held**
SIC: 4911 Generation, electric power; distribution, electric power

(G-13312)
PIONEER TELEPHONE ASSN INC (PA)
Also Called: Pioneer Communications
120 W Kansas Ave (67880-2036)
P.O. Box 707 (67880-0707)
PHONE..................................620 356-3211
Catherine Moyer, *CEO*
EMP: 102 **EST:** 1950
SQ FT: 33,000
SALES (est): 52.1MM **Privately Held**
SIC: 4813 4841 4812 Local telephone communications; ; cable television services; radio telephone communication

(G-13313)
PIONEER TELEPHONE ASSN INC
Also Called: Pioneer Lan Assistance
120 W Kansas Ave (67880-2036)
P.O. Box 707 (67880-0707)
PHONE..................................620 356-1985
Kelly Johnson, *Manager*
EMP: 15
SALES (corp-wide): 52.1MM **Privately Held**
SIC: 4813 Local telephone communications;
PA: The Pioneer Telephone Association Inc
120 W Kansas Ave
Ulysses KS 67880
620 356-3211

(G-13314)
PRAIRIE VISTA DENTAL LLC
209 W Central Ave (67880-2404)
PHONE..................................620 424-4311
Bret J Holman, *Principal*
Vicki R Holman, *Mng Member*
EMP: 11
SALES (est): 541.6K **Privately Held**
SIC: 8021 Dental clinic

(G-13315)
RILEY FORD MERCURY CO
715 E Oklahoma Ave (67880-2821)
PHONE..................................620 356-1206
Sherry Riley, *Partner*
Gary Riley, *Partner*
EMP: 11
SQ FT: 10,000
SALES (est): 1.7MM **Privately Held**
SIC: 5511 5531 7538 Automobiles, new & used; automotive parts; general automotive repair shops

(G-13316)
RIVER BEND FEED YARD INC
17 Mi S & 5 Mi W (67880)
P.O. Box 448 (67880-0448)
PHONE..................................620 356-4100
Patrick Staats, *President*
EMP: 15
SALES (est): 1.4MM **Privately Held**
SIC: 0211 Beef cattle feedlots

(G-13317)
SANDS MOTOR INN
622 W Oklahoma Ave (67880-2452)
PHONE..................................620 356-1404
P J Patel, *Owner*
EMP: 11
SALES: 160K **Privately Held**
SIC: 7011 Motels

(G-13318)
SINGLE TREE INN
2033 W Oklahoma Ave (67880-8415)
PHONE..................................620 356-1500
Gary Cheek, *Partner*
EMP: 20 **EST:** 1996
SALES (est): 519.5K **Privately Held**
WEB: www.singletreeinn.net
SIC: 7011 Inns

(G-13319)
SMYTH OIL AND GAS SERVICES
2398 W Rd 10 (67880)
P.O. Box 905 (67880-0905)
PHONE..................................620 356-4091
Stan Smyth, *President*
Leona Smyth, *Vice Pres*
EMP: 25
SALES (est): 2.4MM **Privately Held**
SIC: 1382 Oil & gas exploration services

(G-13320)
SOUTHERN PIONEER ELECTRIC CO (HQ)
1850 W Oklahoma Ave (67880-8569)
P.O. Box 368 (67880-0368)
PHONE..................................620 356-3370
Randall Magnison, *President*
EMP: 18
SALES: 69.7MM
SALES (corp-wide): 77.4MM **Privately Held**
SIC: 1731 General electrical contractor
PA: Pioneer Electric Cooperative, Inc.
1850 W Oklahoma Ave
Ulysses KS 67880
620 356-1211

(G-13321)
TARBET CONSTRUCTION CO INC (PA)
Also Called: Tarbet Ready-Mix
303 S Road I (67880-8506)
PHONE..................................620 356-2110
Steve Tarbet, *President*
Carol Tarbet, *Treasurer*
EMP: 10 **EST:** 1946
SQ FT: 6,000
SALES (est): 8MM **Privately Held**
WEB: www.tarbertdrilling.com
SIC: 1771 3273 5211 Concrete work; ready-mixed concrete; concrete & cinder block

(G-13322)
TATRO PLUMBING CO INC
1325 E Oklahoma Ave (67880-2906)
P.O. Box 705 (67880-0705)
PHONE..................................620 356-5319
Rob Kreustzer, *Branch Mgr*
EMP: 21
SALES (corp-wide): 13MM **Privately Held**
SIC: 1711 Plumbing contractors
PA: Tatro Plumbing Co., Inc.
1285 Acraway St Ste 300
Garden City KS 67846
620 277-2167

(G-13323)
TEDS PLUMBING LLC
1325 E Oklahoma Ave Ste 1 (67880-2906)
PHONE..................................620 356-5319
Dexter Peters,
EMP: 11

SALES (est): 412.9K **Privately Held**
SIC: 1711 Plumbing contractors

(G-13324)
TEETER IRRIGATION INC (PA)
2729 W Oklahoma Ave (67880-8467)
P.O. Box 987 (67880-0987)
PHONE..................................620 353-1111
Monty Teeter, *CEO*
Terry Winkelman, *President*
Rebecca Teeter, *Corp Secy*
Kenneth Teeter, *Vice Pres*
Michelle Reppart, *Warehouse Mgr*
▲ **EMP:** 70 **EST:** 1977
SQ FT: 17,000
SALES (est): 9.7MM **Privately Held**
WEB: www.teeterirrigation.com
SIC: 7699 Agricultural equipment repair services

(G-13325)
TRECO INC (PA)
2871 W Oklahoma (67880)
PHONE..................................620 356-4785
Richard Trejo, *President*
Janice Trejo, *Corp Secy*
EMP: 60
SQ FT: 6,900
SALES (est): 27.8MM **Privately Held**
WEB: www.treco-inc.com
SIC: 1389 Oil field services

(G-13326)
ULYSSES FAMILY PHYSICIANS
505 N Main St (67880-2135)
PHONE..................................620 356-1261
Asa Wilson, *CEO*
Bruce Birchell, *President*
Steve Daniel, *President*
Patrick N Barker, *Med Doctor*
EMP: 120
SALES (est): 4.1MM **Privately Held**
WEB: www.stevemedeiros.com
SIC: 8011 Clinic, operated by physicians; general & family practice, physician/surgeon

(G-13327)
ULYSSES STANDARD SUPPLY INC
Also Called: Big R
502 S Colorado St (67880-2609)
P.O. Box 408 (67880-0408)
PHONE..................................620 356-4171
Kent Carmichael, *President*
Bruce Anderson, *Corp Secy*
Robert C Anderson, *Vice Pres*
EMP: 13 **EST:** 1961
SQ FT: 18,600
SALES (est): 2MM **Privately Held**
SIC: 5251 5083 5231 Hardware; agricultural machinery & equipment; farm equipment parts & supplies; paint; paint brushes, rollers, sprayers & other supplies

(G-13328)
UNIFIED SCHOOL DISTRICT 214
Also Called: High Plains Educational Coop
207 N Main St (67880-2130)
PHONE..................................620 356-4577
Gail Villespie, *Director*
EMP: 59
SALES (corp-wide): 11MM **Privately Held**
SIC: 8211 8049 Specialty education; clinical psychologist
PA: Unified School District 214
111 S Baughman St
Ulysses KS 67880
620 356-3655

(G-13329)
UNITED PRAIRIE AG LLC
7119 E Highway 160 (67880-8131)
PHONE..................................620 356-2212
Mike Franco, *Branch Mgr*
EMP: 62
SALES (corp-wide): 22.7MM **Privately Held**
SIC: 2873 Nitrogenous fertilizers
PA: United Prairie Ag, Llc
1125 W Oklahoma Ave
Ulysses KS 67880
620 356-1241

(G-13330)
UNITED PRAIRIE AG LLC (PA)
1125 W Oklahoma Ave (67880-2362)
PHONE..................................620 356-1241
Kelly Baptist, *Mng Member*
Don Wiseman, *Manager*
EMP: 44
SALES (est): 22.7MM **Privately Held**
SIC: 2873 Fertilizers: natural (organic), except compost

(G-13331)
WAL-MAC INC
Also Called: Lathem Water Service
902 S Colorado St (67880-2662)
P.O. Box 1105 (67880-1105)
PHONE..................................620 356-3422
Grant Florence, *President*
Sam Minks, *Principal*
EMP: 15
SQ FT: 5,500
SALES: 3.5MM **Privately Held**
SIC: 4212 Liquid transfer services

(G-13332)
WT CONTRACTORS
2214 W Rd 10 (67880)
P.O. Box 604 (67880-0604)
PHONE..................................620 356-4801
Dave Tarbet, *Owner*
EMP: 25
SQ FT: 3,000
SALES (est): 1.9MM **Privately Held**
SIC: 1771 Concrete work

Uniontown
Bourbon County

(G-13333)
UNION STATE BANCSHARES INC (PA)
204 Sherman St (66779-7101)
P.O. Box 100 (66779-0100)
PHONE..................................620 756-4305
Kenneth R Holt, *President*
Susan J Eldridge, *Vice Pres*
Kent L Holt, *Vice Pres*
Susan Eldridge, *Shareholder*
Marilyn J Holt, *Shareholder*
EMP: 31
SQ FT: 6,000
SALES: 2.2MM **Privately Held**
SIC: 6022 State commercial banks

Utica
Ness County

(G-13334)
AEROSWINT
Rr 1 Box 63 (67584)
PHONE..................................785 391-2276
Randy Swint, *Owner*
EMP: 10
SALES (est): 453.4K **Privately Held**
SIC: 5531 7532 5012 Automotive & home supply stores; truck painting & lettering; trucks, commercial

(G-13335)
RANDY SCHWINDT
Also Called: Aeroswint
1 S Hwy 4 (67584)
PHONE..................................785 391-2277
Randy Schwindt, *Owner*
EMP: 12
SQ FT: 6,800
SALES: 2.5MM **Privately Held**
WEB: www.randyschwindt.com
SIC: 3713 7539 7699 7692 Truck bodies (motor vehicles); frame repair shops, automotive; industrial truck repair; welding repair

Valley Center
Sedgwick County

(G-13336)
BARTELS INC
Also Called: True Value
230 N Abilene Ave (67147-2315)
P.O. Box 96 (67147-0096)
PHONE..................................316 755-1853
Tom Bartel, *President*
Michael Bartel, *Treasurer*
EMP: 14
SQ FT: 12,000
SALES (est): 1.2MM **Privately Held**
WEB: www.bartelshardware.com
SIC: 5251 5722 7359 Hardware; household appliance stores; equipment rental & leasing

(G-13337)
BETTER HAULING CO
608 S Ramsey Dr (67147-2164)
PHONE..................................316 943-5865
Mike Davis, *Principal*
EMP: 10 **EST:** 2009
SALES (est): 769.4K **Privately Held**
SIC: 4953 4212 Refuse collection & disposal services; garbage collection & transport, no disposal

(G-13338)
BRYANS HEATING & AC
700 S Ramsey Dr (67147-2168)
PHONE..................................316 755-2447
Bryan Naccarato, *President*
Shelby Naccarato, *Vice Pres*
EMP: 11
SQ FT: 5,000
SALES (est): 1.9MM **Privately Held**
SIC: 1711 Warm air heating & air conditioning contractor

(G-13339)
CENTRAL KANSAS TRUSS CO INC
231 W Industrial St (67147-4913)
P.O. Box 257 (67147-0257)
PHONE..................................316 755-3114
Jeff St Clair, *President*
James Hedden, *Corp Secy*
EMP: 65
SQ FT: 34,000
SALES (est): 6.3MM **Privately Held**
SIC: 2439 Trusses, wooden roof

(G-13340)
DAYSTAR PETROLEUM INC
1321 W 93rd St N (67147-9136)
P.O. Box 360 (67147-0360)
PHONE..................................316 755-3492
Charles D Schmidt, *President*
Colleen Schmidt, *Treasurer*
EMP: 6
SALES: 2MM **Privately Held**
SIC: 6211 1311 Mineral, oil & gas leasing & royalty dealers; crude petroleum & natural gas production

(G-13341)
ELDERSLIE LLC
Also Called: Elderslie Farm
3501 E 101st St N (67147-8902)
PHONE..................................316 680-2637
Katharine Wencel, *Mng Member*
George Elder,
EMP: 12
SQ FT: 1,800
SALES: 150K **Privately Held**
SIC: 0214 2022 5431 5812 Goat farm; natural cheese; fruit & vegetable markets; American restaurant

(G-13342)
FIRST UNITED METHODIST CHURCH
Also Called: Valley Center Pre School
560 N Park Ave (67147-2561)
PHONE..................................316 755-1112
Ji Ju, *Pastor*
EMP: 15
SALES (est): 704.6K **Privately Held**
WEB: www.fumcvc.com
SIC: 8351 8661 Preschool center; religious organizations; Methodist Church

(G-13343)
HORNET CUTTING SYSTEMS LLC
430 W Clay St (67147-2247)
P.O. Box 500 (67147-0500)
PHONE..................................316 755-3683
Brice Turner, *President*
Alan Hamilton, *Vice Pres*
Angela Marsteller, *Purch Agent*
Gerie Byrum, *Controller*
Brandi Smith, *Human Res Mgr*
▼ **EMP:** 42
SQ FT: 96,000
SALES (est): 11.3MM **Privately Held**
SIC: 3541 Plasma process metal cutting machines

(G-13344)
INTRUST BANK NA
142 N Ash Ave (67147-2535)
P.O. Box 185 (67147-0185)
PHONE..................................316 755-1225
Donna Jacob, *Branch Mgr*
EMP: 11
SALES (corp-wide): 134.2MM **Privately Held**
WEB: www.intrustbank.com
SIC: 6021 National commercial banks
HQ: Intrust Bank National Association
105 N Main St
Wichita KS 67202
316 383-1111

(G-13345)
IWP LLC
234 S Sheridan Ct (67147-4704)
PHONE..................................316 308-8507
Shane Isham, *Mng Member*
EMP: 10
SALES (est): 726.5K **Privately Held**
SIC: 1771 1799 Concrete work; waterproofing

(G-13346)
K & N MOTORCYCLES CORPORATION
Also Called: Mid America Power Sports
2537 Sunnydale Ct (67147-8657)
PHONE..................................316 945-8221
Keith Harris, *President*
Ross Reed, *Vice Pres*
EMP: 40
SALES (est): 11.2MM **Privately Held**
WEB: www.mapowersports.com
SIC: 5571 7699 5551 Motorcycles; motorcycle repair service; jet skis

(G-13347)
KANSAS TRAPSHOOTERS ASSN INC
3432 E 117th N (67147)
PHONE..................................316 755-2933
Joe Randle, *Branch Mgr*
EMP: 12
SALES (corp-wide): 1.2MM **Privately Held**
SIC: 8699 Athletic organizations
PA: Kansas Trapshooters Association, Inc.
959 Sw 10th St
Macksville KS 67557
620 546-3519

(G-13348)
MEDICALODGES INC
Also Called: New Horizons of Valley Center
821 W 3rd St (67147-2402)
P.O. Box 186 (67147-0186)
PHONE..................................316 755-1288
Tammi Travis, *Manager*
EMP: 64
SALES (corp-wide): 100.2MM **Privately Held**
WEB: www.medicalodges.com
SIC: 8051 8361 8331 8052 Skilled nursing care facilities; residential care; job training & vocational rehabilitation services; intermediate care facilities

PA: Medicalodges, Inc.
201 W 8th St
Coffeyville KS 67337
620 251-6700

(G-13349)
NATIONAL PLASTICS COLOR INC
Also Called: N P C
100 W Industrial St (67147-4912)
P.O. Box 127 (67147-0127)
PHONE..................................316 755-1273
Steven Sutherland, *President*
Michael Cummings, *Purch Mgr*
Mike McLain, *VP Finance*
Lisa Sutherland, *Sales Staff*
◆ **EMP:** 111
SQ FT: 71,000
SALES (est): 61.2MM **Privately Held**
WEB: www.nationalplasticscolor.com
SIC: 2821 Molding compounds, plastics

(G-13350)
PROFESSIONAL MACHINE & TOOL
Also Called: Stearman Aircraft
510 E 5th St (67147-2605)
P.O. Box 156 (67147-0156)
PHONE..................................316 755-1271
Marc Stearman, *President*
Clint Price, *General Mgr*
Larry G Widmer, *Corp Secy*
EMP: 13
SQ FT: 15,000
SALES (est): 1.5MM **Privately Held**
WEB: www.pmt.kscoxmail.com
SIC: 3728 3599 Aircraft parts & equipment; machine shop, jobbing & repair

(G-13351)
RICOH USA INC
209 W Main St Ste D (67147-2248)
PHONE..................................316 558-5488
Roger Maris, *Principal*
EMP: 23 **Privately Held**
SIC: 5044 Photocopy machines
HQ: Ricoh Usa, Inc.
300 Eagleview Blvd # 200
Exton PA 19341
610 296-8000

(G-13352)
SAFARIK TOOL CO INC
Also Called: STC Aerospace
400 W Clay St (67147-2247)
PHONE..................................316 755-4800
Robert Boorigie, *President*
Allan Safarik, *President*
Ken Best, *General Mgr*
Donald Smith, *Prgrmr*
EMP: 20
SQ FT: 14,000
SALES (est): 1.8MM **Privately Held**
WEB: www.safariktool.com
SIC: 3599 Machine shop, jobbing & repair

(G-13353)
SHARP CONSTRUCTION COMPANY
505 W Clay St (67147-2241)
PHONE..................................316 943-9511
Todd Herman, *Branch Mgr*
EMP: 35
SALES (est): 4.4MM
SALES (corp-wide): 1.7MM **Privately Held**
WEB: www.sharpconstruction.net
SIC: 1542 Commercial & office building contractors
PA: Sharp Construction Company Inc
W Us Hwy 36
Norton KS

(G-13354)
STEARMAN AIRCRAFT PDTS CORP
510 E 5th St (67147-2605)
P.O. Box 156 (67147-0156)
PHONE..................................316 755-1271
Marc Stearman, *CEO*
EMP: 7
SALES (est): 628.2K **Privately Held**
SIC: 3599 Machine shop, jobbing & repair

(G-13355)
SUPERIOR EXCAVATING LLC
10401 N Woodlawn St (67147-8667)
PHONE..................................316 260-1829
Christopher Barnhart,
EMP: 13
SQ FT: 5,760
SALES (est): 1.3MM **Privately Held**
SIC: 1794 1771 Excavation & grading, building construction; concrete work

(G-13356)
TIMBER ROOTS
131 W Industrial St (67147-4912)
PHONE..................................316 755-3114
Jim Hedden, *Owner*
Jerry Hatcher, *Technician*
EMP: 5
SALES (est): 427.7K **Privately Held**
SIC: 2439 Trusses, except roof: laminated lumber

(G-13357)
TRIPLE T PALLETS
11500 N Broadway St (67147-8244)
PHONE..................................316 772-9155
EMP: 22
SALES (est): 2.8MM **Privately Held**
SIC: 2448 Mfg Wood Pallets/Skids

(G-13358)
VALLEY CENTER CITY YARD
545 W Clay St (67147-2241)
P.O. Box 188 (67147-0188)
PHONE..................................316 755-7320
Richard Dunn, *Superintendent*
EMP: 15
SALES (est): 399.3K **Privately Held**
SIC: 7349 Building & office cleaning services

(G-13359)
VALLEY MACHINERY INC
Also Called: Ditch Witch of Kansas
11402 N Broadway St (67147-8228)
PHONE..................................316 755-1911
John Rogers, *President*
Denise Rogers, *Vice Pres*
◆ **EMP:** 15
SQ FT: 10,000
SALES (est): 1.8MM **Privately Held**
WEB: www.ditchwitchofkansas.com
SIC: 5082 Excavating machinery & equipment

(G-13360)
VALLEY OFFSET PRINTING INC
160 S Sheridan Ave (67147-4701)
P.O. Box 298 (67147-0298)
PHONE..................................316 755-0061
Fred Bryant, *President*
Robert Souter, *Prdtn Mgr*
Kevin Kester, *Safety Mgr*
Kenny Haas, *Warehouse Mgr*
Travis Bryant, *Treasurer*
EMP: 50
SQ FT: 37,000
SALES (est): 12MM **Privately Held**
WEB: www.valleyoffset.com
SIC: 2752 2791 2789 Commercial printing, offset; typesetting; bookbinding & related work

Valley Falls
Jefferson County

(G-13361)
BAIN MILLWRIGHTS INC
1508 Willow St (66088-9740)
P.O. Box 67 (66088-0067)
PHONE..................................785 945-3778
Steven M Bain, *CEO*
EMP: 18
SALES (est): 2.4MM **Privately Held**
WEB: www.bainmillwrights.com
SIC: 8711 Building construction consultant

(G-13362)
DAVIS PUBLICATIONS INC (PA)
Also Called: Oskaloosa Independent
416 Broadway St (66088-1304)
P.O. Box 187 (66088-0187)
PHONE..................................785 945-6170
Clark Davis, *CEO*
Marveta Davis, *President*
EMP: 12
SQ FT: 3,500
SALES (est): 959.6K **Privately Held**
SIC: 2711 2752 2791 2789 Newspapers: publishing only, not printed on site; commercial printing, offset; typesetting; bookbinding & related work; secretarial & court reporting

(G-13363)
GRAHEM-HRBERS VFW POST NO 3084
405 Walnut St (66088-1231)
PHONE..................................785 213-6232
Jerry Tullis, *Pt Cmdr*
EMP: 62
SALES (est): 43.8K **Privately Held**
SIC: 8641 Veterans' organization

(G-13364)
HEINEN CUSTOM OPERATIONS INC
13424 Edwards Rd (66088-5103)
P.O. Box 182 (66088-0182)
PHONE..................................785 945-6759
Daniel Heinen, *President*
Marietta Heinen, *Corp Secy*
Douglas Wildeman, *Vice Pres*
EMP: 18
SALES (est): 1.5MM **Privately Held**
SIC: 1521 1542 New construction, single-family houses; commercial & office buildings, renovation & repair; commercial & office building, new construction; farm building construction

(G-13365)
HEINEN P-H-E SERVICES INC
1808 Linn St (66088-1190)
PHONE..................................785 945-6668
Gerald W Heinen, *President*
Karen L Heinen, *Treasurer*
EMP: 12
SQ FT: 30,000
SALES (est): 1.1MM **Privately Held**
SIC: 1711 1731 Plumbing contractors; warm air heating & air conditioning contractor; electrical work

(G-13366)
KENDALL STATE BANK (PA)
406 Broadway St (66088-1304)
P.O. Box 188 (66088-0188)
PHONE..................................785 945-3231
Jayne L Coleman, *President*
Duane Stoskopf, *Chairman*
Gary M Coleman, *Exec VP*
Gary Coleman, *Exec VP*
Kristina J Edwards, *Vice Pres*
EMP: 12 **EST:** 1900
SQ FT: 7,000
SALES: 1.8MM **Privately Held**
WEB: www.kendallstatebank.com
SIC: 6022 State trust companies accepting deposits, commercial

(G-13367)
LINN WOOD PLACE INCORPORATED
Also Called: Linnwood Place
1509 Linn St (66088-1185)
PHONE..................................785 945-3634
Ken Hartle, *President*
Dennis Casey, *Vice Pres*
EMP: 25 **EST:** 1998
SALES (est): 656K **Privately Held**
WEB: www.linnwoodplace.com
SIC: 8322 Senior citizens' center or association

(G-13368)
MIDWEST HEALTH SERVICES INC
Also Called: Valley Health Care Center
400 12th St (66088-1366)
P.O. Box 189 (66088-0189)
PHONE..................................785 945-3832
William Boldridge, *Manager*
EMP: 40
SALES (corp-wide): 32.7MM **Privately Held**
WEB: www.halsteadhealthrehab.com
SIC: 8051 8059 Convalescent home with continuous nursing care; nursing home, except skilled & intermediate care facility
PA: Midwest Health, Inc
3024 Sw Wanamaker Rd # 300
Topeka KS 66614
785 272-1535

(G-13369)
ST FRANCIS HOSPITAL
Also Called: Valley Falls Medical Clinic
403 Sycamore St (66088-1318)
P.O. Box 216 (66088-0216)
PHONE..................................785 945-3263
James Rider, *President*
Frederick Russer, *Principal*
EMP: 20
SALES (est): 1.2MM **Privately Held**
SIC: 8031 Offices & clinics of osteopathic physicians

(G-13370)
VALLEY TRUCKING TRAILER
1401 K4 Hwy (66088-4259)
PHONE..................................785 945-3554
Bill Metzger, *Owner*
EMP: 12
SALES (est): 1.2MM **Privately Held**
SIC: 4212 Local trucking, without storage

Vassar
Osage County

(G-13371)
LAMONT HILL RESORT INC
22975 Highway 368 (66543-9173)
PHONE..................................785 828-3131
Keith Persinger, *President*
EMP: 24
SALES (est): 877.3K **Privately Held**
SIC: 5812 7992 7999 7215 Eating places; public golf courses; tennis courts, outdoor/indoor: non-membership; laundry, coin-operated; trailer park

(G-13372)
U S ARMY CORPS OF ENGINEERS
5260 Pomona Dam Rd (66543-9212)
PHONE..................................785 453-2201
Dave Green, *Branch Mgr*
EMP: 13 **Publicly Held**
WEB: www.sac.usace.army.mil
SIC: 9711 8711 Army; ; building construction consultant
HQ: U.S. Army Corps Of Engineers
441 G St Nw
Washington DC 20314
202 761-0001

Victoria
Ellis County

(G-13373)
DEVELOPMENTAL SVCS NW KANS
604 8th St (67671-9569)
PHONE..................................785 735-2262
Jerry Michaud, *President*
EMP: 11
SALES (est): 126.2K **Privately Held**
SIC: 8322 8399 Social services for the handicapped; health systems agency

(G-13374)
DINKELS CUSTOM WOOD PRODUCTS
Also Called: Dinkel, Dan
1003 390th Ave (67671-9671)
PHONE..................................785 735-2461
Danny Dinkel, *President*
Tracy Dinkel, *Supervisor*
EMP: 10
SALES: 100K **Privately Held**
SIC: 2511 5712 Tables, household: wood; furniture stores

(G-13375)
EXPRESS WELL SERVICE & SUP INC
1110 Us Highway 40 (67671-9517)
P.O. Box 19 (67671-0019)
PHONE..................................785 735-9405
Stephen C Robben, *President*
EMP: 36
SQ FT: 6,000
SALES (est): 2MM **Privately Held**
SIC: 1389 Oil field services

(G-13376)
HEARTLAND COCA-COLA BTLG LLC
1310 Cathedral (67671-9654)
PHONE..................................785 735-9498
EMP: 3433
SALES (corp-wide): 23.9B **Privately Held**
SIC: 5149 2086 Beverages, except coffee & tea; carbonated beverages, nonalcoholic: bottled & canned
PA: Heartland Coca-Cola Bottling Company Llc
9000 Marshall Dr
Lenexa KS

(G-13377)
SMOKEY HILL MEAT PROCESSING
108 Ball Park Rd (67671-9678)
PHONE..................................785 735-2278
Jerry Anzenbach, *President*
EMP: 5
SALES (est): 290K **Privately Held**
SIC: 2011 Meat packing plants

Viola
Sedgwick County

(G-13378)
FARMERS COOPERATIVE ELEV CO
7115 S 183rd St W (67149-9542)
PHONE..................................620 545-7138
Jim Schmitz, *Manager*
EMP: 10
SALES (corp-wide): 15.6MM **Privately Held**
WEB: www.gardenplaincoop.com
SIC: 5153 5191 Grain elevators; animal feeds
PA: Farmers Cooperative Elevator Co Inc
401 N Main St
Garden Plain KS 67050
316 535-2291

(G-13379)
GORGES DAIRY INC
6555 S 183rd St W (67149-9757)
PHONE..................................620 545-7297
Bill Gorges, *President*
Martin Maus, *Vice Pres*
EMP: 15 **EST:** 1949
SALES (est): 1.6MM **Privately Held**
SIC: 4212 Liquid haulage, local

(G-13380)
YOUNG MENS CHRISTIAN ASSOCIAT
Also Called: Camp Hyde
26201 W 71st St S (67149-9729)
PHONE..................................620 545-7290
Sean Amore, *Assoc VP*
Jon Mc Reynolds, *Manager*
Warren Balthazor, *Director*
Bryan Goff, *Director*
Derek Helmers, *Director*
EMP: 135
SALES (corp-wide): 44.6MM **Privately Held**
SIC: 8641 7991 8351 7032 Youth organizations; physical fitness facilities; child day care services; youth camps; individual & family services
PA: The Young Men's Christian Association Of Wichita Kansas
402 N Market St
Wichita KS 67202
316 219-9622

(G-13381)
YOUNGERS AND SONS MFG CO INC
Also Called: None
19223 W State Road 42 (67149-9557)
PHONE..................................620 545-7133
Wayne Youngers, *President*
Neil Youngers, *Vice Pres*
Mike Schippers, *CFO*
▲ **EMP:** 75
SQ FT: 50,000
SALES (est): 16MM **Privately Held**
WEB: www.youngersmfg.com
SIC: 3599 Machine shop, jobbing & repair

WA Keeney
Trego County

(G-13382)
CARGILL INCORPORATED
Old Hwy 40 (67672)
P.O. Box 67, Wakeeney (67672-0067)
PHONE..................................785 743-2288
Brian Ring, *Branch Mgr*
EMP: 44
SALES (corp-wide): 113.4B **Privately Held**
WEB: www.cargill.com
SIC: 5153 2075 2046 2011 Grains; corn; rice, unpolished; wheat; soybean oil, cake or meal; corn oil, meal; corn oil, refined; gluten meal; high fructose corn syrup (HFCS); meat packing plants; beef products from beef slaughtered on site; pork products from pork slaughtered on site; poultry slaughtering & processing
PA: Cargill, Incorporated
15407 Mcginty Rd W
Wayzata MN 55391
952 742-7575

(G-13383)
MIDWEST CONTRACTING & MFG
Also Called: McM
2 Rte 2 (67672)
PHONE..................................785 743-2026
James R Funk, *President*
Bob Funk, *Corp Secy*
EMP: 6
SQ FT: 15,000
SALES: 350K **Privately Held**
SIC: 3523 3449 3944 3842 Farm machinery & equipment; miscellaneous metalwork; tricycles; surgical appliances & supplies

Wakarusa
Shawnee County

(G-13384)
GLACIERS EDGE WINERY & VINYRD
1636 Se 85th St (66546-9640)
PHONE..................................785 862-2298
EMP: 7
SALES (est): 442.8K **Privately Held**
SIC: 2084 Wines

Wakeeney
Trego County

(G-13385)
COUNTY OF TREGO
Also Called: Emergency Medical Services
525 Warren Ave (67672-1809)
PHONE..................................785 743-5337
Sherry Hafliger, *Director*
EMP: 15 **Privately Held**
SIC: 4119 9199 Ambulance service;
PA: County Of Trego
216 N Main St
Wakeeney KS 67672
785 743-5773

(G-13386)
COUNTY OF TREGO
120 S Main St (67672-2423)
PHONE..................................785 743-6441
Dale Pfannenstiel, *Director*
EMP: 21 **Privately Held**
SIC: 4953 9111 Sanitary landfill operation; county supervisors' & executives' offices
PA: County Of Trego
216 N Main St
Wakeeney KS 67672
785 743-5773

(G-13387)
FIRE ALARM SPECIALIST INC
29073 S Rd (67672-2740)
PHONE..................................785 743-5287
Galen Waggoner, *President*
Kathi Waggoner, *CFO*
EMP: 10
SALES: 1MM **Privately Held**
SIC: 3669 Fire alarm apparatus, electric

(G-13388)
FIRST FEDERAL SAVINGS & LOAN
229 N Main St (67672-2136)
P.O. Box 457 (67672-0457)
PHONE..................................785 743-5751
Darrell Gottschalk, *President*
Lori Mattke, *Vice Pres*
Don MAI, *Vice Pres*
Deb Purinton, *Vice Pres*
EMP: 10
SALES: 767K **Privately Held**
SIC: 6022 State commercial banks

(G-13389)
LUTHERAN HOME WA KEENEY
320 South Ave (67672-2649)
PHONE..................................785 743-5787
Steven Sphlipht, *Pastor*
EMP: 40
SALES (est): 1.7MM **Privately Held**
SIC: 8741 Nursing & personal care facility management

(G-13390)
SOLUTIONS NORTH BANK
134 N Main St (67672-2101)
P.O. Box 187 (67672-0187)
PHONE..................................785 743-2104
EMP: 30
SALES (corp-wide): 10.9MM **Privately Held**
SIC: 6022 State commercial banks
PA: Solutions North Bank
123 N Cedar St
Stockton KS 67669
785 425-6721

(G-13391)
SUPER 8 MOTEL
709 S 13th St (67672-2801)
PHONE..................................785 743-6442
Sirena Schneider, *General Mgr*
EMP: 20
SALES (est): 835.7K **Privately Held**
SIC: 7011 Hotels & motels

(G-13392)
TREGO HOSPITAL ENDOWMENT FNDTN
320 N 13th St (67672-2002)
P.O. Box 236 (67672-0236)
PHONE..................................785 743-2182
Ernest J Deines, *Director*
EMP: 25
SALES (est): 118K **Privately Held**
SIC: 6732 Trusts: educational, religious, etc.

(G-13393)
W W DRILLING LLC
675 S 13th St (67672-2800)
P.O. Box 307 (67672-0307)
PHONE..................................785 743-6774
JD Hafliger, *COO*
Dusty Rhoades, *Info Tech Mgr*
EMP: 66
SALES (est): 7MM **Privately Held**
SIC: 1781 Water well drilling

(G-13394)
WAKEENEY TRUCK LINE INC
324 N 4th St (67672-1822)
P.O. Box 296 (67672-0296)
PHONE..................................785 743-6778
Bernie Beydler, *President*
Larry Beydler, *Vice Pres*
Twila Beydler, *Treasurer*
EMP: 15
SALES (est): 1.1MM **Privately Held**
SIC: 4212 4213 Local trucking, without storage; contract haulers

(G-13395)
WESTERN COOPERATIVE ELC ASSN
635 S 13th St (67672-2800)
P.O. Box 278 (67672-0278)
PHONE..................................785 743-5561
Larry Evans, *President*
David L Schneider, *General Mgr*
EMP: 32 **EST:** 1945
SQ FT: 30,000
SALES (est): 37.7MM **Privately Held**
SIC: 4911 Distribution, electric power

(G-13396)
WESTERN KANSAS WORLD INC
Also Called: World Office
205 N Main St (67672-2104)
P.O. Box 218 (67672-0218)
PHONE..................................785 743-2155
Jack Millard, *President*
Jerry Millard, *Vice Pres*
La Vanche Millard, *Treasurer*
Cathy Millard, *Admin Sec*
EMP: 6
SALES: 300K **Privately Held**
SIC: 2711 Newspapers: publishing only, not printed on site

Wakefield
Clay County

(G-13397)
A&L HAY FARMS INC
2255 3rd Rd (67487-9261)
PHONE..................................785 461-5339
Gary Luttman, *President*
Sam Ault, *Vice Pres*
EMP: 11
SALES (est): 1.6MM **Privately Held**
SIC: 0723 Hay baling services

(G-13398)
BEVERLY ENTERPRISES-KANSAS LLC
Also Called: Wakefield Rehabilitation Ctr
509 Grove St (67487-9159)
PHONE..................................785 461-5417
Cheryl Blanken, *Exec Dir*
EMP: 44
SALES (corp-wide): 393.8MM **Privately Held**
SIC: 8051 Skilled nursing care facilities
HQ: Beverly Enterprises-Kansas, Llc
1 1000 Beverly Way
Fort Smith AR 72919
479 201-2000

(G-13399)
ZOOK CONSTRUCTION
1454 3600 Ave (67487-9039)
PHONE..................................785 388-2183
Verl Zook, *Partner*
Vernon Zook, *Partner*
EMP: 10
SALES (est): 972.6K **Privately Held**
SIC: 1623 Telephone & communication line construction

Walton
Harvey County

(G-13400)
FARMERS GRAIN COOPERATIVE
E Hwy 50 (67151)
PHONE..................................620 837-3313
Dave Studibaker, *General Mgr*

GEOGRAPHIC

Terri Washburn, *Production*
Larry Raskopf, *Credit Mgr*
Phil Timken, *Manager*
Bradley Ryan, *E-Business*
EMP: 41 **EST:** 1958
SQ FT: 720
SALES: 14.6MM **Privately Held**
SIC: 5153 5191 5541 Grains; feed; seeds: field, garden & flower; fertilizer & fertilizer materials; chemicals, agricultural; filling stations, gasoline

(G-13401)
MID-KANSAS COOPERATIVE ASSN
100 Main St (67151)
PHONE..................................620 837-3313
Brad Daniels, *Manager*
EMP: 15
SALES (corp-wide): 371.5MM **Privately Held**
WEB: www.mkcoop.com
SIC: 5153 5191 Grain elevators; farm supplies; chemicals, agricultural; fertilizer & fertilizer materials
PA: Mid-Kansas Cooperative Association
307 W Cole St
Moundridge KS 67107
620 345-6328

Wamego
Pottawatomie County

(G-13402)
ADVOCATE HOME SPECIALTY CARE
Also Called: Advacare
811 Poplar St (66547-1506)
P.O. Box 63 (66547-0063)
PHONE..................................785 456-8910
Rhonda Platt, *CEO*
Lori Rogers, *Administration*
EMP: 65
SALES (est): 1MM **Privately Held**
WEB: www.advocarehomecare.com
SIC: 8082 Visiting nurse service

(G-13403)
AT HOME ASSISTED CARE
503 Lincoln Ave (66547-1655)
PHONE..................................785 473-7007
Woody Shoemaker,
EMP: 50
SALES (est): 56.7K **Privately Held**
SIC: 8082 Home health care services

(G-13404)
BANK OF FLINT HILLS (PA)
806 5th St (66547-1460)
P.O. Box 226 (66547-0226)
PHONE..................................785 456-2221
Lance White, *President*
Charles White, *President*
Margo Pray, *COO*
Matt Bulk, *Vice Pres*
Jacque Ekart, *Vice Pres*
EMP: 26 **EST:** 1875
SALES: 12.2MM **Privately Held**
WEB: www.fnbofwamego.com
SIC: 6022 State commercial banks

(G-13405)
BENNINGTON STATE BANK
1800 Farrell Dr (66547-9778)
P.O. Box 21 (66547-0021)
PHONE..................................785 456-1806
Rod George, *Manager*
EMP: 11
SALES (corp-wide): 33.3MM **Privately Held**
SIC: 6022 State trust companies accepting deposits, commercial
PA: Bennington State Bank
2130 S Ohio St
Salina KS 67401
785 827-5522

(G-13406)
BLUESTEM ELECTRIC COOP INC (PA)
614 E Hwy 24 (66547)
P.O. Box 513, Clay Center (67432-0513)
PHONE..................................785 456-2212
Michael M Morton, *Manager*
EMP: 13 **EST:** 1941
SQ FT: 5,000
SALES: 17.1MM **Privately Held**
WEB: www.bluestemelectric.com
SIC: 4911 Distribution, electric power

(G-13407)
BUTLER PLUMBING & HEATING
315 Lincoln Ave (66547-1629)
PHONE..................................785 456-8345
Dennis Butler, *President*
Betty Butler, *Vice Pres*
EMP: 10
SQ FT: 5,000
SALES (est): 1.1MM **Privately Held**
SIC: 1711 Plumbing contractors; warm air heating & air conditioning contractor

(G-13408)
CARLEY CONSTRUCTION CO INC
16875 Ebel Rd (66547-9691)
PHONE..................................785 456-2882
Thad Carley, *President*
EMP: 10
SALES (est): 1.4MM **Privately Held**
SIC: 1521 General remodeling, single-family houses

(G-13409)
CATERPILLAR INC
400 Work Tool Rd (66547-1299)
PHONE..................................309 675-1000
Brandi Herman, *Sales Staff*
Michele March, *Branch Mgr*
EMP: 55
SALES (corp-wide): 54.7B **Publicly Held**
SIC: 3519 3511 6153 Internal combustion engines; turbines & turbine generator sets; short-term business credit
PA: Caterpillar Inc.
510 Lake Cook Rd Ste 100
Deerfield IL 60015
224 551-4000

(G-13410)
CATERPILLAR WORK TOOLS INC (HQ)
400 Work Tool Rd (66547-1299)
P.O. Box 6 (66547-0006)
PHONE..................................785 456-2224
Paolo Fellin, *President*
Chris Langbardt, *Vice Pres*
Warren Wereaui, *Vice Pres*
Mike Guyer, *Treasurer*
Phil Richards, *Marketing Mgr*
◆ **EMP:** 280
SQ FT: 100,000
SALES (est): 75MM
SALES (corp-wide): 54.7B **Publicly Held**
SIC: 3531 Construction machinery attachments
PA: Caterpillar Inc.
510 Lake Cook Rd Ste 100
Deerfield IL 60015
224 551-4000

(G-13411)
CATERPILLAR WORK TOOLS INC
600 Balderson Blvd (66547-1836)
PHONE..................................785 456-2224
Steve Oshea, *Engineer*
Chris C Langbardt, *Branch Mgr*
EMP: 19
SALES (corp-wide): 54.7B **Publicly Held**
SIC: 3531 Construction machinery attachments
HQ: Caterpillar Work Tools, Inc.
400 Work Tool Rd
Wamego KS 66547
785 456-2224

(G-13412)
CITY OF WAMEGO
Also Called: City Elec & Water Dept
430 Lincoln Ave (66547-1632)
P.O. Box 86 (66547-0086)
PHONE..................................785 456-9598
Nerl Page, *Manager*
EMP: 40 **Privately Held**
WEB: www.wamegocityhospital.com
SIC: 4931 Electric & other services combined
PA: City Of Wamego
530 Lincoln Ave
Wamego KS 66547
785 456-9697

(G-13413)
CITY OF WAMEGO
Also Called: Wamego City Hospital
711 Genn Dr (66547-1179)
PHONE..................................785 456-2295
Debbie Sobriss, *Manager*
Michelle Crisler, *Exec Sec*
EMP: 50 **Privately Held**
WEB: www.wamegocityhospital.com
SIC: 8062 8011 7991 General medical & surgical hospitals; clinic, operated by physicians; aerobic dance & exercise classes
PA: City Of Wamego
530 Lincoln Ave
Wamego KS 66547
785 456-9697

(G-13414)
DICKS THRIFTWAY
1009 Lincoln Ave (66547-1501)
P.O. Box 191 (66547-0191)
PHONE..................................785 456-2525
Richard D Dreher, *Owner*
EMP: 25
SQ FT: 10,000
SALES (est): 2MM **Privately Held**
SIC: 5411 7841 Grocery stores, independent; video disk/tape rental to the general public

(G-13415)
DYMAX INC
402 Miller Dr (66547-1209)
P.O. Box 297 (66547-0297)
PHONE..................................785 456-2705
Clark Balderson, *Ch of Bd*
Scott Balderson, *President*
Mary A Balderson, *Corp Secy*
Kevin Baker, *Foreman/Supr*
Carl Williams, *Purch Dir*
◆ **EMP:** 48
SQ FT: 32,000
SALES (est): 12.8MM **Privately Held**
WEB: www.dikenga.com
SIC: 3531 Construction machinery

(G-13416)
DYNAMIC MANAGEMENT SOLUTIONS
5566 Maefield Dr Ste B (66547-9109)
PHONE..................................785 456-1794
Jay Hildreth, *President*
EMP: 30
SALES (est): 1.6MM **Privately Held**
SIC: 8741 Management services

(G-13417)
E & R MACHINE INC
315 Sandusky Ave (66547-1600)
P.O. Box 91 (66547-0091)
PHONE..................................785 456-2373
Todd Ebert, *President*
Janet Ebert, *Vice Pres*
EMP: 6
SQ FT: 2,400
SALES: 950K **Privately Held**
SIC: 3599 Machine shop, jobbing & repair

(G-13418)
EBERT CONSTRUCTION CO INC
103 E Valley St (66547-9513)
P.O. Box 198 (66547-0198)
PHONE..................................785 456-2455
James E Ebert, *Ch of Bd*
Dirk Riniker, *President*
Lisa Diederich, *Vice Pres*
James E Ebert II, *Vice Pres*
EMP: 50 **EST:** 1958
SQ FT: 13,000
SALES: 12.1MM **Privately Held**
WEB: www.ebertconstruction.com
SIC: 1794 1611 Excavation & grading, building construction; general contractor, highway & street construction

(G-13419)
EBI CONSTRUCTION INC
4745 N Highway 99 (66547-9110)
PHONE..................................785 456-7449
Dennis Weixelman, *President*
Dennis Pat Weixelman, *President*
Susan Weixelman, *Vice Pres*
Angela Purkeypyle, *Admin Sec*
EMP: 15
SQ FT: 3,800
SALES (est): 1.2MM **Privately Held**
SIC: 1771 Foundation & footing contractor

(G-13420)
ELECTRICAL CONCEPTS INC
Also Called: Eci Systems
4525 Horizon Trl (66547-9245)
PHONE..................................785 456-8896
Christian Dodge, *President*
EMP: 16
SALES (est): 1.9MM **Privately Held**
SIC: 1731 1711 General electrical contractor; plumbing, heating, air-conditioning contractors

(G-13421)
EVANGELICAL LTHRN GOOD SMRTN (PA)
Also Called: Good Samaritan Center
2011 Grandview Dr (66547-1159)
PHONE..................................785 456-9482
Kandi Bullock, *Technology*
Bea Morris, *Director*
Amy Steiner, *Nursing Dir*
Linda Hensley, *Food Svc Dir*
Candi Bullock, *Executive*
EMP: 62 **EST:** 1969
SQ FT: 20,000
SALES (est): 917.3K **Privately Held**
SIC: 8051 6513 Convalescent home with continuous nursing care; apartment building operators

(G-13422)
EVANGELICAL LUTHERAN
Also Called: Good Samaritan Soc - Vly Vista
2011 Grandview Dr (66547-1159)
P.O. Box 5038, Sioux Falls SD (57117-5038)
PHONE..................................785 456-9482
Justin Williams, *Branch Mgr*
EMP: 77 **Privately Held**
WEB: www.good-sam.com
SIC: 8059 8361 Nursing home, except skilled & intermediate care facility; residential care
HQ: The Evangelical Lutheran Good Samaritan Society
4800 W 57th St
Sioux Falls SD 57108
866 928-1635

(G-13423)
FRANK E SEUFERT & ASSOCIATES
411 Lincoln Ave Ste B (66547-1654)
P.O. Box 170 (66547-0170)
PHONE..................................785 456-2782
Frank Seufert, *CEO*
EMP: 10
SALES (est): 832.3K **Privately Held**
SIC: 6411 Insurance agents

(G-13424)
GRAN VILLAS OF WAMEGO
Also Called: Medica Lodges
1607 4th St (66547-1915)
PHONE..................................785 456-8997
Jan Debord, *Administration*
EMP: 20
SALES (est): 215K **Privately Held**
SIC: 8059 Rest home, with health care

(G-13425)
INDEPENDENT ORDER ODDFELLOWS
Also Called: Wamego Lodge No 80
17165 Elm Slough Rd (66547-9632)
PHONE..................................785 456-9493
Rolland Wohler, *President*
Kennthe McCarter, *Admin Sec*
Kennteh McCarter, *Admin Sec*
EMP: 20 **EST:** 1872
SALES (est): 302K **Privately Held**
SIC: 8641 Civic social & fraternal associations

(G-13426)
KANEQUIP INC (PA)
Also Called: Kubota Authorized Dealer
18035 E Us Highway 24 (66547-9790)
P.O. Box 310 (66547-0310)
PHONE..................................785 456-2041
James Meinhardt, *President*
Jim Burke, *Vice Pres*
Debbie Figge, *Opers Staff*
Michelle Morton, *Accountant*
Judy Jones, *Bookkeeper*
▲ **EMP**: 35
SQ FT: 56,000
SALES (est): 117MM **Privately Held**
SIC: **5999** 5083 Farm machinery; farm & garden machinery

(G-13427)
KAW VALLEY EXTERMINATOR
411 Lincoln Ave (66547-1653)
P.O. Box 275 (66547-0275)
PHONE..................................785 456-7357
Paul Bearmen, *Owner*
Trace Bearmen, *Manager*
EMP: 44
SALES (est): 2MM **Privately Held**
SIC: **7342** Exterminating & fumigating

(G-13428)
KAW VALLEY STATE BANK & TR CO (PA)
1015 Kaw Valley Park Cir (66547-9763)
P.O. Box 245 (66547-0245)
PHONE..................................785 456-2025
Edward Martin, *President*
Lanny B Exec, *Exec VP*
Casey Blume, *Senior VP*
Shawn Branfort, *Vice Pres*
Lacinda Heller, *Vice Pres*
EMP: 17 **EST**: 1914
SALES: 8.4MM **Privately Held**
WEB: www.kvsb.net
SIC: **6022** State trust companies accepting deposits, commercial

(G-13429)
MS BIOTEC LLC
1300 Kaw Valley Rd (66547-9663)
PHONE..................................785 456-1388
Leander Van Der Walt, *CEO*
Celine Aperce, *Research*
EMP: 27
SALES (est): 2MM
SALES (corp-wide): 3.6MM **Privately Held**
SIC: **2836** Biological products, except diagnostic
PA: Ms Biotech, Inc.
6025 S Quebec St Ste 250
Englewood CO 80111
303 551-9244

(G-13430)
NEK CAP INC
Also Called: Nek-Cap Headstart
714 Plum St (66547-1834)
PHONE..................................785 456-9165
Rose Sigmund, *Director*
EMP: 14
SALES (corp-wide): 10.1MM **Privately Held**
SIC: **8351** Head start center, except in conjunction with school
PA: Nek Cap, Inc.
1260 220th St
Hiawatha KS 66434
785 742-2222

(G-13431)
OZ WINERY
417 Lincoln Ave Ste A (66547-1631)
P.O. Box 342 (66547-0342)
PHONE..................................785 456-7417
Brooke Balderson, *Owner*
Noah Wright, *Owner*
EMP: 10 **EST**: 2010
SALES (est): 1MM **Privately Held**
SIC: **2084** Wines

(G-13432)
P & F SERVICES INC
Also Called: B & B Outservices
16375 6th Street Rd (66547-9247)
PHONE..................................785 456-9401
Ruthann Boatwright, *President*
Ted Baotwright, *General Mgr*
EMP: 10
SQ FT: 900
SALES: 310K **Privately Held**
SIC: **1522** Residential construction

(G-13433)
PATRICK A BLANCHARD MD
711 Genn Dr (66547-1179)
PHONE..................................785 456-8778
Patrick A Blanchard, *Owner*
EMP: 10
SALES (est): 236.7K **Privately Held**
SIC: **8011** General & family practice, physician/surgeon

(G-13434)
POTTAWATOMIE CNTY EMRGNCY SVCS
Also Called: Pottawtmie Cnty Ambulance Svcs
514 Plum St (66547-1830)
PHONE..................................785 456-0911
Brian Smith, *Director*
Brett F Howard, *Director*
EMP: 45
SALES: 71.5K **Privately Held**
SIC: **4119** Ambulance service

(G-13435)
PREFERRED REGISTRY OF NURSES
Also Called: Prn Home Health Hospice
1010 Lincoln Ave (66547-1502)
PHONE..................................785 456-8628
Ronda Platt, *President*
Pam Sulmer, *Administration*
EMP: 15
SALES (est): 985.5K **Privately Held**
WEB: www.prnhomehealthhospice.com
SIC: **8082** Visiting nurse service

(G-13436)
PRIZM INCORPORATED
1304 Kaw Valley Rd (66547-9663)
PHONE..................................785 456-1831
Gary Meidinger, *President*
Michele Johnson, *Vice Pres*
▲ **EMP**: 14
SALES (est): 1.5MM **Privately Held**
SIC: **5199** 8661 Gifts & novelties; religious organizations

(G-13437)
R W MILLING COMPANY INC
Also Called: R W H Farms
18124 Military Trail Rd (66547)
P.O. Box 263 (66547-0263)
PHONE..................................785 456-7866
Norman Hupe, *President*
Chris Hupe, *Vice Pres*
Jeanette Hupe, *Treasurer*
EMP: 7
SQ FT: 15,000
SALES (est): 1.2MM **Privately Held**
WEB: www.rwmilling.com
SIC: **2048** Livestock feeds; alfalfa or alfalfa meal, prepared as animal feed

(G-13438)
R-TECH TOOL & MACHINE INC
403 Miller Dr (66547-1209)
P.O. Box 293 (66547-0293)
PHONE..................................785 456-9541
Douglas Routh, *President*
Jeff Wade, *Supervisor*
Rachelle Routh, *Admin Sec*
EMP: 15
SQ FT: 15,000
SALES: 9MM **Privately Held**
SIC: **3599** Machine shop, jobbing & repair

(G-13439)
REED COMPANY LLC
4455 N Highway 99 (66547-9106)
PHONE..................................785 456-7333
Dave Williams,
Donald Ebert,
Rhonda Trudo,
EMP: 20
SALES: 7.2MM **Privately Held**
WEB: www.reedco.net
SIC: **5082** 5521 General construction machinery & equipment; pickups & vans, used

(G-13440)
REESE & NOVELLY PA (PA)
Also Called: Reese & Novelly Cpa's PA
514 Lincoln Ave (66547-1634)
PHONE..................................785 456-2000
Rick Reese, *Partner*
Carol McCullough, *Partner*
Nick Novelly, *Partner*
EMP: 12
SQ FT: 800
SALES (est): 1.7MM **Privately Held**
SIC: **8721** Certified public accountant

(G-13441)
SOMETHING DIFFERENT INC (PA)
Also Called: A Uniform For You
1008 Kaw Valley Park Cir # 501 (66547-9707)
PHONE..................................785 537-1171
Josephine Smith, *President*
Stephanie Chitwood, *Vice Pres*
EMP: 5 **EST**: 1979
SQ FT: 1,500
SALES (est): 669.4K **Privately Held**
SIC: **5699** 2395 7219 Uniforms; embroidery & art needlework; garment alteration & repair shop

(G-13442)
STORMONT-VAIL HEALTHCARE INC
Also Called: Cotton O'Neil Wamego
1704 Commercial Cir (66547-9690)
PHONE..................................785 456-2207
Gina Suther, *Principal*
EMP: 25
SALES (corp-wide): 719MM **Privately Held**
SIC: **8062** 8011 General medical & surgical hospitals; general & family practice, physician/surgeon
PA: Stormont-Vail Healthcare, Inc.
1500 Sw 10th Ave
Topeka KS 66604
785 354-6000

(G-13443)
TALLGRASS COMMODITIES LLC
420 Lincoln Ave (66547-1632)
P.O. Box 110 (66547-0110)
PHONE..................................855 494-8484
Justin Heim, *CFO*
Richard Wollenberg, *Mng Member*
Joe Ish,
Jason Shamburg,
EMP: 20 **EST**: 2007
SQ FT: 5,000
SALES (est): 109.2MM **Privately Held**
SIC: **0119** Feeder grains

(G-13444)
THREE RIVERS INC (PA)
Also Called: THREE RIVERS INDEPENDENT LIVIN
504 Miller Dr (66547-1280)
P.O. Box 408 (66547-0408)
PHONE..................................785 456-9915
Linda Mackey, *Office Mgr*
Audrey Schremmer, *Exec Dir*
EMP: 12
SQ FT: 5,000
SALES: 3.3MM **Privately Held**
SIC: **8322** Social services for the handicapped

(G-13445)
VALLEY MOVING COMPANY LLC
18162 Hwy 24 Ste 1 (66547)
P.O. Box 261 (66547-0261)
PHONE..................................785 456-2400
Randal Hupe, *Owner*
EMP: 12
SALES (est): 968K **Privately Held**
SIC: **4213** 1799 Heavy hauling; building mover, including houses

(G-13446)
VIA CHRISTI HEALTH INC
711 Genn Dr (66547-1179)
PHONE..................................785 456-6288
Stacia Robinson, *Office Mgr*
EMP: 53
SALES (corp-wide): 25.3B **Privately Held**
SIC: **8011** Internal medicine, physician/surgeon
HQ: Via Christi Health, Inc.
2622 W Central Ave # 102
Wichita KS 67203

(G-13447)
VINTAGE PARK ASSISTED LIVING
1607 4th St (66547-1915)
PHONE..................................785 456-8997
Jennifer Payton, *Director*
EMP: 12
SALES (est): 403.3K **Privately Held**
SIC: **8051** Skilled nursing care facilities

(G-13448)
WAMEGO CHMBER CMMRCE MINSTREET
529 Lincoln Ave (66547-1633)
PHONE..................................785 456-7849
Jody Price, *President*
Chris Hupe, *Vice Pres*
Dwight Faulkner, *Treasurer*
EMP: 14
SALES: 166.8K **Privately Held**
WEB: www.wamegochamber.com
SIC: **8611** Chamber of Commerce

(G-13449)
WAMEGO COUNTRY CLUB INC
1900 Country Club Dr (66547-1101)
P.O. Box 177 (66547-0177)
PHONE..................................785 456-2649
Daryn Soldan, *President*
Trampis Nickel, *Superintendent*
EMP: 20
SQ FT: 200
SALES: 869.4K **Privately Held**
WEB: www.wamegogolf.com
SIC: **7997** Country club, membership; golf club, membership

(G-13450)
WAMEGO DENTAL CENTER INC
1519 W Us Highway 24 (66547-1322)
P.O. Box 26 (66547-0026)
PHONE..................................785 456-2330
Steven Bates, *President*
Timothy Woods, *Corp Secy*
EMP: 11
SALES (est): 763.3K **Privately Held**
SIC: **8021** Offices & clinics of dentists

(G-13451)
WAMEGO HOSPITAL ASSOCIATION
Also Called: WAMEGO HEALTH CENTER
711 Genn Dr (66547-1179)
PHONE..................................785 456-2295
Shannon Flach, *CEO*
Sara Powers, *Director*
EMP: 70
SALES: 12.2MM **Privately Held**
SIC: **8062** General medical & surgical hospitals

(G-13452)
WAMEGO INN AND SUITES
1300 Lilac Ln (66547-1218)
P.O. Box 183 (66547-0183)
PHONE..................................785 458-8888
Tom Doperalski, *President*
Tom Debraski, *President*
EMP: 10
SALES (est): 394.2K **Privately Held**
SIC: **7011** Motels

(G-13453)
WAMEGO LUMBER CO INC
Also Called: Valley Moving
18612 E Highway 24 Ste 1 (66547)
PHONE..................................785 456-2400
Penny Hupe, *President*
Randall Hupe, *Vice Pres*
EMP: 14
SALES (est): 1.1MM **Privately Held**
SIC: **1521** New construction, single-family houses; general remodeling, single-family houses

(G-13454)
WAMEGO RECREATION DEPT
430 Lincoln Ave (66547-1632)
P.O. Box 86 (66547-0086)
PHONE..................................785 456-8810
Merl Page, *Manager*
Kristen Jones, *Director*
EMP: 26
SALES (est): 367K **Privately Held**
WEB: www.wamego.com
SIC: 7999 Recreation center

(G-13455)
WAMEGO RECYCLING LLC
18070 E Us Highway 24 (66547-9790)
P.O. Box 378 (66547-0378)
PHONE..................................785 456-2439
Scott Dinger, *Owner*
EMP: 20
SALES (est): 3.6MM **Privately Held**
SIC: 3569 Baling machines, for scrap metal, paper or similar material

(G-13456)
WAMEGO TELEPHONE COMPANY INC (PA)
Also Called: Wamego Telecom Comapny
1009 Lincoln Ave (66547-1501)
P.O. Box 25 (66547-0025)
PHONE..................................785 456-1001
Steven Sackrider, *President*
Alfred Eichman, *Vice Pres*
Ken Blew, *Plant Mgr*
Alan D Weber, *Treasurer*
Jim Jones, *IT/INT Sup*
EMP: 25 **EST:** 1912
SQ FT: 5,600
SALES: 10.6MM **Privately Held**
WEB: www.usd320.org
SIC: 4813 Local telephone communications

(G-13457)
WOLFGANG CONSTRUCTION LLC
17755 High St (66547-9563)
PHONE..................................785 456-8729
Kyle Wolfgang,
EMP: 12 **EST:** 2007
SALES (est): 1.1MM **Privately Held**
SIC: 1521 Single-family housing construction

(G-13458)
WTC COMMUNICATIONS INC
1009 Lincoln Ave (66547-1501)
P.O. Box 25 (66547-0025)
PHONE..................................785 456-1000
Steve Sackrider, *President*
Wayne Ubel, *Treasurer*
Earl Daylor, *Admin Sec*
EMP: 10
SQ FT: 5,550
SALES (est): 369.5K
SALES (corp-wide): 10.6MM **Privately Held**
WEB: www.usd320.org
SIC: 4813 Local telephone communications
PA: Wamego Telephone Company, Inc.
1009 Lincoln Ave
Wamego KS 66547
785 456-1001

Washington
Washington County

(G-13459)
BEKEMEYER ENTERPRISES INC
1497 17th Rd (66968-8407)
PHONE..................................785 325-2274
Glen Bekemeyer, *President*
Gregory Bekemeyer, *Vice Pres*
Gayle Beckemeyer, *Treasurer*
Patricia Beckenmeyer, *Admin Sec*
EMP: 10
SQ FT: 1,200
SALES (est): 1.7MM **Privately Held**
SIC: 0212 5191 0191 0213 Beef cattle except feedlots; feed; seeds: field, garden & flower; general farms, primarily crop; hog feedlot; agricultural machinery & equipment; farm to market haulage, local

(G-13460)
BRADFORD BUILT INC
303 C St (66968-1908)
PHONE..................................785 325-3300
Brad Portenier, *President*
EMP: 20
SALES (est): 5.9MM **Privately Held**
WEB: www.bradfordbuilt.com
SIC: 3523 5511 3715 3446 Hog feeding, handling & watering equipment; trailers & wagons, farm; new & used car dealers; truck trailers; architectural metalwork; sheet metalwork; fabricated plate work (boiler shop)

(G-13461)
BRUNA BROTHERS IMPLEMENT LLC
Also Called: Bruna Implement Co
1613 Quivira Rd (66968-2335)
P.O. Box 162 (66968-0162)
PHONE..................................785 325-2232
Ted F Bruna, *Manager*
EMP: 20
SALES (corp-wide): 26.5MM **Privately Held**
WEB: www.brunaimplementco.com
SIC: 5083 5072 5191 7699 Farm equipment parts & supplies; agricultural machinery & equipment; tractors, agricultural; hardware; farm supplies; agricultural equipment repair services; lawnmowers & tractors
PA: Bruna Brothers Implement, Llc
1128 Pony Express Hwy
Marysville KS 66508
785 562-5304

(G-13462)
CENTENNIAL HOMESTEAD INC
311 E 2nd St (66968-2028)
PHONE..................................785 325-2361
Michael Kongs, *Principal*
Mark Chapin, *Vice Pres*
Deloris Syring, *Director*
EMP: 55
SALES: 1.6MM **Privately Held**
SIC: 8052 Intermediate care facilities

(G-13463)
EARTHMOVERS INC
Also Called: Earthmovers International
1802 Industrial Park Dr (66968-2337)
PHONE..................................785 325-2236
Richard T Bailey, *President*
▼ **EMP:** 18 **EST:** 1993
SQ FT: 9,600
SALES: 267.7K **Privately Held**
WEB: www.earthtrucks.com
SIC: 1629 Earthmoving contractor

(G-13464)
HERRS MACHINE
1745 Prospect Blvd (66968-1840)
PHONE..................................785 325-2875
Lawrence Herrs, *Owner*
Cara Herrs, *Co-Owner*
EMP: 7
SQ FT: 16,350
SALES (est): 663.4K **Privately Held**
SIC: 7699 7539 3519 3599 Hydraulic equipment repair; machine shop, automotive; diesel engine rebuilding; machine shop, jobbing & repair

(G-13465)
HOMESTEAD INC
Also Called: Homestead Nursing Home
311 E 2nd St (66968-2028)
PHONE..................................785 325-2361
Deloris Syring, *Director*
EMP: 54
SQ FT: 10,000
SALES (est): 1MM **Privately Held**
SIC: 8059 8051 Convalescent home; skilled nursing care facilities

(G-13466)
KEESECKER AGRI BUSINESS INC
2069 Prairie Rd (66968-8620)
PHONE..................................785 325-3134
Dale Keesecker, *President*
Lila Keesecker, *Corp Secy*
EMP: 20
SQ FT: 2,000
SALES (est): 3.3MM **Privately Held**
WEB: www.keesecker.com
SIC: 0213 0119 5083 Hogs; feeder grains; livestock equipment

(G-13467)
KIER ENTERPRISES INC (PA)
Also Called: Kier's Thriftway
126 E 2nd St (66968-1916)
PHONE..................................785 325-2150
Travis Kier, *President*
EMP: 50 **EST:** 1951
SQ FT: 10,000
SALES (est): 4.6MM **Privately Held**
SIC: 5411 5421 5431 7841 Grocery stores, independent; meat markets, including freezer provisioners; fruit stands or markets; vegetable stands or markets; video tape rental; filling stations, gasoline

(G-13468)
KSDS INC
120 W 7th St (66968-2222)
PHONE..................................785 325-2256
Roger Post, *President*
Ed Henry, *Vice Pres*
Annette Kohlmeyer, *Technician*
Mary Sawin, *Assistant*
EMP: 10
SALES: 381.5K **Privately Held**
WEB: www.ksds.org
SIC: 0752 Animal specialty services

(G-13469)
MID CONTINENT FARMS
400 E College St (66968-2005)
PHONE..................................785 325-2089
Greg Stewart, *Partner*
Conrad Stewart, *Partner*
Deanna Stewart, *Partner*
Debra Stewart, *Partner*
Kent Stewart, *Partner*
EMP: 10
SALES (est): 570K **Privately Held**
SIC: 0219 5154 0191 5153 General livestock; cattle; general farms, primarily crop; grains

(G-13470)
WASHINGTON 1ST BANCO INC (PA)
Also Called: 1st National Bank
101 C St (66968-1904)
P.O. Box 215 (66968-0215)
PHONE..................................785 325-2221
Tim Matlock, *President*
Paul Judd, *Director*
Roger Judd, *Director*
EMP: 11
SQ FT: 16,000
SALES (est): 2.8MM **Privately Held**
SIC: 6022 State commercial banks

(G-13471)
WASHINGTON FNB
101 C St (66968-1904)
P.O. Box 215 (66968-0215)
PHONE..................................785 325-2221
Tim Matlack, *President*
EMP: 10 **EST:** 1883
SQ FT: 16,000
SALES (est): 2.8MM **Privately Held**
WEB: www.fnbwashington.com
SIC: 6022 7371 State commercial banks; computer software development & applications
PA: Washington 1st Banco, Inc.
101 C St
Washington KS 66968
785 325-2221

Waterville
Marshall County

(G-13472)
CITIZENS STATE BANK
124 E Commercial St (66548-8918)
P.O. Box 10 (66548-0010)
PHONE..................................785 363-2521
Stephen Hendrickson, *Vice Pres*
EMP: 15
SALES (corp-wide): 1.7MM **Privately Held**
WEB: www.csbmarysville.com
SIC: 6022 State trust companies accepting deposits, commercial
HQ: Citizens State Bank
800 Broadway
Marysville KS 66508
785 562-2186

(G-13473)
CITY OF WATERVILLE
Also Called: Waterville Fire Department
136 E Commercial St (66548-8918)
P.O. Box 387 (66548-0387)
PHONE..................................785 363-2367
Don King, *Mayor*
Colby Hearn, *Council Mbr*
Tony Mann, *Council Mbr*
Alex Nolte, *Council Mbr*
Jim Oatney, *Council Mbr*
EMP: 26 **Privately Held**
SIC: 9121 9511 1623 9199 ; ; water, sewer & utility lines; general government administration

Wathena
Doniphan County

(G-13474)
FARMERS STATE BANK
211 Saint Joseph St (66090-1284)
P.O. Box 219 (66090-0219)
PHONE..................................785 989-4431
Lambert A Libel III, *President*
EMP: 14 **EST:** 1903
SALES: 2.8MM **Privately Held**
SIC: 6022 State trust companies accepting deposits, commercial

(G-13475)
MCON LLC
1004 Vernon Rd (66090)
P.O. Box 403 (66090-0403)
PHONE..................................785 989-4550
Jim Miller,
Lindsey Miller,
Tyler Miller,
EMP: 15
SALES (est): 4.4MM **Privately Held**
SIC: 1542 Commercial & office building contractors

(G-13476)
MIDLAND STEEL COMPANY (PA)
202 Boeh Ln (66090)
P.O. Box 527 (66090-0527)
PHONE..................................785 989-4442
Douglas Bibens, *President*
Calvin Bibens, *Chairman*
Bob Housh, *Corp Secy*
Donald Jones, *Exec VP*
Don Weingartner, *Project Mgr*
EMP: 55
SQ FT: 28,000
SALES (est): 12.1MM **Privately Held**
WEB: www.midlandsteelco.com
SIC: 3441 Building components, structural steel

(G-13477)
MK MINERALS INC
1025 Vernon Rd (66090-1258)
PHONE..................................785 989-4566
Arlene Robinson, *Manager*
EMP: 7
SALES (corp-wide): 6MM **Privately Held**
WEB: www.mkminerals.com
SIC: 3274 Lime
PA: Mk Minerals Inc.
1025 Vernon Rd
Wathena KS 66090
785 989-4566

(G-13478)
ST JOSEPH TRUSS COMPANY INC (PA)
2257 169th Rd (66090-4211)
PHONE..................................785 989-4496
Robert Poirier, *Ch of Bd*
Glenn Poirier, *President*
Glenda Poirier, *Corp Secy*
EMP: 16 **EST:** 1975

SQ FT: 10,000
SALES (est): 1.6MM **Privately Held**
WEB: www.trussme.com
SIC: 2439 Trusses, wooden roof; trusses, except roof: laminated lumber

(G-13479)
WATHENA HEALTHCARE
2112 Highway 36 (66090-4126)
PHONE..................................785 989-3141
David Haneke,
EMP: 50
SALES: 3.4MM **Publicly Held**
SIC: 8051 Skilled nursing care facilities
HQ: Genesis Healthcare Llc
101 E State St
Kennett Square PA 19348

(G-13480)
WATHENA HEIGHTS APARTMENTS
509 N 3rd St (66090-4109)
PHONE..................................417 883-7887
William Hamilton, *Vice Pres*
EMP: 16
SALES (est): 520.4K **Privately Held**
SIC: 6513 Apartment building operators

Waverly
Coffey County

(G-13481)
COFFEY COUNTY HOSPITAL
Also Called: Sunset Nursing Home
128 S Pearson Ave (66871-9673)
PHONE..................................785 733-2744
Pam Deville, *Manager*
EMP: 50
SALES (corp-wide): 21.4MM **Privately Held**
SIC: 8062 8052 General medical & surgical hospitals; intermediate care facilities
PA: Coffey County Hospital
801 N 4th St
Burlington KS 66839
620 364-5655

(G-13482)
THOMPSON TAX & ASSOCIATES LLC
406 Kelly St (66871-9542)
P.O. Box 96 (66871-0096)
PHONE..................................916 346-7829
Daniel Thompson, *President*
EMP: 18
SALES: 2MM **Privately Held**
SIC: 7291 7389 Tax return preparation services; legal & tax services

(G-13483)
WHEELER CONSOLIDATED INC
Also Called: Wheeler Lumber
1959 Old Highway 50 (66871-9321)
PHONE..................................785 733-2848
Nick Bailey, *Manager*
EMP: 30
SALES (corp-wide): 38MM **Privately Held**
WEB: www.erickson-eng.com
SIC: 2439 Trusses, wooden roof; trusses, except roof: laminated lumber
PA: Wheeler Consolidated, Inc
3620 Sw 61st St Ste 330
Des Moines IA 50321
515 223-1584

Webber
Jewell County

(G-13484)
LOVEWELL MARINA & GRILL INC
2400 250 Rd (66970-5013)
PHONE..................................785 753-4351
Gary Charbonneau, *President*
Lyndell Charbonneau, *Treasurer*
EMP: 10
SALES: 200K **Privately Held**
SIC: 0919 Miscellaneous marine products

Weir
Cherokee County

(G-13485)
CBW BANK
Also Called: Citizens Bank
109 E Main St (66781-4344)
P.O. Box 287 (66781-0287)
PHONE..................................620 396-8221
Joe W Fowler, *President*
Janet Hogard, *President*
Andy Prescott, *Vice Pres*
Suzanne Fowler, *Treasurer*
Phil Martin, *Director*
EMP: 10 **EST:** 1892
SALES (est): 522.7K **Privately Held**
SIC: 6022 State trust companies accepting deposits, commercial

(G-13486)
TRINITY STEEL AND PIPE INC
204 S Madison Ave (66781-4291)
P.O. Box 288 (66781-0288)
PHONE..................................620 396-8900
David Stricklin, *President*
Gary Engelman, *Vice Pres*
EMP: 16 **EST:** 1997
SQ FT: 13,000
SALES (est): 3.5MM **Privately Held**
WEB: www.trinitysteelandpipe.com
SIC: 3444 3441 Pipe, sheet metal; fabricated structural metal for ships

Welda
Anderson County

(G-13487)
SOUTHERN STAR CENTRAL GAS PIPE
19209 Sw Maryland Rd (66091-3133)
P.O. Box 550 (66091-0550)
PHONE..................................785 448-4800
Freddie Partida, *Branch Mgr*
EMP: 21
SALES (corp-wide): 216.1MM **Privately Held**
WEB: www.sscgp.com
SIC: 4924 Natural gas distribution
HQ: Southern Star Central Gas Pipeline, Inc.
4700 Highway 56
Owensboro KY 42301
270 852-5000

Wellington
Sumner County

(G-13488)
AIR PLAINS SERVICES CORP
439 N West Rd (67152-8047)
P.O. Box 541 (67152-0541)
PHONE..................................620 326-8581
Michael Kelley, *President*
Carolyn Kelley, *Vice Pres*
Mike James, *Opers Mgr*
Rafael Soldan, *Engineer*
Katie Church, *Sales Staff*
EMP: 13
SQ FT: 13,000
SALES: 3.5MM **Privately Held**
WEB: www.airplains.com
SIC: 4581 Aircraft maintenance & repair services; aircraft servicing & repairing

(G-13489)
AMERICAN METAL FABRICATION INC
2000 N Vandenburgh Ave (67152-4433)
PHONE..................................620 399-8508
Marvin Dunnegan, *President*
Krisanna Wolken, *General Mgr*
Vicki Wolken, *Manager*
Patricia Dunnegan, *Admin Sec*
EMP: 11
SQ FT: 18,000
SALES (est): 660K **Privately Held**
SIC: 3441 Fabricated structural metal

(G-13490)
BANK OF CMMRCE TR OF WLLNGTON (PA)
Also Called: BANK COMMERCE AND TRUST
201 W Harvey Ave (67152-3895)
P.O. Box 529 (67152-0529)
PHONE..................................620 326-7471
W C Long Jr, *President*
J C Long, *President*
James Ramsey, *Vice Pres*
Heidi Theurer, *Vice Pres*
EMP: 15 **EST:** 1906
SQ FT: 2,000
SALES: 3.1MM **Privately Held**
WEB: www.bankofcommerce.ws
SIC: 6022 State trust companies accepting deposits, commercial

(G-13491)
BNSF RAILWAY COMPANY
Also Called: Burlington Northern
1315 E 1st St (67152-8411)
PHONE..................................620 399-4201
Betty Cornett, *Principal*
EMP: 200
SALES (corp-wide): 225.3B **Publicly Held**
WEB: www.billpurdy.com
SIC: 4011 Railroads, line-haul operating
HQ: Bnsf Railway Company
2650 Lou Menk Dr
Fort Worth TX 76131
800 795-2673

(G-13492)
BROOKDALE SENIOR LIVING COMMUN
Also Called: Sterling House of Wellington
500 N Plum St (67152-3574)
PHONE..................................620 326-3031
Tish Schwerdtfeger, *Branch Mgr*
EMP: 15
SALES (corp-wide): 4.5B **Publicly Held**
WEB: www.assisted.com
SIC: 8051 Skilled nursing care facilities
HQ: Brookdale Senior Living Communities, Inc.
6737 W Wa St Ste 2300
Milwaukee WI 53214
414 918-5000

(G-13493)
BSB MAUNFACTURING INC
20 Industrial Ave (67152-4524)
P.O. Box 544 (67152-0544)
PHONE..................................620 326-3152
Jay Neal, *President*
Yvette Neal, *Vice Pres*
▲ **EMP:** 8
SQ FT: 11,250
SALES (est): 967.1K **Privately Held**
WEB: www.bsb-mfg.com
SIC: 3599 Machine shop, jobbing & repair

(G-13494)
CANCER CENTER OF KANSAS PA
1323 N A St (67152-4350)
PHONE..................................620 399-1224
Shaker Dakhil, *Branch Mgr*
EMP: 17
SALES (corp-wide): 24.4MM **Privately Held**
SIC: 8011 8069 Oncologist; cancer hospital
PA: Cancer Center Of Kansas, P.A.
818 N Emporia St Ste 403
Wichita KS 67214
316 262-4467

(G-13495)
CHERISHED FRIENDS LLC
924 S Washington Ave Ofc (67152-2203)
P.O. Box 9 (67152-0009)
PHONE..................................620 326-3700
Marsha Bunyan, *Principal*
EMP: 11
SALES (est): 284.5K **Privately Held**
SIC: 8361 Home for destitute men & women

(G-13496)
COUNTY OF SUMNER
Also Called: Sumner County Home Health Agcy
217 W 8th St Ste 1 (67152-3967)
PHONE..................................316 262-2686
Becky Harbison, *Manager*
Rebecca Payne, *Director*
Laura Rettig, *Hlthcr Dir*
Laura Reddid, *Administration*
EMP: 40 **Privately Held**
SIC: 8082 Home health care services
PA: County Of Sumner
110 E 10th St
Wellington KS 67152
620 399-1300

(G-13497)
DAY FUNERAL HOME INC
Also Called: Day Funeral Home & Crematory
1030 Mission Rd (67152-3235)
PHONE..................................620 326-5100
Bryce Day, *President*
Sally Day, *Vice Pres*
EMP: 12
SALES (est): 543K **Privately Held**
SIC: 7261 Funeral director; funeral home

(G-13498)
ELKHORN VALLEY PACKING
1509 E 16th St (67152)
P.O. Box 488 (67152-0488)
PHONE..................................620 326-3443
Jeff Venn, *Regional Mgr*
Troy Bennington, *Sales Associate*
EMP: 35
SALES (est): 4.3MM **Privately Held**
WEB: www.elkhornvalleypacking.com
SIC: 2011 Meat packing plants

(G-13499)
FARMERS COOPERATIVE GRAIN (PA)
9011 N A St (67152-8112)
PHONE..................................620 326-7496
Dennis Tencleve, *President*
Curt Guinn, *General Mgr*
Ken Fitzpatrick, *Exec VP*
Doris Lawrence, *Officer*
EMP: 19 **EST:** 1957
SQ FT: 20,000
SALES (est): 12.7MM **Privately Held**
WEB: www.wellingtoncoop.com
SIC: 5153 5191 4221 Grains; feed; seeds: field, garden & flower; fertilizer & fertilizer materials; grain elevator, storage only

(G-13500)
FIRST NATIONAL BANK NA (HQ)
206 E Harvey Ave (67152-3028)
P.O. Box 398 (67152-0398)
PHONE..................................620 326-3361
John T Stewart III, *Ch of Bd*
Robert Leftwich, *President*
David Carr, *Vice Chairman*
David M Carr, *Exec VP*
Eldon Lawless, *Exec VP*
EMP: 24 **EST:** 1883
SALES: 5.9MM
SALES (corp-wide): 3.5MM **Privately Held**
WEB: www.fnbwellington.com
SIC: 6022 State commercial banks
PA: First Financial Corporation
206 E Harvey Ave
Wellington KS 67152
620 326-3361

(G-13501)
FUTURES UNLIMITED INC (PA)
2410 N A St (67152-9799)
PHONE..................................620 326-8906
Thomas L Kohmetscher, *President*
Doug Norris, *Opers Staff*
◆ **EMP:** 43 **EST:** 1974
SQ FT: 10,000
SALES: 4.8MM **Privately Held**
SIC: 8331 8361 8211 8351 Sheltered workshop; home for the physically handicapped; school for physically handicapped; preschool center; head start center, except in conjunction with school

GEOGRAPHIC

(G-13502)
GATEHOUSE MEDIA LLC
Also Called: Wellington Daily News
113 W Harvey Ave (67152-3840)
PHONE....................................620 326-3326
Jennifer Wilson, *Sales Mgr*
Jackie Fullerton, *Director*
EMP: 25
SALES (corp-wide): 1.5B **Publicly Held**
SIC: 2711 Newspapers, publishing & printing
HQ: Gatehouse Media, Llc
175 Sullys Trl Fl 3
Pittsford NY 14534
585 598-0030

(G-13503)
GENERAL GRND CHPTER ESTRN STAR
Also Called: Order of The Eastern Star
14 Shadybrook Dr (67152-4729)
P.O. Box 81 (67152-0081)
PHONE....................................620 326-3797
Gloria Klima, *Admin Sec*
EMP: 115
SALES (corp-wide): 1.7MM **Privately Held**
WEB: www.easternstar.org
SIC: 8641 Civic associations
PA: General Grand Chapter Order Of The Eastern Star
1618 New Hampshire Ave Nw
Washington DC 20009
202 667-4737

(G-13504)
GGNSC WELLINGTON LLC
Also Called: Golden Livingcenter-Wellington
102 W Botkin St (67152-2302)
PHONE....................................620 326-7437
Tamara Mc Cue, *Director*
Randy Chuchy,
EMP: 40
SALES: 2.6MM
SALES (corp-wide): 2.6B **Privately Held**
SIC: 8051 Extended care facility
HQ: Ggnsc Holdings Llc
1000 Fianna Way
Fort Smith AR 72919

(G-13505)
GKN AEROSPACE PRECISION MACHIN
429 N West Rd (67152-8047)
PHONE....................................620 326-5952
Marcus Bryson, *CEO*
Kevin Cummings, *President*
Brian Decant, *President*
Stephen A Marshall, *President*
Mike McCann, *President*
▲ **EMP:** 255
SALES (est): 27.2MM
SALES (corp-wide): 11.3B **Privately Held**
SIC: 7539 Machine shop, automotive
HQ: Gkn Limited
Po Box 4128
Redditch WORCS

(G-13506)
GOLDEN LIVINGCENTER WELLINGTON
102 W Botkin St (67152-2302)
PHONE....................................620 326-7437
Holly A Rasmussen-Jones, *Principal*
EMP: 14
SALES (est): 479.9K **Privately Held**
SIC: 8082 Home health care services

(G-13507)
GRANT PHIPPS DDS
Also Called: Carnahan, John R DDS
119 E Lincoln Ave (67152-3046)
PHONE....................................620 326-7983
Grant Phipps DDS, *Owner*
EMP: 10 **EST:** 1972
SQ FT: 2,500
SALES (est): 690K **Privately Held**
SIC: 8021 Dentists' office

(G-13508)
KANSAS TURNPIKE AUTHORITY
850 E 10th Ave (67152-8000)
P.O. Box 1 (67152-0001)
PHONE....................................620 326-5044
Eric Becker, *Branch Mgr*
EMP: 40
SALES (corp-wide): 124.8MM **Privately Held**
WEB: www.ksturnpike.com
SIC: 4785 Toll road operation
PA: Kansas Turnpike Authority
9401 E Kellogg Dr
Wichita KS 67207
316 682-4537

(G-13509)
L B WHITE TRUCKING INC
510 E Hillside St (67152-8117)
P.O. Box 487 (67152-0487)
PHONE....................................620 326-8921
Ronald White, *President*
Terry White, *Corp Secy*
EMP: 20
SALES (est): 2.7MM **Privately Held**
SIC: 4213 Contract haulers

(G-13510)
LARRY THEURER
Also Called: Theurer Auction & Realty
802 E 16th St (67152-2807)
P.O. Box 601 (67152-0601)
PHONE....................................620 326-2715
Larry Theurer, *Owner*
Mandy Thomson, *Bookkeeper*
EMP: 11
SALES (est): 780.8K **Privately Held**
SIC: 6531 7389 Real estate brokers & agents; auctioneers, fee basis

(G-13511)
LENA M RUSH SCHOLARSHIP TRUST
Also Called: IMPACT BANK
P.O. Box 398 (67152-0398)
PHONE....................................620 326-3361
Robert Leftwich, *President*
EMP: 24
SALES: 1.7K **Privately Held**
SIC: 6021 National commercial banks

(G-13512)
LODGING ENTERPRISES INC
Also Called: Oak Tree Inn, The
1177 E 16th St (67152-2814)
PHONE....................................620 326-8191
William Burgess, *President*
Dan Abramczak, *General Mgr*
EMP: 34
SALES (est): 724.1K **Privately Held**
WEB: www.theoaktreeinn.com
SIC: 7011 Hotel, franchised

(G-13513)
LONG TERM CARE SPECIALISTS LLC
22 Sunset Rd (67152-4707)
PHONE....................................620 326-0251
Tamara L McCue, *Principal*
EMP: 10
SALES (est): 144K **Privately Held**
SIC: 8051 Skilled nursing care facilities

(G-13514)
MAC-TECH INC (DH)
Also Called: Pre-Mac
429 N West Rd (67152-8047)
PHONE....................................620 326-5952
Doug Whitlock, *President*
William G Tehel, *Vice Pres*
EMP: 12 **EST:** 1966
SQ FT: 380,000
SALES (est): 8MM
SALES (corp-wide): 11.3B **Privately Held**
SIC: 3599 Machine shop, jobbing & repair

(G-13515)
MCALISTER TRANSPORTATION LLC
312 N Washington Ave (67152-3953)
P.O. Box 69 (67152-0069)
PHONE....................................620 326-2491
Jenny Roe, *Office Mgr*
Scott Shank,
Heather Shank,
EMP: 34
SALES: 1.2MM **Privately Held**
SIC: 4213 Contract haulers

(G-13516)
METAL FINISHING COMPANY INC
Also Called: Diversified Services
27 Clark Ave (67152-9797)
PHONE....................................620 326-7655
Dale Crouch, *Manager*
EMP: 34
SALES (corp-wide): 27.7MM **Privately Held**
SIC: 3398 Metal heat treating
PA: The Metal Finishing Company Inc
1423 S Mclean Blvd
Wichita KS 67213
316 267-7289

(G-13517)
METAL IMPROVEMENT COMPANY LLC
440 N West Rd (67152-8047)
PHONE....................................620 326-5509
Roy Branam, *Branch Mgr*
EMP: 20
SALES (corp-wide): 2.4B **Publicly Held**
WEB: www.mic-houston.com
SIC: 3398 Shot peening (treating steel to reduce fatigue)
HQ: Metal Improvement Company, Llc
80 E Rte 4 Ste 310
Paramus NJ 07652
201 843-7800

(G-13518)
MIRROR INC
1014 W 8th St (67152-3421)
PHONE....................................620 326-8822
EMP: 10
SALES (corp-wide): 11.2MM **Privately Held**
SIC: 8093 Substance abuse clinics (outpatient)
PA: The Mirror Inc
130 E 5th St
Newton KS 67114
316 283-6743

(G-13519)
NATIONAL EXPRESS LLC
Also Called: Durham School Services
14 Industrial Ave (67152-4524)
P.O. Box 602 (67152-0602)
PHONE....................................620 326-3318
Heather Heltingspine, *Manager*
EMP: 12 **Privately Held**
SIC: 4151 4141 School buses; local bus charter service
HQ: National Express Llc
2601 Navistar Dr
Lisle IL 60532

(G-13520)
ORSCHELN FARM AND HOME LLC
1201 W 8th St (67152-3402)
PHONE....................................620 326-2804
Dave George, *Branch Mgr*
EMP: 10
SALES (corp-wide): 822.7MM **Privately Held**
WEB: www.orschelnfarmhome.com
SIC: 5191 Farm supplies
PA: Orscheln Farm And Home Llc
1800 Overcenter Dr
Moberly MO 65270
800 577-2580

(G-13521)
OXWELL INC
600 E 16th St (67152-2803)
P.O. Box 588 (67152-0588)
PHONE....................................620 326-7481
H J Thompson, *President*
Jay Thompson, *Vice Pres*
Donna Etter, *Account Dir*
EMP: 55 **EST:** 1951
SQ FT: 47,000
SALES (est): 9MM **Privately Held**
WEB: www.oxwell.com
SIC: 3728 3312 3444 3443 Aircraft parts & equipment; tool & die steel & alloys; sheet metalwork; fabricated plate work (boiler shop)

(G-13522)
PANHANDLE FEDERAL CREDIT UNION
403 N Washington Ave (67152-4029)
P.O. Box 26 (67152-0026)
PHONE....................................620 326-2285
Lonnie Hays, *Vice Chairman*
Karen Horinek, *Vice Pres*
EMP: 10
SQ FT: 5,000
SALES: 1.4MM **Privately Held**
WEB: www.panhandlefcu.com
SIC: 6061 6163 Federal credit unions; loan brokers

(G-13523)
RENN & COMPANY INC (PA)
Also Called: Nationwide
209 S Washington Ave (67152-3037)
P.O. Box 40 (67152-0040)
PHONE....................................620 326-2271
Greg S Renn, *President*
Marilyn McLain, *Corp Secy*
Lyndsey Metzen, *Agent*
EMP: 10 **EST:** 1933
SQ FT: 4,700
SALES (est): 1.7MM **Privately Held**
SIC: 6411 6531 Insurance agents; real estate brokers & agents

(G-13524)
RICKS AUTO RESTORATION
Hwy 81 Rr 1 Rt 1 (67152)
PHONE....................................620 326-5635
EMP: 50
SQ FT: 3,000
SALES (est): 891.7K **Privately Held**
SIC: 7532 Auto Body Repair/Painting

(G-13525)
ROHRER CUSTOM AND FABRICATION
161 S Hillside Rd (67152-8418)
PHONE....................................620 359-1707
Lance Rohrer, *Principal*
EMP: 5 **EST:** 2015
SALES (est): 45.5K **Privately Held**
SIC: 7538 3499 General automotive repair shops; fabricated metal products

(G-13526)
SAINT FRANCIS CMNTY SVCS INC
Also Called: Saint Frncis Acdemy Wellington
1421 W 8th St (67152-4736)
PHONE....................................620 326-6373
Christie Underwood, *Branch Mgr*
EMP: 14
SALES (corp-wide): 108.2MM **Privately Held**
SIC: 8741 8322 Hospital management; individual & family services
PA: Saint Francis Community Services, Inc.
509 E Elm St
Salina KS 67401
785 825-0541

(G-13527)
SECURITY 1ST TITLE LLC
116 E Harvey Ave (67152-3044)
P.O. Box 548 (67152-0548)
PHONE....................................620 326-7460
James Leftwich, *Branch Mgr*
EMP: 16 **Privately Held**
SIC: 6541 Title abstract offices
PA: Security 1st Title Llc
727 N Waco Ave Ste 300
Wichita KS 67203

(G-13528)
SECURITY STATE BANK
101 N Washington Ave (67152-3950)
P.O. Box 160 (67152-0160)
PHONE....................................620 326-7417
Don Ott, *President*
Terry G Dupree, *Senior VP*
Duane Schwartz, *Assistant VP*
EMP: 16
SQ FT: 5,000
SALES: 2.1MM **Privately Held**
WEB: www.securitystbank.com
SIC: 6022 State commercial banks
PA: Ssb Holdings, Inc.
101 N Washington Ave
Wellington KS 67152

(G-13529)
SHUTTLE BUS GENERAL PUB TRNSP
2410 N A St (67152-9799)
PHONE..................................620 326-3953
Tom K Kohmetscher, *Owner*
EMP: 99
SALES (est): 1.2MM **Privately Held**
SIC: 4131 Intercity & rural bus transportation

(G-13530)
ST LUKES HOSPITAL INC
Also Called: Sumner Regional Medical Center
1323 N A St Ste 2 (67152-4350)
PHONE..................................620 326-7451
Darlene Cooney, *Principal*
Pat Gleason, *Manager*
Susan Davidson, *Director*
Amy Walker, *Director*
Kris Weir, *Director*
EMP: 148
SQ FT: 89,664
SALES (est): 13.1MM **Privately Held**
SIC: 8062 Hospital, affiliated with AMA residency

(G-13531)
SUMNER CABLE TV INC
Also Called: WELLINGTON CABLE TV
117 W Harvey Ave (67152-3840)
P.O. Box 468 (67152-0468)
PHONE..................................620 326-8989
Judson Mitchell, *President*
Jack Mitchell, *Shareholder*
EMP: 10
SQ FT: 750
SALES: 2.5MM **Privately Held**
SIC: 4841 Cable television services

(G-13532)
SUMNER COUNTY APPRAISER
500 N Wash Ave Ste 102 (67152)
PHONE..................................620 326-8986
Della Rowley, *Manager*
Joseph Buresh, *Info Tech Dir*
John Tracy, *Director*
Brad Macy, *Executive*
EMP: 11
SALES (est): 661.1K **Privately Held**
SIC: 6531 Appraiser, real estate

(G-13533)
SUMNER COUNTY FAMILY CARE CTR (PA)
507 E 16th St Ste 1 (67152-2828)
PHONE..................................620 326-3301
Larry Anderson MD, *Partner*
Stephen Hawks, *Partner*
Steven Stheusler, *Partner*
Joe Wiegand, *Partner*
EMP: 20
SALES (est): 2.8MM **Privately Held**
SIC: 8011 General & family practice, physician/surgeon

(G-13534)
SUMNER MENTAL HEALTH CENTER (PA)
1601 W 16th St (67152-8125)
P.O. Box 607 (67152-0607)
PHONE..................................620 326-7448
Greg Olson, *CEO*
Darlene Ferguson, *Office Mgr*
Richard Gaskill, *Psychologist*
Jennie Pinion, *Psychologist*
David Robinson, *Info Tech Dir*
EMP: 60
SALES (est): 3.7MM **Privately Held**
SIC: 8322 General counseling services

(G-13535)
TAYLORMADE PROFORMANCE
2710 N A St (67152-9767)
PHONE..................................620 326-3537
Kent Taylor, *Principal*
EMP: 5
SALES (est): 385.8K **Privately Held**
SIC: 3465 Body parts, automobile: stamped metal

(G-13536)
TECT AEROSPACE WELLINGTON INC (HQ)
1515 N A St (67152-4534)
PHONE..................................620 359-5000
Patrick Blackwell, *General Mgr*
Jerry Little, *Opers Staff*
Moran Metz, *Production*
Erin Cox, *Purch Mgr*
Afrose Kadir, *Engineer*
▲ **EMP:** 240
SQ FT: 600,000
SALES (est): 27.7MM
SALES (corp-wide): 39.5MM **Privately Held**
SIC: 3728 Aircraft assemblies, subassemblies & parts
PA: Tect Aerospace Kansas Holdings, Llc
300 W Douglas Ave Ste 100
Wichita KS 67202
620 395-5000

(G-13537)
TRAMEC SLOAN LLC
Also Called: Kansas Plastics
32 Clark Ave (67152-9797)
PHONE..................................620 326-5007
Richard Bloomer, *Manager*
EMP: 35
SALES (corp-wide): 110MM **Privately Held**
SIC: 3089 Plastic processing
HQ: Sloan L Tramec L C
534 E 48th St
Holland MI 49423
616 395-5600

(G-13538)
TRIUMPH GROUP OPERATIONS INC
Also Called: Triumph Accessory Services
411 N West Rd (67152-8047)
PHONE..................................620 326-5761
Angelie Macias, *Purchasing*
Amy Norris, *Purchasing*
Billy Martin, *Marketing Staff*
Jim Berberet, *Branch Mgr*
Jim Beberrate, *Manager*
EMP: 100 **Publicly Held**
WEB: www.triumphairrepair.com
SIC: 3728 4581 3724 3494 Aircraft parts & equipment; airports, flying fields & services; aircraft engines & engine parts; valves & pipe fittings
HQ: The Triumph Group Operations Inc
899 Cassatt Rd Ste 210
Berwyn PA 19312

(G-13539)
WELLINGTON FMLY PRACT CLINC
399 S Seneca Rd (67152-8385)
PHONE..................................620 399-1222
EMP: 20
SALES (est): 1.2MM **Privately Held**
SIC: 8011 Primary care medical clinic

Wellsville
Franklin County

(G-13540)
ANIMAL CHIROPRACTIC CENTER
Also Called: Options For Animals
4267 Virginia Rd (66092-8860)
P.O. Box 3682, Cartersville GA (30120-1712)
PHONE..................................309 658-2920
Sharon Willoughby Dvm, *Owner*
EMP: 25 **EST:** 1990
SALES (est): 500.7K **Privately Held**
SIC: 0742 8041 0741 Veterinarian, animal specialties; offices & clinics of chiropractors; veterinary services for livestock

(G-13541)
CENTRAL FIBER LLC (PA)
4814 Fiber Ln (66092-8873)
PHONE..................................785 883-4600
Darren Traub, *CEO*
▼ **EMP:** 36
SQ FT: 75,000
SALES (est): 12.8MM **Privately Held**
WEB: www.centralfiber.com
SIC: 2493 2611 2679 Insulation board, cellular fiber; pulp manufactured from waste or recycled paper; paper products, converted

(G-13542)
D E EXPLORATION INC
4595 Highway K 33 (66092-8505)
P.O. Box 128 (66092-0128)
PHONE..................................785 883-4057
Douglas Evans, *President*
EMP: 17 **EST:** 1992
SALES (est): 2.4MM **Privately Held**
SIC: 1382 Oil & gas exploration services

(G-13543)
HUGHES DRILLING CO
122 Main St (66092-8522)
PHONE..................................785 883-2235
Beatrice Hughes, *Partner*
Carl Clayton Hughes, *Partner*
Roger A Hughes, *Partner*
Ronald K Hughes, *Partner*
EMP: 7
SALES (est): 680K **Privately Held**
SIC: 1311 1381 Crude petroleum production; directional drilling oil & gas wells

(G-13544)
LANDMARK NATIONAL BANK
112 W 6th St (66092-9205)
P.O. Box 308 (66092-0308)
PHONE..................................785 883-2145
Patrick Alexander, *Branch Mgr*
EMP: 10
SALES (corp-wide): 48.7MM **Publicly Held**
SIC: 6035 Federal savings & loan associations
HQ: Landmark National Bank
701 Poyntz Ave
Manhattan KS 66502
620 225-1745

(G-13545)
Q SOLUTIONS LLC
Also Called: Merchants First Pymnt Systems
406 E 4th St (66092-8606)
PHONE..................................913 948-5931
Troy D Calderwood, *CEO*
Taryn Robbs, *Office Admin*
EMP: 13
SALES (est): 922.2K **Privately Held**
SIC: 7389 Credit card service

Westmoreland
Pottawatomie County

(G-13546)
CROSS COUNTRY GENETICS INC
8855 Michaels Rd (66549-9530)
P.O. Box 637, Manhattan (66505-0637)
PHONE..................................785 457-3336
Kirk Gray, *President*
Cristy Gray, *Corp Secy*
EMP: 13 **EST:** 1992
SALES: 280K **Privately Held**
SIC: 0751 Artificial insemination services, livestock

(G-13547)
FARMERS STATE BNK OF WSTMRLAND (PA)
307 Main St (66549-9684)
P.O. Box 330 (66549-0330)
PHONE..................................785 457-3316
James Moore, *President*
Roxanne Zoeller, *Principal*
Steven Ebert, *Vice Pres*
EMP: 22 **EST:** 1898
SALES: 6.9MM **Privately Held**
WEB: www.fsbwesty.com
SIC: 6022 State trust companies accepting deposits, commercial

(G-13548)
GALEN BLENN TRUCKING
308 N 4th St (66549-9591)
P.O. Box 307 (66549-0307)
PHONE..................................785 457-3995
Galen Blenn, *Owner*
EMP: 25
SALES (est): 1.4MM **Privately Held**
SIC: 4212 Dump truck haulage

(G-13549)
WESTY COMMUNITY CARE HOME INC
105 N Highway 99 (66549-9695)
PHONE..................................785 457-2806
Tim Minges, *Podiatrist*
Phyllis Hupe, *Administration*
EMP: 60
SALES: 2.7MM **Privately Held**
SIC: 8052 Intermediate care facilities

Westwood
Johnson County

(G-13550)
BAR METHOD WEST PLAZA
4722 Rainbow Blvd (66205-1835)
PHONE..................................913 499-1468
Hoedy Potter, *Owner*
EMP: 30
SALES (est): 198.6K **Privately Held**
SIC: 7991 Physical fitness clubs with training equipment

(G-13551)
BOYD DELIVERY SYSTEMS INC
2803 W 47th St (66205-1602)
P.O. Box 413806, Kansas City MO (64141-3806)
PHONE..................................913 677-6700
Randolph F Misejka, *President*
Randy F Misejka, *President*
EMP: 62
SQ FT: 8,000
SALES (est): 6.6MM **Privately Held**
SIC: 4215 4212 Parcel delivery, vehicular; light haulage & cartage, local
PA: Total Distribution System Inc
2803 W 47th St
Westwood KS 66205
913 677-2292

(G-13552)
COOPERTIVE CPON RDEMPTION ASSN
2809 W 47th St (66205-1602)
PHONE..................................913 384-3830
James Sheehan, *President*
Connor Haegerty, *Manager*
EMP: 10
SQ FT: 4,000
SALES (est): 248.4K **Privately Held**
SIC: 8611 Trade associations

(G-13553)
EXPERT ALTERATION
4759 Rainbow Blvd Ste B (66205-1804)
PHONE..................................913 322-2242
Nicolette Lewis, *Owner*
EMP: 5
SALES (est): 367.4K **Privately Held**
SIC: 2395 5949 7219 Embroidery & art needlework; sewing, needlework & piece goods; tailor shop, except custom or merchant tailor

(G-13554)
JAYHAWK PRIMARY CARE INC (PA)
2330 Shawnee Mission Pkwy (66205-2005)
PHONE..................................913 588-9000
E Christian Hansen, *CEO*
Irene Cumming, *President*
Scott Glasrud, *Treasurer*
◆ **EMP:** 80
SALES (est): 13.5MM **Privately Held**
SIC: 8011 Offices & clinics of medical doctors

(G-13555)
LLC BLACK STONE
4759 Rainbow Blvd Ste A (66205-1804)
PHONE..................................816 519-5650
Darryl Muhammad, *Mng Member*
Nicolette Lewis,
EMP: 10 **EST:** 2012

GEOGRAPHIC

SALES (est): 208.7K Privately Held
SIC: 6531 Real estate agents & managers

(G-13556)
MID AMERICA CARDIOLOGY
2330 Shawnee Mission Pkwy
(66205-2005)
PHONE..................................913 588-9549
Chris Hansen, *Principal*
EMP: 14
SALES (est): 1.5MM Privately Held
SIC: 8011 Cardiologist & cardio-vascular specialist

(G-13557)
MID AMERICA CRDIOLGY ASSOC PC
2330 Shawnee Mission Pkwy
(66205-2005)
PHONE..................................913 588-9600
Tracy Rasmussen, *CEO*
EMP: 25
SALES (corp-wide): 13.5MM Privately Held
SIC: 8011 Cardiologist & cardio-vascular specialist
PA: Mid America Cardiology Associates Pc Inc
3901 Rainbow Blvd G600
Kansas City KS 66160
913 588-9600

(G-13558)
RETAIL GROC ASSN GRTER KANS CY (PA)
Also Called: Food Industry Services
2809 W 47th St (66205-1602)
PHONE..................................913 384-3830
John Cunningham, *Treasurer*
James G Sheehan, *Exec Dir*
EMP: 15
SQ FT: 6,000
SALES: 201.2K Privately Held
SIC: 8611 8741 7812 Contractors' association; management services; audio-visual program production

(G-13559)
SPRINT INTERNATIONAL INC (DH)
2330 Shawnee Mission Pkwy
(66205-2005)
PHONE..................................800 259-3755
William T Esrey, *CEO*
▲ EMP: 159
SALES (est): 1.1B Publicly Held
WEB: www.spradling.net
SIC: 4813 Long distance telephone communications; telephone cable service, land or submarine

(G-13560)
ST AGNES MONTESSORI PRE SCHOOL
5149 Mission Rd (66205-1628)
PHONE..................................913 262-2400
Jim Byfield, *Principal*
Barbra Burgoon, *Principal*
EMP: 40
SALES (est): 452.7K Privately Held
SIC: 8351 Preschool center; Montessori child development center

(G-13561)
TOTAL DISTRIBUTION SYSTEM INC (PA)
Also Called: Total Courier
2803 W 47th St (66205-1602)
P.O. Box 413806, Kansas City MO (64141-3806)
PHONE..................................913 677-2292
Randolph F Misejka, *President*
Randy Misejka, *President*
EMP: 60
SQ FT: 7,500
SALES (est): 6.6MM Privately Held
SIC: 4215 4213 Courier services, except by air; trucking, except local

(G-13562)
UNIVERSITY OF KANSAS MED CTR
Also Called: Medical ADM Svcs Ku Med Ctr
2330 Shawnee Mission Pkwy
(66205-2005)
PHONE..................................913 945-5598
Chris Hansen, *Branch Mgr*
EMP: 39
SALES (corp-wide): 1.2B Privately Held
SIC: 8741 8011 Administrative management; medical centers
HQ: The University Of Kansas Medical Center
3901 Rainbow Blvd
Kansas City KS 66160
913 588-1443

(G-13563)
WESTWOOD ANIMAL HOSPITAL
Also Called: Animal Behavior Consultations
4820 Rainbow Blvd (66205-1941)
PHONE..................................913 362-2512
Wayne Hunthausen, *Owner*
EMP: 10
SALES (est): 401.6K Privately Held
SIC: 0742 0752 Veterinarian, animal specialties; training services, pet & animal specialties (not horses)

(G-13564)
YOUTHFRONT INC (PA)
Also Called: YOUTHFRONT ASSOCIATION
4715 Rainbow Blvd (66205-1832)
PHONE..................................913 262-3900
Rev Ronnie Metsker, *President*
Caleb Wood, *Manager*
Dylan Aebersold, *Director*
Rodolfo Armendariz, *Director*
Marta Clewett, *Director*
EMP: 68
SQ FT: 16,000
SALES: 3.9MM Privately Held
WEB: www.youthfrontzone.net
SIC: 8641 Youth organizations

Westwood Hills
Johnson County

(G-13565)
RFS ASSOCIATES LLC
2107 W 49th Ter (66205-1954)
PHONE..................................913 871-0456
Elizabeth Ray,
EMP: 30
SALES (est): 1.5MM Privately Held
SIC: 8742 Management consulting services

Wetmore
Nemaha County

(G-13566)
GIRARD NATIONAL BANK
314 2nd St (66550-9618)
PHONE..................................785 866-2920
John Morsey, *President*
EMP: 10 Privately Held
SIC: 6021 National commercial banks
HQ: Girard National Bank
100 E Forest Ave
Girard KS 66743
620 724-8223

White City
Morris County

(G-13567)
JAMES R BARBER
Also Called: Barber Construction
422 S 6th St (66872-9315)
PHONE..................................785 349-2801
James R Barber, *Owner*
EMP: 12 EST: 1973
SALES: 969.7K Privately Held
SIC: 1794 Excavation work

White Cloud
Doniphan County

(G-13568)
H B J FARMS INC
Also Called: Taylor Seed Farms
2467 Highway 7 (66094-4217)
PHONE..................................785 595-3236
Howard Taylor, *President*
Jason Taylor, *Corp Secy*
Brad Taylor, *Vice Pres*
Rick Madl, *Sales Mgr*
EMP: 11
SALES (est): 3.7MM Privately Held
WEB: www.taylorseedfarms.com
SIC: 5191 Seeds: field, garden & flower

(G-13569)
IOWA TRIBE KANSAS & NEBRASKA
Also Called: Casino White Cloud
5 Miles Nw Of White Cloud (66094)
PHONE..................................785 595-3430
Bill Clisbee, *General Mgr*
EMP: 12
SALES (est): 187.2K Privately Held
SIC: 7999 5541 Bingo hall; gasoline service stations

Whitewater
Butler County

(G-13570)
EDWIN MYERS
Also Called: Providence Project, The
14566 Nw 110th St (67154-8853)
PHONE..................................316 799-2112
Edwin Meyers, *Owner*
Ed Myers, *COO*
EMP: 5
SALES: 120K Privately Held
SIC: 2731 2741 Books: publishing only; miscellaneous publishing

(G-13571)
F & R SWINE INC
13652 Nw Butler Rd (67154-8910)
P.O. Box 38 (67154-0038)
PHONE..................................316 799-1983
Brian Brandt, *President*
Jeanne R Penner, *Treasurer*
Kenneth Penner, *Admin Sec*
EMP: 22
SALES: 5MM Privately Held
SIC: 0213 Hogs

(G-13572)
RAVENSCRAFT IMPLEMENT INC
Also Called: Kubota Authorized Dealer
223 S Main St (67154-8879)
P.O. Box 309 (67154-0309)
PHONE..................................316 799-2141
Jay Ravenscraft, *President*
Ron Ferry, *Finance Mgr*
EMP: 11 EST: 1963
SQ FT: 5,500
SALES (est): 6.2MM Privately Held
WEB: www.ravenscraftimpl.com
SIC: 5083 7699 Agricultural machinery & equipment; agricultural equipment repair services

(G-13573)
WHEAT STATE MANOR INC
601 S Main St (67154-9700)
PHONE..................................316 799-2181
Michael E Smith, *Principal*
Marsha Horter, *Bookkeeper*
EMP: 90
SALES: 3.9MM Privately Held
WEB: www.wheatstatemanor.org
SIC: 8052 8361 8051 Personal care facility; residential care; skilled nursing care facilities

Whiting
Jackson County

(G-13574)
BERNARD D OHLSEN CNSTR CO
30337 V Rd (66552-9428)
PHONE..................................785 873-3462
Bernard D Ohlsen, *Partner*
EMP: 10
SALES (est): 573.5K Privately Held
SIC: 1629 Waterway construction

(G-13575)
WILLIAMS COMPANY INC
137 S Whiting St (66552-9411)
P.O. Box 137 (66552-0137)
PHONE..................................785 873-3260
Roland Dean Williams, *President*
Carol Williams, *Treasurer*
EMP: 11
SALES (est): 1.8MM Privately Held
SIC: 3599 Machine & other job shop work

Wichita
Sedgwick County

(G-13576)
1010 N WEBB ROAD LLC
8333 W 21st St N (67205-1749)
PHONE..................................316 722-7529
Ron Cornejo, *Branch Mgr*
EMP: 20
SALES (corp-wide): 9.8MM Privately Held
WEB: www.allstarwichita.com
SIC: 7996 Amusement parks
HQ: 1010 N. Webb Road, Llc
1010 N Webb Rd
Wichita KS

(G-13577)
1038 PRODUCTIONS
1820 N Woodrow Ave (67203-2931)
PHONE..................................316 644-6883
Jordan Langhofer, *Principal*
EMP: 10
SALES (est): 119.2K Privately Held
SIC: 7822 Motion picture & tape distribution

(G-13578)
21ST ST STEEL
1007 E 21st St N (67214-1439)
PHONE..................................316 265-6661
M J Ryan, *Mng Member*
EMP: 11
SQ FT: 8,000
SALES (est): 1.1MM Privately Held
SIC: 4953 Recycling, waste materials

(G-13579)
3 S ENGINEERING LLC
Also Called: 3s Engineering
9111 E Douglas Ave # 100 (67207-1246)
PHONE..................................316 260-2258
Randy Eno, *General Mgr*
William Shields, *General Mgr*
Robert Lysen, *Principal*
Tim Cox, *Pub Rel Mgr*
Jill Johnson, *Social Dir*
EMP: 15
SALES (est): 2.2MM
SALES (corp-wide): 1.9B Privately Held
SIC: 8711 Consulting engineer
PA: Sierra Nevada Corporation
444 Salomon Cir
Sparks NV 89434
775 331-0222

(G-13580)
360 DOCUMENT SOLUTIONS LLC (PA)
8201 E 34th Cir N Ste 901 (67226-1364)
PHONE..................................316 630-8334
Mark Lindquist,
EMP: 10 EST: 2012
SQ FT: 2,500
SALES (est): 1.5MM Privately Held
SIC: 8748 Business consulting

(G-13581)
360DIRECTORIES LLC
Also Called: 360 Kc.com
400 S Commerce St (67202-4618)
PHONE..................................316 269-6920
Nicole Graszl, *General Mgr*
Paul Badke, *Production*
James Mock, *Mng Member*
EMP: 40
SALES (est): 2.8MM **Privately Held**
WEB: www.360wichita.com
SIC: 8742 Marketing consulting services

(G-13582)
6 MERIDIAN LLC
1635 N Waterfront Pkwy # 250
(67206-6630)
PHONE..................................316 776-4601
Andrew Mies, *CFO*
Margaret Dechant, *Mng Member*
Steve Bahm, *Mng Member*
Sarah Hampton, *Mng Member*
Thomas Kirk, *Mng Member*
EMP: 17
SALES (est): 125.5K **Privately Held**
SIC: 6282 Investment advisory service

(G-13583)
A & H ELECTRIC INC
3939 N Bridgeport Cir (67219-3300)
P.O. Box 3436 (67201-3436)
PHONE..................................316 838-3003
David Bowlin, *President*
Rick Lowez, *Corp Secy*
Steve Jamis, *Project Mgr*
EMP: 76
SQ FT: 6,000
SALES: 21.1MM **Privately Held**
SIC: 1731 General electrical contractor

(G-13584)
A CARING DOCTOR MINNESOTA PA
Also Called: Banfield Pet Hospital 246
533 S Tracy St (67209-2660)
PHONE..................................316 946-0920
EMP: 20
SALES (corp-wide): 37.6B **Privately Held**
WEB: www.banfield.net
SIC: 0742 Animal hospital services, pets & other animal specialties
HQ: A Caring Doctor Minnesota Pa
8000 Ne Tillamook St
Portland OR 97213
503 922-5000

(G-13585)
A CARING DOCTOR MINNESOTA PA
Also Called: Banfield Pet Hospital 245
3615 N Rock Rd (67226-1322)
PHONE..................................316 631-3939
Mark Ekerberg, *Branch Mgr*
EMP: 20
SALES (corp-wide): 37.6B **Privately Held**
WEB: www.banfield.net
SIC: 0742 Animal hospital services, pets & other animal specialties
HQ: A Caring Doctor Minnesota Pa
8000 Ne Tillamook St
Portland OR 97213
503 922-5000

(G-13586)
A CLEAR DIRECTION INC
345 S Hydraulic St (67211-1908)
PHONE..................................316 260-9101
Mario Williams, *Principal*
EMP: 11
SALES (est): 557.2K **Privately Held**
SIC: 8069 Drug addiction rehabilitation hospital

(G-13587)
A L C ENTERPRISES INC
Also Called: J & J Fence
824 N West St (67203-1215)
PHONE..................................316 943-6500
Leroy Christiansen, *President*
Anna Christiansen, *Principal*
EMP: 10
SQ FT: 1,100
SALES (est): 1MM **Privately Held**
WEB: www.alcenterprises.com
SIC: 1799 5211 Fence construction; fencing

(G-13588)
A M CASTLE & CO
3050 S Hydraulic St (67216-2405)
PHONE..................................316 943-0277
Fax: 316 522-2043
EMP: 23
SALES (corp-wide): 979.8MM **Publicly Held**
SIC: 5051 Wholesaler Of Plastic Material/Shapes & Metals Service Center
PA: A. M. Castle & Co.
1420 Kensington Rd # 220
Oak Brook IL 60523
847 455-7111

(G-13589)
A M PLUMBING INC
1414 S Bebe St (67209-2610)
PHONE..................................316 945-8326
Leon Breedlove, *President*
Sandra Breedlove, *Admin Sec*
EMP: 22
SALES (est): 2.5MM **Privately Held**
SIC: 1711 Plumbing contractors

(G-13590)
A M S DIAGNOSTIC LLC
3636 N Ridge Rd Ste 100 (67205-1229)
PHONE..................................316 462-2020
Charles Janzen,
EMP: 32
SALES (est): 1.8MM
SALES (corp-wide): 25.3B **Privately Held**
SIC: 8011 Medical centers
HQ: Via Christi Health Partners, Inc.
8200 E Thorn Dr Ste 300
Wichita KS 67226

(G-13591)
AAA PORTABLE SERVICES LLC
3730 S Broadway Ave (67216-1032)
PHONE..................................316 522-6442
Mark Ysidro, *Mng Member*
Amanda Nettleton, *Manager*
EMP: 17
SQ FT: 8,000
SALES (est): 3MM **Privately Held**
WEB: www.aaaportojon.com
SIC: 7359 Portable toilet rental

(G-13592)
AAA RESTAURANT SUPPLY LLC
611 E Central Ave (67202-1061)
PHONE..................................316 265-4365
Fred Erdman,
Debbie Erdman,
Tanner Erdman,
EMP: 10 **EST:** 1982
SQ FT: 15,000
SALES (est): 4.6MM **Privately Held**
SIC: 5046 5722 5087 Restaurant equipment & supplies; household appliance stores; vacuum cleaning systems

(G-13593)
AARON & PAGE PAINTING INC
1831 N Mosley Ave (67214-1347)
P.O. Box 2078 (67201-2078)
PHONE..................................316 267-2224
Steve Aaron, *President*
Greg Page, *Vice Pres*
EMP: 14
SQ FT: 3,000
SALES: 900K **Privately Held**
SIC: 1721 Commercial painting; commercial wallcovering contractor

(G-13594)
AAT AERO INC
Also Called: Aat Group
946 W 53rd St N (67204-2253)
PHONE..................................316 832-1412
Larry Gardner, *Administration*
EMP: 12
SQ FT: 20,000
SALES: 5MM **Privately Held**
SIC: 7389 3544 Design services; special dies, tools, jigs & fixtures

(G-13595)
ABAY NEUROSCIENCE CENTER PA
3223 N Webb Rd Ste 1 (67226-8176)
PHONE..................................316 609-2600
Eustaquio Abay, *Principal*
Raymond W Grundmeyer, *Med Doctor*
EMP: 34
SALES (est): 4.4MM **Privately Held**
WEB: www.abayneurosciencecenter.com
SIC: 8011 Primary care medical clinic; neurologist

(G-13596)
ABC TAXI CAB COMPANY INC
400 S Greenwood St (67211-1820)
PHONE..................................316 264-4222
Ted Hill, *President*
EMP: 12 **EST:** 1998
SALES (est): 1.3MM **Privately Held**
SIC: 4212 Delivery service, vehicular

(G-13597)
ABERDEEN VILLAGE INC
Also Called: PMMA
2414 N Woodlawn Blvd (67220-3902)
P.O. Box 20440 (67208-1440)
PHONE..................................316 685-1100
Bruce H Shogren, *President*
William Taylor, *COO*
Sherry K Hind, *Admin Sec*
EMP: 40
SALES: 11.4MM
SALES (corp-wide): 8.6MM **Privately Held**
SIC: 8051 Convalescent home with continuous nursing care
PA: Presbyterian Manors Of Mid-America Inc
2414 N Woodlawn Blvd
Wichita KS 67220
316 685-1100

(G-13598)
ABF FREIGHT SYSTEM INC
3833 S West St (67217-3805)
PHONE..................................316 943-1241
Grant Banks, *Manager*
EMP: 15
SALES (corp-wide): 3B **Publicly Held**
WEB: www.abfs.com
SIC: 4213 Contract haulers
HQ: Abf Freight System, Inc.
3801 Old Greenwood Rd
Fort Smith AR 72903
479 785-8700

(G-13599)
ABSOLUTE DIMENSIONS LLC
3838 W May St (67213-1235)
PHONE..................................316 944-2211
Stephen Brittain,
Michael G Rickords,
EMP: 24
SQ FT: 25,000
SALES: 3.4MM **Privately Held**
WEB: www.absolutedimensions.com
SIC: 3599 Machine shop, jobbing & repair

(G-13600)
ABSOLUTE HOME HEALTH CARE
1619 S Rutan Ave (67218-3917)
PHONE..................................316 832-1347
Carol Beltz, *President*
Carol Cravens, *President*
EMP: 25
SALES: 2.3MM **Privately Held**
WEB: www.absolutehomehealthcare.net
SIC: 8082 Visiting nurse service

(G-13601)
ACCENT LIGHTING INC
2020 N Woodlawn St # 220 (67208-1882)
PHONE..................................316 636-1278
Pat Graf, *President*
Paul Graf, *Vice Pres*
Scott Archer, *Sales Staff*
EMP: 19
SQ FT: 1,000
SALES: 10MM **Privately Held**
WEB: www.accentlightinginc.com
SIC: 5063 5719 Lighting fixtures; lighting fixtures

(G-13602)
ACCESS GROUP LLC
982 N Tyler Rd Ste D (67212-3271)
PHONE..................................316 264-0270
John Marstall, *Technology*
Pat Gaughan,
Bruce E Kline,
EMP: 19
SQ FT: 8,000
SALES: 2.3MM **Privately Held**
WEB: www.accessgroupllc.com
SIC: 7373 Local area network (LAN) systems integrator

(G-13603)
ACCOUNT RCVERY SPECIALISTS INC (PA)
Also Called: Arsi
3505 N Topeka St (67219-3641)
P.O. Box 136, Dodge City (67801-0136)
PHONE..................................620 227-8510
Kecia Kesler, *President*
EMP: 42 **EST:** 1992
SALES (est): 5.7MM **Privately Held**
SIC: 7322 Collection agency, except real estate

(G-13604)
ACCURUS AEROSPACE WICHITA LLC
4011 E 31st St S (67210-1509)
PHONE..................................316 683-0266
Brad Julius, *President*
EMP: 35
SQ FT: 6,000
SALES (est): 7.9MM
SALES (corp-wide): 149.4MM **Privately Held**
WEB: www.ztm.com
SIC: 3599 3728 Machine shop, jobbing & repair; aircraft parts & equipment
PA: Accurus Aerospace Corporation
12716 E Pine St
Tulsa OK 74116
918 438-3121

(G-13605)
ACI MOTOR FREIGHT INC (PA)
4545 Palisade St (67217)
PHONE..................................316 522-5559
Robert N Carriker, *President*
Sandra L Carriker, *Corp Secy*
Laura A Hopkins, *Vice Pres*
Kathy Berg, *Sales Staff*
EMP: 24
SQ FT: 11,000
SALES: 12MM **Privately Held**
SIC: 4213 Contract haulers

(G-13606)
ACM REMOVAL LLC
8610 E 34th St N Ste 2 (67226-2634)
PHONE..................................316 684-1800
Paul Ryan, *Mng Member*
EMP: 15
SALES (est): 1.2MM **Privately Held**
SIC: 1799 Asbestos removal & encapsulation

(G-13607)
ACOSTA SALES CO INC
Also Called: Acosta Sales & Marketing
550 N 159th St E Ste 301 (67230-7523)
PHONE..................................316 733-0248
Fax: 316 265-3521
EMP: 20
SALES (corp-wide): 7B **Privately Held**
SIC: 5141 Whol General Groceries
HQ: Acosta Sales Co., Inc.
6600 Corporate Ctr Pkwy
Jacksonville FL 32216
904 281-9800

(G-13608)
ACROBATIC ACADMY FTNS/EDUC CTR
2111 N Maize Rd (67212-5207)
PHONE..................................316 721-2230
Barbara Matous, *President*
Eric Wilson, *Vice Pres*
EMP: 40
SALES (est): 498.3K **Privately Held**
SIC: 7999 7911 Gymnastic instruction, non-membership; dance instructor & school services

GEOGRAPHIC

(G-13609)
ACS IIIIII - KS LLC
Also Called: American Chemical Systems
3505 W 29th St S (67217-1001)
PHONE..................................316 683-3489
Brad Wickham, *Mng Member*
EMP: 14
SALES: 2.5MM **Privately Held**
SIC: 2841 Soap & other detergents

(G-13610)
ACTORS LLC
Also Called: Mosley Street Melodrama
234 N Mosley St (67202-2806)
PHONE..................................316 263-0222
Scott D Noah,
Patty Reeder,
EMP: 20
SQ FT: 5,500
SALES (est): 612.5K **Privately Held**
WEB: www.mosleystreet.com
SIC: 5812 7922 Dinner theater; theatrical producers & services

(G-13611)
AD ASTRA RECOVER SERVICE
7330 W 33rd St N Ste 118 (67205-9370)
PHONE..................................316 941-5448
David H Newman, *President*
Doug Rippel, *Corp Secy*
EMP: 12
SALES (est): 920.4K **Privately Held**
SIC: 8999 7322 Actuarial consultant; adjustment bureau, except insurance

(G-13612)
ADAMS BROWN BRAN BALL CHRTERED
545 N Woodlawn St (67208-3645)
PHONE..................................316 683-2067
Danielle M Kaiser, *Branch Mgr*
EMP: 11
SALES (corp-wide): 9.4MM **Privately Held**
SIC: 8721 Certified public accountant
PA: Adams, Brown, Beran & Ball Chartered Inc
2006 Broadway Ave
Great Bend KS 67530
620 549-3271

(G-13613)
ADAMS JONES LAW FIRM PA
1635 N Waterfront Pkwy # 200 (67206-6623)
PHONE..................................316 265-8591
Brad Stout, *President*
Kate Cass, *Legal Staff*
Linda Higgins, *Legal Staff*
Monte Vines,
EMP: 16
SALES (est): 1.9MM **Privately Held**
WEB: www.adamsjones.com
SIC: 8111 General practice law office

(G-13614)
ADOLESCENT ADULT FMLY RECOVERY
Also Called: Preferred Family Healthcare
830 S Hillside St (67211-3004)
PHONE..................................316 943-2051
William H Morris, *President*
Jacqueline Morris, *Vice Pres*
EMP: 13
SALES (est): 411.7K **Privately Held**
SIC: 8093 8322 8069 Substance abuse clinics (outpatient); general counseling services; drug addiction rehabilitation hospital
PA: Preferred Family Healthcare, Incorporated
900 E Laharpe St
Kirksville MO 63501

(G-13615)
ADORERS OF BLD OF CHRST
Also Called: ASC Formation
1165 Southwest Blvd (67213-1419)
PHONE..................................316 942-2201
Joe N Morton, *Administration*
EMP: 18
SALES (corp-wide): 1.2MM **Privately Held**
SIC: 8741 Administrative management
PA: Adorers Of The Blood Of Christ Of Wichita, Inc
1400 S Sheridan St
Wichita KS 67213
316 943-1203

(G-13616)
ADR INC
Also Called: Adr Book Print
2012 E Northern St (67216-2431)
PHONE..................................316 522-5599
Patrick Tuttle, *Ch of Bd*
Grace Rishel, *President*
James E Rishel, *Vice Pres*
EMP: 65
SQ FT: 30,000
SALES (est): 12.2MM **Privately Held**
WEB: www.adrbookprint.com
SIC: 2752 2732 2789 Commercial printing, offset; book printing; bookbinding & related work

(G-13617)
ADT LLC
Also Called: ADT Security Services
800 E Waterman St (67202-4730)
PHONE..................................316 858-6628
Jamie Haenggi, *Chief Mktg Ofcr*
Madhavi Lee, *Manager*
Manoj Shah, *Manager*
EMP: 200
SALES (corp-wide): 4.5B **Publicly Held**
SIC: 7382 Security systems services
HQ: Adt Llc
1501 W Yamato Rd
Boca Raton FL 33431
561 988-3600

(G-13618)
ADT LLC
Also Called: Protection One
8200 E 34th Street Cir N (67226-1349)
PHONE..................................316 858-4300
Mark Stang, *Principal*
Mike Mondi, *Vice Pres*
Tamara Lipps, *Sales Staff*
Greg Lashay, *Technician*
EMP: 22
SALES (corp-wide): 4.5B **Publicly Held**
SIC: 7382 5999 Burglar alarm maintenance & monitoring; fire alarm maintenance & monitoring; alarm & safety equipment stores
HQ: Adt Llc
1501 W Yamato Rd
Boca Raton FL 33431
561 988-3600

(G-13619)
ADT SECURITY CORPORATION
800 E Waterman St (67202-4730)
PHONE..................................612 721-3690
Connie Schieder, *Branch Mgr*
Kendrick Wilson, *Manager*
Lisa Cole, *Supervisor*
Gay Cox, *Supervisor*
Tyrel Mallett, *Supervisor*
EMP: 24
SALES (corp-wide): 4.5B **Publicly Held**
WEB: www.protectionone.com
SIC: 7382 Burglar alarm maintenance & monitoring
HQ: The Adt Security Corporation
1501 W Yamato Rd
Boca Raton FL 33431
561 988-3600

(G-13620)
ADULT CHILD & FMLY COUNSELING
6700 W Central Ave # 106 (67212-6334)
PHONE..................................316 945-5200
Delores Greene, *Owner*
Andrew Bogner, *Counsel*
Ann Swenson, *Human Res Mgr*
Sidney Funk, *Administration*
EMP: 16
SALES (est): 811K **Privately Held**
WEB: www.adultchildfamilycounseling.com
SIC: 8322 Family (marriage) counseling; family counseling services

(G-13621)
ADVANCE ELECTRIC INC
353 N Indiana Ave (67214-4034)
PHONE..................................316 263-1300
Larry Madson, *President*
Roger Michler, *Director*
EMP: 35
SQ FT: 10,000
SALES: 4.5MM **Privately Held**
WEB: www.advanceelectricinc.biz
SIC: 1731 General electrical contractor

(G-13622)
ADVANCED ANESTHESIA ASSOC
3715 N Oliver St (67220-3404)
PHONE..................................316 942-4519
Jon Parks, *Principal*
EMP: 17
SALES (est): 609.7K **Privately Held**
WEB: www.advanced-anesthesia.com
SIC: 8011 Anesthesiologist

(G-13623)
ADVANCED MACHINE INC
2621 S Custer Ave (67217-1323)
PHONE..................................316 942-9002
Thiem Lam, *President*
Richard Dana, *Vice Pres*
Linda Downs, *Sales Associate*
Kathleen Nguyen, *Manager*
EMP: 8 **EST:** 1999
SALES (est): 1.3MM **Privately Held**
WEB: www.advancedmachine-inc.com
SIC: 3599 Machine shop, jobbing & repair

(G-13624)
ADVANCED MEDICAL RESOURCES
8015 Manor Rd (67208)
PHONE..................................316 687-3071
Craig Meyer, *President*
EMP: 28
SALES (est): 10MM **Privately Held**
SIC: 8742 Industry specialist consultants

(G-13625)
ADVANCED ORTHOPEDIC ASSOC INC
2778 N Webb Rd (67226-8112)
PHONE..................................316 631-1600
Harry Morris, *President*
Dr Kenneth Jansson, *Vice Pres*
Paul Pappademos, *Med Doctor*
Dee Larson, *Receptionist*
EMP: 51 **EST:** 1975
SQ FT: 40,000
SALES (est): 9.5MM **Privately Held**
WEB: www.ksknee.com
SIC: 8011 Orthopedic physician

(G-13626)
ADVANCED PAIN MDCINE ASSOC LLC
3715 N Oliver St (67220-3404)
PHONE..................................316 942-4519
Jon C Parks,
EMP: 10
SALES (est): 1.4MM **Privately Held**
SIC: 8011 Anesthesiologist

(G-13627)
ADVANCED WELDING TECH LLC
2020 W 2nd St N (67203-5716)
PHONE..................................316 295-2333
Cindy Langlois, *CEO*
Marc Langlois, *President*
Mac Leis,
EMP: 25
SALES (est): 5.3MM **Privately Held**
SIC: 3728 Aircraft assemblies, subassemblies & parts

(G-13628)
ADVANTAGE SALES & MKTG LLC
1407 N Armour St (67206-1127)
PHONE..................................316 721-7727
Timothy O'Keeffe, *Manager*
EMP: 17
SALES (corp-wide): 11.7B **Privately Held**
SIC: 8742 Marketing consulting services
HQ: Advantage Sales & Marketing Llc
2201 E 6th St
Austin TX 78702
949 797-2900

(G-13629)
ADVENTURE RV AND TRUCK CTR LLC
4650 S Broadway Ave (67216-1736)
PHONE..................................316 721-1333
Doug Williams,
Shari Williams,
EMP: 25
SALES (est): 5.2MM **Privately Held**
WEB: www.adventurervs.com
SIC: 5561 7538 7519 Recreational vehicle parts & accessories; recreational vehicle repairs; recreational vehicle rental

(G-13630)
ADVENTURELAND RV RENTALS INC
4650 S Broadway Ave (67216-1736)
PHONE..................................800 333-8821
Douglas C Williams, *Principal*
EMP: 16
SALES (est): 1.1MM **Privately Held**
SIC: 7519 Recreational vehicle rental

(G-13631)
ADVISORS ASSET MANAGEMENT INC
Also Called: Matrix Capital Group
8100 E 22nd St N 900-B (67226-2309)
PHONE..................................316 858-1766
Cyndi Wiles, *Vice Pres*
Michael De Luz, *Vice Pres*
EMP: 16 **Privately Held**
WEB: www.matrixunittrust.com
SIC: 6211 Security brokers & dealers
PA: Advisors Asset Management, Inc.
18925 Base Camp Rd
Monument CO 80132

(G-13632)
ADVOCTES FOR BHAVIORAL HLTH PA
1861 N Rock Rd Ste 203 (67206-1264)
PHONE..................................316 630-8444
Christine E Hebert, *President*
EMP: 14
SALES (est): 523.5K **Privately Held**
SIC: 8082 Home health care services

(G-13633)
AEI INVESTMENT HOLDINGS INC
1804 W 2nd St N (67203-5703)
PHONE..................................817 283-3722
Phil Milazzo, *CEO*
Marc Szczerba, *CFO*
EMP: 99 **EST:** 2014
SALES (est): 3.5MM **Privately Held**
SIC: 3728 Aircraft parts & equipment

(G-13634)
AERO METAL FORMS INC
2649 W Esthner Ct (67213-1897)
PHONE..................................316 942-0909
James N Zaudke, *President*
EMP: 30
SQ FT: 26,000
SALES: 4MM **Privately Held**
SIC: 3728 Aircraft parts & equipment

(G-13635)
AERO SPACE CONTROLS CORP
1050 N Mosley St (67214-3097)
PHONE..................................316 264-2875
Steven Keith, *Ch of Bd*
Don Simon, *General Mgr*
Margaret Grossardt, *COO*
Suni Baby, *Project Mgr*
▲ **EMP:** 20
SQ FT: 9,000
SALES: 2.3MM **Privately Held**
WEB: www.aerospace-controls.com
SIC: 3728 Aircraft parts & equipment

(G-13636)
AERO-MACH LABORATORIES INC (PA)
Also Called: Aeromach.com
7707 E Funston St (67207-3121)
PHONE..................................316 682-7707
Don P Bolain, *Ch of Bd*
Chuck Perkins, *President*
Charry Charles Perkins, *Business Mgr*
Jeff Carnley, *Vice Pres*

Marlin Staley, *Opers Mgr*
▲ **EMP:** 120
SQ FT: 51,000
SALES (est): 25.9MM **Privately Held**
WEB: www.aeromach.com
SIC: 3728 Aircraft parts & equipment

(G-13637)
AEROSPACE PRODUCTS COMPANY
260 N Rock Rd Ste 120 (67206-2239)
PHONE....................................316 733-4440
Kenneth Stultz, *Principal*
EMP: 8
SALES (est): 816.5K **Privately Held**
SIC: 3728 Aircraft power transmission equipment

(G-13638)
AEROSPACE SYSTEMS CMPNENTS INC
5201 E 36th St N (67220-3206)
PHONE....................................316 686-7392
Ken Seaman, *Ch of Bd*
Lance Schroeder, *General Mgr*
Jon Currier, *Project Engr*
Vicki D Hickman, *Treasurer*
EMP: 79
SQ FT: 40,000
SALES: 18MM
SALES (corp-wide): 90.8MM **Privately Held**
SIC: 3728 3612 3564 3494 Aircraft parts & equipment; transformers, except electric; blowers & fans; valves & pipe fittings
PA: Great Plains Ventures, Inc.
3504 N Great Plains Dr # 100
Wichita KS 67220
316 684-1540

(G-13639)
AEROSPACE TURBINE ROTABLES INC
1919 E Northern St (67216-2430)
PHONE....................................316 943-6100
Aaron Hollander, *CEO*
Dr Ahmed M Metwalli, *COO*
Dave Seavey, *Vice Pres*
Jason Dumler, *Engineer*
Jason Dumlermechanica, *Engineer*
▲ **EMP:** 62 **EST:** 1972
SQ FT: 30,000
SALES (est): 21.4MM **Privately Held**
SIC: 3728 Aircraft parts & equipment
PA: First Aviation Services Inc.
15 Riverside Ave
Westport CT 06880

(G-13640)
AEROTEK INC
727 N Waco Ave Ste 140 (67203-3952)
PHONE....................................316 448-4500
Deborah Mitchell, *Principal*
Kyle Meyer, *Accounts Mgr*
EMP: 25
SALES (corp-wide): 13.4B **Privately Held**
SIC: 7363 Temporary help service
HQ: Aerotek, Inc.
7301 Parkway Dr
Hanover MD 21076
410 694-5100

(G-13641)
AFFILIATED MEDICAL SVCS LAB
Also Called: AMS
2916 E Central Ave (67214-4717)
PHONE....................................316 265-4533
Edward Harned, *President*
Beth Davis, *Engineer*
Amy Cahill, *Accounts Mgr*
EMP: 85
SQ FT: 18,000
SALES (est): 5MM
SALES (corp-wide): 25.3B **Privately Held**
WEB: www.viachristi.org
SIC: 8071 Testing laboratories
HQ: Via Christi Health, Inc.
2622 W Central Ave # 102
Wichita KS 67203

(G-13642)
AFRICAN AMERICANS RENEWING INT
Also Called: A.R.I.S.E.
2420 N Dellrose St (67220-2903)
PHONE....................................316 312-0183
Dr Sharon Cranford, *Principal*
EMP: 36
SALES: 0 **Privately Held**
SIC: 7389

(G-13643)
AGAPE CENTER OF HOPE LLC
1707 N Piatt Ave (67214-1827)
PHONE....................................316 393-7252
Kevin D Andrews,
EMP: 10
SALES (est): 70.7K **Privately Held**
SIC: 8361 Residential care for children

(G-13644)
AGVANTIS INC
245 N Waco St Ste 270 (67202-1157)
PHONE....................................316 266-5400
David A Oles, *President*
Karla K Rhodes, *Vice Pres*
Aaron J Sanchez, *Vice Pres*
Peter Swenson, *Project Mgr*
Sheri Resa, *Marketing Staff*
EMP: 68
SALES: 16MM **Privately Held**
WEB: www.agvantis.com
SIC: 7379 Computer related consulting services

(G-13645)
AI INDUSTRIES PROF CORP
832 N Country Acres Ave (67212-3134)
PHONE....................................918 401-9641
Eric Bell, *President*
EMP: 10
SALES (est): 338K **Privately Held**
SIC: 3999 Manufacturing industries

(G-13646)
AIR CAPITAL BUILDING MAINT
2822 E 31st St S (67216-2701)
PHONE....................................316 838-3828
Steve Hecox, *President*
Scot Wilken, *President*
EMP: 15 **EST:** 1977
SQ FT: 800
SALES (est): 401.1K **Privately Held**
SIC: 7349 Office cleaning or charring

(G-13647)
AIR CAPITAL EQUIPMENT INC (PA)
806 E Boston St (67211-3313)
PHONE....................................316 522-1111
David A McGee, *President*
Marc McGee, *Vice Pres*
Marcia McGee, *Treasurer*
▲ **EMP:** 22
SQ FT: 6,000
SALES (est): 12MM **Privately Held**
WEB: www.aircapitalequipment.com
SIC: 5084 Fans, industrial

(G-13648)
AIR CAPITAL INTERIORS INC
9424 E 37th St N Ste 300 (67226-2024)
P.O. Box 780168 (67278-0168)
PHONE....................................316 633-4790
Matthew Henry, *CEO*
Rod Wilson, *President*
Terry Crumrine, *Opers Staff*
EMP: 10
SALES (est): 1.2MM **Privately Held**
SIC: 3721 Aircraft

(G-13649)
AIR CAPITOL DIAL INC
220 N Vine St (67203-5841)
PHONE....................................316 264-2483
Steven McKinney, *President*
Jean E Mc Kinney, *Corp Secy*
EMP: 12
SQ FT: 7,200
SALES (est): 1.1MM **Privately Held**
WEB: www.aircapitoldial.com
SIC: 7336 3728 Silk screen design; panel assembly (hydromatic propeller test stands), aircraft

(G-13650)
AIRBUS AMERICAS INC
213 N Mead St (67202-2707)
PHONE....................................316 264-0552
William Greer, *General Mgr*
Bernhard Brenner, *Exec VP*
Ben Bridge, *Exec VP*
Nicolas Chamussy, *Exec VP*
Alain Flourens, *Exec VP*
EMP: 200
SALES (corp-wide): 70.6B **Privately Held**
SIC: 3721 Aircraft
HQ: Airbus Americas, Inc.
2550 Wasser Ter Ste 9100
Herndon VA 20171
703 834-3400

(G-13651)
AIRCRAFT INSTR & RDO CO INC (PA)
Also Called: Airco Group
1853 S Eisenhower Ct (67209-2845)
P.O. Box 9487 (67277-0487)
PHONE....................................316 945-9820
Martin Potash, *President*
Jerry Ward, *COO*
Melanie Combs, *Vice Pres*
Cor Tjalsma, *Director*
EMP: 29
SQ FT: 13,000
SALES (est): 11.2MM **Privately Held**
WEB: www.airco-ict.com
SIC: 5088 5065 7622 7629 Aircraft equipment & supplies; radio parts & accessories; radio repair shop; aircraft electrical equipment repair

(G-13652)
AIRCRAFT INSTRUMENT & RDO SVCS
1851 S Eisenhower Ct (67209-2845)
P.O. Box 9487 (67277-0487)
PHONE....................................316 945-9820
Melanie Combs, *Vice Pres*
EMP: 15
SQ FT: 5,000
SALES (est): 925.9K
SALES (corp-wide): 11.2MM **Privately Held**
WEB: www.airco-ict.com
SIC: 7699 Aircraft flight instrument repair
PA: Aircraft Instrument And Radio Company, Incorporated
1853 S Eisenhower Ct
Wichita KS 67209
316 945-9820

(G-13653)
AIRGAS USA LLC
4115 W 33rd St S (67215-1015)
PHONE....................................316 941-9162
Gregory Begay, *Branch Mgr*
EMP: 24
SALES (corp-wide): 121.9MM **Privately Held**
SIC: 5085 7699 5999 5084 Welding supplies; welding equipment repair; welding supplies; welding machinery & equipment
HQ: Airgas Usa, Llc
259 N Radnor Chester Rd
Radnor PA 19087
610 687-5253

(G-13654)
AIRMD LLC (PA)
Also Called: Lifesave
3445 N Webb Rd (67226-8125)
PHONE....................................316 932-1440
Shawn S Emt, *Engineer*
Tonia Groves, *Accounting Mgr*
Dylan Lincoln, *Corp Comm Staff*
Kyle Perry, *Med Doctor*
Martin E Sellberg, *Mng Member*
EMP: 26
SQ FT: 14,000
SALES (est): 20.7MM **Privately Held**
SIC: 4119 Ambulance service

(G-13655)
AIRPORT RED COACH INN OF WICHI
Also Called: Best Western
6815 W Kellogg Dr (67209-2217)
PHONE....................................316 942-5600
Kim Madison, *General Mgr*
Harry Bledsoe,
EMP: 70
SALES (est): 3.3MM **Privately Held**
SIC: 7011 Hotels & motels

(G-13656)
AIRXCEL INC (HQ)
Also Called: R V Products Div
3050 N Saint Francis St (67219-4045)
P.O. Box 4020 (67204-0020)
PHONE....................................316 832-3400
Jeff Rutherford, *President*
Debra Jones, *CFO*
Steve Smith, *Sales Staff*
Courtney Nickerson, *Admin Asst*
▲ **EMP:** 300
SQ FT: 153,000
SALES (est): 349MM **Privately Held**
SIC: 3585 Heating & air conditioning combination units

(G-13657)
ALADDIN PETROLEUM CORPORATION (PA)
123 S Market St (67202-3801)
P.O. Box 3916 (67201-3916)
PHONE....................................316 265-9602
George Bruce, *President*
EMP: 5 **EST:** 1921
SQ FT: 1,000
SALES (est): 828.5K **Privately Held**
SIC: 1311 Crude petroleum production; natural gas production

(G-13658)
ALAN MOSKOWITZ MD PC
Also Called: Cally, Donald J
10100 E Shannon Woods St (67226-4104)
PHONE....................................316 858-1900
EMP: 65
SALES (est): 3.6MM **Privately Held**
SIC: 8011 Medical Doctor's Office

(G-13659)
ALBERTSON & HEIN INC
3617 W Walker St (67213-1690)
PHONE....................................316 943-7441
Joseph Hein, *President*
Jim Hein, *President*
Alberta Hein, *Vice Pres*
EMP: 20 **EST:** 1951
SQ FT: 33,000
SALES (est): 3.4MM **Privately Held**
SIC: 3599 Machine shop, jobbing & repair

(G-13660)
ALCOHOLICS ANONYMOUS
Also Called: Aa Central Office
2812 E English St (67211-2109)
PHONE....................................316 684-3661
Jo Anne Dickson, *Director*
EMP: 14
SALES (corp-wide): 9.7MM **Privately Held**
WEB: www.alcoholics-anonymous.org
SIC: 8399 Social service information exchange
PA: Alcoholics Anonymous World Services, Inc.
475 Riverside Dr
New York NY 10115
212 870-3400

(G-13661)
ALDERWOODS (KANSAS) INC (PA)
Also Called: Hillside Funeral Home
2929 W 13th St N (67203-6618)
PHONE....................................316 682-5575
Leo Ramsey, *Owner*
EMP: 18 **EST:** 1945
SQ FT: 18,000
SALES (est): 1.5MM **Privately Held**
SIC: 5999 7261 Monuments, finished to custom order; funeral home

(G-13662)
ALL AMERICAN AUTOMOTIVE INC
8630 W Kellogg Dr (67209-1873)
PHONE....................................316 721-3600
Greg Norris, *President*
Russell Norris, *Corp Secy*
▲ **EMP:** 10
SQ FT: 7,500

GEOGRAPHIC

SALES (est): 1.4MM **Privately Held**
SIC: 7538 General automotive repair shops

(G-13663)
ALL CRTRES VETERINARY HOSP P A
8414 W 13th St N Ste 170 (67212-2979)
PHONE..................................316 721-3993
Randy Ohmke, *Principal*
EMP: 15
SALES (est): 568.3K **Privately Held**
SIC: 0742 5999 3999 0752 Animal hospital services, pets & other animal specialties; pet food; pet supplies; boarding services, kennels

(G-13664)
ALL IN CUT
11940 W Central Ave # 112 (67212-5180)
PHONE..................................316 722-4962
Gina Moon, *Owner*
Joleen M Stephens, *Owner*
EMP: 14 **EST:** 1999
SALES (est): 178.2K **Privately Held**
SIC: 7231 Hairdressers

(G-13665)
ALL SAINTS HOME CARE INC
3425 W Central Ave (67203-4919)
P.O. Box 48397 (67201-8397)
PHONE..................................316 755-1076
Darlene Castleman, *Administration*
Daron Castleman, *Administration*
Holly Castleman, *Administration*
EMP: 12
SALES (est): 831.3K **Privately Held**
WEB: www.allsaintshomecare.com
SIC: 8082 Home health care services

(G-13666)
ALL STATES WINDOWS SIDING LLC (PA)
776 N West St (67203-1235)
PHONE..................................316 444-1220
Cris A Keeter, *Mng Member*
Daryn Keeter,
EMP: 22
SALES (est): 4.9MM **Privately Held**
SIC: 1761 Siding contractor

(G-13667)
ALLEN GIBBS & HOULIK LLC
Also Called: A G H
301 N Main St Ste 1700 (67202-4868)
PHONE..................................316 267-7231
Kurt Breitenbach, *Exec VP*
Donald Glenn, *Exec VP*
Steve Houlik, *Exec VP*
Nicole Alexander, *Vice Pres*
Bradly Bechtel, *Vice Pres*
EMP: 140
SALES: 18MM **Privately Held**
WEB: www.aghlc.com
SIC: 8721 Certified public accountant

(G-13668)
ALLEN AND SONS WASTE SVCS LLC
3645 W Esthner Ave (67213-1214)
PHONE..................................316 558-8050
Gerald W Allen,
EMP: 11
SALES (est): 486.2K **Privately Held**
SIC: 4953 Recycling, waste materials

(G-13669)
ALLEN TRENCHING INC
8222 W Irving St (67209-1839)
PHONE..................................316 721-6300
Vicki L Allen, *President*
Bobby E Allen, *Admin Sec*
EMP: 15 **EST:** 1977
SQ FT: 1,900
SALES: 1.5MM **Privately Held**
SIC: 1629 Trenching contractor

(G-13670)
ALLIANCE MONITORING TECH LLC (PA)
Also Called: All-Call
355 S Ellis St (67211-1811)
PHONE..................................316 263-7775
Scott Tucker, *Mng Member*
James Lindamood, *Mng Member*
EMP: 14
SQ FT: 4,500
SALES: 2.7MM **Privately Held**
SIC: 8731 7382 Commercial physical research; security systems services

(G-13671)
ALLIANT BANK
3711 N Ridge Rd (67205-1216)
PHONE..................................316 772-5111
EMP: 11
SALES: 918K **Privately Held**
SIC: 6022 State Commercial Bank

(G-13672)
ALLIED ENVIRONMENTAL CONS INC
214 N Saint Francis Ave (67202-2610)
P.O. Box 234 (67201-0234)
PHONE..................................316 262-5698
Paul R Clark, *President*
Dawn A Breit, *Vice Pres*
Steven M Linehan, *Treasurer*
Theodore B Francis, *Director*
Theodore Francis, *Director*
EMP: 10
SQ FT: 3,500
SALES (est): 1.2MM **Privately Held**
SIC: 8711 8748 Consulting engineer; environmental consultant

(G-13673)
ALLIED OIL & TIRE COMPANY
3619 N Poplar St (67219-2302)
PHONE..................................316 530-5221
Kim Holtz, *Manager*
EMP: 10
SALES (corp-wide): 139.9MM **Privately Held**
SIC: 5014 Automobile tires & tubes
PA: Allied Oil & Tire Company
2209 S 24th St
Omaha NE 68108
402 344-4343

(G-13674)
ALLIED SALES AND MARKETING INC
550 N 159th St E Ste 301 (67230-7523)
PHONE..................................316 617-2160
Albert Crawford, *President*
EMP: 19 **EST:** 1996
SQ FT: 1,000
SALES (est): 78.6K **Privately Held**
SIC: 5141 Groceries, general line

(G-13675)
ALLMETAL RECYCLING LLC (PA)
800 E 21st St N (67214-1326)
PHONE..................................316 558-9914
Angelo Cornejo, *Opers Spvr*
Bob Nash, *Sales Staff*
Clint Cornejo, *Mng Member*
Kolby Cornejo,
Matt Polzin,
EMP: 70
SALES (est): 36.6MM **Privately Held**
SIC: 4953 Recycling, waste materials

(G-13676)
ALLMETAL RECYCLING LLC
410 E 25th St N (67219-4409)
PHONE..................................316 838-9381
EMP: 51
SALES (corp-wide): 36.6MM **Privately Held**
SIC: 4953 5093 1311 Recycling, waste materials; metal scrap & waste materials; crude petroleum production
PA: Allmetal Recycling, Llc
800 E 21st St N
Wichita KS 67214
316 558-9914

(G-13677)
ALLOY ARCHITECTURE PA
Also Called: Howard & Helmer Architects PA
3500 N Rock Rd Bldg 500 (67226-1338)
PHONE..................................316 634-1111
David White, *President*
Rodney Sondergard, *Corp Secy*
Eileen Wagner, *Controller*
Andrew Faires, *Internal Med*
EMP: 21
SQ FT: 4,500
SALES (est): 3.5MM **Privately Held**
WEB: www.howardandhelmer.com
SIC: 8712 Architectural engineering

(G-13678)
ALLTITE INC (PA)
Also Called: Mobilecal
1600 E Murdock St (67214-3477)
P.O. Box 20195 (67208-1195)
PHONE..................................316 686-3010
Thomas Smith, *CEO*
Andrew Smith, *President*
John R Smith, *VP Opers*
Ben White, *Buyer*
Levi Robillard, *Accounts Mgr*
EMP: 43
SQ FT: 62,629
SALES: 12.3MM **Privately Held**
WEB: www.alltite.net
SIC: 5084 1796 7629 3546 Hydraulic systems equipment & supplies; machinery dismantling; aircraft electrical equipment repair; power-driven handtools; sockets (machine tool accessories); tool rental

(G-13679)
ALLY SERVICING LLC
9111 E Douglas Ave 200b (67207-1241)
PHONE..................................316 652-6301
Phil Gibbs, *Branch Mgr*
EMP: 180
SALES (corp-wide): 10.4B **Publicly Held**
WEB: www.accutelinc.com
SIC: 1389 8742 Roustabout service; management consulting services
HQ: Ally Servicing Llc
500 Woodward Ave Fl 1
Detroit MI 48226
248 948-7702

(G-13680)
ALPHA BIOSYSTEMS INC
9912 W York St (67215-8946)
PHONE..................................316 265-7929
Randy Kressler, *President*
Terry Loucks, *Vice Pres*
▲ **EMP:** 8
SALES (est): 1.5MM
SALES (corp-wide): 28.1MM **Privately Held**
WEB: www.alpha-bugs.com
SIC: 2836 Biological products, except diagnostic
PA: Lubrication Engineers, Inc.
1919 E Tulsa St
Wichita KS 67216
800 537-7683

(G-13681)
ALWAYS THERE SENIOR CARE INC
2260 N Ridge Rd Ste 220 (67205-1130)
PHONE..................................316 946-9222
Greg Feldman, *President*
Zach Henson, *Vice Pres*
EMP: 70
SQ FT: 1,200
SALES (est): 1.8MM **Privately Held**
SIC: 8322 Homemakers' service

(G-13682)
AMBASSADOR HOTEL WICHITA LLC
104 S Broadway Ave (67202-4116)
PHONE..................................316 239-7100
Michael Frimel, *Principal*
EMP: 35
SALES (est): 2.5MM **Privately Held**
SIC: 7011 Hotels

(G-13683)
AMERICAN BAPTIST ESTATES INC
Also Called: PRAIRIE HOMESTEAD
1605 W May St (67213-3511)
PHONE..................................316 263-8264
Rev Bill Shook, *Administration*
Diane Hull, *Administration*
EMP: 31
SQ FT: 130,000
SALES: 1.9MM **Privately Held**
WEB: www.prairiehomestead.com
SIC: 8361 Home for the aged

(G-13684)
AMERICAN BLDRS CONTRS SUP INC
Also Called: ABC Supply 113
1321 E 1st St N (67214-4015)
PHONE..................................316 265-8276
Frank Novascone, *Manager*
EMP: 20
SALES (corp-wide): 3.5B **Privately Held**
WEB: www.abcsupply.com
SIC: 5033 5031 Roofing & siding materials; windows
HQ: American Builders & Contractors Supply Co., Inc.
1 Abc Pkwy
Beloit WI 53511
608 362-7777

(G-13685)
AMERICAN BONANZA SOCIETY INC
Also Called: ABS-AIR SAFETY FOUNDATION
3595 N Webb Rd Ste 200 (67226-8191)
P.O. Box 12888 (67277-2888)
PHONE..................................316 945-1700
Coy Cross, *Controller*
Nancy Johnson, *Exec Dir*
Dara Quastad,
EMP: 16
SQ FT: 1,600
SALES: 323.5K **Privately Held**
SIC: 8699 Personal interest organization

(G-13686)
AMERICAN BOTTLING COMPANY
1240 W Macarthur Rd (67217-2726)
PHONE..................................316 529-3777
Steven Browne, *Branch Mgr*
EMP: 70 **Publicly Held**
SIC: 2086 Soft drinks: packaged in cans, bottles, etc.
HQ: The American Bottling Company
5301 Legacy Dr
Plano TX 75024

(G-13687)
AMERICAN CAB INC
Also Called: ABC American Taxi
400 S Greenwood St (67211-1820)
PHONE..................................316 262-7511
Ted Hill, *President*
EMP: 12 **EST:** 1975
SQ FT: 2,400
SALES (est): 505.7K **Privately Held**
SIC: 4121 Taxicabs

(G-13688)
AMERICAN CANCER SOCTY HEARTLND
236 S Topeka Ave (67202-4308)
PHONE..................................316 265-3400
Stephanie Weiter, *Vice Pres*
EMP: 18
SALES (corp-wide): 26.1MM **Privately Held**
SIC: 8733 Noncommercial research organizations
PA: American Cancer Society, Heartland Division, Inc.
1100 Pennsylvania Ave
Kansas City MO 64105

(G-13689)
AMERICAN CHEM SYSTEMS II LLC (PA)
3505 W 29th St S (67217-1001)
P.O. Box 782647 (67278-2647)
PHONE..................................316 263-4448
Brad Wickham,
EMP: 25
SQ FT: 2,000
SALES (est): 4.8MM **Privately Held**
SIC: 5169 Industrial chemicals

(G-13690)
AMERICAN COMM & RESIDENTL SVCS
2408 S Pattie St (67216-1238)
P.O. Box 16353 (67216-0353)
PHONE..................................316 633-5866
Doug Drinnen, *Mng Member*
EMP: 10

SALES: 1MM **Privately Held**
SIC: 1711 7389 Plumbing, heating, air-conditioning contractors;

(G-13691)
AMERICAN FENCE AND SEC CO INC
2909 S West St (67217-1031)
PHONE..................................316 945-5001
Pam Cox, *Finance*
Kerry Schneck, *Branch Mgr*
EMP: 8
SQ FT: 3,600 **Privately Held**
SIC: 3949 1799 Fencing equipment (sporting goods); fence construction
PA: American Fence And Security Company, Inc.
2502 N 27th Ave
Phoenix AZ 85009

(G-13692)
AMERICAN GOLF CORPORATION
Also Called: Tallgrass Country Club
2400 N Tallgrass St (67226-1912)
PHONE..................................316 684-4110
Katie Schwartz, *General Mgr*
EMP: 55
SQ FT: 3,000 **Publicly Held**
WEB: www.americangolf.com
SIC: 7997 Golf club, membership
HQ: American Golf Corporation
909 N Pacific Coast Hwy
El Segundo CA 90245
310 664-4000

(G-13693)
AMERICAN OVERSEAS SCHOOLS HIST
704 W Douglas Ave (67203-6104)
PHONE..................................316 265-6837
Thomas T Drysdale, *President*
EMP: 23
SALES: 64.3K **Privately Held**
SIC: 8412 Historical society

(G-13694)
AMERICAN TIRE DISTRIBUTORS
5015 S Water Cir (67217-4900)
PHONE..................................316 616-9600
Mike Riddle, *Branch Mgr*
EMP: 21
SALES (corp-wide): 5B **Privately Held**
SIC: 5531 5014 3011 Automotive tires; tires & tubes; tires & inner tubes
HQ: American Tire Distributors Inc.
12200 Herbert Wayne Ct # 150
Huntersville NC 28078
704 992-2000

(G-13695)
AMERICAN WTR PURIFICATION INC
7701 E Kellogg Dr Ste 670 (67207-1705)
PHONE..................................316 685-3333
Dan Gates, *President*
Richard Devore, *Principal*
Kathy Gordon, *Vice Pres*
Jim Loewen, *Vice Pres*
Lisa Sawyer, *Vice Pres*
EMP: 12
SQ FT: 1,200
SALES (est): 2.9MM **Privately Held**
SIC: 5074 Water purification equipment

(G-13696)
AMERICOLD LOGISTICS LLC
2707 N Mead St (67219-4238)
PHONE..................................316 838-9317
Eric Schaffer, *Opers Mgr*
Scott Groshann, *Manager*
EMP: 40
SALES (corp-wide): 1.6B **Publicly Held**
WEB: www.americoldlogistics.com
SIC: 4222 Warehousing, cold storage or refrigerated
HQ: Americold Logistics, Llc
10 Glenlake Pkwy Ste 324
Atlanta GA 30328
678 441-1400

(G-13697)
AMERIPRISE FINANCIAL INC
Also Called: Ameriprice Financial
10333 E 21st St N Ste 402 (67206-3547)
PHONE..................................316 858-1506
Deborah Gdisis, *CFO*
Thomas McMillen, *Executive*
Richard Campbell, *Advisor*
EMP: 23
SALES (corp-wide): 12.8B **Publicly Held**
SIC: 6282 Investment advice
PA: Ameriprise Financial, Inc.
55 Ameriprise Fincl Ctr
Minneapolis MN 55474
612 671-3131

(G-13698)
AMETEK ADVANCED INDUSTRIES INC
4550 S Southeast Blvd (67210-1623)
PHONE..................................316 522-0424
Keith Reazin, *Vice Pres*
Alan Stevens, *Engineer*
Glenn Kidd, *Sales Dir*
Randy Rockett, *Supervisor*
EMP: 90
SQ FT: 24,500
SALES (est): 22.1MM
SALES (corp-wide): 4.8B **Publicly Held**
SIC: 3621 7694 Motors, electric; rewinding stators
PA: Ametek, Inc.
1100 Cassatt Rd
Berwyn PA 19312
610 647-2121

(G-13699)
AMETEK ARCFT PARTS & ACC INC
Also Called: B & S Aircraft
1414 S Mosley Ave (67211-3330)
PHONE..................................316 264-2397
Richard Lewallan, *Business Mgr*
Calvin Ringer, *Accountant*
EMP: 47 **EST:** 1965
SQ FT: 16,000
SALES (est): 6.4MM
SALES (corp-wide): 4.8B **Publicly Held**
WEB: www.bsaircraft.com
SIC: 7699 5088 Aircraft flight instrument repair; aircraft & parts
PA: Ametek, Inc.
1100 Cassatt Rd
Berwyn PA 19312
610 647-2121

(G-13700)
AMI METALS INC
2300 S Hoover Rd (67209-2843)
PHONE..................................316 945-7771
John Edwardson, *Production*
EMP: 30
SALES (corp-wide): 11.5B **Publicly Held**
WEB: www.amimetals.com
SIC: 5051 Steel; aluminum bars, rods, ingots, sheets, pipes, plates, etc.
HQ: Ami Metals, Inc.
1738 Gen George Patton Dr
Brentwood TN 37027
615 377-0400

(G-13701)
ANATOMI IMAGING
Also Called: A M S Diagnostics
2734 N Woodlawn Blvd (67220-2730)
PHONE..................................316 858-4091
Kevin Streaker, *CEO*
EMP: 12
SALES (est): 1.1MM **Privately Held**
WEB: www.anatomiimaging.com
SIC: 8011 Radiologist

(G-13702)
ANCIENT FORMULAS INC
1235 S Santa Fe St (67211-3223)
PHONE..................................316 838-5600
Mark Aghakhani, *President*
EMP: 10
SQ FT: 3,000
SALES (est): 1.2MM **Privately Held**
SIC: 2023 Dietary supplements, dairy & non-dairy based

(G-13703)
ANDALE CONSTRUCTION INC
3170 N Ohio St (67219-4134)
PHONE..................................316 832-0063
Lori Payne, *CFO*
Katie Thimesch, *Admin Sec*
EMP: 99
SALES (est): 22.2MM **Privately Held**
SIC: 3273 Ready-mixed concrete

(G-13704)
ANDALE READY MIX CENTRAL INC
3170 N Ohio St (67219-4134)
PHONE..................................316 832-0063
Peter J Molitor, *President*
EMP: 81 **EST:** 2005
SALES (est): 23.9MM **Privately Held**
WEB: www.andalereadymix.com
SIC: 3273 Ready-mixed concrete

(G-13705)
ANDERSON INDUSTRIES INC
3246 W 13th St N (67203-6623)
P.O. Box 4348 (67204-0348)
PHONE..................................316 945-4488
Thomas Anderson, *President*
EMP: 10
SQ FT: 15,000
SALES: 1MM **Privately Held**
WEB: www.pioneercable.com
SIC: 3679 Harness assemblies for electronic use: wire or cable

(G-13706)
ANDERSON MANAGEMENT COMPANY (PA)
3450 N Rock Rd Ste 201 (67226-1352)
PHONE..................................316 681-1711
Norman Foster, *President*
EMP: 16
SQ FT: 3,042
SALES (est): 2.5MM **Privately Held**
SIC: 6531 Real estate managers

(G-13707)
ANDOVER STATE BANK
1718 N Webb Rd (67206-3420)
PHONE..................................316 219-1600
Brian Chamberlin, *Branch Mgr*
EMP: 10
SALES (corp-wide): 4.2MM **Privately Held**
SIC: 6022 State commercial banks
PA: Andover State Bank
511 N Andover Rd
Andover KS 67002
316 733-1375

(G-13708)
ANDREW INC (PA)
2310 E Douglas Ave (67214-4437)
PHONE..................................316 267-3328
Lyle Tanquary, *President*
Janet Tanquary, *Corp Secy*
David Hagan, *Sales Staff*
EMP: 14 **EST:** 1948
SQ FT: 15,000
SALES (est): 5.4MM **Privately Held**
WEB: www.andrew.net
SIC: 5198 5231 Paints; wallcoverings; paint; wallpaper

(G-13709)
ANGEL WINGS LEARNING CTR LLC
770 S Greenwich Rd (67207-4314)
PHONE..................................316 249-4818
Marissa Harris, *CEO*
EMP: 13
SALES (est): 151.8K **Privately Held**
SIC: 8351 Child day care services

(G-13710)
ANGELS CARE HOME HEALTH
8200 E 34th Cir N # 1601 (67226-1349)
PHONE..................................316 636-4000
C Deffencaugh, *Administration*
EMP: 10 **EST:** 2009
SALES: 5.6MM **Privately Held**
SIC: 8082 Visiting nurse service

(G-13711)
ANIMAL CLINIC WICHITA PA
Also Called: Pet Clinic At Webb Village
10712 E Harry St (67207-5024)
PHONE..................................316 686-8516
Brian Dotson, *President*
EMP: 10
SQ FT: 3,300
SALES (est): 519.4K **Privately Held**
SIC: 0742 Animal hospital services, pets & other animal specialties

(G-13712)
ANSWERING EXCHANGE INC
1443 S George Wash Dr (67211-3903)
PHONE..................................316 262-8282
Joni Sadowski, *President*
Joni Sadowske, *Executive*
EMP: 32
SQ FT: 1,200
SALES (est): 2.9MM **Privately Held**
SIC: 7389 Telephone answering service

(G-13713)
ANTOINE E WAKIM INC
Also Called: Antoine E Wakim DDS PA
710 N Woodchuck St (67212-3628)
PHONE..................................316 721-4477
Antoine E Wakim, *President*
EMP: 12
SALES (est): 1.4MM **Privately Held**
SIC: 8021 Dentists' office

(G-13714)
ANTRIM & ASSOC
7303 E Bayley St (67207-2708)
PHONE..................................316 267-2753
Jason L Antrim, *Owner*
EMP: 10
SALES: 101K **Privately Held**
SIC: 6531 1521 Broker of manufactured homes, on site; single-family home remodeling, additions & repairs

(G-13715)
APAC-KANSAS INC
3511 S West St (67217-1043)
P.O. Box 17470 (67217-0470)
PHONE..................................316 522-4881
Neal Kearnes, *Branch Mgr*
EMP: 100
SALES (corp-wide): 29.7B **Privately Held**
SIC: 1799 5032 Parking lot maintenance; paving materials
HQ: Apac-Kansas, Inc.
9660 Legler Rd
Lenexa KS 66219

(G-13716)
APAC-KANSAS INC
3615 S West St (67217-3801)
P.O. Box 17470 (67217-0470)
PHONE..................................316 524-5200
Jim Olson, *President*
Bobby Philipi, *Manager*
EMP: 100
SALES (corp-wide): 29.7B **Privately Held**
SIC: 1799 2951 1611 Parking lot maintenance; asphalt paving mixtures & blocks; surfacing & paving
HQ: Apac-Kansas, Inc.
9660 Legler Rd
Lenexa KS 66219

(G-13717)
APARTMENT MOVERS INC
Also Called: Aarons Wichita Mvg & Stor Co
150 N Osage St (67203-6132)
PHONE..................................316 267-5300
Jim Towey, *President*
Kelly Towey, *Vice Pres*
EMP: 25
SQ FT: 20,000
SALES (est): 2.5MM **Privately Held**
SIC: 4214 4212 Furniture moving & storage, local; delivery service, vehicular

(G-13718)
APEX ENGINEERING INTL LLC (HQ)
Also Called: A E I
1804 W 2nd St N (67203-5703)
PHONE..................................316 262-1494
Debbie Hawley, *General Mgr*
Katie McNatt, *Production*

GEOGRAPHIC

Christina Ohmart, *Production*
Jan Edwards, *Purchasing*
Jennifer Frank, *Purchasing*
EMP: 165
SQ FT: 159,000
SALES (est): 30.9MM
SALES (corp-wide): 200.2MM **Privately Held**
WEB: www.aeillc.com
SIC: 3728 Aircraft assemblies, subassemblies & parts
PA: Hm Dunn Aerosystems, Inc.
3301 House Anderson Rd
Euless TX 76040
817 283-3722

(G-13719)
APOLLON COMPUTERS INC
8351 E 35th St N (67226-1326)
PHONE..................................316 264-2329
David Sasson, *President*
Al Smucker, *Corp Secy*
Brent Hanson, *Vice Pres*
Evangelos Nantsis, *Vice Pres*
David Turner, *Production*
EMP: 27 **EST:** 1996
SQ FT: 30,000
SALES (est): 5.6MM **Privately Held**
WEB: www.apollonpc.com
SIC: 3575 Computer terminals, monitors & components

(G-13720)
APPH WICHITA INC
1445 S Sierra Dr (67209-2933)
PHONE..................................316 943-5752
Mike Meshey, *President*
Curtis Hibarger, *Engineer*
Jon Sharrock, *CFO*
▲ **EMP:** 50
SQ FT: 60,000
SALES (est): 9.1MM
SALES (corp-wide): 365.8MM **Privately Held**
WEB: www.airightinc.com
SIC: 7699 3594 3728 Aircraft & heavy equipment repair services; fluid power pumps & motors; aircraft parts & equipment
PA: Heroux-Devtek Inc
1111 Rue Saint-Charles O Bureau 600
Longueuil QC J4K 5
450 679-5450

(G-13721)
APPLE CENTRAL LLC APPLEBE
P.O. Box 780732 (67278-0732)
PHONE..................................203 987-6162
EMP: 5
SALES (est): 486.2K **Privately Held**
SIC: 3571 Mfg Electronic Computers

(G-13722)
APPLE EGHT HOSPITALITY MGT INC
Also Called: Courtyard Wichita East
2975 N Webb Rd (67226-8115)
PHONE..................................316 636-4600
Ed Diagle, *Manager*
EMP: 43 **Privately Held**
SIC: 7011 Hotels & motels
HQ: Apple Eight Hospitality Management, Inc.
814 E Main St
Richmond VA 23219

(G-13723)
APPLIANCE DOCTOR INC
Also Called: Appliance Doctor, The
1123 E Pawnee St (67211-5127)
PHONE..................................316 263-0005
Terry W Conway, *President*
Tammy Rico, *Treasurer*
EMP: 30
SQ FT: 1,600
SALES (est): 4.6MM **Privately Held**
SIC: 1542 7699 Commercial & office building, new construction; household appliance repair services

(G-13724)
APPRENTICE PERSONNEL INC
328 S Laura Ave (67211-1517)
PHONE..................................316 267-4781
Patti Blanks-Clark, *Opers Mgr*
Christy Golden, *Branch Mgr*
EMP: 100
SALES (est): 2.3MM **Privately Held**
SIC: 7363 Temporary help service

(G-13725)
APRIA HEALTHCARE LLC
318 N Cleveland Ave (67214-4026)
PHONE..................................316 689-4500
Dustin Stos, *Manager*
EMP: 27 **Privately Held**
WEB: www.apria.com
SIC: 7352 5047 Medical equipment rental; hospital equipment & furniture
HQ: Apria Healthcare Llc
26220 Enterprise Ct
Lake Forest CA 92630
949 639-2000

(G-13726)
ARAMARK UNF & CAREER AP LLC
521 W Walker St (67213-4334)
PHONE..................................316 262-5467
Lydell Brandon, *Manager*
EMP: 100 **Publicly Held**
WEB: www.aramark-uniform.com
SIC: 7218 7213 Industrial launderers; uniform supply
HQ: Aramark Uniform & Career Apparel, Llc
115 N First St Ste 203
Burbank CA 91502
818 973-3700

(G-13727)
ARC DOCUMENT SOLUTIONS
Also Called: Www.kbp.com
518 W Douglas Ave (67203-6102)
P.O. Box 793 (67201-0793)
PHONE..................................316 264-9344
EMP: 35
SQ FT: 14,500
SALES (est): 3.7MM **Privately Held**
SIC: 5049 7334 2741 Engineers' equipment & supplies; photocopying & duplicating services; maps: publishing only, not printed on site

(G-13728)
ARC DOCUMENT SOLUTIONS INC
518 W Douglas Ave (67203-6102)
PHONE..................................316 264-9344
Joe Lafever, *President*
EMP: 27
SALES (corp-wide): 400.7MM **Publicly Held**
SIC: 7334 Photocopying & duplicating services
PA: Arc Document Solutions, Inc.
12657 Alcosta Blvd # 200
San Ramon CA 94583
925 949-5100

(G-13729)
ARC OF SEDGWICK COUNTY INC
2919 W 2nd St N (67203-5319)
PHONE..................................316 943-1191
Anita Buchanan, *President*
Terry Finger, *Vice Pres*
Leonal Kilgore, *Vice Pres*
Steven Peiffer, *Treasurer*
Linda Calven, *Supervisor*
EMP: 31
SQ FT: 6,500
SALES: 1.9MM **Privately Held**
WEB: www.arc-sedgwickcounty.org
SIC: 8322 Association for the handicapped

(G-13730)
ARCHEIN AEROSPACE LLC
4601 E Douglas Ave # 321 (67218-1011)
PHONE..................................682 499-2150
Michael Kaufhold,
Shelley Wombacher, *Admin Sec*
Kyle Barker,
Rich Cole Chair,
Robert D Moreau,
EMP: 21 **EST:** 2016
SQ FT: 35,000
SALES: 2MM **Privately Held**
SIC: 3728 7363 8711 8742 Research & dev by manuf., aircraft parts & auxiliary equip; pilot service, aviation; aviation &/or aeronautical engineering; marketing consulting services; business consulting

(G-13731)
ARCHITECTURAL CAST STONE INC
Also Called: Architectural Concrete Pdts
1918 N Wabash Ave (67214-1454)
PHONE..................................316 262-5543
Bob Bales, *President*
Cathey Bales, *Vice Pres*
Michelle Schiefer, *Vice Pres*
▲ **EMP:** 32 **EST:** 1998
SQ FT: 17,000
SALES (est): 5.3MM **Privately Held**
WEB: www.architecturalcaststone.com
SIC: 3272 Stone, cast concrete

(G-13732)
ARCTIC GLACIER TEXAS INC
Also Called: Arctic Glacier Ice
215 E 27th St S (67216-1041)
PHONE..................................316 529-2173
Kevin Coe, *Manager*
EMP: 20
SALES (corp-wide): 2.4B **Publicly Held**
SIC: 5999 4222 2097 Ice; refrigerated warehousing & storage; manufactured ice
HQ: Arctic Glacier Texas Inc.
130 E 42nd St
Lubbock TX

(G-13733)
ARKO MANUFACTURING CO INC
3545 N Broadway Ave (67219-3611)
PHONE..................................316 838-7162
Ronald Koepsel, *President*
Roger Koepsel, *Vice Pres*
EMP: 8
SQ FT: 12,000
SALES (est): 1.2MM **Privately Held**
SIC: 3442 3444 Screens, window, metal; storm doors or windows, metal; awnings, sheet metal

(G-13734)
ARMSTRONG PLUMBING INC
7540 W Northwind St # 300 (67205-2597)
PHONE..................................316 942-9535
Robert J Armstrong, *President*
Dana Armstrong, *Treasurer*
EMP: 17
SALES (est): 2.5MM **Privately Held**
SIC: 1711 5999 Plumbing contractors; plumbing & heating supplies

(G-13735)
ARNOLD & ASSOCIATES OF WICHITA (PA)
Also Called: The Arnold Group
530 S Topeka Ave (67202-4419)
PHONE..................................316 263-9283
George Arnold, *CEO*
Jill Staats, *President*
Marion Arnold, *Vice Pres*
Phil Hayes, *Vice Pres*
Tara Breiding, *Marketing Staff*
EMP: 15
SALES (est): 3.2MM **Privately Held**
WEB: www.the-arnold-group.com
SIC: 7363 Temporary help service

(G-13736)
ARROW LABORATORY INC
1333 N Main St (67203-3436)
P.O. Box 248 (67201-0248)
PHONE..................................316 267-2893
James Nick Roark, *President*
William Bochman, *Vice Pres*
Dale Roark, *Admin Sec*
EMP: 12 **EST:** 1947
SALES (est): 1.3MM **Privately Held**
WEB: www.arrowlab.com
SIC: 8734 Metallurgical testing laboratory

(G-13737)
ARROW WRECKER SERVICE INC
Also Called: Arrow Towing & Recovery
531 E Macarthur Rd (67216-1622)
PHONE..................................316 267-6621
Eugene N Richardson, *President*
Diane Richardson, *Corp Secy*
EMP: 27
SALES (est): 2.2MM **Privately Held**
SIC: 7549 Towing service, automotive

(G-13738)
ARROWHEAD WEST INC
613 N Ridge Rd Ste 105 (67212-3391)
PHONE..................................316 722-4554
Kathy Walter, *Manager*
EMP: 40
SALES (corp-wide): 13.9MM **Privately Held**
SIC: 8331 Vocational rehabilitation agency
PA: Arrowhead West, Inc.
1100 E Wyatt Earp Blvd
Dodge City KS 67801
620 227-8803

(G-13739)
ART OF ESCAPE ICT
3540 W Douglas Ave Ste 4 (67203-5455)
PHONE..................................316 768-2588
Joshua Goldwin, *General Ptnr*
EMP: 9
SALES: 9.8K **Privately Held**
SIC: 7372 Home entertainment computer software

(G-13740)
ARTEYEVIEW PRODUCTIONS
2280 N Williamsgate Ct (67228-8064)
PHONE..................................316 737-7080
EMP: 13
SALES (est): 178.7K **Privately Held**
SIC: 7822 Motion picture & tape distribution

(G-13741)
ARTHRITIS AND RHEUMATOLOGY (PA)
1921 N Webb Rd (67206-3405)
PHONE..................................316 612-4815
Timothy Shaver MD,
Rebecca Hamilton, *Administration*
Maya Estephan, *Internal Med*
Melanie Rohr, *Rheumtlgy Spec*
James Anderson MD,
EMP: 26
SQ FT: 3,300
SALES (est): 4.3MM **Privately Held**
WEB: www.arck.org
SIC: 8011 Clinic, operated by physicians

(G-13742)
ARTHRITIS RES CTR FOUNDATION
1035 N Emporia St Ste 288 (67214-2939)
PHONE..................................316 263-2125
Frederick Wolfe, *Chairman*
Rebecca Shoemaker, *Manager*
Has Hassan, *Info Tech Mgr*
Rebecca Schumacher, *Exec Dir*
EMP: 25
SQ FT: 5,000
SALES: 1.4MM **Privately Held**
SIC: 8011 Rheumatology specialist, physician/surgeon

(G-13743)
ARTISTIC MARBLE LLC
Also Called: Artistic Marble & Bath
4325 W Harry St (67209-2731)
PHONE..................................316 944-8713
Jeff Pritchard,
EMP: 15
SALES (est): 1.6MM **Privately Held**
SIC: 3281 Marble, building: cut & shaped

(G-13744)
ARWOOD WASTE INC
4100 N West St (67205-6509)
PHONE..................................316 448-1576
EMP: 18
SALES (corp-wide): 12.9MM **Privately Held**
SIC: 8741 Management services
PA: Arwood Waste, Inc.
13255 Lanier Rd
Jacksonville FL 32226
904 751-2177

▲ = Import ▼=Export
◆ =Import/Export

(G-13745)
ASCENSION ARIZONA
Also Called: St. Joseph Surgery
3600 E Harry St (67218-3713)
PHONE..................................316 689-5360
Randy Farenholtz MD, *Principal*
EMP: 167
SALES (corp-wide): 25.3B **Privately Held**
SIC: **8062** General medical & surgical hospitals
HQ: Ascension Arizona
2202 N Forbes Blvd
Tucson AZ 85745

(G-13746)
ASCENSION VIA CHRISTI HOME MED (DH)
555 S Washington Ave # 101 (67211-2424)
PHONE..................................316 265-4991
Brian Hess, *IT/INT Sup*
Lori Billesbach, *Lab Dir*
Joy Scott,
Aimee Esparza, *Technician*
EMP: 69
SALES (est): 4.8MM
SALES (corp-wide): 25.3B **Privately Held**
WEB: www.homemedicalservices.com
SIC: **5999** 7352 Medical apparatus & supplies; medical equipment rental

(G-13747)
ASCENSION VIA CHRISTI HOSPITAL (DH)
Also Called: Via Chrsti Hsptals Wichita Inc
929 N St Francis St (67214-3821)
PHONE..................................316 268-5880
Michael Mullis, *CEO*
Michael McCullough, *Vice Pres*
Nicholas Cahoj, *Med Doctor*
Keith Maurath, *Manager*
Lori Campbell, *Nursing Dir*
EMP: 4000
SQ FT: 1,250,000
SALES: 538.8MM
SALES (corp-wide): 25.3B **Privately Held**
SIC: **8062** General medical & surgical hospitals

(G-13748)
ASCENSION VIA CHRISTI HOSPITAL
Also Called: Preferred Diagnostic Services
848 N St Francis St # 1962 (67214-3800)
PHONE..................................316 687-1555
Lynn Batchellor, *Manager*
EMP: 38
SALES (corp-wide): 25.3B **Privately Held**
SIC: **8011** General & family practice, physician/surgeon; radiologist
HQ: Ascension Via Christi Hospitals Wichita, Inc.
929 N St Francis St
Wichita KS 67214
316 268-5880

(G-13749)
ASCENSION VIA CHRISTI HOSPITAL
Also Called: Preferred Medical Associates
8444 W 21st St N (67205-1752)
PHONE..................................316 721-9500
Carol Delk, *Branch Mgr*
EMP: 17
SALES (corp-wide): 25.3B **Privately Held**
SIC: **8062** General medical & surgical hospitals
HQ: Ascension Via Christi Hospitals Wichita, Inc.
929 N St Francis St
Wichita KS 67214
316 268-5880

(G-13750)
ASCENSION VIA CHRISTI HOSPITAL
Also Called: St Francis Publications
929 N St Francis St (67214-3821)
PHONE..................................316 268-6096
Frank Creeden, *CEO*
EMP: 10
SALES (corp-wide): 25.3B **Privately Held**
SIC: **5192** Newspapers
HQ: Ascension Via Christi Hospitals Wichita, Inc.
929 N St Francis St
Wichita KS 67214
316 268-5880

(G-13751)
ASCENSION VIA CHRISTI HOSPITAL
Also Called: Lady Lords Rehabilitaion Hosp
1151 N Rock Rd (67206-1262)
PHONE..................................316 634-3400
Laurie Labarca, *Principal*
Carrie Amershek, *Director*
Kayla Joy, *Director*
EMP: 150
SALES (corp-wide): 25.3B **Privately Held**
SIC: **8069** Specialty hospitals, except psychiatric
HQ: Ascension Via Christi Hospitals Wichita, Inc.
929 N St Francis St
Wichita KS 67214
316 268-5880

(G-13752)
ASCENSION VIA CHRISTI HOSPITAL
848 N St Francis St (67214-3800)
PHONE..................................316 268-5040
Randall Nyp, *President*
EMP: 4000
SALES (corp-wide): 25.3B **Privately Held**
SIC: **8062** 8011 General medical & surgical hospitals; offices & clinics of medical doctors
HQ: Ascension Via Christi Hospitals Wichita, Inc.
929 N St Francis St
Wichita KS 67214
316 268-5880

(G-13753)
ASHLEYS HOUSE LEARNING CENTER (PA)
7150 W Harry St (67209-2925)
PHONE..................................316 941-9877
Alyson Farris, *CEO*
EMP: 31
SALES (est): 810.4K **Privately Held**
WEB: www.ashleyshouse.net
SIC: **8351** Preschool center

(G-13754)
ASSISTANCE LEAGUE WICHITA INC
Also Called: ASSISTANCE LEAGUE THRIFT SHOP
2431 E Douglas Ave (67211-1614)
P.O. Box 8072 (67208-0072)
PHONE..................................316 687-6107
Carolyn May, *President*
Helene Longhofer, *Chairman*
Vivian Kenney, *Vice Pres*
Sue Dunlop, *Treasurer*
Maxine Rhodes, *Admin Sec*
EMP: 120
SQ FT: 3,250
SALES: 505.2K **Privately Held**
SIC: **8322** Service league

(G-13755)
ASSOCIATED INTERGRATED MKTG
330 N Mead St Ste 220 (67202-2830)
PHONE..................................316 683-4691
William Fialka, *CEO*
Susan K Leasure, *Exec VP*
EMP: 40
SQ FT: 15,000
SALES (est): 8MM **Privately Held**
WEB: www.MeetAssociated.com
SIC: **7311** Advertising consultant

(G-13756)
ASSOCIATED MATERIAL & SUP CO (PA)
5600 W 53rd St N (67205-9100)
P.O. Box 4476 (67204-0476)
PHONE..................................316 721-3848
Nadine Stannard, *President*
EMP: 10 **EST**: 1933
SQ FT: 980
SALES (est): 2.9MM **Privately Held**
SIC: **1442** Construction sand & gravel

(G-13757)
ASSOCIATED MATERIALS LLC
Also Called: Alside
3002 W Pawnee St Ste 106 (67213-1830)
PHONE..................................888 544-9774
Randy Cook, *Sales Staff*
Matthew King, *Branch Mgr*
EMP: 10 **Privately Held**
SIC: **5033** Roofing & siding materials
HQ: Associated Materials, Llc
3773 State Rd
Cuyahoga Falls OH 44223
330 929-1811

(G-13758)
ASSOCIATED MATERIALS LLC
3002 W Pawnee St (67213-1828)
PHONE..................................316 944-0800
John Penny, *Manager*
EMP: 10 **Privately Held**
SIC: **5033** Roofing & siding materials; siding, except wood; roofing, asphalt & sheet metal; insulation materials
HQ: Associated Materials, Llc
3773 State Rd
Cuyahoga Falls OH 44223
330 929-1811

(G-13759)
ASSOCIATES IN WOMENS HEALTH PA (PA)
3232 E Murdock St (67208-3003)
PHONE..................................316 219-6777
Travis Stembridge, *President*
Deborah Messamore MD, *Principal*
Jo Marsh, *Business Mgr*
Darin Jensen MD, *Treasurer*
Debra Messamore, *Obstetrician*
EMP: 30
SQ FT: 7,800
SALES (est): 5.5MM **Privately Held**
SIC: **8011** Obstetrician

(G-13760)
AT&T CORP
154 N Broadway Ave # 1260 (67202-2104)
PHONE..................................316 268-3380
Rick Ruff, *Area Mgr*
Jan Beaver, *Sales & Mktg St*
EMP: 566
SALES (corp-wide): 170.7B **Publicly Held**
WEB: www.swbell.com
SIC: **4813** Telephone communication, except radio
HQ: At&T Corp.
1 At&T Way
Bedminster NJ 07921
800 403-3302

(G-13761)
AT&T CORP
2526 W 31st St S Ofc (67217-1600)
PHONE..................................316 383-0380
Tammy Erwin,
EMP: 69
SALES (corp-wide): 170.7B **Publicly Held**
WEB: www.swbell.com
SIC: **4813** Telephone communication, except radio
HQ: At&T Corp.
1 At&T Way
Bedminster NJ 07921
800 403-3302

(G-13762)
ATLANTIC DEV CORP OF PA
Also Called: General Distributors
800 E Indianapolis St (67211-2405)
P.O. Box 396 (67201-0396)
PHONE..................................316 267-2255
Mickey Wilson, *Manager*
EMP: 19
SALES (corp-wide): 18.9MM **Privately Held**
WEB: www.adcpa.net
SIC: **5023** Resilient floor coverings: tile or sheet
PA: Atlantic Development Corp Of Pennsylvania Inc
1445 N Rock Rd Ste 200
Wichita KS 67206
316 634-2133

(G-13763)
ATLAS AEROSPACE LLC (DH)
Also Called: Product Manufacturing
4425 W May St Bldg 1 (67209-2872)
PHONE..................................316 977-7398
Lori Zehr, *Principal*
Curtis Sullivan, *Vice Pres*
Keith Kranzow, *CFO*
Phil Stephens, *CFO*
Ryan Sleffel, *Business Anlyst*
EMP: 5
SALES (est): 10.8MM **Privately Held**
SIC: **3728** Aircraft assemblies, subassemblies & parts

(G-13764)
ATLAS AEROSPACE LLC
Also Called: Wasi, Inc.
4626 W May St D (67209-2806)
PHONE..................................316 219-5862
Rick Wolf,
Keith Kranzow,
Kelli Stroh,
Lori Zehr,
EMP: 15
SALES (est): 10.8MM **Privately Held**
SIC: **3728** Aircraft parts & equipment
HQ: Atlas Aerospace, Llc
4425 W May St Bldg 1
Wichita KS 67209
316 977-7398

(G-13765)
ATLAS ELECTRIC LLC
1607 N Wabash Ave (67214-1447)
PHONE..................................316 858-1560
Doug Grosch,
Bryan Grosch,
Jeremy Page,
EMP: 80
SQ FT: 12,000
SALES: 20MM **Privately Held**
WEB: www.atlaselectricllc.com
SIC: **1731** General electrical contractor

(G-13766)
ATLAS PAINTING
2061 E Wassall St (67216-2147)
PHONE..................................316 686-1546
John Karagianis, *President*
George Karagianis, *Vice Pres*
EMP: 25 **EST**: 1972
SQ FT: 1,500
SALES: 1MM **Privately Held**
SIC: **1721** Residential painting

(G-13767)
ATLAS SPRING & AXLE CO INC
4500 W Irving St (67209-2693)
PHONE..................................316 943-2386
Robert Loyd, *President*
EMP: 17 **EST**: 1944
SQ FT: 10,500
SALES (est): 1.4MM **Privately Held**
SIC: **7539** Automotive springs, rebuilding & repair; front end repair, automotive; frame & front end repair services; frame repair shops, automotive

(G-13768)
AUGUSTA L LAKEPOINT L C
600 N 127th St E (67206-2807)
PHONE..................................316 733-8100
EMP: 13
SALES (est): 423K
SALES (corp-wide): 8.3MM **Privately Held**
SIC: **8051** Skilled nursing care facilities
PA: Augusta L Lakepoint L C
901 Lakepoint Dr
Augusta KS 67010
316 775-6333

(G-13769)
AUSTIN A-7 LTD
Also Called: A7
1835 S Florence St (67209-2832)
PHONE..................................316 945-8892
Dennis Woodward, *Opers-Prdtn-Mfg*
EMP: 11

SALES (corp-wide): 63.9MM **Privately Held**
WEB: www.austindistributing.com
SIC: 5085 5084 3492 Pistons & valves; hydraulic systems equipment & supplies; hose & tube fittings & assemblies, hydraulic/pneumatic
PA: Austin A-7 Ltd
4018 Sw 50th Ave
Amarillo TX 79109
806 350-8020

(G-13770)
AUTO-CRAFT INC (PA)
Also Called: Auto Craft Body & Paint
1427 E 1st St N (67214-4113)
PHONE..................................316 265-6828
Phil Turner, *CEO*
Jaden Randle, *Vice Pres*
Paul Blissett, *Marketing Staff*
Thomas Patten, *Manager*
EMP: 20
SQ FT: 15,000
SALES: 4.9MM **Privately Held**
WEB: www.autocraftinc.com
SIC: 7532 Body shop, automotive

(G-13771)
AUTO-CRAFT INC
Also Called: Auto Craft Body & Paint
8532 E 32nd St N (67226-2610)
PHONE..................................316 630-9494
Jordan Harter, *Facilities Mgr*
Vickie Lohmann, *Accountant*
Ron Lovell, *Manager*
Amber Mertens, *Director*
Jen Edwards, *Assistant*
EMP: 15
SALES (corp-wide): 4.9MM **Privately Held**
WEB: www.autocraftinc.com
SIC: 7532 Body shop, automotive
PA: Auto-Craft, Inc.
1427 E 1st St N
Wichita KS 67214
316 265-6828

(G-13772)
AUTOFLAME
4601 S Palisade Ave (67217-4923)
PHONE..................................620 229-8048
Dennis Wood, *Director*
Paul Cooper, *Administration*
EMP: 7
SALES (est): 1MM **Privately Held**
SIC: 3823 Boiler controls: industrial, power & marine type

(G-13773)
AUTOMATIC DATA PROCESSING INC
Also Called: ADP
7701 E Kellogg Dr Ste 630 (67207-1705)
PHONE..................................515 875-3160
Ron Harley, *Branch Mgr*
EMP: 117
SALES (corp-wide): 14.1B **Publicly Held**
SIC: 7374 8721 Data processing service; payroll accounting service
PA: Automatic Data Processing, Inc.
1 Adp Blvd Ste 1 # 1
Roseland NJ 07068
973 974-5000

(G-13774)
AUTOMOBILE CLUB OF MISSOURI
Also Called: AAA Auto Club
7130 W Maple St Ste 200 (67209-2101)
PHONE..................................316 942-0008
Ken Broadhead, *Manager*
EMP: 10
SALES (corp-wide): 101.5MM **Privately Held**
SIC: 8699 6411 4724 Travel club; insurance agents, brokers & service; travel agencies
PA: Automobile Club Of Missouri
12901 N 40 Dr
Saint Louis MO 63141
314 523-7350

(G-13775)
AUTOMOTIVE SUPPLY INC
Also Called: AUTOMOTIVE WAREHOUSE CO
4410 W Central Ave (67212-2265)
PHONE..................................316 942-8285
David R Jacobs, *President*
Henry Jacobs, *Vice Pres*
Robert Jacobs, *Treasurer*
EMP: 25 **EST:** 1954
SQ FT: 35,000
SALES: 3.9MM **Privately Held**
SIC: 5013 5531 3599 Automotive supplies & parts; automotive parts; machine shop, jobbing & repair

(G-13776)
AUTOMOTIVE SUPPLY INC
706 Dougherty St (67212)
PHONE..................................316 942-8287
Robert Jacobs, *President*
David Jacobs, *Vice Pres*
EMP: 29 **EST:** 1954
SQ FT: 60,000
SALES: 3.9MM **Privately Held**
SIC: 5013 Automotive supplies & parts

(G-13777)
AUTOMOTIVE WAREHOUSE COMPANY
706 N Dougherty Ave (67212-2003)
PHONE..................................316 942-8285
David R Jacobs, *President*
Henry Jacobs, *Vice Pres*
Robert Jacobs, *Admin Sec*
EMP: 29
SALES (est): 6MM **Privately Held**
SIC: 5013 5531 Automotive supplies & parts; automotive & home supply stores

(G-13778)
AUTOTECH COLLISION & SERVICE
4411 W Central Ave (67212-2264)
PHONE..................................316 942-0707
Fred Jelich, *Business Mgr*
EMP: 11
SALES: 800K **Privately Held**
SIC: 7532 Body shop, automotive

(G-13779)
AVIS RENT A CAR SYSTEM INC
Also Called: Avis Rent A Car Systems
Airport Rd (67209-1980)
PHONE..................................316 946-4882
Peggy Paul, *Branch Mgr*
EMP: 17
SALES (corp-wide): 9.1B **Publicly Held**
SIC: 7514 Rent-a-car service
HQ: Avis Rent A Car System, Inc.
6 Sylvan Way Ste 1
Parsippany NJ 07054
973 496-3500

(G-13780)
AXA ADVISORS LLC
301 N Main St Ste 1400 (67202-4814)
PHONE..................................316 263-5761
Mark Miles, *Principal*
John Mastio, *Advisor*
EMP: 25
SALES (corp-wide): 12B **Publicly Held**
SIC: 6411 Insurance agents
HQ: Axa Advisors, Llc
1290 Ave Of Amrcs Fl Cnc1
New York NY 10104
212 554-1234

(G-13781)
AXIUS GROUP LLC
100 S Market St Ste 100 # 100 (67202-3824)
P.O. Box 1385 (67201-1385)
PHONE..................................316 285-0858
Lacy Tedman, *Mng Member*
EMP: 14
SALES (est): 774.3K **Privately Held**
SIC: 8711 Engineering services

(G-13782)
AXLE & WHEEL ALIGNING CO INC
126 N Washington Ave (67202-2816)
PHONE..................................316 263-0213
Michael Standiford, *CEO*
Roger Standiford, *CEO*
Larry J Standiford, *President*
EMP: 12 **EST:** 1937
SQ FT: 11,400
SALES: 480K **Privately Held**
SIC: 7539 Wheel alignment, automotive; frame repair shops, automotive; front end repair, automotive; automotive springs, rebuilding & repair

(G-13783)
AYHAM J FARHA MD
Also Called: Wichita Urology Group
2626 N Webb Rd (67226-8110)
PHONE..................................316 636-6100
Ayham J Farha MD, *Owner*
Jenny Hutson, *Buyer*
Alysha Saenger, *Hum Res Coord*
Diane Cordoba, *Admin Sec*
Twila Puritty, *Administration*
EMP: 47
SALES (est): 11.4MM **Privately Held**
WEB: www.wichitaurology.com
SIC: 8011 Urologist

(G-13784)
B & B AIRPARTS INC
1831 S Hoover Ct (67209-2853)
PHONE..................................316 946-0300
Dan Barnard, *CEO*
Kristin White, *Contract Mgr*
EMP: 130 **EST:** 1998
SQ FT: 85,000
SALES: 3.2MM **Privately Held**
WEB: www.bbairparts.com
SIC: 3444 Sheet metalwork

(G-13785)
B 5 INC
P.O. Box 771071 (67277-1071)
PHONE..................................316 721-3222
Kasey Beltz, *President*
Valerie Beltz, *Vice Pres*
EMP: 5
SALES (est): 249.5K **Privately Held**
SIC: 3489 Guns or gun parts, over 30 mm.

(G-13786)
B&B ELECTRIC MOTOR CO
332 S Lulu Ave (67211-1713)
PHONE..................................316 267-1238
Robert D Giesen, *President*
EMP: 10 **EST:** 1969
SQ FT: 13,000
SALES (est): 3.9MM **Privately Held**
WEB: www.bbelectricmotor.com
SIC: 5063 7629 Motors, electric; electronic equipment repair

(G-13787)
B/E AEROSPACE INC
10900 E 26th St N (67226-4607)
PHONE..................................316 609-3360
Chuck Robinson, *Manager*
EMP: 60
SALES (corp-wide): 66.5B **Publicly Held**
SIC: 3728 Aircraft parts & equipment
HQ: B/E Aerospace, Inc.
1400 Corporate Center Way
Wellington FL 33414
561 791-5000

(G-13788)
B/E AEROSPACE INC
8110 E 32nd St N (67226-2623)
PHONE..................................316 609-4300
Amin J Khoury, *Ch of Bd*
EMP: 6
SALES (corp-wide): 66.5B **Publicly Held**
SIC: 2531 3728 3647 Seats, aircraft; aircraft parts & equipment; aircraft lighting fixtures
HQ: B/E Aerospace, Inc.
1400 Corporate Center Way
Wellington FL 33414
561 791-5000

(G-13789)
BACHUS & SON INC
Also Called: Yard, The
725 E Central Ave (67202-1063)
PHONE..................................316 265-4673
Gary L Bachus, *President*
▲ **EMP:** 30 **EST:** 1946
SQ FT: 250,000
SALES (est): 4.3MM **Privately Held**
WEB: www.store.com
SIC: 5399 5199 Surplus & salvage goods; general merchandise, non-durable

(G-13790)
BACKWOODS EQUIPMENT COMPANY
1900 N Rock Rd Ste 108 (67206-1256)
PHONE..................................316 267-0350
EMP: 24
SALES (corp-wide): 13.4MM **Privately Held**
SIC: 5084 Whol Industrial Equipment
PA: Backwoods Equipment Company
3300 N Interstate 35
Austin TX 78705
817 877-3147

(G-13791)
BACM 2005-3 MAIN WOODLAWN LLC
301 N Main St Ste 145 (67202-4834)
PHONE..................................316 291-8450
Stephanie Palmer,
EMP: 25
SALES (est): 1.2MM **Privately Held**
SIC: 6512 Nonresidential building operators

(G-13792)
BACO CORPORATION
2426 S Hoover Rd (67215-1291)
PHONE..................................316 945-5300
Douglas E Bauer, *President*
Clinton Bauer, *Vice Pres*
Daniel Bauer, *Treasurer*
Cathy Holmes, *Manager*
▲ **EMP:** 17
SQ FT: 60,000
SALES (est): 2.4MM **Privately Held**
SIC: 3999 2448 Carpet tackles; wood pallets & skids

(G-13793)
BAGATELLE INC
Also Called: Bagatelle French Bakery
6801 E Harry St (67207-2908)
PHONE..................................316 684-5662
Naji Toubia, *President*
EMP: 30
SQ FT: 2,000
SALES (est): 1MM **Privately Held**
SIC: 5461 2051 2052 Bread; bread, all types (white, wheat, rye, etc): fresh or frozen; cookies & crackers

(G-13794)
BAISCH & SKINNER INC
3413 W 29th St S (67217-1000)
PHONE..................................316 945-0074
Jessica Christi, *Manager*
EMP: 10
SALES (corp-wide): 38MM **Privately Held**
SIC: 5193 Florists' supplies
PA: Baisch & Skinner, Inc.
2721 Lasalle St
Saint Louis MO 63104
314 664-1212

(G-13795)
BAKER SR MARCELLUS
1201 N Jackson Ave (67203-3566)
PHONE..................................316 670-6329
Marcellus Baker, *Owner*
EMP: 10
SALES (est): 63.9K **Privately Held**
SIC: 8999 Author

(G-13796)
BAKERY PROJECTS INC
Also Called: Delano
1025 W 29th St N (67204-4817)
PHONE..................................316 831-9434
Kelly Dumford, *President*
EMP: 8 **EST:** 1997
SQ FT: 4,800
SALES: 320K **Privately Held**
WEB: www.bakeryprojects.com
SIC: 2051 Bread, cake & related products

(G-13797)
BAKKEN OIL EXPRESS LLC
8301 E 21st St N Ste 420 (67206-2936)
PHONE..................................316 630-0287
Gerald E O'Shaughnessy, *Chairman*
EMP: 15
SALES (est): 3.3MM **Privately Held**
SIC: 4013 Switching & terminal services

(G-13798)
BALCO INC (HQ)
Also Called: Balco-Metalines
2626 S Sheridan Ave (67217-1341)
P.O. Box 17249 (67217-0249)
PHONE..................................800 767-0082
Ronnie Lenard, *CEO*
Ron Knak, *Vice Pres*
Tom Shupe, *Mfg Staff*
Andy Hoss, *Purch Mgr*
Andrea Atkinson, *Purch Agent*
◆ **EMP:** 125
SQ FT: 30,000
SALES (est): 27.2MM
SALES (corp-wide): 350.1MM **Publicly Held**
WEB: www.balcousa.com
SIC: 3441 3089 3496 3446 Expansion joints (structural shapes), iron or steel; plastic hardware & building products; bearings, plastic; mats & matting; architectural metalwork; fabricated plate work (boiler shop)
PA: Csw Industrials, Inc.
5420 Lyndon B Johnson Fwy
Dallas TX 75240
214 884-3777

(G-13799)
BALDRIDGE ELECTRIC INC
1542 S Market St (67211-3119)
PHONE..................................316 267-0058
Judy J Baldridge, *President*
Rebecca Baldridge, *Corp Secy*
George Baldridge, *Vice Pres*
EMP: 20
SQ FT: 3,000
SALES (est): 2.8MM **Privately Held**
SIC: 1731 General electrical contractor

(G-13800)
BANK AMERICA NATIONAL ASSN
2959 N Rock Rd Ste 1 (67226-1117)
PHONE..................................316 261-2025
EMP: 15
SALES (corp-wide): 110.5B **Publicly Held**
WEB: www.bofa.com
SIC: 6021 National commercial banks
HQ: Bank Of America, National Association
100 S Tryon St
Charlotte NC 28202
704 386-5681

(G-13801)
BANK AMERICA NATIONAL ASSN
8304 W Central Ave (67212-3652)
PHONE..................................316 261-2274
Vickie McMillin, *Branch Mgr*
EMP: 15
SALES (corp-wide): 110.5B **Publicly Held**
WEB: www.bofa.com
SIC: 6021 National commercial banks
HQ: Bank Of America, National Association
100 S Tryon St
Charlotte NC 28202
704 386-5681

(G-13802)
BANK AMERICA NATIONAL ASSN
3193 S Seneca St (67217-3234)
PHONE..................................316 261-4359
Tammy Coughin, *Manager*
EMP: 24
SALES (corp-wide): 110.5B **Publicly Held**
WEB: www.bofa.com
SIC: 6021 National commercial banks
HQ: Bank Of America, National Association
100 S Tryon St
Charlotte NC 28202
704 386-5681

(G-13803)
BANK AMERICA NATIONAL ASSN
100 N Broadway Ave Fl 3 (67202-2212)
PHONE..................................316 261-4216
EMP: 19
SALES (corp-wide): 110.5B **Publicly Held**
WEB: www.bofa.com
SIC: 6021 National commercial banks
HQ: Bank Of America, National Association
100 S Tryon St
Charlotte NC 28202
704 386-5681

(G-13804)
BANK AMERICA NATIONAL ASSN
7310 W 21st St N (67205-1728)
PHONE..................................316 261-2210
Rob Rawling, *Manager*
EMP: 15
SALES (corp-wide): 110.5B **Publicly Held**
WEB: www.bofa.com
SIC: 6021 National commercial banks
HQ: Bank Of America, National Association
100 S Tryon St
Charlotte NC 28202
704 386-5681

(G-13805)
BANK AMERICA NATIONAL ASSN
2151 N Hillside St (67214-2359)
PHONE..................................316 261-4040
Chris Davis, *Manager*
EMP: 15
SALES (corp-wide): 110.5B **Publicly Held**
WEB: www.bofa.com
SIC: 6021 National commercial banks
HQ: Bank Of America, National Association
100 S Tryon St
Charlotte NC 28202
704 386-5681

(G-13806)
BANK AMERICA NATIONAL ASSN
1617 S Rock Rd (67207-5148)
PHONE..................................316 261-2143
Kelly Davis, *Manager*
EMP: 15
SALES (corp-wide): 110.5B **Publicly Held**
WEB: www.bofa.com
SIC: 6021 National commercial banks
HQ: Bank Of America, National Association
100 S Tryon St
Charlotte NC 28202
704 386-5681

(G-13807)
BANK OF WEST
255 N Main St (67202-3798)
PHONE..................................316 292-5840
Mandi Martinson, *Manager*
EMP: 10
SQ FT: 1,000
SALES (corp-wide): 2.7B **Privately Held**
SIC: 6022 State trust companies accepting deposits, commercial
HQ: Bank Of The West
180 Montgomery St # 1400
San Francisco CA 94104
415 765-4800

(G-13808)
BANK OF WEST
757 N West St (67203-1240)
PHONE..................................316 292-5870
Brad Heyen, *Vice Pres*
Mandi Martinson, *Branch Mgr*
EMP: 15
SALES (corp-wide): 2.7B **Privately Held**
SIC: 6022 State trust companies accepting deposits, commercial
HQ: Bank Of The West
180 Montgomery St # 1400
San Francisco CA 94104
415 765-4800

(G-13809)
BANK OF WEST
2123 N Maize Rd (67212-5207)
PHONE..................................316 729-7999
Brad Heyen, *Manager*
EMP: 13
SALES (corp-wide): 2.7B **Privately Held**
SIC: 6022 State trust companies accepting deposits, commercial
HQ: Bank Of The West
180 Montgomery St # 1400
San Francisco CA 94104
415 765-4800

(G-13810)
BANK SNB
8415 E 21st St N Ste 150 (67206-2952)
PHONE..................................316 315-1600
Pat Gearheart, *President*
EMP: 13
SALES (corp-wide): 824.5MM **Publicly Held**
WEB: www.snbbankofwichita.com
SIC: 6021 National commercial banks
HQ: Bank Snb
608 S Main St
Stillwater OK 74074
405 372-2230

(G-13811)
BANKERS BANK OF KANSAS NA
555 N Woodlawn St Bldg 5 (67208-3675)
P.O. Box 20810 (67208-6810)
PHONE..................................316 681-2265
Calvin Coady, *CEO*
Grant Paitz, *Assistant VP*
Peg Baldwin, *Vice Pres*
Terry Puett, *Vice Pres*
Chris Gilbert, *VP Opers*
EMP: 49
SQ FT: 4,300
SALES: 15.3MM **Privately Held**
WEB: www.bbok.com
SIC: 6021 National commercial banks

(G-13812)
BARKLEY CONSTRUCTION
1357 S Sierra Dr (67209-2934)
P.O. Box 12087 (67277-2087)
PHONE..................................316 945-6500
Ronald Barkley, *Owner*
EMP: 10
SALES (est): 909.1K **Privately Held**
WEB: www.barkleyconcrete.com
SIC: 1771 1611 Blacktop (asphalt) work; surfacing & paving

(G-13813)
BARONE ELECTRIC INC
5341 N Athenian Ave (67204-2531)
P.O. Box 979 (67201-0979)
PHONE..................................316 263-9579
Debbie Barone, *President*
Danny Barone, *Treasurer*
EMP: 10
SALES: 740K **Privately Held**
SIC: 1731 Electrical work

(G-13814)
BARTLETT GRAIN COMPANY LP
3311 N Emporia St (67219-4019)
PHONE..................................316 838-7421
Rick Vasquez, *Vice Pres*
Andrew Fullerton, *Manager*
EMP: 10
SALES (corp-wide): 1B **Privately Held**
SIC: 5153 Grains
HQ: Bartlett Grain Company, L.P.
4900 Main St Ste 1200
Kansas City MO 64112
816 753-6300

(G-13815)
BARTON INDUSTRIES INC
Also Called: Intermarc Signs
1236 N Mosley St (67214-2714)
PHONE..................................316 262-3171
Eric Becker, *President*
Rae Lynn Barton, *Corp Secy*
Tonya Stroud, *Vice Pres*
EMP: 9
SQ FT: 750
SALES (est): 1.2MM **Privately Held**
WEB: www.intermarcsigns.com
SIC: 3993 Name plates: except engraved, etched, etc.: metal

(G-13816)
BASHAM FURNITURE RENTAL INC (PA)
2141 N Market St (67214-1045)
PHONE..................................316 263-5821
James L Basham, *President*
EMP: 18 **EST:** 1978
SQ FT: 7,500
SALES (est): 1.1MM **Privately Held**
SIC: 7359 Furniture rental

(G-13817)
BASHAM HOME STORE INC
103 E 21st St N (67214-1031)
PHONE..................................316 263-5821
Joseph Basham, *President*
EMP: 14
SALES (est): 1.1MM **Privately Held**
WEB: www.bashamrto.com
SIC: 7359 Furniture rental

(G-13818)
BASIC BEGINNINGS EDUCATIONAL
2111 N Maize Rd (67212-5207)
PHONE..................................316 721-7946
Barb Matous, *President*
Michelle Pacha, *Director*
EMP: 11
SALES (est): 215.1K **Privately Held**
SIC: 8351 Nursery school

(G-13819)
BASIC ENERGY SERVICES INC
100 S Main St Ste 607 (67202-3738)
PHONE..................................316 262-3699
Pat Hutyra, *Sales Mgr*
Timothy Sanders, *Branch Mgr*
Kevin Gordley, *Manager*
EMP: 34
SALES (corp-wide): 964.7MM **Publicly Held**
SIC: 1389 Construction, repair & dismantling services; oil field services
PA: Basic Energy Services, Inc.
801 Cherry St Unit 2
Fort Worth TX 76102
817 334-4100

(G-13820)
BAUGHMAN CO PA
315 S Ellis St (67211-1811)
PHONE..................................316 262-7271
N Brent Wooten, *President*
Denise Vaughn, *Partner*
Jerry Kingsley, *Project Mgr*
Tim Aziere, *Engineer*
Russ Ewy, *Consultant*
EMP: 48
SQ FT: 4,000
SALES (est): 4.1MM **Privately Held**
SIC: 8713 8711 Photogrammetric engineering; civil engineering

(G-13821)
BAYSINGER POLICE SUPPLY INC
430 E Central Ave (67202-1058)
PHONE..................................316 262-5663
Brian Carduff, *President*
Patricia Vickers, *Shareholder*
EMP: 15
SQ FT: 3,800
SALES (est): 3MM **Privately Held**
WEB: www.baysingers.com
SIC: 5049 Law enforcement equipment & supplies

(G-13822)
BBH LLC
Also Called: Cook's Heating & AC
2215 S West St (67213-1113)
PHONE..................................316 945-8208
Kevin Graves, *General Mgr*
Michael J Brand,
EMP: 58 **EST:** 1973
SQ FT: 13,000

GEOGRAPHIC

SALES: 8.2MM **Privately Held**
WEB: www.cooksheatingandcooling.com
SIC: 1711 Warm air heating & air conditioning contractor

(G-13823)
BEACON HILL HOTEL OPERATOR LLC
125 N Emporia Ave Ste 202 (67202-2519)
PHONE..................................316 260-9088
S Shawn Whitney,
EMP: 15
SALES (est): 107.4K **Privately Held**
SIC: 7011 Hotels

(G-13824)
BEAVER EXPRESS SERVICE LLC
2620 Mccormick St (67213)
PHONE..................................316 946-5700
John Guffey, *Manager*
EMP: 33
SALES (corp-wide): 125MM **Privately Held**
WEB: www.beaverexpress.com
SIC: 4213 Trucking, except local
PA: Beaver Express Service, Llc
4310 Oklahoma Ave
Woodward OK 73801
580 256-6460

(G-13825)
BECKER TIRE & TREADING INC
Also Called: Becker Tire of Wichita
3608 W 30th St S (67217-1016)
PHONE..................................316 943-7979
Randy Shumway, *Manager*
EMP: 17
SALES (corp-wide): 96.3MM **Privately Held**
WEB: www.beckertire.com
SIC: 5014 5531 Automobile tires & tubes; automotive tires
PA: Becker Tire & Treading, Inc.
904 Washington St
Great Bend KS 67530
620 793-5414

(G-13826)
BEECHCRAFT HOLDINGS LLC (DH)
10511 E Central Ave (67206-2557)
PHONE..................................316 676-7111
Robert S Miller, *President*
Gina E Vascsinec, *Vice Pres*
Karin-Joyce Tjon Sien Fat, *CFO*
EMP: 29
SQ FT: 3,900,000
SALES (est): 511.4MM
SALES (corp-wide): 13.9B **Publicly Held**
SIC: 3721 3728 6719 Airplanes, fixed or rotary wing; aircraft parts & equipment; investment holding companies, except banks
HQ: Textron Aviation Inc.
1 Cessna Blvd
Wichita KS 67215
316 517-6000

(G-13827)
BEECHCRAFT INTL SVC CO (DH)
10511 E Central Ave (67206-2557)
PHONE..................................316 676-7111
Shawn Vick, *President*
EMP: 5 **EST:** 2007
SALES (est): 94.5K
SALES (corp-wide): 13.9B **Publicly Held**
SIC: 3728 Aircraft parts & equipment
HQ: Textron Aviation Inc.
1 Cessna Blvd
Wichita KS 67215
316 517-6000

(G-13828)
BELFORD ELECTRIC INC
800 E 3rd St N (67202-2720)
PHONE..................................316 267-7060
John Belford, *President*
EMP: 28
SQ FT: 2,800
SALES (est): 2.4MM **Privately Held**
SIC: 1731 General electrical contractor

(G-13829)
BELGER CARTAGE SERVICE INC
2555 S Kessler St (67217-1044)
PHONE..................................316 943-0101
Jim Taylor, *Human Res Mgr*
Mike Foster, *Manager*
John Doesken, *Manager*
EMP: 50
SALES (corp-wide): 49.5MM **Privately Held**
SIC: 7353 7389 4213 Cranes & aerial lift equipment, rental or leasing; crane & aerial lift service; heavy hauling
HQ: Belger Cartage Service, Inc.
2100 Walnut St
Kansas City MO 64108
816 474-3250

(G-13830)
BERAN CONCRETE INC
3530 N Topeka St (67219-3605)
PHONE..................................316 425-7600
EMP: 148
SALES (corp-wide): 34.1MM **Privately Held**
SIC: 1771 Concrete work
PA: Beran Concrete, Inc.
8401 E Oak Knoll St
Wichita KS 67207
316 618-6089

(G-13831)
BERAN CONCRETE INC (PA)
8401 E Oak Knoll St (67207-5439)
PHONE..................................316 618-6089
Brock Beran, *President*
Randy Perry, *Superintendent*
EMP: 82
SQ FT: 2,700
SALES (est): 34.1MM **Privately Held**
WEB: www.beranconcrete.com
SIC: 1771 Concrete work

(G-13832)
BERAN ICF SOLUTIONS LLC
8401 E Oak Knoll St (67207-5439)
PHONE..................................316 944-2131
Kent Webber, *Vice Pres*
Kenneth Beran, *Mng Member*
Brock Beran,
EMP: 12
SQ FT: 3,000
SALES (est): 844.2K **Privately Held**
SIC: 1771 5211 Concrete work; concrete & cinder block

(G-13833)
BERRY COMPANIES INC (PA)
Also Called: Berry Tractor & Equipment Co
3223 N Hydraulic St (67219-3893)
P.O. Box 829 (67201-0829)
PHONE..................................316 838-3321
Fred F Berry Jr, *Ch of Bd*
Walter Berry, *President*
John Engels, *Vice Pres*
Bob Young, *Vice Pres*
Kim Lauffer, *Parts Mgr*
EMP: 50
SQ FT: 3,000
SALES (est): 181.7MM **Privately Held**
WEB: www.berrycompaniesinc.com
SIC: 5251 5084 7699 5082 Hardware; industrial machinery & equipment; industrial machinery & equipment repair; general construction machinery & equipment

(G-13834)
BERRY COMPANIES INC
Also Called: Berry Tractor & Equipment Co
930 S West St (67213-1626)
P.O. Box 12288 (67277-2288)
PHONE..................................316 943-4246
Clayton Shively, *District Mgr*
Sean Wallace, *District Mgr*
Steve Sanders, *Materials Mgr*
Allan Bell, *Parts Mgr*
Randy Spear, *Sales Mgr*
EMP: 40
SALES (corp-wide): 181.7MM **Privately Held**
WEB: www.berrycompaniesinc.com
SIC: 5082 General construction machinery & equipment
PA: Berry Companies, Inc.
3223 N Hydraulic St
Wichita KS 67219
316 838-3321

(G-13835)
BERRY COMPANIES INC
White Star Machinery & Sup Co
3223 N Hydraulic St (67219-3893)
PHONE..................................316 838-3321
Glenn Engels, *Manager*
EMP: 100
SALES (corp-wide): 181.7MM **Privately Held**
WEB: www.berrycompaniesinc.com
SIC: 5084 5082 Industrial machinery & equipment; general construction machinery & equipment
PA: Berry Companies, Inc.
3223 N Hydraulic St
Wichita KS 67219
316 838-3321

(G-13836)
BEST CABS INC
2555 N Market St (67219-4426)
PHONE..................................316 838-2233
George Amburst, *President*
Francis Amburst, *Vice Pres*
EMP: 13
SQ FT: 1,800
SALES (est): 740.5K **Privately Held**
WEB: www.bestcabsinc.com
SIC: 4121 Taxicabs

(G-13837)
BEST CORPORATION INC (PA)
Also Called: ServiceMaster
729 E Boston St (67211-3312)
P.O. Box 48639 (67201-8639)
PHONE..................................316 687-1895
David Lazarus, *President*
Sam Lazarus, *Vice Pres*
Wynonne Beall, *Bookkeeper*
EMP: 30
SALES: 2.5MM **Privately Held**
SIC: 7349 Building maintenance services

(G-13838)
BEST HOME GUYS HOLDING CO
Also Called: Best Home Guys, The
12610 W Hardtner Cir (67235-1344)
PHONE..................................316 681-2639
Philip C Davis, *President*
Kaylee Davis, *Manager*
EMP: 11
SQ FT: 3,000
SALES (est): 1MM **Privately Held**
SIC: 1522 Remodeling, multi-family dwellings

(G-13839)
BEST VALUE SERVICES LLC
200 W Douglas Ave Ste 600 (67202-3006)
P.O. Box 780184 (67278-0184)
PHONE..................................316 440-1048
Solomon Tafesse,
EMP: 60
SALES: 1.5MM **Privately Held**
SIC: 7389 7349 7219 4953 Financial services; document & office record destruction; building maintenance, except repairs; laundry, except power & coin-operated; refuse collection & disposal services; recycling, waste materials

(G-13840)
BETTS PEST CONTROL INC
3015 W Central Ave (67203-4911)
PHONE..................................316 943-3555
Chad K Betts, *President*
Lori Betts, *Corp Secy*
Craig Betts, *Vice Pres*
EMP: 17
SQ FT: 9,600
SALES: 1.3MM **Privately Held**
WEB: www.bettspc.com
SIC: 7342 Pest control in structures

(G-13841)
BETZEN TRENCHING INC
1410 S Walnut St (67213-4349)
P.O. Box 13095 (67213-0095)
PHONE..................................316 269-9331
Russell Betzen, *President*
Patricia S Betzen, *Vice Pres*
EMP: 25
SALES (est): 4.5MM **Privately Held**
WEB: www.betzentrenching.com
SIC: 1794 Excavation work

(G-13842)
BEVAN-RABELL INC
1880 S Airport Rd (67209-1977)
PHONE..................................316 946-4870
Kent McIntyre, *President*
Tad Keller, *Vice Pres*
Russell Parker, *Vice Pres*
Anita Zoglman, *Treasurer*
Mike Gros, *Manager*
EMP: 20
SQ FT: 24,000
SALES: 2.5MM **Privately Held**
WEB: www.bevanrabell.com
SIC: 7622 5065 Aircraft radio equipment repair; communication equipment

(G-13843)
BEVER DYE LC
Also Called: Flesher, Jack D
301 N Main St Ste 600 (67202-4806)
PHONE..................................316 263-8294
Chris Robe, *Partner*
Greg Frankan, *Partner*
Holly Sadowski, *Admin Sec*
Robert Hughes,
Coy Martin,
EMP: 26
SALES (est): 2.3MM **Privately Held**
WEB: www.beverdye.com
SIC: 8111 General practice law office

(G-13844)
BEVERLY ENTERPRISES-KANSAS LLC
Also Called: Lincoln East Nursing Home
4007 E Lincoln St (67218-2111)
PHONE..................................316 683-7588
David Fise, *Director*
EMP: 50
SQ FT: 12,000
SALES (corp-wide): 393.8MM **Privately Held**
SIC: 8051 8741 Convalescent home with continuous nursing care; nursing & personal care facility management
HQ: Beverly Enterprises-Kansas, Llc
1 1000 Beverly Way
Fort Smith AR 72919
479 201-2000

(G-13845)
BG PRODUCTS INCORPORATED (PA)
740 S Wichita St (67213-5496)
P.O. Box 1282 (67201-1282)
PHONE..................................316 265-2686
Galen R Myers, *President*
Darin Greseth, *President*
Ray Connell, *Corp Secy*
Steve Terrell, *Project Mgr*
Jeremy Lee, *Opers Mgr*
◆ **EMP:** 50 **EST:** 1971
SALES (est): 76.3MM **Privately Held**
WEB: www.bgprod.com
SIC: 2992 2899 2911 Lubricating oils & greases; chemical preparations; fuel additives

(G-13846)
BG PRODUCTS INCORPORATED
701 S Wichita St (67213-5429)
PHONE..................................316 265-2686
Kolin G Anglin, *Branch Mgr*
EMP: 60
SALES (corp-wide): 76.3MM **Privately Held**
SIC: 2911 Fuel additives
PA: Bg Products, Incorporated
740 S Wichita St
Wichita KS 67213
316 265-2686

(G-13847)
BIEHLER COMPANIES INC
Also Called: Suburban Landscape Management
1100 E Macarthur Rd (67216-1837)
P.O. Box 16005 (67216-0005)
PHONE..................................316 529-0002

John D Biehler, *President*
James Biehler, *Vice Pres*
Jim Biehler, *Vice Pres*
Kelly Kerans, *Vice Pres*
Paul Bethel, *Accounts Mgr*
EMP: 55
SALES (est): 6.1MM **Privately Held**
WEB: www.landscapeitnow.com
SIC: 0781 7311 5999 5063 Landscape services; advertising consultant; Christmas lights & decorations; lighting fixtures; snowplowing; landscape contractors

(G-13848)
BIG SUR WATERBEDS INC
555 S Hoover Rd Ste 2400 (67209-2357)
PHONE..................................316 944-6225
Bruce Webster, *Branch Mgr*
EMP: 13
SALES (corp-wide): 485.2MM **Privately Held**
SIC: 5712 5047 Furniture stores; beds, hospital
HQ: Big Sur Waterbeds, Inc.
5603 Brdwy
Denver CO 80216
303 566-8700

(G-13849)
BIMBO BAKERIES USA INC
2536 S Southeast Dr (67216-2138)
PHONE..................................620 218-2365
Ben Brockway, *Manager*
EMP: 200 **Privately Held**
SIC: 2051 Bread, all types (white, wheat, rye, etc): fresh or frozen; rolls, bread type: fresh or frozen
HQ: Bimbo Bakeries Usa, Inc
255 Business Center Dr # 200
Horsham PA 19044
215 347-5500

(G-13850)
BINDERY EXPRESS INC
1930 N Ohio Ave (67214-1532)
PHONE..................................316 944-8163
Kim Roberts, *Owner*
EMP: 5
SALES (est): 565.1K **Privately Held**
SIC: 2789 Bookbinding & related work

(G-13851)
BIO-NEXT INC
611 E 13th St N (67214-1204)
P.O. Box 3029 (67201-3029)
PHONE..................................316 260-1540
Scott Norris, *President*
EMP: 6
SQ FT: 900
SALES (est): 1MM **Privately Held**
SIC: 2836 Biological products, except diagnostic

(G-13852)
BKD LLP
1551 N Waterfront Pkwy # 300 (67206-6601)
PHONE..................................316 265-2811
Barry Davis, *Managing Prtnr*
Douglas M Gaston, *Partner*
Bill Pickert, *Partner*
Leigh Sinn, *Finance Mgr*
Carrie Emberson, *CPA*
EMP: 60
SQ FT: 2,800
SALES (corp-wide): 422.5MM **Privately Held**
SIC: 8721 Certified public accountant
PA: Bkd, Llp
910 E Saint Louis St # 400
Springfield MO 65806
417 831-7283

(G-13853)
BLACK & WINSOR INC
7106 W Pueblo Dr (67209-2900)
P.O. Box 12344 (67277-2344)
PHONE..................................316 943-0703
Henry Winsor, *President*
Mary Lue Winsor, *Corp Secy*
EMP: 64
SALES (est): 3.3MM **Privately Held**
SIC: 4212 Local trucking, without storage

(G-13854)
BLACK AND JENSEN INC
729 S Emporia Ave (67211-2307)
P.O. Box 1298 (67201-1298)
PHONE..................................316 262-7277
Carolyn Black, *President*
Paul Jensen, *Vice Pres*
Gary Douglass, *Sales Staff*
Donnie Magnuson, *Consultant*
EMP: 30
SQ FT: 25,000
SALES (est): 6.9MM **Privately Held**
WEB: www.donlevylitho.com
SIC: 2752 Maps, lithographed; commercial printing, offset

(G-13855)
BLACK HILLS/KANSAS GAS
Also Called: Black Hills Energy
2330 N Hoover Rd (67205-1026)
PHONE..................................605 721-1700
EMP: 39
SALES (corp-wide): 1.7B **Publicly Held**
SIC: 4924 Natural gas distribution
HQ: Black Hills/Kansas Gas Utility Company, Llc
7001 Mount Rushmore Rd
Rapid City SD 57702

(G-13856)
BLAIR DOON VETERINARY HOSPITAL
10804 E 31st St S (67210-1833)
PHONE..................................316 685-7300
Jennifer Sullivan, *President*
EMP: 25
SALES (est): 1.5MM **Privately Held**
SIC: 0742 Animal hospital services, pets & other animal specialties

(G-13857)
BLEND TECH INC
1819 S Meridian Ave (67213-1923)
PHONE..................................316 941-9660
Mike Casamento, *President*
Derick Hargrave, *Research*
Nick Palozzi, *Marketing Staff*
▲ **EMP:** 15
SALES (est): 6.9MM **Privately Held**
WEB: www.blendtech.com
SIC: 5149 Spices & seasonings

(G-13858)
BLUE CROSS BLUE SHELD KANS INC
220 W Douglas Ave Ste 200 (67202-3107)
PHONE..................................316 269-1666
Tamila Eslin, *Sales/Mktg Mgr*
Ryan Tandy, *Consultant*
EMP: 100
SALES (corp-wide): 636.3MM **Privately Held**
WEB: www.bcbsks.com
SIC: 6324 Hospital & medical service plans
PA: Blue Cross And Blue Shield Of Kansas, Inc.
1133 Sw Topeka Blvd
Topeka KS 66629
785 291-7000

(G-13859)
BOB BERGKAMP CNSTR CO INC
3709 S West St (67217-3898)
PHONE..................................316 522-3471
Jim Snook, *CEO*
Scott Bergkamp, *President*
Jarret Gowdy, *Project Mgr*
EMP: 80
SQ FT: 13,000
SALES (est): 16.8MM **Privately Held**
SIC: 1629 Earthmoving contractor

(G-13860)
BOB EISEL POWDER COATINGS
1703 N Barrier Cv (67206-3321)
PHONE..................................316 942-8870
Robert L Eisel, *President*
Susie Eisel, *Corp Secy*
EMP: 50
SQ FT: 32,000
SALES (est): 4.8MM **Privately Held**
SIC: 3479 Coating of metals & formed products; painting, coating & hot dipping

(G-13861)
BOB STITH HEATING AND COOLING (PA)
Also Called: Stith Bob Heating Coolg & Plbg
1411 S Handley St (67213-4318)
PHONE..................................316 262-1802
Robert D Stith, *President*
Rochelle Stith, *Corp Secy*
Roger Stith, *Exec VP*
EMP: 15
SQ FT: 2,400
SALES (est): 825K **Privately Held**
SIC: 1711 Warm air heating & air conditioning contractor

(G-13862)
BODYCOTE THERMAL PROC INC
1009 S West St (67213-1627)
PHONE..................................316 943-3288
Douglas Bruce, *Sales Staff*
Gordon Ritter, *Marketing Staff*
EMP: 35
SALES (corp-wide): 960MM **Privately Held**
WEB: www.mic-houston.com
SIC: 3398 Metal heat treating
HQ: Bodycote Thermal Processing, Inc.
12700 Park Central Dr # 700
Dallas TX 75251
214 904-2420

(G-13863)
BODYCOTE THERMAL PROC INC
1019 S Mclean Blvd (67213-4524)
PHONE..................................316 267-6264
Alan Walcher, *Manager*
EMP: 33
SQ FT: 5,000
SALES (corp-wide): 960MM **Privately Held**
WEB: www.mic-houston.com
SIC: 3398 Metal heat treating
HQ: Bodycote Thermal Processing, Inc.
12700 Park Central Dr # 700
Dallas TX 75251
214 904-2420

(G-13864)
BOEING COMPANY
8602 W Shadow Lakes St (67205-1978)
PHONE..................................316 523-7084
Mike Monfared, *Principal*
EMP: 895
SALES (corp-wide): 101.1B **Publicly Held**
SIC: 3721 Airplanes, fixed or rotary wing
PA: The Boeing Company
100 N Riverside Plz
Chicago IL 60606
312 544-2000

(G-13865)
BOEING COMPANY
4174 S Oliver St (67210-2127)
PHONE..................................480 509-5449
EMP: 17
SALES (est): 1.8MM **Privately Held**
SIC: 3721 Aircraft

(G-13866)
BOEING COMPANY
4140 S Oliver St (67210-2127)
PHONE..................................312 544-2000
Christopher Kempf, *Engineer*
Ron Estes, *Manager*
Tina Fox, *Manager*
Renee Jennings, *Manager*
EMP: 19
SALES (corp-wide): 101.1B **Publicly Held**
SIC: 3721 Aircraft
PA: The Boeing Company
100 N Riverside Plz
Chicago IL 60606
312 544-2000

(G-13867)
BOEING DISTRIBUTION SVCS INC
10900 E 26th St N (67226-4607)
PHONE..................................316 630-4900
Chuck Robinson, *Manager*
EMP: 40
SALES (corp-wide): 101.1B **Publicly Held**
SIC: 5088 Aircraft equipment & supplies
HQ: Boeing Distribution Services, Inc.
3760 W 108th St Unit 1
Hialeah FL 33018
561 383-5100

(G-13868)
BOGE IRON & METAL CO INC
10600 E 13th St N Apt 117 (67206-3707)
P.O. Box 286 (67201-0286)
PHONE..................................316 263-8241
Allen Boge, *President*
EMP: 20 **EST:** 1939
SALES (est): 4.3MM **Privately Held**
SIC: 5093 Ferrous metal scrap & waste; nonferrous metals scrap

(G-13869)
BOGUE ANIMAL HOSPITAL WEST PA
429 N Maize Rd (67212-4695)
PHONE..................................316 722-1085
Greg Bogue, *Owner*
Richard J Bogue, *Owner*
EMP: 20 **EST:** 1961
SQ FT: 2,000
SALES (est): 772.6K **Privately Held**
SIC: 0742 Animal hospital services, pets & other animal specialties

(G-13870)
BORDER STATES INDUSTRIES INC
3800 W Dora Ave (67213-1211)
P.O. Box 13281 (67213-0281)
PHONE..................................316 945-1313
Bryan Mason, *Manager*
EMP: 13
SALES (corp-wide): 2B **Privately Held**
WEB: www.krizdavis.com
SIC: 5063 Electrical supplies
PA: Border States Industries, Inc.
2400 38th St S
Fargo ND 58104
701 293-5834

(G-13871)
BOSLEYS TIRE SERVICE CO INC
Also Called: Bosley's Tire & Wheel
3948 S Broadway Ave (67216-1036)
PHONE..................................316 524-8511
Lonnie H Bosley, *President*
Randy Bosley, *Manager*
EMP: 27
SQ FT: 30,000
SALES (est): 4.1MM **Privately Held**
WEB: www.bosley.kscoxmail.com
SIC: 5531 7539 Automotive tires; axle straightening, automotive; electrical services; radiator repair shop, automotive; automotive air conditioning repair

(G-13872)
BOTANICA INC
Also Called: BOTANICA, THE WICHITA GARDENS
701 N Amidon Ave (67203-3162)
PHONE..................................316 264-0448
Marty Miller, *Director*
Barbara Chamberlin, *Director*
Kathy Sweeney, *Director*
EMP: 18
SQ FT: 10,000
SALES: 3MM **Privately Held**
WEB: www.botanica.org
SIC: 8422 Botanical garden

(G-13873)
BOULEVARD ONE INC (PA)
Also Called: Joma Bowling
3200 N Rock Rd (67226-1313)
PHONE..................................316 636-9494
John Crum, *President*
Martha Ann Crum, *Treasurer*
EMP: 48
SALES (est): 2.6MM **Privately Held**
SIC: 7933 Ten pin center

(G-13874)
BOULEVARD ONE INC
Also Called: West Acres Bowl
749 N Ridge Rd (67212-3324)
PHONE..................................316 722-5211
Ray Baty, *General Mgr*

GEOGRAPHIC

Diann Sturgeon, *Manager*
EMP: 30
SALES (est): 770K
SALES (corp-wide): 2.6MM **Privately Held**
SIC: 7933 Ten pin center
PA: Boulevard One, Inc
3200 N Rock Rd
Wichita KS 67226
316 636-9494

(G-13875)
BOX CENTRAL INC (PA)
7130 W Maple St Ste 230 (67209-2101)
PHONE..................................316 689-8484
Clifford Elder, *President*
EMP: 11 **EST:** 2006
SALES (est): 1MM **Privately Held**
SIC: 7389 5932 4731 4213 Packaging & labeling services; antiques; freight forwarding; trucking, except local

(G-13876)
BOYNTON FAMILY DENTAL ARTS LLC
1901 N Webb Rd Ste D (67206-3416)
PHONE..................................316 685-8881
Kreg Boynton, *Fmly & Gen Dent*
Sherie Boynton,
EMP: 20
SALES (est): 1.2MM **Privately Held**
SIC: 8021 Dentists' office

(G-13877)
BOYS & GIRLS CLUB OF S CENTRAL (PA)
2400 N Opportunity Dr (67219-5529)
PHONE..................................316 687-5437
Jordan Weins, *Principal*
Ian Adair, *Exec Dir*
Lauren Hirsh, *Instructor*
Lashonder Harrison,
EMP: 35
SALES: 1MM **Privately Held**
SIC: 8641 8322 Youth organizations; Boy Scout organization; Girl Scout organization; youth center

(G-13878)
BRACE INTEGRATED SERVICES INC (DH)
2112 S Custer Ave (67213-1500)
PHONE..................................316 832-0292
Todd Rouw, *President*
Tim Alexander, *Vice Pres*
Timothy L Blackwell, *Treasurer*
EMP: 30 **EST:** 1979
SQ FT: 16,500
SALES (est): 34.5MM
SALES (corp-wide): 265.1MM **Privately Held**
SIC: 1799 5033 Insulation of pipes & boilers; roofing, siding & insulation; roofing & siding materials; insulation materials
HQ: Brace Industrial Group, Inc.
14950 Heathrow Fore
Houston TX 77032
281 749-1020

(G-13879)
BRAD MURRAY INC
3082 S All Hallows Ave (67217-1055)
PHONE..................................316 943-2516
John Murray, *President*
EMP: 15
SALES (est): 2MM **Privately Held**
WEB: www.bradmurrayinc.com
SIC: 1771 Concrete work

(G-13880)
BRADBURN WRECKING COMPANY
3233 S Southeast Blvd (67216-2658)
P.O. Box 234 (67201-0234)
PHONE..................................316 686-1959
Darren Bradburn, *President*
EMP: 45
SQ FT: 25,000
SALES (est): 5.4MM **Privately Held**
SIC: 1795 1794 Demolition, buildings & other structures; excavation work

(G-13881)
BRADLEY HOTEL WICHITA
Also Called: Hilton Garden Inn Wichita
2041 N Bradley Fair Pkwy (67206-2940)
PHONE..................................316 262-2841
Matt Dolan, *Manager*
William Hamrick,
EMP: 45
SALES (est): 2.1MM **Privately Held**
SIC: 7011 Hotels & motels

(G-13882)
BRADLEY MACHINE INC
130 N Millwood St (67203-5850)
PHONE..................................316 262-3221
Delbert E Bradley, *President*
Jesse Bradley, *Vice Pres*
Nancy Bradley, *Vice Pres*
EMP: 12 **EST:** 1965
SQ FT: 3,840
SALES (est): 1.9MM **Privately Held**
WEB: www.bradleymachine.net
SIC: 3599 Machine shop, jobbing & repair

(G-13883)
BRADY NURSERY INC
11200 W Kellogg St (67209-1289)
PHONE..................................316 722-7516
Joseph J Brady, *President*
Catherine Brady, *Corp Secy*
EMP: 48
SQ FT: 29,000
SALES (est): 3.9MM **Privately Held**
WEB: www.bradynursery.com
SIC: 0181 0781 Nursery stock, growing of; landscape planning services

(G-13884)
BRAND PLUMBING INC
2418 S Hoover Rd (67215-1293)
PHONE..................................316 942-2306
Marc Brand, *President*
Mary R Brand, *Corp Secy*
Michael J Brand, *Vice Pres*
Mary Brand, *Office Mgr*
EMP: 15
SQ FT: 10,000
SALES (est): 2.2MM **Privately Held**
WEB: www.brandplbg.kscoxmail.com
SIC: 1711 Plumbing contractors

(G-13885)
BRANDON HOSPITALITY LLC
Also Called: Staybridge Suites
2250 N Greenwich Rd (67226-8211)
PHONE..................................316 613-1995
Michael Brungardt, *General Mgr*
EMP: 20
SALES (corp-wide): 640.6K **Privately Held**
SIC: 7011 Hotels & motels
PA: Brandon Hospitality Llc
7405 S Bitterroot Pl
Sioux Falls SD 57108
605 770-4933

(G-13886)
BREAKTHROUGH CLB SEDGWICK CNTY
1010 N Main St (67203-3609)
P.O. Box 670 (67201-0670)
PHONE..................................316 269-2534
Steve Benjamin, *President*
Rod Eaton, *Controller*
Douglas Winkley, *Exec Dir*
Katie Gibbons, *Director*
EMP: 23
SQ FT: 10,000
SALES: 195.2K **Privately Held**
WEB: www.btcwichita.com
SIC: 8093 Mental health clinic, outpatient

(G-13887)
BRIDGESTONE RET OPERATIONS LLC
Also Called: Tires Plus Total Car Care
3745 N Rock Rd (67226-1307)
PHONE..................................316 315-0363
Joseph McCaffrey, *Manager*
EMP: 30 **Privately Held**
WEB: www.tiresplus.com
SIC: 7534 Tire retreading & repair shops
HQ: Bridgestone Retail Operations, Llc
333 E Lake St Ste 300
Bloomingdale IL 60108
630 259-9000

(G-13888)
BRIDGESTONE RET OPERATIONS LLC
Also Called: Tires Plus Total Car Care
6500 W Kellogg Dr (67209-2212)
PHONE..................................316 942-1332
John McCaffrey, *Manager*
EMP: 30 **Privately Held**
WEB: www.tiresplus.com
SIC: 7534 Tire retreading & repair shops
HQ: Bridgestone Retail Operations, Llc
333 E Lake St Ste 300
Bloomingdale IL 60108
630 259-9000

(G-13889)
BRIDGESTONE RET OPERATIONS LLC
Also Called: Firestone
7700 E Kellogg Dr Ste K (67207-1700)
PHONE..................................316 684-2682
John Silhan, *Manager*
EMP: 18 **Privately Held**
WEB: www.bfis.com
SIC: 5531 7534 Automotive tires; rebuilding & retreading tires
HQ: Bridgestone Retail Operations, Llc
333 E Lake St Ste 300
Bloomingdale IL 60108
630 259-9000

(G-13890)
BRIJ SYSTEMS LLC
700 E 10th St N (67214-2919)
PHONE..................................316 262-6969
Christina D Smith, *Sls & Mktg Exec*
Nital P Ghosh,
Bijal Parikh,
Yogesh Parikh,
EMP: 8
SQ FT: 28,000
SALES: 700K **Privately Held**
WEB: www.brijsystems.com
SIC: 3599 Machine shop, jobbing & repair

(G-13891)
BRINKS INCORPORATED
2145 S Meridian Ave (67213)
PHONE..................................316 945-0244
James McElwain, *Manager*
EMP: 16
SALES (corp-wide): 3.4B **Publicly Held**
WEB: www.brinksinc.com
SIC: 7381 Armored car services
HQ: Brink's, Incorporated
1801 Bayberry Ct Ste 400
Richmond VA 23226
804 289-9600

(G-13892)
BRITTAIN MACHINE INC (DH)
2520 S Sheridan Ave (67217-1340)
P.O. Box 17227 (67217-0227)
PHONE..................................316 942-8223
Mark Heasely, *CEO*
David Hilter, *COO*
Gene Fibert, *Vice Pres*
◆ **EMP:** 50 **EST:** 1965
SQ FT: 153,000
SALES (est): 16.8MM
SALES (corp-wide): 225.3B **Publicly Held**
WEB: www.brittainmachine.com
SIC: 3544 3769 3812 3599 Special dies & tools; guided missile & space vehicle parts & auxiliary equipment; search & navigation equipment; machine shop, jobbing & repair
HQ: Stratoflight
25540 Rye Canyon Rd
Valencia CA 91355
949 622-0700

(G-13893)
BROADMOOR ONE LLC
Also Called: Gracious Senior Living
9435 E Central Ave (67206-2500)
PHONE..................................316 683-0562
Max Cole,
EMP: 90
SALES (est): 3.6MM **Privately Held**
SIC: 6798 Realty investment trusts

(G-13894)
BROADVIEW HSPTLITY HLDINGS LLC
Also Called: Broadview Hotel
400 W Douglas Ave (67202-2902)
PHONE..................................316 262-5000
Mordechai Boaziz, *Partner*
EMP: 63 **EST:** 2001
SALES (est): 1.8MM **Privately Held**
WEB: www.broadview-hotel.com
SIC: 7011 Hotels

(G-13895)
BROADWAY HOME MEDICAL INC
808 S Hillside St (67211-3004)
PHONE..................................316 264-8600
Mike Lindsey, *President*
Jake Tillman, *General Mgr*
Brenda Fankhouser, *Store Mgr*
Brian Lindsey, *Admin Sec*
EMP: 12
SQ FT: 6,000
SALES (est): 2.3MM **Privately Held**
SIC: 5999 7352 7699 5169 Hospital equipment & supplies; medical equipment rental; medical equipment repair, non-electric; oxygen; medical equipment & supplies

(G-13896)
BROADWAY MORTUARY INC
1147 S Broadway Ave (67211-2285)
PHONE..................................316 262-3435
W Ashley Cozine, *President*
S Susan Cozine, *Corp Secy*
William L Cozine, *Vice Pres*
Vic Graves, *Director*
EMP: 11
SQ FT: 5,000
SALES (est): 1.1MM **Privately Held**
WEB: www.broadwaymortuary.com
SIC: 7261 Funeral home

(G-13897)
BROOKDALE SENIOR LIVING COMMUN
Also Called: Sterling House of Wichita
8600 E 21st St N Ofc Ofc (67206-2990)
PHONE..................................316 684-3100
Micheal Agpoon, *Manager*
EMP: 15
SALES (corp-wide): 4.5B **Publicly Held**
WEB: www.assisted.com
SIC: 8051 Skilled nursing care facilities
HQ: Brookdale Senior Living Communities, Inc.
6737 W Wa St Ste 2300
Milwaukee WI 53214
414 918-5000

(G-13898)
BROOKDALE SNIOR LVING CMMNTIES
Also Called: Clare Bridge of Wichita
9191 E 21st St N (67206-2923)
PHONE..................................316 630-0788
Tom Broderick, *Manager*
EMP: 20
SALES (corp-wide): 4.5B **Publicly Held**
WEB: www.assisted.com
SIC: 8059 8051 Rest home, with health care; extended care facility
HQ: Brookdale Senior Living Communities, Inc.
6737 W Wa St Ste 2300
Milwaukee WI 53214
414 918-5000

(G-13899)
BRP US INC
Also Called: Bomgardier Flight Test Center
1530 S Tyler Rd (67209-1851)
PHONE..................................316 946-2000
Adel Hosny, *Principal*
EMP: 475
SALES (corp-wide): 3.9B **Privately Held**
SIC: 4581 Airports, flying fields & services
HQ: Brp Us Inc.
10101 Science Dr
Sturtevant WI 53177
450 532-5100

(G-13900)
BRUCE BRUCE & LEHMAN LLC
3330 W Douglas Ave # 100 (67203-5415)
P.O. Box 75037 (67275-0037)
PHONE..................................316 722-3391
Eric Bruce, *Mng Member*
Elizabeth Carson,
J Micheal Lehman,
EMP: 10
SALES (est): 1MM **Privately Held**
WEB: www.ksadvocates.com
SIC: 8111 General practice attorney, lawyer

(G-13901)
BRUCE OCHSNER MD
Also Called: Ochsner Eye Center
1100 N Topeka St (67214-2810)
PHONE..................................316 263-6273
Bruce Ochsner MD, *Partner*
David A Kingrey, *Partner*
EMP: 21
SQ FT: 7,000
SALES (est): 1.2MM **Privately Held**
WEB: www.ochsnereye.com
SIC: 8011 Ophthalmologist

(G-13902)
BSREP II WS HOTEL TRS SUB LLC
8621 E 21st St N Ste 230 (67206-2993)
PHONE..................................443 569-7053
Ryan Willey,
EMP: 20
SALES (est): 109.1K **Privately Held**
SIC: 7011 Hotels & motels

(G-13903)
BUCHANAN TECHNOLOGIES INC
3450 N Rock Rd Ste 705 (67226-1357)
PHONE..................................316 219-0124
Lori Parker, *Branch Mgr*
EMP: 25
SALES (corp-wide): 88.6MM **Privately Held**
WEB: www.clickright.com
SIC: 7379 ; computer related consulting services
PA: Buchanan Technologies, Inc.
1026 Texan Trl Ste 200
Grapevine TX 76051
972 869-3966

(G-13904)
BUCKLEY ROOFING COMPANY INC
3601 N Hydraulic St (67219-3898)
PHONE..................................316 838-9321
Ed Frederick, *President*
Teare Moare, *President*
Jane Frederick, *Corp Secy*
Evan Frederick, *Vice Pres*
Jim Duncan, *Project Mgr*
EMP: 70
SQ FT: 27,500
SALES (est): 10.7MM **Privately Held**
WEB: www.buckleyroofing.com
SIC: 1761 Roofing contractor; sheet metalwork

(G-13905)
BUD PALMER AUCTION
101 W 29th St N (67204-4889)
PHONE..................................316 838-4141
Walter F Palmer, *Owner*
EMP: 25
SQ FT: 10,080
SALES (est): 1.1MM **Privately Held**
SIC: 7389 5712 5932 Auctioneers, fee basis; furniture stores; furniture, secondhand

(G-13906)
BUD ROAT INC
Also Called: Roat Bud Standard Service
310 N Handley St (67203-5908)
PHONE..................................316 683-9072
Arlan Roat, *President*
Lois M Roat, *Corp Secy*
EMP: 11
SALES (est): 1.4MM **Privately Held**
WEB: www.budroattowing.com
SIC: 7549 Towing service, automotive

(G-13907)
BUDGET CAR TRCK RENTL WICHITA
Also Called: Budget Rent-A-Car
2250 N Ridge Rd Ste 100 (67205-1141)
PHONE..................................316 729-7979
Monica Hartley, *General Mgr*
EMP: 30
SALES (est): 713.8K **Privately Held**
SIC: 7514 7519 Rent-a-car service; trailer rental

(G-13908)
BUDGET RENT-A-CAR OF KANSAS (PA)
1895 Midfield Rd (67209-1989)
PHONE..................................316 946-4891
Jerry H Green, *President*
John Steinberg, *President*
Howard Steinberg, *Vice Pres*
EMP: 24 **EST:** 1962
SQ FT: 9,000
SALES (est): 2.1MM **Privately Held**
SIC: 7514 7513 Rent-a-car service; truck rental, without drivers

(G-13909)
BUILDERS INC (PA)
1081 S Glendale St (67218-3229)
P.O. Box 20050 (67208-1050)
PHONE..................................316 684-1400
Michael Garvey, *President*
Bradley Smisor, *Corp Secy*
James Garvey, *Senior VP*
Kevin Sanborn, *Vice Pres*
Larry Shoemaker, *Vice Pres*
EMP: 30
SQ FT: 12,000
SALES (est): 6.3MM **Privately Held**
WEB: www.buildersinc.com
SIC: 6512 6514 Commercial & industrial building operation; residential building, four or fewer units: operation

(G-13910)
BUILDERS INC
Also Called: Garvey Industrial Park
5755 S Hoover Rd (67215-9300)
PHONE..................................316 522-6104
Jack Brooks, *Manager*
EMP: 15
SALES (corp-wide): 6.3MM **Privately Held**
WEB: www.buildersinc.com
SIC: 4225 General warehousing
PA: Builders, Inc.
1081 S Glendale St
Wichita KS 67218
316 684-1400

(G-13911)
BUILDERS APARTMENTS INC
1081 S Glendale St (67218-3229)
P.O. Box 20050 (67208-1050)
PHONE..................................316 684-1400
James W Garvey, *President*
EMP: 10
SQ FT: 12,000
SALES (est): 644.8K
SALES (corp-wide): 6.3MM **Privately Held**
SIC: 6513 Apartment building operators
PA: Builders, Inc.
1081 S Glendale St
Wichita KS 67218
316 684-1400

(G-13912)
BUILDERS COMMERCIALS INC
Also Called: Parklane Shopping Center
1081 S Glendale St (67218-3229)
P.O. Box 20050 (67208-1050)
PHONE..................................316 686-3107
Jim Garbey, *President*
Bradley Smiso, *Exec VP*
EMP: 12
SALES (est): 927.5K
SALES (corp-wide): 6.3MM **Privately Held**
WEB: www.shopparklane.com
SIC: 6512 Commercial & industrial building operation
PA: Builders, Inc.
1081 S Glendale St
Wichita KS 67218
316 684-1400

(G-13913)
BUILDERS DEVELOPMENT INC (HQ)
1081 S Glendale St (67218-3229)
P.O. Box 20050 (67208-1050)
PHONE..................................316 684-1400
James W Garvey, *President*
Elton V Parsons, *Vice Pres*
Elton Parsons, *Vice Pres*
Bradley K Smisor, *Treasurer*
EMP: 31
SQ FT: 12,000
SALES (est): 2.7MM
SALES (corp-wide): 6.3MM **Privately Held**
SIC: 6552 1531 Subdividers & developers; speculative builder, multi-family dwellings
PA: Builders, Inc.
1081 S Glendale St
Wichita KS 67218
316 684-1400

(G-13914)
BULK CONVEYORS INC
Also Called: BCI
1850 N (67214)
PHONE..................................316 201-3158
Van Buchanan, *CEO*
Samuel Buchanan, *CEO*
Kevin Doll, *President*
Ty Quillin, *General Mgr*
Steve Cloud, *Vice Pres*
EMP: 50
SQ FT: 40,000
SALES (est): 19.8MM **Privately Held**
SIC: 3535 Conveyors & conveying equipment

(G-13915)
BURGESS MANUFACTURING INC
3443 N Topeka St (67219-3639)
P.O. Box 3809 (67201-3809)
PHONE..................................316 838-5748
Robert L Burgess, *President*
EMP: 25
SALES (est): 4.6MM **Privately Held**
WEB: www.mfginfo.com
SIC: 2448 Wood pallets & skids

(G-13916)
BURNELLS CREATIVE GOLD INC
550 N Rock Rd Ste 104 (67206-1745)
PHONE..................................316 634-2822
Jerry Burnell, *President*
Robin Lies, *General Mgr*
Johnna Burnell, *Office Mgr*
EMP: 9
SQ FT: 2,250
SALES: 1.4MM **Privately Held**
WEB: www.burnells.com
SIC: 5944 3911 7631 Jewelry, precious stones & precious metals; pearl jewelry, natural or cultured; jewelry repair services

(G-13917)
BURNHAM CMPSITE STRUCTURES INC
6262 W 34th St S (67215-1814)
PHONE..................................316 946-5900
Todd Dugan, *President*
Rick Warner, *Opers Mgr*
Glen Kohler, *Controller*
Craig Dugan, *Train & Dev Mgr*
Darrel Dugan, *Director*
▼ **EMP:** 30
SQ FT: 65,000
SALES (est): 5.8MM **Privately Held**
SIC: 3728 Aircraft parts & equipment

(G-13918)
BURNHAM COMPOSITES INC
6262 W 34th St S (67215-1814)
PHONE..................................316 946-5900
Todd Dugan, *President*
Craig Dugan, *Vice Pres*
Ellen Stewart, *Buyer*
Shu Hayes, *Purchasing*
Richard Manriquez, *Purchasing*
EMP: 40
SQ FT: 40,000
SALES (est): 5.7MM **Privately Held**
WEB: www.burnhamcomposites.com
SIC: 3769 Guided missile & space vehicle parts & auxiliary equipment

(G-13919)
BUSCH JOHNSON & MANK
359 S Hydraulic St (67211-1908)
PHONE..................................316 263-5661
Fred A Johnson, *Owner*
EMP: 10
SALES (est): 639.3K **Privately Held**
SIC: 8111 General practice attorney, lawyer

(G-13920)
BUSINESS TECHNOLOGY CAREER
Also Called: BTCO
5111 E 21st St N (67208-1606)
P.O. Box 8217 (67208-0217)
PHONE..................................316 688-1888
Joey Jackson, *President*
TW Anderson, *President*
Mary Jenkins, *Human Resources*
Katey Marshall, *Supervisor*
EMP: 12
SALES: 5.4MM **Privately Held**
SIC: 7389 Personal service agents, brokers & bureaus

(G-13921)
BUTLER & MCILVAIN INC
Also Called: SERVPRO
3225 S Oliver St (67210-1532)
PHONE..................................316 684-6700
Patrick Butler, *Principal*
Craig McIlvain, *Principal*
EMP: 11
SALES: 1MM **Privately Held**
SIC: 7349 Building maintenance services

(G-13922)
BUZZ BUILDING MAINTENANCE INC
3112 N 124th St W (67223-6905)
PHONE..................................316 773-9860
Sonya Busby, *President*
Mike Busby, *Director*
EMP: 20
SALES (est): 490.9K **Privately Held**
WEB: www.buzzclean.com
SIC: 7349 Janitorial service, contract basis

(G-13923)
BWI OF KS INC
6919 E Harry St (67207-2910)
PHONE..................................316 831-0488
Cathy Wolfe, *President*
Kathy Wolf, *President*
William C Wolf, *Vice Pres*
Dallas Wolf, *Director*
EMP: 40 **EST:** 2000
SQ FT: 1,200
SALES (est): 7.2MM **Privately Held**
WEB: www.bwiofksinc.com
SIC: 2241 Strapping webs

(G-13924)
C & B EQUIPMENT MIDWEST INC (PA)
Also Called: Douglas Pump Service, Inc.
3717 N Ridgewood St (67220-4418)
PHONE..................................316 262-5156
Dennis Noyes, *President*
Tucker Noyes, *Sales Staff*
Jeff Shinkle, *Manager*
Dane Winter, *Manager*
Barb Viramontez, *Admin Asst*
EMP: 13
SQ FT: 15,000
SALES: 8MM **Privately Held**
WEB: www.cullumandbrown.com
SIC: 5084 Pumps & pumping equipment

(G-13925)
C E MACHINE CO INC
1741 S Hoover Ct (67209-2871)
PHONE..................................316 942-0411
Brian Eck, *President*
Julia Wiley, *Accounts Mgr*
Tammy Counts, *Office Mgr*
Clay Spexarth, *Manager*

Keith Eck, *IT/INT Sup*
EMP: 70
SQ FT: 55,000
SALES (est): 12.8MM **Privately Held**
WEB: www.cemachine.com
SIC: 3599 Machine shop, jobbing & repair

(G-13926)
CABLECOM INC
800 E 3rd St N (67202-2720)
PHONE..................................316 267-4777
Joel Kelley, *President*
EMP: 12
SQ FT: 3,500
SALES (est): 1.4MM **Privately Held**
WEB: www.cablecomks.com
SIC: 1731 Fiber optic cable installation

(G-13927)
CALIFORNIA NAIL SALON
4600 W Kellogg Dr Ofc (67209-2546)
PHONE..................................316 942-5400
Binh Le, *Owner*
EMP: 10
SALES (est): 210K **Privately Held**
SIC: 7231 Manicurist, pedicurist

(G-13928)
CALVIN OPP CONCRETE INC
1375 S Bebe St (67209-2607)
PHONE..................................316 944-4600
Calvin Opp, *President*
EMP: 60
SALES (est): 6.1MM **Privately Held**
WEB: www.oppconcrete.com
SIC: 1771 Foundation & footing contractor

(G-13929)
CAMBRIDGE FAMILY DENTISTRY
2020 N Webb Rd Ste 301 (67206-3410)
PHONE..................................316 687-2110
Dean Wright DDS, *Owner*
EMP: 17
SALES (est): 1.2MM **Privately Held**
WEB: www.cambridgefamilydentistry.com
SIC: 8021 Dentists' office; dental clinic

(G-13930)
CAMBRIDGE SUITES HOTEL
711 S Main St (67213-5413)
PHONE..................................316 263-1061
Jack Deboer, *Owner*
EMP: 15
SALES (est): 318K **Privately Held**
SIC: 7011 Hotels

(G-13931)
CAMPBELLS PHOENIX GREENHOUSE
Also Called: Plant Kingdom Garden Center
3560 S Broadway St (67216)
PHONE..................................316 524-5311
Gene M Campbell, *Partner*
Nicholas A Campbell, *Partner*
Timothy B Campbell, *Partner*
EMP: 15
SQ FT: 50,000
SALES (est): 980K **Privately Held**
SIC: 5193 Flowers & nursery stock

(G-13932)
CANCER CENTER OF KANSAS PA
3243 E Murdock St Ste 300 (67208-3006)
PHONE..................................316 262-4467
Yoosef Abraham, *CEO*
Phu Truong, *Hematology*
EMP: 90
SALES (corp-wide): 24.4MM **Privately Held**
SIC: 8011 Oncologist
PA: Cancer Center Of Kansas, P.A.
818 N Emporia St Ste 403
Wichita KS 67214
316 262-4467

(G-13933)
CANCER CENTER OF KANSAS PA (PA)
818 N Emporia St Ste 403 (67214-3728)
PHONE..................................316 262-4467
Yoosef Abraham, *CEO*
Shaker Dakhil, *Principal*
Paul Orourke, *Office Mgr*
Mark Humphries, *Director*
Laura Monahan, *Officer*
EMP: 124
SALES (est): 24.4MM **Privately Held**
SIC: 8011 Hematologist; oncologist

(G-13934)
CANLAN ICE SPT CTR WICHITA LLC
505 W Maple St (67213-4616)
PHONE..................................316 337-9199
Jim McCain, *General Mgr*
Carlos Galvan, *Director*
EMP: 60
SALES (est): 3.2MM **Privately Held**
SIC: 6531 7999 Real estate managers; skating rink operation services

(G-13935)
CANYON OIL & GAS CO
Also Called: Slawson Co
727 N Waco Ave Ste 400 (67203-3900)
P.O. Box 2907 (67201-2907)
PHONE..................................316 263-3201
Donald C Slawson, *President*
Bill Wohlford, *Admin Sec*
EMP: 7
SQ FT: 1,000
SALES (est): 1.2MM **Privately Held**
SIC: 1311 Crude petroleum production; natural gas production

(G-13936)
CAP CARPET INC (PA)
Also Called: Carpet One
535 S Emerson St (67209-2161)
PHONE..................................316 262-3496
Aaron Pirner, *CEO*
La Vone J Pirner, *Ch of Bd*
Tony Greco, *Vice Pres*
Robert Lindsey, *Controller*
Josh Shelton, *Sales Associate*
▲ **EMP:** 35
SQ FT: 16,000
SALES (est): 38.8MM **Privately Held**
WEB: www.capcarpetinc.com
SIC: 5713 5023 Carpets; carpets

(G-13937)
CAPITOL FEDERAL SAVINGS BANK
10404 W Central Ave (67212-5102)
PHONE..................................316 689-0200
Kendall Ducksworth, *Vice Pres*
Mark Brookstein, *Buyer*
Tina Hann, *Manager*
Anya Leonard, *Executive Asst*
Brandy Mitchell, *Loan*
EMP: 12
SALES (corp-wide): 351.9MM **Publicly Held**
WEB: www.capfed.com
SIC: 6035 Federal savings banks
HQ: Capitol Federal Savings Bank
700 S Kansas Ave Fl 1
Topeka KS 66603
785 235-1341

(G-13938)
CAPITOL FEDERAL SAVINGS BANK
8103 E 21st St N (67206)
PHONE..................................316 689-3104
Sherry Carlisle, *Manager*
EMP: 32
SALES (corp-wide): 351.9MM **Publicly Held**
WEB: www.capfed.com
SIC: 6035 Federal savings & loan associations
HQ: Capitol Federal Savings Bank
700 S Kansas Ave Fl 1
Topeka KS 66603
785 235-1341

(G-13939)
CAPITOL FEDERAL SAVINGS BANK
4000 E Harry St (67218-3718)
PHONE..................................316 689-0200
Marian Hurst, *Manager*
EMP: 15
SALES (corp-wide): 351.9MM **Publicly Held**
WEB: www.capfed.com
SIC: 6035 Federal savings banks
HQ: Capitol Federal Savings Bank
700 S Kansas Ave Fl 1
Topeka KS 66603
785 235-1341

(G-13940)
CAPPS MANUFACTURING INC
2122 S Custer Ave (67213-1500)
PHONE..................................316 942-9351
Barney L Capps, *Branch Mgr*
EMP: 85
SALES (corp-wide): 27.3MM **Privately Held**
SIC: 3728 Aircraft assemblies, subassemblies & parts
PA: Capps Manufacturing, Incorporated
2121 S Edwards St
Wichita KS 67213
316 942-9351

(G-13941)
CAPPS MANUFACTURING INC (PA)
2121 S Edwards St (67213-1868)
PHONE..................................316 942-9351
Barney L Capps, *President*
Cynthia Davies, *General Mgr*
Donald Smith, *Vice Pres*
Terry Bastow, *Prdtn Mgr*
Matthew Urban, *Purchasing*
▲ **EMP:** 80
SQ FT: 244,000
SALES: 27.3MM **Privately Held**
WEB: www.cappsmfg.com
SIC: 3728 4899 Aircraft assemblies, subassemblies & parts; satellite earth stations

(G-13942)
CAR PARK INC
121 S Emporia Ave (67202-4501)
PHONE..................................316 265-0553
Ryan Wagner, *Branch Mgr*
Troy Harris, *Branch Mgr*
EMP: 20
SALES (corp-wide): 600K **Privately Held**
SIC: 7521 7299 Parking garage; valet parking
PA: The Car Park Inc
702 W Idaho St Ste 650
Boise ID 83702
208 336-6597

(G-13943)
CARDINAL BUFFING CO INC
1432 S Walnut St (67213-4349)
PHONE..................................316 263-8475
Steven W Winfrey, *President*
EMP: 7 **EST:** 1981
SQ FT: 3,600
SALES (est): 450K **Privately Held**
SIC: 3471 Buffing for the trade

(G-13944)
CARDINAL HEALTH INC
536 N St Francis St (67214-3808)
PHONE..................................316 264-6275
EMP: 74
SALES (corp-wide): 145.5B **Publicly Held**
SIC: 5122 Pharmaceuticals
PA: Cardinal Health, Inc.
7000 Cardinal Pl
Dublin OH 43017
614 757-5000

(G-13945)
CARDIOVASCULAR CONS KANS PA
9350 E 35th St N Ste 101 (67226-2022)
PHONE..................................316 440-0845
Richard Steckley MD, *President*
Gregory Duick MD, *President*
Gerard Bieker, *CFO*
Aziz Maksoud, *Cardiology*
EMP: 60
SQ FT: 8,700
SALES (est): 9.1MM **Privately Held**
SIC: 8011 Cardiologist & carcio-vascular specialist

(G-13946)
CARGILL INCORPORATED
1417 N Barwise St (67214-1327)
P.O. Box 2696 (67201-2696)
PHONE..................................316 292-2380
Rajiu Datar, *Branch Mgr*
EMP: 87
SALES (corp-wide): 113.4B **Privately Held**
WEB: www.cargill.com
SIC: 2079 2075 Soybean oil, refined: not made in soybean oil mills; soybean oil mills
PA: Cargill, Incorporated
15407 Mcginty Rd W
Wayzata MN 55391
952 742-7575

(G-13947)
CARGILL INCORPORATED
825 E Douglas Ave (67202-3512)
PHONE..................................316 291-1939
Andrea Epperson, *Manager*
Travis Ackerman, *Analyst*
EMP: 19
SALES (corp-wide): 113.4B **Privately Held**
SIC: 5153 2075 2046 2048 Grain & field beans; soybean oil, cake or meal; corn oil, refined; prepared feeds; meat packing plants; poultry slaughtering & processing
PA: Cargill, Incorporated
15407 Mcginty Rd W
Wayzata MN 55391
952 742-7575

(G-13948)
CARGILL INCORPORATED
1401 N Mosley St (67214-1339)
P.O. Box 2696 (67201-2696)
PHONE..................................316 292-2719
Rob Boardman, *Manager*
EMP: 91
SALES (corp-wide): 113.4B **Privately Held**
WEB: www.cargill.com
SIC: 2075 Soybean oil mills
PA: Cargill, Incorporated
15407 Mcginty Rd W
Wayzata MN 55391
952 742-7575

(G-13949)
CARGILL MT LGSTICS SLTIONS INC (DH)
250 N Water St (67202-1213)
P.O. Box 8183 (67208-0183)
PHONE..................................877 596-4062
John A Keating, *President*
Jonathan E Meier, *Vice Pres*
David A Robertson, *Vice Pres*
James B Sikes, *Vice Pres*
Leasa K Wilch, *Treasurer*
EMP: 41
SQ FT: 5,000
SALES (est): 15.6MM
SALES (corp-wide): 113.4B **Privately Held**
WEB: www.exceltransportationinc.com
SIC: 4213 Contract haulers
HQ: Cargill Meat Solutions Corp
151 N Main St Ste 900
Wichita KS 67202
316 291-2500

(G-13950)
CARL HARRIS CO INC
1245 S Santa Fe St (67211-3223)
PHONE..................................316 267-8700
Carl Harris, *President*
Lori Harris, *Office Mgr*
Brad Hamill, *Manager*
Francis Harris, *Admin Sec*
EMP: 24
SQ FT: 1,620
SALES (est): 2.4MM **Privately Held**
WEB: www.carlharriscompany.com
SIC: 1791 1771 Iron work, structural; concrete work

(G-13951)
CARNEY DANIEL M REHAB ENGINEER
5130 E 20th St N (67208-2546)
PHONE..................................316 651-5200

▲ = Import ▼=Export
◆ =Import/Export

Daniel M Carney, *Chairman*
EMP: 14
SALES (est): 911.5K **Privately Held**
SIC: 8711 Engineering services

(G-13952)
CARO CONSTRUCTION CO INC
527 N Walnut St (67203-5936)
PHONE..................................316 267-7505
David Caro, *President*
Deonne Caro, *Corp Secy*
EMP: 25
SQ FT: 20,000
SALES (est): 4.3MM **Privately Held**
WEB: www.caroconstruction.com
SIC: 1542 1521 Commercial & office building contractors; single-family housing construction

(G-13953)
CAROUSEL SKATE CENTER INC
312 N West St (67203-1205)
PHONE..................................316 942-4505
Herbert J Ottaway, *President*
K Scott Ottaway, *President*
EMP: 20
SQ FT: 20,000
SALES (est): 640K **Privately Held**
SIC: 7999 Roller skating rink operation

(G-13954)
CARRINGTON HOUSE LLC
Also Called: Carriage House Central
1432 N Waco Ave (67203-2649)
PHONE..................................316 262-5516
Dennis Bush, *Mng Member*
Debie Bush,
EMP: 30
SALES (est): 1.1MM **Privately Held**
SIC: 8059 Nursing home, except skilled & intermediate care facility

(G-13955)
CARSTAR INC
606 N Webb Rd (67206-1804)
PHONE..................................316 652-7821
Jeremy J Edwards, *Manager*
EMP: 10
SALES (corp-wide): 136.9MM **Privately Held**
WEB: www.carstar.com
SIC: 7532 Body shop, automotive
HQ: Carstar, Inc.
440 S Church St Ste 700
Charlotte NC 28202

(G-13956)
CARTER-WATERS LLC
4311 W 29th Cir S (67215-1019)
PHONE..................................316 942-6712
Bernard Budenbenber, *Branch Mgr*
EMP: 11
SALES (corp-wide): 482.9MM **Privately Held**
WEB: www.carter-waters.com
SIC: 5031 5032 Building materials, exterior; concrete building products
HQ: Carter-Waters Llc
2435 Jefferson St
Kansas City MO 64108
816 471-2570

(G-13957)
CASE MSES ZIMMERMAN MARTIN PA
200 W Douglas Ave Ste 900 (67202-3009)
PHONE..................................316 303-0100
Michael Case, *Partner*
Thomas Wilson, *Admin Sec*
D Case, *Author*
EMP: 12
SALES (est): 1.1MM **Privately Held**
WEB: www.cmzwlaw.com
SIC: 8111 Criminal law

(G-13958)
CATACOMBS YOUTH MINISTRY
255 S Estelle St (67211-2008)
PHONE..................................316 689-8410
Vic Calcote, *Pastor*
EMP: 50
SALES (est): 591.7K **Privately Held**
SIC: 8322 Youth center

(G-13959)
CATHOLIC CHARITIES INC (PA)
437 N Topeka Ave (67202-2413)
PHONE..................................316 264-8344
Matt Onofrio, *Treasurer*
Teresa Kunze, *Mktg Dir*
Janet Valente Pape, *Exec Dir*
Cynthia N Colbert, *Exec Dir*
Lyndon Drew, *Director*
EMP: 103
SALES: 8.2MM **Privately Held**
SIC: 8322 Family service agency

(G-13960)
CATHOLIC CHARITIES INC
Also Called: Anthony Family Shelter
256 N Ohio Ave (67214-3934)
PHONE..................................316 264-7233
Kate Sins, *Branch Mgr*
EMP: 15
SALES (est): 334.6K
SALES (corp-wide): 8.2MM **Privately Held**
SIC: 8322 Family service agency
PA: Catholic Charities, Inc.
437 N Topeka Ave
Wichita KS 67202
316 264-8344

(G-13961)
CATHOLIC CHARITIES ADULT SVCS
5920 W Central Ave (67212-2841)
PHONE..................................316 942-2008
Tonya Knipp, *Info Tech Dir*
Joyce Mauier, *Director*
EMP: 23 **EST:** 1976
SALES: 4.2MM **Privately Held**
SIC: 8322 Adult day care center

(G-13962)
CATHOLIC CHARITIES OF WICHITA
Also Called: Harbor House
437 N Topeka Ave (67202-2413)
P.O. Box 3759 (67201-3759)
PHONE..................................316 263-6000
Lisa Odell Davis, *Director*
EMP: 12
SALES (est): 470.4K **Privately Held**
SIC: 8322 Crisis intervention center

(G-13963)
CATHOLIC DIOCESE OF WICHITA (PA)
Also Called: Catholic Care Center
424 N Broadway Ave (67202-2377)
PHONE..................................316 269-3900
Bishop Michael O Jackels, *President*
Dave Degenhardt, *Principal*
Fr John Brungardt, *Chancellor*
Laurie Labarca, *COO*
Robert Hemberger, *Treasurer*
EMP: 30
SQ FT: 8,000
SALES (est): 45.5MM **Privately Held**
WEB: www.cdowk.org
SIC: 8661 8051 Catholic Church; skilled nursing care facilities

(G-13964)
CATHOLIC FAMILY FEDERAL CR UN
1902 W Douglas Ave (67203-5732)
PHONE..................................316 264-9163
Mayra Reveles, *Loan Officer*
Cindy Hand, *Mktg Dir*
Marilyn Wells, *Manager*
EMP: 12
SALES (est): 1.9MM **Privately Held**
WEB: www.cffcu.com
SIC: 6061 Federal credit unions

(G-13965)
CBIZ MED MGT PROFESSIONALS INC
8080 E Central Ave # 250 (67206-2368)
PHONE..................................316 686-7327
Mary Lou Tate, *Manager*
EMP: 26
SALES (corp-wide): 144.1MM **Privately Held**
WEB: www.llms.net
SIC: 8721 Billing & bookkeeping service
HQ: Cbiz Medical Management Professionals, Inc.
5959 Shallowford Rd # 575
Chattanooga TN 37421

(G-13966)
CCH INCORPORATED
Also Called: C C H Computax
9111 E Douglas Ave 200a (67207-1241)
PHONE..................................316 612-5000
Brian Diffin, *Vice Pres*
Jim Bryant, *Vice Pres*
Amy Lyon, *Technical Mgr*
Noparuj Kaewsai, *Manager*
EMP: 500
SALES (corp-wide): 4.7B **Privately Held**
WEB: www.cch.com
SIC: 7371 Computer software development
HQ: Cch Incorporated
2700 Lake Cook Rd
Riverwoods IL 60015
847 267-7000

(G-13967)
CCM COUNTERTOP & CAB MFG LLC
2945 S Kansas Ave (67216-2416)
PHONE..................................316 554-0113
Thomas E Traylor, *President*
EMP: 12
SQ FT: 7,500
SALES (est): 2.2MM **Privately Held**
WEB: www.ccmcountertops.com
SIC: 5211 1799 1751 Cabinets, kitchen; counter top installation; cabinet & finish carpentry

(G-13968)
CEC ENTERTAINMENT INC
Also Called: Chuck E. Cheese's
3223 N Rock Rd (67226-1346)
PHONE..................................316 636-2225
Rick Gordon, *General Mgr*
EMP: 60
SALES (corp-wide): 886.7MM **Privately Held**
WEB: www.chuckecheese.com
SIC: 5812 7299 Pizzeria, chain; party planning service
HQ: Cec Entertainment, Inc.
1707 Market Pl Ste 200
Irving TX 75063
972 258-8507

(G-13969)
CECO INC
4125 W Pawnee St (67209-2823)
P.O. Box 2216 (67201-2216)
PHONE..................................316 942-7431
Maurice J Edwards III, *President*
E M Barnett, *Vice Pres*
Norma Womack, *Vice Pres*
EMP: 22 **EST:** 1957
SQ FT: 21,000
SALES (est): 5.4MM **Privately Held**
WEB: www.cecoinc.net
SIC: 3728 3544 Aircraft parts & equipment; special dies & tools; jigs & fixtures

(G-13970)
CELLCO PARTNERSHIP
Also Called: Verizon
2161 N Rock Rd Ste 120 (67206-1360)
PHONE..................................316 636-5155
EMP: 76
SALES (corp-wide): 130.8B **Publicly Held**
SIC: 4812 Cellular telephone services
HQ: Cellco Partnership
1 Verizon Way
Basking Ridge NJ 07920

(G-13971)
CELLCO PARTNERSHIP
Also Called: Verizon Wireless
2441 N Maize Rd Ste 1509 (67205-7951)
PHONE..................................316 722-4532
EMP: 76
SALES (corp-wide): 130.8B **Publicly Held**
SIC: 4812 Cellular telephone services
HQ: Cellco Partnership
1 Verizon Way
Basking Ridge NJ 07920

(G-13972)
CENTER FOR RPRDUCTIVE MEDICINE
Also Called: Tjaden, Bruce L Do
9300 E 29th St N Ste 102 (67226-3007)
PHONE..................................316 687-2112
Bruce Tjaden, *Med Doctor*
David Grainger, *Director*
EMP: 30
SQ FT: 7,000
SALES (est): 2.1MM **Privately Held**
WEB: www.wichita-ivf.com
SIC: 8093 8011 Family planning & birth control clinics; offices & clinics of medical doctors

(G-13973)
CENTER FOR SAME DAY SURGERY
818 N Emporia St Ste 108 (67214-3725)
PHONE..................................316 262-7263
Leori Beamer, *Principal*
Shaun Bachman, *Administration*
Shelly Le Gate, *Administration*
EMP: 35
SALES (est): 2MM
SALES (corp-wide): 25.3B **Privately Held**
WEB: www.centerforsamedaysurgery.com
SIC: 8011 Surgeon
HQ: Via Christi Health Partners, Inc.
8200 E Thorn Dr Ste 300
Wichita KS 67226

(G-13974)
CENTER FOR WOMAN HLTH WICHITA
1855 N Webb Rd (67206-3413)
PHONE..................................316 634-0060
Dan Breit, *Principal*
Sharon K Breit, *Obstetrician*
EMP: 15
SALES (est): 893.6K **Privately Held**
SIC: 8099 Health & allied services

(G-13975)
CENTER FOR WOMENS HEALTH LLC
10111 E 21st St N Ste 301 (67206-3581)
PHONE..................................316 634-0060
Sharon K Breit, *Mng Member*
Daniel L Breit,
EMP: 14
SALES (est): 375.2K **Privately Held**
SIC: 8011 Gynecologist

(G-13976)
CENTER INDUSTRIES CORPORATION
2505 S Custer Ave (67217-1321)
P.O. Box 17364 (67217-0364)
PHONE..................................316 942-8255
Robert J Jackson, *President*
Peter J Jonas, *Vice Pres*
Andrea Reedy, *Prdtn Mgr*
Byron Folkerts, *Opers Staff*
Brenda Braden, *QC Mgr*
EMP: 162
SQ FT: 143,000
SALES: 40MM **Privately Held**
SIC: 3469 3523 3728 Machine parts, stamped or pressed metal; farm machinery & equipment; aircraft parts & equipment

(G-13977)
CENTRAL AG WHEEL & TIRE
4106 W Esthner Ave (67209-2713)
PHONE..................................316 942-1408
Tom Puetz, *Owner*
▲ **EMP:** 10
SALES (est): 1MM **Privately Held**
SIC: 5531 3011 Automotive tires; agricultural tires, pneumatic

(G-13978)
CENTRAL CONSOLIDATED INC
3435 W Harry St (67213-1407)
PHONE..................................316 945-0797
Joe Samia, *President*
Layman Ray, *Vice Pres*
EMP: 130 **EST:** 1959
SQ FT: 20,000

GEOGRAPHIC

SALES (est): 26.4MM **Privately Held**
WEB: www.centralairco.com
SIC: 1711 7389 Plumbing contractors; warm air heating & air conditioning contractor; fire protection service other than forestry or public

(G-13979)
CENTRAL DENTAL CENTER PA
Also Called: Central Dental & Pioneer Lab
4805 W Central Ave (67212-2348)
P.O. Box 12557 (67277-2557)
PHONE..................................316 945-9845
David Steele, *President*
Barbara Williams, *Corp Secy*
EMP: 13
SALES (est): 577.8K **Privately Held**
SIC: 8021 Dentists' office

(G-13980)
CENTRAL MARKETING INC
Also Called: Central Equipment
1702 S West St (67213-1121)
P.O. Box 72, Goddard (67052-0072)
PHONE..................................316 613-2404
Stoney Mott, *President*
Karen Mott, *Vice Pres*
EMP: 10
SALES (est): 2MM **Privately Held**
WEB: www.centralequipment.net
SIC: 5531 5999 5013 Automotive parts; water purification equipment; automotive servicing equipment

(G-13981)
CENTRAL MECHANICAL WICHITA LLC
Also Called: Cmw LLC
806 E Skinner St (67211-4334)
P.O. Box 47343 (67201-7343)
PHONE..................................316 267-7676
Jesse Prier,
Chad Carpenter,
Jamie Conner,
Matt Smith,
EMP: 80
SALES (est): 2.3MM **Privately Held**
SIC: 1711 Mechanical contractor

(G-13982)
CENTRAL PLAINS EYE MDS LLC
7717 E 29th St N Ste 100 (67226-3444)
PHONE..................................316 712-4970
John Pedersen, *General Mgr*
C Joseph Beck,
Kim Darden PA,
Francis Soans MD,
EMP: 10
SALES (est): 740K **Privately Held**
SIC: 8011 Ophthalmologist

(G-13983)
CENTRAL PLAINS MAINTENANCE
3601 W Harry St Ste 2 (67213-1424)
P.O. Box 9224 (67277-0224)
PHONE..................................316 945-4774
Nick Kennedy, *President*
Doran Rhoades, *Vice Pres*
EMP: 70
SQ FT: 5,000
SALES (est): 1.7MM **Privately Held**
SIC: 7349 7521 Building maintenance services; parking lots

(G-13984)
CENTRAL PWR SYSTEMS & SVCS LLC
Also Called: Allison Transmissions
4501 W Irving St (67209-2616)
PHONE..................................316 943-1231
EMP: 35
SALES (corp-wide): 80MM **Privately Held**
SIC: 5084 7538 7537 5063 Engines & parts, diesel; general automotive repair shops; automotive transmission repair shops; generators
PA: Central Power Systems & Services, Llc
9200 Liberty Dr
Pleasant Valley MO 64068
816 781-8070

(G-13985)
CENTRAL STAR CREDIT UNION (PA)
9555 E Corporate Hills Dr (67207-1392)
PHONE..................................316 685-9555
Lee Williams, *President*
EMP: 29
SALES: 4.3MM **Privately Held**
WEB: www.aacu.com
SIC: 6062 State credit unions

(G-13986)
CENTRAL STATE SERVICES
1401 E Douglas Ave (67211-1607)
PHONE..................................316 613-3989
Tim Brecheisen, *President*
EMP: 11
SALES (est): 738.8K **Privately Held**
SIC: 5999 8099 Hearing aids; hearing testing service

(G-13987)
CENTRAL STATES ELECTRIC INC
1660 S Baehr St (67209-2702)
PHONE..................................316 942-6640
J Duane Schneider, *President*
Jamie K Schneider, *Treasurer*
EMP: 20
SQ FT: 1,400
SALES (est): 3.4MM **Privately Held**
SIC: 1731 General electrical contractor

(G-13988)
CENTRAL STEEL INC (PA)
240 W 10th St N (67203-3805)
P.O. Box 1773 (67201-1773)
PHONE..................................316 265-8639
James Aaby, *President*
Stewart Aaby, *Corp Secy*
Les Aaby, *Vice Pres*
Robert Green, *Engineer*
EMP: 52
SQ FT: 44,000
SALES: 10.3MM **Privately Held**
SIC: 3444 3441 Sheet metalwork; fabricated structural metal

(G-13989)
CENTRAL TRANSPORT INTL INC
2225 Southwest Blvd (67213-1443)
PHONE..................................877 446-3795
Kerry AST, *Branch Mgr*
EMP: 16
SALES (corp-wide): 273.6MM **Privately Held**
WEB: www.centraltransportinternational.com
SIC: 4213 Trucking, except local
HQ: Central Transport International, Inc.
12225 Stephens Rd
Warren MI 48089
586 467-0100

(G-13990)
CENTRAL TRNSP SVCS INC
Also Called: CTS Logistics
1820 N Mosley St (67214-1348)
P.O. Box 8263 (67208-0263)
PHONE..................................316 263-3333
Steve Cullins, *Ch of Bd*
Robert K Wagner, *Vice Pres*
EMP: 55
SALES (est): 13.7MM **Privately Held**
WEB: www.ctsco.com
SIC: 4213 4731 Trucking, except local; brokers, shipping

(G-13991)
CENTURY INSTRUMENT CORP
4440 S Southeast Blvd # 2 (67210-1689)
PHONE..................................316 683-7571
Paul G Austin, *President*
Kathryn M Austin, *Treasurer*
EMP: 10 **EST:** 1968
SQ FT: 10,000
SALES (est): 1.9MM **Privately Held**
WEB: www.centuryinst.com
SIC: 5088 7699 Aircraft & parts; aircraft flight instrument repair

(G-13992)
CEREBRAL PALSY RESEARCH FO
5111 E 21st St N (67208-1606)
P.O. Box 8217 (67208-0217)
PHONE..................................316 688-5314
Marsha Anderson, *CFO*
Connie Heckman, *Accountant*
Mary Jenkins, *Human Res Dir*
Kacee Shuler, *Pub Rel Dir*
Dennis Martinez, *Technology*
EMP: 85
SQ FT: 142,000
SALES: 6.2MM **Privately Held**
SIC: 8322 Association for the handicapped

(G-13993)
CESSNA AIRCRAFT COMPANY
5213 E Pawnee St (67218-5530)
PHONE..................................316 686-3961
Fax: 316 686-1022
EMP: 15
SALES (corp-wide): 13.4B **Publicly Held**
SIC: 4581 Aircraft Cleaning And Janitorial Service
HQ: The Cessna Aircraft Company
1 Cessna Blvd
Wichita KS 67215
316 517-6000

(G-13994)
CGF INVESTMENTS INC (PA)
Also Called: Cgf Industries
2420 N Woodlawn Blvd # 500 (67220-3970)
PHONE..................................316 691-4500
Pat Diger, *President*
Chris Widrig, *CFO*
Joanne Ruggiero, *Taxation*
▲ **EMP:** 35
SQ FT: 10,000
SALES: 57.9MM **Privately Held**
SIC: 3442 7379 5031 1389 Metal doors, sash & trim; computer related consulting services; lumber, plywood & millwork; oil field services; gas field services

(G-13995)
CH ROBINSON COMPANY INC
Also Called: C.H. Robinson 46
245 N Waco St Ste 400 (67202-1117)
PHONE..................................316 267-3300
Tim Whistler, *Manager*
Blake Solomon, *Manager*
Jeremy Lasseter, *Supervisor*
EMP: 21
SALES (corp-wide): 16.6B **Publicly Held**
SIC: 4731 Freight forwarding
HQ: C.H. Robinson Company Inc.
14701 Charlson Rd Ste 900
Eden Prairie MN 55347

(G-13996)
CHAMPION OPCO LLC
Also Called: Champion Window Co
1835 S West St (67213-1105)
PHONE..................................316 636-4200
Tad Albright, *Partner*
EMP: 11
SALES (corp-wide): 517.2MM **Privately Held**
SIC: 1761 5211 1751 1521 Siding contractor; door & window products; window & door (prefabricated) installation; patio & deck construction & repair
PA: Champion Opco, Llc
12121 Champion Way
Cincinnati OH 45241
513 327-7338

(G-13997)
CHANCE RIDES MANUFACTURING INC (PA)
4219 W Irving St (67209-2613)
P.O. Box 9046 (67277-0046)
PHONE..................................316 945-6555
Richard G Chance, *CEO*
Michael Chance, *President*
Shawn Lytton, *Materials Mgr*
Jeff Roth, *Admin Sec*
▲ **EMP:** 107
SQ FT: 60,000
SALES (est): 19.7MM **Privately Held**
SIC: 3599 3711 1771 Amusement park equipment; bus & other large specialty vehicle assembly; concrete work

(G-13998)
CHANCE TRANSMISSIONS INC
6325 S Seneca St (67217-5125)
PHONE..................................316 529-1883
David Long, *President*
EMP: 18
SQ FT: 2,800
SALES (est): 2.2MM **Privately Held**
WEB: www.chancetrans.com
SIC: 7537 Automotive transmission repair shops

(G-13999)
CHANNEL NEWS DEPARTMENT
Also Called: Ksnw Channel 3
833 N Main St (67203-3606)
PHONE..................................316 292-1111
John Dawson, *Manager*
EMP: 12 **EST:** 2008
SALES (est): 427.9K **Privately Held**
SIC: 4833 Television broadcasting stations

(G-14000)
CHAUCER ESTATES LLC
10550 E 21st St N Ofc (67206-3590)
PHONE..................................316 630-8111
Donald Schmidt,
Kent Schmidt,
EMP: 55
SALES (est): 2.4MM **Privately Held**
SIC: 8361 Home for the aged

(G-14001)
CHEMSTATION OF KANSAS INC
2355 S Edwards St Ste D (67213-1809)
PHONE..................................316 201-1851
Kevin Lage, *President*
Lacretia Lage, *Admin Sec*
EMP: 10
SALES (est): 1.1MM **Privately Held**
WEB: www.chemstation.com
SIC: 5169 Chemical additives

(G-14002)
CHEYENNE MFG INC
3713 W 30th St S (67217-1017)
PHONE..................................316 942-7665
David Eckerman, *Principal*
Ron Holzman, *Principal*
EMP: 22
SQ FT: 7,500
SALES (est): 4.4MM **Privately Held**
WEB: www.cheyennemfg.com
SIC: 3728 Aircraft parts & equipment

(G-14003)
CHEZ BELLE
550 N Rock Rd Ste 109 (67206-1745)
PHONE..................................316 682-7323
Michelle Burns, *Owner*
EMP: 11
SALES (est): 267.3K **Privately Held**
SIC: 7231 Hairdressers

(G-14004)
CHICAGO TITLE INSURANCE CO
434 N Main St (67202-1604)
PHONE..................................316 267-8371
Roger Bell, *President*
EMP: 50
SALES (corp-wide): 7.5B **Publicly Held**
SIC: 6361 Title insurance
HQ: Chicago Title Insurance Company
601 Riverside Ave
Jacksonville FL 32204

(G-14005)
CHILD ADVCACY CTR SDGWICK CNTY
Also Called: CACSC
1211 S Emporia Ave (67211-3211)
PHONE..................................316 660-9494
Diana Schunn, *Exec Dir*
EMP: 12
SALES: 1.1MM **Privately Held**
SIC: 8322 Child related social services

▲ = Import ▼=Export
◆ =Import/Export

(G-14006)
CHILD START INC
Also Called: Early Head Start
4600 S Clifton Ave Ste B (67216-3077)
PHONE....................................316 522-8677
Glenda Wilcox, *Director*
Tanya Bulluck, *Director*
EMP: 37
SALES (est): 646.1K
SALES (corp-wide): 13.2MM **Privately Held**
SIC: 8351 Head start center, except in conjunction with school
PA: Child Start, Inc.
1002 S Oliver St
Wichita KS 67218
316 682-1853

(G-14007)
CHILD START INC (PA)
Also Called: CHILS START
1002 S Oliver St (67218-3293)
PHONE....................................316 682-1853
Tina Viramontez, *Finance Dir*
Virginia Habash, *Accountant*
Chris G Lewis, *Finance*
Vicky Berberick, *Manager*
Debbie Boldea, *Manager*
EMP: 252
SQ FT: 8,500
SALES: 13.2MM **Privately Held**
SIC: 8351 Head start center, except in conjunction with school

(G-14008)
CHILD START INC
1002 S Oliver St (67218-3293)
PHONE....................................316 682-1853
Diane Gross, *Principal*
Marvin Landes, *Principal*
Larry Tate, *Principal*
Marilee Williams, *Principal*
Teresa Rupp, *Director*
EMP: 60
SALES (est): 264.8K
SALES (corp-wide): 13.2MM **Privately Held**
SIC: 8351 Head start center, except in conjunction with school
PA: Child Start, Inc.
1002 S Oliver St
Wichita KS 67218
316 682-1853

(G-14009)
CHILDHOOD MEMORIES TODDLER
11229 W Peter Ave (67215-8538)
PHONE....................................316 554-1646
Misti Stephen, *Executive*
EMP: 10
SALES (est): 420K **Privately Held**
SIC: 8351 Child day care services

(G-14010)
CHILDRENS MERCY HOSPITAL
3243 E Murdock St Ste 201 (67208-3005)
PHONE....................................316 500-8900
Sandy Fricket, *Principal*
EMP: 605
SALES (corp-wide): 826.4MM **Privately Held**
SIC: 8062 General medical & surgical hospitals
PA: Mercy Children's Hospital
2401 Gillham Rd
Kansas City MO 64108
816 234-3000

(G-14011)
CHILTON VENDING & BILLD INC
Also Called: Chilton Vending & Billiard Sup
700 S Broadway Ave (67211-2224)
PHONE....................................316 262-3539
Toll Free:..888 -
Stan Chilton, *President*
EMP: 12 **EST:** 1940
SQ FT: 40,000
SALES (est): 1.3MM **Privately Held**
SIC: 5962 5941 6512 Merchandising machine operators; pool & billiard tables; commercial & industrial building operation

(G-14012)
CHIRO PLUS INC
Also Called: Wichita Kinesiology Group PA
5205 E Kellogg Dr Ste 101 (67218-1634)
PHONE....................................316 684-0550
Milton Dowty, *Owner*
EMP: 11
SQ FT: 5,000
SALES (est): 549.9K **Privately Held**
SIC: 8041 Offices & clinics of chiropractors

(G-14013)
CHOOSE NETWORKS INC
Also Called: River City Digital
410 N Saint Francis Ave (67202-2624)
PHONE....................................316 773-0920
Christopher T Hoose, *President*
Paula Kirk, *Treasurer*
Blake Heinemann, *Manager*
Dawn May, *Office Admin*
Dawn McCallie, *Office Admin*
EMP: 19
SQ FT: 3,700
SALES (est): 3.5MM **Privately Held**
WEB: www.choosenetworks.com
SIC: 7379 Computer related consulting services

(G-14014)
CHRIS ARCHER GROUP INC (PA)
Also Called: Precise Racing
3801 W Pawnee St Ste 200 (67213-1857)
PHONE....................................316 945-4000
John C Archer, *President*
EMP: 34
SQ FT: 25,000
SALES (est): 6MM **Privately Held**
SIC: 5531 5014 Automotive tires; tires & tubes

(G-14015)
CHRISTIAN RAINBOW KNOWLEDGE
2117 N Parkwood Ln (67208-2555)
PHONE....................................316 686-2169
Nicola Dickinson, *Director*
EMP: 10 **EST:** 2010
SALES (est): 159.7K **Privately Held**
SIC: 8351 Child day care services

(G-14016)
CHRISTOPHER MOELLER
Also Called: Moeller Dermatology
1911 N Webb Rd (67206-3405)
PHONE....................................316 682-7546
Christopher Moeller, *Owner*
Landon Johnson, *Dermatology*
EMP: 15
SALES (est): 2MM **Privately Held**
WEB: www.moellerdermatology.com
SIC: 8011 Dermatologist

(G-14017)
CHROME PLUS INTERNATIONAL INC
3939 W 29th St S (67217-1009)
PHONE....................................316 944-3600
Jorge Della Costa, *CEO*
Jorge Della-Costa, *President*
Michael T Mills, *Corp Secy*
Claudia Della-Costa, *Vice Pres*
EMP: 17
SQ FT: 7,500
SALES (est): 4.6MM **Privately Held**
WEB: www.chromeplusinternational.com
SIC: 3471 Electroplating of metals or formed products

(G-14018)
CHUCK PIERSON DDS PA
9339 E 21st St N Ste 200 (67206-2973)
PHONE....................................316 634-1333
Chuck Pierson, *President*
EMP: 50
SALES (est): 290.6K **Privately Held**
SIC: 8021 Dentists' office

(G-14019)
CHURCH OF MAGDALEN
Also Called: School of The Magdalen
2221 N 127th St E (67226-8301)
PHONE....................................316 634-1572
Eva Williams, *Principal*
Father Ken Vanhaberbeke, *Pastor*
Terri Hessman, *Teacher*
Beth Shepherd, *Teacher*
EMP: 30
SALES (est): 1.9MM **Privately Held**
SIC: 8211 8351 Catholic elementary school; Catholic junior high school; preschool center

(G-14020)
CIAC LLC
Also Called: Clinic In A Can
3545 N Santa Fe St (67219-3633)
PHONE....................................316 262-0953
Michael Wawrzewski,
Cory Simons,
EMP: 5
SALES (est): 215.3K **Privately Held**
SIC: 3448 Prefabricated metal buildings

(G-14021)
CIRCLE ENTERPRISES INC
Also Called: ServiceMaster
3351 W Central Ave (67203-4917)
P.O. Box 48639 (67201-8639)
PHONE....................................316 943-9834
Daniel Kreis, *President*
Annette Kreis, *Corp Secy*
EMP: 10
SQ FT: 3,500
SALES (est): 440.8K **Privately Held**
SIC: 7349 7641 Building maintenance services; upholstery work

(G-14022)
CITIGROUP GLOBAL MARKETS INC
Also Called: Morgan Stanley Smith Barney
1617 N Wtrfrnt Pkwy # 200 (67206-6642)
PHONE....................................316 630-4400
John Dunlop, *Manager*
EMP: 40
SALES (corp-wide): 72.8B **Publicly Held**
WEB: www.salomonsmithbarney.com
SIC: 7389 Brokers' services
HQ: Citigroup Global Markets Inc.
388 Greenwich St Fl 18
New York NY 10013
212 816-6000

(G-14023)
CITY BLUE PRINT INC
1400 E Waterman St (67211-1896)
P.O. Box 544 (67201-0544)
PHONE....................................316 265-6224
Ruth Stearns, *President*
Deborah L Gronniger, *General Mgr*
EMP: 70 **EST:** 1975
SALES (est): 10.6MM **Privately Held**
WEB: www.cityblue.com
SIC: 7334 Photocopying & duplicating services

(G-14024)
CITY OF WICHITA
Also Called: Metropolitan Area Plannin
455 N Main St Fl 4 (67202-1601)
PHONE....................................316 268-4421
John Schlegel, *Director*
EMP: 26 **Privately Held**
WEB: www.cityofwichita.net
SIC: 8748 City planning
PA: Wichita, City Of (Inc)
455 N Main St Fl 5
Wichita KS 67202
316 268-4351

(G-14025)
CITY OF WICHITA
Also Called: Budget Office
455 N Main St Ste 1221 (67202-1605)
PHONE....................................316 942-4482
John Hale, *Opers Staff*
Robert Layton, *Manager*
Adam Zimmerman, *Officer*
EMP: 50 **Privately Held**
WEB: www.cityofwichita.net
SIC: 8741 Management services
PA: Wichita, City Of (Inc)
455 N Main St Fl 5
Wichita KS 67202
316 268-4351

(G-14026)
CITY OF WICHITA
Controllers Office
455 N Main St Fl 12 (67202-1623)
PHONE....................................316 268-4651
Carol McMillan, *Manager*
Bryan Frye, *Council Mbr*
EMP: 20
SQ FT: 80,000 **Privately Held**
WEB: www.cityofwichita.net
SIC: 8721 9111 Accounting services, except auditing;
PA: Wichita, City Of (Inc)
455 N Main St Fl 5
Wichita KS 67202
316 268-4351

(G-14027)
CITY OF WICHITA
Also Called: Edgemore Recreation Centers
5815 E 9th St N (67208-3651)
PHONE....................................316 744-9719
Barbara McGuire, *Director*
EMP: 35 **Privately Held**
WEB: www.cityofwichita.net
SIC: 7999 Recreation center
PA: Wichita, City Of (Inc)
455 N Main St Fl 5
Wichita KS 67202
316 268-4351

(G-14028)
CITY OF WICHITA
Also Called: City Wichita Evironmental Hlth
1900 E 9th St N (67214-3115)
PHONE....................................316 268-8351
Shawn Maloney, *Branch Mgr*
EMP: 35 **Privately Held**
WEB: www.cityofwichita.net
SIC: 8399 9111 Health & welfare council;
PA: Wichita, City Of (Inc)
455 N Main St Fl 5
Wichita KS 67202
316 268-4351

(G-14029)
CITY OF WICHITA
Also Called: Clapp Memorial Park Golf Crse
4611 E Harry St (67218-3727)
PHONE....................................316 688-9341
Cody Lack, *Manager*
EMP: 20 **Privately Held**
WEB: www.cityofwichita.net
SIC: 7992 Public golf courses
PA: Wichita, City Of (Inc)
455 N Main St Fl 5
Wichita KS 67202
316 268-4351

(G-14030)
CITY OF WICHITA
Also Called: Tex Cnslver Mniciple Golf Crse
1931 S Tyler Rd (67209-3011)
PHONE....................................316 337-9494
Paul Oropasa, *Branch Mgr*
EMP: 10 **Privately Held**
WEB: www.cityofwichita.net
SIC: 7992 9111 Public golf courses; mayors' offices
PA: Wichita, City Of (Inc)
455 N Main St Fl 5
Wichita KS 67202
316 268-4351

(G-14031)
CITY OF WICHITA
Also Called: Wichita Transit
777 E Waterman St (67202-4615)
PHONE....................................316 265-7221
V Fields, *VP Human Res*
Jay Banasiak, *Director*
EMP: 120 **Privately Held**
WEB: www.cityofwichita.net
SIC: 4131 9111 Intercity & rural bus transportation; mayors' offices
PA: Wichita, City Of (Inc)
455 N Main St Fl 5
Wichita KS 67202
316 268-4351

(G-14032)
CITY PRINT INC
235 S Ellis St (67211-1802)
PHONE....................................316 267-5555
Laura Vogel, *Sales Staff*
Connie Harshbarger, *Manager*

GEOGRAPHIC

EMP: 6
SALES (est): 926.3K **Privately Held**
SIC: 2752 Commercial printing, offset

(G-14033)
CK CONTRACTING LLC
1444 S Saint Clair Ave B (67213-2938)
PHONE..................................316 267-1996
Kent Hagman,
EMP: 12
SALES (est): 1.8MM **Privately Held**
SIC: 1522 Apartment building construction

(G-14034)
CLARIOS
Also Called: Johnson Controls
404 S Holland St Ste 1 (67209-2169)
PHONE..................................316 721-2777
Chris Stingo, *Manager*
EMP: 30
SQ FT: 5,000 **Privately Held**
SIC: 5084 5075 1731 1711 Controlling instruments & accessories; thermostats; fire detection & burglar alarm systems specialization; heating & air conditioning contractors
HQ: Johnson Controls Inc
5757 N Green Bay Ave
Milwaukee WI 53209
414 524-1200

(G-14035)
CLARIOS
Also Called: Johnson Controls
3110 N Mead St Dock 1/4 (67219-4057)
P.O. Box 19014 (67204-9014)
PHONE..................................316 655-7578
Bryan Rocky, *Vice Pres*
Joleen Loflin, *Purch Agent*
Eric Newberg, *Director*
EMP: 46 **Privately Held**
SIC: 1711 Heating & air conditioning contractors
HQ: Johnson Controls Inc
5757 N Green Bay Ave
Milwaukee WI 53209
414 524-1200

(G-14036)
CLARIOS
Also Called: Johnson Controls
8909 E 35th St N (67226-2002)
PHONE..................................316 634-1309
Jeffrey Troxel, *Mfg Staff*
Frank Kern, *Branch Mgr*
EMP: 9 **Privately Held**
SIC: 2531 Seats, automobile
HQ: Johnson Controls Inc
5757 N Green Bay Ave
Milwaukee WI 53209
414 524-1200

(G-14037)
CLARK INVESTMENT GROUP
1223 N Rock Rd Ste E200 (67206-1272)
PHONE..................................316 634-1112
Steve Clark, *Owner*
Stephen Clark, *Vice Pres*
Robert Baker, *Treasurer*
Sharon Pack, *Manager*
Jennifer Nestelroad, *Executive Asst*
EMP: 20
SQ FT: 2,800
SALES: 30MM **Privately Held**
WEB: www.clarkinvestment.com
SIC: 6512 6513 6552 Nonresidential building operators; apartment building operators; subdividers & developers

(G-14038)
CLC GROUP INC
8111 E 32nd St N Ste 300 (67226-2619)
PHONE..................................316 636-5055
George Hansen, *CEO*
Kevin Bauer, *Exec VP*
Gary Shaw, *Exec VP*
Erick Patton, *Manager*
Matt Rogers, *Manager*
EMP: 125
SALES (est): 6.9MM
SALES (corp-wide): 2.4B **Publicly Held**
WEB: www.fleetcor.com
SIC: 8742 Industry specialist consultants
PA: Fleetcor Technologies, Inc.
3280 Peachtree Rd Ne # 2400
Atlanta GA 30305
770 449-0479

(G-14039)
CLEAN HARBORS WICHITA LLC (HQ)
Also Called: Universal Lubricants
2808 N Ohio St (67219-4319)
P.O. Box 2920 (67201-2920)
PHONE..................................316 832-0151
Michael B Maloney, *Mng Member*
Dennis Maloney,
John Wesley,
Randall Wilson,
▲ **EMP:** 165
SQ FT: 88,000
SALES (est): 119.9MM **Privately Held**
WEB: www.universallubes.com
SIC: 2992 5169 5172 Oils & greases, blending & compounding; anti-freeze compounds; lubricating oils & greases

(G-14040)
CLEAN TECH INC
7453 W 33rd St N (67205-9356)
PHONE..................................316 729-8100
Austin Brumley, *CEO*
EMP: 120
SQ FT: 17,500
SALES (est): 6.2MM **Privately Held**
SIC: 8322 7349 Disaster service; building maintenance, except repairs

(G-14041)
CLEANING AUTHORITY OF CENTRAL
318 S Greenwood St (67211-1818)
PHONE..................................316 733-7890
Robin Schoolfields, *Owner*
Robins Schoolfields, *Owner*
Jennifer Voth, *CFO*
EMP: 18
SALES (est): 437.4K **Privately Held**
SIC: 7349 Maid services, contract or fee basis

(G-14042)
CLINTON ENTERPRISES LLC
9320 E Central Ave (67206-2555)
PHONE..................................316 636-1801
Tom Steven, *Principal*
EMP: 5
SALES (est): 316K **Privately Held**
SIC: 1389 Oil & gas field services

(G-14043)
CLK INC
Also Called: Stanley Steemer
914 E Gilbert St Ste 200 (67211-2412)
PHONE..................................316 686-3238
Michael Baker, *President*
EMP: 13
SALES (est): 962K **Privately Held**
SIC: 7217 Carpet & furniture cleaning on location

(G-14044)
CLUB RODEO LLC
10001 E Kellogg Dr (67207-1906)
PHONE..................................316 613-2424
Eric Reagen, *Principal*
EMP: 15
SALES (est): 445K **Privately Held**
SIC: 7997 Membership sports & recreation clubs

(G-14045)
CMX INC (PA)
1700 N Waterfront Pkwy 300b
(67206-6610)
PHONE..................................316 269-9052
Douglas McGiness II, *President*
Douglas McGinness II, *President*
Douglas H McGinness II, *President*
Curtis F Clark, *Treasurer*
Donna L May-Murray, *Office Mgr*
EMP: 5
SALES (est): 2.7MM **Privately Held**
WEB: www.cmxinc.com
SIC: 1382 Oil & gas exploration services

(G-14046)
CNH INDUSTRIAL AMERICA LLC
Also Called: Case New Holland
3301 S Hoover Rd (67215-1215)
P.O. Box 9228 (67277-0228)
PHONE..................................316 945-0111
Chad Burkholder, *Engineer*
Emory Frey, *Engineer*
Maurizio Giacoma, *Engineer*
Josh Morton, *Engineer*
Nathan Wilhelm, *Engineer*
EMP: 60
SALES (corp-wide): 29.7B **Privately Held**
SIC: 3531 Entrenching machines; loaders, shovel: self-propelled
HQ: Cnh Industrial America Llc
700 State St
Racine WI 53404
262 636-6011

(G-14047)
COAST TO COAST BUILDERS INC
750 E Funston St (67211-4307)
PHONE..................................316 265-2515
Todd A Womacks, *Principal*
EMP: 10
SQ FT: 8,000
SALES (est): 3.4MM **Privately Held**
SIC: 1542 Commercial & office building contractors

(G-14048)
COBANK ACB
245 N Waco St Ofc (67202-1121)
PHONE..................................316 290-2000
David Janish, *Branch Mgr*
EMP: 14
SALES (corp-wide): 4.3B **Privately Held**
SIC: 6163 Mortgage brokers arranging for loans, using money of others
PA: Cobank, Acb
6340 S Fiddlers Green Cir
Greenwood Village CO 80111
303 740-6527

(G-14049)
COBANK ACB
Fcs of Central Kansas, Aca
7940 W Kellogg Dr (67209-2006)
P.O. Box 12800 (67277-2800)
PHONE..................................316 721-1100
Alan Jaax, *CEO*
EMP: 24
SALES (corp-wide): 4.3B **Privately Held**
WEB: www.usagbank.com
SIC: 6111 Federal Land Banks
PA: Cobank, Acb
6340 S Fiddlers Green Cir
Greenwood Village CO 80111
303 740-6527

(G-14050)
COFFEE TIME INC
10821 E 26th St N (67226-4524)
PHONE..................................316 267-3771
Darren Cox, *Principal*
EMP: 63
SALES (est): 1.7MM **Privately Held**
SIC: 7389 Coffee service

(G-14051)
COHOON CHIROPRACTIC
Also Called: Allied Medical
3300 N Rock Rd Ste A-2 (67226-1375)
PHONE..................................316 612-0600
Randy Babcock, *Owner*
EMP: 10 **EST:** 2001
SALES (est): 304K **Privately Held**
SIC: 8041 Offices & clinics of chiropractors

(G-14052)
COIN MACHINE DISTRIBUTORS INC
Also Called: Billiards Sports Plaza
1940 S Oliver St (67218-4211)
PHONE..................................316 652-0361
Theodore W Maisch Jr, *President*
Sue Ann Halliday, *Treasurer*
▲ **EMP:** 10
SQ FT: 23,500
SALES (est): 657.4K **Privately Held**
SIC: 7993 5962 Coin-operated amusement devices; cigarettes vending machines

(G-14053)
COLEMAN COMPANY INC
3600 N Hydraulic St (67219-3812)
PHONE..................................800 835-3278
Hope Korte, *Superintendent*
Richard Bishop, *Vice Pres*
Richard Wilson, *Facilities Mgr*
Denis Wangari, *Transportation*
Gil Bergkamp, *Purch Agent*
EMP: 7
SALES (corp-wide): 8.6B **Publicly Held**
SIC: 3086 5941 Ice chests or coolers (portable), foamed plastic; sporting goods & bicycle shops
HQ: The Coleman Company Inc
180 N Lasalle St Ste 700
Chicago IL 60601

(G-14054)
COLEMAN MATERIALS LLC
3702 W Dora St (67213-1209)
P.O. Box 771481 (67277-1481)
PHONE..................................316 267-9812
Dan Huyett, *Vice Pres*
Ronald Coleman,
EMP: 17
SALES (est): 8.2MM **Privately Held**
SIC: 5032 Concrete building products

(G-14055)
COLLEGE HILL CLEANERS INC (PA)
4618 E Central Ave # 100 (67208-3956)
PHONE..................................316 683-3331
Ferdinand Ortiz, *Owner*
EMP: 12
SALES (est): 603.4K **Privately Held**
SIC: 7216 Drycleaning plants, except rugs

(G-14056)
COLLEGE HILL OB/GYN INC (PA)
Also Called: Wyatt-Harris, Patricia G MD
3233 E 2nd St N (67208-3202)
PHONE..................................316 683-6766
Michael P Brown MD, *President*
Douglas Deboise MD, *Treasurer*
Elizabeth Cox, *Med Doctor*
Teresa Craddock, *Med Doctor*
Anna Stork-Fury, *OB/GYN*
EMP: 25
SQ FT: 3,500
SALES (est): 3.3MM **Privately Held**
SIC: 8011 Gynecologist; obstetrician

(G-14057)
COLLEGE HL NRSING RHBILITATION
5005 E 21st St N (67208-1604)
PHONE..................................316 685-9291
Doug Wyckoff, *Principal*
EMP: 21
SALES (est): 1.3MM **Privately Held**
SIC: 8051 Skilled nursing care facilities

(G-14058)
COLLISION WORKS LLC
1427 E 1st St N (67214-4113)
PHONE..................................316 265-6828
EMP: 20
SALES (corp-wide): 2.5MM **Privately Held**
SIC: 7532 Body shop, automotive
PA: Collision Works Llc
3224 Se 29th St
Oklahoma City OK 73115
405 670-2500

(G-14059)
COMCARE OF SEDGWICK COUNTY
1720 E Morris St Ste 101 (67211-2755)
PHONE..................................316 660-1900
Rita Snider, *Director*
Carli Sanchez, *Analyst*
EMP: 27
SALES (est): 596.1K **Privately Held**
SIC: 8093 Mental health clinic, outpatient

(G-14060)
COMCARE OF SEDGWICK COUNTY
Also Called: Addiction Treatment Service
4035 E Harry St (67218-3724)
PHONE..................................316 660-7550
Richard Morris, *Manager*

▲ = Import ▼=Export
◆ =Import/Export

EMP: 16
SALES (est): 457.3K Privately Held
SIC: 8069 9111 Drug addiction rehabilitation hospital; county supervisors' & executives' offices
PA: Comcare Of Sedgwick County
635 N Main St
Wichita KS 67203

(G-14061)
COMCARE OF SEDGWICK COUNTY (PA)
Also Called: Dept of Mental Health
635 N Main St (67203-3602)
PHONE................................316 660-7600
Marylynn Cook, *Exec Dir*
EMP: 300
SALES (est): 21.4MM Privately Held
SIC: 8011 8322 8093 Offices & clinics of medical doctors; crisis intervention center; specialty outpatient clinics

(G-14062)
COMCARE OF SEDGWICK COUNTY
1929 W 21st St N (67203-2106)
PHONE................................316 660-7700
Richard Morris, *Branch Mgr*
EMP: 244 Privately Held
SIC: 8322 8011 Crisis intervention center; psychiatrist
PA: Comcare Of Sedgwick County
635 N Main St
Wichita KS 67203

(G-14063)
COMFORT CARE HOMES INC (PA)
Also Called: Comfortcare Homes
7701 E Kellogg Dr Ste 490 (67207-1716)
PHONE................................316 685-3322
Douglas Stark, *President*
Mary Louise Stark, *Vice Pres*
EMP: 28
SQ FT: 1,400
SALES (est): 3.5MM Privately Held
SIC: 8059 8051 Nursing home, except skilled & intermediate care facility; skilled nursing care facilities

(G-14064)
COMMERCE BANK
1845 Fairmount St (67260-9700)
PHONE................................316 261-4795
Mooley Caylor, *Manager*
EMP: 20
SALES (corp-wide): 1.3B Publicly Held
SIC: 6021 National commercial banks
HQ: Commerce Bank
1000 Walnut St Fl 700
Kansas City MO 64106
816 234-2000

(G-14065)
COMMERCE BANK
6424 E 13th St N (67206-1358)
PHONE................................316 261-4927
Kristy Krok, *Manager*
EMP: 15
SALES (corp-wide): 1.3B Publicly Held
SIC: 6022 State commercial banks
HQ: Commerce Bank
1000 Walnut St Fl 700
Kansas City MO 64106
816 234-2000

(G-14066)
COMMERCE BANK
1551 N Waterfront Pkwy # 200 (67206-6609)
P.O. Box 637 (67201-0637)
PHONE................................316 261-4700
Marilyn Pauly, *Vice Chairman*
Brad Dieck, *Assistant VP*
John Meyer, *Vice Pres*
EMP: 80
SALES (corp-wide): 1.3B Publicly Held
SIC: 6021 National commercial banks
HQ: Commerce Bank
1000 Walnut St Fl 700
Kansas City MO 64106
816 234-2000

(G-14067)
COMMERCE BANK
1250 S Woodlawn Blvd (67218-3637)
PHONE................................316 261-5590
Rhonda Maass, *Manager*
EMP: 10
SALES (corp-wide): 1.3B Publicly Held
SIC: 6021 National commercial banks
HQ: Commerce Bank
1000 Walnut St Fl 700
Kansas City MO 64106
816 234-2000

(G-14068)
COMMERCE CONSTRUCTION SVCS INC
2225 Southwest Blvd (67213-1443)
PHONE................................316 262-0547
Doug Henning, *President*
Joan Henning, *Corp Secy*
Rob Monson, *Project Mgr*
Debby Cullimore,
EMP: 42
SQ FT: 3,000
SALES (est): 11.3MM Privately Held
WEB: www.commconst.com
SIC: 1542 Commercial & office building, new construction; commercial & office buildings, renovation & repair

(G-14069)
COMMERCIAL LAWN MGT WCHITA INC
3215 E 9th St N (67208-3024)
PHONE................................316 688-0722
James Herrman, *President*
EMP: 10
SALES (est): 725.6K Privately Held
SIC: 0782 Lawn care services

(G-14070)
COMMERCIAL MECHANICAL INC KANS
Also Called: CMI
1655 N Wabash Ave (67214-1447)
PHONE................................316 262-1230
Douglas E Kirkland, *President*
EMP: 80
SQ FT: 20,000
SALES (est): 15MM Privately Held
WEB: www.commercialmechanical.net
SIC: 1711 Mechanical contractor

(G-14071)
COMMERCIAL PROPERTY SERVICES
7707 E Osie St Ste 406 (67207-3100)
PHONE................................316 688-5200
Bob Wells, *President*
EMP: 16 EST: 1997
SALES (est): 975.9K Privately Held
SIC: 6531 Real estate agent, commercial

(G-14072)
COMMERCIAL ROFG SPCIALISTS LLC
2717 N Lake Ridge St (67205-1680)
P.O. Box 4505 (67204-0505)
PHONE................................316 304-1423
Jessica Massey, *Principal*
Thomas Triana,
EMP: 12
SALES (est): 921.9K Privately Held
SIC: 1761 7389 Roofing contractor;

(G-14073)
COMMERCIAL TRADE SERVICES LLC
510 E 46th St S (67216-1745)
PHONE................................316 721-5432
Blaine Tharp, *President*
Nic Word, *President*
Nicholas Word, *General Mgr*
Mike Watts, *CFO*
EMP: 11
SALES: 1.5MM Privately Held
SIC: 3825 1711 Frequency meters: electrical, mechanical & electronic; plumbing contractors

(G-14074)
COMMERCL-NDSTRIAL ELE CONT INC
819 E Indianapolis St (67211-2406)
PHONE................................316 263-1291
Philip W Smith, *President*
EMP: 27
SQ FT: 20,800
SALES: 3.5MM Privately Held
SIC: 1731 General electrical contractor

(G-14075)
COMMTECH INC
9011 E 37th St N (67226-2006)
PHONE................................316 636-1131
Arthur Alvis, *President*
Glen Avis, *Marketing Staff*
▼ EMP: 16
SQ FT: 22,000
SALES: 1.7MM Privately Held
WEB: www.commtech-fastcom.com
SIC: 3672 Printed circuit boards

(G-14076)
COMMUNICATIONS TECH ASSOC (PA)
Also Called: CTA
2007 S Hydraulic St (67211-5307)
P.O. Box 16160 (67216-0160)
PHONE................................316 267-5016
Anthony Estosito, *President*
James Richardson, *Vice Pres*
Stacey Sheridan, *Project Mgr*
David Burdick, *CFO*
Brent Moore, *Manager*
EMP: 36
SQ FT: 11,000
SALES (est): 4.8MM Privately Held
WEB: www.cta-inc.com
SIC: 5065 7622 1731 Communication equipment; communication equipment repair; communications specialization

(G-14077)
COMMUNITIES IN SCHOOL
412 S Main St Ste 212 (67202-3720)
PHONE................................316 973-5110
Mary Galvin, *President*
EMP: 45 EST: 1990
SALES: 777.6K Privately Held
WEB: www.ciswichita.org
SIC: 8322 Individual & family services

(G-14078)
COMMUNITY BANK WICHITA INC (PA)
11330 E 21st St N (67206-3515)
P.O. Box 782320 (67278-2320)
PHONE................................316 634-1600
Steven Carr, *President*
Christine Harrell, *Assistant VP*
Bradley S Bugner, *Vice Pres*
Stephanie Farber, *Vice Pres*
Kelly Gerber, *Vice Pres*
EMP: 10
SALES: 4.1MM Privately Held
WEB: www.communitybankwichita.com
SIC: 6022 State commercial banks

(G-14079)
COMPANION ANIMAL HOSPITAL
10555 W Maple St (67209-4011)
PHONE................................316 722-1004
Tamara Truesdell, *President*
Steve Byers, *Vice Pres*
EMP: 10
SQ FT: 4,000
SALES (est): 916.5K Privately Held
SIC: 0742 0752 Veterinarian, animal specialties; boarding services, kennels

(G-14080)
COMPLETE HOME HEALTH CARE INC
400 N Woodlawn St Ste 15 (67208-4333)
PHONE................................316 260-5012
Fay Cole, *Administration*
Fae Cole, *Administration*
EMP: 10
SALES: 390K Privately Held
SIC: 8082 Home health care services

(G-14081)
COMPLETE LANDSCAPING SYSTEMS
1347 S Washington Ave (67211-3445)
PHONE................................316 832-0061
Peter X Salmeron, *Ch of Bd*
Laura E Ackerman, *President*
Laura McMurray, *President*
EMP: 100
SQ FT: 15,000
SALES (est): 5.2MM Privately Held
SIC: 0782 Lawn care services; landscape contractors

(G-14082)
COMPRESSED GASES INC
602 E 29th St N (67219-4112)
P.O. Box 1456 (67201-1456)
PHONE................................316 838-3222
EMP: 10
SQ FT: 24,000
SALES (corp-wide): 1.2MM Privately Held
SIC: 5169 Whol Chemicals/Products
PA: Compressed Gases, Inc.
602 E 29th St N
Wichita KS
316 838-3222

(G-14083)
COMPTON CONSTRUCTION SVCS LLC
1802 N Washington Ave (67214-1466)
P.O. Box 3097 (67201-3097)
PHONE................................316 262-8885
Gib Compton, *President*
Mark Wagner, *Project Mgr*
EMP: 22
SALES (est): 3.6MM Privately Held
WEB: www.comptonconstruction.com
SIC: 1521 1542 Single-family housing construction; commercial & office building contractors

(G-14084)
COMTRSYS INC
Also Called: Computer Training Systems
200 W Douglas Ave Ste 230 (67202-3002)
PHONE................................316 265-1585
Frank Lichtlin, *President*
Dorine Karlin, *President*
Mark Karlin, *President*
Bob Brown, *Vice Pres*
Jessica Euwer, *Vice Pres*
EMP: 17
SALES (est): 1.8MM Privately Held
WEB: www.ctsys.com
SIC: 7379 Computer related consulting services

(G-14085)
CONCO INC
3051 N Ohio St (67219-4132)
P.O. Box 9166 (67277-0166)
PHONE................................316 943-7111
Craig Nelson, *President*
Aaron Korte, *Superintendent*
Dan J Waller, *Vice Pres*
Kyle Blasdel, *Project Mgr*
Luke Kunkel, *Project Mgr*
EMP: 140
SQ FT: 18,000
SALES (est): 57MM Privately Held
WEB: www.conco.net
SIC: 1542 1541 Commercial & office building, new construction; institutional building construction; industrial buildings, new construction

(G-14086)
CONCORDNCE HLTHCARE SLTONS LLC
1970 S West St Ste 360 (67213-1124)
PHONE................................316 945-6941
Cindy Sipe, *Sales/Mktg Mgr*
EMP: 13
SALES (corp-wide): 504MM Privately Held
WEB: www.mmsmedical.com
SIC: 5047 Medical equipment & supplies
PA: Concordance Healthcare Solutions Llc
85 Shaffer Park Dr
Tiffin OH 44883
419 455-2153

(G-14087)
CONCRETE PUMPING SERVICE INC
Also Called: Brundage-Bone Concrete Pumping
3131 N Hillside Ave (67219-3903)
PHONE..................................316 612-8515
Ron Vudenkas, *President*
Chuck Odiorne, *Manager*
EMP: 18
SALES (est): 2.1MM
SALES (corp-wide): 154.2MM **Privately Held**
SIC: 1771 Concrete pumping
PA: Brundage-Bone Concrete Pumping, Inc.
6461 Downing St
Denver CO 80229
303 289-4444

(G-14088)
CONEQTEC CORP (PA)
3348 S Hoover Rd (67215-1216)
P.O. Box 9102 (67277-0102)
PHONE..................................316 943-8889
Gary Cochran, *President*
Jerri Cochran, *Corp Secy*
David Little, *Manager*
Adam Runner, *Manager*
EMP: 25
SQ FT: 4,000
SALES (est): 9.1MM **Privately Held**
SIC: 3531 5082 Construction machinery attachments; contractors' materials

(G-14089)
CONNOISSEUR MEDIA LLC
Also Called: Wolf 100.5 The
1938 N Woodlawn St # 150 (67208-1857)
PHONE..................................316 558-8800
Doug Downs, *General Mgr*
EMP: 16
SALES (corp-wide): 62.7MM **Privately Held**
SIC: 4832 Radio broadcasting stations, music format
PA: Connoisseur Media, Llc
180 Post Rd E Ste 201
Westport CT 06880
203 293-8349

(G-14090)
CONRADY WESTERN INC
2218 S West St (67213-1114)
PHONE..................................316 943-4261
Steve Apple, *Manager*
EMP: 26
SALES (corp-wide): 10MM **Privately Held**
WEB: www.conradys.com
SIC: 5083 Agricultural machinery & equipment
PA: Conrady Western Inc
501 W Main St
Anthony KS 67003
620 842-5137

(G-14091)
CONSOLIDATED ELEC DISTRS INC
Also Called: American Electrical
411 S Washington Ave (67202-4727)
P.O. Box 7 (67201-0007)
PHONE..................................316 267-5311
Chris Barker, *Sales Staff*
Brad Russell, *Sales Staff*
Stanley D Wilson, *Branch Mgr*
Jerod Hatch, *Manager*
EMP: 20
SALES (corp-wide): 4.1B **Privately Held**
SIC: 5063 Electrical supplies
PA: Consolidated Electrical Distributors, Inc.
1920 Westridge Dr
Irving TX 75038
972 582-5300

(G-14092)
CONSOLIDATED ELEC DISTRS INC
C E D
1134 N Washington Ave (67214-3059)
P.O. Box 4250 (67204-0250)
PHONE..................................316 262-3541
Renee Hoagland, *Finance*
Bruce Harris, *Sales Staff*
Brandon McLey, *Manager*
EMP: 22
SQ FT: 40,000
SALES (corp-wide): 4.1B **Privately Held**
SIC: 5063 Electrical supplies
PA: Consolidated Electrical Distributors, Inc.
1920 Westridge Dr
Irving TX 75038
972 582-5300

(G-14093)
CONSTRUCTION SVCS BRYANT INC
Also Called: Csbi
2748 N North Shore Ct (67205-1072)
P.O. Box 475 (67201-0475)
PHONE..................................316 262-1010
EMP: 12
SQ FT: 3,200
SALES (est): 3.3MM **Privately Held**
SIC: 1542 Nonresidential Construction

(G-14094)
CONTEMPRARY COMMUNICATIONS INC
630 N Pennsylvania Ave (67214-4157)
PHONE..................................316 265-0879
Kay Dawson, *President*
EMP: 67
SQ FT: 100,000
SALES (est): 11.2MM **Privately Held**
WEB: www.mailcci.com
SIC: 7331 Mailing list compilers

(G-14095)
CONVERGYS CORPORATION
4600 W Kellogg Dr Ste 106 (67209-2546)
PHONE..................................316 681-4800
Atila Csech, *CEO*
EMP: 500
SALES (corp-wide): 20B **Publicly Held**
WEB: www.convergys.com
SIC: 7374 Data processing service
HQ: Concentrix Cvg Corporation
201 E 4th St
Cincinnati OH 45202
513 723-7000

(G-14096)
CONWAY BANK N A
121 E Kellogg St (67202-3713)
PHONE..................................316 263-6767
Blake Hemberger, *Vice Pres*
Jerod Heiman, *Manager*
Ronald Carr, *Officer*
EMP: 15
SALES (corp-wide): 5MM **Privately Held**
WEB: www.conwaybank.net
SIC: 6021 National commercial banks
PA: Conway Bank
124 W Spring Ave
Conway Springs KS 67031
620 456-2255

(G-14097)
COONROD & ASSOC CNSTR CO INC
Also Called: C & A
3550 S Hoover Rd (67215-1213)
P.O. Box 12589 (67277-2589)
PHONE..................................316 942-8430
Randall R Coonrod, *President*
Justin Parks, *Vice Pres*
Ray D Penner, *Vice Pres*
Scot E Wolfington, *Vice Pres*
Mary Joerg, *Controller*
EMP: 125
SQ FT: 7,500
SALES (est): 22.5MM **Privately Held**
WEB: www.coonrod.com
SIC: 1542 1541 1521 Commercial & office building, new construction; industrial buildings & warehouses; single-family housing construction

(G-14098)
COOPER MALONE MCCLAIN INC
Also Called: Cooper, John
7701 E Kellogg Dr Ste 700 (67207-1704)
P.O. Box 781684 (67278-1684)
PHONE..................................316 685-5777
John Cooper, *President*
Louis McClain, *Exec VP*
Dave Malone, *Senior VP*
Rick Ensz, *Vice Pres*
EMP: 22
SQ FT: 4,500
SALES (est): 3.5MM **Privately Held**
WEB: www.cmmci.com
SIC: 6211 Stock brokers & dealers

(G-14099)
COPY PRODUCTS INC
8200 E 34th Cir N # 1801 (67226-1362)
PHONE..................................316 315-0102
EMP: 21
SALES (corp-wide): 23.5MM **Privately Held**
SIC: 5044 Whol Office Equipment
PA: Copy Products, Inc.
2103 W Vista St
Springfield MO 65807
417 889-5665

(G-14100)
COPY SHOP INC
Also Called: Mail Right
1815 E Douglas Ave (67211-1611)
P.O. Box 513 (67201-0513)
PHONE..................................316 262-8200
Fax: 316 262-8203
EMP: 6
SQ FT: 3,500
SALES (est): 490K **Privately Held**
SIC: 2752 Offset Printing & Photocoping Service

(G-14101)
CORNEJO & SONS LLC (DH)
2060 E Tulsa St (67216-2440)
P.O. Box 16204 (67216-0204)
PHONE..................................316 522-5100
Ronald Cornejo, *CEO*
Marty Cornejo, *President*
Patrick Short, *General Mgr*
Richard Cornejo, *Vice Pres*
Kirk Howie, *Vice Pres*
EMP: 127 **EST:** 1952
SQ FT: 35,000
SALES (est): 106.8MM
SALES (corp-wide): 2.1B **Publicly Held**
SIC: 1542 1794 1795 1611 Commercial & office building, new construction; excavation & grading, building construction; demolition, buildings & other structures; surfacing & paving
HQ: Summit Materials, Llc
1550 Wynkoop St Ste 300
Denver CO 80202
303 893-0012

(G-14102)
CORNERSTONE FINANCIAL LLC
13111 E 21st St N (67230-7400)
PHONE..................................316 630-0670
Carolyn Denning, *Opers Staff*
Mike Nelson,
Ron Chronister,
Les Morris,
Kerwin Thiessen,
EMP: 14
SQ FT: 2,500
SALES (est): 1.3MM **Privately Held**
SIC: 6211 Security brokers & dealers

(G-14103)
CORNERSTONE RIDGE PLAZA
3636 N Ridge Rd Ste 400 (67205-1221)
PHONE..................................316 462-3636
Doug Friehart, *CEO*
Larry Nanny, *Exec Dir*
EMP: 40
SALES (est): 2.4MM **Privately Held**
SIC: 8052 Intermediate care facilities

(G-14104)
CORPORATE HILLS LLC
Also Called: Wichita Marriott
9100 E Corporate Hills Dr (67207-1317)
PHONE..................................316 651-0333
Phillip G Ruffin, *General Ptnr*
Carl Fry, *Engineer*
Tamera Sherman, *Director*
EMP: 250
SALES (est): 14.4MM **Privately Held**
WEB: www.wichitamarriott.com
SIC: 7011 5812 5813 Hotels; eating places; drinking places

(G-14105)
COSMIC PET LLC (PA)
1315 W Macarthur Rd (67217-2736)
PHONE..................................316 941-1100
Timothy Blurton,
EMP: 25 **EST:** 2015
SQ FT: 90,000
SALES (est): 28.2MM **Publicly Held**
SIC: 5199 Pet supplies

(G-14106)
COUNSELING & MEDIATION CENTER
200 W Douglas Ave Ste 560 (67202-3020)
PHONE..................................316 269-2322
Mike Nichols, *Director*
▲ **EMP:** 18
SALES: 406.8K **Privately Held**
WEB: www.counselingandmediation.org
SIC: 8049 8322 Clinical psychologist; social worker

(G-14107)
COUNTRY ACRES SENIOR RESIDENCE
343 N Country Acres Ave (67212-6138)
PHONE..................................316 773-3900
Barbara Kasson, *Principal*
Margaret Rudy, *Principal*
Rebecca Scuka, *Principal*
Rita Duster, *Director*
EMP: 12
SALES (est): 475.7K **Privately Held**
SIC: 8361 Home for the aged

(G-14108)
COUNTRY INN SUITES
Also Called: Country Suites By Carlson
7824 E 32nd St N (67226-1245)
PHONE..................................316 634-3900
EMP: 12
SALES (est): 435.3K **Privately Held**
SIC: 7011 Hotels & motels

(G-14109)
COUNTY OF SEDGWICK
Also Called: Sedgwick County Regional
1109 N Minneapolis St (67214-3129)
PHONE..................................316 660-4800
Jaime Oeberst, *Director*
EMP: 37 **Privately Held**
WEB: www.kansas-hazmat.com
SIC: 8049 9111 ; county supervisors' & executives' offices
PA: County Of Sedgwick
525 N Main St Ste 823
Wichita KS 67203
316 660-9000

(G-14110)
COUNTY OF SEDGWICK
Also Called: Juvenile Residential Facility
881 S Minnesota Ave (67211-2700)
PHONE..................................316 660-9775
Linda Lambert, *Director*
EMP: 30 **Privately Held**
WEB: www.kansas-hazmat.com
SIC: 8361 9111 Juvenile correctional facilities; county supervisors' & executives' offices
PA: County Of Sedgwick
525 N Main St Ste 823
Wichita KS 67203
316 660-9000

(G-14111)
COUNTY OF SEDGWICK
Also Called: Sedgwick County EXT Council
7001 W 21st St N (67205-1759)
PHONE..................................316 660-0100
Beverly Dunning, *Director*
Angela Jones, *Director*
EMP: 40 **Privately Held**
WEB: www.kansas-hazmat.com
SIC: 9641 8322 Agriculture extension service; youth center
PA: County Of Sedgwick
525 N Main St Ste 823
Wichita KS 67203
316 660-9000

▲ = Import ▼=Export
◆ =Import/Export

(G-14112)
COUNTY OF SEDGWICK
Also Called: Public Works
1144 S Seneca St (67213-4443)
PHONE..................................316 685-2035
David Spears, *Director*
EMP: 50 **Privately Held**
WEB: www.kansas-hazmat.com
SIC: 1611 Highway & street maintenance
PA: County Of Sedgwick
525 N Main St Ste 823
Wichita KS 67203
316 660-9000

(G-14113)
COUNTY OF SEDGWICK
Also Called: Youth Aftercare Program
622 E Central Ave (67202-1062)
PHONE..................................316 660-9500
Mark Masterson, *Manager*
EMP: 40 **Privately Held**
WEB: www.kansas-hazmat.com
SIC: 9431 8361 ; residential care
PA: County Of Sedgwick
525 N Main St Ste 823
Wichita KS 67203
316 660-9000

(G-14114)
COUNTY OF SEDGWICK
Department of Aging
2622 W Central Ave # 500 (67203-4974)
PHONE..................................316 660-7060
Annette Graham, *Director*
EMP: 40 **Privately Held**
WEB: www.kansas-hazmat.com
SIC: 7299 9111 Information services, consumer; county supervisors' & executives' offices
PA: County Of Sedgwick
525 N Main St Ste 823
Wichita KS 67203
316 660-9000

(G-14115)
COURT REPORTING SERVICE INC
1999 N Amidon Ave Ste 224 (67203-2123)
PHONE..................................800 794-8798
Michael J Zarich, *President*
EMP: 10
SALES (est): 589.1K **Privately Held**
WEB: www.crsreporting.com
SIC: 7338 Court reporting service

(G-14116)
COURTYARD-OLD TOWN
Also Called: Courtyard Wichita At Old Town
820 E 2nd St N (67202-2733)
PHONE..................................316 264-5300
Deric Eubanks, *President*
James Gilliam,
EMP: 45
SQ FT: 21,760
SALES (est): 763.8K **Privately Held**
SIC: 7011 Hotels & motels

(G-14117)
COVENTRY HEALTH CARE KANS INC
Principal Health Care
8535 E 21st St N (67206-2910)
PHONE..................................316 634-1222
Jan Dolmeyer, *Manager*
EMP: 14
SALES (corp-wide): 194.5B **Publicly Held**
WEB: www.chckansas.com
SIC: 6324 Health maintenance organization (HMO), insurance only
HQ: Coventry Health Care Of Kansas, Inc.
9401 Indian Creek Pkwy # 1300
Overland Park KS 66210
800 969-3343

(G-14118)
COWBOY INN LLC
642 N Saint Paul St (67203-5035)
PHONE..................................316 943-3869
Judith Short, *President*
Judith A Short,
EMP: 10
SALES (est): 205K **Privately Held**
SIC: 7997 Membership sports & recreation clubs

(G-14119)
COX COMMUNICATIONS INC
901 George Wash Blvd (67211-3901)
PHONE..................................316 260-7392
Nicholas Diponzio, *Branch Mgr*
EMP: 86
SALES (corp-wide): 29.2B **Privately Held**
SIC: 4841 Cable television services
HQ: Cox Communications, Inc.
6205 B Pchtree Dnwody Rd
Atlanta GA 30328

(G-14120)
COX COMMUNICATIONS INC
8924 E 35th St N (67226-2001)
PHONE..................................316 219-5000
Steve Trammel, *Manager*
EMP: 200
SALES (corp-wide): 29.2B **Privately Held**
SIC: 4841 Cable television services
HQ: Cox Communications, Inc.
6205 B Pchtree Dnwody Rd
Atlanta GA 30328

(G-14121)
COX MACHINE INC (PA)
5338 W 21st St N Ste 100 (67205-1789)
PHONE..................................316 943-1342
Steve Cox, *CEO*
Jason Cox, *President*
Janis Cox, *Corp Secy*
Brenna Davis, *COO*
Craig Avagian, *Vice Pres*
EMP: 87
SQ FT: 135,000
SALES (est): 44.9MM **Privately Held**
WEB: www.coxmachine.com
SIC: 3599 3728 Machine shop, jobbing & repair; aircraft parts & equipment

(G-14122)
COX MEDIA LLC
901 S George Wash Blvd (67211-3901)
PHONE..................................623 322-2000
Julianna Burget, *Sales Staff*
Stacy Morris, *Marketing Mgr*
Curt McMurphy, *Branch Mgr*
EMP: 30
SALES (corp-wide): 29.2B **Privately Held**
WEB: www.coxmedia.com
SIC: 4899 Data communication services
HQ: Cox Media, L.L.C.
1400 Lake Hearn Dr Ne
Brookhaven GA 30319

(G-14123)
COX-KENT & ASSOCIATES INC
2807 W Pawnee St (67213-1819)
PHONE..................................316 946-5596
Jeff Kent, *President*
Brian Cox, *Corp Secy*
EMP: 15
SQ FT: 3,000
SALES (est): 2.2MM **Privately Held**
SIC: 1731 General electrical contractor

(G-14124)
CPM TECHNOLOGIES INC
9911 E 21st St N (67206-3551)
PHONE..................................256 777-9869
David Vanderwiel, *President*
Paul Grassoy, *Vice Pres*
Wayne Shea, *Admin Sec*
EMP: 13 **EST:** 2000
SALES: 2MM **Privately Held**
WEB: www.cpmtechnologies.com
SIC: 8742 7389 Management consulting services;

(G-14125)
CRAIG RESOURCES INC (PA)
Also Called: Craig Homecare
1100 E 1st St N (67214-3905)
P.O. Box 2241 (67201-2241)
PHONE..................................316 264-9988
Richard Giblin, *President*
Sean Balke, *COO*
Joanne Giblin, *Vice Pres*
Brian Koehn, *CFO*
EMP: 29
SALES (est): 13.9MM **Privately Held**
WEB: www.craighomecare.com
SIC: 8082 Visiting nurse service

(G-14126)
CRATETECH INCORPORATED
8110 E Marion St (67210-4400)
PHONE..................................316 682-6223
Ray Fricks, *President*
EMP: 25 **Privately Held**
WEB: www.cratetech.com
SIC: 2449 2441 Rectangular boxes & crates, wood; nailed wood boxes & shook
HQ: Cratetech, Incorporated
8247 S 194th St
Kent WA 98032

(G-14127)
CREATIVITY PLACE INC (PA)
Also Called: DISCOVERY PLACE
9112 E Central Ave B (67206-2506)
PHONE..................................316 684-1860
Dene Nelson, *Director*
EMP: 55
SALES: 1.2MM **Privately Held**
WEB: www.creativity-portal.com
SIC: 8351 Preschool center

(G-14128)
CREDIT UNION OF AMERICA (PA)
711 W Douglas Ave (67213-4703)
P.O. Box 47528 (67201-7528)
PHONE..................................316 265-3272
Bob Thurman, *President*
Kelly Higgins, *Assistant VP*
Jim Jacobs, *Assistant VP*
Glenda Burkett, *Vice Pres*
Paul Meissner, *Vice Pres*
EMP: 52
SQ FT: 8,500
SALES: 36.1MM **Privately Held**
SIC: 6061 Federal credit unions

(G-14129)
CREEK ELECTRIC INCORPORATED
2811 W Pawnee St (67213-1819)
PHONE..................................316 943-5888
Galen Schawe, *President*
Steve Vanderhoff, *Superintendent*
Perry Overstake, *Vice Pres*
Nancy Clark, *Project Mgr*
EMP: 45
SALES: 6.6MM **Privately Held**
WEB: www.creekelectric.com
SIC: 1731 General electrical contractor

(G-14130)
CRICKET COMMUNICATIONS LLC
3165 S Seneca St (67217-3234)
PHONE..................................316 636-6387
EMP: 11
SALES (corp-wide): 170.7B **Publicly Held**
WEB: www.cricketcommunications.com
SIC: 4812 Cellular telephone services
HQ: Cricket Communications, Llc
7337 Trade St
San Diego CA 92121
858 882-6000

(G-14131)
CRISS OPTICAL MFG CO INC
3628 S West St (67217-3802)
P.O. Box 12267 (67277-2267)
PHONE..................................316 529-0414
Diane Loveall, *CEO*
EMP: 6
SQ FT: 27,000
SALES: 1.3MM **Privately Held**
SIC: 3089 3851 Molding primary plastic; frames & parts, eyeglass & spectacle

(G-14132)
CRITICAL ELC SYSTEMS GROUP LLC
Also Called: McBride Electric
3215 E 9th St N (67208-3024)
PHONE..................................316 684-0193
Harold Ragland, *Branch Mgr*
EMP: 30
SALES (corp-wide): 12.1MM **Privately Held**
WEB: www.mcbrideinc.com
SIC: 1731 General electrical contractor
PA: System Electric Co.
5700 Gran Pkwy Ste 960
Plano TX 75024
469 453-0997

(G-14133)
CROSS CREEK FURNITURE LLC
13303 W Maple St Ste 139 (67235-8709)
PHONE..................................316 943-0286
Larry Musselman, *Mng Member*
Willie Cole,
EMP: 45
SALES (est): 4.1MM **Privately Held**
WEB: www.crosscreekfurniture.com
SIC: 5021 Furniture

(G-14134)
CROSSFIRST BANK
9451 E 13th St N (67206-9300)
PHONE..................................316 494-4844
Steve Peterson, *Branch Mgr*
EMP: 41 **Privately Held**
SIC: 6022 State commercial banks
PA: Crossfirst Bank
4707 W 135th St
Overland Park KS 66224

(G-14135)
CROSSLAND CONSTRUCTION CO INC
3017 N Cypress St (67226-4024)
PHONE..................................316 942-9090
Rachelle Camacho, *Administration*
EMP: 34
SALES (corp-wide): 567.9MM **Privately Held**
SIC: 1521 Single-family housing construction
PA: Crossland Construction Company, Inc.
833 S East Ave
Columbus KS 66725
620 429-1414

(G-14136)
CROWN EQUIPMENT CORPORATION
2113 S West St Ste 300 (67213-1136)
PHONE..................................316 942-4400
Jim Bicky, *CEO*
EMP: 22
SALES (est): 4.5MM **Privately Held**
SIC: 3537 5084 Forklift trucks; lift trucks & parts

(G-14137)
CSL PLASMA INC
1515 E Central Ave (67214-4131)
PHONE..................................316 264-6973
Erica Michaelson, *Branch Mgr*
EMP: 65 **Privately Held**
WEB: www.zlbplasma.com
SIC: 8099 Blood bank
HQ: Csl Plasma Inc.
900 Broken Sound Pkwy Nw # 400
Boca Raton FL 33487
561 981-3700

(G-14138)
CSS GROUP INC
1550 N Broadway Ave 200 (67214-1100)
P.O. Box 1103 (67201-1103)
PHONE..................................316 269-9090
Don Stearns, *President*
EMP: 10
SQ FT: 5,250
SALES (est): 908.2K **Privately Held**
WEB: www.cssgroup.com
SIC: 7371 Computer software systems analysis & design, custom

(G-14139)
CTMD LLC
Also Called: Rent A Center
940 N Tyler Rd Ste 101 (67212-3265)
PHONE..................................316 686-6116
EMP: 30 **EST:** 2011
SQ FT: 1,300
SALES: 4MM **Privately Held**
SIC: 7299 Rental of personal items, except for recreation & medical

(G-14140)
CTR IMPRVMNT HMN FNCTNNG INT
Also Called: Gift of Health, The
3100 N Hillside Ave (67219-3904)
PHONE..................................316 682-3100
Laura Benson, *COO*
Jean Van Ness, *Office Mgr*
EMP: 50
SALES (est): 337.6K **Privately Held**
WEB: www.brightspot.org
SIC: 8099 Health & allied services

(G-14141)
CURO FINANCIAL TECH CORP (HQ)
Also Called: Speedy Cash
3527 N Ridge Rd (67205-1212)
P.O. Box 780408 (67278-0408)
PHONE..................................316 722-3801
Don Gayhardt, *CEO*
Dorinda Henits, *Vice Pres*
Todd Wessel, *Project Mgr*
Edwina Bartmier, *Store Mgr*
Daniel Morgette, *Store Mgr*
EMP: 20
SALES (est): 158.5MM
SALES (corp-wide): 651MM **Publicly Held**
SIC: 6099 Check cashing agencies
PA: Curo Group Holdings Corp.
3527 N Ridge Rd
Wichita KS 67205
316 772-3801

(G-14142)
CURO GROUP HOLDINGS CORP (PA)
3527 N Ridge Rd (67205-1212)
PHONE..................................316 772-3801
Douglas R Rippel, *Ch of Bd*
Don Gayhardt, *President*
Donald F Gayhardt, *President*
William Baker, *COO*
Terry Pittman, *Exec VP*
EMP: 17
SALES: 651MM **Publicly Held**
SIC: 6163 Loan brokers

(G-14143)
CURO MANAGEMENT LLC
6300 E 21st St N (67208-1808)
PHONE..................................316 771-0000
EMP: 34
SALES (corp-wide): 62.3MM **Privately Held**
SIC: 8741 Management services
PA: Curo Management Llc
3527 N Ridge Rd
Wichita KS 67205
316 722-3801

(G-14144)
CURO MANAGEMENT LLC
3133 E Douglas Ave (67211-1626)
PHONE..................................316 683-2274
Tammy White, *Vice Pres*
EMP: 51
SALES (corp-wide): 62.3MM **Privately Held**
SIC: 6099 Check cashing agencies
PA: Curo Management Llc
3527 N Ridge Rd
Wichita KS 67205
316 722-3801

(G-14145)
CURO MANAGEMENT LLC (PA)
Also Called: Speedy and Rapid Cash
3527 N Ridge Rd (67205-1212)
PHONE..................................316 722-3801
Chad Faulkner, *Principal*
Rosie Laureano, *District Mgr*
Bill Baker, *COO*
William Deer, *Counsel*
Troy Jones, *Vice Pres*
EMP: 89
SALES (est): 62.3MM **Privately Held**
SIC: 8741 Management services

(G-14146)
CUSTOM LAWN SERVICE INC
3333 N Hillside Ave (67219-3907)
P.O. Box 49354 (67201-9354)
PHONE..................................316 321-1563
Kelly Fankhauser, *President*
EMP: 10
SALES (est): 716K **Privately Held**
SIC: 0782 Lawn care services

(G-14147)
CUSTOM VINYL & PAINT INC
1802 Roanoke St (67218-4630)
PHONE..................................316 651-6180
Daniel Lawrence, *President*
EMP: 5
SALES (est): 125K **Privately Held**
SIC: 3711 Automobile assembly, including specialty automobiles

(G-14148)
CUTTING EDGE LAWN CARE INC
3425 N Broadway Ave (67219-3609)
P.O. Box 4108 (67204-0108)
PHONE..................................316 390-1443
Nicholas Thomas, *President*
EMP: 12
SALES: 647K **Privately Held**
SIC: 0781 Landscape services

(G-14149)
CUTTING EDGE TILE & GROUT
121 S Bonnie Brae St (67207-1101)
PHONE..................................316 648-5516
Lance Toguchi, *Owner*
EMP: 6
SALES (est): 682.2K **Privately Held**
SIC: 2952 Asphalt felts & coatings

(G-14150)
CYBERTRON INTERNATIONAL INC
4747 S Emporia St (67216-1765)
PHONE..................................316 303-1022
Shadi Marcos, *President*
Jake Sowders, *Opers Staff*
Dick Graham, *Accounts Mgr*
Jorge Percival, *Marketing Staff*
Chris Fisher, *Manager*
▼ **EMP:** 97
SQ FT: 50,000
SALES: 30MM **Privately Held**
WEB: www.cybertronpc.com
SIC: 3571 7371 Electronic computers; custom computer programming services

(G-14151)
CYPRESS HEART (PA)
9300 E 29th St N Ste 310 (67226-2160)
PHONE..................................316 858-5200
Roger W Evans, *CEO*
Ryan Beard, *Cardiovascular*
EMP: 40
SQ FT: 10,000
SALES (est): 4.7MM **Privately Held**
SIC: 8011 Cardiologist & cardio-vascular specialist

(G-14152)
CYPRESS SURGERY CENTER LLC
9300 E 29th St N Ste 100 (67226-3007)
PHONE..................................316 634-0404
Misty Sachs, *Administration*
EMP: 57 **EST:** 2006
SQ FT: 22,000
SALES (est): 7.7MM **Privately Held**
WEB: www.cypresssurgerycenter.com
SIC: 8011 Surgeon
HQ: Symbion, Inc.
310 Seven Springs Way
Brentwood TN 37027
615 234-5900

(G-14153)
CZARNIECKIS CONSTRUCTION INC
1550 Yucca Pl Wichita (67209)
P.O. Box 771172 (67277-1172)
PHONE..................................316 946-9991
John T Czarniecki, *President*
EMP: 18
SQ FT: 8,000
SALES (est): 1.4MM **Privately Held**
SIC: 1542 Commercial & office building, new construction

(G-14154)
D & D ROLAND ENTERPRISES LLC
Also Called: Steamatic
1120 S Florence St (67209-2642)
PHONE..................................316 942-6474
Darrel Roland, *President*
Diane Roland, *Vice Pres*
EMP: 35
SQ FT: 16,000
SALES: 1.5MM **Privately Held**
WEB: www.calldougforacleanrug.com
SIC: 7349 Building maintenance services

(G-14155)
D & H MACHINE AND TOOL INC
1408 S Osage St (67213-4394)
PHONE..................................316 267-3906
James C Wheeler, *President*
Carol Ann Wheeler, *Admin Sec*
EMP: 6
SQ FT: 4,500
SALES (est): 299.4K **Privately Held**
SIC: 3599 Machine shop, jobbing & repair

(G-14156)
D & S MANUFACTURING INC
319 S Oak St (67213-4637)
PHONE..................................316 685-5337
Scott Ta, *Vice Pres*
Diana Ta, *Vice Pres*
EMP: 8
SQ FT: 18,420
SALES (est): 1.3MM **Privately Held**
SIC: 3728 Aircraft parts & equipment

(G-14157)
D H PACE COMPANY INC
Also Called: Overhead Door South Centl Kans
3506 W Harry St (67213-1410)
PHONE..................................316 944-3667
Jeff Cocking, *Sales Mgr*
Chad Peed, *Regl Sales Mgr*
John Swinford, *Branch Mgr*
Desiree Wilson, *Executive*
EMP: 29
SALES (corp-wide): 433.8MM **Privately Held**
WEB: www.dhpace.com
SIC: 5031 7699 5063 Doors; door & window repair; burglar alarm systems
HQ: D. H. Pace Company, Inc.
1901 E 119th St
Olathe KS 66061
816 221-0543

(G-14158)
D J COMPANY
Also Called: First Place, The
2929 N Rock Rd Ste 165 (67226-5101)
PHONE..................................316 685-3241
Helen J Galloway, *Owner*
Helen Dodson Galloway, *Owner*
EMP: 17 **EST:** 1973
SQ FT: 3,200
SALES (est): 1.9MM **Privately Held**
WEB: www.djcompany.com
SIC: 5944 5947 5932 7389 Jewelry, precious stones & precious metals; gift shop; antiques; interior designer

(G-14159)
D P ENTERPRISES INC
Also Called: Quality Printing
2413 S Laura St (67216-1212)
PHONE..................................316 263-4234
Danny Penachio, *President*
Jan Hauber, *Corp Secy*
EMP: 10
SQ FT: 12,000
SALES (est): 1.2MM **Privately Held**
SIC: 2752 Commercial printing, offset

(G-14160)
D W NEWCOMERS SONS INC
Also Called: Lakeview Funeral Home
12100 E 13th St N (67206-2828)
PHONE..................................316 684-8200
Sean Myers, *Sales/Mktg Mgr*
EMP: 20
SALES (corp-wide): 3.1B **Publicly Held**
WEB: www.dwnewcomers.com
SIC: 7261 Funeral home
HQ: D W Newcomer's Sons Inc
7000 Blue Ridge Blvd
Raytown MO 64133
816 353-1218

(G-14161)
D&A SERVICES INC
926 E Douglas Ave (67202-3510)
P.O. Box 771141 (67277-1141)
PHONE..................................316 943-8857
EMP: 60
SALES (est): 1.7MM **Privately Held**
SIC: 7349 Janitorial service, contract basis

(G-14162)
D&D MACHINE INC
1714 S Baehr St (67209-2704)
PHONE..................................316 269-1553
Dan Slates, *President*
EMP: 18
SQ FT: 15,000
SALES (est): 992.3K **Privately Held**
SIC: 3599 Machine shop, jobbing & repair

(G-14163)
DAN A BURTON DDS
219 S Hillside St (67211-2128)
PHONE..................................316 684-5511
Dan A Burton DDS, *Owner*
EMP: 11
SALES (est): 692.8K **Privately Held**
SIC: 8021 Dentists' office

(G-14164)
DANA MANWEILER MILBY PA
300 W Douglas Ave Ste 600 (67202-2917)
PHONE..................................316 267-8677
Ronald K Badger, *Principal*
EMP: 13
SALES (est): 1.2MM **Privately Held**
SIC: 8111 General practice attorney, lawyer; bankruptcy law

(G-14165)
DANDURAND DRUG COMPANY INC
Also Called: Health Mart
7732 E Central Ave # 108 (67206-2155)
PHONE..................................316 685-2353
Michael F Dandurand, *President*
Mathew Perrey, *Principal*
Lou Ann Dandurand, *Corp Secy*
Ben Dandurand, *Pharmacist*
EMP: 26 **EST:** 1947
SQ FT: 5,500
SALES (est): 6.3MM **Privately Held**
SIC: 5912 8011 Drug stores; offices & clinics of medical doctors

(G-14166)
DANIEL A TATPATI MD
1515 S Clifton Ave # 460 (67218-2900)
PHONE..................................316 689-6803
Daniel A Tatpati, *Owner*
Phyllis J Weber, *Office Mgr*
Olga A Tatpati, *Endocrinology*
Abraham D Tatpati, *Internal Med*
EMP: 12
SALES (est): 1.1MM **Privately Held**
SIC: 8011 Cardiologist & cardio-vascular specialist; thoracic physician

(G-14167)
DANNY SATTERFIELD DRYWALL CORP
4317 W 29th Cir S (67215-1019)
PHONE..................................316 942-5155
Danny Satterfield, *President*
Connie D Satterfield, *Vice Pres*
EMP: 42
SQ FT: 18,000
SALES: 6.2MM **Privately Held**
WEB: www.dannysatterfielddrywall.com
SIC: 1742 1751 Drywall; lightweight steel framing (metal stud) installation

(G-14168)
DANS HEATING & COOLING INC
242 N New York Ave (67214-4140)
PHONE..................................316 522-0372
Wayne Gile, *CEO*
Maureen Gile, *Principal*
Junior Stock, *Vice Pres*
Ken Gile, *Project Mgr*
EMP: 22

▲ = Import ▼=Export
◆ =Import/Export

SQ FT: 4,000
SALES (est): 3.5MM **Privately Held**
SIC: 1711 Heating systems repair & maintenance; warm air heating & air conditioning contractor

(G-14169)
DARLING INGREDIENTS INC
2155 N Mosley Ave (67214-1353)
PHONE..................................316 264-6951
Thomas Menousek, *Branch Mgr*
EMP: 60
SALES (corp-wide): 3.3B **Publicly Held**
WEB: www.darlingii.com
SIC: 2077 5191 2048 2047 Animal & marine fats & oils; farm supplies; prepared feeds; dog & cat food
PA: Darling Ingredients Inc.
5601 N Macarthur Blvd
Irving TX 75038
972 717-0300

(G-14170)
DARRAH OIL COMPANY LLC
125 N Market St Ste 1425 (67202-1720)
P.O. Box 2786 (67201-2786)
PHONE..................................316 219-3390
William Darrah, *General Mgr*
Deann Stagner, *Accountant*
John J Darrah Jr, *Mng Member*
EMP: 6
SQ FT: 2,000
SALES: 4MM **Privately Held**
SIC: 1382 Oil & gas exploration services

(G-14171)
DARRELL BYBEE CONSTRUCTION LLC
Also Called: Bybee Electric
1341 S Ellis St (67211-3526)
PHONE..................................316 409-4186
Darrell Bybee, *Principal*
EMP: 10
SALES (est): 452.8K **Privately Held**
SIC: 1521 1731 Single-family housing construction; general electrical contractor

(G-14172)
DAVID E DISHOP
Also Called: Culligan
10821 E (67226)
PHONE..................................614 861-5440
David E Dishop, *Owner*
EMP: 15
SQ FT: 2,450
SALES (est): 749.3K **Privately Held**
SIC: 5074 7389 Water softeners; water softener service

(G-14173)
DAVID KOEPSEL DDS LLC
8150 E Douglas Ave Ste 10 (67206-2362)
PHONE..................................316 686-7395
David Koepsel, *Principal*
EMP: 10
SALES (est): 99K **Privately Held**
SIC: 8021 Dentists' office

(G-14174)
DAVID LIES PLUMBING INC
1420 S Sabin St (67209-2636)
PHONE..................................316 945-0117
David Lies, *President*
Patricia Lies, *Corp Secy*
EMP: 10 **EST:** 1955
SQ FT: 1,600
SALES (est): 982.4K **Privately Held**
SIC: 1711 Plumbing contractors

(G-14175)
DAVIS & JACK LLC
2121 W Maple St (67213-3315)
P.O. Box 12686 (67277-2686)
PHONE..................................316 945-8251
Kenneth Jack,
Carl B Davis,
EMP: 13
SALES (est): 1.4MM **Privately Held**
WEB: www.davisandjack.com
SIC: 8111 General practice law office

(G-14176)
DAYS INN INC
550 S Florence St (67209-2501)
PHONE..................................316 942-1717
Robert Patel, *President*
EMP: 11
SALES (est): 680K **Privately Held**
SIC: 7011 Hotels & motels

(G-14177)
DBI INC
3707 N Topeka St (67219-3645)
PHONE..................................316 831-9323
Brandon Cahoone, *Branch Mgr*
EMP: 40 **Privately Held**
SIC: 8734 7389 Testing laboratories; inspection & testing services
PA: Dbi, Inc.
15440 W 109th St
Lenexa KS 66219

(G-14178)
DCCCA INC
1319 W May St (67213-3505)
PHONE..................................316 267-2030
Mary Poling, *Principal*
Ernesto T Hodison, *Vice Pres*
Diane Born, *Opers Staff*
Kerye Jackson, *CFO*
Jeff Davis, *Treasurer*
EMP: 21 **Privately Held**
SIC: 8322 General counseling services
PA: Dccca, Inc.
3312 Clinton Pkwy
Lawrence KS

(G-14179)
DCCCA INC
Also Called: Options
122 N Millwood St (67203-5850)
PHONE..................................316 265-6011
Sharon Laudick, *Director*
EMP: 40 **Privately Held**
SIC: 8093 8069 Alcohol clinic, outpatient; alcoholism rehabilitation hospital
PA: Dccca, Inc.
3312 Clinton Pkwy
Lawrence KS

(G-14180)
DEAN E NORRIS INC
2929 S Minneapolis Ave (67216-2424)
P.O. Box 47719 (67201-7719)
PHONE..................................316 688-1901
David Norris, *CEO*
Mike Porch, *CEO*
Dusty Meyer, *General Mgr*
Buck Swaim, *Project Mgr*
Bryan Daniels, *Foreman/Supr*
EMP: 60
SQ FT: 25,000
SALES (est): 13.4MM
SALES (corp-wide): 10.4MM **Privately Held**
WEB: www.denmgmt.com
SIC: 1711 Mechanical contractor
PA: Den Management Co., Inc.
4053 E Navajo Ln
Wichita KS 67210
316 686-1964

(G-14181)
DEANS DESIGNS INC
3555 E Douglas Ave Ste 35 (67218-1097)
PHONE..................................316 686-6674
Dean O White, *Ch of Bd*
K Brad White, *President*
Teresa White, *Vice Pres*
Kris Cranston, *Controller*
EMP: 17
SQ FT: 9,000
SALES (est): 1.1MM **Privately Held**
WEB: www.vasevalet.com
SIC: 5992 7389 5947 5999 Flowers, fresh; interior designer; gift shop; art dealers

(G-14182)
DEBORAH JOHN & ASSOCIATES
Also Called: Dja Financial Aid Services
3000 W Kellogg Dr (67213-2204)
PHONE..................................316 777-0903
Alan John, *CEO*
Deborah John, *President*
Latisha Creekmore, *QC Mgr*
Thomas John, *CFO*
EMP: 26
SQ FT: 3,600
SALES: 820K **Privately Held**
WEB: www.gotodja.com
SIC: 7389 Financial services

(G-14183)
DECKER ELECTRIC INC
4500 W Harry St (67209-2736)
PHONE..................................316 265-8182
Stephen A Decker, *President*
Jesse Perez, *Superintendent*
Jason Seiwert, *Exec VP*
Jeff Easterby, *Project Mgr*
James Kelley, *Project Mgr*
EMP: 75
SQ FT: 15,000
SALES (est): 29.8MM **Privately Held**
WEB: www.decker-electric.com
SIC: 1731 5065 General electrical contractor; electronic parts & equipment

(G-14184)
DECORATOR AND CRAFT CORP (PA)
Also Called: Dcc
428 S Zelta St (67207-1499)
PHONE..................................316 685-6265
Robert L Jennings, *President*
Jeff Jennings, *Vice Pres*
Fleeta Jennings, *Treasurer*
Scott Depriest, *Manager*
▲ **EMP:** 75
SQ FT: 40,000
SALES (est): 11.3MM **Privately Held**
WEB: www.d-cc.com
SIC: 5092 5947 Arts & crafts equipment & supplies; gift, novelty & souvenir shop

(G-14185)
DEER LK ESTTES HOMEOWNERS ASSN
4236 E Wildflower Cir (67210-1645)
PHONE..................................316 640-6592
Tom Pryor, *President*
Denice Alligood, *Treasurer*
EMP: 99
SALES (est): 548.9K **Privately Held**
SIC: 8641 Homeowners' association

(G-14186)
DEERE & COMPANY
2256 S West St (67213-1114)
PHONE..................................316 945-0501
John Roy, *Manager*
EMP: 20
SALES (corp-wide): 39.2B **Publicly Held**
WEB: www.deere.com
SIC: 5083 Farm & garden machinery
PA: Deere & Company
1 John Deere Pl
Moline IL 61265
309 765-8000

(G-14187)
DELIGHT TB INDIANA LLC
P.O. Box 780023 (67278-0023)
PHONE..................................561 301-6257
Andrew Krumholz,
EMP: 500
SALES (est): 4.2MM **Privately Held**
SIC: 8741 Restaurant management

(G-14188)
DELTA DENTAL OF KANSAS INC (PA)
1619 N Waterfront Pkwy (67206-6602)
P.O. Box 789769 (67278-9769)
PHONE..................................316 264-4511
Michael Herbert, *CEO*
Linda Branter, *CEO*
Dean Newton, *Managing Dir*
Michael Fowler, *Counsel*
Keith Asplund, *Vice Pres*
EMP: 81
SQ FT: 40,000
SALES: 305.3MM **Privately Held**
SIC: 6324 Dental insurance

(G-14189)
DELTA ELECTRIC CO INC
2442 S Saint Francis St (67216-1099)
PHONE..................................316 267-2869
Alex Whittit Jr, *President*
James Whittit, *Vice Pres*
EMP: 25
SQ FT: 3,200
SALES: 6MM **Privately Held**
WEB: www.deltaelectricco.com
SIC: 1731 General electrical contractor

(G-14190)
DELTA UPSILON HOUSE CORP (PA)
Also Called: Delta Upsilon Fraternity
1720 N Vassar Ave (67208-2006)
PHONE..................................316 295-4320
Mathew Wedel, *President*
Zach Kettenan, *Treasurer*
Ashley Martin, *Comms Dir*
Ryan King, *Exec Dir*
Nicole Belinsky, *Director*
EMP: 27
SALES (est): 622.3K **Privately Held**
SIC: 8641 University club

(G-14191)
DEN MANAGEMENT CO INC (PA)
4053 E Navajo Ln (67210-1542)
P.O. Box 47719 (67201-7719)
PHONE..................................316 686-1964
David Norris, *CEO*
Michael Porch, *Vice Pres*
EMP: 110
SQ FT: 25,000
SALES (est): 10.4MM **Privately Held**
SIC: 1711 8711 8741 Mechanical contractor; engineering services; management services

(G-14192)
DENNIS P WETTA
200 W Douglas Ave Ste 830 (67202-3008)
PHONE..................................316 267-5293
Dennis Wetta, *Owner*
EMP: 11
SALES (est): 389.7K **Privately Held**
SIC: 8111 General practice attorney, lawyer

(G-14193)
DENTAL ASSOCIATES W WICHITA PA
444 N Ridge Rd (67212-6574)
PHONE..................................316 942-5358
Jeff Miles, *Principal*
Dr David Hall, *Principal*
Dr Sabina May, *Principal*
EMP: 40
SALES (est): 2.9MM **Privately Held**
WEB: www.dentalassociatesks.com
SIC: 8021 Dentists' office

(G-14194)
DENTAL CORNER
2046 N Oliver Ave (67208-2503)
PHONE..................................316 681-2425
Jay Warren Hildreth, *Owner*
EMP: 23
SQ FT: 600
SALES (est): 1MM **Privately Held**
WEB: www.dentalcorner.com
SIC: 8021 Dentists' office

(G-14195)
DEPARTMENT OF KANSAS DISABLED (PA)
5455 E Central Ave (67208-4133)
P.O. Box 16261 (67216-0261)
PHONE..................................316 681-1948
Franklin Bergquise, *Exec Dir*
EMP: 42
SALES (est): 413.1K **Privately Held**
SIC: 8611 Business associations

(G-14196)
DEPEW GLLEN RTHBUN MCINTEER LC
8301 E 21st St N Ste 450 (67206-2936)
PHONE..................................316 262-4000
Jack McInteer, *Counsel*
Kimberly Green, *Manager*
Lon Smith, *Exec Dir*
Dennis Gillen, *Executive*
Janet Stucky, *Legal Staff*
EMP: 17
SALES (est): 1.9MM **Privately Held**
WEB: www.depewgillen.com
SIC: 8111 General practice law office

GEOGRAPHIC

(G-14197)
DEPT LINCOLN SERVICE
Also Called: Davis Moore Lincoln
7675 E Kellogg Dr (67207-1613)
PHONE..................................316 928-7331
Shawn Muth, *General Mgr*
EMP: 25
SALES (est): 164.4K **Privately Held**
SIC: 5511 7538 Automobiles, new & used; general automotive repair shops

(G-14198)
DERMATOLOGY CLINIC
835 N Hillside St (67214-4913)
PHONE..................................316 685-4395
Steven Passman, *Owner*
EMP: 30
SALES (est): 1MM **Privately Held**
WEB: www.dermclin.com
SIC: 8011 Dermatologist

(G-14199)
DESERT STEEL CORPORATION
Also Called: Desert Steel Company
312 N Mosley St (67202-2812)
PHONE..................................316 282-2244
Jason McClintock, *President*
Eric Carroll, *Vice Pres*
Richard Turner, *Vice Pres*
Angie Carroll, *Sales Staff*
Shelly Stilger, *Manager*
▲ **EMP:** 15
SQ FT: 15,000
SALES (est): 3MM **Privately Held**
SIC: 5712 3524 Customized furniture & cabinets; lawn & garden mowers & accessories

(G-14200)
DESIGN BENEFITS
404 S Holland St Ste 2 (67209-2169)
PHONE..................................316 729-7676
Jim Jasnoski, *Owner*
Kevin Gustafson, *Marketing Mgr*
Rachael Osman, *Office Admin*
Theresa Higgins, *Administration*
EMP: 10
SALES (est): 920.8K **Privately Held**
SIC: 8742 6411 Financial consultant; insurance agents, brokers & service

(G-14201)
DESIGNBUILD CONSTRUCTION INC
2822 N Mead St (67219-4241)
PHONE..................................316 722-8180
Louis Eftink, *President*
David Jones, *Vice Pres*
Steve Gillespie, *Treasurer*
Robin Roberts, *Sales Dir*
EMP: 35
SALES: 5MM **Privately Held**
SIC: 1542 Commercial & office building, new construction; commercial & office building contractors

(G-14202)
DEVELOPERS AND MANAGEMENT INC (PA)
11800 W Kellogg St (67209-1243)
PHONE..................................316 682-6770
James March, *President*
Daniel Delahanty, *Treasurer*
Emmet Blaes, *Admin Sec*
EMP: 27
SQ FT: 2,000
SALES (est): 3.6MM **Privately Held**
SIC: 6719 Personal holding companies, except banks

(G-14203)
DEVLIN ENTERPRISES INC
1313 N Webb Rd Ste 100 (67206-4070)
P.O. Box 782170 (67278-2170)
PHONE..................................316 634-1800
Thomas R Devlin, *President*
David C Nesbitt, *Executive*
EMP: 16 **EST:** 1977
SQ FT: 11,000
SALES (est): 2MM **Privately Held**
WEB: www.devlinenterprises.net
SIC: 7359 Equipment rental & leasing

(G-14204)
DEVLIN MANAGEMENT INC
1313 N Webb Rd Ste 100 (67206-4070)
PHONE..................................316 634-1800
David Nesbitt, *President*
Tom Mack, *Vice Pres*
EMP: 14
SQ FT: 11,000
SALES (est): 2.1MM **Privately Held**
SIC: 6282 8741 Investment counselors; business management

(G-14205)
DEVORE & SONS INC
Also Called: Hertel Bible Publishers
9020 E 35th St N (67226-2017)
P.O. Box 780189 (67278-0189)
PHONE..................................316 267-3211
Ross Devore, *President*
William Devore, *Chairman*
Mark Brosz, *Sales Executive*
EMP: 25
SQ FT: 40,000
SALES (est): 6.4MM **Privately Held**
WEB: www.devoreandsons.com
SIC: 2731 Books: publishing & printing

(G-14206)
DEWAAY FINANCIAL NETWORK LLC
245 N Waco St Ste 525 (67202-1154)
PHONE..................................316 303-1985
Don Dewaay, *Branch Mgr*
EMP: 11 **Privately Held**
SIC: 6029 Commercial banks
PA: Dewaay Financial Network, L.L.C.
13001 University Ave
Clive IA

(G-14207)
DHL EXPRESS (USA) INC
2163 S Air Cargo Rd (67209-2177)
PHONE..................................316 943-7683
Scott Ewert, *Branch Mgr*
EMP: 11
SALES (corp-wide): 68.2B **Privately Held**
SIC: 4513 Air courier services
HQ: Dhl Express (Usa), Inc.
1210 S Pine Island Rd
Plantation FL 33324
954 888-7000

(G-14208)
DIAMOND ENGINEERING COMPANY
3512 W Pawnee St (67213-1887)
P.O. Box B (67213)
PHONE..................................316 943-5701
Chad Hinton, *Branch Mgr*
EMP: 50
SALES (corp-wide): 11.9MM **Privately Held**
SIC: 1623 Water & sewer line construction
PA: The Diamond Engineering Company
1521 W Anna St
Grand Island NE 68801
308 382-8362

(G-14209)
DIAMOND SECURITY LC
220 W Douglas Ave Ste 150 (67202-3104)
PHONE..................................316 263-3883
W Michael Hartup, *Partner*
John M Rayburn, *Partner*
EMP: 40
SQ FT: 1,500
SALES: 700K **Privately Held**
SIC: 7381 Security guard service

(G-14210)
DIGGS CONSTRUCTION COMPANY
Also Called: Diggs Holding Company
3101 E 9th St N (67214-3253)
P.O. Box 2742 (67201-2742)
PHONE..................................316 691-1255
Dale G Diggs Jr, *President*
Corelia Diggs, *Admin Sec*
EMP: 30
SALES (est): 4.3MM **Privately Held**
WEB: www.diggsbuilds.com
SIC: 1542 1541 Commercial & office building, new construction; commercial & office buildings, renovation & repair; industrial buildings, new construction; renovation, remodeling & repairs: industrial buildings

(G-14211)
DIGITAL OFFICE SYSTEMS INC
530 S Hydraulic St (67211-2749)
PHONE..................................316 262-7700
Kenneth Brasted, *COO*
Brian Wilbert, *CFO*
Tara Wilbert, *Human Resources*
Tj Stewart, *Accounts Mgr*
Rosalie Schroeder, *Marketing Staff*
EMP: 36
SQ FT: 20,000
SALES (est): 10.3MM **Privately Held**
WEB: www.digitalofficesys.com
SIC: 5044 Office equipment

(G-14212)
DINNING BEARD INC (HQ)
Also Called: Prudential
12021 E 13th St N Ste 100 (67206-2844)
PHONE..................................316 636-1115
Williams Keihle, *President*
G Barry West, *President*
Jane Doughty, *Vice Pres*
Mona Stein, *Vice Pres*
Linda Sloan, *Manager*
EMP: 10
SQ FT: 10,000
SALES (est): 4.8MM
SALES (corp-wide): 62.9B **Publicly Held**
WEB: www.prugo.com
SIC: 6531 Real estate agent, residential
PA: Prudential Financial, Inc.
751 Broad St
Newark NJ 07102
973 802-6000

(G-14213)
DIRECT MAIL PRINTERS INC
231 S Ida St (67211-1507)
PHONE..................................316 263-1855
Randy Brown, *President*
Neil Holley, *President*
Steve Ukena, *Marketing Staff*
Toby Brown, *Admin Sec*
Zach Ferris, *Analyst*
EMP: 11 **EST:** 1952
SQ FT: 6,000
SALES (est): 629.4K **Privately Held**
WEB: www.dmprinters.com
SIC: 2752 7331 Commercial printing, offset; direct mail advertising services

(G-14214)
DIRTY WORK
2077 S Capri Ln (67207-5209)
PHONE..................................316 652-9104
EMP: 12
SALES (est): 200K **Privately Held**
SIC: 7363 Help Supply Services

(G-14215)
DIVERSIFIED FAMILY SVCS LLC
Also Called: Loving Touch Home Healthcare
1631 E 17th St N Ste 100 (67214-1612)
PHONE..................................316 269-3368
Carrie Williams, *President*
EMP: 60
SALES (est): 1.6MM **Privately Held**
SIC: 8082 Home health care services

(G-14216)
DOC GRENS GOURMET SALADS GRILL
10096 E 13th St N Ste 102 (67206-2670)
PHONE..................................316 636-8997
Scott Kuthan, *Manager*
EMP: 11
SALES (est): 256K **Privately Held**
SIC: 5812 6794 Sandwiches & submarines shop; franchises, selling or licensing

(G-14217)
DOCS FRIENDS INC
1788 S Airport Rd (67209)
P.O. Box 771089 (67277-1089)
PHONE..................................316 943-3246
Jeffrey Turner, *Ch of Bd*
EMP: 14
SQ FT: 30,000
SALES: 4.4MM **Privately Held**
SIC: 8412 Museum

(G-14218)
DOCUFORCE INC (PA)
6435 E 34th St N 109 (67226-2525)
PHONE..................................316 636-5400
Michael E Ward, *President*
Kenneth Botts, *Vice Pres*
Dawn Marx, *Controller*
EMP: 15
SALES (est): 2.6MM **Privately Held**
WEB: www.rkblackkansas.com
SIC: 5044 Office equipment

(G-14219)
DOCUMENT RESOURCES INC (HQ)
707 E 33rd St N (67219-4009)
PHONE..................................316 683-1444
David J Kreller, *President*
EMP: 17 **EST:** 1998
SALES (est): 3.1MM
SALES (corp-wide): 18.8MM **Privately Held**
SIC: 7389 Document storage service
PA: Underground Vaults & Storage, Inc.
906 N Halstead St
Hutchinson KS 67501
620 662-6769

(G-14220)
DOCUPLEX INC
Also Called: Copyrite Printing
630 N Pennsylvania Ave (67214-4157)
PHONE..................................316 262-2662
Gerald K Ewy, *President*
Jay C Ewy, *Vice Pres*
Anita Schmidt, *Mfg Staff*
Brent Hardin, *Accounts Mgr*
Jim Hudson, *Accounts Mgr*
EMP: 20
SQ FT: 5,000
SALES (est): 4.8MM **Privately Held**
WEB: www.docu-plex.com
SIC: 2752 7334 Commercial printing, offset; photocopying & duplicating services

(G-14221)
DOLD FOODS LLC
2929 N Ohio St (67219-4320)
P.O. Box 4339 (67204-0339)
PHONE..................................316 838-9101
Al Lieberum, *President*
Terry Hadden, *Plant Mgr*
Brad Blum, *Purch Mgr*
Michael Scott, *Plant Engr*
Gary J Ray, *Director*
EMP: 250
SALES (est): 29.8MM
SALES (corp-wide): 9.5B **Publicly Held**
WEB: www.hormel.com
SIC: 2011 2013 Bacon, slab & sliced from meat slaughtered on site; hams & picnics from meat slaughtered on site; sausages & other prepared meats
PA: Hormel Foods Corporation
1 Hormel Pl
Austin MN 55912
507 437-5611

(G-14222)
DOMINION MANAGEMENT SVCS INC
Also Called: Cashpoint Car Title Loans
240 S West St Ste H (67213-2116)
PHONE..................................571 408-4770
EMP: 11
SALES (corp-wide): 3.8MM **Privately Held**
SIC: 6141 Automobile loans, including insurance
PA: Dominion Management Services, Inc.
240 S West St Ste H
Wichita KS 67213
703 765-2274

(G-14223)
DOMINION MANAGEMENT SVCS INC (PA)
Also Called: Cash Point
240 S West St Ste H (67213-2116)
PHONE.....703 765-2274
Michael H Lester, *President*
EMP: 12
SALES (est): 3.8MM **Privately Held**
SIC: 6141 Automobile loans, including insurance

(G-14224)
DON KLAUSMEYER CNSTR LLC
10008 W York St (67215-8945)
PHONE.....316 554-0001
Don Klaus-Meyer, *Mng Member*
EMP: 25
SALES (est): 2.9MM **Privately Held**
WEB: www.klausmeyer.com
SIC: 1521 1531 New construction, single-family houses; speculative builder, single-family houses

(G-14225)
DONALD B SCRAFFORD
Also Called: Grene Vision Group
3607 N Ridge Rd (67205-1230)
PHONE.....316 721-2701
EMP: 20
SALES (est): 93K **Privately Held**
SIC: 8011 Medical Doctor's Office

(G-14226)
DONDLINGER & SONS CNSTR CO INC (PA)
2656 S Sheridan Ave (67217-1341)
P.O. Box 398 (67201-0398)
PHONE.....316 945-0555
Thomas Dondlinger, *President*
Raymond Dondlinger, *General Mgr*
Greg Phillips, *Corp Secy*
James Dondlinger, *Vice Pres*
Martin C Dondlinger Jr, *Vice Pres*
EMP: 151
SQ FT: 20,000
SALES: 119.1MM **Privately Held**
WEB: www.alliedcrane.net
SIC: 1622 1541 1542 Bridge construction; industrial buildings, new construction; warehouse construction; commercial & office building contractors

(G-14227)
DONDLINGER & SONS CNSTR CO INC
3201 W Casado St (67217-1309)
P.O. Box 398 (67201-0398)
PHONE.....316 943-9393
Ed Helten, *Branch Mgr*
EMP: 12
SALES (est): 843.7K
SALES (corp-wide): 119.1MM **Privately Held**
WEB: www.alliedcrane.net
SIC: 1522 Residential construction
PA: Dondlinger & Sons Construction Co., Inc.
2656 S Sheridan Ave
Wichita KS 67217
316 945-0555

(G-14228)
DONDLINGER COMPANIES INC
2656 S Sheridan Ave (67217-1341)
P.O. Box 398 (67201-0398)
PHONE.....316 945-0555
Thomas Dondlinger, *President*
James Dondlinger, *Vice Pres*
Raymond Dondlinger, *Vice Pres*
Jeff Mullen, *CFO*
EMP: 99
SQ FT: 22,000
SALES (est): 3.1MM **Privately Held**
SIC: 8741 Construction management

(G-14229)
DORMAKABA USA INC
734 S Washington Ave (67211-2426)
PHONE.....316 267-6891
Lance Parr, *Branch Mgr*
EMP: 6
SQ FT: 1,000
SALES (corp-wide): 2.8B **Privately Held**
WEB: www.doorcontrolsinc.com
SIC: 3429 Builders' hardware
HQ: Dormakaba Usa Inc.
100 Dorma Dr
Reamstown PA 17567
717 336-3881

(G-14230)
DOUBLE TREE HILTON
2098 S Airport Rd (67209-1941)
PHONE.....316 945-5272
Michael Phipps, *General Mgr*
Traci Montgomery, *General Mgr*
Paul Ades, *Opers Staff*
Carla Forbes, *Controller*
Kendrick Tucker, *Financial Analy*
EMP: 16 **EST:** 2012
SALES (est): 1MM **Privately Held**
SIC: 7011 Resort hotel

(G-14231)
DOUGLAS V OXLER DDS
900 N Tyler Rd Ste 2 (67212-3249)
PHONE.....316 722-2596
Douglas V Oxler DDS, *President*
EMP: 10
SALES (est): 1.1MM **Privately Held**
SIC: 8021 Dentists' office

(G-14232)
DOUGLAS WEBB CO LP
Also Called: Fairfield Inn
333 S Webb Rd (67207-1305)
PHONE.....316 685-3777
Karl Kahihikolo, *Manager*
EMP: 17
SALES (est): 1.3MM **Privately Held**
SIC: 7011 Hotels & motels
PA: Douglas Webb Co Lp
1522 S Florence St
Wichita KS 67209

(G-14233)
DOUGLAS WEBB LLC
333 S Webb Rd (67207-1305)
PHONE.....316 685-0333
Phillip Ruffin, *Mng Member*
EMP: 18
SALES (est): 501K **Privately Held**
SIC: 1522 Hotel/motel & multi-family home construction

(G-14234)
DOWNING & LAHEY INC
6555 E Central Ave (67206-1924)
PHONE.....316 733-2740
Jack Morris, *CEO*
Thomas R Morris, *President*
Marlane Morris, *Corp Secy*
EMP: 18
SQ FT: 12,000
SALES (est): 1.6MM **Privately Held**
WEB: www.downinglahey.com
SIC: 7261 Funeral home

(G-14235)
DOWNTOWN STATION
330 W 2nd St N (67202-9998)
PHONE.....316 267-7747
Ralph Brown, *Manager*
EMP: 80
SALES (est): 2.1MM **Privately Held**
SIC: 7389 Post office contract stations

(G-14236)
DRAFTING ROOM INC
Also Called: Central Forms & Printing
1608 E Central Ave (67214-4134)
PHONE.....316 267-2291
Lee D Greiving, *President*
EMP: 5
SQ FT: 4,000
SALES (est): 626.7K **Privately Held**
SIC: 2759 5113 5049 Commercial printing; bags, paper & disposable plastic; drafting supplies

(G-14237)
DREAM WAVES LLC
6803 W Taft Ave Ste 401 (67209-2365)
PHONE.....316 942-9283
EMP: 13
SALES (est): 330K **Privately Held**
SIC: 7231 Beauty Shop

(G-14238)
DRS ALLEY AND BRAMMER LC
1601 N Willow Ln (67208-2426)
PHONE.....316 265-0856
Fax: 316 265-0988
EMP: 16
SALES (est): 1.2MM **Privately Held**
SIC: 8021 Dentist's Office

(G-14239)
DRURY HOTELS COMPANY LLC
Also Called: Drury Plaza Hotel Broadview
400 W Douglas Ave (67202-2902)
PHONE.....316 267-1961
Greg Dumars, *Vice Pres*
Ira Harrison, *Production*
Bob Mills, *Treasurer*
Scott Ragatz, *Branch Mgr*
Tyson McGreer, *City Mgr*
EMP: 50
SALES (corp-wide): 389.3MM **Privately Held**
SIC: 7011 Hotels
PA: Drury Hotels Company, Llc
721 Emerson Rd Ste 400
Saint Louis MO 63141
314 429-2255

(G-14240)
DRYWALL SUPPLY
3420 N Ohio St (67219-3720)
PHONE.....316 269-3304
Larry Higgins, *President*
Duane Williams, *Opers Mgr*
Mark Smith, *Sales Staff*
EMP: 11
SQ FT: 16,000
SALES (est): 3.9MM **Privately Held**
SIC: 5032 1742 Drywall materials; drywall

(G-14241)
DRYWALL SYSTEMS INC (PA)
3919 S West St (67217-3807)
PHONE.....316 832-0233
Lawrence Higgins, *Ch of Bd*
Dale Meyer, *COO*
Matt Lashley, *Safety Dir*
Anderson Montgomery, *Opers Mgr*
Steven Mc Callum, *Financial Exec*
EMP: 58
SQ FT: 10,000
SALES (est): 26.9MM **Privately Held**
WEB: www.drywallsystemsks.com
SIC: 1742 Drywall

(G-14242)
DRYWALL SYSTEMS INC
3901 S West St (67217-3807)
PHONE.....316 260-9411
Randy Ogborn, *Branch Mgr*
EMP: 160
SALES (corp-wide): 26.9MM **Privately Held**
SIC: 1793 Glass & glazing work
PA: Drywall Systems, Inc.
3919 S West St
Wichita KS 67217
316 832-0233

(G-14243)
DUDLEY WILLIAMS AND ASSOC PA
230 S Laura Ave Ste 206 (67211-1530)
PHONE.....316 263-7591
Ronald Brown, *President*
Mark McAfee, *Vice Pres*
Vicki Boone, *Office Mgr*
EMP: 13
SQ FT: 2,250
SALES (est): 1.6MM **Privately Held**
WEB: www.dwase.com
SIC: 8711 Structural engineering; designing: ship, boat, machine & product

(G-14244)
DUGAN TRUCK LINE LLC (PA)
3520 S Hoover Rd (67215-1213)
P.O. Box 771380 (67277-1380)
PHONE.....316 946-5985
Ken Case, *Sales Mgr*
John Dugan, *Mng Member*
Glenn Dugan,
EMP: 15
SQ FT: 2,000
SALES (est): 25MM **Privately Held**
SIC: 4213 Trucking, except local

(G-14245)
DURASAFE PRODUCTS INC
Also Called: Oil Field Shelters
1380 S Bebe St (67209-2608)
PHONE.....316 942-3282
Keith Wiggins Jr, *President*
EMP: 12
SALES (est): 1MM **Privately Held**
WEB: www.durasafestalls.com
SIC: 5999 0752 Canvas products; animal specialty services

(G-14246)
DYNAMIC CONTROL SYSTEMS INC
450 S Greenwood St (67211-1820)
P.O. Box 48803 (67201-8803)
PHONE.....316 262-2525
Michael Keys, *President*
Mike Keys, *General Mgr*
Rita Abney, *Manager*
EMP: 11
SALES: 1.6MM **Privately Held**
SIC: 3822 Auto controls regulating residntl & coml environmt & applncs

(G-14247)
DYNAMIC DRYWALL INC
3921 N Bridgeport Cir (67219-3300)
P.O. Box 780787 (67278-0787)
PHONE.....316 945-7087
Randall G Salyer, *President*
Roger Roper, *President*
Ryan Nelson, *Vice Pres*
EMP: 85
SALES (est): 8.5MM **Privately Held**
SIC: 1742 Drywall

(G-14248)
DYNAMIC MACHINE LLC
202 W 11th St N (67203-3809)
PHONE.....316 941-4005
Huy Huynh,
Lydia Nguyen,
EMP: 12
SQ FT: 8,600
SALES: 207.7K **Privately Held**
SIC: 3728 Aircraft parts & equipment

(G-14249)
E & J RENTAL & LEASING INC
Also Called: Dollar Sales
8535 W Kellogg Dr (67209-1846)
P.O. Box 12203 (67277-2203)
PHONE.....316 721-0442
David Johnson, *President*
EMP: 10
SALES (est): 699.1K **Privately Held**
SIC: 7514 5511 7299 Rent-a-car service; automobiles, new & used; valet parking

(G-14250)
EAGLE ENVIRONMENTAL SVCS LLC
5909 W Harry St (67209-2930)
P.O. Box 771106 (67277-1106)
PHONE.....316 944-2445
Star Troyer, *CEO*
John Troyer,
EMP: 21 **EST:** 1999
SQ FT: 4,000
SALES: 2MM **Privately Held**
WEB: www.eagleks.com
SIC: 7349 7389 7699 1799 Cleaning service, industrial or commercial; chemical cleaning services; building cleaning service; telephone services; tank truck cleaning service; waste cleaning services; construction site cleanup; exterior cleaning, including sandblasting; hazardous waste transport; liquid transfer services

(G-14251)
EAGLEMED LLC (HQ)
6601 W Pueblo Dr (67209-2926)
P.O. Box 708, West Plains MO (65775-0708)
PHONE.....316 613-4855
Larry Bugg, *Mng Member*
Dewayne Kimbrough,
EMP: 34
SALES (est): 15.5MM **Privately Held**
SIC: 4522 Ambulance services, air

GEOGRAPHIC

(G-14252)
EARLY LEARNING CENTER
9333 E Douglas Ave (67207-1203)
PHONE..................................316 685-2059
Sherry Syakhasone, *Director*
EMP: 10
SALES (est): 213.4K **Privately Held**
SIC: 8641 Youth organizations

(G-14253)
EAST HEIGHTS UNITED METHDST CH
4407 E Douglas Ave (67218-1009)
PHONE..................................316 682-6518
J C Kelley, *Pastor*
Charles Claycomb, *Pastor*
Moira Lee Murfin, *Director*
EMP: 26
SQ FT: 30,000
SALES (est): 1.7MM **Privately Held**
WEB: www.ehumc.org
SIC: 8661 8351 Methodist Church; child day care services

(G-14254)
EASY CREDIT AUTO SALES INC
3101 S Broadway Ave (67216-1021)
PHONE..................................316 522-3279
Samuel F Hudson, *President*
Jerod Heimen, *Managing Prtnr*
Jeff Heimen, *Corp Secy*
EMP: 20
SQ FT: 1,200
SALES (est): 3.6MM **Privately Held**
SIC: 5521 5012 Automobiles, used cars only; automobiles

(G-14255)
EASY MONEY PAWN SHOP INC
Also Called: Hand Controls & Van Lifts
2525 S Oliver St (67210-1200)
PHONE..................................316 687-2727
Elliott Werbin, *President*
Elliot Werbin, *Owner*
EMP: 7
SQ FT: 11,000
SALES (est): 398.6K **Privately Held**
SIC: 5932 5511 5261 5082 Pawnshop; trucks, tractors & trailers: new & used; lawnmowers & tractors; contractors' materials; tires, used; wheelchair lifts

(G-14256)
EBY CORPORATION (PA)
2525 E 36th Cir N (67219-2303)
PHONE..................................316 268-3500
James R Greir III, *Ch of Bd*
James R Grier III, *Ch of Bd*
Michael A Grier, *President*
Kurt T Grier, *Exec VP*
Kurt Grier, *Exec VP*
EMP: 13
SALES: 93.2MM **Privately Held**
SIC: 1629 1623 1622 1541 Dam construction; dock construction; waterway construction; waste water & sewage treatment plant construction; sewer line construction; bridge construction; tunnel construction; industrial buildings, new construction; warehouse construction; commercial & office building, new construction; heavy construction equipment rental

(G-14257)
ECI ELECTRICAL CONTRACTORS
Also Called: E C I
4009 W Saint Louis Ave (67212-2142)
PHONE..................................316 722-0204
Ken Syler, *President*
Alan Kline, *Admin Sec*
EMP: 10
SALES (est): 980K **Privately Held**
SIC: 1731 General electrical contractor

(G-14258)
ECK & ECK MACHINE COMPANY INC
4606 W Harry St (67209-2738)
PHONE..................................316 942-5924
Paul A Eck, *President*
Brad Somes, *General Mgr*
Bettie L Eck, *Vice Pres*
EMP: 36 **EST:** 1966
SQ FT: 34,500
SALES (est): 9.2MM **Privately Held**
WEB: www.eckeck.com
SIC: 3728 Aircraft assemblies, subassemblies & parts

(G-14259)
EDISON OPERATING COMPANY LLC
1625 N Waterfront Pkwy (67206-6621)
PHONE..................................316 201-1744
EMP: 5
SALES (est): 757.1K **Privately Held**
SIC: 1382 Oil & gas exploration services

(G-14260)
EDMISTON OIL COMPANY INC (PA)
125 N Market St Ste 1420 (67202-1714)
PHONE..................................316 265-5241
Jon M Callen, *President*
Kathlien E Massey, *Vice Pres*
Kelly E Callen, *Admin Sec*
EMP: 10
SALES (est): 2.2MM **Privately Held**
SIC: 1311 Crude petroleum production

(G-14261)
EDWARD ROSE & SONS LLC
Also Called: Stoney Pointe Apartment
2925 N Boulder Dr (67226-3148)
PHONE..................................316 202-3920
EMP: 16 **EST:** 2002
SALES (est): 118.3K
SALES (corp-wide): 1.1MM **Privately Held**
SIC: 1741 Masonry & other stonework
PA: Edward Rose & Sons
31170 Wellington Dr
Novi MI 48377
248 669-5490

(G-14262)
EDWARDS COUNTY GAS COMPANY
Also Called: Great Plains
1710 N Waterfront Pkwy (67206-6603)
PHONE..................................316 682-3022
John Wear, *Partner*
Diana Richeky, *Office Mgr*
EMP: 12
SQ FT: 500
SALES (est): 2.2MM **Privately Held**
SIC: 4923 Gas transmission & distribution

(G-14263)
ELEC-TRON INC
2050 E Northern St (67216-2485)
PHONE..................................316 522-3401
Rose A Rohleder, *President*
Lowell Wiebe, *Vice Pres*
EMP: 57
SQ FT: 30,000
SALES: 7.6MM **Privately Held**
SIC: 3644 3613 3643 3575 Terminal boards; fuse clips & blocks, electric; control panels, electric; current-carrying wiring devices; computer terminals; manufactured hardware (general)

(G-14264)
ELECTRI TECH
11828 E Lewis St (67207-1424)
PHONE..................................316 683-2841
Scott Kelley, *Owner*
EMP: 11
SALES (est): 1.3MM **Privately Held**
SIC: 1731 General electrical contractor

(G-14265)
ELECTRICAL SYSTEMS INC
1815 S Pattie St (67211-4428)
PHONE..................................316 263-2415
David Dauffenbach, *President*
EMP: 13
SQ FT: 2,500
SALES (est): 2.1MM **Privately Held**
SIC: 1731 General electrical contractor

(G-14266)
ELECTROMECH TECHNOLOGIES LLC (DH)
2600 S Custer Ave (67217-1324)
PHONE..................................316 941-0400
Randy Fayette, *Opers Mgr*
Jay Belling, *Production*
Billie Buchana, *Senior Buyer*
Bryce Childs, *Buyer*
Tracy Diaz, *Buyer*
▲ **EMP:** 341
SALES (est): 59.3MM
SALES (corp-wide): 5.2B **Publicly Held**
WEB: www.tyeeair.com
SIC: 3441 Fabricated structural metal
HQ: Mckechnie Aerospace Investments, Inc.
20 Pacifica Ste 200
Irvine CA
859 887-6200

(G-14267)
ELECTROMECH TECHNOLOGIES LLC
2600 S Custer Ave (67217-1324)
PHONE..................................316 941-0400
EMP: 139
SALES (corp-wide): 5.2B **Publicly Held**
WEB: www.tyeeair.com
SIC: 3441 Fabricated structural metal
HQ: Electromech Technologies Llc
2600 S Custer Ave
Wichita KS 67217
316 941-0400

(G-14268)
ELECTRONIC SENSORS INC
Also Called: Level Devil
2063 S Edwards St (67213-1808)
PHONE..................................316 267-2807
Gerald Rues, *President*
Odetta H Howard, *Corp Secy*
John L Howard, *Vice Pres*
Jerry Rues, *Manager*
EMP: 15
SQ FT: 4,000
SALES (est): 3.7MM **Privately Held**
WEB: www.leveldevil.com
SIC: 3699 8742 Electrical equipment & supplies; management consulting services

(G-14269)
ELITE CLEANERS
6161 E 13th St N (67208-2653)
P.O. Box 950411, Oklahoma City OK (73195-0411)
PHONE..................................316 651-5997
Don Tennock, *Owner*
EMP: 12
SQ FT: 2,800
SALES (est): 454.9K **Privately Held**
SIC: 7216 Cleaning & dyeing, except rugs

(G-14270)
ELITE TRANSPORTATION LLC
200 W Douglas Ave Ste 520 (67202-3005)
PHONE..................................316 295-4829
Elvis Lindquist, *Mng Member*
EMP: 25
SALES (est): 6.6MM **Privately Held**
SIC: 4213 4731 Less-than-truckload (LTL) transport; freight forwarding; domestic freight forwarding

(G-14271)
ELITEGEAR4UCOM LLC
3242 W 13th St N Ste 500 (67203-6659)
PHONE..................................316 993-4398
Christopher White, *Mng Member*
EMP: 5
SALES: 1.1MM **Privately Held**
SIC: 2759 3469 Decals: printing; automobile license tags, stamped metal

(G-14272)
ELLIS GRUBB MARTENS COML GROUP (PA)
435 S Broadway Ave (67202-3909)
PHONE..................................316 262-0000
Steven Martens, *President*
EMP: 35
SALES (est): 1.9MM **Privately Held**
WEB: www.martenscos.com
SIC: 6531 6411 6512 8742 Real estate managers; selling agent, real estate; escrow agent, real estate; appraiser, real estate; real estate insurance agents; commercial & industrial building operation; real estate consultant

(G-14273)
EMBERHOPE INC
Also Called: Youthville
4505 E 47th St S (67210-1651)
P.O. Box 210, Newton (67114-0210)
PHONE..................................316 529-9100
Donna Rozell, *Manager*
EMP: 200
SALES (corp-wide): 8MM **Privately Held**
SIC: 8361 Residential care for children
PA: Emberhope, Inc.
900 W Broadway St
Newton KS 67114
316 529-9100

(G-14274)
EMERALD AEROSPACE HOLDINGS LLC
4174 S Oliver St (67210-2127)
PHONE..................................316 440-6966
Ahmed Bashir, *CEO*
Larry Pope, *VP Bus Dvlpt*
EMP: 99
SALES (est): 273.5K **Privately Held**
SIC: 3721 4581 3812 1799 Aircraft; hangars & other aircraft storage facilities; defense systems & equipment; renovation of aircraft interiors

(G-14275)
EMERALD AEROSPACE SERVICES LLC
Also Called: Eas
4174 S Oliver St (67210-2127)
PHONE..................................316 644-4284
Michael Kaufhold, *President*
EMP: 50
SQ FT: 80,000
SALES (est): 1.6MM **Privately Held**
SIC: 3812 1799 3724 8711 Airspeed instrumentation (aeronautical instruments); defense systems & equipment; renovation of aircraft interiors; research & development on aircraft engines & parts; aviation &/or aeronautical engineering

(G-14276)
EMERGENCY SERVICES PA
550 N Hillside St (67214-4910)
PHONE..................................316 962-2239
Rodney Staats, *President*
EMP: 40
SALES (est): 4.5MM **Privately Held**
SIC: 3842 8011 Prosthetic appliances; offices & clinics of medical doctors

(G-14277)
EMMIS COMMUNICATIONS CORP
Also Called: Ksnc-Tv2
833 N Main St (67203-3606)
PHONE..................................620 793-7868
Shawn Oswald, *Sales/Mktg Mgr*
EMP: 12
SALES (corp-wide): 114.1MM **Publicly Held**
WEB: www.emmis.com
SIC: 4832 Radio broadcasting stations
PA: Emmis Communications Corp
40 Monument Cir Ste 700
Indianapolis IN 46204
317 266-0100

(G-14278)
EMPAC INC
300 W Douglas Ave Ste 930 (67202-2912)
PHONE..................................316 265-9922
Gordan W Rogers, *CEO*
Blake Buhrman, *Counsel*
EMP: 12
SQ FT: 2,000
SALES: 1MM **Privately Held**
WEB: www.empac-eap.com
SIC: 8631 8331 Employees' association; community service employment training program

(G-14279)
EMPLOYERS MUTUAL CASUALTY CO
Also Called: EMC Insurance Companies
245 N Waco St Ste 330 (67202-1116)
P.O. Box 1739 (67201-1739)
PHONE..................................316 352-5700
Brian Walker, *Marketing Staff*

Mike Akin, *Branch Mgr*
Lynn Broadhurst, *Underwriter*
Kasey Haley, *Underwriter*
Judi Winter, *Underwriter*
EMP: 178
SALES (corp-wide): 1.1B **Privately Held**
SIC: 6411 6321 6311 6519 Insurance agents; reinsurance carriers, accident & health; life insurance carriers; real property lessors
PA: Employers Mutual Casualty Company
717 Mulberry St
Des Moines IA 50309
515 280-2511

(G-14280)
EMPRISE BANK (HQ)
257 N Broadway Ave (67202-2315)
P.O. Box 247 (67201-0247)
PHONE..................................316 383-4400
Matthew Michaelis, *Ch of Bd*
Trey Cunningham, *President*
Tom Page, *President*
Susan Fra Koslowsky, *Vice Chairman*
Lora Barry, *Exec VP*
EMP: 60 **EST:** 1910
SQ FT: 16,000
SALES: 87.1MM
SALES (corp-wide): 80MM **Privately Held**
WEB: www.emprisebank.com
SIC: 6022 State trust companies accepting deposits, commercial
PA: Emprise Financial Corporation
211 N Broadway Ave
Wichita KS 67202
316 264-8394

(G-14281)
EMPRISE BANK
2140 N Woodlawn St (67208-1842)
PHONE..................................316 383-4301
Trish Guse, *Branch Mgr*
EMP: 11
SALES (corp-wide): 80MM **Privately Held**
SIC: 6022 State trust companies accepting deposits, commercial
HQ: Emprise Bank
257 N Broadway Ave
Wichita KS 67202
316 383-4400

(G-14282)
EMPRISE BANK
2323 S Hydraulic St (67211-5297)
PHONE..................................316 264-1569
Neil Dickson, *Branch Mgr*
EMP: 11
SALES (corp-wide): 80MM **Privately Held**
SIC: 6022 State commercial banks
HQ: Emprise Bank
257 N Broadway Ave
Wichita KS 67202
316 383-4400

(G-14283)
EMPRISE BANK
11111 E Harry St (67207-5035)
PHONE..................................316 689-0717
Tom Page, *Branch Mgr*
EMP: 11
SALES (corp-wide): 80MM **Privately Held**
SIC: 6022 State commercial banks
HQ: Emprise Bank
257 N Broadway Ave
Wichita KS 67202
316 383-4400

(G-14284)
EMPRISE BANK
Also Called: Westlink Branch
8807 W Central Ave (67212-3803)
PHONE..................................316 383-4498
Margie McFrederick, *Branch Mgr*
EMP: 10
SALES (corp-wide): 80MM **Privately Held**
WEB: www.emprisebank.com
SIC: 6022 State trust companies accepting deposits, commercial
HQ: Emprise Bank
257 N Broadway Ave
Wichita KS 67202
316 383-4400

(G-14285)
EMPRISE BANK
2433 S Seneca St (67217-2801)
PHONE..................................316 383-4131
Justine Moore, *Manager*
EMP: 10
SALES (corp-wide): 80MM **Privately Held**
WEB: www.emprisebank.com
SIC: 6022 State commercial banks
HQ: Emprise Bank
257 N Broadway Ave
Wichita KS 67202
316 383-4400

(G-14286)
ENCORE RECEIVABLE MGT INC
4600 W Kellogg Dr Ste 200 (67209-2544)
PHONE..................................913 782-3333
Doug Jones, *President*
EMP: 1000
SALES (est): 42MM
SALES (corp-wide): 20B **Publicly Held**
WEB: www.encorermi.com
SIC: 7322 Adjustment & collection services
HQ: Convergys Customer Management Group Inc.
201 E 4th St Bsmt
Cincinnati OH 45202
513 723-6104

(G-14287)
ENDOSCOPIC SERVICES PA
1431 S Bluffview Dr # 215 (67218-3000)
PHONE..................................316 687-0234
Jace W Hyder MD, *CEO*
EMP: 17
SQ FT: 2,600
SALES (est): 1.7MM **Privately Held**
SIC: 8011 Ambulatory surgical center

(G-14288)
ENGINEERED DOOR PRODUCTS INC
1040 S Santa Fe St (67211-2436)
PHONE..................................316 267-1984
Michelle Winter, *President*
Wayne Winter, *President*
Mack Hudson, *Manager*
EMP: 15
SQ FT: 52,000
SALES (est): 5.4MM **Privately Held**
WEB: www.engineereddoor.com
SIC: 5031 5072 Doors; builders' hardware

(G-14289)
ENGINEERED MACHINE TOOL CO
2950 S All Hallows St (67217-1053)
PHONE..................................316 942-6147
Tim Pohlenz, *President*
Timothy Pohlenz, *President*
Lyle Sherbon, *Vice Pres*
EMP: 10
SQ FT: 16,000
SALES: 1.8MM **Privately Held**
WEB: www.emtco.com
SIC: 3599 Custom machinery

(G-14290)
ENSIGNAL INC (PA)
800 E 1st St N Ste 240 (67202-2740)
PHONE..................................316 265-8311
Greg Reed, *President*
Dan McKenzie, *COO*
Heath Parsons, *Info Tech Mgr*
EMP: 23
SALES: 25MM **Privately Held**
WEB: www.ensignal.net
SIC: 4812 Cellular telephone services

(G-14291)
ENTERCOM COMMUNICATIONS CORP
Also Called: K E Y N FM
9111 E Douglas Ave # 130 (67207-1241)
PHONE..................................316 685-2121
Jackie Wise, *General Mgr*
Jack Oliver, *Director*
EMP: 55
SALES (corp-wide): 1.4B **Publicly Held**
WEB: www.entercom.com
SIC: 4832 Radio broadcasting stations, music format
PA: Entercom Communications Corp.
2400 Market St Fl 4
Philadelphia PA 19103
610 660-5610

(G-14292)
ENTERTAINMENT ENTERPRISES INC
Also Called: Cotillion Ballroom, The
905 N Stratford Ln (67206-1458)
PHONE..................................316 722-4201
Richard H Leslie, *President*
Catherine Leslie, *Vice Pres*
Ryan Stevenson, *Manager*
EMP: 30
SQ FT: 28,500
SALES (est): 1.2MM **Privately Held**
WEB: www.thecotillion.com
SIC: 7911 Dance hall or ballroom operation

(G-14293)
ENVISION INC
610 N Main St Ste 400 (67203-3619)
PHONE..................................316 440-1600
Michael Monteferrante, *Branch Mgr*
▲ **EMP:** 20
SALES (corp-wide): 207.3MM **Privately Held**
SIC: 8011 Clinic, operated by physicians
PA: Envision, Inc.
610 N Main St Ste 400
Wichita KS 67203
316 440-1500

(G-14294)
ENVISION INC
Also Called: Envision Print
2301 S Water St (67213-4819)
PHONE..................................316 425-7123
Fred Cabala, *Manager*
EMP: 14
SALES (corp-wide): 207.3MM **Privately Held**
WEB: www.envisionus.com
SIC: 2673 2676 Plastic bags: made from purchased materials; towels, paper: made from purchased paper
PA: Envision, Inc.
610 N Main St Ste 400
Wichita KS 67203
316 440-1500

(G-14295)
ENVISION INC
2050 S Edwards St Ste B (67213-1866)
PHONE..................................316 440-3737
Linda Merrill, *Manager*
EMP: 30
SALES (corp-wide): 207.3MM **Privately Held**
WEB: www.envisionus.com
SIC: 2711 Commercial printing & newspaper publishing combined
PA: Envision, Inc.
610 N Main St Ste 400
Wichita KS 67203
316 440-1500

(G-14296)
ENVISION INDUSTRIES INC
2301 S Water St (67213-4819)
PHONE..................................316 267-2244
Michael Monteferrante, *President*
Mark Eaton, *CFO*
EMP: 80
SALES: 19.3MM
SALES (corp-wide): 207.3MM **Privately Held**
SIC: 2752 2673 Business form & card printing, lithographic; plastic bags: made from purchased materials
PA: Envision, Inc.
610 N Main St Ste 400
Wichita KS 67203
316 440-1500

(G-14297)
EPISCOPAL SOCIAL SERVICES INC
Also Called: Breakthrough
1010 N Main St (67203-3609)
P.O. Box 670 (67201-0670)
PHONE..................................316 269-4160
Barb Andres, *CEO*
Denise Hinson, *President*
Phil Richardson, *Vice Pres*
Gail Johnson, *Treasurer*
Sharon Atherton, *Admin Sec*
EMP: 29
SQ FT: 20,000
SALES: 1.3MM **Privately Held**
WEB: www.esswichita.org
SIC: 8322 Social service center

(G-14298)
EPRO SERVICES INC (PA)
1328 E Kellogg Dr Ste 1 (67211-2672)
P.O. Box 347, Derby (67037-0347)
PHONE..................................316 262-2513
David M Polk, *President*
William S Osterman, *Vice Pres*
Peter Grant, *VP Mktg*
Bob Couch, *Manager*
Phyllis Jane Polk, *Admin Sec*
◆ **EMP:** 14 **EST:** 1993
SQ FT: 2,200
SALES (est): 3.1MM **Privately Held**
SIC: 2851 2899 Paints, asphalt or bituminous; paints, waterproof; waterproofing compounds

(G-14299)
EQUITY BANK NA (HQ)
7701 E Kellogg Dr Ste 300 (67207-1708)
P.O. Box 730, Andover (67002-0730)
PHONE..................................316 612-6000
Brad Elliott, *CEO*
Lori Kelley, *President*
David King, *President*
Jeremy Machain, *President*
Joshua Means, *President*
EMP: 10
SQ FT: 10,000
SALES: 182MM **Publicly Held**
WEB: www.equitywebbank.com
SIC: 6021 National commercial banks

(G-14300)
ERIC FISHER SALON (PA)
2441 N Maize Rd Ste 113 (67205-7948)
PHONE..................................316 729-0777
Eric Fisher, *Owner*
EMP: 12
SALES (est): 864.6K **Privately Held**
WEB: www.ericfishersalon.com
SIC: 7231 Unisex hair salons

(G-14301)
ERIN IS HOPE FOUNDATION INC
Also Called: Pollard Licklider Clinic
4921 E 21st St N (67208-1602)
PHONE..................................316 681-3204
Judy Pollard-Licklider, *President*
EMP: 25
SALES: 1.2MM **Privately Held**
SIC: 8049 Speech pathologist

(G-14302)
ERNST & YOUNG LLP
Also Called: Ey
1625 N Waterfront Pkwy # 170 (67206-6633)
PHONE..................................316 636-4900
Judith Duggan, *Manager*
EMP: 228
SALES (corp-wide): 4.2B **Privately Held**
WEB: www.ey.com
SIC: 8721 Certified public accountant
PA: Ernst & Young Llp
5 Times Sq Fl Conlv1
New York NY 10036
212 773-3000

(G-14303)
ERNSTMANN MACHINE CO INC
151 S Westfield St (67209-1442)
PHONE..................................316 943-5282
William H Riggins, *President*
EMP: 6
SQ FT: 7,200

GEOGRAPHIC

SALES (est): 676.5K **Privately Held**
WEB: www.ernstmannmachine.com
SIC: 3599 5084 Machine shop, jobbing & repair; industrial machinery & equipment

(G-14304)
ESA P PRTFOLIO OPER LESSEE LLC
Also Called: Extended Stay America, Inc.
9450 E Corporate Hills Dr (67207-1321)
PHONE..................................316 652-8844
Selexte Horynack, *Branch Mgr*
EMP: 10
SALES (corp-wide): 1.2B **Publicly Held**
WEB: www.extendedstayhotels.com
SIC: 7011 Hotels & motels
HQ: Esa P Portfolio Operating Lessee, Llc
11525 N Community House R
Charlotte NC 28277
980 345-1600

(G-14305)
ESTATES UNLIMITED INC
Also Called: Laurence Volbrecht and Assoc
310 S Ellis St (67211-1810)
PHONE..................................316 262-7600
Fax: 316 262-4207
EMP: 15
SALES (corp-wide): 1.4MM **Privately Held**
SIC: 6531 Real Estate Agent
PA: Estates Unlimited Inc
733 N Baltimore Ave
Derby KS
316 788-6717

(G-14306)
ESTES EXPRESS LINES INC
3838 S Gold St (67217-3606)
PHONE..................................316 554-0864
Ellen Crowll, *Branch Mgr*
EMP: 58
SALES (corp-wide): 3.1B **Privately Held**
WEB: www.estes-express.com
SIC: 4213 Contract haulers
PA: Estes Express Lines
3901 W Broad St
Richmond VA 23230
804 353-1900

(G-14307)
ETEZAZI INDUSTRIES INC
2101 E 21st St N (67214-1942)
PHONE..................................316 831-9937
Amir Etezazi, *CEO*
Masoud Etezazi, *President*
EMP: 29
SQ FT: 20,000
SALES: 19.1MM **Privately Held**
SIC: 3728 Aircraft assemblies, subassemblies & parts

(G-14308)
ETHANOL PRODUCTS LLC
Also Called: Poet Ethanol Products
3939 N Webb Rd (67226-8100)
PHONE..................................316 303-1380
Garry Shanks, *Business Mgr*
Corey Bevan, *Opers Staff*
Bob Whiteman, *CFO*
Damaris Hubbell, *Controller*
Gloria Carrell, *Accountant*
EMP: 245
SQ FT: 29,000
SALES (est): 221.8MM **Privately Held**
WEB: www.ethanolproducts.com
SIC: 5172 5169 Gasoline; alcohols
PA: Poet, Llc
4615 N Lewis Ave
Sioux Falls SD 57104

(G-14309)
EUROPEAN WAX CENTER
10096 E 13th St N Ste 122 (67206-2668)
PHONE..................................316 425-0909
David Petty, *Owner*
EMP: 14
SALES (est): 31.4K **Privately Held**
SIC: 7231 Beauty shops

(G-14310)
EVANS INDUSTRIES INC
Also Called: Evans Ceramic Supply
1518 S Washington Ave (67211-3336)
P.O. Box 654 (67201-0654)
PHONE..................................316 262-2551
Donald E Evans, *President*
Kennenth B Evans, *Treasurer*
Cindy Buentello, *Admin Sec*
EMP: 6
SQ FT: 30,000
SALES (est): 850K **Privately Held**
WEB: www.evansceramics.com
SIC: 5092 5193 3999 5945 Arts & crafts equipment & supplies; artificial flowers; artificial flower arrangements; ceramics supplies

(G-14311)
EVCON HOLDINGS INC (DH)
3110 N Mead St (67219-4057)
P.O. Box 19014 (67204-9014)
PHONE..................................316 832-6300
Al Rodriquez, *Controller*
EMP: 20
SALES (est): 3.2MM **Privately Held**
SIC: 3585 5074 Heating equipment, complete; air conditioning units, complete: domestic or industrial; fireplaces, prefabricated
HQ: York International Corporation
631 S Richland Ave
York PA 17403
717 771-7890

(G-14312)
EVEN TEMP OF WICHITA INC
Also Called: Disrigadan Craftman
216 S Commerce St (67202-4604)
PHONE..................................316 469-5321
Howard McDaniel, *President*
Jana McDaniel, *Vice Pres*
EMP: 15
SQ FT: 15,000
SALES: 2.5MM **Privately Held**
WEB: www.eventemp.com
SIC: 5075 1711 7623 Air conditioning & ventilation equipment & supplies; heating & air conditioning contractors; refrigeration repair service

(G-14313)
EVENT ELEMENTS LLC
230 S Topeka Ave (67202-4308)
PHONE..................................316 440-2829
Brandy Zoglmean, *Principal*
▲ **EMP:** 9
SALES (est): 1.1MM **Privately Held**
SIC: 2819 Industrial inorganic chemicals

(G-14314)
EVENT SYSTEMS INC
811 E 10th St N (67214-3017)
P.O. Box 49101 (67201-9101)
PHONE..................................316 641-1848
Joshua D Gordon, *President*
EMP: 10
SQ FT: 40,000
SALES: 900K **Privately Held**
SIC: 8741 Management services

(G-14315)
EVERGY KANSAS CENTRAL INC
100 N Broadway Ave # 800 (67202-2212)
PHONE..................................316 299-7155
Amy Honer, *Branch Mgr*
EMP: 11
SALES (corp-wide): 4.2B **Publicly Held**
SIC: 4911 Electric services
HQ: Evergy Kansas Central, Inc.
818 S Kansas Ave
Topeka KS 66612
785 575-6300

(G-14316)
EW & 7 PRODUCTS LLC
300 W Murdock St (67203-3926)
PHONE..................................316 440-7486
Chad Hessen, *Plant Mgr*
Jayme Regier, *Parts Mgr*
Haylie Corcoran, *Manager*
Emily Strong, *Manager*
Barry Wilson,
EMP: 15
SALES (est): 2.7MM **Privately Held**
SIC: 2591 Drapery hardware & blinds & shades

(G-14317)
EW SCRIPPS COMPANY
Also Called: Kfdi FM
4200 N Old Lawrence Rd (67219-3211)
P.O. Box 1402 (67201-1402)
PHONE..................................316 436-1045
Eric McCart, *General Mgr*
EMP: 50
SALES (corp-wide): 1.2B **Publicly Held**
WEB: www.journalbroadcastgroup.com
SIC: 4832 7313 Radio broadcasting stations; radio advertising representative
PA: The E W Scripps Company
312 Walnut St Ste 2800
Cincinnati OH 45202
513 977-3000

(G-14318)
EXACTA AEROSPACE INC
4200 W Harry St (67209-2730)
PHONE..................................316 941-4200
Bonnie Voegeli, *CEO*
Randall Voegeli, *President*
Craig Bakel, *CTO*
Mark Vancamp, *CTO*
▲ **EMP:** 160 **EST:** 1979
SQ FT: 175,000
SALES (est): 41.9MM
SALES (corp-wide): 225.3B **Publicly Held**
WEB: www.exactaaerospace.com
SIC: 3599 3728 Machine shop, jobbing & repair; aircraft parts & equipment
HQ: Precision Castparts Corp.
4650 Sw Mcdam Ave Ste 300
Portland OR 97239
503 946-4800

(G-14319)
EXALTIA LLC
Also Called: Intra Care
8415 E 21st St N Ste 100 (67206-2959)
PHONE..................................316 616-6200
Tim Buchanan,
EMP: 13
SALES (est): 1.3MM **Privately Held**
SIC: 4813

(G-14320)
EXECUTIVES INC
Also Called: Executive Inn
250 N Rock Rd Ste 300 (67206-2263)
PHONE..................................316 685-8131
Harry Pollack, *President*
Darrel Schmidt, *General Mgr*
EMP: 14
SALES (est): 361.8K **Privately Held**
SIC: 7011 Motels

(G-14321)
EXHIBIT ARTS LLC
326 N Athenian Ave (67203-5737)
PHONE..................................316 264-2915
Elizabeth Harshfield, *President*
Vernon Harshfield, *President*
Christie Thorton, *Project Mgr*
Scott Nicholson, *Opers Staff*
Melissa Huntley, *CFO*
EMP: 42
SQ FT: 32,000
SALES (est): 9.2MM **Privately Held**
WEB: www.exhibitarts.net
SIC: 7363 4225 8742 4226 Temporary help service; general warehousing & storage; management consulting services; special warehousing & storage; facilities support services

(G-14322)
EXPERT AUTO CENTER
Also Called: Auto Maintenance Expert
5230 E Central Ave (67208-4111)
PHONE..................................316 440-6600
Faissal Abou-Faissal, *Sales Staff*
EMP: 15
SALES (est): 587.4K **Privately Held**
SIC: 7538 General automotive repair shops

(G-14323)
EXPLORATION PLACE INC
300 N Mclean Blvd (67203-5901)
PHONE..................................316 660-0600
Janice Luth, *President*
Rick Cain, *Facilities Mgr*
Christina Bluml, *Marketing Staff*
Chaille Blount, *Director*
Lynn Corona, *Director*
EMP: 68
SQ FT: 100,000
SALES: 7MM **Privately Held**
WEB: www.exploration.org
SIC: 8412 Museum

(G-14324)
EXTENDED STAY AMERICA
9450 E Corporate Hills Dr (67207-1321)
PHONE..................................316 652-8844
Fax: 316 652-8882
EMP: 10
SALES (est): 170.4K **Privately Held**
SIC: 7011 Hotel/Motel Operation

(G-14325)
EXTREME TANNING INC (PA)
Also Called: E T I
10646 W Central Ave # 110 (67212-5181)
PHONE..................................316 712-0190
Matthieu C Smith, *President*
EMP: 10
SQ FT: 6,295
SALES (est): 759.6K **Privately Held**
SIC: 7299 7231 4813 Tanning salon; beauty shops;

(G-14326)
EYE ASSOCIATES OF WICHITA
4600 W Kellogg Dr Ste 215 (67209-2546)
PHONE..................................316 943-0433
Carla J Mosteller, *Owner*
EMP: 10
SALES (est): 1.1MM **Privately Held**
SIC: 8042 5995 Specialized optometrists; contact lenses, prescription

(G-14327)
EYE CARE ASSOCIATES
321 S Hillside St (67211-2130)
PHONE..................................316 685-1898
Phillip Ernzen, *President*
Rebecca H Hawk, *Principal*
Jason Eubank, *Med Doctor*
EMP: 11
SALES (est): 917.5K **Privately Held**
SIC: 8042 Specialized optometrists

(G-14328)
EYE SURGERY CENTER WICHITA LLC
Also Called: Team Vision Surgery Center
6100 E Central Ave Ste 5 (67208-4237)
PHONE..................................316 681-2020
Phillip A Clendenin, *President*
Patricia Kusnerus, *Principal*
Judy Williams, *Purch Dir*
Samuel Amstutz, *Med Doctor*
Lacey Vogts,
EMP: 30
SALES (est): 2.4MM **Privately Held**
SIC: 8011 Surgeon

(G-14329)
F G HOLL COMPANY LLC (PA)
9431 E Central Ave # 100 (67206-2563)
PHONE..................................316 684-8481
Margery Nagel, *Financial Exec*
Margery L Nagel, *Manager*
Jacqueline Nagel,
EMP: 9 **EST:** 1926
SALES (est): 1.5MM **Privately Held**
SIC: 1311 Crude petroleum production; natural gas production

(G-14330)
FACC SOLUTIONS INC
800 E 37th St N (67219-3512)
PHONE..................................316 425-4040
John Pasquale, *President*
Steve Clamp, *Principal*
Manuel Taverne, *Director*
EMP: 5
SALES (est): 1.3MM
SALES (corp-wide): 43.3B **Privately Held**
SIC: 3724 7389 Aircraft engines & engine parts; interior designer
HQ: Facc Ag
FischerstraBe 9
Ried Im Innkreis 4910
596 160-

(G-14331)
FACIAL EXPRESSIONS LLC
1025 S Stagecoach St (67230-9106)
PHONE.....316 390-0417
Carmen Trissal, *Branch Mgr*
EMP: 10
SALES (corp-wide): 350.3K **Privately Held**
SIC: 7231 Facial salons
PA: Facial Expressions, Llc
109 W Central Ave
Andover KS 67002
316 295-3887

(G-14332)
FAGRON COMPOUNDING SVCS LLC
Also Called: Fagron Sterile Services
8710 E 34th St N (67226-2636)
PHONE.....316 773-0405
Brian Williamson, *President*
Steve Strickland, *Principal*
Gregory Rockers, *Vice Pres*
Kirsten Van Bockstaele, *Vice Pres*
EMP: 40
SQ FT: 49,000
SALES (est): 6.3MM **Privately Held**
SIC: 2834 Water, sterile: for injections

(G-14333)
FAIRBANK EQUIPMENT INC (PA)
3700 W Jewell St (67213-1217)
P.O. Box 13237 (67213-0237)
PHONE.....316 943-2247
Cody Wray, *President*
Tammy L Keith, *Corp Secy*
Billie M Wray, *Vice Pres*
Scott Depriest, *Marketing Staff*
Chris May, *Manager*
EMP: 27 **EST:** 1969
SQ FT: 12,000
SALES (est): 25.6MM **Privately Held**
WEB: www.fairbankequipment.com
SIC: 5085 5083 Industrial supplies; agricultural machinery & equipment

(G-14334)
FAIRFIELD INN BY MARRTT WICHTA
333 S Webb Rd (67207-1305)
PHONE.....316 685-3777
Webb Douglas, *Director*
EMP: 23
SALES (est): 888.1K **Privately Held**
SIC: 7011 Hotels & motels

(G-14335)
FAIRMOUNT TECHNOLOGIES LLC
Also Called: Cncform
1845 Fairmount St 35 (67260-9700)
PHONE.....316 978-3313
Vis Madhavan, *Partner*
Mahdi S Kashani, *General Mgr*
Mahdi Saket-Kashani, *General Mgr*
Hal Pluenneke, *Mktg Dir*
EMP: 11
SALES (est): 643.8K **Privately Held**
SIC: 8731 Commercial physical research

(G-14336)
FALCON ENTERPRISES INC
1520 S Tyler Rd (67209-1851)
PHONE.....727 579-1233
Steve Holtje, *President*
William Barnes, *Vice Pres*
EMP: 140
SQ FT: 44,000
SALES (est): 10.5MM **Privately Held**
WEB: www.falcongraphix.com
SIC: 2759 Screen printing; decals: printing

(G-14337)
FAMILY HLTH RHBLTATION CTR LLC
639 S Maize Ct (67209-1337)
PHONE.....316 425-5600
Fred Hermes, *Mng Member*
EMP: 84
SALES: 8MM **Privately Held**
SIC: 8051 Convalescent home with continuous nursing care

(G-14338)
FAMILY MEDICINE EAST CHARTERED
Also Called: Heartland Research
1709 S Rock Rd (67207-5150)
PHONE.....316 689-6630
Terry Poling, *President*
Tom Kline, *Corp Secy*
Terry Kline, *Vice Pres*
Becky Reheis, *Office Mgr*
Vickie Jackson, *Manager*
EMP: 30
SALES (est): 6.4MM **Privately Held**
WEB: www.familymedicineeast.com
SIC: 8011 General & family practice, physician/surgeon

(G-14339)
FARHA CONSTRUCTION INC
303 S Broadway Ave # 100 (67202-4311)
PHONE.....316 943-0000
Edward Frank Farha, *President*
Ed Farha, *President*
Ted Farha, *Corp Secy*
Ted A Farha Jr, *Vice Pres*
EMP: 45 **EST:** 1978
SQ FT: 7,000
SALES (est): 9.7MM **Privately Held**
SIC: 1521 Single-family housing construction

(G-14340)
FARM BUR PROPERTY CSLTY INSUR
Also Called: Farm Bureau Insurance
300 W Douglas Ave (67202-2916)
PHONE.....316 978-9950
Adam Jones, *Branch Mgr*
EMP: 21 **Publicly Held**
SIC: 6411 Insurance agents
HQ: Farm Bureau Property & Casualty Insurance Company
5400 University Ave
West Des Moines IA 50266
515 225-5400

(G-14341)
FARM BUREAU MUTL INSUR CO INC
Also Called: E. Wichita Claims Office
7421 E 21st St N (67206-1072)
PHONE.....316 652-1800
Jack Holowell, *Manager*
EMP: 11
SALES (corp-wide): 137.3MM **Privately Held**
SIC: 6411 Insurance claim processing, except medical
PA: The Farm Bureau Mutual Insurance Company Inc
2627 Kfb Plz
Manhattan KS 66503
785 587-6000

(G-14342)
FARMERS GROUP INC
Also Called: Farmers Insurance
12627 E Central Ave # 301 (67206-2838)
PHONE.....316 682-4500
Eric Sigg, *Manager*
EMP: 35
SALES (corp-wide): 48.2B **Privately Held**
WEB: www.farmers.com
SIC: 6411 Insurance agents, brokers & service
HQ: Farmers Group, Inc.
6301 Owensmouth Ave
Woodland Hills CA 91367
323 932-3200

(G-14343)
FARMERS GROUP INC
Also Called: Farmers Insurance
7230 W 13th St N Ste 4 (67212-2982)
PHONE.....316 263-4927
EMP: 32
SALES (corp-wide): 68.4B **Privately Held**
SIC: 6411 Ins Agnts And Brkrs
HQ: Farmers Group, Inc.
6301 Owensmouth Ave
Woodland Hills CA 91367
323 932-3200

(G-14344)
FAST PRINT
Also Called: Fast Print of Wichita
7710 E Harry St (67207-3130)
PHONE.....316 688-1242
Patrick M Doom, *Partner*
Linda Doom, *Partner*
EMP: 6 **EST:** 1975
SQ FT: 2,400
SALES (est): 774K **Privately Held**
WEB: www.fastprintkansas.com
SIC: 2752 Commercial printing, offset

(G-14345)
FASTENAIR CORPORATION
10800 E Central Ave (67206-2597)
PHONE.....316 684-2875
John Stanley, *President*
EMP: 28
SQ FT: 17,000
SALES (est): 5.1MM **Privately Held**
SIC: 3728 Aircraft parts & equipment

(G-14346)
FEDERAL DEPOSIT INSURANCE CORP
Also Called: F D I C
2118 N Tyler Rd Ste 100d (67212-4919)
PHONE.....316 729-0301
Richard Urban, *Manager*
EMP: 21
SALES (corp-wide): 11.6B **Privately Held**
WEB: www.fdic.gov
SIC: 6399 9311 Federal Deposit Insurance Corporation (FDIC); finance, taxation & monetary policy;
PA: Federal Deposit Insurance Corporation
550 17th St Nw
Washington DC 20429
877 275-3342

(G-14347)
FEDERAL EXPRESS CORPORATION
Also Called: Fedex
2073 S Air Cargo Rd (67209-1959)
PHONE.....316 941-4438
EMP: 54
SALES (corp-wide): 69.6B **Publicly Held**
WEB: www.federalexpress.com
SIC: 4212 Local trucking, without storage
HQ: Federal Express Corporation
3610 Hacks Cross Rd
Memphis TN 38125
901 369-3600

(G-14348)
FEDEX FREIGHT CORPORATION
3560 S Maize Rd (67215-8904)
PHONE.....800 426-0104
EMP: 90
SALES (corp-wide): 69.6B **Publicly Held**
SIC: 4213 4215 Trucking, except local; courier services, except by air
HQ: Fedex Freight Corporation
1715 Aaron Brenner Dr
Memphis TN 38120

(G-14349)
FEDEX GROUND PACKAGE SYS INC
5180 N Industry Dr (67226-2339)
PHONE.....800 463-3339
Rachel Kirkendoll, *Commercial*
EMP: 66
SALES (corp-wide): 69.6B **Publicly Held**
WEB: www.fedex.com
SIC: 4215 Courier services, except by air
HQ: Fedex Ground Package System, Inc.
1000 Fed Ex Dr
Coraopolis PA 15108
800 463-3339

(G-14350)
FEDEX OFFICE & PRINT SVCS INC
3605 N Rock Rd Ste 111 (67226-1368)
PHONE.....316 636-5443
EMP: 20
SALES (corp-wide): 69.6B **Publicly Held**
WEB: www.kinkos.com
SIC: 7334 Photocopying & duplicating services
HQ: Fedex Office And Print Services, Inc.
7900 Legacy Dr
Plano TX 75024
800 463-3339

(G-14351)
FEDEX OFFICE & PRINT SVCS INC
7701 E Kellogg Dr Ste 200 (67207-1717)
PHONE.....316 682-1327
Kristopher Shogren, *Manager*
EMP: 15
SALES (corp-wide): 69.6B **Publicly Held**
WEB: www.kinkos.com
SIC: 7334 Photocopying & duplicating services
HQ: Fedex Office And Print Services, Inc.
7900 Legacy Dr
Plano TX 75024
800 463-3339

(G-14352)
FEDEX OFFICE & PRINT SVCS INC
240 S West St Ste 10a (67213-2116)
PHONE.....316 941-9909
EMP: 15
SALES (corp-wide): 69.6B **Publicly Held**
WEB: www.kinkos.com
SIC: 7334 2789 Photocopying & duplicating services; bookbinding & related work
HQ: Fedex Office And Print Services, Inc.
7900 Legacy Dr
Plano TX 75024
800 463-3339

(G-14353)
FEDEX OFFICE & PRINT SVCS INC
2441 N Maize Rd Ste 2507 (67205-7949)
PHONE.....316 721-6529
EMP: 34
SALES (corp-wide): 69.6B **Publicly Held**
SIC: 7334 Photocopying & duplicating services
HQ: Fedex Office And Print Services, Inc.
7900 Legacy Dr
Plano TX 75024
800 463-3339

(G-14354)
FENIX COMPANY INCORPORATED
Also Called: Fenix Heating & Cooling
802 W 2nd St N (67203-6005)
PHONE.....316 945-4842
Luke Parhemer, *President*
Robert A Prigmore, *Corp Secy*
EMP: 25
SQ FT: 13,500
SALES (est): 4.4MM **Privately Held**
WEB: www.fenixheat.com
SIC: 1711 Warm air heating & air conditioning contractor

(G-14355)
FERGUSON ENTERPRISES LLC
Also Called: Ferguson 216
2222 W Harry St (67213-2970)
PHONE.....316 262-0681
Jeremy Zellers, *Branch Mgr*
Josh Peterson, *Branch Mgr*
EMP: 25
SALES (corp-wide): 20.7B **Privately Held**
WEB: www.ferguson.com
SIC: 5074 5999 Plumbing fittings & supplies; heating equipment (hydronic); plumbing & heating supplies
HQ: Ferguson Enterprises, Llc
12500 Jefferson Ave
Newport News VA 23602
757 874-7795

(G-14356)
FERGUSON PAVING INC
3600 W Esthner Ave (67213-1215)
PHONE.....316 942-3374
Wayne J Ferguson, *President*
Beniteo San Roman, *Vice Pres*
EMP: 15
SQ FT: 3,600
SALES (est): 1.3MM **Privately Held**
SIC: 1611 Concrete construction: roads, highways, sidewalks, etc.; highway & street paving contractor

(G-14357)
FERGUSON-PHILLIPS LLC
Also Called: Ferguson-Phillips Homeware
4801 E Douglas Ave (67218-1013)
PHONE..................................316 612-4663
Brenda S Kauffman-Cody, *President*
Jeff Cody, *Vice Pres*
Maureen Scheer, *Sales Staff*
Brenda Cody, *Mng Member*
EMP: 10 **EST:** 2000
SALES (est): 1MM **Privately Held**
WEB: www.fergusonphillips.com
SIC: 5712 5021 Furniture stores; furniture

(G-14358)
FERROLOY INC
515 E 29th St N (67219-4109)
PHONE..................................316 838-0897
Mark Soucie, *President*
Richard Hicks, *COO*
John Rockey, *Vice Pres*
Philla Smith, *Administration*
EMP: 35
SQ FT: 26,000
SALES (est): 8.4MM **Privately Held**
SIC: 3321 3398 3471 Gray iron castings; metal heat treating; plating & polishing

(G-14359)
FETAL WELL-BEING LLC
9300 E 29th St N Ste 102 (67226-3007)
PHONE..................................316 644-8919
David Grainger, *Principal*
EMP: 5
SALES (est): 198.4K **Privately Held**
SIC: 3841 Diagnostic apparatus, medical

(G-14360)
FH KAYSING COMPANY LLC (PA)
1950 S Florence St (67209-2833)
P.O. Box 12497 (67277-2497)
PHONE..................................316 721-8980
Tammi Buss, *Auditor*
Winnie Hilger, *Accounts Mgr*
Jeanie Metzen, *Mng Member*
Jan Albertin, *Info Tech Mgr*
Mary Sapien, *Director*
EMP: 30
SQ FT: 10,000
SALES (est): 5.4MM **Privately Held**
WEB: www.fhkaysing.com
SIC: 4731 Customhouse brokers

(G-14361)
FHR BIOFUELS & INGREDIENTS LLC (DH)
4111 E 37th St N (67220-3203)
PHONE..................................316 828-2400
Bradley J Razook,
EMP: 6
SALES (est): 2.4MM
SALES (corp-wide): 40.6B **Privately Held**
SIC: 2869 Ethanolamines
HQ: Flint Hills Resources, Lp
4111 E 37th St N
Wichita KS 67220
800 292-3133

(G-14362)
FIBER GLASS SYSTEMS LP
2501 S West St (67217-1025)
PHONE..................................316 946-3900
Scott Reichenborn, *Manager*
Paul Rhoten, *Executive*
EMP: 12
SALES (corp-wide): 8.4B **Publicly Held**
WEB: www.fiberglasssystems.com
SIC: 5074 Pipes & fittings, plastic
HQ: Fiber Glass Systems, L.P.
2425 Sw 36th St
San Antonio TX 78237
210 477-7500

(G-14363)
FIDELITY BANK
2251 N Maize Rd Ste 101 (67205-7300)
PHONE..................................316 265-2261
Kimberly Kirk, *Manager*
EMP: 12
SALES (corp-wide): 100.1MM **Privately Held**
SIC: 6022 State commercial banks
HQ: Fidelity Bank
100 E English St
Wichita KS 67202
316 265-2261

(G-14364)
FIDELITY BANK
8442 W 13th St N (67212-2992)
PHONE..................................316 722-1460
EMP: 11
SALES (corp-wide): 100.1MM **Privately Held**
SIC: 6029 Commercial Bank
HQ: Fidelity Bank
100 E English St
Wichita KS 67202
316 265-2261

(G-14365)
FIDELITY MANAGEMENT CORP (DH)
100 E English St Ste 500 (67202-3706)
PHONE..................................316 291-5950
Justin Demel, *President*
M Clark Bastian, *Vice Pres*
Bruce Wilgers, *Treasurer*
Shirley Biggins, *Admin Sec*
EMP: 46
SQ FT: 46,000
SALES (est): 6.6MM
SALES (corp-wide): 100.1MM **Privately Held**
WEB: www.fidelitymgmt.com
SIC: 8741 Management services
HQ: The Fidelity Investment Company
100 E English St
Wichita KS 67202
316 265-2261

(G-14366)
FIGEAC AERO NORTH AMERICA INC
Also Called: National Metal Finishing
9313 E 39th St N (67226-2909)
PHONE..................................316 634-2500
Jean-Claude Maillard, *President*
Jeff Russell, *Vice Pres*
EMP: 81
SQ FT: 64,000
SALES (est): 26.7MM **Privately Held**
WEB: www.sonacanmf.com
SIC: 4581 1721 3728 Aircraft maintenance & repair services; aircraft painting; aircraft body assemblies & parts
PA: Figeac Aero
Zone Industrielle De L
Figeac 46100

(G-14367)
FINANCIAL CONSULTANTS AMERICA
Also Called: Pacific 1 Mortgage
6700 W Central Ave # 110 (67212-6302)
PHONE..................................316 943-7307
Jim Riley, *Owner*
Tracey Lee, *Office Mgr*
EMP: 38
SQ FT: 2,000
SALES (est): 1.4MM **Privately Held**
SIC: 7389 6211 Financial services; investment firm, general brokerage

(G-14368)
FINCH HOLLOW SENIOR RESIDENCES
707 N Golden Hls Apt 101 (67212-6581)
PHONE..................................316 721-9596
Andrew Bias, *CEO*
EMP: 52
SALES: 167.9K **Privately Held**
SIC: 8322 Senior citizens' center or association

(G-14369)
FIRE PROTECTION SERVICES INC
1117 N Santa Fe St (67214-2928)
PHONE..................................316 262-2452
Mark P Carpenter, *President*
EMP: 20
SQ FT: 9,300
SALES (est): 3.4MM **Privately Held**
SIC: 1711 Fire sprinkler system installation

(G-14370)
FIRST AMERICAN TITLE COMPANY
10100 W Maple St (67209-3117)
PHONE..................................316 554-2872
EMP: 24
SALES (corp-wide): 8MM **Privately Held**
SIC: 6541 6411 Title & trust companies;
PA: First American Title Company
727 N Waco Ave Ste 300
Wichita KS 67203
316 267-8371

(G-14371)
FIRST AMERICAN TITLE COMPANY (PA)
727 N Waco Ave Ste 300 (67203-3954)
PHONE..................................316 267-8371
Craig Burns, *Senior VP*
Jennifer B Weas, *Vice Pres*
EMP: 65 **EST:** 1944
SQ FT: 12,000
SALES (est): 8MM **Privately Held**
SIC: 6541 Title abstract offices

(G-14372)
FIRST CHOICE CREDIT UNION (PA)
1401 N Maize Rd (67212-1201)
PHONE..................................316 425-5712
Linda Nicholson, *President*
Gary Howard, *Principal*
EMP: 10
SALES (est): 2.5MM **Privately Held**
SIC: 6062 State credit unions, not federally chartered

(G-14373)
FIRST CLASS HAIR
2260 N Ridge Rd Ste 220 (67205-1130)
PHONE..................................316 721-2662
Danelle Farver, *Owner*
EMP: 10
SALES (est): 135.8K **Privately Held**
SIC: 7231 Hairdressers

(G-14374)
FIRST CON INCORPORATED
3242 W 13th St N Ste 300 (67203-6657)
PHONE..................................316 425-7690
Aaron Heck, *President*
EMP: 10
SALES (est): 1.2MM **Privately Held**
SIC: 1542 Commercial & office building contractors

(G-14375)
FIRST GRADE EXCAVATING INC
430 E 63rd St S (67216-3925)
PHONE..................................316 524-0900
Richard Hancock, *President*
EMP: 10
SALES (est): 950K **Privately Held**
SIC: 1771 Concrete work

(G-14376)
FIRST UNITED METHODIST CHURCH
Also Called: First Untd Methdst Pre-School
330 N Broadway Ave (67202-2370)
PHONE..................................316 263-6244
Cindy Watson, *Pastor*
Kay Sanchez, *Director*
Katrin Enright, *Director*
Tara Dawson, *Assistant*
Tara Novotny, *Assistant*
EMP: 47
SALES (est): 1.5MM **Privately Held**
SIC: 8661 8351 Methodist Church; child day care services

(G-14377)
FISCH BOWL INC
524 S Commerce St (67202-4610)
PHONE..................................316 200-5200
Elizabeth Stevenson, *Principal*
EMP: 13
SALES: 3K **Privately Held**
SIC: 8412 Museums & art galleries

(G-14378)
FISHER RONALD OD PA
Also Called: Drs Fisher & Yarrow PA
2635 W Douglas Ave (67213-2605)
PHONE..................................316 942-7496
Ronald Fisher, *Partner*
EMP: 11
SALES (est): 555.2K **Privately Held**
SIC: 8042 Offices & clinics of optometrists

(G-14379)
FIT PHYSIQUE
Also Called: Acrobatic Academy
2111 N Maize Rd (67212-5207)
PHONE..................................316 721-2230
Barbara Matous, *Partner*
Eric Wilson, *Partner*
EMP: 50 **EST:** 1994
SALES (est): 1.4MM **Privately Held**
WEB: www.acrobaticacademy.com
SIC: 7991 7999 Health club; martial arts school

(G-14380)
FIVE STAR HOTEL MANAGEMENT
Also Called: Hawthorn Suites
411 S Webb Rd (67207-1307)
PHONE..................................316 686-7331
Laura Resor, *Manager*
EMP: 13 **EST:** 2008
SALES (est): 679.1K **Privately Held**
SIC: 7011 Hotels & motels

(G-14381)
FIVE STAR MECHANICAL INC
1707 S Hoover Rd (67209-2813)
PHONE..................................316 943-7827
Jeff Erdman, *President*
Stacey Richards, *Vice Pres*
Drew Schon, *Manager*
Ryan Woodard, *Info Tech Mgr*
EMP: 15
SQ FT: 3,000
SALES (est): 4.4MM **Privately Held**
SIC: 1711 Mechanical contractor

(G-14382)
FLATLAND FOOD DISTRIBUTORS LLC
3930 W 29th St S Ste 90 (67217-1070)
PHONE..................................316 945-5171
Horstdieter Blank,
Kenneth K Blank,
Kristine R Franzen,
EMP: 11
SQ FT: 12,000
SALES (est): 2.6MM **Privately Held**
SIC: 5147 Meats & meat products

(G-14383)
FLATLANDS TRANSPORTATION ICT
3151 N Den Hollow St (67205-8741)
PHONE..................................316 250-1280
Matt Fellows, *Administration*
EMP: 10 **EST:** 2014
SALES (est): 393.6K **Privately Held**
SIC: 4789 Transportation services

(G-14384)
FLEESON GING COULSON KITCH LLC
Also Called: Fleeson.com
301 N Main St Ste 1900 (67202-4819)
P.O. Box 997 (67201-0997)
PHONE..................................316 267-7361
Gregory Stuckey, *Mng Member*
Eric Reusser, *Info Tech Dir*
Ron Campbell,
J Eric Engstrom,
Thomas D Kitch,
EMP: 53
SQ FT: 23,000
SALES (est): 7.4MM **Privately Held**
WEB: www.fleeson.com
SIC: 8111 General practice attorney, lawyer; general practice law office

(G-14385)
FLEETPRIDE INC
Also Called: Power Drive
4401 W Esthner Ave (67209-2718)
PHONE..................................316 942-4227
Jim Carpenter, *Vice Pres*
EMP: 10 **Privately Held**
SIC: 5013 5531 Truck parts & accessories; truck equipment & parts
HQ: Fleetpride, Inc.
600 Las Colinas Blvd E # 400
Irving TX 75039
469 249-7500

(G-14386)
FLEETPRIDE INC
Also Called: Truck Parts & Equipment
4501 W Esthner Ave (67209-2719)
PHONE..............................800 362-2600
EMP: 80 **Privately Held**
SIC: 5013 5531 Truck parts & accessories; truck equipment & parts
HQ: Fleetpride, Inc.
600 Las Colinas Blvd E # 400
Irving TX 75039
469 249-7500

(G-14387)
FLIC LUMINARIES LLC
719 N Brookfield St (67206-1533)
PHONE..............................888 550-3542
David Bayouth, *Manager*
EMP: 10
SALES (est): 180.6K **Privately Held**
SIC: 7389

(G-14388)
FLIGHTSAFETY INTERNATIONAL
Also Called: FLIGHTSAFETY INTERNATIONAL INC
9721 E Central Ave (67206-2507)
PHONE..............................316 612-5300
EMP: 12
SALES (corp-wide): 225.3B **Publicly Held**
SIC: 7363 Pilot service, aviation
HQ: Flightsafety International Inc.
Marine A Trml Lgrdia Arpr
Flushing NY 11371
718 565-4100

(G-14389)
FLIGHTSAFETY INTERNATIONAL INC
Also Called: Cessna Learning Center
1951 S Airport Rd (67209-1950)
PHONE..............................316 220-3200
EMP: 18
SALES (corp-wide): 225.3B **Publicly Held**
SIC: 4581 Airport
HQ: Flightsafety International Inc.
Marine A Trml Lgrdia Arpr
Flushing NY 11371
718 565-4100

(G-14390)
FLINT HILLS RESOURCES LLC (HQ)
8415 E 21st St N Ste 200 (67206-2954)
P.O. Box 2917 (67201-2917)
PHONE..............................316 828-5500
Jeffrey P Ramsey, *CEO*
David Robertson, *President*
Jeremy Ferguson, *General Mgr*
Brett Webb, *General Mgr*
Larry Wielgot, *General Mgr*
◆ **EMP:** 300
SALES (est): 3.2B
SALES (corp-wide): 40.6B **Privately Held**
WEB: www.flinthillsresources.com
SIC: 5169 5084 Industrial chemicals; oil refining machinery, equipment & supplies
PA: Koch Industries, Inc.
4111 E 37th St N
Wichita KS 67220
316 828-5500

(G-14391)
FLINT HILLS RESOURCES CENTRAL (DH)
4111 E 37th St N (67220-3203)
PHONE..............................316 828-5500
Bradley Razook, *President*
EMP: 6
SALES (est): 523.9K
SALES (corp-wide): 40.6B **Privately Held**
SIC: 2911 Gases & liquefied petroleum gases
HQ: Flint Hills Resources, Lp
4111 E 37th St N
Wichita KS 67220
800 292-3133

(G-14392)
FLINT HILLS RESOURCES PORT (DH)
8415 E 21st St N Ste 200 (67206-2954)
P.O. Box 2917 (67201-2917)
PHONE..............................316 828-5500
Phil Gaarder, *Vice Pres*
James Rhame, *Site Mgr*
Barrett Ellis, *Engineer*
Akshay Patil, *Engineer*
Ibrahim Bawi, *Plant Engr*
EMP: 69
SALES (est): 18MM
SALES (corp-wide): 40.6B **Privately Held**
SIC: 2869 Industrial organic chemicals
HQ: Flint Hills Resources, Lp
4111 E 37th St N
Wichita KS 67220
800 292-3133

(G-14393)
FLINT HLLS RSRCES LONGVIEW LLC (DH)
8415 E 21st St N Ste 200 (67206-2954)
P.O. Box 2917 (67201-2917)
PHONE..............................316 828-5500
Jeffrey P Ramsey, *President*
EMP: 14
SALES (est): 8.8MM
SALES (corp-wide): 40.6B **Privately Held**
SIC: 2821 Polyethylene resins
HQ: Flint Hills Resources, Llc
8415 E 21st St N Ste 200
Wichita KS 67206
316 828-5500

(G-14394)
FLOYD MECHANICAL CORPORATION
1635 E 37th St N Ste 4 (67219-3557)
P.O. Box 8211 (67208-0211)
PHONE..............................316 262-3556
Tarrance C Floyd, *President*
Jacqueline Floyd, *Vice Pres*
EMP: 12 **EST:** 1996
SQ FT: 3,000
SALES (est): 1.4MM **Privately Held**
SIC: 1711 Plumbing contractors

(G-14395)
FMC CORPORATION
750 N Socora St Ste 500 (67212-3795)
PHONE..............................316 729-5321
EMP: 91
SALES (corp-wide): 4.7B **Publicly Held**
SIC: 2812 2879 2869 Soda ash, sodium carbonate (anhydrous); agricultural chemicals; pesticides, agricultural or household; insecticides, agricultural or household; fungicides, herbicides; industrial organic chemicals
PA: Fmc Corporation
2929 Walnut St
Philadelphia PA 19104
215 299-6000

(G-14396)
FMS MIDWEST DIALYSIS CTRS LLC
Also Called: Renal Care Group Wichita East
9341 E 21st St N (67206-2927)
PHONE..............................316 634-6760
Jacquie George, *Manager*
EMP: 13
SALES (corp-wide): 18.3B **Privately Held**
WEB: www.bamap.com
SIC: 8092 Kidney dialysis centers
HQ: Fms Midwest Dialysis Centers, Llc
920 Winter St
Waltham MA 02451
781 699-9000

(G-14397)
FMS MIDWEST DIALYSIS CTRS LLC
Also Called: Renal Care Group Wichita West
750 N Socora St Ste 500 (67212-3795)
PHONE..............................316 729-5321
Bobbie Sullivan, *Manager*
EMP: 10
SALES (corp-wide): 18.3B **Privately Held**
SIC: 8092 Kidney dialysis centers
HQ: Fms Midwest Dialysis Centers, Llc
920 Winter St
Waltham MA 02451
781 699-9000

(G-14398)
FMW INC
7016 W Pueblo Dr Ste A (67209-2913)
PHONE..............................316 943-4217
Roger Nelson, *President*
Christie Nelson, *Vice Pres*
EMP: 14
SQ FT: 20,000
SALES (est): 2.1MM **Privately Held**
WEB: www.fmw.com
SIC: 3728 3599 Aircraft parts & equipment; machine shop, jobbing & repair

(G-14399)
FOLEY INDUSTRIES INC (PA)
Also Called: Foley Tractor
1550 S West St (67213-1638)
PHONE..............................316 943-4211
Ann Foley-Konecny, *President*
Paul Foley Jr, *Chairman*
Kerry Miller, *Warehouse Mgr*
Chris McCurry, *Parts Mgr*
Kevin Hoops, *CFO*
EMP: 100
SQ FT: 35,600
SALES (est): 124.2MM **Privately Held**
WEB: www.foleytractor.com
SIC: 5082 5084 7353 6512 General construction machinery & equipment; industrial machinery & equipment; heavy construction equipment rental; nonresidential building operators

(G-14400)
FOLEY SUPPLY LLC
Also Called: Caterpillar Authorized Dealer
1210 S West St (67213-1632)
PHONE..............................316 944-7368
Michael Phelps, *Managing Dir*
Charlotte Kerner, *CFO*
Foley Mankin, *Sales Staff*
John Pamperin, *Manager*
Ann Foley Konecny,
EMP: 38
SALES (est): 6.3MM **Privately Held**
SIC: 7359 7353 5082 Tool rental; heavy construction equipment rental; construction & mining machinery

(G-14401)
FOLGERS GYMNASTICS INC
241 N Lancaster Ct (67230-7807)
PHONE..............................316 733-7525
Mark Folger, *President*
Penny Folger, *Vice Pres*
EMP: 17
SQ FT: 8,800
SALES (est): 419K **Privately Held**
SIC: 7999 7991 Gymnastic instruction, non-membership; aerobic dance & exercise classes

(G-14402)
FORSHEE PAINTING CONTRACTORS
7200 W 13th St N Ste 217 (67212-2943)
PHONE..............................316 263-7777
Dennis Forshee, *President*
EMP: 85
SALES: 3.5MM **Privately Held**
SIC: 1721 Commercial painting; residential painting

(G-14403)
FOSTER DESIGN INC
200 W Douglas Ave Ste 110 (67202-3001)
PHONE..............................316 832-9700
Gene Foster, *President*
Rheba Castillo, *COO*
EMP: 150
SQ FT: 7,200
SALES (est): 10.3MM **Privately Held**
WEB: www.fosterdes.com
SIC: 8711 8741 8748 Labor contractors (employment agency)

(G-14404)
FOULSTON CONLEE SCHMIDT EMERSO
200 W Douglas Ave Ste 300 (67202-3003)
PHONE..............................316 264-3300
John Foulston, *Partner*
John Conlee, *Partner*
Jeff Emerson, *Partner*
Kari Schmidt, *Partner*
Cathy Brown, *Legal Staff*
EMP: 10
SQ FT: 3,555
SALES: 341K **Privately Held**
WEB: www.fcse.net
SIC: 8111 General practice law office

(G-14405)
FOULSTON SIEFKIN LLP
700 Bank Of America Cente (67202)
PHONE..............................316 291-9514
Darrell Warta, *Branch Mgr*
EMP: 52
SALES (corp-wide): 19MM **Privately Held**
SIC: 8111 General practice attorney, lawyer
PA: Foulston Siefkin Llp
1551 N Waterfront Pkwy # 100
Wichita KS 67206
316 267-6371

(G-14406)
FOULSTON SIEFKIN LLP (PA)
1551 N Waterfront Pkwy # 100 (67206-4466)
PHONE..............................316 267-6371
Heidi Ahlstedt, *President*
Melissa Baier, *President*
Lauren Blick, *President*
Lynda Brittingham, *President*
Narla Mance, *President*
EMP: 120
SQ FT: 55,000
SALES (est): 19MM **Privately Held**
WEB: www.foulston.com
SIC: 8111 General practice attorney, lawyer

(G-14407)
FOUR OF WICHITA INC
Also Called: Wichita Inn-West
6335 W Kellogg Dr (67209-2329)
PHONE..............................316 943-2373
Jackie Williams, *General Mgr*
EMP: 25
SALES (corp-wide): 4.6MM **Privately Held**
SIC: 7011 Motels
PA: Four Of Wichita, Inc.
3741 N Rock Rd
Wichita KS 67226
316 636-2022

(G-14408)
FOUR OF WICHITA INC (PA)
Also Called: Wichita Inn-North
3741 N Rock Rd (67226-1307)
PHONE..............................316 636-2022
Harry Pollak, *Principal*
Lindy Andeel, *Vice Pres*
Eugene Coombs, *Admin Sec*
EMP: 30
SALES (est): 4.6MM **Privately Held**
SIC: 7011 Motels

(G-14409)
FOUR OF WICHITA INC
Also Called: Northrock Suites
7856 E 36th St N (67226-3808)
PHONE..............................316 634-2303
EMP: 22
SALES (corp-wide): 4.6MM **Privately Held**
SIC: 7011 Motels
PA: Four Of Wichita, Inc.
3741 N Rock Rd
Wichita KS 67226
316 636-2022

(G-14410)
FOUR OF WICHITA INC
Also Called: Wesley Inn
3343 E Central Ave (67208-3105)
PHONE..............................316 858-3343
Ginger Yager, *Branch Mgr*
EMP: 19
SALES (corp-wide): 4.6MM **Privately Held**
SIC: 7011 Hotels

PA: Four Of Wichita, Inc.
3741 N Rock Rd
Wichita KS 67226
316 636-2022

(G-14411)
FOUR STAR TOOL AND DIE INC
1612 S Mead St (67211-4311)
PHONE..................................316 264-2913
Ron Miller, *President*
Shawna Miller, *Vice Pres*
EMP: 6
SQ FT: 2,500
SALES (est): 820.2K **Privately Held**
SIC: 3544 Special dies & tools

(G-14412)
FOX REALTY INC
9330 E Central Ave # 200 (67206-2561)
PHONE..................................316 681-1313
Sue Fox, *President*
EMP: 10
SALES (est): 894.1K **Privately Held**
SIC: 6531 Real estate agent, residential

(G-14413)
FRAMEWORKS
Also Called: Graphic Impressions
9103 E 37th St N (67226-2010)
PHONE..................................316 636-4470
Marshall Millsap, *President*
David Mason, *Vice Pres*
EMP: 15
SQ FT: 11,000
SALES (est): 2.2MM **Privately Held**
SIC: 5023 Frames & framing, picture & mirror

(G-14414)
FRAX
110 S Main St Ste 200 (67202-3700)
PHONE..................................888 987-3729
Rene Lathrop, *Asst Director*
Bruce Berglind, *Administration*
EMP: 10
SALES (est): 334.6K **Privately Held**
SIC: 8082 Home health care services

(G-14415)
FREDDIE WAYNE LONG
Also Called: Aero Comm Machining
925 E Murdock St (67214-3844)
PHONE..................................316 263-8941
EMP: 14 **EST:** 1969
SQ FT: 33,000
SALES (est): 1.6MM **Privately Held**
SIC: 3728 3599 Mfg Aircraft Parts/Equipment Mfg Industrial Machinery

(G-14416)
FREDERICK PLUMBING & HEATING
815 N Main St (67203-3686)
PHONE..................................316 262-3713
Ray R Frederick Jr, *President*
Russell Frederick, *Vice Pres*
J D Frederick, *Admin Sec*
EMP: 10
SQ FT: 3,000
SALES (est): 1.2MM **Privately Held**
SIC: 1711 5999 Plumbing contractors; plumbing & heating supplies

(G-14417)
FREEDOM 1ST FEDERAL CREDIT UN
57915 Leavenworth St (67221-3508)
PHONE..................................316 685-0205
Ronda Posch, *President*
Lori Schrier, *Loan*
EMP: 18
SALES: 774.5K **Privately Held**
WEB: www.freedom1st.org
SIC: 6061 Federal credit unions

(G-14418)
FREEPORT-MCMORAN OIL & GAS LLC
9320 E Central Ave (67206-2555)
PHONE..................................316 636-1801
Tom Steven, *Manager*
EMP: 27
SALES (corp-wide): 18.6B **Publicly Held**
SIC: 1311 1382 Crude petroleum & natural gas; oil & gas exploration services
HQ: Freeport-Mcmoran Oil & Gas Llc
700 Milam St Ste 3100
Houston TX 77002
713 579-6000

(G-14419)
FREESTATE ADVISORS LLC
10333 E 21st St N (67206-3543)
PHONE..................................888 735-2724
Tom Halvorson, *Branch Mgr*
EMP: 22
SALES (corp-wide): 4.8MM **Privately Held**
SIC: 6726 Investment offices
PA: Freestate Advisors, Llc
4400 College Blvd Ste 125
Leawood KS 66211
913 890-2065

(G-14420)
FREESTYLE SIGN CO INC
1925 N Broadway Ave (67214-1124)
PHONE..................................316 267-5507
Orlando Aratea, *President*
Ken Phan, *Vice Pres*
EMP: 6
SQ FT: 2,000
SALES (est): 878K **Privately Held**
SIC: 3993 1799 Electric signs; sign installation & maintenance

(G-14421)
FREIGHT LOGISTICS INC
3404 N Emporia St (67219-3615)
PHONE..................................316 719-2074
Amanda Sudermann, *President*
Dave Gaggero, *Vice Pres*
EMP: 15
SALES (est): 3.7MM **Privately Held**
WEB: www.flitrans.com
SIC: 4213 Liquid petroleum transport, non-local

(G-14422)
FRENCH QUARTER LLC
2145 N Topeka St (67214-1140)
PHONE..................................316 440-7004
EMP: 6
SALES (est): 325.5K **Privately Held**
SIC: 3131 Quarters

(G-14423)
FRESENIUS MEDICAL SERVICE
1007 N Emporia St (67214-2908)
PHONE..................................316 264-3115
Tracey Austin, *Manager*
EMP: 10
SALES (est): 538.9K **Privately Held**
SIC: 8062 General medical & surgical hospitals

(G-14424)
FRIENDS UNIVERSITY
Also Called: Center On Family Living
2100 W University Ave (67213-3397)
PHONE..................................316 295-5638
Steve Rathdun, *Administration*
EMP: 10
SALES (corp-wide): 31.6MM **Privately Held**
WEB: www.friends.edu
SIC: 8322 8221 Family counseling services; university
PA: Friends University
2100 W University Ave
Wichita KS 67213
316 295-5000

(G-14425)
FRIESEN TOOL CO INC
233 N Ohio Ave (67214-3933)
PHONE..................................316 262-6808
Joachim Friesen, *President*
Kurt Friesen, *Vice Pres*
EMP: 5
SQ FT: 3,400
SALES (est): 604.4K **Privately Held**
SIC: 3544 Special dies & tools

(G-14426)
FRITO-LAY NORTH AMERICA INC
3815 W 30th St S (67217-1098)
PHONE..................................316 942-8764
Dean Miller, *Manager*
EMP: 36
SQ FT: 4,000
SALES (corp-wide): 64.6B **Publicly Held**
WEB: www.fritolay.com
SIC: 5145 Snack foods
HQ: Frito-Lay North America, Inc.
7701 Legacy Dr
Plano TX 75024

(G-14427)
FRUHAUF UNIFORMS INC
800 E Gilbert St (67211-2440)
P.O. Box 16159 (67216-0159)
PHONE..................................316 263-7500
Fred Fruhauf, *Chairman*
Ken Fruhauf, *Vice Pres*
Richard Fruhauf, *Vice Pres*
Drew Teinert, *CFO*
Tausha Bomholt, *Graphic Designe*
EMP: 210
SQ FT: 60,000
SALES (est): 20.9MM **Privately Held**
WEB: www.fruhauf.com
SIC: 2311 2337 Men's & boys' uniforms; uniforms, except athletic: women's, misses' & juniors'

(G-14428)
FUGATE ENTERPRISES
Also Called: Blockbuster
208 S Maize Rd (67209-3110)
PHONE..................................316 722-5670
Kendra Jarvis, *Branch Mgr*
EMP: 11
SALES (corp-wide): 5.6MM **Privately Held**
WEB: www.fugatelaw.com
SIC: 7841 Video disk/tape rental to the general public
PA: Fugate Leasing, Inc.
208 S Maize Rd
Wichita KS 67209
316 722-5670

(G-14429)
FUGATE LEASING INC (PA)
Also Called: Fugate Enterprises
208 S Maize Rd (67209-3110)
PHONE..................................316 722-5670
Larry Fugate, *Principal*
Zach Fugate, *Asst Director*
Kelly Kendall, *Assistant*
EMP: 111
SQ FT: 8,000
SALES (est): 5.6MM **Privately Held**
WEB: www.fugatelaw.com
SIC: 5812 6512 Pizzeria, chain; commercial & industrial building operation

(G-14430)
FUL TECH DENTAL LAB INC
Also Called: F T I Dental Lab
522 N St Francis St (67214-3808)
PHONE..................................316 681-3546
John Michael Fulton, *President*
Lorraine Fulton, *Admin Sec*
EMP: 10
SALES (est): 814.1K **Privately Held**
SIC: 8072 Crown & bridge production

(G-14431)
G & D METALS INC
725 E Skinner St (67211-4333)
PHONE..................................316 303-9090
Randy Gale, *President*
EMP: 8
SALES (est): 1MM **Privately Held**
SIC: 3444 Sheet metalwork

(G-14432)
G & F CONSTRUCTION CO LLC
118 E Harry St (67211-4103)
PHONE..................................316 260-3313
Filiberto Pinon, *Mng Member*
EMP: 20
SALES (est): 2.8MM **Privately Held**
SIC: 1542 1522 Commercial & office building contractors; residential construction

(G-14433)
G AND S MECHANICAL USA INC
3409 W Harry St (67213-1407)
PHONE..................................316 946-9988
Cathy Goertz, *President*
Jim Goertz, *Vice Pres*
EMP: 11
SALES (est): 1.6MM **Privately Held**
SIC: 3613 Control panels, electric

(G-14434)
G T SALES & MANUFACTURING INC (PA)
Also Called: Hewitt USA
2202 S West St (67213-1114)
P.O. Box 9408 (67277-0408)
PHONE..................................316 943-2171
N M Onofrio Jr, *CEO*
Tony Cunningham, *General Mgr*
Rick Mullen, *Engineer*
Sally Blasi, *Controller*
▲ **EMP:** 60
SQ FT: 57,000
SALES (est): 35.4MM **Privately Held**
WEB: www.gtsales.com
SIC: 3053 3052 5085 Gaskets, all materials; hose, pneumatic: rubber or rubberized fabric; rubber goods, mechanical

(G-14435)
G W INC (PA)
Also Called: Wickham Glass Co
4747 N Webb Rd (67226-8153)
PHONE..................................316 262-3403
Gary D Wickham, *President*
David Wickham, *Vice Pres*
Phil Gee, *Project Mgr*
EMP: 21
SQ FT: 18,500
SALES (est): 5.9MM **Privately Held**
WEB: www.itiglass.com
SIC: 1793 3211 5231 Glass & glazing work; insulating glass, sealed units; tempered glass; glass

(G-14436)
GAELIC MANAGEMENT INC
400 N Woodlawn St Ste 210 (67208-4332)
PHONE..................................316 683-5150
Daniel Carney, *President*
George Flynn, *Admin Sec*
EMP: 10
SQ FT: 4,850
SALES (est): 710K **Privately Held**
SIC: 8741 Hotel or motel management; restaurant management

(G-14437)
GALAXY AUDIO INC
601 E Pawnee St Frnt (67211-4946)
P.O. Box 16285 (67216-0285)
PHONE..................................316 263-2852
Brock Jabara, *CEO*
Alison Scheffer, *Accountant*
Chris Locke, *Information Mgr*
▲ **EMP:** 11 **EST:** 1969
SQ FT: 19,000
SALES: 2.5MM **Privately Held**
SIC: 3651 Public address systems

(G-14438)
GALICHIA MEDICAL GROUP PA
9415 E Harry St Ste 407 (67207-5083)
PHONE..................................316 684-3838
Cathy McCaleb, *Med Doctor*
Aunna Dover, *Manager*
Michael Phillips, *Manager*
Charlie Fletcher, *Physician Asst*
Joan Wasser,
EMP: 42 **EST:** 1983
SALES (est): 4.5MM **Privately Held**
SIC: 8099 Medical services organization

(G-14439)
GALICHIA MEDICAL GROUP KANS PA (PA)
Also Called: Gmed
9415 E Harry St Ste 407 (67207-5083)
PHONE..................................316 684-3838
EMP: 205
SQ FT: 27,343
SALES (est): 13.1MM **Privately Held**
SIC: 8011 Medical Doctor's Office

(G-14440)
GALLERY XII INC
412 E Douglas Ave Ste A (67202-3417)
PHONE..................................316 267-5915
John Ellerg, *President*
EMP: 22
SALES (est): 1.8MM **Privately Held**
SIC: 5999 8999 Art dealers; artist

(G-14441)
GALT VENTURES LLC (PA)
Also Called: Speedy Cash
3527 N Ridge Rd (67205-1212)
PHONE..................................316 722-3801
Doug R Rippel, *CEO*
Chad Faulkner, *Vice Pres*
Mike McKnight, *Vice Pres*
Jaquelin Murillo, *Store Mgr*
▲ **EMP:** 15 **EST:** 1996
SQ FT: 1,800
SALES (est): 36.4MM **Privately Held**
WEB: www.galtventures.com
SIC: 6141 Personal credit institutions

(G-14442)
GALT VENTURES LLC
Also Called: Speedy Cash
701 N West St (67203-1214)
PHONE..................................316 942-2211
Barbara Frederick, *Branch Mgr*
EMP: 10
SALES (corp-wide): 36.4MM **Privately Held**
SIC: 6099 Check cashing agencies
PA: Galt Ventures, Llc
3527 N Ridge Rd
Wichita KS 67205
316 722-3801

(G-14443)
GAMOICT INC
Also Called: Get A Move On
1008 S Washington Ave (67211-2428)
PHONE..................................316 262-2123
Eric Kimler, *President*
EMP: 10
SALES (est): 736.6K **Privately Held**
SIC: 4214 Furniture moving & storage, local

(G-14444)
GAO QIZHI
Also Called: Kccm
9235 E Harry St Ste 1a (67207-5073)
PHONE..................................316 691-8811
Janet Gao, *Vice Pres*
Gao Qizhi,
EMP: 10
SALES (est): 450K **Privately Held**
SIC: 8049 Acupuncturist

(G-14445)
GARDA CL WEST INC
Also Called: Pro Securtiy
2018 S Kessler St (67213-1229)
PHONE..................................316 942-9700
Eric Widrig, *Manager*
EMP: 140
SALES (corp-wide): 16.5MM **Privately Held**
SIC: 7381 Armored car services
PA: Garda Cl West Inc
20325 E Walnut Dr N
Walnut CA 91789
323 668-2712

(G-14446)
GARDEN PLAIN BANCSHARES INC (PA)
Also Called: GARDEN PLAIN STATE BANK
10526 W Maple St (67209-4012)
P.O. Box 75009 (67275-0009)
PHONE..................................316 721-1500
Patrick Walden, *President*
EMP: 20
SALES: 4.1MM **Privately Held**
WEB: www.gpsbank.com
SIC: 6022 State commercial banks

(G-14447)
GARDEN PLAIN STATE BANK (PA)
10526 W Maple St (67209-4012)
PHONE..................................316 721-1500
Patrick Walden, *President*
Deneen Fayette, *Vice Pres*
Karissa Richmond, *Vice Pres*
Karl Staats, *Branch Mgr*
Mark Bhar, *Executive*
EMP: 21
SQ FT: 6,500
SALES: 3.4MM **Privately Held**
SIC: 6022 State commercial banks

(G-14448)
GARDN-WISE DISTRIBUTORS INC (PA)
1515 E 29th St N (67219-4129)
PHONE..................................316 838-6104
Robert S Wise, *Ch of Bd*
Stephen T Wise, *President*
David Scott Wise, *Vice Pres*
Marc Wise, *Treasurer*
▲ **EMP:** 16 **EST:** 1953
SQ FT: 30,000
SALES (est): 37.5MM **Privately Held**
SIC: 5191 Garden supplies

(G-14449)
GARNETT AUTO SUPPLY INC (PA)
801 E Zimmerly St (67211-3342)
PHONE..................................316 267-4393
Larry Boehringer, *President*
John C Beal, *President*
John Winter, *Vice Pres*
Kay Rothfelder, *CFO*
EMP: 25
SQ FT: 100,000
SALES (est): 3.8MM **Privately Held**
SIC: 5013 5531 Automotive supplies & parts; automotive parts; automotive accessories

(G-14450)
GARVEY PUBLIC WAREHOUSE INC
Also Called: Builders
5755 S Hoover Rd Bldg 5 (67215-9300)
PHONE..................................316 522-4745
James W Garvey, *President*
Brad Smisor, *Vice Pres*
EMP: 10
SQ FT: 250,000
SALES (est): 1.5MM
SALES (corp-wide): 6.3MM **Privately Held**
WEB: www.garveypublicwarehouse.com
SIC: 4225 General warehousing
PA: Builders, Inc.
1081 S Glendale St
Wichita KS 67218
316 684-1400

(G-14451)
GATEWAY WIRELESS SERVICES LLC (PA)
121 S Lulu Ave (67211-1710)
PHONE..................................316 264-0037
Gary Renberger, *General Mgr*
Scott Sellers, *Sales Staff*
EMP: 10
SQ FT: 7,000
SALES (est): 1.6MM **Privately Held**
WEB: www.gatewaywireless.net
SIC: 5731 3825 7622 Radios, two-way, citizens' band, weather, short-wave, etc.; analog-digital converters, electronic instrumentation type; radio repair shop

(G-14452)
GATEWAY WRELESS NETWRK SVCS LC
Also Called: Gateway Wireless Services
121 S Lulu Ave (67211-1710)
PHONE..................................316 264-0037
Gary Renberger, *President*
EMP: 15 **EST:** 1995
SALES (est): 147.5K **Privately Held**
SIC: 4812 1731 Cellular telephone services; fiber optic cable installation; voice, data & video wiring contractor; access control systems specialization

(G-14453)
GAVILON GRAIN LLC
5755 S Hoover Rd Unit 2 (67215-9300)
PHONE..................................316 226-7250
Neil Schwemmer, *Branch Mgr*
EMP: 22 **Privately Held**
WEB: www.debruce.com
SIC: 5153 Grains
HQ: Gavilon Grain, Llc
1331 Capitol Ave
Omaha NE 68102

(G-14454)
GENE OSWALD COMPANY
519 N Hydraulic St (67214-4223)
PHONE..................................316 263-7191
David Vest, *President*
Debra Vest, *Corp Secy*
EMP: 12
SQ FT: 5,000
SALES: 1.5MM **Privately Held**
SIC: 5063 Electrical apparatus & equipment

(G-14455)
GENERAL DISTRIBUTORS INC (PA)
1445 N Rock Rd Ste 200 (67206-1292)
PHONE..................................316 634-2133
Larry K Arbuckle, *Ch of Bd*
Don Christy, *President*
Sally Arbuckle, *Shareholder*
◆ **EMP:** 28
SALES (est): 7.3MM **Privately Held**
SIC: 5023 Floor coverings; carpets

(G-14456)
GENERAL FINANCIAL SERVICES INC
8441 E 32nd St N Ste 200 (67226-2617)
PHONE..................................316 636-1070
Steve K Miller, *President*
Fadi Mashnouk, *Vice Pres*
EMP: 6
SQ FT: 9,000
SALES (est): 1.1MM **Privately Held**
SIC: 6552 2034 Subdividers & developers; potato products, dried & dehydrated

(G-14457)
GENESIS HEALTH CLUB INC
854 N Socora St Ste B (67212-3277)
PHONE..................................316 721-8938
Rodney Steven II, *Branch Mgr*
EMP: 40
SALES (corp-wide): 5.8MM **Privately Held**
SIC: 7991 Health club
PA: Genesis Health Club, Inc.
3725 W 13th St N
Wichita KS 67203
316 945-8331

(G-14458)
GENESIS HEALTH CLUB INC (PA)
3725 W 13th St N (67203-4499)
PHONE..................................316 945-8331
Rodney L Steven II, *President*
EMP: 45
SALES (est): 5.8MM **Privately Held**
WEB: www.genesishealthclub.com
SIC: 7991 7999 7299 5941 Health club; tennis services & professionals; personal appearance services; tennis goods & equipment

(G-14459)
GENESIS HEALTH CLUBS MGT LLC
Also Called: Genesis Health Club Rock Road
1551 N Rock Rd (67206-1255)
PHONE..................................316 634-0094
Johnny Steven, *General Mgr*
Jason Hardy, *Accountant*
Bobbi Fine, *Accounts Mgr*
Jake McCabe, *VP Mktg*
David Butto, *Manager*
EMP: 50
SQ FT: 104,800
SALES (est): 2.6MM
SALES (corp-wide): 5.8MM **Privately Held**
WEB: www.genesishealthclub.com
SIC: 7997 5941 7991 Tennis club, membership; tennis goods & equipment; physical fitness facilities
PA: Genesis Health Club, Inc.
3725 W 13th St N
Wichita KS 67203
316 945-8331

(G-14460)
GERBER GROUP INC
5617 W Kellogg Dr (67209-2343)
PHONE..................................316 945-7007
EMP: 21
SALES (corp-wide): 1.4B **Privately Held**
SIC: 7532 Collision shops, automotive
HQ: The Gerber Group Inc
400 W Grand Ave
Elmhurst IL 60126
877 743-7237

(G-14461)
GET A MOVE ON INC
1008 S Washington Ave (67211-2428)
PHONE..................................316 729-4897
Paul C Wells, *President*
Paul Wells, *President*
EMP: 32
SQ FT: 2,400
SALES (est): 4.1MM **Privately Held**
WEB: www.getamoveonkansas.com
SIC: 4212 4214 Moving services; local trucking with storage

(G-14462)
GFE LLC
519 N Hydraulic St (67214-4223)
PHONE..................................316 260-8433
Chris Nichols,
EMP: 15
SALES (est): 2.5MM **Privately Held**
SIC: 8711 5531 Mechanical engineering; automotive parts

(G-14463)
GIBSON WHOLESALE CO INC (PA)
Also Called: Barney's Discount Center
3104 W Central Ave (67203-4912)
PHONE..................................316 945-3471
Victor Riffel, *President*
Victor Riffel III, *Vice Pres*
Scott Riffel, *CFO*
EMP: 15
SQ FT: 20,000
SALES: 2.2MM **Privately Held**
SIC: 5912 5122 Drug stores; drugs, proprietaries & sundries

(G-14464)
GILLIAN & HAYES LLP
301 N Main St Ste 1300 (67202-4824)
PHONE..................................316 264-7321
Kenneth P Stewart, *Partner*
Pamela E Bailey, *Partner*
Leland E Cox, *Partner*
John H Gibson, *Partner*
James R Hanson, *Partner*
EMP: 15
SQ FT: 3,000
SALES (est): 786.6K **Privately Held**
SIC: 8111 General practice attorney, lawyer

(G-14465)
GILLILAND & HAYES PA
301 N Main St Ste 1300 (67202-4824)
PHONE..................................316 264-7321
Mark Maloney, *Manager*
EMP: 16
SALES (est): 1.1MM
SALES (corp-wide): 6MM **Privately Held**
WEB: www.gillilandandhayes.com
SIC: 8111 General practice attorney, lawyer
PA: Gilliland & Hayes Pa
20 W 2nd Ave Ste 200
Hutchinson KS 67501
620 662-0537

(G-14466)
GILMORE & BELL A PROF CORP
Also Called: Lacey, Phillip
100 N Main St Ste 800 (67202-1398)
PHONE..................................316 267-2091
Joe Norton, *Manager*
Johnna Middleton, *Legal Staff*
Christine Klinker, *Associate*
EMP: 14
SALES (corp-wide): 12.8MM **Privately Held**
SIC: 8111 General practice law office
PA: Gilmore & Bell, A Professional Corporation
2405 Grand Blvd Ste 1100
Kansas City MO 64108
816 221-1000

GEOGRAPHIC

(G-14467)
GIRL SCOUTS KANS HEARTLAND INC (PA)
360 Lexington Rd (67218-1700)
PHONE..................................316 684-6531
Liz Workman, *CEO*
EMP: 25 **EST:** 1921
SALES: 4.9MM **Privately Held**
SIC: 8641 Girl Scout organization

(G-14468)
GIVENS CLEANING CONTRACTORS
Also Called: Givens Carpet Cleaning Service
250 N Pennsylvania Ave (67214-4149)
PHONE..................................316 265-1315
Ed Givens, *President*
Darryl Givens, *Vice Pres*
EMP: 15
SQ FT: 5,000
SALES (est): 1.3MM **Privately Held**
WEB: www.4givens.net
SIC: 7217 7349 1799 Carpet & upholstery cleaning; building maintenance services; air duct cleaning; post-disaster renovations

(G-14469)
GKN ARMSTRONG WHEELS INC
Also Called: GKN Wichita
801 E Skinner St (67211-4335)
PHONE..................................316 943-3571
Bill Ramsey, *General Mgr*
EMP: 23
SALES (corp-wide): 11.3B **Privately Held**
WEB: www.gknoffhighwaysystems.com
SIC: 3714 Motor vehicle wheels & parts
HQ: Gkn Armstrong Wheels, Inc.
5453 6th Ave
Armstrong IA 50514
712 362-4934

(G-14470)
GLAXOSMITHKLINE LLC
518 N Bracken St (67206-7800)
PHONE..................................316 214-4811
EMP: 26
SALES (corp-wide): 40.6B **Privately Held**
SIC: 2834 Pharmaceutical preparations
HQ: Glaxosmithkline Llc
5 Crescent Dr
Philadelphia PA 19112
215 751-4000

(G-14471)
GLENN PK CHRISTN CH PRESCHOOL
2757 S Glenn Ave (67217-1841)
PHONE..................................316 943-4283
Craig Estet, *Principal*
Tom Hawks, *Pastor*
Jeremy Albert, *Info Tech Mgr*
Janice Peisser, *Director*
EMP: 23
SALES (est): 891.6K **Privately Held**
WEB: www.glennpark.com
SIC: 8661 8351 Christian & Reformed Church; preschool center

(G-14472)
GLMV ARCHITECTURE INC (PA)
1525 E Douglas Ave (67211-1608)
PHONE..................................316 265-9367
William B Livingston, *CEO*
Carol Wooten, *Senior VP*
Matt Cortez, *Vice Pres*
Mac McKee, *Vice Pres*
Craig Rhodes, *Vice Pres*
EMP: 50
SQ FT: 19,000
SALES (est): 15MM **Privately Held**
WEB: www.gossenlivingston.com
SIC: 8712 0781 7389 Architectural engineering; landscape architects; interior designer

(G-14473)
GLOBAL AVIATION TECH LLC
6545 W Pueblo Ct (67209-3213)
PHONE..................................316 425-0999
Woody Cottner, *Vice Pres*
Jerome Cottner, *Prdtn Mgr*
Dawn Sullivan, *Human Resources*
Karla Molina, *Program Mgr*
Chris Bradley, *Director*
EMP: 16
SQ FT: 14,750
SALES (est): 3.7MM **Privately Held**
WEB: www.globalaviationtechnologies.com
SIC: 8711 3728 4581 Engineering services; aircraft parts & equipment; aircraft maintenance & repair services

(G-14474)
GLOBAL CNC CORPORATION
1029 N Wichita St Ste 2 (67203-3846)
PHONE..................................316 516-3400
Lucia Antonio, *Opers Staff*
EMP: 5
SQ FT: 2,000
SALES (est): 471.2K **Privately Held**
SIC: 3724 Aircraft engines & engine parts

(G-14475)
GLOBAL PARTNER SOLUTIONS LLC
100 S Market St Ste 2b (67202-3824)
PHONE..................................316 263-1288
Dave Wardle, *Vice Pres*
Robert Hachey, *Mng Member*
William Wilson, *Manager*
Lacy McDowell, *Business Dir*
Sandro De Ciccio,
EMP: 116
SQ FT: 10,000
SALES (est): 11MM **Privately Held**
SIC: 7361 8711 Employment agencies; engineering services

(G-14476)
GLOBE ENGINEERING CO INC
1539 S Saint Paul St (67213-1797)
P.O. Box 12407 (67277-2407)
PHONE..................................316 943-1266
Jeff Teague, *President*
Jon Tiffany, *General Mgr*
Dave Holt, *Engineer*
Kevin Gerstenkorn, *Treasurer*
Gary Counts, *Human Res Mgr*
EMP: 230
SQ FT: 220,000
SALES: 50MM **Privately Held**
WEB: www.globeeng.com
SIC: 3728 3444 Aircraft body assemblies & parts; sheet metalwork

(G-14477)
GLOW GOLF
7570 W 21st St N 1026c (67205-1734)
PHONE..................................316 685-1040
Elizabeth Barnett, *Branch Mgr*
EMP: 18
SALES (corp-wide): 1.9MM **Privately Held**
SIC: 7929 Entertainment service
PA: Glow Golf
750 Citadel Dr E Ste 2072
Colorado Springs CO 80909
719 597-2720

(G-14478)
GODDARD MACHINE LLC
1738 N Mosley Ave (67214-1346)
PHONE..................................316 838-1381
Kent Beals, *Sales Mgr*
Allen Huang, *Marketing Staff*
Xeng Lam, *Mng Member*
Kent Peals,
EMP: 15 **EST:** 2001
SQ FT: 20,000
SALES (est): 2.1MM **Privately Held**
WEB: www.goddardmachine.com
SIC: 3599 Machine shop, jobbing & repair

(G-14479)
GOENTZEL CONSTRUCTION INC
Also Called: Bgs Company
7570 W 21st St N 1050f (67205-1734)
P.O. Box 487 (67201-0487)
PHONE..................................316 264-6333
Denise Bennett, *Corp Secy*
Marcia Goentzel, *Corp Secy*
Jeff Bennett, *Vice Pres*
EMP: 10
SQ FT: 2,000
SALES (est): 1.1MM **Privately Held**
WEB: www.goentzelhomes.com
SIC: 1521 New construction, single-family houses; general remodeling, single-family houses

(G-14480)
GOLD KEY INC
Also Called: Gold Key Realtors
5212 N Saint Clair Ave (67204-2527)
PHONE..................................316 942-1925
Gerald W Jackson, *President*
EMP: 15
SQ FT: 1,200
SALES (est): 1.1MM **Privately Held**
WEB: www.goldkey.com
SIC: 6531 Real estate agent, residential

(G-14481)
GOLDEN BOOMERS HOME
9306 E Carson St (67210-2430)
PHONE..................................316 730-3110
Christine Nguyen, *Principal*
EMP: 13
SALES (est): 204.5K **Privately Held**
SIC: 8051 Skilled nursing care facilities

(G-14482)
GOLDEN LIVING CENTER WICHITA
4007 E Lincoln St (67218-2111)
PHONE..................................316 683-7588
Victoria Crenshaw, *Principal*
Mary E Olson, *Exec Dir*
EMP: 14
SALES (est): 851.3K **Privately Held**
SIC: 8051 Convalescent home with continuous nursing care

(G-14483)
GOODMAN MANUFACTURING CO LP
1749 S Sabin St (67209-2750)
PHONE..................................316 946-9145
Russ Johnson, *Branch Mgr*
EMP: 292 **Privately Held**
WEB: www.goodmanmfg.com
SIC: 5075 Warm air heating & air conditioning
HQ: Goodman Manufacturing Company, Lp
5151 San Felipe St # 500
Houston TX 77056
713 861-2500

(G-14484)
GOODRICH
P.O. Box 75157 (67275-0157)
PHONE..................................316 448-4282
EMP: 10 **EST:** 2010
SALES (est): 500K **Privately Held**
SIC: 7389 Business Services

(G-14485)
GOODRICH CORPORATION
7016 W Pueblo Dr Ste B (67209-2913)
PHONE..................................316 943-3322
Joe Norsworthy, *Opers Staff*
John Kaiser, *Manager*
EMP: 15
SALES (corp-wide): 66.5B **Publicly Held**
WEB: www.bfgoodrich.com
SIC: 3728 Aircraft parts & equipment
HQ: Goodrich Corporation
2730 W Tyvola Rd 4
Charlotte NC 28217
704 423-7000

(G-14486)
GOODRICH CORPORATION
Goodrich Corp - Cabin Systems
1643 S Maize Rd (67209-1922)
PHONE..................................316 721-3100
Brian Sartain, *Vice Pres*
EMP: 567
SALES (corp-wide): 66.5B **Publicly Held**
SIC: 3728 Aircraft parts & equipment
HQ: Goodrich Corporation
2730 W Tyvola Rd 4
Charlotte NC 28217
704 423-7000

(G-14487)
GORE OIL COMPANY (PA)
202 S Saint Francis Ave (67202-4518)
PHONE..................................316 263-3535
Andrew E Gore, *President*
Michael Harms, *Treasurer*
Kay P La Gree, *Admin Sec*
EMP: 9
SQ FT: 13,800
SALES (est): 16.2MM **Privately Held**
SIC: 1311 Crude petroleum production; natural gas production

(G-14488)
GRABAR VOICE AND DATA INC
8555 E 32nd St N (67226-2611)
PHONE..................................701 258-3528
John T Grabar, *President*
EMP: 9 **EST:** 1998
SALES (est): 1.4MM **Privately Held**
SIC: 3579 Dictating machines

(G-14489)
GRACE OF WICHITA KS LLC
Also Called: Merry Maids
6803 W Taft Ave Ste 305 (67209-2365)
P.O. Box 12413 (67277-2413)
PHONE..................................316 832-9009
David Lazarus, *Mng Member*
EMP: 19 **EST:** 2016
SQ FT: 2,000
SALES: 1.2MM **Privately Held**
SIC: 7349 Maid services, contract or fee basis

(G-14490)
GRACEMED HEALTH CLINIC INC
1905 S Laura Ave (67211-4422)
PHONE..................................316 440-7938
Sharol Sullivan, *Branch Mgr*
EMP: 13
SALES (corp-wide): 26.2MM **Privately Held**
SIC: 8021 Offices & clinics of dentists
PA: Gracemed Health Clinic, Inc.
1122 N Topeka St
Wichita KS 67214
316 866-2001

(G-14491)
GRACEMED HEALTH CLINIC INC (PA)
1122 N Topeka St (67214-2810)
PHONE..................................316 866-2001
David Sanford, *CEO*
Sharol Sullivan, *CFO*
Doreen Eyler, *Manager*
Alice Weingartner, *Director*
Amanda Marceau, *Recruiter*
EMP: 55
SALES: 26.2MM **Privately Held**
WEB: www.gracemed.org
SIC: 8021 Offices & clinics of dentists

(G-14492)
GRACO SUPPLY COMPANY
2056 S Edwards St Ste C (67213-1865)
PHONE..................................316 943-4200
Ron Becker, *Branch Mgr*
EMP: 15
SALES (corp-wide): 24.1MM **Privately Held**
WEB: www.gracosupply.com
SIC: 5088 Aircraft equipment & supplies
PA: Graco Supply Company
1001 Miller Ave
Fort Worth TX 76105
817 535-3200

(G-14493)
GRAF & ASSOCIATES INC (PA)
Also Called: Graf Electric
2445 S Glendale St (67210-1202)
PHONE..................................316 686-2090
David Graf, *President*
Constance Adams, *Corp Secy*
Tim Graf, *Vice Pres*
Tom Rieg, *Manager*
EMP: 12
SQ FT: 4,300
SALES (est): 3.6MM **Privately Held**
WEB: www.grafelectric.com
SIC: 1731 General electrical contractor

(G-14494)
GRAIN CRAFT INC
701 E 17th St N (67214-1311)
PHONE..................................316 267-7311
Jack Keltz, *Superintendent*
Brent Reed, *Plant Mgr*
Charlie Jackson, *Branch Mgr*
EMP: 50

SALES (corp-wide): 288.5MM **Privately Held**
WEB: www.cerealfood.com
SIC: 8721 5149 Accounting, auditing & bookkeeping; flour
PA: Grain Craft, Inc.
201 W Main St Ste 203
Chattanooga TN 37408
423 265-2313

(G-14495)
GRAND MESA OPERATING COMPANY
1700 N Waterfront Pkwy # 600 (67206-5514)
PHONE..................................316 634-0699
Ronald N Sinclair, *CEO*
Michael J Reilly, *President*
James P Reilly, *Corp Secy*
Sandra Reilly, *Shareholder*
EMP: 10
SQ FT: 3,700
SALES (est): 1.2MM **Privately Held**
SIC: 1311 Crude petroleum production; natural gas production

(G-14496)
GRANT THORNTON LLP
1617 N Waterfront Pkwy # 100 (67206-6639)
PHONE..................................316 265-3231
Gary Allerheiligen, *Manager*
Durrel Kelley, *Executive*
EMP: 58
SALES (corp-wide): 65.1MM **Privately Held**
WEB: www.gt.com
SIC: 8721 8742 Certified public accountant; financial consultant
HQ: Grant Thornton Llp
171 N Clark St Ste 200
Chicago IL 60601
312 856-0200

(G-14497)
GRAPHICS SYSTEMS INC (HQ)
Also Called: Mid America Graphics
313 S Ida St (67211-1588)
PHONE..................................316 267-4171
Mike Allen, *CEO*
Brad Wolf, *Principal*
Martin W Fresh, *Principal*
Brian Mogensen, *CFO*
EMP: 90
SQ FT: 40,000
SALES (est): 15.5MM
SALES (corp-wide): 259.3MM **Privately Held**
WEB: www.gsi-graphics.com
SIC: 2672 3993 3999 2752 Tape, pressure sensitive: made from purchased materials; signs, not made in custom sign painting shops; name plates: except engraved, etched, etc.: metal; buttons: Red Cross, union, identification; badges, metal: policemen, firemen, etc.; plaques, picture, laminated; commercial printing, lithographic
PA: Identity Group Holdings Corp.
1480 Gould Dr
Cookeville TN 38506
931 432-4000

(G-14498)
GRAY CONSTRUCTION INC
204 N Woodchuck St (67212-3777)
PHONE..................................316 721-3000
Billy Gray, *President*
Denise Gray, *Vice Pres*
EMP: 27
SALES (est): 2MM **Privately Held**
WEB: www.graycustomhomes.com
SIC: 1521 Single-family housing construction

(G-14499)
GRAY TELEVISION GROUP INC
Also Called: Kwch
2815 E 37th St N (67219-3545)
PHONE..................................316 838-1212
EMP: 10
SALES (corp-wide): 1B **Publicly Held**
SIC: 4833 Television broadcasting stations
HQ: Gray Television Group, Inc.
4370 Peachtree Rd Ne # 500
Brookhaven GA 30319
404 266-8333

(G-14500)
GRAYBAR ELECTRIC COMPANY INC
3609 W Pawnee St (67213-1835)
PHONE..................................316 265-8964
Dewayne Voth, *Sales Staff*
Steve Nadbeu, *Branch Mgr*
Michael Estell, *Supervisor*
EMP: 18
SALES (corp-wide): 7.2B **Privately Held**
WEB: www.graybar.com
SIC: 5063 Electrical supplies
PA: Graybar Electric Company, Inc.
34 N Meramec Ave
Saint Louis MO 63105
314 573-9200

(G-14501)
GREAT AMERCN HARDWOOD FLRG CO
157 S Washington Ave (67202-4721)
PHONE..................................316 264-3660
Jeffrey Bally, *President*
EMP: 15
SALES (est): 2.4MM **Privately Held**
SIC: 5713 1752 Carpets; floor laying & floor work

(G-14502)
GREAT PLAINS HLTH ALIANCE INC
250 N Rock Rd Ste 160 (67206-2241)
PHONE..................................316 685-1523
Eldon Schumacher, *Vice Pres*
Dave Dellasega, *Manager*
EMP: 10
SQ FT: 1,000
SALES (corp-wide): 112.9MM **Privately Held**
WEB: www.gpha.com
SIC: 8742 Productivity improvement consultant
PA: Great Plains Health Alliance, Inc.
625 3rd St
Phillipsburg KS 67661
785 543-2111

(G-14503)
GREAT PLAINS INDUSTRIES INC
Also Called: (OF GREAT PLAINS VENTURES, INC, WICHITA, KS)
5252 E 36th St N (67220-3205)
P.O. Box 8901 (67208-0901)
PHONE..................................316 686-7361
Victor Lukic, *President*
Jack Kratzer, *Vice Pres*
Rodolfo Esparza, *Buyer*
Gary Beach, *Treasurer*
Pat Corcoran, *Manager*
◆ **EMP:** 280
SALES: 64.4MM
SALES (corp-wide): 90.8MM **Privately Held**
WEB: www.gpi.net
SIC: 3586 3824 Measuring & dispensing pumps; gasoline pumps, measuring or dispensing; liquid meters; gasoline dispensing meters
PA: Great Plains Ventures, Inc.
3504 N Great Plains Dr # 100
Wichita KS 67220
316 684-1540

(G-14504)
GREAT PLAINS LOCATING SVC INC
1550 N Broadway Ave (67214-1100)
PHONE..................................316 263-1200
Steve Preifter, *General Mgr*
EMP: 40 **Privately Held**
SIC: 1623 Underground utilities contractor
PA: Great Plains Locating Service, Inc.
11640 Arbor St Ste 200
Omaha NE 68144

(G-14505)
GREAT PLAINS VENTURES INC (PA)
3504 N Great Plains Dr # 100 (67220-3407)
PHONE..................................316 684-1540
Susayn Brandes, *CEO*
Jack Kratzer, *Vice Pres*
Marque Peer, *Vice Pres*
Mike Dugan, *Prdtn Mgr*
Bob Ohlson, *Facilities Mgr*
EMP: 11
SALES: 90.8MM **Privately Held**
SIC: 6719 Investment holding companies, except banks

(G-14506)
GREAT PLINS TRNSPRATION MUSEUM
700 E Douglas Ave (67202-3506)
PHONE..................................316 263-0944
John Grease, *President*
Harvey Koehn, *Director*
EMP: 11
SQ FT: 2,000
SALES: 30.1K **Privately Held**
WEB: www.gptm.us
SIC: 8412 Museum

(G-14507)
GREAT SALT PLINS MIDSTREAM LLC
8301 E 21st St N Ste 370 (67206-2955)
PHONE..................................316 262-2819
EMP: 27
SALES (est): 1.4MM
SALES (corp-wide): 3B **Privately Held**
SIC: 5172 Crude oil
PA: Mvp Holdings, Llc
8301 E 21st St N Ste 370
Wichita KS 67206
316 262-2819

(G-14508)
GREATER WICHITA PARTNR INC
501 E Douglas Ave (67202-3501)
PHONE..................................316 500-6650
Jeff Fluhr, *President*
Evan Rosell, *Vice Pres*
Nick Bishop, *Comms Dir*
EMP: 12
SALES: 2.4MM **Privately Held**
SIC: 8748 Economic consultant

(G-14509)
GREEN HILLS INC
Also Called: Green Earth
3623 E Harry St Bldg 1 (67218-3712)
PHONE..................................316 686-7673
EMP: 11
SQ FT: 4,000
SALES: 500K **Privately Held**
SIC: 0181 0781 1521 6531 Landscape Services Ornamental Nursery Real Estate Agent/Mgr Single-Family House Cnst

(G-14510)
GREEN LANTERN INC
10510 W 21st St N (67205-1842)
PHONE..................................316 721-9242
Brad Rais, *Manager*
Keynan Gibson, *Manager*
EMP: 50
SALES (est): 702.5K **Privately Held**
WEB: www.greenlanterncarwash.com
SIC: 7542 Washing & polishing, automotive

(G-14511)
GREEN MEDICAL GROUP
Also Called: Green Vision Group
655 N Woodlawn St (67208-3648)
PHONE..................................316 691-3937
EMP: 45 **EST:** 2000
SALES (est): 2.5MM **Privately Held**
SIC: 8011 7231 Medical Doctor's Office Beauty Shop

(G-14512)
GREENWICH HOTEL LLC
Also Called: Tru Wichita Northeast
1236 N Greenwich Rd (67206-2665)
PHONE..................................316 925-5100
Richard Huffman, *Manager*
EMP: 28
SALES (est): 35.8K **Privately Held**
SIC: 7011 Hotels

(G-14513)
GRENE VISION GROUP LLC
Also Called: Hanson, Suzanne Sweetman
3910 N Ridge Rd (67205-7800)
PHONE..................................316 721-2701
Lisa Arebalo, *Manager*
Jennifer Taylor, *Manager*
EMP: 30 **Privately Held**
WEB: www.grenevisiongroup.com
SIC: 8042 Offices & clinics of optometrists
PA: Grene Vision Group, L.L.C.
1851 N Webb Rd
Wichita KS 67206

(G-14514)
GRENE VISION GROUP LLC
Also Called: Amstutz, Samuel W
834 1277 N Maize Rd (67212)
PHONE..................................316 722-8883
Marsha Allen, *Manager*
EMP: 20 **Privately Held**
WEB: www.grenevisiongroup.com
SIC: 8042 Offices & clinics of optometrists
PA: Grene Vision Group, L.L.C.
1851 N Webb Rd
Wichita KS 67206

(G-14515)
GRENE VISION GROUP LLC (PA)
Also Called: G.V.g
1851 N Webb Rd (67206-3413)
PHONE..................................316 691-4444
Kayli Smith, *COO*
Crystal Page, *CFO*
Randy Phelps, *Director*
Brian Pond, *Director*
C E Shrader,
EMP: 60
SALES (est): 15.8MM **Privately Held**
WEB: www.grenevisiongroup.com
SIC: 8042 Offices & clinics of optometrists

(G-14516)
GRENE VISION GROUP LLC
Also Called: Amstutz, Samuel W MD
655 N Woodlawn St (67208-3648)
PHONE..................................316 684-5158
Susan Brown, *Manager*
EMP: 55 **Privately Held**
WEB: www.grenevisiongroup.com
SIC: 8042 Offices & clinics of optometrists
PA: Grene Vision Group, L.L.C.
1851 N Webb Rd
Wichita KS 67206

(G-14517)
GRETEMAN GROUP INC
1425 E Douglas Ave Fl 2 (67211-1640)
PHONE..................................316 263-1004
Sonia Greteman, *President*
Joshua Wood, *Editor*
Diana Harms, *Exec VP*
Stephanie Stover, *Marketing Mgr*
Jordan Walker, *Director*
EMP: 19
SQ FT: 4,000
SALES (est): 2.3MM **Privately Held**
WEB: www.gretemangroup.com
SIC: 7336 7311 8742 Graphic arts & related design; advertising agencies; marketing consulting services

(G-14518)
GRIFFITH DEVELEPEMENT
Also Called: Aragon Apts
8909 E Harry St (67207-4702)
P.O. Box 780710 (67278-0710)
PHONE..................................316 686-1831
Leslie W Griffith, *Owner*
EMP: 10
SALES (est): 820.4K **Privately Held**
SIC: 6513 Apartment building operators

(G-14519)
GRIFFITH STEEL ERECTION INC
1355 S Anna St (67209-2601)
P.O. Box 275, Maize (67101-0275)
PHONE..................................316 941-4455
Jerry Griffith, *President*
Jim Griffith, *Vice Pres*
Aaron Sheeley, *Admin Sec*
EMP: 40

SQ FT: 600
SALES: 3MM Privately Held
SIC: 1791 Structural steel erection

(G-14520)
GROENDYKE TRANSPORT INC
3350 N Ohio St (67219-4135)
PHONE....................316 755-1266
Marty Moulton, *Terminal Mgr*
EMP: 45
SALES (corp-wide): 292.7MM Privately Held
WEB: www.groendyke.com
SIC: 4213 Trucking, except local
PA: Groendyke Transport Inc.
2510 Rock Island Blvd
Enid OK 73701
580 234-4663

(G-14521)
GSI ENGINEERING LLC
4503 E 47th St S (67210-1651)
PHONE....................316 554-0725
Chuck Brewer, *President*
Charles Brewer, *Branch Mgr*
EMP: 43
SQ FT: 20,000
SALES: 6MM
SALES (corp-wide): 28.7MM Privately Held
SIC: 8711 Acoustical engineering
PA: Alt & Witzig Engineering Inc
4105 W 99th St
Carmel IN 46032
317 875-7000

(G-14522)
GSI ENGINEERING LLC
4503 E 47th St S (67210-1651)
PHONE....................515 270-6542
Charles Brewer,
EMP: 65
SALES (est): 1.5MM Privately Held
SIC: 8711 Engineering services

(G-14523)
GSI ENGINEERING NTHRN DIV LLC
4503 E 47th St S (67210-1651)
PHONE....................316 554-0725
Charles Brewer, *Branch Mgr*
EMP: 12
SALES (est): 782.2K
SALES (corp-wide): 4.4MM Privately Held
SIC: 8711 8734 8999 7389 Engineering services; soil analysis; earth science services; geological consultant; inspection & testing services
PA: Gsi Engineering Northern Division Llc
2960 N Diers Ave
Grand Island NE 68803
308 381-1987

(G-14524)
GUARDIAN TITLE & TRUST COMPANY
8621 E 21st St N Ste 150 (67206-2991)
PHONE....................620 223-3330
Brandon Knowles, *Vice Pres*
Virginia Black, *Controller*
EMP: 27
SALES (est): 1.2MM Privately Held
WEB: www.guardiantt.com
SIC: 6541 Title & trust companies

(G-14525)
GUARDSMARK LLC
144 N Oliver Ave Ste 301 (67208-4050)
PHONE....................316 440-6646
EMP: 118
SALES (corp-wide): 608.3MM Privately Held
WEB: www.guardsmark.com
SIC: 7381 Security guard service
HQ: Guardsmark, Llc
1551 N Tustin Ave Ste 650
Santa Ana CA 92705
714 619-9700

(G-14526)
GUILD MORTGAGE COMPANY
300 N Main St Ste 200 (67202-1522)
PHONE....................316 749-2789
EMP: 19
SALES (corp-wide): 1.3B Privately Held
SIC: 6162 Mortgage bankers & correspondents
PA: Guild Mortgage Company
5898 Copley Dr Fl 4
San Diego CA 92111
800 365-4441

(G-14527)
GULFSIDE SUPPLY INC
Also Called: Gulfeagle Supply
2424 S Sheridan St (67217-1358)
PHONE....................316 941-9322
Vicki Hargrave, *Office Admin*
EMP: 10
SALES (corp-wide): 642.5MM Privately Held
SIC: 5033 Roofing & siding materials
PA: Gulfside Supply, Inc.
2900 E 7th Ave Ste 100
Tampa FL 33605
813 636-9808

(G-14528)
GUPTONS PETS & SUPPLIES INC
2815 S George Wash Blvd (67210-2198)
PHONE....................316 682-8111
Betty Gupton, *President*
Cammy Lees, *Corp Secy*
EMP: 25 EST: 1966
SALES: 750K Privately Held
SIC: 5999 0213 Pets; tropical fish; pet food; hogs

(G-14529)
GUTHRIDGE/NIGHSWONGER CORP (PA)
Also Called: G & N Cabinets
1702 S Laura Ave (67211-4417)
PHONE....................316 264-7900
Ditmar Guthridge, *President*
Larry Nighswonger, *Treasurer*
Guthridge Corp, *E-Business*
EMP: 15
SALES (est): 3.6MM Privately Held
SIC: 1542 1521 5712 5211 Commercial & office buildings, renovation & repair; general remodeling, single-family houses; cabinet work, custom; cabinets, kitchen; cabinet & finish carpentry

(G-14530)
H & C INSULATION CO INC
418 W 54th St S (67217-5540)
P.O. Box 422, Haysville (67060-0422)
PHONE....................316 522-0236
Randy Tucker, *President*
Sheri Tucker, *Treasurer*
EMP: 19
SALES: 1.2MM Privately Held
SIC: 1742 Insulation, buildings

(G-14531)
H & R PARTS CO INC
3066 S Hoover Rd (67215-1295)
PHONE....................316 942-6984
Lonnie Legleiter, *President*
Brandi Chadwell, *Treasurer*
EMP: 30
SQ FT: 34,618
SALES: 3.3MM Privately Held
SIC: 3728 3444 Aircraft body & wing assemblies & parts; sheet metalwork

(G-14532)
H M DUNN COMPANY INC
4201 S 119th St W (67215-9100)
PHONE....................316 522-5426
Phil Milazzo, *CEO*
Marc Szczerba, *CFO*
Robert Hoheisel, *Accounting Mgr*
▲ EMP: 131 EST: 1978
SQ FT: 80,000
SALES (est): 36.6MM Privately Held
WEB: www.nex-techaerospace.com
SIC: 3599 3728 Machine shop, jobbing & repair; aircraft parts & equipment

(G-14533)
H M DUNN COMPANY INC
1804 W 2nd St N (67203-5703)
PHONE....................314 535-6684
Chris Ross, *General Mgr*
EMP: 125
SALES (corp-wide): 200.2MM Privately Held
WEB: www.nex-techaerospace.com
SIC: 3599 3812 3544 3728 Machine shop, jobbing & repair; search & navigation equipment; special dies, tools, jigs & fixtures; aircraft parts & equipment
HQ: H. M. Dunn Company, Inc.
3301 House Anderson Rd
Euless TX 76040
817 283-3722

(G-14534)
H M DUNN COMPANY INC
4201 S 119th St W (67215-9100)
PHONE....................316 522-5426
James E Fultz, *Branch Mgr*
EMP: 40
SALES (corp-wide): 200.2MM Privately Held
SIC: 3599 Machine shop, jobbing & repair
HQ: H. M. Dunn Company, Inc.
3301 House Anderson Rd
Euless TX 76040
817 283-3722

(G-14535)
H&R BLOCK INC
Also Called: H & R Block
1223 N Rock Rd Ste A100 (67206-1271)
PHONE....................316 636-4009
Daniel Lien, *Manager*
EMP: 12
SALES (corp-wide): 3B Publicly Held
WEB: www.hrblock.com
SIC: 7291 Tax return preparation services
PA: H&R Block, Inc.
1 H&R Block Way
Kansas City MO 64105
816 854-3000

(G-14536)
H&R BLOCK INC
Also Called: H & R Block
2561 S Seneca St Ste 30 (67217-2866)
PHONE....................316 267-8257
Janice Frazee, *Manager*
EMP: 12
SALES (corp-wide): 3B Publicly Held
WEB: www.hrblock.com
SIC: 7291 Tax return preparation services
PA: H&R Block, Inc.
1 H&R Block Way
Kansas City MO 64105
816 854-3000

(G-14537)
H&R BLOCK INC
Also Called: H & R Block
534 S Rock Rd (67207-2366)
PHONE....................316 683-4211
Janice Frazee, *Branch Mgr*
EMP: 12
SALES (corp-wide): 3B Publicly Held
WEB: www.hrblock.com
SIC: 7291 Tax return preparation services
PA: H&R Block, Inc.
1 H&R Block Way
Kansas City MO 64105
816 854-3000

(G-14538)
H2 PLAINS LLC
10500 E Berkeley Square P (67206-6815)
PHONE....................785 798-3995
Kenneth Koerner, *General Mgr*
EMP: 12
SALES: 380K Privately Held
SIC: 1382 Oil & gas exploration services

(G-14539)
HADDOCK CORPORATION (PA)
Also Called: Haddock Computer Center
8625 E 37th St N Ste 104 (67226-2008)
P.O. Box 844118, Kansas City MO (64184-4118)
PHONE....................316 558-3849
Richard Haddock, *President*
Donna Ford, *Technology*
Stephanie Danielson, *Education*
Jan Shiever, *Education*
EMP: 50
SALES (est): 9.5MM Privately Held
WEB: www.gohaddock.com
SIC: 5734 7378 Personal computers; computer software & accessories; computer maintenance & repair

(G-14540)
HAHNER FOREMAN & HARNESS LLC (PA)
423 N Saint Francis Ave (67202-2623)
PHONE....................316 264-0306
David Foreman,
EMP: 20
SQ FT: 2,000
SALES (est): 2.5MM Privately Held
SIC: 1541 1542 Industrial buildings & warehouses; nonresidential construction

(G-14541)
HAIR CONNECTION
2424 N Woodlawn Blvd # 105 (67220-3957)
PHONE....................316 685-7213
Janet Corbett, *Owner*
EMP: 18
SQ FT: 2,300
SALES (est): 414.6K Privately Held
SIC: 7231 Unisex hair salons

(G-14542)
HAIR FORCE
1113 S Rock Rd (67207-3317)
PHONE....................316 684-3361
John Diprima, *Partner*
Joanne Diprima, *Partner*
EMP: 10 EST: 1977
SQ FT: 2,500
SALES (est): 242.7K Privately Held
SIC: 7231 Unisex hair salons

(G-14543)
HAIVALA CONCRETE TOOLS INC
1330 S Walnut St (67213-4347)
P.O. Box 1055 (67201-1055)
PHONE....................316 263-1683
Kerry Huckins, *President*
Paul Griggs, *President*
Kerry Huchins, *Corp Secy*
Beverly Ann Griggs, *Vice Pres*
EMP: 8 EST: 1946
SQ FT: 4,000
SALES: 500K Privately Held
WEB: www.haivala.com
SIC: 3423 3531 Shovels, spades (hand tools); drags, road (construction & road maintenance equipment)

(G-14544)
HAJOCA CORPORATION
711 N Hydraulic St (67214-3470)
P.O. Box 2017 (67201-2017)
PHONE....................316 262-2471
Rick Klau, *President*
Tim Snyder, *Manager*
EMP: 50
SQ FT: 35,000
SALES (corp-wide): 2.3B Privately Held
WEB: www.hajoca.com
SIC: 5074 5075 5085 Plumbing fittings & supplies; heating equipment (hydronic); air conditioning equipment, except room units; industrial supplies
PA: Hajoca Corporation
2001 Joshua Rd
Lafayette Hill PA 19444
610 649-1430

(G-14545)
HALL INDUSTRIAL DEV LLC
1221 E Murdock St Ste D (67214-3456)
PHONE....................316 264-7268
Lindsey Hall, *President*
Scott Hall, *Principal*
EMP: 19 EST: 1997
SALES (est): 1.3MM Privately Held
SIC: 4225 General warehousing

(G-14546)
HALL INDUSTRIAL SERVICES INC
1221 E Murdock St (67214-3456)
PHONE....................316 945-4255
Scott Hall, *Principal*
Doyle Lyon, *Sales Staff*

Lindsey Hall,
EMP: 40 **EST:** 2007
SALES (est): 446.7K **Privately Held**
SIC: 1796 Installing building equipment

(G-14547)
HALL STEEL & FABRICATION INC
1221 E Murdock St (67214-3456)
PHONE..................................316 263-4222
Scott Hall, *President*
Lindsey Hall, *Vice Pres*
EMP: 5
SALES (est): 563.8K **Privately Held**
SIC: 3441 5051 3444 Fabricated structural metal; steel; sheet metalwork

(G-14548)
HAMMEL SCALE CO INC (PA)
1530 N Mosley Ave (67214-1385)
PHONE..................................316 264-1358
Ross Runneabum, *President*
Alice Elam, *Corp Secy*
Craig Bartlett, *Sales Mgr*
Kyle Berg, *Accounts Mgr*
Todd Rice, *Sales Engr*
EMP: 23
SQ FT: 2,500
SALES (est): 4.6MM **Privately Held**
WEB: www.hammelscale.com
SIC: 5046 Scales, except laboratory

(G-14549)
HAMPEL OIL DISTRIBUTORS INC (PA)
3727 S West St (67217-3803)
P.O. Box 12346 (67277-2346)
PHONE..................................316 529-1162
William Hampel, *President*
Ed Hampel, *Vice Pres*
Ken Hampel, *Vice Pres*
Chris Marsh, *Opers Mgr*
Dustin Ruth, *Opers Mgr*
EMP: 30
SQ FT: 20,000
SALES (est): 135.4MM **Privately Held**
WEB: www.hampeloil.com
SIC: 5171 Petroleum bulk stations

(G-14550)
HAMPEL OIL DISTRIBUTORS INC
1245 N West St (67203-1241)
PHONE..................................800 530-5848
William J Hampel, *President*
EMP: 17
SALES (corp-wide): 135.4MM **Privately Held**
SIC: 5171 Petroleum bulk stations
PA: Hampel Oil Distributors, Inc.
3727 S West St
Wichita KS 67217
316 529-1162

(G-14551)
HAMPTON INN
2433 N Greenwich Rd (67226-8205)
PHONE..................................316 636-5594
Don Ross, *Principal*
EMP: 19
SALES (est): 883.9K **Privately Held**
SIC: 7011 Hotels & motels

(G-14552)
HAND CENTER PA
625 N Carriage Pkwy # 125 (67208-4599)
PHONE..................................316 688-5656
J Mark Melhorn, *President*
EMP: 15
SALES (est): 1.4MM **Privately Held**
SIC: 8011 Orthopedic physician

(G-14553)
HANDY MAILING SERVICE
3839 W Dora St (67213-1210)
PHONE..................................316 944-6258
Virgil E Esau, *President*
EMP: 12
SQ FT: 5,000
SALES: 1.1MM **Privately Held**
SIC: 7331 Mailing service

(G-14554)
HANGER PROSTHETICS &
Also Called: Hanger Clinic
410 N Hillside St Ste 100 (67214-4931)
PHONE..................................316 609-3000
Sam Liang, *President*
EMP: 7
SALES (corp-wide): 1B **Publicly Held**
SIC: 3842 Surgical appliances & supplies
HQ: Hanger Prosthetics & Orthotics East, Inc.
33 North Ave Ste 101
Tallmadge OH 44278

(G-14555)
HANGER PRSTHETCS & ORTHO INC
410 N Hillside St Ste 100 (67214-4931)
PHONE..................................316 685-1268
Sam Liang, *President*
Ken Schuldt, *Manager*
EMP: 16
SALES (corp-wide): 1B **Publicly Held**
SIC: 3842 Orthopedic appliances
HQ: Hanger Prosthetics & Orthotics, Inc.
10910 Domain Dr Ste 300
Austin TX 78758
512 777-3800

(G-14556)
HANNA HEATING & AC (PA)
220 N West St (67203-1203)
PHONE..................................316 945-3481
Carl Hanna, *President*
EMP: 23
SQ FT: 4,800
SALES (est): 4MM **Privately Held**
WEB: www.hannaheatingandair.com
SIC: 1711 Warm air heating & air conditioning contractor

(G-14557)
HANNEMAN & HEWITT CPA
Also Called: Hanneman & Hewitt PA
205 W 2nd St N Ste A (67202-1205)
PHONE..................................316 269-4500
Scott Hewitt, *President*
Delbert Hanneman, *Corp Secy*
EMP: 10
SALES: 650K **Privately Held**
WEB: www.hewittcpa.com
SIC: 8721 Certified public accountant

(G-14558)
HAPPY HEARTS CHILD DEVELOPMENT
5833 E 37th St N (67220-1988)
PHONE..................................316 613-3550
EMP: 11 **EST:** 2009
SALES (est): 253.9K **Privately Held**
SIC: 8351 Child Day Care Services

(G-14559)
HARBOR FREIGHT TOOLS USA INC
2487 S Seneca St (67217-2801)
PHONE..................................316 269-2779
Jay Watkins, *Branch Mgr*
EMP: 16
SALES (corp-wide): 2.3B **Privately Held**
SIC: 5251 5084 5072 Tools; processing & packaging equipment; hand tools
PA: Harbor Freight Tools Usa, Inc.
26541 Agoura Rd
Calabasas CA 91302
818 836-5001

(G-14560)
HARLAN HERMANSON
Also Called: Comm Tronix
1735 W Mccormick Ave (67213-3809)
PHONE..................................316 263-5958
Harlan Hermanson, *Owner*
EMP: 5 **EST:** 1981
SQ FT: 1,000
SALES: 500K **Privately Held**
WEB: www.comm-tronix.com
SIC: 3823 Telemetering instruments, industrial process type

(G-14561)
HARLOW AEROSTRUCTURES LLC (PA)
1501 S Mclean Blvd (67213-4303)
P.O. Box 304 (67201-0304)
PHONE..................................316 265-5268
Phillip C Friedman, *CEO*
Jim Barnes, *President*
Daniel Aron, *Vice Pres*
Kevin Alcorn, *Engineer*
Barry Fulmer, *Engineer*
EMP: 129
SQ FT: 130,000
SALES (est): 118.6MM **Privately Held**
WEB: www.harlowair.com
SIC: 3728 3452 Aircraft parts & equipment; bolts, nuts, rivets & washers

(G-14562)
HARP WELL PUMP SVC CORPORATED
215 S Tyler Rd (67209-1436)
PHONE..................................316 722-1411
Lloyd L Harp, *President*
EMP: 19
SQ FT: 1,500
SALES (est): 2.4MM **Privately Held**
SIC: 1781 1623 Water well servicing; pumping station construction

(G-14563)
HARPER TRUCKS INC
1522 S Florence St (67209-2634)
P.O. Box 12330 (67277-2330)
PHONE..................................316 942-1381
Phillip G Ruffin, *CEO*
Gary Leiker, *Vice Pres*
Emmitt Johnson, *Opers Staff*
Darrell Neugebauer, *Natl Sales Mgr*
Susie Ellis, *Cust Mgr*
◆ **EMP:** 130 **EST:** 1953
SQ FT: 170,000
SALES: 30MM **Privately Held**
WEB: www.harpertrucks.com
SIC: 3537 Forklift trucks

(G-14564)
HARRIS HEALTHCARE LLC
5240 N Sullivan Rd (67204-2640)
PHONE..................................316 721-4828
Fax: 316 721-4844
EMP: 13
SQ FT: 1,000
SALES: 200K **Privately Held**
SIC: 8082 Health Care Services

(G-14565)
HARRY B RUSK COMPANY INC
352 N New York Ave (67214-4142)
PHONE..................................316 263-4680
Kenneth Rusk, *President*
Benjamin Rusk, *Manager*
EMP: 8 **EST:** 1968
SQ FT: 3,000
SALES (est): 1MM **Privately Held**
SIC: 3844 X-ray apparatus & tubes

(G-14566)
HARTWOOD PAINTING
3937 S Baehr St (67215-1104)
PHONE..................................316 554-7510
Jim Robinson, *President*
Brian Robinson, *Vice Pres*
EMP: 25
SALES (est): 1.2MM **Privately Held**
SIC: 1721 Industrial painting

(G-14567)
HARVEST FACILITY HOLDINGS LP
Also Called: Grasslands Estates
10665 W 13th St N (67212-5600)
PHONE..................................316 722-5100
Randy Swanson, *Manager*
EMP: 31 **Publicly Held**
WEB: www.holidaytouch.com
SIC: 6513 Retirement hotel operation
HQ: Harvest Facility Holdings Lp
5885 Meadows Rd Ste 500
Lake Oswego OR 97035
503 370-7070

(G-14568)
HAVE IT MAID
737 S Washington Ave # 1 (67211-2411)
PHONE..................................316 264-0110
Mark Danahy, *President*
EMP: 18
SALES (est): 790.6K **Privately Held**
SIC: 7363 7349 Domestic help service; maid services, contract or fee basis

(G-14569)
HAWKS INTERSTATE PESTMASTERS
814 N Main St (67203-3605)
PHONE..................................316 267-8331
Bill J Hawks, *President*
Mary A Hawks, *Corp Secy*
Brad Hawks, *Vice Pres*
EMP: 32
SQ FT: 3,000
SALES (est): 2.3MM **Privately Held**
WEB: www.callhawks.com
SIC: 7342 Pest control in structures

(G-14570)
HAYES COMPANY LLC (PA)
Also Called: Hayes Retail Services
559 W Douglas Ave (67213-4701)
PHONE..................................316 838-8000
Paul Bush, *Project Mgr*
William Hayes, *Mng Member*
Rick Randall, *Info Tech Mgr*
Phillip M Hayes,
Robert J Hayes,
◆ **EMP:** 15
SQ FT: 11,492
SALES (est): 24.8MM **Privately Held**
SIC: 4225 General warehousing

(G-14571)
HAYFORD EAST
129 E 2nd St N (67202-2004)
PHONE..................................316 267-6259
David Holly, *Owner*
EMP: 10
SALES (est): 479.4K **Privately Held**
SIC: 8111 General practice attorney, lawyer

(G-14572)
HCA HOSPITAL SVCS SAN DIEGO (DH)
Also Called: Columbia HCA
550 N Hillside St (67214-4910)
PHONE..................................316 962-2000
David S Nevill, *CEO*
Nancy McMaster, *Purch Dir*
Jeff Schauf, *Info Tech Dir*
EMP: 2500
SQ FT: 1,000,000
SALES (est): 86.7MM **Publicly Held**
WEB: www.wesleymedicalcenter.com
SIC: 8062 Hospital, medical school affiliated with residency
HQ: Hca Inc.
1 Park Plz
Nashville TN 37203
615 344-9551

(G-14573)
HCW WICHITA HOTEL LLC
Also Called: Hampton Inn Wichita Northwest
10047 W 29th St N (67205-7915)
PHONE..................................316 925-6600
Richard Huffman, *Principal*
Derek Q Nguyen, *Principal*
EMP: 25
SALES (est): 246.2K **Privately Held**
SIC: 7011 Hotels & motels

(G-14574)
HEAD START CHILD DEV CNCIL INC
238 N Waco St (67202-1108)
PHONE..................................316 267-1997
Fax: 316 262-2425
EMP: 11
SALES (corp-wide): 20MM **Privately Held**
SIC: 8351 Child Day Care Services
PA: Head Start Child Development, Council, Inc.
5361 N Pershing Ave Ste A
Stockton CA 95207

GEOGRAPHIC

(G-14575)
HEALTH FACILITIES GROUP LLC (PA)
142 N Mosley St Fl 3 (67202-2826)
PHONE.....316 262-2500
Stephen L Lewallen, *CEO*
Kathy Clements, *Business Mgr*
David Wright, *COO*
Ginee Stiverson, *Marketing Staff*
Dana Taylor-Perry, *Marketing Staff*
EMP: 18
SALES (est): 2.2MM **Privately Held**
WEB: www.healthfacilitiesgroup.com
SIC: 8712 Architectural engineering

(G-14576)
HEALTH IN SYNC HOME INC
1107 S Glendale St # 224 (67218-3230)
PHONE.....316 295-4692
Patricia Muthoni, *President*
EMP: 25
SQ FT: 340
SALES (est): 571.2K **Privately Held**
SIC: 8082 Home health care services

(G-14577)
HEALTHBACK OF WICHITA
1133 S Rock Rd Ste 7 (67207-3357)
PHONE.....316 687-0340
Christy Evans, *Principal*
EMP: 12
SALES (est): 253.7K **Privately Held**
SIC: 8082 Home health care services

(G-14578)
HEALTHCORE CLINIC INC
2707 E 21st St N (67214-2249)
PHONE.....316 691-0249
Teresa Lovelady, *CEO*
Jamil Moody, *Ch of Bd*
EMP: 42
SALES: 3.7MM **Privately Held**
WEB: www.wichitawellness.org
SIC: 8011 General & family practice, physician/surgeon

(G-14579)
HEALTHPEAK PROPERTIES INC
Also Called: Cherry Creek Vlg Rtirement Ctr
8200 E Pawnee St Ofc (67207-5445)
PHONE.....316 733-2645
Gennie Davis, *Director*
EMP: 19
SQ FT: 16,000
SALES (corp-wide): 1.8B **Publicly Held**
WEB: www.hcpi.com
SIC: 6512 Nonresidential building operators
PA: Healthpeak Properties, Inc.
1920 Main St Ste 1200
Irvine CA 92614
949 407-0700

(G-14580)
HEARTLAND AT-CHLOR SYSTEMS LLC
1733 Southwest Blvd (67213-1433)
P.O. Box 9005, Amarillo TX (79105-9005)
PHONE.....806 373-4277
Donnell Blake, *Principal*
EMP: 14
SALES (est): 2.6MM **Privately Held**
SIC: 2842 7216 Laundry cleaning preparations; drycleaning collecting & distributing agency

(G-14581)
HEARTLAND CARDIOLOGY LLC
3535 N Webb Rd (67226-8127)
PHONE.....316 686-5300
Barry Reynolds, *CEO*
Assem Farhat, *President*
Lan Phu, *Superintendent*
Ghiyath Al-Tabbal, *Principal*
Ravi Bajaj, *Principal*
EMP: 17 **EST:** 2015
SALES (est): 350.4K **Privately Held**
SIC: 8011 Physicians' office, including specialists; cardiologist & cardio-vascular specialist

(G-14582)
HEARTLAND COCA-COLA BTLG LLC
3151 S West St (67217-1035)
PHONE.....316 942-3838
EMP: 3433
SALES (corp-wide): 23.9B **Privately Held**
SIC: 5149 2086 Beverages, except coffee & tea; carbonated beverages, nonalcoholic: bottled & canned
PA: Heartland Coca-Cola Bottling Company Llc
9000 Marshall Dr
Lenexa KS

(G-14583)
HEARTLAND CREDIT UNION ASSN
2544 N Maize Ct Ste 100 (67205-7358)
PHONE.....316 942-7965
Susan Dyer, *Branch Mgr*
EMP: 10
SALES (corp-wide): 1.4MM **Privately Held**
SIC: 8611 Trade associations
PA: Heartland Credit Union Association
6800 College Blvd Ste 300
Overland Park KS 66211
913 297-2480

(G-14584)
HEARTLAND HM HLTH & HOSPICE PA
Also Called: Hcr Manicure
2872 N Ridge Rd Ste 122 (67205-1144)
PHONE.....316 788-7626
Elliott Lekawa, *CEO*
EMP: 81
SQ FT: 12,000
SALES (est): 1.4MM **Privately Held**
SIC: 8082 Home health care services

(G-14585)
HEARTLAND HOSPICE SERVICES LLC
Also Called: Heartland HM Hlth Care Hospice
2872 N Ridge Rd Ste 122 (67205-1144)
PHONE.....419 252-5743
Rina Lawson, *Manager*
EMP: 55
SALES (corp-wide): 8.2B **Privately Held**
SIC: 8052 Personal care facility
HQ: Heartland Hospice Services, Llc
333 N Summit St
Toledo OH 43604

(G-14586)
HEARTLAND MOVING & STORAGE
2111 E Industrial St (67216-2414)
P.O. Box 16284 (67216-0284)
PHONE.....316 554-0224
Britt King, *Owner*
EMP: 10
SALES (est): 120.3K **Privately Held**
SIC: 4212 Moving services

(G-14587)
HEARTLAND PAYMENT SYSTEMS LLC
3500 N Rock Rd Bldg 1300 (67226-1335)
PHONE.....316 390-1988
Minde Baumgartner, *Mktg Dir*
Minde Baumtartner, *Manager*
EMP: 99
SALES (corp-wide): 3.3B **Publicly Held**
SIC: 7389 Personal service agents, brokers & bureaus
HQ: Heartland Payment Systems, Llc
10 Glenlake Pkwy Ste 324
Atlanta GA 30328
609 683-3831

(G-14588)
HEARTLAND TECHNOLOGIES INC
5200a E 35th St N (67220-3400)
PHONE.....316 932-8001
Mael Hernandez, *President*
Tony Hampton, *Vice Pres*
Jim Stevens, *Manager*
EMP: 7
SALES (est): 963.3K **Privately Held**
WEB: www.purifan.com
SIC: 3564 Air purification equipment

(G-14589)
HEARTLAND WOMENS GROUP AT WES
3243 E Murdock St Ste 401 (67208-3007)
PHONE.....316 962-7175
Andrew Hare, *Principal*
EMP: 30
SALES (est): 1.7MM **Publicly Held**
SIC: 8011 Gynecologist
PA: Hca Healthcare, Inc.
1 Park Plz
Nashville TN 37203

(G-14590)
HEARTSPRING INC
8700 E 29th St N (67226-2169)
PHONE.....316 634-8700
Gary Singleton, *President*
David Stupay, *President*
Paul Faber, *Vice Pres*
Patty Allsbury, *Purch Mgr*
David Dorf, *CFO*
EMP: 320 **EST:** 1934
SQ FT: 88,000
SALES: 18.8MM **Privately Held**
WEB: www.heartspring.com
SIC: 8211 8093 8049 School for physically handicapped; specialty outpatient clinics; audiologist

(G-14591)
HEARTSTONE INC
1651 S Eisenhower St (67209-2807)
PHONE.....316 942-1135
Kirby Jantz, *CEO*
Chad Jantz, *President*
EMP: 10
SQ FT: 1,800
SALES (est): 2.4MM **Privately Held**
WEB: www.heartstone.net
SIC: 1611 Surfacing & paving

(G-14592)
HEAVEN ENGINEERING LLC
340 S Pattie Ave (67211-1721)
PHONE.....316 262-1244
Mark Odonnell, *Manager*
EMP: 10 **Privately Held**
WEB: www.heavenengineering.com
SIC: 5075 Warm air heating equipment & supplies
PA: Heaven Engineering, L.L.C.
4331 Merriam Dr
Overland Park KS 66203

(G-14593)
HENRY L BUMGARDNER JR OD
2205 S Seneca St (67213-4224)
PHONE.....316 264-4648
Henry L Bumgardner, *Owner*
Bruce Will, *Principal*
EMP: 10
SQ FT: 2,600
SALES (est): 600K **Privately Held**
SIC: 8042 Offices & clinics of optometrists

(G-14594)
HERITAGE GROUP LC
7309 E 21st St N Ste 120 (67206-1178)
PHONE.....316 261-5301
Debi Foster, *Accountant*
Todd Connell,
EMP: 17
SALES (est): 1MM **Privately Held**
SIC: 8721 8742 Accounting services, except auditing; billing & bookkeeping service; business consultant

(G-14595)
HERITAGE INN WICHITA OPCO LLC
Also Called: Wichita Comfort Inn
9525 E Corporate Hills Dr (67207-1324)
PHONE.....316 686-2844
Lauris Molbert, *President*
EMP: 20
SALES (est): 130.7K **Privately Held**
SIC: 7011 Hotels & motels
PA: Tmi Hospitality, L.P.
4850 32nd Ave S
Fargo ND 58104

(G-14596)
HERITAGE RESTAURANT INC
4551 S Broadway Ave (67216-1735)
PHONE.....316 524-7495
Michael Choi, *President*
EMP: 27
SQ FT: 5,000
SALES: 2.7MM **Privately Held**
WEB: www.heritage4u.net
SIC: 7999 5812 Lottery tickets, sale of; restaurant, family: independent

(G-14597)
HERTZ CORPORATION
550 N Webb Rd Ste D (67206-1857)
PHONE.....316 689-3773
Steve Off, *Manager*
EMP: 22
SALES (corp-wide): 9.5B **Publicly Held**
SIC: 7514 Rent-a-car service
HQ: The Hertz Corporation
8501 Williams Rd
Estero FL 33928
239 301-7000

(G-14598)
HERTZ CORPORATION
1590 S Airport Rd (67209-1903)
PHONE.....316 946-4860
Richard Kirkham, *Branch Mgr*
EMP: 23
SALES (corp-wide): 9.5B **Publicly Held**
SIC: 7514 Rent-a-car service
HQ: The Hertz Corporation
8501 Williams Rd
Estero FL 33928
239 301-7000

(G-14599)
HERTZ CORPORATION
2010 S Airport Rd (67209-1941)
PHONE.....316 946-4860
EMP: 23
SALES (corp-wide): 9.5B **Publicly Held**
SIC: 7514 Rent-a-car service
HQ: The Hertz Corporation
8501 Williams Rd
Estero FL 33928
239 301-7000

(G-14600)
HERTZ CORPORATION
2121 S Hoover Rd (67209-2821)
PHONE.....316 946-4860
EMP: 23
SALES (corp-wide): 9.5B **Publicly Held**
SIC: 7514 Rent-a-car service
HQ: The Hertz Corporation
8501 Williams Rd
Estero FL 33928
239 301-7000

(G-14601)
HERTZ CORPORATION
1760 S Airport Rd (67209-1944)
PHONE.....316 946-4860
EMP: 23
SALES (corp-wide): 9.5B **Publicly Held**
SIC: 7514 Rent-a-car service
HQ: The Hertz Corporation
8501 Williams Rd
Estero FL 33928
239 301-7000

(G-14602)
HEUBEL MATERIAL HANDLING INC
1220 E Central Ave (67214-3925)
PHONE.....316 941-4115
David Baker, *Branch Mgr*
EMP: 10 **Privately Held**
WEB: www.heubelmaterial.com
SIC: 5084 Lift trucks & parts; materials handling machinery
HQ: Heubel Material Handling, Inc.
6311 Equitable Rd
Kansas City MO 64120
816 231-6900

(G-14603)
HI HRITG INN WCHITA OPCO LLC
Also Called: Wichita Hampton Inn
9449 E Corporate Hills Dr (67207-1322)
PHONE.....316 686-3576

Lauris Molbert, *CEO*
EMP: 20
SALES (est): 294.4K **Privately Held**
SIC: 7011 Hotels & motels
PA: Tmi Hospitality, L.P.
4850 32nd Ave S
Fargo ND 58104

(G-14604)
HIGH QUALITY TECH INC
2302 N Hood Ave Ste 200 (67204-5733)
PHONE.................................316 448-3559
Milton Reagans, *CEO*
EMP: 5
SQ FT: 1,500
SALES (est): 415.3K **Privately Held**
SIC: 8742 3571 Management information systems consultant; electronic computers

(G-14605)
HIGH REACH EQUIPMENT LLC (PA)
3624 W 30th St S (67217-1016)
PHONE.................................316 942-5438
Keith Bomolt,
Todd Leiker,
EMP: 12
SALES (est): 3.8MM **Privately Held**
SIC: 7359 7353 5251 Stores & yards equipment rental; heavy construction equipment rental; hardware

(G-14606)
HIGH TOUCH INC (PA)
Also Called: High Touch Tech Solutions
110 S Main St Ste 600 (67202-3746)
PHONE.................................316 462-4001
Wayne Chambers, *President*
David Oles, *COO*
Dave Glover, *Vice Pres*
Jason Mock, *Vice Pres*
Amy Mounts, *Vice Pres*
EMP: 90
SQ FT: 63,000
SALES (est): 57.4MM **Privately Held**
WEB: www.hightouchinc.com
SIC: 7373 Value-added resellers, computer systems

(G-14607)
HIGHER GROUND
247 N Market St (67202-2003)
PHONE.................................316 262-2060
Mary San Martin, *Director*
Shawn Biberdorf, *Administration*
EMP: 15
SALES (est): 394K **Privately Held**
SIC: 8322 8742 Substance abuse counseling; training & development consultant

(G-14608)
HILAND DAIRY FOODS COMPANY LLC
700 E Central Ave (67202-1064)
P.O. Box 2199 (67201-2199)
PHONE.................................316 267-4221
Greg Thomas, *General Mgr*
Tim Little, *Plant Mgr*
Ginger Penn, *Human Resources*
Jason Hoopes, *Manager*
EMP: 200
SALES (corp-wide): 1.7B **Privately Held**
SIC: 2026 2023 Milk processing (pasteurizing, homogenizing, bottling); dry, condensed, evaporated dairy products
HQ: Hiland Dairy Foods Company., Llc
1133 E Kearney St
Springfield MO 65803
417 862-9311

(G-14609)
HILL TOP CENTER
Also Called: Childcare Association
1329 S Terrace Dr (67218-3127)
PHONE.................................316 686-9095
Deidre Rankin, *Controller*
EMP: 16
SALES (est): 270.3K **Privately Held**
SIC: 8351 Child day care services

(G-14610)
HILLCREST APARTMENT BLDG CO
115 S Rutan Ave (67218-1135)
PHONE.................................316 684-7204
Bill Landis, *Manager*
EMP: 14
SQ FT: 181,000
SALES: 876.9K **Privately Held**
SIC: 6513 Apartment building operators

(G-14611)
HILLER INC
630 N Washington Ave (67214-3894)
PHONE.................................316 264-5231
Horst K Hiller, *President*
Vincent Wade, *Planning*
◆ **EMP:** 40
SQ FT: 54,000
SALES (est): 6.6MM **Privately Held**
WEB: www.hillerinc.com
SIC: 3728 Aircraft parts & equipment

(G-14612)
HILLSHIRE BRANDS COMPANY
Also Called: Cain's Coffee
427 S Washington Ave (67202-4735)
P.O. Box 457 (67201-0457)
PHONE.................................316 262-5443
Mike Stout, *Branch Mgr*
EMP: 30
SALES (corp-wide): 42.4B **Publicly Held**
SIC: 5149 5499 Coffee & tea; beverage stores
HQ: The Hillshire Brands Company
400 S Jefferson St Fl 1
Chicago IL 60607
312 614-6000

(G-14613)
HILLSIDE MEDICAL OFFICE
855 N Hillside St (67214-4982)
PHONE.................................316 685-1381
Hugh Haengern, *Partner*
Kim Hartwell, *Partner*
Rick Hartwell, *Partner*
David Gordon, *General Mgr*
Dave Gordon, *Principal*
EMP: 40
SALES (est): 4.8MM **Privately Held**
SIC: 8011 8621 General & family practice, physician/surgeon; physicians' office, including specialists; professional membership organizations

(G-14614)
HILLSIDE NURSERY INC
2200 S Hillside St (67211-5697)
PHONE.................................316 686-6414
Mark McHenry, *President*
EMP: 19
SQ FT: 5,000
SALES: 1.2MM **Privately Held**
SIC: 5261 0782 Nursery stock, seeds & bulbs; landscape contractors

(G-14615)
HILLTOP MANOR MUTAL HSING CORP
1411 S Oliver St (67218-3225)
PHONE.................................316 684-5141
Jane Tanner, *Treasurer*
Paunee Rohr, *Admin Sec*
EMP: 10
SALES: 390K **Privately Held**
SIC: 6531 Real estate managers

(G-14616)
HINKLE LAW FIRM LLC (PA)
1617 N Waterfront Pkwy # 400
(67206-6639)
PHONE.................................316 267-2000
Gerry Raine, *President*
Peter Collins, *Counsel*
Ruhe Rutter, *Counsel*
Laura Mossman, *CPA*
Anna Foster, *Human Res Mgr*
EMP: 80
SQ FT: 12,000
SALES (est): 13.2MM **Privately Held**
SIC: 8111 Administrative & government law; taxation law; corporate, partnership & business law; real estate law

(G-14617)
HISTORIC PRESRVTN ALIANCE OF W
Also Called: H P A
230 N Market St Ste 201 (67202-2006)
PHONE.................................316 269-9432
Greg Kite, *President*
Sam Nance, *Vice Pres*
Kandi Crenshaw, *Treasurer*
Jo Anne Corbett, *Admin Sec*
EMP: 75
SALES (est): 855.9K **Privately Held**
WEB: www.hpa.com
SIC: 8412 Historical society

(G-14618)
HISTORIC WICHITA SEDQWICK CNTY
Also Called: OLD COWTOWN MUSEUM
1865 W Museum Blvd (67203-3600)
PHONE.................................316 219-1871
Hugh D Gurney, *Principal*
Gregory Hunt, *Manager*
Lisa Dodson, *Consultant*
EMP: 35
SQ FT: 3,000
SALES: 117.9K **Privately Held**
SIC: 8412 Museum

(G-14619)
HITE FANNING & HONEYMAN LLP
100 N Broadway Ave # 950 (67202-2216)
PHONE.................................316 265-7741
Sheila Regene, *President*
Linda Parks, *Managing Prtnr*
Jennifer Skliris, *Counsel*
Alicia M Lange, *Admin Sec*
Elizabeth Satterly, *Admin Sec*
EMP: 40
SALES (est): 4.8MM **Privately Held**
WEB: www.hitefanning.com
SIC: 8111 General practice attorney, lawyer

(G-14620)
HOC INDUSTRIES INC
3511 N Ohio St (67219-3721)
P.O. Box 2609 (67201-2609)
PHONE.................................316 838-4663
William R Nath, *President*
Tom Olsen, *Exec VP*
Harold Befort, *Plant Mgr*
Tharen Spahr, *CFO*
▲ **EMP:** 28
SQ FT: 80,000
SALES (est): 46.5MM **Privately Held**
WEB: www.hocindustries.com
SIC: 5171 Petroleum bulk stations

(G-14621)
HOELKER TOOLING
355 N Martinson St (67203-5960)
PHONE.................................316 744-7777
Donald W Hoelker, *Owner*
Joanna Hoelker, *Co-Owner*
EMP: 5
SQ FT: 3,000
SALES (est): 125K **Privately Held**
SIC: 3544 Special dies & tools

(G-14622)
HOFFMAN INC
Also Called: Richard Hoffman Trucking
3703 W 30th St S (67217-1017)
PHONE.................................316 942-8011
Catherine Deal, *President*
Kathrine Deal, *President*
Richard Hoffman, *Corp Secy*
EMP: 12
SALES (est): 600K **Privately Held**
WEB: www.rhoffmantrucking.com
SIC: 4213 1794 Heavy machinery transport; excavation work

(G-14623)
HOFFMANN FABRICATING LLC
909 E Waterman St (67202-4731)
P.O. Box 3546 (67201-3546)
PHONE.................................316 262-6041
Janice Hoffman, *Partner*
Janice Hoffmann,
Amanda Hoffman, *Administration*
EMP: 15
SQ FT: 6,000
SALES (est): 1.7MM **Privately Held**
SIC: 7389 Sewing contractor

(G-14624)
HOFFMANNS GREEN INDUSTRIES
Also Called: Tropical Designs
1120 E 26th St (67206)
PHONE.................................316 634-1500
Barbara Hoffmann, *President*
John Hoffman, *Corp Secy*
Mary Wacker, *Manager*
EMP: 25
SQ FT: 12,580
SALES (est): 1.4MM **Privately Held**
SIC: 7389 5992 5261 5947 Plant care service; plants, potted; flowers, fresh; nurseries & garden centers; gift shop; live plant rental

(G-14625)
HOLLAND PAVING INC
1255 S Tyler Rd (67209-1830)
P.O. Box 771102 (67277-1102)
PHONE.................................316 722-7114
George Holland, *Principal*
EMP: 42
SALES (est): 9.8MM **Privately Held**
WEB: www.hollandpaving.net
SIC: 1611 Surfacing & paving

(G-14626)
HOLY FAMILY MEDICAL INC
144 S Hillside St Ste A (67211-2155)
PHONE.................................316 682-9900
Brenda Thanel, *CEO*
Ronald Ferris, *Medical Dir*
Catherine Barba Abay, *Bd of Directors*
Michael Dandurand, *Bd of Directors*
Ken Kern, *Bd of Directors*
EMP: 32
SALES (est): 650.9K **Privately Held**
SIC: 7389

(G-14627)
HOLY FAMILY MEDICAL ASSOC LLP
144 S Hillside St Ste A (67211-2155)
PHONE.................................316 682-9900
Ronald Ferris MD, *Principal*
Brenda Thanel, *Administration*
Carolyn Bland, *Physician Asst*
EMP: 22
SALES (est): 2.2MM **Privately Held**
SIC: 8011 General & family practice, physician/surgeon

(G-14628)
HOME DEPOT USA INC
Also Called: Home Depot, The
3350 N Woodlawn Blvd (67220-2202)
PHONE.................................316 681-0899
Dooug Wetcel, *Branch Mgr*
EMP: 200
SALES (corp-wide): 108.2B **Publicly Held**
WEB: www.homerentalsdepot.com
SIC: 5211 7359 Home centers; tool rental
HQ: Home Depot U.S.A., Inc.
2455 Paces Ferry Ave
Atlanta GA 30339

(G-14629)
HOME DEPOT USA INC
Also Called: Home Depot, The
8444 W Mccormick Ave (67209-1700)
PHONE.................................316 773-1988
Louis Peters, *Manager*
EMP: 150
SALES (corp-wide): 108.2B **Publicly Held**
WEB: www.homerentalsdepot.com
SIC: 5211 7359 Home centers; tool rental
HQ: Home Depot U.S.A., Inc.
2455 Paces Ferry Ave
Atlanta GA 30339

(G-14630)
HOME HEALTH OF KANSAS LLC
7607 E Harry St (67207-3111)
PHONE.................................316 684-5122
Anthony Ndungu, *Administration*
Emma Ndungu,
EMP: 30 **EST:** 2005
SALES: 1.8MM **Privately Held**
SIC: 8082 Visiting nurse service

GEOGRAPHIC

(G-14631)
HOME INSTEAD SENIOR CARE
3062 N Cranberry St (67226-1209)
PHONE..................................316 612-7541
Rick Brixius, *President*
EMP: 20
SALES (est): 670K **Privately Held**
SIC: 8082 8322 Home health care services; geriatric social service

(G-14632)
HOMELAND ROOFING AND CNSTR LLC
1107 S West St (67213-1629)
PHONE..................................316 832-9901
Cliff Williams,
EMP: 12
SQ FT: 3,300
SALES: 2.7MM **Privately Held**
SIC: 1761 1542 Roofing contractor; nonresidential construction

(G-14633)
HOMESTEAD HEALTH CENTER INC
2133 S Elizabeth St (67213-3403)
PHONE..................................316 262-4473
Bill Shook, *Director*
Ashley Welch, *Director*
Heather Hayes, *Food Svc Dir*
EMP: 100 **EST:** 1976
SQ FT: 20,000
SALES: 4.8MM **Privately Held**
SIC: 8052 Personal care facility

(G-14634)
HONEYWELL INTERNATIONAL INC
7227 W Harry St (67209-1993)
PHONE..................................316 522-8172
Terry Karst, *General Mgr*
EMP: 220
SALES (corp-wide): 41.8B **Publicly Held**
WEB: www.honeywell.com
SIC: 3724 Aircraft engines & engine parts
PA: Honeywell International Inc.
300 S Tryon St
Charlotte NC 28202
973 455-2000

(G-14635)
HONGS LANDSCAPE & NURSERY INC
8904 E 31st St S (67210-1837)
PHONE..................................316 687-3492
IL Sik Hong, *President*
Debbie Hong, *Treasurer*
Lori Hong, *Retailers*
EMP: 10
SQ FT: 3,000
SALES (est): 1.4MM **Privately Held**
WEB: www.hongslandscape.com
SIC: 5261 0782 Nurseries; landscape contractors

(G-14636)
HOPPERS GLASS INC
880 E Bayley St (67211-3309)
PHONE..................................316 262-0497
Dwight Hooper, *President*
Britt Hopper, *Principal*
Rick Hopper, *Corp Secy*
Larry Hopper, *Project Mgr*
EMP: 30
SQ FT: 15,000
SALES (est): 5.1MM **Privately Held**
WEB: www.hopperglass.com
SIC: 1793 Glass & glazing work

(G-14637)
HOSPICE INCORPORATED (PA)
Also Called: HARRY HYNES MEMORIAL HOSPICE
313 S Market St (67202-3805)
PHONE..................................316 265-9441
Jerry Kerschen, *President*
Steve Gillies, *Vice Pres*
Renee Hahn, *CFO*
Heather Petty, *Accountant*
Gayvon Cassity, *Finance*
EMP: 58
SALES: 18.1MM **Privately Held**
SIC: 8082 7261 Home health care services; funeral service & crematories

(G-14638)
HOSPICE CARE OF KANSAS LLC (PA)
2622 W Central Ave # 501 (67203-4969)
PHONE..................................316 721-8803
EMP: 31
SALES (est): 2MM **Privately Held**
SIC: 8052 Intermediate Care Facility

(G-14639)
HOSPITALITY MANAGEMENT LLC
Also Called: Marten's Company, The
435 S Broadway Ave (67202-3909)
PHONE..................................316 262-0000
Steven Martens,
EMP: 30 **EST:** 2001
SALES (est): 1.1MM **Privately Held**
SIC: 7349 Building maintenance services

(G-14640)
HOTEL AT OLD TOWN INC
830 E 1st St N (67202-2737)
PHONE..................................316 267-4800
Jack Deboer, *CEO*
Jennifer Finlay, *General Mgr*
Steve Butcher, *Vice Pres*
Michael Frimel, *Vice Pres*
Michael Gordon, *Sales Mgr*
EMP: 50 **EST:** 1997
SALES (est): 1.9MM **Privately Held**
WEB: www.hotelatoldtown.com
SIC: 7011 Hotels

(G-14641)
HOTEL WICHITA GREENWICH
1220 N Greenwich Rd (67206-2665)
PHONE..................................316 681-1800
Talia Patterson, *Manager*
EMP: 12
SALES (est): 569.7K **Privately Held**
SIC: 7011 Hotels & motels

(G-14642)
HOUSE OF SCHWAN INC
3636 N Comotara St (67226-1301)
PHONE..................................316 636-9100
Barry L Schwan, *President*
Dale Baalman, *CFO*
EMP: 90
SQ FT: 50,848
SALES (est): 30.2MM **Privately Held**
WEB: www.houseofschwan.com
SIC: 5181 Beer & other fermented malt liquors

(G-14643)
HOWARD JOHNSON EXPRESS INN
6575 W Kellogg Dr (67209-2211)
PHONE..................................316 943-8165
Sal Bhakta, *Owner*
Brenda Smith, *Manager*
EMP: 11
SALES (est): 579.1K **Privately Held**
SIC: 7011 Hotels & motels

(G-14644)
HPT TRS IHG 2 INC
Also Called: Candlewood Suites
570 S Julia St (67209-2301)
PHONE..................................316 942-0400
Chuck Sourbeer, *Branch Mgr*
EMP: 13 **Privately Held**
SIC: 7011 Hotels
HQ: Intercontinental Hotels Group Resources, Inc.
3 Ravinia Dr Ste 100
Atlanta GA 30346
770 604-5000

(G-14645)
HPT TRS IHG-2 INC
Also Called: Candlewood Suites
3141 N Webb Rd (67226-8119)
PHONE..................................316 634-6070
Nina Duke, *General Mgr*
EMP: 13 **Publicly Held**
SIC: 7011 Hotel, franchised
HQ: Hpt Trs Ihg-2, Inc.
255 Washington St Ste 300
Newton MA 02458
617 964-8389

(G-14646)
HUBER INC
117 N Handley St (67203-6114)
P.O. Box 3520 (67201-3520)
PHONE..................................316 267-0289
EMP: 15
SALES (est): 3.8MM **Privately Held**
SIC: 5087 Whol Service Establishment Equipment

(G-14647)
HUBRIS COMMUNICATIONS
266 N Main St Ste 150 (67202-1516)
PHONE..................................316 858-3000
Chris Owen, *President*
EMP: 11
SALES (est): 850.1K **Privately Held**
WEB: www.hubris.com
SIC: 4813

(G-14648)
HUDSON HOLDING INC
Also Called: Preston Pharmacy
14301 W Hardtner Ct (67235-7541)
PHONE..................................866 404-3300
Elliot Lekawa, *Owner*
EMP: 55
SALES (est): 11.7MM **Privately Held**
SIC: 5122 Pharmaceuticals

(G-14649)
HUGHES MACHINERY COMPANY
11021 E 28th St N Ste 1 (67226-7827)
PHONE..................................316 612-0868
Kent Calvert, *Principal*
Joe Reeder, *Engineer*
Nancy Mills, *Consultant*
EMP: 7
SALES (corp-wide): 3.4B **Publicly Held**
WEB: www.hughesmachinery.com
SIC: 5084 5074 3491 3443 Industrial machinery & equipment; heating equipment (hydronic); steam traps; heat exchangers, condensers & components
HQ: Hughes Machinery Company
14400 College Blvd
Lenexa KS 66215
913 492-0355

(G-14650)
HULLINGS JON G DDS MS PA
1700 N Waterfront Pkwy (67206-6614)
PHONE..................................316 636-1980
Jon Hullings, *Owner*
EMP: 12 **EST:** 2001
SALES (est): 264.3K **Privately Held**
SIC: 8021 Orthodontist

(G-14651)
HUMANA INC
601 S Greenwich Rd # 111 (67207-2508)
PHONE..................................316 612-6820
Kelly Quickly, *Manager*
EMP: 42
SALES (corp-wide): 56.9B **Publicly Held**
SIC: 6324 Health maintenance organization (HMO), insurance only
PA: Humana Inc.
500 W Main St Ste 300
Louisville KY 40202
502 580-1000

(G-14652)
HUMANKIND MNSTRIES WICHITA INC (PA)
829 N Market St (67214-3519)
PHONE..................................316 264-9303
Latasha St Arnault, *CEO*
Caroline Kell, *Principal*
Susan Castile, *Director*
EMP: 26
SALES (est): 2.8MM **Privately Held**
WEB: www.ifmnet.org
SIC: 8322 8661 Social service center; family service agency; religious organizations

(G-14653)
HUMANKIND MNSTRIES WICHITA INC
Also Called: Homeless & Housing Services
320 E Central Ave (67202-1056)
PHONE..................................316 264-8051
Sam Muyskens, *Exec Dir*
EMP: 18
SALES (corp-wide): 2.8MM **Privately Held**
WEB: www.ifmnet.org
SIC: 8322 Social service center
PA: Humankind Ministries Wichita, Inc.
829 N Market St
Wichita KS 67214
316 264-9303

(G-14654)
HUMIDOR EAST
2221 N Woodlawn Blvd (67220-3947)
PHONE..................................316 688-0112
Richard Daugherty, *Owner*
EMP: 20
SALES (est): 851.8K **Privately Held**
SIC: 5199 Art goods & supplies

(G-14655)
HUMPHREY PRODUCTS INC (PA)
719 E Zimmerly St (67211-3340)
P.O. Box 16856 (67216-0856)
PHONE..................................316 267-2201
Fax: 316 267-0961
EMP: 25
SQ FT: 30,000
SALES (est): 2.2MM **Privately Held**
SIC: 3442 Mfg Metal Doors/Sash/Trim

(G-14656)
HUNTER HEALTH CLINIC INC (PA)
2318 E Central Ave (67214-4436)
PHONE..................................316 262-2415
Susette Schwartz, *President*
Joshua Reed, *Nurse*
EMP: 86
SQ FT: 15,000
SALES: 8.2MM **Privately Held**
WEB: www.hunterhealthclinic.org
SIC: 8011 Clinic, operated by physicians

(G-14657)
HURRICANE SERVICES INC (PA)
250 N Water St Ste 200 (67202-1215)
PHONE..................................316 303-9515
Darrel Walters, *President*
Johnnie Riley, *Opers Staff*
Renee Duke, *Office Mgr*
Derek Michael, *Manager*
EMP: 32
SALES (est): 12.1MM **Privately Held**
SIC: 1382 Oil & gas exploration services

(G-14658)
HUTTON & HUTTON
8100 E 22nd St N # 1200 (67226-2389)
PHONE..................................316 688-1166
Mark Hutton, *Partner*
Andrew Hutton, *Partner*
EMP: 20
SQ FT: 3,000
SALES (est): 1.7MM **Privately Held**
SIC: 8111 Specialized law offices, attorneys

(G-14659)
HUTTON & HUTTON LAW FIRM
8100 E 22nd St N # 1200 (67226-2389)
P.O. Box 638 (67201-0638)
PHONE..................................316 688-1166
Mark Hutton, *Partner*
Andrew Hutton, *Partner*
Anne Hull, *Manager*
Sharon Fornshell, *Admin Sec*
Nancey Weber, *Admin Sec*
EMP: 21 **EST:** 1979
SALES (est): 2.4MM **Privately Held**
WEB: www.huttonlaw.com
SIC: 8111 General practice attorney, lawyer

(G-14660)
HUTTON CONSTRUCTION CORP (PA)
2229 S West St (67213-1113)
PHONE..................................316 942-8855
Ben Hutton, *President*
Lynn Harrison, *Superintendent*
Mike McBee, *Superintendent*
Josh Herrman, *Vice Pres*
Brandon Brungardt, *Project Mgr*
EMP: 121

SQ FT: 20,000
SALES (est): 82.4MM **Privately Held**
WEB: www.huttonconstruction.com
SIC: 1542 Commercial & office building, new construction; commercial & office buildings, renovation & repair

(G-14661)
HYATT CORPORATION
Also Called: Hyatt Regency Wichita
400 W Waterman St (67202-3600)
PHONE..................................316 293-1234
Justin Stulhsatz, *General Mgr*
Mike Frey, *Vice Pres*
Omar Romero, *Purch Mgr*
Jeff Pace, *Manager*
EMP: 250
SALES (corp-wide): 4.4B **Publicly Held**
WEB: www.hyatt.com
SIC: 7011 7299 5812 Hotels & motels; banquet hall facilities; caterers
HQ: Hyatt Corporation
150 N Riverside Plz
Chicago IL 60606
312 750-1234

(G-14662)
HYSPECO INC (PA)
1729 S Sabin St (67209-2750)
PHONE..................................316 943-0254
Dave Zavala, *CEO*
Ted Barney, *Vice Pres*
Bryan J Webb, *Vice Pres*
Taylor Dotson, *Store Mgr*
Buddy Tucker, *Prdtn Mgr*
EMP: 35
SQ FT: 10,000
SALES (est): 80.8MM **Privately Held**
WEB: www.hyspeco.com
SIC: 5084 Hydraulic systems equipment & supplies; pneumatic tools & equipment

(G-14663)
I A M A W DISTRICT LODGE 70
Also Called: INTERNATIONAL ASSOCIATION OF M
3830 S Meridian Ave (67217-3704)
PHONE..................................316 522-1591
Steve Rooney, *President*
EMP: 17
SALES: 6.5MM
SALES (corp-wide): 61.4MM **Privately Held**
WEB: www.d70iam.org
SIC: 8631 Labor union
PA: International Association Of Machinists And Aerospace Workers
9000 Machinists Pl
Upper Marlboro MD 20772
301 967-4500

(G-14664)
I P H F H A INC
Also Called: International Pizza Hut Franch
7829 E Rockhill St # 201 (67206-3920)
PHONE..................................316 685-1200
Ken McCarren, *Principal*
Mike Jenry, *Vice Pres*
Tom Kennalley, *CFO*
Jill Buchanan, *Executive Asst*
EMP: 14
SALES (est): 2MM **Privately Held**
WEB: www.iphfha.com
SIC: 8611 Merchants' association

(G-14665)
ICE-MASTERS INC
2569 W Pawnee St (67213-1813)
PHONE..................................316 945-6900
Jay Melver, *Manager*
EMP: 16
SALES (corp-wide): 7.7MM **Privately Held**
SIC: 7359 7623 5046 Equipment rental & leasing; ice making machinery repair service; commercial cooking & food service equipment
HQ: Ice-Masters, Inc
6218 Melrose Ln
Shawnee Mission KS 66203
660 827-6900

(G-14666)
ICT BILLET LLC
1107 S West St Unit 2 (67213-1629)
PHONE..................................316 300-0833
Alan Burdue,
EMP: 8
SALES (est): 116.1K **Privately Held**
SIC: 3714 Motor vehicle parts & accessories

(G-14667)
IFR SYSTEMS INC
10200 W York St (67215-8935)
PHONE..................................316 522-4981
Jeffrey A Bloomer, *President*
Jeff Gillum, *President*
EMP: 500
SALES (est): 22.2MM
SALES (corp-wide): 2.4B **Privately Held**
SIC: 4581 Aircraft servicing & repairing
HQ: Aeroflex Incorporated
35 S Service Rd
Plainview NY 11803
516 694-6700

(G-14668)
IHEARTCOMMUNICATIONS INC
9323 E 37th St N (67226-2000)
PHONE..................................316 494-6600
Dick Harlow, *Branch Mgr*
EMP: 60 **Publicly Held**
SIC: 4832 4833 7312 Radio broadcasting stations; television broadcasting stations; outdoor advertising services
HQ: Iheartcommunications, Inc.
20880 Stone Oak Pkwy
San Antonio TX 78258
210 822-2828

(G-14669)
IHEARTCOMMUNICATIONS INC
Also Called: Kkrd
2402 E 37th St N (67219-3538)
PHONE..................................316 832-9600
Dick Harlow, *General Mgr*
EMP: 60 **Publicly Held**
SIC: 4832 Radio broadcasting stations
HQ: Iheartcommunications, Inc.
20880 Stone Oak Pkwy
San Antonio TX 78258
210 822-2828

(G-14670)
ILM 1 HOLDING INC
Also Called: Sedgwick Plz Rtrment Residence
2455 N Woodlawn Blvd Ofc (67220-3996)
PHONE..................................316 687-3741
Kim Sanders, *Exec Dir*
Elaine Riley, *Exec Dir*
EMP: 50
SQ FT: 142,070
SALES (est): 3.6MM **Privately Held**
WEB: www.sedgplaza.com
SIC: 6513 Apartment building operators

(G-14671)
IMA INC
8200 E 32nd St N (67226-2606)
PHONE..................................316 267-9221
William C Cohen Jr, *Ch of Bd*
George M Humphries III, *Principal*
EMP: 255
SALES (est): 35.5MM
SALES (corp-wide): 53.4MM **Privately Held**
SIC: 6411 Insurance agents, brokers & service
PA: The Ima Financial Group Inc
8200 E 32nd St N
Wichita KS 67226
316 267-9221

(G-14672)
IMA FINANCIAL GROUP INC (PA)
8200 E 32nd St N (67226-2606)
P.O. Box 2992 (67201-2992)
PHONE..................................316 267-9221
William C Cohen, *Ch of Bd*
Jeff Grace, *President*
Kevin Hawkins, *President*
Mark Ware, *President*
Leisha Cadwallader, *Vice Pres*
EMP: 15
SQ FT: 35,000
SALES (est): 53.4MM **Privately Held**
SIC: 6411 Insurance brokers

(G-14673)
IMA OF KANSAS INC
8200 E 32nd St N (67226-2606)
P.O. Box 2992 (67201-2992)
PHONE..................................316 267-9221
Jeff Grace, *President*
Raymond J Merz, *Vice Pres*
Bret Burton, *Broker*
Stacey Faber, *Admin Mgr*
Sueann V Schultz, *Admin Sec*
EMP: 196
SALES (est): 32.6MM **Privately Held**
SIC: 6411 Insurance brokers

(G-14674)
IMA SELECT LLC (HQ)
Also Called: Signature Select LLC
8200 E 32nd St N (67226-2606)
P.O. Box 2996 (67201-2996)
PHONE..................................316 266-6203
Lisa Pfannenstiel, *Vice Pres*
Luke Proctor,
Mike Nolan,
EMP: 26 **EST:** 2009
SALES (est): 10.9MM
SALES (corp-wide): 53.4MM **Privately Held**
SIC: 6331 Automobile insurance
PA: The Ima Financial Group Inc
8200 E 32nd St N
Wichita KS 67226
316 267-9221

(G-14675)
IMA WEALTH INC
8200 E 32nd St N Ste 100 (67226-2618)
PHONE..................................316 266-6582
C Weston Cooper, *President*
EMP: 20
SALES (est): 747.7K **Privately Held**
SIC: 6282 Investment advice

(G-14676)
IMAGE QUEST INC (DH)
11021 E 26th St N (67226-3387)
PHONE..................................316 686-3200
Michael Shea, *CEO*
Jack Boucher, *President*
Robert Hughey, *Vice Pres*
EMP: 37
SQ FT: 18,000
SALES (est): 35.2MM
SALES (corp-wide): 9.8B **Publicly Held**
WEB: www.imagequestks.com
SIC: 5044 Office equipment

(G-14677)
IMAGING SOLUTIONS COMPANY
201 N Mead St (67202-2707)
PHONE..................................316 630-0440
Kenra Black, *President*
Paul Black, *Treasurer*
EMP: 27
SQ FT: 10,000
SALES (est): 1.9MM **Privately Held**
SIC: 5999 7389 Business machines & equipment; microfilm recording & developing service

(G-14678)
IMPERIAL AMERICAN OIL CORP
13906 W Onewood St (67235-3408)
PHONE..................................316 721-0036
Hal Porter, *Owner*
EMP: 5
SALES (est): 423.6K **Privately Held**
SIC: 1381 Drilling oil & gas wells

(G-14679)
IMPRESA AEROSPACE LLC
2232 S Custer Ave (67213-1515)
PHONE..................................316 942-9100
EMP: 100
SALES (corp-wide): 88MM **Privately Held**
SIC: 3728 3444 Mfg Aircraft Parts/Equipment Mfg Sheet Metalwork
PA: Impresa Aerospace, Llc
344 W 157th St
Gardena CA 90248
310 354-1200

(G-14680)
INDEPENDENT OIL & GAS SVC INC
Also Called: Independent Digital Printing
226 N Emporia Ave (67202-2598)
P.O. Box 193 (67201-0193)
PHONE..................................316 263-8281
John H Morrison III, *CEO*
Patricia Hanson, *CFO*
EMP: 6
SQ FT: 7,000
SALES: 800K **Privately Held**
WEB: www.iogsi.com
SIC: 1382 2711 2752 7334 Oil & gas exploration services; newspapers, publishing & printing; commercial printing, lithographic; photocopying & duplicating services

(G-14681)
INDEPNDENT LIVING RESOURCE CTR
3033 W 2nd St N Ste 1 (67203-5360)
PHONE..................................316 942-6300
Michael Streit, *Finance*
Cindi Unruh, *Manager*
Judy Weigel, *Exec Dir*
EMP: 35
SQ FT: 26,000
SALES: 14.1MM **Privately Held**
WEB: www.ilrcks.org
SIC: 8322 Association for the handicapped; self-help organization

(G-14682)
INDIAN HILLS ANIMAL CLINIC
3223 W 13th St N (67203-6624)
PHONE..................................316 942-3900
Douglas Winter, *Owner*
Jenna Hill,
Douglas K Winter,
EMP: 25
SALES (est): 1.4MM **Privately Held**
WEB: www.indianhillsanimalclinic.com
SIC: 0742 Animal hospital services, pets & other animal specialties

(G-14683)
INDIAN HILLS MEAT AND PLTY INC
1200 N Mosley Ave (67214-2714)
P.O. Box 145 (67201-0145)
PHONE..................................316 264-1644
Brian E Smith, *President*
Larry Smith, *Exec Dir*
EMP: 20
SALES (est): 5.4MM **Privately Held**
SIC: 5147 2015 2013 2011 Meats, fresh; poultry slaughtering & processing; sausages & other prepared meats; meat packing plants

(G-14684)
INDIGENTS DEFENSE SVCS KANS BD
Also Called: South Central Pub Defender Off
604 N Main St Ste D (67203-3672)
PHONE..................................316 264-8700
Charles S Osburn, *Branch Mgr*
EMP: 31 **Privately Held**
SIC: 8111 9222 General practice attorney, lawyer; legal counsel & prosecution;
HQ: Kansas Board Of Indigents' Defense Services
700 Sw Jackson St
Topeka KS 66603
785 296-6631

(G-14685)
INDUSTRIAL MAINTENANCE INC
708 E 18th St N (67214-1382)
PHONE..................................316 267-7933
Randy Neises, *President*
Rodney Neises, *Vice Pres*
Scott Neises, *Vice Pres*
Dan Nolte, *Vice Pres*
EMP: 30
SQ FT: 24,000
SALES (est): 6MM **Privately Held**
SIC: 1541 Grain elevator construction; renovation, remodeling & repairs: industrial buildings

GEOGRAPHIC

(G-14686)
INDUSTRIAL PROCESS EQP CO
Also Called: I P E Co
8974 W Monroe Cir (67209-3313)
PHONE..................................316 722-7800
Terry Glover, *Branch Mgr*
EMP: 6
SALES (corp-wide): 450MM **Privately Held**
WEB: www.ipegstl.com
SIC: 3728 3599 Aircraft parts & equipment; machine shop, jobbing & repair
HQ: Industrial Process Equipment Company
6823 Hazelwood Ave
Saint Louis MO 63134
314 534-3100

(G-14687)
INDUSTRIAL ROOFG MET WORKS INC
Also Called: Kansas Guttering
2209 W Harry St (67213-2932)
PHONE..................................316 262-4758
Darren Ward, *President*
Jill Ward, *Vice Pres*
EMP: 12
SQ FT: 6,000
SALES (est): 970K **Privately Held**
SIC: 1761 Roofing contractor; sheet metalwork

(G-14688)
INDUSTRIAL UNIFORM COMPANY LLC
Also Called: Logo Depot
3550 N Comotara St (67226-1303)
PHONE..................................316 264-2871
Kim Nivens, *Purch Mgr*
Susan Adams, *Accounting Mgr*
Rob Regier, *Accounts Mgr*
Jeff Johnson, *Mng Member*
Brian Burrus,
EMP: 19 **EST:** 1938
SQ FT: 22,000
SALES (est): 2MM **Privately Held**
WEB: www.industrialuniform.com
SIC: 2395 Embroidery & art needlework

(G-14689)
INFECTIOUS DISEASE CONS PA (PA)
1100 N St Francis St # 130 (67214-2865)
PHONE..................................316 264-3505
Jerry D Peterie, *President*
Jerry Peterie MD, *President*
Keck Hartman MD, *Vice Pres*
Tom Moore MD, *Treasurer*
EMP: 20
SQ FT: 5,500
SALES (est): 2.4MM **Privately Held**
SIC: 8011 8093 8322 8071 Infectious disease specialist, physician/surgeon; immunologist; specialty outpatient clinics; travelers' aid; medical laboratories

(G-14690)
INFECTIOUS DISEASE CONSULTANTS
1100 N St Francis St # 130 (67214-2865)
PHONE..................................316 264-3505
Hewitt Goodpasture, *President*
Jerry Peterie, *Med Doctor*
EMP: 30
SALES (est): 3.2MM **Privately Held**
SIC: 8011 Infectious disease specialist, physician/surgeon

(G-14691)
INFINIA AT WICHITA INC
1600 S Woodlawn Blvd (67218-4728)
PHONE..................................316 691-9999
Brian Robey, *President*
EMP: 50
SALES (est): 497K **Privately Held**
SIC: 8052 Intermediate care facilities

(G-14692)
INFOSYNC SERVICES LLC
1938 N Woodlawn St # 110 (67208-1857)
PHONE..................................316 685-1622
Dale Hoyer, *CEO*
Joshua Bartel, *Vice Pres*
Amy Greenwood, *Accountant*
Katrina Krichati, *Accountant*
Glenda Parker, *Human Resources*
EMP: 500
SALES (est): 10.6MM **Privately Held**
SIC: 8721 Payroll accounting service

(G-14693)
INFUSION LLC
1909 E Central Ave (67214-4304)
PHONE..................................316 686-1610
Chase Reed, *Pharmacist*
Steve Austin, *Mng Member*
Ilyssa Deponte, *Manager*
EMP: 17
SALES (est): 1MM **Privately Held**
SIC: 8082 Home health care services

(G-14694)
INITYAERO INC
1935 W Walker St (67213-3365)
PHONE..................................316 265-0603
David May, *President*
EMP: 35
SQ FT: 32,500
SALES (est): 5.5MM **Privately Held**
WEB: www.midcentral-mfg.com
SIC: 3728 3714 3523 3769 Aircraft parts & equipment; motor vehicle parts & accessories; farm machinery & equipment; guided missile & space vehicle parts & auxiliary equipment

(G-14695)
INNOVATIVE CNSTR SVCS INC
1725 E Wassall St (67216-2143)
PHONE..................................316 260-1644
Bradley Haedt, *President*
Theresa McCullough, *CFO*
EMP: 10
SALES (est): 2MM **Privately Held**
SIC: 8712 Architectural services

(G-14696)
INNTEL CORPORATION OF AMERICA
Also Called: Inn At Tallgrass, The
2280 N Tara Cir (67226-1914)
PHONE..................................316 684-3466
Don Kennedy, *President*
Randy Sebastian, *President*
Toni Doshier, *Accounts Mgr*
Amy Christman, *Accounts Exec*
EMP: 30
SALES (est): 2.4MM **Privately Held**
WEB: www.theinnattallgrass.com
SIC: 7011 Resort hotel; hotels

(G-14697)
INSTRUMENTS AND FLIGHT RES INC
2716 S George Wash Blvd (67210-1520)
PHONE..................................316 684-5177
James F Garufo, *President*
Anna Garufo, *Treasurer*
EMP: 8
SQ FT: 15,000
SALES (est): 1MM **Privately Held**
SIC: 3647 Aircraft lighting fixtures

(G-14698)
INTEGRA HOLDINGS INC (PA)
3450 N Rock Rd Ste 100 (67226-1351)
PHONE..................................316 630-6805
Becky Craft, *CEO*
Brett Robinson, *VP Opers*
Wayne Lam, *Engineer*
EMP: 99
SALES (est): 39.1MM **Privately Held**
SIC: 3674 Semiconductors & related devices

(G-14699)
INTEGRA TECHNOLOGIES LLC (HQ)
3450 N Rock Rd Ste 100 (67226-1351)
PHONE..................................316 630-6800
Mark Marshall, *President*
Dave Bass, *Officer*
Becky Craft,
▲ **EMP:** 104
SALES (est): 35.7MM **Privately Held**
WEB: www.integra-tech.com
SIC: 3674 Semiconductors & related devices

(G-14700)
INTEGRATED COMPONENTS INC
2525 S Leonine Rd (67217-1072)
PHONE..................................316 942-6600
Larry Shorter, *President*
EMP: 12
SQ FT: 7,500
SALES (est): 1.3MM **Privately Held**
SIC: 3599 Machine shop, jobbing & repair

(G-14701)
INTEGRATED ELECTRICAL TECH LLC
Also Called: Iet
2406 W Timbercreek Cir (67204-2567)
PHONE..................................316 684-0193
Harold Ragland, *Mng Member*
Brad Cherry,
Brad Ragland,
EMP: 10
SQ FT: 5,000
SALES (est): 1MM **Privately Held**
SIC: 1731 General electrical contractor

(G-14702)
INTEGRATED FACILITIES GROUP
125 S Washington Ave # 200 (67202-4704)
P.O. Box 781049 (67278-1049)
PHONE..................................316 262-1417
Marsha Geisert, *Owner*
Ken Hobart, *Opers Mgr*
Lori Goodwin, *Bookkeeper*
Preston Gonsalves, *Manager*
EMP: 10
SQ FT: 6,800
SALES (est): 1.4MM **Privately Held**
WEB: www.ifgwichita.com
SIC: 5021 Office furniture

(G-14703)
INTEGRATED MEDIA GROUP LLC
1300 E Central Ave (67214-4002)
PHONE..................................316 425-8333
Jason Opat, *Sales Staff*
EMP: 12
SQ FT: 8,000
SALES (est): 822.8K **Privately Held**
SIC: 7336 Graphic arts & related design

(G-14704)
INTEGRATED SOLUTIONS INC (PA)
Also Called: ISI Environmental Services
215 S Laura Ave (67211-1516)
PHONE..................................316 264-7050
Toll Free:..................................888
Karma Mason, *President*
Allen Sill, *Project Mgr*
Denise Obr, *Engineer*
Gary Mason, *Treasurer*
Casey Moore, *Sales Staff*
EMP: 64
SQ FT: 11,000
SALES (est): 46.1MM **Privately Held**
WEB: www.isienvironmental.com
SIC: 8742 8748 Industry specialist consultants; environmental consultant

(G-14705)
INTEGRATED STADIUM SEATING INC
7330 W 33rd St N Ste 112 (67205-9370)
PHONE..................................316 494-6514
Doug Rippel, *Principal*
EMP: 10
SALES (est): 510K **Privately Held**
SIC: 2531 Stadium seating

(G-14706)
INTEGRITY SIDING & WINDOW CO
2538 N Lake Ridge Ct (67205-1321)
PHONE..................................316 993-6426
Jeffrey Johnson,
EMP: 12
SALES: 1MM **Privately Held**
SIC: 1521 General remodeling, single-family houses

(G-14707)
INTEGRTED CNSLTING ENGNERS INC
349 S Hydraulic St (67211-1908)
PHONE..................................316 264-3588
Scott Smith, *President*
Dwayne Vaughn, *Consultant*
EMP: 15
SALES: 500K **Privately Held**
SIC: 8711 Consulting engineer

(G-14708)
INTEGRTED HLTHCARE SYSTEMS INC
3311 E Murdock St (67208-3054)
PHONE..................................316 689-9111
Kimiberly Shank, *Director*
EMP: 1000
SALES (est): 59.2MM **Privately Held**
SIC: 7359 Equipment rental & leasing

(G-14709)
INTERNATIONAL PAPER COMPANY
4300 W 29th St S (67215-1017)
PHONE..................................316 943-1033
Bridgett Lemon, *Manager*
EMP: 24
SALES (corp-wide): 23.3B **Publicly Held**
WEB: www.internationalpaper.com
SIC: 2621 Paper mills
PA: International Paper Company
6400 Poplar Ave
Memphis TN 38197
901 419-9000

(G-14710)
INTERNTNAL RSCUE COMMITTEE INC
Also Called: Irc Kansas Office For Refugees
245 N Waco St Ste 500 (67202-1118)
PHONE..................................316 201-1804
Danusia Dzierzbinski, *Principal*
Jennifer Doran, *Principal*
David Miliband, *Principal*
Olga Mogollon, *Associate*
EMP: 25 **EST:** 2016
SALES (est): 185.9K **Privately Held**
SIC: 8322 Social service center

(G-14711)
INTERSTATE SUPPLY COMPANY
2140 W Harry St (67213-3254)
PHONE..................................316 265-6653
Gary Morrow, *Manager*
EMP: 20
SALES (corp-wide): 42.9MM **Privately Held**
SIC: 5032 5039 Ceramic construction materials, excluding refractory; prefabricated structures
PA: Interstate Supply Company
9245 Dielman Indus Dr
Saint Louis MO 63132
314 994-7100

(G-14712)
INTERSTATE WRECKER SERVICE
1026 N Mosley St Ste 1028 (67214-3041)
PHONE..................................316 269-1133
Kevin Williams, *President*
Diana Chaffin, *Admin Sec*
EMP: 13
SQ FT: 10,000
SALES (est): 880.5K **Privately Held**
SIC: 7549 Towing service, automotive

(G-14713)
INTRUST BANK NA
500 E Waterman St (67202-4509)
PHONE..................................316 440-9000
Stacy Schraeder, *Opers Staff*
Kenzie Myers, *Marketing Staff*
Christine Pileckas, *Branch Mgr*
EMP: 16
SALES (corp-wide): 134.2MM **Privately Held**
SIC: 6021 National commercial banks
HQ: Intrust Bank National Association
105 N Main St
Wichita KS 67202
316 383-1111

(G-14714)
INTRUST BANK NA
1435 N Waco Ave (67203-2650)
PHONE..................................316 383-1731
Brock Davis, *Branch Mgr*
EMP: 16
SALES (corp-wide): 134.2MM **Privately Held**
WEB: www.intrustbank.com
SIC: **6021** National trust companies with deposits, commercial
HQ: Intrust Bank National Association
105 N Main St
Wichita KS 67202
316 383-1111

(G-14715)
INTRUST BANK NA
2005 W 21st St N (67203-2108)
PHONE..................................316 383-1816
Sherri Hess, *Branch Mgr*
EMP: 16
SALES (corp-wide): 134.2MM **Privately Held**
WEB: www.intrustbank.com
SIC: **6021** National trust companies with deposits, commercial
HQ: Intrust Bank National Association
105 N Main St
Wichita KS 67202
316 383-1111

(G-14716)
INTRUST BANK NA
8202 E 21st St N (67206-2906)
PHONE..................................316 383-1563
Aaron Waller, *Manager*
EMP: 12
SALES (corp-wide): 134.2MM **Privately Held**
WEB: www.intrustbank.com
SIC: **6021** National trust companies with deposits, commercial
HQ: Intrust Bank National Association
105 N Main St
Wichita KS 67202
316 383-1111

(G-14717)
INTRUST BANK NA
2244 N Rock Rd (67226-2352)
PHONE..................................316 383-1342
Kimberely Luckert, *Principal*
EMP: 16
SALES (corp-wide): 134.2MM **Privately Held**
WEB: www.intrustbank.com
SIC: **6021** National trust companies with deposits, commercial
HQ: Intrust Bank National Association
105 N Main St
Wichita KS 67202
316 383-1111

(G-14718)
INTRUST BANK NA
3801 N Rock Rd (67226-3003)
PHONE..................................316 383-1549
Sandi Rhoadman, *Manager*
EMP: 10
SALES (corp-wide): 134.2MM **Privately Held**
WEB: www.intrustbank.com
SIC: **6021** National trust companies with deposits, commercial
HQ: Intrust Bank National Association
105 N Main St
Wichita KS 67202
316 383-1111

(G-14719)
INTRUST BANK NA
4747 S Broadway Ave (67216-1739)
PHONE..................................316 383-1096
Joel Carson, *Branch Mgr*
EMP: 16
SALES (corp-wide): 134.2MM **Privately Held**
WEB: www.intrustbank.com
SIC: **6021** National trust companies with deposits, commercial
HQ: Intrust Bank National Association
105 N Main St
Wichita KS 67202
316 383-1111

(G-14720)
INTRUST BANK NA
10515 W Central Ave (67212-5103)
PHONE..................................316 383-1194
Cynthia Rekoske, *Branch Mgr*
Mindy Kiser, *Representative*
EMP: 16
SALES (corp-wide): 134.2MM **Privately Held**
WEB: www.intrustbank.com
SIC: **6021** National trust companies with deposits, commercial
HQ: Intrust Bank National Association
105 N Main St
Wichita KS 67202
316 383-1111

(G-14721)
INTRUST BANK NA
3433 E Central Ave (67208-3298)
PHONE..................................316 383-1960
Lou Ann Draper, *Branch Mgr*
EMP: 16
SALES (corp-wide): 134.2MM **Privately Held**
WEB: www.intrustbank.com
SIC: **6021** National trust companies with deposits, commercial
HQ: Intrust Bank National Association
105 N Main St
Wichita KS 67202
316 383-1111

(G-14722)
INTRUST BANK NA
1544 S Webb Rd (67207-4208)
PHONE..................................316 383-1505
Sandra Rhodeman, *Branch Mgr*
EMP: 16
SALES (corp-wide): 134.2MM **Privately Held**
WEB: www.intrustbank.com
SIC: **6021** National trust companies with deposits, commercial
HQ: Intrust Bank National Association
105 N Main St
Wichita KS 67202
316 383-1111

(G-14723)
INTRUST BANK NATIONAL ASSN (HQ)
105 N Main St (67202-1401)
P.O. Box 1 (67201-5001)
PHONE..................................316 383-1111
C Q Chandler IV, *Ch of Bd*
Jay Smith, *President*
Bruce A Long, *Exec VP*
John Goff, *Senior VP*
Troy Jordan, *Senior VP*
▲ **EMP**: 300 **EST**: 1876
SQ FT: 176,000
SALES: 251.9MM
SALES (corp-wide): 134.2MM **Privately Held**
WEB: www.intrustbank.com
SIC: **6021** National commercial banks
PA: Intrust Financial Corporation
105 N Main St
Wichita KS 67202
316 383-1111

(G-14724)
INTRUST BANK NATIONAL ASSN
7800 E Central Ave (67206-2156)
P.O. Box 1 (67201-5001)
PHONE..................................316 383-1339
John Bates, *Branch Mgr*
EMP: 21
SALES (corp-wide): 134.2MM **Privately Held**
WEB: www.intrustbank.com
SIC: **6021** National commercial banks
HQ: Intrust Bank National Association
105 N Main St
Wichita KS 67202
316 383-1111

(G-14725)
INTRUST BANK NATIONAL ASSN
123 N Main St (67202-1412)
PHONE..................................316 383-1040
Michele Ballard, *Plant Mgr*
Michael Mitchell, *Manager*
EMP: 10
SALES (corp-wide): 134.2MM **Privately Held**
WEB: www.intrustbank.com
SIC: **6021** National commercial banks
HQ: Intrust Bank National Association
105 N Main St
Wichita KS 67202
316 383-1111

(G-14726)
INTRUST BANK NATIONAL ASSN
3932 W 13th St N (67203-4437)
P.O. Box 427 (67201-0427)
PHONE..................................316 383-1234
Michele Ballard, *Branch Mgr*
EMP: 12
SALES (corp-wide): 134.2MM **Privately Held**
WEB: www.intrustbank.com
SIC: **6022** State commercial banks
HQ: Intrust Bank National Association
105 N Main St
Wichita KS 67202
316 383-1111

(G-14727)
INTRUST FINANCIAL CORPORATION (PA)
105 N Main St (67202-1412)
P.O. Box 1 (67201-5001)
PHONE..................................316 383-1111
Charles Q Chandler III, *CEO*
C Q Chandler III, *Ch of Bd*
C Q Chandler IV, *President*
Rick L Beach, *COO*
Steve L Hipp, *Exec VP*
EMP: 25
SQ FT: 3,500
SALES: 134.2MM **Privately Held**
SIC: **6712** 6022 Bank holding companies; state commercial banks

(G-14728)
INVISTA EQUITIES LLC (HQ)
4111 E 37th St N (67220-3203)
PHONE..................................770 792-4221
Jeff Gentry, *CEO*
Robert Kirkwood, *Vice Pres*
Chris Moore, *CIO*
EMP: 15
SALES (est): 279MM
SALES (corp-wide): 40.6B **Privately Held**
SIC: **2295** 2221 Chemically coated & treated fabrics; textile mills, broadwoven: silk & manmade, also glass
PA: Koch Industries, Inc.
4111 E 37th St N
Wichita KS 67220
316 828-5500

(G-14729)
IPECO WICHITA INC
8974 W Monroe Cir (67209-3313)
PHONE..................................316 722-7800
Darren Wilderman, *Manager*
▲ **EMP**: 25
SALES (est): 2.5MM **Privately Held**
SIC: **5088** Aircraft & parts

(G-14730)
ISF LLC
Also Called: Infinitech Surface Finishing
4420 W 29th Cir S (67215-1018)
PHONE..................................316 945-4040
Lindsay Dieker, *Office Mgr*
John Hankins,
Jeanne Middleton,
EMP: 28 **EST**: 1976
SQ FT: 25,000
SALES (est): 3.8MM **Privately Held**
WEB: www.infinitechfinishing.com
SIC: **3471** Plating of metals or formed products

(G-14731)
ISG TECHNOLOGY LLC
Also Called: Integrated Solutions Group
8201 E 34th Cir N Ste 807 (67226-1398)
PHONE..................................316 636-5655
Jeff Rankin, *Project Mgr*
Tiffany Hawkins, *Accounts Exec*
Mike Davis Wichita, *Accounts Exec*
Robin Cowell, *Sales Staff*
Bret Heinz, *Branch Mgr*
EMP: 20
SALES (corp-wide): 75MM **Privately Held**
WEB: www.isgtech.com
SIC: **7379** Computer related consulting services
PA: Isg Technology, Llc
3030 Cortland Cir 300
Salina KS 67401
785 823-1555

(G-14732)
ISLAND HOSPITALITY MGT LLC
Also Called: TownePlace Suites
9444 E 29th St N (67226-2178)
PHONE..................................316 631-3773
Jed Schanz, *Branch Mgr*
EMP: 35
SALES (corp-wide): 764.3MM **Privately Held**
SIC: **7011** Hotel, franchised
PA: Island Hospitality Management, Llc
222 Lakeview Ave Ste 200
West Palm Beach FL 33401

(G-14733)
ISODYNE INC
7706 E Osie St (67207-3138)
PHONE..................................316 682-5634
Brenda L Reed, *CEO*
Rees Lahman, *QC Mgr*
Bill Fohlbrook, *Regl Sales Mgr*
EMP: 13
SQ FT: 19,000
SALES (est): 3.7MM **Privately Held**
WEB: www.isodyneinc.com
SIC: **5065** Electronic parts

(G-14734)
J B L INC (PA)
Also Called: Lange Homes
4911 S Meridian Ave (67217-3709)
PHONE..................................316 529-3100
Jeff M Lange, *President*
Teri Haynes, *Principal*
Lee Schnyder, *Director*
Colin Busey, *Real Est Agnt*
EMP: 19
SQ FT: 1,200
SALES (est): 5.6MM **Privately Held**
WEB: www.jefflangere.com
SIC: **6531** Real estate agent, residential

(G-14735)
J DIAMOND INC
2020 W Harry St (67213-3256)
P.O. Box 9526 (67277-0526)
PHONE..................................316 264-9505
Joseph Harris Sr, *President*
Jason Harris, *Vice Pres*
Joseph C Harris Jr, *Vice Pres*
Mark Fiedler, *Engineer*
Tepajni Harris, *Engineer*
EMP: 25
SQ FT: 15,000
SALES (est): 4.6MM **Privately Held**
WEB: www.diamondjinc.net
SIC: **3812** Aircraft/aerospace flight instruments & guidance systems

(G-14736)
J HUSTON HOWERY
Also Called: Mid-Continent Mfg & Sales
3900 W Rita St (67213-1249)
PHONE..................................316 945-0023
Joe Howery, *Branch Mgr*
EMP: 5
SALES (corp-wide): 1.7MM **Privately Held**
WEB: www.midcontinentmfg.com
SIC: **3491** Gas valves & parts, industrial; compressed gas cylinder valves
PA: J Huston Howery
3900 W Rita St
Wichita KS 67213
316 945-0023

(G-14737)
J HUSTON HOWERY (PA)
Also Called: Mid Continent Mfg.
3900 W Rita St (67213-1249)
P.O. Box 12887 (67277-2887)
PHONE..................................316 945-0023
Huston J Howery, *Owner*
Lance Howery, *General Mgr*

GEOGRAPHIC

◆ **EMP:** 11
SQ FT: 23,550
SALES (est): 1.7MM **Privately Held**
WEB: www.midcontinentmfg.com
SIC: 3491 Gas valves & parts, industrial; compressed gas cylinder valves

(G-14738)
J P WEIGAND & SONS INC (PA)
150 N Market St (67202-1985)
PHONE..................................316 686-3773
Nestor R Weigand Jr, *CEO*
Connie Simcox, *President*
Michael C Weigand, *Senior VP*
EMP: 217
SQ FT: 12,000
SALES (est): 10.6MM **Privately Held**
WEB: www.jpweigand.com
SIC: 6531 Real estate agent, residential

(G-14739)
J P WEIGAND & SONS INC
2872 N Ridge Rd Ste 112 (67205-1144)
PHONE..................................316 722-6182
Delaine Lacey, *Manager*
EMP: 60
SALES (est): 1.8MM
SALES (corp-wide): 10.6MM **Privately Held**
WEB: www.jpweigand.com
SIC: 6531 Real estate agent, residential
PA: J P Weigand & Sons Inc
150 N Market St
Wichita KS 67202
316 686-3773

(G-14740)
J P WEIGAND AND SONS INC (PA)
150 N Market St (67202-1985)
PHONE..................................316 292-3991
Nestor Weigand Jr, *Ch of Bd*
Roger Weast, *President*
Nester Weigand, *Principal*
Jean Walker, *Sales Staff*
EMP: 45
SQ FT: 400
SALES (est): 22.7MM **Privately Held**
WEB: www.weigand.com
SIC: 7389 Brokers, business: buying & selling business enterprises

(G-14741)
J2 DESIGN SOLUTIONS LLC
Also Called: Lifeboat Creative
120 E 1st St N Ste 270 (67202-2007)
PHONE..................................316 303-9460
Jeremy Luginbill, *Principal*
Tara Battreal, *Accounts Mgr*
Katie Dody, *Office Mgr*
Colt Cox, *Web Dvlpr*
Jennifer Whitney, *Creative Dir*
EMP: 13
SALES (est): 527.6K **Privately Held**
WEB: www.j2designsolutions.com
SIC: 7336 Graphic arts & related design

(G-14742)
JACK FOSTER CO ERECTORS
1119 S Santa Fe St (67211-2439)
PHONE..................................316 263-2901
Martin L Little, *President*
Don Prockish, *Corp Secy*
Kevin Litzner, *Vice Pres*
EMP: 30
SQ FT: 1,200
SALES (est): 3.8MM **Privately Held**
SIC: 1791 Structural steel erection

(G-14743)
JACKSON & BAALMAN
982 N Tyler Rd Ste A (67212-3271)
PHONE..................................316 722-6452
Ronald Jackson, *Owner*
EMP: 15
SALES (est): 1.3MM **Privately Held**
SIC: 8042 5999 5995 Contact lense specialist optometrist; sunglasses; contact lenses, prescription

(G-14744)
JACO GENERAL CONTRACTOR INC
420 S Emporia Ave Ste 200 (67202-4514)
PHONE..................................316 252-8200
John L Walker Jr, *Principal*
Carrie Lindholm, *Principal*
Michael Miller, *Principal*
Joshua Kippenberger, *Exec VP*
EMP: 40
SQ FT: 10,000
SALES: 36.5MM **Privately Held**
SIC: 8711 1541 1542 Building construction consultant; warehouse construction; commercial & office building, new construction; commercial & office building contractors

(G-14745)
JAJO INC
131 N Rock Island St (67202-2709)
PHONE..................................316 267-6700
Steve Randa, *President*
Brian Seitz, *Web Dvlpr*
Mike Gangwere, *Art Dir*
Annelise Muret, *Graphic Designe*
Ashley Yearout, *Associate*
EMP: 23
SQ FT: 2,617
SALES (est): 3.1MM **Privately Held**
SIC: 7311 Advertising agencies

(G-14746)
JAMES MASON ENTERPRISES INC
3810 N Bridgeport Cir (67219-3395)
PHONE..................................316 838-7399
Dorothy Mason, *President*
EMP: 20 **EST:** 1975
SQ FT: 5,000
SALES (est): 4MM **Privately Held**
SIC: 4213 Heavy hauling

(G-14747)
JARAY SOFTWARE INC
245 N Waco St Ste 230 (67202-1131)
PHONE..................................316 267-5758
EMP: 5
SALES (est): 320.1K **Privately Held**
SIC: 7372 7371 Prepackaged Software Computer Programming Services

(G-14748)
JARDEN CORP OUTDOOR SOLUTIONS
2111 E 37th St N (67219-3532)
PHONE..................................316 832-2441
Kenneth Bell, *Senior VP*
EMP: 15
SALES (est): 1MM **Privately Held**
SIC: 8748 Business consulting

(G-14749)
JARDEN CORPORATION
3600 N Hydraulic St (67219-3812)
PHONE..................................316 390-1343
Kenneth R Bell, *Principal*
EMP: 86
SALES (corp-wide): 8.6B **Publicly Held**
SIC: 3089 Plastic containers, except foam
HQ: Jarden Llc
221 River St
Hoboken NJ 07030

(G-14750)
JAY HATFIELD MOBILITY LLC
11922 E Kellogg Dr (67207-1936)
PHONE..................................785 452-9888
Jay F Hatfield, *Branch Mgr*
EMP: 11 **Privately Held**
SIC: 5047 Medical equipment & supplies
PA: Jay Hatfield Mobility, Llc
200 S East Ave
Columbus KS 66725

(G-14751)
JCI INDUSTRIES INC
1335 S Young St (67209-2629)
PHONE..................................316 942-6200
Mike Colgan, *Sales Engr*
Tom Blake, *Manager*
EMP: 19
SALES (corp-wide): 66.3MM **Privately Held**
WEB: www.jciind.com
SIC: 5084 7699 Pumps & pumping equipment; pumps & pumping equipment repair
PA: Jci Industries, Inc.
1161 Se Hamblen Rd
Lees Summit MO 64081
816 525-3320

(G-14752)
JDB ENTERPRISES INC
Also Called: Copy Express
111 S Main St (67202-3701)
PHONE..................................316 263-2411
Jeremy D Bolander, *President*
EMP: 6
SALES (est): 243.6K **Privately Held**
SIC: 2752 Commercial printing, lithographic

(G-14753)
JEFF L KREHBIEL
Also Called: Jeff L Krehbiel Associates
1300 E Lewis St (67211-1707)
PHONE..................................316 267-8233
Jeff Krehbiel, *Owner*
Betty Krehbiel, *Manager*
EMP: 12
SQ FT: 7,240
SALES (est): 2.2MM **Privately Held**
WEB: www.jkaarchitecture.com
SIC: 8712 Architectural engineering

(G-14754)
JENSEN DESIGN INC
933 S West St (67213-1615)
PHONE..................................316 943-7900
Galen Jensen, *President*
Donna Jensen, *Vice Pres*
EMP: 8
SQ FT: 6,000
SALES (est): 1.2MM **Privately Held**
WEB: www.jenseniron.com
SIC: 3645 2511 5712 Residential lighting fixtures; wood household furniture; custom made furniture, except cabinets

(G-14755)
JET DIGITAL PRINTING & COPIES
6410 E Central Ave (67206-1923)
PHONE..................................316 685-2679
Nick Lava, *Owner*
EMP: 10
SALES (est): 550K **Privately Held**
SIC: 7334 Photocopying & duplicating services

(G-14756)
JFAONLINECOM LLC
5550 S West St (67217-3968)
P.O. Box 17188 (67217-0188)
PHONE..................................316 554-1222
Patrick R Manning,
EMP: 6
SALES: 1.7MM **Privately Held**
SIC: 2752 Business form & card printing, lithographic

(G-14757)
JIM STARKEY MUSIC CENTER INC
1318 W 18th St N (67203-2298)
PHONE..................................316 262-2351
Fax: 316 262-0058
EMP: 10 **EST:** 1954
SQ FT: 8,000
SALES (est): 1.1MM **Privately Held**
SIC: 5736 7699 8299 Ret & Repairs Musical Instruments & Operates Music School

(G-14758)
JMT INDUSTRIES INC
8310 E Oak Knoll St (67207-5412)
PHONE..................................316 267-1221
Jorge Montoya-Blas, *President*
EMP: 7
SQ FT: 5,200
SALES: 700K **Privately Held**
SIC: 3728 Aircraft assemblies, subassemblies & parts

(G-14759)
JOBBERS AUTOMOTIVE WHSE INC (PA)
Also Called: Auto Value
801 E Zimmerly St (67211-3342)
P.O. Box 161009 (67216-8009)
PHONE..................................316 267-4393
Bob Evans, *President*
Larry Boehringer, *President*
John R Washbish, *President*
Alfred J Winter, *Vice Pres*
John Winter, *Vice Pres*
EMP: 100 **EST:** 1954
SQ FT: 108,000
SALES (est): 49.7MM **Privately Held**
WEB: www.jawinc.com
SIC: 5013 5015 Automotive supplies; motor vehicle parts, used

(G-14760)
JOE SELF CHEVROLET INC (PA)
8801 E Kellogg Dr (67207-1823)
PHONE..................................316 689-4390
Joe Self, *President*
John Bell, *Vice Pres*
EMP: 110
SQ FT: 63,000
SALES (est): 39.1MM **Privately Held**
WEB: www.joeselfbmw.com
SIC: 5511 5531 7538 7515 Automobiles, new & used; automotive parts; general automotive repair shops; passenger car leasing; top & body repair & paint shops

(G-14761)
JOES SEAT COVER CAR WASH CTR
Also Called: Joe's Express Lube & Oil
206 N Seneca St (67203-6092)
PHONE..................................316 262-2486
Bradley Steven, *President*
Brad Steven, *President*
EMP: 36
SQ FT: 15,000
SALES: 1.5MM **Privately Held**
SIC: 7542 7532 7549 Washing & polishing, automotive; upholstery & trim shop, automotive; lubrication service, automotive

(G-14762)
JOHN B BAKER
Also Called: Advertising Images
447 S Greenwood St (67211-1821)
P.O. Box 20510 (67208-6510)
PHONE..................................316 263-2820
John B Baker, *Owner*
EMP: 5
SQ FT: 6,000
SALES: 850K **Privately Held**
WEB: www.advertisingimg.com
SIC: 2397 5199 2396 Schiffli machine embroideries; advertising specialties; automotive & apparel trimmings

(G-14763)
JOHN T ARNOLD ASSOCIATES INC
100 S Main St Ste 100 # 100 (67202-3734)
PHONE..................................316 263-7242
Marlin Penner, *CEO*
Don Arnold Jr, *Vice Pres*
Lisa Thompson, *Opers Staff*
Evan Larue, *Asst Broker*
Stephanie Wise, *Associate*
EMP: 10
SQ FT: 1,200
SALES (est): 530K **Privately Held**
WEB: www.johntarnold.com
SIC: 6531 6799 Real estate agent, commercial; investors

(G-14764)
JOHN ZINK COMPANY LLC
4111 E 37th St N (67220-3203)
PHONE..................................316 828-7380
Tim Webster, *Vice Pres*
Chris Foster, *Project Mgr*
James Honeyman, *Project Mgr*
Mike Leonard, *Project Mgr*
Shuho McKeon, *Project Mgr*
EMP: 15
SALES (corp-wide): 40.6B **Privately Held**
SIC: 3822 Auto controls regulating residntl & coml environmt & applncs
HQ: John Zink Company, Llc
11920 E Apache St
Tulsa OK 74116
918 234-1800

(G-14765)
JOHNSON CNTRLS SEC SLTIONS LLC
3450 N Rock Rd Ste 509 (67226-1355)
PHONE..................................316 634-1792
Boe McCall, *Manager*

EMP: 40 **Privately Held**
WEB: www.adt.com
SIC: 7382 Burglar alarm maintenance & monitoring
HQ: Johnson Controls Security Solutions Llc
6600 Congress Ave
Boca Raton FL 33487
561 264-2071

(G-14766)
JOHNSON CONTROLS
625 N Carriage Pkwy # 140 (67208-4510)
PHONE..................................316 686-6363
Donald Hull, *Manager*
EMP: 35 **Privately Held**
WEB: www.simplexgrinnell.com
SIC: 3669 1731 1711 Emergency alarms; fire detection & burglar alarm systems specialization; fire sprinkler system installation
HQ: Johnson Controls Fire Protection Lp
6600 Congress Ave
Boca Raton FL 33487
561 988-7200

(G-14767)
JOHNSON DUNCAN & HOLLOWELL CPA
Also Called: Johnson, Pamela J
535 S Emporia Ave Ste 103 (67202-4534)
PHONE..................................316 267-3402
Darrell Duncan, *Partner*
Michael Hollowel, *Partner*
Michael Hollowell, *CPA*
EMP: 10 **EST:** 1980
SQ FT: 2,200
SALES (est): 730.2K **Privately Held**
WEB: www.jdhcpa.net
SIC: 8721 Accounting services, except auditing; certified public accountant

(G-14768)
JOHNSON GAGE & INSPECTION INC
5920 W 21st St N (67205-1722)
PHONE..................................316 943-7532
Ed Johnson, *President*
Steven Cox, *Corp Secy*
EMP: 12
SALES (est): 1.5MM **Privately Held**
WEB: www.jgimte.com
SIC: 8734 Calibration & certification

(G-14769)
JOHNSONS GARDEN CENTER INC (PA)
2707 W 13th St N (67203-1897)
PHONE..................................316 942-3751
Jeremy Johnson, *President*
Sallie Strole, *Store Mgr*
Joanna Ediger, *Asst Mgr*
Nancy Johnson, *Admin Sec*
EMP: 40
SQ FT: 8,875
SALES (est): 13.4MM **Privately Held**
WEB: www.johnsonsgarden.com
SIC: 5261 0782 Garden supplies & tools; nursery stock, seeds & bulbs; landscape contractors

(G-14770)
JONES JANITORIAL SERVICE
1124 N Emerson Ave (67212-3016)
PHONE..................................316 722-5520
Rick Jones, *Owner*
EMP: 10
SALES: 10K **Privately Held**
SIC: 7349 Janitorial service, contract basis

(G-14771)
JORDAN COMPANIES INC
Also Called: Jordan Spray Insulation
1133 S Gordon St (67213-1715)
P.O. Box 2516 (67201-2516)
PHONE..................................316 943-6222
Toll Free:..877 -
Stephen M Jordan, *President*
EMP: 35
SQ FT: 15,000
SALES (est): 3.9MM **Privately Held**
WEB: www.jordaninc.com
SIC: 1761 1742 Siding contractor; insulation, buildings

(G-14772)
JOSEPH & HOLLANDER PA (PA)
500 N Market St (67214-3514)
PHONE..................................316 262-9400
Stephen M Joseph, *Partner*
Ross A Hollander, *Partner*
Christopher M Joseph, *Partner*
Diane Bellquist, *Counsel*
Julia Craft,
EMP: 14
SALES (est): 1.7MM **Privately Held**
WEB: www.josephhollander.com
SIC: 8111 Criminal law

(G-14773)
JOSEPH P STEVEN DDS PA
232 N Seneca St (67203-6023)
PHONE..................................316 262-5273
Joseph Steven, *Owner*
EMP: 18 **EST:** 2001
SALES (est): 576.1K **Privately Held**
SIC: 8021 Dentists' office

(G-14774)
JOSEPH T RYERSON & SON INC
1874 S Florence Ct (67209-2831)
PHONE..................................316 942-6061
Kevin Hebert, *Branch Mgr*
EMP: 33 **Publicly Held**
SIC: 5051 Metals service centers & offices
HQ: Joseph T. Ryerson & Son, Inc.
227 W Monroe St Fl 27
Chicago IL 60606
312 292-5000

(G-14775)
JOYFUL NOISE ACADEMY
2900 N Rock Rd (67226-1144)
PHONE..................................316 688-5060
Pam Harrod, *Director*
Jessica Bengman, *Asst Director*
EMP: 30
SALES (est): 669K **Privately Held**
SIC: 8351 Preschool center

(G-14776)
JR CUSTOM METAL PRODUCTS INC
2237 S West Street Ct (67213-1100)
PHONE..................................316 263-1318
Patricia Koehler, *President*
Jesus Raul Martinez Jr, *Vice Pres*
Kim Martinez, *Purch Mgr*
Don Burton, *Engineer*
Jorge Martinez, *Treasurer*
EMP: 150
SQ FT: 80,000
SALES (est): 43.4MM **Privately Held**
WEB: www.jrcustommetal.com
SIC: 3535 3537 3531 3444 Conveyors & conveying equipment; platforms, stands, tables, pallets & similar equipment; construction machinery; sheet metalwork

(G-14777)
JRI INVESTMENTS LLC
Also Called: Accounting Department
2313 N Zoo Park Cir (67205-6500)
PHONE..................................785 404-2210
EMP: 2988
SALES (corp-wide): 91.3MM **Privately Held**
SIC: 8721 Accounting services, except auditing
PA: Jri Investments, Llc
621 Wetsport Blvd
Salina KS 67401
785 404-2210

(G-14778)
JUNIPER PAYMENTS LLC
9440 E Boston St Ste 150 (67207-3600)
PHONE..................................316 267-3200
Jon Budd, *CEO*
Tracy Hearson, *Mktg Coord*
EMP: 21
SALES (est): 3.8MM **Privately Held**
WEB: www.lendingtools.com
SIC: 5211 7371 Lumber & other building materials; software programming applications

(G-14779)
KAHRS NELSON FANNING HITE KLLG
100 N Broadway Ave # 950 (67202-2212)
PHONE..................................316 265-7741
Richard C Hite, *Partner*
Richard Honeyman, *Partner*
Linda Parks, *Partner*
Betty Ewing, *Technology*
Gary A Winfrey,
EMP: 55
SQ FT: 17,000
SALES (est): 3.6MM **Privately Held**
SIC: 8111 General practice attorney, lawyer

(G-14780)
KAMAN COMPOSITES - WICHITA
1650 S Mccomas St (67213-1239)
PHONE..................................316 942-1241
James C Larwood Jr, *President*
Alphonse J Lariviere Jr, *Division Pres*
Michael L Lafluer, *Vice Pres*
Christopher Simmons, *Vice Pres*
Robert D Starr, *Treasurer*
EMP: 140 **EST:** 1949
SQ FT: 150,000
SALES (est): 22.5MM
SALES (corp-wide): 1.8B **Publicly Held**
SIC: 3082 Unsupported plastics profile shapes
HQ: Kaman Aerospace Group, Inc.
1332 Blue Hills Ave
Bloomfield CT 06002

(G-14781)
KAMMERER AUTO BODY & PAINT
307 S Washington Ave (67202-4725)
PHONE..................................316 265-0211
John Wheeler, *President*
EMP: 15
SQ FT: 13,600
SALES (est): 1.3MM **Privately Held**
SIC: 7532 Body shop, automotive; paint shop, automotive

(G-14782)
KAN PAK LLC (HQ)
Also Called: Mixology
151 S Whittier Rd (67207-1063)
PHONE..................................620 442-6820
Larry McGill, *CEO*
Dennis J Cohlmia, *Ch of Bd*
Dennis Cohlmia, *Ch of Bd*
James Steinbacher, *Engineer*
Pam Osgood, *Admin Asst*
◆ **EMP:** 60
SALES (est): 27.1MM
SALES (corp-wide): 1.3B **Privately Held**
WEB: www.mixology.com
SIC: 2024 Ice cream & frozen desserts
PA: Golden State Foods Corp.
18301 Von Karman Ave # 1
Irvine CA 92612
949 247-8000

(G-14783)
KAN PAK INTERNATIONAL INC
151 S Whittier Rd (67207-1063)
PHONE..................................316 201-4210
Larry McGill, *Principal*
EMP: 49
SALES (est): 16.4MM **Privately Held**
SIC: 2038 Ethnic foods, frozen

(G-14784)
KAN-AM PRODUCTS INC (PA)
1830 W Harry St (67213-3272)
PHONE..................................316 943-8806
Terry Donovan, *President*
Dennis Donovan, *Owner*
Tyler Chapman, *General Mgr*
EMP: 16
SQ FT: 12,000
SALES (est): 6MM **Privately Held**
SIC: 5031 Building materials, exterior; siding, wood

(G-14785)
KANSAS AFFORDABLE HOUSING CORP (PA)
Also Called: MENNONITE HOUSING
2145 N Topeka St (67214-1140)
PHONE..................................316 942-4848
Andrew L Bias, *CEO*
Byron Adrian, *CFO*
Penny Herron, *Director*
EMP: 25
SALES (est): 98.4K **Privately Held**
WEB: www.mennonitehousing.com
SIC: 1521 8322 General remodeling, single-family houses; individual & family services

(G-14786)
KANSAS ASSET RECOVERY INC
921 E Douglas Ave (67202-3509)
PHONE..................................316 303-1000
Jihane Dhayne, *President*
EMP: 47
SALES (est): 5.8MM **Privately Held**
SIC: 5045 Computers, peripherals & software

(G-14787)
KANSAS BIG BROS BIG SSTERS INC (PA)
310 E 2nd St N (67202-2404)
PHONE..................................316 263-3300
Daniel Soliday, *CEO*
Dan Soliday, *President*
Brandon Russell, *COO*
Judi Lemaire, *Accountant*
Jason Runnalls, *Director*
EMP: 52
SQ FT: 10,000
SALES: 4.1MM **Privately Held**
SIC: 8322 Helping hand service (Big Brother, etc.)

(G-14788)
KANSAS BODY WORKS INC
1137 N Mosley Ave (67214-3099)
PHONE..................................316 263-5506
Palma Menges, *President*
Mathew Menges, *Vice Pres*
EMP: 14
SQ FT: 11,000
SALES (est): 1.6MM **Privately Held**
SIC: 7532 Body shop, automotive

(G-14789)
KANSAS CANDY & TOBACCO INC
4430 W 29th Cir S (67215-1018)
PHONE..................................316 942-9081
Scott Larkin, *President*
Julie Daugherty, *Corp Secy*
EMP: 14
SQ FT: 8,000
SALES (est): 18.2MM **Privately Held**
SIC: 5145 5194 Candy; cigarettes

(G-14790)
KANSAS CARPET & TILE INC
2411 S Leonine Rd (67217-1069)
PHONE..................................316 942-2111
Karl Schraider, *President*
Linda Schrader, *Admin Sec*
EMP: 20
SQ FT: 26,000
SALES (est): 2.9MM **Privately Held**
SIC: 5713 1752 Carpets; wood floor installation & refinishing

(G-14791)
KANSAS CENTER ENTREPRNRSHP
Also Called: Network Kansas
550 N 159th St E Ste 208 (67230-7522)
P.O. Box 877, Andover (67002-0877)
PHONE..................................316 425-8808
Steve Radley, *President*
Kristi Pedersen, *Manager*
EMP: 20
SALES (est): 63.7K **Privately Held**
SIC: 8748 Business consulting

(G-14792)
KANSAS CHILDRENS SERVICE LEAG (PA)
1365 N Custer St (67203-6694)
PHONE..................................316 942-4261
Janet Schalansky, *CEO*
Joe Whitaker, *CEO*
Tessa Smith, *Asst Director*
Cindy Dundas, *Executive Asst*
Caryl Clanton, *Receptionist*

EMP: 60
SQ FT: 18,000
SALES: 15MM **Privately Held**
WEB: www.kcsl.org+kansas+childrens+service+garde
SIC: **8322** 8351 Adoption services; head start center, except in conjunction with school

(G-14793)
KANSAS CORPORATE CREDIT UNION
8615 W Frazier Ln Ste 1 (67212-3835)
PHONE..................................316 721-2600
Larry Eisenhower, *CEO*
Kent Gleason, *Exec VP*
Kip Poe, *Vice Pres*
Chris Hageman, *Financial Analy*
Circe Gleeson, *Marketing Mgr*
EMP: 15 **EST:** 2000
SALES: 9.3MM **Privately Held**
WEB: www.kansascorporate.org
SIC: **6062** State credit unions

(G-14794)
KANSAS COUNSELORS INC
1421 N Saint Paul St (67203-1799)
PHONE..................................316 942-8335
Janet Smith, *President*
EMP: 55
SQ FT: 7,000
SALES (est): 2.9MM **Privately Held**
SIC: **7322** Collection agency, except real estate

(G-14795)
KANSAS CREDIT UNION ASSN (PA)
2544 N Maize Ct Ste 100 (67205-7358)
PHONE..................................316 942-7965
Marla Marsh, *President*
Donnell Mihalik, *Vice Pres*
Kim Wheelock, *Vice Pres*
EMP: 25
SQ FT: 19,000
SALES: 1.3MM **Privately Held**
WEB: www.cuachonline.com
SIC: **8611** 8742 Business associations; administrative services consultant

(G-14796)
KANSAS DEPARTMENT TRNSP
Also Called: Area 5
3200 E 45th St N Bldg 2 (67220-1497)
PHONE..................................316 744-1271
Benny Tarberdi, *Manager*
EMP: 125 **Privately Held**
WEB: www.nwwichitabypass.com
SIC: **9621** 1611 Regulation, administration of transportation; ; highway & street maintenance
HQ: Kansas Department Of Transportation
700 Sw Harrison St # 500
Topeka KS 66603
785 296-3501

(G-14797)
KANSAS ELKS TRAINING (PA)
Also Called: KETCH
1006 E Waterman St (67211-1525)
PHONE..................................316 383-8700
Ron Pasmore, *President*
Sheila Brown, *Vice Pres*
Laura Roberds, *Vice Pres*
Raymond Toupin, *Maint Spvr*
Dan Krug, *Treasurer*
EMP: 300
SQ FT: 25,000
SALES: 12MM **Privately Held**
WEB: www.ketch.org
SIC: **8331** Vocational rehabilitation agency

(G-14798)
KANSAS FIBER NETWORK LLC
Also Called: Kfn
8201 E 34th Street Cir N # 1500
(67226-1395)
PHONE..................................316 712-6030
Mike Brigman, *President*
Brian Christiansen, *Vice Pres*
Bob Wallentine, *Opers Staff*
Terry Talken, *VP Finance*
EMP: 24
SQ FT: 17,000
SALES: 16MM **Privately Held**
SIC: **4813** Local telephone communications

(G-14799)
KANSAS FIREFIGHTERS MUSEUM
1300 S Broadway Ave (67211-3126)
PHONE..................................316 264-5990
Bk Owens, *President*
EMP: 16
SALES: 11.7K **Privately Held**
SIC: **8412** Museum

(G-14800)
KANSAS FMLY ADVSORY NETWRK INC
333 E English St Ste 215 (67202-4317)
PHONE..................................316 264-2400
Nina Shaw-Woody, *Exec Dir*
EMP: 10
SALES (est): 35.6K **Privately Held**
SIC: **7389** Business services

(G-14801)
KANSAS FOOD BANK WAREHOUSE INC (PA)
1919 E Douglas Ave (67211-1627)
PHONE..................................316 265-3663
Brian Walker, *President*
Bruce Bartel, *Opers Staff*
Larry Gunkel, *Program Mgr*
Melissa Koehn, *Program Mgr*
Kevin Enz, *Manager*
EMP: 20
SQ FT: 50,000
SALES: 23.3MM **Privately Held**
SIC: **8399** Council for social agency

(G-14802)
KANSAS FORKLIFT INC (PA)
1750 W Harry St (67213-3656)
PHONE..................................316 262-1426
Linda Large, *President*
EMP: 15 **EST:** 1977
SQ FT: 15,000
SALES: 2.4MM **Privately Held**
WEB: www.ksforklift.com
SIC: **5084** 7699 Lift trucks & parts; materials handling machinery; industrial machinery & equipment repair

(G-14803)
KANSAS GUN DRILLING INC
2204 W Harry Ct (67213-2904)
PHONE..................................316 943-4241
Sharron L Walker, *President*
Floyd L Walker, *Vice Pres*
EMP: 10
SQ FT: 8,000
SALES: 600K **Privately Held**
WEB: www.kansasgundrilling.com
SIC: **3599** Machine shop, jobbing & repair

(G-14804)
KANSAS HEALTH FOUNDATION
309 E Douglas Ave (67202-3405)
PHONE..................................316 262-7676
Reginald Robinson, *President*
Doug Clasen, *Principal*
Kristi Zukovich, *Vice Pres*
Evan Meyers, *CFO*
Stephen Webster, *CFO*
EMP: 27
SQ FT: 23,000
SALES: 6.1MM **Privately Held**
SIC: **8699** Charitable organization

(G-14805)
KANSAS HEART HOSPITAL LLC
3601 N Webb Rd (67226-8129)
PHONE..................................800 574-3278
Thomas Ashcom, *CEO*
Gregory F Duick, *President*
Joyce Heismeyer, *COO*
Stephanie Costello, *Vice Pres*
Glenn Leonard, *Plant Mgr*
EMP: 235
SQ FT: 56,000
SALES: 46.6MM **Privately Held**
WEB: www.kansasheart.com
SIC: **8069** 8062 Specialty hospitals, except psychiatric; general medical & surgical hospitals

(G-14806)
KANSAS HUMANE SOC WICHITA KANS
3313 N Hillside Ave (67219-3907)
PHONE..................................316 524-9196
Mark EBY, *President*
Sheri Confield, *Exec Dir*
Karla Hartlep, *Officer*
Pam Cornwell, *Assistant*
EMP: 15
SALES: 3.9MM **Privately Held**
WEB: www.kshumane.org
SIC: **8699** 0742 Animal humane society; veterinary services, specialties

(G-14807)
KANSAS IMAGING CONSULTANTS
929 N St Francis St (67214-3821)
PHONE..................................316 268-5000
Timothy Benning, *Partner*
EMP: 17
SALES (est): 1.1MM **Privately Held**
SIC: **8011** Radiologist

(G-14808)
KANSAS IMAGING CONSULTANTS PA
3600 E Harry St (67218-3713)
PHONE..................................316 689-5043
Hemangini Shah, *Principal*
Kuet Kuan H Fang-Yen, *Diag Radio*
EMP: 17
SALES (est): 841.6K **Privately Held**
SIC: **8011** Radiologist

(G-14809)
KANSAS INN LIMITED PARTNERSHIP
Also Called: Kansas Inn, The
1011 N Topeka St (67214-2913)
PHONE..................................316 269-9999
Raymond Clark, *Partner*
Raymond E Clark, *Partner*
EMP: 16
SQ FT: 25,000
SALES (est): 723.3K **Privately Held**
SIC: **7011** Motels

(G-14810)
KANSAS INTRSCHLSTC ATHLTC ADMN
2301 E Douglas Ave (67211-1613)
PHONE..................................316 655-8929
Marc Haught, *Principal*
EMP: 55 **EST:** 2008
SALES: 80.3K **Privately Held**
SIC: **8699** Membership organizations

(G-14811)
KANSAS INVESTIGATIVE SERVICES
250 S Laura Ave (67211-1515)
PHONE..................................316 267-1357
Emery L Goad, *President*
Jackie Goad, *Principal*
EMP: 10
SALES (est): 400K **Privately Held**
SIC: **7381** Private investigator

(G-14812)
KANSAS LEGAL SERVICES INC
Also Called: Wichita Lawyers Care
340 S Broadway Ave (67202-4301)
PHONE..................................316 265-9681
Marilyn Harp, *CEO*
Shannon Crane, *Director*
EMP: 30
SALES (est): 2.2MM **Privately Held**
SIC: **8111** Legal aid service

(G-14813)
KANSAS LONG TERM CARE PHYS
1131 S Clifton Ave Ste B (67218-2963)
PHONE..................................316 315-0145
Adam F D,
John W D,
EMP: 97
SALES (est): 670.9K
SALES (corp-wide): 287.4MM **Privately Held**
SIC: **8051** Skilled nursing care facilities
HQ: Ipc Healthcare, Inc.
4605 Lankershim Blvd
North Hollywood CA 91602
888 447-2362

(G-14814)
KANSAS MASONIC HOME
401 S Seneca St (67213-5541)
PHONE..................................316 269-7500
Mathew Bogner, *CEO*
Kevin Cronkleton, *CFO*
EMP: 250
SQ FT: 250,000
SALES: 13.9MM **Privately Held**
WEB: www.kansasmasonichome.com
SIC: **8051** 6513 8082 8052 Skilled nursing care facilities; apartment building operators; home health care services; intermediate care facilities

(G-14815)
KANSAS MEDICAL MUTUAL INSUR CO
3020 N Cypress St Ste 100 (67226-4010)
PHONE..................................316 681-8119
Darrell McCool, *Principal*
EMP: 11 **Privately Held**
SIC: **6411** 6399 Insurance agents; health insurance for pets
PA: Kansas Medical Mutual Insurance Co Inc
623 Sw 10th Ave Fl 2
Topeka KS 66612

(G-14816)
KANSAS NPHROLOGY PHYSICIANS PA
Also Called: Dennis L Ross MD
1035 N Emporia St Ste 105 (67214-2943)
PHONE..................................316 263-7285
Jason R Taylor, *Partner*
Kim Fowler, *Office Mgr*
Kenneth Kovach, *Med Doctor*
Dennis Ross, *Med Doctor*
Jason Taylor, *Med Doctor*
EMP: 36
SALES (est): 4.4MM **Privately Held**
SIC: **8011** Nephrologist

(G-14817)
KANSAS ORTHOPEDIC CENTER PA
Also Called: Lewonowski, Kris MD
7550 W Village Cir Ste 1 (67205-9364)
PHONE..................................316 838-2020
Steve Howell, *President*
Brian E D, *Surgeon*
Prince T D, *Surgeon*
Lora Johnston, *Director*
James L D, *Admin Sec*
EMP: 55
SQ FT: 11,334
SALES (est): 5.8MM **Privately Held**
SIC: **8011** Clinic, operated by physicians; orthopedic physician

(G-14818)
KANSAS PATHOLOGY CONS PA
8201 E 34th Cir N # 1301 (67226-1395)
PHONE..................................316 681-2741
Ward Newcomb MD, *President*
EMP: 27 **EST:** 1976
SQ FT: 800
SALES (est): 2.5MM **Privately Held**
WEB: www.kansaspath.com
SIC: **8071** Medical laboratories

(G-14819)
KANSAS PRFFSNL ANESTHESIA
Also Called: Kansas Prof Anesthesia Pain Mg
1515 S Clifton Ave # 200 (67218-2958)
PHONE..................................316 618-1515
Greg Meister, *Partner*
Vickie Smalley, *Partner*
EMP: 21
SALES (est): 2MM **Privately Held**
SIC: **8011** Anesthesiologist

(G-14820)
KANSAS PUBLIC TELECOM SVC INC
Also Called: KPTS
320 W 21st St N (67203-2413)
PHONE..................................316 838-3090
Michele Gors, *CEO*

Kathy Webb, *Ch of Bd*
Michael Norton, *Vice Chairman*
Katelyn Weber, *Manager*
Ted Ayres, *Bd of Directors*
EMP: 31
SQ FT: 8,000
SALES: 2.7MM **Privately Held**
WEB: www.kpts.org
SIC: 4833 Television broadcasting stations

(G-14821)
KANSAS REST HOSPITALITY ASSN
Also Called: Krha
3500 N Rock Rd Bldg 1300 (67226-1335)
PHONE..................................316 267-8383
Donald Sayler, *President*
EMP: 16
SQ FT: 2,000
SALES: 514.4K **Privately Held**
WEB: www.krha.org
SIC: 8611 2721 Trade associations; periodicals

(G-14822)
KANSAS SCHL FOR EFFECTIVE LRNG
Also Called: KANSEL
1650 N Fairview Ave (67203-2636)
PHONE..................................316 263-9620
Carolyn Bunch, *Exec Dir*
Thomas Montiel, *Exec Dir*
Lisa Fitzrow, *Business Dir*
EMP: 22
SALES: 521.9K **Privately Held**
WEB: www.kansel.org
SIC: 8299 8331 8699 Tutoring school; reading & speaking schools; personal development school; job training services; charitable organization

(G-14823)
KANSAS SECURED TITLE SEDGWICK (PA)
232 N Mead St (67202-2708)
PHONE..................................316 262-8261
Kim May, *President*
Harold Siemans, *President*
Judy Cachard, *Vice Pres*
Kevin Mohr, *Vice Pres*
Laurie Witten, *Vice Pres*
EMP: 15
SQ FT: 10,000
SALES (est): 3.4MM **Privately Held**
SIC: 6541 Title abstract offices

(G-14824)
KANSAS SPINE SPCIALTY HOSP LLC
3333 N Webb Rd (67226-8123)
PHONE..................................316 462-5000
Thomas M Schmitt, *CEO*
Theresa Gassett, *Manager*
Timothy Schlittenhardt, *Manager*
John Coslett, *Ch Nursing Ofcr*
Watie McGlothlin, *Lab Dir*
EMP: 125
SALES: 42.1MM **Privately Held**
WEB: www.kansasspinehospital.com
SIC: 8062 8071 General medical & surgical hospitals; neurological laboratory

(G-14825)
KANSAS SRGERY RECOVERY CTR LLC
2770 N Webb Rd (67226-8112)
PHONE..................................316 634-0090
Ely Bartal, *Mng Member*
EMP: 150
SQ FT: 36,000
SALES (est): 3MM
SALES (corp-wide): 25.3B **Privately Held**
WEB: www.ksrc.net
SIC: 8062 General medical & surgical hospitals
HQ: Via Christi Health Partners, Inc.
8200 E Thorn Dr Ste 300
Wichita KS 67226

(G-14826)
KANSAS SURGICAL CONSULTANTS (PA)
Also Called: Waswick, William A MD
3243 E Murdock St Ste 404 (67208-3007)
PHONE..................................316 685-6222
Scott Porter MD, *Partner*
Paul Harrison MD, *Partner*
Andrew Hentzen, *Partner*
John L Kiser, *Partner*
William Waswick MD, *Partner*
EMP: 20 **EST:** 1967
SALES (est): 3.8MM **Privately Held**
WEB: www.kansassurgical.com
SIC: 8011 Surgeon

(G-14827)
KANSAS SURGICAL CONSULTANTS
9300 E 29th St N Ste 203 (67226-2183)
PHONE..................................316 219-9360
William Wafwick, *Branch Mgr*
EMP: 20
SALES (corp-wide): 3.8MM **Privately Held**
WEB: www.kansassurgical.com
SIC: 8011 Surgeon
PA: Kansas Surgical Consultants
3243 E Murdock St Ste 404
Wichita KS 67208
316 685-6222

(G-14828)
KANSAS TRUCK EQUIPMENT CO INC
1521 S Tyler Rd (67209-1889)
PHONE..................................316 722-4291
Maurice R Linnens, *President*
Randall L Underwood, *Corp Secy*
Doug R Maryott, *Vice Pres*
EMP: 24 **EST:** 1959
SQ FT: 16,000
SALES (est): 11MM **Privately Held**
WEB: www.kansastruck.net
SIC: 5012 5084 5047 Buses; industrial machinery & equipment; technical aids for the handicapped

(G-14829)
KANSAS TURNPIKE AUTHORITY (PA)
9401 E Kellogg Dr (67207-1804)
PHONE..................................316 682-4537
Michael L Johnston, *President*
Les Donovan, *Corp Secy*
Alan Bakaitis, *COO*
David Jacobson, *Chief Engr*
Blake Butterworth, *Manager*
EMP: 99
SQ FT: 25,000
SALES: 124.8MM **Privately Held**
WEB: www.ksturnpike.com
SIC: 4785 Toll road operation

(G-14830)
KANSASLAND TIRE INC (HQ)
2904 S Spruce St (67216-2434)
PHONE..................................316 522-5434
Gary K Wright, *President*
Nancy Wright, *Corp Secy*
Scott Samway, *CFO*
▲ **EMP:** 183
SQ FT: 6,000
SALES (est): 49.4MM
SALES (corp-wide): 94.3MM **Privately Held**
WEB: www.nktiregroup.com
SIC: 5531 7538 Automotive tires; general automotive repair shops
PA: Nebraskaland Tire, Inc.
Hwy 283 & Hwy I 80
Lexington NE 68850
308 324-2338

(G-14831)
KANZA BANK
2233 N Greenwich Rd (67226-8209)
PHONE..................................316 636-5821
Barry Purdy, *Vice Pres*
EMP: 14
SALES (corp-wide): 9.6MM **Privately Held**
SIC: 6022 State trust companies accepting deposits, commercial
PA: Kanza Bank
151 N Main St
Kingman KS 67068
620 532-5821

(G-14832)
KANZA BANK
13605 W Maple St Ste 101 (67235-8753)
PHONE..................................316 773-7007
Alyssa Lytle, *Credit Staff*
Susie Alderson, *Manager*
EMP: 10
SALES (corp-wide): 9.6MM **Privately Held**
SIC: 6022 6029 State trust companies accepting deposits, commercial; commercial banks
PA: Kanza Bank
151 N Main St
Kingman KS 67068
620 532-5821

(G-14833)
KARLS TIRE & AUTO SERVICE INC
Also Called: Goodyear
401 S Market St (67202-3903)
PHONE..................................316 685-5338
Joseph R Doubrava, *President*
EMP: 15
SQ FT: 7,000
SALES (est): 1.9MM **Privately Held**
SIC: 5531 7538 5261 Automotive tires; automotive accessories; general automotive repair shops; lawnmowers & tractors

(G-14834)
KAW VALLEY ENGINEERING INC
200 N Emporia Ave (67202-2550)
PHONE..................................316 440-4304
Tim Austin, *Branch Mgr*
EMP: 10
SALES (est): 420.9K
SALES (corp-wide): 24.8MM **Privately Held**
SIC: 8713 8711 Surveying services; construction & civil engineering
PA: Kaw Valley Engineering, Inc.
2319 N Jackson St
Junction City KS 66441
785 762-5040

(G-14835)
KAYLOR DENTAL LABORATORY INC
619 N Florence St (67212-2136)
P.O. Box 7725 (67277-7725)
PHONE..................................316 943-3226
Donald G Kaylor, *President*
Dennis Kaylor, *Vice Pres*
Thomas E Kaylor, *Vice Pres*
EMP: 68 **EST:** 1961
SQ FT: 14,000
SALES (est): 3.8MM **Privately Held**
WEB: www.kaylordental.com
SIC: 8072 8021 Crown & bridge production; offices & clinics of dentists

(G-14836)
KB PROPERTIES OF KANSAS LLC
Also Called: Jtweigand
150 N Market St (67202-1900)
PHONE..................................316 292-3924
Nestor Weigand, *Mng Member*
Steven R Barrett,
EMP: 50
SALES (est): 1.6MM **Privately Held**
SIC: 6531 Real estate brokers & agents

(G-14837)
KC CORING & CUTNG CNSTR INC
Also Called: Kansas Cutting Concrete
3410 N Ohio St (67219-3720)
PHONE..................................316 832-1580
Charles Phillips, *Manager*
EMP: 10
SQ FT: 3,600
SALES (corp-wide): 3.1MM **Privately Held**
SIC: 1799 5082 Core drilling & cutting; contractors' materials
PA: K.C. Coring And Cutting Construction, Inc.
7240 Central St
Kansas City MO 64114
816 523-2015

(G-14838)
KCC CONSERVATION DISTRICT II
3450 N Rock Rd Ste 601 (67226-1356)
PHONE..................................316 630-4000
EMP: 10
SALES (est): 186.4K **Privately Held**
SIC: 8611 Business Association

(G-14839)
KCOE ISOM LLP
1605 N Waterfront Pkwy # 200 (67206-6634)
PHONE..................................316 685-0222
Katherine Hale, *Accountant*
Donna Funk, *CPA*
Dixie Larson, *Sales Staff*
Dave Burger, *Manager*
Sandy Sporleder, *Manager*
EMP: 35
SALES (corp-wide): 48MM **Privately Held**
WEB: www.kcoe.com
SIC: 8721 Certified public accountant
PA: Kcoe Isom, Llp
3030 Courtland Cir
Salina KS
785 825-1561

(G-14840)
KEARNEY REGIONAL MED CTR LLC
200 W Douglas Ave Ste 950 (67202-3033)
PHONE..................................316 682-6770
Dr Sean Denney, *Ch of Bd*
Steve Regier, *CFO*
Dani Peisiger, *Manager*
Randy Gehrt, *Administration*
EMP: 45 **EST:** 2014
SALES (est): 5.2MM **Privately Held**
SIC: 8099 Blood related health services

(G-14841)
KEITH SHAW
Also Called: Avenue Style
220 W Douglas Ave Ste 155 (67202-3104)
PHONE..................................316 262-7297
Keith Shaw, *Owner*
EMP: 10
SALES (est): 320K **Privately Held**
SIC: 7231 Hairdressers

(G-14842)
KELLER WILLIAMS DAVE NEAL
Also Called: Keller Williams Realtors
1635 N Waterfront Pkwy # 150 (67206-6625)
PHONE..................................316 681-3600
Christine Anderson, *Principal*
Susan Langston-Ames, *Real Est Agnt*
EMP: 10
SALES (est): 650.2K **Privately Held**
SIC: 6531 Real estate agent, residential

(G-14843)
KELLEY INSTRUMENTS INC
4131 W May St (67209-2838)
PHONE..................................316 945-7171
Loren Kirk Ellis, *President*
EMP: 13
SQ FT: 7,500
SALES: 975.1K **Privately Held**
WEB: www.kelleyinstruments.com
SIC: 7699 5088 Aircraft flight instrument repair; aircraft equipment & supplies

(G-14844)
KELLEY YORK & ASSOCIATES LTD
515 S Main St Ste 105 (67202-3752)
PHONE..................................316 267-8200
Darlene Kelley, *President*
Vesta York, *Vice Pres*
EMP: 11
SQ FT: 2,500
SALES (est): 740K **Privately Held**
WEB: www.kelleyyork.com
SIC: 7338 Court reporting service

(G-14845)
KELLOGG HOSPITALITY LLC
6815 W Kellogg Dr (67209-2217)
PHONE..................................316 942-5600
Jigna Patel,
EMP: 20

GEOGRAPHIC

SALES (est): 109.1K **Privately Held**
SIC: 7011 Hotels & motels

(G-14846)
KELLY MANUFACTURING COMPANY (PA)
555 S Topeka Ave (67202-4418)
PHONE.....316 265-6868
Justin Kelly, *President*
EMP: 60
SQ FT: 60,000
SALES (est): 9.3MM **Privately Held**
WEB: www.kellymfg.com
SIC: 3812 Aircraft control instruments

(G-14847)
KELLYS CORPORATE APPAREL
355 Pattie St (67211)
PHONE.....316 263-5858
Jim Behring, *President*
EMP: 6
SALES: 300K **Privately Held**
WEB: www.kellyscorporate.com
SIC: 2261 5611 5699 2759 Embossing cotton broadwoven fabrics; clothing, sportswear, men's & boys'; uniforms & work clothing; screen printing; embroidery products, except schiffli machine

(G-14848)
KENCO TRUCKING INC (PA)
1405 N Shefford St (67212-5716)
PHONE.....316 943-4881
Phil Smith, *President*
Cindy Weaver, *Treasurer*
EMP: 24
SALES: 3MM **Privately Held**
SIC: 4212 Dump truck haulage

(G-14849)
KENNEDY & WILLIS
Also Called: Johnson, Douglas D
727 N Waco Ave Ste 585 (67203-3956)
PHONE.....316 263-4921
David Dahl, *Partner*
Douglas D Johnson, *Partner*
Jeff Willis, *Partner*
Craig Kennedy, *Principal*
Chris Leetch, *Manager*
EMP: 10
SALES (est): 857.7K **Privately Held**
SIC: 8111 General practice law office

(G-14850)
KENS AUTO TOW
3760 S Broadway Ave (67216-1032)
PHONE.....316 941-4300
Monty Yfidro, *Owner*
EMP: 10 **EST:** 2000
SALES (est): 484.1K **Privately Held**
WEB: www.kensautotow.com
SIC: 7549 Towing service, automotive

(G-14851)
KENT BUSINESS SYSTEMS CORP
Also Called: Kent Audio Visual
1131 E 1st St N (67214-3904)
PHONE.....316 262-4487
Ron L Bowring, *President*
April King, *Office Mgr*
Olivia Bowring, *Admin Sec*
EMP: 15
SQ FT: 8,500
SALES (est): 4.5MM
SALES (corp-wide): 195.5MM **Publicly Held**
WEB: www.kentav.com
SIC: 5099 7359 7812 7622 Video & audio equipment; audio-visual equipment & supply rental; video tape production; video repair
HQ: Presentation Technologies Inc
9150 N Royal Ln
Irving TX 75063
972 241-5444

(G-14852)
KEY CONSTRUCTION INC (PA)
741 W 2nd St N (67203-6004)
PHONE.....316 263-9515
Kenneth A Wells, *CEO*
David E Wells, *President*
Larry Bodley, *Superintendent*
Richard McCafferty, *Exec VP*
John Walker, *Office Mgr*
EMP: 105
SQ FT: 40,000
SALES: 170.5MM **Privately Held**
SIC: 1542 1541 Commercial & office building, new construction; industrial buildings, new construction

(G-14853)
KEY CONSTRUCTION MISSOURI LLC
741 W 2nd St N (67203-6004)
PHONE.....816 221-7171
Ted Odell, *Owner*
EMP: 17 **EST:** 2007
SQ FT: 5,000
SALES (est): 1.1MM **Privately Held**
SIC: 1521 New construction, single-family houses

(G-14854)
KEYCENTRIX INC
2420 N Woodlawn Blvd 100a (67220-3960)
PHONE.....316 262-2231
Brandon Shuey, *President*
Paula Johnson, *Train & Dev Mgr*
Tony Avery, *Manager*
Marilyn Lawson, *Software Engr*
EMP: 23
SQ FT: 5,000
SALES (est): 2.7MM
SALES (corp-wide): 57.9MM **Privately Held**
WEB: www.keycentrix.com
SIC: 7371 Computer software development
PA: Cgf Investments, Inc.
2420 N Woodlawn Blvd # 500
Wichita KS 67220
316 691-4500

(G-14855)
KEYSTONE AUTOMOTIVE INDS INC
3002 W Pawnee St Ste 100 (67213-1830)
PHONE.....316 262-0500
Rick Higler, *Manager*
EMP: 13
SALES (corp-wide): 11.8B **Publicly Held**
WEB: www.kool-vue.com
SIC: 5013 Automotive supplies & parts
HQ: Keystone Automotive Industries, Inc.
5846 Crossings Blvd
Antioch TN 37013
615 781-5200

(G-14856)
KIDCARE CONNECTION INC
3059 W 13th St N (67203-6620)
PHONE.....316 944-6434
Holly Donaldson, *President*
EMP: 25
SALES (est): 521.4K **Privately Held**
WEB: www.kidcareconnection.net
SIC: 8351 Group day care center

(G-14857)
KILIAN ELECTRICAL SERVICE INC (PA)
4107 W Harry St (67209-2754)
PHONE.....316 942-4600
Mike Kilian, *President*
EMP: 45
SQ FT: 6,600
SALES (est): 6.6MM **Privately Held**
SIC: 1731 General electrical contractor

(G-14858)
KINDERCARE EDUCATION LLC
Also Called: Knowledge Learning
805 N Socora St (67212-3237)
PHONE.....316 721-0168
Dawn Bidwell, *Director*
EMP: 14
SALES (corp-wide): 963.9MM **Privately Held**
WEB: www.knowledgelearning.com
SIC: 8351 Group day care center
PA: Kindercare Education Llc
650 Ne Holladay St # 1400
Portland OR 97232
503 872-1300

(G-14859)
KINDERCARE EDUCATION LLC
9500 E Boston St (67207-3636)
PHONE.....316 684-4574
Tiffany Cox, *Branch Mgr*
Angel Meyer, *Branch Mgr*
EMP: 14
SALES (corp-wide): 963.9MM **Privately Held**
WEB: www.knowledgelearning.com
SIC: 8351 Group day care center
PA: Kindercare Education Llc
650 Ne Holladay St # 1400
Portland OR 97232
503 872-1300

(G-14860)
KINDERCARE LEARNING CTRS LLC
Also Called: Kindercare Center 729
8722 W Thurman St (67212-5816)
PHONE.....316 721-0168
Jennifer Robinson, *Director*
EMP: 20
SALES (corp-wide): 963.9MM **Privately Held**
WEB: www.kindercare.com
SIC: 8351 Nursery school
HQ: Kindercare Learning Centers, Llc
650 Ne Holladay St # 1400
Portland OR 97232
503 872-1300

(G-14861)
KING OF FREIGHT LLC
651 S Quentin St (67218-2027)
PHONE.....316 409-4024
Todd Cheek,
EMP: 20
SALES (est): 764.5K **Privately Held**
SIC: 4731 Freight forwarding

(G-14862)
KING OF FREIGHT LLC (PA)
110 S Main St Ste 300 (67202-3751)
PHONE.....316 440-4661
Chad Warren, *General Mgr*
Grant Kocher, *Broker*
Kaylee Jackson, *Accounts Mgr*
Mark Ricklefs, *Mng Member*
Jacob Pote, *Manager*
EMP: 27
SQ FT: 10,000
SALES (est): 17MM **Privately Held**
SIC: 4731 Freight forwarding

(G-14863)
KINGS MOVING & STORAGE INC (PA)
Also Called: Kings North American
2111 E Industrial St (67216-2414)
P.O. Box 16284 (67216-0284)
PHONE.....316 247-6528
Britt King, *CEO*
Tod King, *Admin Sec*
EMP: 30
SQ FT: 25,000
SALES (est): 14.8MM **Privately Held**
WEB: www.kingms.com
SIC: 4214 4213 Local trucking with storage; trucking, except local

(G-14864)
KINSETH HOSPITALITY CO INC
Also Called: Holiday Inn
549 S Rock Rd (67207-2365)
PHONE.....316 686-7131
Peter Berman, *Branch Mgr*
EMP: 80
SALES (corp-wide): 17.3MM **Privately Held**
WEB: www.kinseth.com
SIC: 7011 Hotels & motels
PA: Kinseth Hospitality Company, Inc.
2 Quail Creek Cir
North Liberty IA 52317
319 626-5600

(G-14865)
KIOWA SERVICE CO INC
8441 E 32nd St N Ste 200 (67226-2617)
PHONE.....316 636-1070
Steve K Miller, *President*
Charline Miller, *Corp Secy*
John Miller, *Vice Pres*
EMP: 12
SALES (est): 2MM **Privately Held**
SIC: 5083 7699 Agricultural machinery & equipment; antique repair & restoration, except furniture, automobiles

(G-14866)
KIRKPATRICK SPRECKER & CO
311 S Hillside St (67211-2195)
PHONE.....316 685-1411
Dam Strunk, *Managing Prtnr*
Daniel Strunk, *Partner*
Emily Jaax, *Accountant*
Kristin Zerger, *Accountant*
Dana Johnson, *Director*
EMP: 11 **EST:** 1963
SQ FT: 3,600
SALES (est): 1.2MM **Privately Held**
WEB: www.kscpa.com
SIC: 8721 Accounting services, except auditing

(G-14867)
KLENDA AUSTERMAN LLC
301 N Main St Ste 1600 (67202-4816)
PHONE.....316 267-0331
Susan McKean, *Controller*
John V Wachtel,
Kimberly Luce, *Admin Sec*
Carlos Nolla,
Teresa Reed, *Legal Staff*
EMP: 50
SQ FT: 20,000
SALES (est): 7.8MM **Privately Held**
WEB: www.kmazlaw.com
SIC: 8111 General practice law office

(G-14868)
KMS INC
811 E Waterman St Ste 1 (67202-4716)
PHONE.....316 264-8833
Michael S Jabara, *President*
Scott Jabara, *President*
Garrell Dombaugh, *Vice Pres*
Larry McKee, *Vice Pres*
◆ **EMP:** 25
SQ FT: 115,000
SALES: 59.5MM **Privately Held**
SIC: 5199 5141 General merchandise, non-durable; groceries, general line

(G-14869)
KNIGHTON OIL CO INC
1700 N Wtrfrnt Pkwy 100a (67206-6627)
PHONE.....316 630-9905
Earl M Knighton Jr, *President*
EMP: 5 **EST:** 1947
SQ FT: 1,500
SALES (est): 548.8K **Privately Held**
SIC: 1311 Crude petroleum production

(G-14870)
KNIGHTS INN
6125 E Kellogg Dr (67218)
PHONE.....316 942-1341
Shaileshkumar Bhakta, *Owner*
John Layne, *Manager*
EMP: 15
SALES (est): 524.7K **Privately Held**
SIC: 7011 Hotels & motels

(G-14871)
KNIPP EQUIPMENT INC
Also Called: Kansas Trane Sales Company
120 S Ida St (67211-1504)
P.O. Box 595 (67201-0595)
PHONE.....316 265-9655
John F Knipp, *President*
Patricia A Knipp, *Vice Pres*
David Sheldon, *Accounts Mgr*
Jonathon Goering, *Marketing Staff*
Andy Knipp, *Manager*
EMP: 35
SQ FT: 13,000
SALES (est): 21.7MM **Privately Held**
SIC: 5075 1711 Warm air heating & air conditioning; warm air heating & air conditioning contractor

(G-14872)
KOCH AG & ENERGY SOLUTIONS LLC (HQ)
4111 E 37th St N (67220-3203)
PHONE.....316 828-5500
Mark Luetters, *President*
EMP: 24

SALES (est): 194.4MM
SALES (corp-wide): 40.6B **Privately Held**
SIC: **5191** Fertilizers & agricultural chemicals
PA: Koch Industries, Inc.
4111 E 37th St N
Wichita KS 67220
316 828-5500

(G-14873)
KOCH BUSINESS HOLDINGS LLC
Also Called: Koch Residential Services
4111 E 37th St N (67220-3203)
P.O. Box 2256 (67201-2256)
PHONE..................................316 828-8943
Phil Glenn,
EMP: 10
SALES (est): 450K
SALES (corp-wide): 40.6B **Privately Held**
WEB: www.kochind.com
SIC: **6719** Investment holding companies, except banks
PA: Koch Industries, Inc.
4111 E 37th St N
Wichita KS 67220
316 828-5500

(G-14874)
KOCH BUSINESS SOLUTIONS LP (HQ)
Also Called: Kbs
4111 E 37th St N (67220-3203)
P.O. Box 2972 (67201-2972)
PHONE..................................316 828-5500
David Robertson, *Partner*
Valerie Jenkins, *Partner*
Craig Highfill, *Vice Pres*
Steve Decker, *Project Mgr*
Sandra McNamee, *Project Mgr*
EMP: 148
SQ FT: 1,000
SALES (est): 133.6MM
SALES (corp-wide): 40.6B **Privately Held**
WEB: www.kochehs.com
SIC: **8748** Business consulting
PA: Koch Industries, Inc.
4111 E 37th St N
Wichita KS 67220
316 828-5500

(G-14875)
KOCH CARBON LLC (DH)
4111 E 37th St N (67220-3203)
P.O. Box 2256 (67201-2256)
PHONE..................................316 828-5500
Ken Hush, *President*
Dan Solomon, *CFO*
◆ **EMP**: 45
SALES (est): 49.1MM
SALES (corp-wide): 40.6B **Privately Held**
WEB: www.kochcarbon.com
SIC: **4731** 5172 4412 4424 Freight transportation arrangement; petroleum products; deep sea foreign transportation of freight; deep sea domestic transportation of freight; coal & other minerals & ores; coke (not from refineries), petroleum
HQ: Koch Mineral Services, Llc
4111 E 37th St N
Wichita KS 67220
316 828-5500

(G-14876)
KOCH COMPANIES PUB SECTOR LLC
4111 E 37th St N (67220-3203)
P.O. Box 2256 (67201-2256)
PHONE..................................316 828-5500
Julie Davis, *Principal*
Jennifer Curfman, *Counsel*
John Orlowski, *Counsel*
Adam Schaeffer, *Counsel*
Raymond Geoffroy, *Vice Pres*
EMP: 8
SALES: 1.2MM **Privately Held**
SIC: **5191** 3295 Fertilizers & agricultural chemicals; minerals, ground or treated

(G-14877)
KOCH ENERGY INC
4111 E 37th St N (67220-3298)
P.O. Box 2256 (67201-2256)
PHONE..................................316 828-5500
Charles G Koch, *CEO*
EMP: 10
SALES (est): 1.3MM **Privately Held**
SIC: **3312** Chemicals & other products derived from coking

(G-14878)
KOCH EXPLORATION COMPANY (DH)
4111 E 37th St N (67220-3203)
P.O. Box 2219 (67201-2219)
PHONE..................................316 828-5508
EMP: 10
SALES (est): 7.1MM
SALES (corp-wide): 115B **Privately Held**
SIC: **1311** 1382 Crude Petroleum/Natural Gas Production Oil/Gas Exploration Services
HQ: Koch Mineral Services, Llc
4111 E 37th St N
Wichita KS 67220
316 828-5500

(G-14879)
KOCH EXPLORATION COMPANY LLC (HQ)
4111 E 37th St N (67220-3203)
P.O. Box 2219 (67201-2219)
PHONE..................................316 828-5508
John Mueller, *President*
Shaun Kolody, *Senior VP*
Byron Lutes, *Vice Pres*
Simon Raven, *Vice Pres*
EMP: 6
SALES (est): 1MM
SALES (corp-wide): 40.6B **Privately Held**
SIC: **1382** Oil & gas exploration services
PA: Koch Industries, Inc.
4111 E 37th St N
Wichita KS 67220
316 828-5500

(G-14880)
KOCH FERTILIZER LLC (DH)
4111 E 37th St N (67220-3203)
P.O. Box 2985 (67201-2985)
PHONE..................................316 828-5010
Steve Packebush,
▲ **EMP**: 31
SQ FT: 100,000
SALES (est): 156MM
SALES (corp-wide): 40.6B **Privately Held**
SIC: **2873** 5169 2813 Nitrogenous fertilizers; chemicals & allied products; industrial gases
HQ: Koch Ag & Energy Solutions, Llc
4111 E 37th St N
Wichita KS 67220
316 828-5500

(G-14881)
KOCH INDUSTRIES INC (PA)
4111 E 37th St N (67220-3298)
P.O. Box 2256 (67201-2256)
PHONE..................................316 828-5500
Charles G Koch, *CEO*
Chris Robertson, *Managing Dir*
Jarrand Blount, *Principal*
Curt Heidecker, *Principal*
Rick Van Cleave, *Business Mgr*
◆ **EMP**: 2100
SQ FT: 500,000
SALES (est): 40.6B **Privately Held**
WEB: www.kochind.com
SIC: **5172** 5169 2911 Petroleum products; chemicals & allied products; petroleum refining

(G-14882)
KOCH INDUSTRIES INC
1760 S Airport Rd (67209-1944)
PHONE..................................316 828-8737
Casey Carlson, *Manager*
EMP: 25
SALES (corp-wide): 40.6B **Privately Held**
WEB: www.kochind.com
SIC: **2911** Petroleum refining
PA: Koch Industries, Inc.
4111 E 37th St N
Wichita KS 67220
316 828-5500

(G-14883)
KOCH MATERIALS LLC
Also Called: Koch Pavement Solutions
4111 E 37th St N (67220-3203)
PHONE..................................316 828-5500
Robert Witte, *Mng Member*
David Dishman,
Chris Hamman,
EMP: 200 **EST**: 1923
SALES (est): 28.8MM
SALES (corp-wide): 40.6B **Privately Held**
WEB: www.kochoil.com
SIC: **2951** 2899 Asphalt & asphaltic paving mixtures (not from refineries); waterproofing compounds
PA: Koch Industries, Inc.
4111 E 37th St N
Wichita KS 67220
316 828-5500

(G-14884)
KOCH MINERAL SERVICES LLC (DH)
4111 E 37th St N (67220-3203)
PHONE..................................316 828-5500
Dan Solomon, *CFO*
Tom Heroneme, *Manager*
◆ **EMP**: 30
SALES (est): 58.7MM
SALES (corp-wide): 40.6B **Privately Held**
SIC: **2999** 2873 2819 4731 Coke (not from refineries), petroleum; nitrogenous fertilizers; industrial inorganic chemicals; freight transportation arrangement; petroleum products; oil & gas exploration services
HQ: Koch Resources, Llc
4111 E 37th St N
Wichita KS 67220
316 828-5500

(G-14885)
KOCH PIPELINE COMPANY LP (DH)
Also Called: Koch Nitrogen Company
4111 E 37th St N (67220-3203)
P.O. Box 2917 (67201-2917)
PHONE..................................316 828-5511
Kim Penner, *President*
Mike Purkey, *Vice Pres*
Corey Dahlin, *Project Mgr*
Patrick Downey, *Project Mgr*
Adam Duhon, *Project Mgr*
EMP: 53
SALES (est): 61.6MM
SALES (corp-wide): 40.6B **Privately Held**
WEB: www.kochpl.com
SIC: **4612** Crude petroleum pipelines
HQ: Flint Hills Resources, Llc
8415 E 21st St N Ste 200
Wichita KS 67206
316 828-5500

(G-14886)
KOCH RAIL LLC
4111 E 37th St N (67220-3203)
PHONE..................................316 828-5500
EMP: 7 **EST**: 2013
SALES (est): 1MM **Privately Held**
SIC: **3443** Fabricated plate work (boiler shop)

(G-14887)
KOCH RESOURCES LLC (HQ)
4111 E 37th St N (67220-3203)
P.O. Box 2256 (67201-2256)
PHONE..................................316 828-5500
Charles G Koch, *CEO*
David L Robertson, *President*
David H Koch, *Exec VP*
EMP: 34
SQ FT: 50,000
SALES (est): 2.4B
SALES (corp-wide): 40.6B **Privately Held**
SIC: **6221** 2911 Commodity traders, contracts; petroleum refining
PA: Koch Industries, Inc.
4111 E 37th St N
Wichita KS 67220
316 828-5500

(G-14888)
KOCH SIEDHOFF HAND & DUNN LLP
3580 W 13th St N (67203-4591)
PHONE..................................316 943-0286
Clarence Koch, *Partner*
Edward P Dunn Jr, *Partner*
James Hand, *Partner*
John Siedhoff, *Partner*
EMP: 20
SQ FT: 4,800
SALES (est): 1.9MM **Privately Held**
WEB: www.kshd.net
SIC: **8721** Certified public accountant

(G-14889)
KOCH SULFUR PRODUCTS CO LLC
4111 E 37th St N (67220-3203)
P.O. Box 2256 (67201-2256)
PHONE..................................316 828-5500
Dan Solomon, *CFO*
Myron J Schuckman,
Steve Carter,
EMP: 20
SQ FT: 100,000
SALES (est): 7.4MM
SALES (corp-wide): 40.6B **Privately Held**
SIC: **2819** 2999 Industrial inorganic chemicals; coke (not from refineries), petroleum
HQ: Koch Mineral Services, Llc
4111 E 37th St N
Wichita KS 67220
316 828-5500

(G-14890)
KOCH SUPPLY & TRADING LP (DH)
Also Called: Koch Supply and Trading
4111 E 37th St N (67220-3203)
P.O. Box 2917 (67201-2917)
PHONE..................................316 828-5500
Charles G Koch, *CEO*
Steve Mawer, *President*
Bradford T Sanders, *Partner*
Kevin Brunton, *Business Anlyst*
Donnie Aschenbrenner, *Info Tech Mgr*
◆ **EMP**: 10
SALES (est): 135.9MM
SALES (corp-wide): 40.6B **Privately Held**
WEB: www.ksandt.com
SIC: **2911** Petroleum refining

(G-14891)
KOCH-GLITSCH LP (HQ)
4111 E 37th St N (67220-3203)
PHONE..................................316 828-5000
Robert Difulgentiz, *Partner*
Vince Dailey, *Partner*
Matt Sherwood, *Partner*
Darran Headley, *Project Mgr*
Charley Tully, *Mfg Staff*
◆ **EMP**: 890 **EST**: 1913
SALES (est): 298.7MM
SALES (corp-wide): 40.6B **Privately Held**
SIC: **3443** Vessels, process or storage (from boiler shops): metal plate
PA: Koch Industries, Inc.
4111 E 37th St N
Wichita KS 67220
316 828-5500

(G-14892)
KOKEN MANUFACTURING CO INC
Also Called: Marble Products
2080 S Edwards St (67213-1869)
PHONE..................................316 942-7600
Bryan Brandis, *Manager*
EMP: 20
SQ FT: 3,000 **Privately Held**
WEB: www.kokenstl.com
SIC: **3281** Cut stone & stone products
HQ: Koken Manufacturing Company, Inc.
1631 Dr Martin L King Dr
Saint Louis MO 63106
314 231-7383

(G-14893)
KONE INC
3450 N Rock Rd Ste 507 (67226-1355)
PHONE..................................316 942-1201
Ted Ragias, *Manager*
EMP: 13
SALES (corp-wide): 10B **Privately Held**
WEB: www.us.kone.com
SIC: **7699** Elevators: inspection, service & repair
HQ: Kone Inc.
4225 Naperville Rd # 400
Lisle IL 60532
630 577-1650

(G-14894)
KPL SOUTH TEXAS LLC
4111 E 37th St N (67220-3203)
PHONE..................................316 828-5500
Sarah Freeman, *Buyer*
Steve Pawlak, *Electrical Engi*
Rick Garcia, *Manager*
Jan Rochelle, *Director*
James Kenner, *Admin Sec*
EMP: 5
SALES (est): 433K **Privately Held**
SIC: 2911 Petroleum refining

(G-14895)
KRUSE CORPORATION (PA)
3636 N Topeka St (67219-3644)
PHONE..................................316 838-7885
Kent Kruse, *President*
Josh McHugh, *General Mgr*
Emily Parker, *General Mgr*
Jarod Pauly, *Superintendent*
Paul McAnerney, *Project Mgr*
▲ **EMP:** 60
SQ FT: 17,500
SALES (est): 19.1MM **Privately Held**
WEB: www.krusecorp.com
SIC: 1711 Warm air heating & air conditioning contractor

(G-14896)
KS&T INTERNATIONAL HOLDINGS LP
Also Called: Koch Supply & Trading
4111 E 37th St N (67220-3203)
PHONE..................................316 828-5500
Charles Koch,
EMP: 5004
SALES (est): 91.7MM
SALES (corp-wide): 40.6B **Privately Held**
SIC: 2911 Petroleum refining
HQ: Koch Resources, Llc
4111 E 37th St N
Wichita KS 67220
316 828-5500

(G-14897)
KTH PROPERTIES CORPORATION (PA)
Also Called: Hyper Pet
3100 S Meridian Ave (67217-2002)
PHONE..................................316 941-1100
Randy Woods, *CEO*
Mary Engelbrecht, *Opers Staff*
Ron Toedman, *Manager*
Warren Vann, *Officer*
▲ **EMP:** 40
SQ FT: 100,000
SALES (est): 8.3MM **Privately Held**
WEB: www.roseam.com
SIC: 3199 5999 Dog furnishings: collars, leashes, muzzles, etc.: leather; pets & pet supplies

(G-14898)
KUHLMAN AND MAJORS DDS
1831 N Rock Road Ct # 101 (67206-1374)
PHONE..................................316 652-0000
Christopher Majors, *Partner*
Larry Kuhlman, *Partner*
EMP: 10
SALES (est): 947.9K **Privately Held**
SIC: 8021 Dentists' office

(G-14899)
KUHLMANN INSTALLATIONS LLC
4465 N Webb Rd (67226-8139)
PHONE..................................316 634-6531
Orvin Kuhlmann,
EMP: 15
SALES: 250K **Privately Held**
SIC: 1542 Stadium construction

(G-14900)
KUHLMANN ROBERTS & JANASEK
8150 E Douglas Ave Ste 50 (67206-2362)
PHONE..................................316 681-0991
Dr A Roy Roberts Od, *Partner*
Dr Jeff Janasek Od, *Partner*
Dr Jim Kuhlmann Od, *Partner*
Jim Kuhlmann, *Principal*
EMP: 25
SQ FT: 6,500
SALES (est): 1.8MM **Privately Held**
SIC: 8042 5995 Specialized optometrists; optical goods stores; eyeglasses, prescription; contact lenses, prescription

(G-14901)
KUTAK ROCK LLP
1605 N Waterfront Pkwy # 150 (67206-6635)
PHONE..................................316 609-7900
Rhonda Wills, *Office Mgr*
EMP: 20
SALES (corp-wide): 105.5MM **Privately Held**
WEB: www.mykutak.com
SIC: 8111 General practice law office
PA: Kutak Rock Llp
1650 Farnam St Fl 2
Omaha NE 68102
402 346-6000

(G-14902)
KVC HEALTH SYSTEMS INC
1507 W 21st St N (67203-2449)
PHONE..................................316 796-5503
EMP: 29 **Privately Held**
SIC: 8361 Residential care for children
PA: Kvc Health Systems, Inc.
21350 W 153rd St
Olathe KS 66061

(G-14903)
L & T MACHINING INC
1827 S Leonine St (67213-1313)
PHONE..................................316 946-9744
Michael Liu, *President*
Vandy Hong, *Vice Pres*
Khamsent Gowing, *Treasurer*
Gai Liu, *Admin Sec*
EMP: 20
SQ FT: 5,200
SALES (est): 3.9MM **Privately Held**
WEB: www.ltmachining.com
SIC: 3599 Machine shop, jobbing & repair

(G-14904)
L C ENTERPRISES (PA)
Also Called: Lc Enterprises
8100 E 22nd St N Bldg 900 (67226-2309)
PHONE..................................316 682-3300
Mathew Shets, *CEO*
Larry Cooley, *President*
Gary Greaves, *COO*
EMP: 12 **EST:** 1977
SQ FT: 8,500
SALES (est): 21.9MM **Privately Held**
WEB: www.lc.cray.com
SIC: 8741 7359 6512 Restaurant management; equipment rental & leasing; commercial & industrial building operation

(G-14905)
L D F COMPANY
10610 E 26th Cir N (67226-4536)
PHONE..................................316 636-5575
Larry D Fleming, *Owner*
EMP: 26
SALES (est): 1.8MM **Privately Held**
SIC: 8741 Business management

(G-14906)
L J HERZBERG ROOFING CO INC
Also Called: Herzberg L J & Sons Roofing Co
15223 E Zimmerly Ct (67230-9244)
P.O. Box 8878 (67208-0878)
PHONE..................................316 529-2222
Brandon Herzberg, *President*
Jerry Herzberg, *Corp Secy*
Brice Herzberg, *Vice Pres*
EMP: 12
SQ FT: 1,500
SALES (est): 1.4MM **Privately Held**
SIC: 1761 Roofing contractor

(G-14907)
L S INDUSTRIES INC
710 E 17th St N (67214-1312)
P.O. Box 1442 (67201-1442)
PHONE..................................316 265-7997
Linda Weir-Enegren, *President*
Darryl Wilson, *Business Mgr*
Phillip Enegren, *Corp Secy*
Phil Enegren, *Vice Pres*
Jerry Kirk, *Manager*
▲ **EMP:** 34
SQ FT: 50,000
SALES (est): 10.6MM **Privately Held**
WEB: www.lsindustries.com
SIC: 3559 3629 Degreasing machines, automotive & industrial; blasting machines, electrical
PA: Machine Works Inc
710 E 17th St N
Wichita KS 67214

(G-14908)
L V S INC (PA)
Also Called: Party City
3411 N Rock Rd Ste 100 (67226-1345)
PHONE..................................316 636-5005
Rekha Reddi, *Owner*
EMP: 28
SQ FT: 8,000
SALES (est): 1.8MM **Privately Held**
SIC: 5947 5699 7299 2759 Gifts & novelties; costumes, masquerade or theatrical; costume rental; invitation & stationery printing & engraving

(G-14909)
LA PETITE ACADEMY INC
7431 E 21st St N (67206-1072)
PHONE..................................316 684-5916
Melissa Breault, *Director*
EMP: 17
SALES (corp-wide): 164MM **Privately Held**
WEB: www.lapetite.com
SIC: 8351 Preschool center
HQ: La Petite Academy, Inc.
21333 Haggerty Rd Ste 300
Novi MI 48375
877 861-5078

(G-14910)
LABORATORY CORPORATION AMERICA
9120 E 37th St N (67226-2009)
PHONE..................................316 636-2300
Dale Mitchell, *Manager*
EMP: 105 **Publicly Held**
WEB: www.labcorp.com
SIC: 8071 Pathological laboratory
HQ: Laboratory Corporation Of America
358 S Main St Ste 458
Burlington NC 27215
336 229-1127

(G-14911)
LADIWALLA HOSPITALITY LLC
Also Called: Comfort Suites
7515 W Taft St (67209-2189)
PHONE..................................316 773-1700
Aaron Herd, *Principal*
EMP: 10 **EST:** 2011
SALES (est): 505K **Privately Held**
SIC: 7011 Hotels & motels

(G-14912)
LAFARGE NORTH AMERICA INC
3500 N West St (67205-6522)
PHONE..................................316 943-3500
Lorie Wilson, *Owner*
EMP: 27
SALES (corp-wide): 4.5B **Privately Held**
SIC: 3241 Cement, hydraulic
HQ: Lafarge North America Inc.
8700 W Bryn Mawr Ave
Chicago IL 60631
773 372-1000

(G-14913)
LAFARGE NORTH AMERICA INC
3600 N West St Ste 100 (67205-6501)
PHONE..................................316 613-5100
Doug Vogt, *Branch Mgr*
EMP: 27
SALES (corp-wide): 4.5B **Privately Held**
SIC: 3241 Cement, hydraulic
HQ: Lafarge North America Inc.
8700 W Bryn Mawr Ave
Chicago IL 60631
773 372-1000

(G-14914)
LAFE T WILLIAMS & ASSOC INC
Also Called: Williams Janitor Supplies
1509 S Washington Ave (67211-3337)
PHONE..................................316 262-0479
Kimberly Hobbie, *President*
EMP: 15
SQ FT: 33,000
SALES (est): 4.6MM **Privately Held**
WEB: www.lafetwilliams.com
SIC: 5087 Janitors' supplies

(G-14915)
LAKEPOINT FAMILY PHYSICIANS
Also Called: Lakepoint Family Physicians PA
8020 E Central Ave # 200 (67206-2382)
PHONE..................................316 636-2662
Cynthia Nash, *Principal*
Virginia Scott, *Manager*
Diana R Crook, *Director*
EMP: 40
SQ FT: 12,165
SALES (est): 2.5MM **Privately Held**
WEB: www.lakepointfamilyphysicians.com
SIC: 8011 Offices & clinics of medical doctors

(G-14916)
LAMINAGE PRODUCTS INC
970 N Santa Fe St (67214-3826)
PHONE..................................316 267-5233
John Maida, *President*
Suzanne Maida, *Vice Pres*
EMP: 5
SALES (est): 324.2K **Privately Held**
WEB: www.laminprint.com
SIC: 5999 3499 2499 Art, picture frames & decorations; picture frames, metal; picture frame molding, finished

(G-14917)
LAMPTON WELDING SUPPLY CO INC (PA)
601 N Washington Ave (67214-3839)
P.O. Box 765 (67201-0765)
PHONE..................................316 263-3293
Marvin E Lampton, *CEO*
Guy Marlin, *President*
Doug Lampton, *Vice Pres*
Sheila Lampton, *Treasurer*
W Brad Lampton, *Admin Sec*
EMP: 35
SQ FT: 30,000
SALES (est): 36.1MM **Privately Held**
WEB: www.lampton.com
SIC: 5084 Welding machinery & equipment

(G-14918)
LANCE ANDERSON DDS
9415 E Harry St Ste 101 (67207-5072)
PHONE..................................316 687-2104
Lance Anderson, *Owner*
EMP: 10
SALES (est): 600.5K **Privately Held**
SIC: 8021 Specialized dental practitioners

(G-14919)
LAND ACQUISITIONS INC
6308 E Ironhorse St (67220-5508)
P.O. Box 5768, Buffalo Grove IL (60089-5768)
PHONE..................................847 749-0675
Gerald Cain, *President*
Lee Courney, *Admin Sec*
EMP: 50
SQ FT: 2,000
SALES: 1MM **Privately Held**
WEB: www.landacquisitionsinc.com
SIC: 8742 6531 8713 8748 Real estate consultant; real estate agents & managers; surveying services; business consulting

(G-14920)
LAND AIR EXPRESS INC
3215 W Pawnee St (67213-1827)
PHONE..................................316 942-0191
Linda Batliner, *Manager*
EMP: 25
SALES (corp-wide): 46.2MM **Privately Held**
WEB: www.landairexpress.com
SIC: 4513 4731 Air courier services; freight transportation arrangement
PA: Land Air Express, Inc.
6377 Cemetery Rd
Bowling Green KY 42103
270 781-0655

(G-14921)
LANDSCAPES INC
Also Called: Winn Enterprise
1100 S West St (67213-1630)
PHONE..................................316 262-7557
Jennifer Winn, *President*
EMP: 45
SALES (est): 1.4MM **Privately Held**
SIC: 0782 7349 8744 7699 Landscape contractors; janitorial service, contract basis; facilities support services; cleaning services

(G-14922)
LANDVEST CORPORATION (PA)
9103 E 37th St N (67226-2010)
PHONE..................................316 634-6510
Marshall Millsap, *President*
David Mason, *Vice Pres*
EMP: 30
SQ FT: 11,000
SALES (est): 3.7MM **Privately Held**
WEB: www.landvestmgmt.com
SIC: 6512 6531 Commercial & industrial building operation; real estate managers

(G-14923)
LANDWEHR MANUFACTURING COMPANY
1332 S Anna St (67209-2602)
PHONE..................................316 942-1719
Ann Landwehr, *Owner*
Martin A Landwehr, *Owner*
EMP: 5
SQ FT: 6,800
SALES (est): 429.6K **Privately Held**
SIC: 3446 Architectural metalwork

(G-14924)
LARIO OIL & GAS COMPANY (HQ)
301 S Market St (67202-3805)
PHONE..................................316 265-5611
Patrick E O Shaughnessy, *Ch of Bd*
Michael W O Shaughnessy, *President*
Rick Stinson, *Vice Pres*
Adam Strunk, *VP Engrg*
Jay Schweikert, *Project Engr*
EMP: 30
SQ FT: 20,000
SALES (est): 63.6MM **Privately Held**
WEB: www.lario.net
SIC: 1311 1382 Crude petroleum production; natural gas production; oil & gas exploration services
PA: O's Companies, Inc.
301 S Market St
Wichita KS 67202
316 265-5611

(G-14925)
LARKSFIELD PLACE
7373 E 29th St N Ofc (67226-3425)
PHONE..................................316 636-1000
Reginald Hislop, *President*
Jason Brenneis, *IT/INT Sup*
EMP: 43
SALES (est): 1.8MM **Privately Held**
SIC: 8361 Residential care

(G-14926)
LARRY BOOZE ROOFING CO INC
13926 W Westport Ct (67235-1562)
P.O. Box 19110 (67204-9110)
PHONE..................................316 263-7796
EMP: 16
SALES (est): 1.6MM **Privately Held**
SIC: 1761 Roofing/Siding Contractor

(G-14927)
LARRYS TRAILER SALES & SVC LLC
4153 N Broadway Ave (67219-3203)
PHONE..................................316 838-1491
Jeffery Hamilton, *Executive*
Sherry Hamilton,
EMP: 15 **EST:** 1954
SQ FT: 10,000
SALES (est): 3.9MM **Privately Held**
WEB: www.larrystrailer.com
SIC: 7539 5012 5078 Trailer repair; trucks, commercial; trailers for trucks, new & used; refrigeration units, motor vehicles

(G-14928)
LARSON & COMPANY PA
200 W Douglas Ave # 1000 (67202-3095)
PHONE..................................316 263-8030
Derry Larson, *Owner*
Linda A Kreuzburg, *Accountant*
Lacie L Lowmaster, *Accountant*
Derek Pippig, *Accountant*
Karl A Rump, *CPA*
EMP: 12
SALES (est): 500K **Privately Held**
SIC: 8721 Accounting services, except auditing

(G-14929)
LAS TARASCAS
5701 E Lincoln St (67218-2739)
PHONE..................................316 941-5511
Eginardo Gonzalez, *Owner*
EMP: 8 **EST:** 2010
SALES (est): 745K **Privately Held**
SIC: 2051 Cakes, bakery: except frozen

(G-14930)
LASH COMPANY LLC
207 N Emporia Ave (67202-2530)
PHONE..................................316 265-5527
Stephanie Rene Struble, *Administration*
EMP: 19
SALES (est): 692.1K **Privately Held**
SIC: 7231 Cosmetology & personal hygiene salons

(G-14931)
LATHROM MANUFACTURING INC
315 E 55th St S (67216-3802)
PHONE..................................316 522-0001
Seyburn Lathrom, *Principal*
EMP: 10
SQ FT: 8,400
SALES (est): 450K **Privately Held**
SIC: 3599 3721 3728 Machine shop, jobbing & repair; motorized aircraft; aircraft assemblies, subassemblies & parts

(G-14932)
LATOUR MANAGEMENT INC
Also Called: Hotel At Old Town Cnfrence Ctr
210 N Mosley St (67202-2806)
PHONE..................................316 262-7300
Goumana Goutoubia, *President*
EMP: 16
SALES (corp-wide): 7MM **Privately Held**
SIC: 7299 Banquet hall facilities
PA: Latour Management, Inc.
2949 N Rock Rd Ste 100
Wichita KS 67226
316 524-2290

(G-14933)
LATOUR MANAGEMENT INC (PA)
2949 N Rock Rd Ste 100 (67226-2279)
PHONE..................................316 524-2290
Naji Toubia, *Ch of Bd*
Joumana Toubia, *President*
EMP: 30
SALES: 7MM **Privately Held**
WEB: www.chelseasbarandgrill.com
SIC: 8741 5812 8742 Restaurant management; Lebanese restaurant; management consulting services

(G-14934)
LAW COMPANY INC (PA)
345 N Rverview St Ste 300 (67203)
P.O. Box 1139 (67201-1139)
PHONE..................................316 268-0200
Dennis Kerschen, *President*
Richard Kerschen, *Chairman*
Marc Porter, *Exec VP*
Bill Reynolds, *Vice Pres*
Dan Alcala, *Project Mgr*
EMP: 152
SQ FT: 80,500
SALES (est): 86.4MM **Privately Held**
WEB: www.law-co.com
SIC: 1542 1522 Commercial & office building, new construction; multi-family dwelling construction

(G-14935)
LAW OFFICES OF M STEVEN WAGLE
301 N Market St (67202-2009)
PHONE..................................316 264-4878
Steven M Wagle, *Owner*
Erin M Daley,
EMP: 15
SALES (est): 1MM **Privately Held**
SIC: 8111 General practice attorney, lawyer

(G-14936)
LAWNWORKS INC
3621 N Santa Fe St (67219-3635)
PHONE..................................316 838-3500
Jess Hiss, *President*
Kurt Hiss, *Vice Pres*
EMP: 15
SALES (est): 1.8MM **Privately Held**
SIC: 0782 Landscape contractors; lawn services

(G-14937)
LAYNE CHRISTENSEN COMPANY
Also Called: Layne-Western
1011 W Harry St (67213-4110)
PHONE..................................316 264-5365
Kent Wartick, *General Mgr*
EMP: 25
SALES (corp-wide): 3.3B **Publicly Held**
WEB: www.laynechristensen.com
SIC: 1623 5084 Water main construction; pumps & pumping equipment
HQ: Layne Christensen Company
9303 New Trils Dr Ste 200
Spring TX 77381
281 475-2600

(G-14938)
LCD UNLIMITED INC
Also Called: Caring Harts For Senior Living
1229 S Byron Rd (67209-1811)
Rural Route 3222 Nw Bay St (67205)
PHONE..................................316 721-4803
EMP: 15
SQ FT: 3,000
SALES (est): 414.7K **Privately Held**
SIC: 8059 Nursing/Personal Care

(G-14939)
LEADING EDGE AEROSPACE LLC
1360 S Anna St (67209-2602)
PHONE..................................316 942-1301
Stan Unruh, *President*
Tammy Russell, *Office Mgr*
EMP: 24
SQ FT: 2,600
SALES (est): 5.7MM **Privately Held**
WEB: www.leadingedgeaerospace.com
SIC: 3544 Special dies & tools

(G-14940)
LEARJET INC (HQ)
Also Called: Bombardier Transportation USA
1 Learjet Way (67209-2924)
P.O. Box 7707 (67277-7707)
PHONE..................................316 946-2000
David Coleal, *President*
Sakhawat Hossain, *Opers Mgr*
Alan Nicholl, *Opers Staff*
August Heard, *Buyer*
Mark Carter, *Engineer*
▲ **EMP:** 750
SQ FT: 891,466
SALES (est): 1.4B
SALES (corp-wide): 16.2B **Privately Held**
WEB: www.bombardier.com
SIC: 3721 3812 Aircraft; search & navigation equipment
PA: Bombardier Inc
800 Boul Rene-Levesque O 29e etage
Montreal QC H3B 1
514 861-9481

(G-14941)
LEARJET INC
Also Called: Business Transformation System
1 Learjet Way (67209-2924)
PHONE..................................316 946-3001
Debbie Winter, *Manager*
EMP: 50
SALES (corp-wide): 16.2B **Privately Held**
SIC: 3721 3769 Aircraft; guided missile & space vehicle parts & auxiliary equipment
HQ: Learjet Inc.
1 Learjet Way
Wichita KS 67209
316 946-2000

(G-14942)
LEARJET INC
Also Called: Bombardier
7761 W Kellogg Dr Bldg 11 (67209-2003)
P.O. Box 7707 (67277-7707)
PHONE..................................316 946-2000
Howard Schmidt, *Vice Pres*
Lloyd Bender, *Project Mgr*
Deb Burbank, *Transportation*
Mike Mitchell, *Opers Staff*
Mike Ayres, *Plant Engr*
EMP: 900
SALES (corp-wide): 16.2B **Privately Held**
SIC: 3721 Aircraft
HQ: Learjet Inc.
1 Learjet Way
Wichita KS 67209
316 946-2000

(G-14943)
LEDIC MANAGEMENT GROUP LLC
Also Called: Sundance Apartments
1945 N Rock Rd (67206-1249)
PHONE..................................316 685-8768
Julie Anderson, *Manager*
EMP: 11
SALES (est): 737.2K **Privately Held**
WEB: www.sundanceapts.com
SIC: 6513 Apartment hotel operation

(G-14944)
LEE WILSON & GURNEY
Also Called: Gurney, Lawrence M
1861 N Rock Rd Ste 320 (67206-1264)
PHONE..................................316 685-2245
Robert R Lee, *Owner*
Chris A Clements,
Larry Gurney,
EMP: 12
SALES (est): 767.3K **Privately Held**
SIC: 8111 General practice attorney, lawyer

(G-14945)
LEE & DEVLIN DDS
387 N Woodlawn St (67208-4330)
PHONE..................................316 685-2309
Benjamin G Lee DDS, *Principal*
EMP: 14
SALES (est): 956.6K **Privately Held**
SIC: 8021 Dentists' office

(G-14946)
LEE AEROSPACE INC
9323 E 34th St N (67226-2621)
PHONE..................................316 636-9200
James Lee, *President*
Greg Piland, *General Mgr*
Jeff Broomhead, *Engineer*
Robert Hart, *CFO*
James Edwards, *Controller*
EMP: 245
SQ FT: 105,000
SALES (est): 55.9MM **Privately Held**
WEB: www.leeaerospace.com
SIC: 3728 Aircraft body assemblies & parts

(G-14947)
LEE AIR INC
3000 S Hydraulic Wichita (67216)
PHONE..................................316 524-4622
Bennie M Lee Jr, *President*
Janet Vann, *Managing Dir*
Kent Tretheway, *Prdtn Mgr*
Don Ausherman, *Design Engr*
Donna Lee, *Accountant*
EMP: 25 **EST:** 1981
SQ FT: 10,000
SALES (est): 3.3MM **Privately Held**
WEB: www.leeair.com
SIC: 3728 Aircraft parts & equipment

(G-14948)
LEE PHILLIPS OIL COMPANY
151 S Whittier Rd # 1400 (67207-1063)
PHONE..................................316 681-4470
Lee Phillips III, *Partner*

GEOGRAPHIC

Innes Phillips, *Partner*
EMP: 5 **EST:** 1936
SQ FT: 1,000
SALES (est): 391.5K **Privately Held**
SIC: 1311 Crude petroleum production

(G-14949)
LEE REED ENGRAVING INC
3417 W Central Ave (67203-4919)
PHONE..................................316 943-9700
Pete Lungwitz, *President*
Sherry Lungwitz, *Corp Secy*
EMP: 5
SQ FT: 5,000
SALES: 310K **Privately Held**
WEB: www.newenglandprintfair.com
SIC: 2759 7389 5999 5199 Engraving; engraving service; trophies & plaques; badges

(G-14950)
LEGACY BANK (HQ)
3711 N Ridge Rd (67205-1216)
P.O. Box 68, Colwich (67030-0068)
PHONE..................................316 796-1221
Leo R Wetta, *Ch of Bd*
Frank A Suellentrop, *President*
Lindsey Wolf, *President*
Gene Suellentrop, *Vice Pres*
Shawn Berschauer, *Loan Officer*
EMP: 51
SALES: 18.8MM **Privately Held**
WEB: www.legacybank.com
SIC: 6022 State trust companies accepting deposits, commercial
PA: Colwich Financial Corp
240 W Wichita Ave
Colwich KS 67030
316 796-1221

(G-14951)
LEGACY BANK
7555 W 21st St N (67205-1733)
PHONE..................................316 260-3755
Lisa Piska, *Branch Mgr*
Teri Parsons, *Manager*
EMP: 10
SALES (corp-wide): 18.8MM **Privately Held**
WEB: www.legacybank.com
SIC: 6022 State trust companies accepting deposits, commercial
HQ: Legacy Bank
3711 N Ridge Rd
Wichita KS 67205
316 796-1221

(G-14952)
LEGACY BANK
3711 N Ridge Rd (67205-1216)
PHONE..................................316 260-3711
Frank A Suellentrop, *President*
Brad Yaeger, *Exec VP*
Brice Malloy, *Vice Pres*
Sam Lines, *Manager*
Katie Haffield, *Officer*
EMP: 36
SALES (corp-wide): 18.8MM **Privately Held**
WEB: www.legacybank.com
SIC: 6022 State trust companies accepting deposits, commercial
HQ: Legacy Bank
3711 N Ridge Rd
Wichita KS 67205
316 796-1221

(G-14953)
LEGEND SENIOR LIVING LLC
Also Called: Regent Pk Rhblttion Healthcare
10604 E 13th St N (67206-3706)
PHONE..................................316 337-5450
Philip Brooks, *CFO*
April Leason, *Sales Dir*
Sue Anderson, *Manager*
EMP: 179
SALES (corp-wide): 44.1MM **Privately Held**
SIC: 8051 8322 Convalescent home with continuous nursing care; rehabilitation services
PA: Senior Legend Living Llc
8415 E 21st St N Ste 100
Wichita KS 67206
316 616-6288

(G-14954)
LEGEND SENIOR LIVING LLC (PA)
8415 E 21st St N Ste 100 (67206-2959)
PHONE..................................316 616-6288
Tim Buchanan, *CEO*
Chris Mahen, *COO*
Catherine Conner, *Vice Pres*
Tonya Hutson, *Sales Dir*
Heather Parsons, *Sales Dir*
EMP: 67
SALES (est): 44.1MM **Privately Held**
SIC: 8361 Residential care

(G-14955)
LENTZ & BAKER EYE CARE (PA)
Also Called: Family Practice Optometry
1223 N Rock Rd Bldg C (67206-1277)
PHONE..................................316 634-2020
Thomas R Lentz, *President*
R Michael Murphy, *Partner*
Dr Tad D Baker, *Principal*
Dr Michael Murphy, *Corp Secy*
Gordon Wiens, *Office Mgr*
EMP: 18
SALES (est): 2MM **Privately Held**
SIC: 8042 Specialized optometrists

(G-14956)
LEWIS BRSBOIS BSGARD SMITH LLP
1605 N Waterfront Pkwy (67206-6634)
PHONE..................................316 609-7900
Alan L Rupe, *Branch Mgr*
EMP: 57
SALES (corp-wide): 284.9MM **Privately Held**
SIC: 8111 General practice law office
PA: Lewis Brisbois Bisgaard & Smith Llp
633 W 5th St Ste 4000
Los Angeles CA 90071
213 250-1800

(G-14957)
LEWIS-GOETZ AND COMPANY INC
Also Called: Wichita Division
2113 S West St Ste 200 (67213-1136)
PHONE..................................316 265-4623
Mark Pyles, *Branch Mgr*
EMP: 12 **Privately Held**
SIC: 5085 Rubber goods, mechanical
HQ: Eriks North America, Inc.
650 Washington Rd Ste 500
Pittsburgh PA 15228
800 937-9070

(G-14958)
LIBERTY TAX SERVICE
1361 N West St (67203-1303)
PHONE..................................316 219-4829
Chris Merchant, *Owner*
EMP: 10
SALES (est): 273.8K **Privately Held**
SIC: 7291 Tax return preparation services

(G-14959)
LIES TRASH SERVICE LLC
4631 S Palisade Ave (67217-4945)
PHONE..................................316 522-1699
David Lies,
EMP: 27
SQ FT: 10,000
SALES (est): 9.1MM
SALES (corp-wide): 14.9B **Publicly Held**
SIC: 4953 Refuse collection & disposal services; recycling, waste materials
PA: Waste Management, Inc.
1001 Fannin St Ste 4000
Houston TX 77002
713 512-6200

(G-14960)
LIF INC
2440 N Fountain St (67220-2842)
P.O. Box 20693 (67208-6693)
PHONE..................................316 260-6092
Lamont Love, *Director*
EMP: 12 **EST:** 2009
SALES (est): 513.2K **Privately Held**
SIC: 8361 Boys' Towns

(G-14961)
LIFE CARE CENTERS AMERICA INC
Also Called: Life Care Center of Wichita
622 N Edgemoor St (67208-3602)
PHONE..................................316 686-5100
Kyle Schaffer, *Director*
Andrea Gutierrez, *Director*
EMP: 150
SALES (corp-wide): 144MM **Privately Held**
SIC: 8051 Convalescent home with continuous nursing care
PA: Life Care Centers Of America, Inc.
3570 Keith St Nw
Cleveland TN 37312
423 472-9585

(G-14962)
LIFETOUCH INC
1803 S Eisenhower St (67209-2810)
PHONE..................................316 262-6611
John Pair, *President*
EMP: 25
SALES (corp-wide): 1.9B **Privately Held**
WEB: www.lifetouch.com
SIC: 7221 Photographic studios, portrait
HQ: Lifetouch Inc.
11000 Viking Dr
Eden Prairie MN 55344
952 826-4000

(G-14963)
LIFT TRUCK CENTER INC (HQ)
4000 W 33rd St S (67215-1009)
P.O. Box 17084 (67217-0084)
PHONE..................................316 942-7465
Bill Bolin, *President*
Robert Young, *Corp Secy*
Eric Haddox, *Sales Mgr*
Jason Maahs, *Sales Staff*
▲ **EMP:** 25
SQ FT: 15,000
SALES (est): 13MM **Privately Held**
WEB: www.ltcenter.com
SIC: 5084 7359 Materials handling machinery; equipment rental & leasing

(G-14964)
LIGHTHOUSE PROPERTIES LLC
Also Called: Homewood Suites
1550 N Waterfront Pkwy (67206-6607)
PHONE..................................316 260-8844
Justine Ratclisic, *Director*
EMP: 50
SALES (corp-wide): 4.5MM **Privately Held**
SIC: 7011 Hotels & motels
PA: Lighthouse Properties, Llc
500 Graves Blvd
Salina KS 67401
785 825-2221

(G-14965)
LINCARE INC
7777 E Osie St Ste 301 (67207-3106)
PHONE..................................316 684-4689
Glabes Beebe, *Manager*
EMP: 15 **Privately Held**
WEB: www.lincare.com
SIC: 5999 5047 Medical apparatus & supplies; medical equipment & supplies
HQ: Lincare Inc.
19387 Us Highway 19 N
Clearwater FL 33764
727 530-7700

(G-14966)
LINDER & ASSOCIATES INC
840 N Main St (67203-3605)
P.O. Box 1202 (67201-1202)
PHONE..................................316 265-1616
Bill Quaney, *President*
Johnna K Hall, *Exec VP*
Randy Sobba, *Vice Pres*
Russell Wedel, *Vice Pres*
Larry Clark, *Project Mgr*
EMP: 121
SQ FT: 13,000
SALES: 21.7MM **Privately Held**
WEB: www.linderandassociates.com
SIC: 1731 General electrical contractor

(G-14967)
LINE MEDICAL INC
825 N Waco Ave (67203-3939)
PHONE..................................316 262-3444
David Saidian, *President*
EMP: 30
SQ FT: 5,000
SALES (est): 8.1MM
SALES (corp-wide): 25.3B **Privately Held**
WEB: www.adamdiagnostics.com
SIC: 5047 7389 Medical laboratory equipment; X-ray film & supplies; courier or messenger service
HQ: Via Christi Health, Inc.
2622 W Central Ave # 102
Wichita KS 67203

(G-14968)
LIQUIDYNAMICS INC
2311 S Edwards St (67213-1871)
PHONE..................................316 943-5477
Frank Russold, *President*
Craig Barth, *General Mgr*
Cheryl McGuire, *Vice Pres*
Mark Pfleeger, *Vice Pres*
Kelly Harbert, *Opers Mgr*
▲ **EMP:** 11
SQ FT: 22,500
SALES (est): 4.2MM **Privately Held**
WEB: www.liquidynamics.com
SIC: 5015 Automotive servicing equipment, used

(G-14969)
LK ARCHITECTURE INC (HQ)
Also Called: Law Kingdon
345 N Rverview St Ste 200 (67203)
P.O. Box 1094 (67201-1094)
PHONE..................................316 268-0230
Dennis Smith, *President*
Roger Brown, *Senior VP*
Dave Hoffman, *Senior VP*
Dan Dokken, *Vice Pres*
Larry Krier, *Vice Pres*
EMP: 90
SALES (est): 19MM
SALES (corp-wide): 86.4MM **Privately Held**
WEB: www.law-kingdon.com
SIC: 8712 Architectural engineering
PA: The Law Company Inc
345 N Rverview St Ste 300
Wichita KS 67203
316 268-0200

(G-14970)
LK ARCHITECTURE/MEAD & HUNT
345 N Riverview St # 200 (67203-4200)
PHONE..................................316 268-0230
Dennis Smith, *Partner*
EMP: 99
SQ FT: 70,000
SALES (est): 1.8MM **Privately Held**
SIC: 8712 Architectural engineering

(G-14971)
LMI AEROSPACE INC
2853 S Hillside St (67216-2546)
PHONE..................................316 944-4143
EMP: 9 **Privately Held**
SIC: 3728 Aircraft parts & equipment
HQ: Lmi Aerospace, Inc.
411 Fountain Lakes Blvd
Saint Charles MO 63301
636 946-6525

(G-14972)
LMI AEROSPACE INC
Also Called: Leonard's Metal
2853 S Hillside St (67216-2546)
PHONE..................................316 943-6059
Phil Lajeunesse, *Manager*
EMP: 120
SQ FT: 17,000 **Privately Held**
WEB: www.lmiaerospace.com
SIC: 3728 3444 Aircraft assemblies, subassemblies & parts; sheet metalwork
HQ: Lmi Aerospace, Inc.
411 Fountain Lakes Blvd
Saint Charles MO 63301
636 946-6525

(G-14973)
LODGEWORKS LP (PA)
8100 E 22nd St N Bldg 500 (67226-2305)
PHONE..................................316 681-5100
Roy R Baker, *Partner*
Tony Isaac, *Partner*
Tami Barocio, *General Mgr*
John R Morse, *Senior VP*
Mike Frey, *Vice Pres*
EMP: 25 **EST:** 2000
SQ FT: 6,000
SALES (est): 42.1MM **Privately Held**
SIC: 7011 Hotels & motels

(G-14974)
LODGEWORKS PARTNERS LP
8100 E 22nd St N Bldg 500 (67226-2305)
PHONE..................................316 681-5100
Mike Daood, *President*
Roy Baker, *CFO*
Seth White, *Controller*
EMP: 60 **EST:** 2011
SALES (est): 798.5K **Privately Held**
SIC: 8741 Hotel or motel management

(G-14975)
LODGING ENTERPRISES LLC (DH)
Also Called: Oak Tree Inn
8080 E Central Ave # 180 (67206-2371)
PHONE..................................316 630-6300
Bruce Pittet, *President*
David Mitchell, *Treasurer*
Barry Downing, *Admin Sec*
EMP: 678
SQ FT: 5,000
SALES (est): 71.4MM
SALES (corp-wide): 52.1MM **Privately Held**
WEB: www.lodgingenterprises.com
SIC: 7011 8741 6552 Hotels & motels; management services; subdividers & developers
HQ: American Hotel Income Properties Reit Inc.
351 W Camden St
Baltimore MD 21201
480 376-7900

(G-14976)
LOGAN STREET FINEWOOD PRODUCTS
1824 E Douglas Ave (67214-4213)
PHONE..................................316 266-4948
Tony Ferraro, *Owner*
EMP: 6
SALES (est): 255.3K **Privately Held**
SIC: 2499 Decorative wood & woodwork

(G-14977)
LOOMIS ARMORED US LLC
419 Wabash St (67214)
PHONE..................................316 267-0269
Matt Guisinger, *Manager*
EMP: 14
SALES (corp-wide): 2B **Privately Held**
WEB: www.loomisfargo.com
SIC: 7381 Armored car services
HQ: Loomis Armored Us, Llc
2500 Citywest Blvd # 900
Houston TX 77042
713 435-6700

(G-14978)
LOPER C-I ELECTRIC
819 E Indianapolis St (67211-2406)
PHONE..................................316 263-1291
Richard Gilpin, *Vice Pres*
EMP: 31
SALES (est): 3.7MM **Privately Held**
SIC: 1731 General electrical contractor

(G-14979)
LORAC COMPANY INC
624 E Harry St (67211-4205)
PHONE..................................316 263-2565
Carol Herring, *President*
Mitchell Herring, *Vice Pres*
Mishelle Whitney, *Sales Staff*
EMP: 17
SQ FT: 12,000
SALES (est): 4.8MM **Privately Held**
WEB: www.loraccompany.com
SIC: 5031 2851 5211 Windows; paints & allied products; door & window products

(G-14980)
LORDS DINER
2825 S Hillside St (67216-2545)
PHONE..................................316 295-2122
Jan Habery, *Exec Dir*
EMP: 12
SALES (est): 151.5K **Privately Held**
SIC: 8699 Charitable organization

(G-14981)
LOVING ARMS CHILD CARE CENTER
1241 N Ridge Rd (67212-2934)
PHONE..................................316 722-1912
Amber Holmens, *Director*
Deb Rockhoff, *Director*
Kathy Lietz, *Admin Sec*
EMP: 20
SALES (est): 628.7K **Privately Held**
SIC: 8351 Preschool center

(G-14982)
LOWES HOME CENTERS LLC
333 S Ridge Rd (67209-2229)
PHONE..................................316 773-1800
Terry Burlson, *Branch Mgr*
EMP: 150
SALES (corp-wide): 71.3B **Publicly Held**
SIC: 5211 5031 5722 5064 Home centers; building materials, exterior; building materials, interior; household appliance stores; electrical appliances, television & radio
HQ: Lowe's Home Centers, Llc
1605 Curtis Bridge Rd
Wilkesboro NC 28697
336 658-4000

(G-14983)
LOWES HOME CENTERS LLC
11959 E Kellogg Dr (67207-1937)
PHONE..................................316 684-3117
Bob Garraux, *Manager*
EMP: 150
SALES (corp-wide): 71.3B **Publicly Held**
SIC: 5211 5031 5722 5064 Home centers; building materials, exterior; building materials, interior; household appliance stores; electrical appliances, television & radio
HQ: Lowe's Home Centers, Llc
1605 Curtis Bridge Rd
Wilkesboro NC 28697
336 658-4000

(G-14984)
LOWES HOME CENTERS LLC
2626 N Maize Rd (67205-7312)
PHONE..................................316 206-1030
Scott Hanika, *Manager*
EMP: 158
SALES (corp-wide): 71.3B **Publicly Held**
SIC: 5211 5031 5722 5064 Home centers; building materials, exterior; building materials, interior; household appliance stores; electrical appliances, television & radio
HQ: Lowe's Home Centers, Llc
1605 Curtis Bridge Rd
Wilkesboro NC 28697
336 658-4000

(G-14985)
LOWRY ELECTRIC CO INC
1524 W 29th St N (67204-4824)
PHONE..................................316 838-4363
Janet Lowry, *Treasurer*
EMP: 15 **EST:** 1976
SQ FT: 15,000
SALES: 1MM **Privately Held**
SIC: 1731 General electrical contractor

(G-14986)
LP TECHNOLOGIES INC
7330 W 13th St N (67212-2964)
PHONE..................................316 831-9696
Samuel Lee, *President*
Alex Mages, *Engineer*
EMP: 10
SALES (est): 979.4K **Privately Held**
WEB: www.lptech.com
SIC: 7379 Computer related consulting services

(G-14987)
LRICO SERVICES LLC
2416 E 37th St N (67219-3538)
PHONE..................................316 847-4800
Leslie Rudd, *CEO*
Darrell Swank, *CFO*
EMP: 110
SQ FT: 2,000
SALES (est): 13.6MM **Privately Held**
SIC: 8741 Business management

(G-14988)
LSI CORPORATION
Also Called: LSI Logic
8200 E 34th Cir N # 2000 (67226-1388)
PHONE..................................316 201-2000
Eric Lamkin, *Branch Mgr*
EMP: 42
SALES (corp-wide): 22.6B **Publicly Held**
SIC: 3674 Microcircuits, integrated (semiconductor)
HQ: Lsi Corporation
1320 Ridder Park Dr
San Jose CA 95131
408 433-8000

(G-14989)
LUBRICATION ENGINEERS INC (PA)
1919 E Tulsa St (67216-2438)
P.O. Box 16025 (67216-0025)
PHONE..................................800 537-7683
Scott A Schwindaman, *President*
Jeffrey Turner, *Exec VP*
Darren G Booth, *Vice Pres*
John Sander, *Vice Pres*
Vincent M Tofani, *Vice Pres*
▼ **EMP:** 42 **EST:** 1951
SQ FT: 18,000
SALES (est): 28.1MM **Privately Held**
WEB: www.le-inc.com
SIC: 5172 Lubricating oils & greases

(G-14990)
LUBRICATION ENGINEERS INC
1919 E Tulsa St (67216-2438)
P.O. Box 16447 (67216-0447)
PHONE..................................316 529-2112
Darren Booth, *COO*
Mike Cooper, *Engineer*
Patrick Kraus, *CFO*
EMP: 50
SALES (corp-wide): 28.1MM **Privately Held**
WEB: www.le-inc.com
SIC: 2992 4225 Oils & greases, blending & compounding; general warehousing & storage
PA: Lubrication Engineers, Inc.
1919 E Tulsa St
Wichita KS 67216
800 537-7683

(G-14991)
LUSTERCRAFT PLASTICS LLC
1818 S Meridian Ave (67213-1924)
P.O. Box 17367 (67217-0367)
PHONE..................................316 942-8451
Lisa Mc Arter, *Manager*
Robert M Veazey,
EMP: 10
SQ FT: 40,000
SALES (est): 1.3MM **Privately Held**
WEB: www.lustercraft.com
SIC: 3081 5162 3089 Unsupported plastics film & sheet; plastics sheets & rods; thermoformed finished plastic products

(G-14992)
M & J ELECTRIC WICHITA LLC (PA)
1444 S Saint Clair Ave D (67213-2937)
PHONE..................................316 831-9879
Eric Parks, *CEO*
EMP: 33
SALES (est): 6.2MM **Privately Held**
SIC: 1731 Communications specialization

(G-14993)
M R IMAGING CENTER LP
Also Called: Anatomi Imaging
928 N St Francis St (67214-3822)
PHONE..................................316 268-6742
Dave Degenhardt, *Managing Prtnr*
EMP: 18
SALES (corp-wide): 25.3B **Privately Held**
SIC: 6719 Investment holding companies, except banks
HQ: Via Christi Health Partners, Inc.
8200 E Thorn Dr Ste 300
Wichita KS 67226

(G-14994)
M W C INC
Also Called: Central Mechanical Wichita
806 E Skinner St (67211-4334)
P.O. Box 47343 (67201-7343)
PHONE..................................316 267-7676
Phil Sewell, *President*
Tom Horner, *Treasurer*
Phil Horner, *Admin Sec*
EMP: 76
SQ FT: 20,000
SALES: 10.5MM **Privately Held**
WEB: www.cenmech.com
SIC: 1711 Mechanical contractor

(G-14995)
M6 CONCRETE ACCESSORIES CO INC (PA)
1040 S West St (67213-1628)
PHONE..................................316 263-7251
John D Munley, *President*
Terry Hegarty, *General Mgr*
Kevin Meyer, *Opers Mgr*
Laura Sears, *Supervisor*
Richard Herb, *Info Tech Mgr*
EMP: 42
SQ FT: 22,000
SALES: 15.5MM **Privately Held**
WEB: www.conacc.com
SIC: 5082 Concrete processing equipment

(G-14996)
MAC ADAMS RECREATION CENTER
1329 E 16th St N (67214-1570)
PHONE..................................316 265-6111
Clifford Normore, *Principal*
EMP: 10
SALES (est): 148K **Privately Held**
SIC: 7999 Recreation center

(G-14997)
MACHINE WORKS INC (PA)
710 E 17th St N (67214-1312)
P.O. Box 1442 (67201-1442)
PHONE..................................316 265-7997
Linda Weir-Enegren, *President*
Phillip Enegren, *Corp Secy*
▲ **EMP:** 50
SQ FT: 50,000
SALES (est): 4.7MM **Privately Held**
SIC: 3629 3559 Blasting machines, electrical; degreasing machines, automotive & industrial

(G-14998)
MACHINING PROGRAMMING MFG INC
Also Called: M P M
2100 S West St (67213-1112)
PHONE..................................316 945-1227
Donald J Gorges, *President*
Chantal Castillo, *Controller*
Larry Watson, *Shareholder*
Shannon Watson, *Maintence Staff*
EMP: 45
SQ FT: 55,000
SALES: 10.8MM **Privately Held**
WEB: www.mpm1.com
SIC: 3728 3599 Aircraft parts & equipment; machine & other job shop work; electrical discharge machining (EDM)

(G-14999)
MADILL CARBIDE INC
1504 E Waterman St (67211-1826)
PHONE..................................316 263-9285
Dennis L Morris, *President*
Lon Trulove, *Vice Pres*
Mitch Davis, *Director*
Carol Molz, *Director*
Cathy Trulove, *Director*
EMP: 13
SQ FT: 5,000
SALES (est): 2.1MM **Privately Held**
WEB: www.madillcarbide.com
SIC: 3545 Cutting tools for machine tools

GEOGRAPHIC

(G-15000)
MADRIGAL & ASSOCIATES INC (PA)
Also Called: Allstate
431 Lulu St (67211)
PHONE..................................316 265-5680
Tony Madrigal, *President*
Brandi Carpenter, *Accounts Mgr*
Gary Short, *Representative*
EMP: 20
SQ FT: 4,000
SALES (est): 4.3MM **Privately Held**
SIC: 6411 Insurance agents, brokers & service

(G-15001)
MAHANEY GROUP INC
Also Called: Charles E Mahaney Roofing Co
2822 N Mead St (67219-4241)
PHONE..................................316 262-4768
Mark Bolt, *President*
◆ **EMP:** 85
SALES: 13MM **Privately Held**
WEB: www.mahaneyroofing.com
SIC: 1761 Roofing contractor; sheet metal-work

(G-15002)
MAJOR INC
1449 S Osage St (67213-4324)
PHONE..................................316 265-7000
Clayton Dickehut, *President*
Kyle Dickehut, *Owner*
Jeremy Sterling, *Superintendent*
Sherri Whitetree, *Office Mgr*
EMP: 50 **EST:** 1971
SQ FT: 480
SALES (est): 6.6MM **Privately Held**
WEB: www.major.com
SIC: 1771 Concrete work

(G-15003)
MANOR CARE OF KANSAS INC
Also Called: Manorcare Health Svcs Wichita
7101 E 21st St N (67206-1037)
PHONE..................................316 684-8018
Debra Houk, *Branch Mgr*
EMP: 120
SALES (corp-wide): 8.2B **Privately Held**
SIC: 8051 Convalescent home with continuous nursing care
HQ: Manor Care Of Kansas, Inc.
333 N Summit St Ste 100
Toledo OH 43604
419 252-5500

(G-15004)
MANOR CARE OF WICHITA KS LLC
7101 E 21st St N (67206-1037)
PHONE..................................316 684-8018
EMP: 13
SALES (est): 757K **Privately Held**
SIC: 8051 Skilled nursing care facilities

(G-15005)
MANPOWERGROUP INC
800 E Douglas Ave (67202-3508)
PHONE..................................316 946-0088
EMP: 12 **Publicly Held**
SIC: 7363 Help Supply Services
PA: Manpowergroup Inc.
100 W Manpower Pl
Milwaukee WI 53212

(G-15006)
MANUFACTURING SERVICES INC
2239 S Mead St (67211-5021)
PHONE..................................316 267-4111
Dick Dague, *President*
Carol Dague, *Vice Pres*
EMP: 5
SALES: 320K **Privately Held**
WEB: www.mfgservs.com
SIC: 3089 Injection molding of plastics

(G-15007)
MAPLE GARDENS ASSOC LTD PARTNR
Also Called: Maple Gardens Apartments
10200 W Maple St Apt B109 (67209-3111)
PHONE..................................316 722-7960
James Durham, *CEO*
EMP: 45
SALES (est): 2.1MM **Privately Held**
SIC: 6513 Apartment building operators

(G-15008)
MARK 8 INN LC
1130 N Broadway Ave (67214-2898)
PHONE..................................316 265-4679
Robert E Peters,
Kenneth C Peters,
EMP: 12
SQ FT: 19,432
SALES: 258K **Privately Held**
SIC: 7011 Motels

(G-15009)
MARK ARTS
1307 N Rock Rd (67206-1203)
PHONE..................................316 634-2787
Kellie Hayden, *Principal*
Katy Dorrah, *Exec Dir*
Dimitris Skliris, *Director*
Kate Sheppard, *Education*
Hayley Hager, *Receptionist*
EMP: 10
SALES: 4MM **Privately Held**
SIC: 8412 Art gallery

(G-15010)
MARK R DAVIS DDS
5805 E Central Ave (67208-4204)
PHONE..................................316 684-8261
Mark R Davis DDS, *Owner*
EMP: 10
SALES (est): 216.3K **Privately Held**
SIC: 8021 Offices & clinics of dentists

(G-15011)
MARTIN INTERCONNECT SVCS INC
Also Called: M I S
3001 E Harry St (67211-4025)
PHONE..................................316 616-1001
Tom Martin, *CEO*
Sharon D Martin, *CEO*
Todd Martin, *Vice Pres*
EMP: 52
SQ FT: 33,000
SALES (est): 12.9MM **Privately Held**
SIC: 3643 Current-carrying wiring devices

(G-15012)
MARTIN K EBY CNSTR CO INC (HQ)
2525 E 36th Cir N (67219-2303)
PHONE..................................316 268-3500
Michael A Grier, *President*
Starla Criser, *Bd of Directors*
Gordon Kessler, *Bd of Directors*
EMP: 150 **EST:** 1937
SQ FT: 11,000
SALES: 93.2MM **Privately Held**
WEB: www.ebycorp.com
SIC: 1542 Commercial & office building, new construction
PA: Eby Corporation
2525 E 36th Cir N
Wichita KS 67219
316 268-3500

(G-15013)
MARTIN PRINGLE OLIVR WALLACE (PA)
Also Called: Martin Pringle Oliver Wallace
100 N Broadway Ave # 500 (67202-2212)
PHONE..................................316 265-9311
Dan Smith, *Managing Prtnr*
Jeff Kennedy, *Managing Prtnr*
Robert Martin, *Partner*
William Oliver Jr, *Partner*
Dwight Wallace, *Partner*
EMP: 68
SQ FT: 13,000
SALES (est): 11.2MM **Privately Held**
WEB: www.mpows.com
SIC: 8111 General practice law office; general practice attorney, lawyer

(G-15014)
MARTIN ROOFING COMPANY INC
102 E Patterson St (67216-1046)
P.O. Box 17206 (67217-0206)
PHONE..................................316 524-3293
Kurt W Baumgartner, *CEO*
Jeff Demott, *President*
Jake Demott, *Project Mgr*
EMP: 25 **EST:** 1961
SQ FT: 2,200
SALES (est): 4MM **Privately Held**
WEB: www.martinroofing.com
SIC: 1761 Roofing contractor

(G-15015)
MARTINEZ INC
5247 N Arkansas Ave (67204-2933)
PHONE..................................316 587-7814
Jeremy Martinez, *CEO*
▲ **EMP:** 5
SQ FT: 1,200
SALES (est): 729.3K **Privately Held**
SIC: 3448 Prefabricated metal components

(G-15016)
MARY KATE & COMPANY LLC
8112 W Central Ave (67212-3640)
PHONE..................................316 721-4101
Megan Deitchler, *Manager*
Rebecca Smith,
Mary Kate Denton,
EMP: 17
SALES (est): 524.9K **Privately Held**
SIC: 7231 Cosmetologist

(G-15017)
MASON STONE INC
540 E 17th St N (67214-1226)
PHONE..................................316 744-3884
Mason Stone, *Principal*
EMP: 12
SALES (est): 1.1MM **Privately Held**
SIC: 1741 Stone masonry

(G-15018)
MATERNAL FETAL MEDICINE INC
551 N Hillside St Ste 330 (67214-4926)
PHONE..................................316 962-7188
Andrew Hare, *Office Mgr*
EMP: 10
SALES (est): 671.4K **Privately Held**
SIC: 8011 Obstetrician

(G-15019)
MATHESON TRI-GAS INC
Also Called: Linweld
1844 S Florence Ct (67209-2831)
PHONE..................................316 554-9353
Jonas Smith, *Principal*
Jeff Mitchell, *Site Mgr*
EMP: 12 **Privately Held**
WEB: www.linweld.net
SIC: 5084 Welding machinery & equipment
HQ: Matheson Tri-Gas, Inc.
150 Allen Rd Ste 302
Basking Ridge NJ 07920
908 991-9200

(G-15020)
MAXIMA PRECISION INC
3616 N Topeka St (67219-3644)
PHONE..................................316 832-2211
Ricardo Nunes, *President*
Steven Nunes, *General Mgr*
Maria Nunes, *Vice Pres*
EMP: 35
SQ FT: 15,000
SALES (est): 6.5MM **Privately Held**
WEB: www.maximaprecision.com
SIC: 3724 3599 3728 Aircraft engines & engine parts; machine shop, jobbing & repair; aircraft parts & equipment

(G-15021)
MCCLELLAND SOUND INC
345 N Ohio Ave (67214-3983)
PHONE..................................316 265-8686
Matthew R Wunderlich, *President*
Richard McClelland, *Principal*
Scott Martin, *Vice Pres*
Janice Wunderlich, *CFO*
Ommanda Trask, *Bookkeeper*
EMP: 16
SQ FT: 9,000
SALES (est): 11.7MM **Privately Held**
WEB: www.macsound.com
SIC: 5065 1731 Communication equipment; sound equipment, electronic; sound equipment specialization

(G-15022)
MCCORMICK-ARMSTRONG CO INC (PA)
1501 E Douglas Ave (67211-1608)
P.O. Box 1377 (67201-1377)
PHONE..................................316 264-1363
Jake Shaffer, *CEO*
Doug Tompkins, *Vice Pres*
Evonne Gaylord, *CFO*
Mildred F Armstrong, *Treasurer*
Bill Pennington, *Accounts Mgr*
▲ **EMP:** 68
SQ FT: 120,000
SALES (est): 13.1MM **Privately Held**
WEB: www.mcaprint.com
SIC: 2752 Commercial printing, offset

(G-15023)
MCCOY PETROLEUM CORPORATION (PA)
Also Called: Chikaskia River Gas Co Div
9342 E Central Ave (67206-2573)
PHONE..................................316 636-2737
Kevin McCoy, *President*
Bruce A Pringle, *Vice Pres*
Ryan J Schweizer, *Vice Pres*
Darlene Reid, *CPA*
EMP: 10
SQ FT: 4,000
SALES (est): 3.7MM **Privately Held**
SIC: 1382 Oil & gas exploration services

(G-15024)
MCCULLOUGH ENTERPRISES INC (PA)
Also Called: Wichita Tractor Company
1750 S West St (67213-1121)
PHONE..................................316 942-8118
Paddy N Mc Cullough, *President*
Sylvia M Mc Cullough, *Corp Secy*
J Donald Mc Cullough, *Vice Pres*
Marty Kuehler, *Parts Mgr*
Clayton R Mc Cullough, *CFO*
EMP: 18
SQ FT: 14,300
SALES: 10MM **Privately Held**
WEB: www.wichitatractor.com
SIC: 5251 5999 7699 Pumps & pumping equipment; farm equipment & supplies; construction equipment repair; farm machinery repair

(G-15025)
MCCULLOUGH EXCAVATION INC
9210 E 34th St N (67226-2612)
PHONE..................................316 634-2199
Jess McCullough, *President*
EMP: 30
SQ FT: 9,000
SALES: 6.2MM **Privately Held**
WEB: www.mcculloughexcavation.com
SIC: 1794 1623 Excavation & grading, building construction; sewer line construction

(G-15026)
MCCURDY AUCTION LLC
12041 E 13th St N (67206-2842)
PHONE..................................316 683-0612
Sylvia McCombs, *CFO*
Casey Stoneman, *Art Dir*
Lonny Mc Curdy,
Eric Gordon, *Internal Med*
Annette McCurdy,
EMP: 20
SQ FT: 8,000
SALES: 1,000K **Privately Held**
WEB: www.mccurdyauction.com
SIC: 6531 7389 Real estate brokers & agents; auctioneers, fee basis

(G-15027)
MCDANIEL CO INC
4301 W Harry St (67209-2731)
P.O. Box 9048 (67277-0048)
PHONE..................................316 942-8325
Mike Mc Guire, *President*
Marla Herdman, *Corp Secy*
EMP: 27
SQ FT: 10,200
SALES: 5.9MM **Privately Held**
WEB: www.mcdaniel.kscoxmail.com
SIC: 1711 Fire sprinkler system installation

▲ = Import ▼=Export
◆ =Import/Export

(G-15028)
MCDONALD TINKER SKAER QUINN
Also Called: Mtsqh
300 W Douglas Ave Ste 500 (67202-2919)
P.O. Box 207 (67201-0207)
PHONE..................................316 440-4882
Richard T Foster, *Partner*
Vincent A Burnett, *Partner*
Alvin Herrington, *Partner*
Robert G Martin, *Partner*
Stacy Ortega, *Counsel*
EMP: 40
SQ FT: 9,500
SALES (est): 3.8MM **Privately Held**
WEB: www.mtsqh.com
SIC: **8111** General practice law office

(G-15029)
MCKISSICK ENTERPRISES LLC (PA)
Also Called: Picture Perfect
5520 E Central Ave (67208-4164)
PHONE..................................316 687-0272
Trent Mc Kissick,
EMP: 15
SALES (est): 1.4MM **Privately Held**
SIC: **7384** 2752 Photographic services; commercial printing, lithographic

(G-15030)
MEADOWLARK ADULT CARE HOME
254 S Robin Rd (67209-1429)
PHONE..................................316 773-2277
Jill Hanes, *President*
EMP: 25
SALES (est): 1.7MM **Privately Held**
WEB: www.meadowlarkcarehomes.com
SIC: **8361** Home for the aged

(G-15031)
MECHANICAL SYSTEMS INC (PA)
625 E 13th St N (67214-1204)
P.O. Box 3029 (67201-3029)
PHONE..................................316 262-2021
Mark Johnson, *President*
Chris Johnson, *Treasurer*
EMP: 65 **EST:** 1976
SQ FT: 9,300
SALES: 11MM **Privately Held**
SIC: **1711** Mechanical contractor

(G-15032)
MECHANICS INC
Also Called: Mechanical Systems
625 E 13th St N (67214-1204)
P.O. Box 3029 (67201-3029)
PHONE..................................316 262-2021
Gregory Johnson, *President*
Christopher Johnson, *Corp Secy*
Mark Johnson, *Vice Pres*
Chris Johnson, *Treasurer*
EMP: 25
SALES: 1.6MM **Privately Held**
SIC: **1711** Mechanical contractor

(G-15033)
MEDICAL SOCIETY SEDGWICK CNTY
1102 S Hillside St (67211-4004)
PHONE..................................316 683-7557
Dennis Ross, *President*
Nicole Bua, *Supervisor*
Carol Jones, *Director*
Sue Seaman, *Director*
Nancy Stuchlik, *Director*
EMP: 35
SQ FT: 9,000
SALES: 555.5K **Privately Held**
SIC: **8621** Health association; medical field-related associations

(G-15034)
MEDOVA HLTHCARE FNCL GROUP LLC (PA)
345 N Rverview St Ste 600 (67203)
PHONE..................................316 616-6160
Michael Floodman, *Consultant*
Dan Whitney,
Amanda Thompson,
EMP: 21
SALES (est): 2.7MM **Privately Held**
WEB: www.medova.com
SIC: **6153** 8742 6411 6799 Purchasers of accounts receivable & commercial paper; hospital & health services consultant; business consultant; insurance agents & brokers; venture capital companies; machinery & equipment finance leasing

(G-15035)
MEL HAMBELTON FORD INC (PA)
11771 W Kellogg St (67209-1240)
P.O. Box 75900 (67275-0900)
PHONE..................................316 462-3673
Mel Hambelton, *President*
Casey Bramlett, *Business Mgr*
Lisa Hambelton, *Vice Pres*
Dave Pratt, *Inv Control Mgr*
Brian Sladek, *Finance Mgr*
EMP: 148 **EST:** 1969
SQ FT: 26,000
SALES (est): 55.9MM **Privately Held**
WEB: www.melhambeltonford.com
SIC: **5511** 7538 7515 5531 Automobiles, new & used; general automotive repair shops; passenger car leasing; automotive & home supply stores; used car dealers

(G-15036)
MEL STEVENSON & ASSOCIATES INC
Also Called: Spec Roofing Contractors Suppl
925 W Harry St (67213-4108)
PHONE..................................316 262-5959
David Ricke, *Manager*
EMP: 15
SALES (corp-wide): 277.2MM **Privately Held**
SIC: **5033** Roofing & siding materials
PA: Mel Stevenson & Associates, Inc.
2840 Roe Ln
Kansas City KS 66103
913 262-0505

(G-15037)
MELISSA WILBERT
7907 W Birdie Lane Cir (67205-1309)
PHONE..................................316 361-2787
Jace Wilbert, *Principal*
EMP: 5
SALES (est): 301.8K **Privately Held**
SIC: **3281** Burial vaults, stone

(G-15038)
MEM INDUSTRIAL LLC (PA)
2939 W Pawnee St (67213-1821)
PHONE..................................316 944-4400
Terry M Rushing,
Mendy Rushing,
EMP: 15
SQ FT: 11,000
SALES: 3MM **Privately Held**
SIC: **5085** Industrial supplies

(G-15039)
MENTAL HEALTH ASSOCIATION OF (PA)
555 N Woodlawn St # 3105 (67208-3673)
PHONE..................................316 685-1821
Carol Manning, *President*
EMP: 59
SQ FT: 21,890
SALES: 8.2MM **Privately Held**
WEB: www.mhasck.org
SIC: **8621** Professional membership organizations

(G-15040)
MENTAL HEALTH ASSOCIATION OF
2332 N Pinecrest St Ofc (67220-3027)
PHONE..................................316 651-5368
EMP: 258
SALES (corp-wide): 8.2MM **Privately Held**
SIC: **8621** Professional membership organizations
PA: The Mental Health Association Of South Central Kansas
555 N Woodlawn St # 3105
Wichita KS 67208
316 685-1821

(G-15041)
MERIDIAN NURSING CENTER INC
1555 N Meridian Ave (67203-1942)
PHONE..................................316 942-8471
David Bise, *President*
Jeannie Schinstock, *Administration*
EMP: 100
SALES: 5.6MM **Privately Held**
SIC: **8059** 8361 8069 8051 Nursing home, except skilled & intermediate care facility; home for the aged; specialty hospitals, except psychiatric; skilled nursing care facilities; rehabilitation services

(G-15042)
MERITRUST CREDIT UNION (PA)
8710 E 32nd St N (67226-4008)
P.O. Box 789757 (67278-9757)
PHONE..................................316 683-1199
Wade Bruendl, *CEO*
Duane Van Camp, *Principal*
Rick Dodds, *Chairman*
Shanda Barnes, *Auditing Mgr*
Ricky Marquez, *Loan Officer*
EMP: 54
SQ FT: 16,000
SALES: 53.9MM **Privately Held**
WEB: www.bwcu.org
SIC: **6062** 6163 State credit unions, not federally chartered; loan brokers

(G-15043)
MERITRUST CREDIT UNION
8015 E 22nd St N (67226-2351)
P.O. Box 789757 (67278-9757)
PHONE..................................316 683-1199
Stephinie Wilcox, *Principal*
Duane Van Camp, *Technology*
Graham Hamilton,
EMP: 10
SALES (corp-wide): 53.9MM **Privately Held**
WEB: www.bwcu.org
SIC: **6062** State credit unions, not federally chartered
PA: Meritrust Credit Union
8710 E 32nd St N
Wichita KS 67226
316 683-1199

(G-15044)
MERITRUST CREDIT UNION
1322 W Pawnee St (67213-3453)
PHONE..................................316 761-4645
Jenni Johnson, *Branch Mgr*
EMP: 10
SALES (corp-wide): 53.9MM **Privately Held**
WEB: www.bwcu.org
SIC: **6062** 6163 State credit unions, not federally chartered; loan brokers
PA: Meritrust Credit Union
8710 E 32nd St N
Wichita KS 67226
316 683-1199

(G-15045)
MERITRUST CREDIT UNION
2900 S Oliver St (67210-1500)
PHONE..................................316 761-4645
Stan Cowan, *Branch Mgr*
Corey Winter, *Manager*
EMP: 10
SALES (corp-wide): 53.9MM **Privately Held**
WEB: www.bwcu.org
SIC: **6062** 6163 State credit unions, not federally chartered; loan brokers
PA: Meritrust Credit Union
8710 E 32nd St N
Wichita KS 67226
316 683-1199

(G-15046)
MERRIFIELD HOTEL ASSOCIATES LP (HQ)
8100 E 22nd St N Bldg 500 (67226-2305)
PHONE..................................316 681-5100
Charles Merrifield, *Principal*
EMP: 35 **EST:** 2010
SALES (est): 3.3MM
SALES (corp-wide): 42.1MM **Privately Held**
SIC: **7011** Hotels
PA: Lodgeworks, L.P.
8100 E 22nd St N Bldg 500
Wichita KS 67226
316 681-5100

(G-15047)
MERRILL LYNCH PIERCE FENNER
2959 N Rock Rd Ste 200 (67226-1193)
PHONE..................................316 631-3500
Ron L Ingle, *Manager*
Charlie Bennett, *Agent*
Cynthia A Laub, *Agent*
Anne Krueger, *Advisor*
EMP: 25
SALES (corp-wide): 110.5B **Publicly Held**
WEB: www.merlyn.com
SIC: **6211** Stock brokers & dealers
HQ: Merrill Lynch, Pierce, Fenner & Smith Incorporated
111 8th Ave
New York NY 10011
800 637-7455

(G-15048)
METAL ARTS LLC
3629 W 30th St S (67217-1015)
P.O. Box 13056 (67213-0056)
PHONE..................................316 942-7958
Jean Gray, *Mng Member*
Kelly Brown,
Don Gray,
EMP: 16 **EST:** 1971
SQ FT: 10,250
SALES: 4.1MM **Privately Held**
WEB: www.metalartsllc.com
SIC: **3441** Fabricated structural metal

(G-15049)
METAL ARTS MACHINE CO LLC
3921 N Bridgeport Cir (67219-3300)
P.O. Box 13056 (67213-0056)
PHONE..................................316 425-2579
Tony Poell, *General Mgr*
Jean Gray,
Dustin Gray,
EMP: 42
SALES (est): 2.3MM **Privately Held**
WEB: www.metalarts-wichita.com
SIC: **3599** Machine shop, jobbing & repair

(G-15050)
METAL FINISHING CO INC (PA)
1423 S Mclean Blvd (67213-4302)
PHONE..................................316 267-7289
Robert H Babst, *President*
Jennifer Babst, *Corp Secy*
EMP: 5
SQ FT: 20,000
SALES (est): 3.1MM **Privately Held**
WEB: www.metalfinishingco.com
SIC: **3471** Finishing, metals or formed products

(G-15051)
METAL FINISHING CO INC
1329 S Mclean Blvd (67213-4301)
PHONE..................................316 267-7289
EMP: 35
SALES (corp-wide): 3.1MM **Privately Held**
SIC: **3471** Plating & polishing
PA: Metal Finishing Co., Inc.
1423 S Mclean Blvd
Wichita KS 67213
316 267-7289

(G-15052)
METAL FINISHING COMPANY INC
721 E Murdock St (67214-3833)
PHONE..................................316 267-7289
EMP: 110
SALES (corp-wide): 27.7MM **Privately Held**
SIC: **3471** Cleaning, polishing & finishing
PA: The Metal Finishing Company Inc
1423 S Mclean Blvd
Wichita KS 67213
316 267-7289

GEOGRAPHIC

(G-15053)
METAL FINISHING COMPANY INC (PA)
1423 S Mclean Blvd (67213-4302)
PHONE..................................316 267-7289
Robert H Babst, *President*
Rene Espinosa, *Plant Mgr*
Jim Walker, *Facilities Mgr*
Edward Dunn Jr, *Treasurer*
Levi Talamantes, *Manager*
EMP: 15
SQ FT: 36,000
SALES (est): 27.7MM **Privately Held**
SIC: 3399 3398 3471 7389 Cryogenic treatment of metal; shot peening (treating steel to reduce fatigue); finishing, metals or formed products; finishing services; product testing laboratory, safety or performance

(G-15054)
METAL PROS LLC
4323 W Bounous St (67209-2751)
PHONE..................................316 942-2238
Ryan Lash, *Manager*
Dan Kilby,
EMP: 25
SALES (est): 8.5MM **Privately Held**
WEB: www.metalprosllc.com
SIC: 3441 Building components, structural steel

(G-15055)
METAL-FAB INC (PA)
Also Called: MICRO AIR - DIVISION OF METAL-
3025 W May St (67213-1536)
P.O. Box 1138 (67201-1138)
PHONE..................................316 943-2351
Kenneth Shannon, *Chairman*
Scott Schmelzer, *Vice Pres*
Denise McGrew, *Engineer*
Mark OHM, *CFO*
Dan Hamel, *Human Res Dir*
◆ **EMP:** 240
SQ FT: 270,000
SALES (est): 62.8MM **Privately Held**
WEB: www.mtlfab.com
SIC: 3444 3564 Flues & pipes, stove or furnace: sheet metal; air cleaning systems

(G-15056)
METAL-FAB INC
2013 S West St (67213)
PHONE..................................316 943-2351
Mark OHM, *President*
EMP: 53
SALES (corp-wide): 62.8MM **Privately Held**
SIC: 3444 Flues & pipes, stove or furnace: sheet metal
PA: Metal-Fab, Inc.
3025 W May St
Wichita KS 67213
316 943-2351

(G-15057)
METAL-FAB INC
Also Called: Micro Air
2009 S West St (67213-1109)
P.O. Box 1138 (67201-1138)
PHONE..................................316 946-5875
John Segal, *Branch Mgr*
EMP: 7
SALES (corp-wide): 62.8MM **Privately Held**
WEB: www.mtlfab.com
SIC: 3444 3564 Flues & pipes, stove or furnace: sheet metal; air cleaning systems
PA: Metal-Fab, Inc.
3025 W May St
Wichita KS 67213
316 943-2351

(G-15058)
METALFORM INDUSTRIES INC
1721 S Eisenhower St (67209-2809)
PHONE..................................316 945-6700
David Monroe, *President*
Val Laetari, *Treasurer*
EMP: 12
SQ FT: 10,000
SALES (est): 1.7MM **Privately Held**
WEB: www.metalformindustries.com
SIC: 3599 3444 Machine shop, jobbing & repair; sheet metalwork

(G-15059)
METRO COMPANIES INC
Also Called: METRO XPRESS
3518 N Ohio St (67219-3722)
P.O. Box 17194 (67217-0194)
PHONE..................................316 838-3345
Kerry Sell, *President*
Cory Sell, *Exec VP*
Diane Sell, *Vice Pres*
Jonathan Winter, *Opers Staff*
Jill Gottschalk, *Receptionist*
EMP: 100
SQ FT: 12,000
SALES: 12.9MM **Privately Held**
WEB: www.metroxpress.com
SIC: 4213 4212 4731 Contract haulers; local trucking, without storage; truck transportation brokers

(G-15060)
METROCALL
2260 N Ridge Rd Ste 100 (67205-1135)
PHONE..................................316 634-1430
Nancy Chadick, *Principal*
EMP: 12
SALES (est): 1.3MM
SALES (corp-wide): 169.4MM **Publicly Held**
WEB: www.metrocall.com
SIC: 5065 Paging & signaling equipment
HQ: Spok Inc.
6850 Versar Ctr Ste 420
Springfield VA 22151
703 269-6850

(G-15061)
METROPOLITAN LIFE INSUR CO
Also Called: MetLife
1938 N Woodlawn St # 304 (67208-1857)
PHONE..................................316 688-5600
Stan Light, *Manager*
EMP: 12
SALES (corp-wide): 67.9B **Publicly Held**
SIC: 6411 Insurance agents & brokers
HQ: Metropolitan Life Insurance Company (Inc)
1095 Ave Of The Americas
New York NY 10036
908 253-1000

(G-15062)
MGMTTV INC
Also Called: Famhost
245 N Waco St Ste 230 (67202-1131)
P.O. Box 6 (67201-0006)
PHONE..................................316 262-4678
Paul Farmer, *President*
Brad White, *Division Mgr*
John Mason, *Opers Staff*
Ron Mason, *Manager*
Ron Nibbelink, *Software Engr*
EMP: 14
SALES (est): 2MM **Privately Held**
WEB: www.famhost.com
SIC: 7372 7374 Application computer software; computer graphics service

(G-15063)
MHA RESIDENTIAL CARE INC
555 N Woodlawn St Ste 120 (67208-3678)
PHONE..................................316 685-1821
Carol Manning, *President*
Bethany Lippe, *Marketing Staff*
Lee Schnyder, *Director*
EMP: 58
SALES (est): 629.6K **Privately Held**
SIC: 8322 Individual & family services

(G-15064)
MICHAEL A DOLD DDS
7570 W 21st St N 1050b (67205-1772)
PHONE..................................316 721-2024
Michael A Dold DDS, *Owner*
EMP: 12
SALES (est): 331.3K **Privately Held**
SIC: 8021 Dentists' office

(G-15065)
MICHEL DRYWALL LLC
1913 N Ohio Ave (67214-1531)
PHONE..................................316 260-6458
Armando Michel, *Manager*
EMP: 24
SALES (est): 1.8MM **Privately Held**
WEB: www.micheldrywall.com
SIC: 1742 Drywall

(G-15066)
MID AMERICA EXTERIORS LLC
1900 E Douglas Ave # 200 (67214-4227)
PHONE..................................316 265-5444
Gregory Schmidt, *President*
Dave Becker, *Admin Sec*
EMP: 15
SQ FT: 8,000
SALES (est): 1.8MM **Privately Held**
WEB: www.midamext.com
SIC: 1751 1761 1521 Window & door (prefabricated) installation; roofing, siding & sheet metal work; patio & deck construction & repair

(G-15067)
MID AMERICAN CREDIT UNION (PA)
8404 W Kellogg Dr (67209-1897)
PHONE..................................316 779-0052
Stan Smith, *Business Mgr*
Rod Calhoun, *Vice Pres*
Brad Herzet, *Vice Pres*
Bradley Herzet, *Vice Pres*
Kristen Spear, *Vice Pres*
EMP: 35 **EST:** 1936
SQ FT: 10,000
SALES: 13.5MM **Privately Held**
SIC: 6062 State credit unions, not federally chartered

(G-15068)
MID CONTINENT ANESTHESIOLOGY
3450 N Rock Rd Ste 208 (67226-1352)
PHONE..................................316 789-8444
G M Bassell, *President*
Chang Yoon, *Anesthesiology*
EMP: 38
SALES (est): 2.7MM **Privately Held**
WEB: www.hcbcinc.com
SIC: 8011 Anesthesiologist

(G-15069)
MID KANSAS PEDIATRIC ASSOC PA
6837 W 37th St N (67205-9355)
PHONE..................................316 773-3100
Amy Gillcrest, *Administration*
EMP: 20
SALES (corp-wide): 3.5MM **Privately Held**
SIC: 8011 Pediatrician
PA: Mid Kansas Pediatric Associates, Pa
9825 E Shannon Woods Cir
Wichita KS 67226
316 634-0057

(G-15070)
MID KANSAS PEDIATRIC ASSOC PA (PA)
9825 E Shannon Woods Cir (67226-4100)
PHONE..................................316 634-0057
Larry Hund MD, *Partner*
Steve Chavez MD, *Partner*
EMP: 21
SQ FT: 11,000
SALES (est): 3.5MM **Privately Held**
SIC: 8011 Pediatrician

(G-15071)
MID KNSAS DRMTOLOGY CLINIC P A
1861 N Rock Rd Ste 310 (67206-1264)
PHONE..................................316 612-1833
Steven Passman, *President*
Christophe Moller MD, *Vice Pres*
EMP: 12
SQ FT: 9,000
SALES (est): 2MM **Privately Held**
SIC: 8011 Dermatologist

(G-15072)
MID STATES HEALTH PRODUCTS
Also Called: Mid States Fitness Equipment
235 S Topeka Ave (67202-4307)
PHONE..................................316 681-3611
Craig Bally, *President*
EMP: 10
SQ FT: 3,500
SALES: 2MM **Privately Held**
WEB: www.midstatesfitness.com
SIC: 5941 5091 Exercise equipment; exercise equipment

(G-15073)
MID-AM BUILDING SUPPLY INC
601 S Anna St (67209-2536)
PHONE..................................316 942-0389
Michael Knaebel, *Sales Staff*
Gary Jacobs, *Manager*
EMP: 11
SALES (corp-wide): 260.3MM **Privately Held**
WEB: www.midambuilding.com
SIC: 5031 5211 Building materials, exterior; building materials, interior; door & window products
PA: Mid-Am Building Supply, Inc.
1615 Omar Bradley Rd
Moberly MO 65270
660 263-2140

(G-15074)
MID-AMERICA AG NETWORK INC
Also Called: Steckline Communications
1632 S Maize Rd Ste 200 (67209-3900)
PHONE..................................316 721-8484
Greg Steckline, *President*
EMP: 30
SQ FT: 8,000
SALES (est): 2MM **Privately Held**
SIC: 4832 News

(G-15075)
MID-AMERICA AUTO AUCTION INC
5817 E Kellogg Dr (67218-1742)
PHONE..................................316 500-7700
Brad Phillips, *President*
Brook Phillips, *Vice Pres*
EMP: 120 **EST:** 1977
SQ FT: 50,000
SALES (est): 14.4MM **Privately Held**
SIC: 5012 Automobile auction

(G-15076)
MID-AMERICA ORTHOPEDICS PA (PA)
1923 N Webb Rd (67206-3405)
PHONE..................................316 262-4886
Matt Quinn, *COO*
Justin Strickland, *Med Doctor*
Cheri Claphan, *Technical Staff*
Kent S Hoffman, *Physician Asst*
Pamela Fruechting, *Nurse*
EMP: 41 **EST:** 2008
SALES (est): 9.5MM **Privately Held**
SIC: 8011 Orthopedic physician

(G-15077)
MID-AMERICA ORTHOPEDICS PA
12112 W Us Highway 54 (67235-1100)
PHONE..................................316 440-1100
Addie Greb, *Branch Mgr*
EMP: 21
SALES (corp-wide): 9.5MM **Privately Held**
SIC: 8049 8011 Physical therapist; orthopedic physician
PA: Mid-America Orthopedics Pa
1923 N Webb Rd
Wichita KS 67206
316 262-4886

(G-15078)
MID-CONTINENT AVI SVCS INC
1640 S Airport Rd (67209-1945)
PHONE..................................316 927-4204
Dave Vander Griend, *President*
J Young, *General Mgr*
John Young, *General Mgr*
Pete Galusha, *Opers Staff*
Mike Nordhus, *QC Mgr*
EMP: 16
SALES (est): 989.1K **Privately Held**
SIC: 4581 Aircraft maintenance & repair services

(G-15079)
MID-CONTINENT THERMAL-GUARD
1516 W 29th St N (67204-4824)
PHONE.................................316 838-4044
Doran Wulf, *President*
EMP: 26
SQ FT: 5,200
SALES (est): 3.9MM **Privately Held**
WEB: www.mctgwindows.com
SIC: 5211 1751 1761 1521 Windows, storm: wood or metal; window & door (prefabricated) installation; siding contractor; patio & deck construction & repair

(G-15080)
MID-KANSAS WOMENS CENTER PA
9300 E 29th St N Ste 201 (67226-2183)
PHONE.................................316 685-3081
Arthur D Dehart, *President*
Taylor Bertschy, *Obstetrician*
EMP: 20
SALES (est): 3.4MM **Privately Held**
SIC: 8011 Gynecologist

(G-15081)
MID-STATES LABORATORIES INC (PA)
216 E 1st St N (67202-2102)
P.O. Box 1140 (67201-1140)
PHONE.................................316 264-6758
Woodrow Rice, *President*
Sherry L Rice Du Perier, *Vice Pres*
Woodrow R Rice Jr, *Vice Pres*
EMP: 18 **EST:** 1951
SQ FT: 2,300
SALES (est): 2.7MM **Privately Held**
SIC: 3089 Molding primary plastic

(G-15082)
MID-STATES LABORATORIES INC
600 N St Francis St (67214-3810)
P.O. Box 1140 (67201-1140)
PHONE.................................316 262-7013
Woodrow Rice, *Manager*
EMP: 15
SALES (corp-wide): 2.7MM **Privately Held**
SIC: 3089 5999 Molding primary plastic; hearing aids
PA: Mid-States Laboratories Inc
216 E 1st St N
Wichita KS 67202
316 264-6758

(G-15083)
MID-WEST ELECTRICAL SUPPLY INC
925 N Mosley St (67214-3423)
PHONE.................................316 265-0562
Randy Cubbage, *President*
Curtis Eaton, *Vice Pres*
Bill Carlson, *Sales Staff*
Jo Cubbage, *Office Mgr*
Darla Jones, *Manager*
EMP: 10
SQ FT: 20,000
SALES: 5MM **Privately Held**
SIC: 5063 Electrical supplies

(G-15084)
MIDAS AUTO SYSTEMS EXPERTS
Also Called: Midas Muffler
3330 N Rock Rd (67226-1315)
PHONE.................................316 636-9299
Tim Hendricks, *Owner*
EMP: 13
SALES (est): 1.2MM **Privately Held**
SIC: 7533 Muffler shop, sale or repair & installation

(G-15085)
MIDCO HOLDINGS LLC (HQ)
8225 E 35th St N (67226-1324)
P.O. Box 780660 (67278-0660)
PHONE.................................316 522-0900
Robert Dool,
EMP: 12
SQ FT: 18,500
SALES (est): 4.8MM **Publicly Held**
WEB: www.midsafe.com
SIC: 5099 Safety equipment & supplies

(G-15086)
MIDCONTINENT CREDIT SVCS INC
3161 N Rock Rd (67226-1452)
P.O. Box 75076 (67275-0076)
PHONE.................................316 721-6467
Paul Matzek, *President*
EMP: 18
SALES (est): 1.6MM **Privately Held**
WEB: www.midccs.com
SIC: 7322 Collection agency, except real estate

(G-15087)
MIDIAN SHRINERS (PA)
130 N Topeka Ave (67202-2406)
PHONE.................................316 265-9676
David Pate, *Principal*
EMP: 17
SALES (est): 1.5MM **Privately Held**
SIC: 8641 Civic social & fraternal associations

(G-15088)
MIDWEST BULK INC
3404 N Emporia St (67219-3615)
PHONE.................................316 831-9700
Amanda Gaggero, *President*
EMP: 20
SALES (est): 2.9MM **Privately Held**
SIC: 4213 Trucking, except local

(G-15089)
MIDWEST CAR CORPORATION
Also Called: National Car Rental
1300 S Airport Rd (67209-2912)
PHONE.................................316 946-4851
Reina Lamprecht, *Manager*
EMP: 16
SQ FT: 2,100
SALES (corp-wide): 75.1MM **Privately Held**
SIC: 7514 7513 Rent-a-car service; truck leasing, without drivers
PA: Midwest Car Corporation
1450 Delanglade St
Kaukauna WI 54130
414 483-9800

(G-15090)
MIDWEST COMBUSTN SOLUTIONS INC
4601 S Palisade Ave (67217-4923)
PHONE.................................316 425-0929
Paul Cooper, *President*
▲ **EMP:** 7 **EST:** 2012
SALES (est): 1.4MM **Privately Held**
SIC: 3822 3433 3443 Flame safety controls for furnaces & boilers; burners, furnaces, boilers & stokers; boiler & boiler shop work

(G-15091)
MIDWEST CORPORATE AVIATION INC
3512 N Webb Rd (67226-8128)
P.O. Box 8067 (67208-0067)
PHONE.................................316 636-9700
Marvin E Autry, *President*
Robert Karslake, *Vice Pres*
Brian Strunk, *Vice Pres*
EMP: 48
SQ FT: 21,600
SALES: 6.7MM **Privately Held**
WEB: www.midwestaviation.com
SIC: 4581 4522 5088 Airport; flying charter service; ambulance services, air; aircraft & parts

(G-15092)
MIDWEST DRYWALL CO INC (PA)
Also Called: Mdc Drywall
1351 S Reca Ct Ste 101 (67209-1815)
P.O. Box 771170 (67277-1170)
PHONE.................................316 722-9559
Steven A Nienke, *President*
Brian Bergman, *Division Mgr*
Gary Everitt, *Warehouse Mgr*
Denis Dieker, *CFO*
Dennis Dieker, *CFO*
EMP: 250
SQ FT: 50,000
SALES (est): 110MM **Privately Held**
SIC: 1742 Drywall; acoustical & ceiling work; plastering, plain or ornamental

(G-15093)
MIDWEST DRYWALL CO INC
1351 S Reca Ct Ste 101 (67209-1815)
PHONE.................................316 722-9559
Bill Wright, *Manager*
EMP: 100
SALES (corp-wide): 110MM **Privately Held**
SIC: 1742 6512 Drywall; acoustical & ceiling work; plastering, plain or ornamental; commercial & industrial building operation
PA: Midwest Drywall Co., Inc.
1351 S Reca Ct Ste 101
Wichita KS 67209
316 722-9559

(G-15094)
MIDWEST HEALTH SERVICES INC
12221 W Maple St Ofc Ofc (67235-8775)
PHONE.................................316 729-2400
EMP: 186
SALES (corp-wide): 32.7MM **Privately Held**
SIC: 8361 Residential care
PA: Midwest Health, Inc
3024 Sw Wanamaker Rd # 300
Topeka KS 66614
785 272-1535

(G-15095)
MIDWEST HEALTH SERVICES INC
Also Called: Great Point Health Alliance
250 N Rock Rd Ste 160 (67206-2241)
PHONE.................................316 685-1587
Roger John, *Manager*
EMP: 12
SALES (corp-wide): 32.7MM **Privately Held**
WEB: www.halsteadhealthrehab.com
SIC: 8051 8742 Extended care facility; hospital & health services consultant
PA: Midwest Health, Inc
3024 Sw Wanamaker Rd # 300
Topeka KS 66614
785 272-1535

(G-15096)
MIDWEST HSTRCAL GNALOGICAL SOC
Also Called: Midwest Historical & Genealogi
1203 N Main St (67203-3614)
P.O. Box 1121 (67201-1121)
PHONE.................................316 264-3611
Sue Bush, *President*
EMP: 25
SQ FT: 3,500
SALES (est): 1MM **Privately Held**
SIC: 8231 7299 Specialized libraries; genealogical investigation service

(G-15097)
MIDWEST ORTHODONTICS INC
4318 W Central Ave (67212-2119)
P.O. Box 75623 (67275-5623)
PHONE.................................316 942-8703
Kent W Nye, *President*
Kent Nye, *President*
Shannon Nye, *Vice Pres*
EMP: 12
SQ FT: 2,800
SALES: 500K **Privately Held**
SIC: 3843 Orthodontic appliances

(G-15098)
MIDWEST PEST CONTROL LLC
2308 E Mount Vernon St (67211-5415)
PHONE.................................316 681-3417
EMP: 12
SQ FT: 2,200
SALES (est): 989.9K **Privately Held**
SIC: 7342 Disinfecting/Pest Services

(G-15099)
MIDWEST ROOFING SERVICES INC (PA)
Also Called: Kansas Guttering
2209 W Harry St (67213-2932)
PHONE.................................316 262-4758
Darren Ward, *President*
EMP: 24 **EST:** 2005
SALES (est): 5.3MM **Privately Held**
SIC: 1761 Roofing contractor

(G-15100)
MIDWEST SERVICE BUREAU INC
625 W Maple St (67213-4618)
P.O. Box 3888 (67201-3888)
PHONE.................................316 263-1051
Salvatore J Manzi, *President*
Micki Kell, *Opers Mgr*
Charles Wilson, *Sales Mgr*
EMP: 30
SQ FT: 3,500
SALES (est): 2.5MM **Privately Held**
SIC: 7322 Collection agency, except real estate

(G-15101)
MIDWEST SEWING & VACUUM CENTER
111 S Pattie Ave (67211-1718)
PHONE.................................316 722-9737
EMP: 38
SALES (est): 3.8MM **Privately Held**
SIC: 5722 7629 Ret Household Appliances Electrical Repair

(G-15102)
MIDWEST SINGLE SOURCE INC (PA)
1501 E 1st St N (67214-4175)
P.O. Box 49380 (67201-9380)
PHONE.................................316 267-6333
John H Osborne, *CEO*
Kevin Ulwelling, *President*
Chris Eckhoff, *Vice Pres*
Angela Williams, *CFO*
Darlene Dunn, *Office Mgr*
EMP: 40
SQ FT: 20,000
SALES (est): 19.3MM **Privately Held**
WEB: www.ssource.com
SIC: 5112 5199 5044 5021 Business forms; advertising specialties; office equipment; furniture; computers, peripherals & software; commercial printing

(G-15103)
MIDWEST STEEL FAB LLC
3690 N Old Lawrence Rd (67219-3659)
P.O. Box 4233 (67204-0233)
PHONE.................................316 832-9669
Tim Sinclair, *President*
Matthew Lazzo, *Vice Pres*
EMP: 15
SQ FT: 14,000
SALES (est): 6.5MM **Privately Held**
SIC: 3441 Building components, structural steel

(G-15104)
MIDWEST SURGERY CENTER LC
825 N Hillside St Ste 100 (67214-4938)
PHONE.................................316 683-3937
Rodney Jones, *Owner*
Kenneth Braun, *Partner*
EMP: 15
SALES (est): 1.8MM **Privately Held**
SIC: 8011 Surgeon

(G-15105)
MIDWEST SURGICAL
1431 S Bluffview Dr # 210 (67218-3010)
PHONE.................................316 687-1090
Jace W Hyder MD, *President*
Jerrod A Conkling, *Physician Asst*
EMP: 15
SALES (est): 1.2MM **Privately Held**
SIC: 8011 Ambulatory surgical center

(G-15106)
MIES CONSTRUCTION INC
1919 Southwest Blvd (67213-1437)
PHONE.................................316 945-7227

Earl L Mies, *President*
Earl Mierzwa, *Project Mgr*
Lindy Sparr, *Office Mgr*
Kathyrn Jost, *Admin Sec*
Kathy L Mies, *Admin Sec*
EMP: 80
SQ FT: 3,500
SALES (est): 11.3MM **Privately Held**
WEB: www.miesconstruction.com
SIC: 1629 1623 Earthmoving contractor; underground utilities contractor

(G-15107)
MIKE GRBIC TEAM REALTORS INC
7309 E 21st St N Ste 200 (67206-1100)
P.O. Box 649 (67201-0649)
PHONE..................................316 684-0000
Mike Grbic, *President*
EMP: 24
SQ FT: 5,100
SALES (est): 2.5MM **Privately Held**
SIC: 6531 Real estate agent, residential

(G-15108)
MILLENIA PRODUCTIONS LLC
Also Called: La Palm Products
3819 N Toben St (67226-2904)
PHONE..................................316 425-2500
Michael Le, *CEO*
▲ **EMP:** 10
SQ FT: 30,000
SALES (est): 4.3MM **Privately Held**
SIC: 2844 Toilet preparations

(G-15109)
MILLENNIUM CONCEPTS INC
8955 W Monroe Cir Ste 300 (67209-3308)
PHONE..................................316 977-8870
Kevin Reifschneider, *President*
Rodney Gorges, *Vice Pres*
Marion Greenlee, *Vice Pres*
Barend Van Beek, *Director*
EMP: 55
SALES (est): 10.9MM **Privately Held**
WEB: www.millennium.aero
SIC: 3728 Aircraft parts & equipment

(G-15110)
MILLENNIUM CONCEPTS INC
9050 W Monroe Cir (67209-3306)
PHONE..................................316 821-9300
Kevin Reifschneider, *President*
Rodney Gorges, *Vice Pres*
EMP: 19 **EST:** 2015
SALES (est): 2.8MM **Privately Held**
SIC: 7389 Design services

(G-15111)
MINI-MAC INC
1703 Southwest Blvd Ste 1 (67213-1406)
P.O. Box 286, Derby (67037-0286)
PHONE..................................316 733-0661
Bob Mc Namee, *President*
Paul Emberson, *Vice Pres*
Dylan Mc Namee, *Vice Pres*
EMP: 6
SQ FT: 1,200
SALES: 1.6MM **Privately Held**
SIC: 3728 Aircraft parts & equipment

(G-15112)
MINIATURE PLASTIC MOLDING LLC
1111 N Washington Ave (67214-3058)
PHONE..................................316 264-2827
Bruce Kester, *Partner*
George Hockett II, *Partner*
Dwan Welty, *Partner*
EMP: 5
SQ FT: 5,600
SALES: 500K **Privately Held**
WEB: www.mpmllc.net
SIC: 3559 3089 5084 8711 Robots, molding & forming plastics; injection molding of plastics; conveyor systems; engineering services

(G-15113)
MINNESOTA PIPE LINE CO LLC (HQ)
4111 E 37th St N (67220-3203)
P.O. Box 2256 (67201-2256)
PHONE..................................316 828-5500
Dave Stecher, *President*
EMP: 10
SQ FT: 100,000
SALES: 195.2MM
SALES (corp-wide): 40.6B **Privately Held**
SIC: 4612 Crude petroleum pipelines
PA: Koch Industries, Inc.
4111 E 37th St N
Wichita KS 67220
316 828-5500

(G-15114)
MIRACLES INC
1015 E 2nd St N (67214-3908)
PHONE..................................316 303-9520
Rhonda Walker, *CEO*
Beverly Goering, *Director*
Bebbie Housler, *Director*
EMP: 15
SALES: 1.2MM **Privately Held**
SIC: 8322 Substance abuse counseling

(G-15115)
MIRACLES HOUSE
1250 N Market St (67214-2835)
PHONE..................................316 264-5900
Rhonda Walker, *Principal*
Angie Shaw, *Principal*
EMP: 12 **EST:** 2004
SALES (est): 170.4K **Privately Held**
SIC: 8322 Alcoholism counseling, nontreatment

(G-15116)
MIRES MACHINE CO INC
4224 W Esthner Ave (67209-2795)
PHONE..................................316 942-6547
Bob Walten, *President*
Ben J Mires, *President*
Carol Mires, *Vice Pres*
Patricia Mires, *Admin Sec*
EMP: 13
SQ FT: 10,000
SALES (est): 2.5MM **Privately Held**
WEB: www.mires.net
SIC: 3599 Machine shop, jobbing & repair

(G-15117)
MIRROR INC
3820 N Toben St (67226-2903)
P.O. Box 711, Newton (67114-0711)
PHONE..................................316 634-3954
Ken McGill, *Vice Pres*
EMP: 15
SALES (corp-wide): 11.2MM **Privately Held**
SIC: 8093 Drug clinic, outpatient
PA: The Mirror Inc
130 E 5th St
Newton KS 67114
316 283-6743

(G-15118)
MKEC ENGINEERING INC (PA)
411 N Webb Rd (67206-2521)
PHONE..................................316 684-9600
Kenneth Bengtson, *President*
Steve Nikkel, *Project Mgr*
Jason Basel, *Engineer*
Jeff Cartwright, *Engineer*
Scott Evans, *Engineer*
EMP: 180
SALES (est): 26.1MM **Privately Held**
WEB: www.mkec.com
SIC: 8711 8713 Civil engineering; surveying services

(G-15119)
MOBILE ADDICTION LLC (PA)
8918 W 21st St N (67205-1885)
PHONE..................................316 773-3463
Charles R Thomas, *Principal*
EMP: 18
SALES (est): 15.1MM **Privately Held**
SIC: 5064 Electrical appliances, television & radio

(G-15120)
MODERN METHODS
439 N Estelle Ave (67214-4620)
P.O. Box 2925 (67201-2925)
PHONE..................................316 686-6391
Richard R Capps, *President*
EMP: 12 **EST:** 1971
SQ FT: 1,000
SALES (est): 863.5K **Privately Held**
SIC: 8072 Crown & bridge production

(G-15121)
MOJACK DISTRIBUTORS LLC
3535 N Rock Rd Ste 300 (67226-1366)
PHONE..................................877 466-5225
Daniel Drake, *Mng Member*
Dan Drake,
Nate Gregory,
Audra Hanson,
Kathy Nguyen, *Assistant*
▲ **EMP:** 15
SALES (est): 3.8MM **Privately Held**
SIC: 3524 Lawn & garden mowers & accessories

(G-15122)
MOLEX LLC
4111 E 37th St N (67220-3203)
PHONE..................................630 969-4550
Dana Bourland, *Branch Mgr*
EMP: 7
SALES (corp-wide): 40.6B **Privately Held**
SIC: 3679 3643 Antennas, receiving; electronic circuits; connectors & terminals for electrical devices
HQ: Molex, Llc
2222 Wellington Ct
Lisle IL 60532
630 969-4550

(G-15123)
MONNAT & SPURRIER CHARTERED
200 W Douglas Ave Ste 830 (67202-3008)
PHONE..................................316 264-2800
Daniel Monnat, *Principal*
Stanley Spurrier, *Principal*
EMP: 12
SALES (est): 1.2MM **Privately Held**
WEB: www.monnat.com
SIC: 8111 General practice attorney, lawyer

(G-15124)
MOONWALKS FOR FUN INC
8545 W Irving St (67209-1890)
P.O. Box 9244 (67277-0244)
PHONE..................................316 522-2224
Duane Zogleman, *President*
Jesse Zoglemen, *Vice Pres*
EMP: 20
SALES (est): 800K **Privately Held**
WEB: www.moonwalksforfun.com
SIC: 7999 Tourist attractions, amusement park concessions & rides

(G-15125)
MOORE JEFF PHD AUDIOLOGIST
9350 E Central Ave (67206-2555)
PHONE..................................316 686-6608
John M Laak MD, *Partner*
Thomas Kryzer MD, *Partner*
EMP: 15
SALES (est): 220.5K **Privately Held**
SIC: 8049 Audiologist

(G-15126)
MORGAN CHANCE INC
4219 W Irving St (67209-2613)
P.O. Box 9046 (67277-0046)
PHONE..................................316 945-6555
Mike Chance, *President*
Jeff Roth, *VP Opers*
▲ **EMP:** 20
SALES (est): 1.1MM **Privately Held**
SIC: 7999 Amusement ride

(G-15127)
MORGAN STANLEY & CO LLC
1617 N Wtrfrnt Pkwy # 200 (67206-6639)
PHONE..................................316 383-8300
David Fancher, *Branch Mgr*
EMP: 15
SALES (corp-wide): 50.1B **Publicly Held**
WEB: www.msvp.com
SIC: 6211 Investment bankers
HQ: Morgan Stanley & Co. Llc
1585 Broadway
New York NY 10036
212 761-4000

(G-15128)
MORRIS LAING EVANS BROCK (PA)
300 N Mead St Ste 200 (67202-2745)
PHONE..................................316 838-1084
Robert I Guenthner, *President*
Jana D Abbott, *Principal*
Robert K Anderson, *Principal*
Richard D Greene, *Principal*
Robert E Nugent, *Principal*
EMP: 60
SQ FT: 21,000
SALES (est): 8.6MM **Privately Held**
SIC: 8111 7389 Will, estate & trust law; labor & employment law; corporate, partnership & business law; financial services

(G-15129)
MORROW & COMPANY LLC
421 E 3rd St N (67202-2509)
PHONE..................................316 263-2223
William Carpenter, *Accountant*
Forrest Morrow, *Accountant*
Frank Morrow, *Mng Member*
Adam W Bennett, *Technology*
Richard Morrow,
EMP: 11
SALES (est): 861.2K **Privately Held**
WEB: www.morrowandcompany.com
SIC: 8721 Certified public accountant

(G-15130)
MORROW ENGINEERING INC
405 S Holland St Ste 100 (67209-2167)
PHONE..................................316 942-0402
James Morrow, *President*
Brian Stratton, *Project Mgr*
Mark Wallsten, *Project Mgr*
Jean Morrow, *Manager*
EMP: 13
SALES: 1.2MM **Privately Held**
WEB: www.morrowengineering.com
SIC: 8711 Electrical or electronic engineering; consulting engineer

(G-15131)
MOTEL 6
465 S Webb Rd (67207)
PHONE..................................316 684-6363
Hemant Patel, *Owner*
EMP: 16
SALES (est): 373.5K **Privately Held**
SIC: 7011 Hotels & motels

(G-15132)
MOTEL 6 OPERATING LP
5736 W Kellogg Dr (67209-2395)
PHONE..................................316 945-8440
George Floyer, *Manager*
EMP: 17
SALES (corp-wide): 579.1MM **Privately Held**
WEB: www.motel6.com
SIC: 7011 Hotels & motels
HQ: Motel 6 Operating L.P.
4001 Intl Pkwy Ste 500
Carrollton TX 75007
972 360-9000

(G-15133)
MOTION INDUSTRIES INC
Also Called: Hub Supply
2546 N Lonaine St (67219)
PHONE..................................316 265-9608
Don Feekes, *Branch Mgr*
EMP: 24
SALES (corp-wide): 18.7B **Publicly Held**
SIC: 5085 5084 Bearings; abrasives & adhesives; machine tools & metalworking machinery
HQ: Motion Industries, Inc.
1605 Alton Rd
Birmingham AL 35210
205 956-1122

(G-15134)
MOTOR MOUTH WIRELESS LLC (PA)
247 S Holyoke St (67218-1123)
PHONE..................................316 260-4660
William E Long, *Administration*
Bill Long,
EMP: 12
SALES (est): 913.5K **Privately Held**
SIC: 4812 Cellular telephone services

▲ = Import ▼=Export
◆ =Import/Export

(G-15135)
MOUFARRIJ NAZIH
818 N Emporia St Ste 200 (67214-3726)
PHONE..................................316 263-0296
Nazih Moufarrij, *Principal*
EMP: 80
SALES (est): 777.5K **Privately Held**
SIC: 8011 General & family practice, physician/surgeon

(G-15136)
MOXLEY &WAGLE DR
825 S Hillside St (67211-3005)
PHONE..................................316 685-2731
Mark Moxley, *Partner*
Jason Wagle, *Partner*
EMP: 19
SALES (est): 1.5MM **Privately Held**
SIC: 8021 Periodontist

(G-15137)
MSI
625 E 13th St N (67214-1204)
P.O. Box 1716 (67201-1716)
PHONE..................................316 262-2021
Mark Johnson, *President*
Chris Johnson, *Treasurer*
EMP: 20
SQ FT: 9,300
SALES (est): 1.9MM
SALES (corp-wide): 11MM **Privately Held**
WEB: www.msiservices.com
SIC: 1711 7699 Warm air heating & air conditioning contractor; boiler repair shop
PA: Mechanical Systems, Inc.
625 E 13th St N
Wichita KS 67214
316 262-2021

(G-15138)
MULL DRILLING COMPANY INC (PA)
1700 N Wtrfrnt Pkwy # 1200 (67206-6637)
PHONE..................................316 264-6366
Lewis M Mull, *Ch of Bd*
Mark Shreve, *President*
Steve Anderson, *Senior VP*
Jennifer Mull, *Treasurer*
Michael Unruh, *CPA*
EMP: 18 **EST:** 1954
SQ FT: 3,391
SALES (est): 8.8MM **Privately Held**
WEB: www.mulldrlg.com
SIC: 1311 1381 Crude petroleum production; drilling oil & gas wells

(G-15139)
MURDOCK COMPANIES INC (PA)
Also Called: Murdock Electric & Supply
1111 E 1st St N (67214-3904)
P.O. Box 2775 (67201-2775)
PHONE..................................316 262-4476
Herbert H Coin, *Ch of Bd*
Brenda Blazer, *President*
Leo Helsel, *Sales Engr*
Bob Friesen, *Sales Staff*
Terry Klein, *Sales Staff*
▲ **EMP:** 27
SQ FT: 23,000
SALES: 14MM **Privately Held**
WEB: www.mcos.com
SIC: 5085 5084 Bearings; industrial machinery & equipment

(G-15140)
MURFIN DRILLING COMPANY INC (HQ)
250 N Water St Ste 300 (67202-1299)
PHONE..................................316 267-3241
David Murfin, *President*
Jerry Abels, *Vice Pres*
David Doyel, *Vice Pres*
Leon Rodak, *Vice Pres*
Richard Koll, *CFO*
EMP: 40
SQ FT: 25,000
SALES (est): 12MM **Privately Held**
SIC: 1311 1381 1382 Crude petroleum production; natural gas production; drilling oil & gas wells; oil & gas exploration services

(G-15141)
MUSTANG SOFTBALL
Also Called: Mustang Softball Academy
2250 N Hoover Rd (67205-1139)
PHONE..................................316 260-9770
Mark Griggs, *Principal*
EMP: 10
SALES (est): 293.1K **Privately Held**
SIC: 7997 Baseball club, except professional & semi-professional

(G-15142)
MV PARTNERS LLC
250 N Water St Ste 300 (67202-1216)
PHONE..................................316 267-3241
David L Murfin, *Partner*
J Michael Vess, *Partner*
EMP: 6
SALES: 51MM **Privately Held**
SIC: 1381 Drilling oil & gas wells

(G-15143)
MV PURCHASING LLC (PA)
8301 E 21st St N Ste 370 (67206-2955)
PHONE..................................316 262-2819
Paul Mangan, *Vice Pres*
Rick Navarro, *Vice Pres*
Gary Navarro, *Mng Member*
Lee Bullock,
Jim Coen,
EMP: 27
SALES (est): 15.1MM **Privately Held**
SIC: 5172 Crude oil

(G-15144)
N J INVESTORS INC
7701 E Kellogg Dr Ste 895 (67207-1711)
PHONE..................................316 652-0616
Allan Joseph, *President*
EMP: 10
SALES (est): 600K **Privately Held**
SIC: 6531 Real estate brokers & agents

(G-15145)
NADIA INC
Also Called: UPS
2250 N Rock Rd Ste 118 (67226-2325)
PHONE..................................316 686-6190
Muhammad Khan, *President*
EMP: 10
SALES (est): 931.9K **Privately Held**
SIC: 7389 4731 Mailbox rental & related service; freight transportation arrangement

(G-15146)
NANCE MANUFACTURING INC (PA)
2005 S West St (67213-1109)
PHONE..................................316 942-8671
James Ruhl, *CEO*
James F McMurry, *Owner*
Lyle Goering, *Business Mgr*
Rob Valdois, *Opers Staff*
EMP: 25
SQ FT: 50,000
SALES (est): 10.6MM **Privately Held**
WEB: www.nancemanufacturing.com
SIC: 3052 3728 3599 3541 Rubber & plastics hose & beltings; aircraft parts & equipment; machine & other job shop work; grinding, polishing, buffing, lapping & honing machines

(G-15147)
NATIONAL BUILDERS INC
7570 W 21st St N 1006e (67205-1773)
PHONE..................................316 729-7445
Steven Gardner, *President*
EMP: 10
SALES (est): 1.8MM **Privately Held**
SIC: 1541 1521 1522 Industrial buildings, new construction; single-family housing construction; residential construction

(G-15148)
NATIONAL CONTRACTORS INC
621 N Birkdale Dr (67230-1528)
P.O. Box 771192 (67277-1192)
PHONE..................................316 722-8484
Clay Davis, *Ch of Bd*
Karen Rumford, *Corp Secy*
Steve Koegeboehn, *Vice Pres*
EMP: 25
SQ FT: 50,000
SALES: 30MM **Privately Held**
WEB: www.natconinc.com
SIC: 1542 Nonresidential construction

(G-15149)
NATIONAL CTSTRPHE RSTRTION INC (PA)
Also Called: Ncri
8447 E 35th St N (67226-1344)
PHONE..................................316 636-5700
Nicholas Easter, *CEO*
Patricia Easter, *President*
EMP: 70
SQ FT: 40,000
SALES (est): 39.2MM **Privately Held**
WEB: www.ncricat.com
SIC: 1542 1541 1521 Commercial & office buildings, renovation & repair; renovation, remodeling & repairs: industrial buildings; repairing fire damage, single-family houses

(G-15150)
NATIONAL OPINION RESEARCH CTR
2021 N Amidon Ave # 1300 (67203-2100)
PHONE..................................316 221-5800
EMP: 96
SALES (corp-wide): 181.4MM **Privately Held**
SIC: 8732 Commercial nonphysical research
PA: National Opinion Research Center
55 E Monroe St Fl 30
Chicago IL 60603
312 759-4266

(G-15151)
NATIONAL RENTAL (US) INC
Also Called: National Rent A Car
1300 S Airport Rd (67209-2912)
PHONE..................................316 946-4851
Rena Lanpery, *Branch Mgr*
EMP: 23
SALES (corp-wide): 4.5B **Privately Held**
WEB: www.specialtyrentals.com
SIC: 7514 Rent-a-car service
HQ: National Rental (Us) Llc
14002 E 21st St Ste 1500
Tulsa OK 74134

(G-15152)
NATIONAL SCREENING BUREAU LLC
515 N Ridge Rd Ste 202 (67212-6389)
PHONE..................................316 263-4400
Troy Trussell, *Mktg Dir*
Joshua Connors, *Research Analys*
EMP: 13
SALES (est): 1.1MM **Privately Held**
WEB: www.natsb.com
SIC: 7389 Personal investigation service

(G-15153)
NATIONAL SOC TOLE/DEC PNTR INC (PA)
393 N Mclean Blvd (67203-5968)
PHONE..................................316 269-9300
Heidy Hadley, *Office Mgr*
EMP: 16
SALES: 887K **Privately Held**
WEB: www.decorativepainters.com
SIC: 8699 Personal interest organization

(G-15154)
NATIONAL-SPENCER INC (PA)
Also Called: Zeeline
9021 W Kellogg Dr (67209-1862)
P.O. Box 57 (67201-0057)
PHONE..................................316 265-5601
Sam L Goode, *CEO*
Harold R England Jr, *President*
Amy Osburn, *Vice Pres*
Sarah Harris, *Office Mgr*
▲ **EMP:** 25
SQ FT: 7,500
SALES (est): 6.9MM **Privately Held**
WEB: www.maximumresponse.com
SIC: 3823 Fluidic devices, circuits & systems for process control

(G-15155)
NATURAL RSOURCE PROTECTION INC
9131 E 37th St N (67226-2010)
PHONE..................................316 303-0505
Gary Morgan, *President*
EMP: 23
SALES (est): 423.2K **Privately Held**
WEB: www.nrp-inc.com
SIC: 8999 Natural resource preservation service

(G-15156)
NCS HEALTHCARE OF KANSAS LLC
Also Called: Omnicare of Wichita
8200 E 34th Cir N (67226-1349)
PHONE..................................316 522-3449
Kathleen Best, *General Mgr*
EMP: 48
SALES (est): 1.9MM
SALES (corp-wide): 194.5B **Publicly Held**
SIC: 8099 Health & allied services
HQ: Neighborcare Pharmacy Services, Inc.
201 E 4th St Ste 900
Cincinnati OH 45202

(G-15157)
NEIGHBORHOOD CONNECTION
200 S Walnut St (67213-4730)
PHONE..................................316 267-0197
Laurel Alkire, *Director*
EMP: 30
SALES (est): 297.4K **Privately Held**
SIC: 8322 Senior citizens' center or association

(G-15158)
NESTEGG CONSULTING INC
100 N Main St Fl 10 (67202-1322)
P.O. Box 1 (67201-5001)
PHONE..................................316 383-1064
Troy Jordan, *President*
EMP: 13 **EST:** 1996
SALES (est): 1.3MM **Privately Held**
SIC: 6411 Pension & retirement plan consultants

(G-15159)
NET SYSTEMS LLC
2709 E Boulevard Plz (67211-3813)
PHONE..................................316 691-9400
Sam Rothe, *Technology*
Dave Perkins,
Stephanie Larkins, *Executive Asst*
Beth Perkins,
EMP: 11
SQ FT: 2,900
SALES (est): 1.3MM **Privately Held**
WEB: www.net-systems.net
SIC: 1731 7379 Computer installation; computer related maintenance services

(G-15160)
NET-ABILITY LLC
2420 N Woodlawn Blvd 100a (67220-3960)
PHONE..................................316 691-4527
Rob Whitmer, *President*
Aaron Stanyer, *Senior Engr*
Chris Douglas, *Info Tech Dir*
EMP: 10
SQ FT: 5,000
SALES: 1.7MM **Privately Held**
SIC: 3571 Electronic computers

(G-15161)
NETAPP INC
3718 N Rock Rd (67226-1308)
PHONE..................................316 636-8000
David Bell, *Engineer*
Kody Fleming, *Engineer*
Shailendra Hebsur, *Engineer*
Keith Holt, *Engineer*
Thomas Kapla, *Engineer*
EMP: 31 **Publicly Held**
SIC: 7373 Computer integrated systems design
PA: Netapp, Inc.
1395 Crossman Ave
Sunnyvale CA 94089

(G-15162)
NETCO CONSTRUCTION CO INC
Also Called: Netco Home Improvement Center
1650 S Meridian Ave Ste 7 (67213-1992)
PHONE..................................316 942-2062
Gaylan Nett, *President*
Gaylan Nett Jr, *Vice Pres*
Tiffany Bass, *Admin Sec*
EMP: 40 **EST:** 1962
SQ FT: 6,000
SALES (est): 4.9MM **Privately Held**
WEB: www.netcoremodeling.com
SIC: 1542 1521 Commercial & office buildings, renovation & repair; general remodeling, single-family houses

(G-15163)
NEUROLOGY ASSOCIATES KANS LLC
Also Called: Neurological Associates Kansas
3243 E Murdock St Ste 104 (67208-3018)
PHONE..................................316 682-5544
Todd A Evans, *CEO*
EMP: 13
SALES (est): 811.2K **Publicly Held**
SIC: 8011 Neurologist
PA: Hca Healthcare, Inc.
1 Park Plz
Nashville TN 37203

(G-15164)
NEUROLOGY CENTER OF WICHITA
220 S Hillside St Ste A (67211-2151)
PHONE..................................316 686-6866
Dr Subhash Shah, *Owner*
Diana Whitson, *Office Mgr*
Maria Garcia, *Assistant*
EMP: 11
SALES (est): 1.2MM **Privately Held**
WEB: www.pedsbrain.com
SIC: 8011 Neurologist

(G-15165)
NEUROLOGY CONSULTANTS KANS LLC
2135 N Collective Ln (67206-3560)
PHONE..................................316 261-3220
Bart A Grelinger MD,
EMP: 20
SALES (est): 3.2MM **Privately Held**
SIC: 8011 Neurologist

(G-15166)
NEW FRONTIER LAWN CARE INC (PA)
Also Called: New Frontier Lawn & Tree Care
2533 E 36th Cir N (67219-2303)
PHONE..................................316 838-0778
Kenneth Matthies, *President*
EMP: 60
SQ FT: 8,000
SALES: 1MM **Privately Held**
WEB: www.newfrontierlawn.com
SIC: 0782 Lawn care services

(G-15167)
NEW IMAGE ROOFING LLC
114 N Wabash Ave (67214-3944)
P.O. Box 610, Andover (67002-0610)
PHONE..................................316 201-1180
Christopher Lent, *President*
EMP: 20
SQ FT: 11,000
SALES: 3.5MM **Privately Held**
SIC: 1761 Roofing contractor

(G-15168)
NEW MARKET HEALTH CARE LLC
2131 N Ridge Rd Ste 101 (67212-1571)
PHONE..................................316 773-1212
Karla Clark, *Mng Member*
EMP: 25
SALES (est): 3.1MM **Privately Held**
WEB: www.newmedicalhealthcare.com
SIC: 8011 General & family practice, physician/surgeon

(G-15169)
NEW SONG ACADEMY INC
Also Called: New Song Academy Preshool
6868 E 32nd St N (67226-1263)
PHONE..................................316 688-1911
Phyllis Lowen, *President*
Donna Leonetti, *Professor*
EMP: 40
SQ FT: 27,000
SALES (est): 1.4MM **Privately Held**
SIC: 8351 Preschool center

(G-15170)
NEW WINDOWS FOR AMERICA LLC
3949 N Bridgeport Cir (67219-3300)
PHONE..................................316 263-0711
Kirby Stucky, *Principal*
Darian Marx, *Principal*
Heath Marx, *Principal*
EMP: 15
SQ FT: 1,600
SALES (est): 805.1K **Privately Held**
SIC: 5031 Windows

(G-15171)
NEW YORK LIFE INSURANCE CO
125 N Market St Ste 1600 (67202-1716)
PHONE..................................316 262-0671
Joseph Tigert, *Manager*
Bernard Zaleski, *Agent*
EMP: 15
SALES (corp-wide): 10.8B **Privately Held**
WEB: www.newyorklife.com
SIC: 6411 Insurance agents & brokers
PA: New York Life Insurance Company
51 Madison Ave Bsmt 1b
New York NY 10010
212 576-7000

(G-15172)
NEXLEARN LLC
100 S Main St Ste 416 (67202-3737)
PHONE..................................316 265-2170
Dennis Rees, *President*
Brandon Andrews, *Vice Pres*
Dean Fouquet, *Vice Pres*
Truc Nguyen, *Vice Pres*
EMP: 28
SALES (est): 2.1MM **Privately Held**
WEB: www.nexlearn.com
SIC: 8243 8249 8748 Software training, computer; business training services; banking school, training; testing service, educational or personnel

(G-15173)
NEXSTAR BROADCASTING INC
Also Called: Ksnw
833 N Main St (67203-3606)
PHONE..................................316 265-3333
Malea Deschner, *Manager*
EMP: 98
SALES (corp-wide): 2.7B **Publicly Held**
SIC: 4833 Television broadcasting stations
HQ: Nexstar Broadcasting, Inc.
545 E John Carpenter Fwy # 700
Irving TX 75062
972 373-8800

(G-15174)
NEXT LED SIGNS LLC
3526 N Comotara St (67226-1303)
PHONE..................................888 263-6530
Jay S Maxwell, *Mng Member*
Luke Luttrell,
EMP: 15 **EST:** 2011
SALES (est): 1.5MM **Privately Held**
SIC: 3993 Signs & advertising specialties

(G-15175)
NIBARGER TOOL SERVICE INC
1765 N Emporia St (67214-1294)
PHONE..................................316 262-6152
Justin Abraham, *President*
EMP: 7 **EST:** 1947
SQ FT: 5,200
SALES: 800K **Privately Held**
WEB: www.nibargertool.com
SIC: 3545 Machine tool accessories

(G-15176)
NICHOLS LAWN SERVICE INC
2516 E 13th St N (67214-2195)
PHONE..................................316 688-0431
Larry Nichols, *President*
Phyllis Nichols, *Corp Secy*
Chavous Nichols Jr, *Vice Pres*
EMP: 11
SQ FT: 3,200
SALES (est): 532.9K **Privately Held**
SIC: 0782 Lawn care services; spraying services, lawn

(G-15177)
NIES CONSTRUCTION INC
Also Called: Nies Remodeling
10333 E 21st St N Ste 303 (67206-3546)
PHONE..................................316 684-0161
Clifford A Nies, *President*
Betty Joan Nies, *Vice Pres*
EMP: 75
SQ FT: 3,000
SALES: 2.5MM **Privately Held**
SIC: 1521 Single-family home remodeling, additions & repairs

(G-15178)
NIES HOMES INC
10333 E 21st St N Ste 303 (67206-3546)
PHONE..................................316 684-0161
Clifford Nies, *Principal*
EMP: 10
SALES (est): 1.2MM **Privately Held**
SIC: 1521 Single-family home remodeling, additions & repairs

(G-15179)
NIES INVESTMENTS LP
Also Called: Nies Properties
10333 E 21st St N Ste 303 (67206-3546)
PHONE..................................316 684-0161
Clifford A Nies, *Partner*
Joan Nies, *Partner*
EMP: 30
SALES (est): 1.3MM **Privately Held**
SIC: 6513 Apartment building operators

(G-15180)
NIFTY NUT HOUSE LLC
537 N St Francis St (67214-3898)
PHONE..................................316 265-0571
Steve Jahn,
EMP: 11 **EST:** 1937
SQ FT: 12,300
SALES (est): 3.6MM **Privately Held**
SIC: 5145 5441 Candy; nuts, salted or roasted; chewing gum; candy, nut & confectionery stores; candy; nuts

(G-15181)
NINNESCAH SAILING ASSOCIATION
Also Called: NINNESCAH YACHT CLUB
9415 E Harry St Ste 107 (67207-5072)
P.O. Box 1587 (67201-1587)
PHONE..................................316 729-5757
Paul Beddow, *Commodore*
Jim Worthington, *Treasurer*
Lynnette Redington, *Manager*
Rodger Brooks, *Admin Sec*
EMP: 11
SALES: 179.8K **Privately Held**
SIC: 8611 Merchants' association

(G-15182)
NK ASPHALT PARTNERS (PA)
Also Called: Koch Asphalt Solutions-Sw
4111 E 37th St N (67220-3203)
PHONE..................................316 828-5500
Rob Witte, *Partner*
Robert Witte, *Partner*
EMP: 5
SALES (est): 4.9MM **Privately Held**
SIC: 2951 Asphalt paving mixtures & blocks

(G-15183)
NOA GROUP LLC
3629 N Hydraulic St (67219-3811)
PHONE..................................316 821-9700
T D O'Connell,
Michael Northrup,
◆ **EMP:** 17
SQ FT: 40,000
SALES (est): 2.1MM **Privately Held**
WEB: www.noagroup.com
SIC: 2329 Hunting coats & vests, men's

(G-15184)
NOKIA OF AMERICA CORPORATION
3450 N Rock Rd Ste 100 (67226-1351)
PHONE..................................316 636-4800
Jon Heard, *Manager*
EMP: 85
SALES (corp-wide): 25B **Privately Held**
WEB: www.lucent.com
SIC: 7373 1731 Computer integrated systems design; electrical work
HQ: Nokia Of America Corporation
600 Mountain Ave Ste 700
New Providence NJ 07974

(G-15185)
NORRIS QUARRIES LLC
P.O. Box 16507 (67216-0507)
PHONE..................................641 682-3427
Charles Norris, *Principal*
EMP: 7
SALES (est): 549.4K **Privately Held**
SIC: 1422 Crushed & broken limestone

(G-15186)
NORTH AMDON FMLY PHYSICIANS PA
3443 N Amidon Ave (67204-4147)
PHONE..................................316 838-8585
David Wall, *President*
EMP: 12
SALES (est): 1.1MM **Privately Held**
WEB: www.davidwall.com
SIC: 8011 Clinic, operated by physicians

(G-15187)
NORTH AMERICAN BUILDINGS INC
9139 E 37th St N (67226-2010)
P.O. Box 12306 (67277-2306)
PHONE..................................316 821-9590
Tommy R Thompson, *President*
Jerry Dieker, *Project Mgr*
EMP: 15
SQ FT: 7,200
SALES (est): 6.3MM **Privately Held**
SIC: 1542 7359 Commercial & office building, new construction; equipment rental & leasing

(G-15188)
NORTH ROCK HOSP FOR ANIMALS PC
Also Called: Schimmels, Alan D Dvm
8338 E 29th St N (67226-2166)
PHONE..................................316 636-1200
Dr Alan Schimmels, *President*
Dr Max Moss, *Vice Pres*
EMP: 13
SQ FT: 1,200
SALES (est): 928.2K **Privately Held**
WEB: www.northrockvet.com
SIC: 0742 0752 Animal hospital services, pets & other animal specialties; veterinarian, animal specialties; boarding services, kennels

(G-15189)
NORTHERN LIGHTS OIL CO L L C
450 N County Line Rd (67230-7704)
P.O. Box 164, Andover (67002-0164)
PHONE..................................316 733-1515
Chris Sutherland, *Ltd Ptnr*
Mark Sutherland, *Ltd Ptnr*
Tom Sutherland, *Ltd Ptnr*
John Sutherland,
EMP: 5
SQ FT: 1,000
SALES (est): 465.8K **Privately Held**
SIC: 1311 Crude petroleum production

(G-15190)
NORTHERN TOOL & EQP CO INC
6610 W Kellogg Dr (67209-2214)
PHONE..................................316 854-9422
Andy Holf, *Manager*
EMP: 13
SALES (corp-wide): 1.4B **Privately Held**
SIC: 5084 Industrial machinery & equipment

▲ = Import ▼=Export
◆ =Import/Export

PA: Northern Tool & Equipment Company, Inc.
2800 Southcross Dr W
Burnsville MN 55306
952 894-9510

(G-15191)
NORTHRDGE PLYCARE BOARDING LLC
7351 W 33rd St N (67205-9368)
PHONE....316 677-8107
Mark James Ekerberg,
Amy Ekerberg,
EMP: 11
SALES (est): 126.1K **Privately Held**
SIC: 0742 Veterinary services, specialties

(G-15192)
NORTHROCK LANES INC
3232 N Rock Rd (67226-1313)
PHONE....316 636-5444
John Crum, *President*
Cathy Desocio, *General Mgr*
Martha Ann Crum, *Treasurer*
EMP: 50
SQ FT: 40,000
SALES (est): 1.6MM **Privately Held**
SIC: 7933 7299 Ten pin center; banquet hall facilities

(G-15193)
NORTHSTAR AUTOMOTIVE GLASS INC (PA)
2326 S Southeast Blvd (67211-5349)
PHONE....316 686-3648
Gary Dunnegan, *President*
▲ **EMP:** 15
SQ FT: 50,000
SALES (est): 12.7MM **Privately Held**
WEB: www.northstarindustrial.com
SIC: 5013 Automobile glass

(G-15194)
NORTHSTAR PROPERTY MANAGEMENT
203 N Mathewson Ave (67214-4040)
PHONE....316 689-8577
Shelly Peaden, *President*
EMP: 12
SALES (est): 1.2MM **Privately Held**
WEB: www.northstarpm.com
SIC: 6531 6519 Real estate managers; real property lessors

(G-15195)
NORTHWEST CENTRE LLC
8111 E 32nd St N Ste 101 (67226-2631)
PHONE....316 262-3331
Gary L Oborny, *Principal*
EMP: 14
SALES: 880K **Privately Held**
SIC: 6719 Holding companies

(G-15196)
NORTHWEST FREIGHT HANDLERS INC
2531 S Kessler St (67217-1044)
P.O. Box 15231, Spokane Valley WA (99215-5231)
PHONE....509 869-7678
Sergio De Leon, *Branch Mgr*
EMP: 15
SALES (corp-wide): 4.6MM **Privately Held**
WEB: www.northwestfreighthandlers.com
SIC: 4731 Freight forwarding
PA: Northwest Freight Handlers, Inc.
102 E Francis Ave
Spokane WA 99208
509 483-1968

(G-15197)
NORTHWESTERN MUTUAL
10500 E Berkeley Square P (67206-6822)
PHONE....316 265-8139
Sean Miller, *Owner*
Geoffrey Stalker, *Officer*
Douglas Leiker, *Advisor*
Gene Fisher, *Representative*
EMP: 22
SALES: 2.3MM **Privately Held**
SIC: 6411 Insurance agents, brokers & service

(G-15198)
NTS TECHNICAL SYSTEMS
7447 W 33rd St N (67205-9356)
PHONE....316 832-1600
Matthew Lutz, *Manager*
EMP: 13
SALES (corp-wide): 301.2MM **Privately Held**
SIC: 8734 8742 Testing laboratories; quality assurance consultant
HQ: Nts Technical Systems
2125 E Katella Ave # 250
Anaheim CA 92806
714 450-9100

(G-15199)
NU-LINE COMPANY INC (PA)
3310 W Central Ave (67203-4916)
PHONE....316 942-0990
James Burleson, *President*
Mike Martin, *Associate*
EMP: 10
SQ FT: 16,000
SALES (est): 1.6MM **Privately Held**
WEB: www.nulinesigns.com
SIC: 1721 3669 Pavement marking contractor; transportation signaling devices; traffic signals, electric

(G-15200)
NUSTAR PIPELINE OPER PARTNR LP
Also Called: Kaneb Pipe Line
7340 W 21st St N Ste 200 (67205-1770)
PHONE....316 773-9000
Anna Kostecki, *Personnel*
Ron Simmons, *Manager*
EMP: 10 **Publicly Held**
WEB: www.kanebpipeline.com
SIC: 8741 Administrative management
HQ: Nustar Pipeline Operating Partnership Lp
2608 E Highway 50
Yankton SD 57078
605 665-4764

(G-15201)
NVT WICHITA LLC (HQ)
Also Called: Ksnw-TV
833 N Main St (67203-3606)
P.O. Box 333 (67201-0333)
PHONE....316 265-3333
Al Buch,
Constance Goodson,
Georgianna Mattke,
Wade O'Hagan,
EMP: 41
SQ FT: 35,000
SALES (est): 16.1MM
SALES (corp-wide): 33.4MM **Privately Held**
WEB: www.ksn.com
SIC: 4833 7313 Television broadcasting stations; television & radio time sales
PA: New Vision Group, Llc
3525 Piedmont Rd Ne
Atlanta GA 30305
404 995-4711

(G-15202)
O2 CORPORATION
235 N Washington Ave (67202-2817)
PHONE....316 634-1240
Sherman Burt Parry Jr, *President*
Arthur Gill, *Director*
EMP: 12
SQ FT: 6,000
SALES: 1.3MM **Privately Held**
WEB: www.o2corporation.com
SIC: 3841 Inhalation therapy equipment

(G-15203)
OAKLAND AVENUE CRAFTSMEN CO
29 N Cypress Dr (67206-2536)
P.O. Box 781714 (67278-1714)
PHONE....316 685-3955
Steve Jacobs, *Owner*
EMP: 12
SALES (est): 786.5K **Privately Held**
SIC: 1521 New construction, single-family houses

(G-15204)
OASIS PRODUCTIONS
8351 E 35th St N (67226-1326)
PHONE....316 210-4488
CJ Wilson, *Principal*
EMP: 11
SALES (est): 124.8K **Privately Held**
SIC: 7822 Motion picture & tape distribution

(G-15205)
OC SERVICES
2126 N Shadybrook (67214)
P.O. Box 8486 (67208-0486)
PHONE....316 655-3952
Richard Holt, *Principal*
EMP: 12
SALES (est): 677.9K **Privately Held**
SIC: 8744 Facilities support services

(G-15206)
OCCIDENTAL CHEMICAL CORP
6200 S Ridge Rd (67215-8822)
P.O. Box 12283 (67277-2283)
PHONE....316 524-4211
John Brenon, *Plant Mgr*
Ed Hoeller, *Human Res Dir*
Paul N Tobia, *Branch Mgr*
EMP: 45
SALES (corp-wide): 18.9B **Publicly Held**
WEB: www.oxychem.com
SIC: 2819 Industrial inorganic chemicals
HQ: Occidental Chemical Corporation
14555 Dallas Pkwy Ste 400
Dallas TX 75254
972 404-3800

(G-15207)
OCONNOR COMPANY INC
5200 E 35th St N Ste B (67220-3400)
PHONE....316 263-3187
Aaron Magnus, *Branch Mgr*
EMP: 15
SALES (corp-wide): 116.3MM **Privately Held**
SIC: 5075 Air conditioning & ventilation equipment & supplies
HQ: O'connor Company, Inc.
16910 W 116th St
Lenexa KS 66219
913 894-8788

(G-15208)
OCONNOR COMPANY INC
Also Called: J M O'Connor Co
811 E Bayley St (67211-3310)
PHONE....316 267-2246
Wendell Miller, *Manager*
EMP: 22
SALES (corp-wide): 116.3MM **Privately Held**
WEB: www.oconnor-hvac.com
SIC: 5075 Warm air heating & air conditioning
HQ: O'connor Company, Inc.
16910 W 116th St
Lenexa KS 66219
913 894-8788

(G-15209)
OCONNOR COMPANY INC
5200 E 35th St N (67220-3400)
PHONE....316 263-3187
Wendall Miller, *Manager*
EMP: 20
SALES (corp-wide): 116.3MM **Privately Held**
WEB: www.oconnor-hvac.com
SIC: 5075 Air conditioning & ventilation equipment & supplies
HQ: O'connor Company, Inc.
16910 W 116th St
Lenexa KS 66219
913 894-8788

(G-15210)
OFC OF US TRUSTEE
301 N Main St Ste 1150 (67202-4811)
PHONE....316 269-6607
Phyllis Creed, *Librarian*
Frank Prevost, *Officer*
Felicia Turner, *Administration*
EMP: 15
SALES (est): 605K **Privately Held**
SIC: 8111 Bankruptcy law

(G-15211)
OFLYNN CONTRACTING INC
Also Called: Midwest Painting
120 N Westfield St (67212-3740)
PHONE....316 524-2500
Rick O'Flynn, *President*
EMP: 13 **EST:** 1971
SQ FT: 8,000
SALES (est): 1MM **Privately Held**
SIC: 1721 Commercial painting

(G-15212)
OIL PRODUCERS INC OF KANSAS
1710 N Waterfront Pkwy (67206-6603)
PHONE....316 681-0231
Melody Fletcher, *President*
Brian McCoy, *Vice Pres*
Greg Gleason, *Controller*
EMP: 13
SQ FT: 1,400
SALES (est): 2.6MM **Privately Held**
SIC: 1311 Crude petroleum production

(G-15213)
OLD DOMINION FREIGHT LINE INC
4520 S Santa Fe St (67216-1752)
PHONE....316 522-3562
Jason Kelly, *Branch Mgr*
EMP: 53
SALES (corp-wide): 4B **Publicly Held**
WEB: www.odfl.com
SIC: 4213 Less-than-truckload (LTL) transport
PA: Old Dominion Freight Line Inc
500 Old Dominion Way
Thomasville NC 27360
336 889-5000

(G-15214)
OLD MISSION MORTUARY
3424 E 21st St N (67208-1513)
PHONE....316 686-7311
Marilyn Nichols, *General Mgr*
Les Kline, *General Mgr*
EMP: 25
SALES (est): 881.1K **Privately Held**
SIC: 7261 Funeral home

(G-15215)
OMEGA SENIOR LIVING LLC
333 S Broadway Ave # 105 (67202-4300)
PHONE....316 260-9494
Lynn Lavallee, *COO*
Lori Prothro, *Human Res Dir*
Craig Hanson, *Mng Member*
Erin Kofoed, *Executive Asst*
Robert Hanson,
EMP: 1000
SALES (est): 13.3MM **Privately Held**
SIC: 8361 Home for the aged

(G-15216)
OMNI AEROSPACE INC
3130 W Pawnee St (67213-1826)
P.O. Box 13278 (67213-0278)
PHONE....316 529-8998
Gretchen O'Neill, *President*
Paul Oneill, *Vice Pres*
Michelle Kline, *Controller*
▲ **EMP:** 31
SALES (est): 8.3MM **Privately Held**
WEB: www.omniks.com
SIC: 3699 3824 5088 3728 Electrical equipment & supplies; mechanical & electromechanical counters & devices; aircraft equipment & supplies; aircraft parts & equipment

(G-15217)
OMNI CENTER II
Also Called: Omni Secretarial Service
111 S Whittier St (67207-1045)
P.O. Box 782253 (67278-2253)
PHONE....316 689-4256
Roger Farrow, *Partner*
EMP: 10
SALES (est): 431.1K **Privately Held**
SIC: 7338 6531 Secretarial & typing service; real estate agents & managers

GEOGRAPHIC

(G-15218)
OMNI CENTER LP (PA)
Also Called: Omni Secretarial
111 S Whittier Rd (67207-1045)
PHONE..................................316 268-9108
Roger Farrow, *Principal*
EMP: 11
SQ FT: 46,000
SALES (est): 1MM **Privately Held**
SIC: 6512 Nonresidential building operators

(G-15219)
ON-LINE COMMUNICATIONS INC
7370 E 37th St N Ste 100 (67226-3241)
PHONE..................................316 831-0500
D'Lisa Barcenas, *Branch Mgr*
EMP: 242
SALES (corp-wide): 12.1MM **Privately Held**
WEB: www.on-linecom.com
SIC: 7389 8732 Telemarketing services; market analysis or research
PA: On-Line Communications, Inc.
2300 Stonewall Dr
Bartlesville OK 74006
918 338-2000

(G-15220)
ONEOK INC
Also Called: Kansas Gas Service
1021 E 26th St N (67219-4308)
PHONE..................................316 821-2722
Brad Dixon, *Manager*
EMP: 22
SALES (corp-wide): 12.5B **Publicly Held**
WEB: www.oneok.com
SIC: 4922 4924 Pipelines, natural gas; natural gas distribution
PA: Oneok, Inc.
100 W 5th St Ste Ll
Tulsa OK 74103
918 588-7000

(G-15221)
OPEN ARMS LTHRAN CHILD DEV CTR
12885 W Maple St (67235-8717)
PHONE..................................316 721-5675
Lynae Reese, *Manager*
EMP: 32
SALES (est): 554.7K **Privately Held**
SIC: 8351 Preschool center

(G-15222)
OPEN ROAD BRANDS LLC
1425 E Douglas Ave # 300 (67211-1640)
PHONE..................................316 337-7550
Robert Hayes, *President*
Christopher Hayes, *Director*
▲ **EMP:** 12
SQ FT: 500,000
SALES (est): 2.7MM **Privately Held**
SIC: 2679 Wallboard, decorated: made from purchased material

(G-15223)
OPPORTUNITY PROJECT LRNG CTR
Also Called: T O P Learning Center
4600 S Clifton Ave (67216-3063)
PHONE..................................316 522-8677
Tammy Blunt, *Finance*
Cornelia Steven, *Exec Dir*
Janice Smith, *Exec Dir*
Cornelia Stevens, *Exec Dir*
EMP: 25
SALES (est): 4.8MM **Privately Held**
SIC: 8699 Charitable organization

(G-15224)
OPTI-LIFE EAST WICHITA LLC
9758 E 21st St N (67206-3201)
PHONE..................................316 927-5959
Matthew J Lillie, *Mng Member*
Kien Huynh,
EMP: 75
SQ FT: 34,000
SALES (est): 182.6K **Privately Held**
SIC: 7991 Physical fitness facilities

(G-15225)
OPTI-LIFE SERVICES LLC
7200 W 13th St N Ste 5 (67212-2968)
PHONE..................................316 518-8757
Matt Lillie, *CEO*
Tien Huynh, *COO*
EMP: 35
SALES (est): 156.8K **Privately Held**
SIC: 7991 Athletic club & gymnasiums, membership

(G-15226)
OPTILEAF INCORPORATED
924 N Main St (67203-3607)
PHONE..................................855 678-4532
Thomas Tran, *President*
Nick Nguyen, *COO*
EMP: 5
SALES: 26.7K **Privately Held**
SIC: 7372 Business oriented computer software

(G-15227)
OPTIMAL PERFORMANCE LLC
11444 E Central Ave (67206-2805)
PHONE..................................316 440-4440
Landon Langston, *Mng Member*
EMP: 18
SALES (est): 622.5K **Privately Held**
SIC: 8331 Community service employment training program

(G-15228)
OPTIMIST INTERNATIONAL
Also Called: Northeast Optimist Club
6215 Clairedon (67220)
P.O. Box 8104 (67208-0104)
PHONE..................................316 744-0849
Billy Berkenridge, *President*
EMP: 27
SALES (corp-wide): 4.6MM **Privately Held**
WEB: www.severnaparkoptimistclub.org
SIC: 8641 Social associations
PA: Optimist International
4494 Lindell Blvd
Saint Louis MO 63108
314 371-6000

(G-15229)
OPTIMUZ MANUFACTURING INC
2331 S Mead St (67211-5023)
PHONE..................................316 519-1354
Oscar Rodriguez, *President*
EMP: 24
SALES (est): 390.8K **Privately Held**
SIC: 3728 3751 3841 Aircraft parts & equipment; motorcycles, bicycles & parts; surgical & medical instruments

(G-15230)
ORAL AND MAXILLA FACIAL ASSOC
1919 N Webb Rd (67206-3405)
PHONE..................................316 634-1414
Kent Nelson, *Partner*
Remy H Blanchaert, *Surgeon*
EMP: 30
SALES (est): 2.4MM **Privately Held**
SIC: 8011 Surgeon

(G-15231)
ORANGETHEORY FITNESS
1423 N Webb Rd Ste 159 (67206-3431)
PHONE..................................316 440-4640
Pat Walsh, *Owner*
EMP: 18
SALES (est): 46.2K **Privately Held**
SIC: 7991 Physical fitness facilities

(G-15232)
OREILLY AUTOMOTIVE STORES INC
3109 E Pawnee St (67211-5605)
PHONE..................................316 685-7900
Eric Workington, *Manager*
EMP: 10 **Publicly Held**
WEB: www.oreillyauto.com
SIC: 5531 5013 Automotive parts; automotive supplies & parts
HQ: O'reilly Automotive Stores, Inc.
233 S Patterson Ave
Springfield MO 65802
417 862-2674

(G-15233)
OREILLY AUTOMOTIVE STORES INC
Also Called: O'Reilly Auto Parts
544 N Tyler Rd (67212-3633)
PHONE..................................316 729-7311
Cody Zimmerman, *Manager*
EMP: 16 **Publicly Held**
WEB: www.oreillyauto.com
SIC: 5013 5531 5063 Motor vehicle supplies & new parts; automotive & home supply stores; automotive parts; storage batteries, industrial
HQ: O'reilly Automotive Stores, Inc.
233 S Patterson Ave
Springfield MO 65802
417 862-2674

(G-15234)
OREILLY AUTOMOTIVE STORES INC
Also Called: O'Reilly Auto Parts
4850 E 13th St N (67208-2853)
PHONE..................................316 686-5536
Jason Riter, *Manager*
EMP: 14 **Publicly Held**
WEB: www.oreillyauto.com
SIC: 5013 5531 5063 Motor vehicle supplies & new parts; automotive parts; storage batteries, industrial
HQ: O'reilly Automotive Stores, Inc.
233 S Patterson Ave
Springfield MO 65802
417 862-2674

(G-15235)
OREILLY AUTOMOTIVE STORES INC
Also Called: O'Reilly Auto Parts
2219 S Seneca St (67213-4224)
PHONE..................................316 264-6422
Tom Vosika, *Manager*
EMP: 30 **Publicly Held**
WEB: www.oreillyauto.com
SIC: 5013 5531 5063 Automotive supplies & parts; automotive parts; storage batteries, industrial
HQ: O'reilly Automotive Stores, Inc.
233 S Patterson Ave
Springfield MO 65802
417 862-2674

(G-15236)
OREILLY AUTOMOTIVE STORES INC
Also Called: O'Reilly Auto Parts
714 W 21st St N (67203-2442)
PHONE..................................316 831-9112
William Smith, *Manager*
EMP: 11 **Publicly Held**
WEB: www.oreillyauto.com
SIC: 5531 5063 Automotive accessories; automotive parts; storage batteries, industrial
HQ: O'reilly Automotive Stores, Inc.
233 S Patterson Ave
Springfield MO 65802
417 862-2674

(G-15237)
ORTHOPEDIC & SPORTS MEDICINE
10100 E Shannon Woods St # 1 (67226-4105)
PHONE..................................316 219-8299
Jennifer L Aleebrahim, *Principal*
EMP: 26
SALES (est): 4.1MM **Privately Held**
SIC: 8011 Orthopedic physician

(G-15238)
OS COMPANIES INC (PA)
301 S Market St (67202-3805)
PHONE..................................316 265-5611
Michael W O'Shaughnessy, *President*
P E Oshaughnessy, *Chairman*
David Loger, *CFO*
EMP: 23
SQ FT: 2,000
SALES (est): 63.6MM **Privately Held**
SIC: 1311 1382 6552 Crude petroleum production; natural gas production; oil & gas exploration services; land subdividers & developers, commercial; land subdividers & developers, residential

(G-15239)
OSI
4316 E Lewis St (67218-1346)
PHONE..................................316 688-5011
Willis Overholt, *Principal*
EMP: 6
SALES (est): 415.4K **Privately Held**
SIC: 2011 Meat packing plants

(G-15240)
OVERHEAD DOOR COMPANY
6215 E Kellogg Dr (67218-1746)
PHONE..................................316 265-4634
Michael J Sweeney, *President*
Deana D Bushell, *Manager*
EMP: 35
SALES (est): 8.4MM **Privately Held**
WEB: www.overheaddoorwichita.com
SIC: 5211 7699 5999 5084 Garage doors, sale & installation; door & window repair; awnings; materials handling machinery; door opening & closing devices, electrical; carpentry work

(G-15241)
OVERLAND CHARTERS INC
3333 N Hillside Ave (67219-3907)
PHONE..................................316 652-9463
Kelly Sankhauser, *President*
Rick Bannister, *Office Mgr*
EMP: 50
SALES (est): 855.4K **Privately Held**
SIC: 4142 Bus charter service, except local

(G-15242)
OWENS BONDING INC
Also Called: Patriot Pawn & Firearms
600 N Main St Ste 200 (67203-3625)
PHONE..................................316 283-3983
Stephen Owens, *Owner*
EMP: 26
SALES (est): 862.4K **Privately Held**
SIC: 7381 7389 Detective services; bail bonding

(G-15243)
OXFORD GRAND ASSISTED LIVING
3051 N Park Pl (67204-6332)
PHONE..................................316 927-2007
Stacy Hawkins, *Director*
EMP: 80
SALES (est): 1MM **Privately Held**
SIC: 8051 Skilled nursing care facilities

(G-15244)
OXFORD MANAGEMENT GROUP LLC (PA)
Also Called: Oxford Senior Living
125 N Market St Ste 1230 (67202-1712)
PHONE..................................316 201-3210
Jason W Wiley, *CEO*
J Chris Dennis, *CFO*
EMP: 21 **EST:** 2010
SALES (est): 2.6MM **Privately Held**
SIC: 8322 Geriatric social service; adult day care center

(G-15245)
OZANAM PATHWAYS
315 N Hillside St (67214-4915)
PHONE..................................316 682-4000
Dorothy Lloyd, *Exec Dir*
EMP: 20
SALES (est): 64.7K **Privately Held**
SIC: 8699 Charitable organization

(G-15246)
P & A INVESTMENTS
Also Called: Northrock Suites
7856 E 36th St N (67226-3808)
P.O. Box 1357 (67201-1357)
PHONE..................................316 634-2303
Harry Pollak, *President*
EMP: 50
SALES (est): 2MM **Privately Held**
SIC: 7011 Motels

(G-15247)
P & W INCORPORATED
Also Called: Roto-Rooter
801 E Mount Vernon St (67211-5035)
PHONE..................................316 267-4277
Wanda N Farmer, *President*
Terrye Stidham, *Managing Dir*

Jane Jantz, *Treasurer*
Paul Farmer II, *Admin Sec*
EMP: 20 **EST:** 1992
SQ FT: 10,500
SALES (est): 1.7MM **Privately Held**
WEB: www.wichitarooter.com
SIC: 7699 1711 Sewer cleaning & rodding; plumbing contractors

(G-15248)
P A HEARTLAND CARDIOLOGY
8710 W 13th St N Ste 102 (67212-6255)
PHONE..................................316 773-5300
Assem Farhat, *President*
Ravi K Bajaj, *Treasurer*
EMP: 11 **Privately Held**
SIC: 8011 Cardiologist & cardio-vascular specialist
PA: P A Heartland Cardiology
3535 N Webb Rd
Wichita KS 67226

(G-15249)
P A HEARTLAND CARDIOLOGY (PA)
3535 N Webb Rd (67226-8127)
PHONE..................................316 686-5300
Ravi K Bajaj, *Director*
EMP: 48
SALES (est): 578.3K **Privately Held**
SIC: 8011 Cardiologist & cardio-vascular specialist

(G-15250)
P B HOIDALE CO INC
3737 W Harry St (67213-1413)
P.O. Box 12104 (67277-2104)
PHONE..................................316 942-1361
Brain Basgall, *Branch Mgr*
EMP: 15
SALES (corp-wide): 26.5MM **Privately Held**
WEB: www.hoidale.com
SIC: 5084 Industrial machinery & equipment
PA: P. B. Hoidale Co., Inc.
3801 W Harry St
Wichita KS 67213
316 942-1361

(G-15251)
P F S GROUP LIMITED
Also Called: Re/Max
1835 N Tony Ln (67212-1579)
PHONE..................................316 722-0001
H Wayne Short, *President*
Beverly Giles, *Manager*
Michelle Briggs, *Real Est Agnt*
Kimberly Wimmer, *Real Est Agnt*
Dixie Ball, *Associate*
EMP: 50
SQ FT: 12,000
SALES (est): 3MM **Privately Held**
SIC: 6531 Real estate agent, residential

(G-15252)
P1 GROUP INC
Also Called: P 1
2333 S West St Ste 319 (67213-1116)
PHONE..................................316 267-3256
Smitty Belcher, *Sales/Mktg Dir*
EMP: 30
SALES (corp-wide): 243.8MM **Privately Held**
WEB: www.p1group.com
SIC: 1711 Warm air heating & air conditioning contractor; refrigeration contractor; plumbing contractors
PA: P1 Group, Inc.
13605 W 96th Ter
Lenexa KS 66215
913 529-5000

(G-15253)
PAINT MASTERS INC
2801 E Kellogg Dr (67211-2922)
PHONE..................................316 683-5203
Scott R Cloud, *President*
Mike Cranston, *Treasurer*
EMP: 17
SALES (est): 1.3MM **Privately Held**
SIC: 1721 1761 1521 1542 Exterior residential painting contractor; interior residential painting contractor; exterior commercial painting contractor; interior commercial painting contractor; siding contractor; general remodeling, single-family houses; commercial & office buildings, renovation & repair

(G-15254)
PARACOM TECHNOLOGIES INC
3020 N Cypress St 200b (67226-4009)
PHONE..................................316 293-2900
Jay Feist, *President*
EMP: 25
SQ FT: 7,032
SALES (est): 1.5MM **Privately Held**
SIC: 7373 Computer integrated systems design

(G-15255)
PARADIGM ALLIANCE INC (PA)
222 S Ridge Rd (67209-2113)
P.O. Box 9123 (67277-0123)
PHONE..................................316 554-9225
Steve McGaffin, *President*
David Wilkerson, *Senior VP*
Tim Friesen, *Prdtn Mgr*
Rob Falconio, *Sales Executive*
Marina King, *Mktg Coord*
EMP: 27
SQ FT: 6,000
SALES (est): 5.8MM **Privately Held**
SIC: 7389 Photogrammatic mapping

(G-15256)
PARADIGM LIAISON SERVICES LLC
222 S Ridge Rd (67209-2113)
P.O. Box 9123 (67277-0123)
PHONE..................................316 554-9225
Greg Klenda, *Principal*
EMP: 30 **EST:** 2007
SALES (est): 831.6K
SALES (corp-wide): 5.8MM **Privately Held**
SIC: 8741 Industrial management
PA: The Paradigm Alliance Inc
222 S Ridge Rd
Wichita KS 67209
316 554-9225

(G-15257)
PARAGON AEROSPACE SERVICES
Also Called: Paragon Services
1015 S West St (67213-1627)
PHONE..................................316 945-5285
Brock Elliot, *President*
EMP: 50
SQ FT: 24,000
SALES (est): 5.1MM **Privately Held**
SIC: 7389 Safety inspection service

(G-15258)
PARAGON GEOPHYSICAL SVCS INC
3500 N Rock Rd Bldg 800b (67226-1347)
PHONE..................................316 636-5552
John H Beury III, *President*
Jeff Logan, *Vice Pres*
Alexandra Beury, *Admin Sec*
EMP: 47
SQ FT: 1,600
SALES (est): 10.9MM **Privately Held**
WEB: www.paragongeo.com
SIC: 1382 Geophysical exploration, oil & gas field

(G-15259)
PARAGON N D T & FINISHES INC
1015 S West St (67213-1694)
PHONE..................................316 945-5285
Dail Graham, *Ch of Bd*
Larry G Elliot, *President*
EMP: 50
SQ FT: 14,000
SALES (est): 2.6MM **Privately Held**
SIC: 8734 3471 7699 8731 Testing laboratories; finishing, metals or formed products; aircraft flight instrument repair; commercial physical research; radio & television repair; paints & allied products

(G-15260)
PARAGON NDT LLC
2210 S Edwards St (67213-1870)
PHONE..................................316 927-4283
Nathan Vandergriend, *Mng Member*
Jim Hallberg,
EMP: 22 **EST:** 2015
SALES (est): 336K **Privately Held**
SIC: 7389 Inspection & testing services

(G-15261)
PARAMOUNT MANAGEMENT CORP (PA)
3413 W 13th St N (67203-4561)
PHONE..................................316 269-4477
Cynthia C Branch, *President*
Sandra D Hudspeth, *Treasurer*
J D White, *Admin Sec*
EMP: 41
SQ FT: 2,000
SALES (est): 2.9MM **Privately Held**
SIC: 6531 Real estate managers

(G-15262)
PARK WEST PLAZA LLC
505 N Maize Rd Ofc (67212-4690)
PHONE..................................316 729-4114
Jay Russell, *Managing Prtnr*
April Leason, *Sales Executive*
John McKay,
EMP: 60
SQ FT: 80,000
SALES (est): 3.4MM **Privately Held**
WEB: www.parkwestplaza.com
SIC: 6513 Apartment hotel operation; retirement hotel operation

(G-15263)
PARKER ENTERPRISES INC
Also Called: Four Seasons Cleaners
858 S Hillside St (67211-3004)
PHONE..................................316 682-4543
John Parker, *CEO*
Billie Sue Parker, *President*
EMP: 20
SALES (est): 250.8K **Privately Held**
SIC: 7216 Drycleaning plants, except rugs

(G-15264)
PARKER OIL CO INC (PA)
4343 S West St (67217-3815)
P.O. Box 17383 (67217-0383)
PHONE..................................316 529-4343
James L Selenke, *President*
Renee Selenke, *Admin Sec*
EMP: 16
SQ FT: 33,600
SALES (est): 18.4MM **Privately Held**
WEB: www.parkeroilco.com
SIC: 5171 5411 Petroleum bulk stations; convenience stores, independent

(G-15265)
PARKLANE AA
1060 S Oliver St (67218-3218)
PHONE..................................316 682-9960
Tim Muir, *Manager*
EMP: 11
SALES (est): 186.6K **Privately Held**
SIC: 8322 Alcoholism counseling, nontreatment

(G-15266)
PARKLANE TOWERS INC
5051 E Lincoln St Ofc Ofc (67218-2499)
PHONE..................................316 684-7247
Kress Fall, *General Mgr*
EMP: 18
SALES (est): 1.2MM **Privately Held**
WEB: www.parklanetowersinc.com
SIC: 6513 Apartment hotel operation

(G-15267)
PARTY BNCE MONWALK RENTALS LLC
4323 W 31st St S (67215-1010)
PHONE..................................316 519-5174
David Clanton,
EMP: 10
SALES (est): 289.6K **Privately Held**
SIC: 7359 Equipment rental & leasing

(G-15268)
PATRICK J PIRROTE OD PA
Also Called: Child & Family Optometry
746 N Maize Rd Ste 100 (67212-4571)
PHONE..................................316 721-8877
Patrick J Pirotte Od, *President*
EMP: 19
SALES (est): 1.2MM **Privately Held**
WEB: www.childandfamilyoptometry.com
SIC: 8042 Offices & clinics of optometrists

(G-15269)
PATTERSON DENTAL SUPPLY INC
Also Called: Patterson Dental 360
8201 E 34th Cir N # 1307 (67226-1490)
PHONE..................................316 315-1800
Pat Crowley, *Branch Mgr*
EMP: 15
SALES (corp-wide): 5.5B **Publicly Held**
WEB: www.pattersondentalsupply.com
SIC: 5047 Dental equipment & supplies
HQ: Patterson Dental Supply, Inc.
1031 Mendota Heights Rd
Saint Paul MN 55120
651 686-1600

(G-15270)
PATTON TERMITE & PEST CTRL INC
7920 W Kellogg Dr Ste 100 (67209-2159)
PHONE..................................316 773-3825
Mike Patton, *President*
Lora Patton, *Vice Pres*
EMP: 10 **EST:** 2002
SALES (est): 1.2MM **Privately Held**
WEB: www.pattonkeehn.com
SIC: 7342 Pest control services

(G-15271)
PAUL W MURPHY MD
1855 N Webb Rd (67206-3413)
PHONE..................................316 686-6303
Paul W Murphy MD, *Principal*
EMP: 25 **EST:** 2001
SALES (est): 675.7K **Privately Held**
SIC: 8063 Psychiatric hospitals

(G-15272)
PAVING CONSTRUCTION INC (PA)
212 N Market St Ste 315 (67202-2016)
PHONE..................................316 684-6161
Doug Hammond, *President*
EMP: 10
SQ FT: 1,000
SALES (est): 2.1MM **Privately Held**
SIC: 1611 1771 Resurfacing contractor; parking lot construction

(G-15273)
PAWNEE AVENUE CHURCH OF GOD
Also Called: Corinthian Nursery School
2611 E Pawnee St (67211-5521)
P.O. Box 16417 (67216-0417)
PHONE..................................316 683-5648
Darrin Early, *Principal*
Dennis Early, *Pastor*
Janet Robertson, *Exec Dir*
EMP: 25
SALES (est): 936.7K **Privately Held**
SIC: 8661 8351 Church of God; child day care services

(G-15274)
PBP MANAGEMENT GROUP INC
Also Called: P B P
4029 N Sweet Bay Ct (67226-3510)
PHONE..................................316 262-2900
Christopher Lee, *President*
EMP: 35
SALES: 2.1MM **Privately Held**
WEB: www.pbpmgmtgroup.com
SIC: 8742 Administrative services consultant

(G-15275)
PEARSON CONSTRUCTION LLC
3450 N Rock Rd Ste 300 (67226-1327)
PHONE..................................316 263-3100
Scott Bratcher, *Superintendent*
Kurtis Cornejo, *Mng Member*
EMP: 150

GEOGRAPHIC

SALES (est): 6MM **Privately Held**
SIC: 1795 1623 1794 1629 Demolition, buildings & other structures; sewer line construction; excavation work; earthmoving contractor

(G-15276)
PEARSON EXCAVATING INC
821 E 25th St N (67219-4433)
P.O. Box 4687 (67204-0687)
PHONE..................................316 263-3100
George Pearson Jr, *President*
Patrick McKean, *Corp Secy*
Coy Johnson, *Vice Pres*
EMP: 48
SQ FT: 5,824
SALES (est): 6.8MM **Privately Held**
SIC: 1794 Excavation & grading, building construction

(G-15277)
PENN MUTUAL LIFE INSURANCE CO
5940 E Central Ave (67208-4239)
PHONE..................................316 685-9296
Bruce Schreck, *Branch Mgr*
Ron Gabel, *Manager*
EMP: 14
SALES (corp-wide): 2.8B **Privately Held**
WEB: www.thepfggroup.com
SIC: 6311 Life insurance
PA: The Penn Mutual Life Insurance Co
600 Dresher Rd
Horsham PA 19044
215 956-8000

(G-15278)
PENSKE TRUCK LEASING CO LP
1440 S Hoover Rd (67209-2945)
PHONE..................................316 943-8500
Mike Forila, *Manager*
EMP: 10
SALES (corp-wide): 9.6B **Privately Held**
WEB: www.pensketruckleasing.com
SIC: 7513 Truck rental & leasing, no drivers
HQ: Penske Truck Leasing Co., L.P.
2675 Morgantown Rd
Reading PA 19607
610 775-6000

(G-15279)
PEPSI BEVERAGES COMPANY
101 W 48th St S (67217-4937)
PHONE..................................316 522-3131
Bill Mikulka, *President*
EMP: 100
SALES (corp-wide): 64.6B **Publicly Held**
SIC: 2086 5181 Carbonated soft drinks, bottled & canned; beer & other fermented malt liquors
HQ: Pepsi Beverages Company
110 S Byhalia Rd
Collierville TN 38017
901 853-5736

(G-15280)
PEPSI-COLA METRO BTLG CO INC
101 W 48th St S (67217-4937)
PHONE..................................316 529-9840
Tim O'Donohue, *Warehouse Mgr*
Allison Stiverson, *Transportation*
Jeff Raney, *Maint Spvr*
Lee Busch, *Manager*
Greg R Archer, *Maintence Staff*
EMP: 200
SALES (corp-wide): 64.6B **Publicly Held**
WEB: www.joy-of-cola.com
SIC: 2086 Soft drinks: packaged in cans, bottles, etc.; water, pasteurized: packaged in cans, bottles, etc.
HQ: Pepsi-Cola Metropolitan Bottling Company, Inc.
1111 Westchester Ave
White Plains NY 10604
914 767-6000

(G-15281)
PERFECT TOUCH INC
Also Called: Fifth Ave
535 W Douglas Ave Ste 120 (67213-1456)
PHONE..................................316 522-9205
Stacey Floyd, *President*
EMP: 10
SALES: 300K **Privately Held**
SIC: 7231 7299 5621 Hairdressers; tanning salon; boutiques

(G-15282)
PERFECTION STRL COMPONENTS LLC
Also Called: STAR FLOORING AND DECORATING
1666 S Saint Clair Ave (67213-2915)
P.O. Box 7712 (67277-7712)
PHONE..................................316 942-8361
Jennifer Stephens, *Treasurer*
Chris Goebel,
Dan Zimmerman,
EMP: 40
SQ FT: 41,000
SALES: 9.3MM
SALES (corp-wide): 121.2MM **Privately Held**
WEB: www.perfectionstructural.com
SIC: 2439 Trusses, wooden roof
PA: Star Lumber & Supply Co., Inc.
325 S West St
Wichita KS 67213
316 942-2221

(G-15283)
PERFEKTA INC (HQ)
Also Called: Perfekta Aerospace
480 E 21st St N (67214-1234)
PHONE..................................316 263-2056
Julian A Guerra II, *President*
Nick Guerra, *Vice Pres*
Matt Smith, *Vice Pres*
Paulino Sanchez, *Opers Mgr*
Darrin Haring, *Engineer*
EMP: 5
SQ FT: 142,000
SALES (est): 25MM **Privately Held**
WEB: www.perfekta-inc.com
SIC: 3312 3599 Forgings, iron & steel; machine shop, jobbing & repair
PA: Cadence Aerospace Finance, Inc.
3130 E Miraloma Ave
Anaheim CA 92806
714 998-6410

(G-15284)
PERKINELMER INC
3108 N Tee Time (67205-1915)
PHONE..................................316 773-0055
Mark Workkey, *Manager*
EMP: 13
SALES (corp-wide): 2.7B **Publicly Held**
WEB: www.perkinelmer.com
SIC: 3826 Analytical instruments
PA: Perkinelmer, Inc.
940 Winter St
Waltham MA 02451
781 663-6900

(G-15285)
PET HAVEN LLC
2524 W 13th St N (67203-1801)
PHONE..................................316 942-2151
David Thompson, *President*
Diana L Thompson, *Vice Pres*
EMP: 16
SQ FT: 10,000
SALES (est): 1.6MM **Privately Held**
WEB: www.pethaven.com
SIC: 5999 5199 Pets; pets & pet supplies

(G-15286)
PETERSON COMPANIES
505 N Rock Rd Ste 200 (67206-1743)
PHONE..................................316 682-4903
Clark Lindstrom, *President*
EMP: 56
SALES (est): 1.6MM **Privately Held**
SIC: 6531 Real estate agent, residential

(G-15287)
PETROLEUM PROPERTY SERVICES
125 N Market St Ste 1251 (67202-1719)
PHONE..................................316 265-3351
Ralph P Duncan, *President*
EMP: 5
SQ FT: 4,925
SALES (est): 648K **Privately Held**
SIC: 1389 1311 Oil field services; crude petroleum & natural gas production

(G-15288)
PETROPOWER LLC
3003 E 37th St N Ste 100 (67219-3504)
PHONE..................................316 361-0222
Wanda James, *General Mgr*
Tahir Ahmad, *Principal*
EMP: 5
SALES (est): 833.6K **Privately Held**
SIC: 1389 7389 Oil field services;

(G-15289)
PHARES PETROLEUM INC
207 N Burr Oak Rd (67206-2105)
PHONE..................................316 682-3349
Alan Phares, *President*
EMP: 5
SALES (est): 411.4K **Privately Held**
SIC: 2911 Petroleum refining

(G-15290)
PHARMCARE HLTH SPECIALISTS LLC
2740 N Regency Park (67226-4527)
PHONE..................................316 681-2181
J L Regan, *Mng Member*
Gary Willms, *Technician*
David Jabara,
Suzanne Regan,
EMP: 10
SQ FT: 4,680
SALES (est): 1.1MM **Privately Held**
WEB: www.pharmacare-wichita.com
SIC: 8082 Home health care services

(G-15291)
PHILLIP G RUFFIN (PA)
Also Called: Ruffin Properties
1522 S Florence St (67209-2634)
P.O. Box 17087 (67217-0087)
PHONE..................................316 942-7940
Phillip G Ruffin, *Owner*
Gail Knott, *CFO*
▲ **EMP:** 10
SQ FT: 20,000
SALES (est): 32.7MM **Privately Held**
WEB: www.ruffinco.com
SIC: 7011 Hotels & motels

(G-15292)
PHILLIPS 66
2400 E 37th St N (67219-3538)
PHONE..................................316 821-2250
Rufpy Lee, *Manager*
EMP: 15
SALES (corp-wide): 114.2B **Publicly Held**
WEB: www.phillipspipeline.com
SIC: 5541 4613 Filling stations, gasoline; refined petroleum pipelines
PA: Phillips 66
2331 Citywest Blvd
Houston TX 77042
281 293-6600

(G-15293)
PHILLIPS SOUTHERN ELC CO INC
650 E Gilbert St (67211-4392)
PHONE..................................316 265-4186
Jason Phillips, *President*
Patrick S Phillips, *Vice Pres*
Lori Ann Phillips, *Shareholder*
EMP: 40 **EST:** 1961
SQ FT: 5,000
SALES: 5.8MM **Privately Held**
SIC: 1731 1623 Lighting contractor; electric power line construction

(G-15294)
PHOENIX SUPPLY INC (PA)
1826 S Pattie St (67211-4493)
PHONE..................................316 262-7241
Dave Fields, *President*
Doug Patry, *Corp Secy*
Nick Patry, *Purchasing*
Mark Patry, *Director*
EMP: 30 **EST:** 1971
SQ FT: 20,000
SALES (est): 11.1MM **Privately Held**
WEB: www.phoenixsupplyinc.com
SIC: 5074 Plumbing fittings & supplies

(G-15295)
PHYSICIANS MEDICAL CLINICS
Also Called: Northeast Family Physicians
3009 N Cypress St (67226-4003)
PHONE..................................316 683-4334
Beatrice Heikes, *Administration*
EMP: 30
SQ FT: 6,000 **Privately Held**
SIC: 8011 Gastronomist
PA: Physicians Medical Clinics, Inc
245 N Waco St Ste 400
Wichita KS

(G-15296)
PHYSICIANS MEDICAL CLINICS
Also Called: Family Med Center Southeast
7150 E Harry St (67207-2914)
PHONE..................................316 687-2651
Connie Johnson, *Principal*
Ramzie Othman, *Director*
EMP: 18 **Privately Held**
SIC: 8011 Gastronomist
PA: Physicians Medical Clinics, Inc
245 N Waco St Ste 400
Wichita KS

(G-15297)
PHYSICIANS MEDICAL CLINICS
Also Called: Pma
848 N St Francis St (67214-3800)
PHONE..................................316 261-3130
Jim Berry, *Branch Mgr*
Estephan Zayat, *Gastroenterlgy*
EMP: 18 **Privately Held**
SIC: 8011 Gastronomist
PA: Physicians Medical Clinics, Inc
245 N Waco St Ste 400
Wichita KS

(G-15298)
PHYSICIANS MEDICAL CLINICS
Also Called: West Wichita Family Physicians
8200 W Central Ave Ste 1 (67212-3661)
PHONE..................................316 721-4910
Sandy Zernickon, *Business Mgr*
Kirk Bliss, *Med Doctor*
EMP: 108 **Privately Held**
SIC: 8011 Gastronomist
PA: Physicians Medical Clinics, Inc
245 N Waco St Ste 400
Wichita KS

(G-15299)
PICKRELL DRILLING CO INC (PA)
100 S Main St Ste 505 (67202-3738)
PHONE..................................316 262-8427
Carl W Sebits, *President*
Jack Gurley, *Vice Pres*
Eugene A Reif, *Vice Pres*
Ruth M Sullivan, *Admin Sec*
EMP: 16 **EST:** 1948
SQ FT: 2,000
SALES (est): 10.4MM **Privately Held**
SIC: 1311 1381 Crude petroleum production; directional drilling oil & gas wells

(G-15300)
PINTAIL PETROLEUM LTD
225 N Market St Ste 300 (67202-2024)
PHONE..................................316 263-2243
Walter Innes Phillips, *President*
Lee E Phillips III, *Corp Secy*
C R Dunne, *Vice Pres*
EMP: 5
SQ FT: 1,500
SALES (est): 630K **Privately Held**
SIC: 1311 Crude petroleum production

(G-15301)
PIONEER - RAM INCORPORATED
5000 E 29th St N (67220-2111)
PHONE..................................316 685-2266
Ted A Vlamis, *President*
Terry McMaster, *Senior VP*
Betty Vlamis, *Vice Pres*
Kenny Eaton, *Warehouse Mgr*
Michael Githens, *Credit Staff*
▲ **EMP:** 600
SQ FT: 27,336

SALES (est): 39.3MM
SALES (corp-wide): 228.7MM **Privately Held**
WEB: www.pioneerram.com
SIC: 3089 3262 3229 Cups, plastic, except foam; vitreous china table & kitchenware; pressed & blown glass
PA: Continental American Corporation
5000 E 29th St N
Wichita KS 67220
316 685-2266

(G-15302)
PIPING & EQUIPMENT COMPANY INC
1111 E 37th St N (67219-3516)
P.O. Box 1065 (67201-1065)
PHONE..................................316 838-7511
John C Wadsworth, *CEO*
Tim Farnham, *President*
Art Farnham, *Senior VP*
Arthur Farnham, *Project Mgr*
Sue Pearce, *CFO*
EMP: 120 **EST:** 1945
SQ FT: 4,200
SALES (est): 36.7MM **Privately Held**
WEB: www.pipingequ.com
SIC: 1623 1711 Pipeline construction; plumbing, heating, air-conditioning contractors

(G-15303)
PIXIUS COMMUNICATIONS LLC (PA)
301 N Saint Francis Ave (67202-2621)
PHONE..................................316 219-8500
Robert Reif, *Prdtn Mgr*
Jen Holler, *Controller*
April Lagnevall, *Accounts Mgr*
Dennis Cernik, *Technology*
Jay Maxwell,
EMP: 51
SQ FT: 21,430
SALES (est): 19.3MM **Privately Held**
WEB: pixius.com
SIC: 4813

(G-15304)
PK TECHNOLOGY LLC
10811 E Harry St (67207-5025)
P.O. Box 336, Augusta (67010-0336)
PHONE..................................316 866-2955
EMP: 13
SALES (est): 1.2MM **Privately Held**
SIC: 8741 Industrial management

(G-15305)
PLANNED PARENTHOOD OF KANSAS (PA)
2226 E Central Ave (67214-4494)
PHONE..................................316 263-7575
Sandy Hill, *Manager*
EMP: 22
SQ FT: 3,000
SALES (est): 676.2K **Privately Held**
SIC: 8093 Family planning clinic

(G-15306)
PLATINUM INC
Also Called: Platinum Salon and Spa
10248 W 13th St N (67212-4377)
PHONE..................................316 773-9700
Tambra Evens, *President*
EMP: 18
SALES (est): 810K **Privately Held**
WEB: www.platinum.com
SIC: 7231 Beauty shops

(G-15307)
PLP INC
Also Called: John Deere Authorized Dealer
2218 S West St (67213-1114)
PHONE..................................316 943-4261
Dave Yoder, *Sales Staff*
Mark Conrady, *Branch Mgr*
EMP: 35
SALES (corp-wide): 66.9MM **Privately Held**
SIC: 5999 5082 Farm equipment & supplies; construction & mining machinery
PA: Plp, Inc
811 E 30th Ave Ste F
Hutchinson KS 67502
620 664-5860

(G-15308)
PLUMBING SPECIALISTS INC
1838 S Anna St (67209-2802)
PHONE..................................316 945-8383
Darrell Hoefling, *President*
EMP: 21
SALES (est): 2.5MM **Privately Held**
SIC: 1711 5999 Plumbing contractors; plumbing & heating supplies

(G-15309)
PLYMOUTH PRESCHOOL LRNG CTR
202 N Clifton Ave (67208-3324)
PHONE..................................316 684-0222
Don Olson, *Principal*
Kristofer Quillin, *Principal*
EMP: 20
SALES (est): 249.9K **Privately Held**
SIC: 8351 Preschool center

(G-15310)
PMA MEDICAL ASSOCIATES PA (PA)
848 N St Francis St (67214-3800)
PHONE..................................316 261-3100
Joe Kasitz, *Manager*
EMP: 58
SQ FT: 17,643
SALES (est): 2.8MM **Privately Held**
SIC: 8011 Internal medicine, physician/surgeon

(G-15311)
PMA TWIN LAKES MEDICAL OFF P A
1900 N Amidon Ave Ste 100 (67203-2125)
PHONE..................................316 832-0465
Edward J Hett MD, *President*
Brian A Johnson, *Partner*
Dennis Phillips MD, *Treasurer*
Michale Grimes, *Med Doctor*
Arthur Windholz MD, *Admin Sec*
EMP: 35
SQ FT: 6,500
SALES (est): 2.1MM **Privately Held**
SIC: 8011 General & family practice, physician/surgeon

(G-15312)
POE & ASSOCIATES INC
5940 E Central Ave # 201 (67208-4239)
PHONE..................................316 685-4114
Bill Fox, *Vice Pres*
James M Thompson, *Manager*
EMP: 23
SALES (corp-wide): 7MM **Privately Held**
WEB: www.poeandassociates.com
SIC: 8711 Civil engineering
HQ: Poe & Associates, Inc.
1601 Nw Expwy St Ste 515
Oklahoma City OK 73118
405 949-1962

(G-15313)
POE & ASSOCIATES OF KANSAS
5940 E Central Ave # 200 (67208-4239)
PHONE..................................316 685-4114
James M Thompson, *President*
Robert C Poe, *Chairman*
EMP: 14 **EST:** 1970
SALES (est): 1.1MM **Privately Held**
WEB: www.poekansas.com
SIC: 8711 Civil engineering

(G-15314)
PONCA PRODUCTS INC
1910 E Northern St (67216-2429)
PHONE..................................316 262-4051
Laverne Schule, *President*
Ken Hamlin, *Sales Staff*
EMP: 20
SQ FT: 15,000
SALES: 1.6MM **Privately Held**
WEB: www.poncaproducts.com
SIC: 2399 2394 Hammocks & other net products; canvas & related products; awnings, fabric: made from purchased materials; tents: made from purchased materials

(G-15315)
POORMAN AUTO SUPPLY INC (PA)
Also Called: Johnson Bros Auto Supply
1400 E Douglas Ave (67214-4135)
PHONE..................................316 265-6284
Toll Free:..................................888 -
Tom T Poorman, *President*
Kenny Palmer, *General Mgr*
Brian Leopold, *Vice Pres*
Mike Poorman, *Treasurer*
Natalie Poorman, *Admin Sec*
EMP: 33 **EST:** 1966
SQ FT: 60,000
SALES (est): 14.5MM **Privately Held**
WEB: www.poormanautosupply.com
SIC: 5013 5531 Automotive supplies & parts; automotive & home supply stores

(G-15316)
POSTAL PRESORT INC
820 W 2nd St N (67203-6005)
PHONE..................................316 262-3333
Bryan Pulliam, *President*
Bryan J Pulliam, *President*
Doug Wenzel, *Prdtn Mgr*
Lynn Grimes, *Sales Staff*
Wilbur Baird, *Consultant*
EMP: 65
SQ FT: 16,000
SALES (est): 9.7MM **Privately Held**
WEB: www.postalpresort.com
SIC: 7331 7374 Mailing service; data processing service

(G-15317)
POWDERTECH LLC
810 E 37th St N (67219)
PHONE..................................316 832-9210
Mark Fawcett, *Controller*
Susan Brandes, *Mng Member*
Charles D Peer,
EMP: 26
SQ FT: 20,000
SALES: 2.2MM
SALES (corp-wide): 90.8MM **Privately Held**
WEB: www.powdertechllc.com
SIC: 3479 Coating of metals & formed products
PA: Great Plains Ventures, Inc.
3504 N Great Plains Dr # 100
Wichita KS 67220
316 684-1540

(G-15318)
POWER CHEMICALS INC
2901 S Kansas Ave (67216-2416)
P.O. Box 15585, Colorado Springs CO (80935-5585)
PHONE..................................316 524-7899
Ray Hinderliter, *President*
Jim Hinderliter, *Owner*
Marjorie Hinderliter, *Corp Secy*
EMP: 18 **EST:** 1971
SQ FT: 12,000
SALES: 1MM **Privately Held**
WEB: www.powerchemicals.com
SIC: 7389 5074 Water softener service; water heaters & purification equipment

(G-15319)
POWER LIFT FOUND REPAIR
9918 E Harry St (67207-5008)
P.O. Box 780852 (67278-0852)
PHONE..................................316 685-0888
EMP: 25
SALES: 1.5MM **Privately Held**
SIC: 1741 1771 Foundation building; foundation & footing contractor

(G-15320)
POWER WASHERS UNLIMITED
1802 W Mccormick Ave (67213-3812)
PHONE..................................316 262-9274
Brad Snyder, *Principal*
EMP: 5
SALES (est): 584.4K **Privately Held**
SIC: 3452 Washers

(G-15321)
PRAIRIE PRINT INC
3748 N Ohio St (67219-3726)
P.O. Box 2833 (67201-2833)
PHONE..................................316 267-1950
Matthew J Devins, *President*
EMP: 7
SQ FT: 6,500
SALES (est): 805.8K **Privately Held**
WEB: www.prairieprint.com
SIC: 2759 2396 Screen printing; automotive & apparel trimmings

(G-15322)
PRATT & WHITNEY ENG SVCS INC
Also Called: Wichita Service Center
1955 Midfield Rd (67209-1961)
PHONE..................................316 945-9763
James L Nelson, *Manager*
EMP: 8
SALES (corp-wide): 66.5B **Publicly Held**
SIC: 7699 3724 5088 4581 Engine repair & replacement, non-automotive; aircraft engines & engine parts; aircraft engines & engine parts; aircraft servicing & repairing
HQ: Pratt & Whitney Engine Services, Inc.
1525 Midway Park Rd
Bridgeport WV 26330
304 842-5421

(G-15323)
PRATT INDUSTRIES USA INC
Also Called: Admin Bldg For Hr/PR & Acct
3600 N Santa Fe St (67219-3636)
PHONE..................................316 838-0851
EMP: 66
SALES (corp-wide): 2.5B **Privately Held**
SIC: 2653 2448 4213 Boxes, corrugated: made from purchased materials; pallets, wood; trucking, except local
PA: Pratt Industries, Inc.
1800 Sarasot Bus Pkwy Ne C
Conyers GA 30013
770 918-5678

(G-15324)
PRATT INDUSTRIES USA INC
700 E 37th St N (67219-3510)
PHONE..................................316 838-0851
Craig Bagley, *General Mgr*
Kevin Harkonen, *General Mgr*
Ron McComas, *General Mgr*
Jeff Sullivan, *General Mgr*
Carl Wright, *General Mgr*
EMP: 66
SALES (corp-wide): 2.5B **Privately Held**
SIC: 2653 Corrugated boxes, partitions, display items, sheets & pad
PA: Pratt Industries, Inc.
1800 Sarasot Bus Pkwy Ne C
Conyers GA 30013
770 918-5678

(G-15325)
PRECISION PRODUCTS
2524 N Lorraine Ave (67219)
PHONE..................................316 943-0477
Scott Warren, *Partner*
George Roberts, *Partner*
EMP: 7
SQ FT: 6,000
SALES (est): 1.2MM **Privately Held**
WEB: www.paulcousa.com
SIC: 3728 3599 Aircraft parts & equipment; machine shop, jobbing & repair

(G-15326)
PREFERRED LAND COMPANY INC
Also Called: Re/Max
3500 N Rock Rd Bldg 100 (67226-1328)
PHONE..................................316 634-1313
Ken Seager, *President*
Jason Garraway, *Real Est Agnt*
EMP: 12
SALES (est): 380.7K **Privately Held**
SIC: 6531 Real estate agent, residential

(G-15327)
PREFERRED MEDICAL ASSOCIATES
1100 N St Francis St # 400 (67214-2884)
PHONE..................................316 268-8080
Edward J Hett, *Principal*
EMP: 13
SALES (est): 736.5K **Privately Held**
SIC: 8099 Blood related health services

GEOGRAPHIC

(G-15328)
PREFERRED MENTAL HEALTH MGT
Also Called: Pmhm
401 E Douglas Ave Ste 300 (67202-3407)
PHONE..................................316 262-0444
Leslie Ruthven, *President*
Dr Courtney Ruthven, *Exec VP*
Tracy Booker, *Director*
EMP: 10
SQ FT: 10,000
SALES (est): 825K **Privately Held**
WEB: www.pmhm.com
SIC: 8741 Nursing & personal care facility management

(G-15329)
PREGNNCY CRISIS CTR OF WICHITA
Also Called: Pregnancy Crises Center
1040 N West St (67203-1226)
PHONE..................................316 945-9400
Roy Roberts, *President*
Karen Fifer, *Manager*
Trisha Smart-Counts, *Director*
EMP: 13
SALES: 499.3K **Privately Held**
WEB: www.pccwichita.org
SIC: 8322 General counseling services

(G-15330)
PREMIER FOOD SERVICE INC
8225 W Irving St (67209-1838)
PHONE..................................316 269-2447
Joseph J Hemmelgarn, *President*
Miguel Grajeda, *Technology*
EMP: 192
SQ FT: 65,000
SALES (est): 13.7MM **Privately Held**
WEB: www.wichitavending.com
SIC: 5087 5962 Vending machines & supplies; merchandising machine operators

(G-15331)
PREMIER LIVING BY WARDEN LLC
234 S Anna St (67209-2404)
PHONE..................................316 945-2028
Brandi Warden,
EMP: 45 **EST:** 2012
SQ FT: 3,000
SALES (est): 807.1K **Privately Held**
SIC: 8051 Skilled nursing care facilities

(G-15332)
PREMIER OPEN MRI INC (HQ)
500 S Main St Ste 100 (67202-3757)
PHONE..................................316 262-1103
Steve Schulman, *President*
EMP: 25 **EST:** 1998
SALES (est): 2.1MM
SALES (corp-wide): 4.7MM **Privately Held**
WEB: www.mri-chicago.net
SIC: 8011 Radiologist

(G-15333)
PREMIER PROCESSING
3002 W Pawnee St Ste 104 (67213-1830)
PHONE..................................316 425-3565
Adam Lynch,
James Brad Hart,
EMP: 15
SQ FT: 36,000
SALES (est): 1.9MM **Privately Held**
SIC: 3471 Plating & polishing

(G-15334)
PREMIER REALTY LLC
Also Called: Re/Max Premier
2243 N Ridge Rd 105 (67205-1054)
PHONE..................................316 773-2707
Marvin L Schellenberg,
EMP: 20
SALES (est): 2.2MM **Privately Held**
WEB: www.premierealty.com
SIC: 6531 Real estate agent, residential

(G-15335)
PRESBYTERIAN MANORS INC
Also Called: Wichita Presbyterian Manor
4700 W 13th St N Ofc (67212-5575)
PHONE..................................316 942-7456
Chad West, *Director*
EMP: 60
SALES (corp-wide): 8.6MM **Privately Held**
SIC: 8059 8051 8052 Rest home, with health care; skilled nursing care facilities; intermediate care facilities
HQ: Presbyterian Manors, Inc.
2414 N Woodlawn Blvd
Wichita KS 67220
316 685-1100

(G-15336)
PRESBYTRIAN MNORS OF MD-MERICA (PA)
Also Called: PMMA
2414 N Woodlawn Blvd (67220-3902)
P.O. Box 20440 (67208-1440)
PHONE..................................316 685-1100
Bruce H Shogren, *Vice Pres*
Jeanne Gerstenkorn, *Vice Pres*
Sherry K Hind, *Vice Pres*
Gary McGuire, *Vice Pres*
Melanie Owens, *Vice Pres*
EMP: 40
SQ FT: 8,000
SALES: 8.6MM **Privately Held**
SIC: 8741 Nursing & personal care facility management

(G-15337)
PRESCRIPTIVE PAYROLL INC
501 S Robin Rd (67209-1620)
PHONE..................................316 247-3166
EMP: 16 **EST:** 2016
SALES (est): 290.3K **Privately Held**
SIC: 8721 Accounting/Auditing/Bookkeeping

(G-15338)
PRESTIGE GRAPHICS INC
500 N Birkdale Cir (67230-1500)
PHONE..................................316 262-3480
EMP: 15 **EST:** 1978
SQ FT: 20,000
SALES (est): 1.8MM **Privately Held**
SIC: 2759 Commercial Printing

(G-15339)
PRESTIGE TRNSP SYSTEMS (PA)
Also Called: Prestige Bus Charters
8620 W 21st St N (67205-1756)
PHONE..................................316 263-9141
Jerry Grover, *President*
Mark Grover, *Vice Pres*
Lori Vinsonhaler, *Admin Sec*
EMP: 50
SQ FT: 530
SALES: 2.7MM **Privately Held**
WEB: www.prestigebuscharters.com
SIC: 4142 Bus charter service, except local

(G-15340)
PRICE BROS EQUIPMENT CO (PA)
Also Called: Kubota Authorized Dealer
619 S Washington Ave (67211-2441)
PHONE..................................316 265-9577
Richard H Price Jr, *President*
Kimberly Hamel, *Corp Secy*
Randall Smith, *Vice Pres*
Lance Waltner, *Vice Pres*
▲ **EMP:** 23 **EST:** 1948
SQ FT: 5,000
SALES (est): 11MM **Privately Held**
WEB: www.pricebroseq.com
SIC: 5083 5084 Agricultural machinery & equipment; farm equipment parts & supplies; industrial machinery & equipment

(G-15341)
PRICE TRUCK LINE INC (PA)
4931 S Victoria St (67216-2004)
PHONE..................................316 945-6915
Ted Toon, *President*
Kathryn Toon, *Vice Pres*
EMP: 185
SQ FT: 11,900
SALES (est): 27MM **Privately Held**
SIC: 4213 Contract haulers

(G-15342)
PRIMARY CARE ASSOCIATES LLC
7111 E 21st St N Ste A (67206-1078)
PHONE..................................316 684-2851
Julie Brost, *Office Mgr*
Paul Davis,
Angela Leiker, *Family Practiti*
Charlene Bui, *Physician Asst*
EMP: 36
SQ FT: 14,935
SALES (est): 6.5MM **Privately Held**
WEB: www.pca-wichita.com
SIC: 8011 General & family practice, physician/surgeon; surgeon

(G-15343)
PRIME CONCEPTS GROUP INC
7570 W 21st St N 1038a (67205-1763)
PHONE..................................316 942-1111
Ford Saeks, *President*
Ronald Jans, *Manager*
EMP: 10
SQ FT: 5,000
SALES: 1.2MM **Privately Held**
WEB: www.primeconcepts.com
SIC: 8742 Business consultant; marketing consulting services

(G-15344)
PRIME DEVELOPMENT COMPANY
8916 E Windwood St (67226-1507)
PHONE..................................316 634-0643
Jerry Newman, *President*
Kathryn Neal, *Corp Secy*
EMP: 12
SALES: 1MM **Privately Held**
SIC: 6552 Subdividers & developers

(G-15345)
PRIMROSE SCHOOL
2072 S 127th St E (67207)
PHONE..................................316 807-8622
Angela Bhakpa, *Owner*
EMP: 45
SALES (est): 343.6K **Privately Held**
SIC: 8351 Preschool center

(G-15346)
PRIMUS INTERNATIONAL INC
4330 W May St (67209-2841)
PHONE..................................316 425-8105
Steven Bumstead, *President*
EMP: 167
SALES (corp-wide): 225.3B **Publicly Held**
WEB: www.primusint.com
SIC: 3728 3769 Aircraft body & wing assemblies & parts; guided missile & space vehicle parts & auxiliary equipment
HQ: Primus International Inc
610 Bllvue Way Ne Ste 200
Auburn WA 98001
425 688-0444

(G-15347)
PRINCETON CHILDRENS CENTER WI
3590 N Woodlawn Blvd (67220-2236)
PHONE..................................316 618-0275
Regina Miller, *Principal*
EMP: 10 **EST:** 2009
SALES (est): 229.4K **Privately Held**
SIC: 8351 Preschool center

(G-15348)
PRINT SOURCE INC
Also Called: Blue Frog Printing
404 S Tracy St (67209-2525)
P.O. Box 12748 (67277-2748)
PHONE..................................316 945-7052
Leon Lungwitz, *Manager*
EMP: 58
SALES (corp-wide): 23.6MM **Privately Held**
WEB: www.ps-printsource.com
SIC: 3993 5072 3496 Signs & advertising specialties; hardware; miscellaneous fabricated wire products
PA: The Print Source Inc
404 S Tracy St
Wichita KS 67209
316 945-7052

(G-15349)
PRINT SOURCE INC (PA)
404 S Tracy St (67209-2525)
P.O. Box 12748 (67277-2748)
PHONE..................................316 945-7052
Stu Lungwitz, *CEO*
Eric Ferrin, *Opers Mgr*
Leon Lungwitz, *Treasurer*
Mary Lungwitz, *Comptroller*
Joe Helms, *Manager*
◆ **EMP:** 72
SQ FT: 40,000
SALES (est): 23.6MM **Privately Held**
WEB: www.ps-printsource.com
SIC: 2752 2759 Commercial printing, offset; screen printing

(G-15350)
PRINTING INC
Also Called: Pix Printing
627 E 3rd St N (67202-2619)
PHONE..................................316 265-1201
Kristin Knoll, *Accounts Mgr*
Carol Maddox, *Branch Mgr*
EMP: 30
SALES (corp-wide): 6.8B **Publicly Held**
SIC: 2752 2789 2759 Commercial printing, offset; bookbinding & related work; commercial printing
HQ: Printing, Inc.
35 W Wacker Dr 36
Chicago IL 60601
316 265-1201

(G-15351)
PRINTINGPLUS INC
231 N Saint Francis Ave (67202-2609)
P.O. Box 1673 (67201-1673)
PHONE..................................316 269-3010
Jerry Vandeventer, *President*
EMP: 8
SQ FT: 7,000
SALES (est): 1.3MM **Privately Held**
SIC: 2752 Commercial printing, offset

(G-15352)
PRO HOME REMODELING LLC
Also Called: Experts Exteriors
616 E 34th St N (67219-3600)
PHONE..................................316 821-9818
Aaron Brown,
EMP: 15 **EST:** 2010
SALES: 1.5MM **Privately Held**
SIC: 1521 General remodeling, single-family houses

(G-15353)
PRO R SALES AND SERVICE INC
4267 S Boyd St (67215-2045)
P.O. Box 12090 (67277-2090)
PHONE..................................316 773-3400
Steven Haigh, *President*
Russ Brown, *Vice Pres*
EMP: 10
SALES (est): 385K **Privately Held**
SIC: 1742 Insulation, buildings

(G-15354)
PRO-WELD LLC
2133 W Rio Vista Dr (67204-1225)
PHONE..................................316 648-6316
Kenneth Burk, *Principal*
EMP: 5
SALES (est): 253.6K **Privately Held**
SIC: 7692 Welding repair

(G-15355)
PROACTIVE HOME CARE INC
3450 N Rock Rd Ste 213 (67226-1352)
PHONE..................................316 688-5511
Jerry Lessard, *President*
Betty Lessard, *Vice Pres*
EMP: 62
SALES: 2.5MM **Privately Held**
WEB: www.proactiveeldercare.com
SIC: 8082 Visiting nurse service

(G-15356)
PROCHASKA HOWELL PROCHASKA LLC
8415 E 21st St N Ste 230 (67206-2956)
PHONE..................................316 683-9080
Bradley Prochaska, *Owner*
James Howell, *Partner*
Walter W Craig,
Gerard C Scott,
EMP: 10
SALES (est): 1.3MM **Privately Held**
WEB: www.prochaskalaw.com
SIC: 8111 General practice attorney, lawyer

(G-15357)
PROFESSIONAL CARGO SVCS INC (PA)
3735 S West St (67217-3803)
P.O. Box 9244 (67277-0244)
PHONE..................................316 522-2224
Duane Zogleman, *President*
Jan Zogleman, *Vice Pres*
EMP: 30 **EST:** 1978
SQ FT: 4,000
SALES (est): 4.4MM **Privately Held**
SIC: 4225 4213 General warehousing & storage; trucking, except local

(G-15358)
PROFESSIONAL DRIVERS GA INC
Also Called: Prodrivers
303 N West St Ste 275 (67203-1299)
PHONE..................................316 945-9700
Sylvia Cruz, *Sales Mgr*
Michael Walden, *Manager*
EMP: 39
SALES (corp-wide): 32B **Privately Held**
SIC: 7363 Temporary help service
HQ: Professional Drivers Of Georgia, Inc.
1040 Crown Pointe Pkwy
Atlanta GA 30338

(G-15359)
PROFESSIONAL ENGRG CONS PA (PA)
Also Called: PEC
303 S Topeka Ave (67202-4309)
PHONE..................................316 262-2691
Rod Young, *President*
Charles Brooksher, *Division Mgr*
Mike Berry, *Principal*
Travis Radford, *Project Mgr*
Sarah Unruh, *Project Mgr*
EMP: 160 **EST:** 1946
SQ FT: 30,000
SALES (est): 66.5MM **Privately Held**
WEB: www.pec.org
SIC: 8711 5049 Consulting engineer; scientific & engineering equipment & supplies

(G-15360)
PROFESSIONAL ENGRG CONS PA
Also Called: Allied Laboratories
350 S Washington Ave (67202-4726)
PHONE..................................316 262-6457
Rod Young, *President*
Calvin Reed, *Transportation*
Kelby Burton, *Electrical Engi*
Gregg Greenwood, *Manager*
Shawn Hendershot, *Administration*
EMP: 49
SALES (corp-wide): 66.5MM **Privately Held**
WEB: www.pec.org
SIC: 8711 Consulting engineer
PA: Professional Engineering Consultants P.A.
303 S Topeka Ave
Wichita KS 67202
316 262-2691

(G-15361)
PROFESSIONAL FLEET SVCS LLC
2650 S Custer Ave (67217-1324)
PHONE..................................316 524-6000
Peggy Lawless, *Mng Member*
EMP: 13
SALES (est): 1.3MM **Privately Held**
SIC: 7538 5084 General truck repair; materials handling machinery

(G-15362)
PROFESSIONAL INSURANCE MGT
4906 N Portwest Cir (67204-2367)
P.O. Box 12750 (67277-2750)
PHONE..................................316 942-0699
Timothy Bonnell, *President*
Janet Bonnell, *President*
William Booris Jr, *President*
EMP: 21
SQ FT: 4,400
SALES: 13.5MM **Privately Held**
WEB: www.pimi.com
SIC: 6411 Insurance agents

(G-15363)
PROFESSIONAL LDSCPG SVCS LLC
1347 S Washington Ave (67211-3445)
PHONE..................................316 832-0061
Peter Salmeron, *Owner*
Jill Reinert, *Vice Pres*
EMP: 20
SQ FT: 60,000
SALES: 1.4MM **Privately Held**
SIC: 0782 0783 Landscape contractors; planting, pruning & trimming services

(G-15364)
PROFESSIONAL MECH CONTRS INC
4053 E Navajo Ln (67210-1542)
P.O. Box 3171 (67201-3171)
PHONE..................................316 684-1927
David Norris, *President*
EMP: 27 **EST:** 1976
SQ FT: 25,000
SALES (est): 5MM
SALES (corp-wide): 10.4MM **Privately Held**
SIC: 1711 Mechanical contractor
PA: Den Management Co., Inc.
4053 E Navajo Ln
Wichita KS 67210
316 686-1964

(G-15365)
PROFESSIONAL PRODUCTS OF KANS
4456 S Clifton Ave (67216-2945)
PHONE..................................316 522-9300
Kenneth W Barry, *President*
Sarah Smith, *Principal*
EMP: 7
SQ FT: 6,000
SALES (est): 1MM **Privately Held**
WEB: www.watersealant.com
SIC: 2899 Waterproofing compounds

(G-15366)
PROFESSIONAL SOFTWARE INC
12401 W Jayson Ct (67235-1439)
P.O. Box 3843 (67201-3843)
PHONE..................................316 269-4264
Douglas D Jenkins, *President*
EMP: 8
SALES (est): 1MM **Privately Held**
WEB: www.pskansas.com
SIC: 7372 Home entertainment computer software

(G-15367)
PROFESSNAL WTRPRFING INSUL LLC
8401 E Oak Knoll St (67207-5439)
PHONE..................................316 264-3101
Carl Goosen,
Mark Hammer,
Paul Woods,
EMP: 14
SQ FT: 3,100
SALES (est): 909.2K
SALES (corp-wide): 34.1MM **Privately Held**
SIC: 1799 Waterproofing
PA: Beran Concrete, Inc.
8401 E Oak Knoll St
Wichita KS 67207
316 618-6089

(G-15368)
PROFILES INC
Also Called: Beau Monde Spa
2939 N Rock Rd Ste 100 (67226-1100)
PHONE..................................316 636-1214
Michele Wheeler, *President*
Olga Abdullayev, *President*
Valeriy Abdullayev, *Vice Pres*
EMP: 12
SQ FT: 2,500
SALES (est): 437.1K **Privately Held**
SIC: 7231 Beauty shops

(G-15369)
PROFILLMENT LLC
1930 S Hoover Rd Ste 200 (67209-2835)
PHONE..................................316 260-7910
Walsh Billy, *Purchasing*
Brian Miller, *Marketing Staff*
Rolf Gunderson,
Chris Trobec,
▲ **EMP:** 14
SQ FT: 53,000
SALES (est): 2.9MM **Privately Held**
WEB: www.profillment.com
SIC: 7389 5064 Design services; electrical appliances, television & radio

(G-15370)
PROFIT BUILDERS INC
2872 N Ridge Rd Ste 201 (67205-1149)
PHONE..................................316 721-3370
Michelle Becker, *President*
Sam Oglesby, *Corp Secy*
Erica Willis, *Accounting Mgr*
Emily Suter, *Accountant*
Betty Herbert, *Accounts Mgr*
EMP: 24
SQ FT: 9,500
SALES (est): 3.2MM **Privately Held**
WEB: www.yourprofitbuilders.com
SIC: 8721 Accounting, auditing & bookkeeping

(G-15371)
PROGRESSIVE HOME HEALTH CARE (PA)
Also Called: Progressive HM Hlth & Hospice
3500 N Rock Rd Bldg 400 (67226-1331)
PHONE..................................316 691-5050
Dorothy McPherson, *President*
Cecllia Wambugu-Davis, *Principal*
Shawn McPherson, *CFO*
Melinda Herzberg, *Mktg Dir*
Marilyn Brandtrn, *Director*
EMP: 50
SALES (est): 4MM **Privately Held**
WEB: www.progressivecare.com
SIC: 8082 Visiting nurse service

(G-15372)
PROHOME INTERNATIONAL LLC (PA)
550 N 159th St E Ste 2000 (67230-7568)
PHONE..................................316 687-6776
Jack Salmans, *President*
Larry Johnson, *Treasurer*
Sue Salmans, *Admin Sec*
EMP: 34
SQ FT: 1,200
SALES (est): 4.6MM **Privately Held**
SIC: 6794 Franchises, selling or licensing

(G-15373)
PUBLIC STORAGE
206 E Macarthur Rd (67216-1746)
PHONE..................................316 522-1162
Brian Maddox, *District Mgr*
EMP: 25
SALES (corp-wide): 2.7B **Publicly Held**
WEB: www.publicstorage.com
SIC: 4225 Warehousing, self-storage
PA: Public Storage
701 Western Ave
Glendale CA 91201
818 244-8080

(G-15374)
PULMONARY SLEEP CONSULTANT
3009 N Cypress St (67226-4003)
PHONE..................................316 440-1010
John D Flesher, *Principal*
Nancy Bettis, *Office Mgr*
Janel Harting, *Med Doctor*
Chloe R Steinshouer, *Med Doctor*
Son V Truong, *Med Doctor*
EMP: 18
SALES (est): 1.9MM **Privately Held**
SIC: 8011 Pulmonary specialist, physician/surgeon

(G-15375)
PULSE SYSTEMS INC (DH)
3020 N Cypress St Ste 200 (67226-4012)
PHONE..................................316 636-5900
Charles Walls, *CEO*
James Isaac, *President*
Elias Hourani, *COO*
Michael Morrison, *Senior VP*
Dave Gordon, *CPA*
EMP: 70
SQ FT: 12,000
SALES (est): 27.2MM
SALES (corp-wide): 7.3MM **Privately Held**
WEB: www.pulseinc.com
SIC: 8741 Hospital management; nursing & personal care facility management

(G-15376)
PUMPHREY MACHINE CO INC
3758 N Old Lawrence Rd (67219-3622)
PHONE..................................316 832-1841
Craig Pumphrey, *President*
Jeanine Pumphrey, *Vice Pres*
Russ Klingsick, *Administration*
EMP: 6
SQ FT: 8,200
SALES (est): 923.5K **Privately Held**
SIC: 3599 Machine shop, jobbing & repair

(G-15377)
PURIFAN INC
5200 E 35th St N (67220-3400)
PHONE..................................316 932-8001
Stan Brannan, *President*
Tony Hampton, *Vice Pres*
◆ **EMP:** 8 **EST:** 2001
SQ FT: 3,200
SALES: 1MM **Privately Held**
SIC: 3564 Air cleaning systems

(G-15378)
PURINA ANIMAL NUTRITION LLC
414 E 18th St N (67214-1228)
PHONE..................................316 265-0624
Troy Smith, *Manager*
EMP: 21
SALES (corp-wide): 6.8B **Privately Held**
WEB: www.landolakesidd.com
SIC: 2048 Prepared feeds
HQ: Purina Animal Nutrition Llc
100 Danforth Dr
Gray Summit MO 63039

(G-15379)
PURINA MILLS LLC
414 E 18th St N (67214-1228)
P.O. Box 1840 (67201-1840)
PHONE..................................316 265-0624
Carl McKettric, *Manager*
EMP: 24
SALES (corp-wide): 6.8B **Privately Held**
WEB: www.purina-mills.com
SIC: 5191 2041 2048 Animal feeds; flour & other grain mill products; feed premixes
HQ: Purina Mills, Llc
555 Maryvle Univ Dr 200
Saint Louis MO 63141

(G-15380)
PWI INC (PA)
109 S Knight St (67213-2417)
PHONE..................................316 942-2811
Miklos Lorik, *CEO*
Robert Lorik, *President*
Bill Steffy, *Plant Engr*
Judy Baldwin, *Treasurer*
Rick Bernhard, *Branch Mgr*
EMP: 50
SQ FT: 6,400
SALES (est): 5.6MM **Privately Held**
WEB: www.pwi-e.com
SIC: 3647 3677 3672 3646 Vehicular lighting equipment; electronic coils, transformers & other inductors; printed circuit boards; commercial indusl & institutional electric lighting fixtures; electric lamps

(G-15381)
PWI INC
3407 W Douglas Ave (67213-2429)
PHONE..................................316 942-2811
Robi Lorik, *General Mgr*
Judith Baldwin, *Purchasing*
Eva Courchaine, *Purchasing*
Tom McGuire,
EMP: 45
SALES (corp-wide): 5.6MM **Privately Held**
WEB: www.pwi-e.com
SIC: 3677 3728 Electronic transformers; aircraft power transmission equipment

PA: Pwi, Inc.
109 S Knight St
Wichita KS 67213
316 942-2811

(G-15382)
PYXIS INC
334 N Topeka Ave (67202-2410)
PHONE..................................316 682-8092
Michael J Kriwiel, *President*
Robert Bragg, *Vice Pres*
Renee McKee, *Receptionist*
EMP: 150
SALES: 5.5MM **Privately Held**
WEB: www.pyxispath.com
SIC: 8331 Community service employment training program

(G-15383)
QUALITY GRANITE & MARBLE INC
1123 S West St (67213-1629)
PHONE..................................316 946-0530
Sally Bauer, *CEO*
James Bauer, *President*
EMP: 23
SALES (est): 2.7MM **Privately Held**
SIC: 1799 Counter top installation

(G-15384)
QUALITY ROOFG INSTALLATION LLC
1218 S Washington Ave (67211-3442)
PHONE..................................316 946-1068
Miguel Garcia,
EMP: 6
SALES (est): 356.2K **Privately Held**
SIC: 2952 Mastic roofing composition

(G-15385)
QUALITY SUITES AIRPORT
Also Called: Quality Inn
658 S Westdale Dr (67209-2527)
PHONE..................................316 945-2600
Mahendra Bhukhan, *President*
Kelly Schmitt, *Vice Pres*
Peter Phakta, *Office Mgr*
EMP: 17
SALES (est): 1.3MM **Privately Held**
SIC: 7011 Hotels & motels

(G-15386)
QUALITY TECH METALS
2518 W May St (67213-1852)
PHONE..................................316 945-4781
Don Bradley, *Owner*
Brent Stoull, *General Mgr*
EMP: 25
SQ FT: 12,000
SALES: 3MM **Privately Held**
SIC: 3728 3599 3444 Aircraft assemblies, subassemblies & parts; machine shop, jobbing & repair; sheet metalwork

(G-15387)
QUALITY TOOL SERVICE INC
1501 S Handley St (67213-4320)
PHONE..................................316 265-0048
Harold Slates, *President*
Rosa Slates, *Corp Secy*
Burt Chrisman, *Sales Mgr*
Jeremy Nelson, *Sales Staff*
EMP: 12
SQ FT: 4,000
SALES (est): 1.2MM **Privately Held**
SIC: 7389 Grinding, precision: commercial or industrial

(G-15388)
QUANTUM CREDIT UNION (PA)
6300 W 21st St N (67205-1762)
PHONE..................................316 263-5756
Charles Bullock, *President*
Vern Nickel, *Vice Pres*
EMP: 14 **EST:** 1938
SQ FT: 4,000
SALES: 5.4MM **Privately Held**
WEB: www.tecu.org
SIC: 6061 Federal credit unions

(G-15389)
QUANTUM CREDIT UNION
6300 W 21st St N (67205-1762)
PHONE..................................316 263-5756
EMP: 15
SALES (corp-wide): 5.4MM **Privately Held**
WEB: www.tecu.org
SIC: 6062 6163 State credit unions, not federally chartered; loan brokers
PA: Quantum Credit Union
6300 W 21st St N
Wichita KS 67205
316 263-5756

(G-15390)
QUARTERS AT CAMBRIDGE LP
9911 E 21st St N Ofc (67206-3550)
PHONE..................................316 636-1277
Sam Catanese, *Partner*
Fred Hanley, *Partner*
Dena Graham, *Asst Mgr*
EMP: 15
SALES (est): 1MM **Privately Held**
WEB: www.quartersatcambridge.com
SIC: 6513 Apartment building operators

(G-15391)
QUEST DIAGNOSTICS INCORPORATED
3100 E Central Ave Ste A (67214-4801)
PHONE..................................316 634-1946
Carol Polly, *Manager*
EMP: 10
SALES (corp-wide): 7.5B **Publicly Held**
WEB: www.questdiagnostics.com
SIC: 8071 Testing laboratories
PA: Quest Diagnostics Incorporated
500 Plaza Dr Ste G
Secaucus NJ 07094
973 520-2700

(G-15392)
QUEST DRILLING SERVICES LLC
607 N Armour St (67206-1515)
PHONE..................................316 260-2196
Timothy J Sanders, *Mng Member*
Renee Chroniscer, *Assistant*
EMP: 20 **EST:** 2015
SALES (est): 713.6K **Privately Held**
SIC: 1381 Drilling oil & gas wells

(G-15393)
QUEST RESEARCH & DEVELOPMENT
1042 N Waco Ave (67203-3915)
PHONE..................................316 267-1216
Clinton S Ash, *President*
EMP: 11
SQ FT: 2,000
SALES (est): 891.2K **Privately Held**
WEB: www.questrd.com
SIC: 8748 7371 Systems engineering consultant, ex. computer or professional; computer software systems analysis & design, custom

(G-15394)
QUICKERTEK INC
777 E Osie St Ste 304a (67207)
PHONE..................................316 691-1585
Rick Estes, *President*
EMP: 8
SALES: 1.1MM **Privately Held**
WEB: www.quickertek.com
SIC: 3612 Signaling transformers, electric

(G-15395)
QUIK TEK MACHINING LLC
1901 Southwest Blvd (67213-1437)
PHONE..................................316 260-9980
Cang Phu, *President*
Paula Harvey, *Opers Mgr*
EMP: 10
SALES (est): 1.2MM **Privately Held**
SIC: 3599 Machine shop, jobbing & repair

(G-15396)
QUIKRETE COMPANIES LLC
Also Called: Quikrete of Wichita
2806 N Ridge Rd (67205-1039)
PHONE..................................316 721-3900
Cary Peaden, *CPA*
Bryan Rebold, *Manager*
EMP: 45 **Privately Held**
WEB: www.quikrete.com
SIC: 3272 Concrete products
HQ: The Quikrete Companies Llc
5 Concourse Pkwy Ste 1900
Atlanta GA 30328
404 634-9100

(G-15397)
QUIVIRA CNCIL BOY SCUTS AMER I (PA)
3247 N Oliver St (67220-2106)
PHONE..................................316 264-4466
Mike Johnson, *Director*
EMP: 20
SQ FT: 3,200
SALES: 2.3MM **Privately Held**
SIC: 8641 Boy Scout organization

(G-15398)
R & L CARRIERS INC
4949 S Victoria St (67216-2046)
PHONE..................................316 529-1222
Larry Roberts, *Owner*
EMP: 27 **Privately Held**
SIC: 4213 Contract haulers
PA: R & L Carriers, Inc.
600 Gilliam Rd
Wilmington OH 45177

(G-15399)
R & R HOLDINGS INC
Also Called: R & R Aerospace
2615 W Esthner Ct (67213-1849)
P.O. Box 17034 (67217-0034)
PHONE..................................316 942-6699
Brett Jacobson, *President*
Mark Norris, *Foreman/Supr*
Karl Nading, *QC Mgr*
Karla Jacobson, *Office Mgr*
Scott Belcher, *Manager*
EMP: 32
SALES (est): 6MM **Privately Held**
SIC: 3728 Aircraft parts & equipment

(G-15400)
R & R PRECISION MACHINE INC
2615 W Esthner Ct (67213-1849)
P.O. Box 17034 (67217-0034)
PHONE..................................316 942-6699
Rick Linnabary, *President*
EMP: 25
SQ FT: 16,500
SALES (est): 3.5MM **Privately Held**
SIC: 3728 Aircraft parts & equipment

(G-15401)
R & T SPECIALTY CNSTR LC
3108 W Maple St (67213-2424)
PHONE..................................316 942-8141
Randy Genteman,
Teri Genteman,
EMP: 5 **EST:** 1965
SQ FT: 10,000
SALES: 817.1K **Privately Held**
SIC: 3613 1799 Control panels, electric; demountable partition installation

(G-15402)
R B P INC
1004 E Murdock St (67214-3453)
P.O. Box 493 (67201-0493)
PHONE..................................316 303-9606
Rodney Beard, *President*
EMP: 15
SALES: 800K **Privately Held**
WEB: www.rbp-inc.com
SIC: 1721 Residential painting

(G-15403)
R D K MACHINE LLC
625 E Pawnee St Ste A (67211-4950)
PHONE..................................316 267-6678
Robert David Klotz, *Owner*
EMP: 15
SQ FT: 5,500
SALES: 675K **Privately Held**
SIC: 3599 Machine shop, jobbing & repair

(G-15404)
R L DIAL CO INC
513 N Covington Ct (67212-5489)
PHONE..................................316 721-0108
Richard L Dial, *President*
Palmer McBride, *President*
Barthlonew Gray, *Group VP*
Cindra Rush, *Vice Pres*
EMP: 380 **Privately Held**
WEB: www.rldial.com
SIC: 6719 Personal holding companies, except banks

(G-15405)
R MESSNER CONSTRUCTION CO
3122 N Cypress St Ste 500 (67226-5402)
PHONE..................................316 634-2381
EMP: 20
SQ FT: 4,500
SALES (est): 3.3MM **Privately Held**
SIC: 1542 8712 5021 Nonresidential Construction Architectural Services

(G-15406)
R R A INC (PA)
100 S Main St Ste 510 (67202-3777)
PHONE..................................316 262-3411
Ronald R Abderhalden, *President*
Sherranna Abderhalden, *Vice Pres*
EMP: 6 **EST:** 1965
SQ FT: 3,000
SALES: 540K **Privately Held**
SIC: 1311 Crude petroleum & natural gas

(G-15407)
R&B SERVICES LLC
Also Called: Meineke Car Care
2344 S Seneca St (67213-4227)
PHONE..................................316 265-7859
Stephen D Blasdal,
Ryan Blasdal,
Ronald Ryan,
Scott Ryan,
EMP: 25
SQ FT: 8,000
SALES (est): 2.5MM **Privately Held**
SIC: 7549 Automotive maintenance services

(G-15408)
R2 CENTER FOR ASSISTING LLC (PA)
13121 E 21st St N Ste 107 (67230-7403)
PHONE..................................316 749-2097
Ty Reusser, *Principal*
EMP: 13
SALES (est): 1MM **Privately Held**
SIC: 8021 Dental clinic

(G-15409)
RADIO SHOP INC
1211 E 1st St N (67214-3906)
PHONE..................................316 265-1851
Robert C Hermreck, *Ch of Bd*
Rick Hermreck, *President*
Twila Hermreck, *Corp Secy*
EMP: 15
SQ FT: 7,500
SALES (est): 2.1MM **Privately Held**
SIC: 5065 5731 7622 Sound equipment, electronic; high fidelity stereo equipment; stereophonic equipment repair

(G-15410)
RADIOLOGICAL WICHITA GROUP PA (PA)
Also Called: Wrg
551 N Hillside St Ste 320 (67214-4926)
P.O. Box 8903 (67208-0903)
PHONE..................................316 685-1367
John Lohnes, *CEO*
Charles McGuire, *President*
Kamran Ali, *Vice Pres*
Akash Joshi, *Treasurer*
Charles W McGuire, *Med Doctor*
EMP: 29
SALES (est): 9.9MM **Privately Held**
WEB: www.wichitarad.com
SIC: 8011 Radiologist

(G-15411)
RADIOLOGICAL WICHITA GROUP PA
Also Called: Cypress Womens Imaging
9300 E 29th St N Ste 202 (67226-2183)
PHONE..................................316 681-1827
Rita Railing, *Manager*
EMP: 15
SALES (corp-wide): 9.9MM **Privately Held**
WEB: www.wichitarad.com
SIC: 8011 Radiologist

PA: Wichita Radiological Group, P.A.
551 N Hillside St Ste 320
Wichita KS 67214
316 685-1367

(G-15412)
RAINBOWS UNITED INC
2901a W Taft St (67213-2304)
PHONE..................................316 684-7060
Karen Markwell, *Human Res Dir*
Lorraine Bockorny, *Exec Dir*
Chris Heiman, *Director*
Cherie Shields, *Director*
EMP: 40
SALES (corp-wide): 9.6MM **Privately Held**
SIC: 8211 8322 School for the retarded; school for physically handicapped; individual & family services
PA: Rainbows United, Inc.
3223 N Oliver St
Wichita KS 67220
316 267-5437

(G-15413)
RALPH BHARATI MD PA
8911 E Orme St Ste A (67207-2424)
PHONE..................................316 686-7884
Ralph Bharati, *General Mgr*
EMP: 15
SALES (est): 1.3MM **Privately Held**
SIC: 8011 8069 Psychiatrist; drug addiction rehabilitation hospital

(G-15414)
RAND GRAPHICS INC
2820 S Hoover Rd (67215-1207)
PHONE..................................316 942-1125
Randy Vautravers, *Branch Mgr*
EMP: 50
SALES (corp-wide): 31.4MM **Privately Held**
SIC: 2759 Screen printing
PA: Rand Graphics, Inc.
500 S Florence St
Wichita KS 67209
316 942-1218

(G-15415)
RANDALL G FORD LLC
534 N Ridge Rd Ste B (67212-6577)
PHONE..................................316 945-1500
Randall G Ford, *Principal*
EMP: 12 **EST:** 2001
SALES (est): 457.5K **Privately Held**
WEB: www.randallford.net
SIC: 8721 Certified public accountant

(G-15416)
RANGE 54 LLC
5725 E Kellogg Dr (67218-1701)
PHONE..................................316 440-2854
Kerry Cox, *Mng Member*
Ken Grommet,
EMP: 14
SALES: 64K **Privately Held**
SIC: 5941 7999 Firearms; shooting range operation

(G-15417)
RAPID PROCESSING SOLUTIONS INC
1367 S Anna St (67209-2601)
PHONE..................................316 265-2001
Phliip Nettleton, *President*
Jeremy Weinman, *Vice Pres*
EMP: 10
SQ FT: 13,000
SALES (est): 1.4MM **Privately Held**
WEB: www.rapidpsi.com
SIC: 3543 2821 Industrial patterns; polyethylene resins

(G-15418)
RAPTOR MANUFACTURING LC
2252 S Hoover Rd (67209-2830)
PHONE..................................316 201-1772
Kevin Payne,
EMP: 35
SQ FT: 35,000
SALES: 5MM **Privately Held**
SIC: 3544 3441 Special dies & tools; fabricated structural metal

(G-15419)
RATZLAFF CRAIG D RATZLAFF DDS
7570 W 21st St N 1020a (67205-1778)
PHONE..................................316 722-7100
Craig D Ratzlaff DDS, *President*
EMP: 12
SALES (est): 1MM **Privately Held**
SIC: 8021 Orthodontist

(G-15420)
RAY HODGE & ASSOCIATES LLC
8558 W 21st St N Ste 300 (67205-1783)
PHONE..................................316 269-1414
Raymond Hodge, *Mng Member*
Ryan Hodge, *Mng Member*
Jennifer Teach, *Legal Staff*
EMP: 10
SALES (est): 1MM **Privately Held**
SIC: 8111 General practice attorney, lawyer

(G-15421)
RAYERS BEARDEN STAINED GL SUP
6205 W Kellogg Dr (67209-2346)
PHONE..................................316 942-2929
Randall D Rayer, *President*
EMP: 14 **EST:** 1978
SQ FT: 7,000
SALES: 1MM **Privately Held**
SIC: 5231 5211 8999 3272 Glass, leaded or stained; door & window products; stained glass art; concrete products

(G-15422)
RAYMOND OIL COMPANY INC (PA)
Also Called: Raymond Development
155 N Market St Ste 800 (67202-1822)
P.O. Box 48788 (67201-8788)
PHONE..................................316 267-4214
William M Raymond, *President*
William S Raymond, *Senior VP*
Patrick R Raymond, *Vice Pres*
Charles D Roach, *Treasurer*
EMP: 13 **EST:** 1956
SQ FT: 3,800
SALES (est): 2.3MM **Privately Held**
SIC: 1311 5082 Crude petroleum production; natural gas production; oil field equipment

(G-15423)
RAYS ELECTRIC INC
1524 W 29th St N (67204-4824)
P.O. Box 4001 (67204-0001)
PHONE..................................316 838-8231
Richard Kretchmar, *President*
EMP: 20
SQ FT: 5,000
SALES (est): 2MM **Privately Held**
WEB: www.rayselectric.com
SIC: 1731 General electrical contractor

(G-15424)
RD HENRY & COMPANY LLC
3738 S Norman St (67215-8943)
PHONE..................................316 529-3431
Raymond Kieliszak, *Principal*
Daniel Henry, *Vice Pres*
▼ **EMP:** 210
SQ FT: 200,000
SALES: 25MM **Privately Held**
WEB: www.customcupboards.com
SIC: 2434 Wood kitchen cabinets

(G-15425)
REALITY EXECUTIVES CENTER
8100 E 22nd St N 2100-4 (67226-2330)
PHONE..................................316 686-4111
Margaret Dewitt, *Partner*
Roderick Jayroe, *Partner*
Shannon McBride, *Broker*
Lana McIntosh, *Sales Associate*
EMP: 25
SALES (est): 1.3MM **Privately Held**
SIC: 6531 Real estate agent, residential

(G-15426)
REALM BRANDS LLC
3629 N Hydraulic St (67219-3811)
PHONE..................................316 821-9700
Michael Northrup, *CEO*
▲ **EMP:** 10
SALES (est): 833.8K **Privately Held**
SIC: 5136 Men's & boys' clothing

(G-15427)
REALTY WORLD ALLIANCE LLC
6100 E Central Ave # 215 (67208-4244)
PHONE..................................316 688-0077
Brady Barnard, *Office Mgr*
Chris Noffert, *Office Mgr*
Jason Adams, *Agent*
Denise Gray, *Agent*
Roberta Hook, *Agent*
EMP: 20
SALES (est): 1.1MM **Privately Held**
WEB: www.realtyworldwichita.com
SIC: 6531 Real estate agent, residential

(G-15428)
RECOVERY UNLIMITED INC
3835 W Douglas Ave (67213-2408)
PHONE..................................316 941-9948
Donna Philbrick, *Exec Dir*
EMP: 18
SALES (est): 1MM **Privately Held**
SIC: 8069 Alcoholism rehabilitation hospital

(G-15429)
RECREATIONAL VEHICLE PRODUCTS
3050 N Saint Francis St (67219-4045)
P.O. Box 4020 (67204-0020)
PHONE..................................316 832-3400
Gregg Guinn, *President*
EMP: 150
SQ FT: 150,000
SALES (est): 25.4MM **Privately Held**
WEB: www.recreationalvehicleproducts.com
SIC: 3585 Air conditioning, motor vehicle

(G-15430)
REDBUD PEDIATRICS LLC
8725 E 32nd St N (67226-4008)
PHONE..................................316 201-1202
Rebecca H Reddy, *Principal*
EMP: 11
SALES (est): 1.2MM **Privately Held**
SIC: 8011 Pediatrician

(G-15431)
REDGUARD LLC (PA)
4340 S West St (67217-3816)
PHONE..................................316 554-9000
Jeff Lange, *Managing Prtnr*
Ross Draney, *General Mgr*
Joey Salome, *Project Mgr*
Gary Reser, *Prdtn Mgr*
Kent Reida, *Foreman/Supr*
EMP: 150
SALES (est): 30.3MM **Privately Held**
WEB: www.abox4u.com
SIC: 3443 Fabricated plate work (boiler shop)

(G-15432)
REDNECK INC
Also Called: Redneck Trailer Supplies
10606 E 26th Cir N (67226-4536)
PHONE..................................316 263-6090
Jason Hancock, *Principal*
EMP: 23
SQ FT: 3,000
SALES (corp-wide): 156.9MM **Privately Held**
WEB: www.redneck-trailer.com
SIC: 5013 5599 5531 5561 Trailer parts & accessories; utility trailers; trailer hitches, automotive; recreational vehicle parts & accessories
PA: Redneck, Inc.
2100 N West Byp
Springfield MO 65803
417 864-5210

(G-15433)
REFLECTION RIDGE GOLF CORP
2300 N Tyler Rd (67205-8766)
PHONE..................................316 721-0500
Matt Maude, *Branch Mgr*
EMP: 24
SALES (corp-wide): 4.1MM **Privately Held**
SIC: 8361 Geriatric residential care
PA: Reflection Ridge Golf Corporation
7700 W Reflection Rd
Wichita KS 67205
316 721-2024

(G-15434)
REFLECTION RIDGE MAINTENANCE
7414 W 21st St N (67205-1730)
PHONE..................................316 721-9483
Andy Randells, *Superintendent*
John Wright, *Director*
EMP: 12
SALES (est): 800K **Privately Held**
SIC: 5941 7997 Golf goods & equipment; golf club, membership

(G-15435)
REGASA AEROSPACE INC
4327 W May St (67209-2874)
PHONE..................................316 425-0079
Rex A Casner, *President*
Jack Casner, *Vice Pres*
EMP: 6
SALES: 750K **Privately Held**
SIC: 3679 Electronic circuits

(G-15436)
REGENT FINANCIAL GROUP INC
10209 W Central Ave Ste 1 (67212-4685)
PHONE..................................316 462-1341
Casey Gates, *Manager*
EMP: 12
SALES (corp-wide): 5.3MM **Privately Held**
WEB: www.regentfinancial.com
SIC: 6163 Mortgage brokers arranging for loans, using money of others
PA: Regent Financial Group Inc
1910 S 72nd St Ste 103
Omaha NE 68124
402 955-0880

(G-15437)
REGIER CARR & MONROE LLP CPA (PA)
300 W Douglas Ave Ste 900 (67202-2994)
PHONE..................................316 264-2335
James W Monroe, *Managing Prtnr*
Brent Curry, *Partner*
Mark Curry, *Partner*
Albert Denny, *Partner*
Gary Freeman, *Partner*
EMP: 14
SALES (est): 3.4MM **Privately Held**
WEB: www.rcmcpa.com
SIC: 8721 Certified public accountant

(G-15438)
REGIONAL INSURANCE SERVICE CO
Also Called: Anico
2400 N Woodlawn Blvd # 110
(67220-3989)
P.O. Box 21020 (67208-7020)
PHONE..................................316 686-6553
William Mc Adoo, *President*
EMP: 10
SALES (est): 1.6MM **Privately Held**
SIC: 6411 Insurance agents, brokers & service

(G-15439)
REGIS CORPORATION
Also Called: Regis Salon
7700 E Kellogg Dr Ste L02 (67207-1763)
PHONE..................................316 685-5333
Sonji Parrotino, *Manager*
EMP: 10
SALES (corp-wide): 1B **Publicly Held**
WEB: www.regiscorp.com
SIC: 7231 Unisex hair salons
PA: Regis Corporation
7201 Metro Blvd
Edina MN 55439
952 947-7777

(G-15440)
RELIANCE STEEL & ALUMINUM CO
Also Called: Central Plains Steel
3900 Comotara Dr (67226)
PHONE..................................316 636-4500
Nick Martin, *Warehouse Mgr*
Steve Thompson, *Finance*

GEOGRAPHIC

Kim Wittsell, *Mktg Dir*
Gary Oneil, *Manager*
EMP: 75
SALES (corp-wide): 11.5B **Publicly Held**
SIC: 5051 3444 3312 Sheets, metal; sheet metalwork; blast furnaces & steel mills
PA: Reliance Steel & Aluminum Co.
350 S Grand Ave Ste 5100
Los Angeles CA 90071
213 687-7700

(G-15441)
RELIANCE STEEL & ALUMINUM CO
Bralco Metals
2750 S Rock Rd (67210-1824)
PHONE..................................316 838-9351
Sharon Stevens, *Safety Mgr*
Stuart Carder, *Branch Mgr*
EMP: 15
SALES (corp-wide): 11.5B **Publicly Held**
WEB: www.rsac.com
SIC: 5051 Steel; aluminum bars, rods, ingots, sheets, pipes, plates, etc.
PA: Reliance Steel & Aluminum Co.
350 S Grand Ave Ste 5100
Los Angeles CA 90071
213 687-7700

(G-15442)
REMEDIATION CONTRACTORS INC
319 N Mathewson Ave (67214-4044)
PHONE..................................316 269-1549
Mark Conway, *President*
Julie Conway, *Corp Secy*
EMP: 15
SQ FT: 7,500
SALES: 1MM **Privately Held**
WEB: www.remediationcontractors.com
SIC: 1799 Asbestos removal & encapsulation

(G-15443)
RENAL TRTMNT CENTERS-WEST INC
Also Called: Wichita Dialysis Center
909 N Topeka St (67214-3620)
PHONE..................................316 263-9090
Jerry B Cohlmia, *Branch Mgr*
EMP: 14 **Publicly Held**
WEB: www.davita.com
SIC: 8092 8011 Kidney dialysis centers; offices & clinics of medical doctors
HQ: Renal Treatment Centers-West, Inc.
2000 16th St
Denver CO 80202

(G-15444)
RENAL TRTMNT CENTERS-WEST INC
Also Called: Ne Wichita Dialysis Cntr
2630 N Webb Rd Ste 100 (67226-8174)
PHONE..................................316 636-5719
EMP: 14 **Publicly Held**
WEB: www.davita.com
SIC: 8092 Kidney dialysis centers
HQ: Renal Treatment Centers-West, Inc.
2000 16th St
Denver CO 80202

(G-15445)
RENAL TRTMNT CENTERS-WEST INC
Also Called: East Wichita Dialysis Center
320 N Hillside St (67214-4918)
PHONE..................................316 684-3200
Shelly Page, *Manager*
EMP: 23 **Publicly Held**
WEB: www.davita.com
SIC: 8092 Kidney dialysis centers
HQ: Renal Treatment Centers-West, Inc.
2000 16th St
Denver CO 80202

(G-15446)
RESCARE KANSAS WICHITA
5112 E 36th St N Ste 100 (67220-3207)
PHONE..................................316 651-2585
Lachalle Shay, *Principal*
EMP: 11
SALES (est): 350.1K **Privately Held**
SIC: 8082 Home health care services

(G-15447)
RESEARCH PARTNERSHIP INC
Also Called: Wichita Market Research
125 N Market St Ste 1810 (67202-1718)
PHONE..................................316 263-6433
Esther Headley, *President*
Robert Ross, *Vice Pres*
Robin Mishler, *Mktg Dir*
EMP: 21
SQ FT: 6,000
SALES (est): 1.6MM **Privately Held**
SIC: 8732 8742 Market analysis or research; marketing consulting services

(G-15448)
RESIDENCE INN BY MARRIOTT LLC
411 S Webb Rd (67207-1397)
PHONE..................................316 686-7331
Kristi Kirchhosf, *Manager*
Troy Hayden, *Manager*
EMP: 167
SALES (corp-wide): 20.7B **Publicly Held**
SIC: 7011 Hotels & motels
HQ: Residence Inn By Marriott, Llc
10400 Fernwood Rd
Bethesda MD 20817
301 380-3000

(G-15449)
RESIDENTIAL SERVICES INC
Also Called: Maids
1525 W 29th St N (67204-4823)
PHONE..................................316 832-9058
Jony Garcia, *CEO*
Joni Garcia, *President*
Ron Garcia, *Treasurer*
EMP: 22
SQ FT: 1,400
SALES: 500K **Privately Held**
SIC: 7349 7363 Maid services, contract or fee basis; domestic help service

(G-15450)
RESTHAVEN GARDENS OF MEMORY
Also Called: Rest Haven Mortuary
11800 W Kellogg St (67209-1243)
PHONE..................................316 722-2100
Mark Hansen, *Principal*
EMP: 26
SQ FT: 5,000
SALES (est): 1.2MM **Privately Held**
SIC: 6553 7261 Cemeteries, real estate operation; funeral home

(G-15451)
RESTHAVEN MORTUARY INC
11800 W Kellogg St (67209-1243)
PHONE..................................316 722-2100
Mark Hanfen, *General Mgr*
EMP: 11
SQ FT: 2,000
SALES (est): 797.2K
SALES (corp-wide): 3.6MM **Privately Held**
SIC: 7261 Crematory; funeral home
PA: Developers And Management Inc
11800 W Kellogg St
Wichita KS 67209
316 682-6770

(G-15452)
RESTORTION WTRPRFING CNTRS INC (PA)
2222 S Hoover Rd (67209-2830)
P.O. Box 771137 (67277-1137)
PHONE..................................316 942-6602
Todd Chapman, *President*
David B Bumpurs, *Vice Pres*
Edward Parr, *Vice Pres*
EMP: 20
SQ FT: 8,900
SALES: 8.5MM **Privately Held**
WEB: www.restoration-waterproof.com
SIC: 1799 1741 Waterproofing; tuckpointing or restoration

(G-15453)
RETEL BROKERAGE SERVICES INC
7701 E Kellogg Dr Ste 670 (67207-1705)
PHONE..................................678 292-5723
Kathy Kelly Jacobs, *President*
William E Jacobs, *COO*
EMP: 45
SQ FT: 2,000
SALES (est): 5MM **Privately Held**
SIC: 6531 8999 Real estate managers; communication services

(G-15454)
REVEST LLC
2002 S Hydraulic St (67211-5306)
PHONE..................................316 262-8460
William Brent Hurst, *Administration*
EMP: 20
SALES (est): 1.5MM **Privately Held**
SIC: 8742 Financial consultant

(G-15455)
RGIS LLC
7777 E Osie St Ste 308 (67207-3106)
PHONE..................................316 685-6233
EMP: 125
SQ FT: 800
SALES (corp-wide): 4.6B **Publicly Held**
SIC: 7389 Business Services
HQ: Rgis, Llc
2000 Taylor Rd
Auburn Hills MI 48326
248 651-2511

(G-15456)
RICHARD E CROWDER DDS
Also Called: Smiles
7015 E Central Ave Uppr (67206-1944)
PHONE..................................316 684-5184
Richard E Crowder, *Owner*
EMP: 12
SALES (est): 726K **Privately Held**
SIC: 8021 Orthodontist

(G-15457)
RICHMOND ELECTRIC INC
246 S Morningside St (67218-1814)
PHONE..................................316 264-2344
John Edwards Jr, *President*
Patricia Van Osdel, *Vice Pres*
Sue Edwards, *Treasurer*
EMP: 8 **EST:** 1948
SQ FT: 8,000
SALES (est): 1.1MM **Privately Held**
WEB: www.richmondelectric.com
SIC: 5999 5251 7694 7629 Motors, electric; tools, power; rewinding stators; tool repair, electric

(G-15458)
RICK WAYLAND & ASSOCIATES
4801 S Cedardale Ave (67216-3403)
PHONE..................................316 524-0079
Rick Wayland, *Mng Member*
EMP: 10
SALES (est): 113K **Privately Held**
SIC: 6531 Real estate leasing & rentals

(G-15459)
RICKMAN MACHINE CO INC
922 N Santa Fe St (67214-3826)
PHONE..................................316 263-0841
Fax: 316 263-0143
EMP: 25 **EST:** 1965
SQ FT: 33,000
SALES (est): 4.6MM **Privately Held**
SIC: 3728 Mfg Aircraft Parts/Equipment

(G-15460)
RICKS APPLIANCE SERVICE INC
Also Called: All Amrican Maytag HM Appl Ctr
1617 W Harry St (67213-3698)
PHONE..................................316 265-2866
Richard L Ott, *President*
EMP: 18
SQ FT: 12,500
SALES (est): 1.8MM **Privately Held**
WEB: www.ricksapplianceservice.com
SIC: 7629 7623 5722 Electrical household appliance repair; refrigerator repair service; household appliance stores

(G-15461)
RICOH USA INC
8200 E 34th Cir N # 1406 (67226-1349)
PHONE..................................316 262-7172
Tobin Acevedo, *Manager*
EMP: 38 **Privately Held**
WEB: www.ikon.com
SIC: 5044 7359 Photocopy machines; office machine rental, except computers
HQ: Ricoh Usa, Inc.
300 Eagleview Blvd # 200
Exton PA 19341
610 296-8000

(G-15462)
RIDGEWOOD SURGERY AND END
4013 N Ridge Rd Ste 100 (67205-8858)
PHONE..................................316 768-4197
Grey Furr,
EMP: 18
SALES (est): 2.2MM **Privately Held**
SIC: 8011 Ambulatory surgical center

(G-15463)
RIEDL FIRST SECURITIES OF KANS
1841 N Rock Road Ct # 400 (67206-4213)
PHONE..................................316 265-9341
Jerry Riedl, *President*
Janis Jansen, *Vice Pres*
Caesar Nastzger, *Vice Pres*
EMP: 15
SALES (est): 1.5MM **Privately Held**
WEB: www.riedlfirstsecurities.net
SIC: 6211 Security brokers & dealers

(G-15464)
RIORDAN CLINIC INC
Also Called: Riordan Bio-Center Laboratory
3100 N Hillside Ave (67219-3904)
PHONE..................................316 682-3100
Brian Riordan, *CEO*
Andrea Rogers, *Principal*
Donna Kramme, *COO*
Nina Mikirova, *Research*
Carol Marsh, *Finance*
EMP: 45 **EST:** 1975
SALES: 3.9MM **Privately Held**
WEB: www.riordanclinic.org
SIC: 8052 8071 Intermediate care facilities; medical laboratories

(G-15465)
RISE VISION USA INC
216 N Mosley St Ste 120 (67202-2837)
PHONE..................................866 770-1150
Byron Darlison, *President*
Ryan Cahoy, *Managing Dir*
Manish Jain, *Controller*
Joe Hawk, *Sales Staff*
Perry Kirk, *Sales Staff*
EMP: 12
SALES: 3.3MM **Privately Held**
WEB: www.risevision.com
SIC: 3993 Electric signs
PA: Rise Vision Incorporated
545 King St W
Toronto ON M5V 1
866 770-1150

(G-15466)
RITCHIE ASSOCIATES INC (PA)
Also Called: Ritchie Building Company
8100 E 22nd St N # 1000 (67226-2388)
PHONE..................................316 684-7300
Jack Ritchie, *CEO*
Kevin Mullen, *President*
Terry Rhea, *Admin Sec*
EMP: 25
SQ FT: 18,000
SALES (est): 3MM **Privately Held**
WEB: www.ritchiebuilding.com
SIC: 6514 6531 1521 Residential building, four or fewer units: operation; real estate brokers & agents; new construction, single-family houses

(G-15467)
RITCHIE BUILDING CO INC
Also Called: Ritchie Associates
8100 E 22nd St N # 1000 (67226-2310)
PHONE..................................316 684-7300
Jack Ritchie, *CEO*
Kevin Mullen, *President*
James Stockman, *Vice Pres*
EMP: 24
SQ FT: 5,800
SALES (est): 1MM
SALES (corp-wide): 3MM **Privately Held**
WEB: www.ritchiebuilding.com
SIC: 1521 New construction, single-family houses

PA: Ritchie Associates Inc
8100 E 22nd St N # 1000
Wichita KS 67226
316 684-7300

(G-15468)
RITCHIE EXPLORATION INC
8100 E 22nd St N Bldg 700 (67226-2328)
P.O. Box 783188 (67278-3188)
PHONE..................................316 691-9500
A Scott Ritchie, *Ch of Bd*
A Scott Ritchie III, *President*
David Jamis, *Treasurer*
Jim Stockton, *Sales Associate*
EMP: 10
SQ FT: 10,000
SALES (est): 2.6MM **Privately Held**
WEB: www.ritchie-exp.com
SIC: 6792 1382 Oil leases, buying & selling on own account; oil & gas exploration services

(G-15469)
RIVER CITY BREWERY INC
150 N Mosley St (67202-2804)
PHONE..................................316 263-2739
William Shea, *Principal*
Ty Issa, *Principal*
EMP: 60
SQ FT: 12,000
SALES (est): 2.1MM **Privately Held**
WEB: www.rivercitybrewingco.com
SIC: 5813 2082 5812 7299 Bar (drinking places); malt beverages; eating places; banquet hall facilities

(G-15470)
RIVER CITY ELEVATOR LLC
428 S Socora St (67209-1732)
PHONE..................................316 773-3161
James Morris,
Rochelle Morris,
EMP: 10 **EST:** 1998
SQ FT: 3,000
SALES: 3MM **Privately Held**
WEB: www.rivercityelevator.biz
SIC: 5084 7699 Elevators; elevators: inspection, service & repair

(G-15471)
RIVER CITY MECHANICAL INC
312 N Indiana Ave (67214-4035)
PHONE..................................316 682-2672
Curt Crager, *Principal*
EMP: 13
SALES (est): 1.7MM **Privately Held**
SIC: 1711 Plumbing contractors

(G-15472)
RIVERSIDE VILLAGE SENIOR LIVIN
777 N Mclean Blvd Ofc (67203-4994)
PHONE..................................316 942-7000
Via Christie, *Owner*
EMP: 60 **EST:** 2000
SALES: 5.8MM **Privately Held**
SIC: 8051 Convalescent home with continuous nursing care

(G-15473)
ROBERT DENTON
Also Called: Haul4u
2019 E 2nd St N (67214-4343)
PHONE..................................316 691-7046
Robert Denton, *Owner*
EMP: 10
SALES (est): 180.6K **Privately Held**
SIC: 7389

(G-15474)
ROCKWELL COLLINS INC
2051 S Airport Rd (67209-1949)
PHONE..................................316 677-4808
Cliff Moore, *Engineer*
Gilles Cochet, *Senior Engr*
Dave Schletzbaum, *Branch Mgr*
Jim Aukofer, *Manager*
EMP: 129
SALES (corp-wide): 66.5B **Publicly Held**
WEB: www.keo.com
SIC: 3812 5088 Search & navigation equipment; aircraft & space vehicle supplies & parts
HQ: Rockwell Collins, Inc.
400 Collins Rd Ne
Cedar Rapids IA 52498

(G-15475)
ROCKY TOP COUNTER TOP LLC
1336 S Mosley Ave (67211-3328)
PHONE..................................316 262-0497
Rocky Hopper, *Mng Member*
EMP: 5
SALES: 100K **Privately Held**
SIC: 1423 Crushed & broken granite

(G-15476)
ROGER A RIEDMILLER
532 N Market St (67214-3514)
PHONE..................................316 448-1028
Roger Riedmiller, *Owner*
EMP: 10
SALES (est): 1.3MM **Privately Held**
SIC: 8111 General practice law office

(G-15477)
ROLLER CITY INC
Also Called: H&H Amusement
3234 S Meridian Ave (67217-2063)
PHONE..................................316 942-4555
Mary Hollaba, *CEO*
EMP: 10
SALES (est): 385.4K **Privately Held**
SIC: 7999 Roller skating rink operation

(G-15478)
ROLLING HILLS COUNTRY CLUB (PA)
223 S Westlink St (67209-1447)
P.O. Box 12388 (67277-2388)
PHONE..................................316 722-4273
Janice Befort, *Controller*
Scott Ronksley, *Manager*
Don Farquhar, *Director*
EMP: 75
SQ FT: 13,500
SALES: 2.7MM **Privately Held**
WEB: www.rollinghillscc.net
SIC: 7997 Country club, membership

(G-15479)
ROLLING HILLS COUNTRY CLUB
Also Called: Maintenance Dept
330 N Maize Rd (67212-4653)
PHONE..................................316 721-6780
Don Farquhar, *Manager*
EMP: 50
SALES (est): 877.8K
SALES (corp-wide): 2.7MM **Privately Held**
WEB: www.rollinghillscc.net
SIC: 7997 Country club, membership
PA: Rolling Hills Country Club Inc
223 S Westlink St
Wichita KS 67209
316 722-4273

(G-15480)
ROLLING HILLS HEALTH AND REHAB
1319 S Seville Ave (67209-1828)
PHONE..................................316 722-6916
EMP: 186
SALES (est): 426.6K
SALES (corp-wide): 32.7MM **Privately Held**
SIC: 8099 Health & allied services
PA: Midwest Health, Inc
3024 Sw Wanamaker Rd # 300
Topeka KS 66614
785 272-1535

(G-15481)
RON J MAREK DO PA
1901 N Maize Rd (67212-5203)
PHONE..................................316 462-1050
Ron J Marek Do, *Owner*
EMP: 12
SALES (est): 1.3MM **Privately Held**
SIC: 8031 Offices & clinics of osteopathic physicians

(G-15482)
RONS SIGN CO INC
1329 S Handley St (67213-4316)
PHONE..................................316 267-8914
John Saindon, *President*
Lareina Lynn Saindon, *Corp Secy*
EMP: 26
SALES (est): 3.6MM **Privately Held**
SIC: 3993 2394 Electric signs; awnings, fabric: made from purchased materials

(G-15483)
ROTEK SERVICES INC
955 N Mosley St (67214-3423)
PHONE..................................316 263-3131
Brian McNeil, *Principal*
EMP: 24
SQ FT: 10,000
SALES: 4MM **Privately Held**
SIC: 7694 Electric motor repair

(G-15484)
ROTH HEATING & AC
4141 W Maple St (67209-2579)
P.O. Box 3727 (67201-3727)
PHONE..................................316 942-4141
James Cole, *President*
Laiketa Brown, *Vice Pres*
Beverly Cole, *Vice Pres*
Brad Freeman, *Opers Mgr*
Jim Cole, *Treasurer*
EMP: 24 **EST:** 1955
SQ FT: 7,300
SALES: 1.8MM **Privately Held**
SIC: 1711 Warm air heating & air conditioning contractor

(G-15485)
ROTH K CHRISTOPHERSON
Also Called: A'Deas
719 S Saint Francis St (67211-2332)
PHONE..................................316 269-2494
Roth K Christopherson, *Principal*
▲ **EMP:** 7 **EST:** 1996
SQ FT: 3,000
SALES (est): 1MM **Privately Held**
WEB: www.adeasprinting.com
SIC: 2752 Publication printing, lithographic

(G-15486)
ROTOR QUALITY LLC
7804 E Funston St Ste 222 (67207-3107)
PHONE..................................316 425-0418
Tuan Nguyen, *Owner*
EMP: 7
SALES (est): 859.5K **Privately Held**
SIC: 3465 Body parts, automobile: stamped metal

(G-15487)
ROYAL CARIBBEAN CRUISES LTD
4729 Palisade St (67217)
PHONE..................................316 554-5000
Mike Semler, *Branch Mgr*
Jeff Carpenter, *Manager*
EMP: 4900
SALES (corp-wide): 9.4B **Publicly Held**
WEB: www.royalcaribbean.com
SIC: 4724 Travel agencies
PA: Royal Caribbean Cruises Ltd.
1050 Caribbean Way
Miami FL 33132
305 539-6000

(G-15488)
ROYAL SPA
7700 E Kellogg Dr Q02a (67207-1715)
PHONE..................................316 681-0002
EMP: 10
SALES (est): 82K **Privately Held**
SIC: 7231 Manicurist, pedicurist

(G-15489)
RPM MOTORSPORTS LLC
10817 W Kellogg St (67209-1223)
P.O. Box 273, Valley Center (67147-0273)
PHONE..................................316 259-4576
Robert Paul Musgrove, *Principal*
EMP: 11
SALES (est): 491.1K **Privately Held**
SIC: 7996 Theme park, amusement

(G-15490)
RS USED OIL SERVICES INC (DH)
2932 N Ohio St (67219-4321)
PHONE..................................866 778-7336
Randall Wilson, *CEO*
Gerald Kutsch, *Manager*
EMP: 39
SQ FT: 12,000
SALES (est): 11.4MM
SALES (corp-wide): 3.3B **Publicly Held**
SIC: 2992 Lubricating oils & greases
HQ: Clean Harbors Environmental Services, Inc.
42 Longwater Dr
Norwell MA 02061
781 792-5000

(G-15491)
RUBBER BELTING & HOSE SUP INC
1850 N Ohio Ave (67214-1530)
PHONE..................................316 269-1151
Steven McNulty, *President*
Samuel Van Buchanan, *Treasurer*
EMP: 36
SQ FT: 36,000
SALES: 15MM **Privately Held**
WEB: www.rbhinc.com
SIC: 5085 Hose, belting & packing; rubber goods, mechanical

(G-15492)
RUFFIN HOTEL OF WICHITA LLC
Also Called: Fairfield Inn
417 S Webb Rd (67207-1307)
PHONE..................................316 685-3777
Michelle Stein, *General Mgr*
Bradley Culp, *Principal*
EMP: 15
SALES (est): 118.2K **Privately Held**
SIC: 7011 Hotels & motels

(G-15493)
RUFFIN RIVERFRONT HOTEL LLC
400 W Waterman St (67202-3600)
PHONE..................................316 293-1234
Michelle Beneke, *Principal*
EMP: 99
SALES (est): 1MM **Privately Held**
SIC: 7011 Hotels

(G-15494)
RV PRODUCTS (DH)
3050 N Saint Francis St (67219-4045)
P.O. Box 4020 (67204-0020)
PHONE..................................316 832-3400
Melvin Adams, *President*
▲ **EMP:** 23
SQ FT: 34,000
SALES (est): 64.4MM **Privately Held**
WEB: www.maxxair.com
SIC: 3714 3585 Motor vehicle parts & accessories; air conditioning equipment, complete
HQ: Airxcel, Inc.
3050 N Saint Francis St
Wichita KS 67219
316 832-3400

(G-15495)
RX PLUS PHARMACIES INC
Also Called: Professional Pharmacy
744 N Waco Ave (67203-3936)
PHONE..................................316 263-5218
Merlin McFarland, *President*
Merlyin McFarrlund, *President*
EMP: 15
SQ FT: 2,000
SALES (est): 3.2MM **Privately Held**
SIC: 5912 5122 Drug stores; pharmaceuticals

(G-15496)
RYAN DEVELOPMENT COMPANY LLC (PA)
8301 E 21st St N (67206-2932)
P.O. Box 47854 (67201-7854)
PHONE..................................316 630-9223
Jeffery Crippen, *President*
David Ray, *COO*
Larry Ryan, *Vice Pres*
Chris Flickenger, *CFO*
EMP: 30 **EST:** 1997
SALES (est): 2.4MM **Privately Held**
SIC: 8732 Research services, except laboratory

(G-15497)
RYDER TRUCK RENTAL INC
3525 N Hydraulic St (67219-3809)
PHONE..................................316 945-8484
Ray Torres, *Manager*

GEOGRAPHIC

EMP: 12
SALES (corp-wide): 8.4B **Publicly Held**
SIC: 7513 7359 Truck rental, without drivers; stores & yards equipment rental
HQ: Ryder Truck Rental, Inc.
11690 Nw 105th St
Medley FL 33178
305 500-3726

(G-15498)
S & A CONSTRUCTION INC
1600 S Topeka Ave (67211-4132)
PHONE..................................316 558-8422
Stuart Nelson, *President*
EMP: 12
SALES (est): 2MM **Privately Held**
SIC: 1521 General remodeling, single-family houses

(G-15499)
S & B MOTELS INC (PA)
Also Called: Hampton Inn
400 N Woodlawn St Ste 205 (67208-4332)
PHONE..................................316 522-3864
Stanley Weilert, *President*
Lee Weilert Price, *Director*
EMP: 165
SQ FT: 2,000
SALES (est): 12MM **Privately Held**
SIC: 7011 Hotels & motels

(G-15500)
S & S EQUIPMENT CO INC
1901 N Broadway Ave (67214-1124)
P.O. Box 4049 (67204-0049)
PHONE..................................316 267-7471
William B Scofield, *President*
Jennifer Lynn Scofield, *Corp Secy*
EMP: 13
SQ FT: 30,000
SALES (est): 4.4MM **Privately Held**
SIC: 5084 7699 Compressors, except air conditioning; compressor repair

(G-15501)
S & S MANUFACTURING INC
2661 W Esthner Ave (67213-1824)
PHONE..................................316 946-5755
Derick Trevor, *Owner*
EMP: 5
SQ FT: 1,500
SALES (est): 322.1K **Privately Held**
SIC: 3365 Aerospace castings, aluminum

(G-15502)
S F B PLASTICS INC
1819 W Harry St (67213-3243)
PHONE..................................800 343-8133
David Long, *President*
John Fosse, *Vice Pres*
Mark Sullivan, *Vice Pres*
Sara Dwyer, *Executive*
Ray Sullivan, *Shareholder*
EMP: 60
SQ FT: 88,000
SALES (est): 14.9MM **Privately Held**
WEB: www.sfbplastics.com
SIC: 3089 Plastic containers, except foam

(G-15503)
S-KMAC INVESTMENTS LLC (PA)
Also Called: Crave Beauty Academy
3804 W Douglas Ave (67203-5428)
PHONE..................................316 990-5095
Stan McIntosh, *CEO*
Kim McIntosh, *President*
EMP: 32
SQ FT: 5,100
SALES (est): 659.2K **Privately Held**
WEB: www.xenonintl.net
SIC: 7231 Cosmetology school

(G-15504)
SAFETY-KLEEN (WT) INC
2549 N New York Ave (67219-4322)
PHONE..................................316 269-7400
Robert M Craycraft II, *President*
Dave Sprinkle, *President*
Dave Eckelbarger, *Exec VP*
Jean Lee, *Senior VP*
Mark Stone, *Senior VP*
EMP: 30
SALES (est): 2MM
SALES (corp-wide): 3.3B **Publicly Held**
SIC: 4953 8748 Refuse systems; environmental consultant
HQ: Safety-Kleen, Inc.
2600 N Central Expy # 400
Richardson TX 75080
800 669-5740

(G-15505)
SAFETY-KLEEN SYSTEMS INC
4801 W Irving St (67209-2620)
PHONE..................................316 942-5001
Mark Jordan, *Manager*
EMP: 15
SALES (corp-wide): 3.3B **Publicly Held**
SIC: 7359 7389 Equipment rental & leasing; solvents recovery service
HQ: Safety-Kleen Systems, Inc.
2600 N Central Expy # 400
Richardson TX 75080
972 265-2000

(G-15506)
SAIA MOTOR FREIGHT LINE LLC
4525 S Palisade Ave (67217-4931)
PHONE..................................316 522-1786
J Rinn, *Branch Mgr*
EMP: 25
SALES (corp-wide): 1.6B **Publicly Held**
WEB: www.saia.com
SIC: 4213 Contract haulers
HQ: Saia Motor Freight Line, Llc
11465 Johns Creek Pkwy # 400
Duluth GA 30097
770 232-5067

(G-15507)
SAINT FRANCIS CMNTY SVCS INC
Also Called: Training Department
1999 N Amidon Ave 100b (67203-2121)
PHONE..................................316 831-0330
Jane Fry, *Principal*
EMP: 10
SALES (corp-wide): 108.2MM **Privately Held**
SIC: 8741 8361 Hospital management; residential care
PA: Saint Francis Community Services, Inc.
509 E Elm St
Salina KS 67401
785 825-0541

(G-15508)
SAINT FRNCIS RADIATION THERAPY
817 N Emporia St (67214-3709)
PHONE..................................316 268-5927
David Gryant, *Principal*
EMP: 20
SALES (est): 615.8K **Privately Held**
SIC: 8011 Oncologist

(G-15509)
SAINT RAPHAEL HOME CARE INC
903 W 18th St N (67203-2306)
PHONE..................................316 269-5400
Pamela S Pirotte, *President*
EMP: 33 **EST:** 1997
SALES (est): 1.5MM **Privately Held**
WEB: www.saintraphaelhomecare.com
SIC: 8082 Home health care services

(G-15510)
SALINA CONCRETE PRODUCTS INC
Kansas Building Products
1600 S Hoover Rd (67209-2812)
P.O. Box 9463 (67277-0463)
PHONE..................................316 943-3241
EMP: 16
SALES (corp-wide): 147MM **Publicly Held**
WEB: www.salinaconcreteproducts.com
SIC: 3251 5032 5211 3272 Brick & structural clay tile; brick, except refractory; tile, structural clay; brick; tile, ceramic; stone, cast concrete; clay chimney products; septic system construction
HQ: Salina Concrete Products, Incorporated
1100 W Ash St
Salina KS 67401
785 827-7281

(G-15511)
SALON KNOTTY
1445 N Rock Rd Ste 175 (67206-1292)
PHONE..................................316 636-4400
Pam Wiemerslage, *Owner*
EMP: 12
SALES (est): 245.7K **Privately Held**
SIC: 7231 Beauty shops

(G-15512)
SALON PROGRESSIONS & DAY SPA
2360 N Maize Rd Ste 100 (67205-7355)
PHONE..................................316 729-1980
Robin Kelly, *Partner*
James Garritson, *Partner*
EMP: 11
SALES (est): 359.5K **Privately Held**
WEB: www.salonprogressionsdayspa.com
SIC: 7231 7991 Unisex hair salons; spas

(G-15513)
SALVATION ARMY
1739 S Elpyco St (67218-4307)
PHONE..................................316 685-8699
Rey Olton, *Manager*
EMP: 45
SALES (corp-wide): 5.8MM **Privately Held**
WEB: www.salvationarmykc.org
SIC: 8661 8641 Miscellaneous denomination church; community membership club
PA: The Salvation Army
1351 E 10th St
Kansas City MO 64106
816 421-5434

(G-15514)
SALVATION ARMY
350 N Market St (67202-2010)
PHONE..................................316 263-2769
M Kaye Barth, *Principal*
EMP: 12
SALES (corp-wide): 2.2B **Privately Held**
WEB: www.salarmychicago.org
SIC: 8322 Emergency shelters
HQ: The Salvation Army
5550 Prairie Stone Pkwy # 130
Hoffman Estates IL 60192
847 294-2000

(G-15515)
SALVATION ARMY NATIONAL CORP
1910 S Everett St (67213-2808)
PHONE..................................316 943-9893
Paul Ferguson, *Manager*
EMP: 38
SALES (corp-wide): 2.2B **Privately Held**
WEB: www.salvationarmyusa.org
SIC: 8661 8322 Miscellaneous denomination church; rehabilitation services
PA: The Salvation Army National Corporation
615 Slaters Ln
Alexandria VA 22314
703 684-5500

(G-15516)
SANDIFER ENGRG & CONTRLS INC
229 S Ellis St (67211-1809)
PHONE..................................316 794-8880
Mike Brumback, *President*
Curtis Johnson, *Vice Pres*
Thomas Aaron Rusher, *Vice Pres*
EMP: 29
SQ FT: 3,000
SALES (est): 8.8MM **Privately Held**
WEB: www.sec-controls.com
SIC: 5075 5065 Warm air heating & air conditioning; security control equipment & systems

(G-15517)
SANDPIPER HEALTHCARE AND
5808 W 8th St N (67212-2802)
PHONE..................................316 945-3606
George V Hager Jr,
EMP: 150
SALES: 8.3MM **Publicly Held**
SIC: 8051 8069 Skilled nursing care facilities; specialty hospitals, except psychiatric
HQ: Genesis Healthcare Llc
101 E State St
Kennett Square PA 19348

(G-15518)
SANDS ENTERPRISES INC
Also Called: Flying Colors
240 S West St Ste 40 (67213-2116)
PHONE..................................316 942-8686
Kay L Sands, *President*
Allan K Sands, *Corp Secy*
EMP: 5
SQ FT: 2,000
SALES: 250K **Privately Held**
WEB: www.flyingcolorsks.com
SIC: 5699 3999 2759 2395 T-shirts, custom printed; buttons: Red Cross, union, identification; screen printing; embroidery products, except schiffli machine

(G-15519)
SARAHLEE COFFEE AND TEA CORP
427 S Washington Ave (67202-4735)
PHONE..................................316 262-0398
Diane Patton, *Manager*
EMP: 27
SALES (est): 901.2K **Privately Held**
SIC: 7389 Coffee service

(G-15520)
SARATOGA CAPITAL INC
Also Called: Twin Lake Apartments
1915 N Porter Ave Apt 162 (67203-2297)
PHONE..................................316 838-1972
Elizabeth Getchell, *Manager*
EMP: 10
SALES (corp-wide): 19.7MM **Privately Held**
WEB: www.saratogacapital.net
SIC: 6513 Apartment building operators
HQ: Saratoga Capital, Inc.
485 Alberto Way Ste 200
Los Gatos CA 95032
408 298-8600

(G-15521)
SASNAK MANAGEMENT CORPORATION (PA)
Also Called: Carlos O'Kelleys
1877 N Rock Rd (67206-1283)
PHONE..................................316 683-2611
Darrel Rolph, *President*
David Rolph, *Vice Pres*
Paul Schwartz, *Treasurer*
Paul Sgontz, *Manager*
EMP: 35 **EST:** 1973
SQ FT: 7,000
SALES (est): 40.6MM **Privately Held**
WEB: www.carlosokelly.com
SIC: 8741 Restaurant management

(G-15522)
SAUERWEIN CONSTRUCTION CO INC
2055 S Edwards St (67213-1858)
P.O. Box 13057 (67213-0057)
PHONE..................................316 942-0028
Frank Sauerwein, *President*
Frank Saurwein, *President*
Mike Sauerwein, *Chairman*
Beverly Sauerwein, *Vice Pres*
Rudolf Sauerwein, *Vice Pres*
EMP: 19
SQ FT: 3,000
SALES (est): 5.5MM **Privately Held**
WEB: www.sauerweinconstruction.com
SIC: 1542 1541 Commercial & office building, new construction; commercial & office buildings, renovation & repair; industrial buildings & warehouses

(G-15523)
SAVOY RGLS BHN ENGNRNG LND SUR
Also Called: Land Surveyor
924 N Main St (67203-3607)
PHONE..................................316 264-8008
Brian Savoy, *President*
Randy Johnson-Assct, *President*

▲ = Import ▼=Export
◆ =Import/Export

EMP: 30
SALES (est): 900.9K **Privately Held**
SIC: 8732 Survey service: marketing, location, etc.

(G-15524)
SB MANUFACTURING INC
3707 W Mccormick St (67213-2025)
PHONE..................................316 941-9591
Tom McBride, *Vice Pres*
Judy Worrell, *Admin Sec*
EMP: 440
SQ FT: 5,000
SALES (est): 68.6MM
SALES (corp-wide): 181.7MM **Privately Held**
WEB: www.sbmfg.com
SIC: 3711 Street sprinklers & sweepers (motor vehicles), assembly of
PA: Berry Companies, Inc.
3223 N Hydraulic St
Wichita KS 67219
316 838-3321

(G-15525)
SC HALL INDUSTRIAL SVCS INC
1221 E Murdock St (67214-3456)
PHONE..................................316 945-4255
Scott Hall, *CEO*
Lindsey Hall,
EMP: 35
SQ FT: 20,000
SALES: 2.5MM **Privately Held**
WEB: www.hallservices.com
SIC: 7359 6531 7629 3444 Equipment rental & leasing; real estate leasing & rentals; electrical repair shops; sheet metalwork

(G-15526)
SCHAEFER JOHNSON COX FREY (PA)
Also Called: Manson Ward Legion/Sjcf
257 N Broadway Ave (67202-2315)
PHONE..................................316 684-0171
Joseph A Johnson, *Senior VP*
J S Frey, *Senior VP*
Matt Hamm, *Vice Pres*
Edward M Koser, *Vice Pres*
Donald Manson, *Vice Pres*
EMP: 71
SALES (est): 7.9MM **Privately Held**
SIC: 8712 8711 Architectural engineering; engineering services

(G-15527)
SCHAEFER JOHNSON COX FREY ARCH
Also Called: Sjcf Architecture
257 N Broadway Ave (67202-2315)
PHONE..................................316 684-0171
Shannon Ferguson-Bohm, *President*
Matt Hamm, *Vice Pres*
Malcolm Watkins, *Associate*
EMP: 36 **EST**: 2009
SQ FT: 10,000
SALES (est): 744.2K **Privately Held**
SIC: 8712 Architectural services

(G-15528)
SCHAMMERHORN INC
124 S Seneca St (67213-4785)
PHONE..................................316 265-8659
Kendall L Wendt, *President*
Lisa Hayse, *Business Mgr*
Peggy Case, *Office Mgr*
EMP: 5
SQ FT: 5,000
SALES (est): 745.1K **Privately Held**
WEB: www.schammerhorn.com
SIC: 5719 5713 5714 5023 Window furnishings; carpets; draperies; carpets; window furnishings; window blinds

(G-15529)
SCHEER DENTISTRY PA
7707 E 29th St N (67226-3403)
PHONE..................................316 636-1222
Brick R Scheer DMD, *President*
Harold M Sheer PA, *Vice Pres*
EMP: 10
SALES (est): 812.4K **Privately Held**
SIC: 8021 Dentists' office

(G-15530)
SCHENDEL SERVICES INC
Also Called: Pest Services
1545 S Broadway Ave (67211-3131)
PHONE..................................316 320-6422
Tim Barlow, *Manager*
EMP: 10
SALES (corp-wide): 1.9B **Publicly Held**
WEB: www.schendelpest.com
SIC: 7342 Pest control in structures
HQ: Schendel Services, Inc.
1035 Se Quincy St
Topeka KS
785 232-9344

(G-15531)
SCHENKER INC
3801 S Oliver St (67210-2112)
PHONE..................................316 260-6367
EMP: 30
SALES (corp-wide): 10.1MM **Privately Held**
WEB: www.schenkerlogisticsusa.com
SIC: 4731 Freight transportation arrangement
HQ: Schenker, Inc.
1305 Executive Blvd # 200
Chesapeake VA 23320
757 821-3400

(G-15532)
SCHENKER INC
1659 S Sabin St (67209-2749)
PHONE..................................316 942-0146
EMP: 28 **Privately Held**
SIC: 4731 Freight Transportation Arrangement
HQ: Schenker, Inc.
41 Pinelawn Rd 110
Melville NY 23320
757 821-3400

(G-15533)
SCHOLFIELD BODY SHOP INC (PA)
11516 E Kellogg Dr (67207-1931)
P.O. Box 781896 (67278-1896)
PHONE..................................316 688-6550
Steve Hatchett, *President*
Victor H Scholfield, *Vice Pres*
Scott Davies, *Shareholder*
Roger Schofield, *Shareholder*
EMP: 40
SQ FT: 28,000
SALES: 5MM **Privately Held**
SIC: 7532 Body shop, automotive

(G-15534)
SCHUELLER JOHN
Also Called: Johns Farm
1230 N Broadway Ave # 125 (67214-2827)
PHONE..................................316 371-7761
John Schueller, *Owner*
EMP: 49 **EST**: 2009
SALES (est): 639K **Privately Held**
SIC: 0191 General farms, primarily crop

(G-15535)
SCHURZ COMMUNICATIONS INC
Also Called: Kwch-CBS TV
2815 E 37th St N (67219-3545)
PHONE..................................316 838-1212
Joan Barrett, *Manager*
EMP: 130
SALES (corp-wide): 1B **Publicly Held**
WEB: www.schurz.com
SIC: 4833 Television broadcasting stations
HQ: Schurz Communications, Inc.
1301 E Douglas Rd Ste 200
Mishawaka IN 46545
574 247-7237

(G-15536)
SCOPE INC
Also Called: Air-Cap Dental
425 S Greenwood St Ste 1 (67211-1841)
PHONE..................................316 393-7414
R Craig Park DDS, *President*
Almeda Park, *Treasurer*
EMP: 8
SALES (est): 877.5K **Privately Held**
SIC: 3843 2434 Hand pieces & parts, dental; dental chairs; cabinets, dental; wood kitchen cabinets

(G-15537)
SCOTSMAN INN WEST LLC
5922 W Kellogg Dr (67209-2338)
Rural Route 7942 E Dublin Ct (67206)
PHONE..................................316 943-3800
EMP: 30
SQ FT: 19,432
SALES (est): 1.3MM **Privately Held**
WEB: www.scotsmaninnwichita.com
SIC: 7011 Motels; hotels

(G-15538)
SCOTT ERICKSON
Also Called: Bax Global
1659 S Sabin St (67209-2749)
PHONE..................................316 942-0146
Fax: 316 942-8320
EMP: 11
SQ FT: 3,000
SALES (est): 1.2MM **Privately Held**
SIC: 4731 Freight Transportation Arrangement

(G-15539)
SCOTTS POWERLINE CONSTRUCTION
9911 E 21st St N Apt 803 (67206-3528)
PHONE..................................316 440-8290
EMP: 10
SALES (est): 985.4K **Privately Held**
SIC: 1623 Water/Sewer/Utility Construction

(G-15540)
SECURITAS SEC SVCS USA INC
Also Called: North Central Region
225 N Market St Ste 310 (67202-2024)
PHONE..................................316 838-2900
Devin Renberger, *Branch Mgr*
Bryan Saindon, *Branch Mgr*
EMP: 220
SALES (corp-wide): 10.6B **Privately Held**
WEB: www.securitasinc.com
SIC: 7381 Security guard service
HQ: Securitas Security Services Usa, Inc.
9 Campus Dr
Parsippany NJ 07054
973 267-5300

(G-15541)
SECURITY 1ST TITLE LLC
2872 N Ridge Rd (67205-1143)
PHONE..................................316 722-2463
Janis Biggs, *Assistant*
EMP: 27 **Privately Held**
SIC: 6541 Title abstract offices
PA: Security 1st Title Llc
727 N Waco Ave Ste 300
Wichita KS 67203

(G-15542)
SECURITY 1ST TITLE LLC (PA)
727 N Waco Ave Ste 300 (67203-3954)
PHONE..................................316 267-8371
Michael Brown, *Vice Pres*
Debby Reed, *Branch Mgr*
Debbie Beck, *Manager*
Lisa Lilja, *Manager*
Deana Henrie, *Officer*
EMP: 25
SALES (est): 64.5MM **Privately Held**
SIC: 6541 Title & trust companies

(G-15543)
SECURITY PORTFOLIO X LP
1223 N Rock Rd Ste E200 (67206-1272)
PHONE..................................316 634-1115
Bill Ard, *Partner*
EMP: 11
SALES (est): 531.1K **Privately Held**
SIC: 7381 Guard services

(G-15544)
SECURITY STORAGE PRPTS LLC
9103 E 37th St N (67226-2010)
PHONE..................................316 634-6510
Marshall Millsap, *Principal*
EMP: 14
SALES (est): 1.3MM **Privately Held**
SIC: 4225 Warehousing, self-storage

(G-15545)
SEDGWICK CNTY DVLPMNTL DSABLTY
615 N Main St (67203-3602)
PHONE..................................316 660-7630
Chad Von Ahnen, *Director*
Karie Hughes, *Administration*
EMP: 20
SALES (est): 396.1K **Privately Held**
SIC: 8322 Social services for the handicapped

(G-15546)
SEDGWICK COUNTRY ANIMAL RESPON
Also Called: Scart
6505 E Central Ave (67206-1924)
PHONE..................................316 619-1723
Christen Skaer, *Director*
EMP: 15
SALES (est): 423.6K **Privately Held**
SIC: 8322 Adoption services

(G-15547)
SEDGWICK COUNTY ACCOUNTING
4035 E Harry St (67218-3724)
PHONE..................................316 383-7184
Teresa Moore, *Manager*
EMP: 18
SALES (est): 1.4MM **Privately Held**
SIC: 8721 Accounting, auditing & bookkeeping

(G-15548)
SEDGWICK COUNTY TRANSPORTATION
1015 W Stillwell St Fl 2 (67213-4450)
PHONE..................................316 660-7070
Valerhy Harmon, *Manager*
Annette Graham, *Exec Dir*
EMP: 50
SALES (est): 2MM **Privately Held**
SIC: 4789 Transportation services

(G-15549)
SEDGWICK COUNTY ZOOLOGICAL SOC
5555 W Zoo Blvd (67212-1643)
PHONE..................................316 660-9453
Sara Jantz, *CFO*
Elyse Trego, *Manager*
Joell Dunham, *Supervisor*
Jeffrey Ettling, *Exec Dir*
Mark Reed, *Director*
EMP: 200
SALES (est): 3.1MM **Privately Held**
WEB: www.kansas-hazmat.com
SIC: 7996 Amusement parks

(G-15550)
SEDGWICK JUVENILE FIELD SVCS
3803 E Harry St Ste 125 (67218-3709)
PHONE..................................316 660-5380
Terri Patterson, *Administration*
EMP: 40 **EST**: 2002
SALES (est): 615.6K **Privately Held**
SIC: 8361 8322 Juvenile correctional facilities; probation office

(G-15551)
SEEDERS INC
4111 S Broad St (67215-1817)
PHONE..................................316 722-8345
Linda Snook, *President*
EMP: 15 **EST**: 1980
SALES (est): 1.4MM **Privately Held**
WEB: www.seeders.com
SIC: 0782 Seeding services, lawn

(G-15552)
SELECT MEDICAL CORPORATION
3243 E Murdock St Ste 101 (67208-3018)
PHONE..................................316 687-4581
Karl Yourdon, *Branch Mgr*
Darci Needham, *Manager*
EMP: 14
SALES (corp-wide): 5B **Publicly Held**
SIC: 8049 Physical therapist

GEOGRAPHIC

HQ: Select Medical Corporation
4714 Gettysburg Rd
Mechanicsburg PA 17055
717 972-1100

(G-15553)
SELECT MEDICAL CORPORATION
929 N St Francis St Sw (67214-3821)
PHONE..................................316 261-8303
Peggy Cliffe, *CEO*
EMP: 13
SALES (corp-wide): 5B **Publicly Held**
WEB: www.selectmedicalcorp.com
SIC: 8093 Rehabilitation center, outpatient treatment
HQ: Select Medical Corporation
4714 Gettysburg Rd
Mechanicsburg PA 17055
717 972-1100

(G-15554)
SELECT MEDICAL CORPORATION
2434 N Woodlawn Blvd # 370
(67220-3997)
PHONE..................................316 687-9227
Brad Begnoche, *Manager*
EMP: 13
SALES (corp-wide): 5B **Publicly Held**
WEB: www.selectmedicalcorp.com
SIC: 8093 Rehabilitation center, outpatient treatment
HQ: Select Medical Corporation
4714 Gettysburg Rd
Mechanicsburg PA 17055
717 972-1100

(G-15555)
SELFS INC (DH)
721 E Mount Vernon St (67211-5093)
PHONE..................................316 267-1295
Eldon L Self, *CEO*
Mitchell Self, *President*
Dave Self, *Vice Pres*
Rob Self, *Controller*
▲ **EMP:** 17
SQ FT: 40,000
SALES: 8MM
SALES (corp-wide): 348.7MM **Privately Held**
WEB: www.selfs.com
SIC: 5023 Floor coverings
HQ: E. J. Welch Co., Inc.
13735 Lakefront Dr
Earth City MO 63045
314 739-2273

(G-15556)
SELLERS EQUIPMENT INC
1645 S West St (67213-1101)
P.O. Box 1940, Salina (67402-1940)
PHONE..................................316 943-9311
Wayne Euker, *Owner*
EMP: 25
SALES (corp-wide): 17MM **Privately Held**
SIC: 5082 5084 General construction machinery & equipment; industrial machinery & equipment
HQ: Sellers Equipment, Inc.
400 N Chicago St
Salina KS 67401
785 823-6378

(G-15557)
SENIHCAM INC
460 E 46th St S (67216-1763)
PHONE..................................316 524-4561
Scott Burke, *President*
Sarah Burke, *Vice Pres*
Joe Vanderhoff, *Project Mgr*
Jacie Sullivan, *Manager*
EMP: 5
SALES (est): 732K **Privately Held**
WEB: www.senihcam.com
SIC: 3599 Machine shop, jobbing & repair

(G-15558)
SENIOR OPERATIONS LLC
Also Called: Senior Aerospace Composites
2700 S Custer Ave (67217-1356)
P.O. Box 12950 (67277-2950)
PHONE..................................316 942-3208
Roy Best, *CEO*
EMP: 200
SALES (corp-wide): 1.4B **Privately Held**
SIC: 3728 Aircraft parts & equipment
HQ: Senior Operations Llc
300 E Devon Ave
Bartlett IL 60103
630 372-3500

(G-15559)
SENIOR SERVICES INC WICHITA (PA)
Also Called: MEALS-ON-WHEELS PROGRAM
200 S Walnut St (67213-4777)
PHONE..................................316 267-0302
Laurel Alkire, *COO*
Karen Dao, *Director*
Chris Heiman, *Director*
Deann Most, *Director*
Diane Nutt, *Director*
EMP: 57
SQ FT: 21,000
SALES: 2.9MM **Privately Held**
SIC: 8322 Old age assistance; general counseling services

(G-15560)
SENIOR SERVICES INC WICHITA
Also Called: Meals On Wheels
200 S Walnut St (67213-4777)
PHONE..................................316 267-0122
Laurel Alkire, *Director*
EMP: 60
SALES (corp-wide): 2.9MM **Privately Held**
SIC: 8322 Senior citizens' center or association
PA: Senior Services, Inc. Of Wichita
200 S Walnut St
Wichita KS 67213
316 267-0302

(G-15561)
SENTAGE CORPORATION
Also Called: Dental Services Group
201 N Emporia Ave (67202-2507)
P.O. Box 760 (67201-0760)
PHONE..................................316 263-0284
Kirby Pickle, *CEO*
Tony Phillips, *Manager*
EMP: 50
SALES (corp-wide): 59MM **Privately Held**
WEB: www.dentalservices.net
SIC: 8072 Artificial teeth production
PA: Sentage Corporation
146 2nd St N Ste 207
Saint Petersburg FL 33701
727 502-2069

(G-15562)
SENTINEL REAL ESTATE CORP
Also Called: Riverpark Plaza Apartments
400 W Central Ave Ofc (67203-4074)
PHONE..................................316 265-9471
Chris Willenbroug, *Principal*
EMP: 11
SALES (corp-wide): 2MM **Privately Held**
WEB: www.andoverplaceapartments.com
SIC: 6513 7382 7349 Apartment building operators; security systems services; building maintenance services
HQ: Sentinel Real Estate Corporation
1251 Ave Of The Americas
New York NY 10020
212 408-2900

(G-15563)
SER CORPORATION (PA)
1020 N Main St Ste D (67203-3617)
PHONE..................................316 264-5372
Richard Lopez, *CEO*
Deb Laviolette, *Marketing Staff*
EMP: 23
SQ FT: 6,000
SALES: 1MM **Privately Held**
WEB: www.sercorp.com
SIC: 8331 Community service employment training program

(G-15564)
SERVICE BODY SHOP
2550 W Pawnee St (67213-1814)
PHONE..................................316 260-5300
Chad Johnson, *Owner*
EMP: 15
SALES (est): 1.1MM **Privately Held**
SIC: 7532 Paint shop, automotive

(G-15565)
SERVICE CORP INTERNATIONAL
Also Called: SCI
11800 W Highway 54 (67209-1243)
PHONE..................................316 722-2100
Mark Hansen, *Branch Mgr*
EMP: 20
SALES (corp-wide): 3.1B **Publicly Held**
WEB: www.sci-corp.com
SIC: 7261 Funeral director
PA: Service Corporation International
1929 Allen Pkwy
Houston TX 77019
713 522-5141

(G-15566)
SERVICE CORP INTERNATIONAL
Also Called: SCI
201 S Hydraulic St (67211-1906)
PHONE..................................316 263-0244
Paul Edmiston, *Branch Mgr*
EMP: 11
SALES (corp-wide): 3.1B **Publicly Held**
SIC: 7261 Funeral home
PA: Service Corporation International
1929 Allen Pkwy
Houston TX 77019
713 522-5141

(G-15567)
SERVICE CORPS RETIRED EXECS
Also Called: S C O R E 143
220 W Douglas Ave Ste 450 (67202-3137)
PHONE..................................316 269-6273
Roger Douthett, *Branch Mgr*
EMP: 12
SALES (corp-wide): 13.1MM **Privately Held**
WEB: www.score199.mv.com
SIC: 8611 8748 8249 Business associations; business consulting; business training services
PA: Service Corps Of Retired Executives Association
1175 Herndon Pkwy Ste 900
Herndon VA 20170
703 487-3612

(G-15568)
SERVICETITAN INC
Also Called: Fam Host
245 N Waco St Ste 230 (67202-1131)
P.O. Box 6 (67201-0006)
PHONE..................................316 267-5758
EMP: 5
SALES (corp-wide): 4.5MM **Privately Held**
SIC: 7372 7371 Prepackaged software; custom computer programming services
PA: Servicetitan, Inc.
801 N Brand Blvd Ste 700
Glendale CA 91203
855 899-0970

(G-15569)
SF HOTEL COMPANY LP
Also Called: Summerfield Hotel Co
8100 E 22nd St N Bldg 500 (67226-2305)
PHONE..................................316 681-5100
Rolf Ruhfus, *Partner*
Roy Baker, *Treasurer*
EMP: 80
SQ FT: 14,000
SALES (est): 2.7MM **Privately Held**
SIC: 7011 Hotels & motels

(G-15570)
SHADOW 7 LLC
1223 N Rock Rd 200 (67206-1269)
PHONE..................................316 687-5777
C Robert Buford, *Mng Member*
Sterling Burner, *Mng Member*
Russell Briggs, *Manager*
EMP: 13
SALES (est): 247.5K **Privately Held**
SIC: 0272 Horse farm

(G-15571)
SHAMROCK RESOURCES INC
4502 N Spyglass Cir (67226-3365)
PHONE..................................316 636-9557
Patrick Denihan, *Principal*
EMP: 5 **EST:** 2008
SALES (est): 340K **Privately Held**
SIC: 1389 1382 Oil & gas field services; oil & gas exploration services

(G-15572)
SHAMROCK TIRE & AUTO SERVICE (PA)
Also Called: Tire Dealers Warehouse
3001 S Broadway Ave (67216-1017)
P.O. Box 472286, Tulsa OK (74147-2286)
PHONE..................................316 522-2297
Gary Sicka, *President*
Kenny Rogers, *General Mgr*
Barbara Sicka, *Corp Secy*
Josh McDonald, *Sales Staff*
▲ **EMP:** 28 **EST:** 1935
SQ FT: 35,000
SALES (est): 5.9MM **Privately Held**
SIC: 5014 5531 Tires & tubes; automotive tires

(G-15573)
SHARON BAPTIST CHURCH
Also Called: Child's Horizon Pre School
2221 S Oliver Ave (67218-5197)
PHONE..................................316 684-5156
Barbara Morgan, *Principal*
Steve Pims, *Pastor*
Rhonda Beasley, *Director*
EMP: 11
SQ FT: 91,000
SALES: 370K **Privately Held**
SIC: 8661 8351 Baptist Church; preschool center

(G-15574)
SHARPE PRINTING CO INC
345 N Waco St (67202-1158)
PHONE..................................316 262-4041
David Sharpe, *President*
Troy Thompson, *Mfg Staff*
EMP: 12 **EST:** 1945
SQ FT: 4,600
SALES (est): 1.6MM **Privately Held**
WEB: www.sharpeprinting.com
SIC: 2752 Commercial printing, offset; offset & photolithographic printing; promotional printing, lithographic; business form & card printing, lithographic

(G-15575)
SHARPENING SPECIALISTS LLC
2124 S Edwards St (67213-1805)
P.O. Box 13322 (67213-0322)
PHONE..................................316 945-0593
Larry J Bell, *Managing Prtnr*
Greta L Bell, *Partner*
David Hudson, *Manager*
EMP: 22
SQ FT: 12,000
SALES (est): 3.1MM **Privately Held**
SIC: 7699 3545 7389 5251 Knife, saw & tool sharpening & repair; cutting tools for machine tools; grinding, precision: commercial or industrial; tools; printing trades machinery, equipment & supplies

(G-15576)
SHARPLINE CONVERTING INC
1520 S Tyler Rd (67209-1851)
P.O. Box 9608 (67277-0608)
PHONE..................................316 722-9080
Jack Snyder, *CEO*
Steve Calvert, *Sales Mgr*
Jenny Hutchison, *Prgrmr*
Buffy Nance, *Representative*
EMP: 308
SQ FT: 120,000
SALES (est): 72.7MM **Privately Held**
WEB: www.sharpline.com
SIC: 2396 Automotive trimmings, fabric

(G-15577)
SHAW GROUP INC
7330 W 33rd St N Ste 106 (67205-9370)
PHONE..................................316 220-8020
EMP: 502

▲ = Import ▼=Export
◆ =Import/Export

SALES (corp-wide): 10.6B **Privately Held**
SIC: 8734 Provides Services To Environmental And Infrastructure
HQ: The Shaw Group Inc
4171 Essen Ln
Baton Rouge LA 70809

(G-15578)
SHAWNEE MISSION TREE SVC INC
Also Called: Arbor Masters Tree Service
3428 N Emporia St (67219-3615)
PHONE..................................316 838-3111
Arlen Bebemeyer, *General Mgr*
EMP: 10
SALES (corp-wide): 56MM **Privately Held**
WEB: www.smtree.com
SIC: 0783 Planting, pruning & trimming services
PA: Shawnee Mission Tree Service, Inc.
8250 Cole Pkwy
Shawnee KS 66227
913 441-8888

(G-15579)
SHEA VISION ASSOCIATES
2251 N Woodlawn Blvd (67220-3947)
PHONE..................................316 686-6071
Fax: 316 686-4214
EMP: 20
SALES (est): 1MM **Privately Held**
SIC: 8042 Optometrist's Office

(G-15580)
SHELL TOPCO LP (DH)
2533 S West St (67217-1025)
P.O. Box 7710 (67277-7710)
PHONE..................................316 942-7266
Jan Kreminski, *Mng Member*
Steve Fricker,
EMP: 12
SQ FT: 100,000
SALES: 100MM
SALES (corp-wide): 1.8MM **Privately Held**
SIC: 3625 1711 Control equipment, electric; mechanical contractor
HQ: Nova Capital Management Usa Llc
401 N Michigan Ave # 1200
Chicago IL 60611
312 822-3380

(G-15581)
SHERWOOD CONSTRUCTION CO INC (PA)
3219 W May St (67213-1540)
P.O. Box 9163 (67277-0163)
PHONE..................................316 943-0211
David Sherwood, *CEO*
Howard Sherwood, *Ch of Bd*
John R Curtis, *President*
Craig Sasser, *Superintendent*
Matt Ritchie, *Vice Pres*
EMP: 197
SQ FT: 4,000
SALES (est): 103.6MM **Privately Held**
SIC: 1794 1622 3273 1611 Excavation & grading, building construction; bridge, tunnel & elevated highway; ready-mixed concrete; highway & street construction; general contractor, highway & street construction

(G-15582)
SHIRLEY ALEXANDER
5500 E Kellogg Dr Bldg 5b (67218-1607)
PHONE..................................316 651-3621
Shirley J Alexander, *Owner*
Donna Cox, *Administration*
EMP: 90 **EST:** 2013
SALES (est): 617.9K **Privately Held**
SIC: 8011 Psychiatrist

(G-15583)
SIEMENS ENERGY INC
1090 E 37th St N (67219-3515)
PHONE..................................316 315-4534
John Logan, *Principal*
EMP: 9
SALES (corp-wide): 96.9B **Privately Held**
SIC: 3511 Turbines & turbine generator sets
HQ: Siemens Energy, Inc.
4400 N Alafaya Trl
Orlando FL 32826
407 736-2000

(G-15584)
SIEMENS INDUSTRY INC
Also Called: B C S
618 E Douglas Ave (67202-3504)
PHONE..................................316 267-5814
Ken Stoppel, *Manager*
EMP: 20
SALES (corp-wide): 96.9B **Privately Held**
WEB: www.sibt.com
SIC: 3829 1711 Measuring & controlling devices; plumbing, heating, air-conditioning contractors
HQ: Siemens Industry, Inc.
1000 Deerfield Pkwy
Buffalo Grove IL 60089
847 215-1000

(G-15585)
SIEMENS INDUSTRY INC
Also Called: S T G
2219b S Air Cargo Rd (67209-1938)
PHONE..................................316 946-4190
Jim Cook, *Manager*
EMP: 43
SALES (corp-wide): 96.9B **Privately Held**
WEB: www.sibt.com
SIC: 7382 Security systems services
HQ: Siemens Industry, Inc.
1000 Deerfield Pkwy
Buffalo Grove IL 60089
847 215-1000

(G-15586)
SIEMENS INDUSTRY INC
740 N Gilda St (67212-4806)
PHONE..................................316 260-4340
EMP: 87
SALES (corp-wide): 96.9B **Privately Held**
SIC: 3822 Air conditioning & refrigeration controls
HQ: Siemens Industry, Inc.
1000 Deerfield Pkwy
Buffalo Grove IL 60089
847 215-1000

(G-15587)
SIERRA HILLS GOLF CLUB
Also Called: Sierra Hills Exec Golf CLB
13420 E Pawnee St (67230-9176)
PHONE..................................316 733-9333
Wayne Larson, *President*
EMP: 18
SALES (est): 550K **Privately Held**
WEB: www.sierrahillsgolfclub.com
SIC: 7992 Public golf courses

(G-15588)
SIGMA DISTRIBUTING COMPANY INC (PA)
901 S Sabin St (67209-2625)
P.O. Box 9226 (67277-0226)
PHONE..................................316 943-4499
Tim Donovan, *President*
Bill Donovan, *Corp Secy*
Christina Donovan, *Vice Pres*
▲ **EMP:** 25
SQ FT: 15,500
SALES (est): 22MM **Privately Held**
WEB: www.sigmadist.com
SIC: 5013 Automobile glass; exhaust systems (mufflers, tail pipes, etc.)

(G-15589)
SIGNAL THEORY INC (PA)
255 N Mead St (67202-2707)
PHONE..................................316 263-0124
Tom Bertels, *Partner*
Randall Mikulecky, *Partner*
Lynell Stucky, *Partner*
Samuel Williams, *Partner*
John January, *Co-CEO*
EMP: 39
SQ FT: 23,000
SALES (est): 12.7MM **Privately Held**
WEB: www.wehatesheep.com
SIC: 7311 Advertising consultant

(G-15590)
SIGNATURE FLIGHT SUPPORT CORP
1980 S Airport Rd (67209-1942)
PHONE..................................316 522-2010
Bryan Orr, *General Mgr*
EMP: 74
SALES (corp-wide): 2.3B **Privately Held**
SIC: 4581 Aircraft servicing & repairing
HQ: Signature Flight Support Corporation
13485 Veterans Way # 600
Orlando FL 32827

(G-15591)
SIGNATURE SPORTSWEAR INC
519 N Turnberry Cir (67230-1522)
PHONE..................................620 421-1871
David Gegen, *President*
John Rigby Carey, *Vice Pres*
Doyle Dodsworth, *Vice Pres*
Jack Ward, *Vice Pres*
EMP: 74 **EST:** 1971
SQ FT: 12,500
SALES (est): 5.2MM **Privately Held**
SIC: 2329 2339 3552 Athletic (warmup, sweat & jogging) suits: men's & boys'; athletic clothing: women's, misses' & juniors'; silk screens for textile industry

(G-15592)
SIGNS & DESIGN LLC
4545 W Central Ave (67212-2223)
P.O. Box 49515 (67201-9515)
PHONE..................................316 264-7446
Michael Janzen, *Owner*
Ariel Davis, *Marketing Staff*
Kenneth Woodruff, *Graphic Designe*
EMP: 5
SQ FT: 4,500
SALES (est): 654K **Privately Held**
WEB: www.signsdesigninc.com
SIC: 3993 Signs & advertising specialties

(G-15593)
SIGNS OF BUSINESS INC (PA)
Also Called: Fastsigns
150 S Rock Rd (67207-1152)
PHONE..................................316 683-5700
Christopher Davis, *President*
Nina Davis, *Corp Secy*
B H Koster, *Vice Pres*
EMP: 13
SALES (est): 1.5MM **Privately Held**
SIC: 3993 5099 Signs & advertising specialties; signs, except electric

(G-15594)
SILVA SECURITY SERVICE
2042 N Gow St (67203-1107)
PHONE..................................316 942-7872
Paul D Silva, *Owner*
EMP: 29
SALES (est): 549.2K **Privately Held**
SIC: 7381 Security guard service

(G-15595)
SIMPLEX TIME RECORDER LLC
Also Called: Simplex Time Recorder 472
625 N Carriage Pkwy # 140 (67208-4510)
PHONE..................................316 686-6363
Donald L Hull, *Branch Mgr*
EMP: 50 **Privately Held**
WEB: www.comtec-alaska.com
SIC: 5063 1731 Power transmission equipment, electric; safety & security specialization
HQ: Simplex Time Recorder Llc
50 Technology Dr
Westminster MA 01441

(G-15596)
SIMPSON CONSTRUCTION SVCS INC
567 W Douglas Ave (67213-4701)
PHONE..................................316 942-3206
Robert Simpson, *President*
Brad Cragun, *Superintendent*
Gary Lubbers, *Superintendent*
Anne Simpson, *Corp Secy*
W Gregg Oblinger, *Exec VP*
EMP: 48
SALES (est): 15MM **Privately Held**
SIC: 1542 1541 Commercial & office building contractors; commercial & office building, new construction; commercial & office buildings, renovation & repair; industrial buildings, new construction; renovation, remodeling & repairs: industrial buildings

(G-15597)
SINCLAIR & SONS CUSTOM WELDING
1023 S Santa Fe St (67211-2437)
PHONE..................................316 263-3500
Rebecca Sinclair, *President*
Ronnie Sinclair, *Vice Pres*
Tina Sinclair-Blazer, *Vice Pres*
Leslie Sinclair, *Treasurer*
EMP: 20
SQ FT: 23,000
SALES: 2MM **Privately Held**
WEB: www.sinclairandsons.com
SIC: 3499 Metal household articles

(G-15598)
SISTERS ST JOSEPH WICHITA KS (HQ)
Also Called: Mount St Mary's Convent
3700 E Lincoln St (67218-2097)
PHONE..................................316 686-7171
Sister Helene Lentz, *President*
Sister Arlys McDonald, *Treasurer*
Patricia Stanley, *CTO*
Sister Pam Young, *Admin Sec*
EMP: 50
SALES (est): 8.4MM
SALES (corp-wide): 16.8MM **Privately Held**
SIC: 8661 8062 8742 Convent; general medical & surgical hospitals; hospital & health services consultant
PA: Sisters Of St Joseph
3430 Rocky River Dr
Cleveland OH 44111
216 252-0440

(G-15599)
SKAER VETERINARY CLINIC P A
404 S Edgemoor St Ste 100 (67218-1632)
PHONE..................................316 683-4641
Dr William C Skaer, *Owner*
Christen L Skaer Dvm, *Principal*
EMP: 19
SALES (est): 977.7K **Privately Held**
SIC: 0742 Animal hospital services, pets & other animal specialties

(G-15600)
SKATE SOUTH INC
1900 E Macarthur Rd (67216-2605)
PHONE..................................316 524-7261
Kelly Little, *President*
EMP: 18
SQ FT: 20,000
SALES (est): 810K **Privately Held**
SIC: 7999 5941 Roller skating rink operation; skating equipment

(G-15601)
SKYWARD CREDIT UNION
4 Cessna Blvd (67215-1423)
P.O. Box 771069 (67277-1069)
PHONE..................................316 517-6578
Larry Damm, *President*
Phil Chronister, *Chairman*
Holly Dixon, *Chairman*
Link Newton, *Chairman*
Misty Randal, *Chairman*
EMP: 37
SALES: 10.2MM **Privately Held**
SIC: 6062 State credit unions, not federally chartered

(G-15602)
SLAPE AND HOWARD CHARTERED
Also Called: Slape, Dale V
1009 S Broadway Ave (67211-2232)
PHONE..................................316 262-3445
Dale V Slape, *President*
Garry Howa, *Partner*
Phillip Slape, *Principal*
Garry L Howard, *Vice Pres*
Delynn Nelson, *Legal Staff*
EMP: 11

SQ FT: 1,950
SALES (est): 1.5MM **Privately Held**
WEB: www.slapehoward.com
SIC: 8111 General practice attorney, lawyer; general practice law office

(G-15603)
SLAWSON EXPLORATION CO INC (PA)
727 N Waco Ave Ste 400 (67203-3900)
PHONE..................................316 263-3201
Donald C Slawson, *President*
Stephen B Slawson, *COO*
Kathy A Atkins, *Vice Pres*
Robert T Slawson, *Vice Pres*
Stuart M Kowalski, *Admin Sec*
EMP: 23
SQ FT: 16,000
SALES (est): 8.7MM **Privately Held**
SIC: 7011 8742 1382 Hotels; real estate consultant; oil & gas exploration services

(G-15604)
SLAWSON INVESTMENT CORPORATION (PA)
727 N Waco Ave Ste 400 (67203-3900)
P.O. Box 2907 (67201-2907)
PHONE..................................316 263-3201
Larry Chambers, *President*
EMP: 26
SQ FT: 16,000
SALES (est): 2.2MM **Privately Held**
SIC: 7011 7997 Hotels & motels; country club, membership

(G-15605)
SMG HOLDINGS INC
500 E Waterman St (67202-4509)
PHONE..................................316 440-9016
EMP: 13
SALES (corp-wide): 23.7B **Privately Held**
SIC: 7929 Entertainment service
HQ: Smg Holdings, Llc
300 Cnshohckn State Rd # 450
Conshohocken PA 19428

(G-15606)
SMITH & SMITH AIRCRAFT INTL
3738 W 29th St S (67217-1006)
PHONE..................................316 945-0204
Linda Mill, *Branch Mgr*
EMP: 14
SQ FT: 7,500 **Privately Held**
SIC: 3724 3721 Aircraft engines & engine parts; research & development on aircraft by the manufacturer
PA: Smith & Smith Aircraft International, Ltd
111 Veterans Memorial Blv
Metairie LA 70005

(G-15607)
SMITH CONSTRUCTION COMPANY INC
4620 W Esthner Ave (67209-2788)
P.O. Box 13213 (67213-0213)
PHONE..................................316 942-7989
W Alan Smith, *President*
Garrett Addison, *Vice Pres*
Jason C Smith, *Treasurer*
Janice J Smith, *Admin Sec*
EMP: 25 **EST:** 1967
SQ FT: 3,200
SALES (est): 7.4MM **Privately Held**
WEB: www.smithconstco.com
SIC: 1542 Commercial & office building, new construction

(G-15608)
SMITH SHAY FARMER & WETTA LLC
200 W Douglas Ave Ste 350 (67202-3019)
PHONE..................................316 267-5293
Dennis E Shay, *Owner*
EMP: 11
SALES (est): 879.4K **Privately Held**
SIC: 8111 General practice attorney, lawyer

(G-15609)
SMITHCON LLC
Also Called: Smithcon Construction
3030 N Ohio St (67219-4131)
PHONE..................................316 744-3406
Erik Smith, *President*
Bruce Richardson, *COO*
EMP: 45
SALES (est): 3.9MM **Privately Held**
SIC: 1771 Concrete work

(G-15610)
SMITHFIELD PACKAGED MEATS CORP
2323 S Sheridan St (67213-1553)
PHONE..................................316 942-8461
Manuel Diaz, *Human Res Mgr*
Randy Dalinghaun, *Manager*
Jason Earhart, *Manager*
EMP: 519 **Privately Held**
WEB: www.farmlandfoods.com
SIC: 2013 5142 Sausages from purchased meat; meat, frozen: packaged
HQ: Smithfield Packaged Meats Corp.
805 E Kemper Rd
Cincinnati OH 45246
513 782-3800

(G-15611)
SNODGRASS & SONS CNSTR CO INC
2700 S George Wash Blvd (67210-1520)
PHONE..................................316 687-3110
David L Snodgrass, *President*
Steve Slusher, *Vice Pres*
Lindsey Koland, *Treasurer*
Aaron Snodgrass, *Manager*
Mark Schmidt, *Info Tech Mgr*
EMP: 58
SQ FT: 24,696
SALES: 16.7MM **Privately Held**
WEB: www.snodgrassconst.com
SIC: 1542 1541 Commercial & office buildings, renovation & repair; industrial buildings, new construction

(G-15612)
SOMNOGRAPH INC
Also Called: Tallgrass
7111 E 21st St N Ste G (67206-1027)
PHONE..................................316 925-4624
Duke Naipohn, *CEO*
EMP: 60
SQ FT: 1,000
SALES: 2.5MM **Privately Held**
WEB: www.somnograph.com
SIC: 8071 Neurological laboratory

(G-15613)
SONAR SANGAM INC
Also Called: Best Western
4510 S Broadway Ave (67216-1734)
PHONE..................................316 529-4911
Neil Patel, *President*
Jan Patel, *Manager*
EMP: 10
SALES (est): 339K **Privately Held**
SIC: 7011 Hotels & motels

(G-15614)
SONNYS INC
1030 S West St (67213-1628)
PHONE..................................316 942-2390
Edward Bosley, *President*
EMP: 10
SALES (est): 1MM **Privately Held**
SIC: 7532 Body shop, automotive

(G-15615)
SONODORA INC
Also Called: Always Best Care of Heart Land
4601 E Douglas Ave (67218-1011)
PHONE..................................316 494-2218
Gweneth Burbank, *President*
EMP: 35
SALES: 350K **Privately Held**
SIC: 8082 Home health care services

(G-15616)
SOS METALS MIDWEST LLC
9800 W York St (67215-8933)
PHONE..................................316 522-0101
Donny Shadrow, *Mng Member*
Janet Pracht, *Manager*
Sandy Shadrow,
EMP: 22
SQ FT: 51,000
SALES (est): 13.2MM **Privately Held**
SIC: 5051 5093 Nonferrous metal sheets, bars, rods, etc.; scrap & waste materials

(G-15617)
SOUTH CENTRAL KS ECON DEV DIST
Also Called: SCKEDD/TAG
9730 E 50th St N (67226-8804)
PHONE..................................316 262-7035
Daniel Bass, *Finance Mgr*
Bill Lampe, *Manager*
Bill Bolin Jr, *Exec Dir*
Arielle Kennedy, *Admin Asst*
Gloria McDowell, *Administration*
EMP: 34
SALES: 4MM **Privately Held**
WEB: www.sckedd.org
SIC: 8733 Noncommercial research organizations

(G-15618)
SOUTH CENTRAL PATHOLOGY LAB PA
Also Called: Stjosephs Via Christy Med Ctr
3600 E Harry St (67218-3713)
PHONE..................................316 689-5668
Phil Stamps, *President*
James Farley, *Vice Pres*
Stanley E Pollman, *Treasurer*
Scott Paxton, *Admin Sec*
EMP: 15
SALES (est): 1MM **Privately Held**
SIC: 8071 Pathological laboratory

(G-15619)
SOUTH ROCK BILLIARD LLC
2020 S Rock Rd Ste 20 (67207-5351)
PHONE..................................316 651-0444
Lori Huysman, *Mng Member*
EMP: 12
SALES (est): 492.1K **Privately Held**
SIC: 7999 Billiard parlor

(G-15620)
SOUTH WICHITA FAMILY MEDICINE
Also Called: Greer, Gregory G
3133 S Seneca St (67217-3234)
PHONE..................................316 524-4338
David Kortge, *Owner*
EMP: 16
SALES (est): 660K **Privately Held**
SIC: 8011 Clinic, operated by physicians; general & family practice, physician/surgeon

(G-15621)
SOUTHBOROUGH PARTNERS
Also Called: Storm Sheltors Plus
4911 S Meridian Ave (67217-3709)
PHONE..................................316 529-3200
Jeff Lang, *Partner*
EMP: 11
SQ FT: 1,700
SALES: 100K **Privately Held**
SIC: 6515 1521 Mobile home site operators; mobile home repair, on site

(G-15622)
SOUTHEAST FAMILY HEALTHCARE
863 N Stagecoach St (67230-7022)
PHONE..................................316 612-1332
Amy E Curry MD, *Partner*
Michael Patton MD, *Partner*
EMP: 18 **EST:** 2001
SALES (est): 995.3K **Privately Held**
SIC: 8011 General & family practice, physician/surgeon

(G-15623)
SOUTHERN FOODS GROUP LLC
Borden Dairy
240 N Handley St (67203-6020)
PHONE..................................316 264-5011
Dale Sinclair, *Manager*
EMP: 8 **Publicly Held**
WEB: www.meadowgold.com
SIC: 2026 Fluid milk
HQ: Southern Foods Group, Llc
3114 S Haskell Ave
Dallas TX 75223
214 824-8163

(G-15624)
SOUTHERN GLAZERS WINE AND SP
4626 S Palisade Ave (67217-4924)
PHONE..................................316 264-1354
Pat Barton, *Branch Mgr*
EMP: 15
SQ FT: 8,000
SALES (corp-wide): 12.3B **Privately Held**
WEB: www.glazer.com
SIC: 5182 Wine
HQ: Southern Glazer's Wine And Spirits Of Texas, Llc
2001 Diplomat Dr
Farmers Branch TX 75234
972 277-2000

(G-15625)
SOUTHERNCARLSON INC
Also Called: Carlson Systems
4245 W 31st St S (67215-1003)
PHONE..................................316 942-1392
Bruce Munsell, *Branch Mgr*
EMP: 16 **Privately Held**
SIC: 5085 5084 Industrial supplies; materials handling machinery
PA: Southerncarlson, Inc.
10840 Harney St
Omaha NE 68154

(G-15626)
SOUTHSIDE HOMES INC
3020 S Broadway Ave (67216-1016)
PHONE..................................316 522-7100
Patrick O'Connor, *President*
EMP: 12
SQ FT: 2,300
SALES: 2.5MM **Privately Held**
SIC: 5039 Mobile homes

(G-15627)
SOUTHWEST NATIONAL BANK (HQ)
400 E Douglas Ave (67202-3408)
P.O. Box 1401 (67201-1401)
PHONE..................................316 291-5299
Jerry Blue, *CEO*
John Naftzger, *Co-COB*
Valerie Parker, *Exec VP*
Keith D Stevens, *Vice Pres*
Mandi Plunk, *Trust Officer*
EMP: 55
SQ FT: 6,000
SALES: 24MM
SALES (corp-wide): 21.8MM **Privately Held**
WEB: www.southwestnb.com
SIC: 6021 National trust companies with deposits, commercial
PA: Republic Financial Corporation
2150 N Woodrow Ave
Wichita KS 67203
316 838-5741

(G-15628)
SOUTHWEST NATIONAL BANK
454 S Tracy St (67209-2525)
P.O. Box 1401 (67201-1401)
PHONE..................................316 942-4004
Nicki Didlake, *Branch Mgr*
EMP: 10
SALES (corp-wide): 21.8MM **Privately Held**
SIC: 6021 National commercial banks
HQ: Southwest National Bank
400 E Douglas Ave
Wichita KS 67202
316 291-5299

(G-15629)
SOUTHWEST NATIONAL BANK
2700 W 13th St N (67203-1805)
PHONE..................................316 941-1335
Pamela Watkins, *Manager*
Palmira Aguilar, *Representative*
EMP: 12
SALES (corp-wide): 21.8MM **Privately Held**
SIC: 6021 National trust companies with deposits, commercial
HQ: Southwest National Bank
400 E Douglas Ave
Wichita KS 67202
316 291-5299

▲ = Import ▼=Export
◆ =Import/Export

(G-15630)
SOUTHWEST NATIONAL BANK
2150 N Woodrow Ave (67203-6214)
PHONE.................................316 838-5741
Vernon Blue, *Branch Mgr*
EMP: 17
SALES (corp-wide): 21.8MM **Privately Held**
SIC: 6021 National trust companies with deposits, commercial
HQ: Southwest National Bank
400 E Douglas Ave
Wichita KS 67202
316 291-5299

(G-15631)
SOUTHWEST PAPER COMPANY INC (PA)
3930 N Bridgeport Cir (67219-3322)
PHONE.................................316 838-7755
Eric Tangeman, *President*
Curt D Clanton, *CFO*
EMP: 29
SQ FT: 80,000
SALES (est): 34.8MM **Privately Held**
WEB: www.swpaper.com
SIC: 5087 5113 5111 Janitors' supplies; industrial & personal service paper; printing paper

(G-15632)
SOUTHWESTERN ELECTRICAL CO INC
1638 E 1st St N (67214-4161)
P.O. Box 1602 (67201-1602)
PHONE.................................316 263-1264
Richard Drake, *President*
Carl Amrine, *Treasurer*
EMP: 120 **EST:** 1908
SQ FT: 21,000
SALES: 10MM **Privately Held**
WEB: www.sw-electric.com
SIC: 1731 5211 General electrical contractor; electrical construction materials

(G-15633)
SOUTHWESTERN REMODELING CONTRS
Also Called: Southwestern Roofing & Siding
134 N Elizabeth St (67203-6126)
PHONE.................................316 263-1239
Art Bryan, *President*
Chad Bryan, *General Mgr*
Rebecca Conner, *Office Mgr*
EMP: 50
SQ FT: 12,000
SALES (est): 6.8MM **Privately Held**
SIC: 1521 1542 General remodeling, single-family houses; commercial & office buildings, renovation & repair

(G-15634)
SPANGENBERG PHILLIPS INC
121 N Mead St Ste 201 (67202-2747)
PHONE.................................316 267-4002
Rebecca Gates, *Partner*
Nancy Steele, *Partner*
Brad Teeter, *Partner*
Greg Tice, *Partner*
Randy Phillips, *Vice Pres*
EMP: 16
SQ FT: 6,000
SALES (est): 2.5MM **Privately Held**
WEB: www.spangenbergphillips.com
SIC: 8712 Architectural engineering

(G-15635)
SPECIALISTS GROUP LLC (PA)
105 S Broadway Ave # 200 (67202-4217)
PHONE.................................316 267-7375
Darren Bean, *General Mgr*
Bim Heineman, *COO*
Greg Foss, *Vice Pres*
Joan Rapp, *Consultant*
J Jerry Holland, *Director*
EMP: 17
SQ FT: 6,000
SALES (est): 1.4MM **Privately Held**
WEB: www.tsgstaff.com
SIC: 7361 7363 Executive placement; temporary help service

(G-15636)
SPECIALTY FABRICATION INC
1517 N Santa Fe St (67214-1257)
PHONE.................................316 264-0603
Daniel J Phillippi, *President*
Daniel J Philippi, *President*
Cheryl Phillippi, *Corp Secy*
EMP: 13
SALES: 2.5MM **Privately Held**
SIC: 7389 3441 3312 1799 Metal slitting & shearing; fabricated structural metal; blast furnaces & steel mills; welding on site; tube fabricating (contract bending & shaping)

(G-15637)
SPECIALTY PATTERNS INC
1300 S Bebe St (67209-2608)
PHONE.................................316 945-8131
Don L Terhune, *President*
Steve Terhune, *General Mgr*
EMP: 10
SQ FT: 5,000
SALES (est): 3.4MM **Privately Held**
SIC: 3724 Engine mount parts, aircraft

(G-15638)
SPECTRUM PROMOTIONAL PDTS INC
9212 E 37th St N (67226-2015)
PHONE.................................316 262-1199
Mike Wood, *President*
Jason Gardner, *General Mgr*
Mike Christman, *Accounts Mgr*
Cindy Miller, *Office Mgr*
EMP: 16
SALES (est): 2.3MM **Privately Held**
SIC: 8743 Promotion service

(G-15639)
SPICE MERCHANT & CO
1300 E Douglas Ave (67214-4029)
PHONE.................................316 263-4121
Robert A Boewe, *Owner*
EMP: 15
SQ FT: 14,000
SALES (est): 540.8K **Privately Held**
WEB: www.thespicemerchant.com
SIC: 5812 5149 5499 Coffee shop; delicatessen (eating places); coffee & tea; coffee

(G-15640)
SPIRIT AEROSYSTEMS INC
3800 S Turnpike Dr (67210)
PHONE.................................316 523-2995
Edwin Fenn, *Manager*
EMP: 21 **Publicly Held**
SIC: 3728 Aircraft parts & equipment
HQ: Spirit Aerosystems, Inc.
3801 S Oliver St
Wichita KS 67210
316 526-9000

(G-15641)
SPIRIT AEROSYSTEMS INC (HQ)
3801 S Oliver St (67210-3000)
P.O. Box 780008 (67278-0008)
PHONE.................................316 526-9000
Tom Gentile, *President*
Bryan Robert, *Business Mgr*
Stacy Cozad, *Counsel*
Sam Marnick, *Exec VP*
Duane Hawkins, *Senior VP*
▲ **EMP:** 224
SALES (est): 3.9B **Publicly Held**
SIC: 3728 Aircraft parts & equipment

(G-15642)
SPIRIT AEROSYSTEMS INNOVATIVE (HQ)
4200 W Macarthur Rd (67215-1107)
P.O. Box 780008 (67278-0008)
PHONE.................................316 526-9000
Tom Gentile, *CEO*
Lindy Hood, *Manager*
Stacy Cozad, *Director*
Kelly Gaide, *Director*
John Gilson, *Director*
EMP: 98
SALES: 86K **Publicly Held**
SIC: 3728 Aircraft parts & equipment

(G-15643)
SPIRIT AROSYSTEMS HOLDINGS INC
4555 E Macarthur Rd (67210-1687)
PHONE.................................316 523-3950
Lynn Wade, *Project Engr*
EMP: 12 **Publicly Held**
SIC: 3728 Aircraft parts & equipment
PA: Spirit Aerosystems Holdings, Inc.
3801 S Oliver St
Wichita KS 67210

(G-15644)
SPIRIT AROSYSTEMS HOLDINGS INC (PA)
3801 S Oliver St (67210-2112)
PHONE.................................316 526-9000
Robert Johnson, *Ch of Bd*
Thomas C Gentile III, *President*
Kristin Miller, *Business Mgr*
Krisstie Kondrotis, *Senior VP*
Michelle J Lohmeier, *Senior VP*
▲ **EMP:** 21
SQ FT: 2,000,000
SALES: 7.2B **Publicly Held**
WEB: www.spiritaero.com
SIC: 3724 3728 Engine mount parts, aircraft; aircraft body assemblies & parts

(G-15645)
SPIRIT/BOEING EMPLOYEES ASSN (PA)
4226 S Gold St (67217-3626)
PHONE.................................316 522-2996
Trish Pulliam, *Exec Dir*
Patricia L Pulliam, *Exec Dir*
EMP: 16 **EST:** 1937
SQ FT: 1,200
SALES: 910.9K **Privately Held**
WEB: www.beatoday.com
SIC: 8641 Social club, membership

(G-15646)
SPOTLESS JANITORIAL SERVICES
1460 N Hillside St (67214-2435)
PHONE.................................316 682-2070
Kelvin Biglow, *Partner*
Kevin Biglow,
EMP: 20
SALES: 700K **Privately Held**
SIC: 7349 Janitorial service, contract basis

(G-15647)
SPRAY EQUIPMENT & SVC CTR LLC (PA)
Also Called: Sesc
311 Pattie St (67211)
P.O. Box 3580 (67201-3580)
PHONE.................................316 264-4349
Mark Hammar, *President*
Jerry Fox, *Engineer*
John Goodman, *Sales Mgr*
Dennis Stover, *Sales Engr*
Randy Merley, *Sales Staff*
EMP: 45
SQ FT: 20,000
SALES (est): 26.6MM **Privately Held**
WEB: www.sprayequipment.com
SIC: 5084 Paint spray equipment, industrial

(G-15648)
SPRINGHILL SUITES
6633 W Kellogg Dr (67209-2213)
PHONE.................................316 260-4404
Ashley Joffe, *Owner*
EMP: 12 **EST:** 2014
SALES (est): 464.6K **Privately Held**
SIC: 7011 Hotels & motels

(G-15649)
SPRINT SPECTRUM LP
3101 N Rock Rd Ste 175 (67226-1339)
PHONE.................................316 634-4900
Pat Mark, *Branch Mgr*
EMP: 23 **Publicly Held**
WEB: www.sprintpcs.com
SIC: 4813 5999 Local & long distance telephone communications; telephone equipment & systems
HQ: Sprint Spectrum L.P.
6800 Sprint Pkwy
Overland Park KS 66251

(G-15650)
SQUIRES CORPORATION
Also Called: Carlson Hydraulics
3414 W 29th St S (67217-1056)
PHONE.................................316 944-0040
Chris Squires, *President*
Cynthia Squires, *Vice Pres*
EMP: 15 **EST:** 1985
SALES (est): 4.3MM **Privately Held**
WEB: www.carlsonhyd.com
SIC: 3561 7699 3593 Cylinders, pump; industrial equipment services; fluid power cylinders & actuators

(G-15651)
SSI INC
Also Called: Ssi Sprinkler Systems
12011 W 34th St S (67227-4107)
PHONE.................................316 722-9631
Jerry C Goodwin Jr, *President*
Sally Goodwin, *Corp Secy*
Jason Goodwin, *Vice Pres*
EMP: 30
SALES: 1.5MM **Privately Held**
WEB: www.ssisprinklers.com
SIC: 1711 Irrigation sprinkler system installation

(G-15652)
STANDARD BEVERAGE CORPORATION (PA)
2526 E 36th Cir N (67219-2300)
PHONE.................................316 838-7707
Leslie Rudd, *President*
Greig Debow, *Exec VP*
Joe Fairchild, *Vice Pres*
Denise Wilkens, *Vice Pres*
Angie Wilhelm, *CFO*
▲ **EMP:** 12 **EST:** 1949
SALES (est): 71.3MM **Privately Held**
WEB: www.beverage-news.com
SIC: 5182 5181 Liquor; wine; beer & other fermented malt liquors

(G-15653)
STANION WHOLESALE ELC CO INC
2710 W Pawnee St (67213-1818)
PHONE.................................316 616-9200
Paul Allsbury, *Sales Staff*
Cay Chavez, *Sales Staff*
Mike Romme, *Branch Mgr*
EMP: 30
SALES (corp-wide): 97.6MM **Privately Held**
WEB: www.stanion.com
SIC: 5063 Electrical supplies
PA: Stanion Wholesale Electric Co., Inc.
812 S Main St
Pratt KS 67124
620 672-5678

(G-15654)
STANS SPRINKLER SERVICE INC
Also Called: Rain Pro Irrigation
3656 S West St (67217-3802)
PHONE.................................800 570-5932
Dennis Dixon, *President*
Shonda Chapa, *Principal*
Wayne Herrmann, *Principal*
Mark Manell, *Treasurer*
EMP: 30
SALES: 1.7MM **Privately Held**
SIC: 1711 5083 Sprinkler contractors; irrigation equipment

(G-15655)
STAR TOOL SERVICE INC
1920 S Florence St (67209-2833)
PHONE.................................316 943-1942
Billy Teter, *President*
Linda Teter, *Corp Secy*
Don Ramu, *Vice Pres*
EMP: 6 **EST:** 1967
SQ FT: 6,000
SALES (est): 1MM **Privately Held**
SIC: 3599 Machine shop, jobbing & repair

(G-15656)
STARFLITE MANUFACTURING CO
1438 S Washington Ave (67211-3397)
P.O. Box 16063 (67216-0063)
PHONE.................................316 267-7297

William Perry, *President*
EMP: 9
SQ FT: 4,800
SALES (est): 1.5MM **Privately Held**
SIC: 3444 1542 Sheet metalwork; commercial & office building contractors

(G-15657)
STARKEY INC (PA)
4500 W Maple St (67209-2567)
PHONE..................................316 942-4221
Cara Ledy, *President*
Eric Larson, *Vice Pres*
Ashley Miller, *Opers Mgr*
Mark Koch, *Treasurer*
Debbie Powell, *Hum Res Coord*
EMP: 127
SALES: 18.3MM **Privately Held**
SIC: 8093 8331 Mental health clinic, outpatient; job training & vocational rehabilitation services

(G-15658)
STARLITE MOLD CO
1518 S Washington Ave (67211-3336)
PHONE..................................316 262-3350
Don Evans, *President*
Jeff Evans, *Principal*
EMP: 10
SALES: 270K **Privately Held**
WEB: www.starlitemolds.com
SIC: 5092 Toys & hobby goods & supplies

(G-15659)
STARWOOD HTLS & RSRTS WRLDWDE
4301 E Harry St (67209)
PHONE..................................888 625-4988
EMP: 300
SALES (corp-wide): 20.7B **Publicly Held**
SIC: 7011 Hotels & motels
HQ: Starwood Hotels & Resorts Worldwide, Llc
1 Star Pt
Stamford CT 06902
203 964-6000

(G-15660)
STELBAR OIL CORPORATION INC (PA)
Also Called: Stelbar Production Company
1625 Nw Fr Pkwy (67206)
PHONE..................................316 264-8378
John C Shawver, *President*
Ed Hill, *Corp Secy*
EMP: 10
SQ FT: 6,000
SALES (est): 4.9MM **Privately Held**
SIC: 1382 1311 Oil & gas exploration services; crude petroleum production

(G-15661)
STEPHEN M CRISER
9415 E Harry St Ste 603 (67207-5082)
PHONE..................................316 685-1040
Stephen M Criser, *President*
Ellen Hittle, *Accountant*
Jacy N Zimmerman, *Bookkeeper*
EMP: 20
SALES (est): 444.4K **Privately Held**
WEB: www.criser.com
SIC: 8721 7291 Certified public accountant; tax return preparation services

(G-15662)
STEPHEN P MOORE DDS
Also Called: Smile Junction
2143 N Collective Ln B (67206-3506)
PHONE..................................316 681-3228
Stephen P Moore DDS, *Owner*
EMP: 10
SALES (est): 568.6K **Privately Held**
SIC: 8021 Dentists' office

(G-15663)
STEPHEN ROHNER DOCTOR OFFICE
1148 S Hillside St # 104 (67211-4005)
PHONE..................................316 687-0006
Serena Metcalf, *Office Mgr*
EMP: 12
SALES (est): 144.8K **Privately Held**
SIC: 8011 Offices & clinics of medical doctors

(G-15664)
STEVE JOHNSON COMPANIES
1555 S Tyler Rd (67209-1850)
P.O. Box 12123 (67277-2123)
PHONE..................................316 722-2660
Steve Johnson, *President*
EMP: 11
SQ FT: 15,000
SALES (est): 2.2MM **Privately Held**
SIC: 3441 Fabricated structural metal

(G-15665)
STEVE KEMP CONCRETE CNSTR
315 N Seneca St (67203-5969)
PHONE..................................316 263-8902
Steve Kemp, *Owner*
EMP: 10
SALES: 445K **Privately Held**
SIC: 1771 Concrete work

(G-15666)
STEVEN BRADON AUTO CENTER
1633 N Rock Rd (67206-1224)
PHONE..................................316 634-0427
Brandon Steven, *Owner*
EMP: 15
SQ FT: 3,000
SALES (est): 1MM **Privately Held**
WEB: www.brandonstevenmotors.com
SIC: 7538 General automotive repair shops

(G-15667)
STEVEN ENTERPRISES LLC
Also Called: Genesis Health Club
6100 E Central Ave Ste 3 (67208-4237)
PHONE..................................316 681-3010
Rodney L Steven II, *President*
EMP: 105
SALES (est): 12.8MM **Privately Held**
SIC: 7991 Physical fitness facilities

(G-15668)
STEVEN F TWIETMEYER DDS
Also Called: Twietmeyer, Rebecca L
3920 W 31st St S (67217-1112)
PHONE..................................316 942-3113
Steven Twietmeyer, *Owner*
EMP: 14
SALES (est): 894.6K **Privately Held**
SIC: 8021 Dentists' office

(G-15669)
STEVEN IMPORT GROUP INC
Also Called: Steven Motors Full Line Collis
650 S Webb Rd (67207-2516)
PHONE..................................316 652-2135
Mike Staeven, *President*
EMP: 15
SALES (corp-wide): 32.5MM **Privately Held**
SIC: 7532 Body shop, automotive
PA: Steven Import Group, Inc.
6601 E Kellogg Dr
Wichita KS 67207
316 652-2277

(G-15670)
STEVEN JOSEPH JR DDS
Also Called: Kisco
232 N Seneca St (67203-6023)
PHONE..................................316 262-5273
Joeseph Steven Jr DDS, *Owner*
▲ **EMP:** 16
SQ FT: 2,000
SALES (est): 1MM **Privately Held**
WEB: www.kiscodental.com
SIC: 8021 5047 Dentists' office; dentists' professional supplies

(G-15671)
STEWART ENTERPRISES INC
12100 E 13th St N (67206-2828)
PHONE..................................316 686-2766
Dennis Christie, *Branch Mgr*
EMP: 15
SALES (corp-wide): 3.1B **Publicly Held**
WEB: www.stewartenterprises.com
SIC: 7261 Funeral home
HQ: Stewart Enterprises, Inc.
1333 S Clearview Pkwy
New Orleans LA 70121
504 729-1400

(G-15672)
STIFEL NICOLAUS & COMPANY INC
301 N Main St Ste 800 (67202-4808)
PHONE..................................316 264-6321
Brent Buller, *Manager*
EMP: 15
SALES (corp-wide): 3.2B **Publicly Held**
SIC: 6211 Brokers, security
HQ: Stifel, Nicolaus & Company Incorporated
501 N Broadway
Saint Louis MO 63102
314 342-2000

(G-15673)
STINSON LASSWELL & WILSON LLC
Also Called: Cranmer, Douglas C
200 W Douglas Ave Ste 100 (67202-3001)
PHONE..................................316 264-9137
Terry Michael Wilson,
Michelle L Anderson, *Legal Staff*
Jennifer R Beck, *Legal Staff*
Lisa Cole, *Legal Staff*
Courtney Ewertz, *Legal Staff*
EMP: 13
SALES (est): 1.5MM **Privately Held**
WEB: www.slwlc.com
SIC: 8111 General practice attorney, lawyer

(G-15674)
STINSON LEONARD STREET LLP
Also Called: Meeker, Larry K
1625 N Wtrfrnt Pkwy # 300 (67206-6621)
PHONE..................................316 265-8800
David Bengtson, *Managing Prtnr*
Alisa Ehrlich, *Counsel*
David Haynes, *Counsel*
David E Bengtson, *Manager*
Erin Udell, *Analyst*
EMP: 35
SALES (corp-wide): 120.9MM **Privately Held**
SIC: 8111 General practice law office
PA: Stinson Llp
1201 Walnut St Ste 2900
Kansas City MO 64106
816 842-8600

(G-15675)
STRATEGIC GLOBAL SERVICES LLC
1910 E Norton (67216)
PHONE..................................316 655-2761
Kam Manyseng, *Mng Member*
EMP: 10
SQ FT: 10,000
SALES: 500K **Privately Held**
SIC: 1761 Skylight installation

(G-15676)
STRUCTRAL INTGRITY SYSTEMS LLC
10302 E Bronco St (67206-8934)
PHONE..................................316 634-1396
Monica Lane, *Partner*
Karl Zhaty, *Partner*
EMP: 10
SALES: 300K **Privately Held**
WEB: www.structuralintegritysys.com
SIC: 8748 Systems engineering consultant, ex. computer or professional

(G-15677)
STRUCTURAL INTEGRITY GROUP LLC
118 Circle Dr (67218-1206)
PHONE..................................316 633-9403
John Lucian,
Grace Lucian,
Jennifer Lucian,
EMP: 26
SALES (est): 383.2K **Privately Held**
SIC: 7389

(G-15678)
STYLE CREST INC
811 E 33rd St N (67219-4011)
PHONE..................................316 832-6303
Bob Berry, *Manager*
EMP: 11
SALES (corp-wide): 168.3MM **Privately Held**
SIC: 5075 Warm air heating & air conditioning
HQ: Style Crest, Inc.
2450 Enterprise St
Fremont OH 43420
419 332-7369

(G-15679)
STYLECRAFT AUTO UPHOLSTERY
1148 N Mosley Ave (67214-3043)
PHONE..................................316 262-0449
Robert G Christian, *President*
EMP: 10
SQ FT: 7,200
SALES (est): 863.8K **Privately Held**
SIC: 7532 Upholstery & trim shop, automotive

(G-15680)
SUBSTANCE ABUSE CENTER KANSAS
940 N Waco Ave (67203-3947)
PHONE..................................316 267-3825
Harold Casey, *CEO*
Bethany Williams, *Receptionist*
EMP: 70
SALES: 5.5MM **Privately Held**
SIC: 8322 Substance abuse counseling

(G-15681)
SUMMER STONE DUPLEXES
Also Called: Remington Apts
7272 E 37th St N Ofc (67226-3204)
PHONE..................................316 636-9000
Nancy Mills, *Manager*
EMP: 10
SALES (corp-wide): 1.9MM **Privately Held**
SIC: 6513 Apartment building operators
PA: Summer Stone Duplexes
1801 S 132nd East Pl
Tulsa OK 74108
918 437-8293

(G-15682)
SUMMERFIELD SUITES MGT CO L P
8100 E 22nd St N Bldg 500 (67226-2305)
PHONE..................................316 681-5100
Anthony Isaac, *President*
Rolf Ruhfus, *Chairman*
Roy Baker, *Treasurer*
EMP: 55
SALES (est): 1.9MM **Privately Held**
WEB: www.lodgeworks.com
SIC: 6531 Real estate managers

(G-15683)
SUNBELT BUSINESS ADVISORS
9920 E Harry St Ste 150 (67207-5008)
P.O. Box 132, Kechi (67067-0132)
PHONE..................................316 684-9040
Brian Slipka, *CEO*
Randy Browning, *President*
Anil Bhatia, *Broker*
Scott Callison, *Broker*
Joshua Covacevich, *Broker*
EMP: 20 **EST:** 2000
SALES (est): 1.1MM **Privately Held**
SIC: 7389 Brokers, business: buying & selling business enterprises

(G-15684)
SUNBELT RENTALS INC
3410 W 30th St S (67217-1012)
PHONE..................................316 789-7000
EMP: 18
SALES (corp-wide): 5.9B **Privately Held**
SIC: 7353 Heavy construction equipment rental
HQ: Sunbelt Rentals, Inc.
2341 Deerfield Dr
Fort Mill SC 29715
803 578-5811

(G-15685)
SUNFIELD LLC
4601 E Douglas Ave # 150 (67218-1011)
PHONE..................................785 338-0314
Shane Feng, *Mng Member*
EMP: 5

▲ = Import ▼=Export
◆ =Import/Export

SALES (est): 442.3K **Privately Held**
SIC: **2521** Wood office desks & tables

(G-15686)
SUNFLOWER BANK NATIONAL ASSN
Also Called: Wichita Northeast Branch
2073 N Webb Rd (67206-3411)
PHONE..................................316 652-1279
Marilyn Smith, *Loan Officer*
Crystal Hervey, *Branch Mgr*
EMP: 10
SALES (corp-wide): 52.4MM **Privately Held**
SIC: **6021** National trust companies with deposits, commercial
HQ: Sunflower Bank, National Association
1400 16th St Ste 250
Denver CO 80202
888 827-5564

(G-15687)
SUNFLOWER BROADCASTING INC
Also Called: Kwch TV
2815 E 37th St N (67219-3545)
PHONE..................................316 838-1212
Joan Barrett, *President*
Joe Miller, *Controller*
EMP: 99
SALES (est): 7.8MM **Privately Held**
WEB: www.kwch.com
SIC: **4833** Television broadcasting stations

(G-15688)
SUNFLOWER TRAVEL CORPORATION (PA)
1223 N Rock Rd Ste G200 (67206-1272)
PHONE..................................316 634-1700
Barbara Hansen, *President*
Karen Mayfield, *Principal*
Devin Hansen, *Vice Pres*
Kenneth Hansen, *Vice Pres*
Angelina Courtney, *Associate*
EMP: 13 **EST**: 1971
SQ FT: 2,800
SALES (est): 2.5MM **Privately Held**
SIC: **4724** Tourist agency arranging transport, lodging & car rental

(G-15689)
SUNSHINE ROOMS INC
Also Called: Crystal Structures
3333 N Mead St Ste B (67219-4088)
PHONE..................................316 838-0033
L Wade Griffith, *President*
Craig Andersen, *Sales Staff*
EMP: 15
SQ FT: 40,000
SALES: 4.2MM **Privately Held**
SIC: **3448** Sunrooms, prefabricated metal

(G-15690)
SUNSTAR WICHITA INC
5500 W Kellogg Dr (67209-2345)
PHONE..................................316 943-2181
Satish Desai, *President*
EMP: 40
SALES (est): 1.3MM **Privately Held**
SIC: **7011** Resort hotel

(G-15691)
SUPER 8 MOTEL
6245 W Kellogg Dr (67209-2331)
PHONE..................................316 945-5261
Hiren Shah, *Manager*
EMP: 15
SALES (est): 799.8K **Privately Held**
SIC: **7011** Hotels & motels

(G-15692)
SUPERIOR BUILDING MAINTENANCE
2007 S West St (67213-1109)
PHONE..................................316 943-2347
Dan Thibault, *President*
EMP: 300
SALES (est): 8.3MM **Privately Held**
SIC: **7349** Janitorial service, contract basis

(G-15693)
SUPERIOR COMPUTER SUPPLY INC
Also Called: Superior Office
2355 S Edwards St Ste A (67213-1894)
PHONE..................................316 942-5577
Jerry Pates, *President*
Charles D Smith, *Corp Secy*
Jessica Parsons, *Opers Staff*
Laura Clevenger, *Representative*
Kim Eaton, *Representative*
EMP: 10
SQ FT: 5,000
SALES (est): 3.7MM **Privately Held**
WEB: www.superiorcomputersupply.com
SIC: **5045** 5112 Computers, peripherals & software; stationery & office supplies

(G-15694)
SUPERIOR HARDWOOD FLOORS LLC
P.O. Box 16628 (67216-0628)
PHONE..................................316 554-9663
Don Mc Greanor, *Branch Mgr*
EMP: 6
SALES (est): 547.7K
SALES (corp-wide): 933.1K **Privately Held**
SIC: **5211** 2426 1771 1752 Flooring, wood; flooring, hardwood; flooring contractor; floor laying & floor work
PA: Superior Hardwood Floors Llc
912 E 43rd St S
Wichita KS 67216
316 761-6361

(G-15695)
SUPERIOR MASONRY & STUCCO LLC
Also Called: Arthur David Garcia
1008 S Santa Fe St (67211-2436)
PHONE..................................316 928-2365
Sherri Garcia, *Office Mgr*
EMP: 30
SALES (est): 1.4MM **Privately Held**
SIC: **1771** 1741 7389 1742 Exterior concrete stucco contractor; concrete block masonry laying; stone masonry; ; exterior insulation & finish (EIFS) applicator

(G-15696)
SUPERIOR PLUMBING OF WICHITA
Also Called: Arco Supply Co
6837 E Harry St (67207-2999)
PHONE..................................316 684-8349
Archie D Conduff, *President*
Patsy Ann Conduff, *Corp Secy*
Steven Conduff, *Vice Pres*
Patsy Conduff, *Treasurer*
EMP: 13 **EST**: 1966
SQ FT: 11,000
SALES (est): 1.2MM **Privately Held**
WEB: www.superiorplumbingict.com
SIC: **1711** 5074 Plumbing contractors; plumbing & hydronic heating supplies

(G-15697)
SUPERIOR POOLS
4811 N Alexander St (67204-2614)
PHONE..................................316 838-4968
Keith Littlejohn, *Owner*
Renee Littlejohn, *Co-Owner*
EMP: 15
SALES (est): 1.2MM **Privately Held**
SIC: **1799** Swimming pool construction

(G-15698)
SUPERIOR RBR STAMP & SEAL INC
2725 E Douglas Ave (67211-1621)
P.O. Box 2258 (67201-2258)
PHONE..................................316 682-5511
Michael Herman, *President*
Mike Herman, *Manager*
◆ **EMP**: 5 **EST**: 1967
SQ FT: 8,000
SALES (est): 598.1K **Privately Held**
WEB: www.superiorrubberstamp.com
SIC: **5999** 3953 Banners, flags, decals & posters; postmark stamps, hand: rubber or metal

(G-15699)
SUPERIOR SCHOOL SUPPLIES INC (PA)
Also Called: Etritionware
1818 W 2nd St N (67203-5703)
PHONE..................................316 265-7683
Fax: 316 265-3387
EMP: 20
SQ FT: 22,000
SALES (est): 7.5MM **Privately Held**
SIC: **5084** 5021 5943 Whol Industrial Equipment Whol Furniture Ret Stationery

(G-15700)
SUPERIOR TOOL SERVICE INC
722 E Zimmerly St (67211-3339)
PHONE..................................316 945-8488
Steve Shofler, *President*
Ellen L Shofler, *Corp Secy*
EMP: 21
SQ FT: 6,500
SALES (est): 5MM **Privately Held**
WEB: www.superiortoolservice.com
SIC: **3545** Cutting tools for machine tools

(G-15701)
SURGICAL SPECIALISTS PA
Also Called: Gaston, Jerry G Do
4013 N Ridge Rd Ste 210 (67205-8860)
PHONE..................................316 945-7309
John P Smith Do, *President*
Bridget Kirk, *Office Mgr*
Jerry Gaston, *Otolaryngology*
EMP: 15
SALES (est): 1.9MM **Privately Held**
SIC: **8031** 8011 Offices & clinics of osteopathic physicians; offices & clinics of medical doctors

(G-15702)
SURGICARE OF WICHITA INC
2818 N Greenwich Rd (67226-8210)
PHONE..................................316 685-2207
Tracie Johanek, *Administration*
EMP: 65
SQ FT: 12,500
SALES (est): 7.3MM **Publicly Held**
WEB: www.surgicareofwichita.com
SIC: **8093** 8011 Specialty outpatient clinics; medical centers
PA: Hca Healthcare, Inc.
1 Park Plz
Nashville TN 37203

(G-15703)
SURVEY COMPANIES LLC
Also Called: Lakewood Senior Living Seville
1319 S Seville Ave (67209-1828)
PHONE..................................316 722-6916
April Puccetti, *Branch Mgr*
EMP: 11 **Privately Held**
SIC: **8713** Surveying services
PA: The Survey Companies Llc
3008 7th Ave S
Birmingham AL 35233

(G-15704)
SUSAN POOL
8200 E 32nd St N Ste 100 (67226-2618)
PHONE..................................316 266-6574
EMP: 11
SALES (est): 759.4K **Privately Held**
SIC: **6282** Investment advisory service

(G-15705)
SUTHERLAND BUILDERS INC
6053 S Seneca St (67217-5119)
PHONE..................................316 529-2620
Paul Sutherland, *President*
Tim Sutherland, *Vice Pres*
John T Sutherland, *Director*
EMP: 10
SQ FT: 4,000
SALES (est): 2.4MM **Privately Held**
WEB: www.builders.kscoxmail.com
SIC: **1542** Commercial & office building, new construction

(G-15706)
SVETAS BODY THERAPY LLC
2141 N Bradley Fair Pkwy (67206-2949)
PHONE..................................316 630-0400
Sveta Yakubovich,
EMP: 14
SQ FT: 1,000
SALES: 300K **Privately Held**
SIC: **8049** 7299 7231 Acupuncturist; hair weaving or replacement; facial salons

(G-15707)
SWEET ADELINES INTRNTNL CHORUS
14105 E Lakeview Ct (67230-9543)
PHONE..................................316 733-4467
Jean Frallic, *Principal*
EMP: 12
SALES (est): 170K **Privately Held**
SIC: **8641** Singing society

(G-15708)
SWINDOLL JANZEN HAWK LLOYD LLC
220 W Douglas Ave Ste 300 (67202-3135)
PHONE..................................316 265-5600
Judy Fenny, *Manager*
EMP: 18
SALES (est): 1.5MM
SALES (corp-wide): 3.5MM **Privately Held**
SIC: **8721** Certified public accountant
PA: Swindoll, Janzen, Hawk & Lloyd Llc
123 S Main St
Mcpherson KS 67460
620 241-1826

(G-15709)
SWISS BURGER BRAND MEAT CO
3763 N Emporia St (67219-3620)
PHONE..................................316 838-7514
Ernestine Fuller, *President*
Wayne Fuller, *Vice Pres*
EMP: 17
SQ FT: 9,800
SALES: 2.9MM **Privately Held**
SIC: **5147** Meats & meat products

(G-15710)
SYNDEO OUTSOURCING LLC
3504 N Great Plains Dr # 200
(67220-3405)
PHONE..................................316 630-9107
Kerry Rasmussen, *Purch Agent*
Mark Fawcett, *Accounting Mgr*
Tonja Sowder, *Human Res Dir*
Heather Price, *Human Res Mgr*
Randy McDonald, *Sales Staff*
EMP: 23
SQ FT: 14,000
SALES: 2.2MM **Privately Held**
WEB: www.syndeogroup.biz
SIC: **8742** 8721 Human resource consulting services; payroll accounting service

(G-15711)
SYSCO KANSAS CITY INC
1001 S Young St (67209-2628)
PHONE..................................316 942-4205
Jim Graham, *President*
Dave Washburn, *Manager*
EMP: 45
SQ FT: 25,000
SALES (corp-wide): 60.1B **Publicly Held**
SIC: **5146** 5023 5148 Seafoods; home furnishings; fruits, fresh; vegetables, fresh
HQ: Sysco Kansas City, Inc.
1915 E Kansas City Rd
Olathe KS 66061
913 829-5555

(G-15712)
T & W TIRE LLC
2280 S Sheridan St (67213-1551)
PHONE..................................316 683-8364
Philip Garrison, *Manager*
EMP: 37
SALES (corp-wide): 189.7MM **Privately Held**
SIC: **5531** 7549 Automotive tires; automotive maintenance services
PA: T & W Tire, L.L.C.
25 N Council Rd
Oklahoma City OK 73127
405 787-6711

(G-15713)
T M H HOTELS INC
Also Called: Hilton Grdn Inn Wichita Dwntwn
401 E Douglas Ave (67202-3407)
PHONE..................................316 669-6175

GEOGRAPHIC

William Hamrick, *President*
EMP: 40
SALES (corp-wide): 4.4MM **Privately Held**
SIC: 7011 Inns
PA: T M H Hotels Inc
8415 E 21st St N Ste 120
Wichita KS 67206
316 262-2841

(G-15714)
T N T MACHINE INC
1300 S Bebe St (67209-2608)
PHONE..................................316 440-6004
Steve Terhune, *CEO*
EMP: 11
SALES (est): 1MM **Privately Held**
SIC: 7539 7699 Machine shop, automotive; industrial machinery & equipment repair

(G-15715)
T V HEPHNER AND ELEC INC
Also Called: Porta-Ad
737 S Washington Ave # 3 (67211-2411)
PHONE..................................316 264-3284
Gregory A Hephner, *President*
Lonnie E Hephner, *Vice Pres*
Bonnie J Hephner, *Treasurer*
Margaret P Hephner, *Info Tech Mgr*
Peggy Hephner, *Admin Sec*
EMP: 14
SQ FT: 10,000
SALES (est): 1.9MM **Privately Held**
WEB: www.hephnertv.com
SIC: 5731 7622 7629 Radio, television & electronic stores; radio repair shop; television repair shop; electrical repair shops

(G-15716)
T-MOBILE USA INC
1918 W 21st St N (67203-2105)
PHONE..................................316 201-6120
EMP: 11
SALES (corp-wide): 83.9B **Publicly Held**
SIC: 4812 Cellular telephone services
HQ: T-Mobile Usa, Inc.
12920 Se 38th St
Bellevue WA 98006
425 378-4000

(G-15717)
TARRANT INC
Also Called: Quik Print
217 N Pennsylvania Ave (67214-4148)
PHONE..................................316 942-2208
Johnny Tarrant, *President*
Rob Galaway, *Prdtn Mgr*
EMP: 20
SQ FT: 13,000
SALES (est): 2.4MM **Privately Held**
WEB: www.qpimaging.com
SIC: 7389 Personal service agents, brokers & bureaus

(G-15718)
TCK- THE TRUST COMPANY KANSAS (PA)
Also Called: T C K Financial Advisors
245 N Waco St Ste 120 (67202-1116)
P.O. Box 3699 (67201-3699)
PHONE..................................316 264-6010
Stephen A English, *President*
Kimberly Ufford, *Exec VP*
Chris English, *Vice Pres*
Jennifer Moore, *Trust Officer*
EMP: 22
SQ FT: 4,000
SALES (est): 5.1MM **Privately Held**
WEB: www.tckansas.com
SIC: 6091 8742 Nondeposit trust facilities; financial consultant

(G-15719)
TCV PUBLISHING INC
2918 E Douglas Ave (67214-4709)
PHONE..................................316 681-1155
Bonita Gooch, *Manager*
EMP: 8
SALES (est): 450.6K **Privately Held**
WEB: www.tcvpub.com
SIC: 2711 Newspapers: publishing only, not printed on site

(G-15720)
TEACHING PARENTS ASSN INC
Also Called: Tpa
1526 N Caddy Ct (67212-1284)
P.O. Box 3968 (67201-3968)
PHONE..................................316 347-9900
Jeff Gorman, *President*
Scott Durkee, *Vice Pres*
Jeff Schaunts, *Treasurer*
David Wells,
EMP: 12
SALES: 6K **Privately Held**
SIC: 8699 Membership organizations

(G-15721)
TEAM VISION SURGERY CENTER
834 N Socora St Ste A (67212-3278)
PHONE..................................316 729-6000
Linda Bitter, *Owner*
EMP: 30
SALES (est): 1.3MM **Privately Held**
SIC: 8011 Clinic, operated by physicians

(G-15722)
TEAMSTERS UNION LOCAL 795
4921 E Cessna Dr (67210-1298)
PHONE..................................316 683-2651
Jesse Castillo, *President*
EMP: 11
SALES: 874K **Privately Held**
SIC: 8631 Labor union

(G-15723)
TEC ENGINEERING INC (PA)
2233 S West Street Ct (67213-1100)
PHONE..................................316 259-8881
Rolland C Eakins, *President*
Larry Pauls, *Engineer*
EMP: 20 **EST:** 1996
SQ FT: 3,500
SALES (est): 1.9MM **Privately Held**
SIC: 8711 3823 3613 Consulting engineer; industrial instrmnts msrmnt display/control process variable; switchgear & switchboard apparatus

(G-15724)
TECH-AIRE INSTRUMENTS INC
1326 S Walnut St (67213-4347)
PHONE..................................316 262-4020
E L Yost, *President*
Darlene Yost, *President*
Tarina C Leslie, *Admin Sec*
EMP: 12
SALES (est): 1.9MM **Privately Held**
WEB: www.tech-aire.com
SIC: 7629 5088 Aircraft electrical equipment repair; aircraft equipment & supplies

(G-15725)
TECHMER PM LLC
7015 W Pueblo Dr (67209-2936)
PHONE..................................316 943-1520
Ramon Reynaga, *Branch Mgr*
EMP: 35
SALES (corp-wide): 39.3MM **Privately Held**
SIC: 2821 Plastics materials & resins
HQ: Techmer Pm, Llc
1 Quality Cir
Clinton TN 37716
865 457-6700

(G-15726)
TECT AEROSPACE LLC (HQ)
300 W Douglas Ave Ste 100 (67202-2905)
PHONE..................................316 425-3638
Bernard Stanek, *President*
Peter Knapper, *President*
Haywood Bower, *Vice Pres*
James R Duncan Jr, *Vice Pres*
Robert Perry, *Vice Pres*
▲ **EMP:** 136
SQ FT: 201,000
SALES (est): 48.8MM **Privately Held**
SIC: 3728 Aircraft parts & equipment
PA: Tect Aerospace Holdings, Llc
300 W Douglas Ave Ste 100
Wichita KS 67202
620 359-5000

(G-15727)
TEE TIME INVESTMENTS INC
Also Called: Ramco Building Maintenance
410 N Saint Francis Ave (67202-2624)
PHONE..................................316 262-7900
Paulette S Kirk, *President*
Chris Hoose, *CFO*
EMP: 85
SQ FT: 3,200
SALES: 2MM **Privately Held**
SIC: 7349 Janitorial service, contract basis

(G-15728)
TEKSYSTEMS INC
727 N Waco Ave Ste 140 (67203-3952)
PHONE..................................316 448-4500
EMP: 30
SALES (corp-wide): 13.4B **Privately Held**
SIC: 7379 Computer related consulting services
HQ: Teksystems, Inc.
7437 Race Rd
Hanover MD 21076

(G-15729)
TENNISON BROTHERS INC
1021 S Washington Ave (67211-2429)
PHONE..................................316 263-7581
James E Tennison, *Opers-Prdtn-Mfg*
EMP: 15
SQ FT: 34,000
SALES (corp-wide): 7.3MM **Privately Held**
SIC: 5039 3444 Structural assemblies, prefabricated: non-wood; prefabricated buildings; metal buildings; sheet metalwork
PA: Tennison Brothers, Inc.
450 N Bellevue Blvd
Memphis TN 38105
901 274-7773

(G-15730)
TERRACON CONSULTANTS INC
Also Called: Terracon Consultants 1
1815 S Eisenhower St (67209-2810)
PHONE..................................316 262-0171
Scott Randle, *Branch Mgr*
EMP: 35
SALES (corp-wide): 751.7MM **Privately Held**
SIC: 8742 8711 Industry specialist consultants; engineering services
HQ: Terracon Consultants, Inc.
10841 S Ridgeview Rd
Olathe KS 66061
913 599-6886

(G-15731)
TETRA MANAGEMENT INC
8100 E 22nd St N Bldg 200 (67226-2396)
P.O. Box 780538 (67278-0538)
PHONE..................................316 685-6221
Jack Shelton, *President*
Doug O Connor, *Corp Secy*
EMP: 17
SQ FT: 6,000
SALES: 1.5MM **Privately Held**
WEB: www.tetramanagement.com
SIC: 8741 Management services

(G-15732)
TEXTRON AIRLAND LLC
5800 E Pawnee Ave Bldg 88 (67218-5541)
PHONE..................................541 390-8888
Eugene Hackett, *Principal*
Bill Anderson, *Vice Pres*
EMP: 8 **EST:** 2011
SALES (est): 750K **Privately Held**
SIC: 3721 Aircraft

(G-15733)
TEXTRON AVIATION DEFENSE LLC
Also Called: Beechcraft Defense Company LLC
201 S Greenwich Rd (67207-1402)
PHONE..................................316 676-2508
Bridgette Thomas Sr, *Mng Member*
Mike Karr,
EMP: 20
SALES (est): 3.2MM
SALES (corp-wide): 13.9B **Publicly Held**
SIC: 7389 Brokers, contract services
HQ: Textron Aviation Inc.
1 Cessna Blvd
Wichita KS 67215
316 517-6000

(G-15734)
TEXTRON AVIATION INC
Also Called: Hawker Beechcraft Parts & Dist
9709 E Central Ave (67206-2507)
P.O. Box 2942 (67201-2942)
PHONE..................................888 727-4344
Charles Dieker, *Director*
EMP: 2055
SALES (corp-wide): 13.9B **Publicly Held**
SIC: 3721 Aircraft
HQ: Textron Aviation Inc.
1 Cessna Blvd
Wichita KS 67215
316 517-6000

(G-15735)
TEXTRON AVIATION INC
Also Called: Cessna Aircraft Company
6263 W 34th St S (67215-1814)
PHONE..................................316 517-8270
Sam Kofoot, *Engineer*
EMP: 91
SALES (corp-wide): 13.9B **Publicly Held**
SIC: 4581 Airports, flying fields & services
HQ: Textron Aviation Inc.
1 Cessna Blvd
Wichita KS 67215
316 517-6000

(G-15736)
TEXTRON AVIATION INC
Also Called: Hawker Beechcraft
1980 S Airport Rd (67209-1942)
PHONE..................................316 517-8270
Skip Madsen, *Branch Mgr*
EMP: 150
SALES (corp-wide): 13.9B **Publicly Held**
SIC: 3721 4581 Aircraft; airports, flying fields & services
HQ: Textron Aviation Inc.
1 Cessna Blvd
Wichita KS 67215
316 517-6000

(G-15737)
TEXTRON AVIATION INC (HQ)
1 Cessna Blvd (67215-1400)
P.O. Box 77130, Fort Worth TX (76177-0130)
PHONE..................................316 517-6000
Ronald Draper, *President*
Mike Van Hart, *Area Mgr*
David Chant, *Counsel*
Brian Howell, *Vice Pres*
Doug May, *Vice Pres*
EMP: 174 **EST:** 2014
SALES (est): 1.7B
SALES (corp-wide): 13.9B **Publicly Held**
SIC: 4581 Airports, flying fields & services
PA: Textron Inc.
40 Westminster St
Providence RI 02903
401 421-2800

(G-15738)
TEXTRON AVIATION INC
2 Cessna Blvd Ste P35 (67215-1423)
PHONE..................................316 517-1375
EMP: 5
SALES (corp-wide): 13.9B **Publicly Held**
SIC: 3728 3721 Aircraft parts & equipment; airplanes, fixed or rotary wing
HQ: Textron Aviation Inc.
1 Cessna Blvd
Wichita KS 67215
316 517-6000

(G-15739)
TEXTRON AVIATION INC
9709 E Central Ave (67206-2507)
PHONE..................................888 727-4344
EMP: 10
SALES (corp-wide): 13.9B **Publicly Held**
SIC: 4581 Airports, flying fields & services
HQ: Textron Aviation Inc.
1 Cessna Blvd
Wichita KS 67215
316 517-6000

(G-15740)
TEXTRON AVIATION INC
1 Cessna Blvd (67215-1400)
PHONE..................................316 517-6000
EMP: 7740
SALES (corp-wide): 13.9B **Publicly Held**
SIC: 3721 Airplanes, fixed or rotary wing
HQ: Textron Aviation Inc.
1 Cessna Blvd
Wichita KS 67215
316 517-6000

(G-15741)
TEXTRON AVIATION INC
10511 E Central Ave (67206-2557)
PHONE..................................316 676-7111
EMP: 1300
SALES (corp-wide): 13.9B **Publicly Held**
SIC: 7699 Aircraft & heavy equipment repair services
HQ: Textron Aviation Inc.
1 Cessna Blvd
Wichita KS 67215
316 517-6000

(G-15742)
TEXTRON AVIATION INC
Also Called: Cessna
7751 E Pawnee St (67207-3027)
PHONE..................................316 831-4021
Mark Dieter, *Principal*
EMP: 15
SALES (corp-wide): 13.9B **Publicly Held**
WEB: www.cessna.com
SIC: 8711 Engineering services
HQ: Textron Aviation Inc.
1 Cessna Blvd
Wichita KS 67215
316 517-6000

(G-15743)
TEXTRON AVIATION INC
2125 S Hoover Rd (67209)
PHONE..................................316 293-9703
Kristin Guthrie, *Manager*
Penny Gilbert, *Manager*
EMP: 91
SALES (corp-wide): 13.9B **Publicly Held**
WEB: www.cessna.com
SIC: 4581 Airports, flying fields & services
HQ: Textron Aviation Inc.
1 Cessna Blvd
Wichita KS 67215
316 517-6000

(G-15744)
TEXTRON AVIATION INC
Hawker Publications Div
9709 E Central Ave (67206-2507)
P.O. Box 85 (67201-0085)
PHONE..................................316 676-7111
Gail E Bachman, *Manager*
EMP: 3000
SALES (corp-wide): 13.9B **Publicly Held**
SIC: 3721 3728 Airplanes, fixed or rotary wing; research & development on aircraft by the manufacturer; aircraft parts & equipment
HQ: Textron Aviation Inc.
1 Cessna Blvd
Wichita KS 67215
316 517-6000

(G-15745)
TEXTRON AVIATION INC
Also Called: Cessna
2617 S Hoover Rd (67215-1200)
P.O. Box 7704 (67277-7704)
PHONE..................................316 517-6000
David Hinote, *Opers Staff*
Tasha Denton, *Buyer*
Jay M Amos, *Engineer*
David Grieve, *Engineer*
Daniel Hoverson, *Engineer*
EMP: 91
SALES (corp-wide): 13.9B **Publicly Held**
WEB: www.cessna.com
SIC: 3721 Aircraft
HQ: Textron Aviation Inc.
1 Cessna Blvd
Wichita KS 67215
316 517-6000

(G-15746)
TEXTRON AVIATION INC
Also Called: Cessna
2625 S Hoover Rd (67215-1200)
PHONE..................................316 517-6081
Mark Patterson, *Principal*
EMP: 500
SALES (corp-wide): 13.9B **Publicly Held**
WEB: www.cessna.com
SIC: 3721 Aircraft
HQ: Textron Aviation Inc.
1 Cessna Blvd
Wichita KS 67215
316 517-6000

(G-15747)
TEXTRON AVIATION INC
5800 E Pawnee Ave (67218-5541)
PHONE..................................316 517-6000
Ernest Scott, *President*
Chris Russell, *Opers Mgr*
Hamilton Daciw, *Analyst*
EMP: 150
SALES (corp-wide): 13.9B **Publicly Held**
WEB: www.cessna.com
SIC: 3728 Aircraft parts & equipment
HQ: Textron Aviation Inc.
1 Cessna Blvd
Wichita KS 67215
316 517-6000

(G-15748)
TEXTRON AVIATION INC
Also Called: Cessna Citation
7121 Southwest Blvd (67215-8725)
PHONE..................................800 835-4090
Gordon Sheffield, *Engineer*
Jack Stiffler, *Branch Mgr*
EMP: 144
SALES (corp-wide): 13.9B **Publicly Held**
SIC: 3721 Airplanes, fixed or rotary wing
HQ: Textron Aviation Inc.
1 Cessna Blvd
Wichita KS 67215
316 517-6000

(G-15749)
TEXTRON AVIATION INC
7603 E Pawnee St (67207-3025)
P.O. Box 7704 (67277-7704)
PHONE..................................316 831-2000
EMP: 144
SALES (corp-wide): 14.2B **Publicly Held**
SIC: 3721 Mfg Aircraft
HQ: Textron Aviation Inc.
1 Cessna Blvd
Wichita KS 67215
316 517-6000

(G-15750)
TEXTRON AVIATION INC
5 Cessna Blvd (67215-1400)
PHONE..................................316 517-6000
Blake Brnrd, *President*
William Adams, *Principal*
Marcelo Casenove, *Director*
EMP: 144
SALES (corp-wide): 13.9B **Publicly Held**
WEB: www.cessna.com
SIC: 3721 Aircraft
HQ: Textron Aviation Inc.
1 Cessna Blvd
Wichita KS 67215
316 517-6000

(G-15751)
TEXTRON AVIATION INC
1643 S Maize Rd (67209-1922)
PHONE..................................316 721-3100
EMP: 300
SALES (corp-wide): 13.9B **Publicly Held**
SIC: 3728 Aircraft parts & equipment
HQ: Textron Aviation Inc.
1 Cessna Blvd
Wichita KS 67215
316 517-6000

(G-15752)
TEXTRON AVIATION INC
10511 E Central Ave (67206-2557)
PHONE..................................316 676-7111
EMP: 1833
SALES (corp-wide): 13.9B **Publicly Held**
SIC: 3721 Aircraft
HQ: Textron Aviation Inc.
1 Cessna Blvd
Wichita KS 67215
316 517-6000

(G-15753)
TEXTRON AVIATION INC
Also Called: Hawker Beechcraft Parts & Dist
515 N Goebel St (67201)
PHONE..................................316 676-5373
EMP: 1833
SALES (corp-wide): 13.9B **Publicly Held**
SIC: 3721 3728 Airplanes, fixed or rotary wing; research & development on aircraft by the manufacturer; aircraft parts & equipment
HQ: Textron Aviation Inc.
1 Cessna Blvd
Wichita KS 67215
316 517-6000

(G-15754)
TGC GREENWICH HOTEL LLC
Also Called: La Quinta Inn
2660 N Greenwich Ct (67226-8226)
PHONE..................................316 500-2660
Nicholas Esterline,
EMP: 27
SALES (est): 808.5K **Privately Held**
SIC: 7011 Hotels & motels

(G-15755)
THAI BINH SUPERMARKET
1530 W 21st St N (67203-2448)
PHONE..................................316 838-8882
Nuot Nguyen, *Owner*
▲ **EMP:** 10
SQ FT: 20,000
SALES (est): 2MM **Privately Held**
WEB: www.thaibinhsupermarket.com
SIC: 5411 5149 Grocery stores; groceries & related products

(G-15756)
THAYER AEROSPACE PLATING INC
4201 S 119th St W (67215-9100)
PHONE..................................316 522-5426
Michael Pompeo, *President*
Brain Bulato, *COO*
Ken Veer, *Manager*
Mark Sims, *Prgrmr*
▲ **EMP:** 175
SALES (est): 10.4MM **Privately Held**
WEB: www.thayeraerospace.com
SIC: 3471 Plating of metals or formed products

(G-15757)
THE NATURE CONSERVANCY
151 S Whittier Rd (67207-1063)
PHONE..................................316 689-4237
Randy Ehrlich, *Branch Mgr*
EMP: 13
SALES (corp-wide): 992.1MM **Privately Held**
SIC: 8641 Environmental protection organization
PA: The Nature Conservancy
4245 Fairfax Dr Ste 100
Arlington VA 22203
703 841-5300

(G-15758)
THERE IS NO PLACE LIKE HOME
Also Called: Right At Home
7348 W 21st St N Ste 101 (67205-1776)
PHONE..................................316 721-6001
Carla Shepard, *President*
EMP: 10 **EST:** 2001
SALES (est): 582.6K **Privately Held**
WEB: www.thereisnoplacelikehome.com
SIC: 8082 Home health care services

(G-15759)
THERMOFORMED PLASTIC PRODUCTS
2148 S Hoover Rd Ste 2 (67209-2829)
PHONE..................................316 214-9623
Christopher J McCosh, *Principal*
EMP: 7
SALES (est): 850.8K **Privately Held**
SIC: 3083 Plastic finished products, laminated

(G-15760)
THOMAS C KLEIN MD
1709 S Rock Rd (67207-5150)
PHONE..................................316 682-7411
Terry Poling MD, *President*
Thomas C Klein, *Med Doctor*
EMP: 52
SALES (est): 1.6MM **Privately Held**
SIC: 8011 General & family practice, physician/surgeon

(G-15761)
THOMAS TRANSFER & STOR CO INC
Also Called: United Van Lines
7701 E Osie St (67207-3137)
PHONE..................................800 835-3300
Brian Crowe, *Branch Mgr*
EMP: 25
SALES (corp-wide): 8MM **Privately Held**
WEB: www.thomasunited.com
SIC: 4213 Trucking, except local
PA: Thomas Transfer And Storage Co., Inc.
906 E 6th Ave
Emporia KS 66801
620 342-2321

(G-15762)
THRASH INC
Also Called: Thrash Floor Maintenance
116 N Martinson St (67203-6128)
P.O. Box 12471 (67277-2471)
PHONE..................................316 265-5331
Russell Thrash, *President*
EMP: 50
SALES: 560K **Privately Held**
SIC: 7349 Floor waxing

(G-15763)
THREE WAY PATTERN INC
1623 S Mccomas St (67213-1297)
PHONE..................................316 942-7421
David Stephenson, *President*
Brandan Stephenson, *President*
Branden Stephenson, *Vice Pres*
EMP: 11
SQ FT: 20,000
SALES: 1.1MM **Privately Held**
SIC: 3544 Special dies & tools

(G-15764)
THYSSENKRUPP ELEVATOR CORP
4939 S Lulu Ct Ste 20 (67216-2066)
PHONE..................................316 529-2233
Dale Donal, *Principal*
Jerry Fofter, *Manager*
EMP: 16
SALES (corp-wide): 46.8B **Privately Held**
WEB: www.tyssenkrupp.com
SIC: 7699 5084 3999 Elevators: inspection, service & repair; elevators; wheelchair lifts
HQ: Thyssenkrupp Elevator Corporation
11605 Haynes Bridge Rd # 650
Alpharetta GA 30009
678 319-3240

(G-15765)
TIMBER CREEK PAPER INC (PA)
520 S Saint Francis Ave (67202-4524)
PHONE..................................316 264-3232
Mahlon Regier, *CEO*
Gregory Regier, *President*
▲ **EMP:** 10
SQ FT: 10,000
SALES (est): 4.2MM **Privately Held**
WEB: www.timbercreekpaper.com
SIC: 5111 5943 Printing paper; stationery stores

(G-15766)
TIMBER PRODUCTS INC
2286 S Custer Ave (67213-1515)
P.O. Box 9028 (67277-0028)
PHONE..................................316 941-9381
Tim N Neff, *President*
EMP: 32
SQ FT: 90,000
SALES (est): 5MM **Privately Held**
WEB: www.timberproductsinc.com
SIC: 2421 Sawmills & planing mills, general

(G-15767)
TIMOTHY M KOEHLER MD
2020 N Tyler Rd (67212-4905)
PHONE..................................316 462-6220
Timothy M Koehler MD, *Owner*
EMP: 20
SALES (est): 351.7K **Privately Held**
SIC: 8011 General & family practice, physician/surgeon

(G-15768)
TIYOSAYE INC HIGHER GROUND
Also Called: TIYOSPAYE PUEBLO PROGRAM
247 N Market St (67202-2003)
PHONE..................................316 262-2060
Mary San Martin, *President*
EMP: 11
SALES: 815.8K **Privately Held**
SIC: 8742 8069 Training & development consultant; alcoholism rehabilitation hospital

(G-15769)
TKFAST INC
437 S Hydraulic St (67211-1911)
PHONE..................................316 260-2500
Steven Anderson, *Exec Dir*
EMP: 31 **EST:** 2005
SALES (est): 3.8MM **Privately Held**
SIC: 7379 Computer related consulting services

(G-15770)
TL ENTERPRISES INC
923 S Doreen St (67207-2720)
PHONE..................................785 448-7100
Twyla D Beinhorn, *President*
Twyla Beinhorn, *President*
EMP: 16
SQ FT: 900
SALES (est): 2.4MM **Privately Held**
WEB: www.tlenterprises.com
SIC: 8711 1711 1623 Construction & civil engineering; plumbing contractors; water, sewer & utility lines

(G-15771)
TLM ENTERPRISES INC
Also Called: Dent Busters
406 S Market St (67202-3904)
P.O. Box 13058 (67213-0058)
PHONE..................................316 265-3833
Tracy Marsh, *President*
EMP: 12
SALES (est): 1.1MM **Privately Held**
WEB: www.mtlenterprises.com
SIC: 7532 Exterior repair services

(G-15772)
TMD TELECOM INC
3534 W 29th St S (67217-1002)
PHONE..................................316 462-0400
Thomas N Pittman, *President*
EMP: 25
SALES (est): 2.5MM **Privately Held**
SIC: 7389 Telephone services

(G-15773)
TORTILLERIA LA TRADICION
1701 N Broadway Ave (67214-1120)
PHONE..................................316 264-3148
Alberto Valvez, *Principal*
EMP: 6
SALES (est): 505.6K **Privately Held**
SIC: 2099 Tortillas, fresh or refrigerated

(G-15774)
TORTILLRIA LOS III PRTLLOS LLC
318 W 29th St N (67204-4806)
PHONE..................................316 831-0811
Jesus Rodriguez, *President*
Esther Orona, *Office Mgr*
EMP: 6
SALES (est): 547.6K **Privately Held**
SIC: 2099 Tortillas, fresh or refrigerated

(G-15775)
TOTAL ELECTRIC INC
1857 N Mosley St (67214-1347)
PHONE..................................316 524-2642
James Pederson, *President*
Mark Smith, *Project Mgr*
Georgia Eakins, *Admin Sec*
EMP: 8
SQ FT: 2,000
SALES (est): 1MM **Privately Held**
SIC: 1731 3613 3823 General electrical contractor; switchgear & switchboard apparatus; industrial instrmnts msrmnt display/control process variable

(G-15776)
TOTAL SECURITY SOLUTIONS LLC
Also Called: Signal 88 Security
934 N Sagebrush Ct (67230-7051)
PHONE..................................316 209-0436
Kris Withrow, *Owner*
Traci Withrow, *VP Admin*
EMP: 50
SALES (est): 200.6K **Privately Held**
SIC: 7381 Security guard service

(G-15777)
TOUCHPOINT DASHBOARD LLC
8918 W 21st St N Pmb 211 Pmb211 (67205-1885)
PHONE..................................512 585-5975
EMP: 5
SALES (est): 266.6K **Privately Held**
SIC: 7372 Business oriented computer software

(G-15778)
TOW SERVICE INC
3760 S Broadway Ave (67216-1032)
PHONE..................................316 522-8908
Mark Ysidro, *President*
EMP: 20
SQ FT: 1,000
SALES (est): 2.6MM **Privately Held**
SIC: 7549 Towing service, automotive

(G-15779)
TOWN AND COUNTRY FOOD MKTS INC
Also Called: Ruffin Oil Co
1522 S Florence St (67209-2634)
P.O. Box 17087 (67217-0087)
PHONE..................................316 942-7940
Phillip G Ruffin, *President*
Lynn Ruffin, *Corp Secy*
Ron Kroeger, *Vice Pres*
John Anderson, *Executive*
EMP: 40 **EST:** 1958
SQ FT: 20,000
SALES (est): 3.6MM **Privately Held**
SIC: 5411 5541 5172 Convenience stores; filling stations, gasoline; petroleum products

(G-15780)
TOWNE EAST SQUARE
7700 E Kellogg Dr Ste 799 (67207-1777)
PHONE..................................316 686-9672
Patty McDonough, *Manager*
EMP: 20 **EST:** 1975
SQ FT: 400
SALES (est): 1.9MM **Publicly Held**
SIC: 6512 Shopping center, property operation only
HQ: Simon Property Group, L.P.
225 W Washington St
Indianapolis IN 46204
317 636-1600

(G-15781)
TRACY PEDIGO
Also Called: Tracy's Automotive
3804 W Maple St (67213-2457)
PHONE..................................316 945-3414
Tracy Pedigo, *Owner*
EMP: 12
SALES (est): 717.8K **Privately Held**
SIC: 7539 Front end repair, automotive

(G-15782)
TRADEMARK INCORPORATED
7540 W Northwind St # 100 (67205-2597)
PHONE..................................316 264-8310
Michael R Strelow, *Principal*
EMP: 13
SALES (est): 1.7MM **Privately Held**
SIC: 8711 Building construction consultant

(G-15783)
TRADESMEN INTERNATIONAL LLC
1117 S Rock Rd Ste 4b (67207-3355)
PHONE..................................316 688-0291
Paul Neuberger, *Manager*
EMP: 30 **Privately Held**
SIC: 7361 Labor contractors (employment agency)
PA: Tradesmen International, Llc
9760 Shepard Rd
Macedonia OH 44056

(G-15784)
TRAFFIC CONTROL SERVICES INC
405 N Cleveland Ave (67214-4027)
PHONE..................................316 448-0402
Brian Foster, *President*
Shawn Koltiska, *Vice Pres*
EMP: 12
SALES (est): 2.5MM **Privately Held**
WEB: www.tcs-ks.com
SIC: 7359 1721 Work zone traffic equipment (flags, cones, barrels, etc.); pavement marking contractor

(G-15785)
TRAILERS N MORE LLC
Also Called: Trailers and More
433 N Maize Rd (67212-4654)
PHONE..................................316 945-8900
Dale Hutchison,
EMP: 32
SALES (est): 3.8MM **Privately Held**
WEB: www.trailersnmore.net
SIC: 5013 Trailer parts & accessories

(G-15786)
TRAN MAJHER AND SHAW OD PA (PA)
2251 N Woodlawn Blvd (67220-3947)
PHONE..................................316 686-6063
Daniel A Shea Od, *President*
EMP: 28
SQ FT: 10,000
SALES (est): 1.5MM **Privately Held**
SIC: 8042 Specialized optometrists

(G-15787)
TRAN AEROSPACE INC
7709 E Harry St (67207-3129)
PHONE..................................316 260-8808
Diep Ho, *President*
Tin Tran, *Principal*
Fred Bogatay, *Manager*
EMP: 5
SALES (est): 807.4K **Privately Held**
SIC: 3441 Fabricated structural metal

(G-15788)
TRANE US INC
120 S Ida St (67211-1504)
PHONE..................................316 265-9655
Emily Weibl, *Finance*
John Knipp, *Sales Dir*
John F Knipp, *Branch Mgr*
Becky Kealey, *Manager*
EMP: 61 **Privately Held**
SIC: 3585 Refrigeration & heating equipment
HQ: Trane U.S. Inc.
3600 Pammel Creek Rd
La Crosse WI 54601
608 787-2000

(G-15789)
TRANS PACIFIC OIL CORPORATION
100 S Main St Ste 200 (67202-3735)
PHONE..................................316 262-3596
Alan D Banta, *President*
Kunihiro Kawamura, *Principal*
Isao Sugiura, *Principal*
Gary Sharp, *Exec VP*
Reiko Trigo, *Treasurer*
EMP: 15
SQ FT: 3,500
SALES (est): 3.8MM **Privately Held**
WEB: www.transpacificoil.com
SIC: 1311 1381 Crude petroleum production; drilling oil & gas wells

(G-15790)
TRANS PACIFIC PROPERTIES LLC
Also Called: Trans Pacific Oil
100 S Main St Ste 200 (67202-3735)
PHONE..................................316 262-3596
Alan Banta,
Gary Sharp,
Reiko Trigo,
EMP: 6
SALES (est): 319.4K **Privately Held**
SIC: 1381 1389 Directional drilling oil & gas wells; oil consultants

(G-15791)
TRANSITIONS GROUP INC (PA)
Also Called: Executay Oakwood Corp Hsing
116 N Cleveland Ave (67214-4022)
PHONE..................................316 262-9100
William R Jackson, *President*
Barney Lehnherr, *President*
Nicole Witherspoon, *COO*
Piper Ayala, *Vice Pres*
Julia Capps, *Controller*
▲ **EMP:** 20
SQ FT: 72,000
SALES: 26.6MM **Privately Held**
WEB: www.transitionsgroup.net
SIC: 7011 Hotels & motels

(G-15792)
TRANSITIONS GROUP INC
Also Called: Furniture Options
1336 E Douglas Ave (67214-4029)
PHONE..................................316 263-5750
Brent Dorrah, *Vice Pres*
Dawn Black, *Opers Mgr*
Dennis Juarez, *Warehouse Mgr*
Brendan Hogan, *Opers Staff*
Jeremy Parks, *Sales Staff*
EMP: 15
SALES (corp-wide): 26.6MM **Privately Held**
WEB: www.transitionsgroup.net
SIC: 7359 5712 Furniture rental; office furniture
PA: Transitions Group, Inc.
116 N Cleveland Ave
Wichita KS 67214
316 262-9100

(G-15793)
TRANSTECS CORPORATION (PA)
2102 E 21st St N (67214-1943)
PHONE..................................316 651-0389
Godwin Opara, *President*
Margaret Opara, *Vice Pres*
Monica Modena, *Purchasing*
Harry Smith, *Engineer*
Darren Rudkin, *Accountant*
EMP: 100
SQ FT: 1,200
SALES (est): 8.9MM **Privately Held**
WEB: www.transtecs.com
SIC: 8744 8711 Facilities support services; engineering services

(G-15794)
TRANSYSTEMS CORPORATION
245 N Waco St Ste 222 (67202-1131)
PHONE..................................316 303-3000
Brett Letkowski, *Vice Pres*
EMP: 10
SALES (corp-wide): 174.5MM **Privately Held**
SIC: 8711 Consulting engineer
PA: Transystems Corporation
2400 Pershing Rd Ste 400
Kansas City MO 64108
816 329-8700

(G-15795)
TREATCO INC
9242 E Lakepoint Dr (67226-2101)
PHONE..................................316 265-7900
Margie Thomas, *President*
Brenda Mason, *Vice Pres*
Ken Thomas, *Vice Pres*
▲ **EMP:** 70
SALES (est): 10.7MM **Privately Held**
WEB: www.treatco.com
SIC: 2047 5199 Dog food; pet supplies

(G-15796)
TREE HOUSE LEARNING CENTER
449 N Maize Rd (67212-4654)
PHONE..................................316 773-3335
Darla Schaller, *Owner*
EMP: 18
SALES (est): 497.4K **Privately Held**
SIC: 8351 Group day care center

(G-15797)
TREE TOP NURSERY AND LANDSCAPE
5910 E 37th St N (67220-1998)
PHONE..................................316 686-7491
Mark Matney, *President*
Jeff Brown, *Vice Pres*
EMP: 50
SQ FT: 6,060
SALES (est): 6MM **Privately Held**
WEB: www.treetop-nursery.com
SIC: 0781 5261 0782 Landscape services; nursery stock, seeds & bulbs; lawn services

(G-15798)
TRENTON AGRI PRODUCTS LLC (PA)
2020 N Bramblewood St (67206-1094)
PHONE..................................316 265-3311
Charles B Wilson, *President*
Robert M Beren, *Chairman*
Adam E Beren, *Vice Chairman*
Charles S Spradlin Jr, *Exec VP*
Peter Willson, *Opers Mgr*
EMP: 5
SALES (est): 4.3MM **Privately Held**
WEB: www.trentonagriproducts.com
SIC: 2869 Ethyl alcohol, ethanol

(G-15799)
TRI-DIM FILTER CORPORATION
1659 S Sabin St (67209-2749)
PHONE..................................316 425-0462
Rik Arguello, *Branch Mgr*
EMP: 8
SALES (corp-wide): 4.3B **Privately Held**
SIC: 3564 Filters, air: furnaces, air conditioning equipment, etc.
HQ: Tri-Dim Filter Corporation
93 Industrial Dr
Louisa VA 23093
540 967-2600

(G-15800)
TRIMARK SIGNWORKS INC
318 S Osage St (67213-5517)
PHONE..................................316 263-2224
Peter Ochs, *President*
Tyler McFadden, *Accounts Exec*
EMP: 25
SQ FT: 38,000
SALES (est): 2.5MM **Privately Held**
WEB: www.trimarksignworks.com
SIC: 3993 Electric signs

(G-15801)
TRINITY DAYCARE & PRESCHOOL
2402 N Arkansas Ave (67204-6020)
P.O. Box 4449 (67204-0449)
PHONE..................................316 838-0909
Jill Grind, *Director*
EMP: 15
SALES: 500K **Privately Held**
SIC: 8351 Preschool center

(G-15802)
TRINITY PRECISION INC
1935 W Walker St (67213-3365)
PHONE..................................316 265-0603
David May, *President*
Wes Hawk, *Vice Pres*
Dave Tice, *Vice Pres*
Steve Ford, *CFO*
▲ **EMP:** 51 **EST:** 2014
SQ FT: 33,000
SALES (est): 9.3MM **Privately Held**
SIC: 3728 Empennage (tail) assemblies & parts, aircraft

(G-15803)
TRINITY SALES LLC
2225 S West St (67213-1113)
PHONE..................................316 942-5555
Gregg Miller, *Mng Member*
Pam Miller, *Office Admin*
EMP: 23
SALES (est): 5.2MM **Privately Held**
WEB: www.trinitysales.biz
SIC: 7353 Heavy construction equipment rental

(G-15804)
TRIPLETT WOOLF & GARRETSON LLC
2959 N Rock Rd Ste 300 (67226-5100)
PHONE..................................316 630-8100
Theron E Fry, *Partner*
Ron H Harnden, *Partner*
Jeffrey Leonard, *Partner*
Eric B Metz, *Partner*
Tad Patton, *Partner*
EMP: 40
SALES (est): 5.8MM **Privately Held**
WEB: www.twgfirm.com
SIC: 8111 Corporate, partnership & business law; general practice attorney, lawyer

(G-15805)
TRIUMPH STRCTRES - WICHITA INC (HQ)
3258 S Hoover Rd (67215-1217)
P.O. Box 12670 (67277-2670)
PHONE..................................316 942-0432
Joe Scheer, *President*
Marwan Hammouri, *President*
M David Kornblatt, *Exec VP*
Kevin E Kindig, *Vice Pres*
John B Wright, *Vice Pres*
▲ **EMP:** 70
SQ FT: 150,000
SALES (est): 39.6MM **Publicly Held**
WEB: www.triumphgrp.com
SIC: 3728 Aircraft body & wing assemblies & parts

(G-15806)
TROPICANA PRODUCTS INC
214 W 21st St N Ste 200 (67203-2405)
PHONE..................................316 838-1000
EMP: 86
SALES (corp-wide): 63B **Publicly Held**
SIC: 2033 Nonclassified Establishment
HQ: Tropicana Products, Inc.
1275 26th Ave E
Bradenton FL 34208
941 747-4461

(G-15807)
TRUCK STUFF INC
427 N Washington Ave (67202-2821)
PHONE..................................316 264-1908
Greg R Bolin, *President*
Julia C Bolin, *Vice Pres*
EMP: 13
SQ FT: 5,000
SALES: 2.5MM **Privately Held**
SIC: 5531 5013 Truck equipment & parts; truck parts & accessories

(G-15808)
TRUE HOME CARE LLC
Also Called: Firstlight Home Care
12828 E 13th St N Ste 6 (67230-1464)
PHONE..................................316 776-4685
Amal Hayyeh,
EMP: 35
SALES (est): 300.3K **Privately Held**
SIC: 8082 Home health care services

(G-15809)
TRUE NORTH INC (PA)
8200 E 32nd St N Ste 100 (67226-2618)
PHONE..................................316 266-6574
West Cooper, *President*
David L Strohm, *Chairman*
Susan Pool, *Manager*
EMP: 15 **EST:** 1999
SALES (est): 2.4MM **Privately Held**
SIC: 6411 6289 Pension & retirement plan consultants; financial reporting

(G-15810)
TRUECARE NURSING SERVICES LLC
4601 E Douglas Ave # 201 (67218-1032)
PHONE..................................626 818-2420
EMP: 48
SALES (corp-wide): 1.5MM **Privately Held**
SIC: 8059 8051 Personal care home, with health care; skilled nursing care facilities
PA: Truecare Nursing Services L.L.C
275 E Green St
Pasadena CA 91101
626 818-2420

(G-15811)
TRUETT & OSBORN CYCLE INC
3345 E 31st St S (67216-2705)
PHONE..................................316 682-4781
Paul Osborn, *President*
Dianne Osborn, *Treasurer*
EMP: 6
SQ FT: 2,400
SALES (est): 1.1MM **Privately Held**
SIC: 5571 7699 5013 3714 Motorcycle parts & accessories; motorcycle repair service; motorcycle parts; motor vehicle parts & accessories

(G-15812)
TRUGREEN LIMITED PARTNERSHIP
Also Called: Tru Green-Chemlawn
1652 S West St (67213-1104)
P.O. Box 13318 (67213-0318)
PHONE..................................316 448-6253
Dan Bleier, *Branch Mgr*
EMP: 40
SQ FT: 4,500
SALES (corp-wide): 3.2B **Privately Held**
SIC: 0782 Lawn care services
HQ: Trugreen Limited Partnership
1790 Kirby Pkwy
Memphis TN 38138
866 417-7866

(G-15813)
TRUJILLO JAN & CRPT CLG SVC
339 S Laura St (67211-1518)
PHONE..................................316 263-8204
EMP: 14 **EST:** 1980
SQ FT: 2,200
SALES (est): 300K **Privately Held**
SIC: 7349 Building And Cleaning

(G-15814)
TSR LLC
325 S West St (67213-2105)
PHONE..................................316 946-1527
Michelle D Riggins,
Travis Riggins,
EMP: 10
SALES (est): 1MM **Privately Held**
SIC: 5072 Hardware

(G-15815)
TURBINE ENG COMP TECH TURNING
Also Called: Tect Power
2019 Southwest Blvd (67213-1439)
PHONE..................................316 925-4020
Robert Cohen, *CEO*
Luke Rankin, *Manager*
Jacob Mullins, *Supervisor*
EMP: 25
SQ FT: 40,000
SALES (est): 3.8MM
SALES (corp-wide): 4.4MM **Privately Held**
SIC: 3724 3728 Aircraft engines & engine parts; aircraft parts & equipment
PA: Tect Corp
334 Beechwood Rd Ste 303
Fort Mitchell KY 41017
859 426-0090

(G-15816)
TURNPIKE INVESTMENTS INC
Also Called: Days Inn
4875 S Laura St (67216-2049)
PHONE..................................316 524-4400
Ken Patel, *President*
Naina Patel, *Vice Pres*
EMP: 12
SALES (est): 898.2K **Privately Held**
SIC: 7011 Hotels & motels

(G-15817)
TUSAR INC
Also Called: Comfort Inn
4849 S Laura St (67216-2049)
PHONE..................................316 522-1800
Jay Bhatka, *President*
EMP: 50
SALES (est): 944.2K **Privately Held**
SIC: 7011 Hotels & motels

(G-15818)
TUTOR TIME LRNG SYSTEMS INC
10710 W Maple St (67209-4016)
PHONE..................................316 721-0848
EMP: 25
SALES (corp-wide): 340.2MM **Privately Held**
SIC: 8351 Child Day Care Services
HQ: Tutor Time Learning Systems, Inc.
621 Nw 53rd St Ste 450
Boca Raton FL

(G-15819)
TUTOR TIME LRNG SYSTEMS INC
7026 W 21st St N (67205-1760)
PHONE..................................316 721-0464
EMP: 20
SALES (corp-wide): 340.2MM **Privately Held**
SIC: 8299 8351 School/Educational Services Child Day Care Services
HQ: Tutor Time Learning Systems, Inc.
621 Nw 53rd St Ste 450
Boca Raton FL

(G-15820)
TWC SERVICES INC
Also Called: Comfort Systems
1840 S West St (67213-1106)
PHONE..................................316 265-7831
Chad Heitman, *Manager*
EMP: 30
SALES (corp-wide): 102.5MM **Privately Held**
WEB: www.comfortsystems.net
SIC: 1711 1761 Mechanical contractor; plumbing contractors; warm air heating & air conditioning contractor; ventilation & duct work contractor; sheet metalwork
PA: Twc Services, Inc.
2601 Bell Ave
Des Moines IA 50321
515 284-1911

(G-15821)
TWICE AS NICE BARBERSHOP
6249 E 21st St N Ste 110 (67208-1861)
PHONE..................................319 201-4542
EMP: 12
SALES (est): 295.8K **Privately Held**
SIC: 7241 Barber Shops, Nsk

(G-15822)
TWOTREES TECHNOLOGIES LLC
Also Called: Water Technology Investments
200 N Emporia Ave Ste 300 (67202-2551)
PHONE..................................800 364-5700
Daryl Woodard, *CEO*
Jim Smith, *President*
Rodney Kramer, *CFO*
EMP: 11
SALES (est): 2.7MM
SALES (corp-wide): 164.2MM **Privately Held**
WEB: www.communico.com
SIC: 4813
PA: Woodard Technology & Investments, L.L.C.
10205 E 61st St Ste D
Tulsa OK 74133
918 270-7000

(G-15823)
TYLER PHYSICIANS PA
10202 W 13th St N (67212-4377)
PHONE..................................316 729-9100
Tristyn Pierce, *President*
EMP: 10
SALES (est): 1.6MM **Privately Held**
SIC: 8011 Pediatrician

GEOGRAPHIC

(G-15824)
U S LOGO INC
520 N West St (67203-1209)
PHONE..................................316 264-1321
T J Smith, *President*
Josh Adams, *Prdtn Mgr*
Lori Wright, *Accounts Mgr*
Joel Smith, *Sales Staff*
Lynne Smith, *Sales Staff*
▲ **EMP:** 10
SQ FT: 6,000
SALES (est): 680K **Privately Held**
WEB: www.uslogo.net
SIC: 7389 2759 2395 Embroidering of advertising on shirts, etc.; screen printing; embroidery products, except schiffli machine

(G-15825)
U S ROAD FREIGHT EXPRESS INC (PA)
Also Called: US Road Freight
3655 S Maize Rd (67215-8925)
P.O. Box 9070 (67277-0070)
PHONE..................................316 942-9944
Shirley Dugan, *President*
Pat Keitel, *President*
Mark Dugan, *Vice Pres*
Jennifer Hare, *Vice Pres*
Tony Antone, *Terminal Mgr*
EMP: 24
SALES (est): 8.9MM **Privately Held**
SIC: 4212 4213 Local trucking, without storage; trucking, except local

(G-15826)
U S S A INC (PA)
Also Called: Alterations By Sarah
1208 S Rock Rd (67207-3320)
PHONE..................................316 686-1653
Sarah Arif, *President*
Abdul A Vice, *Vice Pres*
EMP: 6
SQ FT: 1,500
SALES (est): 359.1K **Privately Held**
SIC: 7219 3993 2759 2395 Garment alteration & repair shop; signs & advertising specialties; screen printing; embroidery products, except schiffli machine

(G-15827)
UBE SERVICES LLC
Also Called: United Bio Energy
2868 N Ridge Rd (67205-1039)
P.O. Box 9610 (67277-0610)
PHONE..................................316 616-3500
Rolf S Peters, *CEO*
Tim Carlson, *COO*
Tom Carlson, *COO*
Bill Hren, *CFO*
EMP: 42
SALES (est): 5.6MM
SALES (corp-wide): 419MM **Privately Held**
WEB: www.unitedbioenergy.com
SIC: 2869 Ethyl alcohol, ethanol
PA: Agmotion, Inc.
730 2nd Ave S Ste 700
Minneapolis MN 55402
612 486-3800

(G-15828)
UBS FINANCIAL SERVICES INC
121 S Whittier Rd (67207-1061)
PHONE..................................316 612-6500
Chris Watkins, *Branch Mgr*
Bryce Flaming, *Agent*
Robert Wilkins, *Agent*
EMP: 40
SALES (corp-wide): 29.9B **Privately Held**
WEB: www.ubs.com
SIC: 6211 Investment bankers; stock brokers & dealers
HQ: Ubs Financial Services Inc.
1285 Ave Of The Americas
New York NY 10019
212 713-2000

(G-15829)
ULTRA MODERN POOL & PATIO INC
Also Called: East Branch
5620 E Kellogg Dr (67218-1717)
PHONE..................................316 681-3011
Jeff Jarvis, *Manager*
EMP: 8
SALES (corp-wide): 5.9MM **Privately Held**
WEB: www.ultramodern.com
SIC: 3446 Architectural metalwork
PA: Ultra Modern Pool & Patio, Inc.
8100 W Kellogg Dr
Wichita KS 67209
316 722-4308

(G-15830)
UMB BANK NATIONAL ASSOCIATION
130 N Market St (67202-1900)
PHONE..................................316 267-1191
Craig L Anderson, *President*
Kaleb Smith, *Manager*
EMP: 15
SALES (corp-wide): 1.1B **Publicly Held**
SIC: 6021 National commercial banks
HQ: Umb Bank, National Association
1010 Grand Blvd Fl 3
Kansas City MO 64106
816 842-2222

(G-15831)
UNDERGROUND VAULTS & STOR INC
Also Called: Record Center of Wichita
3333 N Mead St Ste B (67219-4060)
P.O. Box 4308 (67204-0308)
PHONE..................................316 838-2121
Mike Mongold, *Manager*
Chris Graham, *IT/INT Sup*
EMP: 10
SALES (corp-wide): 18.8MM **Privately Held**
WEB: www.undergroundvaults.com
SIC: 4226 Document & office records storage
PA: Underground Vaults & Storage, Inc.
906 N Halstead St
Hutchinson KS 67501
620 662-6769

(G-15832)
UNDERHILL FINISH CARPENTRY LLC
14350 W Hardtner Ct (67235-7541)
P.O. Box 12871 (67277-2871)
PHONE..................................316 253-7129
Justin Underhill,
Stephanie Underhill,
EMP: 13
SALES (est): 875.6K **Privately Held**
SIC: 2499 Decorative wood & woodwork

(G-15833)
UNIFIED SCHOOL DISTRICT 259 (PA)
Also Called: WICHITA PUBLIC SCHOOLS
903 S Edgemoor St (67218-3337)
PHONE..................................316 973-4000
John Allison, *Superintendent*
Jim Freeman, *CFO*
Linda Jones, *Treasurer*
Sharon Hoyme, *Supervisor*
Mary Halley, *Technician*
EMP: 200 **EST:** 1871
SQ FT: 10,000
SALES: 668.7MM **Privately Held**
SIC: 8211 8249 8331 Public elementary & secondary schools; high school, junior or senior; vocational schools; job training & vocational rehabilitation services

(G-15834)
UNIFIED SCHOOL DISTRICT 259
Also Called: East High Sch Child Lrng Ctr
2301 E Douglas Ave (67211-1613)
PHONE..................................316 973-7292
Katie McHenry, *Principal*
EMP: 275
SALES (corp-wide): 668.7MM **Privately Held**
SIC: 8351 Child day care services
PA: Unified School District 259
903 S Edgemoor St
Wichita KS 67218
316 973-4000

(G-15835)
UNIFIED SCHOOL DISTRICT 259
Also Called: Urban League of Mid Plains
2418 E 9th St N (67214-3150)
PHONE..................................316 683-3315
Brian Black, *Director*
EMP: 10
SALES (corp-wide): 668.7MM **Privately Held**
SIC: 8322 Individual & family services
PA: Unified School District 259
903 S Edgemoor St
Wichita KS 67218
316 973-4000

(G-15836)
UNIFIED SCHOOL DISTRICT 259
Also Called: Witchita Public School Mngt In
201 N Water St (67202-1226)
PHONE..................................316 973-4200
EMP: 54
SALES (corp-wide): 668.7MM **Privately Held**
SIC: 8999 8211 Information bureau; elementary & secondary schools
PA: Unified School District 259
903 S Edgemoor St
Wichita KS 67218
316 973-4000

(G-15837)
UNIFIRST CORPORATION
1707 N Mosley St (67214-1345)
PHONE..................................316 264-2342
Michael Williams, *Principal*
Ryan Lucas, *Manager*
EMP: 10
SALES (corp-wide): 1.8B **Publicly Held**
WEB: www.unifirst.com
SIC: 7218 Industrial launderers
PA: Unifirst Corporation
68 Jonspin Rd
Wilmington MA 01887
978 658-8888

(G-15838)
UNION PACIFIC RAILROAD COMPANY
2646 New York Ave (67219)
PHONE..................................316 268-9446
Lester Pierce, *Office Mgr*
James Ellsworth, *Manager*
EMP: 76
SALES (corp-wide): 22.8B **Publicly Held**
WEB: www.uprr.com
SIC: 4011 Railroads, line-haul operating
HQ: Union Pacific Railroad Company Inc
1400 Douglas St
Omaha NE 68179
402 544-5000

(G-15839)
UNION RESCUE MISSION INC
Also Called: Men's Shelter
2800 N Hillside Ave (67219-4702)
PHONE..................................316 687-4673
Alvin Manning, *Treasurer*
Martin Moody, *Asst Treas*
Dennis Bender, *Exec Dir*
Dennis Benber, *Director*
John McLaughlin, *Director*
EMP: 30 **EST:** 1951
SQ FT: 3,000
SALES (est): 876.6K **Privately Held**
SIC: 8322 Social service center

(G-15840)
UNITED AUTO PARTS INC
Also Called: United Engine Specialists
14801 W Us Highway 54 (67235-8925)
PHONE..................................316 721-6868
Jerry D Livingston, *President*
Jeff Livingston, *Vice Pres*
Richard Livingston, *Vice Pres*
Mary Kay Livingston, *Treasurer*
EMP: 30 **EST:** 1962
SQ FT: 50,000
SALES (est): 4.3MM **Privately Held**
SIC: 3519 5013 Gas engine rebuilding; automotive supplies & parts

(G-15841)
UNITED DISTRIBUTORS INC (PA)
Also Called: Amusement Service Division
420 S Seneca St (67213-5596)
P.O. Box 1995 (67201-1995)
PHONE..................................316 712-2174
Mark Y Blum Jr, *President*
Nancy Blum, *Admin Sec*
EMP: 10 **EST:** 1943
SQ FT: 25,000
SALES: 2MM **Privately Held**
WEB: www.united420.com
SIC: 7359 5046 5621 7993 Vending machine rental; coin-operated equipment; women's clothing stores; coin-operated amusement devices

(G-15842)
UNITED DISTRIBUTORS INC
Also Called: Parrot-Fa-Nalia
420 S Seneca St (67213-5596)
P.O. Box 1995 (67201-1995)
PHONE..................................316 263-6181
Nancy Blum, *Branch Mgr*
EMP: 10
SQ FT: 1,500
SALES (corp-wide): 2MM **Privately Held**
WEB: www.united420.com
SIC: 5621 5632 7299 Women's clothing stores; women's accessory & specialty stores; tuxedo rental
PA: United Distributors, Inc.
420 S Seneca St
Wichita KS 67213
316 712-2174

(G-15843)
UNITED MACHINE COMPANY INC
602 N Hydraulic St (67214-4226)
PHONE..................................316 264-3367
Tim McGinty, *President*
Mike Wright, *Vice Pres*
Theresa Lopez, *Treasurer*
Graydon Winegamer, *Manager*
EMP: 48 **EST:** 1953
SQ FT: 50,000
SALES: 10.6MM **Privately Held**
WEB: www.united-machine.com
SIC: 3599 Machine shop, jobbing & repair

(G-15844)
UNITED METHODIST OPEN DOOR
402 E 2nd St N 220 (67202-2504)
P.O. Box 2756 (67201-2756)
PHONE..................................316 265-9371
Mary Kauffman, *Managing Dir*
Deann Smith Rev, *Exec Dir*
EMP: 25
SALES: 2.6MM **Privately Held**
SIC: 8399 Social service information exchange

(G-15845)
UNITED PARCEL SERVICE INC
Also Called: UPS
1935 S Air Cargo Rd (67209-1926)
PHONE..................................316 946-4074
EMP: 158
SALES (corp-wide): 71.8B **Publicly Held**
SIC: 4215 Package delivery, vehicular
HQ: United Parcel Service, Inc.
55 Glenlake Pkwy
Atlanta GA 30328
404 828-6000

(G-15846)
UNITED PARCEL SERVICE INC
Also Called: UPS
3003 S West St (67217-1033)
PHONE..................................316 941-2010
Ted Thulin, *Opers Mgr*
EMP: 400
SALES (corp-wide): 71.8B **Publicly Held**
WEB: www.upsscs.com
SIC: 4215 Package delivery, vehicular
HQ: United Parcel Service, Inc.
55 Glenlake Pkwy
Atlanta GA 30328
404 828-6000

(G-15847)
UNITED RENTALS NORTH AMER INC
9127 W Kellogg Dr (67209-1860)
PHONE..................................316 722-7368
Penney Simpson, *Opers Staff*
Austin Sharp, *Sales Associate*
Shannon Farr, *Branch Mgr*
EMP: 15
SALES (corp-wide): 8B **Publicly Held**
SIC: 7359 Rental store, general
HQ: United Rentals (North America), Inc.
100 Frederick St 700
Stamford CT 06902
203 622-3131

(G-15848)
UNITED RENTALS NORTH AMER INC
9127 W Kellogg Dr (67209-1860)
PHONE..................................316 682-7368
Fax: 316 682-0254
EMP: 12
SALES (corp-wide): 5.7B **Publicly Held**
SIC: 7353 Heavy Construction Equipment Rental
HQ: United Rentals (North America), Inc.
100 Frist Stamford 700
Stamford CT 06902
203 622-3131

(G-15849)
UNITED STATES AVIATION UNDERWR
Also Called: Usaig
301 N Main St Ste 1450 (67202-4840)
PHONE..................................316 267-1325
EMP: 14
SQ FT: 900
SALES (corp-wide): 225.3B **Publicly Held**
WEB: www.usau.com
SIC: 6411 Insurance agents
HQ: United States Aviation Underwriters, Incorporated
199 Water St
New York NY 10038
212 952-0100

(G-15850)
UNITED TECH AROSPC SYSTEMS
Also Called: UTC Aerospace Systems
1643 S Maize Rd (67209-1922)
PHONE..................................316 721-3100
EMP: 12
SALES (est): 1.5MM **Privately Held**
SIC: 3728 Aircraft parts & equipment

(G-15851)
UNIVAR SOLUTIONS USA INC
2041 N Mosley Ave (67214-1351)
P.O. Box 2201 (67201-2201)
PHONE..................................316 267-1002
Glenn Sims, *Manager*
EMP: 13
SQ FT: 9,000
SALES (corp-wide): 8.6B **Publicly Held**
SIC: 5169 Industrial chemicals
HQ: Univar Solutions Usa Inc.
3075 Highland Pkwy # 200
Downers Grove IL 60515
331 777-6000

(G-15852)
UNIVERSAL AVONICS SYSTEMS CORP
3815 Midco St (67215-8942)
PHONE..................................316 524-9500
Spencer Tepe, *Manager*
Mike Michalski, *Instructor*
EMP: 9
SALES (corp-wide): 1B **Privately Held**
WEB: www.uasc-id.com
SIC: 3728 Aircraft assemblies, subassemblies & parts
HQ: Universal Avionics Systems Corporation
3260 E Universal Way
Tucson AZ 85756
520 295-2300

(G-15853)
UNIVERSAL CONSTRUCTION PDTS
3348 S Hoover Rd (67215-1216)
P.O. Box 9102 (67277-0102)
PHONE..................................316 946-5885
Gary Cochran, *President*
Dennis Skraba, *Vice Pres*
Jerri Cochran, *CFO*
EMP: 50
SALES (est): 5.3MM **Privately Held**
SIC: 3545 5082 Milling machine attachments (machine tool accessories); contractors' materials

(G-15854)
UNIVERSAL MACHINING SHTMTL INC
116 S Lulu Ave (67211-1709)
PHONE..................................316 425-7610
John Darbyshire, *President*
Wes Alexander, *Plant Mgr*
Courtney Cason, *Production*
Guylene Montgomery, *Production*
Susan Yates, *QC Mgr*
EMP: 27
SQ FT: 12,000
SALES: 2.5MM **Privately Held**
SIC: 3728 3599 Research & dev by manuf., aircraft parts & auxiliary equip; machine shop, jobbing & repair

(G-15855)
UNIVERSAL MOTOR FUELS INC
2824 N Ohio St (67219-4319)
P.O. Box 2920 (67201-2920)
PHONE..................................316 832-0151
Dennis Maloney, *President*
Michael B Maloney, *Treasurer*
EMP: 12 **EST:** 1957
SQ FT: 12,000
SALES (est): 5MM **Privately Held**
SIC: 5171 5541 6512 Petroleum bulk stations; filling stations, gasoline; commercial & industrial building operation

(G-15856)
UNIVERSITY OF KANSAS
Also Called: School of Medicine
1010 N Kansas St Ste 3007 (67214-3124)
PHONE..................................316 293-2607
Garold Minnf, *Treasurer*
EMP: 200
SALES (corp-wide): 1.2B **Privately Held**
WEB: www.ukans.edu
SIC: 8062 8221 Hospital, medical school affiliation; university
PA: University Of Kansas
1450 Jayhawk Blvd Rm 225
Lawrence KS 66045
785 864-4868

(G-15857)
UNIVERSITY OF KANSAS
Also Called: School of Medicine
1010 N Kansas St (67214-3124)
PHONE..................................316 293-2620
S Edward Mismuek, *Dean*
EMP: 40
SALES (corp-wide): 1.2B **Privately Held**
WEB: www.ukans.edu
SIC: 8221 8621 University; medical field-related associations
PA: University Of Kansas
1450 Jayhawk Blvd Rm 225
Lawrence KS 66045
785 864-4868

(G-15858)
UNIVERSITY OF KANSAS SCHOOL OF
Also Called: UKSM-W MEDICAL PRACTICE ASSOCI
1010 N Kansas St Rm 3049 (67214-3124)
PHONE..................................316 293-3432
Paige Harwell, *Surgeon*
Lorene Valentine, *Exec Dir*
Diana McPhail, *Admin Sec*
EMP: 100
SALES: 25.6MM **Privately Held**
SIC: 8011 Medical centers

(G-15859)
UNLIMITED SERVICE OPTIONS LLC
Also Called: Usoc
1920 E Northern St (67216-2429)
PHONE..................................316 522-1503
Ronald Pore,
EMP: 15
SALES: 600K **Privately Held**
SIC: 1771 1721 Flooring contractor; painting & paper hanging

(G-15860)
UNXMED-IMMEDIATE MEDICAL CARE
4722 W Kellogg Dr (67209-2508)
PHONE..................................316 440-2565
Grover D Hershberger, *Owner*
Sherry Martinez, *Manager*
Daniel Summerfeld, *Manager*
EMP: 12
SALES (est): 734.7K **Privately Held**
SIC: 8093 Rehabilitation center, outpatient treatment

(G-15861)
URBAN LEAGUE OF KANSAS INC
2418 E 9th St N (67214-3150)
PHONE..................................316 440-9217
Desmond Blake, *CEO*
Kevin Andrews, *Senior VP*
Frankie M Kirkendoll, *Vice Pres*
Sandy Free, *CFO*
Derrick Simmonds, *Accountant*
EMP: 15
SALES: 194.5K **Privately Held**
SIC: 8399 Community development groups

(G-15862)
US ATTORNEYS OFFICE - DST KANS
301 N Main St Ste 1200 (67202-4812)
PHONE..................................316 269-6481
R L Miller, *President*
EMP: 83
SALES (est): 4.1MM **Privately Held**
SIC: 8744 Facilities support services

(G-15863)
US FOODS INC
3409 W 29th St S (67217-1000)
PHONE..................................316 942-9679
Dan Pfannenstiel, *Principal*
EMP: 160 **Publicly Held**
SIC: 5141 Food brokers
HQ: Us Foods, Inc.
9399 W Higgins Rd Ste 500
Rosemont IL 60018

(G-15864)
USI INSURANCE SERVICES LLC
Also Called: Nationwide
245 N Waco St Ste 412 (67202-1117)
PHONE..................................316 263-3211
Eric McCurley, *Manager*
Trent Nichols, *Producer*
EMP: 64 **Privately Held**
SIC: 6411 Insurance agents, brokers & service
HQ: Usi Insurance Services Llc
100 Summit Lake Dr # 400
Valhalla NY 10595

(G-15865)
UTILITIES PLUS INC
3505 W 30th St S (67217-1013)
P.O. Box 385, Haysville (67060-0385)
PHONE..................................316 946-9416
Susan King, *President*
EMP: 25
SALES: 2.5MM **Privately Held**
SIC: 1623 Underground utilities contractor

(G-15866)
UTILITY CONTRACTORS INC (PA)
Also Called: UCI
1930 S Hoover Rd Ste 100 (67209-2835)
P.O. Box 9592 (67277-0592)
PHONE..................................316 942-1253
Charles F Grier, *CEO*
Jeff Barley, *Vice Pres*
Eric Estep, *Vice Pres*
Louise Gerwick, *Treasurer*
David McKee, *Accountant*
EMP: 35 **EST:** 1950
SALES: 42.4MM **Privately Held**
WEB: www.ucict.com
SIC: 1623 1799 1629 Water & sewer line construction; petroleum storage tanks, pumping & draining; chemical plant & refinery construction

(G-15867)
UTILITY MAINTENANCE CONTRS LLC
4151 N Seneca St (67204-3103)
P.O. Box 4780 (67204-0780)
PHONE..................................316 945-8833
Jeremy Ruff, *Project Mgr*
Greg Bruggeman, *Asst Mgr*
Shari Berry, *Executive Asst*
EMP: 13
SQ FT: 5,000
SALES (est): 4.2MM
SALES (corp-wide): 69.5MM **Privately Held**
WEB: www.umcllc.com
SIC: 1623 4952 Sewer line construction; sewerage systems
PA: Wildcat Construction Co., Inc.
3219 W May St
Wichita KS 67213
316 945-9408

(G-15868)
V W C INC
Also Called: Cochran Mortuary
1411 N Broadway Ave (67214-1103)
P.O. Box 3607 (67201-3607)
PHONE..................................316 262-4422
W Robert Phifer, *President*
Todd Phifer, *General Mgr*
Teryl Cochran Phifer, *Corp Secy*
Brandi Phifer, *Office Mgr*
John Rodda, *Director*
EMP: 14 **EST:** 1928
SQ FT: 12,000
SALES (est): 820K **Privately Held**
WEB: www.cochranmortuary.com
SIC: 7261 Funeral home

(G-15869)
VAL ENERGY INC
125 N Market St Ste 1710 (67202-1721)
PHONE..................................316 263-6688
K Todd Allam, *President*
EMP: 5 **EST:** 1961
SQ FT: 1,000
SALES (est): 1.4MM **Privately Held**
WEB: www.valenergy.com
SIC: 1381 1311 Drilling oil & gas wells; crude petroleum production

(G-15870)
VALENT AEROSTRUCTURES LLC
2853 S Hillside St (67216-2546)
PHONE..................................316 682-4551
Mike Clift, *General Mgr*
EMP: 88
SALES (est): 13.2MM **Privately Held**
WEB: www.precisionmetalcraft.com
SIC: 3728 Aircraft parts & equipment

(G-15871)
VALLEY FLORAL COMPANY LLC (PA)
4619 N Arkansas Ave (67204-2921)
P.O. Box 2884 (67201-2884)
PHONE..................................316 838-3355
Gerald Yocum, *President*
Carlos Ramos, *General Mgr*
EMP: 50 **EST:** 1941
SQ FT: 50,000
SALES (est): 7.7MM **Privately Held**
WEB: www.valleyfloral.com
SIC: 5193 5992 Flowers, fresh; florists' supplies; planters & flower pots; plants, potted; florists

(G-15872)
VCHP WICHITA LLC
Also Called: Red Roof Wichita
7335 E Kellogg Dr (67207-1628)
PHONE..................................316 685-1281
Kamini Patel, *Principal*
EMP: 20

GEOGRAPHIC

SALES (est): 194.4K **Privately Held**
SIC: 7011 Hotels & motels

(G-15873)
VEND-TECH ENTERPRISE LLC
250 N Rock Rd Ste 360 (67206-2243)
PHONE..................................316 689-6850
David Edmonds, *Opers Staff*
Cheryl E Etheredge, *Manager*
Cheryl Etheredge, *Info Tech Mgr*
Curtis L Whitten,
EMP: 20
SQ FT: 480
SALES: 300K **Privately Held**
WEB: www.vendtechenterprise.com
SIC: 7389 Personal investigation service

(G-15874)
VERITIV OPERATING COMPANY
Also Called: Southwest Market Area
4700 S Palisade Ave (67217-4926)
PHONE..................................316 522-3494
Joe Robenson, *Manager*
EMP: 48
SALES (corp-wide): 8.7B **Publicly Held**
WEB: www.unisourcelink.com
SIC: 5113 Industrial & personal service paper
HQ: Veritiv Operating Company
1000 Abernathy Rd Bldg 4
Atlanta GA 30328
770 391-8200

(G-15875)
VERMILLION INCORPORATED
4754 S Palisade St (67217-4926)
PHONE..................................316 524-3100
Bill Davis, *President*
Steve Groppe, *Design Engr*
Steve Shook, *CFO*
Cherie Warchuck, *CFO*
G Allen Penniman Jr, *Director*
EMP: 72
SQ FT: 43,800
SALES (est): 24MM **Privately Held**
WEB: www.vermillioninc.com
SIC: 3769 3694 3357 3351 Guided missile & space vehicle parts & auxiliary equipment; engine electrical equipment; communication wire; wire, copper & copper alloy

(G-15876)
VERSASPORT OF KANSAS INC
Also Called: Versacourt Multi Sport Game Co
6801 N Meridian Ave (67204-1100)
PHONE..................................316 393-0487
Lance Pierce, *President*
Brent Carlson, *Partner*
EMP: 20 **EST:** 2007
SALES: 2.4MM **Privately Held**
SIC: 1629 1799 7389 Tennis court construction; court construction, indoor athletic;

(G-15877)
VESS OIL CORPORATION
1700 N Waterfront Pkwy # 500
(67206-5504)
PHONE..................................316 682-1537
Barry Hill, *CEO*
J Michael Vess, *Ch of Bd*
Ronnie Nutt, *COO*
EMP: 10
SQ FT: 1,600
SALES: 1.4MM **Privately Held**
WEB: www.vessoil.com
SIC: 1311 Crude petroleum production; natural gas production

(G-15878)
VETERANS HEALTH ADMINISTRATION
Also Called: Robert J Dole V A Medical Ctr
5500 E Kellogg Dr (67218-1607)
PHONE..................................316 685-2221
Thomas Suduors, *Branch Mgr*
Vicki Bondie, *Program Dir*
EMP: 650 **Publicly Held**
WEB: www.veterans-ru.org
SIC: 8011 9451 Medical centers; administration of veterans' affairs;
HQ: Veterans Health Administration
810 Vermont Ave Nw
Washington DC 20420

(G-15879)
VIA CHRISTI
1947 N Founders Cir (67206-3548)
PHONE..................................316 613-4931
Suzann M Wright, *Principal*
EMP: 16
SALES (est): 1MM **Privately Held**
SIC: 8099 Health & allied services

(G-15880)
VIA CHRISTI CLINIC PA
1947 N Founders Cir (67206-3548)
PHONE..................................316 613-4680
Richard A Desplinter, *Director*
EMP: 37
SALES (corp-wide): 25.3B **Privately Held**
SIC: 8011 Pathologist
HQ: Via Christi Clinic, P.A.
3311 E Murdock St
Wichita KS 67208
316 689-9111

(G-15881)
VIA CHRISTI CLINIC PA (DH)
Also Called: Wichita Clinic Pharmacy
3311 E Murdock St (67208-3054)
PHONE..................................316 689-9111
Noel Sanchez MD, *President*
John Shellipio, *Principal*
Mark L Wencel MD, *Vice Pres*
Ahmad Izard, *Med Doctor*
Bang Chau Nguyen, *Med Doctor*
EMP: 500
SQ FT: 130,000
SALES (est): 80.7MM
SALES (corp-wide): 25.3B **Privately Held**
SIC: 8011 Clinic, operated by physicians

(G-15882)
VIA CHRISTI CLINIC PA
14700 W Saint Teresa St (67235-9601)
PHONE..................................316 945-5400
Stan Noffsinger, *Branch Mgr*
John Dupuis, *Pediatrics*
EMP: 15
SALES (corp-wide): 25.3B **Privately Held**
SIC: 8011 Clinic, operated by physicians
HQ: Via Christi Clinic, P.A.
3311 E Murdock St
Wichita KS 67208
316 689-9111

(G-15883)
VIA CHRISTI CLINIC PA
Also Called: Wichita Clinic
9211 E 21st St N Ste 100 (67206-2968)
PHONE..................................316 609-4440
Cherri Murray, *Principal*
Denise Huskey, *Family Practiti*
Stanley Capper, *Dermatology*
Robert Harrington, *Post Master*
EMP: 37
SALES (corp-wide): 25.3B **Privately Held**
SIC: 8011 Primary care medical clinic
HQ: Via Christi Clinic, P.A.
3311 E Murdock St
Wichita KS 67208
316 689-9111

(G-15884)
VIA CHRISTI CLINIC PA
Also Called: W C Imaging Center
3311 E Murdock St (67208-3054)
P.O. Box 1300 (67201-1300)
PHONE..................................316 689-9111
Rick Conklin, *Branch Mgr*
EMP: 91
SALES (corp-wide): 25.3B **Privately Held**
SIC: 8011 Clinic, operated by physicians
HQ: Via Christi Clinic, P.A.
3311 E Murdock St
Wichita KS 67208
316 689-9111

(G-15885)
VIA CHRISTI CLINIC PA
3243 E Murdock St Ste 300 (67208-3006)
PHONE..................................316 689-9111
Dwight Wheeler, *Manager*
EMP: 35
SALES (corp-wide): 25.3B **Privately Held**
SIC: 8011 5912 Clinic, operated by physicians; drug stores & proprietary stores
HQ: Via Christi Clinic, P.A.
3311 E Murdock St
Wichita KS 67208
316 689-9111

(G-15886)
VIA CHRISTI CLINIC PA
Also Called: The Wichita Clinic
818 N Carriage Pkwy Ste 2 (67208-4511)
PHONE..................................316 651-2252
Paul Zuercher, *Branch Mgr*
EMP: 50
SALES (corp-wide): 25.3B **Privately Held**
SIC: 8011 Clinic, operated by physicians
HQ: Via Christi Clinic, P.A.
3311 E Murdock St
Wichita KS 67208
316 689-9111

(G-15887)
VIA CHRISTI FOUNDATION INC
Also Called: Children's Miracle Network
8200 E Thorn Dr Ste 200 (67226-2719)
PHONE..................................316 239-3520
James N Barber, *President*
Marian Girrens, *Vice Pres*
Joan Parnell, *Manager*
EMP: 10
SQ FT: 4,300
SALES: 4.4MM **Privately Held**
SIC: 7389 Fund raising organizations

(G-15888)
VIA CHRISTI HEALTH INC
Also Called: Samuel Heck
13610 W Maple St (67235-8776)
PHONE..................................316 773-4500
Sharon Reeves, *President*
Dan McCarty, *Family Practiti*
EMP: 53
SALES (corp-wide): 25.3B **Privately Held**
SIC: 8011 Primary care medical clinic
HQ: Via Christi Health, Inc.
2622 W Central Ave # 102
Wichita KS 67203

(G-15889)
VIA CHRISTI HEALTH INC
14800 W Saint Teresa St (67235-9602)
PHONE..................................316 268-7000
Kevin Strecker, *Branch Mgr*
EMP: 10
SALES (corp-wide): 25.3B **Privately Held**
SIC: 8062 General medical & surgical hospitals
HQ: Via Christi Health, Inc.
2622 W Central Ave # 102
Wichita KS 67203

(G-15890)
VIA CHRISTI HEALTH INC
Also Called: Georgetown Village Associates
1655 S Georgetown St Ofc (67218-4140)
PHONE..................................316 685-0400
Janell Moerer, *President*
Denise Cochran, *Office Mgr*
Maggie Rader, *Manager*
Bethany Leland, *Director*
Lana Wyckoff, *Director*
EMP: 80
SALES (corp-wide): 25.3B **Privately Held**
WEB: www.viachristi.org
SIC: 8011 8361 Medical centers; geriatric residential care
HQ: Via Christi Health, Inc.
2622 W Central Ave # 102
Wichita KS 67203

(G-15891)
VIA CHRISTI HEALTH INC (HQ)
2622 W Central Ave # 102 (67203-4970)
PHONE..................................316 858-4900
David Hadley, *Principal*
Marianne Moore, *Human Res Dir*
Judy Hollinger, *Manager*
EMP: 50
SALES (est): 706.7MM
SALES (corp-wide): 25.3B **Privately Held**
WEB: www.viachristi.org
SIC: 8011 8741 Medical centers; hospital management
PA: Ascension Health Alliance
101 S Hanley Rd Ste 450
Saint Louis MO 63105
314 733-8000

(G-15892)
VIA CHRISTI HLTH PARTNERS INC (DH)
8200 E Thorn Dr Ste 300 (67226-2711)
PHONE..................................316 719-3240
Allan Allford, *President*
Renee Hanrahan, *Director*
Kris Langrehr, *Director*
Colleen Pate, *Director*
Robert Heath, *Admin Sec*
EMP: 10
SQ FT: 3,200
SALES: 19.5MM
SALES (corp-wide): 25.3B **Privately Held**
SIC: 8011 Medical centers

(G-15893)
VIA CHRISTI HOPE INC
2622 W Central Ave # 101 (67203-4969)
PHONE..................................316 858-1111
Mark Bailey, *President*
EMP: 50
SALES: 15MM **Privately Held**
SIC: 8322 Old age assistance

(G-15894)
VIA CHRISTI HOSPITAL
14800 W Saint Teresa St (67235-9602)
PHONE..................................316 796-7000
Jim Barber, *President*
Carl Rider, *Senior VP*
Kevin Chiles, *Vice Pres*
Mike Wegner, *CFO*
EMP: 55
SALES: 36.3MM **Privately Held**
SIC: 8062 General medical & surgical hospitals

(G-15895)
VIA CHRISTI MEDICAL MANAGEMENT
1100 N St Francis St # 200 (67214-2878)
PHONE..................................316 268-8123
Leroy Rheault, *President*
John McGreavy, *COO*
Chuck Radabaugh, *Manager*
Samuel Henderson, *Admin Sec*
EMP: 15
SALES (est): 843.7K **Privately Held**
SIC: 8011 Clinic, operated by physicians

(G-15896)
VIA CHRISTI REHABILITATION CTR
1151 N Rock Rd (67206-1262)
PHONE..................................316 634-3400
Laurie Labarca, *COO*
Becky Johnson, *Nursing Dir*
Carla Yost, *Ch Nursing Ofcr*
▲ **EMP:** 200
SALES (est): 24.3MM
SALES (corp-wide): 25.3B **Privately Held**
WEB: www.viachristi.org
SIC: 8069 Specialty hospitals, except psychiatric
HQ: Via Christi Health, Inc.
2622 W Central Ave # 102
Wichita KS 67203

(G-15897)
VIA CHRISTI RESEARCH
1035 N Emporia St Ste 230 (67214-2972)
PHONE..................................316 291-4774
Peggy Gardner, *President*
Ragnar Peterson, *Med Doctor*
Richa Sharma, *Med Doctor*
Michael Good, *Director*
Joe Carrithers, *Director*
EMP: 20
SALES (est): 1.4MM
SALES (corp-wide): 25.3B **Privately Held**
WEB: www.preskorn.com
SIC: 8733 Research institute
HQ: Ascension Via Christi Hospitals Wichita, Inc.
929 N St Francis St
Wichita KS 67214
316 268-5880

(G-15898)
VIA CHRISTI VILLAGES INC (DH)
2622 W Central Ave # 100 (67203-4969)
PHONE..................................316 946-5200
Jerry Cardley, *President*
Kevin Conlin, *Vice Pres*

Robert Harvey, *Vice Pres*
Lynette Rauvolabouta, *Vice Pres*
Arlan Yoder, *Vice Pres*
EMP: 29
SQ FT: 127,656
SALES: 9.8MM
SALES (corp-wide): 25.3B **Privately Held**
SIC: 8322 Senior citizens' center or association

(G-15899)
VIA CHRISTY ST FRANCIS
929 N St Francis St (67214-3821)
PHONE..................................316 613-6511
Hemanth K Reddy, *Med Doctor*
Jim Garrelts, *Exec Dir*
EMP: 43 **EST:** 2012
SALES (est): 3.7MM **Privately Held**
SIC: 8062 Hospital, affiliated with AMA residency

(G-15900)
VIA CHRSTI HM HLTH WICHITA INC
1035 N Emporia St Ste 230 (67214-2972)
PHONE..................................316 268-8588
Joy Scott, *Director*
EMP: 70
SQ FT: 16,000
SALES: 5.7MM **Privately Held**
SIC: 8082 8049 8322 Visiting nurse service; nurses, registered & practical; individual & family services

(G-15901)
VIA CHRSTI REHABILITATION HOSP (DH)
8200 E Thorn Dr (67226-2709)
PHONE..................................316 268-5000
Margo McDonald, *COO*
Kathi Beeton, *Vice Pres*
Diana M Kidd, *Vice Pres*
Darren Orme, *Vice Pres*
Shelly Trent, *Controller*
EMP: 21
SALES (est): 18.3MM
SALES (corp-wide): 25.3B **Privately Held**
SIC: 8093 Rehabilitation center, outpatient treatment

(G-15902)
VIA CHRSTI RHBLTATION HOSP INC
Also Called: Via Christi Hospital
929 N St Francis St (67214-3821)
PHONE..................................316 268-8040
Bassem El Nabbout, *Neurology*
EMP: 19
SALES (corp-wide): 25.3B **Privately Held**
SIC: 8062 General medical & surgical hospitals
HQ: Via Chrsti Rehabilitation Hosp Inc
8200 E Thorn Dr
Wichita KS 67226
316 268-5000

(G-15903)
VIA CHRSTI RHBLTATION HOSP INC
750 N Socora St Ste 100 (67212-3794)
PHONE..................................316 946-1790
EMP: 6
SALES (corp-wide): 25.3B **Privately Held**
SIC: 2834 8011 Medicines, capsuled or ampuled; offices & clinics of medical doctors
HQ: Via Chrsti Rehabilitation Hosp Inc
8200 E Thorn Dr
Wichita KS 67226
316 268-5000

(G-15904)
VIA CHRSTI RVRSIDE MED CTR INC
3600 E Harry St (67218-3713)
PHONE..................................316 689-5335
Jeff Korsmo, *CEO*
EMP: 250
SALES (est): 1.8MM
SALES (corp-wide): 25.3B **Privately Held**
SIC: 8011 Medical centers
HQ: Via Christi Health, Inc.
2622 W Central Ave # 102
Wichita KS 67203

(G-15905)
VIAVI SOLUTIONS LLC (HQ)
Also Called: Viavi Solutions Avcomm
10200 W York St (67215-8935)
PHONE..................................316 522-4981
Oleg Khaykin, *President*
EMP: 350
SQ FT: 156,000
SALES (est): 85.9MM
SALES (corp-wide): 1.1B **Publicly Held**
SIC: 3825 Instruments to measure electricity
PA: Viavi Solutions Inc.
6001 America Center Dr # 6
San Jose CA 95002
408 404-3600

(G-15906)
VICTOR L PHILLIPS COMPANY
3250 N Hydraulic St (67219-3892)
PHONE..................................316 854-1118
Kim Carnegy, *Branch Mgr*
EMP: 13
SALES (est): 1.6MM
SALES (corp-wide): 56MM **Privately Held**
WEB: www.vlpco.com
SIC: 5082 5211 General construction machinery & equipment; lumber & other building materials
HQ: The Victor L Phillips Company
4100 Gardner Ave
Kansas City MO 64120
816 241-9290

(G-15907)
VIGILIAS LLC
Also Called: Vigiias Telehealth
4704 E Oakland (67218-1180)
PHONE..................................800 924-8140
Elisha Yaghmai, *President*
Zana Patrick Desgranges, *Vice Pres*
EMP: 36
SALES (est): 165.8K **Privately Held**
SIC: 8742 8011 8093 7371 Hospital & health services consultant; internal medicine practitioners; pediatrician; mental health clinic, outpatient; computer software development; electromedical equipment

(G-15908)
VISION COMMUNICATIONS KS INC
1235 S Mead St (67211-3321)
PHONE..................................316 634-6747
Jared Kelly, *President*
Bobbie Dixon, *CFO*
EMP: 10
SALES: 950K **Privately Held**
SIC: 1731 Fiber optic cable installation

(G-15909)
VITRE-RETINAL CONS SURGEONS PA
530 N Lorraine Ave # 100 (67214-4837)
PHONE..................................316 683-5611
Michael P Varenhorst, *President*
Liz Berg, *Principal*
John Borrego, *Opers Staff*
Paul Weishaar, *Treasurer*
Kumar Dalla, *Med Doctor*
EMP: 30
SQ FT: 22,000
SALES: 6.8MM **Privately Held**
SIC: 8011 Physicians' office, including specialists; surgeon

(G-15910)
VIZWORX INC (HQ)
2420 N Woodlawn Blvd # 500 (67220-3970)
PHONE..................................316 691-4589
Toll Free:..................................866 -
Eric Shelly, *President*
EMP: 20
SQ FT: 20,000
SALES (est): 1MM
SALES (corp-wide): 57.9MM **Privately Held**
SIC: 7384 Photofinishing laboratory
PA: Cgf Investments, Inc.
2420 N Woodlawn Blvd # 500
Wichita KS 67220
316 691-4500

(G-15911)
VOICE PRODUCTS INC
8555 E 32nd St N (67226-2611)
PHONE..................................316 616-1111
Dean Tullis, *President*
Stuart Peters, *Vice Pres*
Donna Dill, *Info Tech Mgr*
David Essary, *Info Tech Mgr*
EMP: 38
SQ FT: 7,000
SALES: 10.1MM **Privately Held**
WEB: www.voiceproductsinc.com
SIC: 5045 Computer software

(G-15912)
W B CARTER CONSTRUCTION CO
2550 S Hoover Rd (67215-1204)
PHONE..................................316 942-4214
EMP: 48
SALES (corp-wide): 6.1MM **Privately Held**
SIC: 1623 Water/Sewer/Utility Construction
PA: W B Carter Construction Co Inc
6015 N Broadway Ave
Park City KS
316 744-1247

(G-15913)
W W MAILS INC
7106 W Pueblo Dr (67209-2900)
P.O. Box 12344 (67277-2344)
PHONE..................................316 943-0703
Henry Winsor, *President*
EMP: 40
SALES (est): 4.8MM **Privately Held**
SIC: 4213 Trucking, except local

(G-15914)
WADDELL & REED INC
Waddell & Reed Office 1613-00
1861 N Rock Rd Ste 100 (67206-1264)
PHONE..................................316 942-9010
Ron Avey, *Admin Mgr*
Timothy Siefer, *Advisor*
EMP: 20 **Publicly Held**
SIC: 6282 Investment counselors
HQ: Waddell & Reed, Inc.
6300 Lamar Ave
Shawnee Mission KS 66202
913 236-2000

(G-15915)
WAGLE PAINTING
342 N Bluff Ave (67208-3727)
PHONE..................................316 682-2531
Sam Wagle, *Owner*
Steve Wagle, *Owner*
EMP: 15
SALES (est): 428.6K **Privately Held**
SIC: 1721 Residential painting

(G-15916)
WALDINGER CORPORATION
Also Called: Honeywell Authorized Dealer
1630 S Baehr St (67209-2702)
PHONE..................................316 942-7722
Larry Dunn, *Branch Mgr*
EMP: 20
SALES (corp-wide): 207.1MM **Privately Held**
WEB: www.comfortsystems.net
SIC: 1711 Warm air heating & air conditioning contractor
PA: The Waldinger Corporation
2601 Bell Ave
Des Moines IA 50321
515 284-1911

(G-15917)
WALGREEN CO
Also Called: Walgreens
1625 S Webb Rd (67207-5601)
PHONE..................................316 652-9147
Johnny Daughterty, *Branch Mgr*
EMP: 30
SALES (corp-wide): 136.8B **Publicly Held**
WEB: www.walgreens.com
SIC: 5912 7384 Drug stores; photofinishing laboratory
HQ: Walgreen Co.
200 Wilmot Rd
Deerfield IL 60015
800 925-4733

(G-15918)
WALGREEN CO
Also Called: Walgreens
5505 E Harry St (67218-3825)
PHONE..................................316 689-0866
Huston Rich, *Manager*
EMP: 30
SALES (corp-wide): 136.8B **Publicly Held**
WEB: www.walgreens.com
SIC: 5912 7384 Drug stores; photofinishing laboratory
HQ: Walgreen Co.
200 Wilmot Rd
Deerfield IL 60015
800 925-4733

(G-15919)
WALGREEN CO
Also Called: Walgreens
555 N Maize Rd (67212-4655)
PHONE..................................316 729-6171
Erin Hirsch, *Manager*
EMP: 30
SALES (corp-wide): 136.8B **Publicly Held**
WEB: www.walgreens.com
SIC: 5912 7384 Drug stores; photofinishing laboratory
HQ: Walgreen Co.
200 Wilmot Rd
Deerfield IL 60015
800 925-4733

(G-15920)
WALGREEN CO
Also Called: Walgreens
710 N West St (67203-1213)
PHONE..................................316 943-2299
Zach Kowalski, *Manager*
EMP: 30
SALES (corp-wide): 136.8B **Publicly Held**
WEB: www.walgreens.com
SIC: 5912 7384 Drug stores; photofinishing laboratory
HQ: Walgreen Co.
200 Wilmot Rd
Deerfield IL 60015
800 925-4733

(G-15921)
WALGREEN CO
Also Called: Walgreens
1330 N Woodlawn St (67208-2647)
PHONE..................................316 684-2828
Don Schmidt, *Manager*
EMP: 25
SALES (corp-wide): 136.8B **Publicly Held**
WEB: www.walgreens.com
SIC: 5912 7384 Drug stores; photofinishing laboratory
HQ: Walgreen Co.
200 Wilmot Rd
Deerfield IL 60015
800 925-4733

(G-15922)
WALLACE SAUNDERS CHARTERED
200 W Douglas Ave Ste 400 (67202-3004)
PHONE..................................316 269-2100
Tim Finnerty, *Branch Mgr*
Donna Miller, *Branch Mgr*
Marsh D Steven,
Michael D Streit,
EMP: 16
SALES (corp-wide): 17.4MM **Privately Held**
SIC: 8111 General practice attorney, lawyer
PA: Wallace Saunders, Chartered
10111 W 87th St
Overland Park KS 66212
913 888-1000

(G-15923)
WALMART INC
6110 W Kellogg Dr Stop 1 (67209-2350)
PHONE..................................316 945-2800
Ken Thomas, *Manager*
Sandy Beyer, *Manager*
EMP: 145
SQ FT: 210,499

GEOGRAPHIC

SALES (corp-wide): 514.4B **Publicly Held**
WEB: www.walmartstores.com
SIC: 5311 4812 5411 Department stores, discount; radio telephone communication; supermarkets, hypermarket
PA: Walmart Inc.
702 Sw 8th St
Bentonville AR 72716
479 273-4000

(G-15924)
WALMART INC
3030 N Rock Rd (67226-1340)
PHONE..................................316 636-5384
Cory Baker, *Branch Mgr*
EMP: 300
SQ FT: 201,091
SALES (corp-wide): 514.4B **Publicly Held**
WEB: www.walmartstores.com
SIC: 5311 5411 5722 5531 Department stores, discount; supermarkets, hypermarket; household appliance stores; automotive & home supply stores; radio telephone communication; bread, cake & related products
PA: Walmart Inc.
702 Sw 8th St
Bentonville AR 72716
479 273-4000

(G-15925)
WALTONS INC (PA)
3639 N Comotara St (67226-1304)
PHONE..................................316 262-0651
Brett Walton, *President*
EMP: 11
SALES (est): 5.1MM **Privately Held**
SIC: 5147 5719 Meats & meat products; barbeque grills

(G-15926)
WARREN OLD TOWN THEATRE GRILL
353 N Mead St (67202-2721)
P.O. Box 782560 (67278-2560)
PHONE..................................316 262-7123
Les Padzensky, *Vice Pres*
Bill Warren,
EMP: 11
SALES (est): 602.1K **Privately Held**
SIC: 7832 Motion picture theaters, except drive-in

(G-15927)
WARREN THEATRES LLC
11611 E 13th St N (67206-3702)
P.O. Box 782560 (67278-2560)
PHONE..................................316 612-0469
Tom Hutton, *Director*
William Warren,
EMP: 60
SALES (est): 3.6MM **Privately Held**
SIC: 7832 Exhibitors, itinerant: motion picture

(G-15928)
WARREN THEATRES LLC
Also Called: 21st Street Warren Imax
9150 W 21st St N (67205-1806)
P.O. Box 782560 (67278-2560)
PHONE..................................316 722-7060
Bill Warren, *President*
EMP: 60
SALES (est): 2.3MM **Privately Held**
SIC: 7832 5812 Exhibitors, itinerant: motion picture; eating places
HQ: Regal Cinemas, Inc.
101 E Blount Ave Ste 100
Knoxville TN 37920
865 922-1123

(G-15929)
WARREN TRAVEL INC
Also Called: Cruise Corner
6903 E Aberdeen St (67206-1169)
PHONE..................................316 685-1118
EMP: 10
SQ FT: 1,500
SALES (est): 1.6MM **Privately Held**
SIC: 4724 Travel Service

(G-15930)
WASHER SPECIALTIES COMPANY
Also Called: Johnson Contrls Authorized Dlr
224 N Indiana Ave (67214-4096)
P.O. Box 3268 (67201-3268)
PHONE..................................316 263-8179
Clarence Lieber, *CEO*
Alan Lieber, *President*
Juanita J Lieber, *Corp Secy*
Dan Williams, *Site Mgr*
Rodney Sporleder, *Sales Staff*
▲ **EMP:** 48 **EST:** 1960
SQ FT: 30,000
SALES (est): 33.1MM **Privately Held**
WEB: www.washer.net
SIC: 5075 5064 Warm air heating & air conditioning; electric household appliances

(G-15931)
WASHINGTON PRIME GROUP INC
Also Called: Towne West Square
4600 W Kellogg Dr Ofc (67209-2546)
PHONE..................................316 945-9374
Shane McWhorter, *General Mgr*
EMP: 21
SALES (corp-wide): 723.3MM **Publicly Held**
WEB: www.shopsimon.com
SIC: 6512 Shopping center, property operation only
PA: Washington Prime Group Inc.
180 E Broad St Fl 21
Columbus OH 43215
614 621-9000

(G-15932)
WASI INC
4425 W May St Bldg B (67209-2873)
PHONE..................................620 782-3337
Chris Lette, *President*
EMP: 42
SALES (est): 6.4MM **Privately Held**
SIC: 3728 Aircraft body assemblies & parts

(G-15933)
WASTE CONNECTIONS INC
4300 W 37th St N (67205-9308)
PHONE..................................316 941-4320
Melissa Martin, *Payroll Mgr*
Edward Ford, *Manager*
Joseph Ross, *Director*
EMP: 37
SALES (corp-wide): 4.6B **Privately Held**
SIC: 4953 Refuse systems
HQ: Waste Connections Us, Inc.
3 Waterway Square Pl # 110
The Woodlands TX 77380

(G-15934)
WASTE CONNECTIONS KANSAS INC (DH)
Also Called: Northon Disposal Callecia
2745 N Ohio St (67219-4399)
PHONE..................................316 838-4920
Ron Mittelstaedt, *President*
Jim Spencer, *Vice Pres*
Mark Gelvin, *Marketing Staff*
EMP: 37
SALES (est): 59.3MM
SALES (corp-wide): 4.6B **Privately Held**
SIC: 4953 Refuse collection & disposal services

(G-15935)
WATCO COMPANIES LLC
Also Called: Kansas & Oklahoma Railroad
1825 W Harry St (67213-3243)
PHONE..................................316 263-3113
Bill Frederick, *Branch Mgr*
EMP: 56
SALES (corp-wide): 997.9MM **Privately Held**
WEB: www.watcocompanies.com
SIC: 4011 Railroads, line-haul operating
PA: Watco Companies, L.L.C.
315 W 3rd St
Pittsburg KS 66762
575 745-2329

(G-15936)
WATERFRONT ASSISTED LIVING
900 N Bayshore Dr Ofc (67212-4807)
PHONE..................................316 945-3344
Gene Miles, *President*
Sue Curtis, *Administration*
EMP: 16
SALES (est): 621.5K **Privately Held**
SIC: 7011 8051 Inns; skilled nursing care facilities

(G-15937)
WATERWALK WICHITA LLC
Also Called: Waterwalk Apartments
411 W Maple St (67213-4605)
PHONE..................................316 201-1899
Sherrill Carper, *Marketing Staff*
Kevin Dombrow, *Director*
David Redfern,
EMP: 20
SALES (est): 1.1MM **Privately Held**
SIC: 6513 Apartment hotel operation

(G-15938)
WAXENE PRODUCTS COMPANY INC
Also Called: Enexaw
2023 N Broadway Ave (67214-1177)
PHONE..................................316 263-8523
Joretta Norris, *President*
Gary Norris, *Vice Pres*
EMP: 5
SQ FT: 2,000
SALES (est): 1MM **Privately Held**
SIC: 7218 2842 5087 5199 Wiping towel supply; sweeping compounds, oil or water absorbent, clay or sawdust; janitors' supplies; packaging materials

(G-15939)
WDM ARCHITECTS PA
105 N Washington Ave (67202-2815)
PHONE..................................316 262-4700
Matt Schindler, *President*
Dan Wilson, *Partner*
Stanley Landwehr, *Principal*
Scott Ramser, *Principal*
Robert Mock, *Director*
EMP: 29
SALES (est): 3.1MM **Privately Held**
WEB: www.wdmdesign.com
SIC: 8712 0781 Architectural engineering; landscape architects

(G-15940)
WE R KIDS LLC
10221 W 13th St N (67212-4381)
PHONE..................................316 729-0172
Mark Newsom, *Owner*
EMP: 11
SALES (est): 426.4K **Privately Held**
SIC: 8351 Preschool center

(G-15941)
WEIGAND-OMEGA ASSOCIATES INC (PA)
333 S Broadway Ave # 105 (67202-4325)
PHONE..................................316 925-6341
Robert G Hanson, *President*
Bonnie Hanson, *Corp Secy*
Craig Hanson, *Vice Pres*
Nestor R Weigand, *Vice Pres*
Yolanda Porter, *Asst Mgr*
EMP: 18
SQ FT: 7,200
SALES (est): 19.7MM **Privately Held**
WEB: www.weigandomega.com
SIC: 6512 Commercial & industrial building operation

(G-15942)
WEIGAND-OMEGA MANAGEMENT INC (PA)
333 S Broadway Ave # 105 (67202-4325)
PHONE..................................316 925-6341
Robert Hanson, *CEO*
Craig Hanson, *President*
Raymond Moore, *Opers Staff*
Christopher Hanson, *Shareholder*
Nestor Weigand, *Shareholder*
EMP: 35
SALES (est): 1.7MM **Privately Held**
SIC: 6531 Rental agent, real estate

(G-15943)
WELCO TECHNOLOGIES
Also Called: Western Sky Industries
2600 S Custer Ave (67217-1324)
PHONE..................................316 941-0400
William Eichenberger, *Vice Pres*
Michael Sheeran, *Manager*
EMP: 5
SALES (est): 930.6K **Privately Held**
SIC: 3621 5063 Motors & generators; electrical supplies

(G-15944)
WELLS FARGO BANK NATIONAL ASSN
6321 E Central Ave (67208-4278)
PHONE..................................316 685-5495
EMP: 15
SALES (corp-wide): 101B **Publicly Held**
SIC: 6021 National commercial banks
HQ: Wells Fargo Bank, National Association
101 N Phillips Ave
Sioux Falls SD 57104
605 575-6900

(G-15945)
WELLS FARGO BANK NATIONAL ASSN
455 S West St (67213-2107)
PHONE..................................316 943-3159
Penny Selves, *Branch Mgr*
EMP: 16
SALES (corp-wide): 101B **Publicly Held**
SIC: 6021 National commercial banks
HQ: Wells Fargo Bank, National Association
101 N Phillips Ave
Sioux Falls SD 57104
605 575-6900

(G-15946)
WELLS FARGO CLEARING SVCS LLC
Also Called: Wells Fargo Advisors
300 S Main St (67202-3718)
P.O. Box 47430 (67201-7430)
PHONE..................................316 267-0300
Wayne Wentling, *Vice Pres*
Roger Buller, *Manager*
Kent Giffin, *Agent*
James Hukle, *Advisor*
Scott Sennett, *Advisor*
EMP: 50
SALES (corp-wide): 101B **Publicly Held**
SIC: 6211 Investment firm, general brokerage
HQ: Wells Fargo Clearing Services, Llc
1 N Jefferson Ave Fl 7
Saint Louis MO 63103
314 955-3000

(G-15947)
WELLS FARGO CLEARING SVCS LLC
Also Called: Wells Fargo Advisors
8301 E 21st St N Ste 320 (67206-2935)
PHONE..................................316 634-6690
Mark Douglass, *Branch Mgr*
Ken Schmiedbauer, *Agent*
Lisa Schmiedbauer, *Agent*
EMP: 20
SALES (corp-wide): 101B **Publicly Held**
WEB: www.wachoviasec.com
SIC: 6211 Security brokers & dealers
HQ: Wells Fargo Clearing Services, Llc
1 N Jefferson Ave Fl 7
Saint Louis MO 63103
314 955-3000

(G-15948)
WELLS FARGO HOME MORTGAGE INC
10616 W Maple St Ste 100 (67209-4008)
PHONE..................................405 475-2880
Peggy Thorne, *Branch Mgr*
EMP: 20
SALES (corp-wide): 101B **Publicly Held**
WEB: www.wfhm.com
SIC: 6162 Mortgage bankers
HQ: Wells Fargo Home Mortgage Inc
1 Home Campus
Des Moines IA 50328
515 324-3707

(G-15949)
WESCO AIRCRAFT HARDWARE CORP
Electronic Products Group
3851 N Webb Rd (67226-8137)
P.O. Box 780048 (67278-0048)
PHONE..................................316 315-1200
Heather McLeod, *Production*
Sue Ulbrich, *Accounts Mgr*
Christina Kukuruda, *Branch Mgr*
Curtis Aikens, *IT/INT Sup*
Tonya Quattlebaum, *Administration*
EMP: 140 **Privately Held**
SIC: 5072 5065 Hardware; electronic parts
HQ: Wesco Aircraft Hardware Corp.
24911 Avenue Stanford
Valencia CA 91355
661 775-7200

(G-15950)
WESCON CONTROLS LLC
2533 S West St (67217-1025)
PHONE..................................316 942-7266
Michael Bright, *President*
Jennifer Wulf, *Controller*
Mike Kennedy, *Manager*
▲ **EMP:** 180
SALES: 35.1MM **Privately Held**
SIC: 3451 3625 Screw machine products; relays & industrial controls
PA: Suprajit Engineering Limited
No.100, Bommasandra Industrial Area
Bengaluru KA 56009

(G-15951)
WESCON PLASTICS LLC
2810 S West St (67217-1030)
PHONE..................................855 731-6055
Jan Acker, *President*
Mathew Mount, *CFO*
Susan Bayles, *Controller*
Michael Milledge,
EMP: 125
SQ FT: 78,000
SALES (est): 44.8MM
SALES (corp-wide): 1.8MM **Privately Held**
SIC: 3089 Injection molding of plastics
HQ: Shell Topco Lp
2533 S West St
Wichita KS 67217
316 942-7266

(G-15952)
WESLEY MEDICAL CENTER LLC (HQ)
550 N Hillside St (67214-4976)
PHONE..................................316 962-2000
Hugh Tappan, *CEO*
Carl Fitch, *Principal*
Bill Voloch, *COO*
Charles McGuire, *Ch Radiology*
James Carney, *Safety Dir*
EMP: 40
SALES: 631.3MM **Publicly Held**
SIC: 8011 Primary care medical clinic

(G-15953)
WESLEY MEDICAL CENTER LLC
2610 N Woodlawn Blvd (67220-2729)
PHONE..................................316 858-2610
EMP: 35 **Publicly Held**
WEB: www.ghhospital.com
SIC: 8062 General medical & surgical hospitals
HQ: Wesley Medical Center, Llc
550 N Hillside St
Wichita KS 67214
316 962-2000

(G-15954)
WESLEY REHABILITATION HOSPITAL
Also Called: ENCOMPASS HEALTH
8338 W 13th St N (67212-2900)
PHONE..................................316 729-9999
Betty Shuman, *Human Res Mgr*
Nancy Danler, *Manager*
Ladessa Forrest, *Director*
Pam Stanberry, *Administration*
EMP: 125
SALES: 18.8MM
SALES (corp-wide): 4.2B **Publicly Held**
WEB: www.healthsouth.com
SIC: 8069 Specialty hospitals, except psychiatric
PA: Encompass Health Corporation
9001 Liberty Pkwy
Birmingham AL 35242
205 967-7116

(G-15955)
WESLEY RETIREMENT COMMUNITY
Also Called: LARKSFIELD PLACE
7373 E 29th St N Apt W118 (67226-3419)
PHONE..................................316 636-1000
Reginald Hislop, *President*
Frank Rajewski, *COO*
EMP: 200
SQ FT: 265,000
SALES: 18.7MM **Privately Held**
WEB: www.larksfieldplace.org
SIC: 6513 8051 Residential hotel operation; skilled nursing care facilities

(G-15956)
WEST SIDE GOOD NEIGHBOR CENTER
3500 W 13th St N (67203)
PHONE..................................316 942-7349
Ron Trache, *Pastor*
EMP: 15 **EST:** 1999
SALES (est): 287.8K **Privately Held**
SIC: 8322 Individual & family services

(G-15957)
WEST WCHITA ASSSTED LIVING LLC
629 S Maize Ct (67209-1325)
PHONE..................................316 361-2500
Mark Schulte, *Exec Dir*
Matt Little,
EMP: 14
SALES (est): 722.4K **Privately Held**
SIC: 8361 Residential care

(G-15958)
WEST WICHITA FMLY OPTOMETRIST (PA)
1202 W Maple St (67213-3916)
PHONE..................................316 262-3716
Jim Herndon, *President*
Charles W Kissling, *Vice Pres*
Monica Allan, *Technician*
EMP: 15
SALES (est): 1.4MM **Privately Held**
SIC: 8042 Group & corporate practice optometrists

(G-15959)
WEST WICHITA PET CLINIC
8615 W 21st St N (67205-1755)
PHONE..................................316 722-0100
Gregg Reichenberger, *Owner*
EMP: 10
SALES (est): 514.2K **Privately Held**
SIC: 0742 3999 0752 Animal hospital services, pets & other animal specialties; pet supplies; grooming services, pet & animal specialties

(G-15960)
WESTAR ENERGY INC
1900 E Central Ave (67214-4305)
P.O. Box 208 (67201-0208)
PHONE..................................316 261-6575
EMP: 15
SALES (corp-wide): 2.5B **Publicly Held**
SIC: 4911 Electric Services
HQ: Westar Energy, Inc.
818 S Kansas Ave
Topeka KS 66612
785 575-6300

(G-15961)
WESTERN PROFESSIONAL ASSOC
Also Called: Metland Group, The
727 N Waco Ave Ste 280 (67203-3988)
PHONE..................................316 264-5628
Jason Van Gotten, *Manager*
EMP: 14 **Privately Held**
WEB: www.midlanddisability.com
SIC: 8111 Legal services
PA: Western Professional Associates Inc
1310 Wakarusa Dr Ste A
Lawrence KS 66049

(G-15962)
WESTLEY WOODLAWN HOSP EMRGNCY
Also Called: Galicia Heart Hospital
2610 N Woodlawn Blvd (67220-2729)
PHONE..................................316 962-2000
Steve Edgar, *CEO*
Bill Wild, *COO*
Troy Biggs, *Vice Pres*
Greg Gawlik, *CFO*
Robyn Merriam, *Lab Dir*
EMP: 40
SQ FT: 6,100
SALES (est): 11.2MM **Publicly Held**
WEB: www.ghhospital.com
SIC: 8062 General medical & surgical hospitals
HQ: Wesley Medical Center, Llc
550 N Hillside St
Wichita KS 67214
316 962-2000

(G-15963)
WHEATLAND MEDICAL CLINIC PA
5735 W Macarthur Rd (67215-8404)
P.O. Box 3378 (67201-3378)
PHONE..................................316 524-9400
Diana Kettermen, *President*
Diana Ketterman, *President*
Mueeza Zasar, *Vice Pres*
EMP: 10
SALES (est): 1.1MM **Privately Held**
SIC: 8011 General & family practice, physician/surgeon

(G-15964)
WHITE & ELLIS DRILLING INC (PA)
10500 E Berkeley Sq Pk210 (67206-6816)
PHONE..................................316 263-1102
Thomas D White, *President*
Greg Henning, *Treasurer*
EMP: 6
SQ FT: 5,500
SALES (est): 1.3MM **Privately Held**
SIC: 1382 Aerial geophysical exploration oil & gas

(G-15965)
WHITE CHAPEL MEMORIAL CORP
1806 N Oliver Ave (67208-2501)
PHONE..................................316 684-1612
George Mc Manness, *Vice Pres*
Beth Glasier, *Administration*
Gail Weep, *Administration*
EMP: 35
SALES (est): 1.1MM
SALES (corp-wide): 3.1B **Publicly Held**
WEB: www.sci-corp.com
SIC: 6553 Cemetery subdividers & developers
PA: Service Corporation International
1929 Allen Pkwy
Houston TX 77019
713 522-5141

(G-15966)
WHOLESALE BEAUTY CLUB INC (PA)
7732 E Central Ave # 102 (67206-2163)
PHONE..................................316 687-9890
Thomas Bowles, *President*
EMP: 15
SALES (est): 3.8MM **Privately Held**
SIC: 5999 5087 Toiletries, cosmetics & perfumes; beauty parlor equipment & supplies

(G-15967)
WHOLESALE BEAUTY CLUB INC
Also Called: Club Beauty
4800 W Maple St Ste 106 (67209-2565)
PHONE..................................316 941-9500
Tina Grant, *Manager*
EMP: 12
SALES (corp-wide): 3.8MM **Privately Held**
SIC: 5087 Beauty parlor equipment & supplies
PA: Wholesale Beauty Club Inc
7732 E Central Ave # 102
Wichita KS 67206
316 687-9890

(G-15968)
WICHITA AIR SERVICES INC (PA)
3324 N Jabara Rd (67226-8901)
PHONE..................................316 631-1332
Jack P De Boer, *President*
Kevin Janson, *Controller*
EMP: 10
SQ FT: 12,000
SALES (est): 1.6MM **Privately Held**
SIC: 4581 Aircraft maintenance & repair services

(G-15969)
WICHITA AIRPORT AUTHORITY (PA)
2173 S Air Cargo Rd (67209-1958)
PHONE..................................316 946-4700
Victor White, *Director*
Tom Nolan, *Deputy Dir*
EMP: 18
SQ FT: 196,000
SALES: 15.7MM **Privately Held**
SIC: 4581 Airport

(G-15970)
WICHITA AIRPORT AUTHORITY
Also Called: Colonel James Jabara Airport
3512 N Webb Rd (67226-8128)
PHONE..................................316 636-9700
Bob Karslake, *President*
EMP: 40
SALES (corp-wide): 15.7MM **Privately Held**
SIC: 4581 Airport
PA: The Wichita Airport Authority
2173 S Air Cargo Rd
Wichita KS 67209
316 946-4700

(G-15971)
WICHITA AIRPORT HT ASSOC L P
Also Called: Wichita Airport Hilton
2098 S Airport Rd (67209-1941)
P.O. Box 12690 (67277-2690)
PHONE..................................316 945-5272
Michael J Phipps, *Manager*
EMP: 200
SALES (corp-wide): 5.4MM **Privately Held**
SIC: 7011 7299 5813 5812 Hotels & motels; banquet hall facilities; drinking places; eating places
PA: Wichita Airport Hotel Associates L P
7300 W 110th St Ste 990
Shawnee Mission KS 66210
913 451-1300

(G-15972)
WICHITA ALOFT
3642 N Oliver St (67220-3403)
PHONE..................................316 744-1100
Steve Butcher, *CEO*
EMP: 12
SALES (est): 626.6K **Privately Held**
SIC: 7011 Hotels

(G-15973)
WICHITA ANSTHSIOLOGY CHARTERED
8080 E Central Ave # 250 (67206-2367)
PHONE..................................316 686-1564
John Jensan, *President*
Mary Lou Tate, *Manager*
Michael Cooper, *Anesthesiology*
Dean Flaten, *Anesthesiology*
Jason R Williams, *Anesthesiology*
EMP: 100
SQ FT: 3,000
SALES (est): 12.6MM **Privately Held**
WEB: www.wacanes.com
SIC: 8011 Anesthesiologist

(G-15974)
WICHITA AREA ASSN OF REALTORS
Also Called: MULTIPLE LISTING SERVICE
170 W Dewey St (67202-5500)
PHONE..................................316 263-3167
Laura Raudonis, *CEO*

GEOGRAPHIC

Tricia Hayes, *Accountant*
Alyssa Peppiatt, *Corp Comm Staff*
Doug Rhoten, *Info Tech Mgr*
Dennis Clary, *Director*
EMP: 11
SQ FT: 5,000
SALES: 623.7K **Privately Held**
WEB: www.wichitarealtors.com
SIC: 8621 Professional membership organizations

(G-15975)
WICHITA AREA CHAMBER COMMERCE
350 W Douglas Ave (67202-2910)
PHONE..................................316 265-7771
Bryan Derreberry, *CEO*
Gerald H Holman, *Senior VP*
Patricia Gallagher, *Manager*
EMP: 30 **EST:** 1917
SQ FT: 21,600
SALES: 4.7MM **Privately Held**
WEB: www.wacc.org
SIC: 8611 Chamber of Commerce; community affairs & services

(G-15976)
WICHITA AREA SXUAL ASSAULT CTR
355 N Waco St Ste 100 (67202-1122)
PHONE..................................316 263-0185
K Williams, *Exec Dir*
Kathy Williams, *Director*
EMP: 31
SQ FT: 288
SALES: 1.3MM **Privately Held**
WEB: www.wichitasac.com
SIC: 8322 Crisis center

(G-15977)
WICHITA ARPRT HOSPITALITY LLC
Also Called: Holiday Inn
1236 S Dugan Rd (67209-2367)
PHONE..................................316 522-0008
Amy Remmert, *General Mgr*
Susanne Christians, *Vice Pres*
EMP: 19
SALES (est): 1MM **Privately Held**
SIC: 7011 Hotels & motels

(G-15978)
WICHITA AWNING CO INC
357 N Wabash Ave (67214-3947)
PHONE..................................316 838-4432
Gordon Stowe, *President*
EMP: 7
SQ FT: 6,000
SALES (est): 1MM **Privately Held**
WEB: www.wichitaawning.com
SIC: 3444 5039 Awnings & canopies; awnings

(G-15979)
WICHITA BAND INSTRUMENT CO
Also Called: EMC Shorts Guitars
2525 E Douglas Ave (67211-1683)
PHONE..................................316 684-0291
Gary L Ray, *President*
Anita Creekmoore, *Persnl Dir*
EMP: 18 **EST:** 1954
SQ FT: 6,000
SALES (est): 1.7MM **Privately Held**
WEB: www.wichitaband.com
SIC: 5736 7699 Musical instrument stores; musical instrument repair services

(G-15980)
WICHITA BAR ASSOCIATION
Also Called: WICHITA BAR FOUNDATION
225 N Market St Ste 200 (67202-2023)
PHONE..................................316 263-2251
Karin Kirk, *Exec Dir*
Robin Burnside, *Asst Director*
EMP: 10
SQ FT: 14,000
SALES: 460.2K **Privately Held**
WEB: www.wichitabar.org
SIC: 8621 8111 Bar association; education & teacher association; legal services

(G-15981)
WICHITA BINDERY INC
622 S Commerce St (67202-4612)
PHONE..................................316 262-3473
John Marshall, *President*
Janet Marshall, *Vice Pres*
Johnny Marshall, *Treasurer*
EMP: 20
SQ FT: 18,000
SALES: 900K **Privately Held**
SIC: 2789 3554 Binding only: books, pamphlets, magazines, etc.; die cutting & stamping machinery, paper converting

(G-15982)
WICHITA BRASS AND ALUM FNDRY
412 E 29th St N (67219-4108)
P.O. Box 4144 (67204-0144)
PHONE..................................316 838-4286
Shara Carter-Howell, *President*
Erik Carter, *Vice Pres*
Jennifer Carter, *Admin Sec*
EMP: 17 **EST:** 1938
SQ FT: 40,000
SALES: 2MM **Privately Held**
SIC: 3369 3365 Magnesium & magnes.-base alloy castings, exc. die-casting; aluminum & aluminum-based alloy castings

(G-15983)
WICHITA BUSINESS JOURNAL INC
121 N Mead St Ste 100 (67202-3781)
PHONE..................................316 267-6406
John Ek, *Principal*
Brittany Schowalter, *Editor*
Stacie Myers, *Executive*
EMP: 17
SALES (est): 934.5K
SALES (corp-wide): 1.3B **Privately Held**
SIC: 2711 7313 Newspapers: publishing only, not printed on site; newspaper advertising representative
HQ: American City Business Journals, Inc.
120 W Morehead St Ste 400
Charlotte NC 28202
704 973-1000

(G-15984)
WICHITA CANTEEN COMPANY INC (PA)
4430 W 29th Cir S (67215-1018)
PHONE..................................316 524-2254
Wayne L Smith, *President*
James S Grady, *Vice Pres*
Kelley F Grady, *Shareholder*
EMP: 41 **EST:** 1992
SQ FT: 6,500
SALES (est): 4.4MM **Privately Held**
WEB: www.canteenks.com
SIC: 5812 5962 7999 Caterers; food vending machines; beverage vending machines; concession operator

(G-15985)
WICHITA CENTER FOR THE ARTS
9112 E Central Ave (67206-2506)
PHONE..................................316 315-0151
Pamela Kelly, *Manager*
Howard Ellington, *Director*
EMP: 18
SQ FT: 45,000
SALES: 4.8MM **Privately Held**
WEB: www.wcfta.com
SIC: 8412 7922 Art gallery, noncommercial; museum; theatrical production services

(G-15986)
WICHITA CHILD GUIDANCE CENTER
1365 N Custer St (67203-6634)
PHONE..................................316 686-6671
Walter Thiessen, *President*
EMP: 58
SQ FT: 13,000
SALES (est): 1.5MM **Privately Held**
WEB: www.child-guidance.com
SIC: 8322 Child related social services; family counseling services

(G-15987)
WICHITA CHILDRENS HOME
7271 E 37th St N (67226-3202)
PHONE..................................316 684-6581
Debbie Kennedy, *CEO*
Fonda Ellis, *Principal*
Angie Carr, *CFO*
Kurt Breitenbach, *Treasurer*
Laura Kelly, *Director*
EMP: 95
SQ FT: 5,000
SALES: 5.7MM **Privately Held**
WEB: www.wch.org
SIC: 8361 Children's home

(G-15988)
WICHITA CNTRY CLB MAINTENNANCE
8501 E 13th St N Ste 1022 (67206-1243)
PHONE..................................316 634-2882
Cary Cozby, *CEO*
EMP: 18
SALES (est): 217.3K **Privately Held**
SIC: 7997 Country club, membership

(G-15989)
WICHITA CONCRETE PIPE INC
221 W 37th St N (67204-3603)
P.O. Box 369, McPherson (67460-0369)
PHONE..................................316 838-8651
Wade Wentling, *CEO*
Chris Anderson, *President*
Nick Wenger, *QC Mgr*
Jeff Herlocker, *Sales Engr*
EMP: 50
SQ FT: 17,500
SALES: 12.3MM **Privately Held**
WEB: www.wichitaconcretepipe.com
SIC: 3272 1791 Pipe, concrete or lined with concrete; precast concrete structural framing or panels, placing of

(G-15990)
WICHITA CONSULTING COMPANY LP
8100 E 22nd St N Bldg 500 (67226-2305)
PHONE..................................316 681-5102
Rolf Ruhfus, *CEO*
EMP: 20
SALES (est): 853.2K **Privately Held**
SIC: 8748 Business consulting

(G-15991)
WICHITA CONVENTION TOURISM BUR
Also Called: GREATER WICHITA CON & VISITORS
515 S Main St Ste 115 (67202-3756)
PHONE..................................316 265-2800
John Rolfe, *President*
Lindsay Gulley, *Sales Staff*
Josh Howell, *Sales Staff*
Jessica Viramontez, *Sales Staff*
Olivia Reynolds, *Marketing Staff*
EMP: 17
SQ FT: 3,800
SALES: 6.4MM **Privately Held**
WEB: www.visitwichita.com
SIC: 7389 Tourist information bureau; convention & show services

(G-15992)
WICHITA CRIME STOPPERS PROGRAM
Also Called: Crime Stpers of Wchta Sdgwck C
455 N Main St Fl 12 (67202-1623)
PHONE..................................316 267-2111
David Haglund, *President*
Jim Todd, *Vice Pres*
EMP: 21
SALES: 5.9K **Privately Held**
SIC: 8699 Personal interest organization

(G-15993)
WICHITA DRYWALL ACOUSTICS LLC
740 N Gilda St (67212-4806)
PHONE..................................316 773-7826
Bryan Kyllonen, *Mng Member*
EMP: 28
SALES: 3MM **Privately Held**
SIC: 1751 1742 Framing contractor; drywall

(G-15994)
WICHITA EAGLE BEACON PUBG INC (HQ)
330 N Mead St (67202-3594)
PHONE..................................316 268-6000
Lou Heldman, *President*
Pam Siddall, *President*
Jeff Rosen, *Editor*
Judy Leis, *Accounts Mgr*
Robyn Marrero, *Marketing Staff*
EMP: 65 **EST:** 1952
SQ FT: 140,800
SALES (est): 67.2MM
SALES (corp-wide): 807.2MM **Publicly Held**
WEB: www.kansas.com
SIC: 2711 Newspapers, publishing & printing
PA: The Mcclatchy Company
2100 Q St
Sacramento CA 95816
916 321-1844

(G-15995)
WICHITA EAR CLINIC PA
9350 E Central Ave (67206-4999)
PHONE..................................316 686-6608
Thomas Kryzer MD, *Owner*
EMP: 15
SQ FT: 2,300
SALES (est): 1.8MM **Privately Held**
WEB: www.wichitaearclinic.com
SIC: 8011 Ears, nose & throat specialist: physician/surgeon

(G-15996)
WICHITA EAST HOTEL ASSOCIATES
Also Called: Holiday Inn
549 S Rock Rd (67207-2365)
PHONE..................................316 686-7131
Will Harrington, *Manager*
EMP: 100
SALES (est): 2.5MM **Privately Held**
SIC: 7011 Hotels & motels

(G-15997)
WICHITA EMRGNCY VETERINARY LLC
Also Called: Veternary Emrgncy Clnic Wchita
727 S Washington Ave (67211-2427)
PHONE..................................316 262-5321
Brock Lofgreen, *Mng Member*
Holly Smith,
EMP: 31
SQ FT: 1,000
SALES (est): 1.6MM **Privately Held**
SIC: 0742 Animal hospital services, pets & other animal specialties; veterinarian, animal specialties

(G-15998)
WICHITA FAMILY CRISIS CTR INC
1111 N Saint Francis Ave (67214-2813)
PHONE..................................316 263-7501
Amanda Walker, *President*
EMP: 15
SALES: 1.1MM **Privately Held**
WEB: www.ywcaofwichita.org
SIC: 8322 8641 Social service center; civic associations

(G-15999)
WICHITA FAMILY MEDICINE SPECIA
800 N Carriage Pkwy (67208-4508)
P.O. Box 9186 (67277-0186)
PHONE..................................316 858-5800
Janice Arnold, *Human Res Dir*
Steven Davis, *Med Doctor*
Ryan Dusek, *Manager*
Connie Davis, *Director*
Tiffany Lieurance, *Director*
EMP: 43
SQ FT: 14,000
SALES (est): 6.5MM **Privately Held**
WEB: www.modernz.net
SIC: 8011 General & family practice, physician/surgeon

(G-16000)
WICHITA FEDERAL CREDIT UNION
3730 W 13th St N (67203-4402)
PHONE..................................316 941-0600
Wayne Warfel, *President*
Penny Quick, *Vice Pres*
Eric Nikkel, *IT/INT Sup*
Leandra Chinn,
EMP: 23
SQ FT: 5,000
SALES: 5.5MM **Privately Held**
WEB: www.wmfcu.com
SIC: 6061 Federal credit unions

(G-16001)
WICHITA FESTIVALS INC
444 E William St (67202-4411)
PHONE..................................316 267-2817
Janet Wright, *President*
Bob Harbison, *President*
Ann Keefer, *Vice Pres*
Ty Stork, *Opers Staff*
Judi Yoder, *Treasurer*
EMP: 11
SALES: 2.4MM **Privately Held**
WEB: www.wichitafestivals.com
SIC: 7999 Festival operation

(G-16002)
WICHITA FMLY VISION CLINIC PA
Also Called: Robert Nelson Od
437 N Tyler Rd (67212-3630)
PHONE..................................316 722-1001
Dr Robert C Nelson, *President*
Andy Stephens Od, *Treasurer*
Jeremy Durham, *Med Doctor*
EMP: 19
SQ FT: 17,500
SALES (est): 1.5MM **Privately Held**
WEB: www.wfvision.com
SIC: 8042 Specialized optometrists

(G-16003)
WICHITA GYMNASTICS CLUB INC
9400 E 37th St N (67226-2012)
PHONE..................................316 634-1900
Daniel Bruring, *Manager*
EMP: 15
SALES (corp-wide): 569.5K **Privately Held**
WEB: www.wichitagym.com
SIC: 7999 Gymnastic instruction, non-membership
PA: Wichita Gymnastics Club Inc
540 N Hydraulic St
Wichita KS

(G-16004)
WICHITA HABITAT FOR HUMANITY
130 E Murdock St Ste 102 (67214-3630)
P.O. Box 114 (67201-0114)
PHONE..................................316 269-0755
Jerry Jones, *Chairman*
Diana Palmer, *Vice Pres*
Linda Steward, *Exec Dir*
Diana Yates, *Admin Sec*
Pam Bohm, *Assistant*
EMP: 13
SQ FT: 585
SALES: 2MM **Privately Held**
WEB: www.wichitahabitat.org
SIC: 1521 Single-family housing construction

(G-16005)
WICHITA HOME HEALTH CARE GROUP
Also Called: Accessdge HM Hlth Care Wichita
505 S Broadway Ave # 209 (67202-3900)
PHONE..................................316 219-0095
Jeffrey Epley, *Principal*
EMP: 10
SALES (est): 482.5K **Privately Held**
SIC: 8011 Offices & clinics of medical doctors

(G-16006)
WICHITA HSPTTLITY HOLDINGS LLC
Also Called: Ramada Inn
400 W Douglas Ave (67202-2902)
PHONE..................................316 685-1281
John Bennett, *Partner*
Gary Keller, *Partner*
Rick Voelzke, *Manager*
EMP: 43
SALES (est): 1.5MM **Privately Held**
SIC: 7011 Hotels & motels

(G-16007)
WICHITA IND NEIGHBORHOODS INC
Also Called: WIN
2755 E 19th St N (67214-2200)
PHONE..................................316 260-8000
James Rosebroro, *President*
Carla Lee, *Vice Pres*
Loretta Buckner, *Treasurer*
Ashlyruth Eckels, *Admin Sec*
EMP: 20 **EST:** 2001
SALES: 6.4K **Privately Held**
SIC: 8699 Charitable organization

(G-16008)
WICHITA INN SUITES INC
Also Called: Wichita Suites Hotel
5211 E Kellogg Dr (67218-1626)
PHONE..................................316 685-2233
Harry Pollak, *President*
EMP: 25
SQ FT: 800
SALES (est): 1.3MM **Privately Held**
SIC: 7011 6163 Hotels; loan brokers

(G-16009)
WICHITA IRON & METALS CORP INC
922 W Merton St (67213-4113)
P.O. Box 13021 (67213-0021)
PHONE..................................316 267-3291
Harlan C Hartstein, *President*
Carol Rosen, *Corp Secy*
Virgina Martin, *Manager*
EMP: 20
SQ FT: 6,000
SALES (est): 4.1MM **Privately Held**
SIC: 5093 5084 Ferrous metal scrap & waste; oil well machinery, equipment & supplies

(G-16010)
WICHITA MACHINE PRODUCTS INC
2930 S Old Lawrence Rd (67217-3336)
PHONE..................................316 522-7401
Jeremy McAsey, *President*
Lane B Hoss, *President*
EMP: 5
SQ FT: 5,000
SALES (est): 674.6K **Privately Held**
SIC: 3599 Machine shop, jobbing & repair

(G-16011)
WICHITA MATERIAL RECOVERY LLC
624 E Morris St (67211-2435)
PHONE..................................316 303-9303
James Wyatt,
William Theime,
EMP: 15
SALES (est): 1.8MM **Privately Held**
SIC: 4953 Recycling, waste materials

(G-16012)
WICHITA MONTESSORI SCHOOL
8311 E Douglas Ave (67207-1213)
PHONE..................................316 686-7265
Linda Amos, *Principal*
Jane Saunders, *Director*
Miranda Stegman, *Teacher*
EMP: 18
SALES: 602.7K **Privately Held**
WEB: www.wichitamontessori.com
SIC: 8351 8211 Montessori child development center; private elementary school

(G-16013)
WICHITA NEPHROLOGY GROUP PA
818 N Emporia St Ste 310 (67214-3727)
PHONE..................................316 263-5891
Jerry Cohlmia, *President*
Howard Day, *Corp Secy*
EMP: 30 **EST:** 1976
SQ FT: 3,200
SALES (est): 5.1MM **Privately Held**
WEB: www.samcohlmia.com
SIC: 8011 Internal medicine, physician/surgeon; medical centers

(G-16014)
WICHITA OB GYN ASSOCIATES PA
Also Called: Christman, Carl M Jr
551 N Hillside St Ste 510 (67214-4928)
PHONE..................................316 685-0559
Carl Christman MD, *President*
Krista Long, *Office Mgr*
Edmond G Feuille Jr, *Director*
EMP: 30
SALES (est): 4.4MM **Privately Held**
SIC: 8011 Gynecologist; obstetrician

(G-16015)
WICHITA ORTHOPAEDIC ASSOC LLC
Also Called: Surgery Center of Kansas
7550 W Village Cir Ste 2 (67205-9364)
PHONE..................................316 838-2020
Karen Gabbert, *Administration*
EMP: 50
SALES (est): 5MM **Privately Held**
SIC: 8011 Orthopedic physician

(G-16016)
WICHITA PARK CMTRY & MAUSOLEUM
3424 E 21st St N (67208-1513)
PHONE..................................316 686-5594
Bill Walsh, *President*
EMP: 25 **EST:** 2001
SALES (est): 1MM **Privately Held**
SIC: 0782 Cemetery upkeep services

(G-16017)
WICHITA PHYSICAL MEDICINE P A
8338 W 13th St N (67212-2900)
PHONE..................................316 729-1030
Philip Mills MD, *Owner*
EMP: 10
SALES (est): 494.8K **Privately Held**
SIC: 8011 Physical medicine, physician/surgeon

(G-16018)
WICHITA PRESS INC
4401 W Irving St (67209-2626)
P.O. Box 12103 (67277-2103)
PHONE..................................316 945-5651
Dennis Dodd, *President*
Jason Dodd, *Treasurer*
EMP: 9 **EST:** 1949
SQ FT: 4,400
SALES: 1MM **Privately Held**
SIC: 2752 Commercial printing, offset

(G-16019)
WICHITA PUMP & SUPPLY COMPANY
1010 E 14th St N (67214-1496)
PHONE..................................316 264-8308
Gordon Sites, *CEO*
Roger B Sites, *President*
EMP: 14
SQ FT: 17,000
SALES (est): 5.3MM **Privately Held**
SIC: 5084 5085 Pumps & pumping equipment; industrial supplies

(G-16020)
WICHITA RESIDENCE ASSOC LP
711 S Main St (67213-5413)
PHONE..................................316 263-1061
Jack Debore, *President*
Christine Allen, *General Mgr*
Allen Christine, *General Mgr*
Michael Gordon, *Sales Mgr*
Ruth Matous, *Sales Staff*
EMP: 31
SALES (est): 2.7MM **Privately Held**
SIC: 7011 Hotels

(G-16021)
WICHITA ROOFING AND RMDLG INC
3821 W Bounous St (67213-1202)
PHONE..................................316 943-0600
Mark A Eaton, *President*
EMP: 14
SQ FT: 1,200
SALES (est): 2MM **Privately Held**
WEB: www.wichitaroofing.net
SIC: 1761 Roofing contractor

(G-16022)
WICHITA RUGBY FOUNDATION INC
727 N Waco Ave Ste 200 (67203-3953)
P.O. Box 47370 (67201-7370)
PHONE..................................316 262-6800
Gene Paulsen, *President*
EMP: 20
SALES (est): 85.1K **Privately Held**
SIC: 8699 Amateur sports promotion

(G-16023)
WICHITA SPORTS FORUM
2668 N Greenwich Ct (67226-8226)
PHONE..................................316 201-1414
EMP: 15
SALES (est): 552K **Privately Held**
SIC: 7997 Membership sports & recreation clubs

(G-16024)
WICHITA SRGICAL SPECIALISTS PA
Also Called: Midkansas Ear Nose Throat Assn
982 N Tyler Rd Ste D (67212-3271)
PHONE..................................316 722-5814
Jackie Stevens, *Manager*
EMP: 30
SALES (corp-wide): 18.2MM **Privately Held**
WEB: www.wsspa.com
SIC: 8011 Surgeon
PA: Wichita Surgical Specialists Pa
818 N Emporia St Ste 200
Wichita KS 67214
316 263-0296

(G-16025)
WICHITA SRGICAL SPECIALISTS PA (PA)
818 N Emporia St Ste 200 (67214-3788)
PHONE..................................316 263-0296
Alex D Ammar, *CEO*
Kari Clark, *CFO*
Sheri Stallard, *Human Res Mgr*
Mark Niederee, *Med Doctor*
Matthew Arneson, *Surgeon*
▲ **EMP:** 75
SQ FT: 21,445
SALES (est): 18.2MM **Privately Held**
WEB: www.wsspa.com
SIC: 8011 General & family practice, physician/surgeon

(G-16026)
WICHITA SRGICAL SPECIALISTS PA
Advanced Orthopaedic Assoc
2778 N Webb Rd (67226-8112)
PHONE..................................316 631-1600
Kimberly Moss, *Manager*
EMP: 50
SALES (corp-wide): 18.2MM **Privately Held**
WEB: www.wsspa.com
SIC: 8011 Orthopedic physician; sports medicine specialist, physician
PA: Wichita Surgical Specialists Pa
818 N Emporia St Ste 200
Wichita KS 67214
316 263-0296

(G-16027)
WICHITA SRGICAL SPECIALISTS PA
Plastic Surgery Center
1861 N Webb Rd (67206-3413)
PHONE..................................316 688-7500

Therese E Cusick, *Med Doctor*
Paulette Levalley, *Manager*
James Shaw, *Plastic Surgeon*
EMP: 21
SALES (corp-wide): 18.2MM **Privately Held**
WEB: www.wsspa.com
SIC: 8011 7231 Plastic surgeon; depilatory salon, electrolysis
PA: Wichita Surgical Specialists Pa
818 N Emporia St Ste 200
Wichita KS 67214
316 263-0296

(G-16028)
WICHITA SRGICAL SPECIALISTS PA
Mid-Knsas Ear/Nose/Throat Assn
310 S Hillside St (67211-2129)
PHONE..................................316 684-2838
Cathy Hill, *Manager*
Jerome E French,
EMP: 30
SALES (corp-wide): 18.2MM **Privately Held**
WEB: www.wsspa.com
SIC: 8011 Surgeon
PA: Wichita Surgical Specialists Pa
818 N Emporia St Ste 200
Wichita KS 67214
316 263-0296

(G-16029)
WICHITA STAMP AND SEAL INC
807 N Main St (67203-3606)
PHONE..................................316 263-4223
Melvin Bird, *President*
Lynne S Bird, *Treasurer*
EMP: 9
SQ FT: 3,000
SALES (est): 1.1MM **Privately Held**
SIC: 3953 7389 Marking devices; engraving service

(G-16030)
WICHITA STATE SUNFLOWER INC
Also Called: Sunflwer Wchita State Unvrstys
1845 Fairmount St (67260-9700)
PHONE..................................316 978-6917
Jan Richard, *Principal*
Glen Sharp, *Principal*
Robbie Norton, *Business Mgr*
EMP: 30
SALES (est): 962.6K
SALES (corp-wide): 230.7MM **Privately Held**
SIC: 2711 2741 2721 Newspapers; miscellaneous publishing; periodicals
PA: The Wichita State University
1845 Fairmount St
Wichita KS 67260
316 978-3456

(G-16031)
WICHITA STATE UNIV INTER CLLGA
Also Called: WSU-ICAA
1845 Fairmount St (67260-9700)
PHONE..................................316 978-3250
Mark Rogers, *General Mgr*
Jim Schaus, *Director*
Susan Domann, *Director*
Alex Johnson, *Director*
Rege Klitzke, *Director*
EMP: 100
SQ FT: 130,190
SALES: 29.8MM **Privately Held**
WEB: www.goshockers.com
SIC: 8699 Athletic organizations

(G-16032)
WICHITA STATE UNIVERSITY
Also Called: NV Fitness Co
1845 Fairmount St (67260-0001)
PHONE..................................316 978-3584
Pal RAO, *Principal*
EMP: 50
SALES (corp-wide): 230.7MM **Privately Held**
WEB: www.wichita.edu
SIC: 7991 Physical fitness facilities
PA: The Wichita State University
1845 Fairmount St
Wichita KS 67260
316 978-3456

(G-16033)
WICHITA STATE UNIVERSITY
Also Called: Kmuw-FM 89.1 Public Radio
121 N Mead St Ste 200 (67202-2747)
PHONE..................................316 978-6789
Michael Holle, *Research*
Mark McCain, *Director*
EMP: 24
SALES (corp-wide): 230.7MM **Privately Held**
WEB: www.wichita.edu
SIC: 4832 8221 Radio broadcasting stations; university
PA: The Wichita State University
1845 Fairmount St
Wichita KS 67260
316 978-3456

(G-16034)
WICHITA STATE UNIVERSITY
Also Called: Duerksen Fine Arts Center
Duerksen Arts Cntr 1845 (67260-0001)
PHONE..................................316 978-3581
Judith Fear, *Director*
Marcus Graeff, *Graphic Designe*
EMP: 30
SALES (corp-wide): 230.7MM **Privately Held**
WEB: www.wichita.edu
SIC: 7911 8221 Dance instructor & school services; university
PA: The Wichita State University
1845 Fairmount St
Wichita KS 67260
316 978-3456

(G-16035)
WICHITA STATE UNVSITY ALMNI AS
1845 Fairmount St (67260-9700)
PHONE..................................316 978-3290
Courtney Marshall, *CEO*
EMP: 11
SALES: 1.1MM **Privately Held**
SIC: 8641 Civic social & fraternal associations

(G-16036)
WICHITA SWIM CLUB
8323 E Douglas Ave (67207-1213)
PHONE..................................316 683-1491
Katie Yevak, *Manager*
Alison Pick, *Asst Director*
EMP: 20
SALES: 790.9K **Privately Held**
WEB: www.wichitaswimclub.org
SIC: 7997 7999 5699 Swimming club, membership; swimming instruction; bathing suits

(G-16037)
WICHITA SYMPHONY SOCIETY
225 W Douglas Ave Ste 207 (67202-3181)
PHONE..................................316 267-7658
Don Reinhold, *Principal*
Leigh Haman, *Business Mgr*
Samantha Davis, *Opers Mgr*
Anne Marie, *Opers Mgr*
Arleigh McCormick, *Pub Rel Mgr*
EMP: 120
SQ FT: 1,000
SALES: 2.3MM **Privately Held**
SIC: 7929 Symphony orchestras

(G-16038)
WICHITA TERMINAL ASSOCIATION
2649 N New York Ave (67219-4315)
PHONE..................................316 262-0441
Danny Miller, *Superintendent*
Joe Caffin, *Superintendent*
Royce Franklin, *Foreman/Supr*
Jason Smith, *Supervisor*
EMP: 16
SQ FT: 2,000
SALES (est): 1.1MM **Privately Held**
SIC: 4013 Switching & terminal services

(G-16039)
WICHITA THNDER PROF HCKEY TEAM
Also Called: Whichita Thunder
505 W Maple St (67213-4616)
PHONE..................................316 264-4625
Chris Presson, *General Mgr*
Grant Wilson, *Vice Pres*
Matt Brokaw, *Manager*
EMP: 10
SALES (est): 551.5K **Privately Held**
WEB: www.wichitathunder.com
SIC: 7941 8699 7999 Ice hockey club; athletic organizations; hockey instruction school

(G-16040)
WICHITA TOBACCO & CANDY CO
924 W 2nd St N (67203-6095)
PHONE..................................316 264-2412
George F Stevens, *President*
Meredith Stevens, *Corp Secy*
Eugenie Stevens, *Vice Pres*
EMP: 12
SQ FT: 7,000
SALES (est): 3MM **Privately Held**
SIC: 5194 5145 5122 Tobacco & tobacco products; candy; druggists' sundries

(G-16041)
WICHITA TOP CHILDRENS FUND
Also Called: OPPORTUNITY PROJECT, THE
1625 N Waterfront Pkwy (67206-6621)
PHONE..................................316 260-9479
Barry L Downing, *Principal*
Chris Thomas, *Principal*
EMP: 80
SALES: 5.5MM **Privately Held**
SIC: 8351 Child day care services

(G-16042)
WICHITA WATER CONDITIONING INC (PA)
Also Called: Culligan
10821 E 26th St N (67226-4525)
PHONE..................................316 267-5287
Cecil R Hall, *President*
Jason Leriche, *General Mgr*
Troy Snider, *General Mgr*
Jason Stehlik, *General Mgr*
Tim Stutts, *General Mgr*
EMP: 80
SALES (est): 34.9MM **Privately Held**
WEB: www.hallswater.com
SIC: 1711 5999 Plumbing, heating, air-conditioning contractors; water purification equipment

(G-16043)
WICHITA WELDING SUPPLY INC (PA)
Also Called: Young Welders
3001 N Broadway Ave (67219-4096)
PHONE..................................316 838-8671
J Carter Frick, *CEO*
Robert Zollinger, *President*
Yvette Zollinger, *Vice Pres*
EMP: 15
SQ FT: 13,000
SALES (est): 4.7MM **Privately Held**
WEB: www.wichitaweldingsupply.com
SIC: 5169 5999 5084 Gases, compressed & liquefied; welding supplies; welding machinery & equipment

(G-16044)
WICHITA WHOLESALE SUPPLY INC
Also Called: Johnson Controls
1320 E 2nd St N (67214-4018)
P.O. Box 3031 (67201-3031)
PHONE..................................316 267-3629
J Peter Schrepferman, *President*
M Catherine Schrepferman, *Corp Secy*
Richard Schrepferman, *Vice Pres*
EMP: 11
SQ FT: 15,000
SALES (est): 3.3MM **Privately Held**
SIC: 5075 5078 5064 Air conditioning & ventilation equipment & supplies; refrigeration equipment & supplies; electrical appliances, television & radio

(G-16045)
WIESE USA INC
Also Called: Wiese Material Handling
1446 S Florence St (67209-2648)
PHONE..................................316 942-1600
Kevin Estes, *Branch Mgr*
Kelly Bell, *Manager*
EMP: 21
SALES (corp-wide): 134.9MM **Privately Held**
SIC: 5084 Materials handling machinery
PA: Wiese Usa, Inc.
1435 Woodson Rd
Saint Louis MO 63132
314 997-4444

(G-16046)
WILBERT FUNERAL SERVICES INC
Also Called: Wichita Wilbert Vault
2532 N Washington Ave (67219-4428)
PHONE..................................316 832-1114
Dave Stewart, *Finance Mgr*
John Habiger, *Manager*
EMP: 20
SALES (corp-wide): 244.6MM **Privately Held**
WEB: www.suhor.com
SIC: 3272 5211 5087 Burial vaults, concrete or precast terrazzo; brick; concrete burial vaults & boxes
PA: Wilbert Funeral Services, Inc.
10965 Granada Ln Ste 300
Overland Park KS 66211
913 345-2120

(G-16047)
WILCO INC
3502 W Harry St (67213-1494)
PHONE..................................316 943-9379
Floyd Walpole, *President*
Ted Barnes, *Corp Secy*
Beverly Fisher, *Accounts Mgr*
EMP: 12
SQ FT: 24,000
SALES (est): 6.8MM **Privately Held**
WEB: www.wilco.to
SIC: 5085 Industrial supplies

(G-16048)
WILCOX ADVANCED PHYSICAL
2243 S Meridian Ave # 100 (67213-1911)
PHONE..................................316 942-5448
Matthew D Wilcox, *Mng Member*
EMP: 10
SALES (est): 152K **Privately Held**
SIC: 8049 Physical therapist

(G-16049)
WILDCAT CONSTRUCTION CO INC (PA)
3219 W May St (67213-1540)
P.O. Box 9163 (67277-0163)
PHONE..................................316 945-9408
Roger McClellan, *President*
Steve Thoendel, *Superintendent*
Stephen Llamas, *Corp Secy*
John Curtis, *Vice Pres*
Alan Farrington, *Vice Pres*
EMP: 120
SALES (est): 69.5MM **Privately Held**
WEB: www.wildcatcompanies.com
SIC: 1623 1622 1771 1611 Underground utilities contractor; bridge construction; concrete work; grading; golf course construction

(G-16050)
WILDCAT PAINTING INC
4500 W Harry St (67209-2736)
PHONE..................................316 263-8076
Stephen Decker, *President*
EMP: 10
SQ FT: 15,000
SALES (est): 521.3K **Privately Held**
WEB: www.wildcatpainting.com
SIC: 1721 Commercial painting

(G-16051)
WILLIAM SONOMA STORE INC
Also Called: Williams-Sonoma Store
2000 N Rock Rd Ste 152 (67206-1250)
PHONE..................................316 636-5990
Julie Cufick, *Manager*
EMP: 20
SALES (corp-wide): 5.6B **Publicly Held**
SIC: 5023 Kitchenware
HQ: Williams-Sonoma Stores, Inc.
3250 Van Ness Ave
San Francisco CA 94109
415 421-7900

(G-16052)
WILLIAMS CONSTRUCTION CO INC
2008 W Harry Ct (67213-3200)
PHONE.................................316 264-1964
Richard Williams, *President*
EMP: 10
SQ FT: 2,000
SALES (est): 1.9MM **Privately Held**
SIC: 1542 Commercial & office building, new construction

(G-16053)
WILSON BUILDING MAINTENANCE
624 E 1st St N (67202-2604)
P.O. Box 2041 (67201-2041)
PHONE.................................316 264-0699
Anita L Oberwortmann, *President*
EMP: 125
SQ FT: 30,000
SALES (est): 3.9MM **Privately Held**
WEB: www.wilsonmaintenance.com
SIC: 7349 5087 Janitorial service, contract basis; building maintenance, except repairs; window cleaning; janitors' supplies

(G-16054)
WINDING SPECIALISTS CO INC
1225 N Wellington Pl (67203-3898)
PHONE.................................316 265-9358
George B Wills, *Ch of Bd*
David Wills, *President*
Doris Wills, *Vice Pres*
EMP: 11
SQ FT: 7,000
SALES (est): 1MM **Privately Held**
WEB: www.wscgp.com
SIC: 3728 Aircraft assemblies, subassemblies & parts

(G-16055)
WINGERT ANIMAL HOSPITAL
4419 S Seneca St (67217-4599)
PHONE.................................316 524-3257
Bart Wingert Dvm, *Owner*
EMP: 10
SALES (est): 324.9K **Privately Held**
SIC: 0742 Animal hospital services, pets & other animal specialties

(G-16056)
WINNING SPIRIT INC
934 S Oliver St (67218-3216)
PHONE.................................316 684-0855
EMP: 20 **EST:** 2000
SALES (est): 1.1MM **Privately Held**
SIC: 2395 2396 Pleating/Stitching Services Mfg Auto/Apparel Trimming

(G-16057)
WINONA VAN NORMAN INC
710 E 17th St N (67214-1312)
P.O. Box 2309 (67201-2309)
PHONE.................................316 219-3500
Linda Weir-Enegren, *President*
Paul Enegren, *Sales Mgr*
Sasha Enegren, *Sales Staff*
▲ **EMP:** 15
SQ FT: 20,000
SALES (est): 3.3MM **Privately Held**
WEB: www.winonavannorman.com
SIC: 3592 Carburetors, pistons, rings, valves

(G-16058)
WINTER ARCHITECTS INC
1024 E 1st St N (67214-3903)
PHONE.................................316 267-7142
Dan Winter, *President*
Charlie W Wilson, *Purch Mgr*
EMP: 12
SQ FT: 3,000
SALES: 740K **Privately Held**
WEB: www.winterusa.com
SIC: 8712 7389 Architectural engineering; design, commercial & industrial

(G-16059)
WIRTHS & SONS INC
109 E 37th St N (67219-3501)
PHONE.................................316 838-0509
James Wirths, *President*
EMP: 14 **EST:** 1965
SQ FT: 21,000
SALES: 1.2MM **Privately Held**
SIC: 2448 Pallets, wood

(G-16060)
WKCSC INC
Also Called: Kansas Coil Spring
4310 S Southeast Blvd (67210-1619)
PHONE.................................316 652-7113
Linda M Peressin, *President*
Courtney Brown, *Manager*
EMP: 9
SALES (est): 1.2MM **Privately Held**
SIC: 3469 5085 3315 Machine parts, stamped or pressed metal; springs; wire & fabricated wire products

(G-16061)
WOLFE ELECTRIC INC
7761 W Kellogg Dr (67209-2003)
P.O. Box 9090 (67277-0090)
PHONE.................................316 943-2751
Ron Wolfe, *President*
Patacia Wolfe, *Corp Secy*
Lloyd Barton, *CFO*
Steven Merseal, *Clerk*
▲ **EMP:** 52 **EST:** 1941
SQ FT: 207,000
SALES (est): 11.7MM **Privately Held**
SIC: 1731 General electrical contractor

(G-16062)
WOLTERS KLUWER HEALTH INC
Also Called: Wolters Kluwer/Cch
9111 E Douglas Ave (67207-1241)
PHONE.................................316 612-5000
Dee Hairgrove, *Vice Pres*
Shara Cohen, *Vice Pres*
Adrian Pina, *Vice Pres*
Dolph Sharp, *Vice Pres*
Maria Afonso, *Technical Mgr*
EMP: 13
SALES (est): 608.8K **Privately Held**
SIC: 8099 8721 Health & allied services; accounting, auditing & bookkeeping

(G-16063)
WOODARD HERNANDEZ ROTH DAY LLC
245 N Waco St Ste 260 (67202-1157)
P.O. Box 127 (67201-0127)
PHONE.................................316 263-4958
James Roth, *Park Mgr*
Matthew Sorochty, *Manager*
Barb Yates, *Legal Staff*
Chistopher Cole,
Steven Day,
EMP: 35
SALES (est): 3.7MM **Privately Held**
WEB: www.woodard-law.com
SIC: 8111 General practice attorney, lawyer

(G-16064)
WOODARD TECH & INVESTMENTS LLC
Also Called: Two Trees Technologies
200 N Emporia Ave Ste 300 (67202-2551)
PHONE.................................316 636-2122
Jim Smith, *Branch Mgr*
EMP: 12
SALES (corp-wide): 164.2MM **Privately Held**
SIC: 5045 Computers, peripherals & software
PA: Woodard Technology & Investments, L.L.C.
10205 E 61st St Ste D
Tulsa OK 74133
918 270-7000

(G-16065)
WOODLAND LAKES COMMUNITY CHURC
770 S Greenwich Rd (67207-4314)
PHONE.................................316 682-9522
Harlan Buettner, *Pastor*
Rod Thelander, *Pastor*
Sue Wagner, *Treasurer*
EMP: 11
SQ FT: 32,000
SALES (est): 454.3K **Privately Held**
WEB: www.woodlandlakescc.com
SIC: 8661 6514 6512 Church of the Nazarene; residential building, four or fewer units: operation; commercial & industrial building operation

(G-16066)
WOODLAND UNITED METHODIST CH
Also Called: Woodland Untd Mthdst Pr-School
1100 W 15th St N (67203-2800)
PHONE.................................316 265-6669
Charles R Claycomb, *Pastor*
EMP: 15
SALES (est): 525.1K **Privately Held**
WEB: www.woodlandumc.com
SIC: 8661 8351 Methodist Church; preschool center

(G-16067)
WOODLAWN CARE AND REHAB LLC
Also Called: Orchard Grdns Hlth Rhblitation
1600 S Woodlawn Blvd (67218-4728)
PHONE.................................316 691-9999
Joseph C Tutera, *Owner*
EMP: 13
SALES (est): 121.4K **Privately Held**
SIC: 8051 Skilled nursing care facilities

(G-16068)
WOODYS AUTOMOTIVE SVC & SLS
2600 N Amidon Ave (67204-4902)
PHONE.................................316 838-8011
Shawn Sarbaum, *President*
EMP: 10
SALES (est): 121.8K **Privately Held**
SIC: 7539 Automotive repair shops

(G-16069)
WOOLSEY PETROLEUM CORPORATION (PA)
125 N Market St Ste 1000 (67202-1775)
PHONE.................................316 267-4379
I Wayne Woolsey, *President*
Kay Woolsey, *Vice Pres*
Scott Frazier, *Treasurer*
William B McKean, *Treasurer*
Stan Evans, *Controller*
▲ **EMP:** 14 **EST:** 1978
SQ FT: 8,689
SALES (est): 9.8MM **Privately Held**
WEB: www.woolseyco.com
SIC: 1382 1311 1321 Oil & gas exploration services; crude petroleum production; natural gas production; natural gasoline production

(G-16070)
WOOTEN PRINTING CO INC
239 N Handley St (67203-6021)
P.O. Box 1218 (67201-1218)
PHONE.................................316 265-8575
Gilbert L Wooten, *President*
Michael L Snapp, *Vice Pres*
EMP: 7
SQ FT: 6,400
SALES: 750K **Privately Held**
WEB: www.wootenprint.com
SIC: 2752 Commercial printing, offset

(G-16071)
WORD OF LIFE PRESCHOOL
3811 N Meridian Cir (67204-3438)
PHONE.................................316 838-5683
Rob Rotola, *Pastor*
Diana Fraser, *Director*
EMP: 23 **EST:** 2012
SALES (est): 825.4K **Privately Held**
SIC: 8351 Preschool center

(G-16072)
WORKFORCE ALLIANCE OF SOUTH
300 W Douglas Ave Ste 850 (67202-2922)
PHONE.................................316 771-6600
Chad Pettera, *COO*
Amanda Duncan, *Vice Pres*
Chad Pattera, *CFO*
Brooks Mantooth, *Human Res Dir*
Cari Warden, *Manager*
EMP: 58
SALES: 6.4MM **Privately Held**
WEB: www.workforce-ks.com
SIC: 8611 Business associations

(G-16073)
WORLD IMPACT INC
Also Called: Urban Ministries Institute
3701 E 13th St N Ofc Ofc (67208-2004)
PHONE.................................316 687-9398
Al Ewert, *Director*
EMP: 40
SALES (corp-wide): 10.3MM **Privately Held**
WEB: www.wiwichita.org
SIC: 8322 8661 8221 Youth center. Nondenominational church; theological seminary
PA: World Impact, Inc.
2001 S Vermont Ave
Los Angeles CA 90007
323 735-2867

(G-16074)
WPPA INC
Also Called: Kansas Prferred Providers Assn
1102 S Hillside St (67211-4004)
PHONE.................................316 683-4111
James Van Milligan, *CEO*
EMP: 13
SALES (est): 1MM **Privately Held**
SIC: 3825 Network analyzers

(G-16075)
WSM INDUSTRIES INC (HQ)
Also Called: Cardinal Supply & Mfg Co
1601 S Sheridan St (67213-1339)
PHONE.................................316 942-9412
Terry Moore, *CEO*
John Griffitt, *President*
Jim Harshfield, *Opers Mgr*
Karla Ellenz, *Human Res Dir*
Karla McGinnis, *Human Res Mgr*
◆ **EMP:** 120 **EST:** 1900
SQ FT: 150,000
SALES: 65MM **Privately Held**
WEB: www.wsm-industries.com
SIC: 5075 1761 Furnaces, warm air; air conditioning equipment, except room units; sheet metalwork
PA: Wsm Investments, Inc
1601 S Sheridan St
Wichita KS 67213
316 942-9412

(G-16076)
WSM INVESTMENTS INC (PA)
1601 S Sheridan St (67213-1339)
PHONE.................................316 942-9412
Terry Moore, *CEO*
John Griffith, *President*
EMP: 130
SQ FT: 95,000
SALES: 65MM **Privately Held**
SIC: 5075 1761 Furnaces, warm air; air conditioning equipment, except room units; sheet metalwork

(G-16077)
WSU SUNFLOWER NEWSPAPER
1845 Fairmount St 134 (67260-9700)
PHONE.................................316 978-6900
Glen Sharp, *Principal*
Nicole Stockdale, *Principal*
Leigh Jackson, *Manager*
Robbie Norton, *Manager*
EMP: 30
SALES (est): 1.8MM **Privately Held**
SIC: 2711 Newspapers, publishing & printing

(G-16078)
WURTH/SERVICE SUPPLY INC
3144 N Ohio St Ste A (67219-4104)
PHONE.................................316 869-2159
Brandon Fraiser, *Branch Mgr*
EMP: 18
SALES (corp-wide): 15.1B **Privately Held**
SIC: 5251 5085 Hardware; fasteners, industrial: nuts, bolts, screws, etc.
HQ: Wurth/Service Supply Inc
598 Chaney Ave
Greenwood IN 46143
317 704-1000

GEOGRAPHIC

(G-16079)
WW GRAINGER INC
Also Called: Grainger 920
1920 S West St (67213-1108)
PHONE..................................316 945-5101
Rick Weidman, *Manager*
EMP: 25
SQ FT: 17,500
SALES (corp-wide): 11.2B **Publicly Held**
WEB: www.grainger.com
SIC: 5084 5085 5063 Industrial machinery & equipment; industrial supplies; motors, electric
PA: W.W. Grainger, Inc.
100 Grainger Pkwy
Lake Forest IL 60045
847 535-1000

(G-16080)
WYNDHAM GARDEN
Also Called: Hotel
221 E Kellogg St (67202-3917)
PHONE..................................316 269-2090
EMP: 10
SALES (est): 340.2K **Privately Held**
SIC: 7011 Hotels

(G-16081)
WYNDHAM INTERNATIONAL INC
Also Called: Hawthorn Suites
2405 N Ridge Rd (67205-1076)
PHONE..................................316 729-5700
Heather Brown, *Manager*
EMP: 12 **Publicly Held**
SIC: 7011 Hotels & motels
HQ: Wyndham International, Inc
22 Sylvan Way
Parsippany NJ 07054
973 753-6000

(G-16082)
X TECH MIDWEST INC
2423 E 13th St N (67214-2101)
PHONE..................................316 777-6648
EMP: 5
SQ FT: 1,200
SALES (est): 519.7K **Privately Held**
SIC: 3661 3651 Mfg Telephone/Telegraph Apparatus Mfg Home Audio/Video Equipment

(G-16083)
X-PRESS SIGNS AND GRAPHICS LLC
5830 W Hendryx Ave (67209-2351)
PHONE..................................316 613-2360
Sandra Wright, *Principal*
Ron Canupp, *Business Dir*
EMP: 5
SALES (est): 603.5K **Privately Held**
SIC: 3993 Signs & advertising specialties

(G-16084)
XPO LOGISTICS FREIGHT INC
4330 W 29th St S (67215-1017)
PHONE..................................316 942-0498
Andy Beversdorf, *Manager*
Tim Welty, *Instructor*
EMP: 28
SALES (corp-wide): 17.2B **Publicly Held**
WEB: www.con-way.com
SIC: 4213 Contract haulers
HQ: Xpo Logistics Freight, Inc.
2211 Old Earhart Rd # 100
Ann Arbor MI 48105
800 755-2728

(G-16085)
YINGLING AIRCRAFT INC
Also Called: Yingling Aviation
2010 S Airport Rd (67209-1941)
P.O. Box 9248 (67277-0248)
PHONE..................................316 943-3246
Lynn Nichols, *President*
▲ **EMP:** 80 **EST:** 1946
SQ FT: 90,000
SALES (est): 39MM **Privately Held**
WEB: www.yinglingaviation.com
SIC: 5599 5088 4522 7359 Aircraft dealers; aircraft & space vehicle supplies & parts; aircraft & parts; flying charter service; aircraft rental; aircraft maintenance & repair services; aircraft fueling services

(G-16086)
YORK INTERNATIONAL CORPORATION
811 E 33rd St N (67219-4011)
P.O. Box 19014 (67204-9014)
PHONE..................................316 832-6400
Bob Sowler, *Manager*
EMP: 100 **Privately Held**
SIC: 3585 Compressors for refrigeration & air conditioning equipment
HQ: York International Corporation
631 S Richland Ave
York PA 17403
717 771-7890

(G-16087)
YORK INTERNATIONAL CORPORATION
3110 N Mead St (67219-4057)
P.O. Box 19014 (67204-9014)
PHONE..................................316 832-6300
Roland Dextradeur, *Branch Mgr*
EMP: 94 **Privately Held**
SIC: 3585 Refrigeration & heating equipment
HQ: York International Corporation
631 S Richland Ave
York PA 17403
717 771-7890

(G-16088)
YOST AUTO SERVICE
1818 E 2nd St N (67214-4207)
PHONE..................................316 264-8482
Russell Yost, *President*
EMP: 15
SALES (est): 1.9MM **Privately Held**
SIC: 7539 Automotive repair shops

(G-16089)
YOUNG BOGLE MCCAUSLAND WELLS
100 N Main St Ste 1001 (67202-3392)
PHONE..................................316 265-7841
Glenn Young, *Partner*
Patrick Blanchard, *Partner*
Jerry Bogle, *Partner*
Paul McCausland, *Partner*
William Wells, *Partner*
EMP: 15
SALES (est): 2.1MM **Privately Held**
SIC: 8111 General practice attorney, lawyer; general practice law office

(G-16090)
YOUNG ELECTRIC INC
3046 E 31st St S (67216-2702)
PHONE..................................316 681-8118
John P Young, *President*
Mr Denny Young, *Owner*
Sherry Young, *Vice Pres*
EMP: 20
SQ FT: 8,000
SALES: 3.7MM **Privately Held**
WEB: www.young-electric.com
SIC: 1731 8711 7389 General electrical contractor; electrical or electronic engineering; drafting service, except temporary help

(G-16091)
YOUNG MENS CHRISTIAN ASSOCIA
Also Called: YMCA
6940 W Newell St (67212-3379)
PHONE..................................316 942-2271
Nikki L Vancuren, *Controller*
Mike Jobe, *Exec Dir*
Jessica Rall, *Exec Dir*
Tyler Johnston, *Director*
EMP: 130
SALES (corp-wide): 44.6MM **Privately Held**
SIC: 8641 7991 Recreation association; physical fitness facilities
PA: The Young Men's Christian Association
Of Wichita Kansas
402 N Market St
Wichita KS 67202
316 219-9622

(G-16092)
YOUNG MENS CHRISTIAN ASSOCIA
Also Called: YMCA Farha Sport Centers
3405 S Meridian Ave (67217-2151)
PHONE..................................316 945-2255
Lianna Bodlak, *Prgrmr*
Sarah Berry, *Director*
Debbie Cruz, *Program Dir*
Autumm Rasmussen, *Admin Asst*
Sherry Henderson, *Training Spec*
EMP: 61
SALES (corp-wide): 44.6MM **Privately Held**
SIC: 8322 7997 Youth center; membership sports & recreation clubs
PA: The Young Men's Christian Association
Of Wichita Kansas
402 N Market St
Wichita KS 67202
316 219-9622

(G-16093)
YOUNG MENS CHRISTIAN ASSOCIA (PA)
Also Called: Greater Wichita YMCA
402 N Market St (67202-2012)
PHONE..................................316 219-9622
Ronn McMahon, *President*
Shelly Prichard, *Vice Pres*
Matt Prichard, *Maintenance Dir*
Larry Snapp, *Maintenance Dir*
Bill Schmitz, *CFO*
EMP: 113
SQ FT: 110,000
SALES: 44.6MM **Privately Held**
SIC: 8641 7991 8351 7032 Youth organizations; physical fitness facilities; child day care services; youth camps; individual & family services

(G-16094)
YOUNG MENS CHRISTIAN ASSOCIA
Also Called: Northwest YMCA
13838 W 21st St N (67235-9600)
PHONE..................................316 260-9622
Dennis Schoenebeck, *Executive Asst*
EMP: 64
SALES (est): 791.9K
SALES (corp-wide): 44.6MM **Privately Held**
SIC: 8641 7991 8351 7032 Youth organizations; physical fitness facilities; child day care services; youth camps; individual & family services
PA: The Young Men's Christian Association
Of Wichita Kansas
402 N Market St
Wichita KS 67202
316 219-9622

(G-16095)
YOUNG MENS CHRISTIAN ASSOCIA
Also Called: South YMCA
3405 S Meridian Ave (67217-2151)
PHONE..................................316 942-5511
Hillary Alexander, *Branch Mgr*
EMP: 150
SALES (corp-wide): 44.6MM **Privately Held**
SIC: 8641 7991 8351 7032 Youth organizations; physical fitness facilities; child day care services; youth camps; individual & family services
PA: The Young Men's Christian Association
Of Wichita Kansas
402 N Market St
Wichita KS 67202
316 219-9622

(G-16096)
YOUNG MENS CHRISTIAN ASSOCIAT
Also Called: East Branch YMCA Preschool
9333 E Douglas Ave (67207-1203)
PHONE..................................316 685-2251
Cherish Johnette, *Manager*
Jonathan Brewer, *Director*
Josh Whitson, *Director*
EMP: 125
SALES (corp-wide): 44.6MM **Privately Held**
SIC: 8641 8322 7991 8351 Youth organizations; youth center; health club; preschool center
PA: The Young Men's Christian Association
Of Wichita Kansas
402 N Market St
Wichita KS 67202
316 219-9622

(G-16097)
YOUNGER ENERGY COMPANY
9415 E Harry St Ste 403 (67207-5083)
PHONE..................................316 681-2542
Gary Younger, *President*
Diane Rebstock, *Exec VP*
London Younger, *Vice Pres*
EMP: 7
SQ FT: 3,600
SALES: 3.8MM **Privately Held**
WEB: www.wellevaluations.com
SIC: 1311 6792 Crude petroleum & natural gas production; oil leases, buying & selling on own account

(G-16098)
YOUTHVILLE FAMILY CNSLTN SVC
560 N Exposition St (67203-5902)
PHONE..................................316 264-8317
Randall M Class, *CEO*
EMP: 46
SQ FT: 3,400
SALES (est): 1MM **Privately Held**
WEB: www.youthville.org
SIC: 8322 Family (marriage) counseling

(G-16099)
YSIDRO TRUCKING INC
3760 S Broadway Ave (67216-1032)
PHONE..................................316 522-3716
Mark Ysidro, *Principal*
EMP: 11
SALES (est): 880K **Privately Held**
SIC: 1389 Excavating slush pits & cellars

(G-16100)
ZENITH DRILLING CORPORATION (PA)
1223 N Rock Rd Ste A200 (67206-1272)
P.O. Box 780428 (67278-0428)
PHONE..................................316 684-9777
C Robert Buford, *President*
Russell D Briggs, *Corp Secy*
EMP: 6
SQ FT: 4,500
SALES (est): 5MM **Privately Held**
WEB: www.zenithdrilling.com
SIC: 1381 1311 Drilling oil & gas wells; crude petroleum production; natural gas production

(G-16101)
ZEPICK CARDIOLOGY
630 S Hillside St (67211-2157)
PHONE..................................316 616-2020
Lyle Zepick, *Owner*
Tim Zepick, *Asst Office Mgr*
EMP: 25
SALES (est): 1.8MM **Privately Held**
SIC: 8011 Cardiologist & cardio-vascular specialist

(G-16102)
ZERNCO
2400 S Greenwich Rd (67210-1813)
PHONE..................................316 775-9991
Ashley Thill, *Principal*
Jeremy Riley, *Info Tech Mgr*
EMP: 60
SQ FT: 2,000
SALES (est): 33.1MM **Privately Held**
WEB: www.zernco.com
SIC: 1542 Commercial & office building, new construction

(G-16103)
ZIEGLER ELECTRIC SERVICE INC
1602 E 2nd St N (67214-4124)
PHONE..................................316 262-2842
Donald D Ziegler, *President*
Karyn C Ziegler, *Corp Secy*
EMP: 14

▲ = Import ▼=Export
◆ =Import/Export

SALES (est): 1.7MM **Privately Held**
WEB: www.zieglerelectric.com
SIC: 1731 General electrical contractor

Wilson
Ellsworth County

(G-16104)
BEVERLY ENTERPRISES-KANSAS LLC
Also Called: Wilson Nursing Home
611 31st St (67490-8740)
P.O. Box 160 (67490-0160)
PHONE..................................785 658-2505
Cherry Johnson, *Manager*
EMP: 43
SALES (corp-wide): 393.8MM **Privately Held**
SIC: 8051 Convalescent home with continuous nursing care
HQ: Beverly Enterprises-Kansas, Llc
1 1000 Beverly Way
Fort Smith AR 72919
479 201-2000

(G-16105)
GEORGE ESCHBAUGH ADVG INC
3946 205th Rd (67490)
P.O. Box 130 (67490-0130)
PHONE..................................785 658-2105
Stephen R Eschbaugh, *President*
EMP: 32 **EST:** 1954
SQ FT: 32,000
SALES (est): 2.8MM **Privately Held**
SIC: 3993 2759 2399 Signs & advertising specialties; decals: printing; banners, made from fabric

(G-16106)
GOLDEN LIVINGCENTER ROOM 132B
611 31st St (67490-8740)
PHONE..................................785 658-2505
EMP: 16 **EST:** 2008
SALES (est): 455.9K **Privately Held**
SIC: 8051 Skilled nursing care facilities

(G-16107)
WILSON COMMUNICATION CO INC
2504 Avenue D (67490-4203)
P.O. Box 190 (67490-0190)
PHONE..................................785 658-2111
Robert Grauer, *President*
EMP: 15
SALES (est): 1.3MM **Privately Held**
SIC: 4813 Telephone communication, except radio
PA: Wilson Telephone Company, Inc.
2504 Avenue D
Wilson KS 67490
785 658-2111

(G-16108)
WILSON STATE BANK (PA)
422 26th St (67490)
P.O. Box 129 (67490-0129)
PHONE..................................785 658-3441
Irv Mitchell, *President*
Diana Brooks, *Vice Pres*
EMP: 10 **EST:** 1886
SALES: 3.9MM **Privately Held**
SIC: 6022 State trust companies accepting deposits, commercial

(G-16109)
WILSON TELEPHONE COMPANY INC (PA)
2504 Avenue D (67490-4203)
P.O. Box 190 (67490-0190)
PHONE..................................785 658-2111
Scott Grauer, *President*
Robert Grauer, *Vice Pres*
EMP: 23 **EST:** 1943
SQ FT: 2,500
SALES (est): 1.3MM **Privately Held**
WEB: www.wilsontelephone.com
SIC: 4813 Local telephone communications

Winchester
Jefferson County

(G-16110)
JEFFERSON COUNTY MEM HOSP INC
Also Called: Jefferson County Geriatric Ctr
408 Delaware St (66097-4003)
PHONE..................................913 774-4340
Lamomt Cook, *CEO*
Sean Wilson, *Purch Dir*
David Schuler, *Engineer*
Christina Aranda, *Food Svc Dir*
EMP: 70 **EST:** 1952
SQ FT: 15,000
SALES: 4.8MM **Privately Held**
WEB: www.jcmhospital.org
SIC: 8062 8052 General medical & surgical hospitals; intermediate care facilities

(G-16111)
WINCHESTER MEAT PROCESSING
203 Winchester St (66097-4160)
P.O. Box R (66097-0417)
PHONE..................................913 774-2860
Edward Knoll, *President*
Angee Knoll, *Treasurer*
EMP: 5 **EST:** 1940
SQ FT: 3,600
SALES: 310K **Privately Held**
SIC: 2011 5421 4222 2013 Meat packing plants; meat markets, including freezer provisioners; warehousing, cold storage or refrigerated; sausages & other prepared meats

Windom
Mcpherson County

(G-16112)
KINDER MRGAN ENRGY PARTNERS LP
420 Us Highway 56 (67491-9309)
PHONE..................................620 834-2211
Alan Buckman, *Engineer*
John Suer, *Manager*
EMP: 18 **Publicly Held**
WEB: www.kindermorgan.com
SIC: 4613 Refined petroleum pipelines
HQ: Kinder Morgan Energy Partners, L.P.
1001 La St Ste 1000
Houston TX 77002
713 369-9000

Winfield
Cowley County

(G-16113)
3C HEALTHCARE INC
Also Called: Medicap Pharmacy
722 Wheat Rd (67156-3216)
PHONE..................................620 221-7850
Van G Coble, *President*
Jeannette L Coble, *Corp Secy*
EMP: 10
SQ FT: 800
SALES: 2.4MM **Privately Held**
SIC: 5912 8742 Drug stores; hospital & health services consultant

(G-16114)
ALBRIGHT INVESTMENT COMPANY (PA)
Also Called: Prudential
1603 Main St (67156-4931)
P.O. Box 642 (67156-0642)
PHONE..................................620 221-7653
Jeff Albright, *President*
Jeff Everhart, *Vice Pres*
Becky Jarvis-Long, *Agent*
Gwen Lumbert, *Agent*
EMP: 20
SQ FT: 3,290
SALES (est): 1.7MM **Privately Held**
SIC: 6531 6162 6411 Real estate agent, residential; appraiser, real estate; mortgage bankers; insurance agents, brokers & service

(G-16115)
AUTO TECHS FRAME & BODY REPAIR
2800 E 9th Ave (67156-3332)
PHONE..................................620 221-6616
Brian Perrigo, *Owner*
Judy Perrigo, *Office Mgr*
Scott Free, *Manager*
EMP: 10
SQ FT: 3,000
SALES (est): 748.1K **Privately Held**
WEB: www.autotechs.com
SIC: 7532 Body shop, automotive

(G-16116)
BARNS TIMBER CREEK B & B
14704 91st Rd (67156-6852)
PHONE..................................620 221-2797
Martin Rude, *Owner*
EMP: 6 **EST:** 2008
SALES (est): 536.2K **Privately Held**
SIC: 2411 Timber, cut at logging camp

(G-16117)
BTR INC
Also Called: Brian Thomas Robotics
620 Industrial Blvd (67156-9122)
PHONE..................................620 221-7071
Brain Pettey, *President*
Brian Pettey, *President*
EMP: 5
SALES (est): 529.3K **Privately Held**
SIC: 3999 Education aids, devices & supplies

(G-16118)
BUTLER BROS INC
2210 Simpson Ave (67156-2530)
PHONE..................................620 221-3570
Vaudene Butler, *President*
Donald Butler, *Corp Secy*
EMP: 11
SALES (est): 752.7K **Privately Held**
SIC: 1389 Oil field services; haulage, oil field

(G-16119)
BYIS MANUFACTURING LLC
318 Cedar Lane Dr (67156-8807)
PHONE..................................620 221-4603
Bradley W Young, *President*
William Young, *Vice Pres*
Riley Floyd, *Bookkeeper*
▲ **EMP:** 14
SALES (est): 6.7MM **Privately Held**
SIC: 3533 Water well drilling equipment

(G-16120)
CITY OF WINFIELD
Also Called: Power Plant
2801 E 12th St (67156)
P.O. Box 646 (67156-0646)
PHONE..................................620 221-5630
Pat McCuoghley, *Principal*
Jim Neal, *Production*
EMP: 12 **Privately Held**
WEB: www.wpl.org
SIC: 4911 Generation, electric power
PA: City Of Winfield
200 E 9th Ave
Winfield KS 67156
620 221-5520

(G-16121)
COCA-COLA BTLG OF WNFIELD KANS
1003 Industrial Blvd (67156-9131)
P.O. Box 730 (67156-0730)
PHONE..................................620 221-2710
Randy Mayo, *President*
Kenney Frazeir, *General Mgr*
Ron Hutto, *Manager*
EMP: 11
SQ FT: 14,000
SALES: 5MM **Privately Held**
SIC: 2086 Bottled & canned soft drinks

(G-16122)
COFFEYVILLE RESOURCES LLC
Also Called: Crude Transportation
3303 E 9th Ave (67156-3420)
PHONE..................................620 221-2107
EMP: 10
SALES (est): 813.5K
SALES (corp-wide): 5.4B **Publicly Held**
SIC: 1623 Water/Sewer/Utility Construction
PA: Cvr Energy, Inc.
2277 Plaza Dr Ste 500
Sugar Land TX 77479
281 207-3200

(G-16123)
COLUMBIA ELEV SOLUTIONS INC
7702 W 5th Ave (67156-7964)
PHONE..................................620 442-2510
L J Bliaotta, *President*
Thomas Hannah, *Engineer*
Jerry Williams, *CFO*
Jerre Williams, *Executive*
▲ **EMP:** 33
SQ FT: 80,000
SALES (est): 14.7MM
SALES (corp-wide): 34.5MM **Privately Held**
SIC: 5084 Elevators
PA: Columbia Elevator Products Co., Inc.
380 Horace St
Bridgeport CT 06610
914 937-7100

(G-16124)
COLUMBIA ELEVATOR PDTS CO INC
7702 Chester Fild Ind Par (67156)
PHONE..................................888 858-1558
EMP: 35
SALES (corp-wide): 18.1MM **Privately Held**
SIC: 3534 Mfg Elevators/Escalators
PA: Columbia Elevator Products Co., Inc.
380 Horace St
Bridgeport CT 06610
914 937-7100

(G-16125)
COMMUNITY HLTH CTR IN CWLEY CN
221 W 8th Ave (67156-2718)
P.O. Box 643 (67156-0643)
PHONE..................................620 221-3350
David Brazil, *CEO*
Carol Hearne, *Ch of Bd*
Melody Vaden, *CFO*
Curtis Freeland, *Treasurer*
Ben Hanne, *Admin Sec*
EMP: 16 **EST:** 2001
SQ FT: 5,010
SALES (est): 756.2K **Privately Held**
SIC: 8011 Primary care medical clinic

(G-16126)
COMMUNITY NATIONAL BANK
1112 Main St (67156-3609)
P.O. Box 637 (67156-0637)
PHONE..................................620 221-1400
Mike Selt, *Branch Mgr*
EMP: 12 **Privately Held**
SIC: 6022 State commercial banks
HQ: Community National Bank & Trust
14 N Lincoln Ave
Chanute KS 66720

(G-16127)
CONTROL COMPONENTS INC
Also Called: CCI Fluid Kinetics
1108 Industrial Blvd (67156-9132)
PHONE..................................620 221-2343
Hari Nair, *General Mgr*
Ann Henstridge, *Executive Asst*
EMP: 9
SALES (corp-wide): 2.5B **Privately Held**
WEB: www.ccivalve.com
SIC: 3612 3443 Transformers, except electric; industrial vessels, tanks & containers
HQ: Control Components Inc.
22591 Avenida Empresa
Rcho Sta Marg CA 92688
949 858-1877

GEOGRAPHIC

(G-16128)
COUNTY OF COWLEY
Also Called: Appraisers Office
311 E 9th Ave Rm 111 (67156-2843)
P.O. Box 641 (67156-0641)
PHONE..........620 221-5430
Greg Kent, *Principal*
EMP: 10 **Privately Held**
WEB: www.cowleycounty.org
SIC: 7389 Appraisers, except real estate
PA: County Of Cowley
311 E 9th Ave Rm 111
Winfield KS 67156
620 221-5400

(G-16129)
COWLEY CNTY MNTL HLTH & CNSLNG
22214 D St (67156-7376)
PHONE..........620 442-4540
Linda Young, *Exec Dir*
EMP: 67
SALES (est): 1.8MM **Privately Held**
WEB: www.ccmhcc.com
SIC: 8322 Individual & family services

(G-16130)
COWLEY COUNTY COUNCIL ON AGING
700 Gary St Ste C (67156-3137)
PHONE..........620 221-7020
Mary Woods, *Exec Dir*
EMP: 14
SALES: 448K **Privately Held**
SIC: 8322 4789 Senior citizens' center or association; cargo loading & unloading services

(G-16131)
COWLEY COUNTY CRIME STOPPERS
812 Millington St (67156-2840)
P.O. Box 40 (67156-0040)
PHONE..........620 221-7777
Frank Owens, *Manager*
EMP: 11
SALES (corp-wide): 1.9MM **Privately Held**
SIC: 8322 Individual & family services
PA: Cowley County Crime Stoppers
117 W Central Ave
Arkansas City KS 67005
620 442-7777

(G-16132)
COWLEY COUNTY CRIME STOPPERS
812 Millington St (67156-2840)
PHONE..........620 221-7777
Tom Nigh, *Branch Mgr*
EMP: 11
SALES (corp-wide): 1.9MM **Privately Held**
SIC: 4911 Electric services
PA: Cowley County Crime Stoppers
117 W Central Ave
Arkansas City KS 67005
620 442-7777

(G-16133)
COWLEY COUNTY JOINT BOARD HLTH (PA)
Also Called: Cowley County Health Dept
320 E 9th Ave Ste 2 (67156-2871)
PHONE..........620 221-1430
David Brazil, *Administration*
EMP: 18
SALES (est): 2.2MM **Privately Held**
SIC: 8621 Health association

(G-16134)
COWLEY COUNTY UNITED WAY INC
P.O. Box 447 (67156-0447)
PHONE..........620 221-9683
EMP: 12
SALES: 140.1K **Privately Held**
SIC: 8399 Social Services

(G-16135)
CREATIVE COMMUNITY LIVING OF E
1500 E 8th Ave Ste 201 (67156-3104)
PHONE..........620 221-9431
Linda Misasi, *Principal*
EMP: 10
SALES: 95.7K **Privately Held**
SIC: 8361 Residential care

(G-16136)
CREATIVE COMMUNITY LIVING S
1500 E 8th Ave Ste 201 (67156-3104)
PHONE..........620 221-1119
Sharon Bird, *President*
Betty Eastman, *Vice Pres*
Bill Medley, *Treasurer*
Linda Misasi, *Exec Dir*
EMP: 300
SQ FT: 7,300
SALES: 9.8MM **Privately Held**
SIC: 8361 Group foster home

(G-16137)
CUMBERNAULD VILLAGE INC
716 Tweed Ofc (67156-1596)
PHONE..........620 221-4141
George Mc Neish, *President*
Juan Andreas,
Bruce Blake,
Jill Long,
Roger Steffen,
EMP: 86
SQ FT: 57,812
SALES: 5.3MM **Privately Held**
SIC: 6513 8059 8052 8051 Retirement hotel operation; rest home, with health care; intermediate care facilities; skilled nursing care facilities

(G-16138)
DARCO INC
Also Called: Comfort Inn
3800 S Pike Rd (67156-8879)
PHONE..........620 221-7529
Darlene Coffey, *President*
EMP: 20
SALES (est): 696.9K **Privately Held**
SIC: 7011 7991 7997 Hotels & motels; physical fitness facilities; membership sports & recreation clubs

(G-16139)
DARLENE COFFEY
Also Called: Super 8 Motel
3803 S Pike Rd (67156-8872)
PHONE..........620 229-8888
Darlene Coffey, *President*
Bill Schlagel, *Owner*
Darlene Schlagel, *Owner*
EMP: 15
SALES (est): 405.5K **Privately Held**
SIC: 7011 Hotels & motels

(G-16140)
DCCCA INC
104 1/2 W 9th Ave Ste 503 (67156-2893)
PHONE..........620 670-2814
EMP: 16 **Privately Held**
SIC: 8093 Alcohol clinic, outpatient; drug clinic, outpatient
PA: Dccca, Inc.
3312 Clinton Pkwy
Lawrence KS

(G-16141)
FAMILY CARE CENTER
1305 E 19th Ave (67156-5201)
PHONE..........620 221-9500
Bryan K Dennett, *Partner*
Bryan Davis, *Partner*
EMP: 13 **EST:** 2008
SALES (est): 1.4MM **Privately Held**
SIC: 8011 General & family practice, physician/surgeon

(G-16142)
GALAXIE BUSINESS EQUIPMENT INC
913 Main St (67156-3604)
PHONE..........620 221-3469
Nathan S French, *President*
Trudy French, *Corp Secy*
Milton Konstantinidis, *Vice Pres*
Lindsay French, *Mktg Dir*
Judy Flock, *Office Mgr*
EMP: 25
SQ FT: 6,500
SALES: 2.7MM **Privately Held**
WEB: www.gbeinc.com
SIC: 5999 7371 5712 5734 Business machines & equipment; computer software systems analysis & design, custom; furniture stores; modems, monitors, terminals & disk drives: computers

(G-16143)
GALAXY TECHNOLOGIES INC
1111 Industrial Blvd (67156-9133)
PHONE..........620 221-6262
Jim Schuster, *Ch of Bd*
John Boyington Jr, *President*
Paul Maples, *Senior VP*
Mike Kelly, *VP Opers*
Wanda Mc Cullough, *Purch Agent*
▲ **EMP:** 200
SQ FT: 166,000
SALES: 30MM **Privately Held**
WEB: www.galaxytool.com
SIC: 3544 Special dies, tools, jigs & fixtures

(G-16144)
GOTTLOB LAWN & LANDSCAPE LLC
5001 E 9th Ave (67156-3435)
PHONE..........620 222-8870
Alex E Gottlob, *Mng Member*
EMP: 20
SALES (est): 125.9K **Privately Held**
SIC: 0782 Lawn care services

(G-16145)
GREIF INC
7604 Railroad Ave (67156-7327)
PHONE..........620 221-2330
Shawn David, *Plant Mgr*
Becca Talbert, *Safety Mgr*
Darrell Trachsel, *Opers-Prdtn-Mfg*
EMP: 40
SALES (corp-wide): 4.6B **Publicly Held**
WEB: www.greif.com
SIC: 5199 Packaging materials
PA: Greif, Inc.
425 Winter Rd
Delaware OH 43015
740 549-6000

(G-16146)
HEALTH PROFESSIONALS WINFIELD
1230 E 6th Ave Ste 1b (67156-3144)
PHONE..........620 221-4000
Wade Turner, *Owner*
Norma Perkins, *Manager*
Richard James, *Podiatrist*
Patrick Bloedel, *Surgeon*
EMP: 12
SALES (est): 739.1K **Privately Held**
SIC: 8011 Internal medicine, physician/surgeon

(G-16147)
HOSPICE INCORPORATED
206 E 9th Ave Ste 1 (67156-2898)
PHONE..........620 229-8398
Harry Hynes, *Branch Mgr*
EMP: 24
SALES (corp-wide): 18.1MM **Privately Held**
SIC: 8052 Personal care facility
PA: Hospice, Incorporated
313 S Market St
Wichita KS 67202
316 265-9441

(G-16148)
HUSKY LINERS INC
22425 D St Strother Fld (67156)
P.O. Box 839 (67156-0839)
PHONE..........620 221-2268
William Reminder, *President*
Kelly Kneifl, *COO*
Jim Bresingham, *CFO*
Maria Zwas, *Admin Sec*
EMP: 100
SQ FT: 167,000
SALES (est): 31.3MM
SALES (corp-wide): 255.3MM **Privately Held**
WEB: www.huskyliners.com
SIC: 3714 Motor vehicle parts & accessories
HQ: Tectum Holdings, Inc.
5400 Data Ct
Ann Arbor MI 48108
734 677-0444

(G-16149)
INTERSKATE 77
515 Main St (67156-2105)
PHONE..........620 229-7655
EMP: 10
SALES: 60K **Privately Held**
SIC: 7999 Amusement/Recreation Services

(G-16150)
JOHN SCHMIDT & SONS INC
2303 W 9th Ave (67156-8907)
PHONE..........620 221-0300
Earry Schmidt, *Manager*
EMP: 15
SALES (est): 1.3MM
SALES (corp-wide): 12.5MM **Privately Held**
SIC: 5083 Agricultural machinery & equipment
PA: John Schmidt & Sons, Inc.
12903 E Silver Lake Rd
Mount Hope KS 67108
316 445-2103

(G-16151)
KANSAS SPECIALTY SERVICES INC
Also Called: Specialty Home Healthcare
814 Main St (67156-2835)
PHONE..........620 221-6040
Ray Clayton, *President*
Teresa Waits, *Vice Pres*
Linda Triplett, *Admin Sec*
EMP: 15 **EST:** 1996
SQ FT: 100,000
SALES (est): 750K **Privately Held**
WEB: www.ksscustom.com
SIC: 5999 8049 5047 3842 Medical apparatus & supplies; occupational therapist; medical equipment & supplies; orthopedic appliances

(G-16152)
KINGS ALCOHOL & DRUG
2720 E 12th Ave (67156-4114)
PHONE..........620 221-6252
Richard Gilchrist, *Exec Dir*
Patricia Gallarda, *Director*
EMP: 23
SALES: 950K **Privately Held**
SIC: 8093 Alcohol clinic, outpatient; drug clinic, outpatient

(G-16153)
KLINE MOTORS INC
Also Called: Ford Lincoln Mercury
1721 Main St (67156-4933)
P.O. Box 737 (67156-0737)
PHONE..........620 221-2040
Patrick A Biddle, *CEO*
Kristi Briddle, *Co-Owner*
EMP: 19
SQ FT: 13,500
SALES (est): 5.3MM **Privately Held**
WEB: www.klinemotors.kscoxmail.com
SIC: 5511 7538 Automobiles, new & used; general automotive repair shops

(G-16154)
LANDSCAPE OUTFITTERS LLC
20480 81st Rd (67156-7295)
PHONE..........620 221-1108
George Snouffer, *Mng Member*
Doreen Johnson,
EMP: 14
SALES (est): 2.5MM **Privately Held**
SIC: 5083 5261 7342 0181 Lawn & garden machinery & equipment; nurseries; pest control services; ornamental nursery products; landscape contractors

(G-16155)
LEGACY COMMUNITY FOUNDATION
Also Called: Legacy Rgonal Cmnty Foundation
1216 Main St (67156-4323)
P.O. Box 713 (67156-0713)
PHONE..........620 221-7224
Pamela Moore, *Director*

▲ = Import ▼=Export
◆ =Import/Export

EMP: 12
SALES: 816.4K **Privately Held**
SIC: 8699 Charitable organization

(G-16156)
MARTIN LUTHER HOMES KANSAS INC
Also Called: Mosaic
2120 E 9th Ave (67156-3318)
PHONE....................................620 229-8702
Sheryl Koman, *Manager*
EMP: 80 **Privately Held**
SIC: 8059 8361 8322 8052 Home for the mentally retarded, exc. skilled or intermediate; residential care; individual & family services; intermediate care facilities
PA: Martin Luther Homes Of Kansas, Inc.
650 J St Ste 305
Lincoln NE

(G-16157)
MATERIAL MANAGEMENT INC
2016 Country Club Rd (67156-6335)
P.O. Box 842 (67156-0842)
PHONE....................................620 221-9060
Robert Steven Ruud, *Principal*
Rolland Hovey, *Vice Pres*
EMP: 15
SALES (est): 954.3K **Privately Held**
SIC: 8741 Management services

(G-16158)
MAXIDIZE PRODUCTION SVCS LLC
12885 132nd Rd (67156-7736)
P.O. Box 542 (67156-0542)
PHONE....................................620 222-1235
Kenneth B Bunch, *Mng Member*
Misty Bunch, *Manager*
EMP: 8 **EST:** 2007
SALES: 900K **Privately Held**
SIC: 1389 2899 Acidizing wells; chemically treating wells; chemical preparations

(G-16159)
MORTON BUILDINGS INC
7748 7th Ave (67156-7319)
PHONE....................................620 221-4180
Joel Hasse, *Project Mgr*
Larry Modrynski, *Project Mgr*
John Cain, *Engineer*
EMP: 72
SALES (corp-wide): 463.7MM **Privately Held**
WEB: www.mortonbuildings.com
SIC: 3448 5039 Buildings, portable: prefabricated metal; prefabricated structures
PA: Morton Buildings, Inc.
252 W Adams St
Morton IL 61550
800 447-7436

(G-16160)
MORTON BUILDINGS INC
7866 7th Ave (67156-7316)
P.O. Box 194 (67156-0194)
PHONE....................................620 221-3265
Mike Legako, *Business Mgr*
Jeff Bonebrake, *Branch Mgr*
EMP: 12
SALES (corp-wide): 463.7MM **Privately Held**
WEB: www.mortonbuildings.com
SIC: 3448 Buildings, portable: prefabricated metal
PA: Morton Buildings, Inc.
252 W Adams St
Morton IL 61550
800 447-7436

(G-16161)
MOSAIC
2120 E 9th Ave (67156-3318)
PHONE....................................620 229-8702
Don Ziegler, *Exec Dir*
EMP: 99
SALES (corp-wide): 257.7MM **Privately Held**
SIC: 8741 Administrative management
PA: Mosaic
4980 S 118th St
Omaha NE 68137
402 896-3884

(G-16162)
NEWTON WILLIAM MEMORIAL HOSP
1305 E 5th Ave (67156-2406)
PHONE....................................620 221-2916
Randy Mayo, *Branch Mgr*
EMP: 11
SALES (est): 318.6K
SALES (corp-wide): 36.1MM **Privately Held**
SIC: 8082 Home health care services
PA: Newton William Memorial Hospital
1300 E 5th Ave
Winfield KS 67156
620 221-2300

(G-16163)
NEWTON WILLIAM MEMORIAL HOSP (PA)
Also Called: W N H
1300 E 5th Ave (67156-2407)
PHONE....................................620 221-2300
Jason Tauke, *Med Doctor*
Micah Norris, *CIO*
Cindy Cline, *Director*
Barbara Humpert, *Director*
Randy Mayo, *Director*
EMP: 303
SQ FT: 103,733
SALES: 36.1MM **Privately Held**
SIC: 8062 General medical & surgical hospitals

(G-16164)
NORTON ENTERPRISES
3221 Central Ave (67156-9153)
PHONE....................................620 221-1987
Jerry W Norton, *Owner*
EMP: 7
SQ FT: 6,300
SALES: 520.6K **Privately Held**
SIC: 2759 Screen printing

(G-16165)
PRAY BUILDING STONE INC
Also Called: Pray Stone
1000 Industrial Blvd (67156-9130)
PHONE....................................620 221-7422
Ron W Pray, *President*
Cindy Pray, *Admin Sec*
EMP: 10
SQ FT: 7,000
SALES (est): 1.1MM **Privately Held**
WEB: www.praystoneco.com
SIC: 5032 Building stone

(G-16166)
PRECISION PALLET
15665 Us Highway 77 (67156-6732)
PHONE....................................620 221-4066
Justin Broom, *President*
Kimberly Broom, *Corp Secy*
EMP: 5
SALES: 1MM **Privately Held**
SIC: 2448 Pallets, wood & wood with metal

(G-16167)
PREFERRED FMLY HEALTHCARE INC
2720 E 12th Ave (67156-4114)
PHONE....................................620 221-6252
Sherry Gilchrist, *Owner*
EMP: 14 **Privately Held**
SIC: 8099 Childbirth preparation clinic
PA: Preferred Family Healthcare, Incorporated
900 E Laharpe St
Kirksville MO 63501

(G-16168)
RES-CARE INC
Also Called: Southwind Residential Services
317 N Viking Blvd (67156-2507)
P.O. Box 727 (67156-0727)
PHONE....................................620 221-4112
Shari Wampler, *Manager*
EMP: 125
SALES (corp-wide): 2B **Privately Held**
WEB: www.rescare.com
SIC: 8082 Home health care services
HQ: Res-Care, Inc.
805 N Whittington Pkwy
Louisville KY 40222
502 394-2100

(G-16169)
RISK COUNSELORS INC
Also Called: Nationwide
808 Millington St (67156-2840)
P.O. Box 293 (67156-0293)
PHONE....................................620 221-1760
Sharon Handlin, *President*
James Buterbaugh, *Vice Pres*
Monica Hidde, *Agent*
EMP: 13
SQ FT: 3,600
SALES (est): 2.9MM **Privately Held**
WEB: www.buterbaughandhandlin.com
SIC: 6411 6531 Insurance agents; real estate brokers & agents

(G-16170)
ROBOTZONE LLC
3850 E 12th Ave (67156-4103)
PHONE....................................620 221-7071
Brian Pettey, *Principal*
▲ **EMP:** 6
SALES (est): 1.1MM **Privately Held**
WEB: www.robotzone.com
SIC: 3569 Robots, assembly line: industrial & commercial

(G-16171)
S AND Y INDUSTRIES INC
606 Industrial Blvd (67156-9122)
P.O. Box 394 (67156-0394)
PHONE....................................620 221-4001
Sandy Foust, *President*
Gary Foust, *President*
Matt Miers, *Business Mgr*
Dan Foust, *Exec VP*
Amanda Jacobs, *Project Mgr*
▲ **EMP:** 110
SQ FT: 50,000
SALES: 16MM **Privately Held**
WEB: www.sandyindustries.com
SIC: 3672 3679 Printed circuit boards; harness assemblies for electronic use: wire or cable

(G-16172)
SOURCE ONE DISTRIBUTORS INC
511 Industrial Blvd (67156-9121)
P.O. Box 701 (67156-0701)
PHONE....................................620 221-8919
Randy Cates, *President*
EMP: 13
SQ FT: 5,100
SALES (est): 3.4MM **Privately Held**
SIC: 5063 Electrical apparatus & equipment

(G-16173)
SOUTH KANSAS AND OKLA RR INC
Also Called: Watco Co
314 E 6th Ave (67156-2804)
PHONE....................................620 221-3470
Anthony Rogers, *Manager*
EMP: 10
SALES (corp-wide): 997.9MM **Privately Held**
SIC: 4011 4013 Railroads, line-haul operating; switching & terminal services
HQ: South Kansas And Oklahoma Railroad, Inc.
315 W 3rd St
Pittsburg KS 66762

(G-16174)
SOUTHERN KANSAS COTTON GROWERS
19493 51st Rd (67156-7013)
PHONE....................................620 221-1370
Gary Feist, *General Mgr*
Carlitos Torres, *Office Mgr*
EMP: 10
SALES: 3.5MM **Privately Held**
SIC: 0724 Cotton ginning

(G-16175)
STEPHENSON EDWARD B & CO CPA
1002 Main St (67156-3607)
P.O. Box 743 (67156-0743)
PHONE....................................620 221-9320
Loren Pontious, *Managing Prtnr*
EMP: 14
SALES (est): 818.1K **Privately Held**
SIC: 8721 Certified public accountant

(G-16176)
SUNSHINE DAY CARE LLC
19789 81st Rd (67156-7396)
PHONE....................................620 221-1177
Fran Bartlett, *Director*
Sarah Hutchinson, *Hlthcr Dir*
EMP: 15
SQ FT: 4,800
SALES (est): 300.2K **Privately Held**
SIC: 8351 Group day care center

(G-16177)
UNION STATE BANK
823 Main St (67156-2834)
PHONE....................................620 221-3040
Michael Niederee, *Principal*
EMP: 19 **Privately Held**
SIC: 6022 State commercial banks
HQ: Union State Bank
127 S Summit St
Arkansas City KS 67005
620 442-5200

(G-16178)
VECTOR TECHNOLOGIES INC
Also Called: Vector Tooling Technologies
22245 C St (67156-7371)
P.O. Box 753 (67156-0753)
PHONE....................................620 262-2700
Stephen Sutton, *President*
EMP: 47
SALES: 7.7MM **Privately Held**
SIC: 3544 Special dies & tools

(G-16179)
WEBSTER COMBUSTION TECH LLC
619 Industrial Blvd (67156-9123)
PHONE....................................620 221-7464
Mark Wehmeier, *Vice Pres*
▲ **EMP:** 76
SALES (est): 21.4MM
SALES (corp-wide): 31.3MM **Privately Held**
WEB: www.webster-engineering.com
SIC: 3433 Heating equipment, except electric
HQ: Selas Heat Technology Co Llc
11012 Aurora Hudson Rd
Streetsboro OH 44241
800 523-6500

(G-16180)
WESTERN INDS PLASTIC PDTS LLC
7727 1st Ave (67156-7709)
PHONE....................................620 221-9464
Richard Haueter, *CEO*
Gage Hotchkiss, *CFO*
Mark Hanna,
EMP: 225
SALES (est): 9.9MM
SALES (corp-wide): 538.2K **Privately Held**
SIC: 3089 Blow molded finished plastic products
PA: Ljc Investments Iv, Llc
116 W Jones St
Savannah GA 31401
912 472-0300

(G-16181)
WESTERN INDUSTRIES INC
Ksq Division
1st & B Sts (67156)
P.O. Box 746 (67156-0746)
PHONE....................................620 221-9464
Joe Messina, *General Mgr*
Doug Hovey, *Maintence Staff*
EMP: 160 **Privately Held**
WEB: www.westernind.com
SIC: 3089 Blow molded finished plastic products
HQ: Western Industries, Inc.
1111 Wheeling Rd
Wheeling IL 60090

(G-16182)
WESTROCK DSPENSING SYSTEMS INC
Also Called: Mwv Calmar Plant
3719 E 12th Ave (67156-4179)
PHONE..................................620 229-5000
Ron Malawy, *President*
EMP: 227
SALES (corp-wide): 18.2B **Publicly Held**
WEB: www.meadwestvaco.com
SIC: 3089 Plastic containers, except foam
HQ: Westrock Dispensing Systems, Inc.
11901 Grandview Rd
Grandview MO 64030
816 986-6000

(G-16183)
WINFIELD AREA E M S
1300 E 5th Ave (67156-2407)
PHONE..................................620 221-2300
EMP: 28
SALES (est): 684.9K **Privately Held**
SIC: 7363 Emergency Medical Services

(G-16184)
WINFIELD AREA HBTAT FOR HMNITY
1004 Clyde (67156-1520)
P.O. Box 335 (67156-0335)
PHONE..................................620 221-7298
Mike Wacker, *President*
EMP: 30
SALES: 60.2K **Privately Held**
SIC: 8399 Social change association

(G-16185)
WINFIELD COUNTRY CLUB
2916 Country Club Rd (67156-6343)
P.O. Box 501 (67156-0501)
PHONE..................................620 221-1570
Craig King, *President*
EMP: 25
SALES: 519.8K **Privately Held**
SIC: 7997 Country club, membership

(G-16186)
WINFIELD MEDICAL ARTS PA
3625 Quail Ridge Rd (67156-8881)
PHONE..................................620 221-6100
John M Winblad, *President*
J K Winblad MD, *Vice Pres*
C C Samuel MD, *Admin Sec*
EMP: 30
SQ FT: 12,000
SALES: 2.1MM **Privately Held**
SIC: 8011 General & family practice, physician/surgeon

(G-16187)
WINFIELD MOTOR COMPANY INC (PA)
1901 Main St (67156-5417)
P.O. Box 629 (67156-0629)
PHONE..................................620 221-2840
Larry Raber, *President*
P John Eck, *Corp Secy*
EMP: 20
SQ FT: 14,000
SALES (est): 5.6MM **Privately Held**
WEB: www.winfieldmotor.com
SIC: 5511 7538 Automobiles, new & used; general automotive repair shops

(G-16188)
WINFIELD PLUMBING & HEATING
Also Called: Honeywell Authorized Dealer
1910 Wheat Rd (67156-5334)
P.O. Box 625 (67156-0625)
PHONE..................................620 221-2210
Jim Lawrence, *CEO*
Diane Lawrence, *Treasurer*
EMP: 12 **EST:** 1952
SQ FT: 11,000
SALES (est): 1.9MM **Privately Held**
SIC: 1711 Plumbing contractors; warm air heating & air conditioning contractor

(G-16189)
WINFIELD PUBLISHING CO INC
Also Called: Winfield Daily Courier
201 E 9th Ave (67156-2817)
P.O. Box 543 (67156-0543)
PHONE..................................620 221-1100
Frederick D Seaton, *President*
Christie Lynes, *Prdtn Mgr*
EMP: 36
SQ FT: 21,000
SALES (est): 2.3MM **Privately Held**
SIC: 2711 2752 Job printing & newspaper publishing combined; commercial printing, lithographic

(G-16190)
WINFIELD REST HAVEN INC
1611 Ritchie St (67156-5299)
PHONE..................................620 221-9290
Rita Endurude, *Director*
Pam McDade, *Director*
Vicki Sims, *Hlthcr Dir*
Ola Utt, *Administration*
EMP: 50
SQ FT: 7,500
SALES: 3.2MM **Privately Held**
SIC: 8059 Nursing home, except skilled & intermediate care facility

(G-16191)
WINFIELD WALNUT KS LLC
1201 Menor St (67156-4242)
PHONE..................................216 520-1250
Frank Sinito,
EMP: 99 **EST:** 2015
SALES (est): 954.8K **Privately Held**
SIC: 6513 Apartment building operators

(G-16192)
ZEECO INC
Also Called: Reliable Power Products Group
22695 D St Strother Fld (67156)
PHONE..................................620 705-5100
Ken Capps, *Branch Mgr*
EMP: 20 **Privately Held**
SIC: 2295 Metallizing of fabrics
HQ: Zeeco, Inc.
22151 E 91st St S
Broken Arrow OK 74014
918 258-8551

Wright
Ford County

(G-16193)
PRAXAIR INC
11547 Us Highway 50 (67882-9510)
PHONE..................................620 225-1368
Gayen Fribell, *Branch Mgr*
EMP: 5 **Privately Held**
SIC: 2813 Carbon dioxide; dry ice, carbon dioxide (solid)
HQ: Praxair, Inc.
10 Riverview Dr
Danbury CT 06810
203 837-2000

(G-16194)
RIGHT COOPERATIVE ASSOCIATION
Also Called: R C A
10881 Main St (67882-9500)
PHONE..................................620 227-8611
Kyle Eberlee, *CEO*
EMP: 40
SQ FT: 2,000
SALES (est): 29.4MM **Privately Held**
SIC: 5153 5541 2875 Grains; filling stations, gasoline; fertilizers, mixing only

Yates Center
Woodson County

(G-16195)
DESERET HLTH RHAB AT YATES LLC
801 S Fry St (66783-1640)
PHONE..................................620 625-2111
Jon Robertson, *Principal*
EMP: 50
SALES (est): 2.4MM **Privately Held**
SIC: 8051 Convalescent home with continuous nursing care

Yoder
Reno County

(G-16196)
WAGGONER ENTERPRISES INC
Also Called: Yoder Meats
3509 E Switzer Rd (67585)
P.O. Box 93 (67585-0093)
PHONE..................................620 465-3807
Allan Wagoner, *President*
Carol Wagoner, *Corp Secy*
Pam Allender, *Finance Mgr*
EMP: 22
SQ FT: 9,800
SALES (est): 4MM **Privately Held**
SIC: 4222 2011 5421 2013 Storage, frozen or refrigerated goods; meat packing plants; meat & fish markets; sausages & other prepared meats

SIC INDEX

Standard Industrial Classification Alphabetical Index

SIC NO *PRODUCT*

A

3291 Abrasive Prdts
6321 Accident & Health Insurance
8721 Accounting, Auditing & Bookkeeping Svcs
2891 Adhesives & Sealants
7322 Adjustment & Collection Svcs
7311 Advertising Agencies
7319 Advertising, NEC
3563 Air & Gas Compressors
3585 Air Conditioning & Heating Eqpt
4513 Air Courier Svcs
4522 Air Transportation, Nonscheduled
4512 Air Transportation, Scheduled
3721 Aircraft
3724 Aircraft Engines & Engine Parts
3728 Aircraft Parts & Eqpt, NEC
4581 Airports, Flying Fields & Terminal Svcs
2812 Alkalies & Chlorine
3363 Aluminum Die Castings
3354 Aluminum Extruded Prdts
3365 Aluminum Foundries
3483 Ammunition, Large
7999 Amusement & Recreation Svcs, NEC
7996 Amusement Parks
3826 Analytical Instruments
0291 Animal Production, NEC
0279 Animal Specialties, NEC
0752 Animal Specialty Svcs, Exc Veterinary
2077 Animal, Marine Fats & Oils
8422 Arboreta, Botanical & Zoological Gardens
3446 Architectural & Ornamental Metal Work
8712 Architectural Services
7694 Armature Rewinding Shops
3292 Asbestos products
2952 Asphalt Felts & Coatings
3822 Automatic Temperature Controls
3581 Automatic Vending Machines
7521 Automobile Parking Lots & Garages
5012 Automobiles & Other Motor Vehicles Wholesale
7533 Automotive Exhaust System Repair Shops
7536 Automotive Glass Replacement Shops
7539 Automotive Repair Shops, NEC
3465 Automotive Stampings
7549 Automotive Svcs, Except Repair & Car Washes
7537 Automotive Transmission Repair Shops
2396 Automotive Trimmings, Apparel Findings, Related Prdts

B

2673 Bags: Plastics, Laminated & Coated
2674 Bags: Uncoated Paper & Multiwall
3562 Ball & Roller Bearings
7929 Bands, Orchestras, Actors & Entertainers
7241 Barber Shops
7231 Beauty Shops
0211 Beef Cattle Feedlots
0212 Beef Cattle, Except Feedlots
5181 Beer & Ale Wholesale
2836 Biological Prdts, Exc Diagnostic Substances
1221 Bituminous Coal & Lignite: Surface Mining
2782 Blankbooks & Looseleaf Binders
3312 Blast Furnaces, Coke Ovens, Steel & Rolling Mills
3564 Blowers & Fans
3732 Boat Building & Repairing
3452 Bolts, Nuts, Screws, Rivets & Washers
2732 Book Printing, Not Publishing
2789 Bookbinding
5192 Books, Periodicals & Newspapers Wholesale
2731 Books: Publishing & Printing
3131 Boot & Shoe Cut Stock & Findings
7933 Bowling Centers
2051 Bread, Bakery Prdts Exc Cookies & Crackers
3251 Brick & Structural Clay Tile
5032 Brick, Stone & Related Construction Mtrls Wholesale
1622 Bridge, Tunnel & Elevated Hwy Construction
3991 Brooms & Brushes
7349 Building Cleaning & Maintenance Svcs, NEC
4142 Bus Charter Service, Except Local
4173 Bus Terminal & Svc Facilities
8611 Business Associations
8748 Business Consulting Svcs, NEC
7389 Business Svcs, NEC
2021 Butter

SIC NO *PRODUCT*

C

4841 Cable & Other Pay TV Svcs
3578 Calculating & Accounting Eqpt
2064 Candy & Confectionery Prdts
2033 Canned Fruits, Vegetables & Preserves
2032 Canned Specialties
2394 Canvas Prdts
7542 Car Washes
3624 Carbon & Graphite Prdts
2895 Carbon Black
3955 Carbon Paper & Inked Ribbons
3592 Carburetors, Pistons, Rings & Valves
1751 Carpentry Work
7217 Carpet & Upholstery Cleaning
2273 Carpets & Rugs
0119 Cash Grains, NEC
3241 Cement, Hydraulic
6553 Cemetery Subdividers & Developers
2043 Cereal Breakfast Foods
2022 Cheese
1479 Chemical & Fertilizer Mining
2899 Chemical Preparations, NEC
5169 Chemicals & Allied Prdts, NEC Wholesale
8351 Child Day Care Svcs
3262 China, Table & Kitchen Articles
2066 Chocolate & Cocoa Prdts
8641 Civic, Social & Fraternal Associations
3255 Clay Refractories
5052 Coal & Other Minerals & Ores Wholesale
1241 Coal Mining Svcs
3479 Coating & Engraving, NEC
2095 Coffee
7215 Coin Operated Laundries & Cleaning
7993 Coin-Operated Amusement Devices & Arcades
4939 Combination Utilities, NEC
7336 Commercial Art & Graphic Design
6029 Commercial Banks, NEC
8732 Commercial Economic, Sociological & Educational Research
5046 Commercial Eqpt, NEC Wholesale
3582 Commercial Laundry, Dry Clean & Pressing Mchs
7335 Commercial Photography
8731 Commercial Physical & Biological Research
2759 Commercial Printing
2754 Commercial Printing: Gravure
2752 Commercial Printing: Lithographic
3646 Commercial, Indl & Institutional Lighting Fixtures
6221 Commodity Contracts Brokers & Dealers
4899 Communication Svcs, NEC
3669 Communications Eqpt, NEC
7376 Computer Facilities Management Svcs
7373 Computer Integrated Systems Design
7378 Computer Maintenance & Repair
3577 Computer Peripheral Eqpt, NEC
7379 Computer Related Svcs, NEC
7377 Computer Rental & Leasing
3572 Computer Storage Devices
3575 Computer Terminals
5045 Computers & Peripheral Eqpt & Software Wholesale
3271 Concrete Block & Brick
3272 Concrete Prdts
1771 Concrete Work
5145 Confectionery Wholesale
5082 Construction & Mining Mach & Eqpt Wholesale
3531 Construction Machinery & Eqpt
5039 Construction Materials, NEC Wholesale
1442 Construction Sand & Gravel
2679 Converted Paper Prdts, NEC
3535 Conveyors & Eqpt
2052 Cookies & Crackers
3366 Copper Foundries
2298 Cordage & Twine
0115 Corn
2653 Corrugated & Solid Fiber Boxes
3961 Costume Jewelry & Novelties
0131 Cotton
2261 Cotton Fabric Finishers
0724 Cotton Ginning
2211 Cotton, Woven Fabric
4215 Courier Svcs, Except Air
6159 Credit Institutions, Misc Business
6153 Credit Institutions, Short-Term Business
7323 Credit Reporting Svcs

SIC NO *PRODUCT*

0191 Crop Farming, Misc
0722 Crop Harvesting By Machine
0723 Crop Preparation, Except Cotton Ginning
1311 Crude Petroleum & Natural Gas
4612 Crude Petroleum Pipelines
1423 Crushed & Broken Granite
1422 Crushed & Broken Limestone
1429 Crushed & Broken Stone, NEC
3643 Current-Carrying Wiring Devices
2391 Curtains & Draperies
3087 Custom Compounding Of Purchased Plastic Resins
7371 Custom Computer Programming Svcs
3281 Cut Stone Prdts
3421 Cutlery
2865 Cyclic-Crudes, Intermediates, Dyes & Org Pigments

D

0241 Dairy Farms
5143 Dairy Prdts, Except Dried Or Canned Wholesale
7911 Dance Studios, Schools & Halls
7374 Data & Computer Processing & Preparation
0175 Deciduous Tree Fruits
4424 Deep Sea Domestic Transportation Of Freight
4412 Deep Sea Foreign Transportation Of Freight
3843 Dental Eqpt & Splys
8072 Dental Laboratories
7381 Detective & Armored Car Svcs
2835 Diagnostic Substances
2675 Die-Cut Paper & Board
3544 Dies, Tools, Jigs, Fixtures & Indl Molds
1411 Dimension Stone
7331 Direct Mail Advertising Svcs
7342 Disinfecting & Pest Control Svcs
2047 Dog & Cat Food
2591 Drapery Hardware, Window Blinds & Shades
2034 Dried Fruits, Vegetables & Soup
1381 Drilling Oil & Gas Wells
7833 Drive-In Motion Picture Theaters
5122 Drugs, Drug Proprietaries & Sundries Wholesale
7216 Dry Cleaning Plants, Except Rug Cleaning
5099 Durable Goods: NEC Wholesale

E

6732 Education, Religious & Charitable Trusts
4931 Electric & Other Svcs Combined
3634 Electric Household Appliances
3641 Electric Lamps
4911 Electric Svcs
7629 Electrical & Elex Repair Shop, NEC
5064 Electrical Appliances, TV & Radios Wholesale
3694 Electrical Eqpt For Internal Combustion Engines
3629 Electrical Indl Apparatus, NEC
3699 Electrical Machinery, Eqpt & Splys, NEC
1731 Electrical Work
5063 Electrl Apparatus, Eqpt, Wiring Splys Wholesale
3845 Electromedical & Electrotherapeutic Apparatus
3675 Electronic Capacitors
3677 Electronic Coils & Transformers
3679 Electronic Components, NEC
3571 Electronic Computers
3678 Electronic Connectors
5065 Electronic Parts & Eqpt Wholesale
3471 Electroplating, Plating, Polishing, Anodizing & Coloring
3534 Elevators & Moving Stairways
7361 Employment Agencies
8711 Engineering Services
2677 Envelopes
7359 Equipment Rental & Leasing, NEC
1794 Excavating & Grading Work
2892 Explosives

F

2241 Fabric Mills, Cotton, Wool, Silk & Man-Made
3499 Fabricated Metal Prdts, NEC
3498 Fabricated Pipe & Pipe Fittings
3443 Fabricated Plate Work
3069 Fabricated Rubber Prdts, NEC
3441 Fabricated Structural Steel
2399 Fabricated Textile Prdts, NEC
2295 Fabrics Coated Not Rubberized
2297 Fabrics, Nonwoven
8744 Facilities Support Mgmt Svcs
5083 Farm & Garden Mach & Eqpt Wholesale
3523 Farm Machinery & Eqpt

SIC INDEX

Standard Industrial Classification Numerical Index

SIC NO — PRODUCT

01 agricultural production-crops

0111 Wheat
0115 Corn
0116 Soybeans
0119 Cash Grains, NEC
0131 Cotton
0133 Sugarcane & Sugar Beets
0134 Irish Potatoes
0139 Field Crops, Except Cash Grains, NEC
0161 Vegetables & Melons
0175 Deciduous Tree Fruits
0179 Fruits & Tree Nuts, NEC
0181 Ornamental Floriculture & Nursery Prdts
0182 Food Crops Grown Under Cover
0191 Crop Farming, Misc

02 agricultural production-livestock and animal specialties

0211 Beef Cattle Feedlots
0212 Beef Cattle, Except Feedlots
0213 Hogs
0214 Sheep & Goats
0219 General Livestock, NEC
0241 Dairy Farms
0254 Poultry Hatcheries
0259 Poultry & Eggs Farms, NEC
0272 Horse & Other Equine Pro duction
0279 Animal Specialties, NEC
0291 Animal Production, NEC

07 agricultural services

0711 Soil Preparation Svcs
0721 Soil Preparation, Planting & Cultivating Svc
0722 Crop Harvesting By Machine
0723 Crop Preparation, Except Cotton Ginning
0724 Cotton Ginning
0741 Veterinary Livestock Svcs
0742 Veterinary Animal Specialties
0751 Livestock Svcs, Except Veterinary
0752 Animal Specialty Svcs, Exc Veterinary
0762 Farm Management Svcs
0781 Landscape Counseling & Planning
0782 Lawn & Garden Svcs
0783 Ornamental Shrub & Tree Svc

08 forestry

0811 Timber Tracts

09 fishing, hunting, and trapping

0919 Marine Fishing, Misc
0921 Finfish Farming & Fish Hatcheries
0971 Hunting & Trapping

10 metal mining

1081 Metal Mining Svcs

12 coal mining

1221 Bituminous Coal & Lignite: Surface Mining
1241 Coal Mining Svcs

13 oil and gas extraction

1311 Crude Petroleum & Natural Gas
1321 Natural Gas Liquids
1381 Drilling Oil & Gas Wells
1382 Oil & Gas Field Exploration Svcs
1389 Oil & Gas Field Svcs, NEC

14 mining and quarrying of nonmetallic minerals, except fuels

1411 Dimension Stone
1422 Crushed & Broken Limestone
1423 Crushed & Broken Granite
1429 Crushed & Broken Stone, NEC
1442 Construction Sand & Gravel
1474 Potash, Soda & Borate Minerals
1479 Chemical & Fertilizer Mining
1499 Miscellaneous Nonmetallic Mining

15 building construction-general contractors and operative builders

1521 General Contractors, Single Family Houses
1522 General Contractors, Residential Other Than Single Family
1531 Operative Builders
1541 General Contractors, Indl Bldgs & Warehouses
1542 General Contractors, Nonresidential & Non-indl Bldgs

16 heavy construction other than building construction-contractors

1611 Highway & Street Construction
1622 Bridge, Tunnel & Elevated Hwy Construction
1623 Water, Sewer & Utility Line Construction
1629 Heavy Construction, NEC

17 construction-special trade contractors

1711 Plumbing, Heating & Air Conditioning Contractors
1721 Painting & Paper Hanging Contractors
1731 Electrical Work
1741 Masonry & Other Stonework
1742 Plastering, Drywall, Acoustical & Insulation Work
1743 Terrazzo, Tile, Marble & Mosaic Work
1751 Carpentry Work
1752 Floor Laying & Other Floor Work, NEC
1761 Roofing, Siding & Sheet Metal Work
1771 Concrete Work
1781 Water Well Drilling
1791 Structural Steel Erection
1793 Glass & Glazing Work
1794 Excavating & Grading Work
1795 Wrecking & Demolition Work
1796 Installation Or Erection Of Bldg Eqpt & Machinery, NEC
1799 Special Trade Contractors, NEC

20 food and kindred products

2011 Meat Packing Plants
2013 Sausages & Meat Prdts
2015 Poultry Slaughtering, Dressing & Processing
2021 Butter
2022 Cheese
2023 Milk, Condensed & Evaporated
2024 Ice Cream
2026 Milk
2032 Canned Specialties
2033 Canned Fruits, Vegetables & Preserves
2034 Dried Fruits, Vegetables & Soup
2035 Pickled Fruits, Vegetables, Sauces & Dressings
2038 Frozen Specialties
2041 Flour, Grain Milling
2043 Cereal Breakfast Foods
2045 Flour, Blended & Prepared
2046 Wet Corn Milling
2047 Dog & Cat Food
2048 Prepared Feeds For Animals & Fowls
2051 Bread, Bakery Prdts Exc Cookies & Crackers
2052 Cookies & Crackers
2053 Frozen Bakery Prdts
2064 Candy & Confectionery Prdts
2066 Chocolate & Cocoa Prdts
2068 Salted & Roasted Nuts & Seeds
2075 Soybean Oil Mills
2076 Vegetable Oil Mills
2077 Animal, Marine Fats & Oils
2079 Shortening, Oils & Margarine
2082 Malt Beverages
2084 Wine & Brandy
2085 Liquors, Distilled, Rectified & Blended
2086 Soft Drinks
2087 Flavoring Extracts & Syrups
2091 Fish & Seafoods, Canned & Cured
2095 Coffee
2096 Potato Chips & Similar Prdts
2097 Ice
2098 Macaroni, Spaghetti & Noodles
2099 Food Preparations, NEC

22 textile mill products

2211 Cotton, Woven Fabric
2221 Silk & Man-Made Fiber
2241 Fabric Mills, Cotton, Wool, Silk & Man-Made
2252 Hosiery, Except Women's
2261 Cotton Fabric Finishers
2262 Silk & Man-Made Fabric Finishers
2273 Carpets & Rugs
2282 Yarn Texturizing, Throwing, Twisting & Winding Mills
2284 Thread Mills
2295 Fabrics Coated Not Rubberized
2296 Tire Cord & Fabric
2297 Fabrics, Nonwoven
2298 Cordage & Twine
2299 Textile Goods, NEC

23 apparel and other finished products made from fabrics and similar material

2311 Men's & Boys' Suits, Coats & Overcoats
2321 Men's & Boys' Shirts
2325 Men's & Boys' Separate Trousers & Casual Slacks
2326 Men's & Boys' Work Clothing
2329 Men's & Boys' Clothing, NEC
2337 Women's & Misses' Suits, Coats & Skirts
2339 Women's & Misses' Outerwear, NEC
2369 Girls' & Infants' Outerwear, NEC
2391 Curtains & Draperies
2392 House furnishings: Textile
2393 Textile Bags
2394 Canvas Prdts
2395 Pleating & Stitching For The Trade
2396 Automotive Trimmings, Apparel Findings, Related Prdts
2397 Schiffli Machine Embroideries
2399 Fabricated Textile Prdts, NEC

24 lumber and wood products, except furniture

2411 Logging
2421 Saw & Planing Mills
2426 Hardwood Dimension & Flooring Mills
2429 Special Prdt Sawmills, NEC
2431 Millwork
2434 Wood Kitchen Cabinets
2439 Structural Wood Members, NEC
2441 Wood Boxes
2448 Wood Pallets & Skids
2449 Wood Containers, NEC
2451 Mobile Homes
2452 Prefabricated Wood Buildings & Cmpnts
2491 Wood Preserving
2493 Reconstituted Wood Prdts
2499 Wood Prdts, NEC

25 furniture and fixtures

2511 Wood Household Furniture
2512 Wood Household Furniture, Upholstered
2514 Metal Household Furniture
2515 Mattresses & Bedsprings
2517 Wood T V, Radio, Phono & Sewing Cabinets
2521 Wood Office Furniture
2522 Office Furniture, Except Wood
2531 Public Building & Related Furniture
2541 Wood, Office & Store Fixtures
2542 Partitions & Fixtures, Except Wood
2591 Drapery Hardware, Window Blinds & Shades
2599 Furniture & Fixtures, NEC

26 paper and allied products

2611 Pulp Mills
2621 Paper Mills
2631 Paperboard Mills
2652 Set-Up Paperboard Boxes
2653 Corrugated & Solid Fiber Boxes
2656 Sanitary Food Containers
2657 Folding Paperboard Boxes
2671 Paper Coating & Laminating for Packaging
2672 Paper Coating & Laminating, Exc for Packaging
2673 Bags: Plastics, Laminated & Coated
2674 Bags: Uncoated Paper & Multiwall
2675 Die-Cut Paper & Board
2676 Sanitary Paper Prdts
2677 Envelopes
2679 Converted Paper Prdts, NEC

27 printing, publishing, and allied industries

2711 Newspapers: Publishing & Printing
2721 Periodicals: Publishing & Printing
2731 Books: Publishing & Printing
2732 Book Printing, Not Publishing
2741 Misc Publishing
2752 Commercial Printing: Lithographic
2754 Commercial Printing: Gravure
2759 Commercial Printing
2761 Manifold Business Forms
2771 Greeting Card Publishing
2782 Blankbooks & Looseleaf Binders
2789 Bookbinding

S I C

SIC NO PRODUCT

2791 Typesetting
2796 Platemaking & Related Svcs

28 chemicals and allied products

2812 Alkalies & Chlorine
2813 Industrial Gases
2816 Inorganic Pigments
2819 Indl Inorganic Chemicals, NEC
2821 Plastics, Mtrls & Nonvulcanizable Elastomers
2822 Synthetic Rubber (Vulcanizable Elastomers)
2833 Medicinal Chemicals & Botanical Prdts
2834 Pharmaceuticals
2835 Diagnostic Substances
2836 Biological Prdts, Exc Diagnostic Substances
2841 Soap & Detergents
2842 Spec Cleaning, Polishing & Sanitation Preparations
2844 Perfumes, Cosmetics & Toilet Preparations
2851 Paints, Varnishes, Lacquers, Enamels
2865 Cyclic-Crudes, Intermediates, Dyes & Org Pigments
2869 Industrial Organic Chemicals, NEC
2873 Nitrogenous Fertilizers
2874 Phosphatic Fertilizers
2875 Fertilizers, Mixing Only
2879 Pesticides & Agricultural Chemicals, NEC
2891 Adhesives & Sealants
2892 Explosives
2893 Printing Ink
2895 Carbon Black
2899 Chemical Preparations, NEC

29 petroleum refining and related industries

2911 Petroleum Refining
2951 Paving Mixtures & Blocks
2952 Asphalt Felts & Coatings
2992 Lubricating Oils & Greases
2999 Products Of Petroleum & Coal, NEC

30 rubber and miscellaneous plastics products

3011 Tires & Inner Tubes
3021 Rubber & Plastic Footwear
3052 Rubber & Plastic Hose & Belting
3053 Gaskets, Packing & Sealing Devices
3061 Molded, Extruded & Lathe-Cut Rubber Mechanical Goods
3069 Fabricated Rubber Prdts, NEC
3081 Plastic Unsupported Sheet & Film
3082 Plastic Unsupported Profile Shapes
3083 Plastic Laminated Plate & Sheet
3084 Plastic Pipe
3085 Plastic Bottles
3086 Plastic Foam Prdts
3087 Custom Compounding Of Purchased Plastic Resins
3088 Plastic Plumbing Fixtures
3089 Plastic Prdts

31 leather and leather products

3131 Boot & Shoe Cut Stock & Findings
3171 Handbags & Purses
3199 Leather Goods, NEC

32 stone, clay, glass, and concrete products

3211 Flat Glass
3221 Glass Containers
3229 Pressed & Blown Glassware, NEC
3231 Glass Prdts Made Of Purchased Glass
3241 Cement, Hydraulic
3251 Brick & Structural Clay Tile
3255 Clay Refractories
3259 Structural Clay Prdts, NEC
3262 China, Table & Kitchen Articles
3264 Porcelain Electrical Splys
3269 Pottery Prdts, NEC
3271 Concrete Block & Brick
3272 Concrete Prdts
3273 Ready-Mixed Concrete
3274 Lime
3275 Gypsum Prdts
3281 Cut Stone Prdts
3291 Abrasive Prdts
3292 Asbestos products
3295 Minerals & Earths: Ground Or Treated
3296 Mineral Wool
3297 Nonclay Refractories

33 primary metal industries

3312 Blast Furnaces, Coke Ovens, Steel & Rolling Mills
3315 Steel Wire Drawing & Nails & Spikes
3317 Steel Pipe & Tubes
3321 Gray Iron Foundries
3322 Malleable Iron Foundries
3324 Steel Investment Foundries
3325 Steel Foundries, NEC
3341 Secondary Smelting & Refining Of Nonferrous Metals
3351 Rolling, Drawing & Extruding Of Copper
3354 Aluminum Extruded Prdts
3357 Nonferrous Wire Drawing
3363 Aluminum Die Castings
3364 Nonferrous Die Castings, Exc Aluminum
3365 Aluminum Foundries
3366 Copper Foundries
3369 Nonferrous Foundries: Castings, NEC
3398 Metal Heat Treating
3399 Primary Metal Prdts, NEC

34 fabricated metal products, except machinery and transportation equipment

3411 Metal Cans
3412 Metal Barrels, Drums, Kegs & Pails
3421 Cutlery
3423 Hand & Edge Tools
3425 Hand Saws & Saw Blades
3429 Hardware, NEC
3432 Plumbing Fixture Fittings & Trim, Brass
3433 Heating Eqpt
3441 Fabricated Structural Steel
3442 Metal Doors, Sash, Frames, Molding & Trim
3443 Fabricated Plate Work
3444 Sheet Metal Work
3446 Architectural & Ornamental Metal Work
3448 Prefabricated Metal Buildings & Cmpnts
3449 Misc Structural Metal Work
3451 Screw Machine Prdts
3452 Bolts, Nuts, Screws, Rivets & Washers
3462 Iron & Steel Forgings
3463 Nonferrous Forgings
3465 Automotive Stampings
3469 Metal Stampings, NEC
3471 Electroplating, Plating, Polishing, Anodizing & Coloring
3479 Coating & Engraving, NEC
3482 Small Arms Ammunition
3483 Ammunition, Large
3484 Small Arms
3489 Ordnance & Access, NEC
3491 Industrial Valves
3492 Fluid Power Valves & Hose Fittings
3494 Valves & Pipe Fittings, NEC
3495 Wire Springs
3496 Misc Fabricated Wire Prdts
3497 Metal Foil & Leaf
3498 Fabricated Pipe & Pipe Fittings
3499 Fabricated Metal Prdts, NEC

35 industrial and commercial machinery and computer equipment

3511 Steam, Gas & Hydraulic Turbines & Engines
3519 Internal Combustion Engines, NEC
3523 Farm Machinery & Eqpt
3524 Garden, Lawn Tractors & Eqpt
3531 Construction Machinery & Eqpt
3532 Mining Machinery & Eqpt
3533 Oil Field Machinery & Eqpt
3534 Elevators & Moving Stairways
3535 Conveyors & Eqpt
3536 Hoists, Cranes & Monorails
3537 Indl Trucks, Tractors, Trailers & Stackers
3541 Machine Tools: Cutting
3542 Machine Tools: Forming
3543 Industrial Patterns
3544 Dies, Tools, Jigs, Fixtures & Indl Molds
3545 Machine Tool Access
3546 Power Hand Tools
3547 Rolling Mill Machinery & Eqpt
3548 Welding Apparatus
3549 Metalworking Machinery, NEC
3552 Textile Machinery
3553 Woodworking Machinery
3554 Paper Inds Machinery
3555 Printing Trades Machinery & Eqpt
3556 Food Prdts Machinery
3559 Special Ind Machinery, NEC
3561 Pumps & Pumping Eqpt
3562 Ball & Roller Bearings
3563 Air & Gas Compressors
3564 Blowers & Fans
3565 Packaging Machinery
3566 Speed Changers, Drives & Gears
3567 Indl Process Furnaces & Ovens
3568 Mechanical Power Transmission Eqpt, NEC
3569 Indl Machinery & Eqpt, NEC
3571 Electronic Computers
3572 Computer Storage Devices
3575 Computer Terminals
3577 Computer Peripheral Eqpt, NEC
3578 Calculating & Accounting Eqpt
3579 Office Machines, NEC
3581 Automatic Vending Machines
3582 Commercial Laundry, Dry Clean & Pressing Mchs
3585 Air Conditioning & Heating Eqpt
3586 Measuring & Dispensing Pumps
3589 Service Ind Machines, NEC
3592 Carburetors, Pistons, Rings & Valves
3593 Fluid Power Cylinders & Actuators
3594 Fluid Power Pumps & Motors
3596 Scales & Balances, Exc Laboratory
3599 Machinery & Eqpt, Indl & Commercial, NEC

36 electronic and other electrical equipment and components, except computer

3612 Power, Distribution & Specialty Transformers
3613 Switchgear & Switchboard Apparatus
3621 Motors & Generators
3624 Carbon & Graphite Prdts
3625 Relays & Indl Controls
3629 Electrical Indl Apparatus, NEC
3631 Household Cooking Eqpt
3634 Electric Household Appliances
3639 Household Appliances, NEC
3641 Electric Lamps
3643 Current-Carrying Wiring Devices
3644 Noncurrent-Carrying Wiring Devices
3645 Residential Lighting Fixtures
3646 Commercial, Indl & Institutional Lighting Fixtures
3647 Vehicular Lighting Eqpt
3648 Lighting Eqpt, NEC
3651 Household Audio & Video Eqpt
3652 Phonograph Records & Magnetic Tape
3661 Telephone & Telegraph Apparatus
3663 Radio & T V Communications, Systs & Eqpt, Broadcast/Studio
3669 Communications Eqpt, NEC
3672 Printed Circuit Boards
3674 Semiconductors
3675 Electronic Capacitors
3677 Electronic Coils & Transformers
3678 Electronic Connectors
3679 Electronic Components, NEC
3691 Storage Batteries
3692 Primary Batteries: Dry & Wet
3694 Electrical Eqpt For Internal Combustion Engines
3695 Recording Media
3699 Electrical Machinery, Eqpt & Splys, NEC

37 transportation equipment

3711 Motor Vehicles & Car Bodies
3713 Truck & Bus Bodies
3714 Motor Vehicle Parts & Access
3715 Truck Trailers
3716 Motor Homes
3721 Aircraft
3724 Aircraft Engines & Engine Parts
3728 Aircraft Parts & Eqpt, NEC
3731 Shipbuilding & Repairing
3732 Boat Building & Repairing
3743 Railroad Eqpt
3751 Motorcycles, Bicycles & Parts
3769 Guided Missile/Space Vehicle Parts & Eqpt, NEC
3792 Travel Trailers & Campers
3795 Tanks & Tank Components
3799 Transportation Eqpt, NEC

38 measuring, analyzing and controlling instruments; photographic, medical an

3812 Search, Detection, Navigation & Guidance Systs & Instrs
3821 Laboratory Apparatus & Furniture
3822 Automatic Temperature Controls
3823 Indl Instruments For Meas, Display & Control
3824 Fluid Meters & Counters
3825 Instrs For Measuring & Testing Electricity
3826 Analytical Instruments
3827 Optical Instruments
3829 Measuring & Controlling Devices, NEC
3841 Surgical & Medical Instrs & Apparatus
3842 Orthopedic, Prosthetic & Surgical Appliances/Splys
3843 Dental Eqpt & Splys
3844 X-ray Apparatus & Tubes
3845 Electromedical & Electrotherapeutic Apparatus
3851 Ophthalmic Goods
3861 Photographic Eqpt & Splys
3873 Watch & Clock Devices & Parts

SIC NO PRODUCT

39 miscellaneous manufacturing industries

3911 Jewelry: Precious Metal
3914 Silverware, Plated & Stainless Steel Ware
3915 Jewelers Findings & Lapidary Work
3931 Musical Instruments
3944 Games, Toys & Children's Vehicles
3949 Sporting & Athletic Goods, NEC
3952 Lead Pencils, Crayons & Artist's Mtrls
3953 Marking Devices
3955 Carbon Paper & Inked Ribbons
3961 Costume Jewelry & Novelties
3965 Fasteners, Buttons, Needles & Pins
3991 Brooms & Brushes
3993 Signs & Advertising Displays
3999 Manufacturing Industries, NEC

40 railroad transportation

4011 Railroads, Line-Hauling Operations
4013 Switching & Terminal Svcs

41 local and suburban transit and interurban highway passenger transportation

4111 Local & Suburban Transit
4119 Local Passenger Transportation: NEC
4121 Taxi Cabs
4131 Intercity & Rural Bus Transportation
4141 Local Bus Charter Svc
4142 Bus Charter Service, Except Local
4151 School Buses
4173 Bus Terminal & Svc Facilities

42 motor freight transportation and warehousing

4212 Local Trucking Without Storage
4213 Trucking, Except Local
4214 Local Trucking With Storage
4215 Courier Svcs, Except Air
4221 Farm Product Warehousing & Storage
4222 Refrigerated Warehousing & Storage
4225 General Warehousing & Storage
4226 Special Warehousing & Storage, NEC
4231 Terminal & Joint Terminal Maint Facilities

44 water transportation

4412 Deep Sea Foreign Transportation Of Freight
4424 Deep Sea Domestic Transportation Of Freight
4493 Marinas

45 transportation by air

4512 Air Transportation, Scheduled
4513 Air Courier Svcs
4522 Air Transportation, Nonscheduled
4581 Airports, Flying Fields & Terminal Svcs

46 pipelines, except natural gas

4612 Crude Petroleum Pipelines
4613 Refined Petroleum Pipelines
4619 Pipelines, NEC

47 transportation services

4724 Travel Agencies
4729 Passenger Transportation Arrangement, NEC
4731 Freight Forwarding & Arrangement
4741 Railroad Car Rental
4783 Packing & Crating Svcs
4785 Fixed Facilities, Inspection, Weighing Svcs Transptn
4789 Transportation Svcs, NEC

48 communications

4812 Radiotelephone Communications
4813 Telephone Communications, Except Radio
4822 Telegraph & Other Message Communications
4832 Radio Broadcasting Stations
4833 Television Broadcasting Stations
4841 Cable & Other Pay TV Svcs
4899 Communication Svcs, NEC

49 electric, gas, and sanitary services

4911 Electric Svcs
4922 Natural Gas Transmission
4923 Natural Gas Transmission & Distribution
4924 Natural Gas Distribution
4925 Gas Production &/Or Distribution
4931 Electric & Other Svcs Combined
4932 Gas & Other Svcs Combined
4939 Combination Utilities, NEC
4941 Water Sply
4952 Sewerage Systems
4953 Refuse Systems
4959 Sanitary Svcs, NEC
4971 Irrigation Systems

SIC NO PRODUCT

50 wholesale trade¨durable goods

5012 Automobiles & Other Motor Vehicles Wholesale
5013 Motor Vehicle Splys & New Parts Wholesale
5014 Tires & Tubes Wholesale
5015 Motor Vehicle Parts, Used Wholesale
5021 Furniture Wholesale
5023 Home Furnishings Wholesale
5031 Lumber, Plywood & Millwork Wholesale
5032 Brick, Stone & Related Construction Mtrls Wholesale
5033 Roofing, Siding & Insulation Mtrls Wholesale
5039 Construction Materials, NEC Wholesale
5043 Photographic Eqpt & Splys Wholesale
5044 Office Eqpt Wholesale
5045 Computers & Peripheral Eqpt & Software Wholesale
5046 Commercial Eqpt, NEC Wholesale
5047 Medical, Dental & Hospital Eqpt & Splys Wholesale
5048 Ophthalmic Goods Wholesale
5049 Professional Eqpt & Splys, NEC Wholesale
5051 Metals Service Centers
5052 Coal & Other Minerals & Ores Wholesale
5063 Electrl Apparatus, Eqpt, Wiring Splys Wholesale
5064 Electrical Appliances, TV & Radios Wholesale
5065 Electronic Parts & Eqpt Wholesale
5072 Hardware Wholesale
5074 Plumbing & Heating Splys Wholesale
5075 Heating & Air Conditioning Eqpt & Splys Wholesale
5078 Refrigeration Eqpt & Splys Wholesale
5082 Construction & Mining Mach & Eqpt Wholesale
5083 Farm & Garden Mach & Eqpt Wholesale
5084 Industrial Mach & Eqpt Wholesale
5085 Industrial Splys Wholesale
5087 Service Establishment Eqpt & Splys Wholesale
5088 Transportation Eqpt & Splys, Except Motor Vehicles Wholesale
5091 Sporting & Recreational Goods & Splys Wholesale
5092 Toys & Hobby Goods & Splys Wholesale
5093 Scrap & Waste Materials Wholesale
5094 Jewelry, Watches, Precious Stones Wholesale
5099 Durable Goods: NEC Wholesale

51 wholesale trade¨nondurable goods

5111 Printing & Writing Paper Wholesale
5112 Stationery & Office Splys Wholesale
5113 Indl & Personal Svc Paper Wholesale
5122 Drugs, Drug Proprietaries & Sundries Wholesale
5131 Piece Goods, Notions & Dry Goods Wholesale
5136 Men's & Boys' Clothing & Furnishings Wholesale
5137 Women's, Children's & Infants Clothing Wholesale
5141 Groceries, General Line Wholesale
5142 Packaged Frozen Foods Wholesale
5143 Dairy Prdts, Except Dried Or Canned Wholesale
5144 Poultry & Poultry Prdts Wholesale
5145 Confectionery Wholesale
5146 Fish & Seafood Wholesale
5147 Meats & Meat Prdts Wholesale
5148 Fresh Fruits & Vegetables Wholesale
5149 Groceries & Related Prdts, NEC Wholesale
5153 Grain & Field Beans Wholesale
5154 Livestock Wholesale
5159 Farm-Prdt Raw Mtrls, NEC Wholesale
5162 Plastics Materials & Basic Shapes Wholesale
5169 Chemicals & Allied Prdts, NEC Wholesale
5171 Petroleum Bulk Stations & Terminals
5172 Petroleum & Petroleum Prdts Wholesale
5181 Beer & Ale Wholesale
5182 Wine & Distilled Alcoholic Beverages Wholesale
5191 Farm Splys Wholesale
5192 Books, Periodicals & Newspapers Wholesale
5193 Flowers, Nursery Stock & Florists' Splys Wholesale
5194 Tobacco & Tobacco Prdts Wholesale
5198 Paints, Varnishes & Splys Wholesale
5199 Nondurable Goods, NEC Wholesale

60 depository institutions

6021 National Commercial Banks
6022 State Commercial Banks
6029 Commercial Banks, NEC
6035 Federal Savings Institutions
6036 Savings Institutions, Except Federal
6061 Federal Credit Unions
6062 State Credit Unions
6091 Nondeposit Trust Facilities
6099 Functions Related To Deposit Banking, NEC

61 nondepository credit institutions

6111 Federal Credit Agencies
6141 Personal Credit Institutions
6153 Credit Institutions, Short-Term Business
6159 Credit Institutions, Misc Business
6162 Mortgage Bankers & Loan Correspondents

SIC NO PRODUCT

6163 Loan Brokers

62 security and commodity brokers, dealers, exchanges, and services

6211 Security Brokers & Dealers
6221 Commodity Contracts Brokers & Dealers
6231 Security & Commodity Exchanges
6282 Investment Advice
6289 Security & Commodity Svcs, NEC

63 insurance carriers

6311 Life Insurance Carriers
6321 Accident & Health Insurance
6324 Hospital & Medical Svc Plans Carriers
6331 Fire, Marine & Casualty Insurance
6351 Surety Insurance Carriers
6361 Title Insurance
6371 Pension, Health & Welfare Funds
6399 Insurance Carriers, NEC

64 insurance agents, brokers, and service

6411 Insurance Agents, Brokers & Svc

65 real estate

6512 Operators Of Nonresidential Bldgs
6513 Operators Of Apartment Buildings
6514 Operators Of Dwellings, Except Apartments
6515 Operators of Residential Mobile Home Sites
6519 Lessors Of Real Estate, NEC
6531 Real Estate Agents & Managers
6541 Title Abstract Offices
6552 Land Subdividers & Developers
6553 Cemetery Subdividers & Developers

67 holding and other investment offices

6712 Offices Of Bank Holding Co's
6719 Offices Of Holding Co's, NEC
6722 Management Investment Offices
6726 Unit Investment Trusts, Face-Amount Certificate Offices
6732 Education, Religious & Charitable Trusts
6733 Trusts Except Educational, Religious & Charitable
6792 Oil Royalty Traders
6794 Patent Owners & Lessors
6798 Real Estate Investment Trusts
6799 Investors, NEC

70 hotels, rooming houses, camps, and other lodging places

7011 Hotels, Motels & Tourist Courts
7021 Rooming & Boarding Houses
7032 Sporting & Recreational Camps
7033 Trailer Parks & Camp Sites
7041 Membership-Basis Hotels

72 personal services

7211 Power Laundries, Family & Commercial
7212 Garment Pressing & Cleaners' Agents
7213 Linen Sply
7215 Coin Operated Laundries & Cleaning
7216 Dry Cleaning Plants, Except Rug Cleaning
7217 Carpet & Upholstery Cleaning
7218 Industrial Launderers
7219 Laundry & Garment Svcs, NEC
7221 Photographic Studios, Portrait
7231 Beauty Shops
7241 Barber Shops
7261 Funeral Svcs & Crematories
7291 Tax Return Preparation Svcs
7299 Miscellaneous Personal Svcs, NEC

73 business services

7311 Advertising Agencies
7312 Outdoor Advertising Svcs
7313 Radio, TV & Publishers Adv Reps
7319 Advertising, NEC
7322 Adjustment & Collection Svcs
7323 Credit Reporting Svcs
7331 Direct Mail Advertising Svcs
7334 Photocopying & Duplicating Svcs
7335 Commercial Photography
7336 Commercial Art & Graphic Design
7338 Secretarial & Court Reporting Svcs
7342 Disinfecting & Pest Control Svcs
7349 Building Cleaning & Maintenance Svcs, NEC
7352 Medical Eqpt Rental & Leasing
7353 Heavy Construction Eqpt Rental & Leasing
7359 Equipment Rental & Leasing, NEC
7361 Employment Agencies
7363 Help Supply Svcs
7371 Custom Computer Programming Svcs
7372 Prepackaged Software

SIC SECTION

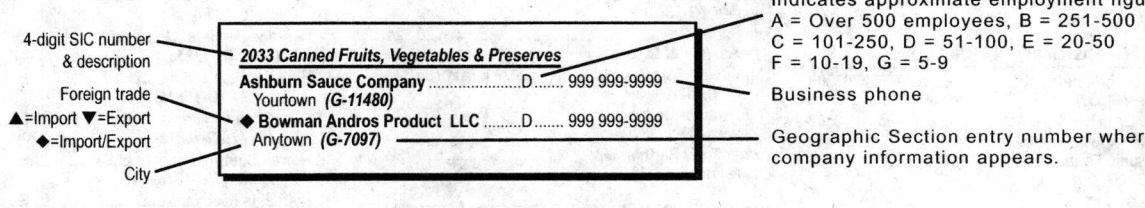

4-digit SIC number & description — *2033 Canned Fruits, Vegetables & Preserves*

Ashburn Sauce Company ....D...... 999 999-9999
Yourtown *(G-11480)*
◆ **Bowman Andros Product LLC** ....D...... 999 999-9999
Anytown *(G-7097)*

Foreign trade: ▲=Import ▼=Export ◆=Import/Export

City

Indicates approximate employment figure
A = Over 500 employees, B = 251-500
C = 101-250, D = 51-100, E = 20-50
F = 10-19, G = 5-9

Business phone

Geographic Section entry number where full company information appears.

See footnotes for symbols and codes identification.

- The SIC codes in this section are from the latest Standard Industrial Classification manual published by the U.S. Government's Office of Management and Budget. For more information regarding SICs, see the Explanatory Notes.
- Companies may be listed under multiple classifications.

01 AGRICULTURAL PRODUCTION-CROPS

0111 Wheat

Brookover Land Enterprises LP ....F....... 620 275-9206
Garden City *(G-2119)*
Chem Till Spray Company Inc ....F....... 620 492-2751
Johnson *(G-3652)*
G H K Farms ....F....... 785 462-6440
Colby *(G-1008)*
Golden Belt Feeders Inc ....D....... 620 549-3241
Saint John *(G-10351)*
Heft & Sons LLC ....E....... 620 723-2495
Greensburg *(G-2679)*
High Choice Feeders LLC ....E....... 620 872-7271
Scott City *(G-10815)*
Kramer Seed Farms ....F....... 620 544-4330
Hugoton *(G-3170)*
Lewis Wheeler Lee Wheeler Ptr ....F....... 620 544-8289
Hugoton *(G-3171)*
Melvin Winger ....F....... 620 492-6214
Johnson *(G-3658)*
Mitchell Farms ....F....... 580 696-4568
Elkhart *(G-1622)*
Pioneer Feedyard LLC ....E....... 785 672-3257
Oakley *(G-7485)*
R Puckett Farms Inc ....F....... 620 378-3342
Fredonia *(G-2043)*
Raymond Baugher ....F....... 620 421-1253
Parsons *(G-9729)*
Roth Farm ....F....... 785 944-3329
Green *(G-2666)*
Sellers Farms Inc ....F....... 620 257-5144
Lyons *(G-6497)*
Winger Cattle Co Inc ....F....... 620 492-6214
Johnson *(G-3666)*

0115 Corn

Chem Till Spray Company Inc ....F....... 620 492-2751
Johnson *(G-3652)*
G H K Farms ....F....... 785 462-6440
Colby *(G-1008)*
Golden Belt Feeders Inc ....D....... 620 549-3241
Saint John *(G-10351)*
Hatcher Land & Cattle Company ....F....... 620 624-1186
Liberal *(G-6319)*
Heft & Sons LLC ....E....... 620 723-2495
Greensburg *(G-2679)*
High Choice Feeders LLC ....E....... 620 872-7271
Scott City *(G-10815)*
J & L Smith Farms Inc ....F....... 620 356-1070
Ulysses *(G-13301)*
Jerry Wray ....G....... 785 255-4644
Pomona *(G-10005)*
Lewis Wheeler Lee Wheeler Ptr ....F....... 620 544-8289
Hugoton *(G-3171)*
Melvin Winger ....F....... 620 492-6214
Johnson *(G-3658)*
Mitchell Farms ....F....... 580 696-4568
Elkhart *(G-1622)*
Pioneer Feedyard LLC ....E....... 785 672-3257
Oakley *(G-7485)*
Raymond Baugher ....F....... 620 421-1253
Parsons *(G-9729)*
S W Agro Center ....F....... 620 563-7264
Kismet *(G-4632)*
Sellers Farms Inc ....F....... 620 257-5144
Lyons *(G-6497)*
Triangle H ....F....... 620 276-4004
Garden City *(G-2301)*
Triangle H Grain & Cattle Co ....F....... 620 276-4004
Garden City *(G-2302)*
Winger Cattle Co Inc ....F....... 620 492-6214
Johnson *(G-3666)*

0116 Soybeans

Lewis Wheeler Lee Wheeler Ptr ....F....... 620 544-8289
Hugoton *(G-3171)*
R Puckett Farms Inc ....F....... 620 378-3342
Fredonia *(G-2043)*
Raymond Baugher ....F....... 620 421-1253
Parsons *(G-9729)*

0119 Cash Grains, NEC

Chem Till Spray Company Inc ....F....... 620 492-2751
Johnson *(G-3652)*
Friends of The Department ....F....... 620 694-2387
Hutchinson *(G-3296)*
G H K Farms ....F....... 785 462-6440
Colby *(G-1008)*
Heft & Sons LLC ....E....... 620 723-2495
Greensburg *(G-2679)*
Herrmann Land & Cattle Co ....F....... 620 369-2252
Ford *(G-1933)*
High Choice Feeders LLC ....E....... 620 872-7271
Scott City *(G-10815)*
Kauffman Seeds Inc ....E....... 620 465-2245
Hutchinson *(G-3348)*
Keesecker Agri Business Inc ....E....... 785 325-3134
Washington *(G-13466)*
Lewis Wheeler Lee Wheeler Ptr ....F....... 620 544-8289
Hugoton *(G-3171)*
Mitchell Farms ....F....... 580 696-4568
Elkhart *(G-1622)*
Raymond Baugher ....F....... 620 421-1253
Parsons *(G-9729)*
Sylvester Ranch Inc ....E....... 785 242-3598
Ottawa *(G-8315)*
Tallgrass Commodities LLC ....E....... 855 494-8484
Wamego *(G-13443)*
Triangle H Grain & Cattle Co ....F....... 620 276-4004
Garden City *(G-2302)*

0131 Cotton

Hatcher Land & Cattle Company ....F....... 620 624-1186
Liberal *(G-6319)*

0133 Sugarcane & Sugar Beets

Seaboard Corporation ....C....... 913 676-8800
Merriam *(G-7103)*

0134 Irish Potatoes

Premium Source Ag LLC ....F....... 620 277-2009
Holcomb *(G-3078)*

0139 Field Crops, Except Cash Grains, NEC

Great Plains Alfalfa Inc ....F....... 620 672-9431
Pratt *(G-10119)*
Innovative Livestock Svcs Inc ....D....... 620 793-9200
Great Bend *(G-2593)*
Mid States Hay Inc ....E....... 620 355-7976
Lakin *(G-4656)*
Pines International Inc ....E....... 800 697-4637
Lawrence *(G-5065)*
Robert Gigstad ....E....... 785 448-6923
Garnett *(G-2387)*
Sebes Hay LLC ....E....... 620 285-6941
Larned *(G-4712)*
Ward Feed Yard Inc ....E....... 620 285-2183
Larned *(G-4715)*

0161 Vegetables & Melons

Gaeddert Farms Sweet Corn Inc ....E....... 620 543-2473
Buhler *(G-616)*
L C Crossfaith ....E....... 620 723-2626
Greensburg *(G-2682)*
Mid-State Farmers Co-Op Inc ....F....... 785 372-4239
Rush Center *(G-10261)*

0175 Deciduous Tree Fruits

Depot Market ....F....... 785 374-4255
Courtland *(G-1180)*

0179 Fruits & Tree Nuts, NEC

Soma By Chicos LLC ....F....... 913 317-8566
Leawood *(G-5554)*

0181 Ornamental Floriculture & Nursery Prdts

Arnolds Greenhouse Inc ....F....... 620 964-2463
Le Roy *(G-5195)*
Bills Tropical Greenhouse ....F....... 913 432-6383
Kansas City *(G-3861)*
Blue Rapids Greenhouse Inc ....E....... 785 363-7300
Blue Rapids *(G-533)*
Brady Nursery Inc ....E....... 316 722-7516
Wichita *(G-13883)*
Cranmer Grass Farms Inc ....E....... 316 722-7230
Maize *(G-6511)*
Dover Sod Farms Inc ....F....... 913 897-2336
Bucyrus *(G-596)*
Gablers Nursery Inc ....F....... 913 642-4164
Shawnee Mission *(G-11389)*
Green Hills Inc ....F....... 316 686-7673
Wichita *(G-14509)*
Greenhouse Effect Inc ....F....... 913 492-7407
Shawnee Mission *(G-11402)*
Halings Florist ....F....... 913 642-5034
Shawnee Mission *(G-11406)*
Hermes Co Inc ....E....... 913 888-2413
Lenexa *(G-5901)*
Landscape Outfitters LLC ....F....... 620 221-1108
Winfield *(G-16154)*
Loma Vista Garden Center Inc ....E....... 913 897-7010
Ottawa *(G-8284)*
Meyers Turf Farms Inc ....D....... 913 533-2456
Bucyrus *(G-603)*
▲ **Neosho Gardens LLC** ....E....... 620 767-6920
Council Grove *(G-1174)*
Pine Howard Grdn Ctr & Grnhse ....E....... 785 749-0302
Lawrence *(G-5064)*
Sod Shop Inc ....F....... 913 814-0044
Lawrence *(G-5113)*
Suburban Lawn & Garden Inc ....E....... 913 649-8700
Shawnee Mission *(G-11906)*
Valley View Greenhouse LLC ....F....... 785 549-3621
Melvern *(G-7077)*
Waters Inc ....E....... 785 822-6540
Salina *(G-10760)*
Waters Inc ....E....... 620 343-2800
Emporia *(G-1849)*
Waters Inc ....E....... 785 537-1340
Manhattan *(G-6847)*
Waters Inc ....E....... 785 238-3114
Junction City *(G-3767)*

SIC

Waters Inc ....E 620 227-2900
Dodge City *(G-1451)*
Whartons For Every ....E 620 276-6000
Garden City *(G-2313)*

0182 Food Crops Grown Under Cover

Blue Rapids Greenhouse Inc ....E 785 363-7300
Blue Rapids *(G-533)*
Pine Howard Grdn Ctr & Grnhse ....E 785 749-0302
Lawrence *(G-5064)*
Rainbow Organic Farms Co ....F 620 939-4933
Bronson *(G-587)*

0191 Crop Farming, Misc

Adams Cattle Company ....F 785 256-4200
Maple Hill *(G-6862)*
Agspring LLC ....E 913 333-3035
Leawood *(G-5314)*
Beachner Bros (kansas) Inc ....F 620 449-2286
Saint Paul *(G-10380)*
Bekemeyer Enterprises Inc ....F 785 325-2274
Washington *(G-13459)*
Bert & Wetta Larned Inc ....E 620 285-7777
Larned *(G-4695)*
C & W Farms ....F 620 375-4429
Leoti *(G-6251)*
Circle Land & Cattle Corp ....F 620 275-6131
Garden City *(G-2124)*
Cross Bell Farms Partners ....E 620 275-1705
Garden City *(G-2140)*
Crown Realty of Kansas Inc ....E 913 795-4555
Mound City *(G-7169)*
Day Farms Inc ....F 620 398-2255
Healy *(G-2965)*
Donohue Ranch ....F 785 867-2160
Greeley *(G-2665)*
Ferguson Zy Farms Inc ....F 785 476-2297
Kensington *(G-4575)*
Frontier Farm Credit ....F 620 421-4030
Parsons *(G-9687)*
Frontier Farm Credit ....F 785 594-2900
Baldwin City *(G-361)*
Henrys Ltd ....F 785 388-2480
Longford *(G-6430)*
Irsik Equities LP ....F 620 335-5454
Garden City *(G-2206)*
J-Six Farms LLC ....F 785 336-2148
Seneca *(G-10869)*
James & Son Farms ....F 620 262-1512
Hugoton *(G-3167)*
Knight Farms Inc ....F 620 257-5106
Lyons *(G-6488)*
L & J Wood Products Inc ....G 620 327-2183
Hesston *(G-2996)*
Livengood Jl Farms Inc ....F 785 399-2251
Kanorado *(G-3773)*
Logan Farms Inc ....E 785 256-6334
Eskridge *(G-1868)*
Meyers Brothers Cnstr Co ....F 913 681-2667
Stilwell *(G-12168)*
Mid Continent Farms ....F 785 325-2089
Washington *(G-13469)*
Mid Kansas Tool & Electric Inc ....F 785 825-9521
Salina *(G-10600)*
Nelson Quarries Inc ....E 620 496-2211
Gas *(G-2392)*
Nemaha County Cooperative Assn ....F 785 456-6924
Belvue *(G-507)*
Nicholson Ventures ....F 620 225-4637
Dodge City *(G-1413)*
Orscheln Farm and Home LLC ....D 620 583-5043
Eureka *(G-1897)*
Palenske Ranch Inc ....F 620 279-4467
Strong City *(G-12194)*
Pizza Ranch ....F 620 662-2066
Hutchinson *(G-3407)*
R Puckett Farms Inc ....E 620 378-3565
Fredonia *(G-2042)*
Saline Valley Farm Inc ....F 785 524-4562
Lincoln *(G-6388)*
Sand and Sage Farm and Ranch ....F 620 723-3052
Greensburg *(G-2684)*
Schueller John ....E 316 371-7761
Wichita *(G-15534)*
Seaboard Foods LLC ....G 620 593-4353
Rolla *(G-10233)*
Security Farms Inc ....F 620 275-4200
Garden City *(G-2278)*
Servicmmber AG Vcation Educatn ....E 785 537-7493
Manhattan *(G-6799)*
Simpson Farm Enterprises Inc ....F 785 731-2700
Ransom *(G-10195)*
Stephen Jr & Kay Irsik ....F 620 335-5363
Ingalls *(G-3580)*
Tdn Farms ....E 620 324-5296
Lewis *(G-6271)*
Timberview Farm ....F 785 336-2399
Bern *(G-524)*
Todd Tractor Co Inc ....F 785 336-2138
Seneca *(G-10884)*
Turner Trust Partnership ....E 620 792-6144
Great Bend *(G-2649)*

02 AGRICULTURAL PRODUCTION-LIVESTOCK AND ANIMAL SPECIALTIES

0211 Beef Cattle Feedlots

2i Feeders LLC ....F 620 528-3740
Allen *(G-60)*
Adams Cattle Company ....F 785 256-4200
Maple Hill *(G-6862)*
▼ Bainter Construction Co Inc ....E 785 675-3297
Hoxie *(G-3135)*
Bartlett Cattle Company LP ....E 620 675-2244
Sublette *(G-12199)*
Barton County Feeders Inc ....E 620 564-2200
Ellinwood *(G-1627)*
Beef Belt LLC ....F 620 872-3059
Scott City *(G-10806)*
Boothill Feeders Inc ....F 620 227-8195
Jetmore *(G-3646)*
Brookover Feed Yards Inc ....D 620 275-9206
Garden City *(G-2117)*
Brookover Feed Yards Inc ....E 620 275-0125
Garden City *(G-2118)*
Cactus Feeders Inc ....E 620 356-1750
Ulysses *(G-13286)*
Cactus Feeders Inc ....E 620 384-7431
Syracuse *(G-12222)*
Cattle Empire LLC ....E 620 649-2235
Satanta *(G-10779)*
Circle Bar Cattle Company Inc ....F 620 275-1182
Satanta *(G-10781)*
Circle Land & Cattle Corp ....F 620 275-6131
Garden City *(G-2124)*
Coake Feeding Co Inc ....F 620 227-2673
Dodge City *(G-1325)*
Decatur County Feed Yard Inc ....E 785 475-2212
Oberlin *(G-7491)*
Deseret Cattle Feeders LLC ....F 620 275-6181
Satanta *(G-10783)*
Dm & M Farms Inc ....E 620 855-3934
Cimarron *(G-823)*
Dudrey Cattle Co Inc ....F 620 549-3234
Saint John *(G-10350)*
Eagle Bar Ranch Inc ....E 620 257-5106
Lyons *(G-6482)*
▲ Finney County Feed Yard Inc ....E 620 275-7163
Garden City *(G-2164)*
Five Rivers Cattle Feeding LLC ....D 620 356-4466
Ulysses *(G-13296)*
Ford Cattle Company Inc ....E 620 369-2252
Ford *(G-1931)*
Ford County Feed Yard Inc ....D 620 369-2252
Ford *(G-1932)*
Fowler Feeders LLC ....F 620 646-5269
Fowler *(G-2019)*
Friona Industries LP ....E 620 649-2235
Sublette *(G-12201)*
Friona Industries LP ....D 620 649-3700
Satanta *(G-10785)*
G H K Farms ....F 785 462-6440
Colby *(G-1008)*
Garden City Feed Yard LLC ....D 620 275-4191
Garden City *(G-2172)*
Golden Belt Feeders Inc ....D 620 549-3241
Saint John *(G-10351)*
Golden Belt Feeders Inc ....E 620 659-2111
Kinsley *(G-4618)*
Great Bend Feeding Inc ....E 620 792-2508
Great Bend *(G-2579)*
Green Plains Cattle Co LLC ....D 620 624-6296
Kismet *(G-4630)*
Green Plains Inc ....D 620 375-2255
Leoti *(G-6252)*
Hatcher Land & Cattle Company ....F 620 624-1186
Liberal *(G-6319)*
Haw Ranch Feedlot 2 LLC ....F 620 752-3221
Potwin *(G-10007)*
Hays Feeder Holdings LLC ....F 785 625-3415
Hays *(G-2830)*
Heritage Feeders LP ....E 620 275-4195
Sublette *(G-12203)*
High Choice Feeders LLC ....E 620 872-7271
Scott City *(G-10815)*
High Choice Feeders LLC ....F 620 872-5376
Scott City *(G-10816)*
Howell Country Feeders LLC ....E 620 227-6612
Dodge City *(G-1376)*
Hy Plains Feedyard LLC ....E 620 846-2226
Montezuma *(G-7156)*
Ingalls Feed Yard ....E 620 335-5174
Ingalls *(G-3576)*
Innovative Livestock Svcs Inc ....D 620 793-9200
Great Bend *(G-2593)*
Irsik & Doll Feed Services Inc ....E 620 872-5371
Scott City *(G-10817)*
Irsik & Doll Feed Services Inc ....E 620 855-3486
Cimarron *(G-831)*
Irsik & Doll Feed Services Inc ....F 620 855-3747
Cimarron *(G-830)*
Kearny County Feeders LLC ....F 620 355-6630
Lakin *(G-4651)*
Lane County Feeders Inc ....E 620 397-5341
Dighton *(G-1286)*
Mid America Ils Inc ....F 620 792-1378
Great Bend *(G-2609)*
Palenske Ranch Inc ....F 620 279-4467
Strong City *(G-12194)*
Pioneer Feedyard LLC ....E 785 672-3257
Oakley *(G-7485)*
Poky Feeders Inc ....D 620 872-7046
Scott City *(G-10828)*
Pratt Feeders LLC ....E 620 672-3401
Pratt *(G-10138)*
Pratt Feeders LLC ....F 620 635-2213
Ashland *(G-197)*
Premier Cattle Co LLC ....E 620 384-5711
Syracuse *(G-12229)*
Premier Cattle Co LLC ....F 620 855-3162
Cimarron *(G-833)*
Premium Feeders Inc ....E 785 335-2221
Scandia *(G-10801)*
Rainbow Organic Farms Co ....F 620 939-4933
Bronson *(G-587)*
Reeve Cattle Co Inc ....F 620 275-0234
Garden City *(G-2265)*
River Bend Feed Yard Inc ....F 620 356-4100
Ulysses *(G-13316)*
Robert Gigstad ....E 785 448-6923
Garnett *(G-2387)*
Roth Farm ....F 785 944-3329
Green *(G-2666)*
Sellers Farms Inc ....F 620 257-5144
Lyons *(G-6497)*
Sherow Cattle Co ....F 620 596-2813
Langdon *(G-4664)*
Solomon Valley Feeders LLC ....F 785 738-2263
Beloit *(G-503)*
Sublette Enterprises Inc ....D 620 668-5501
Sublette *(G-12210)*
T-Bone Feeders Inc ....F 785 899-6551
Goodland *(G-2488)*
Triangle H Grain & Cattle Co ....F 620 276-4004
Garden City *(G-2302)*
Trinity Feedyard LLC ....E 620 275-4191
Garden City *(G-2303)*
Valley Feeds Inc ....E 785 854-7611
Long Island *(G-6429)*
Ward Feed Yard Inc ....E 620 285-2183
Larned *(G-4715)*
We Land & Cattle Co Inc ....F 620 675-2747
Sublette *(G-12213)*
Western Feed Yard Inc ....E 620 492-6256
Johnson *(G-3665)*
Whitham Farms Feedyard Inc ....E 620 375-4684
Leoti *(G-6260)*
Wilroads Feed Yard LLC ....E 620 225-3960
Dodge City *(G-1457)*
Winger Cattle Co Inc ....F 620 492-6214
Johnson *(G-3666)*
Winner Cir Feedyard Dodge LLC ....F 620 227-2246
Dodge City *(G-1459)*
Winter Feed Yard Inc ....E 620 225-4128
Dodge City *(G-1460)*

0212 Beef Cattle, Except Feedlots

Adams Cattle Company ... F ... 785 256-4200 — Maple Hill (G-6862)
Bekemeyer Enterprises Inc ... F ... 785 325-2274 — Washington (G-13459)
Brookover Land Enterprises LP ... F ... 620 275-9206 — Garden City (G-2119)
Callicrate Cattle Co LLC ... F ... 785 332-3344 — Saint Francis (G-10338)
Donohue Ranch ... F ... 785 867-2160 — Greeley (G-2665)
Fairleigh Corporation ... D ... 620 872-1111 — Scott City (G-10809)
Ferguson Ranch ... F ... 620 467-2265 — Cambridge (G-663)
Frank Bills ... E ... 620 736-2875 — Severy (G-10890)
Gardiner Angus Ranch ... F ... 620 635-2932 — Ashland (G-194)
Great Bend Feeding Inc ... E ... 620 792-2508 — Great Bend (G-2579)
Livengood Jl Farms Inc ... F ... 785 399-2251 — Kanorado (G-3773)
Melvin Winger ... F ... 620 492-6214 — Johnson (G-3658)
Midwest Feeders Inc ... E ... 620 335-5790 — Ingalls (G-3579)
Pioneer Feedyard LLC ... E ... 785 672-3257 — Oakley (G-7485)
Ronald Carlile ... F ... 620 624-2632 — Liberal (G-6361)
Sylvester Ranch Inc ... E ... 785 242-3598 — Ottawa (G-8315)
Tdn Farms ... E ... 620 324-5296 — Lewis (G-6271)
Thomas County Feeders Inc ... E ... 785 462-3947 — Colby (G-1046)
Winger Cattle Co Inc ... F ... 620 492-6214 — Johnson (G-3666)

0213 Hogs

Bekemeyer Enterprises Inc ... F ... 785 325-2274 — Washington (G-13459)
F & R Swine Inc ... E ... 316 799-1983 — Whitewater (G-13571)
Grain Sorghum Hogs Inc ... F ... 620 872-3866 — Scott City (G-10813)
Guptons Pets & Supplies Inc ... E ... 316 682-8111 — Wichita (G-14528)
Haverkamp Brothers Inc ... D ... 785 858-4457 — Bern (G-523)
Henrys Ltd ... F ... 785 388-2480 — Longford (G-6430)
Husky Hogs LLC ... E ... 785 854-7666 — Long Island (G-6427)
J-Six Farms LLC ... F ... 785 336-2148 — Seneca (G-10869)
K C Pork Inc ... F ... 785 455-3410 — Clifton (G-901)
Kansas-Smith Farms LLC ... D ... 620 417-6765 — Plains (G-9976)
Keesecker Agri Business Inc ... E ... 785 325-3134 — Washington (G-13466)
Livingston Enterprises Inc ... E ... 402 247-3323 — Mahaska (G-6506)
Poky Feeders Inc ... D ... 620 872-7046 — Scott City (G-10828)
Roth Farm ... F ... 785 944-3329 — Green (G-2666)
Seaboard Corporation ... C ... 913 676-8800 — Merriam (G-7103)
Seaboard Foods LLC ... E ... 620 375-4523 — Leoti (G-6258)
◆ Seaboard Foods LLC ... D ... 913 261-2600 — Shawnee Mission (G-11842)
Seaboard Foods LLC ... E ... 620 375-4431 — Leoti (G-6259)
Summit Producers Company Inc ... F ... 785 827-9331 — Salina (G-10721)
Zoltenko Farms Inc ... E ... 785 278-5405 — Courtland (G-1181)

0214 Sheep & Goats

Elderslie LLC ... F ... 316 680-2637 — Valley Center (G-13341)

0219 General Livestock, NEC

Mid Continent Farms ... F ... 785 325-2089 — Washington (G-13469)

0241 Dairy Farms

Anderson Erickson Dairy Co ... D ... 913 621-4801 — Kansas City (G-3810)
Bird City Dairy LLC ... E ... 785 734-2295 — Bird City (G-529)
Frontier Dairy LLC ... E ... 620 372-2156 — Syracuse (G-12225)
High Plains Dairy LLC ... E ... 620 563-9441 — Plains (G-9975)
High Plains Ranch LLC ... E ... 559 805-5636 — Satanta (G-10786)
Hiland Dairy Foods Company LLC ... F ... 620 225-4111 — Dodge City (G-1373)
Hiland Dairy Foods Company LLC ... F ... 785 539-7541 — Manhattan (G-6657)
KDI Operating Company LLC ... E ... 620 544-4114 — Hugoton (G-3168)
Lakin Dairy ... E ... 620 355-6640 — Lakin (G-4655)
Little Creek Dairy ... E ... 785 348-5576 — Linn (G-6410)
Mas Cow Dairy LLC ... E ... 620 626-7151 — Liberal (G-6340)
McCarty Dairy LLC ... E ... 785 465-9002 — Rexford (G-10201)
McCarty Family Farms LLC ... F ... 785 465-9006 — Rexford (G-10202)
McCarty Farms Scott City LLC ... E ... 620 872-5661 — Scott City (G-10821)
Meadowlark Dairy Nutrition LLC ... D ... 620 765-7700 — Garden City (G-2230)
Midwest Dairy Association ... F ... 913 345-2225 — Overland Park (G-9032)
Milk Palace Dairy LLC ... E ... 620 372-2021 — Coolidge (G-1146)
Ohldes Dairy Inc ... F ... 785 348-5697 — Linn (G-6411)
Powerline Dairy LLC ... D ... 620 855-2844 — Cimarron (G-832)
R & K Horn LLC ... E ... 620 241-5083 — McPherson (G-7021)
RC Geven Farms LLC ... D ... 620 372-2021 — Syracuse (G-12231)
Royal Farms Dairy LLC ... E ... 620 335-5704 — Garden City (G-2269)
Southwest Plains Dairy LLC ... E ... 620 384-6813 — Syracuse (G-12233)
Stone Post Dairy LLC ... E ... 620 357-8634 — Jetmore (G-3648)
Syracuse Dairy II LLC ... E ... 620 492-2525 — Syracuse (G-12234)
Time Line Dairy LLC ... E ... 620 492-3232 — Syracuse (G-12235)
Tuls Dairy Farms LLC ... E ... 620 624-6455 — Liberal (G-6375)

0254 Poultry Hatcheries

BS Cvf Inc ... F ... 785 448-2239 — Garnett (G-2370)
▲ Nelson Poultry Farms Inc ... F ... 785 587-0399 — Manhattan (G-6758)

0259 Poultry & Eggs Farms, NEC

Livingston Enterprises Inc ... E ... 402 247-3323 — Mahaska (G-6506)

0272 Horse & Other Equine Pro duction

Kgj Quarter Horses ... F ... 316 775-0954 — Augusta (G-330)
Shadow 7 LLC ... F ... 316 687-5777 — Wichita (G-15570)

0279 Animal Specialties, NEC

Flint Oak ... E ... 620 658-4401 — Fall River (G-1927)
Ryan Farms Inc ... F ... 785 263-1613 — Abilene (G-53)
Wayne R Ward & Associates ... F ... 785 263-7272 — Abilene (G-57)

0291 Animal Production, NEC

Beachner Bros (kansas) Inc ... F ... 620 449-2286 — Saint Paul (G-10380)
BS Cvf Inc ... F ... 785 448-2239 — Garnett (G-2370)
Fullmer Cattle Co KS LLC ... E ... 620 384-7499 — Syracuse (G-12226)
Ghost Lake Corporation ... F ... 816 809-9411 — Stilwell (G-12149)
Hedrick Exotic Animal Farm ... E ... 620 422-3245 — Nickerson (G-7433)
Holton Livestock Exchange Inc ... E ... 785 364-4114 — Holton (G-3097)
Irsik Family Partnership ... F ... 620 335-5363 — Ingalls (G-3577)
Orscheln Farm and Home LLC ... F ... 620 662-8867 — Hutchinson (G-3397)
Ringneck Ranch Incorporated ... E ... 785 373-4835 — Tipton (G-12249)
Saline Valley Farm Inc ... F ... 785 524-4562 — Lincoln (G-6388)
Todd Tractor Co Inc ... F ... 785 336-2138 — Seneca (G-10884)
Victor Ritter ... F ... 785 678-2423 — Jennings (G-3644)

07 AGRICULTURAL SERVICES

0711 Soil Preparation Svcs

Baker Services Inc ... F ... 913 367-1657 — Atchison (G-212)
County of Douglas ... E ... 785 331-1330 — Lawrence (G-4813)
Hodges Farms & Dredging LLC ... F ... 620 343-0513 — Lebo (G-5606)
Kansas State University ... E ... 620 421-4826 — Parsons (G-9697)
Kaw Valley Engineering Inc ... E ... 785 762-5040 — Junction City (G-3714)
Lange Company LLC ... F ... 620 456-2996 — Conway Springs (G-1143)
Mid-Kansas Cooperative Assn ... F ... 785 227-3361 — Lindsborg (G-6403)
Natures Way Inc ... G ... 785 486-3302 — Horton (G-3132)
Servi Tech Inc ... C ... 620 227-7509 — Dodge City (G-1429)
Surefire AG Systems Inc ... E ... 785 626-3670 — Atwood (G-292)
Undergrund Cvern Stblztion LLC ... F ... 620 662-6367 — Great Bend (G-2651)

0721 Soil Preparation, Planting & Cultivating Svc

Baker Services Inc ... F ... 913 367-1657 — Atchison (G-212)
Central Prairie Co-Op ... F ... 620 278-2470 — Sterling (G-12113)
Chem Till Spray Company Inc ... F ... 620 492-2751 — Johnson (G-3652)
Chem-Trol Inc ... F ... 913 342-3006 — Kansas City (G-3909)
Clark Flying Service Inc ... F ... 620 348-2685 — Macksville (G-6499)
Comanche County ... F ... 620 582-2933 — Coldwater (G-1054)
County of Barber ... E ... 620 886-5087 — Medicine Lodge (G-7059)
County of Jefferson ... F ... 785 863-2581 — Oskaloosa (G-8221)
Crop Service Center Inc ... F ... 785 479-2204 — Abilene (G-22)
Pine Howard Grdn Ctr & Grnhse ... E ... 785 749-0302 — Lawrence (G-5064)
Plainjans Feedlot Service ... F ... 620 872-5777 — Scott City (G-10827)
Pro Tech Spraying Service Inc ... F ... 620 855-7793 — Cimarron (G-834)
Servi Tech Inc ... C ... 620 227-7509 — Dodge City (G-1429)

0722 Crop Harvesting By Machine

Clayton J Befort ... F ... 785 625-7628 — Hays (G-2770)
Custom Harvest Insurance ... F ... 620 259-6996 — Hutchinson (G-3252)
Frederick Harvesting ... F ... 620 534-2211 — Alden (G-58)
Keller Bros Harvesting & Trckg ... F ... 785 726-3555 — Ellis (G-1648)
Logan Farms Inc ... E ... 785 256-6334 — Eskridge (G-1868)
Mike Keimig Harvesting ... F ... 620 278-2334 — Sterling (G-12126)
Morrill Hay Company Inc ... F ... 620 285-6941 — Paola (G-9576)

Mull Family Farms Oper Partnr.....F....620 982-4336
Pawnee Rock *(G-9753)*
Mull Investments LP.....F....620 982-4336
Pawnee Rock *(G-9754)*
Norag LLC.....D....913 851-7200
Bucyrus *(G-605)*
Palenske Ranch Inc.....F....620 279-4467
Strong City *(G-12194)*
Producers Coop Assn Girard.....E....620 724-8241
Girard *(G-2415)*

0723 Crop Preparation, Except Cotton Ginning

A&L Hay Farms Inc.....F....785 461-5339
Wakefield *(G-13397)*
ADM Milling Co.....F....913 266-6300
Shawnee Mission *(G-11077)*
Archer-Daniels-Midland Company.....E....785 899-3700
Goodland *(G-2462)*
Bestifor Hay Co.....F....785 527-2450
Belleville *(G-454)*
Cropland Co-Op Inc.....F....620 356-1241
Ulysses *(G-13294)*
Farmer Direct Foods Inc.....F....785 823-8787
New Cambria *(G-7270)*
Kansas Grain Inspection Svc.....F....785 827-3671
Salina *(G-10565)*
Kauffman Seeds Inc.....F....877 664-3526
Haven *(G-2733)*
Norag LLC.....D....913 851-7200
Bucyrus *(G-605)*
Red River Commodities Inc.....E....785 462-3911
Colby *(G-1035)*
Rice Precision Mfg Inc.....E....785 594-2670
Baldwin City *(G-367)*
Seaboard Corporation.....C....913 676-8800
Merriam *(G-7103)*
Valley View Milling LLC.....F....785 858-4777
Seneca *(G-10887)*

0724 Cotton Ginning

Northwest Cot Growers Coop Inc.....E....620 598-2008
Moscow *(G-7168)*
Southern Kansas Cotton Growers.....F....620 221-1370
Winfield *(G-16174)*

0741 Veterinary Livestock Svcs

Abilene Animal Hospital PA.....E....785 263-2301
Abilene *(G-1)*
Allen Veterinary Center.....F....620 421-1341
Parsons *(G-9665)*
Animal Chiropractic Center.....E....309 658-2920
Wellsville *(G-13540)*
Auburn Animal Clinic Inc.....F....785 256-2476
Auburn *(G-293)*
Direct Vet Marketing Inc.....E....888 280-2221
Manhattan *(G-6614)*
Dodge City Veterinary Clinic.....F....620 227-8651
Dodge City *(G-1352)*
Emporia Veterinary Hospital.....F....620 342-6515
Emporia *(G-1746)*
Eudora Animal Hospital Inc.....F....785 542-3265
Eudora *(G-1873)*
Girard Animal Hospital PA.....F....620 724-6068
Girard *(G-2406)*
Goddard Veterinary Clinic.....F....316 794-8022
Goddard *(G-2441)*
Kansas State University.....E....620 421-4826
Parsons *(G-9697)*
Welborn Animal Hospital.....E....913 334-6770
Kansas City *(G-4533)*

0742 Veterinary Animal Specialties

A Caring Doctor Minnesota PA.....E....913 393-4654
Olathe *(G-7505)*
A Caring Doctor Minnesota PA.....E....785 272-1541
Topeka *(G-12278)*
A Caring Doctor Minnesota PA.....E....913 962-2901
Shawnee *(G-10904)*
A Caring Doctor Minnesota PA.....E....316 946-0920
Wichita *(G-13584)*
A Caring Doctor Minnesota PA.....E....913 345-8383
Shawnee Mission *(G-11061)*
A Caring Doctor Minnesota PA.....E....316 631-3939
Wichita *(G-13585)*
Abilene Animal Hospital PA.....E....785 263-2301
Abilene *(G-1)*
All Crtres Veterinary Hosp P A.....F....316 721-3993
Wichita *(G-13663)*
Allcare Animal Hospital Inc.....E....913 268-5011
Shawnee Mission *(G-11095)*
Allen Veterinary Center.....F....620 421-1341
Parsons *(G-9665)*
Animal Care Center of Top.....F....785 232-2205
Topeka *(G-12329)*
Animal Chiropractic Center.....E....309 658-2920
Wellsville *(G-13540)*
Animal Clinic North Topeka PA.....F....785 357-5188
Topeka *(G-12330)*
Animal Clinic Wichita PA.....F....316 686-8516
Wichita *(G-13711)*
Animal Hospital of Lawrence.....F....785 842-0609
Lawrence *(G-4736)*
Animal Medical Center LLC.....F....620 792-1265
Great Bend *(G-2510)*
Apple Lane Animal Hospital.....F....620 662-0515
Hutchinson *(G-3203)*
Ark Valley Veterinary Hospital.....F....620 793-5457
Great Bend *(G-2512)*
Ark Veterinary Associates PA.....F....620 442-3306
Arkansas City *(G-146)*
Auburn Animal Clinic Inc.....F....785 256-2476
Auburn *(G-293)*
Blackbob Pet Hospital.....E....913 829-7387
Olathe *(G-7556)*
Blair Doon Veterinary Hospital.....E....316 685-7300
Wichita *(G-13856)*
Blue Valley Animal Hospital.....F....913 681-2818
Overland Park *(G-8468)*
Bluepearl Vtrinary Partners LLC.....E....913 642-9563
Shawnee Mission *(G-11172)*
Bogue Animal Hospital West PA.....E....316 722-1085
Wichita *(G-13869)*
Bradley Animal Hospital.....F....785 843-9533
Lawrence *(G-4765)*
Burlingame Road Animal Hosp.....E....785 267-1012
Topeka *(G-12414)*
Camelot Court Animal Clinic.....F....913 469-9330
Shawnee Mission *(G-11200)*
Cat Calls.....F....913 642-2024
Shawnee Mission *(G-11205)*
Cat Clinic of Johnson County.....F....913 541-0478
Lenexa *(G-5732)*
▲ Ceva Animal Health LLC.....C....913 894-0230
Lenexa *(G-5745)*
Ceva Animal Health LLC.....D....800 999-0297
Lenexa *(G-5744)*
Cherokee Animal Clinic PA.....E....913 649-0440
Overland Park *(G-8545)*
Cherokee Cat Clinic.....E....913 649-0446
Shawnee Mission *(G-11218)*
Chisholm Trail Animal Care Ctr.....F....316 744-0501
Park City *(G-9609)*
Clinton Parkway Animal Hosp.....E....785 841-3131
Lawrence *(G-4794)*
College Blvd Animal Hosp PA.....F....913 469-5869
Shawnee Mission *(G-11247)*
Companion Animal Clinic.....F....785 271-7387
Topeka *(G-12494)*
Companion Animal Hospital.....F....316 722-1004
Wichita *(G-14079)*
Countryside Pet Clinic PA.....E....316 733-8433
Andover *(G-88)*
Dallas Caster DDS.....F....785 256-2476
Topeka *(G-12544)*
Davy Harkins Dvm.....F....316 321-1050
El Dorado *(G-1555)*
Dean E Small.....F....913 642-2714
Shawnee Mission *(G-11297)*
Dearborn Animal Clinic PA.....F....913 722-2800
Shawnee Mission *(G-11298)*
▲ Dechra Veterinary Products LLC.....F....913 327-0015
Overland Park *(G-8645)*
Dodge City Veterinary Clinic.....F....620 227-8651
Dodge City *(G-1352)*
El Paso Animal Clinic.....F....316 788-1561
Derby *(G-1243)*
Emporia Veterinary Hospital.....F....620 342-6515
Emporia *(G-1746)*
Eudora Animal Hospital Inc.....F....785 542-3265
Eudora *(G-1873)*
Ewy Animal Hosp Inc.....G....785 823-8428
Salina *(G-10487)*
Gardner Animal Hospital PA.....F....913 856-6255
Gardner *(G-2347)*
Gentle Care Animal Hospital.....F....785 841-1919
Lawrence *(G-4872)*
Girard Animal Hospital PA.....F....620 724-6068
Girard *(G-2406)*
Goddard Veterinary Clinic.....F....316 794-8022
Goddard *(G-2441)*
Greg Ketzner.....E....913 334-6770
Kansas City *(G-4051)*
Hawthorne Animal Hospital.....F....913 345-8147
Shawnee Mission *(G-11417)*
Hays Veterinary Hosp Prof Assn.....F....785 625-2719
Hays *(G-2839)*
Heartland Animal Clinic PA.....F....913 648-1662
Shawnee Mission *(G-11421)*
Heartland Animal Hospital.....F....316 744-8160
Bel Aire *(G-435)*
Hires Gage Dvm.....E....913 432-7611
Fairway *(G-1910)*
Indian Hills Animal Clinic.....E....316 942-3900
Wichita *(G-14682)*
Johnson County Animal Clinic.....F....913 642-2714
Shawnee Mission *(G-11496)*
Kansas Humane Soc Wichita Kans.....F....316 524-9196
Wichita *(G-14806)*
Kansas State University.....E....785 532-5640
Manhattan *(G-6689)*
Kansas State University.....C....785 532-5654
Manhattan *(G-6693)*
Libel & Ripple Dvm.....F....620 227-2751
Dodge City *(G-1399)*
Lionsgate Pet Hospital.....F....913 402-8300
Overland Park *(G-8961)*
Metcalf 107 Animal Clinic Inc.....F....913 642-1077
Overland Park *(G-9014)*
Meyer Veterinary Hospital.....F....913 682-6000
Leavenworth *(G-5270)*
Mill Creek Animal Clinic PA.....F....913 268-0900
Shawnee Mission *(G-11640)*
Miller Veterinary Services PA.....F....913 592-2770
Spring Hill *(G-12090)*
Mission Animal Clinic PA.....F....913 432-3341
Shawnee Mission *(G-11643)*
Mission Medvet.....F....913 722-5566
Shawnee Mission *(G-11646)*
Mission Road Animal Clinic.....F....913 649-0552
Leawood *(G-5486)*
Nall Hills Animal Hospital.....F....913 341-8836
Shawnee Mission *(G-11667)*
National Veterinary Associates.....F....913 782-0173
Olathe *(G-7912)*
North Rock Hosp For Animals PC.....F....316 636-1200
Wichita *(G-15188)*
Northrdge Plycare Boarding LLC.....F....316 677-8107
Wichita *(G-15191)*
Oakbrook Animal Hospital Inc.....F....913 884-8778
Gardner *(G-2356)*
Olathe Animal Hospital Inc.....F....913 764-1415
Olathe *(G-7927)*
Overland Park Veterinary Ctr.....F....913 642-9371
Overland Park *(G-9124)*
Oxford Animal Hospital P A.....F....913 681-2600
Overland Park *(G-9130)*
Paw Prints Animal Hospital.....F....785 267-1918
Berryton *(G-528)*
Petworks Inc.....F....913 381-3131
Shawnee Mission *(G-11730)*
Prairie Village Animal Hosp PA.....F....913 642-7060
Prairie Village *(G-10061)*
Ridgeview Animal Hospital.....F....913 780-0078
Olathe *(G-8035)*
Sdk Laboratories Inc.....E....620 665-5661
Hutchinson *(G-3439)*
Shane Paul Inc.....F....316 283-1650
Newton *(G-7417)*
Shane Paul LLC.....F....316 283-1650
Newton *(G-7418)*
Skaer Veterinary Clinic P A.....F....316 683-4641
Wichita *(G-15599)*
Southside Pet Hospital.....F....913 782-0173
Olathe *(G-8074)*
Stannley Veterinary Clinic.....E....913 897-2080
Shawnee Mission *(G-11894)*
State Line Animal Hospital.....F....913 381-3272
Leawood *(G-5562)*
Stone House Animal Hospital.....E....785 228-9411
Topeka *(G-13100)*
Swartz Veterinary Hospital.....F....785 460-1078
Colby *(G-1044)*
Town & Country Animal Clinic.....F....316 283-1650
Newton *(G-7420)*
Town & Country Animal Hospital.....F....785 823-2217
Salina *(G-10736)*
University of Kansas.....E....913 588-7015
Kansas City *(G-4503)*

Van Petten Animal Health Inc ....F 785 484-3358
Meriden *(G-7083)*

Vet Medical Surgery ....F 785 267-6060
Topeka *(G-13220)*

Veterinary Clinic ....E 785 242-4780
Ottawa *(G-8319)*

Wakarusa Veterinary Hospital ....F 785 843-5577
Lawrence *(G-5176)*

Welborn Animal Hospital ....E 913 334-6770
Kansas City *(G-4533)*

West Wichita Pet Clinic ....F 316 722-0100
Wichita *(G-15959)*

Westside Vet Clnic Mnhattan PA ....F 785 539-7922
Manhattan *(G-6853)*

Westwood Animal Hospital ....F 913 362-2512
Westwood *(G-13563)*

Wichita Emrgncy Veterinary LLC ....E 316 262-5321
Wichita *(G-15997)*

Winchester Place Pet Care Ctr ....F 913 451-2827
Olathe *(G-8155)*

Wingert Animal Hospital ....F 316 524-3257
Wichita *(G-16055)*

0751 Livestock Svcs, Except Veterinary

Butterball LLC ....C 620 597-2800
Columbus *(G-1063)*

Cross Country Genetics Inc ....F 785 457-3336
Westmoreland *(G-13546)*

Harvest Brands Stockade ....E 620 231-6700
Pittsburg *(G-9873)*

Heartland Feeders Inc ....F 620 872-0800
Scott City *(G-10814)*

Heft & Sons LLC ....E 620 723-2495
Greensburg *(G-2679)*

Ils Farm Partnership ....F 620 792-6166
Great Bend *(G-2592)*

Irsik & Doll Feed Services Inc ....E 620 275-7131
Garden City *(G-2205)*

Kansas State University ....F 785 564-7459
Manhattan *(G-6684)*

Kiowa Locker System LLC ....F 620 825-4538
Kiowa *(G-4626)*

Krehbiels Specialty Meats Inc ....E 620 241-0103
McPherson *(G-6985)*

Plankenhorn Inc ....F 620 276-3791
Garden City *(G-2256)*

Rawhide Portable Corral Inc ....E 785 263-3436
Abilene *(G-50)*

Shaw Feedyard Inc ....F 620 635-2670
Ashland *(G-198)*

0752 Animal Specialty Svcs, Exc Veterinary

All Crtres Veterinary Hosp P A ....F 316 721-3993
Wichita *(G-13663)*

Animal Care Center of Top ....F 785 232-2205
Topeka *(G-12329)*

Barks N Bows Dog Grooming ....G 785 823-1627
Salina *(G-10421)*

Blackbob Pet Hospital ....E 913 829-7387
Olathe *(G-7556)*

Bradley Animal Hospital ....F 785 843-9533
Lawrence *(G-4765)*

Camelot Court Animal Clinic ....F 913 469-9330
Shawnee Mission *(G-11200)*

Cherokee Cat Clinic ....E 913 649-0446
Shawnee Mission *(G-11218)*

Clinton Parkway Animal Hosp ....E 785 841-3131
Lawrence *(G-4794)*

College Blvd Animal Hosp PA ....F 913 469-5869
Shawnee Mission *(G-11247)*

Companion Animal Hospital ....F 316 722-1004
Wichita *(G-14079)*

Countryside Pet Clinic PA ....E 316 733-8433
Andover *(G-88)*

Dodge City Veterinary Clinic ....F 620 227-8651
Dodge City *(G-1352)*

Durasafe Products Inc ....F 316 942-3282
Wichita *(G-14245)*

El Paso Animal Clinic ....F 316 788-1561
Derby *(G-1243)*

Garden City Kansas Kennel Club ....E 620 275-4739
Garden City *(G-2174)*

Gentle Care Animal Hospital ....F 785 841-1919
Lawrence *(G-4872)*

Heartland Animal Clinic PA ....F 913 648-1662
Shawnee Mission *(G-11421)*

Howl-A-Dayz Inn LLC ....F 785 539-7849
Manhattan *(G-6661)*

Johnson County Animal Clinic ....F 913 642-2714
Shawnee Mission *(G-11496)*

K C K Animal Control ....F 913 321-1445
Kansas City *(G-4133)*

Kennel Creek ....E 913 498-9900
Overland Park *(G-8915)*

Kgj Quarter Horses ....F 316 775-0954
Augusta *(G-330)*

Ksds Inc ....F 785 325-2256
Washington *(G-13468)*

Lambert Vet Supply LLC ....F 785 527-2209
Belleville *(G-459)*

Land of Paws LLC ....F 913 341-1011
Shawnee Mission *(G-11547)*

Martin Peck Bea Anmal Shlter I ....E 785 248-3454
Ottawa *(G-8290)*

National Greyhound Association ....F 785 263-4660
Abilene *(G-48)*

North Rock Hosp For Animals PC ....F 316 636-1200
Wichita *(G-15188)*

Pawsh Wash ....F 785 856-7297
Lawrence *(G-5059)*

Pete & Macs Recreational Reso ....E 913 888-8889
Lenexa *(G-6055)*

Petsmart Inc ....E 913 393-4111
Olathe *(G-7980)*

Petsmart Inc ....E 913 338-5544
Shawnee Mission *(G-11728)*

Petsmart Inc ....E 785 272-3323
Topeka *(G-12973)*

Petsmart Inc ....E 913 384-4445
Shawnee Mission *(G-11729)*

Petworks Inc ....F 913 381-3131
Shawnee Mission *(G-11730)*

Proud Anmal Lovers Shelter Inc ....F 620 421-0445
Parsons *(G-9726)*

R C Kennels ....F 785 238-7000
Junction City *(G-3747)*

Ridgeview Animal Hospital ....F 913 780-0078
Olathe *(G-8035)*

Town & Country Animal Hospital ....F 785 823-2217
Salina *(G-10736)*

U Bathe Pets ....F 913 829-3275
Olathe *(G-8128)*

Wakarusa Veterinary Hospital ....F 785 843-5577
Lawrence *(G-5176)*

West Wichita Pet Clinic ....F 316 722-0100
Wichita *(G-15959)*

Westwood Animal Hospital ....F 913 362-2512
Westwood *(G-13563)*

Winchester Place Pet Care Ctr ....F 913 451-2827
Olathe *(G-8155)*

Woofs Play & Stay Inc ....F 913 768-9663
Olathe *(G-8161)*

0762 Farm Management Svcs

Citizens State Bank and Tr Co ....E 785 742-2101
Hiawatha *(G-3006)*

Kansas Farm Mgt Assoc SC ....F 620 662-7868
Hutchinson *(G-3345)*

Lazer Spot Inc ....D 913 839-2654
Olathe *(G-7857)*

Triple T Farms ....F 620 355-6707
Lakin *(G-4661)*

0781 Landscape Counseling & Planning

Adki Group LLC ....F 913 208-7899
Olathe *(G-7509)*

All-N-1 Landscape LLC ....F 785 856-5296
Lawrence *(G-4726)*

Arensman Services ....F 620 430-1106
Kinsley *(G-4615)*

Barnds Brothers Inc ....E 913 897-2340
Shawnee Mission *(G-11152)*

Biehler Companies Inc ....D 316 529-0002
Wichita *(G-13847)*

Blackburn Nursery Inc ....E 785 272-2707
Topeka *(G-12387)*

Brady Nursery Inc ....E 316 722-7516
Wichita *(G-13883)*

Brightview Landscapes LLC ....E 913 371-2661
Lenexa *(G-5714)*

Creative Landscaping Inc ....F 785 286-0015
Topeka *(G-12527)*

Cut-N-Edge Inc ....F 785 232-9800
Topeka *(G-12541)*

Cutting Edge Lawn Care Inc ....F 316 390-1443
Wichita *(G-14148)*

Dllc - Dupree Landscap ....F 913 856-0120
Gardner *(G-2339)*

Dlr Group Inc ....D 913 897-7811
Overland Park *(G-8659)*

Doctors Inc ....E 913 681-8041
Stilwell *(G-12145)*

Earth Designs Inc ....G 913 791-2858
Shawnee Mission *(G-11325)*

Elevated Living LLC ....F 316 619-7690
Lenexa *(G-5832)*

Environmental View LLC ....F 913 432-5011
Kansas City *(G-3990)*

Epic Landscape Productions ....F 913 897-3858
Gardner *(G-2341)*

Glmv Architecture Inc ....E 316 265-9367
Wichita *(G-14472)*

Green Hills Inc ....F 316 686-7673
Wichita *(G-14509)*

Howe Landscape Inc ....F 785 485-2857
Riley *(G-10206)*

Kansas State University ....E 785 532-5961
Manhattan *(G-6683)*

Konradys Lawn & Ldscpg Inc ....E 913 722-1163
Olathe *(G-7843)*

Landgenuity LLC ....E 913 594-1845
Louisburg *(G-6455)*

Landmark Landscape LLC ....E 785 608-6907
Topeka *(G-12833)*

Landmasters Landscape ....F 913 667-3382
Olathe *(G-7854)*

Landplan Engineering PA ....D 785 843-7530
Lawrence *(G-4954)*

Lawrence Landscape ....E 785 749-7554
Lawrence *(G-4971)*

Lawrence Landscape Inc ....E 785 843-4370
Lawrence *(G-4972)*

Luka Irrigation Systems Inc ....E 913 248-0400
Shawnee *(G-10990)*

Luxury Lawn & Landscape Inc ....F 785 233-5296
Topeka *(G-12854)*

McKee Pool & Landscaping Inc ....F 785 843-9119
Lawrence *(G-5018)*

Messenger Lawn and Ldscpg LLC ....E 913 681-6165
Stilwell *(G-12166)*

Midwest Turf & Landscape LLC ....F 785 383-7839
Auburn *(G-296)*

Natural Creations Inc ....F 913 390-8058
Olathe *(G-7913)*

Next To Nature Landscape LLC ....E 913 963-8180
Olathe *(G-7919)*

Paramount Landscape Inc ....F 913 375-1697
Kansas City *(G-4311)*

Principal Landscape Group LLC ....F 913 362-0089
Kansas City *(G-4338)*

Quentin Mc Kee & Son Ldscpg ....F 785 827-5155
Salina *(G-10648)*

Reed Dillon & Associates ....F 785 832-0083
Lawrence *(G-5091)*

Riedel Garden Center ....F 785 628-2877
Hays *(G-2900)*

Rolling Meadows Landscape ....F 913 839-0229
Kansas City *(G-4387)*

Rothwell Landscape Inc ....E 785 238-2647
Manhattan *(G-6795)*

Seasonal Solutions LLC ....F 913 685-4222
Overland Park *(G-9287)*

Sheldon C Clayton ....D 913 927-9248
Ottawa *(G-8311)*

Signature Landscape LLC ....C 913 829-8181
Olathe *(G-8066)*

TLC Lawn Care Inc ....D 913 780-5296
Olathe *(G-8112)*

Topeka Landscape Inc ....E 785 232-8873
Topeka *(G-13180)*

Total Turfcare Inc ....F 785 827-6983
Salina *(G-10735)*

Tree Top Nursery and Landscape ....E 316 686-7491
Wichita *(G-15797)*

Treescape Inc ....E 316 733-6388
Andover *(G-112)*

Tuff Turf Inc ....F 913 362-4545
Shawnee Mission *(G-11948)*

Turf Design Inc ....D 913 764-6531
Lenexa *(G-6194)*

Waters Inc ....E 785 822-6540
Salina *(G-10760)*

Waters Inc ....E 620 343-2800
Emporia *(G-1849)*

Waters Inc ....E 785 537-1340
Manhattan *(G-6847)*

Waters Inc ....E 785 238-3114
Junction City *(G-3767)*

Waters Inc ....E 620 227-2900
Dodge City *(G-1451)*

SIC

Wdm Architects PA E 316 262-4700
Wichita (G-15939)
White Lawn and Landscape LLC F 913 709-1472
Edwardsville (G-1521)
Younie Lawnscapes F 620 672-3301
Pratt (G-10165)

0782 Lawn & Garden Svcs

4t Total Lawn Inc E 913 888-0997
Shawnee Mission (G-11059)
Acentric LLC F 913 787-4856
Louisburg (G-6435)
Adki Group LLC F 913 208-7899
Olathe (G-7509)
Aspen Lawn Landscaping Inc E 913 829-6135
Olathe (G-7535)
B J F Inc F 913 837-2726
Paola (G-9540)
Barnds Brothers Inc E 913 897-2340
Shawnee Mission (G-11152)
Biehler Companies Inc D 316 529-0002
Wichita (G-13847)
Bornholdt Plantland Inc F 620 662-0544
Hutchinson (G-3218)
Challenger Construction Corp F 316 680-3036
Girard (G-2396)
Commercial Landscapers Inc F 913 721-5455
Kansas City (G-3930)
Commercial Lawn MGT Wchita Inc F 316 688-0722
Wichita (G-14069)
Complete Landscaping Systems D 316 832-0061
Wichita (G-14081)
Complete Outdoors Inc E 785 565-4077
Manhattan (G-6600)
Cranmer Grass Farms Inc E 316 722-7230
Maize (G-6511)
Curbys Lawn & Garden LLC F 913 764-6159
Gardner (G-2336)
Custom Lawn & Landscape Inc E 913 782-8315
Olathe (G-7631)
Custom Lawn Service Inc F 316 321-1563
Wichita (G-14146)
Davis Contracting LP E 620 331-3922
Independence (G-3510)
Doctors Inc E 913 681-8041
Stilwell (G-12145)
Dover Sod Farms Inc F 913 897-2336
Bucyrus (G-596)
Ellsworth County Highway Dept E 785 472-4182
Ellsworth (G-1669)
Emergent Care Plus LLC E 913 428-8000
Leawood (G-5386)
Epic Irrigation Inc C 913 764-0178
Olathe (G-7690)
Epic Landscape Productions F 913 897-3858
Gardner (G-2341)
Epic Landscape Productions Lc F 913 856-0113
Gardner (G-2342)
First Start Rentl Sls Svc Inc G 620 343-0983
Emporia (G-1756)
G F Enterprises G 785 539-7113
Manhattan (G-6642)
Goodwin Pro Turf Inc E 913 685-1000
Shawnee Mission (G-11399)
Gottlob Lawn & Landscape LLC E 620 222-8870
Winfield (G-16144)
Grass Pad Inc E 913 681-8948
Bucyrus (G-597)
Green Expectations Ldscpg Inc F 913 897-8076
Kansas City (G-4049)
Green Lawn Inc E 913 393-2238
Shawnee (G-10965)
Green Meadows Lawn Landscaping F 316 788-0282
Derby (G-1250)
H & R Lawn & Landscape Inc D 913 897-9705
Bucyrus (G-598)
H B Landscaping & Septic Tanks F 620 793-3985
Great Bend (G-2586)
Hauer Turf Farms Inc F 913 837-2400
Paola (G-9564)
Heimen Ldscp & Irrigation LLC E 913 432-5011
Kansas City (G-4078)
Hermes Co Inc E 913 888-2413
Lenexa (G-5901)
Hillside Nursery Inc F 316 686-6414
Wichita (G-14614)
Hongs Landscape & Nursery Inc F 316 687-3492
Wichita (G-14635)
J B Hinz F 913 492-5566
Shawnee Mission (G-11476)
Jacksons Greenhouse & Grdn Ctr F 785 232-3416
Topeka (G-12735)
Jerry Boresow F 913 441-1111
Shawnee Mission (G-11484)
Johnsons Garden Center Inc E 316 942-3751
Wichita (G-14769)
Jojacs Landscape & Mowing F 316 945-3525
Haysville (G-2950)
K-State Hrtclture Ntral Rsrces E 785 532-6170
Manhattan (G-6670)
Karcher Investments Inc F 785 452-2850
Salina (G-10568)
Konradys Ldscp Winter Svc Inc F 913 647-0286
Kansas City (G-4179)
Landscape Outfitters LLC F 620 221-1108
Winfield (G-16154)
Landscapes Inc E 316 262-7557
Wichita (G-14921)
Landworks Inc E 913 422-9300
Edwardsville (G-1507)
Lawns By Beck Inc F 913 631-8873
Shawnee Mission (G-11549)
Lawnworks Inc F 316 838-3500
Wichita (G-14936)
Lawrence Landscape Inc E 785 843-4370
Lawrence (G-4972)
Lightning Grounds Services Inc E 913 441-3900
Shawnee Mission (G-11572)
Luka Irrigation Systems Inc E 913 248-0400
Shawnee (G-10990)
Luxury Lawn & Landscape Inc F 785 233-5296
Topeka (G-12854)
Messenger Lawn and Ldscpg LLC D 913 681-6165
Stilwell (G-12167)
Meyers Brothers Cnstr Co F 913 681-2667
Stilwell (G-12168)
Midwest Legacy LLC F 316 518-9350
Park City (G-9631)
Mw Lawn & Landscape E 913 829-4949
Olathe (G-7908)
New Frontier Lawn Care Inc D 316 838-0778
Wichita (G-15166)
Nichols Lawn Service Inc F 316 688-0431
Wichita (G-15176)
Personalized Lawn Care Inc F 913 727-3977
Lansing (G-4689)
Pinnacle Lawn Care Inc E 913 851-0423
Shawnee Mission (G-11734)
Prairie Hills Nursery Inc F 620 665-5500
Hutchinson (G-3410)
Preferred Lawn Service F 785 379-8873
Tecumseh (G-12240)
Preferred Lawn Service E 785 887-9900
Lecompton (G-5613)
Premier Landscaping Inc F 316 733-4773
Andover (G-107)
Primary Care Landscape Inc F 913 768-8880
Olathe (G-8006)
Pro Tech Spraying Service Inc F 620 855-7793
Cimarron (G-834)
Professional Ldscpg Svcs LLC E 316 832-0061
Wichita (G-15363)
Proscape Inc F 785 263-7104
Abilene (G-49)
Reed Dillon & Associates F 785 832-0083
Lawrence (G-5091)
Ryan Lawn & Tree Inc D 913 381-1505
Overland Park (G-9265)
Sarto Countertops E 785 437-3344
Saint Marys (G-10375)
Schellers Inc F 620 342-3990
Emporia (G-1824)
Seeders Inc F 316 722-8345
Wichita (G-15551)
Shawnee Mission Tree Svc Inc D 913 441-8888
Shawnee (G-11029)
Signature Landscape LLC C 913 829-8181
Olathe (G-8066)
Skyton Lawn & Landscape LLC F 913 302-9056
Olathe (G-8067)
Sod Shop Inc F 913 814-0044
Bucyrus (G-609)
Stauffer Lawn and Ldscp LLC F 785 256-7300
Auburn (G-297)
Suburban Lawn & Garden Inc E 913 649-8700
Shawnee Mission (G-11906)
Tendercare Lawn and Landscape F 316 788-5416
Derby (G-1275)
TLC Lawn Care Inc D 913 780-5296
Olathe (G-8112)
Tno LLC E 913 278-1911
Kansas City (G-4469)
Topeka Landscape Inc E 785 232-8873
Topeka (G-13180)
Total Turfcare Inc F 785 827-6983
Salina (G-10735)
Town & Country Landscaping F 816 358-4511
Overland Park (G-9420)
Tree Top Nursery and Landscape E 316 686-7491
Wichita (G-15797)
Tree-Rific Landscaping Inc F 316 733-0900
Andover (G-111)
Treescape Inc E 316 733-6388
Andover (G-112)
Trugreen Limited Partnership E 316 448-6253
Wichita (G-15812)
Trugreen Limited Partnership E 785 267-4121
Lenexa (G-6193)
Tuff Turf Inc F 913 362-4545
Shawnee Mission (G-11948)
Turf Management LLC F 785 410-0394
Manhattan (G-6833)
Valley View Greenhouse LLC F 785 549-3621
Melvern (G-7077)
Van Booven Lawn & Landscaping F 913 722-3275
Edwardsville (G-1520)
Wichita Park Cmtry & Mausoleum E 316 686-5594
Wichita (G-16016)
William Barnes F 316 321-3094
El Dorado (G-1614)
William F Frey Inc E 913 541-1000
Shawnee Mission (G-12008)
Willowridge Landscape Inc F 785 842-7022
Lawrence (G-5186)
Wolfert Landscape Co LLC F 913 592-4189
Olathe (G-8158)
Wright Landscaping LLC F 816 225-1050
Lenexa (G-6235)

0783 Ornamental Shrub & Tree Svc

Asplundh Tree Expert LLC A 913 469-5440
Lenexa (G-5668)
Browns Tree Service LLC F 785 379-9212
Topeka (G-12410)
Custom Tree Care Inc E 785 478-9805
Topeka (G-12540)
Kansas City Tree Care LLC E 913 722-4048
Shawnee Mission (G-11513)
Midwest Legacy LLC F 316 518-9350
Park City (G-9631)
Professional Ldscpg Svcs LLC E 316 832-0061
Wichita (G-15363)
Royer Brothers Tree Svc LLC D 620 899-7621
Hutchinson (G-3433)
Ryan Lawn & Tree Inc D 913 381-1505
Overland Park (G-9265)
Shawnee Mission Tree Svc Inc F 316 838-3111
Wichita (G-15578)
Shawnee Mission Tree Svc Inc D 913 441-8888
Shawnee (G-11029)
Solida John & Sons Tree Svc F 785 543-2810
Phillipsburg (G-9799)
Thornes Tree Service Inc F 913 845-2387
Tonganoxie (G-12271)
Town & Country Landscaping F 816 358-4511
Overland Park (G-9420)
Wellnitz Tree Care Inc F 620 340-2484
Emporia (G-1850)

08 FORESTRY

0811 Timber Tracts

Pl Timberline LLC F 913 674-0438
Overland Park (G-9166)
Waters Inc E 785 822-6540
Salina (G-10760)
Waters Inc E 620 343-2800
Emporia (G-1849)
Waters Inc E 785 537-1340
Manhattan (G-6847)
Waters Inc E 785 238-3114
Junction City (G-3767)
Waters Inc E 620 227-2900
Dodge City (G-1451)

09 FISHING, HUNTING, AND TRAPPING

0919 Marine Fishing, Misc

Lovewell Marina & Grill Inc ......F 785 753-4351
Webber *(G-13484)*

0921 Finfish Farming & Fish Hatcheries

Culver Fish Farm Inc ......G 620 241-5200
McPherson *(G-6954)*

0971 Hunting & Trapping

Blue HI Gamebirds & Htchy LLC ......F 785 373-4965
Tipton *(G-12247)*

Flint Oak ......E 620 658-4401
Fall River *(G-1927)*

Show ME Birds Hunting Resort ......F 620 674-8863
Baxter Springs *(G-413)*

10 METAL MINING

1081 Metal Mining Svcs

Triple J Machining LLC ......F 316 214-2414
Augusta *(G-349)*

12 COAL MINING

1221 Bituminous Coal & Lignite: Surface Mining

Harbour Construction Inc ......F 913 441-2555
Kansas City *(G-4067)*

Health and Envmt Kans Dept ......F 620 231-8540
Frontenac *(G-2055)*

1241 Coal Mining Svcs

Continental Coal Inc ......E 913 491-1717
Shawnee Mission *(G-11263)*

13 OIL AND GAS EXTRACTION

1311 Crude Petroleum & Natural Gas

Aladdin Petroleum Corporation ......G 316 265-9602
Wichita *(G-13657)*

Allmetal Recycling LLC ......D 316 838-9381
Wichita *(G-13676)*

Anadarko Petroleum Corporation ......E 620 544-4344
Hugoton *(G-3148)*

Apollo Energies Inc ......F 620 672-5071
Pratt *(G-10097)*

Baird Oil Co Inc ......G 785 689-7456
Logan *(G-6420)*

Berexco Incorporated ......G 620 582-2575
Coldwater *(G-1051)*

Berexco LLC ......F 785 628-6101
Hays *(G-2757)*

Black Diamond Oil Inc ......G 785 625-5891
Hays *(G-2759)*

Bobcat Oil Field Service Inc ......F 913 980-3858
Louisburg *(G-6441)*

Buckeye Corporation ......G 316 321-1060
El Dorado *(G-1539)*

Buckeye Corporation ......G 785 483-3111
Russell *(G-10267)*

Butterfly Supply Inc ......F 620 793-7156
Great Bend *(G-2525)*

Canyon Oil & Gas Co ......G 316 263-3201
Wichita *(G-13935)*

Castle Resources Inc ......E 785 625-5155
Schoenchen *(G-10802)*

CHS Inc ......D 620 241-4247
McPherson *(G-6948)*

Crown Consulting Inc ......F 620 624-0156
Liberal *(G-6300)*

Damar Resources Inc ......G 785 625-0020
Hays *(G-2781)*

Daystar Petroleum Inc ......G 316 755-3492
Valley Center *(G-13340)*

Daystar Petroleum Inc ......G 620 583-5527
Eureka *(G-1883)*

Dreiling Oil Inc ......G 785 625-8327
Hays *(G-2791)*

Edmiston Oil Company Inc ......F 316 265-5241
Wichita *(G-14260)*

Egbert Oil Operations Inc ......F 620 662-4533
Hutchinson *(G-3275)*

Excalibur Production Co Inc ......G 620 241-1265
McPherson *(G-6961)*

F G Holl Company LLC ......G 316 684-8481
Wichita *(G-14329)*

F G Holl Company LLC ......F 620 995-3171
Belpre *(G-505)*

▲ Ferrell Companies Inc ......D 913 661-1500
Overland Park *(G-8712)*

Freeport-Mcmoran Oil & Gas LLC ......E 316 636-1801
Wichita *(G-14418)*

Glacier Petroleum Inc ......F 620 342-1148
Emporia *(G-1762)*

Gore Oil Company ......G 316 263-3535
Wichita *(G-14487)*

Grady Bolding Corporation ......G 620 564-2240
Ellinwood *(G-1633)*

Grand Mesa Operating Company ......F 316 634-0699
Wichita *(G-14495)*

H K W Oil Company Inc ......G 785 483-6185
Salina *(G-10525)*

Hess Oil Company ......E 620 241-4640
McPherson *(G-6973)*

Hughes Drilling Co ......G 785 883-2235
Wellsville *(G-13543)*

Hummon Corporation ......G 620 930-2645
Medicine Lodge *(G-7064)*

J-W Operating Company ......F 620 626-7243
Liberal *(G-6324)*

John O Farmer Inc ......F 785 483-3144
Russell *(G-10277)*

Kanzou Explorations Inc ......E 913 294-2125
Paola *(G-9568)*

Kinder Morgan Kansas Inc ......G 620 384-7830
Syracuse *(G-12228)*

Knighton Oil Co Inc ......G 316 630-9905
Wichita *(G-14869)*

Koch Exploration Company ......F 316 828-5508
Wichita *(G-14878)*

L D Drilling Inc ......E 620 793-3051
Great Bend *(G-2601)*

L-K Wireline Inc ......G 785 625-6877
Hays *(G-2861)*

Lario Oil & Gas Company ......E 316 265-5611
Wichita *(G-14924)*

Lario Oil & Gas Company ......F 785 625-5023
Hays *(G-2862)*

Lee Phillips Oil Company ......G 316 681-4470
Wichita *(G-14948)*

Linn Energy Inc ......E 620 657-8310
Ulysses *(G-13305)*

Merit Energy Company LLC ......G 620 675-8372
Sublette *(G-12205)*

Messenger Petroleum Inc ......G 620 532-5400
Kingman *(G-4606)*

Mull Drilling Company Inc ......F 316 264-6366
Wichita *(G-15138)*

Murfin Drilling Company Inc ......E 316 267-3241
Wichita *(G-15140)*

Murfin Drilling Company Inc ......E 785 421-2101
Hill City *(G-3036)*

Murfin Drilling Company Inc ......E 785 483-5371
Russell *(G-10282)*

Murfin Drilling Company Inc ......F 785 462-7541
Colby *(G-1031)*

N & B Enterprises Inc ......G 620 431-6424
Chanute *(G-744)*

Natural Gas Pipeline Amer LLC ......G 620 885-4505
Minneola *(G-7127)*

Natural Gas Pipeline Amer LLC ......G 785 568-2231
Glasco *(G-2422)*

Northern Lights Oil Co L L C ......G 316 733-1515
Wichita *(G-15189)*

Oil Producers Inc of Kansas ......F 316 681-0231
Wichita *(G-15212)*

One Gas Inc ......C 913 319-8617
Overland Park *(G-9103)*

Oneok Inc ......E 620 562-4205
Bushton *(G-654)*

OS Companies Inc ......E 316 265-5611
Wichita *(G-15238)*

OXY Inc ......F 620 629-4200
Liberal *(G-6351)*

Petroleum Property Services ......G 316 265-3351
Wichita *(G-15287)*

Petrosantander (usa) Inc ......F 620 272-7187
Garden City *(G-2253)*

Pickrell Drilling Co Inc ......F 316 262-8427
Wichita *(G-15299)*

Pintail Petroleum Ltd ......G 316 263-2243
Wichita *(G-15300)*

Prater Oil Gas Operations Inc ......G 620 672-7600
Pratt *(G-10134)*

R & S Pipe Supply ......G 620 365-8114
Iola *(G-3629)*

R P Nixon Operations Inc ......G 785 628-3834
Hays *(G-2896)*

R R A Inc ......G 316 262-3411
Wichita *(G-15406)*

Rama Operating Co Inc ......G 620 234-6034
Stafford *(G-12108)*

Raymond Oil Company Inc ......F 316 267-4214
Wichita *(G-15422)*

Red Hills Resources Inc ......G 620 669-9996
Hutchinson *(G-3421)*

Shawmar Oil & Gas Co Inc ......E 620 382-2932
Marion *(G-6876)*

Shields Oil Producers Inc ......E 785 483-3141
Russell *(G-10299)*

Stelbar Oil Corporation Inc ......F 316 264-8378
Wichita *(G-15660)*

Sterling Drilling Company ......D 620 672-9508
Pratt *(G-10154)*

Strata Drilling Inc ......E 620 793-7971
Great Bend *(G-2640)*

Summit Drilling Co Inc ......F 620 343-3278
Emporia *(G-1832)*

Tengasco Inc ......E 785 625-6374
Hays *(G-2919)*

Town & Country Super Market ......E 620 653-2330
Hoisington *(G-3072)*

Town Oil Company ......F 913 294-2125
Paola *(G-9593)*

Trans Pacific Oil Corporation ......F 316 262-3596
Wichita *(G-15789)*

Tri Resources Inc ......F 620 672-9425
Pratt *(G-10162)*

Val Energy Inc ......G 316 263-6688
Wichita *(G-15869)*

Verde Oil Company ......G 620 754-3800
Savonburg *(G-10793)*

Vess Oil Corporation ......F 316 682-1537
Wichita *(G-15877)*

W-W Production Co ......G 620 431-4137
Chanute *(G-773)*

Westmore Drilling Company Inc ......G 785 749-3712
Lawrence *(G-5184)*

▲ Woolsey Petroleum Corporation ......F 316 267-4379
Wichita *(G-16069)*

Xto Energy Inc ......D 620 355-7838
Lakin *(G-4662)*

Younger Energy Company ......G 316 681-2542
Wichita *(G-16097)*

Zenith Drilling Corporation ......G 316 684-9777
Wichita *(G-16100)*

1321 Natural Gas Liquids

Oneok Inc ......E 620 562-4205
Bushton *(G-654)*

Oneok Field Services Co LLC ......F 620 248-3258
Pratt *(G-10128)*

Oneok Field Services Co LLC ......D 620 356-2231
Ulysses *(G-13309)*

Panhandle Eastrn Pipe Line LP ......E 620 624-7241
Liberal *(G-6353)*

Robinson Supply LLC ......G 620 251-0490
Coffeyville *(G-973)*

Southern Star Central Gas Pipe ......E 620 657-2130
Satanta *(G-10791)*

Tri Resources Inc ......G 620 982-4568
Pawnee Rock *(G-9755)*

▲ Woolsey Petroleum Corporation ......F 316 267-4379
Wichita *(G-16069)*

1381 Drilling Oil & Gas Wells

Associated Environmental Inc ......F 785 776-7755
Manhattan *(G-6547)*

Bruce Oil Co LLC ......G 620 241-2938
McPherson *(G-6939)*

Canary Resources Inc ......G 913 239-8960
Stilwell *(G-12138)*

Chase Contractors Inc ......G 620 431-2142
Chanute *(G-714)*

Cheyenne Well Service Inc ......F 785 798-2282
Ness City *(G-7256)*

Crown Consulting Inc ......F 620 624-0156
Liberal *(G-6300)*

Discovery Drilling Co Inc ......E 785 623-2920
Hays *(G-2789)*

Duke Drilling Co Inc ......D 620 793-8366
Great Bend *(G-2556)*

S I C

Empire Energy E&P LLC ....G.... 785 434-4900
Plainville *(G-9987)*
Fossil Drilling Inc ....F.... 620 672-5625
Pratt *(G-10115)*
Freddy Van Inc ....G.... 620 231-1127
Pittsburg *(G-9863)*
H-40 Drilling Inc ....F.... 316 773-3640
Medicine Lodge *(G-7063)*
Hughes Drilling Co ....G.... 785 883-2235
Wellsville *(G-13543)*
Hurricane Services Inc ....E.... 620 437-2661
Madison *(G-6501)*
Imperial American Oil Corp ....G.... 316 721-0036
Wichita *(G-14678)*
Jones & Buck Development Oil ....F.... 620 725-3636
Sedan *(G-10844)*
Kepley Well Service LLC ....F.... 620 431-9212
Chanute *(G-735)*
L D Drilling Inc ....E.... 620 793-3051
Great Bend *(G-2601)*
Mull Drilling Company Inc ....F.... 316 264-6366
Wichita *(G-15138)*
Murfin Drilling Company Inc ....E.... 785 483-5371
Russell *(G-10282)*
Murfin Drilling Company Inc ....F.... 785 462-7541
Colby *(G-1031)*
Murfin Drilling Company Inc ....E.... 316 267-3241
Wichita *(G-15140)*
Murfin Drilling Company Inc ....E.... 785 421-2101
Hill City *(G-3036)*
Mv Partners LLC ....G.... 316 267-3241
Wichita *(G-15142)*
Pickrell Drilling Co Inc ....F.... 316 262-8427
Wichita *(G-15299)*
Quest Drilling Services LLC ....E.... 316 260-2196
Wichita *(G-15392)*
R & B Oil & Gas Inc ....F.... 620 254-7251
Attica *(G-278)*
Rig 6 Drilling Inc ....G.... 620 365-6294
Bronson *(G-588)*
Shawnee Well Service Inc ....F.... 620 254-7893
Attica *(G-279)*
Shields Oil Producers Inc ....E.... 785 483-3141
Russell *(G-10299)*
Southwind Drilling Inc ....D.... 620 564-3800
Ellinwood *(G-1638)*
Sterling Drilling Company ....D.... 620 672-9508
Pratt *(G-10154)*
Town Oil Company ....F.... 913 294-2125
Paola *(G-9593)*
Trans Pacific Oil Corporation ....F.... 316 262-3596
Wichita *(G-15789)*
Trans Pacific Properties LLC ....G.... 316 262-3596
Wichita *(G-15790)*
Val Energy Inc ....G.... 316 263-6688
Wichita *(G-15869)*
W-W Production Co ....G.... 620 431-4137
Chanute *(G-773)*
Well Refined Drilling Co Inc ....F.... 620 763-2619
Thayer *(G-12246)*
Whitham Frank E Trust 2 ....F.... 620 375-2229
Leoti *(G-6261)*
Zenith Drilling Corporation ....G.... 316 684-9777
Wichita *(G-16100)*

1382 Oil & Gas Field Exploration Svcs

Allied Ofs LLC ....F.... 785 483-2627
Russell *(G-10266)*
Baird Oil Co Inc ....G.... 785 689-7456
Logan *(G-6420)*
Berexco LLC ....F.... 620 275-0320
Garden City *(G-2108)*
Bow Creek Oil Company LLC ....G.... 785 650-1738
Hays *(G-2760)*
Castle Resources Inc ....E.... 785 625-5155
Schoenchen *(G-10802)*
Cmx Inc ....G.... 316 269-9052
Wichita *(G-14045)*
Colt Energy Inc ....G.... 913 236-0016
Shawnee Mission *(G-11251)*
CST Oil & Gas Corporation ....G.... 620 829-5307
Fort Scott *(G-1963)*
D E Exploration Inc ....F.... 785 883-4057
Wellsville *(G-13542)*
Damar Resources Inc ....G.... 785 625-0020
Hays *(G-2781)*
Darrah Oil Company LLC ....G.... 316 219-3390
Wichita *(G-14170)*
Dart Cherokee Basin Oper LLC ....G.... 620 331-7870
Independence *(G-3509)*

Edison Operating Company LLC ....G.... 316 201-1744
Wichita *(G-14259)*
Edmiston Oil Company Inc ....G.... 620 792-6924
Great Bend *(G-2558)*
Freeport-Mcmoran Oil & Gas LLC ....E.... 316 636-1801
Wichita *(G-14418)*
H2 Plains LLC ....F.... 785 798-3995
Wichita *(G-14538)*
Hurricane Services Inc ....E.... 316 303-9515
Wichita *(G-14657)*
Independent Oil & Gas Svc Inc ....G.... 316 263-8281
Wichita *(G-14680)*
Kanzou Explorations Inc ....E.... 913 294-2125
Paola *(G-9568)*
Klm Exploration Co Inc ....F.... 913 796-6763
Mc Louth *(G-6928)*
Koch Exploration Company ....F.... 316 828-5508
Wichita *(G-14878)*
Koch Exploration Company LLC ....G.... 316 828-5508
Wichita *(G-14879)*
◆ **Koch Mineral Services LLC** ....E.... 316 828-5500
Wichita *(G-14884)*
Lario Oil & Gas Company ....E.... 316 265-5611
Wichita *(G-14924)*
Lockhart Geophysical Company ....F.... 785 625-9175
Hays *(G-2865)*
Lockhart Geophysical Kans Inc ....G.... 620 277-7771
Garden City *(G-2226)*
Lr Energy ....G.... 620 627-2499
Independence *(G-3535)*
McCoy Petroleum Corporation ....F.... 316 636-2737
Wichita *(G-15023)*
Murfin Drilling Company Inc ....E.... 316 267-3241
Wichita *(G-15140)*
MWM Oil Co Inc ....G.... 316 265-1992
Towanda *(G-13265)*
OS Companies Inc ....E.... 316 265-5611
Wichita *(G-15238)*
Paragon Geophysical Svcs Inc ....E.... 316 636-5552
Wichita *(G-15258)*
Postrock Energy Corporation ....F.... 620 432-4200
Chanute *(G-756)*
Redbud E&P Inc ....E.... 620 331-7870
Independence *(G-3551)*
Ritchie Exploration Inc ....F.... 316 691-9500
Wichita *(G-15468)*
Shamrock Resources Inc ....G.... 316 636-9557
Wichita *(G-15571)*
Slawson Exploration Co Inc ....E.... 316 263-3201
Wichita *(G-15603)*
Smyth Oil and Gas Services ....E.... 620 356-4091
Ulysses *(G-13319)*
Stelbar Oil Corporation Inc ....F.... 316 264-8378
Wichita *(G-15660)*
Tengasco Inc ....E.... 785 625-6374
Hays *(G-2919)*
Viva International ....G.... 913 859-0438
Shawnee Mission *(G-11983)*
White & Ellis Drilling Inc ....G.... 316 263-1102
Wichita *(G-15964)*
▲ **Woolsey Petroleum Corporation** ....F.... 316 267-4379
Wichita *(G-16069)*
Woolsey Petroleum Corporation ....G.... 620 886-5606
Medicine Lodge *(G-7076)*

1389 Oil & Gas Field Svcs, NEC

Abes Oilfield Service LLC ....E.... 620 532-5551
Spivey *(G-12072)*
Albert G Hogoboom ....E.... 316 321-1397
El Dorado *(G-1527)*
Alliance Inc ....G.... 785 445-3701
Russell *(G-10264)*
Alliance Well Service Inc ....G.... 620 672-1065
Pratt *(G-10095)*
Allied of Kansas Inc ....F.... 785 483-2627
Russell *(G-10265)*
Allied of Kansas Inc ....G.... 620 793-5861
Great Bend *(G-2503)*
Allied of Kansas Inc ....F.... 620 624-5937
Liberal *(G-6276)*
Allied Ofs LLC ....F.... 785 483-2627
Russell *(G-10266)*
Ally Servicing LLC ....C.... 316 652-6301
Wichita *(G-13679)*
Alpha Services and Production ....G.... 620 624-8318
Liberal *(G-6277)*
American Well Service LLC ....G.... 620 672-5625
Pratt *(G-10096)*
Archrock Inc ....E.... 620 241-8740
McPherson *(G-6937)*

B & B Oil Tools Co LLC ....G.... 785 673-4828
Grainfield *(G-2494)*
B&B Cooperative Ventures LLC ....E.... 620 364-1311
Burlington *(G-625)*
Bachman Production Specialties ....F.... 620 792-2549
Great Bend *(G-2513)*
Baker Hghes Olfld Oprtions LLC ....C.... 785 650-0182
Hays *(G-2754)*
Baker Petrolite LLC ....D.... 620 793-3546
Great Bend *(G-2514)*
Bakken Well Service Inc ....F.... 620 276-3442
Garden City *(G-2104)*
Basic Energy Services Inc ....E.... 316 262-3699
Wichita *(G-13819)*
Basic Energy Services LLC ....G.... 620 624-2277
Liberal *(G-6283)*
Bogner Oil Field Service Inc ....G.... 620 276-9453
Garden City *(G-2114)*
Bojack Roustabout LLC ....G.... 785 798-3504
Ness City *(G-7252)*
Brackeen Line Cleaning Inc ....F.... 620 587-3351
Claflin *(G-839)*
Brians Hot Oil Service LLC ....G.... 620 629-5933
Liberal *(G-6287)*
Butler Bros Inc ....F.... 620 221-3570
Winfield *(G-16118)*
C & R Well Service ....G.... 785 448-8792
Garnett *(G-2371)*
C&J Well Services Inc ....E.... 785 628-6395
Hays *(G-2763)*
▲ **Cgf Investments Inc** ....E.... 316 691-4500
Wichita *(G-13994)*
Chaosland Services LLC ....G.... 620 356-1259
Ulysses *(G-13288)*
Chase Tubing Testing ....G.... 620 356-4314
Ulysses *(G-13289)*
Chase Well Service Inc ....F.... 620 793-9556
Great Bend *(G-2535)*
Chem-Tech LLC ....G.... 785 625-1141
Hays *(G-2768)*
Cheyenne Oil Services Inc ....E.... 785 798-2282
Ness City *(G-7255)*
Cheyenne Well Service Inc ....F.... 785 798-2282
Ness City *(G-7256)*
Chitos Well Service LLC ....F.... 785 434-4942
Plainville *(G-9979)*
Clinton Enterprises LLC ....G.... 316 636-1801
Wichita *(G-14042)*
Consolidated Oil Well Ser ....F.... 620 431-9217
Chanute *(G-722)*
Crown Consulting Inc ....F.... 620 624-0156
Liberal *(G-6300)*
Cyclone Well Service Inc ....G.... 620 628-4428
Canton *(G-680)*
D S & W Well Servicing Inc ....E.... 620 793-5838
Great Bend *(G-2551)*
Damm Pipe Testing LLC ....G.... 620 617-8990
Great Bend *(G-2552)*
DC Oilfield Services ....G.... 620 598-2643
Moscow *(G-7167)*
Dillco Fluid Service Inc ....E.... 620 544-2929
Hugoton *(G-3159)*
Dreiling Oil Inc ....G.... 785 625-8327
Hays *(G-2791)*
Eatherly Constructors Inc ....F.... 913 685-9026
Overland Park *(G-8669)*
Eldredge Well Service LLC ....E.... 620 649-2841
Satanta *(G-10784)*
Elite Cementing Acidizing ....G.... 620 583-5561
Eureka *(G-1884)*
Elite Pipe Testing ....G.... 785 726-4366
Ellis *(G-1643)*
Ellinwood Tank Service Inc ....G.... 620 793-0246
Ellinwood *(G-1630)*
Excel Wireline LLC ....G.... 785 764-9557
Pratt *(G-10112)*
Express Well Service & Sup Inc ....E.... 785 735-9405
Victoria *(G-13375)*
Fischer Pipe Testing Inc ....F.... 785 726-3411
Ellis *(G-1645)*
Fischer Well Service Inc ....G.... 785 628-3837
Hays *(G-2808)*
Francis Casing Crews Inc ....G.... 620 793-9630
Great Bend *(G-2567)*
Francis Casing Crews Inc ....E.... 620 275-0443
Garden City *(G-2166)*
G & L Well Service Inc ....G.... 620 278-3105
Sterling *(G-12118)*
G & S Roustabout Service LLC ....G.... 620 213-0172
Medicine Lodge *(G-7061)*

▲ Gabel Lease Service Inc ... G ... 785 798-3122
Ness City (G-7263)

Gary Gorby ... E ... 620 879-5243
Caney (G-668)

Geres ... G ... 620 276-6179
Garden City (G-2187)

Gilmores Roustabout Service ... F ... 620 624-0452
Liberal (G-6313)

Glacier Petroleum Inc ... F ... 620 342-1148
Emporia (G-1762)

Global Oilfield Services LLC ... F ... 785 445-3525
Russell (G-10275)

Grandview Water Disposal Inc ... G ... 785 335-2649
Scandia (G-10799)

Great Plins Gas Cmpression LLC ... C ... 620 544-3578
Hugoton (G-3164)

Gressel Oil Field Service LLC ... G ... 316 524-1225
Peck (G-9763)

Gyp Hills Roustabout LLC ... G ... 620 886-0931
Medicine Lodge (G-7062)

H2 Oil Field Services ... G ... 620 792-7115
Great Bend (G-2588)

Hertel Tank Service Inc ... G ... 785 628-2445
Hays (G-2841)

Horizon Pipe Testing Inc ... G ... 785 726-3773
Ellis (G-1647)

Jakubs Ladder Inc ... G ... 316 214-8932
Derby (G-1255)

Kansas Acid Inc ... G ... 785 625-5599
Hays (G-2857)

Kelly Maclaskey ... E ... 316 321-9011
El Dorado (G-1578)

Kepley Well Service LLC ... F ... 620 431-9212
Chanute (G-735)

Key Energy Services Inc ... G ... 620 649-2368
Satanta (G-10787)

Key Energy Services Inc ... E ... 620 353-1002
Ulysses (G-13302)

Key Energy Services Inc ... D ... 620 353-1002
Ulysses (G-13303)

Kizzar Well Servicing Inc ... F ... 620 938-2555
Chase (G-784)

L & D Oilfield Service Inc ... G ... 620 624-3329
Liberal (G-6330)

L-K Wireline Inc ... G ... 785 625-6877
Hays (G-2861)

Leiker Well Service Inc ... G ... 620 793-2336
Great Bend (G-2602)

Log-Tech Inc ... F ... 785 625-3858
Hays (G-2866)

Lone Star Services LLC ... E ... 620 626-7100
Liberal (G-6337)

M & D Excavating Inc ... F ... 785 628-3169
Hays (G-2867)

MAI Excavating Inc ... G ... 785 483-3387
Russell (G-10280)

Maxidize Production Svcs LLC ... G ... 620 222-1235
Winfield (G-16158)

MBC Well Logging & Leasing ... G ... 620 873-2953
Meade (G-7051)

Mercury Wireline ... G ... 785 625-1182
Hays (G-2872)

Merit Energy Company LLC ... E ... 620 356-3032
Ulysses (G-13306)

Merit Energy Company LLC ... E ... 620 629-4200
Liberal (G-6341)

Mid-West Oilfield Service ... G ... 620 930-2051
Medicine Lodge (G-7068)

Midwest Surveys Inc ... G ... 913 755-2128
Osawatomie (G-8199)

Midwestern Oilfield Svcs LLC ... G ... 620 309-7027
Liberal (G-6342)

Midwestern Well Service Inc ... E ... 620 624-8203
Liberal (G-6343)

Mikes Pipe Inspection Inc ... E ... 620 624-9245
Liberal (G-6344)

Mikes Testing & Salvage Inc ... F ... 620 938-2943
Chase (G-785)

Monster Pump Operations Inc ... G ... 785 623-4488
Hays (G-2875)

MTS Quanta LLC ... E ... 913 383-0800
Overland Park (G-9061)

Nicholas Water Service LLC ... F ... 620 930-7511
Medicine Lodge (G-7070)

Nichols Water Svc An Okla Corp ... F ... 620 624-5582
Liberal (G-6350)

Palmer Oil Inc ... E ... 620 275-2963
Garden City (G-2246)

Panhandle Eastrn Pipe Line LP ... E ... 620 624-8661
Liberal (G-6354)

Passmore Bros Inc ... E ... 620 544-2189
Hugoton (G-3175)

Petroleum Property Services ... G ... 316 265-3351
Wichita (G-15287)

Petropower LLC ... G ... 316 361-0222
Wichita (G-15288)

Phillips Well Service Inc ... G ... 316 321-6650
El Dorado (G-1590)

Piqua Petro Inc ... G ... 620 468-2681
Piqua (G-9802)

Poe Well Service Inc ... F ... 785 475-3422
Oberlin (G-7499)

Post & Mastin Well Service ... F ... 620 276-3442
Garden City (G-2257)

Professional Pulling Svc LLC ... F ... 785 625-8928
Hays (G-2892)

Q Conslidated Oil Well Svcs LLC ... G ... 620 431-9210
Chanute (G-757)

Qes Pressure Pumping LLC ... E ... 620 431-9210
Chanute (G-758)

Qes Pressure Pumping LLC ... F ... 785 242-4044
Ottawa (G-8307)

Qes Pressure Pumping LLC ... F ... 785 672-8822
Oakley (G-7486)

Quality Oilwell Cementing Inc ... F ... 785 483-1071
Russell (G-10285)

Rawhide Well Service LLC ... E ... 620 624-2902
Liberal (G-6358)

Reinhardt Services Inc ... G ... 785 483-2556
Russell (G-10287)

Richs Roustabout Service Inc ... G ... 785 798-3323
Ness City (G-7266)

Rome Corporation ... E ... 785 625-1182
Hays (G-2901)

S & G Water Service Inc ... G ... 620 246-5212
Nashville (G-7230)

Schankie Well Service Inc ... G ... 620 437-2595
Madison (G-6504)

Schippers Oil Field Svcs LLC ... G ... 785 675-9991
Hoxie (G-3141)

Schlumberger Technology Corp ... C ... 785 841-5610
Lawrence (G-5103)

Schulz Welding Service Inc ... F ... 620 628-4431
Canton (G-681)

Scotts Well Service Inc ... G ... 785 254-7828
Roxbury (G-10257)

Shamrock Resources Inc ... G ... 316 636-9557
Wichita (G-15571)

Spivey Oil Field Service LLC ... E ... 620 532-5178
Spivey (G-12073)

Sterling Food Mart Inc ... G ... 620 278-3371
Hutchinson (G-3446)

Sterling Trucking Inc ... F ... 620 534-2461
Alden (G-59)

Steves Electric Roustabout Co ... F ... 785 434-7590
Plainville (G-9992)

Swift Services Inc ... E ... 785 798-2380
Ness City (G-7267)

T & C Mfg & Operating Inc ... E ... 620 793-5483
Great Bend (G-2646)

T R Service & Rental ... F ... 620 672-9100
Pratt (G-10158)

Thornton Air Rotary LLC ... G ... 620 879-2073
Caney (G-675)

Total Lease Service Inc ... G ... 785 735-9520
Hays (G-2920)

Tr Services Inc ... G ... 785 623-1066
Pratt (G-10160)

Trans Pacific Properties LLC ... G ... 316 262-3596
Wichita (G-15790)

Treco Inc ... E ... 620 544-2606
Hugoton (G-3178)

Treco Inc ... D ... 620 356-4785
Ulysses (G-13325)

Trilobite Testing Inc ... E ... 785 625-4778
Hays (G-2921)

Walton Swathing ... G ... 620 492-6827
Johnson (G-3664)

Werner Pipe Service Inc ... F ... 620 331-7384
Independence (G-3572)

Wyoming Casing Service Inc ... F ... 620 793-9630
Great Bend (G-2664)

X-Pert Service Tools Inc ... G ... 785 421-5600
Hill City (G-3039)

Ysidro Trucking Inc ... F ... 316 522-3716
Wichita (G-16099)

14 MINING AND QUARRYING OF NONMETALLIC MINERALS, EXCEPT FUELS

1411 Dimension Stone

Ash Grove Materials Corp ... D ... 913 345-2030
Overland Park (G-8404)

Hamm Inc ... G ... 785 597-5111
Perry (G-9769)

Mulberry Limestone Quarry Co ... F ... 620 764-3337
Mulberry (G-7208)

Rapid Rubble Removal ... G ... 785 862-8875
Topeka (G-12998)

Trendstone LLC ... G ... 913 599-5492
Lenexa (G-6191)

1422 Crushed & Broken Limestone

Ash Grove Aggregates Inc ... D ... 660 679-4128
Overland Park (G-8402)

◆ Ash Grove Cement Company ... C ... 913 451-8900
Overland Park (G-8403)

Bayer Construction Company Inc ... C ... 785 776-8839
Manhattan (G-6553)

Cornejo & Sons LLC ... D ... 620 231-8120
Pittsburg (G-9846)

Cornejo & Sons LLC ... E ... 620 336-3534
Cherryvale (G-804)

Hamm Inc ... E ... 785 597-5111
Perry (G-9768)

Johnson County Aggregates ... E ... 913 764-2127
Olathe (G-7814)

L G Everist Incorporated ... F ... 913 302-5394
Kansas City (G-4189)

Marietta Martin Materials Inc ... E ... 620 736-2962
Severy (G-10891)

Martin Marietta Materials Inc ... G ... 913 390-8396
Olathe (G-7875)

Martin Marietta Materials Inc ... E ... 785 242-3232
Ottawa (G-8289)

Martin Marietta Materials Inc ... F ... 913 583-3311
De Soto (G-1207)

Mid-States Materials LLC ... G ... 785 887-6038
Scranton (G-10839)

Midwest Concrete Materials Inc ... C ... 785 776-8811
Manhattan (G-6746)

Nelson Quarries Inc ... E ... 620 496-2211
Gas (G-2392)

Norris Quarries LLC ... G ... 641 682-3427
Wichita (G-15185)

Wade Agricultural Products Inc ... G ... 913 757-2255
La Cygne (G-4646)

1423 Crushed & Broken Granite

Apac-Kansas Inc ... F ... 620 392-5771
Hartford (G-2726)

Rocky Top Counter Top LLC ... G ... 316 262-0497
Wichita (G-15475)

1429 Crushed & Broken Stone, NEC

Apac-Kansas Inc ... E ... 785 524-4413
Lincoln (G-6379)

Martin Marietta Materials Inc ... E ... 316 775-5458
Augusta (G-334)

Ngc Industries LLC ... F ... 620 248-3248
Sun City (G-12218)

South West Butler Quarry LLC ... F ... 316 775-1737
Augusta (G-347)

1442 Construction Sand & Gravel

Alsop Sand Co Inc ... E ... 785 243-4249
Concordia (G-1101)

Associated Material & Sup Co ... F ... 316 721-3848
Wichita (G-13756)

Cornejo & Sons LLC ... G ... 620 455-3720
Oxford (G-9532)

Dodge City Sand Company Inc ... F ... 620 227-6091
Dodge City (G-1351)

Gravel & Concrete Inc ... G ... 620 422-3249
Nickerson (G-7432)

Hardrock Sand & Gravel LLC ... G ... 620 408-4030
Dodge City (G-1369)

Heft & Sons LLC ... E ... 620 723-2495
Greensburg (G-2679)

Holliday Sand & Gravel Co LLC ... E ... 913 492-5920
Lenexa (G-5905)

Huber Sand Company ... F ... 620 275-7601
Garden City (G-2200)

Midwest Materials By Mueller...F ... 785 337-2252
Hanover *(G-2713)*
OBrien Rock Company Inc...D ... 620 449-2257
Saint Paul *(G-10382)*
Stone Sand Co Inc...E ... 620 793-7864
Great Bend *(G-2639)*
Unruh Sand & Gravel...G ... 620 582-2774
Coldwater *(G-1058)*

1474 Potash, Soda & Borate Minerals

Compass Minerals...B ... 913 344-9200
Overland Park *(G-8585)*
◆ **Compass Minerals Intl Inc**...C ... 913 344-9200
Overland Park *(G-8589)*

1479 Chemical & Fertilizer Mining

▲ **Compass Minerals America Inc**...C ... 913 344-9100
Overland Park *(G-8587)*
◆ **Compass Minerals Intl Inc**...C ... 913 344-9200
Overland Park *(G-8589)*
Hutchinson Salt Company Inc...E ... 620 662-3341
Hutchinson *(G-3324)*
Namsco Inc...D ... 913 344-9100
Shawnee Mission *(G-11669)*
◆ **Searles Valley Minerals Inc**...E ... 913 344-9500
Overland Park *(G-9286)*

1499 Miscellaneous Nonmetallic Mining

National Gympson...F ... 620 248-3247
Sun City *(G-12217)*
New Ngc Inc...C ... 620 886-5613
Medicine Lodge *(G-7069)*

15 BUILDING CONSTRUCTION-GENERAL CONTRACTORS AND OPERATIVE BUILDERS

1521 General Contractors, Single Family Houses

A Lert Corp...F ... 620 378-4153
Coyville *(G-1182)*
Acklin Construction...F ... 316 321-6648
El Dorado *(G-1525)*
Advanced Systems Homes Inc...E ... 620 431-3320
Chanute *(G-702)*
Alenco Inc...E ... 913 438-1902
Lenexa *(G-5638)*
All Things Exterior Inc...E ... 785 738-5015
Beloit *(G-472)*
American Exteriors LLC...F ... 913 712-9668
Mount Hope *(G-7203)*
AMZ Construction Inc...F ... 913 915-7867
Olathe *(G-7529)*
Antes Concrete Inc...F ... 913 856-4535
Olathe *(G-7530)*
Antrim & Assoc...F ... 316 267-2753
Wichita *(G-13714)*
Apex Construction Inc...E ... 913 341-3688
Lenexa *(G-5657)*
Appletech Design & Cnstr Inc...F ... 785 776-3530
Manhattan *(G-6543)*
Arrow Renovation & Cnstr LLC...E ... 913 703-3000
Olathe *(G-7534)*
Augustine Home Improvement Co...E ... 913 362-4707
Shawnee Mission *(G-11134)*
B L Rieke & Associates Inc...F ... 913 599-3393
Shawnee Mission *(G-11141)*
Bartec Construction LLC...E ... 913 208-0015
Tonganoxie *(G-12252)*
Benchmark Construction LLC...F ... 785 862-0340
Eudora *(G-1870)*
Benchmark Enterprises...F ... 785 537-4447
Manhattan *(G-6555)*
Birch Contracting Group LLC...F ... 913 400-3975
Overland Park *(G-8452)*
BKM Construction LLC...F ... 913 297-0049
Leavenworth *(G-5212)*
Blecha Enterprises LLC...F ... 785 539-6640
Manhattan *(G-6563)*
Borton Corporation...D ... 620 669-8211
South Hutchinson *(G-12056)*
Budreau Construction Inc...F ... 785 446-3665
Clyde *(G-904)*
C & P Enterprises Inc...E ... 785 628-6712
Hays *(G-2762)*
Carley Construction Co Inc...F ... 785 456-2882
Wamego *(G-13408)*
Caro Construction Co Inc...E ... 316 267-7505
Wichita *(G-13952)*
Cdh Enterprises...F ... 316 320-7187
El Dorado *(G-1545)*
Champion Opco LLC...F ... 316 636-4200
Wichita *(G-13996)*
Clark Dargal Builders Inc...F ... 785 478-4811
Topeka *(G-12479)*
Compton Construction Svcs LLC...E ... 316 262-8885
Wichita *(G-14083)*
Construction Systems Inc...F ... 913 208-6401
Shawnee Mission *(G-11260)*
Construction Technologies LLC...F ... 913 671-3440
Shawnee Mission *(G-11261)*
Coonrod & Assoc Cnstr Co Inc...C ... 316 942-8430
Wichita *(G-14097)*
Cornerstone Cnstr Svcs LLC...F ... 913 207-1751
Olathe *(G-7616)*
Coyote Investment & Networking...E ... 785 550-6028
Lawrence *(G-4815)*
Crossland Construction Co Inc...E ... 316 942-9090
Wichita *(G-14135)*
Custom Renovation...F ... 620 544-2653
Hugoton *(G-3158)*
D & R Construction Inc...E ... 785 776-1087
Manhattan *(G-6608)*
Dade Construction LLC...F ... 913 208-1968
Kansas City *(G-3951)*
Damage Ctrl & Restoration Inc...E ... 913 722-0228
Kansas City *(G-3954)*
Darrell Bybee Construction LLC...F ... 316 409-4186
Wichita *(G-14171)*
Dennis R Sumner Construction...F ... 785 478-1701
Topeka *(G-12552)*
Discount Siding Supply LP...F ... 785 625-4619
Hays *(G-2788)*
Don Julian Builders Inc...E ... 913 894-6300
Lenexa *(G-5822)*
Don Klausmeyer Cnstr LLC...E ... 316 554-0001
Wichita *(G-14224)*
Double K Cnstr of Mound Cy...F ... 913 795-3147
Mound City *(G-7171)*
Empire Construction Group LLC...F ... 913 375-8886
Shawnee Mission *(G-11335)*
Emporia Construction & Rmdlg...E ... 620 341-3131
Emporia *(G-1738)*
Farha Construction Inc...E ... 316 943-0000
Wichita *(G-14339)*
Four Corners Construction LLC...G ... 620 662-8163
Hutchinson *(G-3290)*
Freund Investment Inc...F ... 620 669-9649
Hutchinson *(G-3295)*
Fuqua Construction Inc...F ... 620 585-2270
Inman *(G-3582)*
G-B Construction LLC...E ... 913 837-5240
Louisburg *(G-6449)*
Genesis Solution LLC...F ... 785 317-5710
Chapman *(G-779)*
Goentzel Construction Inc...F ... 316 264-6333
Wichita *(G-14479)*
Grace Construction & Assoc Inc...F ... 316 617-1729
Derby *(G-1249)*
Gray Construction Inc...E ... 316 721-3000
Wichita *(G-14498)*
Great Western Dining Svc Inc...F ... 620 792-9224
Great Bend *(G-2585)*
Green Hills Inc...F ... 316 686-7673
Wichita *(G-14509)*
Greenamyre Construction LLC...F ... 913 772-1776
Leavenworth *(G-5248)*
Guthridge/Nighswonger Corp...F ... 316 264-7900
Wichita *(G-14529)*
Heartland Midwest LLC...E ... 913 471-4840
Pleasanton *(G-9996)*
Heinen Custom Operations Inc...F ... 785 945-6759
Valley Falls *(G-13364)*
Heritage Builders Inc...F ... 785 776-6011
Manhattan *(G-6655)*
Heritage Home Works LLC...F ... 316 288-9033
Newton *(G-7360)*
Home Center Construction Inc...E ... 620 231-5607
Pittsburg *(G-9877)*
Hudson Inc...E ... 620 232-1145
Pittsburg *(G-9879)*
Indel Corporation...F ... 785 478-9719
Topeka *(G-12715)*
Integrity Siding & Window Co...F ... 316 993-6426
Wichita *(G-14706)*
J Graham Construction Inc...E ... 620 252-2395
Coffeyville *(G-949)*
Jakubs Ladder Inc...G ... 316 214-8932
Derby *(G-1255)*
James Gruver Construction Inc...E ... 620 663-7982
Hutchinson *(G-3340)*
Jim Haas Builders Inc...F ... 913 897-9721
Stilwell *(G-12157)*
Jmar Construction Inc...F ... 620 922-3690
Edna *(G-1494)*
Joel Fritzel Construction Co...E ... 785 843-0566
Lawrence *(G-4925)*
Kansas Affordable Housing Corp...E ... 316 942-4848
Wichita *(G-14785)*
Kansas Heavy Construction LLC...E ... 913 845-2121
Tonganoxie *(G-12264)*
Key Construction Missouri LLC...F ... 816 221-7171
Wichita *(G-14853)*
Klein Construction Inc...F ... 316 262-3313
Park City *(G-9626)*
Koehn Construction...F ... 620 345-6457
Moundridge *(G-7187)*
Lee Haworth Construction Co...F ... 785 823-7168
Salina *(G-10580)*
Line Construction Company...F ... 913 341-1212
Shawnee Mission *(G-11575)*
Mack Pickens General Cont...E ... 316 778-1131
Benton *(G-519)*
Mark Borecky Construction...F ... 620 259-6655
Hutchinson *(G-3364)*
Mark C Jones...F ... 620 375-2357
Leoti *(G-6256)*
Martens Enterprises Inc...F ... 913 851-2772
Stilwell *(G-12165)*
McBride Construction Inc...F ... 620 544-7146
Hugoton *(G-3173)*
McCullough Development Inc...E ... 888 776-3010
Manhattan *(G-6737)*
McPherson Development Co Inc...F ... 785 272-9521
Topeka *(G-12874)*
McQuaid Brothers Rmdlg Co Inc...E ... 913 894-9128
Shawnee Mission *(G-11610)*
Michael S Hundley Cnstr Inc...F ... 913 367-7059
Atchison *(G-249)*
Mid America Exteriors LLC...F ... 316 265-5444
Wichita *(G-15066)*
Mid-Continent Thermal-Guard...E ... 316 838-4044
Wichita *(G-15079)*
Midland Exteriors LLC...F ... 785 537-5130
Manhattan *(G-6743)*
Midwest Siding Inc...E ... 785 825-0606
Salina *(G-10603)*
Mill Valley Construction Inc...F ... 913 764-6539
Olathe *(G-7900)*
Miller Building Services Inc...E ... 913 649-5599
Shawnee *(G-10996)*
Miller Construction...F ... 785 448-6788
Garnett *(G-2383)*
Miller Homebuilders Inc...E ... 620 662-1687
Hutchinson *(G-3381)*
Mitchell-Markowitz Cnstr...E ... 620 343-6840
Emporia *(G-1796)*
Mm Property MGT & Rmdlg LLC...F ... 913 871-6867
Kansas City *(G-4265)*
My Contracting LLC...F ... 913 747-9015
Olathe *(G-7910)*
National Builders Inc...F ... 316 729-7445
Wichita *(G-15147)*
National Ctstrphe Rstrtion Inc...F ... 913 663-4111
Shawnee Mission *(G-11673)*
National Ctstrphe Rstrtion Inc...D ... 316 636-5700
Wichita *(G-15149)*
Nb Remodeling LLC...F ... 785 749-1855
Lawrence *(G-5036)*
Netco Construction Co Inc...E ... 316 942-2062
Wichita *(G-15162)*
New Dimension Pdts Emporia Inc...E ... 620 342-6412
Emporia *(G-1801)*
Nies Construction Inc...D ... 316 684-0161
Wichita *(G-15177)*
Nies Homes Inc...F ... 316 684-0161
Wichita *(G-15178)*
Oakland Avenue Craftsmen Co...F ... 316 685-3955
Wichita *(G-15203)*
Oetinger-Lloyd Construction...F ... 785 632-2106
Clay Center *(G-874)*
Page Corporation...F ... 316 262-7200
Augusta *(G-335)*
Paint Masters Inc...F ... 316 683-5203
Wichita *(G-15253)*
Paint Pro Inc...F ... 913 685-4089
Overland Park *(G-9138)*

Paul Davis Restoratio of Great ... E ... 785 842-0351
Lawrence *(G-5058)*
Paul-Wertenberger Cnstr Inc ... E ... 785 625-8220
Hays *(G-2885)*
PDQ Construction Inc ... F ... 785 842-6844
Topeka *(G-12966)*
Ponton Construction Inc ... F ... 785 823-9584
Salina *(G-10635)*
Pools Plus ... F ... 785 823-7665
Salina *(G-10636)*
Preferred Contg Systems Co ... F ... 913 341-0111
Leawood *(G-5525)*
Premier Housing Inc ... E ... 620 277-0707
Holcomb *(G-3077)*
Prime Place LLC ... F ... 785 317-5265
Manhattan *(G-6781)*
Pro Home Remodeling LLC ... F ... 316 821-9818
Wichita *(G-15352)*
Quality Homes Inc ... E ... 402 248-6218
Summerfield *(G-12216)*
Quality Remodeler ... F ... 785 823-7665
Salina *(G-10646)*
Quality Trust Inc ... E ... 785 375-6372
Junction City *(G-3745)*
R & R Builders Inc ... D ... 913 682-1234
Leavenworth *(G-5282)*
R & R Developers Inc ... F ... 785 762-2255
Junction City *(G-3746)*
Rdcs Inc ... F ... 913 238-5377
Lenexa *(G-6094)*
Reliable Construction Svcs Inc ... F ... 913 764-7274
Olathe *(G-8025)*
Repairs Unlimited Inc ... F ... 913 262-6937
Kansas City *(G-4370)*
Rf Construction Inc ... E ... 785 776-8855
Manhattan *(G-6791)*
Rhino Builders Inc ... F ... 913 722-4353
Kansas City *(G-4376)*
Riley Communities LLC ... D ... 785 717-2210
Fort Riley *(G-1949)*
Ritchie Associates Inc ... E ... 316 684-7300
Wichita *(G-15466)*
Ritchie Building Co Inc ... E ... 316 684-7300
Wichita *(G-15467)*
Robinson Js Construction Inc ... E ... 913 441-2988
Shawnee Mission *(G-11811)*
Rodrock Homes LLC ... F ... 913 851-0347
Lenexa *(G-6112)*
Roeser Homes LLC ... F ... 913 220-7477
Overland Park *(G-9255)*
S & A Construction Inc ... F ... 316 558-8422
Wichita *(G-15498)*
Sears Home Imprv Pdts Inc ... E ... 913 438-5911
Shawnee Mission *(G-11845)*
Shawnee Mission Builders LLC ... G ... 913 631-7020
Shawnee Mission *(G-11854)*
Short Creek Construction ... F ... 620 783-2896
Galena *(G-2085)*
Smart Home Innovations LLC ... F ... 913 339-8641
Kansas City *(G-4426)*
Southborough Partners ... F ... 316 529-3200
Wichita *(G-15621)*
Southwestern Remodeling Contrs ... E ... 316 263-1239
Wichita *(G-15633)*
Still Builders Inc ... F ... 913 780-0702
Olathe *(G-8083)*
Strate Construction Inc ... F ... 620 659-2251
Kinsley *(G-4621)*
Suther Building Supply Inc ... F ... 785 336-2255
Seneca *(G-10883)*
Tommy J Kemp ... E ... 316 522-7255
Derby *(G-1276)*
Total Renovation Group Inc ... F ... 913 491-5000
Lenexa *(G-6186)*
Tribe Construction LLC ... F ... 913 850-0211
Mound City *(G-7176)*
Wamego Lumber Co Inc ... F ... 785 456-2400
Wamego *(G-13453)*
Wardcraft Homes Inc ... D ... 785 632-5664
Clay Center *(G-886)*
Weisbender Contracting Inc ... G ... 785 776-5034
Manhattan *(G-6849)*
Wichita Habitat For Humanity ... F ... 316 269-0755
Wichita *(G-16004)*
Window Design Company ... G ... 785 582-2888
Silver Lake *(G-12030)*
Winston-Brown Construction Co ... E ... 785 271-1661
Topeka *(G-13246)*
Wolfgang Construction LLC ... F ... 785 456-8729
Wamego *(G-13457)*
Wood RE New Joco Inc ... G ... 913 661-9663
Olathe *(G-8159)*
Yoder Builders Inc ... E ... 620 669-8542
South Hutchinson *(G-12068)*

1522 General Contractors, Residential Other Than Single Family

Arrow Renovation & Cnstr LLC ... E ... 913 703-3000
Olathe *(G-7534)*
Baronda Supplies & Service ... F ... 785 466-2501
Herington *(G-2971)*
Best Home Guys Holding Co ... F ... 316 681-2639
Wichita *(G-13838)*
Birch Contracting Group LLC ... F ... 913 400-3975
Overland Park *(G-8452)*
BKM Construction LLC ... F ... 913 297-0049
Leavenworth *(G-5212)*
Building Solutions LLC ... F ... 620 225-1199
Dodge City *(G-1314)*
Central Gc Construction Inc ... F ... 913 484-2400
Spring Hill *(G-12081)*
City Wide Holding Company Inc ... C ... 913 888-5700
Lenexa *(G-5757)*
CK Contracting LLC ... F ... 316 267-1996
Wichita *(G-14033)*
CU - Once Joint Venture LLC ... F ... 913 707-2165
Stilwell *(G-12143)*
DF Osborne Construction Inc ... F ... 785 862-0333
Topeka *(G-12554)*
Dondlinger & Sons Cnstr Co Inc ... F ... 316 943-9393
Wichita *(G-14227)*
Douglas Webb LLC ... F ... 316 685-0333
Wichita *(G-14233)*
Ebco Construction Group LLC ... F ... 866 297-2185
Olathe *(G-7667)*
Econo Lodge ... F ... 785 625-4839
Hays *(G-2797)*
Epic Homes of Kansas Inc ... E ... 785 537-3773
Manhattan *(G-6622)*
G & F Construction Co LLC ... E ... 316 260-3313
Wichita *(G-14432)*
◆ GBA Builders Llc ... E ... 913 492-0400
Lenexa *(G-5870)*
Heartland Hbtat For Hmnity Inc ... F ... 913 342-3047
Kansas City *(G-4075)*
Iqvia Phase One Services LLC ... D ... 913 708-6000
Overland Park *(G-8861)*
Jakubs Ladder Inc ... G ... 316 214-8932
Derby *(G-1255)*
Kdc Construction Inc ... F ... 913 677-1920
Leawood *(G-5447)*
Lang Builders LLC ... F ... 620 331-5850
Independence *(G-3532)*
Law Company Inc ... C ... 316 268-0200
Wichita *(G-14934)*
Mastercraft Corporation ... E ... 785 842-4455
Lawrence *(G-5013)*
MCN Shawnee LLC ... D ... 913 631-2100
Shawnee *(G-10992)*
McPherson Development Co Inc ... F ... 785 272-9521
Topeka *(G-12874)*
Mill Valley Construction Inc ... F ... 913 764-6539
Olathe *(G-7900)*
Mitchell-Markowitz Cnstr ... E ... 620 343-6840
Emporia *(G-1796)*
Mm Property MGT & Rmdlg LLC ... F ... 913 871-6867
Kansas City *(G-4265)*
National Builders Inc ... F ... 316 729-7445
Wichita *(G-15147)*
Neals Foundations Inc ... E ... 316 744-0064
Kechi *(G-4573)*
Neighbors Construction Co Inc ... E ... 913 422-5555
Lenexa *(G-6021)*
Nfi Management Co Inc ... F ... 913 642-3700
Shawnee Mission *(G-11684)*
P & F Services Inc ... F ... 785 456-9401
Wamego *(G-13432)*
Patrick S Kearney ... F ... 913 367-3161
Atchison *(G-255)*
Prairie Landworks Inc ... F ... 620 504-5049
Mcpherson *(G-7017)*
Quality Structures Inc ... E ... 785 835-6100
Richmond *(G-10203)*
R & R Developers Inc ... F ... 785 762-2255
Junction City *(G-3746)*
Rd Thomann Contracting ... F ... 913 268-5580
Shawnee Mission *(G-11780)*
Spartan Installation Repr LLC ... F ... 816 237-0017
Lenexa *(G-6145)*
▲ Titan Construction Inc ... C ... 913 782-6700
Olathe *(G-8111)*
Tommy J Kemp ... E ... 316 522-7255
Derby *(G-1276)*
Wieneke Construction Co Inc ... F ... 620 632-4529
Mc Cune *(G-6923)*
Wildcat Services Inc ... F ... 785 922-6466
Chapman *(G-781)*

1531 Operative Builders

A G Spanos Development Inc ... F ... 913 663-2400
Overland Park *(G-8335)*
B L Rieke & Associates Inc ... F ... 913 599-3393
Shawnee Mission *(G-11141)*
Builders Development Inc ... E ... 316 684-1400
Wichita *(G-13913)*
Don Klausmeyer Cnstr LLC ... E ... 316 554-0001
Wichita *(G-14224)*
Home Center Construction Inc ... E ... 620 231-5607
Pittsburg *(G-9877)*
R & R Developers Inc ... F ... 785 762-2255
Junction City *(G-3746)*
Rooks County Holdings LLC ... F ... 785 261-0455
Stockton *(G-12186)*
Suther Building Supply Inc ... F ... 785 336-2255
Seneca *(G-10883)*
Woodstone Inc ... F ... 913 685-2282
Shawnee Mission *(G-12018)*

1541 General Contractors, Indl Bldgs & Warehouses

All-Steel Building Systems LLC ... F ... 785 271-5559
Topeka *(G-12306)*
Arrowhead Contracting Inc ... D ... 913 814-9994
Lenexa *(G-5664)*
Awad Nicola ... E ... 913 381-6969
Overland Park *(G-8417)*
Berry Holdings LP ... B ... 620 251-4400
Coffeyville *(G-911)*
Bhs Construction Inc ... E ... 785 537-2068
Manhattan *(G-6557)*
BJ Koetting Inc ... F ... 785 823-8580
Salina *(G-10425)*
BKM Construction LLC ... F ... 913 297-0049
Leavenworth *(G-5212)*
Black Hawk Inc ... E ... 785 539-8240
Manhattan *(G-6562)*
Building Erection Svcs Co Inc ... E ... 913 764-5560
Olathe *(G-7568)*
Busboom & Rauh Construction Co ... E ... 785 825-4664
Salina *(G-10434)*
Conco Inc ... C ... 316 943-7111
Wichita *(G-14085)*
Coonrod & Assoc Cnstr Co Inc ... C ... 316 942-8430
Wichita *(G-14097)*
Decker Construction Inc ... E ... 620 251-7693
Coffeyville *(G-933)*
Diggs Construction Company ... E ... 316 691-1255
Wichita *(G-14210)*
Dondlinger & Sons Cnstr Co Inc ... C ... 316 945-0555
Wichita *(G-14226)*
Eby Corporation ... F ... 316 268-3500
Wichita *(G-14256)*
▼ Ernest-Spencer Inc ... E ... 785 484-3165
Meriden *(G-7080)*
Evergreen Design Build LLC ... E ... 620 342-6622
Emporia *(G-1752)*
Ewell Construction Inc ... F ... 913 499-7331
Topeka *(G-12585)*
Excel Constructors Inc ... D ... 913 261-1000
Overland Park *(G-8699)*
Feyerherm Construction Inc ... F ... 913 962-5888
Shawnee *(G-10955)*
◆ GBA Builders Llc ... E ... 913 492-0400
Lenexa *(G-5870)*
Gsr Construction Inc ... F ... 785 749-1770
Lawrence *(G-4883)*
Hahner Foreman & Harness LLC ... E ... 316 264-0306
Wichita *(G-14540)*
Harbin Construction LLC ... E ... 785 825-1651
Salina *(G-10535)*
Haren & Laughlin Cnstr Co Inc ... E ... 913 495-9558
Lenexa *(G-5890)*
Hastco Inc ... E ... 785 235-8718
Topeka *(G-12666)*
Hudson Inc ... E ... 620 232-1145
Pittsburg *(G-9879)*
Industrial Maintenance Inc ... E ... 316 267-7933
Wichita *(G-14685)*

Jaco General Contractor Inc................E....... 316 252-8200
Wichita *(G-14744)*
Julius Kaaz Cnstr Co Inc....................E....... 913 682-3550
Leavenworth *(G-5259)*
Ken Babcock Sales Inc.........................F....... 785 544-6592
Hiawatha *(G-3013)*
Key Construction Inc..........................C....... 316 263-9515
Wichita *(G-14852)*
Laforge and Budd Cnstr Co Inc...........D....... 620 421-4470
Parsons *(G-9706)*
Leavcon II Inc.......................................E....... 913 351-1430
Lansing *(G-4681)*
Lee Construction Inc............................E....... 620 276-6811
Garden City *(G-2222)*
Lee Shafer Ricky..................................E....... 620 252-9126
Coffeyville *(G-955)*
Loyd Builders Inc..................................F....... 785 242-1213
Ottawa *(G-8286)*
Manning Construction Co Inc...............E....... 913 390-1007
Olathe *(G-7873)*
Merit General Contractors....................F....... 913 747-7400
Olathe *(G-7883)*
Midwest Mill Modernization.................F....... 620 583-6883
Eureka *(G-1895)*
Miller - Stauch Cnstr Co Inc................E....... 913 599-1040
Kansas City *(G-4260)*
Mohan Construction Inc........................E....... 785 233-1615
Topeka *(G-12909)*
Morton Buildings Inc............................F....... 620 275-4105
Garden City *(G-2239)*
National Builders Inc............................F....... 316 729-7445
Wichita *(G-15147)*
National Ctstrphe Rstrtion Inc.............D....... 316 636-5700
Wichita *(G-15149)*
North Enterprises LLC..........................F....... 913 592-4025
Spring Hill *(G-12093)*
Overland Park Heating & Coolg............E....... 913 649-0303
Overland Park *(G-9119)*
Paronto Mall Construction Inc..............F....... 785 632-2484
Clay Center *(G-875)*
Paul Davis Restoratio of Great.............E....... 785 842-0351
Lawrence *(G-5058)*
Qti Inc..F....... 913 579-3131
Olathe *(G-8013)*
R M Baril General Contr Inc..................E....... 785 537-2190
Manhattan *(G-6785)*
Roofmasters Roofing Co Inc..................E....... 785 462-6642
Colby *(G-1036)*
Rose Companies Inc..............................F....... 913 782-0777
Olathe *(G-8042)*
Rose Construction Co Inc.....................F....... 913 782-0777
Olathe *(G-8043)*
Rylie Equipment & Contg Co................D....... 913 621-2725
Kansas City *(G-4394)*
Salina Building Systems Inc.................E....... 785 823-6812
Salina *(G-10666)*
Sauerwein Construction Co Inc............F....... 316 942-0028
Wichita *(G-15522)*
Sharper Images Company LLC.............F....... 620 331-7646
Independence *(G-3559)*
Simpson Construction Svcs Inc............E....... 316 942-3206
Wichita *(G-15596)*
Snodgrass & Sons Cnstr Co Inc............D....... 316 687-3110
Wichita *(G-15611)*
Strickland Construction Co...................E....... 913 764-7000
Olathe *(G-8085)*
Team Construction LLC.........................F....... 913 469-9990
Overland Park *(G-9396)*
Titan Cnstr Organization Inc.................F....... 913 782-6700
Olathe *(G-8110)*
Treb Construction Inc............................F....... 785 373-4935
Tipton *(G-12250)*
Universal Construction Co Inc..............E....... 913 342-1150
Kansas City *(G-4494)*
Wds Inc..D....... 913 894-1881
Lenexa *(G-6223)*
Weigel Construction Inc.........................F....... 913 780-1274
Spring Hill *(G-12103)*
Wolf Construction Inc............................D....... 785 862-2474
Topeka *(G-13247)*

1542 General Contractors, Nonresidential & Non-indl Bldgs

2point Construction Co LLC..................E....... 913 749-1855
Shawnee *(G-10903)*
96 Agri Sales Inc....................................F....... 316 661-2281
Mount Hope *(G-7202)*
A G Spanos Development Inc...............F....... 913 663-2400
Overland Park *(G-8335)*
A L Huber Inc..E....... 913 341-4880
Shawnee Mission *(G-11064)*
Accel Construction LLC.........................E....... 316 866-2885
Bel Aire *(G-425)*
Action Plumbing of Lawrence...............F....... 785 843-5670
Lawrence *(G-4718)*
AL Huber Construction Inc....................E....... 913 341-4880
Shawnee Mission *(G-11091)*
Allied Retail Concepts LLC....................F....... 913 492-8008
Shawnee *(G-10908)*
Altmar Inc..E....... 785 233-0053
Topeka *(G-12311)*
American Construction Svcs LLC..........F....... 913 754-3777
Lenexa *(G-5647)*
Appliance Doctor Inc..............................E....... 316 263-0005
Wichita *(G-13723)*
Arrowhead Contracting Inc....................D....... 913 814-9994
Lenexa *(G-5664)*
B & G Construction.................................F....... 620 431-0849
Chanute *(G-704)*
B A Green Construction Co Inc.............E....... 785 843-5277
Lawrence *(G-4747)*
Baker Construction Inc...........................E....... 913 682-6302
Leavenworth *(G-5206)*
Benchmark Construction LLC...............F....... 785 862-0340
Eudora *(G-1870)*
Benchmark Enterprises..........................F....... 785 537-4447
Manhattan *(G-6555)*
Bhs Construction Inc..............................E....... 785 537-2068
Manhattan *(G-6557)*
Bolivar Contracting Inc..........................E....... 913 533-2240
Bucyrus *(G-594)*
Borton Lc...E....... 620 669-8211
South Hutchinson *(G-12057)*
Bowden Contracting Company Inc.........F....... 913 342-5112
Kansas City *(G-3872)*
Bratton Bros Contracting Inc.................F....... 913 422-7771
Shawnee *(G-10920)*
Building Erection Svcs Co Inc...............E....... 913 764-5560
Olathe *(G-7568)*
Busboom & Rauh Construction Co.........E....... 785 825-4664
Salina *(G-10434)*
Caro Construction Co Inc......................E....... 316 267-7505
Wichita *(G-13952)*
Carrothers Construction Co Inc.............E....... 913 294-2361
Paola *(G-9544)*
Chambless Roofing Inc..........................F....... 620 275-8410
Scott City *(G-10807)*
Cmg Construction Inc............................E....... 913 384-2883
Paola *(G-9548)*
Coal Creek Construction Co..................F....... 785 256-7171
Auburn *(G-294)*
Coast To Coast Builders Inc..................F....... 316 265-2515
Wichita *(G-14047)*
Commerce Construction Svcs Inc..........E....... 316 262-0547
Wichita *(G-14068)*
Commercial Builders Inc........................D....... 785 625-6272
Hays *(G-2774)*
Compton Construction Svcs LLC...........E....... 316 262-8885
Wichita *(G-14083)*
Conco Inc...C....... 316 943-7111
Wichita *(G-14085)*
Confederated Builders Supply...............E....... 316 788-3913
Derby *(G-1232)*
Construction Svcs Bryant Inc.................F....... 316 262-1010
Wichita *(G-14093)*
Coonrod & Assoc Cnstr Co Inc..............C....... 316 942-8430
Wichita *(G-14097)*
Cornejo & Sons LLC...............................C....... 316 522-5100
Wichita *(G-14101)*
Crookham Construction LLC..................E....... 913 369-3341
Tonganoxie *(G-12259)*
▲ **Crossland Construction Co Inc**.........C....... 620 429-1414
Columbus *(G-1071)*
Czarnieckis Construction Inc................F....... 316 946-9991
Wichita *(G-14153)*
D & R Construction Inc..........................E....... 785 776-1087
Manhattan *(G-6608)*
D J Carpenter Building Systems............F....... 785 537-9789
Manhattan *(G-6609)*
Damage Ctrl & Restoration Inc..............E....... 913 722-0228
Kansas City *(G-3954)*
Davidson & Associates Inc....................E....... 913 271-6859
Leawood *(G-5372)*
Davis Construction LLC.........................F....... 620 674-3100
Columbus *(G-1074)*
Decker Construction Inc........................E....... 620 251-7693
Coffeyville *(G-933)*
Designbuild Construction Inc................E....... 316 722-8180
Wichita *(G-14201)*
DF Osborne Construction Inc................F....... 785 862-0333
Topeka *(G-12554)*
Dick Construction Inc.............................F....... 620 275-1806
Garden City *(G-2147)*
Diggs Construction Company...............E....... 316 691-1255
Wichita *(G-14210)*
Dondlinger & Sons Cnstr Co Inc...........C....... 316 945-0555
Wichita *(G-14226)*
Duffy Construction Company Inc...........F....... 913 381-1668
Shawnee Mission *(G-11321)*
Ebco Construction Group LLC...............F....... 866 297-2185
Olathe *(G-7667)*
Eby Corporation......................................F....... 316 268-3500
Wichita *(G-14256)*
Emporia Construction & Rmdlg..............E....... 620 341-3131
Emporia *(G-1738)*
EMR-Pcg Construction Group...............E....... 406 249-7730
Lawrence *(G-4853)*
Epic Homes of Kansas Inc......................E....... 785 537-3773
Manhattan *(G-6622)*
Evans Building Co Inc............................E....... 316 524-0103
Maize *(G-6513)*
Excel Constructors Inc...........................D....... 913 261-1000
Overland Park *(G-8699)*
Fagan Construction Co..........................F....... 913 238-5903
Prairie Village *(G-10028)*
Feyerherm Construction Inc..................F....... 913 962-5888
Shawnee *(G-10955)*
Finley Construction & Rdymx................G....... 785 626-3282
Atwood *(G-286)*
Firelake-Arrowhead...............................D....... 913 312-9540
Lenexa *(G-5854)*
Firelk-Diversified Joint Ventr................E....... 913 312-9540
Lenexa *(G-5855)*
First Con Incorporated...........................F....... 316 425-7690
Wichita *(G-14374)*
First Construction LLC...........................E....... 785 749-0006
Lawrence *(G-4859)*
Flex Build LLC..F....... 913 890-2500
Shawnee Mission *(G-11374)*
Flinthills Construction Inc......................F....... 785 379-5499
Tecumseh *(G-12239)*
▲ **Fox Ceramic Tile Inc**..........................E....... 785 437-2792
Saint Marys *(G-10365)*
Frazier Brothers Plbg & Contg...............F....... 785 452-9707
Salina *(G-10506)*
Frontr-Rrwhead Joint Ventr LLC...........E....... 913 461-3804
Olathe *(G-7719)*
Fuqua Construction Inc..........................F....... 620 585-2270
Inman *(G-3582)*
G & F Construction Co LLC....................E....... 316 260-3313
Wichita *(G-14432)*
Golconda Group LLC...............................F....... 913 579-4795
Shawnee *(G-10963)*
Grace Construction & Assoc Inc.............F....... 316 617-1729
Derby *(G-1249)*
Grayling Inc...F....... 913 341-5444
Overland Park *(G-8769)*
Guthridge/Nighswonger Corp..................F....... 316 264-7900
Wichita *(G-14529)*
Hahner Foreman & Harness LLC.............E....... 316 264-0306
Wichita *(G-14540)*
Harbin Construction LLC.........................E....... 785 825-1651
Salina *(G-10535)*
Haren & Laughlin Cnstr Co Inc...............E....... 913 495-9558
Lenexa *(G-5890)*
Haren Laughlin Restoration Inc..............E....... 913 495-9558
Overland Park *(G-8794)*
Harman Huffman Cnstr Group Inc...........E....... 316 744-2081
Kechi *(G-4569)*
Harmon Construction Inc.........................E....... 913 962-5888
Olathe *(G-7753)*
Hastco Inc..E....... 785 235-8718
Topeka *(G-12666)*
Heinen Custom Operations Inc...............F....... 785 945-6759
Valley Falls *(G-13364)*
Hieb & Associates LLC............................F....... 620 663-9430
Hutchinson *(G-3311)*
Hofer & Hofer & Associates Inc..............E....... 620 473-3919
Humboldt *(G-3185)*
Hog Slat Incorporated.............................F....... 580 338-5003
Liberal *(G-6321)*
Home Center Construction Inc................E....... 620 231-5607
Pittsburg *(G-9877)*
Homeland Roofing and Cnstr LLC...........F....... 316 832-9901
Wichita *(G-14632)*
Howell Construction Co Inc.....................E....... 816 474-7766
Stilwell *(G-12153)*
Hudson Inc..E....... 620 232-1145
Pittsburg *(G-9879)*

Hutton Construction Corp....C.... 316 942-8855
Wichita (G-14660)
J & M Contracting Inc....F.... 913 397-0272
Olathe (G-7804)
J A G II Inc....E.... 620 276-8409
Garden City (G-2207)
J A Lyden Construction Co....F.... 785 286-1427
Topeka (G-12730)
J-A-G Construction Company....C.... 620 225-0061
Dodge City (G-1380)
J-A-G Construction Company....E.... 620 225-0061
Dodge City (G-1381)
Jackson Agrobuilders LLC....F.... 913 909-6391
Shawnee (G-10976)
Jaco General Contractor Inc....E.... 316 252-8200
Wichita (G-14744)
Jahnke & Sons Construction Inc....F.... 800 351-2525
Overland Park (G-8870)
James Gruver Construction Inc....E.... 620 663-7982
Hutchinson (G-3340)
Jay McConnell Construction Inc....F.... 913 492-9300
Kansas City (G-4119)
Jayhawk Plumbing Inc....F.... 785 865-5225
Lawrence (G-4920)
Joel Fritzel Construction Co....E.... 785 843-0566
Lawrence (G-4925)
JP Murray Company Inc....F.... 913 451-1279
Overland Park (G-8880)
Julius Kaaz Cnstr Co Inc....E.... 913 682-3550
Leavenworth (G-5259)
K Construction Inc....F.... 785 499-5296
Alta Vista (G-70)
Kbs Constructors Inc....E.... 785 266-4222
Topeka (G-12813)
Kdc Construction Inc....F.... 913 677-1920
Leawood (G-5447)
Kearney Construction Inc....F.... 913 367-1200
Atchison (G-238)
Kelley Construction Co Inc....E.... 785 235-6040
Topeka (G-12815)
Ken Babcock Sales Inc....F.... 785 544-6592
Hiawatha (G-3013)
Kendall Construction Inc....E.... 785 246-1207
Topeka (G-12817)
Key Construction Inc....C.... 316 263-9515
Wichita (G-14852)
Keystone Construction Inc....F.... 316 778-1566
Benton (G-516)
Kiewit Corporation....D.... 913 928-7000
Lenexa (G-5948)
Klein Construction Inc....F.... 316 262-3313
Park City (G-9626)
Koehn Construction Svcs LLC....E.... 620 378-3002
Fredonia (G-2036)
Kuhlmann Installations LLC....F.... 316 634-6531
Wichita (G-14899)
Laforge and Budd Cnstr Co Inc....D.... 620 421-4470
Parsons (G-9706)
Law Company Inc....C.... 316 268-0200
Wichita (G-14934)
Leavcon II Inc....E.... 913 351-1430
Lansing (G-4681)
Lee Construction Inc....E.... 620 276-6811
Garden City (G-2222)
Lee Haworth Construction Co....F.... 785 823-7168
Salina (G-10580)
Line Construction Company....F.... 913 341-1212
Shawnee Mission (G-11575)
Loyd Builders Inc....F.... 785 242-1213
Ottawa (G-8286)
Ls Construction Services Inc....E.... 913 681-5888
Shawnee Mission (G-11580)
Main Street Chanute Inc....F.... 620 431-0056
Chanute (G-741)
Manning Construction Co Inc....E.... 913 390-1007
Olathe (G-7873)
Mar Lan Construction LC....F.... 785 749-2647
Lawrence (G-5010)
Martin K EBY Cnstr Co Inc....C.... 316 268-3500
Wichita (G-15012)
Mastercraft Corporation....E.... 785 842-4455
Lawrence (G-5013)
McBride Construction Inc....F.... 620 544-7146
Hugoton (G-3173)
McCarthy Bldg Companies Inc....E.... 913 202-7002
Overland Park (G-9000)
McCullough Development Inc....E.... 888 776-3010
Manhattan (G-6737)
McOn LLC....F.... 785 989-4550
Wathena (G-13475)
McPherson Con Stor Systems Inc....F.... 620 241-4362
McPherson (G-6994)
▲ McPherson Contractors Inc....D.... 785 273-3880
Topeka (G-12873)
McPherson Development Co Inc....F.... 785 272-9521
Topeka (G-12874)
Merit General Contractors....F.... 913 747-7400
Olathe (G-7883)
Michael S Hundley Cnstr Inc....F.... 913 367-7059
Atchison (G-249)
Midland Restoration Company....F.... 620 223-6855
Fort Scott (G-1991)
Midwest Masonry Construction....E.... 785 861-7500
Topeka (G-12902)
Mill Creek LLC....F.... 785 364-2328
Holton (G-3105)
Miller - Stauch Cnstr Co Inc....E.... 913 599-1040
Kansas City (G-4260)
Miller Construction....F.... 785 448-6788
Garnett (G-2383)
Miller Homebuilders Inc....E.... 620 662-1687
Hutchinson (G-3381)
Minick Gambrell Contrs LLC....F.... 913 538-5391
Olathe (G-7902)
Mitchell-Markowitz Cnstr....E.... 620 343-6840
Emporia (G-1796)
Mm Property MGT & Rmdlg LLC....F.... 913 871-6867
Kansas City (G-4265)
MMC Corp....E.... 913 469-0101
Overland Park (G-9046)
Mohan Construction Inc....E.... 785 233-1615
Topeka (G-12909)
Murray and Sons Cnstr Co Inc....E.... 785 267-1961
Topeka (G-12920)
Mw Builders Inc....C.... 913 469-0101
Lenexa (G-6016)
Nabholz Construction Corp....D.... 913 393-6500
Lenexa (G-6017)
National Commercial Bldrs Inc....F.... 913 599-0200
Lenexa (G-6018)
National Contractors Inc....E.... 316 722-8484
Wichita (G-15148)
National Ctstrphe Rstrtion Inc....D.... 316 636-5700
Wichita (G-15149)
Netco Construction Co Inc....E.... 316 942-2062
Wichita (G-15162)
Nieder Contracting Inc....E.... 785 842-0094
Lawrence (G-5040)
North American Buildings Inc....F.... 316 821-9590
Wichita (G-15187)
Oetinger-Lloyd Construction....F.... 785 632-2106
Clay Center (G-874)
Page Corporation....F.... 316 262-7200
Augusta (G-335)
Paint Masters Inc....F.... 316 683-5203
Wichita (G-15253)
Paul-Wertenberger Cnstr Inc....E.... 785 625-8220
Hays (G-2885)
PDQ Construction Inc....F.... 785 842-6844
Topeka (G-12966)
Pemco Inc....F.... 913 294-2361
Paola (G-9582)
Pkc Construction Co....E.... 913 782-4646
Lenexa (G-6061)
Ponton Construction Inc....F.... 785 823-9584
Salina (G-10635)
Prairie Landworks Inc....F.... 620 504-5049
Mcpherson (G-7017)
Preferred Contg Systems Co....F.... 913 341-0111
Leawood (G-5525)
Profitt Builders and Supply....F.... 620 278-3667
Sterling (G-12129)
Prosser Wilbert Cnstr Inc....F.... 913 906-0104
Lenexa (G-6077)
Purdum Inc....E.... 913 766-0835
Overland Park (G-9204)
Quality Structures Inc....E.... 785 835-6100
Richmond (G-10203)
Quality Trust Inc....E.... 785 375-6372
Junction City (G-3745)
Quinter Mfg & Cnstr Inc....F.... 785 754-3310
Quinter (G-10186)
R D H Electric Inc....E.... 785 625-3833
Hays (G-2895)
R M Baril General Contr Inc....E.... 785 537-2190
Manhattan (G-6785)
R Messner Construction Co....E.... 316 634-2381
Wichita (G-15405)
Rau Construction Company....E.... 913 642-6000
Overland Park (G-9227)
Redmon Housing LLC....F.... 913 432-4945
Overland Park (G-9229)
Regarding Kitchens Inc....F.... 913 642-6184
Olathe (G-8023)
Retrochem Inc....F.... 913 422-8810
Shawnee (G-11018)
Rf Construction Inc....E.... 785 776-8855
Manhattan (G-6791)
Rhino Builders Inc....F.... 913 722-4353
Kansas City (G-4376)
Rhw Construction Inc....F.... 913 451-1222
Shawnee Mission (G-11797)
Rose Companies Inc....F.... 913 782-0777
Olathe (G-8042)
Rose Construction Co Inc....F.... 913 782-0777
Olathe (G-8043)
Rylie Equipment & Contg Co....D.... 913 621-2725
Kansas City (G-4394)
Sauerwein Construction Co Inc....F.... 316 942-0028
Wichita (G-15522)
Sca Construction Inc....E.... 620 331-8247
Independence (G-3557)
Senne and Company Inc....E.... 785 235-1015
Topeka (G-13058)
Service Technologies Midwest....E.... 913 671-3340
Overland Park (G-9299)
Shamburg Unlimited LLC....F.... 785 379-0760
Tecumseh (G-12241)
Sharp Construction Company....E.... 316 943-9511
Valley Center (G-13353)
Simpson Construction Svcs Inc....E.... 316 942-3206
Wichita (G-15596)
Sky Blue Inc....D.... 785 842-9013
Lawrence (G-5112)
Skyline Construction Company....D.... 913 642-7100
Overland Park (G-9316)
Smith Construction Company Inc....E.... 316 942-7989
Wichita (G-15607)
Snodgrass & Sons Cnstr Co Inc....D.... 316 687-3110
Wichita (G-15611)
Southwestern Remodeling Contrs....E.... 316 263-1239
Wichita (G-15633)
Spartan Installation Repr LLC....F.... 816 237-0017
Lenexa (G-6145)
Starflite Manufacturing Co....G.... 316 267-7297
Wichita (G-15656)
Strate Construction Inc....F.... 620 659-2251
Kinsley (G-4621)
Strickland Construction Co....E.... 913 764-7000
Olathe (G-8085)
Sturdi-Bilt Storage Barns Inc....E.... 620 663-5998
Hutchinson (G-3453)
Sutherland Builders Inc....F.... 316 529-2620
Wichita (G-15705)
Titan Built LLC....E.... 913 782-6700
Overland Park (G-9413)
Titan Cnstr Organization Inc....F.... 913 782-6700
Olathe (G-8110)
▲ Titan Construction Inc....C.... 913 782-6700
Olathe (G-8111)
Tommy J Kemp....E.... 316 522-7255
Derby (G-1276)
Treb Construction Inc....F.... 785 373-4935
Tipton (G-12250)
Tutera Group Inc....E.... 913 851-0215
Shawnee Mission (G-11951)
Universal Construction Co Inc....E.... 913 342-1150
Kansas City (G-4494)
Venture Construction Company....E.... 913 642-2972
Overland Park (G-9461)
▲ Wc Construction LLC....E.... 816 741-4810
Merriam (G-7110)
Wiens & Company Construction....E.... 620 665-1155
Hutchinson (G-3488)
Wildcat Services Inc....F.... 785 922-6466
Chapman (G-781)
Williams Construction Co Inc....F.... 316 264-1964
Wichita (G-16052)
Winston-Brown Construction Co....E.... 785 271-1661
Topeka (G-13246)
Wise Construction Inc....F.... 785 781-4383
Cawker City (G-691)
Wood RE New Joco Inc....G.... 913 661-9663
Olathe (G-8159)
Woofter Cnstr & Irrigation Inc....E.... 785 462-8653
Colby (G-1049)
Xec Inc....E.... 913 563-4260
Overland Park (G-9511)
Zernco....D.... 316 775-9991
Wichita (G-16102)

SIC

Zieson Construction Co LLC ....F 785 783-8335
Topeka *(G-13261)*
Zimmerman Construction Company ....F 913 685-2255
Overland Park *(G-9528)*

16 HEAVY CONSTRUCTION OTHER THAN BUILDING CONSTRUCTION-CONTRACTORS

1611 Highway & Street Construction

Amino Bros Co Inc ....C 913 334-2330
Kansas City *(G-3807)*
Andrews Asphalt & Cnstr Inc ....G 785 232-0188
Topeka *(G-12326)*
Apac-Kansas Inc ....E 620 662-3307
Hutchinson *(G-3200)*
Apac-Kansas Inc ....D 785 625-3459
Hays *(G-2749)*
Apac-Kansas Inc ....E 620 342-2047
Emporia *(G-1695)*
Apac-Kansas Inc ....E 785 823-5537
Salina *(G-10406)*
Apac-Kansas Inc ....E 620 662-2112
Hutchinson *(G-3202)*
Apac-Kansas Inc ....E 316 775-7639
Augusta *(G-300)*
Apac-Kansas Inc ....D 316 524-5200
Wichita *(G-13716)*
B & B Bridges Company LLC ....F 620 449-2286
Saint Paul *(G-10379)*
B & H Paving Inc ....F 620 872-3146
Scott City *(G-10805)*
Ballou Pavement Solutions Inc ....C 785 827-4439
Salina *(G-10416)*
Banzet Concrete Inc ....F 316 776-9961
Rose Hill *(G-10236)*
Barkley Construction ....F 316 945-6500
Wichita *(G-13812)*
Bettis Asphalt & Cnstr Inc ....E 785 235-8444
Topeka *(G-12377)*
Central Paving Inc ....E 316 778-1194
Benton *(G-514)*
Circle C Paving and Cnstr LLC ....E 316 794-5070
Goddard *(G-2432)*
City of Junction City ....E 785 238-7142
Junction City *(G-3682)*
City of Liberal ....E 620 626-0135
Liberal *(G-6292)*
City of Overland Park ....E 913 895-6040
Overland Park *(G-8556)*
City of Parsons ....E 620 421-7025
Parsons *(G-9671)*
City of Topeka ....D 785 295-3803
Topeka *(G-12474)*
Concrete Service Co Inc ....E 620 792-2558
Great Bend *(G-2545)*
Concrete Service Co Inc ....G 785 628-2100
Hays *(G-2776)*
Conspec Inc ....D 316 832-0828
Park City *(G-9612)*
Cornejo & Sons LLC ....C 316 522-5100
Wichita *(G-14101)*
County of Chautauqua ....F 620 725-5860
Sedan *(G-10841)*
County of Dickinson ....F 785 263-3193
Abilene *(G-21)*
County of Douglas ....E 785 832-5293
Lawrence *(G-4814)*
County of Finney ....D 620 272-3564
Garden City *(G-2135)*
County of Kiowa ....F 620 723-2531
Greensburg *(G-2673)*
County of Labette ....E 620 784-5391
Altamont *(G-72)*
County of Leavenworth ....D 913 727-1800
Leavenworth *(G-5228)*
County of Morton ....E 620 593-4288
Elkhart *(G-1618)*
County of Pawnee ....E 620 285-6141
Larned *(G-4700)*
County of Reno ....D 620 694-2976
South Hutchinson *(G-12058)*
County of Russell ....E 785 483-4032
Russell *(G-10270)*
County of Sedgwick ....E 316 685-2035
Wichita *(G-14112)*
County of Shawnee ....D 785 862-2071
Topeka *(G-12520)*
County of Shawnee ....D 785 233-7702
Topeka *(G-12521)*
County of Stevens ....E 620 544-8782
Hugoton *(G-3154)*
Cutler Repaving Inc ....D 785 843-1524
Lawrence *(G-4821)*
Diversified Contracting LLC ....F 913 898-4722
Parker *(G-9657)*
Dudley Construction Co Inc ....F 620 665-1166
Hutchinson *(G-3270)*
Dustrol Inc ....D 316 536-2262
Towanda *(G-13264)*
Ebert Construction Co Inc ....E 785 456-2455
Wamego *(G-13418)*
Ferguson Paving Inc ....F 316 942-3374
Wichita *(G-14356)*
Fulsom Brothers Inc ....F 620 758-2828
Cedar Vale *(G-694)*
Goodart Consrtuction Inc ....F 913 557-0044
Paola *(G-9562)*
Gunter Construction Company ....F 913 362-7844
Kansas City *(G-4059)*
Hall Brothers Inc ....F 785 562-2386
Marysville *(G-6890)*
Hamm Inc ....G 785 597-5111
Perry *(G-9769)*
Hamm Asphalt Inc ....F 785 597-5421
Perry *(G-9770)*
Harbour Construction Inc ....F 913 441-2555
Kansas City *(G-4067)*
Haupt Construction Company ....F 913 686-4411
Spring Hill *(G-12085)*
Hazen Construction Services ....F 316 777-0206
Mulvane *(G-7216)*
Heartstone Inc ....F 316 942-1135
Wichita *(G-14591)*
Heckert Construction Co Inc ....F 620 231-6090
Pittsburg *(G-9874)*
Holland Paving Inc ....E 316 722-7114
Wichita *(G-14625)*
Hwa Davis Cnstr & Sup Inc ....F 316 283-0330
Newton *(G-7364)*
Inland Corporation ....F 620 478-2450
Norwich *(G-7470)*
J & J Contractors Inc ....F 620 365-5500
Iola *(G-3613)*
J Corp ....F 785 628-8101
Hays *(G-2854)*
J J Martiny Concrete Co ....D 913 268-7775
Kansas City *(G-4115)*
Jcor Inc ....F 913 461-8804
Overland Park *(G-8873)*
Julius Kaaz Cnstr Co Inc ....E 913 682-3550
Leavenworth *(G-5259)*
Kansas Asphalt Inc ....D 877 384-2280
Bucyrus *(G-601)*
Kansas Department Trnsp ....D 785 672-3113
Oakley *(G-7478)*
Kansas Department Trnsp ....E 316 321-3370
El Dorado *(G-1575)*
Kansas Department Trnsp ....B 785 823-3754
Salina *(G-10564)*
Kansas Department Trnsp ....E 785 486-2142
Horton *(G-3128)*
Kansas Department Trnsp ....D 620 583-5661
Eureka *(G-1893)*
Kansas Department Trnsp ....C 316 744-1271
Wichita *(G-14796)*
Kaw Valley Companies Inc ....C 913 281-9950
Kansas City *(G-4160)*
Kiewit Power Constructors Co ....C 913 928-7800
Lenexa *(G-5950)*
Killough Construction Inc ....F 785 242-1500
Ottawa *(G-8281)*
King Construction Company Inc ....D 620 327-4251
Hesston *(G-2995)*
▼ Konza Constr Co Inc ....D 785 762-2995
Junction City *(G-3717)*
Laforge and Budd Cnstr Co Inc ....D 620 421-4470
Parsons *(G-9706)*
Lee Shafer Ricky ....E 620 252-9126
Coffeyville *(G-955)*
Lrm Industries Inc ....E 785 843-1688
Lawrence *(G-5001)*
Max Rieke & Brothers Inc ....D 913 631-7111
Shawnee *(G-10991)*
McAnany Construction Inc ....D 913 631-5440
Shawnee Mission *(G-11606)*
Miles Excavating Inc ....C 913 724-1934
Basehor *(G-384)*
N R Hamm Contractor Inc ....D 785 597-5111
Perry *(G-9773)*
Ness County Engineers Office ....E 785 798-3350
Ness City *(G-7264)*
ODonnell-Way Cnstr Co Inc ....F 913 498-3355
Prairie Village *(G-10053)*
Oldcastle Infrastructure Inc ....F 620 662-3307
Hutchinson *(G-3392)*
Page Enterprise LLC ....F 913 898-4722
Parker *(G-9659)*
Pavers Inc ....E 785 825-6771
Salina *(G-10632)*
Paving Construction Inc ....F 316 684-6161
Wichita *(G-15272)*
Pyramid Contractors Inc ....E 913 764-6225
Olathe *(G-8012)*
R D Johnson Excavating Co Inc ....E 785 842-9100
Lawrence *(G-5085)*
R Puckett Farms Inc ....E 620 378-3565
Fredonia *(G-2042)*
Recycling Enterprises Inc ....F 316 536-2262
Towanda *(G-13266)*
RFB Construction Co Inc ....E 620 232-2900
Pittsburg *(G-9928)*
Sherwood Construction Co Inc ....C 316 943-0211
Wichita *(G-15581)*
Shilling Construction Co Inc ....E 785 776-5077
Manhattan *(G-6800)*
Skillman Construction LLC ....D 620 364-2505
New Strawn *(G-7305)*
Sporer Land Development Inc ....E 785 672-4319
Oakley *(G-7487)*
Sunflower Paving Inc ....D 785 856-4590
Lawrence *(G-5129)*
Surface Protection Svcs LLC ....F 316 322-5135
El Dorado *(G-1606)*
T & T Flatworks Inc ....E 620 794-0619
Lebo *(G-5609)*
Tri State Construction Inc ....E 620 231-5260
Pittsburg *(G-9948)*
Venture Corporation ....D 620 792-5921
Great Bend *(G-2654)*
W R King Contracting Inc ....E 913 238-7496
Shawnee Mission *(G-11985)*
Wade Agricultural Products Inc ....G 913 757-2255
La Cygne *(G-4646)*
Western Contracting Corp ....D 620 449-2286
Saint Paul *(G-10385)*
Wildcat Construction Co Inc ....C 316 945-9408
Wichita *(G-16049)*
Wyandtte Cnty Unfied Gvernment ....E 913 573-8300
Kansas City *(G-4554)*

1622 Bridge, Tunnel & Elevated Hwy Construction

American Bridge Company ....F 913 948-5800
Overland Park *(G-8375)*
Ballou Pavement Solutions Inc ....C 785 827-4439
Salina *(G-10416)*
BRB Contractors Inc ....C 785 232-1245
Topeka *(G-12403)*
Bridges Inc ....E 316 283-9350
Newton *(G-7322)*
Bryan-Ohlmeier Construction ....E 913 557-9972
Paola *(G-9543)*
County of Ellis ....D 785 628-9455
Hays *(G-2778)*
County of Greenwood ....E 620 583-8112
Eureka *(G-1882)*
Crossland Heavy Contrs Inc ....D 620 429-1410
Columbus *(G-1072)*
Dondlinger & Sons Cnstr Co Inc ....C 316 945-0555
Wichita *(G-14226)*
Eby Corporation ....F 316 268-3500
Wichita *(G-14256)*
J & J Contractors Inc ....F 620 365-5500
Iola *(G-3613)*
King Construction Company Inc ....D 620 327-4251
Hesston *(G-2995)*
Klaver Construction Co Inc ....D 620 532-3183
Kingman *(G-4603)*
L & M Contractors Inc ....D 620 793-8137
Great Bend *(G-2600)*
▼ L G Barcus and Sons Inc ....D 913 621-1100
Kansas City *(G-4188)*
▲ Massman Construction Co ....E 913 291-2600
Leawood *(G-5468)*
Pyramid Contractors Inc ....E 913 764-6225
Olathe *(G-8012)*

RA Knapp Construction Inc ....E.... 913 287-8700
Lenexa *(G-6088)*
Sherwood Construction Co Inc ....C.... 316 943-0211
Wichita *(G-15581)*
Wildcat Construction Co Inc ....C.... 316 945-9408
Wichita *(G-16049)*

1623 Water, Sewer & Utility Line Construction

Ace Construction Corporation ....E.... 316 536-2202
Towanda *(G-13262)*
Alea Communications LLC ....F.... 913 439-7391
Gardner *(G-2323)*
American Energies Gas Svc LLC ....F.... 620 628-4424
Canton *(G-679)*
Amerine Utilities Construction ....E.... 620 792-1223
Great Bend *(G-2508)*
ANR Pipeline Company ....F.... 785 479-5814
Enterprise *(G-1853)*
Bayer Construction Company Inc ....C.... 785 776-8839
Manhattan *(G-6553)*
Becker Construction Inc ....F.... 316 744-6800
Park City *(G-9603)*
Bennett Rgers Pipe Coating Inc ....E.... 913 371-3880
Kansas City *(G-3854)*
Bob Hull Inc ....E.... 785 292-4790
Frankfort *(G-2021)*
BRB Contractors Inc ....C.... 785 232-1245
Topeka *(G-12403)*
Bsj Power Services Inc ....F.... 417 850-1707
Cherokee *(G-799)*
Carrothers Construction Co LLC ....E.... 913 294-8120
Paola *(G-9545)*
Chase Contractors Inc ....G.... 620 431-2142
Chanute *(G-714)*
Cimarron Underground Inc ....E.... 913 438-2981
Overland Park *(G-8552)*
City of Waterville ....E.... 785 363-2367
Waterville *(G-13473)*
Coffeyville Resources LLC ....F.... 620 221-2107
Winfield *(G-16122)*
Coxmontgomery Inc ....F.... 620 508-6260
Pratt *(G-10104)*
Cronister & Company Inc ....E.... 785 862-5003
Topeka *(G-12531)*
D L Smith Electrical Cnstr ....C.... 785 267-4920
Topeka *(G-12543)*
Diamond Engineering Company ....E.... 316 943-5701
Wichita *(G-14208)*
Dobson-Davis Co ....F.... 913 894-4922
Shawnee Mission *(G-11311)*
Dreiling Construction LLC ....F.... 620 275-9433
Garden City *(G-2149)*
Eatherly Constructors Inc ....F.... 620 276-6611
Garden City *(G-2151)*
Eby Corporation ....F.... 316 268-3500
Wichita *(G-14256)*
Emerson Construction Inc ....F.... 785 235-0555
Topeka *(G-12574)*
Gerard Tank & Steel Inc ....E.... 785 243-3895
Concordia *(G-1116)*
Great Plains Locating Svc Inc ....E.... 316 263-1200
Wichita *(G-14504)*
Harp Well Pump Svc Corporated ....F.... 316 722-1411
Wichita *(G-14562)*
Hayden Tower Service Inc ....D.... 785 232-1840
Topeka *(G-12668)*
Herrmans Excavating Inc ....E.... 785 233-4146
Topeka *(G-12687)*
Huston Contracting Inc ....F.... 913 782-1333
Olathe *(G-7782)*
Integrity Locating Svcs LLC ....E.... 913 530-6315
Olathe *(G-7797)*
J & J Powerline Contractors ....E.... 620 227-2467
Dodge City *(G-1379)*
J Corp ....F.... 785 628-8101
Hays *(G-2854)*
Jomax Construction Company Inc ....F.... 620 792-3686
Great Bend *(G-2596)*
K & W Underground Incorporated ....D.... 913 782-7387
Olathe *(G-7821)*
K C Construction Inc ....F.... 913 724-1474
Basehor *(G-382)*
Larson Construction Inc ....E.... 785 537-0160
Manhattan *(G-6710)*
Layne Christensen Company ....E.... 316 264-5365
Wichita *(G-14937)*
◆ **Legacy Technologies LLC** ....E.... 913 432-2020
Shawnee Mission *(G-11559)*
Linaweaver Construction Inc ....F.... 913 351-3474
Lansing *(G-4686)*
▲ **Lowe-North Construction Inc** ....E.... 913 592-4025
Spring Hill *(G-12087)*
Lrm Industries Inc ....E.... 785 843-1688
Lawrence *(G-5001)*
MAI Excavating Inc ....G.... 785 483-3387
Russell *(G-10280)*
Max Rieke & Brothers Inc ....D.... 913 631-7111
Shawnee *(G-10991)*
McCullough Excavation Inc ....E.... 316 634-2199
Wichita *(G-15025)*
Meadows Const Co Inc ....E.... 913 369-3335
Tonganoxie *(G-12266)*
Mels Pump & Plumbing ....F.... 785 632-3392
Clay Center *(G-872)*
Midwest Contractors Inc ....E.... 785 877-3565
Norton *(G-7449)*
Mies Construction Inc ....D.... 316 945-7227
Wichita *(G-15106)*
Miller Paving & Cnstr LLC ....C.... 913 334-5579
Kansas City *(G-4261)*
Northern Pipeline Construction ....F.... 785 232-0034
Topeka *(G-12937)*
Nowak Construction Co Inc ....D.... 316 794-8898
Goddard *(G-2449)*
Npl Construction Co ....D.... 785 232-0034
Topeka *(G-12940)*
Ohlsen Right of Way and Maint ....F.... 785 336-6112
Seneca *(G-10878)*
Pearson Construction LLC ....C.... 316 263-3100
Wichita *(G-15275)*
Phillips Southern Elc Co Inc ....E.... 316 265-4186
Wichita *(G-15293)*
Piping & Equipment Company Inc ....C.... 316 838-7511
Wichita *(G-15302)*
Prairie Landworks Inc ....F.... 620 504-5049
Mcpherson *(G-7017)*
Precision Boring Tech Inc ....F.... 913 735-4728
Olathe *(G-7999)*
R D Johnson Excavating Co Inc ....E.... 785 842-9100
Lawrence *(G-5085)*
RA Knapp Construction Inc ....E.... 913 287-8700
Lenexa *(G-6088)*
Rodriguez Mech Contrs Inc ....D.... 913 281-1814
Kansas City *(G-4386)*
Ron Weers Construction Inc ....E.... 913 681-5575
Bucyrus *(G-608)*
Rylie Equipment & Contg Co ....D.... 913 621-2725
Kansas City *(G-4394)*
Scotts Powerline Construction ....F.... 316 440-8290
Wichita *(G-15539)*
Shawnee Mission Tree Svc Inc ....D.... 913 441-8888
Shawnee *(G-11029)*
Smoky Hill LLC ....D.... 785 825-0810
Salina *(G-10710)*
Teledata Communications LLC ....E.... 913 663-2010
Lenexa *(G-6175)*
Tl Enterprises Inc ....F.... 785 448-7100
Wichita *(G-15770)*
Toms Ditching & Backhoe Inc ....F.... 620 879-2215
Caney *(G-676)*
Total Lease Service Inc ....G.... 785 735-9520
Hays *(G-2920)*
Tri Star Utilities Inc ....F.... 620 331-7159
Independence *(G-3569)*
Utilities Plus Inc ....E.... 316 946-9416
Wichita *(G-15865)*
Utility Contractors Inc ....E.... 316 942-1253
Wichita *(G-15866)*
Utility Maintenance Contrs LLC ....F.... 316 945-8833
Wichita *(G-15867)*
W B Carter Construction Co ....E.... 316 942-4214
Wichita *(G-15912)*
Wildcat Construction ....E.... 316 945-9408
Topeka *(G-13245)*
Wildcat Construction Co Inc ....C.... 316 945-9408
Wichita *(G-16049)*
Zook Construction ....F.... 785 388-2183
Wakefield *(G-13399)*

1629 Heavy Construction, NEC

Allen Trenching Inc ....F.... 316 721-6300
Wichita *(G-13669)*
Amsted Rail Company Inc ....F.... 913 299-2223
Kansas City *(G-3808)*
Ballou Pavement Solutions Inc ....C.... 785 827-4439
Salina *(G-10416)*
Barnharts Excavation LLC ....F.... 620 431-0959
Chanute *(G-706)*
Bernard D Ohlsen Cnstr Co ....F.... 785 873-3462
Whiting *(G-13574)*
Black & Veatch Cnstr Inc ....E.... 913 458-2000
Overland Park *(G-8454)*
Blackburn Construction Inc ....C.... 316 321-5358
El Dorado *(G-1538)*
Bob Bergkamp Cnstr Co Inc ....D.... 316 522-3471
Wichita *(G-13859)*
BRB Contractors Inc ....C.... 785 232-1245
Topeka *(G-12403)*
C-Tech Industrial Group Inc ....F.... 316 321-5358
El Dorado *(G-1542)*
Callaway Electric ....G.... 785 632-5588
Clay Center *(G-847)*
CD&h Inc ....F.... 316 320-7187
El Dorado *(G-1544)*
CDI Industrial Mech Contrs Inc ....C.... 913 287-0334
Kansas City *(G-3898)*
City of Liberal ....F.... 620 626-0138
Liberal *(G-6293)*
Crystal Trenching Inc ....F.... 913 677-1233
Shawnee *(G-10937)*
CS Carey LLC ....F.... 913 432-4877
Kansas City *(G-3947)*
Doctors Inc ....E.... 913 681-8041
Stilwell *(G-12145)*
▼ **Earthmovers Inc** ....F.... 785 325-2236
Washington *(G-13463)*
Eby Corporation ....F.... 316 268-3500
Wichita *(G-14256)*
Enpower Operations Corp ....F.... 913 441-3633
Shawnee *(G-10948)*
Freddy Van Inc ....G.... 620 231-1127
Pittsburg *(G-9863)*
Hdb Construction Inc ....E.... 785 232-5444
Topeka *(G-12670)*
Jmar Construction Inc ....F.... 620 922-3690
Edna *(G-1494)*
Kiewit Power Group Inc ....F.... 913 227-3600
Lenexa *(G-5951)*
Kings Construction Co Inc ....D.... 785 863-2534
Oskaloosa *(G-8228)*
L Blixt Construction Inc ....F.... 785 922-6180
Chapman *(G-780)*
▼ **L G Barcus and Sons Inc** ....D.... 913 621-1100
Kansas City *(G-4188)*
Lawns By Beck Inc ....F.... 913 631-8873
Shawnee Mission *(G-11549)*
Lightning Grounds Services Inc ....E.... 913 441-3900
Shawnee Mission *(G-11572)*
Lrm Industries Inc ....E.... 785 843-1688
Lawrence *(G-5001)*
Luka Irrigation Systems Inc ....E.... 913 248-0400
Shawnee *(G-10990)*
Luxury Lawn & Landscape Inc ....F.... 785 233-5296
Topeka *(G-12854)*
M & D Excavating Inc ....F.... 785 628-3169
Hays *(G-2867)*
▲ **Massman Construction Co** ....E.... 913 291-2600
Leawood *(G-5468)*
Max Rieke & Brothers Inc ....D.... 913 631-7111
Shawnee *(G-10991)*
Mies Construction Inc ....D.... 316 945-7227
Wichita *(G-15106)*
Pearson Construction LLC ....C.... 316 263-3100
Wichita *(G-15275)*
Pexco Company Llc ....E.... 913 907-5022
Leawood *(G-5520)*
Railway Construction ....F.... 620 663-9233
Hutchinson *(G-3419)*
Rdr Excavating Inc ....F.... 785 582-4645
Topeka *(G-13001)*
Ronnie Diehl Construction Inc ....E.... 785 823-7800
Salina *(G-10653)*
Rosencrantz Bemis Enterprises ....E.... 620 792-2488
Great Bend *(G-2632)*
Sporer Land Development Inc ....E.... 785 672-4319
Oakley *(G-7487)*
Tangent Rail Energy Inc ....D.... 913 948-9478
Lenexa *(G-6166)*
Tindle Construction Inc ....D.... 620 378-2046
Fredonia *(G-2047)*
Toms Ditching & Backhoe Inc ....F.... 620 879-2215
Caney *(G-676)*
Torgeson Trenching Inc ....E.... 785 233-3060
Topeka *(G-13193)*
Utility Contractors Inc ....E.... 316 942-1253
Wichita *(G-15866)*
Versasport of Kansas Inc ....E.... 316 393-0487
Wichita *(G-15876)*

S I C

Walters-Morgan Cnstr Inc ....D....... 785 539-7513
Manhattan *(G-6846)*
Western Irrigation Inc ....E....... 620 275-4033
Garden City *(G-2311)*
Western Kansas Valley Inc........F....... 785 852-4606
Sharon Springs *(G-10902)*
Wildcat Construction Co Inc........C....... 316 945-9408
Wichita *(G-16049)*

17 CONSTRUCTION-SPECIAL TRADE CONTRACTORS

1711 Plumbing, Heating & Air Conditioning Contractors

A & H AC & Htg Inc ....F....... 785 594-3357
Baldwin City *(G-352)*
A D J-Hux Service Inc........D....... 913 529-5200
Lenexa *(G-5616)*
A M Mechanical Service Co ....F....... 913 829-5885
Kansas City *(G-3778)*
A M Plumbing Inc........E....... 316 945-8326
Wichita *(G-13589)*
A-1 Electric Inc........F....... 620 431-7500
Chanute *(G-701)*
A1air Heating & Cooling LLC........F....... 620 235-0600
Frontenac *(G-2050)*
AC Professional LLC ....E....... 816 668-4760
Olathe *(G-7508)*
Acentric LLC........F....... 913 787-4856
Louisburg *(G-6435)*
Action Plumbing Inc ....F....... 913 631-1188
Shawnee Mission *(G-11071)*
Action Plumbing of Lawrence ....F....... 785 843-5670
Lawrence *(G-4718)*
Adamson Brothers Sheet Metal........F....... 785 242-9273
Ottawa *(G-8243)*
Air Care Heating & Cooling Co........F....... 913 362-5274
Shawnee Mission *(G-11087)*
Airtech Engineering Inc........F....... 913 888-5900
Overland Park *(G-8363)*
American Comm & Residentl Svcs ....F....... 316 633-5866
Wichita *(G-13690)*
American Fire Sprinkler Corp........F....... 620 792-1909
Great Bend *(G-2505)*
American Mechanical Inc........E....... 316 262-1100
Andover *(G-79)*
Anthony Inc ....E....... 913 384-4440
Lenexa *(G-5656)*
Armstrong Plumbing Inc........F....... 316 942-9535
Wichita *(G-13734)*
Auman Co Inc........F....... 785 628-2833
Hays *(G-2752)*
Automated Control Systems Corp........D....... 913 766-2336
Leawood *(G-5337)*
B & B Plumbing Heating & AC........F....... 785 472-5239
Ellsworth *(G-1657)*
B & W Electric Inc ....F....... 785 337-2598
Hanover *(G-2709)*
B&C Mechanical Services LLC ....F....... 913 681-0088
Paola *(G-9541)*
Bamford Fire Sprinkler Co Inc........E....... 785 825-7710
Salina *(G-10417)*
Bamford Fire Sprinkler Co Inc........E....... 913 432-6688
Shawnee Mission *(G-11145)*
Barnds Brothers Inc ....E....... 913 897-2340
Shawnee Mission *(G-11152)*
Barnes & Dodge Inc........E....... 913 321-6444
Lenexa *(G-5687)*
Baxter Mechanical Contractors........F....... 913 281-6303
Kansas City *(G-3849)*
Bbh LLC........D....... 316 945-8208
Wichita *(G-13822)*
BCI Mechanical Inc ....F....... 913 856-6747
Gardner *(G-2329)*
Beavers Plumbing L L C........F....... 316 619-6119
Augusta *(G-311)*
Becker Bros Inc........F....... 316 531-2264
Garden Plain *(G-2321)*
Beebe Heating & AC Inc ....F....... 913 541-1222
Overland Park *(G-8438)*
Bills Plumbing Service LLC........F....... 913 829-8213
Olathe *(G-7555)*
BKM Construction LLC ....F....... 913 297-0049
Leavenworth *(G-5212)*
Blackburn Nursery Inc........E....... 785 272-2707
Topeka *(G-12387)*
Bob Stith Heating and Cooling........F....... 316 262-1802
Wichita *(G-13861)*
Bobs Plumbing & Heating Inc........F....... 785 539-4155
Manhattan *(G-6565)*
Brand Plumbing Inc........F....... 316 942-2306
Wichita *(G-13884)*
Brite Energy Solar Inc ....E....... 785 856-9936
Lawrence *(G-4768)*
Bryans Heating & AC ....F....... 316 755-2447
Valley Center *(G-13338)*
Budget Plumbing & Heating ....F....... 620 231-5232
Pittsburg *(G-9826)*
Building Control Solutions LLC ....G....... 816 439-6046
Merriam *(G-7087)*
Burnap Bros Inc........F....... 620 342-2645
Emporia *(G-1712)*
Butler Plumbing & Heating ....F....... 785 456-8345
Wamego *(G-13407)*
C & C Group of Companies........D....... 913 492-8414
Lenexa *(G-5723)*
Callabresi Heating & Coolg Inc........E....... 785 825-2599
Salina *(G-10435)*
Carlisle Heating & AC ....F....... 316 321-6230
El Dorado *(G-1543)*
Cates Heating & AC Svc Co ....E....... 913 888-4470
Lenexa *(G-5734)*
CDI Industrial Mech Contrs Inc........C....... 913 287-0334
Kansas City *(G-3898)*
Central Consolidated Inc........C....... 316 945-0797
Wichita *(G-13978)*
Central Mech Cnstr Co Inc ....C....... 785 537-2437
Manhattan *(G-6581)*
Central Mech Svcs Mnhattan Inc........F....... 785 776-9206
Manhattan *(G-6582)*
Central Mechanical Wichita LLC ....D....... 316 267-7676
Wichita *(G-13981)*
Central States Contg Svcs Inc........F....... 913 788-1100
Kansas City *(G-3903)*
Central States Mechanical Inc ....F....... 620 353-1797
Ulysses *(G-13287)*
Chad Briney........F....... 785 462-2445
Colby *(G-993)*
Cimarron Valley Irrigation LLC ....F....... 620 544-7323
Hugoton *(G-3151)*
City of Hutchinson........B....... 620 694-2632
Hutchinson *(G-3240)*
City of Topeka ....D....... 785 368-3851
Topeka *(G-12470)*
City Plumbing Heating & AC Inc........F....... 785 472-3001
Ellsworth *(G-1661)*
City Wide Service Inc........F....... 913 927-6124
Kansas City *(G-3913)*
City Wide Sheet Metal Inc ....F....... 913 871-7464
Kansas City *(G-3914)*
CJ Industries LLC ....F....... 913 788-1104
Kansas City *(G-3915)*
Clarios........E....... 316 655-7578
Wichita *(G-14035)*
Clarios........E....... 785 827-6829
Salina *(G-10454)*
Clarios........E....... 316 721-2777
Wichita *(G-14034)*
Clouds Heating and AC ....E....... 785 842-2258
Lawrence *(G-4795)*
Comfort Contractors Inc ....E....... 620 431-4780
Chanute *(G-718)*
Comfort Management Inc........F....... 620 442-5610
Arkansas City *(G-149)*
Commercial Mechanical Inc Kans........D....... 316 262-1230
Wichita *(G-14070)*
Commercial Trade Services LLC ....F....... 316 721-5432
Wichita *(G-14073)*
Conklin Plumbing LLC ....F....... 785 806-5827
Osage City *(G-8182)*
Custom Sheet Metal & Roofg Inc ....E....... 785 357-6200
Topeka *(G-12539)*
DAgostino Mech Contrs Inc........D....... 913 384-5170
Kansas City *(G-3952)*
Dans Heating & Cooling Inc........E....... 316 522-0372
Wichita *(G-14168)*
Daves Service & Repair Inc........G....... 620 662-8285
Hutchinson *(G-3257)*
David Cobler........F....... 785 234-3384
Topeka *(G-12547)*
David Lies Plumbing Inc ....F....... 316 945-0117
Wichita *(G-14174)*
Dean E Norris Inc........D....... 316 688-1901
Wichita *(G-14180)*
Debackers Inc........E....... 785 232-6999
Topeka *(G-12550)*
Den Management Co Inc ....C....... 316 686-1964
Wichita *(G-14191)*
Dennys Heating & Cooling........F....... 316 283-1598
North Newton *(G-7435)*
Design Mechanical Inc ....C....... 913 281-7200
Kansas City *(G-3970)*
Doctors Inc........E....... 913 681-8041
Stilwell *(G-12145)*
E & M Plumbing Inc ....F....... 620 662-1281
Hutchinson *(G-3271)*
Earl Bryant Enterprises Inc........F....... 913 724-4100
Basehor *(G-374)*
Eisenbarth Plumbing Inc........F....... 785 336-2361
Seneca *(G-10865)*
Electrical Concepts Inc ....F....... 785 456-8896
Wamego *(G-13420)*
Environmental Mech Contrs Inc........D....... 913 829-0100
Olathe *(G-7688)*
Epic Irrigation Inc........C....... 913 764-0178
Olathe *(G-7690)*
Even Temp of Wichita Inc........F....... 316 469-5321
Wichita *(G-14312)*
Fagan Company........C....... 913 621-4444
Kansas City *(G-4002)*
Fenix Company Incorporated ....E....... 316 945-4842
Wichita *(G-14354)*
Fire Protection Services Inc........E....... 316 262-2452
Wichita *(G-14369)*
Firelk-Diversified Joint Ventr ....E....... 913 312-9540
Lenexa *(G-5855)*
Five Star Mechanical Inc ....F....... 316 943-7827
Wichita *(G-14381)*
Flamings Plumbing Heating & AC........F....... 620 382-2181
Marion *(G-6869)*
Floyd Mechanical Corporation ....F....... 316 262-3556
Wichita *(G-14394)*
Fred Pflumm Plumbing Inc ....E....... 913 441-6309
Shawnee Mission *(G-11379)*
Frederick Plumbing & Heating........F....... 316 262-3713
Wichita *(G-14416)*
Fsig LLC........D....... 785 784-2566
Fort Riley *(G-1948)*
G Coopers Inc ....F....... 785 267-4100
Topeka *(G-12630)*
G K Smith & Sons Inc........F....... 913 294-5379
Paola *(G-9560)*
Garrison Plumbing Inc ....F....... 913 768-1311
Olathe *(G-7723)*
General Automatic Sprinkler Fl ....E....... 913 390-1105
Overland Park *(G-8750)*
General Fire Sprinkler Co LLC........F....... 913 390-1105
Shawnee *(G-10960)*
Genesis Solution LLC........F....... 785 317-5710
Chapman *(G-779)*
Glassman Corporation ....D....... 785 625-2115
Hays *(G-2817)*
Grabill Plumbing Inc........E....... 913 432-9660
Kansas City *(G-4042)*
H & R Lawn & Landscape Inc ....D....... 913 897-9705
Bucyrus *(G-598)*
H & R Plumbing Inc........F....... 785 233-4427
Topeka *(G-12655)*
Hanna Heating & AC ....E....... 316 945-3481
Wichita *(G-14556)*
Hanover Electric Inc ....F....... 785 337-2711
Hanover *(G-2711)*
Harrington Bros Htg & Coolg........F....... 913 422-5444
Shawnee Mission *(G-11410)*
Hartley Sheet Metal Co Inc........F....... 620 251-4330
Coffeyville *(G-943)*
Heartland Plumbing Inc........F....... 913 856-5846
Gardner *(G-2350)*
Heinen P-H-E Services Inc ....F....... 785 945-6668
Valley Falls *(G-13365)*
Henry Steckman Plumbing ....F....... 785 388-2782
Manchester *(G-6524)*
Henton Plumbing & AC Inc ....F....... 785 776-5548
Manhattan *(G-6654)*
Hermes Co Inc........E....... 913 888-2413
Lenexa *(G-5901)*
Hertel Tank Service Inc........G....... 785 628-2445
Hays *(G-2841)*
Honeywell International Inc ....E....... 402 597-2279
Olathe *(G-7775)*
Hood Htg Air Plg Electric Inc ....F....... 785 243-1489
Concordia *(G-1118)*
Huxtable & Associates Inc ....C....... 785 843-2910
Lawrence *(G-4907)*
Interstate Elec Cnstr Inc........E....... 620 421-5510
Parsons *(G-9693)*
J-DOT Inc........E....... 785 272-1633
Topeka *(G-12734)*

Jayhawk Fire Sprinkler Co Inc ... E ... 913 422-3770
Olathe (G-7809)
Jayhawk Plumbing Inc ... F ... 785 865-5225
Lawrence (G-4920)
Jf Denney Inc ... E ... 913 772-8994
Leavenworth (G-5257)
Jim Jam Inc ... F ... 913 268-6700
Shawnee (G-10979)
Johnson Controls ... E ... 316 686-6363
Wichita (G-14766)
K & K Industries Inc ... E ... 906 293-5242
Junction City (G-3709)
Kansas City Mechanical Inc ... E ... 913 334-1101
Kansas City (G-4147)
Karcher Investments Inc ... F ... 785 452-2850
Salina (G-10568)
Kastl Plumbing Inc ... E ... 785 841-2112
Lawrence (G-4938)
KB Complete Inc ... F ... 913 722-6835
Shawnee Mission (G-11522)
Kc Solar LLC ... F ... 913 444-9593
Overland Park (G-8909)
King Enterprises Inc ... F ... 620 624-3332
Liberal (G-6329)
Kinney Plumbing Co Inc ... E ... 913 782-2840
Olathe (G-7841)
Knipp Equipment Inc ... E ... 316 265-9655
Wichita (G-14871)
Knopke Company LLC ... E ... 816 231-1001
Leawood (G-5451)
Kruse Corporation ... E ... 785 320-7990
Manhattan (G-6700)
▲ Kruse Corporation ... D ... 316 838-7885
Wichita (G-14895)
Kuhn Mechanical Inc ... F ... 620 441-9339
Arkansas City (G-163)
L T Huxtable Service Inc ... E ... 785 235-5331
Topeka (G-12826)
Lba Air Cndtoning Htg Plbg Inc ... E ... 816 454-5515
Shawnee Mission (G-11551)
Liebert Brothers Electric Co ... F ... 620 251-0299
Coffeyville (G-956)
Locke Equipment Sales Co ... E ... 913 782-8500
Olathe (G-7864)
Lower Heating & AC Inc ... E ... 785 357-5123
Topeka (G-12851)
M & D of Hays Incorporated ... E ... 785 628-3169
Hays (G-2868)
M W C Inc ... D ... 316 267-7676
Wichita (G-14994)
Marick Inc ... E ... 316 941-9575
Colwich (G-1098)
McCann Plumbing & Heating Inc ... E ... 913 727-6225
Leavenworth (G-5268)
McCarty Mechanical Inc ... F ... 913 432-5100
Shawnee Mission (G-11607)
McDaniel Co Inc ... E ... 316 942-8325
Wichita (G-15027)
McElroys Inc ... C ... 785 266-4870
Topeka (G-12871)
Mechanical Systems Inc ... D ... 316 262-2021
Wichita (G-15031)
Mechanics Inc ... E ... 316 262-2021
Wichita (G-15032)
Mels Pump & Plumbing ... F ... 785 632-3392
Clay Center (G-872)
Metro Air Conditioning Co ... D ... 913 888-3991
Lenexa (G-5995)
Mid-American Water & Plbg Inc ... E ... 785 537-1072
Manhattan (G-6741)
Midstate Mechanical Inc ... F ... 785 537-4343
Manhattan (G-6744)
Midwest Energy Inc ... E ... 785 462-8251
Colby (G-1028)
Mikes Heating & Cooling LLC ... E ... 913 441-7807
Olathe (G-7899)
Miller Plumbing Co Inc ... F ... 913 851-1333
Bucyrus (G-604)
Mini Maid Joco Incorporated ... F ... 913 894-2200
Lenexa (G-6005)
Mission Heating and AC ... F ... 913 631-6506
Shawnee Mission (G-11645)
MMC Corp ... E ... 913 469-0101
Overland Park (G-9046)
Modern Air Conditioning Inc ... E ... 620 342-7577
Emporia (G-1797)
MSI ... E ... 316 262-2021
Wichita (G-15137)
MWM Group Inc ... C ... 913 469-0101
Shawnee Mission (G-11662)

Newtons Inc ... F ... 620 336-2276
Cherryvale (G-811)
Niehoff Heating & Air Inc ... E ... 785 594-7137
Lawrence (G-5041)
Overland Park Heating & Coolg ... E ... 913 649-0303
Overland Park (G-9119)
P & W Incorporated ... E ... 316 267-4277
Wichita (G-15247)
P1 Group Inc ... E ... 316 267-3256
Wichita (G-15252)
P1 Group Inc ... F ... 785 235-5331
Topeka (G-12958)
P1 Group Inc ... D ... 785 843-2910
Lawrence (G-5054)
P1 Group International Inc ... C ... 913 529-5000
Lenexa (G-6041)
Paronto Mall Construction Inc ... F ... 785 632-2484
Clay Center (G-875)
Payne and Jones Chartered ... C ... 913 469-4100
Overland Park (G-9147)
Pestinger Heating & AC Inc ... E ... 785 827-6361
Salina (G-10634)
Piping & Equipment Company Inc ... C ... 316 838-7511
Wichita (G-15302)
Piping Contractors Kansas Inc ... E ... 785 233-2010
Topeka (G-12977)
Piping Contractors Kansas Inc ... F ... 785 233-4321
Topeka (G-12976)
Piping Technology Co ... D ... 620 241-3592
McPherson (G-7016)
Plumbing By Carlson Inc ... E ... 785 232-0515
Topeka (G-12981)
Plumbing Specialists Inc ... E ... 316 945-8383
Wichita (G-15308)
Polestar AC & Plbg Htg ... F ... 913 432-3342
Olathe (G-7991)
Premium Heating & Cooling Inc ... F ... 913 780-5639
Olathe (G-8004)
Professional Mech Contrs Inc ... E ... 316 684-1927
Wichita (G-15364)
Pryor Autmtc Fire Sprnklr Inc ... F ... 620 792-6400
Great Bend (G-2625)
R & R Street Plbg Htg & Elec ... F ... 785 524-4551
Lincoln (G-6385)
R P 3 Inc ... F ... 620 827-6136
Mc Cune (G-6921)
Randal J Steiner ... F ... 785 539-4155
Manhattan (G-6786)
Ray Omo Inc ... E ... 620 227-3101
Lenexa (G-6091)
Reddi Services Inc ... D ... 913 287-5005
Shawnee Mission (G-11783)
Reid Plumbing Heating & AC Inc ... F ... 785 537-2869
Manhattan (G-6789)
Resource Service Solutions LLC ... E ... 913 338-5050
Lenexa (G-6107)
Richard Nachbar Plumbing Inc ... F ... 913 268-9488
Lenexa (G-6109)
Riden Service Company Inc ... F ... 913 432-8495
Overland Park (G-9241)
River City Mechanical Inc ... F ... 316 682-2672
Wichita (G-15471)
Robert J Hamilton Inc ... E ... 913 888-4262
Overland Park (G-9250)
Rodriguez Mech Contrs Inc ... D ... 913 281-1814
Kansas City (G-4386)
Roth Heating & AC ... E ... 316 942-4141
Wichita (G-15484)
Royal Flush Plumbing LLC ... F ... 316 794-2656
Goddard (G-2453)
Salina Concrete Products Inc ... F ... 316 943-3241
Wichita (G-15510)
Samco Inc ... E ... 785 234-4000
Topeka (G-13035)
Santa Fe AC & Rfrgn Inc ... F ... 913 856-5801
Gardner (G-2362)
Santa Fe Trails Plumbing Inc ... F ... 913 441-1441
Shawnee Mission (G-11834)
Schnell & Pestinger Inc ... F ... 785 738-3624
Beloit (G-502)
Schuler Heating and Cooling ... F ... 913 262-2969
Kansas City (G-4405)
Shawnee Heating and Cooling ... F ... 913 492-0824
Lenexa (G-6131)
Shell Topco LP ... F ... 316 942-7266
Wichita (G-15580)
Siemens Industry Inc ... E ... 316 267-5814
Wichita (G-15584)
Signature Landscape LLC ... C ... 913 829-8181
Olathe (G-8066)

Srh Mechanical Contractors Inc ... F ... 785 842-0301
Lawrence (G-5116)
Ssi Inc ... E ... 316 722-9631
Wichita (G-15651)
Standard Plumbing Inc ... F ... 785 776-5012
Manhattan (G-6807)
Stans Sprinkler Service Inc ... E ... 800 570-5932
Wichita (G-15654)
Stryker Services Inc ... E ... 785 357-1281
Topeka (G-13115)
Stueder Contractors Inc ... E ... 620 792-6044
Great Bend (G-2642)
Superior Plumbing & Heating Co ... E ... 785 827-5611
Salina (G-10728)
Superior Plumbing of Wichita ... F ... 316 684-8349
Wichita (G-15696)
Systems 4 Inc ... E ... 785 823-9119
Salina (G-10730)
Tatro Plumbing Co Inc ... F ... 620 277-2167
Garden City (G-2296)
Tatro Plumbing Co Inc ... E ... 620 356-5319
Ulysses (G-13322)
Teds Plumbing LLC ... F ... 620 356-5319
Ulysses (G-13323)
Thermal Comfort Air Inc ... E ... 785 537-2436
Manhattan (G-6824)
Tl Enterprises Inc ... F ... 785 448-7100
Wichita (G-15770)
Top Notch Inc ... F ... 913 441-8900
Lenexa (G-6185)
Trigard Vaults ... F ... 785 527-5595
Belleville (G-468)
TWC Services Inc ... E ... 316 265-7831
Wichita (G-15820)
U Priority Inc ... F ... 913 712-8524
Lenexa (G-6197)
Universal Mechanical LLC ... E ... 573 636-8373
Leawood (G-5590)
Vhc Van Hoecke Contracting Inc ... E ... 913 888-0036
Lenexa (G-6212)
Vielhauer Plumbing Inc ... F ... 913 268-9385
Shawnee Mission (G-11978)
W H Debrick Co Inc ... F ... 913 294-3281
Paola (G-9595)
Waddles Heating & Cooling ... E ... 785 827-2621
Salina (G-10755)
Waldinger Corporation ... E ... 316 942-7722
Wichita (G-15916)
Walton Plumbing & Heating Inc ... F ... 620 278-3462
Sterling (G-12132)
Weber Refrigeration & Htg Inc ... E ... 580 338-7338
Garden City (G-2309)
Weber Refrigeration & Htg Inc ... F ... 620 225-7700
Dodge City (G-1452)
Welker Heating and Cooling ... F ... 913 669-7555
Overland Park (G-9487)
Werth Htg Plbg Airconditioning ... F ... 785 628-8088
Hays (G-2930)
West Side Mechanical Inc ... F ... 913 788-1800
Manhattan (G-6852)
Western Enterprise Inc ... F ... 913 342-0505
Kansas City (G-4535)
Western Irrigation Inc ... E ... 620 275-4033
Garden City (G-2311)
Western Kansas Valley Inc ... F ... 785 852-4606
Sharon Springs (G-10902)
Western States Fire Protection ... D ... 913 321-9208
Kansas City (G-4537)
Wheatland Contracting LLC ... F ... 913 833-2304
Effingham (G-1524)
Wichita Water Conditioning Inc ... D ... 316 267-5287
Wichita (G-16042)
Williams-Carver Company Inc ... E ... 913 236-4949
Kansas City (G-4544)
Willowridge Landscape Inc ... F ... 785 842-7022
Lawrence (G-5186)
Winfield Plumbing & Heating ... F ... 620 221-2210
Winfield (G-16188)

1721 Painting & Paper Hanging Contractors

1st Nation Painting Inc ... F ... 785 966-2935
Mayetta (G-6913)
Aaron & Page Painting Inc ... F ... 316 267-2224
Wichita (G-13593)
Albers Finshg & Solutions LLC ... F ... 316 542-0405
Cheney (G-788)
AP Roofing Specialty Codings ... F ... 620 532-1076
Kingman (G-4582)
Atlas Painting ... E ... 316 686-1546
Wichita (G-13766)

SIC

Ben Kitchens Painting Co Inc F 785 375-3288
Junction City (G-3673)
Birch Contracting Group LLC F 913 400-3975
Overland Park (G-8452)
C-Hawkk Construction Inc F 785 542-1800
Eudora (G-1872)
Citywide Painting & Rmdlg LLC F 913 238-9749
Leawood (G-5352)
Columbia Construction Inc E 913 247-3114
Olathe (G-7601)
D&K Painting Inc F 785 537-4779
Manhattan (G-6610)
DA Painting Inc E 913 829-2075
Olathe (G-7639)
Design Source Flooring LLC E 913 387-5858
Lenexa (G-5813)
Figeac Aero North America Inc D 316 634-2500
Wichita (G-14366)
Forshee Painting Contractors D 316 263-7777
Wichita (G-14402)
Gecko Painting Inc E 913 782-7000
Olathe (G-7725)
Genesis Solution LLC F 785 317-5710
Chapman (G-779)
Gray & Company Inc E 785 232-0913
Topeka (G-12644)
Hardister Painting and Dctg F 785 842-2832
Lawrence (G-4889)
Hartwood Painting E 316 554-7510
Wichita (G-14566)
J F McGivern Inc E 785 354-1787
Topeka (G-12731)
Johnson County Pntg & Hm Repr E 913 631-5252
Fairway (G-1911)
Joseph Stowers Painting Inc E 913 722-2534
Shawnee Mission (G-11502)
K5 Painting Inc F 316 283-9612
Newton (G-7368)
Kdoll Koatings Inc G 620 456-2588
Conway Springs (G-1142)
Koehn Painting Co LLC E 316 283-9612
Newton (G-7373)
Kushs Painting F 913 888-0230
Kansas City (G-4185)
Luke Kushs Painting F 913 888-0230
Shawnee Mission (G-11581)
Maas Paint and Paper LLC F 785 643-4790
Hutchinson (G-3362)
Nu-Line Company Inc F 316 942-0990
Wichita (G-15199)
OFlynn Contracting Inc F 316 524-2500
Wichita (G-15211)
Paint Masters Inc F 316 683-5203
Wichita (G-15253)
Paint Pro Inc F 913 685-4089
Overland Park (G-9138)
Parsons Aaron Painting LLC G 620 532-1076
Kingman (G-4609)
Pelton Painting Inc F 785 242-7363
Ottawa (G-8303)
Performance Contracting Inc E 913 928-2850
Lenexa (G-6053)
Pishny Real Estate Services F 913 227-0251
Lenexa (G-6059)
Premier Painting Co LLC F 913 897-7000
Overland Park (G-9181)
Pro-Kleen Inc E 316 775-6898
Augusta (G-339)
R B P Inc F 316 303-9606
Wichita (G-15402)
Ral Contractors F 913 888-8128
Shawnee Mission (G-11777)
Roadsafe Traffic Systems Inc E 316 322-3070
El Dorado (G-1600)
Rob Carrolls Sndblst & Pntg E 620 442-1361
Arkansas City (G-175)
Rt Painting Inc F 913 390-6650
Olathe (G-8046)
Supernova Painting LLC F 785 850-0158
Atchison (G-265)
Total Renovation Group Inc F 913 491-5000
Lenexa (G-6186)
Traffic Control Services Inc F 316 448-0402
Wichita (G-15784)
Twin Traffic Marking Corp E 913 428-2575
Kansas City (G-4480)
Unlimited Service Options LLC F 316 522-1503
Wichita (G-15859)
Wagle Painting F 316 682-2531
Wichita (G-15915)
Warren Moore Painting LLC F 913 558-8549
Shawnee Mission (G-11993)
Wildcat Painting Inc F 316 263-8076
Wichita (G-16050)
Window Design Company G 785 582-2888
Silver Lake (G-12030)
Woods Painting Co Inc F 913 897-3741
Stilwell (G-12180)
Zack Taylor Contracting Inc F 785 235-8704
Topeka (G-13260)

1731 Electrical Work

4 Rivers Electric Coop Inc E 620 364-2116
Lebo (G-5605)
4pc LLC G 316 833-6906
Augusta (G-299)
A & H Electric Inc D 316 838-3003
Wichita (G-13583)
A D J-Hux Service Inc D 913 529-5200
Lenexa (G-5616)
Accurate Electric Inc G 785 825-4010
Salina (G-10391)
Ace Electric-Jones Company Inc E 785 862-8200
Topeka (G-12284)
Adams Electric & Plumbing LLC E 620 672-7279
Pratt (G-10092)
Advance Electric Inc E 316 263-1300
Wichita (G-13621)
AG Services LLC F 620 662-5406
Hutchinson (G-3194)
Alan Bitter F 620 353-7407
Ulysses (G-13281)
Alea Communications LLC F 913 439-7391
Gardner (G-2323)
All Systems Dsgned Sltions Inc E 913 281-5100
Kansas City (G-3800)
Alliance Technologies Inc F 913 262-7977
Overland Park (G-8371)
Apple Electric Inc F 913 837-5285
Louisburg (G-6439)
Atlas Electric LLC D 316 858-1560
Wichita (G-13765)
Atronic Alarms Inc E 913 432-4545
Lenexa (G-5674)
B & W Electric Inc F 785 337-2598
Hanover (G-2709)
B A Barnes Electric Inc E 913 764-4455
Olathe (G-7544)
Baldridge Electric Inc E 316 267-0058
Wichita (G-13799)
Barone Electric Inc F 316 263-9579
Wichita (G-13813)
Bear Communications LLC E 913 441-3355
Lenexa (G-5693)
Belford Electric Inc E 316 267-7060
Wichita (G-13828)
Brunner Electric Inc F 913 268-5463
Shawnee Mission (G-11187)
Cablecom Inc F 316 267-4777
Wichita (G-13926)
Callaway Electric G 785 632-5588
Clay Center (G-847)
Capital Electric Cnstr Co Inc E 816 472-9500
Kansas City (G-3888)
Carlisle Heating & AC F 316 321-6230
El Dorado (G-1543)
CDL Electric Company Inc C 620 232-1242
Pittsburg (G-9829)
Central States Electric Inc E 316 942-6640
Wichita (G-13987)
Cimarron Underground Inc E 913 438-2981
Overland Park (G-8552)
City of Mulvane D 316 777-0191
Mulvane (G-7213)
Citywide Electric Inc E 913 631-1189
Shawnee Mission (G-11234)
Clarios D 913 307-4200
Shawnee Mission (G-11237)
Clarios E 316 721-2777
Wichita (G-14034)
Cnc Underground LLC F 913 744-0485
Gardner (G-2333)
Comfort Contractors Inc E 620 431-4780
Chanute (G-718)
Commercl-Ndstrial Ele Cont Inc E 316 263-1291
Wichita (G-14074)
Communications Tech Assoc E 316 267-5016
Wichita (G-14076)
Computer Cable Connection Inc E 913 390-5141
Lenexa (G-5781)
Convergeone Inc C 913 307-2300
Overland Park (G-8597)
Cox-Kent & Associates Inc F 316 946-5596
Wichita (G-14123)
Creek Electric Incorporated E 316 943-5888
Wichita (G-14129)
Critical Elc Systems Group LLC E 316 684-0193
Wichita (G-14132)
Current Electrical Co Inc E 785 267-2108
Topeka (G-12535)
D L Smith Electrical Cnstr C 785 267-4920
Topeka (G-12543)
Darrell Bybee Construction LLC F 316 409-4186
Wichita (G-14171)
Davin Electric Inc E 785 234-2350
Topeka (G-12548)
Decker Electric Inc D 316 265-8182
Wichita (G-14183)
Delta Electric Co Inc E 316 267-2869
Wichita (G-14189)
Diversified Contracting LLC F 913 898-4722
Parker (G-9657)
Eci Electrical Contractors F 316 722-0204
Wichita (G-14257)
Electri Tech F 316 683-2841
Wichita (G-14264)
Electrical Associates LLC E 913 825-2537
Olathe (G-7674)
Electrical Concepts Inc F 785 456-8896
Wamego (G-13420)
Electrical Enterprises Inc E 785 242-7971
Ottawa (G-8269)
Electrical Systems Inc F 316 263-2415
Wichita (G-14265)
Electronic Technology Inc F 913 962-8083
Shawnee Mission (G-11330)
Elite Electric Inc E 913 724-1645
Basehor (G-375)
Entertainment Specialties F 620 342-3322
Emporia (G-1750)
Facility Solutions Group Inc E 913 422-8400
Shawnee (G-10952)
Faith Technologies Inc D 913 541-4700
Lenexa (G-5847)
Faith Technologies Inc B 785 938-4499
Gove (G-2493)
G Coopers Inc F 785 267-4100
Topeka (G-12630)
G E V Investment Inc E 913 677-5333
Kansas City (G-4024)
G K Smith & Sons Inc F 913 294-5379
Paola (G-9560)
Garwin Electric LLC F 913 780-1200
Olathe (G-7724)
Gateway Wreless Netwrk Svcs Lc F 316 264-0037
Wichita (G-14452)
General Electric Company E 785 229-3710
Ottawa (G-8275)
General Electric Company D 913 541-1839
Lenexa (G-5871)
Gjo Inc E 913 621-6611
Kansas City (G-4035)
Gonzales Cmmunications Inc GCI E 913 685-4866
Overland Park (G-8765)
Graf & Associates Inc F 316 686-2090
Wichita (G-14493)
Hanover Electric Inc F 785 337-2711
Hanover (G-2711)
Harvey & Son Electric F 620 624-3688
Liberal (G-6318)
Haynes Electric Inc E 620 285-2242
Larned (G-4704)
Heartland Electric Inc E 785 233-9546
Topeka (G-12677)
▲ Hedlund Electric Inc E 620 241-3757
McPherson (G-6972)
Heineken Electric Co Inc E 785 738-3831
Beloit (G-486)
Heineken Electric Company Inc F 785 404-3157
Salina (G-10541)
Heineken Electric Company Inc F 785 539-7400
Manhattan (G-6653)
Heinen P-H-E Services Inc F 785 945-6668
Valley Falls (G-13365)
Heritage Electric LLC E 913 747-0528
Olathe (G-7765)
Hood Htg Air Plg Electric Inc F 785 243-1489
Concordia (G-1118)
Huxtable & Associates Inc C 785 843-2910
Lawrence (G-4907)

- **Industrial Battery Pdts Inc** F 913 236-6500 Merriam *(G-7096)*
- **Integrated Electrical Tech LLC** F 316 684-0193 Wichita *(G-14701)*
- **International Electric Inc** D 913 451-8458 Lenexa *(G-5919)*
- **Interstate Elec Cnstr Inc** E 620 421-5510 Parsons *(G-9693)*
- **Italk Telecontracting Inc** F 816 436-8080 Mission *(G-7131)*
- **Jims Electric Inc** F 785 460-2844 Colby *(G-1017)*
- **Johnson Cmmunications Svcs Inc** F 913 681-5505 Stilwell *(G-12159)*
- **Johnson Controls** E 316 686-6363 Wichita *(G-14766)*
- **Johnson Controls Fire** G 785 267-9675 Topeka *(G-12748)*
- **K & K Industries Inc** E 906 293-5242 Junction City *(G-3709)*
- **Kanokla Telephone Association** E 620 845-5682 Caldwell *(G-660)*
- **Kansas Electric Inc** D 316 283-4750 Newton *(G-7369)*
- **Kennys Electrical Co Inc** F 620 662-2359 Hutchinson *(G-3350)*
- **Kiewit Power Group Inc** F 913 227-3600 Lenexa *(G-5951)*
- **Kilian Electrical Service Inc** E 316 942-4600 Wichita *(G-14857)*
- **King Enterprises Inc** F 620 624-3332 Liberal *(G-6329)*
- **L T Huxtable Service Inc** E 785 235-5331 Topeka *(G-12826)*
- **Liebert Brothers Electric Co** F 620 251-0299 Coffeyville *(G-956)*
- **Linder & Associates Inc** C 316 265-1616 Wichita *(G-14966)*
- **Loper C-I Electric** E 316 263-1291 Wichita *(G-14978)*
- **Lowry Electric Co Inc** F 316 838-4363 Wichita *(G-14985)*
- **Lynn Elc & Communications Inc** E 785 843-5079 Lawrence *(G-5003)*
- **M & J Electric Wichita LLC** E 316 831-9879 Wichita *(G-14992)*
- **Mc Electric** E 913 721-2988 Kansas City *(G-4223)*
- **McClelland Sound Inc** F 316 265-8686 Wichita *(G-15021)*
- **McElroy Electric Inc** E 785 266-7111 Topeka *(G-12870)*
- **Mid Kansas Cable Services Inc** F 620 345-2832 Moundridge *(G-7189)*
- **Mid-States Energy Works Inc** F 785 827-3631 Salina *(G-10601)*
- **Midwest Electric Service Inc** F 620 241-8655 McPherson *(G-7006)*
- **Midwest Electrical Cnstr Inc** F 785 215-8902 Topeka *(G-12896)*
- **Midwest Tinting Inc** F 913 384-2665 Overland Park *(G-9036)*
- **Mill-Tel Inc** E 316 262-7171 Park City *(G-9634)*
- **Modus Group LLC** E 785 584-6057 Rossville *(G-10254)*
- **Mvp Electric Llc** F 913 322-0868 Shawnee *(G-11001)*
- **Mvp Electric LLC** E 913 322-0868 Shawnee Mission *(G-11661)*
- **Nelson Electric Inc** F 316 794-8025 Goddard *(G-2447)*
- **Net Systems LLC** F 316 691-9400 Wichita *(G-15159)*
- **Networks Plus** E 785 825-0400 Salina *(G-10611)*
- **Networks Plus** E 785 825-0400 Manhattan *(G-6759)*
- **Newtons Inc** F 620 336-2276 Cherryvale *(G-811)*
- **Nokia of America Corporation** D 316 636-4800 Wichita *(G-15184)*
- **Norse LLC** E 620 225-0778 Dodge City *(G-1414)*
- **Oliver Electric Cnstr Inc** E 785 748-0777 Lawrence *(G-5043)*
- **Outdoor Lighting Services LP** F 913 422-8400 Shawnee *(G-11006)*
- **Overfield Corporation** F 785 843-3434 Lawrence *(G-5052)*
- **P & S Elc & Roustabout Svc Inc** F 620 792-7426 Great Bend *(G-2621)*
- **P1 Group Inc** B 913 529-5000 Lenexa *(G-6040)*
- **P1 Group Inc** F 785 235-5331 Topeka *(G-12958)*
- **P1 Group Inc** D 785 843-2910 Lawrence *(G-5054)*
- **Performance Electric LLC** F 785 242-5748 Ottawa *(G-8305)*
- **Pestinger Heating & AC Inc** E 785 827-6361 Salina *(G-10634)*
- **Phillips Southern Elc Co Inc** E 316 265-4186 Wichita *(G-15293)*
- **Precision Elec Contrs LLC** E 785 309-0094 Salina *(G-10640)*
- **Pro Electric LC** C 913 621-6611 Kansas City *(G-4340)*
- **Qti Inc** F 913 579-3131 Olathe *(G-8013)*
- **Quality Elc Douglas Cnty Inc** E 785 843-9211 Lawrence *(G-5083)*
- **R D H Electric Inc** E 785 625-3833 Hays *(G-2895)*
- **R F Fisher Holdings Inc** C 913 384-1500 Kansas City *(G-4357)*
- **Rays Electric Inc** E 316 838-8231 Wichita *(G-15423)*
- **Reddy Electric Systems Inc** F 913 764-0840 Olathe *(G-8020)*
- **Redi Systems Inc** F 785 587-9100 Manhattan *(G-6788)*
- **S N C Inc** E 620 665-6651 Hutchinson *(G-3434)*
- **Schmidtlein Electric Inc** E 785 357-4572 Topeka *(G-13039)*
- **Schultz Brothers Elc Co Inc** E 913 321-8338 Kansas City *(G-4406)*
- **Seward and Wilson Electric** F 620 232-1696 Pittsburg *(G-9937)*
- **Shelley Electric Inc** E 785 862-0507 Topeka *(G-13066)*
- **Simplex Time Recorder LLC** E 316 686-6363 Wichita *(G-15595)*
- **Southern Pioneer Electric Co** F 620 356-3370 Ulysses *(G-13320)*
- **Southwestern Electrical Co Inc** C 316 263-1264 Wichita *(G-15632)*
- **Stueder Contractors Inc** E 620 792-6044 Great Bend *(G-2642)*
- **Tann Electric Inc** F 913 236-7337 Lenexa *(G-6167)*
- **Td Electric Services LLC** F 913 722-5560 Overland Park *(G-9393)*
- ▲ **Teague Electric Cnstr Inc** C 913 529-4600 Lenexa *(G-6169)*
- **Teague Electric Company Inc** D 913 529-4600 Lenexa *(G-6170)*
- **Tee & Bee Electric Company** F 913 782-8161 Olathe *(G-8105)*
- **Toms Ditching & Backhoe Inc** F 620 879-2215 Caney *(G-676)*
- **Torgeson Electric Company** C 785 233-3060 Topeka *(G-13192)*
- **Total Electric Inc** G 316 524-2642 Wichita *(G-15775)*
- **Total Electric Construction Co** F 913 441-0192 Edwardsville *(G-1517)*
- **Total Electric Contractors** F 913 441-0192 Edwardsville *(G-1518)*
- **Touchton Electric Inc** E 620 232-9294 Pittsburg *(G-9946)*
- **Tracy Electric Inc** E 316 522-8408 Haysville *(G-2962)*
- **Universal Communications LLC** E 913 839-1634 Olathe *(G-8135)*
- **Universal Electric Inc** E 913 238-3024 Olathe *(G-8136)*
- **V & V Electric Company Inc** E 785 539-1975 Manhattan *(G-6840)*
- **V & V Electric Inc** F 785 468-3364 Olsburg *(G-8170)*
- **Vision Communications Ks Inc** F 316 634-6747 Wichita *(G-15908)*
- **Wachter Inc** C 913 541-2500 Lenexa *(G-6219)*
- **Wachter Tech Solutions Inc** D 856 222-0643 Lenexa *(G-6220)*
- **Watson Electric Inc** F 785 827-2924 Salina *(G-10761)*
- **Westar Industries Inc** C 785 575-6507 Topeka *(G-13240)*
- **Winavie LLC** E 913 789-8169 Kansas City *(G-4547)*
- ▲ **Wolfe Electric Inc** D 316 943-2751 Wichita *(G-16061)*
- **Yost Electric Inc** G 785 637-5454 Gorham *(G-2492)*
- **Young Electric Inc** E 316 681-8118 Wichita *(G-16090)*
- **Zenor Electric Company Inc** E 620 662-4694 Hutchinson *(G-3496)*
- **Ziegler Electric Service Inc** F 316 262-2842 Wichita *(G-16103)*
- **Zimmerman Electric Service** G 620 431-2260 Chanute *(G-775)*

1741 Masonry & Other Stonework

- **Alonge Stone Masonry** F 785 832-1438 Tonganoxie *(G-12251)*
- **ATM Concrete Inc** F 785 484-2013 Meriden *(G-7078)*
- **B W Foundations Company Inc** F 913 764-8222 Olathe *(G-7545)*
- ▼ **Berkel & Company Contrs Inc** D 913 422-5125 Bonner Springs *(G-540)*
- **Boan Masonry Company Inc** F 913 592-5369 Spring Hill *(G-12080)*
- **BPW Masonry Inc** E 785 485-2840 Riley *(G-10205)*
- **Builders Stone & Masonry Inc** D 913 764-4446 Olathe *(G-7567)*
- **Cleland Masonry Inc** F 620 347-8546 Arma *(G-189)*
- **Edward Rose & Sons LLC** F 316 202-3920 Wichita *(G-14261)*
- **Five Star Masonry LLC** E 785 484-9737 Meriden *(G-7081)*
- **Fuller Foundation Company Inc** E 913 764-8222 Olathe *(G-7720)*
- **Grimmett Masonry Inc** F 620 342-6582 Emporia *(G-1765)*
- **Hartman Masonry LLC** E 620 767-5286 Council Grove *(G-1169)*
- **Hudson Inc** E 620 232-1145 Pittsburg *(G-9879)*
- **Klaus Masonry LLC** F 785 650-3854 Hays *(G-2860)*
- **Konradys Lawn & Ldscpg Inc** E 913 722-1163 Olathe *(G-7843)*
- **Larry Lawrenz Construction** F 785 258-2056 Herington *(G-2978)*
- **Lawrenz Masonry LLC** E 785 366-0866 Herington *(G-2979)*
- **Lindsey Masonry Co Inc** F 913 721-2458 Kansas City *(G-4204)*
- **Lusker Masonry** F 620 231-9899 Frontenac *(G-2058)*
- **Maderak Construction Co Inc** F 913 299-3929 Kansas City *(G-4212)*
- **Mason Stone Inc** F 316 744-3884 Wichita *(G-15017)*
- **Mid-Cntinental Restoration Inc** C 620 223-3700 Fort Scott *(G-1990)*
- **Midwest Siding Inc** E 785 825-0606 Salina *(G-10603)*
- **ML Nevius Builders Inc** F 620 662-7767 Hutchinson *(G-3383)*
- **Newell & Associates** F 913 592-4421 Olathe *(G-7918)*
- **Perfection II Masonry Inc** F 785 499-6307 Alta Vista *(G-71)*
- **Power Lift Found Repair** E 316 685-0888 Wichita *(G-15319)*
- **Prestige Masonry LLC** F 785 925-3090 Topeka *(G-12985)*
- **Restortion Wtrprfing Cntrs Inc** E 316 942-6602 Wichita *(G-15452)*
- **Retrochem Inc** F 913 422-8810 Shawnee *(G-11018)*
- **Richard L Pride** F 785 485-2900 Riley *(G-10207)*
- **Robert Vanlerberg Foundations** E 913 441-6823 Shawnee Mission *(G-11809)*
- **S&K** E 913 634-2234 Overland Park *(G-9268)*
- **Scott Masonry Inc** F 785 286-3513 Topeka *(G-13043)*
- **Superior Masonry & Stucco LLC** E 316 928-2365 Wichita *(G-15695)*

SIC

1742 Plastering, Drywall, Acoustical & Insulation Work

- **Acoustical Stretched Fabric** G 913 345-1520 — Shawnee Mission *(G-11069)*
- **Allied Construction Svcs Inc** F 913 321-3170 — Roeland Park *(G-10216)*
- **Associated Insulation Inc** D 785 776-0145 — Manhattan *(G-6548)*
- **Black Gold Inc** E 785 354-4000 — Topeka *(G-12386)*
- **Capital Insulation Inc** E 785 246-1775 — Topeka *(G-12432)*
- **Cleaning By Lamunyon Inc** F 785 632-1259 — Clay Center *(G-855)*
- **Custom Stucco LLC** F 913 294-3100 — Paola *(G-9550)*
- **D and D Insulation Inc** E 913 492-1346 — Shawnee Mission *(G-11289)*
- **D V Douglass Roofing Inc** E 620 276-7474 — Garden City *(G-2141)*
- **Danny Satterfield Drywall Corp** E 316 942-5155 — Wichita *(G-14167)*
- **Delbert Chopp Co Inc** F 785 825-8530 — Salina *(G-10472)*
- **Douglas A Firebaugh Cnstr** C 913 451-8599 — Overland Park *(G-8660)*
- **Drewco Inc** E 913 384-6226 — Shawnee Mission *(G-11318)*
- **Drywall Inc** F 620 662-3454 — Hutchinson *(G-3269)*
- **Drywall Supply** F 316 269-3304 — Wichita *(G-14240)*
- **Drywall Systems Inc** D 316 832-0233 — Wichita *(G-14241)*
- **Dynamic Drywall Inc** D 316 945-7087 — Wichita *(G-14247)*
- **Empyre Construction LLC** E 316 558-8186 — Shawnee *(G-10947)*
- **Epic Insulation Inc** F 316 500-1650 — Goddard *(G-2438)*
- **F & H Abatement Services Inc** C 316 264-2208 — Kechi *(G-4567)*
- **Ferguson Dry Wall Company Inc** E 913 334-5658 — Kansas City *(G-4009)*
- **Fh Companies Inc** C 316 264-2208 — Kechi *(G-4568)*
- **Florence Bob Contractor Inc** D 785 357-0341 — Topeka *(G-12618)*
- **Greg E Ross Drywall** F 785 478-9557 — Topeka *(G-12650)*
- **H & C Insulation Co Inc** F 316 522-0236 — Wichita *(G-14530)*
- **Hi-Tech Interiors Inc** D 785 742-1766 — Hiawatha *(G-3009)*
- **Hi-Tech Interiors Inc** E 785 539-7266 — Manhattan *(G-6656)*
- **Home Stl Siding & Windows LLC** F 785 625-8622 — Hays *(G-2849)*
- **Howard Stultz Construction** F 785 842-4796 — Baldwin City *(G-364)*
- **Insco Industries Inc** E 913 422-8001 — Shawnee Mission *(G-11459)*
- **Insulation Drywall Contrs Inc** E 785 862-0554 — Topeka *(G-12725)*
- **Jay Henges Enterprises Inc** E 913 764-4600 — Olathe *(G-7808)*
- **Jordan Companies Inc** E 316 943-6222 — Wichita *(G-14771)*
- **Kd Christian Construction Co** E 913 451-0466 — Stilwell *(G-12161)*
- **Michel Drywall LLC** E 316 260-6458 — Wichita *(G-15065)*
- **Midwest Drywall Co Inc** C 316 722-9559 — Wichita *(G-15092)*
- **Midwest Drywall Co Inc** D 316 722-9559 — Wichita *(G-15093)*
- **Paredes Construction Inc** F 913 334-9662 — Kansas City *(G-4312)*
- ▲ **Performance Contracting Inc** A 913 888-8600 — Lenexa *(G-6051)*
- **Pro R Sales and Service Inc** F 316 773-3400 — Wichita *(G-15353)*
- **Randy Johnson** F 316 775-6786 — Augusta *(G-341)*
- **Rew Materials Inc** F 785 233-3651 — Topeka *(G-13013)*
- **Reynolds Construction Inc** E 913 780-6624 — Olathe *(G-8029)*
- **Rosas Drywall Co** F 620 665-6959 — Hutchinson *(G-3431)*
- **Samco Drywall Company** F 620 864-2289 — Severy *(G-10892)*
- **Superior Masonry & Stucco LLC** E 316 928-2365 — Wichita *(G-15695)*
- **Wagner Interior Systems Inc** E 913 647-6622 — Kansas City *(G-4528)*
- **Wallboard Specialties Inc** E 913 422-5023 — Shawnee Mission *(G-11991)*
- **Washington Companies Inc** F 620 792-2430 — Great Bend *(G-2656)*
- **Wichita Drywall Acoustics LLC** E 316 773-7826 — Wichita *(G-15993)*
- **Wray Roofing Inc** D 316 283-6840 — Newton *(G-7430)*

1743 Terrazzo, Tile, Marble & Mosaic Work

- **Austin Tile Inc** F 913 829-6607 — Olathe *(G-7542)*
- **Carpet Factory Outlet Inc** E 913 261-6800 — Kansas City *(G-3892)*
- ▲ **Fox Ceramic Tile Inc** E 785 437-2792 — Saint Marys *(G-10365)*
- **Interior Surface Entps LLC** F 913 397-8100 — Olathe *(G-7799)*
- **Kc Restoration LLC** F 913 766-2200 — Olathe *(G-7832)*
- **Metro Tile Contractors Inc** E 913 381-7770 — Lenexa *(G-5996)*
- **Romero Custom** F 913 548-3852 — Gardner *(G-2360)*
- ▲ **Turner Ceramic Tile Inc** F 913 441-6161 — Kansas City *(G-4477)*

1751 Carpentry Work

- **Advantage Framing Systems Inc** E 913 592-4150 — Spring Hill *(G-12075)*
- **Alenco Inc** E 913 438-1902 — Lenexa *(G-5638)*
- **All Wther Win Doors Siding Inc** F 913 262-4380 — Overland Park *(G-8367)*
- **Andersen Corporation** F 913 385-1300 — Lenexa *(G-5654)*
- **Apac-Kansas Inc** E 316 321-3221 — El Dorado *(G-1528)*
- **Barnes Millworks Inc** F 620 232-8746 — Pittsburg *(G-9822)*
- **Ben Kitchens Painting Co Inc** F 785 375-3288 — Junction City *(G-3673)*
- **Bhjllc Inc** E 785 272-8800 — Topeka *(G-12379)*
- **Byrne Custom Wood Products Inc** F 913 894-4777 — Lenexa *(G-5722)*
- **Cabinet Shopof Basehor Inc** E 913 845-2182 — Tonganoxie *(G-12255)*
- **CCM Countertop & Cab Mfg LLC** F 316 554-0113 — Wichita *(G-13967)*
- **Champion Opco LLC** F 316 636-4200 — Wichita *(G-13996)*
- **Columbia Industries Inc** E 785 227-3351 — Lindsborg *(G-6396)*
- ▲ **D H Pace Company Inc** A 816 221-0543 — Olathe *(G-7637)*
- **Dade Construction LLC** F 913 208-1968 — Kansas City *(G-3951)*
- **Dahmer Contracting Group LLC** D 816 795-3332 — Overland Park *(G-8630)*
- **Danny Satterfield Drywall Corp** E 316 942-5155 — Wichita *(G-14167)*
- **Delbert Chopp Co Inc** F 785 825-8530 — Salina *(G-10472)*
- **Discount Siding Supply LP** F 785 625-4619 — Hays *(G-2788)*
- **Doubrava Woodworking Inc** G 785 472-4204 — Ellsworth *(G-1666)*
- **Douglas A Firebaugh Cnstr** C 913 451-8599 — Overland Park *(G-8660)*
- **EE Newcomer Enterprises Inc** B 816 221-0543 — Olathe *(G-7671)*
- **Four Corners Construction LLC** G 620 662-8163 — Hutchinson *(G-3290)*
- **Garage Door Group Inc** F 757 253-0522 — Junction City *(G-3691)*
- **Glass Services Inc** F 785 823-5444 — Salina *(G-10511)*
- **Guthridge/Nighswonger Corp** F 316 264-7900 — Wichita *(G-14529)*
- **Halstontine Corp** F 913 780-2171 — Overland Park *(G-8787)*
- **Hays Planing Mill Inc** G 785 625-6507 — Hays *(G-2838)*
- **Hi-Plains Door Systems Inc** F 785 462-6352 — Colby *(G-1013)*
- **Home Stl Siding & Windows LLC** F 785 625-8622 — Hays *(G-2849)*
- **K C Wood Products** F 913 422-3320 — Edwardsville *(G-1505)*
- **King Wood Products Inc** F 913 837-5300 — Louisburg *(G-6453)*
- **Mid America Exteriors LLC** F 316 265-5444 — Wichita *(G-15066)*
- **Mid-AM Building Supply Inc** D 913 592-4313 — Spring Hill *(G-12089)*
- **Mid-Continent Thermal-Guard** E 316 838-4044 — Wichita *(G-15079)*
- **Midway Sales & Distrg Inc** F 785 537-4665 — Manhattan *(G-6745)*
- **Midwest Siding Incorporated** E 785 825-5576 — Salina *(G-10602)*
- **Midwest Siding Inc** E 785 825-0606 — Salina *(G-10603)*
- **Norcraft Companies LP** B 316 283-2859 — Newton *(G-7398)*
- **Ovation Cabinetry Inc** D 785 452-9000 — Salina *(G-10625)*
- **Overhead Door Company** E 316 265-4634 — Wichita *(G-15240)*
- **Overhead Door N Centl Kans Inc** F 785 823-3786 — Salina *(G-10626)*
- **Pratt Glass Inc** F 620 672-6463 — Pratt *(G-10139)*
- **Ray Anderson Co Inc** E 785 233-7454 — Topeka *(G-13000)*
- **Roys Custom Cabinets** G 785 625-6724 — Hays *(G-2902)*
- **Sarin Energy Inc** F 913 912-3235 — Overland Park *(G-9281)*
- **Tuff Shed Inc** F 913 541-8833 — Shawnee Mission *(G-11947)*
- **Wichita Drywall Acoustics LLC** E 316 773-7826 — Wichita *(G-15993)*
- **Wood RE New Joco Inc** G 913 661-9663 — Olathe *(G-8159)*
- **Worldwide Windows** F 785 826-1701 — Salina *(G-10773)*

1752 Floor Laying & Other Floor Work, NEC

- ▲ **Acme Floor Company Inc** D 913 888-3200 — Lenexa *(G-5624)*
- **Aegis Business Solutions LLC** G 913 307-9922 — Olathe *(G-7512)*
- **Austin Tile Inc** F 913 829-6607 — Olathe *(G-7542)*
- **Better Life Technology LLC** E 620 343-2212 — Emporia *(G-1703)*
- **Bills Floor Covering Inc** F 913 492-1964 — Shawnee Mission *(G-11166)*
- **Classic Floors & Design Center** E 913 780-2171 — Overland Park *(G-8561)*
- **Commercial Floors** E 913 583-3525 — De Soto *(G-1197)*
- **Corporate Flooring Inc** F 913 859-9180 — Shawnee Mission *(G-11266)*
- **Custom Renovation** F 620 544-2653 — Hugoton *(G-3158)*
- **Db Flooring LLC** E 913 663-9922 — Lenexa *(G-5806)*
- **Delta Homes Inc** E 316 777-0009 — Mulvane *(G-7215)*
- **Design Source Flooring LLC** E 913 387-5858 — Lenexa *(G-5813)*
- **Furst In Tile Inc** F 913 962-4599 — Shawnee Mission *(G-11386)*
- **Great Amercn Hardwood Flrg Co** F 316 264-3660 — Wichita *(G-14501)*
- **Halstontine Corp** F 913 780-2171 — Overland Park *(G-8787)*
- **Interior Surface Entps LLC** F 913 397-8100 — Olathe *(G-7799)*
- **Kansas Carpet & Tile Inc** E 316 942-2111 — Wichita *(G-14790)*
- **Kaw Valley Hardwood Inc** E 785 925-0142 — Topeka *(G-12812)*
- **L & L Floor Covering Inc** F 620 275-0499 — Garden City *(G-2221)*
- **Mo-Can Flooring Inc** E 913 362-0711 — Shawnee *(G-10999)*
- **Regents Flooring Co Inc** F 913 663-9922 — Lenexa *(G-6098)*
- **Ron Stierly Floor Services** F 913 724-4822 — Basehor *(G-388)*

Sam Carlini ....F 913 416-1280
Shawnee *(G-11024)*
Superior Hardwood Floors LLC ....G 316 554-9663
Wichita *(G-15694)*
UNI Floor Inc ....F 913 238-4633
Overland Park *(G-9439)*
Zack Taylor Contracting Inc ....F 785 235-8704
Topeka *(G-13260)*

1761 Roofing, Siding & Sheet Metal Work

A/R Roofing LLC ....F 620 672-2999
Pratt *(G-10090)*
Aegis Business Solutions LLC ....G 913 307-9922
Olathe *(G-7512)*
Alenco Inc ....E 913 438-1902
Lenexa *(G-5638)*
All States Windows Siding LLC ....E 913 800-5211
Overland Park *(G-8366)*
All States Windows Siding LLC ....E 316 444-1220
Wichita *(G-13666)*
Allstate Roofing Inc ....F 913 782-2000
Olathe *(G-7521)*
American Metals Supply Co Inc ....E 913 754-0616
Lenexa *(G-5651)*
American Roofing Inc ....E 913 772-1776
Leavenworth *(G-5201)*
▲ API Americas Inc ....D 732 382-6800
Lawrence *(G-4737)*
AR Commercial Roofing LLC ....F 620 672-3332
Pratt *(G-10098)*
Arch Design Builders LLC ....E 913 599-5565
Overland Park *(G-8392)*
Arr Roofing LLC ....D 913 829-0447
Olathe *(G-7533)*
Arrow Renovation & Cnstr LLC ....E 913 703-3000
Olathe *(G-7534)*
Barnes & Dodge Inc ....E 913 321-6444
Lenexa *(G-5687)*
Beck Roofing & Construction ....F 316 684-7663
Derby *(G-1223)*
Bill Davis Roofing ....F 913 764-4449
Olathe *(G-7554)*
Blackburns All Star Roofing ....E 913 321-3456
Kansas City *(G-3863)*
Borens Roofing Inc ....F 620 365-7663
Iola *(G-3588)*
Brad H Allen Roofing Inc ....F 785 423-3861
Lawrence *(G-4764)*
Buckley Roofing Company Inc ....D 316 838-9321
Wichita *(G-13904)*
Canadian West Inc ....E 913 422-0099
Kansas City *(G-3887)*
CD Custom Enterprises LLC ....F 316 804-4520
Newton *(G-7327)*
Centurion Industries Inc ....B 620 378-4401
Fredonia *(G-2028)*
Chambless Roofing Inc ....F 620 275-8410
Scott City *(G-10807)*
Champion Opco LLC ....F 316 636-4200
Wichita *(G-13996)*
Commercial Rofg Spcialists LLC ....F 316 304-1423
Wichita *(G-14072)*
Custom Sheet Metal & Roofg Inc ....E 785 357-6200
Topeka *(G-12539)*
D V Douglass Roofing Inc ....E 620 276-7474
Garden City *(G-2141)*
DAgostino Mech Contrs Inc ....D 913 384-5170
Kansas City *(G-3952)*
▼ Davinci Roofscapes LLC ....E 913 599-0766
Lenexa *(G-5804)*
Debackers Inc ....E 785 232-6999
Topeka *(G-12550)*
Delta Innovative Services Inc ....D 913 371-7100
Kansas City *(G-3967)*
Discount Siding Supply LP ....F 785 625-4619
Hays *(G-2788)*
Dm Roofing ....F 620 515-0015
Coffeyville *(G-934)*
E3 Roofing Group Inc ....F 913 782-3332
Olathe *(G-7664)*
Expert Roofing LLC ....F 785 286-1999
Topeka *(G-12588)*
Flint Hills Roof Service ....F 785 238-8609
Chapman *(G-778)*
Geisler Roofing Inc ....F 785 243-7298
Concordia *(G-1114)*
Givens Investments LLC ....F 620 662-1784
Hutchinson *(G-3300)*
Great Plains Roofg Shtmtl Inc ....D 913 677-4679
Kansas City *(G-4046)*
Guilfoyle Roofing ....F 785 233-9315
Topeka *(G-12653)*
Gwaltney Inc ....D 620 225-2622
Dodge City *(G-1368)*
Gwaltney Inc ....E 785 537-8008
Manhattan *(G-6648)*
Hartley Sheet Metal Co Inc ....F 620 251-4330
Coffeyville *(G-943)*
Home Stl Siding & Windows LLC ....F 785 625-8622
Hays *(G-2849)*
Homeland Roofing and Cnstr LLC ....F 316 832-9901
Wichita *(G-14632)*
Industrial Roofg Met Works Inc ....F 316 262-4758
Wichita *(G-14687)*
J B Turner Sons ....E 785 233-9603
Herington *(G-2977)*
Jayhawk Roofing & Supply Co ....E 785 825-5466
Salina *(G-10552)*
Jet Stream Guttering Corp ....F 913 262-2913
Shawnee Mission *(G-11485)*
Jordan Companies Inc ....E 316 943-6222
Wichita *(G-14771)*
L J Herzberg Roofing Co Inc ....F 316 529-2222
Wichita *(G-14906)*
Larry Booze Roofing Co Inc ....F 316 263-7796
Wichita *(G-14926)*
LG Pike Construction Co Inc ....D 620 442-9150
Arkansas City *(G-164)*
Luminous Neon Inc ....E 913 780-3330
Olathe *(G-7867)*
◆ Mahaney Group Inc ....D 316 262-4768
Wichita *(G-15001)*
Martin Roofing Company Inc ....E 316 524-3293
Wichita *(G-15014)*
Martinek & Flynn Wholesale Inc ....E 785 233-6666
Topeka *(G-12862)*
Maxines Inc ....F 620 669-8189
Hutchinson *(G-3367)*
McLaughlin Roofing LLC ....F 785 764-9582
Oskaloosa *(G-8229)*
Mid America Exteriors LLC ....F 316 265-5444
Wichita *(G-15066)*
Mid-Continent Thermal-Guard ....E 316 838-4044
Wichita *(G-15079)*
Midwest Coating Inc ....E 785 232-4276
Topeka *(G-12895)*
Midwest Roofing Services Inc ....E 316 262-4758
Wichita *(G-15099)*
Midwest Siding Incorporated ....E 785 825-5576
Salina *(G-10602)*
Midwest Siding Inc ....E 785 825-0606
Salina *(G-10603)*
Modern Air Conditioning Inc ....E 620 342-7577
Emporia *(G-1797)*
Mt 3 Corporation ....E 785 843-3433
Perry *(G-9772)*
Murphy & Sons Roofing ....F 913 287-2116
Kansas City *(G-4273)*
New Image Roofing LLC ....E 316 201-1180
Wichita *(G-15167)*
Nieder Contracting Inc ....E 785 842-0094
Lawrence *(G-5040)*
Paint Masters Inc ....F 316 683-5203
Wichita *(G-15253)*
Paint Pro Inc ....F 913 685-4089
Overland Park *(G-9138)*
Pestinger Heating & AC Inc ....E 785 827-6361
Salina *(G-10634)*
Ponton Construction Inc ....F 785 823-9584
Salina *(G-10635)*
Premier Contracting Inc ....D 913 362-4141
Kansas City *(G-4330)*
Professional Roofing Systems ....E 785 392-0603
Minneapolis *(G-7122)*
Protec Construction & Sup LLC ....E 913 441-2121
Edwardsville *(G-1513)*
Ray Omo Inc ....E 620 227-3101
Lenexa *(G-6091)*
Reno Fabricating & Sls Co Inc ....E 620 663-1269
Hutchinson *(G-3426)*
Rhino Builders Inc ....F 913 722-4353
Kansas City *(G-4376)*
Rice Precision Mfg Inc ....E 785 594-2670
Baldwin City *(G-367)*
Ronans Roofing Inc ....E 913 384-0901
Lenexa *(G-6113)*
Roofing Services Unlimited ....F 316 284-9900
Newton *(G-7411)*
Roofing Solutions Inc ....F 913 897-1840
Overland Park *(G-9256)*
Roofmasters Roofing Co Inc ....E 785 462-6642
Colby *(G-1036)*
Scott Mesler ....F 785 749-0462
Lawrence *(G-5106)*
Sheet Metal Contractors Inc ....E 913 397-9130
Olathe *(G-8061)*
Stevenson Company Inc ....F 785 233-0691
Topeka *(G-13097)*
Stevenson Company Inc ....F 785 233-1303
Topeka *(G-13098)*
Strategic Global Services LLC ....F 316 655-2761
Wichita *(G-15675)*
Summit Roofing & Contg LLC ....F 417 873-9191
Frontenac *(G-2065)*
Superior Sheet Metal Co Inc ....F 913 831-9900
Kansas City *(G-4449)*
Systems 4 Inc ....E 785 823-9119
Salina *(G-10730)*
T R Management Inc ....E 785 233-9603
Topeka *(G-13130)*
Total Renovation Group Inc ....F 913 491-5000
Lenexa *(G-6186)*
Town & Country Guttering Inc ....F 913 441-0003
Shawnee Mission *(G-11935)*
TWC Services Inc ....E 316 265-7831
Wichita *(G-15820)*
Vincent Roofing Inc ....E 785 233-9603
Topeka *(G-13225)*
Waddles Heating & Cooling ....E 785 827-2621
Salina *(G-10755)*
Washington Companies Inc ....F 620 792-2430
Great Bend *(G-2656)*
Weddle and Sons Inc ....E 785 532-8347
Manhattan *(G-6848)*
Western Aluminum & Glass Co ....F 785 625-2418
Hays *(G-2931)*
Western Roofing Co Services ....E 816 931-1075
Kansas City *(G-4536)*
Westpro Construction Solutions ....F 816 561-7667
Kansas City *(G-4539)*
Wichita Roofing and Rmdlg Inc ....F 316 943-0600
Wichita *(G-16021)*
Wildcat Gttering Exteriors Inc ....F 785 485-2194
Manhattan *(G-6855)*
Wilson Ielah ....F 913 954-9798
Kansas City *(G-4546)*
Wood Haven Inc ....G 785 597-5618
Perry *(G-9775)*
Wray & Sons Roofing Inc ....F 620 663-7107
Hutchinson *(G-3493)*
Wray Roofing Inc ....D 316 283-6840
Newton *(G-7430)*
◆ Wsm Industries Inc ....C 316 942-9412
Wichita *(G-16075)*
Wsm Investments Inc ....C 316 942-9412
Wichita *(G-16076)*

1771 Concrete Work

▲ Aci Cncrete Placement Kans LLC ....E 913 281-3700
Lenexa *(G-5623)*
Andrews Asphalt & Cnstr Inc ....G 785 232-0188
Topeka *(G-12326)*
Apac-Kansas Inc ....F 785 823-8944
Salina *(G-10405)*
ATM Concrete Inc ....F 785 484-2013
Meriden *(G-7078)*
B & B Redimix Inc ....F 785 543-5133
Phillipsburg *(G-9777)*
B & H Construction Company ....F 620 231-0326
Pittsburg *(G-9820)*
Banzet Concrete Inc ....F 316 776-9961
Rose Hill *(G-10236)*
Barkley Construction ....F 316 945-6500
Wichita *(G-13812)*
Beran Concrete Inc ....C 316 425-7600
Wichita *(G-13830)*
Beran Concrete Inc ....D 316 618-6089
Wichita *(G-13831)*
Beran Icf Solutions LLC ....F 316 944-2131
Wichita *(G-13832)*
▼ Berkel & Company Contrs Inc ....D 913 422-5125
Bonner Springs *(G-540)*
Better Concrete Construction ....F 913 390-8500
Olathe *(G-7552)*
Bottorff Construction Inc ....D 913 874-5681
Atchison *(G-219)*
Brad Murray Inc ....F 316 943-2516
Wichita *(G-13879)*
Brak-Hard Concrete Cnstr Co ....F 620 225-1957
Dodge City *(G-1311)*

SIC

Bruce Davis Construction LLC..............E....... 620 342-5001
Emporia *(G-1710)*
Brulez Foundation Inc..............E....... 913 422-3355
Olathe *(G-7562)*
Brundage-Bone Con Pmpg Inc..............E....... 785 823-7706
Salina *(G-10433)*
Bryant and Bryant Cnstr Inc..............E....... 316 835-3322
Halstead *(G-2696)*
Calvin Opp Concrete Inc..............D....... 316 944-4600
Wichita *(G-13928)*
Carl Harris Co Inc..............E....... 316 267-8700
Wichita *(G-13950)*
Carpenter Construction Company..............F....... 620 386-4155
Moundridge *(G-7179)*
Ceco Concrete Cnstr Del LLC..............F....... 913 362-1855
Olathe *(G-7581)*
Chad Eakin Concrete..............F....... 620 285-2097
Larned *(G-4698)*
▲ Chance Rides Manufacturing Inc..............C....... 316 945-6555
Wichita *(G-13997)*
Concrete Inc..............F....... 785 594-4838
Lawrence *(G-4808)*
Concrete Pumping Service Inc..............F....... 316 612-8515
Wichita *(G-14087)*
Concrete Unlimited Cnstr Inc..............E....... 785 232-8636
Topeka *(G-12499)*
Concrete Unlimited Inc..............D....... 785 232-8636
Topeka *(G-12500)*
Creten Basement Contractors..............F....... 913 441-3333
Olathe *(G-7626)*
Creten John G Basement Contr..............F....... 913 441-3333
Olathe *(G-7627)*
Custom Flatwork Inc..............F....... 316 794-8282
Goddard *(G-2435)*
CW Concrete Inc..............E....... 913 780-2316
Olathe *(G-7632)*
D JS Foundation & Flatwork..............F....... 913 441-1909
Bonner Springs *(G-547)*
Designer Construction Inc..............D....... 785 776-9878
Manhattan *(G-6613)*
Dinkel Construction Inc..............F....... 785 232-3377
Topeka *(G-12558)*
Ebi Construction Inc..............F....... 785 456-7449
Wamego *(G-13419)*
Emerson Construction Inc..............F....... 785 235-0555
Topeka *(G-12574)*
Emporia Construction & Rmdlg..............E....... 620 341-3131
Emporia *(G-1738)*
Eslinger Construction & Rdymx..............F....... 620 659-2371
Kinsley *(G-4617)*
Finley Construction & Rdymx..............G....... 785 626-3282
Atwood *(G-286)*
First Grade Excavating Inc..............F....... 316 524-0900
Wichita *(G-14375)*
▲ Fox Ceramic Tile Inc..............E....... 785 437-2792
Saint Marys *(G-10365)*
Freeman Concrete Cnstr LLC..............E....... 913 825-0744
Lenexa *(G-5865)*
George Goracke Basement..............F....... 785 388-9542
Solomon *(G-12051)*
Gold Star Concrete Cnstr..............E....... 785 478-4495
Topeka *(G-12640)*
Gray & Company Inc..............E....... 785 232-0913
Topeka *(G-12644)*
Graybeal Construction Co Inc..............E....... 785 232-1033
Lenexa *(G-5882)*
Gunter Construction Company..............F....... 913 362-7844
Kansas City *(G-4059)*
Gustafson Concrete Inc..............F....... 785 238-7747
Junction City *(G-3697)*
Hamm Inc..............F....... 785 242-1045
Ottawa *(G-8277)*
Hamm Inc..............G....... 785 597-5111
Perry *(G-9769)*
Hett Construction..............F....... 620 382-2236
Marion *(G-6871)*
HMK Concrete..............F....... 913 262-1555
Shawnee Mission *(G-11435)*
Holmes Basement Construction..............F....... 785 823-6770
Salina *(G-10545)*
Industrial Cleaning and Maint..............E....... 785 246-9262
Topeka *(G-12722)*
▲ Interstate Flooring LLC..............F....... 913 541-9700
Lenexa *(G-5921)*
Iwp LLC..............F....... 316 308-8507
Valley Center *(G-13345)*
J Corp..............F....... 785 628-8101
Hays *(G-2854)*
James Voegeli Construction..............E....... 316 721-6800
Maize *(G-6514)*
Jeff Hoge Concrete LLC..............E....... 913 239-0903
Stilwell *(G-12156)*
John Rohrer Contracting Co Inc..............E....... 913 236-5005
Kansas City *(G-4126)*
Klaver Construction Co Inc..............D....... 620 532-3183
Kingman *(G-4603)*
Koehn Painting Co LLC..............E....... 316 283-9612
Newton *(G-7373)*
Kolde Construction Inc..............E....... 785 437-3730
Saint Marys *(G-10370)*
L M C C Inc..............E....... 913 371-1070
Kansas City *(G-4190)*
Leavcon II Inc..............E....... 913 351-1430
Lansing *(G-4681)*
Leo J Debrabander Foundation..............F....... 913 780-1600
Olathe *(G-7858)*
Leslie D Boeckner..............F....... 785 741-1036
Hiawatha *(G-3016)*
Lithko Contracting LLC..............F....... 913 281-2700
Lenexa *(G-5975)*
Little Joes Asphalt Inc..............F....... 913 721-3261
Bonner Springs *(G-560)*
▲ Longfellow Foundation Inc..............F....... 620 662-1228
Hutchinson *(G-3356)*
Madison Brothers Concrete Inc..............F....... 620 224-6098
Fort Scott *(G-1983)*
Major Inc..............E....... 316 265-7000
Wichita *(G-15002)*
Mark Debrabander Foundation Co..............F....... 913 856-4044
Olathe *(G-7874)*
Max Rieke & Brothers Inc..............D....... 913 631-7111
Shawnee *(G-10991)*
McNish Foundations Inc..............F....... 785 865-2413
Lawrence *(G-5019)*
Meadows Const Co Inc..............E....... 913 369-3335
Tonganoxie *(G-12266)*
Miles Excavating Inc..............C....... 913 724-1934
Basehor *(G-384)*
Modern Paving Systems Inc..............F....... 913 962-7208
Shawnee Mission *(G-11652)*
Morgan Concrete Services Inc..............E....... 785 842-1686
Lawrence *(G-5031)*
Nate Apple Concrete Inc..............E....... 913 837-3022
Louisburg *(G-6459)*
New Image Concrete Design LLC..............F....... 913 489-1699
Shawnee *(G-11005)*
Overland Concrete Cnstr Inc..............F....... 913 393-4200
Olathe *(G-7968)*
Paronto Mall Construction Inc..............F....... 785 632-2484
Clay Center *(G-875)*
Paving Construction Inc..............F....... 316 684-6161
Wichita *(G-15272)*
Pfefferkorn Engrg & Envmtl LLC..............F....... 913 490-3967
Olathe *(G-7982)*
Power Lift Found Repair..............E....... 316 685-0888
Wichita *(G-15319)*
Prairie Landworks Inc..............F....... 620 504-5049
Mcpherson *(G-7017)*
R & H Concrete Inc..............E....... 785 286-0335
Lawrence *(G-5084)*
R & S Construction Inc..............F....... 620 325-2130
Neodesha *(G-7247)*
R O K K Concrete Inc..............F....... 785 286-0662
Topeka *(G-12996)*
Restortion Wtrprfing Cntrs Inc..............F....... 785 478-9538
Topeka *(G-13011)*
Rieke Concrete Systems Inc..............F....... 913 492-0270
Shawnee Mission *(G-11803)*
Robert Vanlerberg Foundations..............E....... 913 441-6823
Shawnee Mission *(G-11809)*
Schreiner M & Sons Cnstr..............F....... 785 246-1130
Topeka *(G-13040)*
Scott Heller Trucking..............E....... 816 591-1638
Lenexa *(G-6119)*
SMC Concrete and Cnstr LLC..............F....... 785 545-5186
Cawker City *(G-690)*
Smithcon LLC..............E....... 316 744-3406
Wichita *(G-15609)*
Smoky Hill LLC..............D....... 785 825-0810
Salina *(G-10710)*
Specchem LLC..............E....... 816 968-5600
Kansas City *(G-4432)*
Spriggs Concrete Inc..............E....... 620 795-4841
Oswego *(G-8237)*
Steve Kemp Concrete Cnstr..............F....... 316 263-8902
Wichita *(G-15665)*
Superior Excavating LLC..............F....... 316 260-1829
Valley Center *(G-13355)*
Superior Hardwood Floors LLC..............G....... 316 554-9663
Wichita *(G-15694)*
Superior Masonry & Stucco LLC..............E....... 316 928-2365
Wichita *(G-15695)*
Surface Protection Svcs LLC..............F....... 316 322-5135
El Dorado *(G-1606)*
T & T Flatworks Inc..............E....... 620 794-0619
Lebo *(G-5609)*
Tarbet Construction Co Inc..............F....... 620 356-2110
Ulysses *(G-13321)*
Tarbet Construction Co Inc..............G....... 785 462-7432
Colby *(G-1045)*
Ted Row Inc..............F....... 816 223-9666
Stilwell *(G-12176)*
Thoele Foundations LLC..............E....... 913 757-2317
La Cygne *(G-4644)*
Thrasher Bsmnt Foundation Repr..............D....... 316 320-1853
El Dorado *(G-1609)*
Unlimited Service Options LLC..............F....... 316 522-1503
Wichita *(G-15859)*
Vannahmen Construction Inc..............E....... 785 494-2354
Saint George *(G-10348)*
Vintage Greenmark Cnstr Inc..............F....... 785 843-2700
Lawrence *(G-5174)*
White William & Sons Cnstr Co..............D....... 913 375-9161
Basehor *(G-391)*
Wieneke Construction Co Inc..............F....... 620 632-4529
Mc Cune *(G-6923)*
Wildcat Concrete Services Inc..............E....... 785 478-9000
Topeka *(G-13244)*
Wildcat Construction Co Inc..............C....... 316 945-9408
Wichita *(G-16049)*
Wise Construction Inc..............F....... 785 781-4383
Cawker City *(G-691)*
Wt Contractors..............E....... 620 356-4801
Ulysses *(G-13332)*

1781 Water Well Drilling

Geocore LLC..............E....... 785 826-1616
Salina *(G-10509)*
Gulick Drilling..............F....... 620 583-5804
Eureka *(G-1890)*
Harp Well Pump Svc Corporated..............F....... 316 722-1411
Wichita *(G-14562)*
Hydro Rsrces - Mid Cntnent Inc..............D....... 620 277-2389
Garden City *(G-2201)*
K & K Water Wells LLC..............F....... 620 675-2222
Sublette *(G-12204)*
Kenai Drilling Limited..............C....... 805 937-7871
Liberal *(G-6328)*
Layne Christensen Company..............E....... 913 321-5000
Kansas City *(G-4196)*
Layne Christensen Company..............F....... 913 321-5000
Kansas City *(G-4197)*
Minter-Wilson Drilling Co Inc..............F....... 620 276-8269
Garden City *(G-2237)*
Patchen Electric & Indus Sup..............G....... 785 843-4522
Lawrence *(G-5057)*
Pickrell Drilling Co Inc..............E....... 620 793-5742
Great Bend *(G-2623)*
Rosencrantz Bemis Enterprises..............E....... 620 792-2488
Great Bend *(G-2632)*
Royal Drilling Inc..............E....... 785 483-6446
Russell *(G-10292)*
W W Drilling LLC..............D....... 785 743-6774
Wakeeney *(G-13393)*
Woofter Pump & Well Inc..............F....... 785 675-3991
Hoxie *(G-3144)*

1791 Structural Steel Erection

Building Erection Svcs Co Inc..............E....... 913 764-5560
Olathe *(G-7568)*
Building Solutions LLC..............F....... 620 225-1199
Dodge City *(G-1314)*
Carl Harris Co Inc..............E....... 316 267-8700
Wichita *(G-13950)*
CDI Industrial Mech Contrs Inc..............C....... 913 287-0334
Kansas City *(G-3898)*
Ceo Enterprises Inc..............F....... 913 432-8046
Shawnee Mission *(G-11214)*
Confab Inc..............E....... 316 321-5358
El Dorado *(G-1548)*
Crossland Prefab LLC..............E....... 620 429-1414
Columbus *(G-1073)*
Energy and Envmtl Systems Inc..............E....... 913 845-3553
Tonganoxie *(G-12260)*
Fh Companies Inc..............C....... 316 264-2208
Kechi *(G-4568)*
Frank Construction Company..............E....... 785 825-4213
Salina *(G-10505)*
Gerard Tank & Steel Inc..............E....... 785 243-3895
Concordia *(G-1116)*

Griffith Steel Erection Inc......E....... 316 941-4455
Wichita *(G-14519)*
Jack Foster Co Erectors......E....... 316 263-2901
Wichita *(G-14742)*
Leiser Construction LLC......F....... 620 437-2747
Madison *(G-6503)*
Lift Inc......F....... 913 287-4343
Kansas City *(G-4203)*
Panhandle Steel Erectors Inc......F....... 620 271-9878
Garden City *(G-2247)*
Schuff Steel Company......F....... 913 677-2485
Overland Park *(G-9284)*
Southwest and Associates Inc......D....... 620 463-5631
Burrton *(G-650)*
Welco Services Inc......E....... 620 241-3000
McPherson *(G-7041)*
Wichita Concrete Pipe Inc......E....... 316 838-8651
Wichita *(G-15989)*
XCEL Erectors Inc......F....... 913 664-7400
Overland Park *(G-9510)*

1793 Glass & Glazing Work

A Glass & Tint Shop Kc Inc......F....... 913 491-8468
Merriam *(G-7085)*
▲ **Byers Glass & Mirror Inc**......E....... 913 441-8717
Bonner Springs *(G-544)*
City Glass and Mirror Inc......F....... 785 233-5650
Topeka *(G-12467)*
Drywall Systems Inc......C....... 316 260-9411
Wichita *(G-14242)*
▲ **Fountain Glass Inc**......E....... 913 764-6014
Lenexa *(G-5864)*
G W Inc......E....... 316 262-3403
Wichita *(G-14435)*
Grey Mountain Partners LLC......E....... 785 776-9482
Manhattan *(G-6646)*
Hoppers Glass Inc......E....... 316 262-0497
Wichita *(G-14636)*
Janssen Glass & Mirror Inc......F....... 913 677-5727
Shawnee *(G-10977)*
Kennedy Glass Inc......E....... 785 843-4416
Lawrence *(G-4942)*
Lawrence Glass & Mirror Co......F....... 913 631-5533
Shawnee Mission *(G-11550)*
Masonry & Glass Systems Inc......G....... 913 748-6142
Shawnee Mission *(G-11601)*
Midwest Glass & Glazing LLC......E....... 913 768-6778
Kansas City *(G-4253)*
Performance Glass Inc......F....... 913 441-1290
Bonner Springs *(G-570)*
Pratt Glass Inc......F....... 620 672-6463
Pratt *(G-10139)*
Southwest Glass & Door Inc......F....... 620 626-7400
Liberal *(G-6369)*
Sowards Glass Inc......F....... 785 233-4466
Topeka *(G-13086)*
W Carter & Assoc Glazing LLC......E....... 913 543-2600
Kansas City *(G-4526)*

1794 Excavating & Grading Work

Apac-Kansas Inc......E....... 620 227-6908
Dodge City *(G-1293)*
Apex Trucking Inc......E....... 316 943-0774
Park City *(G-9601)*
Barnharts Excavation LLC......F....... 620 431-0959
Chanute *(G-706)*
Bayer Construction Company Inc......C....... 785 776-8839
Manhattan *(G-6553)*
Betzen Trenching Inc......E....... 316 269-9331
Wichita *(G-13841)*
Bradburn Wrecking Company......E....... 316 686-1959
Wichita *(G-13880)*
Bratton Bros Contracting Inc......F....... 913 422-7771
Shawnee *(G-10920)*
Breason Excavating & Trucking......F....... 785 597-5596
Perry *(G-9766)*
Buck Construction Co......F....... 913 796-6510
Mc Louth *(G-6925)*
Cornejo & Sons LLC......C....... 316 522-5100
Wichita *(G-14101)*
D B Excavating Inc......E....... 913 208-7100
Spring Hill *(G-12083)*
Diversified Contracting LLC......F....... 913 898-4722
Parker *(G-9657)*
E4 Excavating Inc......F....... 785 379-5111
Berryton *(G-526)*
Ebert Construction Co Inc......E....... 785 456-2455
Wamego *(G-13418)*
Emerson Construction Inc......F....... 785 235-0555
Topeka *(G-12574)*
Ferco Inc......E....... 785 825-6380
Salina *(G-10500)*
Firelk-Diversified Joint Ventr......E....... 913 312-9540
Lenexa *(G-5855)*
Frank Construction Company......E....... 785 825-4213
Salina *(G-10505)*
Freddy Van Inc......G....... 620 231-1127
Pittsburg *(G-9863)*
Frederick Excavating Inc......F....... 913 772-0225
Leavenworth *(G-5240)*
Gary Gorby......E....... 620 879-5243
Caney *(G-668)*
Greg Bair Track Hoe Svc Inc......F....... 913 897-1243
Shawnee Mission *(G-11403)*
Hayes Bros Const Co Inc......F....... 913 685-3636
Bucyrus *(G-599)*
Herrmans Excavating Inc......E....... 785 233-4146
Topeka *(G-12687)*
Hoffman Inc......F....... 316 942-8011
Wichita *(G-14622)*
James R Barber......F....... 785 349-2801
White City *(G-13567)*
Jims Electric Inc......F....... 785 460-2844
Colby *(G-1017)*
Kaw Valley Companies Inc......C....... 913 281-9950
Kansas City *(G-4160)*
Killough Construction Inc......F....... 785 242-1500
Ottawa *(G-8281)*
King Enterprises Inc......F....... 620 624-3332
Liberal *(G-6329)*
Knight Trenching & Excvtg Inc......E....... 913 599-6999
Lenexa *(G-5954)*
L Blixt Construction Inc......F....... 785 922-6180
Chapman *(G-780)*
Larkin Excavating, Inc.......D....... 913 727-3772
Leavenworth *(G-5264)*
Larry Bair Excavating Inc......E....... 913 947-7222
Louisburg *(G-6456)*
Leavenworth Excvtg Eqp Co Inc......E....... 913 727-1234
Leavenworth *(G-5265)*
Linaweaver Construction Inc......F....... 913 351-3474
Lansing *(G-4686)*
M & D Excavating Inc......F....... 785 628-3169
Hays *(G-2867)*
M & D of Hays Incorporated......E....... 785 628-3169
Hays *(G-2868)*
Malm Construction Co......F....... 785 227-3190
Lindsborg *(G-6402)*
Manhattan Trenching Inc......E....... 785 537-2330
Manhattan *(G-6728)*
Marlatt Construction Co Inc......F....... 913 367-3342
Atchison *(G-242)*
Mary Carr......E....... 913 207-0900
Kansas City *(G-4221)*
Max Jantz Excavating Inc......C....... 620 846-2634
Montezuma *(G-7158)*
Max Rieke & Brothers Inc......D....... 913 631-7111
Shawnee *(G-10991)*
McCullough Excavation Inc......E....... 316 634-2199
Wichita *(G-15025)*
Meadows Const Co Inc......E....... 913 369-3335
Tonganoxie *(G-12266)*
Midwest Concrete Materials Inc......C....... 785 776-8811
Manhattan *(G-6746)*
Miles Excavating Inc......C....... 913 724-1934
Basehor *(G-384)*
Muller Construction Inc......E....... 620 251-1110
Coffeyville *(G-964)*
Paronto Mall Construction Inc......F....... 785 632-2484
Clay Center *(G-875)*
Pearson Construction LLC......C....... 316 263-3100
Wichita *(G-15275)*
Pearson Excavating Inc......E....... 316 263-3100
Wichita *(G-15276)*
Prairie Landworks Inc......F....... 620 504-5049
Mcpherson *(G-7017)*
Prockish Trucking & Excavating......F....... 785 456-7320
Louisville *(G-6470)*
R D Johnson Excavating Co Inc......E....... 785 842-9100
Lawrence *(G-5085)*
R Puckett Farms Inc......F....... 620 378-3342
Fredonia *(G-2043)*
Rdr Excavating Inc......F....... 785 582-4645
Topeka *(G-13001)*
Rieke Grading Inc......F....... 913 441-2669
Shawnee Mission *(G-11804)*
Rippels Inc......F....... 620 674-1944
Scammon *(G-10797)*
RL Duncan Cnstr Co Inc......D....... 913 583-1160
De Soto *(G-1212)*
Ron Weers Construction Inc......E....... 913 681-5575
Bucyrus *(G-608)*
Sherwood Construction Co Inc......C....... 316 943-0211
Wichita *(G-15581)*
Stoppel Dirt Inc......E....... 620 675-2653
Sublette *(G-12208)*
Superior Excavating LLC......F....... 316 260-1829
Valley Center *(G-13355)*
Ted Row Inc......F....... 816 223-9666
Stilwell *(G-12176)*
Total Lease Service Inc......G....... 785 735-9520
Hays *(G-2920)*
Unruh Excavating LLC......F....... 620 345-3344
Moundridge *(G-7200)*
Vilela Rndy Auto Bdy Repr Pntg......F....... 620 231-6350
Pittsburg *(G-9957)*
W H Debrick Co Inc......F....... 913 294-3281
Paola *(G-9595)*

1795 Wrecking & Demolition Work

Automotive Associates......E....... 620 231-6350
Pittsburg *(G-9818)*
B-3 Construction Inc......F....... 620 479-2323
Columbus *(G-1060)*
Bradburn Wrecking Company......E....... 316 686-1959
Wichita *(G-13880)*
Cornejo & Sons LLC......C....... 316 522-5100
Wichita *(G-14101)*
Greg Bair Track Hoe Svc Inc......F....... 913 897-1243
Shawnee Mission *(G-11403)*
Gunter Construction Company......F....... 913 362-7844
Kansas City *(G-4059)*
Kaw Valley Companies Inc......C....... 913 281-9950
Kansas City *(G-4160)*
L Blixt Construction Inc......F....... 785 922-6180
Chapman *(G-780)*
Marlatt Construction Co Inc......F....... 913 367-3342
Atchison *(G-242)*
Mc Pherson Wrecking Inc......F....... 785 246-3012
Grantville *(G-2497)*
Pearson Construction LLC......C....... 316 263-3100
Wichita *(G-15275)*
Ricks Concrete Sawing Inc......F....... 785 862-5400
Topeka *(G-13016)*
Scott Heller Trucking......E....... 816 591-1638
Lenexa *(G-6119)*
Ted Row Inc......F....... 816 223-9666
Stilwell *(G-12176)*
Vilela Rndy Auto Bdy Repr Pntg......F....... 620 231-6350
Pittsburg *(G-9957)*

1796 Installation Or Erection Of Bldg Eqpt & Machinery, NEC

Adelphi Construction Lc......D....... 913 384-5511
Shawnee Mission *(G-11075)*
Alltite Inc......E....... 316 686-3010
Wichita *(G-13678)*
Beachner Grain Inc......F....... 620 244-3277
Erie *(G-1856)*
Bear Communications LLC......E....... 913 441-3355
Lenexa *(G-5693)*
Belger Cartage Service Inc......E....... 913 541-9100
Shawnee Mission *(G-11158)*
Bl Brooks & Sons Inc......G....... 913 829-5494
Olathe *(G-7553)*
Borton Lc......E....... 620 669-8211
South Hutchinson *(G-12057)*
Burns Boys Co Inc......F....... 913 788-8654
Kansas City *(G-3881)*
CDI Industrial Mech Contrs Inc......C....... 913 287-0334
Kansas City *(G-3898)*
Centurion Industries Inc......B....... 620 378-4401
Fredonia *(G-2028)*
Habco Inc......E....... 785 823-0440
Salina *(G-10528)*
Hall Industrial Services Inc......E....... 316 945-4255
Wichita *(G-14546)*
Jade Millwrights Inc......E....... 785 544-7771
Hiawatha *(G-3011)*
Jayhawk Millwright Erectors Inc......E....... 913 371-5212
Kansas City *(G-4120)*
Masthead International Inc......E....... 913 888-8600
Lenexa *(G-5989)*
Mid-America Millwright Svc Inc......E....... 620 275-6796
Garden City *(G-2232)*
Otis Elevator Company......F....... 316 682-6886
Bel Aire *(G-437)*
P1 Group Inc......B....... 913 529-5000
Lenexa *(G-6040)*

S
I
C

Performance Contg Intl Inc ....D 913 888-8600
Shawnee Mission *(G-11726)*
Pioneer Automation Technology ....F 316 322-0123
El Dorado *(G-1591)*
Senne and Company Inc ....E 785 235-1015
Topeka *(G-13058)*
Southwest and Associates Inc ....D 620 463-5631
Burrton *(G-650)*
Taylor Crane & Rigging Inc ....D 620 251-1530
Coffeyville *(G-981)*
Temp-Con Inc ....D 913 768-4888
Olathe *(G-8106)*
Thyssenkrupp Elevator Corp ....F 913 888-8046
Overland Park *(G-9408)*
Welco Services Inc ....E 620 241-3000
McPherson *(G-7041)*

1799 Special Trade Contractors, NEC

A L C Enterprises Inc ....F 316 943-6500
Wichita *(G-13587)*
Accurate Construction Inc ....F 620 275-0429
Garden City *(G-2097)*
Acm Removal LLC ....F 316 684-1800
Wichita *(G-13606)*
American Fence and SEC Co Inc ....G 316 945-5001
Wichita *(G-13691)*
American Fence Company LLC ....E 913 307-0306
Overland Park *(G-8376)*
Apac-Kansas Inc ....D 316 522-4881
Wichita *(G-13715)*
Apac-Kansas Inc ....D 316 524-5200
Wichita *(G-13716)*
Arg Contracting LLC ....F 913 441-1992
Lenexa *(G-5660)*
Arrowhead Contracting Inc ....D 913 814-9994
Lenexa *(G-5664)*
Associated Insulation Inc ....D 785 776-0145
Manhattan *(G-6548)*
B & R Insulation Inc ....E 913 492-1346
Shawnee Mission *(G-11139)*
Banks Swimming Pool Company ....E 913 897-9290
Overland Park *(G-8431)*
Belfor USA Group Inc ....E 316 260-4087
Park City *(G-9604)*
Brace Integrated Services Inc ....E 316 832-0292
Wichita *(G-13878)*
Browing Gayla ....E 620 343-2274
Emporia *(G-1709)*
Broyles Inc ....F 620 473-3835
Humboldt *(G-3182)*
C2i Inc ....E 620 259-6610
Hutchinson *(G-3227)*
CCM Countertop & Cab Mfg LLC ....F 316 554-0113
Wichita *(G-13967)*
Ceco Concrete Cnstr Del LLC ....F 913 362-1855
Olathe *(G-7581)*
Challenger Fence Co Inc ....F 913 432-3535
Shawnee Mission *(G-11215)*
Cleaning By Lamunyon Inc ....F 785 632-1259
Clay Center *(G-855)*
Cliffs Welding Shop Inc ....G 785 543-5895
Phillipsburg *(G-9780)*
Coffelt Sign Co Inc ....G 620 343-6411
Emporia *(G-1724)*
Continental Pools Inc ....F 913 856-2841
Gardner *(G-2334)*
Cunningham Sndblst Pntg Co Inc ....F 620 848-3030
Riverton *(G-10211)*
D & D Services Inc ....D 913 492-1346
Shawnee Mission *(G-11288)*
Damage Ctrl & Restoration Inc ....E 913 722-0228
Kansas City *(G-3954)*
Desco Coatings LLC ....D 913 782-3330
Olathe *(G-7650)*
Designplast Inc ....E 785 825-7714
Salina *(G-10475)*
Dimensional Stonework LLC ....F 913 851-9390
Shawnee Mission *(G-11307)*
Discount Siding Supply LP ....F 785 625-4619
Hays *(G-2788)*
Discovery Drilling Shop ....E 785 650-0029
Hays *(G-2790)*
Eagle Environmental Svcs LLC ....E 316 944-2445
Wichita *(G-14250)*
Earl Resse Welding ....G 620 624-6141
Liberal *(G-6306)*
Emerald Aerospace Holdings LLC ....D 316 440-6966
Wichita *(G-14274)*
Emerald Aerospace Services LLC ....E 316 644-4284
Wichita *(G-14275)*
Epoxy Coating Specialists Inc ....E 913 362-4141
Kansas City *(G-3993)*
Evologic LLC ....E 913 599-5292
Lenexa *(G-5839)*
F & H Abatement Services Inc ....C 316 264-2208
Kechi *(G-4567)*
Finch Sign Company Inc ....G 785 423-3213
Baldwin City *(G-360)*
Freestyle Sign Co Inc ....G 316 267-5507
Wichita *(G-14420)*
Givens Cleaning Contractors ....F 316 265-1315
Wichita *(G-14468)*
Gleason & Son Signs Inc ....G 785 823-8615
Salina *(G-10512)*
Granite Transformation Kans Cy ....F 913 492-7600
Lenexa *(G-5880)*
Granite Trnsfrmtion Wchita LLC ....F 316 681-1900
Bel Aire *(G-434)*
Green Meadows Lawn Landscaping ....F 316 788-0282
Derby *(G-1250)*
Hayden Tower Service Inc ....D 785 232-1840
Topeka *(G-12668)*
Hayward Baker Inc ....D 913 390-0085
Olathe *(G-7758)*
Hutchinson Theatre Guild ....F 620 662-9202
Hutchinson *(G-3326)*
Icg Inc ....E 913 461-8759
Leawood *(G-5433)*
Industrial Insulation Svcs Inc ....D 316 321-5358
El Dorado *(G-1570)*
Industrial Mfg & Repr Svc ....G 620 275-0481
Garden City *(G-2202)*
Insco Environmental Inc ....F 912 422-8001
Shawnee *(G-10974)*
Iwp LLC ....F 316 308-8507
Valley Center *(G-13345)*
Janssen Glass & Mirror Inc ....F 913 677-5727
Shawnee *(G-10977)*
JED Installation LLC ....E 913 724-4600
Basehor *(G-381)*
Jeffrey A Harris ....E 785 823-8760
Salina *(G-10553)*
K B Machine Shop Inc ....F 913 829-3100
Olathe *(G-7822)*
KC Coring & Cutng Cnstr Inc ....F 316 832-1580
Wichita *(G-14837)*
▲ **Kc Granite & Cabinetry LLC** ....E 913 888-0003
Lenexa *(G-5941)*
Kdoll Koatings Inc ....G 620 456-2588
Conway Springs *(G-1142)*
Kiewit Power Nuclear Co ....F 913 928-7800
Lenexa *(G-5952)*
Koehn Painting Co LLC ....E 316 283-9612
Newton *(G-7373)*
Lamunyon Clg & Restoration ....F 785 632-1259
Clay Center *(G-870)*
Leons Welding & Fabrication ....F 785 625-5736
Hays *(G-2863)*
Luminous Neon Inc ....G 785 842-4930
Lawrence *(G-5002)*
Luminous Neon Inc ....G 785 823-1789
Salina *(G-10586)*
Luminous Neon Inc ....E 913 780-3330
Olathe *(G-7867)*
M C M Restoration Company Inc ....E 620 223-6602
Fort Scott *(G-1982)*
Manko Window Systems Inc ....F 785 238-3188
Junction City *(G-3724)*
▲ **Manko Window Systems Inc** ....B 785 776-9643
Manhattan *(G-6730)*
Mann Fence Company Inc ....F 913 782-2332
Olathe *(G-7872)*
Marlatt Construction Co Inc ....F 913 367-3342
Atchison *(G-242)*
Martin Welding ....G 620 545-7311
Clearwater *(G-894)*
Mc Janitorial LLC ....F 913 780-0731
Olathe *(G-7879)*
McKee Pool & Landscaping Inc ....F 785 843-9119
Lawrence *(G-5018)*
Merit General Contractors ....F 913 747-7400
Olathe *(G-7883)*
Michael Downey ....F 316 540-6166
Maize *(G-6517)*
Midland Restoration Company ....F 620 223-6855
Fort Scott *(G-1991)*
Midwest Tinting Inc ....F 913 384-2665
Overland Park *(G-9036)*
Miller Welding Inc ....F 785 454-3425
Downs *(G-1472)*
Mm Property MGT & Rmdlg LLC ....F 913 871-6867
Kansas City *(G-4265)*
Multi Systems Installation Inc ....D 913 422-8282
Shawnee Mission *(G-11658)*
National Park Service ....F 620 285-6911
Larned *(G-4708)*
Noonshine Window Cleaning Svc ....F 913 381-9666
Shawnee Mission *(G-11687)*
Noonshine Window Cleaning Svc ....F 913 381-3780
Overland Park *(G-9092)*
O I C Inc ....E 816 471-5400
Hesston *(G-2998)*
Panel Systems Plus Inc ....E 913 321-0111
Kansas City *(G-4309)*
Performance Abatement Svcs Inc ....D 913 888-8600
Lenexa *(G-6050)*
Phoenix Restoration Service ....E 620 276-6994
Garden City *(G-2254)*
Phoenix Rnvtion Rstoration Inc ....E 913 599-0055
Stilwell *(G-12171)*
Pihl Repair & Fabrication LLC ....G 785 668-2014
Falun *(G-1928)*
Pishny Real Estate Services ....F 913 227-0251
Lenexa *(G-6059)*
Platinum Contracting LLC ....F 913 210-2003
Shawnee Mission *(G-11737)*
Pool & Patio Supply Inc ....F 913 888-2226
Shawnee Mission *(G-11744)*
Pools Plus ....F 785 823-7665
Salina *(G-10636)*
Preferred Contg Systems Co ....F 913 341-0111
Leawood *(G-5525)*
Premier Tillage Inc ....E 785 754-2381
Quinter *(G-10184)*
Pro Carwash Systems Inc ....F 316 788-9933
Derby *(G-1266)*
Pro-Kleen Inc ....E 316 775-6898
Augusta *(G-339)*
Pro-Kleen Inc ....F 316 253-7556
Augusta *(G-340)*
Professional Service Inds Inc ....E 913 310-1600
Kansas City *(G-4343)*
Professnal Wtrprfing Insul LLC ....F 316 264-3101
Wichita *(G-15367)*
Progressive Contractors Inc ....D 785 235-3032
Topeka *(G-12991)*
Quality Granite & Marble Inc ....E 316 946-0530
Wichita *(G-15383)*
R & T Specialty Cnstr Lc ....G 316 942-8141
Wichita *(G-15401)*
R L C Inc ....F 913 352-8744
Pleasanton *(G-10001)*
Rdr Excavating Inc ....F 785 582-4645
Topeka *(G-13001)*
Remediation Contractors Inc ....F 316 269-1549
Wichita *(G-15442)*
Remediation Services Inc ....E 800 335-1201
Independence *(G-3553)*
Repairs Unlimited Inc ....F 913 262-6937
Kansas City *(G-4370)*
Resource Service Solutions LLC ....E 913 338-5050
Lenexa *(G-6107)*
Restortion Wtr Proofing Contrs ....E 913 321-6226
Kansas City *(G-4373)*
Restortion Wtrprfing Cntrs Inc ....E 316 942-6602
Wichita *(G-15452)*
Restortion Wtrprfing Cntrs Inc ....F 785 478-9538
Topeka *(G-13011)*
Rhino Builders Inc ....F 913 722-4353
Kansas City *(G-4376)*
Rice Precision Mfg Inc ....E 785 594-2670
Baldwin City *(G-367)*
Rigdon Inc ....F 913 322-9274
Overland Park *(G-9242)*
Rob Carrolls Sndblst & Pntg ....E 620 442-1361
Arkansas City *(G-175)*
Schellers Inc ....F 620 342-3990
Emporia *(G-1824)*
Specialty Fabrication Inc ....F 316 264-0603
Wichita *(G-15636)*
Spectrum Construction Co ....F 785 232-3407
Topeka *(G-13088)*
Star Signs LLC ....E 785 842-4892
Lawrence *(G-5119)*
Stoner Door & Dock Corporation ....F 785 478-3074
Topeka *(G-13101)*
Stovers Restoration Inc ....F 316 686-5005
Maize *(G-6521)*
▲ **Suhor Industries Inc** ....A 620 421-4434
Overland Park *(G-9371)*

Summer Snow LLC...E....... 785 706-1003
Manhattan *(G-6816)*
Superior Pools...F....... 316 838-4968
Wichita *(G-15697)*
Surface Solutions Intl Inc...E....... 913 742-7744
Overland Park *(G-9378)*
Tom Burge Fence & Iron Inc...E....... 913 681-7600
Shawnee Mission *(G-11933)*
Total Installation Management...F....... 316 267-0584
Bel Aire *(G-441)*
Tractor Supply Company...F....... 620 663-7607
Hutchinson *(G-3465)*
Unique Design Inc...F....... 785 272-6044
Topeka *(G-13205)*
Utility Contractors Inc...E....... 316 942-1253
Wichita *(G-15866)*
Valley Moving Company LLC...F....... 785 456-2400
Wamego *(G-13445)*
Versasport of Kansas Inc...E....... 316 393-0487
Wichita *(G-15876)*
Western Kansas and Supply...F....... 620 792-4731
Great Bend *(G-2661)*
Wichita Fence Co Inc...F....... 316 838-1342
Park City *(G-9654)*
Wildcat Gttering Exteriors Inc...F....... 785 485-2194
Manhattan *(G-6855)*
Wilkerson Crane Rental Inc...E....... 913 238-7030
Lenexa *(G-6230)*
Window Design Company...G....... 785 582-2888
Silver Lake *(G-12030)*

20 FOOD AND KINDRED PRODUCTS

2011 Meat Packing Plants

APC Inc...E....... 620 675-8691
Sublette *(G-12197)*
B&B Quality Meats LLC...G....... 620 285-8988
Larned *(G-4694)*
Browns Processing...G....... 620 378-2441
Fredonia *(G-2027)*
Cargill Incorporated...E....... 785 743-2288
WA Keeney *(G-13382)*
Cargill Incorporated...F....... 316 291-1939
Wichita *(G-13947)*
Cargill Meat Solutions Corp...E....... 620 225-2610
Dodge City *(G-1317)*
Cargill Mt Lgstics Sltions Inc...F....... 620 225-2610
Dodge City *(G-1318)*
◆ **Creekstone Farm Prem**...A....... 620 741-3100
Arkansas City *(G-152)*
Diecks Inc...E....... 785 632-5550
Clay Center *(G-860)*
Dold Foods LLC...C....... 316 838-9101
Wichita *(G-14221)*
Duis Meat Processing Inc...F....... 785 243-7850
Concordia *(G-1109)*
Ehresman Packing Co...F....... 620 276-3791
Garden City *(G-2152)*
Elkhorn Valley Packing...E....... 620 326-3443
Wellington *(G-13498)*
Elkhorn Valley Packing Co...D....... 620 896-2300
Harper *(G-2721)*
Empirical Technology Inc...C....... 620 277-2753
Holcomb *(G-3074)*
Farview Farms Meat Co...G....... 785 246-1154
Topeka *(G-12597)*
Indian Hills Meat and Plty Inc...E....... 316 264-1644
Wichita *(G-14683)*
Jacksons Frozen Food Center...G....... 620 662-4465
Hutchinson *(G-3339)*
Kensington Lockers Inc...F....... 785 476-2834
Kensington *(G-4577)*
Kiowa Locker System LLC...F....... 620 825-4538
Kiowa *(G-4626)*
Kirby Meat Co Inc...G....... 620 225-0031
Dodge City *(G-1392)*
Moran Meat Locker...G....... 620 237-4331
Moran *(G-7163)*
National Beef Packing Co LLC...F....... 800 449-2333
Liberal *(G-6348)*
National Beef Packing Co LLC...C....... 620 624-1851
Liberal *(G-6349)*
National Beef Packing Co LLC...D....... 620 227-7135
Dodge City *(G-1410)*
Nordic Foods Inc...D....... 913 281-1167
Kansas City *(G-4289)*
Olpe Locker...G....... 620 475-3375
Emporia *(G-1809)*
OSI...G....... 316 688-5011
Wichita *(G-15239)*
Plankenhorn Inc...F....... 620 276-3791
Garden City *(G-2256)*
S&S Quality Meats LLC...D....... 620 342-6354
Emporia *(G-1818)*
Seaboard Corporation...C....... 913 676-8800
Merriam *(G-7103)*
Seaboard Foods LLC...G....... 620 593-4353
Rolla *(G-10233)*
◆ **Seaboard Foods LLC**...D....... 913 261-2600
Shawnee Mission *(G-11842)*
Smithfield Foods Inc...F....... 785 762-3306
Junction City *(G-3756)*
Smokey Hill Meat Processing...G....... 785 735-2278
Victoria *(G-13377)*
Stroot Locker Inc...G....... 316 777-4421
Mulvane *(G-7227)*
Sugar Creek Packing Co...C....... 620 232-2700
Frontenac *(G-2064)*
Tyson Fresh Meats Inc...D....... 620 277-2614
Holcomb *(G-3082)*
Tyson Fresh Meats Inc...G....... 620 343-3640
Emporia *(G-1843)*
Waggoner Enterprises Inc...E....... 620 465-3807
Yoder *(G-16196)*
Walnut Valley Packing LLC...G....... 866 421-3595
El Dorado *(G-1613)*
Winchester Meat Processing...G....... 913 774-2860
Winchester *(G-16111)*

2013 Sausages & Meat Prdts

Alma Foods LLC...F....... 785 765-3396
Alma *(G-61)*
Cargill Mt Lgstics Sltions Inc...F....... 620 225-2610
Dodge City *(G-1318)*
Diecks Inc...E....... 785 632-5550
Clay Center *(G-860)*
Dold Foods LLC...C....... 316 838-9101
Wichita *(G-14221)*
Empirical Technology Inc...C....... 620 277-2753
Holcomb *(G-3074)*
Fritzs Mt Superior Sausage LLC...G....... 913 381-4618
Shawnee Mission *(G-11383)*
Grinnell Locker Plant Inc...F....... 785 824-3400
Grinnell *(G-2693)*
Hams Pool Service LLC...G....... 913 927-0882
Overland Park *(G-8789)*
Indian Hills Meat and Plty Inc...E....... 316 264-1644
Wichita *(G-14683)*
Jacksons Frozen Food Center...G....... 620 662-4465
Hutchinson *(G-3339)*
Johnsonville LLC...C....... 785 364-3126
Holton *(G-3102)*
Kiowa Locker System LLC...F....... 620 825-4538
Kiowa *(G-4626)*
Luthers Smokehouse Inc...G....... 620 964-2222
Le Roy *(G-5197)*
National Beef Packing Co LLC...D....... 620 227-7135
Dodge City *(G-1410)*
Nordic Foods Inc...D....... 913 281-1167
Kansas City *(G-4289)*
Plankenhorn Inc...F....... 620 276-3791
Garden City *(G-2256)*
S&S Quality Meats LLC...D....... 620 342-6354
Emporia *(G-1818)*
Smithfield Packaged Meats Corp...A....... 316 942-8461
Wichita *(G-15610)*
Sugar Creek Packing Co...C....... 620 232-2700
Frontenac *(G-2064)*
Tyson Foods Inc...B....... 620 663-6141
South Hutchinson *(G-12067)*
Tyson Fresh Meats Inc...D....... 620 277-2614
Holcomb *(G-3082)*
Waggoner Enterprises Inc...E....... 620 465-3807
Yoder *(G-16196)*
Winchester Meat Processing...G....... 913 774-2860
Winchester *(G-16111)*

2015 Poultry Slaughtering, Dressing & Processing

Cal-Maine Foods Inc...D....... 620 938-2300
Chase *(G-782)*
Cargill Incorporated...E....... 785 743-2288
WA Keeney *(G-13382)*
Cargill Incorporated...F....... 316 291-1939
Wichita *(G-13947)*
Hitchin Post Steak Co...D....... 913 647-0543
Olathe *(G-7770)*
Hybrid Turkeys LLC...G....... 620 951-4705
Newton *(G-7365)*
Indian Hills Meat and Plty Inc...E....... 316 264-1644
Wichita *(G-14683)*
National Beef Packing Co LLC...C....... 620 624-1851
Liberal *(G-6349)*
Pilgrims Pride Corporation...E....... 620 597-2820
Columbus *(G-1085)*
Simmons Prepared Foods Inc...C....... 479 524-8151
Emporia *(G-1829)*
Tyson Foods Inc...C....... 620 669-8761
Hutchinson *(G-3471)*
Tyson Foods Inc...E....... 620 343-3640
Emporia *(G-1842)*

2021 Butter

▼ **Dairy Farmers America Inc**...B....... 816 801-6455
Kansas City *(G-3953)*

2022 Cheese

▼ **Dairy Farmers America Inc**...B....... 816 801-6455
Kansas City *(G-3953)*
Elderslie LLC...F....... 316 680-2637
Valley Center *(G-13341)*

2023 Milk, Condensed & Evaporated

Ancient Formulas Inc...F....... 316 838-5600
Wichita *(G-13702)*
Cardiotabs Inc...G....... 816 753-4298
Overland Park *(G-8514)*
◆ **Corbion America Holdings Inc**...D....... 913 890-5500
Lenexa *(G-5787)*
▼ **Dairy Farmers America Inc**...B....... 816 801-6455
Kansas City *(G-3953)*
Hiland Dairy Foods Company LLC...C....... 316 267-4221
Wichita *(G-14608)*
Kerry Inc...C....... 913 780-1212
New Century *(G-7290)*

2024 Ice Cream

Braumss...G....... 620 340-8169
Emporia *(G-1707)*
Culvers Frozen Custard...E....... 913 402-9777
Overland Park *(G-8623)*
▼ **Dairy Farmers America Inc**...B....... 816 801-6455
Kansas City *(G-3953)*
◆ **Kan Pak LLC**...D....... 620 442-6820
Wichita *(G-14782)*
Paleteria Tarahumara...G....... 620 805-6509
Garden City *(G-2245)*
Peachwave...G....... 620 624-2045
Liberal *(G-6356)*
Twisted Cow LLC...G....... 316 804-4949
Newton *(G-7422)*

2026 Milk

▼ **Dairy Farmers America Inc**...B....... 816 801-6455
Kansas City *(G-3953)*
Hiland Dairy Foods Company LLC...C....... 316 267-4221
Wichita *(G-14608)*
Kerry Inc...C....... 913 780-1212
New Century *(G-7290)*
Southern Foods Group LLC...G....... 316 264-5011
Wichita *(G-15623)*

2032 Canned Specialties

E-Z Salsa Inc...G....... 620 521-9097
Garden City *(G-2150)*
La Superior Food Products Inc...E....... 913 362-6611
Shawnee Mission *(G-11544)*
Mama Socorros...G....... 913 541-1074
Overland Park *(G-8982)*
Pedro Lopez Co Inc...F....... 785 220-1509
Lebo *(G-5608)*
Resers Fine Foods Inc...B....... 785 233-6431
Topeka *(G-13009)*
Spanish Gardens Food Mfg Co...F....... 913 831-4242
Kansas City *(G-4430)*

2033 Canned Fruits, Vegetables & Preserves

Eastside Mkt Westside Mkt LLC...G....... 785 532-8686
Manhattan *(G-6619)*
Grandma Hoerners Foods Inc...E....... 785 765-2300
Alma *(G-63)*
Smart Beverage Inc...F....... 785 656-2166
Olathe *(G-8068)*
Spicin Foods Inc...D....... 913 432-5228
Kansas City *(G-4435)*
Tropicana Products Inc...D....... 316 838-1000
Wichita *(G-15806)*

S I C

Wyldewood Cellars Inc..........F....... 316 554-9463
Peck *(G-9764)*

2034 Dried Fruits, Vegetables & Soup

General Financial Services Inc..........G....... 316 636-1070
Wichita *(G-14456)*
Good Life Snacks Inc..........G....... 913 220-2117
Lenexa *(G-5878)*
Pines International Inc..........E....... 800 697-4637
Lawrence *(G-5065)*
Rabbit Creek Products Inc..........F....... 913 837-3073
Louisburg *(G-6463)*

2035 Pickled Fruits, Vegetables, Sauces & Dressings

◆ **Gourmet Specialties Inc**..........D....... 913 432-5228
Kansas City *(G-4041)*
Grannies Homemade Mustard..........G....... 620 947-3259
Newton *(G-7351)*
▲ **Old World Spices Seasoning Inc**..........E....... 816 861-0400
Overland Park *(G-9098)*
Resers Fine Foods Inc..........B....... 785 233-6431
Topeka *(G-13009)*
▲ **Williams Foods Inc**..........C....... 913 888-4343
Lenexa *(G-6231)*

2038 Frozen Specialties

Custom Foods Inc..........E....... 913 585-1900
De Soto *(G-1198)*
Dew - Drink Eat Well LLC..........E....... 785 856-3399
Lawrence *(G-4834)*
Kan Pak International Inc..........E....... 316 201-4210
Wichita *(G-14783)*
Sfc Global Supply Chain Inc..........B....... 785 825-1671
Salina *(G-10705)*

2041 Flour, Grain Milling

ADM Milling Co..........D....... 620 442-6200
Arkansas City *(G-139)*
ADM Milling Co..........E....... 620 442-5500
Arkansas City *(G-140)*
ADM Milling Co..........E....... 620 227-8101
Dodge City *(G-1289)*
ADM Milling Co..........D....... 913 491-9400
Overland Park *(G-8348)*
ADM Milling Co..........D....... 785 825-1541
Salina *(G-10395)*
ADM Milling Co..........E....... 785 263-1631
Abilene *(G-11)*
Archer-Daniels-Midland Company..........D....... 785 825-1541
Salina *(G-10407)*
Archer-Daniels-Midland Company..........G....... 620 375-4811
Leoti *(G-6250)*
Archer-Daniels-Midland Company..........F....... 620 872-2174
Scott City *(G-10804)*
Archer-Daniels-Midland Company..........E....... 785 820-8019
Salina *(G-10408)*
Archer-Daniels-Midland Company..........G....... 913 321-1696
Kansas City *(G-3817)*
Archer-Daniels-Midland Company..........G....... 620 357-8733
Jetmore *(G-3645)*
Archer-Daniels-Midland Company..........G....... 620 675-2226
Sublette *(G-12198)*
Archer-Daniels-Midland Company..........F....... 620 657-3411
Satanta *(G-10776)*
Archer-Daniels-Midland Company..........E....... 913 491-9400
Overland Park *(G-8394)*
Archer-Daniels-Midland Company..........E....... 620 663-7957
Hutchinson *(G-3204)*
Archer-Daniels-Midland Company..........F....... 620 663-7278
Hutchinson *(G-3205)*
Archer-Daniels-Midland Company..........F....... 785 671-3171
Oakley *(G-7471)*
Archer-Daniels-Midland Company..........G....... 785 694-2286
Brewster *(G-582)*
Archer-Daniels-Midland Company..........G....... 785 820-8831
New Cambria *(G-7269)*
Archer-Daniels-Midland Company..........G....... 785 737-4135
Palco *(G-9537)*
Archer-Daniels-Midland Company..........E....... 785 899-3700
Goodland *(G-2462)*
Archer-Daniels-Midland Company..........E....... 785 263-2260
Abilene *(G-13)*
Bartlett Milling Company LP..........E....... 620 251-4650
Coffeyville *(G-910)*
CHS Inc..........D....... 620 241-4247
McPherson *(G-6948)*
◆ **Corbion America Holdings Inc**..........D....... 913 890-5500
Lenexa *(G-5787)*
Custom Foods Inc..........E....... 913 585-1900
De Soto *(G-1198)*
Fairview Mills LLC..........F....... 785 336-2148
Elwood *(G-1687)*
Farmer Direct Foods Inc..........F....... 785 823-8787
New Cambria *(G-7270)*
Farmers Union Coop Assn..........F....... 785 632-5632
Clay Center *(G-863)*
Grain Craft Inc..........B....... 913 890-6300
Leawood *(G-5417)*
Grain Craft Inc..........E....... 913 262-1779
Kansas City *(G-4044)*
Grain Craft Inc..........E....... 620 241-2410
McPherson *(G-6970)*
Heartland Mill Inc..........E....... 620 379-4472
Modoc *(G-7153)*
Long Island Grain Co Inc..........F....... 785 854-7431
Long Island *(G-6428)*
◆ **McShares Inc**..........E....... 785 825-2181
Salina *(G-10597)*
Mgp Ingredients Inc..........F....... 913 367-1480
Atchison *(G-246)*
◆ **Mgp Ingredients Inc**..........C....... 913 367-1480
Atchison *(G-245)*
◆ **Mgpi Processing Inc**..........E....... 913 367-1480
Atchison *(G-247)*
Morrill Hay Company Inc..........F....... 620 285-6941
Paola *(G-9576)*
Purina Mills LLC..........E....... 316 265-0624
Wichita *(G-15379)*
Stafford County Flour Mills Co..........E....... 620 458-4121
Hudson *(G-3146)*
Stafford County Flour Mills Co..........F....... 620 486-2493
Sylvia *(G-12221)*

2043 Cereal Breakfast Foods

Inclusion Technologies LLC..........F....... 913 370-8070
Atchison *(G-236)*

2045 Flour, Blended & Prepared

Kansas Maid Inc..........G....... 620 437-2958
Madison *(G-6502)*
Pantry Shelf Company..........G....... 620 662-9342
Hutchinson *(G-3400)*

2046 Wet Corn Milling

ADM Grain River System Inc..........F....... 913 788-7226
Kansas City *(G-3785)*
Cargill Incorporated..........F....... 316 291-1939
Wichita *(G-13947)*
Cargill Incorporated..........E....... 785 743-2288
WA Keeney *(G-13382)*
Chemstar Products Company..........E....... 620 241-2611
McPherson *(G-6947)*
Sergeants Pet Care Pdts Inc..........G....... 913 627-1245
Kansas City *(G-4417)*

2047 Dog & Cat Food

Ainsworth Pet Nutrition LLC..........C....... 620 231-7779
Frontenac *(G-2051)*
Big Heart Pet Brands..........C....... 785 312-3662
Lawrence *(G-4757)*
Big Heart Pet Brands..........C....... 785 338-9240
Topeka *(G-12380)*
Cargill Incorporated..........E....... 913 299-2326
Kansas City *(G-3890)*
Darling Ingredients Inc..........E....... 620 276-7618
Garden City *(G-2142)*
Darling Ingredients Inc..........D....... 316 264-6951
Wichita *(G-14169)*
Emporia Pet Products Inc..........E....... 620 342-1650
Emporia *(G-1741)*
Hills Pet Nutrition Inc..........C....... 785 231-2812
Topeka *(G-12691)*
◆ **Hills Pet Nutrition Inc**..........B....... 800 255-0449
Topeka *(G-12690)*
Simmons Pet Food Inc..........C....... 620 342-1323
Emporia *(G-1828)*
▲ **Treatco Inc**..........D....... 316 265-7900
Wichita *(G-15795)*
Ziwi USA Incorporated..........F....... 913 291-0189
Overland Park *(G-9529)*

2048 Prepared Feeds For Animals & Fowls

Alfalfa Inc..........G....... 620 675-8686
Sublette *(G-12196)*
Alternative Building Tech..........F....... 913 856-4536
Gardner *(G-2325)*
APC Inc..........E....... 620 675-8691
Sublette *(G-12197)*
Archer-Daniels-Midland Company..........E....... 785 263-2260
Abilene *(G-12)*
Ashland Feed & Seed Co..........G....... 620 635-2856
Ashland *(G-193)*
Becker Alfalfa..........G....... 620 275-5567
Garden City *(G-2106)*
Bern Meat Plant Incorporated..........F....... 785 336-2165
Bern *(G-521)*
Bert & Wetta Larned Inc..........E....... 620 285-7777
Larned *(G-4695)*
▼ **Bert and Wetta Sales Inc**..........E....... 620 285-7777
Larned *(G-4696)*
Bert and Wetta Sales Inc..........E....... 785 263-2258
Abilene *(G-14)*
▲ **Blair Milling & Elev Co Inc**..........E....... 913 367-2310
Atchison *(G-216)*
Cargill Incorporated..........F....... 620 241-5120
McPherson *(G-6940)*
Cargill Incorporated..........E....... 620 277-2558
Garden City *(G-2121)*
Cargill Incorporated..........F....... 316 291-1939
Wichita *(G-13947)*
Ceva Animal Health LLC..........D....... 800 999-0297
Lenexa *(G-5744)*
Ceva USA Inc..........E....... 800 999-0297
Lenexa *(G-5748)*
▲ **Cross Brand Feed & Alfalfa Inc**..........E....... 620 324-5571
Lewis *(G-6266)*
Cross Brand Office Inc..........E....... 620 324-5571
Lewis *(G-6267)*
Darling Ingredients Inc..........D....... 316 264-6951
Wichita *(G-14169)*
Elite Endeavors LLC..........F....... 620 391-1577
Plains *(G-9974)*
Elnicki Inc..........F....... 620 232-5800
Pittsburg *(G-9857)*
Fairleigh Ranch Corporation..........F....... 620 872-2111
Scott City *(G-10810)*
Feedex Companies LLC..........F....... 620 500-5016
Hutchinson *(G-3284)*
Harvest Fuel Inc..........G....... 785 486-2626
Horton *(G-3127)*
HI Plains Feed LLC..........G....... 620 277-2886
Garden City *(G-2196)*
Hills Pet Nutrition Inc..........D....... 620 340-6920
Emporia *(G-1772)*
◆ **Hills Pet Nutrition Inc**..........B....... 800 255-0449
Topeka *(G-12690)*
Hills Pet Nutrition Inc..........C....... 785 231-2812
Topeka *(G-12691)*
Hills Pet Nutrition Inc..........C....... 785 286-1451
Topeka *(G-12692)*
Jak 3 Inc..........G....... 785 336-2148
Seneca *(G-10870)*
Kansas Feeds Inc..........F....... 620 225-3500
Dodge City *(G-1385)*
Manna Pro Products LLC..........E....... 913 621-2355
Kansas City *(G-4216)*
Micro-Lite LLc..........F....... 620 537-7025
Buffalo *(G-613)*
Mid-South Milling Company Inc..........E....... 913 621-5442
Kansas City *(G-4246)*
Midwest PMS LLC..........E....... 620 872-2189
Scott City *(G-10824)*
Midwest PMS LLC..........G....... 620 276-0970
Garden City *(G-2235)*
Natures Way Inc..........G....... 785 486-3302
Horton *(G-3132)*
Performix High Plains LLC..........E....... 620 225-0080
Garden City *(G-2250)*
Performix Nutrition Systems..........E....... 620 277-2886
Garden City *(G-2251)*
Provimi North America Inc..........E....... 620 327-2280
Hesston *(G-2999)*
Purina Animal Nutrition LLC..........E....... 316 265-0624
Wichita *(G-15378)*
Purina Mills LLC..........E....... 316 265-0624
Wichita *(G-15379)*
Quality Milling LLC..........F....... 620 724-4900
Girard *(G-2416)*
R W Milling Company Inc..........G....... 785 456-7866
Wamego *(G-13437)*
Ranch-Aid Inc..........F....... 620 583-5585
Eureka *(G-1898)*
Reeve Agri-Energy Inc..........F....... 620 275-7541
Garden City *(G-2264)*
Ridley USA Inc..........E....... 620 231-6700
Pittsburg *(G-9929)*

Ridley USA Inc ....E.... 785 738-2215
Beloit *(G-500)*
Stockade Brands Incorporated ....E.... 620 231-6700
Pittsburg *(G-9941)*
Suther Feeds Inc ....F.... 785 292-4414
Frankfort *(G-2023)*
Western Feed Mills Inc ....E.... 620 758-2283
Cedar Vale *(G-695)*
Woods Alfalfa ....G.... 620 376-4999
Tribune *(G-13272)*
X F Enterprises Inc ....F.... 620 672-5616
Pratt *(G-10164)*

2051 Bread, Bakery Prdts Exc Cookies & Crackers

B Four Corp ....C.... 913 648-1441
Prairie Village *(G-10012)*
B Four Corp ....C.... 913 432-1107
Shawnee Mission *(G-11140)*
Bagatelle Inc ....E.... 316 684-5662
Wichita *(G-13793)*
Bakery Projects Inc ....G.... 316 831-9434
Wichita *(G-13796)*
Bernices Foods Inc ....G.... 913 334-8283
Olathe *(G-7550)*
▲ **Best Harvest LLC** ....D.... 913 287-6300
Kansas City *(G-3856)*
Bimbo Bakeries Usa Inc ....G.... 913 328-1234
Kansas City *(G-3862)*
Bimbo Bakeries Usa Inc ....C.... 620 218-2365
Wichita *(G-13849)*
Bimbo Bakeries Usa Inc ....G.... 620 276-6308
Garden City *(G-2111)*
Bobs Super Saver Inc ....D.... 620 251-6820
Coffeyville *(G-913)*
◆ **Cereal Ingredients Inc** ....D.... 913 727-3434
Leavenworth *(G-5217)*
Dillon Companies Inc ....C.... 620 663-4464
Hutchinson *(G-3263)*
Dillon Companies Inc ....C.... 785 272-0661
Topeka *(G-12557)*
Dillon Companies Inc ....D.... 785 823-9403
Salina *(G-10478)*
Donut X-Press ....G.... 620 544-4700
Hugoton *(G-3160)*
▲ **Drubers Donut Shop** ....G.... 316 283-1206
Newton *(G-7338)*
Flowers Baking Co Lenexa LLC ....C.... 913 564-1100
Lenexa *(G-5858)*
Golden Boy Pies Inc ....E.... 913 384-6460
Overland Park *(G-8763)*
Hostess Brands LLC ....G.... 620 342-6811
Emporia *(G-1776)*
Johnny Schwindt Inc ....G.... 620 275-0633
Garden City *(G-2209)*
Kansas Maid Inc ....G.... 620 437-2958
Madison *(G-6502)*
Keebler Company ....D.... 913 342-2300
Kansas City *(G-4168)*
Las Tarascas ....G.... 316 941-5511
Wichita *(G-14929)*
M & K Daylight Donuts ....G.... 913 495-2529
Shawnee Mission *(G-11588)*
Queen-Morris Ventures LLC ....C.... 913 383-2563
Shawnee Mission *(G-11765)*
Sara Lee Corp ....G.... 913 233-3200
Kansas City *(G-4401)*
Strawberry Hill Povitica Inc ....G.... 800 631-1002
Merriam *(G-7107)*
Walmart Inc ....B.... 316 636-5384
Wichita *(G-15924)*
▲ **Williams Foods Inc** ....C.... 913 888-4343
Lenexa *(G-6231)*

2052 Cookies & Crackers

Bagatelle Inc ....E.... 316 684-5662
Wichita *(G-13793)*
Dots Pretzels LLC ....D.... 913 274-1705
Lenexa *(G-5823)*
Keebler Company ....D.... 913 342-2300
Kansas City *(G-4168)*

2053 Frozen Bakery Prdts

Custom Foods Inc ....E.... 913 585-1900
De Soto *(G-1198)*
Kansas Maid Inc ....G.... 620 437-2958
Madison *(G-6502)*
Sugar Rush Inc ....G.... 913 839-2158
Olathe *(G-8087)*

2064 Candy & Confectionery Prdts

◆ **Cereal Ingredients Inc** ....D.... 913 727-3434
Leavenworth *(G-5217)*
Mars Chocolate North Amer LLC ....G.... 785 861-1800
Topeka *(G-12861)*
Sunflower Hills Inc ....F.... 913 894-2233
Lenexa *(G-6158)*

2066 Chocolate & Cocoa Prdts

Chocolate Specialty Corp ....D.... 816 941-3088
Stilwell *(G-12140)*
Kerry Inc ....C.... 913 780-1212
New Century *(G-7290)*
Mars Chocolate North Amer LLC ....G.... 785 861-1800
Topeka *(G-12861)*
Russell Stover Chocolates LLC ....E.... 785 263-0463
Abilene *(G-52)*

2068 Salted & Roasted Nuts & Seeds

Red River Commodities Inc ....E.... 785 462-3911
Colby *(G-1035)*

2075 Soybean Oil Mills

Archer-Daniels-Midland Company ....C.... 913 782-8800
Olathe *(G-7532)*
Cargill Incorporated ....D.... 316 292-2719
Wichita *(G-13948)*
Cargill Incorporated ....D.... 316 292-2380
Wichita *(G-13946)*
Cargill Incorporated ....F.... 316 291-1939
Wichita *(G-13947)*
Cargill Incorporated ....E.... 785 743-2288
WA Keeney *(G-13382)*
CHS Inc ....D.... 620 241-4247
McPherson *(G-6948)*

2076 Vegetable Oil Mills

Cargill Incorporated ....E.... 620 663-4401
Hutchinson *(G-3230)*

2077 Animal, Marine Fats & Oils

Central Kansas Rendering Inc ....G.... 620 792-2059
Great Bend *(G-2532)*
Darling Ingredients Inc ....E.... 913 321-9328
Kansas City *(G-3956)*
Darling Ingredients Inc ....D.... 316 264-6951
Wichita *(G-14169)*
Darling Ingredients Inc ....G.... 913 371-7083
Kansas City *(G-3957)*
Darling Ingredients Inc ....E.... 620 276-7618
Garden City *(G-2142)*
Darling Ingredients Inc ....F.... 785 336-2535
Seneca *(G-10864)*

2079 Shortening, Oils & Margarine

Cargill Incorporated ....D.... 316 292-2380
Wichita *(G-13946)*
Kerry Inc ....C.... 913 780-1212
New Century *(G-7290)*
Sauer Brands Inc ....C.... 913 324-3700
New Century *(G-7297)*
▲ **Sunflower Vegetable Oil Inc** ....G.... 913 541-8882
Lenexa *(G-6159)*

2082 Malt Beverages

Bishop Brew ....G.... 785 242-8920
Ottawa *(G-8249)*
Brew Lab ....G.... 913 400-2343
Overland Park *(G-8484)*
Dodge City Brewing Co LLC ....G.... 620 338-7247
Dodge City *(G-1342)*
Free State Brewing Co Inc ....D.... 785 843-4555
Lawrence *(G-4865)*
Granite City Food & Brewry Ltd ....D.... 913 334-2255
Kansas City *(G-4045)*
Little Apple Brewing Company ....C.... 785 539-5500
Manhattan *(G-6714)*
River City Brewery Inc ....D.... 316 263-2739
Wichita *(G-15469)*
Tallgrass Brewing Company ....E.... 785 537-1131
Manhattan *(G-6821)*

2084 Wine & Brandy

Ad Astra Selections LLC ....G.... 913 307-0272
Lenexa *(G-5627)*
Bluejcket Crssing Vnyrd Winery ....G.... 785 542-1764
Eudora *(G-1871)*
Emporia Winery LLC ....G.... 620 481-7129
Emporia *(G-1748)*
Glaciers Edge Winery & Vinyrd ....G.... 785 862-2298
Wakarusa *(G-13384)*
Kc Wine Co ....G.... 913 908-3039
Olathe *(G-7834)*
Kuglers Vineyard ....G.... 785 843-8516
Lawrence *(G-4950)*
Oz Winery ....F.... 785 456-7417
Wamego *(G-13431)*
Prairie Fire Winery LLC ....G.... 785 636-5533
Paxico *(G-9757)*
Sommerset Ridge Vineyard ....F.... 913 491-0038
Paola *(G-9587)*
Wyldewood Cellars Inc ....F.... 316 554-9463
Peck *(G-9764)*

2085 Liquors, Distilled, Rectified & Blended

Dark Horse Distillery LLC ....F.... 913 492-3275
Lenexa *(G-5801)*
High Plains Inc ....G.... 913 773-5780
Atchison *(G-235)*
◆ **Lansing Trade Group LLC** ....C.... 913 748-3000
Overland Park *(G-8945)*
◆ **Mgp Ingredients Inc** ....C.... 913 367-1480
Atchison *(G-245)*
◆ **Mgpi Processing Inc** ....E.... 913 367-1480
Atchison *(G-247)*
Mgpi Processing Inc ....G.... 913 367-1480
Atchison *(G-248)*
Ml Rancho Tequila Usa Inc ....G.... 913 530-7260
Kansas City *(G-4241)*
Pernod Ricard Usa LLC ....D.... 913 393-2015
Olathe *(G-7979)*
Union Horse Distilling Co LLC ....F.... 913 492-3275
Lenexa *(G-6200)*

2086 Soft Drinks

American Bottling Company ....E.... 785 233-7471
Topeka *(G-12314)*
American Bottling Company ....D.... 785 625-4488
Hays *(G-2746)*
American Bottling Company ....C.... 913 894-6777
Lenexa *(G-5645)*
American Bottling Company ....D.... 316 529-3777
Wichita *(G-13686)*
American Bottling Company ....E.... 785 537-2100
Manhattan *(G-6540)*
City of Spring Hill ....F.... 913 592-3781
Spring Hill *(G-12082)*
Coca Cola Bottling Co Mid Amer ....E.... 785 243-1071
Topeka *(G-12483)*
Coca-Cola Bottling Emporia Inc ....E.... 239 444-1746
Emporia *(G-1723)*
Coca-Cola Btlg of Wnfield Kans ....F.... 620 221-2710
Winfield *(G-16121)*
Coca-Cola Company ....F.... 913 492-8100
Lenexa *(G-5768)*
Coca-Cola Refreshments USA Inc ....B.... 913 492-8100
Shawnee Mission *(G-11243)*
Heartland Coca-Cola Btlg LLC ....A.... 785 735-9498
Victoria *(G-13376)*
Heartland Coca-Cola Btlg LLC ....A.... 785 232-9372
Topeka *(G-12675)*
Heartland Coca-Cola Btlg LLC ....A.... 785 243-1071
Concordia *(G-1117)*
Heartland Coca-Cola Btlg LLC ....A.... 913 599-9142
Lenexa *(G-5896)*
Heartland Coca-Cola Btlg LLC ....A.... 620 276-3221
Garden City *(G-2194)*
Heartland Coca-Cola Btlg LLC ....A.... 316 942-3838
Wichita *(G-14582)*
Keurig Dr Pepper Inc ....D.... 913 894-6777
Lenexa *(G-5946)*
Keurig Dr Pepper Inc ....D.... 620 223-6166
Fort Scott *(G-1978)*
P-Americas LLC ....B.... 913 791-3000
Olathe *(G-7970)*
Pepsi Beverages Company ....D.... 316 522-3131
Wichita *(G-15279)*
Pepsi-Cola Btlg Co Topeka Inc ....D.... 785 232-9389
Topeka *(G-12969)*
Pepsi-Cola Btlg Marysville Inc ....E.... 785 537-4730
Manhattan *(G-6773)*
Pepsi-Cola Btlg of Pittsburg ....E.... 620 231-3800
Pittsburg *(G-9912)*
Pepsi-Cola Metro Btlg Co Inc ....E.... 620 251-2890
Coffeyville *(G-971)*
Pepsi-Cola Metro Btlg Co Inc ....C.... 316 529-9840
Wichita *(G-15280)*

SIC

Revhoney Inc....F....785 778-2006
Haddam (G-2695)
Seneca Wholesale Company Inc....F....785 336-2118
Seneca (G-10882)
Shasta Beverages Inc....D....913 888-6777
Lenexa (G-6127)
Shasta Midwest Inc....E....913 888-6777
Lenexa (G-6128)
Water Depot Inc....G....913 782-7277
Olathe (G-8148)
Z Bottling Corp....G....620 872-0100
Scott City (G-10837)

2087 Flavoring Extracts & Syrups

◆ Cereal Ingredients Inc....D....913 727-3434
Leavenworth (G-5217)

2091 Fish & Seafoods, Canned & Cured

Culver Fish Farm Inc....G....620 241-5200
McPherson (G-6954)

2095 Coffee

Cardona Coffee LLP....G....785 554-6060
Topeka (G-12446)
Heartland Coffee & Packg Corp....G....785 232-0383
Topeka (G-12676)

2096 Potato Chips & Similar Prdts

Frito-Lay North America Inc....A....785 267-2600
Topeka (G-12629)
La Superior Food Products Inc....E....913 362-6611
Shawnee Mission (G-11544)
Sunflower Hills Inc....F....913 894-2233
Lenexa (G-6158)

2097 Ice

Arctic Glacier Inc....F....620 275-5751
Garden City (G-2102)
Arctic Glacier Texas Inc....E....316 529-2173
Wichita (G-13732)
Berrys Arctic Ice LLC....F....785 357-4466
Topeka (G-12376)
MidAmerican Sales Group....G....913 689-8505
Overland Park (G-9029)
Pepsi Cola Btlg Co of Salina....D....785 827-7297
Salina (G-10633)

2098 Macaroni, Spaghetti & Noodles

Resers Fine Foods Inc....B....785 233-6431
Topeka (G-13009)
Thai Noodle....G....785 320-2899
Manhattan (G-6823)

2099 Food Preparations, NEC

Advanced Food Services Inc....E....913 888-8088
Lenexa (G-5632)
Arts Mexican Products Inc....F....913 371-2163
Kansas City (G-3820)
◆ Barkman Honey LLC....D....620 947-3173
Hillsboro (G-3042)
Brown Honey Farms....G....785 778-2002
Haddam (G-2694)
Central Soyfoods....F....785 312-8638
Lawrence (G-4781)
City of Fredonia....F....620 378-2802
Fredonia (G-2029)
Country Fresh Foods....E....316 283-4414
Newton (G-7336)
▼ Danisco Ingredients Usa Inc....F....913 764-8100
New Century (G-7275)
◆ Danisco USA Inc....C....913 764-8100
New Century (G-7276)
El Taquito Inc....G....913 371-0452
Kansas City (G-3984)
Frito-Lay North America Inc....A....785 267-2600
Topeka (G-12629)
▼ Heartland Food Products Inc....F....866 571-0222
Shawnee Mission (G-11424)
Kerry Inc....C....913 780-1212
New Century (G-7290)
La Nena Tortilleria Rostiseria....G....913 281-8993
Kansas City (G-4191)
La Superior Food Products Inc....E....913 362-6611
Shawnee Mission (G-11544)
▲ Old World Spices Seasoning Inc....E....816 861-0400
Overland Park (G-9098)
Premier Custom Foods LLC....D....913 225-9505
Kansas City (G-4331)
Rabbit Creek Products Inc....F....913 837-3073
Louisburg (G-6463)
Resers Fine Foods Inc....B....785 233-6431
Topeka (G-13009)
Safely Delicious LLC....F....913 963-5140
Overland Park (G-9270)
Sfc Global Supply Chain Inc....B....785 825-1671
Salina (G-10705)
Tortilla King Inc....C....620 345-2674
Moundridge (G-7199)
Tortilleria La Tradicion....G....316 264-3148
Wichita (G-15773)
Tortillria Los III Prtllos LLC....G....316 831-0811
Wichita (G-15774)
▲ Williams Foods Inc....C....913 888-4343
Lenexa (G-6231)
Wyldewood Cellars Inc....F....316 554-9463
Peck (G-9764)

22 TEXTILE MILL PRODUCTS

2211 Cotton, Woven Fabric

Acoustical Stretched Fabric....G....913 345-1520
Shawnee Mission (G-11069)
Classic Cloth Inc....F....785 434-7200
Plainville (G-9980)
Jockey International Globl Inc....G....913 334-4455
Kansas City (G-4125)
King Louie America Lc....F....913 338-5212
Leawood (G-5450)

2221 Silk & Man-Made Fiber

Invista Equities LLC....F....770 792-4221
Wichita (G-14728)

2241 Fabric Mills, Cotton, Wool, Silk & Man-Made

BWI of Ks Inc....E....316 831-0488
Wichita (G-13923)

2252 Hosiery, Except Women's

Notes To Self LLC....G....913 730-0037
Mission (G-7133)
Tradehome Shoe Stores Inc....G....785 539-4003
Manhattan (G-6830)

2261 Cotton Fabric Finishers

CP Partnerships Inc....F....785 625-7388
Hays (G-2779)
Express Print and Signs LLC....E....785 825-8434
Salina (G-10491)
Guerrilla Marketing Inc....G....800 946-9150
Newton (G-7353)
Kellys Corporate Apparel....G....316 263-5858
Wichita (G-14847)
New Wave Enterprises Inc....F....913 287-7671
Kansas City (G-4287)
Spirit Industries Inc....F....913 749-5858
Lawrence (G-5115)
Stewarts Sports & Awards....G....620 241-5990
McPherson (G-7028)
Sun Creations Inc....E....785 830-0403
Lawrence (G-5127)

2262 Silk & Man-Made Fabric Finishers

Sun Creations Inc....E....785 830-0403
Lawrence (G-5127)

2273 Carpets & Rugs

Golden Star Inc....D....913 874-2178
Atchison (G-231)
More Floods Inc....G....913 469-9464
Lenexa (G-6012)
Selfs Inc....E....913 962-7353
Shawnee Mission (G-11847)

2282 Yarn Texturizing, Throwing, Twisting & Winding Mills

Polymer Group Inc....C....620 532-4000
Kingman (G-4612)

2284 Thread Mills

Team Threads....G....620 429-4402
Columbus (G-1089)

2295 Fabrics Coated Not Rubberized

HBD Industries Inc....D....620 431-9100
Chanute (G-730)
Invista Equities LLC....F....770 792-4221
Wichita (G-14728)
Zeeco Inc....E....620 705-5100
Winfield (G-16192)

2296 Tire Cord & Fabric

Polymer Group Inc....C....620 532-5141
Kingman (G-4611)

2297 Fabrics, Nonwoven

Polymer Group Inc....C....620 532-5141
Kingman (G-4611)

2298 Cordage & Twine

Custom Rope A Div Williams....E....620 825-4196
Kiowa (G-4623)
▲ Great Lakes Polymer Tech LLC....C....620 532-5141
Kingman (G-4591)
Great Lakes Polymer Tech LLC....C....507 320-7000
Kingman (G-4592)
Great Lakes Polymer Tech LLC....E....208 324-2120
Kingman (G-4593)
Great Lkes Plymers Hldngs Corp....F....507 320-7000
Kingman (G-4594)
Polymer Group Inc....C....620 532-4000
Kingman (G-4612)

2299 Textile Goods, NEC

Golden Star Inc....D....913 874-2178
Atchison (G-231)
◆ Hix Corporation....D....620 231-8568
Pittsburg (G-9876)
▲ Precision Cut Inc....E....913 422-0777
Shawnee Mission (G-11747)

23 APPAREL AND OTHER FINISHED PRODUCTS MADE FROM FABRICS AND SIMILAR MATERIAL

2311 Men's & Boys' Suits, Coats & Overcoats

Fruhauf Uniforms Inc....C....316 263-7500
Wichita (G-14427)
Todds Clothiers & Tailor Shop....G....913 681-8633
Overland Park (G-9418)

2321 Men's & Boys' Shirts

Rfc Logo Inc....A....913 319-3100
Shawnee Mission (G-11794)

2325 Men's & Boys' Separate Trousers & Casual Slacks

Lee Apparel Company Inc....B....913 789-0330
Shawnee Mission (G-11557)
Lee Apparel Company Inc....C....913 384-4000
Shawnee Mission (G-11558)
Lee Jeans Company Inc....E....913 384-4000
Merriam (G-7099)
McCown Marketing LLC....F....913 284-5584
Bucyrus (G-602)

2326 Men's & Boys' Work Clothing

Deyno LLC....F....785 551-8949
Lawrence (G-4835)

2329 Men's & Boys' Clothing, NEC

Action Custom Sportswear LLC....G....913 433-9900
Overland Park (G-8344)
CC Products LLC....B....913 693-3200
Lenexa (G-5737)
▲ Challenger Sports Teamwear LLC....E....913 599-4884
Lenexa (G-5750)
Custom Branded Sportswear Inc....F....866 441-7464
Overland Park (G-8625)
Gfsi Inc....F....913 693-3200
Lenexa (G-5874)
◆ Gfsi LLC....B....913 693-3200
Lenexa (G-5875)
Lee Apparel Company Inc....C....913 384-4000
Shawnee Mission (G-11558)
Maurices Incorporated....E....620 275-1210
Garden City (G-2229)

◆ **Noa Group LLC** .... F 316 821-9700
Wichita *(G-15183)*
▲ **Outdoor Custom Sportswear LLC** ... E 866 288-5070
Overland Park *(G-9116)*
Signature Sportswear Inc .... D 620 421-1871
Wichita *(G-15591)*

2337 Women's & Misses' Suits, Coats & Skirts

Deyno LLC .... F 785 551-8949
Lawrence *(G-4835)*
Fruhauf Uniforms Inc .... C 316 263-7500
Wichita *(G-14427)*

2339 Women's & Misses' Outerwear, NEC

CC Products LLC .... B 913 693-3200
Lenexa *(G-5737)*
▲ **Challenger Sports Teamwear LLC** .... E 913 599-4884
Lenexa *(G-5750)*
Gfsi Inc .... F 913 693-3200
Lenexa *(G-5874)*
◆ **Gfsi LLC** .... B 913 693-3200
Lenexa *(G-5875)*
Lee Apparel Company Inc .... B 913 789-0330
Shawnee Mission *(G-11557)*
Lee Apparel Company Inc .... C 913 384-4000
Shawnee Mission *(G-11558)*
Lee Jeans Company Inc .... E 913 384-4000
Merriam *(G-7099)*
▲ **Outdoor Custom Sportswear LLC** ... E 866 288-5070
Overland Park *(G-9116)*
Signature Sportswear Inc .... D 620 421-1871
Wichita *(G-15591)*

2369 Girls' & Infants' Outerwear, NEC

Lee Apparel Company Inc .... C 913 384-4000
Shawnee Mission *(G-11558)*
Lee Jeans Company Inc .... E 913 384-4000
Merriam *(G-7099)*

2391 Curtains & Draperies

Alderman Acres Mfg Inc .... F 620 251-4095
Coffeyville *(G-909)*
Andrews and Abbey Riley LLC .... F 913 262-2212
Kansas City *(G-3811)*
Long Shot Enterprises LLC .... F 785 493-0171
Salina *(G-10584)*
Window Flair Draperies .... G 913 722-6070
Shawnee *(G-11054)*

2392 House furnishings: Textile

▲ **Direct Mop Sales Inc** .... E 913 367-3087
Atchison *(G-224)*
Golden Star Inc .... D 913 874-2178
Atchison *(G-231)*
▼ **Splintek Inc** .... E 816 531-1900
Lenexa *(G-6148)*

2393 Textile Bags

▲ **Central Bag Company** .... E 913 250-0325
Leavenworth *(G-5215)*
▲ **Hubco Inc** .... E 620 663-8301
Hutchinson *(G-3315)*
◆ **Tdc Filter Manufacturing Inc** .... C 630 410-6200
Overland Park *(G-9394)*

2394 Canvas Prdts

Colby Supply & Mfg Co .... F 785 462-3981
Colby *(G-999)*
Girard Tarps Inc .... G 620 724-8909
Girard *(G-2410)*
Home Stl Siding & Windows LLC .... F 785 625-8622
Hays *(G-2849)*
Infinity Tents Inc .... E 913 820-3700
Kansas City *(G-4100)*
Midwest Siding Inc .... E 785 825-0606
Salina *(G-10603)*
Ponca Products Inc .... E 316 262-4051
Wichita *(G-15314)*
Rons Sign Co Inc .... E 316 267-8914
Wichita *(G-15482)*
USA Gym Supply .... F 620 792-2800
Great Bend *(G-2652)*
USA Gym Supply Inc .... G 620 792-2209
Great Bend *(G-2653)*

2395 Pleating & Stitching For The Trade

4th Generation Promotional Pdts .... G 913 393-0837
Olathe *(G-7502)*
CP Partnerships Inc .... F 785 625-7388
Hays *(G-2779)*
D Rockey Holdings Inc .... E 816 474-9423
Kansas City *(G-3950)*
▲ **David Camp Inc** .... C 913 648-0573
Overland Park *(G-8641)*
Expert Alteration .... G 913 322-2242
Westwood *(G-13553)*
Express Yourself Digital .... G 620 724-8389
Girard *(G-2404)*
Expressions Embroidery LLC .... F 913 764-7070
Olathe *(G-7698)*
◆ **Gfsi LLC** .... B 913 693-3200
Lenexa *(G-5875)*
Gregory A Scott Inc .... E 913 677-0414
Kansas City *(G-4053)*
Industrial Uniform Company LLC .... F 316 264-2871
Wichita *(G-14688)*
Kellys Corporate Apparel .... G 316 263-5858
Wichita *(G-14847)*
Plainjans Feedlot Service .... F 620 872-5777
Scott City *(G-10827)*
Prairie Patches Inc .... G 785 749-4565
Lawrence *(G-5072)*
Prairie Point .... E 913 322-1222
Lenexa *(G-6068)*
SA Imprints Inc .... F 620 421-6380
Parsons *(G-9734)*
Sands Enterprises Inc .... G 316 942-8686
Wichita *(G-15518)*
Shirts Plus Inc .... F 316 788-1550
Derby *(G-1272)*
Signature Logo Embroidery Inc .... G 913 671-8548
Shawnee Mission *(G-11868)*
Something Different Inc .... G 785 537-1171
Wamego *(G-13441)*
Stewarts Sports & Awards .... G 620 241-5990
McPherson *(G-7028)*
Sunflwer Pcemakers Quilt Guild .... D 913 727-1870
Leavenworth *(G-5295)*
Tioga Territory Ltd .... F 620 431-2479
Chanute *(G-770)*
▲ **U S Logo Inc** .... F 316 264-1321
Wichita *(G-15824)*
U S S A Inc .... G 316 686-1653
Wichita *(G-15826)*
United States Awards Inc .... E 620 231-8470
Pittsburg *(G-9951)*
Walson Ink Inc .... G 785 537-7370
Manhattan *(G-6845)*
Winning Spirit Inc .... E 316 684-0855
Wichita *(G-16056)*

2396 Automotive Trimmings, Apparel Findings, Related Prdts

Falcon Design and Mfg .... E 913 441-1074
Shawnee *(G-10953)*
Finchers Findings Inc .... G 620 886-5952
Medicine Lodge *(G-7060)*
First Edition Inc .... G 620 232-6002
Pittsburg *(G-9861)*
◆ **Gfsi LLC** .... B 913 693-3200
Lenexa *(G-5875)*
Golden Sea Graphics Inc .... G 785 747-2822
Greenleaf *(G-2669)*
Graphic Impressions Inc .... E 620 663-5939
Hutchinson *(G-3305)*
Guerrilla Marketing Inc .... G 800 946-9150
Newton *(G-7353)*
◆ **Hasty Awards Inc** .... D 785 242-5297
Ottawa *(G-8278)*
John B Baker .... G 316 263-2820
Wichita *(G-14762)*
Kansas Graphics Inc .... G 620 273-6111
Cottonwood Falls *(G-1155)*
Koller Enterprises Inc .... D 913 422-2027
Lenexa *(G-5957)*
Navrats Inc .... F 620 342-2092
Emporia *(G-1800)*
Nill Brothers Silkscreen Inc .... F 913 384-4242
Kansas City *(G-4288)*
Prairie Print Inc .... G 316 267-1950
Wichita *(G-15321)*
Ragland Specialty Printing .... E 785 542-3058
Eudora *(G-1879)*
◆ **Screen-It Grphics Lawrence Inc** .... C 785 843-8888
Lawrence *(G-5107)*
Seen Merchandising LLC .... F 913 233-1981
Shawnee *(G-11026)*
Sharpline Converting Inc .... B 316 722-9080
Wichita *(G-15576)*
Shirts Plus Inc .... F 316 788-1550
Derby *(G-1272)*
◆ **Stouse LLC** .... C 913 764-5757
New Century *(G-7301)*
Sun Creations Inc .... E 785 830-0403
Lawrence *(G-5127)*
Sunflwer Pcemakers Quilt Guild .... D 913 727-1870
Leavenworth *(G-5295)*
▲ **USA Inc** .... F 785 825-6247
Salina *(G-10748)*
Winning Spirit Inc .... E 316 684-0855
Wichita *(G-16056)*

2397 Schiffli Machine Embroideries

John B Baker .... G 316 263-2820
Wichita *(G-14762)*
Sun Creations Inc .... E 785 830-0403
Lawrence *(G-5127)*

2399 Fabricated Textile Prdts, NEC

George Eschbaugh Advg Inc .... E 785 658-2105
Wilson *(G-16105)*
Ponca Products Inc .... E 316 262-4051
Wichita *(G-15314)*
United States Awards Inc .... E 620 231-8470
Pittsburg *(G-9951)*
▲ **Winning Streak Sports LLC** .... F 913 768-8868
Lenexa *(G-6232)*

24 LUMBER AND WOOD PRODUCTS, EXCEPT FURNITURE

2411 Logging

Barns Timber Creek B & B .... G 620 221-2797
Winfield *(G-16116)*
Black Jack Tree Lawn and Ldscp .... G 785 865-8536
Baldwin City *(G-356)*
◆ **International Forest Pdts LLC** .... D 913 451-6945
Overland Park *(G-8857)*
Martin James .... G 785 525-7761
Lucas *(G-6474)*
Newton Healthcare Corporation .... A 316 283-2700
Newton *(G-7393)*

2421 Saw & Planing Mills

Advantage Framing Systems Inc .... E 913 592-4150
Spring Hill *(G-12075)*
Barton Keller Sawmill LLC .... G 620 331-8206
Independence *(G-3499)*
Kansas Hardwoods Inc .... F 785 456-8141
Belvue *(G-506)*
McCray Lumber Company .... E 913 780-0060
Olathe *(G-7882)*
Timber Products Inc .... E 316 941-9381
Wichita *(G-15766)*

2426 Hardwood Dimension & Flooring Mills

Bell and Carlson Incorporated .... E 620 225-6688
Dodge City *(G-1306)*
Eubanks Custom Woodworks .... G 785 364-4377
Holton *(G-3088)*
Hays Planing Mill Inc .... G 785 625-6507
Hays *(G-2838)*
McCray Lumber Company .... E 913 780-0060
Olathe *(G-7882)*
R Miller Sales Co Inc .... E 913 341-3727
Shawnee Mission *(G-11772)*
Superior Hardwood Floors LLC .... G 316 554-9663
Wichita *(G-15694)*

2429 Special Prdt Sawmills, NEC

Delmarva Pad Co .... F 620 665-9757
Hutchinson *(G-3261)*

2431 Millwork

Cabinetry & Mllwk Concepts Inc .... F 785 232-1234
Topeka *(G-12417)*
Columbia Industries Inc .... E 785 227-3351
Lindsborg *(G-6396)*
Doubrava Woodworking Inc .... G 785 472-4204
Ellsworth *(G-1666)*
▼ **Goddard Manufacturing Inc** .... G 785 689-4341
Logan *(G-6424)*

Grandview Products Co ....D.... 620 336-2309
Cherryvale *(G-808)*
Hardwood Manufacturing LLC ....F.... 620 463-2663
Burrton *(G-649)*
Hays Planing Mill Inc ....G.... 785 625-6507
Hays *(G-2838)*
Innotech LLC ....G.... 913 888-4646
Lenexa *(G-5915)*
Koch & Co Inc ....B.... 785 336-6022
Seneca *(G-10871)*
McCray Lumber Company ....D.... 913 321-8840
Kansas City *(G-4226)*
▲ Olathe Millwork LLC ....G.... 913 738-8074
Olathe *(G-7947)*
Salina Planing Mill Inc ....E.... 785 825-0588
Salina *(G-10683)*
Shawnee Woodwork Inc ....E.... 785 354-1163
Topeka *(G-13065)*
Ta Millwork LLC ....G.... 316 744-3440
Park City *(G-9646)*
Technique Manufacturing Inc ....F.... 620 663-6360
Hutchinson *(G-3463)*
Tischlerei-Fine Wdwkg LLC ....F.... 785 404-3322
Salina *(G-10734)*
Tracker Door Systems LLC ....G.... 913 585-3100
De Soto *(G-1214)*
Weisbender Contracting Inc ....G.... 785 776-5034
Manhattan *(G-6849)*
Westhoff Interiors Inc ....E.... 620 449-2900
Saint Paul *(G-10386)*
Window Design Company ....G.... 785 582-2888
Silver Lake *(G-12030)*
Wood Haven Inc ....G.... 785 597-5618
Perry *(G-9775)*
Woodwork Mfg & Sup Inc ....E.... 620 663-3393
Hutchinson *(G-3492)*
Wooten Enterprises LLC ....G.... 316 830-2328
Halstead *(G-2707)*

2434 Wood Kitchen Cabinets

Cabinet Shopof Basehor Inc ....E.... 913 845-2182
Tonganoxie *(G-12255)*
Cambridge Cabinetry ....G.... 816 795-5082
Stilwell *(G-12137)*
Century Wood Products Inc ....G.... 913 839-8725
Olathe *(G-7587)*
Creative Hardwoods ....G.... 620 249-4160
Scammon *(G-10795)*
Crestwood Inc ....C.... 785 823-1532
Salina *(G-10467)*
Crestwood Inc ....G.... 785 827-0317
Salina *(G-10468)*
Crooks Floor Covering ....G.... 785 242-4153
Ottawa *(G-8262)*
Crown Tl Inc ....G.... 785 263-7061
Abilene *(G-23)*
Custom Cbnets By Lwrence Cnstr ....F.... 913 208-9797
Kansas City *(G-3948)*
Eubanks Custom Woodworks ....G.... 785 364-4377
Holton *(G-3088)*
Global Engineering & Tech Inc ....C.... 316 729-9232
Goddard *(G-2439)*
Grandview Products Co ....D.... 620 336-2309
Cherryvale *(G-808)*
Grandview Products Co Inc ....C.... 620 421-6950
Parsons *(G-9688)*
Hays Planing Mill Inc ....G.... 785 625-6507
Hays *(G-2838)*
Jay Henges Enterprises Inc ....E.... 913 764-4600
Olathe *(G-7808)*
Jerry Wray ....G.... 785 255-4644
Pomona *(G-10005)*
Kitchens Inc ....F.... 620 225-0208
Dodge City *(G-1393)*
Koch & Co Inc ....B.... 785 336-6022
Seneca *(G-10871)*
Mingo Custom Woods ....G.... 785 462-2200
Colby *(G-1029)*
Norcraft Companies LP ....F.... 316 283-8804
Newton *(G-7397)*
Norcraft Companies LP ....B.... 316 283-2859
Newton *(G-7398)*
Old World Cabinets Inc ....G.... 913 723-3740
Linwood *(G-6417)*
Ovation Cabinetry Inc ....D.... 785 452-9000
Salina *(G-10625)*
Overland Cabinet Company Inc ....F.... 913 441-1985
Bonner Springs *(G-569)*
▼ RD Henry & Company LLC ....C.... 316 529-3431
Wichita *(G-15424)*
Scope Inc ....G.... 316 393-7414
Wichita *(G-15536)*
Stanley Wood Products Inc ....E.... 913 681-2804
Shawnee Mission *(G-11893)*
Technical Services LLC ....G.... 785 825-1250
Salina *(G-10732)*
Technique Manufacturing Inc ....F.... 620 663-6360
Hutchinson *(G-3463)*
Timberline Cabinetry Mllwk LLC ....G.... 785 323-0206
Manhattan *(G-6827)*
Vision Woodworks LLC ....F.... 620 336-2158
Cherryvale *(G-814)*
Wichita Cabinet Company ....G.... 316 617-0176
Udall *(G-13280)*
Wooden Stuff Cabinets Inc ....F.... 785 887-6003
Lecompton *(G-5614)*

2439 Structural Wood Members, NEC

Axtell Truss Manufacturing Inc ....G.... 785 736-2291
Axtell *(G-350)*
Central Kansas Truss Co Inc ....D.... 316 755-3114
Valley Center *(G-13339)*
Component Fabricators Inc ....G.... 785 776-5081
Manhattan *(G-6601)*
Indevco Inc ....D.... 913 236-7222
Shawnee Mission *(G-11454)*
◆ International Forest Pdts LLC ....D.... 913 451-6945
Overland Park *(G-8857)*
Parker Truss & Stuff ....G.... 913 898-2775
Parker *(G-9660)*
Perfection Strl Components LLC ....E.... 316 942-8361
Wichita *(G-15282)*
Precision Truss Inc ....F.... 785 244-6456
Summerfield *(G-12215)*
St Joseph Truss Company Inc ....F.... 785 989-4496
Wathena *(G-13478)*
Timber Roots ....G.... 316 755-3114
Valley Center *(G-13356)*
Weisbender Contracting Inc ....G.... 785 776-5034
Manhattan *(G-6849)*
Wheeler Consolidated Inc ....E.... 785 733-2848
Waverly *(G-13483)*

2441 Wood Boxes

Cratetech Incorporated ....E.... 316 682-6223
Wichita *(G-14126)*
Industrial Crating Inc ....E.... 620 449-2003
Saint Paul *(G-10381)*
L & J Wood Products Inc ....G.... 620 327-2183
Hesston *(G-2996)*
United Manufacturing Inc ....E.... 913 780-0056
New Century *(G-7302)*

2448 Wood Pallets & Skids

▼ Asset Lifecycle LLC ....F.... 785 861-3100
Topeka *(G-12341)*
B J Best Buy Pallets ....G.... 785 488-2923
Solomon *(G-12047)*
▲ Baco Corporation ....F.... 316 945-5300
Wichita *(G-13792)*
Burgess Manufacturing Inc ....E.... 316 838-5748
Wichita *(G-13915)*
Companion Industries Inc ....E.... 620 345-3277
Moundridge *(G-7180)*
Containercraft Inc ....F.... 620 663-1168
Hutchinson *(G-3246)*
Hoyt Pallet Co ....E.... 785 986-6785
Hoyt *(G-3145)*
Industrial Crating Inc ....E.... 620 449-2003
Saint Paul *(G-10381)*
Kansas Hardwoods Inc ....F.... 785 456-8141
Belvue *(G-506)*
Mrg Holdings Inc ....F.... 913 371-3555
Kansas City *(G-4269)*
Palleton of Kansas Inc ....F.... 620 257-3571
Lyons *(G-6496)*
Pratt Industries USA Inc ....D.... 316 838-0851
Wichita *(G-15323)*
Precision Pallet ....G.... 620 221-4066
Winfield *(G-16166)*
▲ R&R Pallet Garden City Inc ....E.... 620 275-2394
Garden City *(G-2262)*
Reardon Pallet Company Inc ....E.... 816 221-3300
Kansas City *(G-4363)*
Southwest Pallets ....G.... 620 275-4343
Garden City *(G-2284)*
Stinnett Timbers LLC ....G.... 620 363-4757
Kincaid *(G-4581)*
Triple T Pallets ....E.... 316 772-9155
Valley Center *(G-13357)*
▼ Whiteleys Inc ....F.... 785 233-3801
Topeka *(G-13243)*
Wirths & Sons Inc ....F.... 316 838-0509
Wichita *(G-16059)*

2449 Wood Containers, NEC

▼ Asset Lifecycle LLC ....F.... 785 861-3100
Topeka *(G-12341)*
Cratetech Incorporated ....E.... 316 682-6223
Wichita *(G-14126)*
United Manufacturing Inc ....E.... 913 780-0056
New Century *(G-7302)*

2451 Mobile Homes

Clayton Homes Inc ....C.... 785 434-4617
Plainville *(G-9981)*
Skyline Corporation ....D.... 620 442-9060
Arkansas City *(G-180)*

2452 Prefabricated Wood Buildings & Cmpnts

Advanced Systems Homes Inc ....E.... 620 431-3320
Chanute *(G-702)*
Clayton Homes Inc ....C.... 785 434-4617
Plainville *(G-9981)*
Countryside of Hays Inc ....G.... 785 625-6539
Hays *(G-2777)*
Tuff Shed Inc ....F.... 913 541-8833
Shawnee Mission *(G-11947)*
Wardcraft Homes Inc ....D.... 785 632-5664
Clay Center *(G-886)*

2491 Wood Preserving

Wood RE New Joco Inc ....G.... 913 661-9663
Olathe *(G-8159)*
Wood Rot Pro ....G.... 913 638-5732
Olathe *(G-8160)*

2493 Reconstituted Wood Prdts

▼ Central Fiber LLC ....E.... 785 883-4600
Wellsville *(G-13541)*
Laminate Works Inc ....E.... 913 281-7474
Kansas City *(G-4194)*
Laminate Works Inc ....D.... 913 800-8263
Lenexa *(G-5963)*
Laminate Works Kansas City LLC ....G.... 913 281-7474
Kansas City *(G-4195)*
Maine Flame LLC ....G.... 913 208-9484
Spring Hill *(G-12088)*

2499 Wood Prdts, NEC

Advance Business Supply ....G.... 785 440-7826
Topeka *(G-12292)*
Capital City Pallet Inc ....F.... 785 379-5099
Topeka *(G-12429)*
Country Accents Inc ....G.... 316 440-1343
Andover *(G-87)*
Country Crafts ....G.... 620 232-1818
Opolis *(G-8180)*
CS Carey LLC ....F.... 913 432-4877
Kansas City *(G-3947)*
Godly Play Resources Inc ....G.... 620 635-4018
Ashland *(G-195)*
Hemslojd Inc ....G.... 785 227-2983
Lindsborg *(G-6399)*
Howell Mouldings LC ....E.... 913 782-0500
New Century *(G-7289)*
Laminage Products Inc ....G.... 316 267-5233
Wichita *(G-14916)*
Logan Street Finewood Products ....G.... 316 266-4948
Wichita *(G-14976)*
Precision Craft Inc ....F.... 913 780-9077
Olathe *(G-8000)*
Roys Custom Cabinets ....G.... 785 625-6724
Hays *(G-2902)*
Sunburst Systems Inc ....F.... 913 383-9309
Kansas City *(G-4446)*
Underhill Finish Carpentry LLC ....F.... 316 253-7129
Wichita *(G-15832)*
Universal Sign & Display LLC ....F.... 785 242-8111
Ottawa *(G-8317)*
Wood Haven Inc ....G.... 785 597-5618
Perry *(G-9775)*
Woodcraft Supply LLC ....G.... 913 599-2800
Shawnee Mission *(G-12016)*
Worship Woodworks Inc ....G.... 620 622-4568
Protection *(G-10177)*

25 FURNITURE AND FIXTURES

2511 Wood Household Furniture

Becker Cabinet Shop ....G 620 327-4448
Newton *(G-7318)*
Corbin Bronze Limited ....G 913 766-4012
Kansas City *(G-3940)*
Country Traditions Inc ....G 620 231-5382
Pittsburg *(G-9847)*
Dinkels Custom Wood Products ....F 785 735-2461
Victoria *(G-13374)*
Four Corners Construction LLC ....G 620 662-8163
Hutchinson *(G-3290)*
Hays Planing Mill Inc ....G 785 625-6507
Hays *(G-2838)*
Jensen Design Inc ....G 316 943-7900
Wichita *(G-14754)*
King Cabinets Inc ....F 913 422-7554
Shawnee Mission *(G-11535)*
Mingo Custom Woods ....G 785 462-2200
Colby *(G-1029)*
Spring Valley Woodworks Inc ....G 620 345-8330
Canton *(G-682)*
Triad Manufacturing Inc ....E 785 825-6050
Salina *(G-10740)*

2512 Wood Household Furniture, Upholstered

Andrews and Abbey Riley LLC ....F 913 262-2212
Kansas City *(G-3811)*
▲ **Dessin Fournir Inc** ....E 785 434-2777
Plainville *(G-9985)*
Dfc Holdings Inc ....F 785 434-2777
Plainville *(G-9986)*
▲ **Lacrosse Furniture Co** ....D 785 222-2541
La Crosse *(G-4635)*
Reimers Furniture Mfg Inc ....G 913 727-5100
Lansing *(G-4691)*
Triad Manufacturing Inc ....E 785 825-6050
Salina *(G-10740)*

2514 Metal Household Furniture

Cabinet Shopof Basehor Inc ....E 913 845-2182
Tonganoxie *(G-12255)*
Corbin Bronze Limited ....G 913 766-4012
Kansas City *(G-3940)*

2515 Mattresses & Bedsprings

Hays Planing Mill Inc ....G 785 625-6507
Hays *(G-2838)*
▲ **Imperial Sleep Products Inc** ....E 620 465-2242
Haven *(G-2732)*
Joe Thoele Foundation ....G 913 685-2282
Stilwell *(G-12158)*
Sealy Inc ....C 913 321-3677
Kansas City *(G-4410)*
Sealy Mattress Co Kans Cy Inc ....D 913 321-3677
Kansas City *(G-4411)*
Sleep Haven Inc ....F 620 465-2242
Haven *(G-2737)*
Ssb Manufacturing Company ....C 913 422-8000
Shawnee Mission *(G-11889)*

2517 Wood T V, Radio, Phono & Sewing Cabinets

Cabinet Shopof Basehor Inc ....E 913 845-2182
Tonganoxie *(G-12255)*
Stanley Wood Products Inc ....E 913 681-2804
Shawnee Mission *(G-11893)*

2521 Wood Office Furniture

Cabinetry & Mllwk Concepts Inc ....F 785 232-1234
Topeka *(G-12417)*
Herman Miller Inc ....G 913 599-4700
Shawnee Mission *(G-11428)*
Old World Cabinets Inc ....G 913 723-3740
Linwood *(G-6417)*
Ovation Cabinetry Inc ....D 785 452-9000
Salina *(G-10625)*
Precision Craft Inc ....F 913 780-9077
Olathe *(G-8000)*
Reimers Furniture Mfg Inc ....G 913 727-5100
Lansing *(G-4691)*
Sunfield LLC ....G 785 338-0314
Wichita *(G-15685)*
Triad Manufacturing Inc ....E 785 825-6050
Salina *(G-10740)*

2522 Office Furniture, Except Wood

Aegis Business Solutions LLC ....G 913 307-9922
Olathe *(G-7512)*
Griffith Lumber Company Inc ....E 785 776-4104
Manhattan *(G-6647)*
Leander Health Tech Inc ....F 785 856-7474
Lawrence *(G-4991)*
Triad Manufacturing Inc ....E 785 825-6050
Salina *(G-10740)*

2531 Public Building & Related Furniture

B/E Aerospace Inc ....G 316 609-4300
Wichita *(G-13788)*
Clarios ....G 316 634-1309
Wichita *(G-14036)*
Clarios ....E 785 827-6829
Salina *(G-10454)*
Federal Prison Industries ....D 913 682-8700
Leavenworth *(G-5238)*
Heartland Leasing Services Inc ....F 913 268-0069
Shawnee *(G-10969)*
Heartland Seating Inc ....F 913 268-0069
Shawnee *(G-10970)*
Integrated Stadium Seating Inc ....F 316 494-6514
Wichita *(G-14705)*
Seat King LLC ....E 620 665-5464
Hutchinson *(G-3440)*
Seats Incorporated ....G 913 686-3137
Spring Hill *(G-12098)*
▲ **Stadium Chair Company LLC** ....E 432 682-4682
Lenexa *(G-6151)*
Triad Manufacturing Inc ....E 785 825-6050
Salina *(G-10740)*
Waggoners Inc ....E 620 662-0181
Hutchinson *(G-3480)*

2541 Wood, Office & Store Fixtures

Alderman Acres Mfg Inc ....F 620 251-4095
Coffeyville *(G-909)*
Cabinet Shopof Basehor Inc ....E 913 845-2182
Tonganoxie *(G-12255)*
Classic Wood Interior Inc ....G 785 392-9937
Minneapolis *(G-7116)*
Grandview Products Co Inc ....C 620 421-6950
Parsons *(G-9688)*
Home Store ....F 620 421-4272
Parsons *(G-9692)*
Kesters Mdsg Display Intl ....E 913 281-4200
Kansas City *(G-4171)*
Keystone Construction Inc ....F 316 778-1566
Benton *(G-516)*
Keystone Financial LLC ....F 620 757-3593
Benton *(G-517)*
Nulook Custom Finishes ....G 913 385-2574
Olathe *(G-7925)*
Top It ....G 620 431-1866
Chanute *(G-771)*

2542 Partitions & Fixtures, Except Wood

Countertop Trends LLC ....E 620 836-2311
Gridley *(G-2689)*
E-Z Shelving Systems Inc ....F 913 384-1331
Shawnee Mission *(G-11324)*
▲ **New Age Industrial Corp Inc** ....C 785 877-5121
Norton *(G-7455)*

2591 Drapery Hardware, Window Blinds & Shades

Alderman Acres Mfg Inc ....F 620 251-4095
Coffeyville *(G-909)*
Ew & 7 Products LLC ....F 316 440-7486
Wichita *(G-14316)*
▲ **King Industries Inc** ....E 785 823-1785
Salina *(G-10575)*
Schammerhorn Inc ....G 316 265-8659
Wichita *(G-15528)*

2599 Furniture & Fixtures, NEC

Caregiver Company LLC ....F 316 247-4005
Andover *(G-85)*

26 PAPER AND ALLIED PRODUCTS

2611 Pulp Mills

▼ **Central Fiber LLC** ....E 785 883-4600
Wellsville *(G-13541)*

2621 Paper Mills

International Paper Company ....E 316 943-1033
Wichita *(G-14709)*
Kansas Business Forms LLC ....E 620 724-5234
Girard *(G-2414)*
Million Packaging Inc ....E 913 402-0055
Overland Park *(G-9039)*

2631 Paperboard Mills

Sonoco Products Company ....C 620 662-2331
Hutchinson *(G-3443)*

2652 Set-Up Paperboard Boxes

Ray Products Inc ....E 620 421-1510
Parsons *(G-9728)*

2653 Corrugated & Solid Fiber Boxes

American Box & Tape Co ....E 913 384-0992
Shawnee *(G-10909)*
International Paper Company ....D 620 272-8318
Garden City *(G-2204)*
Pratt Industries USA Inc ....D 316 838-0851
Wichita *(G-15323)*
Pratt Industries USA Inc ....D 316 838-0851
Wichita *(G-15324)*
Westrock Cp LLC ....C 816 746-0403
Kansas City *(G-4540)*

2656 Sanitary Food Containers

◆ **Huhtamaki Inc** ....B 913 583-3025
De Soto *(G-1202)*

2657 Folding Paperboard Boxes

Russell Stover Chocolates LLC ....E 785 263-0463
Abilene *(G-52)*

2671 Paper Coating & Laminating for Packaging

Bagcraftpapercon I LLC ....C 620 856-4615
Baxter Springs *(G-395)*
◆ **Gunze Plas & Engrg Corp Amer** ....D 913 829-5577
Olathe *(G-7743)*
Kendall Packaging Corporation ....E 620 231-9804
Pittsburg *(G-9891)*
Polynova (usa) LLC ....G 913 309-6977
Lenexa *(G-6062)*
Superior School Supplies Inc ....F 620 421-3190
Parsons *(G-9743)*

2672 Paper Coating & Laminating, Exc for Packaging

Bagcraftpapercon I LLC ....C 620 856-4615
Baxter Springs *(G-395)*
Gary Bell ....G 785 233-6677
Holton *(G-3090)*
Graphics Systems Inc ....D 316 267-4171
Wichita *(G-14497)*
Peavey Corporation ....D 913 888-0600
Lenexa *(G-6047)*
Reliance Label Solutions Inc ....E 913 294-1600
Paola *(G-9585)*
RGI Publications Inc ....E 913 829-8723
Olathe *(G-8030)*
Roll Products Inc ....F 785 437-6000
Saint Marys *(G-10374)*
Spectragraphics Inc ....E 913 888-6828
Lenexa *(G-6147)*
Tabco Incorporated ....E 913 287-3333
Kansas City *(G-4457)*
▲ **Ward-Kraft Inc** ....B 800 821-4021
Fort Scott *(G-2017)*

2673 Bags: Plastics, Laminated & Coated

Bagcraftpapercon I LLC ....C 620 856-4615
Baxter Springs *(G-395)*
▲ **Deelliotte Company Inc** ....D 913 764-0606
New Century *(G-7278)*
Envision Inc ....F 316 425-7123
Wichita *(G-14294)*
Envision Inc ....E 316 267-2244
Kansas City *(G-3991)*
Envision Industries Inc ....D 316 267-2244
Wichita *(G-14296)*
Kendall Packaging Corporation ....E 620 231-9804
Pittsburg *(G-9891)*
Midco Plastics Inc ....E 785 263-8999
Enterprise *(G-1855)*

Nichols Enterprises Inc ....F 913 706-4581
Leawood (G-5502)
▲ Pitt Plastics Inc ....B 620 231-4030
Pittsburg (G-9918)
▲ Plastic Packaging Tech LLC ....C 913 287-3383
Kansas City (G-4325)
Ppt Holdings LLC ....G 913 287-3383
Kansas City (G-4328)

2674 Bags: Uncoated Paper & Multiwall

Bagcraftpapercon I LLC ....C 620 856-4615
Baxter Springs (G-395)
◆ Tdc Filter Manufacturing Inc ....C 630 410-6200
Overland Park (G-9394)

2675 Die-Cut Paper & Board

Leslie Company Inc ....D 913 764-6660
Olathe (G-7859)
Tabco Incorporated ....E 913 287-3333
Kansas City (G-4457)

2676 Sanitary Paper Prdts

Envision Inc ....F 316 425-7123
Wichita (G-14294)
Envision Inc ....E 316 267-2244
Kansas City (G-3991)

2677 Envelopes

Tension Envelope Corporation ....D 785 562-2307
Marysville (G-6911)

2679 Converted Paper Prdts, NEC

▼ Central Fiber LLC ....E 785 883-4600
Wellsville (G-13541)
Creative Mktg Unlimited Inc ....G 913 894-0077
Overland Park (G-8611)
GC Labels Inc ....F 913 897-6966
Stilwell (G-12148)
Illinois Tool Works Inc ....E 913 856-2546
Gardner (G-2351)
Kc Digical ....G 913 541-2688
Lenexa (G-5940)
Ken OKelly ....G 816 868-6028
Prairie Village (G-10042)
▼ Lowen Corporation ....B 620 663-2161
Hutchinson (G-3358)
Lynn Tape & Label ....F 913 422-0484
Kansas City (G-4210)
▲ Open Road Brands LLC ....F 316 337-7550
Wichita (G-15222)
Partners Kan-Verting LLC ....G 913 894-2700
Lenexa (G-6044)
◆ Phenix Label Company Inc ....D 913 327-7000
Olathe (G-7984)
Rickerson Pipe Lining LLC ....F 785 448-5401
Garnett (G-2386)
◆ Rite-Made Paper Converters LLC ....C 913 621-5000
Kansas City (G-4379)
Roll Products Inc ....F 785 437-6000
Saint Marys (G-10374)
Stephanie Wilson ....G 913 563-1240
Paola (G-9591)

27 PRINTING, PUBLISHING, AND ALLIED INDUSTRIES

2711 Newspapers: Publishing & Printing

Abilene Rflctor Chronicle Pubg ....E 785 263-1000
Abilene (G-8)
Advocate Publishing Co Inc ....E 785 562-2317
Marysville (G-6878)
AG Press Inc ....D 785 539-7558
Manhattan (G-6536)
Beloit Call ....G 785 738-3537
Beloit (G-475)
Blade Empire Publishing Co ....E 785 243-2424
Concordia (G-1103)
Chanute Publishing Company ....A 620 431-4100
Chanute (G-712)
City of Anthony ....G 620 842-5123
Anthony (G-123)
Clay Center Publishing Co Inc ....G 785 632-2127
Clay Center (G-852)
Cnhi LLC ....E 620 421-9450
Parsons (G-9673)
Council Grove Republican ....G 620 767-5123
Council Grove (G-1161)
Dan Diehl ....G 785 336-2175
Seneca (G-10863)
Davis Publications Inc ....F 785 945-6170
Valley Falls (G-13362)
Dighton Herald ....G 620 397-5347
Dighton (G-1284)
Ellsworth Reporter Inc ....G 785 472-5085
Ellsworth (G-1672)
Envision Inc ....E 316 440-3737
Wichita (G-14295)
Faimon Publications Inc ....F 620 364-5325
Burlington (G-634)
Galena Sentinel Times ....G 620 783-5034
Galena (G-2074)
Gannett Co Inc ....C 785 832-6319
Lawrence (G-4868)
Garden City Telegram ....E 620 275-8500
Garden City (G-2177)
Garnett Publishing Inc ....F 785 448-3121
Garnett (G-2373)
Gatehouse Media LLC ....D 913 682-0305
Leavenworth (G-5241)
Gatehouse Media LLC ....E 620 326-3326
Wellington (G-13502)
Gatehouse Media LLC ....F 620 241-2422
McPherson (G-6968)
Gatehouse Media LLC ....E 620 672-5512
Pratt (G-10117)
Gatehouse Media LLC ....E 913 682-0305
Leavenworth (G-5242)
Gatehouse Media Inc ....G 913 367-0583
Atchison (G-229)
Gatehuse Mdia Kans Hldings Inc ....F 316 321-6136
El Dorado (G-1564)
Golden Plains Publishers Inc ....G 620 855-3902
Cimarron (G-827)
Greeley County Republican ....G 620 376-4264
Tribune (G-13271)
Hall Publications Inc ....G 785 232-8600
Topeka (G-12659)
Harris Enterprises Group ....F 785 827-6035
Salina (G-10536)
Harvey County Independent ....G 316 835-2235
Halstead (G-2702)
Haynes Publishing Co ....G 785 475-2206
Oberlin (G-7496)
Haynes Publishing Co ....G 785 475-2206
Oberlin (G-7497)
Haynes Publishing Co ....E 785 899-2338
Goodland (G-2475)
Haynes Publishing Co ....F 785 462-3963
Colby (G-1011)
Herald Sabetha Inc ....G 785 284-3300
Sabetha (G-10313)
Hesston Record ....G 620 327-4831
Hesston (G-2992)
High Plains Publishers Inc ....D 620 227-7171
Dodge City (G-1372)
Hoch Publishing Co Inc ....G 620 382-2165
Marion (G-6872)
Hutchinson Publishing Co ....C 620 694-5700
Hutchinson (G-3322)
Independent Oil & Gas Svc Inc ....G 316 263-8281
Wichita (G-14680)
Inland Industries Inc ....G 913 492-9050
Bucyrus (G-600)
Iola Register Inc ....E 620 365-2111
Iola (G-3611)
Julie K Samuelson ....G 785 852-4900
Sharon Springs (G-10899)
Kansas Newspaper Foundation ....E 785 271-5304
Topeka (G-12794)
Kingman Leader Courier ....G 620 532-3151
Kingman (G-4602)
Labette Avenue ....F 620 795-2550
Oswego (G-8234)
Lee Enterprises Incorporated ....G 620 276-2311
Garden City (G-2223)
Lewis Legal News Inc ....G 913 780-5790
Olathe (G-7860)
Lincoln Sentinel Republican ....G 785 524-4200
Lincoln (G-6384)
Linn County Publishing Inc ....F 913 352-6235
Pleasanton (G-9997)
Louisburg Herald ....G 913 837-4321
Paola (G-9570)
Lyons Daily News ....G 620 257-2368
Lyons (G-6489)
Marshall Publishing Inc ....G 620 278-2114
Sterling (G-12125)
McClatchy Newspapers Inc ....D 816 234-4636
Shawnee Mission (G-11608)
McGrath Publishing Company ....G 785 738-2424
Beloit (G-492)
Miami County Publishing Co ....E 913 294-2311
Paola (G-9573)
Minneapolis Messenger Pubg Co ....G 785 392-2129
Minneapolis (G-7118)
Montgomery Communications Inc ....D 785 762-5000
Junction City (G-3727)
Montgomery County Chronicle ....G 620 879-2156
Caney (G-672)
Montgomery County Media LLC ....E 620 331-3550
Independence (G-3541)
Morris Communications Co LLC ....E 316 283-1500
Newton (G-7390)
Morris Communications Co LLC ....D 620 231-2600
Pittsburg (G-9908)
Morris Communications Co LLC ....E 620 225-4151
Dodge City (G-1407)
Morris Communications Co LLC ....E 620 442-4200
Arkansas City (G-167)
Morris Communications Co LLC ....E 785 823-1111
Salina (G-10604)
Morris Newspaper Corp Kansas ....E 620 792-1211
Great Bend (G-2613)
Mt Pleasant News Inc ....F 913 492-9050
Shawnee Mission (G-11657)
Mulvane News and Bandwagon ....G 316 777-4233
Mulvane (G-7225)
News Publishing Co Inc ....D 785 628-1081
Hays (G-2877)
Nor West Newspaper Inc ....G 785 332-3162
Saint Francis (G-10343)
NPS Sales Inc ....G 913 406-1454
Olathe (G-7924)
Osage County Herald ....G 785 528-3511
Osage City (G-8186)
Ottawa Herald Inc ....E 785 242-4700
Ottawa (G-8298)
Ottaway Amusement Co Inc ....G 316 529-0086
Onaga (G-8179)
Parsons Publishing Company LLC ....E 620 421-2000
Parsons (G-9721)
Powls Publishing Company Inc ....F 785 364-3141
Holton (G-3108)
Prairie Dog Press ....F 785 669-2009
Almena (G-68)
Rawlins County Sq Deal Pubg ....G 785 626-3600
Atwood (G-290)
Record Publications ....G 913 362-1988
Kansas City (G-4365)
Russell Publishing Co ....G 785 483-2116
Russell (G-10297)
Salina Journal Inc ....C 785 823-6363
Salina (G-10678)
Seaton Publishing Co Inc ....D 785 776-2200
Manhattan (G-6798)
Senate United States ....F 620 227-2244
Dodge City (G-1428)
Seward County Publishing LLC ....E 620 626-0840
Liberal (G-6367)
Smith County Pioneer ....G 785 282-3371
Smith Center (G-12043)
Star Communication Corporation ....F 620 285-3111
Larned (G-4713)
Tcv Publishing Inc ....G 316 681-1155
Wichita (G-15719)
Telescope Inc ....F 785 527-2244
Belleville (G-467)
Times Sentinel Newspapers ....G 316 540-0500
Cheney (G-797)
Topeka Capital Journal ....E 785 295-1111
Topeka (G-13170)
Tri-County Newspapers Inc ....F 913 856-7615
Gardner (G-2366)
University Daily Kansan ....C 785 864-4358
Lawrence (G-5154)
Walker Publishing Inc ....G 913 352-6700
Pleasanton (G-10003)
Western Kansas World Inc ....G 785 743-2155
Wakeeney (G-13396)
White Corporation Inc ....E 620 342-4800
Emporia (G-1851)
Wichita Business Journal Inc ....F 316 267-6406
Wichita (G-15983)
Wichita Eagle Beacon Pubg Inc ....D 316 268-6000
Wichita (G-15994)
Wichita State Sunflower Inc ....E 316 978-6917
Wichita (G-16030)

Willgrattten Publications LLC ... E ... 785 762-5000
Junction City *(G-3769)*
Wilson County Citizen Inc ... G ... 620 378-4415
Fredonia *(G-2049)*
Winfield Publishing Co Inc ... E ... 620 221-1100
Winfield *(G-16189)*
Worldwest Ltd Liability Co ... C ... 785 843-1000
Lawrence *(G-5192)*
Wsu Sunflower Newspaper ... E ... 316 978-6900
Wichita *(G-16077)*

2721 Periodicals: Publishing & Printing

435 Magazine LLC ... F ... 913 469-6700
Overland Park *(G-8330)*
Advanstar Communications Inc ... E ... 913 871-3800
Shawnee Mission *(G-11079)*
Advocate Publishing Co Inc ... E ... 785 562-2317
Marysville *(G-6878)*
▼ **Allen Press Inc** ... D ... 785 843-1234
Lawrence *(G-4729)*
Anthem Motorsports Inc ... F ... 913 894-6923
Leawood *(G-5328)*
Bank News Publications Inc ... F ... 913 261-7000
Roeland Park *(G-10217)*
Century Marketing Inc ... F ... 913 696-9758
Lenexa *(G-5742)*
Claflin Books & Copies ... F ... 785 776-3771
Manhattan *(G-6591)*
Cpg Communications Group LLC ... G ... 913 317-2888
Shawnee Mission *(G-11276)*
East Kansas Quartly Cnfrce Fre ... G ... 785 272-1843
Topeka *(G-12568)*
Family Media Group Inc ... E ... 913 815-6600
Overland Park *(G-8703)*
Feed-Lot Magazine Inc ... G ... 620 397-2838
Dighton *(G-1285)*
Foil Stamping & Embossing Assn ... G ... 785 271-5816
Topeka *(G-12621)*
Good News Publishing Co Inc ... E ... 620 879-5460
Caney *(G-669)*
Half Price Bks Rec Mgzines Inc ... F ... 913 829-9959
Olathe *(G-7748)*
Hall Publications Inc ... G ... 785 232-8600
Topeka *(G-12659)*
Herald and Banner Press ... F ... 913 432-0331
Overland Park *(G-8811)*
Informa Business Media Inc ... D ... 913 341-1300
Olathe *(G-7789)*
Interstate Publishers Inc ... F ... 913 341-4445
Prairie Village *(G-10036)*
Kansas Electric Cooperatives ... E ... 785 478-4554
Topeka *(G-12775)*
Kansas Rest Hospitality Assn ... F ... 316 267-8383
Wichita *(G-14821)*
McCall Pattern Company ... B ... 785 776-4041
Manhattan *(G-6735)*
Mennonite Weekly Review Inc ... G ... 316 283-3670
Newton *(G-7381)*
Morris Communications Co LLC ... E ... 620 442-4200
Arkansas City *(G-167)*
Morris Communications Co LLC ... D ... 785 295-1111
Topeka *(G-12914)*
Multi-Media International LLC ... G ... 913 469-6800
Shawnee Mission *(G-11659)*
National Publishers Group Inc ... F ... 316 788-6271
Haysville *(G-2953)*
Patient Resource Pubg LLC ... F ... 913 725-1000
Overland Park *(G-9145)*
Peterson Publications Inc ... G ... 785 271-5801
Topeka *(G-12972)*
Wichita State Sunflower Inc ... E ... 316 978-6917
Wichita *(G-16030)*

2731 Books: Publishing & Printing

▲ **Aapc Inc** ... G ... 877 277-8254
Shawnee *(G-10905)*
Aircraft Bluebook ... C ... 913 967-1719
Shawnee Mission *(G-11088)*
Cookbook Publishers Inc ... E ... 913 689-3038
Overland Park *(G-8598)*
Devore & Sons Inc ... E ... 316 267-3211
Wichita *(G-14205)*
Edwin Myers ... G ... 316 799-2112
Whitewater *(G-13570)*
McCall Pattern Company ... B ... 785 776-4041
Manhattan *(G-6735)*
Monaco & Associates Inc ... G ... 785 272-5501
Topeka *(G-12910)*
Premiere Marketing Group Inc ... G ... 913 362-9100
Overland Park *(G-9183)*
Purplefrogintl ... G ... 816 510-0871
Shawnee *(G-11014)*
Schroff Development Corp ... F ... 913 262-2664
Shawnee Mission *(G-11838)*
▲ **Terrell Publishing Co** ... G ... 913 948-8226
Kansas City *(G-4464)*
University of Kansas ... E ... 785 864-4154
Lawrence *(G-5166)*
University Press of Kansas ... E ... 785 864-4155
Lawrence *(G-5168)*

2732 Book Printing, Not Publishing

Adr Inc ... D ... 316 522-5599
Wichita *(G-13616)*
L & L Manufacturing Inc ... E ... 816 257-8411
Kansas City *(G-4187)*
Printing Services Inc ... G ... 913 492-1500
Lenexa *(G-6070)*
Scholastic Book Fairs Inc ... F ... 913 599-5700
Shawnee Mission *(G-11836)*

2741 Misc Publishing

▲ **Aapc Inc** ... G ... 877 277-8254
Shawnee *(G-10905)*
Abilene Rflctor Chronicle Pubg ... E ... 785 263-1000
Abilene *(G-8)*
Anthem Media LLC ... E ... 913 894-6923
Leawood *(G-5327)*
ARC Document Solutions ... E ... 316 264-9344
Wichita *(G-13727)*
AT&T Inc ... F ... 913 676-1136
Lenexa *(G-5673)*
Central Publishing Co Inc ... G ... 620 365-2106
Iola *(G-3591)*
Chanute Publishing Company ... A ... 620 431-4100
Chanute *(G-712)*
Converg Media LLC ... G ... 913 871-0453
Olathe *(G-7613)*
▲ **Davies Communications Inc** ... F ... 620 241-1504
McPherson *(G-6956)*
Edwin Myers ... G ... 316 799-2112
Whitewater *(G-13570)*
Fontastik Inc ... G ... 816 474-4366
Kansas City *(G-4015)*
Franklin Covey Co ... G ... 800 819-1812
Overland Park *(G-8737)*
Gatehuse Mdia Kans Hldings Inc ... F ... 316 321-6136
El Dorado *(G-1564)*
Glover Inc ... E ... 800 654-1511
Olathe *(G-7735)*
Good News Publishing Co Inc ... E ... 620 879-5460
Caney *(G-669)*
Gospel Publishers ... G ... 620 345-2532
Moundridge *(G-7183)*
Guest Communications Corp ... E ... 913 888-1217
Shawnee Mission *(G-11405)*
Hall Publications Inc ... G ... 785 232-8600
Topeka *(G-12659)*
Haynes Publishing Co ... G ... 785 475-2206
Oberlin *(G-7496)*
Herff Jones LLC ... D ... 913 432-8100
Edwardsville *(G-1502)*
Interstate Publishers Inc ... F ... 913 341-4445
Prairie Village *(G-10036)*
K W Brock Directories Inc ... C ... 620 231-4000
Pittsburg *(G-9884)*
Linux New Media Usa LLC ... G ... 785 856-3080
Lawrence *(G-4998)*
▲ **Master Teacher Inc** ... E ... 785 539-0555
Manhattan *(G-6733)*
McCall Pattern Company ... B ... 785 776-4041
Manhattan *(G-6735)*
McGrath Publishing Company ... G ... 785 738-2424
Beloit *(G-492)*
Miracorp Inc ... G ... 913 322-8000
Lenexa *(G-6006)*
Nationwide Learning LLC ... C ... 785 862-2292
Topeka *(G-12925)*
Ogden Publications Inc ... C ... 785 274-4300
Topeka *(G-12943)*
Propane Resources LLC ... E ... 913 262-8345
Shawnee Mission *(G-11756)*
RGI Publications Inc ... E ... 913 829-8723
Olathe *(G-8030)*
Rockhurst University Continuin ... D ... 913 432-7755
Shawnee Mission *(G-11812)*
Salina Journal Inc ... C ... 785 823-6363
Salina *(G-10678)*
Squad It Services LLC ... E ... 785 844-3114
Herington *(G-2981)*
Tristar Publishing Inc ... G ... 913 491-4200
Overland Park *(G-9430)*
Viralnova LLC ... E ... 913 706-9710
Overland Park *(G-9465)*
Walsworth Publishing Co Inc ... E ... 800 265-6795
Overland Park *(G-9483)*
Wichita State Sunflower Inc ... E ... 316 978-6917
Wichita *(G-16030)*

2752 Commercial Printing: Lithographic

A C Printing Co Inc ... G ... 913 780-3377
Olathe *(G-7504)*
Abilene Printing Co Inc ... G ... 785 263-2330
Abilene *(G-7)*
Ace Forms of Kansas Inc ... D ... 620 232-9290
Pittsburg *(G-9805)*
Administration Kansas Dept ... D ... 785 296-3631
Topeka *(G-12289)*
Adr Inc ... D ... 316 522-5599
Wichita *(G-13616)*
Advocate Publishing Co Inc ... E ... 785 562-2317
Marysville *(G-6878)*
AG Press Inc ... D ... 785 539-7558
Manhattan *(G-6536)*
Arrow Printing Company Inc ... G ... 785 825-8124
Salina *(G-10409)*
Art Craft Printers & Design ... G ... 785 776-9151
Manhattan *(G-6545)*
Award Decals Inc ... F ... 913 677-6681
Overland Park *(G-8418)*
Back Room Printing LLC ... G ... 620 873-2900
Meade *(G-7046)*
Baker Bros Printing Co Inc ... G ... 620 947-3520
Hillsboro *(G-3041)*
Barker Printing and Copy Svcs ... G ... 785 233-5533
Topeka *(G-12365)*
Bisel Inc ... G ... 785 842-2656
Lawrence *(G-4758)*
Black and Jensen Inc ... E ... 316 262-7277
Wichita *(G-13854)*
Blade Empire Publishing Co ... E ... 785 243-2424
Concordia *(G-1103)*
Brad Vignatelli ... G ... 913 541-9777
Lenexa *(G-5711)*
Brush Group LLC ... D ... 785 454-3383
Downs *(G-1470)*
Burns Publishing Company Inc ... E ... 913 782-0321
Olathe *(G-7569)*
Caraway Printing Company Inc ... G ... 913 727-5223
Lansing *(G-4670)*
Cds Inc ... F ... 913 541-1166
Overland Park *(G-8532)*
Central Printing & Binding ... G ... 620 665-7251
Hutchinson *(G-3233)*
Chanute Publishing Company ... A ... 620 431-4100
Chanute *(G-712)*
Chester Press Inc ... G ... 620 342-8792
Emporia *(G-1719)*
City Print Inc ... G ... 316 267-5555
Wichita *(G-14032)*
Cliff Hix Engineering Inc ... E ... 620 232-3000
Pittsburg *(G-9836)*
Consolidated Prtg & Sty Co Inc ... E ... 785 825-5426
Salina *(G-10460)*
Cookbook Publishers Inc ... E ... 913 689-3038
Overland Park *(G-8598)*
Copy Center of Topeka Inc ... E ... 785 233-6677
Topeka *(G-12507)*
Copy Shop Inc ... G ... 316 262-8200
Wichita *(G-14100)*
Copy Shoppe ... G ... 785 232-0403
Topeka *(G-12508)*
Creative Printing Company Inc ... E ... 913 262-5000
Merriam *(G-7089)*
D & B Print Shop Inc ... G ... 913 782-6688
Olathe *(G-7634)*
D P Enterprises Inc ... F ... 316 263-4234
Wichita *(G-14159)*
Davis Publications Inc ... F ... 785 945-6170
Valley Falls *(G-13362)*
Deluxe Corporation ... C ... 913 888-3801
Lenexa *(G-5810)*
Dimension Graphics Inc ... D ... 913 469-6800
Lenexa *(G-5820)*
Direct Mail Printers Inc ... F ... 316 263-1855
Wichita *(G-14213)*
Dla Document Services ... G ... 913 684-5591
Fort Leavenworth *(G-1937)*
Docuplex Inc ... E ... 316 262-2662
Wichita *(G-14220)*

S I C

Donnelley Financial LLC F 913 541-4099
Shawnee Mission *(G-11316)*
Ejrex Inc D 620 421-6200
Parsons *(G-9683)*
Envision Industries Inc D 316 267-2244
Wichita *(G-14296)*
Express Print and Signs LLC E 785 825-8434
Salina *(G-10491)*
Fast Print G 316 688-1242
Wichita *(G-14344)*
Federal Prison Industries D 913 682-8700
Leavenworth *(G-5238)*
Fedex Office & Print Svcs Inc E 785 272-2500
Topeka *(G-12603)*
Financial Printing Resource F 913 599-6979
Lenexa *(G-5852)*
Food Trends Inc G 913 383-3600
Overland Park *(G-8732)*
Gary Bell G 785 233-6677
Holton *(G-3090)*
Gatehuse Mdia Kans Hldings Inc F 316 321-6136
El Dorado *(G-1564)*
▲ **Gill Bebco LLC** E 816 942-3100
Lenexa *(G-5876)*
Go-Modern LLC G 785 271-1445
Topeka *(G-12639)*
Golden Belt Printing II LLC F 620 793-6351
Great Bend *(G-2572)*
Graphic Images Inc F 316 283-3776
Newton *(G-7352)*
Graphic Impressions Inc E 620 663-5939
Hutchinson *(G-3305)*
Graphics Four Inc G 913 268-0564
Shawnee *(G-10964)*
Graphics Systems Inc D 316 267-4171
Wichita *(G-14497)*
Greeley County Republican G 620 376-4264
Tribune *(G-13271)*
Guerrilla Marketing Inc G 800 946-9150
Newton *(G-7353)*
Happy Shirt Printing Co LLC G 785 371-1660
Lawrence *(G-4888)*
Harvest Graphics LLC E 913 438-5556
Shawnee Mission *(G-11415)*
High Plains Printing G 785 460-6350
Colby *(G-1015)*
Holderman Printing LLC G 913 557-6848
Garnett *(G-2378)*
Images G 785 827-0824
Salina *(G-10549)*
Independent Oil & Gas Svc Inc G 316 263-8281
Wichita *(G-14680)*
Iola Register Inc E 620 365-2111
Iola *(G-3611)*
J-Con Reprographics Inc F 913 859-0800
Lenexa *(G-5927)*
Jdb Enterprises Inc G 316 263-2411
Wichita *(G-14752)*
Jfaonlinecom LLc G 316 554-1222
Wichita *(G-14756)*
Kansas Graphics Inc G 620 273-6111
Cottonwood Falls *(G-1155)*
Kelsey Construction Inc G 913 894-0330
Shawnee Mission *(G-11528)*
Key Office Products Inc G 620 227-2101
Dodge City *(G-1390)*
Koller Enterprises Inc D 913 422-2027
Lenexa *(G-5957)*
Kopco Inc D 620 879-2117
Caney *(G-671)*
La Dow & Spohn Inc F 620 378-2541
Fredonia *(G-2037)*
Lawrence Printing and Design F 785 843-4600
Lawrence *(G-4984)*
Lees Printing Company Inc G 913 371-0569
Kansas City *(G-4200)*
Legal Printing Company Inc G 913 369-1623
Bonner Springs *(G-559)*
Legends Printing & Graphics G 620 225-0020
Dodge City *(G-1396)*
Leroy Cook G 316 321-0844
El Dorado *(G-1583)*
Liberal Office Machines Co G 620 624-5653
Liberal *(G-6334)*
Linn County Publishing Inc F 913 352-6235
Pleasanton *(G-9997)*
Lockwood Company Inc E 913 367-0110
Atchison *(G-241)*
Louisburg Herald G 913 837-4321
Paola *(G-9570)*
Lowen Corporation G 620 663-2161
Hutchinson *(G-3357)*
▼ **Lowen Corporation** B 620 663-2161
Hutchinson *(G-3358)*
▲ **Mainline Printing Inc** D 785 233-2338
Topeka *(G-12856)*
Martin Dysart Enterprises Inc G 785 776-6731
Manhattan *(G-6732)*
▲ **McCormick-Armstrong Co Inc** D 316 264-1363
Wichita *(G-15022)*
McKissick Enterprises LLC F 316 687-0272
Wichita *(G-15029)*
Mennonite Church USA G 316 283-5100
Newton *(G-7378)*
Mennonite Press Inc E 316 283-3060
Newton *(G-7380)*
Mid West Color Graphics Inc E 620 429-1088
Columbus *(G-1084)*
Midwestern Litho G 620 378-2912
Fredonia *(G-2040)*
Minneapolis Messenger Pubg Co G 785 392-2129
Minneapolis *(G-7118)*
Minuteman Press G 913 829-0300
Olathe *(G-7903)*
Morris Communications Co LLC D 620 231-2600
Pittsburg *(G-9908)*
Morris Communications Co LLC E 620 225-4151
Dodge City *(G-1407)*
Navrats Inc F 620 342-2092
Emporia *(G-1800)*
Northwestern Printers Inc F 785 625-1110
Hays *(G-2881)*
▲ **On Demand Technologies LLC** F 913 438-1800
Overland Park *(G-9102)*
Osage Graphics F 785 654-3939
Burlingame *(G-624)*
Paper Graphics Inc G 620 276-7641
Garden City *(G-2248)*
Par Forms Corporation F 620 421-0970
Parsons *(G-9716)*
Patterson Advertising Agency G 785 232-0533
Topeka *(G-12964)*
Petersen Printing Inc G 620 275-7331
Garden City *(G-2252)*
Pittcraft Printing Inc E 620 231-6200
Pittsburg *(G-9920)*
Pps Inc D 913 791-0164
Olathe *(G-7996)*
◆ **Print Source Inc** D 316 945-7052
Wichita *(G-15349)*
Print Time Inc E 913 345-8900
Leawood *(G-5528)*
Printery Inc F 785 632-5501
Clay Center *(G-877)*
Printery Inc G 785 762-5112
Junction City *(G-3740)*
Printing Inc E 316 265-1201
Wichita *(G-15350)*
Printing Dynamics Inc G 816 524-0444
Olathe *(G-8008)*
Printing Services Inc G 913 492-1500
Lenexa *(G-6070)*
Printing Solutions Kansas Inc G 785 841-8336
Lawrence *(G-5077)*
Printingplus Inc G 316 269-3010
Wichita *(G-15351)*
Professional Graphics Inc F 913 663-3330
Shawnee Mission *(G-11755)*
Pronto Print G 785 823-2285
Salina *(G-10644)*
Proprint Incorporated G 785 272-0070
Topeka *(G-12992)*
Proprint Incorporated E 785 842-3610
Lawrence *(G-5080)*
Quad/Graphics Inc B 816 936-8536
Lenexa *(G-6083)*
Quality Litho Inc E 913 262-5341
Kansas City *(G-4352)*
Quality Printing & Gift Shop G 620 654-3487
Galva *(G-2095)*
▲ **Quality Printing and Off Sups** F 913 491-6366
Lenexa *(G-6084)*
Quality Printing Inc G 620 421-0630
Parsons *(G-9727)*
Ravin Printing LLC G 620 431-5830
Chanute *(G-759)*
RGI Publications Inc E 913 829-8723
Olathe *(G-8030)*
Roberts Hutch-Line Inc E 620 662-3356
Hutchinson *(G-3428)*
▲ **Roth K Christopherson** G 316 269-2494
Wichita *(G-15485)*
Rps Inc F 620 342-3026
Emporia *(G-1817)*
Screen Machine LLC F 785 762-3081
Junction City *(G-3750)*
Seaton Publishing Co Inc D 785 776-2200
Manhattan *(G-6798)*
Sekan Printing Company Inc E 620 223-5190
Fort Scott *(G-2003)*
Shahrokhi Inc G 913 764-5775
Olathe *(G-8060)*
Sharpe Printing Co Inc F 316 262-4041
Wichita *(G-15574)*
Shawnee Copy Center Inc F 913 268-4343
Shawnee Mission *(G-11851)*
Sky Printing and Pubg Inc G 913 362-9292
Shawnee Mission *(G-11873)*
Southwest Holding Corporation E 785 233-5662
Topeka *(G-13083)*
▲ **Spangler Graphics LLC** D 913 722-4500
Overland Park *(G-9332)*
Specialty Projects Corp Inc G 620 429-1086
Columbus *(G-1086)*
◆ **Stouse LLC** C 913 764-5757
New Century *(G-7301)*
Super Speed Printing Inc F 316 283-5828
North Newton *(G-7439)*
Superior Printing Co G 913 682-3313
Leavenworth *(G-5296)*
Tarrant Enterprises Inc F 785 273-8503
Topeka *(G-13142)*
Taylor Printing Inc G 620 672-3656
Pratt *(G-10159)*
Telescope Inc F 785 527-2244
Belleville *(G-467)*
Topeka Blue Print & Sup Co Inc G 785 232-7209
Topeka *(G-13169)*
Valley Offset Printing Inc E 316 755-0061
Valley Center *(G-13360)*
Waynes Printing & Copying G 620 662-4655
Hutchinson *(G-3482)*
Wichita Press Inc G 316 945-5651
Wichita *(G-16018)*
Wilbert Screen Printing Inc G 620 231-1730
Pittsburg *(G-9970)*
Winfield Publishing Co Inc E 620 221-1100
Winfield *(G-16189)*
Wooten Printing Co Inc G 316 265-8575
Wichita *(G-16070)*
Z3 Graphix Inc E 913 599-3355
Overland Park *(G-9525)*

2754 Commercial Printing: Gravure

Ace Forms of Kansas Inc D 620 232-9290
Pittsburg *(G-9805)*
Superior Printing Co G 913 682-3313
Leavenworth *(G-5296)*
▲ **W/K Holding Company Inc** F 620 223-5500
Fort Scott *(G-2016)*

2759 Commercial Printing

4th Gneration Promotional Pdts G 913 393-0837
Olathe *(G-7502)*
Abilene Printing Co Inc G 785 263-2330
Abilene *(G-7)*
Administration Kansas Dept D 785 296-3631
Topeka *(G-12289)*
Arrow Printing Company Inc G 785 825-8124
Salina *(G-10409)*
Art Craft Printers & Design G 785 776-9151
Manhattan *(G-6545)*
B Scott Studio Inc G 316 321-1225
El Dorado *(G-1533)*
Baker Bros Printing Co Inc G 620 947-3520
Hillsboro *(G-3041)*
Blue Eagle Productions Inc F 816 225-2980
Overland Park *(G-8466)*
Bolen Office Supply Inc F 620 672-7535
Pratt *(G-10100)*
▲ **Brightmarks LLC** E 913 338-1131
Lenexa *(G-5713)*
Brileys Designs & Signs E 913 579-7533
Shawnee Mission *(G-11182)*
Capital Label LLC G 785 291-9702
Topeka *(G-12433)*
CB Grduation Announcements LLC E 785 776-5018
Manhattan *(G-6578)*
Central Printing & Binding G 620 665-7251
Hutchinson *(G-3233)*

Coffeyville Printing Center G 620 251-6040
Coffeyville *(G-920)*
Copy Co Corporation G 785 832-2679
Lawrence *(G-4811)*
Copy Co Corporation E 785 823-2679
Salina *(G-10463)*
Creative Design TS Inc F 316 681-1868
Bel Aire *(G-431)*
Creative Signs & Design Inc G 785 233-8000
Topeka *(G-12528)*
Custom Color Corp E 913 730-3100
Lenexa *(G-5798)*
D Rockey Holdings Inc E 816 474-9423
Kansas City *(G-3950)*
Dataco Derex Inc F 913 438-2444
Leawood *(G-5370)*
▲ **David Camp Inc** C 913 648-0573
Overland Park *(G-8641)*
▲ **Davies Communications Inc** F 620 241-1504
McPherson *(G-6956)*
Daymark Solutions Inc F 913 541-8980
Shawnee Mission *(G-11294)*
Deluxe Corporation C 913 888-3801
Lenexa *(G-5810)*
▲ **Digital Lagoon Inc** F 913 648-6900
Overland Park *(G-8656)*
Documart Inc F 913 649-3800
Shawnee Mission *(G-11312)*
Donmar Inc F 913 432-2700
Shawnee Mission *(G-11315)*
Drafting Room Inc G 316 267-2291
Wichita *(G-14236)*
Drexel Technologies Inc E 913 371-4430
Lenexa *(G-5826)*
Edoc Printing G 913 469-0071
Shawnee Mission *(G-11328)*
Ejrex Inc D 620 421-6200
Parsons *(G-9683)*
Elitegear4ucom LLC G 316 993-4398
Wichita *(G-14271)*
Epi Holdings Inc E 816 474-9423
Kansas City *(G-3992)*
Express Card and Label Co Inc E 785 233-0369
Topeka *(G-12589)*
Falcon Design and Mfg E 913 441-1074
Shawnee *(G-10953)*
Falcon Enterprises Inc C 727 579-1233
Wichita *(G-14336)*
Federal Prison Industries D 913 682-8700
Leavenworth *(G-5238)*
Fedex Office & Print Svcs Inc F 913 677-4488
Shawnee Mission *(G-11365)*
Fedex Office & Print Svcs Inc E 785 272-2500
Topeka *(G-12603)*
Fontastik Inc G 816 474-4366
Kansas City *(G-4015)*
Garnett Publishing Inc F 785 448-3121
Garnett *(G-2373)*
Gary Bell G 785 233-6677
Holton *(G-3090)*
GC Labels Inc F 913 897-6966
Stilwell *(G-12148)*
Genigraphics LLC F 913 441-1410
Shawnee *(G-10961)*
George Eschbaugh Advg Inc E 785 658-2105
Wilson *(G-16105)*
Gone Logo Screen Printing G 785 625-3070
Hays *(G-2820)*
Goodwin Sporting Goods Inc G 785 625-2419
Hays *(G-2821)*
Graphic Impressions Inc E 620 663-5939
Hutchinson *(G-3305)*
Gray County Printers G 620 855-2467
Cimarron *(G-828)*
Greeley County Republican G 620 376-4264
Tribune *(G-13271)*
Gregory A Scott Inc E 913 677-0414
Kansas City *(G-4053)*
Guerrilla Marketing Inc G 800 946-9150
Newton *(G-7353)*
Holderman Printing LLC G 913 557-6848
Paola *(G-9567)*
Iola Register Inc E 620 365-2111
Iola *(G-3611)*
Iris Strgc Mktg Support Inc E 913 232-4825
Lenexa *(G-5923)*
▲ **Its Greek To Me Inc** C 800 336-4486
Manhattan *(G-6666)*
Kc Digical G 913 541-2688
Lenexa *(G-5940)*
Kellys Corporate Apparel G 316 263-5858
Wichita *(G-14847)*
Kelsey Construction Inc G 913 894-0330
Shawnee Mission *(G-11528)*
Kendall Packaging Corporation E 620 231-9804
Pittsburg *(G-9891)*
Khaos Apparel LLC F 316 804-4900
Newton *(G-7370)*
Kingston Printing & Design Inc F 785 690-7222
Eudora *(G-1878)*
L V S Inc E 316 636-5005
Wichita *(G-14908)*
Last Chance Graphics Inc G 785 263-4470
Abilene *(G-44)*
Lee Reed Engraving Inc G 316 943-9700
Wichita *(G-14949)*
Leroy Cook G 316 321-0844
El Dorado *(G-1583)*
Linn County Publishing Inc F 913 352-6235
Pleasanton *(G-9997)*
▼ **Lowen Corporation** B 620 663-2161
Hutchinson *(G-3358)*
Lynn Tape & Label F 913 422-0484
Kansas City *(G-4210)*
▲ **Mainline Printing Inc** D 785 233-2338
Topeka *(G-12856)*
Marketing Technologies Inc D 913 342-9111
Kansas City *(G-4218)*
McCartys G 620 251-6169
Coffeyville *(G-957)*
Mennonite Press Inc E 316 283-3060
Newton *(G-7380)*
Midwest Single Source Inc E 316 267-6333
Wichita *(G-15102)*
Mr PS Party Outlet Inc F 785 537-1804
Manhattan *(G-6753)*
National Bd For Rspratory Care F 913 895-4900
Overland Park *(G-9069)*
National Engraving E 785 776-5757
Manhattan *(G-6757)*
Navrats Inc F 620 342-2092
Emporia *(G-1800)*
New Wave Enterprises Inc F 913 287-7671
Kansas City *(G-4287)*
Niffie Printing Inc F 913 592-3040
Spring Hill *(G-12091)*
Northwest Awards & Signs G 785 621-2116
Hays *(G-2880)*
Norton Enterprises G 620 221-1987
Winfield *(G-16164)*
▲ **On Demand Technologies LLC** F 913 438-1800
Overland Park *(G-9102)*
Paper Graphics Inc G 620 276-7641
Garden City *(G-2248)*
Perfect Output LLC D 913 317-8400
Overland Park *(G-9154)*
Pinnacle Plotting and Sup Lc G 913 766-1822
Shawnee *(G-11011)*
Pittcraft Printing Inc E 620 231-6200
Pittsburg *(G-9920)*
Prairie Print Inc G 316 267-1950
Wichita *(G-15321)*
Prestige Graphics Inc F 316 262-3480
Wichita *(G-15338)*
◆ **Print Source Inc** D 316 945-7052
Wichita *(G-15349)*
Print Tech Inc G 913 894-6644
Olathe *(G-8007)*
Print Time Inc E 913 345-8900
Leawood *(G-5528)*
Printery Inc F 785 632-5501
Clay Center *(G-877)*
Printing Inc E 316 265-1201
Wichita *(G-15350)*
Printing Services Inc G 913 492-1500
Lenexa *(G-6070)*
Priority Envelope Inc E 913 859-9710
Lenexa *(G-6071)*
Professional Bank Forms G 620 455-2205
Oxford *(G-9534)*
Professional Printing Kans Inc F 620 343-7125
Emporia *(G-1813)*
PSI Services Inc C 913 895-4600
Olathe *(G-8011)*
Quality Litho Inc E 913 262-5341
Kansas City *(G-4352)*
Quality Printing & Gift Shop G 620 654-3487
Galva *(G-2095)*
Quality Printing Inc G 620 421-0630
Parsons *(G-9727)*
R Miller Sales Co Inc E 913 341-3727
Shawnee Mission *(G-11772)*
Ragland Specialty Printing E 785 542-3058
Eudora *(G-1879)*
Rand Graphics Inc E 316 942-1125
Wichita *(G-15414)*
▲ **Resellers Edge LLC** F 620 364-3398
Burlington *(G-642)*
Sands Enterprises Inc G 316 942-8686
Wichita *(G-15518)*
◆ **Screen-It Grphics Lawrence Inc** C 785 843-8888
Lawrence *(G-5107)*
Shahrokhi Inc G 913 764-5775
Olathe *(G-8060)*
Shire Signs LLC G 316 838-1362
Park City *(G-9643)*
Shirts Plus Inc F 316 788-1550
Derby *(G-1272)*
Sign Solutions F 620 442-5649
Arkansas City *(G-179)*
Simon & Simon Inc G 913 888-9889
Overland Park *(G-9311)*
Southwest Holding Corporation E 785 233-5662
Topeka *(G-13083)*
▲ **Spangler Graphics LLC** D 913 722-4500
Overland Park *(G-9332)*
Special Tee Graphics G 620 227-8160
Dodge City *(G-1434)*
Spectragraphics Inc E 913 888-6828
Lenexa *(G-6147)*
Sterling Screen Printing Inc F 913 441-4411
Shawnee *(G-11034)*
Stewarts Sports & Awards G 620 241-5990
McPherson *(G-7028)*
Superior School Supplies Inc F 620 421-3190
Parsons *(G-9743)*
Tabco Incorporated E 913 287-3333
Kansas City *(G-4457)*
Taylor Printing Inc G 620 672-3656
Pratt *(G-10159)*
Tioga Territory Ltd F 620 431-2479
Chanute *(G-770)*
Tmi Corp F 785 232-8705
Topeka *(G-13161)*
Trainwreck Tees LLC G 620 224-2480
Fort Scott *(G-2011)*
Tritats LLC G 913 219-5949
Overland Park *(G-9431)*
▲ **U S Logo Inc** F 316 264-1321
Wichita *(G-15824)*
U S S A Inc G 316 686-1653
Wichita *(G-15826)*
▲ **Universal Manufacturing Co** C 816 231-2771
Shawnee *(G-11044)*
▲ **Universal Products Inc** C 316 794-8601
Goddard *(G-2455)*
Walson Ink Inc G 785 537-7370
Manhattan *(G-6845)*
Witzkes Screen Printing G 913 839-8270
Olathe *(G-8156)*

2761 Manifold Business Forms

Ace Forms of Kansas Inc D 620 232-9290
Pittsburg *(G-9805)*
▲ **Calibrated Forms** C 620 429-1120
Columbus *(G-1064)*
Ennis Inc D 620 223-6500
Fort Scott *(G-1965)*
Ennis Business Forms of Kansas D 620 223-6500
Fort Scott *(G-1966)*
Federal Prison Industries D 913 682-8700
Leavenworth *(G-5238)*
Flesh Company D 620 421-6120
Parsons *(G-9686)*
General Dynamics Info Tech Inc E 785 832-0207
Lawrence *(G-4871)*
Kansas Business Forms LLC E 620 724-5234
Girard *(G-2414)*
▲ **Ward-Kraft Inc** B 800 821-4021
Fort Scott *(G-2017)*

2771 Greeting Card Publishing

Hallmark Cards Incorporated E 785 843-9050
Lawrence *(G-4886)*
World Publishing Inc E 785 221-8174
Topeka *(G-13252)*

2782 Blankbooks & Looseleaf Binders

Deluxe Corporation C 913 888-3801
Lenexa *(G-5810)*

Employee Codes: A=Over 500 employees, B=251-500
C=101-250, D=51-100, E=20-50, F=10-19, G=5-9

Leslie Company Inc .... D 913 764-6660
Olathe *(G-7859)*

2789 Bookbinding

Administration Kansas Dept .... D 785 296-3631
Topeka *(G-12289)*
Adr Inc .... D 316 522-5599
Wichita *(G-13616)*
Bindery Express Inc .... G 316 944-8163
Wichita *(G-13850)*
Cookbook Publishers Inc .... E 913 689-3038
Overland Park *(G-8598)*
Copy Center of Topeka Inc .... E 785 233-6677
Topeka *(G-12507)*
Davis Publications Inc .... F 785 945-6170
Valley Falls *(G-13362)*
Deluxe Corporation .... C 913 888-3801
Lenexa *(G-5810)*
Documart Inc .... F 913 649-3800
Shawnee Mission *(G-11312)*
Ejrex Inc .... D 620 421-6200
Parsons *(G-9683)*
Fedex Office & Print Svcs Inc .... F 316 941-9909
Wichita *(G-14352)*
Gary Bell .... G 785 233-6677
Holton *(G-3090)*
Graphic Images Inc .... F 316 283-3776
Newton *(G-7352)*
J-Con Reprographics Inc .... F 913 859-0800
Lenexa *(G-5927)*
Kelsey Construction Inc .... G 913 894-0330
Shawnee Mission *(G-11528)*
Kopco Inc .... D 620 879-2117
Caney *(G-671)*
Mennonite Press Inc .... E 316 283-3060
Newton *(G-7380)*
Midwestern Litho .... G 620 378-2912
Fredonia *(G-2040)*
Navrats Inc .... F 620 342-2092
Emporia *(G-1800)*
▲ **On Demand Technologies LLC** .... F 913 438-1800
Overland Park *(G-9102)*
Pittcraft Printing Inc .... E 620 231-6200
Pittsburg *(G-9920)*
Print Time Inc .... E 913 345-8900
Leawood *(G-5528)*
Printery Inc .... F 785 632-5501
Clay Center *(G-877)*
Printing Inc .... E 316 265-1201
Wichita *(G-15350)*
Proprint Incorporated .... E 785 842-3610
Lawrence *(G-5080)*
Quality Litho Inc .... E 913 262-5341
Kansas City *(G-4352)*
Quality Printing Inc .... G 620 421-0630
Parsons *(G-9727)*
RGI Publications Inc .... E 913 829-8723
Olathe *(G-8030)*
Taylor Printing Inc .... G 620 672-3656
Pratt *(G-10159)*
Valley Offset Printing Inc .... E 316 755-0061
Valley Center *(G-13360)*
Wichita Bindery Inc .... E 316 262-3473
Wichita *(G-15981)*

2791 Typesetting

Administration Kansas Dept .... D 785 296-3631
Topeka *(G-12289)*
Art Craft Printers & Design .... G 785 776-9151
Manhattan *(G-6545)*
Consolidated Prtg & Sty Co Inc .... E 785 825-5426
Salina *(G-10460)*
Cookbook Publishers Inc .... E 913 689-3038
Overland Park *(G-8598)*
Copy Center of Topeka Inc .... E 785 233-6677
Topeka *(G-12507)*
Davis Publications Inc .... F 785 945-6170
Valley Falls *(G-13362)*
Deluxe Corporation .... C 913 888-3801
Lenexa *(G-5810)*
Ejrex Inc .... D 620 421-6200
Parsons *(G-9683)*
Gary Bell .... G 785 233-6677
Holton *(G-3090)*
Graphic Images Inc .... F 316 283-3776
Newton *(G-7352)*
J-Con Reprographics Inc .... F 913 859-0800
Lenexa *(G-5927)*
Kelsey Construction Inc .... G 913 894-0330
Shawnee Mission *(G-11528)*
Kopco Inc .... D 620 879-2117
Caney *(G-671)*
Mennonite Press Inc .... E 316 283-3060
Newton *(G-7380)*
Mid West Color Graphics Inc .... E 620 429-1088
Columbus *(G-1084)*
Midwestern Litho .... G 620 378-2912
Fredonia *(G-2040)*
Par Forms Corporation .... F 620 421-0970
Parsons *(G-9716)*
Print Time Inc .... E 913 345-8900
Leawood *(G-5528)*
Printery Inc .... F 785 632-5501
Clay Center *(G-877)*
Proprint Incorporated .... E 785 842-3610
Lawrence *(G-5080)*
Quality Printing Inc .... G 620 421-0630
Parsons *(G-9727)*
R Miller Sales Co Inc .... E 913 341-3727
Shawnee Mission *(G-11772)*
Taylor Printing Inc .... G 620 672-3656
Pratt *(G-10159)*
Valley Offset Printing Inc .... E 316 755-0061
Valley Center *(G-13360)*

2796 Platemaking & Related Svcs

Abilene Printing Co Inc .... G 785 263-2330
Abilene *(G-7)*
Copy Center of Topeka Inc .... E 785 233-6677
Topeka *(G-12507)*
Ejrex Inc .... D 620 421-6200
Parsons *(G-9683)*
Mid West Color Graphics Inc .... E 620 429-1088
Columbus *(G-1084)*
Printery Inc .... F 785 632-5501
Clay Center *(G-877)*
▲ **Universal Engraving Inc** .... C 913 599-0600
Overland Park *(G-9447)*

28 CHEMICALS AND ALLIED PRODUCTS

2812 Alkalies & Chlorine

Clorox Company .... F 913 664-9000
Overland Park *(G-8568)*
FMC Corporation .... D 316 729-5321
Wichita *(G-14395)*

2813 Industrial Gases

Air Products and Chemicals Inc .... F 620 626-7062
Liberal *(G-6274)*
Air Products and Chemicals Inc .... E 316 522-8181
Haysville *(G-2935)*
Air Products and Chemicals Inc .... D 620 626-5700
Liberal *(G-6275)*
Koch Fertilizer LLC .... E 620 227-8631
Dodge City *(G-1394)*
▲ **Koch Fertilizer LLC** .... E 316 828-5010
Wichita *(G-14880)*
Linde Gas North America LLC .... G 785 387-2281
Otis *(G-8240)*
Messer LLC .... E 785 387-2281
Otis *(G-8241)*
Messer LLC .... G 620 251-9190
Coffeyville *(G-962)*
Praxair Inc .... G 620 225-1368
Wright *(G-16193)*
Praxair Inc .... E 620 562-4500
Lorraine *(G-6434)*
Praxair Distribution Inc .... E 913 492-1551
Lenexa *(G-6069)*

2816 Inorganic Pigments

Standridge Color Corporation .... F 316 283-5061
Newton *(G-7419)*

2819 Indl Inorganic Chemicals, NEC

American Phoenix Inc .... E 785 862-7722
Topeka *(G-12320)*
Ce Water Management Inc .... G 913 621-7047
Kansas City *(G-3899)*
Chemtrade Refinery Svcs Inc .... D 785 843-2290
Lawrence *(G-4785)*
Compass Minerals America Inc .... C 620 257-2324
Lyons *(G-6480)*
◆ **Compass Minerals Group Inc** .... C 913 344-9100
Overland Park *(G-8588)*
◆ **Compass Minerals Intl Inc** .... C 913 344-9200
Overland Park *(G-8589)*
Conspec Marketing and Mfg Co .... A 913 287-1700
Kansas City *(G-3933)*
◆ **Corbion America Holdings Inc** .... D 913 890-5500
Lenexa *(G-5787)*
▲ **Event Elements LLC** .... G 316 440-2829
Wichita *(G-14313)*
Harcros Chemicals Inc .... C 913 621-7721
Kansas City *(G-4069)*
Helena Chemical Company .... G 620 375-2073
Leoti *(G-6253)*
Kemira Chemicals Inc .... G 785 434-2474
Plainville *(G-9988)*
◆ **Koch Mineral Services LLC** .... E 316 828-5500
Wichita *(G-14884)*
Koch Sulfur Products Co LLC .... E 316 828-5500
Wichita *(G-14889)*
Meridian Chemicals LLC .... G 913 253-2220
Overland Park *(G-9011)*
Mineral-Right Inc .... F 785 543-6571
Phillipsburg *(G-9791)*
Nalco Company .... G 620 624-1594
Liberal *(G-6347)*
Occidental Chemical Corp .... E 316 524-4211
Wichita *(G-15206)*
Perimeter Solutions LP .... C 785 749-8100
Lawrence *(G-5061)*
PQ Corporation .... D 913 371-3020
Kansas City *(G-4329)*
PQ Corporation .... F 913 227-0561
Lenexa *(G-6065)*

2821 Plastics, Mtrls & Nonvulcanizable Elastomers

Ach Foam Technologies Inc .... D 913 321-4114
Kansas City *(G-3782)*
DOT Green Bioplastics Inc .... F 620 273-8919
Emporia *(G-1730)*
DOT Green Bioplastics LLC .... G 785 889-4600
Onaga *(G-8175)*
Flint Hlls Rsrces Longview LLC .... F 316 828-5500
Wichita *(G-14393)*
McPu Polymer Engineering LLC .... G 620 231-4239
Pittsburg *(G-9901)*
◆ **National Plastics Color Inc** .... C 316 755-1273
Valley Center *(G-13349)*
North Amrcn Specialty Pdts LLC .... F 620 241-5511
McPherson *(G-7010)*
Rapid Processing Solutions Inc .... F 316 265-2001
Wichita *(G-15417)*
▲ **Sunbelt Chemicals Inc** .... F 972 296-3920
Shawnee *(G-11035)*
Techmer Pm LLC .... E 316 943-1520
Wichita *(G-15725)*
Zell-Metall Usa Inc .... F 913 327-0300
Lenexa *(G-6240)*

2822 Synthetic Rubber (Vulcanizable Elastomers)

▲ **Everseal Gasket Inc** .... E 913 441-9232
Shawnee Mission *(G-11351)*

2833 Medicinal Chemicals & Botanical Prdts

Ivy Animal Health Inc .... F 913 888-2192
Lenexa *(G-5925)*
Suther Feeds Inc .... F 785 292-4414
Frankfort *(G-2023)*

2834 Pharmaceuticals

Alixa Rx LLC .... G 913 307-8150
Lenexa *(G-5640)*
Aratana Therapeutics Inc .... D 913 353-1000
Leawood *(G-5329)*
Arconic Inc .... G 620 665-2932
Hutchinson *(G-3206)*
▲ **B F Ascher & Company Inc** .... E 913 888-1880
Lenexa *(G-5680)*
Baxter Drug Inc .... G 620 856-5858
Baxter Springs *(G-396)*
Bayer Healthcare LLC .... E 913 268-2000
Shawnee Mission *(G-11154)*
Bayer Hlthcare Animal Hlth Inc .... E 913 268-2731
Shawnee *(G-10915)*
Biomed Kansas Inc .... G 913 661-0100
Lenexa *(G-5705)*
Carefusion 213 LLC .... B 800 523-0502
Leawood *(G-5347)*

Celgene Corporation ....F 913 266-0300
Overland Park *(G-8534)*
Centaur Inc ....G....... 913 390-6184
Olathe *(G-7583)*
Crititech Particle Engg ....F 785 841-7120
Lawrence *(G-4818)*
Cydex Pharmaceuticals Inc ....F 913 685-8850
Lawrence *(G-4822)*
◆ **Diversified Sports Tech LLC**........G....... 949 466-2393
Baxter Springs *(G-404)*
E I Du Pont De Nemours & Co ....F 302 774-1000
New Century *(G-7282)*
Elias Animal Health LLC........G....... 913 492-2221
Olathe *(G-7676)*
Fagron Compounding Svcs LLC ....E 316 773-0405
Wichita *(G-14332)*
Genzada Pharmaceuticals LLC ....G....... 620 204-7150
Sterling *(G-12119)*
Glaxosmithkline LLC ....E 316 214-4811
Wichita *(G-14470)*
Hospira Inc ....B 620 241-6200
McPherson *(G-6976)*
Ivy Animal Health Inc........E 913 310-7900
Lenexa *(G-5924)*
Ligand Pharmaceuticals Inc ....G....... 785 856-2346
Lawrence *(G-4996)*
McShares Inc........E 785 825-2181
Salina *(G-10598)*
Med Care of Kansas Inc ....F 785 295-8548
Topeka *(G-12876)*
Med Care of Kansas Inc ....G....... 785 295-8548
Topeka *(G-12877)*
Merck Sharp & Dohme Corp ....D....... 913 422-6001
De Soto *(G-1208)*
Norbrook Inc........G....... 913 802-5050
Overland Park *(G-9093)*
◆ **Norbrook Inc** ....E 913 599-5777
Lenexa *(G-6026)*
OBrien Pharmacy........F 913 322-0001
Shawnee Mission *(G-11693)*
Parnell Corporate Svcs US Inc ....E 913 274-2100
Leawood *(G-5515)*
Pfizer Inc........C 913 897-3054
Leawood *(G-5521)*
Pharmion Corporation........E 913 266-0300
Overland Park *(G-9161)*
Prescription Centre........G....... 620 364-5523
Burlington *(G-641)*
Rd2rx LLC........F 816 754-8047
Lenexa *(G-6093)*
Sparhawk Laboratories Inc ....D....... 913 888-7500
Lenexa *(G-6144)*
Teva Neuroscience Inc ....D....... 913 777-3000
Leawood *(G-5573)*
Teva Pharmaceuticals ....G....... 610 727-6055
Leawood *(G-5574)*
Via Chrsti Rhbltation Hosp Inc ....G....... 316 946-1790
Wichita *(G-15903)*

2835 Diagnostic Substances

Abaxis Inc........E 913 787-7400
Olathe *(G-7506)*
George King Bio-Medical Inc ....F 913 469-5464
Shawnee Mission *(G-11396)*
K State Rabies Laboratory ....F 785 532-4472
Manhattan *(G-6668)*
Petnet Solutions Inc ....G....... 913 310-9270
Overland Park *(G-9160)*
Plastikon Healthcare LLC........E 785 330-7100
Lawrence *(G-5069)*
Progene Biomedical Inc ....F 913 492-2224
Lenexa *(G-6074)*
Remel........G....... 913 895-4362
Lenexa *(G-6101)*

2836 Biological Prdts, Exc Diagnostic Substances

▲ **Alpha Biosystems Inc**........G....... 316 265-7929
Wichita *(G-13680)*
Aratana Therapeutics Inc........D 913 353-1000
Leawood *(G-5329)*
Bio-Next Inc........G....... 316 260-1540
Wichita *(G-13851)*
Biomune Company........F 913 894-0230
Lenexa *(G-5706)*
◆ **Biomune Company**........D....... 913 894-0230
Lenexa *(G-5707)*
Central Biomedia Inc ....E 913 541-0090
Shawnee Mission *(G-11212)*
Ceva Biomune........E 913 894-0230
Lenexa *(G-5746)*
Csl Plasma Inc........E 785 749-5750
Lawrence *(G-4819)*
Csl Plasma Inc........F 785 776-9177
Manhattan *(G-6607)*
Ms Biotec LLC........E 785 456-1388
Wamego *(G-13429)*
Phytotech Labs Inc........F 913 341-5343
Lenexa *(G-6056)*
▲ **Phytotechnology Labs LLC** ....F 913 341-5343
Lenexa *(G-6057)*
◆ **Remel Inc**........A....... 800 255-6730
Lenexa *(G-6102)*
◆ **Safc Biosciences Inc**........E 913 469-5580
Lenexa *(G-6116)*
Xenotech LLC........C....... 913 438-7450
Kansas City *(G-4559)*

2841 Soap & Detergents

ACS Iiiiii - Ks LLC........F 316 683-3489
Wichita *(G-13609)*
Procter & Gamble Mfg Co ....B 913 573-0200
Kansas City *(G-4341)*
Product Dev & Designers........F 913 783-4364
Paola *(G-9584)*
Prosoco Inc........D....... 785 865-4200
Lawrence *(G-5081)*
▲ **Vvf Intervest LLC** ....F 913 281-7444
Kansas City *(G-4523)*
▲ **Vvf Kansas LLC**........E 913 281-7444
Kansas City *(G-4524)*
▲ **Vvf Kansas Services LLC**........C....... 913 529-2292
Kansas City *(G-4525)*

2842 Spec Cleaning, Polishing & Sanitation Preparations

Clorox Company........F 913 664-9000
Overland Park *(G-8568)*
Clorox Products Mfg Co........G....... 913 620-1777
Overland Park *(G-8569)*
Heartland At-Chlor Systems LLC ....F 806 373-4277
Wichita *(G-14580)*
Illinois Tool Works Inc ....D....... 913 397-9889
Olathe *(G-7784)*
ITW Dymon........F 913 397-9889
Olathe *(G-7803)*
Product Dev & Designers........F 913 783-4364
Paola *(G-9584)*
Prosoco Inc........D....... 785 865-4200
Lawrence *(G-5081)*
Pur-O-Zone Inc........E 785 843-0771
Lawrence *(G-5082)*
Rehrig Penn Logistics Inc........G....... 620 624-5171
Liberal *(G-6359)*
Sani Wax Inc........G....... 913 383-9703
Prairie Village *(G-10065)*
Thrift Marketing Inc........G....... 913 236-7474
Shawnee Mission *(G-11931)*
Ultra-Chem Inc ....C....... 913 492-2929
Shawnee Mission *(G-11955)*
W F Leonard Co Inc ....G....... 785 484-3342
Meriden *(G-7084)*
Waxene Products Company Inc ....G....... 316 263-8523
Wichita *(G-15938)*

2844 Perfumes, Cosmetics & Toilet Preparations

▲ **Central Solutions Inc**........E 913 621-6542
Kansas City *(G-3902)*
Conopco Inc ....C....... 913 782-7171
New Century *(G-7274)*
▲ **Millenia Productions LLC**........F 316 425-2500
Wichita *(G-15108)*
Product Dev & Designers........F 913 783-4364
Paola *(G-9584)*

2851 Paints, Varnishes, Lacquers, Enamels

AMBS and Associates Inc........G....... 913 599-5939
Lenexa *(G-5644)*
◆ **Epro Services Inc** ....F 316 262-2513
Wichita *(G-14298)*
Lorac Company Inc........F 316 263-2565
Wichita *(G-14979)*
Master Pnt Indus Coating Corp........F 316 283-3999
Newton *(G-7377)*
Paragon N D T & Finishes Inc........E 316 945-5285
Wichita *(G-15259)*
PPG Industries Inc........E 316 262-2456
Bel Aire *(G-438)*
PPG Industries Inc........E 913 681-5573
Overland Park *(G-9174)*
Prosoco Inc........D....... 785 865-4200
Lawrence *(G-5081)*
Raven Lining Systems Inc ....F 918 615-0020
Kansas City *(G-4362)*
▲ **Superior Products Intl II Inc**........G....... 913 962-4848
Shawnee Mission *(G-11912)*
Vanberg Specialized Coatings........G....... 913 948-9825
Lenexa *(G-6208)*
▲ **Versaflex Inc**........E 913 321-9000
Kansas City *(G-4519)*

2865 Cyclic-Crudes, Intermediates, Dyes & Org Pigments

Standridge Color Corporation ....F 316 283-5061
Newton *(G-7419)*

2869 Industrial Organic Chemicals, NEC

Abengoa Bnergy Hybrid Kans LLC ....F 316 796-1234
Colwich *(G-1091)*
Arkalon Energy LLC ....E 620 624-2901
Liberal *(G-6279)*
Bonanza Bioenergy LLC ....E 620 276-4741
Garden City *(G-2115)*
◆ **Corbion America Holdings Inc**........D....... 913 890-5500
Lenexa *(G-5787)*
East Kansas Agri-Energy LLC ....E 785 448-2888
Garnett *(G-2372)*
Emergent Green Energy Inc........F 620 450-4320
Minneola *(G-7124)*
Energy Tech Unlimited LLC ....G....... 913 837-4616
Louisburg *(G-6447)*
Fhr Biofuels & Ingredients LLC........G....... 316 828-2400
Wichita *(G-14361)*
Flint Hills Resources Port........D....... 316 828-5500
Wichita *(G-14392)*
FMC Corporation........D....... 316 729-5321
Wichita *(G-14395)*
Gateway Ethanol LLC........E 620 933-2288
Pratt *(G-10118)*
◆ **Harcros Chemicals Inc**........C....... 913 321-3131
Kansas City *(G-4068)*
Jacam Chemicals 2013 LLC........C....... 620 278-3355
Sterling *(G-12123)*
Kansas Ethanol LLC ....D....... 620 257-2300
Lyons *(G-6487)*
Kemira Chemicals Inc........G....... 785 434-2474
Plainville *(G-9988)*
Koch Industries Inc........G....... 620 834-2204
McPherson *(G-6984)*
Koch Industries Inc........F 620 662-6691
Hutchinson *(G-3352)*
Labone Inc........G....... 913 577-1643
Shawnee Mission *(G-11545)*
◆ **Lansing Trade Group LLC** ....C 913 748-3000
Overland Park *(G-8945)*
Midwest Fuels LLC ....G....... 913 299-3331
Kansas City *(G-4252)*
Natures Way Inc........G....... 785 486-3302
Horton *(G-3132)*
Nesika Energy LLC ....G....... 785 335-2054
Scandia *(G-10800)*
Pbi-Gordon Corporation........E 816 421-4070
Kansas City *(G-4317)*
Phytotech Labs Inc........F 913 341-5343
Lenexa *(G-6056)*
Prairie Horzn Agri-Energy LLC ....E 785 543-6719
Phillipsburg *(G-9794)*
Pratt Energy LLC........E 620 933-2288
Pratt *(G-10136)*
◆ **Purac America Inc** ....E 913 890-5500
Lenexa *(G-6081)*
Reeve Agri-Energy Inc........F 620 275-7541
Garden City *(G-2264)*
S&K Fuels LLC ....G....... 785 454-6219
Cawker City *(G-689)*
Seaboard Energy Oklahoma LLC ....E 913 261-2620
Shawnee Mission *(G-11841)*
Simply Fuel LLC........G....... 913 269-1889
Overland Park *(G-9312)*
Trenton Agri Products LLC ....G 316 265-3311
Wichita *(G-15798)*
Ube Services LLC ....E 316 616-3500
Wichita *(G-15827)*
Western Plains Energy LLC ....E 785 672-8810
Oakley *(G-7488)*

2873 Nitrogenous Fertilizers

Biostar Systems LLC ... G ... 913 438-3002
Overland Park *(G-8451)*

Coffeyville Acquisition LLC ... E ... 913 982-0500
Kansas City *(G-3922)*

Coffeyville Resources LLC ... E ... 913 982-0500
Kansas City *(G-3923)*

Coffeyvlle Ntrgn Frtlizers Inc ... C ... 913 982-0500
Kansas City *(G-3924)*

Coffeyvlle Rsrces Ref Mktg LLC ... D ... 620 251-4000
Coffeyville *(G-925)*

Isp Technologies Inc ... G ... 785 760-1572
Lawrence *(G-4916)*

Koch Fertilizer LLC ... E ... 620 227-8631
Dodge City *(G-1394)*

▲ Koch Fertilizer LLC ... E ... 316 828-5010
Wichita *(G-14880)*

Koch Industries Inc ... E ... 620 227-8631
Dodge City *(G-1395)*

◆ Koch Mineral Services LLC ... E ... 316 828-5500
Wichita *(G-14884)*

Tessenderlo Kerley Inc ... F ... 620 241-1727
McPherson *(G-7031)*

United Prairie Ag LLC ... D ... 620 356-2212
Ulysses *(G-13329)*

United Prairie Ag LLC ... E ... 620 356-1241
Ulysses *(G-13330)*

2874 Phosphatic Fertilizers

Blicks Phsphate Cnversions LLC ... G ... 800 932-5425
Garden City *(G-2113)*

Mid-West Fertilizer Inc ... G ... 620 431-3430
Chanute *(G-743)*

2875 Fertilizers, Mixing Only

Archer-Daniels-Midland Company ... G ... 620 675-2226
Sublette *(G-12198)*

Cropland Co-Op Inc ... F ... 620 649-2230
Satanta *(G-10782)*

Farmers Union Coop Assn ... F ... 785 632-5632
Clay Center *(G-863)*

Helena Agri-Enterprises LLC ... E ... 620 275-9531
Garden City *(G-2195)*

Kugler Oil Company ... G ... 620 356-4347
Ulysses *(G-13304)*

Leroy Cooperative Assn Inc ... E ... 620 964-2225
Le Roy *(G-5196)*

Pbi-Gordon Corporation ... E ... 620 848-3849
Crestline *(G-1184)*

Pbi-Gordon Corporation ... E ... 816 421-4070
Kansas City *(G-4317)*

R & R Manufacturing Inc ... F ... 620 672-7461
Pratt *(G-10147)*

Right Cooperative Association ... E ... 620 227-8611
Wright *(G-16194)*

2879 Pesticides & Agricultural Chemicals, NEC

C5 Manufacturing LLC ... E ... 620 532-3675
Kingman *(G-4584)*

Dupont ... F ... 913 327-3518
Overland Park *(G-8666)*

FMC Corporation ... D ... 316 729-5321
Wichita *(G-14395)*

◆ Jayhawk Fine Chemicals Corp ... C ... 620 783-1321
Galena *(G-2075)*

◆ Pbi-Gordon Corporation ... D ... 816 421-4070
Shawnee *(G-11009)*

Pbi-Gordon Corporation ... E ... 816 421-4070
Kansas City *(G-4317)*

Pbi-Gordon Corporation ... E ... 620 848-3849
Galena *(G-2080)*

Pbi-Gordon Corporation ... E ... 620 848-3849
Crestline *(G-1184)*

▼ Specialty Fertilizer Pdts LLC ... F ... 913 956-7500
Leawood *(G-5556)*

2891 Adhesives & Sealants

Barker B&C Investments LLC ... F ... 620 669-0145
Hutchinson *(G-3215)*

▼ Certanteed Gyps Fnshg Pdts Inc ... F ... 785 762-2994
Junction City *(G-3680)*

Evonik Corporation ... A ... 316 529-9670
Haysville *(G-2942)*

Prosoco Inc ... D ... 785 865-4200
Lawrence *(G-5081)*

Specchem LLC ... F ... 913 371-8705
Kansas City *(G-4431)*

2892 Explosives

Detacorp Inc LLC ... E ... 620 597-2552
Columbus *(G-1075)*

Hodgdon Powder Company Inc ... D ... 785 258-3388
Herington *(G-2976)*

Wimase International Inc ... G ... 620 783-1361
Riverton *(G-10214)*

2893 Printing Ink

Cartridge King of Kansas ... E ... 620 241-7746
McPherson *(G-6941)*

◆ Fujifilm Sericol USA Inc ... C ... 913 342-4060
Kansas City *(G-4022)*

Hubergroup Usa Inc ... F ... 913 262-2510
Kansas City *(G-4088)*

◆ Inkcycle Inc ... D ... 913 894-8387
Shawnee *(G-10973)*

Inland Industries Inc ... G ... 913 492-9050
Bucyrus *(G-600)*

INX International Ink Co ... D ... 913 441-0057
Edwardsville *(G-1504)*

◆ Nazdar Company ... C ... 913 422-1888
Shawnee *(G-11003)*

Nazdar Company ... F ... 913 422-1888
Shawnee *(G-11004)*

2895 Carbon Black

Birla Carbon USA Inc ... E ... 620 356-3151
Ulysses *(G-13283)*

2899 Chemical Preparations, NEC

Akrofire Inc ... E ... 913 888-7172
Shawnee Mission *(G-11090)*

◆ Bg Products Incorporated ... E ... 316 265-2686
Wichita *(G-13845)*

Boyer Industries Corporation ... D ... 785 865-4200
Lawrence *(G-4762)*

British Salt Holdings LLC ... C ... 913 253-2203
Overland Park *(G-8486)*

Cargill Incorporated ... D ... 620 663-2141
Hutchinson *(G-3229)*

Chemtrade Phosphorous Spc LLC ... E ... 785 843-2290
Lawrence *(G-4784)*

Compass Minerals America Inc ... C ... 913 344-9100
Overland Park *(G-8586)*

▲ Compass Minerals America Inc ... C ... 913 344-9100
Overland Park *(G-8587)*

◆ Compass Minerals Group Inc ... C ... 913 344-9100
Overland Park *(G-8588)*

◆ Compass Minerals Intl Inc ... C ... 913 344-9200
Overland Park *(G-8589)*

Dayton Superior Corporation ... D ... 913 596-9784
Kansas City *(G-3960)*

E I Du Pont De Nemours & Co ... F ... 302 774-1000
New Century *(G-7282)*

Enviro-Health Corp ... F ... 785 235-8300
Topeka *(G-12579)*

◆ Epro Services Inc ... F ... 316 262-2513
Wichita *(G-14298)*

Howell Mouldings LLC ... E ... 913 782-0500
New Century *(G-7289)*

Hutchinson Salt Company Inc ... G ... 620 856-3332
Baxter Springs *(G-409)*

Hutchinson Salt Company Inc ... E ... 620 662-3341
Hutchinson *(G-3324)*

Independent Salt Company ... E ... 785 472-4421
Kanopolis *(G-3772)*

Jacam Chemicals LLC ... F ... 620 275-1500
Garden City *(G-2208)*

◆ Jayhawk Fine Chemicals Corp ... C ... 620 783-1321
Galena *(G-2075)*

Kissner Group Holdings LP ... G ... 913 713-0600
Overland Park *(G-8920)*

Koch Industries Inc ... F ... 620 662-6691
Hutchinson *(G-3352)*

Koch Materials LLC ... C ... 316 828-5500
Wichita *(G-14883)*

Maxidize Production Svcs LLC ... G ... 620 222-1235
Winfield *(G-16158)*

Meridian Chemicals LLC ... G ... 913 253-2220
Overland Park *(G-9011)*

Mineral-Right Inc ... F ... 785 543-6571
Phillipsburg *(G-9791)*

Morton Salt Inc ... F ... 620 669-0401
South Hutchinson *(G-12063)*

Nunik Engineering ... F ... 913 384-0010
Shawnee Mission *(G-11691)*

Optic Fuel Clean Inc ... G ... 913 712-8373
Olathe *(G-7960)*

Pbi-Gordon Corporation ... E ... 816 421-4070
Kansas City *(G-4317)*

Peavey Corporation ... D ... 913 888-0600
Lenexa *(G-6047)*

PQ Corporation ... D ... 913 371-3020
Kansas City *(G-4329)*

Professional Products of Kans ... G ... 316 522-9300
Wichita *(G-15365)*

Prosoco Inc ... D ... 785 865-4200
Lawrence *(G-5081)*

Southwest Salt Company LLC ... G ... 913 755-1955
Paola *(G-9588)*

▲ Sportsgear Outdoor Products ... G ... 913 888-0379
Lenexa *(G-6149)*

Stress Panel Manufacturers ... G ... 620 347-8200
Arma *(G-191)*

Undergrund Cvern Stblztion LLC ... G ... 620 617-0302
Hutchinson *(G-3474)*

W R Grace & Co - Conn ... G ... 913 764-8040
Olathe *(G-8144)*

29 PETROLEUM REFINING AND RELATED INDUSTRIES

2911 Petroleum Refining

Bg Products Incorporated ... D ... 316 265-2686
Wichita *(G-13846)*

◆ Bg Products Incorporated ... E ... 316 265-2686
Wichita *(G-13845)*

Capital City Oil Inc ... E ... 785 233-8008
Topeka *(G-12428)*

Chc McPherson Refinery Inc ... F ... 785 543-5246
Phillipsburg *(G-9779)*

Chc McPherson Refinery Inc ... E ... 620 793-3111
Great Bend *(G-2536)*

Chc McPherson Refinery Inc ... G ... 785 798-3684
Ness City *(G-7254)*

CHS Inc ... D ... 620 241-4247
McPherson *(G-6948)*

CHS McPherson Refinery Inc ... B ... 620 241-2340
McPherson *(G-6949)*

Coffeyville Acquisition LLC ... E ... 913 982-0500
Kansas City *(G-3922)*

Coffeyville Resources LLC ... G ... 785 434-4832
Plainville *(G-9982)*

Coffeyville Resources LLC ... F ... 785 434-4832
Plainville *(G-9983)*

Coffeyville Resources LLC ... F ... 620 252-4781
Coffeyville *(G-921)*

Coffeyville Resources LLC ... E ... 913 982-0500
Kansas City *(G-3923)*

Coffeyvlle Rsrces Ref Mktg LLC ... G ... 913 982-0500
Kansas City *(G-3925)*

Coffeyvlle Rsrces Ref Mktg LLC ... D ... 620 251-4252
Coffeyville *(G-926)*

Equilon Enterprises LLC ... F ... 913 648-0535
Shawnee Mission *(G-11346)*

Flint Hills Resources Central ... G ... 316 828-5500
Wichita *(G-14391)*

Gerald A Wallace ... G ... 620 275-2484
Garden City *(G-2186)*

Green Energy Products LLC ... G ... 316 416-4106
Sedgwick *(G-10850)*

▲ Hollyfrntier El Dorado Ref LLC ... B ... 316 321-2200
El Dorado *(G-1567)*

Hpb Biodiesel Inc ... F ... 800 262-7907
Shawnee Mission *(G-11441)*

Koch Hydrocarbon Southwes ... G ... 620 662-6691
Hutchinson *(G-3351)*

Koch Industries Inc ... E ... 316 828-8737
Wichita *(G-14882)*

◆ Koch Industries Inc ... A ... 316 828-5500
Wichita *(G-14881)*

Koch Resources LLC ... E ... 316 828-5500
Wichita *(G-14887)*

◆ Koch Supply & Trading LP ... F ... 316 828-5500
Wichita *(G-14890)*

Kpl South Texas LLC ... G ... 316 828-5500
Wichita *(G-14894)*

KS&t International Holdings LP ... A ... 316 828-5500
Wichita *(G-14896)*

▲ Midcontinental Chemical Co Inc ... E ... 913 390-5556
Olathe *(G-7893)*

Murphy USA Inc ... F ... 620 664-9479
Hutchinson *(G-3386)*

Murphy USA Inc ... F ... 620 227-5607
Dodge City *(G-1409)*

Oneok Hydrocarbon LP ... D ... 620 669-3759
Hutchinson *(G-3395)*

Phares Petroleum Inc..........G....... 316 682-3349
Wichita *(G-15289)*
Sinclair Companies..........D....... 785 799-3116
Home *(G-3120)*
Southwest Kansas Coop Svcs LLC......E....... 620 492-2126
Johnson *(G-3661)*
Tpi Petroleum Inc..........D....... 913 831-3145
Shawnee Mission *(G-11938)*
Wynnewood Refining Company LLC....D....... 913 982-0500
Kansas City *(G-4558)*

2951 Paving Mixtures & Blocks

Apac-Kansas Inc..........D....... 316 524-5200
Wichita *(G-13716)*
Asphalt Sales Company..........E....... 913 788-8806
Olathe *(G-7536)*
County of McPherson..........E....... 620 241-0466
McPherson *(G-6952)*
CPB Materials LLC..........G....... 316 833-1146
Haysville *(G-2938)*
Ergon Asphalt & Emulsions Inc..........G....... 913 788-5300
Kansas City *(G-3995)*
◆ **Husqvrna Cnstr Pdts N Amer Inc**......A....... 913 928-1000
Olathe *(G-7781)*
Koch Materials LLC..........C....... 316 828-5500
Wichita *(G-14883)*
▼ **Mm Distribution LLC**..........G....... 800 689-2098
Douglass *(G-1467)*
Nk Asphalt Partners..........G....... 316 828-5500
Wichita *(G-15182)*
Semcrude LP..........F....... 620 234-5532
Stafford *(G-12109)*
Semmaterials LP..........G....... 785 825-1535
Salina *(G-10704)*

2952 Asphalt Felts & Coatings

Cutting Edge Tile & Grout..........G....... 316 648-5516
Wichita *(G-14149)*
▼ **Davinci Roofscapes LLC**..........E....... 913 599-0766
Lenexa *(G-5804)*
Industrial Coatings Inc..........G....... 913 321-2116
Kansas City *(G-4098)*
Innovative Adhesives Company..........F....... 913 371-8555
Kansas City *(G-4101)*
▼ **Mm Distribution LLC**..........G....... 800 689-2098
Douglass *(G-1467)*
Parsons Aaron Painting LLC..........G....... 620 532-1076
Kingman *(G-4609)*
Quality Roofg Installation LLC..........G....... 316 946-1068
Wichita *(G-15384)*
Superior Home Improvements LLC.......G....... 620 225-3560
Dodge City *(G-1437)*
Tamko Building Products Inc..........C....... 785 543-2144
Phillipsburg *(G-9800)*
Tamko Building Products Inc..........D....... 620 429-1800
Columbus *(G-1088)*

2992 Lubricating Oils & Greases

◆ **Bg Products Incorporated**..........E....... 316 265-2686
Wichita *(G-13845)*
Bg Products Incorporated..........C....... 316 265-2686
El Dorado *(G-1537)*
▲ **Clean Harbors Wichita LLC**..........C....... 316 832-0151
Wichita *(G-14039)*
Crossfaith Ventures Lc..........E....... 620 662-8365
Hutchinson *(G-3251)*
Fuchs Lubricants Co..........D....... 913 422-4022
Kansas City *(G-4020)*
▲ **Kcg Inc**..........E....... 913 438-4142
Lenexa *(G-5942)*
Kcg Inc..........G....... 913 888-0882
Lenexa *(G-5943)*
Koch Industries Inc..........F....... 620 662-6691
Hutchinson *(G-3352)*
Lubrication Engineers Inc..........E....... 316 529-2112
Wichita *(G-14990)*
Nalco Company LLC..........F....... 785 885-4161
Natoma *(G-7232)*
Petronomics Mfg Group Inc..........E....... 620 663-8559
Hutchinson *(G-3405)*
Rs Used Oil Services Inc..........E....... 866 778-7336
Wichita *(G-15490)*

2999 Products Of Petroleum & Coal, NEC

◆ **Koch Carbon LLC**..........E....... 316 828-5500
Wichita *(G-14875)*
◆ **Koch Mineral Services LLC**..........E....... 316 828-5500
Wichita *(G-14884)*

Koch Sulfur Products Co LLC..........E....... 316 828-5500
Wichita *(G-14889)*

30 RUBBER AND MISCELLANEOUS PLASTICS PRODUCTS

3011 Tires & Inner Tubes

American Tire Distributors..........E....... 316 616-9600
Wichita *(G-13694)*
Carlstar Group LLC..........E....... 913 667-1000
Kansas City *(G-3891)*
▲ **Central AG Wheel & Tire**..........F....... 316 942-1408
Wichita *(G-13977)*
Premium Ventures LLC..........F....... 785 842-5500
Lawrence *(G-5073)*

3021 Rubber & Plastic Footwear

Sid Bdeker Safety Shoe Svc Inc..........G....... 913 599-6463
Lenexa *(G-6134)*

3052 Rubber & Plastic Hose & Belting

▲ **G T Sales & Manufacturing Inc**.........D....... 316 943-2171
Wichita *(G-14434)*
HBD Industries Inc..........D....... 620 431-9100
Chanute *(G-730)*
Nance Manufacturing Inc..........E....... 316 942-8671
Wichita *(G-15146)*
▲ **Prairie Belting Inc**..........E....... 620 842-5147
Anthony *(G-133)*

3053 Gaskets, Packing & Sealing Devices

▲ **Everseal Gasket Inc**..........E....... 913 441-9232
Shawnee Mission *(G-11351)*
▲ **G T Sales & Manufacturing Inc**.........D....... 316 943-2171
Wichita *(G-14434)*
Liberal Gasket Mfg Co..........G....... 620 624-4921
Liberal *(G-6333)*

3061 Molded, Extruded & Lathe-Cut Rubber Mechanical Goods

▲ **Everseal Gasket Inc**..........E....... 913 441-9232
Shawnee Mission *(G-11351)*
Moore Rubber Co Inc..........F....... 913 422-5679
Shawnee Mission *(G-11654)*

3069 Fabricated Rubber Prdts, NEC

American Phoenix Inc..........E....... 785 862-7722
Topeka *(G-12320)*
Continental American Corp..........C....... 316 321-4551
El Dorado *(G-1550)*
▼ **Davinci Roofscapes LLC**..........E....... 913 599-0766
Lenexa *(G-5804)*
Longford Water Company LLC..........G....... 785 388-2233
Longford *(G-6432)*
Novation Iq LLC..........E....... 913 492-6000
Lenexa *(G-6029)*
T & C Mfg & Operating Inc..........E....... 620 793-5483
Great Bend *(G-2646)*
▼ **Topps Products Inc**..........F....... 913 685-2500
Bucyrus *(G-611)*

3081 Plastic Unsupported Sheet & Film

Berry Global Inc..........C....... 800 777-3080
Lawrence *(G-4754)*
▲ **Better Life Technology LLC**..........F....... 913 894-0403
Lenexa *(G-5699)*
Lustercraft Plastics LLC..........F....... 316 942-8451
Wichita *(G-14991)*
Midco Plastics Inc..........E....... 785 263-8999
Enterprise *(G-1855)*
◆ **Vanguard Shrink Films Inc**..........F....... 913 599-1111
Lenexa *(G-6209)*

3082 Plastic Unsupported Profile Shapes

Kaman Composites - Wichita..........C....... 316 942-1241
Wichita *(G-14780)*

3083 Plastic Laminated Plate & Sheet

Mid America Products Inc..........C....... 913 856-6550
Gardner *(G-2355)*
Novation Iq LLC..........E....... 913 492-6000
Lenexa *(G-6029)*
Thermoformed Plastic Products..........G....... 316 214-9623
Wichita *(G-15759)*
Worldwide Windows..........F....... 785 826-1701
Salina *(G-10773)*

3084 Plastic Pipe

▲ **Formufit Lc**..........G....... 913 782-0444
Lenexa *(G-5863)*
Mc Coy Company Inc..........C....... 913 342-1653
Kansas City *(G-4222)*
Vanguard Industries Inc..........G....... 620 241-6369
McPherson *(G-7037)*
▲ **Vanguard Piping Systems Inc**..........C....... 620 241-6369
McPherson *(G-7038)*
Vanguard Plastics Inc..........C....... 620 241-6369
McPherson *(G-7039)*
Vinylplex Inc..........E....... 620 231-8290
Pittsburg *(G-9959)*
Werner Pipe Service Inc..........F....... 620 331-7384
Independence *(G-3572)*

3085 Plastic Bottles

Container Services Inc..........D....... 620 947-2664
Hillsboro *(G-3046)*
Pepsi-Cola Btlg of Pittsburg..........E....... 620 231-3800
Pittsburg *(G-9912)*

3086 Plastic Foam Prdts

Ach Foam Technologies Inc..........F....... 913 371-1973
Kansas City *(G-3783)*
Ach Foam Technologies Inc..........D....... 913 321-4114
Kansas City *(G-3782)*
▲ **Buckley Industries Inc**..........D....... 316 744-7587
Park City *(G-9606)*
Coleman Company Inc..........D....... 316 832-3015
Olathe *(G-7597)*
Coleman Company Inc..........G....... 800 835-3278
Wichita *(G-14053)*
Future Foam Inc..........D....... 316 283-8600
Newton *(G-7350)*
Novation Iq LLC..........E....... 913 492-6000
Lenexa *(G-6029)*
Tasler Inc..........G....... 785 885-4533
Natoma *(G-7233)*

3087 Custom Compounding Of Purchased Plastic Resins

Continental American Corp..........C....... 316 321-4551
El Dorado *(G-1550)*
J and J Plastics..........F....... 620 660-9048
Rosalia *(G-10234)*

3088 Plastic Plumbing Fixtures

Arlwin Mfg Co Inc..........F....... 785 282-6487
Smith Center *(G-12031)*
▲ **Bultman Company Inc Mfg**..........F....... 620 544-8004
Hugoton *(G-3149)*
Charloma Inc..........E....... 620 364-2701
Burlington *(G-626)*
▲ **Formufit Lc**..........G....... 913 782-0444
Lenexa *(G-5863)*
▲ **KBK Industries LLC**..........C....... 785 372-4331
Rush Center *(G-10260)*
Onyx Collection Inc..........B....... 785 456-8604
Belvue *(G-508)*
Vanguard Industries Inc..........G....... 620 241-6369
McPherson *(G-7037)*

3089 Plastic Prdts

Advanced Extrusions Co LLC..........F....... 620 241-2006
McPherson *(G-6932)*
▼ **B P E Inc**..........G....... 620 343-3783
Emporia *(G-1700)*
◆ **Balco Inc**..........C....... 800 767-0082
Wichita *(G-13798)*
Berry Global Inc..........C....... 800 777-3080
Lawrence *(G-4754)*
▲ **Century Manufacturing Inc**..........C....... 316 636-5423
Bel Aire *(G-430)*
Certainteed Corporation..........C....... 316 554-9638
McPherson *(G-6945)*
▲ **Charloma Inc**..........E....... 620 336-2124
Cherryvale *(G-801)*
Charloma Inc..........E....... 620 364-2701
Burlington *(G-626)*
Classic Shower Door Inc..........G....... 913 492-9670
Overland Park *(G-8562)*
Consolidated Container Co LP..........C....... 913 888-9494
Shawnee Mission *(G-11259)*
▲ **Converting Technologies Inc**..........F....... 316 722-6907
Goddard *(G-2433)*
Cope Plastics Inc..........F....... 785 267-0552
Topeka *(G-12506)*

S
I
C

Criss Optical Mfg Co Inc ....G.... 316 529-0414
Wichita (G-14131)
Esslinger Manufacturing ....G.... 620 431-4338
Chanute (G-726)
▲ Etco Specialty Products Inc ....E.... 620 724-6463
Girard (G-2403)
Fabpro Oriented Polymers LLC ....F.... 620 532-5141
Kingman (G-4590)
▲ Ferguson Production Inc ....C.... 620 241-2400
McPherson (G-6965)
Fittings Export LLC ....G.... 620 364-2930
Burlington (G-636)
Formation Plastics Inc ....E.... 785 754-3828
Hoxie (G-3138)
▲ Formufit Lc ....G.... 913 782-0444
Lenexa (G-5863)
▲ Gemtech LLC ....E.... 913 782-3080
Olathe (G-7726)
Glass King Manufacturing Co ....F.... 620 793-7838
Great Bend (G-2570)
Good Riddance Corporation ....G.... 620 633-5222
Fredonia (G-2034)
GVL Polymers Inc ....F.... 320 693-8411
Hesston (G-2991)
Hayes Tooling & Plastics Inc ....F.... 913 782-0046
Olathe (G-7757)
Hayesbrand Molding Inc ....F.... 913 238-0424
Garnett (G-2377)
Heartland Plastics Inc ....G.... 316 775-2199
Augusta (G-324)
Hi-Line Plastics Inc ....D.... 913 782-3535
Olathe (G-7767)
▲ Huhtamaki Americas Inc ....B.... 913 583-3025
De Soto (G-1203)
◆ Huhtamaki Films Inc ....A.... 913 583-3025
De Soto (G-1204)
Illinois Tool Works Inc ....G.... 800 262-7907
Shawnee Mission (G-11453)
Jarden Corporation ....D.... 316 390-1343
Wichita (G-14749)
Jem Industries Inc ....G.... 913 837-3202
Louisburg (G-6452)
Koller Enterprises Inc ....D.... 913 422-2027
Lenexa (G-5957)
Lustercraft Plastics LLC ....F.... 316 942-8451
Wichita (G-14991)
Manufacturing Services Inc ....G.... 316 267-4111
Wichita (G-15006)
Masonite International Corp ....E.... 620 231-8200
Pittsburg (G-9899)
McDonald Tank II ....G.... 620 792-3661
Great Bend (G-2607)
Mid America Products Inc ....C.... 913 856-6550
Gardner (G-2355)
Mid-States Laboratories Inc ....F.... 316 264-6758
Wichita (G-15081)
Mid-States Laboratories Inc ....F.... 316 262-7013
Wichita (G-15082)
Miniature Plastic Molding LLC ....G.... 316 264-2827
Wichita (G-15112)
Monarch Molding Inc ....G.... 620 767-5115
Council Grove (G-1171)
Monoflo International Inc ....G.... 785 242-2928
Ottawa (G-8292)
▼ Neodesha Plastics Inc ....E.... 620 325-3096
Neodesha (G-7245)
Neodesha Plastics Inc ....E.... 620 325-3096
Neodesha (G-7246)
North American Aviation Inc ....E.... 316 744-6450
Park City (G-9639)
Orbis Corporation ....C.... 785 528-4875
Osage City (G-8185)
▼ Osborne Industries Inc ....D.... 785 346-2192
Osborne (G-8216)
▲ Packerware LLC ....A.... 785 331-4236
Lawrence (G-5055)
▲ Pioneer - Ram Incorporated ....A.... 316 685-2266
Wichita (G-15301)
Plastikon Industries Inc ....F.... 785 749-1630
Lawrence (G-5070)
Plex Plus ....G.... 913 888-6223
Leawood (G-5523)
Preferred Seamless Guttering ....G.... 620 663-7600
Hutchinson (G-3414)
Quality Profile Services Inc ....E.... 620 767-6757
Council Grove (G-1175)
Rehrig Pacific Company ....E.... 913 585-1175
De Soto (G-1211)
▲ Reifenhauser Incorporated ....F.... 316 260-2122
Maize (G-6518)
Reliable Caps LLC ....E.... 913 764-2277
Olathe (G-8024)
Roberts Group Inc ....G.... 913 381-3930
Overland Park (G-9252)
▲ Rutland Inc ....F.... 913 782-8862
Olathe (G-8049)
S F B Plastics Inc ....D.... 800 343-8133
Wichita (G-15502)
▲ Scientific Plastics Co Inc ....E.... 913 432-0322
Kansas City (G-4407)
▲ Spears Caney Inc ....C.... 620 879-2131
Caney (G-673)
Spears Manufacturing Co ....B.... 620 879-2131
Caney (G-674)
Stealth Technologies LLC ....F.... 913 228-2214
Olathe (G-8082)
▲ Stm Inc ....E.... 316 775-2223
Augusta (G-348)
T & C Mfg & Operating Inc ....E.... 620 793-5483
Great Bend (G-2646)
Thermovac Inc ....G.... 620 431-3270
Chanute (G-769)
Tramec Sloan LLC ....E.... 620 326-5007
Wellington (G-13537)
▲ Ventra Kansas LLC ....D.... 913 334-0614
Kansas City (G-4515)
Wescon Plastics LLC ....C.... 855 731-6055
Wichita (G-15951)
Western Inds Plastic Pdts LLC ....C.... 620 221-9464
Winfield (G-16180)
Western Industries Inc ....C.... 620 221-9464
Winfield (G-16181)
Westirland Industries Inc ....G.... 620 795-4421
Oswego (G-8239)
Westrock Dspensing Systems Inc ....C.... 620 229-5000
Winfield (G-16182)

31 LEATHER AND LEATHER PRODUCTS

3131 Boot & Shoe Cut Stock & Findings

French Quarter LLC ....G.... 316 440-7004
Wichita (G-14422)
Vorona LLC ....G.... 913 888-4646
Lenexa (G-6217)

3171 Handbags & Purses

Too Cute Totes ....G.... 775 423-5907
Lenexa (G-6184)

3199 Leather Goods, NEC

▲ Kth Properties Corporation ....E.... 316 941-1100
Wichita (G-14897)

32 STONE, CLAY, GLASS, AND CONCRETE PRODUCTS

3211 Flat Glass

AGC Flat Glass North Amer Inc ....B.... 913 592-6100
Spring Hill (G-12076)
G W Inc ....E.... 316 262-3403
Wichita (G-14435)
▲ Insulite Glass Co Inc ....D.... 800 452-7721
Olathe (G-7795)
Lippert Components Mfg Inc ....D.... 316 283-0627
North Newton (G-7438)

3221 Glass Containers

Jarden Branded Consumable ....G.... 913 856-1177
Olathe (G-7807)
Sands Level and Tool Company ....F.... 989 428-4141
Lenexa (G-6117)

3229 Pressed & Blown Glassware, NEC

▼ B P E Inc ....G.... 620 343-3783
Emporia (G-1700)
Hutchens Corporation ....G.... 785 252-3423
Holyrood (G-3117)
▲ Karg Art Glass ....E.... 316 744-2442
Kechi (G-4571)
▲ Pioneer - Ram Incorporated ....A.... 316 685-2266
Wichita (G-15301)

3231 Glass Prdts Made Of Purchased Glass

Champion Window Co Kans Cy Inc ....E.... 913 541-8282
Lenexa (G-5751)
Hoefer Enterprises Inc ....G.... 620 663-1778
South Hutchinson (G-12059)
Lippert Components Mfg Inc ....D.... 316 283-0627
North Newton (G-7438)
Masonry & Glass Systems Inc ....G.... 913 748-6142
Shawnee Mission (G-11601)
Petty Products Inc ....G.... 913 782-0028
Olathe (G-7981)
PQ Corporation ....F.... 913 227-0561
Lenexa (G-6065)
Rellec Apparel Graphics LLC ....G.... 913 707-5249
Lenexa (G-6100)

3241 Cement, Hydraulic

◆ Ash Grove Cement Company ....C.... 913 451-8900
Overland Park (G-8403)
Ash Grove Cement Company ....E.... 620 433-3500
Chanute (G-703)
Ash Grove Cement Company ....E.... 913 422-2523
Kansas City (G-3821)
Ash Grove Cement Company ....E.... 785 267-1996
Topeka (G-12339)
Heartland Cement Company ....F.... 620 331-0200
Independence (G-3525)
Lafarge North America Inc ....D.... 620 378-4458
Fredonia (G-2038)
Lafarge North America Inc ....E.... 620 455-3720
Oxford (G-9533)
Lafarge North America Inc ....E.... 316 943-3500
Wichita (G-14912)
Lafarge North America Inc ....E.... 316 613-5100
Wichita (G-14913)
Lafarge North America Inc ....E.... 816 365-9143
Kansas City (G-4192)
Lone Star Industries Inc ....F.... 913 422-1050
Bonner Springs (G-561)
▲ Monarch Cement Company ....C.... 620 473-2222
Humboldt (G-3187)

3251 Brick & Structural Clay Tile

General Finance Incorporated ....D.... 785 243-1284
Concordia (G-1115)
Kansas Brick and Tile Co Inc ....E.... 620 653-2157
Hoisington (G-3068)
Paint Glaze & Fire ....G.... 913 661-2529
Overland Park (G-9137)
Salina Concrete Products Inc ....F.... 316 943-3241
Wichita (G-15510)

3255 Clay Refractories

Harbisonwalker Intl Inc ....E.... 913 888-0425
Lenexa (G-5889)

3259 Structural Clay Prdts, NEC

Salina Concrete Products Inc ....F.... 316 943-3241
Wichita (G-15510)

3262 China, Table & Kitchen Articles

▲ Pioneer - Ram Incorporated ....A.... 316 685-2266
Wichita (G-15301)

3264 Porcelain Electrical Splys

◆ Bunting Group Inc ....C.... 316 284-2020
Newton (G-7325)

3269 Pottery Prdts, NEC

Discovery Concepts Inc ....G.... 913 814-7100
Shawnee Mission (G-11309)
Flint Hills Clay Works Inc ....F.... 620 382-3620
Marion (G-6870)
Pfaltzgraff Co ....F.... 316 283-7754
Newton (G-7404)

3271 Concrete Block & Brick

◆ Ash Grove Cement Company ....C.... 913 451-8900
Overland Park (G-8403)
Big Block Inc ....F.... 913 927-2135
Lenexa (G-5702)
Capitol Concrete Pdts Co Inc ....F.... 785 233-3271
Topeka (G-12436)
Cemex Materials LLC ....D.... 913 287-5725
Kansas City (G-3900)
Form Systems Inc ....F.... 316 522-9285
Haysville (G-2945)
Midwest Concrete Materials Inc ....C.... 785 776-8811
Manhattan (G-6746)
Salina Concrete Products Inc ....E.... 785 827-7281
Salina (G-10668)

3272 Concrete Prdts

▲ **Architectural Cast Stone Inc** ....E.... 316 262-5543
Wichita *(G-13731)*

Ash Grove Materials Corp ....D.... 913 345-2030
Overland Park *(G-8404)*

Canyon Stone Inc ....E.... 913 254-9300
Olathe *(G-7575)*

Cemex Materials LLC ....D.... 913 287-5725
Kansas City *(G-3900)*

Chemsystems Kansas Inc ....G.... 913 422-4443
Shawnee *(G-10927)*

▲ **Concrete Vaults Inc** ....F.... 316 283-3790
Newton *(G-7333)*

Concrete Vaults Inc ....G.... 620 792-6687
Great Bend *(G-2546)*

Coreslab Structures Kansas Inc ....D.... 913 287-5725
Kansas City *(G-3942)*

Cretex Concrete Products Inc ....F.... 785 863-3300
Oskaloosa *(G-8224)*

Dayton Superior Corporation ....D.... 913 596-9784
Kansas City *(G-3960)*

Fairlawn Burial Park Assn ....F.... 620 662-3431
Hutchinson *(G-3282)*

Finley Construction & Rdymx ....G.... 785 626-3282
Atwood *(G-286)*

First Imprssons Crbscaping LLC ....G.... 913 620-5164
Stilwell *(G-12147)*

Forterra Concrete Products Inc ....E.... 913 422-3634
Shawnee *(G-10957)*

Glen-Gery Corporation ....G.... 913 281-2800
Kansas City *(G-4038)*

King Luminaire Company Inc ....G.... 913 255-3112
Atchison *(G-240)*

Los Primos Inc ....G.... 785 527-5535
Belleville *(G-460)*

M6 Concrete Accessories Co Inc ....G.... 316 452-5466
El Dorado *(G-1584)*

McPherson Concrete Pdts Inc ....D.... 620 241-1678
McPherson *(G-6995)*

Midwest Cast Stone Kansas Inc ....E.... 913 371-3300
Kansas City *(G-4250)*

Mound City Vault Co Inc ....G.... 913 795-2529
Mound City *(G-7173)*

Nips LLC ....G.... 913 592-2365
Spring Hill *(G-12092)*

Old Castle Precast Inc ....E.... 785 232-2982
Topeka *(G-12944)*

Omega Concrete Systems Inc ....E.... 913 287-4343
Kansas City *(G-4293)*

Pappas Concrete Inc ....E.... 620 277-2127
Lakin *(G-4657)*

Permanent Paving Inc ....F.... 913 451-7834
Overland Park *(G-9157)*

▲ **Pretech Corporation** ....E.... 913 441-4600
Kansas City *(G-4334)*

Quikrete Companies Inc ....E.... 913 441-6525
Kansas City *(G-4355)*

Quikrete Companies LLC ....E.... 316 721-3900
Wichita *(G-15396)*

Rayers Bearden Stained GL Sup ....F.... 316 942-2929
Wichita *(G-15421)*

Reliable Concrete Products ....G.... 913 321-8108
Kansas City *(G-4369)*

Russell Block Company Inc ....F.... 785 483-6271
Russell *(G-10294)*

Salina Concrete Products Inc ....F.... 316 943-3241
Wichita *(G-15510)*

Salina Concrete Products Inc ....E.... 785 827-7281
Salina *(G-10668)*

St Joe Concrete Products ....E.... 913 365-7281
Elwood *(G-1691)*

Stresscrete Inc ....F.... 913 255-3112
Atchison *(G-264)*

▲ **Suhor Industries Inc** ....A.... 620 421-4434
Overland Park *(G-9371)*

Vogts-Parga Construction LLC ....F.... 316 284-2801
Newton *(G-7425)*

W H Debrick Co Inc ....F.... 913 294-3281
Paola *(G-9595)*

Wichita Concrete Pipe Inc ....E.... 316 838-8651
Wichita *(G-15989)*

Wilbert Funeral Services Inc ....E.... 316 832-1114
Wichita *(G-16046)*

▲ **Wilbert Funeral Services Inc** ....B.... 913 345-2120
Overland Park *(G-9494)*

3273 Ready-Mixed Concrete

Alsop Sand Co Inc ....E.... 785 243-4249
Concordia *(G-1101)*

American Concrete Co Inc ....G.... 620 231-1520
Pittsburg *(G-9807)*

Andale Construction Inc ....D.... 316 832-0063
Wichita *(G-13703)*

Andale Ready Mix Central Inc ....D.... 316 832-0063
Wichita *(G-13704)*

Andale Ready Mix Central Inc ....F.... 316 832-0063
Andale *(G-77)*

◆ **Ash Grove Cement Company** ....C.... 913 451-8900
Overland Park *(G-8403)*

Ash Grove Materials Corp ....D.... 913 345-2030
Overland Park *(G-8404)*

B & B Redimix Inc ....G.... 785 543-5133
Phillipsburg *(G-9776)*

B & B Redimix Inc ....F.... 785 543-5133
Phillipsburg *(G-9777)*

B&B Redi Mix ....F.... 785 543-5133
Phillipsburg *(G-9778)*

Beloit Ready Mix Incorporated ....G.... 785 738-4683
Beloit *(G-478)*

Builders Concrete & Supply ....F.... 316 283-4540
Newton *(G-7324)*

Century Concrete Inc ....E.... 913 451-8900
Shawnee Mission *(G-11213)*

Century Concrete Inc ....F.... 913 764-4264
Olathe *(G-7585)*

Concrete Enterprises Inc ....F.... 620 662-1219
Hutchinson *(G-3244)*

Concrete Enterprises Inc ....E.... 620 532-1165
Kingman *(G-4587)*

Concrete Express Inc ....F.... 805 643-2992
Olathe *(G-7610)*

Concrete Products Co Inc ....F.... 620 947-5921
Hillsboro *(G-3045)*

Concrete Service Co Inc ....E.... 620 792-2558
Great Bend *(G-2545)*

Concrete Service Co Inc ....G.... 785 628-2100
Hays *(G-2776)*

Cornejo & Sons LLC ....G.... 620 251-1690
Coffeyville *(G-931)*

Dodge City Concrete Inc ....F.... 620 227-3041
Dodge City *(G-1343)*

Eslinger Construction & Rdymx ....F.... 620 659-2371
Kinsley *(G-4617)*

Finley Construction & Rdymx ....G.... 785 626-3282
Atwood *(G-286)*

Freedom Ready Mix Inc ....G.... 620 224-2800
Fort Scott *(G-1973)*

Geiger Ready-Mix Co Inc ....E.... 913 772-4010
Leavenworth *(G-5243)*

Geiger Ready-Mix Co Inc ....E.... 913 281-0111
Kansas City *(G-4029)*

Gravel & Concrete Inc ....G.... 620 422-3249
Nickerson *(G-7432)*

H & P Inc ....G.... 785 263-4183
Abilene *(G-36)*

Hamm Inc ....E.... 785 235-6568
Topeka *(G-12661)*

Hamm Inc ....G.... 785 233-7263
Topeka *(G-12662)*

Heft & Sons LLC ....E.... 620 723-2495
Greensburg *(G-2679)*

Independence Ready Mix Inc ....G.... 620 331-4150
Independence *(G-3529)*

J-A-G Construction Company ....C.... 620 225-0061
Dodge City *(G-1380)*

J-A-G Construction Company ....E.... 620 225-0061
Dodge City *(G-1381)*

Kansas Ready Mix LLC ....E.... 316 832-0828
Park City *(G-9623)*

Kansas Sand and Concrete Inc ....E.... 785 235-6284
Topeka *(G-12803)*

Klaver Construction Pdts LLC ....E.... 620 532-3661
Kingman *(G-4604)*

Lafarge North America Inc ....E.... 816 365-9143
Kansas City *(G-4192)*

Lrm Industries Inc ....E.... 785 843-1688
Lawrence *(G-5001)*

McPherson Concrete Pdts Inc ....D.... 620 241-1678
McPherson *(G-6995)*

Meiers Ready Mix Inc ....E.... 785 233-9900
Topeka *(G-12882)*

Mid West Ready Mix & Bldg Sups ....G.... 785 284-2911
Sabetha *(G-10319)*

Mid West Ready Mix & Bldg Sups ....G.... 785 742-3678
Hiawatha *(G-3018)*

Mid-America Redi-Mix Inc ....F.... 620 663-1559
Hutchinson *(G-3377)*

Midwest Concrete Materials Inc ....C.... 785 776-8811
Manhattan *(G-6746)*

Midwest Materials By Mueller ....F.... 785 337-2252
Hanover *(G-2713)*

Mo-Kan Transit Mix Inc ....G.... 913 367-1332
Atchison *(G-250)*

▲ **Monarch Cement Company** ....C.... 620 473-2222
Humboldt *(G-3187)*

OBrien Rock Company Inc ....D.... 620 449-2257
Saint Paul *(G-10382)*

OBrien Rock Company Inc ....G.... 620 231-4940
Frontenac *(G-2061)*

OBrien Rock Company Inc ....G.... 620 421-5127
Parsons *(G-9711)*

Pappas Concrete Inc ....E.... 620 277-2127
Lakin *(G-4657)*

Payless Concrete Products Inc ....F.... 620 365-5588
Iola *(G-3622)*

Pennys Concrete Inc ....E.... 913 441-8781
Shawnee Mission *(G-11724)*

Pennys Concrete Inc ....F.... 913 441-8781
Paola *(G-9583)*

Pennys Concrete Inc ....E.... 913 441-8781
Louisburg *(G-6462)*

Pennys Concrete & Rdymx LLC ....F.... 785 242-1045
Ottawa *(G-8304)*

Quikrete Companies Inc ....E.... 913 441-6525
Kansas City *(G-4355)*

R A Ruud & Son Inc ....F.... 316 788-5000
Haysville *(G-2957)*

Salina Concrete Products Inc ....E.... 785 827-7281
Salina *(G-10668)*

Schlosser Inc ....G.... 785 899-6535
Goodland *(G-2486)*

Sek Ready Mix Inc ....E.... 620 252-8699
Coffeyville *(G-976)*

Seneca Ready Mix Concrete Inc ....F.... 785 336-3511
Seneca *(G-10881)*

Sherwood Construction Co Inc ....C.... 316 943-0211
Wichita *(G-15581)*

Smoky Valley Concrete Inc ....G.... 785 820-8113
Salina *(G-10711)*

Tarbet Construction Co Inc ....F.... 620 356-2110
Ulysses *(G-13321)*

Tarbet Construction Co Inc ....G.... 785 462-7432
Colby *(G-1045)*

Tri-County Concrete Inc ....E.... 913 764-7700
Olathe *(G-8121)*

Walker Products Company Inc ....F.... 785 524-4107
Lincoln *(G-6390)*

3274 Lime

Florence Rock Company LLC ....G.... 620 878-4544
Newton *(G-7346)*

Mk Minerals Inc ....G.... 785 989-4566
Wathena *(G-13477)*

Quikrete Companies Inc ....E.... 913 441-6525
Kansas City *(G-4355)*

3275 Gypsum Prdts

Certainteed Gypsum Mfg Inc ....G.... 785 762-2994
Junction City *(G-3679)*

Georgia-Pacific LLC ....C.... 785 363-7767
Blue Rapids *(G-536)*

New Ngc Inc ....C.... 620 886-5613
Medicine Lodge *(G-7069)*

3281 Cut Stone Prdts

Artistic Marble LLC ....F.... 316 944-8713
Wichita *(G-13743)*

Braco Sales Inc ....E.... 816 471-5005
Kansas City *(G-3874)*

Continental Cast Stone LLC ....E.... 800 989-7866
Shawnee *(G-10933)*

Evolve Gran Natural Stone Inc ....F.... 913 254-1800
Olathe *(G-7696)*

Global Stone LLC ....G.... 913 310-9500
Olathe *(G-7733)*

H J Born Stone Inc ....F.... 316 838-7788
Arkansas City *(G-158)*

J T Lardner Cut Stone Inc ....F.... 785 234-8634
Topeka *(G-12732)*

Koken Manufacturing Co Inc ....E.... 316 942-7600
Wichita *(G-14892)*

Los Primos Inc ....G.... 785 527-5535
Belleville *(G-460)*

Melissa Wilbert ....G.... 316 361-2787
Wichita *(G-15037)*

▲ **Sandstone Inc** ....F.... 913 422-0794
Shawnee Mission *(G-11827)*

▲ **Surface Center Interiors LLC** ....F.... 913 422-0500
Shawnee *(G-11037)*

U S Stone Industries LLC....C....913 529-4154
Herington (G-2982)

3291 Abrasive Prdts

◆ Husqvrna Cnstr Pdts N Amer Inc....A....913 928-1000
Olathe (G-7781)
▲ K C Abrasive Co LLC....E....913 342-2900
Kansas City (G-4131)
US Minerals Inc....G....219 798-5472
La Cygne (G-4645)

3292 Asbestos products

Patriot Abatement Services LLC....F....913 397-6181
Olathe (G-7975)
Precision Pipe Cover Inc....E....785 233-2000
Topeka (G-12982)

3295 Minerals & Earths: Ground Or Treated

A&M Products Manufacturing Co....E....913 592-4344
Spring Hill (G-12074)
Calvert Corporation....G....785 877-5221
Almena (G-67)
Koch Companies Pub Sector LLC....G....316 828-5500
Wichita (G-14876)
McShares Inc....E....785 825-2181
Salina (G-10598)
Reed Mineral Division....G....913 757-4561
La Cygne (G-4642)

3296 Mineral Wool

Certainteed Corporation....B....913 342-6624
Kansas City (G-3906)
Johns Manville Corporation....B....620 241-6260
McPherson (G-6979)
Owens Corning Sales LLC....E....913 281-9495
Kansas City (G-4304)
Owens Corning Sales LLC....B....419 248-8000
Kansas City (G-4305)
Premier Mechanical Pdts LLC....F....913 271-5002
Kansas City (G-4332)

3297 Nonclay Refractories

▲ Rex Materials of Kansas Inc....D....620 767-5119
Council Grove (G-1176)
Thermal Ceramics Inc....E....620 343-2308
Emporia (G-1837)

33 PRIMARY METAL INDUSTRIES

3312 Blast Furnaces, Coke Ovens, Steel & Rolling Mills

Bradken Inc....D....913 367-2121
Atchison (G-220)
Brown Honey Farms....G....785 778-2002
Haddam (G-2694)
Brown Industries LLC....D....785 842-6506
Lawrence (G-4770)
Concordia Technologies LLC....E....785 262-4066
Concordia (G-1108)
Contech Engnered Solutions LLC....E....785 234-1000
Topeka (G-12504)
Cromwell Builders Mfg....F....785 949-2433
Carlton (G-686)
▼ Earth Contact Products LLC....F....913 393-0007
Olathe (G-7665)
◆ Full Vision Inc....D....316 283-3344
Newton (G-7349)
Geo Form International Inc....G....913 782-1166
Olathe (G-7728)
Koch Energy Inc....F....316 828-5500
Wichita (G-14877)
Larue Machine Inc....F....620 431-3303
Chanute (G-738)
Maico Industries Inc....D....785 472-5390
Ellsworth (G-1677)
Oswald Manufacturing Co Inc....G....785 258-2877
Herington (G-2980)
Oxwell Inc....D....620 326-7481
Wellington (G-13521)
PDQ Tools and Equipment Inc....G....913 492-5800
Shawnee Mission (G-11721)
Perfekta Inc....G....316 263-2056
Wichita (G-15283)
Pitt Steel LLC....G....620 231-8100
Pittsburg (G-9919)
R & S Pipe Supply LLC....F....785 448-5401
Garnett (G-2385)
Reliance Steel & Aluminum Co....D....316 636-4500
Wichita (G-15440)
Shostak Iron and Metal Co Inc....E....913 321-9210
Overland Park (G-9309)
Specialty Fabrication Inc....F....316 264-0603
Wichita (G-15636)
Steel Ventures LLC....D....785 587-5100
Manhattan (G-6810)
Tartan Manufacturing Inc....C....913 432-7100
Kansas City (G-4458)
US Pipe Fabrication LLC....F....785 242-6284
Ottawa (G-8318)
Werner Pipe Service Inc....F....620 331-7384
Independence (G-3572)

3315 Steel Wire Drawing & Nails & Spikes

▲ A-1 Scaffold Mfg Inc....E....785 621-5121
Hays (G-2743)
Emco Specialty Products Inc....G....913 281-4555
Kansas City (G-3986)
Lane Myers Company Inc....E....620 622-4310
Protection (G-10175)
Valent Arstrctres - Lenexa LLC....E....913 469-6400
Shawnee Mission (G-11972)
Wkcsc Inc....G....316 652-7113
Wichita (G-16060)

3317 Steel Pipe & Tubes

◆ Alexander Manufacturing Co Inc....F....620 421-5010
Parsons (G-9664)
Contech Engnered Solutions LLC....E....913 294-2131
Paola (G-9549)
Progressive Products Inc....E....620 235-1712
Pittsburg (G-9925)
Werner Pipe Service Inc....F....620 331-7384
Independence (G-3572)

3321 Gray Iron Foundries

▲ Acme Foundry Inc....B....620 251-6800
Coffeyville (G-907)
Acme Foundry Inc....E....620 251-4920
Coffeyville (G-908)
Bradken Inc....D....913 367-2121
Atchison (G-220)
Farrar Corporation....E....620 478-2212
Norwich (G-7468)
Farrar Corporation....B....785 537-7733
Norwich (G-7466)
◆ Fastfittingscom....G....913 709-4467
Overland Park (G-8706)
Ferroloy Inc....E....316 838-0897
Wichita (G-14358)
◆ Kice Industries Inc....C....316 744-7148
Park City (G-9625)
Star Pipe Usa LLC....C....281 558-3000
Coffeyville (G-979)
Star Pipe Usa LLC....D....620 251-5700
Coffeyville (G-980)

3322 Malleable Iron Foundries

Farrar Corporation....B....785 537-7733
Norwich (G-7466)

3324 Steel Investment Foundries

Buffco Engineering Inc....E....316 558-5390
Mulvane (G-7211)

3325 Steel Foundries, NEC

Bradken Inc....D....913 367-2121
Atchison (G-220)
Hampton Hydraulics Llc....D....620 792-4368
Great Bend (G-2590)

3341 Secondary Smelting & Refining Of Nonferrous Metals

Custom Alloy Sales 34p LLC....D....913 471-4800
Prescott (G-10166)
Erman Corporation Inc....E....913 287-4800
Kansas City (G-3996)
Eureka Technology LLC....G....913 557-9639
Paola (G-9557)
Shostak Iron and Metal Co Inc....E....913 321-9210
Overland Park (G-9309)
Tower Metal Products LP....E....620 215-2622
Fort Scott (G-2009)

3351 Rolling, Drawing & Extruding Of Copper

Vermillion Incorporated....D....316 524-3100
Wichita (G-15875)

3354 Aluminum Extruded Prdts

Aero Space Manufacturing Corp....F....620 378-4441
Fredonia (G-2026)
Anodizing Inc....D....620 223-1111
Fort Scott (G-1955)
Bmg of Kansas Inc....D....620 327-4038
Hesston (G-2985)
D-J Extruding LLC....E....620 456-3211
Conway Springs (G-1139)
Extrusions Inc....D....620 223-1111
Fort Scott (G-1967)
Reno Fabricating & Sls Co Inc....E....620 663-1269
Hutchinson (G-3426)

3357 Nonferrous Wire Drawing

Essex Group Inc....B....620 653-2191
Hoisington (G-3063)
▲ Mize & Co Inc....E....620 532-3191
Kingman (G-4607)
Schlumberger Technology Corp....C....785 841-5610
Lawrence (G-5103)
Standard Motor Products Inc....B....913 441-6500
Edwardsville (G-1516)
Superior Essex Inc....E....620 653-2191
Hoisington (G-3071)
Vermillion Incorporated....D....316 524-3100
Wichita (G-15875)

3363 Aluminum Die Castings

Dempsey Inc....G....913 371-3107
Kansas City (G-3968)

3364 Nonferrous Die Castings, Exc Aluminum

Dempsey Inc....G....913 371-3107
Kansas City (G-3968)
National Almnm-Brass Fndry Inc....E....816 833-4500
Leawood (G-5498)

3365 Aluminum Foundries

Denco Aluminum Inc....F....620 724-6325
Girard (G-2402)
National Almnm-Brass Fndry Inc....E....816 833-4500
Leawood (G-5498)
S & S Manufacturing Inc....G....316 946-5755
Wichita (G-15501)
Wichita Brass and Alum Fndry....F....316 838-4286
Wichita (G-15982)

3366 Copper Foundries

National Almnm-Brass Fndry Inc....E....816 833-4500
Leawood (G-5498)
Smith Monuments Inc....G....785 425-6762
Stockton (G-12187)

3369 Nonferrous Foundries: Castings, NEC

National Almnm-Brass Fndry Inc....E....816 833-4500
Leawood (G-5498)
Tc Industries Inc....F....913 371-7922
Kansas City (G-4460)
Wichita Brass and Alum Fndry....F....316 838-4286
Wichita (G-15982)

3398 Metal Heat Treating

Bodycote Thermal Proc Inc....E....316 943-3288
Wichita (G-13862)
Bodycote Thermal Proc Inc....E....316 267-6264
Wichita (G-13863)
Ferroloy Inc....E....316 838-0897
Wichita (G-14358)
Metal Finishing Company Inc....E....620 326-7655
Wellington (G-13516)
Metal Finishing Company Inc....F....316 267-7289
Wichita (G-15053)
Metal Improvement Company LLC....E....620 326-5509
Wellington (G-13517)

3399 Primary Metal Prdts, NEC

Metal Finishing Company Inc....F....316 267-7289
Wichita (G-15053)
Ram Metal Products Inc....G....913 422-0099
Leawood (G-5532)

34 FABRICATED METAL PRODUCTS, EXCEPT MACHINERY AND TRANSPORTATION EQUIPMENT

3411 Metal Cans

Jacks Food Market ....G.... 785 348-5411
Linn (G-6407)
Mid-West Conveyor Company ....C.... 734 288-4400
Kansas City (G-4247)
▲ No Spill Inc ....G.... 913 888-9200
Lenexa (G-6025)

3412 Metal Barrels, Drums, Kegs & Pails

Bmg of Kansas Inc ....D.... 620 327-4038
Hesston (G-2985)
Mobile Mini Inc ....F.... 316 838-2663
Park City (G-9636)
United Manufacturing Inc ....E.... 913 780-0056
New Century (G-7302)

3421 Cutlery

Agra Axe International Inc ....E.... 620 879-5858
Caney (G-664)
▲ Ary Inc ....F.... 913 214-4813
Overland Park (G-8398)
Dunns Custom Knives Inc ....G.... 785 584-6856
Rossville (G-10251)
PB&j ....G.... 913 648-6033
Overland Park (G-9148)

3423 Hand & Edge Tools

Bushton Manufacturing LLC ....G.... 620 562-3557
Bushton (G-652)
▲ Finishpro Tools LLC ....E.... 913 631-0804
Olathe (G-7709)
Great Plains Manufacturing Inc ....C.... 785 263-2486
Abilene (G-34)
Haivala Concrete Tools Inc ....G.... 316 263-1683
Wichita (G-14543)
J&M Tools LLC ....G.... 785 608-3343
Topeka (G-12733)
◆ Kraft Tool Company ....C.... 913 422-4848
Shawnee Mission (G-11538)
McM Manufacturing Inc ....G.... 785 235-1015
Topeka (G-12872)
Russell Steel Products Inc ....E.... 913 831-4600
Kansas City (G-4391)
▲ Sands Level and Tool Company ....D.... 620 325-2687
Neodesha (G-7248)
Triple B Investments Inc ....F.... 913 681-2500
Overland Park (G-9429)
Wilde Tool Co Inc ....E.... 785 742-7171
Hiawatha (G-3028)

3425 Hand Saws & Saw Blades

Barrow Tooling Systems Inc ....G.... 785 364-4306
Holton (G-3085)
▲ Diteq Corporation ....E.... 816 246-5515
Lenexa (G-5821)
◆ Husqvrna Cnstr Pdts N Amer Inc ....A.... 913 928-1000
Olathe (G-7781)

3429 Hardware, NEC

Dormakaba USA Inc ....F.... 913 831-3001
Kansas City (G-3975)
Dormakaba USA Inc ....G.... 316 267-6891
Wichita (G-14229)
Elec-Tron Inc ....D.... 316 522-3401
Wichita (G-14263)
Elite Fireplace Facings Inc ....G.... 913 631-5443
Shawnee Mission (G-11332)
Kmi Inc ....E.... 316 777-0146
Mulvane (G-7217)
Koehn Machine Inc ....G.... 316 282-2298
Newton (G-7372)
Mac Fasteners Inc ....E.... 785 242-2538
Ottawa (G-8287)
Niece Products of Kansas Inc ....E.... 620 223-0340
Fort Scott (G-1994)
North American Aviation Inc ....E.... 316 744-6450
Park City (G-9639)
Schlage Lock Company LLC ....C.... 888 805-9837
Olathe (G-8057)
▲ Vektek LLC ....C.... 620 342-7637
Emporia (G-1845)

3432 Plumbing Fixture Fittings & Trim, Brass

Daves Service & Repair Inc ....G.... 620 662-8285
Hutchinson (G-3257)
Mc Coy Company Inc ....C.... 913 342-1653
Kansas City (G-4222)
▲ Mid-America Fittings LLC ....E.... 913 962-7277
Overland Park (G-9024)
Vanguard Industries Inc ....G.... 620 241-6369
McPherson (G-7037)

3433 Heating Eqpt

A/C Enterprises Inc ....G.... 620 767-5695
Council Grove (G-1157)
▲ Airtex Manufacturing Lllp ....C.... 913 583-3181
De Soto (G-1192)
Cvr Manufacturing Inc ....G.... 620 763-2500
Galesburg (G-2091)
Ernstings Incorporated ....G.... 620 564-2793
Ellinwood (G-1631)
Jorban-Riscoe Associates Inc ....E.... 913 438-1244
Lenexa (G-5932)
▼ Kansas City Deaerator Inc ....F.... 913 312-5800
Overland Park (G-8894)
▲ Midwest Combustn Solutions Inc ....G.... 316 425-0929
Wichita (G-15090)
◆ Power Flame Incorporated ....C.... 620 421-0480
Parsons (G-9724)
◆ Vornado Air LLC ....D.... 316 733-0035
Andover (G-115)
▲ Webster Combustion Tech LLC ....D.... 620 221-7464
Winfield (G-16179)

3441 Fabricated Structural Steel

Advantage Building Systems LLC ....F.... 785 233-1393
Topeka (G-12296)
American Metal Fabrication Inc ....F.... 620 399-8508
Wellington (G-13489)
◆ Balco Inc ....C.... 800 767-0082
Wichita (G-13798)
Bennett Tool & Die LLC ....D.... 913 371-4641
Kansas City (G-3855)
CDI Industrial Mech Contrs Inc ....C.... 913 287-0334
Kansas City (G-3898)
Central Steel Inc ....D.... 316 265-8639
Wichita (G-13988)
Ceo Enterprises Inc ....F.... 913 432-8046
Shawnee Mission (G-11214)
Cook Pump Company ....E.... 620 251-0880
Coffeyville (G-930)
Custom Metal Fabricators Inc ....E.... 785 258-3744
Herington (G-2973)
Danny Axe ....E.... 620 767-5211
Council Grove (G-1162)
Derby Trailer Technologies LLC ....F.... 316 788-3331
Derby (G-1239)
Doherty Steel Inc ....C.... 913 557-9200
Paola (G-9553)
▲ Electromech Technologies LLC ....B.... 316 941-0400
Wichita (G-14266)
Electromech Technologies LLC ....C.... 316 941-0400
Wichita (G-14267)
Ernest-Spencer Metals Inc ....E.... 785 242-8538
Ottawa (G-8271)
Fab Works LLC ....G.... 620 585-2626
Inman (G-3581)
Fcs Manufacturing ....G.... 620 427-4200
Gridley (G-2690)
Genco Manufacturing ....G.... 785 448-2501
Garnett (G-2374)
Goodwill Wstn MO & Eastrn Kans ....F.... 785 331-3908
Lawrence (G-4875)
Goodwill Wstn MO & Eastrn Kans ....E.... 913 768-9540
Olathe (G-7737)
Grain Belt Supply Company Inc ....C.... 785 827-4491
Salina (G-10514)
Hall Steel & Fabrication Inc ....G.... 316 263-4222
Wichita (G-14547)
▼ Haven Steel Products Inc ....D.... 620 465-2573
Haven (G-2731)
Heckendorn Eqp Co of Kans ....G.... 620 983-2186
Peabody (G-9760)
Industrial Maint Topeka Inc ....E.... 785 842-6252
Topeka (G-12723)
Industrial Mtal Fbrication Inc ....D.... 316 283-3303
Newton (G-7366)
Jarit Manufacturing Inc ....G.... 785 448-2501
Garnett (G-2379)
Kasa Companies Inc ....D.... 785 825-5612
Salina (G-10569)
Kdoll Koatings Inc ....G.... 620 456-2588
Conway Springs (G-1142)
◆ Kice Industries Inc ....C.... 316 744-7148
Park City (G-9625)
Lippert Components Inc ....G.... 785 282-6366
Smith Center (G-12037)
M E H Inc ....D.... 785 235-1524
Topeka (G-12855)
M-C Fabrication Inc ....D.... 913 764-5454
Olathe (G-7869)
Magna Tech Inc ....E.... 620 431-3490
Chanute (G-740)
MAI Sky Systems Inc ....G.... 785 825-9151
Salina (G-10588)
Maico Industries Inc ....D.... 785 472-5390
Ellsworth (G-1677)
Matsu Manufacturing Inc ....C.... 620 331-8737
Independence (G-3536)
Mdf Industries Inc ....F.... 785 827-4450
Salina (G-10599)
Mellies Products Inc ....G.... 785 926-4331
Morganville (G-7165)
Metal Arts LLC ....F.... 316 942-7958
Wichita (G-15048)
Metal Pros LLC ....E.... 316 942-2238
Wichita (G-15054)
Mid-West Conveyor Company ....C.... 734 288-4400
Kansas City (G-4247)
Midland Steel Company ....D.... 785 989-4442
Wathena (G-13476)
Midwest Steel Fab LLC ....F.... 316 832-9669
Wichita (G-15103)
Midwestern Metals Inc ....E.... 785 232-1582
Topeka (G-12904)
Mobile Mini Inc ....F.... 316 838-2663
Park City (G-9636)
Needham & Associates Inc ....G.... 913 385-5300
Lenexa (G-6019)
▲ New Age Industrial Corp Inc ....C.... 785 877-5121
Norton (G-7455)
North Topeka Fabrication LLC ....E.... 785 233-4430
Topeka (G-12934)
Pittsburg Steel & Mfg Co Inc ....F.... 620 231-8100
Leawood (G-5522)
Popup Industries Inc ....E.... 620 431-9196
Chanute (G-755)
Ptmw Inc ....C.... 785 232-7792
Topeka (G-12994)
Raptor Manufacturing Lc ....E.... 316 201-1772
Wichita (G-15418)
Rgs Industries Inc ....G.... 913 780-9033
Olathe (G-8031)
Schuff Steel Company ....F.... 913 677-2485
Overland Park (G-9284)
Shawnee Steel & Welding Inc ....E.... 913 432-8046
Shawnee Mission (G-11863)
Southwest and Associates Inc ....D.... 620 463-5631
Burrton (G-650)
Southwest Stl Fabrication LLC ....E.... 913 422-5500
Bonner Springs (G-573)
Specialty Fabrication Inc ....F.... 316 264-0603
Wichita (G-15636)
Steel Fabrications Inc ....G.... 785 625-3075
Hays (G-2913)
Steve Johnson Companies ....F.... 316 722-2660
Wichita (G-15664)
TEC Fab Parts Inc ....F.... 913 369-0882
Tonganoxie (G-12270)
Tindle Construction Inc ....D.... 620 378-2046
Fredonia (G-2047)
Tran Aerospace Inc ....G.... 316 260-8808
Wichita (G-15787)
Trinity Steel and Pipe Inc ....F.... 620 396-8900
Weir (G-13486)
Twin Oaks Industries Inc ....E.... 785 827-4839
Salina (G-10743)
Unique Metal Fabrication Inc ....E.... 620 232-3060
Pittsburg (G-9949)
US Pipe Fabrication LLC ....F.... 785 242-6284
Ottawa (G-8318)
▲ US Tower Corp ....E.... 785 524-9966
Lincoln (G-6389)
Valmont Industries Inc ....D.... 316 321-1201
El Dorado (G-1611)
Valmont Industries Inc ....D.... 785 452-9630
Salina (G-10749)
Viking Industries Inc ....F.... 620 795-2143
Oswego (G-8238)

SIC

3442 Metal Doors, Sash, Frames, Molding & Trim

Arko Manufacturing Co Inc ....G.... 316 838-7162
Wichita *(G-13733)*
Carlson Products LLC ....D.... 316 722-0265
Maize *(G-6509)*
▲ **Cgf Investments Inc** ....E.... 316 691-4500
Wichita *(G-13994)*
Champion Window Co Kans Cy Inc ....E.... 913 541-8282
Lenexa *(G-5751)*
Columbia Industries Inc ....E.... 785 227-3351
Lindsborg *(G-6396)*
Columbia Metal Products Co ....E.... 620 365-3166
Iola *(G-3594)*
Elco Manufacturing Inc ....E.... 620 896-7333
Harper *(G-2720)*
Humphrey Products Inc ....E.... 316 267-2201
Wichita *(G-14655)*
Koch & Co Inc ....B.... 785 336-6022
Seneca *(G-10871)*
Lippert Components Mfg Inc ....C.... 323 663-1261
North Newton *(G-7437)*
▲ **Manko Window Systems Inc** ....B.... 785 776-9643
Manhattan *(G-6730)*
Masonite International Corp ....E.... 620 231-8200
Pittsburg *(G-9899)*
Mpressions ....G.... 913 897-4401
Stilwell *(G-12169)*
▲ **Peerless Products Inc** ....B.... 620 223-4610
Fort Scott *(G-1998)*
Reno Fabricating & Sls Co Inc ....E.... 620 663-1269
Hutchinson *(G-3426)*
Tracker Door Systems LLC ....G.... 913 585-3100
De Soto *(G-1214)*
Western Aluminum & Glass Co ....F.... 785 625-2418
Hays *(G-2931)*
▼ **Wheatbelt Inc** ....G.... 620 947-2323
Hillsboro *(G-3058)*

3443 Fabricated Plate Work

▲ **Abbott Aluminum Inc** ....E.... 785 776-8555
Manhattan *(G-6529)*
Air Products and Chemicals Inc ....F.... 620 626-7062
Liberal *(G-6274)*
American Energy Products Inc ....G.... 913 351-3388
Lansing *(G-4666)*
◆ **Balco Inc** ....C.... 800 767-0082
Wichita *(G-13798)*
Blackmore and Glunt Inc ....F.... 913 469-5715
Shawnee Mission *(G-11168)*
Bmg of Kansas Inc ....D.... 620 327-4038
Hesston *(G-2985)*
Boss Industries LLC ....E.... 620 795-2143
Oswego *(G-8231)*
Bradford Built Inc ....E.... 785 325-3300
Washington *(G-13460)*
CD Custom Enterprises LLC ....F.... 316 804-4520
Newton *(G-7327)*
Contech Engnered Solutions LLC ....E.... 785 234-1000
Topeka *(G-12504)*
Control Components Inc ....G.... 620 221-2343
Winfield *(G-16127)*
Cromwell Builders Mfg ....F.... 785 949-2433
Carlton *(G-686)*
Custom Metal Fabricators Inc ....E.... 785 258-3744
Herington *(G-2973)*
Double T Ind Inc ....E.... 620 593-4357
Rolla *(G-10232)*
Eaton Corporation ....B.... 620 663-5751
Hutchinson *(G-3274)*
▲ **Evaptech Inc** ....D.... 913 322-5165
Edwardsville *(G-1499)*
Glass King Manufacturing Co ....F.... 620 793-7838
Great Bend *(G-2570)*
▼ **Hammersmith Mfg & Sales Inc** ....D.... 785 486-2121
Horton *(G-3126)*
Hammersmith Mfg & Sales Inc ....G.... 785 364-4140
Holton *(G-3095)*
Hammersmith Mfg & Sales Inc ....G.... 913 338-0754
Overland Park *(G-8788)*
Harbison-Fischer Inc ....G.... 620 624-9042
Liberal *(G-6317)*
HBD Industries Inc ....D.... 620 431-9100
Chanute *(G-730)*
Hess Services Inc ....D.... 785 625-9295
Hays *(G-2843)*
◆ **Hix Corporation** ....D.... 620 231-8568
Pittsburg *(G-9876)*
Hughes Machinery Company ....G.... 316 612-0868
Wichita *(G-14649)*
▲ **KBK Industries LLC** ....C.... 785 372-4331
Rush Center *(G-10260)*
Koch Rail LLC ....G.... 316 828-5500
Wichita *(G-14886)*
◆ **Koch-Glitsch LP** ....A.... 316 828-5000
Wichita *(G-14891)*
Marley Cooling Tower Co Inc ....G.... 913 664-7400
Overland Park *(G-8993)*
▲ **Mid America Pipe Fabg Sup LLC** ....C.... 620 827-6121
Scammon *(G-10796)*
▲ **Midwest Combustn Solutions Inc** ....G.... 316 425-0929
Wichita *(G-15090)*
Niece Products of Kansas Inc ....E.... 620 223-0340
Fort Scott *(G-1994)*
▲ **Optimized Process Furnaces Inc** ....F.... 620 431-1260
Chanute *(G-750)*
Optimus Industries LLC ....C.... 620 431-3100
Chanute *(G-751)*
Oxwell Inc ....D.... 620 326-7481
Wellington *(G-13521)*
Pioneer Tank & Steel Inc ....G.... 620 672-2153
Pratt *(G-10133)*
Redguard LLC ....C.... 316 554-9000
Wichita *(G-15431)*
▲ **Sauder Custom Fabrication Inc** ....D.... 620 342-2550
Emporia *(G-1823)*
SPX Cooling Technologies Inc ....G.... 913 722-3600
Overland Park *(G-9345)*
SPX Cooling Technologies Inc ....C.... 913 782-1600
Olathe *(G-8079)*
SPX Dry Cooling Usa LLC ....G.... 913 685-0009
Overland Park *(G-9346)*
Superior Holding Inc ....F.... 620 662-6693
Hutchinson *(G-3458)*
◆ **Tank Connection LLC** ....F.... 620 423-0251
Parsons *(G-9744)*
Tank Wind-Down Corp ....C.... 620 421-0200
Parsons *(G-9745)*
◆ **Taylor Forge Engineered** ....C.... 785 867-2590
Paola *(G-9592)*
Taylor Forge Engineered ....E.... 785 448-6803
Garnett *(G-2390)*
Twin Oaks Industries Inc ....E.... 785 827-4839
Salina *(G-10743)*
◆ **Wall-Ties & Forms Inc** ....C.... 913 441-0073
Shawnee *(G-11049)*
We-Mac Manufacturing Co ....F.... 913 367-3778
Atchison *(G-270)*
We-Mac Manufacturing Co ....F.... 620 879-2187
Caney *(G-678)*
Worthington Cylinder Corp ....C.... 316 529-6950
Maize *(G-6523)*
Worthington Cylinder Corp ....C.... 620 275-7461
Garden City *(G-2318)*

3444 Sheet Metal Work

Accu-Fab Inc ....F.... 785 862-0100
Topeka *(G-12283)*
Adapa Incorporated ....F.... 785 862-2060
Topeka *(G-12286)*
AG Growth International Inc ....C.... 785 632-2161
Clay Center *(G-842)*
Arko Manufacturing Co Inc ....G.... 316 838-7162
Wichita *(G-13733)*
B & B Airparts Inc ....C.... 316 946-0300
Wichita *(G-13784)*
Barnes & Dodge Inc ....E.... 913 321-6444
Lenexa *(G-5687)*
Bmg of Kansas Inc ....D.... 620 327-4038
Hesston *(G-2985)*
Bradford Built Inc ....E.... 785 325-3300
Washington *(G-13460)*
Central Steel Inc ....D.... 316 265-8639
Wichita *(G-13988)*
Centurion Industries Inc ....E.... 620 244-3201
Erie *(G-1857)*
Centurion Industries Inc ....B.... 620 378-4401
Fredonia *(G-2028)*
Champion Window Co Kans Cy Inc ....E.... 913 541-8282
Lenexa *(G-5751)*
Contech Engnered Solutions LLC ....E.... 785 234-1000
Topeka *(G-12504)*
Contractors Engineer Inc ....F.... 620 568-2391
Neodesha *(G-7238)*
Curbs Plus Inc ....E.... 888 639-2872
El Dorado *(G-1554)*
Custom Metal Fabricators Inc ....E.... 785 258-3744
Herington *(G-2973)*
Dandee Air Inc ....F.... 620 663-4341
Hutchinson *(G-3253)*
Daniel Todd Industries Inc ....G.... 913 780-0382
Olathe *(G-7641)*
Dayton Superior Corporation ....C.... 937 866-0711
Parsons *(G-9681)*
Db2 Services Inc ....F.... 913 677-2408
Kansas City *(G-3961)*
Debackers Inc ....E.... 785 232-6999
Topeka *(G-12550)*
▲ **Etco Specialty Products Inc** ....E.... 620 724-6463
Girard *(G-2403)*
Fashion Inc ....E.... 785 242-8111
Ottawa *(G-8272)*
G & D Metals Inc ....G.... 316 303-9090
Wichita *(G-14431)*
General Repair & Supply Inc ....G.... 620 365-5954
Iola *(G-3604)*
Globe Engineering Co Inc ....C.... 316 943-1266
Wichita *(G-14476)*
Gmls Industries Inc ....G.... 620 983-2136
Peabody *(G-9759)*
Goodwill Wstn MO & Eastrn Kans ....E.... 785 228-9774
Topeka *(G-12642)*
Goodwill Wstn MO & Eastrn Kans ....F.... 785 331-3908
Lawrence *(G-4875)*
Goodwill Wstn MO & Eastrn Kans ....E.... 913 768-9540
Olathe *(G-7737)*
Grain Belt Supply Company Inc ....C.... 785 827-4491
Salina *(G-10514)*
H & R Parts Co Inc ....E.... 316 942-6984
Wichita *(G-14531)*
Hall Steel & Fabrication Inc ....G.... 316 263-4222
Wichita *(G-14547)*
Impresa Aerospace LLC ....D.... 316 942-9100
Wichita *(G-14679)*
J & J Drainage Products Co ....E.... 620 663-1575
Hutchinson *(G-3337)*
JR Custom Metal Products Inc ....C.... 316 263-1318
Wichita *(G-14776)*
Kasa Companies Inc ....D.... 785 825-5612
Salina *(G-10569)*
Kemlee Manufacturing Inc ....D.... 620 783-5035
Galena *(G-2076)*
◆ **Kice Industries Inc** ....C.... 316 744-7148
Park City *(G-9625)*
Labconco Corporation ....E.... 620 223-5700
Fort Scott *(G-1980)*
Lb Steel LLC ....B.... 785 862-1071
Topeka *(G-12836)*
Lippert Components Mfg Inc ....C.... 323 663-1261
North Newton *(G-7437)*
LMI Aerospace Inc ....C.... 316 943-6059
Wichita *(G-14972)*
Manufacturing Development Inc ....E.... 316 542-0182
Cheney *(G-793)*
Metal Panels Inc ....E.... 913 766-7200
Kansas City *(G-4236)*
◆ **Metal-Fab Inc** ....C.... 316 943-2351
Wichita *(G-15055)*
Metal-Fab Inc ....D.... 316 943-2351
Wichita *(G-15056)*
Metal-Fab Inc ....G.... 316 946-5875
Wichita *(G-15057)*
Metalform Industries Inc ....F.... 316 945-6700
Wichita *(G-15058)*
▲ **Millett Industries** ....G.... 913 752-3572
Overland Park *(G-9038)*
▲ **New Age Industrial Corp Inc** ....C.... 785 877-5121
Norton *(G-7455)*
Oxwell Inc ....D.... 620 326-7481
Wellington *(G-13521)*
Progressive Manufacturing Co ....F.... 913 383-2239
Leawood *(G-5530)*
Progressive Products Inc ....E.... 620 235-1712
Pittsburg *(G-9925)*
Quality Tech Metals ....E.... 316 945-4781
Wichita *(G-15386)*
▲ **R P M Smith Corporation** ....F.... 913 888-0695
Lenexa *(G-6087)*
Reliance Steel & Aluminum Co ....D.... 316 636-4500
Wichita *(G-15440)*
Rppg Inc ....E.... 620 705-5100
Arkansas City *(G-176)*
SC Hall Industrial Svcs Inc ....E.... 316 945-4255
Wichita *(G-15525)*
Sheet Metal Contractors Inc ....E.... 913 397-9130
Olathe *(G-8061)*
Southwest and Associates Inc ....D.... 620 463-5631
Burrton *(G-650)*
Star Pipe Usa LLC ....C.... 281 558-3000
Coffeyville *(G-979)*

Starflite Manufacturing Co ....G.... 316 267-7297
Wichita (G-15656)
◆ Systemair Mfg Inc....E.... 913 752-6000
Lenexa (G-6164)
Tartan Manufacturing Inc ....C.... 913 432-7100
Kansas City (G-4458)
Tennison Brothers Inc....F.... 316 263-7581
Wichita (G-15729)
Tk Metals Inc ....G.... 913 667-3055
Lenexa (G-6183)
Tower Metal Works Inc ....E.... 785 256-4281
Maple Hill (G-6865)
Town & Country Guttering Inc ....F.... 913 441-0003
Shawnee Mission (G-11935)
Trieb Sheet Metal Co....E.... 913 831-1166
Kansas City (G-4474)
Trinity Steel and Pipe Inc ....F.... 620 396-8900
Weir (G-13486)
Twin Oaks Industries Inc....E.... 785 827-4839
Salina (G-10743)
U-Tek Cnc Solutions LLC ....F.... 888 317-6503
Hiawatha (G-3026)
◆ Vista Manufacturing Company....E.... 913 342-4939
Kansas City (G-4521)
◆ Wall-Ties & Forms Inc ....C.... 913 441-0073
Shawnee (G-11049)
Webco Manufacturing Inc ....D.... 913 764-7111
Olathe (G-8149)
▼ Weis Fire Safety Equip Co Inc ....F.... 785 825-9527
Salina (G-10765)
Western Aluminum & Glass Co ....F.... 785 625-2418
Hays (G-2931)
Wholesale Sheet Metal Inc....C.... 913 432-7100
Kansas City (G-4543)
Wichita Awning Co Inc ....G.... 316 838-4432
Wichita (G-15978)

3446 Architectural & Ornamental Metal Work

Architectural Cast Metals Inc....G.... 785 221-6901
Topeka (G-12337)
◆ Balco Inc ....C.... 800 767-0082
Wichita (G-13798)
Bradford Built Inc....E.... 785 325-3300
Washington (G-13460)
Corbin Bronze Limited ....G.... 913 766-4012
Kansas City (G-3940)
Designer Palms Inc....F.... 316 733-2284
Andover (G-89)
▼ Goddard Manufacturing Inc ....G.... 785 689-4341
Logan (G-6424)
Landwehr Manufacturing Company....G.... 316 942-1719
Wichita (G-14923)
Linders Welding Inc....G.... 913 681-2394
Stilwell (G-12164)
Mc Kinnes Iron & Metal Inc ....G.... 620 257-3821
Lyons (G-6494)
Southwest Stl Fabrication LLC ....E.... 913 422-5500
Bonner Springs (G-573)
Tindle Construction Inc....D.... 620 378-2046
Fredonia (G-2047)
Town & Country Sheetmetal Inc ....F.... 913 441-1208
Shawnee (G-11041)
Ultra Modern Pool & Patio Inc ....G.... 316 681-3011
Wichita (G-15829)
Unique Metal Fabrication Inc ....E.... 620 232-3060
Pittsburg (G-9949)

3448 Prefabricated Metal Buildings & Cmpnts

Ciac LLC ....G.... 316 262-0953
Wichita (G-14020)
Gmls Industries Inc....G.... 620 983-2136
Peabody (G-9759)
Jahnke & Sons Construction Inc....F.... 800 351-2525
Overland Park (G-8870)
L & M Steel & Mfg....G.... 785 462-8216
Colby (G-1023)
▲ Martinez Inc ....G.... 316 587-7814
Wichita (G-15015)
Mobile Mini Inc ....F.... 316 838-2663
Park City (G-9636)
Morton Buildings Inc ....E.... 785 364-4177
Holton (G-3106)
Morton Buildings Inc ....D.... 620 221-4180
Winfield (G-16159)
Morton Buildings Inc ....F.... 620 221-3265
Winfield (G-16160)
Sunshine Rooms Inc ....F.... 316 838-0033
Wichita (G-15689)

3449 Misc Structural Metal Work

AMBS and Associates Inc....G.... 913 599-5939
Lenexa (G-5644)
▼ Custom Rollforming Corp ....E.... 800 457-8837
Moundridge (G-7182)
▲ Femco Inc ....D.... 620 241-3513
McPherson (G-6964)
Lane Myers Company Inc....E.... 620 622-4310
Protection (G-10175)
Midwest Contracting & Mfg....G.... 785 743-2026
WA Keeney (G-13383)
Performance Contracting Inc....E.... 913 928-2800
Lenexa (G-6054)
Performance Contracting Inc....E.... 913 928-2832
Lenexa (G-6052)
Southwest Stl Fabrication LLC ....E.... 913 422-5500
Bonner Springs (G-573)
Southwest Stl Fabricators Inc ....E.... 913 422-5500
Bonner Springs (G-574)
Structura ....F.... 913 390-8787
Olathe (G-8086)

3451 Screw Machine Prdts

Timken Smo LLC....B.... 620 223-0080
Fort Scott (G-2008)
▲ Wescon Controls LLC ....C.... 316 942-7266
Wichita (G-15950)

3452 Bolts, Nuts, Screws, Rivets & Washers

Gaskell Machine & Metal Inc....F.... 785 486-2674
Horton (G-3123)
Harlow Aerostructures LLC ....C.... 316 265-5268
Wichita (G-14561)
Heartland Precision Fas Inc....D.... 913 829-4447
New Century (G-7286)
K-W Manufacturing LLC....F.... 785 548-7454
Everest (G-1900)
Milacron Marketing Company LLC....D.... 620 241-1624
McPherson (G-7008)
Power Washers Unlimited....G.... 316 262-9274
Wichita (G-15320)

3462 Iron & Steel Forgings

▲ Brierton Engineering Inc ....E.... 785 263-7711
Abilene (G-16)
Gear Headquarters Inc ....F.... 913 831-1700
Kansas City (G-4028)
Griffin Wheel Company ....E.... 913 299-2223
Kansas City (G-4054)
◆ Pro-Dig LLC ....F.... 785 856-2661
Elwood (G-1689)
Voestalpine Nortrak Inc....D.... 316 284-0088
Newton (G-7424)

3463 Nonferrous Forgings

GE Steam Power Inc....G.... 785 243-3300
Concordia (G-1113)

3465 Automotive Stampings

Alan Grove Components Inc....G.... 913 837-4368
Louisburg (G-6437)
Amphenol Adronics Inc....D.... 785 625-3000
Hays (G-2747)
Rotor Quality LLC ....G.... 316 425-0418
Wichita (G-15486)
Taylormade Proformance....G.... 620 326-3537
Wellington (G-13535)

3469 Metal Stampings, NEC

Bennett Tool & Die LLC ....D.... 913 371-4641
Kansas City (G-3855)
Carlson Products LLC....D.... 316 722-0265
Maize (G-6509)
Center Industries Corporation....C.... 316 942-8255
Wichita (G-13976)
Cft LLC....E.... 620 431-0885
Chanute (G-710)
Elitegear4ucom LLC ....G.... 316 993-4398
Wichita (G-14271)
▲ Florence Corporation Kansas....C.... 785 323-4400
Manhattan (G-6636)
Kearney Equipment LLC ....F.... 316 722-8710
Maize (G-6515)
Neosho Small Parts LLC ....F.... 620 244-3263
Erie (G-1862)
◆ Schroer Manufacturing Company....C.... 913 281-1500
Kansas City (G-4404)

◆ Vita Craft Corporation ....D.... 913 631-6265
Shawnee Mission (G-11982)
Wkcsc Inc ....G.... 316 652-7113
Wichita (G-16060)

3471 Electroplating, Plating, Polishing, Anodizing & Coloring

101st Earthborn Envmtl Tech LP....G.... 785 691-8918
Colby (G-987)
Alternative Chrome Creations ....G.... 316 680-1209
Haysville (G-2936)
C & R Plating Inc....F.... 785 392-2626
Minneapolis (G-7115)
Cardinal Buffing Co Inc....G.... 316 263-8475
Wichita (G-13943)
▲ Central Electropolishing Inc ....E.... 620 842-3701
Anthony (G-122)
Chrome Plus International Inc....F.... 316 944-3600
Wichita (G-14017)
Disco Machine Liberal Company....E.... 620 624-0179
Liberal (G-6305)
Ferroloy Inc ....E.... 316 838-0897
Wichita (G-14358)
Hampton Hydraulics Llc....D.... 620 792-4368
Great Bend (G-2590)
Ics Inc....E.... 620 654-3020
McPherson (G-6977)
◆ Industrial Chrome Inc ....D.... 785 235-3463
Topeka (G-12721)
Isf LLC....E.... 316 945-4040
Wichita (G-14730)
Kansas City Hydraulics Inc....G.... 913 371-6151
Kansas City (G-4145)
Kc Restoration LLC ....F.... 913 766-2200
Olathe (G-7832)
Metal Finishing Co Inc....G.... 316 267-7289
Wichita (G-15050)
Metal Finishing Co Inc....E.... 316 267-7289
Wichita (G-15051)
Metal Finishing Company Inc ....C.... 316 267-7289
Wichita (G-15052)
Metal Finishing Company Inc ....F.... 316 267-7289
Wichita (G-15053)
Paragon N D T & Finishes Inc....E.... 316 945-5285
Wichita (G-15259)
Precision Industries Inc ....E.... 620 241-5010
McPherson (G-7019)
Premier Processing ....F.... 316 425-3565
Wichita (G-15333)
Right Stuff Co....G.... 913 722-4002
Prairie Village (G-10064)
Specialty Technology Inc....F.... 620 241-6307
McPherson (G-7027)
▲ Thayer Aerospace Plating Inc....C.... 316 522-5426
Wichita (G-15756)
True Spec Finishes LLC ....G.... 620 254-7733
Attica (G-280)

3479 Coating & Engraving, NEC

A Plus Galvanizing....E.... 785 820-9823
Salina (G-10388)
Bob Eisel Powder Coatings ....E.... 316 942-8870
Wichita (G-13860)
Hobby Monster Customs LLC ....G.... 913 417-7088
Tonganoxie (G-12263)
Jayhawk Trophy Company Inc ....G.... 785 843-3900
Lawrence (G-4921)
Landoll Corporation....E.... 785 738-6613
Beloit (G-490)
Powdertech Llc ....E.... 316 832-9210
Wichita (G-15317)
Pro-Kleen Inc....E.... 316 775-6898
Augusta (G-339)
R Miller Sales Co Inc....E.... 913 341-3727
Shawnee Mission (G-11772)
Rogers Manufacturing Inc....E.... 843 423-4680
Olathe (G-8040)

3482 Small Arms Ammunition

Swift Bullet Co....F.... 785 754-2374
Quinter (G-10187)
▲ Velocity Manufacturing Co LLC....F.... 620 223-1277
Fort Scott (G-2015)

3483 Ammunition, Large

Day and Zimmermann Inc ....C.... 620 421-7400
Parsons (G-9680)
Endless Ideas Inc....F.... 913 766-0680
Olathe (G-7681)

SIC

Employee Codes: A=Over 500 employees, B=251-500
C=101-250, D=51-100, E=20-50, F=10-19, G=5-9

Vista Outdoor Inc....C....913 752-3400
Overland Park *(G-9467)*

3484 Small Arms

Bell and Carlson Incorporated....E....620 225-6688
Dodge City *(G-1306)*
▲ Carlsons Choke Tube/NW Arms....F....785 626-3078
Atwood *(G-282)*
▲ Cz-USA....D....913 321-1811
Kansas City *(G-3949)*
Endless Ideas Inc....F....913 766-0680
Olathe *(G-7681)*
Joe Bob Outfitters LLC....F....785 639-7121
Hays *(G-2856)*
▲ Millett Industries....G....913 752-3572
Overland Park *(G-9038)*

3489 Ordnance & Access, NEC

B 5 Inc....G....316 721-3222
Wichita *(G-13785)*

3491 Industrial Valves

Arrow Valve Co Inc....G....620 879-2126
Caney *(G-665)*
Associated Cylinder SE....G....951 776-9915
Kansas City *(G-3823)*
◆ Cashco Inc....C....785 472-4461
Ellsworth *(G-1659)*
◆ Forum Energy Tecnhologies....D....620 437-2440
Madison *(G-6500)*
Hughes Machinery Company....G....316 612-0868
Wichita *(G-14649)*
J Huston Howery....G....316 945-0023
Wichita *(G-14736)*
◆ J Huston Howery....F....316 945-0023
Wichita *(G-14737)*
Powerline Machine Works Inc....F....620 824-6204
Chase *(G-786)*
▲ Salina Vortex Corp....C....785 825-7177
Salina *(G-10696)*
V Mach Inc....E....913 894-2001
Shawnee Mission *(G-11971)*
Waddles Manufacturing & Mch Co....G....785 825-6166
Salina *(G-10756)*

3492 Fluid Power Valves & Hose Fittings

Austin A-7 Ltd....F....316 945-8892
Wichita *(G-13769)*
Cross Manufacturing Inc....D....785 625-2585
Hays *(G-2780)*
Experitec Inc....F....913 894-4044
Shawnee Mission *(G-11356)*
Great Bend Industries Inc....D....620 792-4368
Great Bend *(G-2581)*
Swan Engineering & Sup Co Inc....F....913 371-7425
Kansas City *(G-4452)*
V Mach Inc....E....913 894-2001
Shawnee Mission *(G-11971)*

3494 Valves & Pipe Fittings, NEC

Aerospace Systems Cmpnents Inc....D....316 686-7392
Wichita *(G-13638)*
Arrow Valve Co Inc....G....620 879-2126
Caney *(G-665)*
Eaton Corporation....B....620 663-5751
Hutchinson *(G-3274)*
◆ Kice Industries Inc....C....316 744-7148
Park City *(G-9625)*
Little Giant Fittings Company....G....620 793-5399
Great Bend *(G-2603)*
▲ Mid-America Fittings LLC....E....913 962-7277
Overland Park *(G-9024)*
Progressive Products Inc....E....620 235-1712
Pittsburg *(G-9925)*
Rickerson Pipe Lining LLC....F....785 448-5401
Garnett *(G-2386)*
▲ Salina Vortex Corp....C....785 825-7177
Salina *(G-10696)*
Triumph Group Operations Inc....D....620 326-5761
Wellington *(G-13538)*

3495 Wire Springs

Coil Springs Specialties LLC....G....785 437-2025
Saint Marys *(G-10359)*

3496 Misc Fabricated Wire Prdts

◆ Balco Inc....C....800 767-0082
Wichita *(G-13798)*
Burlingame Wire Products Inc....F....785 483-3138
Russell *(G-10268)*
Certainteed LLC....E....620 241-5511
McPherson *(G-6946)*
Colby Supply & Mfg Co....F....785 462-3981
Colby *(G-999)*
Dayton Superior Corporation....C....937 866-0711
Parsons *(G-9681)*
▲ Farris Burns Corp....G....913 262-0555
Shawnee Mission *(G-11361)*
Hydeman Company Inc....G....913 384-2620
Kansas City *(G-4090)*
Lane Myers Company Inc....E....620 622-4310
Protection *(G-10175)*
▲ Lynk Inc....F....913 492-9202
Shawnee Mission *(G-11586)*
Print Source Inc....D....316 945-7052
Wichita *(G-15348)*
Quality Steel & Wire Pdts Co....G....913 888-2929
Lenexa *(G-6085)*
Wireco Worldgroup Inc....E....816 270-4700
Prairie Village *(G-10084)*
◆ Wireco Worldgroup Inc....B....816 270-4700
Prairie Village *(G-10085)*
▲ Wireco Wrldgroup US Hldngs Inc....F....816 270-4700
Prairie Village *(G-10086)*

3497 Metal Foil & Leaf

▲ API Americas Inc....D....732 382-6800
Lawrence *(G-4737)*

3498 Fabricated Pipe & Pipe Fittings

Bennett Rgers Pipe Coating Inc....E....913 371-3880
Kansas City *(G-3854)*
Callaway Electric....G....785 632-5588
Clay Center *(G-847)*
CDI Industrial Mech Contrs Inc....C....913 287-0334
Kansas City *(G-3898)*
Little Giant Fittings Company....G....620 793-5399
Great Bend *(G-2603)*
▲ Mid America Pipe Fabg Sup LLC....C....620 827-6121
Scammon *(G-10796)*
Premier Mechanical Pdts LLC....F....913 271-5002
Kansas City *(G-4332)*
Reintjes & Hiter Co Inc....F....913 371-1872
Kansas City *(G-4368)*
Spears Manufacturing Co....B....620 879-2131
Caney *(G-674)*
Specialty Fabrication Inc....F....316 264-0603
Wichita *(G-15636)*
US Pipe Fabrication LLC....F....785 242-6284
Ottawa *(G-8318)*

3499 Fabricated Metal Prdts, NEC

A & R Cstm Frms Fbrcations LLC....E....620 423-0401
Parsons *(G-9661)*
Best West Fabrication LLC....G....785 527-2450
Belleville *(G-453)*
Carlson Products LLC....D....316 722-0265
Maize *(G-6509)*
Concordia Technologies LLC....E....785 262-4066
Concordia *(G-1108)*
Custom Fabrication LLC....G....785 331-9460
Lawrence *(G-4820)*
DI Machine LLC....G....913 557-2000
Paola *(G-9552)*
◆ Hasty Awards Inc....D....785 242-5297
Ottawa *(G-8278)*
Kan Fab Inc....G....620 342-5669
Emporia *(G-1783)*
Laminage Products Inc....G....316 267-5233
Wichita *(G-14916)*
Lb Steel LLC....B....785 862-1071
Topeka *(G-12836)*
Locknclimb LLC....G....620 331-8247
Independence *(G-3534)*
Mad Dog Metal Inc....G....620 275-9685
Garden City *(G-2227)*
▲ Multiprens Usa Inc....E....913 371-6999
Kansas City *(G-4271)*
R Miller Sales Co Inc....E....913 341-3727
Shawnee Mission *(G-11772)*
Ram Metal Products Inc....G....913 422-0099
Leawood *(G-5532)*
Rohrer Custom and Fabrication....G....620 359-1707
Wellington *(G-13525)*
SA Consumer Products Inc....G....888 792-4264
Leawood *(G-5544)*
Simon & Simon Inc....G....913 888-9889
Overland Park *(G-9311)*
Sinclair & Sons Custom Welding....E....316 263-3500
Wichita *(G-15597)*
Stouse LLC....E....913 384-0014
Kansas City *(G-4441)*

35 INDUSTRIAL AND COMMERCIAL MACHINERY AND COMPUTER EQUIPMENT

3511 Steam, Gas & Hydraulic Turbines & Engines

Accessible Technologies Inc....D....913 338-2886
Lenexa *(G-5621)*
Caterpillar Inc....D....309 675-1000
Wamego *(G-13409)*
GE Oil & Gas Compression....D....785 823-9211
Salina *(G-10508)*
▲ Kanamak Hydraulics Inc....E....800 473-5843
Garden City *(G-2212)*
Siemens Energy Inc....G....316 315-4534
Wichita *(G-15583)*

3519 Internal Combustion Engines, NEC

Caterpillar Inc....D....309 675-1000
Wamego *(G-13409)*
Cummins - Allison Corp....G....913 894-2266
Lenexa *(G-5797)*
Cummins Central Power LLC....F....785 462-3945
Colby *(G-1002)*
◆ Detroit Diesel Remanufacturing....C....620 343-3790
Emporia *(G-1729)*
Engquist Tractor Service Inc....E....620 654-3651
McPherson *(G-6959)*
Herrs Machine....G....785 325-2875
Washington *(G-13464)*
United Auto Parts Inc....E....316 721-6868
Wichita *(G-15840)*

3523 Farm Machinery & Eqpt

A & B Machine Inc....F....785 827-5171
Salina *(G-10387)*
Adrian Manufacturing Inc....G....507 381-9746
Newton *(G-7307)*
AGCO Corporation....C....620 327-6413
Hesston *(G-2984)*
AGCO Corporation....B....785 738-2261
Beloit *(G-470)*
▲ Agsynergy LLC....G....785 336-6333
Seneca *(G-10857)*
Bar Six Manufaturing Inc....G....620 622-4456
Protection *(G-10174)*
Beck Sales Company....G....620 225-1770
Dodge City *(G-1305)*
Bestway Inc....E....785 742-2949
Hiawatha *(G-3003)*
Bradford Built Inc....E....785 325-3300
Washington *(G-13460)*
Broce Manufacturing Co Inc....G....620 227-8811
Dodge City *(G-1312)*
▲ Bultman Company Inc Mfg....F....620 544-8004
Hugoton *(G-3149)*
Buster Crust Inc....D....620 227-7106
Dodge City *(G-1315)*
Buster Crust Inc....E....620 385-2651
Spearville *(G-12070)*
▲ Cannonball Engineering LLC....F....620 532-3675
Kingman *(G-4585)*
Center Industries Corporation....C....316 942-8255
Wichita *(G-13976)*
Central Plains Coop....G....785 282-6813
Smith Center *(G-12032)*
Cliffs Welding Shop Inc....G....785 543-5895
Phillipsburg *(G-9780)*
Custom Metal Fabricators Inc....E....785 258-3744
Herington *(G-2973)*
Donahue Corporation....E....620 924-5500
Durham *(G-1474)*
Donahue Manufacturing LLC....F....620 732-2665
Durham *(G-1475)*
Excel Industries Inc....F....800 942-4911
Hesston *(G-2989)*
▲ Express Scale Parts Inc....E....913 441-4787
Lenexa *(G-5844)*
▲ Extru-Tech Inc....D....785 284-2153
Sabetha *(G-10309)*
Golden Plains AG Tech....G....785 462-6753
Colby *(G-1009)*

Grain Belt Supply Company Inc ....C 785 827-4491
Salina (G-10514)
▲ Great Plains International LLC ....F 785 823-3276
Salina (G-10516)
Great Plains Manufacturing Inc ....C 785 263-2486
Abilene (G-34)
Great Plains Manufacturing Inc ....B 785 825-1509
Salina (G-10519)
Great Plains Manufacturing Inc ....E 785 373-4145
Tipton (G-12248)
Great Plains Manufacturing Inc ....G 785 472-3508
Ellsworth (G-1675)
Great Plains Manufacturing Inc ....G 785 823-2255
Salina (G-10520)
Great Plains Manufacturing Inc ....E 785 525-6128
Lucas (G-6471)
◆ Great Plains Manufacturing Inc ....C 785 823-3276
Salina (G-10518)
▲ Green Line Inc ....F 620 896-7372
Harper (G-2722)
▼ Gt Mfg Inc ....E 785 632-2151
Clay Center (G-867)
▼ H C Davis Sons Mfg Co ....F 913 422-3000
Bonner Springs (G-554)
Haarslev Inc ....F 785 527-5641
Belleville (G-457)
▲ Harper Industries Inc ....D 620 896-7381
Harper (G-2723)
Heckendorn Eqp Co of Kans ....G 620 983-2186
Peabody (G-9760)
Hoelscher Inc ....F 620 562-3575
Bushton (G-653)
▲ Hutchinson/Mayrath ....E 785 632-2161
Clay Center (G-868)
Inityaero Inc ....E 316 265-0603
Wichita (G-14694)
Irrigation & Turf Equipment ....G 620 365-2121
Iola (G-3612)
▲ J D Skiles Inc ....F 785 626-9338
Atwood (G-287)
▲ Kejr Inc ....C 785 825-1842
Salina (G-10573)
Kiser AG Service LLC ....G 785 689-4292
Logan (G-6425)
▲ Kmw Ltd ....C 620 278-3641
Sterling (G-12124)
Ksi Conveyor Inc ....D 785 284-0600
Sabetha (G-10314)
◆ Landoll Corporation ....B 785 562-5381
Marysville (G-6893)
Lang Diesel Inc ....F 785 462-2412
Colby (G-1024)
LDB Inc ....G 620 532-2236
Kingman (G-4605)
Liberty Inc ....D 785 770-8788
Manhattan (G-6713)
Limestone Feeders LLC ....E 402 770-4118
Beloit (G-491)
Linn Post & Pipe Inc ....E 785 348-5526
Linn (G-6409)
Luco Manufacturing Co Inc ....F 620 273-6723
Strong City (G-12193)
▲ Magnum ....E 913 783-4600
Hillsdale (G-3059)
Mega Manufacturing Inc ....E 620 663-1127
Hutchinson (G-3371)
Mid-Continent Industries Inc ....F 316 283-9648
Newton (G-7384)
Midwest Contracting & Mfg ....G 785 743-2026
WA Keeney (G-13383)
Midwest Mill Modernization ....F 620 583-6883
Eureka (G-1895)
Midwest Mixer Service LLC ....F 620 225-7150
Dodge City (G-1405)
▲ Moly Manufacturing Inc ....E 785 472-3388
Lorraine (G-6433)
◆ Moridge Manufacturing Inc ....B 620 345-6301
Moundridge (G-7193)
Nance Manufacturing Inc ....E 620 842-3761
Anthony (G-130)
▲ Neville Welding Inc ....E 620 532-3487
Kingman (G-4608)
Oswald Manufacturing Co Inc ....G 785 258-2877
Herington (G-2980)
Peters-Howell Lujeana ....G 785 415-2125
Stockton (G-12183)
Prairie Products ....G 620 947-3922
Hillsboro (G-3054)
R & R Industries Inc ....F 620 672-7463
Pratt (G-10146)
Rhs Inc ....E 785 742-2949
Hiawatha (G-3023)
◆ Roto-Mix LLC ....D 620 225-1142
Dodge City (G-1425)
Roto-Mix LLC ....G 620 872-1100
Scott City (G-10830)
Roto-Mix LLC ....E 620 653-7323
Hoisington (G-3070)
Rvc Enterprises Inc ....F 785 937-4386
Princeton (G-10170)
Schaben Industries Inc ....E 316 283-4444
Newton (G-7415)
◆ Schroer Manufacturing Company ....C 913 281-1500
Kansas City (G-4404)
Scoular Company ....E 785 823-6301
Salina (G-10699)
▲ Shield Industries Inc ....E 620 662-7221
Hutchinson (G-3441)
Simpson Farm Enterprises Inc ....F 785 731-2700
Ransom (G-10195)
▲ Stinger Ltd ....E 620 465-2683
Burrton (G-651)
Stroberg Equipment Co Inc ....G 620 662-7650
Hutchinson (G-3452)
Tatge Manufacturing Inc ....G 785 965-7213
Ramona (G-10189)
Titan West Inc ....E 785 348-5660
Linn (G-6412)
Tribine Harvester LLC ....G 316 282-8011
Newton (G-7421)
Triple C Manufacturing Inc ....E 785 284-3674
Sabetha (G-10334)
United States Cstm Harvesters ....G 620 664-6297
Hutchinson (G-3477)
Usc LLC ....F 785 431-7900
Sabetha (G-10336)
Westheffer Company Inc ....E 785 843-1633
Lawrence (G-5183)
Wilkens Manufacturing Inc ....D 785 425-7070
Stockton (G-12190)
Winkel Manufacturing Co ....F 785 545-3297
Glen Elder (G-2428)

3524 Garden, Lawn Tractors & Eqpt

Century Partners LLC ....F 913 642-2489
Olathe (G-7586)
Danville Industries ....G 620 896-7126
Harper (G-2719)
▲ Desert Steel Corporation ....F 316 282-2244
Wichita (G-14199)
First Start Rentl Sls Svc Inc ....G 620 343-0983
Emporia (G-1756)
Great Plains Manufacturing Inc ....C 785 263-2486
Abilene (G-34)
▲ Harper Industries Inc ....D 620 896-7381
Harper (G-2723)
Heritage Tractor Inc ....E 785 235-5100
Topeka (G-12686)
Lippert Components Inc ....G 785 282-6366
Smith Center (G-12037)
▲ Mojack Distributors LLC ....F 877 466-5225
Wichita (G-15121)
◆ Moridge Manufacturing Inc ....B 620 345-6301
Moundridge (G-7193)
Prohoe Mfg LLC ....F 785 987-5450
Munden (G-7229)
Taylor Implement Co Inc ....E 785 675-3272
Hoxie (G-3143)

3531 Construction Machinery & Eqpt

Andrews Asphalt & Cnstr Inc ....G 785 232-0188
Topeka (G-12326)
▼ Bainter Construction Co Inc ....E 785 675-3297
Hoxie (G-3135)
Broce Manufacturing Co Inc ....G 620 227-8811
Dodge City (G-1312)
◆ Broderson Manufacturing Corp ....D 913 888-0606
Lenexa (G-5718)
◆ Caterpillar Work Tools Inc ....B 785 456-2224
Wamego (G-13410)
Caterpillar Work Tools Inc ....F 785 456-2224
Wamego (G-13411)
Cnh Industrial America LLC ....D 316 945-0111
Wichita (G-14046)
Coneqtec Corp ....E 316 943-8889
Wichita (G-14088)
CPB Materials LLC ....G 316 833-1146
Haysville (G-2938)
Crane Sales & Service Co Inc ....F 913 621-7040
Kansas City (G-3944)
▲ Diteq Corporation ....E 816 246-5515
Lenexa (G-5821)
◆ Dymax Inc ....E 785 456-2705
Wamego (G-13415)
◆ Full Vision Inc ....D 316 283-3344
Newton (G-7349)
▼ H C Davis Sons Mfg Co ....F 913 422-3000
Bonner Springs (G-554)
Haivala Concrete Tools Inc ....G 316 263-1683
Wichita (G-14543)
Icon Industries Inc ....E 785 738-3547
Beloit (G-488)
JR Custom Metal Products Inc ....C 316 263-1318
Wichita (G-14776)
Lafarge North America Inc ....B 913 780-6809
Olathe (G-7852)
Lynns Heavy Hauling LLC ....F 913 393-3863
Olathe (G-7868)
Neosho County Road and Bridge ....E 620 244-3855
Erie (G-1861)
Nesco Holdings Inc ....G 913 287-0001
Kansas City (G-4286)
▼ Peerless Conveyor and Mfg Corp ....F 913 342-2240
Kansas City (G-4318)
R & R Equipment Inc ....G 620 223-2450
Fort Scott (G-2000)
R O Terex Corporation ....D 913 782-1200
Olathe (G-8018)
Rgs Industries Inc ....G 913 780-9033
Olathe (G-8031)
Roto-Mix LLC ....E 620 653-7323
Hoisington (G-3070)
Shannahan Crane & Hoist Inc ....F 816 746-9822
Kansas City (G-4419)
Vernon L Goedecke Company Inc ....E 913 621-1284
Kansas City (G-4518)
▲ Weller Tractor Salvage Inc ....F 620 792-5243
Great Bend (G-2659)
Wsm Industries Inc ....E 913 492-9299
Lenexa (G-6236)

3532 Mining Machinery & Eqpt

AG Growth International Inc ....C 785 632-2161
Clay Center (G-842)
▲ Atkinson Industries Inc ....D 620 231-6900
Pittsburg (G-9816)
Midwestern Metals Inc ....E 785 232-1582
Topeka (G-12904)
▼ Rimpull Corporation ....C 913 782-4000
Olathe (G-8036)
▼ Royal Tractor Company Inc ....E 913 782-2598
New Century (G-7296)

3533 Oil Field Machinery & Eqpt

▲ BYIS Manufacturing LLC ....F 620 221-4603
Winfield (G-16119)
Conrad Machine Inc ....E 620 231-9458
Pittsburg (G-9844)
Ernstings Incorporated ....G 620 564-2793
Ellinwood (G-1631)
FMC Technologies Inc ....E 913 214-4300
Lenexa (G-5862)
Harbison-Fischer Inc ....G 620 624-9042
Liberal (G-6317)
Invena Corporation ....E 620 583-8630
Eureka (G-1892)
Oilpure Technologies Inc ....G 913 906-0400
Leawood (G-5508)
Parmac LLC ....E 620 251-5000
Coffeyville (G-969)
◆ Precision International ....D 620 365-7255
Iola (G-3625)
Quality Connectionz Inc ....G 620 380-6262
Iola (G-3628)
Ridge Enterprises LLC ....G 620 491-2141
Kingman (G-4613)
▲ Schwabs Tinker Shop Intl Inc ....G 620 624-7611
Liberal (G-6363)
Schwabs Tinker Shop Intl Inc ....G 620 564-2547
Ellinwood (G-1636)
Star Pipe Usa LLC ....C 281 558-3000
Coffeyville (G-979)
U S Weatherford L P ....F 620 624-9324
Liberal (G-6376)
Vulcan Machine & Repair ....G 620 796-2190
Great Bend (G-2655)
Wsi Holdings LLC ....E 785 421-2255
Hill City (G-3038)

3534 Elevators & Moving Stairways

Columbia Elevator Pdts Co Inc............E....... 888 858-1558
Winfield *(G-16124)*
Interstate Elevator Inc..........................F....... 785 234-2817
Topeka *(G-12727)*

3535 Conveyors & Eqpt

Adapa Incorporated..............................F....... 785 862-2060
Topeka *(G-12286)*
Advanced Machine Solutions LLC........F....... 620 724-6220
Girard *(G-2394)*
Bl Brooks & Sons Inc.............................G....... 913 829-5494
Olathe *(G-7553)*
Bulk Conveyors Inc................................E....... 316 201-3158
Wichita *(G-13914)*
Cargotec USA Inc...................................G....... 785 229-7111
Ottawa *(G-8252)*
Clean Air Management Co Inc...............E....... 913 831-0740
Lenexa *(G-5760)*
▲ **Coperion K-Tron Salina Inc**.............C....... 785 825-1611
Salina *(G-10462)*
Custom Metal Fabricators Inc..............E....... 785 258-3744
Herington *(G-2973)*
Dearborn Mid West Conveyor Co..........G....... 913 261-2428
Overland Park *(G-8644)*
▲ **Express Scale Parts Inc**....................E....... 913 441-4787
Lenexa *(G-5844)*
Grain Belt Supply Company Inc............C....... 785 827-4491
Salina *(G-10514)*
Horizonpsi Inc..D....... 785 842-1299
Lawrence *(G-4902)*
JR Custom Metal Products Inc..............C....... 316 263-1318
Wichita *(G-14776)*
Mac Equipment Inc.................................F....... 785 284-2191
Sabetha *(G-10317)*
Magnatech Engineering Inc...................G....... 913 845-3553
Tonganoxie *(G-12265)*
Mid-West Conveyor Company...............C....... 734 288-4400
Kansas City *(G-4247)*
▼ **Peerless Conveyor and Mfg Corp**....F....... 913 342-2240
Kansas City *(G-4318)*
R & R Industries Inc..............................F....... 620 672-7463
Pratt *(G-10146)*
Rhs Inc...E....... 785 742-2949
Hiawatha *(G-3023)*
Schenck Accurate Inc............................G....... 262 473-2441
Sabetha *(G-10330)*
Schenck Process LLC............................C....... 785 284-2191
Sabetha *(G-10331)*
Tech-Air Inc..G....... 913 677-5777
Shawnee Mission *(G-11923)*
Thomas Manufacturing Inc....................F....... 620 724-6220
Girard *(G-2421)*
United States Systems Inc....................F....... 913 281-1010
Kansas City *(G-4490)*

3536 Hoists, Cranes & Monorails

◆ **Broderson Manufacturing Corp**........D....... 913 888-0606
Lenexa *(G-5718)*
Collis Craneworks Inc...........................E....... 913 764-1315
Olathe *(G-7599)*
Mid-West Conveyor Company...............C....... 734 288-4400
Kansas City *(G-4247)*
Nesco Holdings Inc................................G....... 913 287-0001
Kansas City *(G-4286)*
R O Terex Corporation...........................D....... 913 782-1200
Olathe *(G-8018)*
Wilkerson Crane Rental Inc...................E....... 913 238-7030
Lenexa *(G-6230)*

3537 Indl Trucks, Tractors, Trailers & Stackers

Adapa Incorporated...............................F....... 785 862-2060
Topeka *(G-12286)*
Adobe Truck & Equipment LLC.............G....... 913 498-9888
Olathe *(G-7510)*
Bones Co Inc..G....... 785 242-3070
Ottawa *(G-8250)*
▲ **Brierton Engineering Inc**...................E....... 785 263-7711
Abilene *(G-16)*
Cargotec Holding Inc.............................B....... 785 242-2200
Ottawa *(G-8251)*
Crown Equipment Corporation..............E....... 316 942-4400
Wichita *(G-14136)*
Crown Equipment Corporation..............E....... 913 888-9777
Lenexa *(G-5795)*
Custom Metal Fabricators Inc...............E....... 785 258-3744
Herington *(G-2973)*
◆ **Full Vision Inc**...................................D....... 316 283-3344
Newton *(G-7349)*
Garrison Transportation LLC................G....... 785 404-6744
Salina *(G-10507)*
General Delivery Inc..............................F....... 913 281-6580
Kansas City *(G-4030)*
◆ **Harper Trucks Inc**.............................C....... 316 942-1381
Wichita *(G-14563)*
JR Custom Metal Products Inc.............C....... 316 263-1318
Wichita *(G-14776)*
◆ **Kalmar Solutions LLC**.......................B....... 785 242-2200
Ottawa *(G-8279)*
▲ **Kmw Ltd**...C....... 620 278-3641
Sterling *(G-12124)*
◆ **Landoll Corporation**..........................B....... 785 562-5381
Marysville *(G-6893)*
Mid-West Conveyor Company...............C....... 734 288-4400
Kansas City *(G-4247)*
▲ **Ottawa Truck Inc**...............................B....... 785 242-2200
Ottawa *(G-8302)*
R O Terex Corporation...........................D....... 913 782-1200
Olathe *(G-8018)*
▼ **Rimpull Corporation**..........................C....... 913 782-4000
Olathe *(G-8036)*
▼ **Royal Tractor Company Inc**..............E....... 913 782-2598
New Century *(G-7296)*
Scrommel Resource Management........G....... 785 825-7771
Salina *(G-10700)*
Tracker Door Systems LLC....................G....... 913 585-3100
De Soto *(G-1214)*

3541 Machine Tools: Cutting

Acsys Lasertechnik US Inc....................G....... 847 468-5302
Lenexa *(G-5626)*
ADM Milling Co.......................................D....... 785 825-1541
Salina *(G-10395)*
Bazin Sawing & Drilling Llc...................F....... 913 764-0843
Louisburg *(G-6440)*
Haarslev Inc...F....... 785 527-5641
Belleville *(G-457)*
▼ **Hornet Cutting Systems LLC**...........E....... 316 755-3683
Valley Center *(G-13343)*
◆ **Husqvrna Cnstr Pdts N Amer Inc**......A....... 913 928-1000
Olathe *(G-7781)*
Nance Manufacturing Inc.......................E....... 316 942-8671
Wichita *(G-15146)*
Steel Fabrications Inc............................G....... 785 625-3075
Hays *(G-2913)*
▲ **Straightline Hdd Inc**..........................D....... 620 802-0200
Hutchinson *(G-3449)*
Valley View Milling.................................F....... 785 858-4777
Seneca *(G-10886)*

3542 Machine Tools: Forming

▲ **Hf Rubber Machinery Inc**..................E....... 785 235-2336
Topeka *(G-12688)*
Jorban-Riscoe Associates Inc..............E....... 913 438-1244
Lenexa *(G-5932)*
Marion Manufacturing Inc.....................E....... 620 382-3751
Marion *(G-6874)*
▲ **Mega Manufacturing Inc**..................E....... 620 663-1127
Hutchinson *(G-3370)*
Mega Manufacturing Inc........................E....... 620 663-1127
Hutchinson *(G-3371)*
Mockry & Sons Machine Co Inc............E....... 316 788-7878
Derby *(G-1263)*
Quality Record Pressings.......................E....... 785 820-2931
Salina *(G-10645)*
S D M Die Cutting Equipment...............G....... 913 782-3737
Shawnee *(G-11022)*

3543 Industrial Patterns

Mastercraft Pattern Inc..........................G....... 620 231-3530
Pittsburg *(G-9900)*
Rapid Processing Solutions Inc.............F....... 316 265-2001
Wichita *(G-15417)*

3544 Dies, Tools, Jigs, Fixtures & Indl Molds

Aat Aero Inc..F....... 316 832-1412
Wichita *(G-13594)*
Bennett Tool & Die LLC..........................D....... 913 371-4641
Kansas City *(G-3855)*
◆ **Brittain Machine Inc**..........................E....... 316 942-8223
Wichita *(G-13892)*
Ceco Inc...E....... 316 942-7431
Wichita *(G-13969)*
Certified Water & Mold Restrtn..............G....... 816 835-4959
Olathe *(G-7588)*
▼ **Creative Paradise Inc**.........................F....... 316 794-8621
Goddard *(G-2434)*
De Hoff Tool & Mfg Co Inc.....................F....... 913 342-2212
Kansas City *(G-3963)*
Dme Electronics......................................G....... 316 529-2441
Haysville *(G-2940)*
Excel Tool and Mfg Inc...........................E....... 913 894-6415
Lenexa *(G-5841)*
Four Star Tool and Die Inc.....................G....... 316 264-2913
Wichita *(G-14411)*
Friesen Tool Co Inc.................................G....... 316 262-6808
Wichita *(G-14425)*
▲ **Galaxy Technologies Inc**....................C....... 620 221-6262
Winfield *(G-16143)*
H M Dunn Company Inc..........................C....... 314 535-6684
Wichita *(G-14533)*
Hayes Tooling & Plastics Inc.................F....... 913 782-0046
Olathe *(G-7757)*
Hoelker Tooling.......................................G....... 316 744-7777
Wichita *(G-14621)*
Kansas American Tooling Inc................F....... 620 241-4200
McPherson *(G-6980)*
◆ **Kocher + Beck USA LP**......................D....... 913 529-4336
Lenexa *(G-5955)*
Kocher + Beck USA LP............................E....... 913 529-4336
Lenexa *(G-5956)*
Larue Machine Inc..................................F....... 620 431-3303
Chanute *(G-738)*
Leading Edge Aerospace LLC................E....... 316 942-1301
Wichita *(G-14939)*
Mastercraft Pattern Inc...........................G....... 620 231-3530
Pittsburg *(G-9900)*
Metal Arts Engravers Inc........................F....... 913 262-1979
Shawnee *(G-10994)*
Mid America Products Inc......................C....... 913 856-6550
Gardner *(G-2355)*
Neosho Small Parts LLC.........................F....... 620 244-3263
Erie *(G-1862)*
Raptor Manufacturing Lc........................E....... 316 201-1772
Wichita *(G-15418)*
Sektam of Independence Inc..................F....... 620 331-5480
Independence *(G-3558)*
Three Way Pattern Inc............................F....... 316 942-7421
Wichita *(G-15763)*
Vector Technologies Inc.........................E....... 620 262-2700
Winfield *(G-16178)*
Wilde Tool Co Inc...................................E....... 785 742-7171
Hiawatha *(G-3028)*

3545 Machine Tool Access

▲ **Abbott Aluminum Inc**..........................E....... 785 776-8555
Manhattan *(G-6529)*
Ach Foam Technologies Inc...................D....... 913 321-4114
Kansas City *(G-3782)*
Alltite Inc..E....... 316 686-3010
Wichita *(G-13678)*
D B Investments Inc................................G....... 913 928-1000
Olathe *(G-7635)*
Madill Carbide Inc...................................F....... 316 263-9285
Wichita *(G-14999)*
Midwest Precision Inc............................F....... 913 307-0211
Lenexa *(G-6003)*
MSI Automation Inc................................F....... 316 681-3566
Bel Aire *(G-436)*
Nibarger Tool Service Inc......................G....... 316 262-6152
Wichita *(G-15175)*
Sharpening Specialists LLC....................E....... 316 945-0593
Wichita *(G-15575)*
Superior Tool Service Inc.......................E....... 316 945-8488
Wichita *(G-15700)*
▲ **Takako America Co Inc**.......................C....... 620 663-1790
Hutchinson *(G-3462)*
Universal Construction Pdts...................E....... 316 946-5885
Wichita *(G-15853)*
▲ **Vektek LLC**..C....... 620 342-7637
Emporia *(G-1845)*

3546 Power Hand Tools

Alltite Inc..E....... 316 686-3010
Wichita *(G-13678)*
Bazin Sawing & Drilling Llc....................F....... 913 764-0843
Louisburg *(G-6440)*
◆ **Broderson Manufacturing Corp**.........D....... 913 888-0606
Lenexa *(G-5718)*
▲ **Diteq Corporation**................................E....... 816 246-5515
Lenexa *(G-5821)*
Husqvarna Chain Saws & Pwr Eqp.......G....... 785 263-7668
Abilene *(G-41)*
Kanequip Inc...F....... 785 632-3441
Clay Center *(G-869)*

Kaw Valley Industrial Inc ....G....... 785 841-9751
Eudora (G-1876)
Masterpiece Engineering LLC ....E....... 928 771-2040
Olathe (G-7877)
Mid Kansas Tool & Electric Inc..............F....... 785 825-9521
Salina (G-10600)

3547 Rolling Mill Machinery & Eqpt

◆ Bradbury Co Inc ....B....... 620 345-6394
Moundridge (G-7178)
Marion Manufacturing Inc ....E....... 620 382-3751
Marion (G-6874)
Utah Machine & Mill Supply...................G....... 801 364-2812
Park City (G-9653)

3548 Welding Apparatus

Hi-Tech Weld Overlay Group LLC ....E....... 816 524-9010
Lenexa (G-5903)
Pac Mig Inc...G....... 316 269-3040
Mulvane (G-7226)
Pmti Inc...E....... 913 432-7500
Shawnee Mission (G-11740)
Polaris Electronics Corp ....E....... 913 764-5210
Olathe (G-7990)

3549 Metalworking Machinery, NEC

A & B Machine Inc...................................F....... 785 827-5171
Salina (G-10387)
◆ Bradbury Co Inc ....B....... 620 345-6394
Moundridge (G-7178)
Concept Machinery Inc.........................G....... 317 845-5588
Overland Park (G-8594)
▲ Converting Technologies Inc...........F....... 316 722-6907
Goddard (G-2433)
Encobotics Inc ....G....... 316 788-5656
Derby (G-1245)

3552 Textile Machinery

Cliff Hix Engineering Inc ....E....... 620 232-3000
Pittsburg (G-9836)
Federal Prison Industries.......................D....... 913 682-8700
Leavenworth (G-5238)
◆ Hix Corporation ....D....... 620 231-8568
Pittsburg (G-9876)
Signature Sportswear Inc......................D....... 620 421-1871
Wichita (G-15591)

3553 Woodworking Machinery

▲ Kc Cabinetwright Inc ....E....... 913 825-6555
Lenexa (G-5939)

3554 Paper Inds Machinery

Buyrollscom Inc.......................................F....... 913 851-7100
Overland Park (G-8500)
Specialty Technology Inc.......................F....... 620 241-6307
McPherson (G-7027)
W + D Machinery Co Inc........................E....... 913 492-9880
Overland Park (G-9473)
Wichita Bindery Inc.................................E....... 316 262-3473
Wichita (G-15981)

3555 Printing Trades Machinery & Eqpt

▲ Baldwin Americas Corporation.........G....... 913 310-3258
Lenexa (G-5683)
◆ Brackett Inc ....G....... 785 862-2205
Topeka (G-12402)
◆ Hix Corporation ....D....... 620 231-8568
Pittsburg (G-9876)
Inland Newspaper Mchy Corp................E....... 913 492-9050
Shawnee Mission (G-11457)
Nazdar Company.....................................F....... 913 422-1888
Shawnee (G-11004)
▲ R P M Smith Corporation...................F....... 913 888-0695
Lenexa (G-6087)
Star Innovations II LLC ....E....... 913 764-7738
New Century (G-7298)
▲ Styers Equipment Company ....F....... 913 681-5225
Overland Park (G-9369)

3556 Food Prdts Machinery

ADM Milling Co..D....... 785 825-1541
Salina (G-10395)
AG Growth International Inc ....C....... 785 632-2161
Clay Center (G-842)
Altura Incorporated.................................G....... 913 492-3701
Lenexa (G-5643)
Archer-Daniels-Midland Company ....D....... 785 825-1541
Salina (G-10407)
▲ Baader Linco Inc ....E....... 913 621-3366
Kansas City (G-3836)
▲ Baader North America Corp.............F....... 913 621-3366
Kansas City (G-3837)
Chad Equipment LLC ....F....... 913 764-0321
Olathe (G-7589)
▼ Engineered Systems & Eqp Inc........D....... 620 879-5841
Caney (G-667)
▲ Extru-Tech Inc ....D....... 785 284-2153
Sabetha (G-10309)
◆ Great Western Mfg Co Inc.................D....... 913 682-2291
Leavenworth (G-5247)
▲ Johnson Food Equipment Inc ....E....... 913 621-3366
Kansas City (G-4127)
Kemlee Manufacturing Inc ....D....... 620 783-5035
Galena (G-2076)
◆ Kice Industries Inc ....C....... 316 744-7148
Park City (G-9625)
Midwest B R D Inc..................................F....... 785 256-6240
Topeka (G-12894)
▲ New Age Industrial Corp Inc ....C....... 785 877-5121
Norton (G-7455)
Norvell Company Inc ....E....... 620 223-3110
Fort Scott (G-1995)
Norvell Company Inc ....E....... 785 825-6663
Salina (G-10615)
Numerical Control Support Inc.............E....... 913 441-3500
Shawnee Mission (G-11690)
Stainless Systems Inc ....E....... 620 663-4346
South Hutchinson (G-12066)
Sterling Manufacturing Co Inc..............G....... 620 783-5234
Galena (G-2087)
◆ Wenger Manufacturing Inc ....C....... 785 284-2133
Sabetha (G-10337)
Williams-Carver Company Inc ....E....... 913 236-4949
Kansas City (G-4544)

3559 Special Ind Machinery, NEC

Aarons Repair & Supply Inc..................G....... 620 792-5361
Great Bend (G-2499)
◆ American Maplan Corporation ....D....... 620 241-6843
McPherson (G-6934)
▲ Converting Technologies Inc...........F....... 316 722-6907
Goddard (G-2433)
Dynamold Corporation...........................F....... 785 667-4626
Assaria (G-201)
Enco of Kansas Inc................................D....... 316 788-4143
Derby (G-1244)
▲ Femco Inc ....D....... 620 241-3513
McPherson (G-6964)
▼ Glendo LLC...E....... 620 343-1084
Emporia (G-1763)
Industrial Ventures Inc ....D....... 316 634-6699
Rose Hill (G-10240)
Kratzer Industries ....G....... 620 824-6405
Geneseo (G-2393)
▲ L S Industries Inc ....E....... 316 265-7997
Wichita (G-14907)
▲ Machine Works Inc ....E....... 316 265-7997
Wichita (G-14997)
▲ McLiney Lumber and Supply LLC ...F....... 913 766-7102
Prairie Village (G-10046)
Miniature Plastic Molding LLC...............G....... 316 264-2827
Wichita (G-15112)
◆ Oasis Car Wash Systems Inc ....E....... 620 783-1355
Galena (G-2077)
▲ Optimized Process Furnaces Inc .....F....... 620 431-1260
Chanute (G-750)
Scientific Engineering Inc ....F....... 785 827-7071
Salina (G-10698)
Scriptpro LLC ....D....... 913 403-5260
Kansas City (G-4409)
▲ Scriptpro LLC ....D....... 913 384-1008
Shawnee Mission (G-11839)
SPX Cooling Technologies Inc ....C....... 913 782-1600
Olathe (G-8079)
Standard Motor Products Inc................B....... 620 331-1000
Independence (G-3562)
Stinger By Axe ....F....... 620 767-7555
Council Grove (G-1177)
Superior Mobile Wash Inc ....F....... 913 915-9642
Kansas City (G-4448)
Trail Worthy Inc......................................G....... 316 337-5311
Halstead (G-2705)
▼ Viking Corporation..............................E....... 316 634-6699
Rose Hill (G-10250)

3561 Pumps & Pumping Eqpt

Allegion S&S US Holding Co ....E....... 913 393-8629
Olathe (G-7518)
Cook Pump Company.............................E....... 620 251-0880
Coffeyville (G-930)
Eaton Corporation ....B....... 620 663-5751
Hutchinson (G-3274)
◆ Fairbanks Morse Pump Corp ....B....... 630 859-7000
Kansas City (G-4003)
Fairbanks Morse Pump Corp ....F....... 913 371-5000
Kansas City (G-4004)
Grundfos CBS Inc....................................G....... 281 994-2830
Overland Park (G-8781)
▲ Hallowell Manufacturing LLC............F....... 620 597-2552
Columbus (G-1077)
Jacks Genuine Mfg Inc ....F....... 620 948-3000
Coffeyville (G-950)
Max Papay LLC ....F....... 620 873-5350
Meade (G-7050)
Schlumberger Technology Corp ....C....... 785 841-5610
Lawrence (G-5103)
▲ Seals Inc ....G....... 913 438-1212
Shawnee Mission (G-11844)
Squires Corporation ....F....... 316 944-0040
Wichita (G-15650)
Star Pipe Usa LLC..................................C....... 281 558-3000
Coffeyville (G-979)
Stenner Sales Company.........................G....... 913 768-4114
New Century (G-7300)
Well Watch LLC......................................G....... 785 798-0020
Ness City (G-7268)

3562 Ball & Roller Bearings

Manko Corporation.................................F....... 785 825-1301
Salina (G-10591)

3563 Air & Gas Compressors

▲ Exline Inc..C....... 785 825-4683
Salina (G-10489)
Westheffer Company Inc.......................E....... 785 843-1633
Lawrence (G-5183)

3564 Blowers & Fans

Aerospace Systems Cmpnents Inc.......D....... 316 686-7392
Wichita (G-13638)
Air Filter Plus Inc ....E....... 785 542-3700
Eudora (G-1869)
▲ Airtex Manufacturing Lllp..................C....... 913 583-3181
De Soto (G-1192)
▲ Bha Altair LLC ....C....... 816 356-8400
Overland Park (G-8445)
Clarcor Air Filtration Pdts ....E....... 785 242-1811
Ottawa (G-8256)
Commercial Fltr Svc Knsas Cty.............G....... 913 384-5858
Kansas City (G-3929)
Eplus Envrmental Solutions LLC..........E....... 913 814-9860
Shawnee Mission (G-11345)
Heartland Technologies Inc ....G....... 316 932-8001
Wichita (G-14588)
◆ Kice Industries Inc ....C....... 316 744-7148
Park City (G-9625)
Mac Equipment Inc.................................F....... 785 284-2191
Sabetha (G-10317)
◆ Metal-Fab Inc ....C....... 316 943-2351
Wichita (G-15055)
Metal-Fab Inc..G....... 316 946-5875
Wichita (G-15057)
◆ Purifan Inc..G....... 316 932-8001
Wichita (G-15377)
Ruskin Company.....................................E....... 620 421-6090
Parsons (G-9733)
Schenck Process LLC ....C....... 785 284-2191
Sabetha (G-10331)
Tech-Air Inc..G....... 913 677-5777
Shawnee Mission (G-11923)
Tech-Air Inc ....F....... 913 677-5777
Osawatomie (G-8204)
▲ Transweb Llc......................................E....... 856 205-1313
Leawood (G-5583)
Tri-Dim Filter Corporation ....G....... 316 425-0462
Wichita (G-15799)
◆ Vornado Air LLC ....D....... 316 733-0035
Andover (G-115)

3565 Packaging Machinery

H&H Design & Manufacturing LLC........F....... 620 421-9800
Parsons (G-9691)
◆ Huhtamaki Inc....................................B....... 913 583-3025
De Soto (G-1202)
Liberty Labels LLC.................................G....... 620 223-2208
Fort Scott (G-1981)

▲ Magnum Systems Inc ....E 620 421-5550
Parsons (G-9707)
▲ Performance Packg Group LLC........E 913 438-2012
Shawnee Mission (G-11727)
Taylor Products Co Inc........E 620 421-5550
Parsons (G-9746)
▲ Tdi Global Solutions Inc........F 877 834-6750
Meriden (G-7082)

3566 Speed Changers, Drives & Gears

Curtis Machine Company Inc........D 620 227-7164
Dodge City (G-1338)

3567 Indl Process Furnaces & Ovens

G S Inc of Kansas ....G....... 620 443-5121
Americus (G-76)
▲ Heatron Inc ....C 913 651-4420
Leavenworth (G-5252)
◆ Hix Corporation ....D 620 231-8568
Pittsburg (G-9876)
MSI Automation Inc ....F 316 681-3566
Bel Aire (G-436)
▲ Optimized Process Furnaces Inc .....F 620 431-1260
Chanute (G-750)
Trimac Industrial Systems LLC ....E 913 441-0043
Bonner Springs (G-578)

3568 Mechanical Power Transmission Eqpt, NEC

Carlson Company Inc........E 316 744-0481
Park City (G-9608)
Curtis Machine Company Inc........D 620 227-7164
Dodge City (G-1338)
▲ Eskridge Inc........D 913 782-1238
Olathe (G-7693)
Ics Inc........E 620 654-3020
McPherson (G-6977)

3569 Indl Machinery & Eqpt, NEC

Abrasive Blast Systems Inc........E 785 263-3786
Abilene (G-10)
Clarcor Air Filtration Pdts ....E 785 242-1811
Ottawa (G-8256)
Earth Designs Inc........G....... 913 791-2858
Shawnee Mission (G-11325)
General Automatic Sprinkler Fl ....E 913 390-1105
Overland Park (G-8750)
P B Hoidale Co Inc........F 913 438-1500
Shawnee (G-11008)
▲ Robotzone LLC ....G....... 620 221-7071
Winfield (G-16170)
Ruskin Company........E 620 421-6090
Parsons (G-9733)
Wamego Recycling LLC ....E 785 456-2439
Wamego (G-13455)
▼ Weis Fire Safety Equip Co Inc ....F 785 825-9527
Salina (G-10765)
Zeroburn LLC ....G....... 877 207-7100
Overland Park (G-9526)

3571 Electronic Computers

Aegis Business Solutions LLC........G....... 913 307-9922
Olathe (G-7512)
Apple Central LLC Applebe ....G....... 203 987-6162
Wichita (G-13721)
▼ Cybertron International Inc........D 316 303-1022
Wichita (G-14150)
Data Max of Kansas City ....E 913 752-2200
Lenexa (G-5803)
Elecsys International Corp........C 913 647-0158
Olathe (G-7673)
High Quality Tech Inc ....G....... 316 448-3559
Wichita (G-14604)
Net-Ability LLC ....F 316 691-4527
Wichita (G-15160)
◆ Stallard Technologies Inc ....E 913 851-2260
Overland Park (G-9351)

3572 Computer Storage Devices

Data Locker Inc ....G....... 913 310-9088
Overland Park (G-8636)
EMC Corporation........D 913 530-0433
Overland Park (G-8677)
Sur-Tec Inc........G....... 913 647-7720
Shawnee (G-11036)

3575 Computer Terminals

Apollon Computers Inc ....E 316 264-2329
Wichita (G-13719)
Computerwise Inc........F 408 389-8241
Olathe (G-7609)
Elec-Tron Inc ....D 316 522-3401
Wichita (G-14263)
Hydeman Company Inc ....G....... 913 384-2620
Kansas City (G-4090)
Igt Global Solutions Corp........E 785 861-7300
Topeka (G-12713)

3577 Computer Peripheral Eqpt, NEC

American Marking Systems Inc........G....... 913 492-6028
Lenexa (G-5650)
Cisco Systems Inc........D 913 344-6100
Shawnee Mission (G-11227)
Computerwise Inc........F 408 389-8241
Olathe (G-7609)
Convergeone Inc........C 913 307-2300
Overland Park (G-8597)
General Dynamics Info Tech Inc........E 785 832-0207
Lawrence (G-4871)
K G Moats & Sons LLC........E 785 437-2021
Saint Marys (G-10368)
◆ Knox Electronic Ltd ....F 316 321-2400
El Dorado (G-1579)
Leavenworth Technical Services........G....... 913 351-3344
Leavenworth (G-5266)

3578 Calculating & Accounting Eqpt

1-Stop LLC........G....... 913 898-6211
Parker (G-9656)
Cummins - Allison Corp ....G....... 913 894-2266
Lenexa (G-5797)

3579 Office Machines, NEC

Cummins - Allison Corp ....G....... 913 894-2266
Lenexa (G-5797)
Grabar Voice and Data Inc ....G....... 701 258-3528
Wichita (G-14488)
Pitney Bowes Inc ....D 913 681-5579
Shawnee Mission (G-11736)
Pitney Bowes Inc ....G....... 785 266-6750
Topeka (G-12978)

3581 Automatic Vending Machines

Online Vend Mch Sls & Svc Inc ....G....... 913 492-1097
Lenexa (G-6037)

3582 Commercial Laundry, Dry Clean & Pressing Mchs

Husqvarna US Holding Inc........F 913 928-1000
Olathe (G-7780)

3585 Air Conditioning & Heating Eqpt

ABB Installation Products Inc ....D 913 755-3181
Osawatomie (G-8191)
Airtex Inc........D 913 583-3181
De Soto (G-1191)
▲ Airtex Manufacturing Lllp........C 913 583-3181
De Soto (G-1192)
▲ Airxcel Inc ....B 316 832-3400
Wichita (G-13656)
Classic Heating and Coolg LLC........F 913 238-1036
Edgerton (G-1482)
Dunco Inc........F 785 594-7137
Lawrence (G-4842)
Evcon Holdings Inc........E 316 832-6300
Wichita (G-14311)
Everidge LLC ....C 316 733-1385
Andover (G-91)
Hussmann Corporation ....E 816 373-1274
Lenexa (G-5907)
Recreational Vehicle Products ....C 316 832-3400
Wichita (G-15429)
▲ Rv Products........E 316 832-3400
Wichita (G-15494)
◆ SPX Cooling Technologies Inc........B 913 664-7400
Overland Park (G-9344)
Trane US Inc ....D 785 272-3224
Topeka (G-13196)
Trane US Inc ....D 316 265-9655
Wichita (G-15788)
Trane US Inc ....C 417 863-2110
Lenexa (G-6189)
York International Corporation ....D 316 832-6400
Wichita (G-16086)
York International Corporation ....D 316 832-6300
Wichita (G-16087)

3586 Measuring & Dispensing Pumps

◆ Great Plains Industries Inc........B 316 686-7361
Wichita (G-14503)
◆ Power Flame Incorporated ....C 620 421-0480
Parsons (G-9724)
▲ Scriptpro LLC ....D 913 384-1008
Shawnee Mission (G-11839)

3589 Service Ind Machines, NEC

▲ Aero-Mod Incorporated ....E 785 537-4995
Manhattan (G-6535)
Ameripure Water Company........F 913 825-6600
Kansas City (G-3806)
◆ Bio-Microbics Inc ....E 913 422-0707
Lenexa (G-5704)
City Wide Window Washing Inc........F 913 888-5700
Lenexa (G-5759)
Dewald Enterprises........G....... 316 655-1155
Andover (G-90)
Evoqua Water Technologies LLC ....E 913 422-7600
Overland Park (G-8697)
Fresh Kc Water Inc ....G....... 913 745-0002
Shawnee (G-10958)
◆ Fuller Industries LLC ....C 620 792-1711
Great Bend (G-2568)
▲ General Tech A Svcs & Pdts Co........G....... 913 766-5566
Olathe (G-7727)
Green Product Solutions LLC........G....... 913 633-1274
Overland Park (G-8778)
Hertel Tank Service Inc........G....... 785 628-2445
Hays (G-2841)
Hi-Tech Weld Overlay Group LLC ....E 816 524-9010
Lenexa (G-5903)
▲ Jesse Inc........F 913 342-4282
Kansas City (G-4123)
Pentair Flow Technologies LLC........C 913 371-5000
Kansas City (G-4319)
◆ Peterson Mch Tl Acqisition Inc ....F 316 634-6699
Rose Hill (G-10245)
Power Vac Inc........E 785 826-8220
Salina (G-10639)
Siemens Industry Inc........E 913 683-9787
Lansing (G-4692)
Siemens Industry Inc........E 785 762-7814
Junction City (G-3754)
◆ Smith and Loveless Inc ....C 913 888-5201
Shawnee Mission (G-11875)
United Industries Inc ....F 620 278-3160
Sterling (G-12131)
Watersource Technologies Inc........G....... 316 927-2100
Haysville (G-2963)
▼ Windtrax Inc ....E 913 789-9100
Shawnee Mission (G-12013)

3592 Carburetors, Pistons, Rings & Valves

Cross Manufacturing Inc........D 785 625-2585
Hays (G-2780)
▲ Winona Van Norman Inc........F 316 219-3500
Wichita (G-16057)

3593 Fluid Power Cylinders & Actuators

Cargotec Holding Inc........B 785 242-2200
Ottawa (G-8251)
▲ Cross Manufacturing Inc........G....... 913 451-1233
Overland Park (G-8616)
Cross Manufacturing Inc........D 785 625-2585
Hays (G-2780)
Eaton Corporation ....B 620 663-5751
Hutchinson (G-3274)
Hampton Hydraulics Llc........D 620 792-4368
Great Bend (G-2590)
Squires Corporation ....F 316 944-0040
Wichita (G-15650)
▲ Vektek LLC........C 620 342-7637
Emporia (G-1845)

3594 Fluid Power Pumps & Motors

▲ Apph Wichita Inc........E 316 943-5752
Wichita (G-13720)
◆ Broderson Manufacturing Corp ....D 913 888-0606
Lenexa (G-5718)
Cross Manufacturing Inc........D 785 625-2585
Hays (G-2780)
▲ Harper Industries Inc........D 620 896-7381
Harper (G-2723)

3596 Scales & Balances, Exc Laboratory

▲ **Express Scale Parts Inc** .... E 913 441-4787
Lenexa *(G-5844)*

Hydeman Company Inc .... G 913 384-2620
Kansas City *(G-4090)*

Northeast Kansas Hydraulics .... G 785 235-0405
Topeka *(G-12936)*

◆ **Schroer Manufacturing Company** ..... C 913 281-1500
Kansas City *(G-4404)*

3599 Machinery & Eqpt, Indl & Commercial, NEC

2r Tool & Machine Inc .... G 620 902-5151
Chanute *(G-700)*

A & B Machine Inc .... F 785 827-5171
Salina *(G-10387)*

Aarons Repair & Supply Inc .... G 620 792-5361
Great Bend *(G-2499)*

▲ **Abbott Aluminum Inc** .... E 785 776-8555
Manhattan *(G-6529)*

Absolute Dimensions LLC .... E 316 944-2211
Wichita *(G-13599)*

Accurus Aerospace Wichita LLC .... E 316 683-0266
Wichita *(G-13604)*

Acme Foundry Inc .... E 620 251-4920
Coffeyville *(G-908)*

Adf LLC .... E 913 825-7400
Lenexa *(G-5630)*

Advanced Machine Inc .... G 316 942-9002
Wichita *(G-13623)*

Aeromotive Inc .... F 913 647-7300
Shawnee Mission *(G-11082)*

Albertson & Hein Inc .... E 316 943-7441
Wichita *(G-13659)*

◆ **Alexander Manufacturing Co Inc** .... F 620 421-5010
Parsons *(G-9664)*

Anderson Machine & Supply Inc .... G 785 668-2233
Smolan *(G-12045)*

Arrow Fork Lift Parts Inc .... G 816 231-4410
Lenexa *(G-5663)*

Automotive Supply Inc .... E 316 942-8285
Wichita *(G-13775)*

Bailey Machine Inc .... F 620 848-3116
Riverton *(G-10210)*

Big Creek Investment Corp Inc .... G 620 431-3445
Chanute *(G-707)*

Bradbury Co Inc .... E 620 382-3775
Marion *(G-6866)*

Bradley Machine Inc .... F 316 262-3221
Wichita *(G-13882)*

Brij Systems LLC .... G 316 262-6969
Wichita *(G-13890)*

◆ **Brittain Machine Inc** .... E 316 942-8223
Wichita *(G-13892)*

Brytam Manufacturing Inc .... G 316 788-3300
Derby *(G-1227)*

▲ **BSB Maunfacturing Inc** .... G 620 326-3152
Wellington *(G-13493)*

C & R Mfg Inc .... F 913 441-4120
Shawnee Mission *(G-11195)*

C E Machine Co Inc .... D 316 942-0411
Wichita *(G-13925)*

Central States Machining Wldg .... G 785 233-1376
Topeka *(G-12457)*

Central Welding & Machine LLC .... F 620 663-9353
Hutchinson *(G-3235)*

▲ **Chance Rides Manufacturing Inc** .... C 316 945-6555
Wichita *(G-13997)*

Coffeyville Sektam Inc .... D 620 251-3880
Coffeyville *(G-922)*

Continental Components LLC .... G 816 547-8325
Lenexa *(G-5784)*

Cox Machine Inc .... D 316 943-1342
Wichita *(G-14121)*

Cox Machine Inc .... D 316 943-1342
Harper *(G-2718)*

▲ **Creason Corrugating McHy Inc** .... F 423 629-5532
Park City *(G-9613)*

D & H Machine and Tool Inc .... G 316 267-3906
Wichita *(G-14155)*

D & S Machine and Welding Inc .... G 785 798-3359
Ness City *(G-7259)*

D&D Machine Inc .... F 316 269-1553
Wichita *(G-14162)*

De Hoff Tool & Mfg Co Inc .... F 913 342-2212
Kansas City *(G-3963)*

Dicks Engine & Machine Service .... F 620 564-2238
Ellinwood *(G-1629)*

Disco Machine Liberal Company .... E 620 624-0179
Liberal *(G-6305)*

Dpp Manufacturing LLC .... G 620 340-7200
Emporia *(G-1732)*

E & R Machine Inc .... G 785 456-2373
Wamego *(G-13417)*

EC Manufacturing LLC .... C 913 825-3077
Paola *(G-9555)*

Engineered Machine Tool Co .... F 316 942-6147
Wichita *(G-14289)*

Ernstmann Machine Co Inc .... G 316 943-5282
Wichita *(G-14303)*

▲ **Exacta Aerospace Inc** .... C 316 941-4200
Wichita *(G-14318)*

▲ **Exline Inc** .... C 785 825-4683
Salina *(G-10489)*

Farrar Corporation .... B 785 537-7733
Norwich *(G-7466)*

Farrar Corporation .... E 620 478-2212
Norwich *(G-7467)*

Farrar Corporation .... C 620 478-2212
Norwich *(G-7469)*

Fmw Inc .... F 316 943-4217
Wichita *(G-14398)*

Freddie Wayne Long .... F 316 263-8941
Wichita *(G-14415)*

Gaskell Machine & Metal Inc .... F 785 486-2674
Horton *(G-3123)*

Gear Headquarters Inc .... F 913 831-1700
Kansas City *(G-4028)*

General Repair & Supply Inc .... G 620 365-5954
Iola *(G-3604)*

Goddard Machine LLC .... F 316 838-1381
Wichita *(G-14478)*

Goodland Machine & Auto LLC .... G 785 899-6628
Goodland *(G-2474)*

Goodwin Industries Inc .... G 620 726-5281
Burns *(G-646)*

▲ **H M Dunn Company Inc** .... C 316 522-5426
Wichita *(G-14532)*

H M Dunn Company Inc .... C 314 535-6684
Wichita *(G-14533)*

H M Dunn Company Inc .... E 316 522-5426
Wichita *(G-14534)*

Harrison Machine Shop & Wldg .... G 913 764-0730
Olathe *(G-7756)*

Harrys Machine Works Inc .... G 620 227-2201
Dodge City *(G-1370)*

Hefner Machine Inc .... G 620 225-4999
Dodge City *(G-1371)*

Herrs Machine .... G 785 325-2875
Washington *(G-13464)*

Hoffs Machine & Welding Inc .... F 785 823-6215
Salina *(G-10542)*

Holst Machine Shop .... F 316 794-8477
Goddard *(G-2442)*

Independent Electric McHy Co .... E 913 362-1155
Kansas City *(G-4097)*

Industrial Mfg & Repr Svc .... G 620 275-0481
Garden City *(G-2202)*

Industrial Process Eqp Co .... G 316 722-7800
Wichita *(G-14686)*

Integrated Components Inc .... F 316 942-6600
Wichita *(G-14700)*

K B Machine Shop Inc .... F 913 829-3100
Olathe *(G-7822)*

Kan Fab Inc .... G 620 342-5669
Emporia *(G-1783)*

Kansas Gun Drilling Inc .... F 316 943-4241
Wichita *(G-14803)*

Kansas Manufacturing Company .... G 785 843-2892
Lawrence *(G-4935)*

Kiser Manufacturing Co Inc .... F 620 435-6981
Argonia *(G-138)*

Kriers Auto Parts Inc .... G 785 738-3526
Beloit *(G-489)*

L & M Steel & Mfg .... G 785 462-8216
Colby *(G-1023)*

L & T Machining Inc .... E 316 946-9744
Wichita *(G-14903)*

Landwehr Machine .... G 316 794-3390
Goddard *(G-2445)*

Larue Machine Inc .... F 620 431-3303
Chanute *(G-738)*

Lathrom Manufacturing Inc .... F 316 522-0001
Wichita *(G-14931)*

Lee Construction Inc .... E 620 276-6811
Garden City *(G-2222)*

Lightning Aerospace LLC .... G 316 295-4670
Park City *(G-9628)*

M & W Mfg Inc .... F 620 365-7456
Iola *(G-3619)*

M-C Fabrication Inc .... D 913 764-5454
Olathe *(G-7869)*

Mac-Tech Inc .... F 620 326-5952
Wellington *(G-13514)*

Machine Design Services Inc .... G 620 663-4949
South Hutchinson *(G-12060)*

Machining Programming Mfg Inc .... E 316 945-1227
Wichita *(G-14998)*

Manufacturing Solutions Inc .... E 316 282-0556
Newton *(G-7375)*

Marion Manufacturing Inc .... E 620 382-3751
Marion *(G-6874)*

Maxima Precision Inc .... E 316 832-2211
Wichita *(G-15020)*

Metal Arts Machine Co LLC .... E 316 425-2579
Wichita *(G-15049)*

Metalform Industries Inc .... F 316 945-6700
Wichita *(G-15058)*

Microtool Inc .... F 913 492-1588
Shawnee Mission *(G-11625)*

Mid Kansas Machine Inc .... E 620 241-2959
McPherson *(G-7003)*

Mid-America Pump LLC .... F 913 287-3900
Kansas City *(G-4244)*

Mid-Continent Industries Inc .... F 316 283-9648
Newton *(G-7384)*

Mid-Kansas Machine & Tool .... G 316 777-1189
Mulvane *(G-7222)*

Midwest B R D Inc .... F 785 256-6240
Topeka *(G-12894)*

Midwest Industries & Dev Ltd .... D 620 241-5996
McPherson *(G-7007)*

Midwest Machining Inc .... F 620 896-5050
Harper *(G-2724)*

▲ **Millennium Machine & Tool Inc** .... E 316 282-0884
Newton *(G-7387)*

Miltech Machine Corporation .... E 785 877-5381
Norton *(G-7450)*

Mires Machine Co Inc .... F 316 942-6547
Wichita *(G-15116)*

Mockry & Sons Machine Co Inc .... E 316 788-7878
Derby *(G-1263)*

Myriad Machine Co .... F 620 624-2962
Liberal *(G-6346)*

Nance Manufacturing Inc .... E 620 842-3761
Anthony *(G-130)*

Nance Manufacturing Inc .... E 316 942-8671
Wichita *(G-15146)*

Natoma Corporation .... D 785 877-3529
Norton *(G-7451)*

Natoma Leasing LLC .... D 785 877-3529
Norton *(G-7452)*

Natoma Manufacturing Corp .... D 785 877-3529
Norton *(G-7453)*

Natoma Realty LLC .... D 785 877-3529
Norton *(G-7454)*

Neosho Small Parts LLC .... F 620 244-3263
Erie *(G-1862)*

▲ **NSA Rv Products Inc** .... G 620 365-7714
Iola *(G-3620)*

Numerical Control Support Inc .... E 913 441-3500
Shawnee Mission *(G-11690)*

Paynes Inc .... F 620 231-3170
Frontenac *(G-2063)*

Perfekta Inc .... G 316 263-2056
Wichita *(G-15283)*

Precision Products .... G 316 943-0477
Wichita *(G-15325)*

Professional Machine & Tool .... F 316 755-1271
Valley Center *(G-13350)*

Pumphrey Machine Co Inc .... G 316 832-1841
Wichita *(G-15376)*

▲ **Quality Power Products Inc** .... G 785 263-0060
Solomon *(G-12052)*

Quality Tech Metals .... E 316 945-4781
Wichita *(G-15386)*

Quik Tek Machining LLC .... F 316 260-9980
Wichita *(G-15395)*

R D K Machine LLC .... F 316 267-6678
Wichita *(G-15403)*

R-Tech Tool & Machine Inc .... F 785 456-9541
Wamego *(G-13438)*

Rice Precision Mfg Inc .... E 785 594-2670
Baldwin City *(G-367)*

Riverside Industries LLC .... G 316 788-4428
Derby *(G-1269)*

Safarik Tool Co Inc .... E 316 755-4800
Valley Center *(G-13352)*

Schlotterbeck Machine Shop .... G 620 678-3210
Hamilton *(G-2708)*

Scientific Engineering Inc ....F 785 827-7071
Salina *(G-10698)*
Sektam of Independence Inc ....F 620 331-5480
Independence *(G-3558)*
Senihcam Inc ....G 316 524-4561
Wichita *(G-15557)*
Shackelford Machine Inc ....E 620 584-2436
Clearwater *(G-896)*
Shuttle Aerospace Inc ....G 316 832-0210
Maize *(G-6519)*
▲ **Sids Corrugating & Machinery** ....G 316 744-0061
Park City *(G-9644)*
Star Tool Service Inc ....G 316 943-1942
Wichita *(G-15655)*
Stearman Aircraft Pdts Corp ....G 316 755-1271
Valley Center *(G-13354)*
Strecker Machine Inc ....G 620 793-7128
Heizer *(G-2968)*
▲ **Takako America Co Inc** ....C 620 663-1790
Hutchinson *(G-3462)*
Thomas Manufacturing Inc ....F 620 724-6220
Girard *(G-2421)*
Toms Machine & Welding Svc ....G 785 434-2800
Plainville *(G-9994)*
Topeka Metal Specialties ....E 785 862-1071
Topeka *(G-13181)*
Tower Metal Works Inc ....E 785 256-4281
Maple Hill *(G-6865)*
Ultra-Tech Aerospace Inc ....E 913 262-7009
Kansas City *(G-4482)*
Union Machine & Tool Works Inc ....F 913 342-6000
Kansas City *(G-4486)*
United Machine Company Inc ....E 316 264-3367
Wichita *(G-15843)*
Universal Machining Shtmtl Inc ....E 316 425-7610
Wichita *(G-15854)*
Waddles Manufacturing & Mch Co ....G 785 825-6166
Salina *(G-10756)*
Welch Machine Inc ....G 620 896-2764
Harper *(G-2725)*
Western Chemical Pumps Inc ....E 913 829-1888
Olathe *(G-8152)*
Wichita Machine Products Inc ....G 316 522-7401
Wichita *(G-16010)*
Wifco Steel Products Inc ....D 620 543-2827
Hutchinson *(G-3489)*
Williams Company Inc ....F 785 873-3260
Whiting *(G-13575)*
▼ **Williams Machine and Tl Co Inc** ....E 620 783-5184
Galena *(G-2089)*
▲ **Youngers and Sons Mfg Co Inc** ....D 620 545-7133
Viola *(G-13381)*

36 ELECTRONIC AND OTHER ELECTRICAL EQUIPMENT AND COMPONENTS, EXCEPT COMPUTER

3612 Power, Distribution & Specialty Transformers

ABB Enterprise Software Inc ....D 913 317-1310
Overland Park *(G-8337)*
Aerospace Systems Cmpnents Inc ....D 316 686-7392
Wichita *(G-13638)*
Control Components Inc ....G 620 221-2343
Winfield *(G-16127)*
Emerald Transformer Kansas LLC ....E 620 251-6380
Coffeyville *(G-936)*
▲ **Everbrite Electronics Inc** ....D 620 431-7383
Chanute *(G-727)*
Experitec Inc ....F 913 894-4044
Shawnee Mission *(G-11356)*
Harpenau Power & Process Inc ....G 913 451-2227
Lenexa *(G-5891)*
Quickertek Inc ....G 316 691-1585
Wichita *(G-15394)*
◆ **Solomon Transformers LLC** ....B 785 655-2191
Solomon *(G-12054)*
Torotel Products Inc ....C 913 747-6111
Olathe *(G-8116)*

3613 Switchgear & Switchboard Apparatus

Cmt Inc ....C 785 762-4400
Junction City *(G-3683)*
Custom Control Mfr Kans Inc ....E 913 722-0343
Shawnee Mission *(G-11286)*
Elec-Tron Inc ....D 316 522-3401
Wichita *(G-14263)*
G and S Mechanical USA Inc ....F 316 946-9988
Wichita *(G-14433)*
Integrated Controls Inc ....F 913 782-9600
Olathe *(G-7796)*
Junction City Wire Harness LLC ....D 785 762-4400
Junction City *(G-3706)*
K G Moats & Sons LLC ....E 785 437-2021
Saint Marys *(G-10368)*
Kasa Companies Inc ....D 785 825-5612
Salina *(G-10569)*
▼ **Kasa Companies Inc** ....C 785 825-7181
Salina *(G-10570)*
Kasa Companies Inc ....D 785 825-5612
Salina *(G-10571)*
R & T Specialty Cnstr Lc ....G 316 942-8141
Wichita *(G-15401)*
Standard Motor Products Inc ....B 620 331-1000
Independence *(G-3562)*
TEC Engineering Inc ....E 316 259-8881
Wichita *(G-15723)*
Total Electric Inc ....G 316 524-2642
Wichita *(G-15775)*
U S Automation Inc ....G 913 894-2410
Shawnee Mission *(G-11953)*

3621 Motors & Generators

Ametek Advanced Industries Inc ....D 316 522-0424
Wichita *(G-13698)*
Cimarron Wind Energy LLC ....G 561 691-7171
Cimarron *(G-822)*
Clare Generator Service Inc ....F 785 827-3321
Salina *(G-10453)*
Dels Alternator & Starter Svc ....G 785 825-4466
Salina *(G-10473)*
Hci Energy LLC ....F 913 283-8855
Lenexa *(G-5893)*
▲ **Power Tech Electric Motors LLC** ....G 913 888-4488
Overland Park *(G-9173)*
Precision Railway Eqp Co LLC ....F 817 737-5885
Independence *(G-3548)*
Welco Technologies ....G 316 941-0400
Wichita *(G-15943)*
West Wind Energy LLC ....F 785 387-2623
Otis *(G-8242)*

3624 Carbon & Graphite Prdts

Birla Carbon USA Inc ....E 620 356-3151
Ulysses *(G-13283)*
◆ **Hiper Technology Inc** ....F 785 749-6011
Lawrence *(G-4898)*

3625 Relays & Indl Controls

Accurate Electric Inc ....G 785 825-4010
Salina *(G-10391)*
Capstan AG Systems Inc ....G 785 232-4477
Topeka *(G-12442)*
▲ **Castle Creations Inc** ....D 913 390-6939
Olathe *(G-7580)*
Control Systems Intl Inc ....D 913 599-5010
Shawnee Mission *(G-11264)*
Elecsys International Corp ....C 913 647-0158
Olathe *(G-7673)*
Exide Technologies ....G 913 321-4600
Kansas City *(G-4001)*
K G Moats & Sons LLC ....E 785 437-2021
Saint Marys *(G-10368)*
▼ **Kasa Companies Inc** ....C 785 825-7181
Salina *(G-10570)*
Kasa Companies Inc ....D 785 825-5612
Salina *(G-10571)*
▲ **Pivot International Inc** ....E 913 312-6900
Lenexa *(G-6060)*
Powerhouse Electric Inc ....G 913 856-4141
Gardner *(G-2359)*
Registered Graphics Inc ....F 913 681-4907
Stilwell *(G-12172)*
Rockwell Automation Inc ....F 913 577-2500
Lenexa *(G-6111)*
Shell Topco LP ....F 316 942-7266
Wichita *(G-15580)*
▲ **Smiths Intrcnnect Americas Inc** ....C 913 342-5544
Kansas City *(G-4429)*
▼ **Ultra Electronics Ice Inc** ....D 785 776-6423
Manhattan *(G-6835)*
▲ **Wescon Controls LLC** ....C 316 942-7266
Wichita *(G-15950)*

3629 Electrical Indl Apparatus, NEC

◆ **Clore Automotive LLC** ....E 913 310-1050
Lenexa *(G-5766)*
Earth Care Products Inc ....F 620 331-0090
Independence *(G-3514)*
▲ **Espi LLC** ....F 785 777-2707
Clay Center *(G-862)*
Exide Technologies ....G 913 321-4600
Kansas City *(G-4001)*
Exide Technologies ....C 913 321-3561
Kansas City *(G-4000)*
Exide Technologies ....D 785 825-6276
Salina *(G-10488)*
▲ **L S Industries Inc** ....E 316 265-7997
Wichita *(G-14907)*
▲ **Machine Works Inc** ....E 316 265-7997
Wichita *(G-14997)*
USP Technical Services ....F 310 517-1800
Derby *(G-1278)*

3631 Household Cooking Eqpt

Yoder Smokers Inc ....D 620 802-0201
Hutchinson *(G-3495)*

3634 Electric Household Appliances

B/E Aerospace Inc ....C 913 338-7292
Shawnee Mission *(G-11142)*
Big W Industries Inc ....E 913 321-2112
Kansas City *(G-3860)*
City of Topeka ....D 785 368-3851
Topeka *(G-12470)*
▲ **Select Brands Inc** ....E 913 663-4500
Lenexa *(G-6123)*
▼ **Splintek Inc** ....E 816 531-1900
Lenexa *(G-6148)*
◆ **Vornado Air LLC** ....D 316 733-0035
Andover *(G-115)*

3639 Household Appliances, NEC

Howies Enterprises LLC ....F 785 776-8352
Manhattan *(G-6660)*
Swiss Made Inc ....F 913 341-6400
Overland Park *(G-9383)*

3641 Electric Lamps

◆ **Advanced Technologies Inc** ....G 316 744-2285
Bel Aire *(G-427)*
Cmt Inc ....C 785 762-4400
Junction City *(G-3683)*
Junction City Wire Harness LLC ....D 785 762-4400
Junction City *(G-3706)*
Led Direct LLC ....G 913 912-3760
Kansas City *(G-4198)*
Occk Inc ....C 785 827-9383
Salina *(G-10617)*
Pwi Inc ....E 316 942-2811
Wichita *(G-15380)*
Signify North America Corp ....D 785 826-5218
Salina *(G-10708)*

3643 Current-Carrying Wiring Devices

Amsted Rail Company Inc ....F 800 621-8442
Atchison *(G-205)*
Coxpowerline Inc ....E 620 508-6260
Pratt *(G-10105)*
Elec-Tron Inc ....D 316 522-3401
Wichita *(G-14263)*
▲ **Etco Specialty Products Inc** ....E 620 724-6463
Girard *(G-2403)*
Falcon Design and Mfg ....E 913 441-1074
Shawnee *(G-10953)*
◆ **Kalmar Solutions LLC** ....B 785 242-2200
Ottawa *(G-8279)*
Martin Interconnect Svcs Inc ....D 316 616-1001
Wichita *(G-15011)*
▲ **Mize & Co Inc** ....E 620 532-3191
Kingman *(G-4607)*
Molex LLC ....G 630 969-4550
Wichita *(G-15122)*
National Almnm-Brass Fndry Inc ....E 816 833-4500
Leawood *(G-5498)*
▲ **Smiths Intrcnnect Americas Inc** ....C 913 342-5544
Kansas City *(G-4429)*
Sterling Food Mart Inc ....G 620 278-3371
Hutchinson *(G-3446)*
Sunflower Elec Systems LLC ....G 913 894-1442
Lenexa *(G-6157)*

Ted Mfg Corporation.....E 913 631-6211
Shawnee Mission *(G-11924)*

3644 Noncurrent-Carrying Wiring Devices

Elec-Tron Inc.....D 316 522-3401
Wichita *(G-14263)*

3645 Residential Lighting Fixtures

◆ **Advanced Technologies Inc**.....G 316 744-2285
Bel Aire *(G-427)*
Corbin Bronze Limited.....G 913 766-4012
Kansas City *(G-3940)*
▲ **Fishing Lights Etc LLC**.....G 785 621-2646
Hays *(G-2809)*
Jensen Design Inc.....G 316 943-7900
Wichita *(G-14754)*

3646 Commercial, Indl & Institutional Lighting Fixtures

◆ **Advanced Technologies Inc**.....G 316 744-2285
Bel Aire *(G-427)*
▲ **Fishing Lights Etc LLC**.....G 785 621-2646
Hays *(G-2809)*
Lightwild Inc.....E 913 851-3000
Overland Park *(G-8959)*
▲ **Lw Holding Lc**.....E 913 851-3000
Overland Park *(G-8975)*
Mges LLC.....G 913 334-6333
Kansas City *(G-4240)*
Pwi Inc.....E 316 942-2811
Wichita *(G-15380)*

3647 Vehicular Lighting Eqpt

◆ **Airfixture LLC**.....E 913 312-1100
Kansas City *(G-3794)*
B/E Aerospace Inc.....G 316 609-4300
Wichita *(G-13788)*
Instruments and Flight Res Inc.....G 316 684-5177
Wichita *(G-14697)*
Pwi Inc.....E 316 942-2811
Wichita *(G-15380)*

3648 Lighting Eqpt, NEC

◆ **Advanced Technologies Inc**.....G 316 744-2285
Bel Aire *(G-427)*
Elecsys Corporation.....C 913 647-0158
Olathe *(G-7672)*
▲ **Fishing Lights Etc LLC**.....G 785 621-2646
Hays *(G-2809)*
Flame Engineering Inc.....E 785 222-2873
La Crosse *(G-4633)*
Led2 Lighting Inc.....G 816 912-2180
Kansas City *(G-4199)*

3651 Household Audio & Video Eqpt

▲ **Flyover Innovations Inc**.....G 913 827-2248
Gardner *(G-2346)*
▲ **Galaxy Audio Inc**.....F 316 263-2852
Wichita *(G-14437)*
▲ **Induction Dynamics LLC**.....F 913 663-5600
Lenexa *(G-5912)*
Keywest Technology Inc.....F 913 492-4666
Lenexa *(G-5947)*
Kustom Signals Inc.....C 620 431-2700
Chanute *(G-736)*
Lyntec Inc.....G 913 529-2233
Shawnee Mission *(G-11587)*
Marketing Services of Kansas.....G 913 888-4555
Shawnee Mission *(G-11599)*
Martin-Logan Ltd.....D 785 749-0133
Lawrence *(G-5012)*
Ms Electronics LLC.....F 866 663-9770
Lenexa *(G-6015)*
R D C Inc.....G 913 529-2233
Shawnee Mission *(G-11771)*
Soundtube Entertainment Inc.....F 913 233-8520
Lenexa *(G-6141)*
▲ **Soundtube Entertainment Inc**.....E 435 647-9555
Overland Park *(G-9328)*
T & M Electronics.....G 785 537-1455
Manhattan *(G-6819)*
X Tech Midwest Inc.....G 316 777-6648
Wichita *(G-16082)*

3652 Phonograph Records & Magnetic Tape

Acoustic Sounds Inc.....E 785 825-8609
Salina *(G-10392)*

3661 Telephone & Telegraph Apparatus

AT&T Inc.....F 913 676-1136
Lenexa *(G-5673)*
Ciena Corporation.....G 913 402-4800
Shawnee Mission *(G-11225)*
Computerwise Inc.....F 408 389-8241
Olathe *(G-7609)*
▲ **Kgp Products Inc**.....C 800 755-1950
New Century *(G-7291)*
S & S Underground LLC.....F 620 704-1397
Pittsburg *(G-9932)*
Special Product Company.....E 972 208-1460
Lenexa *(G-6146)*
▲ **Special Product Company**.....F 913 491-8088
Shawnee *(G-11031)*
Spectrum Elite Corp.....G 913 579-7037
Olathe *(G-8076)*
X Tech Midwest Inc.....G 316 777-6648
Wichita *(G-16082)*

3663 Radio & T V Communications, Systs & Eqpt, Broadcast/Studio

AT&T Inc.....F 913 676-1136
Lenexa *(G-5673)*
◆ **Brg Precision Products Inc**.....E 316 788-2000
Derby *(G-1225)*
Childrens Mercy Hospital.....D 913 696-8000
Shawnee Mission *(G-11221)*
▲ **Digital Ally Inc**.....D 913 814-7774
Lenexa *(G-5816)*
Frank Communications Hays Inc.....G 785 623-1500
Hays *(G-2812)*
Ka-Comm Inc.....G 785 776-8177
Manhattan *(G-6672)*
Kustom Signals Inc.....C 620 431-2700
Chanute *(G-736)*
Lg Elctrnics Mbilecomm USA Inc.....E 913 234-3701
Leawood *(G-5457)*
Networks International Corp.....E 913 685-3400
Overland Park *(G-9078)*
Overfield Corporation.....F 785 843-3434
Lawrence *(G-5052)*
Schell Electronics Inc.....G 620 431-2350
Chanute *(G-761)*
Tfmcomm Inc.....G 785 841-2924
Lawrence *(G-5135)*

3669 Communications Eqpt, NEC

Ademco Inc.....G 913 438-1111
Lenexa *(G-5629)*
Certified Life Safety LLC.....G 913 837-5319
Louisburg *(G-6442)*
City Traffic Operation.....F 785 368-3913
Topeka *(G-12477)*
Darrow Company.....G 800 525-6084
Overland Park *(G-8635)*
Dragnet Enterprises.....F 913 362-8378
Kansas City *(G-3977)*
Fire Alarm Specialist Inc.....F 785 743-5287
Wakeeney *(G-13387)*
◆ **Garmin International Inc**.....A 913 397-8200
Olathe *(G-7722)*
Honeywell International Inc.....E 402 597-2279
Olathe *(G-7775)*
▲ **Howard Electronic Instrs Inc**.....G 316 321-2800
El Dorado *(G-1568)*
Johnson Controls.....G 913 894-0010
Lenexa *(G-5930)*
Johnson Controls.....E 316 686-6363
Wichita *(G-14766)*
Johnson Controls Fire.....G 785 267-9675
Topeka *(G-12748)*
Lifeline.....G 800 635-6156
Topeka *(G-12844)*
Nu-Line Company Inc.....F 316 942-0990
Wichita *(G-15199)*
Special Product Company.....E 972 208-1460
Lenexa *(G-6146)*
▲ **Special Product Company**.....F 913 491-8088
Shawnee *(G-11031)*

3672 Printed Circuit Boards

Avatar Engineering Inc.....F 913 897-6757
Lenexa *(G-5676)*
Colt Tech LLC.....G 913 839-8198
Olathe *(G-7600)*
▼ **Commtech Inc**.....F 316 636-1131
Wichita *(G-14075)*
Compass Controls Mfg Inc.....E 913 213-5748
Lenexa *(G-5779)*
Elecsys Corporation.....C 913 647-0158
Olathe *(G-7672)*
Electronic Contrls Assembly Co.....G 913 780-0036
Olathe *(G-7675)*
Pivot-Digittron Inc.....F 913 441-0221
Shawnee *(G-11012)*
Pwi Inc.....E 316 942-2811
Wichita *(G-15380)*
▲ **S and Y Industries Inc**.....C 620 221-4001
Winfield *(G-16171)*
◆ **Vista Manufacturing Company**.....E 913 342-4939
Kansas City *(G-4521)*

3674 Semiconductors

Evonik Corporation.....A 316 529-9670
Haysville *(G-2942)*
Integra Holdings Inc.....D 316 630-6805
Wichita *(G-14698)*
▲ **Integra Technologies LLC**.....C 316 630-6800
Wichita *(G-14699)*
Leidos Inc.....G 913 317-5120
Shawnee Mission *(G-11560)*
LSI Corporation.....E 316 201-2000
Wichita *(G-14988)*
Research Concepts Inc.....F 913 422-0210
Lenexa *(G-6106)*
Telecommunication Systems Inc.....E 913 593-9489
Overland Park *(G-9401)*

3675 Electronic Capacitors

Regal Audio Video.....G 785 628-2700
Hays *(G-2898)*

3677 Electronic Coils & Transformers

Cooper Electronics Inc.....E 913 782-0012
Olathe *(G-7615)*
Kneisley Manufacturing Company.....F 620 365-6628
Iola *(G-3618)*
Networks International Corp.....E 913 685-3400
Overland Park *(G-9078)*
Pwi Inc.....E 316 942-2811
Wichita *(G-15381)*
Pwi Inc.....E 316 942-2811
Wichita *(G-15380)*
Torotel Inc.....E 913 747-6111
Olathe *(G-8115)*
Torotel Products Inc.....C 913 747-6111
Olathe *(G-8116)*

3678 Electronic Connectors

Dme Electronics.....G 316 529-2441
Haysville *(G-2940)*
Wildcat Connectors Inc.....G 785 937-4385
Princeton *(G-10171)*

3679 Electronic Components, NEC

Anderson Industries Inc.....F 316 945-4488
Wichita *(G-13705)*
B & C Specialty Products Inc.....F 316 283-8000
Newton *(G-7315)*
Caliber Electronics Inc.....E 913 782-7787
Olathe *(G-7573)*
▲ **Celltron Inc**.....B 620 783-1333
Galena *(G-2070)*
Control Vision Corporation.....E 620 231-5816
Pittsburg *(G-9845)*
EC Manufacturing LLC.....C 913 825-3077
Paola *(G-9555)*
Elecsys Corporation.....C 913 647-0158
Olathe *(G-7672)*
Elecsys International Corp.....C 913 647-0158
Olathe *(G-7673)*
Electrex Inc.....C 620 662-4866
Hutchinson *(G-3276)*
Electronic Contrls Assembly Co.....G 913 780-0036
Olathe *(G-7675)*
▲ **Inficon Edc Inc**.....D 913 888-1750
Overland Park *(G-8842)*
▲ **Legacy Technologies Inc**.....D 913 432-2487
Shawnee *(G-10986)*
Leidos Inc.....G 913 317-5120
Shawnee Mission *(G-11560)*
Marche Associates Inc.....F 785 749-2925
Lawrence *(G-5011)*
Molex LLC.....G 630 969-4550
Wichita *(G-15122)*

SIC

Networks International Corp....E....913 685-3400
Overland Park (G-9078)
▲ Pivot International Inc....E....913 312-6900
Lenexa (G-6060)
Power Control Devices Inc....E....913 829-1900
Olathe (G-7995)
Quality Intrcnnect Systems Inc....E....620 783-5087
Galena (G-2081)
Regasa Aerospace Inc....G....316 425-0079
Wichita (G-15435)
▲ S and Y Industries Inc....C....620 221-4001
Winfield (G-16171)
Schell Electronics Inc....G....620 431-2350
Chanute (G-761)
Smiths Intrcnnect Americas Inc....G....913 342-5544
Kansas City (G-4428)
▲ Smiths Intrcnnect Americas Inc....C....913 342-5544
Kansas City (G-4429)
▲ Tecnet International Inc....F....913 859-9515
Lenexa (G-6173)
Xsis Electronics Inc....F....913 631-0448
Shawnee (G-11056)

3691 Storage Batteries

Enersys....C....785 625-3355
Hays (G-2799)
Exide Technologies....C....913 321-3561
Kansas City (G-4000)
Exide Technologies....D....785 825-6276
Salina (G-10488)

3692 Primary Batteries: Dry & Wet

Exide Technologies....C....913 321-3561
Kansas City (G-4000)
Spectrum Brands Inc....G....949 279-4099
Edgerton (G-1490)

3694 Electrical Eqpt For Internal Combustion Engines

Clare Generator Service Inc....F....785 827-3321
Salina (G-10453)
Cmt Inc....C....785 762-4400
Junction City (G-3683)
Dels Alternator & Starter Svc....G....785 825-4466
Salina (G-10473)
Electrex Inc....C....620 662-4866
Hutchinson (G-3276)
Junction City Wire Harness LLC....D....785 762-4400
Junction City (G-3706)
Standard Motor Products Inc....B....913 441-6500
Edwardsville (G-1516)
Vermillion Incorporated....D....316 524-3100
Wichita (G-15875)

3695 Recording Media

Data Locker Inc....G....913 310-9088
Overland Park (G-8636)
Magtek Inc....F....913 451-1151
Lenexa (G-5981)
Nuvidia LLC....F....913 599-5200
Lenexa (G-6030)

3699 Electrical Machinery, Eqpt & Splys, NEC

4pc LLC....G....316 833-6906
Augusta (G-299)
Advance Systems International....E....913 888-3578
Lenexa (G-5631)
Advanced Infrared Systems....G....913 888-3578
Lenexa (G-5633)
Azz Inc....E....620 231-6900
Pittsburg (G-9819)
Cheney Door Co Inc....F....620 669-9306
Hutchinson (G-3236)
City of Shawnee....F....913 631-1080
Shawnee Mission (G-11233)
Colt Tech LLC....G....913 839-8198
Olathe (G-7600)
Corrpro Companies Inc....E....620 544-4411
Hugoton (G-3153)
▲ Direct Voltage....F....713 485-9999
Pratt (G-10108)
Electronic Sensors Inc....F....316 267-2807
Wichita (G-14268)
Novatech LLC....E....913 451-1880
Lenexa (G-6028)
Occk Inc....C....785 827-9383
Salina (G-10617)
▲ Omni Aerospace Inc....E....316 529-8998
Wichita (G-15216)
Overhead Door Company....E....316 265-4634
Wichita (G-15240)
▼ Paragon Holdings Lc....E....620 343-0920
Emporia (G-1811)
Prime SEC Svcs Borrower LLC....F....630 410-0662
Lawrence (G-5076)
Raynor Gar Door Co Inc Kans Cy....F....913 422-0441
Shawnee Mission (G-11779)
SNC Alarm Service....E....620 665-6651
Hutchinson (G-3442)
United Manufacturing Inc....E....913 780-0056
New Century (G-7302)
Valiant Global Def Svcs Inc....D....913 651-9782
Leavenworth (G-5304)
Weathercraft Company N Platte....G....785 899-3064
Goodland (G-2490)
Wilbur Inc....F....913 207-6535
Olathe (G-8154)

37 TRANSPORTATION EQUIPMENT

3711 Motor Vehicles & Car Bodies

Broce Manufacturing Co Inc....G....620 227-8811
Dodge City (G-1312)
Brown Industries LLC....D....785 842-6506
Lawrence (G-4770)
▲ Chance Rides Manufacturing Inc....C....316 945-6555
Wichita (G-13997)
◆ Collins Bus Corporation....C....620 662-9000
Hutchinson (G-3242)
Custom Vinyl & Paint Inc....G....316 651-6180
Wichita (G-14147)
Diamond Coach Corporation....D....620 795-2191
Oswego (G-8233)
▼ Eldorado National Kansas Inc....C....785 827-1033
Salina (G-10486)
General Motors LLC....A....913 573-7981
Kansas City (G-4031)
Henke Manufacturing Corp....C....913 682-9000
Leavenworth (G-5254)
◆ Legacy Technologies LLC....E....913 432-2020
Shawnee Mission (G-11559)
Midwest Motorsports Inc....E....913 334-0477
Kansas City (G-4254)
New Horizons Rv Corp....E....785 238-7575
Junction City (G-3731)
P-Ayr Products....F....913 651-5543
Leavenworth (G-5278)
Reinke Manufacturing Co Inc....G....785 527-8024
Belleville (G-463)
Sb Manufacturing Inc....B....316 941-9591
Wichita (G-15524)
Unruh Fire Inc....G....316 772-5400
Sedgwick (G-10854)
Wichita Body & Equipment Co....G....316 522-1080
Haysville (G-2964)

3713 Truck & Bus Bodies

B & W Custom Truck Beds Inc....C....800 810-4918
Humboldt (G-3181)
Big Creek Investment Corp Inc....G....620 431-3445
Chanute (G-707)
Diamond Acquisition LLC....E....620 795-2191
Oswego (G-8232)
Economy Mfg Co Inc....E....620 725-3520
Sedan (G-10842)
▲ Frigiquip International Inc....G....316 321-2400
El Dorado (G-1563)
◆ Full Vision Inc....D....316 283-3344
Newton (G-7349)
◆ Kalmar Solutions LLC....B....785 242-2200
Ottawa (G-8279)
Midwest Truck Equipment Inc....F....316 744-2889
Park City (G-9633)
Nesco Holdings Inc....G....913 287-0001
Kansas City (G-4286)
R B Manufacturing Company....G....913 829-3233
Olathe (G-8016)
Randy Schwindt....F....785 391-2277
Utica (G-13335)
◆ Skymark Refuelers LLC....D....913 653-8100
Kansas City (G-4424)
Star Pipe Usa LLC....C....281 558-3000
Coffeyville (G-979)
▲ Unruh Fab Inc....E....316 772-5400
Sedgwick (G-10853)
Vernies Trux-N-Equip Inc....G....785 625-5087
Hays (G-2923)
VT Hackney Inc....C....620 331-6600
Independence (G-3571)
Western Truck Equipment Co....F....620 793-8464
Great Bend (G-2662)
Wichita Body & Equipment Co....G....316 522-1080
Haysville (G-2964)

3714 Motor Vehicle Parts & Access

▲ Abilene Machine LLC....C....785 655-9455
Solomon (G-12046)
Accessible Technologies Inc....D....913 338-2886
Lenexa (G-5621)
Aeromotive Inc....F....913 647-7300
Shawnee Mission (G-11082)
B & W Custom Truck Beds Inc....C....800 810-4918
Humboldt (G-3181)
▲ Blaylock Diesel Service Inc....F....620 856-5227
Baxter Springs (G-399)
▲ Brierton Engineering Inc....E....785 263-7711
Abilene (G-16)
◆ Clore Automotive LLC....E....913 310-1050
Lenexa (G-5766)
Cromwell Builders Mfg....F....785 949-2433
Carlton (G-686)
Cross Manufacturing Inc....C....620 324-5525
Lewis (G-6268)
Frankenstein Trikes LLC....G....913 352-6788
Pleasanton (G-9995)
▲ Frigiquip International Inc....G....316 321-2400
El Dorado (G-1563)
GKN Armstrong Wheels Inc....E....316 943-3571
Wichita (G-14469)
Haldex Brake Products Corp....D....620 365-5275
Iola (G-3606)
Hampton Hydraulics Llc....D....620 792-4368
Great Bend (G-2590)
◆ Hopkins Manufacturing Corp....B....620 342-7320
Emporia (G-1775)
Husky Liners Inc....D....620 221-2268
Winfield (G-16148)
Ict Billet LLC....G....316 300-0833
Wichita (G-14666)
◆ Industrial Chrome Inc....D....785 235-3463
Topeka (G-12721)
Inityaero Inc....E....316 265-0603
Wichita (G-14694)
▲ John Dere Cffeyville Works Inc....B....620 251-3400
Coffeyville (G-951)
◆ Kalmar Solutions LLC....B....785 242-2200
Ottawa (G-8279)
▼ Kasa Companies Inc....C....785 825-7181
Salina (G-10570)
Kasa Companies Inc....D....785 825-5612
Salina (G-10571)
Kasa Companies Inc....D....785 825-5612
Salina (G-10569)
▲ Mize & Co Inc....E....620 532-3191
Kingman (G-4607)
Precision Manifold Systems Inc....E....913 829-1221
Olathe (G-8001)
Roll Out Inc....G....620 347-4753
Arma (G-190)
▲ Rv Products....E....316 832-3400
Wichita (G-15494)
Standard Motor Products Inc....B....620 331-1000
Independence (G-3562)
Standard Motor Products Inc....B....913 441-6500
Edwardsville (G-1516)
Thunder Struck Inc....E....785 200-6680
Abilene (G-54)
Timken Smo LLC....B....620 223-0080
Fort Scott (G-2008)
Truett & Osborn Cycle Inc....G....316 682-4781
Wichita (G-15811)
Youngs Products LLC....D....620 431-2199
Chanute (G-774)

3715 Truck Trailers

Bradford Built Inc....E....785 325-3300
Washington (G-13460)
Brown Industries LLC....D....785 842-6506
Lawrence (G-4770)
Doonan Specialized Trailer LLC....E....620 792-6222
Great Bend (G-2554)
Dunning Express Inc....E....785 806-3915
Elwood (G-1685)
Eagle Trailer Company Inc....G....785 841-3200
Lawrence (G-4844)
Flint Hills Industries Inc....G....620 947-3127
Hillsboro (G-3048)
High Plains Machine Works Inc....F....785 625-4672
Hays (G-2845)

Landoll Corporation F 785 562-4780
Marysville *(G-6894)*

◆ **Landoll Corporation** B 785 562-5381
Marysville *(G-6893)*

R B Manufacturing Company G 913 829-3233
Olathe *(G-8016)*

Roadruner Manufacturing LLC G 785 586-2228
Levant *(G-6265)*

Sharp Manufacturing LLC F 785 363-7336
Blue Rapids *(G-537)*

Short Go Inc D 620 223-2866
Fort Scott *(G-2004)*

Sun Valley Inc E 620 662-0101
Hutchinson *(G-3456)*

▲ **Unruh Fab Inc** E 316 772-5400
Sedgwick *(G-10853)*

VT Hackney Inc C 620 331-6600
Independence *(G-3571)*

Wabash National Corporation C 913 621-7298
Kansas City *(G-4527)*

Western Truck Equipment Co F 620 793-8464
Great Bend *(G-2662)*

William R Harris Trucking F 913 422-5551
Shawnee Mission *(G-12010)*

3716 Motor Homes

Zodiac Industries Inc E 620 783-5041
Galena *(G-2090)*

3721 Aircraft

Air Capital Interiors Inc F 316 633-4790
Wichita *(G-13648)*

Airbus Americas Inc C 316 264-0552
Wichita *(G-13650)*

Avcon Industries Inc E 913 780-9595
Newton *(G-7313)*

Beechcraft Holdings LLC E 316 676-7111
Wichita *(G-13826)*

Boeing Company A 316 523-7084
Wichita *(G-13864)*

Boeing Company F 480 509-5449
Wichita *(G-13865)*

Boeing Company F 312 544-2000
Wichita *(G-13866)*

Butler National Corporation E 913 780-9595
Olathe *(G-7571)*

Emerald Aerospace Holdings LLC D 316 440-6966
Wichita *(G-14274)*

Lathrom Manufacturing Inc F 316 522-0001
Wichita *(G-14931)*

▲ **Learjet Inc** A 316 946-2000
Wichita *(G-14940)*

Learjet Inc E 316 946-3001
Wichita *(G-14941)*

Learjet Inc A 316 946-2000
Wichita *(G-14942)*

Smith & Smith Aircraft Intl F 316 945-0204
Wichita *(G-15606)*

Textron Airland LLC G 541 390-8888
Wichita *(G-15732)*

Textron Aviation Inc A 316 676-7111
Salina *(G-10733)*

Textron Aviation Inc A 888 727-4344
Wichita *(G-15734)*

Textron Aviation Inc C 316 517-8270
Wichita *(G-15736)*

Textron Aviation Inc A 316 517-6000
Wichita *(G-15740)*

Textron Aviation Inc A 316 676-7111
Wichita *(G-15744)*

Textron Aviation Inc D 316 517-6000
Wichita *(G-15745)*

Textron Aviation Inc B 316 517-6081
Wichita *(G-15746)*

Textron Aviation Inc C 800 835-4090
Wichita *(G-15748)*

Textron Aviation Inc C 316 831-2000
Wichita *(G-15749)*

Textron Aviation Inc C 316 517-6000
Wichita *(G-15750)*

Textron Aviation Inc C 620 332-0228
Independence *(G-3564)*

Textron Aviation Inc A 316 676-7111
Wichita *(G-15752)*

Textron Aviation Inc A 316 676-5373
Wichita *(G-15753)*

Textron Aviation Inc G 316 517-1375
Wichita *(G-15738)*

3724 Aircraft Engines & Engine Parts

Dcs Inc G 316 806-4899
Derby *(G-1233)*

Emerald Aerospace Services LLC E 316 644-4284
Wichita *(G-14275)*

▲ **Eurot Verti Fligh Solut LLC** G 785 331-2220
Eudora *(G-1875)*

Facc Solutions Inc G 316 425-4040
Wichita *(G-14330)*

▼ **Garsite Progress LLC** D 913 342-5600
Kansas City *(G-4025)*

GE Engine Services LLC A 316 264-4741
Arkansas City *(G-157)*

Global Cnc Corporation G 316 516-3400
Wichita *(G-14474)*

Hiperformance LLC G 913 829-3400
New Century *(G-7287)*

Honeywell International Inc C 316 522-8172
Wichita *(G-14634)*

Honeywell International Inc A 816 997-7149
Olathe *(G-7773)*

Honeywell International Inc A 316 204-5503
Derby *(G-1251)*

Honeywell International Inc E 913 712-6017
New Century *(G-7288)*

Honeywell International Inc D 913 712-3000
Olathe *(G-7774)*

Honeywell International Inc D 620 783-1343
Pittsburg *(G-9878)*

Kansas AVI Independence LLC D 620 331-7716
Independence *(G-3530)*

Maxima Precision Inc E 316 832-2211
Wichita *(G-15020)*

Pratt & Whitney Eng Svcs Inc G 316 945-9763
Wichita *(G-15322)*

Smith & Smith Aircraft Intl F 316 945-0204
Wichita *(G-15606)*

Specialty Patterns Inc F 316 945-8131
Wichita *(G-15637)*

▲ **Spirit Arosystems Holdings Inc** E 316 526-9000
Wichita *(G-15644)*

Triumph Group Operations Inc D 620 326-5761
Wellington *(G-13538)*

Triumph Strctres - Kans Cy Inc D 913 882-7200
Edgerton *(G-1491)*

Turbine Eng Comp Tech Turning E 316 925-4020
Wichita *(G-15815)*

3728 Aircraft Parts & Eqpt, NEC

AAA Air Support Mfg LLC G 316 946-9299
Haysville *(G-2934)*

Accurus Aerospace Wichita LLC E 316 683-0266
Wichita *(G-13604)*

Advanced Welding Tech LLC E 316 295-2333
Wichita *(G-13627)*

Aei Investment Holdings Inc D 817 283-3722
Wichita *(G-13633)*

Aero Metal Forms Inc E 316 942-0909
Wichita *(G-13634)*

▲ **Aero Space Controls Corp** E 316 264-2875
Wichita *(G-13635)*

Aero Space Manufacturing Corp F 620 378-4441
Fredonia *(G-2026)*

▲ **Aero-Mach Laboratories Inc** C 316 682-7707
Wichita *(G-13636)*

Aero-Tech Engineering Inc D 316 942-8604
Maize *(G-6507)*

Aerospace Products Company G 316 733-4440
Wichita *(G-13637)*

Aerospace Systems Cmpnents Inc D 316 686-7392
Wichita *(G-13638)*

▲ **Aerospace Turbine Rotables Inc** D 316 943-6100
Wichita *(G-13639)*

Air Capitol Dial Inc F 316 264-2483
Wichita *(G-13649)*

Apex Engineering Intl LLC C 316 262-1494
Wichita *(G-13718)*

▲ **Apph Wichita Inc** E 316 943-5752
Wichita *(G-13720)*

Archein Aerospace LLC E 682 499-2150
Wichita *(G-13730)*

Atlas Aerospace LLC G 316 977-7398
Wichita *(G-13763)*

Atlas Aerospace LLC F 316 219-5862
Wichita *(G-13764)*

Avcon Industries Inc E 913 780-9595
Newton *(G-7313)*

B/E Aerospace Inc D 316 609-3360
Wichita *(G-13787)*

B/E Aerospace Inc D 913 338-9800
Lenexa *(G-5681)*

B/E Aerospace Inc G 316 609-4300
Wichita *(G-13788)*

B/E Aerospace Inc C 913 338-7292
Shawnee Mission *(G-11142)*

Beechcraft Holdings LLC E 316 676-7111
Wichita *(G-13826)*

Beechcraft Intl Svc Co G 316 676-7111
Wichita *(G-13827)*

▼ **Burnham Cmpsite Structures Inc** E 316 946-5900
Wichita *(G-13917)*

Butler National Corporation E 913 780-9595
Olathe *(G-7571)*

Capps Manufacturing Inc D 316 942-9351
Wichita *(G-13940)*

▲ **Capps Manufacturing Inc** D 316 942-9351
Wichita *(G-13941)*

Ceco Inc E 316 942-7431
Wichita *(G-13969)*

Center Industries Corporation C 316 942-8255
Wichita *(G-13976)*

Charles Engineering Inc E 620 584-2381
Clearwater *(G-887)*

Cheyenne Mfg Inc E 316 942-7665
Wichita *(G-14002)*

▲ **Clearwater Engineering Inc** E 316 425-0202
Derby *(G-1230)*

Cmj Manufacturing Inc F 316 777-9692
Mulvane *(G-7214)*

Cox Machine Inc D 316 943-1342
Wichita *(G-14121)*

Cox Machine Inc D 316 943-1342
Harper *(G-2718)*

D & S Manufacturing Inc G 316 685-5337
Wichita *(G-14156)*

D-J Engineering Inc G 620 456-3211
Conway Springs *(G-1138)*

▲ **D-J Engineering Inc** C 316 775-1212
Augusta *(G-316)*

Ducommun Aerostructures Inc E 620 421-3401
Parsons *(G-9682)*

Dynamic Machine LLC F 316 941-4005
Wichita *(G-14248)*

Dynamic N/C LLC D 316 712-5028
Rose Hill *(G-10237)*

Eck & Eck Machine Company Inc E 316 942-5924
Wichita *(G-14258)*

Enjet Aero LLC F 913 717-7396
Overland Park *(G-8683)*

Etezazi Industries Inc E 316 831-9937
Wichita *(G-14307)*

▲ **Exacta Aerospace Inc** C 316 941-4200
Wichita *(G-14318)*

Fastenair Corporation E 316 684-2875
Wichita *(G-14345)*

Figeac Aero North America Inc D 316 634-2500
Wichita *(G-14366)*

Flame Engineering Inc E 785 222-2873
La Crosse *(G-4633)*

Fmw Inc F 316 943-4217
Wichita *(G-14398)*

Forming Specialists Inc G 620 488-3243
Belle Plaine *(G-446)*

Freddie Wayne Long F 316 263-8941
Wichita *(G-14415)*

Global Aviation Tech LLC F 316 425-0999
Wichita *(G-14473)*

Global Engineering & Tech Inc C 316 729-9232
Goddard *(G-2439)*

◆ **Global Ground Support LLC** D 913 780-0300
Olathe *(G-7732)*

Globe Engineering Co Inc C 316 943-1266
Wichita *(G-14476)*

Goodrich Corporation F 316 943-3322
Wichita *(G-14485)*

Goodrich Corporation A 316 721-3100
Wichita *(G-14486)*

H & R Parts Co Inc E 316 942-6984
Wichita *(G-14531)*

▲ **H M Dunn Company Inc** C 316 522-5426
Wichita *(G-14532)*

H M Dunn Company Inc C 314 535-6684
Wichita *(G-14533)*

Harlow Aerostructures LLC C 316 265-5268
Wichita *(G-14561)*

◆ **Hiller Inc** E 316 264-5231
Wichita *(G-14611)*

Hisonic LLC E 913 782-0012
Olathe *(G-7769)*

Impresa Aerospace LLC ..... D 316 942-9100
Wichita *(G-14679)*

Industrial Process Eqp Co ..... G 316 722-7800
Wichita *(G-14686)*

Inityaero Inc ..... E 316 265-0603
Wichita *(G-14694)*

Jmt Industries Inc ..... G 316 267-1221
Wichita *(G-14758)*

Kelly Manufacturing Company ..... F 620 358-3826
Grenola *(G-2687)*

Kmi Inc ..... E 316 777-0146
Mulvane *(G-7217)*

◆ Landoll Corporation ..... B 785 562-5381
Marysville *(G-6893)*

Lathrom Manufacturing Inc ..... F 316 522-0001
Wichita *(G-14931)*

Lee Aerospace Inc ..... C 316 636-9200
Wichita *(G-14946)*

Lee Air Inc ..... E 316 524-4622
Wichita *(G-14947)*

LMI Aerospace Inc ..... F 913 469-6400
Lenexa *(G-5976)*

LMI Aerospace Inc ..... F 620 378-4441
Fredonia *(G-2039)*

LMI Aerospace Inc ..... G 316 944-4143
Wichita *(G-14971)*

LMI Aerospace Inc ..... C 316 943-6059
Wichita *(G-14972)*

LMI Lenexa ..... G 913 491-6975
Lenexa *(G-5977)*

Lyons Manufacturing Co Inc ..... E 620 257-2331
Lyons *(G-6491)*

M I F Inc ..... D 316 838-3970
Park City *(G-9629)*

Machining Programming Mfg Inc ..... E 316 945-1227
Wichita *(G-14998)*

Manufacturing Development Inc ..... E 316 542-0182
Cheney *(G-793)*

Maxima Precision Inc ..... E 316 832-2211
Wichita *(G-15020)*

McFarlane Aviation Inc ..... D 785 594-2741
Baldwin City *(G-366)*

Metal Forming Incorporated ..... F 620 488-3930
Belle Plaine *(G-447)*

Mid Continent Controls Inc ..... E 316 789-0088
Derby *(G-1262)*

Millennium Concepts Inc ..... D 316 977-8870
Wichita *(G-15109)*

Mini-Mac Inc ..... G 316 733-0661
Wichita *(G-15111)*

Mockry & Sons Machine Co Inc ..... E 316 788-7878
Derby *(G-1263)*

Nance Manufacturing Inc ..... E 620 842-3761
Anthony *(G-130)*

Nance Manufacturing Inc ..... E 316 942-8671
Wichita *(G-15146)*

Old Ppp Inc ..... D 620 421-3400
Parsons *(G-9713)*

▲ Omni Aerospace Inc ..... E 316 529-8998
Wichita *(G-15216)*

Optimuz Manufacturing Inc ..... E 316 519-1354
Wichita *(G-15229)*

Orizon Arostructures - Nkc LLC ..... E 620 431-4037
Chanute *(G-752)*

Orizon Arostructures - Nkc LLC ..... F 816 788-7800
Olathe *(G-7964)*

Orizon Arstrctres - Chnute Inc ..... D 816 788-7800
Chanute *(G-753)*

Oxwell Inc ..... D 620 326-7481
Wellington *(G-13521)*

◆ Park Aerospace Tech Corp ..... D 316 283-6500
Newton *(G-7403)*

Precision Aviation Controls ..... D 620 331-8180
Independence *(G-3547)*

Precision Products ..... G 316 943-0477
Wichita *(G-15325)*

Primus International Inc ..... C 316 425-8105
Wichita *(G-15346)*

Professional Machine & Tool ..... F 316 755-1271
Valley Center *(G-13350)*

Pwi Inc ..... E 316 942-2811
Wichita *(G-15381)*

Quality Tech Metals ..... E 316 945-4781
Wichita *(G-15386)*

R & R Holdings Inc ..... E 316 942-6699
Wichita *(G-15399)*

R & R Precision Machine Inc ..... E 316 942-6699
Wichita *(G-15400)*

R O Terex Corporation ..... D 913 782-1200
Olathe *(G-8018)*

Rickman Machine Co Inc ..... E 316 263-0841
Wichita *(G-15459)*

Senior Operations LLC ..... C 316 942-3208
Wichita *(G-15558)*

Sigma Tek Inc ..... E 316 775-6373
Augusta *(G-345)*

Spirit Aerosystems Inc ..... E 316 523-2995
Wichita *(G-15640)*

▲ Spirit Aerosystems Inc ..... C 316 526-9000
Wichita *(G-15641)*

Spirit Aerosystems Innovative ..... D 316 526-9000
Wichita *(G-15642)*

Spirit Arosystems Holdings Inc ..... F 316 523-3950
Wichita *(G-15643)*

▲ Spirit Arosystems Holdings Inc ..... E 316 526-9000
Wichita *(G-15644)*

▲ Tect Aerospace LLC ..... C 316 425-3638
Wichita *(G-15726)*

▲ Tect Aerospace Wellington Inc ..... C 620 359-5000
Wellington *(G-13536)*

Tect Hypervelocity Inc ..... D 316 529-5000
Park City *(G-9647)*

▲ Tect Hypervelocity Inc ..... D 316 529-5000
Park City *(G-9648)*

Textron Aviation Inc ..... G 316 517-1375
Wichita *(G-15738)*

Textron Aviation Inc ..... C 316 517-6000
Wichita *(G-15747)*

Textron Aviation Inc ..... B 316 721-3100
Wichita *(G-15751)*

Textron Aviation Inc ..... A 316 676-7111
Salina *(G-10733)*

Textron Aviation Inc ..... A 316 676-7111
Wichita *(G-15744)*

Textron Aviation Inc ..... A 316 676-5373
Wichita *(G-15753)*

Torotel Products Inc ..... C 913 747-6111
Olathe *(G-8116)*

▲ Trinity Precision Inc ..... D 316 265-0603
Wichita *(G-15802)*

Triumph Group Operations Inc ..... D 620 326-5761
Wellington *(G-13538)*

▲ Triumph Strctres - Wichita Inc ..... D 316 942-0432
Wichita *(G-15805)*

Turbine Eng Comp Tech Turning ..... E 316 925-4020
Wichita *(G-15815)*

▼ Ultra Electronics Ice Inc ..... D 785 776-6423
Manhattan *(G-6835)*

United Tech Arospc Systems ..... F 316 721-3100
Wichita *(G-15850)*

Universal Avonics Systems Corp ..... G 316 524-9500
Wichita *(G-15852)*

Universal Machining Shtmtl Inc ..... E 316 425-7610
Wichita *(G-15854)*

Valent Aerostructures LLC ..... D 316 682-4551
Wichita *(G-15870)*

▲ Valent Aerostructures LLC ..... E 816 423-5600
Lenexa *(G-6207)*

Valent Aerostructures LLC ..... G 620 378-4441
Fredonia *(G-2048)*

Vinland Aerodrome Inc ..... G 785 594-2741
Baldwin City *(G-369)*

Wasi Inc ..... E 620 782-3337
Wichita *(G-15932)*

Webco Air Craft ..... G 316 283-7929
Newton *(G-7426)*

Winding Specialists Co Inc ..... F 316 265-9358
Wichita *(G-16054)*

3731 Shipbuilding & Repairing

North Shore Marina MGT LLC ..... G 785 453-2240
Quenemo *(G-10178)*

3732 Boat Building & Repairing

Accessible Technologies Inc ..... D 913 338-2886
Lenexa *(G-5621)*

▼ Cobalt Boats LLC ..... B 620 325-2653
Neodesha *(G-7236)*

Scs Tech LLC ..... G 785 424-4478
Topeka *(G-13045)*

3743 Railroad Eqpt

Aero Transportation Pdts Inc ..... D 620 241-7010
Mc Pherson *(G-6930)*

▲ Amsted Rail Company Inc ..... D 913 956-2400
Overland Park *(G-8384)*

Amsted Rail Company Inc ..... E 913 367-7200
Atchison *(G-204)*

Millennium Rail Inc ..... F 620 231-2230
Pittsburg *(G-9905)*

Railroad Group ..... G 913 375-1157
Kansas City *(G-4359)*

Voestalpine Nortrak Inc ..... D 316 284-0088
Newton *(G-7424)*

3751 Motorcycles, Bicycles & Parts

Burke Inc ..... E 913 722-5658
Kansas City *(G-3880)*

Cosentino Group II Inc ..... G 913 422-2130
Shawnee *(G-10935)*

Holthaus Autohaus LLC ..... G 785 467-3101
Fairview *(G-1904)*

Optimuz Manufacturing Inc ..... E 316 519-1354
Wichita *(G-15229)*

3769 Guided Missile/Space Vehicle Parts & Eqpt, NEC

B/E Aerospace Inc ..... C 913 338-7292
Shawnee Mission *(G-11142)*

◆ Brittain Machine Inc ..... E 316 942-8223
Wichita *(G-13892)*

Burnham Composites Inc ..... E 316 946-5900
Wichita *(G-13918)*

Inityaero Inc ..... E 316 265-0603
Wichita *(G-14694)*

Learjet Inc ..... E 316 946-3001
Wichita *(G-14941)*

Numerical Control Support Inc ..... E 913 441-3500
Shawnee Mission *(G-11690)*

Primus International Inc ..... C 316 425-8105
Wichita *(G-15346)*

Torotel Products Inc ..... C 913 747-6111
Olathe *(G-8116)*

Triumph Strctres - Kans Cy Inc ..... D 913 882-7200
Edgerton *(G-1491)*

Vermillion Incorporated ..... D 316 524-3100
Wichita *(G-15875)*

3792 Travel Trailers & Campers

Astro Truck Covers Inc ..... D 785 448-5577
Ottawa *(G-8246)*

▲ Bultman Company Inc Mfg ..... F 620 544-8004
Hugoton *(G-3149)*

Custom Campers Inc ..... C 620 431-3990
Chanute *(G-723)*

Lacy Rv Ranch Inc ..... G 620 245-9608
McPherson *(G-6986)*

Nu-WA Industries Inc ..... C 620 431-2088
Chanute *(G-748)*

3795 Tanks & Tank Components

Atec Steel LLC ..... C 877 457-5352
Baxter Springs *(G-394)*

3799 Transportation Eqpt, NEC

Circle D Corporation Inc ..... E 620 947-2385
Hillsboro *(G-3044)*

Cromwell Builders Mfg ..... F 785 949-2433
Carlton *(G-686)*

Eagle Trailer Company Inc ..... G 785 841-3200
Lawrence *(G-4844)*

Flint Hills Powersports Inc ..... G 785 336-3901
Bern *(G-522)*

JM Tran-Sport LLC ..... G 785 545-3756
Glen Elder *(G-2426)*

Landoll Corporation ..... E 785 738-6613
Beloit *(G-490)*

Magna Tech Inc ..... E 620 431-3490
Chanute *(G-740)*

Motivational Tubing LLC ..... G 316 283-7301
Newton *(G-7391)*

38 MEASURING, ANALYZING AND CONTROLLING INSTRUMENTS; PHOTOGRAPHIC, MEDICAL AN

3812 Search, Detection, Navigation & Guidance Systs & Instrs

Advance Systems International ..... E 913 888-3578
Lenexa *(G-5631)*

Airfield Technology Inc ..... G 913 780-9800
Olathe *(G-7515)*

B/E Aerospace Inc ..... C 913 338-7292
Shawnee Mission *(G-11142)*

◆ Brittain Machine Inc ..... E 316 942-8223
Wichita *(G-13892)*

Cooper Electronics Inc....E....913 782-0012
Olathe (G-7615)
Emerald Aerospace Holdings LLC....D....316 440-6966
Wichita (G-14274)
Emerald Aerospace Services LLC....E....316 644-4284
Wichita (G-14275)
Garmin International Inc....G....913 440-8462
New Century (G-7285)
Garmin International Inc....E....312 787-3221
Olathe (G-7721)
◆ Garmin International Inc....A....913 397-8200
Olathe (G-7722)
H M Dunn Company Inc....C....314 535-6684
Wichita (G-14533)
J Diamond Inc....E....316 264-9505
Wichita (G-14735)
Kelly Manufacturing Company....D....316 265-4271
Independence (G-3531)
Kelly Manufacturing Company....D....316 265-6868
Wichita (G-14846)
Kustom Signals Inc....C....620 431-2700
Chanute (G-736)
▲ Learjet Inc....A....316 946-2000
Wichita (G-14940)
Lyons Manufacturing Co Inc....E....620 257-2331
Lyons (G-6491)
Numerical Control Support Inc....E....913 441-3500
Shawnee Mission (G-11690)
Orizon Arstructures - Proc Inc....E....620 305-2402
Chanute (G-754)
Peavey Corporation....D....913 888-0600
Lenexa (G-6047)
Rockwell Collins Inc....C....316 677-4808
Wichita (G-15474)
▼ Selex Es Inc....D....913 945-2600
Overland Park (G-9293)
Sigma Tek Inc....E....316 775-6373
Augusta (G-345)
Telecommunication Systems Inc....E....913 593-9489
Overland Park (G-9401)

3821 Laboratory Apparatus & Furniture

Jeffrey A Harris....E....785 823-8760
Salina (G-10553)
Labconco Corporation....E....620 223-5700
Fort Scott (G-1980)
Phytotech Labs Inc....F....913 341-5343
Lenexa (G-6056)
◆ Schroer Manufacturing Company....C....913 281-1500
Kansas City (G-4404)
▲ T Kennel Systems Inc....D....816 668-8995
Kansas City (G-4454)

3822 Automatic Temperature Controls

Ademco Inc....G....913 438-1111
Lenexa (G-5629)
Bingham Canyon Corporation....G....913 353-4560
Lenexa (G-5703)
Building Control Solutions LLC....G....816 439-6046
Merriam (G-7087)
Clean Air Management Co Inc....E....913 831-0740
Lenexa (G-5760)
Dynamic Control Systems Inc....F....316 262-2525
Wichita (G-14246)
Honeywell International Inc....E....402 597-2279
Olathe (G-7775)
John Zink Company LLC....F....316 828-7380
Wichita (G-14764)
▲ Midwest Combustn Solutions Inc....G....316 425-0929
Wichita (G-15090)
◆ Power Flame Incorporated....C....620 421-0480
Parsons (G-9724)
Siemens Industry Inc....D....316 260-4340
Wichita (G-15586)

3823 Indl Instruments For Meas, Display & Control

Autoflame....G....620 229-8048
Wichita (G-13772)
Emerson Electric Co....C....913 752-6000
Shawnee Mission (G-11334)
Eurotech Inc....E....913 549-1000
Overland Park (G-8693)
Focalpoint Imaging LLC....G....620 325-2298
Neodesha (G-7241)
Harlan Hermanson....G....316 263-5958
Wichita (G-14560)
Kustom Signals Inc....C....620 431-2700
Chanute (G-736)
▲ National-Spencer Inc....E....316 265-5601
Wichita (G-15154)
Pinnacle Technology Inc....E....785 832-8866
Lawrence (G-5066)
Power Admin LLC....G....800 401-2339
Olathe (G-7994)
Ruskin Company....E....620 421-6090
Parsons (G-9733)
TEC Engineering Inc....E....316 259-8881
Wichita (G-15723)
Torotel Inc....E....913 747-6111
Olathe (G-8115)
Total Electric Inc....G....316 524-2642
Wichita (G-15775)

3824 Fluid Meters & Counters

BP America Production Company....E....620 657-4300
Satanta (G-10777)
▲ Digital Ally Inc....D....913 814-7774
Lenexa (G-5816)
◆ Great Plains Industries Inc....B....316 686-7361
Wichita (G-14503)
▲ Omni Aerospace Inc....E....316 529-8998
Wichita (G-15216)
Tank Wind-Down Corp....C....620 421-0200
Parsons (G-9745)

3825 Instrs For Measuring & Testing Electricity

Commercial Trade Services LLC....F....316 721-5432
Wichita (G-14073)
Design Concepts Inc....F....913 782-5672
Olathe (G-7651)
Ecs Inc International....F....913 782-7787
Lenexa (G-5829)
Firemon LLC....E....913 948-9570
Overland Park (G-8717)
Frugal Inc....G....785 776-9088
Saint George (G-10347)
Gateway Wireless Services LLC....F....316 264-0037
Wichita (G-14451)
▲ Howard Electronic Instrs Inc....G....316 321-2800
El Dorado (G-1568)
Landis+gyr Inc....G....913 312-4710
Lenexa (G-5964)
◆ Legacy Technologies LLC....E....913 432-2020
Shawnee Mission (G-11559)
Mid West Elc Transformers Inc....F....316 283-7500
Newton (G-7382)
Midamerica Meter....G....913 441-0790
Shawnee (G-10995)
▲ Smiths Intrcnnect Americas Inc....C....913 342-5544
Kansas City (G-4429)
▼ Steinlite Corporation....E....913 367-3945
Atchison (G-261)
Steinlite Corporation....F....913 367-3945
Atchison (G-262)
Technical Mfg Concepts Inc....E....913 764-1011
Olathe (G-8104)
Viavi Solutions LLC....B....316 522-4981
Wichita (G-15905)
Viavi Solutions LLC....C....913 764-2452
Lenexa (G-6213)
Wppa Inc....F....316 683-4111
Wichita (G-16074)

3826 Analytical Instruments

Aviation Cnslting Engrg Sltons....G....316 265-8335
Maize (G-6508)
▲ Medical Positioning Inc....E....816 474-1555
Kansas City (G-4229)
Perkinelmer Inc....F....316 773-0055
Wichita (G-15284)
Pinnacle Technology Inc....E....785 832-8866
Lawrence (G-5066)
▲ Sunlite Science & Technology....G....785 832-8818
Lawrence (G-5130)
Thermo Fisher Scientific Inc....D....800 255-6730
Lenexa (G-6178)

3827 Optical Instruments

Bushnell Inc....C....913 752-6178
Overland Park (G-8498)
◆ Bushnell Inc....C....913 752-3400
Overland Park (G-8499)
Viavi Solutions LLC....C....913 764-2452
Lenexa (G-6213)

3829 Measuring & Controlling Devices, NEC

Aviation Cnslting Engrg Sltons....G....316 265-8335
Maize (G-6508)
Fireboard Labs LLC....G....816 945-2232
Olathe (G-7710)
Hail Signature Tech LLC....G....913 620-4928
Stilwell (G-12150)
Kohlman Systems Research Inc....F....785 843-4099
Lawrence (G-4948)
Networks International Corp....E....913 685-3400
Overland Park (G-9078)
▲ Point Inc....F....913 928-2720
Olathe (G-7989)
Radiation Oncology....E....913 588-3600
Kansas City (G-4358)
▲ Sands Level and Tool Company....D....620 325-2687
Neodesha (G-7248)
Siemens Industry Inc....E....316 267-5814
Wichita (G-15584)
Solid State Sonics & Elec....G....785 232-0497
Topeka (G-13080)
Tradewind Energy Inc....E....913 888-9463
Lenexa (G-6188)
Weather Metrics Inc....G....913 438-7666
Overland Park (G-9486)

3841 Surgical & Medical Instrs & Apparatus

B/E Aerospace Inc....C....913 338-7292
Shawnee Mission (G-11142)
Bayer Healthcare LLC....E....913 268-2000
Shawnee Mission (G-11154)
Biomedical Devices of KS LLC....G....913 845-3851
Tonganoxie (G-12254)
Cardinal Health Inc....D....800 523-0502
Shawnee Mission (G-11202)
Disposable Instrument Co Inc....F....913 492-6492
Shawnee Mission (G-11310)
▲ Entracare LLC....G....913 451-2234
Shawnee Mission (G-11343)
Fetal Well-Being LLC....G....316 644-8919
Wichita (G-14359)
▲ Hans Rudolph Inc....E....913 422-7788
Shawnee (G-10967)
Innara Health Inc....G....913 742-7770
Olathe (G-7793)
Ivy Animal Health Inc....E....913 310-7900
Lenexa (G-5924)
▲ Nexus Medical LLC....D....913 451-2234
Shawnee Mission (G-11682)
O2 Corporation....F....316 634-1240
Wichita (G-15202)
Optimuz Manufacturing Inc....E....316 519-1354
Wichita (G-15229)
Ross Manufacturing Inc....G....785 332-3012
Saint Francis (G-10345)
◆ Schroer Manufacturing Company....C....913 281-1500
Kansas City (G-4404)
Stannley Veterinary Clinic....E....913 897-2080
Shawnee Mission (G-11894)

3842 Orthopedic, Prosthetic & Surgical Appliances/Splys

Acustep LLC....G....785 826-2500
Salina (G-10393)
▲ Arveda Llc....E....785 625-4674
Hays (G-2750)
Assistive Technology For Kans....E....620 421-8367
Parsons (G-9667)
B/E Aerospace Inc....C....913 338-7292
Shawnee Mission (G-11142)
Burke Inc....E....913 722-5658
Kansas City (G-3880)
Cramer Products Inc....F....913 856-7511
Gardner (G-2335)
Dentec Safety Specialists....F....905 953-9946
Lenexa (G-5811)
Emergency Services PA....E....316 962-2239
Wichita (G-14276)
Hanger Inc....F....913 677-1488
Merriam (G-7094)
Hanger Prosthetics &....G....316 609-3000
Wichita (G-14554)
Hanger Prosthetics &....G....913 498-1540
Shawnee Mission (G-11407)
Hanger Prosthetics &....G....913 341-8897
Overland Park (G-8790)
Hanger Prosthetics &....G....913 588-6548
Kansas City (G-4065)

SIC

Hanger Prosthetics & ....G.... 785 232-5382
Topeka *(G-12664)*
Hanger Prsthetcs & Ortho Inc....F.... 316 685-1268
Wichita *(G-14555)*
Kansas Specialty Services Inc....F.... 620 221-6040
Winfield *(G-16151)*
▲ Knit-Rite Inc....D.... 913 279-6310
Kansas City *(G-4178)*
LSI International Inc....E.... 913 894-4493
Kansas City *(G-4208)*
Midwest Contracting & Mfg....G.... 785 743-2026
WA Keeney *(G-13383)*
Pos-T-Vac LLC....F.... 800 279-7434
Dodge City *(G-1420)*
Primus Sterilizer Company LLC....E.... 620 793-7177
Great Bend *(G-2624)*
▲ Rayes Inc....D.... 785 726-4885
Ellis *(G-1651)*
Rayes Inc....D.... 785 726-4885
Hays *(G-2897)*
Scott Specialties Inc....C.... 785 527-5627
Belleville *(G-466)*
Scott Specialties Inc....E.... 785 632-3161
Clay Center *(G-881)*
Turntine Oclar Prosthetics Inc....E.... 913 962-6299
Shawnee Mission *(G-11949)*
Zimmer Inc....G.... 913 888-1024
Lenexa *(G-6242)*

3843 Dental Eqpt & Splys

Beyond 21st Century Inc....G.... 913 631-4790
Shawnee *(G-10916)*
Chameleon Dental Products....E.... 913 281-5552
Kansas City *(G-3908)*
Henry Schein Inc....F.... 913 894-8444
Shawnee Mission *(G-11427)*
Midwest Orthodontics Inc....F.... 316 942-8703
Wichita *(G-15097)*
Myrons Dental Laboratories....E.... 800 359-7111
Kansas City *(G-4276)*
Scope Inc....G.... 316 393-7414
Wichita *(G-15536)*
▼ Splintek Inc....E.... 816 531-1900
Lenexa *(G-6148)*

3844 X-ray Apparatus & Tubes

Harry B Rusk Company Inc....G.... 316 263-4680
Wichita *(G-14565)*
LSI International Inc....E.... 913 894-4493
Kansas City *(G-4208)*

3845 Electromedical & Electrotherapeutic Apparatus

Care 4 All Home Medical Eqp....G.... 620 223-4141
Fort Scott *(G-1957)*
Hearttraining LLC....G.... 913 402-6012
Overland Park *(G-8809)*
Lifesource Inc....G.... 913 660-9275
Lenexa *(G-5972)*
LSI International Inc....E.... 913 894-4493
Kansas City *(G-4208)*
M R I of Rock Creek....E.... 913 351-4674
Lansing *(G-4687)*
Relevium Labs Inc....F.... 614 568-7000
Dodge City *(G-1423)*
Revolutionary Bus Concepts Inc....D.... 913 385-5700
Shawnee Mission *(G-11793)*
Solid State Sonics & Elec....G.... 785 232-0497
Topeka *(G-13080)*
Vigilias LLC....E.... 800 924-8140
Wichita *(G-15907)*

3851 Ophthalmic Goods

Bushnell Group Holdings Inc....B.... 913 894-4224
Overland Park *(G-8496)*
Bushnell Holdings Inc....G.... 913 981-1929
Olathe *(G-7570)*
◆ Bushnell Holdings Inc....C.... 913 752-3400
Overland Park *(G-8497)*
Criss Optical Mfg Co Inc....G.... 316 529-0414
Wichita *(G-14131)*
▲ Donegan Optical Company Inc....E.... 913 492-2500
Shawnee Mission *(G-11314)*
Duffens Opticals....D.... 785 234-3481
Overland Park *(G-8663)*
Duffins-Langley Optical Co....D.... 913 492-5379
Shawnee Mission *(G-11320)*
Essilor Laboratories Amer Inc....D.... 800 397-2020
Overland Park *(G-8691)*
Midwest Lens Inc....F.... 913 894-1030
Shawnee Mission *(G-11634)*

3861 Photographic Eqpt & Splys

Canon Solutions America Inc....G.... 913 323-5010
Overland Park *(G-8508)*
◆ Inkcycle Inc....D.... 913 894-8387
Shawnee *(G-10973)*
Salina Microfilm....F.... 785 827-6648
Salina *(G-10680)*

3873 Watch & Clock Devices & Parts

◆ Brg Precision Products Inc....E.... 316 788-2000
Derby *(G-1225)*

39 MISCELLANEOUS MANUFACTURING INDUSTRIES

3911 Jewelry: Precious Metal

Burnells Creative Gold Inc....G.... 316 634-2822
Wichita *(G-13916)*
James Avery Craftsman Inc....F.... 913 307-0419
Overland Park *(G-8871)*
Mark Boose....G.... 785 234-4808
Topeka *(G-12860)*
Paco Designs Inc....G.... 913 541-1708
Shawnee Mission *(G-11713)*

3914 Silverware, Plated & Stainless Steel Ware

Stewarts Sports & Awards....G.... 620 241-5990
McPherson *(G-7028)*
◆ Vita Craft Corporation....D.... 913 631-6265
Shawnee Mission *(G-11982)*

3915 Jewelers Findings & Lapidary Work

Diamond Ethanol LLC....G.... 620 626-2026
Liberal *(G-6304)*

3931 Musical Instruments

▼ Reuter Organ Co Inc....E.... 785 843-2622
Lawrence *(G-5094)*

3944 Games, Toys & Children's Vehicles

Advanced Engine Machine Inc....G.... 785 825-6684
Salina *(G-10397)*
Bruces Woodworks LLC....F.... 913 441-1432
Bonner Springs *(G-543)*
Kansas Assn For Conserv & Envr....G.... 785 889-4384
Onaga *(G-8177)*
Midwest Contracting & Mfg....G.... 785 743-2026
WA Keeney *(G-13383)*
▲ Step2 Discovery LLC....E.... 620 232-2400
Pittsburg *(G-9940)*
World Publishing Inc....E.... 785 221-8174
Topeka *(G-13252)*

3949 Sporting & Athletic Goods, NEC

Aj Investors LLC....F.... 316 321-0580
El Dorado *(G-1526)*
American Fence and SEC Co Inc....G.... 316 945-5001
Wichita *(G-13691)*
▼ B P E Inc....G.... 620 343-3783
Emporia *(G-1700)*
▲ Backyard Adventures LLC....E.... 620 308-6863
Pittsburg *(G-9821)*
▲ Carlsons Choke Tube/NW Arms....F.... 785 626-3078
Atwood *(G-282)*
◆ Combat Brands LLC....E.... 913 689-2300
Lenexa *(G-5770)*
DVC Training Specialists LLC....G.... 913 908-3393
Gardner *(G-2340)*
◆ Epic Sports....C.... 316 612-0150
Bel Aire *(G-432)*
▲ First Team Sports Inc....G.... 620 663-6080
Hutchinson *(G-3289)*
GP Traps LLC....G.... 620 394-2341
Atlanta *(G-274)*
Herron Inc....G.... 913 731-2507
Paola *(G-9566)*
▼ Jayhawk Bowling Sup & Eqp Inc....F.... 785 842-3237
Lawrence *(G-4919)*
Lake Garnett Sporting Club....G.... 785 448-5803
Garnett *(G-2380)*
▲ Magnus Inc....G.... 620 793-9222
Great Bend *(G-2604)*
Oswald Manufacturing Co Inc....G.... 785 258-2877
Herington *(G-2980)*
Pro-Bound Sports LLC....F.... 785 666-4207
Dorrance *(G-1465)*
Rings and Cages Inc....G.... 816 945-7772
Bucyrus *(G-607)*
Rnn Enterprises LLC....F.... 913 499-1230
Overland Park *(G-9246)*
Rusty S Baits & Lures....F.... 620 842-5301
Anthony *(G-134)*
Shawnee Mission Builders LLC....G.... 913 631-7020
Shawnee Mission *(G-11854)*
Sports Nutz of Kansas Inc....F.... 913 400-7733
Kansas City *(G-4436)*
Star Innovations II LLC....E.... 913 764-7738
New Century *(G-7298)*
◆ Title Boxing LLC....C.... 913 438-4427
Lenexa *(G-6182)*

3952 Lead Pencils, Crayons & Artist's Mtrls

Company Business Intl Sarl....G.... 913 286-9771
Olathe *(G-7606)*

3953 Marking Devices

Advance Business Supply....G.... 785 440-7826
Topeka *(G-12292)*
E-Z Info Inc....F.... 913 367-5020
Atchison *(G-226)*
Snow Inc....G.... 785 869-2021
Lane *(G-4663)*
◆ Superior Rbr Stamp & Seal Inc....G.... 316 682-5511
Wichita *(G-15698)*
Wichita Stamp and Seal Inc....G.... 316 263-4223
Wichita *(G-16029)*

3955 Carbon Paper & Inked Ribbons

Perfect Output LLC....D.... 913 317-8400
Overland Park *(G-9154)*

3961 Costume Jewelry & Novelties

Swarovski North America Ltd....G.... 913 599-3791
Overland Park *(G-9381)*

3965 Fasteners, Buttons, Needles & Pins

Domestic Fastener & Forge Inc....F.... 913 888-9447
New Century *(G-7280)*

3991 Brooms & Brushes

Mobile Products Inc....C.... 903 759-0610
Hutchinson *(G-3384)*
▲ United Rotary Brush Corp....D.... 913 888-8450
Lenexa *(G-6203)*
▲ West Coast Equipment Inc....F.... 623 842-0978
Lenexa *(G-6226)*

3993 Signs & Advertising Displays

Allsigns LLC....G.... 785 232-5512
Topeka *(G-12308)*
Artstudio Signs & Design....F.... 620 663-3950
Hutchinson *(G-3207)*
Ballyhoo Banners....G.... 913 385-5050
Lenexa *(G-5684)*
Bandy Enterprises Inc....F.... 785 462-3361
Colby *(G-988)*
Barton Industries Inc....G.... 316 262-3171
Wichita *(G-13815)*
Brileys Designs & Signs....E.... 913 579-7533
Shawnee Mission *(G-11182)*
Coffelt Sign Co Inc....G.... 620 343-6411
Emporia *(G-1724)*
Commercial Sign Company Hay....F.... 785 625-1765
Hays *(G-2775)*
Creative Signs & Design Inc....G.... 785 233-8000
Topeka *(G-12528)*
Custom Neon & Vinyl Graphics....G.... 785 233-3218
Topeka *(G-12538)*
Cvr Manufacturing Inc....G.... 620 763-2500
Galesburg *(G-2091)*
E-Z Info Inc....F.... 913 367-5020
Atchison *(G-226)*
Excel Lighting LLC....G.... 816 461-4694
Kansas City *(G-3998)*
Excell Art Sign Products LLC....G.... 620 378-4477
Fredonia *(G-2031)*
Excellart Sign Products LLC....F.... 913 764-2364
Olathe *(G-7697)*
Express Print and Signs LLC....E.... 785 825-8434
Salina *(G-10491)*

Fast Signs Inc G 785 271-8899
Topeka *(G-12598)*
Fastsigns Inc G 913 649-3600
Overland Park *(G-8707)*
File A Gem Inc G 620 856-3800
Baxter Springs *(G-407)*
Finch Sign Company Inc G 785 423-3213
Baldwin City *(G-360)*
Freestyle Sign Co Inc G 316 267-5507
Wichita *(G-14420)*
George Eschbaugh Advg Inc E 785 658-2105
Wilson *(G-16105)*
Gleason & Son Signs Inc G 785 823-8615
Salina *(G-10512)*
Graphics Systems Inc D 316 267-4171
Wichita *(G-14497)*
Halfpricebannerscom Inc G 913 441-9299
Shawnee *(G-10966)*
◆ Hasty Awards Inc D 785 242-5297
Ottawa *(G-8278)*
Hedges Neon Sales Inc G 785 827-9341
Salina *(G-10540)*
Hightech Signs LLC E 913 894-4422
Kansas City *(G-4079)*
Hmong Manufacturing Inc E 913 371-2752
Kansas City *(G-4083)*
Hutch Sign G 620 663-6108
Hutchinson *(G-3317)*
Js Sign & Awning LLC G 785 776-8860
Manhattan *(G-6667)*
▲ K C Sign Express Inc G 913 432-2500
Shawnee Mission *(G-11506)*
Kansas Graphics Inc G 620 273-6111
Cottonwood Falls *(G-1155)*
▼ Lowen Corporation B 620 663-2161
Hutchinson *(G-3358)*
Luminous Neon Inc D 620 662-2363
Hutchinson *(G-3360)*
Luminous Neon Inc G 785 842-4930
Lawrence *(G-5002)*
Luminous Neon Inc G 785 823-1789
Salina *(G-10586)*
Luminous Neon Inc E 913 780-3330
Olathe *(G-7867)*
Midtown Signs LLC F 816 561-7446
Kansas City *(G-4249)*
Midwest Sign Company LLC F 913 568-7552
Kansas City *(G-4258)*
Millers Sign Shoppe LLC G 913 441-6883
Bonner Springs *(G-563)*
National Sign Company Inc F 785 242-4111
Ottawa *(G-8293)*
Next Led Signs LLC F 888 263-6530
Wichita *(G-15174)*
Northwest Awards & Signs G 785 621-2116
Hays *(G-2880)*
Occk Inc E 785 738-3490
Beloit *(G-498)*
Oversize Warning Products Inc G 620 792-5266
Great Bend *(G-2620)*
Power Ad Company Inc E 785 823-9483
Salina *(G-10638)*
Print Source Inc D 316 945-7052
Wichita *(G-15348)*
Rise Vision USA Inc F 866 770-1150
Wichita *(G-15465)*
Rons Sign Co Inc E 316 267-8914
Wichita *(G-15482)*
Schurle Signs Inc G 785 832-9897
Lawrence *(G-5104)*
Schurle Signs Inc F 785 485-2885
Riley *(G-10209)*
▼ Selex Es Inc D 913 945-2600
Overland Park *(G-9293)*
Sign Here Inc G 913 856-0148
Gardner *(G-2363)*
Sign House Inc E 785 827-2729
Salina *(G-10707)*
Sign Solutions F 620 442-5649
Arkansas City *(G-179)*
Signs & Design LLC G 316 264-7446
Wichita *(G-15592)*
Signs By Shire Inc G 316 838-1362
Park City *(G-9645)*
Signs of Business Inc F 316 683-5700
Wichita *(G-15593)*
Simon & Simon Inc G 913 888-9889
Overland Park *(G-9311)*
Star Signs & Graphics Inc E 785 842-2881
Lawrence *(G-5120)*
◆ Stouse LLC C 913 764-5757
New Century *(G-7301)*
Thomas Outdoor Advertising Inc G 785 537-2010
Manhattan *(G-6825)*
◆ Tradenet Publishing Inc C 913 856-4070
Gardner *(G-2365)*
Trimark Signworks Inc E 316 263-2224
Wichita *(G-15800)*
U S S A Inc G 316 686-1653
Wichita *(G-15826)*
Vital Sign Center G 913 262-4447
Kansas City *(G-4522)*
Welch Sign Co Inc G 913 831-4499
Shawnee Mission *(G-11998)*
Wrap Factory G 913 667-3010
Edwardsville *(G-1522)*
X-Press Signs and Graphics LLC G 316 613-2360
Wichita *(G-16083)*
Young Hoins Service Group LLC F 913 772-0708
Leavenworth *(G-5309)*
Young Sign Co Inc E 913 651-5432
Leavenworth *(G-5310)*

3999 Manufacturing Industries, NEC

Al Industries Prof Corp F 918 401-9641
Wichita *(G-13645)*
All American Pet Brands Inc G 913 951-4999
Shawnee *(G-10907)*
All Crtres Veterinary Hosp P A F 316 721-3993
Wichita *(G-13663)*
▲ Baco Corporation F 316 945-5300
Wichita *(G-13792)*
Barks N Bows Dog Grooming G 785 823-1627
Salina *(G-10421)*
Brightwell Dispensers Inc G 913 956-4909
Lenexa *(G-5715)*
BTR Inc G 620 221-7071
Winfield *(G-16117)*
Centurion Manufacturing G 316 210-3504
Benton *(G-515)*
Countryside Pet Clinic PA E 316 733-8433
Andover *(G-88)*
▲ Creason Corrugating McHy Inc F 423 629-5532
Park City *(G-9613)*
Crosswind Industries Inc G 785 380-8668
Topeka *(G-12532)*
D J Inc F 785 667-4651
Assaria *(G-200)*
Dw Industries LLC G 913 782-7575
Olathe *(G-7662)*
E C Manufacturing D 913 825-3077
Shawnee *(G-10942)*
Easy Money Pawn Shop Inc G 316 687-2727
Wichita *(G-14255)*
El Paso Animal Clinic F 316 788-1561
Derby *(G-1243)*
Emco Specialty Products Inc G 913 281-4555
Kansas City *(G-3986)*
Empire Candle Co LLC G 913 621-4555
Kansas City *(G-3987)*
Empire Candle Co LLC F 913 621-4555
Kansas City *(G-3988)*
◆ Empire Candle Co LLC C 913 621-4555
Kansas City *(G-3989)*
Evans Industries Inc G 316 262-2551
Wichita *(G-14310)*
Ewy Animal Hosp Inc G 785 823-8428
Salina *(G-10487)*
Fairview Mills LLC E 785 336-2148
Seneca *(G-10866)*
Fremont Industries Inc G 913 962-7676
Olathe *(G-7718)*
Fur Is Flying LLC G 785 621-7300
Hays *(G-2815)*
Graphics Systems Inc D 316 267-4171
Wichita *(G-14497)*
Kls Industries LLC G 877 952-2548
Shawnee *(G-10983)*
Memory and Music Inc F 913 449-4473
Overland Park *(G-9009)*
Mkc Golf 3 LLC G 913 526-3312
Lenexa *(G-6009)*
Oneok Hydrocarbon LP G 620 834-2204
Conway *(G-1135)*
Orange Industries LLC G 816 694-1919
Mission *(G-7134)*
Orthman Mfg E 785 754-9985
Quinter *(G-10183)*
Peavey Corporation D 913 888-0600
Lenexa *(G-6047)*
Percision Mfg G 913 362-9244
Shawnee *(G-11010)*
▲ Pop-A-Shot Enterprise LLC G 785 827-6229
Salina *(G-10637)*
Rokenn Enterprises Inc G 785 523-4251
Delphos *(G-1217)*
Sands Enterprises Inc G 316 942-8686
Wichita *(G-15518)*
Signature Manufacturing F 913 766-0680
Merriam *(G-7104)*
Sparker Industries Inc G 913 963-5261
Bucyrus *(G-610)*
Thyssenkrupp Elevator Corp F 316 529-2233
Wichita *(G-15764)*
Tr Sales & Distribution Inc F 800 478-5468
Olathe *(G-8118)*
Warren Consulting Inc E 620 727-2468
Hutchinson *(G-3481)*
Waxman Candles Inc G 785 843-8593
Lawrence *(G-5181)*
▼ Weis Fire Safety Equip Co Inc F 785 825-9527
Salina *(G-10765)*
West Wichita Pet Clinic F 316 722-0100
Wichita *(G-15959)*

40 RAILROAD TRANSPORTATION

4011 Railroads, Line-Hauling Operations

Alabama Southern Railroad LLC E 620 231-2230
Pittsburg *(G-9806)*
American Refrigerated Ex Inc F 913 406-8562
Olathe *(G-7527)*
Ann Arbor Railroad Inc D 620 231-2230
Pittsburg *(G-9809)*
Austin Western Railroad E 620 231-2230
Pittsburg *(G-9817)*
B N S F Inc A 316 284-3260
Newton *(G-7316)*
Bnsf Railway Company C 316 284-3224
Newton *(G-7320)*
Bnsf Railway Company E 620 227-5977
Dodge City *(G-1310)*
Bnsf Railway Company F 913 551-4882
Kansas City *(G-3868)*
Bnsf Railway Company E 620 441-2276
Arkansas City *(G-148)*
Bnsf Railway Company D 913 893-4295
Edgerton *(G-1480)*
Bnsf Railway Company E 913 551-2604
Kansas City *(G-3869)*
Bnsf Railway Company C 620 203-2586
Emporia *(G-1706)*
Bnsf Railway Company D 785 435-7021
Topeka *(G-12392)*
Bnsf Railway Company D 620 429-3850
Columbus *(G-1061)*
Bnsf Railway Company F 913 888-5250
Shawnee Mission *(G-11173)*
Bnsf Railway Company B 785 435-2000
Topeka *(G-12393)*
Bnsf Railway Company C 620 399-4201
Wellington *(G-13491)*
Bnsf Railway Company D 817 352-1000
Shawnee Mission *(G-11174)*
Bnsf Railway Company E 316 708-4472
Augusta *(G-312)*
Burlington Nthrn Santa Fe LLC D 913 577-5521
Lenexa *(G-5721)*
Genesee & Wyoming Inc F 785 899-2307
Goodland *(G-2473)*
Great Northwest Railroad F 620 231-2230
Pittsburg *(G-9868)*
Kanawha River Railroad LLC E 620 231-2030
Pittsburg *(G-9885)*
Kansas & Oklahoma Railroad LLC F 620 231-2230
Pittsburg *(G-9887)*
Louisiana Southern Railroad F 620 235-7360
Pittsburg *(G-9895)*
Railamerica Inc D 785 543-6527
Phillipsburg *(G-9796)*
South Kansas and Okla RR Inc E 620 336-2291
Cherryvale *(G-813)*
South Kansas and Okla RR Inc E 620 231-2230
Pittsburg *(G-9939)*
South Kansas and Okla RR Inc F 620 221-3470
Winfield *(G-16173)*
Union Pacific Railroad Company D 316 250-0260
McPherson *(G-7034)*
Union Pacific Railroad Company D 316 268-9446
Wichita *(G-15838)*

S I C

Union Pacific Railroad Company ....D....... 785 232-7814
Topeka *(G-13204)*
Union Pacific Railroad Company ....C....... 209 642-1032
Pratt *(G-10163)*
Watco Companies LLC ....C....... 575 745-2329
Pittsburg *(G-9963)*
Watco Companies LLC ....D....... 316 263-3113
Wichita *(G-15935)*
Watco Companies LLC ....D....... 620 336-2291
Cherryvale *(G-815)*
Watco Railroad Co Holdings ....F....... 620 231-2230
Pittsburg *(G-9964)*

4013 Switching & Terminal Svcs

Bakken Oil Express LLC ....F....... 316 630-0287
Wichita *(G-13797)*
Bnsf Railway Company ....D....... 620 896-2096
Harper *(G-2716)*
RJ Crman Derailment Svcs LLC ....F....... 913 371-1537
Kansas City *(G-4381)*
South Kansas and Okla RR Inc ....E....... 620 336-2291
Cherryvale *(G-813)*
South Kansas and Okla RR Inc ....F....... 620 221-3470
Winfield *(G-16173)*
Watco Inc ....D....... 208 734-4644
Pittsburg *(G-9962)*
Watco Transloading LLC ....D....... 620 231-2230
Pittsburg *(G-9966)*
Wichita Terminal Association ....F....... 316 262-0441
Wichita *(G-16038)*

41 LOCAL AND SUBURBAN TRANSIT AND INTERURBAN HIGHWAY PASSENGER TRANSPORTATION

4111 Local & Suburban Transit

Bell Taxi and Trnsp Inc ....F....... 785 238-6161
Junction City *(G-3672)*
County of Johnson ....F....... 913 782-2210
Olathe *(G-7620)*
CTI Freight Systems Inc ....F....... 913 236-7400
Bucyrus *(G-595)*
Ds Bus Lines Inc ....D....... 913 384-1190
Bonner Springs *(G-551)*
Durham School Services L P ....E....... 620 331-7088
Independence *(G-3512)*
Extreme Limousine LLC ....F....... 913 831-2039
Shawnee *(G-10951)*
Finney Cnty Committee On Aging ....E....... 620 272-3626
Garden City *(G-2160)*
First Student Inc ....D....... 913 422-8501
Lenexa *(G-5857)*
Flint Hlls Area Trnsp Agcy Inc ....E....... 785 537-6345
Manhattan *(G-6635)*
Greyhound Lines Inc ....E....... 785 827-9754
Salina *(G-10523)*
Lafarge North America Inc ....B....... 913 780-6809
Olathe *(G-7852)*
Lansing Unified Schl Dst 469 ....E....... 913 250-0749
Lansing *(G-4680)*
Mv Transportation Inc ....E....... 785 312-7054
Lawrence *(G-5034)*
Rnw Transit LLC ....F....... 785 285-0083
Sabetha *(G-10326)*
Southwest KS Coord Trans Counc ....E....... 620 227-8803
Dodge City *(G-1432)*
Topeka Metropolitan Trnst Auth ....D....... 785 233-2011
Topeka *(G-13182)*
Tri-Valley Developmental Svcs ....D....... 620 223-3990
Fort Scott *(G-2012)*
Tri-Valley Developmental Svcs ....D....... 620 365-3307
Iola *(G-3637)*
Wheatland Enterprises Inc ....E....... 816 756-1700
Leawood *(G-5599)*
Yellowfin Transportation Inc ....F....... 913 645-4834
Shawnee *(G-11057)*

4119 Local Passenger Transportation: NEC

9 Line Medical Solutions LLC ....F....... 402 470-1696
Manhattan *(G-6526)*
A & A Medical Trnsp Inc ....F....... 785 233-8212
Topeka *(G-12277)*
Agenda Usa Inc ....E....... 913 268-4466
Shawnee Mission *(G-11084)*
Airmd LLC ....E....... 316 932-1440
Wichita *(G-13654)*
American Medical Response Inc ....C....... 913 227-0911
Kansas City *(G-3805)*
Bennington Ambulance Service ....F....... 785 488-3768
Bennington *(G-512)*
Chase County Ems ....F....... 620 273-6590
Cottonwood Falls *(G-1152)*
Cherokee Cnty Ambulance & Assn ....E....... 620 429-3018
Columbus *(G-1065)*
Cherokee County Ambulance ....F....... 620 856-2561
Baxter Springs *(G-402)*
City of Galena ....F....... 620 783-5065
Galena *(G-2071)*
City of Salina ....D....... 785 826-7340
Salina *(G-10451)*
Claflin Ambulance Service Assn ....E....... 620 587-3498
Claflin *(G-840)*
County of Clay ....E....... 785 632-2166
Clay Center *(G-858)*
County of Ford ....F....... 620 227-4556
Dodge City *(G-1332)*
County of Franklin ....F....... 785 229-7300
Ottawa *(G-8260)*
County of Norton ....E....... 785 877-5784
Norton *(G-7442)*
County of Osborne ....F....... 785 346-2379
Osborne *(G-8207)*
County of Pratt ....E....... 620 672-4130
Pratt *(G-10103)*
County of Russell ....E....... 785 445-3720
Russell *(G-10269)*
County of Stevens ....E....... 620 544-2562
Hugoton *(G-3156)*
County of Thomas ....E....... 785 460-4585
Colby *(G-1001)*
County of Trego ....F....... 785 743-5337
Wakeeney *(G-13385)*
Crescent Limousines ....F....... 785 232-2236
Topeka *(G-12530)*
Critical Care Transfer Inc ....F....... 620 353-4145
Ulysses *(G-13293)*
Developmental Svcs NW Kans Inc ....F....... 785 621-2078
Hays *(G-2787)*
Ellsworth County Ambulance ....E....... 785 472-3454
Ellsworth *(G-1668)*
Extreme Limousine LLC ....F....... 913 831-2039
Shawnee *(G-10951)*
Finney County Emergency Med ....E....... 620 272-3822
Garden City *(G-2163)*
Jewell County Ems ....E....... 785 378-3069
Mankato *(G-6858)*
Kingman Emergency Medical Svcs ....E....... 620 532-5624
Kingman *(G-4601)*
Kiowa County Ems ....F....... 620 723-3112
Greensburg *(G-2681)*
Life Touch Ems Inc ....F....... 785 825-5115
Salina *(G-10582)*
Marysville Chamber Commerce ....F....... 785 562-2359
Marysville *(G-6896)*
Medevac Midamerica Inc ....C....... 785 233-2400
Topeka *(G-12878)*
Medi Coach LLC ....E....... 913 825-1945
Shawnee *(G-10993)*
Miami County Emergency Med Svc ....E....... 913 294-5010
Paola *(G-9571)*
Nmrmc Ems ....E....... 620 244-3522
Erie *(G-1863)*
Otl Logistics Inc ....D....... 816 918-7688
Basehor *(G-386)*
Plainville Ambulance Service ....F....... 785 434-2530
Plainville *(G-9989)*
Pottawatomie Cnty Emrgncy Svcs ....E....... 785 456-0911
Wamego *(G-13434)*
Quinter Ambulance Service Inc ....E....... 785 754-3734
Quinter *(G-10185)*
Reno County Ambulance Service ....E....... 620 665-2120
Hutchinson *(G-3424)*
Renzenberger Inc ....C....... 913 631-0450
Lenexa *(G-6104)*
Republic County Ems ....F....... 785 527-7149
Belleville *(G-464)*
S&S Limousine LLC ....F....... 316 794-3340
Goddard *(G-2454)*
Saint Lukes Hosp Garnett Inc ....C....... 785 448-3131
Garnett *(G-2388)*
Security Transport Service ....E....... 785 267-3030
Topeka *(G-13056)*
Sedan AR Egy Mdl Sv Dt 2 Inc ....E....... 620 725-5670
Sedan *(G-10847)*
Stretch It Limousine Service ....F....... 913 269-1955
Shawnee Mission *(G-11903)*
Techs Inc ....D....... 785 364-1911
Holton *(G-3112)*
Transcare of Ks LLC ....E....... 620 431-6300
Chanute *(G-772)*
Wheatland Enterprises Inc ....E....... 913 381-3504
Leawood *(G-5598)*
Wheatland Enterprises Inc ....E....... 816 756-1700
Leawood *(G-5599)*
Yellowfin Transportation Inc ....F....... 913 645-4834
Shawnee *(G-11057)*

4121 Taxi Cabs

American Cab Inc ....F....... 316 262-7511
Wichita *(G-13687)*
Bell Taxi and Trnsp Inc ....F....... 785 238-6161
Junction City *(G-3672)*
Best Cabs Inc ....F....... 316 838-2233
Wichita *(G-13836)*
Capitol City Taxi Inc ....F....... 785 267-3777
Topeka *(G-12435)*
Coffey County Trnsp Inc ....F....... 620 364-1935
Burlington *(G-631)*
Edward French Loy ....F....... 785 825-4646
Salina *(G-10485)*
Gorydz Inc ....F....... 913 486-1665
Kansas City *(G-4040)*
Lafarge North America Inc ....B....... 913 780-6809
Olathe *(G-7852)*
Sunflower Taxi Courier Svc LLC ....F....... 785 826-1881
Salina *(G-10727)*
Yellow Cab Taxi Tpeka Kans LLC ....E....... 785 357-4444
Topeka *(G-13254)*

4131 Intercity & Rural Bus Transportation

City of Wichita ....C....... 316 265-7221
Wichita *(G-14031)*
Kincaid Coach Lines Inc ....D....... 913 441-6200
Edwardsville *(G-1506)*
Railcrew Xpress LLC ....A....... 913 928-5000
Lenexa *(G-6089)*
Renzenberger Inc ....C....... 913 631-0450
Lenexa *(G-6104)*
Shuttle Bus General Pub Trnsp ....D....... 620 326-3953
Wellington *(G-13529)*
Yellowfin Transportation Inc ....F....... 913 645-4834
Shawnee *(G-11057)*

4141 Local Bus Charter Svc

Agenda Usa Inc ....E....... 913 268-4466
Shawnee Mission *(G-11084)*
Just For Kids Express ....F....... 785 238-8555
Junction City *(G-3708)*
Mercer Bus Service ....F....... 785 836-7174
Carbondale *(G-684)*
National Express LLC ....E....... 913 837-4470
Louisburg *(G-6460)*
National Express LLC ....E....... 620 662-1299
Hutchinson *(G-3388)*
National Express LLC ....F....... 620 326-3318
Wellington *(G-13519)*

4142 Bus Charter Service, Except Local

Busco Inc ....F....... 816 453-8727
Manhattan *(G-6573)*
Durham School Services L P ....E....... 620 331-7088
Independence *(G-3512)*
First Student Inc ....E....... 620 251-8441
Coffeyville *(G-938)*
Just For Kids Express ....F....... 785 238-8555
Junction City *(G-3708)*
Ottawa Bus Service Inc ....E....... 913 829-6644
Olathe *(G-7966)*
Overland Charters Inc ....E....... 316 652-9463
Wichita *(G-15241)*
Prestige Trnsp Systems ....E....... 316 263-9141
Wichita *(G-15339)*

4151 School Buses

All Point Transportation LLC ....F....... 785 273-4730
Topeka *(G-12305)*
Apple Bus Company ....D....... 913 592-5121
Spring Hill *(G-12077)*
Derby Public Schools ....D....... 316 788-8450
Derby *(G-1237)*
Durham School Services L P ....E....... 913 755-3593
Osawatomie *(G-8192)*
Durham School Services L P ....E....... 620 331-7088
Independence *(G-3512)*

Easton Bus Service Inc .... D 913 682-2244
Leavenworth *(G-5235)*
First Student Inc .... C 785 841-3594
Lawrence *(G-4864)*
First Student Inc .... F 913 856-5650
Gardner *(G-2345)*
First Student Inc .... C 913 782-1050
Olathe *(G-7713)*
Junction CT-Ft Rly Mht Trnsinc .... F 785 762-2219
Junction City *(G-3707)*
National Express LLC .... E 913 837-4470
Louisburg *(G-6460)*
National Express LLC .... E 620 662-1299
Hutchinson *(G-3388)*
National Express LLC .... F 620 326-3318
Wellington *(G-13519)*
Pratt Unified 12th Dist Transp .... F 620 672-4590
Pratt *(G-10145)*
Unified School District 383 .... D 785 587-2190
Manhattan *(G-6838)*

4173 Bus Terminal & Svc Facilities

Fleet Services Topeka .... E 785 368-3735
Topeka *(G-12616)*
Hutchinson Usd 308 .... F 620 615-5575
Hutchinson *(G-3327)*
Reload Express Inc .... F 620 231-2230
Pittsburg *(G-9926)*

42 MOTOR FREIGHT TRANSPORTATION AND WAREHOUSING

4212 Local Trucking Without Storage

A&Atruck Rental/3 Men With .... F 785 236-0003
Topeka *(G-12280)*
A-Plus Logistics LLC .... E 316 945-5757
Park City *(G-9598)*
ABC Taxi Cab Company Inc .... F 316 264-4222
Wichita *(G-13596)*
Allied Courier Systems Inc .... F 913 383-8666
Stilwell *(G-12134)*
Allied Services LLC .... D 620 783-5841
Galena *(G-2068)*
American Trucking Inc .... F 620 594-2481
Sawyer *(G-10794)*
Anderson & Sons Trucking Inc .... E 913 422-3171
Kansas City *(G-3809)*
Apartment Movers Inc .... E 316 267-5300
Wichita *(G-13717)*
Apex Trucking Inc .... E 316 943-0774
Park City *(G-9601)*
Ash Grove Materials Corp .... D 913 345-2030
Overland Park *(G-8404)*
Automotive Associates .... E 620 231-6350
Pittsburg *(G-9818)*
B & B Delivery Enterprise LLC .... F 913 541-9090
Kansas City *(G-3832)*
Bekemeyer Enterprises Inc .... F 785 325-2274
Washington *(G-13459)*
Better Hauling Co .... F 316 943-5865
Valley Center *(G-13337)*
Bettys Trucking Incorporated .... F 913 583-3666
De Soto *(G-1194)*
Bingham Transportation Inc .... D 620 679-9810
Treece *(G-13267)*
Black & Winsor Inc .... D 316 943-0703
Wichita *(G-13853)*
Bourbon Trucking LLC .... E 785 428-3030
Jewell *(G-3649)*
Boyd Delivery Systems Inc .... D 913 677-6700
Westwood *(G-13551)*
Brady Fluid Service Inc .... F 620 275-5827
Garden City *(G-2116)*
Briggs Trucking Inc .... E 620 699-3448
Reading *(G-10198)*
Butler Transport Inc .... C 913 321-0047
Kansas City *(G-3882)*
C & C Truck Line .... F 785 243-3719
Concordia *(G-1104)*
C & H Trucking LLC .... F 316 794-8282
Goddard *(G-2430)*
C Bar P Trucking Inc .... E 316 722-2019
Goddard *(G-2431)*
CD&h Inc .... F 316 320-7187
El Dorado *(G-1544)*
Classic Motor Freight LLC .... E 913 586-5911
Leawood *(G-5353)*
Clayton J Befort .... F 785 625-7628
Hays *(G-2770)*
Coleman American Moving Svcs .... F 785 537-7284
Manhattan *(G-6592)*
Coomes Inc .... D 785 543-2759
Phillipsburg *(G-9781)*
Cutting Edge Trucking Inc .... E 913 837-2249
Louisburg *(G-6445)*
D & A Trucking Inc .... F 620 465-3370
Haven *(G-2729)*
D Doubled Inc .... F 913 334-1075
Shawnee *(G-10938)*
Deffenbaugh Industries Inc .... A 913 631-3300
Kansas City *(G-3965)*
Double T Ind Inc .... E 620 593-4357
Rolla *(G-10232)*
Eagle Environmental Svcs LLC .... E 316 944-2445
Wichita *(G-14250)*
Everetts Inc .... F 785 263-4172
Abilene *(G-28)*
Federal Express Corporation .... D 316 941-4438
Wichita *(G-14347)*
Fedex Ground Package Sys Inc .... B 913 422-3161
Shawnee Mission *(G-11363)*
Fedex Ground Package Sys Inc .... E 800 463-3339
Topeka *(G-12602)*
Feed Mercantile Transport Inc .... F 620 275-4158
Garden City *(G-2159)*
Ferco Inc .... E 785 825-6380
Salina *(G-10500)*
Fexp Inc .... E 785 336-2148
Seneca *(G-10867)*
Galen Blenn Trucking .... E 785 457-3995
Westmoreland *(G-13548)*
Get A Move On Inc .... E 316 729-4897
Wichita *(G-14461)*
Girton Propane Service Inc .... D 785 632-6273
Clay Center *(G-866)*
Gorges Dairy Inc .... F 620 545-7297
Viola *(G-13379)*
Haag Oil Company LLC .... F 785 357-0270
Topeka *(G-12657)*
Harris Quality Inc .... D 402 332-5857
Olathe *(G-7755)*
Hdb Construction Inc .... E 785 232-5444
Topeka *(G-12669)*
Heartland Moving & Storage .... F 316 554-0224
Wichita *(G-14586)*
Herrmans Excavating Inc .... E 785 233-4146
Topeka *(G-12687)*
Hit Inc .... E 913 281-4040
Kansas City *(G-4082)*
J & B Inc .... F 816 590-1174
Shawnee Mission *(G-11470)*
J S Transportation LLC .... E 816 651-1827
Lenexa *(G-5926)*
Jack B Kelley Inc .... D 620 792-8205
Great Bend *(G-2594)*
Jack Cooper Transport Co Inc .... C 913 321-8500
Kansas City *(G-4116)*
Jantz Inc .... F 620 345-2783
Moundridge *(G-7186)*
Jim Mitten Trucking Inc .... F 785 672-3279
Oakley *(G-7477)*
K & L Tank Truck Service Inc .... F 620 277-0101
Garden City *(G-2210)*
K C I Roadrunner Express Inc .... D 785 238-6161
Junction City *(G-3710)*
Kansas City Coml Whsng Co .... E 913 287-3800
Kansas City *(G-4144)*
Kansas Trucking LLC .... F 913 586-5911
De Soto *(G-1205)*
Kenco Trucking Inc .... E 316 943-4881
Wichita *(G-14848)*
Kings Moving & Storage Inc .... E 785 238-7341
Junction City *(G-3715)*
Knight Trucking LLC .... E 620 256-6525
Lebo *(G-5607)*
Korte Trucking Inc .... F 620 276-8873
Garden City *(G-2220)*
L & S Scott Inc .... F 785 643-1488
Salina *(G-10577)*
Long Island Grain Co Inc .... F 785 854-7431
Long Island *(G-6428)*
Lrm Industries Inc .... E 785 843-1688
Lawrence *(G-5001)*
Macconnell Enterprises LLC .... E 785 885-8081
Natoma *(G-7231)*
Magna Tech Inc .... E 620 431-3490
Chanute *(G-740)*
Mail Contractors of America .... D 913 287-9811
Kansas City *(G-4215)*
Marroquin Express Inc .... F 316 295-0595
Maize *(G-6516)*
Mary Carr .... E 913 207-0900
Kansas City *(G-4221)*
Materials Transport Company .... B 913 345-2030
Shawnee Mission *(G-11602)*
Max Rieke & Brothers Inc .... D 913 631-7111
Shawnee *(G-10991)*
Meemaws Country Kitchen .... F 913 352-6297
Pleasanton *(G-9998)*
Metro Companies Inc .... D 316 838-3345
Wichita *(G-15059)*
Michael Bennett Trucking Inc .... F 785 336-2942
Seneca *(G-10873)*
Midwest Concrete Materials Inc .... C 785 776-8811
Manhattan *(G-6746)*
Moonlite Trucking Inc .... F 620 767-5499
Council Grove *(G-1172)*
Moving Kings LLC .... E 913 882-2121
Overland Park *(G-9058)*
Mr PS Truckn Inc .... E 785 372-4371
Rush Center *(G-10262)*
Myfreightworld Carrier MGT Inc .... E 877 549-9438
Overland Park *(G-9066)*
N T S LLC .... E 913 281-5353
Kansas City *(G-4277)*
New Image Concrete Design LLC .... F 913 489-1699
Shawnee *(G-11005)*
Nichols Water Svc An Okla Corp .... F 620 624-5582
Liberal *(G-6350)*
NL Wilson Moving Inc .... E 913 652-9488
Olathe *(G-7923)*
NTS LLC .... E 913 321-3838
Kansas City *(G-4291)*
Penner Trucking Inc .... F 620 353-8475
Sublette *(G-12206)*
Price Truck Line Inc .... F 785 625-2603
Hays *(G-2888)*
Prockish Trucking & Excavating .... F 785 456-7320
Louisville *(G-6470)*
Quality Carriers Inc .... F 913 281-0901
Kansas City *(G-4351)*
Quicksilver Ex Courier of MO .... D 913 321-5959
Kansas City *(G-4354)*
Ramon E Guardiola .... F 620 355-4266
Lakin *(G-4658)*
Randolph Carter Entps Inc .... F 913 837-3955
Louisburg *(G-6464)*
Richman Helstrom Trucking Inc .... F 785 478-3186
Topeka *(G-13014)*
Rick Sauceda Trucking LLC .... F 913 231-8584
Centerville *(G-696)*
Riverside Transport Inc .... D 913 233-5500
Kansas City *(G-4380)*
Roady Trucking .... F 785 562-1221
Marysville *(G-6908)*
Robinsons Delivery Service .... E 913 281-4952
Kansas City *(G-4385)*
Ronald Carlile .... F 620 624-2632
Liberal *(G-6361)*
S Noble Trucking Inc .... F 620 704-0886
Mc Cune *(G-6922)*
S P D Transfer Service Lc .... F 913 321-0333
Shawnee Mission *(G-11820)*
Sallee Inc .... D 620 227-3320
Dodge City *(G-1426)*
Satchell Creek Express Inc .... E 316 775-1300
Augusta *(G-342)*
Schueman Transfer .... E 785 378-3114
Mankato *(G-6861)*
Scott Heller Trucking .... E 816 591-1638
Lenexa *(G-6119)*
SD & S Trucking LLC .... E 316 744-2318
Park City *(G-9642)*
Speedway Service Corporation .... F 913 488-6695
Olathe *(G-8077)*
Steve Hilker Trucking Inc .... E 620 855-3257
Cimarron *(G-837)*
Studer Truck Line Inc .... F 785 353-2241
Beattie *(G-420)*
Sunflower Taxi Courier Svc LLC .... F 785 826-1881
Salina *(G-10727)*
Supervan Service Co Inc .... E 913 281-4044
Kansas City *(G-4450)*
T L C Trucking LLC .... F 620 277-0140
Holcomb *(G-3081)*
Tandem Truck Service Inc .... F 913 782-5454
Olathe *(G-8101)*

S I C

Taylor Crane & Rigging Inc....D....620 251-1530
Coffeyville *(G-981)*
Terry Trucking & Wrecking LLC....F....913 281-3854
Kansas City *(G-4465)*
Thomas and Sons Trucking LLC....E....785 454-3839
Downs *(G-1473)*
Trans Services Inc....E....913 592-3878
Spring Hill *(G-12102)*
Transervice Logistics Inc....D....785 493-4295
Salina *(G-10739)*
Transwood Inc....E....620 331-5699
Independence *(G-3567)*
Transwood Edwardsville66....E....913 745-1773
Kansas City *(G-4473)*
U S Road Freight Express Inc....E....316 942-9944
Wichita *(G-15825)*
United Petro Transports Inc....E....316 263-6868
Park City *(G-9651)*
Unlimited Logistics LLC....F....913 851-4900
Stilwell *(G-12178)*
Valley Trucking Trailer....F....785 945-3554
Valley Falls *(G-13370)*
Wakeeney Truck Line Inc....F....785 743-6778
Wakeeney *(G-13394)*
Wal-Mac Inc....F....620 356-3422
Ulysses *(G-13331)*
Warren Davidson Trucking....F....785 625-5126
Hays *(G-2929)*
William R Harris Trucking....F....913 422-5551
Shawnee Mission *(G-12010)*
Wynne Transport Service Inc....E....316 321-3900
El Dorado *(G-1615)*
Yrc Inc....B....913 696-6100
Kansas City *(G-4565)*

4213 Trucking, Except Local

A Arnold of Kansas City LLC....E....913 829-8267
Olathe *(G-7503)*
A-Plus Logistics LLC....E....316 945-5757
Park City *(G-9598)*
ABF Freight System Inc....F....316 943-1241
Wichita *(G-13598)*
Accord Services Inc....E....913 281-1879
Kansas City *(G-3781)*
Aci Motor Freight Inc....E....316 522-5559
Wichita *(G-13605)*
ADM Trucking Inc....F....785 899-6500
Goodland *(G-2459)*
Albert G Hogoboom....E....316 321-1397
El Dorado *(G-1527)*
All Freight Systems Inc....E....913 281-1203
Kansas City *(G-3797)*
Ark City Warehouse Truckline....F....620 442-7305
Arkansas City *(G-144)*
Austin Trucking....F....316 323-0313
Augusta *(G-310)*
B & B Redimix Inc....F....785 543-5133
Phillipsburg *(G-9777)*
B & H Freight Line Inc....F....913 621-1840
Kansas City *(G-3834)*
B C A /fry-wagner Inc....E....573 499-0000
Lenexa *(G-5679)*
Bar K Bar Trucking Inc....F....620 257-5118
Lyons *(G-6479)*
Beaver Express Service LLC....E....316 946-5700
Wichita *(G-13824)*
Belger Cartage Service Inc....E....316 943-0101
Wichita *(G-13829)*
Bennet Rogers Pipe Coating....F....913 371-5288
Kansas City *(G-3853)*
Bestmark Express Inc....E....620 273-7018
Strong City *(G-12191)*
Bills Frank Trucking Inc....E....620 736-2875
Severy *(G-10889)*
Box Central Inc....F....316 689-8484
Wichita *(G-13875)*
Briggs Trucking Inc....E....620 699-3448
Reading *(G-10198)*
Brisk Transportation....E....620 669-3481
Hutchinson *(G-3225)*
Browns Super Service Inc....F....785 267-1080
Topeka *(G-12409)*
Butler Transport Inc....C....913 321-0047
Kansas City *(G-3882)*
C & C Truck Line....F....785 243-3719
Concordia *(G-1104)*
C & H Trucking LLC....F....316 794-8282
Goddard *(G-2430)*
Cal Southern Transport Co....E....785 232-4202
Topeka *(G-12418)*
Cargill Mt Lgstics Sltions Inc....E....877 596-4062
Wichita *(G-13949)*
Cargill Mt Lgstics Sltions Inc....F....620 225-2610
Dodge City *(G-1318)*
Central Transport Intl Inc....E....913 371-7500
Kansas City *(G-3904)*
Central Transport Intl Inc....F....877 446-3795
Wichita *(G-13989)*
Central Trnsp Svcs Inc....D....316 263-3333
Wichita *(G-13990)*
Century Van Lines Inc....E....913 651-3600
Leavenworth *(G-5216)*
Chc McPherson Refinery Inc....E....620 793-3111
Great Bend *(G-2536)*
Chc McPherson Refinery Inc....G....785 798-3684
Ness City *(G-7254)*
Chc McPherson Refinery Inc....F....785 543-5246
Phillipsburg *(G-9779)*
CHS McPherson Refinery Inc....B....620 241-2340
McPherson *(G-6949)*
Clinton L Williams....E....316 775-1300
Leon *(G-6246)*
Convoy Equipment Leasing LLC....D....913 371-6500
Kansas City *(G-3937)*
Coomes Inc....D....785 543-2759
Phillipsburg *(G-9781)*
Coomes Brothers Ltd....E....785 543-5896
Phillipsburg *(G-9782)*
Coover Trucking Inc....F....620 244-3572
Erie *(G-1858)*
Core Carrier Corporation....C....913 621-3434
Kansas City *(G-3941)*
Cowan Systems LLC....C....913 393-0110
Olathe *(G-7625)*
D & A Trucking Inc....F....620 465-3370
Haven *(G-2729)*
D & R Trucking Co....E....620 672-7713
Pratt *(G-10106)*
Darling Ingredients Inc....F....785 336-2535
Seneca *(G-10864)*
Debrick Truck Line Company....F....913 294-5020
Paola *(G-9551)*
Doll Truck Line....F....620 456-2519
Conway Springs *(G-1140)*
Double T Ind Inc....E....620 593-4357
Rolla *(G-10232)*
Doug Bradley Trucking Inc....D....785 826-9681
Salina *(G-10481)*
Dredge Transport Service Inc....F....785 506-8285
Topeka *(G-12561)*
Dugan Truck Line LLC....F....316 946-5985
Wichita *(G-14244)*
E S Wilson Transport Inc....F....785 263-9845
Abilene *(G-25)*
Eagel Transit Inc....E....620 343-3444
Emporia *(G-1735)*
Elite Transportation LLC....E....316 295-4829
Wichita *(G-14270)*
Emporia Freight and Dlvry Svc....F....785 862-1611
Topeka *(G-12575)*
Estes Express Lines....D....620 260-9580
Garden City *(G-2153)*
Estes Express Lines Inc....D....316 554-0864
Wichita *(G-14306)*
Estes Express Lines Inc....D....913 281-1723
Kansas City *(G-3997)*
Everetts Inc....F....785 263-4172
Abilene *(G-28)*
Federal Express Corporation....F....800 463-3339
Manhattan *(G-6626)*
Fedex Freight Corporation....C....800 872-7028
Edwardsville *(G-1500)*
Fedex Freight Corporation....D....800 426-0104
Wichita *(G-14348)*
Fedex Freight Corporation....E....800 752-0047
Topeka *(G-12601)*
Fedex Freight Corporation....F....800 752-0045
Cherryvale *(G-806)*
Fedex Freight Corporation....F....888 399-4737
Great Bend *(G-2564)*
Fedex Freight Corporation....F....800 541-2032
Salina *(G-10498)*
Fedex Ground Package Sys Inc....C....800 463-3339
Olathe *(G-7706)*
Freight Brokers America LLC....A....913 438-4300
Overland Park *(G-8740)*
Freight Logistics Inc....F....316 719-2074
Wichita *(G-14421)*
Fry-Wagner Systems Inc....D....913 438-2925
Lenexa *(G-5867)*
G & R Trucking Inc....F....620 356-4500
Ulysses *(G-13297)*
GP Express Inc....F....620 223-1244
Fort Scott *(G-1974)*
Graham Ship By Truck Co....D....913 621-7500
Prairie Village *(G-10033)*
Graham Ship By Truck Company....E....913 621-7575
Prairie Village *(G-10034)*
Great Plains Mobile HM Movers....F....620 463-2420
Burrton *(G-648)*
Great Plains Trucking Inc....D....785 823-2261
Salina *(G-10522)*
Greg Smith Enterprises Inc....E....913 543-7614
Kansas City *(G-4052)*
Groendyke Transport Inc....E....316 755-1266
Wichita *(G-14520)*
Groendyke Transport Inc....E....913 621-2200
Kansas City *(G-4055)*
Gs Enterprises Inc....F....913 543-7614
Kansas City *(G-4057)*
Hadley Transit LLC....F....620 726-5853
Burns *(G-647)*
Hnry Logistics Inc....F....833 810-4679
Overland Park *(G-8819)*
Hoffman Inc....F....316 942-8011
Wichita *(G-14622)*
Intercity Direct LLC....F....913 647-7550
Lenexa *(G-5917)*
International Ex Trckg Inc....E....913 621-1525
Kansas City *(G-4106)*
Irish Express Inc....E....785 765-2500
Alma *(G-64)*
J & J Martin Trucking....F....620 544-7976
Hugoton *(G-3166)*
J and S Trucking Inc....F....785 973-2768
Prairie View *(G-10011)*
J Marquez Trucking....F....620 335-5872
Ingalls *(G-3578)*
J&J Driveaway Systems LLC....E....913 387-0158
Overland Park *(G-8868)*
Jacam Carriers 2013 LLC....F....620 278-3355
Sterling *(G-12122)*
Jack B Kelley Inc....D....620 792-8205
Great Bend *(G-2594)*
Jack Cooper Transport Co Inc....C....913 321-8500
Kansas City *(G-4116)*
James B Stddard Trnsf Stor Inc....E....913 727-3627
Leavenworth *(G-5256)*
James Mason Enterprises Inc....E....316 838-7399
Wichita *(G-14746)*
Jantz Inc....F....620 345-2783
Moundridge *(G-7186)*
Jesse Latham & Sons Inc....F....785 361-4281
Republic *(G-10200)*
Jessee Trucking Incorporated....E....620 389-2546
Columbus *(G-1080)*
Jim Mitten Trucking Inc....F....785 672-3279
Oakley *(G-7477)*
Jim Ogrady Trucking....F....620 624-5343
Liberal *(G-6325)*
John E Jones Oil Co Inc....F....785 425-6746
Stockton *(G-12182)*
K C I Roadrunner Express Inc....D....785 238-6161
Junction City *(G-3710)*
Kansas Continental Express Inc....F....620 343-7100
Emporia *(G-1786)*
Kenny Livingston Trucking Inc....F....785 598-2493
Abilene *(G-43)*
Kindsvater Inc....D....620 227-6191
Dodge City *(G-1391)*
Kings Moving & Storage Inc....E....316 247-6528
Wichita *(G-14863)*
Knight-Swift Trnsp Hldings Inc....D....913 535-5155
Kansas City *(G-4177)*
Korte Trucking Inc....F....620 276-8873
Garden City *(G-2220)*
Kunshek Chat & Coal Inc....E....620 231-8270
Pittsburg *(G-9893)*
▲ **Kustom Karriers LLC**....D....316 283-1060
Newton *(G-7374)*
Kw Trucking Inc....E....785 346-5881
Osborne *(G-8210)*
L B White Trucking Inc....E....620 326-8921
Wellington *(G-13509)*
Little Creek Trucking Inc....F....316 778-1873
Benton *(G-518)*
Lone Star Services LLC....E....620 626-7100
Liberal *(G-6337)*
Ludwig Truck Line Inc....E....620 878-4243
Florence *(G-1929)*

Lvt Trucking Inc F 913 233-2111
Kansas City *(G-4209)*

Lynns Heavy Hauling LLC F 913 393-3863
Olathe *(G-7868)*

M & A Barnett Trucking Inc F 785 673-4700
Grainfield *(G-2495)*

MAI Excavating Inc G 785 483-3387
Russell *(G-10280)*

Marroquin Express Inc F 316 295-0595
Maize *(G-6516)*

Marten Transport Ltd B 913 535-5255
Kansas City *(G-4219)*

Marten Transport Ltd E 913 535-5259
Kansas City *(G-4220)*

Martin Trucking Inc E 620 544-4920
Hugoton *(G-3172)*

Mast Trucking Inc F 620 668-5121
Copeland *(G-1150)*

McAlister Transportation LLC E 620 326-2491
Wellington *(G-13515)*

Mel Rick Inc F 785 284-3577
Sabetha *(G-10318)*

Metro Companies Inc D 316 838-3345
Wichita *(G-15059)*

Michael Bennett Trucking Inc F 785 336-2942
Seneca *(G-10873)*

Michael Downey F 316 540-6166
Maize *(G-6517)*

Midwest Bulk Inc E 316 831-9700
Wichita *(G-15088)*

Midwest Express Corporation F 913 573-1400
Lenexa *(G-6001)*

Midwest Trnspt Specialists Inc D 913 281-1003
Kansas City *(G-4259)*

Mies & Sons Trucking Inc E 316 796-0186
Colwich *(G-1099)*

Miller Trucking Ltd E 785 222-3170
La Crosse *(G-4636)*

Mj Transportation Inc E 316 832-1321
Park City *(G-9635)*

Mss Transport Inc E 785 825-7291
Salina *(G-10609)*

N T S LLC E 913 281-5353
Kansas City *(G-4277)*

Nationwide Transportation and F 913 888-1685
Shawnee *(G-11002)*

Old Dominion Freight Line Inc D 316 522-3562
Wichita *(G-15213)*

Old Dominion Freight Line Inc F 785 354-7336
Topeka *(G-12946)*

Old Dominion Freight Line Inc E 620 421-4121
Parsons *(G-9712)*

Old Dominion Freight Line Inc F 620 792-2006
Great Bend *(G-2617)*

P & B Trucking Inc F 316 283-6868
Newton *(G-7402)*

Passmore Bros Inc E 620 544-2189
Hugoton *(G-3175)*

Penner Feed & Supply Inc F 620 585-6612
Inman *(G-3583)*

Penner Trucking Inc F 620 353-8475
Sublette *(G-12206)*

Pratt Industries USA Inc D 316 838-0851
Wichita *(G-15323)*

Price Truck Line Inc C 316 945-6915
Wichita *(G-15341)*

Price Truck Line Inc E 913 596-9779
Kansas City *(G-4335)*

Price Truck Line Inc F 785 232-1183
Topeka *(G-12988)*

Price Truck Line Inc F 785 625-2603
Hays *(G-2888)*

Price Truck Line Inc F 620 365-6626
Iola *(G-3627)*

Pro-Tow LLC F 913 262-3300
Shawnee Mission *(G-11752)*

Professional Cargo Svcs Inc E 316 522-2224
Wichita *(G-15357)*

Propane Resources Trnsp Inc E 913 262-8345
Shawnee Mission *(G-11757)*

Quality Carriers Inc F 913 281-0901
Kansas City *(G-4351)*

R & L Carriers Inc E 316 529-1222
Wichita *(G-15398)*

▲ R&R Pallet Garden City Inc E 620 275-2394
Garden City *(G-2262)*

Red Line Inc F 620 343-1000
Emporia *(G-1815)*

Riverside Transport Inc D 913 233-5500
Kansas City *(G-4380)*

Robson Oil Co Inc F 785 263-2470
Abilene *(G-51)*

Ruan Trnsp MGT Systems Inc E 785 274-6672
Topeka *(G-13030)*

Run-R-Way Express Co Inc F 785 346-2900
Portis *(G-10006)*

RVB Trucking Inc E 620 365-6823
Iola *(G-3631)*

Saia Motor Freight Line LLC E 316 522-1786
Wichita *(G-15506)*

Sallee Inc D 620 227-3320
Dodge City *(G-1426)*

Schmuhl Brothers Inc E 913 422-1111
Kansas City *(G-4403)*

Seaboard Transport LLC F 913 676-8800
Shawnee Mission *(G-11843)*

Skillett & Sons Incorporated E 785 222-3611
La Crosse *(G-4639)*

Smart Truck Line Inc F 785 353-2411
Beattie *(G-419)*

Smith Brothers Inc F 620 754-3958
Stark *(G-12112)*

Smith Transportation Inc F 913 543-7614
Kansas City *(G-4427)*

Snell Harvesting Inc F 620 564-3312
Ellinwood *(G-1637)*

Sourdough Express Incorporated F 907 452-1181
Medicine Lodge *(G-7072)*

Southern Plains Co-Op At Lewis E 620 324-5536
Lewis *(G-6270)*

Southwest Express Inc F 620 544-7500
Hugoton *(G-3176)*

State Tractor Trucking Inc F 913 287-3322
Shawnee *(G-11033)*

Studdard Moving & Storage Inc E 913 341-4600
Leavenworth *(G-5293)*

Studer Truck Line Inc F 785 353-2241
Beattie *(G-420)*

T & M Contracting Inc F 913 393-1087
Olathe *(G-8094)*

T S Keim Inc C 785 284-2147
Sabetha *(G-10333)*

Taylor Crane & Rigging Inc D 620 251-1530
Coffeyville *(G-981)*

Thomas and Sons Trucking LLC E 785 454-3839
Downs *(G-1473)*

▲ Thomas Transfer & Stor Co Inc D 620 342-2321
Emporia *(G-1838)*

Thomas Transfer & Stor Co Inc E 800 835-3300
Wichita *(G-15761)*

Tim R Schwab Inc E 316 772-9055
Sedgwick *(G-10852)*

Time Inc F 816 288-5394
Olathe *(G-8109)*

Total Distribution System Inc D 913 677-2292
Westwood *(G-13561)*

Traditional Trucking Corp D 785 456-8604
Belvue *(G-509)*

Transam Trucking Inc A 913 782-5300
Olathe *(G-8119)*

Transwood Edwardsville66 E 913 745-1773
Kansas City *(G-4473)*

Triangle Trucking Inc D 785 827-5500
Salina *(G-10741)*

Trucking By George Inc F 620 879-2117
Caney *(G-677)*

Tsi Kansas Inc E 785 632-5183
Clay Center *(G-884)*

Tyson Fresh Meats Inc E 620 343-8010
Emporia *(G-1844)*

U S Road Freight Express Inc E 316 942-9944
Wichita *(G-15825)*

United Petro Transports Inc E 316 263-6868
Park City *(G-9651)*

UPS Ground Freight Inc F 913 281-0055
Kansas City *(G-4510)*

USF Holland LLC C 913 287-1770
Kansas City *(G-4512)*

V & M Transport Inc E 620 662-7281
Hutchinson *(G-3478)*

Valley Moving Company LLC F 785 456-2400
Wamego *(G-13445)*

Vernon Enterprises E 620 343-9111
Emporia *(G-1846)*

W W Mails Inc E 316 943-0703
Wichita *(G-15913)*

Wakeeney Truck Line Inc F 785 743-6778
Wakeeney *(G-13394)*

West Plains Transport Inc E 620 563-7665
Plains *(G-9978)*

Wichita Southeast Kansas Trnst C 620 421-2272
Parsons *(G-9750)*

Wilson Transportation Inc F 913 851-7900
Overland Park *(G-9497)*

Wtg Hugoton LP E 620 544-4381
Hugoton *(G-3180)*

Wynne Transport Service Inc E 316 321-3900
El Dorado *(G-1615)*

Xpo Logistics Freight Inc D 913 281-3535
Kansas City *(G-4560)*

Xpo Logistics Freight Inc D 785 823-3926
Salina *(G-10774)*

Xpo Logistics Freight Inc E 316 942-0498
Wichita *(G-16084)*

Yellow Frt Sys Employees CLB F 913 344-3000
Overland Park *(G-9516)*

Yrc Enterprise Services Inc F 913 696-6100
Overland Park *(G-9521)*

Yrc Global F 913 696-6100
Overland Park *(G-9522)*

▼ Yrc Inc B 913 696-6100
Overland Park *(G-9523)*

Yrc Inc B 620 856-2161
Baxter Springs *(G-416)*

Yrc Inc B 913 696-6100
Kansas City *(G-4565)*

Yrc Worldwide Inc B 913 696-6100
Overland Park *(G-9524)*

Yrc Worldwide Technologies Inc D 913 344-3000
Shawnee Mission *(G-12025)*

4214 Local Trucking With Storage

A Arnold of Kansas City LLC E 913 829-8267
Olathe *(G-7503)*

Air Capitol Dlvry & Whse LLC D 316 303-9005
Park City *(G-9599)*

Apartment Movers Inc E 316 267-5300
Wichita *(G-13717)*

Bailey Moving & Storage Co LLC E 785 232-0521
Topeka *(G-12357)*

Beelman Truck Co E 913 362-0553
Kansas City *(G-3852)*

Beltmann Group Incorporated E 913 888-9105
Lenexa *(G-5698)*

Century Van Lines Inc E 913 651-3600
Leavenworth *(G-5216)*

Coleman American Mvg Svcs Inc E 913 631-1440
Shawnee Mission *(G-11246)*

Coleman American Mvg Svcs Inc E 913 248-1766
Shawnee *(G-10930)*

Coleman American Mvg Svcs Inc E 785 537-7284
Manhattan *(G-6593)*

Diamond Transfer & Dist Co F 785 825-1531
Salina *(G-10476)*

Gamoict Inc F 316 262-2123
Wichita *(G-14443)*

Get A Move On Inc E 316 729-4897
Wichita *(G-14461)*

James B Stddard Trnsf Stor Inc E 913 727-3627
Leavenworth *(G-5256)*

Kansas Van & Stor Criqui Corp E 785 266-6992
Topeka *(G-12809)*

Kings Moving & Storage Inc E 316 247-6528
Wichita *(G-14863)*

Kings Moving & Storage Inc E 785 238-7341
Junction City *(G-3715)*

M & S Trucks Inc F 620 842-3764
Anthony *(G-129)*

Midwest Trnspt Specialists Inc D 913 281-1003
Kansas City *(G-4259)*

Professional Moving & Storage E 785 842-1115
Lawrence *(G-5078)*

Reliable Transfer & Storage F 785 776-4887
Manhattan *(G-6790)*

Schmuhl Brothers Inc E 913 422-1111
Kansas City *(G-4403)*

Studdard Moving & Storage Inc E 913 341-4600
Leavenworth *(G-5293)*

Studdard Relocation Svcs LLC E 816 524-2772
Leavenworth *(G-5294)*

Taylor Crane & Rigging Inc D 620 251-1530
Coffeyville *(G-981)*

4215 Courier Svcs, Except Air

Boyd Delivery Systems Inc D 913 677-6700
Westwood *(G-13551)*

Fedex Freight Corporation D 800 426-0104
Wichita *(G-14348)*

Fedex Ground Package Sys Inc E 800 463-3339
Salina *(G-10499)*

SIC

Fedex Ground Package Sys Inc ....D....... 800 463-3339
Wichita (G-14349)
Step Two Investments LLC ....E....... 913 888-9000
Overland Park (G-9357)
Total Distribution System Inc ....D....... 913 677-2292
Westwood (G-13561)
United Parcel Service Inc.....................D....... 620 421-1346
Parsons (G-9747)
United Parcel Service Inc.....................C....... 785 354-1111
Topeka (G-13207)
United Parcel Service Inc.....................C....... 785 628-3253
Hays (G-2922)
United Parcel Service Inc.....................D....... 620 662-5961
Hutchinson (G-3476)
United Parcel Service Inc.....................D....... 785 843-6530
Lawrence (G-5151)
United Parcel Service Inc.....................C....... 316 946-4074
Wichita (G-15845)
United Parcel Service Inc.....................B....... 316 941-2010
Wichita (G-15846)
United Parcel Service Inc.....................C....... 913 599-0899
Shawnee Mission (G-11964)
United Parcel Service Inc.....................C....... 913 573-4701
Kansas City (G-4488)
United Parcel Service Inc.....................D....... 913 894-0255
Lenexa (G-6202)
United Parcel Service Inc.....................E....... 620 235-1220
Pittsburg (G-9950)

4221 Farm Product Warehousing & Storage

ADM Milling Co...D....... 620 442-6200
Arkansas City (G-139)
Agco Inc...F....... 785 483-2128
Russell (G-10263)
Agri Trails Coop Inc...............................F....... 785 258-2286
Herington (G-2969)
Alliance AG and Grain LLC...................F....... 785 798-3775
Ness City (G-7251)
Anthony Frmrs Coop Elev Cmpnys ......F....... 620 842-5181
Anthony (G-119)
Archer-Daniels-Midland Company ....E....... 785 263-2260
Abilene (G-13)
Beachner Grain Inc................................F....... 620 244-3277
Erie (G-1856)
Beaver Grain Corporation Inc................F....... 620 587-3417
Beaver (G-424)
Cargill Incorporated...............................E....... 785 825-8128
Salina (G-10436)
Cargill Incorporated...............................F....... 913 367-3579
Cummings (G-1186)
Central Prairie Co-Op ....F....... 620 278-2470
Sterling (G-12113)
CHS McPherson Refinery Inc ....F....... 785 421-2157
Hill City (G-3030)
Cropland Co-Op Inc................................F....... 620 356-1241
Ulysses (G-13294)
Cropland Co-Op Inc................................F....... 620 649-2230
Satanta (G-10782)
D E Bondurant Grain Co Inc ....E....... 785 798-3322
Ness City (G-7260)
Dodge City Cooperative Exch................E....... 620 225-4193
Dodge City (G-1344)
Ellsworth Coop..F....... 785 472-3261
Ellsworth (G-1667)
Farmers Co-Operative Union ....D....... 620 278-2141
Sterling (G-12116)
Farmers Coop Grn Assn Inc ....F....... 620 456-2222
Conway Springs (G-1141)
Farmers Cooperative Grain.....................F....... 620 326-7496
Wellington (G-13499)
Golden Valley Inc ....E....... 620 527-4216
Rozel (G-10258)
Great Bend Cooperative Assn ....E....... 620 793-3531
Great Bend (G-2576)
Irsik & Doll Feed Services Inc................F....... 620 855-3747
Cimarron (G-830)
Kanza Cooperative Association ....F....... 620 546-2231
Iuka (G-3640)
Kanza Cooperative Association ....E....... 316 444-2141
Andale (G-78)
Nemaha County Cooperative Assn ....F....... 785 456-6924
Belvue (G-507)
Norag LLC...D....... 913 851-7200
Bucyrus (G-605)
O K Coop Grn & Merc Co ....F....... 620 825-4212
Kiowa (G-4628)
Piqua Farmers Coop Assn Incthe ....F....... 620 468-2535
Piqua (G-9801)
Randall Farmers Coop Un Inc.................F....... 785 739-2312
Randall (G-10190)

Skyland Grain LLC.................................F....... 620 492-2126
Johnson (G-3660)
Strong City Elevator ....F....... 620 273-6483
Strong City (G-12195)
United Prarie AG ....F....... 620 544-2017
Hugoton (G-3179)

4222 Refrigerated Warehousing & Storage

Americold Logistics LLC.........................E....... 316 838-9317
Wichita (G-13696)
Americold Logistics LLC.........................E....... 620 276-2304
Garden City (G-2100)
Arctic Glacier Texas Inc ....E....... 316 529-2173
Wichita (G-13732)
Berrys Arctic Ice LLC ....F....... 785 357-4466
Topeka (G-12376)
Browns Processing ....G....... 620 378-2441
Fredonia (G-2027)
Cookbook Publishers Inc........................D....... 913 706-6069
Shawnee Mission (G-11265)
Emporia Cold Storage Co ....F....... 620 343-8010
Emporia (G-1736)
Grinnell Locker Plant Inc.........................F....... 785 824-3400
Grinnell (G-2693)
Kensington Lockers Inc ....F....... 785 476-2834
Kensington (G-4577)
Midwest Refrigerated Svcs LLC ....F....... 913 621-1111
Kansas City (G-4255)
Olpe Locker ....G....... 620 475-3375
Emporia (G-1809)
Waggoner Enterprises Inc ....E....... 620 465-3807
Yoder (G-16196)
Winchester Meat Processing..................G....... 913 774-2860
Winchester (G-16111)

4225 General Warehousing & Storage

Advance Stores Company Inc................C....... 785 826-2400
Salina (G-10396)
Aldi Inc...B....... 913 768-1119
Olathe (G-7517)
American Eagle Outfitters Inc.................B....... 724 779-5209
Ottawa (G-8244)
Archrock Inc..E....... 620 241-8740
McPherson (G-6937)
◆ Associated Wholesale Groc Inc........A....... 913 288-1000
Kansas City (G-3825)
Associated Wholesale Groc Inc ....C....... 913 319-8500
Kansas City (G-3826)
Attic Management Group LLC...............F....... 913 269-4583
Olathe (G-7541)
Bayer Healthcare LLC..............................E....... 913 268-2000
Shawnee Mission (G-11154)
Berger Company.......................................D....... 913 367-3700
Atchison (G-215)
Bold LLC...F....... 620 663-3300
Hutchinson (G-3217)
Builders Inc ....F....... 316 522-6104
Wichita (G-13910)
Comprehensive Logistics Co Inc...........E....... 913 371-0770
Kansas City (G-3932)
Dd Traders Inc...F....... 913 402-6800
Gardner (G-2337)
Dillards Inc...B....... 913 791-6400
Olathe (G-7654)
Exhibit Arts LLC..E....... 316 264-2915
Wichita (G-14321)
Flexcon Company Inc................................F....... 913 768-8669
Olathe (G-7714)
Garvey Public Warehouse Inc ....F....... 316 522-4745
Wichita (G-14450)
Hall Industrial Dev LLC.............................F....... 316 264-7268
Wichita (G-14545)
◆ Hayes Company LLC ....F....... 316 838-8000
Wichita (G-14570)
Hummert International Inc ....F....... 785 234-5652
Topeka (G-12707)
Illinois Auto Electric Co...........................F....... 913 543-7600
Edwardsville (G-1503)
International Code Council Inc...............F....... 913 888-0304
Shawnee Mission (G-11464)
Kansas City Coml Whsng Co..................E....... 913 287-3800
Kansas City (G-4144)
Kubota Tractor Corporation.....................F....... 913 215-5298
Edgerton (G-1486)
Kuhn Co LLC..E....... 316 788-6500
Derby (G-1257)
▲ Kustom Karriers LLC.........................D....... 316 283-1060
Newton (G-7374)
Lubrication Engineers Inc........................E....... 316 529-2112
Wichita (G-14990)

Meritex Enterprises Inc ....F....... 913 888-0601
Shawnee Mission (G-11617)
Metro Park Warehouses Inc....................E....... 913 621-3116
Kansas City (G-4237)
Metro Park Warehouses Inc....................E....... 913 342-8141
Kansas City (G-4238)
Metro Park Warehouses Inc....................E....... 913 287-7366
Kansas City (G-4239)
Midpoint National Inc..............................E....... 913 362-7400
Kansas City (G-4248)
Mud-Co/Service Mud Inc.........................F....... 620 672-2957
Pratt (G-10126)
National Cold Storage Inc ....E....... 913 422-4050
Bonner Springs (G-566)
National Cold Storage Kc Inc..................E....... 913 422-4050
Bonner Springs (G-567)
Professional Cargo Svcs Inc ....E....... 316 522-2224
Wichita (G-15357)
Public Storage..E....... 316 522-1162
Wichita (G-15373)
Ronald Carlile..F....... 620 624-2632
Liberal (G-6361)
Security Storage Prpts LLC ....F....... 316 634-6510
Wichita (G-15544)
▲ Smart Warehousing LLC ....E....... 913 888-3222
Edgerton (G-1489)
Southwest Pallets......................................G....... 620 275-4343
Garden City (G-2284)
Standard Motor Products Inc..................B....... 913 441-6500
Edwardsville (G-1516)
Suther Feeds Inc..F....... 785 292-4415
Frankfort (G-2024)
TFT Global Inc...F....... 519 842-4540
Kansas City (G-4467)
Unified School District 383 ....D....... 785 587-2850
Manhattan (G-6837)
▲ United Warehouse Company ....D....... 316 712-1000
Park City (G-9652)
UPS Srvice Parts Logistics Inc...............A....... 800 451-4550
Overland Park (G-9449)
Vf Outdoor Inc...D....... 913 384-4000
Shawnee Mission (G-11976)
Watco Transportation Svcs LLC.............E....... 620 231-2230
Pittsburg (G-9967)
Wilbur Inc...F....... 913 207-6535
Olathe (G-8154)

4226 Special Warehousing & Storage, NEC

Access Info MGT Shred Svcs LLC ....E....... 913 492-4581
Lenexa (G-5620)
Exhibit Arts LLC ....E....... 316 264-2915
Wichita (G-14321)
Helena Agri-Enterprises LLC..................E....... 620 275-9531
Garden City (G-2195)
Magellan Midstream Partners LP ....F....... 620 834-2205
McPherson (G-6987)
Mass Medical Storage LLC.....................F....... 913 438-8835
Lenexa (G-5988)
Medart Inc...F....... 636 282-2300
Kansas City (G-4227)
Mini Warehouse Limited II.......................F....... 785 273-4004
Topeka (G-12906)
Mixture LLC..F....... 913 944-2441
Shawnee (G-10997)
Northern Natural Gas Company ....E....... 620 675-2239
Kismet (G-4631)
Northern Natural Gas Company ....E....... 785 455-3311
Clifton (G-902)
Northern Natural Gas Company ....E....... 620 723-2151
Mullinville (G-7210)
Northern Natural Gas Company ....F....... 620 277-2364
Holcomb (G-3076)
Northern Natural Gas Company ....E....... 620 298-5111
Cunningham (G-1188)
Pepsico Inc...F....... 620 275-5312
Garden City (G-2249)
Salina Microfilm ....F....... 785 827-6648
Salina (G-10680)
Standard Motor Products Inc..................B....... 913 441-6500
Edwardsville (G-1516)
Target Corporation.....................................C....... 785 274-6500
Topeka (G-13141)
Taylor Crane & Rigging Inc.....................D....... 620 251-1530
Coffeyville (G-981)
▲ Thomas Transfer & Stor Co Inc ....D....... 620 342-2321
Emporia (G-1838)
Underground Vaults & Stor Inc..............E....... 620 662-6769
Hutchinson (G-3472)
Underground Vaults & Stor Inc..............F....... 316 838-2121
Wichita (G-15831)

Underground Vaults & Stor Inc..............E....... 620 663-5434
Hutchinson *(G-3473)*

4231 Terminal & Joint Terminal Maint Facilities

Core Carrier Corporation ....C....... 913 621-3434
Kansas City *(G-3941)*
Jts Transports Inc.................................E....... 316 554-0706
Haysville *(G-2951)*

44 WATER TRANSPORTATION

4412 Deep Sea Foreign Transportation Of Freight

◆ Koch Carbon LLC.............................E....... 316 828-5500
Wichita *(G-14875)*
Seaboard Corporation ....C....... 913 676-8800
Merriam *(G-7103)*

4424 Deep Sea Domestic Transportation Of Freight

◆ Koch Carbon LLC.............................E....... 316 828-5500
Wichita *(G-14875)*

4493 Marinas

Clinton Marina Inc.................................E....... 785 749-3222
Lawrence *(G-4793)*
Lake Perry Yacht & Marina LLC.............F....... 785 783-4927
Perry *(G-9771)*
North Shore Marina MGT LLC................G....... 785 453-2240
Quenemo *(G-10178)*

45 TRANSPORTATION BY AIR

4512 Air Transportation, Scheduled

United Parcel Service Inc ....F....... 800 742-5877
Salina *(G-10746)*

4513 Air Courier Svcs

Dhl Express (usa) Inc ....F....... 316 943-7683
Wichita *(G-14207)*
Federal Express Corporation................F....... 800 463-3339
Topeka *(G-12599)*
Federal Express Corporation................C....... 800 463-3339
Salina *(G-10497)*
Land Air Express Inc ....E....... 316 942-0191
Wichita *(G-14920)*
▲ Noatum Logistics Usa LLC ....E....... 913 696-7100
Overland Park *(G-9089)*
UPS Srvice Parts Logistics Inc.............A....... 800 451-4550
Overland Park *(G-9449)*

4522 Air Transportation, Nonscheduled

Collins Industries Inc.............................E....... 620 663-5551
Hutchinson *(G-3243)*
Eagle Med Inc...F....... 785 899-3810
Goodland *(G-2468)*
Eaglemed LLC..E....... 316 613-4855
Wichita *(G-14251)*
Executive Airshare LLC.........................F....... 816 221-7200
Lenexa *(G-5842)*
Kansas Air Center Inc............................F....... 785 776-1991
Manhattan *(G-6674)*
Kansas City Aviation Ctr Inc..................D....... 913 782-0530
Olathe *(G-7823)*
Lyddon Aero Center Inc ....F....... 620 624-1646
Liberal *(G-6338)*
Midwest Corporate Aviation Inc ....E....... 316 636-9700
Wichita *(G-15091)*
Topeka Air Ambulance Inc ....E....... 785 862-5433
Topeka *(G-13165)*
▲ Yingling Aircraft Inc ....D....... 316 943-3246
Wichita *(G-16085)*

4581 Airports, Flying Fields & Terminal Svcs

Aero Interior Maintenance Inc ....F....... 316 990-5088
Cheney *(G-787)*
Air Plains Services Corp ....F....... 620 326-8581
Wellington *(G-13488)*
Alliance Jantr Advisors Inc ....F....... 913 815-8807
Olathe *(G-7520)*
AvFlight Salina Corporation ....F....... 734 663-6466
Salina *(G-10415)*
Brp US Inc..B....... 316 946-2000
Wichita *(G-13899)*
Cav Ice Protection Inc ....E....... 913 738-5391
New Century *(G-7272)*
Cessna Aircraft Company ....F....... 316 686-3961
Wichita *(G-13993)*
Crotts Aircraft Service Inc......................F....... 620 227-3553
Dodge City *(G-1336)*
Emerald Aerospace Holdings LLC ....D....... 316 440-6966
Wichita *(G-14274)*
Executive Beechcraft Inc ....E....... 913 782-9003
New Century *(G-7284)*
Figeac Aero North America Inc..............D....... 316 634-2500
Wichita *(G-14366)*
Flightsafety International Inc.................F....... 316 220-3200
Wichita *(G-14389)*
Freeman Holdings LLC..........................F....... 785 862-0950
Topeka *(G-12627)*
Freeman Holdings LLC..........................F....... 913 951-5600
Topeka *(G-12628)*
General Electric Company ....D....... 785 320-2350
Manhattan *(G-6644)*
Global Aviation Tech LLC.......................F....... 316 425-0999
Wichita *(G-14473)*
Global Engineering and Tech ....E....... 620 664-6268
Hutchinson *(G-3301)*
Global Parts Aero Mfg ....E....... 316 775-9292
Augusta *(G-320)*
Global Parts Group Inc..........................D....... 316 733-9240
Augusta *(G-321)*
Hetrick Air Services Inc ....F....... 785 842-0000
Lawrence *(G-4896)*
Honeywell International Inc ....E....... 913 712-0400
Olathe *(G-7776)*
IFR Systems Inc ....B....... 316 522-4981
Wichita *(G-14667)*
Jet Airwerks LLC...................................E....... 620 442-3625
Arkansas City *(G-161)*
Jrm Enterprises Inc ....E....... 785 404-1328
Salina *(G-10557)*
Kansas Air Center Inc............................F....... 785 776-1991
Manhattan *(G-6674)*
Kansas City Aviation Ctr Inc..................D....... 913 782-0530
Olathe *(G-7823)*
Lawrence Municipal Airport-Lwc...........F....... 785 842-0000
Lawrence *(G-4977)*
Lyddon Aero Center Inc ....F....... 620 624-1646
Liberal *(G-6338)*
Metropolitan Topeka Arprt Auth ....E....... 785 862-2362
Topeka *(G-12885)*
Mid-Continent AVI Svcs Inc...................F....... 316 927-4204
Wichita *(G-15078)*
Midwest A Traffic Ctrl Svc Inc...............F....... 913 782-7082
Overland Park *(G-9030)*
Midwest Corporate Aviation Inc ....E....... 316 636-9700
Wichita *(G-15091)*
Midwest Malibu Center Inc....................F....... 620 728-1356
Hutchinson *(G-3379)*
New Century Air ....F....... 913 768-9400
New Century *(G-7294)*
Pratt & Whitney Eng Svcs Inc...............G....... 316 945-9763
Wichita *(G-15322)*
Salina Airport Authority..........................F....... 785 827-3914
Salina *(G-10664)*
Signature Flight Support Corp ....D....... 316 522-2010
Wichita *(G-15590)*
T and C Aviation Enterprises.................E....... 913 764-4800
Olathe *(G-8095)*
Textron Aviation Inc................................D....... 316 517-8270
Wichita *(G-15735)*
Textron Aviation Inc................................C....... 316 517-6000
Wichita *(G-15737)*
Textron Aviation Inc................................F....... 888 727-4344
Wichita *(G-15739)*
Textron Aviation Inc................................D....... 316 293-9703
Wichita *(G-15743)*
Textron Aviation Inc................................C....... 316 517-8270
Wichita *(G-15736)*
Triumph Group Operations Inc..............D....... 620 326-5761
Wellington *(G-13538)*
Webco Air Craft......................................G....... 316 283-7929
Newton *(G-7426)*
Wells Aircraft Inc....................................E....... 620 663-1546
Hutchinson *(G-3483)*
Wichita Air Services Inc ....F....... 316 631-1332
Wichita *(G-15968)*
Wichita Airport Authority ....F....... 316 946-4700
Wichita *(G-15969)*
Wichita Airport Authority ....E....... 316 636-9700
Wichita *(G-15970)*
▲ Yingling Aircraft Inc ....D....... 316 943-3246
Wichita *(G-16085)*

46 PIPELINES, EXCEPT NATURAL GAS

4612 Crude Petroleum Pipelines

CHS McPherson Refinery Inc ....B....... 620 241-2340
McPherson *(G-6949)*
Jayhawk Pipeline LLC ....F....... 620 241-9270
McPherson *(G-6978)*
Jayhawk Pipeline LLC ....E....... 620 938-2971
Chase *(G-783)*
Koch Pipeline Company LP ....F....... 620 834-2309
Conway *(G-1134)*
Koch Pipeline Company LP ....D....... 316 828-5511
Wichita *(G-14885)*
Magellan Pipeline Company LP.............E....... 913 647-8400
Kansas City *(G-4213)*
Magellan Pipeline Company LP.............F....... 913 647-8504
Kansas City *(G-4214)*
Minnesota Pipe Line Co LLC ....F....... 316 828-5500
Wichita *(G-15113)*
Panhandle Eastrn Pipe Line LP ....E....... 620 624-8661
Liberal *(G-6352)*
Panhandle Eastrn Pipe Line LP ....F....... 620 723-2185
Greensburg *(G-2683)*
Panhandle Eastrn Pipe Line LP ....E....... 913 906-1500
Overland Park *(G-9139)*
Plains Marketing LP..............................F....... 620 365-3208
Iola *(G-3623)*
Plains Marketing LP..............................F....... 785 483-3171
Russell *(G-10284)*
Semcrude LP..F....... 620 234-5532
Stafford *(G-12109)*

4613 Refined Petroleum Pipelines

CHS Inc ....D....... 620 241-4247
McPherson *(G-6948)*
Kinder Mrgan Enrgy Partners LP ....F....... 785 543-6602
Phillipsburg *(G-9790)*
Kinder Mrgan Enrgy Partners LP ....F....... 620 834-2211
Windom *(G-16112)*
Koch Industries Inc.................................F....... 316 321-6380
El Dorado *(G-1580)*
Magellan Pipeline Company LP.............F....... 913 310-7710
Shawnee Mission *(G-11590)*
Magellan Pipeline Company LP.............F....... 316 321-3730
El Dorado *(G-1585)*
Nustar Pipeline Oper Partnr LP ....F....... 316 321-3500
El Dorado *(G-1586)*
Phillips 66 ....F....... 316 821-2250
Wichita *(G-15292)*
Tessenderlo Kerley Inc..........................F....... 620 251-3111
Coffeyville *(G-982)*
Trailblazer Pipeline Co LLC...................F....... 913 928-6060
Leawood *(G-5582)*

4619 Pipelines, NEC

Nowak Pipe Reaming Inc ....D....... 316 794-8898
Goddard *(G-2450)*

47 TRANSPORTATION SERVICES

4724 Travel Agencies

A & P Cruises & Tours ....F....... 913 248-9800
Shawnee Mission *(G-11060)*
AAA Allied Group Inc.............................F....... 785 233-0222
Topeka *(G-12281)*
Automobile Club of Missouri ....F....... 316 942-0008
Wichita *(G-13774)*
Brennco Travel Services Inc..................F....... 913 660-0121
Shawnee Mission *(G-11179)*
City of Dodge City..................................E....... 620 225-8186
Dodge City *(G-1323)*
Eidsons Florist..F....... 913 721-2775
Kansas City *(G-3981)*
Global Connections Inc..........................E....... 913 498-0960
Leawood *(G-5413)*
Hoover Stores Inc ....D....... 620 364-5444
Burlington *(G-637)*
Jade Travel Center Inc...........................F....... 785 273-1226
Topeka *(G-12736)*
K C I Roadrunner Express Inc ....D....... 785 238-6161
Junction City *(G-3710)*
Loves Travel Stops ....F....... 785 263-3390
Abilene *(G-45)*
Loves Travel Stops ....F....... 620 872-5727
Scott City *(G-10820)*
Royal Caribbean Cruises Ltd.................A....... 316 554-5000
Wichita *(G-15487)*

Shorts Travel Management Inc ... E ... 319 234-5577
Overland Park *(G-9308)*

Sunflower Travel Corporation ... F ... 316 634-1700
Wichita *(G-15688)*

Warren Travel Inc ... F ... 316 685-1118
Wichita *(G-15929)*

4729 Passenger Transportation Arrangement, NEC

Jade Travel Center Inc ... F ... 785 273-1226
Topeka *(G-12736)*

Vidtronix LLC ... F ... 913 441-9777
Shawnee *(G-11047)*

4731 Freight Forwarding & Arrangement

212 Logistics LLC ... E ... 620 563-7656
Plains *(G-9973)*

Affton Trucking Company Inc ... F ... 913 871-1315
Kansas City *(G-3791)*

AG Source Inc ... F ... 785 841-1315
Lawrence *(G-4724)*

Alliance Shippers Inc ... E ... 913 262-7060
Shawnee Mission *(G-11098)*

ASAP Transport Solutions LLC ... E ... 800 757-1178
Lenexa *(G-5666)*

Box Central Inc ... F ... 316 689-8484
Wichita *(G-13875)*

Bruenger Trucking Company ... E ... 316 744-0494
Park City *(G-9605)*

Burlington Nthrn Santa Fe LLC ... F ... 785 435-5065
Topeka *(G-12415)*

Butler Transport Inc ... C ... 913 321-0047
Kansas City *(G-3882)*

C L Nationwide Inc ... F ... 913 492-5200
Shawnee Mission *(G-11198)*

Catapult International LLC ... E ... 913 232-2389
Lenexa *(G-5733)*

Central Trnsp Svcs Inc ... D ... 316 263-3333
Wichita *(G-13990)*

CH Robinson Company Inc ... E ... 316 267-3300
Wichita *(G-13995)*

Coldpoint Logistics LLC ... E ... 816 888-7380
Edgerton *(G-1483)*

D & L Transport LLC ... D ... 913 402-4514
Overland Park *(G-8626)*

Data2logistics LLC ... C ... 816 483-9000
Shawnee Mission *(G-11291)*

Dynamic Logistix LLC ... E ... 913 274-3800
Overland Park *(G-8668)*

Efreightship LLC ... F ... 913 871-9309
Overland Park *(G-8671)*

Elite Transportation LLC ... E ... 316 295-4829
Wichita *(G-14270)*

FH Kaysing Company LLC ... E ... 316 721-8980
Wichita *(G-14360)*

Fli Inc ... E ... 913 851-2247
Overland Park *(G-8729)*

Gold Star Transportation Inc ... E ... 913 341-0081
Overland Park *(G-8762)*

Great Plains Logistics Inc ... D ... 785 823-2261
Salina *(G-10517)*

Greg Orscheln Trnsp Co ... E ... 913 371-1260
Lenexa *(G-5884)*

Hannebaum Grain Co Inc ... F ... 785 825-8205
Salina *(G-10534)*

Headhaulcom LLC ... E ... 913 905-5189
Overland Park *(G-8802)*

In Terminal Consolidation Co ... E ... 913 671-7755
Kansas City *(G-4096)*

Itransport & Logistics Inc ... E ... 316 665-7653
Haysville *(G-2948)*

J & H Transportation Inc ... F ... 316 733-8200
Andover *(G-96)*

J&J Driveaway Systems LLC ... E ... 913 387-0158
Overland Park *(G-8868)*

Jasper Investments Inc ... F ... 913 599-0899
Lenexa *(G-5928)*

Jts Transports Inc ... E ... 316 554-0706
Haysville *(G-2951)*

Kansota Transport Inc ... E ... 620 792-9100
Great Bend *(G-2598)*

King of Freight LLC ... E ... 316 409-4024
Wichita *(G-14861)*

King of Freight LLC ... E ... 316 440-4661
Wichita *(G-14862)*

◆ Koch Carbon LLC ... E ... 316 828-5500
Wichita *(G-14875)*

◆ Koch Mineral Services LLC ... E ... 316 828-5500
Wichita *(G-14884)*

Land Air Express Inc ... E ... 316 942-0191
Wichita *(G-14920)*

Metro Companies Inc ... D ... 316 838-3345
Wichita *(G-15059)*

◆ Miq Logistics LLC ... C ... 913 696-7100
Overland Park *(G-9041)*

Myfreightworld Tech Inc ... E ... 913 677-6691
Leawood *(G-5495)*

Nadia Inc ... F ... 316 686-6190
Wichita *(G-15145)*

Nicholas Water Service LLC ... F ... 620 930-7511
Medicine Lodge *(G-7070)*

▲ Noatum Logistics Usa LLC ... E ... 913 696-7100
Overland Park *(G-9089)*

Northwest Freight Handlers Inc ... F ... 509 869-7678
Wichita *(G-15196)*

Northwind Merchant Company ... F ... 785 856-1183
Lawrence *(G-5042)*

P1 Transportation LLC ... F ... 913 249-1505
Overland Park *(G-9134)*

Preferred Cartage Service Inc ... D ... 620 276-8080
Garden City *(G-2259)*

Priority Logistics Inc ... E ... 913 991-7281
Overland Park *(G-9186)*

Professional Cargo Svcs Inc ... E ... 785 625-2249
Hays *(G-2890)*

Raudin McCormick Inc ... C ... 913 928-5000
Lenexa *(G-6090)*

Redstone Logistics LLC ... E ... 913 998-7905
Overland Park *(G-9230)*

▲ Return Products Management Inc ... F ... 913 768-1747
Olathe *(G-8028)*

Ryan Transportation Svc Inc ... C ... 800 860-7926
Overland Park *(G-9266)*

Schenker Inc ... E ... 316 260-6367
Wichita *(G-15531)*

Schenker Inc ... E ... 316 942-0146
Wichita *(G-15532)*

Scott Erickson ... F ... 316 942-0146
Wichita *(G-15538)*

Shamrock Trading Corporation ... B ... 877 642-8553
Overland Park *(G-9302)*

Smartway Transportation Inc ... F ... 877 537-2681
Overland Park *(G-9320)*

Team Drive-Away Inc ... C ... 913 825-4776
Olathe *(G-8103)*

Tiger Cool Express LLC ... F ... 913 305-3510
Overland Park *(G-9411)*

Traffic Tech Inc ... C ... 888 592-2009
Spring Hill *(G-12101)*

Transportation Inc ... E ... 785 242-3660
Ottawa *(G-8316)*

U P S Stores ... F ... 913 829-3750
Olathe *(G-8129)*

UPS Supply Chain Solutions Inc ... B ... 800 714-8779
Overland Park *(G-9450)*

Waechter LLC ... E ... 620 342-1080
Emporia *(G-1848)*

Xpo Stacktrain LLC ... F ... 913 422-6400
Kansas City *(G-4561)*

Yusen Logistics Americas Inc ... E ... 913 768-4484
Olathe *(G-8165)*

4741 Railroad Car Rental

Alliance Jantr Advisors Inc ... F ... 913 815-8807
Olathe *(G-7520)*

Watco Inc ... D ... 208 734-4644
Pittsburg *(G-9962)*

Watco Switching Inc ... D ... 620 231-2230
Pittsburg *(G-9965)*

4783 Packing & Crating Svcs

Jasper Investments Inc ... F ... 913 599-0899
Lenexa *(G-5928)*

4785 Fixed Facilities, Inspection, Weighing Svcs Transptn

Advance Systems International ... E ... 913 888-3578
Lenexa *(G-5631)*

Advanced Infrared Systems ... G ... 913 888-3578
Lenexa *(G-5633)*

County of Kingman ... F ... 620 532-5241
Kingman *(G-4588)*

Dodge City International Inc ... E ... 620 225-4177
Dodge City *(G-1348)*

International Trans Logis Inc ... F ... 913 621-2750
Kansas City *(G-4108)*

Kansas Turnpike Authority ... E ... 620 326-5044
Wellington *(G-13508)*

Kansas Turnpike Authority ... F ... 785 266-9414
Topeka *(G-12808)*

Kansas Turnpike Authority ... D ... 316 682-4537
Wichita *(G-14829)*

Kansas Turnpike Authority ... E ... 316 321-0631
El Dorado *(G-1577)*

4789 Transportation Svcs, NEC

4g Express Inc ... F ... 316 619-3888
Colwich *(G-1090)*

Anderson County Council ... F ... 785 448-4237
Garnett *(G-2368)*

Ash Grove Resources LLC ... F ... 785 267-1996
Topeka *(G-12340)*

Cardinal Logistics ... E ... 620 223-4903
Fort Scott *(G-1956)*

Carrier Logistics LLC ... E ... 913 681-2780
Olathe *(G-7579)*

Cowley County Council On Aging ... F ... 620 221-7020
Winfield *(G-16130)*

Fcg Inc ... F ... 620 545-8300
Clearwater *(G-892)*

Fedex Freight Corporation ... F ... 888 880-1320
Goodland *(G-2470)*

First Class Transportation ... F ... 785 266-1331
Topeka *(G-12613)*

Flatlands Transportation Ict ... F ... 316 250-1280
Wichita *(G-14383)*

Flint Hills Area Trnsp Agcy Bd ... D ... 787 537-6345
Manhattan *(G-6630)*

Gbw Railcar Services LLC ... E ... 844 364-7403
Coffeyville *(G-942)*

Gbw Railcar Services LLC ... E ... 888 968-4364
Overland Park *(G-8749)*

Gbw Railcar Services LLC ... D ... 620 325-3001
Neodesha *(G-7243)*

Gbw Railcar Services LLC ... E ... 866 785-4082
Atchison *(G-230)*

Greenbrier Companies Inc ... E ... 866 722-7068
Topeka *(G-12647)*

Greenbrier Railcar LLC ... E ... 913 342-0010
Kansas City *(G-4050)*

Gunderson Rail Services LLC ... F ... 913 827-3536
Osawatomie *(G-8194)*

Hallcon Corporation ... F ... 913 890-6105
Lenexa *(G-5887)*

Intermodal Acquisition LLC ... B ... 708 225-2400
Edgerton *(G-1485)*

Interntnal Mtr Coach Group Inc ... F ... 913 906-0111
Lenexa *(G-5920)*

Kansas City Railcar Svc Inc ... E ... 913 621-0326
Kansas City *(G-4150)*

KS Transit Inc ... F ... 281 841-6078
Overland Park *(G-8931)*

L L L Transport Inc ... F ... 913 777-5400
Shawnee Mission *(G-11540)*

LG Pike Construction Co Inc ... D ... 620 442-9150
Arkansas City *(G-164)*

Mid Continent Transportation ... F ... 620 793-3573
Great Bend *(G-2610)*

Millennium Rail Inc ... F ... 620 231-2230
Pittsburg *(G-9905)*

Nebraska Transport Co Inc ... E ... 913 281-9991
Kansas City *(G-4284)*

Propak Logistics Inc ... D ... 913 213-3896
Kansas City *(G-4346)*

PSI Transport LLC ... E ... 785 675-3881
Hoxie *(G-3140)*

Railserve Inc ... E ... 316 321-3816
El Dorado *(G-1595)*

Sarik LLC ... F ... 785 379-1235
Topeka *(G-13036)*

Sedgwick County Transportation ... E ... 316 660-7070
Wichita *(G-15548)*

Watco Inc ... D ... 208 734-4644
Pittsburg *(G-9962)*

Watco Switching Inc ... D ... 620 231-2230
Pittsburg *(G-9965)*

Western Transport ... F ... 620 271-0540
Garden City *(G-2312)*

48 COMMUNICATIONS

4812 Radiotelephone Communications

ABC Phones North Carolina Inc ... E ... 785 243-4099
Concordia *(G-1100)*

ABC Phones North Carolina Inc ... E ... 785 263-3553
Manhattan *(G-6530)*

ABC Phones North Carolina Inc ... E ... 620 508-6167
Pratt *(G-10091)*

Aka Wireless Inc ....D.... 785 823-6605
Salina *(G-10399)*
Answer Topeka Inc ....E.... 785 234-4444
Topeka *(G-12331)*
AT&T Corp ....D.... 620 272-0383
Garden City *(G-2103)*
AT&T Corp ....E.... 785 272-4002
Topeka *(G-12349)*
AT&T Corp ....D.... 913 383-4943
Overland Park *(G-8407)*
AT&T Corp ....F.... 913 894-0800
Overland Park *(G-8408)*
AT&T Corp ....E.... 785 832-2700
Lawrence *(G-4742)*
AT&T Corp ....F.... 913 254-0303
Olathe *(G-7538)*
AT&T Corp ....B.... 913 676-1261
Shawnee Mission *(G-11128)*
AT&T Corp ....F.... 913 334-9615
Kansas City *(G-3829)*
AT&T Corp ....F.... 620 421-7612
Parsons *(G-9668)*
AT&T Corp ....D.... 620 626-5168
Liberal *(G-6280)*
AT&T Inc ....F.... 913 676-1136
Lenexa *(G-5673)*
AT&T Mobility LLC ....E.... 913 254-0303
Olathe *(G-7539)*
Cellco Partnership ....D.... 316 636-5155
Wichita *(G-13970)*
Cellco Partnership ....D.... 620 276-6776
Garden City *(G-2122)*
Cellco Partnership ....D.... 785 820-6311
Salina *(G-10438)*
Cellco Partnership ....D.... 316 722-4532
Wichita *(G-13971)*
Cellco Partnership ....D.... 913 631-0677
Overland Park *(G-8536)*
Cellco Partnership ....F.... 913 897-5022
Overland Park *(G-8535)*
Cellco Partnership ....F.... 316 789-9911
Derby *(G-1228)*
Cellco Partnership ....F.... 785 537-6159
Manhattan *(G-6580)*
Clearwire LLC ....F.... 202 628-3544
Overland Park *(G-8564)*
Cricket Communications Inc ....F.... 913 341-2799
Overland Park *(G-8614)*
Cricket Communications LLC ....F.... 316 636-6387
Wichita *(G-14130)*
Cricket Communications LLC ....F.... 913 999-0163
Roeland Park *(G-10222)*
Discount Tobacco & Cellular ....F.... 913 281-3067
Kansas City *(G-3972)*
Ensignal Inc ....E.... 316 265-8311
Wichita *(G-14290)*
▲ Flint Telecom Group Inc ....F.... 913 815-1570
Overland Park *(G-8730)*
Gateway Wreless Netwrk Svcs Lc ....F.... 316 264-0037
Wichita *(G-14452)*
Hightech Solutions Inc ....C.... 620 228-2216
Fredonia *(G-2035)*
Informtion Cmmunications Group ....E.... 913 469-6767
Leawood *(G-5437)*
Ka-Comm Inc ....G.... 785 776-8177
Manhattan *(G-6672)*
Motor Mouth Wireless LLC ....F.... 316 260-4660
Wichita *(G-15134)*
New Cingular Wireless Svcs Inc ....F.... 785 832-2700
Lawrence *(G-5038)*
New Cingular Wireless Svcs Inc ....B.... 913 344-2845
Shawnee Mission *(G-11679)*
Nex-Tech Wireless LLC ....D.... 785 567-4281
Hays *(G-2879)*
Nextel of California Inc ....E.... 866 505-2385
Overland Park *(G-9083)*
Nextel Partners Operating Corp ....C.... 800 829-0965
Overland Park *(G-9084)*
Overfield Corporation ....F.... 785 843-3434
Lawrence *(G-5052)*
Pioneer Telephone Assn Inc ....C.... 620 356-3211
Ulysses *(G-13312)*
▲ Sprint Communications Inc ....A.... 855 848-3280
Overland Park *(G-9337)*
Sprint Communications NH Inc ....E.... 800 829-0965
Overland Park *(G-9339)*
Sprint Corporation ....C.... 877 564-3166
Overland Park *(G-9340)*
Sprint Spectrum LP ....F.... 913 671-7007
Merriam *(G-7105)*
Sprint Spectrum LP ....F.... 785 537-3500
Manhattan *(G-6804)*
T-Mobile Usa Inc ....D.... 913 402-6500
Shawnee Mission *(G-11916)*
T-Mobile Usa Inc ....F.... 316 201-6120
Wichita *(G-15716)*
T-Mobile Usa Inc ....F.... 913 268-4414
Shawnee *(G-11038)*
T-Mobile Usa Inc ....F.... 913 262-2789
Shawnee Mission *(G-11917)*
T-Mobile Usa Inc ....F.... 785 273-5021
Topeka *(G-13131)*
T-Mobile Usa Inc ....F.... 913 254-1674
Olathe *(G-8098)*
T2 Wireless Inc ....F.... 785 537-8034
Manhattan *(G-6820)*
Ubiquitel Inc ....D.... 913 315-5800
Overland Park *(G-9437)*
United States Cellular Corp ....F.... 620 231-2444
Pittsburg *(G-9952)*
United Wrless Cmmnications Inc ....E.... 620 227-8127
Dodge City *(G-1445)*
United Wrlss Arina Mgrk Conf C ....F.... 620 371-7390
Dodge City *(G-1446)*
Walmart Inc ....C.... 316 945-2800
Wichita *(G-15923)*
Walmart Inc ....B.... 316 636-5384
Wichita *(G-15924)*

4813 Telephone Communications, Except Radio

1&1 Internet Inc ....F.... 816 621-4795
Lenexa *(G-5615)*
Allegiant Networks LLC ....E.... 913 599-6900
Leawood *(G-5316)*
American Telephone Inc ....F.... 913 780-3166
Gardner *(G-2326)*
AT&T Corp ....B.... 785 276-8201
Topeka *(G-12348)*
AT&T Corp ....A.... 316 268-3380
Wichita *(G-13760)*
AT&T Corp ....D.... 785 276-8514
Topeka *(G-12350)*
AT&T Corp ....D.... 316 383-0380
Wichita *(G-13761)*
AT&T Corp ....E.... 785 625-0120
Hays *(G-2751)*
AT&T Corp ....F.... 620 231-9941
Pittsburg *(G-9815)*
AT&T Corp ....E.... 913 676-1000
Shawnee Mission *(G-11129)*
AT&T Corp ....C.... 913 676-1000
Shawnee Mission *(G-11130)*
AT&T Corp ....F.... 800 403-3022
Topeka *(G-12352)*
AT&T Corp ....E.... 785 749-7155
Lawrence *(G-4743)*
AT&T Corp ....D.... 620 665-1946
Hutchinson *(G-3209)*
AT&T Inc ....F.... 913 676-1136
Lenexa *(G-5673)*
AT&T Mobility LLC ....E.... 913 254-0303
Olathe *(G-7539)*
Blue Vly Tl-Communications Inc ....D.... 785 799-3311
Home *(G-3119)*
Cellco Partnership ....F.... 785 537-6159
Manhattan *(G-6580)*
Centurylink Inc ....E.... 913 791-4971
New Century *(G-7273)*
Civicplus LLC ....F.... 785 267-6800
Manhattan *(G-6589)*
◆ Clearwire Corporation ....E.... 425 216-7600
Overland Park *(G-8563)*
Columbus Telephone Company ....F.... 620 429-3132
Columbus *(G-1067)*
Connex International Inc ....C.... 785 749-9500
Lawrence *(G-4810)*
Cox Communications Inc ....D.... 785 236-1606
Manhattan *(G-6605)*
Cox Communications Inc ....D.... 785 233-3383
Topeka *(G-12523)*
Craw-Kan Telephone Coop Inc ....D.... 620 724-8235
Girard *(G-2399)*
Cunningham Communications Inc ....F.... 785 545-3215
Glen Elder *(G-2424)*
Cunningham Telephone Company ....F.... 785 545-3215
Glen Elder *(G-2425)*
Direct Communications Inc ....F.... 913 599-5577
Overland Park *(G-8657)*
Eagle Bradband Investments LLC ....F.... 785 625-5910
Hays *(G-2792)*
Eagle Communications Inc ....F.... 785 726-3291
Hays *(G-2794)*
Eagle Communications Inc ....E.... 785 483-3244
Russell *(G-10273)*
Elkhart Telephone Company Inc ....E.... 620 697-2111
Elkhart *(G-1620)*
Euronet Worldwide Inc ....D.... 913 327-4200
Leawood *(G-5389)*
Exaltia LLC ....F.... 316 616-6200
Wichita *(G-14319)*
Extreme Tanning Inc ....F.... 316 712-0190
Wichita *(G-14325)*
▲ Flint Telecom Group Inc ....F.... 913 815-1570
Overland Park *(G-8730)*
Giant Communications Inc ....E.... 785 362-9331
Holton *(G-3091)*
Golden Belt Telephone Assn Inc ....E.... 785 372-4236
Rush Center *(G-10259)*
Golden Wheat Inc ....E.... 620 782-3341
Udall *(G-13277)*
H & B Communications Inc ....F.... 620 562-3598
Holyrood *(G-3115)*
Haviland Telephone Company Inc ....F.... 620 862-5211
Haviland *(G-2741)*
Home Telephone Co Inc ....F.... 620 654-3381
Galva *(G-2094)*
Hubris Communications ....F.... 316 858-3000
Wichita *(G-14647)*
Ideatek Telecom LLC ....E.... 620 543-2580
Buhler *(G-617)*
Internet Svc Prvders Ntwrk Inc ....E.... 913 859-9500
Shawnee Mission *(G-11465)*
Iq Group Inc ....F.... 913 722-6700
Lenexa *(G-5922)*
Iris Data Services Inc ....D.... 913 937-0590
Kansas City *(G-4112)*
It21 Inc ....F.... 913 393-4821
Overland Park *(G-8864)*
JBN Telephone Company Inc ....F.... 785 362-3323
Holton *(G-3101)*
Kanokla Communications LLC ....D.... 620 845-5682
Caldwell *(G-659)*
Kanokla Telephone Association ....E.... 620 845-5682
Caldwell *(G-660)*
Kansas Broadband Internet ....F.... 785 825-0199
Salina *(G-10563)*
Kansas Fiber Network LLC ....E.... 316 712-6030
Wichita *(G-14798)*
Kca Internet ....F.... 913 735-7206
Stilwell *(G-12160)*
Knology Inc ....C.... 785 841-2100
Lawrence *(G-4947)*
Mavicor LLC ....E.... 888 387-1620
Overland Park *(G-8995)*
Mercury Wireless Kansas LLC ....F.... 800 354-4915
Topeka *(G-12883)*
Midcontinent Communications ....C.... 785 841-2100
Lawrence *(G-5025)*
Mokan Dial Inc ....F.... 913 837-2219
Louisburg *(G-6458)*
Motorola Solutions Inc ....E.... 913 317-3020
Overland Park *(G-9057)*
Moundridge Telephone Company ....F.... 620 345-2831
Moundridge *(G-7194)*
▲ Nex-Tech LLC ....C.... 785 625-7070
Hays *(G-2878)*
Nex-Tech LLC ....F.... 785 421-4197
Hill City *(G-3037)*
Nexlynx ....F.... 785 232-5969
Topeka *(G-12930)*
Papa Murphys Take N Bake ....F.... 913 897-0008
Overland Park *(G-9140)*
Payspot LLC ....D.... 913 327-4200
Leawood *(G-5518)*
Pcs Incorporated ....F.... 913 981-1100
Olathe *(G-7977)*
Peoples Telecommunications LLC ....F.... 913 757-2500
La Cygne *(G-4641)*
Pioneer Telephone Assn Inc ....C.... 620 356-3211
Ulysses *(G-13312)*
Pioneer Telephone Assn Inc ....F.... 620 356-1985
Ulysses *(G-13313)*
Pixius Communications LLC ....D.... 316 219-8500
Wichita *(G-15303)*
Prime Communications LP ....F.... 785 371-4990
Lawrence *(G-5075)*
Qwest Corporation ....D.... 913 851-9024
Overland Park *(G-9220)*

SIC

Rainbow Telecom Assn Inc....................F........ 785 548-7511
Everest (G-1902)
Regional Media Corporation Inc............F........ 316 320-1120
El Dorado (G-1598)
Rural Telephone Service Co Inc ....D....... 785 567-4281
Lenora (G-6245)
Rural Telephone Service Co Inc ....F 785 483-5555
Russell (G-10293)
S & T Telephone Coop Assn ....F 785 460-7300
Colby (G-1038)
S & T Telephone Coop Assn.................E........ 785 890-7400
Goodland (G-2485)
S & T Telephone Coop Assn ....E 785 694-2256
Brewster (G-586)
Savage Holdings Inc...............................F 913 583-1007
Lenexa (G-6118)
South Central Tele Assn Inc..................E 620 933-1000
Pratt (G-10149)
Southern Kansas Tele Co Inc ....E 620 584-2255
Clearwater (G-898)
Southern Kansas Tele Co Inc ....E 620 584-2255
Clearwater (G-899)
Southwestern Bell Telephone Co...........E 785 862-5538
Topeka (G-13085)
Sprint..E 703 433-4000
Overland Park (G-9336)
▲ Sprint Communications Inc ....A....... 855 848-3280
Overland Park (G-9337)
Sprint Communications Co LP ....A....... 800 829-0965
Overland Park (G-9338)
Sprint Corporation ....C....... 877 564-3166
Overland Park (G-9340)
▲ Sprint International Inc.....................C....... 800 259-3755
Westwood (G-13559)
Sprint Solutions Inc..................................D....... 800 829-0965
Overland Park (G-9341)
Sprint Spectrum Holding Co LP ....A....... 800 829-0965
Shawnee Mission (G-11885)
Sprint Spectrum LP ....E 913 962-7777
Shawnee Mission (G-11886)
Sprint Spectrum LP ....E 316 634-4900
Wichita (G-15649)
Sprint Spectrum LP ....F 913 894-1375
Overland Park (G-9342)
▲ Sprint Spectrum LP ....C....... 703 433-4000
Overland Park (G-9343)
Sprint Spectrum LP ....E 913 323-5000
Shawnee Mission (G-11887)
Sprint Spectrum LP ....F 785 537-3500
Manhattan (G-6804)
Surewest Communications....................F 913 825-2882
Lenexa (G-6162)
Surewest Kans Connections LLC ....D....... 913 890-4483
Lenexa (G-6163)
Teledata Communications LLC ....E 913 663-2010
Lenexa (G-6175)
Tri-County Telephone Assn Inc ....D....... 785 366-7000
Council Grove (G-1178)
Twin Valley Telephone Inc.....................E 785 427-2211
Miltonvale (G-7112)
Twotrees Technologies LLC ....F 800 364-5700
Wichita (G-15822)
United Communications Assn Inc.........E 620 227-8645
Dodge City (G-1442)
United Telephone Assn Inc ....E 620 227-8641
Dodge City (G-1443)
Viralnova LLC...E 913 706-9710
Overland Park (G-9465)
Wamego Telephone Company Inc........E 785 456-1001
Wamego (G-13456)
Wheat State Telephone Inc ....F 620 782-3341
Udall (G-13279)
Wheatland Broadband Services............F 620 872-0006
Scott City (G-10836)
Wildflower Internet LLC.........................E 620 543-2580
Buhler (G-619)
Wilson Communication Co Inc..............F 785 658-2111
Wilson (G-16107)
Wilson Telephone Company Inc...........E 785 658-2111
Wilson (G-16109)
Windstream Nuvox Kansas LLC...........E 913 747-7000
Shawnee Mission (G-12012)
Wtc Communications Inc......................F 785 456-1000
Wamego (G-13458)

4822 Telegraph & Other Message Communications

1&1 Internet Inc.......................................F 816 621-4795
Lenexa (G-5615)
Em Sales LLC ....F 913 486-6762
Kansas City (G-3985)
Wise Connect ....C 913 276-4100
Overland Park (G-9500)

4832 Radio Broadcasting Stations

94 5 Country Inc.......................................D....... 785 272-3456
Topeka (G-12275)
Ad Astra Per Aspera Broadcasti.............E 620 665-5758
Hutchinson (G-3190)
Alpha Media LLC.....................................F 785 823-1111
Salina (G-10400)
Alpha Media LLC.....................................F 785 272-3456
Topeka (G-12310)
American Media Investments Inc ....E 620 231-7200
Pittsburg (G-9808)
Bott Communications Inc ....F 913 642-7770
Shawnee Mission (G-11176)
Bott Radio Network Inc ....D....... 913 642-7770
Overland Park (G-8475)
CM Wind Down Topco Inc.......................D....... 785 272-2122
Topeka (G-12481)
Community Broadcasting Inc.................F 913 642-7770
Overland Park (G-8581)
Connoisseur Media LLC.........................F 316 558-8800
Wichita (G-14089)
Cumulus Media Inc..................................E 913 514-3000
Shawnee Mission (G-11285)
▲ Davies Communications Inc..............F 620 241-1504
McPherson (G-6956)
Eagle Communications Inc....................F 785 625-5910
Hays (G-2793)
Eagle Communications Inc....................F 620 792-3101
Great Bend (G-2557)
Eagle Communications Inc....................F 785 726-3291
Hays (G-2794)
Eagle Communications Inc....................D....... 785 650-5349
Hays (G-2795)
Eagle Communications Inc....................F 785 587-0103
Manhattan (G-6618)
Eagle Communications Inc....................E 785 483-3244
Russell (G-10273)
Eagle Communications Inc....................E 620 662-4486
Hutchinson (G-3272)
Eagle Communications Inc....................F 785 825-4631
Salina (G-10482)
Emmis Communications Corp................F 620 793-7868
Wichita (G-14277)
Emporias Radio Stations Inc..................F 620 342-1400
Emporia (G-1749)
Entercom Communications Corp...........D....... 316 685-2121
Wichita (G-14291)
Entercom Kansas City LLC....................C....... 913 744-3600
Shawnee Mission (G-11338)
EW Scripps Company.............................E 316 436-1045
Wichita (G-14317)
Great Plains Christian Radio ....F 620 873-2991
Meade (G-7049)
Iheartcommunications Inc ....D....... 316 494-6600
Wichita (G-14668)
Iheartcommunications Inc ....D....... 316 832-9600
Wichita (G-14669)
Ingstad Broadcasting Inc.......................E 620 276-2366
Garden City (G-2203)
Innovative Broadcasting Corp................F 620 232-5993
Pittsburg (G-9880)
Iola Broadcasting Inc..............................F 620 365-3151
Iola (G-3609)
K H U T F M Country Music....................E 620 662-4486
Hutchinson (G-3344)
K J H K 907 FM..E 785 864-4745
Lawrence (G-4928)
K N Z A Inc ....F 785 547-3461
Hiawatha (G-3012)
K S A J Oldies..D....... 785 823-1111
Salina (G-10559)
Kccv Am 760..E 913 642-7600
Shawnee Mission (G-11525)
Kggf K U S N Broadcasting Stn.............F 620 251-3800
Coffeyville (G-952)
Knck Inc...F 785 243-1414
Concordia (G-1120)
Kvco ....E 785 243-4444
Concordia (G-1122)
Kxbz B 104 7 FM......................................E 785 539-1047
Manhattan (G-6706)
M Rocking Radio Inc...............................F 785 565-0406
Manhattan (G-6716)
M Rocking Radio Inc...............................D....... 620 225-8080
Dodge City (G-1400)
M Rocking Radio Inc...............................F 785 460-3306
Colby (G-1027)
Manhattan Broadcasting Co Inc ....E 785 776-1350
Manhattan (G-6718)
Mid-America AG Network Inc...............E 316 721-8484
Wichita (G-15074)
Morris Communications Co LLC ....E 785 823-1111
Salina (G-10604)
Morris Communications Co LLC ....D....... 785 272-3456
Topeka (G-12913)
Praise Network Inc..................................F 785 694-2877
Brewster (G-585)
Q 1035 ....F 785 762-5525
Junction City (G-3743)
Radio Kansas ....E 620 662-6646
Hutchinson (G-3418)
Reyes Media Group Inc ....E 913 287-1480
Kansas City (G-4375)
Seaton Publishing Co Inc.......................D....... 785 776-2200
Manhattan (G-6798)
Seward County Broadcasting Co ....F 620 624-3891
Liberal (G-6364)
Taylor Communications Inc ....E 785 632-5661
Clay Center (G-883)
Training & Educational Service ....E 913 498-1914
Overland Park (G-9423)
Union Broadcasting Inc...........................E 913 344-1500
Shawnee Mission (G-11961)
Waitt Media Inc..F 620 225-8080
Dodge City (G-1448)
Wichita State University ....E 316 978-6789
Wichita (G-16033)
Zimmer Radio Group ....E 785 843-1320
Lawrence (G-5194)

4833 Television Broadcasting Stations

Channel News Department ....F 316 292-1111
Wichita (G-13999)
Evening Telegram Company..................D....... 417 624-0233
Pittsburg (G-9858)
Gray Television Group Inc ....F 316 838-1212
Wichita (G-14499)
Gray Television Group Inc ....E 785 272-6397
Topeka (G-12645)
Iheartcommunications Inc ....D....... 316 494-6600
Wichita (G-14668)
Kansas Public Telecom Svc Inc ....E 316 838-3090
Wichita (G-14820)
Meredith Corporation ....C....... 913 677-5555
Fairway (G-1914)
Montgomery Communications Inc.........D....... 785 762-5000
Junction City (G-3727)
Nexstar Broadcasting Inc......................F 785 582-4000
Topeka (G-12931)
Nexstar Broadcasting Inc......................D....... 316 265-3333
Wichita (G-15173)
Nvt Wichita LLC ....E 316 265-3333
Wichita (G-15201)
Schurz Communications Inc.................C....... 316 838-1212
Wichita (G-15535)
Smoky Hills Public TV Corp...................F 785 483-6990
Bunker Hill (G-620)
Sunflower Broadcasting Inc ....D....... 316 838-1212
Wichita (G-15687)
Waitt Media Inc..F 785 462-3305
Colby (G-1047)
Washburn University of Topeka ....E 785 670-1111
Topeka (G-13233)

4841 Cable & Other Pay TV Svcs

Cequel Communications LLC................E 620 223-1804
Fort Scott (G-1958)
Clearwater Cable Vision Inc...................E 620 584-2077
Clearwater (G-888)
Comcast Corporation ....C....... 800 934-6489
Olathe (G-7602)
Cox Communications..............................F 620 474-4318
Hutchinson (G-3250)
Cox Communications Inc.......................D....... 316 260-7392
Wichita (G-14119)
Cox Communications Inc.......................F 620 227-3361
Dodge City (G-1333)
Cox Communications Inc.......................C....... 316 219-5000
Wichita (G-14120)
Cox Communications Inc.......................F 620 275-5552
Garden City (G-2137)
Cox Communications Inc.......................D....... 785 238-6165
Junction City (G-3686)
Cox Communications Inc.......................E 785 368-1000
Topeka (G-12524)

Cox Enterprises Inc ....E.... 913 825-6124
Overland Park *(G-8607)*
Directv Group Inc ....C.... 620 235-0743
Pittsburg *(G-9853)*
Directv Group Inc ....C.... 620 663-8132
Hutchinson *(G-3266)*
Dish Network Corporation ....D.... 816 256-5622
Kansas City *(G-3973)*
Eagle Communications Inc ....F.... 785 625-5910
Hays *(G-2793)*
Eagle Communications Inc ....F.... 785 726-3291
Hays *(G-2794)*
Eagle Communications Inc ....E.... 785 483-3244
Russell *(G-10273)*
▲ Globl Adams Communications LLC .E.... 913 402-4499
Lenexa *(G-5877)*
Golden Wheat Inc ....E.... 620 782-3341
Udall *(G-13277)*
H & B Cable Service Inc ....E.... 785 252-4000
Holyrood *(G-3114)*
Multimedia Cablevision ....F.... 620 251-6610
Coffeyville *(G-965)*
Pioneer Telephone Assn Inc ....C.... 620 356-3211
Ulysses *(G-13312)*
Rainbow Communications LLC ....E.... 785 548-7511
Everest *(G-1901)*
S & T Telephone Coop Assn ....E.... 785 694-2256
Brewster *(G-586)*
S & T Telephone Coop Assn ....F.... 785 460-7300
Colby *(G-1038)*
Skycom Inc ....F.... 785 273-1000
Topeka *(G-13076)*
Spectrum MGT Holdg Co LLC ....F.... 913 682-2113
Leavenworth *(G-5290)*
Sumner Cable Tv Inc ....F.... 620 326-8989
Wellington *(G-13531)*
United Communications Assn Inc ....E.... 620 227-8645
Dodge City *(G-1442)*
Universal Cable Services Inc ....F.... 913 481-7839
Olathe *(G-8134)*
Windjammer Communications LLC ....C.... 913 563-5450
Overland Park *(G-9498)*

4899 Communication Svcs, NEC

Alltech Communications Inc ....F.... 785 267-0316
Topeka *(G-12309)*
Bear Communications LLC ....C.... 785 856-3333
Lawrence *(G-4753)*
▲ Capps Manufacturing Inc ....D.... 316 942-9351
Wichita *(G-13941)*
Cox Media LLC ....A.... 785 215-8880
Topeka *(G-12525)*
Cox Media LLC ....E.... 623 322-2000
Wichita *(G-14122)*
Envision Technology Group LLC ....E.... 913 390-5141
Overland Park *(G-8685)*
Evans Media Group ....F.... 913 489-7364
Lenexa *(G-5837)*
Jmz Corporation ....E.... 620 365-7782
Iola *(G-3616)*
Rare Moon Media ....F.... 913 951-8360
Overland Park *(G-9226)*
Zillner Mktg Cmmunications Inc ....E.... 913 599-3230
Lenexa *(G-6241)*

49 ELECTRIC, GAS, AND SANITARY SERVICES

4911 Electric Svcs

Ark Valley Electric Coop Assn ....F.... 620 662-6661
South Hutchinson *(G-12055)*
Augusta Electric Plant 2 ....F.... 316 775-4527
Augusta *(G-303)*
Bluestem Electric Coop Inc ....F.... 785 456-2212
Wamego *(G-13406)*
Bluestem Electric Cooperative ....E.... 785 632-3111
Clay Center *(G-844)*
Bradley R Lewis ....F.... 816 453-7198
Overland Park *(G-8479)*
Brown-Atchinson Elc Coop Assn ....F.... 785 486-2117
Horton *(G-3122)*
Butler Rural Elc Coop Assn Inc ....E.... 316 321-9600
El Dorado *(G-1541)*
Caney Valley Elc Coop Assn ....F.... 620 758-2262
Cedar Vale *(G-692)*
City of Chanute ....F.... 620 431-5270
Chanute *(G-716)*
City of Coffeyville ....F.... 620 252-6180
Coffeyville *(G-915)*
City of Goodland ....F.... 785 890-4555
Goodland *(G-2465)*
City of Pratt ....F.... 620 672-3831
Pratt *(G-10101)*
City of Winfield ....F.... 620 221-5630
Winfield *(G-16120)*
Cowley County Crime Stoppers ....F.... 620 221-7777
Winfield *(G-16132)*
DS&o Electric Cooperative ....E.... 785 655-2011
Solomon *(G-12050)*
Duke Energy Corporation ....F.... 620 855-6830
Cimarron *(G-824)*
Empire District Electric Co ....D.... 620 848-3456
Riverton *(G-10212)*
Empire District Electric Co ....F.... 620 856-2121
Baxter Springs *(G-405)*
Enel Green Power N Amer Inc ....F.... 785 524-4900
Lincoln *(G-6381)*
Etc Endure Energy LLC ....E.... 913 956-4500
Overland Park *(G-8692)*
Evergy Kansas Central Inc ....A.... 785 575-6300
Topeka *(G-12583)*
Evergy Kansas Central Inc ....D.... 785 587-2350
Manhattan *(G-6624)*
Evergy Kansas Central Inc ....F.... 620 793-3515
Great Bend *(G-2560)*
Evergy Kansas Central Inc ....E.... 785 742-2185
Hiawatha *(G-3007)*
Evergy Kansas Central Inc ....F.... 316 299-7155
Wichita *(G-14315)*
Evergy Kansas Central Inc ....F.... 800 383-1183
El Dorado *(G-1560)*
Evergy Kansas Central Inc ....E.... 800 383-1183
Independence *(G-3516)*
Evergy Kansas Central Inc ....E.... 913 667-5134
Shawnee *(G-10950)*
Evergy Kansas Central Inc ....F.... 800 794-6101
Pratt *(G-10111)*
Evergy Kansas Central Inc ....B.... 785 456-6125
Saint Marys *(G-10363)*
Evergy Kansas Central Inc ....F.... 620 820-8205
Parsons *(G-9685)*
Evergy Kansas Central Inc ....F.... 620 532-2782
Kingman *(G-4589)*
Evergy Kansas Central Inc ....D.... 785 575-1352
Topeka *(G-12584)*
Evergy Kansas Central Inc ....F.... 785 263-2023
Abilene *(G-29)*
Evergy Kansas Central Inc ....C.... 785 331-4700
Lawrence *(G-4854)*
Evergy Kansas Central Inc ....E.... 316 291-8626
Colwich *(G-1095)*
Evergy Kansas Central Inc ....E.... 316 291-8612
Colwich *(G-1096)*
Evergy Kansas Central Inc ....D.... 620 341-7020
Emporia *(G-1753)*
Evergy Kansas Central Inc ....D.... 316 283-5521
Newton *(G-7342)*
Evergy Kansas South Inc ....E.... 620 441-2427
Arkansas City *(G-155)*
Evergy Metro Inc ....C.... 913 757-4451
La Cygne *(G-4640)*
Evergy Metro Inc ....E.... 913 294-6200
Paola *(G-9558)*
Evergy Metro Inc ....D.... 913 894-3000
Lenexa *(G-5838)*
Evergy Missouri West Inc ....F.... 620 793-1279
Great Bend *(G-2561)*
Federated Rural Elc MGT Corp ....E.... 913 541-0150
Lenexa *(G-5849)*
Flint Hlls Rur Elc Coop Assn I ....E.... 620 767-5144
Council Grove *(G-1167)*
Freestate Electric Coop Inc ....E.... 913 796-6111
Mc Louth *(G-6927)*
Heartland Rural Elc Coop Inc ....E.... 620 724-8251
Girard *(G-2411)*
▲ Itc Great Plains LLC ....F.... 785 783-2226
Topeka *(G-12729)*
▲ Jeffrey Energy ....F.... 785 456-2035
Saint Marys *(G-10367)*
Kansas City Bd Pub Utilities ....C.... 913 573-9675
Kansas City *(G-4139)*
Kansas City Bd Pub Utilities ....E.... 913 573-6810
Kansas City *(G-4142)*
Kansas City Bd Pub Utilities ....C.... 913 573-9556
Kansas City *(G-4138)*
Kansas City Bd Pub Utilities ....A.... 913 573-9143
Kansas City *(G-4141)*
Kansas Electric Power Coop Inc ....E.... 785 273-7010
Topeka *(G-12776)*
Kansas Gas Service ....F.... 800 794-4780
Overland Park *(G-8902)*
Kansas Municipal Energy Agency ....F.... 913 677-2884
Overland Park *(G-8904)*
L Kcp ....F.... 913 894-3009
Lenexa *(G-5959)*
Merit Energy Company LLC ....E.... 620 629-4200
Liberal *(G-6341)*
Midwest Energy Inc ....E.... 620 792-1301
Great Bend *(G-2611)*
Midwest Energy Inc ....D.... 785 625-3437
Hays *(G-2873)*
Midwest Energy Inc ....E.... 785 462-8251
Colby *(G-1028)*
Nemaha-Marshall Electric ....F.... 785 736-2345
Axtell *(G-351)*
Personal Membership ....F.... 785 979-7812
Lawrence *(G-5062)*
Pioneer Electric Coop Inc ....D.... 620 356-1211
Ulysses *(G-13311)*
Powell Electrical Systems Inc ....F.... 785 856-5863
Lawrence *(G-5071)*
Prairie Land Electric Coop Inc ....D.... 785 877-3323
Norton *(G-7461)*
Radiant Electric Cooperative ....F.... 620 378-2161
Fredonia *(G-2044)*
Rolling Hills Electric Coop ....F.... 785 534-1601
Beloit *(G-501)*
Rolling Hills Electric Coop ....E.... 785 472-4021
Ellsworth *(G-1680)*
Sedgwick County Elc Coop Assn ....F.... 316 542-3131
Cheney *(G-796)*
Sunflower Electric Power Corp ....C.... 620 277-2590
Holcomb *(G-3080)*
Sunflower Electric Power Corp ....E.... 785 628-2845
Hays *(G-2916)*
Sunflower Electric Power Corp ....E.... 620 275-0161
Garden City *(G-2293)*
Sunflower Electric Power Corp ....F.... 620 657-4400
Satanta *(G-10792)*
Twin Valley Electric Coop ....F.... 620 784-5500
Altamont *(G-73)*
Victory Electric Coop Assn Inc ....D.... 620 227-2139
Dodge City *(G-1447)*
Westar Energy Inc ....F.... 316 261-6575
Wichita *(G-15960)*
Western Cooperative Elc Assn ....E.... 785 743-5561
Wakeeney *(G-13395)*
Wheatland Electric Coop Inc ....E.... 620 275-0261
Garden City *(G-2314)*
Wheatland Electric Coop Inc ....F.... 620 793-4223
Great Bend *(G-2663)*
▲ Wolf Creek Nuclear Oper Corp ....A.... 620 364-4141
Burlington *(G-645)*

4922 Natural Gas Transmission

ANR Pipeline Company ....F.... 620 723-2381
Greensburg *(G-2672)*
ANR Pipeline Company ....F.... 785 948-2670
Havensville *(G-2739)*
ANR Pipeline Company ....F.... 785 479-5814
Enterprise *(G-1853)*
Colorado Interstate Gas Co LLC ....F.... 620 355-7955
Lakin *(G-4648)*
Kinder Morgan Kansas Inc ....G.... 620 384-7830
Syracuse *(G-12228)*
Natural Gas Pipeline Amer LLC ....F.... 620 793-7118
Great Bend *(G-2615)*
Natural Gas Pipeline Amer LLC ....G.... 785 568-2231
Glasco *(G-2422)*
Natural Gas Pipeline Amer LLC ....G.... 620 885-4505
Minneola *(G-7127)*
Northern Natural Gas Company ....E.... 620 675-2239
Kismet *(G-4631)*
Northern Natural Gas Company ....E.... 785 455-3311
Clifton *(G-902)*
Northern Natural Gas Company ....E.... 620 723-2151
Mullinville *(G-7210)*
Northern Natural Gas Company ....E.... 620 298-5111
Cunningham *(G-1188)*
Oneok Inc ....E.... 785 483-2501
Russell *(G-10283)*
Oneok Inc ....F.... 620 341-7054
Emporia *(G-1810)*
Oneok Inc ....F.... 913 599-8936
Ottawa *(G-8295)*
Oneok Inc ....D.... 785 431-4201
Topeka *(G-12947)*
Oneok Inc ....E.... 785 575-8554
Topeka *(G-12948)*

Oneok Inc.......E....... 620 792-0603
Great Bend *(G-2618)*
Oneok Inc.......F....... 620 669-2300
Hutchinson *(G-3394)*
Oneok Inc.......F....... 785 223-5408
Junction City *(G-3733)*
Oneok Inc.......F....... 620 241-0837
McPherson *(G-7011)*
Oneok Inc.......E....... 620 672-6706
Pratt *(G-10127)*
Oneok Inc.......E....... 785 822-3522
Salina *(G-10622)*
Oneok Inc.......F....... 316 322-8131
El Dorado *(G-1587)*
Oneok Inc.......E....... 316 821-2722
Wichita *(G-15220)*
Oneok Field Services Co LLC.......F....... 620 544-2179
Hugoton *(G-3174)*
Panhandle Eastrn Pipe Line LP.......E....... 620 465-2201
Haven *(G-2735)*
Panhandle Eastrn Pipe Line LP.......F....... 620 475-3226
Olpe *(G-8167)*
Panhandle Eastrn Pipe Line LP.......E....... 913 837-5163
Louisburg *(G-6461)*
▲ **Rockies Express Pipeline LLC**.......F....... 913 928-6060
Leawood *(G-5542)*
Tallgrass Development LP.......E....... 513 941-0500
Leawood *(G-5565)*
Tallgrass Energy LP.......F....... 913 928-6060
Leawood *(G-5566)*
Tallgrass Energy Partners LP.......F....... 620 355-7122
Lakin *(G-4660)*
◆ **Tallgrass Energy Partners LP**.......E....... 913 928-6060
Leawood *(G-5567)*
Tallgrass Interstate Gas Trans.......F....... 913 928-6060
Leawood *(G-5568)*
Tallgrass Operations LLC.......E....... 913 928-6060
Leawood *(G-5569)*
West Wichita Gas Gathering LLC.......F....... 970 764-6653
Cheney *(G-798)*

4923 Natural Gas Transmission & Distribution

Dcp Operating Company LP.......E....... 620 626-1201
Liberal *(G-6301)*
Edwards County Gas Company.......F....... 316 682-3022
Wichita *(G-14262)*
Evergy Kansas Central Inc.......D....... 785 575-1352
Topeka *(G-12584)*
Southern Star Central Gas Pipe.......E....... 620 657-2130
Satanta *(G-10791)*
Southern Star Central Gas Pipe.......F....... 620 257-7800
Lyons *(G-6498)*
Star Transport LLC.......E....... 913 396-5070
Overland Park *(G-9355)*
◆ **Tallgrass Energy Partners LP**.......E....... 913 928-6060
Leawood *(G-5567)*

4924 Natural Gas Distribution

Atmos Energy Corporation.......F....... 785 258-2300
Herington *(G-2970)*
Atmos Energy Corporation.......D....... 913 254-6300
Olathe *(G-7540)*
Black Hills/Kansas Gas.......E....... 605 721-1700
Lawrence *(G-4759)*
Black Hills/Kansas Gas.......F....... 605 721-1700
Garden City *(G-2112)*
Black Hills/Kansas Gas.......E....... 605 721-1700
Wichita *(G-13855)*
Black Hills/Kansas Gas.......F....... 605 721-1700
Dodge City *(G-1309)*
Black Hills/Kansas Gas.......F....... 605 721-1700
Liberal *(G-6284)*
Duke Energy Corporation.......F....... 620 855-6830
Cimarron *(G-824)*
Kinder Morgan Kansas Inc.......G....... 620 384-7830
Syracuse *(G-12228)*
Midwest Energy Inc.......F....... 620 872-2179
Scott City *(G-10822)*
Northern Natural Gas Company.......F....... 620 277-2364
Holcomb *(G-3076)*
Oneok Inc.......E....... 913 319-8600
Overland Park *(G-9104)*
Oneok Inc.......F....... 800 794-4780
Kansas City *(G-4295)*
Oneok Inc.......F....... 785 738-9700
Beloit *(G-499)*
Oneok Inc.......E....... 620 728-4303
Hutchinson *(G-3393)*
Oneok Inc.......D....... 785 431-4201
Topeka *(G-12947)*
Oneok Inc.......E....... 316 821-2722
Wichita *(G-15220)*
Oneok Energy Services Co II.......E....... 785 274-4900
Topeka *(G-12949)*
Southern Star Central Gas Pipe.......E....... 913 422-6304
Lenexa *(G-6142)*
Southern Star Central Gas Pipe.......E....... 785 448-4800
Welda *(G-13487)*
Sterling Energy Resources Inc.......F....... 913 469-9072
Overland Park *(G-9360)*
Williams Natural Gas Company.......F....... 913 422-4496
Shawnee Mission *(G-12011)*

4925 Gas Production &/Or Distribution

American Energies Gas Svc LLC.......F....... 620 628-4424
Canton *(G-679)*
Dcp Operating Company LP.......E....... 620 626-1201
Liberal *(G-6301)*
Evergy Kansas Central Inc.......D....... 316 283-5521
Newton *(G-7342)*

4931 Electric & Other Svcs Combined

Biostar Renewables LLC.......E....... 913 369-4100
Overland Park *(G-8450)*
City of Clay Center.......E....... 785 632-2139
Clay Center *(G-849)*
City of Wamego.......E....... 785 456-9598
Wamego *(G-13412)*
Duke Energy Corporation.......F....... 620 855-6830
Cimarron *(G-824)*
▲ **Kansas City Bd Pub Utilities**.......C....... 913 573-9000
Kansas City *(G-4134)*
Kansas City Bd Pub Utilities.......C....... 913 573-9000
Kansas City *(G-4136)*
Kansas City Bd Pub Utilities.......D....... 913 573-9300
Kansas City *(G-4137)*
Kansas City Bd Pub Utilities.......C....... 913 573-9556
Kansas City *(G-4138)*
Kansas City Bd Pub Utilities.......A....... 913 573-9143
Kansas City *(G-4141)*
Web Creations & Consulting LLC.......G....... 785 823-7630
Salina *(G-10762)*

4932 Gas & Other Svcs Combined

Chips Inc.......F....... 785 842-6921
Lawrence *(G-4787)*
Msip-Sscc Holdings LLC.......F....... 620 657-4166
Satanta *(G-10788)*
MTS Quanta LLC.......E....... 913 383-0800
Overland Park *(G-9061)*

4939 Combination Utilities, NEC

Campus Electric Power Company.......E....... 785 271-4824
Topeka *(G-12420)*
City of Iola.......C....... 620 365-4900
Iola *(G-3593)*
City of Ottawa.......F....... 785 229-3750
Ottawa *(G-8254)*
City of Ottawa.......E....... 785 229-3710
Ottawa *(G-8255)*
Heartland Midwest LLC.......C....... 913 397-9911
Olathe *(G-7763)*

4941 Water Sply

City of Conway Springs.......E....... 620 456-2345
Conway Springs *(G-1136)*
City of Dodge City.......F....... 620 225-8176
Dodge City *(G-1322)*
City of Garden City.......F....... 620 276-1291
Garden City *(G-2126)*
City of Great Bend.......F....... 620 793-4170
Great Bend *(G-2542)*
City of Lawrence.......E....... 785 832-7840
Lawrence *(G-4791)*
City of Leavenworth.......E....... 913 682-1513
Leavenworth *(G-5222)*
City of Salina.......E....... 785 826-7305
Salina *(G-10448)*
City of Sedan.......E....... 620 725-3193
Sedan *(G-10840)*
Coffey County District 2.......F....... 620 836-4080
Gridley *(G-2688)*
Consolidated Rur Wtr District 4.......F....... 785 286-1729
Topeka *(G-12502)*
County of Ellsworth.......F....... 785 472-4486
Ellsworth *(G-1665)*
Dickinson County Rur Wtr Dst 1.......F....... 785 388-2290
Talmage *(G-12237)*
Greenwood Cnty Rur Wtr Dst 1.......F....... 620 583-7181
Eureka *(G-1889)*
Kansas City Bd Pub Utilities.......E....... 913 573-9280
Kansas City *(G-4135)*
Kansas City Bd Pub Utilities.......D....... 913 573-9700
Kansas City *(G-4140)*
▲ **Kansas City Bd Pub Utilities**.......C....... 913 573-9000
Kansas City *(G-4134)*
Kansas City Bd Pub Utilities.......D....... 913 573-9300
Kansas City *(G-4137)*
Kansas City Bd Pub Utilities.......A....... 913 573-9143
Kansas City *(G-4141)*
McPherson Bd of Pub Utilities.......D....... 620 245-2515
McPherson *(G-6992)*
Mitchell County Rur Wtr Dst 2.......F....... 785 545-3341
Glen Elder *(G-2427)*
Public Whl Wtr Sup Dst No 13.......F....... 913 795-2503
Mound City *(G-7174)*
Rural Water Distribution 3.......F....... 913 755-4503
Osawatomie *(G-8203)*
Rural Water Dst 3 Cowley Cnty.......F....... 620 442-7131
Arkansas City *(G-177)*
Rural Water Dst 7 Osage Cnty.......F....... 785 528-5090
Osage City *(G-8189)*
Water Dst No1 Jhnson Cnty Kans.......C....... 913 895-5500
Lenexa *(G-6222)*
Water Dst No1 Jhnson Cnty Kans.......D....... 913 895-5800
Kansas City *(G-4532)*

4952 Sewerage Systems

Carson Mobile HM Pk Sewer Dst.......D....... 785 537-6330
Manhattan *(G-6577)*
City of Leavenworth.......F....... 913 682-1090
Leavenworth *(G-5221)*
City of Topeka.......E....... 785 368-3860
Topeka *(G-12472)*
Johnson County Unified Wstwtr.......D....... 913 715-8500
Olathe *(G-7819)*
Operations Management Intl Inc.......E....... 913 367-5563
Atchison *(G-252)*
Ray Lindsey Co.......F....... 913 339-6666
Olathe *(G-8019)*
Utility Maintenance Contrs LLC.......F....... 316 945-8833
Wichita *(G-15867)*

4953 Refuse Systems

21st St Steel.......F....... 316 265-6661
Wichita *(G-13578)*
Allen and Sons Waste Svcs LLC.......F....... 316 558-8050
Wichita *(G-13668)*
Allied Services LLC.......D....... 620 783-5841
Galena *(G-2068)*
Allied Waste Inds Ariz Inc.......F....... 620 336-3678
Cherryvale *(G-800)*
Allmetal Recycling LLC.......D....... 316 558-9914
Wichita *(G-13675)*
Allmetal Recycling LLC.......D....... 316 838-9381
Wichita *(G-13676)*
▼ **Asset Lifecycle LLC**.......F....... 785 861-3100
Topeka *(G-12341)*
Best Value Services LLC.......D....... 316 440-1048
Wichita *(G-13839)*
Better Hauling Co.......F....... 316 943-5865
Valley Center *(G-13337)*
Budget Equipment Inc.......E....... 316 284-9994
Newton *(G-7323)*
Champlin Tire Recycling Inc.......E....... 785 243-3345
Concordia *(G-1105)*
City of Manhattan.......F....... 785 587-4555
Manhattan *(G-6588)*
Commercial Metals Company.......E....... 620 331-1710
Independence *(G-3507)*
County of Finney.......F....... 620 275-4421
Garden City *(G-2136)*
County of Reno.......E....... 620 694-2587
Hutchinson *(G-3248)*
County of Seward.......F....... 620 626-3266
Liberal *(G-6298)*
County of Shawnee.......D....... 785 233-4774
Topeka *(G-12517)*
County of Trego.......E....... 785 743-6441
Wakeeney *(G-13386)*
Deffenbaugh Industries Inc.......A....... 913 631-3300
Kansas City *(G-3965)*
Emerald Transformer Ppm LLC.......E....... 620 251-6380
Coffeyville *(G-937)*
Enserv LLC.......F....... 316 283-5943
Newton *(G-7341)*

Evergreen Pallet LLC ....E 316 821-9991
Park City *(G-9617)*
F & F Iron & Metal Co ....E 785 877-3830
Norton *(G-7445)*
Greenpoint Cnstr Dem Proc Ctr ....F 785 234-6000
Topeka *(G-12648)*
Hamm Inc ....E 785 597-5111
Perry *(G-9768)*
Healy Biodiesel Inc ....F 620 545-7800
Clearwater *(G-893)*
Hodges Farms & Dredging LLC ....F 620 343-0513
Lebo *(G-5606)*
Honey Creek Disposal Service ....F 913 369-8999
Lawrence *(G-4901)*
Howies Enterprises LLC ....F 785 776-8352
Manhattan *(G-6660)*
Images ....G 785 827-0824
Salina *(G-10549)*
Itgs Shipping ....E 316 322-3000
El Dorado *(G-1574)*
John F Hafner LLC ....F 620 244-5393
Erie *(G-1859)*
Johnson County Landfill ....E 913 631-8181
Shawnee Mission *(G-11499)*
Laser Recycling Company ....F 785 865-4075
Lawrence *(G-4956)*
Lies Trash Service LLC ....E 316 522-1699
Wichita *(G-14959)*
Lrm Industries Inc ....E 785 843-1688
Lawrence *(G-5001)*
Macquarie Infrastructure ....C 620 638-4339
Arcadia *(G-137)*
Mc Pherson Area Solid Wast ....E 620 585-2321
McPherson *(G-6988)*
Meridian Chemicals LLC ....G 913 253-2220
Overland Park *(G-9011)*
N R Hamm Quarry Inc ....E 785 842-3236
Lawrence *(G-5035)*
National Fiber Supply LLC ....F 913 321-0066
Kansas City *(G-4280)*
Nisly Brothers Inc ....E 620 662-6561
Hutchinson *(G-3391)*
Ottawa Sanitation Service ....F 785 242-3227
Ottawa *(G-8301)*
Pcdisposalcom LLC ....E 913 980-4750
New Century *(G-7295)*
Premier Contracting Inc ....D 913 362-4141
Kansas City *(G-4330)*
Recall Secure Destruction Serv ....F 913 310-0811
Shawnee Mission *(G-11782)*
Reconserve of Kansas Inc ....E 913 621-5619
Kansas City *(G-4364)*
Republic Services Inc ....E 620 336-3678
Cherryvale *(G-812)*
Republic Services Inc ....E 620 783-5841
Galena *(G-2082)*
Resource Management Co Inc ....F 785 398-2240
Brownell *(G-589)*
Safety-Kleen (wt) Inc ....E 316 269-7400
Wichita *(G-15504)*
Salina Iron & Metal Company ....E 785 826-9838
Salina *(G-10677)*
Scrap Management Kansas Inc ....F 316 832-1198
Park City *(G-9641)*
Sea Coast Disposal Inc ....E 785 784-5308
Junction City *(G-3751)*
Siemens Industry Inc ....E 620 252-4223
Coffeyville *(G-977)*
Stericycle Inc ....F 913 321-3928
Kansas City *(G-4440)*
Superior Disposal Service Inc ....F 913 938-4552
Gardner *(G-2364)*
Superior Disposal Service Inc ....F 913 406-9460
Eudora *(G-1881)*
Temps Disposal Service Inc ....F 785 562-5360
Marysville *(G-6910)*
United States Dept of Army ....E 785 239-2385
Fort Riley *(G-1951)*
Veolia Water North America Ope ....F 785 762-5855
Junction City *(G-3765)*
Waste Connections Inc ....E 316 941-4320
Wichita *(G-15933)*
Waste Connections Kansas Inc ....E 785 827-3939
Salina *(G-10759)*
Waste Connections Kansas Inc ....E 316 838-4920
Wichita *(G-15934)*
Waste Connections Us Inc ....E 620 227-3371
Dodge City *(G-1449)*
Waste Corporation Kansas LLC ....D 713 292-2400
Parsons *(G-9749)*
Waste Management of Kansas ....D 785 233-3541
Topeka *(G-13234)*
Waste Management of Kansas ....D 913 631-3300
Kansas City *(G-4531)*
Waste Management of Kansas ....F 785 246-0413
Topeka *(G-13235)*
Waste Management of Kansas ....F 785 238-3293
Junction City *(G-3766)*
Wichita Material Recovery LLC ....F 316 303-9303
Wichita *(G-16011)*

4959 Sanitary Svcs, NEC

4t Total Lawn Inc ....E 913 888-0997
Shawnee Mission *(G-11059)*
Andax Industries LLC ....E 785 437-0604
Saint Marys *(G-10358)*
Biehler Companies Inc ....D 316 529-0002
Wichita *(G-13847)*
County of Cherokee ....E 620 429-3954
Columbus *(G-1070)*
County of Osage ....F 785 828-4444
Lyndon *(G-6476)*
D L P Services Inc ....F 913 685-1477
Overland Park *(G-8628)*
Frontr-Rrwhead Joint Ventr LLC ....E 913 461-3804
Olathe *(G-7719)*
Geocore LLC ....E 785 826-1616
Salina *(G-10509)*
Haz-Mat Response Inc ....E 913 782-5151
Olathe *(G-7759)*
Jojacs Landscape & Mowing ....F 316 945-3525
Haysville *(G-2950)*
Kans Dept Health and Envmt ....A 785 296-0461
Topeka *(G-12755)*
Karcher Investments Inc ....F 785 452-2850
Salina *(G-10568)*
Reconserve of Kansas Inc ....E 913 621-5619
Kansas City *(G-4364)*
Signature Landscape LLC ....C 913 829-8181
Olathe *(G-8066)*
Total Lease Service Inc ....G 785 735-9520
Hays *(G-2920)*
True North Outdoor LLC ....E 913 322-1340
Kansas City *(G-4476)*
True North Services LLC ....E 888 478-9470
Shawnee Mission *(G-11945)*
Tuff Turf Inc ....F 913 362-4545
Shawnee Mission *(G-11948)*
Turf Management LLC ....F 785 410-0394
Manhattan *(G-6833)*
W R King Contracting Inc ....E 913 238-7496
Shawnee Mission *(G-11985)*
Wab Co Road & Bridge ....F 785 765-3432
Alma *(G-66)*
Willowridge Landscape Inc ....F 785 842-7022
Lawrence *(G-5186)*

4971 Irrigation Systems

Kc Irrigation Specialist ....F 913 406-0670
Leawood *(G-5446)*
Premier Landscaping Inc ....F 316 733-4773
Andover *(G-107)*
T-L Irrigation Co ....F 620 675-2253
Sublette *(G-12212)*

50 WHOLESALE TRADE¨DURABLE GOODS

5012 Automobiles & Other Motor Vehicles Wholesale

Aeroswint ....F 785 391-2276
Utica *(G-13334)*
Bme Inc ....E 785 274-5116
Topeka *(G-12391)*
Briggs Auto Group Inc ....C 785 776-7799
Manhattan *(G-6568)*
Briggs Auto Group Inc ....C 785 537-8330
Manhattan *(G-6570)*
Briggs Auto Group Inc ....E 785 776-3677
Manhattan *(G-6569)*
Brown Industries LLC ....D 785 842-6506
Lawrence *(G-4770)*
Chuck Henry Sales Inc ....F 785 655-9430
Solomon *(G-12049)*
Contract Trailer Service Inc ....F 913 281-2589
Kansas City *(G-3936)*
▼ Copart of Kansas Inc ....F 913 287-6200
Kansas City *(G-3939)*
Coyson Transportation LLC ....E 620 336-2846
Cherryvale *(G-805)*
Cstk Inc ....F 316 744-2061
Park City *(G-9614)*
Doonan Truck & Equipment Inc ....E 620 792-2491
Great Bend *(G-2555)*
Easy Credit Auto Sales Inc ....E 316 522-3279
Wichita *(G-14254)*
Fleetpride Inc ....F 785 862-1540
Topeka *(G-12617)*
Hays Mack Sales and Svc Inc ....F 785 625-7343
Hays *(G-2832)*
Iaa Inc ....F 316 832-1101
Park City *(G-9620)*
Iaa Inc ....F 913 422-9303
Kansas City *(G-4092)*
Iowa Kenworth Inc ....E 816 483-6444
Leawood *(G-5440)*
J & D Equipment Inc ....E 913 342-1450
Kansas City *(G-4113)*
Kansas Auto Auction Inc ....E 913 365-0460
Elwood *(G-1688)*
Kansas City Peterbilt Inc ....D 913 441-2888
Kansas City *(G-4148)*
Kansas Cy Freightliner Sls Inc ....E 913 780-6606
Olathe *(G-7828)*
Kansas Kenworth Inc ....E 785 823-9700
Salina *(G-10566)*
Kansas Truck Equipment Co Inc ....E 316 722-4291
Wichita *(G-14828)*
Larrys Trailer Sales & Svc LLC ....F 316 838-1491
Wichita *(G-14927)*
Meyer Truck Center Inc ....F 913 764-2000
Olathe *(G-7887)*
Mid-America Auto Auction Inc ....C 316 500-7700
Wichita *(G-15075)*
Midwest Bus Sales Inc ....E 913 422-1000
Bonner Springs *(G-562)*
Midwest Services & Towing Inc ....E 913 281-1003
Kansas City *(G-4257)*
Midwest Truck Equipment Inc ....F 316 744-2889
Park City *(G-9633)*
Moss Enterprises Inc ....E 620 277-2646
Garden City *(G-2241)*
North Carolina Kenworth Inc ....E 816 483-6444
Leawood *(G-5503)*
Olathe Ford Sales Inc ....E 913 782-0881
Olathe *(G-7936)*
Omaha Truck Center Inc ....E 785 823-2204
Salina *(G-10619)*
Roberts Truck Ctr Holdg Co LLC ....D 316 262-8413
Park City *(G-9640)*
Rush Truck Centers Kansas Inc ....E 913 764-6000
Olathe *(G-8047)*
Sunflower Auto Auction LLC ....E 785 862-2900
Topeka *(G-13117)*
Tennessee Kenworth Inc ....E 816 483-6444
Leawood *(G-5571)*
Western Trailer Service Inc ....E 913 281-2226
Kansas City *(G-4538)*
Wilkens Manufacturing Inc ....D 785 425-7070
Stockton *(G-12190)*
Wilson Trailer Sales Kans Inc ....F 620 225-6220
Dodge City *(G-1458)*
Zodiac Industries Inc ....E 620 783-5041
Galena *(G-2090)*

5013 Motor Vehicle Splys & New Parts Wholesale

1-800 Radiator & A/C ....E 913 677-1799
Kansas City *(G-3774)*
A-One Auto Salvage of Wichita ....F 316 524-3273
Haysville *(G-2933)*
Advance Stores Company Inc ....C 785 826-2400
Salina *(G-10396)*
Automotive Associates ....E 620 231-6350
Pittsburg *(G-9818)*
Automotive Equipment Services ....E 913 254-2600
Olathe *(G-7543)*
Automotive Supply Inc ....E 316 942-8285
Wichita *(G-13775)*
Automotive Supply Inc ....E 316 942-8287
Wichita *(G-13776)*
Automotive Warehouse Company ....E 316 942-8285
Wichita *(G-13777)*
▲ Blackjack Tire Supplies Inc ....F 816 872-1158
Kansas City *(G-3865)*
▲ Boettcher Supply Inc ....E 785 738-5781
Beloit *(G-479)*

S I C

Burnett Automotive Inc ....F 785 539-8970
Manhattan (G-6572)
Burnett Automotive Inc ....F 913 681-8824
Overland Park (G-8494)
Central Marketing Inc ....F 316 613-2404
Wichita (G-13980)
▲ Clancey Co ....F 913 894-4444
Overland Park (G-8559)
Clare Generator Service Inc ....F 785 827-3321
Salina (G-10453)
Cline Auto Supply Inc ....E 620 343-6000
Emporia (G-1721)
Commercial Fltr Svc Knsas Cty ....G 913 384-5858
Kansas City (G-3929)
◆ Computer Distribution Corp ....E 785 354-1086
Topeka (G-12498)
Cross Manufacturing Inc ....C 620 324-5525
Lewis (G-6268)
Errol E Engel Inc ....E 785 625-3195
Hays (G-2800)
Farneys Inc ....F 316 522-7248
Haysville (G-2943)
Fleetpride Inc ....F 785 862-1540
Topeka (G-12617)
Fleetpride Inc ....F 316 942-4227
Wichita (G-14385)
Fleetpride Inc ....D 800 362-2600
Wichita (G-14386)
Garnett Auto Supply Inc ....E 316 267-4393
Wichita (G-14449)
Genuine Parts Company ....F 913 631-4329
Shawnee Mission (G-11395)
Hays Mack Sales and Svc Inc ....F 785 625-7343
Hays (G-2832)
◆ Hiper Technology Inc ....F 785 749-6011
Lawrence (G-4898)
Hub Cap & Wheel Store Inc ....F 913 432-0002
Kansas City (G-4087)
Inland Truck Parts Company ....F 913 492-7559
Olathe (G-7792)
Jobbers Automotive Whse Inc ....D 316 267-4393
Wichita (G-14759)
Keystone Auto Holdings Inc ....F 913 371-3249
Kansas City (G-4173)
Keystone Automotive Inds Inc ....F 785 235-1920
Topeka (G-12820)
Keystone Automotive Inds Inc ....F 316 262-0500
Wichita (G-14855)
Keystone Automotive Inds Inc ....E 816 921-8929
Kansas City (G-4174)
◆ LAd Global Enterprises Inc ....F 913 768-0888
Olathe (G-7851)
Lewis Auto Salvage LLC ....F 785 233-0561
Topeka (G-12841)
◆ Long Motor Corporation ....C 913 541-1525
Lenexa (G-5978)
Long Motor Corporation ....C 913 541-1525
Lenexa (G-5979)
Magna Tech Inc ....E 620 431-3490
Chanute (G-740)
Manko Window Systems Inc ....F 785 238-3188
Junction City (G-3724)
Maupin Truck Parts Inc ....E 620 225-4433
Dodge City (G-1401)
Medart Inc ....F 636 282-2300
Kansas City (G-4227)
Mid-Amrcan Dstrbtrs/Jyhawk RAD ....F 913 321-9664
Kansas City (G-4245)
▲ Mikes Equipment Company ....F 620 543-2535
Buhler (G-618)
▲ Northstar Automotive Glass Inc ....F 316 686-3648
Wichita (G-15193)
Oldham Sales Inc ....F 785 625-2547
Hays (G-2882)
Omaha Truck Center Inc ....E 785 823-2204
Salina (G-10619)
OReilly Automotive Stores Inc ....F 620 664-6800
Hutchinson (G-3396)
OReilly Automotive Stores Inc ....F 620 421-6070
Parsons (G-9714)
OReilly Automotive Stores Inc ....F 913 268-6001
Shawnee Mission (G-11702)
OReilly Automotive Stores Inc ....F 785 235-9241
Topeka (G-12951)
OReilly Automotive Stores Inc ....F 620 251-5280
Coffeyville (G-967)
OReilly Automotive Stores Inc ....F 913 829-6188
Olathe (G-7963)
OReilly Automotive Stores Inc ....F 316 729-7311
Wichita (G-15233)
OReilly Automotive Stores Inc ....F 316 686-5536
Wichita (G-15234)
OReilly Automotive Stores Inc ....F 785 235-5658
Topeka (G-12952)
OReilly Automotive Stores Inc ....F 785 862-4749
Topeka (G-12953)
OReilly Automotive Stores Inc ....F 785 266-3688
Topeka (G-12954)
OReilly Automotive Stores Inc ....F 913 621-6939
Kansas City (G-4297)
OReilly Automotive Stores Inc ....F 785 832-0408
Lawrence (G-5049)
OReilly Automotive Stores Inc ....F 913 367-4138
Atchison (G-253)
OReilly Automotive Stores Inc ....E 316 264-6422
Wichita (G-15235)
OReilly Automotive Stores Inc ....F 316 685-7900
Wichita (G-15232)
OReilly Automotive Stores Inc ....F 785 842-9800
Lawrence (G-5048)
OReilly Automotive Stores Inc ....F 913 287-2409
Kansas City (G-4296)
OReilly Automotive Stores Inc ....F 913 381-0451
Overland Park (G-9111)
OReilly Automotive Stores Inc ....E 913 764-8685
Olathe (G-7962)
OReilly Automotive Stores Inc ....F 620 331-1018
Independence (G-3545)
Patterson Racing Inc ....F 316 775-7771
Augusta (G-337)
Paynes Inc ....F 620 231-3170
Frontenac (G-2063)
PDQ Tools and Equipment Inc ....G 913 492-5800
Shawnee Mission (G-11721)
Pgw Auto Glass LLC ....F 913 927-2753
Kansas City (G-4320)
Poorman Auto Supply Inc ....E 316 265-6284
Wichita (G-15315)
Popup Industries Inc ....E 620 431-9196
Chanute (G-755)
Redneck Inc ....E 316 263-6090
Wichita (G-15432)
Rose Motor Supply Inc ....F 620 662-1254
Hutchinson (G-3432)
S & W Supply Company Inc ....E 785 625-7363
Hays (G-2904)
▲ Sigma Distributing Company Inc ....E 316 943-4499
Wichita (G-15588)
Smith Auto & Truck Parts Inc ....F 620 275-9145
Garden City (G-2282)
◆ Sparkle Auto LLC ....F 620 272-9559
Garden City (G-2286)
Standard Motor Products Inc ....B 913 441-6500
Edwardsville (G-1516)
Tennessee Kenworth Inc ....E 816 483-6444
Leawood (G-5571)
Trailers n More LLC ....E 316 945-8900
Wichita (G-15785)
Truck Stuff Inc ....F 316 264-1908
Wichita (G-15807)
Truett & Osborn Cycle Inc ....G 316 682-4781
Wichita (G-15811)
Two-Bee Inc ....F 785 364-2162
Holton (G-3113)
United Auto Parts Inc ....E 316 721-6868
Wichita (G-15840)
Vee Village Parts Inc ....F 816 421-6441
Basehor (G-390)
Vernies Trux-N-Equip Inc ....G 785 625-5087
Hays (G-2923)
W Carter Orvil Inc ....E 620 251-4700
Coffeyville (G-984)
Wescorp Ltd ....F 913 281-1833
Kansas City (G-4534)
▲ Wholesale Batteries Inc ....F 913 342-0113
Kansas City (G-4542)
Williams Automotive Inc ....F 620 343-0086
Emporia (G-1852)
Williams Service Inc ....E 620 878-4225
Florence (G-1930)

5014 Tires & Tubes Wholesale

Allied Oil & Tire Company ....F 316 530-5221
Wichita (G-13673)
American Tire Distributors ....E 316 616-9600
Wichita (G-13694)
Becker Tire & Treading Inc ....D 620 793-5414
Great Bend (G-2519)
Becker Tire & Treading Inc ....F 316 943-7979
Wichita (G-13825)
Bridgestone Americas ....F 785 267-0074
Topeka (G-12405)
Bridgestone Ret Operations LLC ....F 913 393-2212
Olathe (G-7560)
Buds Tire Service Inc ....F 785 632-2135
Clay Center (G-846)
Burnett Automotive Inc ....F 913 681-8824
Overland Park (G-8494)
Burnett Automotive Inc ....F 785 539-8970
Manhattan (G-6572)
Camso Manufacturing Usa Ltd ....E 620 340-6500
Emporia (G-1715)
Carrolls LLC ....F 913 321-2233
Kansas City (G-3893)
Chris Archer Group Inc ....E 316 945-4000
Wichita (G-14014)
Clingan Tires Incorporated ....E 620 624-5649
Liberal (G-6294)
D & D Tire Inc ....F 785 843-0191
Lawrence (G-4823)
Easy Money Pawn Shop Inc ....G 316 687-2727
Wichita (G-14255)
Garden City Tire Center Inc ....F 620 276-7652
Garden City (G-2178)
Great Western Tire of Dodge Cy ....F 620 225-1343
Dodge City (G-1367)
Gregg Tire Co Inc ....F 785 233-4156
Topeka (G-12651)
▲ O K Thompsons Tire Inc ....E 785 738-2283
Beloit (G-497)
O K Tire of Dodge City Inc ....F 620 225-0204
Dodge City (G-1415)
Pomps Tire Service Inc ....F 913 621-5200
Kansas City (G-4326)
Rakies Oil LLC ....F 620 442-2210
Arkansas City (G-171)
▲ Shamrock Tire & Auto Service ....E 316 522-2297
Wichita (G-15572)
▲ Shore Tire Co Inc ....E 913 541-9300
Lenexa (G-6132)
Super Oil Co Inc ....F 785 354-1410
Topeka (G-13125)
T O Haas LLC ....F 620 662-0261
Hutchinson (G-3461)
▲ Tech Inc ....E 913 492-6440
Lenexa (G-6171)
Tire Town Inc ....E 913 682-3201
Leavenworth (G-5298)
Wiebe Tire & Automotive ....F 316 283-4242
Newton (G-7429)

5015 Motor Vehicle Parts, Used Wholesale

A & A Auto Salvage ....F 785 286-2728
Topeka (G-12276)
Diamond Coach Corporation ....D 620 795-2191
Oswego (G-8233)
Griffin Wheel Company ....E 913 299-2223
Kansas City (G-4054)
Hess & Son Salvage Inc ....F 785 238-3382
Junction City (G-3699)
Jobbers Automotive Whse Inc ....D 316 267-4393
Wichita (G-14759)
◆ LAd Global Enterprises Inc ....F 913 768-0888
Olathe (G-7851)
▲ Liquidynamics Inc ....F 316 943-5477
Wichita (G-14968)
Lkq Corporation ....E 785 862-0000
Topeka (G-12847)
Piland Auto Dismantling ....F 620 275-5506
Garden City (G-2255)
S & W Supply Company Inc ....E 785 625-7363
Hays (G-2904)
Smith Auto & Truck Parts Inc ....F 620 275-9145
Garden City (G-2282)
Vilela Rndy Auto Bdy Repr Pntg ....F 620 231-6350
Pittsburg (G-9957)

5021 Furniture Wholesale

Aegis Business Solutions LLC ....G 913 307-9922
Olathe (G-7512)
Avcorp Business Systems LLC ....E 913 888-0333
Overland Park (G-8415)
Bolen Office Supply Inc ....F 620 672-7535
Pratt (G-10100)
Consolidated Prtg & Sty Co Inc ....E 785 825-5426
Salina (G-10460)
Cross Creek Furniture LLC ....E 316 943-0286
Wichita (G-14133)
Custom Cabinet & Rack Inc ....E 785 862-2271
Topeka (G-12537)

Design Central Inc F 785 825-4131
Salina (G-10474)
Designed Bus Intros Tpeka Inc F 785 233-2078
Topeka (G-12553)
Designers Library Inc F 913 227-0010
Shawnee Mission (G-11303)
Ferguson-Phillips LLC F 316 612-4663
Wichita (G-14357)
Global Industries Inc F 913 310-9963
Overland Park (G-8758)
Integrated Facilities Group F 316 262-1417
Wichita (G-14702)
▼ Jakobe Furniture LLC D 913 371-8900
Kansas City (G-4117)
McCartys G 620 251-6169
Coffeyville (G-957)
Mfl Inc E 785 862-2767
Topeka (G-12886)
Midwest Single Source Inc E 316 267-6333
Wichita (G-15102)
▲ Mittelmans Furniture Co Inc E 913 897-5505
Overland Park (G-9044)
Navrats Inc F 620 342-2092
Emporia (G-1800)
Office Works LLC F 785 462-2222
Colby (G-1032)
OfficeMax Incorporated E 913 667-5300
Edwardsville (G-1511)
R Messner Construction Co E 316 634-2381
Wichita (G-15405)
Roberts Hutch-Line Inc E 620 662-3356
Hutchinson (G-3428)
Sleep One Inc F 913 859-0001
Overland Park (G-9317)
Spaces Inc E 913 894-8900
Lenexa (G-6143)
Ssb Manufacturing Company C 913 422-8000
Shawnee Mission (G-11889)
Superior School Supplies Inc E 316 265-7683
Wichita (G-15699)
United Office Products Inc E 913 782-4441
Olathe (G-8132)
▲ Unruh Fab Inc E 316 772-5400
Sedgwick (G-10853)

5023 Home Furnishings Wholesale

Atlantic Dev Corp of PA F 316 267-2255
Wichita (G-13762)
Big W Industries Inc E 913 321-2112
Kansas City (G-3860)
▲ Cap Carpet Inc E 316 262-3496
Wichita (G-13936)
Cap Carpet Inc F 785 273-1402
Topeka (G-12422)
Ceramic Cafe F 913 383-0222
Overland Park (G-8540)
Classic Floors & Design Center E 913 780-2171
Overland Park (G-8561)
Country Carpet Inc F 785 256-4800
Maple Hill (G-6863)
Crawford Supply Co F 785 434-4631
Plainville (G-9984)
◆ Design Materials Inc E 913 342-9796
Kansas City (G-3969)
Designed Bus Intros Tpeka Inc F 785 233-2078
Topeka (G-12553)
Frameworks F 316 636-4470
Wichita (G-14413)
Frank Colladay Hardware Co F 620 663-4477
Hutchinson (G-3292)
Gardner Floor Covering Inc E 785 266-6220
Topeka (G-12632)
◆ General Distributors Inc E 316 634-2133
Wichita (G-14455)
Home Depot USA Inc B 913 871-1221
Overland Park (G-8824)
Image Flooring LLC D 314 432-3000
Lenexa (G-5910)
▲ Interstate Flooring LLC C 913 573-0600
Kansas City (G-4110)
▲ King Industries Inc E 785 823-1785
Salina (G-10575)
◆ LAd Global Enterprises Inc F 913 768-0888
Olathe (G-7851)
▼ Mel Stevenson & Associates Inc D 913 262-0505
Kansas City (G-4232)
▲ Olathe Glass Company Inc E 913 782-7444
Olathe (G-7938)
Petty Products Inc G 913 782-0028
Olathe (G-7981)
◆ Phantom Enterprises Inc F 316 264-7070
Newton (G-7405)
▲ Picture & Frame Industries Inc E 913 384-3751
Kansas City (G-4322)
Pools Plus F 785 823-7665
Salina (G-10636)
R P Products Inc E 913 492-6380
Shawnee Mission (G-11773)
Rigdon Floor Coverings Inc E 913 362-9829
Kansas City (G-4378)
◆ Robert Wilson Co Inc E 913 642-1500
Overland Park (G-9251)
Schammerhorn Inc G 316 265-8659
Wichita (G-15528)
Sebring & Co F 913 888-8141
Overland Park (G-9288)
▲ Selfs Inc F 316 267-1295
Wichita (G-15555)
Sysco Kansas City Inc E 316 942-4205
Wichita (G-15711)
Tapco Products Co E 913 492-2777
Shawnee Mission (G-11920)
Tile Shop LLC F 913 631-8453
Shawnee (G-11040)
▼ Weber Carpet Inc C 913 469-5430
Lenexa (G-6224)
William Sonoma Store Inc E 316 636-5990
Wichita (G-16051)
Window Flair Draperies G 913 722-6070
Shawnee (G-11054)

5031 Lumber, Plywood & Millwork Wholesale

American Bldrs Contrs Sup Inc D 913 722-4747
Kansas City (G-3803)
American Bldrs Contrs Sup Inc F 785 354-7398
Topeka (G-12313)
American Bldrs Contrs Sup Inc E 316 265-8276
Wichita (G-13684)
American Drect Procurement Inc C 913 677-5588
Lenexa (G-5648)
American Wholesale Corporation F 785 364-4901
Holton (G-3084)
Beacon Sales Acquisition Inc D 913 262-7663
Shawnee Mission (G-11155)
Carter-Waters LLC E 913 671-1870
Overland Park (G-8523)
Carter-Waters LLC F 316 942-6712
Wichita (G-13956)
Century Building Solutions Inc F 913 422-5555
Lenexa (G-5740)
Century Wood Products Inc G 913 839-8725
Olathe (G-7587)
▲ Cgf Investments Inc E 316 691-4500
Wichita (G-13994)
Confederated Builders Supply E 316 788-3913
Derby (G-1232)
D H Pace Company Inc C 816 221-0072
Olathe (G-7636)
D H Pace Company Inc E 316 944-3667
Wichita (G-14157)
D H Pace Company Inc B 816 480-2600
Olathe (G-7638)
Dahmer Contracting Group LLC D 816 795-3332
Overland Park (G-8630)
▲ Diebolt LLC E 620 496-2222
Iola (G-3598)
Dormakaba USA Inc F 717 335-4334
Topeka (G-12560)
Duranotic Door Inc F 913 764-3408
Olathe (G-7661)
E D Bishop Lumber Muncie Inc F 913 441-2691
Bonner Springs (G-552)
Engineered Door Products Inc F 316 267-1984
Wichita (G-14288)
Galyon Lumber Inc F 620 897-6290
Little River (G-6418)
Georgia-Pacific LLC C 785 363-7767
Blue Rapids (G-536)
Griffith Lumber Company Inc E 785 776-4104
Manhattan (G-6647)
Hardman Wholesale LLC E 785 346-2131
Osborne (G-8209)
Hd Supply Inc E 816 283-3687
Kansas City (G-4071)
Home Stl Siding & Windows LLC F 785 625-8622
Hays (G-2849)
Kan-AM Products Inc F 316 943-8806
Wichita (G-14784)
Kansas Builders Supply Co Inc F 913 831-1511
Shawnee Mission (G-11508)
Kansas Building Supply Co Inc D 913 962-5227
Overland Park (G-8888)
Kansas City Millwork Company E 913 768-0068
Olathe (G-7825)
Kansas City Millwork Company E 913 768-0068
Olathe (G-7826)
Kansas Door Inc F 620 793-7600
Great Bend (G-2597)
▲ Kc Cabinetwright Inc E 913 825-6555
Lenexa (G-5939)
L & J Wood Products Inc G 620 327-2183
Hesston (G-2996)
Lorac Company Inc F 316 263-2565
Wichita (G-14979)
Lowes Home Centers LLC C 913 631-3003
Shawnee Mission (G-11579)
Lowes Home Centers LLC C 316 773-1800
Wichita (G-14982)
Lowes Home Centers LLC C 785 452-9303
Salina (G-10585)
Lowes Home Centers LLC C 620 513-2000
Hutchinson (G-3359)
Lowes Home Centers LLC C 316 684-3117
Wichita (G-14983)
Lowes Home Centers LLC C 913 397-7070
Olathe (G-7866)
Lowes Home Centers LLC C 785 273-0888
Topeka (G-12852)
Lowes Home Centers LLC C 316 206-0000
Derby (G-1259)
Lowes Home Centers LLC C 913 328-7170
Kansas City (G-4207)
Lowes Home Centers LLC C 913 261-1040
Roeland Park (G-10227)
Lowes Home Centers LLC C 316 206-1030
Wichita (G-14984)
Macs Fence Inc E 913 287-6173
Kansas City (G-4211)
McCray Lumber Company E 913 780-0060
Olathe (G-7882)
McCray Lumber Company D 913 321-8840
Kansas City (G-4226)
Miami Lumber Inc F 913 294-2041
Paola (G-9574)
Mid-AM Building Supply Inc D 913 592-4313
Spring Hill (G-12089)
Mid-AM Building Supply Inc F 316 942-0389
Wichita (G-15073)
Mid-States Millwork Inc F 913 492-6300
Overland Park (G-9028)
Midway Sales & Distrg Inc D 785 233-7406
Topeka (G-12893)
Midway Sales & Distrg Inc F 785 537-4665
Manhattan (G-6745)
Midwest Siding Inc E 785 825-0606
Salina (G-10603)
Neighbors Construction Co Inc E 913 422-5555
Lenexa (G-6021)
New Windows For America LLC F 316 263-0711
Wichita (G-15170)
Northwest Hardwoods Inc E 913 894-9790
Lenexa (G-6027)
▲ Olathe Glass Company Inc E 913 782-7444
Olathe (G-7938)
▲ Olathe Millwork LLC G 913 738-8074
Olathe (G-7947)
▲ Olathe Millwork Company E 913 894-5010
Lenexa (G-6035)
Pella Products Kansas City Inc E 913 492-7927
Lenexa (G-6048)
Pratt Glass Inc F 620 672-6463
Pratt (G-10139)
Probuild Company LLC F 785 827-2644
Salina (G-10643)
▲ Pwd Inc E 316 283-0335
Newton (G-7409)
Roberts Products Inc F 913 780-1702
Olathe (G-8039)
Roys Custom Cabinets G 785 625-6724
Hays (G-2902)
Southard Corporation E 620 793-5434
Great Bend (G-2637)
Superior Door Service Inc F 913 381-1767
Kansas City (G-4447)
T H Rogers Lumber Company F 620 231-0900
Pittsburg (G-9944)
Vos Window & Door Inc D 913 962-5227
Shawnee Mission (G-11984)
Weyerhaeuser Company E 316 284-6700
Newton (G-7428)

S I C

Wichita Fence Co Inc....F....316 838-1342
Park City (G-9654)
Window Design Company....G....785 582-2888
Silver Lake (G-12030)
Woodwork Mfg & Sup Inc....E....620 663-3393
Hutchinson (G-3492)

5032 Brick, Stone & Related Construction Mtrls Wholesale

Air Capital Stucco L L C....E....316 650-2450
Newton (G-7308)
AMBS and Associates Inc....G....913 599-5939
Lenexa (G-5644)
Apac-Kansas Inc....E....785 625-3459
Hutchinson (G-3201)
Apac-Kansas Inc....D....316 522-4881
Wichita (G-13715)
Apac-Kansas Inc....E....620 662-3307
Hutchinson (G-3200)
Ash Grove Cement Company....E....620 433-3500
Chanute (G-703)
▲ Bedrock International LLC....E....913 438-7625
Lenexa (G-5697)
Braco Sales Inc....E....816 471-5005
Kansas City (G-3874)
Capitol Concrete Pdts Co Inc....F....785 233-3271
Topeka (G-12436)
Carter-Waters LLC....F....316 942-6712
Wichita (G-13956)
Classic Floors & Design Center....E....913 780-2171
Overland Park (G-8561)
Coleman Materials LLC....F....316 267-9812
Wichita (G-14054)
Deffenbaugh Industries Inc....E....913 208-1000
Olathe (G-7647)
▲ Direct Source Gran & Stone Imp....F....913 766-9200
Overland Park (G-8658)
Drywall Supply....F....316 269-3304
Wichita (G-14240)
▲ Emotorpro....F....785 437-2046
Saint Marys (G-10362)
Flint Hills Clay Works Inc....F....620 382-3620
Marion (G-6870)
Florence Rock Company LLC....G....620 878-4544
Newton (G-7346)
Glen-Gery Corporation....G....913 281-2800
Kansas City (G-4038)
Global Stone LLC....G....913 310-9500
Olathe (G-7733)
House of Rocks Inc....E....913 432-5990
Kansas City (G-4086)
Huber Sand Company....F....620 275-7601
Garden City (G-2200)
▲ Interstate Flooring LLC....C....913 573-0600
Kansas City (G-4110)
Interstate Supply Company....E....316 265-6653
Wichita (G-14711)
J T Lardner Cut Stone Inc....F....785 234-8634
Topeka (G-12732)
Kansas Sand and Concrete Inc....E....785 235-6284
Topeka (G-12803)
Kaw Valley Companies Inc....C....913 281-9950
Kansas City (G-4160)
Kaw Valley Sand and Gravel Inc....E....913 281-9950
Kansas City (G-4162)
▲ Kcg Inc....E....913 438-4142
Lenexa (G-5942)
Kcg Inc....G....913 888-0882
Lenexa (G-5943)
Kcg Inc....E....913 236-4909
Kansas City (G-4167)
Kunshek Chat & Coal Inc....E....620 231-8270
Pittsburg (G-9893)
L & W Supply Corporation....E....913 782-1777
Olathe (G-7847)
OBrien Rock Company Inc....G....620 421-5127
Parsons (G-9711)
Pray Building Stone Inc....F....620 221-7422
Winfield (G-16165)
Quikrete Companies Inc....E....913 441-6525
Kansas City (G-4355)
R A Ruud & Son Inc....F....316 788-5000
Haysville (G-2957)
Rew Materials Inc....D....913 236-4909
Kansas City (G-4374)
Salina Concrete Products Inc....E....785 827-7281
Salina (G-10668)
Salina Concrete Products Inc....F....316 943-3241
Wichita (G-15510)
South West Butler Quarry LLC....F....316 775-1737
Augusta (G-347)
Stone Sand Co Inc....E....620 793-7864
Great Bend (G-2639)
Sturgis Materials Inc....E....913 371-7757
Kansas City (G-4442)
▲ Sun Marble LLC....F....913 438-3366
Lenexa (G-6156)
U S Stone Industries LLC....C....913 529-4154
Herington (G-2982)
Williams Diversified Mtls Inc....E....620 679-9810
Baxter Springs (G-415)

5033 Roofing, Siding & Insulation Mtrls Wholesale

American Bldrs Contrs Sup Inc....F....785 354-7398
Topeka (G-12313)
American Bldrs Contrs Sup Inc....E....316 265-8276
Wichita (G-13684)
American Wholesale Corporation....F....785 364-4901
Holton (G-3084)
Arrow Renovation & Cnstr LLC....E....913 703-3000
Olathe (G-7534)
Associated Materials LLC....F....888 544-9774
Wichita (G-13757)
Associated Materials LLC....F....316 944-0800
Wichita (G-13758)
Beacon Sales Acquisition Inc....D....913 262-7663
Shawnee Mission (G-11155)
Beacon Sales Acquisition Inc....F....785 234-8406
Topeka (G-12368)
Beacon Sales Acquisition Inc....F....913 871-1949
Lenexa (G-5692)
Brace Integrated Services Inc....E....316 832-0292
Wichita (G-13878)
▲ Buckley Industries Inc....D....316 744-7587
Park City (G-9606)
Cameron Ashley Bldg Pdts Inc....F....913 621-3111
Kansas City (G-3886)
Discount Siding Supply LP....F....785 625-4619
Hays (G-2788)
Gulfside Supply Inc....F....913 384-9610
Kansas City (G-4058)
Gulfside Supply Inc....F....316 941-9322
Wichita (G-14527)
▼ Mel Stevenson & Associates Inc....D....913 262-0505
Kansas City (G-4232)
Mel Stevenson & Associates Inc....F....913 262-0505
Kansas City (G-4233)
Mel Stevenson & Associates Inc....F....316 262-5959
Wichita (G-15036)
Mid-AM Building Supply Inc....D....913 592-4313
Spring Hill (G-12089)
Midway Sales & Distrg Inc....D....785 233-7406
Topeka (G-12893)
Midway Sales & Distrg Inc....F....785 537-4665
Manhattan (G-6745)
Protec Construction & Sup LLC....E....913 441-2121
Edwardsville (G-1513)
Roofing Sup Grup-Kansas Cy LLC....F....913 281-4300
Kansas City (G-4388)
Scott Mesler....F....785 749-0462
Lawrence (G-5106)

5039 Construction Materials, NEC Wholesale

Adelhardt Enterprises Inc....F....620 672-6463
Pratt (G-10093)
Binswanger Enterprises LLC....F....785 267-4090
Topeka (G-12382)
City Glass and Mirror Inc....F....785 233-5650
Topeka (G-12467)
Clayton Homes Inc....C....785 434-4617
Plainville (G-9981)
Curb Appeal of Kansas Inc....E....620 488-5214
Belle Plaine (G-445)
Dayton Superior Corporation....E....913 279-4800
Kansas City (G-3959)
Erosion Control Inc....F....913 397-7324
Paola (G-9556)
▲ Insulite Glass Co Inc....D....800 452-7721
Olathe (G-7795)
Interstate Supply Company....E....316 265-6653
Wichita (G-14711)
Lippert Components Mfg Inc....D....316 283-0627
North Newton (G-7438)
▲ Manko Window Systems Inc....B....785 776-9643
Manhattan (G-6730)
Masonry & Glass Systems Inc....G....913 748-6142
Shawnee Mission (G-11601)
Mdf Industries Inc....F....785 827-4450
Salina (G-10599)
Morton Buildings Inc....F....785 823-6359
Salina (G-10606)
Morton Buildings Inc....D....620 221-4180
Winfield (G-16159)
Morton Buildings Inc....F....620 275-4105
Garden City (G-2239)
▲ Olathe Glass Company Inc....E....913 782-7444
Olathe (G-7938)
◆ Pro-Dig LLC....F....785 856-2661
Elwood (G-1689)
Southside Homes Inc....F....316 522-7100
Wichita (G-15626)
Tennison Brothers Inc....F....316 263-7581
Wichita (G-15729)
Topeka Foundry and Ir Works Co....D....785 232-8212
Topeka (G-13176)
Tuff Shed Inc....F....913 541-8833
Shawnee Mission (G-11947)
Wagner Intr Sup Kans Cy Inc....F....913 647-6622
Kansas City (G-4529)
We-Mac Manufacturing Co....F....913 367-3778
Atchison (G-270)
Weigel Construction Inc....F....913 780-1274
Spring Hill (G-12103)
Western Metal Company Inc....F....913 681-8787
Louisburg (G-6469)
Wichita Awning Co Inc....G....316 838-4432
Wichita (G-15978)

5043 Photographic Eqpt & Splys Wholesale

Daymark Solutions Inc....F....913 541-8980
Shawnee Mission (G-11294)
Fujifilm North America Corp....F....816 914-5942
Kansas City (G-4021)
Heartland Imaging Companies....B....913 621-1211
Kansas City (G-4076)
Meridianpro Inc....E....620 421-1107
Parsons (G-9709)
▲ R E B Inc....E....620 365-5701
Iola (G-3630)
Wolfes Camera Shops Inc....E....785 235-1386
Topeka (G-13248)

5044 Office Eqpt Wholesale

American Paper Products Inc....F....913 681-5777
Shawnee Mission (G-11107)
Avcorp Business Systems LLC....E....913 888-0333
Overland Park (G-8415)
Bolen Office Supply Inc....F....620 672-7535
Pratt (G-10100)
Canon Solutions America Inc....G....913 323-5010
Overland Park (G-8508)
Canon Solutions America Inc....F....785 232-8222
Topeka (G-12421)
Central Office Svc & Sup Inc....F....785 632-2177
Clay Center (G-848)
Century Business Systems Inc....F....785 776-0495
Manhattan (G-6583)
Century Business Technologies....E....785 267-4555
Topeka (G-12458)
Century Office Pdts Inc Topeka....E....785 267-4555
Topeka (G-12460)
Consolidated Prtg & Sty Co Inc....E....785 825-5426
Salina (G-10460)
Copy Products Inc....E....316 315-0102
Wichita (G-14099)
Copy Products Inc....D....620 365-7611
Iola (G-3596)
Daniksco Office Interiors LLC....F....620 259-8009
Hutchinson (G-3254)
Daniksco Office Interiors LLC....F....316 491-2607
Park City (G-9616)
Data Systems Inc....F....913 281-1333
Overland Park (G-8637)
Digital Office Systems Inc....E....316 262-7700
Wichita (G-14211)
Docuforce Inc....F....316 636-5400
Wichita (G-14218)
Evolv Solutions LLC....E....913 469-8900
Shawnee Mission (G-11352)
Faimon Publications Inc....F....620 364-5325
Burlington (G-634)
Gibbs Technology Company....E....913 621-2424
Kansas City (G-4034)
▲ I M S of Kansas City Inc....F....913 599-6007
Shawnee Mission (G-11446)
Image Quest Inc....E....316 686-3200
Wichita (G-14676)

Key Office Products Inc ....G....... 620 227-2101
Dodge City (G-1390)
Kingman Leader Courier.......................G....... 620 532-3151
Kingman (G-4602)
Knighton Bus Solutions LLC.................E....... 913 747-2818
Overland Park (G-8924)
Konica Minolta Business Soluti ....E....... 913 563-1800
Lenexa (G-5958)
Logan Business Machines Inc.............E....... 785 233-1102
Topeka (G-12848)
Midwest Office Technologies................E....... 785 272-7704
Topeka (G-12903)
Midwest Office Technology..................E....... 913 894-9600
Overland Park (G-9034)
Midwest Single Source Inc..................E....... 316 267-6333
Wichita (G-15102)
Office Works LLC.................................F....... 785 462-2222
Colby (G-1032)
R K Black Missouri LLC ....F....... 913 577-8100
Olathe (G-8017)
Ricoh Usa Inc ....E....... 316 262-7172
Wichita (G-15461)
Ricoh Usa Inc ....E....... 316 558-5488
Valley Center (G-13351)
Ricoh Usa Inc ....C....... 913 890-5100
Shawnee Mission (G-11802)
Ricoh Usa Inc ....E....... 785 272-0248
Topeka (G-13017)
Sta-Mot-Ks LLC ....E....... 913 894-9600
Overland Park (G-9349)
Toshiba Amer Bus Solutions Inc..........E....... 785 242-4942
Lawrence (G-5142)

5045 Computers & Peripheral Eqpt & Software Wholesale

Arrow Electronics Inc...........................E....... 913 242-3012
Overland Park (G-8396)
Asi Computer Technologies Inc...........E....... 913 888-8843
Lenexa (G-5667)
Avcorp Business Systems LLC............E....... 913 888-0333
Overland Park (G-8415)
Cisco Systems Inc...............................D....... 913 344-6100
Shawnee Mission (G-11227)
▲ Cloud Storage Corporation..............F....... 785 621-4350
Hays (G-2772)
Cobalt Iron Inc.....................................E....... 888 584-4766
Lawrence (G-4796)
Communication Cable Company..........D....... 610 644-5155
Leawood (G-5356)
Computech Service of Kansas ....E....... 785 266-2585
Topeka (G-12497)
◆ Computer Distribution Corp ....E....... 785 354-1086
Topeka (G-12498)
Control Systems Intl Inc.......................D....... 913 599-5010
Shawnee Mission (G-11264)
Control Vision Corporation..................E....... 620 231-5816
Pittsburg (G-9845)
Convergeone Inc..................................C....... 913 307-2300
Overland Park (G-8597)
Copy Products Inc ....D....... 620 365-7611
Iola (G-3596)
Cytek Media Systems Inc.....................E....... 785 295-4200
Topeka (G-12542)
Danco Systems Inc...............................F....... 913 962-0600
Shawnee (G-10939)
Data Max of Kansas City......................E....... 913 752-2200
Lenexa (G-5803)
Dataco Derex Inc.................................F....... 913 438-2444
Leawood (G-5370)
Digital Simplistics Inc...........................E....... 913 643-2445
Lenexa (G-5818)
Direct Communications Inc ....F....... 913 599-5577
Overland Park (G-8657)
Environmental Systems Research........D....... 913 383-8235
Leawood (G-5387)
Fujifilm North America Corp ....F....... 816 914-5942
Kansas City (G-4021)
Gateway Solutions Inc.........................F....... 913 851-1055
Overland Park (G-8748)
Globalink Inc ....D....... 785 823-8284
Salina (G-10513)
Hospitality Management Systems........F....... 913 438-5040
Overland Park (G-8828)
Inland Associates Inc ....F....... 913 764-7977
Olathe (G-7791)
Integrated Health Systems LLC............F....... 913 647-9020
Stilwell (G-12155)
Iris Strgc Mktg Support Inc.................E....... 913 232-4825
Lenexa (G-5923)

J & M Industries Inc.............................E....... 913 362-8994
Prairie Village (G-10037)
Jack Henry & Associates Inc ....C....... 913 422-3233
Shawnee Mission (G-11479)
Kanokla Telephone Association...........E....... 620 845-5682
Caldwell (G-660)
Kansas Asset Recovery Inc ....E....... 316 303-1000
Wichita (G-14786)
Keltech Solutions LLC..........................F....... 785 841-4611
Lawrence (G-4940)
Micro Electronics Inc...........................E....... 913 341-4297
Shawnee Mission (G-11624)
◆ Microtech Computers Inc ....E....... 785 841-9513
Lawrence (G-5024)
Midwest Single Source Inc...................E....... 316 267-6333
Wichita (G-15102)
▲ On Demand Technologies LLC ....F....... 913 438-1800
Overland Park (G-9102)
Optiv Security Inc................................F....... 816 421-6611
Overland Park (G-9110)
Results Technology Inc........................E....... 913 928-8300
Overland Park (G-9238)
Rural Telephone Service Co Inc ....D....... 785 567-4281
Lenora (G-6245)
Shi International Corp ....F....... 512 226-3984
Overland Park (G-9307)
Shoroeders Jim Sftwr & Video ....F....... 620 227-7628
Dodge City (G-1430)
◆ Stallard Technologies Inc ....E....... 913 851-2260
Overland Park (G-9351)
Stone Lock Global Inc ....E....... 800 970-6168
Olathe (G-8084)
Superior Computer Supply Inc.............F....... 316 942-5577
Wichita (G-15693)
Voice Products Inc...............................E....... 316 616-1111
Wichita (G-15911)
Woodard Tech & Investments LLC........F....... 316 636-2122
Wichita (G-16064)
Word-Tech Inc ....E....... 913 722-3334
Shawnee Mission (G-12019)

5046 Commercial Eqpt, NEC Wholesale

AAA Restaurant Supply LLC ....F....... 316 265-4365
Wichita (G-13592)
American Fun Food Company Inc.........F....... 316 838-9329
Park City (G-9600)
Arrow Fork Lift Parts Inc......................G....... 816 231-4410
Lenexa (G-5663)
B & J Food Service Eqp Inc ....E....... 913 621-6165
Kansas City (G-3835)
Bar Code Systems ....F....... 913 894-6368
Shawnee Mission (G-11151)
Concepts For Business LLC..................F....... 913 888-8686
Shawnee Mission (G-11258)
Custom Cabinet & Rack Inc..................E....... 785 862-2271
Topeka (G-12537)
Dee Jays Enterprises............................F....... 620 227-3126
Dodge City (G-1340)
▲ Express Scale Parts Inc ....E....... 913 441-4787
Lenexa (G-5844)
Fsw Subtech Holdings LLC ....F....... 816 795-9955
Kansas City (G-4019)
Hammel Scale Co Inc...........................E....... 316 264-1358
Wichita (G-14548)
Hammel Scale Kansas City Inc.............F....... 913 321-5428
Kansas City (G-4062)
▼ Heartland Food Products Inc............F....... 866 571-0222
Shawnee Mission (G-11424)
Hobart Sales and Service Inc...............E....... 913 469-9600
Lenexa (G-5904)
▼ Hockenbergs Restaurant Supply .....F....... 913 696-9773
Shawnee Mission (G-11436)
Ice-Masters Inc....................................F....... 316 945-6900
Wichita (G-14665)
▲ K C Sign Express Inc........................G....... 913 432-2500
Shawnee Mission (G-11506)
Kanequip Inc ....C....... 785 562-2377
Marysville (G-6892)
Kansas Powertrain & Eqp LLC ....F....... 785 861-7034
Topeka (G-12797)
▲ Marel Inc ....E....... 913 888-9110
Lenexa (G-5986)
Muckenthaler Incorporated..................F....... 620 342-5653
Emporia (G-1799)
Norvell Company Inc ....E....... 785 825-6663
Salina (G-10615)
Pitsco Inc...F....... 620 231-0010
Pittsburg (G-9917)
Salina Scale Sales & Service ....F....... 785 827-4441
Salina (G-10690)

Sorella Group Inc.................................F....... 913 390-9544
Lenexa (G-6140)
Stevenson Company Inc ....F....... 785 233-1303
Topeka (G-13098)
◆ Sub-Technologies Inc ....E....... 816 795-9955
Kansas City (G-4443)
▲ Sunflower Medical LLC ....F....... 785 726-2486
Ellis (G-1654)
Sunflower Restaurant Sup Inc..............F....... 785 823-6394
Salina (G-10726)
United Distributors Inc ....F....... 316 712-2174
Wichita (G-15841)
Veteran Fdsrvice Solutions LLC...........F....... 913 307-9922
Lenexa (G-6211)

5047 Medical, Dental & Hospital Eqpt & Splys Wholesale

Advanced Medical Dme LLC.................F....... 913 814-7464
Kansas City (G-3787)
Animal Health Intl Inc ....E....... 620 276-8289
Garden City (G-2101)
Apria Healthcare LLC ....B....... 913 492-2212
Lenexa (G-5658)
Apria Healthcare LLC ....F....... 949 616-2606
Dodge City (G-1295)
Apria Healthcare LLC ....E....... 316 689-4500
Wichita (G-13725)
Big Sur Waterbeds Inc..........................F....... 316 944-6225
Wichita (G-13848)
Briovarx LLC ....F....... 913 307-9900
Lenexa (G-5716)
Broadway Home Medical Inc ....F....... 316 264-8600
Wichita (G-13895)
Browns Medical Imaging......................F....... 913 888-6710
Lenexa (G-5719)
C A Titus Inc ....D....... 913 888-1024
Lenexa (G-5724)
Carefore Medical Inc............................E....... 913 327-5445
Olathe (G-7578)
Centaur Inc ....G....... 913 390-6184
Olathe (G-7583)
Central Plins Rsprtory Med LLC............F....... 785 527-8727
Belleville (G-455)
Cherub Medical Supply LLC ....F....... 913 227-0440
Shawnee (G-10928)
Concordnce Hlthcare Sltons LLC..........F....... 316 945-6941
Wichita (G-14086)
Contourmd Marketing Group LLC........E....... 913 541-9200
Lenexa (G-5786)
Cramer Products Inc............................F....... 913 856-7511
Gardner (G-2335)
▲ Ddi Holdings Inc...............................E....... 913 371-2200
Kansas City (G-3962)
Finucane Enterprises Inc ....F....... 913 829-5665
De Soto (G-1199)
First Biomedical Inc.............................E....... 800 962-9656
Lenexa (G-5856)
Hanger Prosthetics & ....G....... 913 588-6548
Kansas City (G-4065)
Henry Schein Inc..................................F....... 913 894-8444
Shawnee Mission (G-11427)
Howmedica Osteonics Corp ....E....... 913 491-3505
Leawood (G-5432)
Jay Hatfield Mobility LLC ....F....... 785 452-9888
Wichita (G-14750)
Jay Hatfield Mobility LLC ....F....... 620 429-2636
Columbus (G-1079)
Kansas Specialty Services Inc ....F....... 620 221-6040
Winfield (G-16151)
Kansas Truck Equipment Co Inc...........E....... 316 722-4291
Wichita (G-14828)
Karis Inc...F....... 620 260-9931
Garden City (G-2215)
◆ LAd Global Enterprises Inc ....F....... 913 768-0888
Olathe (G-7851)
Lincare Inc..E....... 913 438-8200
Lenexa (G-5973)
Lincare Inc..F....... 316 684-4689
Wichita (G-14965)
Line Medical Inc ....E....... 316 262-3444
Wichita (G-14967)
Medical Eqp Solutions Inc ....F....... 816 241-3334
Leawood (G-5471)
Medical Equipment Exchange ....F....... 913 451-2888
Shawnee Mission (G-11613)
▲ Medical Positioning Inc ....E....... 816 474-1555
Kansas City (G-4229)
Medventures International Inc.............F....... 785 862-2300
Topeka (G-12881)

Merry X-Ray Chemical Corp .... E .... 858 565-4472 Overland Park *(G-9013)*
Mwi Veterinary Supply Co .... F .... 913 422-3900 Edwardsville *(G-1509)*
Newman Mem Hosp Foundation .... F .... 620 343-1800 Emporia *(G-1804)*
Newman Mem Hosp Foundation .... B .... 620 343-6800 Emporia *(G-1803)*
Patterson Dental Supply Inc .... E .... 913 492-6100 Lenexa *(G-6045)*
Patterson Dental Supply Inc .... F .... 316 315-1800 Wichita *(G-15269)*
Peavey Corporation .... D .... 913 888-0600 Lenexa *(G-6047)*
Pharmacy Dist Partners LLC .... F .... 903 357-3391 Mission Hills *(G-7147)*
Pulse Needlefree Systems Inc .... F .... 913 599-1590 Lenexa *(G-6080)*
Relevium Labs Inc .... F .... 614 568-7000 Dodge City *(G-1423)*
Sizewise Rentals LLC .... E .... 785 726-4371 Ellis *(G-1653)*
Somnicare Inc .... E .... 913 498-1331 Overland Park *(G-9326)*
Spectrum Medical Equipment Inc .... F .... 913 831-2979 Kansas City *(G-4434)*
Spinal Simplicity LLC .... F .... 913 451-4414 Leawood *(G-5558)*
Stecklein Enterprises LLC .... F .... 785 625-2529 Hays *(G-2912)*
▲ Steven Joseph Jr DDS .... F .... 316 262-5273 Wichita *(G-15670)*
Suture Express Inc .... E .... 913 384-2220 Overland Park *(G-9380)*
▲ Unimed II Inc .... C .... 913 533-2202 Stilwell *(G-12177)*
Vitalograph Inc .... E .... 913 888-4221 Lenexa *(G-6215)*

5048 Ophthalmic Goods Wholesale

Duffins-Langley Optical Co .... D .... 913 492-5379 Shawnee Mission *(G-11320)*
Essilor Laboratories Amer Inc .... D .... 800 397-2020 Overland Park *(G-8691)*

5049 Professional Eqpt & Splys, NEC Wholesale

ARC Document Solutions .... E .... 316 264-9344 Wichita *(G-13727)*
Baysinger Police Supply Inc .... F .... 316 262-5663 Wichita *(G-13821)*
◆ Bushnell Holdings Inc .... C .... 913 752-3400 Overland Park *(G-8497)*
Continental Equipment Company .... F .... 913 845-2148 Tonganoxie *(G-12258)*
Cretex .... E .... 785 863-3300 Oskaloosa *(G-8223)*
Drafting Room Inc .... G .... 316 267-2291 Wichita *(G-14236)*
Guardian Business Services .... F .... 785 823-1635 Salina *(G-10524)*
Kc Tool LLC .... F .... 913 440-9766 Olathe *(G-7833)*
Kneisley Manufacturing Company .... F .... 620 365-6628 Iola *(G-3618)*
Midwest Lens Inc .... F .... 913 894-1030 Shawnee Mission *(G-11634)*
O H Gerry Optical Company .... E .... 913 362-8822 Overland Park *(G-9095)*
Oppliger Banking Systems Inc .... E .... 913 829-6300 Olathe *(G-7959)*
▲ Pitsco Inc .... C .... 620 231-0000 Pittsburg *(G-9914)*
▲ Pitsco Inc .... F .... 800 835-0686 Pittsburg *(G-9915)*
Professional Engrg Cons PA .... C .... 316 262-2691 Wichita *(G-15359)*
Shimadzu Scientific Instrs Inc .... F .... 913 888-9449 Shawnee Mission *(G-11864)*
▲ Sokkia Corporation .... E .... 816 322-0939 Olathe *(G-8071)*
Superior School Supplies Inc .... F .... 620 421-3190 Parsons *(G-9743)*
U S Toy Co Inc .... E .... 913 642-8247 Leawood *(G-5587)*

5051 Metals Service Centers

A M Castle & Co .... E .... 316 943-0277 Wichita *(G-13588)*
Al Stevens Construction LLC .... F .... 913 897-0688 Overland Park *(G-8364)*
Alcoa Inc .... C .... 620 665-5281 Hutchinson *(G-3195)*
American Metals Supply Co Inc .... E .... 913 754-0616 Lenexa *(G-5651)*
AMI Metals Inc .... E .... 316 945-7771 Wichita *(G-13700)*
Brown Strauss Inc .... E .... 913 621-4000 Kansas City *(G-3879)*
Butterfly Supply Inc .... F .... 620 793-7156 Great Bend *(G-2525)*
Custom Alloy Sales 34p LLC .... D .... 913 471-4800 Prescott *(G-10166)*
Eagle Trailer Company Inc .... G .... 785 841-3200 Lawrence *(G-4844)*
Frank Black Pipe & Supply Co .... F .... 620 241-2582 McPherson *(G-6966)*
Hajoca Corporation .... F .... 785 825-1333 Salina *(G-10531)*
Hall Steel & Fabrication Inc .... G .... 316 263-4222 Wichita *(G-14547)*
Joseph T Ryerson & Son Inc .... E .... 316 942-6061 Wichita *(G-14774)*
Kemlee Manufacturing Inc .... D .... 620 783-5035 Galena *(G-2076)*
L & M Steel & Mfg .... G .... 785 462-8216 Colby *(G-1023)*
Metalwest LLC .... D .... 913 829-8585 New Century *(G-7293)*
Midwest Iron & Metal Co Inc .... E .... 620 662-5663 Hutchinson *(G-3378)*
Norfolk Iron & Metal Co .... C .... 620 342-9202 Emporia *(G-1807)*
P K M Steel Service Inc .... D .... 785 827-3638 Salina *(G-10629)*
Phoenix Corporation .... E .... 913 321-5200 Kansas City *(G-4321)*
Pioneer Tank & Steel Inc .... G .... 620 672-2153 Pratt *(G-10133)*
▲ Piping Alloys Inc .... E .... 913 677-3833 Lenexa *(G-6058)*
Reliance Steel & Aluminum Co .... D .... 316 636-4500 Wichita *(G-15440)*
Reliance Steel & Aluminum Co .... F .... 316 838-9351 Wichita *(G-15441)*
Rgs Industries Inc .... G .... 913 780-9033 Olathe *(G-8031)*
Rock Ridge Steel Company LLC .... F .... 913 365-5200 Elwood *(G-1690)*
Royal Metal Industries Inc .... E .... 913 829-3000 Olathe *(G-8044)*
Salina Steel Supply Inc .... E .... 785 825-2138 Salina *(G-10692)*
SOS Metals Midwest LLC .... E .... 316 522-0101 Wichita *(G-15616)*
◆ Steel and Pipe Supply Co Inc .... C .... 785 587-5100 Manhattan *(G-6809)*
Steel and Pipe Supply Co Inc .... D .... 913 768-4333 New Century *(G-7299)*
Steel Building Sales LLC .... F .... 316 733-5380 Rose Hill *(G-10249)*
Teeter Irrigation Inc .... F .... 620 276-8257 Garden City *(G-2297)*
Thyssenkrupp Materials NA Inc .... F .... 620 802-0900 Hutchinson *(G-3464)*
TW Metals Inc .... E .... 316 744-5000 Park City *(G-9650)*
Welborn Sales Inc .... F .... 785 823-2394 Salina *(G-10766)*
Wessel Iron & Supply Inc .... F .... 620 225-0568 Dodge City *(G-1453)*
Wholesale Sheet Metal Inc .... C .... 913 432-7100 Kansas City *(G-4543)*
Wifco Steel Products Inc .... D .... 620 543-2827 Hutchinson *(G-3489)*

5052 Coal & Other Minerals & Ores Wholesale

◆ Koch Carbon LLC .... E .... 316 828-5500 Wichita *(G-14875)*
Pride AG Resources .... F .... 620 227-8671 Dodge City *(G-1422)*
Tessenderlo Kerley Inc .... F .... 620 251-3111 Coffeyville *(G-982)*

5063 Electrl Apparatus, Eqpt, Wiring Splys Wholesale

A-1 Electric Inc .... F .... 620 431-7500 Chanute *(G-701)*
ABB Motors and Mechanical Inc .... F .... 816 587-0272 Lenexa *(G-5618)*
Accent Lighting Inc .... F .... 316 636-1278 Wichita *(G-13601)*
Ademco Inc .... G .... 913 438-1111 Lenexa *(G-5629)*
Aggreko LLC .... F .... 913 281-9782 Shawnee Mission *(G-11085)*
American Sentry Security Sys .... E .... 785 232-1525 Topeka *(G-12323)*
Anixter Inc .... F .... 620 365-7161 Iola *(G-3587)*
Anixter Inc .... F .... 913 492-2622 Overland Park *(G-8386)*
Anixter Power Solutions Inc .... F .... 913 202-6945 Kansas City *(G-3812)*
Atronic Alarms Inc .... E .... 913 432-4545 Lenexa *(G-5674)*
Autozone Inc .... F .... 785 452-9790 Salina *(G-10414)*
B&B Electric Motor Co .... F .... 316 267-1238 Wichita *(G-13786)*
Barr-Thorp Electric Company .... E .... 913 789-8840 Merriam *(G-7086)*
Bhjllc Inc .... D .... 913 888-8028 Lenexa *(G-5701)*
Bhjllc Inc .... E .... 785 272-8800 Topeka *(G-12379)*
Biehler Companies Inc .... D .... 316 529-0002 Wichita *(G-13847)*
▲ Boettcher Supply Inc .... E .... 785 738-5781 Beloit *(G-479)*
Border States Industries Inc .... F .... 785 827-4497 Salina *(G-10430)*
Border States Industries Inc .... E .... 785 354-9532 Topeka *(G-12398)*
Border States Industries Inc .... F .... 316 945-1313 Wichita *(G-13870)*
C & O Elec Sales Co Inc .... F .... 913 981-0008 Shawnee Mission *(G-11194)*
Calkins Electric Supply Co Inc .... F .... 913 631-6363 Shawnee *(G-10923)*
Central Pwr Systems & Svcs LLC .... E .... 316 943-1231 Wichita *(G-13984)*
Company Business Intl Sarl .... G .... 913 286-9771 Olathe *(G-7606)*
Consolidated Elec Distrs Inc .... F .... 785 823-7161 Salina *(G-10459)*
Consolidated Elec Distrs Inc .... E .... 316 267-5311 Wichita *(G-14091)*
Consolidated Elec Distrs Inc .... E .... 316 262-3541 Wichita *(G-14092)*
D H Pace Company Inc .... C .... 816 221-0072 Olathe *(G-7636)*
D H Pace Company Inc .... E .... 316 944-3667 Wichita *(G-14157)*
D H Pace Company Inc .... B .... 816 480-2600 Olathe *(G-7638)*
Eaton Corporation .... E .... 913 451-6314 Lenexa *(G-5828)*
Eiko Global LLC .... F .... 913 441-8500 Shawnee *(G-10944)*
▲ Eiko Global LLC .... E .... 800 852-2217 Shawnee *(G-10945)*
▲ Emotorpro .... F .... 785 437-2046 Saint Marys *(G-10362)*
Endacott Lighting Inc .... F .... 785 776-4472 Manhattan *(G-6620)*
Enersys .... C .... 785 625-3355 Hays *(G-2799)*
Exide Technologies .... D .... 785 825-6276 Salina *(G-10488)*
Facility Solutions Group Inc .... E .... 913 422-8400 Shawnee *(G-10952)*
▲ Farris Burns Corp .... G .... 913 262-0555 Shawnee Mission *(G-11361)*
Flex-N-Gate Missouri LLC .... D .... 913 387-3857 Kansas City *(G-4012)*
Foley Group Inc .... F .... 913 342-3336 Kansas City *(G-4014)*
French-Gerleman Electric Co .... E .... 314 569-3122 Lenexa *(G-5866)*
Gene Oswald Company .... F .... 316 263-7191 Wichita *(G-14454)*
Gibson Industrial Controls Inc .... G .... 620 241-3551 McPherson *(G-6969)*

Graybar Electric Company Inc F 316 265-8964
Wichita (G-14500)
Green Expectations Ldscpg Inc F 913 897-8076
Kansas City (G-4049)
Headco Industries Inc F 913 831-1444
Kansas City (G-4072)
Hill & Company Inc F 785 235-5374
Topeka (G-12689)
▲ Himoinsa Power Systems Inc E 913 495-5557
Olathe (G-7768)
Independent Electric McHy Co E 913 362-1155
Kansas City (G-4097)
Industrial Battery Pdts Inc F 913 236-6500
Merriam (G-7096)
Kansas City Electrical Sup Co E 913 563-7002
Lenexa (G-5936)
Klemp Electric Machinery Co F 913 371-4330
Kansas City (G-4176)
Led2 Lighting Inc G 816 912-2180
Kansas City (G-4199)
Liebert Brothers Electric Co F 620 251-0299
Coffeyville (G-956)
▼ Light Bulbs Etc Inc F 913 894-9030
Shawnee Mission (G-11571)
▲ Meico Lamp Parts Company F 913 469-5888
Shawnee Mission (G-11616)
Mercer-Zimmerman Inc F 913 438-4546
Overland Park (G-9010)
Meter Engineers Inc F 316 721-4214
Kechi (G-4572)
Mid Kansas Tool & Electric Inc F 785 825-9521
Salina (G-10600)
Mid-West Electrical Supply Inc F 316 265-0562
Wichita (G-15083)
Naab Electric Inc F 620 276-8101
Garden City (G-2242)
Okonite Company F 913 441-4465
Edwardsville (G-1512)
OReilly Automotive Stores Inc F 316 321-4371
El Dorado (G-1588)
OReilly Automotive Stores Inc F 316 831-9112
Wichita (G-15236)
OReilly Automotive Stores Inc F 316 729-7311
Wichita (G-15233)
OReilly Automotive Stores Inc F 316 686-5536
Wichita (G-15234)
OReilly Automotive Stores Inc E 316 264-6422
Wichita (G-15235)
Overfield Corporation F 785 843-3434
Lawrence (G-5052)
Power Equipment Sales Co F 913 384-3848
Kansas City (G-4327)
Quality Steel & Wire Pdts Co G 913 888-2929
Lenexa (G-6085)
RE Pedrotti Company Inc F 913 677-7754
Shawnee Mission (G-11781)
Rensen House of Lights Inc E 913 888-0888
Lenexa (G-6103)
◆ Robert Wilson Co Inc E 913 642-1500
Overland Park (G-9251)
Satellite Engrg Group Inc E 913 324-6000
Overland Park (G-9282)
Simplex Time Recorder LLC E 316 686-6363
Wichita (G-15595)
Source One Distributors Inc F 620 221-8919
Winfield (G-16172)
Spectrum Elite Corp G 913 579-7037
Olathe (G-8076)
Standard Electric Co Inc F 913 782-5409
Olathe (G-8080)
Stanion Wholesale Elc Co Inc E 316 616-9200
Wichita (G-15653)
Stanion Wholesale Elc Co Inc E 620 672-5678
Pratt (G-10153)
Stanion Wholesale Elc Co Inc F 785 841-8420
Lawrence (G-5118)
Stanion Wholesale Elc Co Inc F 913 829-8111
Olathe (G-8081)
Stanion Wholesale Elc Co Inc F 785 823-2323
Salina (G-10715)
Stanion Wholesale Elc Co Inc F 785 537-4600
Manhattan (G-6808)
Stanion Wholesale Elc Co Inc F 913 342-1177
Kansas City (G-4438)
Sunflwer Elc Sup Htchinson Inc E 620 662-0531
Hutchinson (G-3457)
▲ Superior Signals Inc E 913 780-1440
Olathe (G-8088)
Tech Electronics Kansas LLC E 785 379-0300
Topeka (G-13149)
Ted Systems LLC E 913 677-5771
Lenexa (G-6174)
Treescape Inc E 316 733-6388
Andover (G-112)
Velociti Inc E 913 233-7230
Kansas City (G-4514)
Welco Technologies G 316 941-0400
Wichita (G-15943)
Western Chandelier Company F 913 685-2000
Overland Park (G-9491)
Western Extralite Company F 913 438-1777
Shawnee Mission (G-12005)
Williams Investigation & SEC E 620 275-1134
Garden City (G-2315)
WW Grainger Inc E 913 492-8550
Lenexa (G-6237)
WW Grainger Inc E 316 945-5101
Wichita (G-16079)

5064 Electrical Appliances, TV & Radios Wholesale

Bhjllc Inc D 913 888-8028
Lenexa (G-5701)
Blackmore and Glunt Inc F 913 469-5715
Shawnee Mission (G-11168)
▲ Clark Enterprises 2000 Inc E 785 825-7172
Salina (G-10455)
Custom Rdo Communications Ltd F 816 561-4100
Leawood (G-5367)
▲ Ermator Inc F 813 684-7091
Olathe (G-7691)
Hajoca Corporation F 785 825-1333
Salina (G-10531)
Jetz Service Co Inc F 785 354-7588
Topeka (G-12744)
Lowes Home Centers LLC C 913 631-3003
Shawnee Mission (G-11579)
Lowes Home Centers LLC C 316 773-1800
Wichita (G-14982)
Lowes Home Centers LLC C 785 452-9303
Salina (G-10585)
Lowes Home Centers LLC C 620 513-2000
Hutchinson (G-3359)
Lowes Home Centers LLC C 316 684-3117
Wichita (G-14983)
Lowes Home Centers LLC C 913 397-7070
Olathe (G-7866)
Lowes Home Centers LLC C 785 273-0888
Topeka (G-12852)
Lowes Home Centers LLC C 316 206-0000
Derby (G-1259)
Lowes Home Centers LLC C 913 328-7170
Kansas City (G-4207)
Lowes Home Centers LLC C 913 261-1040
Roeland Park (G-10227)
Lowes Home Centers LLC C 316 206-1030
Wichita (G-14984)
Mobile Addiction LLC F 316 773-3463
Wichita (G-15119)
▲ Profillment LLC F 316 260-7910
Wichita (G-15369)
Rensen House of Lights Inc E 913 888-0888
Lenexa (G-6103)
◆ Robert Wilson Co Inc E 913 642-1500
Overland Park (G-9251)
◆ Vornado Air LLC D 316 733-0035
Andover (G-115)
▲ Washer Specialties Company E 316 263-8179
Wichita (G-15930)
Wichita Wholesale Supply Inc F 316 267-3629
Wichita (G-16044)

5065 Electronic Parts & Eqpt Wholesale

Accu-Tech Corporation F 913 894-0444
Shawnee Mission (G-11066)
◆ Adams Cable Equipment Inc E 913 888-5100
Lenexa (G-5628)
Aircraft Instr & Rdo Co Inc E 316 945-9820
Wichita (G-13651)
All Systems Inc E 913 281-5100
Kansas City (G-3799)
Answernet Inc F 785 301-2810
Hays (G-2748)
Arrow Electronics Inc E 913 242-3012
Overland Park (G-8396)
▼ Asset Lifecycle LLC F 785 861-3100
Topeka (G-12341)
AVI Systems Inc E 913 495-9494
Lenexa (G-5677)
Bevan-Rabell Inc E 316 946-4870
Wichita (G-13842)
Border States Industries Inc E 785 354-9532
Topeka (G-12398)
Caliber Electronics Inc E 913 782-7787
Olathe (G-7573)
Carlton-Bates Company F 913 375-1160
Overland Park (G-8518)
Cellco Partnership F 913 897-5022
Overland Park (G-8535)
Cellco Partnership F 785 537-6159
Manhattan (G-6580)
Cellco Partnership F 316 789-9911
Derby (G-1228)
Communications Tech Assoc E 316 267-5016
Wichita (G-14076)
Cooper Electronics Inc E 913 782-0012
Olathe (G-7615)
Cytek Media Systems Inc E 785 295-4200
Topeka (G-12542)
Data Locker Inc G 913 310-9088
Overland Park (G-8636)
Decker Electric Inc D 316 265-8182
Wichita (G-14183)
Direct Communications Inc F 913 599-5577
Overland Park (G-8657)
Future Electronics Corp F 913 498-1531
Shawnee Mission (G-11388)
G E V Investment Inc E 913 677-5333
Kansas City (G-4024)
Honeywell International Inc C 913 782-0400
Olathe (G-7772)
Isodyne Inc F 316 682-5634
Wichita (G-14733)
K and C Technical Service LLC F 316 650-4464
Reading (G-10199)
Ka-Comm Inc F 785 827-8555
Salina (G-10560)
Kanokla Telephone Association E 620 845-5682
Caldwell (G-660)
Kgp Telecommunications Inc D 800 755-1950
New Century (G-7292)
Lg Elctrnics Mbilecomm USA Inc E 913 234-3701
Leawood (G-5457)
McClelland Sound Inc F 316 265-8686
Wichita (G-15021)
Metrocall F 316 634-1430
Wichita (G-15060)
Mitel Technologies Inc E 913 752-9100
Lenexa (G-6008)
Ms Electronics LLC F 913 233-8518
Lenexa (G-6014)
Optiv Security Inc F 816 421-6611
Overland Park (G-9110)
Radio Shop Inc F 316 265-1851
Wichita (G-15409)
Ricoh Usa Inc C 913 890-5100
Shawnee Mission (G-11802)
S N C Inc E 620 665-6651
Hutchinson (G-3434)
Sandifer Engrg & Contrls Inc E 316 794-8880
Wichita (G-15516)
▲ Santa Fe Distributing Inc E 913 492-8288
Shawnee Mission (G-11831)
Satellite Engrg Group Inc E 913 324-6000
Overland Park (G-9282)
▲ Skc Communication Products LLC C 913 422-4222
Shawnee Mission (G-11870)
Smith Audio Visual Inc E 785 235-3481
Topeka (G-13079)
Sound Products Inc F 913 599-3666
Olathe (G-8073)
South Centl Communications Inc E 620 930-1000
Medicine Lodge (G-7073)
Southern Kansas Tele Co Inc E 620 584-2255
Clearwater (G-899)
Southern Kansas Tele Co Inc E 620 584-2255
Clearwater (G-898)
▲ Special Product Company F 913 491-8088
Shawnee (G-11031)
Talley Inc F 913 390-8484
Olathe (G-8100)
▲ Tecnet International Inc F 913 859-9515
Lenexa (G-6173)
Teledata Communications LLC E 913 663-2010
Lenexa (G-6175)
Tfmcomm Inc E 785 233-2343
Topeka (G-13156)
Wesco Aircraft Hardware Corp C 316 315-1200
Wichita (G-15949)

Williams Investigation & SEC ....E 620 275-1134
Garden City *(G-2315)*
◆ Wireless Lifestyle LLC ....D 913 962-0002
Overland Park *(G-9499)*

5072 Hardware Wholesale

▲ Ary Inc ....F 913 214-4813
Overland Park *(G-8398)*
▲ Assembly Component Systems Inc .E 913 492-9500
Lenexa *(G-5669)*
Blish-Mize Co ....E 913 367-1250
Atchison *(G-217)*
Blish-Mize Co ....C 913 367-1250
Atchison *(G-218)*
Bruna Brothers Implement LLC ....E 785 325-2232
Washington *(G-13461)*
CBS Manhattan LLC ....F 785 537-4935
Manhattan *(G-6579)*
▲ Clancey Co ....F 913 894-4444
Overland Park *(G-8559)*
Engineered Door Products Inc ....F 316 267-1984
Wichita *(G-14288)*
Frank Colladay Hardware Co ....F 620 663-4477
Hutchinson *(G-3292)*
Harbor Freight Tools Usa Inc ....F 316 269-2779
Wichita *(G-14559)*
Indian Hills Hardware Inc ....E 785 841-1479
Lawrence *(G-4911)*
▲ Infinity Fasteners Inc ....E 913 438-8547
Lenexa *(G-5914)*
J & S Tool and Fastener Inc ....F 913 677-2000
Kansas City *(G-4114)*
K-W Manufacturing LLC ....F 785 548-7454
Everest *(G-1900)*
Kc Tool LLC ....F 913 440-9766
Olathe *(G-7833)*
Locks & Pulls Inc ....F 913 381-1335
Overland Park *(G-8967)*
Mid Kansas Tool & Electric Inc ....F 785 825-9521
Salina *(G-10600)*
Nifast Corporation ....F 913 888-9344
Lenexa *(G-6024)*
Overland Tool & Machinery Inc ....E 913 599-4044
Shawnee *(G-11007)*
Print Source Inc ....D 316 945-7052
Wichita *(G-15348)*
Smallwood Lock Supply Inc ....F 913 371-5678
Kansas City *(G-4425)*
T W Lacy & Associates Inc ....F 913 706-7625
Prairie Village *(G-10073)*
Tsr LLC ....F 316 946-1527
Wichita *(G-15814)*
Wesco Aircraft Hardware Corp ....C 316 315-1200
Wichita *(G-15949)*
WW Grainger Inc ....E 913 492-8550
Lenexa *(G-6237)*

5074 Plumbing & Heating Splys Wholesale

Ambrose Sales Inc ....E 913 780-5666
Olathe *(G-7526)*
American Wtr Purification Inc ....F 316 685-3333
Wichita *(G-13695)*
▲ Boettcher Supply Inc ....E 785 738-5781
Beloit *(G-479)*
Callaway Electric ....G 785 632-5588
Clay Center *(G-847)*
Clarios ....E 785 827-6829
Salina *(G-10454)*
David E Dishop ....F 614 861-5440
Wichita *(G-14172)*
Design Concepts Inc ....F 913 782-5672
Olathe *(G-7651)*
Dxp Enterprises Inc ....F 913 888-0108
Lenexa *(G-5827)*
Evcon Holdings Inc ....E 316 832-6300
Wichita *(G-14311)*
Ferguson Enterprises LLC ....E 316 262-0681
Wichita *(G-14355)*
Ferguson Enterprises LLC ....F 785 354-4305
Topeka *(G-12604)*
Ferguson Enterprises LLC ....D 913 752-5660
Lenexa *(G-5851)*
Fiber Glass Systems LP ....F 316 946-3900
Wichita *(G-14362)*
Frank Colladay Hardware Co ....F 620 663-4477
Hutchinson *(G-3292)*
Hajoca Corporation ....E 316 262-2471
Wichita *(G-14544)*
Hajoca Corporation ....F 785 825-1333
Salina *(G-10531)*
Harrington Industrial Plas LLC ....F 816 400-9438
Lenexa *(G-5892)*
Heating and Cooling Distrs Inc ....F 913 262-5848
Stilwell *(G-12152)*
Home Depot USA Inc ....E 913 310-0204
Overland Park *(G-8823)*
Hughes Machinery Company ....E 913 492-0355
Lenexa *(G-5906)*
Hughes Machinery Company ....G 316 612-0868
Wichita *(G-14649)*
Industrial Sales Company Inc ....E 913 829-3500
Olathe *(G-7787)*
John G Levin ....E 785 234-5551
Topeka *(G-12746)*
Johnson & White Sales Company ....F 913 390-9808
Olathe *(G-7812)*
K & K Industries Inc ....E 906 293-5242
Junction City *(G-3709)*
Kansas City Winnelson Co ....F 913 262-6868
Kansas City *(G-4152)*
Locke Equipment Sales Co ....E 913 782-8500
Olathe *(G-7864)*
Mack McClain & Associates Inc ....F 913 339-6677
Olathe *(G-7871)*
Mc Coy Company Inc ....C 913 342-1653
Kansas City *(G-4222)*
▲ Mid-America Fittings LLC ....E 913 962-7277
Overland Park *(G-9024)*
Mid-American Water & Plbg Inc ....E 785 537-1072
Manhattan *(G-6741)*
Phoenix Supply Inc ....E 316 262-7241
Wichita *(G-15294)*
Power Chemicals Inc ....F 316 524-7899
Wichita *(G-15318)*
Salina Supply Company ....E 785 823-2221
Salina *(G-10693)*
◆ Smith and Loveless Inc ....C 913 888-5201
Shawnee Mission *(G-11875)*
Superior Plumbing of Wichita ....F 316 684-8349
Wichita *(G-15696)*
United Pipe & Supply ....F 785 357-0612
Topeka *(G-13208)*
▲ Vanguard Piping Systems Inc ....C 620 241-6369
McPherson *(G-7038)*
Viega LLC ....F 678 447-1882
McPherson *(G-7040)*
Western Supply Co Inc ....E 620 663-9082
Hutchinson *(G-3486)*
Wheatland Waters Inc ....D 785 267-0512
Olathe *(G-8153)*

5075 Heating & Air Conditioning Eqpt & Splys Wholesale

A-1 Electric Inc ....F 620 431-7500
Chanute *(G-701)*
Aggreko LLC ....F 913 281-9782
Shawnee Mission *(G-11085)*
▲ Airtex Manufacturing Lllp ....C 913 583-3181
De Soto *(G-1192)*
American Metals Supply Co Inc ....E 913 754-0616
Lenexa *(G-5651)*
Automated Control Systems Corp ....D 913 766-2336
Leawood *(G-5337)*
Clarios ....D 913 307-4200
Shawnee Mission *(G-11237)*
Clarios ....F 785 267-0801
Topeka *(G-12478)*
Clarios ....E 316 721-2777
Wichita *(G-14034)*
Commercial Fltr Svc Knsas Cty ....G 913 384-5858
Kansas City *(G-3929)*
Daikin Applied Americas Inc ....F 913 492-8885
Shawnee Mission *(G-11290)*
Even Temp of Wichita Inc ....F 316 469-5321
Wichita *(G-14312)*
Foley Group Inc ....F 913 342-3336
Kansas City *(G-4014)*
Freeman Supply Inc ....F 620 662-2330
Hutchinson *(G-3294)*
▲ Frigiquip International Inc ....G 316 321-2400
El Dorado *(G-1563)*
Goodman Manufacturing Co LP ....B 316 946-9145
Wichita *(G-14483)*
Hajoca Corporation ....E 316 262-2471
Wichita *(G-14544)*
Hajoca Corporation ....F 785 825-1333
Salina *(G-10531)*
Heating and Cooling Distrs Inc ....F 913 262-5848
Stilwell *(G-12152)*
Heaven Engineering LLC ....F 316 262-1244
Wichita *(G-14592)*
IAC Systems Inc ....E 913 384-5511
Shawnee Mission *(G-11449)*
Industrial Accessories Company ....D 913 384-5511
Shawnee Mission *(G-11455)*
▲ J M OConnor Inc ....F 913 438-7867
Shawnee Mission *(G-11477)*
Jorban-Riscoe Associates Inc ....E 913 438-1244
Lenexa *(G-5932)*
Knipp Equipment Inc ....E 316 265-9655
Wichita *(G-14871)*
Lba Air Cndtoning Htg Plbg Inc ....E 816 454-5515
Shawnee Mission *(G-11551)*
Lennox Industries Inc ....E 913 339-9993
Shawnee Mission *(G-11564)*
Mac Equipment Inc ....F 785 284-2191
Sabetha *(G-10317)*
McQueeny Group Inc ....F 913 396-4700
Overland Park *(G-9004)*
OConnor Company Inc ....F 316 263-3187
Wichita *(G-15207)*
OConnor Company Inc ....E 913 894-8788
Lenexa *(G-6033)*
OConnor Company Inc ....E 316 267-2246
Wichita *(G-15208)*
OConnor Company Inc ....E 316 263-3187
Wichita *(G-15209)*
Piping Contractors Kansas Inc ....F 785 233-4321
Topeka *(G-12976)*
Salina Supply Company ....E 785 823-2221
Salina *(G-10693)*
Sandifer Engrg & Contrls Inc ....E 316 794-8880
Wichita *(G-15516)*
Style Crest Inc ....F 316 832-6303
Wichita *(G-15678)*
Triangle Sales Inc ....E 913 541-1800
Shawnee Mission *(G-11942)*
▲ Washer Specialties Company ....E 316 263-8179
Wichita *(G-15930)*
Weber Refrigeration & Htg Inc ....E 580 338-7338
Garden City *(G-2309)*
▼ Weis Fire Safety Equip Co Inc ....F 785 825-9527
Salina *(G-10765)*
Western Supply Co Inc ....E 620 663-9082
Hutchinson *(G-3486)*
Wichita Wholesale Supply Inc ....F 316 267-3629
Wichita *(G-16044)*
◆ Wsm Industries Inc ....C 316 942-9412
Wichita *(G-16075)*
Wsm Investments Inc ....C 316 942-9412
Wichita *(G-16076)*
WW Grainger Inc ....E 913 492-8550
Lenexa *(G-6237)*

5078 Refrigeration Eqpt & Splys Wholesale

▲ Cstk Inc ....E 913 233-7220
Overland Park *(G-8621)*
Larrys Trailer Sales & Svc LLC ....F 316 838-1491
Wichita *(G-14927)*
Refrigeration Technologies ....F 316 542-0397
Cheney *(G-795)*
Tresko Inc ....E 913 631-6900
Shawnee Mission *(G-11941)*
▲ Tyson Foods Inc ....F 913 393-7000
Olathe *(G-8127)*
Velociti Inc ....E 913 233-7230
Kansas City *(G-4514)*
Weber Refrigeration & Htg Inc ....E 580 338-7338
Garden City *(G-2309)*
Wichita Wholesale Supply Inc ....F 316 267-3629
Wichita *(G-16044)*
WW Grainger Inc ....E 913 492-8550
Lenexa *(G-6237)*

5082 Construction & Mining Mach & Eqpt Wholesale

◆ American Crane & Tractor Parts ....D 913 551-8223
Kansas City *(G-3804)*
B&B Redi Mix ....F 785 543-5133
Phillipsburg *(G-9778)*
Baxter Mechanical Contractors ....F 913 281-6303
Kansas City *(G-3849)*
Berry Companies Inc ....F 785 266-9509
Topeka *(G-12373)*
Berry Companies Inc ....F 785 228-2225
Topeka *(G-12374)*
Berry Companies Inc ....E 316 943-4246
Wichita *(G-13834)*

Berry Companies Inc.......E....... 785 232-7731
Topeka *(G-12375)*
Berry Companies Inc.......D....... 316 838-3321
Wichita *(G-13835)*
Berry Companies Inc.......E....... 316 838-3321
Wichita *(G-13833)*
Berry Companies Inc.......F....... 620 277-2290
Garden City *(G-2109)*
Brandsafway Services LLC.......F....... 913 342-9000
Kansas City *(G-3876)*
Bti Ness City.......E....... 785 798-2251
Ness City *(G-7253)*
Buckeye Corporation.......G....... 316 321-1060
El Dorado *(G-1539)*
Buckeye Corporation.......G....... 785 483-3111
Russell *(G-10267)*
Concordia Tractor Inc.......E....... 785 632-3181
Clay Center *(G-856)*
Coneqtec Corp.......E....... 316 943-8889
Wichita *(G-14088)*
Crane Sales & Service Co Inc.......F....... 913 621-7040
Kansas City *(G-3944)*
Crawford Supply Co.......F....... 785 434-4631
Plainville *(G-9984)*
Ditch Witch Sales Inc.......F....... 913 782-5223
Olathe *(G-7657)*
Easy Money Pawn Shop Inc.......G....... 316 687-2727
Wichita *(G-14255)*
Environmental Mfg Inc.......E....... 785 587-0807
Manhattan *(G-6621)*
Ferco Inc.......E....... 785 825-6380
Salina *(G-10500)*
Foley Equipment Company.......E....... 620 225-4121
Dodge City *(G-1361)*
Foley Equipment Company.......E....... 785 825-4661
Salina *(G-10503)*
Foley Equipment Company.......D....... 913 393-0303
Olathe *(G-7716)*
Foley Equipment Company.......F....... 316 943-4211
Park City *(G-9619)*
Foley Equipment Company.......D....... 620 626-6555
Liberal *(G-6309)*
Foley Equipment Company.......D....... 785 266-5784
Topeka *(G-12622)*
Foley Equipment Company.......F....... 620 792-5246
Great Bend *(G-2566)*
Foley Equipment Company.......C....... 785 266-5770
Topeka *(G-12623)*
Foley Industries Inc.......D....... 316 943-4211
Wichita *(G-14399)*
Foley Supply LLC.......E....... 316 944-7368
Wichita *(G-14400)*
Francis Casing Crews Inc.......E....... 620 275-0443
Garden City *(G-2166)*
Heritage Tractor Inc.......E....... 785 235-5100
Topeka *(G-12686)*
◆ **Htc Inc**.......E....... 865 689-2311
Olathe *(G-7779)*
◆ **Husqvrna Cnstr Pdts N Amer Inc**.......A....... 913 928-1000
Olathe *(G-7781)*
Kanequip Inc.......F....... 785 632-3441
Clay Center *(G-869)*
KC Coring & Cutng Cnstr Inc.......F....... 316 832-1580
Wichita *(G-14837)*
Laser Specialists Inc.......E....... 913 780-9990
Olathe *(G-7856)*
Logan Contractors Supply Inc.......E....... 913 768-1551
Olathe *(G-7865)*
M6 Concrete Accessories Co Inc.......E....... 316 263-7251
Wichita *(G-14995)*
Mather Flare Rental Inc.......F....... 785 478-9696
Topeka *(G-12863)*
▼ **Mel Stevenson & Associates Inc**.......D....... 913 262-0505
Kansas City *(G-4232)*
Midway Sales & Distrg Inc.......F....... 785 537-4665
Manhattan *(G-6745)*
Midwest Truck Equipment Inc.......F....... 316 744-2889
Park City *(G-9633)*
Mud-Co/Service Mud Inc.......F....... 620 672-2957
Pratt *(G-10126)*
Murphy Tractor & Eqp Co Inc.......F....... 620 227-3139
Dodge City *(G-1408)*
Murphy Tractor & Eqp Co Inc.......F....... 620 792-2748
Great Bend *(G-2614)*
◆ **Murphy Tractor & Eqp Co Inc**.......E....... 855 246-9124
Park City *(G-9638)*
Nesco Holdings Inc.......G....... 913 287-0001
Kansas City *(G-4286)*
Plp Inc.......E....... 620 842-5137
Anthony *(G-132)*
Plp Inc.......E....... 620 382-3794
Marion *(G-6875)*
Plp Inc.......E....... 620 342-5000
Emporia *(G-1812)*
Plp Inc.......C....... 620 664-5860
Hutchinson *(G-3408)*
Plp Inc.......E....... 316 943-4261
Wichita *(G-15307)*
Raymond Oil Company Inc.......F....... 316 267-4214
Wichita *(G-15422)*
Reed Company LLC.......E....... 785 456-7333
Wamego *(G-13439)*
Road Builders McHy & Sup Co.......F....... 913 371-3822
Kansas City *(G-4383)*
▼ **Road Builders Mchy & Sup Co**.......D....... 913 371-3822
Kansas City *(G-4384)*
Rogers Contracting.......F....... 316 613-2002
Haysville *(G-2958)*
Sellers Companies Inc.......E....... 785 823-6378
Salina *(G-10702)*
▲ **Sellers Equipment Inc**.......E....... 785 823-6378
Salina *(G-10703)*
Sellers Equipment Inc.......E....... 316 943-9311
Wichita *(G-15556)*
Shears Shop.......F....... 785 823-6201
Salina *(G-10706)*
U S Weatherford L P.......D....... 620 624-6273
Liberal *(G-6377)*
United Rentals North Amer Inc.......F....... 913 696-5628
Olathe *(G-8133)*
United Water Works Co.......E....... 913 287-1280
Kansas City *(G-4491)*
Universal Construction Pdts.......E....... 316 946-5885
Wichita *(G-15853)*
◆ **Valley Machinery Inc**.......F....... 316 755-1911
Valley Center *(G-13359)*
Vermeer Great Plains Inc.......E....... 913 782-3655
Olathe *(G-8139)*
Victor L Phillips Company.......F....... 316 854-1118
Wichita *(G-15906)*
Victor L Phillips Company.......F....... 785 380-0678
Topeka *(G-13223)*
◆ **Wall-Ties & Forms Inc**.......C....... 913 441-0073
Shawnee *(G-11049)*
Welborn Sales Inc.......F....... 785 823-2394
Salina *(G-10766)*
▲ **Weller Tractor Salvage Inc**.......F....... 620 792-5243
Great Bend *(G-2659)*
Wilkerson Crane Rental Inc.......E....... 913 238-7030
Lenexa *(G-6230)*

5083 Farm & Garden Mach & Eqpt Wholesale

96 Agri Sales Inc.......F....... 316 661-2281
Mount Hope *(G-7202)*
▲ **Abilene Machine LLC**.......C....... 785 655-9455
Solomon *(G-12046)*
AG Power Equipment Co.......F....... 785 899-3432
Goodland *(G-2460)*
AG Power Equipment Co.......F....... 785 852-4235
Sharon Springs *(G-10894)*
American Implement Inc.......E....... 620 275-4114
Garden City *(G-2098)*
American Implement Inc.......F....... 620 544-4351
Hugoton *(G-3147)*
American Implement Inc.......E....... 620 872-7244
Scott City *(G-10803)*
American Implement Inc.......E....... 620 697-2182
Elkhart *(G-1617)*
American Implement Main Office.......F....... 620 356-3460
Ulysses *(G-13282)*
Animal Health Intl Inc.......E....... 620 276-8289
Garden City *(G-2101)*
B & D Equipment Co Inc.......F....... 913 367-1744
Atchison *(G-211)*
▲ **Baker Abilene Machine Inc**.......E....... 785 565-9455
Solomon *(G-12048)*
▲ **Beaver Valley Supply Co Inc**.......E....... 800 982-1280
Atwood *(G-281)*
Bekemeyer Enterprises Inc.......F....... 785 325-2274
Washington *(G-13459)*
Berry Companies Inc.......F....... 620 277-2290
Garden City *(G-2109)*
Bill Harmon.......E....... 620 275-9597
Garden City *(G-2110)*
▲ **Boettcher Supply Inc**.......E....... 785 738-5781
Beloit *(G-479)*
Bretz Inc.......F....... 620 397-5329
Dighton *(G-1283)*
Bruna Brothers Implement LLC.......E....... 785 325-2232
Washington *(G-13461)*
Bruna Brothers Implement LLC.......F....... 785 562-5304
Marysville *(G-6881)*
Bruna Brothers Implement LLC.......F....... 785 632-5621
Clay Center *(G-845)*
Bruna Brothers Implement LLC.......F....... 785 742-2261
Hiawatha *(G-3005)*
Bruna Brothers Implement LLC.......F....... 785 336-2111
Seneca *(G-10858)*
Bucklin Tractor & Impt Co Inc.......E....... 620 826-3271
Bucklin *(G-591)*
C & W Farm Supply Inc.......F....... 785 374-4521
Courtland *(G-1179)*
Callaway Electric.......G....... 785 632-5588
Clay Center *(G-847)*
Carrico Implement Co Inc.......D....... 785 738-5744
Beloit *(G-480)*
Carrico Implement Co Inc.......F....... 785 472-4400
Ellsworth *(G-1658)*
Carrico Implement Co Inc.......E....... 785 625-2219
Hays *(G-2765)*
Century Partners LLC.......F....... 913 642-2489
Olathe *(G-7586)*
Colby A G Center LLC.......F....... 785 462-6132
Colby *(G-995)*
Concordia Tractor Inc.......F....... 785 263-3051
Abilene *(G-20)*
Conrady Western Inc.......E....... 620 842-5137
Anthony *(G-124)*
Conrady Western Inc.......E....... 316 943-4261
Wichita *(G-14090)*
Crustbuster/Speed King Inc.......D....... 620 227-7106
Dodge City *(G-1337)*
▼ **Dairy Farmers America Inc**.......B....... 816 801-6455
Kansas City *(G-3953)*
Dauer Implement Company Inc.......F....... 785 825-2141
Salina *(G-10470)*
Deer Trail Implement Inc.......E....... 620 342-5000
Emporia *(G-1728)*
Deere & Company.......E....... 309 765-4826
Olathe *(G-7644)*
Deere & Company.......F....... 913 310-8344
Olathe *(G-7646)*
Deere & Company.......E....... 800 665-4620
Hutchinson *(G-3260)*
Deere & Company.......E....... 316 945-0501
Wichita *(G-14186)*
Delaney Implement Co Inc.......F....... 620 525-6221
Burdett *(G-621)*
Fairbank Equipment Inc.......E....... 316 943-2247
Wichita *(G-14333)*
Foley Equipment Company.......C....... 785 266-5770
Topeka *(G-12623)*
Fort Scott Truck & Tractor.......F....... 620 223-6506
Fort Scott *(G-1972)*
Foster Unruh Inc.......E....... 620 227-2165
Dodge City *(G-1362)*
Frank Colladay Hardware Co.......F....... 620 663-4477
Hutchinson *(G-3292)*
▲ **General Tech A Svcs & Pdts Co**.......G....... 913 766-5566
Olathe *(G-7727)*
Gigot Agra Services Inc.......F....... 620 276-8444
Cheney *(G-792)*
Glen-Gery Corporation.......G....... 913 281-2800
Kansas City *(G-4038)*
Golden Plains AG Tech.......G....... 785 462-6753
Colby *(G-1009)*
Great Bend Farm Equipment Inc.......F....... 620 793-3509
Great Bend *(G-2578)*
◆ **Great Plains Manufacturing Inc**.......C....... 785 823-3276
Salina *(G-10518)*
Heritage Tractor Inc.......E....... 620 231-0950
Pittsburg *(G-9875)*
▲ **Heritage Tractor Inc**.......D....... 785 594-6486
Baldwin City *(G-363)*
Heritage Tractor Inc.......E....... 913 529-2376
Olathe *(G-7766)*
Hiplains Farm Equipment Inc.......F....... 620 225-0064
Dodge City *(G-1374)*
Hog Slat Incorporated.......F....... 580 338-5003
Liberal *(G-6321)*
▲ **Hoxie Implement Co Inc**.......E....... 785 675-3201
Hoxie *(G-3139)*
Industrial Sales Company Inc.......E....... 913 829-3500
Olathe *(G-7787)*
J & W Equipment Inc.......F....... 620 365-2341
Iola *(G-3614)*
Jdamc Inc.......A....... 913 310-8100
Olathe *(G-7810)*
Jewell Implement Company Inc.......F....... 785 428-3261
Jewell *(G-3650)*

S I C

Jies LLC F 620 668-5585
Copeland *(G-1149)*

John Schmidt & Sons Inc E 316 445-2103
Mount Hope *(G-7205)*

John Schmidt & Sons Inc F 620 221-0300
Winfield *(G-16150)*

▲ **Kalvesta Implement Co Inc** F 620 855-3567
Kalvesta *(G-3771)*

Kanequip Inc E 785 472-3114
Ellsworth *(G-1676)*

Kanequip Inc F 785 632-3441
Clay Center *(G-869)*

Kanequip Inc F 620 225-0016
Dodge City *(G-1384)*

Kanequip Inc F 785 562-2377
Marysville *(G-6891)*

Kanequip Inc F 785 267-9200
Topeka *(G-12754)*

▲ **Kanequip Inc** E 785 456-2041
Wamego *(G-13426)*

Kanequip Inc C 785 562-2377
Marysville *(G-6892)*

Kearney Equipment LLC F 316 722-8710
Maize *(G-6515)*

Keating Tractor & Eqp Inc E 620 624-1668
Liberal *(G-6327)*

Keesecker Agri Business Inc E 785 325-3134
Washington *(G-13466)*

Kincheloe Inc F 620 672-6401
Pratt *(G-10123)*

Kiowa Service Co Inc F 316 636-1070
Wichita *(G-14865)*

Kubota Tractor Corporation F 913 215-5298
Edgerton *(G-1486)*

Landmark Implement Inc E 785 282-6601
Smith Center *(G-12036)*

Landscape Outfitters LLC F 620 221-1108
Winfield *(G-16154)*

Lang Diesel Inc F 620 947-3182
Hillsboro *(G-3051)*

Lang Diesel Inc F 620 431-6700
Chanute *(G-737)*

Lang Diesel Inc F 785 284-3401
Sabetha *(G-10316)*

Lawrence Landscape Inc E 785 843-4370
Lawrence *(G-4972)*

Leoti Greentech Incorporated F 620 375-2621
Leoti *(G-6255)*

Liberty Inc D 785 770-8788
Manhattan *(G-6713)*

Lightning Grounds Services Inc E 913 441-3900
Shawnee Mission *(G-11572)*

Linn Post & Pipe Inc E 785 348-5526
Linn *(G-6409)*

Luka Irrigation Systems Inc E 913 248-0400
Shawnee *(G-10990)*

▲ **Magnum** E 913 783-4600
Hillsdale *(G-3059)*

McConnell Machinery Co Inc F 785 843-2676
Lawrence *(G-5016)*

McLaughlin Leasing Inc F 316 542-0303
Cheney *(G-794)*

Mid-Continent Industries Inc F 316 283-9648
Newton *(G-7384)*

Midwest Mixer Service LLC E 620 872-7251
Scott City *(G-10823)*

▲ **Mikes Equipment Company** F 620 543-2535
Buhler *(G-618)*

Miller Welding Inc F 785 454-3425
Downs *(G-1472)*

Minter-Wilson Drilling Co Inc E 620 275-7471
Garden City *(G-2238)*

Murphy Tractor & Eqp Co Inc F 785 233-0556
Topeka *(G-12919)*

Norvell Company Inc E 785 825-6663
Salina *(G-10615)*

Oakley Motors Inc E 785 672-3238
Oakley *(G-7484)*

Oregon Trail Equipment LLC F 785 562-2346
Marysville *(G-6905)*

Orscheln Farm and Home LLC F 620 930-3276
Medicine Lodge *(G-7071)*

Pankratz Implement Co E 620 662-8681
Hutchinson *(G-3399)*

Plp Inc E 620 532-3106
Kingman *(G-4610)*

Prairieland Partners LLC D 620 664-6552
Hutchinson *(G-3412)*

▲ **Price Bros Equipment Co** E 316 265-9577
Wichita *(G-15340)*

Professnal Turf Pdts Ltd Prtnr E 913 599-1449
Lenexa *(G-6073)*

▲ **Quality Power Products Inc** G 785 263-0060
Solomon *(G-12052)*

R & F Farm Supply Inc F 620 244-3275
Erie *(G-1864)*

R & H Implement Company Inc F 620 384-7421
Syracuse *(G-12230)*

Radke Implement Inc F 620 935-4310
Russell *(G-10286)*

Ravenscraft Implement Inc F 316 799-2141
Whitewater *(G-13572)*

Rhs Inc E 785 742-2949
Hiawatha *(G-3023)*

Romans Outdoor Power Inc F 620 331-2970
Independence *(G-3556)*

Romans Outdoor Power Inc E 913 837-5225
Louisburg *(G-6466)*

Roto-Mix LLC G 620 872-1100
Scott City *(G-10830)*

Roto-Mix LLC E 620 653-7323
Hoisington *(G-3070)*

Shaw Motor Co Inc F 785 673-4228
Grainfield *(G-2496)*

Shepherds Truck & Tractor F 620 331-2970
Independence *(G-3560)*

Simpson Farm Enterprises Inc F 785 731-2700
Ransom *(G-10195)*

Stans Sprinkler Service Inc E 800 570-5932
Wichita *(G-15654)*

▲ **Storrer Implement Inc** F 620 365-5692
Iola *(G-3636)*

Straub International Inc F 620 672-2998
Pratt *(G-10156)*

Straub International Inc E 620 792-5256
Great Bend *(G-2641)*

Straub International Inc F 620 662-0211
Hutchinson *(G-3451)*

Straub International Inc F 785 825-1300
Salina *(G-10717)*

T & C Mfg & Operating Inc E 620 793-5483
Great Bend *(G-2646)*

Taylor Implement Co Inc E 785 675-3272
Hoxie *(G-3143)*

Teeter Irrigation Inc F 620 276-8257
Garden City *(G-2297)*

TLC Lawn Care Inc D 913 780-5296
Olathe *(G-8112)*

Todd Tractor Co Inc F 785 336-2138
Seneca *(G-10884)*

Treescape Inc E 316 733-6388
Andover *(G-112)*

Ulysses Standard Supply Inc F 620 356-4171
Ulysses *(G-13327)*

Underground Specialists Inc F 620 276-3344
Garden City *(G-2305)*

Unruh-Foster Inc E 620 846-2215
Montezuma *(G-7161)*

▲ **Upu Industries Inc** D 785 238-6990
Junction City *(G-3762)*

Van-Wall Equipment Inc E 913 397-6009
Olathe *(G-8138)*

Western Kansas Valley Inc F 785 852-4606
Sharon Springs *(G-10902)*

Western Sprinklers Inc F 785 462-6755
Colby *(G-1048)*

Western Supply Co Inc E 620 663-9082
Hutchinson *(G-3486)*

Woofter Cnstr & Irrigation Inc E 785 462-8653
Colby *(G-1049)*

▲ **Zeitlow Distributing Co Inc** F 620 241-4279
McPherson *(G-7045)*

5084 Industrial Mach & Eqpt Wholesale

Accent Erection & Maint Co Inc F 913 371-1600
Kansas City *(G-3780)*

Ach Foam Technologies Inc D 913 321-4114
Kansas City *(G-3782)*

Adelphi Construction Lc D 913 384-5511
Shawnee Mission *(G-11075)*

▲ **Air Capital Equipment Inc** E 316 522-1111
Wichita *(G-13647)*

Air Products and Chemicals Inc E 620 624-8151
Liberal *(G-6273)*

Airgas Usa LLC E 785 823-8100
Salina *(G-10398)*

Airgas Usa LLC E 316 941-9162
Wichita *(G-13653)*

Alltite Inc E 316 686-3010
Wichita *(G-13678)*

American Equipment Sales Inc F 785 843-4500
Lawrence *(G-4734)*

▲ **Arrow Acquisition LLC** D 913 495-4869
Lenexa *(G-5662)*

▼ **Asset Lifecycle LLC** F 785 861-3100
Topeka *(G-12341)*

Associated Air Products Inc F 913 894-5600
Lenexa *(G-5670)*

Associated Eqp Sls Co LLC F 913 894-4455
Lenexa *(G-5671)*

Austin A-7 Ltd F 316 945-8892
Wichita *(G-13769)*

AW Schultz Inc F 913 307-0399
Shawnee Mission *(G-11136)*

B & B Hydraulics Inc E 620 662-2552
Hutchinson *(G-3210)*

▲ **Baader Linco Inc** E 913 621-3366
Kansas City *(G-3836)*

▲ **Baader North America Corp** F 913 621-3366
Kansas City *(G-3837)*

Backwoods Equipment Company E 316 267-0350
Wichita *(G-13790)*

Barton Solvents Inc F 316 321-1540
El Dorado *(G-1534)*

Bedeschi Mid-West Conveyor LLC E 913 384-9950
Lenexa *(G-5696)*

Berry Companies Inc D 316 838-3321
Wichita *(G-13835)*

Berry Companies Inc E 316 838-3321
Wichita *(G-13833)*

Berry Companies Inc F 785 228-2225
Topeka *(G-12374)*

Berry Companies Inc F 620 277-2290
Garden City *(G-2109)*

▲ **Beumer Kansas City LLC** E 816 245-7260
Overland Park *(G-8443)*

Bl Brooks & Sons Inc G 913 829-5494
Olathe *(G-7553)*

Black Stag Brewery LLC D 785 764-1628
Lawrence *(G-4760)*

Blackmore and Glunt Inc F 913 469-5715
Shawnee Mission *(G-11168)*

Buckeye Corporation G 785 483-3111
Russell *(G-10267)*

Butterfly Supply Inc F 620 793-7156
Great Bend *(G-2525)*

C & B Equipment Midwest Inc F 316 262-5156
Wichita *(G-13924)*

C W Mill Equipment Co Inc E 785 284-3454
Sabetha *(G-10308)*

Callaway Electric G 785 632-5588
Clay Center *(G-847)*

Central Pwr Systems & Svcs LLC E 316 943-1231
Wichita *(G-13984)*

Central Pwr Systems & Svcs LLC F 785 462-8211
Colby *(G-992)*

Clarios E 316 721-2777
Wichita *(G-14034)*

Classic Well Service Inc F 620 587-3402
Claflin *(G-841)*

▲ **Columbia Elev Solutions Inc** E 620 442-2510
Winfield *(G-16123)*

◆ **Continental-Agra Equip Inc** F 316 283-9602
Newton *(G-7334)*

Cross Manufacturing Inc D 785 625-2585
Hays *(G-2780)*

Cross Manufacturing Inc C 620 324-5525
Lewis *(G-6268)*

Crown Equipment Corporation E 316 942-4400
Wichita *(G-14136)*

Crown Packaging Corp E 913 888-1951
Shawnee Mission *(G-11283)*

▲ **Cstk Inc** E 913 233-7220
Overland Park *(G-8621)*

Cummins Central Power LLC E 316 838-0875
Park City *(G-9615)*

Cummins Central Power LLC F 785 462-3945
Colby *(G-1002)*

▲ **Custom Mobile Equipment Inc** E 785 594-7475
Baldwin City *(G-358)*

Darwin Industries Inc F 620 251-8438
Coffeyville *(G-932)*

DCS Sanitation Management Inc C 620 624-5533
Liberal *(G-6302)*

Denison Inc F 620 378-4148
Fredonia *(G-2030)*

Dicks Engine & Machine Service F 620 564-2238
Ellinwood *(G-1629)*

Dxp Enterprises Inc F 913 888-0108
Lenexa *(G-5827)*

Eaton Corporation ....B 620 663-5751
Hutchinson (G-3274)
Economy Mfg Co Inc ....E 620 725-3520
Sedan (G-10842)
Engquist Tractor Service Inc ....E 620 654-3651
McPherson (G-6959)
Ernstmann Machine Co Inc ....G 316 943-5282
Wichita (G-14303)
Exline Leasing Inc ....C 785 825-4683
Salina (G-10490)
Ferrellgas Inc ....F 913 661-1500
Overland Park (G-8713)
Ferrellgas Partners LP ....D 913 661-1500
Overland Park (G-8714)
◆ Flint Hills Resources LLC ....B 316 828-5500
Wichita (G-14390)
Fluidtech LLC ....E 913 492-3300
Lenexa (G-5859)
Fluidtech LLC ....E 913 492-3300
Lenexa (G-5860)
Fluidtech LLC ....F 913 492-3300
Lenexa (G-5861)
Foley Equipment Company ....D 785 537-2101
Manhattan (G-6637)
Foley Equipment Company ....C 785 266-5770
Topeka (G-12623)
Foley Industries Inc ....D 316 943-4211
Wichita (G-14399)
Fujifilm North America Corp ....F 816 914-5942
Kansas City (G-4021)
◆ Fujifilm Sericol USA Inc ....C 913 342-4060
Kansas City (G-4022)
General Machinery & Sup Co Inc ....F 620 231-1550
Pittsburg (G-9865)
Gibson Industrial Controls Inc ....G 620 241-3551
McPherson (G-6969)
Global Systems Incorporated ....F 913 829-5900
Olathe (G-7734)
Gressel Oil Field Service LLC ....G 316 524-1225
Peck (G-9763)
Hajoca Corporation ....F 785 825-1333
Salina (G-10531)
◆ Hantover Inc ....C 913 214-4800
Overland Park (G-8792)
Harbison-Fischer Inc ....G 620 624-9042
Liberal (G-6317)
Harbor Freight Tools Usa Inc ....F 316 269-2779
Wichita (G-14559)
Hartfiel Automation Inc ....F 913 894-6545
Overland Park (G-8797)
Hertel Tank Service Inc ....G 785 628-2445
Hays (G-2841)
Heubel Material Handling Inc ....F 316 941-4115
Wichita (G-14602)
Hughes Machinery Company ....E 913 492-0355
Lenexa (G-5906)
Hughes Machinery Company ....G 316 612-0868
Wichita (G-14649)
Hydro Rsrces - Mid Cntnent Inc ....D 620 277-2389
Garden City (G-2201)
Hydrochem LLC ....E 316 321-7541
El Dorado (G-1569)
Hyspeco Inc ....E 316 943-0254
Wichita (G-14662)
▲ I2 Asia LLC ....F 913 422-1600
Shawnee (G-10972)
IAC Systems Inc ....E 913 384-5511
Shawnee Mission (G-11449)
Industrial Accessories Company ....D 913 384-5511
Shawnee Mission (G-11455)
Inland Industries Inc ....G 913 492-9050
Bucyrus (G-600)
Inland Newspaper Mchy Corp ....E 913 492-9050
Shawnee Mission (G-11457)
Innovative Fluid Power ....F 913 768-7008
Olathe (G-7794)
Invena Corporation ....E 620 583-8630
Eureka (G-1892)
J-W Operating Company ....F 620 626-7243
Liberal (G-6324)
Jci Industries Inc ....F 316 942-6200
Wichita (G-14751)
◆ Jem International Inc ....F 913 441-4788
Shawnee (G-10978)
K Young Inc ....F 785 475-3888
Colby (G-1019)
Kaeser Compressors Inc ....F 913 599-5100
Overland Park (G-8884)
▲ Kanamak Hydraulics Inc ....E 800 473-5843
Garden City (G-2212)
▲ Kansas City Power Products Inc ....F 913 321-7040
Kansas City (G-4149)
Kansas Forklift Inc ....F 316 262-1426
Wichita (G-14802)
Kansas Truck Equipment Co Inc ....E 316 722-4291
Wichita (G-14828)
Kaw Valley Industrial Inc ....G 785 841-9751
Eudora (G-1876)
Key Equipment & Supply Co ....F 913 788-2546
Kansas City (G-4172)
Lampton Welding Supply Co Inc ....E 316 263-3293
Wichita (G-14917)
Layne Christensen Company ....F 913 321-5000
Kansas City (G-4197)
Layne Christensen Company ....E 316 264-5365
Wichita (G-14937)
▲ Lift Truck Center Inc ....E 316 942-7465
Wichita (G-14963)
Locke Equipment Sales Co ....E 913 782-8500
Olathe (G-7864)
Mack McClain & Associates Inc ....F 913 339-6677
Olathe (G-7871)
Magnatech Engineering Inc ....G 913 845-3553
Tonganoxie (G-12265)
▲ Marlen Research Corp ....F 913 888-3333
Lenexa (G-5987)
Matheson Tri-Gas Inc ....F 785 537-0395
Manhattan (G-6734)
Matheson Tri-Gas Inc ....F 316 554-9353
Wichita (G-15019)
Matheson Tri-Gas Inc ....F 785 493-8200
Salina (G-10594)
Matheson Tri-Gas Inc ....E 785 234-3424
Topeka (G-12864)
McDonald Tank and Eqp Co Inc ....E 620 793-3555
Great Bend (G-2606)
McLaughlin Leasing Inc ....F 316 542-0303
Cheney (G-794)
Medart Inc ....F 636 282-2300
Kansas City (G-4227)
Mid-West Conveyor Company ....C 734 288-4400
Kansas City (G-4247)
Miller Welding Inc ....F 785 454-3425
Downs (G-1472)
Miniature Plastic Molding LLC ....G 316 264-2827
Wichita (G-15112)
Motion Industries Inc ....E 316 265-9608
Wichita (G-15133)
▲ Murdock Companies Inc ....E 316 262-4476
Wichita (G-15139)
Murphy Tractor & Eqp Co Inc ....F 785 233-0556
Topeka (G-12919)
Neighbors & Associates Inc ....F 620 423-3010
Parsons (G-9710)
Northeast Kansas Hydraulics ....G 785 235-0405
Topeka (G-12936)
Northern Tool & Eqp Co Inc ....F 316 854-9422
Wichita (G-15190)
◆ Oasis Car Wash Systems Inc ....E 620 783-1355
Galena (G-2077)
Oil Patch Pump and Supply Inc ....F 620 431-1890
Chanute (G-749)
Orscheln Farm and Home LLC ....F 785 825-1681
Salina (G-10624)
Orscheln Farm and Home LLC ....F 913 367-2261
Atchison (G-254)
Orscheln Farm and Home LLC ....F 785 625-7316
Hays (G-2884)
Otis Elevator Company ....F 316 682-6886
Bel Aire (G-437)
Otis Elevator Company ....E 913 621-8800
Kansas City (G-4300)
Overhead Door Company ....E 316 265-4634
Wichita (G-15240)
P B Hoidale Co Inc ....F 316 942-1361
Wichita (G-15250)
P B Hoidale Co Inc ....F 913 438-1500
Shawnee (G-11008)
Pac Mig Inc ....G 316 269-3040
Mulvane (G-7226)
Palmer Johnson Pwr Systems LLC ....F 913 268-2941
Olathe (G-7972)
▼ Peerless Conveyor and Mfg Corp ....F 913 342-2240
Kansas City (G-4318)
Pentair Flow Technologies LLC ....C 913 371-5000
Kansas City (G-4319)
Pmti Inc ....E 913 432-7500
Shawnee Mission (G-11740)
Praxair Inc ....E 620 657-2711
Satanta (G-10789)
Praxair Distribution Inc ....E 913 492-1551
Lenexa (G-6069)
Precision Manifold Systems Inc ....E 913 829-1221
Olathe (G-8001)
▲ Price Bros Equipment Co ....E 316 265-9577
Wichita (G-15340)
Pro Carwash Systems Inc ....F 316 788-9933
Derby (G-1266)
Professional Fleet Svcs LLC ....F 316 524-6000
Wichita (G-15361)
Raab Sales Inc ....F 913 227-0814
Shawnee Mission (G-11775)
RE Pedrotti Company Inc ....F 913 677-7754
Shawnee Mission (G-11781)
Reinhardt Services Inc ....G 785 483-2556
Russell (G-10287)
Reintjes & Hiter Co Inc ....F 913 371-1872
Kansas City (G-4368)
River City Elevator LLC ....F 316 773-3161
Wichita (G-15470)
Roberts Group Inc ....G 913 381-3930
Overland Park (G-9252)
▼ Royal Tractor Company Inc ....E 913 782-2598
New Century (G-7296)
Ryko Solutions Inc ....F 913 451-3719
Lenexa (G-6115)
S & S Equipment Co Inc ....F 316 267-7471
Wichita (G-15500)
▲ Salina Vortex Corp ....C 785 825-7177
Salina (G-10696)
Sanden North America Inc ....A 913 888-6667
Shawnee Mission (G-11826)
Schenck Process LLC ....C 785 284-2191
Sabetha (G-10331)
▲ Seals Inc ....G 913 438-1212
Shawnee Mission (G-11844)
Sellers Companies Inc ....E 785 823-6378
Salina (G-10702)
▲ Sellers Equipment Inc ....E 785 823-6378
Salina (G-10703)
Sellers Equipment Inc ....E 316 943-9311
Wichita (G-15556)
Shannahan Crane & Hoist Inc ....F 816 746-9822
Kansas City (G-4419)
Sharpening Specialists LLC ....E 316 945-0593
Wichita (G-15575)
Southerncarlson Inc ....F 316 942-1392
Wichita (G-15625)
Spray Equipment & Svc Ctr LLC ....E 316 264-4349
Wichita (G-15647)
Spsi Inc ....F 913 541-8304
Lenexa (G-6150)
▲ Styers Equipment Company ....F 913 681-5225
Overland Park (G-9369)
Superior School Supplies Inc ....E 316 265-7683
Wichita (G-15699)
◆ Tank Connection LLC ....F 620 423-0251
Parsons (G-9744)
Teeter Irrigation Inc ....F 620 276-8257
Garden City (G-2297)
Thompson Bros Supplies Inc ....E 620 251-1740
Coffeyville (G-983)
Thompson Pump Co ....E 913 788-2583
Kansas City (G-4468)
Thyssenkrupp Elevator Corp ....F 913 888-8046
Overland Park (G-9408)
Thyssenkrupp Elevator Corp ....F 316 529-2233
Wichita (G-15764)
Tractor Supply Company ....F 785 827-3300
Salina (G-10738)
◆ Tvh Parts Co ....B 913 829-1000
Olathe (G-8125)
U S Automation Inc ....G 913 894-2410
Shawnee Mission (G-11953)
Velociti Inc ....E 913 233-7230
Kansas City (G-4514)
Veritiv Operating Company ....C 913 667-1500
Kansas City (G-4516)
Voestalpine Nortrak Inc ....D 316 284-0088
Newton (G-7424)
▲ W + D North America Inc ....E 913 492-9880
Overland Park (G-9474)
▲ Weber Manufacturing LLC ....F 620 251-9800
Coffeyville (G-985)
Weis Fire & Safety Eqp LLC ....E 303 421-2001
Shawnee (G-11051)
Wes Material Handling Inc ....F 913 369-9375
Tonganoxie (G-12273)
Western Hydro LLC ....F 620 277-2132
Garden City (G-2310)

Wichita Iron & Metals Corp Inc E 316 267-3291
Wichita *(G-16009)*
Wichita Pump & Supply Company F 316 264-8308
Wichita *(G-16019)*
Wichita Welding Supply Inc F 316 838-8671
Wichita *(G-16043)*
Wiese Usa Inc E 316 942-1600
Wichita *(G-16045)*
Wilkerson Crane Rental Inc E 913 238-7030
Lenexa *(G-6230)*
Wki Operations Inc F 316 838-0867
Dodge City *(G-1462)*
Woodcraft Supply LLC G 913 599-2800
Shawnee Mission *(G-12016)*
WW Grainger Inc E 316 945-5101
Wichita *(G-16079)*
WW Grainger Inc E 913 492-8550
Lenexa *(G-6237)*

5085 Industrial Splys Wholesale

Air Filter Plus Inc E 785 542-3700
Eudora *(G-1869)*
Airgas Usa LLC E 785 823-8100
Salina *(G-10398)*
Airgas Usa LLC E 316 941-9162
Wichita *(G-13653)*
Applied Industrial Tech Inc F 785 232-5508
Topeka *(G-12334)*
Austin A-7 Ltd F 316 945-8892
Wichita *(G-13769)*
Bamford Fire Sprinkler Co Inc E 913 432-6688
Shawnee Mission *(G-11145)*
Barrow Tooling Systems Inc G 785 364-4306
Holton *(G-3085)*
Beaver Drill & Tool Company F 913 384-2400
Kansas City *(G-3851)*
Big Springs Sports Center E 785 887-6700
Lecompton *(G-5610)*
Chada Sales Inc F 785 842-1199
Lawrence *(G-4783)*
Crown Packaging Corp E 913 888-1951
Shawnee Mission *(G-11283)*
Custom Rope A Div Williams E 620 825-4196
Kiowa *(G-4623)*
▲ Diteq Corporation E 816 246-5515
Lenexa *(G-5821)*
Domestic Fastener & Forge Inc F 913 888-9447
New Century *(G-7280)*
Experitec Inc F 913 894-4044
Shawnee Mission *(G-11356)*
Fairbank Equipment Inc E 316 943-2247
Wichita *(G-14333)*
Fastenal Company F 316 283-2266
Newton *(G-7344)*
Fastenal Company F 316 320-2223
El Dorado *(G-1561)*
▲ Flinthills Trading Company C 785 392-3017
Minneapolis *(G-7117)*
◆ Fujifilm Sericol USA Inc C 913 342-4060
Kansas City *(G-4022)*
▲ G T Sales & Manufacturing Inc D 316 943-2171
Wichita *(G-14434)*
Gates Corporation A 620 365-4100
Iola *(G-3603)*
Glantz Holdings Inc F 913 722-1000
Kansas City *(G-4037)*
Great Lakes Polymer Tech LLC E 208 324-2120
Kingman *(G-4593)*
H & P Inc G 785 263-4183
Abilene *(G-36)*
Hajoca Corporation E 316 262-2471
Wichita *(G-14544)*
Headco Industries Inc F 913 831-1444
Kansas City *(G-4072)*
◆ Husqvrna Cnstr Pdts N Amer Inc A 913 928-1000
Olathe *(G-7781)*
Ibt Inc F 913 428-4958
Kansas City *(G-4093)*
Ibt Inc C 913 677-3151
Shawnee Mission *(G-11450)*
Inventory Sales Co E 913 371-7002
Kansas City *(G-4111)*
INX International Ink Co D 913 441-0057
Edwardsville *(G-1504)*
Kc Tool LLC F 913 440-9766
Olathe *(G-7833)*
▲ Kenneth R Johnson Inc E 913 599-1133
Lenexa *(G-5945)*
Koller Enterprises Inc D 913 422-2027
Lenexa *(G-5957)*
Kuhn Co LLC E 316 788-6500
Derby *(G-1257)*
Lewis-Goetz and Company Inc F 316 265-4623
Wichita *(G-14957)*
Manko Corporation F 785 825-1301
Salina *(G-10591)*
Matheson Tri-Gas Inc E 785 234-3424
Topeka *(G-12864)*
Mem Industrial LLC F 316 944-4400
Wichita *(G-15038)*
Menard Incorporated F 620 364-3600
Burlington *(G-640)*
Mid-America Pump LLC F 913 287-3900
Kansas City *(G-4244)*
◆ Missouri-Kansas Supply Co Inc E 816 842-6513
Kansas City *(G-4263)*
▲ Mize & Co Inc E 620 532-3191
Kingman *(G-4607)*
Motion Industries Inc E 316 265-9608
Wichita *(G-15133)*
▲ Murdock Companies Inc E 316 262-4476
Wichita *(G-15139)*
Nazdar Company F 913 422-1888
Shawnee *(G-11004)*
O Ring Sales and Service Inc F 913 310-0001
Lenexa *(G-6031)*
Parker-Hannifin Corporation C 785 537-4181
Manhattan *(G-6768)*
Perfect Output LLC D 913 317-8400
Overland Park *(G-9154)*
Professional Sales Svcs Inc F 316 941-4542
El Dorado *(G-1594)*
Ragland Specialty Printing E 785 542-3058
Eudora *(G-1879)*
Rubber Belting & Hose Sup Inc E 316 269-1151
Wichita *(G-15491)*
Southerncarlson Inc F 316 942-1392
Wichita *(G-15625)*
Supply Technologies LLC E 913 982-4016
Lenexa *(G-6161)*
Swan Engineering & Sup Co Inc F 913 371-7425
Kansas City *(G-4452)*
Timken Company F 913 492-4848
Lenexa *(G-6181)*
◆ Tompkins Industries Inc E 913 764-8088
Olathe *(G-8113)*
Total Tool Supply Inc F 913 722-7879
Kansas City *(G-4471)*
V Mach Inc E 913 894-2001
Shawnee Mission *(G-11971)*
Westheffer Company Inc E 785 843-1633
Lawrence *(G-5183)*
Wichita Pump & Supply Company F 316 264-8308
Wichita *(G-16019)*
Wilco Inc F 316 943-9379
Wichita *(G-16047)*
Wilde Tool Co Inc E 785 742-7171
Hiawatha *(G-3028)*
Wkcsc Inc G 316 652-7113
Wichita *(G-16060)*
Wurth/Service Supply Inc F 316 869-2159
Wichita *(G-16078)*
WW Grainger Inc E 316 945-5101
Wichita *(G-16079)*
WW Grainger Inc E 913 492-8550
Lenexa *(G-6237)*

5087 Service Establishment Eqpt & Splys Wholesale

AAA Restaurant Supply LLC F 316 265-4365
Wichita *(G-13592)*
Ahn Marketing Incorporated F 913 342-2176
Kansas City *(G-3793)*
Artco Casket Co Inc E 913 438-2655
Lenexa *(G-5665)*
Bamford Fire Sprinkler Co Inc E 913 432-6688
Shawnee Mission *(G-11145)*
Bhjllc Inc D 913 888-8028
Lenexa *(G-5701)*
Bhjllc Inc E 785 272-8800
Topeka *(G-12379)*
Blackburn Nursery Inc E 785 272-2707
Topeka *(G-12387)*
City Wide Holding Company Inc C 913 888-5700
Lenexa *(G-5757)*
Clean-Rite LLC F 785 628-1945
Hays *(G-2771)*
Comet 1 H R Cleaners Inc F 620 626-8100
Liberal *(G-6295)*
Edwards Chemicals Inc F 913 365-5158
Elwood *(G-1686)*
Emporia Wholesale Coffee Co C 620 343-7000
Emporia *(G-1747)*
▲ Fabriclean Supply Kansas Lc F 913 492-1743
Lenexa *(G-5845)*
Four State Maintenance Sup Inc E 620 251-7033
Coffeyville *(G-940)*
Gaia Inc F 785 539-2622
Manhattan *(G-6643)*
Haynes Salon and Supply Inc F 785 539-5512
Manhattan *(G-6651)*
Hertel Tank Service Inc G 785 628-2445
Hays *(G-2841)*
Huber Inc F 316 267-0289
Wichita *(G-14646)*
Hugos Industrial Supply Inc E 620 331-4846
Independence *(G-3526)*
Jayhawk Fire Sprinkler Co Inc E 913 422-3770
Olathe *(G-7809)*
Keller Fire & Safety Inc D 913 371-8494
Kansas City *(G-4169)*
Lafe T Williams & Assoc Inc F 316 262-0479
Wichita *(G-14914)*
McAfee Enterprises LLC F 913 839-3328
Olathe *(G-7880)*
Netzer Sales Inc F 913 599-6464
Shawnee Mission *(G-11676)*
Premier Food Service Inc C 316 269-2447
Wichita *(G-15330)*
Pro Carwash Systems Inc F 316 788-9933
Derby *(G-1266)*
Raintree Inc E 913 262-7013
Shawnee Mission *(G-11776)*
Ryan D&M Inc F 620 231-4559
Pittsburg *(G-9930)*
Ryko Solutions Inc F 913 451-3719
Lenexa *(G-6115)*
Scriptpro USA Inc B 913 384-1008
Shawnee Mission *(G-11840)*
Southwest Paper Company Inc E 316 838-7755
Wichita *(G-15631)*
T D C Ltd E 913 780-9631
Olathe *(G-8096)*
TDS Allocation Co E 800 857-2906
Topeka *(G-13146)*
Treat America Limited B 913 384-4900
Shawnee Mission *(G-11940)*
Ultra-Chem Inc C 913 492-2929
Shawnee Mission *(G-11955)*
Waxene Products Company Inc G 316 263-8523
Wichita *(G-15938)*
Wholesale Beauty Club Inc F 316 941-9500
Wichita *(G-15967)*
Wholesale Beauty Club Inc F 316 687-9890
Wichita *(G-15966)*
Wilbert Funeral Services Inc E 316 832-1114
Wichita *(G-16046)*
Wilson Building Maintenance C 316 264-0699
Wichita *(G-16053)*
▼ Windtrax Inc E 913 789-9100
Shawnee Mission *(G-12013)*

5088 Transportation Eqpt & Splys, Except Motor Vehicles Wholesale

A & K Railroad Materials Inc D 913 375-1810
Kansas City *(G-3776)*
Aircraft Instr & Rdo Co Inc E 316 945-9820
Wichita *(G-13651)*
Ametek Arcft Parts & ACC Inc E 316 264-2397
Wichita *(G-13699)*
Amsted Rail Company Inc F 913 299-2223
Kansas City *(G-3808)*
Boeing Distribution Svcs Inc E 316 630-4900
Wichita *(G-13867)*
Cav Ice Protection Inc E 913 738-5391
New Century *(G-7272)*
Century Instrument Corp F 316 683-7571
Wichita *(G-13991)*
◆ Dodson International Parts Inc D 785 878-8000
Rantoul *(G-10196)*
◆ Dodson Investments Inc D 785 878-4000
Rantoul *(G-10197)*
◆ Global Ground Support LLC D 913 780-0300
Olathe *(G-7732)*
◆ Global Parts Inc D 316 733-9240
Augusta *(G-319)*
Graco Supply Company F 316 943-4200
Wichita *(G-14492)*

- Honeywell International Inc ... E ... 913 712-0400 Olathe *(G-7776)*
- ▲ Ipeco Wichita Inc ... E ... 316 722-7800 Wichita *(G-14729)*
- Kansas Golf and Turf Inc ... F ... 316 267-9111 Park City *(G-9622)*
- Kelley Instruments Inc ... F ... 316 945-7171 Wichita *(G-14843)*
- McFarlane Aviation Inc ... D ... 785 594-2741 Baldwin City *(G-366)*
- Mid-State Aerospace Inc ... F ... 913 764-3600 Olathe *(G-7892)*
- Midwest Corporate Aviation Inc ... E ... 316 636-9700 Wichita *(G-15091)*
- ▲ Omni Aerospace Inc ... E ... 316 529-8998 Wichita *(G-15216)*
- Pratt & Whitney Eng Svcs Inc ... G ... 316 945-9763 Wichita *(G-15322)*
- Progress Rail Services Corp ... E ... 913 345-4807 Overland Park *(G-9191)*
- Progress Rail Services Corp ... C ... 913 352-6613 Pleasanton *(G-10000)*
- Rockwell Collins Inc ... C ... 316 677-4808 Wichita *(G-15474)*
- Tech-Aire Instruments Inc ... F ... 316 262-4020 Wichita *(G-15724)*
- Textron Aviation Inc ... C ... 620 332-0228 Independence *(G-3564)*
- Wm F Hurst Co LLC ... F ... 800 741-0543 Shawnee *(G-11055)*
- ▲ Yingling Aircraft Inc ... D ... 316 943-3246 Wichita *(G-16085)*

5091 Sporting & Recreational Goods & Splys Wholesale

- Abraham Jacob Gorelick ... F ... 913 371-0459 Kansas City *(G-3779)*
- Bills Outdoor Sports ... F ... 620 241-7130 McPherson *(G-6938)*
- ◆ Bushnell Holdings Inc ... C ... 913 752-3400 Overland Park *(G-8497)*
- ◆ Combat Brands LLC ... E ... 913 689-2300 Lenexa *(G-5770)*
- County of Johnson ... E ... 913 829-4653 Olathe *(G-7623)*
- Don Coffey Company Inc ... F ... 913 764-2108 Olathe *(G-7659)*
- Glen Thurber ... E ... 785 233-9541 Topeka *(G-12638)*
- Grand Prairie Ht & Convention ... C ... 620 669-9311 Hutchinson *(G-3303)*
- Great Plains Supply Inc ... F ... 913 492-1520 Shawnee Mission *(G-11400)*
- ▼ Jayhawk Bowling Sup & Eqp Inc ... F ... 785 842-3237 Lawrence *(G-4919)*
- Joe Bob Outfitters LLC ... F ... 785 639-7121 Hays *(G-2856)*
- Lo-Mar Bowling Supply Inc ... F ... 785 483-2222 Russell *(G-10279)*
- Ludwikoski & Associates Inc ... F ... 913 879-2224 Overland Park *(G-8974)*
- Mid States Health Products ... F ... 316 681-3611 Wichita *(G-15072)*
- Nill Bros Sporting Goods Inc ... F ... 913 345-8655 Overland Park *(G-9087)*
- Olathe Billiards Inc ... F ... 913 780-5740 Olathe *(G-7928)*
- Pools Plus ... F ... 785 823-7665 Salina *(G-10636)*
- R T Sporting Goods Inc ... F ... 620 275-5507 Garden City *(G-2261)*
- ▲ RC Sports Inc ... E ... 913 894-5177 Lenexa *(G-6092)*
- Scp Distributors LLC ... F ... 913 660-0061 Lenexa *(G-6120)*
- United Industries Inc ... F ... 620 278-3160 Sterling *(G-12131)*
- USA Gym Supply Inc ... G ... 620 792-2209 Great Bend *(G-2653)*
- ▲ USA Inc ... F ... 785 825-6247 Salina *(G-10748)*

5092 Toys & Hobby Goods & Splys Wholesale

- Continental American Corp ... C ... 316 321-4551 El Dorado *(G-1550)*
- ▲ Decorator and Craft Corp ... D ... 316 685-6265 Wichita *(G-14184)*
- Evans Industries Inc ... G ... 316 262-2551 Wichita *(G-14310)*
- Fun Services of Kansas City ... E ... 913 631-3772 Shawnee Mission *(G-11385)*
- ▲ Jakes Fireworks Inc ... F ... 620 231-2264 Pittsburg *(G-9881)*
- Starlite Mold Co ... F ... 316 262-3350 Wichita *(G-15658)*
- ◆ Winco Fireworks Intl LLC ... E ... 913 649-2071 Prairie Village *(G-10083)*

5093 Scrap & Waste Materials Wholesale

- Advantage Metals Recycling LLC ... D ... 620 674-3800 Columbus *(G-1059)*
- Advantage Metals Recycling LLC ... E ... 913 621-2711 Kansas City *(G-3788)*
- Advantage Metals Recycling LLC ... E ... 913 321-3358 Kansas City *(G-3789)*
- Advantage Metals Recycling LLC ... E ... 816 861-2700 Kansas City *(G-3790)*
- Advantage Metals Recycling LLC ... E ... 620 342-1122 Emporia *(G-1692)*
- Advantage Metals Recycling LLC ... E ... 785 841-0396 Lawrence *(G-4723)*
- Advantage Metals Recycling LLC ... F ... 785 232-5152 Topeka *(G-12297)*
- Allmetal Recycling LLC ... D ... 316 838-9381 Wichita *(G-13676)*
- Asner Iron and Metal Co ... F ... 913 281-4000 Kansas City *(G-3822)*
- Batliner Paper Stock Company ... F ... 913 233-1367 Kansas City *(G-3848)*
- Boge Iron & Metal Co Inc ... E ... 316 263-8241 Wichita *(G-13868)*
- Bohm Farm & Ranch Inc ... E ... 785 823-0303 Salina *(G-10429)*
- Environmental Protection Agcy ... B ... 913 551-7118 Lenexa *(G-5835)*
- Erman Corporation Inc ... E ... 913 287-4800 Kansas City *(G-3996)*
- F & F Iron & Metal Co ... E ... 785 877-3830 Norton *(G-7445)*
- Garden City Iron & Metal ... F ... 620 277-0227 Garden City *(G-2173)*
- Mc Kinnes Iron & Metal Inc ... G ... 620 257-3821 Lyons *(G-6494)*
- Midwest Iron & Metal Co Inc ... E ... 620 662-5663 Hutchinson *(G-3378)*
- National Fiber Supply LLC ... F ... 913 321-0066 Kansas City *(G-4280)*
- Salina Iron & Metal Company ... E ... 785 826-9838 Salina *(G-10677)*
- Scrap Management LLC ... F ... 913 573-1000 Kansas City *(G-4408)*
- Shostak Iron and Metal Co Inc ... E ... 913 321-9210 Overland Park *(G-9309)*
- ◆ Solomon Transformers LLC ... B ... 785 655-2191 Solomon *(G-12054)*
- SOS Metals Midwest LLC ... E ... 316 522-0101 Wichita *(G-15616)*
- ◆ Stallard Technologies Inc ... E ... 913 851-2260 Overland Park *(G-9351)*
- Wessel Iron & Supply Inc ... F ... 620 225-0568 Dodge City *(G-1453)*
- Wichita Iron & Metals Corp Inc ... E ... 316 267-3291 Wichita *(G-16009)*

5094 Jewelry, Watches, Precious Stones Wholesale

- Dee Jays Enterprises ... F ... 620 227-3126 Dodge City *(G-1340)*
- Ehlers Industries Inc ... E ... 913 381-7884 Leawood *(G-5384)*
- Jayhawk Trophy Company Inc ... G ... 785 843-3900 Lawrence *(G-4921)*
- ▲ Meico Lamp Parts Company ... F ... 913 469-5888 Shawnee Mission *(G-11616)*
- Simon & Simon Inc ... G ... 913 888-9889 Overland Park *(G-9311)*

5099 Durable Goods: NEC Wholesale

- Airgas Usa LLC ... E ... 785 823-8100 Salina *(G-10398)*
- Amsted Rail Company Inc ... F ... 913 299-2223 Kansas City *(G-3808)*
- Ballyhoo Banners ... G ... 913 385-5050 Lenexa *(G-5684)*
- Bell Memorials LLC ... F ... 785 738-2257 Beloit *(G-474)*
- Conrad Fire Equipment Inc ... F ... 913 780-5521 Olathe *(G-7611)*
- Cytek Media Systems Inc ... E ... 785 295-4200 Topeka *(G-12542)*
- FP Supply LLC ... F ... 316 284-6700 Newton *(G-7347)*
- ◆ Hantover Inc ... C ... 913 214-4800 Overland Park *(G-8792)*
- Keller Fire & Safety Inc ... D ... 913 371-8494 Kansas City *(G-4169)*
- Kent Business Systems Corp ... F ... 316 262-4487 Wichita *(G-14851)*
- Kiefs Cds & Tapes ... E ... 785 842-1544 Lawrence *(G-4945)*
- Lumber One LLC ... E ... 913 583-9889 De Soto *(G-1206)*
- Magtek Inc ... F ... 913 451-1151 Lenexa *(G-5981)*
- Martin James ... G ... 785 525-7761 Lucas *(G-6474)*
- Midco Holdings LLC ... F ... 316 522-0900 Wichita *(G-15085)*
- Norder Supply Inc ... E ... 620 805-5972 Garden City *(G-2243)*
- ▲ Pop-A-Shot Enterprise LLC ... G ... 785 827-6229 Salina *(G-10637)*
- R Miller Sales Co Inc ... E ... 913 341-3727 Shawnee Mission *(G-11772)*
- Raymarr Inc ... F ... 913 648-3480 Shawnee Mission *(G-11778)*
- ◆ Sevo Systems Inc ... E ... 913 677-1112 Lenexa *(G-6125)*
- Signs of Business Inc ... F ... 316 683-5700 Wichita *(G-15593)*
- Smith Monuments Inc ... G ... 785 425-6762 Stockton *(G-12187)*
- ▲ Suhor Industries Inc ... A ... 620 421-4434 Overland Park *(G-9371)*
- Sunburst Systems Inc ... F ... 913 383-9309 Kansas City *(G-4446)*
- ▲ Superior Signals Inc ... E ... 913 780-1440 Olathe *(G-8088)*
- ▲ Terrell Publishing Co ... G ... 913 948-8226 Kansas City *(G-4464)*
- ▲ Therien & Company Inc ... F ... 415 956-8850 Plainville *(G-9993)*
- Traftec Inc ... F ... 913 621-2919 Kansas City *(G-4472)*
- U S Toy Co Inc ... E ... 913 642-8247 Leawood *(G-5587)*
- Ultimate Tan ... F ... 785 842-4949 Lawrence *(G-5148)*
- ▲ Wolf Memorial Co Inc ... F ... 785 726-4430 Ellis *(G-1655)*

51 WHOLESALE TRADE¨NONDURABLE GOODS

5111 Printing & Writing Paper Wholesale

- Digital Printing Services Inc ... F ... 913 492-1500 Lenexa *(G-5817)*
- Southwest Paper Company Inc ... E ... 316 838-7755 Wichita *(G-15631)*
- ▲ Timber Creek Paper Inc ... F ... 316 264-3232 Wichita *(G-15765)*
- Veritiv Operating Company ... D ... 913 492-5050 Kansas City *(G-4517)*
- Ward-Kraft Inc ... E ... 620 223-1104 Fort Scott *(G-2018)*
- Westfall Newco LLC ... E ... 844 663-5939 Hutchinson *(G-3487)*

5112 Stationery & Office Splys Wholesale

- ◆ Amanda Blu & Co LLC ... F ... 913 381-9494 Olathe *(G-7524)*
- Blade Empire Publishing Co ... E ... 785 243-2424 Concordia *(G-1103)*
- Bolen Office Supply Inc ... F ... 620 672-7535 Pratt *(G-10100)*
- Consolidated Prtg & Sty Co Inc ... E ... 785 825-5426 Salina *(G-10460)*
- DCI Studios ... F ... 913 385-9550 Prairie Village *(G-10026)*
- Ennis Inc ... D ... 620 223-6500 Fort Scott *(G-1965)*
- Ennis Business Forms of Kansas ... D ... 620 223-6500 Fort Scott *(G-1966)*
- Evolv Solutions LLC ... E ... 913 469-8900 Shawnee Mission *(G-11352)*

Food Trends Inc ....G.... 913 383-3600
Overland Park *(G-8732)*
Graphic Impressions Inc ....E.... 620 663-5939
Hutchinson *(G-3305)*
Images ....G.... 785 827-0824
Salina *(G-10549)*
Kalos Inc ....E.... 785 232-3606
Topeka *(G-12752)*
Kansas Business Forms LLC ....E.... 620 724-5234
Girard *(G-2414)*
Key Office Products Inc ....G.... 620 227-2101
Dodge City *(G-1390)*
McCartys ....G.... 620 251-6169
Coffeyville *(G-957)*
Midwest Office Technology ....E.... 913 894-9600
Overland Park *(G-9034)*
Midwest Single Source Inc ....E.... 316 267-6333
Wichita *(G-15102)*
Million Packaging Inc ....E.... 913 402-0055
Overland Park *(G-9039)*
Navrats Inc ....F.... 620 342-2092
Emporia *(G-1800)*
Office Works LLC ....F.... 785 462-2222
Colby *(G-1032)*
OfficeMax Incorporated ....E.... 913 667-5300
Edwardsville *(G-1511)*
Perfect Output LLC ....D.... 913 317-8400
Overland Park *(G-9154)*
Polynova (usa) LLC ....G.... 913 309-6977
Lenexa *(G-6062)*
Professional Bank Forms ....G.... 620 455-2205
Oxford *(G-9534)*
Shawnee Copy Center Inc ....F.... 913 268-4343
Shawnee Mission *(G-11851)*
Sta-Mot-Ks LLC ....E.... 913 894-9600
Overland Park *(G-9349)*
Superior Computer Supply Inc ....F.... 316 942-5577
Wichita *(G-15693)*
Tension Envelope Corporation ....D.... 785 562-2307
Marysville *(G-6911)*
Topeka Blue Print & Sup Co Inc ....G.... 785 232-7209
Topeka *(G-13169)*
United Office Products Inc ....E.... 913 782-4441
Olathe *(G-8132)*

5113 Indl & Personal Svc Paper Wholesale

▲ **Central Bag Company** ....E.... 913 250-0325
Leavenworth *(G-5215)*
Creative Mktg Unlimited Inc ....G.... 913 894-0077
Overland Park *(G-8611)*
Crown Packaging Corp ....E.... 913 888-1951
Shawnee Mission *(G-11283)*
Drafting Room Inc ....G.... 316 267-2291
Wichita *(G-14236)*
Earp Meat Company ....C.... 913 287-3311
Edwardsville *(G-1497)*
Joe Smith Company ....E.... 620 231-3610
Pittsburg *(G-9883)*
Ken OKelly ....G.... 816 868-6028
Prairie Village *(G-10042)*
McLane Company Inc ....E.... 913 492-7090
Shawnee Mission *(G-11609)*
Medina Logistics LLC ....D.... 785 506-4002
Topeka *(G-12880)*
National Fiber Supply LLC ....F.... 913 321-0066
Kansas City *(G-4280)*
Northview Development Services ....C.... 316 281-3213
Newton *(G-7399)*
Q4 Industries LLC ....F.... 913 894-6240
Overland Park *(G-9205)*
Shaughnsy-Knp-Hw-ppr Co St ....E.... 913 541-0080
Lenexa *(G-6129)*
Southwest Paper Company Inc ....E.... 316 838-7755
Wichita *(G-15631)*
Streeter Enterprises LLC ....F.... 785 537-0100
Manhattan *(G-6815)*
Sunflower Supply Company Inc ....E.... 620 783-5473
Galena *(G-2088)*
▲ **Universal Products Inc** ....C.... 316 794-8601
Goddard *(G-2455)*
Veritiv Operating Company ....D.... 913 492-5050
Kansas City *(G-4517)*
Veritiv Operating Company ....F.... 785 862-2233
Topeka *(G-13219)*
Veritiv Operating Company ....E.... 316 522-3494
Wichita *(G-15874)*
Veritiv Operating Company ....F.... 620 231-2508
Pittsburg *(G-9955)*

5122 Drugs, Drug Proprietaries & Sundries Wholesale

Asd Specialty Healthcare LLC ....E.... 913 492-5505
Shawnee Mission *(G-11122)*
▲ **Bill Barr & Company** ....F.... 913 599-6668
Overland Park *(G-8448)*
Briovarx Infusion Svcs 305 LLC ....D.... 913 747-3700
Lenexa *(G-5717)*
C & W Operations Ltd ....C.... 913 438-6400
Shawnee Mission *(G-11196)*
Cardinal Health Inc ....D.... 316 264-6275
Wichita *(G-13944)*
▲ **Gdm Enterprises LLC** ....F.... 816 753-2900
Fairway *(G-1908)*
Genzada Pharmaceuticals Usa ....F.... 620 204-7150
Sterling *(G-12120)*
Gibson Wholesale Co Inc ....F.... 316 945-3471
Wichita *(G-14463)*
Hudson Holding Inc ....D.... 866 404-3300
Wichita *(G-14648)*
Mane Event ....F.... 785 827-1999
Salina *(G-10590)*
Rx Plus Pharmacies Inc ....F.... 316 263-5218
Wichita *(G-15495)*
Scp Specialty Infusion LLC ....B.... 913 747-3700
Lenexa *(G-6121)*
Sera Inc ....F.... 913 541-1307
Shawnee Mission *(G-11848)*
Stecklein Enterprises LLC ....F.... 785 625-2529
Hays *(G-2912)*
Wichita Tobacco & Candy Co ....F.... 316 264-2412
Wichita *(G-16040)*

5131 Piece Goods, Notions & Dry Goods Wholesale

◆ **Berger Company** ....F.... 913 367-3700
Atchison *(G-214)*
Classic Cloth Inc ....F.... 785 434-7200
Plainville *(G-9980)*
Crown Packaging Corp ....E.... 913 888-1951
Shawnee Mission *(G-11283)*
Designers Library Inc ....F.... 913 227-0010
Shawnee Mission *(G-11303)*
John K Burch Company ....F.... 800 365-1988
Shawnee Mission *(G-11492)*
◆ **LAd Global Enterprises Inc** ....F.... 913 768-0888
Olathe *(G-7851)*
Ray Bechard Inc ....E.... 785 864-5077
Lawrence *(G-5087)*
Sebring & Co ....F.... 913 888-8141
Overland Park *(G-9288)*
Spirit Industries Inc ....F.... 913 749-5858
Lawrence *(G-5115)*
Stephanie Wilson ....G.... 913 563-1240
Paola *(G-9591)*
Tell Industries LLC ....F.... 316 260-3297
Park City *(G-9649)*

5136 Men's & Boys' Clothing & Furnishings Wholesale

▲ **Acres Inc** ....F.... 785 776-3234
Manhattan *(G-6532)*
Branded Custom Sportswear Inc ....E.... 913 663-6800
Overland Park *(G-8481)*
Dcm Wichita Inc ....F.... 800 662-9573
Towanda *(G-13263)*
▲ **Design Resources Inc** ....D.... 913 652-6522
Overland Park *(G-8651)*
Dri Duck Traders Inc ....F.... 913 648-8222
Overland Park *(G-8661)*
Finchers Findings Inc ....G.... 620 886-5952
Medicine Lodge *(G-7060)*
▲ **Its Greek To Me Inc** ....C.... 800 336-4486
Manhattan *(G-6666)*
▲ **Key Industries Inc** ....E.... 620 223-2000
Fort Scott *(G-1979)*
▲ **Promotional Headwear Intl Inc** ....F.... 913 541-0901
Lenexa *(G-6076)*
▲ **Realm Brands LLC** ....F.... 316 821-9700
Wichita *(G-15426)*
Stardust Corporation ....F.... 913 894-1966
Kansas City *(G-4439)*

5137 Women's, Children's & Infants Clothing Wholesale

▲ **Acres Inc** ....F.... 785 776-3234
Manhattan *(G-6532)*
▼ **Baldwin LLC** ....F.... 913 312-2375
Leawood *(G-5338)*
Branded Custom Sportswear Inc ....E.... 913 663-6800
Overland Park *(G-8481)*
Dri Duck Traders Inc ....F.... 913 648-8222
Overland Park *(G-8661)*
Five Clothes LLC ....F.... 913 713-6216
Overland Park *(G-8726)*
▲ **Its Greek To Me Inc** ....C.... 800 336-4486
Manhattan *(G-6666)*
Stardust Corporation ....F.... 913 894-1966
Kansas City *(G-4439)*
▲ **Strasburg-Jarvis Inc** ....B.... 913 888-1115
Shawnee Mission *(G-11902)*
Urban Outfitters Inc ....E.... 785 331-2885
Lawrence *(G-5169)*

5141 Groceries, General Line Wholesale

Acosta Inc ....D.... 913 227-1000
Shawnee Mission *(G-11068)*
Acosta Sales Co Inc ....E.... 316 733-0248
Wichita *(G-13607)*
Advantage Sales & Mktg LLC ....F.... 913 696-1700
Overland Park *(G-8351)*
Allied Sales and Marketing Inc ....F.... 316 617-2160
Wichita *(G-13674)*
American Fun Food Company Inc ....F.... 316 838-9329
Park City *(G-9600)*
Arts Mexican Products Inc ....F.... 913 371-2163
Kansas City *(G-3820)*
Cosentino Group Inc ....E.... 913 749-1500
Prairie Village *(G-10022)*
Crossmark Inc ....E.... 913 338-1133
Lenexa *(G-5794)*
CSC Gold Inc ....F.... 913 664-8100
Shawnee Mission *(G-11284)*
Dgs-Re LLC ....E.... 913 288-1000
Kansas City *(G-3971)*
Dillon Companies Inc ....D.... 620 275-0151
Garden City *(G-2148)*
Earp Meat Company ....C.... 913 287-3311
Edwardsville *(G-1497)*
Emporia Wholesale Coffee Co ....C.... 620 343-7000
Emporia *(G-1747)*
Food Service Specialists Inc ....F.... 913 648-6611
Shawnee Mission *(G-11376)*
Food Trends Inc ....G.... 913 383-3600
Overland Park *(G-8732)*
Great Western Dining Svc Inc ....F.... 620 792-9224
Great Bend *(G-2585)*
Key Impact Sales & Systems Inc ....E.... 913 648-6611
Olathe *(G-7835)*
◆ **Kms Inc** ....E.... 316 264-8833
Wichita *(G-14868)*
Marrones Inc ....E.... 620 231-6610
Pittsburg *(G-9897)*
McLane Foodservice Inc ....C.... 913 422-6100
Lenexa *(G-5992)*
Mueller-Yurgae Associates Inc ....F.... 913 362-7777
Overland Park *(G-9062)*
Pallucca and Sons ....F.... 620 231-7700
Frontenac *(G-2062)*
Reese Group Inc ....F.... 913 383-8260
Merriam *(G-7102)*
Regan Marketing Inc ....F.... 816 531-5111
Lenexa *(G-6097)*
Rheuark FSI Sales Inc ....F.... 913 432-9500
Shawnee Mission *(G-11795)*
Schraad & Associates ....F.... 913 661-2404
Overland Park *(G-9283)*
Streeter Enterprises LLC ....F.... 785 537-0100
Manhattan *(G-6815)*
Sysco Corporation ....E.... 913 829-5555
Olathe *(G-8091)*
Sysco Kansas City Inc ....A.... 913 829-5555
Olathe *(G-8092)*
Trans-Pak Inc ....F.... 620 275-1758
Garden City *(G-2300)*
US Foods Inc ....C.... 316 942-9679
Wichita *(G-15863)*
US Foods Inc ....C.... 913 894-6161
Lenexa *(G-6205)*

5142 Packaged Frozen Foods Wholesale

◆ **Associated Wholesale Groc Inc** ....A.... 913 288-1000
Kansas City *(G-3825)*
Earp Meat Company ....C.... 913 287-3311
Edwardsville *(G-1497)*
Foodbrands Sup Chain Svcs Inc ....C.... 913 393-7000
Olathe *(G-7717)*

Jacksons Frozen Food Center ..... G 620 662-4465
Hutchinson *(G-3339)*
Scavuzzos Inc ..... D 816 231-1517
Kansas City *(G-4402)*
Smithfield Packaged Meats Corp ..... A 316 942-8461
Wichita *(G-15610)*

5143 Dairy Prdts, Except Dried Or Canned Wholesale

Anderson Erickson Dairy Co ..... D 913 621-4801
Kansas City *(G-3810)*
◆ Associated Wholesale Groc Inc ..... A 913 288-1000
Kansas City *(G-3825)*
Bern Meat Plant Incorporated ..... F 785 336-2165
Bern *(G-521)*
Hiland Dairy Foods Company LLC ..... F 620 225-4111
Dodge City *(G-1373)*
Hiland Dairy Foods Company LLC ..... F 785 539-7541
Manhattan *(G-6657)*
KDI Operating Company LLC ..... E 620 453-1034
Leawood *(G-5448)*
Roberts Dairy Company LLC ..... F 785 232-1274
Topeka *(G-13022)*
Southwest Dairy Quality Svc ..... F 620 384-6953
Syracuse *(G-12232)*

5144 Poultry & Poultry Prdts Wholesale

Cal-Maine Foods Inc ..... D 620 938-2300
Chase *(G-782)*
▲ Nelson Poultry Farms Inc ..... F 785 587-0399
Manhattan *(G-6758)*

5145 Confectionery Wholesale

Frito-Lay North America Inc ..... E 620 251-4367
Coffeyville *(G-941)*
Frito-Lay North America Inc ..... F 785 625-6581
Hays *(G-2814)*
Frito-Lay North America Inc ..... E 316 942-8764
Wichita *(G-14426)*
Frito-Lay North America Inc ..... D 913 261-4700
Shawnee Mission *(G-11382)*
Happy Food Co LLC ..... F 816 835-3600
Overland Park *(G-8793)*
Joe Smith Company ..... E 620 231-3610
Pittsburg *(G-9883)*
Kansas Candy & Tobacco Inc ..... F 316 942-9081
Wichita *(G-14789)*
Nifty Nut House LLC ..... F 316 265-0571
Wichita *(G-15180)*
Schmidt Vending Inc ..... F 785 354-7397
Topeka *(G-13038)*
Seneca Wholesale Company Inc ..... F 785 336-2118
Seneca *(G-10882)*
Shawnee Biscuit Inc ..... E 913 441-7306
Lenexa *(G-6130)*
Wichita Tobacco & Candy Co ..... F 316 264-2412
Wichita *(G-16040)*

5146 Fish & Seafood Wholesale

◆ Associated Wholesale Groc Inc ..... A 913 288-1000
Kansas City *(G-3825)*
Qins International Inc ..... E 913 342-4488
Kansas City *(G-4350)*
Sysco Kansas City Inc ..... E 316 942-4205
Wichita *(G-15711)*

5147 Meats & Meat Prdts Wholesale

◆ Associated Wholesale Groc Inc ..... A 913 288-1000
Kansas City *(G-3825)*
Bern Meat Plant Incorporated ..... F 785 336-2165
Bern *(G-521)*
Bichelmeyer Meats A Corp ..... F 913 342-5945
Kansas City *(G-3859)*
Duis Meat Processing Inc ..... F 785 243-7850
Concordia *(G-1109)*
Flatland Food Distributors LLC ..... F 316 945-5171
Wichita *(G-14382)*
Harvest Meat Company Inc ..... F 913 371-2333
Kansas City *(G-4070)*
Hormel Foods Corp Svcs LLC ..... F 913 888-8744
Shawnee Mission *(G-11440)*
Indian Hills Meat and Plty Inc ..... E 316 264-1644
Wichita *(G-14683)*
Jacksons Frozen Food Center ..... G 620 662-4465
Hutchinson *(G-3339)*
Kiowa Locker System LLC ..... F 620 825-4538
Kiowa *(G-4626)*
Krehbiels Specialty Meats Inc ..... E 620 241-0103
McPherson *(G-6985)*
Plankenhorn Inc ..... F 620 276-3791
Garden City *(G-2256)*
Qins International Inc ..... E 913 342-4488
Kansas City *(G-4350)*
Rons Market ..... F 620 277-2073
Holcomb *(G-3079)*
◆ Seaboard Foods LLC ..... D 913 261-2600
Shawnee Mission *(G-11842)*
Smithfield Direct LLC ..... E 785 762-3306
Junction City *(G-3755)*
Swiss Burger Brand Meat Co ..... F 316 838-7514
Wichita *(G-15709)*
Waltons Inc ..... F 316 262-0651
Wichita *(G-15925)*

5148 Fresh Fruits & Vegetables Wholesale

◆ Associated Wholesale Groc Inc ..... A 913 288-1000
Kansas City *(G-3825)*
Chlorofields LLC ..... F 785 304-3226
Overbrook *(G-8323)*
Depot Market ..... F 785 374-4255
Courtland *(G-1180)*
Earl Barnes ..... F 620 662-6761
Hutchinson *(G-3273)*
Keith Connell Inc ..... F 913 681-5585
Stilwell *(G-12162)*
▲ Liberty Fruit Company Inc ..... B 913 281-5200
Kansas City *(G-4202)*
Martinous Produce Company Inc ..... E 620 231-5840
Pittsburg *(G-9898)*
Sysco Kansas City Inc ..... E 316 942-4205
Wichita *(G-15711)*

5149 Groceries & Related Prdts, NEC Wholesale

ADM Milling Co ..... D 785 825-1541
Salina *(G-10395)*
American Bottling Company ..... F 620 223-6166
Fort Scott *(G-1954)*
American Bottling Company ..... C 913 894-6777
Lenexa *(G-5645)*
Bagel Works Cafe Inc ..... F 913 789-7333
Kansas City *(G-3838)*
▲ Blend Tech Inc ..... F 316 941-9660
Wichita *(G-13857)*
Cardona Coffee LLP ..... G 785 554-6060
Topeka *(G-12446)*
Cargill Incorporated ..... D 620 663-2141
Hutchinson *(G-3229)*
Coca-Cola Company ..... F 785 243-1071
Concordia *(G-1107)*
Coca-Cola Refreshments USA Inc ..... B 913 492-8100
Shawnee Mission *(G-11243)*
Country Fresh Foods ..... E 316 283-4414
Newton *(G-7336)*
CSM Bakery Solutions LLC ..... C 913 441-7216
Bonner Springs *(G-546)*
Eastside Mkt Westside Mkt LLC ..... G 785 532-8686
Manhattan *(G-6619)*
Grain Craft Inc ..... E 316 267-7311
Wichita *(G-14494)*
Grandma Hoerners Foods Inc ..... E 785 765-2300
Alma *(G-63)*
Heartland Coca-Cola Btlg LLC ..... A 785 735-9498
Victoria *(G-13376)*
Heartland Coca-Cola Btlg LLC ..... A 785 232-9372
Topeka *(G-12675)*
Heartland Coca-Cola Btlg LLC ..... A 785 243-1071
Concordia *(G-1117)*
Heartland Coca-Cola Btlg LLC ..... A 913 599-9142
Lenexa *(G-5896)*
Heartland Coca-Cola Btlg LLC ..... A 620 276-3221
Garden City *(G-2194)*
Heartland Coca-Cola Btlg LLC ..... A 316 942-3838
Wichita *(G-14582)*
◆ Hills Pet Nutrition Inc ..... B 800 255-0449
Topeka *(G-12690)*
▼ Hills Pet Nutrition Sales Inc ..... E 785 354-8523
Topeka *(G-12693)*
Hillshire Brands Company ..... E 316 262-5443
Wichita *(G-14612)*
Hutchinson Salt Company Inc ..... E 620 662-3341
Hutchinson *(G-3324)*
International Food Pdts Corp ..... F 913 788-7720
Kansas City *(G-4107)*
John G Levin ..... E 785 234-5551
Topeka *(G-12746)*
Kerry Inc ..... C 913 780-1212
New Century *(G-7290)*
◆ Manildra Milling Corporation ..... F 913 362-0777
Leawood *(G-5464)*
▲ Old World Spices Seasoning Inc ..... E 816 861-0400
Overland Park *(G-9098)*
P-Americas LLC ..... B 913 791-3000
Olathe *(G-7970)*
Pepsi Cola Btlg Co of Salina ..... D 785 827-7297
Salina *(G-10633)*
Pepsi-Cola Metro Btlg Co Inc ..... E 620 227-8123
Dodge City *(G-1419)*
Pepsi-Cola Metro Btlg Co Inc ..... F 620 624-0287
Liberal *(G-6357)*
Pepsi-Cola Metro Btlg Co Inc ..... C 785 628-3024
Hays *(G-2886)*
Quality Water Inc ..... F 785 825-4912
Salina *(G-10647)*
Seneca Wholesale Company Inc ..... F 785 336-2118
Seneca *(G-10882)*
Shasta Midwest Inc ..... E 913 888-6777
Lenexa *(G-6128)*
Shawnee Biscuit Inc ..... E 913 441-7306
Lenexa *(G-6130)*
Spice Merchant & Co ..... F 316 263-4121
Wichita *(G-15639)*
Sysco Kansas City Inc ..... A 913 829-5555
Olathe *(G-8092)*
Tasty Pastry Bakery ..... E 785 632-2335
Clay Center *(G-882)*
▲ Thai Binh Supermarket ..... F 316 838-8882
Wichita *(G-15755)*
Wheatland Waters Inc ..... D 785 267-0512
Olathe *(G-8153)*
Ziwi USA Incorporated ..... F 913 291-0189
Overland Park *(G-9529)*

5153 Grain & Field Beans Wholesale

ADM Grain River System Inc ..... F 913 788-7226
Kansas City *(G-3785)*
ADM Milling Co ..... E 620 227-8101
Dodge City *(G-1289)*
ADM Milling Co ..... E 785 263-1631
Abilene *(G-11)*
ADM Milling Co ..... D 785 825-1541
Salina *(G-10395)*
AG Partners Cooperative Inc ..... E 785 742-2196
Hiawatha *(G-3001)*
AG Valley Coop Non-Stock ..... F 785 877-5131
Norton *(G-7440)*
Agco Inc ..... F 785 483-2128
Russell *(G-10263)*
Agmark LLC ..... F 785 738-9641
Beloit *(G-471)*
◆ Agrex Inc ..... E 913 851-6300
Overland Park *(G-8358)*
Agri Trails Coop Inc ..... F 785 258-2286
Herington *(G-2969)*
Agspring Idaho LLC ..... F 952 956-6720
Leawood *(G-5315)*
Alliance AG and Grain LLC ..... F 785 798-3775
Ness City *(G-7251)*
Alliance AG and Grain LLC ..... C 620 385-2898
Spearville *(G-12069)*
Alliance AG and Grain LLC ..... F 620 723-3351
Greensburg *(G-2671)*
Alliance AG and Grain LLC ..... F 620 622-4511
Protection *(G-10172)*
Anthony Frmrs Coop Elev Cmpnys ..... F 620 842-5181
Anthony *(G-119)*
Archer-Daniels-Midland Company ..... F 620 675-8520
Copeland *(G-1148)*
Archer-Daniels-Midland Company ..... F 620 846-2218
Montezuma *(G-7154)*
Archer-Daniels-Midland Company ..... C 913 491-9400
Overland Park *(G-8393)*
Archer-Daniels-Midland Company ..... F 620 659-2099
Kinsley *(G-4614)*
Archer-Daniels-Midland Company ..... E 620 663-7957
Hutchinson *(G-3204)*
Archer-Daniels-Midland Company ..... G 785 737-4135
Palco *(G-9537)*
Bartlett Cooperative Assn ..... E 620 226-3311
Bartlett *(G-371)*
Bartlett Grain Company LP ..... F 316 838-7421
Wichita *(G-13814)*
Bartlett Grain Company LP ..... F 913 321-0900
Kansas City *(G-3845)*
Bartlett Grain Company LP ..... F 913 321-1696
Kansas City *(G-3846)*
Beachner Grain Inc ..... E 620 820-8600
Parsons *(G-9669)*

SIC

Beattie Farmers Un Coop Assn ....E 785 353-2237
Beattie (G-418)
Bunge Milling Inc ....C 913 367-3251
Atchison (G-221)
Bunge North America Inc ....D 620 342-7270
Emporia (G-1711)
Cargill Incorporated ....E 785 357-1989
Topeka (G-12448)
Cargill Incorporated ....E 913 236-0346
Overland Park (G-8517)
Cargill Incorporated ....F 316 291-1939
Wichita (G-13947)
Cargill Incorporated ....F 785 235-3003
Topeka (G-12449)
Cargill Incorporated ....E 620 663-4401
Hutchinson (G-3230)
Cargill Incorporated ....F 806 659-3554
Shawnee Mission (G-11204)
Cargill Incorporated ....E 785 743-2288
WA Keeney (G-13382)
Cargill Incorporated ....E 785 825-8128
Salina (G-10436)
Cargill Incorporated ....F 913 367-3579
Cummings (G-1186)
Central Planes Coop ....F 785 695-2216
Athol (G-273)
Central Prairie Co-Op ....F 620 278-2470
Sterling (G-12113)
Central Soyfoods ....F 785 312-8638
Lawrence (G-4781)
Central Valley AG Cooperative ....C 785 738-2241
Beloit (G-481)
CGB Diversified Services Inc ....F 785 235-5566
Topeka (G-12462)
CHS Inc ....F 785 386-4546
Selden (G-10855)
CHS Inc ....E 785 852-4241
Sharon Springs (G-10895)
CHS Inc ....D 620 241-4247
McPherson (G-6948)
Cooperative Elevator & Sup Co ....E 620 873-2161
Meade (G-7047)
Cornerstone Ag LLC ....F 785 462-3354
Colby (G-1000)
Cropland Co-Op Inc ....F 620 356-1241
Ulysses (G-13294)
Cropland Co-Op Inc ....F 620 649-2230
Satanta (G-10782)
D E Bondurant Grain Co Inc ....E 785 798-3322
Ness City (G-7260)
Decatur Cooperative Assn ....F 785 475-2234
Oberlin (G-7490)
Delphos Cooperative Assn ....E 785 523-4213
Delphos (G-1216)
Dm & M Farms Inc ....E 620 855-3934
Cimarron (G-823)
Dodge City Cooperative Exch ....E 620 225-4193
Dodge City (G-1344)
Elkhart Coop Equity Exchnge ....E 620 697-2135
Elkhart (G-1619)
Ellsworth Coop ....F 785 472-3261
Ellsworth (G-1667)
Farmers Co-Operative Equity Co ....F 620 739-4335
Isabel (G-3639)
Farmers Co-Operative Union ....D 620 278-2141
Sterling (G-12116)
Farmers Coop Grn Assn Inc ....F 620 456-2222
Conway Springs (G-1141)
Farmers Cooperative Assn ....F 620 856-2365
Baxter Springs (G-406)
Farmers Cooperative Elev Assn ....F 785 747-2236
Greenleaf (G-2668)
Farmers Cooperative Elev Co ....F 620 545-7138
Viola (G-13378)
Farmers Cooperative Elev Inc ....F 785 284-2185
Sabetha (G-10310)
Farmers Cooperative Grain ....F 620 326-7496
Wellington (G-13499)
Farmers Cooperative Grain Co ....F 620 845-6441
Caldwell (G-658)
Farmers Grain Cooperative ....E 620 837-3313
Walton (G-13400)
Farmers Union Coop Assn ....F 785 632-5632
Clay Center (G-863)
Farmway Cooperative Inc ....E 785 439-6457
Scottsville (G-10838)
Faulkner Grain Inc ....F 620 597-2636
Chetopa (G-817)
Fleming Feed & Grain Inc ....E 316 742-3411
Leon (G-6247)
Frontier Ag Inc ....E 785 734-7011
Goodland (G-2472)
Frontier Ag Inc ....F 785 734-2331
Bird City (G-530)
Frontier Ag Inc ....E 785 824-3201
Grinnell (G-2692)
Garden City Co-Op Inc ....F 620 356-1219
Ulysses (G-13298)
Gavilon Grain LLC ....E 316 226-7250
Wichita (G-14453)
Gfg AG Services LLC ....F 913 233-0001
Kansas City (G-4032)
Golden Belt Coop Assn Inc ....F 785 726-3115
Ellis (G-1646)
Great Bend Cooperative Assn ....E 620 793-3531
Great Bend (G-2576)
Green Plains Cattle Co LLC ....D 620 624-6296
Kismet (G-4630)
Hannebaum Grain Co Inc ....F 785 825-8205
Salina (G-10534)
Haven Commodities Inc ....E 620 345-6328
Moundridge (G-7185)
Healy Cooperative Elevator Co ....E 620 398-2211
Healy (G-2966)
HI Plains Cooperative Assn ....F 785 462-3351
Colby (G-1012)
Irsik & Doll Feed Services Inc ....F 620 855-3747
Cimarron (G-830)
Jackson Farmers Inc ....F 785 364-3161
Holton (G-3100)
Johnson Cooperative Grn Co Inc ....F 620 492-6210
Johnson (G-3654)
Johnson Cooperative Grn Co Inc ....F 620 492-2297
Johnson (G-3655)
Kanza Cooperative Association ....F 620 234-5252
Stafford (G-12104)
Kanza Cooperative Association ....F 620 546-2231
luka (G-3640)
Kanza Cooperative Association ....E 316 444-2141
Andale (G-78)
Kanza Cooperative Association ....F 620 234-5252
Stafford (G-12105)
Kanza Cooperative Association ....F 620 672-6761
Pratt (G-10122)
Kanza Cooperative Association ....D 620 546-2593
luka (G-3641)
Lange Company LLC ....F 620 456-2996
Conway Springs (G-1143)
Lansing Grain Company LLC ....F 913 748-4320
Overland Park (G-8944)
◆ Lansing Trade Group LLC ....C 913 748-3000
Overland Park (G-8945)
Leroy Cooperative Assn Inc ....E 620 964-2225
Le Roy (G-5196)
Long Island Grain Co Inc ....F 785 854-7431
Long Island (G-6428)
McCune Farmers Union Coop ....F 620 632-4226
Mc Cune (G-6920)
Mid Continent Farms ....F 785 325-2089
Washington (G-13469)
Mid-Kansas Cooperative Assn ....E 620 345-6328
Moundridge (G-7190)
Mid-Kansas Cooperative Assn ....F 785 776-9467
Manhattan (G-6742)
Mid-Kansas Cooperative Assn ....F 620 837-3313
Walton (G-13401)
Mid-Kansas Cooperative Assn ....F 620 465-2292
Haven (G-2734)
Mid-Kansas Cooperative Assn ....F 620 345-6361
Moundridge (G-7191)
Minneola Co-Op Inc ....F 620 885-4361
Minneola (G-7125)
Mulvane Cooperative Union Inc ....F 316 777-1121
Mulvane (G-7223)
Nemaha County Cooperative Assn ....D 785 336-6153
Seneca (G-10874)
Norton County Co-Op Assn Inc ....F 785 877-5900
Norton (G-7456)
O K Coop Grn & Merc Co ....F 620 825-4212
Kiowa (G-4628)
Offerle Coop Grn & Sup Co ....F 620 659-2165
Offerle (G-7500)
Palmer Grain Inc ....F 785 692-4212
Palmer (G-9538)
Plains Equity Exch & Coop Un ....E 620 563-9566
Plains (G-9977)
Pride AG Resources ....F 620 227-8671
Dodge City (G-1422)
Producers Coop Assn Girard ....E 620 724-8241
Girard (G-2415)
Randall Farmers Coop Un Inc ....F 785 739-2312
Randall (G-10190)
Rangeland Cooperatives Inc ....E 785 543-2114
Phillipsburg (G-9797)
Redwood Group LLC ....D 816 979-1786
Mission (G-7137)
Right Cooperative Association ....E 620 227-8611
Wright (G-16194)
Scott Cooperative Association ....E 620 872-5823
Scott City (G-10831)
Scoular Company ....E 785 823-6301
Salina (G-10699)
Scoular Company ....F 785 392-9024
Minneapolis (G-7123)
Scoular Company ....F 620 372-8611
Coolidge (G-1147)
Severy Cooperative Association ....F 620 736-2211
Severy (G-10893)
Skyland Grain LLC ....F 620 672-3961
Cunningham (G-1189)
Southern Plains Co-Op At Lewis ....E 620 324-5536
Lewis (G-6270)
Stafford County Flour Mills Co ....E 620 458-4121
Hudson (G-3146)
Sublette Cooperative Inc ....E 620 675-2297
Sublette (G-12209)
Sublette Enterprises Inc ....D 620 668-5501
Sublette (G-12210)
Team Marketing Alliance LLC ....F 620 345-3560
Moundridge (G-7198)
Two Rivers Consumers Coop Assn ....E 620 442-2360
Arkansas City (G-185)
United AG Service Inc ....F 785 525-6455
Lucas (G-6475)
United Plains AG ....E 785 852-4241
Sharon Springs (G-10901)
Walker Products Company Inc ....F 785 524-4107
Lincoln (G-6390)
White Cloud Grain Company Inc ....F 785 235-5381
Topeka (G-13242)
Windriver Grain LLC ....E 620 275-2101
Garden City (G-2316)

5154 Livestock Wholesale

Anderson County Sales Co ....F 785 448-3811
Garnett (G-2369)
Anthony Livestock Sales Co ....F 620 842-3757
Anthony (G-120)
Atchison County Auction Co ....E 913 367-5278
Atchison (G-208)
Colby Livestock Auction ....F 785 460-3231
Colby (G-998)
El Dorado Livestock Auction ....E 316 320-3212
El Dorado (G-1559)
Farmers Rnchers Livstock Cmnty ....D 785 825-0211
Salina (G-10496)
Fort Scott Livestock Market ....E 620 223-4600
Fort Scott (G-1970)
Fredonia Livestock Auction LLC ....E 620 378-2212
Fredonia (G-2033)
Hays Livestock Market Center ....E 785 628-8206
Hays (G-2831)
Herington Livestock Market ....E 785 258-2205
Herington (G-2974)
Holton Livestock Exchange Inc ....E 785 364-4114
Holton (G-3097)
La Crosse Livestock Market ....E 785 222-2586
La Crosse (G-4634)
Livestock Nutrition Center LLC ....F 913 725-0300
Overland Park (G-8963)
Mankato Livestock Inc ....E 785 378-3283
Mankato (G-6860)
Marysville Livestock Inc ....F 785 562-1015
Marysville (G-6900)
Michael L Sebes ....F 620 324-5509
Lewis (G-6269)
Mid Continent Farms ....F 785 325-2089
Washington (G-13469)
Oberlin Livestock Auction Inc ....F 785 475-2323
Oberlin (G-7498)
Overbrook Livestock Comm Co ....E 785 665-7181
Overbrook (G-8327)
Parsons Livestock Market Inc ....E 620 421-2900
Parsons (G-9720)
Pratt Livestock Inc ....E 620 672-5961
Sterling (G-12127)
Pratt Livestock Inc ....E 620 672-5961
Pratt (G-10142)
Premiere Pork Inc ....F 620 872-7073
Scott City (G-10829)

R and P Calf Ranch LLC .... F 620 855-2550
Cimarron (G-835)
Rezac Sales Barn .... E 785 437-2785
Saint Marys (G-10373)
Russell Livestock Commission .... E 785 483-2961
Russell (G-10295)
Russell Livestock LLC .... E 785 483-2961
Russell (G-10296)
Sylvan Sales Commission LLC .... E 785 526-7123
Sylvan Grove (G-12220)
Winter Livestock Inc .... E 620 525-6271
Hanston (G-2715)
Winter Livestock Inc .... F 620 225-4159
Dodge City (G-1461)

5159 Farm-Prdt Raw Mtrls, NEC Wholesale

Cargill Incorporated .... E 913 752-1200
Lenexa (G-5730)
Redwood Group LLC .... D 816 979-1786
Mission (G-7137)

5162 Plastics Materials & Basic Shapes Wholesale

Bagcraftpapercon I LLC .... C 620 856-4615
Baxter Springs (G-395)
Koller Enterprises Inc .... D 913 422-2027
Lenexa (G-5957)
Lustercraft Plastics LLC .... F 316 942-8451
Wichita (G-14991)
Univar Solutions USA Inc .... F 913 621-7494
Kansas City (G-4493)

5169 Chemicals & Allied Prdts, NEC Wholesale

Air Products and Chemicals Inc .... E 620 624-8151
Liberal (G-6273)
Airgas Usa LLC .... E 785 823-8100
Salina (G-10398)
▲ Airosol Co Inc .... E 620 325-2666
Neodesha (G-7234)
American Chem Systems II LLC .... E 316 263-4448
Wichita (G-13689)
Baker Petrolite LLC .... D 620 793-3546
Great Bend (G-2514)
Barton Solvents Inc .... F 316 321-1540
El Dorado (G-1534)
Barton Solvents Inc .... F 913 287-5500
Kansas City (G-3847)
Blue Valley Chemical LLC .... F 816 984-2125
Overland Park (G-8469)
Bobs Janitorial Service & Sup .... C 785 271-6600
Topeka (G-12395)
Broadway Home Medical Inc .... F 316 264-8600
Wichita (G-13895)
▲ Buckley Industries Inc .... D 316 744-7587
Park City (G-9606)
Chemical Services Inc .... F 620 792-6886
Great Bend (G-2537)
Chemstation of Kansas Inc .... F 316 201-1851
Wichita (G-14001)
Clarke Enterprises LLC .... E 913 601-3830
Kansas City (G-3917)
▲ Clean Harbors Wichita LLC .... C 316 832-0151
Wichita (G-14039)
Cleaning By Lamunyon Inc .... F 785 632-1259
Clay Center (G-855)
Compressed Gases Inc .... F 316 838-3222
Wichita (G-14082)
Crown Packaging Corp .... E 913 888-1951
Shawnee Mission (G-11283)
Danisco USA Inc .... C 913 764-8100
New Century (G-7277)
Denison Inc .... F 620 378-4148
Fredonia (G-2030)
E I Du Pont De Nemours & Co .... C 913 764-8100
New Century (G-7283)
Edwards Chemicals Inc .... F 913 365-5158
Elwood (G-1686)
Ethanol Products LLC .... C 316 303-1380
Wichita (G-14308)
◆ Flint Hills Resources LLC .... B 316 828-5500
Wichita (G-14390)
Fujifilm North America Corp .... F 816 914-5942
Kansas City (G-4021)
▲ General Tech A Svcs & Pdts Co .... G 913 766-5566
Olathe (G-7727)
◆ Harcros Chemicals Inc .... C 913 321-3131
Kansas City (G-4068)
Helena Chemical Company .... F 913 441-0676
Shawnee (G-10971)
Koch Fertilizer LLC .... E 620 227-8631
Dodge City (G-1394)
▲ Koch Fertilizer LLC .... E 316 828-5010
Wichita (G-14880)
◆ Koch Industries Inc .... A 316 828-5500
Wichita (G-14881)
Lyons Salt Company .... D 620 257-5626
Lyons (G-6492)
Matheson Tri-Gas Inc .... F 785 537-0395
Manhattan (G-6734)
Meridian Chemicals LLC .... G 913 253-2220
Overland Park (G-9011)
▲ Midcontinental Chemical Co Inc .... E 913 390-5556
Olathe (G-7893)
Mud-Co/Service Mud Inc .... F 620 672-2957
Pratt (G-10126)
Nalco Company LLC .... E 785 625-3822
Hays (G-2876)
Power Vac Inc .... E 785 826-8220
Salina (G-10639)
Prosoco Inc .... D 785 865-4200
Lawrence (G-5081)
Pur-O-Zone Inc .... E 785 843-0771
Lawrence (G-5082)
Q4 Industries LLC .... F 913 894-6240
Overland Park (G-9205)
▲ Scotwood Industries Inc .... E 913 851-3500
Overland Park (G-9285)
Ultra-Chem Inc .... C 913 492-2929
Shawnee Mission (G-11955)
Univar Solutions USA Inc .... F 913 621-7494
Kansas City (G-4493)
Univar Solutions USA Inc .... F 316 267-1002
Wichita (G-15851)
Wichita Welding Supply Inc .... F 316 838-8671
Wichita (G-16043)
Wilbur-Ellis Company LLC .... F 785 582-4052
Silver Lake (G-12029)
Wilbur-Ellis Company LLC .... F 785 359-6569
Leona (G-6248)
▲ Wilke Resources Inc .... F 913 438-5544
Lenexa (G-6229)

5171 Petroleum Bulk Stations & Terminals

Bartlett Cooperative Assn .... E 620 226-3311
Bartlett (G-371)
Bennington Oil Co Inc .... F 785 392-3031
Minneapolis (G-7113)
Berwick Cooperative Oil Co .... F 785 284-2227
Sabetha (G-10307)
Brecheisens Stop 2 Shop Inc .... E 620 392-5577
Hartford (G-2727)
Brown - Dupree Oil Co Inc .... F 620 353-1874
Ulysses (G-13285)
Capital City Oil Inc .... E 785 233-8008
Topeka (G-12428)
Clark-Timmons Oil Company .... F 816 229-0228
Kansas City (G-3916)
Clough Oil Company Inc .... F 620 251-0521
Coffeyville (G-916)
Consumer Oil Company Inc .... F 785 988-4459
Bendena (G-511)
Decatur Cooperative Assn .... F 785 475-2234
Oberlin (G-7490)
Farmers Co-Operative Equity Co .... F 620 739-4335
Isabel (G-3639)
Great Bend Cooperative Assn .... E 620 793-3531
Great Bend (G-2576)
Haag Oil Co LLC .... D 785 357-0270
Topeka (G-12656)
Hallauer Oil Co Inc .... F 785 364-3140
Holton (G-3094)
Hampel Oil Inc .... E 913 321-0139
Kansas City (G-4063)
Hampel Oil Distributors Inc .... E 316 529-1162
Wichita (G-14549)
Hampel Oil Distributors Inc .... F 800 530-5848
Wichita (G-14550)
▲ Hoc Industries Inc .... E 316 838-4663
Wichita (G-14620)
Jim Woods Marketing Inc .... F 620 856-3554
Baxter Springs (G-410)
L C McClain Inc .... F 785 584-6151
Rossville (G-10253)
Leavenworth County Coop Assn .... F 913 727-1900
Lansing (G-4683)
Leiszler Oil Co Inc .... E 785 632-5648
Manhattan (G-6712)
McCune Farmers Union Coop .... F 620 632-4226
Mc Cune (G-6920)
Mike Groves Oil Inc .... F 620 442-0480
Arkansas City (G-166)
Mitten Inc .... E 785 672-3062
Oakley (G-7481)
Mulvane Cooperative Union Inc .... F 316 777-1121
Mulvane (G-7223)
Nusser Oil Company Inc .... E 620 697-4624
Elkhart (G-1625)
Parker Oil Co Inc .... F 316 529-4343
Wichita (G-15264)
Rakies Oil LLC .... F 620 442-2210
Arkansas City (G-171)
Robson Oil Co Inc .... F 785 263-2470
Abilene (G-51)
Semcrude LP .... F 620 234-5532
Stafford (G-12109)
Service Oil Company .... F 785 462-3441
Colby (G-1040)
Severy Cooperative Association .... F 620 736-2211
Severy (G-10893)
Stuhlsatz Service Inc .... F 316 531-2282
Garden Plain (G-2322)
Triplett Inc .... F 785 823-7839
Salina (G-10742)
Universal Motor Fuels Inc .... F 316 832-0151
Wichita (G-15855)
Wenger Oil Inc .... F 316 283-8795
Newton (G-7427)
World Fuel Services Inc .... C 913 643-2300
Overland Park (G-9505)

5172 Petroleum & Petroleum Prdts Wholesale

Andax Industries LLC .... E 785 437-0604
Saint Marys (G-10358)
Barton Solvents Inc .... F 316 321-1540
El Dorado (G-1534)
Barton Solvents Inc .... F 913 287-5500
Kansas City (G-3847)
Casillas Petroleum Corp .... E 620 276-3693
Satanta (G-10778)
Central Valley AG Cooperative .... C 785 738-2241
Beloit (G-481)
Chc McPherson Refinery Inc .... E 620 793-3111
Great Bend (G-2536)
Clean Harbors Wichita LLC .... E 913 287-6880
Kansas City (G-3919)
▲ Clean Harbors Wichita LLC .... C 316 832-0151
Wichita (G-14039)
Clough Oil Company Inc .... E 620 251-0103
Coffeyville (G-917)
Collingwood Grain Inc .... D 785 899-3636
Goodland (G-2466)
Crossfaith Ventures Lc .... E 620 662-8365
Hutchinson (G-3251)
Ethanol Products LLC .... C 316 303-1380
Wichita (G-14308)
Executive Beechcraft Inc .... E 913 782-9003
New Century (G-7284)
Farmers Cooperative Elev Co .... F 316 835-2261
Halstead (G-2699)
Farneys Inc .... F 316 522-7248
Haysville (G-2943)
Fbo Air - Garden City Inc .... F 620 275-5055
Garden City (G-2158)
Ferrellgas Inc .... F 913 661-1500
Overland Park (G-8713)
Ferrellgas Partners LP .... D 913 661-1500
Overland Park (G-8714)
Fleming Feed & Grain Inc .... E 316 742-3411
Leon (G-6247)
Frontier Ag Inc .... F 785 734-2331
Bird City (G-530)
Fuchs Lubricants Co .... D 913 422-4022
Kansas City (G-4020)
G H K Farms .... F 785 462-6440
Colby (G-1008)
Garden City Co-Op Inc .... F 620 275-6161
Garden City (G-2170)
Garden City Co-Op Inc .... F 620 276-8903
Garden City (G-2171)
Geo Bit Exploration Inc .... F 940 888-3134
Council Grove (G-1168)
Girton Propane Service Inc .... D 785 632-6273
Clay Center (G-866)
Golden Belt Coop Assn Inc .... F 785 726-3115
Ellis (G-1646)

Great Salt Plins Midstream LLC ....E....... 316 262-2819
Wichita *(G-14507)*
Industrial Sling Lbrcation Inc ....F....... 913 294-3001
Olathe *(G-7788)*
John E Jones Oil Co Inc......................F....... 785 425-6746
Stockton *(G-12182)*
Johnson Cooperative Grn Co Inc............F....... 620 492-6210
Johnson *(G-3654)*
Jrm Enterprises Inc ....E....... 785 404-1328
Salina *(G-10557)*
Kelly Maclaskey ....E....... 316 321-9011
El Dorado *(G-1578)*
Kinder Morgan Kansas Inc...................G....... 620 384-7830
Syracuse *(G-12228)*
◆ **Koch Carbon LLC**...............................E....... 316 828-5500
Wichita *(G-14875)*
◆ **Koch Industries Inc**............................A....... 316 828-5500
Wichita *(G-14881)*
◆ **Koch Mineral Services LLC**..............E....... 316 828-5500
Wichita *(G-14884)*
L & M Oil Company...............................F....... 913 856-8502
Gardner *(G-2352)*
L & M Oil Company...............................F....... 913 893-9789
Gardner *(G-2353)*
L C McClain Inc......................................F....... 785 584-6151
Rossville *(G-10253)*
▼ **Lubrication Engineers Inc**.................E....... 800 537-7683
Wichita *(G-14989)*
Lybarger Oil Inc......................................F....... 785 448-5512
Garnett *(G-2381)*
Lydcon Aero Center Inc ....F....... 620 624-1646
Liberal *(G-6338)*
Mackie Clemens Fuel Company ....F....... 785 242-2177
Ottawa *(G-8288)*
Mid-Kansas Cooperative Assn ....F....... 785 227-3343
Lindsborg *(G-6404)*
Mv Purchasing LLC ....E....... 316 262-2819
Wichita *(G-15143)*
Norton County Co-Op Assn Inc............F....... 785 877-5900
Norton *(G-7456)*
P B Hoidale Co Inc.................................F....... 913 438-1500
Shawnee *(G-11008)*
Parker Oil Co Inc....................................F....... 316 529-4343
Kansas City *(G-4313)*
Parker Oil Company Inc ....F....... 913 596-6247
Kansas City *(G-4314)*
Plains Marketing LP...............................F....... 620 365-3208
Iola *(G-3624)*
Propane Central......................................F....... 785 762-5160
Junction City *(G-3742)*
Redwood Group LLC..............................D....... 816 979-1786
Mission *(G-7137)*
Robinson Oil Co Inc...............................F....... 620 275-4237
Garden City *(G-2268)*
Skyland Grain LLC.................................F....... 620 492-2126
Johnson *(G-3660)*
Southern Plains Co-Op At Lewis...........E....... 620 324-5536
Lewis *(G-6270)*
T & E Oil Company Inc 1 ....E....... 620 663-3777
Hutchinson *(G-3460)*
Tex-Ok-Kan Oil Field Svcs LLC ....E....... 620 271-7310
Garden City *(G-2298)*
Town and Country Food Mkts Inc ....E....... 316 942-7940
Wichita *(G-15779)*
Volz Oil Company - Kinsley Inc ....F....... 620 659-2979
Greensburg *(G-2685)*
Wallis Oil Company ....F....... 913 621-6521
Kansas City *(G-4530)*
▲ **Yingling Aircraft Inc**...........................D....... 316 943-3246
Wichita *(G-16085)*

5181 Beer & Ale Wholesale

Ark Valley Distributing Inc ....F....... 620 221-6500
Arkansas City *(G-145)*
Best Beverage Sales Inc ....F....... 620 331-7100
Independence *(G-3500)*
Big Sky Distributors Kans LLC.............C....... 913 897-4488
Shawnee Mission *(G-11164)*
City Beverage Co Inc..............................E....... 620 662-6271
Hutchinson *(G-3239)*
Demo Sales Inc ....F....... 316 320-6670
El Dorado *(G-1556)*
Eagle Beverage Co Inc............................F....... 620 231-7970
Frontenac *(G-2054)*
Flint Hills Beverage LLC........................F....... 785 776-2337
Manhattan *(G-6631)*
Glazers Beer and Beverage LLC ....E....... 620 227-8168
Dodge City *(G-1365)*
House of Schwan Inc..............................D....... 316 636-9100
Wichita *(G-14642)*
Jayhawk Beverage Inc...........................E....... 785 234-8611
Topeka *(G-12741)*
▲ **Midwest Distributors Co Inc** ....D....... 913 287-2020
Kansas City *(G-4251)*
OMalley Beverage of Kansas................E....... 785 843-8816
Lawrence *(G-5044)*
Pepsi Beverages Company...................D....... 316 522-3131
Wichita *(G-15279)*
Seneca Wholesale Company Inc..........F....... 785 336-2118
Seneca *(G-10882)*
▲ **Southern Glazer SPI KS** ....C....... 913 745-2900
Edwardsville *(G-1515)*
▲ **Standard Beverage Corporation**.......F....... 316 838-7707
Wichita *(G-15652)*
Strathman Sales Company Inc ....E....... 785 354-8537
Topeka *(G-13114)*
Vidricksen Distributing Co....................F....... 785 827-2386
Salina *(G-10753)*
Western Beverage Inc ....E....... 620 227-7641
Dodge City *(G-1454)*
Western Beverage-Hays........................F....... 785 625-3712
Hays *(G-2932)*

5182 Wine & Distilled Alcoholic Beverages Wholesale

Blacks Retail Liquor LLC ....F....... 913 281-1551
Kansas City *(G-3866)*
Handcrafted Wines LLC ....F....... 913 829-4500
Lenexa *(G-5888)*
Lion Nathan Usa Inc ....E....... 913 338-4433
Overland Park *(G-8960)*
▲ **Southern Glazer SPI KS** ....C....... 913 745-2900
Edwardsville *(G-1515)*
Southern Glazers Wine and Sp............D....... 913 396-4900
Overland Park *(G-9331)*
Southern Glazers Wine and Sp............F....... 316 264-1354
Wichita *(G-15624)*
▲ **Standard Beverage Corporation**.......F....... 316 838-7707
Wichita *(G-15652)*
Standard Beverage Corporation...........C....... 800 999-8797
Lawrence *(G-5117)*
Standard Beverage Corporation...........E....... 913 888-7200
Lenexa *(G-6152)*

5191 Farm Splys Wholesale

Ackerman Supply Inc ....F....... 785 738-5733
Beloit *(G-469)*
AG Connection Sales Inc ....F....... 785 336-2121
Seneca *(G-10856)*
Ag-Service Inc..F....... 620 947-3166
Hillsboro *(G-3040)*
Agco Inc..F....... 785 483-2128
Russell *(G-10263)*
Agri Trails Coop Inc..............................D....... 785 479-5870
Chapman *(G-776)*
Agri Trails Coop Inc..............................F....... 785 258-2286
Herington *(G-2969)*
Alfalfa Inc...G....... 620 675-8686
Sublette *(G-12196)*
Alliance AG and Grain LLC ....F....... 620 723-3351
Greensburg *(G-2671)*
Alternative Building Tech......................F....... 913 856-4536
Gardner *(G-2325)*
American Midwest Distrs LLC ....F....... 816 842-1905
Overland Park *(G-8379)*
Archer-Daniels-Midland Company ....G....... 620 375-4811
Leoti *(G-6250)*
Archer-Daniels-Midland Company ....F....... 620 872-2174
Scott City *(G-10804)*
Archer-Daniels-Midland Company ....G....... 620 357-8733
Jetmore *(G-3645)*
Archer-Daniels-Midland Company ....F....... 785 671-3171
Oakley *(G-7471)*
Archer-Daniels-Midland Company ....G....... 785 694-2286
Brewster *(G-582)*
Atwood Distributing LP ....E....... 316 789-1800
Derby *(G-1218)*
Atwood Distributing LP ....F....... 316 744-8888
Park City *(G-9602)*
Bartlett Cooperative Assn.....................E....... 620 226-3311
Bartlett *(G-371)*
Beachner Seed Co Inc...........................F....... 913 686-2090
Spring Hill *(G-12078)*
Beattie Farmers Un Coop Assn ....E....... 785 353-2237
Beattie *(G-418)*
Beaver Grain Corporation Inc...............F....... 620 587-3417
Beaver *(G-424)*
▲ **Beaver Valley Supply Co Inc**............E....... 800 982-1280
Atwood *(G-281)*
Bekemeyer Enterprises Inc...................F....... 785 325-2274
Washington *(G-13459)*
Bert and Wetta Sales Inc......................E....... 785 263-2258
Abilene *(G-14)*
Bestifor Hay Co......................................F....... 785 527-2450
Belleville *(G-454)*
Bluestem Farm and Rnch Sup Inc.........D....... 620 342-5502
Emporia *(G-1705)*
Bruna Brothers Implement LLC............F....... 785 632-5621
Clay Center *(G-845)*
Bruna Brothers Implement LLC............E....... 785 325-2232
Washington *(G-13461)*
Cargill Incorporated..............................E....... 620 277-2558
Garden City *(G-2121)*
Cargill Animal Nutrition........................E....... 620 342-1650
Emporia *(G-1717)*
Carl Leatherwood Inc ....E....... 620 855-3850
Cimarron *(G-820)*
Central Planes Coop..............................F....... 785 695-2216
Athol *(G-273)*
Central Prairie Co-Op ....F....... 620 278-2470
Sterling *(G-12113)*
Central Valley AG Cooperative ....C....... 785 738-2241
Beloit *(G-481)*
Chisholm Trail Country Str LLC ....F....... 316 283-3276
Newton *(G-7328)*
CHS Inc...F....... 785 754-3318
Quinter *(G-10180)*
CHS Inc...D....... 620 663-5711
Hutchinson *(G-3238)*
CHS Inc...E....... 785 852-4241
Sharon Springs *(G-10895)*
City of Great Bend ....D....... 620 793-5031
Great Bend *(G-2543)*
Cooperative Elevator & Sup Co............E....... 620 873-2161
Meade *(G-7047)*
Countryside Feed LLC..........................E....... 620 947-3111
Hillsboro *(G-3047)*
Countryside Feed LLC..........................F....... 785 336-6777
Seneca *(G-10861)*
Crazy House Inc.....................................F....... 620 275-2153
Garden City *(G-2138)*
Cropland Co-Op Inc...............................F....... 620 649-2230
Satanta *(G-10782)*
Cropland Co-Op Inc...............................F....... 620 356-1241
Ulysses *(G-13294)*
CSC Gold Inc..F....... 913 664-8100
Shawnee Mission *(G-11284)*
Darling Ingredients Inc..........................D....... 316 264-6951
Wichita *(G-14169)*
Darling Ingredients Inc..........................G....... 913 371-7083
Kansas City *(G-3957)*
Decatur Cooperative Assn....................F....... 785 475-2234
Oberlin *(G-7490)*
Delange Seed House Inc........................E....... 620 724-6223
Girard *(G-2401)*
Delphos Cooperative Assn ....E....... 785 523-4213
Delphos *(G-1216)*
Dodge City Cooperative Exch...............F....... 620 227-8671
Dodge City *(G-1345)*
Donohue Ranch ....F....... 785 867-2160
Greeley *(G-2665)*
Ellsworth Coop.......................................F....... 785 472-3261
Ellsworth *(G-1667)*
Farmers Co-Operative Equity Co ....F....... 620 739-4335
Isabel *(G-3639)*
Farmers Co-Operative Union................D....... 620 278-2141
Sterling *(G-12116)*
Farmers Coop Grn Assn Inc ....F....... 620 456-2222
Conway Springs *(G-1141)*
Farmers Cooperative Elev Assn............F....... 785 747-2236
Greenleaf *(G-2668)*
Farmers Cooperative Elev Co...............F....... 316 835-2261
Halstead *(G-2699)*
Farmers Cooperative Elev Co...............F....... 620 545-7138
Viola *(G-13378)*
Farmers Cooperative Elev Inc ....F....... 785 284-2185
Sabetha *(G-10310)*
Farmers Cooperative Grain...................F....... 620 326-7496
Wellington *(G-13499)*
Farmers Cooperative Grain Co.............F....... 620 845-6441
Caldwell *(G-658)*
Farmers Grain Cooperative...................E....... 620 837-3313
Walton *(G-13400)*
Faulkner Grain Inc ....F....... 620 597-2636
Chetopa *(G-817)*
Fleming Feed & Grain Inc......................E....... 316 742-3411
Leon *(G-6247)*
Frontier Ag Inc ....E....... 785 462-2063
Oakley *(G-7475)*

Frontier Ag Inc F 785 694-2281
Brewster *(G-583)*

Frontier Ag Inc E 785 824-3201
Grinnell *(G-2692)*

Garden City Co-Op Inc F 620 275-6161
Garden City *(G-2170)*

Garden City Co-Op Inc F 620 356-1219
Ulysses *(G-13298)*

▲ Gardn-Wise Distributors Inc F 316 838-6104
Wichita *(G-14448)*

▲ General Tech A Svcs & Pdts Co G 913 766-5566
Olathe *(G-7727)*

Golden Belt Coop Assn Inc F 785 726-3115
Ellis *(G-1646)*

Golden Valley Inc E 620 527-4216
Rozel *(G-10258)*

Grass Pad Inc D 913 764-4100
Olathe *(G-7739)*

Great Bend Cooperative Assn E 620 793-3531
Great Bend *(G-2576)*

H B J Farms Inc F 785 595-3236
White Cloud *(G-13568)*

Heartland Hay F 785 525-6331
Lucas *(G-6472)*

Helena Agri-Enterprises LLC F 785 899-2391
Goodland *(G-2476)*

Helena Agri-Enterprises LLC E 620 275-9531
Garden City *(G-2195)*

Helena Chemical Company G 620 375-2073
Leoti *(G-6253)*

Hi Plains Cooperative Assn F 785 462-3351
Colby *(G-1012)*

Hunn Leather Products Inc F 316 775-6300
Augusta *(G-326)*

J B Pearl Sales & Svc Inc E 785 437-2772
Saint Marys *(G-10366)*

Jackson Farmers Inc F 785 364-3161
Holton *(G-3100)*

Johnson Cooperative Grn Co Inc F 620 492-6210
Johnson *(G-3654)*

Kanza Cooperative Association F 620 546-2231
Iuka *(G-3640)*

Kanza Cooperative Association E 316 444-2141
Andale *(G-78)*

Kauffman Seeds Inc F 877 664-3526
Haven *(G-2733)*

Koch AG & Energy Solutions LLC E 316 828-5500
Wichita *(G-14872)*

Koch Companies Pub Sector LLC G 316 828-5500
Wichita *(G-14876)*

Koch Industries Inc E 620 227-8631
Dodge City *(G-1395)*

Kugler Oil Company G 620 356-4347
Ulysses *(G-13304)*

Land OLakes Inc E 785 445-4030
Russell *(G-10278)*

Lange Company LLC F 620 456-2996
Conway Springs *(G-1143)*

Lawrence Feed & Farm Sup Inc F 785 843-4311
Lawrence *(G-4966)*

Leavenworth County Coop Assn F 913 727-1900
Lansing *(G-4683)*

Leroy Cooperative Assn Inc E 620 964-2225
Le Roy *(G-5196)*

Lone Pine AG Services Inc F 785 887-6559
Lecompton *(G-5612)*

Long Island Grain Co Inc F 785 854-7431
Long Island *(G-6428)*

Manna Pro Products LLC E 913 621-2355
Kansas City *(G-4216)*

McCune Farmers Union Coop F 620 632-4226
Mc Cune *(G-6920)*

MFA Enterprises Inc F 620 237-4668
Moran *(G-7162)*

Mid-Kansas Cooperative Assn E 620 345-6328
Moundridge *(G-7190)*

Mid-Kansas Cooperative Assn F 785 776-9467
Manhattan *(G-6742)*

Mid-Kansas Cooperative Assn F 620 837-3313
Walton *(G-13401)*

Mid-West Fertilizer Inc G 620 431-3430
Chanute *(G-743)*

Minneola Co-Op Inc F 620 885-4361
Minneola *(G-7125)*

Morrill Hay Company Inc F 620 285-6941
Paola *(G-9576)*

Mulvane Cooperative Union Inc F 316 777-1121
Mulvane *(G-7223)*

Nemaha County Cooperative Assn D 785 336-6153
Seneca *(G-10874)*

Norder Supply Inc E 620 872-3058
Scott City *(G-10825)*

Norton County Co-Op Assn Inc F 785 877-5900
Norton *(G-7456)*

Nutrien AG Solutions Inc F 316 794-2231
Goddard *(G-2451)*

Nutrien AG Solutions Inc F 620 872-2174
Scott City *(G-10826)*

Nutrien AG Solutions Inc E 620 275-4271
Garden City *(G-2244)*

O K Coop Grn & Merc Co F 620 825-4212
Kiowa *(G-4628)*

Offerle Coop Grn & Sup Co F 620 659-2165
Offerle *(G-7500)*

Orscheln Farm and Home LLC F 620 241-0707
McPherson *(G-7012)*

Orscheln Farm and Home LLC F 620 331-2551
Independence *(G-3546)*

Orscheln Farm and Home LLC F 785 825-1681
Salina *(G-10624)*

Orscheln Farm and Home LLC F 620 442-5760
Arkansas City *(G-168)*

Orscheln Farm and Home LLC E 913 728-2014
Basehor *(G-385)*

Orscheln Farm and Home LLC F 785 562-2459
Marysville *(G-6906)*

Orscheln Farm and Home LLC F 785 762-4411
Junction City *(G-3734)*

Orscheln Farm and Home LLC F 913 367-2261
Atchison *(G-254)*

Orscheln Farm and Home LLC E 620 421-0555
Parsons *(G-9715)*

Orscheln Farm and Home LLC F 785 282-3272
Smith Center *(G-12038)*

Orscheln Farm and Home LLC F 785 243-6071
Concordia *(G-1126)*

Orscheln Farm and Home LLC F 620 662-8867
Hutchinson *(G-3397)*

Orscheln Farm and Home LLC F 620 251-2950
Coffeyville *(G-968)*

Orscheln Farm and Home LLC F 785 838-3184
Lawrence *(G-5050)*

Orscheln Farm and Home LLC F 620 227-8700
Dodge City *(G-1416)*

Orscheln Farm and Home LLC F 620 792-5480
Great Bend *(G-2619)*

Orscheln Farm and Home LLC F 316 283-2969
Newton *(G-7401)*

Orscheln Farm and Home LLC E 785 776-1476
Manhattan *(G-6766)*

Orscheln Farm and Home LLC F 785 460-1551
Colby *(G-1033)*

Orscheln Farm and Home LLC F 785 899-7132
Goodland *(G-2481)*

Orscheln Farm and Home LLC F 620 326-2804
Wellington *(G-13520)*

Orscheln Farm and Home LLC F 620 365-7695
Iola *(G-3621)*

Orscheln Farm and Home LLC F 316 321-4004
El Dorado *(G-1589)*

Orscheln Farm and Home LLC F 785 625-7316
Hays *(G-2884)*

Orscheln Farm and Home LLC E 785 242-3133
Ottawa *(G-8296)*

Orscheln Farm and Home LLC F 785 228-9688
Topeka *(G-12955)*

Orscheln Farm and Home LLC F 620 930-3276
Medicine Lodge *(G-7071)*

Palmer Grain Inc F 785 692-4212
Palmer *(G-9538)*

Pioneer Hi-Bred Intl Inc F 785 776-1335
Manhattan *(G-6777)*

Plains Equity Exch & Coop Un E 620 563-9566
Plains *(G-9977)*

Polansky Seed Inc F 785 527-2271
Belleville *(G-462)*

Preferred AG Services Inc F 620 271-7366
Garden City *(G-2258)*

Prime Feeders LLC F 620 492-6674
Johnson *(G-3659)*

Progressive AG Coop Assn F 620 962-5238
Danville *(G-1190)*

Provimi North America Inc E 620 327-2280
Hesston *(G-2999)*

Purina Mills LLC E 316 265-0624
Wichita *(G-15379)*

R & F Farm Supply Inc F 620 244-3275
Erie *(G-1864)*

R Puckett Farms Inc F 620 378-3342
Fredonia *(G-2043)*

Ranch-Aid Inc F 620 583-5585
Eureka *(G-1898)*

Randall Farmers Coop Un Inc F 785 739-2312
Randall *(G-10190)*

Rangeland Cooperatives Inc E 785 543-2114
Phillipsburg *(G-9797)*

Schendel Services Inc F 913 498-1811
Olathe *(G-8056)*

▲ Scotwood Industries Inc E 913 851-3500
Overland Park *(G-9285)*

Seaboard Feed Mill E 620 375-3300
Leoti *(G-6257)*

Severy Cooperative Association F 620 736-2211
Severy *(G-10893)*

▼ Sharp Bros Seed Company E 620 398-2231
Healy *(G-2967)*

Simpson Farm Enterprises Inc F 785 731-2700
Ransom *(G-10195)*

Sims Fertilizer and Chem Co F 785 346-5681
Osborne *(G-8218)*

Skyland Grain LLC F 620 492-2126
Johnson *(G-3660)*

Skyland Grain LLC F 620 672-3961
Cunningham *(G-1189)*

Southern Plains Co-Op At Lewis E 620 324-5536
Lewis *(G-6270)*

▼ Specialty Fertilizer Pdts LLC F 913 956-7500
Leawood *(G-5556)*

Stafford County Flour Mills Co E 620 458-4121
Hudson *(G-3146)*

Star Seed Inc F 800 782-7311
Osborne *(G-8219)*

Sublette Cooperative Inc E 620 675-2297
Sublette *(G-12209)*

Syngenta Seeds Inc F 785 210-0218
Junction City *(G-3759)*

Tarwaters Inc E 785 286-2390
Topeka *(G-13143)*

Tractor Supply Company F 620 408-9119
Dodge City *(G-1439)*

Tractor Supply Company F 620 672-1102
Pratt *(G-10161)*

Tractor Supply Company F 785 587-8949
Manhattan *(G-6829)*

Tractor Supply Company F 620 223-4900
Fort Scott *(G-2010)*

Two Rivers Consumers Coop Assn E 620 442-2360
Arkansas City *(G-185)*

Two-Bee Inc F 785 364-2162
Holton *(G-3113)*

United Plains AG E 785 852-4241
Sharon Springs *(G-10901)*

Western AG Enterprises Inc E 620 793-8355
Great Bend *(G-2660)*

Wilbur-Ellis Company LLC F 785 582-4052
Silver Lake *(G-12029)*

Wilbur-Ellis Company LLC F 785 359-6569
Leona *(G-6248)*

William G Woods F 620 285-6971
Larned *(G-4716)*

Winfield Solutions LLC F 620 277-2231
Garden City *(G-2317)*

5192 Books, Periodicals & Newspapers Wholesale

435 Magazine LLC F 913 469-6700
Overland Park *(G-8330)*

Ascension Via Christi Hospital F 316 268-6096
Wichita *(G-13750)*

Design Analysis and RES Corp F 785 832-0434
Lawrence *(G-4833)*

Everhance LLC F 785 218-1406
Overland Park *(G-8696)*

▲ Florists Review Entps Inc E 785 266-0888
Topeka *(G-12620)*

Main Street Media Inc F 785 483-2116
Russell *(G-10281)*

Mennonite Mission Network F 540 434-6701
Newton *(G-7379)*

Scholastic Book Fairs Inc F 913 599-5700
Shawnee Mission *(G-11836)*

Subscription Ink Co D 913 248-1800
Shawnee Mission *(G-11905)*

Western International Inc F 785 856-1840
Lawrence *(G-5182)*

S I C

5193 Flowers, Nursery Stock & Florists' Splys Wholesale

Absolutely Flowers..........F....... 620 728-0266
Hutchinson *(G-3189)*
▲ **Alex R Masson Inc**..........D....... 913 301-3281
Linwood *(G-6415)*
Arnolds Greenhouse Inc..........F....... 620 964-2463
Le Roy *(G-5195)*
Baisch & Skinner Inc..........F....... 785 267-6931
Topeka *(G-12358)*
Baisch & Skinner Inc..........F....... 316 945-0074
Wichita *(G-13794)*
Campbells Phoenix Greenhouse..........F....... 316 524-5311
Wichita *(G-13931)*
Eureka Greenhouses Inc..........F....... 620 583-8676
Eureka *(G-1886)*
Evans Industries Inc..........G....... 316 262-2551
Wichita *(G-14310)*
Grass Pad Inc..........D....... 913 764-4100
Olathe *(G-7739)*
Hermes Nursery Inc..........E....... 913 441-2400
Shawnee Mission *(G-11429)*
Jerrys Nursery and Ldscpg Inc..........F....... 913 721-1444
Kansas City *(G-4122)*
Loma Vista Garden Center Inc..........E....... 913 897-7010
Ottawa *(G-8284)*
Overland Park Garden Ctr Inc..........E....... 913 788-7974
Kansas City *(G-4303)*
Stutzman Greenhouse Inc..........E....... 620 662-0559
Hutchinson *(G-3454)*
Valley Floral Company LLC..........E....... 316 838-3355
Wichita *(G-15871)*
William O Broeker Enterprises..........E....... 913 682-2022
Leavenworth *(G-5306)*

5194 Tobacco & Tobacco Prdts Wholesale

Joe Smith Company..........E....... 620 231-3610
Pittsburg *(G-9883)*
Kansas Candy & Tobacco Inc..........F....... 316 942-9081
Wichita *(G-14789)*
Philip Morris USA Inc..........F....... 913 339-9317
Shawnee Mission *(G-11731)*
Sunflower Supply Company Inc..........E....... 620 783-5473
Galena *(G-2088)*
Wichita Tobacco & Candy Co..........F....... 316 264-2412
Wichita *(G-16040)*

5198 Paints, Varnishes & Splys Wholesale

Andrew Inc..........F....... 316 267-3328
Wichita *(G-13708)*
Blish-Mize Co..........C....... 913 367-1250
Atchison *(G-218)*
◆ **Design Materials Inc**..........E....... 913 342-9796
Kansas City *(G-3969)*
Designed Bus Intrors Tpeka Inc..........F....... 785 233-2078
Topeka *(G-12553)*
Designers Library Inc..........F....... 913 227-0010
Shawnee Mission *(G-11303)*
Master Pnt Indus Coating Corp..........F....... 316 283-3999
Newton *(G-7377)*
Sherwin-Williams Company..........F....... 913 782-0126
Olathe *(G-8062)*
▲ **Sunbelt Chemicals Inc**..........F....... 972 296-3920
Shawnee *(G-11035)*

5199 Nondurable Goods, NEC Wholesale

4th Gneration Promotional Pdts..........G....... 913 393-0837
Olathe *(G-7502)*
▲ **Ambrose Packaging Inc**..........E....... 913 780-5666
Olathe *(G-7525)*
Ambrose Sales Inc..........E....... 913 780-5666
Olathe *(G-7526)*
▲ **Bachus & Son Inc**..........E....... 316 265-4673
Wichita *(G-13789)*
◆ **Berger Company**..........F....... 913 367-3700
Atchison *(G-214)*
◆ **Computer Distribution Corp**..........E....... 785 354-1086
Topeka *(G-12498)*
Cosmic Pet LLC..........E....... 316 941-1100
Wichita *(G-14105)*
▲ **Creative Consumer Concepts Inc**..........E....... 913 491-6444
Overland Park *(G-8610)*
◆ **Dd Traders Inc**..........B....... 913 402-6800
Leawood *(G-5376)*
▲ **Diligence Inc**..........E....... 913 254-0500
New Century *(G-7279)*
▲ **Express Scale Parts Inc**..........E....... 913 441-4787
Lenexa *(G-5844)*
Finchers Findings Inc..........G....... 620 886-5952
Medicine Lodge *(G-7060)*
Fittings Export LLC..........G....... 620 364-2930
Burlington *(G-636)*
Gibson Products Co Salina Inc..........E....... 785 827-4474
Salina *(G-10510)*
Gibsons Ace Hardware..........E....... 785 632-3147
Clay Center *(G-865)*
Glover Inc..........E....... 800 654-1511
Olathe *(G-7735)*
Greif Inc..........E....... 620 221-2330
Winfield *(G-16145)*
▲ **Hairuwear Inc**..........E....... 954 835-2200
Lenexa *(G-5886)*
Heritage Cmpt Consulting Inc..........F....... 913 529-4227
Overland Park *(G-8812)*
Hills Pet Nutrition Inc..........C....... 785 286-1451
Topeka *(G-12692)*
Humidor East..........E....... 316 688-0112
Wichita *(G-14654)*
Iris Strgc Mktg Support Inc..........E....... 913 232-4825
Lenexa *(G-5923)*
John B Baker..........G....... 316 263-2820
Wichita *(G-14762)*
John G Levin..........E....... 785 234-5551
Topeka *(G-12746)*
▲ **Joseph F Beaver**..........F....... 620 872-2395
Scott City *(G-10818)*
K & F Distributors Inc..........F....... 316 213-2030
Kechi *(G-4570)*
◆ **Kid Stuff Marketing Inc**..........E....... 785 862-3707
Topeka *(G-12821)*
◆ **Kms Inc**..........E....... 316 264-8833
Wichita *(G-14868)*
Lambriars Inc..........D....... 785 245-3231
Mahaska *(G-6505)*
Lawrence Feed & Farm Sup Inc..........F....... 785 843-4311
Lawrence *(G-4966)*
▲ **Lawrence Paper Company**..........C....... 785 843-8111
Lawrence *(G-4982)*
Lee Reed Engraving Inc..........G....... 316 943-9700
Wichita *(G-14949)*
Long Shot Enterprises LLC..........F....... 785 493-0171
Salina *(G-10584)*
▲ **Mediacorp LLC**..........E....... 913 317-8900
Overland Park *(G-9006)*
▲ **Mer-Sea & Co LLC**..........E....... 816 974-3115
Lenexa *(G-5994)*
Mfl Inc..........E....... 785 862-2767
Topeka *(G-12886)*
Midwest Single Source Inc..........E....... 316 267-6333
Wichita *(G-15102)*
▲ **Nathan Weiner & Associates**..........F....... 913 390-0508
Olathe *(G-7911)*
National Fabric Co Inc..........F....... 913 281-1833
Kansas City *(G-4279)*
Nazdar Company..........F....... 913 422-1888
Shawnee *(G-11004)*
▲ **Neff Sales Co Inc**..........F....... 913 371-0777
Kansas City *(G-4285)*
Novation Iq LLC..........E....... 913 492-6000
Lenexa *(G-6029)*
Omc Distribution Center..........F....... 913 791-3592
Olathe *(G-7957)*
Peavey Corporation..........D....... 913 888-0600
Lenexa *(G-6047)*
Pet Haven LLC..........F....... 316 942-2151
Wichita *(G-15285)*
▲ **Power Sales and Advertising**..........D....... 913 324-4900
Lenexa *(G-6063)*
Prairie Patches Inc..........G....... 785 749-4565
Lawrence *(G-5072)*
▼ **Premium Nutritional Pdts Inc**..........F....... 913 962-8887
Shawnee Mission *(G-11750)*
▲ **Prizm Incorporated**..........F....... 785 456-1831
Wamego *(G-13436)*
▲ **Redemption Plus LLC**..........D....... 913 563-4331
Lenexa *(G-6095)*
Regal Distributing Co..........E....... 913 894-8787
Lenexa *(G-6096)*
Rfc Logo Inc..........A....... 913 319-3100
Shawnee Mission *(G-11794)*
Rjs Discount Sales Inc..........F....... 785 267-7476
Topeka *(G-13020)*
▲ **Robbie Transcontinental Inc**..........C....... 913 492-3400
Lenexa *(G-6110)*
Rods Food Stores Inc..........E....... 785 243-2035
Concordia *(G-1127)*
▲ **Tdi Global Solutions Inc**..........F....... 877 834-6750
Meriden *(G-7082)*
Touch Enterprises LLC..........E....... 913 638-2130
Olathe *(G-8117)*
▲ **Treatco Inc**..........D....... 316 265-7900
Wichita *(G-15795)*
Treescape Inc..........E....... 316 733-6388
Andover *(G-112)*
▲ **Tytan International LLC**..........F....... 913 492-3222
Lenexa *(G-6196)*
U S Toy Co Inc..........E....... 913 642-8247
Leawood *(G-5587)*
United States Awards Inc..........E....... 620 231-8470
Pittsburg *(G-9951)*
Valu Merchandisers Company..........F....... 620 223-1313
Fort Scott *(G-2014)*
▲ **Valu Merchandisers Company**..........E....... 913 319-8500
Kansas City *(G-4513)*
▲ **Victorian Paper Company**..........D....... 913 438-3995
Lenexa *(G-6214)*
Waxene Products Company Inc..........G....... 316 263-8523
Wichita *(G-15938)*
Wds Inc..........D....... 913 894-1881
Lenexa *(G-6223)*

60 DEPOSITORY INSTITUTIONS

6021 National Commercial Banks

1st National Bank of Dighton..........F....... 620 397-5324
Dighton *(G-1282)*
Armed Forces Bank Nat Assn..........B....... 913 682-9090
Fort Leavenworth *(G-1934)*
Armed Forces Bank Nat Assn..........F....... 913 651-2992
Fort Leavenworth *(G-1935)*
Armed Forces Bank Nat Assn..........F....... 785 238-2241
Junction City *(G-3667)*
Arvest Bank Operations Inc..........E....... 913 261-2265
Shawnee Mission *(G-11121)*
Banccentral National Assn..........F....... 620 842-1000
Anthony *(G-121)*
Bank America National Assn..........F....... 316 788-2811
Derby *(G-1222)*
Bank America National Assn..........F....... 785 625-3413
Hays *(G-2755)*
Bank America National Assn..........F....... 913 768-1340
Olathe *(G-7546)*
Bank America National Assn..........F....... 316 261-4242
Dodge City *(G-1302)*
Bank America National Assn..........F....... 816 979-8482
Prairie Village *(G-10013)*
Bank America National Assn..........F....... 316 261-4242
Liberal *(G-6281)*
Bank America National Assn..........F....... 816 979-8561
Olathe *(G-7547)*
Bank America National Assn..........F....... 785 235-1532
Topeka *(G-12362)*
Bank America National Assn..........F....... 316 261-2025
Wichita *(G-13800)*
Bank America National Assn..........F....... 816 979-8215
Kansas City *(G-3839)*
Bank America National Assn..........F....... 785 842-1000
Lawrence *(G-4749)*
Bank America National Assn..........F....... 785 227-3344
Lindsborg *(G-6391)*
Bank America National Assn..........F....... 316 261-2274
Wichita *(G-13801)*
Bank America National Assn..........F....... 785 238-8012
Junction City *(G-3671)*
Bank America National Assn..........E....... 816 979-4592
Overland Park *(G-8425)*
Bank America National Assn..........E....... 316 261-4359
Wichita *(G-13802)*
Bank America National Assn..........E....... 620 331-4800
Independence *(G-3498)*
Bank America National Assn..........F....... 816 979-8200
Overland Park *(G-8426)*
Bank America National Assn..........F....... 316 261-4242
Liberal *(G-6282)*
Bank America National Assn..........E....... 785 235-1532
Lawrence *(G-4750)*
Bank America National Assn..........F....... 816 979-8608
Shawnee Mission *(G-11146)*
Bank America National Assn..........F....... 816 979-8257
Kansas City *(G-3840)*
Bank America National Assn..........F....... 316 529-6730
Andover *(G-84)*
Bank America National Assn..........F....... 816 979-8219
Lenexa *(G-5685)*
Bank America National Assn..........F....... 913 897-1470
Overland Park *(G-8427)*
Bank America National Assn..........F....... 316 261-4216
Wichita *(G-13803)*

Bank America National Assn D 620 694-4395 Hutchinson *(G-3212)*
Bank America National Assn F 316 261-2210 Wichita *(G-13804)*
Bank America National Assn F 316 261-4040 Wichita *(G-13805)*
Bank America National Assn F 316 261-2143 Wichita *(G-13806)*
Bank America National Assn F 913 441-1067 Shawnee *(G-10913)*
Bank of Blue Valley F 913 888-7852 Shawnee Mission *(G-11147)*
Bank of Flint Hills F 785 765-2220 Alma *(G-62)*
Bank of Tescott E 785 825-1621 Salina *(G-10418)*
Bank Snb F 316 315-1600 Wichita *(G-13810)*
Bank Snb F 620 728-3000 Hutchinson *(G-3214)*
Bankers Bank of Kansas NA E 316 681-2265 Wichita *(G-13811)*
Bok Financial Corporation E 785 273-9993 Topeka *(G-12396)*
Cbi-Kansas Inc E 785 625-6542 Hays *(G-2766)*
Centera Bank F 620 227-6370 Dodge City *(G-1320)*
Central National Bank E 785 238-4114 Junction City *(G-3676)*
Central National Bank F 620 382-2129 Marion *(G-6868)*
Central National Bank F 785 838-1960 Lawrence *(G-4779)*
Central National Bank F 785 238-4114 Junction City *(G-3677)*
Central National Bank F 785 838-1893 Lawrence *(G-4780)*
Central National Bank F 785 234-2265 Topeka *(G-12456)*
Central of Kansas Inc D 785 238-4114 Junction City *(G-3678)*
Citizens Bank NA F 913 239-2700 Overland Park *(G-8553)*
Citizens Bank NA E 620 223-1200 Fort Scott *(G-1959)*
Citizens Bank of Kansas NA F 316 788-1111 Derby *(G-1229)*
Citizens Bank of Kansas NA F 620 886-5686 Medicine Lodge *(G-7058)*
Citizens National Bank D 785 747-2261 Greenleaf *(G-2667)*
Citizens National Bank F 913 727-3266 Lansing *(G-4671)*
Citizens State Bank E 316 518-6621 Hugoton *(G-3152)*
Commerce Bank F 816 234-2000 Kansas City *(G-3927)*
Commerce Bank E 620 276-5600 Garden City *(G-2129)*
Commerce Bank E 316 261-4795 Wichita *(G-14064)*
Commerce Bank F 785 865-4799 Lawrence *(G-4799)*
Commerce Bank D 316 261-4700 Wichita *(G-14066)*
Commerce Bank F 785 532-3500 Manhattan *(G-6596)*
Commerce Bank F 316 261-5590 Wichita *(G-14067)*
Commerce Bank F 816 234-2000 Olathe *(G-7603)*
Commerce Bank F 816 234-2000 Lawrence *(G-4801)*
Commerce Bank E 785 537-1234 Manhattan *(G-6598)*
Community National Bank F 913 369-0100 Tonganoxie *(G-12256)*
Community National Bank F 620 423-0314 Parsons *(G-9677)*
Community National Bank F 316 775-6068 Augusta *(G-314)*
Community National Bank F 913 724-9901 Basehor *(G-373)*
Community National Bank F 620 922-3294 Edna *(G-1492)*
Community National Bank E 620 235-1345 Pittsburg *(G-9842)*
Community National Bank & Tr F 620 365-6000 Iola *(G-3595)*
Community National Bank & Tr F 316 283-0059 Newton *(G-7332)*
Community National Bank & Tr F 620 336-2145 Cherryvale *(G-803)*
Condon National Bank E 620 251-5500 Coffeyville *(G-929)*
Conway Bank E 620 456-2255 Conway Springs *(G-1137)*
Conway Bank N A F 316 263-6767 Wichita *(G-14096)*
Corefirst Bank & Trust F 913 248-7000 Shawnee *(G-10934)*
Country Club Bank E 913 682-0001 Leavenworth *(G-5226)*
Country Club Bank F 913 682-2300 Leavenworth *(G-5227)*
Enterprise Bank & Trust F 913 791-9950 Olathe *(G-7682)*
Equity Bank NA F 731 989-2161 Shawnee *(G-10949)*
Equity Bank NA D 620 624-1971 Liberal *(G-6307)*
Equity Bank NA F 316 612-6000 Wichita *(G-14299)*
Exchange National Bank & Tr Co E 913 367-6000 Atchison *(G-227)*
Exchange National Bank & Tr Co F 913 833-5560 Effingham *(G-1523)*
Exchange National Bank Inc F 620 273-6389 Cottonwood Falls *(G-1153)*
Farmers & Merchants Bank Colby E 785 460-3321 Colby *(G-1007)*
Farmers Bank & Trust F 913 402-7257 Overland Park *(G-8705)*
Farmers National Bank F 785 543-6541 Phillipsburg *(G-9785)*
First Bank of Newton E 316 283-2600 Newton *(G-7345)*
First Heritage Bank F 785 857-3341 Centralia *(G-699)*
First Horizon Bank E 913 317-2000 Overland Park *(G-8719)*
First Nat Bnk of Hutchinson D 620 663-1521 Hutchinson *(G-3285)*
First Nat Bnk of Hutchinson E 620 662-7858 Hutchinson *(G-3286)*
First Nat Bnk of Hutchinson E 620 465-2225 Haven *(G-2730)*
First Nat Bnk of Hutchinson F 620 694-2304 Hutchinson *(G-3287)*
First Nat Bnk of Hutchinson E 620 663-1521 Hutchinson *(G-3288)*
First Nat Bnk Syracuse Inc F 620 384-7441 Syracuse *(G-12224)*
First Nat Bnk Syracuse Inc F 620 276-6971 Garden City *(G-2165)*
First Nat Bnk Syracuse Inc F 620 492-1754 Johnson *(G-3653)*
First Nat Bnkshares Beloit Inc F 785 738-2251 Beloit *(G-484)*
First Nat Bnkshres of Scott Cy E 620 872-2143 Scott City *(G-10811)*
First National Bank D 785 890-2000 Goodland *(G-2471)*
First National Bank F 785 852-2000 Sharon Springs *(G-10897)*
First National Bank E 620 855-3416 Cimarron *(G-825)*
First National Bank & Trust E 785 543-6511 Phillipsburg *(G-9786)*
First National Bank Clifton F 785 437-6585 Saint Marys *(G-10364)*
First National Bank In Pratt E 620 672-6421 Pratt *(G-10113)*
First National Bank Louisburg F 913 766-6701 Shawnee Mission *(G-11373)*
First National Bank Louisburg F 913 837-5191 Louisburg *(G-6448)*
First National Bank of Girard F 620 724-6111 Girard *(G-2405)*
First National Bank of Hutchin E 316 661-2471 Mount Hope *(G-7204)*
First National Bank of Kansas F 785 733-2564 Burlington *(G-635)*
First National Bank of Omaha D 913 768-1120 Olathe *(G-7712)*
First National Bank of Omaha D 913 451-5824 Overland Park *(G-8721)*
First National Bank of Omaha D 913 631-0016 Shawnee *(G-10956)*
First National Bnk of Scott Cy E 620 872-2143 Scott City *(G-10812)*
First National Bnk of Sedan KS F 620 725-3106 Sedan *(G-10843)*
First Option Bank and Trust F 913 294-3811 Osawatomie *(G-8193)*
First Pratt Bankshares Inc E 620 672-6421 Pratt *(G-10114)*
First Security Bank & Trust Co E 785 877-3313 Norton *(G-7446)*
Firstoak Bank F 620 331-2265 Independence *(G-3519)*
Gardner Bancshares Inc E 855 856-0233 Lenexa *(G-5868)*
Generations Bank F 913 928-6181 Overland Park *(G-8752)*
Girard National Bank F 620 724-8223 Girard *(G-2409)*
Girard National Bank F 785 866-2920 Wetmore *(G-13566)*
Girard National Bank F 785 486-2124 Horton *(G-3124)*
Girard National Bank F 785 742-7120 Hiawatha *(G-3008)*
Intrust Bank NA F 316 440-9000 Wichita *(G-14713)*
Intrust Bank NA F 316 383-3350 Andover *(G-95)*
Intrust Bank NA F 316 383-3340 Augusta *(G-328)*
Intrust Bank NA F 316 383-1767 Derby *(G-1252)*
Intrust Bank NA F 316 321-1640 El Dorado *(G-1573)*
Intrust Bank NA F 785 565-5400 Manhattan *(G-6665)*
Intrust Bank NA F 316 755-1225 Valley Center *(G-13344)*
Intrust Bank NA F 316 383-1731 Wichita *(G-14714)*
Intrust Bank NA F 316 383-1816 Wichita *(G-14715)*
Intrust Bank NA F 316 383-1563 Wichita *(G-14716)*
Intrust Bank NA F 316 383-1342 Wichita *(G-14717)*
Intrust Bank NA F 316 383-1549 Wichita *(G-14718)*
Intrust Bank NA F 316 383-1096 Wichita *(G-14719)*
Intrust Bank NA F 316 383-1194 Wichita *(G-14720)*
Intrust Bank NA F 316 383-1960 Wichita *(G-14721)*
Intrust Bank NA F 316 383-1505 Wichita *(G-14722)*
▲ **Intrust Bank National Assn** B 316 383-1111 Wichita *(G-14723)*
Intrust Bank National Assn D 913 385-8200 Shawnee Mission *(G-11466)*
Intrust Bank National Assn E 316 383-1339 Wichita *(G-14724)*
Intrust Bank National Assn F 316 383-1040 Wichita *(G-14725)*
Intrust Bank National Assn F 785 830-2600 Lawrence *(G-4915)*
Landmark Bancorp Inc F 785 565-2000 Manhattan *(G-6708)*
Landmark National Bank F 913 239-2719 Overland Park *(G-8942)*
Landmark National Bank D 620 225-1745 Manhattan *(G-6709)*
Lena M Rush Scholarship Trust E 620 326-3361 Wellington *(G-13511)*
Midland National Bank F 316 283-1700 Newton *(G-7386)*
Millennium Bancshares Inc F 785 761-2265 Junction City *(G-3726)*
Peoples Bank & Trust Co E 620 585-2265 Inman *(G-3584)*
Rcb Bank Service Inc D 620 442-4040 Arkansas City *(G-173)*
Small Business Bank E 913 856-7199 Lenexa *(G-6139)*
Southwest National Bank D 316 291-5299 Wichita *(G-15627)*
Southwest National Bank F 316 942-4004 Wichita *(G-15628)*
Southwest National Bank F 316 941-1335 Wichita *(G-15629)*

Southwest National Bank.......F....... 316 838-5741
Wichita (G-15630)
Stanley Bank.......F....... 913 681-8800
Overland Park (G-9353)
Stock Exchange Bank.......F....... 620 442-2400
Caldwell (G-661)
Stockton National Bank.......E....... 785 425-6721
Stockton (G-12189)
Sunflower Bank Inc.......E....... 620 225-0086
Dodge City (G-1436)
Sunflower Bank National Assn.......F....... 785 312-7274
Lawrence (G-5128)
Sunflower Bank National Assn.......F....... 316 652-1279
Wichita (G-15686)
Sunflower Bank National Assn.......F....... 785 827-5564
Salina (G-10724)
Sunflower Bank National Assn.......F....... 785 537-0550
Manhattan (G-6817)
Sunflower Bank National Assn.......E....... 785 625-8888
Hays (G-2914)
Sunflower Bank National Assn.......F....... 785 825-6900
Salina (G-10725)
Sunflower Bank National Assn.......F....... 785 238-3177
Junction City (G-3758)
Sunflower Bank National Assn.......F....... 620 624-2063
Liberal (G-6374)
Sunflower Holdings Inc.......F....... 620 241-1220
McPherson (G-7029)
Tricentury Bank.......F....... 913 648-8010
De Soto (G-1215)
Truist Bank.......E....... 913 491-6700
Leawood (G-5586)
Umb Bank National Association.......F....... 785 263-1130
Abilene (G-55)
Umb Bank National Association.......F....... 620 223-1255
Fort Scott (G-2013)
Umb Bank National Association.......F....... 785 838-2500
Lawrence (G-5150)
Umb Bank National Association.......E....... 785 776-9400
Manhattan (G-6836)
Umb Bank National Association.......F....... 785 483-6800
Russell (G-10300)
Umb Bank National Association.......E....... 913 234-2070
Shawnee Mission (G-11956)
Umb Bank National Association.......F....... 913 791-6600
Olathe (G-8131)
Umb Bank National Association.......F....... 913 360-6060
Atchison (G-266)
Umb Bank National Association.......F....... 913 236-0300
Prairie Village (G-10078)
Umb Bank National Association.......F....... 913 402-3600
Shawnee Mission (G-11957)
Umb Bank National Association.......F....... 913 667-5400
Shawnee Mission (G-11958)
Umb Bank National Association.......F....... 913 621-8002
Kansas City (G-4483)
Umb Bank National Association.......F....... 913 894-4088
Shawnee Mission (G-11959)
Umb Bank National Association.......F....... 316 267-1191
Wichita (G-15830)
Umb Financial Corporation.......F....... 785 826-4000
Salina (G-10744)
United National Bank.......F....... 785 483-2146
Russell (G-10301)
University Nat Bnk of Lawrence.......E....... 785 841-1988
Lawrence (G-5157)
US Bank National Association.......F....... 785 312-5280
Lawrence (G-5170)
US Bank National Association.......F....... 785 312-5060
Lawrence (G-5171)
US Bank National Association.......F....... 913 432-9633
Overland Park (G-9451)
US Bank National Association.......E....... 913 261-5663
Prairie Village (G-10079)
US Bank National Association.......F....... 913 323-5314
Overland Park (G-9452)
US Bank National Association.......F....... 913 338-0646
Overland Park (G-9453)
US Bank National Association.......F....... 620 231-4040
Pittsburg (G-9953)
US Bank National Association.......F....... 913 725-7000
Overland Park (G-9454)
US Bank National Association.......F....... 913 383-2126
Leawood (G-5592)
US Bank National Association.......F....... 913 248-1001
Shawnee (G-11045)
US Bank National Association.......F....... 913 402-6919
Overland Park (G-9455)
US Bank National Association.......F....... 785 312-6880
Lawrence (G-5172)
US Bank National Association.......F....... 913 671-2723
Merriam (G-7108)
US Bank National Association.......F....... 913 239-8204
Overland Park (G-9456)
US Bank National Association.......F....... 913 261-5401
Roeland Park (G-10230)
US Bank National Association.......F....... 785 276-6300
Topeka (G-13214)
Wells Fargo & Company.......F....... 913 782-9603
Olathe (G-8150)
Wells Fargo Bank NA.......F....... 913 631-6600
Shawnee (G-11052)
Wells Fargo Bank National Assn.......F....... 816 234-2929
Overland Park (G-9488)
Wells Fargo Bank National Assn.......F....... 316 685-5495
Wichita (G-15944)
Wells Fargo Bank National Assn.......F....... 913 341-4774
Leawood (G-5596)
Wells Fargo Bank National Assn.......F....... 316 943-3159
Wichita (G-15945)
Wells Fargo Bank National Assn.......E....... 785 271-2492
Topeka (G-13237)
Wells Fargo Bank National Assn.......E....... 913 663-6040
Shawnee Mission (G-12001)
Wells Fargo Home Mortgage Inc.......E....... 785 565-2900
Manhattan (G-6850)
Wilson State Bank.......F....... 620 653-4113
Hoisington (G-3073)

6022 State Commercial Banks

Alliance Bank.......E....... 785 271-1800
Topeka (G-12307)
Alliant Bank.......F....... 316 772-5111
Wichita (G-13671)
Alta Vista State Bank.......F....... 785 499-6304
Alta Vista (G-69)
American Bank Baxter Springs.......F....... 620 856-2301
Baxter Springs (G-393)
American State Bank & Trust Co.......F....... 620 793-5900
Great Bend (G-2506)
American State Bank & Trust Co.......F....... 620 271-0123
Garden City (G-2099)
American State Bank & Trust Co.......F....... 620 549-3244
Saint John (G-10349)
Andover State Bank.......F....... 316 733-1375
Andover (G-82)
Andover State Bank.......F....... 316 219-1600
Wichita (G-13707)
Arvest Bank.......F....... 417 627-8000
Pittsburg (G-9810)
Arvest Bank.......F....... 913 953-4070
Leawood (G-5330)
Arvest Bank.......F....... 913 953-4000
Overland Park (G-8397)
Arvest Bank.......F....... 785 229-3950
Ottawa (G-8245)
Arvest Bank.......F....... 913 279-3300
Gardner (G-2327)
Arvest Bank.......F....... 620 879-5811
Caney (G-666)
Astra Bank.......E....... 785 335-2243
Scandia (G-10798)
Baldwin State Bank.......E....... 785 594-6421
Baldwin City (G-355)
Bank 7.......F....... 620 846-2221
Montezuma (G-7155)
Bank of Blue Valley.......F....... 785 284-3433
Sabetha (G-10306)
Bank of Blue Valley.......E....... 785 742-2121
Hiawatha (G-3002)
Bank of Blue Valley.......E....... 913 338-1000
Overland Park (G-8428)
Bank of Blue Valley.......E....... 785 889-4211
Onaga (G-8171)
Bank of Cmmrce Tr of Wllngton.......F....... 620 326-7471
Wellington (G-13490)
Bank of Commerce.......E....... 620 431-1400
Chanute (G-705)
Bank of Flint Hills.......E....... 785 456-2221
Wamego (G-13404)
Bank of Flint Hills.......F....... 785 539-8322
Manhattan (G-6552)
Bank of Hays.......F....... 785 621-2265
Hays (G-2756)
Bank of Labor.......F....... 913 321-4242
Overland Park (G-8429)
Bank of Labor.......E....... 913 321-4242
Shawnee (G-10914)
Bank of Labor.......E....... 913 321-4242
Kansas City (G-3841)
Bank of Labor.......E....... 913 321-4242
Kansas City (G-3842)
Bank of Labor.......E....... 913 321-6800
Kansas City (G-3843)
Bank of Prairie.......F....... 785 353-2298
Olathe (G-7548)
Bank of Prairie Village.......F....... 913 713-0300
Prairie Village (G-10014)
Bank of Protection Inc.......F....... 620 622-4224
Protection (G-10173)
Bank of Tescott.......F....... 785 283-4217
Tescott (G-12244)
Bank of Tescott.......F....... 785 227-8830
Lindsborg (G-6392)
Bank of Tescott.......E....... 785 825-1621
Salina (G-10418)
Bank of West.......F....... 316 292-5840
Wichita (G-13807)
Bank of West.......F....... 913 362-8900
Shawnee Mission (G-11148)
Bank of West.......F....... 620 225-4147
Dodge City (G-1303)
Bank of West.......F....... 316 292-5870
Wichita (G-13808)
Bank of West.......F....... 620 662-0543
Hutchinson (G-3213)
Bank of West.......F....... 316 283-7310
Newton (G-7317)
Bank of West.......F....... 913 642-5212
Shawnee Mission (G-11149)
Bank of West.......F....... 316 729-7999
Wichita (G-13809)
Bank of West.......F....... 785 242-2804
Ottawa (G-8248)
Bank of West.......F....... 620 792-1771
Great Bend (G-2515)
Bank VI.......F....... 785 825-4321
Salina (G-10419)
Bankwest of Kansas.......E....... 785 899-2342
Goodland (G-2463)
Baxter State Bank.......F....... 620 856-2323
Baxter Springs (G-397)
Bendena State Bank.......F....... 785 988-4453
Bendena (G-510)
Bennington State Bank.......F....... 785 392-2136
Minneapolis (G-7114)
Bennington State Bank.......E....... 785 827-5522
Salina (G-10423)
Bennington State Bank.......F....... 785 456-1806
Wamego (G-13405)
Bennington State Bank.......F....... 785 488-3344
Bennington (G-513)
Bern Bancshares Inc.......F....... 785 336-6121
Bern (G-520)
Busey Bank.......E....... 913 338-4300
Overland Park (G-8495)
Cbi-Kansas Inc.......F....... 620 341-7420
Emporia (G-1718)
Cbw Bank.......F....... 620 396-8221
Weir (G-13485)
Centera Bank.......F....... 620 675-8611
Sublette (G-12200)
Centera Bank.......F....... 620 649-2220
Satanta (G-10780)
Central Bank and Trust Co.......E....... 620 663-0666
Hutchinson (G-3231)
Central Bank of Midwest.......F....... 913 268-3202
Shawnee (G-10925)
Central Bank of Midwest.......D....... 913 856-7715
Gardner (G-2331)
Central Bank of Midwest.......D....... 913 893-6049
Edgerton (G-1481)
Central Bank of Midwest.......D....... 913 791-9988
Overland Park (G-8537)
Central Bank of Midwest.......D....... 913 791-9288
Shawnee Mission (G-11211)
Chisholm Trail State Bank.......E....... 316 744-1293
Park City (G-9610)
Citizens Bank of Kansas.......E....... 620 532-5162
Kingman (G-4586)
Citizens Bank of Kansas NA.......F....... 620 886-5686
Medicine Lodge (G-7058)
Citizens State Bank.......E....... 316 518-6621
Hugoton (G-3152)
Citizens State Bank.......F....... 785 363-2521
Waterville (G-13472)
Citizens State Bank.......F....... 316 542-3142
Cheney (G-791)
Citizens State Bank.......E....... 785 562-2186
Marysville (G-6882)

Citizens State Bank F 620 327-4941
Hesston *(G-2986)*
Citizens State Bank and Tr Co E 785 742-2101
Hiawatha *(G-3006)*
Citizens State Bnk Tr Ellswrth E 785 472-3141
Ellsworth *(G-1660)*
City State Bank F 620 223-1600
Fort Scott *(G-1960)*
City State Bank F 620 223-1600
Fort Scott *(G-1961)*
Colt Investments Inc E 913 385-5010
Prairie Village *(G-10020)*
Colwich Financial Corp E 316 796-1221
Colwich *(G-1092)*
Commerce Bank F 620 429-2515
Columbus *(G-1068)*
Commerce Bank E 913 381-2386
Overland Park *(G-8578)*
Commerce Bank F 816 234-2000
Shawnee Mission *(G-11252)*
Commerce Bank E 316 321-1250
El Dorado *(G-1546)*
Commerce Bank F 316 261-4927
Wichita *(G-14065)*
Commerce Bank F 785 625-6542
Hays *(G-2773)*
Commerce Bank F 913 682-8282
Leavenworth *(G-5224)*
Commerce Bank F 913 888-0700
Lenexa *(G-5773)*
Commerce Bank F 816 234-2000
Lawrence *(G-4800)*
Commerce Bank F 816 234-2000
Leawood *(G-5355)*
Commerce Bank F 785 587-1696
Manhattan *(G-6597)*
Commerce Bank F 816 234-2000
Olathe *(G-7604)*
Commerce Bank F 816 234-2000
Overland Park *(G-8579)*
Commerce Bank F 816 234-2000
Shawnee *(G-10931)*
Commerce Bank E 816 234-2000
Shawnee *(G-10932)*
Commerce Bank F 816 234-2000
Shawnee Mission *(G-11253)*
Commerce Bank F 620 231-8400
Pittsburg *(G-9839)*
Commerce Bank F 816 234-2000
Kansas City *(G-3928)*
Commercial Bank E 620 423-0770
Parsons *(G-9674)*
Commercial Bank E 620 423-0770
Parsons *(G-9675)*
Commercial Bank F 620 423-0750
Independence *(G-3506)*
Commercial Bank F 620 431-3200
Chanute *(G-719)*
Community Bank F 620 624-6898
Liberal *(G-6296)*
Community Bank E 785 440-4400
Topeka *(G-12491)*
Community Bank and Trust F 620 783-1395
Galena *(G-2072)*
Community Bank Wichita Inc F 316 634-1600
Wichita *(G-14078)*
Community First National Bank E 785 323-1111
Manhattan *(G-6599)*
Community National Bank E 785 336-6143
Seneca *(G-10859)*
Community National Bank F 620 724-4446
Girard *(G-2398)*
Community National Bank F 620 325-2900
Neodesha *(G-7237)*
Community National Bank F 620 221-1400
Winfield *(G-16126)*
Community National Bank & Tr E 620 431-2265
Chanute *(G-721)*
Community State Bank F 620 251-1313
Coffeyville *(G-928)*
Corefirst Bank & Trust E 785 267-8900
Topeka *(G-12509)*
Corefirst Bank & Trust F 785 286-5100
Topeka *(G-12510)*
Corefirst Bank & Trust F 620 341-7420
Emporia *(G-1725)*
Corefirst Bank & Trust F 785 267-8900
Topeka *(G-12511)*
Cornerstone Bank D 913 239-8100
Overland Park *(G-8599)*
Crossfirst Bank E 316 494-4844
Wichita *(G-14134)*
Crossfirst Bank D 913 327-1212
Overland Park *(G-8617)*
Douglas County Bank D 785 865-1000
Lawrence *(G-4836)*
Douglas County Bank E 785 865-1022
Lawrence *(G-4837)*
Emprise Bank D 316 383-4400
Wichita *(G-14280)*
Emprise Bank F 316 776-9584
Rose Hill *(G-10238)*
Emprise Bank F 316 383-4301
Wichita *(G-14281)*
Emprise Bank F 316 775-4233
Augusta *(G-318)*
Emprise Bank F 316 264-1569
Wichita *(G-14282)*
Emprise Bank F 316 689-0717
Wichita *(G-14283)*
Emprise Bank F 316 794-2258
Goddard *(G-2437)*
Emprise Bank F 620 767-5128
Council Grove *(G-1164)*
Emprise Bank F 620 241-7113
McPherson *(G-6958)*
Emprise Bank F 316 383-4498
Wichita *(G-14284)*
Emprise Bank F 316 383-4131
Wichita *(G-14285)*
Emprise Bank F 785 838-2001
Lawrence *(G-4852)*
Emprise Bank F 620 584-2201
Clearwater *(G-891)*
Emprise Bank F 316 522-2222
Haysville *(G-2941)*
Emprise Bank National Assn E 785 625-6595
Hays *(G-2798)*
Enterprise Bank E 913 663-5525
Shawnee Mission *(G-11339)*
Enterprise Bank & Trust F 620 431-7070
Chanute *(G-725)*
Enterprise Bank & Trust E 913 782-3211
Olathe *(G-7683)*
Enterprise Bank & Trust F 913 791-9300
Olathe *(G-7684)*
Enterprise Bank & Trust F 913 791-9100
Olathe *(G-7685)*
Equity Bank NA E 913 371-1242
Kansas City *(G-3994)*
Esb Financial E 620 342-3454
Emporia *(G-1751)*
Everest Bancshares Inc F 785 863-2267
Oskaloosa *(G-8225)*
Exchange Bank F 785 762-4121
Junction City *(G-3688)*
Exchange National Bank & Tr Co D 913 833-5560
Atchison *(G-228)*
Exchange National Bank & Tr Co F 913 833-5560
Effingham *(G-1523)*
Farmers & Merchants Bank Colby E 785 460-3321
Colby *(G-1007)*
Farmers & Merchants Bank Hl Cy F 785 421-2131
Hill City *(G-3034)*
Farmers Bank & Trust F 785 626-3233
Atwood *(G-285)*
Farmers Bank & Trust E 620 792-2411
Great Bend *(G-2563)*
Farmers Bank & Trust F 620 285-3177
Larned *(G-4702)*
Farmers Nat Bnk of Canfield F 785 346-2000
Osborne *(G-8208)*
Farmers State Bank F 785 989-4431
Wathena *(G-13474)*
Farmers State Bank Blue Mound E 913 756-2221
Blue Mound *(G-532)*
Farmers State Bank of Bucklin F 620 826-3231
Bucklin *(G-592)*
Farmers State Bank of Oakley F 785 672-3251
Oakley *(G-7474)*
Farmers State Bankshares Inc E 785 924-3311
Circleville *(G-838)*
Farmers State Bankshares Inc E 785 364-4691
Holton *(G-3089)*
Farmers State Bnk of Wstmrland E 785 457-3316
Westmoreland *(G-13547)*
Farmers State Bnk of Wstmrland F 785 889-4211
Onaga *(G-8176)*
Fidelity Bank F 316 265-2261
Wichita *(G-14363)*
Fidelity Kansas Bankshares E 785 295-2100
Topeka *(G-12605)*
Fidelity State Bank and Tr Co E 785 295-2100
Topeka *(G-12607)*
Fidelity State Bnk Tr Ddge Cy E 620 227-8586
Dodge City *(G-1359)*
First Bancshares Inc E 913 371-1242
Kansas City *(G-4010)*
First Bank F 620 278-2161
Sterling *(G-12117)*
First Bank Kansas D 785 825-2211
Salina *(G-10501)*
First Bank of Newton E 316 283-2600
Newton *(G-7345)*
First Business Bank F 913 681-2223
Leawood *(G-5402)*
First Business Bank F 913 681-2223
Leawood *(G-5403)*
First Commerce Bank F 785 562-5558
Marysville *(G-6889)*
First Federal Savings & Loan F 785 743-5751
Wakeeney *(G-13388)*
First Kansas Bank E 620 653-4921
Hoisington *(G-3064)*
First National Bank & Trust Co F 785 762-4121
Junction City *(G-3690)*
First National Bank Elkhart F 620 697-2777
Elkhart *(G-1621)*
First National Bank Inc E 785 263-1090
Abilene *(G-31)*
First National Bank NA E 620 326-3361
Wellington *(G-13500)*
First Neodesha Bank F 620 325-2632
Neodesha *(G-7240)*
First Security Bank F 785 665-7155
Overbrook *(G-8324)*
First Security Bank & Trust Co E 785 877-3313
Norton *(G-7446)*
First State Bank F 785 798-2212
Ness City *(G-7262)*
First State Bank F 785 675-3241
Hoxie *(G-3137)*
First State Bank E 785 877-3341
Norton *(G-7447)*
First State Bank & Trust D 913 845-2500
Tonganoxie *(G-12261)*
First State Bank & Trust E 785 749-0400
Lawrence *(G-4863)*
First State Bank & Trust E 785 597-5151
Perry *(G-9767)*
First State Bank & Trust F 913 724-2121
Basehor *(G-378)*
First State Bank (inc) E 785 654-2421
Burlingame *(G-623)*
First State Bank of Edna Inc E 620 922-3294
Edna *(G-1493)*
First State Bnk Tr of Larned F 620 285-6931
Larned *(G-4703)*
First-Citizens Bank & Trust Co F 913 312-5108
Overland Park *(G-8723)*
Flint Hills Bank E 785 449-2266
Eskridge *(G-1866)*
Garden Plain Bancshares Inc E 316 721-1500
Wichita *(G-14446)*
Garden Plain State Bank E 316 721-1500
Wichita *(G-14447)*
Goppert State Service Bank E 785 448-3111
Garnett *(G-2375)*
Grant County Bank E 620 356-4142
Ulysses *(G-13300)*
Great American Bank F 913 585-1131
De Soto *(G-1200)*
Great American Bank F 785 838-9704
Lawrence *(G-4880)*
Great Southern Bank F 620 365-3101
Iola *(G-3605)*
Great Southern Bank E 620 421-5700
Parsons *(G-9689)*
Great Southern Bank C 913 557-4311
Paola *(G-9563)*
Great Western Bank F 913 248-3300
Shawnee Mission *(G-11401)*
Greensburg State Bank F 620 723-2131
Greensburg *(G-2678)*
Guaranty State Bnk Tr Bloit Ka E 785 738-3501
Beloit *(G-485)*
Harris Bmo Bank National Assn F 913 441-7900
Shawnee Mission *(G-11411)*
Harris Bmo Bank National Assn F 620 231-2000
Pittsburg *(G-9871)*

Harris Bmo Bank National Assn............E....... 913 307-0707
Overland Park *(G-8796)*
Harris Bmo Bank National Assn............F....... 913 693-1600
Leawood *(G-5419)*
Harris Bmo Bank National Assn............F....... 913 254-6600
Olathe *(G-7754)*
Harris Bmo Bank National Assn............F....... 620 235-7250
Pittsburg *(G-9872)*
Harris Bmo Bank National Assn............E....... 913 962-1400
Shawnee Mission *(G-11412)*
Haviland Bancshares Inc.....................F....... 620 862-5222
Haviland *(G-2740)*
Hillsboro State Bank..............................F....... 620 947-3961
Hillsboro *(G-3050)*
Holton National Bank..............................F....... 785 364-2166
Holton *(G-3098)*
Home Bank and Trust Company............F....... 620 583-5516
Eureka *(G-1891)*
Home Savings Bank................................F....... 620 431-1100
Chanute *(G-733)*
Home State Bank & Trust Co................E....... 620 241-3732
McPherson *(G-6974)*
Industrial State Bank..............................E....... 913 831-2000
Kansas City *(G-4099)*
Intrust Bank NA......................................F....... 785 761-2265
Junction City *(G-3700)*
Intrust Bank National Assn....................F....... 785 238-1121
Junction City *(G-3701)*
Intrust Bank National Assn....................F....... 913 385-8330
Olathe *(G-7802)*
Intrust Bank National Assn....................F....... 316 383-1234
Wichita *(G-14726)*
Intrust Bank National Assn....................E....... 316 524-3251
Haysville *(G-2947)*
Intrust Financial Corporation................E....... 316 383-1111
Wichita *(G-14727)*
Jamestown State Bank............................F....... 785 439-6224
Jamestown *(G-3643)*
Johnson State Bank.................................E....... 620 492-6200
Johnson *(G-3656)*
Kansas State Bank...................................E....... 785 364-2166
Holton *(G-3103)*
Kansas State Bank...................................E....... 785 242-1011
Ottawa *(G-8280)*
Kansas State Bank...................................F....... 785 665-7121
Overbrook *(G-8325)*
Kansasland Bank.....................................F....... 785 754-2500
Quinter *(G-10182)*
Kanza Bank..E....... 620 532-5821
Kingman *(G-4596)*
Kanza Bank..F....... 316 636-5821
Wichita *(G-14831)*
Kanza Bank..F....... 316 773-7007
Wichita *(G-14832)*
Kaw Valley Bank.......................................E....... 785 232-2700
Topeka *(G-12810)*
Kaw Valley Bank.......................................F....... 785 272-8100
Topeka *(G-12811)*
Kaw Valley State Bank.............................F....... 785 542-4200
Eudora *(G-1877)*
Kaw Valley State Bank & Tr Co..............F....... 785 437-6585
Saint Marys *(G-10369)*
Kaw Valley State Bank & Tr Co..............F....... 785 456-2025
Wamego *(G-13428)*
Kearny County Bank................................F....... 620 355-6222
Lakin *(G-4650)*
Kendall State Bank..................................F....... 785 945-3231
Valley Falls *(G-13366)*
King Bancshares Inc...............................E....... 620 532-5162
Kingman *(G-4597)*
KS Statebank...E....... 785 587-4000
Manhattan *(G-6701)*
KS Statebank...E....... 785 762-5050
Junction City *(G-3719)*
KS Statebank...E....... 785 587-4000
Manhattan *(G-6702)*
Lakin Bancshares Inc..............................E....... 620 355-6222
Lakin *(G-4654)*
Legacy Bank...D....... 316 796-1221
Wichita *(G-14950)*
Legacy Bank...F....... 316 260-3755
Wichita *(G-14951)*
Legacy Bank...E....... 316 260-3711
Wichita *(G-14952)*
Liberty Bank and Trust Company..........F....... 913 321-7200
Kansas City *(G-4201)*
Lyndon State Bank..................................E....... 785 828-4411
Lyndon *(G-6477)*
Lyon County State Bank.........................E....... 620 342-3523
Emporia *(G-1787)*
Lyon County State Bank.........................F....... 620 343-4444
Emporia *(G-1788)*
Lyons State Bank.....................................E....... 620 257-3775
Lyons *(G-6493)*
Metcalf Bank...E....... 913 648-4540
Shawnee Mission *(G-11618)*
Metcalf Bank...F....... 913 685-3801
Shawnee Mission *(G-11619)*
Metcalf Bank...F....... 913 782-6522
Olathe *(G-7885)*
Metcalf Bank...F....... 913 451-1199
Shawnee Mission *(G-11620)*
Midland National Bank............................E....... 316 283-1700
Newton *(G-7385)*
Morley Bancshares Corporation............D....... 620 488-2211
Belle Plaine *(G-448)*
Nbh Bank...F....... 785 842-4300
Lawrence *(G-5037)*
Nbh Bank...E....... 785 242-2900
Ottawa *(G-8294)*
Nbh Bank...F....... 913 782-5400
Olathe *(G-7914)*
Nbh Bank...F....... 913 831-4184
Kansas City *(G-4282)*
Nbh Bank...F....... 913 441-6800
Edwardsville *(G-1510)*
Nbh Bank...F....... 913 299-9700
Kansas City *(G-4283)*
Olpe State Bank Inc.................................F....... 620 475-3213
Olpe *(G-8166)*
Osawatomie Agency Inc..........................D....... 913 755-3811
Osawatomie *(G-8201)*
Osawatomie Agency Inc..........................F....... 913 294-3811
Paola *(G-9577)*
Peabody State Bank................................F....... 620 983-2181
Peabody *(G-9762)*
Peoples Bank...E....... 620 672-5611
Pratt *(G-10132)*
Peoples Bank...F....... 620 582-2166
Coldwater *(G-1056)*
Peoples Bank...F....... 785 282-6682
Smith Center *(G-12039)*
Peoples Bank & Trust Co.........................E....... 620 241-2100
McPherson *(G-7013)*
Peoples Bank & Trust Co.........................D....... 620 662-6502
Hutchinson *(G-3401)*
Peoples Bank & Trust Co.........................E....... 620 669-0234
Hutchinson *(G-3402)*
Peoples Bank & Trust Co.........................E....... 620 241-6908
McPherson *(G-7014)*
Peoples Bank & Trust Co.........................E....... 620 241-7664
McPherson *(G-7015)*
Peoples Bank & Trust Co.........................F....... 620 663-4000
Hutchinson *(G-3403)*
PNC Bank National Association.............F....... 913 253-9490
Overland Park *(G-9172)*
Prairie Bank of Kansas............................E....... 620 234-5226
Stafford *(G-12107)*
Premier Bank...E....... 913 888-8490
Shawnee Mission *(G-11748)*
Premier Bank...F....... 913 541-6180
Shawnee Mission *(G-11749)*
Prescott State Bnk Holdg Inc..................F....... 913 471-4321
Prescott *(G-10167)*
Rcb Bank...F....... 620 860-7797
Hutchinson *(G-3420)*
Riley State Bank of Riley Kans...............F....... 785 485-2811
Riley *(G-10208)*
Rose Hill Bank..E....... 316 776-2131
Rose Hill *(G-10247)*
Security Bank of Kansas City.................D....... 913 281-3165
Kansas City *(G-4412)*
Security Bank of Kansas City.................F....... 913 621-8423
Kansas City *(G-4413)*
Security Bank of Kansas City.................F....... 913 621-8465
Kansas City *(G-4414)*
Security Bank of Kansas City.................F....... 913 621-8462
Kansas City *(G-4415)*
Security Bank of Kansas City.................D....... 913 299-6200
Kansas City *(G-4416)*
Security Bank of Kansas City.................F....... 913 621-8430
Shawnee Mission *(G-11846)*
Security Bank of Kansas City.................F....... 913 384-3300
Fairway *(G-1919)*
Security State Bank.................................D....... 620 872-7224
Scott City *(G-10834)*
Security State Bank.................................F....... 620 326-7417
Wellington *(G-13528)*
Silver Lake Bank......................................E....... 785 232-0102
Topeka *(G-13072)*
Sjn Banc Co...F....... 620 549-3225
Saint John *(G-10356)*
Sjn Bank of Kansas.................................F....... 620 549-3225
Saint John *(G-10357)*
Solomon State Bank.................................F....... 785 655-2941
Solomon *(G-12053)*
Solutions North Bank...............................E....... 785 425-6721
Stockton *(G-12188)*
Solutions North Bank...............................E....... 785 743-2104
Wakeeney *(G-13390)*
Southeast Bancshares Inc......................F....... 620 325-2632
Neodesha *(G-7249)*
Southeast Bancshares Inc......................E....... 620 431-1400
Chanute *(G-763)*
St Marys State Bank................................E....... 785 437-2271
Saint Marys *(G-10377)*
State Bank..F....... 785 675-3261
Hoxie *(G-3142)*
State Bank of Canton...............................F....... 620 628-4425
Canton *(G-683)*
State Bank of Kansas..............................F....... 620 378-2114
Fredonia *(G-2045)*
State Bank of Spring Hill.........................F....... 913 592-3326
Spring Hill *(G-12100)*
Stockgrowers State Bank........................E....... 800 772-2265
Ashland *(G-199)*
Stockgrowers State Bank........................F....... 785 256-4241
Maple Hill *(G-6864)*
Stockgrowers State Bank........................F....... 620 873-2123
Meade *(G-7054)*
Union Bank and Trust Company.............D....... 913 491-0909
Leawood *(G-5589)*
Union State Bancshares Inc...................E....... 620 756-4305
Uniontown *(G-13333)*
Union State Bank.....................................E....... 620 442-5200
Arkansas City *(G-186)*
Union State Bank.....................................F....... 620 221-3040
Winfield *(G-16177)*
Union State Bank.....................................E....... 785 632-3122
Clay Center *(G-885)*
Union State Bank Inc...............................E....... 785 468-3341
Olsburg *(G-8169)*
Union State Bank Inc...............................F....... 785 293-5516
Randolph *(G-10191)*
Union State Bank of Everest..................F....... 785 548-7521
Everest *(G-1903)*
Union State Bank of Everest..................E....... 913 367-2700
Atchison *(G-267)*
United Bank & Trust.................................F....... 785 284-2187
Sabetha *(G-10335)*
United Bank & Trust.................................F....... 785 336-2123
Seneca *(G-10885)*
United Bank & Trust.................................E....... 785 562-4330
Marysville *(G-6912)*
Valley State Bank.....................................E....... 620 488-2211
Belle Plaine *(G-449)*
Valley State Bank.....................................F....... 620 384-7451
Syracuse *(G-12236)*
Valley View State Bank............................C....... 913 381-3311
Shawnee Mission *(G-11973)*
Valley View State Bank............................F....... 913 381-3311
Overland Park *(G-9458)*
Valley View State Bank............................F....... 913 381-3311
Shawnee Mission *(G-11974)*
Vision Bank...F....... 785 357-4669
Topeka *(G-13226)*
Washington 1st Banco Inc......................F....... 785 325-2221
Washington *(G-13470)*
Washington FNB.......................................F....... 785 325-2221
Washington *(G-13471)*
Western State Bank.................................F....... 785 899-2393
Goodland *(G-2491)*
Wilson State Bank....................................F....... 785 658-3441
Wilson *(G-16108)*

6029 Commercial Banks, NEC

Country Club Bank....................................F....... 913 438-5660
Lenexa *(G-5790)*
Country Club Bank....................................F....... 816 751-4270
Kansas City *(G-3943)*
Country Club Bank....................................F....... 816 931-4060
Shawnee Mission *(G-11268)*
Country Club Bank....................................F....... 816 931-4060
Leawood *(G-5360)*
Country Club Bank....................................F....... 913 441-2444
Shawnee *(G-10936)*
Dewaay Financial Network LLC..............F....... 316 303-1985
Wichita *(G-14206)*
Exchange National Bank & Tr Co............F....... 913 833-5560
Effingham *(G-1523)*

Farm Credit of Western Kansas ....E 785 462-6714
Colby *(G-1006)*
Farmers Bank & Trust ....F 913 402-7257
Overland Park *(G-8705)*
Fidelity Bank ....F 316 722-1460
Wichita *(G-14364)*
Kanza Bank ....F 316 773-7007
Wichita *(G-14832)*
Osawatomie Agency Inc ....E 913 592-3811
Spring Hill *(G-12095)*
Osawatomie Agency Inc ....F 913 294-3811
Paola *(G-9577)*
Sunflower Bank ....A 785 827-5564
Salina *(G-10723)*
Sunflower Bank National Assn ....F 785 827-5564
Salina *(G-10724)*
Wells Fargo Bank National Assn ....F 816 234-2929
Overland Park *(G-9488)*

6035 Federal Savings Institutions

A Divis of P Midla Loan Servi ....B 913 253-9000
Overland Park *(G-8334)*
Argentine Savings and Ln Assn ....F 913 831-2004
Kansas City *(G-3818)*
Bankwest of Kansas ....F 785 462-7557
Colby *(G-989)*
Capitol Federal Financial Inc ....D 785 235-1341
Topeka *(G-12437)*
Capitol Federal Savings Bank ....F 316 689-0200
Wichita *(G-13937)*
Capitol Federal Savings Bank ....E 785 235-1341
Topeka *(G-12438)*
Capitol Federal Savings Bank ....C 785 235-1341
Topeka *(G-12439)*
Capitol Federal Savings Bank ....E 316 689-3104
Wichita *(G-13938)*
Capitol Federal Savings Bank ....F 913 782-5100
Olathe *(G-7577)*
Capitol Federal Savings Bank ....F 785 749-9100
Lawrence *(G-4775)*
Capitol Federal Savings Bank ....F 620 342-0125
Emporia *(G-1716)*
Capitol Federal Savings Bank ....F 785 539-9976
Manhattan *(G-6575)*
Capitol Federal Savings Bank ....F 316 689-0200
Wichita *(G-13939)*
Citizens Savings & Loan Assn ....E 913 727-1040
Leavenworth *(G-5218)*
First Federal Bank Kansas City ....F 913 233-6100
Kansas City *(G-4011)*
First Independence Corporation ....E 620 331-1660
Independence *(G-3517)*
First Independence Corporation ....F 620 331-1660
Independence *(G-3518)*
First Manhattan Bancorporation ....E 785 537-0200
Manhattan *(G-6629)*
First Seacoast Bank ....F 913 766-2500
Overland Park *(G-8722)*
Golden Belt Banking & Sav Assn ....E 785 625-7345
Hays *(G-2818)*
Landmark National Bank ....F 785 883-2145
Wellsville *(G-13544)*
Lyons Federal Savings Assn ....F 620 257-2316
Lyons *(G-6490)*
Mutual Savings Association ....F 913 441-5555
Bonner Springs *(G-564)*
Mutual Savings Association ....D 913 682-3491
Leavenworth *(G-5272)*
Sunflower Bank National Assn ....F 785 537-0550
Manhattan *(G-6817)*

6036 Savings Institutions, Except Federal

Chisholm Trail State Bank ....E 316 744-1293
Park City *(G-9610)*
Golden Belt Banking & Sav Assn ....E 785 625-7345
Hays *(G-2818)*
Silver Lake Bank ....E 785 232-0102
Topeka *(G-13072)*

6061 Federal Credit Unions

Augusta White Eagle Credit Un ....E 316 775-5747
Augusta *(G-309)*
Azura Credit Union ....E 785 233-5556
Topeka *(G-12354)*
Catholic Family Federal Cr Un ....F 316 264-9163
Wichita *(G-13964)*
Central Kansas Credit Union ....F 620 663-1566
Hutchinson *(G-3232)*
Country Club Bank ....F 816 751-4251
Leawood *(G-5361)*
Credit Union of America ....D 316 265-3272
Wichita *(G-14128)*
Educational Credit Union ....E 785 271-6900
Topeka *(G-12571)*
Emporia State Federal Cr Un ....E 620 342-2336
Emporia *(G-1744)*
Farmway Credit Union ....E 785 738-2224
Beloit *(G-483)*
Freedom 1st Federal Credit Un ....F 316 685-0205
Wichita *(G-14417)*
Great Plains Federal Cr Un ....F 620 331-4060
Independence *(G-3524)*
Great Plains Federal Cr Un ....F 620 241-4181
McPherson *(G-6971)*
Great Plains Federal Cr Un ....F 785 823-9226
Salina *(G-10515)*
Heartland Credit Union ....E 620 669-0177
Hutchinson *(G-3310)*
Kansas State Univ Federal Cr ....F 785 776-3003
Manhattan *(G-6678)*
Kansas Teachers Cmnty Cr Un ....F 620 223-1475
Fort Scott *(G-1977)*
Mainstreet Credit Union ....F 785 856-5200
Lawrence *(G-5007)*
Mainstreet Federal Credit Un ....E 785 856-5200
Lawrence *(G-5008)*
Mainstreet Federal Credit Un ....D 913 599-1010
Lenexa *(G-5982)*
Mainstreet Federal Credit Un ....F 785 842-5657
Lawrence *(G-5009)*
Mainstreet Federal Credit Un ....E 913 754-3926
Shawnee Mission *(G-11591)*
Mazuma Credit Union ....C 913 574-5000
Overland Park *(G-8999)*
Meritrust Credit Union ....F 785 856-7878
Lawrence *(G-5022)*
Mid-Kansas Credit Union ....F 620 543-2662
Moundridge *(G-7192)*
Navy Federal Credit Union ....C 888 842-6328
Leavenworth *(G-5275)*
Panhandle Federal Credit Union ....F 620 326-2285
Wellington *(G-13522)*
Quantum Credit Union ....F 316 263-5756
Wichita *(G-15388)*
Truity Credit Union ....F 785 749-2224
Lawrence *(G-5147)*
United West Community Cr Un ....F 620 227-7181
Dodge City *(G-1444)*
Wichita Federal Credit Union ....E 316 941-0600
Wichita *(G-16000)*

6062 State Credit Unions

Central Star Credit Union ....E 316 685-9555
Wichita *(G-13985)*
Communityamerica Credit Union ....C 913 905-7000
Lenexa *(G-5778)*
Communityamerica Credit Union ....F 913 397-6600
Olathe *(G-7605)*
Communityamerica Credit Union ....F 785 232-6900
Topeka *(G-12493)*
Dillon Credit Union ....F 620 669-8500
Hutchinson *(G-3264)*
Educational Credit Union ....F 785 267-4900
Topeka *(G-12572)*
First Choice Credit Union ....F 316 425-5712
Wichita *(G-14372)*
Fort Leavenworth Credit Union ....E 913 651-6575
Fort Leavenworth *(G-1938)*
Golden Plains Credit Union ....E 620 275-8187
Garden City *(G-2188)*
Golden Plains Credit Union ....F 620 624-8491
Liberal *(G-6314)*
Golden Plains Credit Union ....F 785 628-1007
Hays *(G-2819)*
Great Plains Federal Cr Un ....F 620 331-4060
Independence *(G-3524)*
Kan Colo Credit Union ....F 620 653-4415
Hoisington *(G-3067)*
Kansas Corporate Credit Union ....F 316 721-2600
Wichita *(G-14793)*
Meritrust Credit Union ....F 785 579-5700
Junction City *(G-3725)*
Meritrust Credit Union ....F 785 320-7222
Manhattan *(G-6740)*
Meritrust Credit Union ....D 316 683-1199
Wichita *(G-15042)*
Meritrust Credit Union ....F 316 219-7614
Derby *(G-1261)*
Meritrust Credit Union ....F 316 683-1199
Wichita *(G-15043)*
Meritrust Credit Union ....F 316 761-4645
Wichita *(G-15044)*
Meritrust Credit Union ....F 316 761-4645
Wichita *(G-15045)*
Mid American Credit Union ....E 316 779-0052
Wichita *(G-15067)*
Midwest Regional Credit Union ....F 913 755-2127
Kansas City *(G-4256)*
Quantum Credit Union ....F 316 263-5756
Wichita *(G-15389)*
Skyward Credit Union ....E 316 517-6578
Wichita *(G-15601)*
Truity Credit Union ....F 785 749-2224
Lawrence *(G-5147)*
U S Central Credit Union ....B 913 227-6000
Lenexa *(G-6198)*

6091 Nondeposit Trust Facilities

Security Benefit Life Insur Co ....B 785 438-3000
Topeka *(G-13054)*
Tck- The Trust Company Kansas ....E 316 264-6010
Wichita *(G-15718)*

6099 Functions Related To Deposit Banking, NEC

Bankers Life & Casualty Co ....F 913 894-6553
Overland Park *(G-8430)*
Core Cashless LLC ....E 913 529-8200
Lenexa *(G-5788)*
Crossfirst Bank ....C 913 312-6800
Leawood *(G-5364)*
Curo Financial Tech Corp ....E 316 722-3801
Wichita *(G-14141)*
Curo Management LLC ....D 316 683-2274
Wichita *(G-14144)*
Electronic Funds Transfer Inc ....E 913 831-2055
Lenexa *(G-5831)*
Euronet Worldwide Inc ....D 913 327-4200
Leawood *(G-5389)*
Fidelity National Fincl Inc ....F 913 422-5122
Leawood *(G-5399)*
Galt Ventures LLC ....F 316 942-2211
Wichita *(G-14442)*
◆ **Qc Financial Services Inc** ....D 913 439-1100
Shawnee Mission *(G-11763)*
Residential Treatment Service ....E 620 421-1155
Parsons *(G-9732)*
United Ptriot Abtment Svcs LLC ....F 785 856-1349
Lawrence *(G-5152)*
Universal Money Centers Inc ....E 913 831-2055
Lenexa *(G-6204)*
Western Union ....F 800 325-6000
Kinsley *(G-4622)*

61 NONDEPOSITORY CREDIT INSTITUTIONS

6111 Federal Credit Agencies

Cobank Acb ....F 620 342-0138
Emporia *(G-1722)*
Cobank Acb ....E 316 721-1100
Wichita *(G-14049)*
Cobank Acb ....F 620 431-0240
Chanute *(G-717)*
Community Nat Bnk of El Dorado ....F 316 320-2265
El Dorado *(G-1547)*
Federal Home Loan Bank Topeka ....D 785 233-0507
Topeka *(G-12600)*
Federal Land Bank Assoc ....F 620 544-4006
Hugoton *(G-3162)*
Jaafar Inc ....F 913 269-5113
Olathe *(G-7805)*

6141 Personal Credit Institutions

Bank of Tescott ....E 785 825-1621
Salina *(G-10418)*
Beneficial Kansas Inc ....E 913 492-1383
Shawnee Mission *(G-11161)*
Capfusion LLC ....E 816 888-5302
Prairie Village *(G-10018)*
Capital Resources LLC ....F 913 469-1630
Overland Park *(G-8511)*
Claro Financiero LLC ....F 913 608-5444
Mission Hills *(G-7141)*
Community National Bank ....E 620 235-1345
Pittsburg *(G-9842)*
Community National Bank ....F 620 431-2265
Chanute *(G-720)*

Dominion Management Svcs Inc ....F 571 408-4770
Wichita *(G-14222)*

Dominion Management Svcs Inc ....F 703 765-2274
Wichita *(G-14223)*

Easy Cash Asap LLC ....E 913 291-1134
Leawood *(G-5383)*

▲ **Galt Ventures LLC** ....F 316 722-3801
Wichita *(G-14441)*

Hsbc Finance Corporation ....F 913 362-1400
Roeland Park *(G-10225)*

Kansas Teachers Cmnty Cr Un ....E 620 231-5719
Pittsburg *(G-9889)*

Kansas Teachers Cmnty Cr Un ....F 620 223-1475
Fort Scott *(G-1977)*

◆ **Qc Financial Services Inc** ....D 913 439-1100
Shawnee Mission *(G-11763)*

Qc Holdings Inc ....C 866 660-2243
Lenexa *(G-6082)*

Toyota Motor Credit Corp ....F 913 661-6800
Shawnee Mission *(G-11937)*

Union State Bank of Everest ....E 913 367-2700
Atchison *(G-267)*

6153 Credit Institutions, Short-Term Business

Alliance Data Systems Corp ....C 214 494-3000
Shawnee Mission *(G-11097)*

Bankwest of Kansas ....F 785 462-7557
Colby *(G-989)*

Capital Resources LLC ....F 913 469-1630
Overland Park *(G-8511)*

Caterpillar Inc ....D 309 675-1000
Wamego *(G-13409)*

Medova Hlthcare Fncl Group LLC ....E 316 616-6160
Wichita *(G-15034)*

Pollen Inc ....D 877 465-4045
Leawood *(G-5524)*

RTS Financial Service Inc ....C 877 642-8553
Overland Park *(G-9263)*

Shamrock Trading Corporation ....B 877 642-8553
Overland Park *(G-9302)*

Speculative Funding LLC ....F 785 267-1996
Topeka *(G-13089)*

Squaretwo Financial Commercial ....F 913 888-8300
Overland Park *(G-9347)*

Tafs Inc ....E 877 898-9797
Olathe *(G-8099)*

Td Auto Finance LLC ....E 913 663-6300
Shawnee Mission *(G-11921)*

Transport Funding LLC ....E 913 319-7400
Overland Park *(G-9425)*

6159 Credit Institutions, Misc Business

Clune & Company Lc ....E 913 498-3000
Shawnee Mission *(G-11241)*

Cobank Acb ....E 620 275-4281
Garden City *(G-2128)*

Cobank Acb ....F 785 798-2278
Ness City *(G-7257)*

Commercial Bank ....F 620 431-3200
Chanute *(G-719)*

Commercial Capital Company LLC ....E 913 341-0053
Lenexa *(G-5774)*

Farm Credit of Western Kansas ....E 785 462-6714
Colby *(G-1005)*

Frontier Farm Credit Aca ....C 785 776-6955
Manhattan *(G-6641)*

Garden City Production Cr Assn ....E 620 275-4281
Garden City *(G-2175)*

Medova Hlthcare Fncl Group LLC ....E 316 616-6160
Wichita *(G-15034)*

Murphy-Hoffman Company ....E 816 483-6444
Leawood *(G-5492)*

Wki Operations Inc ....F 316 838-0867
Dodge City *(G-1462)*

6162 Mortgage Bankers & Loan Correspondents

A Divis of P Midla Loan Servi ....B 913 253-9000
Overland Park *(G-8334)*

Affinity Mortgage LLC ....F 913 469-0777
Lenexa *(G-5637)*

Albright Investment Company ....E 620 221-7653
Winfield *(G-16114)*

Arvest Bank Operations Inc ....E 913 261-2265
Shawnee Mission *(G-11121)*

Ballyhoo Banners ....G 913 385-5050
Lenexa *(G-5684)*

BNC National Bank ....E 913 647-7000
Overland Park *(G-8471)*

Bok Financial Corporation ....D 913 234-6632
Overland Park *(G-8474)*

Citizens Bank of Kansas NA ....F 620 886-5686
Medicine Lodge *(G-7058)*

Citywide Mortgage Associates ....F 913 498-8822
Overland Park *(G-8558)*

Collateral RE Capitl LLC ....F 913 677-2001
Mission Woods *(G-7150)*

Cornerstone Home Lending Inc ....F 913 317-5626
Overland Park *(G-8600)*

Emprise Bank ....F 785 838-2001
Lawrence *(G-4852)*

Fairway Independent Mrtg Corp ....F 785 841-4434
Lawrence *(G-4855)*

First Horizon Bank ....E 913 317-2000
Overland Park *(G-8719)*

First Nat Bncshres of Fredonia ....F 620 378-2151
Fredonia *(G-2032)*

First Seacoast Bank ....F 913 766-2500
Overland Park *(G-8722)*

Firstrust Mortgage Inc ....E 913 312-2000
Fairway *(G-1907)*

Guild Mortgage Company ....F 316 749-2789
Wichita *(G-14526)*

High Plains Farm Credit Flca ....E 620 285-6978
Larned *(G-4705)*

High Plains Farm Credit Flca ....F 785 625-2110
Hays *(G-2844)*

Leader One Financial Corp ....E 913 747-4000
Overland Park *(G-8950)*

M Squared Financial LLC ....F 913 745-7000
Prairie Village *(G-10045)*

Metropolitan Mortgage Corp ....F 913 642-8300
Overland Park *(G-9017)*

Mortgage Company ....F 785 825-8100
Salina *(G-10605)*

Prime Lending ....E 913 327-5507
Leawood *(G-5527)*

Security National Fincl Corp ....B 620 241-3400
McPherson *(G-7025)*

Triad Capital Advisors Inc ....F 816 561-7000
Fairway *(G-1922)*

Tru Home Solutions LLC ....E 913 219-7547
Lenexa *(G-6192)*

Wells Fargo Home Mortgage Inc ....E 913 319-7900
Shawnee Mission *(G-12003)*

Wells Fargo Home Mortgage Inc ....E 405 475-2880
Wichita *(G-15948)*

Western State Bank ....F 785 899-2393
Goodland *(G-2491)*

6163 Loan Brokers

Advantage Commercial Lending ....F 316 215-0115
Sedgwick *(G-10849)*

Affinity Mortgage LLC ....F 913 469-0777
Lenexa *(G-5637)*

Agape Mortgage Partners Corp ....F 913 871-7377
Louisburg *(G-6436)*

Bank Commssnr Kansas Offce ....D 785 296-2266
Topeka *(G-12363)*

Baystone Financial Group ....F 785 587-4050
Manhattan *(G-6554)*

Citizens Bank of Kansas NA ....F 620 886-5686
Medicine Lodge *(G-7058)*

Cobank Acb ....F 316 290-2000
Wichita *(G-14048)*

Communityamerica Credit Union ....C 913 905-7000
Lenexa *(G-5778)*

Curo Group Holdings Corp ....F 316 772-3801
Wichita *(G-14142)*

Himalaya Mortgage Inc ....F 913 649-9700
Shawnee Mission *(G-11434)*

Kansas Assistive Tech Corp ....E 620 341-9002
Emporia *(G-1784)*

Meritrust Credit Union ....D 316 683-1199
Wichita *(G-15042)*

Meritrust Credit Union ....F 316 219-7614
Derby *(G-1261)*

Meritrust Credit Union ....F 316 761-4645
Wichita *(G-15044)*

Meritrust Credit Union ....F 316 761-4645
Wichita *(G-15045)*

Metcalf Bank ....F 913 685-3801
Shawnee Mission *(G-11619)*

Metcalf Bank ....F 913 782-6522
Olathe *(G-7885)*

Midland National Bank ....F 316 283-1700
Newton *(G-7386)*

Mission Mortgage LLC ....F 913 469-1999
Overland Park *(G-9042)*

Panhandle Federal Credit Union ....F 620 326-2285
Wellington *(G-13522)*

Plaza Mortgage ....F 913 671-1865
Shawnee Mission *(G-11739)*

Quantum Credit Union ....F 316 263-5756
Wichita *(G-15389)*

Regent Financial Group Inc ....F 316 462-1341
Wichita *(G-15436)*

Sunbelt Business Brokers ....F 913 383-2671
Overland Park *(G-9373)*

Wichita Inn Suites Inc ....E 316 685-2233
Wichita *(G-16008)*

Zillow Group Inc ....E 913 491-4299
Leawood *(G-5604)*

Zillow Home Loans LLC ....E 913 491-4299
Overland Park *(G-9527)*

62 SECURITY AND COMMODITY BROKERS, DEALERS, EXCHANGES, AND SERVICES

6211 Security Brokers & Dealers

Advisors Asset Management Inc ....F 316 858-1766
Wichita *(G-13631)*

Bats Trading Inc ....D 913 815-7000
Lenexa *(G-5690)*

Client One Securities LLC ....F 913 814-6097
Leawood *(G-5354)*

Cooper Malone McClain Inc ....E 316 685-5777
Wichita *(G-14098)*

Cornerstone Financial LLC ....F 316 630-0670
Wichita *(G-14102)*

CU Capital Mkt Solutions LLC ....F 913 402-2627
Overland Park *(G-8622)*

David M King & Associates ....F 785 841-9517
Lawrence *(G-4827)*

David M King & Associates ....F 319 377-4636
Hays *(G-2782)*

Daystar Petroleum Inc ....G 316 755-3492
Valley Center *(G-13340)*

Financial Consultants America ....E 316 943-7307
Wichita *(G-14367)*

First Horizon Bank ....F 913 339-5400
Shawnee Mission *(G-11371)*

Great Plains Financial Group ....F 785 843-7070
Lawrence *(G-4882)*

Hokanson Lehman & Stevens ....F 913 338-2525
Leawood *(G-5430)*

Infinity Insur Solutions LLC ....E 913 338-3200
Leawood *(G-5436)*

Jack M Schwartz ....F 785 823-3035
Salina *(G-10551)*

Kansas City Brokerage Inc ....E 913 384-4994
Overland Park *(G-8890)*

Kansas Development Fin Auth ....F 785 357-4445
Topeka *(G-12773)*

Members Mortgage Services LLC ....E 620 665-7713
Hutchinson *(G-3373)*

Merrill Lynch Pierce Fenner ....E 316 631-3500
Wichita *(G-15047)*

Merrill Lynch Pierce Fenner ....D 913 906-5200
Leawood *(G-5475)*

Mil-Spec Security Group LLC ....F 785 832-1351
Lawrence *(G-5027)*

Morgan Stanley ....F 913 402-5200
Leawood *(G-5491)*

Morgan Stanley & Co LLC ....F 316 383-8300
Wichita *(G-15127)*

Morgan Stanley & Co LLC ....F 785 749-1111
Lawrence *(G-5032)*

Ofg Financial Services Inc ....F 785 233-4071
Topeka *(G-12941)*

Perkins Smart & Boyd Inc ....F 800 344-1621
Fairway *(G-1916)*

Prosperity Netwrk Advisors LLC ....E 913 451-4501
Overland Park *(G-9197)*

Qts Finance Corporation ....F 913 814-9988
Overland Park *(G-9208)*

Raymond James Fincl Svcs Inc ....F 785 383-1893
Lawrence *(G-5088)*

Raymond James Fincl Svcs Inc ....F 620 442-1198
Arkansas City *(G-172)*

Raymond James Fincl Svcs Inc ....E 785 537-0366
Manhattan *(G-6787)*

Rbc Capital Markets LLC ....F 913 451-3500
Leawood *(G-5533)*

Riedl First Securities of Kans F 316 265-9341
Wichita *(G-15463)*
Securities Commissioner Kansas E 785 296-3307
Topeka *(G-13050)*
Security Benefit Group Inc B 785 438-3000
Topeka *(G-13053)*
Security Benefit Life Insur Co B 785 438-3000
Topeka *(G-13054)*
Stifel Nicolaus & Company Inc F 316 264-6321
Wichita *(G-15672)*
Stifel Nicolaus & Company Inc F 785 271-1300
Topeka *(G-13099)*
Stifel Nicolaus & Company Inc F 913 345-4200
Overland Park *(G-9362)*
UBS Financial Services Inc E 913 345-3200
Shawnee Mission *(G-11954)*
UBS Financial Services Inc E 316 612-6500
Wichita *(G-15828)*
UBS Securities LLC E 913 345-3200
Leawood *(G-5588)*
W & R Corporate LLC E 913 236-2000
Overland Park *(G-9472)*
Waddell & Reed Inc A 913 236-2000
Shawnee Mission *(G-11987)*
Waddell & Reed Inc F 913 491-9202
Leawood *(G-5593)*
Waddell & Reed Inc E 785 537-4505
Manhattan *(G-6844)*
Waddell & Reed Financial Inc D 913 236-2000
Overland Park *(G-9477)*
Waddell & Reed Fincl Svcs Inc B 913 236-2000
Overland Park *(G-9478)*
Waddell & Reed Inv MGT Co E 913 491-9202
Leawood *(G-5594)*
Wells Fargo Clearing Svcs LLC E 785 271-2492
Topeka *(G-13238)*
Wells Fargo Clearing Svcs LLC E 316 267-0300
Wichita *(G-15946)*
Wells Fargo Clearing Svcs LLC D 913 267-7200
Shawnee Mission *(G-12002)*
Wells Fargo Clearing Svcs LLC F 785 825-4636
Salina *(G-10767)*
Wells Fargo Clearing Svcs LLC F 620 665-0659
Hutchinson *(G-3484)*
Wells Fargo Clearing Svcs LLC E 316 634-6690
Wichita *(G-15947)*
Wells Fargo Clearing Svcs LLC D 913 402-5100
Overland Park *(G-9489)*

6221 Commodity Contracts Brokers & Dealers

Baxter Cmmdts-Dntity Grins LLC F 620 492-4040
Johnson *(G-3651)*
Gavilon Grain LLC F 785 263-7275
Abilene *(G-33)*
Koch Resources LLC E 316 828-5500
Wichita *(G-14887)*
Lansing Ethanol Services LLC E 913 748-3000
Overland Park *(G-8943)*
Schwieterman Inc F 620 275-4100
Garden City *(G-2277)*
Seaboard Corporation C 913 676-8800
Merriam *(G-7103)*
Southern Plains Co-Op At Lewis E 620 324-5536
Lewis *(G-6270)*
Wells Fargo Clearing Svcs LLC F 620 665-0659
Hutchinson *(G-3484)*

6231 Security & Commodity Exchanges

Cboe Bats LLC E 913 815-7000
Lenexa *(G-5736)*

6282 Investment Advice

6 Meridian LLC F 316 776-4601
Wichita *(G-13582)*
Ameriprise Financial Inc E 316 858-1506
Wichita *(G-13697)*
Ameriprise Financial Svcs Inc E 913 451-2811
Shawnee Mission *(G-11109)*
Ameriprise Fincl Ameriprise F 913 451-2811
Leawood *(G-5324)*
Compass Fincl Resources LLC F 913 747-2000
Olathe *(G-7607)*
Creative Planning Inc E 913 341-0900
Overland Park *(G-8612)*
David M King & Associates F 319 377-4636
Hays *(G-2782)*
Demarche Associates Inc D 913 384-4994
Overland Park *(G-8648)*
Devlin Management Inc F 316 634-1800
Wichita *(G-14204)*
Esb Financial F 785 539-3553
Manhattan *(G-6623)*
Eveans Bash Klein Inc F 913 345-7000
Overland Park *(G-8694)*
Fidelity Investments Instituti E 913 345-8079
Leawood *(G-5398)*
Financial Counselors Inc F 816 329-1500
Leawood *(G-5401)*
Financial Institution Tech Inc F 785 273-5578
Topeka *(G-12609)*
First Command Fincl Plg Inc F 785 537-0497
Manhattan *(G-6628)*
First Command Fincl Plg Inc F 913 651-6820
Leavenworth *(G-5239)*
First Horizon National Corp D 913 339-5400
Overland Park *(G-8720)*
Foresters Financial Svcs Inc E 913 310-0435
Leawood *(G-5408)*
Great Plains Trust Company F 913 831-7999
Overland Park *(G-8775)*
Ima Wealth Inc E 316 266-6582
Wichita *(G-14675)*
Insight Financial Services LLC F 913 402-2020
Overland Park *(G-8853)*
Kwmg LLC F 913 624-1841
Overland Park *(G-8933)*
Lawing Financial Group Inc D 913 491-6226
Overland Park *(G-8948)*
Legacy Financial Strategy LLC F 913 403-0600
Leawood *(G-5456)*
Lincoln Fincl Advisors Corp E 913 451-1505
Shawnee Mission *(G-11573)*
Mariner LLC E 913 647-9700
Leawood *(G-5465)*
McDaniel Knutson Inc F 785 841-4664
Lawrence *(G-5017)*
Midwest Trust Company F 913 319-0300
Shawnee Mission *(G-11638)*
Mitchell Capital Management Co F 913 428-3222
Leawood *(G-5489)*
Mutual Fund Store Inc E 913 338-2323
Shawnee Mission *(G-11660)*
Mutual Fund Store LLC F 913 319-8181
Overland Park *(G-9064)*
Nasb Financial Inc E 913 327-2000
Leawood *(G-5497)*
New England Life Insurance Co E 620 754-3725
Elsmore *(G-1683)*
Pacific Investment Inc F 785 827-1271
Salina *(G-10630)*
Susan Pool F 316 266-6574
Wichita *(G-15704)*
Tortoise Capital Advisors LLC E 913 981-1020
Leawood *(G-5578)*
Trust Company of Manhattan F 785 537-7200
Manhattan *(G-6832)*
Umb Bank National Association E 785 776-9400
Manhattan *(G-6836)*
Umb Bank National Association F 785 483-6800
Russell *(G-10300)*
Umb Bank National Association E 913 234-2070
Shawnee Mission *(G-11956)*
Waddell & Reed Inc A 913 236-2000
Shawnee Mission *(G-11987)*
Waddell & Reed Inc E 316 942-9010
Wichita *(G-15914)*
Waddell & Reed Inc E 785 827-3606
Salina *(G-10754)*
Waddell & Reed Inc F 785 263-7496
Abilene *(G-56)*
Waddell & Reed Financial Inc D 913 236-2000
Overland Park *(G-9477)*
Waddell & Reed Inv MGT Co E 913 491-9202
Leawood *(G-5594)*
Waddell & Reed Inv Mgt Co E 913 236-2000
Shawnee Mission *(G-11988)*
Wesbanco Inc D 785 539-3553
Manhattan *(G-6851)*

6289 Security & Commodity Svcs, NEC

True North Inc F 316 266-6574
Wichita *(G-15809)*
Waddell & Reed Inc A 913 236-2000
Shawnee Mission *(G-11987)*

63 INSURANCE CARRIERS

6311 Life Insurance Carriers

American Income Life Insurance E 402 699-3366
Overland Park *(G-8378)*
Ameritas Life Insurance Corp F 785 273-3504
Topeka *(G-12325)*
Arrowood Indemnity Company E 913 345-1776
Shawnee Mission *(G-11120)*
Clinical Reference Lab Inc B 913 492-3652
Lenexa *(G-5765)*
Employers Mutual Casualty Co E 913 663-0119
Overland Park *(G-8679)*
Employers Mutual Casualty Co C 316 352-5700
Wichita *(G-14279)*
Financial Designs Inc F 913 451-4747
Overland Park *(G-8715)*
Foster Callanan Financial Svc E 866 363-9595
Topeka *(G-12624)*
Great Plains Annuity Marketing F 913 888-0488
Overland Park *(G-8772)*
Hawks Funeral Home Inc F 620 442-0220
Arkansas City *(G-159)*
Keller Leopold Insurance LLC F 620 276-7671
Garden City *(G-2218)*
Massachusetts Mutl Lf Insur Co E 913 234-0300
Overland Park *(G-8994)*
New York Life Insurance Co E 913 451-9100
Overland Park *(G-9081)*
New York Life Insurance Co D 913 906-4000
Leawood *(G-5501)*
Penn Mutual Life Insurance Co F 316 685-9296
Wichita *(G-15277)*
Penn Mutual Life Insurance Co F 913 322-9177
Leawood *(G-5519)*
Pinnacle Consulting Group LLC E 913 254-3030
Overland Park *(G-9168)*
Scor Globl Lf USA Reinsurance E 913 901-4600
Leawood *(G-5549)*
Security Benefit Corporation C 785 438-3000
Topeka *(G-13052)*
Security Benefit Life Insur Co B 785 438-3000
Topeka *(G-13054)*
Standard Insurance Company F 913 661-9241
Overland Park *(G-9352)*
Swiss RE America Holding Corp A 913 676-5200
Overland Park *(G-9384)*
Swiss Reinsurance America Corp A 913 676-5200
Overland Park *(G-9387)*
Unified Life Insur Co Texas E 913 685-2233
Shawnee Mission *(G-11960)*
United Omaha Life Insurance Co E 913 402-1191
Shawnee Mission *(G-11963)*
United Services Auto Assn B 913 451-6100
Shawnee Mission *(G-11965)*
Waddell & Reed Inc E 785 537-4505
Manhattan *(G-6844)*
Waddell & Reed Fincl Svcs Inc B 913 236-2000
Overland Park *(G-9478)*
Zurich Agency Services Inc B 913 339-1000
Overland Park *(G-9530)*

6321 Accident & Health Insurance

American National Insurance Co E 913 722-2232
Shawnee Mission *(G-11106)*
Bcbsks E 785 291-7498
Topeka *(G-12367)*
Blue Cross Blue Sheld Kans Inc A 785 291-7000
Topeka *(G-12390)*
Employers Mutual Casualty Co E 913 663-0119
Overland Park *(G-8679)*
Employers Mutual Casualty Co C 316 352-5700
Wichita *(G-14279)*
Federated Mutual Insurance Co D 913 906-9363
Leawood *(G-5397)*
Health and Benefit Systems LLC E 913 642-1666
Leawood *(G-5422)*
Healthcare Alliance Group LLC F 913 956-2080
Lenexa *(G-5894)*
Kammco Health Solutions Inc F 800 435-2104
Topeka *(G-12753)*
Kansas Medical Mutual Insur Co E 785 232-2224
Topeka *(G-12790)*
Medicare Advisors 365 LLC F 866 956-0745
Lenexa *(G-5993)*
Mennonite Union Aid F 620 846-2286
Montezuma *(G-7159)*
New Drctons Bhavioral Hlth LLC C 816 237-2300
Overland Park *(G-9080)*

Rx Power ......E 913 696-0691
Shawnee Mission *(G-11817)*

Scor Globl Lf USA Reinsurance ......E 913 901-4600
Leawood *(G-5549)*

Streamline Benefits Group LLC ......F 913 744-2900
Lenexa *(G-6155)*

United Omaha Life Insurance Co ......E 913 402-1191
Shawnee Mission *(G-11963)*

6324 Hospital & Medical Svc Plans Carriers

Blue Cross and Blue Shield of ......E 785 291-4180
Topeka *(G-12389)*

Blue Cross Blue Sheld Kans Inc ......D 316 269-1666
Wichita *(G-13858)*

Blue Cross Blue Sheld Kans Inc ......A 785 291-7000
Topeka *(G-12390)*

Centene Corporation ......D 913 599-3078
Lenexa *(G-5738)*

Cigna Dental Health Kansas Inc ......F 913 339-4700
Overland Park *(G-8551)*

Coventry Health Care Kans Inc ......C 800 969-3343
Overland Park *(G-8606)*

Coventry Health Care Kans Inc ......F 316 634-1222
Wichita *(G-14117)*

Delta Dental of Kansas Inc ......F 913 381-4928
Leawood *(G-5377)*

Delta Dental of Kansas Inc ......D 316 264-4511
Wichita *(G-14188)*

Heart of America Bone Marrow D ......F 913 901-3131
Shawnee Mission *(G-11420)*

Humana Inc ......E 316 612-6820
Wichita *(G-14651)*

Humana Inc ......E 913 217-3300
Overland Park *(G-8834)*

New Drctons Bhavioral Hlth LLC ......C 816 237-2300
Overland Park *(G-9080)*

Sunflower State Hlth Plan Inc ......C 877 644-4623
Overland Park *(G-9374)*

United Healthcare Services Inc ......D 888 340-9716
Overland Park *(G-9443)*

United Omaha Life Insurance Co ......E 913 402-1191
Shawnee Mission *(G-11963)*

Unitedhealth Group Inc ......E 952 936-1300
Overland Park *(G-9445)*

6331 Fire, Marine & Casualty Insurance

Agri-Risk Services Inc ......F 913 897-1699
Stilwell *(G-12133)*

Amtrust AG Insurance Svcs LLC ......D 844 350-2767
Leawood *(G-5325)*

Armed Forces Insurance Exhange ......C 913 651-5000
Leavenworth *(G-5204)*

Bituminous Casualty Corp ......F 913 262-4664
Fairway *(G-1905)*

Bituminous Casualty Corp ......E 913 268-9176
Shawnee Mission *(G-11167)*

Bremen Farmers Mutual Insur Co ......F 785 337-2203
Bremen *(G-581)*

California Casualty MGT Co ......D 913 266-3000
Leawood *(G-5345)*

CGB Enterprises Inc ......E 913 367-5450
Atchison *(G-222)*

Federated Mutual Insurance Co ......D 913 906-9363
Leawood *(G-5397)*

First Excess Reinsurance Corp ......A 913 676-5524
Shawnee Mission *(G-11369)*

Great American Insurance Co ......D 785 840-1100
Lawrence *(G-4881)*

Great Plains Mutual Insur Co ......E 785 825-5531
Salina *(G-10521)*

Hudson Crop Insurance Svcs Inc ......C 866 450-1446
Overland Park *(G-8833)*

Ima Select LLC ......E 316 266-6203
Wichita *(G-14674)*

Kansas Mutual Insurance Co ......F 785 354-1076
Topeka *(G-12792)*

Liberty Mutual Insurance Co ......D 913 648-5900
Shawnee Mission *(G-11567)*

Old United Casualty Company ......E 913 432-6400
Shawnee Mission *(G-11695)*

Progressive Casualty Insur Co ......F 913 202-6600
Kansas City *(G-4344)*

Swiss RE America Holding Corp ......A 913 676-5200
Overland Park *(G-9384)*

▲ **Swiss RE Solutions Holdg Corp** ......A 913 676-5200
Overland Park *(G-9386)*

Transatlantic Reinsurance Co ......E 913 319-2510
Overland Park *(G-9424)*

United Services Auto Assn ......B 913 451-6100
Shawnee Mission *(G-11965)*

W Ralph Wilkerson Jr Inc ......C 913 432-4400
Shawnee Mission *(G-11986)*

Westport Insurance Corporation ......C 913 676-5270
Overland Park *(G-9492)*

Zurich Agency Services Inc ......B 913 339-1000
Overland Park *(G-9530)*

Zurich American Insurance Co ......D 913 339-1000
Overland Park *(G-9531)*

6351 Surety Insurance Carriers

CNA Financial Corporation ......D 913 661-2700
Overland Park *(G-8570)*

Newcomer Funeral Svc Group Inc ......F 785 233-6655
Topeka *(G-12928)*

Progressive Casualty Insur Co ......F 913 202-6600
Kansas City *(G-4344)*

R & R Builders Inc ......D 913 682-1234
Leavenworth *(G-5282)*

Reece and Nichols Realtors Inc ......B 913 945-3704
Leawood *(G-5536)*

6361 Title Insurance

Chicago Title and Trust Co ......F 913 451-1200
Leawood *(G-5351)*

Chicago Title Insurance Co ......F 913 385-9307
Shawnee Mission *(G-11219)*

Chicago Title Insurance Co ......F 913 782-0041
Olathe *(G-7592)*

Chicago Title Insurance Co ......F 913 451-1200
Overland Park *(G-8546)*

Chicago Title Insurance Co ......E 316 267-8371
Wichita *(G-14004)*

Koehler Bortnick Team LLC ......E 913 239-2069
Leawood *(G-5452)*

Lawyers Title of Kansas Inc ......F 785 271-9500
Topeka *(G-12835)*

6371 Pension, Health & Welfare Funds

Bukaty Companies ......E 913 345-0440
Leawood *(G-5344)*

Sra Benefits ......F 913 236-3090
Shawnee Mission *(G-11888)*

Taben Group LLC ......F 913 649-0468
Shawnee Mission *(G-11918)*

6399 Insurance Carriers, NEC

Ameritrust Group Inc ......F 913 339-5000
Overland Park *(G-8381)*

Farmers Group Inc ......E 913 227-3200
Olathe *(G-7704)*

Federal Deposit Insurance Corp ......E 316 729-0301
Wichita *(G-14346)*

Ima Financial Group Inc ......E 785 232-2202
Topeka *(G-12714)*

Kansas Medical Mutual Insur Co ......F 316 681-8119
Wichita *(G-14815)*

Livestock Marketing Assn ......E 816 891-0502
Leawood *(G-5458)*

Uniformed Services Beneft Assn ......F 913 327-5500
Overland Park *(G-9440)*

64 INSURANCE AGENTS, BROKERS, AND SERVICE

6411 Insurance Agents, Brokers & Svc

Advance Insurance Company Kans ......F 785 273-9804
Topeka *(G-12293)*

Agency Services Corp Kansas ......F 785 232-0561
Topeka *(G-12301)*

Agri-Risk Services Inc ......F 913 897-1699
Stilwell *(G-12133)*

Agrilogic Insurance Svcs LLC ......F 913 982-2450
Overland Park *(G-8359)*

Albright Investment Company ......E 620 221-7653
Winfield *(G-16114)*

Alternative Claims Services ......F 816 298-7506
Olathe *(G-7523)*

American Academy Family Physcn ......F 913 906-6000
Shawnee Mission *(G-11101)*

American Fidelity Assurance Co ......D 785 232-8100
Topeka *(G-12316)*

American Gen Lf Insur Co Del ......E 913 402-5000
Overland Park *(G-8377)*

American Home Life Insur Co ......E 785 235-6276
Topeka *(G-12318)*

American National Insurance Co ......E 913 722-2232
Shawnee Mission *(G-11106)*

American Senior Benefits ......E 785 273-8200
Topeka *(G-12322)*

American Trust Administrators ......D 913 378-9860
Overland Park *(G-8380)*

American Underwriters Lf Insur ......D 316 794-2200
Goddard *(G-2429)*

Ameritrust Group Inc ......F 913 339-5000
Overland Park *(G-8381)*

Ascension Insur Holdings LLC ......B 800 955-1991
Overland Park *(G-8400)*

Assurance Partners LLC ......E 785 825-0286
Salina *(G-10411)*

Auditing For Cmpliance Educatn ......F 913 648-8572
Shawnee Mission *(G-11133)*

Automobile Club of Missouri ......F 316 942-0008
Wichita *(G-13774)*

Axa Advisors LLC ......E 913 345-2800
Shawnee Mission *(G-11137)*

Axa Advisors LLC ......E 316 263-5761
Wichita *(G-13780)*

Bankers and Investors Co ......F 913 299-5008
Kansas City *(G-3844)*

Bankers Life & Casualty Co ......F 785 820-8815
Salina *(G-10420)*

Benefit Management LLC ......E 620 792-1779
Great Bend *(G-2520)*

Berkley Risk ADM Co LLC ......F 913 385-4960
Overland Park *(G-8440)*

Berkshire Risk Services LLC ......E 913 433-7000
Overland Park *(G-8441)*

Bituminous Casualty Corp ......F 913 262-4664
Fairway *(G-1905)*

Blue Valley Insurance Agencies ......F 785 337-2268
Hanover *(G-2710)*

Boulevard Insurance LLC ......F 785 865-0077
Overland Park *(G-8476)*

Bukaty Companies ......E 913 345-0440
Leawood *(G-5344)*

Burnham Builders ......F 620 343-2047
Emporia *(G-1713)*

C & T Enterprises Inc ......E 913 782-1404
Olathe *(G-7572)*

Calvin Eddy & Kappelman Inc ......E 785 843-2772
Lawrence *(G-4774)*

Cappers Insurance Service Inc ......E 785 274-4300
Topeka *(G-12441)*

Cbiz Benefits & Insur Svcs Inc ......F 913 234-1000
Leawood *(G-5350)*

CC Services Inc ......F 913 894-0700
Shawnee Mission *(G-11209)*

CC Services Inc ......F 913 381-1995
Overland Park *(G-8529)*

Central of Kansas Inc ......D 785 238-4114
Junction City *(G-3678)*

Century Health Solutions Inc ......F 785 233-1816
Topeka *(G-12459)*

Charlson & Wilson Bonded Abstr ......F 785 565-4800
Manhattan *(G-6584)*

Charlson Wilsin Insurance Agcy ......F 785 537-1600
Manhattan *(G-6585)*

Chris-Leef General Agency Inc ......E 913 631-1232
Shawnee Mission *(G-11222)*

Chubb US Holding Inc ......D 913 491-2000
Shawnee Mission *(G-11224)*

Cjd & Associates LLC ......F 913 469-1188
Shawnee Mission *(G-11235)*

Claim Solution Inc ......E 913 322-2300
Shawnee Mission *(G-11236)*

Cliff Tozier Insurance Agency ......F 913 385-5000
Overland Park *(G-8566)*

CNA Financial Corporation ......D 913 661-2700
Overland Park *(G-8570)*

Cobbs Allen & Hall Inc ......E 913 267-5600
Overland Park *(G-8571)*

Colt Investments Inc ......E 913 385-5010
Prairie Village *(G-10020)*

Comptech Group LLC ......F 913 341-7600
Overland Park *(G-8592)*

CPI Qualified Plan Cons Inc ......B 620 793-8473
Great Bend *(G-2549)*

Crawford & Company ......F 913 909-4552
Shawnee Mission *(G-11277)*

Crawford & Company ......F 913 323-0300
Great Bend *(G-2550)*

Creative One Marketing Corp ......C 913 814-0510
Leawood *(G-5363)*

Crop USA Hutson Insur Group ......E 913 345-1515
Overland Park *(G-8615)*

D & K Insurance Services Inc ......F 785 540-4133
Phillipsburg *(G-9784)*

Davis G Sam Insurance ....F 913 451-1800
Shawnee Mission (G-11293)
Dee Jays Enterprises....F....... 620 227-3126
Dodge City (G-1340)
Demarche Associates Inc ....D....... 913 384-4994
Overland Park (G-8648)
Demars Pnsion Cnslting Svcs In....E....... 913 469-6111
Overland Park (G-8649)
Design Benefits....F 316 729-7676
Wichita (G-14200)
Dorothy Rush Realty Inc ....F 620 442-7851
Arkansas City (G-153)
Eck Agency Inc ....E....... 620 254-7222
Attica (G-277)
Elliott Insurance Inc....F....... 913 294-2110
Louisburg (G-6446)
Ellis Grubb Martens Coml Group ....E....... 316 262-0000
Wichita (G-14272)
Employers Mutual Casualty Co ....E 913 663-0119
Overland Park (G-8679)
Employers Mutual Casualty Co ....C....... 316 352-5700
Wichita (G-14279)
Employers Reassurance Corp....D....... 913 676-5200
Shawnee Mission (G-11336)
Farm and Family Insur Assoc....E....... 785 823-5071
Salina (G-10495)
Farm Bur Property Cslty Insur....E....... 316 978-9950
Wichita (G-14340)
Farm Bureau Claims....F 620 275-9195
Garden City (G-2156)
Farm Bureau Mutl Insur Co Inc....C....... 785 587-6000
Manhattan (G-6625)
Farm Bureau Mutl Insur Co Inc....F 620 275-9195
Garden City (G-2157)
Farm Bureau Mutl Insur Co Inc....F 316 652-1800
Wichita (G-14341)
Farmers & Drovers Bank....E....... 620 767-2265
Council Grove (G-1166)
Farmers Alliance Mutl Insur Co ....A....... 620 241-2200
McPherson (G-6963)
Farmers Group Inc....E....... 785 271-8088
Topeka (G-12595)
Farmers Group Inc....E....... 785 267-4653
Topeka (G-12596)
Farmers Group Inc....E....... 316 682-4500
Wichita (G-14342)
Farmers Group Inc....E....... 316 263-4927
Wichita (G-14343)
Farmers Group Inc....E....... 913 227-2000
Olathe (G-7703)
Farmers Group Inc....E....... 913 227-3200
Olathe (G-7704)
Farmers National Bank....F 785 543-6541
Phillipsburg (G-9785)
Federated Rural Elc Insur Exch....E....... 913 541-0150
Shawnee (G-10954)
Fee Insurance Group Inc....F 620 662-2381
Hutchinson (G-3283)
Financial Benefits of Kansas ....F 913 385-7000
Leawood (G-5400)
Financial Insurance Corp....F 913 631-7441
Overland Park (G-8716)
First American Title Company ....E....... 316 554-2872
Wichita (G-14370)
First State Bank....E....... 785 877-3341
Norton (G-7447)
Fmh Benefit Services Inc ....C....... 913 685-4740
Overland Park (G-8731)
Frank E Seufert & Associates....F 785 456-2782
Wamego (G-13423)
G H C Associates Inc....F 785 243-1555
Concordia (G-1112)
Garden City Co-Op Inc ....F 620 275-6161
Garden City (G-2170)
Genex Services LLC ....E....... 913 310-0303
Lenexa (G-5872)
Gerber Insurance Group ....F 913 649-7800
Prairie Village (G-10031)
Great-West Financial Retiremen....A 847 857-3000
Overland Park (G-8776)
Haas Wilkerson & Wohlberg Inc....E....... 913 432-4400
Fairway (G-1909)
Harlan C Parker Insurance Agcy ....F 913 782-3310
Olathe (G-7752)
Hartford Fire Insurance Co ....D....... 913 693-8500
Shawnee Mission (G-11414)
Health and Benefit Systems LLC....E....... 913 642-1666
Leawood (G-5422)
Heartland Adjustments Inc ....F....... 785 823-5100
Salina (G-10539)
Henry Scherer Crop Insurance ....F 785 847-6843
Atchison (G-234)
Hokanson Lehman & Stevens ....F 913 338-2525
Leawood (G-5430)
Hooper Holmes Inc....D....... 913 764-1045
Olathe (G-7777)
Ima Inc....B....... 316 267-9221
Wichita (G-14671)
Ima Financial Group Inc ....F 316 267-9221
Wichita (G-14672)
Ima of Kansas Inc ....C....... 316 267-9221
Wichita (G-14673)
Insurance Center Inc ....E....... 316 321-5600
El Dorado (G-1571)
Insurance Designer Kansas City....F 913 451-3960
Shawnee Mission (G-11461)
Insurance Guys LLC ....F 316 775-0606
Augusta (G-327)
Insurance Planning Inc....E....... 785 625-5605
Hays (G-2853)
Inter-Americas Insurance Corp ....D....... 316 794-2200
Goddard (G-2443)
John C Gross III ....F 620 223-2550
Fort Scott (G-1976)
John Jaco Inc....F 620 792-2541
Great Bend (G-2595)
Johnston Insurance Agency....E....... 913 396-0800
Shawnee Mission (G-11501)
Kansas City Financial Group....E....... 913 649-7447
Overland Park (G-8895)
Kansas Department of Labor....F 913 680-2200
Leavenworth (G-5260)
Kansas Health Solutions Inc....D....... 785 575-9393
Topeka (G-12780)
Kansas Hospital Association....E....... 785 233-7436
Topeka (G-12781)
Kansas Medical Mutual Insur Co....F....... 316 681-8119
Wichita (G-14815)
Kansas Mutual Insurance Co....F 785 354-1076
Topeka (G-12792)
Keating & Associates Inc ....E....... 785 537-0366
Manhattan (G-6698)
Keller Leopold Insurance LLC ....F 620 276-7671
Garden City (G-2218)
Keller RE & Insur Agcy....F 620 792-2128
Great Bend (G-2599)
Kermit Cottrell Allstate Agcy ....E....... 785 843-2532
Lawrence (G-4943)
L J Gliem & Associates LLC ....E....... 913 557-9402
Overland Park (G-8935)
▲ Labone Inc....A....... 913 888-1770
Lenexa (G-5961)
Lewer Agency Inc ....D....... 816 753-4390
Overland Park (G-8954)
Lewis & Ellis Inc....E....... 913 491-3388
Overland Park (G-8955)
Lockton Affinity LLC....C....... 913 652-7500
Overland Park (G-8968)
Madrigal & Associates Inc ....E....... 316 265-5680
Wichita (G-15000)
Marino & Associates Inc ....F....... 816 478-1122
Leawood (G-5466)
Marsh & McLennan Agency LLC ....D....... 913 451-3900
Leawood (G-5467)
Marysville Mutual Insurance Co ....F 785 562-2379
Marysville (G-6901)
Max Share Fund Inc....E 913 338-1100
Overland Park (G-8996)
McInnes Group Inc....F 913 831-0999
Fairway (G-1913)
Med James Inc ....D....... 913 663-5500
Overland Park (G-9005)
Medova Hlthcare Fncl Group LLC ....E 316 616-6160
Wichita (G-15034)
Medplans Partners Inc....D....... 620 223-8200
Shawnee Mission (G-11615)
Metropolitan Life Insur Co ....E....... 913 234-4800
Overland Park (G-9016)
Metropolitan Life Insur Co ....E....... 913 451-8282
Shawnee Mission (G-11621)
Metropolitan Life Insur Co ....F 316 688-5600
Wichita (G-15061)
Mid West Pnsion Administrators....F 913 663-2777
Shawnee Mission (G-11628)
Missouri Livestock Mktg Assn ....E 816 891-0502
Leawood (G-5488)
Mitchell County Farm Bur Assn ....F 785 738-2551
Beloit (G-494)
Mobile Health Clinics LLC....D....... 913 383-0991
Leawood (G-5490)
Msaver Resources Llc ....E....... 913 663-4672
Overland Park (G-9059)
Mutualaid Exchange ....E 913 338-1100
Overland Park (G-9065)
National Crop Insur Svcs Inc....E....... 913 685-2767
Overland Park (G-9070)
Nations Title Agency....E....... 913 341-2705
Prairie Village (G-10051)
Nestegg Consulting Inc....F 316 383-1064
Wichita (G-15158)
New Mountain Capital I LLC....D....... 913 451-3222
Shawnee Mission (G-11680)
New York Life Insurance Co....F 316 262-0671
Wichita (G-15171)
Newkirk Dennis & Buckles....F 620 331-3700
Independence (G-3543)
Nolan Company....E....... 913 888-3500
Overland Park (G-9091)
Northwestern Mutual ....E....... 316 265-8139
Wichita (G-15197)
Oliver Insurance Agency Inc....F 913 341-1900
Overland Park (G-9099)
Overland Solutions Inc....C....... 913 451-3222
Overland Park (G-9127)
Parker Hafkins Insurance Inc....F 620 225-2888
Dodge City (G-1417)
Parkway Insurance Agency Inc ....F 913 385-5000
Shawnee Mission (G-11718)
Peoples Bank ....F 620 582-2166
Coldwater (G-1056)
Peoples/Commercial Insur LLC....F 785 271-8097
Topeka (G-12968)
Ppm Services Inc ....E....... 913 262-2585
Overland Park (G-9175)
Preferred Physicians Mdcl Rrg....E....... 913 262-2585
Overland Park (G-9179)
Prevail Strategies LLC....E....... 913 295-9500
Leawood (G-5526)
Professional Benefit Cons ....F....... 913 268-0515
Shawnee Mission (G-11754)
Professional Insurance Mgt....E....... 316 942-0699
Wichita (G-15362)
Provalue Insurance LLC....E....... 620 662-5406
Hutchinson (G-3417)
Prudential Insur Co of Amer ....E....... 913 327-1060
Shawnee Mission (G-11759)
Quest Capital Management Inc....F 913 599-6422
Shawnee Mission (G-11766)
Ralph S Passman & Associates ....F 913 642-5432
Overland Park (G-9221)
Regional Insurance Service Co ....F 316 686-6553
Wichita (G-15438)
Reilly Company LLC....D....... 913 682-1234
Leavenworth (G-5284)
Relation Insurance Services ....E 800 955-1991
Overland Park (G-9233)
Relation Insurance Services ....F 800 955-1991
Overland Park (G-9234)
Renn & Company Inc....F 620 326-2271
Wellington (G-13523)
Resnick Associates ....F 913 681-5454
Shawnee Mission (G-11790)
Risk Counselors Inc ....F 620 221-1760
Winfield (G-16169)
Robert E Miller Insurance Agcy....E....... 816 333-3000
Leawood (G-5540)
Rutter Cline Associates Inc ....F 620 276-8274
Garden City (G-2271)
SBS Insurance....F 785 336-2821
Seneca (G-10880)
Se2 LLC....B....... 800 747-3940
Topeka (G-13047)
Security Benefit Group Inc....B 785 438-3000
Topeka (G-13053)
Senio Livin Retir Commu LLC ....C....... 913 534-8872
Overland Park (G-9294)
Shelter Insurance....E 785 272-7181
Topeka (G-13067)
Sims Insurance Services I....F 316 722-9977
Maize (G-6520)
Smart Money Concepts Inc....F 913 962-9806
Overland Park (G-9318)
St Paul Fire and Mar Insur Co....B....... 913 469-2720
Shawnee Mission (G-11891)
Stephens Realestate Inc....D....... 785 841-4500
Lawrence (G-5122)
Sunburst Properties Inc ....F 913 393-4747
Stilwell (G-12174)
Swiss RE Management US Corp ....F 913 676-5200
Overland Park (G-9385)

SIC

Employee Codes: A=Over 500 employees, B=251-500
C=101-250, D=51-100, E=20-50, F=10-19, G=5-9

T & M Financial Inc ....F 785 266-8333
Topeka (G-13129)
T S A Inc ....F 913 322-2800
Prairie Village (G-10072)
Target Insurance Services LLC ....E 913 384-6300
Overland Park (G-9391)
Tax Favored Benefits Inc ....E 913 648-5526
Overland Park (G-9392)
Tfwilson LLC ....E 913 327-0200
Shawnee Mission (G-11927)
Thrivent Financial For Luthera ....E 620 364-2177
Burlington (G-643)
Tic International Corporation ....E 913 236-5490
Overland Park (G-9409)
Tri-County Title & Abstract Co ....F 913 682-8911
Leavenworth (G-5301)
Truck Insurance Mart Inc ....F 913 441-0349
Edwardsville (G-1519)
Truck Insurance Mart Inc ....F 620 654-3921
Galva (G-2096)
True North Inc ....F 316 266-6574
Wichita (G-15809)
Truenorth Companies Lc ....D 913 307-0838
Overland Park (G-9432)
Trustpoint Services Inc ....F 620 364-5665
Burlington (G-644)
United Agency Inc ....E 620 442-0400
Arkansas City (G-187)
United States Aviation Underwr ....F 316 267-1325
Wichita (G-15849)
Upland Mutual Insurance Inc ....F 785 762-4324
Junction City (G-3761)
USI Insurance Services LLC ....D 316 263-3211
Wichita (G-15864)
Virtus LLC ....E 816 919-2323
Overland Park (G-9466)
W Ralph Wilkerson Jr Inc ....C 913 432-4400
Shawnee Mission (G-11986)
Waddell & Reed Inc ....F 913 491-9202
Leawood (G-5593)
Waddell & Reed Inc ....A 913 236-2000
Shawnee Mission (G-11987)
Waddell & Reed Financial Inc ....D 913 236-2000
Overland Park (G-9477)
Wells Fargo Clearing Svcs LLC ....F 785 825-4636
Salina (G-10767)
Willis North America Inc ....D 913 339-0800
Overland Park (G-9495)

65 REAL ESTATE

6512 Operators Of Nonresidential Bldgs

7600 College Partnr Ted Greene ....F 913 341-1000
Overland Park (G-8332)
All American Indoor Sports ....D 913 888-5425
Shawnee Mission (G-11093)
Associates Gould-Evens ....E 785 842-3800
Lawrence (G-4739)
Bacm 2005-3 Main Woodlawn LLC ....E 316 291-8450
Wichita (G-13791)
Builders Inc ....E 316 684-1400
Wichita (G-13909)
Builders Commercials Inc ....F 316 686-3107
Wichita (G-13912)
Calvin Investments LLC ....F 785 266-8755
Topeka (G-12419)
Central Mall Realty Holdg LLC ....E 785 825-7733
Salina (G-10443)
Chilton Vending & Billd Inc ....F 316 262-3539
Wichita (G-14011)
City of Salina ....E 785 826-7200
Salina (G-10449)
City Oil Company Inc ....E 913 321-1764
Kansas City (G-3912)
Clark Investment Group ....E 316 634-1112
Wichita (G-14037)
Clonmel Community Club Inc ....E 620 545-7136
Clearwater (G-890)
Cloverleaf Office Park ....F 913 831-3200
Shawnee Mission (G-11240)
Complete Music Inc ....E 913 432-1111
Leawood (G-5357)
Coyotes Inc ....E 785 842-2295
Lawrence (G-4816)
Crossfirst Bankshares Inc ....C 913 754-9700
Overland Park (G-8618)
Ellis Grubb Martens Coml Group ....E 316 262-0000
Wichita (G-14272)
First National Bank ....F 785 366-7225
Hope (G-3121)
Flint Hills Mall LLC ....F 620 342-4631
Emporia (G-1759)
Foley Industries Inc ....D 316 943-4211
Wichita (G-14399)
Forest City Enterprises Inc ....E 785 539-3500
Manhattan (G-6638)
Fugate Leasing Inc ....C 316 722-5670
Wichita (G-14429)
Gcb Holdings LLC ....D 785 841-5185
Lawrence (G-4869)
Great Plains Investments Ltd ....D 913 492-9880
Overland Park (G-8773)
Greenamyre Rentals Inc ....F 913 651-9717
Leavenworth (G-5249)
Health Care Inc ....A 620 665-2000
Hutchinson (G-3309)
Healthpeak Properties Inc ....F 316 733-2645
Wichita (G-14579)
Inland Industries Inc ....G 913 492-9050
Bucyrus (G-600)
J A Peterson Enterprises Inc ....E 913 384-3800
Shawnee Mission (G-11471)
J A Peterson Realty Co Inc ....F 913 384-3800
Shawnee Mission (G-11473)
Kansas State University ....E 785 532-7600
Manhattan (G-6687)
Kuhn Co LLC ....E 316 788-6500
Derby (G-1257)
L C Enterprises ....F 316 682-3300
Wichita (G-14904)
Landvest Corporation ....E 316 634-6510
Wichita (G-14922)
Loyalty Properties LLC ....F 913 323-6850
Overland Park (G-8971)
Mallon Family LLC ....F 620 342-6622
Emporia (G-1789)
Manhattan Medical Center Inc ....F 785 537-2651
Manhattan (G-6724)
Marc Gorges ....E 316 630-0689
Eastborough (G-1476)
March Inc ....E 913 449-7640
Overland Park (G-8987)
MD Associates 4 Inc ....F 913 831-2996
Shawnee Mission (G-11612)
Melvin Simon & Associates Inc ....D 620 665-5307
Hutchinson (G-3372)
Mid Amrica Prpts Pittsburg LLC ....F 620 232-1678
Frontenac (G-2060)
Midland Theater Foundation Inc ....F 901 501-6832
Coffeyville (G-963)
Midwest Drywall Co Inc ....D 316 722-9559
Wichita (G-15093)
Mtc Development LLC ....E 785 539-3500
Manhattan (G-6755)
Nallwood Heights Corporation ....F 913 341-4880
Shawnee Mission (G-11668)
Oak Park Mall ....E 913 888-4400
Overland Park (G-9096)
Omni Center LP ....F 316 268-9108
Wichita (G-15218)
Parkview Joint Venture ....F 785 267-3410
Topeka (G-12962)
Patrick Properties Services ....F 913 262-6824
Overland Park (G-9146)
Pauline Food Center ....F 785 862-2774
Topeka (G-12965)
Price Brothers Realty Inc ....C 913 381-2280
Shawnee Mission (G-11751)
Quality Tech Svcs Lenexa LLC ....E 913 814-9988
Overland Park (G-9215)
Rainbow Village Management ....E 913 677-3060
Kansas City (G-4361)
Ranch Mart Inc ....F 913 649-0123
Overland Park (G-9223)
Real Estate Corporation Inc ....F 913 642-5134
Prairie Village (G-10062)
Roach Building Co Inc ....F 785 233-9606
Topeka (G-13021)
Rubenstein Real Estate Co LLC ....F 913 362-1999
Shawnee Mission (G-11815)
Sagar Inc ....E 620 241-5343
McPherson (G-7024)
Santa Fe Law Building ....F 913 648-3220
Shawnee Mission (G-11832)
Southwest Bowl ....F 785 272-1324
Topeka (G-13082)
Timothy D White ....F 620 331-7060
Independence (G-3565)
Town Center Plaza LLC ....F 913 498-1111
Leawood (G-5581)
Towne East Square ....E 316 686-9672
Wichita (G-15780)
United Wrlss Arina Mgrk Conf C ....F 620 371-7390
Dodge City (G-1446)
Universal Motor Fuels Inc ....F 316 832-0151
Wichita (G-15855)
Vista Franchise Inc ....E 785 537-0100
Manhattan (G-6843)
Warmack and Company LLC ....E 785 825-0122
Salina (G-10758)
Washington Prime Group Inc ....E 316 945-9374
Wichita (G-15931)
Weigand-Omega Associates Inc ....F 316 925-6341
Wichita (G-15941)
Woodland Lakes Community Churc ....F 316 682-9522
Wichita (G-16065)

6513 Operators Of Apartment Buildings

A G Spanos Development Inc ....F 913 663-2400
Overland Park (G-8335)
Abilene Housing Inc ....F 785 263-1080
Abilene (G-5)
Active Prime Timers Inc ....F 785 272-0237
Topeka (G-12285)
Anchor Properties Inc ....D 913 661-2250
Shawnee Mission (G-11112)
Archon Residential MGT LP ....F 913 631-2100
Shawnee Mission (G-11118)
Aspen Place Apartments ....F 913 856-8185
Gardner (G-2328)
Atriums Retirement Home ....D 913 381-9133
Shawnee Mission (G-11132)
Barrington Park Town Homes ....F 913 469-5449
Shawnee Mission (G-11153)
Bethany Home Cottage Complex ....F 785 227-2721
Lindsborg (G-6395)
Bloom Living Senior Apartments ....D 913 738-4335
Olathe (G-7557)
Boulevard Apprtments Townhomes ....F 913 722-3171
Roeland Park (G-10219)
Brookdale Senior Living Inc ....E 913 345-9339
Overland Park (G-8488)
Builders Apartments Inc ....F 316 684-1400
Wichita (G-13911)
Cedars Inc ....C 620 241-0919
McPherson (G-6942)
Chase Manhattan Apartment ....F 785 776-3663
Manhattan (G-6586)
Clark Investment Group ....E 316 634-1112
Wichita (G-14037)
Colorado Plaza Management ....F 785 776-7994
Manhattan (G-6595)
Contemprary Hsing Altrntves of ....E 785 271-9594
Topeka (G-12505)
Cumbernauld Village Inc ....D 620 221-4141
Winfield (G-16137)
Delmar Gardens of Lenexa Inc ....E 913 492-8682
Shawnee Mission (G-11299)
Delmar Gardens of Lenexa Inc ....C 913 492-1130
Lenexa (G-5809)
Double T Enterprises ....F 620 342-2655
Emporia (G-1731)
Eaglecrest Retirement Cmnty ....E 785 309-1501
Salina (G-10484)
Eden West Inc ....E 913 384-3800
Shawnee Mission (G-11327)
Edr Lawrence Ltd Partnership ....F 785 842-0032
Lawrence (G-4846)
Emeritus Corporation ....D 620 663-9195
Hutchinson (G-3279)
Emporia Prsbt Mnor of Mid Amer ....D 620 412-2019
Emporia (G-1743)
Evangelical Lthrn Good Smrtn ....D 785 456-9482
Wamego (G-13421)
Evangelical Lutheran ....D 785 472-3167
Ellsworth (G-1674)
Evergreen Apartments ....F 913 341-5572
Overland Park (G-8695)
Fidelity Management Corp ....F 785 266-8010
Topeka (G-12606)
First Management Inc ....F 785 232-5555
Topeka (G-12614)
Fogelman Management Group LLC ....F 913 345-2888
Shawnee Mission (G-11375)
Fort Leavenworth Frontier ....F 913 682-6300
Fort Leavenworth (G-1939)
Fox Ridge Coop Townhouses Inc ....F 785 273-0640
Topeka (G-12626)
Gateway Housing LP ....E 913 621-3840
Kansas City (G-4026)

Griffith Developement ....F 316 686-1831
Wichita *(G-14518)*
Hanover Rs Limited Partnership ....F 913 851-4200
Overland Park *(G-8791)*
Harvest Facility Holdings LP ....E 316 722-5100
Wichita *(G-14567)*
Harvest Facility Holdings LP ....E 785 228-0555
Topeka *(G-12665)*
Highlands Highpoint Village ....F 913 381-0335
Overland Park *(G-8814)*
Hill Investment & Rental Co ....F 785 537-9064
Manhattan *(G-6658)*
Hillcrest Apartment Bldg Co ....F 316 684-7204
Wichita *(G-14610)*
Ilm 1 Holding Inc ....E 316 687-3741
Wichita *(G-14670)*
J A Peterson Enterprises Inc ....F 913 642-9020
Shawnee Mission *(G-11472)*
J A Peterson Realty Co Inc ....F 913 384-3800
Shawnee Mission *(G-11473)*
J A Peterson Realty Co Inc ....F 913 631-2332
Shawnee Mission *(G-11474)*
J A Peterson Realty Co Inc ....F 785 842-1455
Lawrence *(G-4917)*
J A Peterson Realty Co Inc ....F 913 432-5050
Shawnee Mission *(G-11475)*
Jefferson Pointe Apartments ....F 913 906-9100
Shawnee Mission *(G-11483)*
Kansas Masonic Home ....C 316 269-7500
Wichita *(G-14814)*
Lakeview Village Inc ....A 913 888-1900
Lenexa *(G-5962)*
Ledic Management Group LLC ....F 316 685-8768
Wichita *(G-14943)*
Lee Construction Co ....F 785 539-7961
Manhattan *(G-6711)*
Liberty Assisted Living Center ....E 785 273-0886
Topeka *(G-12842)*
Liberty Assisted Living Center ....F 785 273-6847
Topeka *(G-12843)*
Lifespace Communities Inc ....C 913 383-2085
Shawnee Mission *(G-11570)*
Living Center Inc ....D 620 665-2170
Hutchinson *(G-3355)*
Lodge of Overland Park LLC ....E 913 648-8000
Overland Park *(G-8969)*
Louisberg Square Apartments ....F 913 381-4997
Overland Park *(G-8970)*
M P M Services Inc ....F 785 841-5797
Lawrence *(G-5005)*
Malkin Properties LLC ....F 913 262-2666
Shawnee Mission *(G-11593)*
Maple Gardens Assoc Ltd Partnr ....E 316 722-7960
Wichita *(G-15007)*
McCrite Retirement Association ....C 785 267-2960
Topeka *(G-12868)*
McCullough Developement Inc ....E 785 776-3010
Manhattan *(G-6736)*
MD Associates 3 Inc ....F 913 831-2996
Shawnee Mission *(G-11611)*
Meadowbrook Apartments ....E 785 842-4200
Lawrence *(G-5020)*
Medicalodges Inc ....D 913 367-2077
Atchison *(G-243)*
Mkt Community Development Inc ....F 913 596-7310
Kansas City *(G-4264)*
Mt Hope Community Development ....D 316 667-2431
Mount Hope *(G-7207)*
Nfi Management Co Inc ....F 913 341-4411
Shawnee Mission *(G-11683)*
Nies Investments LP ....E 316 684-0161
Wichita *(G-15179)*
Nolan Real Estate Services Inc ....F 913 362-1920
Shawnee Mission *(G-11686)*
Npi Property Management Corp ....F 913 648-4339
Shawnee Mission *(G-11689)*
Oak Park Village ....F 913 888-1500
Lenexa *(G-6032)*
Park West Plaza LLC ....D 316 729-4114
Wichita *(G-15262)*
Parklane Towers Inc ....F 316 684-7247
Wichita *(G-15266)*
Parkway 4000 LP ....F 785 749-2555
Lawrence *(G-5056)*
Parkwood Village ....E 620 672-5541
Pratt *(G-10130)*
Perserve At Overland Park ....F 913 685-3700
Overland Park *(G-9158)*
Price Brothers Realty Inc ....C 913 381-2280
Shawnee Mission *(G-11751)*
Quarters At Cambridge LP ....F 316 636-1277
Wichita *(G-15390)*
Rane Management ....F 620 663-3341
Pretty Prairie *(G-10169)*
Real Estate Corporation Inc ....F 913 642-5134
Prairie Village *(G-10062)*
Retreat of Shawnee Apartments ....F 913 624-1326
Shawnee Mission *(G-11792)*
Santa Marta Retirement Cmnty ....F 913 906-0990
Olathe *(G-8054)*
Saratoga Capital Inc ....F 316 838-1972
Wichita *(G-15520)*
Sentinel Real Estate Corp ....F 913 451-8976
Overland Park *(G-9295)*
Sentinel Real Estate Corp ....F 316 265-9471
Wichita *(G-15562)*
Southeast Kansas Lutherans Inc ....F 620 331-8010
Independence *(G-3561)*
Spearville District Hospital ....F 620 385-2632
Spearville *(G-12071)*
Summer Stone Duplexes ....F 316 636-9000
Wichita *(G-15681)*
Sunset Home Inc ....D 785 243-2720
Concordia *(G-1131)*
Tiehen Group ....F 913 648-1188
Leawood *(G-5575)*
Vintage Prk Assistd Lvng Rsdnc ....F 913 837-5133
Louisburg *(G-6468)*
Waddell & Reed Inc ....F 785 233-6400
Topeka *(G-13229)*
Waterwalk Wichita LLC ....E 316 201-1899
Wichita *(G-15937)*
Wathena Heights Apartments ....F 417 883-7887
Wathena *(G-13480)*
Wesley Retirement Community ....C 316 636-1000
Wichita *(G-15955)*
Wesley Towers Inc ....B 620 663-9175
Hutchinson *(G-3485)*
Windsor Estates Inc ....F 785 825-8183
Salina *(G-10770)*
Winfield Walnut KS LLC ....D 216 520-1250
Winfield *(G-16191)*
Wiston Property Management ....F 913 383-8100
Shawnee Mission *(G-12014)*
Wood View Apartments LLC ....F 913 262-8733
Kansas City *(G-4549)*
Wyncroft Hill Apartments ....F 913 829-1404
Olathe *(G-8162)*
Yarco Company Inc ....C 620 564-2180
Ellinwood *(G-1640)*

6514 Operators Of Dwellings, Except Apartments

Builders Inc ....E 316 684-1400
Wichita *(G-13909)*
Cof Residential Authority Inc ....F 785 242-5035
Ottawa *(G-8257)*
E State Management LLC ....F 785 312-9945
Lawrence *(G-4843)*
Fogelman Management Group LLC ....F 913 345-2888
Shawnee Mission *(G-11375)*
Greenamyre Rentals Inc ....F 913 651-9717
Leavenworth *(G-5249)*
O K Electric Work Inc ....G 620 251-2270
Coffeyville *(G-966)*
Riley Communities LLC ....D 785 717-2210
Fort Riley *(G-1949)*
Ritchie Associates Inc ....E 316 684-7300
Wichita *(G-15466)*
Timothy D White ....F 620 331-7060
Independence *(G-3565)*
Woodland Lakes Community Churc ....F 316 682-9522
Wichita *(G-16065)*

6515 Operators of Residential Mobile Home Sites

American Rsdntial Cmmnties LLC ....F 785 776-4440
Manhattan *(G-6542)*
Bartos Enterprises Inc ....F 620 232-9813
Frontenac *(G-2053)*
Martin Mobile Home Park Inc ....F 620 275-4722
Garden City *(G-2228)*
Mid-America Mnfct Hsng Cmmnts ....D 913 441-0194
Kansas City *(G-4243)*
Southborough Partners ....F 316 529-3200
Wichita *(G-15621)*

6519 Lessors Of Real Estate, NEC

Bent Tree Partners LLC ....F 417 206-7846
Galena *(G-2069)*
Blecha Enterprises LLC ....F 785 539-6640
Manhattan *(G-6563)*
Circle Land & Cattle Corp ....F 620 275-6131
Garden City *(G-2124)*
Employers Mutual Casualty Co ....E 913 663-0119
Overland Park *(G-8679)*
Employers Mutual Casualty Co ....C 316 352-5700
Wichita *(G-14279)*
Fairleigh Ranch Corporation ....F 620 872-2111
Scott City *(G-10810)*
Home Town Real ....F 620 271-9500
Garden City *(G-2198)*
KS Commercial RE Svcs Inc ....F 785 272-2525
Topeka *(G-12824)*
Northstar Property Management ....F 316 689-8577
Wichita *(G-15194)*
Qae Acquisition Company LLC ....F 913 814-9988
Overland Park *(G-9206)*
Quality Technology Svcs NJ LLC ....F 913 814-9988
Overland Park *(G-9218)*
Reece & Nichols Realtors Inc ....F 913 247-3064
Spring Hill *(G-12097)*
Sheila M Burdett Agency LLC ....F 785 762-2451
Junction City *(G-3753)*
Wallace Saunders Chartered ....C 913 888-1000
Shawnee Mission *(G-11990)*
Walnut Ridge Group Inc ....F 620 232-3359
Pittsburg *(G-9961)*

6531 Real Estate Agents & Managers

Adamson and Associates ....F 913 722-5432
Shawnee *(G-10906)*
Adamson and Associates Inc ....E 913 722-5432
Overland Park *(G-8347)*
Albright Investment Company ....E 620 221-7653
Winfield *(G-16114)*
American Rsdntial Cmmnties LLC ....F 785 776-4440
Manhattan *(G-6542)*
Amli Management Company ....F 913 851-3200
Overland Park *(G-8383)*
Amli Management Company ....F 913 685-3700
Shawnee Mission *(G-11110)*
Anderson Management Company ....F 316 681-1711
Wichita *(G-13706)*
Antrim & Assoc ....F 316 267-2753
Wichita *(G-13714)*
Appraisal Office Ford County ....F 620 227-4570
Dodge City *(G-1294)*
Archon Residential MGT LP ....F 913 631-2100
Shawnee Mission *(G-11118)*
Associated Commercial Brks Co ....E 785 228-9494
Topeka *(G-12343)*
Associated Management Services ....F 785 228-9494
Topeka *(G-12344)*
Astle Realty Inc ....F 620 662-0576
Hutchinson *(G-3208)*
Avery Capital LLC ....F 913 742-3002
Overland Park *(G-8416)*
B&G Group LLC ....F 816 616-4034
Overland Park *(G-8422)*
BA Karbank & Co LLP ....F 816 221-4488
Shawnee Mission *(G-11143)*
Barnds Brothers Inc ....E 913 897-2340
Shawnee Mission *(G-11152)*
Berkshire Hthway Frst Realtors ....F 785 271-2888
Topeka *(G-12371)*
Blackfin LLC ....F 816 985-4850
Kansas City *(G-3864)*
Block Real Estate Services LLC ....E 816 746-9922
Overland Park *(G-8465)*
Block Real Estate Services LLC ....E 816 412-8409
Lenexa *(G-5708)*
Bulk Industrial Group LLC ....F 913 362-6000
Prairie Village *(G-10017)*
Canlan Ice Spt Ctr Wichita LLC ....D 316 337-9199
Wichita *(G-13934)*
Capital Realty LLC ....E 913 469-4600
Overland Park *(G-8510)*
Carr Auction & Realestate ....E 620 285-3148
Larned *(G-4697)*
Cbre Inc ....F 785 435-2399
Topeka *(G-12455)*
Cek Real Estate Inc ....F 785 843-2055
Lawrence *(G-4778)*
Chuck Krte Rlty Est Auctn Svcs ....E 316 775-2201
Augusta *(G-313)*

Circle C Country Supply Inc ....F 785 398-2571
Louisburg *(G-6443)*
Clearview City Inc ....F 913 583-1451
De Soto *(G-1196)*
Cohen-Esrey LLC ....E 913 671-3300
Overland Park *(G-8573)*
Cohen-Esrey Communities LLC ....D 913 671-3300
Overland Park *(G-8574)*
Coldwell Banker Advantage ....D 913 345-9999
Overland Park *(G-8575)*
Coldwell Banker RE Corp ....E 620 331-2950
Independence *(G-3504)*
Coldwell Banker Regan Realtors ....E 913 631-2900
Shawnee Mission *(G-11245)*
Coldwell Bnkr Psternak Johnson ....F 620 331-5510
Independence *(G-3505)*
Colliers Intl Neng LLC ....E 785 865-5100
Lawrence *(G-4798)*
Commercial Management Company ....F 785 234-2882
Topeka *(G-12489)*
Commercial Property Services ....F 316 688-5200
Wichita *(G-14071)*
Commercial Real Estate News ....E 913 345-2378
Overland Park *(G-8580)*
Connection At Lawrence ....E 785 842-3336
Lawrence *(G-4809)*
County of Riley ....F 785 537-6310
Manhattan *(G-6604)*
County of Shawnee ....E 785 233-2882
Topeka *(G-12519)*
Crossroads Shop Ctr LLC ....F 913 362-1999
Shawnee Mission *(G-11282)*
Crown Realty of Kansas Inc ....E 913 782-1155
Olathe *(G-7628)*
Crown Realty of Kansas Inc ....F 785 242-7700
Ottawa *(G-8263)*
Crown Realty of Kansas Inc ....E 913 837-5155
Louisburg *(G-6444)*
CSM-Csi Joint Venture ....D 913 227-9609
Overland Park *(G-8620)*
Cushman & Wakefield Ill Inc ....F 913 440-0420
Overland Park *(G-8624)*
D D I Realty Services Inc ....F 913 685-4100
Overland Park *(G-8627)*
David W Head ....D 913 402-0057
Overland Park *(G-8642)*
Dddi Commercial Inc ....F 913 685-4100
Shawnee Mission *(G-11295)*
Destination Properties Inc ....F 913 583-1515
Overland Park *(G-8652)*
Development Inc ....F 913 651-9717
Leavenworth *(G-5233)*
Devlin Partners LLC ....F 913 894-1300
Lenexa *(G-5814)*
Diamond Partners Inc ....E 913 322-7500
Olathe *(G-7653)*
Dinning Beard Inc ....F 316 636-1115
Wichita *(G-14212)*
Dinning Beard Inc ....F 316 775-2201
Augusta *(G-317)*
Dorothy Rush Realty Inc ....F 620 442-7851
Arkansas City *(G-153)*
Duke Realty Corporation ....D 913 829-1453
New Century *(G-7281)*
Dunes Residential Services Inc ....E 913 955-2900
Leawood *(G-5380)*
E F Hadel Realty Inc ....F 913 681-1600
Shawnee Mission *(G-11322)*
Ebco Construction Group LLC ....F 866 297-2185
Olathe *(G-7667)*
EBY Realty Group LLC ....E 913 782-3200
Olathe *(G-7669)*
Eden West Inc ....E 913 384-3800
Shawnee Mission *(G-11327)*
Ellis Grubb Martens Coml Group ....E 316 262-0000
Wichita *(G-14272)*
Estates Unlimited Inc ....F 316 262-7600
Wichita *(G-14305)*
Executive Hills Management ....D 913 451-9000
Leawood *(G-5391)*
Facility Mgmt Svs Grp of Kc ....D 913 888-7600
Lenexa *(G-5846)*
Fairways of Ironhorse ....D 913 396-7931
Leawood *(G-5394)*
Farm & Ranch Realty Inc ....F 785 462-3904
Colby *(G-1004)*
Faulkner Real Estate ....F 620 356-5808
Ulysses *(G-13295)*
Fishman and Co Realtors Inc ....F 913 782-9000
Overland Park *(G-8724)*
Fox Realty Inc ....F 316 681-1313
Wichita *(G-14412)*
G H C Associates Inc ....F 785 243-1555
Concordia *(G-1112)*
Glenwood Estate Inc ....D 620 331-2260
Independence *(G-3523)*
Gold Key Inc ....F 316 942-1925
Wichita *(G-14480)*
Green Hills Inc ....F 316 686-7673
Wichita *(G-14509)*
Gt Kansas LLC ....E 913 266-1106
Shawnee Mission *(G-11404)*
H Schwaller & Sons Inc ....F 785 628-6162
Hays *(G-2822)*
Heartland Multiple Ll ....F 913 661-1600
Leawood *(G-5426)*
Heritage Management Corp ....F 785 273-2995
Topeka *(G-12685)*
Hilltop Manor Mutal Hsing Corp ....F 316 684-5141
Wichita *(G-14615)*
Home Rental Services Inc ....F 913 469-6633
Overland Park *(G-8825)*
Home Town Real ....F 620 271-9500
Garden City *(G-2198)*
Hughes Development Company Inc ....F 913 321-2262
Kansas City *(G-4089)*
Integra Realty Resources ....E 913 236-4700
Shawnee Mission *(G-11462)*
J B L Inc ....F 316 529-3100
Wichita *(G-14734)*
J P Weigand & Sons Inc ....C 316 686-3773
Wichita *(G-14738)*
J P Weigand & Sons Inc ....D 316 722-6182
Wichita *(G-14739)*
J P Weigand & Sons Inc ....E 316 788-5581
Derby *(G-1254)*
J P Weigand and Sons Inc ....F 620 663-4458
Hutchinson *(G-3338)*
J P Weigand and Sons Inc ....E 316 283-1330
Newton *(G-7367)*
JC Nchols Dnton Rbrts Rltors ....F 913 299-1600
Kansas City *(G-4121)*
Jim Bishop & Associates ....F 620 231-4370
Pittsburg *(G-9882)*
Joe Barns ....F 785 842-2772
Lawrence *(G-4924)*
John C Gross III ....F 620 223-2550
Fort Scott *(G-1976)*
John H Moffitt & Co Inc ....E 913 491-6800
Shawnee Mission *(G-11491)*
John T Arnold Associates Inc ....F 316 263-7242
Wichita *(G-14763)*
Jones Lang Lasalle Inc ....F 816 531-2323
Overland Park *(G-8879)*
Jury & Associates Inc ....E 913 642-5656
Shawnee Mission *(G-11504)*
KB Properties of Kansas LLC ....E 316 292-3924
Wichita *(G-14836)*
Kc Commercial Realty Group ....F 913 232-5100
Prairie Village *(G-10041)*
Keller RE & Insur Agcy ....F 620 792-2128
Great Bend *(G-2599)*
Keller Williams Dave Neal ....F 316 681-3600
Wichita *(G-14842)*
Kelly Enterprise Inc ....F 913 685-1800
Overland Park *(G-8912)*
Kessinger/Hunter & Company Lc ....C 816 842-2690
Shawnee Mission *(G-11529)*
Keybank Real Estate ....F 216 813-4756
Leawood *(G-5449)*
Kirk & Cobb Realty ....E 785 272-5555
Topeka *(G-12823)*
Knickerbocker Properties Inc ....E 913 451-4466
Shawnee Mission *(G-11536)*
KS Commercial RE Svcs Inc ....F 785 272-2525
Topeka *(G-12824)*
L L C Fun Services of K C ....F 913 441-9200
Shawnee *(G-10984)*
Land Acquisitions Inc ....E 847 749-0675
Wichita *(G-14919)*
Landvest Corporation ....E 316 634-6510
Wichita *(G-14922)*
Larry Theurer ....F 620 326-2715
Wellington *(G-13510)*
Lawrence Realty Associates ....D 785 841-2727
Lawrence *(G-4986)*
Lee & Associates Kansas Cy LLC ....F 913 890-2000
Leawood *(G-5455)*
Lenexa FDA Oc LLC ....D 913 894-9735
Lenexa *(G-5969)*
Licausi-Styers Company ....E 913 681-5888
Shawnee Mission *(G-11568)*
Little Creek Dairy ....E 785 348-5576
Linn *(G-6410)*
LLC Black Stone ....F 816 519-5650
Westwood *(G-13555)*
Ls Construction Services Inc ....E 913 681-5888
Shawnee Mission *(G-11580)*
M H P Management Services ....E 913 441-0194
Edwardsville *(G-1508)*
Maccallum Char RE Group ....F 913 782-8857
Olathe *(G-7870)*
Marcus Mllchap RE Inv Svcs Inc ....E 816 410-1010
Overland Park *(G-8989)*
Mastercraft Corporation ....E 785 842-4455
Lawrence *(G-5013)*
Max RE Professional Inc ....F 620 227-3629
Dodge City *(G-1402)*
Mc Grew Realestate Inc ....F 785 843-2055
Lawrence *(G-5015)*
Mc Real Estate Service Inc ....F 913 451-4466
Shawnee Mission *(G-11605)*
McCullough Development Inc ....E 888 776-3010
Manhattan *(G-6737)*
McCurdy Auction LLC ....E 316 683-0612
Wichita *(G-15026)*
Mid-Land Management Inc ....D 785 272-1398
Topeka *(G-12890)*
Midamerica Appraisals Inc ....F 620 231-0939
Pittsburg *(G-9904)*
Midland Properties Inc ....F 913 677-5300
Mission Woods *(G-7151)*
Midland Property Management ....F 913 677-5300
Mission Woods *(G-7152)*
Mike Grbic Team Realtors Inc ....E 316 684-0000
Wichita *(G-15107)*
Miller & Midyett Realtor Inc ....F 785 843-8566
Lawrence *(G-5029)*
Mission Place Ltd LP ....E 620 662-8731
Hutchinson *(G-3382)*
Montara LLC ....F 785 862-1030
Topeka *(G-12911)*
N J Investors Inc ....F 316 652-0616
Wichita *(G-15144)*
Nations Title Agency ....E 913 341-2705
Prairie Village *(G-10051)*
Neighborhood Group Inc ....E 913 362-0000
Shawnee Mission *(G-11675)*
Newcomer Funeral Svc Group Inc ....F 785 233-6655
Topeka *(G-12928)*
Northstar Property Management ....F 316 689-8577
Wichita *(G-15194)*
Och Regional Office ....E 913 599-6137
Shawnee Mission *(G-11694)*
Omni Center II ....F 316 689-4256
Wichita *(G-15217)*
P F S Group Limited ....E 316 722-0001
Wichita *(G-15251)*
P K C Realty Company LLC ....C 913 491-1550
Overland Park *(G-9133)*
Paramount Management Corp ....E 316 269-4477
Wichita *(G-15261)*
Partners Inc ....F 913 906-5400
Overland Park *(G-9143)*
Peterson Companies ....D 316 682-4903
Wichita *(G-15286)*
Preferred Land Company Inc ....F 316 634-1313
Wichita *(G-15326)*
Premier Realty LLC ....E 316 773-2707
Wichita *(G-15334)*
Prestige Property Co ....E 800 730-1249
Topeka *(G-12986)*
Prestige Real Estate ....F 785 242-1167
Ottawa *(G-8306)*
Price Brothers Realty Inc ....C 913 381-2280
Shawnee Mission *(G-11751)*
Prism Real Estate Services LLC ....F 913 674-0438
Overland Park *(G-9187)*
Pro X Property Solutions LLC ....F 620 249-5767
Pittsburg *(G-9923)*
Prudential Henry & Burrows ....E 913 345-3000
Shawnee Mission *(G-11758)*
Prudential Kansas City Realty ....D 913 491-1550
Overland Park *(G-9200)*
Quality Group Companies LLC ....E 913 814-9988
Overland Park *(G-9211)*
R & R Builders Inc ....D 913 682-1234
Leavenworth *(G-5282)*
RE Max Professionals L L C ....F 785 843-9393
Lawrence *(G-5089)*

Re/Max Excel ...F ... 785 856-8484
Lawrence (G-5090)
Real Estate Ctr Indpndence LLC ...F ... 620 331-7550
Independence (G-3550)
Reality Executives Center ...E ... 316 686-4111
Wichita (G-15425)
Realty Associates Inc ...F ... 785 827-0331
Salina (G-10651)
Realty Professionals LLC ...F ... 785 271-8400
Topeka (G-13002)
Realty World Alliance LLC ...E ... 316 688-0077
Wichita (G-15427)
Reece & Nichols Alliance Inc ...D ... 913 262-7755
Prairie Village (G-10063)
Reece & Nichols Alliance Inc ...D ... 913 451-4415
Shawnee Mission (G-11784)
Reece & Nichols Alliance Inc ...D ... 913 782-8822
Olathe (G-8022)
Reece & Nichols Realtors Inc ...D ... 913 851-8082
Leawood (G-5534)
Reece & Nichols Realtors Inc ...E ... 913 620-3419
Overland Park (G-9231)
Reece & Nichols Realtors Inc ...E ... 913 351-5600
Basehor (G-387)
Reece & Nichols Realtors Inc ...E ... 913 491-1001
Leawood (G-5535)
Reece & Nichols Realtors Inc ...E ... 913 307-4000
Shawnee (G-11016)
Reece & Nichols Realtors Inc ...E ... 913 339-6800
Shawnee Mission (G-11785)
Reece & Nichols Realtors Inc ...F ... 913 247-3064
Spring Hill (G-12097)
Reece and Nichols Realtors Inc ...B ... 913 945-3704
Leawood (G-5536)
Reib Inc ...F ... 620 662-0583
Hutchinson (G-3422)
Reilly Company LLC ...D ... 913 682-1234
Leavenworth (G-5284)
Renn & Company Inc ...F ... 620 326-2271
Wellington (G-13523)
Retel Brokerage Services Inc ...E ... 678 292-5723
Wichita (G-15453)
Rick Wayland & Associates ...F ... 316 524-0079
Wichita (G-15458)
Risk Counselors Inc ...F ... 620 221-1760
Winfield (G-16169)
Ritchie Associates Inc ...E ... 316 684-7300
Wichita (G-15466)
Rodrock & Associates Inc ...E ... 913 533-9980
Overland Park (G-9254)
Rubenstein Real Estate Co LLC ...F ... 913 362-1999
Shawnee Mission (G-11815)
Salina Homes ...F ... 785 820-5900
Salina (G-10675)
Salina Housing Authority ...F ... 785 827-0441
Salina (G-10676)
Sandstone Creek Apartments ...F ... 913 402-8282
Shawnee Mission (G-11828)
SC Hall Industrial Svcs Inc ...E ... 316 945-4255
Wichita (G-15525)
Shaner Appraisals Inc ...F ... 913 451-1451
Overland Park (G-9303)
Sharon Sigma Realtors LLC ...E ... 913 381-6794
Overland Park (G-9304)
Sheets Adams Realtors Inc ...F ... 620 241-3648
McPherson (G-7026)
Sheila M Burdett Agency LLC ...F ... 785 762-2451
Junction City (G-3753)
Stephens Realestate Inc ...D ... 785 841-4500
Lawrence (G-5122)
Stewart Realty Co Inc ...F ... 620 223-6700
Fort Scott (G-2007)
Stoltz Realty Delaware Inc ...E ... 913 451-4466
Overland Park (G-9364)
Summerfield Suites Mgt Co L P ...D ... 316 681-5100
Wichita (G-15682)
Sumner County Appraiser ...F ... 620 326-8986
Wellington (G-13532)
Sunburst Properties Inc ...F ... 913 393-4747
Stilwell (G-12174)
T & J Holdings Inc ...F ... 785 841-4935
Lawrence (G-5131)
Tiehen Group Inc ...F ... 913 648-1188
Leawood (G-5576)
Timothy D White ...F ... 620 331-7060
Independence (G-3565)
Tjk Inc ...F ... 785 841-0110
Lawrence (G-5139)
Tom Jones Real Estate Company ...F ... 913 341-7777
Shawnee Mission (G-11934)
Town & Country Super Market ...E ... 620 653-2330
Hoisington (G-3072)
Trail Wood Company Inc ...F ... 316 321-6500
El Dorado (G-1610)
Trammell Crow Company ...F ... 913 722-1155
Prairie Village (G-10076)
Trinity Property Group LLC ...E ... 620 342-8723
Emporia (G-1840)
Trustpoint Services Inc ...F ... 620 364-5665
Burlington (G-644)
Tutera Group Inc ...E ... 913 851-0215
Shawnee Mission (G-11951)
United Agency Inc ...E ... 620 442-0400
Arkansas City (G-187)
Universal Management Inc ...E ... 913 321-3521
Kansas City (G-4495)
Valley Realtors Inc ...F ... 785 233-4222
Topeka (G-13218)
Vic Regnier Builders Inc ...E ... 913 649-0123
Overland Park (G-9463)
Waddell & Reed Fincl Svcs Inc ...B ... 913 236-2000
Overland Park (G-9478)
Weigand-Omega Management Inc ...E ... 316 925-6341
Wichita (G-15942)
Wesley Management Inc ...F ... 913 682-6844
Leavenworth (G-5305)
Winbury Group of KC LLC ...F ... 785 865-5100
Lawrence (G-5187)
Woodstone Inc ...F ... 913 685-2282
Shawnee Mission (G-12018)
Wyncroft Hill Apartments ...F ... 913 829-1404
Olathe (G-8162)
Xec Inc ...E ... 913 563-4260
Overland Park (G-9511)
Yarco Company Inc ...C ... 913 225-8733
Kansas City (G-4563)

6541 Title Abstract Offices

Accurate Title Company LLC ...F ... 913 338-0100
Overland Park (G-8343)
Capital Title Insurance Co Lc ...F ... 785 272-2900
Topeka (G-12434)
Chicago Title and Trust Co ...F ... 913 451-1200
Leawood (G-5351)
Chicago Title Insurance Co ...F ... 913 782-0041
Olathe (G-7592)
Fidelity National Fincl Inc ...F ... 913 422-5122
Leawood (G-5399)
First American Title Company ...E ... 316 554-2872
Wichita (G-14370)
First American Title Company ...D ... 316 267-8371
Wichita (G-14371)
Guardian Title & Trust Company ...E ... 620 223-3330
Wichita (G-14524)
Kansas Secured Title ...F ... 316 320-2410
El Dorado (G-1576)
Kansas Secured Title Sedgwick ...F ... 316 262-8261
Wichita (G-14823)
Kansas Secured Ttle Inc ...F ... 785 232-9349
Topeka (G-12804)
Land Title Services Inc ...F ... 785 823-7223
Salina (G-10579)
Lawyers Title of Kansas Inc ...F ... 785 271-9500
Topeka (G-12835)
Metro Title Services LLC ...D ... 913 236-9923
Lenexa (G-5997)
Midwest Title Co Inc ...F ... 913 393-2511
Olathe (G-7898)
Moon Abstract Company ...F ... 620 342-1917
Overland Park (G-9050)
Nations Title Agency ...E ... 913 341-2705
Prairie Village (G-10051)
Reno County Abstract & Title ...F ... 620 662-5455
Hutchinson (G-3423)
Security 1st Title LLC ...F ... 620 442-7029
Arkansas City (G-178)
Security 1st Title LLC ...E ... 620 842-3333
Anthony (G-135)
Security 1st Title LLC ...F ... 316 322-8164
El Dorado (G-1601)
Security 1st Title LLC ...E ... 316 722-2463
Wichita (G-15541)
Security 1st Title LLC ...F ... 620 326-7460
Wellington (G-13527)
Security 1st Title LLC ...E ... 316 260-5634
Augusta (G-344)
Security 1st Title LLC ...E ... 316 267-8371
Wichita (G-15542)
Title Midwest Inc ...F ... 785 232-9110
Fairway (G-1920)
Tm Holdings Inc ...F ... 785 232-9110
Fairway (G-1921)
Tri-County Title & Abstract Co ...F ... 913 682-8911
Leavenworth (G-5301)

6552 Land Subdividers & Developers

Alvamar Inc ...E ... 785 842-2929
Lawrence (G-4732)
Builders Development Inc ...E ... 316 684-1400
Wichita (G-13913)
Clark Investment Group ...E ... 316 634-1112
Wichita (G-14037)
Corvias Military Living LLC ...F ... 785 717-2200
Fort Riley (G-1947)
General Financial Services Inc ...G ... 316 636-1070
Wichita (G-14456)
Haren & Laughlin Cnstr Co Inc ...E ... 913 495-9558
Lenexa (G-5890)
J A Peterson Enterprises Inc ...E ... 913 384-3800
Shawnee Mission (G-11471)
John H Moffitt & Co Inc ...E ... 913 491-6800
Shawnee Mission (G-11491)
Jones & Jones Development LLC ...F ... 913 422-9477
Bonner Springs (G-557)
Kdc Construction Inc ...F ... 913 677-1920
Leawood (G-5447)
Kessinger/Hunter & Company Lc ...C ... 816 842-2690
Shawnee Mission (G-11529)
Licausi-Styers Company ...E ... 913 681-5888
Shawnee Mission (G-11568)
Lodging Enterprises LLC ...A ... 316 630-6300
Wichita (G-14975)
Mark IV Associates LLC ...E ... 913 345-2120
Shawnee Mission (G-11595)
McCullough Development Inc ...E ... 888 776-3010
Manhattan (G-6737)
Midland Properties Inc ...F ... 913 677-5300
Mission Woods (G-7151)
Nai Heartland Co ...F ... 913 362-1000
Leawood (G-5496)
OS Companies Inc ...E ... 316 265-5611
Wichita (G-15238)
Petersen Development Corp ...F ... 785 228-9494
Topeka (G-12971)
Prime Development Company ...F ... 316 634-0643
Wichita (G-15344)
Quality Inv Prpts Land Co LLC ...F ... 913 312-5500
Overland Park (G-9212)
Sheets Adams Realtors Inc ...F ... 620 241-3648
McPherson (G-7026)
Southwind Development Co ...E ... 620 275-2117
Garden City (G-2285)
Summit Group of Salina KS LP ...F ... 785 826-1711
Salina (G-10718)
Turkey Creek Golf Course ...F ... 620 241-8530
McPherson (G-7032)
Tutera Group Inc ...E ... 913 851-0215
Shawnee Mission (G-11951)
Woodstone Inc ...F ... 913 685-2282
Shawnee Mission (G-12018)

6553 Cemetery Subdividers & Developers

Catholic Cemteries Inc ...E ... 913 371-4040
Kansas City (G-3894)
Fairlawn Burial Park Assn ...F ... 620 662-3431
Hutchinson (G-3282)
Hawks Funeral Home Inc ...F ... 620 442-0220
Arkansas City (G-159)
Mount Hope Cemetery Company ...F ... 785 272-1122
Topeka (G-12917)
National Cemetery ADM ...F ... 913 758-4105
Leavenworth (G-5273)
National Cemetery ADM ...F ... 913 758-4105
Leavenworth (G-5274)
Resthaven Gardens of Memory ...E ... 316 722-2100
Wichita (G-15450)
Service Corp International ...E ... 913 334-3366
Kansas City (G-4418)
Topeka Cemetery Association ...F ... 785 233-4132
Topeka (G-13171)
White Chapel Memorial Corp ...E ... 316 684-1612
Wichita (G-15965)

67 HOLDING AND OTHER INVESTMENT OFFICES

6712 Offices Of Bank Holding Co's

Coronado Inc ...F ... 620 278-2161
Sterling (G-12115)

S I C

Cunningham Agency Inc .... F 913 795-2212
Mound City *(G-7170)*
First Nat Bncshres of Fredonia .... F 620 378-2151
Fredonia *(G-2032)*
Hnb Corporation .... D 620 442-4040
Arkansas City *(G-160)*
Holyrood Bancshares Inc .... F 785 252-3239
Holyrood *(G-3116)*
Intrust Financial Corporation .... E 316 383-1111
Wichita *(G-14727)*
Johnson State Bankshares Inc .... F 620 492-6200
Johnson *(G-3657)*
Peabody State Bancorp Inc .... F 620 983-2810
Peabody *(G-9761)*
Republic Bancshares Inc .... F 785 483-2300
Russell *(G-10288)*
Wheatland Investments Inc .... F 620 465-2225
Haven *(G-2738)*

6719 Offices Of Holding Co's, NEC

Beechcraft Holdings LLC .... E 316 676-7111
Wichita *(G-13826)*
Bicknell Family Holding Co LLC .... E 913 387-2743
Overland Park *(G-8447)*
Developers and Management Inc .... E 316 682-6770
Wichita *(G-14202)*
EBY Group Inc .... A 913 782-3200
Olathe *(G-7668)*
Eldridge Holding LLC .... F 785 749-5011
Lawrence *(G-4849)*
Frontier Farm Credit Aca .... C 785 776-6955
Manhattan *(G-6641)*
Giant Kfn Holding Company LLC .... E 785 362-2532
Holton *(G-3092)*
Gjo Holdings Inc .... E 913 621-6611
Kansas City *(G-4036)*
Great Plains Ventures Inc .... F 316 684-1540
Wichita *(G-14505)*
Koch Business Holdings LLC .... F 316 828-8943
Wichita *(G-14873)*
M R Imaging Center LP .... F 316 268-6742
Wichita *(G-14993)*
Mariner Wealth Advisors LLC .... E 913 904-5700
Overland Park *(G-8991)*
Mrv Holding Company .... F 785 272-1398
Topeka *(G-12918)*
Mtc Holding Corporation .... F 913 319-0300
Overland Park *(G-9060)*
Nations Holding Company .... E 913 383-8185
Prairie Village *(G-10050)*
Northwest Centre LLC .... F 316 262-3331
Wichita *(G-15195)*
Prairie Band LLC .... F 785 364-2463
Holton *(G-3109)*
R L Dial Co Inc .... B 316 721-0108
Wichita *(G-15404)*
Spoon Creek Holdings LLC .... F 913 375-2275
Olathe *(G-8078)*
Tech Investments III LLC .... D 816 674-9993
Mission Hills *(G-7149)*

6722 Management Investment Offices

Buffalo Balanced Fund Inc .... F 913 677-7778
Shawnee Mission *(G-11189)*
Buffalo Funds .... E 913 677-7778
Shawnee Mission *(G-11190)*
Ivy Funds Distributor Inc .... F 913 261-2800
Shawnee Mission *(G-11469)*
Ivy Funds VIP Small Cap Growth .... F 800 777-6472
Overland Park *(G-8866)*
Palmer Square Capital MGT LLC .... E 816 994-3201
Shawnee Mission *(G-11714)*
Rydex Fund Services Inc .... C 301 296-5100
Topeka *(G-13031)*
SBC Funding LLC .... A 785 438-3000
Topeka *(G-13037)*
Security Benefit Life Insur Co .... B 785 438-3000
Topeka *(G-13054)*
Tortoise Energy Capital Corp .... F 913 981-1020
Leawood *(G-5579)*
Tortoise Energy Independenc .... E 913 981-1020
Leawood *(G-5580)*
Waddell & Reed Fincl Svcs Inc .... B 913 236-2000
Overland Park *(G-9478)*

6726 Unit Investment Trusts, Face-Amount Certificate Offices

Bridge Capital Management LLC .... F 913 283-7804
Lenexa *(G-5712)*
Freestate Advisors LLC .... E 888 735-2724
Wichita *(G-14419)*

6732 Education, Religious & Charitable Trusts

Community Fndtion Sthwest Kans .... F 620 225-0959
Dodge City *(G-1326)*
Oak Ridge Youth Dev Corp .... E 913 788-5657
Kansas City *(G-4292)*
Trego Hospital Endowment Fndtn .... E 785 743-2182
Wakeeney *(G-13392)*
University of Kansas .... A 913 588-5436
Kansas City *(G-4502)*
Washburn University Foundation .... E 785 670-4483
Topeka *(G-13232)*

6733 Trusts Except Educational, Religious & Charitable

Great Plains Trust Company .... F 913 831-7999
Overland Park *(G-8775)*
Mercy Hlth Fndtion Sthstern PA .... F 620 223-2200
Fort Scott *(G-1987)*
Midwest Trust Company .... F 913 319-0300
Shawnee Mission *(G-11638)*
National Advisors Holdings Inc .... E 913 234-8200
Overland Park *(G-9068)*
Trust Sourcing Solutions LLC .... E 913 319-0300
Shawnee Mission *(G-11946)*
Whitham Frank E Trust 2 .... F 620 375-2229
Leoti *(G-6261)*

6792 Oil Royalty Traders

Castle Resources Inc .... E 785 625-5155
Schoenchen *(G-10802)*
Ritchie Exploration Inc .... F 316 691-9500
Wichita *(G-15468)*
Younger Energy Company .... G 316 681-2542
Wichita *(G-16097)*

6794 Patent Owners & Lessors

Big Bobs Outlets Kansas Cy Inc .... F 913 362-2627
Shawnee Mission *(G-11163)*
Capital City Corral Inc .... D 785 273-5354
Topeka *(G-12425)*
Coverall North America Inc .... F 913 888-5009
Leawood *(G-5362)*
Doc Grens Gourmet Salads Grill .... F 316 636-8997
Wichita *(G-14216)*
Majestic Franchising Inc .... F 913 385-1440
Lenexa *(G-5983)*
Mr Goodcents Franchise Systems .... E 913 583-8400
De Soto *(G-1209)*
Mriglobal - Kansas LLC .... A 816 753-7600
Manhattan *(G-6754)*
Myron International Inc .... F 913 281-5552
Kansas City *(G-4275)*
Myrons Dental Laboratories .... E 800 359-7111
Kansas City *(G-4276)*
Npc Quality Burgers Inc .... F 913 327-5555
Overland Park *(G-9094)*
Prohome International LLc .... E 316 687-6776
Wichita *(G-15372)*
Stanley Dairy Queen .... E 913 851-1850
Shawnee Mission *(G-11892)*
Stockade Companies LLC .... D 620 669-9372
Hutchinson *(G-3448)*
Title Boxing Club LLC .... E 913 991-8285
Overland Park *(G-9415)*
Vista Franchise Inc .... E 785 537-0100
Manhattan *(G-6843)*

6798 Real Estate Investment Trusts

Broadmoor One LLC .... D 316 683-0562
Wichita *(G-13893)*
Midwest Bioscience RES Pk LLC .... E 913 319-0300
Leawood *(G-5482)*
Qts Invstmnt Props Carpathia .... E 913 814-9988
Overland Park *(G-9209)*
Qts Realty Trust Inc .... E 913 814-9988
Overland Park *(G-9210)*
Quality Investment Properties .... F 913 814-9988
Overland Park *(G-9213)*
Reeble Inc .... D 620 342-0404
Emporia *(G-1816)*

6799 Investors, NEC

Awg Acquisition LLC .... A 913 288-1000
Kansas City *(G-3831)*
Big Creek Investment Corp Inc .... G 620 431-3445
Chanute *(G-707)*
Brittany Court Inv Partner LP .... F 816 300-0685
Gardner *(G-2330)*
Cambridgen Inc .... E 913 384-3800
Overland Park *(G-8507)*
Capital City Investments Inc .... E 785 274-5600
Topeka *(G-12427)*
Cassian Energy LLC .... F 913 948-1107
Overland Park *(G-8525)*
Central States Capital Markets .... F 913 766-6565
Prairie Village *(G-10019)*
Cg Investments .... E 816 398-5862
Kansas City *(G-3907)*
Dean Development Inc .... F 913 685-4100
Shawnee Mission *(G-11296)*
Eighteen Capital Group .... F 866 799-5157
Leawood *(G-5385)*
GE Capital Montgomery Ward .... A 913 676-4100
Shawnee Mission *(G-11391)*
John T Arnold Associates Inc .... F 316 263-7242
Wichita *(G-14763)*
Licausi-Styers Company .... E 913 681-5888
Shawnee Mission *(G-11568)*
Medova Hlthcare Fncl Group LLC .... E 316 616-6160
Wichita *(G-15034)*
Midland Properties Inc .... F 913 677-5300
Mission Woods *(G-7151)*
Midwest Legacy LLC .... F 316 518-9350
Park City *(G-9631)*
Mkl Acquisitions LLC .... F 620 704-5228
Pittsburg *(G-9907)*
Prias Prairie View LLC .... F 816 437-9636
Overland Park *(G-9185)*
Prime SEC Svcs Borrower LLC .... F 630 410-0662
Lawrence *(G-5076)*
Resources Inv Advisors Inc .... E 913 338-5300
Leawood *(G-5538)*
S J Investments Inc of Topeka .... F 785 233-1568
Topeka *(G-13032)*
Stone Investment Inc .... E 913 367-0276
Atchison *(G-263)*
Vfs Acquisition Corp .... F 913 422-4088
Bonner Springs *(G-579)*

70 HOTELS, ROOMING HOUSES, CAMPS, AND OTHER LODGING PLACES

7011 Hotels, Motels & Tourist Courts

17th Street Properties LLC .... F 785 320-5440
Manhattan *(G-6525)*
7240 Shawnee Mission Hospitali .... E 913 217-7283
Overland Park *(G-8331)*
7th Street Casino .... E 913 371-3500
Kansas City *(G-3775)*
A Scampis Bar & Grill .... E 785 539-5311
Manhattan *(G-6527)*
Abilene Super Eight .... F 785 263-4545
Abilene *(G-9)*
Absecon SW Hotel Inc .... E 913 345-2111
Lenexa *(G-5619)*
AHP H6 Topeka .... E 785 273-0066
Topeka *(G-12302)*
Airport Red Coach Inn of Wichi .... D 316 942-5600
Wichita *(G-13655)*
Allen County Lodging LLC .... F 620 365-3030
Iola *(G-3586)*
Ambassador Hotel Wichita LLC .... E 316 239-7100
Wichita *(G-13682)*
Americal Inc .... F 785 890-7566
Goodland *(G-2461)*
Americas Best Value Inn .... F 620 793-8486
Great Bend *(G-2507)*
AmericInn Motel & Suites .... F 913 367-4000
Atchison *(G-203)*
Andrea Investments LLC .... E 785 823-1739
Salina *(G-10402)*
Angus Inn Best Western Motel .... D 620 792-3541
Great Bend *(G-2509)*
Apple Eght Hospitality MGT Inc .... E 913 338-3600
Overland Park *(G-8389)*
Apple Eght Hospitality MGT Inc .... E 316 636-4600
Wichita *(G-13722)*
Apple Eght Hospitality MGT Inc .... E 913 491-0010
Shawnee Mission *(G-11113)*
Apple Eght Svcs Ovrland Pk Inc .... E 913 327-7484
Overland Park *(G-8390)*

Apple Tree Inn F 620 331-5500
Independence *(G-3497)*
Ascend Learning Holdings LLC F 800 667-7531
Leawood *(G-5332)*
Atchison Hospitality Group LLC F 913 674-0033
Atchison *(G-210)*
B & L Motels Inc F 785 628-8008
Hays *(G-2753)*
B and L Motels E 913 451-5874
Overland Park *(G-8421)*
Bartlesville SW Hotel Inc D 913 345-2111
Lenexa *(G-5688)*
Beacon Hill Hotel Operator LLC F 316 260-9088
Wichita *(G-13823)*
Belleville Super 8 Motel F 785 527-2112
Belleville *(G-452)*
Belmont Hotels LLC F 785 823-6939
Salina *(G-10422)*
Best Western Bricktown Lodge F 620 251-3700
Coffeyville *(G-912)*
Best Western of Manhattan F 785 537-8300
Manhattan *(G-6556)*
Best Western Red Coach Inn F 316 283-9120
Newton *(G-7319)*
Best Wstn Cntry Inn & Suites F 620 225-7378
Dodge City *(G-1307)*
Best Wstn K C Spdway Inn Sites F 913 334-4440
Kansas City *(G-3857)*
Bethany College D 785 227-3380
Lindsborg *(G-6393)*
Bhakta LLC F 620 532-3118
Kingman *(G-4583)*
Bhcmc LLC B 620 682-7777
Dodge City *(G-1308)*
Booth Hotel LLC F 620 331-1704
Independence *(G-3501)*
Bradley Hotel Wichita E 316 262-2841
Wichita *(G-13881)*
Branding Iron Restaurant & CLB E 620 624-7254
Liberal *(G-6286)*
Brandon Hospitality LLC E 316 613-1995
Wichita *(G-13885)*
Bristol Hotel & Resorts Inc E 785 462-8787
Colby *(G-991)*
Bristol Hotel & Resorts Inc D 785 823-1739
Salina *(G-10431)*
Broadview Hsptlity Hldings LLC D 316 262-5000
Wichita *(G-13894)*
Bsrep II Ws Hotel Trs Sub LLC E 443 569-7053
Wichita *(G-13902)*
C & I LLC F 316 214-7308
Park City *(G-9607)*
C B H Consultants Inc E 620 624-9700
Liberal *(G-6289)*
Cambridge Suites Hotel F 316 263-1061
Wichita *(G-13930)*
Candlewood Suites Hotel F 913 768-8888
Olathe *(G-7574)*
Cave Inn LLC E 785 749-6010
Lawrence *(G-4777)*
Chaudhrys Investment Group F 913 856-8887
Gardner *(G-2332)*
Chaudhrys Investment Group Inc E 913 393-1111
Olathe *(G-7590)*
Cni Thl Propco Fe LLC E 785 271-6165
Topeka *(G-12482)*
Cobblestoner Inn and Suites F 620 896-2400
Harper *(G-2717)*
Comfort Inn F 620 793-9000
Great Bend *(G-2544)*
Comfort Inn F 316 744-7711
Park City *(G-9611)*
Comfort Inn & Suites E 620 231-8800
Pittsburg *(G-9838)*
Comfort Inn and Suites E 316 804-4866
Newton *(G-7331)*
Comfort Inn Kansas City F 913 299-5555
Kansas City *(G-3926)*
Comfort Suites F 620 672-9999
Pratt *(G-10102)*
Condor Hospitality Trust Inc F 620 232-1881
Pittsburg *(G-9843)*
Corporate East LLC F 620 356-5010
Ulysses *(G-13290)*
Corporate Hills LLC C 316 651-0333
Wichita *(G-14104)*
Cottage House Hotel and Motel F 620 767-6828
Council Grove *(G-1159)*
Cottonwood Inn E 785 543-2125
Phillipsburg *(G-9783)*
Country Inn Suites F 316 634-3900
Wichita *(G-14108)*
Courtyard By Marriott F 785 309-1300
Salina *(G-10466)*
Courtyard By Marriott F 913 339-9900
Shawnee Mission *(G-11274)*
Courtyard Kansas City Olathe E 913 839-4500
Olathe *(G-7624)*
Courtyard-Old Town E 316 264-5300
Wichita *(G-14116)*
Crystal Hospitality LLC E 913 680-1500
Leavenworth *(G-5229)*
Dab of Lenexa KS I LLC E 605 275-9499
Lenexa *(G-5799)*
Dab of Lenexa KS II LLC E 913 492-4516
Lenexa *(G-5800)*
Darco Inc E 620 221-7529
Winfield *(G-16138)*
Darlene Coffey F 620 229-8888
Winfield *(G-16139)*
Days Inn F 785 823-9791
Salina *(G-10471)*
Days Inn Inc F 316 942-1717
Wichita *(G-14176)*
Days Inn of Overland Park F 913 341-0100
Leawood *(G-5375)*
Days Inn Suites Hutchinson LLC F 620 665-3700
Hutchinson *(G-3259)*
Derby Hotel Inc F 316 425-7900
Derby *(G-1236)*
Derrick Inn E 785 798-3617
Ness City *(G-7261)*
Dodge Enteprise Inc E 620 227-2125
Dodge City *(G-1356)*
Double Tree Hilton F 316 945-5272
Wichita *(G-14230)*
Douglas Webb Co LP F 316 685-3777
Wichita *(G-14232)*
Drury Hotels Company LLC E 316 267-1961
Wichita *(G-14239)*
Drury Hotels Company LLC E 913 345-1500
Overland Park *(G-8662)*
Drury Hotels Company LLC E 913 236-9200
Shawnee Mission *(G-11319)*
Earth Rising Inc F 913 796-2141
Mc Louth *(G-6926)*
Econo Lodge E 785 242-3400
Ottawa *(G-8268)*
Econo Lodge F 785 625-4839
Hays *(G-2797)*
Eldridge House Invest Ltd Ptnr E 785 749-5011
Lawrence *(G-4850)*
Embassy Suites Olathe F 913 353-9280
Olathe *(G-7677)*
Englewood Beach House LLC F 913 385-5400
Prairie Village *(G-10027)*
Ep Resorts Inc E 970 586-5958
Olathe *(G-7689)*
Eqh - Leavenworth LLC F 913 651-8600
Leavenworth *(G-5236)*
ESA P Prtfolio Oper Lessee LLC F 316 652-8844
Wichita *(G-14304)*
ESA P Prtfolio Oper Lessee LLC F 913 661-9299
Overland Park *(G-8689)*
ESA P Prtfolio Oper Lessee LLC F 913 541-4000
Lenexa *(G-5836)*
ESA P Prtfolio Oper Lessee LLC F 913 236-6006
Merriam *(G-7092)*
Executive Mnor Leavenworth Inc F 785 234-5400
Topeka *(G-12586)*
Executives Inc F 316 685-8131
Wichita *(G-14320)*
Extended Stay America F 316 652-8844
Wichita *(G-14324)*
Extra Inn Inc E 620 232-2800
Pittsburg *(G-9859)*
Fairfeld Inn Suites Hutchinson F 620 259-8787
Hutchinson *(G-3281)*
Fairfield Inn By Marriott E 913 768-7000
Olathe *(G-7700)*
Fairfield Inn By Marrtt Wichta E 316 685-3777
Wichita *(G-14334)*
Farmers Dream Inc F 785 562-5588
Marysville *(G-6888)*
Ferguson Properties Inc E 785 625-3344
Hays *(G-2805)*
First Call Hospitality LLC E 913 345-2661
Shawnee Mission *(G-11368)*
Five Star Hotel Management F 316 686-7331
Wichita *(G-14380)*
Flint Hills Hospitality LLC F 785 320-7995
Manhattan *(G-6634)*
Flint Oak E 620 658-4401
Fall River *(G-1927)*
Fossil Creek Hotel & Suites E 785 483-4200
Russell *(G-10274)*
Four of Wichita Inc E 316 943-2373
Wichita *(G-14407)*
Four of Wichita Inc E 316 636-2022
Wichita *(G-14408)*
Four of Wichita Inc E 316 634-2303
Wichita *(G-14409)*
Four of Wichita Inc F 316 858-3343
Wichita *(G-14410)*
Four Points By Sheraton F 785 539-5311
Manhattan *(G-6639)*
Frontier Lodging Concordia LLC F 785 243-2700
Concordia *(G-1111)*
Frontier Lodging Liberal LLC E 620 624-9700
Liberal *(G-6310)*
Fryslie Inc F 620 672-6407
Pratt *(G-10116)*
Gardner Hospitality LLC E 913 856-2100
Gardner *(G-2349)*
Gary Dean Anderson E 785 475-2340
Oberlin *(G-7495)*
Gateway Inn D 620 624-0242
Liberal *(G-6311)*
Gbk Ventures LLC F 620 603-6565
Great Bend *(G-2569)*
Gli LLC F 913 648-7858
Overland Park *(G-8757)*
Golden Eagle Casino B 785 486-6601
Horton *(G-3125)*
Grand Central Hotel Corp E 620 273-6763
Cottonwood Falls *(G-1154)*
Grand Prairie Ht & Convention C 620 669-9311
Hutchinson *(G-3303)*
Great Wolf Kansas Spe LLC B 913 299-7001
Kansas City *(G-4047)*
Great Wolf Lodge Kansas Cy LLC F 913 299-7001
Kansas City *(G-4048)*
Greenwich Hotel LLC E 316 925-5100
Wichita *(G-14512)*
H Schwaller & Sons Inc F 785 628-6162
Hays *(G-2822)*
Hampton Inn F 316 636-5594
Wichita *(G-14551)*
Hampton Inn F 620 272-0454
Garden City *(G-2191)*
Hampton Inn F 785 460-2333
Colby *(G-1010)*
Hampton Inn E 913 328-1400
Kansas City *(G-4064)*
Hampton Inn F 785 228-0111
Topeka *(G-12663)*
Hampton Inn Hays-North I-70 F 785 621-4444
Hays *(G-2825)*
Hampton Inn Junction City F 785 579-4633
Junction City *(G-3698)*
Hampton Inn Suites F 620 604-0699
Liberal *(G-6316)*
Hampton Inns LLC E 785 823-9800
Salina *(G-10533)*
Hardage Hotels I LLC F 913 491-3333
Shawnee Mission *(G-11409)*
Hawthorn Suites F 913 344-8100
Overland Park *(G-8799)*
HCW Wichita Hotel LLC E 316 925-6600
Wichita *(G-14573)*
Heart America Management LLC E 913 397-0100
Olathe *(G-7762)*
Heart of America Inn Inc E 785 827-9315
Salina *(G-10538)*
Hedrick Exotic Animal Farm E 620 422-3245
Nickerson *(G-7433)*
Heritage Inn Wichita Opco LLC E 316 686-2844
Wichita *(G-14595)*
HI Hritg Inn Wchita Opco LLC E 316 686-3576
Wichita *(G-14603)*
Hi-Plains Motel & Restaurant F 620 375-4438
Leoti *(G-6254)*
Highland Lodging LLC F 620 792-2431
Great Bend *(G-2591)*
Hilltop Lodge C 785 738-2509
Beloit *(G-487)*
Hilton Garden Inn 23930 D 913 342-7900
Kansas City *(G-4081)*
Hit Portfolio I Hil Trs LLC E 816 464-5454
Overland Park *(G-8816)*

S I C

Hit Portfolio I Trs LLC F 913 451-2553
Overland Park *(G-8817)*
Holiday Inn & Suites F 620 508-6350
Pratt *(G-10120)*
Holiday Inn Ex Ht & Suites E 785 263-4049
Abilene *(G-38)*
Holiday Inn Ex Suites Topeka N F 785 861-7200
Topeka *(G-12697)*
Holiday Inn Express F 913 250-1000
Lansing *(G-4675)*
Holiday Inn Express F 785 625-8000
Hays *(G-2848)*
Holiday Inn Express F 785 890-9060
Goodland *(G-2478)*
Holiday Inn Express & Suites F 316 804-7040
Newton *(G-7362)*
Holiday Inn Express & Suites E 785 404-3300
Salina *(G-10544)*
Holiday Inn Express & Suites E 620 431-0817
Chanute *(G-732)*
Holiday Inn Express and Suites F 316 322-7275
El Dorado *(G-1566)*
Holiday Inn Express Village W F 913 328-1024
Kansas City *(G-4084)*
Hospice Incorporated E 316 283-1103
Newton *(G-7363)*
Hospitality Oakley Group LLC F 785 671-1111
Oakley *(G-7476)*
Hotel At Old Town Inc E 316 267-4800
Wichita *(G-14640)*
Hotel Clubs Corp Woods Inc D 913 451-6100
Overland Park *(G-8829)*
Hotel Wichita Greenwich F 316 681-1800
Wichita *(G-14641)*
Howard Johnson Express Inn F 316 943-8165
Wichita *(G-14643)*
Hpt Trs Ihg 2 Inc F 316 942-0400
Wichita *(G-14644)*
Hpt Trs Ihg-2 Inc F 913 469-5557
Shawnee Mission *(G-11442)*
Hpt Trs Ihg-2 Inc F 316 634-6070
Wichita *(G-14645)*
Hulsing Hotels Kansas Inc D 785 841-7077
Lawrence *(G-4906)*
Hulsing Hotels Kansas Inc D 785 539-5311
Manhattan *(G-6662)*
Hyatt Corporation C 316 293-1234
Wichita *(G-14661)*
I Samco Investments Ltd D 913 345-2111
Shawnee Mission *(G-11447)*
Im Olathe LP E 913 829-6700
Olathe *(G-7786)*
Inland Industries Inc G 913 492-9050
Bucyrus *(G-600)*
Inn Hampton and Suites F 620 225-0000
Dodge City *(G-1378)*
Inntel Corporation of America E 316 684-3466
Wichita *(G-14696)*
Innworks Inc F 620 342-7567
Emporia *(G-1777)*
Island Hospitality MGT LLC E 316 631-3773
Wichita *(G-14732)*
Janki Inc F 620 225-7373
Dodge City *(G-1382)*
Jay Maa Ambe LLC E 785 554-1044
Kansas City *(G-4118)*
Jefferson St Ht Partners LLC D 785 234-5400
Topeka *(G-12742)*
Jnn LLC E 785 843-9100
Lawrence *(G-4923)*
Jrko LLC E 913 648-7858
Shawnee Mission *(G-11503)*
Junction City Lodging LLC E 785 579-5787
Junction City *(G-3705)*
K & S LLC D 620 275-7471
Garden City *(G-2211)*
Kan Tex Hospitality Inc F 785 404-1870
Salina *(G-10561)*
Kandarpam Hotels LLC E 785 762-4200
Lenexa *(G-5935)*
Kansas Entertaiment LLC E 913 288-9300
Kansas City *(G-4154)*
Kansas Global Hotel LLC E 913 722-0800
Merriam *(G-7098)*
Kansas Inn Limited Partnership F 316 269-9999
Wichita *(G-14809)*
Kansas Investment Corporation F 785 843-6611
Lawrence *(G-4933)*
Kcai LP E 913 596-6000
Kansas City *(G-4166)*
Kellogg Hospitality LLC E 316 942-5600
Wichita *(G-14845)*
Kickapoo Tribe In Kansas Inc C 785 486-2131
Horton *(G-3130)*
Kinseth Hospitality Co Inc D 316 686-7131
Wichita *(G-14864)*
Knights Inn F 316 942-1341
Wichita *(G-14870)*
Krina Corporation F 620 251-1034
Coffeyville *(G-953)*
KS City Marriott Overland Park E 913 338-8627
Overland Park *(G-8930)*
Ladiwalla Hospitality LLC F 316 773-1700
Wichita *(G-14911)*
Lake Perry Yacht & Marina LLC F 785 783-4927
Perry *(G-9771)*
Lake Pointe Hotel Co LLC F 913 451-1222
Shawnee Mission *(G-11546)*
Laquinta Inn and Suites F 913 648-5555
Overland Park *(G-8946)*
Laxminarayan Lodging Llc F 785 462-3933
Colby *(G-1025)*
Leisure Hotel Corporation E 913 250-1000
Lansing *(G-4685)*
Leisure Hotel Corporation D 913 905-1460
Lenexa *(G-5966)*
Leisure Hotel Corporation D 316 832-9387
Park City *(G-9627)*
Leisure Hotel Corporation F 620 225-3924
Dodge City *(G-1397)*
Leisure Hotel Corporation E 620 227-5000
Dodge City *(G-1398)*
Leisure Hotel Corporation E 620 275-5900
Garden City *(G-2224)*
Lenexa City Center Hotel Corp E 913 742-7777
Lenexa *(G-5968)*
Lenexa Hotel LP A 785 841-3100
Lawrence *(G-4993)*
Lenexa Hotel LP D 913 217-1000
Lenexa *(G-5970)*
Liberal Super 8 Motel E 620 624-8880
Liberal *(G-6336)*
Lighthouse Properties LLC E 785 825-2221
Salina *(G-10583)*
Lighthouse Properties LLC E 316 260-8844
Wichita *(G-14964)*
Lilken Lllp E 785 749-7555
Lawrence *(G-4997)*
Lodge F 785 594-0574
Baldwin City *(G-365)*
Lodgeworks LP E 316 681-5100
Wichita *(G-14973)*
Lodgian Inc E 785 841-7077
Lawrence *(G-5000)*
Lodging Enterprises Inc E 620 326-8191
Wellington *(G-13512)*
Lodging Enterprises LLC F 785 852-4664
Sharon Springs *(G-10900)*
Lodging Enterprises LLC A 316 630-6300
Wichita *(G-14975)*
Lq Management LLC E 913 492-5500
Lenexa *(G-5980)*
Maa Santoshi LLC E 620 665-9800
Hutchinson *(G-3361)*
Magers Lodgings Inc E 785 841-4994
Lawrence *(G-5006)*
Mark 8 Inn Lc F 316 265-4679
Wichita *(G-15008)*
Mark Randolf F 620 431-7788
Chanute *(G-742)*
Marriott International Inc B 913 451-8000
Shawnee Mission *(G-11600)*
Masonic Lodge F 620 662-7012
Hutchinson *(G-3366)*
Mclcv Courtyard By Marriott F 913 317-8500
Overland Park *(G-9002)*
Merrifield Hotel Associates LP E 316 681-5100
Wichita *(G-15046)*
Microtel Inn & Suites F 620 331-0088
Independence *(G-3540)*
Midas Lenexa LLC D 913 225-9955
Lenexa *(G-5999)*
Midland Properties Inc F 913 677-5300
Mission Woods *(G-7151)*
Midwest Heritage Inn F 785 273-6800
Topeka *(G-12901)*
Midwest Star Equities LLC F 620 225-3000
Dodge City *(G-1406)*
Minter-Wilson Drilling Co Inc E 620 275-7471
Garden City *(G-2238)*
Minter-Wilson Drilling Co Inc F 620 276-8269
Garden City *(G-2237)*
Mokan Hospitality LLC E 913 541-9999
Olathe *(G-7907)*
Motel 6 F 316 684-6363
Wichita *(G-15131)*
Motel 6 Operating LP F 316 945-8440
Wichita *(G-15132)*
Motel 6 Operating LP F 785 827-8397
Salina *(G-10607)*
Motel 6 Operating LP F 913 541-8558
Shawnee Mission *(G-11655)*
Motel 6 Operating LP F 785 537-1022
Manhattan *(G-6752)*
Motel 6 Operating LP F 785 273-2896
Topeka *(G-12915)*
Motel 6 Operating LP F 785 272-8283
Topeka *(G-12916)*
Motel 6 Operating LP F 620 343-1240
Emporia *(G-1798)*
Nebco Inc F 785 462-3943
Salina *(G-10610)*
News Publishing Co Inc D 785 628-1081
Hays *(G-2877)*
Nogales Hotel Company LLC E 785 238-1454
Junction City *(G-3732)*
Oak Tree and Pennys Diner F 785 562-1234
Marysville *(G-6904)*
Olathe Hotels LLC F 913 829-6700
Olathe *(G-7939)*
Oread Hotel E 785 843-1200
Lawrence *(G-5046)*
Overland Park Development Corp D 913 234-2100
Overland Park *(G-9117)*
Overland Park Hospitality LLC E 913 312-0900
Shawnee Mission *(G-11708)*
Overland Park Hotel Assoc Lc C 913 888-8440
Overland Park *(G-9120)*
Oz Accommodations Inc F 913 894-8400
Overland Park *(G-9131)*
P & A Investments E 316 634-2303
Wichita *(G-15246)*
Paola Inn and Suites F 913 294-3700
Paola *(G-9580)*
Park Hotels & Resorts Inc D 913 649-7060
Shawnee Mission *(G-11716)*
Park-Rn Overland Park LLC F 913 850-5400
Overland Park *(G-9142)*
Payal Hotels LLC F 785 579-5787
Junction City *(G-3736)*
▲ Phillip G Ruffin F 316 942-7940
Wichita *(G-15291)*
Pillar Hotels and Resorts LLC E 785 271-6165
Topeka *(G-12974)*
Prairie Band Casino and Resort A 785 966-7777
Mayetta *(G-6916)*
Prairie Inn Inc E 316 283-3330
Newton *(G-7406)*
Pssk LLC F 620 277-7100
Garden City *(G-2260)*
Quality Inn F 785 784-5106
Junction City *(G-3744)*
Quality Inn F 785 770-8000
Manhattan *(G-6784)*
Quality Inn D 620 663-4444
South Hutchinson *(G-12064)*
Quality Suites Airport F 316 945-2600
Wichita *(G-15385)*
Rainbow Village Management E 913 677-3060
Kansas City *(G-4361)*
Ramada Conference Center Salin F 785 823-1739
Salina *(G-10650)*
Red Coach Inn E 316 321-6900
El Dorado *(G-1597)*
Regency Midwest Ventures Limit E 785 273-8888
Topeka *(G-13004)*
Relax Investments Inc F 785 838-4242
Lawrence *(G-5092)*
Residence Inn By Marriott LLC C 316 686-7331
Wichita *(G-15448)*
Rest Easy LLC E 913 684-4091
Fort Leavenworth *(G-1941)*
Revocable Trust B 785 210-1500
Junction City *(G-3748)*
Rhw Hotel Holdings Company LLC F 913 451-1222
Shawnee Mission *(G-11798)*
Rhw Management Inc E 785 776-8829
Manhattan *(G-6792)*
Rhw Management Inc F 913 451-1222
Shawnee Mission *(G-11799)*

Rhw Management Inc ....E 913 768-7000
Olathe (G-8033)
Rhw Management Inc ....E 913 631-8800
Shawnee (G-11019)
Rhw Management Inc ....E 913 722-0800
Shawnee Mission (G-11800)
Rhw Management Inc ....F 913 397-9455
Olathe (G-8034)
Rl Heritage Inn of Kc LLC ....E 913 788-5650
Kansas City (G-4377)
Riley Hotel Suites LLC ....E 785 539-2400
Manhattan (G-6793)
Rockgate Management Company ....E 402 331-0101
Overland Park (G-9253)
Rothfuss Motels ....F 785 632-2148
Clay Center (G-878)
Rothfuss Motels ....F 785 632-5611
Clay Center (G-879)
Ruffin Hotel of Wichita LLC ....F 316 685-3777
Wichita (G-15492)
Ruffin Riverfront Hotel LLC ....D 316 293-1234
Wichita (G-15493)
Russells America Inn LLC ....F 785 483-4200
Russell (G-10298)
S & B Motels Inc ....E 785 899-7181
Goodland (G-2484)
S & B Motels Inc ....C 316 522-3864
Wichita (G-15499)
S & B Motels Inc ....F 785 823-8808
Salina (G-10656)
Sabetha Country Inn Inc ....E 785 284-2300
Sabetha (G-10327)
Sady Vijay Inc ....F 620 343-7750
Emporia (G-1819)
Sagar Inc ....D 620 241-5566
McPherson (G-7022)
Sagar Inc ....E 620 241-5343
McPherson (G-7023)
Sagar Inc ....E 620 241-5343
McPherson (G-7024)
Salina KS Lodging LLC ....E 785 827-1271
Salina (G-10679)
Salina Red Coach Inn ....F 785 825-2111
Salina (G-10684)
Sana Hospitality Corp ....F 620 342-7567
Emporia (G-1822)
Sand Dollar Hospitality 2 LLC ....E 913 299-4700
Kansas City (G-4400)
Sands Motor Inn ....F 620 356-1404
Ulysses (G-13317)
Schwartz Inc ....F 620 275-5800
Garden City (G-2276)
Scotsman Inn West LLC ....E 316 943-3800
Wichita (G-15537)
Select Hotels Group LLC ....E 913 491-9002
Overland Park (G-9289)
Senate Luxury Suites Inc ....F 785 233-5050
Topeka (G-13057)
Service Oil Company ....F 785 462-3441
Colby (G-1040)
Settle Inn ....F 913 381-5700
Overland Park (G-9300)
SF Hotel Company LP ....D 316 681-5100
Wichita (G-15569)
Shamir Corp ....E 785 266-8880
Topeka (G-13062)
Shawnee Inn Inc ....E 913 248-1900
Shawnee Mission (G-11852)
Shirconn Investments Inc ....F 913 390-9500
Olathe (G-8064)
Show ME Birds Hunting Resort ....F 620 674-8863
Baxter Springs (G-413)
Shree Ram Investments of Pltte ....F 913 948-9000
Olathe (G-8065)
Shree-Guru Investments Inc ....F 785 273-0003
Topeka (G-13071)
Shreeji Investments Inc ....F 785 838-4242
Lawrence (G-5110)
Shri Ram Corp ....F 248 477-3200
Lenexa (G-6133)
Shriji Inc ....F 785 242-9898
Ottawa (G-8312)
Si Overland Park LP ....D 913 345-2661
Overland Park (G-9310)
Single Tree Inn ....E 620 356-1500
Ulysses (G-13318)
Six Continents Hotels Inc ....D 785 827-9000
Salina (G-10709)
Six Continents Hotels Inc ....D 620 792-2431
Great Bend (G-2636)
Six Continents Hotels Inc ....E 785 462-8787
Colby (G-1041)
Skyline Motel ....F 620 431-1500
Chanute (G-762)
Slawson Exploration Co Inc ....E 316 263-3201
Wichita (G-15603)
Slawson Investment Corporation ....E 316 263-3201
Wichita (G-15604)
Sleep Inn & Suites ....F 620 223-2555
Fort Scott (G-2005)
Sleep Inn & Suites Parsons ....F 620 421-6126
Parsons (G-9738)
Sleep Inn and Suite ....F 620 688-6400
Coffeyville (G-978)
Sleep Inn and Suites 07 ....F 620 805-6535
Garden City (G-2281)
Sleep Inn Inn & Suites ....F 785 625-2700
Hays (G-2908)
Sleep Inn Suite ....F 316 425-6077
Haysville (G-2960)
Sonar Sangam Inc ....F 316 529-4911
Wichita (G-15613)
Springhill Suites ....F 316 260-4404
Wichita (G-15648)
Starwood Htls & Rsrts Wrldwde ....B 888 625-4988
Wichita (G-15659)
Sterling Centrecorp Inc ....E 785 841-6500
Lawrence (G-5124)
Sterling Centrecorp Inc ....E 913 651-6000
Leavenworth (G-5291)
Sterling Centrecorp Inc ....F 785 242-7000
Ottawa (G-8314)
Sugarcat Hospitality Inc ....F 620 275-5800
Garden City (G-2292)
Summit Group of Salina KS LP ....F 785 826-1711
Salina (G-10718)
Summit Hospitality LLC ....E 970 765-5690
Salina (G-10719)
Summit Hotel Properties Inc ....E 785 826-1711
Salina (G-10720)
Summit Hotel Properties LLC ....F 620 341-9393
Emporia (G-1833)
Sunflower Partners Inc ....E 785 462-3933
Colby (G-1042)
Sunset Inn ....F 316 321-9172
El Dorado (G-1605)
Sunstar Wichita Inc ....E 316 943-2181
Wichita (G-15690)
Super 8 Hotel In Colby Kansas ....F 785 462-8248
Colby (G-1043)
Super 8 Motel ....F 913 721-3877
Bonner Springs (G-576)
Super 8 Motel ....E 785 743-6442
Wakeeney (G-13391)
Super 8 Motel ....F 316 945-5261
Wichita (G-15691)
Super 8 Motel ....F 620 421-8000
Parsons (G-9742)
Super 8 Motel of Beloit ....F 785 738-4300
Beloit (G-504)
Super 8 Motel of Concordia ....F 785 243-4200
Concordia (G-1132)
Super 8 Motel of Pratt Inc ....F 620 672-5945
Pratt (G-10157)
Swami Inc ....F 785 228-2500
Topeka (G-13128)
Swami Investment Inc ....F 913 788-9929
Kansas City (G-4451)
Swedish Country Inn ....F 785 227-2985
Lindsborg (G-6406)
T M H Hotels Inc ....E 316 669-6175
Wichita (G-15713)
Tenth Street Ht Partners LLC ....F 785 233-5411
Topeka (G-13150)
Tenth Street Ht Partners LLC ....E 785 228-9500
Topeka (G-13151)
Tgc Greenwich Hotel LLC ....E 316 500-2660
Wichita (G-15754)
Tirupati Balaji LLC ....F 913 262-9600
Overland Park (G-9412)
Tps Leavenworth Lp ....E 913 297-5400
Leavenworth (G-5299)
▲ Transitions Group Inc ....E 316 262-9100
Wichita (G-15791)
True North Hotel Group Inc ....F 913 341-4440
Shawnee Mission (G-11944)
Tucson Hotels LP ....C 785 431-7200
Topeka (G-13201)
Tucson Hotels LP ....C 785 210-1500
Junction City (G-3760)
Turnpike Investments Inc ....F 316 524-4400
Wichita (G-15816)
Tusar Inc ....E 316 522-1800
Wichita (G-15817)
V & R Motel LLC ....F 620 331-8288
Independence (G-3570)
Value Place Hotel ....F 913 831-1417
Shawnee Mission (G-11975)
Value Place Topeka ....F 785 271-8862
Overland Park (G-9459)
Vchp Wichita LLC ....E 316 685-1281
Wichita (G-15872)
Ventura Hotel Corp ....C 785 841-3100
Lawrence (G-5173)
Venture Hotels LLC ....E 620 231-1177
Pittsburg (G-9954)
W2005/Fargo Hotels (pool C) ....E 785 271-6165
Topeka (G-13228)
Wamego Inn and Suites ....F 785 458-8888
Wamego (G-13452)
Waterfront Assisted Living ....F 316 945-3344
Wichita (G-15936)
Wichita Airport Ht Assoc L P ....C 316 945-5272
Wichita (G-15971)
Wichita Aloft ....F 316 744-1100
Wichita (G-15972)
Wichita Arprt Hospitality LLC ....F 316 522-0008
Wichita (G-15977)
Wichita East Hotel Associates ....D 316 686-7131
Wichita (G-15996)
Wichita Hspttlity Holdings LLC ....E 316 685-1281
Wichita (G-16006)
Wichita Inn Suites Inc ....E 316 685-2233
Wichita (G-16008)
Wichita Residence Assoc LP ....E 316 263-1061
Wichita (G-16020)
Wingate Inns International Inc ....E 620 241-5566
McPherson (G-7043)
Wingate Inns International Inc ....E 316 733-8833
Andover (G-117)
Woods of Cherry Creek Inc ....F 913 491-3030
Overland Park (G-9504)
Woofter Woofter Stupka Inc ....E 785 460-6683
Colby (G-1050)
Ww Kc Metcalf LLC ....F 913 956-0234
Leawood (G-5602)
Wyndham Garden ....F 316 269-2090
Wichita (G-16080)
Wyndham International Inc ....E 913 383-2550
Overland Park (G-9509)
Wyndham International Inc ....F 316 729-5700
Wichita (G-16081)

7021 Rooming & Boarding Houses

Blue Valley Partners LP ....E 913 963-5534
Prairie Village (G-10016)
College Park Univ Xing Fully ....F 785 539-0500
Manhattan (G-6594)
Hutchinson Community College ....F 620 665-3500
Hutchinson (G-3320)
Kansas State University ....B 785 532-6376
Manhattan (G-6681)
Lbubs 2003-C5 Nismith Hall LLC ....F 785 832-8676
Lawrence (G-4990)
Leisure Hotel Corporation ....F 620 225-3924
Dodge City (G-1397)
Visiting Nurses Association ....D 785 843-3738
Lawrence (G-5175)

7032 Sporting & Recreational Camps

Alexander Camp ....E 620 342-1386
Emporia (G-1694)
Association of Kansas Nebraska ....F 785 468-3638
Olsburg (G-8168)
Earth Rising Inc ....F 913 796-2141
Mc Louth (G-6926)
Junction City Family YMCA Inc ....E 785 762-4780
Junction City (G-3704)
Kings Camp & Retreat Center ....E 316 794-2913
Goddard (G-2444)
Lakeside Camp of The United ....F 620 872-2021
Scott City (G-10819)
Show ME Birds Hunting Resort ....F 620 674-8863
Baxter Springs (G-413)
Volley Ball Inc ....E 913 422-4070
Shawnee (G-11048)
YMCA Topeaka Downtown Branch ....E 785 354-8591
Topeka (G-13256)
Young Mens Christian ....F 785 233-9815
Topeka (G-13258)

S I C

Young Mens Christian Assn..................E....... 620 275-1199
Garden City *(G-2319)*
Young Mens Christian Associa..............C....... 316 219-9622
Wichita *(G-16093)*
Young Mens Christian Associa..............D....... 316 320-9622
El Dorado *(G-1616)*
Young Mens Christian Associa..............D....... 316 260-9622
Wichita *(G-16094)*
Young Mens Christian Associa..............C....... 316 942-5511
Wichita *(G-16095)*
Young Mens Christian Associat............C....... 620 545-7290
Viola *(G-13380)*
Young Mens Christian Gr Kansas.........D....... 913 362-3489
Prairie Village *(G-10088)*
Young Mens Christian Gr Kansas.........C....... 913 393-9622
Olathe *(G-8163)*
Young Mens Christian Gr Kansas.........D....... 913 782-7707
Olathe *(G-8164)*
Young MNS Chrstn Assn of Tpeka.......C....... 785 354-8591
Topeka *(G-13259)*
Young MNS Chrstn Assn Pttsburg........D....... 620 231-1100
Pittsburg *(G-9972)*

7033 Trailer Parks & Camp Sites

Association of Kansas Nebraska..........E....... 785 478-4726
Topeka *(G-12345)*
Four Seasons Rv Acres Inc..................E....... 785 598-2221
Abilene *(G-32)*
Kansas 4-H Foundation Inc...................F....... 785 257-3221
Junction City *(G-3712)*
Lamont Hill Resort Inc..........................E....... 785 828-3131
Vassar *(G-13371)*
North Shore Marina MGT LLC..............G....... 785 453-2240
Quenemo *(G-10178)*
Saint Francis Acdmy Inc Atchsn...........E....... 913 367-5005
Atchison *(G-259)*
Water Spt Rcreation Campground........F....... 620 225-9003
Dodge City *(G-1450)*

7041 Membership-Basis Hotels

Alpha CHI Omega...................................F....... 785 843-7600
Lawrence *(G-4731)*
Beta Theta PHI.......................................F....... 785 843-9188
Lawrence *(G-4756)*
Delta Gamma..F....... 785 830-9945
Lawrence *(G-4831)*
Delta Omega of Delta Zeta Bldg...........E....... 785 625-3719
Hays *(G-2784)*
Linn Valley Lake Property Assn............E....... 913 757-4591
Linn Valley *(G-6414)*
Masonic Order..E....... 785 625-3127
Hays *(G-2870)*

72 PERSONAL SERVICES

7211 Power Laundries, Family & Commercial

Cintas Corporation No 2........................C....... 913 782-8333
Olathe *(G-7596)*
Just Our Laundry Inc.............................F....... 913 649-8364
Shawnee Mission *(G-11505)*
Penn Enterprises Inc.............................E....... 785 762-3600
Junction City *(G-3737)*
Scotch Industries Inc.............................E....... 785 843-8585
Lawrence *(G-5105)*

7212 Garment Pressing & Cleaners' Agents

Band Box Corporation...........................E....... 785 272-6646
Topeka *(G-12361)*

7213 Linen Sply

Ameripride Services Inc.......................D....... 785 234-3475
Topeka *(G-12324)*
Aramark Unf & Career AP LLC..............E....... 913 351-3534
Lansing *(G-4667)*
Aramark Unf & Career AP LLC..............D....... 316 262-5467
Wichita *(G-13726)*
Cintas Corporation................................C....... 913 782-8333
Olathe *(G-7595)*
Excel Linen Supply................................E....... 816 842-6565
Kansas City *(G-3999)*
Hospital Linen Services Inc..................D....... 913 621-2228
Kansas City *(G-4085)*
Ineeda Laundry & Dry Cleaners.............D....... 620 662-6450
Hutchinson *(G-3332)*
N C K Commercial Laundry Inc.............F....... 785 243-4432
Concordia *(G-1124)*
Unifirst Corporation..............................F....... 785 233-1550
Topeka *(G-13203)*
Unifirst Corporation..............................F....... 785 825-8766
Salina *(G-10745)*
Whiteway Inc..D....... 816 842-6565
Kansas City *(G-4541)*

7215 Coin Operated Laundries & Cleaning

Bubble Rm Coin Ldry Dry Clean...........F....... 913 962-4046
Shawnee Mission *(G-11188)*
Just Our Laundry Inc.............................F....... 913 649-8364
Shawnee Mission *(G-11505)*
Lamont Hill Resort Inc...........................E....... 785 828-3131
Vassar *(G-13371)*

7216 Dry Cleaning Plants, Except Rug Cleaning

Al Morris..F....... 620 225-5611
Dodge City *(G-1291)*
Band Box Corporation...........................E....... 785 272-6646
Topeka *(G-12361)*
Bayless Dry Cleaning Inc.......................F....... 620 793-3576
Great Bend *(G-2517)*
College Hill Cleaners Inc.......................F....... 316 683-3331
Wichita *(G-14055)*
Comet 1 H R Cleaners Inc.....................F....... 620 626-8100
Liberal *(G-6295)*
Dry Clean City.......................................F....... 785 776-1515
Manhattan *(G-6617)*
Elite Cleaners..F....... 316 651-5997
Wichita *(G-14269)*
Heartland At-Chlor Systems LLC..........F....... 806 373-4277
Wichita *(G-14580)*
Holiday Cleaners....................................F....... 913 631-6181
Overland Park *(G-8822)*
Hygienic Dry Cleaners Inc.....................E....... 785 478-0066
Topeka *(G-12710)*
Ineeda Laundry & Dry Cleaners.............D....... 620 662-6450
Hutchinson *(G-3332)*
Ineeda Laundry and Drycleaners...........E....... 620 663-5688
Hutchinson *(G-3333)*
Just Our Laundry Inc.............................F....... 913 649-8364
Shawnee Mission *(G-11505)*
Mjv Holdings LLC..................................F....... 913 432-5348
Shawnee Mission *(G-11650)*
Oak Park Cleaners Inc..........................F....... 913 599-3040
Shawnee Mission *(G-11692)*
Parker Enterprises Inc..........................E....... 316 682-4543
Wichita *(G-15263)*
Scotch Industries Inc.............................E....... 785 235-3401
Topeka *(G-13042)*
Scotch Industries Inc.............................E....... 785 843-8585
Lawrence *(G-5105)*
Stickels Inc..E....... 785 539-5722
Manhattan *(G-6812)*
Stovers Restoration Inc.........................F....... 316 686-5005
Maize *(G-6521)*

7217 Carpet & Upholstery Cleaning

All-Pro Services Inc...............................F....... 785 842-1402
Lawrence *(G-4727)*
Alliance Jantr Advisors Inc....................F....... 913 815-8807
Olathe *(G-7520)*
Bluestreak Enterprises Inc....................F....... 785 550-8179
Lawrence *(G-4761)*
Clean-Rite LLC......................................F....... 785 628-1945
Hays *(G-2771)*
Clk Inc...F....... 316 686-3238
Wichita *(G-14043)*
Dalan Inc..E....... 913 384-5662
Overland Park *(G-8631)*
Design Source Flooring LLC..................E....... 913 387-5858
Lenexa *(G-5813)*
First Response..F....... 913 557-2187
Paola *(G-9559)*
Givens Cleaning Contractors..................F....... 316 265-1315
Wichita *(G-14468)*
McGinleys Crpt Pro Jantr Svcs.............E....... 785 825-2627
Salina *(G-10596)*
Mid-America Maintenance Kansas........F....... 620 365-3872
Gas *(G-2391)*
Phoenix Restoration Service..................E....... 620 276-6994
Garden City *(G-2254)*
Pro Carpet Building Svcs LLC...............E....... 620 331-4304
Independence *(G-3549)*
Resource Service Solutions LLC............E....... 913 338-5050
Lenexa *(G-6107)*
ServiceMaster North Centl Kans...........F....... 785 243-1965
Concordia *(G-1130)*
Steam Action Restoration......................F....... 620 276-0622
Garden City *(G-2291)*
Steam Way Carpet Restorations............F....... 620 331-9553
Independence *(G-3563)*
Stovers Restoration Inc.........................F....... 316 686-5005
Maize *(G-6521)*

7218 Industrial Launderers

Ameripride Services Inc.......................D....... 785 234-3475
Topeka *(G-12324)*
Aramark Unf & Career AP LLC..............D....... 316 262-5467
Wichita *(G-13726)*
N C K Commercial Laundry Inc.............F....... 785 243-4432
Concordia *(G-1124)*
Penn Enterprises Inc.............................E....... 785 762-3600
Junction City *(G-3737)*
Unifirst Corporation..............................F....... 785 233-1550
Topeka *(G-13203)*
Unifirst Corporation..............................F....... 316 264-2342
Wichita *(G-15837)*
Unifirst Corporation..............................F....... 785 825-8766
Salina *(G-10745)*
Unifirst Corporation..............................D....... 620 275-0231
Garden City *(G-2306)*
Waxene Products Company Inc............G....... 316 263-8523
Wichita *(G-15938)*

7219 Laundry & Garment Svcs, NEC

Alaskan Fur Company Inc......................E....... 913 649-4000
Overland Park *(G-8365)*
Bayless Dry Cleaning Inc.......................F....... 620 793-3576
Great Bend *(G-2517)*
Best Value Services LLC........................D....... 316 440-1048
Wichita *(G-13839)*
Comet 1 H R Cleaners Inc.....................F....... 620 626-8100
Liberal *(G-6295)*
Expert Alteration....................................G....... 913 322-2242
Westwood *(G-13553)*
Mias Bridal & Tailoring LLC...................F....... 913 764-9114
Olathe *(G-7890)*
Scotch Industries Inc.............................E....... 785 843-8585
Lawrence *(G-5105)*
Something Different Inc........................G....... 785 537-1171
Wamego *(G-13441)*
U S S A Inc..G....... 316 686-1653
Wichita *(G-15826)*

7221 Photographic Studios, Portrait

Inter-State Studio & Pubg Co................D....... 913 745-6700
Bonner Springs *(G-556)*
Lifetouch Inc..E....... 316 262-6611
Wichita *(G-14962)*
Scholastic Photography Inc...................F....... 913 384-9126
Shawnee Mission *(G-11837)*
Sears Roebuck and Co..........................C....... 785 826-4378
Salina *(G-10701)*
Tpp Acquisition Inc................................F....... 913 317-5591
Overland Park *(G-9421)*
Walmart Inc...B....... 620 275-0775
Garden City *(G-2308)*

7231 Beauty Shops

A Total Image..F....... 785 272-2855
Topeka *(G-12279)*
All In Cut..F....... 316 722-4962
Wichita *(G-13664)*
Bath & Body Works LLC........................F....... 620 338-8409
Dodge City *(G-1304)*
Bath & Body Works LLC........................F....... 785 749-0214
Lawrence *(G-4751)*
Beauty Brands LLC................................E....... 816 505-2800
Kansas City *(G-3850)*
Beauty Brands LLC................................E....... 913 492-7900
Lenexa *(G-5694)*
Beauty Brands LLC................................E....... 913 393-4800
Olathe *(G-7549)*
Beauty Brands LLC................................E....... 785 228-9778
Topeka *(G-12369)*
Beauty Brands LLC................................E....... 913 663-4848
Shawnee Mission *(G-11157)*
Beauty Brands LLC................................E....... 816 531-2266
Lenexa *(G-5695)*
Beauty Escntuals Salon Day Spa..........E....... 913 851-4644
Overland Park *(G-8437)*
Bella Vita Salon & Day Spa Inc.............E....... 913 651-6161
Leavenworth *(G-5207)*
Bijin For Hair..D....... 913 671-7777
Shawnee Mission *(G-11165)*
C & W Operations Ltd...........................C....... 913 438-6400
Shawnee Mission *(G-11196)*

C & W Operations Ltd.....F 913 299-8820
Kansas City *(G-3884)*
C & W Operations Ltd.....F 913 268-1032
Shawnee Mission *(G-11197)*
California Nail Salon.....F 316 942-5400
Wichita *(G-13927)*
Capelli Hair & Nail Salon.....F 785 271-6811
Topeka *(G-12423)*
Chez Belle.....F 316 682-7323
Wichita *(G-14003)*
Courtland Day Spa.....F 620 223-0098
Fort Scott *(G-1962)*
Creative Hairlines Inc.....E 620 241-3535
McPherson *(G-6953)*
Design Court.....F 620 276-3019
Garden City *(G-2145)*
Diane Londene.....F 785 233-1991
Topeka *(G-12556)*
Dream Waves LLC.....F 316 942-9283
Wichita *(G-14237)*
Eastside Barbershop & Salon.....E 800 857-2906
Topeka *(G-12569)*
Eric Fisher Salon.....F 316 729-0777
Wichita *(G-14300)*
European Wax Center.....F 316 425-0909
Wichita *(G-14309)*
Executive Hills Style Shop.....F 913 451-1204
Shawnee Mission *(G-11355)*
Exsalonce LLC.....F 785 823-1724
Salina *(G-10493)*
Extreme Tanning Inc.....F 316 712-0190
Wichita *(G-14325)*
Facial Expressions LLC.....F 316 390-0417
Wichita *(G-14331)*
First Class Hair.....F 316 721-2662
Wichita *(G-14373)*
Gaia Inc.....F 785 539-2622
Manhattan *(G-6643)*
Geesu Inc.....F 913 648-0087
Shawnee Mission *(G-11392)*
Golden Key Salon.....F 316 744-0230
Bel Aire *(G-433)*
Gq Inc.....F 785 843-2138
Lawrence *(G-4878)*
Gram Enterprises Inc.....E 913 888-3689
Lenexa *(G-5879)*
Great Clips.....F 913 727-1917
Leavenworth *(G-5246)*
Great Clips For Hair.....F 913 888-7447
Lenexa *(G-5883)*
Great Clips For Hair.....E 913 888-3400
Overland Park *(G-8770)*
Great Clips For Hair.....F 913 338-2580
Overland Park *(G-8771)*
Green Medical Group.....E 316 691-3937
Wichita *(G-14511)*
Hair Affaire.....F 785 827-0445
Salina *(G-10529)*
Hair Connection.....F 316 685-7213
Wichita *(G-14541)*
Hair Cutting Company.....F 316 283-0532
Newton *(G-7356)*
Hair Design Company.....F 913 897-4776
Overland Park *(G-8784)*
Hair E Clips Ltd.....F 620 793-9050
Great Bend *(G-2589)*
Hair Experts.....E 785 776-4455
Manhattan *(G-6650)*
Hair Experts Design Team.....F 785 841-6886
Lawrence *(G-4885)*
Hair Force.....F 316 684-3361
Wichita *(G-14542)*
Hair Loft.....F 785 827-2306
Salina *(G-10530)*
Hair Productions Inc.....F 785 273-2881
Topeka *(G-12658)*
Hair Shop & Retailing Center.....E 913 397-9888
Olathe *(G-7745)*
Hair Shop West Inc.....E 913 829-4868
Olathe *(G-7746)*
Hair Wear and Co.....F 785 625-2875
Hays *(G-2824)*
Hairem of Olathe LLC.....F 913 829-1260
Olathe *(G-7747)*
Haydens Salon and Day Spa.....F 620 663-2179
Hutchinson *(G-3308)*
Haynes Salon and Supply Inc.....F 785 539-5512
Manhattan *(G-6651)*
Hays Academy of Hair Design.....F 785 628-6624
Hays *(G-2827)*
His and Her Hairstyling Inc.....F 785 232-9724
Topeka *(G-12694)*
Images Salon & Day Spa.....F 785 843-2138
Lawrence *(G-4909)*
Jhon-Josephsons Salon.....E 913 338-4443
Shawnee Mission *(G-11490)*
K C D Inc.....F 785 827-0445
Salina *(G-10558)*
Kansas State University.....D 785 826-2646
Salina *(G-10567)*
Karen Tobin.....F 913 341-1976
Shawnee Mission *(G-11520)*
Keith Shaw.....F 316 262-7297
Wichita *(G-14841)*
Krizmans Beauty Salons Inc.....F 913 648-6080
Prairie Village *(G-10043)*
Lash Company LLC.....F 316 265-5527
Wichita *(G-14930)*
Lulu Salon & Spa.....F 913 648-3658
Shawnee Mission *(G-11583)*
Mane Event.....F 785 827-1999
Salina *(G-10590)*
Mane Thing.....E 785 762-2397
Junction City *(G-3723)*
Mary Kate & Company LLC.....F 316 721-4101
Wichita *(G-15016)*
Midland Clippers.....F 913 962-7070
Shawnee Mission *(G-11630)*
Monarch Skin Care.....E 913 317-9386
Shawnee Mission *(G-11653)*
Nail Perfection LLC.....F 913 722-0799
Roeland Park *(G-10228)*
Nail Pro.....F 913 402-0882
Shawnee Mission *(G-11665)*
Nailery.....F 913 599-2225
Overland Park *(G-9067)*
Nailery Too.....F 913 599-3331
Shawnee Mission *(G-11666)*
Oliver P Steinnagel Inc.....E 913 338-2266
Shawnee Mission *(G-11696)*
Par Exsalonce.....E 913 469-9532
Shawnee Mission *(G-11715)*
Perfect Details Inc.....F 913 592-5022
Spring Hill *(G-12096)*
Perfect Touch Inc.....F 316 522-9205
Wichita *(G-15281)*
Platinum Inc.....F 316 773-9700
Wichita *(G-15306)*
Prim and Polished LLC.....F 316 516-2537
Derby *(G-1265)*
Professional Hairstyling.....F 913 888-3536
Lenexa *(G-6072)*
Profiles Inc.....F 316 636-1214
Wichita *(G-15368)*
Regis Corporation.....F 316 685-5333
Wichita *(G-15439)*
Regis Corporation.....F 785 273-2992
Topeka *(G-13005)*
Regis Corporation.....F 785 628-2111
Hays *(G-2899)*
Regis Salon Corp.....E 785 273-2992
Topeka *(G-13006)*
Royal Spa.....F 316 681-0002
Wichita *(G-15488)*
Ruth Grimsley.....F 913 393-1711
Olathe *(G-8048)*
S-Kmac Investments LLC.....E 316 990-5095
Wichita *(G-15503)*
Salon 103.....F 913 383-9040
Overland Park *(G-9276)*
Salon Avanti.....F 913 829-2424
Olathe *(G-8051)*
Salon Brands.....F 785 301-2984
Hays *(G-2906)*
Salon Knotty.....F 316 636-4400
Wichita *(G-15511)*
Salon Mission Inc.....E 913 642-8333
Overland Park *(G-9277)*
Salon One 19 & Spa.....F 913 451-7119
Leawood *(G-5546)*
Salon Progressions & Day Spa.....F 316 729-1980
Wichita *(G-15512)*
Salon Ten O Seven.....E 785 628-6000
Hays *(G-2907)*
Salon X.....F 620 343-8634
Emporia *(G-1820)*
Sams Fantastic.....F 913 856-4247
Gardner *(G-2361)*
Shear Designers.....F 620 342-5393
Emporia *(G-1826)*
Stem 2 LLC.....E 913 236-9368
Merriam *(G-7106)*
Strands.....F 620 663-6397
Hutchinson *(G-3450)*
Styling Studios.....E 913 685-8800
Shawnee Mission *(G-11904)*
Supercuts Inc.....F 316 218-1400
Andover *(G-109)*
Svetas Body Therapy LLC.....F 316 630-0400
Wichita *(G-15706)*
Thairapy Salon.....F 316 321-6263
El Dorado *(G-1608)*
Tresses Hair Salon.....F 620 662-2299
Hutchinson *(G-3469)*
Ultimate Escape Day Spa LLC.....E 913 851-3385
Overland Park *(G-9438)*
Wave Review Salon.....F 913 345-9252
Shawnee Mission *(G-11997)*
Wichita Srgical Specialists PA.....E 316 688-7500
Wichita *(G-16027)*
Xiphium Hair Salon.....F 913 696-1616
Leawood *(G-5603)*

7241 Barber Shops

Crisp Cuts & Styles Etcllc.....F 816 916-1841
Shawnee Mission *(G-11280)*
Hair Experts Design Team.....F 785 841-6886
Lawrence *(G-4885)*
Professional Hairstyling.....F 913 888-3536
Lenexa *(G-6072)*
Ricks Barbr Sp & Natural Hair.....F 913 268-3944
Shawnee *(G-11020)*
Salon 103.....F 913 383-9040
Overland Park *(G-9276)*
Twice As Nice Barbershop.....F 319 201-4542
Wichita *(G-15821)*

7261 Funeral Svcs & Crematories

Alderwoods (kansas) Inc.....F 316 682-5575
Wichita *(G-13661)*
Amos Family Inc.....E 913 631-7314
Shawnee Mission *(G-11111)*
Bath-Naylor Inc.....F 620 231-4700
Pittsburg *(G-9823)*
Broadway Mortuary Inc.....F 316 262-3435
Wichita *(G-13896)*
Bryant-Funeral Home.....F 620 793-3525
Great Bend *(G-2523)*
Carriage Services Inc.....F 785 242-3550
Ottawa *(G-8253)*
Carriage Services Inc.....F 913 682-2820
Leavenworth *(G-5214)*
Charter Funerals Kansas LLC.....F 913 671-7222
Merriam *(G-7088)*
D W Newcomers Sons Inc.....F 913 451-1860
Overland Park *(G-8629)*
D W Newcomers Sons Inc.....E 316 684-8200
Wichita *(G-14160)*
Day Funeral Home Inc.....F 620 326-5100
Wellington *(G-13497)*
Downing & Lahey Inc.....F 316 733-2740
Wichita *(G-14234)*
Elliott Mortuary Inc.....F 620 663-3327
Hutchinson *(G-3277)*
Feuerborn Fmly Fnrl Svc.....F 620 365-2948
Iola *(G-3600)*
First Call.....F 785 234-2881
Topeka *(G-12612)*
Garnand Funeral Home Inc.....F 620 276-3219
Garden City *(G-2185)*
Hays Veterinary Hosp Prof Assn.....F 785 625-2719
Hays *(G-2839)*
Hospice Incorporated.....D 316 265-9441
Wichita *(G-14637)*
Johnson Bowser Funeral Chapel.....F 785 233-3039
Topeka *(G-12747)*
Johnson Mortuary Inc.....F 620 431-1220
Chanute *(G-734)*
Kimple Inc.....F 620 564-2300
Ellinwood *(G-1635)*
Larrison-Forsyth Fnrl HM LLC.....F 620 886-5641
Medicine Lodge *(G-7065)*
Lawrence Funeral Chapel Inc.....F 785 841-3822
Lawrence *(G-4967)*
Logan Funeral Home.....F 785 689-4211
Logan *(G-6426)*
Louis Dengel & Son Mortuary.....F 785 242-2323
Ottawa *(G-8285)*
Morris Newspaper Corp Kansas.....E 620 792-1211
Great Bend *(G-2613)*

SIC

Newcomer Funeral Svc Group Inc ....F 785 233-6655
Topeka *(G-12928)*
Newcomer Funeral Svc Group Inc ....F 785 354-8558
Topeka *(G-12929)*
Old Mission Mortuary ....E 316 686-7311
Wichita *(G-15214)*
Penwell Gbl Frl Wlf Brns Chpl ....F 620 251-3100
Coffeyville *(G-970)*
Preferred Mortuary Svcs LLC ....E 316 522-7300
Haysville *(G-2955)*
Resthaven Gardens of Memory ....E 316 722-2100
Wichita *(G-15450)*
Resthaven Mortuary Inc ....F 316 722-2100
Wichita *(G-15451)*
Rumsey-Yost Funeral Inc ....F 785 843-5111
Lawrence *(G-5099)*
Ryan Mortuary Inc ....F 785 825-4242
Salina *(G-10655)*
Service Corp International ....E 316 722-2100
Wichita *(G-15565)*
Service Corp International ....F 913 782-0582
Olathe *(G-8059)*
Service Corp International ....F 316 263-0244
Wichita *(G-15566)*
Service Corp International ....E 913 334-3366
Kansas City *(G-4418)*
Stewart Enterprises Inc ....F 316 686-2766
Wichita *(G-15671)*
▲ **Suhor Industries Inc** ....A 620 421-4434
Overland Park *(G-9371)*
Swaim Funeral Home Inc ....F 620 227-2136
Dodge City *(G-1438)*
Turnbull Corporation ....F 620 342-2134
Emporia *(G-1841)*
V W C Inc ....F 316 262-4422
Wichita *(G-15868)*
Warren McElwain Mortuary LLC ....F 785 843-1120
Lawrence *(G-5180)*
Yorgensen-Meloan Inc ....F 785 539-7481
Manhattan *(G-6857)*

7291 Tax Return Preparation Svcs

AC Professional LLC ....E 816 668-4760
Olathe *(G-7508)*
Bob Thornton ....E 620 624-7691
Liberal *(G-6285)*
Dave Tarter ....F 620 227-8031
Dodge City *(G-1339)*
H & R Block ....F 316 321-6960
El Dorado *(G-1565)*
H & R Block ....F 620 421-2850
Parsons *(G-9690)*
H & R Block Inc ....F 785 271-0706
Topeka *(G-12654)*
H & R Block Tax Services LLC ....F 316 775-7331
Augusta *(G-322)*
H & R Block Tax Services LLC ....F 913 648-1040
Olathe *(G-7744)*
H & R Block Tax Services LLC ....F 620 231-5563
Pittsburg *(G-9870)*
H & R Block Tax Services LLC ....F 785 749-1649
Lawrence *(G-4884)*
H&R Block Inc ....F 316 636-4009
Wichita *(G-14535)*
H&R Block Inc ....F 316 267-8257
Wichita *(G-14536)*
H&R Block Inc ....F 913 837-5418
Ottawa *(G-8276)*
H&R Block Inc ....F 785 827-4253
Salina *(G-10527)*
H&R Block Inc ....F 316 683-4211
Wichita *(G-14537)*
H&R Block Inc ....E 913 788-7779
Kansas City *(G-4060)*
H&R Block Inc ....F 620 793-9361
Great Bend *(G-2587)*
H&R Block Inc ....F 785 776-7531
Manhattan *(G-6649)*
H&R Block Inc ....E 316 283-1495
Newton *(G-7355)*
H&R Block Inc ....F 620 336-2750
Cherryvale *(G-809)*
H&R Block Inc ....F 913 788-5222
Kansas City *(G-4061)*
I 70 Tax Services LLC ....F 785 539-5240
Manhattan *(G-6663)*
J L D J Inc ....F 785 625-6316
Hays *(G-2855)*
Keller & Miller Cpas LLP ....F 620 275-6883
Garden City *(G-2217)*
Keller & Owens LLC ....E 913 338-3500
Overland Park *(G-8911)*
Kramer & Associates Cpas LLC ....F 913 680-1690
Leavenworth *(G-5263)*
Liberty Tax ....F 913 384-1040
Roeland Park *(G-10226)*
Liberty Tax Service ....F 316 219-4829
Wichita *(G-14958)*
Mize Houser & Company PA ....D 785 233-0536
Topeka *(G-12908)*
Paycor Inc ....D 913 262-9484
Shawnee Mission *(G-11719)*
R & J Salina Tax Service Inc ....E 785 827-1304
Salina *(G-10649)*
Sckats Inc ....F 620 662-2368
Hutchinson *(G-3438)*
Sharon Miller ....F 620 856-3377
Baxter Springs *(G-412)*
Shemar Inc ....F 620 342-5787
Emporia *(G-1827)*
Stephen M Criser ....E 316 685-1040
Wichita *(G-15661)*
Tax 911com Incorporated ....F 913 712-8539
Olathe *(G-8102)*
Thompson Tax & Associates LLC ....F 916 346-7829
Waverly *(G-13482)*
Topeka Income Tax Service Inc ....F 785 478-2833
Topeka *(G-13178)*
V G Electracon Inc ....F 913 780-9995
Olathe *(G-8137)*
Y & M Business Services LLC ....F 620 331-4600
Independence *(G-3575)*

7299 Miscellaneous Personal Svcs, NEC

A Total Image ....F 785 272-2855
Topeka *(G-12279)*
Ah Tannery Inc ....F 913 772-1111
Leavenworth *(G-5200)*
Ase Group Inc ....F 913 339-9333
Leawood *(G-5333)*
B & C Restaurant Corporation ....C 913 327-0800
Shawnee Mission *(G-11138)*
Bday Parties ....F 913 961-1857
De Soto *(G-1193)*
Bobby TS Bar & Grill Inc ....F 785 537-8383
Manhattan *(G-6564)*
Bockers Two Catering Inc ....F 785 539-9431
Manhattan *(G-6566)*
Brown Management Inc ....F 785 528-3769
Osage City *(G-8181)*
Car Park Inc ....E 316 265-0553
Wichita *(G-13942)*
Cec Entertainment Inc ....E 913 648-4920
Overland Park *(G-8533)*
Cec Entertainment Inc ....D 316 636-2225
Wichita *(G-13968)*
Charles Ritz Inc ....F 913 685-2600
Overland Park *(G-8542)*
Chase Manhattan Apartment ....F 785 776-3663
Manhattan *(G-6586)*
China Palace ....F 620 365-3723
Iola *(G-3592)*
City of Leawood ....D 913 685-4550
Shawnee Mission *(G-11228)*
City of Salina ....E 785 826-7200
Salina *(G-10449)*
County of Sedgwick ....E 316 660-7060
Wichita *(G-14114)*
Courtland Day Spa ....F 620 223-0098
Fort Scott *(G-1962)*
Ctmd LLC ....E 316 686-6116
Wichita *(G-14139)*
Dcm Wichita Inc ....F 800 662-9573
Towanda *(G-13263)*
Dick Construction Inc ....F 620 275-1806
Garden City *(G-2147)*
E & J Rental & Leasing Inc ....F 316 721-0442
Wichita *(G-14249)*
Eldridge House Invest Ltd Ptnr ....E 785 749-5011
Lawrence *(G-4850)*
Extreme Tanning Inc ....F 316 712-0190
Wichita *(G-14325)*
Falcon Ridge Golf Club ....F 913 393-4653
Shawnee Mission *(G-11359)*
Free State Brewing Co Inc ....D 785 843-4555
Lawrence *(G-4865)*
Friend That Cooks LLC ....E 913 660-0790
Shawnee *(G-10959)*
Garozzos III Inc ....D 913 491-8300
Shawnee Mission *(G-11390)*
Genesis Health Club Inc ....E 316 945-8331
Wichita *(G-14458)*
Gram Enterprises Inc ....E 913 888-3689
Lenexa *(G-5879)*
Hair Club For Men Ltd Inc ....F 888 888-8986
Overland Park *(G-8783)*
Hair Shop & Retailing Center ....E 913 397-9888
Olathe *(G-7745)*
Hair Shop West Inc ....E 913 829-4868
Olathe *(G-7746)*
Hartzler Lorenda ....E 785 749-2424
Lawrence *(G-4891)*
Heart America Management LLC ....E 913 397-0100
Olathe *(G-7762)*
Hedricks Promotions Inc ....E 620 422-3296
Nickerson *(G-7434)*
Herbs & More Inc ....F 785 865-4372
Lawrence *(G-4895)*
Hulsing Hotels Kansas Inc ....D 785 539-5311
Manhattan *(G-6662)*
Hyatt Corporation ....C 316 293-1234
Wichita *(G-14661)*
Ice Sports Kansas City LLC ....E 913 441-3033
Shawnee Mission *(G-11451)*
Images Salon & Day Spa ....F 785 843-2138
Lawrence *(G-4909)*
Jaafar Inc ....F 913 269-5113
Olathe *(G-7805)*
Jims Formal Wear LLC ....E 785 825-1529
Salina *(G-10555)*
Joco Barking Club ....E 913 558-2625
Overland Park *(G-8876)*
L V S Inc ....E 316 636-5005
Wichita *(G-14908)*
La Mesa Mexican Restaurant ....F 913 837-3455
Louisburg *(G-6454)*
Latour Management Inc ....F 316 262-7300
Wichita *(G-14932)*
Lawrence Gymnastics Academy ....E 785 865-0856
Lawrence *(G-4968)*
Leisure Hotel Corporation ....E 620 227-5000
Dodge City *(G-1398)*
Leisure Hotel Corporation ....E 620 275-5900
Garden City *(G-2224)*
Liberty Hall Inc ....F 785 749-1972
Lawrence *(G-4994)*
Little Apple Brewing Company ....C 785 539-5500
Manhattan *(G-6714)*
M P M Services Inc ....F 785 841-5797
Lawrence *(G-5005)*
Mane Thing ....E 785 762-2397
Junction City *(G-3723)*
Midas Touch Golden Tans ....F 620 340-1011
Emporia *(G-1795)*
Midwest Hstrcal Gnalogical Soc ....E 316 264-3611
Wichita *(G-15096)*
Northrock Lanes Inc ....E 316 636-5444
Wichita *(G-15192)*
Old Fort Genealgcl Socty SE KS ....F 620 223-3300
Fort Scott *(G-1996)*
Overland Park Hotel Assoc Lc ....C 913 888-8440
Overland Park *(G-9120)*
Perfect Touch Inc ....F 316 522-9205
Wichita *(G-15281)*
Rekat Recreation Inc ....E 785 272-1881
Topeka *(G-13007)*
River City Brewery Inc ....D 316 263-2739
Wichita *(G-15469)*
Round Hill Bath &TEnnis Club ....F 913 381-2603
Shawnee Mission *(G-11814)*
S S of Kansas Inc ....E 620 663-5951
Hutchinson *(G-3435)*
S S of Kansas Inc ....D 785 823-2787
Salina *(G-10657)*
Salina Red Coach Inn ....F 785 825-2111
Salina *(G-10684)*
Second Hand Enterprises Inc ....F 316 775-7627
Augusta *(G-343)*
Sharks Investment Inc ....F 785 841-8289
Lawrence *(G-5109)*
Skilled Saws Inc ....F 785 249-5084
Silver Lake *(G-12028)*
Svetas Body Therapy LLC ....F 316 630-0400
Wichita *(G-15706)*
T & J Holdings Inc ....F 785 841-4935
Lawrence *(G-5131)*
T L C Professional LLC ....E 785 823-7444
Salina *(G-10731)*
Tellers ....D 785 843-4111
Lawrence *(G-5133)*

Thermal King Windows Inc..................E....... 913 451-2300
Shawnee Mission *(G-11928)*
Two Guys & A Grill..........................F....... 913 393-4745
Olathe *(G-8126)*
U S Toy Co Inc..................................E....... 913 642-8247
Leawood *(G-5587)*
Ultimate Tan......................................F....... 785 842-4949
Lawrence *(G-5148)*
United Distributors Inc.....................F....... 316 263-6181
Wichita *(G-15842)*
Unity Church of Overland Park..........E....... 913 649-1750
Shawnee Mission *(G-11966)*
Walgreen Co......................................E....... 913 393-2757
Olathe *(G-8146)*
Wichita Airport Ht Assoc L P..............C....... 316 945-5272
Wichita *(G-15971)*
Windmill Inn Inc.................................F....... 785 336-3696
Seneca *(G-10888)*
Ww North America Holdings Inc..........E....... 913 227-0152
Overland Park *(G-9507)*
Ww North America Holdings Inc..........E....... 913 495-1400
Overland Park *(G-9508)*

73 BUSINESS SERVICES

7311 Advertising Agencies

Anthem Media LLC..............................E....... 913 894-6923
Leawood *(G-5327)*
Armstrong Creative Services...............F....... 316 522-3000
Haysville *(G-2937)*
Associated Intergrated Mktg...............E....... 316 683-4691
Wichita *(G-13755)*
Biehler Companies Inc........................D....... 316 529-0002
Wichita *(G-13847)*
Brush Art Corporation.........................E....... 785 454-3415
Downs *(G-1469)*
Callahan Creek Inc..............................D....... 785 838-4774
Lawrence *(G-4772)*
Frank Agency Inc.................................D....... 913 648-8333
Overland Park *(G-8736)*
Greteman Group Inc............................F....... 316 263-1004
Wichita *(G-14517)*
Hss IT Management Inc.......................C....... 913 498-9988
Overland Park *(G-8832)*
Huyett Jones Partners..........................F....... 785 228-0900
Topeka *(G-12709)*
Insideresponse LLC.............................E....... 855 969-0812
Overland Park *(G-8851)*
Jajo Inc..E....... 316 267-6700
Wichita *(G-14745)*
Kuhn and Wittenborn Inc.....................E....... 816 471-7888
Overland Park *(G-8932)*
Making The Mark Inc............................G....... 913 402-8000
Shawnee Mission *(G-11592)*
MBB Inc..E....... 816 531-1992
Leawood *(G-5469)*
Media Partners Inc...............................F....... 316 652-2210
Eastborough *(G-1477)*
Montgomery County Media LLC...........E....... 620 331-3550
Independence *(G-3541)*
Patterson Advertising Agency..............G....... 785 232-0533
Topeka *(G-12964)*
Platform Advertising............................E....... 913 254-6000
Olathe *(G-7988)*
Rba Associates Inc..............................F....... 816 444-4270
Mission *(G-7136)*
Rhycom Advertising.............................F....... 913 451-9102
Overland Park *(G-9240)*
Security Benefit Group Inc...................B....... 785 438-3000
Topeka *(G-13053)*
Signal Theory Inc.................................E....... 316 263-0124
Wichita *(G-15589)*
Stephens & Associates Advg Inc..........E....... 913 661-0910
Overland Park *(G-9358)*
Walz Tetrick Advertising Inc................E....... 913 789-8778
Mission *(G-7140)*
ZMC Inc..E....... 913 599-3230
Shawnee Mission *(G-12027)*

7312 Outdoor Advertising Svcs

Boyles Portable Sign Rent....................F....... 785 266-5401
Topeka *(G-12399)*
Iheartcommunications Inc....................D....... 316 494-6600
Wichita *(G-14668)*
Lamar Advertising Company................F....... 785 234-0501
Topeka *(G-12832)*
Lamar Advertising Company................F....... 913 438-4048
Overland Park *(G-8940)*
Partners N Promotion Inc.....................F....... 913 397-9500
Olathe *(G-7974)*

7313 Radio, TV & Publishers Adv Reps

Answer Media LLC...............................F....... 816 984-8853
Leawood *(G-5326)*
Eagle Communications Inc..................F....... 785 726-3291
Hays *(G-2794)*
Eagle Communications Inc..................D....... 785 650-5349
Hays *(G-2795)*
Eagle Communications Inc..................F....... 785 587-0103
Manhattan *(G-6618)*
Eagle Communications Inc..................E....... 785 483-3244
Russell *(G-10273)*
Eagle Communications Inc..................F....... 785 825-4631
Salina *(G-10482)*
EW Scripps Company...........................E....... 316 436-1045
Wichita *(G-14317)*
Great Plains Christian Radio................F....... 620 873-2991
Meade *(G-7049)*
Innovative Broadcasting Corp..............F....... 620 232-5993
Pittsburg *(G-9880)*
K S A J Oldies......................................D....... 785 823-1111
Salina *(G-10559)*
Morris Communications Co LLC...........E....... 316 283-1500
Newton *(G-7390)*
Nvt Wichita LLC...................................E....... 316 265-3333
Wichita *(G-15201)*
Praise Network Inc................................F....... 785 694-2877
Brewster *(G-585)*
Printing Services Inc............................G....... 913 492-1500
Lenexa *(G-6070)*
Viralnova LLC......................................E....... 913 706-9710
Overland Park *(G-9465)*
Waitt Media Inc....................................F....... 620 225-8080
Dodge City *(G-1448)*
Wichita Business Journal Inc...............F....... 316 267-6406
Wichita *(G-15983)*

7319 Advertising, NEC

AP Roofing Specialty Codings..............F....... 620 532-1076
Kingman *(G-4582)*
Beauty Brands LLC...............................F....... 913 227-0797
Shawnee Mission *(G-11156)*
▲ **Davies Communications Inc**............F....... 620 241-1504
McPherson *(G-6956)*
Feet On Ground Marketing Inc.............F....... 913 242-5558
Lawrence *(G-4858)*
New Media Samurai LLC......................F....... 785 856-6673
Lawrence *(G-5039)*
Old World Balloonery LLC....................F....... 913 338-2628
Overland Park *(G-9097)*
Partners N Promotion Inc.....................F....... 913 397-9500
Olathe *(G-7974)*
Proforma Marketing..............................F....... 913 685-9098
Overland Park *(G-9190)*
Trainwreck Tees LLC............................G....... 620 224-2480
Fort Scott *(G-2011)*
Wds Inc..D....... 913 894-1881
Lenexa *(G-6223)*

7322 Adjustment & Collection Svcs

A/R Allegiance Group LLC...................F....... 913 338-4790
Leawood *(G-5311)*
Account Rcvery Specialists Inc............E....... 620 227-8510
Wichita *(G-13603)*
Account Rcvery Specialists Inc............F....... 620 227-8510
Dodge City *(G-1288)*
Ad Astra Recover Service.....................F....... 316 941-5448
Wichita *(G-13611)*
Affiliated Management Svcs Inc...........F....... 913 677-9470
Shawnee Mission *(G-11083)*
Aih Receivable Management Svcs.......F....... 800 666-4606
Shawnee Mission *(G-11086)*
Berlin-Wheeler Inc................................C....... 785 271-1000
Topeka *(G-12372)*
C B C S Inc...F....... 620 343-6220
Emporia *(G-1714)*
Central States Recovery Inc..................E....... 620 663-8811
Hutchinson *(G-3234)*
Collection Bureau Kansas Inc...............E....... 785 228-3636
Topeka *(G-12486)*
Credit Bureau Services.........................E....... 620 276-7631
Garden City *(G-2139)*
Credit World Services Inc.....................E....... 913 362-3950
Shawnee Mission *(G-11278)*
Creditors Service Bureau Inc................F....... 785 266-3223
Topeka *(G-12529)*
Encore Receivable MGT Inc..................A....... 913 782-3333
Wichita *(G-14286)*
Golden Plains Credit Union..................E....... 620 275-8187
Garden City *(G-2188)*
International Fincl Svcs Inc..................E....... 620 665-7708
Hutchinson *(G-3336)*
Kansas Counselors Inc.........................D....... 316 942-8335
Wichita *(G-14794)*
Kansas Counselors Kans Cy Inc...........E....... 913 541-9704
Lenexa *(G-5938)*
Mid America Credit Bureau LLC...........E....... 913 307-0551
Lenexa *(G-5998)*
Midcontinent Credit Svcs Inc................F....... 316 721-6467
Wichita *(G-15086)*
Midwest Service Bureau Inc..................E....... 316 263-1051
Wichita *(G-15100)*
National Credit Adjusters LLC..............C....... 888 768-0674
Hutchinson *(G-3387)*
Portfolio Recovery Assoc LLC..............C....... 620 662-2800
Hutchinson *(G-3409)*
Sure Check Brokerage Inc....................F....... 785 823-1334
Salina *(G-10729)*
Ui Benefit Overpayments.....................F....... 785 296-5000
Topeka *(G-13202)*
Yellow Roadway Receivables Fun.........F....... 913 491-6363
Overland Park *(G-9517)*

7323 Credit Reporting Svcs

1138 Inc..E....... 913 322-5900
Overland Park *(G-8328)*
ACS Data Search LLC...........................F....... 913 649-1771
Shawnee Mission *(G-11070)*
C B C S Inc...F....... 620 343-6220
Emporia *(G-1714)*
Collection of Lawrence Inc...................E....... 785 843-4210
Lawrence *(G-4797)*
Computer Sciences Corporation...........C....... 913 469-8700
Overland Park *(G-8593)*
Credit Bureau Services.........................E....... 620 276-7631
Garden City *(G-2139)*
Credit Restart LLC................................F....... 888 670-7709
Lenexa *(G-5792)*
N A C M Credit Services Inc.................E....... 913 383-9300
Shawnee Mission *(G-11663)*
Shamrock Trading Corporation............B....... 877 642-8553
Overland Park *(G-9302)*

7331 Direct Mail Advertising Svcs

Adkins Systems Inc..............................F....... 913 438-8440
Shawnee Mission *(G-11076)*
Aegis Processing Solutions Inc.............D....... 785 232-0061
Topeka *(G-12300)*
Burdiss Lettershop Services Co............F....... 913 492-0545
Overland Park *(G-8492)*
Cahill Business Services LLC...............F....... 913 515-8398
Shawnee Mission *(G-11199)*
Consolidated Mailing Corp...................E....... 913 262-4400
Tonganoxie *(G-12257)*
Contemprary Communications Inc.......D....... 316 265-0879
Wichita *(G-14094)*
Direct Mail Printers Inc.......................F....... 316 263-1855
Wichita *(G-14213)*
Handy Mailing Service.........................F....... 316 944-6258
Wichita *(G-14553)*
Kc Presort..F....... 913 432-0866
Kansas City *(G-4165)*
Knight Enterprises Ltd.........................E....... 785 843-5511
Lawrence *(G-4946)*
Lexinet Corporation.............................E....... 620 767-6346
Council Grove *(G-1170)*
Lionshare Marketing Inc.......................F....... 913 631-8400
Lenexa *(G-5974)*
Marketing Concepts..............................F....... 785 364-4611
Holton *(G-3104)*
Marketing Technologies Inc..................D....... 913 342-9111
Kansas City *(G-4218)*
Midpoint National Inc..........................E....... 913 362-7400
Kansas City *(G-4248)*
Occk Inc...E....... 785 243-1977
Concordia *(G-1125)*
Personal Marketing Company Inc.........E....... 913 492-0377
Overland Park *(G-9159)*
Postal Presort Inc................................D....... 316 262-3333
Wichita *(G-15316)*
Professional Printing Kans Inc.............F....... 620 343-7125
Emporia *(G-1813)*
Southwest Holding Corporation............E....... 785 233-5662
Topeka *(G-13083)*
Southwest Pubg & Mailing Corp...........C....... 785 233-5662
Topeka *(G-13084)*
Step Two Investments LLC...................E....... 913 888-9000
Overland Park *(G-9357)*
U P S Stores..F....... 913 829-3750
Olathe *(G-8129)*

S I C

7334 Photocopying & Duplicating Svcs

Administration Kansas Dept...C... 785 296-3001
Topeka *(G-12290)*
ARC Document Solutions...E... 316 264-9344
Wichita *(G-13727)*
ARC Document Solutions Inc...E... 816 300-6600
Kansas City *(G-3814)*
ARC Document Solutions Inc...E... 314 231-5025
Kansas City *(G-3815)*
ARC Document Solutions Inc...E... 316 264-9344
Wichita *(G-13728)*
Barker Printing and Copy Svcs...G... 785 233-5533
Topeka *(G-12365)*
Capitol LLC...E... 602 462-5888
Olathe *(G-7576)*
City Blue Print Inc...D... 316 265-6224
Wichita *(G-14023)*
Copy Center of Topeka Inc...E... 785 233-6677
Topeka *(G-12507)*
Copy Co Corporation...G... 785 832-2679
Lawrence *(G-4811)*
Copy Co Corporation...E... 785 823-2679
Salina *(G-10463)*
Copy Shoppe...G... 785 232-0403
Topeka *(G-12508)*
Documart Inc...F... 913 649-3800
Shawnee Mission *(G-11312)*
Docuplex Inc...E... 316 262-2662
Wichita *(G-14220)*
Evolv Solutions LLC...E... 913 469-8900
Shawnee Mission *(G-11352)*
Fedex Office & Print Svcs Inc...F... 913 239-9399
Overland Park *(G-8710)*
Fedex Office & Print Svcs Inc...E... 913 894-2010
Lenexa *(G-5850)*
Fedex Office & Print Svcs Inc...E... 316 636-5443
Wichita *(G-14350)*
Fedex Office & Print Svcs Inc...F... 316 682-1327
Wichita *(G-14351)*
Fedex Office & Print Svcs Inc...F... 785 537-7340
Manhattan *(G-6627)*
Fedex Office & Print Svcs Inc...F... 316 941-9909
Wichita *(G-14352)*
Fedex Office & Print Svcs Inc...E... 913 661-0192
Shawnee Mission *(G-11364)*
Fedex Office & Print Svcs Inc...F... 913 677-4488
Shawnee Mission *(G-11365)*
Fedex Office & Print Svcs Inc...E... 316 721-6529
Wichita *(G-14353)*
Fedex Office & Print Svcs Inc...F... 913 383-2178
Overland Park *(G-8711)*
Fedex Office & Print Svcs Inc...E... 785 272-2500
Topeka *(G-12603)*
Fedex Office & Print Svcs Inc...F... 913 393-0953
Olathe *(G-7707)*
Fedex Office & Print Svcs Inc...F... 913 780-6010
Olathe *(G-7708)*
Independent Oil & Gas Svc Inc...G... 316 263-8281
Wichita *(G-14680)*
Jet Digital Printing & Copies...F... 316 685-2679
Wichita *(G-14755)*
Marathon Reprographics Inc...F... 816 221-7881
Kansas City *(G-4217)*
Optimation Holographics Inc...E... 785 233-6000
Topeka *(G-12950)*
Perfect Output LLC...D... 913 317-8400
Overland Park *(G-9154)*
Print Time Inc...E... 913 345-8900
Leawood *(G-5528)*
Proprint Incorporated...G... 785 272-0070
Topeka *(G-12992)*
Scanning America Inc...D... 785 749-7471
Lawrence *(G-5102)*
Shahrokhi Inc...G... 913 764-5775
Olathe *(G-8060)*
Topeka Blue Print & Sup Co Inc...G... 785 232-7209
Topeka *(G-13169)*

7335 Commercial Photography

Graphics Four Inc...G... 913 268-0564
Shawnee *(G-10964)*
Ranieri Camera & Video Inc...F... 785 336-3719
Seneca *(G-10879)*

7336 Commercial Art & Graphic Design

A G I Inc...F... 913 281-5533
Shawnee Mission *(G-11063)*
Air Capitol Dial Inc...F... 316 264-2483
Wichita *(G-13649)*
Astronomical Society Kansas Cy...F... 913 631-8413
Shawnee Mission *(G-11127)*
Copy Co Corporation...E... 785 823-2679
Salina *(G-10463)*
Custom Design Inc...F... 913 764-6511
Olathe *(G-7630)*
Davinci Reprographics...F... 913 371-0014
Kansas City *(G-3958)*
Greteman Group Inc...F... 316 263-1004
Wichita *(G-14517)*
Harvest Graphics LLC...E... 913 438-5556
Shawnee Mission *(G-11415)*
Infusion Design Incorporated...E... 913 422-0317
Bonner Springs *(G-555)*
Integrated Media Group LLC...F... 316 425-8333
Wichita *(G-14703)*
J2 Design Solutions LLC...F... 316 303-9460
Wichita *(G-14741)*
Jack Jones Inc...F... 620 342-4221
Emporia *(G-1779)*
Kca Internet...F... 913 735-7206
Stilwell *(G-12160)*
Khaos Apparel LLC...F... 316 804-4900
Newton *(G-7370)*
Last Chance Graphics Inc...G... 785 263-4470
Abilene *(G-44)*
Legends Printing & Graphics...G... 620 225-0020
Dodge City *(G-1396)*
MBB Inc...E... 816 531-1992
Leawood *(G-5469)*
Plainjans Feedlot Service...F... 620 872-5777
Scott City *(G-10827)*
Printery Inc...F... 785 632-5501
Clay Center *(G-877)*
Service Pak Inc...D... 913 438-3500
Lenexa *(G-6124)*
Sgl LLC...E... 800 835-0588
Parsons *(G-9737)*
▲ **Terrell Publishing Co**...G... 913 948-8226
Kansas City *(G-4464)*
Wilbert Screen Printing Inc...G... 620 231-1730
Pittsburg *(G-9970)*

7338 Secretarial & Court Reporting Svcs

Answer Link...F... 620 662-4427
Hutchinson *(G-3199)*
Appino Biggs Reporting Svc Inc...F... 785 273-3063
Topeka *(G-12333)*
ARS Reporting LLC...E... 913 422-5198
Shawnee *(G-10911)*
Copy Center of Topeka Inc...E... 785 233-6677
Topeka *(G-12507)*
Court Reporting Service Inc...F... 800 794-8798
Wichita *(G-14115)*
Davis Publications Inc...F... 785 945-6170
Valley Falls *(G-13362)*
Graphic Images Inc...F... 316 283-3776
Newton *(G-7352)*
Jay E Suddreth & Associates...E... 913 451-5820
Leawood *(G-5441)*
Kelley York & Associates Ltd...F... 316 267-8200
Wichita *(G-14844)*
Metropolitan Court Reporters...E... 913 317-8800
Overland Park *(G-9015)*
Omni Center II...F... 316 689-4256
Wichita *(G-15217)*
Reporting Services Company...E... 913 385-2699
Overland Park *(G-9235)*
Superior Crt Reporting Svc LLC...F... 913 262-0100
Overland Park *(G-9377)*
Transcription Unlimited Inc...E... 816 350-3800
Shawnee *(G-11042)*

7342 Disinfecting & Pest Control Svcs

Advance Termite & Pest Control...F... 620 662-3616
Hutchinson *(G-3192)*
Augustine Exterminators Inc...E... 913 362-4399
Overland Park *(G-8413)*
Bats Inc...F... 785 526-7185
Sylvan Grove *(G-12219)*
Betts Pest Control Inc...F... 316 943-3555
Wichita *(G-13840)*
Browns Tree Service LLC...F... 785 379-9212
Topeka *(G-12410)*
Central States Enterprises LLC...E... 785 827-8215
Salina *(G-10445)*
Edge Pest Control Kans Cy LLC...F... 913 262-3343
Shawnee *(G-10943)*
F/X Termite and Pest Control...F... 913 599-5990
Shawnee Mission *(G-11357)*
Frechin Pest Control LLC...F... 816 358-5776
Overland Park *(G-8739)*
General Pest Control LLC...F... 620 855-7768
Cimarron *(G-826)*
Gunter Pest Management Inc...E... 913 397-0220
Olathe *(G-7742)*
Hawks Interstate Pestmasters...E... 316 267-8331
Wichita *(G-14569)*
Industrial Fumigant Collc...E... 913 782-7600
Lenexa *(G-5913)*
Kaw Valley Exterminator...E... 785 456-7357
Wamego *(G-13427)*
Landscape Outfitters LLC...F... 620 221-1108
Winfield *(G-16154)*
Midwest Pest Control LLC...F... 316 681-3417
Wichita *(G-15098)*
Moxie Services LLC...E... 913 416-1205
Lenexa *(G-6013)*
Orkin LLC...F... 785 827-0314
Salina *(G-10623)*
Orkin LLC...F... 913 492-4029
Lenexa *(G-6038)*
Parker Pest Control Inc...F... 316 524-4311
Augusta *(G-336)*
Patton Termite & Pest Ctrl Inc...F... 316 773-3825
Wichita *(G-15270)*
Plainjans Feedlot Service...F... 620 872-5777
Scott City *(G-10827)*
Schendel Services Inc...F... 913 498-1811
Olathe *(G-8056)*
Schendel Services Inc...F... 316 320-6422
Wichita *(G-15530)*
Tapco Products Co...E... 913 492-2777
Shawnee Mission *(G-11920)*
Terminix Intl Co Ltd Partnr...E... 913 696-0351
Lenexa *(G-6176)*
Terminix Intl Co Ltd Partnr...F... 785 266-2600
Topeka *(G-13152)*
Terminix Intl Co Ltd Partnr...E... 913 696-0351
Overland Park *(G-9402)*
Tox-Eol Pest Management Inc...F... 785 825-5143
Salina *(G-10737)*

7349 Building Cleaning & Maintenance Svcs, NEC

Air Capital Building Maint...F... 316 838-3828
Wichita *(G-13646)*
Alert Enterprises Inc...F... 785 862-9800
Topeka *(G-12304)*
Alliance Jantr Advisors Inc...F... 913 815-8807
Olathe *(G-7520)*
American Superclean...F... 913 815-3257
Olathe *(G-7528)*
B A Barnes Electric Inc...E... 913 764-4455
Olathe *(G-7544)*
Best Corporation Inc...E... 316 687-1895
El Dorado *(G-1536)*
Best Corporation Inc...E... 316 687-1895
Wichita *(G-13837)*
Best Value Services LLC...D... 316 440-1048
Wichita *(G-13839)*
Bobs Janitorial Service & Sup...C... 785 271-6600
Topeka *(G-12395)*
Buckingham Palace Inc...D... 785 842-6264
Lawrence *(G-4771)*
Burkhart Enterprises Inc...E... 620 662-8678
Hutchinson *(G-3226)*
Butler & McIlvain Inc...F... 316 684-6700
Wichita *(G-13921)*
Buzz Building Maintenance Inc...E... 316 773-9860
Wichita *(G-13922)*
C & P Enterprises Inc...E... 785 628-6712
Hays *(G-2762)*
C & S Maintenance Inc...E... 913 227-9609
Overland Park *(G-8503)*
CD McCormick & Company Inc...E... 913 541-0106
Overland Park *(G-8531)*
Central Maintenance System...E... 913 621-6545
Kansas City *(G-3901)*
Central Plains Maintenance...D... 316 945-4774
Wichita *(G-13983)*
Chavez Restoration & Cleaning...F... 785 232-3779
Topeka *(G-12463)*
Circle Enterprises Inc...F... 316 943-9834
Wichita *(G-14021)*
City of Halstead...E... 316 835-3492
Halstead *(G-2698)*
City of Leavenworth...F... 913 684-1560
Leavenworth *(G-5219)*

City Wide Franchise Co Inc....E....913 888-5700
Lenexa (G-5756)
City Wide Holding Company Inc....C....913 888-5700
Lenexa (G-5757)
City Wide Maintenance Co Inc....C....913 888-5700
Lenexa (G-5758)
Clean Tech Inc....C....316 729-8100
Wichita (G-14040)
Clean-Rite LLC....F....785 628-1945
Hays (G-2771)
Cleaning Authority of Central....F....316 733-7890
Wichita (G-14041)
Cleaning Up LLC....E....913 327-7226
Lenexa (G-5761)
Cleansweep Janitorial Inc....F....785 856-8617
Lawrence (G-4792)
Clear View Inc....E....785 286-2070
Topeka (G-12480)
◆ Cogen Cleaning Technology Inc....E....281 339-5751
Stilwell (G-12142)
Consociates Group LLC....F....316 321-7500
El Dorado (G-1549)
Contract Services Inc....D....785 239-9069
Fort Riley (G-1946)
Cottagecare Inc....F....913 469-8778
Overland Park (G-8603)
Coverall North America Inc....F....913 888-5009
Leawood (G-5362)
Cs Cleaners Inc....F....785 825-8636
Salina (G-10469)
D & D Roland Enterprises Llc....E....316 942-6474
Wichita (G-14154)
D&A Services Inc....D....316 943-8857
Wichita (G-14161)
Dalan Inc....E....913 384-5662
Overland Park (G-8631)
DCS Sanitation Management Inc....C....620 624-5533
Liberal (G-6302)
Development Inc....F....913 651-9717
Leavenworth (G-5233)
Eagle Environmental Svcs LLC....E....316 944-2445
Wichita (G-14250)
Ermc II LP....E....913 859-9621
Overland Park (G-8688)
Fluebrothers LLC....F....913 236-7141
Kansas City (G-4013)
Franchise Development Inc....E....620 662-3283
Hutchinson (G-3291)
Fsig LLC....D....785 784-2566
Fort Riley (G-1948)
Givens Cleaning Contractors....F....316 265-1315
Wichita (G-14468)
Goodwill Wstn MO & Eastrn Kans....F....785 331-3908
Lawrence (G-4875)
Goodwill Wstn MO & Eastrn Kans....E....913 768-9540
Olathe (G-7737)
Grace of Wichita Ks LLC....F....316 832-9009
Wichita (G-14489)
Have It Maid....F....316 264-0110
Wichita (G-14568)
Hawk Wash Window Cleaning....F....785 749-0244
Lawrence (G-4893)
Heartland Building Maintenance....D....913 268-7132
Shawnee Mission (G-11422)
Helping Hands Services-Kansas....E....417 438-6102
Baxter Springs (G-408)
Hospitality Management LLC....E....316 262-0000
Wichita (G-14639)
Housekeeping Unlimited....E....785 842-2444
Lawrence (G-4905)
Hutchinson Usd 308....F....620 615-5575
Hutchinson (G-3327)
Hydrochem LLC....E....316 321-7541
El Dorado (G-1569)
I B S Industries Inc....F....913 281-0787
Kansas City (G-4091)
Icg Inc....E....913 461-8759
Leawood (G-5433)
Jeff Goldman....F....785 842-0351
Lawrence (G-4922)
Jenkins Building Maintenance....F....316 529-1263
Haysville (G-2949)
Jones Janitorial Service....F....316 722-5520
Wichita (G-14770)
Jt Maintenance Inc....F....913 642-5656
Overland Park (G-8881)
Kc Cleaning Solutions....C....913 236-0040
Overland Park (G-8905)
Lamunyon Clg & Restoration....F....785 632-1259
Clay Center (G-870)
Landscapes Inc....E....316 262-7557
Wichita (G-14921)
Lenere LLC....F....785 320-0208
Saint Marys (G-10371)
LMS Company LLC....F....913 648-4123
Shawnee Mission (G-11576)
Lulu Mimi Hsclners Extrrdnaire....F....913 649-6022
Shawnee Mission (G-11582)
Maid Services Inc....E....785 537-6243
Manhattan (G-6717)
Majestic Franchising Inc....F....913 385-1440
Lenexa (G-5983)
Mc Janitorial LLC....F....913 780-0731
Olathe (G-7879)
Merry Maids 391....F....785 273-3422
Topeka (G-12884)
Merry Maids Ltd Partnership....E....913 403-0813
Overland Park (G-9012)
Merry Maids Ltd Partnership....F....785 842-2410
Lawrence (G-5023)
Mid Central Contract Svcs Inc....E....620 231-1166
Pittsburg (G-9903)
Mini Maid Joco Incorporated....F....913 894-2200
Lenexa (G-6005)
Modern Maintenance Inc....B....913 345-9777
Shawnee Mission (G-11651)
Noonshine Window Cleaning Svc....F....913 381-3780
Overland Park (G-9092)
Noonshine Window Cleaning Svc....F....913 381-9666
Shawnee Mission (G-11687)
Olathe Unified School Dst 233....D....913 780-7011
Olathe (G-7951)
Phoenix Restoration Service....E....620 276-6994
Garden City (G-2254)
Piat Inc....F....913 782-4693
Olathe (G-7986)
Pioneer Janitorial LLC....E....785 379-5101
Topeka (G-12975)
Prairie Cleaning Service....E....785 539-4997
Manhattan (G-6778)
Progreen Window Cleaning Inc....F....913 387-3210
Lenexa (G-6075)
Residential Services Inc....E....316 832-9058
Wichita (G-15449)
Resource Service Solutions LLC....E....913 338-5050
Lenexa (G-6107)
Restore It Systems LLC....F....620 331-3997
Independence (G-3555)
Rigdon Inc....F....913 322-9274
Overland Park (G-9242)
S & H Inc....F....620 251-4422
Coffeyville (G-974)
Sage Restoration LLC....F....913 905-0500
Overland Park (G-9271)
Sanibel Investments Inc....E....913 422-7949
Shawnee Mission (G-11829)
Sentinel Real Estate Corp....F....316 265-9471
Wichita (G-15562)
ServiceMaster Company LLC....F....620 260-9994
Garden City (G-2279)
ServiceMaster Consumer Service....F....316 283-5404
Newton (G-7416)
ServiceMaster North Centl Kans....F....785 243-1965
Concordia (G-1130)
Servimster Prof Rstoration Clg....F....785 832-0055
Bonner Springs (G-572)
Smart Way....F....913 764-3071
Olathe (G-8069)
Source Building Services Inc....F....913 341-7500
Overland Park (G-9329)
Spotless Janitorial Services....E....316 682-2070
Wichita (G-15646)
Steam Way Carpet Restorations....F....620 331-9553
Independence (G-3563)
Stovers Restoration Inc....F....316 686-5005
Maize (G-6521)
Superior Building Maintenance....B....316 943-2347
Wichita (G-15692)
T D C Ltd....E....913 780-9631
Olathe (G-8096)
T W Lacy & Associates Inc....F....913 706-7625
Prairie Village (G-10073)
Tee Time Investments Inc....D....316 262-7900
Wichita (G-15727)
Thorman Enterprises LLC....F....913 772-1818
Leavenworth (G-5297)
Thrash Inc....E....316 265-5331
Wichita (G-15762)
Tidy Up Angels LLC....F....913 642-2006
Overland Park (G-9410)
Tk & Company Inc of Kansas....F....785 472-3226
Ellsworth (G-1682)
Trujillo Jan & Crpt Clg Svc....F....316 263-8204
Wichita (G-15813)
Valley Center City Yard....F....316 755-7320
Valley Center (G-13358)
Wilson Building Maintenance....C....316 264-0699
Wichita (G-16053)
Wyandtte Cnty Unfied Gvernment....C....913 281-3300
Kansas City (G-4555)
Xtreme Clean 88 LLC....F....913 451-9274
Overland Park (G-9514)
Xxtra Clean....F....785 210-5255
Junction City (G-3770)

7352 Medical Eqpt Rental & Leasing

American Homepatient Inc....E....913 495-9545
Lenexa (G-5649)
Apria Healthcare LLC....E....316 689-4500
Wichita (G-13725)
Apria Healthcare LLC....F....785 272-8411
Topeka (G-12335)
Ascension Via Christi Home Med....D....316 265-4991
Wichita (G-13746)
Broadway Home Medical Inc....F....316 264-8600
Wichita (G-13895)
First Biomedical Inc....E....800 962-9656
Lenexa (G-5856)
Health Care Inc....A....620 665-2000
Hutchinson (G-3309)
Hutchinson Hlth Care Svcs Inc....E....620 665-0528
Hutchinson (G-3321)
Kingman Drug Inc....F....620 532-5113
Kingman (G-4600)

7353 Heavy Construction Eqpt Rental & Leasing

AAF Fleet Service Inc....F....913 683-3816
Mc Louth (G-6924)
Belger Cartage Service Inc....E....316 943-0101
Wichita (G-13829)
Berry Companies Inc....E....785 232-7731
Topeka (G-12375)
Building Erection Svcs Co Inc....E....913 764-5560
Olathe (G-7568)
Cillessen Equipment Co LLC....F....316 682-2400
Kechi (G-4566)
Crane Sales & Service Co Inc....F....913 621-7040
Kansas City (G-3944)
Duke Aerial Inc....F....785 494-8001
Saint George (G-10346)
Eby Corporation....F....316 268-3500
Wichita (G-14256)
Ferco Inc....E....785 825-6380
Salina (G-10500)
Foley Equipment Company....D....785 537-2101
Manhattan (G-6637)
Foley Industries Inc....D....316 943-4211
Wichita (G-14399)
Foley Supply LLC....E....316 944-7368
Wichita (G-14400)
Gerard Tank & Steel Inc....E....785 243-3895
Concordia (G-1116)
High Reach Equipment LLC....F....316 942-5438
Wichita (G-14605)
Midwest Crane and Rigging LLC....E....913 747-5100
Olathe (G-7894)
Midwest Siding Incorporated....E....785 825-5576
Salina (G-10602)
Nesco Holdings Inc....G....913 287-0001
Kansas City (G-4286)
Panhandle Steel Erectors Inc....F....620 271-9878
Garden City (G-2247)
Reinhardt Services Inc....G....785 483-2556
Russell (G-10287)
▼ Road Builders Mchy & Sup Co....D....913 371-3822
Kansas City (G-4384)
Russell & Russell LLC....F....785 827-4878
Salina (G-10654)
Sunbelt Rentals Inc....F....316 789-7000
Wichita (G-15684)
T & C Tank Rental & Anchor Svc....E....806 592-3286
Overland Park (G-9389)
Trimble & Maclaskey Oil LLC....F....620 836-2000
Gridley (G-2691)
Trinity Sales LLC....E....316 942-5555
Wichita (G-15803)
U S Weatherford L P....D....620 624-6273
Liberal (G-6377)

S I C

U-Haul Co of Kansas Inc ....D 913 287-1327
Kansas City *(G-4481)*
United Rentals North Amer Inc ....F 316 682-7368
Wichita *(G-15848)*
Wilkerson Crane Rental Inc ....E 913 238-7030
Lenexa *(G-6230)*

7359 Equipment Rental & Leasing, NEC

AAA Party Rental Inc ....F 816 333-1767
Lenexa *(G-5617)*
AAA Portable Services LLC ....F 316 522-6442
Wichita *(G-13591)*
ABC Leasing Co Inc ....E 785 267-4555
Topeka *(G-12282)*
Aggreko LLC ....F 913 281-9782
Shawnee Mission *(G-11085)*
Ahern Rentals Inc ....E 913 281-7555
Kansas City *(G-3792)*
▲ **All Seasons Party Rental Inc** ....C 816 765-1444
Kansas City *(G-3798)*
Alltite Inc ....E 316 686-3010
Wichita *(G-13678)*
Anderson Rentals Inc ....F 785 843-2044
Lawrence *(G-4735)*
Augusta Rental Inc ....F 316 775-5050
Augusta *(G-308)*
B & K Enterprises Inc ....F 785 238-3076
Junction City *(G-3670)*
Bartels Inc ....F 316 755-1853
Valley Center *(G-13336)*
Basham Furniture Rental Inc ....F 316 263-5821
Wichita *(G-13816)*
Basham Home Store Inc ....F 316 263-5821
Wichita *(G-13817)*
Berry Companies Inc ....F 620 277-2290
Garden City *(G-2109)*
Big DS Rent All ....F 785 625-2443
Hays *(G-2758)*
Bli Rentals LLC ....E 620 342-7847
Emporia *(G-1704)*
Building Erection Svcs Co Inc ....E 913 764-5560
Olathe *(G-7568)*
C-Hawkk Construction Inc ....F 785 542-1800
Eudora *(G-1872)*
Capital City Pallet Inc ....F 785 379-5099
Topeka *(G-12429)*
Century Business Technologies ....E 785 267-4555
Topeka *(G-12458)*
Clune & Company Lc ....F 913 498-3000
Shawnee Mission *(G-11242)*
Commercial Capital Company LLC ....E 913 341-0053
Lenexa *(G-5774)*
Cort Business Services Corp ....E 913 888-0100
Overland Park *(G-8601)*
Devlin Enterprises Inc ....F 316 634-1800
Wichita *(G-14203)*
Family Video Movie Club Inc ....F 913 254-7219
Olathe *(G-7702)*
First Financial Leasing Inc ....E 913 236-8800
Shawnee Mission *(G-11370)*
Foley Supply LLC ....E 316 944-7368
Wichita *(G-14400)*
Gerken Rent-All Inc ....F 913 294-3783
Paola *(G-9561)*
Hedges Neon Sales Inc ....G 785 827-9341
Salina *(G-10540)*
High Reach Equipment LLC ....F 316 942-5438
Wichita *(G-14605)*
Hoffmanns Green Industries ....E 316 634-1500
Wichita *(G-14624)*
Home Depot USA Inc ....C 913 789-8899
Merriam *(G-7095)*
Home Depot USA Inc ....F 785 217-2260
Topeka *(G-12700)*
Home Depot USA Inc ....C 316 681-0899
Wichita *(G-14628)*
Home Depot USA Inc ....C 316 773-1988
Wichita *(G-14629)*
Home Depot USA Inc ....C 785 749-2074
Lawrence *(G-4900)*
Home Depot USA Inc ....D 620 275-5943
Garden City *(G-2197)*
Home Depot USA Inc ....C 785 272-5949
Topeka *(G-12701)*
Home Depot USA Inc ....C 913 648-7811
Shawnee Mission *(G-11438)*
Hume Music Inc ....F 816 474-1960
Stilwell *(G-12154)*
Ice-Masters Inc ....F 660 827-6900
Shawnee Mission *(G-11452)*
Ice-Masters Inc ....F 316 945-6900
Wichita *(G-14665)*
Integrted Hlthcare Systems Inc ....A 316 689-9111
Wichita *(G-14708)*
J & A Rentals Inc ....F 316 788-4540
Derby *(G-1253)*
Jetz Service Co Inc ....F 785 354-7588
Topeka *(G-12744)*
Jrm Enterprises Inc ....E 785 404-1328
Salina *(G-10557)*
K-State Union Corporation ....C 785 532-6575
Manhattan *(G-6671)*
Kanequip Inc ....F 785 632-3441
Clay Center *(G-869)*
Kansas Rental Inc ....F 785 272-1232
Topeka *(G-12801)*
Kent Business Systems Corp ....F 316 262-4487
Wichita *(G-14851)*
Kraft Leasing LLC ....E 913 601-6999
Kansas City *(G-4180)*
L C Enterprises ....F 316 682-3300
Wichita *(G-14904)*
Laser Specialists Inc ....E 913 780-9990
Olathe *(G-7856)*
▲ **Lift Truck Center Inc** ....E 316 942-7465
Wichita *(G-14963)*
Lyddon Aero Center Inc ....F 620 624-1646
Liberal *(G-6338)*
Maid Services Inc ....E 785 537-6243
Manhattan *(G-6717)*
Manning Music Inc ....F 785 272-1740
Topeka *(G-12857)*
Marc Gorges ....E 316 630-0689
Eastborough *(G-1476)*
Mather Flare Rental Inc ....F 785 478-9696
Topeka *(G-12863)*
Midwest Office Technology ....E 913 894-9600
Overland Park *(G-9034)*
Mobile Mini Inc ....F 316 838-2663
Park City *(G-9636)*
Nisly Brothers Inc ....E 620 662-6561
Hutchinson *(G-3391)*
North American Buildings Inc ....F 316 821-9590
Wichita *(G-15187)*
Panhandle Steel Erectors Inc ....F 620 271-9878
Garden City *(G-2247)*
Party Bnce Monwalk Rentals LLC ....F 316 519-5174
Wichita *(G-15267)*
Perrys Inc ....F 620 662-2375
Hutchinson *(G-3404)*
Pitney Bowes Inc ....D 913 681-5579
Shawnee Mission *(G-11736)*
Pitney Bowes Inc ....G 785 266-6750
Topeka *(G-12978)*
Rental Station LLC ....E 620 431-7368
Chanute *(G-760)*
Ricoh Usa Inc ....E 316 262-7172
Wichita *(G-15461)*
Ryder Truck Rental Inc ....F 316 945-8484
Wichita *(G-15497)*
Ryder Truck Rental Inc ....E 913 492-4420
Lenexa *(G-6114)*
Safety-Kleen Systems Inc ....F 316 942-5001
Wichita *(G-15505)*
SC Hall Industrial Svcs Inc ....E 316 945-4255
Wichita *(G-15525)*
Scheopners Water Cond LLC ....F 620 275-5121
Garden City *(G-2275)*
Sizewise Rentals LLC ....F 800 814-9389
Ellis *(G-1652)*
Sta-Mot-Ks LLC ....E 913 894-9600
Overland Park *(G-9349)*
▲ **Styers Equipment Company** ....F 913 681-5225
Overland Park *(G-9369)*
Sunflower Rents Inc ....F 785 233-9489
Topeka *(G-13120)*
Textron Aviation Inc ....A 316 676-7111
Salina *(G-10733)*
Traffic Control Services Inc ....F 316 448-0402
Wichita *(G-15784)*
Traftec Inc ....F 913 621-2919
Kansas City *(G-4472)*
Transitions Group Inc ....F 913 327-0700
Lenexa *(G-6190)*
Transitions Group Inc ....F 316 263-5750
Wichita *(G-15792)*
Tresko Inc ....E 913 631-6900
Shawnee Mission *(G-11941)*
U S Weatherford L P ....D 620 624-6273
Liberal *(G-6377)*
U-Haul Co of Kansas Inc ....D 913 287-1327
Kansas City *(G-4481)*
United Distributors Inc ....F 316 712-2174
Wichita *(G-15841)*
United Rentals North Amer Inc ....F 785 272-6006
Topeka *(G-13209)*
United Rentals North Amer Inc ....F 785 838-4110
Lawrence *(G-5153)*
United Rentals North Amer Inc ....F 316 722-7368
Wichita *(G-15847)*
United Rentals North Amer Inc ....E 620 245-0550
McPherson *(G-7035)*
United Rentals North Amer Inc ....F 913 696-5628
Olathe *(G-8133)*
Wheatland Waters Inc ....D 785 267-0512
Olathe *(G-8153)*
▲ **Yingling Aircraft Inc** ....D 316 943-3246
Wichita *(G-16085)*

7361 Employment Agencies

A1 Staffing ....F 913 652-0005
Overland Park *(G-8336)*
Ace Personnel Inc ....F 913 384-1100
Shawnee Mission *(G-11067)*
Advantage Tech Inc ....D 913 888-5050
Overland Park *(G-8352)*
Amazing Grace Staffing Inc ....E 785 432-2920
Hays *(G-2745)*
Aquent LLC ....E 913 345-9119
Shawnee Mission *(G-11115)*
Atterro Inc ....F 913 338-3020
Overland Park *(G-8412)*
Bartunek Group Inc ....E 913 327-8800
Overland Park *(G-8435)*
Bradford and Galt Incorporated ....E 913 663-1264
Shawnee Mission *(G-11177)*
Chase Group Inc ....F 913 696-6300
Overland Park *(G-8543)*
Excel Personnel Services Inc ....E 913 341-1150
Shawnee Mission *(G-11353)*
Experis Us Inc ....F 913 800-3027
Overland Park *(G-8700)*
Express Services Inc ....D 785 825-4545
Salina *(G-10492)*
Global Partner Solutions LLC ....C 316 263-1288
Wichita *(G-14475)*
Grafton Inc ....A 913 498-0701
Overland Park *(G-8768)*
Healthstaff Dental LLC ....D 913 402-4334
Leawood *(G-5423)*
Ingenium Solutions Inc ....E 913 239-0050
Overland Park *(G-8844)*
Jt2 Inc ....F 913 323-4915
Overland Park *(G-8882)*
Kansas Department of Labor ....F 913 680-2200
Leavenworth *(G-5260)*
Kansas Ltd Liability Company ....F 888 222-6359
Overland Park *(G-8903)*
Kansas Personnel Services Inc ....C 785 272-9999
Topeka *(G-12796)*
Kansas State University ....E 785 532-6506
Manhattan *(G-6692)*
Kforce Inc ....E 913 890-5000
Overland Park *(G-8916)*
Krucial Staffing LLC ....F 913 802-2560
Overland Park *(G-8928)*
Labor Source LLC ....F 913 764-5333
Olathe *(G-7850)*
Lynn Care LLC ....E 913 707-4639
Overland Park *(G-8977)*
Lynn Care LLC ....C 913 491-3562
Overland Park *(G-8978)*
Macfarlane Group LLC ....E 913 825-1200
Shawnee Mission *(G-11589)*
McGhee and Associates LLC ....E 785 341-2550
Manhattan *(G-6738)*
Midwest Consulting Group Inc ....C 913 693-8200
Overland Park *(G-9031)*
Morgan Hunter Corporation ....E 913 491-3434
Overland Park *(G-9053)*
National Greyhound Association ....F 785 263-4660
Abilene *(G-48)*
Nextaff LLC ....E 913 562-5620
Overland Park *(G-9082)*
Onsite Solutions LLC ....C 913 912-7384
Shawnee Mission *(G-11698)*
Pivot Companies LLC ....F 800 581-6398
Overland Park *(G-9170)*
Premier Personnel Inc ....D 785 273-9944
Topeka *(G-12983)*

Q S Nurses Kansas LLC .... D 620 793-7262
Great Bend *(G-2627)*
Quantum Health Professionals .... D 913 894-1910
Mission *(G-7135)*
Randstad Technologies LLC .... F 913 696-0808
Overland Park *(G-9225)*
Robert Half International Inc .... D 913 451-7600
Overland Park *(G-9247)*
Robert Half International Inc .... D 816 421-6623
Overland Park *(G-9248)*
Robert Half International Inc .... E 913 339-9849
Shawnee Mission *(G-11808)*
Robert Half International Inc .... F 913 451-1014
Overland Park *(G-9249)*
Shc Services Inc .... C 913 652-9229
Overland Park *(G-9306)*
Spec Personnel LLC .... D 913 534-8430
Overland Park *(G-9333)*
Specialists Group LLC .... F 316 267-7375
Wichita *(G-15635)*
Spencer Reed Group LLC .... E 913 722-7860
Shawnee Mission *(G-11884)*
Spencer Reed Group LLC .... C 913 663-4400
Leawood *(G-5557)*
Squadbuilders Inc .... D 913 649-4401
Leawood *(G-5559)*
Srg III LLC .... F 913 663-4400
Overland Park *(G-9348)*
Supported Employment Services .... F 620 431-1805
Chanute *(G-766)*
Tarc Inc .... D 785 266-2323
Topeka *(G-13140)*
Tdb Communications Inc .... C 913 327-7400
Lenexa *(G-6168)*
Tradesmen International LLC .... E 316 688-0291
Wichita *(G-15783)*
Transerve Inc .... D 620 231-2230
Pittsburg *(G-9947)*
Ultimate Group LLP .... F 816 813-8182
Prairie Village *(G-10077)*
Velocity Staff Inc .... E 913 693-4626
Overland Park *(G-9460)*
Vertical 1 Inc .... E 913 829-8100
Lenexa *(G-6210)*
Waterman Group Inc .... F 913 685-4900
Overland Park *(G-9484)*

7363 Help Supply Svcs

Addiction and Prevention Svcs .... F 785 296-6807
Topeka *(G-12287)*
Adkore Staffing Group LLC .... F 913 402-8031
Leawood *(G-5312)*
Ado Staffing Inc .... F 785 842-1515
Lawrence *(G-4719)*
Advantage Tech Inc .... D 913 888-5050
Overland Park *(G-8352)*
Aerotek Inc .... F 913 905-3000
Overland Park *(G-8355)*
Aerotek Inc .... E 316 448-4500
Wichita *(G-13640)*
Aerotek Inc .... E 913 981-1970
Lenexa *(G-5636)*
Apprentice Personnel Inc .... D 316 267-4781
Wichita *(G-13724)*
APS Staffing Services Inc .... F 913 327-7605
Overland Park *(G-8391)*
Archein Aerospace LLC .... E 682 499-2150
Wichita *(G-13730)*
Arnold & Associates of Wichita .... F 316 263-9283
Wichita *(G-13735)*
Asgn Incorporated .... F 913 341-9100
Overland Park *(G-8401)*
Atterro Inc .... F 913 338-3020
Overland Park *(G-8412)*
Career Athletes LLC .... E 913 538-6259
Lenexa *(G-5729)*
Carestaf Inc .... B 913 498-2888
Overland Park *(G-8516)*
Cbiz M&S Consulting Svcs LLC .... E 785 228-6700
Topeka *(G-12454)*
County of Seward .... E 620 626-3275
Liberal *(G-6299)*
Dirty Work .... F 316 652-9104
Wichita *(G-14214)*
Excel Personnel Services Inc .... E 913 341-1150
Shawnee Mission *(G-11353)*
Exhibit Arts LLC .... E 316 264-2915
Wichita *(G-14321)*
Favorite Hlthcare Staffing Inc .... C 913 383-9733
Overland Park *(G-8708)*
Favorite Hlthcare Staffing Inc .... A 913 648-6563
Leawood *(G-5396)*
Flightsafety International .... F 316 612-5300
Wichita *(G-14388)*
Grafton Inc .... A 913 498-0701
Overland Park *(G-8768)*
Have It Maid .... F 316 264-0110
Wichita *(G-14568)*
Housekeeping Unlimited .... E 785 842-2444
Lawrence *(G-4905)*
Interim Healthcare Inc .... C 785 272-1616
Topeka *(G-12726)*
Interim Healthcare Inc .... E 620 663-2423
Hutchinson *(G-3335)*
Interim Healthcare Kansas City .... E 913 381-3100
Leawood *(G-5439)*
▼ **John A Marshall Company** .... C 913 599-4700
Lenexa *(G-5929)*
Kansas Air Center Topeka Inc .... E 785 234-2602
Topeka *(G-12757)*
Kansas City Transcription Inc .... F 913 469-1000
Shawnee Mission *(G-11512)*
Kansas Personnel Services Inc .... C 785 272-9999
Topeka *(G-12796)*
Kelly Services Inc .... A 913 451-1400
Overland Park *(G-8913)*
Kleeb Services Inc .... F 913 253-7000
Overland Park *(G-8922)*
Kwik Staff LLC .... F 785 430-5806
Topeka *(G-12825)*
Lulu Mimi Hsclners Extrrdnaire .... F 913 649-6022
Shawnee Mission *(G-11582)*
Manchester Inc .... F 913 262-0440
Overland Park *(G-8983)*
Manpowergroup Inc .... F 316 946-0088
Wichita *(G-15005)*
Maxim Healthcare Services Inc .... F 913 383-2220
Overland Park *(G-8998)*
MB Health Specialist Inc .... F 913 438-6337
Shawnee Mission *(G-11603)*
Merry Maids Ltd Partnership .... F 785 842-2410
Lawrence *(G-5023)*
Mobile Health Clinics LLC .... D 913 383-0991
Leawood *(G-5490)*
Nexus It Group Inc .... F 913 815-1750
Overland Park *(G-9085)*
On Demand Employment Svcs LLC .... F 913 371-3212
Kansas City *(G-4294)*
Ortho Innovations LLC .... F 913 449-8376
Overland Park *(G-9115)*
Pivot Companies LLC .... F 800 581-6398
Overland Park *(G-9170)*
Premier Personnel Inc .... D 785 273-9944
Topeka *(G-12983)*
Professional Drivers GA Inc .... E 316 945-9700
Wichita *(G-15358)*
Rebel Staffing LLC .... D 888 372-3302
Phillipsburg *(G-9798)*
Residential Services Inc .... E 316 832-9058
Wichita *(G-15449)*
Sebes Hay LLC .... E 620 285-6941
Larned *(G-4712)*
Specialists Group LLC .... F 316 267-7375
Wichita *(G-15635)*
Spencer Reed Group LLC .... C 913 663-4400
Leawood *(G-5557)*
Squadbuilders Inc .... D 913 649-4401
Leawood *(G-5559)*
Starfire Enterprises Inc .... F 785 842-1111
Lawrence *(G-5121)*
Tdb Communications Inc .... C 913 327-7400
Lenexa *(G-6168)*
Team International Inc .... F 913 681-0740
Overland Park *(G-9397)*
Temporary Employment Corp .... E 785 749-2800
Lawrence *(G-5134)*
Topeka Services Inc .... F 785 228-7800
Lawrence *(G-5141)*
Trac Staffing Service Inc .... F 913 341-1150
Shawnee Mission *(G-11939)*
USP Technical Services .... F 310 517-1800
Derby *(G-1278)*
Vintage Place of Pittsburg .... E 620 231-4554
Pittsburg *(G-9958)*
Volt Management Corp .... D 913 906-9568
Overland Park *(G-9471)*
Winfield Area E M S .... E 620 221-2300
Winfield *(G-16183)*
Yoh Services LLC .... F 913 648-4004
Overland Park *(G-9518)*

7371 Custom Computer Programming Svcs

911 Datamaster Inc .... E 913 469-6401
Overland Park *(G-8333)*
Aceware Systems Inc .... F 785 537-2937
Manhattan *(G-6531)*
Actuarial Resources Corp Kans .... E 913 451-0044
Overland Park *(G-8345)*
Ad Astra Info Systems LLC .... E 913 652-4100
Shawnee Mission *(G-11073)*
Advantage Computer Entps Inc .... E 620 365-5156
Iola *(G-3585)*
Adventuretech Group Inc .... F 913 402-9600
Overland Park *(G-8354)*
Agelix Consulting LLC .... E 913 708-8145
Overland Park *(G-8357)*
All of E Solutions LLC .... E 785 832-2900
Lawrence *(G-4725)*
American Gvrnment Slutions LLC .... F 913 428-2550
Leawood *(G-5320)*
Apex Innovations Inc .... F 913 254-0250
Olathe *(G-7531)*
Applied Content RES Tech LLC .... F 785 422-4980
Morland *(G-7166)*
Aquent LLC .... E 913 345-9119
Shawnee Mission *(G-11115)*
AT&T Corp .... E 785 276-5553
Topeka *(G-12351)*
Atonix Digital LLC .... E 913 458-2000
Overland Park *(G-8411)*
Bardavon Hlth Innovations LLC .... E 913 236-1020
Overland Park *(G-8433)*
Bowman Systems LLC .... D 318 213-8780
Overland Park *(G-8478)*
Builder Designs Inc .... F 913 393-3367
Olathe *(G-7566)*
Bungii LLC .... E 913 353-6683
Overland Park *(G-8491)*
Cactus Software LLC .... D 913 677-0092
Overland Park *(G-8506)*
Catapult International LLC .... E 913 232-2389
Lenexa *(G-5733)*
CCH Incorporated .... B 316 612-5000
Wichita *(G-13966)*
Centralized Showing Svc Inc .... D 913 851-8405
Overland Park *(G-8538)*
Certtech LLC .... E 913 814-9770
Lenexa *(G-5743)*
Chelsoft Solutions Co .... D 913 579-1399
Olathe *(G-7591)*
Chocolatey Software Inc .... F 785 783-4720
Topeka *(G-12465)*
Clarus Group LLC .... E 913 599-5255
Overland Park *(G-8560)*
Command Alkon Incorporated .... E 913 384-0880
Lenexa *(G-5772)*
Computer Instruments Inc .... E 913 307-8850
Lenexa *(G-5782)*
Computerwise Inc .... F 408 389-8241
Olathe *(G-7609)*
Control Vision Corporation .... E 620 231-5816
Pittsburg *(G-9845)*
Cowley College & Area .... B 620 442-0430
Arkansas City *(G-150)*
Creative Capsule LLC .... D 816 421-1714
Overland Park *(G-8608)*
CSS Group Inc .... F 316 269-9090
Wichita *(G-14138)*
▼ **Cybertron International Inc** .... D 316 303-1022
Wichita *(G-14150)*
Datateam Systems Inc .... E 785 843-8150
Lawrence *(G-4826)*
Ddsports Inc .... G 913 636-0432
Merriam *(G-7090)*
Dg Business Solutions Inc .... F 913 766-0163
Lenexa *(G-5815)*
Digital Evolution Group LLC .... C 913 498-9988
Overland Park *(G-8655)*
Distributorcentral LLC .... F 888 516-7401
Gardner *(G-2338)*
Dunami Inc .... E 303 981-3303
Overland Park *(G-8665)*
E-Consultsusa LLC .... F 913 696-1001
Leawood *(G-5381)*
Esolutions Inc .... D 866 633-4726
Overland Park *(G-8690)*
Faithlink LLC .... F 913 904-1070
Overland Park *(G-8702)*
Fannect LLC .... F 913 271-2346
Overland Park *(G-8704)*

S I C

Firemon LLC E 913 948-9570
Overland Park *(G-8717)*

Fujitsu America Inc E 913 327-2800
Shawnee Mission *(G-11384)*

Fundamental Technologies LLC F 785 840-0800
Lawrence *(G-4866)*

Fusion Global Solutions LLC E 913 707-2866
Overland Park *(G-8743)*

Galaxie Business Equipment Inc E 620 221-3469
Winfield *(G-16142)*

Global Soft Systems Inc E 913 338-1400
Overland Park *(G-8760)*

Gorydz Inc F 913 486-1665
Kansas City *(G-4040)*

Healthcare Prfmce Group Inc D 316 796-0337
Spring Hill *(G-12086)*

Heritage Cmpt Consulting Inc F 913 529-4227
Overland Park *(G-8812)*

I T Power LLC E 913 384-5800
Shawnee Mission *(G-11448)*

Information Tech Intl Inc F 913 579-8079
Hays *(G-2852)*

Innova Consulting LLC F 913 210-2002
Overland Park *(G-8845)*

Innovative Technology Services E 785 271-2070
Topeka *(G-12724)*

Innovision Corporation E 913 438-3200
Overland Park *(G-8847)*

Inscyt LLC A 913 579-7335
Overland Park *(G-8848)*

Iq Group Inc F 913 722-6700
Lenexa *(G-5922)*

Itedium Inc E 913 499-4850
Overland Park *(G-8865)*

J & M Industries Inc E 913 362-8994
Prairie Village *(G-10037)*

Jack Henry & Associates Inc C 913 422-3233
Shawnee Mission *(G-11479)*

Jaray Software Inc G 316 267-5758
Wichita *(G-14747)*

Juniper Payments LLC E 316 267-3200
Wichita *(G-14778)*

Jupiter Esources LLC F 405 488-3886
Kansas City *(G-4129)*

K2b Incorporated E 913 663-3311
Shawnee Mission *(G-11507)*

Kaliaperumal Mamalay G 816 210-1248
Overland Park *(G-8885)*

Kalos Inc E 785 232-3606
Topeka *(G-12752)*

Kansys Inc E 913 780-5291
Olathe *(G-7830)*

Keycentrix Inc E 316 262-2231
Wichita *(G-14854)*

Leidos Inc G 913 317-5120
Shawnee Mission *(G-11560)*

Lexinet Corporation E 620 767-6346
Council Grove *(G-1170)*

Lockpath Inc D 913 601-4800
Overland Park *(G-8966)*

LPI Information Systems G 913 381-9118
Overland Park *(G-8972)*

Lucity Inc E 800 492-2468
Overland Park *(G-8973)*

Marathon Reprographics Inc F 816 221-7881
Kansas City *(G-4217)*

Mobile Reasoning Inc G 913 888-2600
Lenexa *(G-6010)*

Moonshot Innovations LLC E 913 815-6611
Overland Park *(G-9051)*

Myfreightworld Carrier MGT Inc E 877 549-9438
Overland Park *(G-9066)*

Netsmart LLC E 913 327-7444
Overland Park *(G-9075)*

Netsmart Technologies Inc C 913 327-7444
Overland Park *(G-9076)*

Networks Plus E 785 825-0400
Manhattan *(G-6759)*

Neural Technologies Inc C 913 831-0273
Shawnee Mission *(G-11677)*

Nic Inc B 877 234-3468
Olathe *(G-7920)*

Nicusa Inc C 913 498-3468
Olathe *(G-7922)*

Object Tech Solutions Inc D 913 345-9080
Leawood *(G-5507)*

▲ On Demand Technologies LLC F 913 438-1800
Overland Park *(G-9102)*

Onspring Technologies LLC F 913 601-4900
Overland Park *(G-9105)*

Orion Information Systems LLC F 913 825-3272
Overland Park *(G-9113)*

Paige Technologies LLC E 913 381-0600
Overland Park *(G-9135)*

Pegasus Communication Solution F 913 937-8552
Overland Park *(G-9153)*

Platform Technologies LLC E 816 285-3874
Fairway *(G-1917)*

Presig Holdings LLC F 913 706-1315
Overland Park *(G-9184)*

Prs Inc F 844 679-2273
Overland Park *(G-9199)*

PS Holdings LLC E 913 599-1600
Overland Park *(G-9201)*

PSC Group LLC E 847 517-7200
Overland Park *(G-9202)*

Quest Research & Development F 316 267-1216
Wichita *(G-15393)*

R & O Partnership E 785 434-4534
Plainville *(G-9991)*

Rhythm Engineering LLC E 913 227-0603
Lenexa *(G-6108)*

Sara It Solutions Inc F 913 269-6980
Overland Park *(G-9280)*

Sara Software Systems LLC E 913 370-4197
Olathe *(G-8055)*

Servicetitan Inc G 316 267-5758
Wichita *(G-15568)*

Signal Kit LLC F 866 297-7585
Leawood *(G-5551)*

Softek Illuminate Inc F 913 981-5300
Overland Park *(G-9321)*

Softek Solutions Inc E 913 649-1024
Prairie Village *(G-10067)*

Sohum Systems LLC E 913 221-7204
Overland Park *(G-9323)*

Solutions North Bank E 785 425-6721
Stockton *(G-12188)*

Solutions Now Inc E 913 327-5805
Overland Park *(G-9325)*

Spatial Data Research Inc F 314 705-0772
Lawrence *(G-5114)*

Stackify LLC F 816 888-5055
Leawood *(G-5560)*

Staffbridge LLC F 913 381-4044
Overland Park *(G-9350)*

Stonelock Global F 800 970-6168
Overland Park *(G-9366)*

Sur-Tec Inc G 913 647-7720
Shawnee *(G-11036)*

Tennessee Info Consortium LLC E 913 498-3468
Olathe *(G-8107)*

Terradatum D 888 212-4793
Overland Park *(G-9403)*

Torch Research LLC E 913 955-2738
Leawood *(G-5577)*

Traq-It Inc F 913 498-1221
Overland Park *(G-9426)*

Tri-Com Technical Services LLC C 913 652-0600
Leawood *(G-5584)*

United States Dept of Army D 785 240-0308
Fort Riley *(G-1952)*

Upg Solutions LLC F 844 737-0365
Leawood *(G-5591)*

Valiant Global Def Svcs Inc D 913 651-9782
Leavenworth *(G-5304)*

Veracity Consulting Inc D 913 945-1912
Overland Park *(G-9462)*

Vigilias LLC E 800 924-8140
Wichita *(G-15907)*

Vinsolutions C 913 825-6124
Shawnee Mission *(G-11980)*

Vos Design Inc F 913 825-6556
Lenexa *(G-6218)*

Washington FNB F 785 325-2221
Washington *(G-13471)*

Xpressotech Solutions LLC F 316 993-9397
Goddard *(G-2457)*

7372 Prepackaged Software

Advanced Technology Group Inc E 913 239-0050
Overland Park *(G-8350)*

Art of Escape Ict G 316 768-2588
Wichita *(G-13739)*

Black Knight Fincl Svcs Inc G 913 693-0000
Leawood *(G-5340)*

Blue Infotech Inc F 816 945-2583
Leawood *(G-5341)*

Bowman Software Systems LLC D 318 213-8780
Overland Park *(G-8477)*

Classone Software G 913 831-4976
Shawnee Mission *(G-11238)*

Control Systems Intl Inc D 913 599-5010
Shawnee Mission *(G-11264)*

Control Vision Corporation E 620 231-5816
Pittsburg *(G-9845)*

Daniel Zimmerman G 303 378-2511
Overland Park *(G-8634)*

Data Locker Inc G 913 310-9088
Overland Park *(G-8636)*

Datateam Systems Inc E 785 843-8150
Lawrence *(G-4826)*

Ddsports Inc G 913 636-0432
Merriam *(G-7090)*

▲ Digital Ally Inc D 913 814-7774
Lenexa *(G-5816)*

Euronet Worldwide Inc D 913 327-4200
Leawood *(G-5389)*

Examfx Inc E 800 586-2253
Leawood *(G-5390)*

Financial Institution Tech Inc E 888 848-7349
Topeka *(G-12610)*

General Dynamics Info Tech Inc E 785 832-0207
Lawrence *(G-4871)*

Hyland Holdings LLC E 913 227-7000
Lenexa *(G-5908)*

Hyland LLC B 440 788-5045
Olathe *(G-7783)*

Igt Global Solutions Corp E 785 861-7300
Topeka *(G-12713)*

J & M Industries Inc E 913 362-8994
Prairie Village *(G-10037)*

Jaray Software Inc G 316 267-5758
Wichita *(G-14747)*

Jayhawk Software G 620 365-8065
Iola *(G-3615)*

Kaliaperumal Mamalay G 816 210-1248
Overland Park *(G-8885)*

Kana Software Inc C 913 802-6756
Overland Park *(G-8886)*

Lockpath Inc D 913 601-4800
Overland Park *(G-8966)*

LPI Information Systems G 913 381-9118
Overland Park *(G-8972)*

Making The Mark Inc G 913 402-8000
Shawnee Mission *(G-11592)*

Medforce Technologies Inc F 845 426-0459
Topeka *(G-12879)*

Mersoft Corporation E 913 871-6200
Leawood *(G-5476)*

Mgmttv Inc F 316 262-4678
Wichita *(G-15062)*

Microsoft Corporation A 913 323-1200
Overland Park *(G-9020)*

Mobile Reasoning Inc G 913 888-2600
Lenexa *(G-6010)*

Netsmart Technologies Inc C 913 327-7444
Overland Park *(G-9076)*

Nortonlifelock Inc E 913 451-6710
Shawnee Mission *(G-11688)*

Optileaf Incorporated G 855 678-4532
Wichita *(G-15226)*

Oracle Systems Corporation D 913 663-3400
Shawnee Mission *(G-11699)*

Orion Communications Inc G 913 538-7110
Overland Park *(G-9112)*

Professional Data Services F 620 663-5282
Hutchinson *(G-3415)*

Professional Software Inc G 316 269-4264
Wichita *(G-15366)*

PSI Services Inc C 913 895-4600
Olathe *(G-8011)*

PSI Services Inc F 843 520-2992
Olathe *(G-8010)*

Redivus Health G 816 582-5428
Olathe *(G-8021)*

Rpms LLC F 800 776-7435
Overland Park *(G-9261)*

S & T Telephone Coop Assn F 785 460-7300
Colby *(G-1038)*

Scott Specialties Inc E 785 243-2594
Concordia *(G-1129)*

Servicetitan Inc G 316 267-5758
Wichita *(G-15568)*

Soleran Inc G 913 647-5900
Overland Park *(G-9324)*

Systems Building Services LLC E 913 385-1496
Lenexa *(G-6165)*

Tbcsoft Inc G 785 272-5993
Topeka *(G-13144)*

Thunderhead Engrg Cons Inc.........F....... 785 770-8511
Manhattan *(G-6826)*
Touchnet Info Systems Inc.........D....... 913 599-6699
Lenexa *(G-6187)*
Touchpoint Dashboard LLC.........G....... 512 585-5975
Wichita *(G-15777)*
U Inc.........F....... 913 814-7708
Overland Park *(G-9436)*
Unitas Global LLC.........D....... 913 339-2300
Overland Park *(G-9441)*
Web Creations & Consulting LLC.........G....... 785 823-7630
Salina *(G-10762)*
Wellsky Corporation.........C....... 913 307-1000
Overland Park *(G-9490)*
Work Comp Specialty Associates.........E....... 785 841-7751
Lawrence *(G-5191)*

7373 Computer Integrated Systems Design

Access Group LLC.........F....... 316 264-0270
Wichita *(G-13602)*
Advantage Computer Entps Inc.........E....... 620 365-5156
Iola *(G-3585)*
Aegis Business Solutions LLC.........G....... 913 307-9922
Olathe *(G-7512)*
Air Power Consultants Inc.........F....... 913 894-0044
Olathe *(G-7514)*
Allegiant Networks LLC.........E....... 913 599-6900
Leawood *(G-5316)*
American Ctrl & Engrg Svc Inc.........F....... 316 776-7500
Rose Hill *(G-10235)*
American Gvrnment Slutions LLC.........F....... 913 428-2550
Leawood *(G-5320)*
Balance Innovations LLC.........D....... 913 599-1177
Lenexa *(G-5682)*
Bartunek Group Inc.........E....... 913 327-8800
Overland Park *(G-8435)*
Cerner Government Services Inc.........E....... 816 201-2273
Kansas City *(G-3905)*
Clarus Group LLC.........E....... 913 599-5255
Overland Park *(G-8560)*
Computer Sciences Corporation.........C....... 913 469-8700
Overland Park *(G-8593)*
Control Systems Intl Inc.........D....... 913 599-5010
Shawnee Mission *(G-11264)*
Convergeone Inc.........C....... 913 307-2300
Overland Park *(G-8597)*
Covansys Corporation.........C....... 913 469-8700
Shawnee Mission *(G-11275)*
Danco Systems Inc.........F....... 913 962-0600
Shawnee *(G-10939)*
Datasystem Solutions Inc.........E....... 913 362-6969
Overland Park *(G-8638)*
Depco LLC.........E....... 620 231-0019
Pittsburg *(G-9852)*
Design Analysis and RES Corp.........F....... 785 832-0434
Lawrence *(G-4833)*
Dynamic Cmpt Sltons Topeka Inc.........F....... 785 354-7000
Topeka *(G-12563)*
Financial Institution Tech Inc.........E....... 888 848-7349
Topeka *(G-12610)*
Fireboard Labs LLC.........G....... 816 945-2232
Olathe *(G-7710)*
Foresite Msp LLC.........E....... 800 940-4699
Overland Park *(G-8734)*
Gorydz Inc.........F....... 913 486-1665
Kansas City *(G-4040)*
GSM Sales LLC.........F....... 816 674-1066
Roeland Park *(G-10223)*
Harris Computer Systems.........D....... 785 843-8150
Lawrence *(G-4890)*
High Touch Inc.........D....... 316 462-4001
Wichita *(G-14606)*
Innova Consulting LLC.........F....... 913 210-2002
Overland Park *(G-8845)*
Isigma Consulting LLC.........F....... 620 757-6363
Overland Park *(G-8863)*
K G Moats & Sons LLC.........E....... 785 437-2021
Saint Marys *(G-10368)*
Kaliaperumal Mamalay.........G....... 816 210-1248
Overland Park *(G-8885)*
Kansas Info Consortium LLC.........F....... 785 296-5059
Topeka *(G-12783)*
Leidos Inc.........G....... 913 317-5120
Shawnee Mission *(G-11560)*
Mersoft Corporation.........E....... 913 871-6200
Leawood *(G-5476)*
Netapp Inc.........E....... 316 636-8000
Wichita *(G-15161)*
Netapp Inc.........C....... 913 451-6718
Overland Park *(G-9073)*
Netchemia LLC.........E....... 913 789-0996
Overland Park *(G-9074)*
Netstandard Inc.........D....... 913 428-4200
Overland Park *(G-9077)*
Networks Plus.........E....... 785 825-0400
Salina *(G-10611)*
Networks Plus.........E....... 785 825-0400
Manhattan *(G-6759)*
Nokia of America Corporation.........D....... 316 636-4800
Wichita *(G-15184)*
Northrop Grumman Systems Corp.........E....... 785 861-3398
Topeka *(G-12939)*
Orion Information Systems LLC.........F....... 913 825-3272
Overland Park *(G-9113)*
Paracom Technologies Inc.........E....... 316 293-2900
Wichita *(G-15254)*
Quark Studios LLC.........F....... 913 871-5154
Olathe *(G-8014)*
Regulatory Consultants Inc.........E....... 785 486-2882
Horton *(G-3133)*
Results Technology Inc.........E....... 913 928-8300
Overland Park *(G-9238)*
Rhythm Engineering LLC.........E....... 913 227-0603
Lenexa *(G-6108)*
Saicon Consultants Inc.........F....... 913 451-1178
Overland Park *(G-9272)*
Sara Software Systems LLC.........E....... 913 370-4197
Olathe *(G-8055)*
Sirius Computer Solutions Inc.........F....... 913 469-7900
Overland Park *(G-9314)*
Softwarfare LLC.........F....... 202 854-9268
Prairie Village *(G-10068)*
Source Incorporated Missouri.........F....... 913 663-2700
Shawnee *(G-11030)*
◆ **Stallard Technologies Inc**.........E....... 913 851-2260
Overland Park *(G-9351)*
Thunderhead Engrg Cons Inc.........F....... 785 770-8511
Manhattan *(G-6826)*
Triple-I Corporation.........D....... 913 563-7227
Leawood *(G-5585)*
Wachter Tech Solutions Inc.........D....... 856 222-0643
Lenexa *(G-6220)*

7374 Data & Computer Processing & Preparation

1&1 Internet Inc.........F....... 816 621-4795
Lenexa *(G-5615)*
Accenture LLP.........C....... 913 319-1000
Overland Park *(G-8340)*
Aegis Processing Solutions Inc.........D....... 785 232-0061
Topeka *(G-12300)*
American Design Inc.........F....... 785 766-0409
Baldwin City *(G-353)*
American Gvrnment Slutions LLC.........F....... 913 428-2550
Leawood *(G-5320)*
Automatic Data Processing Inc.........F....... 913 492-4200
Lenexa *(G-5675)*
Automatic Data Processing Inc.........C....... 515 875-3160
Wichita *(G-13773)*
Bradford and Galt Incorporated.........E....... 913 663-1264
Shawnee Mission *(G-11177)*
Capital Graphics Inc.........E....... 785 233-6677
Topeka *(G-12431)*
Casey Associates Inc.........F....... 913 276-3200
Lenexa *(G-5731)*
Central of Kansas Inc.........D....... 785 238-4114
Junction City *(G-3678)*
Century Business Technologies.........E....... 785 267-4555
Topeka *(G-12458)*
Civicplus LLC.........C....... 888 228-2233
Manhattan *(G-6590)*
Computer Sciences Corporation.........C....... 913 469-8700
Overland Park *(G-8593)*
Convergys Corporation.........E....... 913 782-3333
Olathe *(G-7614)*
Convergys Corporation.........B....... 316 681-4800
Wichita *(G-14095)*
Covansys Corporation.........C....... 913 469-8700
Shawnee Mission *(G-11275)*
Data Center Inc.........C....... 620 694-6800
Hutchinson *(G-3255)*
Data Center Inc.........F....... 913 492-2468
Lenexa *(G-5802)*
Data Center Inc.........E....... 620 694-6800
Hutchinson *(G-3256)*
Digital Evolution Group LLC.........C....... 913 498-9988
Overland Park *(G-8655)*
▲ **Digital Lagoon Inc**.........F....... 913 648-6900
Overland Park *(G-8656)*
Dimension X Design LLC.........F....... 913 908-3824
Olathe *(G-7655)*
Farmobile Inc.........F....... 844 337-2255
Leawood *(G-5395)*
Florida Information Consortium.........F....... 913 498-3468
Olathe *(G-7715)*
General Dynamics Info Tech Inc.........E....... 785 832-0207
Lawrence *(G-4871)*
Infutor Data Solutions LLC.........F....... 913 782-8544
Olathe *(G-7790)*
Insysiv LLC.........F....... 816 694-9397
Kansas City *(G-4102)*
Iq Group Inc.........F....... 913 722-6700
Lenexa *(G-5922)*
Iris Data Services Inc.........D....... 913 937-0590
Kansas City *(G-4112)*
Jack Henry & Associates Inc.........E....... 913 341-3434
Shawnee Mission *(G-11480)*
Jupiter Esources LLC.........F....... 405 488-3886
Kansas City *(G-4129)*
Megaforce LLC.........D....... 913 402-0800
Leawood *(G-5472)*
Mgmttv Inc.........F....... 316 262-4678
Wichita *(G-15062)*
Mize Houser & Company PA.........D....... 785 233-0536
Topeka *(G-12908)*
Neufinancial Inc.........E....... 913 825-0000
Overland Park *(G-9079)*
Nic Solutions LLC.........F....... 913 498-3468
Olathe *(G-7921)*
Northrop Grumman Systems Corp.........C....... 785 861-3375
Topeka *(G-12938)*
Northrop Grumman Systems Corp.........B....... 913 651-8311
Fort Leavenworth *(G-1940)*
Perspecta Entp Solutions LLC.........F....... 785 274-4200
Topeka *(G-12970)*
Physicians Business Netwrk LLC.........E....... 913 381-5200
Overland Park *(G-9164)*
Postal Presort Inc.........D....... 316 262-3333
Wichita *(G-15316)*
Qts Realty Trust Inc.........E....... 913 814-9988
Overland Park *(G-9210)*
Qualitytech LP.........E....... 877 787-3282
Overland Park *(G-9219)*
R & S Digital Services Inc.........F....... 620 792-6171
Great Bend *(G-2628)*
Servervault LLC.........F....... 913 814-9988
Overland Park *(G-9298)*
Systronics Inc.........F....... 913 829-9229
Olathe *(G-8093)*
Teracrunch LLC.........F....... 214 405-7158
Leawood *(G-5572)*
Trinity Animation Inc.........F....... 816 525-0103
Overland Park *(G-9428)*
Tsunami Surf Riders LLC.........F....... 913 498-3468
Olathe *(G-8123)*
Universal Money Centers Inc.........E....... 913 831-2055
Lenexa *(G-6204)*
Web Creations & Consulting LLC.........G....... 785 823-7630
Salina *(G-10762)*
Whale Ventures LLC.........C....... 913 814-9988
Overland Park *(G-9493)*
Xcellence Inc.........D....... 913 362-8662
Shawnee Mission *(G-12021)*

7375 Information Retrieval Svcs

Blue Infotech Inc.........F....... 816 945-2583
Leawood *(G-5341)*
Building Solutions LLC.........F....... 620 225-1199
Dodge City *(G-1314)*
Company Kitchen LLC.........E....... 913 384-4900
Shawnee Mission *(G-11255)*
Elavon Inc.........B....... 913 648-6444
Overland Park *(G-8672)*
Fusion Telecom Intl Inc.........F....... 913 262-4638
Shawnee Mission *(G-11387)*
General Dynamics Info Tech Inc.........E....... 785 832-0207
Lawrence *(G-4871)*
Hooper Holmes Inc.........D....... 913 764-1045
Olathe *(G-7777)*
Infutor Data Solutions LLC.........F....... 913 782-8544
Olathe *(G-7790)*
Kansas African American Aff.........F....... 785 296-4874
Topeka *(G-12756)*
Kansas Info Consortium LLC.........F....... 785 296-5059
Topeka *(G-12783)*
Marketing Technologies Inc.........D....... 913 342-9111
Kansas City *(G-4218)*
Qts Realty Trust Inc.........E....... 913 814-9988
Overland Park *(G-9210)*

S I C

Topeka Unified School Dst 501 ......E 785 438-4750
Topeka (G-13190)

7376 Computer Facilities Management Svcs

Computer Sciences Corporation ......C 913 469-8700
Overland Park (G-8593)

Convergeone Inc ......C 913 307-2300
Overland Park (G-8597)

Quality Tech Svcs Frt Worth II ......F 913 814-9988
Overland Park (G-9214)

Quality Tech Svcs Nrtheast LLC ......F 913 814-9988
Overland Park (G-9216)

Quality Technology Svcs LLC ......D 913 814-9988
Overland Park (G-9217)

Sara Software Systems LLC ......E 913 370-4197
Olathe (G-8055)

Topeka Unified School Dst 501 ......E 785 438-4750
Topeka (G-13190)

7377 Computer Rental & Leasing

Evolv Solutions LLC ......E 913 469-8900
Shawnee Mission (G-11352)

7378 Computer Maintenance & Repair

ADI Systems Inc ......F 785 825-5975
Salina (G-10394)

Alliance Technologies Inc ......F 913 262-7977
Overland Park (G-8371)

Computech Service of Kansas ......E 785 266-2585
Topeka (G-12497)

Dataco Derex Inc ......F 913 438-2444
Leawood (G-5370)

Fox Computer Inc ......E 785 776-1452
Manhattan (G-6640)

Haddock Corporation ......E 316 558-3849
Wichita (G-14539)

Heritage Cmpt Consulting Inc ......F 913 529-4227
Overland Park (G-8812)

Installation and Svc Tech Inc ......C 913 652-7000
Leawood (G-5438)

Iris Data Services Inc ......D 913 937-0590
Kansas City (G-4112)

Isigma Consulting LLC ......F 620 757-6363
Overland Park (G-8863)

Jack Henry & Associates Inc ......C 913 422-3233
Shawnee Mission (G-11479)

Kanokla Telephone Association ......E 620 845-5682
Caldwell (G-660)

Keltech Solutions LLC ......F 785 841-4611
Lawrence (G-4940)

Loquient Inc ......F 913 221-0430
Shawnee Mission (G-11577)

Maps Inc ......E 913 599-0500
Lenexa (G-5984)

Network Management Group Inc ......E 620 665-3611
Hutchinson (G-3389)

Niffie Printing Inc ......F 913 592-3040
Spring Hill (G-12091)

Repair Shack Inc ......E 913 732-0514
Lenexa (G-6105)

Resq Systems LLC ......F 913 390-1030
Olathe (G-8027)

Ricoh Usa Inc ......C 913 890-5100
Shawnee Mission (G-11802)

Tech Gurus LLC ......F 913 299-8700
Kansas City (G-4462)

Wolfes Camera Shops Inc ......E 785 235-1386
Topeka (G-13248)

Word-Tech Inc ......E 913 722-3334
Shawnee Mission (G-12019)

7379 Computer Related Svcs, NEC

A R Systems Inc ......E 620 564-3790
Ellinwood (G-1626)

Acceligent Inc ......F 972 504-6660
Overland Park (G-8339)

Advisors Tech LLC ......F 844 671-6071
Topeka (G-12299)

Agelix Consulting LLC ......E 913 708-8145
Overland Park (G-8357)

Agvantis Inc ......D 316 266-5400
Wichita (G-13644)

ASK Associates Inc ......E 785 841-8194
Lawrence (G-4738)

Avazpour Networking Svcs Inc ......E 913 323-1411
Overland Park (G-8414)

Buchanan Technologies Inc ......E 316 219-0124
Wichita (G-13903)

▲ Cgf Investments Inc ......E 316 691-4500
Wichita (G-13994)

Choose Networks Inc ......F 316 773-0920
Wichita (G-14013)

Clarus Group LLC ......E 913 599-5255
Overland Park (G-8560)

Communication Cable Company ......D 610 644-5155
Leawood (G-5356)

Computer Sciences Corporation ......C 913 469-8700
Overland Park (G-8593)

Comtrsys Inc ......F 316 265-1585
Wichita (G-14084)

Dave McDermott ......F 785 354-8233
Topeka (G-12546)

Digital Printing Services Inc ......F 913 492-1500
Lenexa (G-5817)

Dunami Inc ......E 303 981-3303
Overland Park (G-8665)

Eagle Software Inc ......E 785 823-7257
Salina (G-10483)

Electronic Technology Inc ......F 913 962-8083
Shawnee Mission (G-11330)

Escoute LLC ......F 816 678-8398
Olathe (G-7692)

Gateway Solutions Inc ......F 913 851-1055
Overland Park (G-8748)

General Dynamics Info Tech Inc ......D 913 684-5770
Leavenworth (G-5244)

Genesis Corp ......C 913 906-9991
Shawnee Mission (G-11393)

Globalink Inc ......D 785 823-8284
Salina (G-10513)

Health Data Specialists LLC ......E 785 242-3419
Pomona (G-10004)

Heartland Cstmer Solutions LLC ......C 913 685-8855
Leawood (G-5424)

Hyr Global Source Inc ......F 913 815-2597
Overland Park (G-8835)

I T G Consulting Inc ......F 785 228-1585
Topeka (G-12711)

Imagintive Cnsulting Group Inc ......F 913 481-1936
Overland Park (G-8839)

Integrated Solutions Group Inc ......E 620 662-5796
Hutchinson (G-3334)

Isg Technology LLC ......C 785 823-1555
Salina (G-10550)

Isg Technology LLC ......F 785 266-2585
Topeka (G-12728)

Isg Technology LLC ......E 316 636-5655
Wichita (G-14731)

Isigma Consulting LLC ......F 620 757-6363
Overland Park (G-8863)

It21 Inc ......F 913 393-4821
Overland Park (G-8864)

Kanokla Telephone Association ......E 620 845-5682
Caldwell (G-660)

Local Gvernment Online Ind LLC ......E 913 498-3468
Olathe (G-7863)

Loquient Inc ......F 913 221-0430
Shawnee Mission (G-11577)

LP Technologies Inc ......F 316 831-9696
Wichita (G-14986)

Magna Infotech Ltd ......D 203 748-7680
Overland Park (G-8979)

Menufycom LLC ......E 913 738-9399
Leawood (G-5473)

Mize Houser & Company PA ......D 785 233-0536
Topeka (G-12908)

Net Systems LLC ......F 316 691-9400
Wichita (G-15159)

Network Management Group Inc ......E 620 665-3611
Hutchinson (G-3389)

Optiv Security Inc ......F 816 421-6611
Overland Park (G-9110)

Progrssive Tech Intgrators LLC ......F 913 663-0870
Overland Park (G-9192)

PSC Group LLC ......E 847 517-7200
Overland Park (G-9202)

Quark Studios LLC ......F 913 871-5154
Olathe (G-8014)

Randel Solutions LLC ......F 703 459-7672
Overland Park (G-9224)

Risenow LLC ......F 913 948-7405
Leawood (G-5539)

Riverpoint Group Illinois LLC ......F 913 663-2002
Overland Park (G-9245)

Rx Savings LLC ......F 913 815-3139
Overland Park (G-9264)

Saicon Consultants Inc ......F 913 451-1178
Overland Park (G-9272)

Shoroeders Jim Sftwr & Video ......F 620 227-7628
Dodge City (G-1430)

Smart Security Solutions Inc ......E 913 568-2573
Overland Park (G-9319)

Softwarfare LLC ......F 202 854-9268
Prairie Village (G-10068)

Sogeti USA LLC ......E 913 451-9600
Overland Park (G-9322)

Sun Microsystems Inc ......F 913 327-7820
Overland Park (G-9372)

Technology Group Solutions LLC ......D 913 451-9900
Lenexa (G-6172)

Teksystems Inc ......E 316 448-4500
Wichita (G-15728)

Tkfast Inc ......E 316 260-2500
Wichita (G-15769)

Twenty-First Century ......F 913 713-2121
Mission (G-7139)

Veracity Consulting Inc ......D 913 945-1912
Overland Park (G-9462)

Vizion Interactive ......F 888 484-9466
Overland Park (G-9469)

White Paladin Group Inc ......E 913 722-4688
Prairie Village (G-10082)

Whiting House Group LLC ......F 816 272-4496
Lenexa (G-6228)

Wood Ribble & Twyman Inc ......D 913 396-4400
Overland Park (G-9503)

Word-Tech Inc ......E 913 722-3334
Shawnee Mission (G-12019)

7381 Detective & Armored Car Svcs

1138 Inc ......E 913 322-5900
Overland Park (G-8328)

Alert 360 ......C 913 599-3439
Lenexa (G-5639)

American Sentry Security Sys ......E 785 232-1525
Topeka (G-12323)

Blue Eagle Investigations Inc ......F 913 685-2583
Paola (G-9542)

Brinks Incorporated ......F 316 945-0244
Wichita (G-13891)

Civil Air Patrol Inc ......E 620 275-6121
Garden City (G-2127)

Clarence M Kelley & Assoc of K ......D 913 647-7700
Shawnee (G-10929)

Clark Security Service ......F 620 225-6577
Dodge City (G-1324)

D & B Legal Services Inc ......D 913 362-8110
Prairie Village (G-10024)

Day & Zimmermann Kansas LLC ......C 620 421-7400
Parsons (G-9679)

Diamond Security Lc ......E 316 263-3883
Wichita (G-14209)

Eagle Security Inc ......D 913 721-1360
Kansas City (G-3979)

Eagle Security Services ......D 620 251-0085
Coffeyville (G-935)

First State Bnk of St Charles ......F 913 469-5400
Leawood (G-5404)

Fishnet Security ......F 816 701-3315
Leawood (G-5405)

Free State Security Svcs LLC ......F 785 843-7073
Shawnee Mission (G-11380)

Garda CL West Inc ......C 316 942-9700
Wichita (G-14445)

Guardsmark LLC ......C 316 440-6646
Wichita (G-14525)

Kansas Investigative Services ......F 316 267-1357
Wichita (G-14811)

Kansas State University ......E 785 532-6412
Manhattan (G-6691)

Livewatch Security LLC ......F 785 844-2130
Saint Marys (G-10372)

Loomis Armored Us LLC ......F 316 267-0269
Wichita (G-14977)

Orion Security Inc ......D 913 385-5657
Overland Park (G-9114)

Owens Bonding Inc ......E 316 283-3983
Wichita (G-15242)

Prime SEC Svcs Borrower LLC ......F 630 410-0662
Lawrence (G-5076)

Rees Contract Service Inc ......B 913 888-0590
Shawnee Mission (G-11786)

Rockwell Security LLC ......F 913 362-3300
Shawnee (G-11021)

Securitas SEC Svcs USA Inc ......C 316 838-2900
Wichita (G-15540)

Security Portfolio X LP ......F 316 634-1115
Wichita (G-15543)

Silva Security Service ...E ... 316 942-7872
Wichita (G-15594)
Strawder Security Service ...F ... 620 343-8392
Emporia (G-1831)
Total Security Solutions LLC ...E ... 316 209-0436
Wichita (G-15776)
Williams Investigation & SEC ...E ... 620 275-1134
Garden City (G-2315)
WSC Services Inc ...F ... 913 660-0454
Prairie Village (G-10087)

7382 Security Systems Svcs

ACS Electronic Systems Inc ...E ... 913 248-8828
Lenexa (G-5625)
ADT 24 7 Alarm and Security ...D ... 620 860-0229
Pratt (G-10094)
ADT LLC ...A ... 785 856-5500
Lawrence (G-4720)
ADT LLC ...C ... 316 858-6628
Wichita (G-13617)
ADT LLC ...E ... 316 858-4300
Wichita (G-13618)
ADT Security Corporation ...E ... 612 721-3690
Wichita (G-13619)
Advance Systems International ...E ... 913 888-3578
Lenexa (G-5631)
Advanced Infrared Systems ...G ... 913 888-3578
Lenexa (G-5633)
Alliance Monitoring Tech LLC ...F ... 316 263-7775
Wichita (G-13670)
CAM-Dex Corporation ...F ... 913 621-6160
Kansas City (G-3885)
Eichhorn Holdings LLC ...F ... 785 843-1426
Lawrence (G-4848)
Foresite Msp LLC ...E ... 800 940-4699
Overland Park (G-8734)
Johnson Cntrls SEC Sltions LLC ...E ... 316 634-1792
Wichita (G-14765)
Optiv Security Inc ...F ... 816 421-6611
Overland Park (G-9110)
Overfield Corporation ...F ... 785 843-3434
Lawrence (G-5052)
Prime SEC Svcs Borrower LLC ...F ... 630 410-0662
Lawrence (G-5076)
Riskanalytics LLC ...E ... 913 685-6526
Overland Park (G-9243)
S N C Inc ...E ... 620 665-6651
Hutchinson (G-3434)
Safelink Security Systems Inc ...E ... 913 338-3888
Tonganoxie (G-12269)
Sentinel Real Estate Corp ...F ... 316 265-9471
Wichita (G-15562)
Siemens Industry Inc ...E ... 316 946-4190
Wichita (G-15585)
Tech Electronics Kansas LLC ...E ... 785 379-0300
Topeka (G-13149)
Titan Monitoring Inc ...E ... 913 441-0911
Overland Park (G-9414)
Wanda America Inv Holdg Co Ltd ...A ... 913 213-2000
Leawood (G-5595)
Westar Industries Inc ...C ... 785 575-6507
Topeka (G-13240)

7384 Photofinishing Labs

CVS Pharmacy Inc ...E ... 913 651-2323
Leavenworth (G-5230)
CVS Pharmacy Inc ...F ... 913 722-3711
Shawnee Mission (G-11287)
Dillon Companies Inc ...C ... 620 225-6130
Dodge City (G-1341)
McKissick Enterprises LLC ...F ... 316 687-0272
Wichita (G-15029)
Millers Inc ...B ... 620 231-8050
Pittsburg (G-9906)
Ranieri Camera & Video Inc ...F ... 785 336-3719
Seneca (G-10879)
Steinle Inc ...C ... 620 421-3940
Parsons (G-9741)
Vizworx Inc ...E ... 316 691-4589
Wichita (G-15910)
Walgreen Co ...E ... 913 393-2757
Olathe (G-8146)
Walgreen Co ...E ... 785 628-1767
Hays (G-2928)
Walgreen Co ...E ... 316 652-9147
Wichita (G-15917)
Walgreen Co ...E ... 316 689-0866
Wichita (G-15918)
Walgreen Co ...E ... 316 729-6171
Wichita (G-15919)
Walgreen Co ...E ... 316 943-2299
Wichita (G-15920)
Walgreen Co ...E ... 913 814-7977
Overland Park (G-9480)
Walgreen Co ...E ... 913 829-3176
Olathe (G-8147)
Walgreen Co ...E ... 913 789-9275
Merriam (G-7109)
Walgreen Co ...E ... 316 218-0819
Andover (G-116)
Walgreen Co ...E ... 913 341-1725
Overland Park (G-9481)
Walgreen Co ...E ... 316 684-2828
Wichita (G-15921)
Walgreen Co ...E ... 785 841-9000
Lawrence (G-5178)
Walgreen Co ...E ... 785 832-8388
Lawrence (G-5179)
Walmart Inc ...B ... 316 347-2092
Goddard (G-2456)
Walmart Inc ...C ... 785 899-2111
Goodland (G-2489)
Walmart Inc ...B ... 620 232-1593
Pittsburg (G-9960)
Wolfes Camera Shops Inc ...E ... 785 235-1386
Topeka (G-13248)

7389 Business Svcs, NEC

1st Due Er Response Solutns LL ...F ... 620 226-3566
Bartlett (G-370)
A Plus Construction LLC ...E ... 620 212-4029
Saint Paul (G-10378)
A S Escort ...F ... 620 655-6613
Liberal (G-6272)
A+ Decor LLC ...F ... 816 699-6817
Pittsburg (G-9803)
A1 Bonding ...D ... 785 539-3950
Manhattan (G-6528)
Aat Aero Inc ...F ... 316 832-1412
Wichita (G-13594)
African Americans Renewing Int ...E ... 316 312-0183
Wichita (G-13642)
▲ All Seasons Party Rental Inc ...C ... 816 765-1444
Kansas City (G-3798)
All-Pro Services Inc ...F ... 785 842-1402
Lawrence (G-4727)
Allsigns LLC ...G ... 785 232-5512
Topeka (G-12308)
Alorica Customer Care Inc ...A ... 215 441-2323
Lenexa (G-5642)
American Comm & Residentl Svcs ...F ... 316 633-5866
Wichita (G-13690)
American Pre Sort Inc ...F ... 785 232-2633
Topeka (G-12321)
Andrews Asphalt & Cnstr Inc ...G ... 785 232-0188
Topeka (G-12326)
Answer Link ...F ... 620 662-4427
Hutchinson (G-3199)
Answer Topeka Inc ...E ... 785 234-4444
Topeka (G-12331)
Answering Exchange Inc ...E ... 316 262-8282
Wichita (G-13712)
Answernet Inc ...F ... 785 301-2810
Hays (G-2748)
Arch Design Builders LLC ...E ... 913 599-5565
Overland Park (G-8392)
Arrow Printing Company Inc ...G ... 785 825-8124
Salina (G-10409)
Ash Grove Materials Corp ...D ... 913 345-2030
Overland Park (G-8404)
Ash Grove Resources LLC ...F ... 785 267-1996
Topeka (G-12340)
Associated Purch Svcs Corp ...F ... 913 327-8730
Overland Park (G-8406)
Atlas Recovery Systems LLC ...F ... 913 281-7000
Overland Park (G-8410)
B A Designs LLC ...E ... 785 267-8110
Topeka (G-12356)
Bailey Showroom 2 LLC ...F ... 913 432-9696
Shawnee Mission (G-11144)
Banks Swimming Pool Company ...E ... 913 897-9290
Overland Park (G-8431)
Bar Code Systems ...F ... 913 894-6368
Shawnee Mission (G-11151)
Barker Printing and Copy Svcs ...G ... 785 233-5533
Topeka (G-12365)
Barrier Compliance Svcs LLC ...F ... 913 905-2695
Overland Park (G-8434)
Basys Processing Inc ...E ... 800 386-0711
Lenexa (G-5689)
Belger Cartage Service Inc ...E ... 316 943-0101
Wichita (G-13829)
Benchmark Rehabilitation Partn ...D ... 913 384-5810
Shawnee Mission (G-11159)
Best Value Services LLC ...D ... 316 440-1048
Wichita (G-13839)
BKM Construction LLC ...F ... 913 297-0049
Leavenworth (G-5212)
Black & Veatch - Er JV ...A ... 913 458-6650
Overland Park (G-8453)
Blue Valley Tele-Marketing ...D ... 785 799-3500
Home (G-3118)
Blue Vly Tl-Communications Inc ...D ... 785 799-3311
Home (G-3119)
Box Central Inc ...F ... 316 689-8484
Wichita (G-13875)
Boyer-Kansas Inc ...E ... 913 307-9400
Lenexa (G-5710)
Brock Maggard ...F ... 417 793-7790
Baxter Springs (G-401)
Bud Palmer Auction ...E ... 316 838-4141
Wichita (G-13905)
Business Technology Career ...F ... 316 688-1888
Wichita (G-13920)
Butler National Corporation ...E ... 913 780-9595
Olathe (G-7571)
C3i ...F ... 913 327-2255
Overland Park (G-8505)
Carlson Auction Service Inc ...E ... 785 478-4250
Topeka (G-12451)
Carr Auction & Realestate ...E ... 620 285-3148
Larned (G-4697)
Carson Mobile HM Pk Sewer Dst ...D ... 785 537-6330
Manhattan (G-6577)
Casa of The Thirty-First Judic ...E ... 620 365-1448
Iola (G-3589)
Casey Associates Inc ...F ... 913 276-3200
Lenexa (G-5731)
Catalyst Artificial Lift LLC ...E ... 620 365-7150
Iola (G-3590)
Central Consolidated Inc ...C ... 316 945-0797
Wichita (G-13978)
Charge It LLC ...E ... 913 341-8772
Paola (G-9546)
Chavey Ventures Inc ...F ... 913 888-5108
Shawnee (G-10926)
Christian Ch of Grater Kans Cy ...F ... 913 301-3004
Linwood (G-6416)
Citigroup Global Markets Inc ...E ... 316 630-4400
Wichita (G-14022)
City Goodland Inspection Dept ...D ... 785 890-4500
Goodland (G-2464)
City of Lawrence ...F ... 785 832-7700
Lawrence (G-4789)
City of Overland Park ...E ... 913 339-3000
Overland Park (G-8555)
City of Overland Park ...E ... 913 895-6040
Overland Park (G-8556)
City of Paola ...D ... 913 259-3600
Paola (G-9547)
City of Salina ...E ... 785 826-7200
Salina (G-10449)
Claim Solution Inc ...E ... 913 322-2300
Shawnee Mission (G-11236)
Clinical Reference Lab Inc ...F ... 913 492-3652
Lenexa (G-5764)
Coffee Time Inc ...D ... 316 267-3771
Wichita (G-14050)
Colby Convention Center ...E ... 785 460-0131
Colby (G-997)
Colt Tech LLC ...G ... 913 839-8198
Olathe (G-7600)
Commercial Rofg Spcialists LLC ...F ... 316 304-1423
Wichita (G-14072)
Consortium Inc ...D ... 785 232-1196
Topeka (G-12503)
Container Services Inc ...D ... 620 947-2664
Hillsboro (G-3046)
Convergys Corporation ...E ... 913 782-3333
Olathe (G-7614)
Country Club Bank ...F ... 816 751-4251
Leawood (G-5361)
County of Cowley ...F ... 620 221-5430
Winfield (G-16128)
CP Engners Land Srveyors Inc ...F ... 785 267-5071
Topeka (G-12526)
CPM Technologies Inc ...F ... 256 777-9869
Wichita (G-14124)
Cr Inspection Inc ...D ... 620 544-2666
Hugoton (G-3157)

SIC

Crane Sales & Service Co Inc...F ... 913 621-7040
Kansas City *(G-3944)*
Creative Signs & Design Inc...G ... 785 233-8000
Topeka *(G-12528)*
Crosswind Conference Center...E ... 620 327-2700
Hesston *(G-2988)*
Crown Recovery Services LLC...F ... 816 777-2366
Overland Park *(G-8619)*
Csd7 Social Medal...D ... 620 203-0477
Burlington *(G-633)*
D J Company...F ... 316 685-3241
Wichita *(G-14158)*
David E Dishop...F ... 614 861-5440
Wichita *(G-14172)*
Dbi Inc...E ... 316 831-9323
Wichita *(G-14177)*
Deans Designs Inc...F ... 316 686-6674
Wichita *(G-14181)*
Deborah John & Associates...E ... 316 777-0903
Wichita *(G-14182)*
Design Central Inc...F ... 785 825-4131
Salina *(G-10474)*
Designed Bus Intrors Tpeka Inc...F ... 785 233-2078
Topeka *(G-12553)*
Digital Sound Systems Inc...E ... 913 492-5775
Lenexa *(G-5819)*
Dion A Daniel Inc...F ... 816 287-1452
Mission *(G-7130)*
Disabled American Veterens Str...F ... 785 827-6477
Salina *(G-10479)*
Display Studios Inc...E ... 913 305-5948
Kansas City *(G-3974)*
Document Resources Inc...F ... 316 683-1444
Wichita *(G-14219)*
Downtown Station...D ... 316 267-7747
Wichita *(G-14235)*
Eagle Environmental Svcs LLC...E ... 316 944-2445
Wichita *(G-14250)*
EKA Consulting LLC...F ... 913 244-2980
Shawnee *(G-10946)*
Elanco Kc...F ... 816 442-4114
Lenexa *(G-5830)*
Elecsys International Corp...C ... 913 647-0158
Olathe *(G-7673)*
Empire Construction Group LLC...F ... 913 375-8886
Shawnee Mission *(G-11335)*
EMR-Pcg Construction Group...E ... 406 249-7730
Lawrence *(G-4853)*
Epay North America...F ... 913 327-4200
Leawood *(G-5388)*
Epic Insulation Inc...F ... 316 500-1650
Goddard *(G-2438)*
Evergance Partners LLC...E ... 913 825-1000
Shawnee Mission *(G-11350)*
Facc Solutions Inc...G ... 316 425-4040
Wichita *(G-14330)*
Fastsigns Inc...G ... 913 649-3600
Overland Park *(G-8707)*
Fcg Inc...F ... 620 545-8300
Clearwater *(G-892)*
Fedex Corporation...F ... 913 393-0953
Olathe *(G-7705)*
Fedex Corporation...F ... 913 677-5005
Shawnee Mission *(G-11362)*
Financial Benefits of Kansas...F ... 913 385-7000
Leawood *(G-5400)*
Financial Consultants America...E ... 316 943-7307
Wichita *(G-14367)*
First Horizon Bank...E ... 913 317-2000
Overland Park *(G-8719)*
Fischer Well Service Inc...G ... 785 628-3837
Hays *(G-2808)*
Flic Luminaries LLC...F ... 888 550-3542
Wichita *(G-14387)*
Flint Hills Ford Inc...E ... 785 776-4004
Manhattan *(G-6632)*
Glmv Architecture Inc...E ... 316 265-9367
Wichita *(G-14472)*
Global Engineering & Tech Inc...C ... 316 729-9232
Goddard *(G-2439)*
Goodrich...F ... 316 448-4282
Wichita *(G-14484)*
Grace Agapes Inc...E ... 913 837-5885
Louisburg *(G-6450)*
▲ **Grapevine Designs LLC**...E ... 913 307-0225
Lenexa *(G-5881)*
Great Plains Insptn & Lining...F ... 620 793-7090
Great Bend *(G-2584)*
Gross PHD Judith M S...F ... 913 645-2437
Kansas City *(G-4056)*

Gsi Engineering Nthrn Div LLC...F ... 316 554-0725
Wichita *(G-14523)*
Guardian Business Services...F ... 785 823-1635
Salina *(G-10524)*
Habitat For Hmanity Ellis Cnty...F ... 785 623-4200
Hays *(G-2823)*
Haskell Foundation...F ... 785 749-8425
Lawrence *(G-4892)*
Heartland Payment Systems LLC...D ... 316 390-1988
Wichita *(G-14587)*
Hoffmann Fabricating LLC...F ... 316 262-6041
Wichita *(G-14623)*
Hoffmanns Green Industries...E ... 316 634-1500
Wichita *(G-14624)*
Holy Family Medical Inc...E ... 316 682-9900
Wichita *(G-14626)*
◆ **Huhtamaki Films Inc**...A ... 913 583-3025
De Soto *(G-1204)*
Humbert Envelope Machinery...F ... 785 845-6085
Topeka *(G-12706)*
Hyr Global Source Inc...F ... 913 815-2597
Overland Park *(G-8835)*
Icg Inc...E ... 913 461-8759
Leawood *(G-5433)*
Icon Integration & Design Inc...F ... 913 221-8801
Overland Park *(G-8837)*
Ils National LLC...F ... 913 888-9191
Olathe *(G-7785)*
Imaging Solutions Company...E ... 316 630-0440
Wichita *(G-14677)*
Informtion Cmmunications Group...E ... 913 469-6767
Leawood *(G-5437)*
Infusion Design Incorporated...E ... 913 422-0317
Bonner Springs *(G-555)*
▲ **Insight 2 Design LLC**...F ... 913 937-9386
Overland Park *(G-8852)*
Insysiv LLC...F ... 816 694-9397
Kansas City *(G-4102)*
International Fincl Svcs Inc...E ... 620 665-7708
Hutchinson *(G-3336)*
J P Weigand and Sons Inc...E ... 316 292-3991
Wichita *(G-14740)*
J-Six Enterprises LLC...F ... 785 336-2149
Seneca *(G-10868)*
J-Six Farms LLC...F ... 785 336-2148
Seneca *(G-10869)*
Jasper Investments Inc...F ... 913 599-0899
Lenexa *(G-5928)*
Jies LLC...F ... 620 668-5585
Copeland *(G-1149)*
Johnson County Communications...E ... 913 764-2876
Olathe *(G-7815)*
Kaliaperumal Mamalay...G ... 816 210-1248
Overland Park *(G-8885)*
Kansas Crop Improvement Assn...F ... 785 532-6118
Manhattan *(G-6675)*
Kansas Fmly Advsory Netwrk Inc...F ... 316 264-2400
Wichita *(G-14800)*
Kansas Grain Inspection Svc...F ... 785 827-3671
Salina *(G-10565)*
Kansas Grain Inspection Svc...D ... 785 233-7063
Topeka *(G-12778)*
Kansas State Univ Foundation...D ... 785 532-6266
Manhattan *(G-6679)*
Kaw Valley Companies Inc...F ... 913 596-9752
Kansas City *(G-4161)*
Kaw Valley Engineering Inc...E ... 785 762-5040
Junction City *(G-3714)*
Kc Blind All-Stars Foundation...F ... 913 281-3308
Kansas City *(G-4163)*
Kcai LP...E ... 913 596-6000
Kansas City *(G-4166)*
Kemper Auction Group...F ... 913 287-3207
Kansas City *(G-4170)*
Khaos Apparel LLC...F ... 316 804-4900
Newton *(G-7370)*
Kingman Cnty Ecnmic Dev Cncil...A ... 620 532-3694
Kingman *(G-4598)*
L L C Fun Services of K C...F ... 913 441-9200
Shawnee *(G-10984)*
Larry Theurer...F ... 620 326-2715
Wellington *(G-13510)*
Lauries Kitchen Inc...F ... 316 777-9198
Mulvane *(G-7218)*
Lee Reed Engraving Inc...G ... 316 943-9700
Wichita *(G-14949)*
Lee Shafer Ricky...E ... 620 252-9126
Coffeyville *(G-955)*
Legacy Home Inspections...E ... 913 484-4157
Lenexa *(G-5965)*

Leisure Hotel Corporation...E ... 620 227-5000
Dodge City *(G-1398)*
Leisure Hotel Corporation...E ... 620 275-5900
Garden City *(G-2224)*
Lil Sprouts Playcare LLC...F ... 785 343-7529
Ottawa *(G-8283)*
Line Medical Inc...E ... 316 262-3444
Wichita *(G-14967)*
Little Soldier...F ... 785 845-1987
Mayetta *(G-6915)*
Luce Press Clippings Inc...D ... 785 232-0201
Topeka *(G-12853)*
Madden-Mcfarland Interiors Ltd...E ... 913 681-2821
Leawood *(G-5462)*
McCurdy Auction LLC...E ... 316 683-0612
Wichita *(G-15026)*
McDonalds Plaza LLC...E ... 913 362-1999
Overland Park *(G-9001)*
Metal Cut To Length...F ... 913 829-8600
Olathe *(G-7884)*
Metal Finishing Company Inc...F ... 316 267-7289
Wichita *(G-15053)*
Michael S Hundley Cnstr Inc...F ... 913 367-7059
Atchison *(G-249)*
Midwest Engraving Inc...F ... 913 294-5348
Paola *(G-9575)*
Midwest Mixer Service LLC...E ... 620 872-7251
Scott City *(G-10823)*
Millennium Concepts Inc...F ... 316 821-9300
Wichita *(G-15110)*
Mm Property MGT & Rmdlg LLC...F ... 913 871-6867
Kansas City *(G-4265)*
Mnvc Financial Services LLC...E ... 816 589-4336
Overland Park *(G-9047)*
Monarch Inventories Services...E ... 913 541-0645
Lenexa *(G-6011)*
Moorekc Enterprises LLC...F ... 316 347-0121
Shawnee *(G-11000)*
Morris Laing Evans Brock...D ... 316 838-1084
Wichita *(G-15128)*
Mosaic...C ... 620 276-7972
Garden City *(G-2240)*
Motivated RE Solutions LLC...D ... 785 842-3530
Lawrence *(G-5033)*
Mr PS Party Outlet Inc...F ... 785 537-1804
Manhattan *(G-6753)*
Multi Svc Tech Solutions Inc...B ... 800 239-1064
Overland Park *(G-9063)*
My1stop LLC...F ... 316 554-9700
Fort Scott *(G-1992)*
Nadia Inc...F ... 316 686-6190
Wichita *(G-15145)*
National Center For Competency...E ... 913 498-1000
Shawnee Mission *(G-11672)*
National Ctstrphe Rstrtion Inc...F ... 913 663-4111
Overland Park *(G-9071)*
National Rgstred Agents Inc NJ...F ... 913 754-0637
Overland Park *(G-9072)*
National Screening Bureau LLC...F ... 316 263-4400
Wichita *(G-15152)*
Nex-Tech LLC...F ... 785 421-4197
Hill City *(G-3037)*
Nn8 LLC...F ... 913 948-1107
Overland Park *(G-9088)*
Ogden Check Approval Network...E ... 785 228-5600
Topeka *(G-12942)*
On-Line Communications Inc...C ... 316 831-0500
Wichita *(G-15219)*
One Power LLC...E ... 913 219-5061
Shawnee Mission *(G-11697)*
Osborne Investment Inc...F ... 785 346-2147
Osborne *(G-8217)*
Overlnd Prk Cnvntn & Vstrs Bre...F ... 913 491-0123
Overland Park *(G-9129)*
Owens Bonding Inc...E ... 316 283-3983
Wichita *(G-15242)*
P A Select Healthcare...F ... 913 948-6400
Leawood *(G-5513)*
PA Acquisition Corp...F ... 913 498-3700
Shawnee Mission *(G-11712)*
Panhandle Steel Erectors Inc...F ... 620 271-9878
Garden City *(G-2247)*
Paola Lifestock Auction Inc...E ... 913 294-3335
Paola *(G-9581)*
Paradigm Alliance Inc...E ... 316 554-9225
Wichita *(G-15255)*
Paragon Aerospace Services...E ... 316 945-5285
Wichita *(G-15257)*
Paragon Ndt LLC...E ... 316 927-4283
Wichita *(G-15260)*

Parsons Livestock Auction LLC ....E 620 421-2900
Parsons (G-9719)
Patriot Abatement Services LLC ....F 913 397-6181
Olathe (G-7975)
Pda of Kansas City Inc ....F 913 631-0711
Overland Park (G-9149)
Pennington Co Fundraising LLC ....E 785 843-1661
Lawrence (G-5060)
Petropower LLC ....G 316 361-0222
Wichita (G-15288)
Pharmacy Dist Partners LLC ....F 903 357-3391
Mission Hills (G-7147)
Phoenix Restoration Service ....E 620 276-6994
Garden City (G-2254)
Picture Perfect Interiors LLC ....F 913 829-3365
Overland Park (G-9167)
Pioneer Industries Intl Inc ....E 913 233-1368
Kansas City (G-4323)
Pitsco Inc ....F 620 231-2424
Pittsburg (G-9916)
Pittsburg State Univ Foundatio ....E 620 235-4764
Pittsburg (G-9922)
Plans Professional Inc ....F 785 357-7777
Topeka (G-12979)
Pool & Patio Inc ....F 913 888-2226
Shawnee Mission (G-11743)
Pool & Patio Supply Inc ....F 913 888-2226
Shawnee Mission (G-11744)
Pools Plus ....F 785 823-7665
Salina (G-10636)
Power Chemicals Inc ....F 316 524-7899
Wichita (G-15318)
Presig Holdings LLC ....F 913 706-1315
Overland Park (G-9184)
Primary Care Landscape Inc ....F 913 768-8880
Olathe (G-8006)
Print Source Direct LLC ....E 620 947-5702
Hillsboro (G-3056)
Professional Express Inc ....F 913 722-6060
Kansas City (G-4342)
▲ Profillment LLC ....F 316 260-7910
Wichita (G-15369)
Propio Ls LLC ....F 913 381-3143
Overland Park (G-9196)
Pt Kansas LLC ....E 620 791-7082
Great Bend (G-2626)
Publishers Delivery Solut ....F 913 894-1299
Lenexa (G-6078)
Pulse Design Group Inc ....E 913 438-9095
Lenexa (G-6079)
Purple Wave Auction ....D 785 537-5057
Manhattan (G-6783)
Q Solutions LLC ....F 913 948-5931
Wellsville (G-13545)
Qc Holdings Inc ....C 866 660-2243
Lenexa (G-6082)
Quality Inventory Services ....F 913 888-7700
Merriam (G-7101)
Quality Tool Service Inc ....F 316 265-0048
Wichita (G-15387)
Quicksilver Ex Courier of MO ....D 913 321-5959
Kansas City (G-4354)
Radiofrquency Saftey Intl Corp ....E 620 825-4600
Kiowa (G-4629)
Rapco Inc ....F 785 524-4232
Lincoln (G-6386)
Rellec Apparel Graphics LLC ....G 913 707-5249
Lenexa (G-6100)
Residential Appraisal Services ....F 913 492-0226
Shawnee Mission (G-11789)
Retail Services Wis Corp ....E 913 831-6400
Shawnee Mission (G-11791)
Retail Services Wis Corp ....E 316 683-3289
Bel Aire (G-439)
Retirement Planning Group Inc ....F 913 498-8898
Overland Park (G-9239)
▲ Return Products Management Inc ....F 913 768-1747
Olathe (G-8028)
Rgis LLC ....C 316 685-6233
Wichita (G-15455)
Richman Helstrom Trucking Inc ....F 785 478-3186
Topeka (G-13014)
Riley Hotel Suites LLC ....E 785 539-2400
Manhattan (G-6793)
Roadsafe Traffic Systems Inc ....D 316 778-2112
El Dorado (G-1599)
Roadsafe Traffic Systems Inc ....E 316 322-3070
El Dorado (G-1600)
Robert Denton ....F 316 691-7046
Wichita (G-15473)
Roberts Group Inc ....G 913 381-3930
Overland Park (G-9252)
Rueschhoff Communications ....E 785 841-0111
Lawrence (G-5098)
Rule Properties LLC ....F 785 621-8000
Hays (G-2903)
S C F Inc ....E 913 722-3473
Overland Park (G-9267)
Safety-Kleen Systems Inc ....E 913 829-6677
Olathe (G-8050)
Safety-Kleen Systems Inc ....F 316 942-5001
Wichita (G-15505)
Salina Microfilm ....F 785 827-6648
Salina (G-10680)
Salina Red Coach Inn ....F 785 825-2111
Salina (G-10684)
Saline Valley Farm Inc ....F 785 524-4562
Lincoln (G-6388)
Sarahlee Coffee and Tea Corp ....E 316 262-0398
Wichita (G-15519)
Scheopners Water Cond LLC ....F 620 275-5121
Garden City (G-2275)
Sewing Workshop ....F 785 357-6231
Topeka (G-13061)
Shadmea Ministries Inc ....E 912 332-0563
Junction City (G-3752)
Shannahan Crane & Hoist Inc ....F 816 746-9822
Kansas City (G-4419)
Sharpening Specialists LLC ....E 316 945-0593
Wichita (G-15575)
Sjh Family Corp ....F 785 856-5296
Lawrence (G-5111)
Skillpath Seminars Inc ....C 913 362-3900
Shawnee Mission (G-11872)
Skyline E3 Inc ....F 913 599-4787
Lenexa (G-6137)
Sooner Oil LLC ....F 785 340-5602
Junction City (G-3757)
South Central Tele Assn Inc ....E 620 930-1000
Medicine Lodge (G-7074)
South Central Wireless Inc ....E 620 930-1000
Medicine Lodge (G-7075)
Specialty Fabrication Inc ....F 316 264-0603
Wichita (G-15636)
▲ Spt Distribution Center ....E 785 862-5226
Topeka (G-13093)
Standees Pv LLC ....D 913 601-5250
Prairie Village (G-10069)
Stericycle Inc ....E 913 307-9400
Lenexa (G-6153)
Strategic Value Media ....E 913 214-5203
Overland Park (G-9367)
Structural Integrity Group LLC ....E 316 633-9403
Wichita (G-15677)
Sunbelt Business Advisors ....E 316 684-9040
Wichita (G-15683)
Sunbelt Business Brokers ....F 913 383-2671
Overland Park (G-9373)
Super 8 Forbes Landing ....F 785 862-2222
Topeka (G-13123)
Super Chief Inc ....F 785 272-7277
Topeka (G-13124)
Superior Masonry & Stucco LLC ....E 316 928-2365
Wichita (G-15695)
T T Companies Inc ....A 913 599-6886
Olathe (G-8097)
T W Lacy & Associates Inc ....F 913 706-7625
Prairie Village (G-10073)
T2 Holdings LLC ....F 913 327-8889
Kansas City (G-4456)
Tantillo Financial Group LLC ....F 913 649-3200
Shawnee Mission (G-11919)
Tarrant Inc ....E 316 942-2208
Wichita (G-15717)
Taylor Crane & Rigging Inc ....D 620 251-1530
Coffeyville (G-981)
Teracrunch LLC ....F 214 405-7158
Leawood (G-5572)
Tevis Architectural Group ....F 913 599-3003
Shawnee (G-11039)
Textron Aviation Defense LLC ....E 316 676-2508
Wichita (G-15733)
▲ Therien & Company Inc ....F 415 956-8850
Plainville (G-9993)
Thompson Tax & Associates LLC ....F 916 346-7829
Waverly (G-13482)
Tjk Inc ....F 785 841-0110
Lawrence (G-5139)
Tk & Company Inc of Kansas ....F 785 472-3226
Ellsworth (G-1682)
Tmd Telecom Inc ....E 316 462-0400
Wichita (G-15772)
Turner Recreation Commission ....D 913 287-2111
Kansas City (G-4479)
U P S Stores ....F 913 829-3750
Olathe (G-8129)
U S Automation Inc ....G 913 894-2410
Shawnee Mission (G-11953)
▲ U S Logo Inc ....F 316 264-1321
Wichita (G-15824)
United Parcel Service Inc ....E 913 541-3700
Lenexa (G-6201)
Unitedlex Corporation ....C 913 685-8900
Overland Park (G-9446)
University Kansas Mem Corp ....D 785 864-4651
Lawrence (G-5156)
University of Kansas ....D 785 864-8885
Lawrence (G-5160)
Upper Lake Processing Services ....F 855 418-9500
Overland Park (G-9448)
US Textiles LLC ....F 913 660-0995
Shawnee Mission (G-11970)
USA Missions Church of God ....E 620 345-2532
Moundridge (G-7201)
Vend-Tech Enterprise LLC ....E 316 689-6850
Wichita (G-15873)
Versasport of Kansas Inc ....E 316 393-0487
Wichita (G-15876)
Via Christi Foundation Inc ....F 316 239-3520
Wichita (G-15887)
Via Express Delivery Systems ....F 913 341-8101
Shawnee Mission (G-11977)
Waisner Inc ....F 913 345-2663
Shawnee Mission (G-11989)
Walker Centrifuge Services LLC ....F 785 826-8265
Salina (G-10757)
Wallabys Inc ....F 913 541-9255
Lenexa (G-6221)
Welco Services Inc ....E 620 241-3000
McPherson (G-7041)
Wellington Experience Inc ....F 913 897-9229
Shawnee Mission (G-11999)
Western Feed Mills Inc ....E 620 758-2283
Cedar Vale (G-695)
Wichita Convention Tourism Bur ....F 316 265-2800
Wichita (G-15991)
Wichita Stamp and Seal Inc ....G 316 263-4223
Wichita (G-16029)
Wilson Inc Engneers Architects ....E 913 652-9911
Overland Park (G-9496)
Winter Architects Inc ....F 316 267-7142
Wichita (G-16058)
Women In Trnstion Together Inc ....F 785 424-7516
Lawrence (G-5189)
World Fuel Services Corp ....B 913 451-2400
Overland Park (G-9506)
Yaeger Architecture Inc ....E 913 742-8000
Lenexa (G-6239)
Young Electric Inc ....E 316 681-8118
Wichita (G-16090)

75 AUTOMOTIVE REPAIR, SERVICES, AND PARKING

7513 Truck Rental & Leasing, Without Drivers

Bud Brown Automotive Inc ....D 913 393-8100
Olathe (G-7564)
Budget Rent-A-Car of Kansas ....E 316 946-4891
Wichita (G-13908)
Central Kansas Auto Rental ....F 785 827-7237
Salina (G-10439)
Convoy Equipment Leasing LLC ....D 913 371-6500
Kansas City (G-3937)
Convoy Leasing Inc ....F 913 371-6500
Kansas City (G-3938)
Garden City Travel Plaza LLC ....E 620 275-4404
Garden City (G-2179)
Hertz Corporation ....E 620 342-6322
Emporia (G-1769)
Idealease of Mo-Kan Inc ....E 785 235-8711
Topeka (G-12712)
Idealease of Mo-Kan Inc ....F 785 379-2300
Kansas City (G-4095)
K & S Eastside Amoco Inc ....F 620 342-3565
Emporia (G-1782)
Mead Rental Center ....F 620 672-7718
Pratt (G-10125)
Mhc Truck Leasing Inc ....F 816 483-0604
Leawood (G-5477)

Midwest Bus Sales Inc .... E 913 422-1000
Bonner Springs *(G-562)*
Midwest Car Corporation .... F 316 946-4851
Wichita *(G-15089)*
Mike Groves Oil Inc .... F 620 442-0480
Arkansas City *(G-166)*
Murphy-Hoffman Company .... E 816 483-6444
Leawood *(G-5492)*
Otl Logistics Inc .... D 816 918-7688
Basehor *(G-386)*
Paccar Leasing Corporation .... E 913 829-1444
Olathe *(G-7971)*
Paynes Inc .... F 620 231-3170
Frontenac *(G-2063)*
Penske Truck Leasing Co LP .... F 316 943-8500
Wichita *(G-15278)*
Penske Truck Leasing Co LP .... F 785 776-3139
Manhattan *(G-6772)*
Roberts Truck Ctr Holdg Co LLC .... D 316 262-8413
Park City *(G-9640)*
Ryder Truck Rental Inc .... F 316 945-8484
Wichita *(G-15497)*
Ryder Truck Rental Inc .... F 913 573-2119
Kansas City *(G-4392)*
Ryder Truck Rental Inc .... E 913 621-3300
Kansas City *(G-4393)*
Ryder Truck Rental Inc .... E 913 888-5040
Shawnee Mission *(G-11818)*
Ryder Truck Rental Inc .... E 913 492-4420
Lenexa *(G-6114)*
Santa Fe Market Inc .... F 785 594-7466
Baldwin City *(G-368)*
Spencer & Company .... F 785 235-3131
Topeka *(G-13090)*
Stewart Truck Leasing Inc .... E 785 827-0336
Salina *(G-10716)*
Success Truck Leasing Inc .... E 913 321-1716
Kansas City *(G-4445)*
U Haul Co Independent Dealers .... F 316 722-0216
Maize *(G-6522)*
U-Haul Co of Kansas Inc .... D 913 287-1327
Kansas City *(G-4481)*
U-Haul Co of Oregon .... F 913 780-4494
Olathe *(G-8130)*

7514 Passenger Car Rental

Avis Budget Group Inc .... F 785 331-0658
Lawrence *(G-4745)*
Avis Rent A Car System Inc .... F 316 946-4882
Wichita *(G-13779)*
Avis Rental Car Systems .... B 785 749-1464
Lawrence *(G-4746)*
Bob Allen Ford Inc .... D 913 381-3000
Overland Park *(G-8473)*
Budget Car Trck Rentl Wichita .... E 316 729-7979
Wichita *(G-13907)*
Budget Rent-A-Car of Kansas .... E 316 946-4891
Wichita *(G-13908)*
Central Kansas Auto Rental .... F 785 827-7237
Salina *(G-10439)*
Classic Enterprises Inc .... F 785 628-6700
Hays *(G-2769)*
E & J Rental & Leasing Inc .... F 316 721-0442
Wichita *(G-14249)*
Elrac LLC .... F 913 642-9669
Overland Park *(G-8675)*
Enterprise Leasing Co KS LLC .... E 913 254-0012
Olathe *(G-7686)*
Enterprise Leasing Co KS LLC .... E 913 782-6381
Olathe *(G-7687)*
Enterprise Leasing Co KS LLC .... E 913 631-7663
Shawnee Mission *(G-11341)*
Enterprise Leasing Co KS LLC .... E 913 402-1322
Overland Park *(G-8684)*
Enterprise Leasing Co KS LLC .... F 913 262-8888
Shawnee Mission *(G-11342)*
Enterprise Leasing Co KS LLC .... C 913 383-1515
Shawnee Mission *(G-11340)*
Hertz Corporation .... E 620 342-6322
Emporia *(G-1769)*
Hertz Corporation .... E 913 962-1226
Shawnee Mission *(G-11430)*
Hertz Corporation .... E 316 689-3773
Wichita *(G-14597)*
Hertz Corporation .... E 913 341-1782
Overland Park *(G-8813)*
Hertz Corporation .... E 316 946-4860
Wichita *(G-14598)*
Hertz Corporation .... E 316 946-4860
Wichita *(G-14599)*
Hertz Corporation .... E 316 946-4860
Wichita *(G-14600)*
Hertz Corporation .... E 316 946-4860
Wichita *(G-14601)*
Hertz Corporation .... E 620 341-9656
Emporia *(G-1770)*
Hertz Corporation .... E 316 284-6084
Newton *(G-7361)*
Hertz Corporation .... E 913 696-0003
Lenexa *(G-5902)*
Hobart Transportation Co Inc .... F 785 267-4468
Topeka *(G-12696)*
Midwest Car Corporation .... F 316 946-4851
Wichita *(G-15089)*
National Rental (us) Inc .... E 316 946-4851
Wichita *(G-15151)*
Priceless .... F 785 625-7664
Hays *(G-2889)*
Ray Shepherd Motors Inc .... E 620 644-2625
Fort Scott *(G-2001)*

7515 Passenger Car Leasing

Bob Allen Ford Inc .... D 913 381-3000
Overland Park *(G-8473)*
Bud Brown Automotive Inc .... D 913 393-8100
Olathe *(G-7564)*
Enterprise Leasing Co KS LLC .... C 913 383-1515
Shawnee Mission *(G-11340)*
Enterprise Leasing Co KS LLC .... F 913 262-8888
Shawnee Mission *(G-11342)*
Fleet Auto Rent Inc .... F 913 901-9900
Overland Park *(G-8727)*
Joe Self Chevrolet Inc .... C 316 689-4390
Wichita *(G-14760)*
Mel Hambelton Ford Inc .... C 316 462-3673
Wichita *(G-15035)*
Merchants Automotive Group Inc .... E 913 901-9900
Leawood *(G-5474)*
Noller Lincoln-Mercury Inc .... E 785 267-2800
Topeka *(G-12932)*
Oakley Motors Inc .... E 785 672-3238
Oakley *(G-7484)*
Ray Shepherd Motors Inc .... E 620 644-2625
Fort Scott *(G-2001)*
South Star Chrysler Inc .... F 785 242-5600
Ottawa *(G-8313)*

7519 Utility Trailers & Recreational Vehicle Rental

Adventure Rv and Truck Ctr LLC .... E 316 721-1333
Wichita *(G-13629)*
Adventureland Rv Rentals Inc .... F 800 333-8821
Wichita *(G-13630)*
Budget Car Trck Rentl Wichita .... E 316 729-7979
Wichita *(G-13907)*
K Young Inc .... F 785 475-3888
Colby *(G-1019)*
Mather Flare Rental Inc .... F 785 478-9696
Topeka *(G-12863)*
Mike Groves Oil Inc .... F 620 442-0480
Arkansas City *(G-166)*
Ryder Truck Rental Inc .... E 913 888-5040
Shawnee Mission *(G-11818)*

7521 Automobile Parking Lots & Garages

Apac-Kansas Inc .... E 620 662-3307
Hutchinson *(G-3200)*
Car Park Inc .... E 316 265-0553
Wichita *(G-13942)*
Central Plains Maintenance .... D 316 945-4774
Wichita *(G-13983)*
City of Newton .... F 316 284-6083
Newton *(G-7329)*
Parking Systems Inc .... F 913 345-9272
Shawnee Mission *(G-11717)*

7532 Top, Body & Upholstery Repair & Paint Shops

A D L M LLC .... F 913 888-0770
Shawnee Mission *(G-11062)*
Aeroswint .... F 785 391-2276
Utica *(G-13334)*
Alan Clark Body Shop Inc .... F 785 776-5333
Manhattan *(G-6538)*
Allied Body Shop Incorporated .... F 785 841-3672
Lawrence *(G-4730)*
Auto Techs Frame & Body Repair .... F 620 221-6616
Winfield *(G-16115)*
Auto-Craft Inc .... E 316 265-6828
Wichita *(G-13770)*
Auto-Craft Inc .... F 316 630-9494
Wichita *(G-13771)*
Auto-Craft Inc .... E 785 579-5997
Junction City *(G-3669)*
Automotive Specialists Inc .... F 316 321-5130
El Dorado *(G-1532)*
Autotech Collision & Service .... F 316 942-0707
Wichita *(G-13778)*
Brenneman & Bremmeman Inc .... F 316 282-8834
Newton *(G-7321)*
Briggs Auto Group Inc .... E 785 776-3677
Manhattan *(G-6569)*
▲ **Butler Enterprises Inc** .... F 913 262-9109
Shawnee Mission *(G-11192)*
Car Star Inc .... F 785 232-2084
Topeka *(G-12443)*
Car Star Spc .... E 201 444-0601
Overland Park *(G-8512)*
Carstar Inc .... F 316 652-7821
Wichita *(G-13955)*
Carstar Inc .... F 913 685-2886
Stilwell *(G-12139)*
Classic Collision Center .... F 913 287-9410
Kansas City *(G-3918)*
College Body Shop .... F 785 235-5628
Topeka *(G-12487)*
Collision Works LLC .... E 316 788-5722
Derby *(G-1231)*
Collision Works LLC .... E 316 265-6828
Wichita *(G-14058)*
Dacus LLC .... F 620 241-6054
McPherson *(G-6955)*
Dick Edwards Ford Lincoln Merc .... D 785 320-4499
Junction City *(G-3687)*
Dons Body Shop Inc .... F 913 782-9255
Olathe *(G-7660)*
Dons Car Care & Body Shop Inc .... F 620 669-8178
Hutchinson *(G-3268)*
Ervs Body Shop Inc .... F 620 225-4015
Dodge City *(G-1358)*
Eveland Brothers Body Shop .... E 913 262-6050
Shawnee Mission *(G-11349)*
Fastsigns Inc .... G 913 649-3600
Overland Park *(G-8707)*
G I P Inc .... F 785 749-0005
Lawrence *(G-4867)*
Georgia Kenworth Inc .... E 816 483-6444
Leawood *(G-5411)*
Gerber Group Inc .... E 316 945-7007
Wichita *(G-14460)*
Hillsboro Ford Inc .... E 620 947-3134
Hillsboro *(G-3049)*
Hite Collision Repair Ctr Inc .... F 785 843-8991
Lawrence *(G-4899)*
Jayhawk Auto Incorporated .... F 785 354-1758
Topeka *(G-12740)*
Joe Self Chevrolet Inc .... C 316 689-4390
Wichita *(G-14760)*
Joes Seat Cover Car Wash Ctr .... E 316 262-2486
Wichita *(G-14761)*
Johns Body Shop Inc .... F 620 225-2213
Dodge City *(G-1383)*
K C Freightliner Body Shop .... F 913 342-4269
Kansas City *(G-4132)*
Kammerer Auto Body & Paint .... F 316 265-0211
Wichita *(G-14781)*
Kansas Body Works Inc .... F 316 263-5506
Wichita *(G-14788)*
Kansas Coachworks Ltd .... F 913 888-0991
Shawnee Mission *(G-11515)*
Kc Colors Auto Body Ltd .... F 913 491-0696
Shawnee Mission *(G-11523)*
Keimig Body Shop .... F 913 367-0184
Atchison *(G-239)*
Laird Noller Ford Inc .... E 785 232-8347
Topeka *(G-12830)*
Lawrence Cllsion Spcalists LLC .... F 785 841-3672
Lawrence *(G-4961)*
Lewis Auto Plaza Inc .... F 785 266-8850
Topeka *(G-12840)*
Lindan Auto Mechanical & Body .... E 913 722-4243
Shawnee Mission *(G-11574)*
Manweiler Chevrolet Co Inc .... F 620 653-2121
Hoisington *(G-3069)*
McKenzie Paint & Body Inc .... F 620 662-3721
South Hutchinson *(G-12061)*
Metro Collision Repair Inc .... F 913 839-1044
Olathe *(G-7886)*

Moore Buick Chevrolet Pontiac ..... F 785 346-5972
Osborne *(G-8213)*
Moores Lnny Collision Repr LLC ..... F 316 744-1151
Park City *(G-9637)*
Nesco Holdings Inc ..... G 913 287-0001
Kansas City *(G-4286)*
Norris Collision Center LLC ..... F 316 794-1161
Goddard *(G-2448)*
Olathe Ford Sales Inc ..... E 913 829-1957
Olathe *(G-7937)*
P & D Inc ..... F 913 782-2247
Olathe *(G-7969)*
PDQ Tools and Equipment Inc ..... G 913 492-5800
Shawnee Mission *(G-11721)*
Pringle Auto Body & Sales Inc ..... F 913 432-6361
Kansas City *(G-4339)*
Quality Trust Inc ..... E 785 375-6372
Junction City *(G-3745)*
Ricks Auto Restoration ..... E 620 326-5635
Wellington *(G-13524)*
S & S Auto Body ..... F 785 524-4641
Lincoln *(G-6387)*
Santa Fe Body Inc ..... F 913 894-6090
Shawnee Mission *(G-11830)*
Santa Fe Tow Service Inc ..... D 417 553-3676
Shawnee Mission *(G-11833)*
Scholfield Body Shop Inc ..... E 316 688-6550
Wichita *(G-15533)*
Service Body Shop ..... F 316 260-5300
Wichita *(G-15564)*
Sharps Auto Bdy Collision Inc ..... F 620 231-6011
Pittsburg *(G-9938)*
Shelton Collision Repair Inc ..... F 316 788-1528
Derby *(G-1271)*
Skeeters Body Shop Inc ..... F 620 275-7255
Garden City *(G-2280)*
Sonnys Inc ..... F 316 942-2390
Wichita *(G-15614)*
Steven Import Group Inc ..... F 316 652-2135
Wichita *(G-15669)*
Stylecraft Auto Upholstery ..... F 316 262-0449
Wichita *(G-15679)*
Tlm Enterprises Inc ..... F 316 265-3833
Wichita *(G-15771)*
Troostwood Garage & Body Shop ..... E 816 444-3800
Kansas City *(G-4475)*
Vernies Trux-N-Equip Inc ..... G 785 625-5087
Hays *(G-2923)*
Vilela Rndy Auto Bdy Repr Pntg ..... F 620 231-6350
Pittsburg *(G-9957)*
Wagner Auto Body & Sales Inc ..... F 913 422-1955
Bonner Springs *(G-580)*
Walt Carstar Auto Inc ..... E 785 273-7701
Topeka *(G-13230)*
Weavers Auto Body Inc ..... F 913 441-0001
Shawnee *(G-11050)*
Williams Automotive Inc ..... F 620 343-0086
Emporia *(G-1852)*
Wiseman Discount Tire Inc ..... F 620 231-5291
Frontenac *(G-2067)*

7533 Automotive Exhaust System Repair Shops

Auto Masters LLC ..... F 316 789-8540
Derby *(G-1219)*
Gregg Tire Co Inc ..... F 785 233-4156
Topeka *(G-12652)*
Midas Auto Systems Experts ..... F 316 636-9299
Wichita *(G-15084)*
Midwest Dynamics Inc ..... F 913 383-9320
Leawood *(G-5483)*

7534 Tire Retreading & Repair Shops

Blizzard Energy Inc ..... F 620 796-2396
Great Bend *(G-2521)*
Bridgestone Ret Operations LLC ..... F 913 498-0880
Shawnee Mission *(G-11180)*
Bridgestone Ret Operations LLC ..... E 316 315-0363
Wichita *(G-13887)*
Bridgestone Ret Operations LLC ..... E 316 942-1332
Wichita *(G-13888)*
Bridgestone Ret Operations LLC ..... F 913 831-9955
Overland Park *(G-8485)*
Bridgestone Ret Operations LLC ..... F 913 299-3090
Kansas City *(G-3877)*
Bridgestone Ret Operations LLC ..... F 913 393-2212
Olathe *(G-7560)*
Bridgestone Ret Operations LLC ..... E 913 334-1555
Kansas City *(G-3878)*
Bridgestone Ret Operations LLC ..... F 913 492-8160
Shawnee Mission *(G-11181)*
Bridgestone Ret Operations LLC ..... F 316 684-2682
Wichita *(G-13889)*
Garden City Tire Center Inc ..... F 620 276-7652
Garden City *(G-2178)*
Goodyear Tire & Rubber Company ..... F 785 266-3862
Topeka *(G-12643)*
Kistler Service Inc ..... E 620 782-3611
Udall *(G-13278)*
Midwest Trailer Supply Inc ..... E 316 744-1515
Park City *(G-9632)*
▲ O K Thompsons Tire Inc ..... E 785 738-2283
Beloit *(G-497)*
Superior Car Care Center LLC ..... F 620 492-6856
Johnson *(G-3663)*

7536 Automotive Glass Replacement Shops

A Glass & Tint Shop Kc Inc ..... F 913 491-8468
Merriam *(G-7085)*
Alan Clark Body Shop Inc ..... F 785 776-5333
Manhattan *(G-6538)*
Dons Car Care & Body Shop Inc ..... F 620 669-8178
Hutchinson *(G-3268)*
G I P Inc ..... F 785 749-0005
Lawrence *(G-4867)*
Kennedy Glass Inc ..... E 785 843-4416
Lawrence *(G-4942)*
Norris Collision Center LLC ..... F 316 794-1161
Goddard *(G-2448)*
Safelite Fulfillment Inc ..... F 913 236-5888
Shawnee *(G-11023)*
Service Auto Glass Inc ..... F 630 628-0398
Mc Louth *(G-6929)*
Southwest Glass & Door Inc ..... F 620 626-7400
Liberal *(G-6369)*

7537 Automotive Transmission Repair Shops

Auto Masters LLC ..... F 316 789-8540
Derby *(G-1219)*
Auto Masters LLC ..... E 316 789-8540
Derby *(G-1220)*
Central Pwr Systems & Svcs LLC ..... E 316 943-1231
Wichita *(G-13984)*
Chance Transmissions Inc ..... F 316 529-1883
Wichita *(G-13998)*
Haag Inc ..... D 785 256-2311
Auburn *(G-295)*
Topeka Transmission Service ..... F 785 234-2597
Topeka *(G-13188)*

7538 General Automotive Repair Shop

A-Plus Logistics LLC ..... E 316 945-5757
Park City *(G-9598)*
Action Tire & Service Inc ..... F 913 631-9600
Shawnee Mission *(G-11072)*
Advance Auto Parts Inc ..... F 913 782-0076
Olathe *(G-7511)*
Adventure Rv and Truck Ctr LLC ..... E 316 721-1333
Wichita *(G-13629)*
▲ All American Automotive Inc ..... F 316 721-3600
Wichita *(G-13662)*
Allen Samuels Waco D C J Inc ..... E 620 860-1869
Hutchinson *(G-3196)*
Auto Masters LLC ..... F 316 789-8540
Derby *(G-1219)*
Auto Service Ctr Shawnee LLC ..... F 913 422-5388
Shawnee *(G-10912)*
▲ Autobody of Lawrence ..... E 785 843-3055
Lawrence *(G-4744)*
Automotive Associates ..... E 620 231-6350
Pittsburg *(G-9818)*
B & B Redimix Inc ..... F 785 543-5133
Phillipsburg *(G-9777)*
Berning Tire Inc ..... F 913 422-3033
Bonner Springs *(G-541)*
Bme Inc ..... E 785 274-5116
Topeka *(G-12391)*
Bob Allen Ford Inc ..... D 913 381-3000
Overland Park *(G-8473)*
Boss Motors Inc ..... F 785 562-3696
Marysville *(G-6880)*
Brets Autoworks Corp ..... F 913 764-8677
Olathe *(G-7559)*
Browns Super Service Inc ..... F 785 267-1080
Topeka *(G-12409)*
Calverts Auto Express ..... E 913 631-9995
Lenexa *(G-5725)*
Calverts Express Auto S ..... E 913 631-9995
Lenexa *(G-5726)*
Central Pwr Systems & Svcs LLC ..... F 785 825-8291
Salina *(G-10444)*
Central Pwr Systems & Svcs LLC ..... E 620 792-1361
Great Bend *(G-2534)*
Central Pwr Systems & Svcs LLC ..... E 316 943-1231
Wichita *(G-13984)*
City of Hutchinson ..... D 620 694-1970
Hutchinson *(G-3241)*
City of Salina ..... F 785 309-5752
Salina *(G-10452)*
Complete Automotive LLC ..... E 620 245-0600
McPherson *(G-6951)*
Conklin Fangman Investment Co ..... C 620 662-4467
Hutchinson *(G-3245)*
Cooperative Elevator & Sup Co ..... F 620 873-2376
Meade *(G-7048)*
Credit Motors Inc ..... F 913 621-1206
Kansas City *(G-3945)*
Cstk Inc ..... F 316 744-2061
Park City *(G-9614)*
Cummins Central Power LLC ..... F 785 462-3945
Colby *(G-1002)*
Dept Lincoln Service ..... E 316 928-7331
Wichita *(G-14197)*
Diamond Intl Trcks Inc ..... E 785 235-8711
Topeka *(G-12555)*
Dick Edwards Ford Lincoln Merc ..... D 785 320-4499
Junction City *(G-3687)*
Dodge City Cooperative Exch ..... E 620 225-4193
Dodge City *(G-1344)*
Dodge City International Inc ..... E 620 225-4177
Dodge City *(G-1348)*
Don Hattan Derby Inc ..... E 316 744-1275
Derby *(G-1240)*
Done With Care Auto Repair LLC ..... F 913 722-3466
Shawnee *(G-10941)*
Dons Body Shop Inc ..... F 913 782-9255
Olathe *(G-7660)*
Doug Reh Chevrolet Inc ..... E 620 672-5633
Pratt *(G-10109)*
Engels Sales & Service Center ..... F 785 877-3391
Norton *(G-7444)*
Engquist Tractor Service Inc ..... E 620 654-3651
McPherson *(G-6959)*
Errol E Engel Inc ..... E 785 625-3195
Hays *(G-2800)*
Expert Auto Center ..... F 316 440-6600
Wichita *(G-14322)*
Express Auto Service Inc ..... E 816 373-9995
Lenexa *(G-5843)*
Foley Equipment Company ..... C 785 266-5770
Topeka *(G-12623)*
Four Seasons Rv Acres Inc ..... E 785 598-2221
Abilene *(G-32)*
Fyrs Car Care ..... F 913 385-3600
Overland Park *(G-8744)*
Garden City Travel Plaza LLC ..... E 620 275-4404
Garden City *(G-2179)*
Georgia Kenworth Inc ..... E 816 483-6444
Leawood *(G-5411)*
Ghumms Auto Center LLC ..... F 620 544-7800
Hugoton *(G-3163)*
Goodland Machine & Auto LLC ..... G 785 899-6628
Goodland *(G-2474)*
Great Western Tire of Dodge Cy ..... F 620 225-1343
Dodge City *(G-1367)*
Gregg Tire Co Inc ..... F 785 233-4156
Topeka *(G-12651)*
Hachmeister Service Center LLC ..... F 785 567-4818
Lenora *(G-6243)*
Harrys Machine Works Inc ..... G 620 227-2201
Dodge City *(G-1370)*
Hertel Tank Service Inc ..... G 785 628-2445
Hays *(G-2841)*
Huntingdon Park Standard Svc ..... F 785 272-4499
Topeka *(G-12708)*
JC Auto ..... F 785 266-1300
Berryton *(G-527)*
Joe Self Chevrolet Inc ..... C 316 689-4390
Wichita *(G-14760)*
Johnson County Investors Inc ..... C 913 631-0000
Shawnee Mission *(G-11498)*
K C Freightliner Body Shop ..... F 913 342-4269
Kansas City *(G-4132)*
Kansas Cy Freightliner Sls Inc ..... E 913 780-6606
Olathe *(G-7828)*
Kansas Tire & Wheel Co LLC ..... F 620 421-0005
Parsons *(G-9698)*
▲ Kansasland Tire Inc ..... C 316 522-5434
Wichita *(G-14830)*

Kansasland Tire Inc ....F 785 243-2706
Concordia (G-1119)
Kansasland Tire Inc ....F 620 231-7210
Pittsburg (G-9890)
Kansasland Tire Inc ....F 316 744-0401
Park City (G-9624)
Karls Tire & Auto Service Inc ....F 316 685-5338
Wichita (G-14833)
Kens Garage Inc ....F 913 651-2433
Leavenworth (G-5262)
Kistler Service Inc ....E 620 782-3611
Udall (G-13278)
Kline Motors Inc ....F 620 221-2040
Winfield (G-16153)
Laird Noller Ford Inc ....C 785 235-9211
Topeka (G-12828)
Laird Noller Ford Inc ....E 785 264-2800
Topeka (G-12829)
Lenexa Automotive Inc ....F 913 492-8250
Shawnee Mission (G-11561)
Macconnell Enterprises LLC ....E 785 885-8081
Natoma (G-7231)
Manweiler Chevrolet Co Inc ....F 620 653-2121
Hoisington (G-3069)
McKenzie Paint & Body Inc ....F 620 662-3721
South Hutchinson (G-12061)
Mel Hambelton Ford Inc ....C 316 462-3673
Wichita (G-15035)
Metro Collision Repair Inc ....F 913 839-1044
Olathe (G-7886)
Meyer Truck Center Inc ....F 913 764-2000
Olathe (G-7887)
Midway Motors Inc ....D 620 241-7737
McPherson (G-7005)
Midwest Services & Towing Inc ....E 913 281-1003
Kansas City (G-4257)
Miles Automotive Inc ....D 785 843-7700
Lawrence (G-5028)
Mitten Inc ....E 785 672-3062
Oakley (G-7481)
Murphy-Hoffman Company ....E 816 483-6444
Leawood (G-5492)
Noller Lincoln-Mercury Inc ....E 785 267-2800
Topeka (G-12932)
O K Tire of Dodge City Inc ....F 620 225-0204
Dodge City (G-1415)
Oakley Motors Inc ....E 785 672-3238
Oakley (G-7484)
Oards Auto & Truck Repr Svcs ....F 785 823-9732
Salina (G-10616)
Olathe Ford Sales Inc ....E 913 856-8145
Gardner (G-2357)
Omaha Truck Center Inc ....E 785 823-2204
Salina (G-10619)
Omaha Truck Center Inc ....E 785 823-2204
Salina (G-10620)
Perl Auto Center Inc ....F 620 251-4050
Coffeyville (G-972)
Plastic Omnium Auto Inergy ....F 913 370-6081
Kansas City (G-4324)
Premium Ventures LLC ....F 785 842-5500
Lawrence (G-5073)
Professional Fleet Svcs LLC ....F 316 524-6000
Wichita (G-15361)
Quality Care ....F 785 228-1118
Topeka (G-12995)
Red Rock Auto Center Inc ....F 620 663-9822
South Hutchinson (G-12065)
▼ Reedy Ford Inc ....E 620 442-4800
Arkansas City (G-174)
Riley Ford Mercury Co ....F 620 356-1206
Ulysses (G-13315)
Robert Brogden Buick Gmc Inc ....E 913 782-1500
Olathe (G-8038)
Rohrer Custom and Fabrication ....G 620 359-1707
Wellington (G-13525)
Ronco Inc ....F 913 362-7200
Mission Hills (G-7148)
S Jackson Service Center Inc ....F 913 422-7438
Edwardsville (G-1514)
Schmidt Haven Ford Sales Inc ....F 620 465-2252
Haven (G-2736)
South Star Chrysler Inc ....F 785 242-5600
Ottawa (G-8313)
Southwest Sterling Inc ....E 816 483-6444
Leawood (G-5555)
▲ Southwest Truck Parts Inc ....D 620 672-5686
Pratt (G-10151)
Spencer & Company ....F 785 235-3131
Topeka (G-13090)
Star Lube Auto Ex Care Inc ....F 620 856-4281
Baxter Springs (G-414)
Steven Bradon Auto Center ....F 316 634-0427
Wichita (G-15666)
Steves Quick Lube ....F 785 742-3500
Hiawatha (G-3025)
Transwood Inc ....E 620 331-5924
Independence (G-3566)
Troostwood Garage & Body Shop ....E 816 444-3800
Kansas City (G-4475)
Vee Village Parts Inc ....F 816 421-6441
Basehor (G-390)
Watco Companies LLC ....C 575 745-2329
Pittsburg (G-9963)
Wichita Kenworth Inc ....D 316 838-0867
Park City (G-9655)
Wiebe Tire & Automotive ....F 316 283-4242
Newton (G-7429)
Williams Automotive Inc ....F 620 343-0086
Emporia (G-1852)
Williams Service Inc ....E 620 878-4225
Florence (G-1930)
Winfield Motor Company Inc ....E 620 221-2840
Winfield (G-16187)
Wiseman Discount Tire Inc ....F 620 231-5291
Frontenac (G-2067)
Yingling Auto Electric Inc ....F 785 232-0484
Topeka (G-13255)

7539 Automotive Repair Shops, NEC

A-Plus Logistics LLC ....E 316 945-5757
Park City (G-9598)
Allied Body Shop Incorporated ....F 785 841-3672
Lawrence (G-4730)
Atlas Spring & Axle Co Inc ....F 316 943-2386
Wichita (G-13767)
Auto Masters LLC ....F 316 789-8540
Derby (G-1219)
Auto Masters LLC ....E 316 789-8540
Derby (G-1220)
Axle & Wheel Aligning Co Inc ....F 316 263-0213
Wichita (G-13782)
Blue Valley Goodyear Service ....F 913 345-1380
Shawnee Mission (G-11170)
Bosleys Tire Service Co Inc ....E 316 524-8511
Wichita (G-13871)
Bridgestone Ret Operations LLC ....F 913 393-2212
Olathe (G-7560)
Bridgestone Ret Operations LLC ....F 913 782-1833
Olathe (G-7561)
Bridgestone Ret Operations LLC ....E 913 334-1555
Kansas City (G-3878)
Bridgestone Ret Operations LLC ....F 913 492-8160
Shawnee Mission (G-11181)
▲ Brierton Engineering Inc ....E 785 263-7711
Abilene (G-16)
Briggs Auto Group Inc ....E 785 776-3677
Manhattan (G-6569)
Calverts Express Auto S ....E 913 631-9995
Lenexa (G-5726)
Car Star Spc ....E 201 444-0601
Overland Park (G-8512)
City of Ellinwood ....F 620 564-3046
Ellinwood (G-1628)
Contract Trailer Service Inc ....F 913 281-2589
Kansas City (G-3936)
Eagle Trailer Company Inc ....G 785 841-3200
Lawrence (G-4844)
Ernstings Incorporated ....G 620 564-2793
Ellinwood (G-1631)
Express Auto Service Inc ....E 816 373-9995
Lenexa (G-5843)
Five Star Service Inc ....E 785 625-9400
Hays (G-2810)
Fowlers LLC ....F 785 475-3451
Oberlin (G-7494)
G F Enterprises ....G 785 539-7113
Manhattan (G-6642)
▲ GKN Aerospace Precision Machin ....B 620 326-5952
Wellington (G-13505)
Great Bend Cooperative Assn ....F 620 792-1281
Great Bend (G-2577)
Herrs Machine ....G 785 325-2875
Washington (G-13464)
Iowa Kenworth Inc ....E 816 483-6444
Leawood (G-5440)
Johnson County Automotive LLC ....F 913 432-1721
Shawnee Mission (G-11497)
Landoll Corporation ....E 785 738-6613
Beloit (G-490)
Larrys Trailer Sales & Svc LLC ....F 316 838-1491
Wichita (G-14927)
Mels Tire LLC ....F 620 342-8473
Emporia (G-1792)
Michael E Fromholtz ....F 913 492-8290
Shawnee Mission (G-11622)
Mid-Amrcan Dstrbtrs/Jyhawk RAD ....F 913 321-9664
Kansas City (G-4245)
Midwest Dynamics Inc ....F 913 383-9320
Leawood (G-5483)
Miller Welding Inc ....F 785 454-3425
Downs (G-1472)
Mobile Fx Inc ....F 913 287-1556
Kansas City (G-4266)
O K Electric Work Inc ....G 620 251-2270
Coffeyville (G-966)
OReilly Automotive Stores Inc ....F 913 287-2409
Kansas City (G-4296)
Orrick Trailer Services LLC ....F 913 321-0400
Kansas City (G-4298)
Pomps Tire Service Inc ....F 913 621-5200
Kansas City (G-4326)
Randy Schwindt ....F 785 391-2277
Utica (G-13335)
Rmvk Enterprises Inc ....E 913 321-1915
Kansas City (G-4382)
Star Motors Ltd ....E 913 432-7800
Shawnee Mission (G-11895)
Super Oil Co Inc ....F 785 354-1410
Topeka (G-13125)
T N T Machine Inc ....F 316 440-6004
Wichita (G-15714)
Topeka Trailer Repair Inc ....F 785 862-6010
Topeka (G-13187)
Tracy Pedigo ....F 316 945-3414
Wichita (G-15781)
Truck Sales Inc ....F 620 225-4155
Dodge City (G-1440)
Ultrafab Inc ....E 620 245-0781
McPherson (G-7033)
Vee Village Parts Inc ....F 816 421-6441
Basehor (G-390)
Weavers Auto Body Inc ....F 913 441-0001
Shawnee (G-11050)
Welco Services Inc ....E 620 241-3000
McPherson (G-7041)
Western Trailer Service Inc ....E 913 281-2226
Kansas City (G-4538)
Wichita Body & Equipment Co ....G 316 522-1080
Haysville (G-2964)
Wilkens Manufacturing Inc ....D 785 425-7070
Stockton (G-12190)
Woodys Automotive Svc & Sls ....F 316 838-8011
Wichita (G-16068)
Yost Auto Service ....F 316 264-8482
Wichita (G-16088)

7542 Car Washes

Auto Masters LLC ....E 316 789-8540
Derby (G-1220)
Auto-Craft Inc ....E 785 579-5997
Junction City (G-3669)
Blue Beacon LP II ....B 785 825-2221
Salina (G-10427)
Blue Beacon USA LP ....A 785 825-2221
Salina (G-10428)
Blue Beacon USA LP II ....E 785 672-3328
Oakley (G-7473)
Car Clinic Auto Salon ....F 913 208-5478
Kansas City (G-3889)
Car Star Spc ....E 201 444-0601
Overland Park (G-8512)
Car Wash Center of Mission Inc ....F 913 236-6886
Shawnee Mission (G-11201)
Eagle Auto Salon Inc ....E 785 272-2886
Topeka (G-12565)
Extreme Detail Kc LLC ....F 913 568-4045
Olathe (G-7699)
Finley Construction & Rdymx ....G 785 626-3282
Atwood (G-286)
Green Lantern Inc ....E 316 721-9242
Wichita (G-14510)
Greggpiercy Inc ....F 913 469-9274
Overland Park (G-8779)
Joes Seat Cover Car Wash Ctr ....E 316 262-2486
Wichita (G-14761)
L & M Oil Company ....F 913 856-8502
Gardner (G-2352)
Lakhani Commercial Corp ....D 913 677-1100
Kansas City (G-4193)

Mission Car Wash LLC ......E 913 236-6886
Shawnee Mission *(G-11644)*
Profab ......E 785 392-3442
Minneapolis *(G-7121)*
Rainbow Car Wash Inc ......F 913 432-1116
Kansas City *(G-4360)*
Rakies Oil LLC ......F 620 442-2210
Arkansas City *(G-171)*
Ronco Inc ......F 913 362-7200
Mission Hills *(G-7148)*
Saragenes Short Stop ......F 620 235-1141
Pittsburg *(G-9935)*
Speedy Falcon LLC ......F 913 451-2100
Shawnee Mission *(G-11883)*
Star Fuel Centers Inc ......E 913 652-9400
Leawood *(G-5561)*
Superior Mobile Wash Inc ......F 913 915-9642
Kansas City *(G-4448)*
Turtle Wax Inc ......E 913 236-6886
Shawnee Mission *(G-11950)*
Waterway Gas & Wash Company ......E 913 897-3111
Overland Park *(G-9485)*
Waterway Gas & Wash Company ......E 913 339-9542
Shawnee Mission *(G-11995)*
Waterway Gas & Wash Company ......D 913 339-9964
Shawnee Mission *(G-11996)*

7549 Automotive Svcs, Except Repair & Car Washes

A & M Towing & Recovery Inc ......F 785 331-3100
Lawrence *(G-4717)*
A Glass & Tint Shop Kc Inc ......F 913 491-8468
Merriam *(G-7085)*
Alan Clark Body Shop Inc ......F 785 776-5333
Manhattan *(G-6538)*
All City Tow Service ......F 913 371-1000
Kansas City *(G-3796)*
Almighty Tow Service LLC ......F 913 362-8697
Overland Park *(G-8372)*
Andrade Auto Sales Inc ......F 620 624-2400
Liberal *(G-6278)*
Arrow Wrecker Service Inc ......E 316 267-6621
Wichita *(G-13737)*
Asurion LLC ......A 816 237-3000
Leawood *(G-5336)*
Auto House Inc ......F 785 825-6644
Salina *(G-10413)*
Auto Masters LLC ......E 316 789-8540
Derby *(G-1220)*
Automotive Specialists Inc ......F 316 321-5130
El Dorado *(G-1532)*
Brenneman & Bremmeman Inc ......F 316 282-8834
Newton *(G-7321)*
Browns Super Service Inc ......F 785 267-1080
Topeka *(G-12409)*
Bud Roat Inc ......F 316 683-9072
Wichita *(G-13906)*
Car Clinic Auto Salon ......F 913 208-5478
Kansas City *(G-3889)*
Chris Carlson Hot Rods LLC ......F 316 777-4774
Mulvane *(G-7212)*
Dales Tow Service Inc ......F 913 782-2289
Olathe *(G-7640)*
Dons Car Care & Body Shop Inc ......F 620 669-8178
Hutchinson *(G-3268)*
Ervs Body Shop Inc ......F 620 225-4015
Dodge City *(G-1358)*
Happy Autos LLC ......F 785 621-4100
Hays *(G-2826)*
Interstate Wrecker Service ......F 316 269-1133
Wichita *(G-14712)*
Jgs Auto Wrecking ......F 913 321-2716
Kansas City *(G-4124)*
Jiffy Lube International Inc ......F 913 682-7020
Leavenworth *(G-5258)*
Joes Seat Cover Car Wash Ctr ......E 316 262-2486
Wichita *(G-14761)*
Kansas Fast Lube Inc ......F 620 241-5656
McPherson *(G-6982)*
Kens Auto Tow ......F 316 941-4300
Wichita *(G-14850)*
Lawrence City Vehicle Maint ......F 785 832-3020
Lawrence *(G-4960)*
Marvins Tow Service Inc ......F 913 764-7630
Olathe *(G-7876)*
McCarthy Collision Center ......E 913 324-7300
Olathe *(G-7881)*
Midwest Dynamics Inc ......F 913 383-9320
Leawood *(G-5483)*
Midwest Services & Towing Inc ......E 913 281-1003
Kansas City *(G-4257)*
Midwest Tinting Inc ......F 913 384-2665
Overland Park *(G-9036)*
Overland Tow Service Inc ......F 913 722-3505
Overland Park *(G-9128)*
Pro-Tow LLC ......F 913 262-3300
Shawnee Mission *(G-11752)*
R&B Services LLC ......E 316 265-7859
Wichita *(G-15407)*
Ridge Auto Center ......F 785 286-1498
Topeka *(G-13018)*
Ritchey Motors LLC ......F 785 380-0222
Topeka *(G-13019)*
Santa Fe Tow Service Inc ......D 417 553-3676
Shawnee Mission *(G-11833)*
Sears Roebuck and Co ......F 785 271-4200
Topeka *(G-13049)*
T & W Tire LLC ......E 316 683-8364
Wichita *(G-15712)*
Team Car Care LLC ......F 913 334-5950
Kansas City *(G-4461)*
Team Car Care LLC ......F 785 266-7696
Topeka *(G-13147)*
Team Car Care LLC ......F 785 228-1824
Topeka *(G-13148)*
Team Car Care LLC ......F 913 362-3349
Shawnee Mission *(G-11922)*
Team Car Care LLC ......F 785 749-1599
Lawrence *(G-5132)*
Team Car Care LLC ......F 913 381-1005
Leawood *(G-5570)*
Tiger Tow & Transport Inc ......F 913 422-7300
Bonner Springs *(G-577)*
Tow All of Kansas City LLC ......E 913 208-0327
Overland Park *(G-9419)*
Tow Service Inc ......E 316 522-8908
Wichita *(G-15778)*
Williams Automotive Inc ......F 620 343-0086
Emporia *(G-1852)*

76 MISCELLANEOUS REPAIR SERVICES

7622 Radio & TV Repair Shops

Aircraft Instr & Rdo Co Inc ......E 316 945-9820
Wichita *(G-13651)*
All Systems Inc ......E 913 281-5100
Kansas City *(G-3799)*
AVI Systems Inc ......E 913 495-9494
Lenexa *(G-5677)*
Bevan-Rabell Inc ......E 316 946-4870
Wichita *(G-13842)*
▲ Clark Enterprises 2000 Inc ......E 785 825-7172
Salina *(G-10455)*
Communications Tech Assoc ......E 316 267-5016
Wichita *(G-14076)*
Custom Rdo Communications Ltd ......F 816 561-4100
Leawood *(G-5367)*
G E V Investment Inc ......E 913 677-5333
Kansas City *(G-4024)*
Gateway Wireless Services LLC ......F 316 264-0037
Wichita *(G-14451)*
Ka-Comm Inc ......G 785 776-8177
Manhattan *(G-6672)*
Ka-Comm Inc ......F 785 827-8555
Salina *(G-10560)*
Kent Business Systems Corp ......F 316 262-4487
Wichita *(G-14851)*
Mobile Radio Service Inc ......F 620 793-3231
Great Bend *(G-2612)*
Northeast Kans Educatn Svc Ctr ......C 913 538-7250
Ozawkie *(G-9536)*
Overland TV Inc ......F 913 648-2222
Shawnee Mission *(G-11711)*
Paragon N D T & Finishes Inc ......E 316 945-5286
Wichita *(G-15259)*
Radio Shop Inc ......F 316 265-1851
Wichita *(G-15409)*
Repair Shack Inc ......E 913 732-0514
Lenexa *(G-6105)*
T V Hephner and Elec Inc ......F 316 264-3284
Wichita *(G-15715)*
Teledata Communications LLC ......E 913 663-2010
Lenexa *(G-6175)*
Tfmcomm Inc ......E 785 233-2343
Topeka *(G-13156)*

7623 Refrigeration & Air Conditioning Svc & Repair Shop

Air Power Consultants Inc ......F 913 894-0044
Olathe *(G-7514)*
Auman Co Inc ......F 785 628-2833
Hays *(G-2752)*
Automated Control Systems Corp ......D 913 766-2336
Leawood *(G-5337)*
CMS Mechanical Services LLC ......E 321 473-0488
Lenexa *(G-5767)*
▲ Cstk Inc ......E 913 233-7220
Overland Park *(G-8621)*
Even Temp of Wichita Inc ......F 316 469-5321
Wichita *(G-14312)*
Ice-Masters Inc ......F 316 945-6900
Wichita *(G-14665)*
Lba Air Cndtoning Htg Plbg Inc ......E 816 454-5515
Shawnee Mission *(G-11551)*
Murphy-Hoffman Company ......F 913 441-6300
Kansas City *(G-4274)*
R & R Street Plbg Htg & Elec ......F 785 524-4551
Lincoln *(G-6385)*
Ricks Appliance Service Inc ......F 316 265-2866
Wichita *(G-15460)*
Temp-Con Inc ......D 913 768-4888
Olathe *(G-8106)*
Thermal Comfort Air Inc ......E 785 537-2436
Manhattan *(G-6824)*
Tresko Inc ......E 913 631-6900
Shawnee Mission *(G-11941)*
Velociti Inc ......E 913 233-7230
Kansas City *(G-4514)*
Vhc Van Hoecke Contracting Inc ......E 913 888-0036
Lenexa *(G-6212)*

7629 Electrical & Elex Repair Shop, NEC

▲ Abilene Machine LLC ......C 785 655-9455
Solomon *(G-12046)*
Accurate Electric Inc ......G 785 825-4010
Salina *(G-10391)*
Aircraft Instr & Rdo Co Inc ......E 316 945-9820
Wichita *(G-13651)*
Alltite Inc ......E 316 686-3010
Wichita *(G-13678)*
Athena Communications Ltd ......F 913 599-3444
Overland Park *(G-8409)*
Audiology Consultants Inc ......F 785 823-3761
Salina *(G-10412)*
B & H Appliance ......F 620 364-8700
New Strawn *(G-7303)*
B&B Electric Motor Co ......F 316 267-1238
Wichita *(G-13786)*
Broyles Petroleum Equipment Co ......E 417 863-6800
Humboldt *(G-3183)*
Century Business Systems Inc ......F 785 776-0495
Manhattan *(G-6583)*
Communication Link LLC ......F 913 681-5400
Lenexa *(G-5776)*
Elecsys International Corp ......C 913 647-0158
Olathe *(G-7673)*
Factory Direct Appliance ......F 785 272-8800
Topeka *(G-12592)*
G F Enterprises ......G 785 539-7113
Manhattan *(G-6642)*
Heartland Services Inc ......E 913 685-8855
Leawood *(G-5427)*
▲ Heartland Services Inc ......E 913 685-8855
Leawood *(G-5428)*
Honeywell International Inc ......C 913 782-0400
Olathe *(G-7772)*
Independent Electric McHy Co ......E 913 362-1155
Kansas City *(G-4097)*
Kansas Communications Inc ......E 913 402-2200
Lenexa *(G-5937)*
Mar-Beck Appliance Svc Co Inc ......E 913 322-4022
Lenexa *(G-5985)*
McCarty Office Machines Inc ......F 620 421-5530
Parsons *(G-9708)*
Mid Kansas Tool & Electric Inc ......F 785 825-9521
Salina *(G-10600)*
Mid West Elc Transformers Inc ......F 316 283-7500
Newton *(G-7382)*
Midwest Office Technologies ......E 785 272-7704
Topeka *(G-12903)*
Midwest Office Technology ......E 913 894-9600
Overland Park *(G-9034)*
Midwest Sewing & Vacuum Center ......E 316 722-9737
Wichita *(G-15101)*
Naab Electric Inc ......F 620 276-8101
Garden City *(G-2242)*

Nation-Wide Repr Holdg Co Inc..........E....... 913 248-1722
Stilwell *(G-12170)*
Networks Plus..........E....... 785 825-0400
Salina *(G-10611)*
Office Products Inc..........E....... 620 793-8180
Great Bend *(G-2616)*
Oswald Manufacturing Co Inc..........G....... 785 258-2877
Herington *(G-2980)*
Ott Electric Inc..........F....... 785 562-2641
Marysville *(G-6907)*
Repair Shack Inc..........E....... 913 732-0514
Lenexa *(G-6105)*
Richmond Electric Inc..........G....... 316 264-2344
Wichita *(G-15457)*
Ricks Appliance Service Inc..........F....... 316 265-2866
Wichita *(G-15460)*
Royal Flush Plumbing LLC..........F....... 316 794-2656
Goddard *(G-2453)*
S D M Die Cutting Equipment..........G....... 913 782-3737
Shawnee *(G-11022)*
S N C Inc..........E....... 620 665-6651
Hutchinson *(G-3434)*
Satellite Engrg Group Inc..........E....... 913 324-6000
Overland Park *(G-9282)*
SC Hall Industrial Svcs Inc..........E....... 316 945-4255
Wichita *(G-15525)*
Skaggs Inc..........E....... 620 672-5312
Pratt *(G-10148)*
Spectrum Elite Corp..........G....... 913 579-7037
Olathe *(G-8076)*
Sta-Mot-Ks LLC..........E....... 913 894-9600
Overland Park *(G-9349)*
T V Hephner and Elec Inc..........F....... 316 264-3284
Wichita *(G-15715)*
Tech-Aire Instruments Inc..........F....... 316 262-4020
Wichita *(G-15724)*
Test and Measurement Inc..........F....... 913 233-2724
Kansas City *(G-4466)*
Tpcks Inc..........F....... 785 776-4429
Manhattan *(G-6828)*
X TEC Repair Inc..........E....... 913 829-3773
Lenexa *(G-6238)*

7631 Watch, Clock & Jewelry Repair

Brimans Leading Jewelers Inc..........F....... 785 357-4438
Topeka *(G-12408)*
Burnells Creative Gold Inc..........G....... 316 634-2822
Wichita *(G-13916)*
Mark Boose..........G....... 785 234-4808
Topeka *(G-12860)*
Noble House Jewelry Ltd..........F....... 913 491-4861
Overland Park *(G-9090)*
Riddles Group Inc..........D....... 620 371-6284
Dodge City *(G-1424)*
Tivol Plaza Inc..........E....... 913 345-0200
Overland Park *(G-9416)*
Vernon Jewelers of Salina Inc..........F....... 785 825-0531
Salina *(G-10751)*

7641 Reupholstery & Furniture Repair

Andrews and Abbey Riley LLC..........F....... 913 262-2212
Kansas City *(G-3811)*
Big Lkes Developmental Ctr Inc..........E....... 785 632-5357
Clay Center *(G-843)*
Circle Enterprises Inc..........F....... 316 943-9834
Wichita *(G-14021)*
De Leon Furniture Inc..........F....... 913 342-9446
Kansas City *(G-3964)*
Design Central Inc..........F....... 785 825-4131
Salina *(G-10474)*
Panel Systems Plus Inc..........E....... 913 321-0111
Kansas City *(G-4309)*

7692 Welding Repair

A&R Custom Form & Fabricatio..........G....... 620 423-0170
Parsons *(G-9662)*
Anna M Kramer..........G....... 785 353-2205
Beattie *(G-417)*
B&B Welding..........G....... 620 253-1023
Dodge City *(G-1300)*
Built-So-Well..........G....... 785 537-5166
Manhattan *(G-6571)*
Central States Machining Wldg..........G....... 785 233-1376
Topeka *(G-12457)*
Central Welding & Machine LLC..........F....... 620 663-9353
Hutchinson *(G-3235)*
Ceo Enterprises Inc..........F....... 913 432-8046
Shawnee Mission *(G-11214)*
Cimarron Welding Inc..........G....... 620 855-3582
Cimarron *(G-821)*
Cliffs Welding Shop Inc..........G....... 785 543-5895
Phillipsburg *(G-9780)*
Earl Resse Welding..........G....... 620 624-6141
Liberal *(G-6306)*
G F Enterprises..........G....... 785 539-7113
Manhattan *(G-6642)*
General Repair & Supply Inc..........G....... 620 365-5954
Iola *(G-3604)*
▼ Hammersmith Mfg & Sales Inc..........D....... 785 486-2121
Horton *(G-3126)*
Hammersmith Mfg & Sales Inc..........G....... 785 364-4140
Holton *(G-3095)*
Harrison Machine Shop & Wldg..........G....... 913 764-0730
Olathe *(G-7756)*
Harrods Blacksmith & Welding..........G....... 620 374-2323
Howard *(G-3134)*
Harvest AG Fabricating LLC..........G....... 620 345-8205
Moundridge *(G-7184)*
Independent Electric McHy Co..........E....... 913 362-1155
Kansas City *(G-4097)*
Kan Fab Inc..........G....... 620 342-5669
Emporia *(G-1783)*
Koehn Customs..........G....... 316 304-7979
Montezuma *(G-7157)*
Larue Machine Inc..........F....... 620 431-3303
Chanute *(G-738)*
Leons Welding & Fabrication..........F....... 785 625-5736
Hays *(G-2863)*
Linders Welding Inc..........G....... 913 681-2394
Stilwell *(G-12164)*
Martin Welding..........G....... 620 545-7311
Clearwater *(G-894)*
Mc Intire Welding Inc..........E....... 785 823-5454
Salina *(G-10595)*
Mid Kansas Machine Inc..........E....... 620 241-2959
McPherson *(G-7003)*
Miller Welding Inc..........F....... 785 454-3425
Downs *(G-1472)*
Mlr Welding LLC..........G....... 785 203-1020
Hays *(G-2874)*
▲ Neville Welding Inc..........E....... 620 532-3487
Kingman *(G-4608)*
Numerical Control Support Inc..........E....... 913 441-3500
Shawnee Mission *(G-11690)*
Pihl Repair & Fabrication LLC..........G....... 785 668-2014
Falun *(G-1928)*
Premier Tillage Inc..........E....... 785 754-2381
Quinter *(G-10184)*
Pro-Weld LLC..........G....... 316 648-6316
Wichita *(G-15354)*
Progressive Manufacturing Co..........F....... 913 383-2239
Leawood *(G-5530)*
Randy Schwindt..........F....... 785 391-2277
Utica *(G-13335)*
Rons Welding & Pipeline Svcs..........G....... 620 935-4275
Russell *(G-10291)*
Schlotterbeck Machine Shop..........G....... 620 678-3210
Hamilton *(G-2708)*
Schulz Welding Service Inc..........F....... 620 628-4431
Canton *(G-681)*
Steel Fabrications Inc..........G....... 785 625-3075
Hays *(G-2913)*
Toms Machine & Welding Svc..........G....... 785 434-2800
Plainville *(G-9994)*
Turon Welding and Fabrication..........G....... 620 388-4458
Turon *(G-13275)*
Vernies Trux-N-Equip Inc..........G....... 785 625-5087
Hays *(G-2923)*
Webco Manufacturing Inc..........D....... 913 764-7111
Olathe *(G-8149)*
Welco Services Inc..........E....... 620 241-3000
McPherson *(G-7041)*

7694 Armature Rewinding Shops

Ametek Advanced Industries Inc..........D....... 316 522-0424
Wichita *(G-13698)*
▲ Atkinson Industries Inc..........D....... 620 231-6900
Pittsburg *(G-9816)*
Gems Inc..........G....... 785 731-2849
Ransom *(G-10192)*
Gibson Industrial Controls Inc..........G....... 620 241-3551
McPherson *(G-6969)*
Independent Electric McHy Co..........G....... 620 257-5375
Lyons *(G-6486)*
Independent Electric McHy Co..........G....... 785 233-4282
Topeka *(G-12716)*
Klemp Electric Machinery Co..........F....... 913 371-4330
Kansas City *(G-4176)*
Kriers Auto Parts Inc..........G....... 785 738-3526
Beloit *(G-489)*
Naab Electric Inc..........F....... 620 276-8101
Garden City *(G-2242)*
O K Electric Work Inc..........G....... 620 251-2270
Coffeyville *(G-966)*
Patchen Electric & Indus Sup..........G....... 785 843-4522
Lawrence *(G-5057)*
Richmond Electric Inc..........G....... 316 264-2344
Wichita *(G-15457)*
Rotek Services Inc..........E....... 316 263-3131
Wichita *(G-15483)*
Yost Electric Inc..........G....... 785 637-5454
Gorham *(G-2492)*
Zimmerman Electric Service..........G....... 620 431-2260
Chanute *(G-775)*

7699 Repair Shop & Related Svcs, NEC

A 1 Sewer & Septic Service..........F....... 913 631-5201
Kansas City *(G-3777)*
Accent Erection & Maint Co Inc..........F....... 913 371-1600
Kansas City *(G-3780)*
Acsys Lasertechnik US Inc..........G....... 847 468-5302
Lenexa *(G-5626)*
Adelphi Construction Lc..........D....... 913 384-5511
Shawnee Mission *(G-11075)*
Air Filter Plus Inc..........E....... 785 542-3700
Eudora *(G-1869)*
Aircraft Instrument & Rdo Svcs..........F....... 316 945-9820
Wichita *(G-13652)*
Airgas Usa LLC..........E....... 316 941-9162
Wichita *(G-13653)*
Allen Commercial Clg Svcs LLC..........E....... 913 322-2900
Lenexa *(G-5641)*
Ametek Arcft Parts & ACC Inc..........E....... 316 264-2397
Wichita *(G-13699)*
▲ Apph Wichita Inc..........E....... 316 943-5752
Wichita *(G-13720)*
Appliance Doctor Inc..........E....... 316 263-0005
Wichita *(G-13723)*
Armdat Inc..........F....... 913 321-4287
Kansas City *(G-3819)*
B & B Hydraulics Inc..........E....... 620 662-2552
Hutchinson *(G-3210)*
B & D Equipment Co Inc..........F....... 913 367-1744
Atchison *(G-211)*
Barrow Tooling Systems Inc..........G....... 785 364-4306
Holton *(G-3085)*
Berry Companies Inc..........E....... 316 838-3321
Wichita *(G-13833)*
Big Twin Inc..........E....... 785 234-6174
Topeka *(G-12381)*
Broadway Home Medical Inc..........F....... 316 264-8600
Wichita *(G-13895)*
Bruna Brothers Implement LLC..........F....... 785 562-5304
Marysville *(G-6881)*
Bruna Brothers Implement LLC..........F....... 785 742-2261
Hiawatha *(G-3005)*
Bruna Brothers Implement LLC..........F....... 785 336-2111
Seneca *(G-10858)*
Bruna Brothers Implement LLC..........E....... 785 325-2232
Washington *(G-13461)*
Butler Avionics Inc..........F....... 913 829-4606
New Century *(G-7271)*
C & B Equipment Midwest Inc..........F....... 913 236-8222
Overland Park *(G-8502)*
Canon Solutions America Inc..........G....... 913 323-5010
Overland Park *(G-8508)*
Capital City Pallet Inc..........F....... 785 379-5099
Topeka *(G-12429)*
Central Plains Contracting Co..........F....... 620 231-2660
Pittsburg *(G-9830)*
Century Instrument Corp..........F....... 316 683-7571
Wichita *(G-13991)*
Century Office Pdts Inc Topeka..........E....... 785 267-4555
Topeka *(G-12460)*
Century Partners LLC..........F....... 913 642-2489
Olathe *(G-7586)*
Cheney Door Co Inc..........F....... 620 669-9306
Hutchinson *(G-3236)*
City Cycle Sales..........F....... 785 238-3411
Junction City *(G-3681)*
City of Topeka..........F....... 785 273-0811
Topeka *(G-12473)*
Clevlun Enterprises Inc..........F....... 913 631-1111
Shawnee Mission *(G-11239)*
Colby A G Center LLC..........F....... 785 462-6132
Colby *(G-995)*
Cook Pump Company..........E....... 620 251-0880
Coffeyville *(G-930)*
Cottagecare Inc..........F....... 913 469-8778
Overland Park *(G-8603)*

D & S Machine and Welding Inc ....G 785 798-3359
Ness City *(G-7259)*
D H Pace Company Inc ....C 816 221-0072
Olathe *(G-7636)*
▲ D H Pace Company Inc ....A 816 221-0543
Olathe *(G-7637)*
D H Pace Company Inc ....E 316 944-3667
Wichita *(G-14157)*
D H Pace Company Inc ....B 816 480-2600
Olathe *(G-7638)*
Daka Inc ....E 913 768-1803
Prairie Village *(G-10025)*
Dauer Implement Company Inc ....F 785 825-2141
Salina *(G-10470)*
Daves Pumping Service Inc ....F 620 343-3081
Emporia *(G-1727)*
David Cobler ....F 785 234-3384
Topeka *(G-12547)*
Delbert Chopp Co Inc ....F 785 825-8530
Salina *(G-10472)*
Dicks Engine & Machine Service ....F 620 564-2238
Ellinwood *(G-1629)*
Doll Cradle ....F 913 631-1900
Shawnee Mission *(G-11313)*
Eagle Environmental Svcs LLC ....E 316 944-2445
Wichita *(G-14250)*
EE Newcomer Enterprises Inc ....B 816 221-0543
Olathe *(G-7671)*
Eichhorn Holdings LLC ....F 785 843-1426
Lawrence *(G-4848)*
Ernstings Incorporated ....G 620 564-2793
Ellinwood *(G-1631)*
Excel Sales Inc ....F 620 327-4911
Hesston *(G-2990)*
Executive Beechcraft Inc ....E 913 782-9003
New Century *(G-7284)*
▲ Exline Inc ....C 785 825-4683
Salina *(G-10489)*
▲ Express Scale Parts Inc ....E 913 441-4787
Lenexa *(G-5844)*
Falcon Industries Inc ....F 620 289-4290
Tyro *(G-13276)*
First Response ....F 913 557-2187
Paola *(G-9559)*
Flint Hills Powersports Inc ....G 785 336-3901
Bern *(G-522)*
Fort Scott Truck & Tractor ....F 620 223-6506
Fort Scott *(G-1972)*
Fresh Apprach Clg Prfessionals ....F 913 707-5500
Shawnee Mission *(G-11381)*
▼ Garsite Progress LLC ....D 913 342-5600
Kansas City *(G-4025)*
GE Engine Services LLC ....A 316 264-4741
Arkansas City *(G-157)*
General Electric Company ....E 816 244-9672
Overland Park *(G-8751)*
Gibson Industrial Controls Inc ....G 620 241-3551
McPherson *(G-6969)*
Girard Tarps Inc ....G 620 724-8909
Girard *(G-2410)*
Glass Services Inc ....F 785 823-5444
Salina *(G-10511)*
Global Aviation Services LLC ....D 913 780-0300
Olathe *(G-7731)*
Green Clean Kc LLC ....F 913 499-7106
Overland Park *(G-8777)*
Hammel Scale Kansas City Inc ....F 913 321-5428
Kansas City *(G-4062)*
Harrods Blacksmith & Welding ....G 620 374-2323
Howard *(G-3134)*
Heartland Cstmer Solutions LLC ....C 913 685-8855
Leawood *(G-5424)*
Heartland Deisel Repair ....F 913 403-0208
Shawnee Mission *(G-11423)*
Heritage Tractor Inc ....E 785 235-5100
Topeka *(G-12686)*
Herrs Machine ....G 785 325-2875
Washington *(G-13464)*
High Plains Machine Works Inc ....F 785 625-4672
Hays *(G-2845)*
Hume Music Inc ....F 816 474-1960
Stilwell *(G-12154)*
Iclean Prof Clg Svcs LLC ....F 913 521-5995
Overland Park *(G-8836)*
Industrial Cleaning and Maint ....E 785 246-9262
Topeka *(G-12722)*
Interstate Cleaning Corp ....C 314 428-0566
Olathe *(G-7801)*
Interstate Elevator Inc ....F 785 234-2817
Topeka *(G-12727)*
Invena Corporation ....E 620 583-8630
Eureka *(G-1892)*
Jade Millwrights Inc ....E 785 544-7771
Hiawatha *(G-3011)*
Janssen Glass & Mirror Inc ....F 913 677-5727
Shawnee *(G-10977)*
Jci Industries Inc ....F 316 942-6200
Wichita *(G-14751)*
Jens House & Coml Clg LLC ....F 785 286-2463
Topeka *(G-12743)*
Jies LLC ....F 620 668-5585
Copeland *(G-1149)*
Jim Starkey Music Center Inc ....F 316 262-2351
Wichita *(G-14757)*
Jmh Cleaning Service ....F 785 819-0725
Salina *(G-10556)*
K & N Motorcycles Corporation ....E 316 945-8221
Valley Center *(G-13346)*
▲ Kanamak Hydraulics Inc ....E 800 473-5843
Garden City *(G-2212)*
Kanequip Inc ....F 785 562-2377
Marysville *(G-6891)*
Kansas City Hydraulics Inc ....G 913 371-6151
Kansas City *(G-4145)*
▲ Kansas City Strings Violin Sp ....E 913 677-0400
Shawnee Mission *(G-11511)*
Kansas Forklift Inc ....F 316 262-1426
Wichita *(G-14802)*
Kansas Kenworth Inc ....E 785 823-9700
Salina *(G-10566)*
Kaw Valley Industrial Inc ....G 785 841-9751
Eudora *(G-1876)*
▲ KBK Industries LLC ....C 785 372-4331
Rush Center *(G-10260)*
Kcsc Space Works Inc ....E 620 662-2305
Hutchinson *(G-3349)*
Kelley Instruments Inc ....F 316 945-7171
Wichita *(G-14843)*
Kiowa Service Co Inc ....F 316 636-1070
Wichita *(G-14865)*
Kone Inc ....F 316 942-1201
Wichita *(G-14893)*
Landscapes Inc ....E 316 262-7557
Wichita *(G-14921)*
Laser Specialists Inc ....E 913 780-9990
Olathe *(G-7856)*
Layne Christensen Company ....E 913 321-5000
Kansas City *(G-4196)*
Lba Air Cndtoning Htg Plbg Inc ....E 816 454-5515
Shawnee Mission *(G-11551)*
Liberal Office Machines Co ....G 620 624-5653
Liberal *(G-6334)*
Logan Business Machines Inc ....E 785 233-1102
Topeka *(G-12848)*
Machine Design Services Inc ....G 620 663-4949
South Hutchinson *(G-12060)*
Mame Inc ....F 620 964-2156
Le Roy *(G-5198)*
Manning Music Inc ....F 785 272-1740
Topeka *(G-12857)*
McCullough Enterprises Inc ....F 316 942-8118
Wichita *(G-15024)*
McDonald Tank and Eqp Co Inc ....E 620 793-3555
Great Bend *(G-2606)*
McLaughlin Leasing Inc ....F 316 542-0303
Cheney *(G-794)*
Merry X-Ray Chemical Corp ....E 858 565-4472
Overland Park *(G-9013)*
Mid Kansas Marine & Rv Inc ....F 620 665-0396
Hutchinson *(G-3376)*
Mid Kansas Tool & Electric Inc ....F 785 825-9521
Salina *(G-10600)*
▲ Mid-American Machine & Eqp Inc ....F 620 964-2156
Le Roy *(G-5199)*
Mid-Continent Harley-Davidson ....F 316 440-5700
Park City *(G-9630)*
Mid-Kansas Cylinder Head Inc ....F 620 241-6800
McPherson *(G-7004)*
Midway Manufacturing Inc ....E 620 659-3631
Kinsley *(G-4620)*
Midwest Duct Cleaning Services ....F 913 648-5300
Shawnee Mission *(G-11633)*
Midwest Merchandising Inc ....C 913 428-8430
Overland Park *(G-9033)*
Midwest Merchandising Inc ....F 913 451-1515
Shawnee Mission *(G-11635)*
Millennium Rail Inc ....F 620 231-2230
Pittsburg *(G-9905)*
MSI ....E 316 262-2021
Wichita *(G-15137)*
Noonshine Window Cleaning Svc ....F 913 381-3780
Overland Park *(G-9092)*
Northeast Kansas Hydraulics ....G 785 235-0405
Topeka *(G-12936)*
Online Vend Mch Sls & Svc Inc ....G 913 492-1097
Lenexa *(G-6037)*
Oswald Manufacturing Co Inc ....G 785 258-2877
Herington *(G-2980)*
Outlaws Group LLC ....F 913 381-5565
Shawnee Mission *(G-11704)*
Overhead Door Company ....E 316 265-4634
Wichita *(G-15240)*
Overland Tool & Machinery Inc ....E 913 599-4044
Shawnee *(G-11007)*
P & W Incorporated ....E 316 267-4277
Wichita *(G-15247)*
Paragon N D T & Finishes Inc ....E 316 945-5285
Wichita *(G-15259)*
Perfect Output LLC ....D 913 317-8400
Overland Park *(G-9154)*
Prairiebrooke Arts Inc ....F 913 341-0333
Overland Park *(G-9178)*
Pratt & Whitney Eng Svcs Inc ....G 316 945-9763
Wichita *(G-15322)*
Premier Casting & Machine Svc ....F 620 241-2040
McPherson *(G-7020)*
R & R Street Plbg Htg & Elec ....F 785 524-4551
Lincoln *(G-6385)*
Randy Schwindt ....F 785 391-2277
Utica *(G-13335)*
Ravenscraft Implement Inc ....F 316 799-2141
Whitewater *(G-13572)*
Reid Plumbing Heating & AC Inc ....F 785 537-2869
Manhattan *(G-6789)*
River City Elevator LLC ....F 316 773-3161
Wichita *(G-15470)*
Rmvk Enterprises Inc ....E 913 321-1915
Kansas City *(G-4382)*
▼ Road Builders Mchy & Sup Co ....D 913 371-3822
Kansas City *(G-4384)*
Romans Outdoor Power Inc ....E 913 837-5225
Louisburg *(G-6466)*
Rueschhoff Communications ....E 785 841-0111
Lawrence *(G-5098)*
Ryans Comet Cleaner ....F 620 231-4559
Pittsburg *(G-9931)*
S & S Equipment Co Inc ....F 316 267-7471
Wichita *(G-15500)*
Salina Scale Sales & Service ....F 785 827-4441
Salina *(G-10690)*
▲ Schwabs Tinker Shop Intl Inc ....G 620 624-7611
Liberal *(G-6363)*
▲ Seals Inc ....G 913 438-1212
Shawnee Mission *(G-11844)*
Sew Easy Sewing Center Inc ....F 913 341-1122
Overland Park *(G-9301)*
Shady Creek Sales Inc ....F 316 321-0943
El Dorado *(G-1602)*
Shannahan Crane & Hoist Inc ....F 816 746-9822
Kansas City *(G-4419)*
Sharpening Specialists LLC ....E 316 945-0593
Wichita *(G-15575)*
Shepherds Truck & Tractor ....F 620 331-2970
Independence *(G-3560)*
Smallwood Lock Supply Inc ....F 913 371-5678
Kansas City *(G-4425)*
Squires Corporation ....F 316 944-0040
Wichita *(G-15650)*
▲ Storrer Implement Inc ....F 620 365-5692
Iola *(G-3636)*
Straub International Inc ....F 620 662-0211
Hutchinson *(G-3451)*
▲ Styers Equipment Company ....F 913 681-5225
Overland Park *(G-9369)*
T and C Aviation Enterprises ....E 913 764-4800
Olathe *(G-8095)*
T N T Machine Inc ....F 316 440-6004
Wichita *(G-15714)*
T W Lacy & Associates Inc ....F 913 706-7625
Prairie Village *(G-10073)*
Taylor Implement Co Inc ....E 785 675-3272
Hoxie *(G-3143)*
▲ Teeter Irrigation Inc ....D 620 353-1111
Ulysses *(G-13324)*
Textron Aviation Inc ....A 316 676-7111
Wichita *(G-15741)*
Thompson Dehydrating Co Inc ....F 785 272-7722
Topeka *(G-13160)*
Thyssenkrupp Elevator Corp ....F 316 529-2233
Wichita *(G-15764)*

SIC

Employee Codes: A=Over 500 employees, B=251-500
C=101-250, D=51-100, E=20-50, F=10-19, G=5-9

Thyssenkrupp Elevator Corp................F....... 913 888-8046
Overland Park (G-9408)
Todd Tractor Co Inc ....F....... 785 336-2138
Seneca (G-10884)
Topeka Foundry and Ir Works Co..........D....... 785 232-8212
Topeka (G-13176)
Total Tool Supply Inc ....F....... 913 722-7879
Kansas City (G-4471)
Trimac Industrial Systems LLC ....E....... 913 441-0043
Bonner Springs (G-578)
Truett & Osborn Cycle Inc......................G....... 316 682-4781
Wichita (G-15811)
Unruh-Foster Inc....................................E....... 620 846-2215
Montezuma (G-7161)
US Boatworks Inc ....F....... 913 342-0011
Kansas City (G-4511)
Van-Wall Equipment Inc ....E....... 913 397-6009
Olathe (G-8138)
▲ Weller Tractor Salvage Inc ....F....... 620 792-5243
Great Bend (G-2659)
Wes Material Handling Inc ....F....... 913 369-9375
Tonganoxie (G-12273)
Wichita Band Instrument Co..................F....... 316 684-0291
Wichita (G-15979)
Wilkerson Crane Rental Inc ....E....... 913 238-7030
Lenexa (G-6230)
Woofter Pump & Well Inc ....F....... 785 675-3991
Hoxie (G-3144)

78 MOTION PICTURES

7812 Motion Picture & Video Tape Production

AVI Systems Inc ....E....... 913 495-9494
Lenexa (G-5677)
Complete Video Production...................F....... 913 888-2383
Shawnee Mission (G-11256)
Digital Sound Systems Inc....................E....... 913 492-5775
Lenexa (G-5819)
Jack Wilson & Associates Inc ....F....... 785 856-4546
Lawrence (G-4918)
Kent Business Systems Corp................F....... 316 262-4487
Wichita (G-14851)
Nuvidia LLC ....F....... 913 599-5200
Lenexa (G-6030)
Retail Groc Assn Grter Kans Cy............F....... 913 384-3830
Westwood (G-13558)
Something Different Media Prod ....F....... 913 764-9500
Olathe (G-8072)

7819 Services Allied To Motion Picture Prdtn

Real Media LLC ....F....... 913 894-8989
Overland Park (G-9228)
Trinity Animation Inc ....F....... 816 525-0103
Overland Park (G-9428)
Twa LLC ....E....... 913 599-5200
Lenexa (G-6195)

7822 Motion Picture & Video Tape Distribution

1038 Productions ....F....... 316 644-6883
Wichita (G-13577)
Arteyeview Productions.........................F....... 316 737-7080
Wichita (G-13740)
Do Good Productions Inc.......................F....... 913 400-3416
Leawood (G-5379)
F&F Productions Inc...............................F....... 785 235-8300
Topeka (G-12591)
K&J Outdoor Products LLC....................F....... 816 769-6060
Cherryvale (G-810)
Leisure Time Products ....F....... 620 308-5224
Pittsburg (G-9894)
Mid America Printed ....F....... 913 432-2700
Merriam (G-7100)
Midwest Sports Productions LLC ....E....... 913 543-6116
Lenexa (G-6004)
Oasis Productions...................................F....... 316 210-4488
Wichita (G-15204)
Over Cat Products LLC ....F....... 913 256-2126
Osawatomie (G-8202)
Purpose Productions...............................F....... 913 620-3508
Kansas City (G-4349)
Santa Fe Products LLC ....F....... 913 362-6611
Overland Park (G-9279)
Yaco Productions.....................................F....... 913 669-7380
Kansas City (G-4562)

7832 Motion Picture Theaters, Except Drive-In

Acme Cinema Inc.....................................E....... 620 421-4404
Parsons (G-9663)
AMC Entertainment Holdings Inc..........D....... 913 213-2000
Leawood (G-5317)
AMC Entertainment Inc ....F....... 913 213-2000
Leawood (G-5318)
American Multi-Cinema Inc...................D....... 913 498-8696
Leawood (G-5321)
American Multi-Cinema Inc...................C....... 913 213-2000
Leawood (G-5322)
Astro 3 Theatre..F....... 785 562-3715
Marysville (G-6879)
B & B Cinemas ....F....... 785 242-0777
Ottawa (G-8247)
B & B Movie Theatres LLC.....................F....... 620 342-0900
Emporia (G-1699)
B & B Movie Theatres LLC.....................F....... 620 227-8100
Dodge City (G-1299)
B & B Movie Theatres LLC.....................F....... 620 669-8510
Hutchinson (G-3211)
Carmike Cinemas LLC............................F....... 913 213-2000
Leawood (G-5348)
Carmike Reviews Holdings LLC............F....... 913 213-2000
Leawood (G-5349)
Cinemark Usa Inc....................................C....... 913 789-7038
Shawnee Mission (G-11226)
Cooper Enterprises.................................F....... 620 225-4347
Dodge City (G-1331)
Dickinson Theatres.................................E....... 913 383-6114
Overland Park (G-8654)
Eastwynn Theatres Inc............................E....... 913 213-2000
Leawood (G-5382)
Finch Theatres ....F....... 785 524-4350
Lincoln (G-6382)
George G Kerasotes Corporation..........A....... 913 213-2000
Leawood (G-5410)
Gkc Michigan Theatres Inc ....B....... 913 213-2000
Leawood (G-5412)
Glenwood Arts Theater ....F....... 913 642-1132
Overland Park (G-8756)
Goodrich Quality Theaters Inc...............F....... 620 232-2256
Pittsburg (G-9867)
Innovtive Cinema Solutions LLC...........F....... 855 401-4567
Lenexa (G-5916)
Liberty Hall Inc..E....... 785 749-1972
Lawrence (G-4995)
Regal Cinemas Inc...................................E....... 925 757-0466
Leawood (G-5537)
State Theatre ....E....... 620 285-3535
Larned (G-4714)
Vbc Enterprises LLC................................E....... 316 789-0114
Derby (G-1279)
Warren Old Town Theatre Grill ....F....... 316 262-7123
Wichita (G-15926)
Warren Theatres LLC...............................D....... 316 612-0469
Wichita (G-15927)
Warren Theatres LLC...............................D....... 316 722-7060
Wichita (G-15928)

7833 Drive-In Motion Picture Theaters

Cooper Enterprises..................................F....... 620 225-4347
Dodge City (G-1331)

7841 Video Tape Rental

B & B Cinemas ....F....... 785 242-0777
Ottawa (G-8247)
Blockbuster LLC ....F....... 913 438-3203
Shawnee Mission (G-11169)
Dicks Thriftway ....E....... 785 456-2525
Wamego (G-13414)
Duncans Movie Magic Inc ....E....... 785 266-3010
Topeka (G-12562)
Family Video Movie Club Inc ....F....... 620 342-4659
Emporia (G-1755)
Family Video Movie Club Inc ....F....... 913 254-7219
Olathe (G-7702)
Family Video Movie Club Inc ....E....... 785 263-3853
Abilene (G-30)
Family Video Movie Club Inc ....E....... 785 478-0606
Topeka (G-12594)
Family Video Movie Club Inc ....F....... 785 762-2377
Junction City (G-3689)
Fugate Enterprises ....F....... 316 722-5670
Wichita (G-14428)
Kier Enterprises Inc ....E....... 785 325-2150
Washington (G-13467)

Liberty Hall Inc ....E....... 785 749-1972
Lawrence (G-4995)
Liberty Hall Inc ....F....... 785 749-1972
Lawrence (G-4994)
Major Video of Kansas Inc ....F....... 913 649-7137
Overland Park (G-8980)
Regal Audio Video ....G....... 785 628-2700
Hays (G-2898)
Sparks Music Co...F....... 620 442-5030
Arkansas City (G-182)

79 AMUSEMENT AND RECREATION SERVICES

7911 Dance Studios, Schools & Halls

Academy of Arts LLC ....F....... 913 441-7300
Shawnee Mission (G-11065)
Acrobatic Acadmy Ftns/Educ Ctr.............E....... 316 721-2230
Wichita (G-13608)
Ballet Midwest Inc.....................................F....... 785 272-5991
Topeka (G-12360)
Barbaras Conservatory Dance ....F....... 785 272-5991
Topeka (G-12364)
Beller Dance Studio Inc.............................E....... 913 648-2626
Overland Park (G-8439)
Byrds Dance & Gymnastics Inc.................E....... 913 788-9792
Kansas City (G-3883)
Dance Factory Inc.......................................F....... 785 272-4548
Topeka (G-12545)
Dance Gallery..F....... 785 838-9100
Lawrence (G-4825)
Entertainment Enterprises Inc...................E....... 316 722-4201
Wichita (G-14292)
Fanchon Ballroom & Supper Club ....F....... 785 628-8154
Hays (G-2804)
House of Dance...F....... 913 839-1962
Olathe (G-7778)
Jody Phillips Dance Company....................E....... 913 897-9888
Overland Park (G-8877)
Miss Mrias Acrbat Dance Studio ....E....... 913 888-0060
Olathe (G-7904)
Raeanns Fancy Footwork ....F....... 316 788-4499
Derby (G-1267)
Shirley Marley Enterprises.........................F....... 913 492-0004
Shawnee Mission (G-11865)
Starstruck Prfrmg Arts Ctr LLC ....F....... 913 492-3186
Shawnee Mission (G-11896)
Wichita State University ....E....... 316 978-3581
Wichita (G-16034)

7922 Theatrical Producers & Misc Theatrical Svcs

Actors LLC..E....... 316 263-0222
Wichita (G-13610)
City of Pittsburg ....F....... 620 231-7827
Pittsburg (G-9833)
Complete Music Inc ....E....... 913 432-1111
Leawood (G-5357)
Granada Theater ....F....... 785 842-1390
Lawrence (G-4879)
Kansas City Blues Society Inc.....................F....... 913 660-4692
Olathe (G-7824)
Lawrence Theatre Inc ....F....... 785 843-7469
Lawrence (G-4988)
Liberty Hall Inc ....F....... 785 749-1972
Lawrence (G-4994)
Liberty Hall Inc ....E....... 785 749-1972
Lawrence (G-4995)
Marysvlle Area Cmnty Thtre Inc ....D....... 785 268-0420
Marysville (G-6903)
McPherson Opera House Company............F....... 620 241-1952
McPherson (G-7001)
New Theatre Company.................................C....... 913 649-7469
Shawnee Mission (G-11681)
Overbudget Productions..............................E....... 913 254-1186
Olathe (G-7967)
Prior Productions Incorporated...................E....... 816 654-5473
Olathe (G-8009)
SNC Alarm Service ....E....... 620 665-6651
Hutchinson (G-3442)
Talent On Parade...F....... 316 522-4836
Haysville (G-2961)
Ticket Solutions LLC ....E....... 913 384-4751
Shawnee Mission (G-11932)
Topeka Civic Theatre & Academy...............F....... 785 357-5211
Topeka (G-13172)
Topeka Performing Arts Center...................F....... 785 234-2787
Topeka (G-13184)

Wichita Center For The Arts..................F 316 315-0151
Wichita *(G-15985)*

7929 Bands, Orchestras, Actors & Entertainers

B & B Backyard..................F 785 246-6348
Topeka *(G-12355)*
Complete Music Inc..................E 913 432-1111
Leawood *(G-5357)*
Glow Golf..................F 316 685-1040
Wichita *(G-14477)*
Hightech Solutions Inc..................C 620 228-2216
Fredonia *(G-2035)*
Hutchinson Symphony Assn..................F 620 543-2511
Hutchinson *(G-3325)*
Little Soldier..................F 785 845-1987
Mayetta *(G-6915)*
Pride of Prairie Orchestra Inc..................E 785 460-5518
Colby *(G-1034)*
Smg Holdings Inc..................F 316 440-9016
Wichita *(G-15605)*
Topeka Performing Arts Center..................F 785 234-2787
Topeka *(G-13184)*
Wichita Symphony Society..................C 316 267-7658
Wichita *(G-16037)*
Wild Wild West Inc..................F 785 827-8938
Salina *(G-10768)*

7933 Bowling Centers

AMF Bowling Centers Inc..................E 913 451-6400
Overland Park *(G-8382)*
Army & Air Force Exchange Svc..................E 785 239-4366
Fort Riley *(G-1945)*
B & E Inc..................F 913 299-1110
Kansas City *(G-3833)*
Bobec Inc..................E 913 248-1110
Shawnee Mission *(G-11175)*
Boulevard One Inc..................E 316 636-9494
Wichita *(G-13873)*
Boulevard One Inc..................E 316 722-5211
Wichita *(G-13874)*
Boyd & Boyd Inc..................D 913 764-4568
Olathe *(G-7558)*
Cheney Lanes Inc..................F 316 542-3126
Cheney *(G-790)*
Coach and Four Bowling Lanes..................F 785 472-5571
Ellsworth *(G-1663)*
Colby Bowl..................F 785 460-2672
Colby *(G-996)*
Frazier Enterprises Inc..................F 316 788-0263
Derby *(G-1247)*
Hutchinson Vending Company..................F 620 662-6474
Hutchinson *(G-3328)*
Incred-A-Bowl LLC..................D 913 851-1700
Overland Park *(G-8841)*
Junction City Bowl Inc..................F 785 238-6813
Junction City *(G-3703)*
Kc Bowl Inc..................F 913 299-1110
Kansas City *(G-4164)*
Little Apple Lanes..................F 785 539-0371
Manhattan *(G-6715)*
Lynco Rec Inc..................F 620 231-2222
Pittsburg *(G-9896)*
Mayberrys Inc..................F 620 793-9400
Great Bend *(G-2605)*
Mission Bowl N Olathe..................E 913 782-0279
Olathe *(G-7905)*
Mission Recreation Inc..................E 913 782-0279
Olathe *(G-7906)*
Northrock Lanes Inc..................E 316 636-5444
Wichita *(G-15192)*
Park Hill Lanes..................F 620 842-5571
Anthony *(G-131)*
Prairie Sports Inc..................F 785 625-2916
Hays *(G-2887)*
Raymire Inc..................F 620 275-4061
Garden City *(G-2263)*
Rekat Recreation Inc..................D 785 272-1881
Topeka *(G-13008)*
Southwest Bowl..................F 785 272-1324
Topeka *(G-13082)*
Spare Tyme LLC..................F 620 225-2695
Dodge City *(G-1433)*
Tins Inc..................E 785 842-1234
Lawrence *(G-5137)*
West Ridge Lanes Fmly Fun Ctr..................E 785 273-3333
Topeka *(G-13239)*

7941 Professional Sports Clubs & Promoters

All American Indoor Sports..................F 913 599-4884
Shawnee Mission *(G-11094)*
All American Indoor Sports..................D 913 888-5425
Shawnee Mission *(G-11093)*
▲ **Challenger Sports Corp**..................E 913 599-4884
Lenexa *(G-5749)*
◆ **Diversified Sports Tech LLC**..................G 949 466-2393
Baxter Springs *(G-404)*
Kansas Coliseum Inc..................F 316 440-0888
Park City *(G-9621)*
Ksu Football Operation..................D 785 532-6832
Manhattan *(G-6704)*
Olathe Soccer Club..................F 913 764-4111
Olathe *(G-7949)*
Smg Holdings Inc..................E 785 235-1986
Topeka *(G-13078)*
Sunflower Soccer Assn..................F 785 233-9700
Topeka *(G-13121)*
T-Bones Baseball Club LLC..................F 913 328-2255
Kansas City *(G-4455)*
Wichita Hoops LLC..................F 316 440-4990
Bel Aire *(G-444)*
Wichita Thnder Prof Hckey Team..................F 316 264-4625
Wichita *(G-16039)*

7948 Racing & Track Operations

B & H Motor Sports..................E 785 966-2575
Mayetta *(G-6914)*
Kansas Speedway Corporation..................E 913 328-3300
Kansas City *(G-4157)*
Patterson Racing Inc..................F 316 775-7771
Augusta *(G-337)*
Thunder Hill Speedway LLC..................E 785 313-2922
Mayetta *(G-6919)*

7991 Physical Fitness Facilities

24 Hour Fitness Usa Inc..................E 913 338-2442
Overland Park *(G-8329)*
24 Hour Fitness Usa Inc..................E 913 248-0724
Shawnee Mission *(G-11058)*
24 Hour Fitness Usa Inc..................E 913 829-4503
Olathe *(G-7501)*
Angus Inn Best Western Motel..................D 620 792-3541
Great Bend *(G-2509)*
Bar Method West Plaza..................E 913 499-1468
Westwood *(G-13550)*
Bella Vita Salon & Day Spa Inc..................E 913 651-6161
Leavenworth *(G-5207)*
Capital Frsght Golf Fitnes LLC..................E 913 648-1600
Overland Park *(G-8509)*
City of Wamego..................E 785 456-2295
Wamego *(G-13413)*
Curves Ahead LLC..................F 785 221-9652
Topeka *(G-12536)*
Darco Inc..................E 620 221-7529
Winfield *(G-16138)*
Dermatology & Skin Cancer Ctr..................F 913 451-7546
Shawnee Mission *(G-11302)*
Egos Salon & Day Spa Inc..................F 785 272-1181
Topeka *(G-12573)*
Element Fitness..................D 913 268-3633
Shawnee Mission *(G-11331)*
Executive Mnor Leavenworth Inc..................F 785 234-5400
Topeka *(G-12586)*
Fit Physique..................E 316 721-2230
Wichita *(G-14379)*
Fitness Plus More LLC..................F 913 383-2636
Overland Park *(G-8725)*
Folgers Gymnastics Inc..................F 316 733-7525
Wichita *(G-14401)*
Geary Rhabilitation Fitnes Ctr..................E 785 238-3747
Junction City *(G-3696)*
Genesis Health Club Inc..................E 316 721-8938
Wichita *(G-14457)*
Genesis Health Club Inc..................E 316 945-8331
Wichita *(G-14458)*
Genesis Health Club Inc..................F 620 663-9090
Hutchinson *(G-3298)*
Genesis Health Clubs MGT LLC..................E 316 634-0094
Wichita *(G-14459)*
Genesis Hlth Clubs Emporia LLC..................B 620 343-6034
Emporia *(G-1761)*
Get After It LLC..................F 402 885-0964
Manhattan *(G-6645)*
Hartzler Lorenda..................E 785 749-2424
Lawrence *(G-4891)*
Health Connection Inc..................F 913 294-1000
Paola *(G-9565)*
Healthridge Fitness Center LLC..................C 913 888-0656
Olathe *(G-7761)*
Heartland Pool & Spa Svc Inc..................F 913 438-2909
Lenexa *(G-5898)*
Hoover Bachman & Assoc Inc..................F 620 342-2348
Emporia *(G-1774)*
Infinite Fitness..................F 913 469-8850
Overland Park *(G-8843)*
Inside Sports and Fitness LLC..................F 913 888-9247
Overland Park *(G-8849)*
Inside Sports and Fitness LLC..................F 913 894-4752
Overland Park *(G-8850)*
James Mirabile..................E 913 888-7546
Overland Park *(G-8872)*
Jewish Cmnty Ctr Grter Kans Cy..................B 913 327-8000
Shawnee Mission *(G-11486)*
Junction City Family YMCA Inc..................E 785 762-4780
Junction City *(G-3704)*
Kansas State University..................F 785 532-6980
Manhattan *(G-6685)*
Kristie Winters..................F 913 648-8946
Park *(G-9597)*
Lees Energy Connection..................F 913 682-3782
Leavenworth *(G-5267)*
Life Time Fitness Inc..................C 913 492-4781
Lenexa *(G-5971)*
Life Time Fitness Inc..................C 913 239-9000
Overland Park *(G-8958)*
Lyerla Associates..................E 913 888-9247
Shawnee Mission *(G-11585)*
Maximus Fitness and Wellness..................F 785 267-2132
Topeka *(G-12865)*
Maximus Fitness and Wellness..................F 785 266-8000
Topeka *(G-12866)*
Maximus Fitness and Wellness..................F 785 232-3133
Topeka *(G-12867)*
Memorial Hospital Fitness Ctr..................F 785 263-3888
Abilene *(G-46)*
Nck Wellness Center Inc..................E 785 738-3995
Beloit *(G-495)*
Oprc Inc..................E 913 642-6880
Overland Park *(G-9108)*
Opti-Life East Wichita LLC..................D 316 927-5959
Wichita *(G-15224)*
Opti-Life Services LLC..................E 316 518-8757
Wichita *(G-15225)*
Orangetheory Fitness..................F 316 440-4640
Wichita *(G-15231)*
P A Therapyworks Inc..................E 785 749-1300
Lawrence *(G-5053)*
Par Exsalonce..................E 913 469-9532
Shawnee Mission *(G-11715)*
Performance Enhancement Center..................F 620 421-2125
Parsons *(G-9723)*
Prairie Lf Ctr of Overland Pk..................F 913 764-5444
Olathe *(G-7998)*
Prairie Lf Ctr of Overland Pk..................E 913 648-8077
Overland Park *(G-9177)*
Punch Boxing Plus Fitness..................E 816 589-2690
Shawnee *(G-11013)*
Quivira Athletic Club L C..................D 913 268-3633
Lenexa *(G-6086)*
R & D Fitness Inc..................E 913 722-2001
Shawnee Mission *(G-11770)*
Refresh Medical Spa LLC..................F 913 681-6200
Overland Park *(G-9232)*
Rsvp Medspa LLC..................F 913 387-1104
Overland Park *(G-9262)*
Sagar Inc..................E 620 241-5343
McPherson *(G-7024)*
Salon Dimarco and Day Spa..................F 785 843-0044
Lawrence *(G-5100)*
Salon One 19 & Spa..................F 913 451-7119
Leawood *(G-5546)*
Salon Progressions & Day Spa..................F 316 729-1980
Wichita *(G-15512)*
Steven Enterprises LLC..................C 316 681-3010
Wichita *(G-15667)*
Topeka Country Club..................D 785 232-2090
Topeka *(G-13173)*
Ultimate Escape Day Spa LLC..................E 913 851-3385
Overland Park *(G-9438)*
Wichita State University..................E 316 978-3584
Wichita *(G-16032)*
Wood Valley Racquet Club Inc..................E 785 506-8928
Topeka *(G-13250)*
Woodside Tennis & Health Club..................C 913 831-0034
Shawnee Mission *(G-12017)*
YMCA of Hutchinson Reno Cnty..................D 620 662-1203
Hutchinson *(G-3494)*

SIC

YMCA Topeaka Downtown Branch........E....... 785 354-8591
Topeka *(G-13256)*
Young Mens Christian...........................F....... 785 233-9815
Topeka *(G-13258)*
Young Mens Christian Assn..................E....... 620 275-1199
Garden City *(G-2319)*
Young Mens Christian Associa.............D....... 316 320-9622
El Dorado *(G-1616)*
Young Mens Christian Associa.............E....... 913 321-9622
Kansas City *(G-4564)*
Young Mens Christian Associa.............C....... 316 942-2271
Wichita *(G-16091)*
Young Mens Christian Associa.............C....... 316 219-9622
Wichita *(G-16093)*
Young Mens Christian Associa.............D....... 316 260-9622
Wichita *(G-16094)*
Young Mens Christian Associa.............C....... 316 942-5511
Wichita *(G-16095)*
Young Mens Christian Associat............C....... 620 545-7290
Viola *(G-13380)*
Young Mens Christian Associat............C....... 316 685-2251
Wichita *(G-16096)*
Young Mens Christian Gr Kansas.........D....... 913 642-6800
Shawnee Mission *(G-12024)*
Young Mens Christian Gr Kansas.........D....... 913 362-3489
Prairie Village *(G-10088)*
Young Mens Christian Gr Kansas.........C....... 913 393-9622
Olathe *(G-8163)*
Young Mens Christian Gr Kansas.........D....... 913 782-7707
Olathe *(G-8164)*
Young MNS Chrstn Assn of Tpeka........C....... 785 354-8591
Topeka *(G-13259)*
Young MNS Chrstn Assn Pttsburg.........D....... 620 231-1100
Pittsburg *(G-9972)*
Young MNS Chrstn Assn Slina Ka.........D....... 785 825-2151
Salina *(G-10775)*

7992 Public Golf Courses

Alvamar Inc..E....... 785 842-2929
Lawrence *(G-4732)*
American Golf Corporation....................E....... 913 681-3100
Shawnee Mission *(G-11103)*
Augusta Country Club...........................E....... 316 775-7281
Augusta *(G-301)*
Capital Frsght Golf Fitnes LLC..............E....... 913 648-1600
Overland Park *(G-8509)*
City of Hesston......................................F....... 620 327-2331
Hesston *(G-2987)*
City of Junction City..............................F....... 785 238-4303
Milford *(G-7111)*
City of Lawrence....................................F....... 785 748-0600
Lawrence *(G-4790)*
City of Leawood.....................................D....... 913 685-4550
Shawnee Mission *(G-11228)*
City of Overland Park.............................F....... 913 897-3806
Shawnee Mission *(G-11230)*
City of Overland Park.............................F....... 913 897-3805
Overland Park *(G-8557)*
City of Pittsburg.....................................F....... 620 231-8070
Pittsburg *(G-9832)*
City of Topeka..F....... 785 291-2670
Topeka *(G-12469)*
City of Wichita..E....... 316 688-9341
Wichita *(G-14029)*
City of Wichita..F....... 316 337-9494
Wichita *(G-14030)*
County of Johnson..................................E....... 913 829-4653
Olathe *(G-7623)*
Falcon Lakes Golf LLC............................E....... 913 724-4653
Basehor *(G-376)*
Falcon Lakes Maintenance......................E....... 913 724-4460
Basehor *(G-377)*
Falcon Ridge Golf Club............................F....... 913 393-4653
Shawnee Mission *(G-11359)*
Flint Hills National Golf Club..................D....... 316 733-4131
Andover *(G-93)*
Golf Operations Management LLC..........E....... 913 897-3809
Overland Park *(G-8764)*
Kangolf Inc...F....... 785 539-7529
Manhattan *(G-6673)*
Kansas State University Golf C..............E....... 785 776-6475
Manhattan *(G-6697)*
Lamont Hill Resort Inc.............................E....... 785 828-3131
Vassar *(G-13371)*
Mayberrys Inc...F....... 620 793-9400
Great Bend *(G-2605)*
National Golf Properties LLC..................E....... 913 721-1333
Kansas City *(G-4281)*
Robin White Hills Inc...............................F....... 785 877-3399
Norton *(G-7462)*
Sand Creek Station Golf Course..............E....... 316 284-6161
Newton *(G-7414)*
Shawnee Country Club............................E....... 785 233-2373
Topeka *(G-13063)*
Sierra Hills Golf Club...............................F....... 316 733-9333
Wichita *(G-15587)*
Stag Hill Golf Club Inc.............................F....... 785 539-1041
Manhattan *(G-6805)*
Sugar Hills Golf Club Inc..........................E....... 785 899-2785
Goodland *(G-2487)*
Sunflower Hills Golf Course....................F....... 913 721-2727
Bonner Springs *(G-575)*
Twin Fiddle Investment Co LLC..............E....... 316 788-2855
Derby *(G-1277)*
Wedgewood Golf Course........................D....... 316 835-2991
Halstead *(G-2706)*
Western Hills Golf Club Inc......................E....... 785 478-4000
Topeka *(G-13241)*

7993 Coin-Operated Amusement Devices & Arcades

B & E Inc...F....... 913 299-1110
Kansas City *(G-3833)*
Bird Music & Amusement Svcs................E....... 785 537-2930
Manhattan *(G-6561)*
▲ Coin Machine Distributors Inc............F....... 316 652-0361
Wichita *(G-14052)*
Hutchinson Vending Company................F....... 620 662-6474
Hutchinson *(G-3328)*
Kangolf Inc...F....... 785 539-7529
Manhattan *(G-6673)*
Memorial Union Corp Emporia...............D....... 620 341-5901
Emporia *(G-1793)*
United Distributors Inc.............................F....... 316 712-2174
Wichita *(G-15841)*

7996 Amusement Parks

1010 N Webb Road LLC............................E....... 316 722-7529
Wichita *(G-13576)*
Dillon Nature Center.................................E....... 620 663-7411
Hutchinson *(G-3265)*
RPM Motorsports LLC..............................F....... 316 259-4576
Wichita *(G-15489)*
Sedgwick County Zoological Soc............C....... 316 660-9453
Wichita *(G-15549)*
Splashtacular Inc......................................F....... 800 844-5334
Paola *(G-9590)*
Widgets Family Fun Center.....................F....... 785 320-5099
Manhattan *(G-6854)*

7997 Membership Sports & Recreation Clubs

Abilene Country Club...............................E....... 785 263-3811
Abilene *(G-3)*
All American Indoor Sports.....................D....... 913 888-5425
Shawnee Mission *(G-11093)*
Alvamar Inc...E....... 785 842-2929
Lawrence *(G-4732)*
Alvamar Inc...E....... 785 843-0196
Lawrence *(G-4733)*
American Golf Corporation......................D....... 316 684-4110
Wichita *(G-13692)*
American Golf Corporation......................E....... 620 663-5301
Hutchinson *(G-3198)*
American Golf Corporation......................E....... 913 681-3100
Shawnee Mission *(G-11103)*
Ann N Hogan LLC.....................................E....... 913 271-7440
Louisburg *(G-6438)*
Augusta Country Club..............................E....... 316 775-7281
Augusta *(G-301)*
Barton County Club Inc............................F....... 620 653-4255
Great Bend *(G-2516)*
Bellevue Golf and Country Club..............E....... 913 367-3022
Atchison *(G-213)*
Beloit Country Club Inc............................E....... 785 738-3163
Beloit *(G-476)*
Bobby TS Bar & Grill Inc.........................F....... 785 537-8383
Manhattan *(G-6564)*
Brookridge Golf & Country Club..............F....... 913 648-1600
Shawnee Mission *(G-11186)*
Central Station Club & Gr........................F....... 620 225-1176
Dodge City *(G-1321)*
▲ Challenger Sports Corp.......................E....... 913 599-4884
Lenexa *(G-5749)*
Club Rodeo LLC.......................................F....... 316 613-2424
Wichita *(G-14044)*
Coffeyville Country Club..........................E....... 620 251-5236
Coffeyville *(G-918)*
Cowboy Inn LLC.......................................F....... 316 943-3869
Wichita *(G-14118)*
Coyotes Inc..E....... 785 842-2295
Lawrence *(G-4816)*
Crestwood Country Club Inc...................E....... 620 231-9697
Pittsburg *(G-9850)*
Darco Inc...E....... 620 221-7529
Winfield *(G-16138)*
Dodge City Country Club.........................E....... 620 225-5231
Dodge City *(G-1346)*
Emporia Country Club Inc........................E....... 620 342-0343
Emporia *(G-1739)*
First Serve Tennis.....................................D....... 785 749-3200
Lawrence *(G-4862)*
Flint Hills National Golf Club...................D....... 316 733-4131
Andover *(G-93)*
Fort Scott Country Club Inc.....................F....... 620 223-5060
Fort Scott *(G-1969)*
Genesis Health Clubs MGT LLC..............E....... 316 634-0094
Wichita *(G-14459)*
Glen Shadow Golf Club............................D....... 913 764-2299
Olathe *(G-7729)*
Glen Shadow Golf Club............................E....... 913 764-6572
Olathe *(G-7730)*
Golden Belt Country Club Inc..................E....... 620 792-4303
Great Bend *(G-2571)*
Golf Club At Southwind LLC....................E....... 620 275-2117
Garden City *(G-2189)*
Hallbrook Country Club............................D....... 913 345-9292
Leawood *(G-5418)*
Homestead Country Club.........................D....... 913 262-4100
Prairie Village *(G-10035)*
Independence Country Club....................E....... 620 331-1270
Independence *(G-3527)*
Indian Hills Country Club.........................D....... 913 362-6200
Mission Hills *(G-7144)*
Ironhorse Golf Club Maint.......................F....... 913 897-8181
Shawnee Mission *(G-11468)*
J R Galley Inc..F....... 785 938-8024
Colby *(G-1016)*
Johnson Cnty Pk Recreation Dst............E....... 913 438-7275
Shawnee Mission *(G-11495)*
Kansas City Country Club.........................C....... 913 236-2100
Mission Hills *(G-7145)*
Kansas City Racquet Club........................F....... 913 789-8000
Shawnee Mission *(G-11510)*
Kansas City SC LLC..................................F....... 913 575-1278
Olathe *(G-7827)*
Lawrence Country Club............................D....... 785 842-0592
Lawrence *(G-4963)*
Leavenworth Country Club......................E....... 913 727-6600
Lansing *(G-4682)*
Leawood South Country Club..................E....... 913 491-1313
Shawnee Mission *(G-11555)*
Liberal Country Club Assn.......................E....... 620 624-3992
Liberal *(G-6332)*
Lil Toledo Lodge LLC................................E....... 620 244-5668
Chanute *(G-739)*
Lindsey Management Co Inc...................F....... 316 788-3070
Derby *(G-1258)*
Manhattan Country Club Inc.....................D....... 785 539-7501
Manhattan *(G-6720)*
McDs Clubhouse 5.....................................F....... 620 504-6044
McPherson *(G-6991)*
McPherson Country Club Inc...................F....... 620 241-3541
Mcpherson *(G-6996)*
McPherson Family Ymca Inc....................D....... 620 241-0363
McPherson *(G-6999)*
Milburn Golf and Country Club................E....... 913 432-0490
Shawnee Mission *(G-11639)*
Mission Hills Country Club Inc.................D....... 913 722-5400
Mission Hills *(G-7146)*
Missouri Vly Tennis Foundation...............F....... 913 322-4800
Overland Park *(G-9043)*
Montes De Areia LLC................................E....... 620 663-5301
Hutchinson *(G-3385)*
Mustang Softball..F....... 316 260-9770
Wichita *(G-15141)*
National Golf Properties LLC...................E....... 913 721-1333
Kansas City *(G-4281)*
Nicklaus Golf Club LP................................D....... 913 402-1000
Overland Park *(G-9086)*
Nicklaus Golf Club Maintenance..............F....... 913 897-1624
Shawnee Mission *(G-11685)*
Olathe Soccer Club....................................F....... 913 764-4111
Olathe *(G-7949)*
Olathe Youth Baseball Inc........................F....... 913 393-9891
Olathe *(G-7955)*
Oprc Inc...E....... 913 642-6880
Overland Park *(G-9108)*
Osage Hills Inc...F....... 620 449-2713
Saint Paul *(G-10383)*

Paola Country Club Inc ....F 913 294-2910
Paola *(G-9579)*
Park Hills Golf & Supper Club ....F 620 672-7541
Pratt *(G-10129)*
Parsons Golf Club Restaurant ....F 620 421-5290
Parsons *(G-9718)*
Prairie Trails Golf Cntry CLB ....E 316 321-4114
El Dorado *(G-1593)*
Quivira Country Club Inc ....E 913 631-4820
Kansas City *(G-4356)*
Ravenwood Hunting Preserve Inc ....F 785 256-6444
Topeka *(G-12999)*
Recreation Commission ....F 620 223-0386
Fort Scott *(G-2002)*
Reflection Ridge Maintenance ....F 316 721-9483
Wichita *(G-15434)*
Riverside Recreation Assn ....F 785 332-3401
Saint Francis *(G-10344)*
Rolling Hills Country Club ....D 316 722-4273
Wichita *(G-15478)*
Rolling Hills Country Club ....E 316 721-6780
Wichita *(G-15479)*
Round Hill Bath &TEnnis Club ....F 913 381-2603
Shawnee Mission *(G-11814)*
Sabetha Golf Club Inc ....F 785 284-2023
Sabetha *(G-10328)*
Salina Country Club ....D 785 827-0388
Salina *(G-10669)*
Shawnee Country Club ....E 785 233-2373
Topeka *(G-13063)*
Shawnee Mission Bch Volleyball ....E 913 422-4070
Shawnee Mission *(G-11853)*
Sherwood Lake Club Inc ....F 785 478-3305
Topeka *(G-13070)*
Slawson Investment Corporation ....E 316 263-3201
Wichita *(G-15604)*
Smoky Hill Country Club Inc ....E 785 625-4021
Hays *(G-2909)*
Stagg Hill Golf Club Inc ....F 785 539-1041
Manhattan *(G-6806)*
Sterling Country Club Inc ....F 620 278-9956
Sterling *(G-12130)*
Sublette Recreation Commission ....F 620 675-8211
Sublette *(G-12211)*
Sugar Hills Golf Club Inc ....E 785 899-2785
Goodland *(G-2487)*
Sunflower Soccer Assn ....F 785 233-9700
Topeka *(G-13121)*
Terradyne Country Club LLC ....E 316 733-2582
Andover *(G-110)*
◆ **Title Boxing LLC** ....C 913 438-4427
Lenexa *(G-6182)*
Title Boxing Club ....F 785 856-2696
Lawrence *(G-5138)*
Title Boxing Club LLC ....E 913 991-8285
Overland Park *(G-9415)*
Topeka Country Club ....D 785 232-2090
Topeka *(G-13173)*
Topeka Round Up Club Inc ....F 785 478-4431
Topeka *(G-13185)*
Town & Country Racquet Club ....E 620 792-1366
Great Bend *(G-2648)*
Tuckers Bar & Grill ....F 785 235-3172
Topeka *(G-13200)*
Turkey Creek Golf Course ....F 620 241-8530
McPherson *(G-7032)*
Twb Inc ....E 620 663-8396
Hutchinson *(G-3470)*
Wamego Country Club Inc ....E 785 456-2649
Wamego *(G-13449)*
Wichita Cntry CLB Maintennance ....F 316 634-2882
Wichita *(G-15988)*
Wichita Sports Forum ....F 316 201-1414
Wichita *(G-16023)*
Wichita Swim Club ....E 316 683-1491
Wichita *(G-16036)*
Winfield Country Club ....E 620 221-1570
Winfield *(G-16185)*
Wolf Creek Golf Links Inc ....E 913 592-3329
Olathe *(G-8157)*
Woodside Tennis & Health Club ....C 913 831-0034
Shawnee Mission *(G-12017)*
YMCA of Hutchinson Reno Cnty ....D 620 662-1203
Hutchinson *(G-3494)*
Young Mens Christian Associa ....D 316 945-2255
Wichita *(G-16092)*
Young MNS Chrstn Assn Slina Ka ....D 785 825-2151
Salina *(G-10775)*

7999 Amusement & Recreation Svcs, NEC

Acrobatic Acadmy Ftns/Educ Ctr ....E 316 721-2230
Wichita *(G-13608)*
AMF Bowling Centers Inc ....E 913 451-6400
Overland Park *(G-8382)*
Between Lnes Elite Spt Academy ....F 913 422-1221
Lenexa *(G-5700)*
Bhcmc LLC ....B 620 682-7777
Dodge City *(G-1308)*
Bishop Rink Holdings LLC ....E 913 268-2625
Shawnee *(G-10918)*
Blue Valley Recreation Comm ....E 913 685-6030
Shawnee Mission *(G-11171)*
Boys Grls CLB Lwrnce Lwrnce K ....D 785 841-5672
Lawrence *(G-4763)*
Byrds Dance & Gymnastics Inc ....E 913 788-9792
Kansas City *(G-3883)*
Canlan Ice Spt Ctr Wichita LLC ....D 316 337-9199
Wichita *(G-13934)*
Capital Area Gymnstics Emprium ....F 785 266-4151
Topeka *(G-12424)*
Capital City Gun Club Inc ....F 785 478-4682
Topeka *(G-12426)*
Carousel Skate Center Inc ....E 316 942-4505
Wichita *(G-13953)*
Cervs Conoco & Convenience ....F 785 625-7777
Hays *(G-2767)*
▲ **Challenger Sports Corp** ....E 913 599-4884
Lenexa *(G-5749)*
Chanute Art Gallery ....F 620 431-7807
Chanute *(G-711)*
Chanute Recreation Commission ....D 620 431-4199
Chanute *(G-713)*
City of Leavenworth ....E 913 651-2132
Leavenworth *(G-5220)*
City of Leawood ....D 913 685-4550
Shawnee Mission *(G-11228)*
City of Manhattan ....E 785 587-2737
Manhattan *(G-6587)*
City of Prairie Village ....F 913 642-6010
Shawnee Mission *(G-11232)*
City of Topeka Employees ....F 785 272-5503
Topeka *(G-12476)*
City of Wichita ....E 316 744-9719
Wichita *(G-14027)*
Coffeyvlle Unfied Schl Dst 445 ....E 620 251-5910
Coffeyville *(G-927)*
Core Cashless LLC ....E 913 529-8200
Lenexa *(G-5788)*
County of Grant ....F 620 356-4233
Ulysses *(G-13292)*
County of Johnson ....F 913 631-5208
Shawnee Mission *(G-11271)*
County of Johnson ....C 913 888-4713
Shawnee Mission *(G-11272)*
County of Johnson ....C 913 403-8069
Shawnee Mission *(G-11273)*
Creative Carnivals Events LLC ....F 913 642-0900
Overland Park *(G-8609)*
Derby Recreation Comm Usd 260 ....D 316 788-3781
Derby *(G-1238)*
Diamond Gymnstics Dnce Academy ....E 913 851-7500
Stilwell *(G-12144)*
Dillon Nature Center ....E 620 663-7411
Hutchinson *(G-3265)*
▲ **Dynamic Discs LLC** ....F 620 208-3472
Emporia *(G-1734)*
Ellis Kinney Swimming Pool ....E 620 672-7724
Cullison *(G-1185)*
Elmdale Community Center ....F 620 663-6170
Hutchinson *(G-3278)*
Emerald City Gymnastics Inc ....E 913 438-4444
Overland Park *(G-8678)*
Entertainment Specialties ....F 620 342-3322
Emporia *(G-1750)*
Executive Mnor Leavenworth Inc ....F 785 234-5400
Topeka *(G-12586)*
Falcon Ridge Golf Club ....F 913 393-4653
Shawnee Mission *(G-11359)*
Festival Grogs Inc ....F 913 721-2110
Bonner Springs *(G-553)*
Fit Physique ....E 316 721-2230
Wichita *(G-14379)*
Flint Oak ....E 620 658-4401
Fall River *(G-1927)*
Folgers Gymnastics Inc ....F 316 733-7525
Wichita *(G-14401)*
Genesis Health Club Inc ....E 316 945-8331
Wichita *(G-14458)*

Golden Eagle Casino ....B 785 486-6601
Horton *(G-3125)*
Golden Prairie Hunting Service ....F 620 675-8490
Sublette *(G-12202)*
Golf Operations Management LLC ....E 913 897-3809
Overland Park *(G-8764)*
Goody Tickets LLC ....F 913 231-2674
Leawood *(G-5415)*
Great Wolf Kansas Spe LLC ....B 913 299-7001
Kansas City *(G-4047)*
Harrahs North Kansas City LLC ....A 816 472-7777
Overland Park *(G-8795)*
Hedrick Exotic Animal Farm ....E 620 422-3245
Nickerson *(G-7433)*
Heritage Restaurant Inc ....E 316 524-7495
Wichita *(G-14596)*
Hesston Unified School Dst 460 ....E 620 327-2989
Hesston *(G-2993)*
Holcomb Recreation Commission ....D 620 277-2152
Holcomb *(G-3075)*
Hugoton Swimming Pool ....E 620 544-2793
Hugoton *(G-3165)*
Hutchinson Recreation Comm ....F 620 663-6179
Hutchinson *(G-3323)*
Ice Sports Kansas City LLC ....E 913 441-3033
Shawnee Mission *(G-11451)*
Igt Global Solutions Corp ....E 785 861-7300
Topeka *(G-12713)*
Incred-A-Bowl LLC ....D 913 851-1700
Overland Park *(G-8841)*
Independence Main Street Inc ....F 620 331-2300
Independence *(G-3528)*
Interskate 77 ....F 620 229-7655
Winfield *(G-16149)*
Iowa Tribe Kansas & Nebraska ....F 785 595-3430
White Cloud *(G-13569)*
K D Sullivan Investments LLC ....F 785 460-0170
Colby *(G-1018)*
K-State Union Corporation ....C 785 532-6575
Manhattan *(G-6671)*
Kangolf Inc ....F 785 539-7529
Manhattan *(G-6673)*
Kansas City Blues Society Inc ....F 913 660-4692
Olathe *(G-7824)*
Kansas Cy Renaissance Festival ....F 913 721-2110
Bonner Springs *(G-558)*
Kansas Gymnastics & Dance Ctr ....E 913 764-8282
Olathe *(G-7829)*
Kansas Starbase Inc ....F 785 861-4709
Topeka *(G-12805)*
Lamont Hill Resort Inc ....E 785 828-3131
Vassar *(G-13371)*
Lawrence Gymnastics Academy ....E 785 865-0856
Lawrence *(G-4968)*
Longford Rodeo LLC ....D 785 388-2330
Longford *(G-6431)*
Mac Adams Recreation Center ....F 316 265-6111
Wichita *(G-14996)*
Mini-Train Gage Park ....F 785 273-6108
Topeka *(G-12907)*
Moonwalks For Fun Inc ....E 316 522-2224
Wichita *(G-15124)*
▲ **Morgan Chance Inc** ....E 316 945-6555
Wichita *(G-15126)*
Newton Recreation Commission ....E 316 283-7330
Newton *(G-7395)*
Olathe Billiards Inc ....F 913 780-5740
Olathe *(G-7928)*
Old World Balloonery LLC ....F 913 338-2628
Overland Park *(G-9097)*
Ottawa Recreation Commission ....C 785 242-1939
Ottawa *(G-8299)*
Prairie Band Potawatomi Bingo ....E 785 966-4000
Mayetta *(G-6917)*
Pride Amusements LLC ....E 417 529-3810
Baxter Springs *(G-411)*
Q Golden Billiards ....F 785 625-6913
Hays *(G-2893)*
Raeanns Fancy Footwork ....F 316 788-4499
Derby *(G-1267)*
Range 54 LLC ....F 316 440-2854
Wichita *(G-15416)*
Rekat Recreation Inc ....E 785 272-1881
Topeka *(G-13007)*
Riverfront Community Center ....E 913 651-2132
Leavenworth *(G-5286)*
Roller City Inc ....F 316 942-4555
Wichita *(G-15477)*
Sac & Fox Ntion MO In Kans Neb ....B 785 467-8000
Powhattan *(G-10010)*

SIC

Side Pockets Inc F 913 888-7665
Shawnee Mission *(G-11867)*
Sk8away Inc E 785 272-0303
Topeka *(G-13075)*
Skate South Inc F 316 524-7261
Wichita *(G-15600)*
South Rock Billiard LLC F 316 651-0444
Wichita *(G-15619)*
Sports Center Inc E 785 272-5522
Topeka *(G-13092)*
Starlite Skate Center South F 785 862-2241
Topeka *(G-13096)*
Sunset Zoological Pk Wildlife E 785 587-2737
Manhattan *(G-6818)*
Team Ko LLC F 913 897-1300
Overland Park *(G-9398)*
Tennis Corporation of America E 913 491-4116
Shawnee Mission *(G-11926)*
Ticket Solutions LLC E 913 384-4751
Shawnee Mission *(G-11932)*
Tobys Carnival Inc E 620 235-6667
Arma *(G-192)*
Tumbleweed Festival Inc F 620 275-9141
Garden City *(G-2304)*
Twin Fiddle Investment Co LLC E 316 788-2855
Derby *(G-1277)*
United States Tennis F 913 322-4823
Overland Park *(G-9444)*
Wamego Recreation Dept E 785 456-8810
Wamego *(G-13454)*
Wichita Canteen Company Inc E 316 524-2254
Wichita *(G-15984)*
Wichita Festivals Inc F 316 267-2817
Wichita *(G-16001)*
Wichita Gymnastics Club Inc F 316 634-1900
Wichita *(G-16003)*
Wichita Swim Club E 316 683-1491
Wichita *(G-16036)*
Wichita Thnder Prof Hckey Team F 316 264-4625
Wichita *(G-16039)*
Wyandotte County Sports Assn F 913 299-9197
Kansas City *(G-4553)*

80 HEALTH SERVICES

8011 Offices & Clinics Of Doctors Of Medicine

A M S Diagnostic LLC E 316 462-2020
Wichita *(G-13590)*
Abay Neuroscience Center PA E 316 609-2600
Wichita *(G-13595)*
Abilene Family Physicians PA F 785 263-7190
Abilene *(G-4)*
Advanced Anesthesia Assoc F 316 942-4519
Wichita *(G-13622)*
Advanced Dermatologic Surgery F 913 661-1755
Shawnee Mission *(G-11078)*
Advanced Dermatology and Skin E 785 537-4990
Manhattan *(G-6533)*
Advanced Orthopedic Assoc Inc D 316 631-1600
Wichita *(G-13625)*
Advanced Orthpdcs & Sprts Med F 620 225-7744
Dodge City *(G-1290)*
Advanced Pain Mdcine Assoc LLC F 316 942-4519
Wichita *(G-13626)*
Alan Moskowitz MD PC D 316 858-1900
Wichita *(G-13658)*
Alexander C Davis F 913 888-5577
Shawnee Mission *(G-11092)*
Allergy & Asthma Care PA E 913 491-3300
Overland Park *(G-8368)*
Allergy Rhmtlogy Clnics Kc LLC F 913 338-3222
Overland Park *(G-8369)*
Anatomi Imaging F 316 858-4091
Wichita *(G-13701)*
Anesthesia Assoc Kans Cy PC C 913 428-2900
Overland Park *(G-8385)*
Anesthesia Associates Topeka E 785 235-3451
Topeka *(G-12327)*
Ark City Clinic P A E 620 442-2100
Arkansas City *(G-143)*
Arla Jean Genstler MD PA F 785 537-3400
Manhattan *(G-6544)*
Arla Jean Genstler MD PA E 785 273-8080
Topeka *(G-12338)*
Arnold Katz MD F 913 888-3231
Shawnee Mission *(G-11119)*
Arthritis and Rheumatology E 316 612-4815
Wichita *(G-13741)*
Arthritis RES Ctr Foundation E 316 263-2125
Wichita *(G-13742)*
Ascension Via Christi D 620 231-6788
Pittsburg *(G-9813)*
Ascension Via Christi Hospital E 316 687-1555
Wichita *(G-13748)*
Ascension Via Christi Hospital A 316 268-5040
Wichita *(G-13752)*
Associate In Family Hlth Care E 913 727-1018
Lansing *(G-4668)*
Associated Orthopedics P A F 913 541-8897
Lenexa *(G-5672)*
Associated Plastic Surgeons PC F 913 451-3722
Shawnee Mission *(G-11126)*
Associated Urologist P A F 785 537-8710
Manhattan *(G-6549)*
Associates Family Medicine PA E 913 596-1313
Kansas City *(G-3827)*
Associates For Female Care PA F 913 299-2229
Kansas City *(G-3828)*
Associates In Internal Medped F 913 393-4888
Olathe *(G-7537)*
Associates In Womens Health PA E 316 219-6777
Wichita *(G-13759)*
Associates In Womens Health PA F 316 283-4153
Newton *(G-7312)*
Asthma & Allergy Associates PA F 785 842-3778
Lawrence *(G-4741)*
Augusta Family Practice PA E 316 775-9191
Augusta *(G-305)*
Axtell Clinic P A D 316 283-2800
Newton *(G-7314)*
Ayham J Farha MD E 316 636-6100
Wichita *(G-13783)*
Belleville Medical Clinic P A F 785 527-2217
Belleville *(G-451)*
Beloit Medical Center P A E 785 738-2246
Beloit *(G-477)*
Bio-Mdcal Applcations Kans Inc E 785 266-3087
Topeka *(G-12383)*
Birth & Women Center Inc F 785 232-6950
Topeka *(G-12385)*
Bluestem Medical LLP F 785 754-2458
Quinter *(G-10179)*
Bradley Kwapiszeski MD F 913 362-3210
Shawnee Mission *(G-11178)*
Braham J Geha E 913 383-9099
Kansas City *(G-3875)*
Brookdale Snior Lving Cmmnties E 913 491-3681
Leawood *(G-5343)*
Bruce Ochsner MD E 316 263-6273
Wichita *(G-13901)*
Bruce Speak F 785 267-6301
Topeka *(G-12411)*
Burkey Richard L DPM P A F 620 793-7624
Great Bend *(G-2524)*
C & S Medical Clinic PA E 620 408-9700
Dodge City *(G-1316)*
Cancer Center of Kansas PA F 620 399-1224
Wellington *(G-13494)*
Cancer Center of Kansas PA F 620 421-2855
Parsons *(G-9670)*
Cancer Center of Kansas PA F 620 629-6727
Liberal *(G-6290)*
Cancer Center of Kansas PA D 316 262-4467
Wichita *(G-13932)*
Cancer Center of Kansas PA C 316 262-4467
Wichita *(G-13933)*
Cancer Center of Kansas PA F 620 431-7580
Chanute *(G-708)*
Candlewood Medical Group PA F 785 539-0800
Manhattan *(G-6574)*
Captify Health Inc E 913 951-2600
Lenexa *(G-5728)*
Cardiology Cons Topeka PA E 785 233-9643
Topeka *(G-12444)*
Cardiovascular Cons Kans PA D 316 440-0845
Wichita *(G-13945)*
Cardiovascular Consultants Inc E 913 491-1000
Shawnee Mission *(G-11203)*
Cardivsclar Thrcic Surgeons PA F 785 270-8625
Topeka *(G-12445)*
Carol J Feltheim D 913 469-5579
Overland Park *(G-8519)*
Carondelet Home Care Services E 913 529-4800
Shawnee *(G-10924)*
Carondelet Orthpdc Srgns Sprts E 913 642-0200
Overland Park *(G-8521)*
Cavanaugh Eye Center PA F 913 897-9200
Overland Park *(G-8527)*
Cedar Surgical LLC F 316 616-6272
Andover *(G-86)*
Cedar Vale Rural Health Clinic F 620 758-2221
Cedar Vale *(G-693)*
Center For Counseling & Cnsltn E 620 792-2544
Great Bend *(G-2526)*
Center For Rprductive Medicine E 316 687-2112
Wichita *(G-13972)*
Center For Same Day Surgery E 316 262-7263
Wichita *(G-13973)*
Center For Woman Health F 913 491-6878
Shawnee Mission *(G-11210)*
Center For Womens Health LLC F 316 634-0060
Wichita *(G-13975)*
Central Care PA E 620 624-4700
Liberal *(G-6291)*
Central Kans Fmly Practice PA E 620 792-5341
Great Bend *(G-2527)*
Central Kansas Ent Assoc PA E 785 823-7225
Salina *(G-10440)*
Central Kansas Orthpd Group F 620 792-4383
Great Bend *(G-2531)*
Central Plains Eye Mds LLC F 316 712-4970
Wichita *(G-13982)*
Charles I Davis MD PA F 913 648-8880
Overland Park *(G-8541)*
Charles L Brroks MD F 913 248-8008
Shawnee Mission *(G-11217)*
Cheyenne County Hospital E 785 332-2682
Saint Francis *(G-10340)*
Christopher B Geha E 913 383-9099
Shawnee Mission *(G-11223)*
Christopher Moeller F 316 682-7546
Wichita *(G-14016)*
City of Wamego E 785 456-2295
Wamego *(G-13413)*
Clay Center Fmly Physicians PA E 785 632-2181
Clay Center *(G-851)*
Coffey County Hospital E 620 364-5395
Burlington *(G-630)*
Coffeyville Doctors Clinic P A E 620 251-7500
Coffeyville *(G-919)*
Coffeyvlle Fmly Prctice Clinic E 620 251-1100
Coffeyville *(G-923)*
Cokingtin Eye Center PA D 913 491-3737
Shawnee Mission *(G-11244)*
Cole & Cooper PA F 785 823-6391
Salina *(G-10457)*
College Hill Ob/Gyn Inc E 316 683-6766
Wichita *(G-14056)*
College Park Fmly Care Ctr Inc E 913 438-6700
Shawnee Mission *(G-11248)*
College Park Fmly Care Ctr Inc C 913 469-5579
Shawnee Mission *(G-11249)*
College Park Fmly Care Ctr Inc F 913 681-8866
Shawnee Mission *(G-11250)*
College Park Fmly Care Ctr Inc D 913 492-8686
Lenexa *(G-5769)*
College Park Fmly Care Ctr Inc E 913 829-0505
Olathe *(G-7598)*
Comanche County F 620 582-2136
Coldwater *(G-1053)*
Comcare of Sedgwick County B 316 660-7600
Wichita *(G-14061)*
Comcare of Sedgwick County C 316 660-7700
Wichita *(G-14062)*
Community Health Center of Sou E 620 231-6788
Pittsburg *(G-9840)*
Community Health Center of Sou F 620 429-2101
Columbus *(G-1069)*
Community Healthcare Sys Inc E 785 364-3205
Holton *(G-3086)*
Community Healthcare Sys Inc F 785 889-4241
Onaga *(G-8172)*
Community Hlth Ctr In Cwley CN F 620 221-3350
Winfield *(G-16125)*
Community Hlth Ctr Sthast Kans D 620 231-9873
Pittsburg *(G-9841)*
Community Memorial Healthcare E 785 562-3942
Marysville *(G-6885)*
Community Memorial Healthcare F 785 363-7202
Blue Rapids *(G-535)*
Community Memorial Hospital E 785 562-2311
Marysville *(G-6886)*
Community Physicians Clinic F 785 562-3942
Marysville *(G-6887)*
Compass Behavioral Health E 620 227-5040
Dodge City *(G-1328)*
Compass Behavioral Health E 620 227-8566
Dodge City *(G-1329)*

Compassionate Family Care LLC ....F 913 744-4300
Lenexa (G-5780)
Compcare ....E 785 823-7470
Salina (G-10458)
Comprehensive Womens Care ....F 913 643-0075
Shawnee Mission (G-11257)
Comptech Group LLC ....F 913 341-7600
Overland Park (G-8592)
Concentra Medical Centers ....F 913 894-6601
Lenexa (G-5783)
Consultants In Neurology PA ....E 913 894-1500
Shawnee Mission (G-11262)
Contemporary Womens Centre ....F 913 345-2322
Overland Park (G-8596)
Cotton Oneil Clinic Endoscopy ....E 785 270-4850
Topeka (G-12512)
Cotton ONeil Osage City ....F 785 528-3161
Osage City (G-8183)
Cotton-Neil Clnic Revocable Tr ....D 785 354-9591
Topeka (G-12513)
Cottonwood Pediatrics ....F 316 283-7100
Newton (G-7335)
County of Finney ....E 620 272-3600
Garden City (G-2134)
County of Geary ....E 785 762-5788
Junction City (G-3684)
County of Harvey ....F 316 283-1637
Newton (G-7337)
County of Kearny ....F 620 355-7501
Lakin (G-4649)
County of Lincoln ....F 785 524-4474
Lincoln (G-6380)
County of Shawnee ....C 785 368-2000
Topeka (G-12522)
County of Smith ....E 785 282-6924
Smith Center (G-12033)
Coventry Health Care Kans Inc ....C 800 969-3343
Overland Park (G-8606)
Cypress Heart ....E 316 858-5200
Wichita (G-14151)
Cypress Surgery Center LLC ....D 316 634-0404
Wichita (G-14152)
Dale P Denning MD Facs ....F 785 856-8346
Lawrence (G-4824)
Dandurand Drug Company Inc ....E 316 685-2353
Wichita (G-14165)
Daniel A Tatpati MD ....F 316 689-6803
Wichita (G-14166)
Daniel Aires MD ....E 913 588-6050
Kansas City (G-3955)
Daniel J Geha MD ....E 913 383-9099
Leawood (G-5369)
▲ David B Lyon MD ....E 913 261-2020
Leawood (G-5371)
Days Inn Olathe Medical Center ....E 913 390-9500
Olathe (G-7642)
Debakey Heart Clinic ....F 785 625-4699
Hays (G-2783)
Debra L Heidgen ....F 913 772-6046
Leavenworth (G-5231)
Deer Creek Surgery Center LLC ....F 913 897-0022
Overland Park (G-8646)
Delaware Hghlnds Assistd Lvng ....F 913 721-1400
Kansas City (G-3966)
Dennis Knudsen Dr ....F 620 624-3811
Liberal (G-6303)
Dennis M Cooley MD ....E 785 235-0335
Topeka (G-12551)
Dermatology & Skin Cancer Ctr ....F 913 451-7546
Shawnee Mission (G-11302)
Dermatology Clinic ....E 316 685-4395
Wichita (G-14198)
Dermatology Cons Midwest ....F 913 469-0110
Overland Park (G-8650)
Diabetes & Endocrinology Assoc ....F 913 676-7585
Overland Park (G-8653)
Diagnostic Imaging Center ....E 913 491-9299
Shawnee Mission (G-11304)
Diagnostic Imaging Center ....F 913 344-9989
Olathe (G-7652)
Diagnostic Imaging Centers PA ....C 913 319-8450
Leawood (G-5378)
Dickson-Diveley Midwest Ortho ....D 913 319-7600
Shawnee Mission (G-11306)
Dodge City Med Ctr Chartered ....C 620 227-8506
Dodge City (G-1349)
Donald B Scrafford ....E 316 721-2701
Wichita (G-14225)
Dr Vernon A Mills ....F 913 772-6046
Leavenworth (G-5234)
Drs Dobbins & Letourneau ....F 785 843-5665
Lawrence (G-4841)
E M Specialist PA ....F 913 676-2214
Shawnee Mission (G-11323)
Edward J Lind II ....E 316 788-6963
Derby (G-1242)
El Dorado Clinic PA ....E 316 321-2010
El Dorado (G-1557)
El Dorado Intrnal Medicine LLC ....F 316 321-2100
El Dorado (G-1558)
Ellsworth Medical Clinic Inc ....E 785 472-3277
Ellsworth (G-1671)
Emergency Dept Physicians ....E 913 469-1411
Shawnee Mission (G-11333)
Emergency Services of Kansas ....E 866 815-9776
Newton (G-7340)
Emergency Services PA ....E 316 962-2239
Wichita (G-14276)
Encompass Medical Group PA ....E 913 495-2000
Lenexa (G-5833)
Endoscopic Associates LLC ....E 913 492-0800
Overland Park (G-8680)
Endoscopic Services PA ....F 316 687-0234
Wichita (G-14287)
Endoscopy & Surgery Ctr Topeka ....F 785 354-1254
Topeka (G-12577)
Ent Assctes Greater Kans Cy PC ....E 816 478-4200
Merriam (G-7091)
▲ Envision Inc ....E 316 440-1600
Wichita (G-14293)
Esther V Rettig ....F 620 245-0556
McPherson (G-6960)
Eye Association Overland Park ....F 913 339-9090
Overland Park (G-8701)
Eye Care PC ....E 816 478-4400
Leawood (G-5392)
Eye Specialists ....F 785 628-8218
Hays (G-2803)
Eye Surgery Center Wichita LLC ....E 316 681-2020
Wichita (G-14328)
Faerber Surgical Arts ....F 913 469-8895
Shawnee Mission (G-11358)
Family Care Center ....F 620 221-9500
Winfield (G-16141)
Family Center For Health Care ....E 785 462-6184
Colby (G-1003)
Family Health Ctr Morris Cnty ....F 620 767-5126
Council Grove (G-1165)
Family Medical Group PA ....E 913 299-9200
Kansas City (G-4007)
Family Medicine Associates PA ....F 785 830-0100
Lawrence (G-4856)
Family Medicine East Chartered ....E 316 689-6630
Wichita (G-14338)
Family Physicians Kansas LLC ....F 316 733-4500
Andover (G-92)
Family Physicians Mgt Corp ....F 620 365-3115
Iola (G-3599)
Family Practice Associates ....E 620 241-7400
McPherson (G-6962)
Family Practice Associates ....F 913 299-2100
Kansas City (G-4008)
Family Practice Associates ....F 913 438-2226
Lenexa (G-5848)
Fandhill Orthpd & Spt Medicine ....F 620 275-8400
Garden City (G-2155)
First Care Clinic Inc ....E 785 621-4990
Hays (G-2807)
First Med PA ....E 785 865-5300
Lawrence (G-4861)
First Point Urgent Care Inc ....F 913 856-1369
Gardner (G-2344)
Flanner & Mc Bratney Mds PA ....F 913 651-3111
Lansing (G-4673)
Flint Hills Cmnty Hlth Ctr Inc ....D 620 342-4864
Emporia (G-1758)
Flint Hills Heart Vascular ....F 785 320-5858
Manhattan (G-6633)
For Women Only Inc ....F 913 541-9495
Leawood (G-5407)
Fry Eye Associates ....E 620 275-7248
Garden City (G-2167)
Fry Eye Associates ....F 620 276-7699
Garden City (G-2168)
Fry Eye Surgery Center LLC ....E 620 276-7699
Garden City (G-2169)
Galichia Medical Group Kans PA ....C 316 684-3838
Wichita (G-14439)
Garden Medical Clinic PA ....C 620 275-3702
Garden City (G-2182)
Garden Surgical Assoc ....E 620 275-3740
Garden City (G-2183)
Gastrointestinal Associates PA ....F 913 495-9600
Overland Park (G-8746)
Geary Community Hospital ....F 785 762-5437
Junction City (G-3692)
Gerstberger Medical Clinic ....F 620 356-2432
Ulysses (G-13299)
Great Bend Childrens Clinic PA ....E 620 792-5437
Great Bend (G-2574)
Great Bend Internists PA ....E 620 793-8429
Great Bend (G-2582)
Greeley Cnty Hosp & Long TRM C ....F 785 852-4230
Sharon Springs (G-10898)
Greeley County Family Practice ....F 620 376-4251
Tribune (G-13269)
Green Medical Group ....E 316 691-3937
Wichita (G-14511)
Grisell Memorial Hospital Assn ....D 785 731-2231
Ransom (G-10194)
Gupta Ganesh ....F 913 451-0000
Overland Park (G-8782)
Hand Center PA ....F 316 688-5656
Wichita (G-14552)
Harder Family Practice PA ....F 316 775-7500
Augusta (G-323)
Hays Family Practice Center ....E 785 623-5095
Hays (G-2829)
Hays Medical Center Inc ....F 785 623-5774
Hays (G-2833)
Hays Orthopedic Clinic PA ....E 785 625-3012
Hays (G-2836)
Haysville Family Medcenter ....F 316 858-4165
Haysville (G-2946)
HCA Holdings Inc ....D 620 365-1330
Iola (G-3607)
HCA Inc ....E 913 498-7409
Overland Park (G-8800)
Head & Neck Surgery Kans Cy PA ....E 913 599-4800
Leawood (G-5420)
Head & Neck Surgical Assoc ....F 913 663-5100
Leawood (G-5421)
Headache & Pain Center PA ....D 913 491-3999
Overland Park (G-8801)
Health Ministries Clinic Inc ....D 316 283-6103
Newton (G-7358)
Health Ministries Clinic Inc ....F 620 727-1183
Newton (G-7359)
Health Options That Matter ....E 913 722-3100
Kansas City (G-4073)
Health Partnership Clinic Inc ....E 913 433-7583
Olathe (G-7760)
Health Professionals Winfield ....F 620 221-4000
Winfield (G-16146)
Healthcare Administrative Svcs ....E 816 763-5446
Overland Park (G-8803)
Healthcore Clinic Inc ....E 316 691-0249
Wichita (G-14578)
Heart America Eye Care PA ....F 913 492-0021
Overland Park (G-8804)
Heart Ctr At Ovrland Pk Rgonal ....E 913 541-5374
Overland Park (G-8806)
Heartland Cardiology LLC ....F 316 686-5300
Wichita (G-14581)
Heartland Clinic ....F 785 263-4131
Abilene (G-37)
▲ Heartland Dental Group PA ....D 913 682-1000
Leavenworth (G-5251)
Heartland Dermatology Center ....E 785 628-3231
Hays (G-2840)
Heartland Medical Clinic Inc ....F 785 841-7297
Lawrence (G-4894)
Heartland Primary Care PA ....E 913 299-3700
Kansas City (G-4077)
Heartland Womens Group At Wes ....E 316 962-7175
Wichita (G-14589)
Henry J Kanarek ....F 913 451-8555
Shawnee Mission (G-11426)
Hess Medical Services PA ....E 785 628-7495
Hays (G-2842)
Hiawatha Hospital Association ....F 785 742-2161
Hiawatha (G-3010)
Hillside Medical Office ....E 316 685-1381
Wichita (G-14613)
Hodes & Nauser Mds PA ....F 913 491-6878
Overland Park (G-8821)
Hoisington Homestead ....F 620 653-4121
Hoisington (G-3066)
Holy Family Medical Assoc LLP ....E 316 682-9900
Wichita (G-14627)

S I C

Hospital Dst 1 of Rice Cnty ......F 620 278-2123
Sterling (G-12121)
Howell Matthew D Dr DDS PA ......F 316 260-6220
Andover (G-94)
Hunkeler Eye Institute PA ......F 913 338-4733
Shawnee Mission (G-11443)
Hunter Health Clinic Inc ......D 316 262-2415
Wichita (G-14656)
Hutchinson Clinic PA ......A 620 669-2500
Hutchinson (G-3319)
Hutchinson Clinic PA ......F 620 486-2985
Saint John (G-10352)
Ian F Yeats MD Chartered ......F 620 624-0142
Liberal (G-6322)
Ian S Kovach MD PHD ......E 620 672-1002
Pratt (G-10121)
Independence Anesthesia Inc ......F 913 707-5294
Lenexa (G-5911)
Infectious Disease Cons PA ......E 316 264-3505
Wichita (G-14689)
Infectious Disease Consultants ......E 316 264-3505
Wichita (G-14690)
Internal Medicine ......E 316 321-2100
El Dorado (G-1572)
Internal Medicine Associates ......E 620 342-2521
Emporia (G-1778)
Internal Medicine Group PA ......E 785 843-5160
Lawrence (G-4912)
James L Ruhlen MD PA ......E 913 829-4001
Olathe (G-7806)
◆ Jayhawk Primary Care Inc ......D 913 588-9000
Westwood (G-13554)
Jewell County Hospital ......D 785 378-3137
Mankato (G-6859)
John D Ebeling MD ......F 785 232-3555
Topeka (G-12745)
John P Gravino Do ......F 785 842-5070
Lawrence (G-4927)
Johnson Cnty Ob-Gyn Chartered ......E 913 236-6455
Shawnee Mission (G-11494)
Johnson County Dermatology ......F 913 764-1125
Olathe (G-7816)
Johnson County Imaging Ctr PA ......E 913 469-8998
Overland Park (G-8878)
Johnson County Pediatrics ......D 913 384-5500
Merriam (G-7097)
Josie Norris MD ......F 785 232-6950
Topeka (G-12749)
K Craig Place MD ......F 913 385-9009
Prairie Village (G-10039)
Kansas Cardiovascular Assoc ......F 913 682-6950
Lansing (G-4676)
Kansas City Bone & Joint Clini ......E 913 381-5225
Overland Park (G-8889)
Kansas City Cancer Center LLC ......F 913 788-8883
Kansas City (G-4143)
Kansas City Cancer Center LLC ......E 913 541-4600
Overland Park (G-8891)
Kansas City Eye Clinic PA ......E 913 341-3100
Shawnee Mission (G-11509)
Kansas City Imaging Center ......F 913 667-5600
Kansas City (G-4146)
Kansas City Urology Care ......F 913 831-1003
Humboldt (G-3186)
Kansas City Urology Care ......E 913 338-5585
Overland Park (G-8897)
Kansas City Urology Care PA ......C 913 341-7985
Overland Park (G-8898)
Kansas City Womens Clinic PA ......D 913 894-8500
Shawnee Mission (G-11514)
Kansas Cy Gen Vscular Surgeons ......E 913 754-2800
Overland Park (G-8899)
Kansas Cy Internal Medicine PA ......E 913 451-8500
Overland Park (G-8900)
Kansas Cy Ob Gyn Pysicians PC ......F 913 648-1840
Overland Park (G-8901)
Kansas Fmly Mdicine Foundation ......E 913 588-1900
Kansas City (G-4155)
Kansas Imaging Consultants ......F 316 268-5000
Wichita (G-14807)
Kansas Imaging Consultants PA ......F 316 689-5043
Wichita (G-14808)
Kansas Medical Clinic PA ......F 785 233-3553
Topeka (G-12786)
Kansas Medical Clinic PA ......F 785 233-3555
Topeka (G-12787)
Kansas Medical Clinic PA ......F 785 233-3555
Topeka (G-12788)
Kansas Nphrology Physicians PA ......E 316 263-7285
Wichita (G-14816)
Kansas Orthopedic Center PA ......D 316 838-2020
Wichita (G-14817)
Kansas Prffsnl Anesthesia ......E 316 618-1515
Wichita (G-14819)
Kansas Rgnrtive Mdcine Ctr LLC ......F 785 320-4700
Manhattan (G-6676)
Kansas Surgical Consultants ......E 316 685-6222
Wichita (G-14826)
Kansas Surgical Consultants ......E 316 219-9360
Wichita (G-14827)
Kansas Univ Physicians Inc ......B 913 742-7611
Shawnee (G-10980)
Kansas Univ Physicians Inc ......C 913 362-2128
Kansas City (G-4158)
Keil Vtrnary Ophthalmology LLC ......F 785 331-4600
Overland Park (G-8910)
Kent W Haverkamp MD ......E 785 267-0744
Topeka (G-12818)
Kevin J Stuever MD ......E 785 843-5160
Lawrence (G-4944)
Kevin Mosier MD ......F 620 421-0881
Parsons (G-9699)
Kevin R McDonald ......F 785 628-6014
Hays (G-2859)
Kickapoo Nation Health Center ......F 785 486-2154
Horton (G-3129)
Kimberly A Allman LLC ......F 316 733-3003
Andover (G-98)
Konza Prairie Cmnty Hlth Ctr ......F 785 238-4711
Junction City (G-3718)
KU Childrens Ctr Foundation ......E 913 588-6301
Kansas City (G-4181)
Ku Midwest Ambulatory Svc Ctr ......E 913 588-8452
Shawnee Mission (G-11539)
Ku Physicians Inc ......F 913 588-3243
Kansas City (G-4182)
Ku Womens Hlth Specialty Ctrs ......F 913 588-6200
Kansas City (G-4183)
Kuhns H Richard Jr Md El ......E 316 320-1917
El Dorado (G-1581)
Kvc Behavioral Healthcare Inc ......D 620 820-7680
Parsons (G-9701)
Kyle Tipton MD LLC ......E 316 321-2100
El Dorado (G-1582)
Labette County Medical Center ......E 620 421-4880
Parsons (G-9703)
Labette Health Foundation Inc ......F 620 922-3838
Coffeyville (G-954)
Lakepoint Family Physicians ......E 316 636-2662
Wichita (G-14915)
Laurie D Fisher MD ......E 913 345-3650
Overland Park (G-8947)
Lawrence Anaesthesia PA ......F 785 842-7026
Lawrence (G-4958)
Lawrence Cancer Center ......F 785 749-3600
Lawrence (G-4959)
Lawrence Family Practice Ctr ......E 785 841-6540
Lawrence (G-4965)
Lawrence Internal Medicine PA ......E 785 842-7200
Lawrence (G-4970)
Lawrence Occpational Hlth Svcs ......F 785 838-1500
Lawrence (G-4978)
Lawrence Orthpaedic Surgery PA ......E 785 843-9125
Lawrence (G-4980)
Lawrence Otlryngology Assoc PA ......F 620 343-6600
Lawrence (G-4981)
Lawrence Pediatrics PA ......F 785 856-9090
Lawrence (G-4983)
Lawrence Surgery Center LLC ......E 785 832-0588
Lawrence (G-4987)
Leavenworth Family Health Ctr ......F 913 682-5588
Lansing (G-4684)
Leavenwrth-Knsas Cy Imaging PA ......E 913 651-6066
Overland Park (G-8951)
Leawood Family Care PA ......F 913 338-4515
Leawood (G-5453)
Leawood Family Physicians ......F 913 451-4443
Shawnee Mission (G-11554)
Leawood Pediatrics LLC ......F 913 825-3627
Leawood (G-5454)
Lincoln Ctr Obstrcs/Gynclgy PA ......E 785 273-4010
Topeka (G-12845)
Lincoln Ctr Obstrcs/Gynclgy PA ......F 785 273-4010
Topeka (G-12846)
Logan County Manor ......F 785 672-8109
Oakley (G-7480)
Lowe Fryldnhoven Mds Chartered ......F 913 677-2508
Shawnee Mission (G-11578)
Mallery Clinic LLC ......F 785 825-9024
Salina (G-10589)
Manhattan Radiology LLP ......F 785 539-7641
Manhattan (G-6726)
Marian Clinic Inc ......E 785 233-2800
Topeka (G-12859)
Marillac Center Inc ......E 816 508-3300
Overland Park (G-8990)
Mark A McCune ......E 913 541-3230
Shawnee Mission (G-11594)
Mark Molos ......F 913 962-2122
Shawnee Mission (G-11596)
Mark S Humphrey MD ......F 913 541-8897
Shawnee Mission (G-11597)
Marysville Clinic ......F 785 562-2744
Marysville (G-6898)
Maternal Fetal Medicine Inc ......F 316 962-7188
Wichita (G-15018)
Meade Rural Health Clinic ......F 620 873-2112
Meade (G-7053)
Medical Administrative K U Med ......E 913 588-8400
Kansas City (G-4228)
▲ Medical Arts Clnic A Prof Assn ......E 620 343-2900
Emporia (G-1791)
Medical Assoc Manhattan PA ......E 785 537-2651
Manhattan (G-6739)
Medical Heights Medical Center ......E 620 227-3141
Dodge City (G-1403)
Medical Plaza Consultants P C ......E 913 945-6900
Overland Park (G-9007)
Medical Specialist ......E 785 623-2312
Hays (G-2871)
Medical-Surgical Eye Care PA ......E 913 299-8800
Kansas City (G-4230)
Mednax Inc ......F 913 599-1396
Shawnee Mission (G-11614)
Mercy Hlth Fndtion Sthstern PA ......F 620 223-2200
Fort Scott (G-1987)
Mercy Kansas Communities Inc ......F 913 352-8379
Pleasanton (G-9999)
Merrill R Conant MD ......E 620 227-6550
Dodge City (G-1404)
Metropolitan Spine Rehab PA ......F 913 387-2800
Overland Park (G-9018)
Mid America Cardiology ......F 913 588-9549
Westwood (G-13556)
Mid America Crdiolgy Assoc PC ......E 913 588-9600
Westwood (G-13557)
Mid America Crdiolgy Assoc PC ......E 913 588-9554
Shawnee Mission (G-11626)
Mid America Crdiolgy Assoc PC ......E 913 588-9600
Kansas City (G-4242)
Mid America Crdiolgy Assoc PC ......E 913 588-9400
Overland Park (G-9021)
Mid America Eye Center Inc ......E 913 384-1441
Prairie Village (G-10048)
Mid America Physicians Charter ......E 913 422-2020
Shawnee Mission (G-11627)
Mid America Polyclinic PA ......E 913 599-2440
Overland Park (G-9023)
Mid America Urology PC ......F 913 948-8365
Leawood (G-5479)
Mid Continent Anesthesiology ......E 316 789-8444
Wichita (G-15068)
Mid Kansas Family Practice ......E 620 327-2440
Hesston (G-2997)
Mid Kansas Pediatric Assoc PA ......E 316 773-3100
Wichita (G-15069)
Mid Kansas Pediatric Assoc PA ......E 316 634-0057
Wichita (G-15070)
Mid Knsas Drmtology Clinic P A ......F 316 612-1833
Wichita (G-15071)
Mid-America Diabetes Assoc PA ......E 316 687-3100
Mount Hope (G-7206)
Mid-America Orthopedics PA ......E 316 262-4886
Wichita (G-15076)
Mid-America Orthopedics PA ......E 316 440-1100
Wichita (G-15077)
Mid-America Surgery Institute ......E 913 906-0855
Overland Park (G-9026)
Mid-Amrca Kdny Stn Assctn LLC ......F 913 766-1860
Leawood (G-5480)
Mid-Amrica Rhumatology Cons PA ......E 913 661-9980
Overland Park (G-9027)
Mid-Kansas Womens Center PA ......E 316 685-3081
Wichita (G-15080)
Midwest Anesthesia Assoc PA ......E 913 642-4900
Leawood (G-5481)
Midwest Cardiology Associates ......F 913 894-9015
Lenexa (G-6000)
Midwest Cardiology Associates ......D 913 253-3045
Shawnee Mission (G-11631)

Midwest Ear Nose Throat PA ....F 913 764-2737
Olathe (G-7895)
Midwest Orthopedics PA ....E 913 362-8317
Shawnee Mission (G-11636)
Midwest Pain Management ....F 620 664-6724
Hutchinson (G-3380)
Midwest Pathology Assoc LLC ....F 913 341-6275
Overland Park (G-9035)
Midwest Reproductive Center PA ....F 913 780-4300
Olathe (G-7897)
Midwest Surgery Center Lc ....F 316 683-3937
Wichita (G-15104)
Midwest Surgical ....F 316 687-1090
Wichita (G-15105)
Milton B Grin MD PA ....E 913 829-5511
Olathe (G-7901)
Minneola Hospital District 2 ....F 620 885-4202
Bloom (G-531)
Monarch Plastic Surgery ....E 913 663-3838
Overland Park (G-9049)
Morton County Hospital ....F 620 697-2175
Elkhart (G-1624)
Mosier Mosier Fmly Physicians ....F 785 539-8700
Manhattan (G-6751)
Moufarrij Nazih ....D 316 263-0296
Wichita (G-15135)
Mowery Clinic LLC ....C 785 827-7261
Salina (G-10608)
Multispecialty Kanza Group PA ....E 913 788-7099
Kansas City (G-4272)
Mulvane Family Medcenter ....F 316 777-0176
Mulvane (G-7224)
Nelson Harmon Kapln WMS MD ....F 913 599-3800
Lenexa (G-6022)
Nemaha County Community Hlth ....F 785 284-2152
Sabetha (G-10320)
Nemaha Valley Community Hosp ....E 785 336-6107
Seneca (G-10877)
Nephrology Associates Inc ....F 913 381-0622
Olathe (G-7915)
Neurology Associates Kans LLC ....F 316 682-5544
Wichita (G-15163)
Neurology Center of Wichita ....F 316 686-6866
Wichita (G-15164)
Neurology Cons Chartered ....F 913 632-9810
Shawnee Mission (G-11678)
Neurology Consultants Kans LLC ....E 316 261-3220
Wichita (G-15165)
Neurosurgery Kansas City PA ....F 913 299-9507
Lenexa (G-6023)
New Frontiers ....F 785 672-3261
Oakley (G-7482)
New Market Health Care LLC ....E 316 773-1212
Wichita (G-15168)
Newman Mem Hosp Foundation ....E 620 342-2521
Emporia (G-1802)
Newman Mem Hosp Foundation ....B 620 343-6800
Emporia (G-1803)
Newton Healthcare Corporation ....A 316 283-2700
Newton (G-7393)
Newton Surgery Ctr ....F 316 283-9977
Newton (G-7396)
North Amdon Fmly Physicians PA ....F 316 838-8585
Wichita (G-15186)
Norton County Hospital ....F 785 877-3305
Norton (G-7458)
Nuehealth Management Svcs LLC ....D 913 387-0510
Leawood (G-5504)
Occupational Hlth Partners LLC ....E 785 823-8381
Salina (G-10618)
Olathe Family Practice PA ....E 913 782-3322
Olathe (G-7933)
Olathe Medical Services Inc ....D 913 780-4900
Olathe (G-7942)
Olathe Medical Services Inc ....F 913 782-3798
Lenexa (G-6034)
Olathe Medical Services Inc ....F 913 755-3044
Osawatomie (G-8200)
Olathe Medical Services Inc ....D 913 782-7515
Olathe (G-7943)
Olathe Medical Services Inc ....F 913 782-8487
Olathe (G-7944)
Olathe Medical Services Inc ....F 913 764-0036
Olathe (G-7945)
Olathe Medical Services Inc ....E 913 782-1610
Olathe (G-7946)
Olathe Regional Oncology Ctr ....F 913 768-7200
Olathe (G-7948)
Olathe Womens Center Inc ....F 913 780-3388
Olathe (G-7954)

Ophthalmic Services PA ....F 913 498-2015
Overland Park (G-9107)
Oral & Facial Surgery Assoc ....E 913 381-5194
Prairie Village (G-10054)
Oral and Maxilla Facial Assoc ....E 316 634-1414
Wichita (G-15230)
Ortho 4-States Real Estate LLC ....F 417 206-7846
Galena (G-2078)
Orthokansas PA ....E 785 843-9125
Lawrence (G-5051)
Orthopaedic MGT Svcs LLC ....D 913 319-7500
Shawnee Mission (G-11703)
Orthopdic Spcalists Four State ....E 620 783-4441
Galena (G-2079)
Orthopdic Spt Mdicine Cons LLC ....E 913 319-7534
Leawood (G-5510)
Orthopdic Spt Medicine Ctr LLP ....E 785 537-4200
Manhattan (G-6767)
Orthopedic & Spo ....F 913 319-7546
Leawood (G-5511)
Orthopedic & Sports Medicine ....E 316 219-8299
Wichita (G-15237)
Orthopedic Professional Assn ....F 913 788-7111
Kansas City (G-4299)
Oswego Medical Center LLC ....E 620 795-2386
Oswego (G-8235)
Otolaryngic Head/Neck Surgry ....E 913 588-6700
Kansas City (G-4301)
Ottawa Fmly Physcans Chartered ....E 785 242-1620
Ottawa (G-8297)
Overland Park Fmly Hlth Prtnr ....F 913 894-6500
Overland Park (G-9118)
Overland Park Surgery Ctr LLC ....D 913 894-7260
Overland Park (G-9123)
P A Comcare ....E 785 392-2144
Minneapolis (G-7120)
P A Comcare ....E 785 825-8221
Salina (G-10627)
P A Comcare ....E 785 827-6453
Salina (G-10628)
P A Family Medcenters ....C 316 771-9999
Derby (G-1264)
P A Heartland Cardiology ....F 316 773-5300
Wichita (G-15248)
P A Heartland Cardiology ....E 316 686-5300
Wichita (G-15249)
P A Med Assist ....F 785 272-2161
Topeka (G-12956)
PA Hays Anesthesiologist Assoc ....F 785 628-8300
Antonino (G-136)
Paincare PA ....E 913 901-8880
Overland Park (G-9136)
Parallel Pkwy Emrgncy Physcans ....E 913 596-4000
Kansas City (G-4310)
Parris R David MD ....E 620 223-8045
Fort Scott (G-1997)
Parsons Eye Clinic PA ....F 620 421-5900
Parsons (G-9717)
Partners Family Practice LLC ....E 620 345-6322
Moundridge (G-7195)
Partners In Pediatrics PA ....F 785 234-4624
Topeka (G-12963)
Partners In Primary Care ....E 913 335-6986
Kansas City (G-4316)
Partners In Primary Care ....E 913 815-5508
Olathe (G-7973)
Patrick A Blanchard MD ....F 785 456-8778
Wamego (G-13433)
Pediatric Care Specialist PA ....E 913 906-0900
Overland Park (G-9151)
Pediatric Orthopedic Surgery ....F 913 451-0000
Prairie Village (G-10057)
Pediatric Partners ....E 913 888-4567
Overland Park (G-9152)
Pediatric Professional Assn ....E 913 541-3300
Shawnee Mission (G-11723)
Pediatrics Associates ....E 785 235-0335
Topeka (G-12967)
Peter J Cristiano Dr ....F 913 682-5588
Lansing (G-4690)
Physician Office Partners LLC ....E 913 754-0467
Overland Park (G-9163)
Physicians Medical Clinics ....E 316 683-4334
Wichita (G-15295)
Physicians Medical Clinics ....F 316 687-2651
Wichita (G-15296)
Physicians Medical Clinics ....F 316 261-3130
Wichita (G-15297)
Physicians Medical Clinics ....C 316 721-4910
Wichita (G-15298)

Physicians Surgery Center ....E 913 384-9600
Shawnee Mission (G-11733)
Pittsburg Internal Medcine PA ....F 620 231-1650
Pittsburg (G-9921)
Pma Andover ....E 316 733-1331
Andover (G-105)
PMa Medical Associates PA ....D 316 261-3100
Wichita (G-15310)
Pma Twin Lakes Medical Off P A ....E 316 832-0465
Wichita (G-15311)
Prairiestar Health Center Inc ....F 620 663-8484
Hutchinson (G-3413)
Pratt Family Practice ....E 620 672-7422
Pratt (G-10137)
Pratt Intrnal Mdicine Group PA ....E 620 672-7417
Pratt (G-10141)
Prefered Medical Associates ....E 620 365-6933
Iola (G-3626)
Preferred Medical Associates ....E 316 733-1331
Andover (G-106)
Preferred Pediatrics PA ....F 913 764-7060
Olathe (G-8002)
Premier Dermatologic ....F 913 327-1117
Overland Park (G-9180)
Premier Open Mri Inc ....E 316 262-1103
Wichita (G-15332)
Premier Pediatrics PA ....F 913 384-5500
Overland Park (G-9182)
Premier Plastic Surgery ....F 913 782-0707
Olathe (G-8003)
Primary Care Associates LLC ....E 316 684-2851
Wichita (G-15342)
Primary Care Physcans Mnhattan ....E 785 537-4940
Manhattan (G-6780)
Pro Partners MD Holbrook ....E 913 451-4776
Leawood (G-5529)
Psychiatry Assoc Kans Cy PC ....E 913 385-7252
Shawnee Mission (G-11762)
Pulmonary Sleep Consultant ....F 316 440-1010
Wichita (G-15374)
Quinn Plastic Surgery Ctr LLC ....F 913 492-3443
Leawood (G-5531)
Quivira Internal Medicine ....E 913 541-3340
Shawnee Mission (G-11769)
Radiation Oncology ....E 913 588-3600
Kansas City (G-4358)
Radiologic Prof Svcs PA ....F 785 841-3211
Lawrence (G-5086)
Radiological Wichita Group PA ....E 316 685-1367
Wichita (G-15410)
Radiological Wichita Group PA ....F 316 681-1827
Wichita (G-15411)
Radiology Nuclear Medicine LLC ....E 785 234-3454
Topeka (G-12997)
Ralph Bharati MD PA ....F 316 686-7884
Wichita (G-15413)
Redbud Pediatrics LLC ....F 316 201-1202
Wichita (G-15430)
Reifschneider Eye Center PC ....F 913 682-2900
Leavenworth (G-5283)
Renal Trtmnt Centers-West Inc ....F 316 263-9090
Wichita (G-15443)
Reproductive Rsrce Ctr of Grtr ....E 913 894-2323
Shawnee Mission (G-11788)
Republic County Family ....F 785 527-2237
Belleville (G-465)
Rheumatology Cons Chartered ....E 913 661-9990
Shawnee Mission (G-11796)
Rhulen & Morgan Prof Assn ....F 913 782-8300
Olathe (G-8032)
Richard A Orchards MD ....F 785 841-2280
Lawrence (G-5095)
Richard F Sosinski ....E 785 843-5160
Lawrence (G-5096)
Rick R Tague MD MPH ....F 785 228-2277
Topeka (G-13015)
Ridgewood Surgery and End ....F 316 768-4197
Wichita (G-15462)
Riverbend Rgnal Hlthcare Fndti ....B 913 367-2131
Atchison (G-258)
Rockhill Womens Care Inc ....E 816 942-3339
Leawood (G-5541)
Rodney Lyles MD ....E 913 894-2323
Shawnee Mission (G-11813)
Rogers Duncan Dillehay DDS PA ....F 316 683-6518
Derby (G-1270)
Rural Hlth Rsurces Jackson Inc ....F 785 364-2126
Holton (G-3111)
S E K Otolaryngology PA ....F 620 232-7500
Pittsburg (G-9933)

SIC

Sabates Eye Centers PC ....F 913 261-2020
Shawnee Mission *(G-11822)*
Sabates Eye Centers PC ....F 913 261-2020
Leawood *(G-5545)*
Sabates Eye Centers PC ....E 913 469-8806
Shawnee Mission *(G-11823)*
Saint Frncis Radiation Therapy ....E 316 268-5927
Wichita *(G-15508)*
Saint Joseph Oncology Inc ....F 913 367-9175
Atchison *(G-260)*
Saint Lkes S Srgery Centre LLC ....F 913 317-3200
Overland Park *(G-9273)*
Saint Lukes Primary Care At ....D 913 317-7990
Overland Park *(G-9274)*
Salina Hlth Educatn Foundation ....D 785 825-7251
Salina *(G-10674)*
Salina Pediatric Care ....F 785 825-2273
Salina *(G-10681)*
Salina Regional Health Ctr Inc ....D 785 452-4850
Salina *(G-10687)*
Salina Sports Med &ORth Clinic ....F 785 823-7213
Salina *(G-10691)*
Salina Urology Associates PA ....F 785 827-9635
Salina *(G-10695)*
Scott County Hospital ....C 620 872-2187
Scott City *(G-10832)*
SE Kansas Orthopedic Clinic ....F 620 421-0881
Parsons *(G-9736)*
Sharon Lee Family Health Care ....D 913 722-3100
Kansas City *(G-4420)*
Shawnee Mission Corp Care LLC ....E 913 492-9675
Shawnee Mission *(G-11855)*
Shawnee Mission Med Ctr Inc ....E 913 422-2020
Shawnee *(G-11028)*
Shawnee Mission Med Ctr Inc ....E 913 789-1980
Shawnee Mission *(G-11859)*
Shawnee Mission Med Ctr Inc ....F 913 676-8400
Shawnee Mission *(G-11860)*
Shawnee Mission Pediatrics PA ....E 913 362-1660
Overland Park *(G-9305)*
Shawnee Mssion Plmnary Cons PA ....F 913 362-0300
Shawnee Mission *(G-11861)*
Shirley Alexander ....D 316 651-3621
Wichita *(G-15582)*
Sisters of Charity of Leavenwo ....E 913 825-0500
Kansas City *(G-4422)*
Skin Renewal ....E 913 722-5551
Overland Park *(G-9315)*
Smith County Family Practice ....F 785 282-6834
Smith Center *(G-12042)*
Somnitech Inc ....E 913 498-8120
Overland Park *(G-9327)*
South Cntl Kans Bone Joint Ctr ....F 620 672-1002
Pratt *(G-10150)*
South Kans Cy Surgical Ctr Lc ....E 913 901-9000
Overland Park *(G-9330)*
South Wichita Family Medicine ....F 316 524-4338
Wichita *(G-15620)*
Southeast Family Healthcare ....F 316 612-1332
Wichita *(G-15622)*
Southeast Kansas Orthpd Clinic ....F 620 421-0881
Parsons *(G-9740)*
Southwest Guidance Center ....F 620 624-8171
Liberal *(G-6370)*
St Francis Medical Clinic ....E 785 232-4248
Topeka *(G-13095)*
St Marys Hosp of Blue Sprng ....B 816 523-4525
Iola *(G-3635)*
Stateline Surgery Center LLC ....E 620 783-4072
Galena *(G-2086)*
Statland Clinic Ltd PA ....E 913 345-8500
Shawnee Mission *(G-11897)*
Stephen Rohner Doctor Office ....F 316 687-0006
Wichita *(G-15663)*
Steve Priddle ....E 785 776-1400
Manhattan *(G-6811)*
Steven D Braun ....F 620 662-1212
Hutchinson *(G-3447)*
Steven Donnenwerth ....E 620 672-7422
Pratt *(G-10155)*
Stonecreek Family Physicians ....E 785 587-4101
Manhattan *(G-6813)*
Stormont Vale Hospital ....E 785 273-8224
Topeka *(G-13102)*
Stormont-Vail Healthcare Inc ....E 785 354-5225
Topeka *(G-13113)*
Stormont-Vail Healthcare Inc ....F 785 836-7111
Carbondale *(G-685)*
Stormont-Vail Healthcare Inc ....E 785 456-2207
Wamego *(G-13442)*
Stormont-Vail Healthcare Inc ....C 785 270-4600
Topeka *(G-13103)*
Student Health Center Psu ....F 620 235-4452
Pittsburg *(G-9942)*
Sugar Scholl Magee Carriker ....E 913 384-4990
Overland Park *(G-9370)*
Summit Surgical LLC ....E 620 663-4800
Hutchinson *(G-3455)*
Sumner County Family Care Ctr ....E 620 326-3301
Wellington *(G-13533)*
Sunflower Medical Group ....E 913 432-2080
Shawnee Mission *(G-11909)*
Sunflower Medical Group PA ....D 913 261-5800
Shawnee Mission *(G-11910)*
Sunflower Medical Group PA ....E 913 722-4240
Shawnee Mission *(G-11911)*
Sunflower Prompt Care ....F 785 246-3733
Topeka *(G-13119)*
Surgery Center of Leawood LLC ....E 913 661-9977
Shawnee Mission *(G-11913)*
Surgery Center Olathe LLC ....F 913 829-4001
Olathe *(G-8089)*
Surgery Ctr S Centl Kans LLC ....F 620 663-7187
Hutchinson *(G-3459)*
Surgical Specialists PA ....F 316 945-7309
Wichita *(G-15701)*
Surgicare of Wichita Inc ....D 316 685-2207
Wichita *(G-15702)*
Surgicenter Johnson County Ltd ....E 913 894-4050
Shawnee Mission *(G-11914)*
Tall Grass Prarie Surg Spclsts ....E 785 233-7491
Topeka *(G-13132)*
Tallgrass Immediate Care LLC ....D 785 234-0880
Topeka *(G-13133)*
Tallgrass Orthpdics Spt Mdcine ....F 785 228-9999
Topeka *(G-13134)*
Tallgrass Orthpdics Spt Mdcine ....E 785 228-4700
Topeka *(G-13135)*
Tallgrass Prairie Surgical ....E 785 234-9830
Topeka *(G-13136)*
Tallgrass Prairie Surgical ....F 785 295-4500
Topeka *(G-13137)*
Tallgrass Surgical Center LLC ....E 785 272-8807
Topeka *(G-13138)*
Tanglewood Family Med Ctr PA ....E 316 788-3787
Derby *(G-1273)*
Tanglewood Family Medical Ctr ....E 316 788-3787
Derby *(G-1274)*
Team Vision Surgery Center ....E 316 729-6000
Wichita *(G-15721)*
Thomas C Klein MD ....D 316 682-7411
Wichita *(G-15760)*
Thomas E Moskow MD ....E 785 273-8224
Topeka *(G-13159)*
Thomas P Eyen ....F 913 663-5100
Shawnee Mission *(G-11929)*
Timothy M Koehler MD ....E 316 462-6220
Wichita *(G-15767)*
Topeka Allrgy Asthma Clinic PA ....F 785 273-9999
Topeka *(G-13166)*
Topeka Ansthsia Pain Trtmnt PA ....E 785 295-8000
Topeka *(G-13167)*
Topeka Ear Nose & Throat ....F 620 340-0168
Topeka *(G-13175)*
Topeka Pathology Group PA ....F 785 354-6031
Topeka *(G-13183)*
Topeka Surgery Center Inc ....E 785 273-8282
Topeka *(G-13186)*
Topeka Urology Clinic PA ....F 785 232-1005
Topeka *(G-13191)*
Trudi R Grin ....F 913 888-1888
Olathe *(G-8122)*
Trustees Indiana University ....E 913 499-6661
Fairway *(G-1923)*
Turner House Clinic Inc ....E 913 342-2552
Kansas City *(G-4478)*
Tyler Physicians PA ....F 316 729-9100
Wichita *(G-15823)*
Ultrasound For Women LLC ....E 785 331-4160
Lawrence *(G-5149)*
Ulysses Family Physicians ....C 620 356-1261
Ulysses *(G-13326)*
United Medical Group LLC ....C 913 287-7800
Kansas City *(G-4487)*
United Rdlgy Group Chartered ....F 785 827-9526
Salina *(G-10747)*
United States Dept of Army ....B 913 684-2747
Fort Leavenworth *(G-1942)*
University of Kansas ....E 785 864-2277
Lawrence *(G-5158)*
University of Kansas ....A 913 677-1590
Fairway *(G-1924)*
University of Kansas ....E 913 588-5900
Kansas City *(G-4497)*
University of Kansas ....A 913 588-1443
Kansas City *(G-4501)*
University of Kansas ....D 913 588-2720
Kansas City *(G-4504)*
University of Kansas ....A 913 588-6000
Kansas City *(G-4505)*
University of Kansas ....E 913 588-6798
Kansas City *(G-4496)*
University of Kansas Hospital ....E 913 682-6950
Leavenworth *(G-5303)*
University of Kansas Hospital ....C 913 588-5000
Kansas City *(G-4507)*
University of Kansas Med Ctr ....E 913 945-5598
Westwood *(G-13562)*
University of Kansas Med Ctr ....F 913 588-6311
Kansas City *(G-4508)*
University of Kansas School of ....D 316 293-3432
Wichita *(G-15858)*
Urologic Surgery Associates PA ....F 913 438-3833
Shawnee Mission *(G-11969)*
Urology Associates Topeka PA ....F 785 233-4256
Topeka *(G-13213)*
US Healthworks Medical Group ....E 913 495-9905
Lenexa *(G-6206)*
Vascular Surgery Associates PA ....F 913 262-9201
Shawnee *(G-11046)*
Vello Kass MD ....E 316 283-3600
Newton *(G-7423)*
Veterans Health Administration ....A 316 685-2221
Wichita *(G-15878)*
Veterans Health Administration ....B 785 826-1580
Salina *(G-10752)*
Veterans Health Administration ....B 620 423-3858
Parsons *(G-9748)*
Via Christi Clinic PA ....E 316 613-4680
Wichita *(G-15880)*
Via Christi Clinic PA ....F 316 789-8222
Derby *(G-1280)*
Via Christi Clinic PA ....B 316 689-9111
Wichita *(G-15881)*
Via Christi Clinic PA ....F 316 945-5400
Wichita *(G-15882)*
Via Christi Clinic PA ....E 316 609-4440
Wichita *(G-15883)*
Via Christi Clinic PA ....D 316 689-9111
Wichita *(G-15884)*
Via Christi Clinic PA ....E 316 689-9111
Wichita *(G-15885)*
Via Christi Clinic PA ....E 316 651-2252
Wichita *(G-15886)*
Via Christi Clinic PA ....F 316 733-6618
Andover *(G-113)*
Via Christi Health Inc ....D 785 456-6288
Wamego *(G-13446)*
Via Christi Health Inc ....D 316 773-4500
Wichita *(G-15888)*
Via Christi Health Inc ....D 316 685-0400
Wichita *(G-15890)*
Via Christi Health Inc ....E 316 858-4900
Wichita *(G-15891)*
Via Christi Hlth Partners Inc ....F 316 719-3240
Wichita *(G-15892)*
Via Christi Medical Management ....F 316 268-8123
Wichita *(G-15895)*
Via Chrsti Rhbltation Hosp Inc ....G 316 946-1790
Wichita *(G-15903)*
Via Chrsti Rvrside Med Ctr Inc ....C 316 689-5335
Wichita *(G-15904)*
Vigilias LLC ....E 800 924-8140
Wichita *(G-15907)*
Village Pediatrics LLC ....E 913 642-2100
Prairie Village *(G-10080)*
Vision Green Group ....E 620 663-7187
Hutchinson *(G-3479)*
Vision Today Inc ....F 913 397-9111
Olathe *(G-8142)*
Vitre-Retinal Cons Surgeons PA ....E 316 683-5611
Wichita *(G-15909)*
Volunteers With Heart Inc ....F 913 563-5100
Olathe *(G-8143)*
Ward Parkway Medical Group ....F 913 383-9099
Shawnee Mission *(G-11992)*
Warren Clinic ....D 785 337-2214
Hanover *(G-2714)*
Wellington Fmly Pract Clinc ....E 620 399-1222
Wellington *(G-13539)*

Wellness Services Inc ....F 913 438-8779
Shawnee Mission *(G-12000)*
Wellness Services Inc ....C 913 894-6600
Lenexa *(G-6225)*
Wesley Medical Center LLC ....E 316 962-2000
Wichita *(G-15952)*
West Central Kansas Assn Inc ....C 785 483-3131
Russell *(G-10303)*
Westglen Endoscopy Center LLC ....E 913 248-8800
Shawnee Mission *(G-12006)*
Wheatland Medical Clinic PA ....F 316 524-9400
Wichita *(G-15963)*
Wichita Ansthsiology Chartered ....D 316 686-1564
Wichita *(G-15973)*
Wichita Ear Clinic PA ....F 316 686-6608
Wichita *(G-15995)*
Wichita Family Medicine Specia ....E 316 858-5800
Wichita *(G-15999)*
Wichita Home Health Care Group ....F 316 219-0095
Wichita *(G-16005)*
Wichita Nephrology Group PA ....E 316 263-5891
Wichita *(G-16013)*
Wichita Ob Gyn Associates PA ....E 316 685-0559
Wichita *(G-16014)*
Wichita Orthopaedic Assoc LLC ....E 316 838-2020
Wichita *(G-16015)*
Wichita Physical Medicine P A ....F 316 729-1030
Wichita *(G-16017)*
Wichita Srgical Specialists PA ....E 316 722-5814
Wichita *(G-16024)*
▲ Wichita Srgical Specialists PA ....D 316 263-0296
Wichita *(G-16025)*
Wichita Srgical Specialists PA ....E 316 631-1600
Wichita *(G-16026)*
Wichita Srgical Specialists PA ....E 316 688-7500
Wichita *(G-16027)*
Wichita Srgical Specialists PA ....E 316 684-2838
Wichita *(G-16028)*
William Unsderfer MD ....E 620 669-6690
Hutchinson *(G-3490)*
Winfield Medical Arts PA ....E 620 221-6100
Winfield *(G-16186)*
Womans Place PA ....F 620 662-2229
Hutchinson *(G-3491)*
Womens Care ....E 913 384-4990
Overland Park *(G-9501)*
Womens Clinic Assoc PA ....F 913 788-9797
Leavenworth *(G-5307)*
Womens Clinic Johnson County ....F 913 491-4020
Leawood *(G-5600)*
Womens Clinic Johnson County ....F 913 491-4020
Overland Park *(G-9502)*
Womens Health Associates Inc ....E 913 677-3113
Shawnee Mission *(G-12015)*
Womens Health Care Group ....F 816 589-2121
Lawrence *(G-5190)*
Womens Health Care Group ....E 913 438-0018
Lenexa *(G-6233)*
Womens Health Group PA ....E 785 776-1400
Manhattan *(G-6856)*
Womens Health Svcs Kans Cy PC ....F 816 941-2700
Leawood *(G-5601)*
Woodich John ....E 620 332-3280
Independence *(G-3574)*
▲ Wyandtte Occpational Hlth Svcs ....F 913 945-9740
Kansas City *(G-4557)*
Zepick Cardiology ....E 316 616-2020
Wichita *(G-16101)*

8021 Offices & Clinics Of Dentists

Accent Dental LLC ....F 620 231-2871
Pittsburg *(G-9804)*
Adams Dental Group PA ....F 913 621-3113
Kansas City *(G-3784)*
Allen K Kelley DDS PA ....F 785 841-5590
Lawrence *(G-4728)*
Ann Barber ....F 913 788-0800
Kansas City *(G-3813)*
Antoine E Wakim Inc ....F 316 721-4477
Wichita *(G-13713)*
Associates In Dentistry ....F 785 843-4333
Lawrence *(G-4740)*
Augusta Family Dentistry PA ....F 316 775-2482
Augusta *(G-304)*
Barden and Thompson LLC ....F 620 343-8000
Emporia *(G-1702)*
Bel-Air Dental Care Chartered ....E 913 649-0310
Prairie Village *(G-10015)*
Bob Durbin DDS ....F 785 267-5010
Topeka *(G-12394)*
Boynton Family Dental Arts LLC ....E 316 685-8881
Wichita *(G-13876)*
Briscoe Richard L DDS PA ....F 620 669-1032
Hutchinson *(G-3224)*
Bruce Speak ....F 785 267-6301
Topeka *(G-12411)*
Bulleigh Orthodontics ....E 913 962-7223
Shawnee *(G-10921)*
Cambridge Family Dentistry ....F 316 687-2110
Wichita *(G-13929)*
Cascade Dental Care ....F 785 841-3311
Lawrence *(G-4776)*
Central Dental Center PA ....F 316 945-9845
Wichita *(G-13979)*
Chuck Pierson DDS PA ....E 316 634-1333
Wichita *(G-14018)*
Clay Center Family Dentistry ....F 785 632-3126
Clay Center *(G-850)*
Community Health Center of Sou ....F 620 856-2900
Baxter Springs *(G-403)*
Complete Dental Care ....F 913 469-5646
Olathe *(G-7608)*
Dalton L Hunt DDS ....F 620 543-2768
Buhler *(G-615)*
Dan A Burton DDS ....F 316 684-5511
Wichita *(G-14163)*
David Koepsel DDS LLC ....F 316 686-7395
Wichita *(G-14173)*
Dennis C McAllister DDS PA ....E 316 788-3736
Derby *(G-1234)*
Dental Associates ....E 785 539-7401
Manhattan *(G-6612)*
Dental Associates W Wichita PA ....E 316 942-5358
Wichita *(G-14193)*
Dental Corner ....E 316 681-2425
Wichita *(G-14194)*
Dental Innovation ....F 913 236-8899
Shawnee Mission *(G-11301)*
Derby Dental Care ....E 316 789-9999
Derby *(G-1235)*
Discover Dental Care ....F 913 268-1337
Shawnee Mission *(G-11308)*
Dlabal & Fellner Gen Denistry ....F 785 537-8484
Manhattan *(G-6615)*
Dodge City Dental ....F 620 225-2650
Dodge City *(G-1347)*
Douglas County Dntl Clinic Inc ....F 785 312-7770
Lawrence *(G-4839)*
Douglas V Oxler DDS ....F 316 722-2596
Wichita *(G-14231)*
Dr Nick Rogers ....F 620 442-5660
Arkansas City *(G-154)*
Dr William E Hartman Assoc PA ....F 913 441-1600
Bonner Springs *(G-550)*
Drs Alley and Brammer LC ....F 316 265-0856
Wichita *(G-14238)*
E Brent Nelson ....F 316 789-9999
Derby *(G-1241)*
Edwards & Wilson Periodontides ....F 785 843-4076
Lawrence *(G-4847)*
Emporia Orthodontics ....F 620 343-7275
Emporia *(G-1740)*
Enchanted Smiles Easthetic ....E 785 246-6300
Topeka *(G-12576)*
Erik J Peterson DDS ....F 785 227-2299
Lindsborg *(G-6398)*
Executive Hills Family Dental ....F 913 451-1606
Shawnee Mission *(G-11354)*
Faerber Surgical Arts ....F 913 469-8895
Shawnee Mission *(G-11358)*
First Care Clinic Inc ....E 785 621-4990
Hays *(G-2807)*
First Dental ....E 620 225-5154
Dodge City *(G-1360)*
Fry Orthodontics Prairie Vlg ....E 913 387-2500
Prairie Village *(G-10030)*
Gage Center Dental Group PA ....D 785 273-4770
Topeka *(G-12631)*
Gardner Dental Care ....F 913 856-7123
Gardner *(G-2348)*
Gary J Newman DDS PA ....F 785 273-1544
Topeka *(G-12633)*
Gentle Dental Service Corp ....E 913 248-8880
Lenexa *(G-5873)*
Gina B Pinamonti DDS ....F 620 231-6910
Pittsburg *(G-9866)*
Glenn V Hemberger DDS ....F 913 345-0331
Shawnee Mission *(G-11397)*
Grace Dental ....F 913 685-9111
Overland Park *(G-8767)*
Gracemed Health Clinic Inc ....F 316 440-7938
Wichita *(G-14490)*
Gracemed Health Clinic Inc ....D 316 866-2001
Wichita *(G-14491)*
Grant D Ringler DDS Inc ....F 620 669-0835
Hutchinson *(G-3304)*
Grant Phipps DDS ....F 620 326-7983
Wellington *(G-13507)*
Greg Cohen DDS ....F 785 273-2350
Topeka *(G-12649)*
Gust Orothondtcs PA G Morrison ....F 620 662-3255
Hutchinson *(G-3306)*
Gust Orthodontics ....F 316 283-1090
Newton *(G-7354)*
Hamilton & Wilson DDS ....F 785 272-3722
Topeka *(G-12660)*
Hannah & Oltjen ....F 913 829-2244
Olathe *(G-7749)*
Hannah & Oltjen ....F 620 343-3000
Emporia *(G-1767)*
Hannah & Oltjen ....F 913 268-5559
Shawnee Mission *(G-11408)*
Heartland Dental Group ....F 913 682-1000
Leavenworth *(G-5250)*
▲ Heartland Dental Group PA ....D 913 682-1000
Leavenworth *(G-5251)*
Heath Family Dentistry ....F 785 234-5410
Topeka *(G-12682)*
Holton Dental ....F 785 364-3038
Holton *(G-3096)*
Howell Matthew D Dr DDS PA ....F 316 260-6220
Andover *(G-94)*
Hullings Jon G DDS Ms PA ....F 316 636-1980
Wichita *(G-14650)*
Interdent Inc ....E 913 248-8880
Lenexa *(G-5918)*
James P Gertken DDS ....F 620 669-0411
Hutchinson *(G-3341)*
James R Kiene Jr DDS PA LLC ....F 913 825-9373
Shawnee Mission *(G-11482)*
Jenkins & Leblanc PA ....E 913 378-9610
Prairie Village *(G-10038)*
Jerry R Lundgrin DDS ....F 785 825-5473
Salina *(G-10554)*
Joe Rosenberg DDS ....F 620 285-3886
Saint John *(G-10353)*
John C Patton DDS ....F 620 342-0673
Emporia *(G-1780)*
John D Meschke DDS PA ....F 620 662-6667
Hutchinson *(G-3342)*
John F Dahm Dr ....F 620 665-5582
Hutchinson *(G-3343)*
John Fales Dr ....F 913 782-2207
Olathe *(G-7811)*
John H Hay DDS ....F 785 749-2525
Lawrence *(G-4926)*
Joseph P Steven DDS PA ....F 316 262-5273
Wichita *(G-14773)*
Joseph Wommack DDS ....F 620 421-0980
Parsons *(G-9694)*
Kaylor Dental Laboratory Inc ....D 316 943-3226
Wichita *(G-14835)*
Kc Smile PA ....F 913 491-6874
Overland Park *(G-8908)*
Keith and Assoc Dentistry LLC ....E 913 384-0044
Mission *(G-7132)*
Kelly B Deeter DDS Chartered ....F 785 267-6120
Topeka *(G-12816)*
Kelly S Henrichs DDS ....F 620 225-6555
Dodge City *(G-1388)*
Kuhlman and Majors DDS ....F 316 652-0000
Wichita *(G-14898)*
Lance Anderson DDS ....F 316 687-2104
Wichita *(G-14918)*
Larry D Sheldon DDS ....F 913 782-7580
Olathe *(G-7855)*
Lawrence Oral Surgery ....F 785 843-5490
Lawrence *(G-4979)*
Le John Minh DDS ....F 913 888-9399
Overland Park *(G-8949)*
Leawood Ctr For Dntl Excllence ....F 913 491-4466
Shawnee Mission *(G-11553)*
Lee & Devlin DDS ....F 316 685-2309
Wichita *(G-14945)*
Lenexa Dental Group Chartered ....F 913 888-8008
Shawnee Mission *(G-11563)*
Lisa R Gonzales DDS P C ....F 913 299-3999
Shawnee *(G-10989)*
Lynne M Schopper DDS PA ....F 913 451-2929
Leawood *(G-5461)*

S I C

Manhattan Oral Surgery & ... F ... 785 477-4038
Manhattan *(G-6725)*
Mark H Armfield DDS ... F ... 316 775-5451
Augusta *(G-333)*
Mark Hungerford MD ... F ... 785 539-5949
Manhattan *(G-6731)*
Mark R Davis DDS ... F ... 316 684-8261
Wichita *(G-15010)*
Mark S Jensen DDS PA ... F ... 913 384-0600
Shawnee Mission *(G-11598)*
Mark Troilo DDS PA ... F ... 316 776-2144
Rose Hill *(G-10242)*
McPherson Dental Care LLC ... F ... 620 241-5000
McPherson *(G-6997)*
Medallion Dental Lab Inc ... F ... 913 642-0039
Prairie Village *(G-10047)*
Michael A Dold DDS ... F ... 316 721-2024
Wichita *(G-15064)*
Michael F Cassidy DDS ... F ... 785 233-0582
Topeka *(G-12887)*
Michael J Randall ... F ... 913 498-3636
Leawood *(G-5478)*
Michael P Harris Inc ... F ... 620 276-7623
Garden City *(G-2231)*
Michael S Klein DDS ... F ... 913 829-4466
Olathe *(G-7891)*
Michael Yowell DDS PA ... F ... 620 241-0842
McPherson *(G-7002)*
Miller Sullivan & Assoc DDS PA ... F ... 913 492-5052
Shawnee Mission *(G-11641)*
Mobilecare 2u LLC ... E ... 913 362-1112
Overland Park *(G-9048)*
Morningstar Family Dental PA ... F ... 913 344-9990
Overland Park *(G-9055)*
Moxley &WAgle Dr ... F ... 316 685-2731
Wichita *(G-15136)*
Murray Clary Anita C DDS ... F ... 785 272-6060
Topeka *(G-12921)*
Nevin K Waters DDS PA ... F ... 913 782-1330
Olathe *(G-7916)*
New Horizons Dental Care ... F ... 785 376-0250
Salina *(G-10612)*
Olathe Dental Care Center ... F ... 913 782-1420
Olathe *(G-7930)*
Olathe Endodontics ... F ... 913 829-0060
Olathe *(G-7931)*
Olathe Family Dentistry PA ... F ... 913 829-1438
Olathe *(G-7932)*
Oral & Facial Surgery Assoc ... E ... 913 381-5194
Prairie Village *(G-10054)*
Oral & Facial Surgery Assoc ... E ... 913 782-1529
Olathe *(G-7961)*
Oral & Facial Surgery Assoc ... E ... 913 541-1888
Shawnee Mission *(G-11700)*
Oral and Facial Associate ... E ... 913 381-5194
Prairie Village *(G-10055)*
Oral Mxilo Ofcial Srgery Assoc ... E ... 913 268-9500
Shawnee Mission *(G-11701)*
Oread Orthodontics ... F ... 785 856-2483
Lawrence *(G-5047)*
Orthodonics Thompson PC ... F ... 913 681-8300
Leawood *(G-5509)*
Orthodontics P A Young ... F ... 913 592-2900
Spring Hill *(G-12094)*
Orthosynetics Inc ... E ... 913 782-1663
Olathe *(G-7965)*
Overland Park Dental ... F ... 913 383-2343
Shawnee Mission *(G-11706)*
Overland Park Dentistry PA ... F ... 913 647-8700
Shawnee Mission *(G-11707)*
Overland Park Smiles ... F ... 913 851-8400
Leawood *(G-5512)*
Pacific Dental Services LLC ... E ... 913 299-8860
Kansas City *(G-4307)*
Palmer Family Dentistry ... F ... 316 453-6918
Haysville *(G-2954)*
Pediatric Dental Specialist PA ... F ... 913 829-0981
Olathe *(G-7978)*
Perfect Smiles Dental Care PA ... F ... 913 631-2677
Lenexa *(G-6049)*
Periodontist PA ... F ... 913 451-6158
Overland Park *(G-9156)*
Prairie Vista Dental LLC ... F ... 620 424-4311
Ulysses *(G-13314)*
R2 Center For Assisting LLC ... F ... 316 749-2097
Wichita *(G-15408)*
Ratzlaff Craig D Ratzlaff DDS ... F ... 316 722-7100
Wichita *(G-15419)*
Rawlins Cnty Dntl Clinic Fund ... F ... 785 626-8290
Atwood *(G-288)*
Richard E Crowder DDS ... F ... 316 684-5184
Wichita *(G-15456)*
Richard Winburn ... F ... 913 492-5180
Shawnee Mission *(G-11801)*
Robert G Smith DDS Chartered ... F ... 913 649-5600
Shawnee Mission *(G-11807)*
Roger D Gausman DDS ... F ... 620 663-5044
Hutchinson *(G-3429)*
Roger L Stevens Dentist ... F ... 785 539-2314
Manhattan *(G-6794)*
Rogers Duncan Dillehay DDS PA ... F ... 316 683-6518
Derby *(G-1270)*
Ronald G Higgins ... F ... 620 584-2223
Clearwater *(G-895)*
Ronald J Burgmeier DDS PA ... F ... 913 764-1169
Olathe *(G-8041)*
Salina Dental Arts ... F ... 785 823-2472
Salina *(G-10671)*
Salina Dental Associates PA ... F ... 785 827-4401
Salina *(G-10672)*
Scheer Dentistry PA ... F ... 316 636-1222
Wichita *(G-15529)*
Smile Centre ... F ... 913 651-9800
Leavenworth *(G-5289)*
Smith Ned E Jr DDS Ms Charter ... F ... 913 383-3233
Leawood *(G-5552)*
Stephen P Moore DDS ... F ... 316 681-3228
Wichita *(G-15662)*
Steven F Twietmeyer DDS ... F ... 316 942-3113
Wichita *(G-15668)*
Steven G Mitchell DDS ... F ... 913 492-9660
Lenexa *(G-6154)*
Steven J Pierce DDS PA ... F ... 913 888-2882
Shawnee Mission *(G-11899)*
▲ Steven Joseph Jr DDS ... F ... 316 262-5273
Wichita *(G-15670)*
Steven L Hechler DDS Ms ... F ... 913 345-0541
Overland Park *(G-9361)*
Steven L Thomas DDS ... F ... 913 451-7680
Shawnee Mission *(G-11900)*
Thomspon R Wayne DDS Inc ... F ... 913 631-0110
Shawnee Mission *(G-11930)*
Todays Dentistry ... F ... 785 267-5010
Topeka *(G-13162)*
Turner House Clinic Inc ... E ... 913 342-2552
Kansas City *(G-4478)*
W Ross Greenlaw DMD ... F ... 207 374-5538
Overland Park *(G-9475)*
Wamego Dental Center Inc ... F ... 785 456-2330
Wamego *(G-13450)*
Webber Webber & Exon ... F ... 785 232-7707
Topeka *(G-13236)*
Wilkerson Anderson & Anderson ... E ... 785 843-6060
Lawrence *(G-5185)*
William E Hoffman DDS ... F ... 913 663-2992
Shawnee Mission *(G-12007)*
William Hoffman ... F ... 913 649-8890
Shawnee Mission *(G-12009)*
Wince Family Dental ... F ... 620 241-0266
McPherson *(G-7042)*
Ziegenhorn & Linneman DDS ... F ... 913 649-7500
Prairie Village *(G-10089)*

8031 Offices & Clinics Of Doctors Of Osteopathy

Anesthia Assn Centl Kans PA ... E ... 785 827-2238
Salina *(G-10403)*
Coffeyvlle Fmly Prctice Clinic ... E ... 620 251-1100
Coffeyville *(G-923)*
Rita Oplotnik DO ... F ... 913 764-0036
Olathe *(G-8037)*
Ron J Marek Do PA ... F ... 316 462-1050
Wichita *(G-15481)*
St Francis Hospital ... E ... 785 945-3263
Valley Falls *(G-13369)*
Surgical Specialists PA ... F ... 316 945-7309
Wichita *(G-15701)*
Witchita Clinic Inc ... F ... 620 583-7436
Eureka *(G-1899)*

8041 Offices & Clinics Of Chiropractors

Advanced Chiropractic Svcs PA ... F ... 785 842-4181
Lawrence *(G-4721)*
Advantage Medical Group ... F ... 785 749-0130
Lawrence *(G-4722)*
Animal Chiropractic Center ... E ... 309 658-2920
Wellsville *(G-13540)*
Chiro Plus Inc ... F ... 316 684-0550
Wichita *(G-14012)*
Chiroserve Inc ... E ... 913 764-6237
Olathe *(G-7594)*
Cleveland University - Kans Cy ... D ... 913 234-0600
Overland Park *(G-8565)*
Cohoon Chiropractic ... F ... 316 612-0600
Wichita *(G-14051)*
Counslman Wade Chrprctic Clnic ... F ... 785 234-0521
Topeka *(G-12514)*
First Choice Chiropractic PA ... F ... 913 402-7444
Overland Park *(G-8718)*
Hall Chiropractic Center ... F ... 785 242-6444
Overland Park *(G-8786)*
Lifeworks Chiropractic ... F ... 913 441-2293
Shawnee *(G-10988)*
Natural Way Chiropractic ... F ... 913 385-1999
Shawnee Mission *(G-11674)*
Robin Chiropractic & Acupnctur ... F ... 913 962-7408
Shawnee Mission *(G-11810)*
Saint Lukes South Hospital Inc ... F ... 913 317-7990
Overland Park *(G-9275)*
Walmart Inc ... B ... 620 232-1593
Pittsburg *(G-9960)*

8042 Offices & Clinics Of Optometrists

Bealmear Bowl Trrey Hoch Reves ... E ... 620 276-3381
Garden City *(G-2105)*
Branstetter & Associates ... F ... 316 788-9290
Derby *(G-1224)*
Brian Strange ... E ... 620 663-8700
Hutchinson *(G-3222)*
Burlingame Vision Associates ... F ... 913 338-1948
Overland Park *(G-8493)*
Chris O D Jacquinot ... F ... 620 235-1737
Pittsburg *(G-9831)*
Cohake Deutscher and Hefner ... E ... 785 271-8181
Topeka *(G-12485)*
Cole & Cooper PA ... F ... 785 823-6391
Salina *(G-10457)*
Daniel S Durrie Cokingtin LLC ... E ... 913 491-3330
Overland Park *(G-8633)*
Drake & Assoc Optometrists ... F ... 913 894-2020
Lenexa *(G-5825)*
Drs Dobbins & Letourneau ... F ... 785 843-5665
Lawrence *(G-4841)*
Drs Price Young Odle Horsch PA ... E ... 620 343-7120
Emporia *(G-1733)*
Eye Associates of Wichita ... F ... 316 943-0433
Wichita *(G-14326)*
Eye Association Overland Park ... F ... 913 339-9090
Overland Park *(G-8701)*
Eye Care Associates ... F ... 785 823-7403
Salina *(G-10494)*
Eye Care Associates ... F ... 316 685-1898
Wichita *(G-14327)*
Fisher Ronald Od PA ... F ... 316 942-7496
Wichita *(G-14378)*
Flintells Eyecare ... E ... 620 343-7120
Emporia *(G-1760)*
Grene Vision Group LLC ... E ... 316 721-2701
Wichita *(G-14513)*
Grene Vision Group LLC ... E ... 316 722-8883
Wichita *(G-14514)*
Grene Vision Group LLC ... D ... 316 691-4444
Wichita *(G-14515)*
Grene Vision Group LLC ... D ... 316 684-5158
Wichita *(G-14516)*
Hawks Bsler Rgers Optmtrist PA ... F ... 913 341-4508
Shawnee Mission *(G-11416)*
Heartland Eye Care LLC ... E ... 785 235-3322
Topeka *(G-12678)*
Henry L Bumgardner Jr Od ... F ... 316 264-4648
Wichita *(G-14593)*
Hopkins & Hopkins ... F ... 620 275-5375
Garden City *(G-2199)*
Jackson & Baalman ... F ... 316 722-6452
Wichita *(G-14743)*
Kannarr Eye Care LLC ... F ... 620 235-1737
Pittsburg *(G-9886)*
Kuhlmann Roberts & Janasek ... E ... 316 681-0991
Wichita *(G-14900)*
Lawrence Eyecare Associates ... F ... 785 841-2280
Lawrence *(G-4964)*
Lentz & Baker Eye Care ... F ... 316 634-2020
Wichita *(G-14955)*
Lynn W ONeal ... F ... 785 841-2280
Lawrence *(G-5004)*
Mc Pherson Eye Care LLP ... F ... 620 241-2262
McPherson *(G-6990)*
Milton B Grin MD PA ... E ... 913 829-5511
Olathe *(G-7901)*

Morrison Optometric Assoc PA ......F 785 462-8231
Colby (G-1030)
Mosier Mosier Fmly Physicians ......F 785 539-8700
Manhattan (G-6751)
Norris & Kelly Drs ......F 913 682-2929
Leavenworth (G-5277)
Olathe Family Vision ......F 913 782-5993
Olathe (G-7934)
Olathe Family Vision ......F 913 254-0200
Olathe (G-7935)
Patrick J Pirrote Od PA ......F 316 721-8877
Wichita (G-15268)
Physicians Optical ......F 913 829-5511
Olathe (G-7985)
Price & Young & Odle ......F 785 223-5777
Junction City (G-3739)
Price & Young & Odle ......F 913 780-3200
Olathe (G-8005)
Price & Young & Odle ......E 785 537-1118
Manhattan (G-6779)
Price & Young & Odle ......F 785 272-0707
Topeka (G-12987)
Ron D Hansen Od Inc ......F 620 662-2355
Hutchinson (G-3430)
Shea Vision Associates ......E 316 686-6071
Wichita (G-15579)
Southwind Eyecare ......F 620 662-2355
Hutchinson (G-3444)
Stiles Glaucoma Cons P A ......F 913 897-9299
Overland Park (G-9363)
The Eye Doctors ......F 785 272-3322
Topeka (G-13157)
Tran Majher and Shaw Od PA ......E 316 686-6063
Wichita (G-15786)
Vincent Pennipede Od ......E 913 825-2600
Overland Park (G-9464)
Vincent Pennipede Od ......E 913 780-9696
Olathe (G-8141)
West Wichita Fmly Optometrist ......F 316 262-3716
Wichita (G-15958)
Wichita Fmly Vision Clinic PA ......F 316 722-1001
Wichita (G-16002)
Wolf & Hatfield Inc ......F 620 227-3071
Dodge City (G-1463)

8043 Offices & Clinics Of Podiatrists

Associated Podiatrist PA ......E 913 321-0522
Kansas City (G-3824)
David B Laha MD Bpm ......F 913 338-4440
Overland Park (G-8640)
Foot Specialist Kansas City ......F 913 677-3600
Overland Park (G-8733)
Heart America Eye Care PA ......E 913 362-3210
Overland Park (G-8805)
Podiatry Associates PA ......F 913 432-5052
Shawnee Mission (G-11741)

8049 Offices & Clinics Of Health Practitioners, NEC

Abilene Physcl Thrpy & Sprts ......F 785 263-3519
Abilene (G-6)
Advance Rehabilitation LLC ......F 785 232-9805
Topeka (G-12294)
Advanced Chiropractic Svcs PA ......F 785 842-4181
Lawrence (G-4721)
Advanced Therapy & Spt Med LLC ......F 620 792-7868
Great Bend (G-2501)
Allstaff Chartered ......E 620 792-4643
Great Bend (G-2504)
Andbe Home Inc ......D 785 877-2601
Norton (G-7441)
ARC Physica Thera Plus Limite ......E 913 831-2721
Shawnee Mission (G-11116)
Associated Audiologists Inc ......E 913 403-0018
Shawnee Mission (G-11125)
Associated Homecare Inc ......C 316 320-0473
El Dorado (G-1529)
Audiology Consultants Inc ......F 785 823-3761
Salina (G-10412)
Bethany HM Assn Lindsborg Kans ......C 785 227-2334
Lindsborg (G-6394)
Bloom & Associates Therapy ......F 785 273-7700
Topeka (G-12388)
Board of Edcatn of Kans Cy Ks ......E 913 627-3913
Kansas City (G-3871)
Capper Foundation ......E 785 272-4060
Topeka (G-12440)
Christian Psychological Svcs ......F 785 843-2429
Lawrence (G-4788)
Clinical Associates ......E 913 677-3553
Lenexa (G-5762)
Clinical Associates PA ......F 913 677-3553
Lenexa (G-5763)
Compass Behavioral Health ......E 620 227-8566
Dodge City (G-1329)
Consultants In Neurology PA ......E 913 894-1500
Shawnee Mission (G-11262)
▲ Counseling & Mediation Center ......F 316 269-2322
Wichita (G-14106)
County of Saline ......F 785 826-6606
Salina (G-10465)
County of Sedgwick ......E 316 660-4800
Wichita (G-14109)
Dermatology & Skin Cancer Ctr ......F 913 451-7546
Shawnee Mission (G-11302)
Dr Vernon Rowe ......E 913 894-1500
Lenexa (G-5824)
Edward J Lind II ......E 316 788-6963
Derby (G-1242)
Erin Is Hope Foundation Inc ......E 316 681-3204
Wichita (G-14301)
Family Therapy Inst Midwest ......F 785 830-8299
Lawrence (G-4857)
Fandhill Orthpd & Spt Medicine ......F 620 275-8400
Garden City (G-2155)
For Women Only Inc ......F 913 541-9495
Leawood (G-5407)
Fss Psychiatric LLC ......F 913 677-0500
Leawood (G-5409)
Gao Qizhi ......F 316 691-8811
Wichita (G-14444)
Geary Rhabilitation Fitnes Ctr ......E 785 238-3747
Junction City (G-3696)
Guidance Center ......E 913 367-1593
Atchison (G-233)
Health Adminisource LLC ......F 913 384-5600
Shawnee Mission (G-11419)
Heartspring Inc ......B 316 634-8700
Wichita (G-14590)
Hodes & Nauser Mds PA ......F 913 491-6878
Overland Park (G-8821)
Horizons Mental Health Ctr Inc ......F 620 532-3895
Kingman (G-4595)
Integral Care Provider Inc ......C 913 384-2273
Shawnee Mission (G-11463)
Kansas Specialty Services Inc ......F 620 221-6040
Winfield (G-16151)
Lawrence Otlryngology Assoc PA ......F 620 343-6600
Lawrence (G-4981)
Michael R Magee ......E 913 339-6551
Shawnee Mission (G-11623)
Mid-America Orthopedics PA ......E 316 440-1100
Wichita (G-15077)
Moore Enterprises Inc ......C 913 451-5900
Overland Park (G-9052)
Moore Jeff PHD Audiologist ......F 316 686-6608
Wichita (G-15125)
Occupational Hlth Partners LLC ......E 785 823-8381
Salina (G-10618)
P A Therapyworks Inc ......E 785 749-1300
Lawrence (G-5053)
Physical Rsprtory Therapy Svcs ......E 785 742-7606
Hiawatha (G-3022)
Physical Rsprtory Therapy Svcs ......F 785 742-2131
Hiawatha (G-3021)
Prairie View Inc ......E 620 947-3200
Hillsboro (G-3055)
Quivira Athletic Club L C ......D 913 268-3633
Lenexa (G-6086)
Rebound Physical Therapy ......E 785 271-5533
Topeka (G-13003)
Salina Physical Therapy Clinic ......F 785 825-1361
Salina (G-10682)
Salina Regional Health Ctr Inc ......D 785 452-4850
Salina (G-10687)
Saltcreek Fitness & Rehab ......F 785 528-1123
Osage City (G-8190)
Select Medical Corporation ......F 316 687-4581
Wichita (G-15552)
Select Medical Corporation ......F 913 239-9539
Overland Park (G-9290)
Select Medical Corporation ......F 913 385-0075
Overland Park (G-9291)
Shc Services Inc ......C 913 652-9229
Overland Park (G-9306)
Sports Rehab/Physl Thrpy Assoc ......E 913 663-2555
Overland Park (G-9335)
Svetas Body Therapy LLC ......F 316 630-0400
Wichita (G-15706)
Trumove Physical Therapy PA ......F 913 642-7746
Overland Park (G-9433)
Unified School District 214 ......D 620 356-4577
Ulysses (G-13328)
Via Chrsti HM Hlth Wichita Inc ......D 316 268-8588
Wichita (G-15900)
Wilcox Advanced Physical ......F 316 942-5448
Wichita (G-16048)

8051 Skilled Nursing Facilities

Aberdeen Village Inc ......E 316 685-1100
Wichita (G-13597)
Accredo Health Group Inc ......E 913 339-7100
Lenexa (G-5622)
Ahc of Overland Park LLC ......F 913 232-2413
Overland Park (G-8360)
Alegria Living & Healthcare ......D 785 665-7124
Overbrook (G-8322)
America Care Quaker Hill Manor ......E 620 848-3797
Baxter Springs (G-392)
American Retirement Corp ......E 913 248-1500
Shawnee Mission (G-11108)
Andbe Home Inc ......D 785 877-2601
Norton (G-7441)
Andover Health Care Center ......C 316 448-4041
Andover (G-80)
Apostolic Christian Home ......C 785 284-3471
Sabetha (G-10305)
Arkansas City Presbt Manor Inc ......F 620 442-8700
Arkansas City (G-147)
Arma Care Center LLC ......E 620 347-4103
Arma (G-188)
Augusta L Lakepoint L C ......F 316 733-8100
Wichita (G-13768)
Augusta L Lakepoint L C ......D 316 775-6333
Augusta (G-307)
Augusta L Lakepoint L C ......E 316 320-4140
El Dorado (G-1531)
Avita Assisted Living At Derby ......F 316 260-4447
Derby (G-1221)
Beaver Dam Health Care Center ......E 620 231-1120
Pittsburg (G-9824)
Beaver Dam Health Care Center ......D 316 321-4444
El Dorado (G-1535)
Beaver Dam Health Care Center ......E 913 592-3100
Spring Hill (G-12079)
Beaver Dam Health Care Center ......D 913 422-5952
Edwardsville (G-1495)
Beaver Dam Health Care Center ......E 620 273-6369
Cottonwood Falls (G-1151)
Bethany HM Assn Lindsborg Kans ......C 785 227-2334
Lindsborg (G-6394)
Bethany Home Cottage Complex ......F 785 227-2721
Lindsborg (G-6395)
Beverly Enterprises-Kansas LLC ......E 316 683-7588
Wichita (G-13844)
Beverly Enterprises-Kansas LLC ......E 913 351-1284
Lansing (G-4669)
Beverly Enterprises-Kansas LLC ......E 785 672-3115
Oakley (G-7472)
Beverly Enterprises-Kansas LLC ......D 785 263-1431
Abilene (G-15)
Beverly Enterprises-Kansas LLC ......D 620 273-6369
Tonganoxie (G-12253)
Beverly Enterprises-Kansas LLC ......D 785 454-3321
Downs (G-1468)
Beverly Enterprises-Kansas LLC ......E 785 449-2294
Eskridge (G-1865)
Beverly Enterprises-Kansas LLC ......E 785 658-2505
Wilson (G-16104)
Beverly Enterprises-Kansas LLC ......E 913 422-5832
Edwardsville (G-1496)
Beverly Enterprises-Kansas LLC ......D 620 231-1120
Pittsburg (G-9825)
Beverly Enterprises-Kansas LLC ......E 785 462-6721
Colby (G-990)
Beverly Enterprises-Kansas LLC ......E 785 461-5417
Wakefield (G-13398)
Blue Valley Health Care ......E 785 363-7777
Blue Rapids (G-534)
Brandon Woods Retirement Cmnty ......C 785 838-8000
Lawrence (G-4766)
Brighton Place W Oper Co LLC ......E 785 232-1212
Topeka (G-12407)
Brookdale Overland Pk Glenwood ......F 913 385-2052
Overland Park (G-8487)
Brookdale Senior Living Commun ......E 785 628-1111
Hays (G-2761)
Brookdale Senior Living Commun ......E 913 894-6979
Shawnee Mission (G-11183)

S I C

Brookdale Senior Living Commun........F....... 316 684-3100
Wichita *(G-13897)*
Brookdale Senior Living Commun........F....... 785 263-7400
Abilene *(G-17)*
Brookdale Senior Living Commun........E....... 620 342-1000
Emporia *(G-1708)*
Brookdale Senior Living Commun........F....... 620 792-7000
Great Bend *(G-2522)*
Brookdale Senior Living Commun........E....... 785 820-2991
Salina *(G-10432)*
Brookdale Senior Living Commun........F....... 620 241-6600
Conway *(G-1133)*
Brookdale Senior Living Commun........F....... 620 326-3031
Wellington *(G-13492)*
Brookdale Senior Living Commun........E....... 620 225-7555
Dodge City *(G-1313)*
Brookdale Snior Lving Cmmnties.........E....... 316 630-0788
Wichita *(G-13898)*
Brookdale Snior Lving Cmmnties.........D....... 913 491-1144
Shawnee Mission *(G-11184)*
Buhler Sunshine Home Inc...................D....... 620 543-2251
Buhler *(G-614)*
Butler County Health Services.............D....... 316 320-4140
El Dorado *(G-1540)*
C & H Health LLC...................................D....... 913 631-8200
Shawnee Mission *(G-11193)*
Caregiver Support System....................E....... 214 207-7273
Marion *(G-6867)*
Catholic Care Center Inc.......................B....... 316 744-8651
Bel Aire *(G-428)*
Catholic Diocese of Wichita..................B....... 316 744-2020
Bel Aire *(G-429)*
Catholic Diocese of Wichita..................E....... 316 269-3900
Wichita *(G-13963)*
Cedars Inc...C....... 620 241-0919
McPherson *(G-6942)*
Centennial Healthcare Corp..................C....... 913 829-2273
Olathe *(G-7584)*
Chapman Adult Care Homes Inc...........D....... 785 922-6525
Chapman *(G-777)*
Cheney Golden Age Home Inc..............D....... 316 540-3691
Cheney *(G-789)*
City of Logan..D....... 785 689-4227
Logan *(G-6421)*
City of Logan..E....... 785 689-4201
Logan *(G-6422)*
City of Stockton......................................E....... 785 425-6754
Stockton *(G-12181)*
CLC Bonner Springs...............................D....... 913 441-2515
Bonner Springs *(G-545)*
Clearwter Nrsing Rhabilitation.............F....... 620 584-2271
Clearwater *(G-889)*
College Hl Nrsing Rhbilitation..............E....... 316 685-9291
Wichita *(G-14057)*
Comfort Care Homes Inc........................E....... 316 685-3322
Wichita *(G-14063)*
Community Healthcare Sys Inc.............D....... 785 437-3734
Saint Marys *(G-10361)*
Congregational Home.............................C....... 785 274-3350
Topeka *(G-12501)*
Country Place Senior Living..................F....... 785 336-6868
Seneca *(G-10860)*
Countryside Health Center....................E....... 785 234-6147
Topeka *(G-12515)*
County of Hamilton.................................E....... 620 384-7780
Syracuse *(G-12223)*
County of Johnson..................................C....... 913 894-8383
Olathe *(G-7621)*
County of Mitchell...................................F....... 785 738-2266
Beloit *(G-482)*
County of Stevens...................................D....... 620 544-2023
Hugoton *(G-3155)*
Crestview Operation Inc........................D....... 785 336-2156
Seneca *(G-10862)*
Cumbernauld Village Inc.......................D....... 620 221-4141
Winfield *(G-16137)*
Delmar Gardens Lenexa Oper LLC.......D....... 913 492-1130
Lenexa *(G-5808)*
Delmar Gardens of Lenexa Inc.............C....... 913 492-1130
Lenexa *(G-5809)*
Deseret Health Group.............................F....... 785 476-2623
Kensington *(G-4574)*
Deseret Hlth Rhab At Onaga LLC..........E....... 785 889-4227
Onaga *(G-8174)*
Deseret Hlth Rhab At Yates LLC............E....... 620 625-2111
Yates Center *(G-16195)*
Dickinson County....................................D....... 785 263-1431
Abilene *(G-24)*
Diversicare Leasing Corp......................F....... 316 524-3211
Haysville *(G-2939)*
Diversicare Leasing Corp......................F....... 620 431-4940
Chanute *(G-724)*
Diversicare Leasing Corp......................F....... 620 767-5172
Council Grove *(G-1163)*
Diversicare of Hutchinson.....................F....... 620 669-9393
Hutchinson *(G-3267)*
Diversicare of Larned LLC....................D....... 620 285-6914
Larned *(G-4701)*
Eagle Care Inc...F....... 785 227-2304
Lindsborg *(G-6397)*
Eaglecrest Operations LLC...................F....... 785 272-1535
Topeka *(G-12566)*
East Orlndo Hlth Rehab Ctr Inc............D....... 913 383-9866
Shawnee Mission *(G-11326)*
Emporia Prsbt Mnor of Mid Amer.........D....... 620 412-2019
Emporia *(G-1743)*
Enterprise Cmnty Nursing Hm..............E....... 785 263-8278
Enterprise *(G-1854)*
Evangelical Lthrn Good Smrtn..............D....... 785 456-9482
Wamego *(G-13421)*
Evangelical Lutheran.............................C....... 785 621-2499
Hays *(G-2802)*
Evangelical Lutheran.............................C....... 785 332-3588
Saint Francis *(G-10341)*
Evangelical Lutheran.............................C....... 620 663-1189
Hutchinson *(G-3280)*
Evangelical Lutheran.............................D....... 620 624-3832
Liberal *(G-6308)*
Evangelical Lutheran.............................D....... 785 472-3167
Ellsworth *(G-1674)*
Eventide Convalescent Center..............D....... 785 233-8918
Topeka *(G-12582)*
Family Hlth Rhbltation Ctr LLC.............D....... 316 425-5600
Wichita *(G-14337)*
Five Star Quality Care-Ks LLC..............D....... 620 564-2337
Ellinwood *(G-1632)*
Five Star Senior Living Inc....................D....... 913 648-4500
Leawood *(G-5406)*
Flint Hills Care Center...........................D....... 620 342-3280
Emporia *(G-1757)*
Fountainview Nursing &.........................F....... 316 776-2194
Rose Hill *(G-10239)*
Fowler Nursing Home.............................E....... 620 646-5215
Fowler *(G-2020)*
Frankfort Community Care Home..........D....... 785 292-4442
Frankfort *(G-2022)*
Friends Kansas Christn HM Inc.............C....... 316 283-6600
Newton *(G-7348)*
Frontline Management...........................D....... 620 227-8551
Dodge City *(G-1363)*
Garden Vly Retirement Vlg LLC.............C....... 620 275-9651
Garden City *(G-2184)*
Genesis Healthcare Corporation...........F....... 785 594-6492
Baldwin City *(G-362)*
Ggnsc Holdings LLC..............................F....... 913 422-5832
Kansas City *(G-4033)*
Ggnsc Wellington LLC............................E....... 620 326-7437
Wellington *(G-13504)*
Glencare/Cherryvale CA Ltd Pt..............E....... 620 336-2102
Cherryvale *(G-807)*
Golden Boomers Home...........................F....... 316 730-3110
Wichita *(G-14481)*
Golden Lc Edwardsvill...........................E....... 913 441-1900
Edwardsville *(G-1501)*
Golden Living Center.............................F....... 913 727-1284
Lansing *(G-4674)*
Golden Living Center Wichita................F....... 316 683-7588
Wichita *(G-14482)*
Golden Livingcenter - Eskridge............F....... 785 449-2294
Eskridge *(G-1867)*
Golden Livingcenter Room 132b...........F....... 785 658-2505
Wilson *(G-16106)*
Golden Oaks Healthcare Inc.................D....... 913 788-2100
Kansas City *(G-4039)*
Good Samaritan Society........................C....... 620 663-1189
Hutchinson *(G-3302)*
Good Shepherd Villages Inc.................E....... 785 244-6418
Summerfield *(G-12214)*
Grace Grdns Assistd Lvng Fclty...........F....... 913 685-4800
Leawood *(G-5416)*
Grace Management Inc..........................A....... 913 367-2655
Atchison *(G-232)*
Gran Villas...F....... 785 528-5095
Osage City *(G-8184)*
Gran Villas of Holton Inc.......................F....... 785 364-5051
Holton *(G-3093)*
Great Bend Manor...................................D....... 620 792-2448
Great Bend *(G-2583)*
Greeley Cnty Hosp & Long TRM C........D....... 620 376-4225
Tribune *(G-13268)*
Hays Medical Center Inc.........................A....... 785 623-5000
Hays *(G-2834)*
Health Management of Kansas..............C....... 620 251-5190
Coffeyville *(G-945)*
Heart Living Centers Colo LLC..............D....... 817 739-8529
Salina *(G-10537)*
Herington Opco LLC...............................F....... 785 789-4750
Herington *(G-2975)*
Heritage House Assisted Living............F....... 620 473-3456
Humboldt *(G-3184)*
Hickory Pointe...F....... 785 863-2108
Oskaloosa *(G-8226)*
Highland Healthcare and........................E....... 785 442-3217
Highland *(G-3029)*
Hillside Village LLC.................................D....... 913 583-1266
De Soto *(G-1201)*
Hilltop Lodge..C....... 785 738-2509
Beloit *(G-487)*
Hodgeman County Health Center...........C....... 620 357-8361
Jetmore *(G-3647)*
Holiday Healthcare LLC..........................D....... 785 825-2201
Salina *(G-10543)*
Homestead Inc..D....... 785 325-2361
Washington *(G-13465)*
Homestead of Augusta............................D....... 316 775-1000
Augusta *(G-325)*
Hospice Care of Kansas..........................E....... 316 283-2116
McPherson *(G-6975)*
Hospice of Graham County.....................C....... 785 421-2121
Hill City *(G-3035)*
Hospice of Reno County Inc...................F....... 620 669-3773
Hutchinson *(G-3313)*
Hospital District 2 Rice Cnty..................D....... 620 897-6266
Little River *(G-6419)*
Hospital Management Corp....................F....... 913 492-0159
Overland Park *(G-8827)*
Hre—Colorado Springs LLC....................D....... 817 739-8529
Salina *(G-10548)*
Hutch Good Samaritan Village...............E....... 620 663-1189
Hutchinson *(G-3316)*
Jackson County Nursing Home...............D....... 785 364-3164
Holton *(G-3099)*
John Knox Village....................................F....... 913 403-8343
Leawood *(G-5443)*
Kansas Long Term Care Phys.................D....... 316 315-0145
Wichita *(G-14813)*
Kansas Masonic Home............................C....... 316 269-7500
Wichita *(G-14814)*
Kingman County Retirement Assn..........D....... 620 532-5801
Kingman *(G-4599)*
Kiowa District Hospital...........................E....... 620 825-4117
Kiowa *(G-4624)*
▲ Lakepint Nrsing Rhbltation Ctr...........E....... 316 776-2194
Rose Hill *(G-10241)*
Lane County Hospital..............................D....... 620 397-5321
Dighton *(G-1287)*
Lansing Care Rhblttion Ctr LLC.............D....... 913 727-1284
Lansing *(G-4679)*
Las Villas Del Norte.................................D....... 760 741-1046
Junction City *(G-3720)*
Lawrence Memorial Hospital End...........A....... 785 505-3315
Lawrence *(G-4974)*
Lcrc..F....... 913 383-2085
Prairie Village *(G-10044)*
Legacy On 10th Opco LLC......................D....... 785 233-8918
Topeka *(G-12838)*
Legend Senior Living LLC.......................C....... 316 337-5450
Wichita *(G-14953)*
Leisure Homestead Association.............E....... 620 234-5208
Stafford *(G-12106)*
Leisure Homestead At St John...............E....... 620 549-3541
Saint John *(G-10355)*
Leisure Operations LLC..........................D....... 718 327-5762
Overland Park *(G-8952)*
Leisureterrace LLC..................................D....... 773 945-1000
Overland Park *(G-8953)*
Liberty Assisted Living Center...............E....... 785 273-0886
Topeka *(G-12842)*
Liberty Healthcare of Oklahoma.............D....... 785 823-7107
Salina *(G-10581)*
Liberty Terrace Care Center...................C....... 816 792-2211
Overland Park *(G-8956)*
Life Care Center Burlington...................D....... 620 364-2117
Burlington *(G-638)*
Life Care Centers America Inc...............E....... 316 733-5376
Andover *(G-103)*
Life Care Centers America Inc...............F....... 423 472-9585
Overland Park *(G-8957)*
Life Care Centers America Inc...............D....... 620 364-2117
Burlington *(G-639)*

Life Care Centers America Inc..............C....... 316 686-5100
Wichita (G-14961)
Life Care Centers America Inc..............C....... 913 755-4165
Osawatomie (G-8198)
Life Care Centers America Inc..............C....... 913 631-2273
Shawnee Mission (G-11569)
Life Care Centers America Inc..............D....... 785 336-3528
Seneca (G-10872)
Life Care Services LLC..............C....... 785 762-2162
Junction City (G-3721)
Lifespace Communities Inc..............C....... 913 383-2085
Shawnee Mission (G-11570)
Lincoln County Hospital..............D....... 785 524-4403
Lincoln (G-6383)
Linn Community Nursing Home..............D....... 785 348-5551
Linn (G-6408)
Logan County Manor..............F....... 785 672-8109
Oakley (G-7480)
Long Term Care Specialists LLC..............F....... 620 326-0251
Wellington (G-13513)
Lsl of Derby Ks LLC..............D....... 316 788-3739
Derby (G-1260)
Manhattan Rtrment Fndation Inc..............B....... 785 537-4610
Manhattan (G-6727)
Manor Care of Kansas Inc..............C....... 316 684-8018
Wichita (G-15003)
Manor Care of Kansas Inc..............D....... 785 271-6808
Topeka (G-12858)
Manor Care of Kansas Inc..............C....... 913 383-2569
Overland Park (G-8984)
Manor Care of Wichita Ks LLC..............F....... 316 684-8018
Wichita (G-15004)
Manor of Garnett Inc..............D....... 785 448-2434
Garnett (G-2382)
Manor of Liberal Inc..............D....... 620 624-0130
Liberal (G-6339)
Marysville Health Corporation..............D....... 785 562-2424
Marysville (G-6899)
McCrite Retirement Association..............C....... 785 267-2960
Topeka (G-12868)
McPherson Care Center LLC..............E....... 620 241-5360
McPherson (G-6993)
Meade Hospital District..............C....... 620 873-2146
Meade (G-7052)
Medicalodges Inc..............C....... 620 223-5085
Fort Scott (G-1984)
Medicalodges Inc..............D....... 913 772-1844
Leavenworth (G-5269)
Medicalodges Inc..............D....... 620 429-4317
Columbus (G-1081)
Medicalodges Inc..............D....... 620 251-6700
Coffeyville (G-958)
Medicalodges Inc..............F....... 785 742-4566
Hiawatha (G-3017)
Medicalodges Inc..............D....... 620 442-9300
Arkansas City (G-165)
Medicalodges Inc..............E....... 620 659-2156
Kinsley (G-4619)
Medicalodges Inc..............D....... 316 794-8635
Goddard (G-2446)
Medicalodges Inc..............D....... 785 632-5696
Clay Center (G-871)
Medicalodges Inc..............E....... 620 251-3705
Coffeyville (G-959)
Medicalodges Inc..............C....... 913 367-6066
Atchison (G-244)
Medicalodges Inc..............D....... 620 251-6700
Coffeyville (G-960)
Medicalodges Inc..............D....... 316 755-1288
Valley Center (G-13348)
Medicalodges Inc..............D....... 620 223-0210
Fort Scott (G-1985)
Medicalodges Inc..............D....... 620 231-0300
Pittsburg (G-9902)
Medicalodges Inc..............D....... 620 429-2134
Columbus (G-1082)
Medicalodges Inc..............D....... 620 583-7418
Eureka (G-1894)
Medicalodges Frontenac..............F....... 620 231-0322
Frontenac (G-2059)
Medicalodges of Kansas City..............E....... 913 334-0200
Kansas City (G-4231)
Mennonite Bethesda Society..............D....... 620 367-2291
Goessel (G-2458)
Mennonite Frndship Communities..............C....... 620 663-7175
South Hutchinson (G-12062)
Meridian Nursing Center Inc..............D....... 316 942-8471
Wichita (G-15041)
Midland Care Connection Inc..............C....... 785 232-2044
Topeka (G-12892)
Midwest Health Services Inc..............C....... 785 440-0399
Topeka (G-12897)
Midwest Health Services Inc..............B....... 913 829-4663
Olathe (G-7896)
Midwest Health Services Inc..............E....... 913 894-0014
Lenexa (G-6002)
Midwest Health Services Inc..............E....... 913 663-3351
Leawood (G-5484)
Midwest Health Services Inc..............E....... 785 537-1065
Manhattan (G-6748)
Midwest Health Services Inc..............E....... 316 835-4810
Halstead (G-2703)
Midwest Health Services Inc..............F....... 785 272-2200
Topeka (G-12898)
Midwest Health Services Inc..............E....... 785 765-3318
Alma (G-65)
Midwest Health Services Inc..............E....... 785 945-3832
Valley Falls (G-13368)
Midwest Health Services Inc..............B....... 913 727-6100
Lansing (G-4688)
Midwest Health Services Inc..............C....... 785 440-0500
Topeka (G-12899)
Midwest Health Services Inc..............D....... 785 776-0065
Manhattan (G-6749)
Midwest Health Services Inc..............D....... 785 233-0544
Topeka (G-12900)
Midwest Health Services Inc..............C....... 620 276-7643
Garden City (G-2234)
Midwest Health Services Inc..............F....... 316 685-1587
Wichita (G-15095)
Midwest Health Services Inc..............C....... 785 665-7124
Overbrook (G-8326)
Minneola Hospital District 2..............D....... 620 885-4238
Minneola (G-7126)
Mt Hope Community Development..............D....... 316 667-2431
Mount Hope (G-7207)
National Healthcare Corp..............D....... 620 767-5172
Council Grove (G-1173)
National Healthcare Corp..............C....... 316 524-3211
Haysville (G-2952)
National Healthcare Corp..............D....... 620 285-6914
Larned (G-4707)
National Healthcare Corp..............D....... 316 772-5185
Sedgwick (G-10851)
National Healthcare Corp..............D....... 620 431-4940
Chanute (G-745)
New Hope Services..............F....... 620 231-9895
Pittsburg (G-9911)
Nhi of Chanute LLC..............D....... 620 431-4940
Chanute (G-746)
Nursing By Numbers LLC..............F....... 913 788-0566
Olathe (G-7926)
Oxford Grand Assisted Living..............D....... 316 927-2007
Wichita (G-15243)
Parkside Homes Inc..............D....... 620 947-2301
Hillsboro (G-3053)
Phillips County Retirement Ctr..............D....... 785 543-2131
Phillipsburg (G-9793)
Pine Village..............C....... 620 345-2901
Moundridge (G-7196)
Pinnacle Hlth Fclties Xviii LP..............D....... 913 441-2515
Bonner Springs (G-571)
Pioneer Ridge Ind Living..............F....... 785 749-6785
Lawrence (G-5067)
Pioneer Ridge Retirement Cmnty..............C....... 785 344-1100
Lawrence (G-5068)
Plaza West Care Center Inc..............C....... 785 271-6700
Topeka (G-12980)
Pleasant Valley Nursing LLC..............F....... 620 725-3154
Sedan (G-10845)
Prairie Haven..............F....... 785 476-2623
Smith Center (G-12040)
Prairie Mission Retirement Vlg..............D....... 620 449-2400
Saint Paul (G-10384)
Pratt Health and Rehab..............D....... 620 672-6541
Pratt (G-10140)
Pratt Regional Med Ctr Corp..............E....... 620 672-3424
Pratt (G-10143)
Premier Living By Warden LLC..............E....... 316 945-2028
Wichita (G-15331)
Presbyterian Manors Inc..............D....... 785 841-4262
Lawrence (G-5074)
Presbyterian Manors Inc..............D....... 620 278-3651
Sterling (G-12128)
Presbyterian Manors Inc..............D....... 316 283-5400
Newton (G-7408)
Presbyterian Manors Inc..............D....... 620 442-8700
Arkansas City (G-170)
Presbyterian Manors Inc..............E....... 620 225-4474
Dodge City (G-1421)
Presbyterian Manors Inc..............D....... 785 272-6510
Topeka (G-12984)
Presbyterian Manors Inc..............D....... 316 942-7456
Wichita (G-15335)
Presbyterian Manors Inc..............D....... 913 334-3666
Kansas City (G-4333)
Presbyterian Manors Inc..............D....... 785 825-1366
Salina (G-10641)
Presbyterian Manors Inc..............D....... 785 632-5646
Clay Center (G-876)
Prime Healthcare Services Inc..............A....... 913 596-4000
Kansas City (G-4337)
Providence Place Inc..............F....... 913 596-4200
Kansas City (G-4348)
Rh Montgomery Properties Inc..............E....... 620 783-1383
Galena (G-2083)
Rh Montgomery Properties Inc..............D....... 913 294-4308
Paola (G-9586)
Rh Montgomery Properties Inc..............E....... 785 445-3732
Russell (G-10290)
Rh Montgomery Properties Inc..............E....... 620 237-4300
Moran (G-7164)
Rh Montgomery Properties Inc..............D....... 913 837-2916
Louisburg (G-6465)
Rh Montgomery Properties Inc..............D....... 620 725-3154
Sedan (G-10846)
Rh Montgomery Properties Inc..............E....... 785 284-3411
Sabetha (G-10324)
Rh Montgomery Properties Inc..............E....... 785 528-3138
Osage City (G-8188)
Richmond Healthcare..............D....... 785 835-6135
Richmond (G-10204)
Riverside Village Senior Livin..............D....... 316 942-7000
Wichita (G-15472)
Riverview Manor Inc..............E....... 620 455-2214
Oxford (G-9535)
Rolling Hills Health Center..............C....... 785 273-5001
Topeka (G-13026)
Rolling Hills Health Center..............E....... 785 273-2202
Topeka (G-13027)
Rossville Healthcare..............D....... 785 584-6104
Rossville (G-10255)
Royal Terrace Healthcare LLC..............D....... 913 829-2273
Olathe (G-8045)
Rush County Nursing Home Soc..............F....... 785 222-2574
La Crosse (G-4638)
Saint Lukes Hosp Garnett Inc..............C....... 785 448-3131
Garnett (G-2388)
Salem Hospital Inc..............D....... 620 947-2272
Hillsboro (G-3057)
Sandpiper Healthcare and..............C....... 316 945-3606
Wichita (G-15517)
Seniortrust of Haysville LLC..............C....... 316 524-3211
Haysville (G-2959)
Shawnee Gardens Health..............C....... 913 631-2146
Shawnee (G-11027)
Shawnee Mission Health Care..............D....... 913 676-2000
Shawnee Mission (G-11856)
Shepherd of Plains Foundation..............E....... 620 855-3498
Cimarron (G-836)
Southwest Medical Center..............E....... 620 624-1651
Liberal (G-6372)
St Catherine Hospital..............F....... 620 272-2519
Garden City (G-2289)
St Johns Rest Home Inc..............D....... 785 628-3241
Hays (G-2911)
Stanton County Hosp Aux Inc..............C....... 620 492-6250
Johnson (G-3662)
Sunbrdge Asssted Lving Rsdnces..............D....... 913 385-2052
Shawnee Mission (G-11907)
Sunrise Senior Living Inc..............D....... 913 262-1611
Prairie Village (G-10070)
Sunrise Senior Living Inc..............D....... 913 307-0665
Lenexa (G-6160)
Sunrise Senior Living LLC..............D....... 913 685-3340
Overland Park (G-9376)
Sunrise Senior Living LLC..............D....... 913 906-0200
Leawood (G-5564)
Sunrise Senior Living Svcs Inc..............E....... 913 262-1611
Prairie Village (G-10071)
Sunset Home Inc..............D....... 785 243-2720
Concordia (G-1131)
Sunset Manor Inc..............C....... 620 231-7340
Frontenac (G-2066)
Survey Companies LLC..............E....... 620 862-5291
Haviland (G-2742)
Susan B Allen Memorial Hosp..............B....... 316 322-4510
El Dorado (G-1607)
Sweet Life At Rosehill..............C....... 913 962-7600
Overland Park (G-9382)

T W G Nursing Home Inc.......D....... 620 724-8288
Girard *(G-2420)*
Thi of Kansas Indian Meadows.......E....... 913 649-5110
Overland Park *(G-9406)*
Topeka Adult Care Center.......F....... 785 233-7397
Topeka *(G-13164)*
Trinity Nursing & Rehab Center.......E....... 913 671-7376
Shawnee Mission *(G-11943)*
Truecare Nursing Services LLC.......E....... 626 818-2420
Wichita *(G-15810)*
Tutera Group Inc.......D....... 913 381-6000
Shawnee Mission *(G-11952)*
Tutera Group Inc.......E....... 913 851-0215
Shawnee Mission *(G-11951)*
United Methodist Homes Inc.......B....... 785 478-9440
Topeka *(G-13206)*
Valley View Senior Life LLC.......D....... 316 733-1144
Junction City *(G-3763)*
Via Christi Vlg Manhattan Inc.......C....... 785 539-7671
Manhattan *(G-6842)*
Via Christi Vlg Pittsburg Inc.......E....... 620 235-0020
Pittsburg *(G-9956)*
Victory Hill Retirement Cmnty.......E....... 913 299-1166
Kansas City *(G-4520)*
Villa St Francis Inc.......C....... 913 254-3264
Olathe *(G-8140)*
Village Villa Inc.......E....... 913 886-6400
Nortonville *(G-7465)*
Vintage Group Inc.......E....... 316 321-7777
El Dorado *(G-1612)*
Vintage Group Inc.......E....... 785 483-5882
Russell *(G-10302)*
Vintage Park Assisted Living.......F....... 785 456-8997
Wamego *(G-13447)*
Vitas Healthcare Corp Midwest.......E....... 913 722-1631
Overland Park *(G-9468)*
Vitas Healthcare Corporation.......E....... 913 722-1631
Lenexa *(G-6216)*
Waterfront Assisted Living.......F....... 316 945-3344
Wichita *(G-15936)*
Wathena Healthcare.......E....... 785 989-3141
Wathena *(G-13479)*
Wesley Retirement Community.......C....... 316 636-1000
Wichita *(G-15955)*
Wheat State Manor Inc.......D....... 316 799-2181
Whitewater *(G-13573)*
Wichita Cnty Long Term Rest Hm.......D....... 620 375-4600
Leoti *(G-6262)*
Windsor Nursing Home Assoc.......D....... 785 825-6757
Salina *(G-10771)*
Windsor of Lawrence.......E....... 785 832-9900
Lawrence *(G-5188)*
Windsor Place.......D....... 620 251-6545
Iola *(G-3638)*
Windsor Place At-Home Care.......E....... 620 331-3388
Independence *(G-3573)*
Woodlawn Care and Rehab LLC.......F....... 316 691-9999
Wichita *(G-16067)*

8052 Intermediate Care Facilities

Andbe Home Inc.......D....... 785 877-2601
Norton *(G-7441)*
Angel Arms.......F....... 620 245-0848
McPherson *(G-6935)*
Apostolic Christian Home.......C....... 785 284-3471
Sabetha *(G-10305)*
Asbury Park Inc.......C....... 316 283-4770
Newton *(G-7311)*
Athletic & Rehabilitation Ctr.......F....... 913 378-0778
Shawnee Mission *(G-11131)*
Attica Hospital District 1.......D....... 620 254-7253
Attica *(G-276)*
Brandon Woods Retirement Cmnty.......C....... 785 838-8000
Lawrence *(G-4766)*
Bucklin Hospital District Inc.......E....... 620 826-3202
Bucklin *(G-590)*
Buhler Sunshine Home Inc.......D....... 620 543-2251
Buhler *(G-614)*
Catholic Charities of Northeas.......E....... 913 621-5090
Overland Park *(G-8526)*
Cedars Inc.......C....... 620 241-0919
McPherson *(G-6942)*
Centennial Homestead Inc.......D....... 785 325-2361
Washington *(G-13462)*
Centrlia Cmmmity Hlth Care Svc.......D....... 785 857-3388
Centralia *(G-697)*
Cherry Village Benevolence.......D....... 620 792-2165
Great Bend *(G-2538)*
Cheyenne Lodge Inc.......E....... 785 439-6211
Jamestown *(G-3642)*
Clp Healthcare Services Inc.......D....... 620 232-9898
Pittsburg *(G-9837)*
Coffey County Hospital.......E....... 785 733-2744
Waverly *(G-13481)*
Community Care Inc.......E....... 785 455-3522
Clifton *(G-900)*
Compass Behavioral Health.......E....... 620 276-6470
Garden City *(G-2131)*
Cornerstone Ridge Plaza.......E....... 316 462-3636
Wichita *(G-14103)*
Country Care Inc.......D....... 913 773-5517
Easton *(G-1478)*
Country Place Senior Living.......F....... 785 632-5052
Clay Center *(G-857)*
County of Atchison.......E....... 913 367-1905
Atchison *(G-223)*
County of Stevens.......D....... 620 544-2023
Hugoton *(G-3155)*
Cumbernauld Village Inc.......D....... 620 221-4141
Winfield *(G-16137)*
Dignity Care Home Inc.......F....... 785 823-3434
Salina *(G-10477)*
Douglass Medicalodges.......E....... 316 747-2157
Douglass *(G-1466)*
Evangelical Lutheran.......D....... 785 472-3167
Ellsworth *(G-1674)*
Evangelical Lutheran.......C....... 785 621-2499
Hays *(G-2802)*
Evangelical Lutheran.......C....... 785 332-3588
Saint Francis *(G-10341)*
Eventide Convalescent Center.......D....... 785 233-8918
Topeka *(G-12582)*
Fowler Nursing Home.......E....... 620 646-5215
Fowler *(G-2020)*
Frankfort Community Care Home.......D....... 785 292-4442
Frankfort *(G-2022)*
Friends Kansas Christn HM Inc.......C....... 316 283-6600
Newton *(G-7348)*
Frontline Management.......D....... 620 227-8551
Dodge City *(G-1363)*
Glenwood Estate Inc.......D....... 620 331-2260
Independence *(G-3523)*
Halstead Place Inc.......E....... 316 830-2424
Halstead *(G-2701)*
Health Management of Kansas.......C....... 620 251-5190
Coffeyville *(G-945)*
Heart America Hospice Kans LLC.......E....... 785 228-0400
Topeka *(G-12674)*
Heartland Assisted Living.......E....... 913 248-6600
Shawnee *(G-10968)*
Heartland Hospice Services LLC.......D....... 419 252-5743
Wichita *(G-14585)*
High Plains Mental Health Ctr.......F....... 785 543-5284
Phillipsburg *(G-9788)*
High Plains Mental Health Ctr.......E....... 785 462-6774
Colby *(G-1014)*
High Plains Mental Health Ctr.......F....... 785 625-2400
Hays *(G-2847)*
Hilltop Manor Inc.......C....... 620 298-2781
Cunningham *(G-1187)*
Homestead Health Center Inc.......D....... 316 262-4473
Wichita *(G-14633)*
Hospice Incorporated.......E....... 620 251-1640
Coffeyville *(G-947)*
Hospice Incorporated.......E....... 620 229-8398
Winfield *(G-16147)*
Hospice Advantage LLC.......F....... 913 859-9582
Overland Park *(G-8826)*
Hospice Care of Kansas LLC.......E....... 316 721-8803
Wichita *(G-14638)*
Hospice of Salina Inc.......F....... 785 825-1717
Salina *(G-10547)*
Hospice of The Prairie Inc.......E....... 620 227-7209
Dodge City *(G-1375)*
Hospice Services Inc.......F....... 785 543-2900
Phillipsburg *(G-9789)*
Infinia At Wichita Inc.......E....... 316 691-9999
Wichita *(G-14691)*
Jefferson County Mem Hosp Inc.......D....... 913 774-4340
Winchester *(G-16110)*
Kansas City Hospice Inc.......E....... 816 363-2600
Overland Park *(G-8896)*
Kansas Masonic Home.......C....... 316 269-7500
Wichita *(G-14814)*
Kingman County Retirement Assn.......D....... 620 532-5801
Kingman *(G-4599)*
Lafayette Life Plan Inc.......D....... 785 742-7465
Hiawatha *(G-3015)*
Lakeview Village Inc.......A....... 913 888-1900
Lenexa *(G-5962)*
Leonardville Nursing Home Inc.......D....... 785 468-3661
Leonardville *(G-6249)*
Life Care Centers America Inc.......D....... 785 336-3528
Seneca *(G-10872)*
Life Care Centers America Inc.......D....... 620 364-2117
Burlington *(G-639)*
Lindsborg House 2.......F....... 785 227-3652
Lindsborg *(G-6401)*
Linn Community Nursing Home.......D....... 785 348-5551
Linn *(G-6408)*
Living Center Inc.......D....... 620 665-2170
Hutchinson *(G-3355)*
Maria Villa Inc.......D....... 316 777-1129
Mulvane *(G-7220)*
Maria Villa Inc.......E....... 316 777-9917
Mulvane *(G-7221)*
Martin Luther Homes Kansas Inc.......D....... 620 229-8702
Winfield *(G-16156)*
Marysville Health Corporation.......D....... 785 562-2424
Marysville *(G-6899)*
McCrite Retirement Association.......C....... 785 267-2960
Topeka *(G-12868)*
Medicalodges Inc.......D....... 620 223-0210
Fort Scott *(G-1985)*
Medicalodges Inc.......D....... 620 231-0300
Pittsburg *(G-9902)*
Medicalodges Inc.......D....... 620 429-2134
Columbus *(G-1082)*
Medicalodges Inc.......D....... 620 583-7418
Eureka *(G-1894)*
Medicalodges Inc.......D....... 620 442-9300
Arkansas City *(G-165)*
Medicalodges Inc.......E....... 620 659-2156
Kinsley *(G-4619)*
Medicalodges Inc.......D....... 316 794-8635
Goddard *(G-2446)*
Medicalodges Inc.......D....... 316 755-1288
Valley Center *(G-13348)*
Mennonite Frndship Communities.......C....... 620 663-7175
Hutchinson *(G-3374)*
Midwest Division - Oprmc LLC.......A....... 913 541-5000
Shawnee Mission *(G-11632)*
Midwest Health Services Inc.......E....... 620 272-9800
Garden City *(G-2233)*
Midwest Health Services Inc.......E....... 785 537-1065
Manhattan *(G-6748)*
Midwest Health Services Inc.......C....... 785 440-0500
Topeka *(G-12899)*
Midwest Health Services Inc.......E....... 785 776-1772
Manhattan *(G-6750)*
Mission Village Living Ctr Inc.......E....... 785 486-2697
Horton *(G-3131)*
Morton County Hospital.......C....... 620 697-2141
Elkhart *(G-1623)*
Multi Community Diversfd Svcs.......F....... 785 227-2712
Lindsborg *(G-6405)*
Nicol Home Inc.......E....... 785 568-2251
Glasco *(G-2423)*
Old Creek Senior Living.......E....... 785 272-2601
Topeka *(G-12945)*
Osborne Development Company.......D....... 785 346-2114
Osborne *(G-8215)*
Park Wheatridge Care Center.......E....... 620 624-0130
Liberal *(G-6355)*
Parkside Homes Inc.......D....... 620 947-2301
Hillsboro *(G-3053)*
Pine Village.......C....... 620 345-2901
Moundridge *(G-7196)*
Prairie Sunset Home Inc.......E....... 620 459-6822
Pretty Prairie *(G-10168)*
Presbyterian Manors Inc.......D....... 913 334-3666
Kansas City *(G-4333)*
Presbyterian Manors Inc.......D....... 785 825-1366
Salina *(G-10641)*
Presbyterian Manors Inc.......D....... 785 632-5646
Clay Center *(G-876)*
Presbyterian Manors Inc.......D....... 316 942-7456
Wichita *(G-15335)*
Protection Valley Manor Inc.......D....... 620 622-4261
Protection *(G-10176)*
Regal Estate.......E....... 305 751-4257
Independence *(G-3552)*
RES-Care Kansas Inc.......F....... 913 342-9426
Kansas City *(G-4372)*
RES-Care Kansas Inc.......E....... 785 728-7198
Goodland *(G-2483)*
RES-Care Kansas Inc.......D....... 620 793-8501
Great Bend *(G-2631)*
Riordan Clinic Inc.......E....... 316 682-3100
Wichita *(G-15464)*

Riverview Estates Inc ....E.... 785 546-2211
Marquette (G-6877)
Rural Health Development Inc ....D.... 785 462-8295
Colby (G-1037)
Sabetha Manor Incorporated ....E.... 785 284-3411
Sabetha (G-10329)
Saint Jude Hospice ....F.... 785 742-3823
Hiawatha (G-3024)
Spring View Manor Inc ....E.... 620 456-2285
Conway Springs (G-1145)
Sunset Home Inc ....D.... 785 243-2720
Concordia (G-1131)
Sunset Manor Inc ....C.... 620 231-7340
Frontenac (G-2066)
Valley Springs ....F.... 785 256-7100
Auburn (G-298)
Via Christi Vlg Manhattan Inc ....C.... 785 539-7671
Manhattan (G-6842)
Villa St Francis Inc ....C.... 913 254-3264
Olathe (G-8140)
Vintage Park of Paola ....E.... 913 557-0202
Paola (G-9594)
Westview Mnor Healthcare Assoc ....D.... 316 788-3739
Derby (G-1281)
Westy Community Care Home Inc ....D.... 785 457-2806
Westmoreland (G-13549)
Wheat State Manor Inc ....D.... 316 799-2181
Whitewater (G-13573)
Wichita Cnty Long Term Rest Hm ....D.... 620 375-4600
Leoti (G-6262)
Windsor Nursing Home Assoc ....D.... 785 825-6757
Salina (G-10771)
Woodridge Estates LLC ....F.... 620 421-2431
Parsons (G-9751)
Woodworth Enterprises Inc ....E.... 620 236-7248
Chetopa (G-818)

8059 Nursing & Personal Care Facilities, NEC

4-B Properties LLC ....E.... 785 364-4643
Holton (G-3083)
Apostolic Christian Home ....C.... 785 284-3471
Sabetha (G-10305)
Applewood Rehabilation Inc ....E.... 620 431-7300
Altoona (G-75)
Benedictine Health System ....C.... 913 498-2700
Shawnee Mission (G-11160)
Brookdale Senior Living Commun ....F.... 620 251-6270
Coffeyville (G-914)
Brookdale Senior Living Commun ....E.... 785 762-3123
Junction City (G-3675)
Brookdale Senior Lving Cmmnties ....E.... 316 630-0788
Wichita (G-13898)
Brookdale Senior Lving Cmmnties ....F.... 785 263-7800
Abilene (G-18)
Brookdale Senior Lving Cmmnties ....F.... 785 832-9900
Lawrence (G-4769)
Brookdale Senior Lving Cmmnties ....D.... 913 491-1144
Shawnee Mission (G-11184)
Brookdale Senior Lving Cmmnties ....E.... 913 491-3681
Leawood (G-5343)
Carondelet Health ....D.... 913 345-1745
Overland Park (G-8520)
Carrington House LLC ....E.... 316 262-5516
Wichita (G-13954)
Cedars Inc ....C.... 620 241-0919
McPherson (G-6942)
Cherry Village Benevolence ....D.... 620 792-2165
Great Bend (G-2538)
City of Stockton ....E.... 785 425-6754
Stockton (G-12181)
Clyde Development Inc ....E.... 785 446-2818
Clyde (G-906)
Comfort Care Homes Inc ....E.... 316 685-3322
Wichita (G-14063)
Community Lving Opprtnties Inc ....F.... 785 832-2332
Lawrence (G-4805)
Community Lving Opprtnties Inc ....E.... 785 843-7072
Lawrence (G-4806)
Cumbernauld Village Inc ....D.... 620 221-4141
Winfield (G-16137)
Dawson Place Inc ....E.... 785 421-3414
Hill City (G-3032)
Deaconess Long Term Care of MI ....C.... 785 242-5399
Ottawa (G-8264)
Deaconess Long Term Care of MI ....F.... 785 242-9378
Ottawa (G-8265)
Developmental Svcs NW Kans Inc ....E.... 785 625-5678
Hays (G-2785)
Developmental Svcs NW Kans Inc ....C.... 785 625-2521
Hays (G-2786)
Developmental Svcs NW Kans Inc ....F.... 785 877-5154
Norton (G-7443)
Developmental Svcs NW Kans Inc ....F.... 785 483-3020
Russell (G-10272)
Dooley Center ....E.... 913 360-6200
Atchison (G-225)
Evangelical Lutheran ....C.... 620 663-1189
Hutchinson (G-3280)
Evangelical Lutheran ....D.... 785 475-2245
Oberlin (G-7493)
Evangelical Lutheran ....D.... 785 626-9015
Atwood (G-284)
Evangelical Lutheran ....C.... 785 625-7331
Hays (G-2801)
Evangelical Lutheran ....D.... 620 624-3832
Liberal (G-6308)
Evangelical Lutheran ....B.... 913 782-1372
Olathe (G-7694)
Evangelical Lutheran ....D.... 620 257-5163
Lyons (G-6483)
Evangelical Lutheran ....D.... 785 726-3101
Ellis (G-1644)
Evangelical Lutheran ....D.... 785 890-7517
Goodland (G-2469)
Evangelical Lutheran ....D.... 785 456-9482
Wamego (G-13422)
Evangelical Lutheran ....D.... 620 421-1110
Parsons (G-9684)
Evangelical Lutheran ....D.... 785 472-3167
Ellsworth (G-1674)
Evergreen Lving Innvations Inc ....D.... 913 477-8227
Olathe (G-7695)
Faith Village Inc ....D.... 913 906-5000
Olathe (G-7701)
Galena Medical Properties LLC ....F.... 620 783-4616
Galena (G-2073)
Ggnsc Spring Hill LLC ....E.... 913 592-3100
Spring Hill (G-12084)
Gran Villas of Wamego ....E.... 785 456-8997
Wamego (G-13424)
Guest Home Estates ....F.... 620 431-7115
Pittsburg (G-9869)
Guest Home Estates ....E.... 620 879-5199
Caney (G-670)
Heritage Healthcare Management ....F.... 785 899-0100
Goodland (G-2477)
Homestead Inc ....D.... 785 325-2361
Washington (G-13465)
Just In Time Adult Care ....F.... 913 371-3391
Kansas City (G-4130)
Lakemary Center Homes Inc ....F.... 913 557-4000
Paola (G-9569)
Lcd Unlimited Inc ....F.... 316 721-4803
Wichita (G-14938)
Liberty Healthcare of Oklahoma ....D.... 785 823-7107
Salina (G-10581)
Liz Gonzalez Examinetics Inc ....E.... 913 748-2042
Overland Park (G-8964)
Lsl of Kansas LLC ....E.... 785 527-5636
Belleville (G-461)
Martin Luther Homes Kansas Inc ....D.... 620 229-8702
Winfield (G-16156)
Meade Hospital District ....C.... 620 873-2146
Meade (G-7052)
Medicalodges Inc ....E.... 620 251-3705
Coffeyville (G-959)
Meridian Nursing Center Inc ....D.... 316 942-8471
Wichita (G-15041)
Midwest Health Services Inc ....F.... 785 272-2200
Topeka (G-12898)
Midwest Health Services Inc ....E.... 785 765-3318
Alma (G-65)
Midwest Health Services Inc ....E.... 785 945-3832
Valley Falls (G-13368)
Mosaic ....E.... 785 472-4081
Ellsworth (G-1679)
Norton Retirement and Assisted ....E.... 785 874-4314
Norton (G-7460)
Nursing Home Legacy At Pk View ....E.... 620 356-3331
Ulysses (G-13308)
Overland Park Senior Living ....E.... 913 912-7800
Overland Park (G-9122)
Overland Pk Nursing Rehab Ctr ....F.... 913 383-9866
Overland Park (G-9125)
Park View ....E.... 620 424-2000
Ulysses (G-13310)
Parkside Homes Inc ....D.... 620 947-2301
Hillsboro (G-3053)
Pinnacle Hlth Fclties Xviii LP ....D.... 913 441-2515
Bonner Springs (G-571)
Pioneer Community Care Inc ....E.... 620 582-2123
Coldwater (G-1057)
Presbyterian Manors Inc ....D.... 913 334-3666
Kansas City (G-4333)
Presbyterian Manors Inc ....D.... 785 825-1366
Salina (G-10641)
Presbyterian Manors Inc ....D.... 785 632-5646
Clay Center (G-876)
Presbyterian Manors Inc ....D.... 316 942-7456
Wichita (G-15335)
Presbyterian Manors Inc ....E.... 620 421-1450
Parsons (G-9725)
Sheltered Living Inc ....E.... 785 233-2566
Topeka (G-13068)
Sheltered Living Inc ....F.... 785 266-8686
Topeka (G-13069)
St Francis Academy Inc ....E.... 785 825-0563
Salina (G-10714)
Sunflower Supports Company ....C.... 785 267-3093
Topeka (G-13122)
Thi of Kansas Indian Meadows ....E.... 913 649-5110
Overland Park (G-9406)
Thriver Services LLC ....F.... 913 955-2555
Lenexa (G-6179)
Top City Healthcare Inc ....D.... 785 272-2124
Topeka (G-13163)
Truecare Nursing Services LLC ....E.... 626 818-2420
Wichita (G-15810)
Trustees of The Baker Univ ....E.... 785 354-5850
Topeka (G-13199)
United Methodist Homes Inc ....B.... 785 478-9440
Topeka (G-13206)
Via Christi Village Hays Inc ....C.... 785 628-3241
Hays (G-2926)
Vintage Park At Hiawatha LLC ....F.... 785 742-4566
Hiawatha (G-3027)
Vintage Park At Osawatomie LLC ....F.... 913 755-2167
Osawatomie (G-8206)
Vintage Park of Lenexa LLC ....F.... 913 894-6979
Shawnee Mission (G-11981)
Volga-Canal Housing Inc ....E.... 785 625-5678
Hays (G-2927)
Winfield Rest Haven Inc ....E.... 620 221-9290
Winfield (G-16190)
Woodland Hlth Ctr Oprtions LLC ....D.... 785 234-6147
Topeka (G-13251)
Woodworth International Inc ....E.... 620 236-7248
Chetopa (G-819)

8062 General Medical & Surgical Hospitals

Adventist Health System/Sunbel ....A.... 913 676-2163
Shawnee Mission (G-11081)
Andover Spine & Health Ctr ....F.... 316 733-9555
Andover (G-81)
Ascension Arizona ....C.... 316 689-5360
Wichita (G-13745)
Ascension Via Christi ....A.... 620 231-6100
Pittsburg (G-9811)
Ascension Via Christi Hospital ....A.... 316 268-5880
Wichita (G-13747)
Ascension Via Christi Hospital ....F.... 316 721-9500
Wichita (G-13749)
Ascension Via Christi Hospital ....A.... 316 268-5040
Wichita (G-13752)
Atchison Hospital Association ....B.... 913 367-2131
Atchison (G-209)
Bob Wilson Mem Grant Cnty Hosp ....C.... 620 356-1266
Ulysses (G-13284)
Cah Acquisition Company 5 LLC ....E.... 620 947-3114
Hillsboro (G-3043)
Central Kansas Medical Center ....B.... 620 792-2511
Great Bend (G-2529)
Central Kansas Medical Center ....F.... 620 792-8171
Great Bend (G-2530)
Cheyenne County Hospital ....D.... 785 332-2104
Saint Francis (G-10339)
Childrens Mercy Hospital ....A.... 316 500-8900
Wichita (G-14010)
Childrens Mercy Hospital ....E.... 913 287-8800
Kansas City (G-3911)
Childrens Mercy Hospital ....E.... 913 696-5767
Shawnee Mission (G-11220)
Childrens Mercy Hospital ....B.... 913 696-8000
Overland Park (G-8548)
Childrens Mercy Hospital ....D.... 913 696-8000
Shawnee Mission (G-11221)
Citizens Medical Center Inc ....B.... 785 462-7511
Colby (G-994)
City of Wamego ....E.... 785 456-2295
Wamego (G-13413)

Clara Barton Hospital ....F 620 653-4191
Hoisington (G-3060)
Clara Barton Hospital ....D 620 653-2114
Hoisington (G-3061)
Clara Barton Hospital ....D 620 653-2114
Hoisington (G-3062)
Clay Center Fmly Physicians PA ....F 785 446-2226
Clyde (G-905)
Cloud County Health Center Inc........C 785 243-1234
Concordia (G-1106)
Coffey County Hospital ....C 620 364-5655
Burlington (G-628)
Coffey County Hospital ....E 785 733-2744
Waverly (G-13481)
Coffey County Hospital ....E 620 364-8861
Burlington (G-629)
Coffey County Hospital ....E 620 364-5395
Burlington (G-630)
Coffey Health Systems ....D 620 364-5118
Burlington (G-632)
Coffeyvlle Rgional Med Ctr Inc........B 620 251-1200
Coffeyville (G-924)
College Park Endoscopy Ctr LLC........A 913 385-4400
Overland Park (G-8577)
Comanche Cnty Hosp Med Clinic........E 620 582-2144
Coldwater (G-1052)
Comanche County ....E 620 582-2144
Coldwater (G-1055)
Community Healthcare Sys Inc........E 785 364-3205
Holton (G-3086)
Community Healthcare Sys Inc........F 785 889-4241
Onaga (G-8172)
Community Healthcare Sys Inc........C 785 889-4274
Onaga (G-8173)
Community Healthcare Sys Inc........B 785 437-3407
Saint Marys (G-10360)
Community Memorial Healthcare........C 785 562-2311
Marysville (G-6884)
Community Memorial Healthcare........F 785 363-7202
Blue Rapids (G-535)
County of Gove ....C 785 754-3335
Quinter (G-10181)
County of Graham........E 785 421-5464
Hill City (G-3031)
County of Hamilton........E 620 384-7780
Syracuse (G-12223)
County of Kiowa........D 620 723-3341
Greensburg (G-2674)
County of Riley........E 785 539-3535
Manhattan (G-6603)
County of Sheridan........F 785 675-3281
Hoxie (G-3136)
County of Sherman........E 785 890-3625
Goodland (G-2467)
Decatur Health Systems Inc........D 785 475-2208
Oberlin (G-7492)
Edwards County Hospital ....D 620 659-2732
Kinsley (G-4616)
Ellsworth County Medical Ctr........C 785 472-3111
Ellsworth (G-1670)
Emporia Physical Therapy ....F 620 342-4100
Emporia (G-1742)
Foundation of Neosho Memorial........E 620 431-4000
Chanute (G-729)
Fresenius Medical Service........F 316 264-3115
Wichita (G-14423)
Geary County Hospital ....B 785 238-4131
Junction City (G-3694)
Girard Medical Center........D 620 724-7288
Girard (G-2407)
Girard Medical Center........D 620 724-8291
Girard (G-2408)
Great Plains Hlth Aliance Inc........D 785 332-2104
Saint Francis (G-10342)
Great Plains Hlth Aliance Inc........D 785 284-2121
Sabetha (G-10311)
Great Plains Kiowa Co Inc ....D 620 723-3341
Greensburg (G-2676)
Great Plains of Sabetha Inc ....C 785 284-2121
Sabetha (G-10312)
Great Plains Smith Co Inc........C 785 282-6845
Smith Center (G-12034)
Greeley County Health Svcs Inc........C 620 376-4221
Tribune (G-13270)
Greenwood Cnty Hosp Foundation........C 620 583-5909
Eureka (G-1888)
Grisell Memorial Hospital Assn........D 785 731-2231
Ransom (G-10193)
Hamilton County Hospital ....D 620 384-7461
Syracuse (G-12227)
Hanover Hospital & Clinic........D 785 337-2214
Hanover (G-2712)
Harper Hospital District 5........C 620 896-7324
Anthony (G-127)
Hays Medical Center Inc........F 785 623-5774
Hays (G-2833)
Hays Medical Center Inc........A 785 623-5000
Hays (G-2834)
Hays Medical Center Inc........A 785 623-6270
Hays (G-2835)
HCA Hospital Svcs San Diego........A 316 962-2000
Wichita (G-14572)
HCA Inc ....C 620 365-1000
Iola (G-3608)
Health Care Inc........A 620 665-2000
Hutchinson (G-3309)
Heartland Health ....A 785 985-2211
Troy (G-13274)
Hiawatha Hospital Association........F 785 742-2161
Hiawatha (G-3010)
Hodgeman County Health Center........C 620 357-8361
Jetmore (G-3647)
Hospital District 1 ....E 620 724-8291
Girard (G-2413)
Hospital District 1 Rice Cnty........C 620 257-5173
Lyons (G-6484)
Hospital District 3 Clark Cnty ....D 620 635-2241
Ashland (G-196)
Hospital Dst 1 Dcknson Cnty Ka ....C 785 263-2100
Abilene (G-40)
Hospital Dst 1 Marion Cnty ....C 620 382-2177
Marion (G-6873)
Hospital Dst 1 of Rice Cnty........D 620 257-5173
Lyons (G-6485)
Hospital Dst 6 Harper Cnty ....C 620 914-1200
Anthony (G-128)
Hutchnson Regional Med Ctr Inc ....A 620 665-2000
Hutchinson (G-3331)
Jefferson County Mem Hosp Inc........D 913 774-4340
Winchester (G-16110)
Jewell County Hospital........D 785 378-3137
Mankato (G-6859)
Kansas City Orthoped ....C 913 338-4100
Leawood (G-5444)
Kansas Heart Hospital LLC ....C 800 574-3278
Wichita (G-14805)
Kansas Spine Spcialty Hosp LLC........C 316 462-5000
Wichita (G-14824)
Kansas Srgery Recovery Ctr LLC ....C 316 634-0090
Wichita (G-14825)
Kearny County Hospital ....C 620 355-7111
Lakin (G-4653)
Kiowa District Hospital........D 620 825-4131
Kiowa (G-4625)
Labette Health Foundation Inc ....B 620 421-4881
Parsons (G-9705)
Labette Health Foundation Inc ....F 620 922-3838
Coffeyville (G-954)
Lane County Hospital ....D 620 397-5321
Dighton (G-1287)
Lawrence Memorial Hospital ....E 785 505-5000
Lawrence (G-4973)
Lawrence Memorial Hospital End........F 785 840-3114
Lawrence (G-4975)
Lawrence Memorial Hospital End........F 785 505-3780
Lawrence (G-4976)
Lawrence Memorial Hospital End........A 785 505-3315
Lawrence (G-4974)
Lincoln County Hospital........D 785 524-4403
Lincoln (G-6383)
Lindsborg Community Hosp Assn........D 785 227-3308
Lindsborg (G-6400)
Logan County Hospital........C 785 672-3211
Oakley (G-7479)
McPherson Hospital Inc ....B 620 241-0917
McPherson (G-7000)
Medicine Lodge Memorial Hosp ....C 620 886-3771
Medicine Lodge (G-7067)
Mercy & Truth Med Missions Inc ....F 913 248-9965
Kansas City (G-4235)
Mercy Health........B 620 223-2200
Fort Scott (G-1986)
Mercy Hosp Fdn of Independence ....F 620 331-2200
Independence (G-3537)
Mercy Hospital Inc ....E 620 345-6391
Moundridge (G-7188)
Mercy Hospital Columbus........F 620 429-2545
Columbus (G-1083)
Mercy Kansas Communities Inc........B 620 223-7075
Fort Scott (G-1989)
Mercy Kansas Communities Inc........B 620 332-3264
Independence (G-3539)
Mercy Kansas Communities Inc........F 913 352-8379
Pleasanton (G-9999)
Miami County Medical Ctr Inc........C 913 294-2327
Paola (G-9572)
Midwest Division - Oprmc LLC........A 913 541-5000
Shawnee Mission (G-11632)
Minneola Hospital District 2........F 620 885-4202
Bloom (G-531)
Minneola Hospital District 2........D 620 885-4238
Minneola (G-7126)
Mitchell Count Hospi Healt Sys........B 785 738-2266
Beloit (G-493)
Morton County Hospital ....C 620 697-2141
Elkhart (G-1623)
Nemaha Valley Community Hosp........C 785 336-6181
Seneca (G-10876)
Ness County Hospital Dst No 2 ....C 785 798-2107
Ness City (G-7265)
Newman Mem Hosp Foundation ....B 620 343-6800
Emporia (G-1803)
Newton Healthcare Corporation........A 316 283-2700
Newton (G-7393)
Newton William Memorial Hosp........B 620 221-2300
Winfield (G-16163)
Norton County Hospital........F 785 877-3351
Norton (G-7457)
Norton County Hospital........F 785 877-3305
Norton (G-7458)
Norton County Hospital........F 785 877-5745
Norton (G-7459)
Nueterra Holdings LLC........E 785 776-5100
Manhattan (G-6763)
Olathe Medical Center Inc........E 913 791-4200
Olathe (G-7940)
On Call Mobile Therapies LLC........E 913 449-1679
Lenexa (G-6036)
Osborne County Memorial Hosp........D 785 346-2121
Osborne (G-8214)
Ottawa County Health Center ....C 785 392-2044
Minneapolis (G-7119)
Overland Park Reg Med Staff Df........F 913 541-5000
Shawnee Mission (G-11709)
Overland Park Regional Hosp ....E 913 541-5406
Overland Park (G-9121)
Overland Pk Rgonal Med Ctr Inc ....A 913 541-0000
Overland Park (G-9126)
Phillips County Hospital........D 785 543-5226
Phillipsburg (G-9792)
Pinnacle Regional Hospital Inc........E 913 541-0230
Overland Park (G-9169)
Plainville Rural Hospital ....C 785 434-2622
Plainville (G-9990)
Pratt Regional Med Ctr Corp........B 620 672-7451
Pratt (G-10144)
Prime Health Servi-Saint John........F 913 680-6000
Leavenworth (G-5280)
Prime Healthcare Services Inc........A 913 596-4000
Kansas City (G-4337)
Prime Healthcare Services Inc........E 913 651-3542
Leavenworth (G-5281)
Promise Hosp Overland Pk Inc........D 913 275-5092
Overland Park (G-9193)
Providence Medical Center ....F 913 596-4870
Kansas City (G-4347)
Ransom Memorial Hospital Chari........C 785 229-8200
Ottawa (G-8308)
Ransom Memorial Hospital Chari........B 785 229-8200
Ottawa (G-8309)
Rawlins County Health Center........D 785 626-3211
Atwood (G-289)
Resurrection Hospital Physn CL ....E 785 483-3333
Russell (G-10289)
Riverbend Rgnal Hlthcare Fndti ....B 913 367-2131
Atchison (G-258)
Rural Hlth Rsurces Jackson Inc........C 785 364-2116
Holton (G-3110)
Rush County Memorial Hospital........D 785 222-2545
La Crosse (G-4637)
Saint Lukes Cushing Hospital ....B 913 684-1100
Leavenworth (G-5288)
Saint Lukes Hosp Garnett Inc........C 785 448-3131
Garnett (G-2388)
Saint Lukes South Hospital Inc ....B 913 317-7000
Shawnee Mission (G-11825)
Saint Lukes South Hospital Inc ....E 913 317-7514
Kansas City (G-4396)
Salina Regional Health Ctr Inc........A 785 452-7000
Salina (G-10686)

Salina Regional Health Ctr Inc....B....785 452-7000
Salina (G-10688)
Salina Regional Health Ctr Inc....D....785 452-4850
Salina (G-10687)
Salina Surgical Center LLC....D....785 827-0610
Salina (G-10694)
Satanta District Hosp & Long T....C....620 649-2761
Satanta (G-10790)
Scott County Hospital Inc....D....620 872-5811
Scott City (G-10833)
Sedan City Hospital....D....620 725-3115
Sedan (G-10848)
Shawnee Mission Med Ctr Inc....F....913 632-9800
Shawnee Mission (G-11857)
Shawnee Mission Med Ctr Inc....A....913 676-2000
Shawnee Mission (G-11858)
Sisters of Charity of Leavenwo....F....785 295-7800
Topeka (G-13073)
Sisters of Charity of Leavenwo....E....785 295-5310
Topeka (G-13074)
Sisters of Charity of Leavenwo....E....913 825-0500
Kansas City (G-4422)
Sisters St Joseph Wichita KS....E....316 686-7171
Wichita (G-15598)
South Cntl Kans Rgonal Med Ctr....C....620 442-2500
Arkansas City (G-181)
Southwest Medical Center....E....620 624-1651
Liberal (G-6372)
St Catherine Hospital....B....620 272-2222
Garden City (G-2288)
St Catherine Hospital....F....620 272-2519
Garden City (G-2289)
St Cathrine Hosp Dev Fundation....F....620 272-2222
Garden City (G-2290)
St Jhns Maude Norton Mem Hosp....D....620 429-2545
Columbus (G-1087)
St Lukes Health Corporation....C....913 250-1244
Lansing (G-4693)
St Lukes Hospital Inc....C....620 326-7451
Wellington (G-13530)
Stafford District Hospital 4....E....620 234-5221
Stafford (G-12111)
Stanton County Hosp Aux Inc....C....620 492-6250
Johnson (G-3662)
Stevens County Hospital....C....620 544-8511
Hugoton (G-3177)
Stormont-Vail Healthcare Inc....C....785 270-4600
Topeka (G-13103)
▲ Stormont-Vail Healthcare Inc....A....785 354-6000
Topeka (G-13104)
Stormont-Vail Healthcare Inc....B....785 584-6705
Rossville (G-10256)
Stormont-Vail Healthcare Inc....B....785 270-4820
Topeka (G-13105)
Stormont-Vail Healthcare Inc....B....785 270-8625
Topeka (G-13106)
Stormont-Vail Healthcare Inc....B....785 863-3417
Oskaloosa (G-8230)
Stormont-Vail Healthcare Inc....B....785 354-9591
Topeka (G-13107)
Stormont-Vail Healthcare Inc....B....785 231-1800
Topeka (G-13108)
Stormont-Vail Healthcare Inc....B....620 343-2900
Emporia (G-1830)
Stormont-Vail Healthcare Inc....B....785 537-2651
Manhattan (G-6814)
Stormont-Vail Healthcare Inc....B....785 273-8224
Topeka (G-13109)
Stormont-Vail Healthcare Inc....B....785 354-6116
Topeka (G-13110)
Stormont-Vail Healthcare Inc....B....785 354-5545
Topeka (G-13111)
Stormont-Vail Healthcare Inc....B....785 270-8605
Topeka (G-13112)
Stormont-Vail Healthcare Inc....E....785 354-5225
Topeka (G-13113)
Stormont-Vail Healthcare Inc....F....785 836-7111
Carbondale (G-685)
Stormont-Vail Healthcare Inc....E....785 456-2207
Wamego (G-13442)
Sumner County Hospital Dst 1....D....620 845-6492
Caldwell (G-662)
Susan B Allen Memorial Hosp....B....316 322-4510
El Dorado (G-1607)
Swope Health Services....F....816 922-7600
Kansas City (G-4453)
Taylor Mih Womens Clinic....F....620 431-0340
Chanute (G-767)
Thi of Kans At Spclty Hosp LLC....C....913 649-3701
Overland Park (G-9405)
Ukhs Great Bend LLC....E....620 792-8833
Great Bend (G-2650)
United States Dept of Army....B....913 684-6000
Fort Leavenworth (G-1943)
United States Dept of Army....A....785 239-7000
Fort Riley (G-1953)
University of Kansas....C....913 588-5238
Shawnee Mission (G-11967)
University of Kansas....E....913 588-5133
Kansas City (G-4499)
University of Kansas....C....913 588-5000
Kansas City (G-4500)
University of Kansas....C....316 293-2607
Wichita (G-15856)
University of Kansas....C....785 864-2700
Lawrence (G-5163)
University of Kansas Hosp Auth....F....913 588-5000
Kansas City (G-4506)
University of Kansas Hospital....C....913 588-8400
Shawnee Mission (G-11968)
University of Kansas Med Ctr....F....913 588-6311
Kansas City (G-4508)
University of Kansas Med Ctr....F....913 588-6805
Kansas City (G-4509)
Veterans Health Administration....A....785 350-3111
Topeka (G-13222)
Via Christi Health Inc....F....316 268-7000
Wichita (G-15889)
Via Christi Hospital....D....316 796-7000
Wichita (G-15894)
Via Christy St Francis....E....316 613-6511
Wichita (G-15899)
Via Chrsti Rhbltation Hosp Inc....F....316 268-8040
Wichita (G-15902)
Wamego Hospital Association....D....785 456-2295
Wamego (G-13451)
Wesley Medical Center LLC....E....316 858-2610
Wichita (G-15953)
West Central Kansas Assn Inc....C....785 483-3131
Russell (G-10303)
Western Plins Rgional Hosp LLC....B....620 225-8400
Dodge City (G-1456)
Westley Woodlawn Hosp Emrgncy....E....316 962-2000
Wichita (G-15962)
Wichita County Health Center....D....620 375-2233
Leoti (G-6263)
Wichita County Health Center....D....620 375-2233
Leoti (G-6264)
Wilson County Hospital....C....620 325-2611
Neodesha (G-7250)
Woodich John....E....620 332-3280
Independence (G-3574)

8063 Psychiatric Hospitals

High Plains Mental Health Ctr....F....785 625-2400
Hays (G-2847)
Kansas Dept For Aging & Disabi....D....620 285-2131
Larned (G-4706)
Kansas Dept For Aging & Disabi....D....913 755-7000
Osawatomie (G-8195)
Paul W Murphy MD....E....316 686-6303
Wichita (G-15271)
Prairie View Inc....B....316 284-6400
Newton (G-7407)
Prairie View Inc....E....620 947-3200
Hillsboro (G-3055)
Providence Living Center Inc....D....785 233-0588
Topeka (G-12993)
Psychiatric Associates....E....913 438-8221
Shawnee Mission (G-11761)
South Cntl Mntal Hlth Cnsling....E....316 321-6036
El Dorado (G-1604)
Stormont-Vail Healthcare Inc....C....785 270-4600
Topeka (G-13103)
Turner House Clinic Inc....E....913 342-2552
Kansas City (G-4478)

8069 Specialty Hospitals, Except Psychiatric

A Clear Direction Inc....F....316 260-9101
Wichita (G-13586)
Adolescent Adult Fmly Recovery....F....316 943-2051
Wichita (G-13614)
Alcoholics Anonyms Bnnr Sprngs....F....913 441-3277
Bonner Springs (G-539)
Ascension Via Christi Hospital....C....316 634-3400
Wichita (G-13751)
Bills Friends AA Group....F....913 722-9801
Roeland Park (G-10218)
Butler County Health Services....D....316 320-4140
El Dorado (G-1540)
Cancer Center....E....620 235-7900
Pittsburg (G-9828)
Cancer Center of Kansas PA....F....620 399-1224
Wellington (G-13494)
Centennial Healthcare Corp....C....913 829-2273
Olathe (G-7584)
Center For Counseling & Cnsltn....E....620 792-2544
Great Bend (G-2526)
Childrens Hospital Association....E....913 262-1436
Overland Park (G-8547)
Childrens Mercy Hospital....B....913 234-8683
Olathe (G-7593)
Childrens Mercy Hospital....D....913 696-8000
Shawnee Mission (G-11221)
Childrens Mercy Specialty Ctr....D....816 234-3000
Overland Park (G-8549)
Comcare of Sedgwick County....F....316 660-7550
Wichita (G-14060)
Community Mntl Hlth Ctr Crwfd....E....620 724-8806
Girard (G-2397)
Compass Behavioral Health....E....620 227-8566
Dodge City (G-1329)
Cottonwood Springs LLC....F....913 353-3000
Olathe (G-7618)
Counseling Ctr For Butlr Cnty....D....316 776-2007
El Dorado (G-1552)
Cypress Recovery Inc....F....913 764-7555
Olathe (G-7633)
Dccca Inc....E....316 265-6011
Wichita (G-14179)
Encompass Health Corporation....D....913 649-3701
Shawnee Mission (G-11337)
For Central Kansas Foundation....D....785 825-6224
Salina (G-10504)
Four Cnty Mental Hlth Ctr Inc....C....620 251-8180
Coffeyville (G-939)
Guidance Center....E....913 367-1593
Atchison (G-233)
Horizons Mental Health Ctr Inc....F....620 532-3895
Kingman (G-4595)
Kansas Heart Hospital LLC....C....800 574-3278
Wichita (G-14805)
Kansas Rehabilitation Hospital....C....785 235-6600
Topeka (G-12800)
Lee Ann Britian Infant Dev Ctr....E....913 676-2253
Shawnee Mission (G-11556)
Livewell Northwest Kansas Inc....F....785 460-8177
Colby (G-1026)
Mary Elizabeth Maternity Home....F....785 625-6800
Hays (G-2869)
Mercy Kansas Communities Inc....B....620 223-7075
Fort Scott (G-1989)
Meridian Nursing Center Inc....D....316 942-8471
Wichita (G-15041)
Mirror Inc....E....316 283-6743
Newton (G-7389)
New Chance Inc....E....620 225-0476
Dodge City (G-1412)
Parsons State Hosp Trining Ctr....B....620 421-6550
Parsons (G-9722)
Pawnee Mental Health Svcs Inc....E....785 587-4344
Manhattan (G-6770)
Radiation Oncology....E....913 588-3600
Kansas City (G-4358)
Ralph Bharati MD PA....F....316 686-7884
Wichita (G-15413)
Recovery Unlimited Inc....F....316 941-9948
Wichita (G-15428)
Sandpiper Healthcare and....C....316 945-3606
Wichita (G-15517)
South Central Mntl Hlth CN....F....316 775-5491
Augusta (G-346)
Summit Surgical LLC....E....620 663-4800
Hutchinson (G-3455)
Tiyosaye Inc Higher Ground....F....316 262-2060
Wichita (G-15768)
Topeka Hospital LLC....F....785 295-8000
Topeka (G-13177)
Valeo Behavioral Hlth Care Inc....E....785 273-2252
Topeka (G-13216)
Valley Hope Association....E....785 877-2421
Norton (G-7463)
Valley Hope Association....E....913 367-1618
Atchison (G-269)
▲ Via Christi Rehabilitation Ctr....C....316 634-3400
Wichita (G-15896)
Wesley Rehabilitation Hospital....C....316 729-9999
Wichita (G-15954)

SIC

8071 Medical Laboratories

Affiliated Medical Svcs Lab D 316 265-4533
Wichita *(G-13641)*
Ameripath Inc E 816 412-7003
Lenexa *(G-5653)*
Anatomical Pathology Services E 620 421-2424
Parsons *(G-9666)*
Aviation Cnslting Engrg Sltons G 316 265-8335
Maize *(G-6508)*
Biodesix Inc E 913 583-9000
De Soto *(G-1195)*
Boyce Bynum Pathology Labs PC E 816 813-2792
Lenexa *(G-5709)*
Central KS Medical Park PA F 620 793-5404
Great Bend *(G-2533)*
Clinical Reference Lab Inc B 913 492-3652
Lenexa *(G-5765)*
Consultants In Neurology PA E 913 894-1500
Shawnee Mission *(G-11262)*
Cytocheck Laboratory LLC E 620 421-2424
Parsons *(G-9678)*
Diagnostic Imaging Center E 913 491-9299
Shawnee Mission *(G-11305)*
Dodge Cy Unified Schl Dst 443 D 620 227-7771
Dodge City *(G-1355)*
General Electric Company A 785 666-4244
Dorrance *(G-1464)*
Great Plains Laboratory Inc D 913 341-8949
Overland Park *(G-8774)*
Hays Pathology Laboratories PA E 785 650-2700
Hays *(G-2837)*
Heartland Health Labs Inc D 913 599-3636
Lenexa *(G-5897)*
Hutchinson Clinic PA A 620 669-2500
Hutchinson *(G-3319)*
Infectious Disease Cons PA E 316 264-3505
Wichita *(G-14689)*
Johnson County Imaging Ctr PA E 913 469-8998
Overland Park *(G-8878)*
Kansas Dialysis Services LLC D 785 234-2277
Topeka *(G-12774)*
Kansas Pathology Cons PA E 316 681-2741
Wichita *(G-14818)*
Kansas Spine Spcialty Hosp LLC C 316 462-5000
Wichita *(G-14824)*
Kansas State University D 785 532-5650
Manhattan *(G-6688)*
Ksu Dprtment of Clncal Science D 785 532-5690
Manhattan *(G-6703)*
Kupi Rprdctive Endcrnology Lab E 913 588-6377
Kansas City *(G-4184)*
▲ Labone Inc A 913 888-1770
Lenexa *(G-5961)*
Laboratory Corporation America E 785 539-2537
Manhattan *(G-6707)*
Laboratory Corporation America B 913 338-4070
Overland Park *(G-8938)*
Laboratory Corporation America C 316 636-2300
Wichita *(G-14910)*
Mercy Kansas Communities Inc F 620 332-3215
Independence *(G-3538)*
Mid America Pathology Lab LLC E 913 341-6275
Overland Park *(G-9022)*
Mid Star Lab Inc F 913 369-8734
Tonganoxie *(G-12268)*
New York Blood Center Inc E 785 233-0195
Topeka *(G-12926)*
Palmer Webber Macy E 785 823-7201
Salina *(G-10631)*
Peterson Laboratory Svcs PA D 785 539-5363
Manhattan *(G-6774)*
PH Enterprises Inc F 620 232-1900
Pittsburg *(G-9913)*
Pipeline Tstg Consortium Inc E 620 669-8800
Hutchinson *(G-3406)*
Progene Biomedical Inc F 913 492-2224
Lenexa *(G-6074)*
Quest Diagnostics Incorporated F 785 621-4300
Hays *(G-2894)*
Quest Diagnostics Incorporated F 913 768-1959
Olathe *(G-8015)*
Quest Diagnostics Incorporated F 913 299-8538
Kansas City *(G-4353)*
Quest Diagnostics Incorporated F 913 982-2900
Shawnee Mission *(G-11767)*
Quest Diagnostics Incorporated F 316 634-1946
Wichita *(G-15391)*
Riordan Clinic Inc E 316 682-3100
Wichita *(G-15464)*
Salina Regional Health Ctr Inc D 785 823-1032
Salina *(G-10685)*
Somnitech Inc E 913 498-8120
Overland Park *(G-9327)*
Somnograph Inc D 316 925-4624
Wichita *(G-15612)*
South Central Pathology Lab PA F 316 689-5668
Wichita *(G-15618)*
Synexis LLC F 816 399-0895
Overland Park *(G-9388)*
Ultrasound For Women LLC E 785 331-4160
Lawrence *(G-5149)*
Weber Palmer & Macy Chartered E 785 823-7201
Salina *(G-10763)*

8072 Dental Laboratories

Dental Concepts Inc F 913 829-0242
Olathe *(G-7648)*
Dentek Inc E 913 262-1717
Lenexa *(G-5812)*
Eurodent Dental Lab Inc F 913 685-9930
Shawnee Mission *(G-11347)*
Ful Tech Dental Lab Inc F 316 681-3546
Wichita *(G-14430)*
Interdent Inc E 913 248-8880
Lenexa *(G-5918)*
Jade Dental Lab Inc E 913 469-9500
Shawnee Mission *(G-11481)*
Kaylor Dental Laboratory Inc D 316 943-3226
Wichita *(G-14835)*
Legends Drive Dental Ctr LLC F 785 841-5590
Lawrence *(G-4992)*
Medallion Dental Lab Inc F 913 642-0039
Prairie Village *(G-10047)*
Modern Methods F 316 686-6391
Wichita *(G-15120)*
Myrons Dental Laboratories E 800 359-7111
Kansas City *(G-4276)*
Root Laboratory Inc C 913 491-3555
Leawood *(G-5543)*
Sentage Corporation D 785 235-9293
Topeka *(G-13059)*
Sentage Corporation E 316 263-0284
Wichita *(G-15561)*
Sokolov Dental Laboratory Inc E 913 262-5444
Shawnee Mission *(G-11879)*
Steve Hnsens Prcision Dntl Lab E 913 432-6951
Shawnee Mission *(G-11898)*
Sunflower Dental Studio Inc F 785 354-1981
Topeka *(G-13118)*

8082 Home Health Care Svcs

Aberdeen Village Inc E 913 599-6100
Olathe *(G-7507)*
Absolute Home Health Care E 316 832-1347
Wichita *(G-13600)*
Accessible Home Care F 785 493-0340
Salina *(G-10390)*
Adult Health Services Inc C 913 788-9896
Kansas City *(G-3786)*
Advanced Homecare MGT Inc E 620 662-9238
Hutchinson *(G-3193)*
Advantaged Home Care E 785 267-4433
Topeka *(G-12298)*
Advocate Home Specialty Care D 785 456-8910
Wamego *(G-13402)*
Advoctes For Bhavioral Hlth PA F 316 630-8444
Wichita *(G-13632)*
Alegria Living & Healthcare D 785 665-7124
Overbrook *(G-8322)*
All Saints Home Care Inc F 316 755-1076
Wichita *(G-13665)*
Alternacare Infusion Phrm Inc F 913 906-9260
Olathe *(G-7522)*
Angel Arms F 620 241-1074
McPherson *(G-6936)*
Angels At Home Care F 785 271-4376
Topeka *(G-12328)*
Angels Care Home Health F 316 636-4000
Wichita *(G-13710)*
Another Day Homecare Inc F 913 599-2221
Lenexa *(G-5655)*
Apria Healthcare LLC E 316 283-1936
Newton *(G-7310)*
APS Staffing Services Inc F 913 327-7605
Overland Park *(G-8391)*
Arbuthnots Inc E 785 527-2146
Belleville *(G-450)*
Archdiocese Kansas Cy In Kans E 913 621-5090
Kansas City *(G-3816)*
Arj Infusion Services Inc E 913 451-8804
Lenexa *(G-5661)*
Ascend Mdia Med Healthcare LLC F 913 469-1110
Overland Park *(G-8399)*
Ascension Via Christi F 620 231-3088
Pittsburg *(G-9812)*
Assisted Transportation Svcs F 785 291-2900
Topeka *(G-12342)*
Associated Homecare Inc C 316 320-0473
El Dorado *(G-1529)*
At Home Assisted Care E 785 473-7007
Wamego *(G-13403)*
At Home Assisted Care Inc F 785 473-7007
Manhattan *(G-6550)*
At Home Support Care Inc E 620 341-9350
Emporia *(G-1696)*
Axelacare Holdings Inc C 877 342-9352
Lenexa *(G-5678)*
Barber County Home Health Agcy F 620 886-3775
Medicine Lodge *(G-7057)*
Brookdale Snior Lving Cmmnties F 785 263-7800
Abilene *(G-18)*
C&L Management LLC E 913 851-4800
Overland Park *(G-8504)*
Caldwell Communicare D 620 845-6492
Caldwell *(G-656)*
Care 4 U Inc E 620 223-1411
Girard *(G-2395)*
Carecentrix Inc D 913 749-5600
Overland Park *(G-8515)*
Caregivers of KS Inc F 785 354-0767
Topeka *(G-12447)*
Carestaf Inc B 913 498-2888
Overland Park *(G-8516)*
Caring Compassionate Care LLC F 785 215-8127
Topeka *(G-12450)*
Carondelet Home Care Services E 913 529-4800
Shawnee *(G-10924)*
Childrens Mercy Home Care E 913 696-8999
Kansas City *(G-3910)*
Childrens Mercy Hospital D 913 696-8000
Shawnee Mission *(G-11221)*
Choicecare LLC D 913 906-9880
Lenexa *(G-5754)*
Coffey County Hospital E 620 364-8861
Burlington *(G-629)*
Comforcare Senior Services E 913 906-9880
Lenexa *(G-5771)*
Comfort Keepers E 785 215-8330
Topeka *(G-12488)*
Community Healthcare Sys Inc C 785 889-4274
Onaga *(G-8173)*
Community Works Inc C 913 789-9900
Shawnee Mission *(G-11254)*
Compassionate Care Community E 785 783-8785
Topeka *(G-12495)*
Complete Home Health Care Inc F 316 260-5012
Wichita *(G-14080)*
Continua Home Health LLC F 913 905-0255
Leawood *(G-5359)*
County of Clay E 785 632-3193
Clay Center *(G-859)*
County of Kiowa D 620 723-3341
Greensburg *(G-2674)*
County of Saline F 785 826-6606
Salina *(G-10465)*
County of Sumner E 316 262-2686
Wellington *(G-13496)*
Craig Homecare E 785 798-4821
Ness City *(G-7258)*
Craig Resources Inc E 316 264-9988
Wichita *(G-14125)*
Diversified Family Svcs LLC D 316 269-3368
Wichita *(G-14215)*
Dodge Cy Healthcare Group LLC F 620 225-8401
Dodge City *(G-1353)*
Enhanced Home Care LLC F 913 327-0000
Overland Park *(G-8682)*
Frax F 888 987-3729
Wichita *(G-14414)*
Garden Vly Retirement Vlg LLC C 620 275-9651
Garden City *(G-2184)*
Genoa Healthcare Kansas LLC F 785 783-0209
Topeka *(G-12634)*
Gentiva Health Services Inc A 913 814-2800
Overland Park *(G-8753)*
Gentiva Health Services Inc E 913 906-0522
Overland Park *(G-8754)*
Golden Livingcenter Wellington F 620 326-7437
Wellington *(G-13506)*

Great Plains Ellinwood Inc........E....... 620 564-2548
Ellinwood (G-1634)
Hand In Hand & Hospice........F....... 620 340-6177
Emporia (G-1766)
Hands 2 Help........D....... 785 832-2515
Lawrence (G-4887)
Harris Healthcare LLC........F....... 316 721-4828
Wichita (G-14564)
Health In Sync Home Inc........E....... 316 295-4692
Wichita (G-14576)
Health Management of Kansas........D....... 620 431-7474
Chanute (G-731)
Health Management of Kansas........D....... 620 251-1866
Coffeyville (G-944)
Health Management of Kansas........D....... 620 429-3803
Columbus (G-1078)
Healthback of Wichita........F....... 316 687-0340
Wichita (G-14577)
Heartland HM Hlth & Hospice PA........D....... 316 788-7626
Wichita (G-14584)
Heartland Hospice Services LLC........F....... 913 362-0044
Leawood (G-5425)
Heartland Hospice Services LLC........E....... 785 271-6500
Topeka (G-12679)
Home Health Agency Hosp Dst........F....... 620 724-8469
Girard (G-2412)
Home Health of Kansas LLC........E....... 316 684-5122
Wichita (G-14630)
Home Instead Senior Care........E....... 316 612-7541
Wichita (G-14631)
Home Instead Senior Care........E....... 785 272-6101
Topeka (G-12702)
Hospice Incorporated........D....... 316 265-9441
Wichita (G-14637)
Hospice of Graham County........C....... 785 421-2121
Hill City (G-3035)
Hospice of Reno County Inc........E....... 620 665-2473
Hutchinson (G-3314)
Hospice Preferred Choice Inc........E....... 785 840-0820
Lawrence (G-4903)
Hospital District 1 of Dcknsn........F....... 785 263-6630
Abilene (G-39)
Independence Inc........E....... 785 841-0333
Lawrence (G-4910)
Individual Support Systems Inc........D....... 785 228-9443
Topeka (G-12720)
Infusion LLC........F....... 316 686-1610
Wichita (G-14693)
Inspire Hospice LLC........F....... 913 521-2727
Overland Park (G-8854)
Integral Care Provider Inc........C....... 913 384-2273
Shawnee Mission (G-11463)
Integrated Behavioral Tech Inc........E....... 913 662-7071
Basehor (G-380)
Integrated Behavioral Tech Inc........D....... 913 662-7071
Basehor (G-379)
Integrity Home Care Inc........F....... 913 685-1616
Overland Park (G-8855)
Interim Healthcare Kansas City........E....... 913 381-3100
Leawood (G-5439)
Jills Helping Hands Inc........D....... 785 622-4254
Lenora (G-6244)
John Knox Village........F....... 913 403-8343
Leawood (G-5443)
Kansas Masonic Home........C....... 316 269-7500
Wichita (G-14814)
Kindred Healthcare Oper LLC........E....... 913 906-0522
Overland Park (G-8919)
Kuderx LLC........F....... 785 760-2298
Concordia (G-1121)
Lenere LLC........F....... 785 320-0208
Saint Marys (G-10371)
Lifespace Communities Inc........C....... 913 383-2085
Shawnee Mission (G-11570)
Locamp LLC........F....... 913 287-4400
Kansas City (G-4206)
Marlene Schoenberger........E....... 785 625-8189
Ellis (G-1650)
Maxim Healthcare Services Inc........C....... 913 381-8233
Overland Park (G-8997)
Medicalodges Inc........C....... 620 223-5085
Fort Scott (G-1984)
Mercy Home Health........F....... 620 223-8090
Fort Scott (G-1988)
MHS Home Health LLC........E....... 913 663-9930
Overland Park (G-9019)
Midland Care........F....... 785 232-2044
Topeka (G-12891)
Midland Care Connection Inc........C....... 785 232-2044
Topeka (G-12892)
Minds Matter LLC........F....... 866 429-6757
Overland Park (G-9040)
Missouri Hospice Holdings LLC........F....... 913 905-0255
Leawood (G-5487)
Moore Enterprises Inc........C....... 913 451-5900
Overland Park (G-9052)
Muve Health LLC........F....... 303 862-9215
Leawood (G-5493)
Newman Mem Hosp Foundation........E....... 620 340-6161
Emporia (G-1805)
Newton William Memorial Hosp........F....... 620 221-2916
Winfield (G-16162)
North Centl Kans Hm Hlth Agcy........F....... 785 738-5175
Beloit (G-496)
Norton County Hospital........F....... 785 877-5745
Norton (G-7459)
Olathe Medical Center Inc........E....... 913 791-4200
Olathe (G-7940)
Olathe Medical Center Inc........E....... 913 791-4315
Olathe (G-7941)
Option Care Enterprises Inc........E....... 913 599-3745
Overland Park (G-9109)
Peace of Mind........F....... 316 260-7046
Rose Hill (G-10244)
Pharmcare Hlth Specialists LLC........F....... 316 681-2181
Wichita (G-15290)
Preferred Registry of Nurses........F....... 785 456-8628
Wamego (G-13435)
Prestige Home Care of Kansas........F....... 913 680-0493
Leavenworth (G-5279)
Proactive Home Care Inc........D....... 316 688-5511
Wichita (G-15355)
Professional Home Health Svcs........F....... 785 625-0055
Hays (G-2891)
Professional Orthc & Prosthtc........E....... 785 375-7458
Manhattan (G-6782)
Progressive Care Prof Hm Care........E....... 785 984-2290
Alton (G-74)
Progressive Home Health Care........E....... 316 691-5050
Wichita (G-15371)
RES-Care Inc........E....... 913 281-1161
Kansas City (G-4371)
RES-Care Inc........E....... 620 421-2454
Parsons (G-9731)
RES-Care Inc........E....... 620 793-8501
Great Bend (G-2630)
RES-Care Inc........E....... 620 271-0176
Garden City (G-2267)
RES-Care Inc........E....... 785 899-2322
Goodland (G-2482)
RES-Care Inc........E....... 620 624-5117
Liberal (G-6360)
RES-Care Inc........E....... 316 283-5170
Newton (G-7410)
RES-Care Inc........C....... 620 221-4112
Winfield (G-16168)
Rescare Kansas Wichita........F....... 316 651-2585
Wichita (G-15446)
Rooney Enterprises Corporation........E....... 913 325-4770
Overland Park (G-9257)
Sacred Heart Home Care........F....... 913 299-4515
Kansas City (G-4395)
Saint Raphael Home Care Inc........E....... 316 269-5400
Wichita (G-15509)
Salina Regional Health Ctr Inc........B....... 785 452-7000
Salina (G-10688)
Sisters Servants of Mary........E....... 913 371-3423
Kansas City (G-4423)
Sleepcair Inc........E....... 913 438-8200
Lenexa (G-6138)
Sonodora Inc........E....... 316 494-2218
Wichita (G-15615)
Southeast KS AR AG Aging........D....... 620 431-2980
Chanute (G-765)
Southern Care Inc........E....... 913 906-9497
Topeka (G-13081)
Southview Homecare........F....... 913 837-5121
Louisburg (G-6467)
Southwind Hospice Inc........F....... 620 672-7553
Pratt (G-10152)
Spectrum Health Foundation Inc........D....... 913 831-2979
Kansas City (G-4433)
Spectrum Private Care Services........D....... 913 299-7100
Shawnee (G-11032)
St Catherine Hospital........F....... 620 272-2660
Garden City (G-2287)
Sunshine Horizons........F....... 620 276-1787
Garden City (G-2294)
Sunshine Nursing Agency Inc........E....... 620 276-8868
Garden City (G-2295)
Teakwood Investments LLC........D....... 913 203-7444
Overland Park (G-9395)
There Is No Place Like Home........F....... 316 721-6001
Wichita (G-15758)
Thoughtful Care Inc........F....... 816 256-8200
Prairie Village (G-10075)
Trinity In-Home Care Inc........C....... 785 842-3159
Lawrence (G-5146)
True Home Care LLC........E....... 316 776-4685
Wichita (G-15808)
Via Chrsti HM Hlth Wichita Inc........D....... 316 268-8588
Wichita (G-15900)
Vintage Park At Tonganoxie LLC........E....... 913 845-2204
Tonganoxie (G-12272)
Visiting Nurses Association........D....... 785 843-3738
Lawrence (G-5175)
Vitalcore Hlth Strategies LLC........F....... 785 246-6840
Topeka (G-13227)
Vitas Healthcare Corp Midwest........E....... 913 722-1631
Overland Park (G-9468)
Vitas Healthcare Corporation........E....... 913 722-1631
Lenexa (G-6216)

8092 Kidney Dialysis Centers

Bio-Mdcal Applcations Kans Inc........F....... 913 498-1780
Overland Park (G-8449)
Bio-Mdcal Applcations Kans Inc........E....... 785 823-6460
Salina (G-10424)
Bladon Dialysis LLC........E....... 620 728-0440
Hutchinson (G-3216)
Davita Healthcare Partners Inc........E....... 316 773-1400
Maize (G-6512)
Davita Inc........E....... 620 331-6117
Independence (G-3511)
Davita Inc........E....... 913 660-8881
Lenexa (G-5805)
Fms Midwest Dialysis Ctrs LLC........F....... 316 634-6760
Wichita (G-14396)
Fms Midwest Dialysis Ctrs LLC........F....... 620 431-1239
Chanute (G-728)
Fms Midwest Dialysis Ctrs LLC........F....... 316 729-5321
Wichita (G-14397)
Fresenius Med Care W Wllow LLC........F....... 785 625-0033
Hays (G-2813)
Kenai Dialysis LLC........E....... 913 649-2671
Overland Park (G-8914)
Nra-Ukmc Kansas LLC........F....... 913 299-1044
Kansas City (G-4290)
Renal Trtmnt Centers-West Inc........F....... 316 788-2899
Derby (G-1268)
Renal Trtmnt Centers-West Inc........F....... 620 421-1081
Parsons (G-9730)
Renal Trtmnt Centers-West Inc........F....... 316 263-9090
Wichita (G-15443)
Renal Trtmnt Centers-West Inc........F....... 316 636-5719
Wichita (G-15444)
Renal Trtmnt Centers-West Inc........F....... 620 331-6117
Independence (G-3554)
Renal Trtmnt Centers-West Inc........E....... 316 684-3200
Wichita (G-15445)
Renal Trtmnt Centers-West Inc........F....... 620 260-9852
Garden City (G-2266)
Salina County Medical Supply........F....... 785 823-6416
Salina (G-10670)
Total Renal Care Inc........E....... 785 235-1094
Topeka (G-13194)
Total Renal Care Inc........E....... 785 841-0490
Lawrence (G-5143)
Total Renal Care Inc........E....... 620 340-8043
Emporia (G-1839)
Total Renal Care Inc........E....... 785 273-1824
Topeka (G-13195)
Total Renal Care Inc........F....... 785 843-2000
Lawrence (G-5144)
Total Renal Care Inc........E....... 913 287-5724
Kansas City (G-4470)
Windcreek Dialysis LLC........E....... 913 294-8417
Paola (G-9596)
Wyandotte Central Dialysis LLC........F....... 913 233-0536
Kansas City (G-4552)

8093 Specialty Outpatient Facilities, NEC

Adolescent Adult Fmly Recovery........F....... 316 943-2051
Wichita (G-13614)
Advantage Medical Group........F....... 785 749-0130
Lawrence (G-4722)
Ascension Via Christi........E....... 620 232-0178
Pittsburg (G-9814)
Bert Nash Cmnty Mntal Hlth Ctr........C....... 785 843-9192
Lawrence (G-4755)

SIC

Big Lkes Developmental Ctr Inc............E....... 785 632-5357
Clay Center (G-843)
Birthright Inc............E....... 913 682-2700
Leavenworth (G-5211)
Breakthrough CLB Sedgwick Cnty............E....... 316 269-2534
Wichita (G-13886)
Brown Cnty Developmental Svcs............E....... 785 742-2053
Hiawatha (G-3004)
Center For Counseling & Cnsltn............E....... 620 792-2544
Great Bend (G-2526)
Center For Rprductive Medicine............E....... 316 687-2112
Wichita (G-13972)
Central Kansas Mental Hlth Ctr............D....... 785 823-6322
Salina (G-10441)
Childrens Therapy Group............F....... 913 383-9014
Mission (G-7129)
Comcare of Sedgwick County............E....... 316 660-1900
Wichita (G-14059)
Comcare of Sedgwick County............B....... 316 660-7600
Wichita (G-14061)
Community Mntl Hlth Ctr Crwfd............E....... 620 724-8806
Girard (G-2397)
Compass Behavioral Health............D....... 620 275-0625
Garden City (G-2132)
Compass Behavioral Health............F....... 620 872-5338
Scott City (G-10808)
Compass Behavioral Health............E....... 620 227-5040
Dodge City (G-1328)
Compass Behavioral Health............E....... 620 227-8566
Dodge City (G-1329)
County of Crawford............E....... 620 231-5130
Pittsburg (G-9848)
County of Crawford............C....... 620 231-5141
Pittsburg (G-9849)
Cowley County Joint Board Hlth............F....... 620 442-3260
Arkansas City (G-151)
Critical Care Systems Intl Inc............E....... 913 789-5560
Shawnee Mission (G-11281)
Dccca Inc............F....... 620 670-2803
Pittsburg (G-9851)
Dccca Inc............F....... 620 672-7546
Pratt (G-10107)
Dccca Inc............F....... 620 670-2814
Winfield (G-16140)
Dccca Inc............F....... 785 830-8238
Lawrence (G-4828)
Dccca Inc............E....... 785 843-9262
Lawrence (G-4829)
Dccca Inc............E....... 316 265-6011
Wichita (G-14179)
Developmental Svcs NW Kans Inc............F....... 785 877-5154
Norton (G-7443)
Developmental Svcs NW Kans Inc............F....... 785 483-6686
Russell (G-10271)
Douglass Medicalodges............E....... 316 747-2157
Douglass (G-1466)
Elizabeth Layton Center Inc............D....... 785 242-3780
Ottawa (G-8270)
Elm Acres Youth & Family Svcs............C....... 620 231-9840
Pittsburg (G-9855)
Family Svc Gdnce Ctr Tpeka Inc............C....... 785 232-5005
Topeka (G-12593)
For Wyandot Center............C....... 913 328-4600
Kansas City (G-4017)
For Wyandot Center............D....... 913 362-0393
Kansas City (G-4016)
Four Cnty Mental Hlth Ctr Inc............C....... 620 331-1748
Independence (G-3520)
Four Cnty Mental Hlth Ctr Inc............F....... 620 325-2141
Neodesha (G-7242)
Four Cnty Mental Hlth Ctr Inc............F....... 620 331-0057
Independence (G-3521)
Four Cnty Mental Hlth Ctr Inc............C....... 620 251-8180
Coffeyville (G-939)
Freeman Srgcl Ctr Pttsbrg LLC............F....... 620 231-9072
Pittsburg (G-9864)
Guidance Center............E....... 913 367-1593
Atchison (G-233)
Heart America Surgery Ctr LLC............E....... 913 334-8935
Kansas City (G-4074)
Heartland Reg Alchl & Drug............E....... 913 789-0951
Roeland Park (G-10224)
Heartland Surgical Care............F....... 913 647-3999
Overland Park (G-8808)
Heartspring Inc............B....... 316 634-8700
Wichita (G-14590)
High Plains Mental Health Ctr............C....... 785 628-2871
Hays (G-2846)
High Plains Mental Health Ctr............F....... 785 543-5284
Phillipsburg (G-9788)
Horizons Mental Health Ctr Inc............F....... 620 532-3895
Kingman (G-4595)
Horizons Mental Health Ctr Inc............C....... 620 663-7595
Hutchinson (G-3312)
Infectious Disease Cons PA............E....... 316 264-3505
Wichita (G-14689)
Integrated Behavioral Tech Inc............D....... 913 662-7071
Basehor (G-379)
Integrated Behavioral Tech Inc............E....... 913 662-7071
Basehor (G-380)
Iroquois Ctr For Humn Dev Inc............E....... 620 723-2272
Greensburg (G-2680)
Kansas City Ctr For Anxty Trmt............F....... 913 649-8820
Overland Park (G-8893)
Kansas Dept For Chldren Fmlies............C....... 913 755-7000
Osawatomie (G-8196)
Kaw Valley Center............F....... 913 334-0294
Kansas City (G-4159)
Key Rehabilitation Inc............F....... 620 231-3887
Pittsburg (G-9892)
Kings Alcohol & Drug............E....... 620 221-6252
Winfield (G-16152)
Kvc Health Systems Inc............D....... 913 621-5753
Kansas City (G-4186)
Kvc Hospitals Inc............E....... 913 322-4900
Olathe (G-7846)
Labette Center For Mental Inc............F....... 620 421-9402
Parsons (G-9702)
Labette Ctr For Mntal Hlth Svc............D....... 620 421-3770
Parsons (G-9704)
Lawrenc-Douglas Cnty Hlth Dept............E....... 785 843-3060
Lawrence (G-4957)
McPherson Family Clinic............E....... 785 861-8800
McPherson (G-6998)
Medi-Weightloss Clinics LLC............E....... 316 733-8505
Andover (G-104)
Medical Center P A............E....... 620 669-9657
Hutchinson (G-3369)
Mental Health Association............E....... 913 281-2221
Kansas City (G-4234)
Mental Hlth Ctr of Est-Cntral............E....... 620 343-2211
Emporia (G-1794)
Midamerica Rehabilitation Ctr............F....... 913 491-2432
Shawnee Mission (G-11629)
Midwest Health Services Inc............E....... 316 835-4810
Halstead (G-2703)
Mirror Inc............F....... 316 634-3954
Wichita (G-15117)
Mirror Inc............F....... 620 326-8822
Wellington (G-13518)
Mirror Inc............F....... 316 283-7829
Newton (G-7388)
Mirror Inc............E....... 316 283-6743
Newton (G-7389)
Mosaic............D....... 620 624-3817
Liberal (G-6345)
New Chance Inc............E....... 620 225-0476
Dodge City (G-1412)
Occupational Hlth Partners LLC............E....... 785 823-8381
Salina (G-10618)
P A Comcare............E....... 785 827-6453
Salina (G-10628)
P A Therapyworks Inc............E....... 785 749-1300
Lawrence (G-5053)
Pawnee Mental Health Svcs Inc............C....... 785 762-5250
Manhattan (G-6769)
Pawnee Mental Health Svcs Inc............E....... 785 762-5250
Junction City (G-3735)
Pawnee Mental Health Svcs Inc............E....... 785 587-4344
Manhattan (G-6770)
Performance Rehab LLC............E....... 913 681-9909
Overland Park (G-9155)
Physical Rsprtory Therapy Svcs............F....... 785 742-2131
Hiawatha (G-3021)
Pinkerton Pain Therapy LLC............F....... 417 649-6406
Olathe (G-7987)
Pipeline Tstg Consortium Inc............E....... 620 669-8800
Hutchinson (G-3406)
Planned Parenthood of Kansas............E....... 316 263-7575
Wichita (G-15305)
Planned Prenthood Great Plains............E....... 913 312-5100
Overland Park (G-9171)
Prairie View Inc............F....... 620 245-5000
McPherson (G-7018)
Prairie View Inc............B....... 316 284-6400
Newton (G-7407)
Professional Renewal Center PA............F....... 785 842-9772
Lawrence (G-5079)
Renew............F....... 913 768-6606
Olathe (G-8026)
Rural Hlth Rsurces Jackson Inc............C....... 785 364-2116
Holton (G-3110)
Rural Hlth Rsurces Jackson Inc............F....... 785 364-2126
Holton (G-3111)
Saint Francis Acdmy Inc Atchsn............E....... 913 367-5005
Atchison (G-259)
Saint Lukes Primary Care At............D....... 913 317-7990
Overland Park (G-9274)
Salina Physical Therapy Clinic............F....... 785 825-1361
Salina (G-10682)
Salina Regional Health Ctr Inc............B....... 785 452-7000
Salina (G-10688)
Select Medical Corporation............F....... 316 261-8303
Wichita (G-15553)
Select Medical Corporation............F....... 316 687-9227
Wichita (G-15554)
Shawnee Gardens Health............C....... 913 631-2146
Shawnee (G-11027)
Shorman & Associates Inc............E....... 913 341-8811
Shawnee Mission (G-11866)
South Cntl Mntal Hlth Cnsling............E....... 316 321-6036
El Dorado (G-1604)
Southeast Kans Mental Hlth Ctr............D....... 620 473-2241
Humboldt (G-3188)
Southeast Kans Mental Hlth Ctr............F....... 913 352-8214
Pleasanton (G-10002)
Southeast Kans Mental Hlth Ctr............E....... 620 223-5030
Fort Scott (G-2006)
Southeast Kans Mental Hlth Ctr............F....... 785 448-6806
Garnett (G-2389)
Southeast Kans Mental Hlth Ctr............F....... 620 431-7890
Chanute (G-764)
Southeast Kans Mental Hlth Ctr............E....... 620 365-5717
Iola (G-3633)
Spring Rver Mntal Hlth Wllness............D....... 620 848-2300
Riverton (G-10213)
Starkey Inc............C....... 316 942-4221
Wichita (G-15657)
Stormont-Vail Healthcare Inc............C....... 785 270-4600
Topeka (G-13103)
Summitt Rest Care LLC............F....... 620 624-5117
Liberal (G-6373)
Surgicare of Wichita Inc............D....... 316 685-2207
Wichita (G-15702)
Unxmed-Immediate Medical Care............F....... 316 440-2565
Wichita (G-15860)
Valeo Behavioral Health Care............E....... 785 233-1730
Topeka (G-13215)
Valeo Behavioral Hlth Care Inc............E....... 785 273-2252
Topeka (G-13216)
Valley Hope Association............E....... 785 877-5101
Norton (G-7464)
Valley Hope Association............E....... 913 367-1618
Atchison (G-269)
Valley Hope Association............E....... 785 877-2421
Norton (G-7463)
Veridian Behavorial Health............E....... 785 452-4930
Salina (G-10750)
Via Christi Vlg Manhattan Inc............C....... 785 539-7671
Manhattan (G-6842)
Via Chrsti Rehabilitation Hosp............E....... 316 268-5000
Wichita (G-15901)
Vigilias LLC............E....... 800 924-8140
Wichita (G-15907)
Wyandot Center For Community B............E....... 913 233-3300
Kansas City (G-4550)
Wyandot Inc............F....... 913 233-3300
Kansas City (G-4551)

8099 Health & Allied Svcs, NEC

Animal Care Center of Top............F....... 785 232-2205
Topeka (G-12329)
Assured Occupational Solutions............F....... 316 321-3313
El Dorado (G-1530)
Biomat Usa Inc............F....... 785 233-0079
Topeka (G-12384)
Center For Woman Hlth Wichita............F....... 316 634-0060
Wichita (G-13974)
Central Care PA............E....... 620 272-2579
Garden City (G-2123)
Central State Services............F....... 316 613-3989
Wichita (G-13986)
Childrens Hospital Association............E....... 913 262-1436
Overland Park (G-8547)
Coliseum Imging Ventures I LLC............F....... 913 338-3344
Overland Park (G-8576)
Community Memorial Healthcare............E....... 785 562-4062
Marysville (G-6883)
Compass Behavioral Health............E....... 620 227-5040
Dodge City (G-1328)

County of Geary ... E ... 785 762-5788
Junction City (G-3684)
Csl Plasma Inc ... D ... 316 264-6973
Wichita (G-14137)
Csl Plasma Inc ... E ... 785 749-5750
Lawrence (G-4819)
Csl Plasma Inc ... F ... 785 776-9177
Manhattan (G-6607)
Ctr Imprvmnt Hmn Fnctnng Int ... E ... 316 682-3100
Wichita (G-14140)
Defy Medical Group LLC ... F ... 913 396-2888
Overland Park (G-8647)
Ellsworth County Ambulance ... E ... 785 472-3454
Ellsworth (G-1668)
Emergency Medical Care ... F ... 913 791-4357
Olathe (G-7679)
Examinetics Inc ... C ... 913 748-2000
Overland Park (G-8698)
Examone World Wide Inc ... E ... 913 888-1770
Lenexa (G-5840)
Finney County Community Hlth ... F ... 620 765-1185
Garden City (G-2162)
Forum Health Care ... C ... 913 648-4980
Shawnee Mission (G-11377)
Fresenius Med Care W Wllow LLC ... F ... 913 491-6341
Overland Park (G-8741)
Galichia Medical Group PA ... E ... 316 684-3838
Wichita (G-14438)
Greensburg Family Practice PA ... F ... 620 723-2127
Greensburg (G-2677)
Health Care Stabilization Fund ... F ... 785 291-3777
Topeka (G-12671)
Health Partnership Clinic Inc ... E ... 913 433-7583
Olathe (G-7760)
Home Health Agency ... F ... 785 826-6600
Salina (G-10546)
Hooper Holmes Inc ... D ... 913 764-1045
Olathe (G-7777)
Hope Planting Intl Inc ... F ... 785 776-8523
Manhattan (G-6659)
Hospital Dst 1 of Rice Cnty ... F ... 620 278-2123
Sterling (G-12121)
Hutchinson Care Center LLC ... D ... 620 662-0597
Hutchinson (G-3318)
Icare Usa Inc ... F ... 919 624-9095
Kansas City (G-4094)
Johnson Cnty Dept Hlth & Envmt ... D ... 913 826-1200
Olathe (G-7813)
Johnson County Med-Act ... F ... 913 715-1950
Olathe (G-7818)
Kansas City Cancer Center LLC ... F ... 913 788-8883
Kansas City (G-4143)
Kansas Medical Assoc Inc ... F ... 316 733-4747
Andover (G-97)
Kdhe Ber Attn R Avila ... E ... 785 291-3121
Topeka (G-12814)
Kearney Regional Med Ctr LLC ... E ... 316 682-6770
Wichita (G-14840)
Maple Hills Healthcare Inc ... E ... 913 383-2001
Overland Park (G-8985)
Marc A Asher Md Comprehensi ... E ... 913 945-9800
Overland Park (G-8986)
Medical Center P A ... D ... 620 669-6690
Hutchinson (G-3368)
Medical Center P A ... E ... 620 669-9657
Hutchinson (G-3369)
Miami County Medical Center ... F ... 913 791-4940
Olathe (G-7889)
Midwest Transplant Network Inc ... D ... 913 262-1668
Shawnee Mission (G-11637)
Ncs Healthcare of Kansas LLC ... E ... 316 522-3449
Wichita (G-15156)
New York Blood Center Inc ... E ... 785 233-0195
Topeka (G-12926)
Preferred Fmly Healthcare Inc ... F ... 620 221-6252
Winfield (G-16167)
Preferred Medical Associates ... F ... 316 268-8080
Wichita (G-15327)
Quality Health Care Inc ... F ... 316 263-8880
Fredonia (G-2041)
Ransom Memorial Hospital Chari ... B ... 785 229-8200
Ottawa (G-8309)
Rolling Hills Health and Rehab ... C ... 316 722-6916
Wichita (G-15480)
Salina Hlth Educatn Foundation ... D ... 785 825-7251
Salina (G-10674)
Sandhill Orthopaedic ... F ... 620 624-7400
Liberal (G-6362)
Tanglewood Hlth Rehabilitation ... E ... 785 273-0886
Topeka (G-13139)
Tria Health LLC ... E ... 888 799-8742
Overland Park (G-9427)
Trumpet Behavioral Health LLC ... F ... 816 802-6969
Overland Park (G-9434)
U S X-Ray LLC ... F ... 913 652-0550
Lenexa (G-6199)
Via Christi ... F ... 316 613-4931
Wichita (G-15879)
Wolters Kluwer Health Inc ... F ... 316 612-5000
Wichita (G-16062)

81 LEGAL SERVICES

8111 Legal Svcs

Adam & McDonald PA ... F ... 913 647-0670
Shawnee Mission (G-11074)
Adams Brown Bran Ball Chrtered ... F ... 620 549-3271
Great Bend (G-2500)
Adams Brown Bran Ball Chrtered ... F ... 620 241-2090
McPherson (G-6931)
Adams Jones Law Firm PA ... F ... 316 265-8591
Wichita (G-13613)
Administration Kansas Dept ... F ... 785 296-3017
Topeka (G-12291)
Adrian & Pankratz PA ... F ... 316 283-8746
Newton (G-7306)
Alderson Alderson Weiler Co ... E ... 785 232-0753
Topeka (G-12303)
Arthur Green LLP ... F ... 785 537-1345
Manhattan (G-6546)
Ausemus Stnley R Esq Chartered ... F ... 620 342-8717
Emporia (G-1697)
Bangerter Rebein PA ... F ... 620 227-8126
Dodge City (G-1301)
Barber Financial Group Inc ... F ... 913 393-1000
Lenexa (G-5686)
Barbera & Watkins LLC ... F ... 913 677-3800
Overland Park (G-8432)
Beam-Ward Kruse Wilson ... F ... 913 339-6888
Overland Park (G-8436)
Beam-Ward Kruse Wilson Wright ... F ... 785 865-1558
Lawrence (G-4752)
Berman & Rabin PA ... F ... 913 649-1555
Overland Park (G-8442)
Bever Dye Lc ... E ... 316 263-8294
Wichita (G-13843)
Blake & Uhlig P A ... E ... 913 321-8884
Kansas City (G-3867)
Bottaro Morefield & Kubin Lc ... F ... 913 948-8200
Leawood (G-5342)
Brenton Financial Group Inc ... F ... 913 451-9072
Overland Park (G-8483)
Bretz & Young Law Office ... F ... 620 662-3435
Hutchinson (G-3221)
Bruce Bruce & Lehman LLC ... F ... 316 722-3391
Wichita (G-13900)
Bryan Lykins Hjtmnek Fncher PA ... F ... 785 428-4566
Topeka (G-12412)
Busch Johnson & Mank ... F ... 316 263-5661
Wichita (G-13919)
Butler & Associates PA ... E ... 785 267-6444
Topeka (G-12416)
Calihan Brwn Burgrdt Wurst ... F ... 620 276-2381
Garden City (G-2120)
Case Mses Zimmerman Martin PA ... F ... 316 303-0100
Wichita (G-13957)
Cavanaugh Biggs and Lemon PA ... F ... 785 440-4000
Topeka (G-12452)
Charles Ritz Inc ... F ... 913 685-2600
Overland Park (G-8542)
City of Overland Park ... B ... 913 895-6080
Overland Park (G-8554)
Clark Mize Linville Chartered ... E ... 785 823-6325
Salina (G-10456)
Coffman Defries & Nothern ... F ... 785 234-3461
Topeka (G-12484)
Cornwell & Scheriff ... F ... 913 254-7600
Olathe (G-7617)
Couch Pierce King & Hoffmeiste ... F ... 913 451-8430
Overland Park (G-8604)
County of Allen ... E ... 620 365-1425
Iola (G-3597)
County of Butler ... F ... 316 322-4130
El Dorado (G-1553)
County of Johnson ... C ... 913 715-3300
Olathe (G-7622)
Crpenter Charted ... F ... 785 357-5251
Topeka (G-12533)
Dana Manweiler Milby PA ... F ... 316 267-8677
Wichita (G-14164)
Davis & Jack LLC ... F ... 316 945-8251
Wichita (G-14175)
Davis Ketchmark McCreight ... F ... 816 842-1515
Leawood (G-5373)
Davis Ktchmark Eschens McCrght ... F ... 816 842-1515
Leawood (G-5374)
Davis Unrein Hummer McCalister ... F ... 785 354-1100
Topeka (G-12549)
Dennis P Wetta ... F ... 316 267-5293
Wichita (G-14192)
Depew Gllen Rthbun McInteer Lc ... F ... 316 262-4000
Wichita (G-14196)
Dowell & Sypher LLC ... E ... 913 451-8833
Shawnee Mission (G-11317)
Duggan Shadwick Doerr Kurlbaum ... F ... 913 498-3536
Overland Park (G-8664)
Elder & Disability Law Firm PA ... F ... 913 338-5713
Overland Park (G-8673)
Eric K Johnson ... F ... 785 267-2410
Topeka (G-12581)
Erise Ip ... F ... 913 777-5600
Overland Park (G-8686)
Evans & Mullinix PA ... E ... 913 962-8700
Shawnee Mission (G-11348)
Ferree Bunn OGrady & Rundberg ... F ... 913 381-8180
Shawnee Mission (G-11366)
Finney County Attorneys Office ... F ... 620 272-3568
Garden City (G-2161)
Fisher Pttrson Syler Smith LLP ... E ... 785 232-7761
Topeka (G-12615)
Fleeson Ging Coulson Kitch LLC ... D ... 316 267-7361
Wichita (G-14384)
Foulston Conlee Schmidt Emerso ... F ... 316 264-3300
Wichita (G-14404)
Foulston Siefkin LLP ... D ... 316 291-9514
Wichita (G-14405)
Foulston Siefkin LLP ... C ... 316 267-6371
Wichita (G-14406)
Foulston Siefkin LLP ... E ... 913 498-2100
Overland Park (G-8735)
Foulston Siefkin LLP ... F ... 785 233-3600
Topeka (G-12625)
Frank C Allison Jr ... E ... 913 648-2080
Shawnee Mission (G-11378)
Franklin L Taylor PA ... F ... 913 782-2350
Overland Park (G-8738)
Fred Spigarelli PA ... F ... 620 231-1290
Pittsburg (G-9862)
Garcia and Antosh LLP ... F ... 620 225-7400
Dodge City (G-1364)
Gates Shields Ferguson Swall H ... F ... 913 661-0222
Overland Park (G-8747)
Gillian & Hayes LLP ... F ... 316 264-7321
Wichita (G-14464)
Gilliland & Hayes PA ... D ... 620 662-0537
Hutchinson (G-3299)
Gilliland & Hayes PA ... F ... 913 317-5100
Overland Park (G-8755)
Gilliland & Hayes PA ... F ... 316 264-7321
Wichita (G-14465)
Gilmore & Bell A Prof Corp ... F ... 316 267-2091
Wichita (G-14466)
Gilmore Shellenberger & Maxwel ... F ... 620 624-5599
Liberal (G-6312)
Glassman Bird Powell LLP ... F ... 785 625-6919
Hays (G-2816)
Goodell Stratton Edmonds & P ... E ... 785 233-0593
Topeka (G-12641)
Greenleaf & Brooks Smith ... F ... 620 624-6266
Liberal (G-6315)
Hampton & Royce Lc ... E ... 785 827-7251
Salina (G-10532)
Hayford East ... F ... 316 267-6259
Wichita (G-14571)
Hinkle Law Firm LLC ... D ... 316 267-2000
Wichita (G-14616)
Hite Fanning & Honeyman LLP ... E ... 316 265-7741
Wichita (G-14619)
Holman Hansen and Colvile PC ... E ... 913 648-7272
Leawood (G-5431)
Hovey Williams LLP ... E ... 913 647-9050
Overland Park (G-8831)
Hutton & Hutton ... E ... 316 688-1166
Wichita (G-14658)
Hutton & Hutton Law Firm ... E ... 316 688-1166
Wichita (G-14659)
Indigents Defense Svcs Kans Bd ... F ... 785 296-1833
Topeka (G-12717)
Indigents Defense Svcs Kans Bd ... F ... 785 296-6631
Topeka (G-12718)

S I C

Indigents Defense Svcs Kans Bd..........E....... 785 296-5484
Topeka (G-12719)
Indigents Defense Svcs Kans Bd..........E....... 316 264-8700
Wichita (G-14684)
Jackson Lewis PC..........................E....... 913 982-5747
Overland Park (G-8869)
James S Willard...........................F....... 785 267-0040
Topeka (G-12737)
Jennifer Brunetti..........................D....... 620 235-0100
Frontenac (G-2056)
Joseph & Hollander PA....................F....... 316 262-9400
Wichita (G-14772)
Judiciary Court of The State..............D....... 785 233-8200
Topeka (G-12751)
Justis Law Firm LLC.......................F....... 913 955-3710
Overland Park (G-8883)
Kahrs Nelson Fanning Hite Kllg...........D....... 316 265-7741
Wichita (G-14779)
Kansas Dept For Chldren Fmlies..........C....... 785 296-1368
Topeka (G-12771)
Kansas Legal Services Inc................E....... 620 227-7349
Dodge City (G-1387)
Kansas Legal Services Inc................F....... 620 694-2955
Hutchinson (G-3346)
Kansas Legal Services Inc................E....... 785 354-8531
Topeka (G-12784)
Kansas Legal Services Inc................E....... 316 265-9681
Wichita (G-14812)
Kansas Legal Services Inc................F....... 913 621-0200
Kansas City (G-4156)
Kansas Medical Mutual Insur Co..........E....... 785 232-2224
Topeka (G-12790)
Kennedy & Willis...........................F....... 316 263-4921
Wichita (G-14849)
Kennedy Brkley Yrnvich Wllmson.........F....... 785 825-4674
Salina (G-10574)
Klenda Austerman LLC....................E....... 316 267-0331
Wichita (G-14867)
Kreamer Kincaid Taylor...................F....... 913 782-2350
Overland Park (G-8927)
Kutak Rock LLP.............................E....... 316 609-7900
Wichita (G-14901)
Lathrop & Gage LLP.......................D....... 913 451-5100
Shawnee Mission (G-11548)
Law Office of Pter A Jouras Jr...........F....... 913 677-1999
Fairway (G-1912)
Law Offices of M Steven Wagle...........F....... 316 264-4878
Wichita (G-14935)
Lee Wilson & Gurney......................F....... 316 685-2245
Wichita (G-14944)
Lewis Brsbois Bsgard Smith LLP.........D....... 316 609-7900
Wichita (G-14956)
Little & Miller Chartered Inc.............F....... 785 841-6245
Lawrence (G-4999)
Lyle Law LLC...............................F....... 913 225-6463
Overland Park (G-8976)
Manhattan-City.............................F....... 785 587-8995
Manhattan (G-6729)
Marietta Kellogg & Price..................F....... 785 825-5403
Salina (G-10592)
Marilyn M Wilder...........................F....... 316 283-8746
Newton (G-7376)
Martin Pringle Olivr Wallace..............D....... 316 265-9311
Wichita (G-15013)
Martindell Swearer Shaffer................E....... 620 662-3331
Hutchinson (G-3365)
Mc Dowell Rice Smith Buchanan.........F....... 913 338-5400
Shawnee Mission (G-11604)
McAnany Van Cleave & Phillips..........F....... 913 371-3838
Kansas City (G-4224)
McAnany Van Cleave Phillips PA.........D....... 913 371-3838
Kansas City (G-4225)
McCullough Wareheim & Labunker......F....... 785 233-2323
Topeka (G-12869)
McDonald Tinker Skaer Quinn............E....... 316 440-4882
Wichita (G-15028)
McPherson & Mcvey Law Offices..........F....... 620 793-3420
Great Bend (G-2608)
Michael J Unrein Atty.....................F....... 785 354-1100
Topeka (G-12888)
Michael W Ryan Atty......................F....... 785 632-5666
Clay Center (G-873)
Midwest Bioscience RES Pk LLC..........E....... 913 319-0300
Leawood (G-5482)
Monnat & Spurrier Chartered.............F....... 316 264-2800
Wichita (G-15123)
Morris Laing Evans Brock.................D....... 316 838-1084
Wichita (G-15128)
Morris Laing Evans Brock.................F....... 785 232-2662
Topeka (G-12912)
Newberry Ungerer & Heckert LLP.........F....... 785 273-5250
Topeka (G-12927)
Northast Kans Chpter 13 Trstee...........F....... 785 234-1551
Topeka (G-12935)
Norton Wssrman Jones Kelly LLC........E....... 785 827-3646
Salina (G-10614)
Ofc of US Trustee..........................F....... 316 269-6607
Wichita (G-15210)
Oswalt Arnold Oswald & Henry...........F....... 620 662-5489
Hutchinson (G-3398)
P C Southlaw...............................C....... 913 663-7600
Overland Park (G-9132)
Palmer Leatherman & White LLP.........F....... 785 233-1836
Topeka (G-12959)
Parker & Hay LLP..........................F....... 785 266-3044
Topeka (G-12961)
Parkview Joint Venture....................F....... 785 267-3410
Topeka (G-12962)
Payne and Jones Chartered...............D....... 816 960-3600
Shawnee Mission (G-11720)
Polsinelli PC................................E....... 913 451-8788
Shawnee Mission (G-11742)
Potts Law Firm LLP........................F....... 816 931-2230
Shawnee Mission (G-11745)
Prochaska Howell Prochaska LLC........F....... 316 683-9080
Wichita (G-15356)
Ray Hodge & Associates LLC.............F....... 316 269-1414
Wichita (G-15420)
Redmon Michael Law Office..............F....... 913 342-5917
Kansas City (G-4366)
Reynold Fork Berkl Suter Rose...........E....... 620 663-7131
Hutchinson (G-3427)
Richeson Anderson Byrd..................F....... 785 242-1234
Ottawa (G-8310)
Robert A Kumin PC........................F....... 913 432-1826
Shawnee Mission (G-11806)
Roger A Riedmiller.........................F....... 316 448-1028
Wichita (G-15476)
Roger Fincher...............................F....... 785 430-5770
Topeka (G-13024)
Rouse Frets White Goss Gentile..........E....... 913 387-1600
Overland Park (G-9259)
Ryan Condray and Wenger LLC...........F....... 785 632-5666
Clay Center (G-880)
Sanders Warren & Russell LLP...........E....... 913 234-6100
Overland Park (G-9278)
Schlagel Kinzer LLC........................F....... 913 782-5885
Olathe (G-8058)
Scott Qinlan Willard Barns LLC...........F....... 785 267-0040
Topeka (G-13044)
Shank & Hamilton PC......................F....... 816 471-0909
Shawnee Mission (G-11849)
Sharon Lee Family Health Care...........D....... 913 722-3100
Kansas City (G-4420)
Sharp McQueen Mckinley Mora...........E....... 620 624-2548
Liberal (G-6368)
Simpson Lgback Lynch Norris PA........E....... 913 342-2500
Overland Park (G-9313)
Slape and Howard Chartered..............F....... 316 262-3445
Wichita (G-15602)
Sloan Eisenbarth Glassman...............E....... 785 357-6311
Topeka (G-13077)
Smith Shay Farmer & Wetta LLC..........F....... 316 267-5293
Wichita (G-15608)
Smithyman & Zakoura Chartered..........F....... 913 661-9800
Shawnee Mission (G-11876)
Snyder Law Firm LLC......................F....... 913 685-3900
Leawood (G-5553)
Southeast Bancshares Inc.................E....... 620 431-1400
Chanute (G-763)
Spencer Fane Britt Browne LLP...........E....... 913 345-8100
Overland Park (G-9334)
Stevens & Brand LLP......................E....... 785 843-0811
Lawrence (G-5125)
Stinson Lasswell & Wilson LLC...........F....... 316 264-9137
Wichita (G-15673)
Stinson Leonard Street LLP...............E....... 913 451-8600
Shawnee Mission (G-11901)
Stinson Leonard Street LLP...............E....... 316 265-8800
Wichita (G-15674)
Sunflwer Child Spport Svcs LLC..........F....... 785 623-4516
Hays (G-2917)
Thompson Ramsdell Qualseth PA.........F....... 785 841-4554
Lawrence (G-5136)
Timothy R Keenan..........................F....... 620 793-7811
Great Bend (G-2647)
Topeka Attorneys...........................F....... 785 267-2410
Topeka (G-13168)
Triplett Woolf & Garretson LLC...........E....... 316 630-8100
Wichita (G-15804)
Vold & Morris LLC..........................F....... 913 696-0001
Overland Park (G-9470)
Wagoner Bankruptcy Group PC............F....... 913 422-0909
Olathe (G-8145)
Waldeck Matteuzzi & Sloan................E....... 913 253-2500
Overland Park (G-9479)
Wallace Saunders Chartered..............D....... 913 888-1000
Overland Park (G-9482)
Wallace Saunders Chartered..............F....... 316 269-2100
Wichita (G-15922)
Wallace Saunders Chartered..............C....... 913 888-1000
Shawnee Mission (G-11990)
Warden Triplett Grier LLP..................F....... 816 877-8100
Prairie Village (G-10081)
Watkins Calcara Rondeau Friede..........F....... 620 792-8231
Great Bend (G-2658)
Weary Davis LLC...........................F....... 785 762-2210
Junction City (G-3768)
Western Professional Assoc...............F....... 316 264-5628
Wichita (G-15961)
Wheeler & Mitchelson Chartered..........F....... 620 231-4650
Pittsburg (G-9968)
Wichita Bar Association....................F....... 316 263-2251
Wichita (G-15980)
Wilbert & Towner PA.......................F....... 620 231-5620
Pittsburg (G-9969)
William H Griffin............................F....... 913 677-1311
Roeland Park (G-10231)
Williamson & Cubbison....................F....... 913 371-1930
Kansas City (G-4545)
Wise & Breymer............................F....... 620 241-0554
McPherson (G-7044)
Woner Glenn Reder Grant Riordn.........F....... 785 235-5371
Topeka (G-13249)
Woodard Hernandez Roth Day LLC......E....... 316 263-4958
Wichita (G-16063)
Work Comp Specialty Associates.........E....... 785 841-7751
Lawrence (G-5191)
Wright Henson Clark & Bakr LLP..........E....... 785 232-2200
Topeka (G-13253)
Yeretsky & Maher LLC.....................F....... 913 897-5813
Shawnee Mission (G-12023)
Young Bogle McCausland Wells...........F....... 316 265-7841
Wichita (G-16089)
Yoxall Antrim & Yoxall....................F....... 620 624-8444
Liberal (G-6378)

83 SOCIAL SERVICES

8322 Individual & Family Social Svcs

Abwa Management LLC....................E....... 913 732-5100
Overland Park (G-8338)
Adolescent Adult Fmly Recovery..........F....... 316 943-2051
Wichita (G-13614)
Adult Child & Fmly Counseling............F....... 316 945-5200
Wichita (G-13620)
Adult Health Services Inc..................C....... 913 788-9896
Kansas City (G-3786)
Advance Catastrophe Tech Inc............E....... 316 262-9992
Bel Aire (G-426)
Alcoholics Anonymous......................E....... 620 793-3962
Great Bend (G-2502)
Alderbrook Village..........................F....... 620 442-4400
Arkansas City (G-141)
Alliance Equities Corporation..............F....... 913 428-8278
Overland Park (G-8370)
Always There Senior Care Inc.............D....... 316 946-9222
Wichita (G-13681)
Alzheimrs Dsease Rltd Dsordrs...........F....... 913 381-3888
Shawnee Mission (G-11100)
American Adoptions Inc....................E....... 913 492-2229
Overland Park (G-8374)
American National Red Cross.............E....... 620 446-0966
Arkansas City (G-142)
American National Red Cross.............E....... 785 309-0263
Salina (G-10401)
American National Red Cross.............E....... 913 245-3565
Lenexa (G-5652)
Andrea Clark.................................D....... 913 683-3061
Leavenworth (G-5203)
Antioch Church..............................F....... 785 232-1937
Topeka (G-12332)
ARC of Sedgwick County Inc..............E....... 316 943-1191
Wichita (G-13729)
Archdiocese Kansas Cy In Kans...........E....... 913 621-5090
Kansas City (G-3816)
Archdiocese of Miami Inc..................E....... 785 233-6300
Topeka (G-12336)
Armed Services YMCA of USA.............F....... 785 238-2972
Junction City (G-3668)

Arrowhead West Inc F 620 225-5177 Dodge City *(G-1298)*
Ashby House Ltd F 785 826-4935 Salina *(G-10410)*
Assistance League Wichita Inc C 316 687-6107 Wichita *(G-13754)*
Athletic & Rehabilitation Ctr F 913 378-0778 Shawnee Mission *(G-11131)*
Augusta Crime Stoppers Inc E 316 775-0055 Augusta *(G-302)*
Auspision LLC E 620 343-3685 Emporia *(G-1698)*
Avenue of Life Inc E 816 519-8419 Kansas City *(G-3830)*
Baptist Senior Ministries E 913 685-4800 Shawnee Mission *(G-11150)*
Bethel Neighborhood Center F 913 371-8218 Kansas City *(G-3858)*
Birthright Inc E 913 682-2700 Leavenworth *(G-5211)*
Boys & Girls Club of S Central E 316 687-5437 Wichita *(G-13877)*
Boys Girls Clubs Huthinson Inc D 620 665-7171 Hutchinson *(G-3220)*
Boys Grls CLB Lwrnce Lwrnce K D 785 841-5672 Lawrence *(G-4763)*
Breakthrough House Inc E 785 232-6807 Topeka *(G-12404)*
Brighthouse Inc E 620 665-3630 Hutchinson *(G-3223)*
Brown Cnty Developmental Svcs E 785 742-2053 Hiawatha *(G-3004)*
Cancer Council of Reno County F 620 665-5555 Hutchinson *(G-3228)*
Caring Hands Humane Society F 316 284-0487 Newton *(G-7326)*
Casa Jhnson Wyndtte Cnties Inc F 913 715-4040 Mission *(G-7128)*
Catacombs Youth Ministry E 316 689-8410 Wichita *(G-13958)*
Catholic Charities E 913 433-2061 Shawnee Mission *(G-11206)*
Catholic Charities Inc C 316 264-8344 Wichita *(G-13959)*
Catholic Charities Inc F 316 264-7233 Wichita *(G-13960)*
Catholic Charities Adult Svcs E 316 942-2008 Wichita *(G-13961)*
Catholic Charities of D 913 721-1570 Kansas City *(G-3895)*
Catholic Charities of Northeas E 913 621-5090 Overland Park *(G-8526)*
Catholic Charities of Salina F 785 825-0208 Salina *(G-10437)*
Catholic Charities of Southwes F 620 227-1562 Dodge City *(G-1319)*
Catholic Charities of Wichita F 316 263-6000 Wichita *(G-13962)*
Catholic Chrties Fndtion Nrtha C 913 621-1504 Kansas City *(G-3896)*
Catholic Chrties Nrthast Kans D 913 433-2100 Kansas City *(G-3897)*
Cawker City Senior Center F 785 781-4763 Cawker City *(G-688)*
Center For Counseling & Cnsltn E 620 792-2544 Great Bend *(G-2526)*
Central Knss Cncil of Grl Sct F 785 827-3679 Salina *(G-10442)*
Cerebral Palsy Research Fo D 316 688-5314 Wichita *(G-13992)*
Cfcc & Associates E 785 272-0778 Topeka *(G-12461)*
Cherry Street Youth Center F 620 431-0818 Chanute *(G-715)*
Child Advcacy Ctr Sdgwick Cnty F 316 660-9494 Wichita *(G-14005)*
Child Support Enforcement F 620 331-7231 Independence *(G-3502)*
Childrens Therapy Group F 913 383-9014 Mission *(G-7129)*
Choices Network Inc B 785 820-8018 Salina *(G-10447)*
Christian Psychological Svcs F 785 843-2429 Lawrence *(G-4788)*
City of Great Bend F 620 792-3906 Great Bend *(G-2541)*
City of Lenexa D 913 541-0209 Lenexa *(G-5755)*
City of McPherson F 620 241-1122 McPherson *(G-6950)*
City of Mission D 913 722-8200 Shawnee Mission *(G-11229)*
City of Neodesha F 620 325-2642 Neodesha *(G-7235)*
Class Ltd E 620 331-8604 Independence *(G-3503)*
Clean Tech Inc C 316 729-8100 Wichita *(G-14040)*
Coalition For Independence E 913 321-5140 Kansas City *(G-3921)*
Comcare of Sedgwick County C 316 660-7700 Wichita *(G-14062)*
Comcare of Sedgwick County B 316 660-7600 Wichita *(G-14061)*
Communities In School E 316 973-5110 Wichita *(G-14077)*
Community Action Inc E 785 235-9561 Topeka *(G-12490)*
Community Foundation of Ellis F 785 726-2660 Ellis *(G-1641)*
Community Living Serv C 620 227-8803 Dodge City *(G-1327)*
Community Lving Opprtnties Inc C 785 865-5520 Lawrence *(G-4804)*
Compass Behavioral Health E 620 276-6470 Garden City *(G-2131)*
Compass Behavioral Health E 620 227-8566 Dodge City *(G-1329)*
Continuity Operation Plg LLC F 913 227-0660 Lenexa *(G-5785)*
Corrections Kansas Department F 620 792-3549 Great Bend *(G-2547)*
Corrections Kansas Department E 620 341-3294 Emporia *(G-1726)*
▲ Counseling & Mediation Center F 316 269-2322 Wichita *(G-14106)*
Counseling Ctr For Butlr Cnty D 316 776-2007 El Dorado *(G-1552)*
Counseling Inc F 785 472-4300 Ellsworth *(G-1664)*
County of Barton F 620 793-1910 Great Bend *(G-2548)*
County of Crawford E 620 231-5130 Pittsburg *(G-9848)*
County of Crawford C 620 231-5141 Pittsburg *(G-9849)*
County of Decatur F 785 475-8113 Oberlin *(G-7489)*
County of Doniphan F 785 985-2380 Troy *(G-13273)*
County of Finney F 620 271-6120 Garden City *(G-2133)*
County of Reno E 620 665-7042 Hutchinson *(G-3249)*
County of Riley F 785 537-4040 Manhattan *(G-6602)*
County of Sedgwick E 316 660-0100 Wichita *(G-14111)*
County of Seward F 620 626-0198 Liberal *(G-6297)*
County of Shawnee E 785 233-8856 Topeka *(G-12518)*
Court Trustee Dept F 785 762-2583 Junction City *(G-3685)*
Cowley Cnty Mntl Hlth & Cnslng D 620 442-4540 Winfield *(G-16129)*
Cowley County Council On Aging F 620 221-7020 Winfield *(G-16130)*
Cowley County Crime Stoppers F 620 221-7777 Winfield *(G-16131)*
Crisis Center Inc E 785 539-7935 Manhattan *(G-6606)*
Crisis Center of Dodge City F 620 225-6987 Dodge City *(G-1334)*
D Kohake E 785 857-3854 Centralia *(G-698)*
Dandelion & Mudd Puddles Cdc E 913 825-0399 Shawnee *(G-10940)*
Daughters & Company Inc E 913 341-2500 Overland Park *(G-8639)*
Dccca Inc E 316 267-2030 Wichita *(G-14178)*
Dccca Inc F 785 830-8238 Lawrence *(G-4828)*
Department Corrections Kansas F 913 829-6207 Olathe *(G-7649)*
Developmental Svcs NW Kans F 785 735-2262 Victoria *(G-13373)*
Developmental Svcs NW Kans Inc F 785 483-6686 Russell *(G-10271)*
Developmental Svcs NW Kans Inc C 785 625-2521 Hays *(G-2786)*
Disability Rights Ctr of Kans F 785 273-9661 Topeka *(G-12559)*
Disablty Spprts of The Grt Pln C 620 241-8411 McPherson *(G-6957)*
Donipan Cnty Svcs & Workskills E 913 365-5561 Elwood *(G-1684)*
Douglas County Child Dev Assn F 785 842-9679 Lawrence *(G-4838)*
Dove Estates Senior Living E 316 550-6343 Goddard *(G-2436)*
Downs Senior Citizens Inc F 785 454-6228 Downs *(G-1471)*
East Central Kansas Economic E 785 242-6413 Ottawa *(G-8266)*
East Cntl Kans Area Agcy On AG E 785 242-7200 Ottawa *(G-8267)*
Economic Opprtunity Foundation E 913 371-7800 Kansas City *(G-3980)*
El Centro Inc F 913 677-0100 Kansas City *(G-3982)*
El Centro Inc F 913 677-1115 Kansas City *(G-3983)*
Eldercare Inc C 620 792-5942 Great Bend *(G-2559)*
Elizabeth B Ballard Comm Ctr F 785 842-0729 Lawrence *(G-4851)*
Emberhope Inc D 620 225-0276 Dodge City *(G-1357)*
Emergency Assistance Sites F 913 782-3640 Olathe *(G-7678)*
Emmanuel United Methodist Ch F 785 263-3342 Abilene *(G-27)*
Episcopal Social Services Inc E 316 269-4160 Wichita *(G-14297)*
Erc/Resource & Referral Inc F 785 357-5171 Topeka *(G-12580)*
Families Together Inc F 620 276-6364 Garden City *(G-2154)*
Family Conservancy Inc D 913 342-1110 Kansas City *(G-4005)*
Family Conservancy Inc F 913 287-1300 Kansas City *(G-4006)*
Family Crisis Center Inc F 620 793-9941 Great Bend *(G-2562)*
Family First Center For Autism E 913 250-5634 Leavenworth *(G-5237)*
Family Life Services Emporia F 620 342-2244 Emporia *(G-1754)*
Family Therapy Inst Midwest F 785 830-8299 Lawrence *(G-4857)*
Finch Hollow Senior Residences D 316 721-9596 Wichita *(G-14368)*
First Choice Support Services F 785 823-3555 Salina *(G-10502)*
Flinthills Services Inc D 316 321-2325 El Dorado *(G-1562)*
Florence Crittenton Services E 785 233-0516 Topeka *(G-12619)*
For Central Kansas Foundation D 785 825-6224 Salina *(G-10504)*
For Wyandot Center D 913 362-0393 Kansas City *(G-4016)*
Fort Scott Presbyterian Vlg E 620 223-5550 Fort Scott *(G-1971)*
Four Cnty Mental Hlth Ctr Inc C 620 251-8180 Coffeyville *(G-939)*
Fourth Judicial Dist Comnity C F 785 229-3510 Ottawa *(G-8273)*
Franklin Cnty Cncer Foundation F 785 242-6703 Ottawa *(G-8274)*
Friends of Yates Inc E 913 321-1566 Kansas City *(G-4018)*
Friends University F 316 295-5638 Wichita *(G-14424)*
Geary Corrections Center E 785 762-4679 Junction City *(G-3693)*
Good Shepherd Villages Inc E 785 244-6418 Summerfield *(G-12214)*
Grayco Over 50 F 620 855-3711 Cimarron *(G-829)*
Great Bend Commission On Aging F 620 792-3906 Great Bend *(G-2575)*
Grenola Senior Citizens F 620 358-3601 Grenola *(G-2686)*
Guidance Center E 913 367-1593 Atchison *(G-233)*
Halstead Place Inc E 316 830-2424 Halstead *(G-2701)*

Hays Area Children Center Inc E 785 625-3257
Hays *(G-2828)*
Hays Medical Center Inc A 785 623-6270
Hays *(G-2835)*
Health and Envmt Kans Dept E 620 272-3600
Garden City *(G-2192)*
Health Management Strategies F 785 233-1165
Topeka *(G-12673)*
Heart Spport Group For Bttred F 620 275-5911
Garden City *(G-2193)*
High Plains Mental Health Ctr F 785 543-5284
Phillipsburg *(G-9788)*
High Plains Mental Health Ctr E 785 462-6774
Colby *(G-1014)*
Higher Ground F 316 262-2060
Wichita *(G-14607)*
Home Instead Senior Care E 316 612-7541
Wichita *(G-14631)*
Home Readers Inc F 913 893-6900
Edgerton *(G-1484)*
Homestead Assisted Living E 785 272-2200
Topeka *(G-12703)*
Horizons Mental Health Ctr Inc F 620 532-3895
Kingman *(G-4595)*
Humankind Mnstries Wichita Inc E 316 264-9303
Wichita *(G-14652)*
Humankind Mnstries Wichita Inc F 316 264-8051
Wichita *(G-14653)*
Hutchnson Hosp Psychiatric Ctr E 620 665-2364
Hutchinson *(G-3330)*
Independence Inc E 785 841-0333
Lawrence *(G-4910)*
Indepndent Living Resource Ctr E 316 942-6300
Wichita *(G-14681)*
Infant Tddler Svcs Jhnson Cnty F 913 432-2900
Shawnee Mission *(G-11456)*
Infectious Disease Cons PA E 316 264-3505
Wichita *(G-14689)*
Interntnal Rscue Committee Inc E 316 201-1804
Wichita *(G-14710)*
Jay Hawk Area Agency On Aging E 785 235-1367
Topeka *(G-12738)*
Jefferson Cnty Svc Orgnization E 785 863-2637
Oskaloosa *(G-8227)*
Jewish Cmnty Ctr Grter Kans Cy B 913 327-8000
Shawnee Mission *(G-11486)*
Jewish Community Campus E 913 327-8200
Shawnee Mission *(G-11487)*
Jewish Family and Chld Svc F 913 327-8250
Shawnee Mission *(G-11488)*
Jewish Family Services E 913 327-8250
Overland Park *(G-8874)*
Jones Foundation F 620 342-1714
Emporia *(G-1781)*
Judiciary Court of The State E 785 296-6290
Topeka *(G-12750)*
Junction City Family YMCA Inc E 785 762-4780
Junction City *(G-3704)*
Kansas Affordable Housing Corp E 316 942-4848
Wichita *(G-14785)*
Kansas Big Bros Big Ssters Inc F 620 231-1145
Pittsburg *(G-9888)*
Kansas Big Bros Big Ssters Inc D 316 263-3300
Wichita *(G-14787)*
Kansas Big Bros Big Ssters Inc F 785 843-7359
Lawrence *(G-4931)*
Kansas Big Bros Big Ssters Inc F 620 421-0472
Parsons *(G-9695)*
Kansas Childrens Service Leag F 620 340-0408
Emporia *(G-1785)*
Kansas Childrens Service Leag D 316 942-4261
Wichita *(G-14792)*
Kansas Childrens Service Leag E 785 274-3100
Topeka *(G-12764)*
Kansas Childrens Service Leag F 785 274-3800
Topeka *(G-12765)*
Kansas Childrens Service Leag F 620 626-5339
Liberal *(G-6326)*
Kansas Childrens Service Leag D 620 276-3232
Garden City *(G-2213)*
Kansas Coalittion Against E 785 232-9784
Topeka *(G-12766)*
Kansas Dept For Aging & Disabi D 785 296-2917
Topeka *(G-12770)*
Kansas Dept For Chldren Fmlies C 913 651-6200
Leavenworth *(G-5261)*
Kansas Dept For Chldren Fmlies D 620 421-4500
Parsons *(G-9696)*
Kansas Dept For Chldren Fmlies E 785 296-3237
Topeka *(G-12772)*

Kansas Dept For Chldren Fmlies E 785 462-6769
Colby *(G-1020)*
Kansas Dept For Chldren Fmlies E 913 755-2162
Osawatomie *(G-8197)*
Kansas Dept For Chldren Fmlies F 620 241-3802
McPherson *(G-6981)*
Kansas Laleche League Inc F 785 865-5919
Lawrence *(G-4934)*
Kansas State University E 785 532-6984
Manhattan *(G-6696)*
Kansas Statewide Homeless F 785 354-4990
Lawrence *(G-4937)*
Kensington Senior Cmnty Ctr F 785 476-2224
Kensington *(G-4578)*
Keys For Networking Inc E 785 233-8732
Topeka *(G-12819)*
Lakemary Center Inc E 913 768-6831
Olathe *(G-7853)*
Lamunyon Clg & Restoration F 785 632-1259
Clay Center *(G-870)*
Lawrence Community Shelter F 785 832-8864
Lawrence *(G-4962)*
Lawrence Wmens Trnstnal Cre S F 785 865-3956
Lawrence *(G-4989)*
Legend Senior Living LLC C 316 337-5450
Wichita *(G-14953)*
Lets Help Inc E 785 234-6208
Topeka *(G-12839)*
Liberal Area Rape Crisis F 620 624-3079
Liberal *(G-6331)*
Link Inc F 785 625-6942
Hays *(G-2864)*
Linn County Nutrition Project F 913 795-2279
Mound City *(G-7172)*
Linn Wood Place Incorporated E 785 945-3634
Valley Falls *(G-13367)*
Loving Heart D 785 783-7200
Topeka *(G-12850)*
Maison De Naissance Foundation F 913 402-6800
Leawood *(G-5463)*
Manhattan Emrgncy Shelter Inc F 785 537-3113
Manhattan *(G-6722)*
Marshall County Agcy On Aging F 785 562-5522
Marysville *(G-6895)*
Martin Luther Homes Kansas Inc D 620 229-8702
Winfield *(G-16156)*
Mc Pherson County Food Bank F 620 241-8050
McPherson *(G-6989)*
Meals On Whls of Shwnee & Jeff E 785 354-5420
Topeka *(G-12875)*
Medical Assistance Progra F 785 842-0726
Lawrence *(G-5021)*
Medicalodges Inc C 620 223-5085
Fort Scott *(G-1984)*
Medicalodges Inc E 620 659-2156
Kinsley *(G-4619)*
Meridian Nursing Center Inc D 316 942-8471
Wichita *(G-15041)*
Mha Residential Care Inc D 316 685-1821
Wichita *(G-15063)*
Mid-America Nutrition Program E 785 242-8341
Ottawa *(G-8291)*
Mid-Amrica Yuth Basketball Inc F 316 284-0354
Newton *(G-7383)*
Midland Care Connection Inc C 785 232-2044
Topeka *(G-12892)*
Mini Bus Service Inc F 620 272-3626
Garden City *(G-2236)*
Miracles Inc F 316 303-9520
Wichita *(G-15114)*
Miracles House F 316 264-5900
Wichita *(G-15115)*
Mission Project Inc F 913 777-6722
Shawnee Mission *(G-11647)*
Mosaic C 620 231-5590
Pittsburg *(G-9909)*
Mount St Scholastica Inc C 913 906-8990
Kansas City *(G-4268)*
Neighborhood Connection E 316 267-0197
Wichita *(G-15157)*
New Beginnings Inc F 620 966-0274
Hutchinson *(G-3390)*
New Directions Emrgncy Shelter E 785 223-0500
Junction City *(G-3730)*
Noahs Ark Christian Day Care F 620 431-1832
Chanute *(G-747)*
North Central Flint Hills Area E 785 323-4300
Manhattan *(G-6762)*
North Shawnee Community Center F 785 286-0676
Topeka *(G-12933)*

Northast Kans Area Agcy On Agi F 785 742-7152
Hiawatha *(G-3020)*
O S S Inc E 620 343-8799
Emporia *(G-1808)*
Occk Inc E 785 243-1977
Concordia *(G-1125)*
Occk Inc E 785 738-3490
Beloit *(G-498)*
Olathe Unified School Dst 233 E 913 780-7002
Olathe *(G-7950)*
Options Dom & Sexual Violenc F 785 625-4202
Hays *(G-2883)*
Oxford Management Group LLC E 316 201-3210
Wichita *(G-15244)*
Paces Wyandot Ctr Youth Svcs E 913 956-3420
Kansas City *(G-4306)*
Parklane AA F 316 682-9960
Wichita *(G-15265)*
Pawnee Mental Health Svcs Inc C 785 762-5250
Manhattan *(G-6769)*
Pawnee Mental Health Svcs Inc E 785 587-4344
Manhattan *(G-6770)*
Prairie Ind Lving Resource Ctr F 620 663-3989
Hutchinson *(G-3411)*
Pregnncy Crisis Ctr of Wichita F 316 945-9400
Wichita *(G-15329)*
Project Eagle E 913 281-2648
Kansas City *(G-4345)*
Rainbows United Inc E 316 684-7060
Wichita *(G-15412)*
Recovery For All Foundation F 316 322-7057
El Dorado *(G-1596)*
Reno County Youth Services E 620 694-2500
Hutchinson *(G-3425)*
Resonate Relationship Clinic F 913 647-8092
Overland Park *(G-9236)*
Resource Center For Ind Living F 785 267-1717
Topeka *(G-13010)*
Resource Center For Ind Living D 785 528-3105
Osage City *(G-8187)*
Restorative Justice Authority F 620 235-7118
Pittsburg *(G-9927)*
Ronald McDnald Hse Chrties Nrt F 785 235-6852
Topeka *(G-13028)*
Safe Home Inc E 913 432-9300
Overland Park *(G-9269)*
Safehouse Crisis Center Inc E 620 231-8692
Pittsburg *(G-9934)*
Safehouse Inc F 620 251-0030
Coffeyville *(G-975)*
Saint Francis Acdmy Inc Atchsn F 785 625-6651
Hays *(G-2905)*
Saint Francis Cmnty Svcs Inc C 785 462-6679
Colby *(G-1039)*
Saint Francis Cmnty Svcs Inc F 620 326-6373
Wellington *(G-13526)*
Saint Francis Cmnty Svcs Inc D 785 243-4215
Concordia *(G-1128)*
Saint Francis Community and RE D 785 825-0541
Salina *(G-10662)*
Saint Frncis Acdemy Great Bend E 620 793-7454
Great Bend *(G-2634)*
Saint Frncis Acdemy Hutchinson E 620 669-3734
Hutchinson *(G-3436)*
Saint Frncis Cmnty Svcs In Ill E 785 825-0541
Salina *(G-10663)*
Saint Vincent Depaul Society D 620 421-8004
Parsons *(G-9735)*
Salina Rescue Mission Inc F 785 823-3317
Salina *(G-10689)*
Saline County Comm On Aging E 785 823-6666
Salina *(G-10697)*
Salvation Army F 316 263-2769
Wichita *(G-15514)*
Salvation Army F 913 232-5400
Kansas City *(G-4397)*
Salvation Army E 785 233-9648
Topeka *(G-13034)*
Salvation Army F 620 276-4027
Garden City *(G-2273)*
Salvation Army F 620 343-3166
Emporia *(G-1821)*
Salvation Army National Corp F 913 299-4822
Kansas City *(G-4399)*
Salvation Army National Corp E 316 943-9893
Wichita *(G-15515)*
Sedgwick Cnty Dvlpmntl Dsablty E 316 660-7630
Wichita *(G-15545)*
Sedgwick Country Animal Respon F 316 619-1723
Wichita *(G-15546)*

Sedgwick Juvenile Field Svcs ....E....... 316 660-5380
Wichita *(G-15550)*

Select Medical Corporation ....F....... 913 385-0075
Overland Park *(G-9291)*

Senior Center ....E....... 316 835-2283
Halstead *(G-2704)*

Senior Rsrce Ctr For Dglas CNT ....F....... 785 842-0543
Lawrence *(G-5108)*

Senior Services Inc Wichita ....D....... 316 267-0302
Wichita *(G-15559)*

Senior Services Inc Wichita ....D....... 316 267-0122
Wichita *(G-15560)*

Senior Svcs of Southeast Kans ....F....... 620 232-7443
Pittsburg *(G-9936)*

Seniorcare Homes LLC ....F....... 913 236-0036
Prairie Village *(G-10066)*

Services Offering Safety ....E....... 620 343-8799
Emporia *(G-1825)*

Seward County Council On Aging ....E....... 620 624-2511
Liberal *(G-6365)*

Silver City Cmnty Resource Ctr ....F....... 913 362-3367
Kansas City *(G-4421)*

Social and Rehabilitation Serv ....D....... 620 272-5800
Garden City *(G-2283)*

South Central Mntl Hlth CN ....F....... 316 775-5491
Augusta *(G-346)*

South Cntl Mntal Hlth Cnseling ....F....... 316 733-5047
Andover *(G-108)*

Southast Kans Ind Lving Rsrce ....E....... 620 421-5502
Parsons *(G-9739)*

Southeast Kans Mental Hlth Ctr ....E....... 620 365-5717
Iola *(G-3633)*

Southeast Kans Mental Hlth Ctr ....F....... 913 352-8214
Pleasanton *(G-10002)*

Southeast KS AR AG Aging ....D....... 620 431-2980
Chanute *(G-765)*

Southwest Developmental Svcs ....F....... 620 793-7604
Great Bend *(G-2638)*

Southwest Guidance Center ....F....... 620 624-8171
Liberal *(G-6370)*

Southwest Guidance Ctr ....F....... 620 624-0280
Liberal *(G-6371)*

Southwest KS Agency On Aging ....F....... 620 225-8230
Dodge City *(G-1431)*

Special Olympics Kansas Inc ....F....... 913 236-9290
Shawnee Mission *(G-11881)*

Spectrum Retirement Shawnee KS ....E....... 913 631-0058
Shawnee Mission *(G-11882)*

Substance Abuse Center Kansas ....D....... 316 267-3825
Wichita *(G-15680)*

Summit Care Inc ....E....... 913 239-8777
Leawood *(G-5563)*

Sumner Mental Health Center ....D....... 620 326-7448
Wellington *(G-13534)*

Sunflower Adult Day Services ....F....... 785 823-6666
Salina *(G-10722)*

Sunflower House ....E....... 913 631-5800
Shawnee Mission *(G-11908)*

Sunporch of Smith Center ....F....... 785 506-6003
Smith Center *(G-12044)*

Sunshine Connections Inc ....F....... 785 625-2093
Hays *(G-2918)*

Supreme Court United States ....E....... 785 295-2790
Topeka *(G-13126)*

Tfi Family Services Inc ....F....... 620 231-0443
Pittsburg *(G-9945)*

Tfi Family Services Inc ....F....... 913 894-2985
Overland Park *(G-9404)*

Three Rivers Inc ....F....... 785 456-9915
Wamego *(G-13444)*

Thriver Services LLC ....F....... 913 955-2555
Lenexa *(G-6179)*

Tonys Pizza ....F....... 620 275-4626
Garden City *(G-2299)*

Topeka Adult Care Center ....F....... 785 233-7397
Topeka *(G-13164)*

Topeka Ind Lving Rsrce Ctr Inc ....E....... 785 233-4572
Topeka *(G-13179)*

Training & Evaluation Cente ....E....... 620 663-2216
Hutchinson *(G-3466)*

Training & Evaluation Cente ....E....... 620 663-1596
Hutchinson *(G-3467)*

Training & Evaluation Cente ....E....... 620 615-5850
Hutchinson *(G-3468)*

Tri-Valley Developmental Svcs ....D....... 620 365-3307
Iola *(G-3637)*

Unified School District 259 ....F....... 316 683-3315
Wichita *(G-15835)*

Union Rescue Mission Inc ....E....... 316 687-4673
Wichita *(G-15839)*

United Disaster Response LLC ....E....... 913 963-8403
Shawnee Mission *(G-11962)*

United Methodist Western Kansa ....E....... 620 275-1766
Garden City *(G-2307)*

United States Courts ADM ....D....... 913 735-2242
Kansas City *(G-4489)*

United Way of McPherson County ....E....... 620 241-5152
McPherson *(G-7036)*

Valeo Behavioral Health Care ....E....... 785 233-1730
Topeka *(G-13215)*

Valeo Behavioral Hlth Care Inc ....E....... 785 233-1730
Topeka *(G-13217)*

Via Christi Hope Inc ....E....... 316 858-1111
Wichita *(G-15893)*

Via Christi Villages Inc ....E....... 316 946-5200
Wichita *(G-15898)*

Via Chrsti HM Hlth Wichita Inc ....D....... 316 268-8588
Wichita *(G-15900)*

Villages Inc ....F....... 785 267-5900
Topeka *(G-13224)*

Webster Conference Center Inc ....E....... 785 827-6565
Salina *(G-10764)*

West Side Good Neighbor Center ....F....... 316 942-7349
Wichita *(G-15956)*

Western First Aid & Safety LLC ....F....... 316 263-0687
Leawood *(G-5597)*

Western Kansas Child Advocacy ....F....... 620 872-3706
Scott City *(G-10835)*

Wichita Area Sxual Assault Ctr ....E....... 316 263-0185
Wichita *(G-15976)*

Wichita Child Guidance Center ....D....... 316 686-6671
Wichita *(G-15986)*

Wichita Family Crisis Ctr Inc ....F....... 316 263-7501
Wichita *(G-15998)*

Womens Chldren Shelter Linwood ....D....... 620 231-0415
Pittsburg *(G-9971)*

World Impact Inc ....E....... 316 687-9398
Wichita *(G-16073)*

Wright Intl Studnt Svcs ....D....... 913 677-1142
Shawnee Mission *(G-12020)*

YMCA Topeka Downtown Branch ....E....... 785 354-8591
Topeka *(G-13256)*

Young Kansas Christian ....C....... 785 233-1750
Topeka *(G-13257)*

Young Mens Christian ....F....... 785 233-9815
Topeka *(G-13258)*

Young Mens Christian Assn ....E....... 620 275-1199
Garden City *(G-2319)*

Young Mens Christian Assoc At ....D....... 913 367-4948
Atchison *(G-272)*

Young Mens Christian Associa ....D....... 316 945-2255
Wichita *(G-16092)*

Young Mens Christian Associa ....C....... 316 219-9622
Wichita *(G-16093)*

Young Mens Christian Associa ....D....... 316 320-9622
El Dorado *(G-1616)*

Young Mens Christian Associa ....D....... 316 260-9622
Wichita *(G-16094)*

Young Mens Christian Associa ....C....... 316 942-5511
Wichita *(G-16095)*

Young Mens Christian Associat ....C....... 316 685-2251
Wichita *(G-16096)*

Young Mens Christian Associat ....C....... 620 545-7290
Viola *(G-13380)*

Young Mens Christian Gr Kansas ....D....... 913 362-3489
Prairie Village *(G-10088)*

Young Mens Christian Gr Kansas ....C....... 913 393-9622
Olathe *(G-8163)*

Young Mens Christian Gr Kansas ....D....... 913 782-7707
Olathe *(G-8164)*

Young MNS Chrstn Assn of Tpeka ....C....... 785 354-8591
Topeka *(G-13259)*

Young MNS Chrstn Assn Pttsburg ....D....... 620 231-1100
Pittsburg *(G-9972)*

Young MNS Chrstn Assn Slina Ka ....D....... 785 825-2151
Salina *(G-10775)*

Youth Crisis Shelter Inc ....E....... 620 421-6941
Parsons *(G-9752)*

Youthville Family Cnsltn Svc ....E....... 316 264-8317
Wichita *(G-16098)*

8331 Job Training & Vocational Rehabilitation Svcs

Achievement Svcs For Ne Kans ....E....... 913 367-2432
Atchison *(G-202)*

Arrowhead West Inc ....E....... 620 225-4061
Dodge City *(G-1296)*

Arrowhead West Inc ....E....... 620 227-8803
Dodge City *(G-1297)*

Arrowhead West Inc ....E....... 316 722-4554
Wichita *(G-13738)*

Arrowhead West Inc ....E....... 620 886-3711
Medicine Lodge *(G-7056)*

Arrowhead West Inc ....F....... 620 225-5177
Dodge City *(G-1298)*

Big Lkes Developmental Ctr Inc ....E....... 785 632-5357
Clay Center *(G-843)*

Class Ltd ....D....... 620 231-3131
Pittsburg *(G-9835)*

Class Ltd ....C....... 620 429-1212
Columbus *(G-1066)*

Class Ltd ....D....... 620 421-2800
Parsons *(G-9672)*

Cof Training Services Inc ....D....... 785 242-5035
Ottawa *(G-8258)*

Cof Training Services Inc ....E....... 620 364-2151
Burlington *(G-627)*

Cof Training Services Inc ....D....... 785 242-6064
Ottawa *(G-8259)*

Cottonwood Incorporated ....C....... 785 842-0550
Lawrence *(G-4812)*

Curtis Klaassen ....F....... 913 661-4616
Leawood *(G-5366)*

Developmental Services of Jack ....E....... 785 364-3534
Holton *(G-3087)*

Developmental Svcs NW Kans Inc ....E....... 785 626-3688
Atwood *(G-283)*

Developmental Svcs NW Kans Inc ....E....... 785 421-2851
Hill City *(G-3033)*

Empac Inc ....F....... 316 265-9922
Wichita *(G-14278)*

◆ **Futures Unlimited Inc** ....E....... 620 326-8906
Wellington *(G-13501)*

Goodwill Industries Ea ....E....... 316 789-8804
Derby *(G-1248)*

Goodwill Industries Ea ....E....... 620 343-3564
Emporia *(G-1764)*

Goodwill Industries Ea ....E....... 620 275-1007
Garden City *(G-2190)*

Goodwill Wstn MO & Eastrn Kans ....E....... 785 228-9774
Topeka *(G-12642)*

Goodwill Wstn MO & Eastrn Kans ....F....... 785 331-3908
Lawrence *(G-4875)*

Goodwill Wstn MO & Eastrn Kans ....E....... 913 768-9540
Olathe *(G-7737)*

Heartland Works Inc ....E....... 785 234-0500
Topeka *(G-12681)*

Hetlinger Dvlopmental Svcs Inc ....E....... 620 342-1087
Emporia *(G-1771)*

Kansas Elks Training ....B....... 316 383-8700
Wichita *(G-14797)*

Kansas Schl For Effective Lrng ....E....... 316 263-9620
Wichita *(G-14822)*

Medicalodges Inc ....D....... 316 755-1288
Valley Center *(G-13348)*

Multi Community Diversfd Svcs ....F....... 620 241-6693
McPherson *(G-7009)*

Nemaha County Training Center ....E....... 785 336-6116
Seneca *(G-10875)*

Nemaha County Training Center ....F....... 785 300-1306
Sabetha *(G-10321)*

New Beginnings Enterprise ....F....... 620 583-6835
Eureka *(G-1896)*

Nickell Barracks Training Ctr ....E....... 785 822-1193
Salina *(G-10613)*

Northview Development Services ....C....... 316 281-3213
Newton *(G-7399)*

Northview Developmental Svcs ....F....... 316 283-5170
Newton *(G-7400)*

Occk Inc ....E....... 785 243-1977
Concordia *(G-1125)*

Occk Inc ....E....... 785 738-3490
Beloit *(G-498)*

Occk Inc ....C....... 785 827-9383
Salina *(G-10617)*

Optimal Performance LLC ....F....... 316 440-4440
Wichita *(G-15227)*

Pryor Learning Solutions Inc ....E....... 913 967-8300
Shawnee Mission *(G-11760)*

Pyxis Inc ....C....... 316 682-8092
Wichita *(G-15382)*

RES-Care Kansas Inc ....F....... 913 342-9426
Kansas City *(G-4372)*

RES-Care Kansas Inc ....D....... 620 793-8501
Great Bend *(G-2631)*

Riverside Resources Inc ....D....... 913 651-6810
Leavenworth *(G-5287)*

Ser Corporation ....E....... 316 264-5372
Wichita *(G-15563)*

S I C

Social and Rehabilitation Serv ....D 620 272-5800
Garden City (G-2283)
Starkey Inc ....C 316 942-4221
Wichita (G-15657)
Sunflower Diversified Svcs Inc ....D 620 792-1321
Great Bend (G-2643)
Sunflower Diversified Svcs Inc ....C 620 792-4087
Great Bend (G-2644)
Sunflower Diversified Svcs Inc ....C 620 792-1325
Great Bend (G-2645)
Tri-Ko Inc ....E 913 755-3025
Osawatomie (G-8205)
Tri-Valley Developmental Svcs ....D 620 223-3990
Fort Scott (G-2012)
Tri-Valley Developmental Svcs ....D 620 365-3307
Iola (G-3637)
Twin Rvers Dvlpmental Supports ....D 620 442-3575
Arkansas City (G-184)
Unified School District 259 ....C 316 973-4000
Wichita (G-15833)

8351 Child Day Care Svcs

A Childs World Day Care Ctr ....F 785 863-2161
Oskaloosa (G-8220)
A Deere Place Inc ....F 913 727-5437
Lansing (G-4665)
A Step Above Academy-Wyandotte ....F 913 721-3770
Bonner Springs (G-538)
Abilene Childcare Learning Ctr ....F 785 263-1799
Abilene (G-2)
Abilene Unified Schl Dst 435 ....F 785 825-9185
Salina (G-10389)
Agape Montessori School ....E 913 768-0812
Olathe (G-7513)
Aldersgate Untd Meth Pre Schl ....E 913 764-2407
Olathe (G-7516)
Allen Preschool LLC ....E 913 451-1066
Shawnee Mission (G-11096)
American Baptist Church ....F 913 236-7067
Shawnee Mission (G-11102)
Ancilla Center For Children ....F 913 758-6113
Leavenworth (G-5202)
Angel Little Learning Ctr Inc ....E 913 724-4442
Basehor (G-372)
Angel Wings Learning Ctr LLC ....F 316 249-4818
Wichita (G-13709)
Angels Little Playgrnd Daycare ....F 785 823-1448
Salina (G-10404)
Apple Tree Kid Day Out/Presch ....E 913 888-3702
Shawnee Mission (G-11114)
Archdiocese Kansas Cy In Kans ....E 913 631-0004
Shawnee Mission (G-11117)
Ashbury Church Pre School ....F 913 432-5573
Shawnee Mission (G-11123)
Ashleys House Learning Center ....E 316 941-9877
Wichita (G-13753)
Assoction Christn Schools Intl ....D 785 232-3878
Topeka (G-12347)
Atchison Child Care Assn ....F 913 367-6441
Atchison (G-207)
Augusta Head Start ....F 316 775-3421
Augusta (G-306)
Basic Beginnings Educational ....F 316 721-7946
Wichita (G-13818)
Bccc Child Development Center ....E 620 786-1131
Great Bend (G-2518)
Board of Edcatn of Kans Cy Ks ....E 913 627-6550
Kansas City (G-3870)
Bonner Springs Head Start ....F 913 441-2828
Bonner Springs (G-542)
Books & Blocks Academy Inc ....F 785 266-5150
Topeka (G-12397)
Boys Girls Clubs Huthinson Inc ....D 620 665-7171
Hutchinson (G-3220)
Bright Circle Montesorri Schl ....F 785 235-1033
Topeka (G-12406)
Brookridge Day School ....E 913 649-2228
Shawnee Mission (G-11185)
BS Family Development LLC ....E 913 961-6579
Olathe (G-7563)
Bugs Early Learning Ctr I ....F 913 254-0088
Olathe (G-7565)
Building Blocks Child Care Ctr ....F 620 767-8029
Council Grove (G-1158)
Building Blocks Child Dev Ctr ....E 913 888-7244
Shawnee Mission (G-11191)
Building Blocks of Topeka Inc ....E 785 232-0441
Topeka (G-12413)
Care A Lot Daycare ....F 785 628-2563
Hays (G-2764)
Caring Connections ....F 620 544-2050
Hugoton (G-3150)
Century School Inc ....E 785 832-0101
Lawrence (G-4782)
Chase Childrens Services Inc ....F 620 273-6650
Strong City (G-12192)
Child Care Services Strlng Inc ....F 620 904-4231
Sterling (G-12114)
Child Start Inc ....E 316 522-8677
Wichita (G-14006)
Child Start Inc ....B 316 682-1853
Wichita (G-14007)
Child Start Inc ....D 316 682-1853
Wichita (G-14008)
Childhood Memories Toddler ....F 316 554-1646
Wichita (G-14009)
Childrens Center LLC ....F 913 432-5114
Roeland Park (G-10220)
Childrens Learning Center Inc ....E 785 841-2185
Lawrence (G-4786)
Christ King Early Educatn Ctr ....E 785 272-2999
Topeka (G-12466)
Christian Rainbow Knowledge ....F 316 686-2169
Wichita (G-14015)
Christs Care Pre-School ....F 620 662-1283
Hutchinson (G-3237)
Christs Kids Childcare ....F 620 654-4567
Galva (G-2092)
Church of Magdalen ....E 316 634-1572
Wichita (G-14019)
Clay County Child Care Ctr Inc ....E 785 632-2195
Clay Center (G-853)
Clay County Child Care Ctr Inc ....F 785 632-5399
Clay Center (G-854)
Clay Jars Childrens Center Inc ....F 785 379-9098
Tecumseh (G-12238)
Community Child Care Center ....E 620 421-6550
Parsons (G-9676)
Community Childrens Center Inc ....F 785 842-2515
Lawrence (G-4803)
Community Day Care Center 1 ....E 620 275-5757
Garden City (G-2130)
Cornerstone Day Care Preschool ....F 620 257-5622
Lyons (G-6481)
Country Child Care Inc ....E 316 722-4500
Maize (G-6510)
Country Kids Day Care Inc ....E 913 888-9400
Shawnee Mission (G-11269)
Countryside United Methdst Ch ....F 785 266-7541
Topeka (G-12516)
Cradle To Cryons Childcare Ctr ....F 620 345-2390
Moundridge (G-7181)
Crazy Girls LLC ....F 913 495-9797
Lenexa (G-5791)
Creativity Place Inc ....D 316 684-1860
Wichita (G-14127)
Creche Academy LLC ....F 785 484-3100
Meriden (G-7079)
Creme De La Creme Kansas Inc ....E 913 451-0858
Shawnee Mission (G-11279)
Dandelion & Mudd Puddles Cdc ....E 913 825-0399
Shawnee (G-10940)
Dinosaur Den Child Dev Ctr ....F 913 780-2626
Olathe (G-7656)
Dodge Cy Unified Schl Dst 443 ....D 620 227-1614
Dodge City (G-1354)
Early Childhood Connections ....E 785 623-2430
Hays (G-2796)
Early Childhood Dev Ctr ....E 620 544-4334
Hugoton (G-3161)
Early Chldhood Cnnection/Pre K ....E 785 726-2413
Ellis (G-1642)
Early Head Start Clay County ....F 877 688-5454
Clay Center (G-861)
Early Headstart Cmnty Action ....D 785 266-3152
Topeka (G-12567)
East Central Kansas Economic ....E 913 294-4880
Paola (G-9554)
East Heights United Methdst Ch ....E 316 682-6518
Wichita (G-14253)
Edwardslle Untd Mthdst Daycare ....F 913 422-5384
Edwardsville (G-1498)
Elizabeth B Ballard Comm Ctr ....F 785 842-0729
Lawrence (G-4851)
Emporia Community Daycare Ctr ....F 620 343-2888
Emporia (G-1737)
Faith Evangelical Lutheran Ch ....E 316 788-1715
Derby (G-1246)
Family First Child Care LLC ....F 316 333-1481
Newton (G-7343)
Family Resource Center Inc ....D 620 235-3150
Pittsburg (G-9860)
First Assembly God Inc ....E 316 524-4981
Haysville (G-2944)
First Baptist Church Olathe ....F 913 764-7088
Olathe (G-7711)
First Steps Childcare and Lear ....F 620 518-1532
Great Bend (G-2565)
First United Methodist Church ....F 316 755-1112
Valley Center (G-13342)
First United Methodist Church ....E 316 263-6244
Wichita (G-14376)
Fleet Early Learning Stn LLC ....E 913 638-7178
Overland Park (G-8728)
Friends of Montessori Assn ....F 913 649-6160
Prairie Village (G-10029)
Full Faith Church of Love ....F 913 262-3145
Kansas City (G-4023)
◆ Futures Unlimited Inc ....E 620 326-8906
Wellington (G-13501)
Garden City Public Schools ....E 620 275-0291
Garden City (G-2176)
Genesis School Inc ....E 913 845-9498
Tonganoxie (G-12262)
Glenn Pk Christn Ch Preschool ....E 316 943-4283
Wichita (G-14471)
Global Montessori Academy ....F 816 561-4533
Prairie Village (G-10032)
Goddard Public Schools ....E 316 794-2281
Goddard (G-2440)
Goddard School ....E 913 764-1331
Olathe (G-7736)
Goddard School ....E 913 451-1066
Shawnee Mission (G-11398)
Good Shepherd Child Care Ctr ....F 620 429-4611
Columbus (G-1076)
Googols of Learning ....E 785 856-6002
Lawrence (G-4876)
Grace Angels Family Service ....F 913 233-2944
Kansas City (G-4043)
Grace United Methodist Church ....E 913 859-0111
Olathe (G-7738)
Grannys ....E 913 837-5222
Louisburg (G-6451)
Great Bend Child Day Care Assn ....F 620 792-2421
Great Bend (G-2573)
Growing Futures Early Educ ....E 913 649-6057
Overland Park (G-8780)
Hadley Day Care Ctr Inc ....E 620 663-9622
Hutchinson (G-3307)
Halstd-Bntley Unfied Schl Dst ....C 316 835-2641
Halstead (G-2700)
Happy Hearts Child Development ....F 316 613-3550
Wichita (G-14558)
Happy Hearts Learning Ctr LLC ....F 913 334-3331
Kansas City (G-4066)
Happy House Day Care ....F 913 782-1115
Olathe (G-7750)
Happy House Day Care ....F 913 782-1115
Olathe (G-7751)
Hays Area Children Center Inc ....E 785 625-3257
Hays (G-2828)
Head Start Child Dev Cncil Inc ....F 316 267-1997
Wichita (G-14574)
Headstart Program ....E 620 341-2260
Emporia (G-1768)
Helpers Inc ....F 913 322-7212
Olathe (G-7764)
Hill Top Center ....F 316 686-9095
Wichita (G-14609)
Hillcrest Chrstn Child Dev Ctr ....E 913 663-1997
Shawnee Mission (G-11432)
Hillcrest Covenant Church ....E 913 901-2300
Shawnee Mission (G-11433)
Hilltop Child Development Ctr ....E 785 864-4940
Lawrence (G-4897)
Hillview Church of God Inc ....F 913 299-4406
Kansas City (G-4080)
Holy Name Catholic Church ....C 785 232-7744
Topeka (G-12698)
Holy Name Church ....E 785 232-1603
Topeka (G-12699)
Hope Lutheran Church Shawnee ....E 913 631-6940
Shawnee Mission (G-11439)
Integrated Behavioral Tech Inc ....D 913 662-7071
Basehor (G-379)
Iola Pre Schl For Excptnl Chld ....F 620 365-6730
Iola (G-3610)
Ivy League Learning Center ....E 913 338-4060
Overland Park (G-8867)

Jack Jill Prschl-Extended Care.............F 913 682-1222
Leavenworth (G-5255)
Jewish Cmnty Ctr Grter Kans Cy ....B 913 327-8000
Shawnee Mission (G-11486)
Joyful Noise Academy..........................E 316 688-5060
Wichita (G-14775)
Junction City Family YMCA Inc ....E 785 762-4780
Junction City (G-3704)
Kansas Association of Child ....E 785 823-3343
Salina (G-10562)
Kansas Childrens Service Leag ....D 620 276-3232
Garden City (G-2213)
Kansas Childrens Service Leag ....D 316 942-4261
Wichita (G-14792)
Kansas Childrens Service Leag ....F 785 274-3800
Topeka (G-12765)
Kansas City Christian School...............D 913 648-5227
Prairie Village (G-10040)
Kansas East Conference United...........E 913 631-2280
Shawnee Mission (G-11516)
Kansas East Conference United...........F 913 383-9146
Shawnee Mission (G-11517)
Kansas Kids Daycare Preschool ....F 785 762-4338
Junction City (G-3713)
Kid Stop LLC ....F 913 422-9999
Shawnee (G-10981)
Kidcare Connection Inc........................E 316 944-6434
Wichita (G-14856)
Kiddi Kollege Inc..................................F 913 814-7770
Overland Park (G-8917)
Kiddi Kollege Inc..................................E 913 764-4423
Olathe (G-7836)
Kiddi Kollege Inc..................................F 913 788-7060
Kansas City (G-4175)
Kiddi Kollege Inc..................................E 913 649-4747
Shawnee Mission (G-11530)
Kiddi Kollege Inc..................................F 913 780-0246
Olathe (G-7837)
Kiddicat Child Care Center ....F 785 272-2001
Topeka (G-12822)
Kids At Heart Inc..................................E 913 648-8577
Overland Park (G-8918)
Kids First Day Care Preschool ....E 620 231-4994
Frontenac (G-2057)
Kids Kampus...E 620 241-8499
Mcpherson (G-6983)
Kids R Kids...E 913 390-0234
Olathe (G-7838)
Kindercare Education LLC....................F 913 631-6910
Shawnee Mission (G-11531)
Kindercare Education LLC....................F 913 441-9202
Shawnee (G-10982)
Kindercare Education LLC....................F 316 721-0168
Wichita (G-14858)
Kindercare Education LLC....................E 316 733-2066
Andover (G-99)
Kindercare Education LLC....................F 316 684-4574
Wichita (G-14859)
Kindercare Education LLC....................F 316 775-7503
Augusta (G-331)
Kindercare Learning Ctrs LLC..............F 316 733-2066
Andover (G-100)
Kindercare Learning Ctrs LLC..............E 913 402-1024
Shawnee Mission (G-11532)
Kindercare Learning Ctrs LLC..............F 913 727-6267
Lansing (G-4677)
Kindercare Learning Ctrs LLC..............E 316 721-0168
Wichita (G-14860)
Kindercare Learning Ctrs LLC..............F 316 788-5925
Derby (G-1256)
Kindercare Learning Ctrs LLC..............F 913 492-3221
Shawnee Mission (G-11533)
Kindercare Learning Ctrs LLC..............F 785 539-7540
Manhattan (G-6699)
Kindercare Learning Ctrs LLC..............E 913 451-6066
Shawnee Mission (G-11534)
Knox Presbt Ch Child Dev Ctr ....F 913 888-0089
Overland Park (G-8925)
La Petite Academy Inc..........................F 913 685-2800
Shawnee Mission (G-11541)
La Petite Academy Inc..........................E 913 441-5100
Shawnee Mission (G-11542)
La Petite Academy Inc..........................F 785 843-5703
Lawrence (G-4951)
La Petite Academy Inc..........................F 316 684-5916
Wichita (G-14909)
La Petite Academy Inc..........................F 785 273-9393
Topeka (G-12827)
La Petite Academy Inc..........................F 913 432-5053
Shawnee Mission (G-11543)
La Petite Academy Inc..........................F 913 764-2345
Olathe (G-7848)
La Petite Academy Inc..........................F 913 492-4183
Lenexa (G-5960)
La Petite Academy Inc..........................F 913 649-5773
Overland Park (G-8936)
La Petite Academy Inc..........................F 785 843-6445
Lawrence (G-4952)
La Petite Academy Inc..........................F 913 780-2318
Olathe (G-7849)
La Petite Academy Inc..........................F 913 469-1006
Overland Park (G-8937)
Lakeshore Learning Center Svcs..........E 785 271-9146
Topeka (G-12831)
Learn & Grow Childcare Center.............F 316 777-0355
Mulvane (G-7219)
Learning Care Group Inc.......................E 913 851-7800
Shawnee Mission (G-11552)
Lets Grow Preschool ....F 913 262-2261
Shawnee Mission (G-11565)
Little Bldg Blocks Daycare LLC.............F 913 856-5633
Gardner (G-2354)
Little Learners Early Childho.................F 913 254-1818
Olathe (G-7861)
Little Tots Montessori Corp ....F 913 602-7923
Kansas City (G-4205)
Little Wnders Christn Day Care.............E 913 393-3035
Olathe (G-7862)
Lord of Life Lutheran Church ....E 913 681-5167
Leawood (G-5459)
Loving Arms Child Care Center.............E 316 722-1912
Wichita (G-14981)
Loving Arms Daycare Ctrs Inc...............F 785 238-2767
Junction City (G-3722)
M L K Child Development Center ....E 785 827-3841
Salina (G-10587)
Manhattan Day Care & Lrng Ctr............F 785 776-5071
Manhattan (G-6721)
Martin Luther King Jr Child De ....E 785 827-3841
Salina (G-10593)
Marysville School District ....D 785 562-5386
Marysville (G-6902)
Mini Adventures.....................................F 913 334-6008
Kansas City (G-4262)
Mini Masters Lrng Academy LLC ....F 785 862-0772
Topeka (G-12905)
Munchkin Village....................................F 620 577-2440
Independence (G-3542)
My Child Advocate PA ....F 913 829-8838
Olathe (G-7909)
N2 Kids Enterprises Inc.........................E 913 648-5457
Shawnee Mission (G-11664)
Nall Ave Baptist Church ....E 913 432-4141
Prairie Village (G-10049)
Neighborhood Learning Ctr LLC ....F 785 238-2321
Junction City (G-3729)
Nek Cap Inc ....F 785 364-4798
Holton (G-3107)
Nek Cap Inc ....E 785 742-2222
Hiawatha (G-3019)
Nek Cap Inc ....F 913 367-7848
Atchison (G-251)
Nek Cap Inc ....F 913 651-5692
Leavenworth (G-5276)
Nek Cap Inc ....F 785 456-9165
Wamego (G-13430)
New Day Educare ....F 913 764-1353
Olathe (G-7917)
New Generation.....................................F 620 223-1506
Fort Scott (G-1993)
New Song Academy Inc ....E 316 688-1911
Wichita (G-15169)
Newton Cmnty Child Care Ctr................E 316 284-6525
Newton (G-7392)
Newton Medical Ctr Child Care..............F 316 804-6094
Newton (G-7394)
Noahs Arkademy....................................F 620 331-7791
Independence (G-3544)
Northridge Family Dev Ctr ....E 785 284-2401
Sabetha (G-10322)
Olathe Unified School Dst 233...............D 913 780-7410
Olathe (G-7953)
Old Mission United Methdst Ch.............F 913 262-1040
Fairway (G-1915)
One of Kind Progressive Chld C ....E 785 830-9040
Lawrence (G-5045)
Open Arms Lthran Child Dev Ctr...........E 316 721-5675
Wichita (G-15221)
Open Arms Lthran Child Dev Ctr...........E 913 856-4250
Gardner (G-2358)
Open Minds Child Dev Ctr LLC..............F 913 703-6736
Olathe (G-7958)
Our Ladys Montessori School ....F 913 403-9550
Kansas City (G-4302)
Pandarama Prschool Toddler Ctr ....F 913 342-9692
Kansas City (G-4308)
Paola Assembly of God Inc....................F 913 294-5198
Paola (G-9578)
Parkdale Pre-School Center..................E 785 235-7240
Topeka (G-12960)
Pawnee Avenue Church of God.............E 316 683-5648
Wichita (G-15273)
Peanut Co LLC ....E 913 647-2240
Overland Park (G-9150)
Peppermint Pttys Mntssori Schl............F 913 631-9376
Shawnee Mission (G-11725)
Pioneer Pre School LLC........................E 913 338-4282
Shawnee Mission (G-11735)
Plymouth Preschool Lrng Ctr ....E 316 684-0222
Wichita (G-15309)
Prairie Bend Ptwtomi Childcare ....E 785 966-2707
Mayetta (G-6918)
Prairie Ctr Christn Childcare..................E 913 390-0230
Olathe (G-7997)
Primrose School ....E 316 807-8622
Wichita (G-15345)
Princeton Childrens Center Wl ....F 316 618-0275
Wichita (G-15347)
Rhum Wee Rockets Pre School.............F 316 776-9330
Rose Hill (G-10246)
Rock Pre-K Center ....F 785 266-2285
Topeka (G-13023)
Rose Hill Unified School Dst.................E 316 776-3340
Rose Hill (G-10248)
Russell Child Dev Ctr Inc ....D 620 275-0291
Garden City (G-2270)
Saint Ann Child Care Center..................F 913 362-4660
Shawnee Mission (G-11824)
Salvation Army ....F 913 782-3640
Olathe (G-8052)
Salvation Army ....F 913 782-3640
Olathe (G-8053)
Sas Childcare Inc ....E 913 897-8900
Leawood (G-5548)
Seaman Unified School Dst 345 ....E 785 286-7103
Topeka (G-13048)
Security Benefit Academy Inc ....E 785 438-3000
Topeka (G-13051)
Sharon Baptist Church..........................F 316 684-5156
Wichita (G-15573)
Shawnee Church of Nazarene ....F 913 631-5555
Shawnee Mission (G-11850)
Shawnee Hts Untd Methdst Ch..............E 785 379-5492
Tecumseh (G-12243)
Shawnee Presbyterian Church..............E 913 631-6689
Shawnee Mission (G-11862)
Shining Stars Daycare Center ....E 913 829-5000
Olathe (G-8063)
Small Beginnings...................................E 913 851-2223
Shawnee Mission (G-11874)
Smart Start of Kansas LLC ....F 620 345-6000
Moundridge (G-7197)
Southeast Kansas Community..............F 620 365-7189
Iola (G-3634)
Southeast Kansas Community..............F 620 795-2102
Oswego (G-8236)
Special Beginnings Inc..........................D 913 894-0131
Shawnee Mission (G-11880)
Special Beginnings Inc..........................D 913 393-2223
Olathe (G-8075)
St Agnes Montessori Pre School ....E 913 262-2400
Westwood (G-13560)
St Johns Child Dev Ctr LLC ....F 620 564-2044
Ellinwood (G-1639)
St Michaels Day School Inc ....E 913 432-1174
Shawnee Mission (G-11890)
Start To Finish Celebration ....F 785 364-2257
Grantville (G-2498)
Stepping Stones Day Care Ctr..............F 913 724-7700
Basehor (G-389)
Stepping Stones Inc ....D 785 843-5919
Lawrence (G-5123)
Sunset Zoological Pk Wildlife................E 785 587-2737
Manhattan (G-6818)
Sunshine Day Care LLC ....F 620 221-1177
Winfield (G-16176)
Suzanna Wesley Child Care..................F 785 478-3703
Topeka (G-13127)
Swan Corporation..................................F 913 390-1411
Olathe (G-8090)

S I C

Swansons Streamway Dog P F 913 422-8242
Shawnee Mission *(G-11915)*
Tdc Learning Centers Inc F 785 234-2273
Topeka *(G-13145)*
Tender Hearts Inc F 913 962-2200
Shawnee Mission *(G-11925)*
Tender Hearts Child Care Ctr F 785 754-3937
Quinter *(G-10188)*
Tender Hearts Inc F 913 788-2273
Kansas City *(G-4463)*
Todays Tomorrows Lrng Ctr LLC F 888 602-1815
Mulvane *(G-7228)*
Top Flight Kids Learning Ctr E 913 768-4661
Olathe *(G-8114)*
Topeka Day Care Inc F 785 272-5051
Topeka *(G-13174)*
Topeka Lutheran Schl Cntr For E 785 272-1704
Lawrence *(G-5140)*
Training & Evaluation Cente E 620 615-5850
Hutchinson *(G-3468)*
Tree House Learning Center F 316 773-3335
Wichita *(G-15796)*
Trinity Daycare & Preschool F 316 838-0909
Wichita *(G-15801)*
Tutor Time Lrng Systems Inc E 316 721-0848
Wichita *(G-15818)*
Tutor Time Lrng Systems Inc E 316 721-0464
Wichita *(G-15819)*
Unified School District 259 B 316 973-7292
Wichita *(G-15834)*
Victoria Flls Sklld Cre & Rhab F 316 733-0654
Andover *(G-114)*
We R Kids LLC F 316 729-0172
Wichita *(G-15940)*
Wee Workshop Inc E 913 681-2191
Stilwell *(G-12179)*
West Side Kids Day Out Program F 913 764-0813
Olathe *(G-8151)*
Wichita Montessori School F 316 686-7265
Wichita *(G-16012)*
Wichita Top Childrens Fund D 316 260-9479
Wichita *(G-16041)*
Womens Community Y F 913 682-6404
Leavenworth *(G-5308)*
Woodland United Methodist Ch F 316 265-6669
Wichita *(G-16066)*
Word of Life Preschool E 316 838-5683
Wichita *(G-16071)*
YMCA of Hutchinson Reno Cnty D 620 662-1203
Hutchinson *(G-3494)*
YMCA Topeaka Downtown Branch E 785 354-8591
Topeka *(G-13256)*
Young Mens Christian F 785 233-9815
Topeka *(G-13258)*
Young Mens Christian Assn E 620 275-1199
Garden City *(G-2319)*
Young Mens Christian Associa D 316 320-9622
El Dorado *(G-1616)*
Young Mens Christian Associa C 316 219-9622
Wichita *(G-16093)*
Young Mens Christian Associa D 316 260-9622
Wichita *(G-16094)*
Young Mens Christian Associa C 316 942-5511
Wichita *(G-16095)*
Young Mens Christian Associat C 620 545-7290
Viola *(G-13380)*
Young Mens Christian Associat C 316 685-2251
Wichita *(G-16096)*
Young Mens Christian Gr Kansas D 913 362-3489
Prairie Village *(G-10088)*
Young Mens Christian Gr Kansas C 913 393-9622
Olathe *(G-8163)*
Young Mens Christian Gr Kansas D 913 782-7707
Olathe *(G-8164)*
Young MNS Chrstn Assn of Tpeka C 785 354-8591
Topeka *(G-13259)*
Young MNS Chrstn Assn Pttsburg D 620 231-1100
Pittsburg *(G-9972)*

8361 Residential Care

Agape Center of Hope LLC F 316 393-7252
Wichita *(G-13643)*
Ala Operations LLC E 785 313-4059
Kansas City *(G-3795)*
American Baptist Estates Inc E 316 263-8264
Wichita *(G-13683)*
Angel Square F 785 534-1080
Concordia *(G-1102)*
Applewood Rehabilation Inc E 620 431-7300
Altoona *(G-75)*
Atria Senior Living Inc E 785 234-6225
Topeka *(G-12353)*
Bethesda Lthran Cmmunities Inc C 913 906-5000
Olathe *(G-7551)*
Bickford Overland Park LLC E 913 782-3200
Shawnee Mission *(G-11162)*
Big Lkes Developmental Ctr Inc D 785 776-9201
Manhattan *(G-6558)*
Big Lkes Developmental Ctr Inc F 785 776-7748
Manhattan *(G-6559)*
Big Lkes Developmental Ctr Inc E 785 632-5357
Clay Center *(G-843)*
Big Lkes Developmental Ctr Inc F 785 776-0777
Manhattan *(G-6560)*
Brad Carson F 620 429-1011
Columbus *(G-1062)*
Brad Carson F 620 856-3999
Baxter Springs *(G-400)*
Brandon Woods Retirement Cmnty C 785 838-8000
Lawrence *(G-4766)*
Bridge Hven Mmory Care Rsdents E 785 856-1630
Lawrence *(G-4767)*
Brookdale Senior Living Commun F 316 788-0370
Derby *(G-1226)*
Brown Memorial Foundation E 785 263-2351
Abilene *(G-19)*
Caney Guest Home Inc F 620 431-7115
Chanute *(G-709)*
Cedars Inc E 620 241-7959
McPherson *(G-6943)*
Chaucer Estates LLC D 316 630-8111
Wichita *(G-14000)*
Cherished Friends LLC F 620 326-3700
Wellington *(G-13495)*
Cherry Vlg Assisted Self-Care F 620 793-5765
Great Bend *(G-2539)*
Choices Network Inc B 785 820-8018
Salina *(G-10447)*
Class Ltd D 620 231-3131
Pittsburg *(G-9835)*
Class Ltd C 620 429-1212
Columbus *(G-1066)*
Cof Training Services Inc D 785 242-5035
Ottawa *(G-8258)*
Comfort Care Homes Kans Cy LLC F 913 643-0111
Prairie Village *(G-10021)*
Community Living Opportunities F 913 341-9316
Overland Park *(G-8582)*
Community Lving Opprtnties Inc E 913 499-8894
Overland Park *(G-8583)*
Community Lving Opprtnties Inc E 785 979-1889
Baldwin City *(G-357)*
Community Lving Opprtnties Inc E 913 341-9316
Lenexa *(G-5777)*
Community Lving Opprtnties Inc C 785 865-5520
Lawrence *(G-4804)*
Community Lving Opprtnties Inc F 785 832-2332
Lawrence *(G-4805)*
Community Lving Opprtnties Inc E 785 843-7072
Lawrence *(G-4806)*
Congregational Home C 785 274-3350
Topeka *(G-12501)*
Corrections Kansas Department C 620 285-0300
Larned *(G-4699)*
Cottonwood Point Inc F 316 775-0368
Augusta *(G-315)*
Country Acres Senior Residence F 316 773-3900
Wichita *(G-14107)*
Country Living Inc F 620 842-5858
Anthony *(G-125)*
Country Place Senior Living F 785 336-6868
Seneca *(G-10860)*
County of Sedgwick E 316 660-9775
Wichita *(G-14110)*
County of Sedgwick E 316 660-9500
Wichita *(G-14113)*
Crawford Cnty Assistd Lvng Com F 620 724-6760
Girard *(G-2400)*
Creative Community Living of E F 620 221-9431
Winfield *(G-16135)*
Creative Community Living S B 620 221-1119
Winfield *(G-16136)*
Douglass Medicalodges E 316 747-2157
Douglass *(G-1466)*
Dove Estates Senior Living E 316 550-6343
Goddard *(G-2436)*
Eagle Estates Inc E 620 331-1662
Independence *(G-3513)*
East Orlndo Hlth Rehab Ctr Inc D 913 383-9866
Shawnee Mission *(G-11326)*
Eb Group E 217 787-9000
Olathe *(G-7666)*
Eldercare Inc C 620 792-5942
Great Bend *(G-2559)*
Elm Acres Youth & Family Svcs C 620 231-9840
Pittsburg *(G-9855)*
Elm Acres Youth & Family Svcs E 620 231-6129
Pittsburg *(G-9856)*
Emberhope Inc C 316 529-9100
Newton *(G-7339)*
Emberhope Inc C 316 529-9100
Wichita *(G-14273)*
Emberhope Inc D 620 225-0276
Dodge City *(G-1357)*
Evangelical Lutheran D 785 456-9482
Wamego *(G-13422)*
Faith Village Inc D 913 856-4607
Gardner *(G-2343)*
Faith Village Inc D 913 906-5000
Olathe *(G-7701)*
Family Crisis Center Inc F 620 793-9941
Great Bend *(G-2562)*
Fountain Villa Inc F 620 365-6002
Iola *(G-3602)*
◆ **Futures Unlimited Inc** E 620 326-8906
Wellington *(G-13501)*
Gansel House LLC F 620 331-7422
Independence *(G-3522)*
Garden Vly Retirement Vlg LLC C 620 275-9651
Garden City *(G-2184)*
Gps Kids Club F 620 282-2288
Hoisington *(G-3065)*
Gran Villa F 620 583-7473
Eureka *(G-1887)*
Guest Home Estates F 620 431-7115
Pittsburg *(G-9869)*
Guest Home Estates VI E 620 223-1620
Fort Scott *(G-1975)*
Help Housing Corporation D 913 651-6810
Leavenworth *(G-5253)*
Holiday Healthcare LLC E 620 343-9285
Emporia *(G-1773)*
Homestead of Hays D 785 628-3200
Hays *(G-2850)*
Homestead of Olathe North C 913 829-1403
Olathe *(G-7771)*
Hospital Dst 1 of Rice Cnty D 620 257-5173
Lyons *(G-6485)*
Hufford House D 620 225-0276
Dodge City *(G-1377)*
Johnson County Dev Support F 913 826-2626
Lenexa *(G-5931)*
Kansas Dept For Aging & Disabi B 785 296-5389
Topeka *(G-12769)*
Kc House of Hope F 913 262-8885
Overland Park *(G-8907)*
Kearny County Home For Aged E 620 355-7836
Lakin *(G-4652)*
Kenwood Plaza Inc F 620 549-6133
Saint John *(G-10354)*
Kidstlc Inc C 913 764-2887
Olathe *(G-7839)*
Kvc Behavioral Healthcare Inc D 913 322-4900
Olathe *(G-7844)*
Kvc Health Systems Inc E 316 796-5503
Wichita *(G-14902)*
Kvc Health Systems Inc D 913 322-4900
Olathe *(G-7845)*
Lakemary Center Inc E 913 768-6831
Olathe *(G-7853)*
Lakeside Terrace E 785 284-0005
Sabetha *(G-10315)*
Larksfield Place E 316 636-1000
Wichita *(G-14925)*
Las Villas Del Norte D 760 741-1046
Junction City *(G-3720)*
Legend Senior Living LLC D 316 616-6288
Wichita *(G-14954)*
Lif Inc F 316 260-6092
Wichita *(G-14960)*
Marquis Place Concordia LLc E 785 243-2255
Concordia *(G-1123)*
Martin Luther Homes Kansas Inc D 620 229-8702
Winfield *(G-16156)*
Meade Hospital District C 620 873-2146
Meade *(G-7052)*
Meadowlark Adult Care Home E 316 773-2277
Wichita *(G-15030)*
Medical Lodges Inc E 620 325-2244
Neodesha *(G-7244)*

Medicalodges Inc.....D..... 316 755-1288
Valley Center *(G-13348)*
Mennonite Frndship Communities.....C..... 620 663-7175
South Hutchinson *(G-12062)*
Meridian Nursing Center Inc.....D..... 316 942-8471
Wichita *(G-15041)*
Midwest Health Services Inc.....C..... 316 729-2400
Wichita *(G-15094)*
Midwest Health Services Inc.....E..... 785 776-1772
Manhattan *(G-6750)*
Midwest Health Services Inc.....E..... 620 272-9800
Garden City *(G-2233)*
Mirror Inc.....F..... 913 248-1943
Shawnee Mission *(G-11642)*
Mirror Inc.....E..... 316 283-6743
Newton *(G-7389)*
Multi Community Diversfd Svcs.....F..... 620 241-6693
McPherson *(G-7009)*
New Hope Services.....F..... 620 231-9895
Pittsburg *(G-9911)*
Northview Developmental Svcs.....F..... 316 283-5170
Newton *(G-7400)*
Occk Inc.....E..... 785 243-1977
Concordia *(G-1125)*
Occk Inc.....E..... 785 738-3490
Beloit *(G-498)*
Occk Inc.....C..... 785 827-9383
Salina *(G-10617)*
Omega Senior Living LLC.....A..... 316 260-9494
Wichita *(G-15215)*
One Hope United - Northern Reg.....E..... 785 827-1756
Salina *(G-10621)*
Ottawa Retirement Plaza Inc.....E..... 785 242-1127
Ottawa *(G-8300)*
Overland Park Seniorcare LLC.....E..... 913 491-1144
Shawnee Mission *(G-11710)*
Park Meadows Senior Living LLC.....D..... 913 901-8200
Overland Park *(G-9141)*
Prairie Elder Homes LLC.....F..... 913 257-5425
Overland Park *(G-9176)*
Prairie View Inc.....B..... 316 284-6400
Newton *(G-7407)*
Prairie Wind Villa Assstant.....F..... 785 543-6180
Phillipsburg *(G-9795)*
Pratt County Achievement Place.....F..... 620 672-6610
Pratt *(G-10135)*
Presbyterian Manors Inc.....D..... 785 841-4262
Lawrence *(G-5074)*
Presbytrian Mnors of MD-Merica.....E..... 620 223-5550
Fort Scott *(G-1999)*
Reflection Ridge Golf Corp.....E..... 316 721-0500
Wichita *(G-15433)*
Reno County Youth Services.....E..... 620 694-2500
Hutchinson *(G-3425)*
RES-Care Kansas Inc.....D..... 620 793-8501
Great Bend *(G-2631)*
Residentialsoultion LLC.....E..... 913 268-2967
Shawnee *(G-11017)*
Rh Montgomery Properties Inc.....F..... 785 284-3418
Sabetha *(G-10325)*
Riverside Resources Inc.....D..... 913 651-6810
Leavenworth *(G-5287)*
Rose Villa Inc.....E..... 785 232-0671
Topeka *(G-13029)*
Saint Francis Academy Newton.....E..... 316 284-2477
Newton *(G-7412)*
Saint Francis Cmnty Svcs Inc.....C..... 785 587-8818
Manhattan *(G-6796)*
Saint Francis Cmnty Svcs Inc.....C..... 620 276-4482
Garden City *(G-2272)*
Saint Francis Cmnty Svcs Inc.....E..... 785 825-0541
Salina *(G-10659)*
Saint Francis Cmnty Svcs Inc.....E..... 785 452-9653
Salina *(G-10660)*
Saint Francis Cmnty Svcs Inc.....F..... 316 831-0330
Wichita *(G-15507)*
Saint Francis Cmnty Svcs Inc.....D..... 785 243-4215
Concordia *(G-1128)*
Salvation Army.....D..... 913 232-5400
Kansas City *(G-4398)*
Schowalter Villa.....E..... 620 327-0400
Hesston *(G-3000)*
Sedgwick Juvenile Field Svcs.....E..... 316 660-5380
Wichita *(G-15550)*
Silver Crest At Deercreek.....F..... 913 681-1101
Shawnee Mission *(G-11869)*
Silvercrest At College View Sr.....F..... 913 915-6041
Lenexa *(G-6135)*
Spearville Senior Living Inc.....E..... 785 506-6003
Topeka *(G-13087)*
Spectrum Retirement Shawnee KS.....E..... 913 631-0058
Shawnee Mission *(G-11882)*
St Johns Rest Home Inc.....D..... 785 735-2208
Hays *(G-2910)*
Substance Abuse Cntr E Kansas.....E..... 913 362-0045
Kansas City *(G-4444)*
Sunrise Senior Living Inc.....D..... 913 262-1611
Prairie Village *(G-10070)*
Sunrise Senior Living LLC.....D..... 913 685-3340
Overland Park *(G-9376)*
Sunrise Senior Living Svcs Inc.....E..... 913 262-1611
Prairie Village *(G-10071)*
Tfi LLC.....F..... 785 235-1524
Topeka *(G-13154)*
Tfi Family Services Inc.....D..... 620 342-2239
Emporia *(G-1834)*
Tfi Family Services Inc.....F..... 913 894-2985
Overland Park *(G-9404)*
Tfi Family Services Inc.....F..... 620 342-2239
Emporia *(G-1835)*
Tfi Family Services Inc.....F..... 620 431-0312
Chanute *(G-768)*
Tfi Family Services Inc.....D..... 785 232-1019
Topeka *(G-13155)*
Town Village Leawood LLC.....E..... 913 491-3681
Shawnee Mission *(G-11936)*
Tri City Assisted Living LLC.....D..... 913 782-3200
Olathe *(G-8120)*
Tri-Valley Developmental Svcs.....D..... 620 223-3990
Fort Scott *(G-2012)*
Tri-Valley Developmental Svcs.....D..... 620 365-3307
Iola *(G-3637)*
Twin Rivers Developmental Supp.....D..... 620 402-6395
Arkansas City *(G-183)*
Twin Vly Dvelopmental Svcs Inc.....F..... 785 747-2611
Greenleaf *(G-2670)*
Twin Vly Dvelopmental Svcs Inc.....E..... 785 353-2347
Beattie *(G-421)*
Twin Vly Dvelopmental Svcs Inc.....E..... 785 353-2347
Beattie *(G-422)*
Twin Vly Dvelopmental Svcs Inc.....F..... 785 353-2226
Beattie *(G-423)*
University of Kansas.....E..... 913 588-6798
Kansas City *(G-4496)*
Valeo Behavioral Health Care.....E..... 785 233-1730
Topeka *(G-13215)*
Via Christi Health Inc.....D..... 316 685-0400
Wichita *(G-15890)*
Village Shalom Inc.....C..... 913 317-2600
Shawnee Mission *(G-11979)*
Villages Inc.....F..... 785 267-5900
Topeka *(G-13224)*
Vintage Group Inc.....E..... 316 321-7777
El Dorado *(G-1612)*
Vintage Park At Ottawa LLC.....F..... 785 242-3715
Ottawa *(G-8320)*
Visiting Nurses Association.....D..... 785 843-3738
Lawrence *(G-5175)*
Welstone.....F..... 913 788-6045
Shawnee Mission *(G-12004)*
West Wchita Asssted Living LLC.....F..... 316 361-2500
Wichita *(G-15957)*
Wheat State Manor Inc.....D..... 316 799-2181
Whitewater *(G-13573)*
Wichita Childrens Home.....D..... 316 684-6581
Wichita *(G-15987)*
Womens Chldren Shelter Linwood.....D..... 620 231-0415
Pittsburg *(G-9971)*
Youth Crisis Shelter Inc.....E..... 620 421-6941
Parsons *(G-9752)*

8399 Social Services, NEC

Alcoholics Anonymous.....F..... 316 684-3661
Wichita *(G-13660)*
Als Assction Md-Merica Chapter.....F..... 913 648-2062
Shawnee Mission *(G-11099)*
Alzheimrs Dsease Rltd Dsordrs.....F..... 913 381-3888
Shawnee Mission *(G-11100)*
Children & Family Services.....D..... 785 296-4653
Topeka *(G-12464)*
City of Topeka Employees.....A..... 785 368-3749
Topeka *(G-12475)*
City of Wichita.....E..... 316 268-8351
Wichita *(G-14028)*
Compresults LLC.....F..... 913 310-9800
Fairway *(G-1906)*
County of Jefferson.....E..... 785 863-2447
Oskaloosa *(G-8222)*
Cowley County United Way Inc.....F..... 620 221-9683
Winfield *(G-16134)*
Cross-Lines Cmnty Outreach Inc.....F..... 913 281-3388
Kansas City *(G-3946)*
Destiny Supports Inc.....F..... 620 272-0564
Garden City *(G-2146)*
Developmental Svcs NW Kans.....F..... 785 735-2262
Victoria *(G-13373)*
Economic & Empolyment Support.....D..... 785 296-4276
Topeka *(G-12570)*
Erc/Resource & Referral Inc.....F..... 785 357-5171
Topeka *(G-12580)*
Harvey County Dv/SA Task Force.....F..... 316 284-6920
Newton *(G-7357)*
Health Partnership Clinic Inc.....E..... 913 433-7583
Olathe *(G-7760)*
▼ Heart To Heart Intl Inc.....E..... 913 764-5200
Lenexa *(G-5895)*
Heartland Hbtat For Hmnity Inc.....F..... 913 342-3047
Kansas City *(G-4075)*
Housing and Credit Counseling.....E..... 785 234-0217
Topeka *(G-12705)*
Jewish Fdrtion Greater Kans Cy.....E..... 913 327-8100
Shawnee Mission *(G-11489)*
Kansas Food Bank Warehouse Inc.....E..... 316 265-3663
Wichita *(G-14801)*
Ku Workgroup For Community Hea.....E..... 785 864-0533
Lawrence *(G-4949)*
L & C Home Health Agency Inc.....F..... 785 465-7444
Colby *(G-1022)*
March of Dimes Inc.....F..... 913 469-3611
Overland Park *(G-8988)*
Mt Carmel Redevelopment Corp.....F..... 913 621-4111
Kansas City *(G-4270)*
National Rural Health Assn.....F..... 913 220-2997
Leawood *(G-5500)*
Project Concern Inc.....F..... 913 367-4655
Atchison *(G-257)*
Purplefrogintl.....G..... 816 510-0871
Shawnee *(G-11014)*
Quest Services Inc.....C..... 620 208-6180
Emporia *(G-1814)*
Rebuilding Together Shawnee/Jo.....F..... 913 558-5079
Shawnee *(G-11015)*
Residential Treatment Service.....E..... 620 421-1155
Parsons *(G-9732)*
Rosewood Services Inc.....E..... 620 793-5888
Great Bend *(G-2633)*
Rsvp of Northeast Kansas Inc.....C..... 785 562-2154
Marysville *(G-6909)*
Saint Francis Cmnty Svcs Inc.....D..... 785 243-4215
Concordia *(G-1128)*
Saint Francis Community.....D..... 785 825-0541
Salina *(G-10661)*
Salvation Army.....F..... 620 343-3166
Emporia *(G-1821)*
Shawnee Regl Prevention An.....F..... 785 266-8666
Topeka *(G-13064)*
Southeast Kansas Community.....E..... 620 724-8204
Girard *(G-2419)*
Southwind Hospice Inc.....F..... 620 672-7553
Pratt *(G-10152)*
Trash Mountain Project Inc.....F..... 785 246-6845
Topeka *(G-13197)*
United Methodist Open Door.....E..... 316 265-9371
Wichita *(G-15844)*
United Way of Greater Topeka.....F..... 785 228-5110
Topeka *(G-13211)*
United Way of Wyandotte County.....E..... 913 371-3674
Kansas City *(G-4492)*
Urban League of Kansas Inc.....F..... 316 440-9217
Wichita *(G-15861)*
Willlowtree Supports Inc.....E..... 913 353-1970
Shawnee *(G-11053)*
Winfield Area Hbtat For Hmnity.....E..... 620 221-7298
Winfield *(G-16184)*
Young Kansas Christian.....C..... 785 233-1750
Topeka *(G-13257)*

84 MUSEUMS, ART GALLERIES, AND BOTANICAL AND ZOOLOGICAL GARDENS

8412 Museums & Art Galleries

Adjutant Generals Dept Kans.....F..... 785 862-1020
Topeka *(G-12288)*
American Overseas Schools Hist.....E..... 316 265-6837
Wichita *(G-13693)*
B-29 Museum Inc.....F..... 620 282-1123
Pratt *(G-10099)*

S I C

Burlingame Historical Preserva............D....... 785 654-3561
Burlingame *(G-622)*
City of Newton..E....... 316 283-3113
Newton *(G-7330)*
City of Salina..F....... 785 309-5775
Salina *(G-10450)*
▲ **Cosmosphere Inc**..................................E....... 620 662-2305
Hutchinson *(G-3247)*
County of Franklin...................................E....... 785 242-1250
Ottawa *(G-8261)*
County of Johnson...................................F....... 913 715-2550
Overland Park *(G-8605)*
Culture House Inc....................................E....... 913 393-3141
Olathe *(G-7629)*
Dane G Hansen Memorial M.....................F....... 785 689-4848
Logan *(G-6423)*
Deaf Cultural Ctr Foundation.................F....... 913 782-5808
Olathe *(G-7643)*
Docs Friends Inc......................................F....... 316 943-3246
Wichita *(G-14217)*
Douglas County Historical Soc..............F....... 785 841-4109
Lawrence *(G-4840)*
Executive Office of Kansas....................F....... 785 272-8681
Topeka *(G-12587)*
Exploration Place Inc...............................D....... 316 660-0600
Wichita *(G-14323)*
Fisch Bowl Inc..F....... 316 200-5200
Wichita *(G-14377)*
Fort Hays State University......................E....... 785 628-4286
Hays *(G-2811)*
Great Plins Trnspration Museum............F....... 316 263-0944
Wichita *(G-14506)*
Greyhound Hall of Fame..........................F....... 785 263-3000
Abilene *(G-35)*
Historic Presrvtn Aliance of W...............D....... 316 269-9432
Wichita *(G-14617)*
Historic Wichita Sedqwick Cnty.............E....... 316 219-1871
Wichita *(G-14618)*
Interntnal Sclpture Foundation...............F....... 785 864-2599
Olathe *(G-7800)*
Kansas Firefighters Museum...................F....... 316 264-5990
Wichita *(G-14799)*
Kansas Genealogical Socie.....................E....... 620 225-1951
Dodge City *(G-1386)*
Kansas Museum of Mltry Histry..............F....... 316 775-1425
Augusta *(G-329)*
Kansas State Historical Soc....................F....... 785 272-8681
Topeka *(G-12807)*
Kansas State University..........................E....... 785 532-7718
Manhattan *(G-6680)*
Kauffman Museum Association..............F....... 316 283-1612
North Newton *(G-7436)*
Lanesfield Schl Historic Site...................F....... 913 893-6645
Edgerton *(G-1487)*
Lecompton Historical Soc Inc.................F....... 785 887-6260
Lecompton *(G-5611)*
Lucas Arts Hmnties Council Inc.............F....... 785 525-6118
Lucas *(G-6473)*
Mark Arts...F....... 316 634-2787
Wichita *(G-15009)*
Medicine Lodge Indian & Peace..............F....... 620 886-9815
Medicine Lodge *(G-7066)*
Midwest Educational Center...................F....... 785 776-1234
Manhattan *(G-6747)*
National AG Ctr & Hall Fame...................F....... 913 721-1075
Bonner Springs *(G-565)*
National Archives and Rec ADM..............D....... 785 263-6700
Abilene *(G-47)*
Pawnee Valley Scouts Inc........................F....... 620 285-6427
Larned *(G-4710)*
Richard Allen Cultural Center.................E....... 913 682-8772
Leavenworth *(G-5285)*
Rolling Hills Zoo Foundation...................E....... 785 827-9488
Salina *(G-10652)*
Rooks County Historical Museum..........F....... 785 425-7217
Stockton *(G-12185)*
Santa Fe Trail Association......................F....... 620 285-2054
Larned *(G-4711)*
Seward County Historical Soc.................E....... 620 624-7624
Liberal *(G-6366)*
Stafford County Historical.......................F....... 620 234-5664
Stafford *(G-12110)*
Sunflower Chapter of The Ameri.............F....... 785 656-0329
Hays *(G-2915)*
University of Kansas...............................C....... 785 864-2451
Lawrence *(G-5164)*
University of Kansas...............................D....... 785 864-4710
Lawrence *(G-5165)*
University of Kansas...............................C....... 785 864-4540
Lawrence *(G-5167)*
Wichita Center For The Arts....................F....... 316 315-0151
Wichita *(G-15985)*

8422 Arboreta, Botanical & Zoological Gardens

Botanica Inc..F....... 316 264-0448
Wichita *(G-13872)*
City of Garden City...................................E....... 620 276-1250
Garden City *(G-2125)*
City of Topeka..E....... 785 368-9180
Topeka *(G-12468)*
Hedricks Promotions Inc...........................E....... 620 422-3296
Nickerson *(G-7434)*
Overland Park Arboretm & Btncl...............E....... 913 685-3604
Bucyrus *(G-606)*
Pine Howard Grdn Ctr & Grnhse...............E....... 785 749-0302
Lawrence *(G-5064)*

86 MEMBERSHIP ORGANIZATIONS

8611 Business Associations

Abwa Management LLC............................E....... 913 732-5100
Overland Park *(G-8338)*
Asian Amrcn Chmber of Commerce.........F....... 913 338-0774
Shawnee Mission *(G-11124)*
Atchison Area Chamber Commerce.........F....... 913 367-2427
Atchison *(G-206)*
Bettis Contractors Inc...............................E....... 785 783-8353
Topeka *(G-12378)*
Bluetooth Sig Inc.......................................F....... 913 317-4700
Overland Park *(G-8470)*
Caldwell Area Chambe..............................F....... 620 845-6914
Caldwell *(G-655)*
Chamber of Commerce..............................F....... 785 258-2115
Herington *(G-2972)*
City of Great Bend.....................................E....... 620 793-4111
Great Bend *(G-2540)*
City of Halstead...E....... 316 835-2286
Halstead *(G-2697)*
City of Overland Park................................C....... 913 895-6000
Shawnee Mission *(G-11231)*
City of Pittsburg...D....... 620 308-6916
Pittsburg *(G-9834)*
Coopertive Cpon Rdemption Assn..........F....... 913 384-3830
Westwood *(G-13552)*
Department of Kansas Disabled..............E....... 316 681-1948
Wichita *(G-14195)*
Diecks Inc...E....... 785 632-5550
Clay Center *(G-860)*
Ellswrth Knplis Chmber Cmmerce..........F....... 785 472-4071
Ellsworth *(G-1673)*
Garden City Co-Op Inc..............................F....... 620 276-8903
Garden City *(G-2171)*
Garden Cy Area Chmber Commerce.......F....... 620 276-3264
Garden City *(G-2181)*
Gcsaa..F....... 800 832-4410
Lawrence *(G-4870)*
Global Prairie Marketing LLC...................E....... 913 722-7244
Mission Hills *(G-7142)*
Greater Topeka Commerce......................E....... 785 234-2644
Topeka *(G-12646)*
Heartland Credit Union Assn...................F....... 913 297-2480
Overland Park *(G-8807)*
Heartland Credit Union Assn...................F....... 316 942-7965
Wichita *(G-14583)*
Hutchinson/Reno County Chamber.........F....... 620 662-3391
Hutchinson *(G-3329)*
I P H F H A Inc...F....... 316 685-1200
Wichita *(G-14664)*
International Assn Plas Dist....................F....... 913 345-1005
Overland Park *(G-8856)*
K U Endowment Association....................F....... 785 830-7600
Lawrence *(G-4929)*
Kansas Assn of Insur Agents....................F....... 785 232-0561
Topeka *(G-12759)*
Kansas Bankers Association....................E....... 785 232-3444
Topeka *(G-12762)*
Kansas Consulting Engineers..................F....... 785 357-1824
Topeka *(G-12767)*
Kansas Credit Union Assn........................E....... 316 942-7965
Wichita *(G-14795)*
Kansas Electric Cooperatives..................E....... 785 478-4554
Topeka *(G-12775)*
Kansas Livestock Association.................E....... 785 273-5115
Topeka *(G-12785)*
Kansas Real Estate Commission.............F....... 785 296-3411
Topeka *(G-12799)*
Kansas Regional Assn Realtors..............E....... 913 498-1100
Shawnee Mission *(G-11519)*
Kansas Rest Hospitality Assn..................F....... 316 267-8383
Wichita *(G-14821)*
Kcc Conservation District II......................F....... 316 630-4000
Wichita *(G-14838)*
Lawrence Home Builders Assn................F....... 785 748-0612
Lawrence *(G-4969)*
League Kansas Municipalities.................F....... 785 354-9565
Topeka *(G-12837)*
Lenexa Chamber of Commerce...............F....... 913 888-1414
Shawnee Mission *(G-11562)*
Louisburg Chamber of Commerce..........F....... 913 837-2826
Louisburg *(G-6457)*
Manhattan Chamber of Commerce..........F....... 785 776-8829
Manhattan *(G-6719)*
Marysville Chamber Commerce..............F....... 785 562-3101
Marysville *(G-6897)*
Midway Co-Op Association.......................F....... 785 346-5401
Osborne *(G-8211)*
Midway Co-Op Association.......................F....... 785 346-5451
Osborne *(G-8212)*
Midwest Energy Inc...................................D....... 785 625-3437
Hays *(G-2873)*
Missouri Livestock Mktg Assn.................E....... 816 891-0502
Leawood *(G-5488)*
National Auctioneers Assn.......................F....... 913 541-8084
Shawnee Mission *(G-11671)*
National Publishers Group Inc.................F....... 316 788-6271
Haysville *(G-2953)*
Ninnescah Sailing Association...............F....... 316 729-5757
Wichita *(G-15181)*
Oakley Area Chamber Commerce............F....... 785 672-4862
Oakley *(G-7483)*
Olathe Chamber of Commerce.................F....... 913 764-1050
Olathe *(G-7929)*
Overland Park Chamber Commerce........F....... 913 491-3600
Shawnee Mission *(G-11705)*
PSI Services Inc..C....... 913 895-4600
Olathe *(G-8011)*
Redbud Village..F....... 785 425-6312
Stockton *(G-12184)*
Retail Groc Assn Grter Kans Cy..............F....... 913 384-3830
Westwood *(G-13558)*
Sac & Fox Gaming Commission...............F....... 785 467-8070
Powhattan *(G-10009)*
Salina Area Chmber Cmmerce Inc...........F....... 785 827-9301
Salina *(G-10665)*
Salina Economic Dev Corp.......................F....... 785 827-9301
Salina *(G-10673)*
Service Corps Retired Execs...................F....... 316 269-6273
Wichita *(G-15567)*
Service Corps Retired Execs...................F....... 620 793-3420
Great Bend *(G-2635)*
Service Corps Retired Execs...................F....... 785 234-3049
Topeka *(G-13060)*
Smith Center Chamber Commerce...........F....... 785 282-3895
Smith Center *(G-12041)*
Spring Hill Chamber Commerce...............F....... 913 592-3893
Spring Hill *(G-12099)*
State Assn of Kans Watersheds...............F....... 785 544-6686
Robinson *(G-10215)*
Treasurer Kansas State...........................E....... 785 296-3171
Topeka *(G-13198)*
Valiant Global Def Svcs Inc.....................D....... 913 651-9782
Leavenworth *(G-5304)*
Wamego Chmber Cmmrce Minstreet........F....... 785 456-7849
Wamego *(G-13448)*
Weishaar Adaptation...............................E....... 913 367-6299
Atchison *(G-271)*
Wichita Area Chamber Commerce...........E....... 316 265-7771
Wichita *(G-15975)*
Workforce Alliance of South....................D....... 316 771-6600
Wichita *(G-16072)*

8621 Professional Membership Organizations

Accreditation Council For Busi................F....... 913 339-9356
Overland Park *(G-8342)*
Adams-Gabbert & Associates LLC...........F....... 913 735-4390
Overland Park *(G-8346)*
Advanced Health Care Corp.....................C....... 913 890-8400
Overland Park *(G-8349)*
American Academy Family Physcn..........F....... 913 906-6000
Shawnee Mission *(G-11101)*
American Acdemy Fmly Physcians..........B....... 913 906-6000
Leawood *(G-5319)*
American Assn Univ Women......................F....... 785 472-5737
Ellsworth *(G-1656)*
American College of Clinical....................E....... 913 492-3311
Lenexa *(G-5646)*

American Heart Association Ka ....E 785 272-7056
Topeka (G-12317)
American Heart Association Ka ....E 913 652-1913
Shawnee Mission (G-11104)
Association of National ....F 785 296-5474
Topeka (G-12346)
Astronomical Society Kansas Cy ....F 913 631-8413
Shawnee Mission (G-11127)
Child Health Corp America ....C 913 262-1436
Lenexa (G-5753)
Clinical Radiology Foundation ....F 913 588-6830
Kansas City (G-3920)
Command and General Staff ....F 913 651-0624
Fort Leavenworth (G-1936)
Community Care Netwrk Kans Inc ....E 785 233-8483
Topeka (G-12492)
Cowley County Joint Board Hlth ....F 620 221-1430
Winfield (G-16133)
Dental Associates ....F 620 276-7681
Garden City (G-2144)
Domestic Vlnce Assn of Cntl Ka ....F 785 827-5862
Salina (G-10480)
Firemans Relief Assoc Inc ....F 620 365-4972
Iola (G-3601)
First Response ....F 913 557-2187
Paola (G-9559)
Health Dpknsas Assn Lcal Depts ....F 785 271-8391
Topeka (G-12672)
Henson Hutton Mudrick Gragson ....F 785 232-2200
Topeka (G-12684)
Hillside Medical Office ....E 316 685-1381
Wichita (G-14613)
Job Board Network LLC ....F 913 238-1181
Overland Park (G-8875)
Kansas Assn of Insur Agents ....F 785 232-0561
Topeka (G-12759)
Kansas Assn of Schl Boards ....E 785 273-3600
Topeka (G-12761)
Kansas Bar Association ....E 785 234-5696
Topeka (G-12763)
Kansas City Blues Society Inc ....F 913 660-4692
Olathe (G-7824)
Kansas Cnty Dst Attys Associat ....D 785 232-5822
Kansas City (G-4153)
Kansas Fndtion For Med Care In ....E 785 273-2552
Topeka (G-12777)
Kansas Hospital Association ....E 785 233-7436
Topeka (G-12781)
Kansas Medical Society ....F 785 235-2383
Topeka (G-12791)
Kansas National Education Assn ....F 913 268-4005
Shawnee Mission (G-11518)
Kansas National Education Assn ....E 785 232-8271
Topeka (G-12793)
Medical Society Sedgwick Cnty ....E 316 683-7557
Wichita (G-15033)
Mental Health Association of ....D 316 685-1821
Wichita (G-15039)
Mental Health Association of ....B 316 651-5368
Wichita (G-15040)
National Bd For Rspratory Care ....F 913 895-4900
Overland Park (G-9069)
National Healthcareer Assn ....E 800 499-9092
Leawood (G-5499)
National Rural Health Assn ....F 913 220-2997
Leawood (G-5500)
Olathe Unified School Dst 233 ....C 913 780-7880
Olathe (G-7952)
Revisor of Statutes ....E 785 296-2321
Topeka (G-13012)
Salina Child Care Association ....E 785 827-6431
Salina (G-10667)
Society of Tchers Fmly Mdicine ....F 913 906-6000
Shawnee Mission (G-11877)
Society of Teachers of Family ....F 913 906-6000
Shawnee Mission (G-11878)
South Centl KS Educatn Svc Ctr ....F 620 584-3300
Clearwater (G-897)
Topeka Unified School Dst 501 ....D 785 295-3750
Topeka (G-13189)
University of Kansas ....E 316 293-2620
Wichita (G-15857)
Wichita Area Assn of Realtors ....F 316 263-3167
Wichita (G-15974)
Wichita Bar Association ....F 316 263-2251
Wichita (G-15980)

8631 Labor Unions & Similar Organizations

American Federation ....F 785 267-0100
Topeka (G-12315)
Calvin Investments LLC ....F 785 266-8755
Topeka (G-12419)
Construction & Gen Labor 1290 ....F 913 432-1903
Kansas City (G-3934)
Empac Inc ....F 316 265-9922
Wichita (G-14278)
Firefighters Bnfit Asn-Sedgwic ....E 316 660-3473
Park City (G-9618)
Go Local LLC ....E 913 231-3083
Overland Park (G-8761)
Harvest America Corporation ....E 913 342-2121
Overland Park (G-8798)
I A M A W District Lodge 70 ....F 316 522-1591
Wichita (G-14663)
International Brotherhood ....E 913 371-2640
Kansas City (G-4103)
International Brotherhood ....F 913 281-5036
Kansas City (G-4104)
International Brotherhood of ....F 913 371-2640
Kansas City (G-4105)
International Union United Au ....A 913 342-7330
Kansas City (G-4109)
International Union United Au ....C 620 251-2022
Coffeyville (G-948)
Kansas Assn of Pub Employees ....F 785 233-1956
Topeka (G-12760)
Kansas Pub Emplyee Rtrment Sys ....D 785 296-1019
Topeka (G-12798)
Kansas State Council of Fire ....F 620 662-1808
Hutchinson (G-3347)
National Assn Ltr Carriers ....E 620 378-3263
Coyville (G-1183)
National Assn Ltr Carriers ....E 620 257-3934
Lyons (G-6495)
National Assn Ltr Carriers ....F 785 232-6835
Topeka (G-12923)
Teamsters Union Local 795 ....F 316 683-2651
Wichita (G-15722)
Ufcw District Union Local 2 ....E 816 842-4086
Bel Aire (G-442)
United Steel Wrkrs of America ....F 785 234-5688
Topeka (G-13210)
United Steelworkers ....E 913 674-5067
Atchison (G-268)

8641 Civic, Social & Fraternal Associations

Alpha CHI Omega ....F 785 843-7600
Lawrence (G-4731)
American Legion ....F 620 241-0343
McPherson (G-6933)
American Legion Post 156 ....E 913 294-4676
Paola (G-9539)
American Legion Post 400 ....F 785 296-9400
Topeka (G-12319)
American Legion Post 95 Inc ....F 620 983-2048
Peabody (G-9758)
Ancient Free & Accepted M ....E 785 284-3169
Sabetha (G-10304)
Ancient Free & Accptd Masons ....D 785 738-5095
Beloit (G-473)
Argonna Post 180 Amercn Legion ....F 620 793-5912
Great Bend (G-2511)
Ball-Mccolm Post No 5 Inc ....E 620 342-1119
Emporia (G-1701)
Benevolent & P O of Elks 1404 ....F 620 276-3732
Garden City (G-2107)
Benevolent/Protectv Order Elks ....F 785 762-2922
Junction City (G-3674)
Beta Theta PHI ....D 785 843-4711
Leavenworth (G-5209)
Blind Pig ....F 785 827-7449
Salina (G-10426)
Blue River Elementary Pto Inc ....E 913 239-6000
Overland Park (G-8467)
Boys & Girls CLB Manhattan Inc ....D 785 539-1947
Manhattan (G-6567)
Boys & Girls Club of S Central ....E 316 687-5437
Wichita (G-13877)
Boys & Girls Clubs of America ....F 913 621-3260
Kansas City (G-3873)
Boys and Girls Club of Topeka ....E 785 234-5601
Topeka (G-12400)
Boys Girls Clubs Huthinson Inc ....F 620 665-7171
Hutchinson (G-3219)
Boys Grls CLB Lwrnce Lwrnce K ....D 785 841-5672
Lawrence (G-4763)
Caldwell Snior Ctizens Ctr Inc ....F 620 845-6926
Caldwell (G-657)
Central Knss Cncil of Grl Sct ....F 785 827-3679
Salina (G-10442)
Cherryvale Alumni Commnty/Educ ....F 620 336-3198
Cherryvale (G-802)
City of Emporia ....E 620 340-6339
Emporia (G-1720)
Corinth Scouts Inc ....E 913 236-8920
Roeland Park (G-10221)
Coronado Area Council Bsa ....F 785 827-4461
Salina (G-10464)
Deaf Cultural Ctr Foundation ....F 913 782-5808
Olathe (G-7643)
Deer Lk Esttes Homeowners Assn ....D 316 640-6592
Wichita (G-14185)
Delta Gamma ....F 785 830-9945
Lawrence (G-4831)
Delta Kappa Gamma Society ....E 620 793-3977
Great Bend (G-2553)
Delta Tau Delta Society ....F 785 843-6866
Lawrence (G-4832)
Delta Upsilon House Corp ....E 316 295-4320
Wichita (G-14190)
Downtown Shareholders ....E 913 371-0705
Kansas City (G-3976)
Early Learning Center ....F 316 685-2059
Wichita (G-14252)
Elks Lodge Inc ....E 620 672-2011
Pratt (G-10110)
Emberhope Inc ....D 620 225-0276
Dodge City (G-1357)
Emporia State Univ Fndtion Inc ....F 620 341-5440
Emporia (G-1745)
Epsilon Sigma Alpha Intl ....E 620 331-1063
Independence (G-3515)
Eudora Lion Club Foundation ....F 785 542-2315
Eudora (G-1874)
Field & Stream Club Inc ....F 785 233-4793
Topeka (G-12608)
Fraternal Order Eagles Inc ....E 785 632-3521
Clay Center (G-864)
Fraternal Order of Police ....D 620 694-2830
Hutchinson (G-3293)
General Grnd Chpter Estrn Star ....C 620 326-3797
Wellington (G-13503)
Girl Scouts Kans Heartland Inc ....E 316 684-6531
Wichita (G-14467)
Girl Scts of Ne Kansas & NW MO ....F 816 358-8750
Topeka (G-12637)
Grahem-Hrbers VFW Post No 3084 ....D 785 213-6232
Valley Falls (G-13363)
Great Bend Foundation Inc ....F 620 792-4217
Great Bend (G-2580)
Independent Order Oddfellows ....E 785 456-9493
Wamego (G-13425)
International Assn Lions Clubs ....E 620 673-8081
Havana (G-2728)
International Assn Lions Clubs ....E 785 388-2764
Abilene (G-42)
International Assn Lions Clubs ....E 785 694-2278
Brewster (G-584)
International Association of ....E 785 842-8847
Lawrence (G-4914)
International Association of ....E 620 327-4271
Hesston (G-2994)
International Association of ....F 785 283-4746
Tescott (G-12245)
International Inst Christian S ....E 913 962-4422
Overland Park (G-8858)
Interntional Forest Friendship ....E 913 367-1419
Atchison (G-237)
Jayhawk Area Cncl Bsa Cncl ....F 785 354-0291
Topeka (G-12739)
Jewish Cmnty Ctr Grter Kans Cy ....B 913 327-8000
Shawnee Mission (G-11486)
Junction City Family YMCA Inc ....E 785 762-4780
Junction City (G-3704)
Kanbrews LLC ....F 913 499-6495
Overland Park (G-8887)
Kansas Assc Home For Aged Inc ....F 785 233-7443
Topeka (G-12758)
Kansas National Education Assn ....F 913 268-4005
Shawnee Mission (G-11518)
Kansas Scholastic Press Assoc ....F 785 864-7612
Lawrence (G-4936)
Kansas State High Schl Actvtie ....F 785 273-5329
Topeka (G-12806)
Kansas State Univ Alumni Assn ....E 785 532-6260
Manhattan (G-6677)
Kings Court Investors ....F 913 764-7500
Olathe (G-7840)
Kiwanis International Inc ....F 620 672-6257
Pratt (G-10124)

SIC

Kiwanis International Inc....F.... 316 733-4984
Andover (G-101)
Kiwanis International Inc....E.... 785 742-2596
Hiawatha (G-3014)
Kiwanis International Inc....F.... 913 724-1120
Basehor (G-383)
Kiwanis International Inc....F.... 913 727-1039
Lansing (G-4678)
Kiwanis International Inc....F.... 620 365-3925
Iola (G-3617)
Kiwanis International Inc....F.... 620 544-8445
Hugoton (G-3169)
Kiwanis International Inc....F.... 785 238-4521
Junction City (G-3716)
Kiwanis International Inc....F.... 785 462-6007
Colby (G-1021)
Kiwanis International Inc....F.... 785 282-6680
Smith Center (G-12035)
Knights of Columbus....E.... 785 636-5453
Paxico (G-9756)
Knights of Columbus....F.... 620 825-4378
Kiowa (G-4627)
Knights of Columbus....F.... 620 251-2891
Parsons (G-9700)
Knights of Columbus....F.... 620 442-7264
Arkansas City (G-162)
Lake Region Resource Conservat....E.... 785 242-2073
Ottawa (G-8282)
Lakewood Middle School Pto....D.... 913 239-5800
Overland Park (G-8939)
Lambda CHI Alpha Frternity Inc....D.... 785 843-1172
Lawrence (G-4953)
Lawrence Public Lib Foundation....D.... 785 843-3833
Lawrence (G-4985)
Manhattan Martin Luther King J....E.... 785 410-4599
Manhattan (G-6723)
Marais Des Cygnes Chapter Daug....E.... 913 898-3088
Parker (G-9658)
Masonic Lodge....F.... 620 662-7012
Hutchinson (G-3366)
Masonic Order....E.... 785 625-3127
Hays (G-2870)
Masonic Temple....F.... 620 342-3913
Emporia (G-1790)
McPherson Family Ymca Inc....D.... 620 241-0363
McPherson (G-6999)
Mid America Assc Computer Ed....F.... 785 273-3680
Topeka (G-12889)
Midian Shriners....F.... 316 265-9676
Wichita (G-15087)
Mize Elementary Pto....F.... 913 441-0880
Shawnee (G-10998)
Nacada The Glbl Comm For Acdm....E.... 785 532-3398
Manhattan (G-6756)
Natio Assoc For The Advan of....D.... 913 334-0366
Kansas City (G-4278)
Natio Assoc For The Advan of....F.... 913 362-2272
Shawnee Mission (G-11670)
National Society Daughters Rev....E.... 785 448-5959
Garnett (G-2384)
Optimist International....E.... 316 744-0849
Wichita (G-15228)
Paul Henson Family YMCA Inc....E.... 913 642-6800
Prairie Village (G-10056)
Pauls Valley Third Additon....F.... 316 733-1648
Rose Hill (G-10243)
Pearce Keller American Legion....F.... 785 776-4556
Manhattan (G-6771)
PHI Kappa Theta....F.... 785 539-7491
Manhattan (G-6775)
PI Beta PHI House Inc....F.... 785 539-1818
Manhattan (G-6776)
PI Kappa PHI House Mother....D.... 785 856-1400
Lawrence (G-5063)
Potwin Lions Club....F.... 620 752-3644
Potwin (G-10008)
Pride/Chapter Intl Assoc....E.... 913 321-2733
Kansas City (G-4336)
Pta Kansas Congress Oxford....F.... 913 897-1719
Overland Park (G-9203)
Quail Ridge Homes Assoc Inc....E.... 913 381-2042
Shawnee Mission (G-11764)
Quivira Cncil Boy Scuts Amer I....E.... 316 264-4466
Wichita (G-15397)
Quivira Falls Community Assn....E.... 913 469-5463
Shawnee Mission (G-11768)
Rebuilding Together Shawnee/Jo....F.... 913 558-5079
Shawnee (G-11015)
Roeland Park Community Center....F.... 913 722-0310
Roeland Park (G-10229)
Rosedale Development Assn Inc....F.... 913 677-5097
Kansas City (G-4389)
Rotary International....F.... 785 626-9444
Atwood (G-291)
Rotary International....F.... 913 299-0466
Kansas City (G-4390)
Salvation Army....E.... 316 685-8699
Wichita (G-15513)
Scooters LLC....F.... 785 284-2978
Sabetha (G-10332)
SE Kansas Nture Ctr Schrmrhorn....E.... 620 783-5207
Galena (G-2084)
Servant Foundation....E.... 913 310-0279
Overland Park (G-9297)
Shawnee Hts Booster CLB Pto....F.... 785 379-5880
Tecumseh (G-12242)
Shawns Foundations....F.... 316 214-1070
Garfield (G-2367)
Soil Conservation Service USDA....E.... 785 823-4500
Salina (G-10712)
Soroptimist International....E.... 316 321-0433
El Dorado (G-1603)
Spirit/Boeing Employees Assn....F.... 316 522-2996
Wichita (G-15645)
St Marys Literary Club....E.... 785 437-6418
Saint Marys (G-10376)
Stilwell Venturing Crew....F.... 913 306-2419
Stilwell (G-12173)
Stone Croft Ministries Inc....D.... 816 763-7800
Overland Park (G-9365)
Sugar Valley Lakes Homes Assn....E.... 913 795-2120
Mound City (G-7175)
Sunrise Point Elementary Pto....F.... 913 239-7500
Overland Park (G-9375)
Sweet Adelines Intrntnl Chorus....F.... 316 733-4467
Wichita (G-15707)
Tanglewood Lk Owners Assn Inc....F.... 913 795-2286
La Cygne (G-4643)
The Nature Conservancy....F.... 785 233-4400
Topeka (G-13158)
The Nature Conservancy....F.... 316 689-4237
Wichita (G-15757)
Union Valley Pto....F.... 620 662-4891
Hutchinson (G-3475)
University Kansas Alumni Assn....E.... 785 864-4760
Lawrence (G-5155)
Upsilon Chapter Alpha PHI Intl....E.... 785 233-7466
Topeka (G-13212)
Veterans Affairs Kans Comm On....F.... 785 350-4489
Topeka (G-13221)
Veterans Fgn Wars Post 9076....F.... 785 625-9940
Hays (G-2924)
Village Elementary School Pto....D.... 620 341-2282
Emporia (G-1847)
Washburn Endowment Association....E.... 785 670-4483
Topeka (G-13231)
Wholmoor Amrcn Lgion Post 237....F.... 785 348-5370
Linn (G-6413)
Wichita Chapter of Links Inc....F.... 316 744-7873
Bel Aire (G-443)
Wichita Family Crisis Ctr Inc....F.... 316 263-7501
Wichita (G-15998)
Wichita State Unvsity Almni As....F.... 316 978-3290
Wichita (G-16035)
YMCA of Hutchinson Reno Cnty....D.... 620 662-1203
Hutchinson (G-3494)
YMCA Topeaka Downtown Branch....E.... 785 354-8591
Topeka (G-13256)
Young Mens Christian....F.... 785 233-9815
Topeka (G-13258)
Young Mens Christian Assn....E.... 620 275-1199
Garden City (G-2319)
Young Mens Christian Associa....C.... 316 733-9622
Andover (G-118)
Young Mens Christian Associa....C.... 316 942-2271
Wichita (G-16091)
Young Mens Christian Associa....C.... 316 219-9622
Wichita (G-16093)
Young Mens Christian Associa....D.... 316 260-9622
Wichita (G-16094)
Young Mens Christian Associa....C.... 316 942-5511
Wichita (G-16095)
Young Mens Christian Associa....D.... 316 320-9622
El Dorado (G-1616)
Young Mens Christian Associat....C.... 316 685-2251
Wichita (G-16096)
Young Mens Christian Associat....C.... 620 545-7290
Viola (G-13380)
Young Mens Christian Gr Kansas....D.... 913 642-6800
Shawnee Mission (G-12024)
Young Mens Christian Gr Kansas....D.... 913 362-3489
Prairie Village (G-10088)
Young Mens Christian Gr Kansas....C.... 913 393-9622
Olathe (G-8163)
Young Mens Christian Gr Kansas....D.... 913 782-7707
Olathe (G-8164)
Young MNS Chrstn Assn of Sthwe....E.... 620 275-1199
Garden City (G-2320)
Young MNS Chrstn Assn of Tpeka....C.... 785 354-8591
Topeka (G-13259)
Young MNS Chrstn Assn Pttsburg....D.... 620 231-1100
Pittsburg (G-9972)
Young MNS Chrstn Assn Slina Ka....D.... 785 825-2151
Salina (G-10775)
Youthfront Inc....D.... 913 262-3900
Westwood (G-13564)

8699 Membership Organizations, NEC

A Adopt Family Inc....F.... 620 378-4458
Fredonia (G-2025)
AAA Allied Group Inc....F.... 785 233-0222
Topeka (G-12281)
Active Prime Timers Inc....F.... 785 272-0237
Topeka (G-12285)
Allen Cnty Anmal Rscue Fndtion....F.... 620 496-3647
La Harpe (G-4647)
Alpha Ministries....F.... 785 597-5235
Perry (G-9765)
American Bonanza Society Inc....F.... 316 945-1700
Wichita (G-13685)
Automobile Club of Missouri....F.... 913 248-1627
Shawnee Mission (G-11135)
Automobile Club of Missouri....F.... 316 942-0008
Wichita (G-13774)
Bartlett Cooperative Assn....E.... 620 236-7143
Chetopa (G-816)
Called To Greatness Ministries....E.... 785 749-2100
Lawrence (G-4773)
Caring Hands Humane Society....F.... 316 284-0487
Newton (G-7326)
Casa of The Thirty-First Judic....E.... 620 365-1448
Iola (G-3589)
Catholic Charities of Southwes....F.... 620 227-1562
Dodge City (G-1319)
Citizens Savings & Loan Assn....E.... 913 727-1040
Leavenworth (G-5218)
Council Grove Area Foundation....F.... 620 767-6653
Council Grove (G-1160)
Elk County Development Corp....E.... 620 325-3333
Neodesha (G-7239)
Elks Club....F.... 785 263-1675
Abilene (G-26)
Foundation For A Christian Civ....F.... 785 584-6251
Rossville (G-10252)
Global Services Inc....D.... 913 451-0960
Leawood (G-5414)
Golf Crse Superintendents Amer....D.... 785 841-2240
Lawrence (G-4874)
Great Plains Spca....E.... 913 831-7722
Merriam (G-7093)
Heartstrings Cmnty Foundation....F.... 913 649-5700
Shawnee Mission (G-11425)
Helping Hands Humane Society....E.... 785 233-7325
Topeka (G-12683)
Hope Planting Intl Inc....F.... 785 776-8523
Manhattan (G-6659)
Humane Soc of High Plains....F.... 785 625-5252
Hays (G-2851)
International Association....F.... 785 760-5005
Lawrence (G-4913)
Interntional Wheat Gluten Assn....F.... 913 381-8180
Overland Park (G-8859)
Interntnal Pnck Day Lberal Inc....E.... 620 624-6423
Liberal (G-6323)
Johnson Cnty Grls Athc Complex....D.... 913 422-7837
Shawnee Mission (G-11493)
Johnson County Kansas Heritage....E.... 913 481-3137
Olathe (G-7817)
Kansas Cattlemens Associate....F.... 785 238-1483
Junction City (G-3711)
Kansas Athletics Incorporated....B.... 785 864-7050
Lawrence (G-4930)
Kansas City Compensation & Ben....F.... 913 381-4458
Overland Park (G-8892)
Kansas City Regional....F.... 913 661-1600
Leawood (G-5445)
Kansas Health Foundation....E.... 316 262-7676
Wichita (G-14804)
Kansas Humane Soc Wichita Kans....F.... 316 524-9196
Wichita (G-14806)

Kansas Intrschlstc Athltc Admn............D....... 316 655-8929
Wichita *(G-14810)*
Kansas Schl For Effective Lrng............E....... 316 263-9620
Wichita *(G-14822)*
Kansas State University........................A....... 785 539-4971
Manhattan *(G-6682)*
Kansas Trapshooters Assn Inc.............F....... 316 755-2933
Valley Center *(G-13347)*
Kaw Valley Rabbit Club.........................F....... 913 764-1531
Olathe *(G-7831)*
Lake Region Resource Conservat..........E....... 785 242-2073
Ottawa *(G-8282)*
Legacy Community Foundation.............F....... 620 221-7224
Winfield *(G-16155)*
Leukemia & Lymphoma Soc Inc.............F....... 913 262-1515
Shawnee Mission *(G-11566)*
Lords Diner..F....... 316 295-2122
Wichita *(G-14980)*
Loves Travel Stops................................E....... 785 726-2561
Ellis *(G-1649)*
Mize Houser & Company PA..................E....... 913 451-1882
Shawnee Mission *(G-11649)*
Mize Houser & Company PA..................F....... 785 842-8844
Lawrence *(G-5030)*
National Soc Tole/Dec Pntr Inc.............F....... 316 269-9300
Wichita *(G-15153)*
National Socty of The Daughtrs............F....... 620 356-2570
Ulysses *(G-13307)*
Nationl Soc Daught AMR Rev................E....... 620 457-8747
Pittsburg *(G-9910)*
Neighborhood Network LLC...................E....... 913 341-9316
Lenexa *(G-6020)*
Neosho County Fair Assn Inc................E....... 620 433-0446
Erie *(G-1860)*
Onaga Historical Society......................E....... 785 889-7104
Onaga *(G-8178)*
Opportunity Project Lrng Ctr................E....... 316 522-8677
Wichita *(G-15223)*
Ozanam Pathways.................................E....... 316 682-4000
Wichita *(G-15245)*
Parkinsons Exercise and.......................F....... 913 276-4665
Leawood *(G-5514)*
Pastorserve Inc.....................................F....... 877 918-4746
Overland Park *(G-9144)*
Pawnee County Humane Soc Inc...........F....... 620 285-8510
Larned *(G-4709)*
Pride/Chapter Intl Assoc.......................E....... 913 321-2733
Kansas City *(G-4336)*
Proud Anmal Lovers Shelter Inc............F....... 620 421-0445
Parsons *(G-9726)*
Rural Water Dist 5 Sumner Cnty............F....... 620 456-2350
Conway Springs *(G-1144)*
Salvation Army.....................................F....... 316 283-3190
Newton *(G-7413)*
Salvation Army.....................................F....... 620 663-3353
Hutchinson *(G-3437)*
Salvation Army.....................................F....... 620 225-4871
Dodge City *(G-1427)*
Salvation Army.....................................E....... 620 276-6622
Garden City *(G-2274)*
Salvation Army.....................................E....... 785 843-1716
Lawrence *(G-5101)*
Salvation Army.....................................F....... 785 233-9648
Topeka *(G-13033)*
Salvation Army.....................................F....... 620 343-3166
Emporia *(G-1821)*
Servant Chrstn Cmnty Fundation..........E....... 913 310-0279
Overland Park *(G-9296)*
Social Security Employees....................F....... 877 840-5741
Manhattan *(G-6803)*
South Central Tele Assn Inc..................E....... 620 930-1000
Medicine Lodge *(G-7074)*
Sports Car Club America Inc.................E....... 785 357-7222
Topeka *(G-13091)*
Taylor Made Visions LLC......................F....... 913 210-0699
Kansas City *(G-4459)*
Teaching Parents Assn Inc...................F....... 316 347-9900
Wichita *(G-15720)*
Tfi Family Services Inc.........................C....... 620 342-2239
Emporia *(G-1836)*
Trash Mountain Project Inc..................F....... 785 246-6845
Topeka *(G-13197)*
Unbound...C....... 913 384-6500
Kansas City *(G-4484)*
United Sttes Bowl Congress Inc............D....... 913 631-7209
Shawnee *(G-11043)*
Veterans Fgn Wars Post 9076...............F....... 785 625-9940
Hays *(G-2924)*
Waldorf Association Lawrence..............F....... 785 841-8800
Lawrence *(G-5177)*
Wichita Crime Stoppers Program..........E....... 316 267-2111
Wichita *(G-15992)*
Wichita Ind Neighborhoods Inc.............E....... 316 260-8000
Wichita *(G-16007)*
Wichita Rugby Foundation Inc..............E....... 316 262-6800
Wichita *(G-16022)*
Wichita State Univ Inter Cllga...............D....... 316 978-3250
Wichita *(G-16031)*
Wichita Thndr Prof Hckey Team............F....... 316 264-4625
Wichita *(G-16039)*

87 ENGINEERING, ACCOUNTING, RESEARCH, MANAGEMENT, AND RELATED SERVICES

8711 Engineering Services

3 S Engineering LLC.............................F....... 316 260-2258
Wichita *(G-13579)*
Abrasive Blast Systems Inc...................E....... 785 263-3786
Abilene *(G-10)*
Advanced Environmental Svcs..............F....... 785 231-9324
Topeka *(G-12295)*
Advanced Manufacturing Inst...............E....... 785 532-7044
Manhattan *(G-6534)*
Advatech LLC.......................................D....... 913 344-1000
Overland Park *(G-8353)*
Affinis Corp..E....... 913 239-1100
Overland Park *(G-8356)*
Agelix Consulting LLC...........................E....... 913 708-8145
Overland Park *(G-8357)*
Air Care Systems Hvac Inc....................F....... 360 403-9939
Berryton *(G-525)*
Alfred Benesch & Company...................F....... 785 539-2202
Manhattan *(G-6539)*
Allenbrand-Drews and Assoc...............E....... 913 764-1076
Olathe *(G-7519)*
Allied Environmental Cons Inc..............F....... 316 262-5698
Wichita *(G-13672)*
Alph Omega Geotech Inc......................E....... 913 371-0000
Kansas City *(G-3801)*
Amec Fster Wheler E C Svcs Inc...........E....... 785 272-6830
Topeka *(G-12312)*
Archein Aerospace LLC.........................E....... 682 499-2150
Wichita *(G-13730)*
Archer-Daniels-Midland Company.........D....... 785 825-1541
Salina *(G-10407)*
Argus Consulting Inc.............................E....... 816 228-7500
Overland Park *(G-8395)*
Asm Engineering Cons LLC..................F....... 316 260-5895
Andover *(G-83)*
Asset MGT Analis Group LLC................E....... 803 270-0996
Leawood *(G-5335)*
Attica Engineering LLC.........................F....... 620 254-7070
Attica *(G-275)*
Avatar Engineering Inc..........................F....... 913 897-6757
Lenexa *(G-5676)*
Aviation Cnslting Engrg Sltons.............G....... 316 265-8335
Maize *(G-6508)*
Axius Group LLC..................................F....... 316 285-0858
Wichita *(G-13781)*
B G Consultants Inc..............................E....... 785 537-7448
Manhattan *(G-6551)*
B G Consultants Inc..............................F....... 785 749-4474
Lawrence *(G-4748)*
B&V E&E JV...D....... 913 458-4300
Overland Park *(G-8423)*
B&V-Baker Guam JV.............................A....... 913 458-4300
Overland Park *(G-8424)*
Bain Millwrights Inc..............................F....... 785 945-3778
Valley Falls *(G-13361)*
Bartlett & West Inc................................C....... 785 272-2252
Topeka *(G-12366)*
Baughman Co PA..................................E....... 316 262-7271
Wichita *(G-13820)*
Benchmark Construction LLC...............F....... 785 862-0340
Eudora *(G-1870)*
Bgr Consulting Engineers Inc...............F....... 816 842-2800
Overland Park *(G-8444)*
Bird Engineering Company PA.............F....... 913 631-2222
Shawnee *(G-10917)*
▲ **Black & Veatch Corporation**.................A....... 913 458-2000
Overland Park *(G-8455)*
Black & Veatch Corporation..................E....... 913 458-2000
Overland Park *(G-8456)*
◆ **Black & Veatch Holding Company**.....D....... 913 458-2000
Overland Park *(G-8457)*
Black & Veatch-GEC Joint Ventr...........B....... 913 458-4300
Overland Park *(G-8458)*
Black & Veatch-Olsson JV....................E....... 913 458-6650
Overland Park *(G-8459)*
Black Veatch-Altan Joint Ventr..............B....... 913 458-4300
Overland Park *(G-8461)*
Black Vtch - Gsyntec Jint Vntr...............D....... 913 458-4300
Overland Park *(G-8462)*
Black Vtch Spcial Prjects Corp..............B....... 913 458-2000
Overland Park *(G-8463)*
Blot Engineering Inc..............................F....... 913 441-1636
Shawnee *(G-10919)*
Brack/Asscts Cnsltng Engnrs PA..........F....... 785 271-6644
Topeka *(G-12401)*
Branchpattern Inc.................................F....... 913 951-8311
Overland Park *(G-8480)*
Bredson and Associates Inc..................E....... 913 663-0100
Overland Park *(G-8482)*
Brungardt Honomichl & Co PA..............D....... 913 663-1900
Overland Park *(G-8490)*
Bse Structural Engineers LLC...............E....... 913 492-7400
Lenexa *(G-5720)*
Bvspc - Envirocon JV...........................D....... 913 458-6665
Overland Park *(G-8501)*
Camcorp Inc..F....... 913 831-0740
Lenexa *(G-5727)*
Carney Daniel M Rehab Engineer..........F....... 316 651-5200
Wichita *(G-13951)*
Charles Engineering Inc........................E....... 620 584-2381
Clearwater *(G-887)*
City of Topeka..E....... 785 295-3842
Topeka *(G-12471)*
◆ **Cogen Cleaning Technology Inc**.........E....... 281 339-5751
Stilwell *(G-12142)*
Colt Tech LLC..G....... 913 839-8198
Olathe *(G-7600)*
Complete LLC..F....... 913 238-0206
Overland Park *(G-8590)*
Construction Design Inc.........................C....... 913 287-0334
Kansas City *(G-3935)*
Constructive Engrg Design....................F....... 913 341-3300
Overland Park *(G-8595)*
Continental Consulting Inc.....................E....... 913 642-6642
Leawood *(G-5358)*
Control Systems Intl Inc.........................D....... 913 599-5010
Shawnee Mission *(G-11264)*
Corps of Engineers Fall River................F....... 620 658-4445
Fall River *(G-1926)*
County of Grant......................................E....... 620 356-4837
Ulysses *(G-13291)*
County of Harper....................................E....... 620 842-5240
Anthony *(G-126)*
County of Johnson..................................D....... 913 782-2640
Olathe *(G-7619)*
County of Republic.................................E....... 785 527-2235
Belleville *(G-456)*
CP Engners Land Srveyors Inc..............F....... 785 267-5071
Topeka *(G-12526)*
Davidson & Associates Inc.....................E....... 913 271-6859
Leawood *(G-5372)*
Davidson Arch Engrg LLC......................F....... 913 451-9390
Overland Park *(G-8643)*
Delich Roth & Goodwillie PA..................F....... 913 441-1100
Bonner Springs *(G-548)*
Delich Roth & Goodwillie PA..................F....... 913 441-1100
Bonner Springs *(G-549)*
Den Management Co Inc........................C....... 316 686-1964
Wichita *(G-14191)*
Design Analysis and RES Corp..............F....... 785 832-0434
Lawrence *(G-4833)*
Dlr Group Inc..D....... 913 897-7811
Overland Park *(G-8659)*
Dudley Williams and Assoc PA...............F....... 316 263-7591
Wichita *(G-14243)*
Ecology and Environment Inc.................F....... 913 339-9519
Overland Park *(G-8670)*
Efi Global Inc..F....... 913 648-5232
Shawnee Mission *(G-11329)*
Emerald Aerospace Services LLC..........E....... 316 644-4284
Wichita *(G-14275)*
En Engineering LLC................................D....... 913 901-4400
Olathe *(G-7680)*
Energy Management & Ctrl Corp............F....... 785 233-0289
Topeka *(G-12578)*
Engie Services US Inc............................E....... 913 225-7081
Overland Park *(G-8681)*
Envirnmntal Advisors Engineers.............E....... 913 599-4326
Shawnee Mission *(G-11344)*
Erm-West Inc...F....... 913 661-0770
Overland Park *(G-8687)*
Finney & Trnp SD Trnsprttn...................F....... 785 235-2393
Topeka *(G-12611)*

S I C

First Layer Communications ....F 913 491-0062
Shawnee Mission *(G-11372)*
Foster Design Inc ....C....... 316 832-9700
Wichita *(G-14403)*
Garver LLC ....E....... 913 696-9755
Overland Park *(G-8745)*
GBA Architects Inc ....E....... 913 492-0400
Lenexa *(G-5869)*
◆ **GBA Builders Llc** ....E....... 913 492-0400
Lenexa *(G-5870)*
Geary County Public Works ....E....... 785 238-3612
Junction City *(G-3695)*
Geosource LLC ....F....... 785 272-7200
Topeka *(G-12635)*
Geotechnology Inc ....E....... 913 438-1900
Shawnee *(G-10962)*
Gfe LLC ....F....... 316 260-8433
Wichita *(G-14462)*
Global Aviation Tech LLC ....F....... 316 425-0999
Wichita *(G-14473)*
Global Partner Solutions LLC ....C....... 316 263-1288
Wichita *(G-14475)*
Global Procurement Corporation ....F....... 913 458-2000
Overland Park *(G-8759)*
Gpw & Associates LLC ....F....... 785 865-2332
Lawrence *(G-4877)*
Green Product Solutions LLC ....G....... 913 633-1274
Overland Park *(G-8778)*
Gsi Engineering LLC ....E....... 316 554-0725
Wichita *(G-14521)*
Gsi Engineering LLC ....D....... 515 270-6542
Wichita *(G-14522)*
Gsi Engineering Nthrn Div LLC ....F....... 316 554-0725
Wichita *(G-14523)*
H W Lochner Inc ....E....... 785 827-3603
Salina *(G-10526)*
H W Lochner Inc ....D....... 816 945-5840
Lenexa *(G-5885)*
Hd Engineering & Design Inc ....F....... 913 631-2222
Shawnee Mission *(G-11418)*
Henderson Engineers Inc ....D....... 913 742-5000
Overland Park *(G-8810)*
Henderson Engineers Inc ....B....... 913 742-5000
Lenexa *(G-5900)*
Hntb Corporation ....D....... 913 491-9333
Overland Park *(G-8820)*
Hoss and Brown Engineers Inc ....E....... 785 832-1105
Lawrence *(G-4904)*
Icm Inc ....C....... 316 796-0900
Colwich *(G-1097)*
Industrial Accessories Company ....D....... 913 384-5511
Shawnee Mission *(G-11455)*
Integrted Cnslting Engners Inc ....F....... 316 264-3588
Wichita *(G-14707)*
Interactive Technologies Inc ....F....... 913 254-0887
Olathe *(G-7798)*
Jaco General Contractor Inc ....E....... 316 252-8200
Wichita *(G-14744)*
Js Westhoff & Company Inc ....F....... 913 663-9900
Lenexa *(G-5933)*
Jvf Enterprises Inc ....F....... 913 888-9111
Lenexa *(G-5934)*
Kansas City Tstg & Engrg LLC ....E....... 913 321-8100
Kansas City *(G-4151)*
Kansas Department Trnsp ....F....... 785 527-2520
Belleville *(G-458)*
Kaw Valley Engineering Inc ....E....... 785 762-5040
Junction City *(G-3714)*
Kaw Valley Engineering Inc ....E....... 913 894-5150
Shawnee Mission *(G-11521)*
Kaw Valley Engineering Inc ....F....... 316 440-4304
Wichita *(G-14834)*
Kiewit Engineering Group Inc ....C....... 402 943-1465
Lenexa *(G-5949)*
Kjww Corp ....E....... 913 952-6636
Overland Park *(G-8921)*
KLA Environmental Services ....F....... 785 823-0097
Salina *(G-10576)*
Kleinfelder Inc ....E....... 913 962-0909
Overland Park *(G-8923)*
Kleinfelder Inc ....D....... 913 962-0909
Lenexa *(G-5953)*
Kruger Technologies Inc ....E....... 913 498-1114
Overland Park *(G-8929)*
Landplan Engineering PA ....D....... 785 843-7530
Lawrence *(G-4954)*
Latimer Sommers and Assoc PA ....E....... 785 233-3232
Topeka *(G-12834)*
Locke Equipment Sales Co ....E....... 913 782-8500
Olathe *(G-7864)*
Loves Enterprise Inc ....F....... 785 235-0479
Topeka *(G-12849)*
Lutz Daily & Brain Llc ....E....... 913 831-0833
Shawnee Mission *(G-11584)*
Malone Finkle Echardt & Clns ....E....... 913 322-1400
Overland Park *(G-8981)*
Marche Associates Inc ....F....... 785 749-2925
Lawrence *(G-5011)*
McAfee Henderson Solutions Inc ....F....... 913 888-4647
Lenexa *(G-5990)*
McAfee Henderson Solutions Inc ....F....... 913 888-4647
Lenexa *(G-5991)*
McPu Polymer Engineering LLC ....G....... 620 231-4239
Pittsburg *(G-9901)*
Messenger Petroleum Inc ....G....... 620 532-5400
Kingman *(G-4606)*
Michael Kirkham & Assoc Inc ....E....... 785 472-3163
Ellsworth *(G-1678)*
Mid-America Mfg Tech Ctr Inc ....F....... 913 649-4333
Overland Park *(G-9025)*
Mid-States Energy Works Inc ....F....... 785 827-3631
Salina *(G-10601)*
Miniature Plastic Molding LLC ....G....... 316 264-2827
Wichita *(G-15112)*
Mkec Engineering Inc ....C....... 316 684-9600
Wichita *(G-15118)*
Mkec Engineering Cons Inc ....E....... 913 317-9390
Overland Park *(G-9045)*
Morrow Engineering Inc ....F....... 316 942-0402
Wichita *(G-15130)*
MTS Quanta LLC ....E....... 913 383-0800
Overland Park *(G-9061)*
MWH Global Inc ....F....... 913 383-2086
Leawood *(G-5494)*
Needham & Associates Inc ....G....... 913 385-5300
Lenexa *(G-6019)*
Northrop Grumman Systems Corp ....C....... 785 861-3375
Topeka *(G-12938)*
Northrop Grumman Systems Corp ....B....... 913 651-8311
Fort Leavenworth *(G-1940)*
Northwind Technical Svcs LLC ....F....... 785 284-0080
Sabetha *(G-10323)*
Nunik Engineering ....F....... 913 384-0010
Shawnee Mission *(G-11691)*
Olsson Inc ....F....... 785 539-6900
Manhattan *(G-6764)*
Olsson Inc ....C....... 913 381-1170
Overland Park *(G-9100)*
Olsson Inc ....E....... 913 829-0078
Olathe *(G-7956)*
Optimus Industries LLC ....C....... 620 431-3100
Chanute *(G-751)*
Orazem & Scalora Engrg PA ....F....... 785 537-2553
Manhattan *(G-6765)*
Pars Consulting Engineers Inc ....E....... 913 432-0107
Leawood *(G-5516)*
Parsons Corporation ....F....... 913 233-3100
Kansas City *(G-4315)*
Pearson Kent McKinley Raaf Eng ....E....... 913 492-2400
Lenexa *(G-6046)*
Performance Contracting Inc ....E....... 913 928-2832
Lenexa *(G-6052)*
▲ **Performance Contracting Inc** ....A....... 913 888-8600
Lenexa *(G-6051)*
Pfefferkorn Engrg & Envmtl LLC ....F....... 913 490-3967
Olathe *(G-7982)*
Phelps Engineering Inc ....E....... 913 393-1155
Olathe *(G-7983)*
Pinnacle Technology Inc ....E....... 785 832-8866
Lawrence *(G-5066)*
Poe & Associates Inc ....E....... 316 685-4114
Wichita *(G-15312)*
Poe & Associates of Kansas ....F....... 316 685-4114
Wichita *(G-15313)*
Ponzeryoungquist PA ....F....... 913 782-0541
Olathe *(G-7992)*
Poole Fire Protection Inc ....F....... 913 747-2044
Olathe *(G-7993)*
Professional Engrg Cons PA ....C....... 316 262-2691
Wichita *(G-15359)*
Professional Engrg Cons PA ....F....... 620 235-0195
Pittsburg *(G-9924)*
Professional Engrg Cons PA ....E....... 785 290-0550
Topeka *(G-12989)*
Professional Engrg Cons PA ....E....... 316 262-6457
Wichita *(G-15360)*
Professional Engrg Cons PA ....E....... 785 233-8300
Topeka *(G-12990)*
Professional Group ....F....... 785 762-5855
Junction City *(G-3741)*
Professional Service Inds Inc ....E....... 913 310-1600
Kansas City *(G-4343)*
Progress Rail Services Corp ....E....... 913 345-4807
Overland Park *(G-9191)*
Rapco Inc ....F....... 785 524-4232
Lincoln *(G-6386)*
Research Concepts Inc ....F....... 913 422-0210
Lenexa *(G-6106)*
Rice Precision Mfg Inc ....E....... 785 594-2670
Baldwin City *(G-367)*
River Oak Mechanical ....F....... 573 338-7203
Overland Park *(G-9244)*
Rock Creek Technologies LLC ....E....... 620 364-1400
New Strawn *(G-7304)*
S C F Inc ....E....... 913 722-3473
Overland Park *(G-9267)*
S K Design Group Inc ....E....... 913 451-1818
Shawnee Mission *(G-11819)*
Sandmeyer Henthorn and Company ....F....... 913 951-2010
Leawood *(G-5547)*
Schaefer Johnson Cox Frey ....D....... 316 684-0171
Wichita *(G-15526)*
Schlagel & Associates PA ....E....... 913 492-5158
Shawnee Mission *(G-11835)*
SD Engineering LLC ....F....... 785 233-8880
Topeka *(G-13046)*
Selective Site Consultants Inc ....E....... 913 438-7700
Overland Park *(G-9292)*
Shafer Kline & Warren Inc ....E....... 913 888-7800
Lenexa *(G-6126)*
Sky Blue Inc ....D....... 785 842-9013
Lawrence *(G-5112)*
SMH Consultants PA ....F....... 785 776-0541
Manhattan *(G-6802)*
Smith & Boucher Inc ....E....... 913 345-2127
Olathe *(G-8070)*
Spencer Reed Group LLC ....E....... 913 722-7860
Shawnee Mission *(G-11884)*
Splashtacular LLC ....F....... 800 844-5334
Paola *(G-9589)*
Stearns Conrad and Schmidt ....D....... 913 681-0030
Overland Park *(G-9356)*
Summers & Spencer Company ....E....... 785 272-4484
Topeka *(G-13116)*
Summers & Spencer Company ....F....... 785 838-4484
Lawrence *(G-5126)*
T & C Mfg & Operating Inc ....E....... 620 793-5483
Great Bend *(G-2646)*
T T Companies Inc ....A....... 913 599-6886
Olathe *(G-8097)*
TEC Engineering Inc ....E....... 316 259-8881
Wichita *(G-15723)*
Telecommunication Systems Inc ....E....... 913 593-9489
Overland Park *(G-9401)*
Terracon Consultants Inc ....E....... 785 539-9099
Manhattan *(G-6822)*
Terracon Consultants Inc ....C....... 913 492-7777
Lenexa *(G-6177)*
Terracon Consultants Inc ....E....... 316 262-0171
Wichita *(G-15730)*
Textron Aviation Inc ....F....... 316 831-4021
Wichita *(G-15742)*
Thompson Dehydrating Co Inc ....F....... 785 272-7722
Topeka *(G-13160)*
Thunderhead Engrg Cons Inc ....F....... 785 770-8511
Manhattan *(G-6826)*
Tl Enterprises Inc ....F....... 785 448-7100
Wichita *(G-15770)*
Trademark Incorporated ....F....... 316 264-8310
Wichita *(G-15782)*
Transtecs Corporation ....D....... 316 651-0389
Wichita *(G-15793)*
Transystems Corporation ....F....... 316 303-3000
Wichita *(G-15794)*
Transystems Corporation ....E....... 620 331-3999
Independence *(G-3568)*
Trideum Corporation ....E....... 913 364-5900
Leavenworth *(G-5302)*
U S Army Corps of Engineers ....D....... 785 537-7392
Manhattan *(G-6834)*
U S Army Corps of Engineers ....F....... 785 597-5144
Perry *(G-9774)*
U S Army Corps of Engineers ....F....... 785 453-2201
Vassar *(G-13372)*
Waters Edge Aquatic Design LLC ....F....... 913 438-4338
Shawnee Mission *(G-11994)*
Wilson Inc Engineers Architects ....D....... 785 827-0433
Salina *(G-10769)*
Wyandtte Cnty Unfied Gvernment ....F....... 913 573-5700
Kansas City *(G-4556)*

Young Electric Inc .... E 316 681-8118
Wichita (G-16090)

8712 Architectural Services

Alloy Architecture PA .... E 316 634-1111
Wichita (G-13677)
Associates Gould-Evens .... E 785 842-3800
Lawrence (G-4739)
B G Consultants Inc .... E 785 537-7448
Manhattan (G-6551)
Bell/Knott and Associates C .... E 913 378-1600
Leawood (G-5339)
Black Veatch-Altan Joint Ventr .... B 913 458-4300
Overland Park (G-8461)
Brr Architecture Inc .... C 913 262-9095
Overland Park (G-8489)
Davidson & Associates Inc .... E 913 271-6859
Leawood (G-5372)
Davidson Architure and Engr .... F 913 451-9390
Shawnee Mission (G-11292)
Dlr Group Inc .... D 913 897-7811
Overland Park (G-8659)
E Architects PA .... F 785 234-6664
Topeka (G-12564)
GBA Architects Inc .... E 913 492-0400
Lenexa (G-5869)
Glmv Architecture Inc .... E 316 265-9367
Wichita (G-14472)
Gossen Livingston Associates .... D 620 225-3300
Dodge City (G-1366)
Gpw & Associates LLC .... F 785 865-2332
Lawrence (G-4877)
H W Lochner Inc .... D 816 945-5840
Lenexa (G-5885)
Health Facilities Group LLC .... F 316 262-2500
Wichita (G-14575)
Hmn Architects Inc .... D 913 451-9075
Overland Park (G-8818)
Hoefer Wysocki Architects LLC .... D 913 307-3700
Leawood (G-5429)
Horst Trrill Krst Archtects PA .... E 785 266-5373
Topeka (G-12704)
Innovative Cnstr Svcs Inc .... F 316 260-1644
Wichita (G-14695)
Jeff L Krehbiel .... F 316 267-8233
Wichita (G-14753)
Johnson Wilson Embers .... E 913 438-9095
Shawnee Mission (G-11500)
Kiewit Engineering Group Inc .... C 402 943-1465
Lenexa (G-5949)
Lk Architecture Inc .... D 316 268-0230
Wichita (G-14969)
Lk Architecture/Mead & Hunt .... D 316 268-0230
Wichita (G-14970)
Mann & Co Architects/Engineers .... F 620 662-4493
Hutchinson (G-3363)
Michael Kirkham & Assoc Inc .... E 785 472-3163
Ellsworth (G-1678)
Monarch Plastic Surgery .... E 913 663-3838
Overland Park (G-9049)
Nearing Staats Prelogar .... E 913 831-1415
Prairie Village (G-10052)
Oldcastle Apg Midwest Inc .... E 913 667-1792
Bonner Springs (G-568)
P A Treanorhl .... F 785 235-0012
Topeka (G-12957)
Peckham Gyton Albers Viets Inc .... E 913 362-6500
Shawnee Mission (G-11722)
Pkhls Architecture PA .... F 316 321-4774
El Dorado (G-1592)
R Messner Construction Co .... E 316 634-2381
Wichita (G-15405)
R S Bickford & Co Inc .... F 913 451-1480
Shawnee Mission (G-11774)
Rees Msilionis Turley Arch LLC .... E 816 842-1292
Shawnee Mission (G-11787)
Schaefer Johnson Cox Frey .... D 316 684-0171
Wichita (G-15526)
Schaefer Johnson Cox Frey Arch .... E 316 684-0171
Wichita (G-15527)
Schwerdt Design Group Inc .... E 785 273-7540
Topeka (G-13041)
Scientific Engineering Inc .... F 785 827-7071
Salina (G-10698)
Shafer Kline & Warren Inc .... E 913 888-7800
Lenexa (G-6126)
Spangenberg Phillips Inc .... F 316 267-4002
Wichita (G-15634)
Tevis Architectural Group .... F 913 599-3003
Shawnee (G-11039)
Treanorhl Inc .... E 785 842-4858
Lawrence (G-5145)
Wdm Architects PA .... E 316 262-4700
Wichita (G-15939)
Wilson Inc Engneers Architects .... D 785 827-0433
Salina (G-10769)
Winter Architects Inc .... F 316 267-7142
Wichita (G-16058)
Yaeger Architecture Inc .... E 913 742-8000
Lenexa (G-6239)
Yaeger-Acuity Solutions .... E 913 742-8000
Overland Park (G-9515)

8713 Surveying Services

Alpha Land Surveys Inc .... F 620 728-0012
Hutchinson (G-3197)
B G Consultants Inc .... E 785 537-7448
Manhattan (G-6551)
Baughman Co PA .... E 316 262-7271
Wichita (G-13820)
Central Kans Surveying Mapping .... F 620 792-2873
Great Bend (G-2528)
Cornerstone Rgnal Srveying LLC .... E 620 331-6767
Independence (G-3508)
CP Engners Land Srveyors Inc .... F 785 267-5071
Topeka (G-12526)
Dolan Technologies Corporation .... E 913 390-5156
Olathe (G-7658)
Focalpoint Imaging LLC .... G 620 325-2298
Neodesha (G-7241)
Garber Surveying Service PA .... F 620 241-4441
McPherson (G-6967)
Garber Surveying Service PA .... E 620 665-7032
Hutchinson (G-3297)
◆ Garmin International Inc .... A 913 397-8200
Olathe (G-7722)
Idea Center Inc .... F 785 320-2400
Manhattan (G-6664)
Infinity Insur Solutions LLC .... E 913 338-3200
Leawood (G-5436)
Kansas Biological Survey .... E 785 864-1505
Lawrence (G-4932)
Kaw Valley Engineering Inc .... F 316 440-4304
Wichita (G-14834)
Kaw Valley Engineering Inc .... E 785 762-5040
Junction City (G-3714)
Land Acquisitions Inc .... E 847 749-0675
Wichita (G-14919)
Landplan Engineering PA .... D 785 843-7530
Lawrence (G-4954)
McAfee Henderson Solutions Inc .... F 913 888-4647
Lenexa (G-5990)
McAfee Henderson Solutions Inc .... F 913 888-4647
Lenexa (G-5991)
Mkec Engineering Inc .... C 316 684-9600
Wichita (G-15118)
MTS Quanta LLC .... E 913 383-0800
Overland Park (G-9061)
Olsson Inc .... C 913 381-1170
Overland Park (G-9100)
Payne & Brockway P A .... E 913 782-4800
Olathe (G-7976)
Phelps Engineering Inc .... E 913 393-1155
Olathe (G-7983)
Ponzeryoungquist PA .... F 913 782-0541
Olathe (G-7992)
Schmitz King & Associates Inc .... F 913 397-6080
Shawnee (G-11025)
Schwab-Eaton PA .... E 785 539-4687
Manhattan (G-6797)
Shafer Kline & Warren Inc .... E 913 888-7800
Lenexa (G-6126)
Survey Companies LLC .... F 316 722-6916
Wichita (G-15703)
Surveying and Mapping LLC .... C 913 344-9933
Overland Park (G-9379)
Surveys Inc .... E 785 472-4456
Ellsworth (G-1681)

8721 Accounting, Auditing & Bookkeeping Svcs

AC Professional LLC .... E 816 668-4760
Olathe (G-7508)
Actuarius LLC .... F 913 908-2830
Bucyrus (G-593)
Adams Brown Bran Ball Chrtered .... F 316 683-2067
Wichita (G-13612)
Adams Brown Bran Ball Chrtered .... F 620 549-3271
Great Bend (G-2500)
Adams Brown Bran Ball Chrtered .... F 620 663-5659
Hutchinson (G-3191)
Adams Brown Bran Ball Chrtered .... E 785 628-3046
Hays (G-2744)
Adams Brown Bran Ball Chrtered .... F 620 241-2090
McPherson (G-6931)
Adams-Gabbert & Associates LLC .... F 913 735-4390
Overland Park (G-8346)
Agler and Gaeddert Chartered .... E 620 342-7641
Emporia (G-1693)
Allen Gibbs & Houlik Llc .... C 316 267-7231
Wichita (G-13667)
Anesthesia Assoc Kans Cy PC .... C 913 428-2900
Overland Park (G-8385)
Anesthesia Billing Inc .... E 316 281-3700
Newton (G-7309)
Automatic Data Processing Inc .... C 515 875-3160
Wichita (G-13773)
Axcet Hr Solutions Inc .... E 913 383-2999
Overland Park (G-8420)
B C C Business Services Inc .... F 913 682-4548
Leavenworth (G-5205)
Berberich Trahan & Co PA .... E 785 234-3427
Topeka (G-12370)
Bhr Inc .... F 913 469-1599
Overland Park (G-8446)
Bkd LLP .... D 316 265-2811
Wichita (G-13852)
Boan Connealy & Houlehan LLC .... F 913 491-9178
Overland Park (G-8472)
Bruce Oil Co LLC .... G 620 241-2938
McPherson (G-6939)
Byron G Bird Assoc Chartered .... F 620 624-1994
Liberal (G-6288)
Cbiz Accounting Tax & A .... E 785 272-3176
Topeka (G-12453)
Cbiz Accounting Tax & Advisor .... F 913 234-1932
Shawnee Mission (G-11207)
Cbiz Med MGT Professionals Inc .... F 913 652-1899
Shawnee Mission (G-11208)
Cbiz Med MGT Professionals Inc .... E 316 686-7327
Wichita (G-13965)
Chance Purinton and Mills LLC .... F 913 491-8200
Shawnee Mission (G-11216)
Choices Network Inc .... B 785 820-8018
Salina (G-10447)
City of Wichita .... E 316 268-4651
Wichita (G-14026)
Cliftonlarsonallen LLP .... F 913 491-6655
Overland Park (G-8567)
Clubine & Rettele .... E 785 472-3915
Ellsworth (G-1662)
Cochran Head Vick & Co PA .... F 913 378-1100
Overland Park (G-8572)
Commercial Bank .... E 620 423-0770
Parsons (G-9674)
Complex Property Advisers Corp .... F 913 498-0790
Overland Park (G-8591)
Compone Services Ltd .... F 785 267-9196
Topeka (G-12496)
County of Wallace .... E 785 852-4282
Sharon Springs (G-10896)
Cummins Coffman & .... F 785 267-2030
Topeka (G-12534)
Dana F Cole & Company LLP .... F 913 341-8200
Overland Park (G-8632)
Demaranville & Assoc Cpas LLC .... F 913 682-4548
Leavenworth (G-5232)
Diehl Banwart Bolton Jarred .... E 620 223-4300
Fort Scott (G-1964)
Ernst & Young LLP .... C 316 636-4900
Wichita (G-14302)
Farm Management Services Inc .... F 785 243-1854
Concordia (G-1110)
Goodencoff & Malone Inc .... F 785 483-6220
Russell (G-10276)
Grain Craft Inc .... E 316 267-7311
Wichita (G-14494)
Grant Thornton LLP .... D 316 265-3231
Wichita (G-14496)
Hanneman & Hewitt CPA .... F 316 269-4500
Wichita (G-14557)
Hay & Rice Assoc Chartered .... F 620 624-8471
Liberal (G-6320)
Heritage Group Lc .... F 316 261-5301
Wichita (G-14594)
Higdon and Hale Cpas P C .... F 913 831-7000
Shawnee Mission (G-11431)
Hinrichszenk + Pesavento .... F 785 691-5407
Overland Park (G-8815)

S I C

Hutchins & Associates ....F 913 338-4455
Shawnee Mission (G-11444)
Ifft & Co PA ....F 913 345-1120
Overland Park (G-8838)
In2itive Bus Solutions LLC ....E 913 344-7002
Leawood (G-5435)
Infosync Services Llc ....B 316 685-1622
Wichita (G-14692)
Johnson Duncan & Hollowell CPA ....F 316 267-3402
Wichita (G-14767)
Jri Investments LLC ....A 785 404-2210
Wichita (G-14777)
Kcoe Isom LLP ....E 316 685-0222
Wichita (G-14839)
Kcoe Isom LLP ....F 785 899-3676
Goodland (G-2479)
Kcoe Isom LLP ....F 913 643-5000
Lenexa (G-5944)
Kcoe Isom LLP ....F 620 672-7476
Garden City (G-2216)
Keller & Miller Cpas LLP ....F 620 275-6883
Garden City (G-2217)
Keller & Owens LLC ....E 913 338-3500
Overland Park (G-8911)
Kennedy Mc Kee and Company LLP ....F 620 227-3135
Dodge City (G-1389)
Kirkpatrick Sprecker & Co ....F 316 685-1411
Wichita (G-14866)
Knudsen Monroe & Company LLC ....F 316 283-5366
Newton (G-7371)
Koch Siedhoff Hand & Dunn LLP ....E 316 943-0286
Wichita (G-14888)
Kramer & Associates Cpas LLC ....F 913 680-1690
Leavenworth (G-5263)
L L C Oasis of Hutchinson ....E 620 663-4800
Hutchinson (G-3353)
Larson & Company PA ....F 316 263-8030
Wichita (G-14928)
Lewis Hooper & Dick LLC ....E 620 275-9267
Garden City (G-2225)
Lindburg Vogel Pierc Faris Ch ....E 620 669-0461
Hutchinson (G-3354)
LLP Moss Adams ....F 913 599-3236
Overland Park (G-8965)
Mapes & Miller CPA ....F 785 877-5833
Norton (G-7448)
Meara Welch Browne PC ....E 816 561-1400
Leawood (G-5470)
Michael E Evans CPA ....E 620 669-0461
Hutchinson (G-3375)
Mize Houser & Company PA ....D 785 233-0536
Topeka (G-12908)
Morrow & Company LLC ....F 316 263-2223
Wichita (G-15129)
Myers and Stauffer Lc ....E 785 228-6700
Topeka (G-12922)
Parman Tnner Soule Jackson CPA ....F 620 442-3700
Arkansas City (G-169)
Patrick Friess LLP ....F 620 227-3135
Dodge City (G-1418)
Patton Cramer & Laprod Charter ....F 620 672-5533
Pratt (G-10131)
Paychex Inc ....D 913 814-7776
Leawood (G-5517)
Paycor Inc ....D 913 262-9484
Shawnee Mission (G-11719)
Payroll Plus ....E 620 846-2658
Montezuma (G-7160)
Physicians Business Netwrk LLC ....E 913 381-5200
Overland Park (G-9164)
Pottberg Gssman Hffman Chrtred ....F 785 238-5166
Junction City (G-3738)
PQ Corporation ....F 913 744-2056
Lenexa (G-6064)
Prescriptive Payroll Inc ....F 316 247-3166
Wichita (G-15337)
Pro Pay LLC ....E 913 826-6300
Salina (G-10642)
Professionals Business MGT Inc ....F 913 888-1444
Overland Park (G-9188)
Profit Builders Inc ....E 316 721-3370
Wichita (G-15370)
Property Tax Advisory Group ....F 913 897-4744
Overland Park (G-9194)
Protiviti Inc ....F 913 685-6200
Overland Park (G-9198)
R & J Salina Tax Service Inc ....E 785 827-1304
Salina (G-10649)
Randall G Ford LLC ....F 316 945-1500
Wichita (G-15415)
Ray A Cheely Chartered ....F 620 793-8436
Great Bend (G-2629)
Reese & Novelly PA ....F 785 456-2000
Wamego (G-13440)
Regier Carr & Monroe LLP CPA ....F 316 264-2335
Wichita (G-15437)
Roark & Associates PA ....F 785 842-3431
Lawrence (G-5097)
Robert E Miller Insurance Agcy ....E 816 333-3000
Leawood (G-5540)
Roger L Johnson ....E 785 233-4226
Topeka (G-13025)
Rolf Perrin & Associates PC ....F 913 671-8600
Fairway (G-1918)
Ruther & Associates LLC ....F 913 894-8877
Shawnee Mission (G-11816)
Sedgwick County Accounting ....F 316 383-7184
Wichita (G-15547)
Sink Gordon & Associates LLP ....E 785 537-0190
Manhattan (G-6801)
Snodgrass Dunlap & Company PA ....E 620 365-3125
Iola (G-3632)
SS&c Wealth MGT Group LLC ....E 785 825-5479
Salina (G-10713)
Stephen M Criser ....E 316 685-1040
Wichita (G-15661)
Stephenson Edward B & Co CPA ....F 620 221-9320
Winfield (G-16175)
Summers & Spencer Company ....E 785 272-4484
Topeka (G-13116)
Summers & Spencer Company ....F 785 838-4484
Lawrence (G-5126)
Swindoll Janzen Hawk Lloyd LLC ....E 620 241-1826
McPherson (G-7030)
Swindoll Janzen Hawk Lloyd LLC ....F 316 265-5600
Wichita (G-15708)
Syndeo Outsourcing LLC ....E 316 630-9107
Wichita (G-15710)
Tax 911com Incorporated ....F 913 712-8539
Olathe (G-8102)
Tpp Crtfied Pub Accntants LLC ....E 913 498-2200
Overland Park (G-9422)
Varney & Associates Cpas LLC ....E 785 537-2202
Manhattan (G-6841)
Wolski & Associates ....F 913 281-3233
Kansas City (G-4548)
Wolters Kluwer Health Inc ....F 316 612-5000
Wichita (G-16062)
Woods & Durham LLC ....E 785 825-5494
Salina (G-10772)
Wright Redden & Associates LLC ....F 620 251-6204
Coffeyville (G-986)

8731 Commercial Physical & Biological Research

Alliance Monitoring Tech LLC ....F 316 263-7775
Wichita (G-13670)
Altasciences Clinical Kans Inc ....D 913 696-1601
Overland Park (G-8373)
American Institute of Baking ....D 785 537-4750
Manhattan (G-6541)
Biodesix Inc ....E 913 583-9000
De Soto (G-1195)
Citoxlab Usa LLC ....D 913 850-5000
Stilwell (G-12141)
Clinical Reference Lab Inc ....B 913 492-3652
Lenexa (G-5765)
Deciphera Pharmaceuticals LLC ....F 785 830-2100
Lawrence (G-4830)
Eaglepicher Technologies LLC ....F 620 232-3631
Pittsburg (G-9854)
Ez2 Technologies Inc ....E 913 498-8872
Leawood (G-5393)
Fairmount Technologies LLC ....F 316 978-3313
Wichita (G-14335)
Heartland Plant Innovations ....F 785 320-4300
Manhattan (G-6652)
Iqvua RDS Inc ....D 913 894-5533
Shawnee Mission (G-11467)
Iqvua RDS Inc ....D 913 708-6000
Overland Park (G-8862)
Kansas State University ....E 620 275-9164
Garden City (G-2214)
Kansas State University ....E 620 421-4826
Parsons (G-9697)
Kcas LLC ....C 913 248-3000
Shawnee Mission (G-11524)
Land Institute ....E 785 823-5376
Salina (G-10578)
Leidos Inc ....G 913 317-5120
Shawnee Mission (G-11560)
Mriglobal - Kansas LLC ....A 816 753-7600
Manhattan (G-6754)
Netchemia LLC ....E 913 789-0996
Overland Park (G-9074)
▲ On Demand Technologies LLC ....F 913 438-1800
Overland Park (G-9102)
Paragon N D T & Finishes Inc ....E 316 945-5285
Wichita (G-15259)
PRA International ....D 913 410-2000
Lenexa (G-6066)
PRA International LLC ....F 913 345-5754
Lenexa (G-6067)
PRA Intrntional Operations Inc ....B 913 410-2000
Shawnee Mission (G-11746)
Revolutionary Bus Concepts Inc ....D 913 385-5700
Shawnee Mission (G-11793)
Secureaire Ltd Liability Co ....F 813 766-0400
Lenexa (G-6122)
Servi Tech Inc ....C 620 227-7509
Dodge City (G-1429)
Solid State Sonics & Elec ....G 785 232-0497
Topeka (G-13080)
United Biosource LLC ....D 913 339-7000
Overland Park (G-9442)
University of Kansas ....B 785 864-4780
Lawrence (G-5162)
University of Kansas ....D 785 864-1500
Lawrence (G-5161)
Veterinary Research and Cnslt ....F 785 324-9200
Hays (G-2925)

8732 Commercial Economic, Sociological & Educational Research

American Gvrnment Slutions LLC ....F 913 428-2550
Leawood (G-5320)
American Indian Health Researc ....F 913 422-7523
Shawnee (G-10910)
Business & Technology Inst ....E 620 235-4920
Pittsburg (G-9827)
Callahan Creek Inc ....D 785 838-4774
Lawrence (G-4772)
Data Source of Kansas LLC ....F 620 735-4353
Cassoday (G-687)
Deere & Company ....E 913 310-8100
Olathe (G-7645)
Dpra Incorporated ....F 785 539-3565
Manhattan (G-6616)
E T C Institute Inc ....E 913 747-0646
Olathe (G-7663)
Education Market Resources Inc ....E 913 390-8110
Olathe (G-7670)
Everhance LLC ....F 785 218-1406
Overland Park (G-8696)
Glover Inc ....E 800 654-1511
Olathe (G-7735)
Harte-Hanks Inc ....B 913 312-8100
Shawnee Mission (G-11413)
Juniper Gardens Childrens Prj ....D 913 321-3143
Kansas City (G-4128)
Kansas Health Institute ....E 785 233-5443
Topeka (G-12779)
Kingman Cnty Ecnmic Dev Cncil ....A 620 532-3694
Kingman (G-4598)
Lionshare Marketing Inc ....F 913 631-8400
Lenexa (G-5974)
Little Hse On Prrie Museum Inc ....F 559 202-8147
Independence (G-3533)
National Opinion Research Ctr ....D 316 221-5800
Wichita (G-15150)
Northrop Grumman Systems Corp ....B 913 651-8311
Fort Leavenworth (G-1940)
On-Line Communications Inc ....C 316 831-0500
Wichita (G-15219)
▲ Pivot International Inc ....E 913 312-6900
Lenexa (G-6060)
Research Partnership Inc ....E 316 263-6433
Wichita (G-15447)
Ryan Development Company LLC ....E 316 630-9223
Wichita (G-15496)
Savoy Rgls BHN Engnrng Lnd Sur ....E 316 264-8008
Wichita (G-15523)
Stratgic Knwldge Solutions Inc ....F 913 682-2002
Leavenworth (G-5292)
Walz Tetrick Advertising Inc ....E 913 789-8778
Mission (G-7140)

8733 Noncommercial Research Organizations

190th Medical Group ....D 785 861-4663
Topeka *(G-12274)*
American Cancer Socty Heartlnd ....F 316 265-3400
Wichita *(G-13688)*
Crititech Inc ....F 785 841-7120
Lawrence *(G-4817)*
Edge Enterprises Inc ....E 785 749-1473
Lawrence *(G-4845)*
Glover Inc ....E 800 654-1511
Olathe *(G-7735)*
Jewish Heritage Fndtn Greater ....E 913 981-8866
Leawood *(G-5442)*
Kansas State University ....D 785 532-6011
Manhattan *(G-6686)*
Kansas State University ....E 785 625-3425
Hays *(G-2858)*
Mitre Corporation ....E 913 946-1900
Leavenworth *(G-5271)*
MSI Automation Inc ....F 316 681-3566
Bel Aire *(G-436)*
Phoenix Medical Research Inc ....F 913 381-7180
Prairie Village *(G-10060)*
South Central KS Econ Dev Dist ....E 316 262-7035
Wichita *(G-15617)*
University of Kansas ....A 913 588-4718
Kansas City *(G-4498)*
University of KS Medcl ....E 913 588-1261
Fairway *(G-1925)*
Ventria Bioscience Inc ....F 785 238-1101
Junction City *(G-3764)*
Via Christi Research ....E 316 291-4774
Wichita *(G-15897)*
Xenotech LLC ....C 913 438-7450
Kansas City *(G-4559)*

8734 Testing Laboratories

Als Marshfield LLC ....F 620 225-4172
Dodge City *(G-1292)*
Als USA Inc ....E 913 281-9881
Kansas City *(G-3802)*
Antech Diagnostics Inc ....E 913 529-4392
Overland Park *(G-8388)*
Arrow Laboratory Inc ....F 316 267-2893
Wichita *(G-13736)*
Certified Environmental Mgt ....E 785 823-0492
Salina *(G-10446)*
Clinical Reference Lab Inc ....B 913 492-3652
Lenexa *(G-5765)*
Colt Tech LLC ....G 913 839-8198
Olathe *(G-7600)*
Continental Analytical Svcs ....E 785 827-1273
Salina *(G-10461)*
County of Johnson ....F 913 432-3868
Shawnee Mission *(G-11270)*
Dbi Inc ....E 316 831-9323
Wichita *(G-14177)*
Dbi Inc ....E 913 888-2321
Lenexa *(G-5807)*
Dvt LLC ....E 913 636-3056
Overland Park *(G-8667)*
Gsi Engineering Nthrn Div LLC ....F 316 554-0725
Wichita *(G-14523)*
Identigen North America Inc ....F 785 856-8800
Lawrence *(G-4908)*
Idexx Laboratories Inc ....D 913 339-4550
Lenexa *(G-5909)*
Johnson Gage & Inspection Inc ....F 316 943-7532
Wichita *(G-14768)*
K State Rabies Laboratory ....F 785 532-4472
Manhattan *(G-6668)*
K-State Diagnostic & Analyticl ....C 785 532-3294
Manhattan *(G-6669)*
Kansas State University ....E 620 421-4826
Parsons *(G-9697)*
Kcas LLC ....C 913 248-3000
Shawnee Mission *(G-11524)*
Kruger Technologies Inc ....E 913 498-1114
Overland Park *(G-8929)*
Ksu National Gas Machinery Lab ....F 785 532-2617
Manhattan *(G-6705)*
Lee Dental Laboratory ....F 913 599-3888
Shawnee *(G-10985)*
Meridian Analytical Labs LLC ....F 620 328-3222
Mound Valley *(G-7177)*
Metal Finishing Company Inc ....F 316 267-7289
Wichita *(G-15053)*
NTS Technical Systems ....F 316 832-1600
Wichita *(G-15198)*
Pace Analytical Services Inc ....D 913 599-5665
Lenexa *(G-6042)*
Paragon N D T & Finishes Inc ....E 316 945-5285
Wichita *(G-15259)*
Professnal Toxicology Svcs Inc ....F 913 599-3535
Overland Park *(G-9189)*
Sdk Laboratories Inc ....E 620 665-5661
Hutchinson *(G-3439)*
Shaw Group Inc ....A 316 220-8020
Wichita *(G-15577)*
Syntech Research Lab Svcs LLC ....E 913 378-0998
Stilwell *(G-12175)*
Veriprime Inc ....E 620 873-7175
Meade *(G-7055)*

8741 Management Services

Adorers of Bld of Chrst ....F 316 942-2201
Wichita *(G-13615)*
Adventist Health Mid-America ....C 913 676-2184
Shawnee Mission *(G-11080)*
Agelix Consulting LLC ....E 913 708-8145
Overland Park *(G-8357)*
▼ **Allen Press Inc** ....D 785 843-1234
Lawrence *(G-4729)*
American Multi-Cinema Inc ....C 913 213-2000
Leawood *(G-5322)*
Archer-Daniels-Midland Company ....D 785 825-1541
Salina *(G-10407)*
Arthur Dogswell LLC ....D 620 231-7779
Frontenac *(G-2052)*
Arwood Waste Inc ....F 316 448-1576
Wichita *(G-13744)*
Bettis Contractors Inc ....E 785 783-8353
Topeka *(G-12378)*
Beverly Enterprises-Kansas LLC ....E 316 683-7588
Wichita *(G-13844)*
Beverly Enterprises-Kansas LLC ....E 913 351-1284
Lansing *(G-4669)*
Beverly Enterprises-Kansas LLC ....E 785 449-2294
Eskridge *(G-1865)*
◆ **Black & Veatch Holding Company** ....D 913 458-2000
Overland Park *(G-8457)*
Bristol Hotel & Resorts Inc ....E 785 462-8787
Colby *(G-991)*
Bristol Hotel & Resorts Inc ....D 785 823-1739
Salina *(G-10431)*
Butler National Corporation ....E 913 780-9595
Olathe *(G-7571)*
Capital Performance MGT LLC ....E 913 381-1481
Leawood *(G-5346)*
Capstone MGT & Dev Group Inc ....F 785 341-2494
Manhattan *(G-6576)*
Carson Development Inc ....F 913 499-1926
Overland Park *(G-8522)*
Centennial Healthcare Corp ....C 913 829-2273
Olathe *(G-7584)*
Centrinex LLC ....F 913 827-9600
Lenexa *(G-5739)*
Century Construction Sup LLC ....F 913 438-3366
Lenexa *(G-5741)*
Ceva US Holdings Inc ....F 913 894-0230
Lenexa *(G-5747)*
Channelview SW Hotel Inc ....E 913 345-2111
Lenexa *(G-5752)*
City of Wichita ....E 316 942-4482
Wichita *(G-14025)*
Commercial Hotel Management Co ....E 913 642-0160
Lenexa *(G-5775)*
Construction MGT Svcs Inc ....E 913 231-5736
Olathe *(G-7612)*
Corvel Corporation ....E 913 253-7200
Overland Park *(G-8602)*
Crestline Hotels & Resorts LLC ....E 913 451-2553
Overland Park *(G-8613)*
Cryo Management Inc ....E 913 362-9005
Prairie Village *(G-10023)*
Cullor Property Management LLC ....F 913 324-5900
Lenexa *(G-5796)*
Curo Management LLC ....E 316 771-0000
Wichita *(G-14143)*
Curo Management LLC ....D 316 722-3801
Wichita *(G-14145)*
Cushman Wkefield Solutions LLC ....C 316 721-3656
Colwich *(G-1093)*
Dalmark Management Group LLC ....F 816 272-0041
Leawood *(G-5368)*
Davidson & Associates Inc ....E 913 271-6859
Leawood *(G-5372)*
Delight Tb Indiana LLC ....B 561 301-6257
Wichita *(G-14187)*
Delmar Gardens of Overland Pk ....C 913 469-4210
Shawnee Mission *(G-11300)*
Den Management Co Inc ....C 316 686-1964
Wichita *(G-14191)*
Deseret Health Group Llc ....B 620 662-0597
Hutchinson *(G-3262)*
Devlin Management Inc ....F 316 634-1800
Wichita *(G-14204)*
Dondlinger Companies Inc ....D 316 945-0555
Wichita *(G-14228)*
Dynamic Management Solutions ....E 785 456-1794
Wamego *(G-13416)*
Eagle Case Management LLC ....E 913 334-9035
Kansas City *(G-3978)*
Event Systems Inc ....F 316 641-1848
Wichita *(G-14314)*
Fidelity Management Corp ....E 316 291-5950
Wichita *(G-14365)*
Firstsource Solutions USA Inc ....F 620 223-8200
Fort Scott *(G-1968)*
Foster Design Inc ....C 316 832-9700
Wichita *(G-14403)*
Gaelic Management Inc ....F 316 683-5150
Wichita *(G-14436)*
◆ **GBA Builders Llc** ....E 913 492-0400
Lenexa *(G-5870)*
Gunter Construction Company ....F 913 362-7844
Kansas City *(G-4059)*
Health Management of Kansas ....D 620 431-7474
Chanute *(G-731)*
Health Management of Kansas ....D 620 251-1866
Coffeyville *(G-944)*
Health Management of Kansas ....D 620 429-3803
Columbus *(G-1078)*
Health Management of Kansas ....C 620 251-5190
Coffeyville *(G-945)*
Health Management of Kansas ....D 620 251-6545
Coffeyville *(G-946)*
Heartland Golf Dev II LLC ....F 913 856-7235
Mission Hills *(G-7143)*
Heartland Management Company ....F 785 233-6655
Topeka *(G-12680)*
Henderson Bldg Solutions LLC ....F 913 894-9720
Lenexa *(G-5899)*
Home Depot USA Inc ....E 913 888-9090
Shawnee Mission *(G-11437)*
Innco Hospitality Inc ....E 913 451-1300
Shawnee Mission *(G-11458)*
Interntnal Mtr Coach Group Inc ....F 913 906-0111
Lenexa *(G-5920)*
J & K Contracting Lc ....F 785 238-3298
Junction City *(G-3702)*
Kansas Asphalt Inc ....D 877 384-2280
Bucyrus *(G-601)*
Kansas Assc Home For Aged Inc ....F 785 233-7443
Topeka *(G-12758)*
Kansas Medical Insur Svcs Corp ....F 785 232-2224
Topeka *(G-12789)*
Kcoe Isom LLP ....E 785 825-1561
Salina *(G-10572)*
Kessinger/Hunter & Company Lc ....C 816 842-2690
Shawnee Mission *(G-11529)*
Kickapoo Tribe In Kansas Inc ....C 785 486-2131
Horton *(G-3130)*
Knight Enterprises Ltd ....E 785 843-5511
Lawrence *(G-4946)*
Koppers Recovery Resources LLC ....E 913 213-6127
Overland Park *(G-8926)*
L C Enterprises ....F 316 682-3300
Wichita *(G-14904)*
L C Epoch Group ....C 855 753-7624
Overland Park *(G-8934)*
L D F Company ....E 316 636-5575
Wichita *(G-14905)*
Lakemary Center Inc ....E 913 768-6831
Olathe *(G-7853)*
Lamar Court ....D 913 906-9696
Overland Park *(G-8941)*
Latour Management Inc ....E 316 524-2290
Wichita *(G-14933)*
Latour Management Inc ....F 316 733-1922
Andover *(G-102)*
Leisure Hotel Corporation ....D 913 905-1460
Lenexa *(G-5966)*
Liberal School District ....E 620 604-2400
Liberal *(G-6335)*
Lodgeworks Partners LP ....D 316 681-5100
Wichita *(G-14974)*
Lodging Enterprises LLC ....A 316 630-6300
Wichita *(G-14975)*

Lrico Services LLC ....C 316 847-4800
Wichita *(G-14987)*
Lutheran Home WA Keeney ....E 785 743-5787
Wakeeney *(G-13389)*
Macfarlane Group LLC ....E 913 825-1200
Shawnee Mission *(G-11589)*
Manning Construction Co Inc ....E 913 390-1007
Olathe *(G-7873)*
Material Management Inc ....F 620 221-9060
Winfield *(G-16157)*
Medtrak Services LLC ....D 913 262-2187
Overland Park *(G-9008)*
Midwest Bioscience RES Pk LLC ....E 913 319-0300
Leawood *(G-5482)*
Mll Management Group Inc ....D 620 947-3608
Hillsboro *(G-3052)*
◆ **Miq Logistics LLC** ....C 913 696-7100
Overland Park *(G-9041)*
Mosaic ....E 913 788-8400
Kansas City *(G-4267)*
Mosaic ....E 785 472-4081
Ellsworth *(G-1679)*
Mosaic ....D 620 229-8702
Winfield *(G-16161)*
Mpp Co Inc ....F 913 895-0269
Shawnee Mission *(G-11656)*
National Bd For Rspratory Care ....F 913 895-4900
Overland Park *(G-9069)*
Natural Gas Pipeline Amer LLC ....G 620 885-4505
Minneola *(G-7127)*
Nueterra DC Holdings LLC ....E 913 387-0689
Leawood *(G-5506)*
Nustar Pipeline Oper Partnr LP ....F 316 773-9000
Wichita *(G-15200)*
Osage Cnty Ecnmic Dev Corp Inc ....D 785 828-3242
Lyndon *(G-6478)*
Paradigm Liaison Services LLC ....E 316 554-9225
Wichita *(G-15256)*
Petl Management Corp Inc ....F 620 792-1717
Great Bend *(G-2622)*
Pk Technology LLC ....F 316 866-2955
Wichita *(G-15304)*
Plaza Belmont MGT Group II LLC ....B 913 381-7177
Shawnee Mission *(G-11738)*
Preferred Mental Health Mgt ....F 316 262-0444
Wichita *(G-15328)*
Presbytrian Mnors of Md-Merica ....E 316 685-1100
Wichita *(G-15336)*
Priority Logistics Inc ....E 913 991-7281
Overland Park *(G-9186)*
Profit Plus Bus Solutions LLC ....F 913 583-8440
De Soto *(G-1210)*
PSI Services Inc ....C 913 895-4600
Olathe *(G-8011)*
Pulse Systems Inc ....D 316 636-5900
Wichita *(G-15375)*
Quality Technology Svcs LLC ....D 913 814-9988
Overland Park *(G-9217)*
R D H Electric Inc ....E 785 625-3833
Hays *(G-2895)*
Reit Management & Research ....F 913 492-4375
Lenexa *(G-6099)*
Resource Service Solutions LLC ....E 913 338-5050
Lenexa *(G-6107)*
Retail Groc Assn Grter Kans Cy ....F 913 384-3830
Westwood *(G-13558)*
Rf Construction Inc ....E 785 776-8855
Manhattan *(G-6791)*
Rhw Hotel Holdings Company LLC ....F 913 451-1222
Shawnee Mission *(G-11798)*
Saint Francis Cmnty Svcs Inc ....F 620 326-6373
Wellington *(G-13526)*
Saint Francis Cmnty Svcs Inc ....E 785 210-1000
Junction City *(G-3749)*
Saint Francis Cmnty Svcs Inc ....E 785 825-0541
Salina *(G-10658)*
Saint Francis Cmnty Svcs Inc ....C 620 276-4482
Garden City *(G-2272)*
Saint Francis Cmnty Svcs Inc ....E 785 825-0541
Salina *(G-10659)*
Saint Francis Cmnty Svcs Inc ....E 785 452-9653
Salina *(G-10660)*
Saint Francis Cmnty Svcs Inc ....F 316 831-0330
Wichita *(G-15507)*
Sasnak Management Corporation ....E 316 683-2611
Wichita *(G-15521)*
Six Continents Hotels Inc ....E 785 462-8787
Colby *(G-1041)*
Sr Food and Beverage Co Inc ....D 913 299-9797
Kansas City *(G-4437)*
T T Companies Inc ....A 913 599-6886
Olathe *(G-8097)*
T W Lacy & Associates Inc ....F 913 706-7625
Prairie Village *(G-10073)*
T-143 Inc ....E 913 681-8313
Overland Park *(G-9390)*
Tetra Management Inc ....F 316 685-6221
Wichita *(G-15731)*
Tmfs Management LLC ....C 913 319-8100
Overland Park *(G-9417)*
Tsvc Inc ....C 913 599-6886
Olathe *(G-8124)*
Tyr Energy Inc ....F 913 754-5800
Overland Park *(G-9435)*
United States Dept of Army ....E 913 684-2151
Fort Leavenworth *(G-1944)*
Universal Construction Co Inc ....E 913 342-1150
Kansas City *(G-4494)*
University of Kansas Med Ctr ....E 913 945-5598
Westwood *(G-13562)*
Via Christi Health Inc ....E 316 858-4900
Wichita *(G-15891)*
Watco Supply Chain Svcs LLC ....F 479 502-3658
Great Bend *(G-2657)*
Westdale Asset Management Ltd ....D 913 307-5900
Lenexa *(G-6227)*
Western Plins Rgional Hosp LLC ....F 620 225-8700
Dodge City *(G-1455)*
Woofter Cnstr & Irrigation Inc ....E 785 462-8653
Colby *(G-1049)*
Young Management Corporation ....D 913 341-3113
Overland Park *(G-9519)*
Young Management Group Inc ....F 913 213-3827
Overland Park *(G-9520)*

8742 Management Consulting Services

360directories LLC ....E 316 269-6920
Wichita *(G-13581)*
3c Healthcare Inc ....F 620 221-7850
Winfield *(G-16113)*
Accenture LLP ....C 913 319-1000
Overland Park *(G-8340)*
Accountable Finance Inc ....F 913 381-4077
Overland Park *(G-8341)*
Adams-Gabbert & Associates LLC ....F 913 735-4390
Overland Park *(G-8346)*
Advanced Medical Resources ....E 316 687-3071
Wichita *(G-13624)*
Advanced Resources LLC ....E 913 207-9998
Leawood *(G-5313)*
Advantage Medical Group ....F 785 749-0130
Lawrence *(G-4722)*
Advantage Sales & Mktg LLC ....F 913 890-0900
Lenexa *(G-5634)*
Advantage Sales & Mktg LLC ....F 316 721-7727
Wichita *(G-13628)*
Advisory Associates Inc ....E 913 829-7323
Lenexa *(G-5635)*
Agelix Consulting LLC ....E 913 708-8145
Overland Park *(G-8357)*
Agenda Usa Inc ....E 913 268-4466
Shawnee Mission *(G-11084)*
Aib International Inc ....D 785 537-4750
Manhattan *(G-6537)*
AIG ....C 503 323-2500
Overland Park *(G-8361)*
Ally Servicing LLC ....C 316 652-6301
Wichita *(G-13679)*
American Gen Lf Insur Co Del ....E 913 402-5000
Overland Park *(G-8377)*
American Gvrnment Slutions LLC ....F 913 428-2550
Leawood *(G-5320)*
American Management Assn Intl ....C 913 451-2700
Shawnee Mission *(G-11105)*
◆ **American Maplan Corporation** ....D 620 241-6843
McPherson *(G-6934)*
Ameriprise Financial Inc ....E 913 239-8140
Leawood *(G-5323)*
Ameriprise Financial Svcs Inc ....E 913 451-2811
Shawnee Mission *(G-11109)*
Annan Marketing Services Inc ....E 913 254-0050
Overland Park *(G-8387)*
Archein Aerospace LLC ....E 682 499-2150
Wichita *(G-13730)*
Arrowhead Intermodal Svcs LLC ....F 816 509-0746
Edgerton *(G-1479)*
Ascend Learning LLC ....B 855 856-7705
Leawood *(G-5331)*
ASK Associates Inc ....E 785 841-8194
Lawrence *(G-4738)*
Asset MGT Analis Group LLC ....E 803 270-0996
Leawood *(G-5335)*
Asset Services Inc ....F 913 383-2738
Overland Park *(G-8405)*
Axa Financial Inc ....E 913 345-2800
Overland Park *(G-8419)*
Axcet Hr Solutions Inc ....E 913 383-2999
Overland Park *(G-8420)*
Bajillion Agency ....E 785 408-5927
Topeka *(G-12359)*
Bankonip ....F 913 928-6297
Stilwell *(G-12135)*
Barber Financial Group Inc ....F 913 393-1000
Lenexa *(G-5686)*
Beshenich Muir & Assoc LLC ....F 913 904-1880
Leavenworth *(G-5208)*
Big Creek Investment Corp Inc ....G 620 431-3445
Chanute *(G-707)*
Black Vatch MGT Consulting LLC ....B 913 458-2000
Overland Park *(G-8460)*
Block Real Estate Services LLC ....F 816 412-8457
Overland Park *(G-8464)*
Bok Financial Corporation ....E 785 273-9993
Topeka *(G-12396)*
Booz Allen Hamilton Inc ....D 913 682-5300
Leavenworth *(G-5213)*
Caenen Castle ....F 913 631-4100
Shawnee *(G-10922)*
Capital Financial Group ....F 785 228-1234
Topeka *(G-12430)*
Cartesian Inc ....E 913 345-9315
Overland Park *(G-8524)*
CCL Construction Consultants ....E 913 491-0807
Overland Park *(G-8530)*
Central States Mktg & Mfg Inc ....E 620 245-9955
McPherson *(G-6944)*
Century Construction Sup LLC ....F 913 438-3366
Lenexa *(G-5741)*
Century Health Solutions Inc ....F 785 233-1816
Topeka *(G-12459)*
Certified Environmental Mgt ....E 785 823-0492
Salina *(G-10446)*
Chelepis & Associates Inc ....E 913 912-7113
Overland Park *(G-8544)*
CLC Group Inc ....C 316 636-5055
Wichita *(G-14038)*
Collateral Services Inc ....F 913 680-1015
Leavenworth *(G-5223)*
Commercial RE Women Netwrk ....F 785 832-1808
Lawrence *(G-4802)*
Communityworks Inc ....D 913 789-9900
Overland Park *(G-8584)*
Complex Property Advisers Corp ....F 913 498-0790
Overland Park *(G-8591)*
Conant Construction LLC ....F 620 408-6784
Dodge City *(G-1330)*
Control Systems Intl Inc ....D 913 599-5010
Shawnee Mission *(G-11264)*
Copy Co Corporation ....G 785 832-2679
Lawrence *(G-4811)*
Corporate Enterprise SEC Inc ....F 913 422-0410
Lenexa *(G-5789)*
Corridor Group Holdings LLC ....E 913 362-0600
Shawnee Mission *(G-11267)*
Cpg Communications Group LLC ....G 913 317-2888
Shawnee Mission *(G-11276)*
CPI Qualified Plan Cons Inc ....B 620 793-8473
Great Bend *(G-2549)*
CPM Technologies Inc ....F 256 777-9869
Wichita *(G-14124)*
Creative Capsule LLC ....D 816 421-1714
Overland Park *(G-8608)*
Cro Magnon Repast LLC ....F 913 747-5559
Lenexa *(G-5793)*
Culture Index LLC ....F 816 361-7575
Leawood *(G-5365)*
Daymon Worldwide Inc ....F 620 669-4200
Hutchinson *(G-3258)*
Deere & Company ....E 913 310-8100
Olathe *(G-7645)*
Design Benefits ....F 316 729-7676
Wichita *(G-14200)*
Dg Business Solutions Inc ....F 913 766-0163
Lenexa *(G-5815)*
DVC Training Specialists LLC ....G 913 908-3393
Gardner *(G-2340)*
E T C Institute Inc ....E 913 747-0646
Olathe *(G-7663)*
EAC Audit Inc ....F 785 594-6707
Baldwin City *(G-359)*

Electronic Sensors Inc ....F 316 267-2807
Wichita *(G-14268)*
Ellis Grubb Martens Coml Group ....E 316 262-0000
Wichita *(G-14272)*
Enterprise Bus Solutions LLC ....F 913 529-4350
Lenexa *(G-5834)*
Eveans Bash Klein Inc ....F 913 345-7000
Overland Park *(G-8694)*
Excel Personnel Services Inc ....E 913 341-1150
Shawnee Mission *(G-11353)*
Exhibit Arts LLC ....E 316 264-2915
Wichita *(G-14321)*
Fbd Consulting Inc ....F 913 319-8850
Overland Park *(G-8709)*
Feet On Ground Marketing Inc ....F 913 242-5558
Lawrence *(G-4858)*
Financial Advisory Service Inc ....F 913 239-2300
Shawnee Mission *(G-11367)*
First Intermark Corporation ....E 620 442-2460
Arkansas City *(G-156)*
First Management Inc ....D 785 749-0006
Lawrence *(G-4860)*
Franklin Covey Co ....G 800 819-1812
Overland Park *(G-8737)*
Fujitsu America Inc ....E 913 327-2800
Shawnee Mission *(G-11384)*
Garden Cy Ammonia Program LLC ....F 620 271-0037
Garden City *(G-2180)*
Genesis Corp ....C 913 906-9991
Shawnee Mission *(G-11393)*
Geneva-Roth Ventures Inc ....E 913 825-1200
Shawnee Mission *(G-11394)*
Genoa Healthcare Mass LLC ....E 913 680-1652
Leavenworth *(G-5245)*
Ghd Services Inc ....E 785 783-8982
Topeka *(G-12636)*
Globalcom Solutions LLC ....F 785 832-8101
Lawrence *(G-4873)*
Glover Inc ....E 800 654-1511
Olathe *(G-7735)*
Gorham Gold Greenwich & Assoc ....F 913 981-4442
Overland Park *(G-8766)*
Grafton Inc ....A 913 498-0701
Overland Park *(G-8768)*
Grant Thornton LLP ....D 316 265-3231
Wichita *(G-14496)*
Great Plains Hlth Aliance Inc ....F 785 543-2111
Phillipsburg *(G-9787)*
Great Plains Hlth Aliance Inc ....F 316 685-1523
Wichita *(G-14502)*
Great Plains Hlth Aliance Inc ....D 620 723-3341
Greensburg *(G-2675)*
Greg Orscheln Trnsp Co ....E 913 371-1260
Lenexa *(G-5884)*
Greteman Group Inc ....F 316 263-1004
Wichita *(G-14517)*
Guerrilla Marketing Inc ....G 800 946-9150
Newton *(G-7353)*
Harte-Hanks Inc ....B 913 312-8100
Shawnee Mission *(G-11413)*
Hatcher Consultants Inc ....F 785 271-5557
Topeka *(G-12667)*
Hayse Management Services ....F 620 548-2369
Mullinville *(G-7209)*
Health Data Specialists LLC ....E 785 242-3419
Pomona *(G-10004)*
Healthcare Prfmce Group Inc ....D 316 796-0337
Spring Hill *(G-12086)*
Healthcare Revenue Group LLC ....F 913 717-4000
Stilwell *(G-12151)*
Heritage Group Lc ....F 316 261-5301
Wichita *(G-14594)*
High Quality Tech Inc ....G 316 448-3559
Wichita *(G-14604)*
Higher Ground ....F 316 262-2060
Wichita *(G-14607)*
HMS Holdings Corp ....E 785 271-9300
Topeka *(G-12695)*
Hss IT Management Inc ....C 913 498-9988
Overland Park *(G-8832)*
Hyr Global Source Inc ....F 913 815-2597
Overland Park *(G-8835)*
Ill Investments Inc ....D 913 262-6500
Leawood *(G-5434)*
Incisive Consultants LLC ....F 800 973-1743
Overland Park *(G-8840)*
Institute For Professional Dev ....E 913 491-4432
Shawnee Mission *(G-11460)*
Integra Realty Resources ....E 913 236-4700
Shawnee Mission *(G-11462)*
Integrated Solutions Inc ....D 316 264-7050
Wichita *(G-14704)*
Intellectual Growth Engrg ....F 913 210-8570
Shawnee *(G-10975)*
Intouch Group LLC ....C 913 317-9700
Overland Park *(G-8860)*
Iris Strgc Mktg Support Inc ....E 913 232-4825
Lenexa *(G-5923)*
J L D J Inc ....F 785 625-6316
Hays *(G-2855)*
J Schmid & Assoc Inc ....F 913 236-8988
Shawnee Mission *(G-11478)*
Kansas City Financial Group ....E 913 649-7447
Overland Park *(G-8895)*
Kansas Credit Union Assn ....E 316 942-7965
Wichita *(G-14795)*
Kansas Medical Society ....F 785 235-2383
Topeka *(G-12791)*
Kansas Rural Housing Service ....E 785 862-4877
Topeka *(G-12802)*
KC Hopps Ltd ....E 913 322-2440
Overland Park *(G-8906)*
Kci Kansas Counselors Inc ....E 913 541-9704
Shawnee Mission *(G-11526)*
Kdjm Consulting Inc ....F 913 362-0600
Shawnee Mission *(G-11527)*
Kea Advisors ....F 913 832-6099
Lawrence *(G-4939)*
Kemira Water Solutions Inc ....F 785 842-7424
Lawrence *(G-4941)*
Kessinger/Hunter & Company Lc ....C 816 842-2690
Shawnee Mission *(G-11529)*
Koesten Hirschmann & Crabtree ....F 913 345-1881
Shawnee Mission *(G-11537)*
Land Acquisitions Inc ....E 847 749-0675
Wichita *(G-14919)*
Latour Management Inc ....E 316 524-2290
Wichita *(G-14933)*
Lawing Financial Group Inc ....D 913 491-6226
Overland Park *(G-8948)*
Leidos Inc ....G 913 317-5120
Shawnee Mission *(G-11560)*
Leisure Hotels LLC ....F 913 905-1460
Lenexa *(G-5967)*
Level Five Solutions Inc ....F 913 400-2014
Stilwell *(G-12163)*
Lionshare Marketing Inc ....F 913 631-8400
Lenexa *(G-5974)*
Lpl Financial ....F 913 345-2908
Leawood *(G-5460)*
Macfarlane Group LLC ....E 913 825-1200
Shawnee Mission *(G-11589)*
Manning Construction Co Inc ....E 913 390-1007
Olathe *(G-7873)*
▼ Mbs Inc ....F 913 393-2525
Olathe *(G-7878)*
McCullough Development Inc ....E 888 776-3010
Manhattan *(G-6737)*
McDaniel Knutson Inc ....F 785 841-4664
Lawrence *(G-5017)*
McMc LLC ....E 913 341-8811
Overland Park *(G-9003)*
Medicalodges Cnstr Co Inc ....F 620 251-6700
Coffeyville *(G-961)*
Medova Hlthcare Fncl Group LLC ....E 316 616-6160
Wichita *(G-15034)*
Menufycom LLC ....E 913 738-9399
Leawood *(G-5473)*
MGM Marketing Inc ....F 913 451-0023
Olathe *(G-7888)*
▲ Midcontinental Chemical Co Inc ....E 913 390-5556
Olathe *(G-7893)*
Midland Professional Services ....E 785 840-9676
Lawrence *(G-5026)*
Midland Properties Inc ....F 913 677-5300
Mission Woods *(G-7151)*
Midwest Division - Oprmc LLC ....A 913 541-5000
Shawnee Mission *(G-11632)*
Midwest Health Services Inc ....F 316 685-1587
Wichita *(G-15095)*
Miller Group ....F 816 333-3000
Leawood *(G-5485)*
Mixon-Hill Inc ....F 913 239-8400
Shawnee Mission *(G-11648)*
Morningstar Communications Co ....F 913 660-9630
Overland Park *(G-9054)*
Motivtion Thrugh Incntives Inc ....E 913 438-2600
Overland Park *(G-9056)*
New Boston Creative Group LLC ....F 785 587-8185
Manhattan *(G-6760)*
New Paradigm Solutions Inc ....F 785 313-0946
Manhattan *(G-6761)*
Nonprofit Solutions Inc ....D 620 343-6111
Emporia *(G-1806)*
NTS Technical Systems ....F 316 832-1600
Wichita *(G-15198)*
Nuesynergy Inc ....F 913 396-0884
Leawood *(G-5505)*
Object Tech Solutions Inc ....D 913 345-9080
Leawood *(G-5507)*
Omni Employment MGT Svc LLC ....E 913 341-2119
Overland Park *(G-9101)*
Onyx Meetings Inc ....F 913 381-1123
Overland Park *(G-9106)*
Parsons Brnckrhoff Hldings Inc ....E 913 310-9943
Lenexa *(G-6043)*
Pbp Management Group Inc ....E 316 262-2900
Wichita *(G-15274)*
Pennington Co Fundraising LLC ....E 785 843-1661
Lawrence *(G-5060)*
Phillips and Associates Inc ....D 913 706-7625
Prairie Village *(G-10059)*
Phillips Resource Network Inc ....E 913 236-7777
Shawnee Mission *(G-11732)*
Pioneer Automation Technology ....F 316 322-0123
El Dorado *(G-1591)*
Prime Concepts Group Inc ....F 316 942-1111
Wichita *(G-15343)*
Pro AG Marketing ....F 785 476-2211
Kensington *(G-4579)*
Proactive Solutions Inc ....E 913 948-8000
Shawnee Mission *(G-11753)*
Professionals Business MGT Inc ....F 913 888-1444
Overland Park *(G-9188)*
Propane Resources LLC ....E 913 262-8345
Shawnee Mission *(G-11756)*
Protiviti Inc ....F 913 685-6200
Overland Park *(G-9198)*
Regan Marketing Inc ....F 816 531-5111
Lenexa *(G-6097)*
Regulatory Consultants Inc ....E 785 486-2882
Horton *(G-3133)*
Research Partnership Inc ....E 316 263-6433
Wichita *(G-15447)*
Restaurant Purchasing Svcs LLC ....F 800 548-2292
Overland Park *(G-9237)*
▲ Return Products Management Inc ....F 913 768-1747
Olathe *(G-8028)*
Revest LLC ....E 316 262-8460
Wichita *(G-15454)*
RFS Associates LLC ....E 913 871-0456
Westwood Hills *(G-13565)*
Right Management Inc ....E 913 451-1100
Shawnee Mission *(G-11805)*
Ross Consultants Inc ....E 213 926-2090
Overland Park *(G-9258)*
Royal Mechanical Services Inc ....E 913 897-3436
Overland Park *(G-9260)*
S T Carter Inc ....E 913 451-1100
Shawnee Mission *(G-11821)*
Selective Site Consultants Inc ....E 913 438-7700
Overland Park *(G-9292)*
Shamrock Trading Corporation ....B 877 642-8553
Overland Park *(G-9302)*
Shc Holdings LLC ....F 620 273-6900
Cottonwood Falls *(G-1156)*
Sisters St Joseph Wichita KS ....E 316 686-7171
Wichita *(G-15598)*
Skutouch Solutions LLC ....F 913 538-5165
Lenexa *(G-6136)*
Slawson Exploration Co Inc ....E 316 263-3201
Wichita *(G-15603)*
State of Kansas ....B 620 225-4804
Dodge City *(G-1435)*
Stepp and Rothwell ....F 913 345-4800
Overland Park *(G-9359)*
Sterling Readiness Rounds LLC ....F 785 542-1405
Eudora *(G-1880)*
Stratgic Knwldge Solutions Inc ....F 913 682-2002
Leavenworth *(G-5292)*
Syndeo Outsourcing LLC ....E 316 630-9107
Wichita *(G-15710)*
T & M Financial Inc ....F 785 266-8333
Topeka *(G-13129)*
T T Companies Inc ....A 913 599-6886
Olathe *(G-8097)*
Tantillo Financial Group LLC ....F 913 649-3200
Shawnee Mission *(G-11919)*
Tck- The Trust Company Kansas ....E 316 264-6010
Wichita *(G-15718)*

SIC

Telcon Associates Inc........F....... 855 864-1571
Overland Park *(G-9400)*
Terracon Consultants Inc........E....... 316 262-0171
Wichita *(G-15730)*
Terracon Consultants Inc........F....... 785 267-3310
Topeka *(G-13153)*
TFT Global Inc........F....... 519 842-4540
Kansas City *(G-4467)*
Thats A Wrap LLC........E....... 913 390-0035
Olathe *(G-8108)*
Thomas G Geha & Associates........F....... 913 563-6707
Prairie Village *(G-10074)*
Three Click Ventres Inc DBA AV........F....... 913 955-3700
Overland Park *(G-9407)*
Thruline Marketing Inc........C....... 913 254-6000
Lenexa *(G-6180)*
Tiyosaye Inc Higher Ground........F....... 316 262-2060
Wichita *(G-15768)*
Training Tech & Support Inc........E....... 913 682-7048
Leavenworth *(G-5300)*
Transerve Inc........D....... 620 231-2230
Pittsburg *(G-9947)*
Tru8 Solutions LLC........F....... 678 451-0264
Manhattan *(G-6831)*
Trust Company of Manhattan........F....... 785 537-7200
Manhattan *(G-6832)*
U Inc........F....... 913 814-7708
Overland Park *(G-9436)*
U S Automation Inc........G....... 913 894-2410
Shawnee Mission *(G-11953)*
V Wealth Advisors LLC........E....... 913 827-4600
Overland Park *(G-9457)*
Varney & Associates Cpas LLC........E....... 785 537-2202
Manhattan *(G-6841)*
Veracity Consulting Inc........D....... 913 945-1912
Overland Park *(G-9462)*
Veterinary Research and Cnslt........F....... 785 324-9200
Hays *(G-2925)*
Vigilias LLC........E....... 800 924-8140
Wichita *(G-15907)*
W S Griffith Inc........E....... 913 451-1855
Overland Park *(G-9476)*
Waddell & Reed Inc........F....... 913 491-9202
Leawood *(G-5593)*
Waddell & Reed Inc........E....... 785 537-4505
Manhattan *(G-6844)*
Waddell & Reed Inc........F....... 785 233-6400
Topeka *(G-13229)*
Waddell & Reed Inv MGT Co........E....... 913 491-9202
Leawood *(G-5594)*
Water Systems Engineering Inc........F....... 785 242-5853
Ottawa *(G-8321)*
Wells Fargo Clearing Svcs LLC........F....... 785 825-4636
Salina *(G-10767)*
Xelocity Inc........F....... 913 647-8660
Overland Park *(G-9512)*
Xk Solutions Inc........E....... 877 954-9656
Overland Park *(G-9513)*
Yaeger Architecture Inc........E....... 913 742-8000
Lenexa *(G-6239)*
Yellow Customer Solutions Inc........F....... 913 696-6100
Shawnee Mission *(G-12022)*
Young Management Corporation........F....... 913 947-3134
Bucyrus *(G-612)*
Zamani Davis and Associate........E....... 913 851-0092
Shawnee Mission *(G-12026)*
Ziegler Corporation........F....... 785 841-4250
Lawrence *(G-5193)*

8743 Public Relations Svcs

Big Creek Investment Corp Inc........G....... 620 431-3445
Chanute *(G-707)*
Cpg Communications Group LLC........G....... 913 317-2888
Shawnee Mission *(G-11276)*
Creative Mktg Unlimited Inc........G....... 913 894-0077
Overland Park *(G-8611)*
Discovery Concepts Inc........G....... 913 814-7100
Shawnee Mission *(G-11309)*
Family Ftres Edtorial Synd Inc........E....... 913 722-0055
Shawnee Mission *(G-11360)*
Frank Agency Inc........D....... 913 648-8333
Overland Park *(G-8736)*
Mennonite Mission Network........F....... 540 434-6701
Newton *(G-7379)*
Morningstar Communications Co........F....... 913 660-9630
Overland Park *(G-9054)*
Pennington Co Fundraising LLC........E....... 785 843-1661
Lawrence *(G-5060)*
Raymarr Inc........F....... 913 648-3480
Shawnee Mission *(G-11778)*
Spectrum Promotional Pdts Inc........F....... 316 262-1199
Wichita *(G-15638)*
Walz Tetrick Advertising Inc........E....... 913 789-8778
Mission *(G-7140)*

8744 Facilities Support Mgmt Svcs

BKM Construction LLC........F....... 913 297-0049
Leavenworth *(G-5212)*
Blackstone Environmental Inc........F....... 913 495-9990
Stilwell *(G-12136)*
Cleaning By Lamunyon Inc........F....... 785 632-1259
Clay Center *(G-855)*
Contract Services Inc........D....... 785 239-9069
Fort Riley *(G-1946)*
Corecivic Inc........C....... 913 727-3246
Leavenworth *(G-5225)*
Corrections Kansas Department........D....... 913 727-3235
Lansing *(G-4672)*
Corrections Kansas Department........D....... 316 321-7284
El Dorado *(G-1551)*
Court Trustee Dept........F....... 785 762-2583
Junction City *(G-3685)*
Envirnmntal Advisors Engineers........E....... 913 599-4326
Shawnee Mission *(G-11344)*
Exhibit Arts LLC........E....... 316 264-2915
Wichita *(G-14321)*
Hydrogeologic Inc........E....... 913 317-8860
Shawnee Mission *(G-11445)*
Kansas Asphalt Inc........D....... 877 384-2280
Bucyrus *(G-601)*
Landscapes Inc........E....... 316 262-7557
Wichita *(G-14921)*
N Central KS Reg Juven Deten........F....... 785 238-4549
Junction City *(G-3728)*
Oc Services........F....... 316 655-3952
Wichita *(G-15205)*
Remediation Services Inc........E....... 800 335-1201
Independence *(G-3553)*
Skookum Educational Programs........C....... 785 307-8180
Fort Riley *(G-1950)*
Sky Blue Inc........D....... 785 842-9013
Lawrence *(G-5112)*
Southast Kans Rgnal Jvnile Dtn........E....... 620 724-4174
Girard *(G-2417)*
Transtecs Corporation........D....... 316 651-0389
Wichita *(G-15793)*
Unified Gvrnment Cmnty Corectn........E....... 913 573-4180
Kansas City *(G-4485)*
US Attorneys Office - Dst Kans........D....... 316 269-6481
Wichita *(G-15862)*
Usd 383 Mnhttan Ogden Schl Dst........D....... 785 587-2180
Manhattan *(G-6839)*

8748 Business Consulting Svcs, NEC

360 Document Solutions LLC........F....... 316 630-8334
Wichita *(G-13580)*
A G 1 Source LLC........E....... 620 327-2205
Hesston *(G-2983)*
Adams-Gabbert & Associates LLC........F....... 913 735-4390
Overland Park *(G-8346)*
Advanced Manufacturing Inst........E....... 785 532-7044
Manhattan *(G-6534)*
Advantage Tech Inc........D....... 913 888-5050
Overland Park *(G-8352)*
Agspring LLC........E....... 913 333-3035
Leawood *(G-5314)*
Air & Waste Management Assn........F....... 913 940-0081
Overland Park *(G-8362)*
Airsource Technologies Inc........F....... 913 422-9001
Shawnee Mission *(G-11089)*
Alea Communications LLC........F....... 913 439-7391
Gardner *(G-2323)*
Allied Business Solutions Inc........F....... 913 856-2323
Gardner *(G-2324)*
Allied Environmental Cons Inc........F....... 316 262-5698
Wichita *(G-13672)*
Anthem Media LLC........E....... 913 894-6923
Leawood *(G-5327)*
Applied Ecological Svcs Inc........F....... 785 594-2245
Baldwin City *(G-354)*
Arcadis US Inc........E....... 913 492-4156
Lenexa *(G-5659)*
Archein Aerospace LLC........E....... 682 499-2150
Wichita *(G-13730)*
Assessment Tech Inst LLC........B....... 800 667-7531
Leawood *(G-5334)*
Associated Environmental Inc........F....... 785 776-7755
Manhattan *(G-6547)*
Auditing For Cmpliance Educatn........F....... 913 648-8572
Shawnee Mission *(G-11133)*
Baxter Vault Company Inc........F....... 620 856-3441
Baxter Springs *(G-398)*
BE Smith Inc........B....... 913 341-9116
Lenexa *(G-5691)*
Billy Murphy & Associates LLC........F....... 913 306-0381
Leavenworth *(G-5210)*
Blue Infotech Inc........F....... 816 945-2583
Leawood *(G-5341)*
Cardinal Health 127 Inc........D....... 913 451-3955
Overland Park *(G-8513)*
CB&i Envmtl Infrastructure Inc........E....... 913 451-1224
Lenexa *(G-5735)*
Cbiz Inc........F....... 913 345-0500
Overland Park *(G-8528)*
Cellint Usa Inc........F....... 913 871-6500
Olathe *(G-7582)*
Central Prairie Co-Op........F....... 620 422-3221
Nickerson *(G-7431)*
Centrinex LLC........B....... 913 744-3410
Overland Park *(G-8539)*
Century Health Solutions Inc........F....... 785 233-1816
Topeka *(G-12459)*
Choice Solutions LLC........E....... 913 338-4950
Overland Park *(G-8550)*
City of Wichita........E....... 316 268-4421
Wichita *(G-14024)*
Clarence M Kelley & Assoc of K........D....... 913 647-7700
Shawnee *(G-10929)*
Community Foundation of Ellis........F....... 785 726-2660
Ellis *(G-1641)*
Community Hsing Wyandotte Cnty........F....... 913 342-7580
Kansas City *(G-3931)*
Computrzed Asssments Lrng LLC........F....... 785 856-1034
Lawrence *(G-4807)*
Convergeone Inc........C....... 913 307-2300
Overland Park *(G-8597)*
Corporate Enterprise SEC Inc........F....... 913 422-0410
Lenexa *(G-5789)*
Cox Communications Inc........F....... 620 227-3361
Dodge City *(G-1333)*
Crop Quest Inc........F....... 620 225-2233
Dodge City *(G-1335)*
Darren Miller........F....... 620 276-4515
Garden City *(G-2143)*
Design Analysis and RES Corp........F....... 785 832-0434
Lawrence *(G-4833)*
Dpra Incorporated........F....... 785 539-3565
Manhattan *(G-6616)*
EAC Audit Inc........F....... 785 594-6707
Baldwin City *(G-359)*
Ecology and Environment Inc........F....... 913 339-9519
Overland Park *(G-8670)*
Educational Resources Inc........D....... 913 262-0448
Stilwell *(G-12146)*
El Centro Inc........F....... 913 677-1115
Kansas City *(G-3983)*
Elm Services LLC........D....... 913 954-4414
Overland Park *(G-8674)*
EMB Statistical Solutions LLC........F....... 913 322-6555
Overland Park *(G-8676)*
Envirnmntal Advisors Engineers........E....... 913 599-4326
Shawnee Mission *(G-11344)*
Eri Solutions Inc........E....... 316 927-4290
Colwich *(G-1094)*
Erm-West Inc........F....... 913 661-0770
Overland Park *(G-8687)*
Eureka Foundation........F....... 620 583-8630
Eureka *(G-1885)*
F & L Enterprises Inc........F....... 785 266-4933
Topeka *(G-12590)*
Fire Cnslting Case Review Intl........F....... 913 262-5200
Lenexa *(G-5853)*
Foster Design Inc........C....... 316 832-9700
Wichita *(G-14403)*
Friedman Group........E....... 310 590-1248
Overland Park *(G-8742)*
Garcia and Antosh LLP........F....... 620 225-7400
Dodge City *(G-1364)*
Gateway Plaza West Ltd........F....... 913 621-3840
Kansas City *(G-4027)*
Geocore LLC........E....... 785 826-1616
Salina *(G-10509)*
Greater Wichita Partnr Inc........F....... 316 500-6650
Wichita *(G-14508)*
Green Expectations Ldscpg Inc........F....... 913 897-8076
Kansas City *(G-4049)*
Groupsource Gpo LLC........F....... 913 888-9191
Olathe *(G-7741)*
Haley & Aldrich Inc........F....... 913 693-1900
Overland Park *(G-8785)*

Hotel MGT & Consulting Inc F 913 602-8470
Overland Park *(G-8830)*
Housing and Credit Counseling E 785 234-0217
Topeka *(G-12705)*
Icm Inc C 316 796-0900
Colwich *(G-1097)*
Innova Consulting LLC F 913 210-2002
Overland Park *(G-8845)*
Innovative Service Solutions F 913 851-7745
Overland Park *(G-8846)*
Integrated Solutions Inc D 316 264-7050
Wichita *(G-14704)*
It21 Inc F 913 393-4821
Overland Park *(G-8864)*
Jarden Corp Outdoor Solutions F 316 832-2441
Wichita *(G-14748)*
Jay Henges Enterprises Inc E 913 764-4600
Olathe *(G-7808)*
Johnson Cmmunications Svcs Inc F 913 681-5505
Stilwell *(G-12159)*
Jurysync LLC F 913 338-4301
Olathe *(G-7820)*
Jvf Enterprises Inc F 913 888-9111
Lenexa *(G-5934)*
K & D Ferguson Partnership F 785 476-2657
Kensington *(G-4576)*
Kansas Center Entreprnrshp E 316 425-8808
Wichita *(G-14791)*
Kansas Department Commerce E 785 296-5298
Topeka *(G-12768)*
Kansas Housing Resources Corp E 785 217-2001
Topeka *(G-12782)*
Kansas Operation Lifesaver F 785 806-8801
Topeka *(G-12795)*
Kansas Secured Title F 316 320-2410
El Dorado *(G-1576)*
Kansas State University F 785 532-5813
Manhattan *(G-6690)*
Kansas State University F 785 532-3900
Manhattan *(G-6694)*
Kansas State University F 785 532-6804
Manhattan *(G-6695)*
Kansys Inc E 913 780-5291
Olathe *(G-7830)*
Kcoe Isom LLP F 620 672-7476
Garden City *(G-2216)*
Keating & Associates Inc E 785 537-0366
Manhattan *(G-6698)*
KLA Environmental Services F 785 823-0097
Salina *(G-10576)*
Kleinfelder Inc D 913 962-0909
Lenexa *(G-5953)*
Knk Telecom Llc E 913 768-8000
Olathe *(G-7842)*
Koch Business Solutions LP C 316 828-5500
Wichita *(G-14874)*
Koers-Turgeon Consulting Svc F 620 272-9131
Garden City *(G-2219)*
Lakepoint Corporate F 316 990-6792
Augusta *(G-332)*
Land Acquisitions Inc E 847 749-0675
Wichita *(G-14919)*
Larsen & Associates Inc F 785 841-8707
Lawrence *(G-4955)*
Led2 Lighting Inc G 816 912-2180
Kansas City *(G-4199)*
Litigation Insights Inc E 913 339-9885
Overland Park *(G-8962)*
Marketsphere Consulting LLC D 913 608-3648
Overland Park *(G-8992)*
Mayhew Envmtl Training Assoc E 800 444-6382
Lawrence *(G-5014)*
Meitler Consulting Inc F 913 422-9339
Tonganoxie *(G-12267)*
Mid-States Energy Works Inc F 785 827-3631
Salina *(G-10601)*
Midwest Consulting Group Inc C 913 693-8200
Overland Park *(G-9031)*
Montgomery County Media LLC E 620 331-3550
Independence *(G-3541)*
National Bd For Rspratory Care F 913 895-4900
Overland Park *(G-9069)*
Needham & Associates Inc G 913 385-5300
Lenexa *(G-6019)*
Netstandard Inc D 913 428-4200
Overland Park *(G-9077)*
Network Consulting Inc F 913 893-4150
Edgerton *(G-1488)*
Nexlearn LLC E 316 265-2170
Wichita *(G-15172)*
P/Strada LLC F 816 256-4577
Lenexa *(G-6039)*
Pendello Solutions F 913 677-6744
Prairie Village *(G-10058)*
Perinatal Consultants PA F 785 354-5952
Goddard *(G-2452)*
Phone Tech Communications Inc F 913 859-9150
Overland Park *(G-9162)*
Pl Arm C 913 661-1662
Overland Park *(G-9165)*
Professional Service Inds Inc E 913 310-1600
Kansas City *(G-4343)*
Professors of Peace LLC F 316 213-7233
Haysville *(G-2956)*
Progress Rail Services F 256 593-1260
Atchison *(G-256)*
Propharma Group LLC D 888 242-0559
Overland Park *(G-9195)*
Provalue Cooperative Inc E 620 662-5406
Hutchinson *(G-3416)*
PSI Services Inc F 843 520-2992
Olathe *(G-8010)*
PSI Services Inc C 913 895-4600
Olathe *(G-8011)*
Purplefrogintl G 816 510-0871
Shawnee *(G-11014)*
Qspec Solutions Inc F 877 467-7732
Overland Park *(G-9207)*
Quest Research & Development F 316 267-1216
Wichita *(G-15393)*
Ramboll Environ US Corporation E 816 891-8228
Overland Park *(G-9222)*
Regency Gas Services LLC F 620 355-7905
Lakin *(G-4659)*
Regulatory Consultants Inc E 785 486-2882
Horton *(G-3133)*
Resolution Services LLC E 785 843-1638
Lawrence *(G-5093)*
Rhythm Engineering LLC E 913 227-0603
Lenexa *(G-6108)*
S C F Inc E 913 722-3473
Overland Park *(G-9267)*
Safety-Kleen (wt) Inc E 316 269-7400
Wichita *(G-15504)*
Schultz Brothers Elc Co Inc E 913 321-8338
Kansas City *(G-4406)*
SE Kansas Nture Ctr Schrmrhorn E 620 783-5207
Galena *(G-2084)*
Security Benefit Life Insur Co B 785 438-3000
Topeka *(G-13054)*
Security Management Co LLC E 785 438-3000
Topeka *(G-13055)*
Selective Site Consultants Inc E 913 438-7700
Overland Park *(G-9292)*
Servi Tech Inc C 620 227-7509
Dodge City *(G-1429)*
Service Corps Retired Execs F 316 269-6273
Wichita *(G-15567)*
Skc Corporation E 800 882-7779
Shawnee Mission *(G-11871)*
Something Different Media Prod F 913 764-9500
Olathe *(G-8072)*
South Central Kansas E 316 262-7035
Bel Aire *(G-440)*
Southeast Kans Educatn Svc Ctr C 620 724-6281
Girard *(G-2418)*
Southwest Plins Rgonal Svc Ctr D 620 675-2241
Sublette *(G-12207)*
Specpro Environmental Svcs LLC F 913 583-3000
De Soto *(G-1213)*
Spectrum Elite Corp G 913 579-7037
Olathe *(G-8076)*
Srd Environmental Services E 620 665-5590
Hutchinson *(G-3445)*
SRS Strategic Development F 785 296-4327
Topeka *(G-13094)*
Stantec Consulting Svcs Inc E 913 202-6867
Overland Park *(G-9354)*
Stratgic Knwldge Solutions Inc F 913 682-2002
Leavenworth *(G-5292)*
Structral Intgrity Systems LLC F 316 634-1396
Wichita *(G-15676)*
Student In Free Enterpris E 620 235-4574
Pittsburg *(G-9943)*
Studio 13 Inc F 913 948-1284
Overland Park *(G-9368)*
Systech Environmental Corp E 620 378-4451
Fredonia *(G-2046)*
T & C Mfg & Operating Inc E 620 793-5483
Great Bend *(G-2646)*
T T Companies Inc A 913 599-6886
Olathe *(G-8097)*
Techncal Trning Prfssonals LLC F 865 312-4189
Overland Park *(G-9399)*
Terracon Consultants Inc F 785 267-3310
Topeka *(G-13153)*
Veracity Consulting Inc D 913 945-1912
Overland Park *(G-9462)*
Veterinary Research and Cnslt F 785 324-9200
Hays *(G-2925)*
Wachter Inc C 913 541-2500
Lenexa *(G-6219)*
Wachter Tech Solutions Inc D 856 222-0643
Lenexa *(G-6220)*
Wichita Consulting Company LP E 316 681-5102
Wichita *(G-15990)*
Worldwide Energy Inc F 913 310-0705
Lenexa *(G-6234)*
XCEL NDT LLC E 785 455-2027
Clifton *(G-903)*

89 SERVICES, NOT ELSEWHERE CLASSIFIED

8999 Services Not Elsewhere Classified

Actuarial Resources Corp Kans E 913 451-0044
Overland Park *(G-8345)*
Ad Astra Recover Service F 316 941-5448
Wichita *(G-13611)*
B Scott Studio Inc G 316 321-1225
El Dorado *(G-1533)*
Baker Sr Marcellus F 316 670-6329
Wichita *(G-13795)*
Corbin Bronze Limited G 913 766-4012
Kansas City *(G-3940)*
Dell Ann Upp F 785 473-7001
Manhattan *(G-6611)*
Dodge City Public Library E 620 225-0248
Dodge City *(G-1350)*
EKA Consulting LLC F 913 244-2980
Shawnee *(G-10946)*
First Call For Help Ellis Cnty E 785 623-2800
Hays *(G-2806)*
Gallery Xii Inc E 316 267-5915
Wichita *(G-14440)*
Grassland Heritage Foundation F 913 856-4784
Olathe *(G-7740)*
Gsi Engineering Nthrn Div LLC F 316 554-0725
Wichita *(G-14523)*
Hawkins Inc E 785 448-1610
Garnett *(G-2376)*
Home Communications Inc F 620 654-3381
Galva *(G-2093)*
Invena Corporation E 620 583-8630
Eureka *(G-1892)*
Lenexa Services Inc D 913 541-0150
Shawnee *(G-10987)*
Lewis & Ellis Inc E 913 491-3388
Overland Park *(G-8955)*
Miller & Newberg Inc F 913 393-2522
Overland Park *(G-9037)*
Mitel (delaware) Inc F 913 752-9100
Lenexa *(G-6007)*
National Weather Service E 785 899-2360
Goodland *(G-2480)*
National Weather Service E 785 234-2592
Topeka *(G-12924)*
National Weather Service E 620 225-6514
Dodge City *(G-1411)*
Natural Rsource Protection Inc E 316 303-0505
Wichita *(G-15155)*
Pk Safety Services Inc D 316 260-4141
Augusta *(G-338)*
Rayers Bearden Stained GL Sup F 316 942-2929
Wichita *(G-15421)*
Regional Prvntion Ctr Wyndotte F 913 288-7685
Kansas City *(G-4367)*
Retel Brokerage Services Inc E 678 292-5723
Wichita *(G-15453)*
Saint Francis Cmnty Svcs Inc D 785 476-3234
Kensington *(G-4580)*
Service USA Inc E 913 543-3844
Leawood *(G-5550)*
Spideroak Inc F 847 564-8900
Mission *(G-7138)*
Tucson Transformer & Appa F 620 227-5100
Dodge City *(G-1441)*
Unified School District 259 D 316 973-4200
Wichita *(G-15836)*

S I C

University of Kansas ....D....... 785 864-9520
Lawrence ***(G-5159)***
Veterinary Research and Cnslt ....F....... 785 324-9200
Hays ***(G-2925)***

ALPHABETIC SECTION

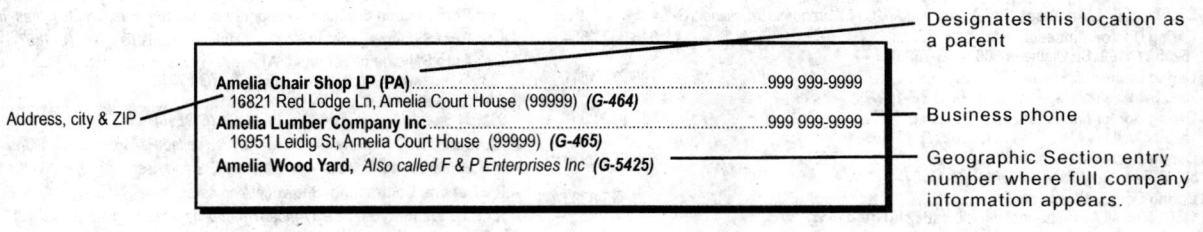

Designates this location as a parent

Address, city & ZIP

Business phone

Geographic Section entry number where full company information appears.

Amelia Chair Shop LP (PA).....999 999-9999
16821 Red Lodge Ln, Amelia Court House (99999) *(G-464)*
Amelia Lumber Company Inc.....999 999-9999
16951 Leidig St, Amelia Court House (99999) *(G-465)*
Amelia Wood Yard, *Also called F & P Enterprises Inc (G-5425)*

See footnotes for symbols and codes identification.

* Companies listed alphabetically.

* Complete physical or mailing address.

1&1 Internet Inc.....816 621-4795
10950 Strang Line Rd Lenexa (66215) *(G-5615)*
1-800 Radiator & A/C.....913 677-1799
2820 Roe Ln Ste A Kansas City (66103) *(G-3774)*
1-Stop LLC.....913 898-6211
423 E Woodward St Parker (66072) *(G-9656)*
1010 N Webb Road LLC.....316 722-7529
8333 W 21st St N Wichita (67205) *(G-13576)*
101st Earthborn Envmtl Tech LP.....785 691-8918
1065 Taylor Ave Colby (67701) *(G-987)*
1038 Productions.....316 644-6883
1820 N Woodrow Ave Wichita (67203) *(G-13577)*
1138 Inc.....913 322-5900
8717 W 110th St Ste 750 Overland Park (66210) *(G-8328)*
17th Street Properties LLC.....785 320-5440
505 S 17th St Manhattan (66502) *(G-6525)*
190th Medical Group.....785 861-4663
5920 Se Coyote Dr Topeka (66619) *(G-12274)*
1st Due E.R.S., Bartlett *Also called 1st Due Er Response Solutns LL (G-370)*
1st Due Er Response Solutns LL.....620 226-3566
1728 7000 Rd Bartlett (67332) *(G-370)*
1st Nation Painting Inc.....785 966-2935
207 S 4th St Mayetta (66509) *(G-6913)*
1st National Bank, Washington *Also called Washington 1st Banco Inc (G-13470)*
1ST NATIONAL BANK IN CIMARRON, Cimarron *Also called First National Bank (G-825)*
1st National Bank of Dighton.....620 397-5324
105 E Long St Dighton (67839) *(G-1282)*
1ST STATE BANK INTEREST, Tonganoxie *Also called First State Bank & Trust (G-12261)*
212 Logistics LLC.....620 563-7656
2063 O Rd Plains (67869) *(G-9973)*
21st St Steel.....316 265-6661
1007 E 21st St N Wichita (67214) *(G-13578)*
21st Street Warren Imax, Wichita *Also called Warren Theatres LLC (G-15928)*
24 7 Transcription, Shawnee Mission *Also called Kansas City Transcription Inc (G-11512)*
24 Hour Fitness Usa Inc.....913 338-2442
12075 Metcalf Ave Overland Park (66213) *(G-8329)*
24 Hour Fitness Usa Inc.....913 248-0724
11311 Shwnee Mission Pkwy Shawnee Mission (66203) *(G-11058)*
24 Hour Fitness Usa Inc.....913 829-4503
13370 S Blackfoot Dr Olathe (66062) *(G-7501)*
24/7 Store, Salina *Also called Triplett Inc (G-10742)*
2i Feeders LLC.....620 528-3740
884 Road 350 Allen (66833) *(G-60)*
2point Construction Co LLC.....913 749-1855
7252 W Frontage Rd Shawnee (66203) *(G-10903)*
2r Tool & Machine Inc.....620 902-5151
915 W Ash St Chanute (66720) *(G-700)*
3 S Engineering LLC.....316 260-2258
9111 E Douglas Ave # 100 Wichita (67207) *(G-13579)*
360 Commercial Cleaning, Overland Park *Also called Rigdon Inc (G-9242)*
360 Document Solutions LLC (PA).....316 630-8334
8201 E 34th Cir N Ste 901 Wichita (67226) *(G-13580)*
360 Kc.com, Wichita *Also called 360directories LLC (G-13581)*
360directories LLC.....316 269-6920
400 S Commerce St Wichita (67202) *(G-13581)*
3c Healthcare Inc.....620 221-7850
722 Wheat Rd Winfield (67156) *(G-16113)*
3s Engineering, Wichita *Also called 3 S Engineering LLC (G-13579)*
4 Rivers Electric Coop Inc.....620 364-2116
2731 Milo Ter Lebo (66856) *(G-5605)*
4 Winds Chapter, Garnett *Also called National Society Daughters Rev (G-2384)*
4-B Properties LLC.....785 364-4643
925 Pennsylvania Ave Holton (66436) *(G-3083)*
435 Magazine LLC.....913 469-6700
11775 W 112th St Ste 200 Overland Park (66210) *(G-8330)*
4g Express Inc.....316 619-3888
549 Homestead Ct Colwich (67030) *(G-1090)*
4pc LLC.....316 833-6906
415 State St Augusta (67010) *(G-299)*
4pc Security Technologies, Augusta *Also called 4pc LLC (G-299)*
4t Total Lawn Inc.....913 888-0997
10960 Eicher Dr Shawnee Mission (66219) *(G-11059)*
4th Gneration Promotional Pdts.....913 393-0837
14470 W 122nd St Olathe (66062) *(G-7502)*
6 Meridian LLC.....316 776-4601
1635 N Waterfront Pkwy # 250 Wichita (67206) *(G-13582)*
66 Food Plaza, Holton *Also called Hallauer Oil Co Inc (G-3094)*
69 Highway Branch, Overland Park *Also called Central Bank of Midwest (G-8537)*
7 Up Snapple Group, Manhattan *Also called American Bottling Company (G-6540)*
7240 Shawnee Mission Hospitali.....913 217-7283
7240 Shawnee Mission Pkwy Overland Park (66202) *(G-8331)*
7600 College Partnr Ted Greene.....913 341-1000
6750 W 93rd St Ste 250 Overland Park (66212) *(G-8332)*
7th Street Casino.....913 371-3500
777 N 7th St Kansas City (66101) *(G-3775)*
8th Jdcial Dst Cmnty Crrctions, Junction City *Also called Geary Corrections Center (G-3693)*
9 Line Medical Solutions LLC.....402 470-1696
620 Zeandale Rd Manhattan (66502) *(G-6526)*
911 Datamaster Inc.....913 469-6401
7500 College Blvd Ste 500 Overland Park (66210) *(G-8333)*
911 Emergency Management, Liberal *Also called County of Seward (G-6297)*
94 5 Country Inc.....785 272-3456
1210 Sw Executive Dr Topeka (66615) *(G-12275)*
96 Agri Sales Inc.....316 661-2281
10400 N 247th St W Mount Hope (67108) *(G-7202)*
9round, Manhattan *Also called Get After It LLC (G-6645)*
A & A Auto and Truck Parts, Topeka *Also called A & A Auto Salvage (G-12276)*
A & A Auto Salvage.....785 286-2728
1440 Se Jefferson St Topeka (66607) *(G-12276)*
A & A Medical Trnsp Inc.....785 233-8212
135 Nw Harrison St Topeka (66603) *(G-12277)*
A & A Services, Topeka *Also called A & A Medical Trnsp Inc (G-12277)*
A & B Machine Inc.....785 827-5171
2259b Centennial Rd Salina (67401) *(G-10387)*
A & E Custom Manufacturing, Kansas City *Also called Bennett Tool & Die LLC (G-3855)*
A & H AC & Htg Inc.....785 594-3357
1717 College St Baldwin City (66006) *(G-352)*
A & H Electric Inc.....316 838-3003
3939 N Bridgeport Cir Wichita (67219) *(G-13583)*
A & K Railroad Materials Inc.....913 375-1810
2131 S 74th St Kansas City (66106) *(G-3776)*
A & M Towing & Recovery Inc.....785 331-3100
529 Maple St Lawrence (66044) *(G-4717)*
A & P Cruises & Tours.....913 248-9800
11800 Shawnee Mission Pkw Shawnee Mission (66203) *(G-11060)*
A & R Cstm Frms Fbrcations LLC.....620 423-0401
2601 Flynn Dr Parsons (67357) *(G-9661)*
A 1 Sewer & Septic Service.....913 631-5201
1891 Merriam Ln Kansas City (66106) *(G-3777)*
A A A Insurance and Travel, Shawnee Mission *Also called Automobile Club of Missouri (G-11135)*
A A P, Lenexa *Also called Associated Air Products Inc (G-5670)*
A Adopt Family Inc.....620 378-4458
1400 S Cement Plant Rd Fredonia (66736) *(G-2025)*
A Arnold of Kansas City LLC.....913 829-8267
15761 S Keeler St Olathe (66062) *(G-7503)*
A B C Midwest Siding, Salina *Also called Midwest Siding Incorporated (G-10602)*
A B C Nursery Schl & Day Camp, Augusta *Also called Kindercare Education LLC (G-331)*
A C E, Lenexa *Also called Adams Cable Equipment Inc (G-5628)*
A C I, Independence *Also called Precision Aviation Controls (G-3547)*
A C I Brokerage, Salina *Also called Great Plains Logistics Inc (G-10517)*

ALPHABETIC

A C Printing Co Inc 913 780-3377
1475 N Winchester St Olathe (66061) *(G-7504)*
A C W Truckline, Arkansas City *Also called Ark City Warehouse Truckline (G-144)*
A Caring Doctor Minnesota PA 913 393-4654
15255 W 119th St Olathe (66062) *(G-7505)*
A Caring Doctor Minnesota PA 785 272-1541
2020 Sw Westport Dr Topeka (66604) *(G-12278)*
A Caring Doctor Minnesota PA 913 962-2901
15200 Shawnee Msn Shawnee (66217) *(G-10904)*
A Caring Doctor Minnesota PA 316 946-0920
533 S Tracy St Wichita (67209) *(G-13584)*
A Caring Doctor Minnesota PA 913 345-8383
11501 Metcalf Ave Shawnee Mission (66210) *(G-11061)*
A Caring Doctor Minnesota PA 316 631-3939
3615 N Rock Rd Wichita (67226) *(G-13585)*
A Childs World Day Care Ctr 785 863-2161
302 Madison St Oskaloosa (66066) *(G-8220)*
A Clear Direction Inc 316 260-9101
345 S Hydraulic St Wichita (67211) *(G-13586)*
A D J-Hux Service Inc 913 529-5200
13605 W 96th Ter Lenexa (66215) *(G-5616)*
A D L M LLC 913 888-0770
8787 Lenexa Dr Shawnee Mission (66214) *(G-11062)*
A Deere Place Inc 913 727-5437
1104 Industrial St Lansing (66043) *(G-4665)*
A Divis of P Midla Loan Servi (HQ) 913 253-9000
10851 Mastin St Ste 300 Overland Park (66210) *(G-8334)*
A E I, Wichita *Also called Apex Engineering Intl LLC (G-13718)*
A G 1 Source LLC 620 327-2205
603 E Lincoln Blvd Hesston (67062) *(G-2983)*
A G H, Wichita *Also called Allen Gibbs & Houlik Llc (G-13667)*
A G I Inc 913 281-5533
8008 Floyd St Ste 300 Shawnee Mission (66204) *(G-11063)*
A G Spanos Development Inc 913 663-2400
8300 College Blvd Ste 350 Overland Park (66210) *(G-8335)*
A Glass & Tint Shop Kc Inc (PA) 913 491-8468
9928 W 62nd Ter Merriam (66203) *(G-7085)*
A I B, Manhattan *Also called American Institute of Baking (G-6541)*
A L C Enterprises Inc 316 943-6500
824 N West St Wichita (67203) *(G-13587)*
A L Huber Inc 913 341-4880
10770 El Monte St Shawnee Mission (66211) *(G-11064)*
A Lert Corp (PA) 620 378-4153
401 N 6th St Coyville (66736) *(G-1182)*
A M Castle & Co 316 943-0277
3050 S Hydraulic St Wichita (67216) *(G-13588)*
A M Mechanical Service Co 913 829-5885
225 S 65th St Kansas City (66111) *(G-3778)*
A M P, Olathe *Also called PSI Services Inc (G-8011)*
A M Plumbing Inc 316 945-8326
1414 S Bebe St Wichita (67209) *(G-13589)*
A M S Diagnostic LLC 316 462-2020
3636 N Ridge Rd Ste 100 Wichita (67205) *(G-13590)*
A M S Diagnostics, Wichita *Also called Anatomi Imaging (G-13701)*
A Plus Construction LLC 620 212-4029
107 Saint Joseph St Saint Paul (66771) *(G-10378)*
A Plus Galvanizing 785 820-9823
1100 N Ohio St Salina (67401) *(G-10388)*
A Plus Mini Market, Park City *Also called A-Plus Logistics LLC (G-9598)*
A R Systems Inc 620 564-3790
13 N Main St Lowr Level Ellinwood (67526) *(G-1626)*
A S Escort 620 655-6613
1431 Road F Liberal (67901) *(G-6272)*
A S I Kansas, Lenexa *Also called Asi Computer Technologies Inc (G-5667)*
A Scampis Bar & Grill 785 539-5311
530 Richards Dr Manhattan (66502) *(G-6527)*
A Step Above Academy-Wyandotte 913 721-3770
600 N 118th St Bonner Springs (66012) *(G-538)*
A Tei, Maize *Also called Aero-Tech Engineering Inc (G-6507)*
A Total Image 785 272-2855
4005 Sw 21st St Topeka (66604) *(G-12279)*
A Uniform For You, Wamego *Also called Something Different Inc (G-13441)*
A W T, Shawnee Mission *Also called Donmar Inc (G-11315)*
A Wireless, Manhattan *Also called ABC Phones North Carolina Inc (G-6530)*
A&Atruck Rental/3 Men With 785 236-0003
200 Sw Jackson St Ste B Topeka (66603) *(G-12280)*
A&L Hay Farms Inc 785 461-5339
2255 3rd Rd Wakefield (67487) *(G-13397)*
A&M Products Manufacturing Co 913 592-4344
705 N Lincoln St Spring Hill (66083) *(G-12074)*
A&R Custom Form & Fabricatio 620 423-0170
24080 Scott Rd Parsons (67357) *(G-9662)*
A'Deas, Wichita *Also called Roth K Christopherson (G-15485)*
A+ Decor LLC 816 699-6817
1146 S 220th St Pittsburg (66762) *(G-9803)*
A-1 Electric Inc 620 431-7500
414 E Main St Chanute (66720) *(G-701)*
A-1 Scaffold Mfg Inc 785 621-5121
590 Commerce Pkwy Hays (67601) *(G-2743)*
A-Lert Construction Services, Fredonia *Also called Centurion Industries Inc (G-2028)*
A-Lert Roof Systems, Erie *Also called Centurion Industries Inc (G-1857)*
A-One Auto Salvage of Wichita (PA) 316 524-3273
7335 S Broadway Ave Haysville (67060) *(G-2933)*
A-Plus Logistics LLC 316 945-5757
6015 N Broadway Ave Park City (67219) *(G-9598)*
A. D. Jacobson Company, Inc., Lenexa *Also called P1 Group International Inc (G-6041)*
A.M.B.S. Marketing, Lenexa *Also called AMBS and Associates Inc (G-5644)*
A.R.c General Contracting, Shawnee *Also called Allied Retail Concepts LLC (G-10908)*
A.R.I.S.E., Wichita *Also called African Americans Renewing Int (G-13642)*
A/C Enterprises Inc 620 767-5695
510 Spencer St Council Grove (66846) *(G-1157)*
A/R Allegiance Group LLC 913 338-4790
6900 College Blvd Ste 550 Leawood (66211) *(G-5311)*
A/R Roofing LLC (PA) 620 672-2999
40100 N Us Highway 281 Pratt (67124) *(G-10090)*
A1 Bonding 785 539-3950
700 Rosencutter Rd Manhattan (66502) *(G-6528)*
A1 Staffing (PA) 913 652-0005
7050 W 107th St Ste 120 Overland Park (66212) *(G-8336)*
A1air Heating & Cooling LLC 620 235-0600
1035 N Highway 69 Frontenac (66763) *(G-2050)*
A7, Wichita *Also called Austin A-7 Ltd (G-13769)*
Aa Central Office, Wichita *Also called Alcoholics Anonymous (G-13660)*
Aa World Services, Roeland Park *Also called Bills Friends AA Group (G-10218)*
AAA Air Support Mfg LLC 316 946-9299
205 Pirner Ste 1 Haysville (67060) *(G-2934)*
AAA Allied Group Inc 785 233-0222
1223 Sw Wanamaker Rd Topeka (66604) *(G-12281)*
AAA Auto Club, Wichita *Also called Automobile Club of Missouri (G-13774)*
AAA Court Reporting Company, Overland Park *Also called Reporting Services Company (G-9235)*
AAA Night Watchman Service, Topeka *Also called American Sentry Security Sys (G-12323)*
AAA Party Rental Inc 816 333-1767
10900 Mid America Dr Lenexa (66219) *(G-5617)*
AAA Portable Services LLC 316 522-6442
3730 S Broadway Ave Wichita (67216) *(G-13591)*
AAA Restaurant Supply LLC 316 265-4365
611 E Central Ave Wichita (67202) *(G-13592)*
AAF Fleet Service Inc 913 683-3816
P.O. Box 358 Mc Louth (66054) *(G-6924)*
Aafp, Leawood *Also called American Acdemy Fmly Physcians (G-5319)*
AAFP FOUNDATION, Shawnee Mission *Also called American Academy Family Physcn (G-11101)*
AAMCO Transmissions, Auburn *Also called Haag Inc (G-295)*
Aamia Enterprises, Great Bend *Also called Highland Lodging LLC (G-2591)*
Aapc Inc 877 277-8254
6448 Vista Dr Shawnee (66218) *(G-10905)*
Aaron & Page Painting Inc 316 267-2224
1831 N Mosley Ave Wichita (67214) *(G-13593)*
Aarons Repair & Supply Inc 620 792-5361
170 Sw 40 Ave Great Bend (67530) *(G-2499)*
Aarons Wichita Mvg & Stor Co, Wichita *Also called Apartment Movers Inc (G-13717)*
Aat Aero Inc 316 832-1412
946 W 53rd St N Wichita (67204) *(G-13594)*
Aat Group, Wichita *Also called Aat Aero Inc (G-13594)*
Aauw Ellsworth, Ellsworth *Also called American Assn Univ Women (G-1656)*
Abaxis Inc 913 787-7400
14830 W 117th St Olathe (66062) *(G-7506)*
Abay Neuroscience Center PA 316 609-2600
3223 N Webb Rd Ste 1 Wichita (67226) *(G-13595)*
ABB Enterprise Software Inc 913 317-1310
12980 Metcalf Ave Ste 400 Overland Park (66213) *(G-8337)*
ABB Installation Products Inc 913 755-3181
820 6th St Osawatomie (66064) *(G-8191)*
ABB Motors and Mechanical Inc 816 587-0272
9810 Industrial Blvd Lenexa (66215) *(G-5618)*
Abbey-Riley Furniture Studio, Kansas City *Also called Andrews and Abbey Riley LLC (G-3811)*
Abbott Aluminum Inc (PA) 785 776-8555
430 Mccall Rd Manhattan (66502) *(G-6529)*
Abbott Workholding Products, Manhattan *Also called Abbott Aluminum Inc (G-6529)*
ABC American Taxi, Wichita *Also called American Cab Inc (G-13687)*
ABC Leasing Co Inc 785 267-4555
401 Sw 30th St Topeka (66611) *(G-12282)*
ABC Phones North Carolina Inc 785 243-4099
1578 Lincoln St Concordia (66901) *(G-1100)*
ABC Phones North Carolina Inc 785 263-3553
202 Nw 2nd St Manhattan (66502) *(G-6530)*
ABC Phones North Carolina Inc 620 508-6167
103 S Parke St Pratt (67124) *(G-10091)*
ABC Seamless, Hays *Also called Western Aluminum & Glass Co (G-2931)*
ABC Supply 113, Wichita *Also called American Bldrs Contrs Sup Inc (G-13684)*

ABC Supply 326, Topeka *Also called American Bldrs Contrs Sup Inc* ***(G-12313)***
ABC Supply 6, Kansas City *Also called American Bldrs Contrs Sup Inc* ***(G-3803)***
ABC Taxi Cab Company Inc 316 264-4222
400 S Greenwood St Wichita (67211) ***(G-13596)***
Abco Wire & Metal Products, Russell *Also called Burlingame Wire Products Inc* ***(G-10268)***
Abengoa Bnergy Hybrid Kans LLC 316 796-1234
523 E Union Ave Colwich (67030) ***(G-1091)***
Aberdeen Village Inc 913 599-6100
17500 W 119th St Olathe (66061) ***(G-7507)***
Aberdeen Village Inc 316 685-1100
2414 N Woodlawn Blvd Wichita (67220) ***(G-13597)***
Abes Oilfield Service LLC 620 532-5551
220 W Stanley St Spivey (67142) ***(G-12072)***
ABF Freight System Inc 316 943-1241
3833 S West St Wichita (67217) ***(G-13598)***
Abilene Animal Hospital PA (PA) 785 263-2301
320 Ne 14th St Abilene (67410) ***(G-1)***
Abilene Childcare Learning Ctr 785 263-1799
504 S Campbell St Abilene (67410) ***(G-2)***
Abilene Concrete & Supply, Abilene *Also called H & P Inc* ***(G-36)***
Abilene Country Club 785 263-3811
1705 Country Club Ln Abilene (67410) ***(G-3)***
Abilene Family Physicians PA 785 263-7190
511 Ne 10th St Abilene (67410) ***(G-4)***
Abilene Housing Inc 785 263-1080
601 N Buckeye Ave Abilene (67410) ***(G-5)***
Abilene Machine LLC (PA) 785 655-9455
407 Old Highway 40 Solomon (67480) ***(G-12046)***
Abilene Physcl Thrpy & Sprts 785 263-3519
103 Nw 15th St Abilene (67410) ***(G-6)***
Abilene Printing & Office Pdts, Abilene *Also called Abilene Printing Co Inc* ***(G-7)***
Abilene Printing Co Inc 785 263-2330
207 Ne 3rd St Abilene (67410) ***(G-7)***
Abilene Rflctor Chronicle Pubg 785 263-1000
303 N Broadway St Abilene (67410) ***(G-8)***
Abilene Super Eight 785 263-4545
2207 N Buckeye Ave Abilene (67410) ***(G-9)***
Abilene Unified Schl Dst 435 785 825-9185
605 E Crawford St Salina (67401) ***(G-10389)***
Able Plumbing, Shawnee Mission *Also called Reddi Services Inc* ***(G-11783)***
Able Program, Salina *Also called Saint Francis Cmnty Svcs Inc* ***(G-10660)***
Abraham Jacob Gorelick 913 371-0459
620 Minnesota Ave Kansas City (66101) ***(G-3779)***
Abrasive Blast Systems Inc 785 263-3786
418 Ne 14th St Abilene (67410) ***(G-10)***
ABS, Abilene *Also called Abrasive Blast Systems Inc* ***(G-10)***
ABS-AIR SAFETY FOUNDATION, Wichita *Also called American Bonanza Society Inc* ***(G-13685)***
Absecon SW Hotel Inc 913 345-2111
9903 Pflumm Rd Lenexa (66215) ***(G-5619)***
Absolute Computer Solutions, Overland Park *Also called Alliance Technologies Inc* ***(G-8371)***
Absolute Dimensions LLC 316 944-2211
3838 W May St Wichita (67213) ***(G-13599)***
Absolute Home Health Care 316 832-1347
1619 S Rutan Ave Wichita (67218) ***(G-13600)***
Absolutely Flowers 620 728-0266
1328 N Main St Hutchinson (67501) ***(G-3189)***
Abwa Management LLC (PA) 913 732-5100
9820 Metcalf Ave Ste 110 Overland Park (66212) ***(G-8338)***
Abz Valve, Madison *Also called Forum Energy Tecnhologies* ***(G-6500)***
AC Blower Wheels Motors & Fans, Kansas City *Also called Klemp Electric Machinery Co* ***(G-4176)***
AC Professional LLC 816 668-4760
1499 E 151st St Olathe (66062) ***(G-7508)***
Academy of Arts LLC 913 441-7300
5413 Martindale Rd Shawnee Mission (66218) ***(G-11065)***
Academy of Children, Kansas City *Also called El Centro Inc* ***(G-3983)***
Acadeus, Overland Park *Also called Propharma Group LLC* ***(G-9195)***
ACBSP, Overland Park *Also called Accreditation Council For Busi* ***(G-8342)***
Acca, Atchison *Also called Atchison Child Care Assn* ***(G-207)***
Accel Construction LLC 316 866-2885
4015 N Woodlawn Ct Ste 1 Bel Aire (67220) ***(G-425)***
Acceligent Inc (PA) 972 504-6660
9415 W 163rd Ter Overland Park (66085) ***(G-8339)***
Accent Dental LLC 620 231-2871
2002 S Rouse St Pittsburg (66762) ***(G-9804)***
Accent Erection & Maint Co Inc 913 371-1600
501 S Valley St Kansas City (66105) ***(G-3780)***
Accent Lighting Inc 316 636-1278
2020 N Woodlawn St # 220 Wichita (67208) ***(G-13601)***
Accent Sales and Service Co, Kansas City *Also called Accent Erection & Maint Co Inc* ***(G-3780)***
Accenture LLP 913 319-1000
7300 W 110th St Ste 850 Overland Park (66210) ***(G-8340)***
Access Group LLC 316 264-0270
982 N Tyler Rd Ste D Wichita (67212) ***(G-13602)***
Access Info MGT Shred Svcs LLC 913 492-4581
17501 W 98th St Lenexa (66219) ***(G-5620)***
Access Information Protected, Lenexa *Also called Access Info MGT Shred Svcs LLC* ***(G-5620)***
Access Kansas, Topeka *Also called Kansas Info Consortium LLC* ***(G-12783)***
Access Van Service, Hays *Also called Developmental Svcs NW Kans Inc* ***(G-2787)***
Accessdge HM Hlth Care Wichita, Wichita *Also called Wichita Home Health Care Group* ***(G-16005)***
Accessible Home Care 785 493-0340
1300 E Iron Ave Ste 121 Salina (67401) ***(G-10390)***
Accessible Technologies Inc (PA) 913 338-2886
14801 W 114th Ter Lenexa (66215) ***(G-5621)***
Accord Services Inc 913 281-1879
4141 Fairbanks Ave Kansas City (66106) ***(G-3781)***
Account Rcvery Specialists Inc (PA) 620 227-8510
3505 N Topeka St Wichita (67219) ***(G-13603)***
Account Rcvery Specialists Inc 620 227-8510
200 W Wyatt Earp Blvd Dodge City (67801) ***(G-1288)***
Accountable Finance Inc 913 381-4077
7733a Metcalf Ave Overland Park (66204) ***(G-8341)***
Accounting Department, Wichita *Also called Jri Investments LLC* ***(G-14777)***
ACCP, Lenexa *Also called American College of Clinical* ***(G-5646)***
Accreditation Council For Busi 913 339-9356
11520 W 119th St Overland Park (66213) ***(G-8342)***
Accredo Health Group Inc 913 339-7100
11411 Strang Line Rd Lenexa (66215) ***(G-5622)***
Accu-Fab Inc 785 862-0100
235 Se 53rd St Topeka (66609) ***(G-12283)***
Accu-Tech Corporation 913 894-0444
15731 W 100th Ter Bldg 3 Shawnee Mission (66219) ***(G-11066)***
Accurate Construction Inc 620 275-0429
3085 W Sagebrush Rd Garden City (67846) ***(G-2097)***
Accurate Electric Inc 785 825-4010
510 N Santa Fe Ave Salina (67401) ***(G-10391)***
Accurate Title Company LLC 913 338-0100
7171 W 95th St Ste 200 Overland Park (66212) ***(G-8343)***
Accurus Aerospace Wichita LLC 316 683-0266
4011 E 31st St S Wichita (67210) ***(G-13604)***
Ace Construction Corporation (PA) 316 536-2202
301 Main St Towanda (67144) ***(G-13262)***
Ace Electric-Jones Company Inc 785 862-8200
223 Se 53rd St Topeka (66609) ***(G-12284)***
Ace Forms of Kansas Inc 620 232-9290
2900 N Rotary Ter Pittsburg (66762) ***(G-9805)***
Ace Hardware, Emporia *Also called Bluestem Farm and Rnch Sup Inc* ***(G-1705)***
Ace Hardware, Pratt *Also called Skaggs Inc* ***(G-10148)***
Ace Hardware, Salina *Also called Gibson Products Co Salina Inc* ***(G-10510)***
Ace Hardware, Clay Center *Also called Gibsons Ace Hardware* ***(G-865)***
Ace Personnel Inc (PA) 913 384-1100
5909 Woodson St Shawnee Mission (66202) ***(G-11067)***
Ace Plumbing & Sewer Service, Topeka *Also called David Cobler* ***(G-12547)***
Ace USA, Shawnee Mission *Also called Chubb US Holding Inc* ***(G-11224)***
Acentric LLC 913 787-4856
26025 Metcalf Rd Louisburg (66053) ***(G-6435)***
Aceware Systems Inc 785 537-2937
7480 Dyer Rd Manhattan (66502) ***(G-6531)***
Ach Foam Technologies Inc 913 321-4114
4001 Kaw Dr Kansas City (66102) ***(G-3782)***
Ach Foam Technologies Inc 913 371-1973
1400 N 3rd St Kansas City (66101) ***(G-3783)***
Achievement Svcs For Ne Kans (PA) 913 367-2432
215 N 5th St Atchison (66002) ***(G-202)***
Aci Cncrete Placement Kans LLC (PA) 913 281-3700
25412 W 95th Ln Unit 1710 Lenexa (66227) ***(G-5623)***
Aci Motor Freight Inc (PA) 316 522-5559
4545 Palisade St Wichita (67217) ***(G-13605)***
Ackerman Supply Inc (PA) 785 738-5733
3147 Us 24 Hwy Beloit (67420) ***(G-469)***
Acklin Construction 316 321-6648
3720 Ne 4th St El Dorado (67042) ***(G-1525)***
Acm Removal LLC 316 684-1800
8610 E 34th St N Ste 2 Wichita (67226) ***(G-13606)***
Acme Cinema Inc 620 421-4404
210 N 17th Parsons (67357) ***(G-9663)***
Acme Floor Company Inc 913 888-3200
10100 Marshall Dr Lenexa (66215) ***(G-5624)***
Acme Foundry Inc (PA) 620 251-6800
1502 Spruce St Coffeyville (67337) ***(G-907)***
Acme Foundry Inc 620 251-4920
1209 Buckeye St Coffeyville (67337) ***(G-908)***
Acorn Underwriters, Overland Park *Also called Ralph S Passman & Associates* ***(G-9221)***
Acosta Inc 913 227-1000
8155 Lenexa Dr Shawnee Mission (66214) ***(G-11068)***
Acosta Sales & Marketing, Shawnee Mission *Also called Acosta Inc* ***(G-11068)***
Acosta Sales & Marketing, Wichita *Also called Acosta Sales Co Inc* ***(G-13607)***
Acosta Sales Co Inc 316 733-0248
550 N 159th St E Ste 301 Wichita (67230) ***(G-13607)***

Acoustic Sounds Inc 785 825-8609
518 N 10th St Salina (67401) **(G-10392)**
Acoustical Stretched Fabric 913 345-1520
14014 W 107th St Shawnee Mission (66215) **(G-11069)**
Acres Inc 785 776-3234
613 Pecan Cir Manhattan (66502) **(G-6532)**
Acro Dishwashing Service, Kansas City *Also called Jesse Inc* **(G-4123)**
Acrobatic Academy, Wichita *Also called Fit Physique* **(G-14379)**
Acrobatic Acadmy Ftns/Educ Ctr 316 721-2230
2111 N Maize Rd Wichita (67212) **(G-13608)**
ACS, Leawood *Also called Automated Control Systems Corp* **(G-5337)**
ACS, Lenexa *Also called American Construction Svcs LLC* **(G-5647)**
ACS Apparel, Overland Park *Also called Action Custom Sportswear LLC* **(G-8344)**
ACS Data Search LLC (PA) 913 649-1771
6701 W 64th St Ste 108 Shawnee Mission (66202) **(G-11070)**
ACS Electronic Systems Inc 913 248-8828
7856 Barton St Lenexa (66214) **(G-5625)**
ACS Iiiiii - Ks LLC 316 683-3489
3505 W 29th St S Wichita (67217) **(G-13609)**
Acsys Lasertechnik US Inc 847 468-5302
8224 Nieman Rd Lenexa (66214) **(G-5626)**
Action Custom Sportswear LLC 913 433-9900
9401 Indian Creek Pkwy Overland Park (66210) **(G-8344)**
Action Mobile Wash, Kansas City *Also called Superior Mobile Wash Inc* **(G-4448)**
Action Plumbing Inc 913 631-1188
6405 Caenen Lake Rd Shawnee Mission (66216) **(G-11071)**
Action Plumbing of Lawrence 785 843-5670
801 Comet Ln Ste D Lawrence (66049) **(G-4718)**
Action Tire & Service Inc 913 631-9600
10823 Shawnee Mission Pkwy Shawnee Mission (66203) **(G-11072)**
Active Prime Timers Inc 785 272-0237
2219 Sw Fairlawn Rd Apt 2 Topeka (66614) **(G-12285)**
Actors LLC 316 263-0222
234 N Mosley St Wichita (67202) **(G-13610)**
Actparts, Kansas City *Also called American Crane & Tractor Parts* **(G-3804)**
Actuarial Resources Corp Kans 913 451-0044
6720 W 121st St Ste 200 Overland Park (66209) **(G-8345)**
Actuarius LLC 913 908-2830
18283 Melrose Dr Bucyrus (66013) **(G-593)**
Acustep LLC (PA) 785 826-2500
2850 Caywood Salina (67401) **(G-10393)**
Ad Astra Info Systems LLC 913 652-4100
6900 W 80th St Ste 300 Shawnee Mission (66204) **(G-11073)**
Ad Astra Per Aspera Broadcasti 620 665-5758
10 E 5th Ave Ste 2 Hutchinson (67501) **(G-3190)**
Ad Astra Recover Service 316 941-5448
7330 W 33rd St N Ste 118 Wichita (67205) **(G-13611)**
Ad Astra Selections LLC 913 307-0272
9892 Pflumm Rd Lenexa (66215) **(G-5627)**
Adam & McDonald PA 913 647-0670
9300 W 110th St Ste 470 Shawnee Mission (66210) **(G-11074)**
Adams Brown Beran Ball, Hays *Also called Adams Brown Bran Ball Chrtered* **(G-2744)**
Adams Brown Bran Ball Chrtered 316 683-2067
545 N Woodlawn St Wichita (67208) **(G-13612)**
Adams Brown Bran Ball Chrtered (PA) 620 549-3271
2006 Broadway Ave Great Bend (67530) **(G-2500)**
Adams Brown Bran Ball Chrtered 620 663-5659
1701 Landon St Hutchinson (67502) **(G-3191)**
Adams Brown Bran Ball Chrtered 785 628-3046
718 Main St Ste 224 Hays (67601) **(G-2744)**
Adams Brown Bran Ball Chrtered 620 241-2090
200 S Main St McPherson (67460) **(G-6931)**
Adams Cable Equipment Inc 913 888-5100
9635 Widmer Rd Lenexa (66215) **(G-5628)**
Adams Cattle Company 785 256-4200
1 Mile Ne Of Town Maple Hill (66507) **(G-6862)**
Adams Dental Group PA 913 621-3113
2119 Minnesota Ave Kansas City (66102) **(G-3784)**
Adams Electric & Plumbing LLC (PA) 620 672-7279
606 N Main St Pratt (67124) **(G-10092)**
Adams Jones Law Firm PA 316 265-8591
1635 N Waterfront Pkwy # 200 Wichita (67206) **(G-13613)**
Adams, John R MD, Manhattan *Also called Advanced Dermatology and Skin* **(G-6533)**
Adams-Gabbert & Associates LLC (PA) 913 735-4390
9200 Indian Creek Pkwy # 205 Overland Park (66210) **(G-8346)**
Adamson and Associates 913 722-5432
7451 Switzer St Ste 100 Shawnee (66203) **(G-10906)**
Adamson and Associates Inc (PA) 913 722-5432
7800 College Blvd Ste 200 Overland Park (66210) **(G-8347)**
Adamson Bros Sheetmetal, Ottawa *Also called Adamson Brothers Sheet Metal* **(G-8243)**
Adamson Brothers Sheet Metal 785 242-9273
102 S Walnut St Ottawa (66067) **(G-8243)**
Adapa Incorporated 785 862-2060
5525 Sw Randolph Ave Topeka (66609) **(G-12286)**
Adaptive Solutions Group, Overland Park *Also called Wood Ribble & Twyman Inc* **(G-9503)**
Addiction and Prevention Svcs 785 296-6807
915 Sw Harrison St Fl 9 Topeka (66612) **(G-12287)**
Addiction Treatment Service, Wichita *Also called Comcare of Sedgwick County* **(G-14060)**
Addictn Treatmnt Ctr SE Kansas, Girard *Also called Community Mntl Hlth Ctr Crwfd* **(G-2397)**
Adelhardt Enterprises Inc 620 672-6463
210 S Jackson St Pratt (67124) **(G-10093)**
Adelphi Construction Lc 913 384-5511
4800 Lamar Ave Ste 104 Shawnee Mission (66202) **(G-11075)**
Ademco Inc 913 438-1111
8055 Flint St Lenexa (66214) **(G-5629)**
Adf LLC 913 825-7400
11042 Strang Line Rd Lenexa (66215) **(G-5630)**
ADI Global Distribution, Lenexa *Also called Ademco Inc* **(G-5629)**
ADI Systems Inc 785 825-5975
628 N Broadway Blvd Salina (67401) **(G-10394)**
Adjutant Generals Dept Kans 785 862-1020
125 Se Airport Dr Topeka (66619) **(G-12288)**
Adki Group LLC 913 208-7899
18730 S Ridgeview Rd Olathe (66062) **(G-7509)**
Adkins Systems Inc 913 438-8440
9714 Rosehill Rd Shawnee Mission (66215) **(G-11076)**
Adkore Staffing Group LLC (PA) 913 402-8031
4200 W 115th St Ste 300 Leawood (66211) **(G-5312)**
ADM, Olathe *Also called Archer-Daniels-Midland Company* **(G-7532)**
ADM, Abilene *Also called Archer-Daniels-Midland Company* **(G-12)**
ADM, Copeland *Also called Archer-Daniels-Midland Company* **(G-1148)**
ADM, Salina *Also called Archer-Daniels-Midland Company* **(G-10407)**
ADM, Leoti *Also called Archer-Daniels-Midland Company* **(G-6250)**
ADM, Scott City *Also called Archer-Daniels-Midland Company* **(G-10804)**
ADM, Kansas City *Also called Archer-Daniels-Midland Company* **(G-3817)**
ADM, Jetmore *Also called Archer-Daniels-Midland Company* **(G-3645)**
ADM, Sublette *Also called Archer-Daniels-Midland Company* **(G-12198)**
ADM, Montezuma *Also called Archer-Daniels-Midland Company* **(G-7154)**
ADM, Overland Park *Also called Archer-Daniels-Midland Company* **(G-8393)**
ADM, Satanta *Also called Archer-Daniels-Midland Company* **(G-10776)**
ADM, Overland Park *Also called Archer-Daniels-Midland Company* **(G-8394)**
ADM, Hutchinson *Also called Archer-Daniels-Midland Company* **(G-3204)**
ADM, Hutchinson *Also called Archer-Daniels-Midland Company* **(G-3205)**
ADM, Oakley *Also called Archer-Daniels-Midland Company* **(G-7471)**
ADM, Brewster *Also called Archer-Daniels-Midland Company* **(G-582)**
ADM, Kinsley *Also called Archer-Daniels-Midland Company* **(G-4614)**
ADM, New Cambria *Also called Archer-Daniels-Midland Company* **(G-7269)**
ADM, Palco *Also called Archer-Daniels-Midland Company* **(G-9537)**
ADM, Goodland *Also called Archer-Daniels-Midland Company* **(G-2462)**
ADM Grain River System Inc 913 788-7226
10520 Wolcott Dr Ste 1 Kansas City (66109) **(G-3785)**
ADM Milling Co 620 442-6200
1200 S Mill Rd Arkansas City (67005) **(G-139)**
ADM Milling Co 620 442-5500
309 W Madison Ave Arkansas City (67005) **(G-140)**
ADM Milling Co 620 227-8101
1901 E Wyatt Earp Blvd Dodge City (67801) **(G-1289)**
ADM Milling Co (HQ) 913 491-9400
8000 W 110th St Ste 300 Overland Park (66210) **(G-8348)**
ADM Milling Co 785 825-1541
850 E Pacific Ave Salina (67401) **(G-10395)**
ADM Milling Co 785 263-1631
210 Ne 3rd St Abilene (67410) **(G-11)**
ADM Milling Co 913 266-6300
8000 W 110th St Ste 220 Shawnee Mission (66210) **(G-11077)**
ADM Trucking Inc 785 899-6500
6425 Road 14 Goodland (67735) **(G-2459)**
Admin Bldg For Hr/PR & Acct, Wichita *Also called Pratt Industries USA Inc* **(G-15323)**
Administration Dept, Kansas City *Also called KU Childrens Ctr Foundation* **(G-4181)**
Administration Kansas Dept 785 296-3631
201 Nw Macvicar Ave Topeka (66606) **(G-12289)**
Administration Kansas Dept 785 296-3001
201 Nw Macvicar Ave Topeka (66606) **(G-12290)**
Administration Kansas Dept 785 296-3017
900 Sw Jackson St Rm 1041 Topeka (66612) **(G-12291)**
Ado Staffing Inc 785 842-1515
100 E 9th St Lawrence (66044) **(G-4719)**
Adobe Truck & Equipment LLC 913 498-9888
11510 S Strang Line Rd Olathe (66062) **(G-7510)**
Adolescent Adult Fmly Recovery 316 943-2051
830 S Hillside St Wichita (67211) **(G-13614)**
Adorers of Bld of Chrst 316 942-2201
1165 Southwest Blvd Wichita (67213) **(G-13615)**
ADP, Lenexa *Also called Automatic Data Processing Inc* **(G-5675)**
ADP, Wichita *Also called Automatic Data Processing Inc* **(G-13773)**
Adr Inc 316 522-5599
2012 E Northern St Wichita (67216) **(G-13616)**
Adr Book Print, Wichita *Also called Adr Inc* **(G-13616)**
Adrian & Pankratz PA 316 283-8746
301 N Main St Ste 400 Newton (67114) **(G-7306)**
Adrian Manufacturing Inc 507 381-9746
191 120th Newton (67114) **(G-7307)**

ADT 24 7 Alarm and Security....620 860-0229
516 E 1st St Pratt (67124) *(G-10094)*
ADT LLC....785 856-5500
1035 N 3rd St Ste 101 Lawrence (66044) *(G-4720)*
ADT LLC....316 858-6628
800 E Waterman St Wichita (67202) *(G-13617)*
ADT LLC....316 858-4300
8200 E 34th Street Cir N Wichita (67226) *(G-13618)*
ADT Security Corporation....612 721-3690
800 E Waterman St Wichita (67202) *(G-13619)*
ADT Security Services, Wichita *Also called ADT LLC (G-13617)*
Adult Child & Fmly Counseling....316 945-5200
6700 W Central Ave # 106 Wichita (67212) *(G-13620)*
Adult Health Services Inc....913 788-9896
1999 N 77th St Kansas City (66112) *(G-3786)*
Advacare, Wamego *Also called Advocate Home Specialty Care (G-13402)*
Advance Auto Parts, Salina *Also called Advance Stores Company Inc (G-10396)*
Advance Auto Parts Inc....913 782-0076
13794 S Blackbob Rd Olathe (66062) *(G-7511)*
Advance Business Supply....785 440-7826
631 Nw Tyler Ct Ste 303 Topeka (66608) *(G-12292)*
Advance Catastrophe Tech Inc....316 262-9992
3835 N Hillcrest St Ste 4 Bel Aire (67220) *(G-426)*
Advance Electric Inc....316 263-1300
353 N Indiana Ave Wichita (67214) *(G-13621)*
Advance Insurance Company Kans (HQ)....785 273-9804
1133 Sw Topeka Blvd Topeka (66629) *(G-12293)*
Advance Printing and Copy Ctr, Olathe *Also called Shahrokhi Inc (G-8060)*
Advance Rehabilitation LLC....785 232-9805
6001 Sw 6th Ave Ste 230 Topeka (66615) *(G-12294)*
Advance Stores Company Inc....785 826-2400
3633 S 9th St Salina (67401) *(G-10396)*
Advance Systems International....913 888-3578
9801 Renner Blvd Ste 250 Lenexa (66219) *(G-5631)*
Advance Termite & Pest Control....620 662-3616
2515 E 14th Ave Hutchinson (67501) *(G-3192)*
Advance Therapy & Spt Medicine, Great Bend *Also called Advanced Therapy & Spt Med LLC (G-2501)*
Advanced Anesthesia Assoc....316 942-4519
3715 N Oliver St Wichita (67220) *(G-13622)*
Advanced Catastrophe Tech, Bel Aire *Also called Advance Catastrophe Tech Inc (G-426)*
Advanced Chiropractic Svcs PA (PA)....785 842-4181
1605 Wakarusa Dr Lawrence (66047) *(G-4721)*
Advanced Dermatologic Surgery....913 661-1755
6901 W 121st St Shawnee Mission (66209) *(G-11078)*
Advanced Dermatology and Skin....785 537-4990
2735 Pembrook Pl Manhattan (66502) *(G-6533)*
Advanced Engine Machine Inc....785 825-6684
1206 N 9th St Salina (67401) *(G-10397)*
Advanced Environmental Svcs....785 231-9324
3825 Sw Dukeries Rd Topeka (66610) *(G-12295)*
Advanced Extrusions Co LLC....620 241-2006
404 N Chestnut St McPherson (67460) *(G-6932)*
Advanced Food Services Inc....913 888-8088
9729 Lackman Rd Lenexa (66219) *(G-5632)*
Advanced Health Care Corp....913 890-8400
4700 Indian Creek Pkwy Overland Park (66207) *(G-8349)*
Advanced Homecare MGT Inc....620 662-9238
1300 N Main St Ste 3 Hutchinson (67501) *(G-3193)*
Advanced Information Systems, Topeka *Also called Northrop Grumman Systems Corp (G-12939)*
Advanced Infrared Systems (PA)....913 888-3578
9324 Greenway Ln Lenexa (66215) *(G-5633)*
Advanced Machine Inc....316 942-9002
2621 S Custer Ave Wichita (67217) *(G-13623)*
Advanced Machine Solutions LLC....620 724-6220
414 S Cherokee St Girard (66743) *(G-2394)*
Advanced Manufacturing Inst....785 532-7044
510 Mccall Rd Manhattan (66502) *(G-6534)*
Advanced Medical Dme LLC....913 814-7464
2040 Hutton Rd Kansas City (66109) *(G-3787)*
Advanced Medical Resources....316 687-3071
8015 Manor Rd Wichita (67208) *(G-13624)*
Advanced Orthopedic Assoc Inc....316 631-1600
2778 N Webb Rd Wichita (67226) *(G-13625)*
Advanced Orthpdcs & Sprts Med....620 225-7744
2300 N 14th Ave Ste 104 Dodge City (67801) *(G-1290)*
Advanced Pain Mdcine Assoc LLC....316 942-4519
3715 N Oliver St Wichita (67220) *(G-13626)*
Advanced Resources LLC....913 207-9998
5400 W 133rd Pl Apt 221 Leawood (66209) *(G-5313)*
Advanced Systems Homes Inc....620 431-3320
4711 S Santa Fe Ave Chanute (66720) *(G-702)*
Advanced Technologies Inc....316 744-2285
4278 Westlake Dr Bel Aire (67220) *(G-427)*
Advanced Technology Group Inc (PA)....913 239-0050
9401 Indian Creek Pkwy # 670 Overland Park (66210) *(G-8350)*
Advanced Therapy & Spt Med LLC....620 792-7868
4801 10th St Great Bend (67530) *(G-2501)*
Advanced Welding Tech LLC....316 295-2333
2020 W 2nd St N Wichita (67203) *(G-13627)*
Advanstar Communications Inc....913 871-3800
8033 Flint St Shawnee Mission (66214) *(G-11079)*
Advantage Building Systems LLC....785 233-1393
2027 Nw Brickyard Rd Topeka (66618) *(G-12296)*
Advantage Commercial Lending....316 215-0115
1410 N Washington Ave Sedgwick (67135) *(G-10849)*
Advantage Computer Entps Inc....620 365-5156
1000 W Miller Rd Iola (66749) *(G-3585)*
Advantage Concrete, Hiawatha *Also called Leslie D Boeckner (G-3016)*
Advantage Dental, Lenexa *Also called Interdent Inc (G-5918)*
Advantage Framing Systems Inc....913 592-4150
701 N Lincoln St Spring Hill (66083) *(G-12075)*
Advantage Medical Group....785 749-0130
1104 E 23rd St Lawrence (66046) *(G-4722)*
Advantage Metals Recycling LLC....620 674-3800
2466 Nw Highway 7 Columbus (66725) *(G-1059)*
Advantage Metals Recycling LLC....913 621-2711
1153 S 12th St Kansas City (66105) *(G-3788)*
Advantage Metals Recycling LLC....913 321-3358
1015 S Packard St Kansas City (66105) *(G-3789)*
Advantage Metals Recycling LLC....816 861-2700
201 N 2nd St Kansas City (66118) *(G-3790)*
Advantage Metals Recycling LLC....620 342-1122
302 Graham St Emporia (66801) *(G-1692)*
Advantage Metals Recycling LLC....785 841-0396
1545 N 3rd St Lawrence (66044) *(G-4723)*
Advantage Metals Recycling LLC....785 232-5152
1628 Nw Gordon St Topeka (66608) *(G-12297)*
Advantage Sales & Mktg LLC....913 696-1700
8001 College Blvd Ste 100 Overland Park (66210) *(G-8351)*
Advantage Sales & Mktg LLC....913 890-0900
14001 Marshall Dr Lenexa (66215) *(G-5634)*
Advantage Sales & Mktg LLC....316 721-7727
1407 N Armour St Wichita (67206) *(G-13628)*
Advantage Tech Inc....913 888-5050
4400 W 107th St Overland Park (66207) *(G-8352)*
Advantaged Home Care....785 267-4433
1940 Sw Gage Blvd Ste C Topeka (66604) *(G-12298)*
Advatech LLC (HQ)....913 344-1000
8300 College Blvd Ste 200 Overland Park (66210) *(G-8353)*
Adventhealth Shawnee Mission, Shawnee Mission *Also called Shawnee Mission Med Ctr Inc (G-11858)*
Adventist Health Mid-America (PA)....913 676-2184
9100 W 74th St Shawnee Mission (66204) *(G-11080)*
Adventist Health System/Sunbel....913 676-2163
7312 Antioch Rd Shawnee Mission (66204) *(G-11081)*
Adventure Rv and Truck Ctr LLC....316 721-1333
4650 S Broadway Ave Wichita (67216) *(G-13629)*
Adventureland Rv Rentals Inc....800 333-8821
4650 S Broadway Ave Wichita (67216) *(G-13630)*
Adventures In Advertising, Shawnee Mission *Also called Making The Mark Inc (G-11592)*
Adventures In Early Lrng Ctr, Topeka *Also called Tdc Learning Centers Inc (G-13145)*
Adventuretech Group Inc....913 402-9600
7450 W 130th St Ste 320 Overland Park (66213) *(G-8354)*
Advertising Images, Wichita *Also called John B Baker (G-14762)*
Advisor's Excel, Topeka *Also called Foster Callanan Financial Svc (G-12624)*
Advisors Asset Management Inc....316 858-1766
8100 E 22nd St N 900-B Wichita (67226) *(G-13631)*
Advisors Tech LLC....844 671-6071
6001 Sw 6th Ave Ste 101 Topeka (66615) *(G-12299)*
Advisory Associates Inc....913 829-7323
14904 W 87th Street Pkwy Lenexa (66215) *(G-5635)*
Advocate Home Specialty Care....785 456-8910
811 Poplar St Wamego (66547) *(G-13402)*
Advocate Publishing Co Inc....785 562-2317
107 S 9th St Marysville (66508) *(G-6878)*
Advoctes For Bhavioral Hlth PA....316 630-8444
1861 N Rock Rd Ste 203 Wichita (67206) *(G-13632)*
Ae Farms, Kansas City *Also called Anderson Erickson Dairy Co (G-3810)*
Aegis Business Solutions LLC (PA)....913 307-9922
14453 Shady Bend Rd Olathe (66061) *(G-7512)*
Aegis Processing Solutions Inc....785 232-0061
240 Se Madison St Topeka (66607) *(G-12300)*
Aei Investment Holdings Inc....817 283-3722
1804 W 2nd St N Wichita (67203) *(G-13633)*
Aero Comm Machining, Wichita *Also called Freddie Wayne Long (G-14415)*
Aero Interior Maintenance Inc....316 990-5088
2120 S 343rd St W Cheney (67025) *(G-787)*
Aero Metal Forms Inc....316 942-0909
2649 W Esthner Ct Wichita (67213) *(G-13634)*
Aero Space Controls Corp....316 264-2875
1050 N Mosley St Wichita (67214) *(G-13635)*
Aero Space Manufacturing Corp....620 378-4441
1075 Fillmore St Fredonia (66736) *(G-2026)*
Aero Transportation Pdts Inc....620 241-7010
1330 N 81 Byp Mc Pherson (67460) *(G-6930)*

ALPHABETIC

Aero-Mach Laboratories Inc (PA)...316 682-7707
7707 E Funston St Wichita (67207) *(G-13636)*
Aero-Mod Incorporated...785 537-4995
7927 E Us Highway 24 Manhattan (66502) *(G-6535)*
Aero-Tech Engineering Inc...316 942-8604
5555 N 119th St W Maize (67101) *(G-6507)*
Aerocharger, New Century *Also called Hiperformance LLC (G-7287)*
Aeromach.com, Wichita *Also called Aero-Mach Laboratories Inc (G-13636)*
Aeromotive Inc...913 647-7300
7805 Barton St Shawnee Mission (66214) *(G-11082)*
Aerospace Products Company...316 733-4440
260 N Rock Rd Ste 120 Wichita (67206) *(G-13637)*
Aerospace Systems Cmpnents Inc...316 686-7392
5201 E 36th St N Wichita (67220) *(G-13638)*
Aerospace Turbine Rotables Inc...316 943-6100
1919 E Northern St Wichita (67216) *(G-13639)*
Aeroswint, Utica *Also called Randy Schwindt (G-13335)*
Aeroswint...785 391-2276
Rr 1 Box 63 Utica (67584) *(G-13334)*
Aerotek Inc...913 905-3000
7900 College Blvd Ste 200 Overland Park (66210) *(G-8355)*
Aerotek Inc...316 448-4500
727 N Waco Ave Ste 140 Wichita (67203) *(G-13640)*
Aerotek Inc...913 981-1970
15200 Santa Fe Dr Ste 100 Lenexa (66219) *(G-5636)*
Aerotek 410, Overland Park *Also called Aerotek Inc (G-8355)*
Aerotek 964, Lenexa *Also called Aerotek Inc (G-5636)*
AES Lawnparts, Olathe *Also called Automotive Equipment Services (G-7543)*
Affiliated Management Svcs Inc...913 677-9470
5651 Broadmoor St Shawnee Mission (66202) *(G-11083)*
Affiliated Medical Svcs Lab...316 265-4533
2916 E Central Ave Wichita (67214) *(G-13641)*
Affinis Corp...913 239-1100
8900 Indian Creek Pkwy # 450 Overland Park (66210) *(G-8356)*
Affinity Mortgage LLC...913 469-0777
8725 Rosehill Rd Ste 109 Lenexa (66215) *(G-5637)*
Affton Trucking Company Inc...913 871-1315
10 Shawnee Ave Ste C Kansas City (66105) *(G-3791)*
Afg Spring Hill Plant, Spring Hill *Also called AGC Flat Glass North Amer Inc (G-12076)*
African Americans Renewing Int...316 312-0183
2420 N Dellrose St Wichita (67220) *(G-13642)*
AG Center, Johnson *Also called Johnson Cooperative Grn Co Inc (G-3655)*
AG Connection Sales Inc...785 336-2121
877 Us Highway 36 Seneca (66538) *(G-10856)*
AG Growth International Inc...785 632-2161
514 W Crawford St Clay Center (67432) *(G-842)*
AG HALL OF HAME, Bonner Springs *Also called National AG Ctr & Hall Fame (G-565)*
AG Partners Cooperative Inc (PA)...785 742-2196
708 S 10th St Hiawatha (66434) *(G-3001)*
AG Power Equipment Co...785 899-3432
124 W Hwy 24 Goodland (67735) *(G-2460)*
AG Power Equipment Co (PA)...785 852-4235
1385 Kansas 27 Sharon Springs (67758) *(G-10894)*
AG Press Inc...785 539-7558
1531 Yuma St Manhattan (66502) *(G-6536)*
AG Research Center- Hayes, Hays *Also called Kansas State University (G-2858)*
AG Services LLC...620 662-5406
1515 E 30th Ave Hutchinson (67502) *(G-3194)*
AG Source Inc (PA)...785 841-1315
4910 Corp Centre Dr # 110 Lawrence (66047) *(G-4724)*
AG Valley Coop Non-Stock...785 877-5131
314 W North St Norton (67654) *(G-7440)*
Ag-Service Inc (PA)...620 947-3166
1830 Kanza Hillsboro (67063) *(G-3040)*
Agape Center of Hope LLC...316 393-7252
1707 N Piatt Ave Wichita (67214) *(G-13643)*
Agape Montessori School...913 768-0812
16550 W 129th St Olathe (66062) *(G-7513)*
Agape Mortgage Partners Corp (PA)...913 871-7377
105 E Amity St Ste 8 Louisburg (66053) *(G-6436)*
AGC, Lenexa *Also called Globl Adams Communications LLC (G-5877)*
AGC Flat Glass North Amer Inc...913 592-6100
20400 Webster St Spring Hill (66083) *(G-12076)*
Agco Inc (PA)...785 483-2128
913 N Fossil St Russell (67665) *(G-10263)*
AGCO Corporation...620 327-6413
420 W Lincoln Blvd Hesston (67062) *(G-2984)*
AGCO Corporation...785 738-2261
3154 Hallie Trl Beloit (67420) *(G-470)*
Agelix Consulting LLC...913 708-8145
8101 College Blvd Ste 100 Overland Park (66210) *(G-8357)*
Agency Services Corp Kansas...785 232-0561
815 Sw Topeka Blvd Ste 2b Topeka (66612) *(G-12301)*
Agenda Usa Inc...913 268-4466
5509 Foxridge Dr Shawnee Mission (66202) *(G-11084)*
Aggie Lounge, Manhattan *Also called Stickels Inc (G-6812)*
Aggreko LLC...913 281-9782
9601 Alden St Shawnee Mission (66215) *(G-11085)*
Aggreko Rental, Shawnee Mission *Also called Aggreko LLC (G-11085)*
Agler and Gaeddert Chartered (PA)...620 342-7641
1225 W 6th Ave Ste A Emporia (66801) *(G-1693)*
Agmark LLC (PA)...785 738-9641
118 W Main St Beloit (67420) *(G-471)*
Agra Axe International Inc...620 879-5858
166e Industrial Park Hwy Caney (67333) *(G-664)*
Agrex Inc (HQ)...913 851-6300
8205 W 108th Ter Ste 200 Overland Park (66210) *(G-8358)*
Agri Trails Coop Inc...785 479-5870
1754 Quail Rd Chapman (67431) *(G-776)*
Agri Trails Coop Inc...785 258-2286
500 N 7th St Herington (67449) *(G-2969)*
Agri-Risk Services Inc...913 897-1699
7540 W 160th St Ste 100 Stilwell (66085) *(G-12133)*
Agrilogic Insurance Svcs LLC...913 982-2450
4551 W 107th St Ste 250 Overland Park (66207) *(G-8359)*
Agris Hardware, Hutchinson *Also called Deere & Company (G-3260)*
Agspring LLC (PA)...913 333-3035
5101 College Blvd Leawood (66211) *(G-5314)*
Agspring Idaho LLC (HQ)...952 956-6720
5101 College Blvd Leawood (66211) *(G-5315)*
Agsynergy LLC...785 336-6333
1183 120th Rd Seneca (66538) *(G-10857)*
Agvantis Inc...316 266-5400
245 N Waco St Ste 270 Wichita (67202) *(G-13644)*
Ah Tannery Inc...913 772-1111
2212 S 4th St Leavenworth (66048) *(G-5200)*
Ahc of Overland Park LLC...913 232-2413
4700 Indian Creek Pkwy Overland Park (66207) *(G-8360)*
Ahern Rentals Inc...913 281-7555
350 N James St Kansas City (66118) *(G-3792)*
Ahn Marketing Incorporated (PA)...913 342-2176
3748 State Ave Kansas City (66102) *(G-3793)*
AHP H6 Topeka...785 273-0066
6021 Sw 6th Ave Topeka (66615) *(G-12302)*
AI Industries Prof Corp...918 401-9641
832 N Country Acres Ave Wichita (67212) *(G-13645)*
Aib International Inc (HQ)...785 537-4750
1213 Bakers Way Manhattan (66502) *(G-6537)*
AIG, Overland Park *Also called American Gen Lf Insur Co Del (G-8377)*
AIG...503 323-2500
P.O. Box 25588 Overland Park (66225) *(G-8361)*
Aih Receivable Management Svcs...800 666-4606
5800 Foxridge Dr Ste 105 Shawnee Mission (66202) *(G-11086)*
Aihrea, Shawnee *Also called American Indian Health Researc (G-10910)*
Ainsworth Pet Nutrition LLC...620 231-7779
1601 W Mckay St Frontenac (66763) *(G-2051)*
Air & Waste Management Assn...913 940-0081
8717 W 110th St Ste 650 Overland Park (66210) *(G-8362)*
Air Associates of Kansas, Olathe *Also called T and C Aviation Enterprises (G-8095)*
Air Capital Building Maint...316 838-3828
2822 E 31st St S Wichita (67216) *(G-13646)*
Air Capital Equipment Inc (PA)...316 522-1111
806 E Boston St Wichita (67211) *(G-13647)*
Air Capital Interiors Inc...316 633-4790
9424 E 37th St N Ste 300 Wichita (67226) *(G-13648)*
Air Capital Stucco L L C...316 650-2450
124 W 8th St Newton (67114) *(G-7308)*
Air Capitol Dial Inc...316 264-2483
220 N Vine St Wichita (67203) *(G-13649)*
Air Capitol Dlvry & Whse LLC...316 303-9005
5841 N Prospect Rd Park City (67204) *(G-9599)*
Air Care Heating & Cooling Co...913 362-5274
6235 Eby Ave Shawnee Mission (66202) *(G-11087)*
Air Care Systems Hvac Inc...360 403-9939
4140 Se 61st St Berryton (66409) *(G-525)*
Air Filter Plus Inc...785 542-3700
1205 Cardinal Dr Eudora (66025) *(G-1869)*
Air Plains Services Corp...620 326-8581
439 N West Rd Wellington (67152) *(G-13488)*
Air Power Consultants Inc...913 894-0044
18903 W 157th Ter Olathe (66062) *(G-7514)*
Air Products and Chemicals Inc...620 624-8151
2701 Road G Liberal (67901) *(G-6273)*
Air Products and Chemicals Inc...620 626-7062
2525 N Country Ests Liberal (67901) *(G-6274)*
Air Products and Chemicals Inc...316 522-8181
6601 S Ridge Rd Haysville (67060) *(G-2935)*
Air Products and Chemicals Inc...620 626-5700
12412 Road R Liberal (67901) *(G-6275)*
Air-Cap Dental, Wichita *Also called Scope Inc (G-15536)*
Airbus Americas Inc...316 264-0552
213 N Mead St Wichita (67202) *(G-13650)*
Airco Group, Wichita *Also called Aircraft Instr & Rdo Co Inc (G-13651)*
Aircraft Bluebook...913 967-1719
9800 Metcalf Ave Shawnee Mission (66212) *(G-11088)*
Aircraft Instr & Rdo Co Inc (PA)...316 945-9820
1853 S Eisenhower Ct Wichita (67209) *(G-13651)*

Aircraft Instrument & Rdo Svcs 316 945-9820
1851 S Eisenhower Ct Wichita (67209) *(G-13652)*

Airfield Technology Inc 913 780-9800
12897 W 151st St Ste A Olathe (66062) *(G-7515)*

Airfixture LLC 913 312-1100
51 Kansas Ave Ste A Kansas City (66105) *(G-3794)*

Airgas Usa LLC 785 823-8100
300 N Santa Fe Ave Salina (67401) *(G-10398)*

Airgas Usa LLC 316 941-9162
4115 W 33rd St S Wichita (67215) *(G-13653)*

Airmd LLC (PA) 316 932-1440
3445 N Webb Rd Wichita (67226) *(G-13654)*

Airosol Co Inc 620 325-2666
1101 Illinois St Neodesha (66757) *(G-7234)*

Airport Red Coach Inn of Wichi 316 942-5600
6815 W Kellogg Dr Wichita (67209) *(G-13655)*

Airsource Technologies Inc 913 422-9001
20505 W 67th St Shawnee Mission (66218) *(G-11089)*

Airtech Engineering Inc 913 888-5900
11936 W 119th St Overland Park (66213) *(G-8363)*

Airtex Inc 913 583-3181
32050 W 83rd St De Soto (66018) *(G-1191)*

Airtex Manufacturing Lllp (HQ) 913 583-3181
32050 W 83rd St De Soto (66018) *(G-1192)*

Airxcel Inc (HQ) 316 832-3400
3050 N Saint Francis St Wichita (67219) *(G-13656)*

Aj Investors LLC 316 321-0580
307 S Haverhill Rd El Dorado (67042) *(G-1526)*

Aka Wireless Inc 785 823-6605
2401 S 9th St Salina (67401) *(G-10399)*

Akro Fireguard Products, Shawnee Mission *Also called Akrofire Inc (G-11090)*

Akrofire Inc 913 888-7172
9001 Rosehill Rd Shawnee Mission (66215) *(G-11090)*

AL Huber Construction Inc 913 341-4880
10770 El Monte St Ste 100 Shawnee Mission (66211) *(G-11091)*

Al Morris 620 225-5611
801 N 2nd Ave Dodge City (67801) *(G-1291)*

Al Stevens Construction LLC (PA) 913 897-0688
6800 W 152nd Ter Overland Park (66223) *(G-8364)*

Ala Operations LLC 785 313-4059
2300 N 113th Ter Kansas City (66109) *(G-3795)*

Alabama Southern Railroad LLC 620 231-2230
315 W 3rd St Pittsburg (66762) *(G-9806)*

Aladdin Petroleum Corporation (PA) 316 265-9602
123 S Market St Wichita (67202) *(G-13657)*

Alan Bitter 620 353-7407
202 E Oklahoma Ave Ulysses (67880) *(G-13281)*

Alan Clark Body Shop Inc 785 776-5333
2160 Pillsbury Dr Manhattan (66502) *(G-6538)*

Alan County Magistrate, Iola *Also called County of Allen (G-3597)*

Alan Grove Components Inc 913 837-4368
27070 Metcalf Rd Louisburg (66053) *(G-6437)*

Alan Moskowitz MD PC 316 858-1900
10100 E Shannon Woods St Wichita (67226) *(G-13658)*

Alaskan Fur Company Inc 913 649-4000
9029 Metcalf Ave Overland Park (66212) *(G-8365)*

Albers Finshg & Solutions LLC 316 542-0405
38628 W 15th St S Cheney (67025) *(G-788)*

Albert G Hogoboom 316 321-1397
767 Oil Hill Rd El Dorado (67042) *(G-1527)*

Albertson & Hein Inc 316 943-7441
3617 W Walker St Wichita (67213) *(G-13659)*

Albright Investment Company (PA) 620 221-7653
1603 Main St Winfield (67156) *(G-16114)*

Alcoa Inc 620 665-5281
1501 Airport Rd Hutchinson (67501) *(G-3195)*

Alcoholics Anonymous 620 793-3962
1620 Hubbard St Great Bend (67530) *(G-2502)*

Alcoholics Anonymous 316 684-3661
2812 E English St Wichita (67211) *(G-13660)*

Alcoholics Anonyms Bnnr Sprngs 913 441-3277
144 N Nettleton Ave Bonner Springs (66012) *(G-539)*

Alderbrook Village 620 442-4400
402 E Windsor Rd Arkansas City (67005) *(G-141)*

Alderman Acres Mfg Inc 620 251-4095
623 Union St Coffeyville (67337) *(G-909)*

Aldersgate Untd Meth Pre Schl 913 764-2407
15315 W 151st St Olathe (66062) *(G-7516)*

ALDERSGATE VILLAGE, Topeka *Also called United Methodist Homes Inc (G-13206)*

Alderson Alderson Weiler Co 785 232-0753
2101 Sw 21st St Topeka (66604) *(G-12303)*

Alderwoods (kansas) Inc (PA) 316 682-5575
2929 W 13th St N Wichita (67203) *(G-13661)*

Aldi Foods Divisional Office, Olathe *Also called Aldi Inc (G-7517)*

Aldi Inc 913 768-1119
10505 S K 7 Hwy Olathe (66061) *(G-7517)*

Alea Communications LLC 913 439-7391
510 N Poplar St Gardner (66030) *(G-2323)*

Alegria Living & Healthcare 785 665-7124
700 W 7th St Overbrook (66524) *(G-8322)*

Alenco Inc (HQ) 913 438-1902
16201 W 110th St Lenexa (66219) *(G-5638)*

Alenco Materials Company, Lenexa *Also called Alenco Inc (G-5638)*

Alert 360 ....913 599-3439
11635 W 83rd Ter Lenexa (66214) *(G-5639)*

Alert Enterprises Inc 785 862-9800
4900 Sw Topeka Blvd Ste 1 Topeka (66609) *(G-12304)*

Alex R Masson Inc (PA) 913 301-3281
12819 198th St Linwood (66052) *(G-6415)*

Alexander C Davis 913 888-5577
5701 W 119th St Ste 345 Shawnee Mission (66209) *(G-11092)*

Alexander Camp 620 342-1386
1783 Road P5 Emporia (66801) *(G-1694)*

Alexander Manufacturing Co Inc 620 421-5010
1407 Corporate Dr Parsons (67357) *(G-9664)*

Alfalfa Inc 620 675-8686
1242 Road 180 Sublette (67877) *(G-12196)*

Alfred Benesch & Company 785 539-2202
3226 Kimball Ave Manhattan (66503) *(G-6539)*

Alfred Benjamin Conseling Svc, Shawnee Mission *Also called Jewish Family and Chld Svc (G-11488)*

Alixa Rx LLC 913 307-8150
11286 Renner Blvd Lenexa (66219) *(G-5640)*

All American Automotive Inc 316 721-3600
8630 W Kellogg Dr Wichita (67209) *(G-13662)*

All American Indoor Sports (PA) 913 888-5425
8875 Rosehill Rd Shawnee Mission (66215) *(G-11093)*

All American Indoor Sports 913 599-4884
8045 Flint St Shawnee Mission (66214) *(G-11094)*

All American Pet Brands Inc 913 951-4999
8310 Hedge Lane Ter Shawnee (66227) *(G-10907)*

All American Supply Co, Lenexa *Also called Wsm Industries Inc (G-6236)*

All Amrican Maytag HM Appl Ctr, Wichita *Also called Ricks Appliance Service Inc (G-15460)*

All City Tow Service 913 371-1000
1015 S Bethany St Kansas City (66105) *(G-3796)*

All Crtres Veterinary Hosp P A 316 721-3993
8414 W 13th St N Ste 170 Wichita (67212) *(G-13663)*

All Freight Systems Inc (PA) 913 281-1203
1134 S 12th St Kansas City (66105) *(G-3797)*

All In Cut 316 722-4962
11940 W Central Ave # 112 Wichita (67212) *(G-13664)*

All of E Solutions LLC 785 832-2900
2510 W 6th St Lawrence (66049) *(G-4725)*

All Point Transportation LLC 785 273-4730
6342 Sw 21st St Ste 100 Topeka (66615) *(G-12305)*

All Radio Cab Co, Salina *Also called Edward French Loy (G-10485)*

All Saints Home Care Inc 316 755-1076
3425 W Central Ave Wichita (67203) *(G-13665)*

All Seasons Party Rental Inc 816 765-1444
5050 Kansas Ave Kansas City (66106) *(G-3798)*

All Seasons Tent Sales, Kansas City *Also called Infinity Tents Inc (G-4100)*

All Service Maint & Rmdlg, Lawrence *Also called M P M Services Inc (G-5005)*

All States Windows Siding LLC 913 800-5211
6414 College Blvd Overland Park (66211) *(G-8366)*

All States Windows Siding LLC (PA) 316 444-1220
776 N West St Wichita (67203) *(G-13666)*

All Systems Inc 913 281-5100
3241 N 7th Street Trfy Kansas City (66115) *(G-3799)*

All Systems Dsgned Sltions Inc 913 281-5100
3241 N 7th Street Trfy Kansas City (66115) *(G-3800)*

All Things Exterior Inc 785 738-5015
3075 Us 24 Hwy Beloit (67420) *(G-472)*

All Wther Win Doors Siding Inc (PA) 913 262-4380
7710 Shawnee Mission Pkwy Overland Park (66202) *(G-8367)*

All-Call, Wichita *Also called Alliance Monitoring Tech LLC (G-13670)*

All-N-1 Landscape LLC 785 856-5296
411 N Iowa St Lawrence (66044) *(G-4726)*

All-Pro Services Inc 785 842-1402
757 Highway 40 Lawrence (66049) *(G-4727)*

All-Steel Building Systems LLC 785 271-5559
1300 Nw Us Highway 24 Topeka (66608) *(G-12306)*

Allcare Animal Hospital Inc 913 268-5011
7252 Renner Rd Shawnee Mission (66217) *(G-11095)*

Allegiant, Lenexa *Also called Kansas Communications Inc (G-5937)*

Allegiant Networks LLC 913 599-6900
10983 Granada Ln 300 Leawood (66211) *(G-5316)*

Allegion S&S US Holding Co 913 393-8629
2119 E Kansas City Rd Olathe (66061) *(G-7518)*

Allen Gibbs & Houlik Llc 316 267-7231
301 N Main St Ste 1700 Wichita (67202) *(G-13667)*

Allen K Kelley DDS PA 785 841-5590
4900 Legends Dr Lawrence (66049) *(G-4728)*

Allen and Sons Waste Svcs LLC 316 558-8050
3645 W Esthner Ave Wichita (67213) *(G-13668)*

Allen Cnty Anmal Rscue Fndtion 620 496-3647
305 E Highway 54 La Harpe (66751) *(G-4647)*

Allen Commercial Clg Svcs LLC 913 322-2900
8194 Nieman Rd Lenexa (66214) *(G-5641)*

Allen County Hospital, Iola *Also called HCA Inc (G-3608)*

A L P H A B E T I C

Allen County Lodging LLC ...620 365-3030
200 Bills Way Iola (66749) *(G-3586)*
Allen Park III, Overland Park *Also called Sweet Life At Rosehill (G-9382)*
Allen Preschool LLC ...913 451-1066
11060 Oakmont St Shawnee Mission (66210) *(G-11096)*
Allen Press Inc (PA) ...785 843-1234
810 E 10th St Lawrence (66044) *(G-4729)*
Allen Samuels Waco D C J Inc ...620 860-1869
1421 E 30th Ave Hutchinson (67502) *(G-3196)*
Allen Smels Ddge Chrysler Jeep, Hutchinson *Also called Allen Samuels Waco D C J Inc (G-3196)*
Allen Trenching Inc ...316 721-6300
8222 W Irving St Wichita (67209) *(G-13669)*
Allen Veterinary Center ...620 421-1341
1425 Us Highway 59 Parsons (67357) *(G-9665)*
Allenbrand-Drews and Assoc (PA) ...913 764-1076
122 N Water St Olathe (66061) *(G-7519)*
Allergy & Asthma Care PA ...913 491-3300
10787 Nall Ave Ste 200 Overland Park (66211) *(G-8368)*
Allergy Rhmtlogy Clnics Kc LLC ...913 338-3222
8401 W 125th St Overland Park (66213) *(G-8369)*
Alliance AG and Grain, Lewis *Also called Southern Plains Co-Op At Lewis (G-6270)*
Alliance AG and Grain LLC ...785 798-3775
918 W Sycamore St Ness City (67560) *(G-7251)*
Alliance AG and Grain LLC (PA) ...620 385-2898
313 N Main St Spearville (67876) *(G-12069)*
Alliance AG and Grain LLC ...620 723-3351
311 N Main St Greensburg (67054) *(G-2671)*
Alliance AG and Grain LLC ...620 622-4511
108 W Chestnut St Protection (67127) *(G-10172)*
Alliance Bank (HQ) ...785 271-1800
3001 Sw Wanamaker Rd Topeka (66614) *(G-12307)*
Alliance Data Systems Corp ...214 494-3000
8035 Quivira Rd Ste 100 Shawnee Mission (66215) *(G-11097)*
Alliance Equities Corporation ...913 428-8278
7227 Metcalf Ave Ste 201 Overland Park (66204) *(G-8370)*
Alliance Inc ...785 445-3701
255 S Vanhouten Russell (67665) *(G-10264)*
Alliance Insurance Co, McPherson *Also called Farmers Alliance Mutl Insur Co (G-6963)*
Alliance Jantr Advisors Inc ...913 815-8807
119 N Parker St Ste 120 Olathe (66061) *(G-7520)*
Alliance Monitoring Tech LLC (PA) ...316 263-7775
355 S Ellis St Wichita (67211) *(G-13670)*
Alliance Shippers Inc ...913 262-7060
5700 Broadmoor St Ste 600 Shawnee Mission (66202) *(G-11098)*
Alliance Technologies Inc ...913 262-7977
10881 Lowell Ave Ste 110 Overland Park (66210) *(G-8371)*
Alliance Well Service Inc ...620 672-1065
271 Lake Rd Pratt (67124) *(G-10095)*
Alliant Bank ...316 772-5111
3711 N Ridge Rd Wichita (67205) *(G-13671)*
Allied Auto Body Carstar, Lawrence *Also called Allied Body Shop Incorporated (G-4730)*
Allied Body Shop Incorporated ...785 841-3672
800 E 23rd St Lawrence (66046) *(G-4730)*
Allied Business Solutions Inc ...913 856-2323
314 E Main St Ste 202 Gardner (66030) *(G-2324)*
Allied Construction Svcs Inc ...913 321-3170
4700 Roe Pkwy Roeland Park (66205) *(G-10216)*
Allied Courier Systems Inc ...913 383-8666
7540 W 160th St Ste 180 Stilwell (66085) *(G-12134)*
Allied Environmental Cons Inc ...316 262-5698
214 N Saint Francis Ave Wichita (67202) *(G-13672)*
Allied Laboratories, Wichita *Also called Professional Engrg Cons PA (G-15360)*
Allied Medical, Wichita *Also called Cohoon Chiropractic (G-14051)*
Allied of Kansas Inc (PA) ...785 483-2627
24 S Lincoln St Russell (67665) *(G-10265)*
Allied of Kansas Inc ...620 793-5861
N Main St Great Bend (67530) *(G-2503)*
Allied of Kansas Inc ...620 624-5937
712 N Country Estates Rd Liberal (67901) *(G-6276)*
Allied Ofs LLC ...785 483-2627
24 S Lincoln St Russell (67665) *(G-10266)*
Allied Oil & Tire Company ...316 530-5221
3619 N Poplar St Wichita (67219) *(G-13673)*
Allied Retail Concepts LLC ...913 492-8008
6205 Goddard St Shawnee (66203) *(G-10908)*
Allied Sales and Marketing Inc ...316 617-2160
550 N 159th St E Ste 301 Wichita (67230) *(G-13674)*
Allied Services LLC ...620 783-5841
1715 E Front St Galena (66739) *(G-2068)*
Allied Waste Inds Ariz Inc ...620 336-3678
4237 Cr 5300 Cherryvale (67335) *(G-800)*
Allied Waste Svcs Cherryvale, Cherryvale *Also called Allied Waste Inds Ariz Inc (G-800)*
Allison Transmissions, Wichita *Also called Central Pwr Systems & Svcs LLC (G-13984)*
Allmetal Recycling LLC (PA) ...316 558-9914
800 E 21st St N Wichita (67214) *(G-13675)*
Allmetal Recycling LLC ...316 838-9381
410 E 25th St N Wichita (67219) *(G-13676)*
Allofe Studio, Lawrence *Also called All of E Solutions LLC (G-4725)*
Alloy Architecture PA ...316 634-1111
3500 N Rock Rd Bldg 500 Wichita (67226) *(G-13677)*
Allsigns LLC ...785 232-5512
414 Se Jefferson St Topeka (66607) *(G-12308)*
Allstaff Chartered ...620 792-4643
2000 Washington St Great Bend (67530) *(G-2504)*
Allstate, Wichita *Also called Madrigal & Associates Inc (G-15000)*
Allstate, Arkansas City *Also called United Agency Inc (G-187)*
Allstate, Garden City *Also called Rutter Cline Associates Inc (G-2271)*
Allstate, Garden City *Also called Keller Leopold Insurance LLC (G-2218)*
Allstate Roofing Inc ...913 782-2000
523 N Mur Len Rd Olathe (66062) *(G-7521)*
Alltech Communications Inc ...785 267-0316
430 W 1st Ave Topeka (66603) *(G-12309)*
Alltech Electrical Service, Ulysses *Also called Alan Bitter (G-13281)*
Alltite Inc (PA) ...316 686-3010
1600 E Murdock St Wichita (67214) *(G-13678)*
Ally Servicing LLC ...316 652-6301
9111 E Douglas Ave 200b Wichita (67207) *(G-13679)*
Alma Foods LLC ...785 765-3396
110 E 1st St Alma (66401) *(G-61)*
Alma Manor, Alma *Also called Midwest Health Services Inc (G-65)*
Almighty Tow Service LLC ...913 362-8697
8787 Lenexa Dr Overland Park (66214) *(G-8372)*
Alonge Stone Masonry ...785 832-1438
23604 Cantrell Rd Tonganoxie (66086) *(G-12251)*
Alorica Customer Care Inc ...215 441-2323
95 Metcalf Sq Bldg J Lenexa (66219) *(G-5642)*
Alph Omega Geotech Inc ...913 371-0000
1701 State Ave Kansas City (66102) *(G-3801)*
Alpha Biosystems Inc ...316 265-7929
9912 W York St Wichita (67215) *(G-13680)*
Alpha CHI Omega ...785 843-7600
1500 Sigma Nu Pl Lawrence (66044) *(G-4731)*
Alpha Land Surveys Inc ...620 728-0012
102 E 4th Ave Hutchinson (67501) *(G-3197)*
Alpha Media LLC ...785 823-1111
131 N Santa Fe Ave Salina (67401) *(G-10400)*
Alpha Media LLC ...785 272-3456
1210 Sw Executive Dr Topeka (66615) *(G-12310)*
Alpha Ministries ...785 597-5235
15017 27th St Perry (66073) *(G-9765)*
Alpha Security Midwest, Overland Park *Also called Weather Metrics Inc (G-9486)*
Alpha Services and Production ...620 624-8318
2511 Hwy 83 Liberal (67901) *(G-6277)*
Als Assction Md-Merica Chapter (PA) ...913 648-2062
6950 Squibb Rd Ste 210 Shawnee Mission (66202) *(G-11099)*
Als Marshfield LLC ...620 225-4172
3201 E Trail St Dodge City (67801) *(G-1292)*
Als Tribology, Kansas City *Also called Als USA Inc (G-3802)*
Als USA Inc ...913 281-9881
935 Sunshine Rd Kansas City (66115) *(G-3802)*
Alside, Wichita *Also called Associated Materials LLC (G-13757)*
Alsop Sand Co Inc (PA) ...785 243-4249
E Hwy 9 Concordia (66901) *(G-1101)*
Alta Vista State Bank ...785 499-6304
619 Main St Alta Vista (66834) *(G-69)*
Altasciences Clinical Kans Inc (HQ) ...913 696-1601
10103 Metcalf Ave Overland Park (66212) *(G-8373)*
Alterations By Sarah, Wichita *Also called U S S A Inc (G-15826)*
Alternacare Infusion Phrm Inc ...913 906-9260
15065 W 116th St Olathe (66062) *(G-7522)*
Alternative Building Tech ...913 856-4536
711 S Sycamore St Gardner (66030) *(G-2325)*
Alternative Chrome Creations ...316 680-1209
8900 S Broadway Ave Haysville (67060) *(G-2936)*
Alternative Claims Services ...816 298-7506
15665 S Mahaffie St Olathe (66062) *(G-7523)*
Altmar Inc ...785 233-0053
3860 Nw 16th St Topeka (66618) *(G-12311)*
Altmar Inc General Contractors, Topeka *Also called Altmar Inc (G-12311)*
Altura Incorporated ...913 492-3701
8411 Renner Blvd Apt 1309 Lenexa (66219) *(G-5643)*
Alvamar Inc (PA) ...785 842-2929
1809 Crossgate Dr Lawrence (66047) *(G-4732)*
Alvamar Golf and Country Club, Lawrence *Also called Alvamar Inc (G-4732)*
Alvamar Inc ...785 843-0196
1611 Saint Andrews Dr Lawrence (66047) *(G-4733)*
Always Best Care of Heart Land, Wichita *Also called Sonodora Inc (G-15615)*
Always Fresh, Kansas City *Also called Valu Merchandisers Company (G-4513)*
Always There Senior Care Inc ...316 946-9222
2260 N Ridge Rd Ste 220 Wichita (67205) *(G-13681)*
Alzheimer's Disease and Relate, Shawnee Mission *Also called Alzheimrs Dsease Rltd Dsordrs (G-11100)*
Alzheimrs Dsease Rltd Dsordrs (HQ) ...913 381-3888
3846 W 75th St Shawnee Mission (66208) *(G-11100)*
Am-Knck, Concordia *Also called Knck Inc (G-1120)*

Amanda Blu & Co LLC 913 381-9494
883 N Jan Mar Ct Olathe (66061) ***(G-7524)***
Amazing Grace Staffing Inc 785 432-2920
2004 Hall St Hays (67601) ***(G-2745)***
Ambassador Hotel Wichita LLC 316 239-7100
104 S Broadway Ave Wichita (67202) ***(G-13682)***
Ambrose Packaging Inc 913 780-5666
1654 S Lone Elm Rd Olathe (66061) ***(G-7525)***
Ambrose Sales Inc 913 780-5666
1654 S Lone Elm Rd Olathe (66061) ***(G-7526)***
AMBS and Associates Inc 913 599-5939
9209 Quivira Rd Lenexa (66215) ***(G-5644)***
Ambulance Service, Colby *Also called County of Thomas* ***(G-1001)***
AMC, Leawood *Also called American Multi-Cinema Inc* ***(G-5321)***
AMC, Leawood *Also called American Multi-Cinema Inc* ***(G-5322)***
AMC Entertainment Holdings Inc (HQ) 913 213-2000
1 Amc Way 11500 Ash St Leawood (66211) ***(G-5317)***
AMC Entertainment Inc (HQ) 913 213-2000
11500 Ash St Leawood (66211) ***(G-5318)***
Amec Fster Wheler E C Svcs Inc 785 272-6830
100 Se 9th St Ste 400 Topeka (66612) ***(G-12312)***
America Care Quaker Hill Manor 620 848-3797
8675 Se 72nd Ter Baxter Springs (66713) ***(G-392)***
America Jet, Salina *Also called Jrm Enterprises Inc* ***(G-10557)***
Americal Inc 785 890-7566
2520 Commerce Rd Goodland (67735) ***(G-2461)***
American Academy Family Physcn (PA) 913 906-6000
11400 Tomahawk Creek Pkwy Shawnee Mission (66211) ***(G-11101)***
American Acdemy Fmly Physcians (PA) 913 906-6000
11400 Tomahawk Creek Pkwy Leawood (66211) ***(G-5319)***
American Adoptions Inc (PA) 913 492-2229
7500 W 110th St Ste 500 Overland Park (66210) ***(G-8374)***
American Assn Univ Women 785 472-5737
606 Webb St Ellsworth (67439) ***(G-1656)***
American Bank Baxter Springs (HQ) 620 856-2301
1201 Military Ave Baxter Springs (66713) ***(G-393)***
American Baptist Church 913 236-7067
7416 Roe Ave Shawnee Mission (66208) ***(G-11102)***
American Baptist Estates Inc 316 263-8264
1605 W May St Wichita (67213) ***(G-13683)***
American Bldrs Contrs Sup Inc 913 722-4747
1262 Southwest Blvd Kansas City (66103) ***(G-3803)***
American Bldrs Contrs Sup Inc 785 354-7398
2031 Nw Us Highway 24 Topeka (66618) ***(G-12313)***
American Bldrs Contrs Sup Inc 316 265-8276
1321 E 1st St N Wichita (67214) ***(G-13684)***
American Bonanza Society Inc 316 945-1700
3595 N Webb Rd Ste 200 Wichita (67226) ***(G-13685)***
American Bottling Company 785 233-7471
3526 Se 21st St Topeka (66607) ***(G-12314)***
American Bottling Company 785 625-4488
723 E 6th St Hays (67601) ***(G-2746)***
American Bottling Company 913 894-6777
9960 Lakeview Ave Lenexa (66219) ***(G-5645)***
American Bottling Company 620 223-6166
425 Marble Rd Fort Scott (66701) ***(G-1954)***
American Bottling Company 316 529-3777
1240 W Macarthur Rd Wichita (67217) ***(G-13686)***
American Bottling Company 785 537-2100
613 Pecan Cir Manhattan (66502) ***(G-6540)***
American Box & Tape Co 913 384-0992
23128 W 43rd St Shawnee (66226) ***(G-10909)***
American Bridge Company 913 948-5800
7301 W 129th St Ste 130 Overland Park (66213) ***(G-8375)***
American Cab Inc 316 262-7511
400 S Greenwood St Wichita (67211) ***(G-13687)***
American Cancer Socty Heartlnd 316 265-3400
236 S Topeka Ave Wichita (67202) ***(G-13688)***
American Chem Systems II LLC (PA) 316 263-4448
3505 W 29th St S Wichita (67217) ***(G-13689)***
American Chemical Systems, Wichita *Also called ACS Iiiiii - Ks LLC* ***(G-13609)***
American College of Clinical (PA) 913 492-3311
13000 W 87th Street Pkwy # 100 Lenexa (66215) ***(G-5646)***
American Comm & Residentl Svcs 316 633-5866
2408 S Pattie St Wichita (67216) ***(G-13690)***
American Concrete Co Inc 620 231-1520
504 N Smelter St Pittsburg (66762) ***(G-9807)***
American Construction Svcs LLC 913 754-3777
11000 Lakeview Ave Lenexa (66219) ***(G-5647)***
American Crane & Tractor Parts (PA) 913 551-8223
2200 State Line Rd Kansas City (66103) ***(G-3804)***
American Ctrl & Engrg Svc Inc 316 776-7500
14433 Sw 150th St Rose Hill (67133) ***(G-10235)***
American Design Inc (PA) 785 766-0409
1015 Firetree Ave Baldwin City (66006) ***(G-353)***
American Disposal Services, Galena *Also called Republic Services Inc* ***(G-2082)***
American Drect Procurement Inc (PA) 913 677-5588
11000 Lakeview Ave Lenexa (66219) ***(G-5648)***
American Eagle Outfitters Inc 724 779-5209
1301 N Davis Ave Ottawa (66067) ***(G-8244)***
American Electric Company, Salina *Also called Consolidated Elec Distrs Inc* ***(G-10459)***
American Electrical, Wichita *Also called Consolidated Elec Distrs Inc* ***(G-14091)***
American Energies Gas Svc LLC 620 628-4424
136 S Main St Canton (67428) ***(G-679)***
American Energy Products Inc 913 351-3388
1105 Industrial St Lansing (66043) ***(G-4666)***
American Equipment, Kansas City *Also called J & D Equipment Inc* ***(G-4113)***
American Equipment Sales Inc 785 843-4500
1723 E 1500 Rd Lawrence (66044) ***(G-4734)***
American Exteriors LLC 913 712-9668
9730 N 215th St W Mount Hope (67108) ***(G-7203)***
American Federation 785 267-0100
2131 Sw 36th St Topeka (66611) ***(G-12315)***
American Fence and SEC Co Inc 316 945-5001
2909 S West St Wichita (67217) ***(G-13691)***
American Fence Company LLC 913 307-0306
7616 Wedd St Overland Park (66204) ***(G-8376)***
American Fidelity Assurance Co 785 232-8100
3100 Sw Huntoon St # 102 Topeka (66604) ***(G-12316)***
American Fire Sprinkler Corp 620 792-1909
4901 8th St Great Bend (67530) ***(G-2505)***
American Fun Food Company Inc 316 838-9329
6010 N Broadway Ave Park City (67219) ***(G-9600)***
American Gen Lf Insur Co Del 913 402-5000
13220 Metcalf Ave Ste 360 Overland Park (66213) ***(G-8377)***
American Golf Corporation 316 684-4110
2400 N Tallgrass St Wichita (67226) ***(G-13692)***
American Golf Corporation 620 663-5301
922 Crazy Horse Rd Hutchinson (67502) ***(G-3198)***
American Golf Corporation 913 681-3100
7000 W 133rd St Shawnee Mission (66209) ***(G-11103)***
American Gvrnment Slutions LLC 913 428-2550
5251 W 116th Pl Ste 200 Leawood (66211) ***(G-5320)***
American Heart Association Ka (PA) 785 272-7056
5375 Sw 7th St Ste 300 Topeka (66606) ***(G-12317)***
American Heart Association Ka 913 652-1913
6800 W 93rd St Shawnee Mission (66212) ***(G-11104)***
American Highway Technology, Parsons *Also called Dayton Superior Corporation* ***(G-9681)***
American Home Life Insur Co 785 235-6276
400 S Kansas Ave Ste 100 Topeka (66603) ***(G-12318)***
American Homepatient Inc 913 495-9545
11427 Strang Line Rd Lenexa (66215) ***(G-5649)***
American Implement Inc (PA) 620 275-4114
2611 W Jones Ave Garden City (67846) ***(G-2098)***
American Implement Inc 620 544-4351
843 E Highway 51 Hugoton (67951) ***(G-3147)***
American Implement Inc 620 872-7244
807 N Main St Scott City (67871) ***(G-10803)***
American Implement Inc 620 697-2182
364 Us Hgwy 56 Elkhart (67950) ***(G-1617)***
American Implement Main Office 620 356-3460
2718 W Oklahoma Ave Ulysses (67880) ***(G-13282)***
American Income Life Insurance 402 699-3366
11235 Mastin St Ste 201 Overland Park (66210) ***(G-8378)***
American Indian Health Researc 913 422-7523
6819 Woodstock Ct Shawnee (66218) ***(G-10910)***
American Institute of Baking (PA) 785 537-4750
1213 Bakers Way Manhattan (66502) ***(G-6541)***
American Legion 620 241-0343
401 N Main St McPherson (67460) ***(G-6933)***
AMERICAN LEGION ARGONNE POST 1, Great Bend *Also called Argonna Post 180 Amercn Legion* ***(G-2511)***
American Legion Post 156 ....913 294-4676
5 Delaware St Paola (66071) ***(G-9539)***
American Legion Post 400 ....785 296-9400
3029 Nw Us Highway 24 Topeka (66618) ***(G-12319)***
American Legion Post 95 Inc 620 983-2048
108 N Walnut St Peabody (66866) ***(G-9758)***
American Management Assn Intl 913 451-2700
11221 Roe Ave Shawnee Mission (66211) ***(G-11105)***
American Maplan Corporation 620 241-6843
823 S Us Highway 81 Byp McPherson (67460) ***(G-6934)***
American Marking Systems Inc 913 492-6028
14609 W 106th St Lenexa (66215) ***(G-5650)***
American Mechanical Inc 316 262-1100
1608 E Us Highway 54 Andover (67002) ***(G-79)***
American Media Investments Inc 620 231-7200
1162 E Highway 126 Pittsburg (66762) ***(G-9808)***
American Medical Response Inc 913 227-0911
1902 Foxridge Dr Kansas City (66106) ***(G-3805)***
American Metal Fabrication Inc 620 399-8508
2000 N Vandenburgh Ave Wellington (67152) ***(G-13489)***
American Metals Supply Co Inc 913 754-0616
15201 W 101st Ter Lenexa (66219) ***(G-5651)***
American Midwest Distrs LLC 816 842-1905
12009 Stearns St Overland Park (66213) ***(G-8379)***
American Multi-Cinema Inc 913 498-8696
11701 Nall Ave Leawood (66211) ***(G-5321)***
American Multi-Cinema Inc (HQ) 913 213-2000
1 Amc Way Leawood (66211) ***(G-5322)***

ALPHABETIC

American National Insurance Co...913 722-2232
6405 Metcalf Ave Ste 314 Shawnee Mission (66202) ***(G-11106)***
American National Red Cross...620 446-0966
110 W Bryant Rd Arkansas City (67005) ***(G-142)***
American National Red Cross...785 309-0263
120 W Prescott Ave Salina (67401) ***(G-10401)***
American National Red Cross...913 245-3565
8053 Bond St Lenexa (66214) ***(G-5652)***
American Oil & Gas Reporter, Haysville *Also called National Publishers Group Inc* ***(G-2953)***
American Overseas Schools Hist...316 265-6837
704 W Douglas Ave Wichita (67203) ***(G-13693)***
American Paper Products Inc...913 681-5777
12333 Wedd St Shawnee Mission (66213) ***(G-11107)***
American Phoenix Inc...785 862-7722
7215 Sw Topeka Blvd Topeka (66619) ***(G-12320)***
American Pre Sort Inc...785 232-2633
540 Nw Tyler Ct Ste 101 Topeka (66608) ***(G-12321)***
American Red Cross, Salina *Also called American National Red Cross* ***(G-10401)***
American Red Cross, Lenexa *Also called American National Red Cross* ***(G-5652)***
American Refrigerated Ex Inc...913 406-8562
505 N Mur Len Rd Olathe (66062) ***(G-7527)***
American Retirement Corp...913 248-1500
11400 W 65th St Shawnee Mission (66203) ***(G-11108)***
American Roofing Inc...913 772-1776
2500 S 2nd St Leavenworth (66048) ***(G-5201)***
American Rsdntial Cmmnties LLC...785 776-4440
3050 Tuttle Creek Blvd Manhattan (66502) ***(G-6542)***
American Senior Benefits...785 273-8200
3745 Sw Wanamaker Rd A Topeka (66610) ***(G-12322)***
American Sentry Security Sys...785 232-1525
120 Se 6th Ave Ste 265 Topeka (66603) ***(G-12323)***
American State Bank & Trust Co (PA)...620 793-5900
1321 Main St Ste A Great Bend (67530) ***(G-2506)***
American State Bank & Trust Co...620 271-0123
1901 E Mary St Garden City (67846) ***(G-2099)***
American State Bank & Trust Co...620 549-3244
216 N Main St Saint John (67576) ***(G-10349)***
American Superclean...913 815-3257
2011 E Crossroads Ln # 301 Olathe (66062) ***(G-7528)***
American Telephone Inc...913 780-3166
17540 Four Corners Rd Gardner (66030) ***(G-2326)***
American Time Products, Olathe *Also called Power Control Devices Inc* ***(G-7995)***
American Tire Distributors...316 616-9600
5015 S Water Cir Wichita (67217) ***(G-13694)***
American Trucking Inc...620 594-2481
204 S Main St Sawyer (67134) ***(G-10794)***
American Trust Administrators (PA)...913 378-9860
7223 W 95th St Ste 301 Overland Park (66212) ***(G-8380)***
American Underwriters Lf Insur (PA)...316 794-2200
1035 S 183rd St W Goddard (67052) ***(G-2429)***
American Well Service LLC...620 672-5625
10213 Bluestem Blvd Pratt (67124) ***(G-10096)***
American Wholesale Corporation...785 364-4901
24000 Us Highway 75 Holton (66436) ***(G-3084)***
American Wtr Purification Inc...316 685-3333
7701 E Kellogg Dr Ste 670 Wichita (67207) ***(G-13695)***
Americas Best Value Inn...620 793-8486
3500 10th St Great Bend (67530) ***(G-2507)***
AmericInn Hotel, Salina *Also called Summit Hotel Properties Inc* ***(G-10720)***
AmericInn Motel & Suites...913 367-4000
500 Us Hwy 73 S Atchison (66002) ***(G-203)***
Americold Logistics LLC...316 838-9317
2707 N Mead St Wichita (67219) ***(G-13696)***
Americold Logistics LLC...620 276-2304
2007 W Mary St Garden City (67846) ***(G-2100)***
Amerine Utilities Construction...620 792-1223
252 Se 10 Ave Great Bend (67530) ***(G-2508)***
Ameripath Inc...816 412-7003
10101 Renner Blvd A Lenexa (66219) ***(G-5653)***
Ameriprice Financial, Wichita *Also called Ameriprise Financial Inc* ***(G-13697)***
Ameripride Linen, Topeka *Also called Ameripride Services Inc* ***(G-12324)***
Ameripride Services Inc...785 234-3475
400 Se 1st Ave Topeka (66607) ***(G-12324)***
Ameriprise Financial Inc...316 858-1506
10333 E 21st St N Ste 402 Wichita (67206) ***(G-13697)***
Ameriprise Financial Inc...913 239-8140
5700 W 112th St Ste 130 Leawood (66211) ***(G-5323)***
Ameriprise Financial Services, Leawood *Also called Ameriprise Fincl Ameriprise* ***(G-5324)***
Ameriprise Financial Svcs Inc...913 451-2811
6800 College Blvd Ste 500 Shawnee Mission (66211) ***(G-11109)***
Ameriprise Fincl Ameriprise...913 451-2811
4550 W 109th St Ste 200 Leawood (66211) ***(G-5324)***
Ameripure Water Company...913 825-6600
2704 W 43rd Ave Kansas City (66103) ***(G-3806)***
Ameritas Life Insurance Corp...785 273-3504
6540 Sw 10th Ave Topeka (66615) ***(G-12325)***
Ameritrust Group Inc...913 339-5000
11880 College Blvd # 500 Overland Park (66210) ***(G-8381)***
Ametek Advanced Industries Inc...316 522-0424
4550 S Southeast Blvd Wichita (67210) ***(G-13698)***
Ametek Arcft Parts & ACC Inc...316 264-2397
1414 S Mosley Ave Wichita (67211) ***(G-13699)***
AMF Bowling Centers Inc...913 451-6400
10201 College Blvd Overland Park (66210) ***(G-8382)***
AMI Metals Inc...316 945-7771
2300 S Hoover Rd Wichita (67209) ***(G-13700)***
Amino Bros Co Inc...913 334-2330
8110 Kaw Dr Kansas City (66111) ***(G-3807)***
Amli At Regents Crest, Shawnee Mission *Also called Amli Management Company* ***(G-11110)***
Amli Management Company...913 851-3200
8500 W 131st Ter Overland Park (66213) ***(G-8383)***
Amli Management Company...913 685-3700
12401 W 120th St Shawnee Mission (66213) ***(G-11110)***
Amos Family Inc (PA)...913 631-7314
10901 Johnson Dr Shawnee Mission (66203) ***(G-11111)***
Amos Family Funeral Home, Shawnee Mission *Also called Amos Family Inc* ***(G-11111)***
Amphenol Adronics Inc...785 625-3000
608 E 13th St Hays (67601) ***(G-2747)***
AMR, Topeka *Also called Medevac Midamerica Inc* ***(G-12878)***
AMS, Wichita *Also called Affiliated Medical Svcs Lab* ***(G-13641)***
Amsted Rail Company Inc (PA)...913 956-2400
8101 College Blvd Ste 200 Overland Park (66210) ***(G-8384)***
Amsted Rail Company Inc...913 299-2223
7111 Griffin Rd Kansas City (66111) ***(G-3808)***
Amsted Rail Company Inc...913 367-7200
2604 Industrial Rd Atchison (66002) ***(G-204)***
Amsted Rail Company Inc...800 621-8442
2604 Industry St Atchison (66002) ***(G-205)***
Amsted RPS, Overland Park *Also called Amsted Rail Company Inc* ***(G-8384)***
Amstutz, Samuel W, Wichita *Also called Grene Vision Group LLC* ***(G-14514)***
Amstutz, Samuel W MD, Wichita *Also called Grene Vision Group LLC* ***(G-14516)***
Amsurg, Topeka *Also called Endoscopy & Surgery Ctr Topeka* ***(G-12577)***
Amtrust AG Insurance Svcs LLC...844 350-2767
11300 Tomahawk Crk Pkwy # 300 Leawood (66211) ***(G-5325)***
Amusement Service Division, Wichita *Also called United Distributors Inc* ***(G-15841)***
AMZ Construction Inc...913 915-7867
14561 Greentree Ln Olathe (66061) ***(G-7529)***
Anadarko Petroleum Corporation...620 544-4344
P.O. Box 40 Hugoton (67951) ***(G-3148)***
Anatomi Imaging, Wichita *Also called M R Imaging Center LP* ***(G-14993)***
Anatomi Imaging...316 858-4091
2734 N Woodlawn Blvd Wichita (67220) ***(G-13701)***
Anatomical Pathology Services...620 421-2424
1902 S Us Highway 59 D Parsons (67357) ***(G-9666)***
Anchor Properties Inc (PA)...913 661-2250
6400 W 110th St Ste 201 Shawnee Mission (66211) ***(G-11112)***
Ancient Formulas Inc...316 838-5600
1235 S Santa Fe St Wichita (67211) ***(G-13702)***
Ancient Free & Accepted M...785 284-3169
708 Jefferson St Sabetha (66534) ***(G-10304)***
Ancient Free & Accptd Masons...785 738-5095
965 Kansas 14 Hwy Beloit (67420) ***(G-473)***
Ancilla Center For Children...913 758-6113
4100 S 4th St Leavenworth (66048) ***(G-5202)***
Andale Construction Inc...316 832-0063
3170 N Ohio St Wichita (67219) ***(G-13703)***
Andale Ready Mix Central Inc...316 832-0063
3170 N Ohio St Wichita (67219) ***(G-13704)***
Andale Ready Mix Central Inc...316 832-0063
430 2nd St Andale (67001) ***(G-77)***
Andax Industries LLC...785 437-0604
613 W Palmer St Saint Marys (66536) ***(G-10358)***
Andbe Home Inc...785 877-2601
201 W Crane St Norton (67654) ***(G-7441)***
Andersen Corporation...913 385-1300
8180 Nieman Rd Lenexa (66214) ***(G-5654)***
Anderson & Sons Trucking Inc...913 422-3171
108 S 102nd St Kansas City (66111) ***(G-3809)***
Anderson Countian, Garnett *Also called Garnett Publishing Inc* ***(G-2373)***
Anderson County Council...785 448-4237
128 W 5th Ave Garnett (66032) ***(G-2368)***
Anderson County Hospital, Garnett *Also called Saint Lukes Hosp Garnett Inc* ***(G-2388)***
Anderson County Sales Co...785 448-3811
Hwy 59 Garnett (66032) ***(G-2369)***
Anderson Erickson Dairy Co...913 621-4801
5341 Speaker Rd Kansas City (66106) ***(G-3810)***
Anderson Industries Inc...316 945-4488
3246 W 13th St N Wichita (67203) ***(G-13705)***
Anderson Machine & Supply Inc...785 668-2233
111 Main St Smolan (67456) ***(G-12045)***
Anderson Management Company (PA)...316 681-1711
3450 N Rock Rd Ste 201 Wichita (67226) ***(G-13706)***
Anderson Rentals Inc...785 843-2044
1312 W 6th St Lawrence (66044) ***(G-4735)***
Andover Family Dentistry PA, Andover *Also called Howell Matthew D Dr DDS PA* ***(G-94)***

Andover Health Care Center......316 448-4041
621 W 21st St Andover (67002) *(G-80)*
Andover Spine & Health Ctr......316 733-9555
149 S Andover Rd Ste 400 Andover (67002) *(G-81)*
Andover State Bank (PA)......316 733-1375
511 N Andover Rd Andover (67002) *(G-82)*
Andover State Bank......316 219-1600
1718 N Webb Rd Wichita (67206) *(G-13707)*
Andover YMCA, Andover *Also called Young Mens Christian Associa (G-118)*
Andrade Auto Sales Inc......620 624-2400
153 W Pancake Blvd Liberal (67901) *(G-6278)*
Andrade Window Tinting, Liberal *Also called Andrade Auto Sales Inc (G-6278)*
Andrea Clark......913 683-3061
200 Osage St Leavenworth (66048) *(G-5203)*
Andrea Investments LLC......785 823-1739
1616 W Crawford St Salina (67401) *(G-10402)*
Andrew Inc (PA)......316 267-3328
2310 E Douglas Ave Wichita (67214) *(G-13708)*
Andrews and Abbey Riley LLC......913 262-2212
4462 State Line Rd Kansas City (66103) *(G-3811)*
Andrews Asphalt & Cnstr Inc......785 232-0188
2327 Nw 39th St Topeka (66618) *(G-12326)*
Anesthesia Assoc Kans Cy PC (PA)......913 428-2900
8717 W 110th St Ste 600 Overland Park (66210) *(G-8385)*
Anesthesia Associates Topeka......785 235-3451
823 Sw Mulvane St Ste 210 Topeka (66606) *(G-12327)*
Anesthesia Billing Inc......316 281-3700
1715 Medical Pkwy Ste 200 Newton (67114) *(G-7309)*
Anesthia Assn Centl Kans PA......785 827-2238
200 S 5th St Ste A Salina (67401) *(G-10403)*
Angel Arms......620 245-0848
318 N Main St McPherson (67460) *(G-6935)*
Angel Arms......620 241-1074
110 S Main St McPherson (67460) *(G-6936)*
Angel Arms Home Health, McPherson *Also called Angel Arms (G-6935)*
ANGEL ARMS HOME HEALTH, McPherson *Also called Angel Arms (G-6936)*
Angel Little Learning Ctr Inc......913 724-4442
1206 N 155th St Basehor (66007) *(G-372)*
Angel Square......785 534-1080
517 Washington St Concordia (66901) *(G-1102)*
Angel Wings Learning Ctr LLC......316 249-4818
770 S Greenwich Rd Wichita (67207) *(G-13709)*
Angels At Home Care......785 271-4376
112 Sw 6th Ave Ste 403 Topeka (66603) *(G-12328)*
Angels Care Home Health......316 636-4000
8200 E 34th Cir N # 1601 Wichita (67226) *(G-13710)*
Angels Little Playgrnd Daycare......785 823-1448
200 W Key Ave Salina (67401) *(G-10404)*
Angus Inn Best Western Motel......620 792-3541
2920 10th St Great Bend (67530) *(G-2509)*
Anico, Shawnee Mission *Also called American National Insurance Co (G-11106)*
Anico, Wichita *Also called Regional Insurance Service Co (G-15438)*
Animal Behavior Consultations, Westwood *Also called Westwood Animal Hospital (G-13563)*
Animal Care Center of Top......785 232-2205
2061 Se California Ave Topeka (66607) *(G-12329)*
Animal Chiropractic Center......309 658-2920
4267 Virginia Rd Wellsville (66092) *(G-13540)*
Animal Clinic North Topeka PA......785 357-5188
625 Nw Us Highway 24 Topeka (66608) *(G-12330)*
Animal Clinic Wichita PA......316 686-8516
10712 E Harry St Wichita (67207) *(G-13711)*
Animal Health Division, Shawnee Mission *Also called Bayer Healthcare LLC (G-11154)*
Animal Health Intl Inc......620 276-8289
2103 W Jones Ave Garden City (67846) *(G-2101)*
Animal Hospital of Lawrence......785 842-0609
701 Michigan St Lawrence (66044) *(G-4736)*
Animal Medical Center LLC......620 792-1265
622 Mckinley St Great Bend (67530) *(G-2510)*
Animal Resource Falicity, Manhattan *Also called Kansas State University (G-6689)*
Anixter Inc......620 365-7161
502 N State St Iola (66749) *(G-3587)*
Anixter Inc......913 492-2622
10457 W 84th Ter Overland Park (66214) *(G-8386)*
Anixter Power Solutions Inc......913 202-6945
4600 Kansas Ave Kansas City (66106) *(G-3812)*
Ann Arbor Railroad Inc......620 231-2230
315 W 3rd St Pittsburg (66762) *(G-9809)*
Ann Barber......913 788-0800
9501 State Ave Ste 7 Kansas City (66111) *(G-3813)*
Ann N Hogan LLC......913 271-7440
6302 W 295th St Louisburg (66053) *(G-6438)*
Anna M Kramer......785 353-2205
2014 Granite Rd Beattie (66406) *(G-417)*
Annan Marketing Services Inc......913 254-0050
12603 Hemlock St Ste B Overland Park (66213) *(G-8387)*
Anodizing Inc......620 223-1111
2401 S Main St Fort Scott (66701) *(G-1955)*
Another Day Homecare Inc......913 599-2221
11802 W 77th St Lenexa (66214) *(G-5655)*
ANR Pipeline Company......620 723-2381
15499 19th Ave Greensburg (67054) *(G-2672)*
ANR Pipeline Company......785 948-2670
19955 English Ridge Rd Havensville (66432) *(G-2739)*
ANR Pipeline Company......785 479-5814
1615 Nail Rd Enterprise (67441) *(G-1853)*
Answer Link......620 662-4427
107 W 1st Ave Hutchinson (67501) *(G-3199)*
Answer Media LLC......816 984-8853
2020 W 89th St Ste 200 Leawood (66206) *(G-5326)*
Answer Topeka Inc......785 234-4444
1717 Sw Gage Blvd Topeka (66604) *(G-12331)*
Answering Exchange Inc......316 262-8282
1443 S George Wash Dr Wichita (67211) *(G-13712)*
Answernet Inc......785 301-2810
2000 E 13th St Hays (67601) *(G-2748)*
Antech Diagnostics Inc......913 529-4392
11950 W 110th St Overland Park (66210) *(G-8388)*
Antes Concrete Inc......913 856-4535
30914 W 119th St Olathe (66061) *(G-7530)*
Anthem Media LLC (PA)......913 894-6923
4303 W 119th St Leawood (66209) *(G-5327)*
Anthem Media Group, Leawood *Also called Anthem Media LLC (G-5327)*
Anthem Motorsports Inc......913 894-6923
4303 W 119th St Leawood (66209) *(G-5328)*
Anthony Inc......913 384-4440
15203 W 99th St Lenexa (66219) *(G-5656)*
Anthony Family Shelter, Wichita *Also called Catholic Charities Inc (G-13960)*
Anthony Frmrs Coop Elev Cmpnys (PA)......620 842-5181
519 W Main St Anthony (67003) *(G-119)*
Anthony Livestock Sales Co......620 842-3757
624 S Jennings Ave Anthony (67003) *(G-120)*
Anthony Plumbing Htg & Coolg, Lenexa *Also called Anthony Inc (G-5656)*
Anthony Police Department, Anthony *Also called City of Anthony (G-123)*
Antioch Church......785 232-1937
1921 Se Indiana Ave Topeka (66607) *(G-12332)*
ANTIOCH FAMILY LIFE CENTER, Topeka *Also called Antioch Church (G-12332)*
Antoine E Wakim DDS PA, Wichita *Also called Antoine E Wakim Inc (G-13713)*
Antoine E Wakim Inc......316 721-4477
710 N Woodchuck St Wichita (67212) *(G-13713)*
Antrim & Assoc......316 267-2753
7303 E Bayley St Wichita (67207) *(G-13714)*
Aoscloud, Overland Park *Also called Unitas Global LLC (G-9441)*
AP Roofing Specialty Codings......620 532-1076
602 N Defonte St Kingman (67068) *(G-4582)*
AP Travel, Shawnee Mission *Also called A & P Cruises & Tours (G-11060)*
Apac-Kansas Inc......620 662-3307
1600 N Lorraine St Ste 1 Hutchinson (67501) *(G-3200)*
Apac-Kansas Inc......785 524-4413
1160 N Highway 14 Lincoln (67455) *(G-6379)*
Apac-Kansas Inc......316 321-3221
5143 Sw Hwy 254 El Dorado (67042) *(G-1528)*
Apac-Kansas Inc......785 823-8944
Rr 3 Salina (67401) *(G-10405)*
Apac-Kansas Inc......785 625-3459
820 Cantebury Rd Hays (67601) *(G-2749)*
Apac-Kansas Inc......620 227-6908
11188 56th Byp Dodge City (67801) *(G-1293)*
Apac-Kansas Inc......620 342-2047
302 Peyton St Emporia (66801) *(G-1695)*
Apac-Kansas Inc......785 823-5537
1622 Sunflower Rd Salina (67401) *(G-10406)*
Apac-Kansas Inc......785 625-3459
5603 E 4th Ave Hutchinson (67501) *(G-3201)*
Apac-Kansas Inc......620 392-5771
669 County Road Z Hartford (66854) *(G-2726)*
Apac-Kansas Inc......316 522-4881
3511 S West St Wichita (67217) *(G-13715)*
Apac-Kansas Inc......316 524-5200
3615 S West St Wichita (67217) *(G-13716)*
Apac-Kansas Inc......620 662-2112
819 W 1st Ave Hutchinson (67501) *(G-3202)*
Apac-Kansas Inc......316 775-7639
11221 Sw Us Highway 54 Augusta (67010) *(G-300)*
Apartment Credit Service, Shawnee Mission *Also called ACS Data Search LLC (G-11070)*
Apartment Movers Inc......316 267-5300
150 N Osage St Wichita (67203) *(G-13717)*
APC Inc......620 675-8691
Hwy 83 N Hc 1 Sublette (67877) *(G-12197)*
Apc-Sublette, Sublette *Also called APC Inc (G-12197)*
Apex Construction Inc......913 341-3688
13315 W 91st St Lenexa (66215) *(G-5657)*
Apex Engineering Intl LLC (HQ)......316 262-1494
1804 W 2nd St N Wichita (67203) *(G-13718)*
Apex Innovations Inc......913 254-0250
19951 W 162nd St Olathe (66062) *(G-7531)*
Apex Trucking Inc (PA)......316 943-0774
6031 N Prospect Rd Park City (67204) *(G-9601)*

ALPHABETIC

API Americas Inc (HQ).......732 382-6800
3841 Greenway Cir Lawrence (66046) ***(G-4737)***
API Foils, Lawrence *Also called API Americas Inc* ***(G-4737)***
Apollo Energies Inc.......620 672-5071
40134 N Us Highway 281 Pratt (67124) ***(G-10097)***
Apollon Computers Inc.......316 264-2329
8351 E 35th St N Wichita (67226) ***(G-13719)***
Apostolic Christian Home.......785 284-3471
511 Paramount St Sabetha (66534) ***(G-10305)***
Apothecare, Pittsburg *Also called Community Hlth Ctr Sthast Kans* ***(G-9841)***
Appellate Defender Office, Topeka *Also called Indigents Defense Svcs Kans Bd* ***(G-12719)***
Apph Wichita Inc.......316 943-5752
1445 S Sierra Dr Wichita (67209) ***(G-13720)***
Appino Biggs Reporting Svc Inc (PA).......785 273-3063
5111 Sw 21st St Topeka (66604) ***(G-12333)***
Apple Bus Company.......913 592-5121
802 S A Line Dr Spring Hill (66083) ***(G-12077)***
Apple Butte Company, Osawatomie *Also called Durham School Services L P* ***(G-8192)***
Apple Central LLC Applebe.......203 987-6162
P.O. Box 780732 Wichita (67278) ***(G-13721)***
Apple Eght Hospitality MGT Inc.......913 338-3600
12440 Blue Valley Pkwy Overland Park (66213) ***(G-8389)***
Apple Eght Hospitality MGT Inc.......316 636-4600
2975 N Webb Rd Wichita (67226) ***(G-13722)***
Apple Eght Hospitality MGT Inc.......913 491-0010
12000 Blue Valley Pkwy Shawnee Mission (66213) ***(G-11113)***
Apple Eght Svcs Ovrland Pk Inc.......913 327-7484
12010 Blue Valley Pkwy Overland Park (66213) ***(G-8390)***
Apple Electric Inc.......913 837-5285
209 N Broadway St Louisburg (66053) ***(G-6439)***
Apple Lane Animal Hospital.......620 662-0515
2909 Apple Ln Hutchinson (67502) ***(G-3203)***
Apple Tree Inn.......620 331-5500
201 N 8th St Independence (67301) ***(G-3497)***
Apple Tree Kid Day Out/Presch.......913 888-3702
10551 Quivira Rd Shawnee Mission (66215) ***(G-11114)***
Appletech Design & Cnstr Inc.......785 776-3530
240 Levee Dr Ste 1 Manhattan (66502) ***(G-6543)***
Applewood Rehabilation Inc.......620 431-7300
20526 1700 Rd Altoona (66710) ***(G-75)***
Appliance Doctor Inc.......316 263-0005
1123 E Pawnee St Wichita (67211) ***(G-13723)***
Appliance Doctor, The, Wichita *Also called Appliance Doctor Inc* ***(G-13723)***
Applied Content RES Tech LLC.......785 422-4980
205 E Main St Morland (67650) ***(G-7166)***
Applied Ecological Svcs Inc.......785 594-2245
224 E 1260th Rd Baldwin City (66006) ***(G-354)***
Applied Industrial Tech 0471, Topeka *Also called Applied Industrial Tech Inc* ***(G-12334)***
Applied Industrial Tech Inc.......785 232-5508
115 Nw Jackson St Topeka (66603) ***(G-12334)***
Appraisal Office Ford County.......620 227-4570
100 Gunsmoke St Dodge City (67801) ***(G-1294)***
Appraisers Office, Winfield *Also called County of Cowley* ***(G-16128)***
Apprentice Personnel Inc.......316 267-4781
328 S Laura Ave Wichita (67211) ***(G-13724)***
Apria Healthcare LLC.......316 689-4500
318 N Cleveland Ave Wichita (67214) ***(G-13725)***
Apria Healthcare LLC.......785 272-8411
6261 Sw 9th St Ste B Topeka (66615) ***(G-12335)***
Apria Healthcare LLC.......913 492-2212
16815 College Blvd Lenexa (66219) ***(G-5658)***
Apria Healthcare LLC.......316 283-1936
2305 S Kansas Rd Newton (67114) ***(G-7310)***
Apria Healthcare LLC.......949 616-2606
2600 Central Ave Ste 7 Dodge City (67801) ***(G-1295)***
APS Staffing Services Inc.......913 327-7605
7015 College Blvd Ste 150 Overland Park (66211) ***(G-8391)***
Apu Solutions, Overland Park *Also called PS Holdings LLC* ***(G-9201)***
Aquent LLC.......913 345-9119
7450 W 130th St Ste 100 Shawnee Mission (66213) ***(G-11115)***
Aquila Networks, Great Bend *Also called Evergy Missouri West Inc* ***(G-2561)***
AR Commercial Roofing LLC.......620 672-3332
40100 N Us Highway 281 Pratt (67124) ***(G-10098)***
Aragon Apts, Wichita *Also called Griffith Developement* ***(G-14518)***
Aramark Unf & Career AP LLC.......316 262-5467
521 W Walker St Wichita (67213) ***(G-13726)***
Aramark Unf & Career AP LLC.......913 351-3534
123 American Ave Lansing (66043) ***(G-4667)***
Aratana Therapeutics Inc (HQ).......913 353-1000
11400 Tomahawk Creek Pkwy # 340 Leawood (66211) ***(G-5329)***
Arbor Masters Tree Service, Wichita *Also called Shawnee Mission Tree Svc Inc* ***(G-15578)***
Arbor Msters/SMC Utility Cnstr, Shawnee *Also called Shawnee Mission Tree Svc Inc* ***(G-11029)***
Arbuthnot Drug, Belleville *Also called Arbuthnots Inc* ***(G-450)***
Arbuthnots Inc.......785 527-2146
1806 M St Belleville (66935) ***(G-450)***
ARC, Arkansas City *Also called American National Red Cross* ***(G-142)***
ARC, Hays *Also called Countryside of Hays Inc* ***(G-2777)***
ARC Document Solutions.......316 264-9344
518 W Douglas Ave Wichita (67203) ***(G-13727)***
ARC Document Solutions Inc.......816 300-6600
1100 W Cambrdg Cir Dr 300 Kansas City (66103) ***(G-3814)***
ARC Document Solutions Inc.......314 231-5025
1100 W Cambrdg Circl 300 Kansas City (66103) ***(G-3815)***
ARC Document Solutions Inc.......316 264-9344
518 W Douglas Ave Wichita (67203) ***(G-13728)***
ARC of Sedgwick County Inc.......316 943-1191
2919 W 2nd St N Wichita (67203) ***(G-13729)***
ARC Physica Thera Plus Limite (PA).......913 831-2721
6400 Glenwood St Ste 111 Shawnee Mission (66202) ***(G-11116)***
Arcadis US Inc.......913 492-4156
Rosehill Offc Pk 1 Lenexa (66215) ***(G-5659)***
Arch Design Builders LLC.......913 599-5565
11100 W 91st St Ste 200 Overland Park (66214) ***(G-8392)***
Arch Roofing, Overland Park *Also called Arch Design Builders LLC* ***(G-8392)***
Archdiocese Kansas Cy In Kans.......913 631-0004
11525 Johnson Dr Shawnee Mission (66203) ***(G-11117)***
Archdiocese Kansas Cy In Kans.......913 621-5090
2220 Central Ave Kansas City (66102) ***(G-3816)***
Archdiocese of Kansas City, Kansas City *Also called Catholic Charities of* ***(G-3895)***
Archdiocese of Miami Inc.......785 233-6300
234 S Kansas Ave Topeka (66603) ***(G-12336)***
Archein Aerospace LLC.......682 499-2150
4601 E Douglas Ave # 321 Wichita (67218) ***(G-13730)***
Archer-Daniels-Midland Company.......913 782-8800
100 S Paniplus Dr Olathe (66061) ***(G-7532)***
Archer-Daniels-Midland Company.......785 263-2260
1000 N Washington St Abilene (67410) ***(G-12)***
Archer-Daniels-Midland Company.......620 675-8520
2502 Hwy 56 Copeland (67837) ***(G-1148)***
Archer-Daniels-Midland Company.......785 825-1541
850 E Pacific Ave Salina (67401) ***(G-10407)***
Archer-Daniels-Midland Company.......620 375-4811
505 N 4th St Leoti (67861) ***(G-6250)***
Archer-Daniels-Midland Company.......620 872-2174
181 N Front St Scott City (67871) ***(G-10804)***
Archer-Daniels-Midland Company.......785 820-8019
124 S 4th St Salina (67401) ***(G-10408)***
Archer-Daniels-Midland Company.......785 263-2260
210 Ne 3rd St Abilene (67410) ***(G-13)***
Archer-Daniels-Midland Company.......913 321-1696
940 Kindleberger Rd Kansas City (66115) ***(G-3817)***
Archer-Daniels-Midland Company.......620 357-8733
1122 Main St Jetmore (67854) ***(G-3645)***
Archer-Daniels-Midland Company.......620 675-2226
1892 Hwy 83 Sublette (67877) ***(G-12198)***
Archer-Daniels-Midland Company.......620 846-2218
28605 12 Rd Montezuma (67867) ***(G-7154)***
Archer-Daniels-Midland Company.......913 491-9400
8000 W 110th St Overland Park (66210) ***(G-8393)***
Archer-Daniels-Midland Company.......620 657-3411
6500 S Road X Satanta (67870) ***(G-10776)***
Archer-Daniels-Midland Company.......913 491-9400
8000 W 110th St Ste 300 Overland Park (66210) ***(G-8394)***
Archer-Daniels-Midland Company.......620 663-7957
1700 N Halstead St Hutchinson (67501) ***(G-3204)***
Archer-Daniels-Midland Company.......620 663-7278
816 N Halstead St Hutchinson (67501) ***(G-3205)***
Archer-Daniels-Midland Company.......785 671-3171
104 S Freeman Ave Oakley (67748) ***(G-7471)***
Archer-Daniels-Midland Company.......785 694-2286
410 Railroad Ave Brewster (67732) ***(G-582)***
Archer-Daniels-Midland Company.......620 659-2099
Hwy 56 & Colony Ave Kinsley (67547) ***(G-4614)***
Archer-Daniels-Midland Company.......785 820-8831
1884a E Old Highway 40 New Cambria (67470) ***(G-7269)***
Archer-Daniels-Midland Company.......785 737-4135
104 S Main St Palco (67657) ***(G-9537)***
Archer-Daniels-Midland Company.......785 899-3700
6425 Road 14 Goodland (67735) ***(G-2462)***
Architectural Cast Metals Inc.......785 221-6901
5600 Sw Topeka Blvd Ste D Topeka (66609) ***(G-12337)***
Architectural Cast Stone Inc.......316 262-5543
1918 N Wabash Ave Wichita (67214) ***(G-13731)***
Architectural Concrete Pdts, Wichita *Also called Architectural Cast Stone Inc* ***(G-13731)***
Archon Residential MGT LP.......913 631-2100
7530 Cody St Shawnee Mission (66214) ***(G-11118)***
Archrock Inc.......620 241-8740
1404 Mohawk Rd McPherson (67460) ***(G-6937)***
Arckc, Overland Park *Also called Allergy Rhmtlogy Clnics Kc LLC* ***(G-8369)***
Arco Supply Co, Wichita *Also called Superior Plumbing of Wichita* ***(G-15696)***
Arconic Inc.......620 665-2932
1501 Airport Rd Hutchinson (67501) ***(G-3206)***
Arctic Glacier Ice, Wichita *Also called Arctic Glacier Texas Inc* ***(G-13732)***
Arctic Glacier Inc.......620 275-5751
102 N 9th St Garden City (67846) ***(G-2102)***
Arctic Glacier Texas Inc.......316 529-2173
215 E 27th St S Wichita (67216) ***(G-13732)***

Area 5, Wichita *Also called Kansas Department Trnsp* ***(G-14796)***
Area Mntl Hlth Cmnty Sprt Svc, Dodge City *Also called Compass Behavioral Health* ***(G-1328)***
Arensman Services 620 430-1106
1003 Briggs Ave Kinsley (67547) ***(G-4615)***
Arg Contracting LLC 913 441-1992
8167 Cole Pkwy Lenexa (66227) ***(G-5660)***
Argentine Savings and Ln Assn (PA) 913 831-2004
3004 Strong Ave Kansas City (66106) ***(G-3818)***
Argonna Post 180 Amercn Legion 620 793-5912
1011 Kansas Ave Great Bend (67530) ***(G-2511)***
Argus Consulting Inc (PA) 816 228-7500
6363 College Blvd Ste 600 Overland Park (66211) ***(G-8395)***
Argyle Winery, Overland Park *Also called Lion Nathan Usa Inc* ***(G-8960)***
Arj Infusion Services Inc (PA) 913 451-8804
7930 Marshall Dr Lenexa (66214) ***(G-5661)***
Ark City Clinic P A 620 442-2100
510 W Radio Ln Arkansas City (67005) ***(G-143)***
Ark City Warehouse Truckline 620 442-7305
1105 W Madison Ave Arkansas City (67005) ***(G-144)***
Ark Valley Distributing Inc 620 221-6500
7748 2nd Ave Arkansas City (67005) ***(G-145)***
Ark Valley Electric Coop Assn 620 662-6661
10 E 10th Ave South Hutchinson (67505) ***(G-12055)***
Ark Valley Veterinary Hospital 620 793-5457
1205 Patton Rd Great Bend (67530) ***(G-2512)***
Ark Veterinary Associates PA 620 442-3306
907 E Kansas Ave Arkansas City (67005) ***(G-146)***
Arkalon Energy LLC 620 624-2901
300 N Lincoln Ave Liberal (67901) ***(G-6279)***
Arkansas City Presbt Manor Inc 620 442-8700
1711 N 4th St Arkansas City (67005) ***(G-147)***
Arkansas City Traveler, Arkansas City *Also called Morris Communications Co LLC* ***(G-167)***
Arko Manufacturing Co Inc 316 838-7162
3545 N Broadway Ave Wichita (67219) ***(G-13733)***
Arla Jean Genstler MD PA 785 537-3400
1502 Browning Pl Manhattan (66502) ***(G-6544)***
Arla Jean Genstler MD PA (PA) 785 273-8080
3630 Sw Fairlawn Rd Topeka (66614) ***(G-12338)***
Arlwin Mfg Co Inc 785 282-6487
720 E Highway 36 Smith Center (66967) ***(G-12031)***
Arma Care Center LLC 620 347-4103
605 E Melvin St Arma (66712) ***(G-188)***
Armdat Inc 913 321-4287
18 Central Ave Kansas City (66118) ***(G-3819)***
Armed Forces Bank Nat Assn (HQ) 913 682-9090
320 Kansas Ave Fort Leavenworth (66027) ***(G-1934)***
Armed Forces Bank Nat Assn 913 651-2992
330 Kansas Ave Bldg 700 Fort Leavenworth (66027) ***(G-1935)***
Armed Forces Bank Nat Assn 785 238-2241
429 W 18th St Junction City (66441) ***(G-3667)***
Armed Forces Insurance Exhange 913 651-5000
550 Eisenhower Rd Leavenworth (66048) ***(G-5204)***
Armed Services YMCA of USA 785 238-2972
111 E 16th St Junction City (66441) ***(G-3668)***
Armfield Dentistry, Augusta *Also called Mark H Armfield DDS* ***(G-333)***
Armstrong Creative Services 316 522-3000
7450 S Seneca St Haysville (67060) ***(G-2937)***
Armstrong Plumbing Inc 316 942-9535
7540 W Northwind St # 300 Wichita (67205) ***(G-13734)***
Armstrong Shank, Haysville *Also called Armstrong Creative Services* ***(G-2937)***
Army & Air Force Exchange Svc 785 239-4366
7485 Fort Riley Campus Fort Riley (66442) ***(G-1945)***
Arnold & Associates of Wichita (PA) 316 263-9283
530 S Topeka Ave Wichita (67202) ***(G-13735)***
Arnold Katz MD 913 888-3231
10550 Quivira Rd Ste 320 Shawnee Mission (66215) ***(G-11119)***
Arnolds Greenhouse Inc 620 964-2463
1430 Highway 58 Le Roy (66857) ***(G-5195)***
Arr Roofing LLC 913 829-0447
1060 W Santa Fe St Olathe (66061) ***(G-7533)***
Arrow Acquisition LLC 913 495-4869
16000 W 108th St Lenexa (66219) ***(G-5662)***
Arrow Dynamics, Topeka *Also called Glen Thurber* ***(G-12638)***
Arrow Electronics Inc 913 242-3012
7500 College Blvd Ste 500 Overland Park (66210) ***(G-8396)***
Arrow Fork Lift Parts Inc 816 231-4410
16000 W 108th St Lenexa (66219) ***(G-5663)***
Arrow Laboratory Inc 316 267-2893
1333 N Main St Wichita (67203) ***(G-13736)***
Arrow Material Handling Pdts, Lenexa *Also called Arrow Acquisition LLC* ***(G-5662)***
Arrow Printing Company Inc 785 825-8124
115 W Woodland Ave Salina (67401) ***(G-10409)***
Arrow Renovation & Cnstr LLC 913 703-3000
305 E Dennis Ave Olathe (66061) ***(G-7534)***
Arrow Stage Lines, Manhattan *Also called Busco Inc* ***(G-6573)***
Arrow Towing & Recovery, Wichita *Also called Arrow Wrecker Service Inc* ***(G-13737)***
Arrow Valve Co Inc 620 879-2126
201 N Foreman St Caney (67333) ***(G-665)***
Arrow Wrecker Service Inc 316 267-6621
531 E Macarthur Rd Wichita (67216) ***(G-13737)***
Arrow Zeus Electronics, Overland Park *Also called Arrow Electronics Inc* ***(G-8396)***
Arrowhead Apartments, Shawnee Mission *Also called Archon Residential MGT LP* ***(G-11118)***
Arrowhead Contracting Inc 913 814-9994
10981 Eicher Dr Lenexa (66219) ***(G-5664)***
Arrowhead Drywall Supply, Olathe *Also called L & W Supply Corporation* ***(G-7847)***
Arrowhead Intermodal Svcs LLC 816 509-0746
32355 W 191st St Edgerton (66021) ***(G-1479)***
Arrowhead West Inc 620 225-4061
231 San Jose Dodge City (67801) ***(G-1296)***
Arrowhead West Inc (PA) 620 227-8803
1100 E Wyatt Earp Blvd Dodge City (67801) ***(G-1297)***
Arrowhead West Inc 316 722-4554
613 N Ridge Rd Ste 105 Wichita (67212) ***(G-13738)***
Arrowhead West Inc 620 886-3711
Hwys 281 & 160 Medicine Lodge (67104) ***(G-7056)***
Arrowhead West Inc 620 225-5177
401 Edgemore St Dodge City (67801) ***(G-1298)***
Arrowood Indemnity Company 913 345-1776
7500 College Blvd Ste 650 Shawnee Mission (66210) ***(G-11120)***
Arroyo, Zeferino J, Garden City *Also called Garden Surgical Assoc* ***(G-2183)***
ARS Reporting LLC 913 422-5198
22052 W 66th St Ste 314 Shawnee (66226) ***(G-10911)***
Arsi, Wichita *Also called Account Rcvery Specialists Inc* ***(G-13603)***
Art Craft Printers & Design 785 776-9151
317 Houston St Ste B Manhattan (66502) ***(G-6545)***
Art of Escape Ict 316 768-2588
3540 W Douglas Ave Ste 4 Wichita (67203) ***(G-13739)***
Art Studio Signs & Design, Hutchinson *Also called Artstudio Signs & Design* ***(G-3207)***
Artco Casket Co Inc (PA) 913 438-2655
16023 W 99th St Lenexa (66219) ***(G-5665)***
Arteyeview Productions 316 737-7080
2280 N Williamsgate Ct Wichita (67228) ***(G-13740)***
Artheritis Specs of Gtr Kns Cy, Shawnee Mission *Also called Arnold Katz MD* ***(G-11119)***
Arthritis and Rheumatology (PA) 316 612-4815
1921 N Webb Rd Wichita (67206) ***(G-13741)***
Arthritis RES Ctr Foundation 316 263-2125
1035 N Emporia St Ste 288 Wichita (67214) ***(G-13742)***
Arthur David Garcia, Wichita *Also called Superior Masonry & Stucco LLC* ***(G-15695)***
Arthur Dogswell LLC 620 231-7779
1601 W Mckay St Frontenac (66763) ***(G-2052)***
Arthur Green LLP 785 537-1345
801 Poyntz Ave Manhattan (66502) ***(G-6546)***
Artistic Marble & Bath, Wichita *Also called Artistic Marble LLC* ***(G-13743)***
Artistic Marble LLC 316 944-8713
4325 W Harry St Wichita (67209) ***(G-13743)***
Arts Mexican Products Inc 913 371-2163
615 Kansas Ave Kansas City (66105) ***(G-3820)***
Artstudio Signs & Design 620 663-3950
3010 N Plum St Hutchinson (67502) ***(G-3207)***
Artz Dee Jay Insurance Agency, Dodge City *Also called Dee Jays Enterprises* ***(G-1340)***
Arveda Llc 785 625-4674
718 Main St Ste 201 Hays (67601) ***(G-2750)***
Arvest Bank 417 627-8000
2313 S Rouse St Pittsburg (66762) ***(G-9810)***
Arvest Bank 913 953-4070
10685 Mission Rd Leawood (66206) ***(G-5330)***
Arvest Bank 913 953-4000
7401 W 135th St Overland Park (66223) ***(G-8397)***
Arvest Bank 785 229-3950
119 E 3rd St Ottawa (66067) ***(G-8245)***
Arvest Bank 913 279-3300
306 E Main St Gardner (66030) ***(G-2327)***
Arvest Bank 620 879-5811
301 W 4th Ave Caney (67333) ***(G-666)***
Arvest Bank Operations Inc 913 261-2265
6300 Nall Ave Ste 100 Shawnee Mission (66202) ***(G-11121)***
Arwood Waste Inc 316 448-1576
4100 N West St Wichita (67205) ***(G-13744)***
Ary Inc (HQ) 913 214-4813
5200 W 110th St Ste 200 Overland Park (66211) ***(G-8398)***
Ary Professional Cutlery Div, Overland Park *Also called Ary Inc* ***(G-8398)***
ASAP Transport Solutions LLC 800 757-1178
11248 Strang Line Rd Lenexa (66215) ***(G-5666)***
Asbury Park Inc 316 283-4770
200 Sw 14th St Newton (67114) ***(G-7311)***
ASC Formation, Wichita *Also called Adorers of Bld of Chrst* ***(G-13615)***
Ascend Learning LLC (HQ) 855 856-7705
11161 Overbrook Rd Leawood (66211) ***(G-5331)***
Ascend Learning Holdings LLC (PA) 800 667-7531
11161 Overbrook Rd Leawood (66211) ***(G-5332)***
Ascend Mdia Med Healthcare LLC 913 469-1110
171 W 95th Ste 300 Overland Park (66212) ***(G-8399)***
Ascension Arizona 316 689-5360
3600 E Harry St Wichita (67218) ***(G-13745)***
Ascension Health, Shawnee *Also called Carondelet Home Care Services* ***(G-10924)***

ALPHABETIC

Ascension Insur Holdings LLC 800 955-1991
9225 Indian Creek Pkwy # 700 Overland Park (66210) ***(G-8400)***
Ascension Via Christi (PA)........620 231-6100
1 Mt Carmel Way Pittsburg (66762) ***(G-9811)***
Ascension Via Christi........620 231-3088
3 Medical Ctr Cir Ste B Pittsburg (66762) ***(G-9812)***
Ascension Via Christi........620 231-6788
411 E 12th St Pittsburg (66762) ***(G-9813)***
Ascension Via Christi........620 232-0178
1 Med Center Cir Ste B Pittsburg (66762) ***(G-9814)***
Ascension Via Christi Home Med (HQ)........316 265-4991
555 S Washington Ave # 101 Wichita (67211) ***(G-13746)***
Ascension Via Christi Hospital (HQ)........316 268-5880
929 N St Francis St Wichita (67214) ***(G-13747)***
Ascension Via Christi Hospital 316 687-1555
848 N St Francis St # 1962 Wichita (67214) ***(G-13748)***
Ascension Via Christi Hospital 316 721-9500
8444 W 21st St N Wichita (67205) ***(G-13749)***
Ascension Via Christi Hospital 316 268-6096
929 N St Francis St Wichita (67214) ***(G-13750)***
Ascension Via Christi Hospital 316 634-3400
1151 N Rock Rd Wichita (67206) ***(G-13751)***
Ascension Via Christi Hospital 316 268-5040
848 N St Francis St Wichita (67214) ***(G-13752)***
Asd Specialty Healthcare LLC........913 492-5505
9652 Loiret Blvd Shawnee Mission (66219) ***(G-11122)***
Ase Group Inc........913 339-9333
6600 College Blvd Ste 310 Leawood (66211) ***(G-5333)***
Aseracare Hospice, Lawrence *Also called Hospice Preferred Choice Inc* ***(G-4903)***
Asgn Incorporated........913 341-9100
7171 W 95th St Overland Park (66212) ***(G-8401)***
Ash Grove Aggregates Inc (HQ)........660 679-4128
11011 Cody St Ste 300 Overland Park (66210) ***(G-8402)***
Ash Grove Cement Company (HQ)........913 451-8900
11011 Cody St Ste 300 Overland Park (66210) ***(G-8403)***
Ash Grove Cement Company........620 433-3500
1801 N Santa Fe Ave Chanute (66720) ***(G-703)***
Ash Grove Cement Company........913 422-2523
8440 Gibbs Rd Kansas City (66111) ***(G-3821)***
Ash Grove Cement Company........785 267-1996
1520 Sw 41st St Topeka (66609) ***(G-12339)***
Ash Grove Materials Corp (HQ)........913 345-2030
11011 Cody St Ste 300 Overland Park (66210) ***(G-8404)***
Ash Grove Resources LLC........785 267-1996
5375 Sw 7th St Ste 400 Topeka (66606) ***(G-12340)***
Ashbury Children Center, Shawnee Mission *Also called Ashbury Church Pre School* ***(G-11123)***
Ashbury Church Pre School........913 432-5573
5400 W 75th St Shawnee Mission (66208) ***(G-11123)***
Ashby House Ltd........785 826-4935
150 S 8th St Salina (67401) ***(G-10410)***
Ashland Feed & Seed Co (PA)........620 635-2856
S Main & Santa Fe St Ashland (67831) ***(G-193)***
Ashland Feeders, Ashland *Also called Pratt Feeders LLC* ***(G-197)***
Ashland Health Center, Ashland *Also called Hospital District 3 Clark Cnty* ***(G-196)***
Ashleys House Learning Center (PA)........316 941-9877
7150 W Harry St Wichita (67209) ***(G-13753)***
Asi Computer Technologies Inc........913 888-8843
15000 W 106th St Lenexa (66215) ***(G-5667)***
Asian Amrcn Chmber of Commerce........913 338-0774
8645 College Blvd Ste 110 Shawnee Mission (66210) ***(G-11124)***
ASK Associates Inc........785 841-8194
1201 Wakarusa Dr Ste C1 Lawrence (66049) ***(G-4738)***
Asm Engineering Cons LLC........316 260-5895
202 E Rhondda Ave Ste C Andover (67002) ***(G-83)***
Asner Iron and Metal Co........913 281-4000
34 N James St Kansas City (66118) ***(G-3822)***
Aspen Lawn Landscaping Inc........913 829-6135
1265 N Winchester St Olathe (66061) ***(G-7535)***
Aspen Place Apartments........913 856-8185
101 Aspen St Gardner (66030) ***(G-2328)***
Asphalt Sales Company (PA)........913 788-8806
23200 W 159th St Olathe (66061) ***(G-7536)***
Asphalt Sealcoating Direct.com, Douglass *Also called Mm Distribution LLC* ***(G-1467)***
Asplundh Tree Expert LLC........913 469-5440
10575 Widmer Rd Lenexa (66215) ***(G-5668)***
Assembly Component Systems Inc (HQ)........913 492-9500
14621 W 112th St Lenexa (66215) ***(G-5669)***
Assessment Tech Inst LLC........800 667-7531
11161 Overbrook Rd Leawood (66211) ***(G-5334)***
Asset Lifecycle LLC (PA)........785 861-3100
7215 Sw Topeka Blvd # 1 Topeka (66619) ***(G-12341)***
Asset MGT Analis Group LLC........803 270-0996
5016 W 108th Ter Apt 517 Leawood (66211) ***(G-5335)***
Asset Services Inc........913 383-2738
6750 Antioch Rd Ste 300 Overland Park (66204) ***(G-8405)***
ASSISTANCE LEAGUE THRIFT SHOP, Wichita *Also called Assistance League Wichita Inc* ***(G-13754)***
Assistance League Wichita Inc........316 687-6107
2431 E Douglas Ave Wichita (67211) ***(G-13754)***
Assisted Transportation Svcs (PA)........785 291-2900
6342 Sw 21st St Ste 100 Topeka (66615) ***(G-12342)***
Assistive Technology For Kans........620 421-8367
2601 Gabriel Ave Parsons (67357) ***(G-9667)***
Associate In Family Hlth Care........913 727-1018
712 1st Ter Ste A Lansing (66043) ***(G-4668)***
Associated Air Products Inc (PA)........913 894-5600
14900 W 107th St Lenexa (66215) ***(G-5670)***
Associated Audiologists Inc (PA)........913 403-0018
8800 W 75th St Ste 101 Shawnee Mission (66204) ***(G-11125)***
Associated Commercial Brks Co (PA)........785 228-9494
1111 Sw Gage Blvd Ste 100 Topeka (66604) ***(G-12343)***
Associated Cylinder SE........951 776-9915
1201 Douglas Ave Kansas City (66103) ***(G-3823)***
Associated Environmental Inc........785 776-7755
404 Pottawatomie Ave Manhattan (66502) ***(G-6547)***
Associated Eqp Sls Co LLC........913 894-4455
14535 W 96th Ter Lenexa (66215) ***(G-5671)***
Associated Grocers, Kansas City *Also called Associated Wholesale Groc Inc* ***(G-3825)***
Associated Homecare Inc........316 320-0473
113 S Main St El Dorado (67042) ***(G-1529)***
Associated Insulation Inc (PA)........785 776-0145
701 Pecan Cir Manhattan (66502) ***(G-6548)***
Associated Intergrated Mktg........316 683-4691
330 N Mead St Ste 220 Wichita (67202) ***(G-13755)***
Associated Management Services........785 228-9494
1111 Sw Gage Blvd Ste 100 Topeka (66604) ***(G-12344)***
Associated Material & Sup Co (PA)........316 721-3848
5600 W 53rd St N Wichita (67205) ***(G-13756)***
Associated Materials LLC........888 544-9774
3002 W Pawnee St Ste 106 Wichita (67213) ***(G-13757)***
Associated Materials LLC........316 944-0800
3002 W Pawnee St Wichita (67213) ***(G-13758)***
Associated Orthopedics P A........913 541-8897
12200 W 106th St Ste 400 Lenexa (66215) ***(G-5672)***
Associated Plastic Surgeons PC (PA)........913 451-3722
11501 Granada St Shawnee Mission (66211) ***(G-11126)***
Associated Podiatrist PA........913 321-0522
8919 Parallel Pkwy # 550 Kansas City (66112) ***(G-3824)***
Associated Purch Svcs Corp........913 327-8730
7015 College Blvd Ste 150 Overland Park (66211) ***(G-8406)***
Associated Urologist P A........785 537-8710
1133 College Ave Ste G100 Manhattan (66502) ***(G-6549)***
Associated Wholesale Groc Inc (PA)........913 288-1000
5000 Kansas Ave Kansas City (66106) ***(G-3825)***
Associated Wholesale Groc Inc........913 319-8500
5000 Kansas Ave Kansas City (66106) ***(G-3826)***
Associates Family Medicine PA........913 596-1313
8940 State Ave Kansas City (66112) ***(G-3827)***
Associates For Female Care PA........913 299-2229
9501 State Ave Ste 3 Kansas City (66111) ***(G-3828)***
Associates Gould-Evens........785 842-3800
706 Massachusetts St Lawrence (66044) ***(G-4739)***
Associates In Dentistry........785 843-4333
306 E 23rd St Lawrence (66046) ***(G-4740)***
Associates In Family Care, Osawatomie *Also called Olathe Medical Services Inc* ***(G-8200)***
Associates In Family Care, Olathe *Also called Olathe Medical Services Inc* ***(G-7943)***
Associates In Internal Medped........913 393-4888
20375 W 151st St Ste 251 Olathe (66061) ***(G-7537)***
Associates In Womens Health PA (PA)........316 219-6777
3232 E Murdock St Wichita (67208) ***(G-13759)***
Associates In Womens Health PA........316 283-4153
700 Medical Center Dr # 120 Newton (67114) ***(G-7312)***
Association of Kansas Nebraska (HQ)........785 478-4726
3440 Sw Urish Rd Topeka (66614) ***(G-12345)***
Association of Kansas Nebraska........785 468-3638
1950 Sagebrush Rd Olsburg (66520) ***(G-8168)***
Association of National........785 296-5474
3107 Sw 21st St Topeka (66604) ***(G-12346)***
Assoction Christn Schools Intl........785 232-3878
635 Sw Clay St Topeka (66606) ***(G-12347)***
Assoction Indvdual Prcttioners, Hutchinson *Also called Oswalt Arnold Oswald & Henry* ***(G-3398)***
Assurance Partners LLC........785 825-0286
201 E Iron Ave Salina (67401) ***(G-10411)***
Assured Occupational Solutions........316 321-3313
111 W Ash Ave El Dorado (67042) ***(G-1530)***
Asthma & Allergy Associates PA........785 842-3778
4601 W 6th St Ste B Lawrence (66049) ***(G-4741)***
Astle Realty Inc........620 662-0576
224 E 30th Ave Hutchinson (67502) ***(G-3208)***
Astra Bank (HQ)........785 335-2243
323 4th St Scandia (66966) ***(G-10798)***
Astro 3 Theatre........785 562-3715
820 Center St Marysville (66508) ***(G-6879)***
Astro Theatre, Marysville *Also called Astro 3 Theatre* ***(G-6879)***
Astro Truck Covers Inc........785 448-5577
801 E North St Ottawa (66067) ***(G-8246)***

Astronomical Society Kansas Cy 913 631-8413
7311 Stearns St Shawnee Mission (66203) ***(G-11127)***
Asurion LLC 816 237-3000
11460 Tomahwk Crk Pkwy # 300 Leawood (66211) ***(G-5336)***
At Home Assisted Care 785 473-7007
503 Lincoln Ave Wamego (66547) ***(G-13403)***
At Home Assisted Care Inc 785 473-7007
400 Poyntz Ave Manhattan (66502) ***(G-6550)***
At Home Support Care Inc 620 341-9350
417 Commercial St Ste 1 Emporia (66801) ***(G-1696)***
AT&T, Topeka *Also called Southwestern Bell Telephone Co* ***(G-13085)***
AT&T Corp 785 276-8201
4112 Nw 16th Topeka (66603) ***(G-12348)***
AT&T Corp 316 268-3380
154 N Broadway Ave # 1260 Wichita (67202) ***(G-13760)***
AT&T Corp 620 272-0383
3104 E Kansas Ave Garden City (67846) ***(G-2103)***
AT&T Corp 785 272-4002
2201 Sw Wanamaker Rd # 101 Topeka (66614) ***(G-12349)***
AT&T Corp 913 383-4943
9444 Nall Ave Overland Park (66207) ***(G-8407)***
AT&T Corp 913 894-0800
9761 Quivira Rd Overland Park (66215) ***(G-8408)***
AT&T Corp 785 832-2700
3310 Iowa St Ste A Lawrence (66046) ***(G-4742)***
AT&T Corp 785 276-8514
220 Se 6th Ave Rm 505 Topeka (66603) ***(G-12350)***
AT&T Corp 913 254-0303
11971 S Blackbob Rd Olathe (66062) ***(G-7538)***
AT&T Corp 316 383-0380
2526 W 31st St S Ofc Wichita (67217) ***(G-13761)***
AT&T Corp 785 625-0120
126 W 11th St Hays (67601) ***(G-2751)***
AT&T Corp 913 676-1261
5400 Foxridge Dr Ste 240 Shawnee Mission (66202) ***(G-11128)***
AT&T Corp 620 231-9941
611 N Locust St Pittsburg (66762) ***(G-9815)***
AT&T Corp 785 276-5553
1622 Nw Saline St Topeka (66618) ***(G-12351)***
AT&T Corp 913 676-1000
13201 W 103rd St Shawnee Mission (66215) ***(G-11129)***
AT&T Corp 913 676-1000
7400 Johnson Dr Shawnee Mission (66202) ***(G-11130)***
AT&T Corp 800 403-3022
714 1/2 Sw Fairlawn Rd Topeka (66606) ***(G-12352)***
AT&T Corp 913 334-9615
1813 Village West Pkwy Kansas City (66111) ***(G-3829)***
AT&T Corp 620 421-7612
5015 Main St Parsons (67357) ***(G-9668)***
AT&T Corp 785 749-7155
547 E 19th St Lawrence (66046) ***(G-4743)***
AT&T Corp 620 665-1946
2519 E 17th Ave Hutchinson (67501) ***(G-3209)***
AT&T Corp 620 626-5168
111 E Tucker Rd Liberal (67901) ***(G-6280)***
AT&T Inc 913 676-1136
10636 Lackman Rd Lenexa (66219) ***(G-5673)***
AT&T Mobility LLC 913 254-0303
20163 W 153rd St Olathe (66062) ***(G-7539)***
AT&T Wireless, Shawnee Mission *Also called New Cingular Wireless Svcs Inc* ***(G-11679)***
ATA BUS, Manhattan *Also called Flint Hlls Area Trnsp Agcy Inc* ***(G-6635)***
Atc Truck Covers, Ottawa *Also called Astro Truck Covers Inc* ***(G-8246)***
Atchison Area Chamber Commerce 913 367-2427
200 S 10th St Atchison (66002) ***(G-206)***
Atchison Child Care Assn 913 367-6441
1326 Kansas Ave Atchison (66002) ***(G-207)***
Atchison County Auction Co 913 367-5278
16971 286th Rd Atchison (66002) ***(G-208)***
Atchison County Headstart, Atchison *Also called Nek Cap Inc* ***(G-251)***
Atchison Globe, Atchison *Also called Gatehouse Media Inc* ***(G-229)***
Atchison Hospital Association (PA) 913 367-2131
800 Ravenhill Dr Atchison (66002) ***(G-209)***
Atchison Hospitality Group LLC 913 674-0033
401 Main St Atchison (66002) ***(G-210)***
Atchison Leather, Atchison *Also called Berger Company* ***(G-215)***
Atchison Senior Village, Atchison *Also called County of Atchison* ***(G-223)***
ATCHSION HOSPITAL, Atchison *Also called Riverbend Rgnal Hlthcare Fndti* ***(G-258)***
Atec Steel LLC 877 457-5352
1000 W 5th St Baxter Springs (66713) ***(G-394)***
Atec Steel Fabrication & Cnstr, Baxter Springs *Also called Atec Steel LLC* ***(G-394)***
Athena Communications Ltd 913 599-3444
4905 Antioch Rd Overland Park (66203) ***(G-8409)***
Athlete Network, Lenexa *Also called Career Athletes LLC* ***(G-5729)***
Athletic & Rehabilitation Ctr 913 378-0778
6405 Metcalf Ave Ste 504 Shawnee Mission (66202) ***(G-11131)***
Athletic Department, Manhattan *Also called Kansas State University* ***(G-6687)***
Athletic Department Bus Off, Manhattan *Also called Kansas State University* ***(G-6682)***
ATI Nursing Education, Leawood *Also called Assessment Tech Inst LLC* ***(G-5334)***
Atipa Technologies, Lawrence *Also called Microtech Computers Inc* ***(G-5024)***
Atkinson Industries Inc 620 231-6900
1801 E 27th Ter Pittsburg (66762) ***(G-9816)***
Atlantic Dev Corp of PA 316 267-2255
800 E Indianapolis St Wichita (67211) ***(G-13762)***
Atlantic States Bank, Overland Park *Also called First-Citizens Bank & Trust Co* ***(G-8723)***
Atlas Aerospace LLC (HQ) 316 977-7398
4425 W May St Bldg 1 Wichita (67209) ***(G-13763)***
Atlas Aerospace LLC 316 219-5862
4626 W May St D Wichita (67209) ***(G-13764)***
Atlas Electric LLC 316 858-1560
1607 N Wabash Ave Wichita (67214) ***(G-13765)***
Atlas Painting 316 686-1546
2061 E Wassall St Wichita (67216) ***(G-13766)***
Atlas Recovery Systems LLC 913 281-7000
7932 Foster St Ste B Overland Park (66204) ***(G-8410)***
Atlas Spring & Axle Co Inc 316 943-2386
4500 W Irving St Wichita (67209) ***(G-13767)***
ATM Concrete Inc 785 484-2013
111 Water St Meriden (66512) ***(G-7078)***
Atmos Energy Corporation 785 258-2300
20 W Main St Herington (67449) ***(G-2970)***
Atmos Energy Corporation 913 254-6300
25090 W 110th Ter Olathe (66061) ***(G-7540)***
Atonix Digital LLC 913 458-2000
11401 Lamar Ave Overland Park (66211) ***(G-8411)***
Atp, Mc Pherson *Also called Aero Transportation Pdts Inc* ***(G-6930)***
Atria Senior Living Inc 785 234-6225
3415 Sw 6th Ave Topeka (66606) ***(G-12353)***
Atriums Retirement Home 913 381-9133
7300 W 107th St Apt 118 Shawnee Mission (66212) ***(G-11132)***
Atriums, The, Shawnee Mission *Also called Atriums Retirement Home* ***(G-11132)***
Atronic Alarms Inc (PA) 913 432-4545
8220 Melrose Dr Lenexa (66214) ***(G-5674)***
Atterro Inc 913 338-3020
10740 Nall Ave Ste 110 Overland Park (66211) ***(G-8412)***
Attic Management Group LLC 913 269-4583
720 S Rogers Rd Olathe (66062) ***(G-7541)***
Attica Engineering LLC 620 254-7070
201 N Main St Attica (67009) ***(G-275)***
Attica Hospital District 1 ....620 254-7253
302 N Botkin St Attica (67009) ***(G-276)***
Attica Long Term Care, Attica *Also called Attica Hospital District 1* ***(G-276)***
Attitudes 902, Junction City *Also called Mane Thing* ***(G-3723)***
Atwood Distributing LP 316 789-1800
333 W Red Powell Dr Derby (67037) ***(G-1218)***
Atwood Distributing LP 316 744-8888
6235 N Broadway Ave Park City (67219) ***(G-9602)***
Auburn Animal Clinic Inc 785 256-2476
8370 Sw Auburn Rd Auburn (66402) ***(G-293)***
Audiology Consultants Inc 785 823-3761
520 S Santa Fe Ave # 400 Salina (67401) ***(G-10412)***
Audiometric Aides, Salina *Also called Central Kansas Ent Assoc PA* ***(G-10440)***
Auditing For Cmpliance Educatn 913 648-8572
8900 State Line Rd # 350 Shawnee Mission (66206) ***(G-11133)***
Augusta Country Club 316 775-7281
1610 Fairway Dr Augusta (67010) ***(G-301)***
Augusta Crime Stoppers Inc 316 775-0055
2100 Ohio St Augusta (67010) ***(G-302)***
Augusta Electric Plant 2 ....316 775-4527
615 12th Ave Augusta (67010) ***(G-303)***
Augusta Family Dentistry PA 316 775-2482
401 State St Augusta (67010) ***(G-304)***
Augusta Family Practice PA 316 775-9191
1306 State St Augusta (67010) ***(G-305)***
Augusta Head Start 316 775-3421
730 Cliff Dr Augusta (67010) ***(G-306)***
Augusta L Lakepoint L C 316 733-8100
600 N 127th St E Wichita (67206) ***(G-13768)***
Augusta L Lakepoint L C (PA) 316 775-6333
901 Lakepoint Dr Augusta (67010) ***(G-307)***
Augusta L Lakepoint L C 316 320-4140
1313 S High St El Dorado (67042) ***(G-1531)***
Augusta Quarry, Augusta *Also called Martin Marietta Materials Inc* ***(G-334)***
Augusta Rental Inc 316 775-5050
9965 Sw Santa Fe Lake Rd Augusta (67010) ***(G-308)***
Augusta White Eagle Credit Un (PA) 316 775-5747
2830 Ohio St Augusta (67010) ***(G-309)***
Augustine Carpenting HM Imprv, Overland Park *Also called Augustine Exterminators Inc* ***(G-8413)***
Augustine Exterminators, Shawnee Mission *Also called Augustine Home Improvement Co* ***(G-11134)***
Augustine Exterminators Inc 913 362-4399
9280 Flint St Overland Park (66214) ***(G-8413)***
Augustine Home Improvement Co 913 362-4707
9280 Flint St Shawnee Mission (66214) ***(G-11134)***
Auman Co Inc 785 628-2833
311 E 11th St Hays (67601) ***(G-2752)***

ALPHABETIC

Ausemus Stnley R Esq Chartered 620 342-8717
413 Commercial St Emporia (66801) ***(G-1697)***
Auspision LLC 620 343-3685
1211 Stanton St Emporia (66801) ***(G-1698)***
Austin A-7 Ltd 316 945-8892
1835 S Florence St Wichita (67209) ***(G-13769)***
Austin Tile Inc (PA) 913 829-6607
704 E Dennis Ave Olathe (66061) ***(G-7542)***
Austin Trucking 316 323-0313
1782 Sw 92nd Ter Augusta (67010) ***(G-310)***
Austin Western Railroad 620 231-2230
315 W 3rd St Pittsburg (66762) ***(G-9817)***
Austin, Robert L, Stafford *Also called Rama Operating Co Inc* ***(G-12108)***
Autism Asperger Publishing Co, Shawnee *Also called Aapc Inc* ***(G-10905)***
Auto Care Center, Topeka *Also called Quality Care* ***(G-12995)***
Auto Craft Body & Paint, Wichita *Also called Auto-Craft Inc* ***(G-13770)***
Auto Craft Body & Paint, Wichita *Also called Auto-Craft Inc* ***(G-13771)***
Auto House Inc 785 825-6644
565 Westport Blvd Salina (67401) ***(G-10413)***
Auto Maintenance Expert, Wichita *Also called Expert Auto Center* ***(G-14322)***
Auto Masters LLC 316 789-8540
945 N K 15 Hwy Derby (67037) ***(G-1219)***
Auto Masters LLC (PA) 316 789-8540
945 N K 15 Hwy Derby (67037) ***(G-1220)***
Auto Masters Service Center, Derby *Also called Auto Masters LLC* ***(G-1220)***
Auto Service Ctr Shawnee LLC 913 422-5388
6590 Vista Dr Shawnee (66218) ***(G-10912)***
Auto Techs Frame & Body Repair 620 221-6616
2800 E 9th Ave Winfield (67156) ***(G-16115)***
Auto Value, Wichita *Also called Jobbers Automotive Whse Inc* ***(G-14759)***
Auto-Craft Inc 785 579-5997
220 E Chestnut St Junction City (66441) ***(G-3669)***
Auto-Craft Inc (PA) 316 265-6828
1427 E 1st St N Wichita (67214) ***(G-13770)***
Auto-Craft Inc 316 630-9494
8532 E 32nd St N Wichita (67226) ***(G-13771)***
Autobody of Lawrence 785 843-3055
2101 W 29th Ter Lawrence (66047) ***(G-4744)***
Autoflame 620 229-8048
4601 S Palisade Ave Wichita (67217) ***(G-13772)***
Automated Control Systems Corp 913 766-2336
5251 W 116th Pl Ste 200 Leawood (66211) ***(G-5337)***
Automatic Data Processing Inc 913 492-4200
16011 College Blvd # 110 Lenexa (66219) ***(G-5675)***
Automatic Data Processing Inc 515 875-3160
7701 E Kellogg Dr Ste 630 Wichita (67207) ***(G-13773)***
Automobile Club of Missouri 913 248-1627
15810b Shwnee Mssion Pkwy Shawnee Mission (66217) ***(G-11135)***
Automobile Club of Missouri 316 942-0008
7130 W Maple St Ste 200 Wichita (67209) ***(G-13774)***
Automotive Associates 620 231-6350
103 S Elm St Pittsburg (66762) ***(G-9818)***
Automotive Equipment Services 913 254-2600
1651 E Kansas City Rd Olathe (66061) ***(G-7543)***
Automotive Specialists Inc 316 321-5130
2150 W Central Ave El Dorado (67042) ***(G-1532)***
Automotive Supply Inc 316 942-8285
4410 W Central Ave Wichita (67212) ***(G-13775)***
Automotive Supply Inc 316 942-8287
706 Dougherty St Wichita (67212) ***(G-13776)***
AUTOMOTIVE WAREHOUSE CO, Wichita *Also called Automotive Supply Inc* ***(G-13775)***
Automotive Warehouse Company 316 942-8285
706 N Dougherty Ave Wichita (67212) ***(G-13777)***
Autotech Collision & Service 316 942-0707
4411 W Central Ave Wichita (67212) ***(G-13778)***
Autotrader Com, Overland Park *Also called Cox Enterprises Inc* ***(G-8607)***
Autozone Inc 785 452-9790
1916 S 9th St Salina (67401) ***(G-10414)***
Autum Place, The, Columbus *Also called Brad Carson* ***(G-1062)***
Autumn Place, Baxter Springs *Also called Brad Carson* ***(G-400)***
Avant Acoustics, Lenexa *Also called Jvf Enterprises Inc* ***(G-5934)***
Avatar Engineering Inc 913 897-6757
14360 W 96th Ter Lenexa (66215) ***(G-5676)***
Avazpour Networking Svcs Inc 913 323-1411
12980 Metcalf Ave Ste 400 Overland Park (66213) ***(G-8414)***
Avcon Industries Inc 913 780-9595
714 N Oliver Rd Newton (67114) ***(G-7313)***
Avcorp Business Systems LLC (HQ) 913 888-0333
8200 Nieman Rd Overland Park (66214) ***(G-8415)***
Avenue of Life Inc 816 519-8419
500 N 7th St Kansas City (66101) ***(G-3830)***
Avenue Style, Wichita *Also called Keith Shaw* ***(G-14841)***
Avery Capital LLC 913 742-3002
7803 W 61st Ter Overland Park (66202) ***(G-8416)***
AvFlight Salina Corporation 734 663-6466
2035 Beechcraft Rd Salina (67401) ***(G-10415)***
AVI Systems Inc 913 495-9494
8019 Bond St Lenexa (66214) ***(G-5677)***
Aviation Cnslting Engrg Sltons 316 265-8335
202 N Park St Maize (67101) ***(G-6508)***
Avis Budget Group Inc 785 331-0658
2201 Saint James Ct Lawrence (66046) ***(G-4745)***
Avis Rent A Car System Inc 316 946-4882
Airport Rd Wichita (67209) ***(G-13779)***
Avis Rent A Car Systems, Wichita *Also called Avis Rent A Car System Inc* ***(G-13779)***
Avis Rental Car Systems 785 749-1464
1216 E 23rd St Lawrence (66046) ***(G-4746)***
Avita Assisted Living At Derby 316 260-4447
731 N Klein Cir Derby (67037) ***(G-1221)***
AW Schultz Inc 913 307-0399
6861 Martindale Rd Shawnee Mission (66218) ***(G-11136)***
Awad Nicola (PA) 913 381-6969
11477 W 95th St Overland Park (66214) ***(G-8417)***
Award Decals Inc 913 677-6681
12507 Hemlock St Overland Park (66213) ***(G-8418)***
Awg, Kansas City *Also called Associated Wholesale Groc Inc* ***(G-3826)***
Awg Acquisition LLC 913 288-1000
5000 Kansas Ave Kansas City (66106) ***(G-3831)***
Axa Advisors LLC 913 345-2800
7400 W 110th St Ste 700 Shawnee Mission (66210) ***(G-11137)***
Axa Advisors LLC 316 263-5761
301 N Main St Ste 1400 Wichita (67202) ***(G-13780)***
Axa Financial Inc 913 345-2800
7400 W 110th St Ste 700 Overland Park (66210) ***(G-8419)***
Axcet Hr Solutions Inc 913 383-2999
10975 Grandview Dr # 200 Overland Park (66210) ***(G-8420)***
Axelacare Health Care, Lenexa *Also called Axelacare Holdings Inc* ***(G-5678)***
Axelacare Holdings Inc (PA) 877 342-9352
15529 College Blvd Lenexa (66219) ***(G-5678)***
Axiom Rligious Fcilty Advisors, Shawnee *Also called Adamson and Associates* ***(G-10906)***
Axius Group LLC 316 285-0858
100 S Market St Ste 100 # 100 Wichita (67202) ***(G-13781)***
Axle & Wheel Aligning Co Inc 316 263-0213
126 N Washington Ave Wichita (67202) ***(G-13782)***
Axtell Clinic P A 316 283-2800
700 Medical Center Dr # 210 Newton (67114) ***(G-7314)***
Axtell Truss Manufacturing Inc 785 736-2291
2828 Pony Express Hwy Axtell (66403) ***(G-350)***
Ayham J Farha MD 316 636-6100
2626 N Webb Rd Wichita (67226) ***(G-13783)***
Aztec Oil Division, El Dorado *Also called Buckeye Corporation* ***(G-1539)***
Azura Credit Union (PA) 785 233-5556
610 Sw 10th Ave Fl 1 Topeka (66612) ***(G-12354)***
Azz Inc 620 231-6900
1801 E 27th St Ter Pittsburg (66762) ***(G-9819)***
B & B Airparts Inc 316 946-0300
1831 S Hoover Ct Wichita (67209) ***(G-13784)***
B & B Backyard 785 246-6348
2134 N Kansas Ave Topeka (66608) ***(G-12355)***
B & B Bridges Company LLC 620 449-2286
411 6th St Saint Paul (66771) ***(G-10379)***
B & B Busing, Junction City *Also called Just For Kids Express* ***(G-3708)***
B & B Cinemas 785 242-0777
209 S Main St Ottawa (66067) ***(G-8247)***
B & B Delivery Enterprise LLC 913 541-9090
29 Woodswether Rd Kansas City (66118) ***(G-3832)***
B & B Hydraulics Inc (PA) 620 662-2552
2400 Line Rd Hutchinson (67501) ***(G-3210)***
B & B Movie Theatres LLC 620 342-0900
1614 Industrial Rd Emporia (66801) ***(G-1699)***
B & B Movie Theatres LLC 620 227-8100
2601 Central Ave Dodge City (67801) ***(G-1299)***
B & B Movie Theatres LLC 620 669-8510
1500 E 11th Ave Hutchinson (67501) ***(G-3211)***
B & B Oil Tools Co LLC 785 673-4828
806 Main St Grainfield (67737) ***(G-2494)***
B & B Outservices, Wamego *Also called P & F Services Inc* ***(G-13432)***
B & B Plumbing Heating & AC 785 472-5239
814 Stanberry St Ellsworth (67439) ***(G-1657)***
B & B Redimix Inc 785 543-5133
1873 1st St Phillipsburg (67661) ***(G-9776)***
B & B Redimix Inc (PA) 785 543-5133
1873 1st St Phillipsburg (67661) ***(G-9777)***
B & B Transfer, Kansas City *Also called B & B Delivery Enterprise LLC* ***(G-3832)***
B & B Wrecker, Newton *Also called Brenneman & Bremmeman Inc* ***(G-7321)***
B & C Restaurant Corporation 913 327-0800
5001 Town Center Dr Shawnee Mission (66211) ***(G-11138)***
B & C Specialty Products Inc 316 283-8000
123 E 4th St Newton (67114) ***(G-7315)***
B & D Equipment Co Inc 913 367-1744
17526 286th Rd Atchison (66002) ***(G-211)***
B & E Inc 913 299-1110
8201 State Ave Kansas City (66112) ***(G-3833)***
B & G Construction 620 431-0849
3914 S Santa Fe Ave Chanute (66720) ***(G-704)***
B & H Appliance 620 364-8700
330 N 3rd St New Strawn (66839) ***(G-7303)***

B & H Construction Company............620 231-0326
2601 E 20th St Pittsburg (66762) *(G-9820)*
B & H Freight Line Inc............913 621-1840
468 S 26th St Kansas City (66105) *(G-3834)*
B & H Motor Sports (PA)............785 966-2575
14212 142nd Rd Mayetta (66509) *(G-6914)*
B & H Paving Inc............620 872-3146
711 E 7th St Scott City (67871) *(G-10805)*
B & J Food Service Eqp Inc (PA)............913 621-6165
236 N 7th St Kansas City (66101) *(G-3835)*
B & K Enterprises Inc............785 238-3076
417 N Franklin St Junction City (66441) *(G-3670)*
B & K Vending & Amusement, Junction City *Also called B & K Enterprises Inc (G-3670)*
B & L Motels Inc (PA)............785 628-8008
2810 Vine St Hays (67601) *(G-2753)*
B & R Insulation Inc............913 492-1346
15001 W 101st Ter Shawnee Mission (66215) *(G-11139)*
B & S Aircraft, Wichita *Also called Ametek Arcft Parts & ACC Inc (G-13699)*
B & W Custom Truck Beds Inc............800 810-4918
1216 Hawaii Rd Humboldt (66748) *(G-3181)*
B & W Electric Inc............785 337-2598
107 W North St Hanover (66945) *(G-2709)*
B & W Trailer Hitches, Humboldt *Also called B & W Custom Truck Beds Inc (G-3181)*
B 5 Inc............316 721-3222
P.O. Box 771071 Wichita (67277) *(G-13785)*
B A Barnes Electric Inc............913 764-4455
2014 E Spruce Cir Olathe (66062) *(G-7544)*
B A Designs LLC............785 267-8110
117 Se 10th Ave Apt 100 Topeka (66612) *(G-12356)*
B A Green Construction Co Inc............785 843-5277
1207 Iowa St Lawrence (66044) *(G-4747)*
B and L Motels (PA)............913 451-5874
10874 Nieman Rd Overland Park (66210) *(G-8421)*
B and R Insulation, Shawnee Mission *Also called D & D Services Inc (G-11288)*
B C A /fry-wagner Inc............573 499-0000
15850 Santa Fe Trail Dr Lenexa (66219) *(G-5679)*
B C C Business Services Inc............913 682-4548
121 Cherokee St Leavenworth (66048) *(G-5205)*
B C S, Wichita *Also called Siemens Industry Inc (G-15584)*
B F Ascher & Company Inc............913 888-1880
15501 W 109th St Lenexa (66219) *(G-5680)*
B Four Corp............913 648-1441
4050 W 83rd St Prairie Village (66208) *(G-10012)*
B Four Corp............913 432-1107
7000 W 75th St Shawnee Mission (66204) *(G-11140)*
B G Consultants Inc (PA)............785 537-7448
4806 Vue Du Lac Pl Manhattan (66503) *(G-6551)*
B G Consultants Inc............785 749-4474
1405 Wakarusa Dr Lawrence (66049) *(G-4748)*
B J Best Buy Pallets............785 488-2923
661 N 240th Rd Solomon (67480) *(G-12047)*
B J F Inc............913 837-2726
31030 Spring Valley Rd Paola (66071) *(G-9540)*
B L Rieke & Associates Inc............913 599-3393
14352 W 96th Ter Shawnee Mission (66215) *(G-11141)*
B M I, Lenexa *Also called Browns Medical Imaging (G-5719)*
B N S F Inc............316 284-3260
301 W 4th St Newton (67114) *(G-7316)*
B P E Inc............620 343-3783
890 Road 160 Emporia (66801) *(G-1700)*
B P O Elks Lodge 1451, Pratt *Also called Elks Lodge Inc (G-10110)*
B Scott Studio Inc............316 321-1225
1717 W Towanda Ave El Dorado (67042) *(G-1533)*
B W Foundations Company Inc............913 764-8222
19125 W 151st Ter Ste C Olathe (66062) *(G-7545)*
B&B Cooperative Ventures LLC............620 364-1311
1044 Us Highway 75 Burlington (66839) *(G-625)*
B&B Electric Motor Co............316 267-1238
332 S Lulu Ave Wichita (67211) *(G-13786)*
B&B Quality Meats LLC............620 285-8988
508 Broadway St Larned (67550) *(G-4694)*
B&B Redi Mix............785 543-5133
1873 1st St Phillipsburg (67661) *(G-9778)*
B&B Welding............620 253-1023
2945 E Trail St Lot 203 Dodge City (67801) *(G-1300)*
B&C Mechanical Services LLC (PA)............913 681-0088
19403 W 335th St Paola (66071) *(G-9541)*
B&G Group LLC............816 616-4034
9930 W 116th Pl Apt 7 Overland Park (66210) *(G-8422)*
B&V E&E JV............913 458-4300
6800 W 115th St Ste 2200 Overland Park (66211) *(G-8423)*
B&V-Baker Guam JV............913 458-4300
6601 College Blvd Overland Park (66211) *(G-8424)*
B-29 Museum Inc............620 282-1123
82 Curran Rd Pratt (67124) *(G-10099)*
B-3 Construction Inc............620 479-2323
1106 S Highschool Ave Columbus (66725) *(G-1060)*
B/E Aerospace Inc............316 609-3360
10900 E 26th St N Wichita (67226) *(G-13787)*
B/E Aerospace Inc............316 609-4300
8110 E 32nd St N Wichita (67226) *(G-13788)*
B/E Aerospace Inc............913 338-9800
10800 Pflumm Rd Lenexa (66215) *(G-5681)*
B/E Aerospace Inc............913 338-7292
10800 Pflumm Rd Shawnee Mission (66215) *(G-11142)*
BA Karbank & Co LLP (PA)............816 221-4488
2000 Shawnee Mission Pkwy Shawnee Mission (66205) *(G-11143)*
Baader Linco Inc (HQ)............913 621-3366
2955 Fairfax Trfy Kansas City (66115) *(G-3836)*
Baader North America Corp (HQ)............913 621-3366
2955 Fairfax Trfy Kansas City (66115) *(G-3837)*
Babcock Sales & Service, Hiawatha *Also called Ken Babcock Sales Inc (G-3013)*
Babock, Julie E DDS, Shawnee Mission *Also called Steven J Pierce DDS PA (G-11899)*
Bachman Production Specialties............620 792-2549
307 C Ave Great Bend (67530) *(G-2513)*
Bachus & Son Inc............316 265-4673
725 E Central Ave Wichita (67202) *(G-13789)*
Back Room Printing LLC............620 873-2900
102 N Fowler St Meade (67864) *(G-7046)*
Backwoods Equipment Company............316 267-0350
1900 N Rock Rd Ste 108 Wichita (67206) *(G-13790)*
Backyard Adventures LLC............620 308-6863
3305 Airport Cir Pittsburg (66762) *(G-9821)*
Backyard Discovery, Pittsburg *Also called Step2 Discovery LLC (G-9940)*
Bacm 2005-3 Main Woodlawn LLC............316 291-8450
301 N Main St Ste 145 Wichita (67202) *(G-13791)*
Baco Corporation............316 945-5300
2426 S Hoover Rd Wichita (67215) *(G-13792)*
Bagatelle French Bakery, Wichita *Also called Bagatelle Inc (G-13793)*
Bagatelle Inc............316 684-5662
6801 E Harry St Wichita (67207) *(G-13793)*
Bagcraftpapercon I LLC............620 856-4615
3400 Bagcraft Blvd Baxter Springs (66713) *(G-395)*
Bagel Works Bread Company, Kansas City *Also called Bagel Works Cafe Inc (G-3838)*
Bagel Works Cafe Inc............913 789-7333
1523 S 45th St Kansas City (66106) *(G-3838)*
Bailey Machine Inc............620 848-3116
1 Mile N On Hwy 69 A Riverton (66770) *(G-10210)*
Bailey Moving & Storage Co LLC............785 232-0521
235 Sw Gage Blvd Topeka (66606) *(G-12357)*
Bailey Showroom 2 LLC............913 432-9696
5301 Johnson Dr Shawnee Mission (66205) *(G-11144)*
Bain Millwrights Inc............785 945-3778
1508 Willow St Valley Falls (66088) *(G-13361)*
Bainter Construction Co Inc............785 675-3297
844 Main St Hoxie (67740) *(G-3135)*
Bair Products, Louisburg *Also called Larry Bair Excavating Inc (G-6456)*
Baird Oil Co Inc............785 689-7456
113 W Main St Logan (67646) *(G-6420)*
Baisch & Skinner Inc............785 267-6931
1720 Sw 42nd St Topeka (66609) *(G-12358)*
Baisch & Skinner Inc............316 945-0074
3413 W 29th St S Wichita (67217) *(G-13794)*
Bajillion Agency............785 408-5927
100 S Kansas Ave Topeka (66603) *(G-12359)*
Baker Abilene Machine Inc............785 565-9455
2150 Daisy Rd Solomon (67480) *(G-12048)*
Baker Bros Printing Co Inc............620 947-3520
113 S Main St Hillsboro (67063) *(G-3041)*
Baker Clinic The, Pittsburg *Also called S E K Otolaryngology PA (G-9933)*
Baker Construction Inc............913 682-6302
714 Oak St Leavenworth (66048) *(G-5206)*
Baker Hghes Olfld Oprtions LLC............785 650-0182
103 E 27th St Hays (67601) *(G-2754)*
Baker Petrolite LLC............620 793-3546
5801 10th St Great Bend (67530) *(G-2514)*
Baker Services Inc............913 367-1657
1699 Highway 59 Atchison (66002) *(G-212)*
Baker Sr Marcellus............316 670-6329
1201 N Jackson Ave Wichita (67203) *(G-13795)*
Bakery Projects Inc............316 831-9434
1025 W 29th St N Wichita (67204) *(G-13796)*
Bakken Oil Express LLC............316 630-0287
8301 E 21st St N Ste 420 Wichita (67206) *(G-13797)*
Bakken Well Service Inc............620 276-3442
3210 W Jones Ave Garden City (67846) *(G-2104)*
Balance Innovations LLC............913 599-1177
11011 Eicher Dr Lenexa (66219) *(G-5682)*
Balco Inc (HQ)............800 767-0082
2626 S Sheridan Ave Wichita (67217) *(G-13798)*
Balco-Metalines, Wichita *Also called Balco Inc (G-13798)*
Baldor Shour & Associates, Lenexa *Also called ABB Motors and Mechanical Inc (G-5618)*
Baldridge Electric Inc............316 267-0058
1542 S Market St Wichita (67211) *(G-13799)*
Baldwin LLC (PA)............913 312-2375
6601 College Blvd Ste 140 Leawood (66211) *(G-5338)*
Baldwin Americas Corporation............913 310-3258
14600 W 106th St Lenexa (66215) *(G-5683)*

Baldwin State Bank 785 594-6421
721 High St Baldwin City (66006) ***(G-355)***
Ball-Mccolm Post No 5 Inc 620 342-1119
2921 W 12th Ave Emporia (66801) ***(G-1701)***
Ballard Aviation, Goodland *Also called Eagle Med Inc* ***(G-2468)***
Ballet Midwest Inc 785 272-5991
4300 Sw Huntoon St Topeka (66604) ***(G-12360)***
Ballou Pavement Solutions Inc 785 827-4439
1100 W Grand Ave Salina (67401) ***(G-10416)***
Ballstars, New Century *Also called Star Innovations II LLC* ***(G-7298)***
Ballyhoo Banners 913 385-5050
8022 Monrovia St Lenexa (66215) ***(G-5684)***
Bamford Fire Sprinkler Co Inc (HQ) 785 825-7710
1383 W North St Salina (67401) ***(G-10417)***
Bamford Fire Sprinkler Co Inc 913 432-6688
5134 Merriam Dr Shawnee Mission (66203) ***(G-11145)***
Banccentral National Assn 620 842-1000
203 W Main St Anthony (67003) ***(G-121)***
Band Box Corporation (PA) 785 272-6646
2033 Sw Seabrook Ave Topeka (66604) ***(G-12361)***
Bandy Enterprises Inc (PA) 785 462-3361
1185 Zelfer Ave Colby (67701) ***(G-988)***
Banfield Pet Hospital 237, Shawnee Mission *Also called A Caring Doctor Minnesota PA* ***(G-11061)***
Banfield Pet Hospital 241, Olathe *Also called A Caring Doctor Minnesota PA* ***(G-7505)***
Banfield Pet Hospital 242, Shawnee *Also called A Caring Doctor Minnesota PA* ***(G-10904)***
Banfield Pet Hospital 244, Topeka *Also called A Caring Doctor Minnesota PA* ***(G-12278)***
Banfield Pet Hospital 245, Wichita *Also called A Caring Doctor Minnesota PA* ***(G-13585)***
Banfield Pet Hospital 246, Wichita *Also called A Caring Doctor Minnesota PA* ***(G-13584)***
Bangerter Rebein PA 620 227-8126
810 W Frontview St Dodge City (67801) ***(G-1301)***
Bank 7 ....620 846-2221
209 N Aztec St Montezuma (67867) ***(G-7155)***
Bank America National Assn 316 788-2811
201 N Baltimore Ave Derby (67037) ***(G-1222)***
Bank America National Assn 785 625-3413
1200 E 27th St Hays (67601) ***(G-2755)***
Bank America National Assn 913 768-1340
15025 W 119th St Olathe (66062) ***(G-7546)***
Bank America National Assn 316 261-4242
619 N 2nd Ave Dodge City (67801) ***(G-1302)***
Bank America National Assn 816 979-8482
7624 State Line Rd Prairie Village (66208) ***(G-10013)***
Bank America National Assn 316 261-4242
300 N Kansas Ave Liberal (67901) ***(G-6281)***
Bank America National Assn 816 979-8561
175 N Clairborne Olathe (66062) ***(G-7547)***
Bank America National Assn 785 235-1532
700 Sw Topeka Blvd Topeka (66603) ***(G-12362)***
Bank America National Assn 316 261-2025
2959 N Rock Rd Ste 1 Wichita (67226) ***(G-13800)***
Bank America National Assn 816 979-8215
7809 State Ave Kansas City (66112) ***(G-3839)***
Bank America National Assn 785 842-1000
900 Ohio St Lawrence (66044) ***(G-4749)***
Bank America National Assn 785 227-3344
118 N Main St Lindsborg (67456) ***(G-6391)***
Bank America National Assn 316 261-2274
8304 W Central Ave Wichita (67212) ***(G-13801)***
Bank America National Assn 785 238-8012
227 W 18th St Junction City (66441) ***(G-3671)***
Bank America National Assn 816 979-4592
8695 College Blvd Ste 100 Overland Park (66210) ***(G-8425)***
Bank America National Assn 316 261-4359
3193 S Seneca St Wichita (67217) ***(G-13802)***
Bank America National Assn 620 331-4800
501 N Penn Ave Independence (67301) ***(G-3498)***
Bank America National Assn 816 979-8200
8440 W 135th St Overland Park (66223) ***(G-8426)***
Bank America National Assn 316 261-4242
1325 N Kansas Ave Liberal (67901) ***(G-6282)***
Bank America National Assn 785 235-1532
900 Ohio St Lawrence (66044) ***(G-4750)***
Bank America National Assn 816 979-8608
12345 W 95th St Shawnee Mission (66215) ***(G-11146)***
Bank America National Assn 816 979-8257
1314 N 38th St Kansas City (66102) ***(G-3840)***
Bank America National Assn 316 529-6730
329 S Andover Rd Andover (67002) ***(G-84)***
Bank America National Assn 816 979-8219
7747 Quivira Rd Lenexa (66216) ***(G-5685)***
Bank America National Assn 913 897-1470
15811 Metcalf Ave Overland Park (66223) ***(G-8427)***
Bank America National Assn 316 261-4216
100 N Broadway Ave Fl 3 Wichita (67202) ***(G-13803)***
Bank America National Assn 620 694-4395
20 2nd Hutchinson (67501) ***(G-3212)***
Bank America National Assn 316 261-2210
7310 W 21st St N Wichita (67205) ***(G-13804)***
Bank America National Assn 316 261-4040
2151 N Hillside St Wichita (67214) ***(G-13805)***
Bank America National Assn 316 261-2143
1617 S Rock Rd Wichita (67207) ***(G-13806)***
Bank America National Assn 913 441-1067
22425 W 66th St Shawnee (66226) ***(G-10913)***
BANK COMMERCE AND TRUST, Wellington *Also called Bank of Cmmrce Tr of Wllngton* ***(G-13490)***
Bank Commssnr Kansas Offce (HQ) 785 296-2266
700 Sw Jackson St Ste 300 Topeka (66603) ***(G-12363)***
Bank Midwest, Lawrence *Also called Nbh Bank* ***(G-5037)***
Bank Midwest, Ottawa *Also called Nbh Bank* ***(G-8294)***
Bank Midwest, Olathe *Also called Nbh Bank* ***(G-7914)***
Bank Midwest, Kansas City *Also called Nbh Bank* ***(G-4282)***
Bank Midwest, Edwardsville *Also called Nbh Bank* ***(G-1510)***
Bank Midwest, Kansas City *Also called Nbh Bank* ***(G-4283)***
Bank News Publications Inc 913 261-7000
5115 Roe Blvd Ste 200 Roeland Park (66205) ***(G-10217)***
Bank of America Lawrence, Lawrence *Also called Bank America National Assn* ***(G-4749)***
Bank of Atchison, Atchison *Also called Union State Bank of Everest* ***(G-267)***
Bank of Blue Valley 785 284-3433
21 Main St Sabetha (66534) ***(G-10306)***
Bank of Blue Valley 785 742-2121
7th & Delaware St Hiawatha (66434) ***(G-3002)***
Bank of Blue Valley (HQ) 913 338-1000
11935 Riley St Overland Park (66213) ***(G-8428)***
Bank of Blue Valley 785 889-4211
301 Leonard St Onaga (66521) ***(G-8171)***
Bank of Blue Valley 913 888-7852
9500 Lackman Rd Shawnee Mission (66219) ***(G-11147)***
Bank of Cmmrce Tr of Wllngton (PA) 620 326-7471
201 W Harvey Ave Wellington (67152) ***(G-13490)***
Bank of Commerce (HQ) 620 431-1400
101 W Main St Chanute (66720) ***(G-705)***
Bank of Flint Hills (PA) 785 456-2221
806 5th St Wamego (66547) ***(G-13404)***
Bank of Flint Hills 785 765-2220
408 Missouri Ave Alma (66401) ***(G-62)***
Bank of Flint Hills 785 539-8322
7860 E Us Highway 24 Manhattan (66502) ***(G-6552)***
Bank of Hays (PA) 785 621-2265
1000 W 27th St Hays (67601) ***(G-2756)***
Bank of Labor 913 321-4242
11810 W 75th St Overland Park (66214) ***(G-8429)***
Bank of Labor 913 321-4242
12500 W 63rd St Shawnee (66216) ***(G-10914)***
Bank of Labor 913 321-4242
7354 State Ave Kansas City (66112) ***(G-3841)***
Bank of Labor 913 321-4242
4431 Shawnee Dr Kansas City (66106) ***(G-3842)***
Bank of Labor (HQ) 913 321-6800
756 Minnesota Ave Kansas City (66101) ***(G-3843)***
Bank of Prairie (HQ) 785 353-2298
18675 W 151st St Olathe (66062) ***(G-7548)***
Bank of Prairie Village 913 713-0300
3515 W 75th St Ste 115 Prairie Village (66208) ***(G-10014)***
Bank of Protection Inc 620 622-4224
302 N Broadway Protection (67127) ***(G-10173)***
Bank of Tescott (PA) 785 283-4217
104 S Main St Tescott (67484) ***(G-12244)***
Bank of Tescott 785 227-8830
202 N Main St Lindsborg (67456) ***(G-6392)***
Bank of Tescott 785 825-1621
600 S Santa Fe Ave Salina (67401) ***(G-10418)***
Bank of West 316 292-5840
255 N Main St Wichita (67202) ***(G-13807)***
Bank of West 913 362-8900
6263 Nall Ave Shawnee Mission (66202) ***(G-11148)***
Bank of West 620 225-4147
400 W Frontview St Dodge City (67801) ***(G-1303)***
Bank of West 316 292-5870
757 N West St Wichita (67203) ***(G-13808)***
Bank of West 620 662-0543
829 E 30th Ave Hutchinson (67502) ***(G-3213)***
Bank of West 316 283-7310
100 W 12th St Newton (67114) ***(G-7317)***
Bank of West 913 642-5212
9400 Antioch Rd Shawnee Mission (66212) ***(G-11149)***
Bank of West 316 729-7999
2123 N Maize Rd Wichita (67212) ***(G-13809)***
Bank of West 785 242-2804
700 S Main St Ottawa (66067) ***(G-8248)***
Bank of West 620 792-1771
1200 Kansas Ave Great Bend (67530) ***(G-2515)***
Bank Snb 316 315-1600
8415 E 21st St N Ste 150 Wichita (67206) ***(G-13810)***
Bank Snb 620 728-3000
100 E 30th Ave Hutchinson (67502) ***(G-3214)***

Bank VI (PA) 785 825-4321
1900 S Ohio St Salina (67401) *(G-10419)*
Bankers and Investors Co 913 299-5008
1300 N 78th St Ste G03 Kansas City (66112) *(G-3844)*
Bankers Bank of Kansas NA 316 681-2265
555 N Woodlawn St Bldg 5 Wichita (67208) *(G-13811)*
Bankers Life, Topeka *Also called American Senior Benefits* *(G-12322)*
Bankers Life & Casualty Co 913 894-6553
8207 Melrose Dr Ste 150 Overland Park (66214) *(G-8430)*
Bankers Life & Casualty Co 785 820-8815
328 N Ohio St Salina (67401) *(G-10420)*
Bankhaven, Haven *Also called Wheatland Investments Inc* *(G-2738)*
Bankonip 913 928-6297
17745 Metcalf Ave Stilwell (66085) *(G-12135)*
Banks Pool & Spa Designs, Overland Park *Also called Banks Swimming Pool Company* *(G-8431)*
Banks Swimming Pool Company (PA) 913 897-9290
8026 W 151st St Overland Park (66223) *(G-8431)*
Bankwest of Kansas 785 462-7557
295 N Franklin Ave Colby (67701) *(G-989)*
Bankwest of Kansas (PA) 785 899-2342
924 Main Ave Goodland (67735) *(G-2463)*
Banner Creek, Holton *Also called Johnsonville LLC* *(G-3102)*
Banzet Concrete Inc 316 776-9961
19664 Sw Butler Rd Rose Hill (67133) *(G-10236)*
Baptist Senior Ministries 913 685-4800
5201 W 143rd St Shawnee Mission (66224) *(G-11150)*
Bar Code Systems 913 894-6368
12230 Santa Fe Trail Dr Shawnee Mission (66215) *(G-11151)*
Bar K Bar Trucking Inc 620 257-5118
1700 E Us Highway 56 Lyons (67554) *(G-6479)*
Bar Method West Plaza 913 499-1468
4722 Rainbow Blvd Westwood (66205) *(G-13550)*
Bar Six Manufaturing Inc 620 622-4456
E Hwy 160 Protection (67127) *(G-10174)*
Barbaras Conservatory Dance 785 272-5991
4300 Sw Huntoon St Topeka (66604) *(G-12364)*
Barber Construction, White City *Also called James R Barber* *(G-13567)*
Barber County Home Health Agcy 620 886-3775
118 E Washington Ave Medicine Lodge (67104) *(G-7057)*
Barber Financial Group Inc (PA) 913 393-1000
13550 W 95th St Lenexa (66215) *(G-5686)*
Barbera & Watkins LLC 913 677-3800
6701 W 64th St Ste 315 Overland Park (66202) *(G-8432)*
Barclay, Andrew M, Andover *Also called Preferred Medical Associates* *(G-106)*
Bardavon Hlth Innovations LLC 913 236-1020
6803 W 64th St Overland Park (66202) *(G-8433)*
Barden and Thompson LLC 620 343-8000
2518 W 15th Ave Emporia (66801) *(G-1702)*
Barker B&C Investments LLC 620 669-0145
1430 W 4th Ave Hutchinson (67501) *(G-3215)*
Barker Printing and Copy Svcs 785 233-5533
925 S Kansas Ave Topeka (66612) *(G-12365)*
Barkley Construction 316 945-6500
1357 S Sierra Dr Wichita (67209) *(G-13812)*
Barkman Honey LLC (PA) 620 947-3173
120 Santa Fe St Hillsboro (67063) *(G-3042)*
Barks N Bows Dog Grooming 785 823-1627
314 S Broadway Blvd Ste B Salina (67401) *(G-10421)*
Barnds Brothers Inc 913 897-2340
10000 W 135th St Shawnee Mission (66221) *(G-11152)*
Barnds Brothers Lawn & Garden, Shawnee Mission *Also called Barnds Brothers Inc* *(G-11152)*
Barnes & Dodge Inc 913 321-6444
17135 W 116th St Lenexa (66219) *(G-5687)*
Barnes Millworks Inc 620 232-8746
2920 N Rotary Ter Pittsburg (66762) *(G-9822)*
Barney's Discount Center, Wichita *Also called Gibson Wholesale Co Inc* *(G-14463)*
Barnharts Excavation LLC 620 431-0959
2082 W 21st St Chanute (66720) *(G-706)*
Barns Timber Creek B & B 620 221-2797
14704 91st Rd Winfield (67156) *(G-16116)*
Baronda Supplies & Service 785 466-2501
1550 S 2700 Rd Herington (67449) *(G-2971)*
Barone Electric Inc 316 263-9579
5341 N Athenian Ave Wichita (67204) *(G-13813)*
Barr-Thorp Electric Company (PA) 913 789-8840
9245 W 53rd St Merriam (66203) *(G-7086)*
Barrier Compliance Svcs LLC 913 905-2695
8245 Nieman Rd Overland Park (66214) *(G-8434)*
Barrington Park Town Homes 913 469-5449
10963 Richards Ct Shawnee Mission (66210) *(G-11153)*
Barrow Tooling Systems Inc 785 364-4306
2000 Frontage Rd Holton (66436) *(G-3085)*
Bartec Construction LLC 913 208-0015
16834 182nd St Tonganoxie (66086) *(G-12252)*
Bartels Inc 316 755-1853
230 N Abilene Ave Valley Center (67147) *(G-13336)*
Bartlesville SW Hotel Inc 913 345-2111
9903 Pflumm Rd Lenexa (66215) *(G-5688)*
Bartlett & West Inc (PA) 785 272-2252
1200 Sw Executive Dr A Topeka (66615) *(G-12366)*
Bartlett Cattle Company LP 620 675-2244
Hc 1 Box 14 Sublette (67877) *(G-12199)*
Bartlett Cooperative Assn (PA) 620 226-3311
4th Main St Bartlett (67332) *(G-371)*
Bartlett Cooperative Assn 620 236-7143
508 S 3rd St Chetopa (67336) *(G-816)*
Bartlett Grain Company LP 316 838-7421
3311 N Emporia St Wichita (67219) *(G-13814)*
Bartlett Grain Company LP 913 321-0900
1310 Fairfax Trfy Kansas City (66115) *(G-3845)*
Bartlett Grain Company LP 913 321-1696
940 Kindleberger Rd Kansas City (66115) *(G-3846)*
Bartlett Milling Company LP 620 251-4650
1307 Maple St Coffeyville (67337) *(G-910)*
Barton County Club Inc 620 653-4255
N Hwy 281 Great Bend (67530) *(G-2516)*
Barton County Cmnty College, Great Bend *Also called Great Western Dining Svc Inc* *(G-2585)*
Barton County Feeders Inc 620 564-2200
1164 Se 40 Rd Ellinwood (67526) *(G-1627)*
Barton Golf Course, Great Bend *Also called Barton County Club Inc* *(G-2516)*
Barton Industries Inc 316 262-3171
1236 N Mosley St Wichita (67214) *(G-13815)*
Barton Keller Sawmill LLC 620 331-8206
2667 W Oak St Independence (67301) *(G-3499)*
Barton Solvents Inc 316 321-1540
2601 Pioneer Dr El Dorado (67042) *(G-1534)*
Barton Solvents Inc 913 287-5500
901 S 66th Ter Kansas City (66111) *(G-3847)*
Bartos Enterprises Inc (PA) 620 232-9813
509 S Cayuga St Frontenac (66763) *(G-2053)*
Bartunek Group Inc 913 327-8800
14137 Nicklaus Dr Overland Park (66223) *(G-8435)*
Basement and Stem Wall Cnstr, Solomon *Also called George Goracke Basement* *(G-12051)*
Basham Furniture Rental Inc (PA) 316 263-5821
2141 N Market St Wichita (67214) *(G-13816)*
Basham Home Store Inc 316 263-5821
103 E 21st St N Wichita (67214) *(G-13817)*
Basic Beginnings Educational 316 721-7946
2111 N Maize Rd Wichita (67212) *(G-13818)*
Basic Energy Services Inc 316 262-3699
100 S Main St Ste 607 Wichita (67202) *(G-13819)*
Basic Energy Services LLC 620 624-2277
1700 S Country Estates Rd Liberal (67901) *(G-6283)*
Basys Processing Inc 800 386-0711
15423 W 100th Ter Lenexa (66219) *(G-5689)*
Bath & Body Works LLC 620 338-8409
2601 Central Ave Ste 2a Dodge City (67801) *(G-1304)*
Bath & Body Works LLC 785 749-0214
3140 Iowa St Ste 105 Lawrence (66046) *(G-4751)*
Bath Body Works 2038, Lawrence *Also called Bath & Body Works LLC* *(G-4751)*
BATH EXPRESSIONS, Emporia *Also called Burnap Bros Inc* *(G-1712)*
Bath Naylor Funeral Home, Pittsburg *Also called Bath-Naylor Inc* *(G-9823)*
Bath-Naylor Inc 620 231-4700
522 S Broadway St Pittsburg (66762) *(G-9823)*
Batliner Paper Converting, Kansas City *Also called Batliner Paper Stock Company* *(G-3848)*
Batliner Paper Stock Company 913 233-1367
305 Sunshine Rd Kansas City (66115) *(G-3848)*
Baton Rouge Southern Railroad, Pittsburg *Also called Watco Companies LLC* *(G-9963)*
Bats Inc 785 526-7185
206 N Main St Sylvan Grove (67481) *(G-12219)*
Bats Trading Inc (HQ) 913 815-7000
8050 Marshall Dr Ste 120 Lenexa (66214) *(G-5690)*
Battenfeld-Cincinnati USA, McPherson *Also called American Maplan Corporation* *(G-6934)*
Baughman Co PA 316 262-7271
315 S Ellis St Wichita (67211) *(G-13820)*
Bauman's Cedar Valley Farms, Garnett *Also called BS Cvf Inc* *(G-2370)*
Bax Global, Wichita *Also called Scott Erickson* *(G-15538)*
Baxter Cmmdts-Dntity Grins LLC 620 492-4040
450 E Road 13 Johnson (67855) *(G-3651)*
Baxter Drug Inc 620 856-5858
1000 Military Ave Baxter Springs (66713) *(G-396)*
Baxter Mechanical Contractors 913 281-6303
565 S 4th St Kansas City (66105) *(G-3849)*
Baxter State Bank (PA) 620 856-2323
1401 Military Ave Baxter Springs (66713) *(G-397)*
Baxter Vault Company Inc 620 856-3441
1325 Grant Ave Baxter Springs (66713) *(G-398)*
Bayer Construction Company Inc 785 776-8839
120 Deep Creek Rd Manhattan (66502) *(G-6553)*
Bayer Healthcare LLC 913 268-2000
12707 Shwnee Mission Pkwy Shawnee Mission (66216) *(G-11154)*
Bayer Hlthcare Animal Hlth Inc 913 268-2731
12809 Shwnee Mission Pkwy Shawnee (66216) *(G-10915)*

ALPHABETIC

Bayless Dry Cleaning Inc...620 793-3576
1110 Kansas Ave Great Bend (67530) *(G-2517)*
Baymont Inn & Suites, Lawrence *Also called Shreeji Investments Inc (G-5110)*
Baymont Inn & Suites, Lawrence *Also called Relax Investments Inc (G-5092)*
Bayouth, William Dr, Lawrence *Also called Animal Hospital of Lawrence (G-4736)*
Baysinger Police Supply Inc...316 262-5663
430 E Central Ave Wichita (67202) *(G-13821)*
Baystone Financial Group (PA)...785 587-4050
2627 Kfb Plz Ste 202e Manhattan (66503) *(G-6554)*
Bazin Sawing & Drilling Llc...913 764-0843
30790 Switzer Rd Louisburg (66053) *(G-6440)*
Bbh LLC...316 945-8208
2215 S West St Wichita (67213) *(G-13822)*
Bcbsks...785 291-7498
1133 Sw Topeka Blvd Topeka (66629) *(G-12367)*
Bccc Child Development Center...620 786-1131
245 Ne 30 Rd Great Bend (67530) *(G-2518)*
BCI, Wichita *Also called Bulk Conveyors Inc (G-13914)*
BCI Manufacturing, Hugoton *Also called Bultman Company Inc Mfg (G-3149)*
BCI Mechanical Inc...913 856-6747
341 S Poplar St Gardner (66030) *(G-2329)*
Bcs Apparel, Overland Park *Also called Branded Custom Sportswear Inc (G-8481)*
Bday Parties (PA)...913 961-1857
32605 W 82nd St De Soto (66018) *(G-1193)*
BE Smith Inc...913 341-9116
8801 Renner Ave Lenexa (66219) *(G-5691)*
Beach Bar and Grill, The, Shawnee Mission *Also called Shawnee Mission Bch Volleyball (G-11853)*
Beachner Bros (kansas) Inc (PA)...620 449-2286
6th & Central Saint Paul (66771) *(G-10380)*
Beachner Grain Inc (PA)...620 820-8600
2600 Flynn Dr Parsons (67357) *(G-9669)*
Beachner Grain Inc...620 244-3277
725 N Main St Erie (66733) *(G-1856)*
Beachner Seed Co Inc...913 686-2090
20300 W 191st St Spring Hill (66083) *(G-12078)*
Beacon Hill Hotel Operator LLC...316 260-9088
125 N Emporia Ave Ste 202 Wichita (67202) *(G-13823)*
Beacon Sales Acquisition Inc...913 262-7663
6000 Merriam Dr Shawnee Mission (66203) *(G-11155)*
Beacon Sales Acquisition Inc...785 234-8406
4008 Nw 14th St Topeka (66618) *(G-12368)*
Beacon Sales Acquisition Inc...913 871-1949
15500 W 108th St Lenexa (66219) *(G-5692)*
Bealmear Bowl Trrey Hoch Reves...620 276-3381
707 E Kansas Plz Garden City (67846) *(G-2105)*
Beam-Ward Kruse Wilson...913 339-6888
8645 College Blvd Ste 250 Overland Park (66210) *(G-8436)*
Beam-Ward Kruse Wilson Wright...785 865-1558
10 E 9th St Ste E Lawrence (66044) *(G-4752)*
Bear Communications LLC...785 856-3333
725 N 2nd St Ste M Lawrence (66044) *(G-4753)*
Bear Communications LLC...913 441-3355
21987 W 83rd St Lenexa (66227) *(G-5693)*
Bearing Headquarters Co, Kansas City *Also called Headco Industries Inc (G-4072)*
Beattie Farmers Un Coop Assn (PA)...785 353-2237
203 Hamilton St Beattie (66406) *(G-418)*
Beau Monde Spa, Wichita *Also called Profiles Inc (G-15368)*
Beauty Brands LLC...913 227-0797
15501 W 99th St Shawnee Mission (66219) *(G-11156)*
Beauty Brands LLC...913 492-7900
9570 Quivira Rd Lenexa (66215) *(G-5694)*
Beauty Brands LLC...913 393-4800
15225 W 119th St Olathe (66062) *(G-7549)*
Beauty Brands LLC...816 505-2800
6519 Nw Barry Rd Kansas City (66106) *(G-3850)*
Beauty Brands LLC...785 228-9778
5820 Sw 21st St Topeka (66604) *(G-12369)*
Beauty Brands LLC...913 663-4848
7501 W 119th St Shawnee Mission (66213) *(G-11157)*
Beauty Brands LLC (PA)...816 531-2266
15507 W 99th St Lenexa (66219) *(G-5695)*
Beauty Brnds Slon Spa Sprstore, Lenexa *Also called Beauty Brands LLC (G-5694)*
Beauty Brnds Slon Spa Sprstore, Olathe *Also called Beauty Brands LLC (G-7549)*
Beauty Brnds Slon Spa Sprstore, Lenexa *Also called Beauty Brands LLC (G-5695)*
Beauty Brnds Slon Spa Sprstres, Shawnee Mission *Also called Beauty Brands LLC (G-11157)*
Beauty Escntuals Salon Day Spa...913 851-4644
12675 Metcalf Ave Overland Park (66213) *(G-8437)*
Beaver Dam Health Care Center...620 231-1120
1005 E Centennial Dr Pittsburg (66762) *(G-9824)*
Beaver Dam Health Care Center...316 321-4444
900 Country Club Ln El Dorado (67042) *(G-1535)*
Beaver Dam Health Care Center...913 592-3100
251 E Wilson St Spring Hill (66083) *(G-12079)*
Beaver Dam Health Care Center...913 422-5952
749 Blake St Edwardsville (66111) *(G-1495)*
Beaver Dam Health Care Center...620 273-6369
612 Walnut St Cottonwood Falls (66845) *(G-1151)*
Beaver Drill & Tool Company...913 384-2400
3995 Mission Rd Kansas City (66103) *(G-3851)*
Beaver Express Service LLC...316 946-5700
2620 Mccormick St Wichita (67213) *(G-13824)*
Beaver Grain Corporation Inc (PA)...620 587-3417
1905 Main St Beaver (67525) *(G-424)*
Beaver Valley Supply Co Inc (PA)...800 982-1280
21366 Highway 36 Atwood (67730) *(G-281)*
Beavers Plumbing L L C...316 619-6119
231 N Walnut St Augusta (67010) *(G-311)*
Beck Roofing & Construction...316 684-7663
400 N River St Derby (67037) *(G-1223)*
Beck Sales Company...620 225-1770
10860 Us Highway 50 Dodge City (67801) *(G-1305)*
Beck's Lawn and Landscaping, Shawnee Mission *Also called Lawns By Beck Inc (G-11549)*
Becker Alfalfa (PA)...620 275-5567
1602 N Van Dittie Dr Garden City (67846) *(G-2106)*
Becker Bros Inc...316 531-2264
514 N Main St Garden Plain (67050) *(G-2321)*
Becker Cabinet & Furniture, Newton *Also called Becker Cabinet Shop (G-7318)*
Becker Cabinet Shop...620 327-4448
9113 N Meridian Rd Newton (67114) *(G-7318)*
Becker Construction Inc...316 744-6800
100 W 61st St N Ste F Park City (67204) *(G-9603)*
Becker Tire & Treading Inc (PA)...620 793-5414
904 Washington St Great Bend (67530) *(G-2519)*
Becker Tire & Treading Inc...316 943-7979
3608 W 30th St S Wichita (67217) *(G-13825)*
Becker Tire of Wichita, Wichita *Also called Becker Tire & Treading Inc (G-13825)*
Becker, James, Garden City *Also called Becker Alfalfa (G-2106)*
Bed Breakfast Inn, Nickerson *Also called Hedrick Exotic Animal Farm (G-7433)*
Bedeschi Mid-West Conveyor LLC...913 384-9950
8245 Nieman Rd Ste 123 Lenexa (66214) *(G-5696)*
Bedrock International LLC (HQ)...913 438-7625
9929 Lackman Rd Lenexa (66219) *(G-5697)*
Beebe Heating & AC Inc...913 541-1222
9104 Cody St Overland Park (66214) *(G-8438)*
Beechcraft Defense Company LLC, Wichita *Also called Textron Aviation Defense LLC (G-15733)*
Beechcraft Holdings LLC (HQ)...316 676-7111
10511 E Central Ave Wichita (67206) *(G-13826)*
Beechcraft Intl Svc Co (HQ)...316 676-7111
10511 E Central Ave Wichita (67206) *(G-13827)*
Beef Belt LLC...620 872-3059
1350 E Road 70 Scott City (67871) *(G-10806)*
Beef Cattle Institute, Manhattan *Also called Kansas State University (G-6684)*
Beelman Truck Co...913 362-0553
51 Silver Ave Kansas City (66103) *(G-3852)*
Befort Harvest and Trucking, Hays *Also called Clayton J Befort (G-2770)*
Bekemeyer Enterprises Inc...785 325-2274
1497 17th Rd Washington (66968) *(G-13459)*
Bel-Air Dental Care Chartered...913 649-0310
5000 W 95th St Ste 300 Prairie Village (66207) *(G-10015)*
Belden Larkin Funeral Home, Leavenworth *Also called Carriage Services Inc (G-5214)*
Belfor USA Group Inc...316 260-4087
100 W 61st St N Park City (67204) *(G-9604)*
Belford Electric Inc...316 267-7060
800 E 3rd St N Wichita (67202) *(G-13828)*
Belger Cartage Co, Shawnee Mission *Also called Belger Cartage Service Inc (G-11158)*
Belger Cartage Service Inc...316 943-0101
2555 S Kessler St Wichita (67217) *(G-13829)*
Belger Cartage Service Inc...913 541-9100
9805 Alden St Shawnee Mission (66215) *(G-11158)*
Bell and Carlson Incorporated...620 225-6688
101 Allen Rd Dodge City (67801) *(G-1306)*
Bell Graphics, Holton *Also called Gary Bell (G-3090)*
Bell Memorials LLC (PA)...785 738-2257
301 S River St Beloit (67420) *(G-474)*
Bell Taxi & K C I Roadrunner, Junction City *Also called Bell Taxi and Trnsp Inc (G-3672)*
Bell Taxi and Trnsp Inc (PA)...785 238-6161
1002 N Washington St Junction City (66441) *(G-3672)*
Bell/Knott and Associates C (PA)...913 378-1600
12730 State Line Rd Leawood (66209) *(G-5339)*
Bella Vita Salon & Day Spa Inc...913 651-6161
4516 S 4th St Leavenworth (66048) *(G-5207)*
Beller Dance Studio Inc...913 648-2626
7820 Foster St Overland Park (66204) *(G-8439)*
Beller, Pattie Dance Studio, Overland Park *Also called Beller Dance Studio Inc (G-8439)*
Belleville Construction, Belleville *Also called Kansas Department Trnsp (G-458)*
BELLEVILLE HEALTHCARE CENTER, Belleville *Also called Lsl of Kansas LLC (G-461)*
Belleville Medical Clinic P A...785 527-2217
2337 G St Ste 100 Belleville (66935) *(G-451)*
Belleville Super 8 Motel...785 527-2112
1410 28th St Belleville (66935) *(G-452)*
Belleville Telescope, Belleville *Also called Telescope Inc (G-467)*

Bellevue Country Club, Atchison *Also called Bellevue Golf and Country Club* ***(G-213)***
Bellevue Golf and Country Club 913 367-3022
1713 Country Club Rd Atchison (66002) ***(G-213)***
Belmont Hotels LLC 785 823-6939
2650 Planet Ave Salina (67401) ***(G-10422)***
Beloit Call 785 738-3537
119 E Main St Beloit (67420) ***(G-475)***
Beloit Country Club Inc 785 738-3163
3167 Hallie Trl Beloit (67420) ***(G-476)***
Beloit Medical Center P A (PA) 785 738-2246
1005 N Lincoln Ave Beloit (67420) ***(G-477)***
Beloit Ready Mix Incorporated (PA) 785 738-4683
2936 K Rd Beloit (67420) ***(G-478)***
Beltmann Group Incorporated 913 888-9105
8101 Lenexa Dr Ste B Lenexa (66214) ***(G-5698)***
Ben Kitchens Painting Co Inc 785 375-3288
611 Country Club Ter Junction City (66441) ***(G-3673)***
Benchmark Construction LLC 785 862-0340
1006 Ash St Eudora (66025) ***(G-1870)***
Benchmark Enterprises 785 537-4447
1181 Rock Springs Ln Manhattan (66502) ***(G-6555)***
Benchmark Rehabilitation Partn 913 384-5810
6640 Johnson Dr Shawnee Mission (66202) ***(G-11159)***
Bendena State Bank (PA) 785 988-4453
933 Friendship Rd Bendena (66008) ***(G-510)***
Bene, Richard J, Overland Park *Also called Monarch Plastic Surgery* ***(G-9049)***
Benedictine Health System 913 498-2700
11901 Rosewood St Shawnee Mission (66209) ***(G-11160)***
Beneficial Kansas Inc (HQ) 913 492-1383
14207 W 95th St Shawnee Mission (66215) ***(G-11161)***
Benefit Comm Insourcing, Leawood *Also called Health and Benefit Systems LLC* ***(G-5422)***
Benefit Management LLC (HQ) 620 792-1779
2015 16th St Great Bend (67530) ***(G-2520)***
Benefit Management Inc, Great Bend *Also called Benefit Management LLC* ***(G-2520)***
Benevolent & P O of Elks 1404 ....620 276-3732
905 E Kansas Plz Garden City (67846) ***(G-2107)***
Benevolent/Protectv Order Elks 785 762-2922
723 S Washington St Junction City (66441) ***(G-3674)***
Bennet Rogers Pipe Coating 913 371-5288
900 Kindleberger Rd Kansas City (66115) ***(G-3853)***
Bennett Rgers Pipe Coating Inc 913 371-3880
900 Kindleberger Rd Kansas City (66115) ***(G-3854)***
Bennett Tool & Die LLC 913 371-4641
3150 Chrysler Rd Kansas City (66115) ***(G-3855)***
Bennington Ambulance Service 785 488-3768
584 N 180th Rd Bennington (67422) ***(G-512)***
Bennington Oil Co Inc 785 392-3031
107 E 2nd St Minneapolis (67467) ***(G-7113)***
Bennington State Bank 785 392-2136
320 W 2nd St Ste 1 Minneapolis (67467) ***(G-7114)***
Bennington State Bank (PA) 785 827-5522
2130 S Ohio St Salina (67401) ***(G-10423)***
Bennington State Bank 785 456-1806
1800 Farrell Dr Wamego (66547) ***(G-13405)***
Bennington State Bank 785 488-3344
104 W Washington St Bennington (67422) ***(G-513)***
Bent Tree Partners LLC 417 206-7846
444 Four States Dr Galena (66739) ***(G-2069)***
Beran Concrete Inc 316 425-7600
3530 N Topeka St Wichita (67219) ***(G-13830)***
Beran Concrete Inc (PA) 316 618-6089
8401 E Oak Knoll St Wichita (67207) ***(G-13831)***
Beran Icf Solutions LLC 316 944-2131
8401 E Oak Knoll St Wichita (67207) ***(G-13832)***
Berberich Trahan & Co PA (PA) 785 234-3427
4301 Sw Huntoon St Topeka (66604) ***(G-12370)***
Berexco Incorporated 620 582-2575
401 S Leavenworth Ave Coldwater (67029) ***(G-1051)***
Berexco LLC 785 628-6101
800a Commerce Pkwy Hays (67601) ***(G-2757)***
Berexco LLC 620 275-0320
808 S Us Hwy 83 Frntage Garden City (67846) ***(G-2108)***
Berger Company (PA) 913 367-3700
104 N 6th St Ste 10 Atchison (66002) ***(G-214)***
Berger Company 913 367-3700
316 Commercial St Ste 10 Atchison (66002) ***(G-215)***
Berkel & Company Contrs Inc (PA) 913 422-5125
2649 S 142nd St Bonner Springs (66012) ***(G-540)***
Berkley Risk ADM Co LLC 913 385-4960
10851 Mastin St Ste 200 Overland Park (66210) ***(G-8440)***
Berkley, Raymond F, Hutchinson *Also called Reynold Fork Berkl Suter Rose* ***(G-3427)***
Berkshire Hthway Frst Realtors 785 271-2888
2858 Sw Vlla W Dr Ste 200 Topeka (66614) ***(G-12371)***
Berkshire Risk Services LLC 913 433-7000
7400 W 132nd St Ste 200 Overland Park (66213) ***(G-8441)***
Berlin-Wheeler Inc 785 271-1000
2942 Sw Wanamaker Rd Topeka (66614) ***(G-12372)***
Berman & Rabin PA 913 649-1555
15280 Metcalf Ave # 200 Overland Park (66223) ***(G-8442)***
Bern Bancshares Inc (PA) 785 336-6121
402 Main St Bern (66408) ***(G-520)***
Bern Meat Plant Incorporated 785 336-2165
411 Main St Bern (66408) ***(G-521)***
Bernard D Ohlsen Cnstr Co 785 873-3462
30337 V Rd Whiting (66552) ***(G-13574)***
Bernices Foods Inc 913 334-8283
15447 W 164th Ter Olathe (66062) ***(G-7550)***
Berning Tire Inc 913 422-3033
306 Oak St Bonner Springs (66012) ***(G-541)***
Berry Companies Inc (PA) 316 838-3321
3223 N Hydraulic St Wichita (67219) ***(G-13833)***
Berry Companies Inc 785 266-9509
1750 Sw 41st St Topeka (66609) ***(G-12373)***
Berry Companies Inc 620 277-2290
3830 W Jones Ave Garden City (67846) ***(G-2109)***
Berry Companies Inc 785 228-2225
1300 Nw Us Highway 24 Topeka (66608) ***(G-12374)***
Berry Companies Inc 316 943-4246
930 S West St Wichita (67213) ***(G-13834)***
Berry Companies Inc 316 838-3321
3223 N Hydraulic St Wichita (67219) ***(G-13835)***
Berry Companies Inc 785 232-7731
835 Ne Us Highway 24 Topeka (66608) ***(G-12375)***
Berry Global Inc 800 777-3080
2401 Lakeview Rd Lawrence (66044) ***(G-4754)***
Berry Holdings LP 620 251-4400
714 Maple St Coffeyville (67337) ***(G-911)***
Berry Material Handling, Topeka *Also called Berry Companies Inc* ***(G-12374)***
Berry Tractor & Equipment Co, Wichita *Also called Berry Companies Inc* ***(G-13833)***
Berry Tractor & Equipment Co, Topeka *Also called Berry Companies Inc* ***(G-12373)***
Berry Tractor & Equipment Co, Wichita *Also called Berry Companies Inc* ***(G-13834)***
Berrys Arctic Ice LLC 785 357-4466
200 N Kansas Ave Topeka (66603) ***(G-12376)***
Bert & Wetta Abilene, Abilene *Also called Bert and Wetta Sales Inc* ***(G-14)***
Bert & Wetta Larned Inc 620 285-7777
1416 Us Highway 56 Larned (67550) ***(G-4695)***
Bert and Wetta Sales Inc (PA) 620 285-7777
1230 Ne Trail St Larned (67550) ***(G-4696)***
Bert and Wetta Sales Inc 785 263-2258
509 Se 4th St Abilene (67410) ***(G-14)***
Bert Nash Cmnty Mntal Hlth Ctr 785 843-9192
200 Maine St Ste A Lawrence (66044) ***(G-4755)***
Berwick Cooperative Oil Co (PA) 785 284-2227
1111 S Us Old Highway 75 Sabetha (66534) ***(G-10307)***
Berwick Oil, Sabetha *Also called Berwick Cooperative Oil Co* ***(G-10307)***
Beshenich Muir & Assoc LLC (PA) 913 904-1880
117 Cherokee St Leavenworth (66048) ***(G-5208)***
Best Beverage, El Dorado *Also called Demo Sales Inc* ***(G-1556)***
Best Beverage Sales Inc 620 331-7100
709 N 20th St Independence (67301) ***(G-3500)***
Best Brands, Bonner Springs *Also called CSM Bakery Solutions LLC* ***(G-546)***
Best Cabs Inc 316 838-2233
2555 N Market St Wichita (67219) ***(G-13836)***
Best Corporation Inc 316 687-1895
225 N Main St El Dorado (67042) ***(G-1536)***
Best Corporation Inc (PA) 316 687-1895
729 E Boston St Wichita (67211) ***(G-13837)***
Best Harvest Bakeries, Kansas City *Also called Best Harvest LLC* ***(G-3856)***
Best Harvest LLC 913 287-6300
530 S 65th St Kansas City (66111) ***(G-3856)***
Best Home Guys Holding Co 316 681-2639
12610 W Hardtner Cir Wichita (67235) ***(G-13838)***
Best Home Guys, The, Wichita *Also called Best Home Guys Holding Co* ***(G-13838)***
Best Value Services LLC 316 440-1048
200 W Douglas Ave Ste 600 Wichita (67202) ***(G-13839)***
Best West Fabrication LLC 785 527-2450
1817 E Frontage Rd Belleville (66935) ***(G-453)***
Best Western, Wichita *Also called Airport Red Coach Inn of Wichi* ***(G-13655)***
Best Western, Wichita *Also called Sonar Sangam Inc* ***(G-15613)***
Best Western, Kansas City *Also called Rainbow Village Management* ***(G-4361)***
Best Western, McPherson *Also called Sagar Inc* ***(G-7022)***
Best Western, Salina *Also called Heart of America Inn Inc* ***(G-10538)***
Best Western, El Dorado *Also called Red Coach Inn* ***(G-1597)***
Best Western, McPherson *Also called Sagar Inc* ***(G-7024)***
Best Western, Lawrence *Also called Jnn LLC* ***(G-4923)***
Best Western Bricktown Lodge 620 251-3700
605 Northeast St Coffeyville (67337) ***(G-912)***
Best Western of Manhattan 785 537-8300
601 Poyntz Ave Manhattan (66502) ***(G-6556)***
Best Western Red Coach Inn 316 283-9120
1301 E 1st St Newton (67114) ***(G-7319)***
Best Western Wichita North, Park City *Also called Leisure Hotel Corporation* ***(G-9627)***
Best Wstn Cntry Inn & Suites 620 225-7378
506 N 14th Ave Dodge City (67801) ***(G-1307)***
Best Wstn K C Spdway Inn Sites 913 334-4440
10401 France Family Dr Kansas City (66111) ***(G-3857)***

A L P H A B E T I C

Best Wstn Plus Emrald Inn Stes, Garden City *Also called Pssk LLC* ***(G-2260)***
Bestifor Hay Co.....785 527-2450
1817 E Frontage Rd Belleville (66935) ***(G-454)***
Bestmark Express Inc.....620 273-7018
2286 Rd U Strong City (66869) ***(G-12191)***
Bestway Inc.....785 742-2949
2021 Iowa St Hiawatha (66434) ***(G-3003)***
Beta Theta PHI.....785 843-4711
P.O. Box 116 Leavenworth (66048) ***(G-5209)***
Beta Theta PHI.....785 843-9188
1425 Tennessee St Lawrence (66044) ***(G-4756)***
Bethany College.....785 227-3380
424 N 1st St Lindsborg (67456) ***(G-6393)***
Bethany HM Assn Lindsborg Kans.....785 227-2334
321 N Chestnut St Lindsborg (67456) ***(G-6394)***
Bethany Home Cottage Complex.....785 227-2721
321 N Chestnut St Lindsborg (67456) ***(G-6395)***
Bethel Neighborhood Center.....913 371-8218
14 S 7th St Kansas City (66101) ***(G-3858)***
BETHESDA HOME, Goessel *Also called Mennonite Bethesda Society* ***(G-2458)***
Bethesda Lthran Cmmunities Inc.....913 906-5000
14150 W 113th St Olathe (66215) ***(G-7551)***
Better Concrete Construction.....913 390-8500
21935 W 122nd St Olathe (66061) ***(G-7552)***
Better Hauling Co.....316 943-5865
603 S Ramsey Dr Valley Center (67147) ***(G-13337)***
Better Life Technology LLC.....620 343-2212
1219 Hatcher St Emporia (66801) ***(G-1703)***
Better Life Technology LLC (PA).....913 894-0403
9736 Legler Rd Lenexa (66219) ***(G-5699)***
Bettis Asphalt & Cnstr Inc.....785 235-8444
1800 Nw Brickyard Rd Topeka (66618) ***(G-12377)***
Bettis Contractors Inc.....785 783-8353
1800 Nw Brickyard Rd Topeka (66618) ***(G-12378)***
Betts Pest Control Inc.....316 943-3555
3015 W Central Ave Wichita (67203) ***(G-13840)***
Bettys Trucking Incorporated.....913 583-3666
9455 Lexington Ave De Soto (66018) ***(G-1194)***
Between Lnes Elite Spt Academy.....913 422-1221
8259 Hedge Lane Ter Lenexa (66227) ***(G-5700)***
Betzen Trenching Inc.....316 269-9331
1410 S Walnut St Wichita (67213) ***(G-13841)***
Beumer Kansas City LLC.....816 245-7260
7300 W 110th St Ste 530 Overland Park (66210) ***(G-8443)***
Bevan-Rabell Inc.....316 946-4870
1880 S Airport Rd Wichita (67209) ***(G-13842)***
Bever Dye Lc.....316 263-8294
301 N Main St Ste 600 Wichita (67202) ***(G-13843)***
Beverly, Spring Hill *Also called Beaver Dam Health Care Center* ***(G-12079)***
Beverly Enterprises-Kansas LLC.....316 683-7588
4007 E Lincoln St Wichita (67218) ***(G-13844)***
Beverly Enterprises-Kansas LLC.....913 351-1284
210 N Plaza Dr Lansing (66043) ***(G-4669)***
Beverly Enterprises-Kansas LLC.....785 672-3115
615 Price Ave Oakley (67748) ***(G-7472)***
Beverly Enterprises-Kansas LLC.....785 263-1431
705 N Brady St Abilene (67410) ***(G-15)***
Beverly Enterprises-Kansas LLC.....620 273-6369
1010 East St Tonganoxie (66086) ***(G-12253)***
Beverly Enterprises-Kansas LLC.....785 454-3321
1218 Kansas St 2 Downs (67437) ***(G-1468)***
Beverly Enterprises-Kansas LLC.....785 449-2294
505 N Main St Eskridge (66423) ***(G-1865)***
Beverly Enterprises-Kansas LLC.....785 658-2505
611 31st St Wilson (67490) ***(G-16104)***
Beverly Enterprises-Kansas LLC.....913 422-5832
750 Blake St Edwardsville (66111) ***(G-1496)***
Beverly Enterprises-Kansas LLC.....620 231-1120
1005 E Centennial Dr Pittsburg (66762) ***(G-9825)***
Beverly Enterprises-Kansas LLC.....785 462-6721
105 E College Dr Colby (67701) ***(G-990)***
Beverly Enterprises-Kansas LLC.....785 461-5417
509 Grove St Wakefield (67487) ***(G-13398)***
Beverly Healthcare, Abilene *Also called Beverly Enterprises-Kansas LLC* ***(G-15)***
Beverly Rehabilitation Center, Pittsburg *Also called Beverly Enterprises-Kansas LLC* ***(G-9825)***
Beyond 21st Century Inc.....913 631-4790
7306 Reeder St Shawnee (66203) ***(G-10916)***
Bfr Metals, Salina *Also called Bohm Farm & Ranch Inc* ***(G-10429)***
Bg Products Incorporated (PA).....316 265-2686
740 S Wichita St Wichita (67213) ***(G-13845)***
Bg Products Incorporated.....316 265-2686
701 S Wichita St Wichita (67213) ***(G-13846)***
Bg Products Incorporated.....316 265-2686
2415 Pioneer Dr El Dorado (67042) ***(G-1537)***
Bgr Consulting Engineers Inc.....816 842-2800
8908 W 106th St Overland Park (66212) ***(G-8444)***
Bgs Company, Wichita *Also called Goentzel Construction Inc* ***(G-14479)***
Bha Altair LLC (HQ).....816 356-8400
11501 Outlook St Ste 100 Overland Park (66211) ***(G-8445)***
Bhakta LLC.....620 532-3118
1113 E Us Highway 54 Kingman (67068) ***(G-4583)***
Bhc Rhodes, Overland Park *Also called Brungardt Honomichl & Co PA* ***(G-8490)***
Bhcmc LLC.....620 682-7777
4000 W Comanche St Dodge City (67801) ***(G-1308)***
Bhjllc Inc (PA).....913 888-8028
14105 Marshall Dr Lenexa (66215) ***(G-5701)***
Bhjllc Inc.....785 272-8800
1145 Sw Wanamaker Rd Topeka (66604) ***(G-12379)***
Bhr Inc.....913 469-1599
7939 Floyd St Overland Park (66204) ***(G-8446)***
Bhs Construction Inc.....785 537-2068
727 S Juliette Ave Manhattan (66502) ***(G-6557)***
Bl Brooks & Sons Inc (PA).....913 829-5494
15625 S Keeler Ter Olathe (66062) ***(G-7553)***
Bichelmeyer Meats A Corp.....913 342-5945
704 Cheyenne Ave Kansas City (66105) ***(G-3859)***
Bichelmeyer's, Kansas City *Also called Bichelmeyer Meats A Corp* ***(G-3859)***
Bickford House, Olathe *Also called Eb Group* ***(G-7666)***
Bickford Overland Park LLC.....913 782-3200
10665 Barkley St Shawnee Mission (66212) ***(G-11162)***
Bickford Senior Living, Olathe *Also called Tri City Assisted Living LLC* ***(G-8120)***
Bicknell Family Holding Co LLC.....913 387-2743
7400 College Blvd Ste 205 Overland Park (66210) ***(G-8447)***
Biehler Companies Inc.....316 529-0002
1100 E Macarthur Rd Wichita (67216) ***(G-13847)***
Big Block Inc.....913 927-2135
8167 Cole Pkwy Lenexa (66227) ***(G-5702)***
Big Bobs Outlets Kansas Cy Inc (PA).....913 362-2627
10001 W 75th St Shawnee Mission (66204) ***(G-11163)***
Big Bobs U Crpt Shops Kans Cy, Shawnee Mission *Also called Big Bobs Outlets Kansas Cy Inc* ***(G-11163)***
Big Creek Investment Corp Inc.....620 431-3445
10280 210th Rd Chanute (66720) ***(G-707)***
Big Creek Sound, Chanute *Also called Big Creek Investment Corp Inc* ***(G-707)***
Big DS Rent All.....785 625-2443
1110 E 22nd St Hays (67601) ***(G-2758)***
Big G Manufacturing, Harper *Also called Green Line Inc* ***(G-2722)***
Big Heart Pet Brands.....785 312-3662
727 N Iowa St Lawrence (66044) ***(G-4757)***
Big Heart Pet Brands.....785 338-9240
2200 Nw Brickyard Rd Topeka (66618) ***(G-12380)***
Big Lkes Developmental Ctr Inc (PA).....785 776-9201
1416 Hayes Dr Manhattan (66502) ***(G-6558)***
Big Lkes Developmental Ctr Inc.....785 776-7748
515 Colorado St Ste 517 Manhattan (66502) ***(G-6559)***
Big Lkes Developmental Ctr Inc.....785 632-5357
302 Lincoln Ave Clay Center (67432) ***(G-843)***
Big Lkes Developmental Ctr Inc.....785 776-0777
2304 Butternut Ln Manhattan (66502) ***(G-6560)***
Big Phils Auto Plaza, Topeka *Also called Ritchey Motors LLC* ***(G-13019)***
Big R, Ulysses *Also called Ulysses Standard Supply Inc* ***(G-13327)***
Big Sky Distributors Kans LLC.....913 897-4488
1900 W 142nd St Shawnee Mission (66224) ***(G-11164)***
Big Springs Sports Center.....785 887-6700
1895 E 56th Rd Lecompton (66050) ***(G-5610)***
Big Sur Waterbeds Inc.....316 944-6225
555 S Hoover Rd Ste 2400 Wichita (67209) ***(G-13848)***
Big Tool Store, Derby *Also called Kuhn Co LLC* ***(G-1257)***
Big Twin Inc.....785 234-6174
2047 Sw Topeka Blvd Frnt Topeka (66612) ***(G-12381)***
Big W Industries Inc.....913 321-2112
200 S 5th St Kansas City (66101) ***(G-3860)***
Bijin For Hair.....913 671-7777
6960 Mission Rd Ste 18 Shawnee Mission (66208) ***(G-11165)***
Bijin Salon & Day Spa, Shawnee Mission *Also called Bijin For Hair* ***(G-11165)***
Bikson, Bruce, Olathe *Also called Complete Dental Care* ***(G-7608)***
Bill Barr & Company (PA).....913 599-6668
8800 Grant Ave Overland Park (66212) ***(G-8448)***
Bill Davis Roofing.....913 764-4449
26359 W 110th St Olathe (66061) ***(G-7554)***
Bill G Goble, Hutchinson *Also called Grant D Ringler DDS Inc* ***(G-3304)***
Bill Harmon.....620 275-9597
5550 N 16 Mile Rd Garden City (67846) ***(G-2110)***
Bill Tropical Greenhouse, Kansas City *Also called Bills Tropical Greenhouse* ***(G-3861)***
Bill White Realty Co, Independence *Also called Timothy D White* ***(G-3565)***
Billiards Sports Plaza, Wichita *Also called Coin Machine Distributors Inc* ***(G-14052)***
Billing Healthcare Resources, Overland Park *Also called Bhr Inc* ***(G-8446)***
Bills Floor Covering Inc.....913 492-1964
14316 W 99th St Shawnee Mission (66215) ***(G-11166)***
Bills Frank Trucking Inc.....620 736-2875
Old Hwy 99 Severy (67137) ***(G-10889)***
Bills Friends AA Group.....913 722-9801
4700 Mission Rd Roeland Park (66205) ***(G-10218)***

Bills Outdoor Sports 620 241-7130
835 S Us Highway 81 Byp McPherson (67460) ***(G-6938)***
Bills Plumbing Service LLC 913 829-8213
308 E Park St Olathe (66061) ***(G-7555)***
Bills Tropical Greenhouse 913 432-6383
2943 S 47th St Kansas City (66106) ***(G-3861)***
Bills, Frank Ranch, Severy *Also called Frank Bills* ***(G-10890)***
Billy Murphy & Associates LLC 913 306-0381
1011 Metropolitan Ave Leavenworth (66048) ***(G-5210)***
Bimbo Bakeries Usa Inc 913 328-1234
7565 State Ave Kansas City (66112) ***(G-3862)***
Bimbo Bakeries Usa Inc 620 218-2365
2536 S Southeast Dr Wichita (67216) ***(G-13849)***
Bimbo Bakeries Usa Inc 620 276-6308
1130 Massey Ferguson Rd Garden City (67846) ***(G-2111)***
Bindery Express Inc 316 944-8163
1930 N Ohio Ave Wichita (67214) ***(G-13850)***
Bingham Canyon Corporation (PA) 913 353-4560
10457 W 84th Ter Lenexa (66214) ***(G-5703)***
Bingham Transportation Inc 620 679-9810
Hwy 69 Treece (66778) ***(G-13267)***
Binswanger Enterprises LLC 785 267-4090
211 Sw 37th St Topeka (66611) ***(G-12382)***
Binswanger Glass, Topeka *Also called Binswanger Enterprises LLC* ***(G-12382)***
Bio-Mdcal Applcations Kans Inc 913 498-1780
6751 W 119th St Overland Park (66209) ***(G-8449)***
Bio-Mdcal Applcations Kans Inc 785 266-3087
3408 Se 29th St Topeka (66605) ***(G-12383)***
Bio-Mdcal Applcations Kans Inc 785 823-6460
700 E Iron Ave Salina (67401) ***(G-10424)***
Bio-Microbics Inc (PA) 913 422-0707
16002 W 110th St Lenexa (66219) ***(G-5704)***
Bio-Next Inc 316 260-1540
611 E 13th St N Wichita (67214) ***(G-13851)***
Biodesix Inc 913 583-9000
8960 Commerce Dr Bldg 6 De Soto (66018) ***(G-1195)***
Biomat Usa Inc 785 233-0079
2120 Sw 6th Ave Topeka (66606) ***(G-12384)***
Biomed Kansas Inc (HQ) 913 661-0100
10633 Rene St Lenexa (66215) ***(G-5705)***
Biomedical Devices of KS LLC 913 845-3851
1205 E Highway 24-40 Tonganoxie (66086) ***(G-12254)***
Biomune Company 913 894-0230
8735 Rosehill Rd Lenexa (66215) ***(G-5706)***
Biomune Company (HQ) 913 894-0230
8906 Rosehill Rd Lenexa (66215) ***(G-5707)***
Biostar Lighting, Overland Park *Also called Biostar Renewables LLC* ***(G-8450)***
Biostar Renewables LLC 913 369-4100
9400 Reeds Rd Ste 150 Overland Park (66207) ***(G-8450)***
Biostar Systems LLC 913 438-3002
9400 Reeds Rd Ste 150 Overland Park (66207) ***(G-8451)***
Birch Contracting Group LLC 913 400-3975
16220 Birch St Overland Park (66085) ***(G-8452)***
Bird City Dairy LLC 785 734-2295
1440 Road 32 Bird City (67731) ***(G-529)***
Bird Engineering Company PA 913 631-2222
6100 Nieman Rd Ste 200 Shawnee (66203) ***(G-10917)***
Bird Music & Amusement Svcs 785 537-2930
5104 Skyway Dr Manhattan (66503) ***(G-6561)***
Birla Carbon USA Inc 620 356-3151
3500 S Road S Ulysses (67880) ***(G-13283)***
Birth & Women Center Inc 785 232-6950
1109 Sw Topeka Blvd Topeka (66612) ***(G-12385)***
Birthright Inc 913 682-2700
221 Delaware St Ste A Leavenworth (66048) ***(G-5211)***
Bisel Inc 785 842-2656
1404 E 24th St Ste B Lawrence (66046) ***(G-4758)***
Bishop Brew 785 242-8920
120 E Dundee St Ottawa (66067) ***(G-8249)***
Bishop Rink Holdings LLC 913 268-2625
5225 Renner Rd Shawnee (66217) ***(G-10918)***
Bituminous Casualty Corp 913 262-4664
4330 Shawnee Mission Pkwy Fairway (66205) ***(G-1905)***
Bituminous Casualty Corp 913 268-9176
6718 Hauser Dr Shawnee Mission (66216) ***(G-11167)***
BJ Koetting Inc 785 823-8580
321 Pine Ridge Dr Salina (67401) ***(G-10425)***
Bkd LLP 316 265-2811
1551 N Waterfront Pkwy # 300 Wichita (67206) ***(G-13852)***
BKM Construction LLC 913 297-0049
501 S 5th St Leavenworth (66048) ***(G-5212)***
Black & Veatch - Er JV 913 458-6650
6800 W 115th St Ste 2200 Overland Park (66211) ***(G-8453)***
Black & Veatch Cnstr Inc 913 458-2000
11880 College Blvd # 410 Overland Park (66210) ***(G-8454)***
Black & Veatch Corporation (HQ) 913 458-2000
11401 Lamar Ave Overland Park (66211) ***(G-8455)***
Black & Veatch Corporation 913 458-2000
6800 W 115th St Ste 600 Overland Park (66211) ***(G-8456)***
Black & Veatch Holding Company (HQ) 913 458-2000
11401 Lamar Ave Overland Park (66211) ***(G-8457)***
Black & Veatch-GEC Joint Ventr 913 458-4300
6800 W 115th St Ste 2200 Overland Park (66211) ***(G-8458)***
Black & Veatch-Olsson JV 913 458-6650
6800 W 115th St Ste 2200 Overland Park (66211) ***(G-8459)***
Black & Winsor Inc 316 943-0703
7106 W Pueblo Dr Wichita (67209) ***(G-13853)***
Black and Jensen Inc 316 262-7277
729 S Emporia Ave Wichita (67211) ***(G-13854)***
Black Bob Banking Center BR, Olathe *Also called Enterprise Bank & Trust* ***(G-7682)***
Black Diamond Oil Inc 785 625-5891
P.O. Box 641 Hays (67601) ***(G-2759)***
Black Gold Inc 785 354-4000
2404 Ne Grantville Rd Topeka (66608) ***(G-12386)***
Black Gold Installation, Topeka *Also called Black Gold Inc* ***(G-12386)***
Black Hawk Inc 785 539-8240
2104 Tamarron Ter Manhattan (66502) ***(G-6562)***
Black Hawkins, Manhattan *Also called Black Hawk Inc* ***(G-6562)***
Black Hills Energy, Lawrence *Also called Black Hills/Kansas Gas* ***(G-4759)***
Black Hills Energy, Garden City *Also called Black Hills/Kansas Gas* ***(G-2112)***
Black Hills Energy, Wichita *Also called Black Hills/Kansas Gas* ***(G-13855)***
Black Hills Energy, Dodge City *Also called Black Hills/Kansas Gas* ***(G-1309)***
Black Hills Energy, Liberal *Also called Black Hills/Kansas Gas* ***(G-6284)***
Black Hills/Kansas Gas 605 721-1700
601 N Iowa St Lawrence (66044) ***(G-4759)***
Black Hills/Kansas Gas 605 721-1700
1810 Buffalo Jones Ave Garden City (67846) ***(G-2112)***
Black Hills/Kansas Gas 605 721-1700
2330 N Hoover Rd Wichita (67205) ***(G-13855)***
Black Hills/Kansas Gas 605 721-1700
11142 Kliesen St Dodge City (67801) ***(G-1309)***
Black Hills/Kansas Gas 605 721-1700
1600 General Welch Blvd Liberal (67901) ***(G-6284)***
Black Jack Tree Lawn and Ldscp 785 865-8536
311 Baker St Baldwin City (66006) ***(G-356)***
Black Knight Fincl Svcs Inc 913 693-0000
4400 College Blvd Leawood (66211) ***(G-5340)***
Black Stag Brewery LLC 785 764-1628
623 Massachusetts St Lawrence (66044) ***(G-4760)***
Black Vatch MGT Consulting LLC 913 458-2000
11401 Lamar Ave Overland Park (66211) ***(G-8460)***
Black Veatch-Altan Joint Ventr 913 458-4300
6800 W 115th St Ste 2200 Overland Park (66211) ***(G-8461)***
Black Vtch - Gsyntec Jint Vntr 913 458-4300
6800 W 115th St Ste 2200 Overland Park (66211) ***(G-8462)***
Black Vtch Spcial Prjects Corp (HQ) 913 458-2000
6800 W 115th St Ste 2200 Overland Park (66211) ***(G-8463)***
Black's Liquor Store, Kansas City *Also called Blacks Retail Liquor LLC* ***(G-3866)***
Blackbird Maintenance, El Dorado *Also called Confab Inc* ***(G-1548)***
Blackbob Pet Hospital 913 829-7387
15200 S Blackbob Rd Olathe (66062) ***(G-7556)***
Blackburn Construction Inc 316 321-5358
2200 W 6th Ave El Dorado (67042) ***(G-1538)***
Blackburn Nursery Inc 785 272-2707
5645 Sw 33rd St Topeka (66614) ***(G-12387)***
Blackburns All Star Roofing 913 321-3456
902 Osage Ave Kansas City (66105) ***(G-3863)***
Blackfin LLC 816 985-4850
537 Central Ave Kansas City (66101) ***(G-3864)***
Blackjack Manufacturing, Kansas City *Also called Blackjack Tire Supplies Inc* ***(G-3865)***
Blackjack Tire Supplies Inc 816 872-1158
3260 N 7th Street Trfy Kansas City (66115) ***(G-3865)***
Blackmore and Glunt Inc 913 469-5715
13835 W 107th St Shawnee Mission (66215) ***(G-11168)***
Blacks Retail Liquor LLC 913 281-1551
1014 Central Ave Kansas City (66102) ***(G-3866)***
Blackstone Environmental Inc (PA) 913 495-9990
16200 Foster St Stilwell (66085) ***(G-12136)***
Blade Empire Publishing Co 785 243-2424
510 Washington St Concordia (66901) ***(G-1103)***
Bladon Dialysis LLC 620 728-0440
1901 N Waldron St Hutchinson (67502) ***(G-3216)***
Blair Doon Veterinary Hospital 316 685-7300
10804 E 31st St S Wichita (67210) ***(G-13856)***
Blair Feeds, Atchison *Also called Blair Milling & Elev Co Inc* ***(G-216)***
Blair Milling & Elev Co Inc 913 367-2310
1000 Main St Atchison (66002) ***(G-216)***
Blake & Uhlig P A (PA) 913 321-8884
753 State Ave Ste 475 Kansas City (66101) ***(G-3867)***
Blaylock Diesel Service Inc 620 856-5227
3100 Military Ave Baxter Springs (66713) ***(G-399)***
Blaylock Turbo, Baxter Springs *Also called Blaylock Diesel Service Inc* ***(G-399)***
Blecha Enterprises LLC 785 539-6640
6130 Tuttle Ter Manhattan (66503) ***(G-6563)***
Blend Tech Inc 316 941-9660
1819 S Meridian Ave Wichita (67213) ***(G-13857)***

ALPHABETIC

Bli Rentals LLC.......620 342-7847
1554 Road 175 Emporia (66801) ***(G-1704)***
Blicks Phsphate Cnversions LLC.......800 932-5425
401 N Campus Dr Garden City (67846) ***(G-2113)***
Blind Pig.......785 827-7449
2501 Market Pl Ste A Salina (67401) ***(G-10426)***
Blish-Mize Co (PA).......913 367-1250
223 S 5th St Atchison (66002) ***(G-217)***
Blish-Mize Co.......913 367-1250
2606 Industrial Rd Atchison (66002) ***(G-218)***
Blizzard Energy Inc.......620 796-2396
9015 8th St Great Bend (67530) ***(G-2521)***
Block Real Estate Services LLC.......816 412-8457
7101 College Blvd Ste 735 Overland Park (66210) ***(G-8464)***
Block Real Estate Services LLC.......816 746-9922
8349 Melrose Dr Overland Park (66214) ***(G-8465)***
Block Real Estate Services LLC.......816 412-8409
10411 W 84th Ter Lenexa (66214) ***(G-5708)***
Blockbuster, Wichita *Also called Fugate Enterprises* ***(G-14428)***
Blockbuster, Overland Park *Also called Major Video of Kansas Inc* ***(G-8980)***
Blockbuster LLC.......913 438-3203
13630 W 87th Street Pkwy Shawnee Mission (66215) ***(G-11169)***
Bloom & Associates Therapy (PA).......785 273-7700
2300 Se Sagis Ct Topeka (66605) ***(G-12388)***
Bloom Living Senior Apartments.......913 738-4335
14001 W 133rd St Olathe (66062) ***(G-7557)***
Blot Engineering Inc (PA).......913 441-1636
5420 Martindale Rd Shawnee (66218) ***(G-10919)***
Blue Beacon LP II.......785 825-2221
500 Graves Blvd Salina (67401) ***(G-10427)***
Blue Beacon Truck Wash, Oakley *Also called Blue Beacon USA LP II* ***(G-7473)***
Blue Beacon USA LP (PA).......785 825-2221
500 Graves Blvd Salina (67401) ***(G-10428)***
Blue Beacon USA LP II.......785 672-3328
1003 Highway 40 Oakley (67748) ***(G-7473)***
Blue Chip Copy & Print, Lenexa *Also called Brad Vignatelli* ***(G-5711)***
Blue Cross and Blue Shield of.......785 291-4180
1133 Sw Topeka Blvd Topeka (66629) ***(G-12389)***
Blue Cross Blue Sheld Kans Inc (PA).......785 291-7000
1133 Sw Topeka Blvd Topeka (66629) ***(G-12390)***
Blue Cross Blue Sheld Kans Inc.......316 269-1666
220 W Douglas Ave Ste 200 Wichita (67202) ***(G-13858)***
Blue DOT Services Company Kans, Topeka *Also called J-DOT Inc* ***(G-12734)***
Blue Eagle Investigations Inc.......913 685-2583
18890 W 252nd St Paola (66071) ***(G-9542)***
Blue Eagle Productions Inc.......816 225-2980
13805 Fontana St Overland Park (66224) ***(G-8466)***
Blue Frog Printing, Wichita *Also called Print Source Inc* ***(G-15348)***
Blue Hill Peninsula Dental, Overland Park *Also called W Ross Greenlaw DMD* ***(G-9475)***
Blue Hl Gamebirds & Htchy LLC.......785 373-4965
517 Grasshopper Tipton (67485) ***(G-12247)***
Blue Infotech Inc.......816 945-2583
5251 W 116th Pl Ste 200 Leawood (66211) ***(G-5341)***
Blue Rapids Greenhouse Inc.......785 363-7300
805 Pomeroy St Blue Rapids (66411) ***(G-533)***
Blue Rapids Medical Clinic, Blue Rapids *Also called Community Memorial Healthcare* ***(G-535)***
Blue River Elementary Pto Inc.......913 239-6000
5101 W 163rd Ter Overland Park (66085) ***(G-8467)***
Blue River Sand and Gravel Co, Marysville *Also called Hall Brothers Inc* ***(G-6890)***
Blue Valley Animal Hospital (PA).......913 681-2818
16200 Metcalf Ave Overland Park (66085) ***(G-8468)***
Blue Valley Chemical LLC.......816 984-2125
5423 W 131st Ter Overland Park (66209) ***(G-8469)***
Blue Valley Goodyear Service.......913 345-1380
6717 W 119th St Shawnee Mission (66209) ***(G-11170)***
Blue Valley Health Care, Marysville *Also called Marysville Health Corporation* ***(G-6899)***
Blue Valley Health Care (PA).......785 363-7777
710 Western Ave Blue Rapids (66411) ***(G-534)***
Blue Valley Insurance Agencies (PA).......785 337-2268
204 W North St Hanover (66945) ***(G-2710)***
Blue Valley Nursing Home, Blue Rapids *Also called Blue Valley Health Care* ***(G-534)***
Blue Valley Partners LP.......913 963-5534
8008 Granada Rd Prairie Village (66208) ***(G-10016)***
Blue Valley Recreation Comm.......913 685-6030
9701 W 137th St Shawnee Mission (66221) ***(G-11171)***
Blue Valley Tan, Overland Park *Also called Blue Valley Chemical LLC* ***(G-8469)***
Blue Valley Tele-Marketing.......785 799-3500
1555 Pony Express Hwy Home (66438) ***(G-3118)***
Blue Vly Tl-Communications Inc (PA).......785 799-3311
1559 Pony Express Hwy Home (66438) ***(G-3119)***
Bluejcket Crssing Vnyrd Winery.......785 542-1764
1969 N 1250th Rd Eudora (66025) ***(G-1871)***
Bluepearl Vtrinary Partners LLC.......913 642-9563
11950 W 110th St Ste B Shawnee Mission (66210) ***(G-11172)***
Bluestem Electric Coop Inc (PA).......785 456-2212
614 E Hwy 24 Wamego (66547) ***(G-13406)***
Bluestem Electric Cooperative.......785 632-3111
524 Dexter St Clay Center (67432) ***(G-844)***
Bluestem Farm and Rnch Sup Inc.......620 342-5502
2611 W Us Highway 50 Emporia (66801) ***(G-1705)***
Bluestem Medical Clinic, P.A., Eureka *Also called Witchita Clinic Inc* ***(G-1899)***
Bluestem Medical LLP.......785 754-2458
501 Garfield St Quinter (67752) ***(G-10179)***
Bluestreak Enterprises Inc.......785 550-8179
808 Lynn St Lawrence (66044) ***(G-4761)***
Bluetooth Sig Inc.......913 317-4700
7300 College Blvd Ste 200 Overland Park (66210) ***(G-8470)***
Blumoo, Gardner *Also called Flyover Innovations Inc* ***(G-2346)***
BMA, Leavenworth *Also called Beshenich Muir & Assoc LLC* ***(G-5208)***
BMA Leawood, Overland Park *Also called Bio-Mdcal Applcations Kans Inc* ***(G-8449)***
Bme Inc.......785 274-5116
3001 S Kansas Ave Topeka (66611) ***(G-12391)***
Bmg of Kansas Inc.......620 327-4038
606 Commerce Dr Hesston (67062) ***(G-2985)***
Bmo Harris Bank, Shawnee Mission *Also called Harris Bmo Bank National Assn* ***(G-11411)***
Bmo Harris Bank, Pittsburg *Also called Harris Bmo Bank National Assn* ***(G-9871)***
Bmo Harris Bank, Leawood *Also called Harris Bmo Bank National Assn* ***(G-5419)***
Bmo Harris Bank, Olathe *Also called Harris Bmo Bank National Assn* ***(G-7754)***
Bmo Harris Bank, Pittsburg *Also called Harris Bmo Bank National Assn* ***(G-9872)***
Bmo Harris Bank, Shawnee Mission *Also called Harris Bmo Bank National Assn* ***(G-11412)***
BNC, Olathe *Also called Butler National Corporation* ***(G-7571)***
BNC National Bank.......913 647-7000
7007 College Blvd Ste 330 Overland Park (66211) ***(G-8471)***
Bnsf Railway Company.......316 284-3224
620 S Boyd Ave Newton (67114) ***(G-7320)***
Bnsf Railway Company.......620 227-5977
804 E Trail St Dodge City (67801) ***(G-1310)***
Bnsf Railway Company.......913 551-4882
2525 Argentine Blvd Kansas City (66106) ***(G-3868)***
Bnsf Railway Company.......620 441-2276
520 E Central Ave Arkansas City (67005) ***(G-148)***
Bnsf Railway Company.......913 893-4295
32880 W 191st St Edgerton (66021) ***(G-1480)***
Bnsf Railway Company.......913 551-2604
4515 Kansas Ave Kansas City (66106) ***(G-3869)***
Bnsf Railway Company.......620 203-2586
1112 W South Ave Emporia (66801) ***(G-1706)***
Bnsf Railway Company.......620 896-2096
210 E 5th St Harper (67058) ***(G-2716)***
Bnsf Railway Company.......785 435-7021
920 Se Quincy St Topeka (66612) ***(G-12392)***
Bnsf Railway Company.......620 429-3850
400 N Tennessee Ave Columbus (66725) ***(G-1061)***
Bnsf Railway Company.......913 888-5250
13301 Santa Fe Trail Dr Shawnee Mission (66215) ***(G-11173)***
Bnsf Railway Company.......785 435-2000
1001 Ne Atchison Ave Topeka (66616) ***(G-12393)***
Bnsf Railway Company.......620 399-4201
1315 E 1st St Wellington (67152) ***(G-13491)***
Bnsf Railway Company.......817 352-1000
12345 College Blvd Shawnee Mission (66210) ***(G-11174)***
Bnsf Railway Company.......316 708-4472
301 E 5th Ave Augusta (67010) ***(G-312)***
Boan Connealy & Houlehan LLC.......913 491-9178
13220 Metcalf Ave Ste 100 Overland Park (66213) ***(G-8472)***
Boan & Connealy, Overland Park *Also called Boan Connealy & Houlehan LLC* ***(G-8472)***
Boan Masonry Company Inc.......913 592-5369
19155 S Hedge Ln Spring Hill (66083) ***(G-12080)***
Board of Edcatn of Kans Cy Ks.......913 627-6550
912 S Baltimore St Kansas City (66105) ***(G-3870)***
Board of Edcatn of Kans Cy Ks.......913 627-3913
2112 N 18th St Kansas City (66104) ***(G-3871)***
Board of Pension Trustees, Kansas City *Also called Kansas City Bd Pub Utilities* ***(G-4136)***
Board of Public Utilities, Kansas City *Also called Kansas City Bd Pub Utilities* ***(G-4142)***
Bob Allen Ford Inc.......913 381-3000
9239 Metcalf Ave Overland Park (66212) ***(G-8473)***
Bob Bergkamp Cnstr Co Inc.......316 522-3471
3709 S West St Wichita (67217) ***(G-13859)***
Bob Boyd, Manhattan *Also called Dry Clean City* ***(G-6617)***
Bob Durbin DDS.......785 267-5010
5310 Sw 37th St Topeka (66614) ***(G-12394)***
Bob Eisel Powder Coatings.......316 942-8870
1703 N Barrier Cv Wichita (67206) ***(G-13860)***
Bob Hull Inc.......785 292-4790
710 N Elm St Frankfort (66427) ***(G-2021)***
Bob Johnson Youth Shelter, Hutchinson *Also called Reno County Youth Services* ***(G-3425)***
Bob Stith Heating and Cooling (PA).......316 262-1802
1411 S Handley St Wichita (67213) ***(G-13861)***
Bob Thornton.......620 624-7691
11 Village Plz Liberal (67901) ***(G-6285)***
Bob Wilson Mem Grant Cnty Hosp.......620 356-1266
415 N Main St Ulysses (67880) ***(G-13284)***
Bob's Fuel, Cawker City *Also called S&K Fuels LLC* ***(G-689)***

Bobby T'S Restaurant & Bar, Manhattan *Also called Bobby TS Bar & Grill Inc* ***(G-6564)***
Bobby TS Bar & Grill Inc.....785 537-8383
3236 Kimball Ave Manhattan (66503) ***(G-6564)***
Bobcat Oil Field Service Inc.....913 980-3858
27260 Normandy Rd Louisburg (66053) ***(G-6441)***
Bobec Inc.....913 248-1110
7701 Renner Rd Shawnee Mission (66217) ***(G-11175)***
Bobs Janitorial Service & Sup (HQ).....785 271-6600
725 Ne Us Highway 24 A Topeka (66608) ***(G-12395)***
Bobs Plumbing, Manhattan *Also called Randal J Steiner* ***(G-6786)***
Bobs Plumbing & Heating Inc (PA).....785 539-4155
5281 Tuttle Creek Blvd Manhattan (66502) ***(G-6565)***
Bobs Super Saver Inc.....620 251-6820
1000 Hall St Coffeyville (67337) ***(G-913)***
Bocker's Two Catering Service, Manhattan *Also called Bockers Two Catering Inc* ***(G-6566)***
Bockers Two Catering Inc.....785 539-9431
1108 Laramie St 1106 Manhattan (66502) ***(G-6566)***
Body Boutique, Lawrence *Also called Hartzler Lorenda* ***(G-4891)***
Bodycote Thermal Proc Inc.....316 943-3288
1009 S West St Wichita (67213) ***(G-13862)***
Bodycote Thermal Proc Inc.....316 267-6264
1019 S Mclean Blvd Wichita (67213) ***(G-13863)***
Boeing Company.....316 523-7084
8602 W Shadow Lakes St Wichita (67205) ***(G-13864)***
Boeing Company.....480 509-5449
4174 S Oliver St Wichita (67210) ***(G-13865)***
Boeing Company.....312 544-2000
4140 S Oliver St Wichita (67210) ***(G-13866)***
Boeing Distribution Svcs Inc.....316 630-4900
10900 E 26th St N Wichita (67226) ***(G-13867)***
Boettcher Supply Inc (PA).....785 738-5781
118 W Court St Beloit (67420) ***(G-479)***
Boge Iron & Metal Co Inc.....316 263-8241
10600 E 13th St N Apt 117 Wichita (67206) ***(G-13868)***
Bogner Oil Field Service Inc.....620 276-9453
606 E Thompson St Garden City (67846) ***(G-2114)***
Bogue Animal Hospital West PA.....316 722-1085
429 N Maize Rd Wichita (67212) ***(G-13869)***
Bohm Farm & Ranch Inc.....785 823-0303
1504 W State St Salina (67401) ***(G-10429)***
Bojack Roustabout LLC.....785 798-3504
11457 R Rd Ness City (67560) ***(G-7252)***
Bok Financial Corporation.....785 273-9993
900 S Kansas Ave Topeka (66612) ***(G-12396)***
Bok Financial Corporation.....913 234-6632
7500 College Blvd Ste 100 Overland Park (66210) ***(G-8474)***
Bok Financial The Private Bank, Topeka *Also called Bok Financial Corporation* ***(G-12396)***
Bold LLC.....620 663-3300
1125 E 4th Ave Hutchinson (67501) ***(G-3217)***
Bolen Office Supply Inc (PA).....620 672-7535
114 S Main St Pratt (67124) ***(G-10100)***
Bolivar Contracting Inc.....913 533-2240
20924 Floyd St Bucyrus (66013) ***(G-594)***
Bomar Designs, Louisburg *Also called Jem Industries Inc* ***(G-6452)***
Bombardier, Wichita *Also called Learjet Inc* ***(G-14942)***
Bombardier Transportation USA, Wichita *Also called Learjet Inc* ***(G-14940)***
Bomgardier Flight Test Center, Wichita *Also called Brp US Inc* ***(G-13899)***
Bonanza Bioenergy LLC.....620 276-4741
2830 E Us Highway 50 Garden City (67846) ***(G-2115)***
Bones Co Inc.....785 242-3070
3557 Highway 59 Ottawa (66067) ***(G-8250)***
Bonner Springs Head Start.....913 441-2828
402 N Neconi Ave Bonner Springs (66012) ***(G-542)***
Bonner Springs Nrsng & Rehab, Bonner Springs *Also called Pinnacle Hlth Fclties Xviii LP* ***(G-571)***
Books & Blocks Academy Inc.....785 266-5150
206 Se Lakewood Ct Topeka (66609) ***(G-12397)***
Boone Brothers Roofing, Olathe *Also called Arr Roofing LLC* ***(G-7533)***
Boot Hill Casino and Resort, Dodge City *Also called Bhcmc LLC* ***(G-1308)***
Booth Hotel LLC.....620 331-1704
201 W Main St Independence (67301) ***(G-3501)***
Boothill Feeders Inc.....620 227-8195
20041 Sw C Rd Jetmore (67854) ***(G-3646)***
Booz Allen Hamilton Inc.....913 682-5300
1122 N 2nd St Leavenworth (66048) ***(G-5213)***
Border States Industries Inc.....785 827-4497
232 N 3rd St Salina (67401) ***(G-10430)***
Border States Industries Inc.....785 354-9532
1516 Nw Saline St Topeka (66618) ***(G-12398)***
Border States Industries Inc.....316 945-1313
3800 W Dora Ave Wichita (67213) ***(G-13870)***
Borens Roofing Inc.....620 365-7663
306 N State St Iola (66749) ***(G-3588)***
Boresow's Lawn Enforcement, Shawnee Mission *Also called Jerry Boresow* ***(G-11484)***
Bornholdt Plantland Inc.....620 662-0544
1508 W 4th Ave Hutchinson (67501) ***(G-3218)***
Borton Corporation.....620 669-8211
21 Des Moines Ave South Hutchinson (67505) ***(G-12056)***
Borton Lc (PA).....620 669-8211
21 Des Moines Ave South Hutchinson (67505) ***(G-12057)***
Bose Bude, Liberal *Also called Comet 1 H R Cleaners Inc* ***(G-6295)***
Bosley's Tire & Wheel, Wichita *Also called Bosleys Tire Service Co Inc* ***(G-13871)***
Bosleys Tire Service Co Inc.....316 524-8511
3948 S Broadway Ave Wichita (67216) ***(G-13871)***
Boss Industries LLC.....620 795-2143
12057 Us Highway 59 Oswego (67356) ***(G-8231)***
Boss Motors Inc.....785 562-3696
605 Broadway Marysville (66508) ***(G-6880)***
Boss Mtrs-Ford Mercury Lincoln, Marysville *Also called Boss Motors Inc* ***(G-6880)***
Boss Tank, Oswego *Also called Boss Industries LLC* ***(G-8231)***
Botanica Inc.....316 264-0448
701 N Amidon Ave Wichita (67203) ***(G-13872)***
BOTANICA, THE WICHITA GARDENS, Wichita *Also called Botanica Inc* ***(G-13872)***
Bott Communications Inc (PA).....913 642-7770
10550 Barkley St Ste 100 Shawnee Mission (66212) ***(G-11176)***
Bott Radio Network, Shawnee Mission *Also called Kccv Am 760* ***(G-11525)***
Bott Radio Network Inc (PA).....913 642-7770
10550 Barkley St Ste 100 Overland Park (66212) ***(G-8475)***
Bottaro Morefield & Kubin Lc.....913 948-8200
11300 Tomahawk Creek Pkwy Leawood (66211) ***(G-5342)***
Bottorff Construction Inc.....913 874-5681
8001 Industrial Park Ln Atchison (66002) ***(G-219)***
Boulevard Apprtments Townhomes.....913 722-3171
5405 Skyline Dr Roeland Park (66205) ***(G-10219)***
Boulevard Insurance LLC.....785 865-0077
7501 College Blvd Ste 115 Overland Park (66210) ***(G-8476)***
Boulevard One Inc (PA).....316 636-9494
3200 N Rock Rd Wichita (67226) ***(G-13873)***
Boulevard One Inc.....316 722-5211
749 N Ridge Rd Wichita (67212) ***(G-13874)***
Bourbon Trucking LLC.....785 428-3030
864 Highway 14 Jewell (66949) ***(G-3649)***
Bow Creek Oil Company LLC.....785 650-1738
1304 Eisenhower Rd Hays (67601) ***(G-2760)***
Bowden Contracting Company Inc.....913 342-5112
1030 Pawnee Ave Kansas City (66105) ***(G-3872)***
Bowman Software Systems LLC.....318 213-8780
11300 Switzer St Overland Park (66210) ***(G-8477)***
Bowman Systems LLC.....318 213-8780
11300 Switzer St Overland Park (66210) ***(G-8478)***
Box Central Inc (PA).....316 689-8484
7130 W Maple St Ste 230 Wichita (67209) ***(G-13875)***
BOY & GIRLS CLUBS, Hutchinson *Also called Boys Girls Clubs Huthinson Inc* ***(G-3220)***
Boyce Bynum Pathology Labs PC.....816 813-2792
8550 Marshall Dr Lenexa (66214) ***(G-5709)***
Boyd & Boyd Inc.....913 764-4568
303 N Lindenwood Dr Olathe (66062) ***(G-7558)***
Boyd Delivery Systems Inc.....913 677-6700
2803 W 47th St Westwood (66205) ***(G-13551)***
Boyer Industries Corporation (PA).....785 865-4200
3741 Greenway Cir Lawrence (66046) ***(G-4762)***
Boyer-Kansas Inc.....913 307-9400
10000 Lackman Rd Lenexa (66219) ***(G-5710)***
Boyles Portable Sign Rent.....785 266-5401
3652 Se Indiana Ave Topeka (66605) ***(G-12399)***
Boynton Family Dental Arts LLC.....316 665-8881
1901 N Webb Rd Ste D Wichita (67206) ***(G-13876)***
Boys & Girls CLB Manhattan Inc.....785 539-1947
220 S 5th St Manhattan (66502) ***(G-6567)***
Boys & Girls Club of S Central (PA).....316 687-5437
2400 N Opportunity Dr Wichita (67219) ***(G-13877)***
Boys & Girls Clubs of America.....913 621-3260
1240 Troup Ave Kansas City (66104) ***(G-3873)***
Boys & Girls of Lawrence, Lawrence *Also called Boys Grls CLB Lwrnce Lwrnce K* ***(G-4763)***
Boys and Girls Club of Topeka.....785 234-5601
550 Se 27th St Topeka (66605) ***(G-12400)***
Boys Girls Clubs Huthinson Inc.....620 665-7171
600 W 2nd Ave Hutchinson (67501) ***(G-3219)***
Boys Girls Clubs Huthinson Inc (PA).....620 665-7171
600 W 2nd Ave Hutchinson (67501) ***(G-3220)***
Boys Grls CLB Htchnsn-Kids Aft, Hutchinson *Also called Boys Girls Clubs Huthinson Inc* ***(G-3219)***
Boys Grls CLB Lwrnce Lwrnce K.....785 841-5672
2910 Haskell Ave Lawrence (66046) ***(G-4763)***
Boys Grls Clubs Grater Kans Ci, Kansas City *Also called Boys & Girls Clubs of America* ***(G-3873)***
BP, Topeka *Also called Huntingdon Park Standard Svc* ***(G-12708)***
BP America Production Company.....620 657-4300
13201 E Hwy 160 Satanta (67870) ***(G-10777)***
BPU, Kansas City *Also called Kansas City Bd Pub Utilities* ***(G-4134)***
Bpu, Kansas City *Also called Kansas City Bd Pub Utilities* ***(G-4139)***
Bpu, Kansas City *Also called Kansas City Bd Pub Utilities* ***(G-4141)***
BPW Masonry Inc.....785 485-2840
7714 Jenkins Rd Riley (66531) ***(G-10205)***
Brace Integrated Services Inc (HQ).....316 832-0292
2112 S Custer Ave Wichita (67213) ***(G-13878)***

ALPHABETIC

Brack/Asscts Cnsltng Engnrs PA 785 271-6644
3501 Sw Gage Blvd Topeka (66614) ***(G-12401)***
Brackeen Line Cleaning Inc 620 587-3351
101 S 6th St Claflin (67525) ***(G-839)***
Brackett Inc 785 862-2205
7115 Se Forbes Ave Topeka (66619) ***(G-12402)***
Braco Sales Inc 816 471-5005
3299 N 7th Street Trfy Kansas City (66115) ***(G-3874)***
Braco Stone, Kansas City *Also called Braco Sales Inc* ***(G-3874)***
Brad Carson 620 429-1011
311 S East Ave Columbus (66725) ***(G-1062)***
Brad Carson (PA) 620 856-3999
120 Aaron Ln Baxter Springs (66713) ***(G-400)***
Brad H Allen Roofing Inc 785 423-3861
776 Grant St Lawrence (66044) ***(G-4764)***
Brad Murray Inc 316 943-2516
3082 S All Hallows Ave Wichita (67217) ***(G-13879)***
Brad Vignatelli 913 541-9777
17501 W 98th St Spc 1855 Lenexa (66219) ***(G-5711)***
Bradburn Wrecking Company 316 686-1959
3233 S Southeast Blvd Wichita (67216) ***(G-13880)***
Bradbury Co Inc (PA) 620 345-6394
1200 E Cole St Moundridge (67107) ***(G-7178)***
Bradbury Co Inc 620 382-3775
421 W Main St Marion (66861) ***(G-6866)***
Bradbury Group, The, Moundridge *Also called Bradbury Co Inc* ***(G-7178)***
Bradford and Galt Incorporated 913 663-1264
9200 Indian Creek Pkwy # 570 Shawnee Mission (66210) ***(G-11177)***
Bradford Built Inc 785 325-3300
303 C St Washington (66968) ***(G-13460)***
Bradford Galt Consulting Svcs, Shawnee Mission *Also called Bradford and Galt Incorporated* ***(G-11177)***
Bradken Inc 913 367-2121
400 S 4th St Atchison (66002) ***(G-220)***
Bradley Animal Hospital 785 843-9533
935 E 23rd St Lawrence (66046) ***(G-4765)***
Bradley Hotel Wichita 316 262-2841
2041 N Bradley Fair Pkwy Wichita (67206) ***(G-13881)***
Bradley Kwapiszeski MD 913 362-3210
8901 W 74th St Ste 285 Shawnee Mission (66204) ***(G-11178)***
Bradley Machine Inc 316 262-3221
130 N Millwood St Wichita (67203) ***(G-13882)***
Bradley R Lewis 816 453-7198
13900 Nicklaus Dr Overland Park (66223) ***(G-8479)***
Brady Fluid Service Inc 620 275-5827
3020 W Oller Rd Garden City (67846) ***(G-2116)***
Brady Nursery Inc 316 722-7516
11200 W Kellogg St Wichita (67209) ***(G-13883)***
Braham J Geha 913 383-9099
8800 State Line Kansas City (66160) ***(G-3875)***
Brak-Hard Concrete Cnstr, Dodge City *Also called Brak-Hard Concrete Cnstr Co* ***(G-1311)***
Brak-Hard Concrete Cnstr Co 620 225-1957
10744 Marshall Rd Dodge City (67801) ***(G-1311)***
Branchpattern Inc 913 951-8311
7400 College Blvd Ste 150 Overland Park (66210) ***(G-8480)***
Brand Plumbing Inc 316 942-2306
2418 S Hoover Rd Wichita (67215) ***(G-13884)***
Branded Custom Sportswear Inc 913 663-6800
7007 College Blvd Ste 700 Overland Park (66211) ***(G-8481)***
Branded Emblem, Overland Park *Also called David Camp Inc* ***(G-8641)***
Branding Iron Restaurant & CLB 620 624-7254
603 E Pancake Blvd Liberal (67901) ***(G-6286)***
Brandon Hospitality LLC 316 613-1995
2250 N Greenwich Rd Wichita (67226) ***(G-13885)***
Brandon Woods Retirement Cmnty 785 838-8000
1501 Inverness Dr Ofc Lawrence (66047) ***(G-4766)***
Brandsafway Services LLC 913 342-9000
548 S 11th St Kansas City (66105) ***(G-3876)***
Brandt, Kenneth MD, Fairway *Also called Trustees Indiana University* ***(G-1923)***
Branson Truck Line, Lyons *Also called Bar K Bar Trucking Inc* ***(G-6479)***
Branstetter & Associates 316 788-9290
1105 N Buckner St Derby (67037) ***(G-1224)***
Branstetter & Sparks, Derby *Also called Branstetter & Associates* ***(G-1224)***
Brass Hat Lawn Maintenance, Coffeyville *Also called S & H Inc* ***(G-974)***
Bratton Bros Contracting Inc 913 422-7771
6091 Woodland Dr Shawnee (66218) ***(G-10920)***
Braumss 620 340-8169
2120 Industrial Rd Emporia (66801) ***(G-1707)***
BRB Contractors Inc (PA) 785 232-1245
3805 Nw 25th St Topeka (66618) ***(G-12403)***
Breakthrough, Wichita *Also called Episcopal Social Services Inc* ***(G-14297)***
Breakthrough CLB Sedgwick Cnty 316 269-2534
1010 N Main St Wichita (67203) ***(G-13886)***
Breakthrough House Inc 785 232-6807
1195 Sw Buchanan St # 202 Topeka (66604) ***(G-12404)***
Breason Excavating & Trucking 785 597-5596
5353 Marion Rd Perry (66073) ***(G-9766)***
Breason Excavating Service, Perry *Also called Breason Excavating & Trucking* ***(G-9766)***
Brecheisen Oil Company, Hartford *Also called Brecheisens Stop 2 Shop Inc* ***(G-2727)***
Brecheisens Stop 2 Shop Inc 620 392-5577
108 E Plumb Ave Hartford (66854) ***(G-2727)***
Bredson & Assoc Consulting Eng, Overland Park *Also called Bredson and Associates Inc* ***(G-8482)***
Bredson and Associates Inc 913 663-0100
9225 Indian Creek Pkwy # 300 Overland Park (66210) ***(G-8482)***
Bremen Farmers Mutual Insur Co 785 337-2203
201 Brenneke St Bremen (66412) ***(G-581)***
Brennco Travel Services Inc 913 660-0121
6600 College Blvd Ste 130 Shawnee Mission (66211) ***(G-11179)***
Brenneman & Bremmeman Inc (PA) 316 282-8834
812 W 1st St Newton (67114) ***(G-7321)***
Brenton Financial Group Inc 913 451-9072
13232 Craig St Overland Park (66213) ***(G-8483)***
Brets Autoworks Corp (PA) 913 764-8677
128 N Mahaffie St Olathe (66061) ***(G-7559)***
Bretz Inc 620 397-5329
640 W Long St Dighton (67839) ***(G-1283)***
Bretz & Young Law Office 620 662-3435
3 Compound Dr Hutchinson (67502) ***(G-3221)***
Brew Lab 913 400-2343
8004 Foster St Overland Park (66204) ***(G-8484)***
BREWSTER PLACE RETIREMENT COM, Topeka *Also called Congregational Home* ***(G-12501)***
Brg Precision Products Inc 316 788-2000
600 N River St Derby (67037) ***(G-1225)***
Brian Strange 620 663-8700
2701 N Main St Ste A Hutchinson (67502) ***(G-3222)***
Brian Thomas Robotics, Winfield *Also called BTR Inc* ***(G-16117)***
Brians Hot Oil Service LLC 620 629-5933
P.O. Box 888 Liberal (67905) ***(G-6287)***
Briarcliff Care Center, Topeka *Also called Old Creek Senior Living* ***(G-12945)***
Bridge Capital Management LLC 913 283-7804
16829 W 116th St Lenexa (66219) ***(G-5712)***
Bridge Hven Mmory Care Rsdents 785 856-1630
1701 Research Park Dr Lawrence (66047) ***(G-4767)***
Bridges Inc 316 283-9350
911 Sw 14th St Newton (67114) ***(G-7322)***
Bridgestone Americas 785 267-0074
1400 Sw 41st St Topeka (66609) ***(G-12405)***
Bridgestone Ret Operations LLC 913 498-0880
7601 W 119th St Shawnee Mission (66213) ***(G-11180)***
Bridgestone Ret Operations LLC 316 315-0363
3745 N Rock Rd Wichita (67226) ***(G-13887)***
Bridgestone Ret Operations LLC 316 942-1332
6500 W Kellogg Dr Wichita (67209) ***(G-13888)***
Bridgestone Ret Operations LLC 913 831-9955
7425 Metcalf Ave Ste B Overland Park (66204) ***(G-8485)***
Bridgestone Ret Operations LLC 913 299-3090
7815 State Ave Kansas City (66112) ***(G-3877)***
Bridgestone Ret Operations LLC 913 393-2212
13512 S Alden St Olathe (66062) ***(G-7560)***
Bridgestone Ret Operations LLC 913 782-1833
15050 W 135th St Olathe (66062) ***(G-7561)***
Bridgestone Ret Operations LLC 913 334-1555
7717 State Ave Kansas City (66112) ***(G-3878)***
Bridgestone Ret Operations LLC 913 492-8160
12380 W 95th St Shawnee Mission (66215) ***(G-11181)***
Bridgestone Ret Operations LLC 316 684-2682
7700 E Kellogg Dr Ste K Wichita (67207) ***(G-13889)***
Brierton Engineering Inc 785 263-7711
1200 S Buckeye Ave Abilene (67410) ***(G-16)***
Briggs Auto Group Inc 785 776-7799
2500 Stagg Hill Rd Manhattan (66502) ***(G-6568)***
Briggs Auto Group Inc 785 776-3677
2312 Stagg Hill Rd Manhattan (66502) ***(G-6569)***
Briggs Auto Group Inc 785 537-8330
2312 Stagg Hill Rd Manhattan (66502) ***(G-6570)***
Briggs Chrysler Jeep Dodge Ram, Lawrence *Also called Autobody of Lawrence* ***(G-4744)***
Briggs Dodge, Topeka *Also called Bme Inc* ***(G-12391)***
Briggs Jeep Eagle Isuzu, Manhattan *Also called Briggs Auto Group Inc* ***(G-6569)***
Briggs Trucking Inc 620 699-3448
2594 Road X Reading (66868) ***(G-10198)***
Briggs Turf Farm, Overland Park *Also called Triple B Investments Inc* ***(G-9429)***
Bright Circle Montesorri Schl 785 235-1033
401 Sw Oakley Ave Topeka (66606) ***(G-12406)***
Brighthouse Inc 620 665-3630
335 N Washington St # 240 Hutchinson (67501) ***(G-3223)***
Brightmarks LLC 913 338-1131
9900 Pflumm Rd Ste 29 Lenexa (66215) ***(G-5713)***
BRIGHTON GARDENS OF PRAIRIE VI, Prairie Village *Also called Sunrise Senior Living Svcs Inc* ***(G-10071)***
Brighton Gardens Prairie Vlg, Prairie Village *Also called Sunrise Senior Living Inc* ***(G-10070)***
Brighton Place W Oper Co LLC 785 232-1212
331 Sw Oakley Ave Topeka (66606) ***(G-12407)***

Brightview Landscapes LLC 913 371-2661
12421 Santa Fe Trail Dr Lenexa (66215) *(G-5714)*
Brightwell Dispensers Inc 913 956-4909
9567 Alden St Lenexa (66215) *(G-5715)*
Brij Systems LLC 316 262-6969
700 E 10th St N Wichita (67214) *(G-13890)*
Brileys Designs & Signs 913 579-7533
14842 Robinson St Shawnee Mission (66223) *(G-11182)*
Brimans Leading Jewelers Inc (PA) 785 357-4438
734 S Kansas Ave Topeka (66603) *(G-12408)*
Brinks Incorporated 316 945-0244
2145 S Meridian Ave Wichita (67213) *(G-13891)*
Briovarx LLC (HQ) 913 307-9900
11142 Renner Blvd Lenexa (66219) *(G-5716)*
Briovarx Infusion Svcs 305 LLC (HQ) 913 747-3700
15529 College Blvd Lenexa (66219) *(G-5717)*
Briscoe Richard L DDS PA 620 669-1032
1710 E 23rd Ave Hutchinson (67502) *(G-3224)*
Brisk Transportation 620 669-3481
2700 E 4th Ave Hutchinson (67501) *(G-3225)*
Bristol Hotel & Resorts Inc 785 462-8787
645 W Willow Ave Colby (67701) *(G-991)*
Bristol Hotel & Resorts Inc 785 823-1739
1616 W Crawford St Salina (67401) *(G-10431)*
Britain Center, The, Shawnee Mission *Also called Lee Ann Britian Infant Dev Ctr (G-11556)*
Brite Energy Solar Inc 785 856-9936
1035 N 3rd St Ste 101 Lawrence (66044) *(G-4768)*
British Salt Holdings LLC 913 253-2203
10955 Lowell Ave Ste 600 Overland Park (66210) *(G-8486)*
Brittain Machine Inc (HQ) 316 942-8223
2520 S Sheridan Ave Wichita (67217) *(G-13892)*
Brittany Court Inv Partner LP 816 300-0685
153 Brittany Ct Gardner (66030) *(G-2330)*
Brms, Atchison *Also called E-Z Info Inc (G-226)*
Broadmoor One LLC 316 683-0562
9435 E Central Ave Wichita (67206) *(G-13893)*
Broadview Hotel, Wichita *Also called Broadview Hsptlity Hldings LLC (G-13894)*
Broadview Hsptlity Hldings LLC 316 262-5000
400 W Douglas Ave Wichita (67202) *(G-13894)*
Broadway Home Medical Inc 316 264-8600
808 S Hillside St Wichita (67211) *(G-13895)*
Broadway Mortuary Inc 316 262-3435
1147 S Broadway Ave Wichita (67211) *(G-13896)*
Broce Manufacturing Co Inc 620 227-8811
1460 S 2nd Ave Dodge City (67801) *(G-1312)*
Broce Manufacturing Fab Div, Dodge City *Also called Broce Manufacturing Co Inc (G-1312)*
Brock Maggard 417 793-7790
2011 Fairview Ave Baxter Springs (66713) *(G-401)*
Broderson Manufacturing Corp (HQ) 913 888-0606
14741 W 106th St Lenexa (66215) *(G-5718)*
Broken Arrow Ranch, Olsburg *Also called Association of Kansas Nebraska (G-8168)*
Brookdale Derby, Derby *Also called Brookdale Senior Living Commun (G-1226)*
Brookdale Overland Pk Glenwood 913 385-2052
9201 Foster St Overland Park (66212) *(G-8487)*
Brookdale Senior Living Commun 785 628-1111
1801 E 27th St Ofc Hays (67601) *(G-2761)*
Brookdale Senior Living Commun 913 894-6979
8710 Caenen Lake Rd Shawnee Mission (66215) *(G-11183)*
Brookdale Senior Living Commun 620 251-6270
3800 Asbury Dr Coffeyville (67337) *(G-914)*
Brookdale Senior Living Commun 316 684-3100
8600 E 21st St N Ofc Ofc Wichita (67206) *(G-13897)*
Brookdale Senior Living Commun 785 263-7400
1100 N Vine St Ofc Abilene (67410) *(G-17)*
Brookdale Senior Living Commun 620 342-1000
1200 W 12th Ave Ofc Emporia (66801) *(G-1708)*
Brookdale Senior Living Commun 785 762-3123
1022 Caroline Ave Ofc Junction City (66441) *(G-3675)*
Brookdale Senior Living Commun 316 788-0370
1709 E Walnut Grove Rd Derby (67037) *(G-1226)*
Brookdale Senior Living Commun 620 792-7000
1206 Patton Rd Ofc Great Bend (67530) *(G-2522)*
Brookdale Senior Living Commun 785 820-2991
1200 E Kirwin Ave Salina (67401) *(G-10432)*
Brookdale Senior Living Commun 620 241-6600
1460 N Main St Conway (67460) *(G-1133)*
Brookdale Senior Living Commun 620 326-3031
500 N Plum St Wellington (67152) *(G-13492)*
Brookdale Senior Living Commun 620 225-7555
2400 N 14th Ave Ofc Dodge City (67801) *(G-1313)*
Brookdale Senior Living Inc 913 345-9339
6101 W 119th St Overland Park (66209) *(G-8488)*
Brookdale Snior Lving Cmmnties 316 630-0788
9191 E 21st St N Wichita (67206) *(G-13898)*
Brookdale Snior Lving Cmmnties 785 263-7800
1102 N Vine St Abilene (67410) *(G-18)*
Brookdale Snior Lving Cmmnties 785 832-9900
3220 Peterson Rd Lawrence (66049) *(G-4769)*
Brookdale Snior Lving Cmmnties 913 491-1144
11000 Oakmont St Shawnee Mission (66210) *(G-11184)*
Brookdale Snior Lving Cmmnties 913 491-3681
4400 W 115th St Leawood (66211) *(G-5343)*
Brookover Feed Yards Inc (PA) 620 275-9206
50 Grandview Dr Garden City (67846) *(G-2117)*
Brookover Feed Yards Inc 620 275-0125
3 1/2 Mile Se 5250 Brkver Garden City (67846) *(G-2118)*
Brookover Land Enterprises LP 620 275-9206
50 Grandview Dr Garden City (67846) *(G-2119)*
Brookover Ranch Feedyard, Garden City *Also called Brookover Feed Yards Inc (G-2118)*
Brookridge Day School, Shawnee Mission *Also called Brookridge Day School (G-11185)*
Brookridge Day School (PA) 913 649-2228
9555 Hadley Dr Shawnee Mission (66212) *(G-11185)*
Brookridge Golf & Country Club (PA) 913 648-1600
8223 W 103rd St Shawnee Mission (66212) *(G-11186)*
Brookridge Golf & Fitness, Overland Park *Also called Capital Frsght Golf Fitnes LLC (G-8509)*
Brookridge Swimming Pool, Shawnee Mission *Also called Brookridge Golf & Country Club (G-11186)*
Brookside Manor, Overbrook *Also called Midwest Health Services Inc (G-8326)*
BROOKSIDE RETIREMENT COMMUNITY, Overbrook *Also called Alegria Living & Healthcare (G-8322)*
Brotherhood Bank & Trust, Overland Park *Also called Bank of Labor (G-8429)*
Browing Gayla 620 343-2274
1731 Whittier St Emporia (66801) *(G-1709)*
Brown - Dupree Oil Co Inc (PA) 620 353-1874
111 E Kansas Ave Ulysses (67880) *(G-13285)*
Brown Cnty Developmental Svcs 785 742-2053
400 S 12th St Hiawatha (66434) *(G-3004)*
Brown Honey Farms 785 778-2002
428 Kent St Haddam (66944) *(G-2694)*
Brown Industries LLC (PA) 785 842-6506
807 E 29th St Lawrence (66046) *(G-4770)*
Brown Management Inc 785 528-3769
Hwy 31 E Osage City (66523) *(G-8181)*
Brown Memorial Foundation 785 263-2351
409 Nw 3rd St Ste G Abilene (67410) *(G-19)*
BROWN MEMORIAL HOME, Abilene *Also called Brown Memorial Foundation (G-19)*
Brown Specialty Vehicles, Lawrence *Also called Brown Industries LLC (G-4770)*
Brown Strauss Inc 913 621-4000
802 Kindleberger Rd Kansas City (66115) *(G-3879)*
Brown, Heath, Shawnee Mission *Also called Mission Animal Clinic PA (G-11643)*
Brown-Atchison Elc Coop Assn (PA) 785 486-2117
1712 Central Ave Horton (66439) *(G-3122)*
Brown-Atchison Electric Co-Op, Horton *Also called Brown-Atchison Elc Coop Assn (G-3122)*
Browns Medical Imaging 913 888-6710
9880 Pflumm Rd Lenexa (66215) *(G-5719)*
Browns Processing 620 378-2441
103 W Jefferson St Fredonia (66736) *(G-2027)*
Browns Super Service Inc 785 267-1080
3812 Sw South Park Ave Topeka (66609) *(G-12409)*
Browns Tree Service LLC 785 379-9212
1801 Se Madison St Topeka (66607) *(G-12410)*
Broyles Inc (PA) 620 473-3835
1303 N 9th St Humboldt (66748) *(G-3182)*
Broyles Petroleum Equipment Co 417 863-6800
1303 N 9th St Humboldt (66748) *(G-3183)*
Brp US Inc 316 946-2000
1530 S Tyler Rd Wichita (67209) *(G-13899)*
Brr Architecture Inc (PA) 913 262-9095
8131 Metcalf Ave Ste 300 Overland Park (66204) *(G-8489)*
Bruce Bruce & Lehman LLC 316 722-3391
3330 W Douglas Ave # 100 Wichita (67203) *(G-13900)*
Bruce Davis Construction LLC 620 342-5001
1201 Graphic Arts Rd Emporia (66801) *(G-1710)*
Bruce Ochsner MD 316 263-6273
1100 N Topeka St Wichita (67214) *(G-13901)*
Bruce Oil Co LLC 620 241-2938
1704 Limestone Rd McPherson (67460) *(G-6939)*
Bruce Speak 785 267-6301
2887 Sw Macvicar Ave # 3 Topeka (66611) *(G-12411)*
Bruces Woodworks LLC 913 441-1432
600 E Front St Bonner Springs (66012) *(G-543)*
Bruenger Trucking Company (HQ) 316 744-0494
6250 N Broadway Ave Park City (67219) *(G-9605)*
Brulez Foundation Inc 913 422-3355
10363 S Highland Cir Olathe (66061) *(G-7562)*
Bruna Brothers Implement LLC 785 325-2232
1613 Quivira Rd Washington (66968) *(G-13461)*
Bruna Brothers Implement LLC (PA) 785 562-5304
1128 Pony Express Hwy Marysville (66508) *(G-6881)*
Bruna Brothers Implement LLC 785 632-5621
1798 18th Rd Clay Center (67432) *(G-845)*
Bruna Brothers Implement LLC 785 742-2261
201 E Miami St Hiawatha (66434) *(G-3005)*
Bruna Brothers Implement LLC 785 336-2111
12 E North St Seneca (66538) *(G-10858)*
Bruna Implement Co, Washington *Also called Bruna Brothers Implement LLC (G-13461)*

ALPHABETIC

Bruna Implement Company, Marysville *Also called Bruna Brothers Implement LLC (G-6881)*
Bruna Implement Company, Clay Center *Also called Bruna Brothers Implement LLC (G-845)*
Bruna Implement Company, Hiawatha *Also called Bruna Brothers Implement LLC (G-3005)*
Brundage-Bone Con Pmpg Inc.......785 823-7706
1265 W Diamond Dr Salina (67401) ***(G-10433)***
Brundage-Bone Concrete Pumping, Wichita *Also called Concrete Pumping Service Inc (G-14087)*
Brungardt Honomichl & Co PA (PA).......913 663-1900
7101 College Blvd Ste 400 Overland Park (66210) ***(G-8490)***
Brunner Electric Inc.......913 268-5463
5730 Reeder St Shawnee Mission (66203) ***(G-11187)***
Brush Art Corporation (PA).......785 454-3415
343 W Highway 24 Downs (67437) ***(G-1469)***
Brush Group LLC.......785 454-3383
343 W Highway 24 Downs (67437) ***(G-1470)***
Brush Reduction, Kansas City *Also called CS Carey LLC (G-3947)*
Bryan Lykins Hjtmnek Fncher PA.......785 428-4566
222 Sw 7th St Topeka (66603) ***(G-12412)***
Bryan-Ohlmeier Construction.......913 557-9972
911 N Pearl St Paola (66071) ***(G-9543)***
Bryans Heating & AC.......316 755-2447
700 S Ramsey Dr Valley Center (67147) ***(G-13338)***
Bryant and Bryant Cnstr Inc.......316 835-3322
703 Mcnair St Halstead (67056) ***(G-2696)***
Bryant Funeral Home, Great Bend *Also called Bryant-Funeral Home (G-2523)*
Bryant-Funeral Home.......620 793-3525
1425 Patton Rd Great Bend (67530) ***(G-2523)***
Brytam Manufacturing Inc.......316 788-3300
229 S Water St Derby (67037) ***(G-1227)***
BS Cvf Inc.......785 448-2239
24161 Nw Kentucky Rd Garnett (66032) ***(G-2370)***
BS Family Development LLC.......913 961-6579
15350 S Constance St Olathe (66062) ***(G-7563)***
BSB Maunfacturing Inc.......620 326-3152
20 Industrial Ave Wellington (67152) ***(G-13493)***
Bse Structural Engineers LLC.......913 492-7400
11320 W 79th St Lenexa (66214) ***(G-5720)***
Bsj Power Services Inc.......417 850-1707
441 W 520th Ave Cherokee (66724) ***(G-799)***
Bsm Wall Systems, Olathe *Also called Builders Stone & Masonry Inc (G-7567)*
Bsrep II Ws Hotel Trs Sub LLC.......443 569-7053
8621 E 21st St N Ste 230 Wichita (67206) ***(G-13902)***
BTCO, Wichita *Also called Business Technology Career (G-13920)*
Bti Ness City.......785 798-2251
118 S 7th St Ness City (67560) ***(G-7253)***
BTR Inc.......620 221-7071
620 Industrial Blvd Winfield (67156) ***(G-16117)***
Bubble Rm Coin Ldry Dry Clean.......913 962-4046
7735 Quivira Rd Shawnee Mission (66216) ***(G-11188)***
Buchanan Technologies Inc.......316 219-0124
3450 N Rock Rd Ste 705 Wichita (67226) ***(G-13903)***
Buck Construction Co.......913 796-6510
18345 46th St Mc Louth (66054) ***(G-6925)***
Buckeye Corporation (PA).......316 321-1060
625 S Main St El Dorado (67042) ***(G-1539)***
Buckeye Corporation.......785 483-3111
1021 E Wichita Ave Russell (67665) ***(G-10267)***
Buckeye Supply, Russell *Also called Buckeye Corporation (G-10267)*
Buckingham Palace House Clg, Lawrence *Also called Buckingham Palace Inc (G-4771)*
Buckingham Palace Inc.......785 842-6264
2441 W 6th St Lawrence (66049) ***(G-4771)***
Buckley Industries Inc (HQ).......316 744-7587
1850 E 53rd St N Park City (67219) ***(G-9606)***
Buckley Roofing Company Inc.......316 838-9321
3601 N Hydraulic St Wichita (67219) ***(G-13904)***
Bucklin Hospital District Inc.......620 826-3202
505 W Elm St Bucklin (67834) ***(G-590)***
Bucklin Tractor & Impt Co Inc (PA).......620 826-3271
115 W Railroad St Bucklin (67834) ***(G-591)***
Bucyrus, Hillsdale *Also called Magnum (G-3059)*
Bud Brown Automotive Inc (PA).......913 393-8100
925 N Rawhide Dr Olathe (66061) ***(G-7564)***
Bud Palmer Auction.......316 838-4141
101 W 29th St N Wichita (67204) ***(G-13905)***
Bud Roat Inc.......316 683-9072
310 N Handley St Wichita (67203) ***(G-13906)***
Bud Smart Janitorial, Olathe *Also called Smart Way (G-8069)*
Budget Car Trck Rentl Wichita.......316 729-7979
2250 N Ridge Rd Ste 100 Wichita (67205) ***(G-13907)***
Budget Equipment Inc.......316 284-9994
1521 Nw 36th St Newton (67117) ***(G-7323)***
Budget Host Inn, Salina *Also called Nebco Inc (G-10610)*
Budget Office, Wichita *Also called City of Wichita (G-14025)*
Budget Plumbing & Heating.......620 231-5232
3706 E 20th St Pittsburg (66762) ***(G-9826)***
Budget Rent-A-Car, Wichita *Also called Budget Car Trck Rentl Wichita (G-13907)*
Budget Rent-A-Car of Kansas (PA).......316 946-4891
1895 Midfield Rd Wichita (67209) ***(G-13908)***
Budget Truck Rental Service, Lawrence *Also called Avis Budget Group Inc (G-4745)*
Budreau Construction Inc.......785 446-3665
132 S Railroad Ave Clyde (66938) ***(G-904)***
Buds Tire Service Inc.......785 632-2135
410 Court St Clay Center (67432) ***(G-846)***
Buffalo Balanced Fund Inc.......913 677-7778
5420 W 61st Pl Shawnee Mission (66205) ***(G-11189)***
Buffalo Funds.......913 677-7778
5420 W 61st Pl Shawnee Mission (66205) ***(G-11190)***
Buffco Engineering Inc.......316 558-5390
200 Industrial Dr Mulvane (67110) ***(G-7211)***
Buffco Engineering Office, Mulvane *Also called Buffco Engineering Inc (G-7211)*
Bugs Early Learning Ctr I.......913 254-0088
1330 W Dennis Ave Olathe (66061) ***(G-7565)***
Buhler Sunshine Home Inc.......620 543-2251
400 S Buhler Rd Buhler (67522) ***(G-614)***
Builder Designs Inc.......913 393-3367
125 S Kansas Ave Olathe (66061) ***(G-7566)***
Builders, Wichita *Also called Garvey Public Warehouse Inc (G-14450)*
Builders Inc (PA).......316 684-1400
1081 S Glendale St Wichita (67218) ***(G-13909)***
Builders Inc.......316 522-6104
5755 S Hoover Rd Wichita (67215) ***(G-13910)***
Builders Apartments Inc.......316 684-1400
1081 S Glendale St Wichita (67218) ***(G-13911)***
Builders Choice Aggregates, Topeka *Also called Hamm Inc (G-12662)*
Builders Commercials Inc.......316 686-3107
1081 S Glendale St Wichita (67218) ***(G-13912)***
Builders Concrete & Supply (PA).......316 283-4540
505 W 1st St Newton (67114) ***(G-7324)***
Builders Development Inc (HQ).......316 684-1400
1081 S Glendale St Wichita (67218) ***(G-13913)***
Builders Stone & Masonry Inc.......913 764-4446
616 N Rogers Rd Olathe (66062) ***(G-7567)***
Building Blocks Child Care Ctr.......620 767-8029
300 N Union St Ste A Council Grove (66846) ***(G-1158)***
Building Blocks Child Dev Ctr.......913 888-7244
15215 College Blvd Shawnee Mission (66219) ***(G-11191)***
Building Blocks of Topeka Inc.......785 232-0441
620 Sw Lane St Topeka (66606) ***(G-12413)***
Building Control Solutions LLC.......816 439-6046
5138 Merriam Dr Merriam (66203) ***(G-7087)***
Building Erection Svcs Co Inc (PA).......913 764-5560
15585 S Keeler St Olathe (66062) ***(G-7568)***
Building Inspection, Hutchinson *Also called City of Hutchinson (G-3240)*
Building Maintenance, Hutchinson *Also called Hutchinson Usd 308 (G-3327)*
Building Solutions LLC.......620 225-1199
11106 Saddle Rd Dodge City (67801) ***(G-1314)***
Built-So-Well.......785 537-5166
1210 Pottawatomie Ave Manhattan (66502) ***(G-6571)***
Bukaty Companies (PA).......913 345-0440
4601 College Blvd Ste 100 Leawood (66211) ***(G-5344)***
Bulk Conveyors Inc.......316 201-3158
1850 N Wichita (67214) ***(G-13914)***
Bulk Industrial Group LLC (PA).......913 362-6000
3500 W 75th St Ste 360 Prairie Village (66208) ***(G-10017)***
Bulleigh Orthodontics.......913 962-7223
6804 Silver Hls Shawnee (66226) ***(G-10921)***
Bultman Company Inc Mfg.......620 544-8004
1550 W 10th St Hugoton (67951) ***(G-3149)***
Bumper Bling Shop, Olathe *Also called Stealth Technologies LLC (G-8082)*
Bunge Milling Inc.......913 367-3251
16755 274th Rd Atchison (66002) ***(G-221)***
Bunge North America Inc.......620 342-7270
701 E 6th Ave Emporia (66801) ***(G-1711)***
Bungii LLC.......913 353-6683
11011 King St Ste 280 Overland Park (66210) ***(G-8491)***
Bunny's Beauty Supply, Kansas City *Also called Ahn Marketing Incorporated (G-3793)*
Bunting Group Inc (PA).......316 284-2020
500 S Spencer Rd Newton (67114) ***(G-7325)***
Burch Fabrics, Shawnee Mission *Also called John K Burch Company (G-11492)*
Burdiss Lettershop Services Co.......913 492-0545
3439 Merriam Dr Overland Park (66203) ***(G-8492)***
Burgess Manufacturing Inc.......316 838-5748
3443 N Topeka St Wichita (67219) ***(G-13915)***
Burgmeier, Ronald J, Olathe *Also called Ronald J Burgmeier DDS PA (G-8041)*
Burke Inc (PA).......913 722-5658
1800 Merriam Ln Kansas City (66106) ***(G-3880)***
Burke, Evans, Allen, Pannell, Shawnee Mission *Also called Oral Mxilo Ofcial Srgery Assoc (G-11701)*
Burkett, Jeffrey L DDS, Topeka *Also called Gage Center Dental Group PA (G-12631)*
Burkey Richard L DPM P A.......620 793-7624
3509 Forest Ave Great Bend (67530) ***(G-2524)***
Burkhart Enterprises Inc.......620 662-8678
808 W 1st Ave Hutchinson (67501) ***(G-3226)***
Burlingame Historical Preserva.......785 654-3561
117 S Dacotah St Burlingame (66413) ***(G-622)***

Burlingame Road Animal Hosp 785 267-1012
3715 Sw Burlingame Rd Topeka (66609) *(G-12414)*
BURLINGAME SCHUYLER MUSEUM, Burlingame *Also called Burlingame Historical Preserva (G-622)*
Burlingame Vision Associates 913 338-1948
11500 W 119th St Overland Park (66213) *(G-8493)*
Burlingame Wire Products Inc (PA) 785 483-3138
535 S Front St Russell (67665) *(G-10268)*
Burlington Division, Burlington *Also called Charloma Inc (G-626)*
Burlington Health Care Ctr, Burlington *Also called Life Care Centers America Inc (G-639)*
BURLINGTON HEALTHCARE CENTER, Burlington *Also called Life Care Center Burlington (G-638)*
Burlington Northern, Newton *Also called Bnsf Railway Company (G-7320)*
Burlington Northern, Arkansas City *Also called Bnsf Railway Company (G-148)*
Burlington Northern, Kansas City *Also called Bnsf Railway Company (G-3869)*
Burlington Northern, Topeka *Also called Bnsf Railway Company (G-12392)*
Burlington Northern, Columbus *Also called Bnsf Railway Company (G-1061)*
Burlington Northern, Shawnee Mission *Also called Bnsf Railway Company (G-11173)*
Burlington Northern, Topeka *Also called Bnsf Railway Company (G-12393)*
Burlington Northern, Wellington *Also called Bnsf Railway Company (G-13491)*
Burlington Northern, Shawnee Mission *Also called Bnsf Railway Company (G-11174)*
Burlington Nthrn Santa Fe LLC 785 435-5065
100 Ne Jefferson Trwy Topeka (66607) *(G-12415)*
Burlington Nthrn Santa Fe LLC 913 577-5521
8310 Nieman Rd Lenexa (66214) *(G-5721)*
Burnap Bros Inc 620 342-2645
722 Commercial St Emporia (66801) *(G-1712)*
Burnells Creative Gold Inc 316 634-2822
550 N Rock Rd Ste 104 Wichita (67206) *(G-13916)*
Burnett Automotive Inc (PA) 785 539-8970
400 Mccall Rd Manhattan (66502) *(G-6572)*
Burnett Automotive Inc 913 681-8824
8210 W 135th St Overland Park (66223) *(G-8494)*
Burnham Builders 620 343-2047
314 Neosho St Emporia (66801) *(G-1713)*
Burnham Cmpsite Structures Inc 316 946-5900
6262 W 34th St S Wichita (67215) *(G-13917)*
Burnham Composites Inc 316 946-5900
6262 W 34th St S Wichita (67215) *(G-13918)*
Burns Boys Co Inc 913 788-8654
6634 Kaw Dr Kansas City (66111) *(G-3881)*
Burns Printing Company, Olathe *Also called Burns Publishing Company Inc (G-7569)*
Burns Publishing Company Inc 913 782-0321
14465 W 140th Ter Olathe (66062) *(G-7569)*
Burrellesluce Information Svcs, Topeka *Also called Luce Press Clippings Inc (G-12853)*
Busboom & Rauh Construction Co 785 825-4664
145 1/2 S Santa Fe Ave Salina (67401) *(G-10434)*
Busch Johnson & Mank 316 263-5661
359 S Hydraulic St Wichita (67211) *(G-13919)*
Busco Inc 816 453-8727
425 Mccall Rd Manhattan (66502) *(G-6573)*
Busey Bank 913 338-4300
4550 W 109th St Ste 100 Overland Park (66211) *(G-8495)*
Busey Schmidtberger Engrg, Lenexa *Also called Bse Structural Engineers LLC (G-5720)*
Bushman & Associates Cpa's, Leavenworth *Also called B C C Business Services Inc (G-5205)*
Bushnell Group Holdings Inc 913 894-4224
9200 Cody St Overland Park (66214) *(G-8496)*
Bushnell Holdings Inc 913 981-1929
22101 W 167th St Olathe (66062) *(G-7570)*
Bushnell Holdings Inc (HQ) 913 752-3400
9200 Cody St Overland Park (66214) *(G-8497)*
Bushnell Inc 913 752-6178
9200 Cody St Overland Park (66214) *(G-8498)*
Bushnell Inc (HQ) 913 752-3400
9200 Cody St Overland Park (66214) *(G-8499)*
Bushnell Outdoor Products, Overland Park *Also called Bushnell Group Holdings Inc (G-8496)*
Bushnell Outdoor Products, Overland Park *Also called Bushnell Holdings Inc (G-8497)*
Bushnell Outdoor Products, Overland Park *Also called Bushnell Inc (G-8499)*
Bushton Manufacturing LLC 620 562-3557
319 S Main St Bushton (67427) *(G-652)*
Business & Technology Inst 620 235-4920
1501 S Joplin St Pittsburg (66762) *(G-9827)*
Business and Indust Hlth Group, Shawnee Mission *Also called Wellness Services Inc (G-12000)*
Business Systems Division, Clearwater *Also called Southern Kansas Tele Co Inc (G-898)*
Business Technology Career 316 688-1888
5111 E 21st St N Wichita (67208) *(G-13920)*
Business Transformation System, Wichita *Also called Learjet Inc (G-14941)*
Buster Crust Inc (PA) 620 227-7106
2300 E Trail St Dodge City (67801) *(G-1315)*
Buster Crust Inc 620 385-2651
Main St Spearville (67876) *(G-12070)*

Butler & Associates PA 785 267-6444
3706 Sw Topeka Blvd # 300 Topeka (66609) *(G-12416)*
Butler & Mcllvain Inc 316 684-6700
3225 S Oliver St Wichita (67210) *(G-13921)*
Butler Avionics Inc 913 829-4606
280 Gardner Dr Ste 3 New Century (66031) *(G-7271)*
Butler Bros Inc 620 221-3570
2210 Simpson Ave Winfield (67156) *(G-16118)*
Butler County Health Services 316 320-4140
1313 S High St El Dorado (67042) *(G-1540)*
Butler Enterprises Inc 913 262-9109
5747 Kessler Ln Shawnee Mission (66203) *(G-11192)*
Butler National Corporation (PA) 913 780-9595
19920 W 161st St Olathe (66062) *(G-7571)*
Butler Plumbing & Heating 785 456-8345
315 Lincoln Ave Wamego (66547) *(G-13407)*
Butler Rural Elc Coop Assn Inc 316 321-9600
216 S Vine St El Dorado (67042) *(G-1541)*
Butler Transport Inc 913 321-0047
347 N James St Kansas City (66118) *(G-3882)*
Butler's C-D Collision/Repair, Shawnee Mission *Also called Butler Enterprises Inc (G-11192)*
Butterball LLC 620 597-2800
6410 Sw Hallowell Rd Columbus (66725) *(G-1063)*
Butterfly Supply Inc 620 793-7156
5858 10th St Great Bend (67530) *(G-2525)*
Butternut Home, Manhattan *Also called Big Lkes Developmental Ctr Inc (G-6560)*
Buyers Guide, Salina *Also called Harris Enterprises Group (G-10536)*
Buyrollscom Inc 913 851-7100
11150 W 163rd Pl Overland Park (66221) *(G-8500)*
Buzz Building Maintenance Inc 316 773-9860
3112 N 124th St W Wichita (67223) *(G-13922)*
Buzzi Uncem USA, Bonner Springs *Also called Lone Star Industries Inc (G-561)*
Bvspc - Envirocon JV 913 458-6665
6800 W 115th St Ste 2200 Overland Park (66211) *(G-8501)*
Bwcu, Lawrence *Also called Meritrust Credit Union (G-5022)*
BWI of Ks Inc 316 831-0488
6919 E Harry St Wichita (67207) *(G-13923)*
Bybee Electric, Wichita *Also called Darrell Bybee Construction LLC (G-14171)*
Byers Glass & Mirror Inc 913 441-8717
11685 Kaw Dr Bonner Springs (66012) *(G-544)*
BYIS Manufacturing LLC 620 221-4603
318 Cedar Lane Dr Winfield (67156) *(G-16119)*
Byrds Dance & Gymnastics Inc 913 788-9792
2929 N 103rd Ter Kansas City (66109) *(G-3883)*
Byrne Custom Wood Products Inc 913 894-4777
17501 W 98th St Spc 2862 Lenexa (66219) *(G-5722)*
Byron Bird & Assoc Chartered, Liberal *Also called Byron G Bird Assoc Chartered (G-6288)*
Byron G Bird Assoc Chartered 620 624-1994
224 N Lincoln Ave Liberal (67901) *(G-6288)*
C & A, Wichita *Also called Coonrod & Assoc Cnstr Co Inc (G-14097)*
C & B Equipment Midwest Inc (PA) 316 262-5156
3717 N Ridgewood St Wichita (67220) *(G-13924)*
C & B Equipment Midwest Inc 913 236-8222
4719 Merriam Dr Overland Park (66203) *(G-8502)*
C & C Group of Companies 913 492-8414
10012 Darnell St Lenexa (66215) *(G-5723)*
C & C Truck Line 785 243-3719
611 E 1st St Concordia (66901) *(G-1104)*
C & H Health LLC 913 631-8200
10315 Johnson Dr Shawnee Mission (66203) *(G-11193)*
C & H Trucking LLC 316 794-8282
18333 W 39th St S Goddard (67052) *(G-2430)*
C & I LLC 316 214-7308
990 N Connolly Ct Park City (67219) *(G-9607)*
C & O Elec Sales Co Inc 913 981-0008
10201 W 105th St Shawnee Mission (66212) *(G-11194)*
C & P Enterprises Inc 785 628-6712
808 Milner St Hays (67601) *(G-2762)*
C & R Mfg Inc 913 441-4120
6790 Martindale Rd Shawnee Mission (66218) *(G-11195)*
C & R Plating Inc 785 392-2626
1120 E 10th St Minneapolis (67467) *(G-7115)*
C & R Well Service 785 448-8792
424 W 10th Ave Garnett (66032) *(G-2371)*
C & S Maintenance Inc 913 227-9609
5705 W 153rd Ter Overland Park (66223) *(G-8503)*
C & S Medical Clinic PA 620 408-9700
2200 Summerlon Cir Ste A Dodge City (67801) *(G-1316)*
C & T Enterprises Inc (PA) 913 782-1404
14812 W 117th St Olathe (66062) *(G-7572)*
C & W Farm Supply Inc 785 374-4521
518 Main St Courtland (66939) *(G-1179)*
C & W Farms 620 375-4429
116 S 4th St Leoti (67861) *(G-6251)*
C & W Operations Ltd (PA) 913 438-6400
9108 Barton St Shawnee Mission (66214) *(G-11196)*
C & W Operations Ltd 913 299-8820
8157 State Ave Kansas City (66112) *(G-3884)*

ALPHABETIC

C & W Operations Ltd ...913 268-1032
7407 Quivira Rd Shawnee Mission (66216) ***(G-11197)***
C A Titus Inc (PA) ...913 888-1024
9545 Alden St Lenexa (66215) ***(G-5724)***
C B C S Inc ...620 343-6220
105 W 5th Ave Emporia (66801) ***(G-1714)***
C B H Consultants Inc ...620 624-9700
1550 N Lincoln Ave Liberal (67901) ***(G-6289)***
C B Heating & Air Conditioning, Colby *Also called Chad Briney* ***(G-993)***
C Bar P Trucking Inc ...316 722-2019
20707 W 21st St N Goddard (67052) ***(G-2431)***
C C H Computax, Wichita *Also called CCH Incorporated* ***(G-13966)***
C C R, Topeka *Also called Custom Cabinet & Rack Inc* ***(G-12537)***
C D I, Kansas City *Also called Construction Design Inc* ***(G-3935)***
C Dean Gigot Farms, Garden City *Also called Circle Land & Cattle Corp* ***(G-2124)***
C Dirt Services, Great Bend *Also called Pickrell Drilling Co Inc* ***(G-2623)***
C E D, Overland Park *Also called Constructive Engrg Design* ***(G-8595)***
C E K Real Estte, Lawrence *Also called Cek Real Estate Inc* ***(G-4778)***
C E Machine Co Inc ...316 942-0411
1741 S Hoover Ct Wichita (67209) ***(G-13925)***
C H S, McPherson *Also called CHS Inc* ***(G-6948)***
C L Nationwide Inc ...913 492-5200
9290 Bond St Ste 203 Shawnee Mission (66214) ***(G-11198)***
C P G, Shawnee Mission *Also called Cpg Communications Group LLC* ***(G-11276)***
C W Associates, Shawnee Mission *Also called Mc Real Estate Service Inc* ***(G-11605)***
C W Mill Equipment Co Inc ...785 284-3454
14 Commerce Dr Sabetha (66534) ***(G-10308)***
C&J Well Services Inc ...785 628-6395
1327 Noose Rd Hays (67601) ***(G-2763)***
C&L Management LLC ...913 851-4800
7400 W 130th St Overland Park (66213) ***(G-8504)***
C-Bar-H Farm & Home, Garden City *Also called Crazy House Inc* ***(G-2138)***
C-Hawkk Construction Inc (PA) ...785 542-1800
527 Main St Eudora (66025) ***(G-1872)***
C-Tech Industrial Group Inc (PA) ...316 321-5358
2200 W 6th Ave El Dorado (67042) ***(G-1542)***
C.H. Robinson 46, Wichita *Also called CH Robinson Company Inc* ***(G-13995)***
C2fo, Leawood *Also called Pollen Inc* ***(G-5524)***
C2i Inc ...620 259-6610
4108 Sherwood Dr Hutchinson (67502) ***(G-3227)***
C3, Overland Park *Also called Creative Consumer Concepts Inc* ***(G-8610)***
C3i ...913 327-2255
10955 Granada Ln Overland Park (66211) ***(G-8505)***
C5 Manufacturing LLC ...620 532-3675
1005 E Us Highway 54 Kingman (67068) ***(G-4584)***
Cabinet Connection, Salina *Also called Technical Services LLC* ***(G-10732)***
Cabinet Shop of Basehor, Tonganoxie *Also called Cabinet Shopof Basehor Inc* ***(G-12255)***
Cabinet Shopof Basehor Inc ...913 845-2182
21522 203rd St Tonganoxie (66086) ***(G-12255)***
Cabinetry & Mllwk Concepts Inc ...785 232-1234
3433 Nw 18th St Topeka (66618) ***(G-12417)***
Cablecom Inc ...316 267-4777
800 E 3rd St N Wichita (67202) ***(G-13926)***
CACSC, Wichita *Also called Child Advcacy Ctr Sdgwick Cnty* ***(G-14005)***
Cactus Feeders Inc ...620 356-1750
1765 E Road 21 Ulysses (67880) ***(G-13286)***
Cactus Feeders Inc ...620 384-7431
Hwy 50 E Syracuse (67878) ***(G-12222)***
Cactus Software LLC ...913 677-0092
10950 Grandview Dr # 200 Overland Park (66210) ***(G-8506)***
Caenen Castle ...913 631-4100
12401 Johnson Dr Shawnee (66216) ***(G-10922)***
Cafe Garozzo, Shawnee Mission *Also called Garozzos III Inc* ***(G-11390)***
Cah Acquisition Company 5 LLC ...620 947-3114
101 Industrial Rd Hillsboro (67063) ***(G-3043)***
Cahill Business Services LLC ...913 515-8398
10003 W 120th St Shawnee Mission (66213) ***(G-11199)***
Cain's Coffee, Wichita *Also called Hillshire Brands Company* ***(G-14612)***
Cair Paravel Latin School, Topeka *Also called Assoction Christn Schools Intl* ***(G-12347)***
Cal, Lawrence *Also called Computrzed Assssments Lrng LLC* ***(G-4807)***
Cal Southern Transport Co ...785 232-4202
3728 Se 6th St Topeka (66607) ***(G-12418)***
Cal-Maine Foods Inc ...620 938-2300
625 Avenue K Chase (67524) ***(G-782)***
Caldwell Area Chambe ...620 845-6914
24 N Main St Caldwell (67022) ***(G-655)***
Caldwell Banker Mc Grew RE, Lawrence *Also called Mc Grew Realestate Inc* ***(G-5015)***
Caldwell Communicare ...620 845-6492
601 S Osage St Caldwell (67022) ***(G-656)***
Caldwell Snior Ctizens Ctr Inc ...620 845-6926
428 N Chisholm St Caldwell (67022) ***(G-657)***
Caliber Electronics Inc ...913 782-7787
1105 S Ridgeview Rd Olathe (66062) ***(G-7573)***
Calibrated Forms ...620 429-1120
537 N East Ave Columbus (66725) ***(G-1064)***
California Casualty MGT Co ...913 266-3000
4000 W 114th St Ste 300 Leawood (66211) ***(G-5345)***
California Casualty Svc Ctr, Leawood *Also called California Casualty MGT Co* ***(G-5345)***
California Nail Salon ...316 942-5400
4600 W Kellogg Dr Ofc Wichita (67209) ***(G-13927)***
Calihan Brwn Burgrdt Wurst ...620 276-2381
212 W Pine St Garden City (67846) ***(G-2120)***
Calkins Electric Supply Co Inc ...913 631-6363
5707 Nieman Rd Shawnee (66203) ***(G-10923)***
Callabresi Heating & Coolg Inc ...785 825-2599
1311 Armory Rd Salina (67401) ***(G-10435)***
Callahan Creek Inc (PA) ...785 838-4774
805 New Hampshire St A Lawrence (66044) ***(G-4772)***
Callaway Electric ...785 632-5588
1803 Limestone Rd Clay Center (67432) ***(G-847)***
Called To Greatness Ministries ...785 749-2100
5836 Robinson Dr Lawrence (66049) ***(G-4773)***
Callicrate Cattle Co LLC ...785 332-3344
940 Road 12 Saint Francis (67756) ***(G-10338)***
Callicrate Feed Yard, Saint Francis *Also called Callicrate Cattle Co LLC* ***(G-10338)***
Cally, Donald J, Wichita *Also called Alan Moskowitz MD PC* ***(G-13658)***
Calvert Corporation ...785 877-5221
22850 Kansas 383 Almena (67622) ***(G-67)***
Calverts Auto Express ...913 631-9995
11490 Strang Line Rd Lenexa (66215) ***(G-5725)***
Calverts Express Auto S (PA) ...913 631-9995
11490 Strang Line Rd Lenexa (66215) ***(G-5726)***
Calvin Eddy & Kappelman Inc (PA) ...785 843-2772
1011 Westdale Rd Lawrence (66049) ***(G-4774)***
Calvin Investments LLC ...785 266-8755
2838 Se 29th St Topeka (66605) ***(G-12419)***
Calvin Opp Concrete Inc ...316 944-4600
1375 S Bebe St Wichita (67209) ***(G-13928)***
CAM-Dex Corporation (PA) ...913 621-6160
10 Central Ave Kansas City (66118) ***(G-3885)***
CAM-Dex Security, Kansas City *Also called CAM-Dex Corporation* ***(G-3885)***
Cambridge Cabinetry ...816 795-5082
6800 W 180th St Stilwell (66085) ***(G-12137)***
Cambridge Family Dentistry ...316 687-2110
2020 N Webb Rd Ste 301 Wichita (67206) ***(G-13929)***
Cambridge Suites Hotel ...316 263-1061
711 S Main St Wichita (67213) ***(G-13930)***
Cambridgen Inc ...913 384-3800
10000 W 75th St Ste 100 Overland Park (66204) ***(G-8507)***
Camcorp Inc ...913 831-0740
9732 Pflumm Rd Lenexa (66215) ***(G-5727)***
Camelot Court Animal Clinic ...913 469-9330
4320 W 119th St Shawnee Mission (66209) ***(G-11200)***
Cameron Ashley Bldg Pdts Inc ...913 621-3111
2801 Fairfax Trfy Kansas City (66115) ***(G-3886)***
Camp Hyde, Viola *Also called Young Mens Christian Associat* ***(G-13380)***
Camp Lakeside, Scott City *Also called Lakeside Camp of The United* ***(G-10819)***
Campbells Phoenix Greenhouse ...316 524-5311
3560 S Broadway St Wichita (67216) ***(G-13931)***
Campus Electric Power Company ...785 271-4824
600 Sw Corporate Vw Topeka (66615) ***(G-12420)***
Camso Manufacturing Usa Ltd ...620 340-6500
1601 E South Ave Emporia (66801) ***(G-1715)***
Canadian West Inc ...913 422-0099
6 S 59th St Kansas City (66102) ***(G-3887)***
Canary Resources Inc (PA) ...913 239-8960
7230 W 162nd St Ste A Stilwell (66085) ***(G-12138)***
Cancer Center ...620 235-7900
1 Mt Carmel Way Pittsburg (66762) ***(G-9828)***
Cancer Center of Kansas PA ...620 399-1224
1323 N A St Wellington (67152) ***(G-13494)***
Cancer Center of Kansas PA ...620 421-2855
1902 S Us Highway 59 Parsons (67357) ***(G-9670)***
Cancer Center of Kansas PA ...620 629-6727
315 W 15th St Liberal (67901) ***(G-6290)***
Cancer Center of Kansas PA ...316 262-4467
3243 E Murdock St Ste 300 Wichita (67208) ***(G-13932)***
Cancer Center of Kansas PA (PA) ...316 262-4467
818 N Emporia St Ste 403 Wichita (67214) ***(G-13933)***
Cancer Center of Kansas PA ...620 431-7580
505 S Plummer Ave Chanute (66720) ***(G-708)***
Cancer Council of Reno County ...620 665-5555
633 Hutchinson Hutchinson (67504) ***(G-3228)***
Cancer Medicine & Hemotology, Topeka *Also called Sisters of Charity of Leavenwo* ***(G-13073)***
Candlewood Medical Center, Manhattan *Also called Candlewood Medical Group PA* ***(G-6574)***
Candlewood Medical Group PA ...785 539-0800
1133 College Ave Ste D200 Manhattan (66502) ***(G-6574)***
Candlewood Suites, Wichita *Also called Hpt Trs Ihg 2 Inc* ***(G-14644)***
Candlewood Suites, Manhattan *Also called Flint Hills Hospitality LLC* ***(G-6634)***
Candlewood Suites, Salina *Also called Belmont Hotels LLC* ***(G-10422)***
Candlewood Suites, Shawnee Mission *Also called Hpt Trs Ihg-2 Inc* ***(G-11442)***
Candlewood Suites, Junction City *Also called Nogales Hotel Company LLC* ***(G-3732)***

Candlewood Suites, Kansas City *Also called Swami Investment Inc* ***(G-4451)***
Candlewood Suites, Wichita *Also called Hpt Trs Ihg-2 Inc* ***(G-14645)***
Candlewood Suites Hotel 913 768-8888
15490 S Rogers Rd Olathe (66062) ***(G-7574)***
Caney Chronicle, Caney *Also called Montgomery County Chronicle* ***(G-672)***
Caney Guest Home Inc 620 431-7115
7440 220th Rd Chanute (66720) ***(G-709)***
Caney Valley Elc Coop Assn 620 758-2262
401 Lawrence St Cedar Vale (67024) ***(G-692)***
Canlan Ice Spt Ctr Wichita LLC 316 337-9199
505 W Maple St Wichita (67213) ***(G-13934)***
Cannonball Engineering LLC (PA) 620 532-3675
1005 E Us Highway 54 Kingman (67068) ***(G-4585)***
Canon Solutions America Inc 913 323-5010
7300 W 110th St Ste 100 Overland Park (66210) ***(G-8508)***
Canon Solutions America Inc 785 232-8222
1131 Sw Winding Rd Ste A Topeka (66615) ***(G-12421)***
Canyon Oil & Gas Co 316 263-3201
727 N Waco Ave Ste 400 Wichita (67203) ***(G-13935)***
Canyon Stone Inc (PA) 913 254-9300
550 E Old Highway 56 B Olathe (66061) ***(G-7575)***
Cap Carpet Inc (PA) 316 262-3496
535 S Emerson St Wichita (67209) ***(G-13936)***
Cap Carpet Inc 785 273-1402
5131 Sw 29th St Topeka (66614) ***(G-12422)***
Capelli Hair & Nail Salon 785 271-6811
2824 Sw Arrowhead Rd Topeka (66614) ***(G-12423)***
Capfusion LLC 816 888-5302
2310 W 75th St Prairie Village (66208) ***(G-10018)***
Capital Area Gymnstics Emprium 785 266-4151
3740 Sw South Park Ave Topeka (66609) ***(G-12424)***
Capital Business Service, Paola *Also called Charge It LLC* ***(G-9546)***
Capital City Corral Inc 785 273-5354
1601 Sw Wanamaker Rd Topeka (66604) ***(G-12425)***
Capital City Gun Club Inc 785 478-4682
Nw 4th St Topeka (66601) ***(G-12426)***
Capital City Investments Inc 785 274-5600
3710 Sw Topeka Blvd Topeka (66609) ***(G-12427)***
Capital City Oil Inc (PA) 785 233-8008
911 Se Adams St Topeka (66607) ***(G-12428)***
Capital City Pallet Inc 785 379-5099
804 Ne Us Highway 24 Topeka (66608) ***(G-12429)***
Capital Electric Cnstr Co Inc (HQ) 816 472-9500
2801 Fairfax Trfy Kansas City (66115) ***(G-3888)***
Capital Federal, Emporia *Also called Capitol Federal Savings Bank* ***(G-1716)***
Capital Financial Group 785 228-1234
2820 Sw Mission Woods Dr # 150 Topeka (66614) ***(G-12430)***
Capital Frsght Golf Fitnes LLC 913 648-1600
8223 W 103rd St Overland Park (66212) ***(G-8509)***
Capital Graphics Inc 785 233-6677
305 Se 17th St Ste C Topeka (66607) ***(G-12431)***
Capital Insulation Inc 785 246-1775
2714 Nw Topeka Blvd # 106 Topeka (66617) ***(G-12432)***
Capital Label LLC 785 291-9702
305 Se 17th St Ste C Topeka (66607) ***(G-12433)***
Capital Performance MGT LLC (PA) 913 381-1481
11835 Roe Ave 236 Leawood (66211) ***(G-5346)***
Capital Realty LLC 913 469-4600
7500 College Blvd Ste 920 Overland Park (66210) ***(G-8510)***
Capital Resources LLC 913 469-1630
7960 W 135th St Ste 200 Overland Park (66223) ***(G-8511)***
Capital Title Insurance Co Lc 785 272-2900
2655 Sw Wanamaker Rd C Topeka (66614) ***(G-12434)***
Capitol LLC 602 462-5888
17795 W 106th St Ste 201 Olathe (66061) ***(G-7576)***
Capitol City Taxi Inc 785 267-3777
2050 Se 30th St Topeka (66605) ***(G-12435)***
Capitol Concrete Pdts Co Inc (PA) 785 233-3271
627 Nw Tyler St Topeka (66608) ***(G-12436)***
Capitol Discovery Services, Olathe *Also called Capitol LLC* ***(G-7576)***
Capitol Federal Financial Inc (PA) 785 235-1341
700 S Kansas Ave Fl 1 Topeka (66603) ***(G-12437)***
Capitol Federal Savings Bank 316 689-0200
10404 W Central Ave Wichita (67212) ***(G-13937)***
Capitol Federal Savings Bank 785 235-1341
2100 Sw Fairlawn Rd Topeka (66614) ***(G-12438)***
Capitol Federal Savings Bank (HQ) 785 235-1341
700 S Kansas Ave Fl 1 Topeka (66603) ***(G-12439)***
Capitol Federal Savings Bank 316 689-3104
8103 E 21st St N Wichita (67206) ***(G-13938)***
Capitol Federal Savings Bank 913 782-5100
1408 E Santa Fe St Olathe (66061) ***(G-7577)***
Capitol Federal Savings Bank 785 749-9100
11th & Vermont Sts Lawrence (66044) ***(G-4775)***
Capitol Federal Savings Bank 620 342-0125
602 Commercial St Emporia (66801) ***(G-1716)***
Capitol Federal Savings Bank 785 539-9976
705 Commons Pl Manhattan (66503) ***(G-6575)***
Capitol Federal Savings Bank 316 689-0200
4000 E Harry St Wichita (67218) ***(G-13939)***
Capitol Plaza Hotel, Topeka *Also called Tucson Hotels LP* ***(G-13201)***
Capper Foundation 785 272-4060
3500 Sw 10th Ave Topeka (66604) ***(G-12440)***
Cappers Insurance Service Inc 785 274-4300
1503 Sw 42nd St Topeka (66609) ***(G-12441)***
Capps Manufacturing Inc 316 942-9351
2122 S Custer Ave Wichita (67213) ***(G-13940)***
Capps Manufacturing Inc (PA) 316 942-9351
2121 S Edwards St Wichita (67213) ***(G-13941)***
Caps Direct, Overland Park *Also called Design Resources Inc* ***(G-8651)***
Capstan AG Systems Inc (HQ) 785 232-4477
4225 Sw Kirklawn Ave Topeka (66609) ***(G-12442)***
Capstone MGT & Dev Group Inc 785 341-2494
1083 Wildcat Creek Rd Manhattan (66503) ***(G-6576)***
Captify Health Inc 913 951-2600
13321 W 98th St Lenexa (66215) ***(G-5728)***
Car Care, Meade *Also called Cooperative Elevator & Sup Co* ***(G-7048)***
Car Clinic Auto Salon 913 208-5478
1270 Southwest Blvd Kansas City (66103) ***(G-3889)***
Car Park Inc 316 265-0553
121 S Emporia Ave Wichita (67202) ***(G-13942)***
Car Star Inc 785 232-2084
313 Sw Jackson St Topeka (66603) ***(G-12443)***
Car Star Spc 201 444-0601
8400 W 110th St Ste 200 Overland Park (66210) ***(G-8512)***
Car Wash Center of Mission Inc 913 236-6886
5960 Barkley St Shawnee Mission (66202) ***(G-11201)***
Caraway Printing Company Inc 913 727-5223
204 N Main St Ste B Lansing (66043) ***(G-4670)***
Cardinal Buffing Co Inc 316 263-8475
1432 S Walnut St Wichita (67213) ***(G-13943)***
Cardinal Health Inc 316 264-6275
536 N St Francis St Wichita (67214) ***(G-13944)***
Cardinal Health Inc 800 523-0502
11400 Tomahawk Crk Pkwy # 310 Shawnee Mission (66211) ***(G-11202)***
Cardinal Health 127 Inc 913 451-3955
7400 W 110th St Overland Park (66210) ***(G-8513)***
Cardinal Logistics 620 223-4903
4805 Campbell Dr Fort Scott (66701) ***(G-1956)***
Cardinal Supply & Mfg Co, Wichita *Also called Wsm Industries Inc* ***(G-16075)***
Cardiology Cons Topeka PA 785 233-9643
600 Sw College Ave Topeka (66606) ***(G-12444)***
Cardiology Service, Olathe *Also called Olathe Medical Services Inc* ***(G-7942)***
Cardiotabs Inc 816 753-4298
6701 W 91st St Overland Park (66212) ***(G-8514)***
Cardiovascular Cons Kans PA 316 440-0845
9350 E 35th St N Ste 101 Wichita (67226) ***(G-13945)***
Cardiovascular Consultants Inc 913 491-1000
12300 Metcalf Ave 280 Shawnee Mission (66213) ***(G-11203)***
Cardivsclar Thrcic Surgeons PA 785 270-8625
830 Sw Mulvane St Topeka (66606) ***(G-12445)***
Cardona Coffee LLP 785 554-6060
6540 Se Johnston St Topeka (66619) ***(G-12446)***
Care 4 All Home Medical Eqp 620 223-4141
2 W 18th St Fort Scott (66701) ***(G-1957)***
Care 4 U Inc 620 223-1411
207 E Prairie Ave Girard (66743) ***(G-2395)***
Care A Lot Daycare 785 628-2563
401 Oak St Hays (67601) ***(G-2764)***
Carecentrix Inc 913 749-5600
6130 Sprint Pkwy Ste 200 Overland Park (66211) ***(G-8515)***
Career Athletes LLC 913 538-6259
10000 Marshall Dr Lenexa (66215) ***(G-5729)***
Career P& Employment Svc, Manhattan *Also called Kansas State University* ***(G-6692)***
Carefore Medical Inc 913 327-5445
11605 S Alden St Olathe (66062) ***(G-7578)***
Carefusion 213 LLC 800 523-0502
11400 Tomahawk Creek Pkwy Leawood (66211) ***(G-5347)***
Caregiver Bed, The, Andover *Also called Caregiver Company LLC* ***(G-85)***
Caregiver Company LLC 316 247-4005
541 S Riverview St Andover (67002) ***(G-85)***
Caregiver Support System 214 207-7273
306 S Roosevelt St Marion (66861) ***(G-6867)***
Caregivers of KS Inc 785 354-0767
3715 Sw 29th St Topeka (66614) ***(G-12447)***
Carestaf Inc 913 498-2888
8001 College Blvd Ste 250 Overland Park (66210) ***(G-8516)***
Cargill, Leoti *Also called Green Plains Inc* ***(G-6252)***
Cargill Incorporated 913 752-1200
15405 College Blvd # 200 Lenexa (66219) ***(G-5730)***
Cargill Incorporated 785 825-8128
1112 N Halstead Rd Salina (67401) ***(G-10436)***
Cargill Incorporated 913 367-3579
15662 258th Rd Cummings (66016) ***(G-1186)***
Cargill Incorporated 620 241-5120
2025 E 1st St McPherson (67460) ***(G-6940)***
Cargill Incorporated 316 292-2380
1417 N Barwise St Wichita (67214) ***(G-13946)***

A L P H A B E T I C

Cargill Incorporated 620 663-2141
609 E Avenue G Hutchinson (67501) ***(G-3229)***
Cargill Incorporated 785 357-1989
1845 Nw Gordon St Topeka (66608) ***(G-12448)***
Cargill Incorporated 913 236-0346
5200 Metcalf Ave Ste 150 Overland Park (66202) ***(G-8517)***
Cargill Incorporated 316 291-1939
825 E Douglas Ave Wichita (67202) ***(G-13947)***
Cargill Incorporated 620 277-2558
3680 W Jones Ave Garden City (67846) ***(G-2121)***
Cargill Incorporated 913 299-2326
6833 Griffin Rd Kansas City (66111) ***(G-3890)***
Cargill Incorporated 785 235-3003
5135 Nw Us Highway 24 Topeka (66618) ***(G-12449)***
Cargill Incorporated 620 663-4401
309 N Halstead St Hutchinson (67501) ***(G-3230)***
Cargill Incorporated 316 292-2719
1401 N Mosley St Wichita (67214) ***(G-13948)***
Cargill Incorporated 806 659-3554
5200 Metcalf Ave Ste 250 Shawnee Mission (66202) ***(G-11204)***
Cargill Incorporated 785 743-2288
Old Hwy 40 WA Keeney (67672) ***(G-13382)***
Cargill Animal Nutrition 620 342-1650
841 Graphic Arts Rd Emporia (66801) ***(G-1717)***
Cargill Meat Solutions Corp 620 225-2610
3201 E Hwy 154 Dodge City (67801) ***(G-1317)***
Cargill Mt Lgstics Sltions Inc (HQ) 877 596-4062
250 N Water St Wichita (67202) ***(G-13949)***
Cargill Mt Lgstics Sltions Inc 620 225-2610
3201 E Hwy 400 Dodge City (67801) ***(G-1318)***
Cargotec Holding Inc (HQ) 785 242-2200
415 E Dundee St Ottawa (66067) ***(G-8251)***
Cargotec USA Inc 785 229-7111
1230 N Mulberry St Ottawa (66067) ***(G-8252)***
Caring Compassionate Care LLC 785 215-8127
220 Sw 33rd St Ste 101 Topeka (66611) ***(G-12450)***
Caring Connections 620 544-2050
516 Northeast Ave Hugoton (67951) ***(G-3150)***
Caring Hands Humane Society 316 284-0487
1400 Se 3rd St Newton (67114) ***(G-7326)***
Caring Harts For Senior Living, Wichita *Also called Lcd Unlimited Inc* ***(G-14938)***
Carl Harris Co Inc 316 267-8700
1245 S Santa Fe St Wichita (67211) ***(G-13950)***
Carl Leatherwood Inc 620 855-3850
215 S Main St Cimarron (67835) ***(G-820)***
Carley Construction Co Inc 785 456-2882
16875 Ebel Rd Wamego (66547) ***(G-13408)***
Carlisle Belts, Fort Scott *Also called Timken Smo LLC* ***(G-2008)***
Carlisle Heating & AC 316 321-6230
1100 N Main St El Dorado (67042) ***(G-1543)***
Carlos O'Kelleys, Wichita *Also called Sasnak Management Corporation* ***(G-15521)***
Carlos Palmeri, Lenexa *Also called Family Practice Associates* ***(G-5848)***
Carlson Auction Service Inc 785 478-4250
11048 Sw Us Highway 40 Topeka (66615) ***(G-12451)***
Carlson Company Inc 316 744-0481
6045 N Broadway Ave Park City (67219) ***(G-9608)***
Carlson Hydraulics, Wichita *Also called Squires Corporation* ***(G-15650)***
Carlson Plumbing, Topeka *Also called Plumbing By Carlson Inc* ***(G-12981)***
Carlson Products LLC 316 722-0265
4601 N Tyler Rd Maize (67101) ***(G-6509)***
Carlson Systems, Wichita *Also called Southerncarlson Inc* ***(G-15625)***
Carlson, Mark MD, Pittsburg *Also called Pittsburg Internal Medcine PA* ***(G-9921)***
Carlsons Choke Tube/NW Arms 785 626-3078
720 S 2nd St Atwood (67730) ***(G-282)***
Carlstar Group LLC 913 667-1000
2701 S 98th St Kansas City (66111) ***(G-3891)***
Carlton-Bates Company 913 375-1160
10814 W 78th St Overland Park (66214) ***(G-8518)***
Carlyle Apartments, Shawnee *Also called MCN Shawnee LLC* ***(G-10992)***
Carmike Cinemas LLC (HQ) 913 213-2000
11500 Ash St Leawood (66211) ***(G-5348)***
Carmike Reviews Holdings LLC 913 213-2000
11500 Ash St Leawood (66211) ***(G-5349)***
Carnahan, John R DDS, Wellington *Also called Grant Phipps DDS* ***(G-13507)***
Carney Daniel M Rehab Engineer 316 651-5200
5130 E 20th St N Wichita (67208) ***(G-13951)***
Caro Construction Co Inc 316 267-7505
527 N Walnut St Wichita (67203) ***(G-13952)***
Carol J Feltheim 913 469-5579
11725 W 112th St Overland Park (66210) ***(G-8519)***
Carondelet Health 913 345-1745
11901 Rosewood St Overland Park (66209) ***(G-8520)***
Carondelet Home Care Services 913 529-4800
7255 Renner Rd Shawnee (66217) ***(G-10924)***
Carondelet Orthpdc Srgns Sprts 913 642-0200
10777 Nall Ave Ste 300 Overland Park (66211) ***(G-8521)***
Carousel Skate Center Inc 316 942-4505
312 N West St Wichita (67203) ***(G-13953)***
Carpenter Chartered, Topeka *Also called Crpenter Charted* ***(G-12533)***
Carpenter Construction Company 620 386-4155
320 S Avenue A Moundridge (67107) ***(G-7179)***
Carpet Factory Outlet Inc (PA) 913 261-6800
3200 S 24th St Kansas City (66106) ***(G-3892)***
Carpet One, Wichita *Also called Cap Carpet Inc* ***(G-13936)***
Carpet One Topeka, Topeka *Also called Cap Carpet Inc* ***(G-12422)***
Carquest Auto Parts, Rossville *Also called L C McClain Inc* ***(G-10253)***
Carquest Auto Parts, Beloit *Also called Kriers Auto Parts Inc* ***(G-489)***
Carr Auction & Realestate 620 285-3148
909 Auction Ave Larned (67550) ***(G-4697)***
Carr Trucking, Kansas City *Also called Mary Carr* ***(G-4221)***
Carriage House Central, Wichita *Also called Carrington House LLC* ***(G-13954)***
Carriage Services Inc 785 242-3550
325 S Hickory St Ottawa (66067) ***(G-8253)***
Carriage Services Inc 913 682-2820
707 S 6th St Leavenworth (66048) ***(G-5214)***
Carrico Implement Co Inc (PA) 785 738-5744
3160 Us 24 Hwy Beloit (67420) ***(G-480)***
Carrico Implement Co Inc 785 472-4400
1104 E 8th St Ellsworth (67439) ***(G-1658)***
Carrico Implement Co Inc 785 625-2219
300 W 48th St Hays (67601) ***(G-2765)***
Carrier Logistics LLC (PA) 913 681-2780
15641 S Mahaffie St Olathe (66062) ***(G-7579)***
Carrington House LLC 316 262-5516
1432 N Waco Ave Wichita (67203) ***(G-13954)***
Carrolls LLC 913 321-2233
625 S Adams St Kansas City (66105) ***(G-3893)***
Carrothers Construction Co Inc 913 294-2361
401 W Wea St Paola (66071) ***(G-9544)***
Carrothers Construction Co LLC 913 294-8120
401 W Wea St Paola (66071) ***(G-9545)***
Carson Development Inc 913 499-1926
7248 W 121st St Overland Park (66213) ***(G-8522)***
Carson Mobile HM Pk Sewer Dst 785 537-6330
6215 Tuttle Creek Blvd Manhattan (66503) ***(G-6577)***
Carstar, Topeka *Also called Car Star Inc* ***(G-12443)***
Carstar, Lawrence *Also called Lawrence Cllsion Spcalists LLC* ***(G-4961)***
Carstar Inc 316 652-7821
606 N Webb Rd Wichita (67206) ***(G-13955)***
Carstar Inc 913 685-2886
7235 W 162nd St Stilwell (66085) ***(G-12139)***
Carter Automotive Warehouse, Coffeyville *Also called W Carter Orvil Inc* ***(G-984)***
Carter Energy, Overland Park *Also called World Fuel Services Inc* ***(G-9505)***
Carter-Waters LLC 913 671-1870
6803 W 64th St Overland Park (66202) ***(G-8523)***
Carter-Waters LLC 316 942-6712
4311 W 29th Cir S Wichita (67215) ***(G-13956)***
Cartesian Inc (HQ) 913 345-9315
6405 Metcalf Ave Ste 417 Overland Park (66202) ***(G-8524)***
Cartridge King of Kansas (PA) 620 241-7746
2107 Industrial Dr McPherson (67460) ***(G-6941)***
Casa Jhnson Wyndtte Cnties Inc 913 715-4040
6950 Squibb Rd Ste 300 Mission (66202) ***(G-7128)***
Casa of The Thirty-First Judic 620 365-1448
1 N Washington Ave Iola (66749) ***(G-3589)***
Cascade Dental Care 785 841-3311
1425 Wakarusa Dr Lawrence (66049) ***(G-4776)***
Case Mses Zimmerman Martin PA 316 303-0100
200 W Douglas Ave Ste 900 Wichita (67202) ***(G-13957)***
Case New Holland, Wichita *Also called Cnh Industrial America LLC* ***(G-14046)***
Casemax, Overland Park *Also called Prs Inc* ***(G-9199)***
Casey Associates Inc 913 276-3200
8307 Melrose Dr Lenexa (66214) ***(G-5731)***
Cash Point, Wichita *Also called Dominion Management Svcs Inc* ***(G-14223)***
Cashco Inc (PA) 785 472-4461
607 W 15th St Ellsworth (67439) ***(G-1659)***
Cashpoint Car Title Loans, Wichita *Also called Dominion Management Svcs Inc* ***(G-14222)***
Casillas Petroleum Corp 620 276-3693
348 Road Dd Satanta (67870) ***(G-10778)***
Casino White Cloud, White Cloud *Also called Iowa Tribe Kansas & Nebraska* ***(G-13569)***
Cassian Energy LLC 913 948-1107
9300 W 110th St Ste 235 Overland Park (66210) ***(G-8525)***
Cassidy Orthodontic, Topeka *Also called Michael F Cassidy DDS* ***(G-12887)***
Castle Creations Inc 913 390-6939
540 N Rogers Rd Olathe (66062) ***(G-7580)***
Castle Resources Inc 785 625-5155
114 Oak St Schoenchen (67667) ***(G-10802)***
Cat Calls 913 642-2024
9621 W 87th St Shawnee Mission (66212) ***(G-11205)***
Cat Clinic of Johnson County 913 541-0478
9421 Pflumm Rd A Lenexa (66215) ***(G-5732)***
Cat Clinic of Johnson, The, Lenexa *Also called Cat Clinic of Johnson County* ***(G-5732)***
Catacombs Youth Ministry 316 689-8410
255 S Estelle St Wichita (67211) ***(G-13958)***
Catalog Dog, Olathe *Also called Tr Sales & Distribution Inc* ***(G-8118)***

Catalyst Artificial Lift LLC (PA)....620 365-7150
2702 N State St Iola (66749) *(G-3590)*
Catapult International LLC (HQ)....913 232-2389
13632 W 95th St Lenexa (66215) *(G-5733)*
Catapult, A Mercator Company, Lenexa *Also called Catapult International LLC (G-5733)*
Caterpillar Authorized Dealer, Dodge City *Also called Foley Equipment Company (G-1361)*
Caterpillar Authorized Dealer, Wichita *Also called Foley Supply LLC (G-14400)*
Caterpillar Authorized Dealer, Great Bend *Also called Foley Equipment Company (G-2566)*
Caterpillar Authorized Dealer, Manhattan *Also called Foley Equipment Company (G-6637)*
Caterpillar Authorized Dealer, Topeka *Also called Foley Equipment Company (G-12623)*
Caterpillar Inc....309 675-1000
400 Work Tool Rd Wamego (66547) *(G-13409)*
Caterpillar Work Tools Inc (HQ)....785 456-2224
400 Work Tool Rd Wamego (66547) *(G-13410)*
Caterpillar Work Tools Inc....785 456-2224
600 Balderson Blvd Wamego (66547) *(G-13411)*
Cates Heating & AC Svc Co....913 888-4470
14361 W 96th Ter Lenexa (66215) *(G-5734)*
Cates Service Co, Lenexa *Also called Cates Heating & AC Svc Co (G-5734)*
Catholic Care Center, Wichita *Also called Catholic Diocese of Wichita (G-13963)*
Catholic Care Center Inc....316 744-8651
6700 E 45th St N Bel Aire (67226) *(G-428)*
Catholic Cemeteries K C K, Kansas City *Also called Catholic Cemteries Inc (G-3894)*
Catholic Cemteries Inc....913 371-4040
1150 N 38th St Kansas City (66102) *(G-3894)*
Catholic Charities, Topeka *Also called Archdiocese of Miami Inc (G-12336)*
Catholic Charities....913 433-2061
9700 W 87th St Shawnee Mission (66212) *(G-11206)*
Catholic Charities Inc (PA)....316 264-8344
437 N Topeka Ave Wichita (67202) *(G-13959)*
Catholic Charities Inc....316 264-7233
256 N Ohio Ave Wichita (67214) *(G-13960)*
Catholic Charities Adult Svcs....316 942-2008
5920 W Central Ave Wichita (67212) *(G-13961)*
Catholic Charities of....913 721-1570
12615 Parallel Pkwy Kansas City (66109) *(G-3895)*
Catholic Charities of Northeas....913 621-5090
9740 W 87th St Overland Park (66212) *(G-8526)*
Catholic Charities of Salina (PA)....785 825-0208
1500 S 9th St Salina (67401) *(G-10437)*
Catholic Charities of Southwes....620 227-1562
906 Central Ave Dodge City (67801) *(G-1319)*
Catholic Charities of Wichita....316 263-6000
437 N Topeka Ave Wichita (67202) *(G-13962)*
Catholic Chrties Fndtion Nrtha....913 621-1504
2220 Central Ave Kansas City (66102) *(G-3896)*
Catholic Chrties Nrthast Kans (PA)....913 433-2100
2220 Central Ave Kansas City (66102) *(G-3897)*
Catholic Cmnty Svc HM Hlth Dp, Kansas City *Also called Archdiocese Kansas Cy In Kans (G-3816)*
Catholic Community Hospice, Overland Park *Also called Catholic Charities of Northeas (G-8526)*
Catholic Community Services, Shawnee Mission *Also called Catholic Charities (G-11206)*
CATHOLIC COMMUNTY SERVICES, Kansas City *Also called Catholic Chrties Fndtion Nrtha (G-3896)*
Catholic Diocese of Wichita (PA)....316 269-3900
424 N Broadway Ave Wichita (67202) *(G-13963)*
Catholic Diocese of Wichita....316 744-2020
6700 E 45th St N Bel Aire (67226) *(G-429)*
Catholic Family Federal Cr Un....316 264-9163
1902 W Douglas Ave Wichita (67203) *(G-13964)*
Cattle Empire LLC....620 649-2235
2425 Road Dd Satanta (67870) *(G-10779)*
Cav Ice Protection Inc....913 738-5391
30 Leawood Dr New Century (66031) *(G-7272)*
Cavanaugh Biggs and Lemon PA....785 440-4000
2942 Sw Wnamaker Dr Ste A Topeka (66614) *(G-12452)*
Cavanaugh Eye Center PA....913 897-9200
6200 W 135th St Ste 300 Overland Park (66223) *(G-8527)*
Cave Inn LLC....785 749-6010
2176 E 23rd St Lawrence (66046) *(G-4777)*
Cavein Techonolgy, Lenexa *Also called Continuity Operation Plg LLC (G-5785)*
Cawker City Senior Center....785 781-4763
521 Wisconson St Cawker City (67430) *(G-688)*
CB Announcement Balfour, Manhattan *Also called CB Grduation Announcements LLC (G-6578)*
CB Grduation Announcements LLC (PA)....785 776-5018
2316 Skyvue Ln Manhattan (66502) *(G-6578)*
CB&i Envmtl Infrastructure Inc....913 451-1224
11206 Thompson Ave Lenexa (66219) *(G-5735)*
Cbcs Collections, Emporia *Also called C B C S Inc (G-1714)*
Cbi-Kansas Inc....785 625-6542
2200 Vine St Hays (67601) *(G-2766)*
Cbi-Kansas Inc....620 341-7420
1440 Industrial Rd Emporia (66801) *(G-1718)*
Cbiz Inc....913 345-0500
6900 College Blvd Ste 300 Overland Park (66211) *(G-8528)*
Cbiz Accounting Tax & A....785 272-3176
990 Sw Fairlawn Rd Topeka (66606) *(G-12453)*
Cbiz Accounting Tax & Advisor....913 234-1932
11440 Tomahawk Creek Pkwy Shawnee Mission (66211) *(G-11207)*
Cbiz Benefits & Insur Svcs Inc....913 234-1000
11440 Tomahawk Creek Pkwy Leawood (66211) *(G-5350)*
Cbiz M&S Consulting Svcs LLC (HQ)....785 228-6700
4123 Sw Gage Center Dr # 200 Topeka (66604) *(G-12454)*
Cbiz Med MGT Professionals Inc....913 652-1899
10100 Santa Fe Ln Ste 100 Shawnee Mission (66212) *(G-11208)*
Cbiz Med MGT Professionals Inc....316 686-7327
8080 E Central Ave # 250 Wichita (67206) *(G-13965)*
Cboe Bats LLC (HQ)....913 815-7000
8050 Marshall Dr Lenexa (66214) *(G-5736)*
Cbre Inc....785 435-2399
920 Se Quincy St Topeka (66612) *(G-12455)*
CBS, Shawnee Mission *Also called Cahill Business Services LLC (G-11199)*
CBS Manhattan LLC (PA)....785 537-4935
9130 Green Valley Dr Manhattan (66502) *(G-6579)*
Cbw Bank....620 396-8221
109 E Main St Weir (66781) *(G-13485)*
CC Account, Lenexa *Also called PQ Corporation (G-6064)*
CC Products LLC....913 693-3200
9700 Commerce Pkwy Lenexa (66219) *(G-5737)*
CC Services Inc....913 894-0700
14867 W 95th St Shawnee Mission (66215) *(G-11209)*
CC Services Inc....913 381-1995
10561 Barkley St Overland Park (66212) *(G-8529)*
Cccs of Topeka/Lawrence, Topeka *Also called Housing and Credit Counseling (G-12705)*
CCDS, Arkansas City *Also called Twin Rvers Dvlpmental Supports (G-184)*
Ccfp, Clay Center *Also called Clay Center Fmly Physicians PA (G-851)*
CCH Incorporated....316 612-5000
9111 E Douglas Ave 200a Wichita (67207) *(G-13966)*
CCHC, Concordia *Also called Cloud County Health Center Inc (G-1106)*
CCI Fluid Kinetics, Winfield *Also called Control Components Inc (G-16127)*
CCL Construction Consultants (PA)....913 491-0807
4600 College Blvd Ste 104 Overland Park (66211) *(G-8530)*
CCM Countertop & Cab Mfg LLC....316 554-0113
2945 S Kansas Ave Wichita (67216) *(G-13967)*
Ccpi, Lenexa *Also called CC Products LLC (G-5737)*
CCT, Stilwell *Also called Cogen Cleaning Technology Inc (G-12142)*
CD Custom Enterprises LLC....316 804-4520
1800 Se 9th St Newton (67114) *(G-7327)*
CD McCormick & Company Inc....913 541-0106
12020 W 87th Street Pkwy Overland Park (66215) *(G-8531)*
CD&h Inc....316 320-7187
2510 W 6th Ave El Dorado (67042) *(G-1544)*
Cdh Enterprises....316 320-7187
2000 W 6th Ave El Dorado (67042) *(G-1545)*
CDI Industrial Mech Contrs Inc....913 287-0334
5621 Kansas Ave Kansas City (66106) *(G-3898)*
CDL Electric Company Inc....620 232-1242
1308 N Walnut St Pittsburg (66762) *(G-9829)*
Cds Inc....913 541-1166
9095 Bond St Overland Park (66214) *(G-8532)*
Ce Water Management Inc....913 621-7047
3250 Brinkerhoff Rd Kansas City (66115) *(G-3899)*
Cec Entertainment, Topeka *Also called Spt Distribution Center (G-13093)*
Cec Entertainment Inc....913 648-4920
10510 Metcalf Ave Overland Park (66212) *(G-8533)*
Cec Entertainment Inc....316 636-2225
3223 N Rock Rd Wichita (67226) *(G-13968)*
Ceco Inc....316 942-7431
4125 W Pawnee St Wichita (67209) *(G-13969)*
Ceco Concrete Cnstr Del LLC....913 362-1855
1290 W 151st St Olathe (66061) *(G-7581)*
Cedar Court Motel, Clay Center *Also called Rothfuss Motels (G-878)*
Cedar Lnscape Maintence Fcilty, Olathe *Also called Glen Shadow Golf Club (G-7730)*
Cedar Surgical LLC....316 616-6272
2237 Keystone Cir Andover (67002) *(G-86)*
Cedar Vale Rural Health Clinic....620 758-2221
501 Walnut St Cedar Vale (67024) *(G-693)*
Cedar Vale Rural Hlth Clinics, Cedar Vale *Also called Cedar Vale Rural Health Clinic (G-693)*
Cedars Inc (PA)....620 241-0919
1021 Cedars Dr McPherson (67460) *(G-6942)*
Cedars Inc....620 241-7959
1071 Darlow Dr McPherson (67460) *(G-6943)*
Cedars Courts The, McPherson *Also called Cedars Inc (G-6943)*
CEDARS HEALTH CARE CENTER, McPherson *Also called Cedars Inc (G-6942)*
Cederlind, Cranston J, Shawnee Mission *Also called Johnson Cnty Ob-Gyn Chartered (G-11494)*
Cek Real Estate Inc....785 843-2055
1501 Kasold Dr Lawrence (66047) *(G-4778)*
Celco, Anthony *Also called Central Electropolishing Inc (G-122)*
Celgene Corporation....913 266-0300
9225 Indian Creek Pkwy # 900 Overland Park (66210) *(G-8534)*

ALPHABETIC

Cellco Partnership...913 897-5022
6925 W 135th St Overland Park (66223) ***(G-8535)***
Cellco Partnership...316 636-5155
2161 N Rock Rd Ste 120 Wichita (67206) ***(G-13970)***
Cellco Partnership...620 276-6776
3010 E Kansas Ave Garden City (67846) ***(G-2122)***
Cellco Partnership...316 789-9911
2100 N Rock Rd Ste 100 Derby (67037) ***(G-1228)***
Cellco Partnership...785 820-6311
621 Westport Blvd Salina (67401) ***(G-10438)***
Cellco Partnership...785 537-6159
100 Bluemont Ave Ste H Manhattan (66502) ***(G-6580)***
Cellco Partnership...316 722-4532
2441 N Maize Rd Ste 1509 Wichita (67205) ***(G-13971)***
Cellco Partnership...913 631-0677
11868 W 95th St Overland Park (66214) ***(G-8536)***
Cellint Usa Inc...913 871-6500
14670 S Kaw Dr Olathe (66062) ***(G-7582)***
Celltron Inc...620 783-1333
1110 W 7th St Galena (66739) ***(G-2070)***
Celsius Tannery, The, Leavenworth *Also called Ah Tannery Inc* ***(G-5200)***
Cemex Materials LLC...913 287-5725
759 S 65th St Kansas City (66111) ***(G-3900)***
Centaur Inc...913 390-6184
1351 W Old Highway 56 F Olathe (66061) ***(G-7583)***
Centene Corporation...913 599-3078
8325 Lenexa Dr Lenexa (66214) ***(G-5738)***
Centennial Healthcare Corp...913 829-2273
201 E Flaming Rd Olathe (66061) ***(G-7584)***
Centennial Homestead Inc...785 325-2361
311 E 2nd St Washington (66968) ***(G-13462)***
Centennial Lanes, Hays *Also called Prairie Sports Inc* ***(G-2887)***
Center Court Assisted Living, Hutchinson *Also called Mennonite Frndship Communities* ***(G-3374)***
Center Feed Co, Parsons *Also called Allen Veterinary Center* ***(G-9665)***
Center For Counseling & Cnsltn (PA)...620 792-2544
5815 Broadway Ave Great Bend (67530) ***(G-2526)***
Center For Design Dev & Prod, Pittsburg *Also called Business & Technology Inst* ***(G-9827)***
Center For Research & Learning, Lawrence *Also called University of Kansas* ***(G-5162)***
Center For Rprductive Medicine...316 687-2112
9300 E 29th St N Ste 102 Wichita (67226) ***(G-13972)***
Center For Same Day Surgery...316 262-7263
818 N Emporia St Ste 108 Wichita (67214) ***(G-13973)***
Center For Woman Health...913 491-6878
4840 College Blvd Shawnee Mission (66211) ***(G-11210)***
Center For Woman Hlth Wichita...316 634-0060
1855 N Webb Rd Wichita (67206) ***(G-13974)***
Center For Womens Health LLC...316 634-0060
10111 E 21st St N Ste 301 Wichita (67206) ***(G-13975)***
Center Industries Corporation...316 942-8255
2505 S Custer Ave Wichita (67217) ***(G-13976)***
Center On Family Living, Wichita *Also called Friends University* ***(G-14424)***
Centera Bank (PA)...620 675-8611
119 S Inman St Sublette (67877) ***(G-12200)***
Centera Bank...620 227-6370
2200 N 14th Ave Dodge City (67801) ***(G-1320)***
Centera Bank...620 649-2220
218 Sequoyah St Satanta (67870) ***(G-10780)***
Central AG Wheel & Tire...316 942-1408
4106 W Esthner Ave Wichita (67209) ***(G-13977)***
Central Bag Company (PA)...913 250-0325
4901 S 4th St Leavenworth (66048) ***(G-5215)***
Central Bank and Trust Co...620 663-0666
700 E 30th Ave Hutchinson (67502) ***(G-3231)***
Central Bank of Midwest...913 268-3202
15100 W 67th St Shawnee (66217) ***(G-10925)***
Central Bank of Midwest...913 856-7715
900 E Main St Gardner (66030) ***(G-2331)***
Central Bank of Midwest...913 893-6049
405 E Nelson St Edgerton (66021) ***(G-1481)***
Central Bank of Midwest...913 791-9988
7960 W 135th St Overland Park (66223) ***(G-8537)***
Central Bank of Midwest...913 791-9288
6114 Nieman Rd Shawnee Mission (66203) ***(G-11211)***
Central Biomedia Inc (PA)...913 541-0090
9900 Pflumm Rd Ste 63 Shawnee Mission (66215) ***(G-11212)***
Central Camp Medical Center, Great Bend *Also called Great Bend Internists PA* ***(G-2582)***
Central Care PA...620 624-4700
305 W 15th St Ste 203 Liberal (67901) ***(G-6291)***
Central Care PA...620 272-2579
410 E Spruce St Garden City (67846) ***(G-2123)***
Central Care Cancer Center, Garden City *Also called Central Care PA* ***(G-2123)***
Central Consolidated Inc...316 945-0797
3435 W Harry St Wichita (67213) ***(G-13978)***
Central Dental & Pioneer Lab, Wichita *Also called Central Dental Center PA* ***(G-13979)***
Central Dental Center PA...316 945-9845
4805 W Central Ave Wichita (67212) ***(G-13979)***
Central Electropolishing Inc...620 842-3701
103 N Lawrence Ave Anthony (67003) ***(G-122)***
Central Equipment, Wichita *Also called Central Marketing Inc* ***(G-13980)***
Central Fiber LLC (PA)...785 883-4600
4814 Fiber Ln Wellsville (66092) ***(G-13541)***
Central Forms & Printing, Wichita *Also called Drafting Room Inc* ***(G-14236)***
Central Garage, Hutchinson *Also called City of Hutchinson* ***(G-3241)***
Central Gc Construction Inc...913 484-2400
22599 Columbia Rd Spring Hill (66083) ***(G-12081)***
CENTRAL INVESTMENT SERVICES, Junction City *Also called Central National Bank* ***(G-3676)***
Central Investment Services, Junction City *Also called Central of Kansas Inc* ***(G-3678)***
Central Kans Fmly Practice PA...620 792-5341
1309 Polk St Ste C Great Bend (67530) ***(G-2527)***
Central Kans Surveying Mapping...620 792-2873
2344 Washington St Great Bend (67530) ***(G-2528)***
Central Kansas Auto Rental (PA)...785 827-7237
3230 Arnold Ave Salina (67401) ***(G-10439)***
Central Kansas Credit Union (PA)...620 663-1566
2616 N Main St Hutchinson (67502) ***(G-3232)***
Central Kansas Ent Assoc PA...785 823-7225
520 S Santa Fe Ave # 200 Salina (67401) ***(G-10440)***
Central Kansas Medical Center (HQ)...620 792-2511
3515 Broadway Ave Great Bend (67530) ***(G-2529)***
Central Kansas Medical Center...620 792-8171
3515 Broadway Ave Ste 102 Great Bend (67530) ***(G-2530)***
Central Kansas Mental Hlth Ctr (PA)...785 823-6322
809 Elmhurst Blvd Salina (67401) ***(G-10441)***
Central Kansas Orthepedics, Great Bend *Also called Central Kansas Orthpd Group* ***(G-2531)***
Central Kansas Orthpd Group...620 792-4383
1514 State Road 96 Ste A Great Bend (67530) ***(G-2531)***
Central Kansas Rendering Inc...620 792-2059
58 Se 20 Rd Great Bend (67530) ***(G-2532)***
Central Kansas Truss Co Inc...316 755-3114
231 W Industrial St Valley Center (67147) ***(G-13339)***
Central Knss Cncil of Grl Sct...785 827-3679
3115 Enterprise Dr Salina (67401) ***(G-10442)***
Central KS Medical Park PA...620 793-5404
1309 Polk St Ste C Great Bend (67530) ***(G-2533)***
Central Maintenance System...913 621-6545
401 Funston Rd Kansas City (66115) ***(G-3901)***
Central Mall, Salina *Also called Warmack and Company LLC* ***(G-10758)***
Central Mall Realty Holdg LLC...785 825-7733
2259 S 9th St Salina (67401) ***(G-10443)***
Central Market Place, Abilene *Also called Abilene Rflctor Chronicle Pubg* ***(G-8)***
Central Marketing Inc...316 613-2404
1702 S West St Wichita (67213) ***(G-13980)***
Central Mech Cnstr Co Inc (HQ)...785 537-2437
631 Pecan Cir Manhattan (66502) ***(G-6581)***
Central Mech Svcs Mnhattan Inc...785 776-9206
1131 Hayes Dr Manhattan (66502) ***(G-6582)***
Central Mechanical Wichita, Wichita *Also called M W C Inc* ***(G-14994)***
Central Mechanical Wichita LLC...316 267-7676
806 E Skinner St Wichita (67211) ***(G-13981)***
Central National Bank (HQ)...785 238-4114
802 N Washington St Junction City (66441) ***(G-3676)***
Central National Bank...620 382-2129
231 E Main St Marion (66861) ***(G-6868)***
Central National Bank...785 838-1960
3140 Nieder Rd Lawrence (66047) ***(G-4779)***
Central National Bank...785 238-4114
540 W 6th St Junction City (66441) ***(G-3677)***
Central National Bank...785 838-1893
711 Wakarusa Dr Lawrence (66049) ***(G-4780)***
Central National Bank...785 234-2265
800 Se Quincy St Topeka (66612) ***(G-12456)***
Central of Kansas Inc (PA)...785 238-4114
802 N Washington St Junction City (66441) ***(G-3678)***
Central Office Svc & Sup Inc...785 632-2177
421 Lincoln Ave Clay Center (67432) ***(G-848)***
Central Paving Inc...316 778-1194
1250 N Main St Benton (67017) ***(G-514)***
Central Plains Contracting Co...620 231-2660
733 E 520th Ave Pittsburg (66762) ***(G-9830)***
Central Plains Coop (PA)...785 282-6813
318 S Madison St Smith Center (66967) ***(G-12032)***
Central Plains Eye Mds LLC...316 712-4970
7717 E 29th St N Ste 100 Wichita (67226) ***(G-13982)***
Central Plains Laboratories, Hays *Also called Hays Pathology Laboratories PA* ***(G-2837)***
Central Plains Maintenance...316 945-4774
3601 W Harry St Ste 2 Wichita (67213) ***(G-13983)***
Central Plains Steel, Wichita *Also called Reliance Steel & Aluminum Co* ***(G-15440)***
Central Planes Coop (PA)...785 695-2216
205 Railway Athol (66932) ***(G-273)***
Central Plins Rsprtory Med LLC...785 527-8727
1331 18th St Belleville (66935) ***(G-455)***
Central Prairie Co-Op...620 278-2470
1775 State Rd 14 Hwy Sterling (67579) ***(G-12113)***
Central Prairie Co-Op...620 422-3221
404 S Nickerson St Nickerson (67561) ***(G-7431)***

Central Printing & Binding 620 665-7251
107 W 1st Ave Hutchinson (67501) *(G-3233)*
Central Publishing Co Inc 620 365-2106
1811 East St Iola (66749) *(G-3591)*
Central Pwr Systems & Svcs LLC 620 792-1361
625 10th St Great Bend (67530) *(G-2534)*
Central Pwr Systems & Svcs LLC 785 825-8291
1944b N 9th St Salina (67401) *(G-10444)*
Central Pwr Systems & Svcs LLC 316 943-1231
4501 W Irving St Wichita (67209) *(G-13984)*
Central Pwr Systems & Svcs LLC 785 462-8211
1920 Thielen Ave Colby (67701) *(G-992)*
Central Region, Overland Park *Also called Ash Grove Materials Corp (G-8404)*
Central Salt, Lyons *Also called Lyons Salt Company (G-6492)*
Central Security Group, Lenexa *Also called Alert 360 (G-5639)*
Central Solutions Inc (PA) 913 621-6542
401 Funston Rd Kansas City (66115) *(G-3902)*
Central Soyfoods 785 312-8638
710 E 22nd St Ste C Lawrence (66046) *(G-4781)*
Central Star Credit Union (PA) 316 685-9555
9555 E Corporate Hills Dr Wichita (67207) *(G-13985)*
Central State Services 316 613-3989
1401 E Douglas Ave Wichita (67211) *(G-13986)*
Central States Capital Markets 913 766-6565
4200 W 83rd St Prairie Village (66208) *(G-10019)*
Central States Contg Svcs Inc 913 788-1100
610 S 78th St Kansas City (66111) *(G-3903)*
Central States Electric Inc 316 942-6640
1660 S Baehr St Wichita (67209) *(G-13987)*
Central States Enterprises LLC 785 827-8215
1908 W Old Highway 40 Salina (67401) *(G-10445)*
Central States Fumigation, Salina *Also called Central States Enterprises LLC (G-10445)*
Central States Machining Wldg 785 233-1376
300 W 1st Ave Topeka (66603) *(G-12457)*
Central States Mechanical Inc 620 353-1797
108 S Main St Ulysses (67880) *(G-13287)*
Central States Mktg & Mfg Inc 620 245-9955
1320 N Us Highway 81 Byp McPherson (67460) *(G-6944)*
Central States Recovery Inc 620 663-8811
1314 N Main St Hutchinson (67501) *(G-3234)*
CENTRAL STATES THERMO KING, Overland Park *Also called Cstk Inc (G-8621)*
Central Station Club & Gr 620 225-1176
207 E Wyatt Earp Blvd Dodge City (67801) *(G-1321)*
Central Steel Inc (PA) 316 265-8639
240 W 10th St N Wichita (67203) *(G-13988)*
Central STS Scout Museum, Larned *Also called Pawnee Valley Scouts Inc (G-4710)*
Central Transport Intl Inc 913 371-7500
615 Miami Ave Kansas City (66105) *(G-3904)*
Central Transport Intl Inc 877 446-3795
2225 Southwest Blvd Wichita (67213) *(G-13989)*
Central Trnsp Svcs Inc 316 263-3333
1820 N Mosley St Wichita (67214) *(G-13990)*
Central Valley AG Cooperative 785 738-2241
204 E Court St Beloit (67420) *(G-481)*
Central Welding & Machine LLC 620 663-9353
218 N Whiteside St Hutchinson (67501) *(G-3235)*
Centralized Showing Svc Inc (PA) 913 851-8405
11225 College Blvd # 450 Overland Park (66210) *(G-8538)*
Centrinex LLC 913 827-9600
10310 W 84th Ter Lenexa (66214) *(G-5739)*
Centrinex LLC 913 744-3410
11933 W 95th St Ste 147 Overland Park (66215) *(G-8539)*
Centrlia Cmmmity Hlth Care Svc 785 857-3388
604 1st St Centralia (66415) *(G-697)*
Centurion Industries Inc 620 378-4401
401 N 6th St Fredonia (66736) *(G-2028)*
Centurion Industries Inc 620 244-3201
810 N Main St Erie (66733) *(G-1857)*
Centurion Manufacturing 316 210-3504
701 N Main St Benton (67017) *(G-515)*
Century 21, Lawrence *Also called Miller & Midyett Realtor Inc (G-5029)*
Century 21, Concordia *Also called G H C Associates Inc (G-1112)*
Century Building Solutions Inc 913 422-5555
9800 Legler Rd Lenexa (66219) *(G-5740)*
Century Business Systems Inc (PA) 785 776-0495
415 Houston St Manhattan (66502) *(G-6583)*
Century Business Technologies (PA) 785 267-4555
401 Sw 30th St Topeka (66611) *(G-12458)*
Century Concrete Inc (HQ) 913 451-8900
11011 Cody St Ste 300 Shawnee Mission (66210) *(G-11213)*
Century Concrete Inc 913 764-4264
1340 W 149th St Olathe (66061) *(G-7585)*
Century Construction Sup LLC 913 438-3366
9600 Dice Ln Lenexa (66215) *(G-5741)*
Century Health Solutions Inc 785 233-1816
2951 Sw Woodside Dr Topeka (66614) *(G-12459)*
Century Instrument Corp 316 683-7571
4440 S Southeast Blvd # 2 Wichita (67210) *(G-13991)*
Century Manufacturing Inc 316 636-5423
9750 E 50th St N Bel Aire (67226) *(G-430)*
Century Marketing Inc 913 696-9758
14631 W 95th St Lenexa (66215) *(G-5742)*
Century Office Pdts Inc Topeka (HQ) 785 267-4555
401 Sw 30th St Topeka (66611) *(G-12460)*
Century Partners LLC 913 642-2489
2300 N Rogers Rd Olathe (66062) *(G-7586)*
Century Ready-Mix, Shawnee Mission *Also called Century Concrete Inc (G-11213)*
Century Roofing, Kansas City *Also called Canadian West Inc (G-3887)*
Century School Inc 785 832-0101
816 Kentucky St Lawrence (66044) *(G-4782)*
Century Van Lines Inc 913 651-3600
211 Marion St Leavenworth (66048) *(G-5216)*
Century Wood Products Inc 913 839-8725
15435 S Keeler St Olathe (66062) *(G-7587)*
Centurylink Inc 913 791-4971
600 New Century Pkwy New Century (66031) *(G-7273)*
Ceo Enterprises Inc (PA) 913 432-8046
6124 Merriam Dr Shawnee Mission (66203) *(G-11214)*
Cepco, Topeka *Also called Campus Electric Power Company (G-12420)*
Cequel Communications LLC 620 223-1804
14 E 2nd St Fort Scott (66701) *(G-1958)*
Ceramic Cafe 913 383-0222
9510 Nall Ave Overland Park (66207) *(G-8540)*
Cereal Ingredients Inc (PA) 913 727-3434
4720 S 13th St Leavenworth (66048) *(G-5217)*
Cerebral Palsy Research Fo 316 688-5314
5111 E 21st St N Wichita (67208) *(G-13992)*
Cerner Government Services Inc 816 201-2273
10200 Abilities Way Kansas City (66111) *(G-3905)*
Certainteed Corporation 913 342-6624
103 Funston Rd Kansas City (66115) *(G-3906)*
Certainteed Corporation 316 554-9638
873 N Hickory St McPherson (67460) *(G-6945)*
Certainteed Gypsum Mfg Inc 785 762-2994
3105 Industrial St Junction City (66441) *(G-3679)*
Certainteed LLC 620 241-5511
500 W 1st St McPherson (67460) *(G-6946)*
Certanteed Gyps Fnshg Pdts Inc (HQ) 785 762-2994
3105 Industrial St Junction City (66441) *(G-3680)*
Certified Environmental Mgt 785 823-0492
3115 Enterprise Dr Ste C Salina (67401) *(G-10446)*
Certified Life Safety LLC 913 837-5319
5880 W 319th St Louisburg (66053) *(G-6442)*
Certified Water & Mold Restrtn 816 835-4959
P.O. Box 880 Olathe (66051) *(G-7588)*
Certtech LLC 913 814-9770
14425 College Blvd # 140 Lenexa (66215) *(G-5743)*
Cervs Conoco & Convenience 785 625-7777
2701 Vine St Hays (67601) *(G-2767)*
Cesco, Shawnee *Also called Calkins Electric Supply Co Inc (G-10923)*
Cessna, Wichita *Also called Textron Aviation Inc (G-15742)*
Cessna, Wichita *Also called Textron Aviation Inc (G-15745)*
Cessna, Wichita *Also called Textron Aviation Inc (G-15746)*
Cessna Aircraft Company, Wichita *Also called Textron Aviation Inc (G-15735)*
Cessna Aircraft Company 316 686-3961
5213 E Pawnee St Wichita (67218) *(G-13993)*
Cessna Citation, Wichita *Also called Textron Aviation Inc (G-15748)*
Cessna Learning Center, Wichita *Also called Flightsafety International Inc (G-14389)*
Ceva Animal Health LLC (HQ) 800 999-0297
8735 Rosehill Rd Ste 300 Lenexa (66215) *(G-5744)*
Ceva Animal Health LLC 913 894-0230
8906 Rosehill Rd Lenexa (66215) *(G-5745)*
Ceva Biomune, Lenexa *Also called Biomune Company (G-5706)*
Ceva Biomune 913 894-0230
8735 Rosehill Rd Lenexa (66215) *(G-5746)*
Ceva US Holdings Inc 913 894-0230
8906 Rosehill Rd Lenexa (66215) *(G-5747)*
Ceva USA Inc 800 999-0297
8735 Rosehill Rd Lenexa (66215) *(G-5748)*
Cfcc & Associates 785 272-0778
2000 Sw Gage Blvd Topeka (66604) *(G-12461)*
Cft LLC 620 431-0885
500 W 21st St Chanute (66720) *(G-710)*
Cg Investments 816 398-5862
421 N 82nd Ter Kansas City (66112) *(G-3907)*
CGB Diversified Services Inc 785 235-5566
120 Se 6th Ave Ste 210 Topeka (66603) *(G-12462)*
CGB Enterprises Inc 913 367-5450
812 Skyway Hwy Atchison (66002) *(G-222)*
Cgf Industries, Wichita *Also called Cgf Investments Inc (G-13994)*
Cgf Investments Inc (PA) 316 691-4500
2420 N Woodlawn Blvd # 500 Wichita (67220) *(G-13994)*
Cgsc Foundation, Fort Leavenworth *Also called Command and General Staff (G-1936)*
CH Robinson Company Inc 316 267-3300
245 N Waco St Ste 400 Wichita (67202) *(G-13995)*

ALPHABETIC

Chad Briney 785 462-2445
1730 W 4th St Colby (67701) ***(G-993)***
Chad Eakin Concrete 620 285-2097
111 Main St Larned (67550) ***(G-4698)***
Chad Equipment LLC 913 764-0321
19950 W 161st St Ste A Olathe (66062) ***(G-7589)***
Chada Sales Inc 785 842-1199
815 E 12th St Ste A Lawrence (66044) ***(G-4783)***
Challenger Construction Corp 316 680-3036
415 E Saint John St Girard (66743) ***(G-2396)***
Challenger Fence Co Inc 913 432-3535
20201 W 55th St Ste B Shawnee Mission (66218) ***(G-11215)***
Challenger Hydroseeding, Girard *Also called Challenger Construction Corp* ***(G-2396)***
Challenger Sports Corp (PA) 913 599-4884
8263 Flint St Lenexa (66214) ***(G-5749)***
Challenger Sports Teamwear LLC 913 599-4884
8263 Flint St Lenexa (66214) ***(G-5750)***
Chalmers Cancer Treatment Ctr, Hutchinson *Also called Steven D Braun* ***(G-3447)***
Chamber of Commerce 785 258-2115
106 N Broadway Ste A Herington (67449) ***(G-2972)***
Chambless Roofing Inc (PA) 620 275-8410
1005 W 5th St Scott City (67871) ***(G-10807)***
Chameleon Dental Products 913 281-5552
200 N 6th St Kansas City (66101) ***(G-3908)***
Champion Opco LLC 316 636-4200
1835 S West St Wichita (67213) ***(G-13996)***
Champion Teamwear, Manhattan *Also called Its Greek To Me Inc* ***(G-6666)***
Champion Win Sding Patio Rooms, Lenexa *Also called Champion Window Co Kans Cy Inc* ***(G-5751)***
Champion Window Co, Wichita *Also called Champion Opco LLC* ***(G-13996)***
Champion Window Co Kans Cy Inc 913 541-8282
9050 Quivira Rd Lenexa (66215) ***(G-5751)***
Champlin Tire Recycling Inc 785 243-3345
301 Cedar St Concordia (66901) ***(G-1105)***
Chance Purinton and Mills LLC 913 491-8200
6900 College Blvd Ste 350 Shawnee Mission (66211) ***(G-11216)***
Chance Rides Manufacturing Inc (PA) 316 945-6555
4219 W Irving St Wichita (67209) ***(G-13997)***
Chance Transmissions Inc 316 529-1883
6325 S Seneca St Wichita (67217) ***(G-13998)***
Channel News Department 316 292-1111
833 N Main St Wichita (67203) ***(G-13999)***
Channelview SW Hotel Inc 913 345-2111
9903 Pflumm Rd Lenexa (66215) ***(G-5752)***
Chanute Art Gallery 620 431-7807
17 N Lincoln Ave Chanute (66720) ***(G-711)***
Chanute Fintube, Chanute *Also called Cft LLC* ***(G-710)***
Chanute First Street Drive Up, Chanute *Also called Community National Bank* ***(G-720)***
Chanute Manufacturing, Chanute *Also called Optimus Industries LLC* ***(G-751)***
Chanute Operations, Chanute *Also called HBD Industries Inc* ***(G-730)***
Chanute Plant, Chanute *Also called Ash Grove Cement Company* ***(G-703)***
Chanute Publishing Company 620 431-4100
15 N Evergreen Ave Chanute (66720) ***(G-712)***
Chanute Recreation Commission 620 431-4199
400 S Highland Ave Ste 2 Chanute (66720) ***(G-713)***
Chanute Tribune, Chanute *Also called Chanute Publishing Company* ***(G-712)***
Chaosland Services LLC 620 356-1259
1020 W Road 19 Ulysses (67880) ***(G-13288)***
Chaotic Customs, LLC, Mulvane *Also called Chris Carlson Hot Rods LLC* ***(G-7212)***
Chapman Adult Care Homes Inc 785 922-6525
1009 N Marshall Ave Chapman (67431) ***(G-777)***
CHAPMAN VALLEY MANOR, Chapman *Also called Chapman Adult Care Homes Inc* ***(G-777)***
Charge It LLC 913 341-8772
14 E Peoria St Paola (66071) ***(G-9546)***
Charles E Mahaney Roofing Co, Wichita *Also called Mahaney Group Inc* ***(G-15001)***
Charles Engineering Inc 620 584-2381
10400 S 119th St W Clearwater (67026) ***(G-887)***
Charles I Davis MD PA 913 648-8880
8312 W 102nd St Overland Park (66212) ***(G-8541)***
Charles L Brroks MD 913 248-8008
6850 Hilltop Rd Ste 170 Shawnee Mission (66226) ***(G-11217)***
Charles Ritz Inc 913 685-2600
5833 W 145th St Overland Park (66223) ***(G-8542)***
Charloma Inc (HQ) 620 336-2124
727 N Liberty St Cherryvale (67335) ***(G-801)***
Charloma Inc 620 364-2701
1290 10th Rd Burlington (66839) ***(G-626)***
Charlson & Wilson Bonded Abstr 785 565-4800
111 N 4th St Manhattan (66502) ***(G-6584)***
Charlson Wilsin Insurance Agcy 785 537-1600
555 Poyntz Ave Ste 205 Manhattan (66502) ***(G-6585)***
Charter American Mortgage Co, Mission Woods *Also called Collateral RE Capitl LLC* ***(G-7150)***
Charter Funerals Kansas LLC (PA) 913 671-7222
10250 Shawnee Mission Pkwy Merriam (66203) ***(G-7088)***
Chase Childrens Services Inc 620 273-6650
410 Palmer St Strong City (66869) ***(G-12192)***
Chase Contractors Inc 620 431-2142
800 W 35th Pkwy Chanute (66720) ***(G-714)***
Chase County Ems 620 273-6590
130 Broadway St Cottonwood Falls (66845) ***(G-1152)***
Chase Group Inc 913 696-6300
10975 Grandview Dr # 100 Overland Park (66210) ***(G-8543)***
Chase Manhattan Apartment 785 776-3663
1409 Chase Pl Manhattan (66502) ***(G-6586)***
Chase Suite Hotel By Woodfin, Shawnee Mission *Also called Hardage Hotels I LLC* ***(G-11409)***
Chase Tubing Testing 620 356-4314
1809 N Easy St Ulysses (67880) ***(G-13289)***
Chase Well Service, Great Bend *Also called Strata Drilling Inc* ***(G-2640)***
Chase Well Service Inc 620 793-9556
5286 Timber Creek Rd Great Bend (67530) ***(G-2535)***
Chateau Avalon, Kansas City *Also called Kcai LP* ***(G-4166)***
Chaucer Estates LLC 316 630-8111
10550 E 21st St N Ofc Wichita (67206) ***(G-14000)***
Chaudhrys Investment Group 913 856-8887
2001 E Santa Fe St Gardner (66030) ***(G-2332)***
Chaudhrys Investment Group Inc 913 393-1111
12081 S Strang Line Rd Olathe (66062) ***(G-7590)***
Chavey Ventures Inc 913 888-5108
6640 Wedd St Shawnee (66203) ***(G-10926)***
Chavez Restoration & Cleaning (PA) 785 232-3779
2400 S Kansas Ave Topeka (66611) ***(G-12463)***
Chc Kansas, Overland Park *Also called Coventry Health Care Kans Inc* ***(G-8606)***
Chc McPherson Refinery Inc 785 543-5246
N H Way 183 Phillipsburg (67661) ***(G-9779)***
Chc McPherson Refinery Inc 620 793-3111
2421 10th St Great Bend (67530) ***(G-2536)***
Chc McPherson Refinery Inc 785 798-3684
2000 S Kansas Ness City (67560) ***(G-7254)***
Chelepis & Associates Inc 913 912-7113
8695 College Blvd Ste 200 Overland Park (66210) ***(G-8544)***
Chelsoft Solutions Co 913 579-1399
527 N Mur Len Rd Ste B Olathe (66062) ***(G-7591)***
Chem Till Spray Company Inc 620 492-2751
609 S Main St Johnson (67855) ***(G-3652)***
Chem-Tech LLC 785 625-1141
1023 Reservation Rd Hays (67601) ***(G-2768)***
Chem-Till, Johnson *Also called Chem Till Spray Company Inc* ***(G-3652)***
Chem-Trol Inc (PA) 913 342-3006
411 S 42nd St Kansas City (66106) ***(G-3909)***
Chemical Services Inc 620 792-6886
32 Ne 40th Ave Great Bend (67530) ***(G-2537)***
Chemstar Products Company 620 241-2611
503 W Hayes St McPherson (67460) ***(G-6947)***
Chemstation of Kansas Inc 316 201-1851
2355 S Edwards St Ste D Wichita (67213) ***(G-14001)***
Chemsystems Kansas Inc 913 422-4443
8329 Monticello Rd Ste E Shawnee (66227) ***(G-10927)***
Chemtrade Phosphorous Spc, Lawrence *Also called Chemtrade Refinery Svcs Inc* ***(G-4785)***
Chemtrade Phosphorous Spc LLC 785 843-2290
440 N 9th St Lawrence (66044) ***(G-4784)***
Chemtrade Refinery Svcs Inc (HQ) 785 843-2290
440 N 9th St Lawrence (66044) ***(G-4785)***
Cheney Door Co Inc 620 669-9306
2701 E 17th Ave Hutchinson (67501) ***(G-3236)***
Cheney Golden Age Home Inc 316 540-3691
724 N Main St Cheney (67025) ***(G-789)***
Cheney Lanes Inc 316 542-3126
1635 S Cheney Rd Cheney (67025) ***(G-790)***
Cherished Friends LLC 620 326-3700
924 S Washington Ave Ofc Wellington (67152) ***(G-13495)***
Cherokee Animal Clinic PA 913 649-0440
9630 Antioch Rd Overland Park (66212) ***(G-8545)***
Cherokee Cat Clinic 913 649-0446
9620 Antioch Rd Shawnee Mission (66212) ***(G-11218)***
Cherokee Cnty Ambulance & Assn 620 429-3018
800 W Powrachute Way Columbus (66725) ***(G-1065)***
Cherokee County Ambulance 620 856-2561
311 Military Ave Baxter Springs (66713) ***(G-402)***
Cherokee County Highway Dept, Columbus *Also called County of Cherokee* ***(G-1070)***
Cherry Creek Vlg Rtirement Ctr, Wichita *Also called Healthpeak Properties Inc* ***(G-14579)***
Cherry Street Youth Center (PA) 620 431-0818
710 N Forest Ave Chanute (66720) ***(G-715)***
Cherry Village Benevolence 620 792-2165
1401 Cherry Ln Great Bend (67530) ***(G-2538)***
Cherry Village Nursing Home, Great Bend *Also called Cherry Vlg Assisted Self-Care* ***(G-2539)***
CHERRY VILLAGE RETIREMENT, Great Bend *Also called Cherry Village Benevolence* ***(G-2538)***
Cherry Vlg Assisted Self-Care 620 793-5765
5926 Eisenhower Ave Ofc Great Bend (67530) ***(G-2539)***
Cherryvale Alumni Commnty/Educ 620 336-3198
404 N Liberty St Cherryvale (67335) ***(G-802)***
Cherryvale Banking Center, Cherryvale *Also called Community National Bank & Tr* ***(G-803)***

Cherryvale Medi-Lodge, Cherryvale *Also called Glencare/Cherryvale CA Ltd Pt* ***(G-807)***
Cherub Medical Supply LLC.....913 227-0440
11217 Johnson Dr Shawnee (66203) ***(G-10928)***
Chester Press Inc.....620 342-8792
2 S Commercial St Emporia (66801) ***(G-1719)***
Chet's Lock & Key, Shawnee Mission *Also called Outlaws Group LLC* ***(G-11704)***
CHETOPA MANOR, Chetopa *Also called Woodworth International Inc* ***(G-819)***
Chetopa Medical Clinic, Coffeyville *Also called Labette Health Foundation Inc* ***(G-954)***
Cheyenne County Hospital (PA).....785 332-2104
210 W 1st St Saint Francis (67756) ***(G-10339)***
Cheyenne County Hospital.....785 332-2682
221 W 1st St Saint Francis (67756) ***(G-10340)***
Cheyenne Lodge Inc.....785 439-6211
716 Cedar St Jamestown (66948) ***(G-3642)***
CHEYENNE LODGE NURSING HOME, Jamestown *Also called Cheyenne Lodge Inc* ***(G-3642)***
Cheyenne Mfg Inc.....316 942-7665
3713 W 30th St S Wichita (67217) ***(G-14002)***
Cheyenne Oil Services Inc.....785 798-2282
118 N Pennsylvania Ave Ness City (67560) ***(G-7255)***
Cheyenne Well Service Inc (PA).....785 798-2282
118 N Pennsylvania Ave Ness City (67560) ***(G-7256)***
Chez Belle.....316 682-7323
550 N Rock Rd Ste 109 Wichita (67206) ***(G-14003)***
Chicago Title and Trust Co.....913 451-1200
6700 College Blvd Ste 300 Leawood (66211) ***(G-5351)***
Chicago Title Insurance Co, Leawood *Also called Fidelity National Fincl Inc* ***(G-5399)***
Chicago Title Insurance Co.....913 385-9307
1900 W 75th St Lowr Ll20 Shawnee Mission (66208) ***(G-11219)***
Chicago Title Insurance Co.....913 782-0041
110 S Cherry St Ste 202 Olathe (66061) ***(G-7592)***
Chicago Title Insurance Co.....913 451-1200
11005 Metcalf Ave Overland Park (66210) ***(G-8546)***
Chicago Title Insurance Co.....316 267-8371
434 N Main St Wichita (67202) ***(G-14004)***
Chiefton Brand Meats, Kiowa *Also called Kiowa Locker System LLC* ***(G-4626)***
Chikaskia River Gas Co Div, Wichita *Also called McCoy Petroleum Corporation* ***(G-15023)***
Child & Family Optometry, Wichita *Also called Patrick J Pirrote Od PA* ***(G-15268)***
CHILD ADULT CARE FOOD PROGRAM, Salina *Also called First Choice Support Services* ***(G-10502)***
Child Advcacy Ctr Sdgwick Cnty.....316 660-9494
1211 S Emporia Ave Wichita (67211) ***(G-14005)***
CHILD CARE AWARE OF KANSAS, Salina *Also called Kansas Association of Child* ***(G-10562)***
Child Care Services Strlng Inc.....620 904-4231
309 N Broadway Ave Sterling (67579) ***(G-12114)***
Child Development Unit, Kansas City *Also called University of Kansas* ***(G-4497)***
Child Health Corp America.....913 262-1436
16011 College Blvd # 250 Lenexa (66219) ***(G-5753)***
Child Start Inc.....316 522-8677
4600 S Clifton Ave Ste B Wichita (67216) ***(G-14006)***
Child Start Inc (PA).....316 682-1853
1002 S Oliver St Wichita (67218) ***(G-14007)***
Child Start Inc.....316 682-1853
1002 S Oliver St Wichita (67218) ***(G-14008)***
Child Support Enforcement, Topeka *Also called Kansas Dept For Chldren Fmlies* ***(G-12772)***
Child Support Enforcement.....620 331-7231
301 N 8th St Independence (67301) ***(G-3502)***
Child's Horizon Pre School, Wichita *Also called Sharon Baptist Church* ***(G-15573)***
Childcare Association, Wichita *Also called Hill Top Center* ***(G-14609)***
Childhood Memories Toddler.....316 554-1646
11229 W Peter Ave Wichita (67215) ***(G-14009)***
Children & Family Policy, Topeka *Also called Children & Family Services* ***(G-12464)***
Children & Family Services.....785 296-4653
915 Sw Harrison St Fl 5 Topeka (66612) ***(G-12464)***
Children's Dental Specialists, Olathe *Also called John Fales Dr* ***(G-7811)***
Children's Home Care, Shawnee Mission *Also called Childrens Mercy Hospital* ***(G-11221)***
Children's Mercy South, Overland Park *Also called Childrens Mercy Hospital* ***(G-8548)***
Children's Mercy West Clinic, Kansas City *Also called Childrens Mercy Hospital* ***(G-3911)***
Children's Miracle Network, Wichita *Also called Via Christi Foundation Inc* ***(G-15887)***
Childrens Center LLC.....913 432-5114
5023 Granada St Roeland Park (66205) ***(G-10220)***
Childrens Hospital Association, Lenexa *Also called Child Health Corp America* ***(G-5753)***
Childrens Hospital Association.....913 262-1436
6803 W 64th St Overland Park (66202) ***(G-8547)***
Childrens Learning Center Inc.....785 841-2185
205 N Michigan St Lawrence (66044) ***(G-4786)***
Childrens Mercy Home Care.....913 696-8999
1900 N 47th St Kansas City (66102) ***(G-3910)***
Childrens Mercy Hospital.....913 234-8683
14943 S Summit St Olathe (66062) ***(G-7593)***
Childrens Mercy Hospital.....316 500-8900
3243 E Murdock St Ste 201 Wichita (67208) ***(G-14010)***
Childrens Mercy Hospital.....913 287-8800
4313 State Ave Kansas City (66102) ***(G-3911)***
Childrens Mercy Hospital.....913 696-5767
5520 College Blvd Ste 415 Shawnee Mission (66211) ***(G-11220)***
Childrens Mercy Hospital.....913 696-8000
1900 W 47th Pl Ste 250 Shawnee Mission (66205) ***(G-11221)***
Childrens Mercy Hospital.....913 696-8000
5808 W 110th St Overland Park (66211) ***(G-8548)***
Childrens Mercy Specialty Ctr, Shawnee Mission *Also called Childrens Mercy Hospital* ***(G-11220)***
Childrens Mercy Specialty Ctr.....816 234-3000
5808 W 110th St Overland Park (66211) ***(G-8549)***
Childrens Therapy Group.....913 383-9014
6223 Slater St Mission (66202) ***(G-7129)***
Childrens Threrapy, Mission *Also called Childrens Therapy Group* ***(G-7129)***
CHILS START, Wichita *Also called Child Start Inc* ***(G-14007)***
Chilton Vending & Billd Inc.....316 262-3539
700 S Broadway Ave Wichita (67211) ***(G-14011)***
Chilton Vending & Billiard Sup, Wichita *Also called Chilton Vending & Billd Inc* ***(G-14011)***
China Palace.....620 365-3723
110 N State St Iola (66749) ***(G-3592)***
Chips Inc.....785 842-6921
2220 Harper St Lawrence (66046) ***(G-4787)***
Chiro Plus Inc.....316 684-0550
5205 E Kellogg Dr Ste 101 Wichita (67218) ***(G-14012)***
Chiropratic Clinic, Topeka *Also called Counslman Wade Chrprctic Clnic* ***(G-12514)***
Chiroserve Inc.....913 764-6237
2110 E Santa Fe St Olathe (66062) ***(G-7594)***
Chisholm Trail Animal Care Ctr.....316 744-0501
1726 E 61st St N Park City (67219) ***(G-9609)***
Chisholm Trail Animal Hospital, Park City *Also called Chisholm Trail Animal Care Ctr* ***(G-9609)***
Chisholm Trail Country Str LLC.....316 283-3276
507 Se 36th St Newton (67114) ***(G-7328)***
Chisholm Trail State Bank (PA).....316 744-1293
6160 N Broadway Ave Park City (67219) ***(G-9610)***
Chitos Well Service LLC.....785 434-4942
111 1/2 N Jefferson St Plainville (67663) ***(G-9979)***
Chlorofields LLC.....785 304-3226
6901 E 149th St Overbrook (66524) ***(G-8323)***
Chocolate Specialty Corp.....816 941-3088
18009 Broadmoor St Stilwell (66085) ***(G-12140)***
Chocolatey Software Inc (PA).....785 783-4720
3620 Sw Fairlawn Rd # 220 Topeka (66614) ***(G-12465)***
Choice Hotels, Haysville *Also called Sleep Inn Suite* ***(G-2960)***
Choice Solutions LLC (PA).....913 338-4950
7015 College Blvd Ste 300 Overland Park (66211) ***(G-8550)***
Choicecare LLC.....913 906-9880
12345 W 95th St Ste 215 Lenexa (66215) ***(G-5754)***
Choicepoint, Shawnee Mission *Also called New Mountain Capital I LLC* ***(G-11680)***
Choices Network Inc.....785 820-8018
2151 Centennial Rd Salina (67401) ***(G-10447)***
Choose Networks Inc.....316 773-0920
410 N Saint Francis Ave Wichita (67202) ***(G-14013)***
Chris Archer Group Inc (PA).....316 945-4000
3801 W Pawnee St Ste 200 Wichita (67213) ***(G-14014)***
Chris Carlson Hot Rods LLC.....316 777-4774
246 Industrial Dr Mulvane (67110) ***(G-7212)***
Chris O D Jacquinot.....620 235-1737
2521 N Broadway St Pittsburg (66762) ***(G-9831)***
Chris-Leef General Agency Inc.....913 631-1232
11503 W 75th St Ste 100 Shawnee Mission (66214) ***(G-11222)***
CHRIST FIRST COUNSELING CENTER, Topeka *Also called Cfcc & Associates* ***(G-12461)***
Christ King Early Educatn Ctr.....785 272-2999
5973 Sw 25th St Topeka (66614) ***(G-12466)***
Christian Ch of Grater Kans Cy.....913 301-3004
12778 189th St Linwood (66052) ***(G-6416)***
Christian Cmnty Fundation Kans, Overland Park *Also called Servant Chrstn Cmnty Fundation* ***(G-9296)***
Christian Psychological Svcs (PA).....785 843-2429
3500 Westridge Dr Lawrence (66049) ***(G-4788)***
Christian Rainbow Knowledge.....316 686-2169
2117 N Parkwood Ln Wichita (67208) ***(G-14015)***
Christianson, Timothy H, Overland Park *Also called Heart America Eye Care PA* ***(G-8804)***
Christman, Carl M Jr, Wichita *Also called Wichita Ob Gyn Associates PA* ***(G-16014)***
Christopher B Geha.....913 383-9099
8800 State Line Rd Shawnee Mission (66206) ***(G-11223)***
Christopher Moeller.....316 682-7546
1911 N Webb Rd Wichita (67206) ***(G-14016)***
Christs Care Pre-School.....620 662-1283
4290 N Monroe St Hutchinson (67502) ***(G-3237)***
Christs Kids Childcare.....620 654-4567
400 Northview Rd Galva (67443) ***(G-2092)***
Chrome Plus International Inc.....316 944-3600
3939 W 29th St S Wichita (67217) ***(G-14017)***
CHS Inc.....785 754-3318
7085 Highway 40 Quinter (67752) ***(G-10180)***
CHS Inc.....785 386-4546
7756 W Us Highway 83 Selden (67757) ***(G-10855)***
CHS Inc.....620 241-4247
1384 Iron Horse Rd McPherson (67460) ***(G-6948)***

ALPHABETIC

CHS Inc...620 663-5711
2701 E 11th Ave Hutchinson (67501) ***(G-3238)***
CHS Inc...785 852-4241
102 N Front St Sharon Springs (67758) ***(G-10895)***
CHS McPherson Refinery Inc (HQ)...620 241-2340
2000 S Main St McPherson (67460) ***(G-6949)***
CHS McPherson Refinery Inc...785 421-2157
721 W Main St Hill City (67642) ***(G-3030)***
Chubb US Holding Inc...913 491-2000
7007 College Blvd Ste 600 Shawnee Mission (66211) ***(G-11224)***
Chuck E. Cheese's, Overland Park *Also called Cec Entertainment Inc* ***(G-8533)***
Chuck E. Cheese's, Wichita *Also called Cec Entertainment Inc* ***(G-13968)***
Chuck Henry Sales Inc...785 655-9430
525 N Poplar St Ste A Solomon (67480) ***(G-12049)***
Chuck Krte Rlty Est Auctn Svcs...316 775-2201
420 N Walnut St Augusta (67010) ***(G-313)***
Chuck Pierson DDS PA...316 634-1333
9339 E 21st St N Ste 200 Wichita (67206) ***(G-14018)***
Church of Magdalen...316 634-1572
2221 N 127th St E Wichita (67226) ***(G-14019)***
Churchill Container, Lenexa *Also called Koller Enterprises Inc* ***(G-5957)***
Chwc, Kansas City *Also called Community Hsing Wyandotte Cnty* ***(G-3931)***
Ciac LLC...316 262-0953
3545 N Santa Fe St Wichita (67219) ***(G-14020)***
Ciena Corporation...913 402-4800
13220 Metcalf Ave Ste 200 Shawnee Mission (66213) ***(G-11225)***
Cigna Dental Health Kansas Inc...913 339-4700
7400 W 110th St Ste 400 Overland Park (66210) ***(G-8551)***
Cillessen Equipment Co LLC...316 682-2400
2300 E Tigua St Kechi (67067) ***(G-4566)***
Cimarron Underground Inc (PA)...913 438-2981
7900 College Blvd Ste 106 Overland Park (66210) ***(G-8552)***
Cimarron Valley Irrigation LLC...620 544-7323
715 E 11th St Hugoton (67951) ***(G-3151)***
Cimarron Welding Inc...620 855-3582
112 N Main St113 # 113 Cimarron (67835) ***(G-821)***
Cimarron Wind Energy LLC...561 691-7171
10001 Rd 19 Cimarron (67835) ***(G-822)***
Cimarron Wind Power 2, Cimarron *Also called Duke Energy Corporation* ***(G-824)***
Cinemark Cinema 20, Shawnee Mission *Also called Cinemark Usa Inc* ***(G-11226)***
Cinemark Usa Inc...913 789-7038
5500 Antioch Rd Shawnee Mission (66202) ***(G-11226)***
Cintas Corporation...913 782-8333
2050 E Kansas City Rd Olathe (66061) ***(G-7595)***
Cintas Corporation No 2...913 782-8333
2050 E Kansas City Rd Olathe (66061) ***(G-7596)***
Cintas-The Uniform People, Olathe *Also called Cintas Corporation* ***(G-7595)***
Circle Bar Cattle Company Inc...620 275-1182
842 Road 60 Satanta (67870) ***(G-10781)***
Circle C Country Supply Inc (PA)...785 398-2571
204 N Broadway St Louisburg (66053) ***(G-6443)***
Circle C Paving and Cnstr LLC...316 794-5070
630 Industrial Rd Goddard (67052) ***(G-2432)***
Circle D Corporation Inc...620 947-2385
613 N Ash St Hillsboro (67063) ***(G-3044)***
Circle E Feeds, Pittsburg *Also called Elnicki Inc* ***(G-9857)***
Circle Enterprises Inc...316 943-9834
3351 W Central Ave Wichita (67203) ***(G-14021)***
Circle Land & Cattle Corp...620 275-6131
955 S Circle Land Rd Garden City (67846) ***(G-2124)***
Cisco Systems Inc...913 344-6100
7400 College Blvd Ste 400 Shawnee Mission (66210) ***(G-11227)***
Citigroup Global Markets Inc...316 630-4400
1617 N Wtrfrnt Pkwy # 200 Wichita (67206) ***(G-14022)***
Citizens Bank, Weir *Also called Cbw Bank* ***(G-13485)***
Citizens Bank NA...913 239-2700
8101 W 135th St Overland Park (66223) ***(G-8553)***
Citizens Bank NA (HQ)...620 223-1200
200 S Main St Fort Scott (66701) ***(G-1959)***
Citizens Bank of Kansas (HQ)...620 532-5162
300 N Main St Kingman (67068) ***(G-4586)***
Citizens Bank of Kansas NA...316 788-1111
1033 N Buckner St Derby (67037) ***(G-1229)***
Citizens Bank of Kansas NA...620 886-5686
120 E Kansas Ave Medicine Lodge (67104) ***(G-7058)***
Citizens Medical Center, Colby *Also called Family Center For Health Care* ***(G-1003)***
Citizens Medical Center Inc...785 462-7511
100 E College Dr Colby (67701) ***(G-994)***
Citizens National Bank (PA)...785 747-2261
417 Commercial St Greenleaf (66943) ***(G-2667)***
Citizens National Bank...913 727-3266
601 N Main St Lansing (66043) ***(G-4671)***
Citizens Savings & Loan Assn (PA)...913 727-1040
5151 S 4th St Leavenworth (66048) ***(G-5218)***
Citizens State Bank...316 518-6621
601 S Main St Hugoton (67951) ***(G-3152)***
Citizens State Bank...785 363-2521
124 E Commercial St Waterville (66548) ***(G-13472)***
Citizens State Bank...316 542-3142
306 N Main St Cheney (67025) ***(G-791)***
Citizens State Bank (HQ)...785 562-2186
800 Broadway Marysville (66508) ***(G-6882)***
Citizens State Bank...620 327-4941
201 N Main St Hesston (67062) ***(G-2986)***
Citizens State Bank and Tr Co (PA)...785 742-2101
610 Oregon St Hiawatha (66434) ***(G-3006)***
Citizens State Bnk Tr Ellswrth (HQ)...785 472-3141
203 N Douglas Ave Ellsworth (67439) ***(G-1660)***
Citoxlab Usa LLC...913 850-5000
17745 Metcalf Ave Stilwell (66085) ***(G-12141)***
City Beverage Co Inc...620 662-6271
2 S Kirby St Hutchinson (67501) ***(G-3239)***
City Blue Print Inc...316 265-6224
1400 E Waterman St Wichita (67211) ***(G-14023)***
City Clerks Office, Conway Springs *Also called City of Conway Springs* ***(G-1136)***
City County Health Department, Garden City *Also called Health and Envmt Kans Dept* ***(G-2192)***
City Cycle Sales...785 238-3411
1021 Goldenbelt Blvd Junction City (66441) ***(G-3681)***
City Cycle Sls Harley Davidson, Junction City *Also called City Cycle Sales* ***(G-3681)***
City Elec & Water Dept, Wamego *Also called City of Wamego* ***(G-13412)***
City Glass and Mirror Inc...785 233-5650
2017 Sw 6th Ave Topeka (66606) ***(G-12467)***
City Goodland Inspection Dept...785 890-4500
204 W 11th St Goodland (67735) ***(G-2464)***
City Maintenance Shop, Ellinwood *Also called City of Ellinwood* ***(G-1628)***
City of Agusta, Augusta *Also called Augusta Electric Plant 2* ***(G-303)***
City of Anthony...620 842-5123
202 S Bluff Ave Anthony (67003) ***(G-123)***
City of Chanute...620 431-5270
1415 S Garfield St Chanute (66720) ***(G-716)***
City of Clay Center...785 632-2139
427 Court St Clay Center (67432) ***(G-849)***
City of Coffeyville...620 252-6180
605 Santa Fe St Coffeyville (67337) ***(G-915)***
City of Conway Springs...620 456-2345
208 W Spring Ave Conway Springs (67031) ***(G-1136)***
City of Dodge City...620 225-8176
705 W Trail St Dodge City (67801) ***(G-1322)***
City of Dodge City...620 225-8186
400 W Wyatt Earp Blvd Dodge City (67801) ***(G-1323)***
City of Ellinwood...620 564-3046
505 E Santa Fe Blvd Ellinwood (67526) ***(G-1628)***
City of Emporia...620 340-6339
1220 Hatcher St Emporia (66801) ***(G-1720)***
City of Fredonia...620 378-2802
1701 Madison St Fredonia (66736) ***(G-2029)***
City of Galena...620 783-5065
210 Turner Dr Galena (66739) ***(G-2071)***
City of Garden City...620 276-1250
312 Finnup Dr Garden City (67846) ***(G-2125)***
City of Garden City...620 276-1291
106 S 11th St Garden City (67846) ***(G-2126)***
City of Goodland...785 890-4555
1701 Cherry Ave Goodland (67735) ***(G-2465)***
City of Great Bend (PA)...620 793-4111
1209 Williams St Great Bend (67530) ***(G-2540)***
City of Great Bend...620 792-3906
2005 Kansas Ave Great Bend (67530) ***(G-2541)***
City of Great Bend...620 793-4170
200 Kiowa Rd Great Bend (67530) ***(G-2542)***
City of Great Bend...620 793-5031
323 S Us Highway 281 Great Bend (67530) ***(G-2543)***
City of Halstead (PA)...316 835-2286
303 Main St Halstead (67056) ***(G-2697)***
City of Halstead...316 835-3492
103 Locust St Halstead (67056) ***(G-2698)***
City of Hesston...620 327-2331
520 Yost Dr Hesston (67062) ***(G-2987)***
City of Hutchinson...620 694-2632
125 E Avenue B Hutchinson (67501) ***(G-3240)***
City of Hutchinson...620 694-1970
1500 S Plum St Hutchinson (67501) ***(G-3241)***
City of Iola...620 365-4900
2 W Jackson Ave Iola (66749) ***(G-3593)***
City of Junction City...785 238-4303
6514 Old Milford Rc Milford (66514) ***(G-7111)***
City of Junction City...785 238-7142
2324 N Jackson St Junction City (66441) ***(G-3682)***
City of Lawrence...785 832-7700
110 Riverfront Rd Lawrence (66044) ***(G-4789)***
City of Lawrence...785 748-0600
1250 E 902nd Rd Lawrence (66047) ***(G-4790)***
City of Lawrence...785 832-7840
1400 E 8th St Lawrence (66044) ***(G-4791)***
City of Leavenworth...913 684-1560
401 S 3rd St Leavenworth (66048) ***(G-5219)***

City of Leavenworth...913 651-2132
123 N Esplanade St Leavenworth (66048) ***(G-5220)***
City of Leavenworth...913 682-1090
1800 S 2nd St Leavenworth (66048) ***(G-5221)***
City of Leavenworth...913 682-1513
601 Cherokee St Leavenworth (66048) ***(G-5222)***
City of Leawood...913 685-4550
15400 Mission Rd Shawnee Mission (66224) ***(G-11228)***
City of Lenexa...913 541-0209
17201 W 87th St Lenexa (66219) ***(G-5755)***
City of Liberal...620 626-0135
405 N Pennsylvania Ave Liberal (67901) ***(G-6292)***
City of Liberal...620 626-0138
1401 E Pine St Liberal (67901) ***(G-6293)***
City of Logan...785 689-4227
302 W Logan St Logan (67646) ***(G-6421)***
City of Logan...785 689-4201
108 S Adams St Logan (67646) ***(G-6422)***
City of Manhattan...785 587-2737
2333 Oak St Manhattan (66502) ***(G-6587)***
City of Manhattan...785 587-4555
7408 E Us Hwy 24 Manhattan (66502) ***(G-6588)***
City of McPherson...620 241-1122
1177 W Woodside St McPherson (67460) ***(G-6950)***
City of Mission...913 722-8200
6200 Martway St Shawnee Mission (66202) ***(G-11229)***
City of Mulvane...316 777-0191
410 W Bridge St Mulvane (67110) ***(G-7213)***
City of Neodesha...620 325-2642
112 S 4th St Neodesha (66757) ***(G-7235)***
City of Newton...316 284-6083
304 Grandview Ave Newton (67114) ***(G-7329)***
City of Newton...316 283-3113
211 E 1st St Newton (67114) ***(G-7330)***
City of Ottawa...785 229-3750
1000 W 2nd St Ottawa (66067) ***(G-8254)***
City of Ottawa...785 229-3710
324 S Beech St Ottawa (66067) ***(G-8255)***
City of Ottawa Power Plant, Ottawa *Also called City of Ottawa* ***(G-8254)***
City of Ottawa Utility Center, Ottawa *Also called City of Ottawa* ***(G-8255)***
City of Overland Park...913 895-6080
8500 Santa Fe Dr Overland Park (66212) ***(G-8554)***
City of Overland Park...913 897-3806
10515 W 135th St Shawnee Mission (66223) ***(G-11230)***
City of Overland Park...913 339-3000
6000 College Blvd Overland Park (66211) ***(G-8555)***
City of Overland Park...913 895-6040
11300 W 91st St Overland Park (66214) ***(G-8556)***
City of Overland Park...913 895-6000
8500 Santa Fe Dr Shawnee Mission (66212) ***(G-11231)***
City of Overland Park...913 897-3805
12698 Nieman Rd Overland Park (66213) ***(G-8557)***
City of Paola...913 259-3600
19 E Peoria St Paola (66071) ***(G-9547)***
City of Parsons...620 421-7025
1000 N 21st St Parsons (67357) ***(G-9671)***
City of Pittsburg...620 231-8070
910 Memorial Dr Pittsburg (66762) ***(G-9832)***
City of Pittsburg...620 231-7827
503 N Pine St Pittsburg (66762) ***(G-9833)***
City of Pittsburg...620 308-6916
201 N Pine St Pittsburg (66762) ***(G-9834)***
City of Prairie Village...913 642-6010
7711 Delmar St Shawnee Mission (66208) ***(G-11232)***
City of Pratt...620 672-3831
321 W 10th St Pratt (67124) ***(G-10101)***
City of Salina...785 826-7305
401 S 5th St Rm 200 Salina (67401) ***(G-10448)***
City of Salina...785 826-7200
800 The Midway Salina (67401) ***(G-10449)***
City of Salina...785 309-5775
211 W Iron Ave Salina (67401) ***(G-10450)***
City of Salina...785 826-7340
222 W Elm St Salina (67401) ***(G-10451)***
City of Salina...785 309-5752
418 E Ash St Salina (67401) ***(G-10452)***
City of Salina Central Garage, Salina *Also called City of Salina* ***(G-10452)***
City of Sedan (PA)...620 725-3193
111 E Cherokee St Sedan (67361) ***(G-10840)***
City of Shawnee...913 631-1080
6501 Quivira Rd Shawnee Mission (66216) ***(G-11233)***
City of Spring Hill...913 592-3781
22400 W 207th St Spring Hill (66083) ***(G-12082)***
City of Stockton...785 425-6754
315 S Ash St Stockton (67669) ***(G-12181)***
City of Topeka...785 368-9180
635 Sw Gage Blvd Topeka (66606) ***(G-12468)***
City of Topeka...785 291-2670
2533 Sw Urish Rd Topeka (66614) ***(G-12469)***
City of Topeka...785 368-3851
1115 Ne Poplar St Topeka (66616) ***(G-12470)***
City of Topeka...785 295-3842
515 S Kansas Ave Ste 301 Topeka (66603) ***(G-12471)***
City of Topeka...785 368-3860
3245 Nw Water Works Dr Topeka (66606) ***(G-12472)***
City of Topeka...785 273-0811
6921 Sw 21st St Topeka (66615) ***(G-12473)***
City of Topeka...785 295-3803
201 Nw Topeka Blvd Ste B Topeka (66603) ***(G-12474)***
City of Topeka Employees...785 368-3749
620 Se Madison St Topeka (66607) ***(G-12475)***
City of Topeka Employees...785 272-5503
4801 Sw Shunga Dr Topeka (66614) ***(G-12476)***
City of Wamego...785 456-9598
430 Lincoln Ave Wamego (66547) ***(G-13412)***
City of Wamego...785 456-2295
711 Genn Dr Wamego (66547) ***(G-13413)***
City of Waterville...785 363-2367
136 E Commercial St Waterville (66548) ***(G-13473)***
City of Wichita...316 268-4421
455 N Main St Fl 4 Wichita (67202) ***(G-14024)***
City of Wichita...316 942-4482
455 N Main St Ste 1221 Wichita (67202) ***(G-14025)***
City of Wichita...316 268-4651
455 N Main St Fl 12 Wichita (67202) ***(G-14026)***
City of Wichita...316 744-9719
5815 E 9th St N Wichita (67208) ***(G-14027)***
City of Wichita...316 268-8351
1900 E 9th St N Wichita (67214) ***(G-14028)***
City of Wichita...316 688-9341
4611 E Harry St Wichita (67218) ***(G-14029)***
City of Wichita...316 337-9494
1931 S Tyler Rd Wichita (67209) ***(G-14030)***
City of Wichita...316 265-7221
777 E Waterman St Wichita (67202) ***(G-14031)***
City of Winfield...620 221-5630
2801 E 12th St Winfield (67156) ***(G-16120)***
City Oil Company Inc...913 321-1764
2011 N 10th St Kansas City (66104) ***(G-3912)***
City Plumbing Heating & AC Inc...785 472-3001
120 N Lincoln Ave Ellsworth (67439) ***(G-1661)***
City Print Inc...316 267-5555
235 S Ellis St Wichita (67211) ***(G-14032)***
City Rent-A-Truck, Overland Park *Also called Bob Allen Ford Inc* ***(G-8473)***
City State Bank...620 223-1600
202 Scott Ave Fort Scott (66701) ***(G-1960)***
City State Bank (HQ)...620 223-1600
1012 Highway 69 Fort Scott (66701) ***(G-1961)***
City Traffic Operation...785 368-3913
927 Nw Harrison St Topeka (66608) ***(G-12477)***
City Wichita Evironmental Hlth, Wichita *Also called City of Wichita* ***(G-14028)***
City Wide Franchise Co Inc...913 888-5700
15447 W 100th Ter Lenexa (66219) ***(G-5756)***
City Wide Heating & Cooling, Kansas City *Also called City Wide Service Inc* ***(G-3913)***
City Wide Holding Company Inc (PA)...913 888-5700
15447 W 100th Ter Lenexa (66219) ***(G-5757)***
City Wide Maintenance Co Inc...913 888-5700
15447 W 100th Ter Lenexa (66219) ***(G-5758)***
City Wide Service Inc...913 927-6124
2820 Roe Ln Ste G Kansas City (66103) ***(G-3913)***
City Wide Sheet Metal Inc...913 871-7464
2824 Roe Ln Kansas City (66103) ***(G-3914)***
City Wide Window Washing Inc...913 888-5700
15447 W 100th Ter Lenexa (66219) ***(G-5759)***
Citywide Electric Inc...913 631-1189
5911 Barton Dr Shawnee Mission (66203) ***(G-11234)***
Citywide Mortgage Associates...913 498-8822
10800 Farley St Ste 300 Overland Park (66210) ***(G-8558)***
Citywide Painting & Rmdlg LLC...913 238-9749
4904 W 114th St Leawood (66211) ***(G-5352)***
Civicplus LLC...785 267-6800
2627 Kfb Plz Ste 206w Manhattan (66503) ***(G-6589)***
Civicplus LLC (PA)...888 228-2233
302 S 4th St Ste 500 Manhattan (66502) ***(G-6590)***
Civil Air Patrol Inc...620 275-6121
2708 N 7th St Garden City (67846) ***(G-2127)***
CJ Industries LLC...913 788-1104
610 S 78th St Ste 1 Kansas City (66111) ***(G-3915)***
Cjd & Associates LLC (PA)...913 469-1188
10875 Benson Dr Ste 110 Shawnee Mission (66210) ***(G-11235)***
CK Contracting LLC...316 267-1996
1444 S Saint Clair Ave B Wichita (67213) ***(G-14033)***
Claflin Academic Publishing, Manhattan *Also called Claflin Books & Copies* ***(G-6591)***
Claflin Ambulance Service Assn...620 587-3498
309 W Front St Claflin (67525) ***(G-840)***
Claflin Books & Copies...785 776-3771
103 N 4th St Manhattan (66502) ***(G-6591)***
Claim Solution Inc...913 322-2300
8900 Indian Creek Pkwy # 450 Shawnee Mission (66210) ***(G-11236)***

ALPHABETIC

Clancey Co (PA)....913 894-4444
8081 Flint St Overland Park (66214) ***(G-8559)***
Clapp Memorial Park Golf Crse, Wichita *Also called City of Wichita* ***(G-14029)***
Clara Barton Hospital....620 653-4191
351 W 10th St Hoisington (67544) ***(G-3060)***
Clara Barton Hospital (PA)....620 653-2114
252 W 9th St Hoisington (67544) ***(G-3061)***
Clara Barton Hospital....620 653-2114
250 W 9th St Hoisington (67544) ***(G-3062)***
Clara Barton Surgical Services, Hoisington *Also called Clara Barton Hospital* ***(G-3060)***
Clarcor Air Filtration Pdts....785 242-1811
1612 N Davis Ave Ottawa (66067) ***(G-8256)***
Clarcor Industrial Air, Overland Park *Also called Bha Altair LLC* ***(G-8445)***
Clare Bridge of Overland Park, Shawnee Mission *Also called Brookdale Snior Lving Cmmnties* ***(G-11184)***
Clare Bridge of Wichita, Wichita *Also called Brookdale Snior Lving Cmmnties* ***(G-13898)***
Clare Generator Service Inc....785 827-3321
801 N 10th St Salina (67401) ***(G-10453)***
Clarence M Kelley & Assoc of K....913 647-7700
6840 Silverheel St Shawnee (66226) ***(G-10929)***
Claridge Court, Shawnee Mission *Also called Lifespace Communities Inc* ***(G-11570)***
Clarion Hotel, Manhattan *Also called Hulsing Hotels Kansas Inc* ***(G-6662)***
Clarion Hotel, Garden City *Also called K & S LLC* ***(G-2211)***
Clarion Hotel Kansas, Lenexa *Also called Lenexa Hotel LP* ***(G-5970)***
Clarios....913 307-4200
9850 Legler Rd Shawnee Mission (66219) ***(G-11237)***
Clarios....316 721-2777
404 S Holland St Ste 1 Wichita (67209) ***(G-14034)***
Clarios....785 267-0801
4024 Sw Topeka Blvd Topeka (66609) ***(G-12478)***
Clarios....316 655-7578
3110 N Mead St Dock 1/4 Wichita (67219) ***(G-14035)***
Clarios....316 634-1309
8909 E 35th St N Wichita (67226) ***(G-14036)***
Clarios....785 827-6829
2001 W Grand Ave Bldg 2-5 Salina (67401) ***(G-10454)***
Clark Dargal Builders Inc....785 478-4811
1324 Sw Auburn Rd Topeka (66615) ***(G-12479)***
Clark Enterprises 2000 Inc....785 825-7172
3603 S Knoll Ln Salina (67401) ***(G-10455)***
Clark Flying Service Inc....620 348-2685
102 Nw 120th Ave Macksville (67557) ***(G-6499)***
Clark Investment Group....316 634-1112
1223 N Rock Rd Ste E200 Wichita (67206) ***(G-14037)***
Clark Mize Linville Chartered....785 823-6325
129 S 8th St Salina (67401) ***(G-10456)***
Clark Security Service....620 225-6577
1701 Avenue C Dodge City (67801) ***(G-1324)***
Clark-Timmons Oil Company (PA)....816 229-0228
445 Sunshine Rd Kansas City (66115) ***(G-3916)***
Clarke Enterprises LLC....913 601-3830
3250 Brinkerhoff Rd Kansas City (66115) ***(G-3917)***
Clarke, Jeffrey A CPA, Garden City *Also called Keller & Miller Cpas LLP* ***(G-2217)***
Claro Financiero LLC....913 608-5444
6612 Willow Ln Mission Hills (66208) ***(G-7141)***
Clarus Group LLC....913 599-5255
9401 Indian Creek Pkwy # 500 Overland Park (66210) ***(G-8560)***
Class Ltd....620 231-3131
2928 N Rouse St Pittsburg (66762) ***(G-9835)***
Class Ltd (PA)....620 429-1212
1200 E Merle Evans Dr Columbus (66725) ***(G-1066)***
Class Ltd....620 331-8604
2801 W Main St Unit B Independence (67301) ***(G-3503)***
Class Ltd....620 421-2800
1207 Partridge Ave Parsons (67357) ***(G-9672)***
Classic Awards, Overland Park *Also called Simon & Simon Inc* ***(G-9311)***
Classic Cloth Inc....785 434-7200
308 W Mill St Plainville (67663) ***(G-9980)***
Classic Collision Center....913 287-9410
4835 Metropolitan Ave Kansas City (66106) ***(G-3918)***
Classic Enterprises Inc....785 628-6700
2719 Plaza Ave Hays (67601) ***(G-2769)***
Classic Floors & Design Center (PA)....913 780-2171
15425 Metcalf Ave Overland Park (66223) ***(G-8561)***
Classic Heating and Coolg LLC....913 238-1036
20944 Spooncreek Rd Edgerton (66021) ***(G-1482)***
Classic Motor Freight LLC....913 586-5911
10777 Barkley St Ste 210 Leawood (66211) ***(G-5353)***
Classic Quality Body Shop, Hays *Also called Classic Enterprises Inc* ***(G-2769)***
Classic Shower Door Inc....913 492-9670
8841 Lenexa Dr Overland Park (66214) ***(G-8562)***
Classic Well Service Inc....620 587-3402
510 W Hamilton St Claflin (67525) ***(G-841)***
Classic Wood Interior Inc....785 392-9937
705 Laurel St Minneapolis (67467) ***(G-7116)***
Classifiedkits.com, Kansas City *Also called Sunburst Systems Inc* ***(G-4446)***
Classone Software....913 831-4976
6316 Riley St Shawnee Mission (66202) ***(G-11238)***
Classy Kids, Overland Park *Also called Awad Nicola* ***(G-8417)***
Clay Center Family Dentistry (PA)....785 632-3126
714 Liberty St Clay Center (67432) ***(G-850)***
Clay Center Fmly Physicians PA (PA)....785 632-2181
609 Liberty St Clay Center (67432) ***(G-851)***
Clay Center Fmly Physicians PA....785 446-2226
815 Campbell Ave Clyde (66938) ***(G-905)***
Clay Center Locker, Clay Center *Also called Diecks Inc* ***(G-860)***
Clay Center Office, Clay Center *Also called Big Lkes Developmental Ctr Inc* ***(G-843)***
Clay Center Publishing Co Inc....785 632-2127
805 5th St Clay Center (67432) ***(G-852)***
Clay County Ambulance Service, Clay Center *Also called County of Clay* ***(G-858)***
Clay County Child Care Ctr Inc (PA)....785 632-2195
314 Court St Clay Center (67432) ***(G-853)***
Clay County Child Care Ctr Inc....785 632-5399
1021 4th St Clay Center (67432) ***(G-854)***
Clay County Health Department, Clay Center *Also called County of Clay* ***(G-859)***
Clay Jars Childrens Center Inc....785 379-9098
2930 Se Tecumseh Rd Tecumseh (66542) ***(G-12238)***
Clayton Homes Inc....785 434-4617
507 N Industrial Park Rd Plainville (67663) ***(G-9981)***
Clayton J Befort....785 625-7628
1177 Commerce Pkwy Hays (67601) ***(G-2770)***
CLC Bonner Springs....913 441-2515
520 E Morse Ave Bonner Springs (66012) ***(G-545)***
CLC Group Inc....316 636-5055
8111 E 32nd St N Ste 300 Wichita (67226) ***(G-14038)***
Clean Air Management Co Inc....913 831-0740
9732 Pflumm Rd Lenexa (66215) ***(G-5760)***
Clean Harbors Wichita LLC (HQ)....316 832-0151
2808 N Ohio St Wichita (67219) ***(G-14039)***
Clean Harbors Wichita LLC....913 287-6880
601 S 66th Ter Kansas City (66111) ***(G-3919)***
Clean Sweep,, Geneseo *Also called Kratzer Industries* ***(G-2393)***
Clean Tech Inc....316 729-8100
7453 W 33rd St N Wichita (67205) ***(G-14040)***
Clean-Rite LLC....785 628-1945
1307 Vine St Hays (67601) ***(G-2771)***
Cleaning Authority of Central....316 733-7890
318 S Greenwood St Wichita (67211) ***(G-14041)***
Cleaning Authority, The, Overland Park *Also called CD McCormick & Company Inc* ***(G-8531)***
Cleaning By Lamunyon Inc....785 632-1259
1541 18th Rd Clay Center (67432) ***(G-855)***
Cleaning Up LLC....913 327-7226
11386 Strang Line Rd Lenexa (66215) ***(G-5761)***
Cleansweep Janitorial Inc....785 856-8617
423 Hutton Cir Lawrence (66049) ***(G-4792)***
Clear View Inc....785 286-2070
5709 Sw 21st St Ste 102 Topeka (66604) ***(G-12480)***
Clearview City Inc....913 583-1451
36000 W 103rd St De Soto (66018) ***(G-1196)***
Clearwater Cable Vision Inc....620 584-2077
112 S Lee St Clearwater (67026) ***(G-888)***
Clearwater Dental Office, Clearwater *Also called Ronald G Higgins* ***(G-895)***
Clearwater Engineering Inc....316 425-0202
301 N River St Derby (67037) ***(G-1230)***
Clearwire Corporation (HQ)....425 216-7600
6200 Sprint Pkwy Overland Park (66251) ***(G-8563)***
Clearwire LLC....202 628-3544
6391 Sprint Pkwy Overland Park (66251) ***(G-8564)***
Clearwter Nrsing Rhabilitation....620 584-2271
620 E Wood St Clearwater (67026) ***(G-889)***
Cleland Masonry Inc....620 347-8546
728 E 640th Ave Arma (66712) ***(G-189)***
Clerk District Crt Ltd Actions, Topeka *Also called Judiciary Court of The State* ***(G-12751)***
Cleveland University - Kans Cy (PA)....913 234-0600
10850 Lowell Ave Overland Park (66210) ***(G-8565)***
Clevlun Enterprises Inc....913 631-1111
13020 Shwnee Mission Pkwy Shawnee Mission (66216) ***(G-11239)***
Cli- Kansas City, Kansas City *Also called Comprehensive Logistics Co Inc* ***(G-3932)***
Client One Securities LLC....913 814-6097
11460 Tomahwk Crk Pkwy # 200 Leawood (66211) ***(G-5354)***
Cliff Hix Engineering Inc....620 232-3000
3411 Airport Rd Pittsburg (66762) ***(G-9836)***
Cliff Tozier Insurance Agency....913 385-5000
5750 W 95th St Ste 105 Overland Park (66207) ***(G-8566)***
Cliff's Welding Service, Phillipsburg *Also called Cliffs Welding Shop Inc* ***(G-9780)***
Cliffs Welding Shop Inc....785 543-5895
45 W Ridge Rd Phillipsburg (67661) ***(G-9780)***
Cliftonlarsonallen LLP....913 491-6655
12721 Metcalf Ave Ste 201 Overland Park (66213) ***(G-8567)***
Cline Auto Supply Inc....620 343-6000
810 Industrial Rd Emporia (66801) ***(G-1721)***
Clingan Tires Incorporated (PA)....620 624-5649
314 S Kansas Ave Liberal (67901) ***(G-6294)***
Clingan Tires Service Center, Liberal *Also called Clingan Tires Incorporated* ***(G-6294)***
Clinic In A Can, Wichita *Also called Ciac LLC* ***(G-14020)***

Clinical Associates 913 677-3553
8629 Bluejacket St # 100 Lenexa (66214) *(G-5762)*
Clinical Associates PA (PA) 913 677-3553
8629 Bluejacket St # 100 Lenexa (66214) *(G-5763)*
Clinical Radiology Foundation 913 588-6830
3901 Rainbow Blvd Rm 2162 Kansas City (66160) *(G-3920)*
Clinical Reference Lab Inc 913 492-3652
11711 W 83rd Ter Lenexa (66214) *(G-5764)*
Clinical Reference Lab Inc (PA) 913 492-3652
8433 Quivira Rd Lenexa (66215) *(G-5765)*
Clinical Research Center, Fairway *Also called University of Kansas (G-1924)*
Clinton Enterprises LLC 316 636-1801
9320 E Central Ave Wichita (67206) *(G-14042)*
Clinton L Williams 316 775-1300
10756 Se Stchell Creek Rd Leon (67074) *(G-6246)*
Clinton Marina Inc 785 749-3222
1329 E 800 Rd Lawrence (66046) *(G-4793)*
Clinton Parkway Animal Hosp 785 841-3131
4340 Clinton Pkwy Lawrence (66047) *(G-4794)*
Clk Inc 316 686-3238
914 E Gilbert St Ste 200 Wichita (67211) *(G-14043)*
Clo, Lawrence *Also called Community Lving Opprtnties Inc (G-4804)*
Clonmel Community Club Inc 620 545-7136
6101 S 167th St W Clearwater (67026) *(G-890)*
Clonmel Hall, Clearwater *Also called Clonmel Community Club Inc (G-890)*
Clore Automotive LLC (PA) 913 310-1050
8735 Rosehill Rd Ste 220 Lenexa (66215) *(G-5766)*
Clorox Company 913 664-9000
7101 College Blvd Ste 320 Overland Park (66210) *(G-8568)*
Clorox Products Mfg Co 913 620-1777
7101 College Blvd Ste 320 Overland Park (66210) *(G-8569)*
Cloud Ceramics Div, Concordia *Also called General Finance Incorporated (G-1115)*
Cloud County Health Center Inc 785 243-1234
1100 Highland Dr Concordia (66901) *(G-1106)*
Cloud Storage Corporation 785 621-4350
1305 Canterbury Dr Hays (67601) *(G-2772)*
Clouds Heating and AC 785 842-2258
920 E 28th St Lawrence (66046) *(G-4795)*
Clough Oil Company Inc 620 251-0521
104 E 4th St Coffeyville (67337) *(G-916)*
Clough Oil Company Inc 620 251-0103
1106 Oak St Coffeyville (67337) *(G-917)*
Cloverleaf Buildings, Shawnee Mission *Also called Cloverleaf Office Park (G-11240)*
Cloverleaf Office Park 913 831-3200
6811 Shwn Mssn Pkwy 104 Shawnee Mission (66202) *(G-11240)*
Clp Healthcare Services Inc 620 232-9898
200 E Centennial Dr Ste 9 Pittsburg (66762) *(G-9837)*
Club Beauty, Wichita *Also called Wholesale Beauty Club Inc (G-15967)*
Club Rodeo LLC 316 613-2424
10001 E Kellogg Dr Wichita (67207) *(G-14044)*
Clubhouse Inn & Suites, Topeka *Also called Regency Midwest Ventures Limit (G-13004)*
Clubine & Rettele 785 472-3915
118 N Lincoln Ave Ellsworth (67439) *(G-1662)*
Clune & Company Lc (PA) 913 498-3000
5950 Roe Ave Shawnee Mission (66205) *(G-11241)*
Clune & Company Lc 913 498-3000
5950 Roe Ave Shawnee Mission (66205) *(G-11242)*
Clyde Development Inc 785 446-2818
114 S High St Clyde (66938) *(G-906)*
CM Wind Down Topco Inc 785 272-2122
825 S Kansas Ave Fl 1 Topeka (66612) *(G-12481)*
CMC Recycling, Independence *Also called Commercial Metals Company (G-3507)*
CMF, Herington *Also called Custom Metal Fabricators Inc (G-2973)*
Cmg Construction Inc 913 384-2883
1601 E Peoria St Paola (66071) *(G-9548)*
CMI, Wichita *Also called Commercial Mechanical Inc Kans (G-14070)*
Cmj Manufacturing Inc 316 777-9692
242 Industrial Dr Mulvane (67110) *(G-7214)*
Cmka, Shawnee *Also called Clarence M Kelley & Assoc of K (G-10929)*
CMS Mechanical Services LLC 321 473-0488
14843 W 95th St Lenexa (66215) *(G-5767)*
Cmt Inc 785 762-4400
1002 Perry St Junction City (66441) *(G-3683)*
Cmw LLC, Wichita *Also called Central Mechanical Wichita LLC (G-13981)*
Cmx Inc (PA) 316 269-9052
1700 N Waterfront Pkwy 300b Wichita (67206) *(G-14045)*
CNA Financial Corporation 913 661-2700
7400 W 110th St Ste 650 Overland Park (66210) *(G-8570)*
CNA Insurance, Overland Park *Also called CNA Financial Corporation (G-8570)*
Cnbs, Overland Park *Also called CU Capital Mkt Solutions LLC (G-8622)*
Cnc Underground LLC 913 744-0485
633 N Oak St Gardner (66030) *(G-2333)*
Cncform, Wichita *Also called Fairmount Technologies LLC (G-14335)*
CNG Developments, Great Bend *Also called Butterfly Supply Inc (G-2525)*
Cnh Industrial America LLC 316 945-0111
3301 S Hoover Rd Wichita (67215) *(G-14046)*
Cnhi LLC 620 421-9450
1801 S 59 Hwy Parsons (67357) *(G-9673)*
Cni Thl Propco Fe LLC 785 271-6165
2033 Sw Wanamaker Rd Topeka (66604) *(G-12482)*
Coach and Four Bowling Lanes 785 472-5571
203213 N Main Ellsworth (67439) *(G-1663)*
Coake Feed Yards, Dodge City *Also called Coake Feeding Co Inc (G-1325)*
Coake Feeding Co Inc 620 227-2673
1406 Highland Ter Dodge City (67801) *(G-1325)*
Coal Creek Construction Co 785 256-7171
8248 Sw 77th St Auburn (66402) *(G-294)*
Coalition For Independence (PA) 913 321-5140
626 Minnesota Ave Fl 2 Kansas City (66101) *(G-3921)*
Coast To Coast Builders Inc 316 265-2515
750 E Funston St Wichita (67211) *(G-14047)*
Cobalt Boats LLC (PA) 620 325-2653
1715 N 8th St Neodesha (66757) *(G-7236)*
Cobalt Iron Inc 888 584-4766
1421 Res Pk Dr Ste 2c Lawrence (66049) *(G-4796)*
Cobalt Iron Vault, Lawrence *Also called Cobalt Iron Inc (G-4796)*
Cobalt Medplans, Overland Park *Also called L C Epoch Group (G-8934)*
Cobank Acb 620 275-4281
1606 E Kansas Ave Garden City (67846) *(G-2128)*
Cobank Acb 316 290-2000
245 N Waco St Ofc Wichita (67202) *(G-14048)*
Cobank Acb 620 342-0138
1221 E 12th Ave Emporia (66801) *(G-1722)*
Cobank Acb 785 798-2278
101 Eagle Dr Ness City (67560) *(G-7257)*
Cobank Acb 316 721-1100
7940 W Kellogg Dr Wichita (67209) *(G-14049)*
Cobank Acb 620 431-0240
725 W Cherry St Chanute (66720) *(G-717)*
Cobblestoner Inn and Suites 620 896-2400
899 Frontage Rd Harper (67058) *(G-2717)*
Cobbs Allen & Hall Inc 913 267-5600
7300 College Blvd Ste 300 Overland Park (66210) *(G-8571)*
Coca Cola Bottling Co Mid Amer (HQ) 785 243-1071
435 Se 70th St Topeka (66619) *(G-12483)*
Coca-Cola, Topeka *Also called Coca Cola Bottling Co Mid Amer (G-12483)*
Coca-Cola Bottling Emporia Inc 239 444-1746
2931 W 15th Ave Emporia (66801) *(G-1723)*
Coca-Cola Btlg of Wnfield Kans 620 221-2710
1003 Industrial Blvd Winfield (67156) *(G-16121)*
Coca-Cola Company 913 492-8100
9000 Marshall Dr Lenexa (66215) *(G-5768)*
Coca-Cola Company 785 243-1071
Hwy 81 & 148 Jct Concordia (66901) *(G-1107)*
Coca-Cola Refreshments USA Inc 913 492-8100
9000 Marshall Dr Shawnee Mission (66215) *(G-11243)*
Cochran Head Vick & Co PA 913 378-1100
7255 W 98th Ter Ste 100 Overland Park (66212) *(G-8572)*
Cochran Mortuary, Wichita *Also called V W C Inc (G-15868)*
Cof Residential Authority Inc 785 242-5035
1516 N Davis Ave Ottawa (66067) *(G-8257)*
Cof Training Services Inc (PA) 785 242-5035
1516 N Davis Ave Ottawa (66067) *(G-8258)*
Cof Training Services Inc 620 364-2151
1415 S 6th St Burlington (66839) *(G-627)*
Cof Training Services Inc 785 242-6064
707 N Cherry St Ottawa (66067) *(G-8259)*
Coffee Rules Lounge, Hays *Also called Rule Properties LLC (G-2903)*
Coffee Time Inc 316 267-3771
10821 E 26th St N Wichita (67226) *(G-14050)*
Coffelt Sign Co Inc 620 343-6411
18 S Commercial St Emporia (66801) *(G-1724)*
Coffey County District 2 620 836-4080
502 Main St Gridley (66852) *(G-2688)*
Coffey County Hospital (PA) 620 364-5655
801 N 4th St Burlington (66839) *(G-628)*
Coffey County Hospital 785 733-2744
128 S Pearson Ave Waverly (66871) *(G-13481)*
Coffey County Hospital 620 364-8861
1201 Martindale St Burlington (66839) *(G-629)*
Coffey County Hospital 620 364-5395
309 Sanders St Burlington (66839) *(G-630)*
Coffey County Medical Center, Burlington *Also called Coffey County Hospital (G-628)*
Coffey County Medical Center, Burlington *Also called Coffey County Hospital (G-630)*
Coffey County Republican, Burlington *Also called Faimon Publications Inc (G-634)*
Coffey County Trnsp Inc 620 364-1935
520 Cross St Burlington (66839) *(G-631)*
Coffey Health Systems 620 364-5118
801 N 4th St Burlington (66839) *(G-632)*
Coffey, Dan Co, Olathe *Also called Don Coffey Company Inc (G-7659)*
Coffeyville, Coffeyville *Also called Four Cnty Mental Hlth Ctr Inc (G-939)*
Coffeyville Acquisition LLC 913 982-0500
10 E Cambridge Circle Dr Kansas City (66103) *(G-3922)*
Coffeyville Concrete, Coffeyville *Also called Cornejo & Sons LLC (G-931)*
Coffeyville Country Club 620 251-5236
1322 Englewood Coffeyville (67337) *(G-918)*

Coffeyville Doctors Clinic P A 620 251-7500
801 W 8th St Coffeyville (67337) *(G-919)*
Coffeyville Power & Light Dept, Coffeyville *Also called City of Coffeyville (G-915)*
Coffeyville Printing Center 620 251-6040
707 Walnut St Coffeyville (67337) *(G-920)*
Coffeyville Recreation Comm, Coffeyville *Also called Coffeyvlle Unfied Schl Dst 445 (G-927)*
Coffeyville Refinery, Kansas City *Also called Coffeyville Resources LLC (G-3923)*
Coffeyville Resources LLC 785 434-4832
606 S Cemetery Rd Plainville (67663) *(G-9982)*
Coffeyville Resources LLC 785 434-4832
606 S Cemetary Rd Plainville (67663) *(G-9983)*
Coffeyville Resources LLC 913 982-0500
10 E Cambridge Circle Dr # 250 Kansas City (66103) *(G-3923)*
Coffeyville Resources LLC 620 252-4781
701 E Martin St Coffeyville (67337) *(G-921)*
Coffeyville Resources LLC 620 221-2107
3303 E 9th Ave Winfield (67156) *(G-16122)*
Coffeyville Sektam Inc 620 251-3880
509 Cline Rd Coffeyville (67337) *(G-922)*
Coffeyvlle Fmly Prctice Clinic 620 251-1100
209 W 7th St Coffeyville (67337) *(G-923)*
Coffeyvlle Ntrgn Frtlizers Inc 913 982-0500
10 E Cambridge Circle Dr Kansas City (66103) *(G-3924)*
Coffeyvlle Rgional Med Ctr Inc 620 251-1200
1400 W 4th St Coffeyville (67337) *(G-924)*
Coffeyvlle Rsrces Ref Mktg LLC 913 982-0500
10 E Cambrdge Cir Dr 250 Kansas City (66103) *(G-3925)*
Coffeyvlle Rsrces Ref Mktg LLC 620 251-4000
701 E North St Coffeyville (67337) *(G-925)*
Coffeyvlle Rsrces Ref Mktg LLC 620 251-4252
400 N Linden St Coffeyville (67337) *(G-926)*
Coffeyvlle Unfied Schl Dst 445 ....620 251-5910
508 Park St Coffeyville (67337) *(G-927)*
Coffman Defries & Nothern 785 234-3461
534 S Kansas Ave Ste 925 Topeka (66603) *(G-12484)*
Cogen Cleaning Technology Inc 281 339-5751
16014 Foster St Stilwell (66085) *(G-12142)*
Cohake Deutscher and Hefner 785 271-8181
4848 Sw 21st St Ste 101 Topeka (66604) *(G-12485)*
Cohen Esrey, Overland Park *Also called Cohen-Esrey LLC (G-8573)*
Cohen-Esrey LLC (PA) 913 671-3300
6800 W 64th St Ste 101 Overland Park (66202) *(G-8573)*
Cohen-Esrey Communities LLC 913 671-3300
6800 W 64th St Ste 101 Overland Park (66202) *(G-8574)*
Cohoon Chiropractic 316 612-0600
3300 N Rock Rd Ste A-2 Wichita (67226) *(G-14051)*
Coil Springs Specialties LLC 785 437-2025
632 W Bertrand Ave Saint Marys (66536) *(G-10359)*
Coin Machine Distributors Inc 316 652-0361
1940 S Oliver St Wichita (67218) *(G-14052)*
Cokingtin Eye Center PA (PA) 913 491-3737
5520 College Blvd Ste 201 Shawnee Mission (66211) *(G-11244)*
Colby A G Center LLC 785 462-6132
305 E Horton Ave Colby (67701) *(G-995)*
Colby Bowl 785 460-2672
1175 S Range Ave Ste 3 Colby (67701) *(G-996)*
Colby Bowl and Fun Center, Colby *Also called Colby Bowl (G-996)*
Colby Canvas Co, Colby *Also called Colby Supply & Mfg Co (G-999)*
Colby Convention Center 785 460-0131
2227 S Range Ave Colby (67701) *(G-997)*
Colby Fertilizer, Colby *Also called G H K Farms (G-1008)*
Colby Free Press, Colby *Also called Haynes Publishing Co (G-1011)*
Colby Livestock Auction 785 460-3231
125 S Country Club Dr Colby (67701) *(G-998)*
Colby Supply & Mfg Co 785 462-3981
285 E 3rd St Colby (67701) *(G-999)*
Coldpoint Logistics LLC 816 888-7380
31301 W 181st St Edgerton (66021) *(G-1483)*
Coldwell Banker, Pittsburg *Also called Jim Bishop & Associates (G-9882)*
Coldwell Banker, Shawnee Mission *Also called John H Moffitt & Co Inc (G-11491)*
Coldwell Banker, Leavenworth *Also called Reilly Company LLC (G-5284)*
Coldwell Banker Advantage 913 345-9999
10865 Grandview Dr # 2050 Overland Park (66210) *(G-8575)*
Coldwell Banker RE Corp 620 331-2950
1921 N Penn Ave Independence (67301) *(G-3504)*
Coldwell Banker Regan Realtors 913 631-2900
11800 Shawnee Mission Pkw Shawnee Mission (66203) *(G-11245)*
Coldwell Bnkr Coml Fishman Co, Overland Park *Also called Fishman and Co Realtors Inc (G-8724)*
Coldwell Bnkr Psternak Johnson 620 331-5510
2001 N Penn Ave Independence (67301) *(G-3505)*
Cole & Cooper PA 785 823-6391
1000 E Cloud St Salina (67401) *(G-10457)*
Coleman American Moving Svcs 785 537-7284
5925 Corp Dr Section B Manhattan (66503) *(G-6592)*
Coleman American Mvg Svcs Inc (HQ) 913 631-1440
12905 Shwnee Mission Pkwy Shawnee Mission (66216) *(G-11246)*
Coleman American Mvg Svcs Inc 913 248-1766
12905 W 63rd St Shawnee (66216) *(G-10930)*
Coleman American Mvg Svcs Inc 785 537-7284
5925b Corporate Dr Manhattan (66503) *(G-6593)*
Coleman Company Inc 316 832-3015
17150 Mercury St Olathe (66061) *(G-7597)*
Coleman Company Inc 800 835-3278
3600 N Hydraulic St Wichita (67219) *(G-14053)*
Coleman Materials LLC 316 267-9812
3702 W Dora St Wichita (67213) *(G-14054)*
Coliseum Imging Ventures I LLC 913 338-3344
8000 College Blvd Overland Park (66210) *(G-8576)*
Collage Pk Fmly Care Ctr Olthe, Olathe *Also called College Park Fmly Care Ctr Inc (G-7598)*
Collateral RE Capitl LLC 913 677-2001
2001 Shawnee Mission Pkwy Mission Woods (66205) *(G-7150)*
Collateral Services Inc 913 680-1015
530 Delaware St Leavenworth (66048) *(G-5223)*
Collection Bureau Kansas Inc 785 228-3636
3615 Sw 29th St Bsmt 101 Topeka (66614) *(G-12486)*
Collection of Lawrence Inc 785 843-4210
303 W 11th St Lawrence (66044) *(G-4797)*
College Blvd Animal Hosp PA 913 469-5869
11733 College Blvd Shawnee Mission (66210) *(G-11247)*
College Body Shop 785 235-5628
1134 Sw Kent Pl Topeka (66604) *(G-12487)*
College Boulevard Animal Hosp, Shawnee Mission *Also called College Blvd Animal Hosp PA (G-11247)*
College Hill Cleaners Inc (PA) 316 683-3331
4618 E Central Ave # 100 Wichita (67208) *(G-14055)*
College Hill Ob/Gyn Inc (PA) 316 683-6766
3233 E 2nd St N Wichita (67208) *(G-14056)*
College Hl Nrsing Rhbilitation 316 685-9291
5005 E 21st St N Wichita (67208) *(G-14057)*
College Park Endoscopy Ctr LLC 913 385-4400
10787 Nall Ave Overland Park (66211) *(G-8577)*
College Park Family Care Ctr, Shawnee Mission *Also called College Park Fmly Care Ctr Inc (G-11248)*
College Park Fmly Care Ctr Inc 913 438-6700
12210 W 87th Street Pkwy Shawnee Mission (66215) *(G-11248)*
College Park Fmly Care Ctr Inc (PA) 913 469-5579
11725 W 112th St Shawnee Mission (66210) *(G-11249)*
College Park Fmly Care Ctr Inc 913 681-8866
15101 Glenwood Ave Shawnee Mission (66223) *(G-11250)*
College Park Fmly Care Ctr Inc 913 492-8686
12200 W 106th St Ste 235 Lenexa (66215) *(G-5769)*
College Park Fmly Care Ctr Inc 913 829-0505
1803 S Ridgeview Rd # 100 Olathe (66062) *(G-7598)*
College Park Univ Xing Fully 785 539-0500
2215 College Ave Manhattan (66502) *(G-6594)*
Colliers Intl Neng LLC 785 865-5100
805 New Hampshire St Lawrence (66044) *(G-4798)*
Collingwood Grain Inc 785 899-3636
17 Wyoming Goodland (67735) *(G-2466)*
Collins Bus Corporation (HQ) 620 662-9000
415 W 6th Ave Hutchinson (67505) *(G-3242)*
Collins Industries Inc (HQ) 620 663-5551
15 Compound Dr Hutchinson (67502) *(G-3243)*
Collis Craneworks Inc 913 764-1315
100 S Paniplus Dr Olathe (66061) *(G-7599)*
Collision Works LLC 316 788-5722
910 N Nelson Dr Derby (67037) *(G-1231)*
Collision Works LLC 316 265-6828
1427 E 1st St N Wichita (67214) *(G-14058)*
Colonel James Jabara Airport, Wichita *Also called Wichita Airport Authority (G-15970)*
Colonial Manor of Lansing, Lansing *Also called Beverly Enterprises-Kansas LLC (G-4669)*
Colorado Interstate Gas Co, Minneola *Also called Natural Gas Pipeline Amer LLC (G-7127)*
Colorado Interstate Gas Co LLC 620 355-7955
W Hwy 50 Lakin (67860) *(G-4648)*
Colorado Plaza Management 785 776-7994
420 Colorado St Apt 5o Manhattan (66502) *(G-6595)*
Colorado-Kansas Division, Olathe *Also called Atmos Energy Corporation (G-7540)*
Colortyme, Derby *Also called J & A Rentals Inc (G-1253)*
Colt Energy Inc 913 236-0016
6299 Nall Ave Ste 100 Shawnee Mission (66202) *(G-11251)*
Colt Investments Inc 913 385-5010
4121 W 83rd St Ste 120 Prairie Village (66208) *(G-10020)*
Colt Tech LLC 913 839-8198
14830 W 117th St Olathe (66062) *(G-7600)*
Colt, Mack V, Prairie Village *Also called Colt Investments Inc (G-10020)*
Columbia Construction Inc 913 247-3114
19965 W 162nd St Olathe (66062) *(G-7601)*
Columbia Elev Solutions Inc 620 442-2510
7702 W 5th Ave Winfield (67156) *(G-16123)*
Columbia Elevator Pdts Co Inc 888 858-1558
7702 Chester Fild Ind Par Winfield (67156) *(G-16124)*
Columbia Glass Window, Lindsborg *Also called Columbia Industries Inc (G-6396)*
Columbia HCA, Wichita *Also called HCA Hospital Svcs San Diego (G-14572)*

Columbia Industries Inc ... 785 227-3351
429 E Mcpherson St Lindsborg (67456) *(G-6396)*
Columbia Insurance Group, Salina *Also called Great Plains Mutual Insur Co (G-10521)*
Columbia Metal Products Co ... 620 365-3166
600 S State Fairgrnd & Ri Iola (66749) *(G-3594)*
Columbia Sportswear, Overland Park *Also called Outdoor Custom Sportswear LLC (G-9116)*
Columbian Tech Tank, Parsons *Also called Tank Wind-Down Corp (G-9745)*
Columbus Clinic, Columbus *Also called Community Health Center of Sou (G-1069)*
Columbus Telephone Company (PA) ... 620 429-3132
224 S Kansas Ave Columbus (66725) *(G-1067)*
Colwich Financial Corp (PA) ... 316 796-1221
240 W Wichita Ave Colwich (67030) *(G-1092)*
Comanche Cnty Hosp Med Clinic ... 620 582-2144
202 S Frisco St Coldwater (67029) *(G-1052)*
Comanche County ... 620 582-2136
301 S Washington St Coldwater (67029) *(G-1053)*
Comanche County ... 620 582-2933
401 S Philadelphia St Coldwater (67029) *(G-1054)*
Comanche County ... 620 582-2144
202 S Frisco St Coldwater (67029) *(G-1055)*
Combat Brands LLC ... 913 689-2300
15850 W 108th St Lenexa (66219) *(G-5770)*
Comcare, Salina *Also called Occupational Hlth Partners LLC (G-10618)*
Comcare of Sedgwick County ... 316 660-1900
1720 E Morris St Ste 101 Wichita (67211) *(G-14059)*
Comcare of Sedgwick County ... 316 660-7550
4035 E Harry St Wichita (67218) *(G-14060)*
Comcare of Sedgwick County (PA) ... 316 660-7600
635 N Main St Wichita (67203) *(G-14061)*
Comcare of Sedgwick County ... 316 660-7700
1929 W 21st St N Wichita (67203) *(G-14062)*
Comcast Corporation ... 800 934-6489
772 N Ridgeview Rd Olathe (66061) *(G-7602)*
Comet 1 H R Cleaners Inc ... 620 626-8100
2361 N Kansas Ave Liberal (67901) *(G-6295)*
Comet Cleaners, Pittsburg *Also called Ryan D&M Inc (G-9930)*
Comforcare Senior Services ... 913 906-9880
12345 W 95th St Ste 215 Lenexa (66215) *(G-5771)*
Comforn Inn and Suites, Overland Park *Also called Gli LLC (G-8757)*
Comfort Care, Lenexa *Also called Choicecare LLC (G-5754)*
Comfort Care Homes Inc (PA) ... 316 685-3322
7701 E Kellogg Dr Ste 490 Wichita (67207) *(G-14063)*
Comfort Care Homes Kans Cy LLC ... 913 643-0111
3848 W 75th St Prairie Village (66208) *(G-10021)*
Comfort Contractors Inc ... 620 431-4780
215 N Lincoln Ave Chanute (66720) *(G-718)*
Comfort Inn, Junction City *Also called Payal Hotels LLC (G-3736)*
Comfort Inn, Ottawa *Also called Shriji Inc (G-8312)*
Comfort Inn, Wichita *Also called Tusar Inc (G-15817)*
Comfort Inn, Shawnee Mission *Also called Jrko LLC (G-11503)*
Comfort Inn, Garden City *Also called Schwartz Inc (G-2276)*
Comfort Inn, Goodland *Also called S & B Motels Inc (G-2484)*
Comfort Inn, Salina *Also called Summit Group of Salina KS LP (G-10718)*
Comfort Inn, Colby *Also called Woofter Woofter Stupka Inc (G-1050)*
Comfort Inn, Winfield *Also called Darco Inc (G-16138)*
Comfort Inn, Hays *Also called B & L Motels Inc (G-2753)*
Comfort Inn, Olathe *Also called Heart America Management LLC (G-7762)*
Comfort Inn ... 620 793-9000
911 Grant St Great Bend (67530) *(G-2544)*
Comfort Inn ... 316 744-7711
990 N Connolly Ct Park City (67219) *(G-9611)*
Comfort Inn & Suites ... 620 231-8800
4009 Parkview Dr Pittsburg (66762) *(G-9838)*
Comfort Inn and Suites ... 316 804-4866
1205 E 1st St Newton (67114) *(G-7331)*
Comfort Inn Kansas City ... 913 299-5555
234 N 78th St Kansas City (66112) *(G-3926)*
Comfort Inn Olathe, Olathe *Also called Shree Ram Investments of Pltte (G-8065)*
Comfort Keepers ... 785 215-8330
2611 Sw 17th St Ste 7 Topeka (66604) *(G-12488)*
Comfort Management Inc ... 620 442-5610
1705 N Summit St Arkansas City (67005) *(G-149)*
Comfort Suites, Wichita *Also called Ladiwalla Hospitality LLC (G-14911)*
Comfort Suites ... 620 672-9999
704 Allison Ln Pratt (67124) *(G-10102)*
Comfort Systems, Wichita *Also called TWC Services Inc (G-15820)*
Comfortcare Homes, Wichita *Also called Comfort Care Homes Inc (G-14063)*
Comm Solutions, Leawood *Also called Communication Cable Company (G-5356)*
Comm Tronix, Wichita *Also called Harlan Hermanson (G-14560)*
Commanche County Med Clinic, Coldwater *Also called Comanche County (G-1053)*
Command Alkon Incorporated ... 913 384-0880
12351 W 96th Ter Ste 300 Lenexa (66215) *(G-5772)*
Command and General Staff ... 913 651-0624
100 Stimson Ave Ste 1149 Fort Leavenworth (66027) *(G-1936)*
Commerce Bank, Hays *Also called Cbi-Kansas Inc (G-2766)*
Commerce Bank ... 620 429-2515
137 W Maple St Columbus (66725) *(G-1068)*
Commerce Bank ... 816 234-2000
4020 Rainbow Blvd Kansas City (66103) *(G-3927)*
Commerce Bank ... 620 276-5600
1111 Fleming St Garden City (67846) *(G-2129)*
Commerce Bank ... 316 261-4795
1845 Fairmount St Wichita (67260) *(G-14064)*
Commerce Bank ... 913 381-2386
9501 Antioch Rd Overland Park (66212) *(G-8578)*
Commerce Bank ... 816 234-2000
4050 W 83rd St Shawnee Mission (66208) *(G-11252)*
Commerce Bank ... 316 321-1250
100 N Main St El Dorado (67042) *(G-1546)*
Commerce Bank ... 316 261-4927
6424 E 13th St N Wichita (67206) *(G-14065)*
Commerce Bank ... 785 625-6542
2200 Vine St Hays (67601) *(G-2773)*
Commerce Bank ... 785 865-4799
955 Iowa St Lawrence (66044) *(G-4799)*
Commerce Bank ... 316 261-4700
1551 N Waterfront Pkwy # 200 Wichita (67206) *(G-14066)*
Commerce Bank ... 785 532-3500
727 Point Ave Manhattan (66502) *(G-6596)*
Commerce Bank ... 316 261-5590
1250 S Woodlawn Blvd Wichita (67218) *(G-14067)*
Commerce Bank ... 816 234-2000
15910 S Mur Len Rd Olathe (66062) *(G-7603)*
Commerce Bank ... 913 682-8282
2830 S 4th St Leavenworth (66048) *(G-5224)*
Commerce Bank ... 913 888-0700
8700 Monrovia St Ste 100 Lenexa (66215) *(G-5773)*
Commerce Bank ... 816 234-2000
1015 W 23rd St Lawrence (66046) *(G-4800)*
Commerce Bank ... 816 234-2000
11405 Nall Ave Leawood (66211) *(G-5355)*
Commerce Bank ... 785 587-1696
2740 Claflin Rd Manhattan (66502) *(G-6597)*
Commerce Bank ... 816 234-2000
11900 S Strang Line Rd Olathe (66062) *(G-7604)*
Commerce Bank ... 816 234-2000
12280 W 135th St Overland Park (66221) *(G-8579)*
Commerce Bank ... 816 234-2000
11000 Shwnee Mission Pkwy Shawnee (66203) *(G-10931)*
Commerce Bank ... 816 234-2000
21800 Midland Dr Shawnee (66218) *(G-10932)*
Commerce Bank ... 816 234-2000
1321 Oread Ave Lawrence (66045) *(G-4801)*
Commerce Bank ... 816 234-2000
4006 W 83rd St Shawnee Mission (66208) *(G-11253)*
Commerce Bank ... 620 231-8400
100 S Broadway St Pittsburg (66762) *(G-9839)*
Commerce Bank ... 816 234-2000
1906 W 43rd Ave Kansas City (66103) *(G-3928)*
Commerce Bank ... 785 537-1234
727 Poyntz Ave Ste 100 Manhattan (66502) *(G-6598)*
Commerce Bank & Trust, Emporia *Also called Cbi-Kansas Inc (G-1718)*
Commerce Construction Svcs Inc ... 316 262-0547
2225 Southwest Blvd Wichita (67213) *(G-14068)*
Commercial Bank (HQ) ... 620 423-0770
1901 Main St Parsons (67357) *(G-9674)*
Commercial Bank ... 620 423-0770
1830 Parsons Plz Parsons (67357) *(G-9675)*
Commercial Bank ... 620 423-0750
121 Peter Pan Rd Independence (67301) *(G-3506)*
Commercial Bank ... 620 431-3200
1315 S Santa Fe Ave Chanute (66720) *(G-719)*
Commercial Builders Inc ... 785 625-6272
2717 Canal Blvd Ste I Hays (67601) *(G-2774)*
Commercial Capital Company LLC ... 913 341-0053
8215 Melrose Dr Lenexa (66214) *(G-5774)*
Commercial Concepts and Furn, Shawnee *Also called Moorekc Enterprises LLC (G-11000)*
Commercial Floors ... 913 583-3525
9055 Hillview Dr De Soto (66018) *(G-1197)*
Commercial Fltr Svc Knsas Cty ... 913 384-5858
1946 Foxridge Dr Kansas City (66106) *(G-3929)*
Commercial Hotel Management Co ... 913 642-0160
11944 W 95th St Lenexa (66215) *(G-5775)*
Commercial Landscapers Inc ... 913 721-5455
10800 Donahoo Rd Kansas City (66109) *(G-3930)*
Commercial Lawn MGT Wchita Inc ... 316 688-0722
3215 E 9th St N Wichita (67208) *(G-14069)*
Commercial Management Company (PA) ... 785 234-2882
6220 Sw 29th St Ste 200 Topeka (66614) *(G-12489)*
Commercial Mechanical Inc Kans ... 316 262-1230
1655 N Wabash Ave Wichita (67214) *(G-14070)*
Commercial Metals Company ... 620 331-1710
501 S 20th St Independence (67301) *(G-3507)*
Commercial Property Services ... 316 688-5200
7707 E Osie St Ste 406 Wichita (67207) *(G-14071)*

ALPHABETIC

Commercial RE Women Netwrk...785 832-1808
1201 Wakarusa Dr Ste D1 Lawrence (66049) ***(G-4802)***
Commercial Real Estate News...913 345-2378
10870 Benson Dr Ste 2160 Overland Park (66210) ***(G-8580)***
Commercial Rofg Spcialists LLC...316 304-1423
2717 N Lake Ridge St Wichita (67205) ***(G-14072)***
Commercial Sign Company, Colby *Also called Bandy Enterprises Inc* ***(G-988)***
Commercial Sign Company Hay...785 625-1765
720 E 7th St Hays (67601) ***(G-2775)***
Commercial Trade Services LLC...316 721-5432
510 E 46th St S Wichita (67216) ***(G-14073)***
Commercl-Ndstrial Ele Cont Inc...316 263-1291
819 E Indianapolis St Wichita (67211) ***(G-14074)***
Commtech Inc...316 636-1131
9011 E 37th St N Wichita (67226) ***(G-14075)***
Communication Cable Company (HQ)...610 644-5155
6130 Sprint Pkwy Ste 400 Leawood (66211) ***(G-5356)***
Communication Link LLC...913 681-5400
16309 W 108th Cir Lenexa (66219) ***(G-5776)***
Communications Tech Assoc (PA)...316 267-5016
2007 S Hydraulic St Wichita (67211) ***(G-14076)***
Communities In School...316 973-5110
412 S Main St Ste 212 Wichita (67202) ***(G-14077)***
Community Action Inc...785 235-9561
1000 Se Hancock St Topeka (66607) ***(G-12490)***
Community America Credit Union, Olathe *Also called Communityamerica Credit Union* ***(G-7605)***
Community Bank...620 624-6898
2320 N Kansas Ave Liberal (67901) ***(G-6296)***
Community Bank (PA)...785 440-4400
5431 Sw 29th St Ste 100 Topeka (66614) ***(G-12491)***
Community Bank and Trust...620 783-1395
215 E 7th St Galena (66739) ***(G-2072)***
Community Bank Wichita Inc (PA)...316 634-1600
11330 E 21st St N Wichita (67206) ***(G-14078)***
Community Broadcasting Inc...913 642-7770
10550 Barkley St Overland Park (66212) ***(G-8581)***
Community Care Connection, Fort Scott *Also called Medicalodges Inc* ***(G-1984)***
Community Care Inc...785 455-3522
310 Strand St Clifton (66937) ***(G-900)***
Community Care Netwrk Kans Inc...785 233-8483
700 Sw Jackson St Ste 600 Topeka (66603) ***(G-12492)***
Community Child Care Center...620 421-6550
2601 Gabriel Ave Parsons (67357) ***(G-9676)***
Community Childrens Center Inc...785 842-2515
925 Vermont St Lawrence (66044) ***(G-4803)***
Community Day Care Center 1...620 275-5757
505 College Dr Garden City (67846) ***(G-2130)***
Community First National Bank (HQ)...785 323-1111
215 S Seth Child Rd Manhattan (66502) ***(G-6599)***
Community Fndtion Sthwest Kans...620 225-0959
208 W Wyatt Earp Blvd Dodge City (67801) ***(G-1326)***
Community Foundation of Ellis...785 726-2660
820 Washington St Ellis (67637) ***(G-1641)***
Community Gates SEC Solutions, Olathe *Also called Wilbur Inc* ***(G-8154)***
Community Health Center of Sou...620 231-6788
924 N Broadway St Pittsburg (66762) ***(G-9840)***
Community Health Center of Sou...620 429-2101
120 W Pine St Columbus (66725) ***(G-1069)***
Community Health Center of Sou...620 856-2900
2990 Military Ave Baxter Springs (66713) ***(G-403)***
Community Health System, Onaga *Also called Community Healthcare Sys Inc* ***(G-8172)***
Community Healthcare Sys Inc...785 364-3205
1603 W 4th St Holton (66436) ***(G-3086)***
Community Healthcare Sys Inc...785 889-4241
120 W 8th St Onaga (66521) ***(G-8172)***
Community Healthcare Sys Inc (PA)...785 889-4274
120 W 8th St Onaga (66521) ***(G-8173)***
Community Healthcare Sys Inc...785 437-3407
206 S Grand Ave Saint Marys (66536) ***(G-10360)***
Community Healthcare Sys Inc...785 437-3734
206 S Grand Ave Saint Marys (66536) ***(G-10361)***
Community Hlth Ctr In Cwley CN...620 221-3350
221 W 8th Ave Winfield (67156) ***(G-16125)***
Community Hlth Ctr Sthast Kans (PA)...620 231-9873
3011 N Michigan St Pittsburg (66762) ***(G-9841)***
Community Hospital Onaga, Saint Marys *Also called Community Healthcare Sys Inc* ***(G-10360)***
Community Hsing Wyandotte Cnty...913 342-7580
2 S 14th St Kansas City (66102) ***(G-3931)***
Community Living Opportunities...913 341-9316
6900 W 80th St Overland Park (66204) ***(G-8582)***
Community Living Serv...620 227-8803
1100 E Wyatt Earp Blvd Dodge City (67801) ***(G-1327)***
Community Lving Opprtnties Inc...913 499-8894
7725 W 87th St Overland Park (66212) ***(G-8583)***
Community Lving Opprtnties Inc...785 979-1889
2084 N 600 Rd Unit B Baldwin City (66006) ***(G-357)***
Community Lving Opprtnties Inc (PA)...913 341-9316
11627 W 79th St Lenexa (66214) ***(G-5777)***
Community Lving Opprtnties Inc...785 865-5520
2113 Delaware St Lawrence (66046) ***(G-4804)***
Community Lving Opprtnties Inc...785 832-2332
1121 Monterey Way Lawrence (66049) ***(G-4805)***
Community Lving Opprtnties Inc...785 843-7072
1311 E 21st Ter Ste 4 Lawrence (66046) ***(G-4806)***
Community Memorial Healthcare...785 562-4062
805 Broadway Marysville (66508) ***(G-6883)***
Community Memorial Healthcare (PA)...785 562-2311
708 N 18th St Marysville (66508) ***(G-6884)***
Community Memorial Healthcare...785 363-7202
607 Lincoln St Blue Rapids (66411) ***(G-535)***
Community Memorial Healthcare...785 562-3942
1902 May St Marysville (66508) ***(G-6885)***
Community Memorial Hospital...785 562-2311
1172 11th Rd Marysville (66508) ***(G-6886)***
Community Mntl Hlth Ctr Crwfd...620 724-8806
810 Cedar St Girard (66743) ***(G-2397)***
Community Nat Bnk of El Dorado...316 320-2265
301 N Main St El Dorado (67042) ***(G-1547)***
Community National Bank...913 369-0100
231 N Main St Tonganoxie (66086) ***(G-12256)***
Community National Bank...620 423-0314
330 N 16th St Parsons (67357) ***(G-9677)***
Community National Bank...620 235-1345
401 E Centennial Dr Pittsburg (66762) ***(G-9842)***
Community National Bank...316 775-6068
645 State St Augusta (67010) ***(G-314)***
Community National Bank (PA)...785 336-6143
210 Main St Seneca (66538) ***(G-10859)***
Community National Bank...913 724-9901
15718 Pinehurst Dr Basehor (66007) ***(G-373)***
Community National Bank...620 431-2265
115 E 1st St Chanute (66720) ***(G-720)***
Community National Bank...620 724-4446
606 W Saint John St Girard (66743) ***(G-2398)***
Community National Bank...620 922-3294
100 Delware Ave Edna (67342) ***(G-1492)***
Community National Bank...620 325-2900
102 N 4th St Neodesha (66757) ***(G-7237)***
Community National Bank...620 221-1400
1112 Main St Winfield (67156) ***(G-16126)***
Community National Bank & Tr...620 365-6000
120 E Madison Ave Iola (66749) ***(G-3595)***
Community National Bank & Tr...316 283-0059
127 N Main St Newton (67114) ***(G-7332)***
Community National Bank & Tr...620 336-2145
333 W Main St Cherryvale (67335) ***(G-803)***
Community National Bank & Tr (HQ)...620 431-2265
14 N Lincoln Ave Chanute (66720) ***(G-721)***
Community National Mortgage Co, Tonganoxie *Also called Community National Bank* ***(G-12256)***
Community Physicians Clinic, Marysville *Also called Community Memorial Healthcare* ***(G-6885)***
Community Physicians Clinic...785 562-3942
1902 May St Marysville (66508) ***(G-6887)***
Community State Bank (PA)...620 251-1313
1414 W 11th St Coffeyville (67337) ***(G-928)***
Community Support Program, Parsons *Also called Labette Center For Mental Inc* ***(G-9702)***
Community Works Inc...913 789-9900
7819 Conser Pl Shawnee Mission (66204) ***(G-11254)***
Communityamerica Credit Union (PA)...913 905-7000
9777 Ridge Dr Lenexa (66219) ***(G-5778)***
Communityamerica Credit Union...913 397-6600
13590 S Blackbob Rd Olathe (66062) ***(G-7605)***
Communityamerica Credit Union...785 232-6900
1129 S Kansas Ave Ste B Topeka (66612) ***(G-12493)***
Communityworks Inc...913 789-9900
7819 Conser Pl Overland Park (66204) ***(G-8584)***
Companion Animal Clinic...785 271-7387
3335 Sw Fairlawn Rd Topeka (66614) ***(G-12494)***
Companion Animal Hospital...316 722-1004
10555 W Maple St Wichita (67209) ***(G-14079)***
Companion Industries Inc...620 345-3277
500 S Drucilla Ave Moundridge (67107) ***(G-7180)***
Company Business Intl Sarl...913 286-9771
988 N Findley St Olathe (66061) ***(G-7606)***
Company Commercial Sign, Hays *Also called Commercial Sign Company Hay* ***(G-2775)***
Company Kitchen LLC...913 384-4900
8500 Shawnee Mission Pkwy Shawnee Mission (66202) ***(G-11255)***
Compass Behavioral Health (PA)...620 276-6470
531 Campus View St Garden City (67846) ***(G-2131)***
Compass Behavioral Health...620 275-0625
1145 E Kansas Plz Garden City (67846) ***(G-2132)***
Compass Behavioral Health...620 872-5338
204 S College St Scott City (67871) ***(G-10808)***
Compass Behavioral Health...620 227-5040
3000 N 14th Ave Dodge City (67801) ***(G-1328)***

Compass Behavioral Health 620 227-8566
Hwy 50 Byp Dodge City (67801) ***(G-1329)***
Compass Controls Mfg Inc 913 213-5748
14343 W 100th St Lenexa (66215) ***(G-5779)***
Compass Fincl Resources LLC 913 747-2000
13095 S Mur Len Rd # 100 Olathe (66062) ***(G-7607)***
Compass Minerals 913 344-9200
9900 W 109th St Ste 600 Overland Park (66210) ***(G-8585)***
Compass Minerals America Inc 913 344-9100
9900 W 109th St Ste 100 Overland Park (66210) ***(G-8586)***
Compass Minerals America Inc (HQ) 913 344-9100
9900 W 109th St Ste 600 Overland Park (66210) ***(G-8587)***
Compass Minerals America Inc 620 257-2324
1662 Avenue N Lyons (67554) ***(G-6480)***
Compass Minerals Group Inc 913 344-9100
9900 W 109th St Ste 600 Overland Park (66210) ***(G-8588)***
Compass Minerals Intl Inc (PA) 913 344-9200
9900 W 109th St Ste 100 Overland Park (66210) ***(G-8589)***
Compassionate Care Community 785 783-8785
6118 Sw 38th St Topeka (66610) ***(G-12495)***
Compassionate Family Care LLC 913 744-4300
15900 College Blvd # 100 Lenexa (66219) ***(G-5780)***
Compcare 785 823-7470
520 S Santa Fe Ave # 300 Salina (67401) ***(G-10458)***
Compdata Surveys & Consulting, Olathe *Also called Dolan Technologies Corporation* ***(G-7658)***
Compeer of Prairie View, Hillsboro *Also called Prairie View Inc* ***(G-3055)***
Complete LLC 913 238-0206
8666 W 96th St Overland Park (66212) ***(G-8590)***
Complete Automotive LLC 620 245-0600
1306 N Us Highway 81 Byp McPherson (67460) ***(G-6951)***
Complete Dental Care 913 469-5646
11150 S Pflumm Rd Olathe (66215) ***(G-7608)***
Complete Home Health Care Inc 316 260-5012
400 N Woodlawn St Ste 15 Wichita (67208) ***(G-14080)***
Complete Landscaping Systems 316 832-0061
1347 S Washington Ave Wichita (67211) ***(G-14081)***
Complete Music Disc Jockey Svc, Leawood *Also called Complete Music Inc* ***(G-5357)***
Complete Music Inc 913 432-1111
6363 W 110th St Leawood (66211) ***(G-5357)***
Complete Outdoors Inc 785 565-4077
600 Zeandale Rd Manhattan (66502) ***(G-6600)***
Complete Video Production 913 888-2383
12209 W 88th St Shawnee Mission (66215) ***(G-11256)***
Complex Property Advisers Corp 913 498-0790
14400 Metcalf Ave Overland Park (66223) ***(G-8591)***
Compone Services Ltd 785 267-9196
2348 Sw Topeka Blvd # 200 Topeka (66611) ***(G-12496)***
Component Fabricators Inc 785 776-5081
5107 Murray Rd Manhattan (66503) ***(G-6601)***
Comprehensive Fincl Plg Svcs, Lenexa *Also called Barber Financial Group Inc* ***(G-5686)***
Comprehensive Logistics Co Inc 913 371-0770
230 Kindleberger Rd Kansas City (66115) ***(G-3932)***
Comprehensive Womens Care 913 643-0075
21624 Midland Dr Shawnee Mission (66218) ***(G-11257)***
Compressed Gases Inc 316 838-3222
602 E 29th St N Wichita (67219) ***(G-14082)***
Compresults LLC 913 310-9800
4330 Shawnee Mission Pkwy # 221 Fairway (66205) ***(G-1906)***
Comptech Group LLC 913 341-7600
3853 W 95th St Overland Park (66206) ***(G-8592)***
Comptech Group The, Overland Park *Also called Comptech Group LLC* ***(G-8592)***
Compton Construction Svcs LLC 316 262-8885
1802 N Washington Ave Wichita (67214) ***(G-14083)***
Computech Service of Kansas 785 266-2585
3301 S Kansas Ave Ste B Topeka (66611) ***(G-12497)***
Computer Cable Connection Inc 913 390-5141
11227 Strang Line Rd Lenexa (66215) ***(G-5781)***
Computer Distribution Corp 785 354-1086
524 Ne Gordon St Topeka (66608) ***(G-12498)***
Computer Instruments Inc 913 307-8850
10591 Widmer Rd Lenexa (66215) ***(G-5782)***
Computer Sciences Corporation 913 469-8700
7701 College Blvd Ste 200 Overland Park (66210) ***(G-8593)***
Computer Training Systems, Wichita *Also called Comtrsys Inc* ***(G-14084)***
Computerwise Inc 408 389-8241
302 N Winchester St Olathe (66062) ***(G-7609)***
Computrzed Assssments Lrng LLC 785 856-1034
1202 E 23rd St Ste D Lawrence (66046) ***(G-4807)***
Comtrsys Inc 316 265-1585
200 W Douglas Ave Ste 230 Wichita (67202) ***(G-14084)***
Con-Way, Salina *Also called Xpo Logistics Freight Inc* ***(G-10774)***
Conant Construction LLC 620 408-6784
10562 Us Highway 50 Dodge City (67801) ***(G-1330)***
Concentra Medical Centers 913 894-6601
14809 W 95th St Lenexa (66215) ***(G-5783)***
Concept Machinery Inc 317 845-5588
6319 W 110th St Overland Park (66211) ***(G-8594)***
Concepts For Business LLC 913 888-8686
8343 Melrose Dr Shawnee Mission (66214) ***(G-11258)***
Concil Grove Publishing, Council Grove *Also called Council Grove Republican* ***(G-1161)***
Conco Inc 316 943-7111
3051 N Ohio St Wichita (67219) ***(G-14085)***
Concordia Technologies LLC 785 262-4066
1830 E 6th St Concordia (66901) ***(G-1108)***
Concordia Tractor Inc 785 632-3181
1181 18th Rd Clay Center (67432) ***(G-856)***
Concordia Tractor Inc 785 263-3051
1300 S Buckeye Ave Abilene (67410) ***(G-20)***
Concordnce Hlthcare Sltons LLC 316 945-6941
1970 S West St Ste 360 Wichita (67213) ***(G-14086)***
Concrete Enterprises Inc (HQ) 620 662-1219
2430 E 1st Ave Hutchinson (67501) ***(G-3244)***
Concrete Enterprises Inc 620 532-1165
319 E Sherman St Kingman (67068) ***(G-4587)***
Concrete Express Inc 805 643-2992
11137 S Crestone St Olathe (66061) ***(G-7610)***
Concrete Inc 785 594-4838
791 E 1500 Rd Lawrence (66046) ***(G-4808)***
Concrete Products Co Inc (PA) 620 947-5921
209 S Cedar St Hillsboro (67063) ***(G-3045)***
Concrete Pumping Service Inc 316 612-8515
3131 N Hillside Ave Wichita (67219) ***(G-14087)***
Concrete Service Co Inc (PA) 620 792-2558
221 Baker Ave Great Bend (67530) ***(G-2545)***
Concrete Service Co Inc 785 628-2100
1648 230th Ave Hays (67601) ***(G-2776)***
Concrete Unlimited Cnstr Inc 785 232-8636
3160 Se 21st St Topeka (66607) ***(G-12499)***
Concrete Unlimited Inc 785 232-8636
3160 Se 21st St Topeka (66607) ***(G-12500)***
Concrete Vaults Inc (PA) 316 283-3790
901 Sharps Dr Newton (67114) ***(G-7333)***
Concrete Vaults Inc 620 792-6687
559 B St Great Bend (67530) ***(G-2546)***
Condon National Bank (PA) 620 251-5500
814 Walnut St Coffeyville (67337) ***(G-929)***
Condor Hospitality Trust Inc 620 232-1881
3108 N Broadway St Pittsburg (66762) ***(G-9843)***
Coneqtec Corp (PA) 316 943-8889
3348 S Hoover Rd Wichita (67215) ***(G-14088)***
Confab Inc 316 321-5358
2200 W 6th Ave El Dorado (67042) ***(G-1548)***
Confederated Builders Supply 316 788-3913
503 N Buckner St Derby (67037) ***(G-1232)***
Conference Center, Junction City *Also called Kansas 4-H Foundation Inc* ***(G-3712)***
Congregational Home 785 274-3350
1205 Sw 29th St Topeka (66611) ***(G-12501)***
Conklin Fangman Investment Co (PA) 620 662-4467
1400 E 11th Ave Hutchinson (67501) ***(G-3245)***
Conklin Plumbing LLC 785 806-5827
512 Main St Osage City (66523) ***(G-8182)***
Connection At Lawrence 785 842-3336
3100 Ousdahl Rd Lawrence (66046) ***(G-4809)***
Connex International Inc 785 749-9500
1800 E 23rd St Lawrence (66046) ***(G-4810)***
Connoisseur Media LLC 316 558-8800
1938 N Woodlawn St # 150 Wichita (67208) ***(G-14089)***
Conoco, Bendena *Also called Consumer Oil Company Inc* ***(G-511)***
Conopco Inc 913 782-7171
27080 W 159th St New Century (66031) ***(G-7274)***
Conrad Fire Equipment Inc 913 780-5521
887 N Jan Mar Ct Olathe (66061) ***(G-7611)***
Conrad Machine Inc 620 231-9458
1627 E 27th Ter Pittsburg (66762) ***(G-9844)***
Conrady Western Inc (PA) 620 842-5137
501 W Main St Anthony (67003) ***(G-124)***
Conrady Western Inc 316 943-4261
2218 S West St Wichita (67213) ***(G-14090)***
CONSERVATION TRUST, Manhattan *Also called Sunset Zoological Pk Wildlife* ***(G-6818)***
Consociates Group LLC 316 321-7500
116 W Pine Ave Ste 105 El Dorado (67042) ***(G-1549)***
Consoldated Rur Wtr District 4 ....785 286-1729
1741 Ne 46th St Topeka (66617) ***(G-12502)***
Consolidated Container Co LP 913 888-9494
11725 W 85th St Shawnee Mission (66214) ***(G-11259)***
Consolidated Elec Distrs Inc 785 823-7161
1103 W South St Salina (67401) ***(G-10459)***
Consolidated Elec Distrs Inc 316 267-5311
411 S Washington Ave Wichita (67202) ***(G-14091)***
Consolidated Elec Distrs Inc 316 262-3541
1134 N Washington Ave Wichita (67214) ***(G-14092)***
Consolidated Industrial Svcs, Ottawa *Also called Qes Pressure Pumping LLC* ***(G-8307)***
Consolidated Mailing Corp (PA) 913 262-4400
16740 259th St Tonganoxie (66086) ***(G-12257)***
Consolidated Oil Well Ser 620 431-9217
1322 S Grant Ave Chanute (66720) ***(G-722)***

ALPHABETIC

Consolidated Prtg & Sty Co Inc (PA) 785 825-5426
319 S 5th St Salina (67401) ***(G-10460)***
Consortium Inc 785 232-1196
2121 Sw Chelsea Dr Topeka (66614) ***(G-12503)***
Conspec Inc 316 832-0828
4880 N Old Lawrence Rd Park City (67219) ***(G-9612)***
Conspec Marketing and Mfg Co 913 287-1700
636 S 66th Ter Kansas City (66111) ***(G-3933)***
Construction & Gen Labor 1290 (PA) 913 432-1903
2600 Merriam Ln Kansas City (66106) ***(G-3934)***
Construction Design Inc (PA) 913 287-0334
5621 Kansas Ave Kansas City (66106) ***(G-3935)***
Construction MGT Svcs Inc 913 231-5736
18901 W 158th St Olathe (66062) ***(G-7612)***
Construction Svcs Bryant Inc 316 262-1010
2748 N North Shore Ct Wichita (67205) ***(G-14093)***
Construction Systems Inc 913 208-6401
14611 W 62nd St Shawnee Mission (66216) ***(G-11260)***
Construction Technologies LLC 913 671-3440
6800 W 64th St Shawnee Mission (66202) ***(G-11261)***
Constructive Engrg Design 913 341-3300
9400 Reeds Rd Ste 200 Overland Park (66207) ***(G-8595)***
Constructive Playthings, Leawood *Also called U S Toy Co Inc* ***(G-5587)***
Consultants In Neurology, Lenexa *Also called Dr Vernon Rowe* ***(G-5824)***
Consultants In Neurology PA 913 894-1500
8550 Marshall Dr Ste 100 Shawnee Mission (66214) ***(G-11262)***
Consulting Engineers, Olathe *Also called Ponzeryoungquist PA* ***(G-7992)***
Consumer Oil Company Inc (PA) 785 988-4459
209 Commercial St Bendena (66008) ***(G-511)***
Container Services Inc 620 947-2664
220 Santa Fe St Hillsboro (67063) ***(G-3046)***
Containercraft Inc 620 663-1168
2507 E 14th Ave Hutchinson (67501) ***(G-3246)***
Contech, Goddard *Also called Converting Technologies Inc* ***(G-2433)***
Contech Engnered Solutions LLC 913 294-2131
702 N Pearl St Paola (66071) ***(G-9549)***
Contech Engnered Solutions LLC 785 234-1000
2707 Ne Seward Ave Topeka (66616) ***(G-12504)***
Contemerary Cleaning Services, Shawnee Mission *Also called Lulu Mimi Hsclners Extrrdnaire* ***(G-11582)***
Contemporary Womens Centre 913 345-2322
8675 College Blvd Ste 100 Overland Park (66210) ***(G-8596)***
Contemprary Communications Inc 316 265-0879
630 N Pennsylvania Ave Wichita (67214) ***(G-14094)***
Contemprary Hsing Altrntves of (HQ) 785 271-9594
1800 Sw Fairmont Rd Topeka (66604) ***(G-12505)***
Continental Agra Grain Eqp, Newton *Also called Continental-Agra Equip Inc* ***(G-7334)***
Continental American Corp 316 321-4551
2400 Pioneer Dr El Dorado (67042) ***(G-1550)***
Continental Analytical Svcs 785 827-1273
525 N 8th St Salina (67401) ***(G-10461)***
Continental Cast Stone LLC 800 989-7866
22001 W 83rd St Shawnee (66227) ***(G-10933)***
Continental Coal Inc 913 491-1717
10801 Mastin St Ste 920 Shawnee Mission (66210) ***(G-11263)***
Continental Components LLC 816 547-8325
15941 W 108th St Lenexa (66219) ***(G-5784)***
Continental Consulting Inc 913 642-6642
9000 State Line Rd Leawood (66206) ***(G-5358)***
Continental Equipment Company (PA) 913 845-2148
315 N Village St Tonganoxie (66086) ***(G-12258)***
Continental Plastic Container, Shawnee Mission *Also called Consolidated Container Co LP* ***(G-11259)***
Continental Pools Inc 913 856-2841
805 E Warren St Gardner (66030) ***(G-2334)***
Continental-Agra Equip Inc 316 283-9602
1400 S Spencer Rd Newton (67114) ***(G-7334)***
Continua Home Health LLC 913 905-0255
13002 State Line Rd Leawood (66209) ***(G-5359)***
Continua Hospice, Leawood *Also called Missouri Hospice Holdings LLC* ***(G-5487)***
Continuity Operation Plg LLC (PA) 913 227-0660
17501 W 98th St Spc 2632 Lenexa (66219) ***(G-5785)***
Contourmd Marketing Group LLC 913 541-9200
15550 W 109th St Lenexa (66219) ***(G-5786)***
Contract Services Inc 785 239-9069
7920 Apennines Dr Fort Riley (66442) ***(G-1946)***
Contract Trailer Service Inc 913 281-2589
47 Kansas Ave Kansas City (66105) ***(G-3936)***
Contractors Engineer Inc 620 568-2391
7563 Quinter Dr Neodesha (66757) ***(G-7238)***
Contractors Traffic Protection, Kansas City *Also called Traftec Inc* ***(G-4472)***
Contractors Waterproofing, Maize *Also called Michael Downey* ***(G-6517)***
Control Components Inc 620 221-2343
1108 Industrial Blvd Winfield (67156) ***(G-16127)***
Control Systems Intl Inc (HQ) 913 599-5010
8040 Nieman Rd Shawnee Mission (66214) ***(G-11264)***
Control Vision Corporation 620 231-5816
1902 E 27th Ter Pittsburg (66762) ***(G-9845)***
Controlvision.com, Pittsburg *Also called Control Vision Corporation* ***(G-9845)***
Converg Media LLC 913 871-0453
804 N Meadowbrook Dr Olathe (66062) ***(G-7613)***
Convergeone Inc 913 307-2300
12980 Foster St Ste 300 Overland Park (66213) ***(G-8597)***
Convergys Corporation 913 782-3333
400 N Rogers Rd Olathe (66062) ***(G-7614)***
Convergys Corporation 316 681-4800
4600 W Kellogg Dr Ste 106 Wichita (67209) ***(G-14095)***
Converting Technologies Inc 316 722-6907
1756 S 151st St W Goddard (67052) ***(G-2433)***
Convoy Equipment Leasing LLC (PA) 913 371-6500
333 N James St Kansas City (66118) ***(G-3937)***
Convoy Leasing Inc 913 371-6500
333 N James St Kansas City (66118) ***(G-3938)***
Conway Bank (PA) 620 456-2255
124 W Spring Ave Conway Springs (67031) ***(G-1137)***
Conway Bank N A 316 263-6767
121 E Kellogg St Wichita (67202) ***(G-14096)***
Cook Pump Company 620 251-0880
1400 W 12th St Coffeyville (67337) ***(G-930)***
Cook's Heating & AC, Wichita *Also called Bbh LLC* ***(G-13822)***
Cookbook Publishers Inc (PA) 913 689-3038
11633 W 83rd Ter Overland Park (66214) ***(G-8598)***
Cookbook Publishers Inc 913 706-6069
9900 Pflumm Rd Ste 17 Shawnee Mission (66215) ***(G-11265)***
Coomes Inc 785 543-2759
1697 E 250 Ln Phillipsburg (67661) ***(G-9781)***
Coomes Brothers Ltd 785 543-5896
1697 E 250 Ln Phillipsburg (67661) ***(G-9782)***
Coonrod & Assoc Cnstr Co Inc 316 942-8430
3550 S Hoover Rd Wichita (67215) ***(G-14097)***
Cooper Electronics Inc 913 782-0012
310 N Marion St Olathe (66061) ***(G-7615)***
Cooper Enterprises (PA) 620 225-4347
911 S 2nd Ave Dodge City (67801) ***(G-1331)***
Cooper Malone McClain Inc 316 685-5777
7701 E Kellogg Dr Ste 700 Wichita (67207) ***(G-14098)***
Cooper, John, Wichita *Also called Cooper Malone McClain Inc* ***(G-14098)***
Cooperative Elevator & Sup Co (PA) 620 873-2161
801 N Fowler St Meade (67864) ***(G-7047)***
Cooperative Elevator & Sup Co 620 873-2376
917 W Carthage St Meade (67864) ***(G-7048)***
Coopers, Topeka *Also called G Coopers Inc* ***(G-12630)***
Coopertive Cpon Rdemption Assn 913 384-3830
2809 W 47th St Westwood (66205) ***(G-13552)***
Coover Trucking Inc 620 244-3572
17670 180th Rd Erie (66733) ***(G-1858)***
Copa Motel, Kingman *Also called Bhakta LLC* ***(G-4583)***
Copart Kansas City Salv Pool, Kansas City *Also called Copart of Kansas Inc* ***(G-3939)***
Copart of Kansas Inc 913 287-6200
6211 Kansas Ave Kansas City (66111) ***(G-3939)***
Cope Plastics Inc 785 267-0552
1751 Sw 41st St Topeka (66609) ***(G-12506)***
Coperion K-Tron Salina Inc 785 825-1611
606 N Front St Salina (67401) ***(G-10462)***
Copy Center of Topeka Inc 785 233-6677
305 Se 17th St Ste C Topeka (66607) ***(G-12507)***
Copy Co Corporation 785 832-2679
540 Fireside Ct Lawrence (66049) ***(G-4811)***
Copy Co Corporation (PA) 785 823-2679
2346 Planet Ave Salina (67401) ***(G-10463)***
Copy Co of Lawrence, Lawrence *Also called Copy Co Corporation* ***(G-4811)***
Copy Express, Wichita *Also called Jdb Enterprises Inc* ***(G-14752)***
Copy Products Inc 316 315-0102
8200 E 34th Cir N # 1801 Wichita (67226) ***(G-14099)***
Copy Products Inc 620 365-7611
207 S Jefferson Ave Iola (66749) ***(G-3596)***
Copy Shop Inc 316 262-8200
1815 E Douglas Ave Wichita (67211) ***(G-14100)***
Copy Shoppe 785 232-0403
715 Se 8th Ave Topeka (66607) ***(G-12508)***
Copyrite Printing, Wichita *Also called Docuplex Inc* ***(G-14220)***
Corbin Bronze Limited 913 766-4012
1166 Southwest Blvd Kansas City (66103) ***(G-3940)***
Corbion America Holdings Inc 913 890-5500
7905 Quivira Rd Lenexa (66215) ***(G-5787)***
Corbion-Purac, Lenexa *Also called Purac America Inc* ***(G-6081)***
Corbys Hair Salon, Overland Park *Also called Hair Design Company* ***(G-8784)***
Core Carrier Corporation 913 621-3434
1020 Sunshine Rd Kansas City (66115) ***(G-3941)***
Core Cashless LLC 913 529-8200
14803 W 95th St Lenexa (66215) ***(G-5788)***
Corecivic Inc 913 727-3246
100 Highway Ter Leavenworth (66048) ***(G-5225)***
Corefirst Bank & Trust (HQ) 785 267-8900
3035 Sw Topeka Blvd Topeka (66611) ***(G-12509)***
Corefirst Bank & Trust 913 248-7000
7430 Switzer St Shawnee (66203) ***(G-10934)***

Corefirst Bank & Trust ... 785 286-5100
2841 Se Croco Rd Ste 2 Topeka (66605) ***(G-12510)***
Corefirst Bank & Trust ... 620 341-7420
1440 Industrial Rd Emporia (66801) ***(G-1725)***
Corefirst Bank & Trust ... 785 267-8900
1205 Sw 29th St Unit 2 Topeka (66611) ***(G-12511)***
Coreslab Structures Kansas Inc ... 913 287-5725
759 S 65th St Kansas City (66111) ***(G-3942)***
Corinth Scouts Inc ... 913 236-8920
5011 Neosho Ln Roeland Park (66205) ***(G-10221)***
Corinthian Nursery School, Wichita *Also called Pawnee Avenue Church of God* ***(G-15273)***
Cornejo & Sons LLC (HQ) ... 316 522-5100
2060 E Tulsa St Wichita (67216) ***(G-14101)***
Cornejo & Sons LLC ... 620 455-3720
1438 122nd Rd Oxford (67119) ***(G-9532)***
Cornejo & Sons LLC ... 620 231-8120
709 N Locust St Pittsburg (66762) ***(G-9846)***
Cornejo & Sons LLC ... 620 251-1690
206 N Linden St Coffeyville (67337) ***(G-931)***
Cornejo & Sons LLC ... 620 336-3534
Rural Route 1 Cherryvale (67335) ***(G-804)***
Cornerstone Ag LLC ... 785 462-3354
2148 County Road Q Colby (67701) ***(G-1000)***
Cornerstone Bank ... 913 239-8100
9120 W 135th St Ste 200 Overland Park (66221) ***(G-8599)***
Cornerstone Cnstr Svcs LLC ... 913 207-1751
106 S Janell Dr Olathe (66061) ***(G-7616)***
Cornerstone Day Care Preschool ... 620 257-5622
803 S Dinsmore Ave Lyons (67554) ***(G-6481)***
Cornerstone Endodontics, Leawood *Also called Michael J Randall* ***(G-5478)***
Cornerstone Financial LLC ... 316 630-0670
13111 E 21st St N Wichita (67230) ***(G-14102)***
Cornerstone Home Lending Inc ... 913 317-5626
9393 W 110th St Ste 250 Overland Park (66210) ***(G-8600)***
Cornerstone Rgnal Srveying LLC ... 620 331-6767
1921 N Penn Ave Independence (67301) ***(G-3508)***
Cornerstone Ridge Plaza ... 316 462-3636
3636 N Ridge Rd Ste 400 Wichita (67205) ***(G-14103)***
Cornwell & Scheriff ... 913 254-7600
201 E Loula St Ste 101 Olathe (66061) ***(G-7617)***
Coronado Inc (PA) ... 620 278-2161
128 S Broadway Ave Sterling (67579) ***(G-12115)***
Coronado Area Council Bsa (PA) ... 785 827-4461
644 S Ohio St Salina (67401) ***(G-10464)***
Corporate Document Service, Overland Park *Also called Cds Inc* ***(G-8532)***
Corporate East LLC ... 620 356-5010
1110 E Oklahoma St Ulysses (67880) ***(G-13290)***
Corporate Enterprise SEC Inc (PA) ... 913 422-0410
11900 W 87th Street Pkwy # 120 Lenexa (66215) ***(G-5789)***
Corporate Flooring Inc ... 913 859-9180
8018 Reeder St Shawnee Mission (66214) ***(G-11266)***
Corporate Hills LLC ... 316 651-0333
9100 E Corporate Hills Dr Wichita (67207) ***(G-14104)***
Corporate Solutions, Paola *Also called Stephanie Wilson* ***(G-9591)***
Corps of Engineers Fall River ... 620 658-4445
2453 Lake Rd Fall River (67047) ***(G-1926)***
Corrections Kansas Department ... 620 285-0300
1301 K264 Hwy Larned (67550) ***(G-4699)***
Corrections Kansas Department ... 913 727-3235
301 E Kansas St Lansing (66043) ***(G-4672)***
Corrections Kansas Department ... 620 792-3549
1806 12th St Great Bend (67530) ***(G-2547)***
Corrections Kansas Department ... 316 321-7284
1737 Se Hwy 54 El Dorado (67042) ***(G-1551)***
Corrections Kansas Department ... 620 341-3294
430 Commercial St Bsmnt Emporia (66801) ***(G-1726)***
Corridor Group Holdings LLC (PA) ... 913 362-0600
6405 Metcalf Ave Ste 108 Shawnee Mission (66202) ***(G-11267)***
Corridor Group, The, Shawnee Mission *Also called Kdjm Consulting Inc* ***(G-11527)***
Corrpro Companies Inc ... 620 544-4411
839 E 11th St Hugoton (67951) ***(G-3153)***
Cort Business Services Corp ... 913 888-0100
9111 Quivira Rd Overland Park (66215) ***(G-8601)***
Cort Furniture Rental, Overland Park *Also called Cort Business Services Corp* ***(G-8601)***
Corvel Corporation ... 913 253-7200
9401 Indian Creek Pkwy # 400 Overland Park (66210) ***(G-8602)***
Corvias Military Living LLC ... 785 717-2200
2460 G St Ste A Fort Riley (66442) ***(G-1947)***
Cosentino Group Inc ... 913 749-1500
3901 W 83rd St Prairie Village (66208) ***(G-10022)***
Cosentino Group II Inc ... 913 422-2130
22210 W 66th St Shawnee (66226) ***(G-10935)***
Cosentino's Food Stores, Prairie Village *Also called Cosentino Group Inc* ***(G-10022)***
Cosmic Pet LLC (PA) ... 316 941-1100
1315 W Macarthur Rd Wichita (67217) ***(G-14105)***
Cosmosphere Inc (PA) ... 620 662-2305
1100 N Plum St Hutchinson (67501) ***(G-3247)***
Cotillion Ballroom, The, Wichita *Also called Entertainment Enterprises Inc* ***(G-14292)***
Cottage Care, Prairie Village *Also called Daka Inc* ***(G-10025)***
Cottage House Hotel and Motel ... 620 767-6828
25 N Neosho St Council Grove (66846) ***(G-1159)***
Cottagecare Inc (PA) ... 913 469-8778
6323 W 110th St Overland Park (66211) ***(G-8603)***
Cotton O'Neil Wamego, Wamego *Also called Stormont-Vail Healthcare Inc* ***(G-13442)***
Cotton Oneil Clinic Endoscopy ... 785 270-4850
720 Sw Lane St Topeka (66606) ***(G-12512)***
Cotton ONeil Osage City ... 785 528-3161
131 W Market St Ste B Osage City (66523) ***(G-8183)***
Cotton-Neil Clinic At Urish Rd, Topeka *Also called Stormont-Vail Healthcare Inc* ***(G-13113)***
Cotton-Neil Clnic Revocable Tr ... 785 354-9591
1500 Sw 10th Ave Topeka (66604) ***(G-12513)***
Cotton-Neil Digestive Hlth Ctr, Topeka *Also called Stormont-Vail Healthcare Inc* ***(G-13105)***
Cotton-O'neil Clinicrossville, Rossville *Also called Stormont-Vail Healthcare Inc* ***(G-10256)***
Cotton-Oneil Cardiot and Vascu, Topeka *Also called Stormont-Vail Healthcare Inc* ***(G-13106)***
Cotton-Oneil Clinicoskaloosa, Oskaloosa *Also called Stormont-Vail Healthcare Inc* ***(G-8230)***
Cottonwood Group The, Overland Park *Also called Cbiz Inc* ***(G-8528)***
Cottonwood Incorporated ... 785 842-0550
2801 W 31st St Lawrence (66047) ***(G-4812)***
Cottonwood Inn ... 785 543-2125
1200 State St Phillipsburg (67661) ***(G-9783)***
Cottonwood Pediatrics ... 316 283-7100
700 Medical Center Dr # 150 Newton (67114) ***(G-7335)***
Cottonwood Point Inc ... 316 775-0368
100 Cottonwood Point Ln Augusta (67010) ***(G-315)***
Cottonwood Springs LLC ... 913 353-3000
13351 S Arapaho Dr Olathe (66062) ***(G-7618)***
Couch Pierce King & Hoffmeiste ... 913 451-8430
10975 Benson Dr Ste 370 Overland Park (66210) ***(G-8604)***
Council Grove Area Foundation ... 620 767-6653
315 W Main St Council Grove (66846) ***(G-1160)***
Council Grove Healthcare, Council Grove *Also called National Healthcare Corp* ***(G-1173)***
Council Grove Republican ... 620 767-5123
302 W Main St Council Grove (66846) ***(G-1161)***
Council Grove Telephone Co, Council Grove *Also called Tri-County Telephone Assn Inc* ***(G-1178)***
Counseling & Mediation Center ... 316 269-2322
200 W Douglas Ave Ste 560 Wichita (67202) ***(G-14106)***
Counseling & Psychological Svc, Lawrence *Also called University of Kansas* ***(G-5158)***
Counseling Ctr For Butlr Cnty, Augusta *Also called South Central Mntl Hlth CN* ***(G-346)***
Counseling Ctr For Butlr Cnty ... 316 776-2007
524 N Main St El Dorado (67042) ***(G-1552)***
Counseling Inc ... 785 472-4300
525 E 3rd St Ellsworth (67439) ***(G-1664)***
Counslman Wade Chrprctic Clnic ... 785 234-0521
1408 Sw Topeka Blvd Topeka (66612) ***(G-12514)***
Countertop Trends LLC ... 620 836-2311
406 Main St Gridley (66852) ***(G-2689)***
Country Accents Inc ... 316 440-1343
16328 Sw 123rd Ter Andover (67002) ***(G-87)***
Country Acres Senior Residence ... 316 773-3900
343 N Country Acres Ave Wichita (67212) ***(G-14107)***
Country Care Inc ... 913 773-5517
515 Dawson St Easton (66020) ***(G-1478)***
Country Carpet Inc ... 785 256-4800
14969 Wterman Crossing Rd Maple Hill (66507) ***(G-6863)***
Country Child Care Inc ... 316 722-4500
404 W Irma St Maize (67101) ***(G-6510)***
Country Club Bank ... 913 682-0001
401 Delaware St Leavenworth (66048) ***(G-5226)***
Country Club Bank ... 913 438-5660
9100 Park St Lenexa (66215) ***(G-5790)***
Country Club Bank ... 816 751-4270
11006 Parallel Pkwy Kansas City (66109) ***(G-3943)***
Country Club Bank ... 816 931-4060
9400 Mission Rd Shawnee Mission (66206) ***(G-11268)***
Country Club Bank ... 816 931-4060
13451 Briar Dr Ste 100 Leawood (66209) ***(G-5360)***
Country Club Bank ... 913 441-2444
21911 W 66th St Ste 100 Shawnee (66226) ***(G-10936)***
Country Club Bank ... 816 751-4251
11181 Overbrook Rd Leawood (66211) ***(G-5361)***
Country Club Bank ... 913 682-2300
2310 S 4th St Leavenworth (66048) ***(G-5227)***
Country Club Restaurant, Independence *Also called Independence Country Club* ***(G-3527)***
Country Crafts ... 620 232-1818
306 S Walnut St Opolis (66760) ***(G-8180)***
Country Fresh Foods ... 316 283-4414
1515 N Main St Newton (67114) ***(G-7336)***
Country Haven Nursing Center, Paola *Also called Rh Montgomery Properties Inc* ***(G-9586)***
Country Inn Suites ... 316 634-3900
7824 E 32nd St N Wichita (67226) ***(G-14108)***
Country Inn Suites By Carlson, Salina *Also called Salina KS Lodging LLC* ***(G-10679)***
Country Kids Day Care Inc ... 913 888-9400
8745 Bourgade St Shawnee Mission (66219) ***(G-11269)***
Country Living Inc ... 620 842-5858
420 N 5th Ave Anthony (67003) ***(G-125)***
Country Mart West, Coffeyville *Also called Bobs Super Saver Inc* ***(G-913)***

ALPHABETIC

Country Place Senior Living...785 632-5052
722 Liberty St Clay Center (67432) ***(G-857)***
Country Place Senior Living...785 336-6868
1700 Community Dr Seneca (66538) ***(G-10860)***
Country Suites By Carlson, Wichita *Also called Country Inn Suites* ***(G-14108)***
Country Suites By Carlson, Lawrence *Also called Cave Inn LLC* ***(G-4777)***
Country Suites By Carlson, Kansas City *Also called Sand Dollar Hospitality 2 LLC* ***(G-4400)***
Country Traditions Inc...620 231-5382
1227 E 540th Ave Pittsburg (66762) ***(G-9847)***
Countryside Feed LLC (PA)...620 947-3111
101 Santa Fe St Hillsboro (67063) ***(G-3047)***
Countryside Feed LLC...785 336-6777
1972 State Highway 187 Seneca (66538) ***(G-10861)***
Countryside Health Center...785 234-6147
440 Se Woodland Ave Topeka (66607) ***(G-12515)***
Countryside of Hays Inc...785 625-6539
1000 Reservation Rd Hays (67601) ***(G-2777)***
Countryside Pet Clinic PA...316 733-8433
1936 N Andover Rd Andover (67002) ***(G-88)***
Countryside United Methdst Ch...785 266-7541
3221 Sw Burlingame Rd Topeka (66611) ***(G-12516)***
County Ambulance Service, Belleville *Also called Republic County Ems* ***(G-464)***
County Attorney, El Dorado *Also called County of Butler* ***(G-1553)***
County Engineer, Ulysses *Also called County of Grant* ***(G-13291)***
County Family Practice, Johnson *Also called Stanton County Hosp Aux Inc* ***(G-3662)***
County Health Department, Arkansas City *Also called Cowley County Joint Board Hlth* ***(G-151)***
County of Allen...620 365-1425
1 N Washington Ave Rm B Iola (66749) ***(G-3597)***
County of Atchison...913 367-1905
1419 N 6th St Atchison (66002) ***(G-223)***
County of Barber...620 886-5087
1027 Ne Isabel Rd Medicine Lodge (67104) ***(G-7059)***
County of Barton...620 793-1910
1806 12th St Great Bend (67530) ***(G-2548)***
County of Butler...316 322-4130
201 W Pine Ave Ste 104 El Dorado (67042) ***(G-1553)***
County of Chautauqua...620 725-5860
215 N Chautauqua St # 10 Sedan (67361) ***(G-10841)***
County of Cherokee...620 429-3954
509 E Country Rd Columbus (66725) ***(G-1070)***
County of Clay...785 632-2166
603 4th St Clay Center (67432) ***(G-858)***
County of Clay...785 632-3193
820 Spellman Cir Clay Center (67432) ***(G-859)***
County of Cowley...620 221-5430
311 E 9th Ave Rm 111 Winfield (67156) ***(G-16128)***
County of Crawford...620 231-5130
911 E Centennial Dr Pittsburg (66762) ***(G-9848)***
County of Crawford...620 231-5141
911 E Cennetial Ave Pittsburg (66762) ***(G-9849)***
County of Decatur...785 475-8113
120 E Hall St Oberlin (67749) ***(G-7489)***
County of Dickinson...785 263-3193
408 Se 2nd St Abilene (67410) ***(G-21)***
County of Doniphan...785 985-2380
Doniphan Cnty Courthouse Troy (66087) ***(G-13273)***
County of Douglas...785 331-1330
711 23rd Lawrence (66046) ***(G-4813)***
County of Douglas...785 832-5293
3755 E 25th St Lawrence (66046) ***(G-4814)***
County of Ellis...785 628-9455
1195 280th Ave Hays (67601) ***(G-2778)***
County of Ellsworth...785 472-4486
103 N Douglas Ave Ellsworth (67439) ***(G-1665)***
County of Finney...620 271-6120
425 N 8th St Garden City (67846) ***(G-2133)***
County of Finney...620 272-3600
919 W Zerr Rd Garden City (67846) ***(G-2134)***
County of Finney...620 272-3564
201 W Maple St Garden City (67846) ***(G-2135)***
County of Finney...620 275-4421
1250 S Raceway Rd Garden City (67846) ***(G-2136)***
County of Ford...620 227-4556
100 Gunsmoke St Ste 38 Dodge City (67801) ***(G-1332)***
County of Franklin...785 229-7300
219 E 14th St Ottawa (66067) ***(G-8260)***
County of Franklin...785 242-1250
135 W Tecumseh St Ottawa (66067) ***(G-8261)***
County of Geary...785 762-5788
1212 W Ash St Junction City (66441) ***(G-3684)***
County of Gove...785 754-3335
520 W 5th St Quinter (67752) ***(G-10181)***
County of Graham...785 421-5464
304 W Prout St Hill City (67642) ***(G-3031)***
County of Grant...620 356-4837
1550 N Rd I Ulysses (67880) ***(G-13291)***
County of Grant...620 356-4233
815 E Oklahoma Ave Ulysses (67880) ***(G-13292)***
County of Greenwood...620 583-8112
510 S Jefferson St Eureka (67045) ***(G-1882)***
County of Hamilton...620 384-7780
E G St Syracuse (67878) ***(G-12223)***
County of Harper...620 842-5240
201 N Jennings Ave Anthony (67003) ***(G-126)***
County of Harvey...316 283-1637
215 S Pine St Newton (67114) ***(G-7337)***
County of Jefferson...785 863-2581
15049 94th St Oskaloosa (66066) ***(G-8221)***
County of Jefferson...785 863-2447
1212 Walnut St Oskaloosa (66066) ***(G-8222)***
County of Johnson...913 782-2640
1800 W Old Highway 56 Olathe (66061) ***(G-7619)***
County of Johnson...913 782-2210
1701 W 56 Hwy Olathe (66061) ***(G-7620)***
County of Johnson...913 894-8383
11875 S Sunset Dr Ste 100 Olathe (66061) ***(G-7621)***
County of Johnson...913 715-3300
100 N Kansas Ave Olathe (66061) ***(G-7622)***
County of Johnson...913 432-3868
4800 Nall Ave Shawnee Mission (66202) ***(G-11270)***
County of Johnson...913 631-5208
7700 Renner Rd Shawnee Mission (66217) ***(G-11271)***
County of Johnson...913 888-4713
7900 Renner Rd Shawnee Mission (66219) ***(G-11272)***
County of Johnson...913 715-2550
8788 Metcalf Ave Overland Park (66212) ***(G-8605)***
County of Johnson...913 829-4653
16445 Lackman St Olathe (66062) ***(G-7623)***
County of Johnson...913 403-8069
9301 W 73rd St Shawnee Mission (66204) ***(G-11273)***
County of Kearny...620 355-7501
506 E Thorpe St Ste 355 Lakin (67860) ***(G-4649)***
County of Kingman...620 532-5241
823 E A Ave Kingman (67068) ***(G-4588)***
County of Kiowa...620 723-2531
1002 S Grove St Greensburg (67054) ***(G-2673)***
County of Kiowa...620 723-3341
501 S Walnut St Greensburg (67054) ***(G-2674)***
County of Labette...620 784-5391
901 S Huston St Altamont (67330) ***(G-72)***
County of Leavenworth...913 727-1800
23690 187th St Leavenworth (66048) ***(G-5228)***
County of Lincoln...785 524-4474
313 E Franklin St Lincoln (67455) ***(G-6380)***
County of Mc Pherson, McPherson *Also called County of McPherson* ***(G-6952)***
County of McPherson...620 241-0466
1115 W Avenue A McPherson (67460) ***(G-6952)***
County of Mitchell...785 738-2266
400 W 8th St Beloit (67420) ***(G-482)***
County of Morton...620 593-4288
1 2 Mile S Of Wilburton16 Elkhart (67950) ***(G-1618)***
County of Norton...785 877-5784
11822 Road W1 Norton (67654) ***(G-7442)***
County of Osage...785 828-4444
1215 Washington Lyndon (66451) ***(G-6476)***
County of Osborne...785 346-2379
117 N 1st St Osborne (67473) ***(G-8207)***
County of Pawnee...620 285-6141
615 E 10th St Larned (67550) ***(G-4700)***
County of Pratt...620 672-4130
1001 E 1st St Pratt (67124) ***(G-10103)***
County of Reno...620 694-2587
703 S Mohawk Rd Hutchinson (67501) ***(G-3248)***
County of Reno...620 665-7042
115 W 1st Ave Hutchinson (67501) ***(G-3249)***
County of Reno...620 694-2976
600 Scott Blvd South Hutchinson (67505) ***(G-12058)***
County of Republic...785 527-2235
702 K St Belleville (66935) ***(G-456)***
County of Riley...785 537-4040
301 N 4th St Manhattan (66502) ***(G-6602)***
County of Riley...785 539-3535
2011 Claflin Rd Manhattan (66502) ***(G-6603)***
County of Riley...785 537-6310
110 Courthouse Plz B302 Manhattan (66502) ***(G-6604)***
County of Russell...785 445-3720
311 S Fossil St Russell (67665) ***(G-10269)***
County of Russell...785 483-4032
4288 Us Highway 40 Russell (67665) ***(G-10270)***
County of Saline...785 826-6606
125 W Elm St Salina (67401) ***(G-10465)***
County of Sedgwick...316 660-4800
1109 N Minneapolis St Wichita (67214) ***(G-14109)***
County of Sedgwick...316 660-9775
881 S Minnesota Ave Wichita (67211) ***(G-14110)***
County of Sedgwick...316 660-0100
7001 W 21st St N Wichita (67205) ***(G-14111)***
County of Sedgwick...316 685-2035
1144 S Seneca St Wichita (67213) ***(G-14112)***

County of Sedgwick...316 660-9500
622 E Central Ave Wichita (67202) ***(G-14113)***
County of Sedgwick...316 660-7060
2622 W Central Ave # 500 Wichita (67203) ***(G-14114)***
County of Seward...620 626-0198
501 N Washington Ave # 101 Liberal (67901) ***(G-6297)***
County of Seward...620 626-3266
89th St Hwy 54 Liberal (67901) ***(G-6298)***
County of Seward...620 626-3275
320 W 18th St Liberal (67901) ***(G-6299)***
County of Shawnee...785 233-4774
1515 Nw Saline St Ste 150 Topeka (66618) ***(G-12517)***
County of Shawnee...785 233-8856
712 S Kansas Ave Ste 3e Topeka (66603) ***(G-12518)***
County of Shawnee...785 233-2882
1515 Nw Saline St Topeka (66618) ***(G-12519)***
County of Shawnee...785 862-2071
1515 Nw Saline St Ste 200 Topeka (66618) ***(G-12520)***
County of Shawnee...785 233-7702
1515 Nw Saline St Ste 200 Topeka (66618) ***(G-12521)***
County of Shawnee...785 368-2000
1615 Nw 8th St Topeka (66608) ***(G-12522)***
County of Sheridan...785 675-3281
826 18th St Hoxie (67740) ***(G-3136)***
County of Sherman...785 890-3625
220 W 2nd St Goodland (67735) ***(G-2467)***
County of Smith...785 282-6924
914 E Highway 36 Smith Center (66967) ***(G-12033)***
County of Stevens...620 544-8782
510 W 6th St Hugoton (67951) ***(G-3154)***
County of Stevens...620 544-2023
6th & Polk Hugoton (67951) ***(G-3155)***
County of Stevens...620 544-2562
109 Northwest Ave Hugoton (67951) ***(G-3156)***
County of Sumner...316 262-2686
217 W 8th St Ste 1 Wellington (67152) ***(G-13496)***
County of Thomas...785 460-4585
1275 S Franklin Ave Colby (67701) ***(G-1001)***
County of Trego...785 743-5337
525 Warren Ave Wakeeney (67672) ***(G-13385)***
County of Trego...785 743-6441
120 S Main St Wakeeney (67672) ***(G-13386)***
County of Wallace (PA)...785 852-4282
313 N Main St Sharon Springs (67758) ***(G-10896)***
Courier Tribune, Seneca *Also called Dan Diehl* ***(G-10863)***
Court of Appeals, Topeka *Also called Judiciary Court of The State* ***(G-12750)***
Court Reporting Service Inc...800 794-8798
1999 N Amidon Ave Ste 224 Wichita (67203) ***(G-14115)***
Court Trustee Dept...785 762-2583
801 N Washington St Ste D Junction City (66441) ***(G-3685)***
Courtland Day Spa...620 223-0098
121 E 1st St Fort Scott (66701) ***(G-1962)***
Courtyard & Patio, Shawnee Mission *Also called Pool & Patio Supply Inc* ***(G-11744)***
Courtyard and Patio, Shawnee Mission *Also called Pool & Patio Inc* ***(G-11743)***
Courtyard By Marriott, Shawnee Mission *Also called Lake Pointe Hotel Co LLC* ***(G-11546)***
Courtyard By Marriott...785 309-1300
3020 Riffel Dr Salina (67401) ***(G-10466)***
Courtyard By Marriott...913 339-9900
11301 Metcalf Ave Shawnee Mission (66210) ***(G-11274)***
Courtyard By Marriott Jct Cy, Junction City *Also called Revocable Trust* ***(G-3748)***
Courtyard Kansas City Olathe...913 839-4500
12151 S Strang Line Ct Olathe (66062) ***(G-7624)***
Courtyard Topeka, Topeka *Also called W2005/Fargo Hotels (pool C)* ***(G-13228)***
Courtyard Topeka, Topeka *Also called Cni Thl Propco Fe LLC* ***(G-12482)***
Courtyard Wichita At Old Town, Wichita *Also called Courtyard-Old Town* ***(G-14116)***
Courtyard Wichita East, Wichita *Also called Apple Eght Hospitality MGT Inc* ***(G-13722)***
Courtyard-Old Town...316 264-5300
820 E 2nd St N Wichita (67202) ***(G-14116)***
Covansys Corporation...913 469-8700
7701 College Blvd Fl 2 Shawnee Mission (66210) ***(G-11275)***
Coventry Health Care Kans Inc (HQ)...800 969-3343
9401 Indian Creek Pkwy # 1300 Overland Park (66210) ***(G-8606)***
Coventry Health Care Kans Inc...316 634-1222
8535 E 21st St N Wichita (67206) ***(G-14117)***
Coverall Cleaning Concepts, Leawood *Also called Coverall North America Inc* ***(G-5362)***
Coverall North America Inc...913 888-5009
8700 State Line Rd # 105 Leawood (66206) ***(G-5362)***
Cowan Systems LLC...913 393-0110
19943 W 162nd St Olathe (66062) ***(G-7625)***
Cowboy Inn LLC...316 943-3869
642 N Saint Paul St Wichita (67203) ***(G-14118)***
Cowley Cnty Mntl Hlth & Cnslng...620 442-4540
22214 D St Winfield (67156) ***(G-16129)***
Cowley College & Area...620 442-0430
125 S 2nd St Arkansas City (67005) ***(G-150)***
Cowley County Council On Aging...620 221-7020
700 Gary St Ste C Winfield (67156) ***(G-16130)***
Cowley County Crime Stoppers...620 221-7777
812 Millington St Winfield (67156) ***(G-16131)***
Cowley County Crime Stoppers...620 221-7777
812 Millington St Winfield (67156) ***(G-16132)***
Cowley County Health Dept, Winfield *Also called Cowley County Joint Board Hlth* ***(G-16133)***
Cowley County Joint Board Hlth...620 442-3260
115 E Radio Ln Arkansas City (67005) ***(G-151)***
Cowley County Joint Board Hlth (PA)...620 221-1430
320 E 9th Ave Ste 2 Winfield (67156) ***(G-16133)***
Cowley County United Way Inc...620 221-9683
P.O. Box 447 Winfield (67156) ***(G-16134)***
Cox Communications, Coffeyville *Also called Multimedia Cablevision* ***(G-965)***
Cox Communications...620 474-4318
1510 E 17th Ave Hutchinson (67501) ***(G-3250)***
Cox Communications Inc...785 236-1606
900 Hayes Dr Ste B Manhattan (66502) ***(G-6605)***
Cox Communications Inc...316 260-7392
901 George Wash Blvd Wichita (67211) ***(G-14119)***
Cox Communications Inc...620 227-3361
2012 1st Ave Dodge City (67801) ***(G-1333)***
Cox Communications Inc...316 219-5000
8924 E 35th St N Wichita (67226) ***(G-14120)***
Cox Communications Inc...620 275-5552
1109 College Dr Garden City (67846) ***(G-2137)***
Cox Communications Inc...785 233-3383
1615 Sw Washburn Ave Topeka (66604) ***(G-12523)***
Cox Communications Inc...785 238-6165
140 W 8th St Junction City (66441) ***(G-3686)***
Cox Communications Inc...785 368-1000
931 Sw Henderson Rd Topeka (66615) ***(G-12524)***
Cox Enterprises Inc...913 825-6124
6405 Metcalf Ave Overland Park (66202) ***(G-8607)***
Cox Machine Inc (PA)...316 943-1342
5338 W 21st St N Ste 100 Wichita (67205) ***(G-14121)***
Cox Machine Inc...316 943-1342
949 N State Road 14 Harper (67058) ***(G-2718)***
Cox Media LLC...785 215-8880
931 Sw Henderson Rd Topeka (66615) ***(G-12525)***
Cox Media LLC...623 322-2000
901 S George Wash Blvd Wichita (67211) ***(G-14122)***
Cox-Kent & Associates Inc...316 946-5596
2807 W Pawnee St Wichita (67213) ***(G-14123)***
Coxmontgomery Inc...620 508-6260
75 Nw 40th Ave Pratt (67124) ***(G-10104)***
Coxpowerline Inc...620 508-6260
75 Nw 40th Ave Pratt (67124) ***(G-10105)***
Coyote Investment & Networking...785 550-6028
2011 Hogan Dr Lawrence (66047) ***(G-4815)***
Coyotes Inc...785 842-2295
1003 E 23rd St Lawrence (66046) ***(G-4816)***
Coyson Transportation LLC...620 336-2846
929 N Liberty St Cherryvale (67335) ***(G-805)***
CP Engners Land Srveyors Inc (PA)...785 267-5071
2710 Oak Ridge Rd Topeka (66617) ***(G-12526)***
CP Partnerships Inc...785 625-7388
1003 Main St Hays (67601) ***(G-2779)***
CPB Materials LLC...316 833-1146
5114 W 87th St S Haysville (67060) ***(G-2938)***
Cpg Communications Group LLC...913 317-2888
7300 W 110th St Ste 700 Shawnee Mission (66210) ***(G-11276)***
CPI Printing and Bindery Svcs, Overland Park *Also called Cookbook Publishers Inc* ***(G-8598)***
CPI Qualified Plan Cons Inc (HQ)...620 793-8473
1809 24th St Great Bend (67530) ***(G-2549)***
CPM Technologies Inc...256 777-9869
9911 E 21st St N Wichita (67206) ***(G-14124)***
Cr Inspection Inc...620 544-2666
621 S Main St Hugoton (67951) ***(G-3157)***
Cradle To Cryons Childcare Ctr...620 345-2390
311 E Thornton St Moundridge (67107) ***(G-7181)***
Craig Homecare, Wichita *Also called Craig Resources Inc* ***(G-14125)***
Craig Homecare...785 798-4821
103 S Iowa Ave Ness City (67560) ***(G-7258)***
Craig Resources Inc (PA)...316 264-9988
1100 E 1st St N Wichita (67214) ***(G-14125)***
Cramer Products Inc...913 856-7511
153 W Warren St Gardner (66030) ***(G-2335)***
Cramer, Dona H CPA, Pratt *Also called Patton Cramer & Laprod Charter* ***(G-10131)***
Crane Sales & Service Co Inc...913 621-7040
1025 S Mill St Kansas City (66105) ***(G-3944)***
Cranmer Grass Farms Inc...316 722-7230
6121 N 119th St W Maize (67101) ***(G-6511)***
Cranmer, Douglas C, Wichita *Also called Stinson Lasswell & Wilson LLC* ***(G-15673)***
Cratetech Incorporated...316 682-6223
8110 E Marion St Wichita (67210) ***(G-14126)***
Crave Beauty Academy, Wichita *Also called S-Kmac Investments LLC* ***(G-15503)***
Craw-Kan Telephone Coop Inc (PA)...620 724-8235
200 N Ozark St Girard (66743) ***(G-2399)***
Crawdad Construction, Emporia *Also called Browing Gayla* ***(G-1709)***
Crawford & Company...913 909-4552
12802 Pembrooke Cir Shawnee Mission (66209) ***(G-11277)***

ALPHABETIC

Crawford & Company.....913 323-0300
1411 Harding St Great Bend (67530) ***(G-2550)***
Crawford Cnty Assistd Lvng Com.....620 724-6760
950 W Saint John St Girard (66743) ***(G-2400)***
Crawford Cnty Mental Hlth Ctr, Pittsburg *Also called County of Crawford* ***(G-9848)***
Crawford Cnty Mental Hlth Ctr, Pittsburg *Also called County of Crawford* ***(G-9849)***
Crawford Supply Co (PA).....785 434-4631
604 Nw 3rd St Plainville (67663) ***(G-9984)***
Crazy Girls LLC.....913 495-9797
9740 Rosehill Rd Lenexa (66215) ***(G-5791)***
Crazy House Inc (PA).....620 275-2153
3502 N Campus Dr Garden City (67846) ***(G-2138)***
Crazy Hrse Spt CLB & Golf Crse, Hutchinson *Also called Montes De Areia LLC* ***(G-3385)***
Creason Corrugating McHy Inc (PA).....423 629-5532
5844 N Broadway Ave 44 Park City (67219) ***(G-9613)***
Creative Capsule LLC.....816 421-1714
10875 Benson Dr Ste 275 Overland Park (66210) ***(G-8608)***
Creative Carnivals Events LLC (PA).....913 642-0900
11121 W 87th Ter Overland Park (66214) ***(G-8609)***
Creative Community Living of E.....620 221-9431
1500 E 8th Ave Ste 201 Winfield (67156) ***(G-16135)***
Creative Community Living S.....620 221-1119
1500 E 8th Ave Ste 201 Winfield (67156) ***(G-16136)***
Creative Consumer Concepts Inc (PA).....913 491-6444
10955 Granada Ln Ste 200 Overland Park (66211) ***(G-8610)***
Creative Design TS Inc.....316 681-1868
3835 N Hillcrest St Ste 2 Bel Aire (67220) ***(G-431)***
Creative Hairlines Inc.....620 241-3535
207 S Main St McPherson (67460) ***(G-6953)***
Creative Hairlines Salon & Spa, McPherson *Also called Creative Hairlines Inc* ***(G-6953)***
Creative Hardwoods.....620 249-4160
2542 Nw Highway 102 Scammon (66773) ***(G-10795)***
Creative Landscaping Inc.....785 286-0015
4100 Sw 40th St Topeka (66610) ***(G-12527)***
Creative Marketing, Leawood *Also called Creative One Marketing Corp* ***(G-5363)***
Creative Mktg Unlimited Inc.....913 894-0077
9548 Buena Vista St Overland Park (66207) ***(G-8611)***
Creative One Marketing Corp.....913 814-0510
11460 Tomahawk Creek Pkwy Leawood (66211) ***(G-5363)***
Creative Paradise Inc.....316 794-8621
415 Industrial Rd Goddard (67052) ***(G-2434)***
Creative Planning Inc (PA).....913 341-0900
5454 W 110th St Overland Park (66211) ***(G-8612)***
Creative Printing Company Inc.....913 262-5000
9014 W 51st Ter Merriam (66203) ***(G-7089)***
Creative Signs & Design Inc.....785 233-8000
2910 S Kansas Ave Topeka (66611) ***(G-12528)***
Creativenergy Options, Overland Park *Also called Bradley R Lewis* ***(G-8479)***
Creativity Place Inc (PA).....316 684-1860
9112 E Central Ave B Wichita (67206) ***(G-14127)***
Creche Academy LLC.....785 484-3100
7043 Wells Rd Meriden (66512) ***(G-7079)***
Credit Bureau Services (PA).....620 276-7631
1135 College Dr Ste L2 Garden City (67846) ***(G-2139)***
Credit Motors Inc (PA).....913 621-1206
1400 State Ave Kansas City (66102) ***(G-3945)***
Credit Restart LLC.....888 670-7709
8700 Monrovia St Ste 310 Lenexa (66215) ***(G-5792)***
Credit Union of America (PA).....316 265-3272
711 W Douglas Ave Wichita (67213) ***(G-14128)***
Credit World Services Inc.....913 362-3950
6000 Martway St Shawnee Mission (66202) ***(G-11278)***
Creditors Service Bureau Inc.....785 266-3223
3410 Sw Van Buren St # 101 Topeka (66611) ***(G-12529)***
Creek Electric Incorporated.....316 943-5888
2811 W Pawnee St Wichita (67213) ***(G-14129)***
Creekstone Farm Prem.....620 741-3100
604 Goff Industrial Pk Rd Arkansas City (67005) ***(G-152)***
Creme De La Creme Kansas Inc.....913 451-0858
4600 W 115th St Shawnee Mission (66211) ***(G-11279)***
Crescent Limousines.....785 232-2236
4216 Ne Seward Ave Topeka (66616) ***(G-12530)***
Crestline Hotels & Resorts LLC.....913 451-2553
6801 W 112th St Overland Park (66211) ***(G-8613)***
Crestview Community Center, Topeka *Also called City of Topeka Employees* ***(G-12476)***
Crestview Operation Inc.....785 336-2156
808 N 8th St Seneca (66538) ***(G-10862)***
Crestwood Inc (PA).....785 823-1532
601 E Water Well Rd Salina (67401) ***(G-10467)***
Crestwood Inc.....785 827-0317
353 E Avenue A Salina (67401) ***(G-10468)***
Crestwood Apartments, Kansas City *Also called Mkt Community Development Inc* ***(G-4264)***
Crestwood Country Club Inc.....620 231-9697
304 W Crestview Ave Pittsburg (66762) ***(G-9850)***
Creten Basement Contractors.....913 441-3333
10212 S Shadow Cir Olathe (66061) ***(G-7626)***
Creten J G Basement Contractor, Olathe *Also called Creten Basement Contractors* ***(G-7626)***
Creten John G Basement Contr.....913 441-3333
10212 S Shadow Cir Olathe (66061) ***(G-7627)***
Cretex.....785 863-3300
5150 Us 59 Hwy Oskaloosa (66066) ***(G-8223)***
Cretex Concrete Products Inc.....785 863-3300
5150 Us Hwy 59 Oskaloosa (66066) ***(G-8224)***
Crew Network, Lawrence *Also called Commercial RE Women Netwrk* ***(G-4802)***
Cricket Communications Inc.....913 341-2799
7620 Metcalf Ave Overland Park (66204) ***(G-8614)***
Cricket Communications LLC.....316 636-6387
3165 S Seneca St Wichita (67217) ***(G-14130)***
Cricket Communications LLC.....913 999-0163
4980 Roe Blvd Roeland Park (66205) ***(G-10222)***
Crime Stoppers Hotline, McPherson *Also called City of McPherson* ***(G-6950)***
Crime Stpers of Wchta Sdgwck C, Wichita *Also called Wichita Crime Stoppers Program* ***(G-15992)***
Crisis Center Inc.....785 539-7935
423 Houston St Manhattan (66502) ***(G-6606)***
Crisis Center of Dodge City.....620 225-6987
605 Central Ave Dodge City (67801) ***(G-1334)***
Crisp Cuts & Styles Etcllc.....816 916-1841
7625 Quivira Rd Shawnee Mission (66216) ***(G-11280)***
Criss Optical Mfg Co Inc.....316 529-0414
3628 S West St Wichita (67217) ***(G-14131)***
Critical Care Systems Intl Inc.....913 789-5560
9100 W 74th St Shawnee Mission (66204) ***(G-11281)***
Critical Care Transfer Inc.....620 353-4145
930 N Joyce Dr Ulysses (67880) ***(G-13293)***
Critical Elc Systems Group LLC.....316 684-0193
3215 E 9th St N Wichita (67208) ***(G-14132)***
Crititech Inc.....785 841-7120
1849 E 1450 Rd Lawrence (66044) ***(G-4817)***
Crititech Particle Engg.....785 841-7120
1849 E 1450 Rd Lawrence (66044) ***(G-4818)***
Crl, Lenexa *Also called Clinical Reference Lab Inc* ***(G-5765)***
Cro Magnon Repast LLC.....913 747-5559
8428 Melrose Dr Lenexa (66214) ***(G-5793)***
Cromwell Builders Mfg.....785 949-2433
665 Eden Rd Carlton (67448) ***(G-686)***
Cronister & Company Inc.....785 862-5003
5612 Sw Fairlawn Rd Topeka (66610) ***(G-12531)***
Crookham Construction LLC.....913 369-3341
325 E Highway 24-40 Tonganoxie (66086) ***(G-12259)***
Crooks Floor Covering.....785 242-4153
636 N Main St Ottawa (66067) ***(G-8262)***
Crop Quest Inc (PA).....620 225-2233
1204 W Frontview St Dodge City (67801) ***(G-1335)***
CROP QUEST AGRONOMIC SERVICES, Dodge City *Also called Crop Quest Inc* ***(G-1335)***
Crop Risk Management Services, Atchison *Also called Henry Scherer Crop Insurance* ***(G-234)***
Crop Service Center Inc (PA).....785 479-2204
1123 Eden Rd Abilene (67410) ***(G-22)***
Crop USA Hutson Insur Group.....913 345-1515
7300 W 110th St Ste 400 Overland Park (66210) ***(G-8615)***
Cropland Co-Op Inc (PA).....620 356-1241
1125 W Oklahoma Ave Ulysses (67880) ***(G-13294)***
Cropland Co-Op Inc.....620 649-2230
506 W Hwy 56 Satanta (67870) ***(G-10782)***
Cross Bell Farms Partners.....620 275-1705
2711 N Rowland Rd Garden City (67846) ***(G-2140)***
Cross Brand Feed, Lewis *Also called Cross Brand Office Inc* ***(G-6267)***
Cross Brand Feed & Alfalfa Inc.....620 324-5571
Hwy 50 E Lewis (67552) ***(G-6266)***
Cross Brand Office Inc (PA).....620 324-5571
Hwy 50 S Lewis (67552) ***(G-6267)***
Cross Country Genetics Inc.....785 457-3336
8855 Michaels Rd Westmoreland (66549) ***(G-13546)***
Cross Creek Furniture LLC.....316 943-0286
13303 W Maple St Ste 139 Wichita (67235) ***(G-14133)***
Cross Manufacturing Inc (PA).....913 451-1233
11011 King St Ste 210 Overland Park (66210) ***(G-8616)***
Cross Manufacturing Inc.....785 625-2585
901 Canterbury Dr Hays (67601) ***(G-2780)***
Cross Manufacturing Inc.....620 324-5525
100 James H Blvd Lewis (67552) ***(G-6268)***
Cross Midwest Tire, Kansas City *Also called Pomps Tire Service Inc* ***(G-4326)***
Cross-Lines Cmnty Outreach Inc.....913 281-3388
736 Shawnee Ave Kansas City (66105) ***(G-3946)***
Crossfaith Ventures Lc.....620 662-8365
1101 W 4th Ave Hutchinson (67501) ***(G-3251)***
Crossfirst Bank.....316 494-4844
9451 E 13th St N Wichita (67206) ***(G-14134)***
Crossfirst Bank.....913 312-6800
11440 Tomahawk Creek Pkwy Leawood (66211) ***(G-5364)***
Crossfirst Bank (PA).....913 327-1212
4707 W 135th St Overland Park (66224) ***(G-8617)***
Crossfirst Bankshares Inc.....913 754-9700
4707 W 135th St Overland Park (66224) ***(G-8618)***
Crossland Construction Co Inc.....316 942-9090
3017 N Cypress St Wichita (67226) ***(G-14135)***

Crossland Construction Co Inc (PA)....620 429-1414
833 S East Ave Columbus (66725) *(G-1071)*
Crossland Heavy Contrs Inc (PA)....620 429-1410
833 S East Ave Columbus (66725) *(G-1072)*
Crossland Prefab LLC....620 429-1414
501 S East Ave Columbus (66725) *(G-1073)*
Crossmark Inc....913 338-1133
11900 W 87th Street Pkwy # 120 Lenexa (66215) *(G-5794)*
Crossroad Tours, Olathe *Also called Ottawa Bus Service Inc (G-7966)*
CROSSROADS CLUB, Salina *Also called Central Kansas Mental Hlth Ctr (G-10441)*
Crossroads Shop Ctr LLC....913 362-1999
6310 Lamar Ave Ste 220 Shawnee Mission (66202) *(G-11282)*
Crosstown Couriers, Topeka *Also called Emporia Freight and Dlvry Svc (G-12575)*
Crosswind Conference Center....620 327-2700
8036 N Hoover Rd Hesston (67062) *(G-2988)*
Crosswind Industries Inc....785 380-8668
2127 Se Lakewood Blvd Topeka (66605) *(G-12532)*
Crotts Aircraft Service Inc....620 227-3553
102 Airport Rd Dodge City (67801) *(G-1336)*
Crown Cabinets, Abilene *Also called Crown Tl Inc (G-23)*
Crown Cleaning, Shawnee Mission *Also called Sanibel Investments Inc (G-11829)*
Crown Consulting Inc....620 624-0156
150 Plaza Dr Ste 103 Liberal (67901) *(G-6300)*
Crown Equipment Corporation....316 942-4400
2113 S West St Ste 300 Wichita (67213) *(G-14136)*
Crown Equipment Corporation....913 888-9777
9500 Widmer Rd Lenexa (66215) *(G-5795)*
Crown Group, Overland Park *Also called Settle Inn (G-9300)*
Crown Lift Trucks, Lenexa *Also called Crown Equipment Corporation (G-5795)*
Crown Packaging Corp....913 888-1951
15301 W 110th St Ste 1 Shawnee Mission (66219) *(G-11283)*
Crown Realty of Kansas Inc....913 782-1155
2099 E 151st St Olathe (66062) *(G-7628)*
Crown Realty of Kansas Inc....913 795-4555
501 Main St Mound City (66056) *(G-7169)*
Crown Realty of Kansas Inc....785 242-7700
336 S Main St Ottawa (66067) *(G-8263)*
Crown Realty of Kansas Inc....913 837-5155
100 Crestview Cir Ste 101 Louisburg (66053) *(G-6444)*
Crown Recovery Services LLC....816 777-2366
12811 W 131st St Overland Park (66213) *(G-8619)*
Crown Tl Inc....785 263-7061
210 N Brady St Abilene (67410) *(G-23)*
Crown Toyota, Lawrence *Also called Miles Automotive Inc (G-5028)*
Crowne Plaza Hotel, Lawrence *Also called Lenexa Hotel LP (G-4993)*
Crpenter Charted....785 357-5251
1525 Sw Topeka Blvd Ste A Topeka (66612) *(G-12533)*
Crude Transportation, Winfield *Also called Coffeyville Resources LLC (G-16122)*
Cruise Corner, Wichita *Also called Warren Travel Inc (G-15929)*
Crustbuster/Speed King Inc (PA)....620 227-7106
2300 E Trail St Dodge City (67801) *(G-1337)*
Cryo Management Inc....913 362-9005
2209 W 72nd Ter Prairie Village (66208) *(G-10023)*
Crystal Company, Overland Park *Also called Welker Heating and Cooling (G-9487)*
Crystal Hospitality LLC....913 680-1500
405 Choctaw St Leavenworth (66048) *(G-5229)*
Crystal Structures, Wichita *Also called Sunshine Rooms Inc (G-15689)*
Crystal Trenching Inc....913 677-1233
4622 Merriam Dr Shawnee (66203) *(G-10937)*
CS Carey LLC....913 432-4877
6225 Kansas Ave Kansas City (66111) *(G-3947)*
Cs Cleaners Inc....785 825-8636
1123 Holiday St Salina (67401) *(G-10469)*
Csbi, Wichita *Also called Construction Svcs Bryant Inc (G-14093)*
CSC Gold Inc....913 664-8100
9300 W 110th St Ste 115 Shawnee Mission (66210) *(G-11284)*
Csd7 Social Medal....620 203-0477
1016 S 6th St Burlington (66839) *(G-633)*
Csi, Hillsboro *Also called Container Services Inc (G-3046)*
Csl Plasma Inc....316 264-6973
1515 E Central Ave Wichita (67214) *(G-14137)*
Csl Plasma Inc....785 749-5750
816 W 24th St Lawrence (66046) *(G-4819)*
Csl Plasma Inc....785 776-9177
1130 Garden Way Manhattan (66502) *(G-6607)*
CSM Bakery Solutions LLC....913 441-7216
2410 Scheidt Ln Bonner Springs (66012) *(G-546)*
CSM Bakery Supplies North Amer, Lenexa *Also called Corbion America Holdings Inc (G-5787)*
CSM-Csi Joint Venture....913 227-9609
6920 W 154th St Ste B Overland Park (66223) *(G-8620)*
Csr, Hutchinson *Also called Central States Recovery Inc (G-3234)*
CSS Group Inc....316 269-9090
1550 N Broadway Ave 200 Wichita (67214) *(G-14138)*
CST Oil & Gas Corporation (PA)....620 829-5307
1690 155th St Fort Scott (66701) *(G-1963)*
Cstk Inc (PA)....913 233-7220
7200 W 132nd St Ste 270 Overland Park (66213) *(G-8621)*
Cstk Inc....316 744-2061
7915 N Hartman Arena Dr Park City (67147) *(G-9614)*
CTA, Wichita *Also called Communications Tech Assoc (G-14076)*
CTI, Clay Center *Also called Concordia Tractor Inc (G-856)*
CTI Freight Systems Inc....913 236-7400
4530 W 207th St Bucyrus (66013) *(G-595)*
Ctmd LLC....316 686-6116
940 N Tyler Rd Ste 101 Wichita (67212) *(G-14139)*
Ctr Imprvmnt Hmn Fnctnng Int....316 682-3100
3100 N Hillside Ave Wichita (67219) *(G-14140)*
CTS Logistics, Wichita *Also called Central Trnsp Svcs Inc (G-13990)*
CU - Once Joint Venture LLC....913 707-2165
7215 W 162nd Ter Stilwell (66085) *(G-12143)*
CU Capital Mkt Solutions LLC....913 402-2627
7200 W 132nd St Ste 240 Overland Park (66213) *(G-8622)*
Culligan, Wichita *Also called David E Dishop (G-14172)*
Culligan, Olathe *Also called Wheatland Waters Inc (G-8153)*
Culligan, Wichita *Also called Wichita Water Conditioning Inc (G-16042)*
Culligan, Salina *Also called Quality Water Inc (G-10647)*
Cullor Property Management LLC....913 324-5900
P.O. Box 14763 Lenexa (66285) *(G-5796)*
Culture House Inc....913 393-3141
14808 W 117th St Olathe (66062) *(G-7629)*
Culture Index LLC....816 361-7575
10200 State Ln Rd 102 Leawood (66206) *(G-5365)*
Culver Fish Farm Inc....620 241-5200
1432 Ranch Rd McPherson (67460) *(G-6954)*
Culvers Frozen Custard....913 402-9777
8600 W 135th St Overland Park (66223) *(G-8623)*
Cumbernauld Village Inc....620 221-4141
716 Tweed Ofc Winfield (67156) *(G-16137)*
Cummins Coffman &....785 267-2030
3706 Sw Topeka Blvd # 302 Topeka (66609) *(G-12534)*
Cummins - Allison Corp....913 894-2266
8851 Long St Lenexa (66215) *(G-5797)*
Cummins Central Power LLC....785 462-3945
1880 S Range Ave Colby (67701) *(G-1002)*
Cummins Central Power LLC....316 838-0875
5101 N Broadway Ave Park City (67219) *(G-9615)*
Cummins Mid-America, Colby *Also called Cummins Central Power LLC (G-1002)*
Cumulus Media Inc....913 514-3000
5800 Foxridge Dr Ste 600 Shawnee Mission (66202) *(G-11285)*
CUNA Mutl Retirement Solutions, Great Bend *Also called CPI Qualified Plan Cons Inc (G-2549)*
Cunningham Agency Inc (PA)....913 795-2212
103 S 5th St Mound City (66056) *(G-7170)*
Cunningham Communications Inc....785 545-3215
220 W Main St Glen Elder (67446) *(G-2424)*
Cunningham Sndblst Pntg Co Inc....620 848-3030
5960 Se Beasley Rd Riverton (66770) *(G-10211)*
Cunningham Tele & Cable Co, Glen Elder *Also called Cunningham Telephone Company (G-2425)*
Cunningham Tele & Cable Svc, Glen Elder *Also called Cunningham Communications Inc (G-2424)*
Cunningham Telephone Company (PA)....785 545-3215
220 W Main St Glen Elder (67446) *(G-2425)*
Curb Appeal of Kansas Inc....620 488-5214
402 N Merchant St Belle Plaine (67013) *(G-445)*
Curbs Plus Inc....888 639-2872
205 Metcalf Rd El Dorado (67042) *(G-1554)*
Curbys Lawn & Garden LLC....913 764-6159
14835 S Gardner Rd Gardner (66030) *(G-2336)*
Curo Financial Tech Corp (HQ)....316 722-3801
3527 N Ridge Rd Wichita (67205) *(G-14141)*
Curo Group Holdings Corp (PA)....316 772-3801
3527 N Ridge Rd Wichita (67205) *(G-14142)*
Curo Management LLC....316 771-0000
6300 E 21st St N Wichita (67208) *(G-14143)*
Curo Management LLC....316 683-2274
3133 E Douglas Ave Wichita (67211) *(G-14144)*
Curo Management LLC (PA)....316 722-3801
3527 N Ridge Rd Wichita (67205) *(G-14145)*
Current Electrical Co Inc....785 267-2108
3811 Sw South Park Ave Topeka (66609) *(G-12535)*
Curtis Klaassen....913 661-4616
2617 W 112th St Leawood (66211) *(G-5366)*
Curtis Machine Company Inc....620 227-7164
4209 Jayhawk Dr Dodge City (67801) *(G-1338)*
Curves Ahead LLC....785 221-9652
109 Nw Woodlawn Ave Topeka (66606) *(G-12536)*
Cushing Memorial Hospital, Leavenworth *Also called Saint Lukes Cushing Hospital (G-5288)*
Cushman & Wakefield III Inc....913 440-0420
7304 W 130th St Ste 150 Overland Park (66213) *(G-8624)*
Cushman Wkefield Solutions LLC....316 721-3656
128 N 1st St Colwich (67030) *(G-1093)*
Custer Hill Bowling Center, Fort Riley *Also called Army & Air Force Exchange Svc (G-1945)*

ALPHABETIC

Custom 1 Construction, Topeka *Also called Clark Dargal Builders Inc* ***(G-12479)***
Custom Alloy Sales 34p LLC..........913 471-4800
4008 Vernon Rd Prescott (66767) ***(G-10166)***
Custom Branded Sportswear Inc..........866 441-7464
7007 College Blvd Overland Park (66211) ***(G-8625)***
Custom Cabinet & Rack Inc..........785 862-2271
5600 Sw Topeka Blvd Ste E Topeka (66609) ***(G-12537)***
Custom Campers Inc..........620 431-3990
3701 S Johnson Rd Chanute (66720) ***(G-723)***
Custom Cbnets By Lwrence Cnstr..........913 208-9797
1427 Merriam Ln Kansas City (66103) ***(G-3948)***
Custom Color Corp..........913 730-3100
14320 W 101st Ter Lenexa (66215) ***(G-5798)***
Custom Control Mfr Kans Inc..........913 722-0343
5601 Merriam Dr Shawnee Mission (66203) ***(G-11286)***
Custom Design Inc..........913 764-6511
14131 S Mur Len Rd Olathe (66062) ***(G-7630)***
Custom Fabrication LLC..........785 331-9460
1017 N 1156 Rd Lawrence (66047) ***(G-4820)***
Custom Fabricators, Council Grove *Also called Danny Axe* ***(G-1162)***
Custom Flatwork Inc..........316 794-8282
18333 W 39th St S Goddard (67052) ***(G-2435)***
Custom Foods Inc..........913 585-1900
9101 Commerce Dr De Soto (66018) ***(G-1198)***
Custom Harvest Insurance..........620 259-6996
1125 E 4th Ave 1 Hutchinson (67501) ***(G-3252)***
Custom Lawn & Landscape Inc..........913 782-8315
15204 S Keeler St Olathe (66062) ***(G-7631)***
Custom Lawn Service Inc..........316 321-1563
3333 N Hillside Ave Wichita (67219) ***(G-14146)***
Custom Metal & Fabrication, Olathe *Also called Rgs Industries Inc* ***(G-8031)***
Custom Metal Fabricators Inc..........785 258-3744
3194 R Ave Herington (67449) ***(G-2973)***
Custom Mobile Equipment Inc..........785 594-7475
439 E High St Baldwin City (66006) ***(G-358)***
Custom Neon & Vinyl Graphics..........785 233-3218
530 Nw Broad St Topeka (66608) ***(G-12538)***
Custom Rdo Communications Ltd..........816 561-4100
6600 College Blvd Ste 317 Leawood (66211) ***(G-5367)***
Custom Renovation..........620 544-2653
600 E 11th St Hugoton (67951) ***(G-3158)***
Custom Rollforming Corp..........800 457-8837
201 S Avenue C Moundridge (67107) ***(G-7182)***
Custom Rope A Div Williams..........620 825-4196
436 Campbell St Kiowa (67070) ***(G-4623)***
Custom Sheet Metal & Roofg Inc..........785 357-6200
828 Nw Buchanan St Topeka (66608) ***(G-12539)***
Custom Stucco LLC..........913 294-3100
1106 Jeff Cir Paola (66071) ***(G-9550)***
Custom Tree Care Inc..........785 478-9805
3431 Se 21st St Topeka Topeka (66607) ***(G-12540)***
Custom Vinyl & Paint Inc..........316 651-6180
1802 Roanoke St Wichita (67218) ***(G-14147)***
Customeyes, Lenexa *Also called Drake & Assoc Optometrists* ***(G-5825)***
Cut-N-Edge Inc..........785 232-9800
3530 Se 21st St Topeka (66607) ***(G-12541)***
Cutler Repaving Inc (PA)..........785 843-1524
921 E 27th St Lawrence (66046) ***(G-4821)***
Cutting Edge Lawn Care Inc..........316 390-1443
3425 N Broadway Ave Wichita (67219) ***(G-14148)***
Cutting Edge Tile & Grout..........316 648-5516
121 S Bonnie Brae St Wichita (67207) ***(G-14149)***
Cutting Edge Trucking Inc..........913 837-2249
8 S 4th St Louisburg (66053) ***(G-6445)***
Cvr Manufacturing Inc..........620 763-2500
6 Center St Galesburg (66740) ***(G-2091)***
CVS Pharmacy Inc..........913 651-2323
390 Limit St Leavenworth (66048) ***(G-5230)***
CVS Pharmacy Inc..........913 722-3711
6300 Johnson Dr Shawnee Mission (66202) ***(G-11287)***
CW Concrete Inc..........913 780-2316
605 S Kansas Ave Olathe (66061) ***(G-7632)***
Cybertron International Inc..........316 303-1022
4747 S Emporia St Wichita (67216) ***(G-14150)***
Cyclone Well Service Inc..........620 628-4428
1504 27th Ave Canton (67428) ***(G-680)***
Cydex Pharmaceuticals Inc..........913 685-8850
2029 Becker Dr Lawrence (66047) ***(G-4822)***
Cynthia's Playhouse, Mulvane *Also called Todays Tomorrows Lrng Ctr LLC* ***(G-7228)***
Cypress Court At Overland Park, Shawnee Mission *Also called Overland Park Seniorcare LLC* ***(G-11710)***
Cypress Heart (PA)..........316 858-5200
9300 E 29th St N Ste 310 Wichita (67226) ***(G-14151)***
Cypress Recovery Inc..........913 764-7555
1009 E Highway 56 Olathe (66061) ***(G-7633)***
Cypress Ridge Golf Course, Topeka *Also called City of Topeka* ***(G-12473)***
Cypress Surgery Center LLC..........316 634-0404
9300 E 29th St N Ste 100 Wichita (67226) ***(G-14152)***
Cypress Womens Imaging, Wichita *Also called Radiological Wichita Group PA* ***(G-15411)***
Cytek Media Systems Inc (PA)..........785 295-4200
126 Nw Jackson St Topeka (66603) ***(G-12542)***
Cyto Check Labor, Parsons *Also called Anatomical Pathology Services* ***(G-9666)***
Cytocheck Laboratory LLC..........620 421-2424
1201 Corporate Dr Parsons (67357) ***(G-9678)***
Cz-USA..........913 321-1811
3341 N 7th Street Trfy Kansas City (66115) ***(G-3949)***
Czarnieckis Construction Inc..........316 946-9991
1550 Yucca Pl Wichita Wichita (67209) ***(G-14153)***
D & A Trucking Inc..........620 465-3370
9304 E Red Rock Rd Haven (67543) ***(G-2729)***
D & B Legal Services Inc..........913 362-8110
5350 W 94th Ter Ste 206 Prairie Village (66207) ***(G-10024)***
D & B Print Shop Inc..........913 782-6688
1175 W Dennis Ave Olathe (66061) ***(G-7634)***
D & D Roland Enterprises Llc..........316 942-6474
1120 S Florence St Wichita (67209) ***(G-14154)***
D & D Services Inc (PA)..........913 492-1346
15001 W 101st Ter Shawnee Mission (66215) ***(G-11288)***
D & D Tire Inc..........785 843-0191
1000 Vermont St Lawrence (66044) ***(G-4823)***
D & G Oil Company, Minneapolis *Also called Bennington Oil Co Inc* ***(G-7113)***
D & H Machine and Tool Inc..........316 267-3906
1408 S Osage St Wichita (67213) ***(G-14155)***
D & K Insurance Services Inc..........785 540-4133
466 State St Phillipsburg (67661) ***(G-9784)***
D & L Transport LLC (PA)..........913 402-4514
8101 College Blvd 110 Overland Park (66210) ***(G-8626)***
D & R Construction Inc..........785 776-1087
210 Southwind Pl Ste 2c Manhattan (66503) ***(G-6608)***
D & R Trucking Co..........620 672-7713
201 Simpson St Pratt (67124) ***(G-10106)***
D & S Machine and Welding Inc..........785 798-3359
N Hwy 283 Ness City (67560) ***(G-7259)***
D & S Manufacturing Inc..........316 685-5337
319 S Oak St Wichita (67213) ***(G-14156)***
D A V, Salina *Also called Disabled American Veterens Str* ***(G-10479)***
D and D Insulation Inc..........913 492-1346
15001 W 101st Ter Shawnee Mission (66215) ***(G-11289)***
D B Excavating Inc..........913 208-7100
802 S A Line Dr Spring Hill (66083) ***(G-12083)***
D B Investments Inc (HQ)..........913 928-1000
17400 W 119th St Olathe (66061) ***(G-7635)***
D C C A, Pittsburg *Also called Elm Acres Youth & Family Svcs* ***(G-9856)***
D D I Realty Services Inc..........913 685-4100
7200 W 132nd St Ste 300 Overland Park (66213) ***(G-8627)***
D Doubled Inc..........913 334-1075
66210 Shawnee (66203) ***(G-10938)***
D E Bondurant Grain Co Inc..........785 798-3322
223 S Iowa Ave Ness City (67560) ***(G-7260)***
D E Exploration Inc..........785 883-4057
4595 Highway K 33 Wellsville (66092) ***(G-13542)***
D H Pace Company Inc..........816 221-0072
1901 E 119th St Olathe (66061) ***(G-7636)***
D H Pace Company Inc (HQ)..........816 221-0543
1901 E 119th St Olathe (66061) ***(G-7637)***
D H Pace Company Inc..........316 944-3667
3506 W Harry St Wichita (67213) ***(G-14157)***
D H Pace Company Inc..........816 480-2600
1901 E 119th St Olathe (66061) ***(G-7638)***
D H Pace Door Services, Olathe *Also called D H Pace Company Inc* ***(G-7637)***
D J Carpenter Building Systems..........785 537-9789
709 Pecan Cir Ste B Manhattan (66502) ***(G-6609)***
D J Company..........316 685-3241
2929 N Rock Rd Ste 165 Wichita (67226) ***(G-14158)***
D J Inc..........785 667-4651
6737 S Tamara Ln Assaria (67416) ***(G-200)***
D JS Foundation & Flatwork..........913 441-1909
16160 174th St Bonner Springs (66012) ***(G-547)***
D Kohake..........785 857-3854
677 120th Rd Centralia (66415) ***(G-698)***
D L P Services Inc..........913 685-1477
8181 W 123rd Ter Overland Park (66213) ***(G-8628)***
D L Smith Electrical Cnstr..........785 267-4920
1405 Sw 41st St Topeka (66609) ***(G-12543)***
D Marios, Cheney *Also called Cheney Lanes Inc* ***(G-790)***
D P Enterprises Inc..........316 263-4234
2413 S Laura St Wichita (67216) ***(G-14159)***
D Rockey Holdings Inc..........816 474-9423
87 Shawnee Ave Kansas City (66105) ***(G-3950)***
D S & W Well Servicing Inc..........620 793-5838
1822 24th St Great Bend (67530) ***(G-2551)***
D V Douglass Roofing Inc..........620 276-7474
1215 W Mary St Garden City (67846) ***(G-2141)***
D W Newcomers Sons Inc..........913 451-1860
11200 Metcalf Ave Overland Park (66210) ***(G-8629)***
D W Newcomers Sons Inc..........316 684-8200
12100 E 13th St N Wichita (67206) ***(G-14160)***
D&A Services Inc..........316 943-8857
926 E Douglas Ave Wichita (67202) ***(G-14161)***

D&D Machine Inc ... 316 269-1553
1714 S Baehr St Wichita (67209) *(G-14162)*
D&K Painting Inc ... 785 537-4779
3986 Foxridge Dr Manhattan (66502) *(G-6610)*
D&M Construction, Kansas City *Also called Wilson Ielah (G-4546)*
D-J Engineering Inc ... 620 456-3211
723 E Spring Ave Conway Springs (67031) *(G-1138)*
D-J Engineering Inc (PA) ... 316 775-1212
219 W 6th Ave Augusta (67010) *(G-316)*
D-J Extruding LLC ... 620 456-3211
723 E Spring Ave Conway Springs (67031) *(G-1139)*
DA Painting Inc ... 913 829-2075
13724 W 158th St Olathe (66062) *(G-7639)*
Dab of Lenexa KS I LLC ... 605 275-9499
9630 Rosehill Rd Lenexa (66215) *(G-5799)*
Dab of Lenexa KS II LLC ... 913 492-4516
9620 Rosehill Rd Lenexa (66215) *(G-5800)*
Dacus Autobody, McPherson *Also called Dacus LLC (G-6955)*
Dacus LLC ... 620 241-6054
2088 E South Front St McPherson (67460) *(G-6955)*
Dade Construction LLC ... 913 208-1968
6352 County Line Rd Kansas City (66106) *(G-3951)*
DAgostino Mech Contrs Inc ... 913 384-5170
4440 Oliver St Kansas City (66106) *(G-3952)*
Dahmer Contracting Group LLC ... 816 795-3332
8375 Nieman Rd Overland Park (66214) *(G-8630)*
Daikin Applied Americas Inc ... 913 492-8885
10623 Rene St Shawnee Mission (66215) *(G-11290)*
Dairy Farmers America Inc (PA) ... 816 801-6455
1405 N 98th St Kansas City (66111) *(G-3953)*
Daka Inc (PA) ... 913 768-1803
8841 Roe Ave Prairie Village (66207) *(G-10025)*
Dalan Inc ... 913 384-5662
8220 Travis St Ste 200 Overland Park (66204) *(G-8631)*
Dale Brothers, Shawnee *Also called D Doubled Inc (G-10938)*
Dale P Denning MD Facs ... 785 856-8346
1130 W 4th St Ste 2051 Lawrence (66044) *(G-4824)*
Dale's Athletic Club, Shawnee Mission *Also called Lyerla Associates (G-11585)*
Dale's Body Shop, Olathe *Also called P & D Inc (G-7969)*
Dales Tow Service Inc ... 913 782-2289
15345 S Keeler St Olathe (66062) *(G-7640)*
Dallas Caster DDS ... 785 256-2476
8370 Sw Auburn Rd Topeka (66699) *(G-12544)*
Dalmark Management Group LLC ... 816 272-0041
12220 State Line Rd Leawood (66209) *(G-5368)*
Dalton L Hunt DDS ... 620 543-2768
115 N Main St Buhler (67522) *(G-615)*
Damage Ctrl & Restoration Inc ... 913 722-0228
413 Division St Kansas City (66103) *(G-3954)*
Damar Resources Inc ... 785 625-0020
234 W 11th St Ste A Hays (67601) *(G-2781)*
Damm Pipe Testing LLC ... 620 617-8990
5548 Oilcenter Rd S Great Bend (67530) *(G-2552)*
Dan A Burton DDS ... 316 684-5511
219 S Hillside St Wichita (67211) *(G-14163)*
Dan Dee Air, Hutchinson *Also called Dandee Air Inc (G-3253)*
Dan Diehl ... 785 336-2175
512 Main St Seneca (66538) *(G-10863)*
Dana F Cole & Company LLP ... 913 341-8200
9300 W 110th St Ste 145 Overland Park (66210) *(G-8632)*
Dana Manweiler Milby PA ... 316 267-8677
300 W Douglas Ave Ste 600 Wichita (67202) *(G-14164)*
Dance Factory Inc ... 785 272-4548
5331 Sw 22nd Pl Ste 42 Topeka (66614) *(G-12545)*
Dance Gallery ... 785 838-9100
4940 Legends Dr Lawrence (66049) *(G-4825)*
Danco Systems Inc (PA) ... 913 962-0600
11101 Johnson Dr Shawnee (66203) *(G-10939)*
Dandee Air Inc ... 620 663-4341
639 W 2nd Ave Hutchinson (67501) *(G-3253)*
Dandelion & Mudd Puddles Cdc ... 913 825-0399
13811 W 63rd St Shawnee (66216) *(G-10940)*
Dandurand Drug Company Inc ... 316 685-2353
7732 E Central Ave # 108 Wichita (67206) *(G-14165)*
Dane G Hansen Memorial M ... 785 689-4848
110 W Main St Logan (67646) *(G-6423)*
Daniel A Tatpati MD ... 316 689-6803
1515 S Clifton Ave # 460 Wichita (67218) *(G-14166)*
Daniel Aires MD ... 913 588-6050
3901 Rainbow Blvd 2027 Kansas City (66160) *(G-3955)*
Daniel J Geha MD ... 913 383-9099
8800 State Line Rd Leawood (66206) *(G-5369)*
Daniel S Durrie Cokingtin LLC ... 913 491-3330
8300 College Blvd Ste 201 Overland Park (66210) *(G-8633)*
Daniel Todd Industries Inc ... 913 780-0382
230 N Monroe St Ste A Olathe (66061) *(G-7641)*
Daniel Zimmerman ... 303 378-2511
12009 W 163rd St Overland Park (66221) *(G-8634)*
Daniksco Office Interiors LLC ... 620 259-8009
1125 E 4th Ave 11 Hutchinson (67501) *(G-3254)*
Daniksco Office Interiors LLC (PA) ... 316 491-2607
6010 N Broadway Ave Park City (67219) *(G-9616)*
Danisco, New Century *Also called E I Du Pont De Nemours & Co (G-7283)*
Danisco Ingredients Usa Inc ... 913 764-8100
4 New Century Pkwy New Century (66031) *(G-7275)*
Danisco USA Inc (HQ) ... 913 764-8100
4 New Century Pkwy New Century (66031) *(G-7276)*
Danisco USA Inc ... 913 764-8100
201 Century Pkwy New Century (66031) *(G-7277)*
Danny Axe ... 620 767-5211
1040 N Union St Council Grove (66846) *(G-1162)*
Danny Satterfield Drywall Corp ... 316 942-5155
4317 W 29th Cir S Wichita (67215) *(G-14167)*
Dans Heating & Cooling Inc ... 316 522-0372
242 N New York Ave Wichita (67214) *(G-14168)*
Danville Industries ... 620 896-7126
124 W Main St Harper (67058) *(G-2719)*
Darco Inc ... 620 221-7529
3800 S Pike Rd Winfield (67156) *(G-16138)*
Darcorporation, Lawrence *Also called Design Analysis and RES Corp (G-4833)*
Dark Horse Distillery LLC ... 913 492-3275
11740 W 86th Ter Lenexa (66214) *(G-5801)*
Darlene Coffey ... 620 229-8888
3803 S Pike Rd Winfield (67156) *(G-16139)*
Darling Ingredients Inc ... 913 321-9328
685 S Adams St Kansas City (66105) *(G-3956)*
Darling Ingredients Inc ... 316 264-6951
2155 N Mosley Ave Wichita (67214) *(G-14169)*
Darling Ingredients Inc ... 913 371-7083
229 N James St Kansas City (66118) *(G-3957)*
Darling Ingredients Inc ... 620 276-7618
755 S Farmland Rd Garden City (67846) *(G-2142)*
Darling Ingredients Inc ... 785 336-2535
1188 144th Rd Seneca (66538) *(G-10864)*
Darrah Oil Company LLC ... 316 219-3390
125 N Market St Ste 1425 Wichita (67202) *(G-14170)*
Darrell Bybee Construction LLC ... 316 409-4186
1341 S Ellis St Wichita (67211) *(G-14171)*
Darren Miller ... 620 276-4515
407 N 7th St Garden City (67846) *(G-2143)*
Darrow Company ... 800 525-6084
9310 W 85th St Overland Park (66212) *(G-8635)*
Dart Cherokee Basin Oper LLC ... 620 331-7870
211 W Myrtle St Independence (67301) *(G-3509)*
Darwin Industries Inc ... 620 251-8438
5184 E Industrial Rd B Coffeyville (67337) *(G-932)*
Data Center Inc (PA) ... 620 694-6800
20 W 2nd Ave Ste 300 Hutchinson (67501) *(G-3255)*
Data Center Inc ... 913 492-2468
10051 Lakeview Ave Lenexa (66219) *(G-5802)*
Data Center Inc ... 620 694-6800
220 E Sherman St Hutchinson (67501) *(G-3256)*
Data Locker Inc ... 913 310-9088
7300 College Blvd Ste 600 Overland Park (66210) *(G-8636)*
Data Max of Kansas City ... 913 752-2200
8030 Flint St Bldg 26 Lenexa (66214) *(G-5803)*
Data Source of Kansas LLC ... 620 735-4353
17000 Ne State Road 177 Cassoday (66842) *(G-687)*
Data Systems Inc ... 913 281-1333
11505 W 79th St Overland Park (66214) *(G-8637)*
Data2logistics LLC ... 816 483-9000
5427 Johnson Dr 265 Shawnee Mission (66205) *(G-11291)*
Dataco Derex Inc (PA) ... 913 438-2444
6217 W 127th Ter Leawood (66209) *(G-5370)*
Datalocker, Overland Park *Also called Data Locker Inc (G-8636)*
Datasystem Solutions Inc ... 913 362-6969
6901 Shawnee Mission Pkwy # 207 Overland Park (66202) *(G-8638)*
Datateam Systems Inc ... 785 843-8150
4911 Legends Dr Lawrence (66049) *(G-4826)*
Dauer Implement Company Inc ... 785 825-2141
1101 E Iron Ave Salina (67401) *(G-10470)*
Daughters & Company Inc ... 913 341-2500
10560 Barkley St Ste 320 Overland Park (66212) *(G-8639)*
Dave Holland Portable Toilets, Emporia *Also called Daves Pumping Service Inc (G-1727)*
Dave McDermott ... 785 354-8233
1130 Sw Winding Rd Topeka (66615) *(G-12546)*
Dave Tarter ... 620 227-8031
710 3rd Ave Dodge City (67801) *(G-1339)*
Daves Pumping Service Inc ... 620 343-3081
1257 Road 137 Emporia (66801) *(G-1727)*
Daves Service & Repair Inc ... 620 662-8285
6005 S Broadacres Rd Hutchinson (67501) *(G-3257)*
David B Laha MD Bpm ... 913 338-4440
7230 W 129th St Overland Park (66213) *(G-8640)*
David B Lyon MD ... 913 261-2020
11261 Nall Ave Leawood (66211) *(G-5371)*
David Camp Inc ... 913 648-0573
7920 Foster St Overland Park (66204) *(G-8641)*
David Cobler ... 785 234-3384
908 N Kansas Ave Topeka (66608) *(G-12547)*

David E Dishop ... 614 861-5440
10821 E Wichita (67226) ***(G-14172)***
David Koepsel DDS LLC ... 316 686-7395
8150 E Douglas Ave Ste 10 Wichita (67206) ***(G-14173)***
David Lies Plumbing Inc ... 316 945-0117
1420 S Sabin St Wichita (67209) ***(G-14174)***
David M King & Associates (PA) ... 785 841-9517
1425 Oread West St # 106 Lawrence (66049) ***(G-4827)***
David M King & Associates ... 319 377-4636
103 W 13th St Bsmt Hays (67601) ***(G-2782)***
David Vodonick MD, Shawnee Mission *Also called E M Specialist PA* ***(G-11323)***
David W Head ... 913 402-0057
12721 W 138th Pl Overland Park (66221) ***(G-8642)***
David's Jewelers, Topeka *Also called Mark Boose* ***(G-12860)***
Davidson & Associates Inc ... 913 271-6859
12701 El Monte St Leawood (66209) ***(G-5372)***
Davidson Arch Engrg LLC ... 913 451-9390
4301 Indian Creek Pkwy Overland Park (66207) ***(G-8643)***
Davidson Archicture and Engr ... 913 451-9390
4301 Indian Creek Pkwy Shawnee Mission (66207) ***(G-11292)***
Davidson-Babcock, Shawnee Mission *Also called Cjd & Associates LLC* ***(G-11235)***
Davies Communications Inc ... 620 241-1504
411 E Euclid St McPherson (67460) ***(G-6956)***
Davin Electric Inc ... 785 234-2350
2131 Ne Grantville Rd Topeka (66608) ***(G-12548)***
Davinci Reprographics ... 913 371-0014
1140 Adams St Kansas City (66103) ***(G-3958)***
Davinci Roofscapes LLC ... 913 599-0766
13890 W 101st St Lenexa (66215) ***(G-5804)***
Davis & Jack LLC ... 316 945-8251
2121 W Maple St Wichita (67213) ***(G-14175)***
Davis Construction LLC ... 620 674-3100
2143 Ne Highway 7 Columbus (66725) ***(G-1074)***
Davis Contracting LP ... 620 331-3922
4775 E Us Highway 160 Independence (67301) ***(G-3510)***
Davis G Sam Insurance ... 913 451-1800
6240 W 135th St Ste 100 Shawnee Mission (66223) ***(G-11293)***
Davis Ketchmark McCreight ... 816 842-1515
11161 Overbrook Rd Leawood (66211) ***(G-5373)***
Davis Ktchmark Eschens McCrght ... 816 842-1515
11161 Overbrook Rd # 210 Leawood (66211) ***(G-5374)***
Davis Manufacturing, Bonner Springs *Also called H C Davis Sons Mfg Co* ***(G-554)***
Davis Moore Lincoln, Wichita *Also called Dept Lincoln Service* ***(G-14197)***
Davis Publications Inc (PA) ... 785 945-6170
416 Broadway St Valley Falls (66088) ***(G-13362)***
Davis Unrein Hummer McCalister ... 785 354-1100
100 Se 9th St Fl 2 Topeka (66612) ***(G-12549)***
Davis, William D, Hutchinson *Also called Medical Center P A* ***(G-3368)***
Davita Healthcare Partners Inc ... 316 773-1400
10001 W Grady Ave Maize (67101) ***(G-6512)***
Davita Inc ... 620 331-6117
801 W Myrtle St Independence (67301) ***(G-3511)***
Davita Inc ... 913 660-8881
8922 Millstone Dr Lenexa (66220) ***(G-5805)***
Davy Harkins Dvm ... 316 321-1050
111 E Locust Ave El Dorado (67042) ***(G-1555)***
Dawson Place Inc ... 785 421-3414
208 W Prout St Hill City (67642) ***(G-3032)***
Day & Zimmermann Kansas LLC ... 620 421-7400
23102 Rush Rd Parsons (67357) ***(G-9679)***
Day and Zimmermann Inc ... 620 421-7400
23102 Rush Rd Parsons (67357) ***(G-9680)***
Day Farms Inc ... 620 398-2255
6008 W Illinois Healy (67850) ***(G-2965)***
Day Funeral Home & Crematory, Wellington *Also called Day Funeral Home Inc* ***(G-13497)***
Day Funeral Home Inc ... 620 326-5100
1030 Mission Rd Wellington (67152) ***(G-13497)***
Daylight Donuts, Garden City *Also called Johnny Schwindt Inc* ***(G-2209)***
Daymark Solutions Inc ... 913 541-8980
7800 Shawnee Mission Pkwy # 14 Shawnee Mission (66202) ***(G-11294)***
Daymon Worldwide Inc ... 620 669-4200
1302 N Grand St Hutchinson (67501) ***(G-3258)***
Days Inn, Lawrence *Also called Sterling Centrecorp Inc* ***(G-5124)***
Days Inn, Wichita *Also called Turnpike Investments Inc* ***(G-15816)***
Days Inn, Leavenworth *Also called Sterling Centrecorp Inc* ***(G-5291)***
Days Inn, Ottawa *Also called Sterling Centrecorp Inc* ***(G-8314)***
Days Inn, Newton *Also called Prairie Inn Inc* ***(G-7406)***
Days Inn ... 785 823-9791
407 W Diamond Dr Salina (67401) ***(G-10471)***
Days Inn Inc ... 316 942-1717
550 S Florence St Wichita (67209) ***(G-14176)***
Days Inn of Overland Park ... 913 341-0100
6800 W 108th St Leawood (66211) ***(G-5375)***
Days Inn Olathe Medical Center ... 913 390-9500
20662 W 151st St Olathe (66061) ***(G-7642)***
Days Inn Suites Hutchinson LLC ... 620 665-3700
1420 N Lorraine St Hutchinson (67501) ***(G-3259)***

Daystar Petroleum Inc ... 316 755-3492
1321 W 93rd St N Valley Center (67147) ***(G-13340)***
Daystar Petroleum Inc ... 620 583-5527
522 N Main St Eureka (67045) ***(G-1883)***
Dayton Superior Corporation ... 937 866-0711
1900 Wilson Ave Parsons (67357) ***(G-9681)***
Dayton Superior Corporation ... 913 279-4800
4226 Kansas Ave Kansas City (66106) ***(G-3959)***
Dayton Superior Corporation ... 913 596-9784
636 S 66th Ter Kansas City (66111) ***(G-3960)***
Db Flooring LLC ... 913 663-9922
9555 Alden St Lenexa (66215) ***(G-5806)***
Db2 Services Inc ... 913 677-2408
508 S 14th St Kansas City (66105) ***(G-3961)***
Dbi Inc ... 316 831-9323
3707 N Topeka St Wichita (67219) ***(G-14177)***
Dbi Inc (PA) ... 913 888-2321
15440 W 109th St Lenexa (66219) ***(G-5807)***
DC Oilfield Services ... 620 598-2643
W Hwy 56 Moscow (67952) ***(G-7167)***
Dcc, Wichita *Also called Decorator and Craft Corp* ***(G-14184)***
Dccca Inc ... 316 267-2030
1319 W May St Wichita (67213) ***(G-14178)***
Dccca Inc ... 620 670-2803
1102 S Rouse St Pittsburg (66762) ***(G-9851)***
Dccca Inc ... 620 672-7546
501 S Ninnescah St Pratt (67124) ***(G-10107)***
Dccca Inc ... 620 670-2814
104 1/2 W 9th Ave Ste 503 Winfield (67156) ***(G-16140)***
Dccca Inc ... 785 830-8238
1739 E 23rd St Lawrence (66046) ***(G-4828)***
Dccca Inc ... 785 843-9262
3015 W 31st St Lawrence (66047) ***(G-4829)***
Dccca Inc ... 316 265-6011
122 N Millwood St Wichita (67203) ***(G-14179)***
DCI, Olathe *Also called Design Concepts Inc* ***(G-7651)***
DCI Studios ... 913 385-9550
8010 State Line Rd # 200 Prairie Village (66208) ***(G-10026)***
Dcm Wichita Inc (PA) ... 800 662-9573
1233 Willowbrook Ln Towanda (67144) ***(G-13263)***
Dcp Operating Company LP ... 620 626-1201
7635 Road 3 Liberal (67901) ***(G-6301)***
Dcs Inc ... 316 806-4899
2300 N Nelson Dr Unit 13 Derby (67037) ***(G-1233)***
DCS Sanitation Management Inc ... 620 624-5533
1406 N Western Ave Liberal (67901) ***(G-6302)***
Dd Sports, Merriam *Also called Ddsports Inc* ***(G-7090)***
Dd Traders Inc (PA) ... 913 402-6800
5000 W 134th St Leawood (66209) ***(G-5376)***
Dd Traders Inc ... 913 402-6800
31426 W 191st St Gardner (66030) ***(G-2337)***
Dda Sales/Service, Great Bend *Also called Central Pwr Systems & Svcs LLC* ***(G-2534)***
Dddi Commercial Inc ... 913 685-4100
7200 W 132nd St Ste 300 Shawnee Mission (66213) ***(G-11295)***
Ddi Holdings Inc (PA) ... 913 371-2200
640 Miami Ave Kansas City (66105) ***(G-3962)***
Ddsports Inc ... 913 636-0432
7220 W Frontage Rd Merriam (66203) ***(G-7090)***
De Hoff Tool & Mfg Co Inc ... 913 342-2212
1021 S Pyle St Kansas City (66105) ***(G-3963)***
De Leon Furniture Inc ... 913 342-9446
1142 Minnesota Ave Kansas City (66102) ***(G-3964)***
Deaconess Long Term Care of MI ... 785 242-5399
1100 W 15th St Ofc Ottawa (66067) ***(G-8264)***
Deaconess Long Term Care of MI ... 785 242-9378
1527 S Twyman St Ottawa (66067) ***(G-8265)***
Deaf Cultural Ctr Foundation ... 913 782-5808
455 E Park St Olathe (66061) ***(G-7643)***
Dean Development Inc ... 913 685-4100
7200 W 132nd St Ste 300 Shawnee Mission (66213) ***(G-11296)***
Dean E Norris Inc ... 316 688-1901
2929 S Minneapolis Ave Wichita (67216) ***(G-14180)***
Dean E Small ... 913 642-2714
9425 W 75th St Shawnee Mission (66204) ***(G-11297)***
Deans Designs Inc ... 316 686-6674
3555 E Douglas Ave Ste 35 Wichita (67218) ***(G-14181)***
Dearborn Animal Clinic PA ... 913 722-2800
6100 Johnson Dr Shawnee Mission (66202) ***(G-11298)***
Dearborn Mid West Conveyor Co ... 913 261-2428
8245 Nieman Rd Ste 123 Overland Park (66214) ***(G-8644)***
Debackers Inc ... 785 232-6999
1520 Se 10th Ave Topeka (66607) ***(G-12550)***
Debakey Heart Clinic ... 785 625-4699
2220 Canterbury Dr Hays (67601) ***(G-2783)***
Deborah John & Associates ... 316 777-0903
3000 W Kellogg Dr Wichita (67213) ***(G-14182)***
Debra L Heidgen ... 913 772-6046
3550 S 4th St Ste 120 Leavenworth (66048) ***(G-5231)***
Debrick Truck Line Company (PA) ... 913 294-5020
33130 Lone Star Rd Paola (66071) ***(G-9551)***

Deca Outpatient, Lawrence *Also called Dccca Inc* ***(G-4828)***
Decatur Coop Assoc, Oberlin *Also called Decatur Cooperative Assn* ***(G-7490)***
Decatur Cooperative Assn (PA)....785 475-2234
305 S York Ave Oberlin (67749) ***(G-7490)***
Decatur County Feed Yard Inc....785 475-2212
2361 Highway 83 Oberlin (67749) ***(G-7491)***
Decatur County Hospital, Oberlin *Also called Decatur Health Systems Inc* ***(G-7492)***
Decatur Health Systems Inc....785 475-2208
810 W Columbia St Oberlin (67749) ***(G-7492)***
Dechra Veterinary Products LLC (HQ)....913 327-0015
7015 College Blvd Ste 525 Overland Park (66211) ***(G-8645)***
Deciphera Pharmaceuticals LLC....785 830-2100
643 Msschsetts St Ste 200 Lawrence (66044) ***(G-4830)***
Decker Construction Inc (PA)....620 251-7693
1215 E 8th St Coffeyville (67337) ***(G-933)***
Decker Electric Inc....316 265-8182
4500 W Harry St Wichita (67209) ***(G-14183)***
Decorative Concrete Supply, Shawnee *Also called Chemsystems Kansas Inc* ***(G-10927)***
Decorator and Craft Corp (PA)....316 685-6265
428 S Zelta St Wichita (67207) ***(G-14184)***
Dee Jays Enterprises....620 227-3126
10764 Us Highway 50 Dodge City (67801) ***(G-1340)***
Dee's Mini Mart, Gardner *Also called L & M Oil Company* ***(G-2353)***
Dee's Mini-Mart, Gardner *Also called L & M Oil Company* ***(G-2352)***
Deelliotte Company Inc....913 764-0606
201 Prairie Village Dr New Century (66031) ***(G-7278)***
Deer Creek Golf Club, Shawnee Mission *Also called American Golf Corporation* ***(G-11103)***
Deer Creek Surgery Center LLC....913 897-0022
7220 W 129th St Overland Park (66213) ***(G-8646)***
Deer Lk Esttes Homeowners Assn....316 640-6592
4236 E Wildflower Cir Wichita (67210) ***(G-14185)***
Deer Trail Implement Inc....620 342-5000
1744 Road F Emporia (66801) ***(G-1728)***
Deer Valley Plaza 16, Leawood *Also called Regal Cinemas Inc* ***(G-5537)***
Deere & Company....309 765-4826
10789 S Ridgeview Rd Olathe (66061) ***(G-7644)***
Deere & Company....913 310-8100
10789 S Ridgeview Rd Olathe (66061) ***(G-7645)***
Deere & Company....913 310-8344
10789 S Ridgeview Rd Olathe (66061) ***(G-7646)***
Deere & Company....800 665-4620
1800 S Lorraine St Hutchinson (67501) ***(G-3260)***
Deere & Company....316 945-0501
2256 S West St Wichita (67213) ***(G-14186)***
Deffenbaugh Industries Inc (HQ)....913 631-3300
2601 Midwest Dr Kansas City (66111) ***(G-3965)***
Deffenbaugh Industries Inc....913 208-1000
1600 E 151st Ter Olathe (66062) ***(G-7647)***
Defy Medical Group LLC....913 396-2888
14105 Kessler St Overland Park (66221) ***(G-8647)***
Deg, Overland Park *Also called Hss IT Management Inc* ***(G-8832)***
Del Monte Foods, Lawrence *Also called Big Heart Pet Brands* ***(G-4757)***
Delaney Implement Co Inc....620 525-6221
502 Broadway Ave Burdett (67523) ***(G-621)***
Delange Seed House Inc (PA)....620 724-6223
537 W 47 Hwy Girard (66743) ***(G-2401)***
Delano, Wichita *Also called Bakery Projects Inc* ***(G-13796)***
Delaware Hghlnds Assistd Lvng....913 721-1400
12600 Delaware Pkwy Kansas City (66109) ***(G-3966)***
Delbert Chopp Co Inc....785 825-8530
448 N Front St Salina (67401) ***(G-10472)***
Delich Roth & Goodwillie PA (PA)....913 441-1100
913 Sheidley Ave Ste 110 Bonner Springs (66012) ***(G-548)***
Delich Roth & Goodwillie PA....913 441-1100
913 Sheidley Ave Ste 110 Bonner Springs (66012) ***(G-549)***
Delight Tb Indiana LLC....561 301-6257
P.O. Box 780023 Wichita (67278) ***(G-14187)***
Dell Ann Upp....785 473-7001
1223 Moro St Manhattan (66502) ***(G-6611)***
Delmar Gardens Lenexa Oper LLC....913 492-1130
9701 Monrovia St Lenexa (66215) ***(G-5808)***
Delmar Gardens of Lenexa Inc (PA)....913 492-1130
9701 Monrovia St Lenexa (66215) ***(G-5809)***
Delmar Gardens of Lenexa Inc....913 492-8682
9705 Monrovia St Ofc Shawnee Mission (66215) ***(G-11299)***
Delmar Gardens of Overland Pk....913 469-4210
12100 W 109th St Shawnee Mission (66210) ***(G-11300)***
Delmarva Pad Co....620 665-9757
406 S Obee Rd Hutchinson (67501) ***(G-3261)***
Delphia Family Practice, Olathe *Also called Olathe Medical Services Inc* ***(G-7946)***
Delphos Cooperative Assn....785 523-4213
413 W 1st St Delphos (67436) ***(G-1216)***
Dels Alternator & Starter Svc....785 825-4466
901 N 8th St Salina (67401) ***(G-10473)***
Delta Dental of Kansas Inc....913 381-4928
11300 Tomahawk Crk Pkwy # 350 Leawood (66211) ***(G-5377)***
Delta Dental of Kansas Inc (PA)....316 264-4511
1619 N Waterfront Pkwy Wichita (67206) ***(G-14188)***
Delta Electric Co Inc....316 267-2869
2442 S Saint Francis St Wichita (67216) ***(G-14189)***
Delta Gamma....785 830-9945
1015 Emery Rd Lawrence (66044) ***(G-4831)***
Delta Homes Inc....316 777-0009
1555 E 120th Ave N Mulvane (67110) ***(G-7215)***
Delta Innovative Services Inc....913 371-7100
508 S 14th St Kansas City (66105) ***(G-3967)***
Delta Kappa Gamma Society....620 793-3977
2331 Garfield St Great Bend (67530) ***(G-2553)***
Delta Omega of Delta Zeta Bldg....785 625-3719
410 W 6th St Hays (67601) ***(G-2784)***
Delta Supply, Garden City *Also called Eatherly Constructors Inc* ***(G-2151)***
Delta Tau Delta of Lawrence, Lawrence *Also called Delta Tau Delta Society* ***(G-4832)***
Delta Tau Delta Society....785 843-6866
1111 W 11th St Lawrence (66044) ***(G-4832)***
Delta Upsilon Fraternity, Wichita *Also called Delta Upsilon House Corp* ***(G-14190)***
Delta Upsilon House Corp (PA)....316 295-4320
1720 N Vassar Ave Wichita (67208) ***(G-14190)***
Deluxe Check Printers, Lenexa *Also called Deluxe Corporation* ***(G-5810)***
Deluxe Corporation....913 888-3801
16505 W 113th St Lenexa (66219) ***(G-5810)***
Demaranville & Assoc Cpas LLC....913 682-4548
121 Cherokee St Leavenworth (66048) ***(G-5232)***
Demarche Associates Inc....913 384-4994
6700 Antioch Rd Ste 420 Overland Park (66204) ***(G-8648)***
Demars Pnsion Cnslting Svcs In....913 469-6111
8700 Indian Creek Pkwy Overland Park (66210) ***(G-8649)***
Demdaco, Leawood *Also called Dd Traders Inc* ***(G-5376)***
Demdaco, Gardner *Also called Dd Traders Inc* ***(G-2337)***
Demo Distributors, Independence *Also called Best Beverage Sales Inc* ***(G-3500)***
Demo Sales Inc....316 320-6670
202 W 5th Ave El Dorado (67042) ***(G-1556)***
Dempsey Foundery, Kansas City *Also called Dempsey Inc* ***(G-3968)***
Dempsey Inc....913 371-3107
72 Central Ave Kansas City (66118) ***(G-3968)***
Den Management Co Inc (PA)....316 686-1964
4053 E Navajo Ln Wichita (67210) ***(G-14191)***
Denco Aluminum Inc....620 724-6325
109 E Southern Blvd Girard (66743) ***(G-2402)***
Denison Inc (PA)....620 378-4148
405 Madison St Fredonia (66736) ***(G-2030)***
Denison Weldings Supplies, Fredonia *Also called Denison Inc* ***(G-2030)***
Dennis C McAllister DDS PA....316 788-3736
1700 E James St Derby (67037) ***(G-1234)***
Dennis Knudsen Dr....620 624-3811
222 W 15th St Liberal (67901) ***(G-6303)***
Dennis L Ross MD, Wichita *Also called Kansas Nphrology Physicians PA* ***(G-14816)***
Dennis M Cooley MD....785 235-0335
3500 Sw 6th Ave Topeka (66606) ***(G-12551)***
Dennis P Wetta....316 267-5293
200 W Douglas Ave Ste 830 Wichita (67202) ***(G-14192)***
Dennis R Sumner Construction....785 478-1701
915 Nw Valencia Rd Topeka (66615) ***(G-12552)***
Dennys Heating & Cooling....316 283-1598
506 W 22nd St North Newton (67117) ***(G-7435)***
Dent Busters, Wichita *Also called Tlm Enterprises Inc* ***(G-15771)***
Dental Associates....620 276-7681
1133 E Kansas Plz Garden City (67846) ***(G-2144)***
Dental Associates....785 539-7401
1133 College Ave Ste D202 Manhattan (66502) ***(G-6612)***
Dental Associates W Wichita PA....316 942-5358
444 N Ridge Rd Wichita (67212) ***(G-14193)***
Dental Care Family, Hutchinson *Also called James P Gertken DDS* ***(G-3341)***
Dental Clinic, Pittsburg *Also called Community Health Center of Sou* ***(G-9840)***
Dental Concepts Inc....913 829-0242
13849 S Mur Len Rd Ste H Olathe (66062) ***(G-7648)***
Dental Corner....316 681-2425
2046 N Oliver Ave Wichita (67208) ***(G-14194)***
Dental Innovation....913 236-8899
11221 Shwnee Mission Pkwy Shawnee Mission (66203) ***(G-11301)***
Dental Services Group, Topeka *Also called Sentage Corporation* ***(G-13059)***
Dental Services Group, Wichita *Also called Sentage Corporation* ***(G-15561)***
Dentec Safety Specialists (PA)....905 953-9946
8101 Lenexa Dr Ste D Lenexa (66214) ***(G-5811)***
Dentek Inc....913 262-1717
8056 Reeder Rd Lenexa (66214) ***(G-5812)***
Department Corrections Kansas....913 829-6207
804 N Meadowbrook Dr # 100 Olathe (66062) ***(G-7649)***
Department of Kansas Disabled (PA)....316 681-1948
5455 E Central Ave Wichita (67208) ***(G-14195)***
Department of Preventive, Kansas City *Also called University of Kansas* ***(G-4504)***
Department of Public Works, Garden City *Also called County of Finney* ***(G-2135)***
Depco LLC....620 231-0019
264 N Industrial Dr Pittsburg (66762) ***(G-9852)***
Depew Gllen Rthbun Mclnteer Lc....316 262-4000
8301 E 21st St N Ste 450 Wichita (67206) ***(G-14196)***

ALPHABETIC

Depot Market...785 374-4255
1101 30 Rd Courtland (66939) ***(G-1180)***
Dept Lincoln Service...316 928-7331
7675 E Kellogg Dr Wichita (67207) ***(G-14197)***
Dept of Mental Health, Wichita *Also called Comcare of Sedgwick County* ***(G-14061)***
Dept of Rehab Medicine, Kansas City *Also called University of Kansas* ***(G-4496)***
Dept of Utilities, Mulvane *Also called City of Mulvane* ***(G-7213)***
Derby Bowl, Derby *Also called Frazier Enterprises Inc* ***(G-1247)***
Derby Dental Care...316 789-9999
1120 N Rock Rd Ste 100 Derby (67037) ***(G-1235)***
Derby Family Medcenter, Derby *Also called P A Family Medcenters* ***(G-1264)***
Derby Golf & Country Club, Derby *Also called Lindsey Management Co Inc* ***(G-1258)***
Derby Hotel Inc...316 425-7900
1701 E Cambridge St Derby (67037) ***(G-1236)***
Derby Machine, Derby *Also called Riverside Industries LLC* ***(G-1269)***
Derby Plaza Theaters, Derby *Also called Vbc Enterprises LLC* ***(G-1279)***
Derby Public Schools...316 788-8450
120 N Westview Dr Derby (67037) ***(G-1237)***
Derby Recreation Comm Usd 260...316 788-3781
801 E Market St Derby (67037) ***(G-1238)***
Derby School Service Center, Derby *Also called Derby Public Schools* ***(G-1237)***
Derby Steel Technologies, Derby *Also called Derby Trailer Technologies LLC* ***(G-1239)***
Derby Trailer Technologies LLC...316 788-3331
449 N Water St Derby (67037) ***(G-1239)***
Dermatology & Skin Cancer Ctr, Shawnee Mission *Also called Dermatology & Skin Cancer Ctr* ***(G-11302)***
Dermatology & Skin Cancer Ctr (PA)...913 451-7546
1'550 Granada St Shawnee Mission (66211) ***(G-11302)***
Dermatology Clinic...316 685-4395
835 N Hillside St Wichita (67214) ***(G-14198)***
Dermatology Cons Midwest...913 469-0110
10777 Nall Ave Ste 220 Overland Park (66211) ***(G-8650)***
Derrick Inn...785 798-3617
409 E Sycamore St Ness City (67560) ***(G-7261)***
Desco Coatings LLC (PA)...913 782-3330
19890 W 156th St Olathe (66062) ***(G-7650)***
Deseret Cattle Feeders LLC...620 275-6181
521 Road 50 Satanta (67870) ***(G-10783)***
Deseret Health Group...785 476-2623
6'3 N Main St Kensington (66951) ***(G-4574)***
Deseret Health Group Llc...620 662-0597
2301 N Severance St Hutchinson (67502) ***(G-3262)***
Deseret Hlth Rhab At Knsington, Kensington *Also called Deseret Health Group* ***(G-4574)***
Deseret Hlth Rhab At Onaga LLC...785 889-4227
500 Western St Onaga (66521) ***(G-8174)***
Deseret Hlth Rhab At Yates LLC...620 625-2111
801 S Fry St Yates Center (66783) ***(G-16195)***
Desert Steel Company, Wichita *Also called Desert Steel Corporation* ***(G-14199)***
Desert Steel Corporation...316 282-2244
312 N Mosley St Wichita (67202) ***(G-14199)***
Design Analysis and RES Corp...785 832-0434
910 E 29th St Lawrence (66046) ***(G-4833)***
Design Benefits...316 729-7676
404 S Holland St Ste 2 Wichita (67209) ***(G-14200)***
Design Build Steel, Lenexa *Also called Needham & Associates Inc* ***(G-6019)***
Design Central Inc...785 825-4131
152 S 5th St Salina (67401) ***(G-10474)***
Design Concepts Inc...913 782-5672
866 N Jan Mar Ct Olathe (66061) ***(G-7651)***
Design Court...620 276-3019
523 N Main St Garden City (67846) ***(G-2145)***
Design Electric, Shawnee *Also called Outdoor Lighting Services LP* ***(G-11006)***
Design Materials Inc (PA)...913 342-9796
241 S 55th St Kansas City (66106) ***(G-3969)***
Design Mechanical Inc...913 281-7200
100 Greystone Ave Kansas City (66103) ***(G-3970)***
Design Resources Inc...913 652-6522
7007 College Blvd Ste 700 Overland Park (66211) ***(G-8651)***
Design Source Flooring LLC (PA)...913 387-5858
10645 Lackman Rd Lenexa (66219) ***(G-5813)***
Designbuild Construction Inc...316 722-8180
2822 N Mead St Wichita (67219) ***(G-14201)***
Designed Bus Intrors Tpeka Inc...785 233-2078
107 Sw 6th Ave Topeka (66603) ***(G-12553)***
Designer Construction Inc...785 776-9878
2716 Eureka Ter Manhattan (66503) ***(G-6613)***
Designer Palms Inc...316 733-2284
12631 Sw Frontr Trail St Andover (67002) ***(G-89)***
Designers Library Inc...913 227-0010
9102 Barton St Shawnee Mission (66214) ***(G-11303)***
Designplast Inc...785 825-7714
431 N 13th St Salina (67401) ***(G-10475)***
Dessin Fournir Inc (HQ)...785 434-2777
308 W Mill St Plainville (67663) ***(G-9985)***
Dessin Fournir Companies, Plainville *Also called Dfc Holdings Inc* ***(G-9986)***
Dessin Fournir Companies, Plainville *Also called Dessin Fournir Inc* ***(G-9985)***
Destination Properties Inc...913 583-1515
7715 Shawnee Mission Pkwy Overland Park (66202) ***(G-8652)***
Destiny Supports Inc...620 272-0564
2508 N John St Garden City (67846) ***(G-2146)***
Detacorp Inc LLC...620 597-2552
3600 Nw 74th St Columbus (66725) ***(G-1075)***
Details Intimate Apparel, Emporia *Also called Salon X* ***(G-1820)***
Detroit Diesel, Colby *Also called Central Pwr Systems & Svcs LLC* ***(G-992)***
Detroit Diesel Remanufacturing...620 343-3790
840 Overlander Rd Emporia (66801) ***(G-1729)***
Developers and Management Inc (PA)...316 682-6770
11800 W Kellogg St Wichita (67209) ***(G-14202)***
Development Inc...913 651-9717
2500 S 2nd St Leavenworth (66048) ***(G-5233)***
Developmental Services NW KS, Russell *Also called Developmental Svcs NW Kans Inc* ***(G-10271)***
Developmental Services of Jack...785 364-3534
625 Vermont Ave Holton (66436) ***(G-3087)***
Developmental Svcs NW Kans...785 735-2262
604 8th St Victoria (67671) ***(G-13373)***
Developmental Svcs NW Kans Inc...785 626-3688
208 S 4th St Atwood (67730) ***(G-283)***
Developmental Svcs NW Kans Inc...785 421-2851
100 W Mcfarland St Hill City (67642) ***(G-3033)***
Developmental Svcs NW Kans Inc (PA)...785 625-5678
2703 Hall St Ste B10 Hays (67601) ***(G-2785)***
Developmental Svcs NW Kans Inc...785 625-2521
317 W 13th St Hays (67601) ***(G-2786)***
Developmental Svcs NW Kans Inc...785 877-5154
1104 N State St Norton (67654) ***(G-7443)***
Developmental Svcs NW Kans Inc...785 621-2078
1205 E 22nd St Hays (67601) ***(G-2787)***
Developmental Svcs NW Kans Inc...785 483-6686
15 N Maple St Russell (67665) ***(G-10271)***
Developmental Svcs NW Kans Inc...785 483-3020
1212 N Krug St Russell (67665) ***(G-10272)***
Devlin Enterprises Inc...316 634-1800
1313 N Webb Rd Ste 100 Wichita (67206) ***(G-14203)***
Devlin Management Inc...316 634-1800
1313 N Webb Rd Ste 100 Wichita (67206) ***(G-14204)***
Devlin Partners LLC...913 894-1300
15617 W 87th St Lenexa (66219) ***(G-5814)***
Devore & Sons Inc...316 267-3211
9020 E 35th St N Wichita (67226) ***(G-14205)***
Dew - Drink Eat Well LLC...785 856-3399
2205 Haskell Ave Lawrence (66046) ***(G-4834)***
Dewaay Financial Network LLC...316 303-1985
245 N Waco St Ste 525 Wichita (67202) ***(G-14206)***
Dewald Enterprises...316 655-1155
224 Cory Dr Andover (67002) ***(G-90)***
Dewalt Interprises., Andover *Also called Dewald Enterprises* ***(G-90)***
Deweze Manufacturing, Harper *Also called Harper Industries Inc* ***(G-2723)***
Deyno LLC...785 551-8949
925 Iowa St Ste K Lawrence (66044) ***(G-4835)***
DF Osborne Construction Inc...785 862-0333
3310 Sw Harrison St Ste 1 Topeka (66611) ***(G-12554)***
Dfc Holdings Inc (PA)...785 434-2777
308 W Mill St Plainville (67663) ***(G-9986)***
Dg Business Solutions Inc...913 766-0163
11008 Rene St Lenexa (66215) ***(G-5815)***
Dgi Print Solutions, Lenexa *Also called Dimension Graphics Inc* ***(G-5820)***
Dgs-Re LLC...913 288-1000
5000 Kansas Ave Kansas City (66106) ***(G-3971)***
Dhl Express (usa) Inc...316 943-7683
2163 S Air Cargo Rd Wichita (67209) ***(G-14207)***
Diabetes & Endocrinology Assoc...913 676-7585
8901 W 74th St Ste 372 Overland Park (66204) ***(G-8653)***
Diabetes and Endocrinology Ctr, Topeka *Also called Stormont-Vail Healthcare Inc* ***(G-13107)***
Diagnostic Imaging Center...913 491-9299
5500 College Blvd Shawnee Mission (66211) ***(G-11304)***
Diagnostic Imaging Center...913 491-9299
5520 College Blvd Ste 100 Shawnee Mission (66211) ***(G-11305)***
Diagnostic Imaging Center...913 344-9989
13795 S Mur Len Rd # 105 Olathe (66062) ***(G-7652)***
Diagnostic Imaging Centers PA...913 319-8450
6650 W 110th St Leawood (66211) ***(G-5378)***
DIALYSIS CENTER OF HUTCHINSON, Hutchinson *Also called Bladon Dialysis LLC* ***(G-3216)***
Diamond Acquisition LLC...620 795-2191
2300 4th St Oswego (67356) ***(G-8232)***
Diamond Coach Corporation...620 795-2191
2300 4th St Oswego (67356) ***(G-8233)***
Diamond Engineering Company...316 943-5701
3512 W Pawnee St Wichita (67213) ***(G-14208)***
Diamond Ethanol LLC...620 626-2026
1701 N Kansas Ave Liberal (67901) ***(G-6304)***
Diamond Finish Car Wash, Shawnee Mission *Also called Mission Car Wash LLC* ***(G-11644)***
Diamond Gymnstics Dnce Academy...913 851-7500
7270 W 161st St Stilwell (66085) ***(G-12144)***

Diamond Idealease, Kansas City *Also called Idealease of Mo-Kan Inc* ***(G-4095)***
Diamond Intl Trcks Inc 785 235-8711
500 E Tenth St Topeka (66607) ***(G-12555)***
Diamond Partners Inc 913 322-7500
13671 S Mur Len Rd Olathe (66062) ***(G-7653)***
Diamond Roofing, Dodge City *Also called Gwaltney Inc* ***(G-1368)***
Diamond Roofing, Manhattan *Also called Gwaltney Inc* ***(G-6648)***
Diamond Security Lc 316 263-3883
220 W Douglas Ave Ste 150 Wichita (67202) ***(G-14209)***
Diamond Tools & Equipment, Lenexa *Also called Diteq Corporation* ***(G-5821)***
Diamond Transfer & Dist Co 785 825-1531
1012 W North St Salina (67401) ***(G-10476)***
Diamond-Everley Roofing Contrs, Perry *Also called Mt 3 Corporation* ***(G-9772)***
Diane Londene 785 233-1991
2926 Sw 10th Ave Topeka (66604) ***(G-12556)***
Dick Construction Inc 620 275-1806
1805 E Mary St Ste A Garden City (67846) ***(G-2147)***
Dick Edwards Ford Lincoln Merc (PA) 785 320-4499
1825 Goldenbelt Blvd Junction City (66441) ***(G-3687)***
Dickinson County 785 263-1431
705 N Brady St Abilene (67410) ***(G-24)***
Dickinson County Learning Exch, Salina *Also called Abilene Unified Schl Dst 435* ***(G-10389)***
Dickinson County Rur Wtr Dst 1 ....785 388-2290
2979 Main St Talmage (67482) ***(G-12237)***
Dickinson Theatres 913 383-6114
6801 W 107th St Overland Park (66212) ***(G-8654)***
Dicks Engine & Machine Service 620 564-2238
803 E Santa Fe Blvd Ellinwood (67526) ***(G-1629)***
Dicks Thriftway 785 456-2525
1009 Lincoln Ave Wamego (66547) ***(G-13414)***
Dickson-Diveley Midwest Ortho 913 319-7600
3651 College Blvd 100c Shawnee Mission (66211) ***(G-11306)***
Diebolt LLC 620 496-2222
214 Sunflower Ln Iola (66749) ***(G-3598)***
Diecks Inc 785 632-5550
212 6th St Clay Center (67432) ***(G-860)***
Diehl Banwart Bolton Jarred (PA) 620 223-4300
7 1/2 E Wall St Fort Scott (66701) ***(G-1964)***
Digestive Health Center, Topeka *Also called Cotton Oneil Clinic Endoscopy* ***(G-12512)***
Diggs Construction Company 316 691-1255
3101 E 9th St N Wichita (67214) ***(G-14210)***
Diggs Holding Company, Wichita *Also called Diggs Construction Company* ***(G-14210)***
Dighton Herald 620 397-5347
113 E Long St Dighton (67839) ***(G-1284)***
Digital Ally Inc 913 814-7774
9705 Loiret Blvd Lenexa (66219) ***(G-5816)***
Digital Evolution Group LLC 913 498-9988
6601 College Blvd 6 Overland Park (66211) ***(G-8655)***
Digital Lagoon Inc 913 648-6900
9121 Bond St Overland Park (66214) ***(G-8656)***
Digital Office Systems Inc 316 262-7700
530 S Hydraulic St Wichita (67211) ***(G-14211)***
Digital Printing Services Inc 913 492-1500
13309 W 98th St Lenexa (66215) ***(G-5817)***
Digital Simplistics Inc 913 643-2445
14207 W 95th St Lenexa (66215) ***(G-5818)***
Digital Sound Systems Inc (PA) 913 492-5775
9721 Loiret Blvd Lenexa (66219) ***(G-5819)***
Digitech Systems, Topeka *Also called Computer Distribution Corp* ***(G-12498)***
Dignity Care Home Inc 785 823-3434
745 Faith Dr Salina (67401) ***(G-10477)***
Diligence Inc 913 254-0500
110 Leawood Dr New Century (66031) ***(G-7279)***
Dillard's Distribution Center, Olathe *Also called Dillards Inc* ***(G-7654)***
Dillards Inc 913 791-6400
700 E 151st St Olathe (66062) ***(G-7654)***
Dillco Fluid Service Inc (HQ) 620 544-2929
513 W 4th St Hugoton (67951) ***(G-3159)***
Dillon Companies Inc 620 225-6130
1700 N 14th Ave Dodge City (67801) ***(G-1341)***
Dillon Companies Inc 620 663-4464
206 W 5th Ave Hutchinson (67501) ***(G-3263)***
Dillon Companies Inc 785 272-0661
2815 Sw 29th St Topeka (66614) ***(G-12557)***
Dillon Companies Inc 785 823-9403
2350 Planet Ave Salina (67401) ***(G-10478)***
Dillon Companies Inc 620 275-0151
1211 Buffalo Jones Ave Garden City (67846) ***(G-2148)***
Dillon Credit Union 620 669-8500
2704 N Lorraine St Hutchinson (67502) ***(G-3264)***
Dillon Nature Center 620 663-7411
3002 E 30th Ave Hutchinson (67502) ***(G-3265)***
Dillon's 00001, Dodge City *Also called Dillon Companies Inc* ***(G-1341)***
Dillon's 00074, Salina *Also called Dillon Companies Inc* ***(G-10478)***
Dillons 25, Hutchinson *Also called Dillon Companies Inc* ***(G-3263)***
Dillons 47, Topeka *Also called Dillon Companies Inc* ***(G-12557)***
Dillons 60, Garden City *Also called Dillon Companies Inc* ***(G-2148)***
Dimas Division, Olathe *Also called Husqvrna Cnstr Pdts N Amer Inc* ***(G-7781)***
Dimension Graphics Inc 913 469-6800
13915 W 107th St Lenexa (66215) ***(G-5820)***
Dimension X Design LLC 913 908-3824
18001 W 106th St Ste 150 Olathe (66061) ***(G-7655)***
Dimensional Stonework LLC 913 851-9390
8301 W 125th St Ste 110 Shawnee Mission (66213) ***(G-11307)***
Dinkel Construction Inc 785 232-3377
3311 Se 21st St Topeka (66607) ***(G-12558)***
Dinkel, Dan, Victoria *Also called Dinkels Custom Wood Products* ***(G-13374)***
Dinkels Custom Wood Products 785 735-2461
1003 390th Ave Victoria (67671) ***(G-13374)***
Dinning Beard Inc (HQ) 316 636-1115
12021 E 13th St N Ste 100 Wichita (67206) ***(G-14212)***
Dinning Beard Inc 316 775-2201
420 N Walnut St Augusta (67010) ***(G-317)***
Dinosaur Den Child Dev Ctr 913 780-2626
14299 S Darnell St Olathe (66062) ***(G-7656)***
Dion A Daniel Inc 816 287-1452
5400 Johnson Dr Ste 214 Mission (66205) ***(G-7130)***
Direct Communications Inc 913 599-5577
11817 Gillette St Overland Park (66210) ***(G-8657)***
Direct Mail Printers Inc 316 263-1855
231 S Ida St Wichita (67211) ***(G-14213)***
Direct Mop Sales Inc 913 367-3087
7700 Schuele Rd Atchison (66002) ***(G-224)***
Direct Source Gran & Stone Imp 913 766-9200
8675 College Blvd Ste 150 Overland Park (66210) ***(G-8658)***
Direct Vet Marketing Inc 888 280-2221
512 Poyntz Ave Manhattan (66502) ***(G-6614)***
Direct Voltage 713 485-9999
323 Illinois Ave Pratt (67124) ***(G-10108)***
Direct Wholesale, Beloit *Also called All Things Exterior Inc* ***(G-472)***
Directv Group Inc 620 235-0743
115 E 23rd St Pittsburg (66762) ***(G-9853)***
Directv Group Inc 620 663-8132
2314 N Wilson Rd Hutchinson (67502) ***(G-3266)***
Dirty Work 316 652-9104
2077 S Capri Ln Wichita (67207) ***(G-14214)***
Disability Rights Ctr of Kans 785 273-9661
214 Sw 6th Ave Ste 100 Topeka (66603) ***(G-12559)***
Disabled American Veterens Str 785 827-6477
901 W Crawford St Salina (67401) ***(G-10479)***
Disablty Spprts of The Grt Pln 620 241-8411
501 E Northview Ave McPherson (67460) ***(G-6957)***
Disco Machine Liberal Company 620 624-0179
2161 N Grant Ave Liberal (67901) ***(G-6305)***
Discount Sding Spply-Hys/Bloit, Hays *Also called Discount Siding Supply LP* ***(G-2788)***
Discount Siding Supply LP 785 625-4619
2706 Plaza Ave Hays (67601) ***(G-2788)***
Discount Tobacco & Cellular 913 281-3067
1017 N 18th St Kansas City (66102) ***(G-3972)***
Discount Toner and Ink, Lawrence *Also called Laser Recycling Company* ***(G-4956)***
Discover Dental Care 913 268-1337
21620 Midland Dr Ste A Shawnee Mission (66218) ***(G-11308)***
Discovery Concepts Inc (PA) 913 814-7100
5201 Johnson Dr Ste 301 Shawnee Mission (66205) ***(G-11309)***
Discovery Drilling Co Inc 785 623-2920
1029 Reservation Rd Hays (67601) ***(G-2789)***
Discovery Drilling Shop 785 650-0029
1029 Reservation Rd Hays (67601) ***(G-2790)***
DISCOVERY PLACE, Wichita *Also called Creativity Place Inc* ***(G-14127)***
Dish Network Corporation 816 256-5622
4701 Parallel Pkwy Kansas City (66104) ***(G-3973)***
Dispatch, The, Clay Center *Also called Clay Center Publishing Co Inc* ***(G-852)***
Display Studios Inc 913 305-5948
5420 Kansas Ave Kansas City (66106) ***(G-3974)***
Disposable Instrument Co Inc 913 492-6492
14248 Santa Fe Trail Dr Shawnee Mission (66215) ***(G-11310)***
Disrigadan Craftman, Wichita *Also called Even Temp of Wichita Inc* ***(G-14312)***
Distributorcentral LLC 888 516-7401
1200 Energy Center Dr Gardner (66030) ***(G-2338)***
District Dourt, Garden City *Also called County of Finney* ***(G-2133)***
Ditch Witch of Kansas, Valley Center *Also called Valley Machinery Inc* ***(G-13359)***
Ditch Witch Sales Inc 913 782-5223
1325 S Enterprise St Olathe (66061) ***(G-7657)***
Ditch Witch Sales Kansas City, Olathe *Also called Ditch Witch Sales Inc* ***(G-7657)***
Diteq Corporation (HQ) 816 246-5515
9876 Pflumm Rd Lenexa (66215) ***(G-5821)***
Diversicare Leasing Corp 316 524-3211
215 N Lamar Ave Haysville (67060) ***(G-2939)***
Diversicare Leasing Corp 620 431-4940
530 W 14th St Chanute (66720) ***(G-724)***
Diversicare Leasing Corp 620 767-5172
400 Sunset Dr Council Grove (66846) ***(G-1163)***
Diversicare of Chanute, Chanute *Also called Diversicare Leasing Corp* ***(G-724)***
Diversicare of Council Grove, Council Grove *Also called Diversicare Leasing Corp* ***(G-1163)***
Diversicare of Haysville, Haysville *Also called Diversicare Leasing Corp* ***(G-2939)***

ALPHABETIC

Diversicare of Hutchinson.....620 669-9393
1202 E 23rd Ave Hutchinson (67502) ***(G-3267)***
Diversicare of Larned LLC.....620 285-6914
1114 W 11th St Larned (67550) ***(G-4701)***
Diversified Contracting LLC.....913 898-4722
21368 Earnest Rd Parker (66072) ***(G-9657)***
Diversified Crop Insur Svcs, Topeka *Also called CGB Diversified Services Inc* ***(G-12462)***
Diversified Family Svcs LLC.....316 269-3368
1631 E 17th St N Ste 100 Wichita (67214) ***(G-14215)***
Diversified Services, Wellington *Also called Metal Finishing Company Inc* ***(G-13516)***
Diversified Sports Tech LLC.....949 466-2393
140 E 10th St Baxter Springs (66713) ***(G-404)***
Dixon Dively Orthopedics, Leawood *Also called Kansas City Orthoped* ***(G-5444)***
Dja Financial Aid Services, Wichita *Also called Deborah John & Associates* ***(G-14182)***
Dl Machine LLC.....913 557-2000
210 N Silver St Paola (66071) ***(G-9552)***
Dla Document Services.....913 684-5591
290 Grant Ave Bldg 77 Fort Leavenworth (66027) ***(G-1937)***
Dlabal & Fellner Gen Denistry.....785 537-8484
1834 Claflin Rd Ste A Manhattan (66502) ***(G-6615)***
Dlabal J Dennis Dntst, Manhattan *Also called Dlabal & Fellner Gen Denistry* ***(G-6615)***
Dllc - Dupree Landscap.....913 856-0120
791 E Warren St Gardner (66030) ***(G-2339)***
Dlr Group Inc (HQ).....913 897-7811
7290 W 133rd St Overland Park (66213) ***(G-8659)***
Dm & M Farms Inc (PA).....620 855-3934
220 S Main St Cimarron (67835) ***(G-823)***
Dm Roofing.....620 515-0015
502 Highland Rd Coffeyville (67337) ***(G-934)***
Dme Electronics.....316 529-2441
170 Cain Dr Haysville (67060) ***(G-2940)***
Do Good Productions Inc.....913 400-3416
12000 Aberdeen Rd Leawood (66209) ***(G-5379)***
Do It Best, Iola *Also called Diebolt LLC* ***(G-3598)***
Do It Best, Seneca *Also called Suther Building Supply Inc* ***(G-10883)***
Do It Best, Summerfield *Also called Quality Homes Inc* ***(G-12216)***
Dobbins, Kent E, Lawrence *Also called Drs Dobbins & Letourneau* ***(G-4841)***
Dobson-Davis Co.....913 894-4922
8521 Richards Rd Shawnee Mission (66215) ***(G-11311)***
Doc Grens Gourmet Salads Grill.....316 636-8997
10096 E 13th St N Ste 102 Wichita (67206) ***(G-14216)***
Dock, The, Topeka *Also called Calvin Investments LLC* ***(G-12419)***
Docs Friends Inc.....316 943-3246
1788 S Airport Rd Wichita (67209) ***(G-14217)***
Docs Whole Care, Olathe *Also called Volunteers With Heart Inc* ***(G-8143)***
Doctors Inc (PA).....913 681-8041
7425 W 161st St Stilwell (66085) ***(G-12145)***
Docuforce Inc (PA).....316 636-5400
6435 E 34th St N 109 Wichita (67226) ***(G-14218)***
Documart Inc.....913 649-3800
10316 W 79th St Shawnee Mission (66214) ***(G-11312)***
Document Resources Inc (HQ).....316 683-1444
707 E 33rd St N Wichita (67219) ***(G-14219)***
Docuplex Inc.....316 262-2662
630 N Pennsylvania Ave Wichita (67214) ***(G-14220)***
Dodge City Brewing Co LLC.....620 338-7247
701 3rd Ave Dodge City (67801) ***(G-1342)***
Dodge City Concrete Inc.....620 227-3041
1105 E Wyatt Earp Blvd Dodge City (67801) ***(G-1343)***
Dodge City Cooperative Exch (PA).....620 225-4193
710 W Trail St Dodge City (67801) ***(G-1344)***
Dodge City Cooperative Exch.....620 227-8671
708 W Trail St Dodge City (67801) ***(G-1345)***
Dodge City Country Club.....620 225-5231
1900 Country Club Dr Dodge City (67801) ***(G-1346)***
Dodge City Daily Globe, Dodge City *Also called Morris Communications Co LLC* ***(G-1407)***
Dodge City Dental.....620 225-2650
2300 N 14th Ave Ste 202 Dodge City (67801) ***(G-1347)***
Dodge City Express, Dodge City *Also called Sallee Inc* ***(G-1426)***
Dodge City International Inc (PA).....620 225-4177
2201 E Wyatt Earp Blvd Dodge City (67801) ***(G-1348)***
Dodge City Kenworth, Park City *Also called Wichita Kenworth Inc* ***(G-9655)***
Dodge City Med Ctr Chartered (PA).....620 227-8506
2020 Central Ave Dodge City (67801) ***(G-1349)***
Dodge City Public Library.....620 225-0248
1001 N 2nd Ave Dodge City (67801) ***(G-1350)***
Dodge City Sand Company Inc.....620 227-6091
801 Lulu Ave Dodge City (67801) ***(G-1351)***
Dodge City Veterinary Clinic.....620 227-8651
1920 E Trail St Dodge City (67801) ***(G-1352)***
Dodge Cy Healthcare Group LLC.....620 225-8401
3001 Avenue A Dodge City (67801) ***(G-1353)***
Dodge Cy Unified Schl Dst 443.....620 227-1614
1000 N 2nd Ave Dodge City (67801) ***(G-1354)***
Dodge Cy Unified Schl Dst 443.....620 227-7771
2601 Central Ave Frnt Dodge City (67801) ***(G-1355)***
Dodge Enteprise Inc.....620 227-2125
1510 W Wyatt Earp Blvd Dodge City (67801) ***(G-1356)***
Dodson International Parts Inc (HQ).....785 878-8000
2155 Vermont Rd Rantoul (66079) ***(G-10196)***
Dodson Investments Inc (PA).....785 878-4000
2155 Vermont Rd Rantoul (66079) ***(G-10197)***
Doherty Steel Inc.....913 557-9200
21110 W 311th St Paola (66071) ***(G-9553)***
Doing Better Inspections, Lenexa *Also called Dbi Inc* ***(G-5807)***
Dolan Technologies Corporation (HQ).....913 390-5156
1713 E 123rd St Olathe (66061) ***(G-7658)***
Dold Foods LLC.....316 838-9101
2929 N Ohio St Wichita (67219) ***(G-14221)***
Doll Cradle.....913 631-1900
10910 Johnson Dr Shawnee Mission (66203) ***(G-11313)***
Doll Truck Line.....620 456-2519
824 E Saint Louis St Conway Springs (67031) ***(G-1140)***
Dollar Sales, Wichita *Also called E & J Rental & Leasing Inc* ***(G-14249)***
Domestic Fastener & Forge Inc.....913 888-9447
150 New Century Pkwy B New Century (66031) ***(G-7280)***
Domestic Vlnce Assn of Cntl Ka.....785 827-5862
148 N Oakdale Ave Salina (67401) ***(G-10480)***
Dominion Management Svcs Inc.....571 408-4770
240 S West St Ste H Wichita (67213) ***(G-14222)***
Dominion Management Svcs Inc (PA).....703 765-2274
240 S West St Ste H Wichita (67213) ***(G-14223)***
Don Coffey Company Inc (PA).....913 764-2108
15375 S Us 169 Hwy Olathe (66062) ***(G-7659)***
Don Hattan Derby Inc.....316 744-1275
2518 N Rock Rd Derby (67037) ***(G-1240)***
Don Julian Builders Inc.....913 894-6300
15521 W 110th St Lenexa (66219) ***(G-5822)***
Don Klausmeyer Cnstr LLC.....316 554-0001
10008 W York St Wichita (67215) ***(G-14224)***
Don's Tow Service, Olathe *Also called Dons Body Shop Inc* ***(G-7660)***
Donahue Corporation.....620 924-5500
946 290th Durham (67438) ***(G-1474)***
Donahue Manufacturing LLC.....620 732-2665
946 290th Durham (67438) ***(G-1475)***
Donald B Scrafford.....316 721-2701
3607 N Ridge Rd Wichita (67205) ***(G-14225)***
Dondlinger & Sons Cnstr Co Inc (PA).....316 945-0555
2656 S Sheridan Ave Wichita (67217) ***(G-14226)***
Dondlinger & Sons Cnstr Co Inc.....316 943-9393
3201 W Casado St Wichita (67217) ***(G-14227)***
Dondlinger Companies Inc.....316 945-0555
2656 S Sheridan Ave Wichita (67217) ***(G-14228)***
Done With Care Auto Repair LLC.....913 722-3466
5810 Merriam Dr Shawnee (66203) ***(G-10941)***
Donegan Optical Company Inc.....913 492-2500
15549 W 108th St Shawnee Mission (66219) ***(G-11314)***
Donipan Cnty Svcs & Workskills.....913 365-5561
203 Roseport Rd Elwood (66024) ***(G-1684)***
Doniphan Cnty Council On Aging, Troy *Also called County of Doniphan* ***(G-13273)***
DONIPHAN COUNTY SERVICES & WOR, Elwood *Also called Donipan Cnty Svcs & Workskills* ***(G-1684)***
Donlevy Lithograph, Parsons *Also called Sgl LLC* ***(G-9737)***
Donlevy Lthograph/Sun Graphics, Downs *Also called Brush Group LLC* ***(G-1470)***
Donmar Inc.....913 432-2700
5401 Hayes St Ste A Shawnee Mission (66203) ***(G-11315)***
Donna Jean's Unique Gift Shop, Assaria *Also called D J Inc* ***(G-200)***
Donnelley Financial LLC.....913 541-4099
14702 W 105th St Shawnee Mission (66215) ***(G-11316)***
Donohue Ranch.....785 867-2160
331 N Vine Greeley (66033) ***(G-2665)***
Dons Body Shop Inc.....913 782-9255
207 W Cedar St Olathe (66061) ***(G-7660)***
Dons Car Care & Body Shop Inc.....620 669-8178
104 E 4th Ave Hutchinson (67501) ***(G-3268)***
Donut X-Press.....620 544-4700
406 W 11th St Hugoton (67951) ***(G-3160)***
Dooley Center.....913 360-6200
801 S 8th St Atchison (66002) ***(G-225)***
Doonan Peterbilt of Great Bend, Great Bend *Also called Doonan Truck & Equipment Inc* ***(G-2555)***
Doonan Specialized Trailer LLC.....620 792-6222
36 Ne Us Highway 156 B Great Bend (67530) ***(G-2554)***
Doonan Truck & Equipment Inc.....620 792-2491
Jct Hwy 56 & 156 Great Bend (67530) ***(G-2555)***
Doric Vaults, Newton *Also called Concrete Vaults Inc* ***(G-7333)***
Dormakaba USA Inc.....717 335-4334
2300 Se Lakewood Blvd Topeka (66605) ***(G-12560)***
Dormakaba USA Inc.....913 831-3001
301 Southwest Blvd Kansas City (66103) ***(G-3975)***
Dormakaba USA Inc.....316 267-6891
734 S Washington Ave Wichita (67211) ***(G-14229)***
Dorothy Rush Realty Inc.....620 442-7851
206 N Summit St Arkansas City (67005) ***(G-153)***
DOROTHY'S HOUSE, Liberal *Also called Seward County Historical Soc* ***(G-6366)***

DOT Green Bioplastics Inc (PA)...620 273-8919
527 Commercial St Ste 310 Emporia (66801) ***(G-1730)***
DOT Green Bioplastics LLC...785 889-4600
210 S Leonard St Onaga (66521) ***(G-8175)***
Dots Pretzels LLC...913 274-1705
16286 W 110th St Lenexa (66219) ***(G-5823)***
Double K Cnstr of Mound Cy...913 795-3147
5624 Knapp Rd Mound City (66056) ***(G-7171)***
Double T Enterprises...620 342-2655
906 E 6th Ave Emporia (66801) ***(G-1731)***
Double T Ind Inc...620 593-4357
980 Hwy 51 N Rolla (67954) ***(G-10232)***
Double Tree Hilton...316 945-5272
2098 S Airport Rd Wichita (67209) ***(G-14230)***
Doubletree By, Overland Park *Also called Hotel Clubs Corp Woods Inc* ***(G-8829)***
Doubltree By Hlton Ht Lawrence, Lawrence *Also called Hulsing Hotels Kansas Inc* ***(G-4906)***
Doubrava Woodworking Inc...785 472-4204
1375 1/2 Avenue K Ellsworth (67439) ***(G-1666)***
Doug Bradley Trucking Inc (PA)...785 826-9681
680 E Water Well Rd Salina (67401) ***(G-10481)***
Doug Reh Chevrolet Inc...620 672-5633
1501 E 1st St Pratt (67124) ***(G-10109)***
Doughxpress, Pittsburg *Also called Hix Corporation* ***(G-9876)***
Douglas A Firebaugh Cnstr...913 451-8599
9393 W 110th St Ste 120 Overland Park (66210) ***(G-8660)***
Douglas County Bank (PA)...785 865-1000
300 W 9th St Lawrence (66044) ***(G-4836)***
Douglas County Bank...785 865-1022
1501 Inverness Dr Ofc Lawrence (66047) ***(G-4837)***
Douglas County Child Dev Assn...785 842-9679
1900 Delaware St Lawrence (66046) ***(G-4838)***
Douglas County Dntl Clinic Inc...785 312-7770
4920 Bob Billings Pkwy Lawrence (66049) ***(G-4839)***
Douglas County Historical Soc...785 841-4109
1047 Massachusetts St Lawrence (66044) ***(G-4840)***
Douglas E Bald, Hutchinson *Also called Ron D Hansen Od Inc* ***(G-3430)***
Douglas J Knop DDS, Shawnee Mission *Also called Overland Park Dental* ***(G-11706)***
Douglas Pump Service, Inc., Wichita *Also called C & B Equipment Midwest Inc* ***(G-13924)***
Douglas Pump Service, Inc., Overland Park *Also called C & B Equipment Midwest Inc* ***(G-8502)***
Douglas V Oxler DDS...316 722-2596
900 N Tyler Rd Ste 2 Wichita (67212) ***(G-14231)***
Douglas Webb Co LP...316 685-3777
333 S Webb Rd Wichita (67207) ***(G-14232)***
Douglas Webb LLC...316 685-0333
333 S Webb Rd Wichita (67207) ***(G-14233)***
Douglass Medicalodges...316 747-2157
619 S Us Highway 77 Douglass (67039) ***(G-1466)***
Douthit Frets Rouse Gentile, Overland Park *Also called Rouse Frets White Goss Gentile* ***(G-9259)***
Dove Estates Senior Living...316 550-6343
1400 S 83rd St W Goddard (67052) ***(G-2436)***
Dover Sod Farms Inc...913 897-2336
10886 W 239th St Bucyrus (66013) ***(G-596)***
Dowell & Sypher LLC...913 451-8833
10955 Lowell Ave Ste 630 Shawnee Mission (66210) ***(G-11317)***
Downing & Lahey Inc...316 733-2740
6555 E Central Ave Wichita (67206) ***(G-14234)***
Downs Nursing Center, Downs *Also called Beverly Enterprises-Kansas LLC* ***(G-1468)***
Downs Senior Citizens Inc...785 454-6228
514 Morgan Ave Downs (67437) ***(G-1471)***
Downtown Branch, Manhattan *Also called KS Statebank* ***(G-6702)***
Downtown Shareholders...913 371-0705
726 Armstrong Ave Ste 201 Kansas City (66101) ***(G-3976)***
Downtown Station...316 267-7747
330 W 2nd St N Wichita (67202) ***(G-14235)***
Dpp Manufacturing LLC...620 340-7200
886 Road 160 Emporia (66801) ***(G-1732)***
Dpra Incorporated...785 539-3565
121 S 4th St Ste 202 Manhattan (66502) ***(G-6616)***
Dr Michelle Robin, Shawnee Mission *Also called Robin Chiropractic & Acupnctur* ***(G-11810)***
Dr Nick Rogers...620 442-5660
1939 N 11th St Arkansas City (67005) ***(G-154)***
Dr Vernon A Mills...913 772-6046
3550 S 4th St Ste 120 Leavenworth (66048) ***(G-5234)***
Dr Vernon Rowe...913 894-1500
8550 Marshall Dr Ste 100 Lenexa (66214) ***(G-5824)***
Dr William E Hartman Assoc PA...913 441-1600
13031 Kansas Ave Bonner Springs (66012) ***(G-550)***
Dr William Mauch, Salina *Also called Salina Urology Associates PA* ***(G-10695)***
Drafting Room Inc...316 267-2291
1608 E Central Ave Wichita (67214) ***(G-14236)***
Dragnet Enterprises...913 362-8378
2507 S 42nd St Kansas City (66106) ***(G-3977)***
Drake & Assoc Optometrists...913 894-2020
15601 W 87th Street Pkwy Lenexa (66219) ***(G-5825)***
DRC, Topeka *Also called Disability Rights Ctr of Kans* ***(G-12559)***
Dream Waves LLC...316 942-9283
6803 W Taft Ave Ste 401 Wichita (67209) ***(G-14237)***
Dreamsteamer, Council Grove *Also called A/C Enterprises Inc* ***(G-1157)***
Dredge Transport Service Inc...785 506-8285
1105-C Nw Lowr Topeka (66608) ***(G-12561)***
Dreiling Construction LLC...620 275-9433
2917 W Mary St Garden City (67846) ***(G-2149)***
Dreiling Oil Inc...785 625-8327
1008 Cody Ave Hays (67601) ***(G-2791)***
Drewco Inc...913 384-6226
14904 W 87th Pkwy 143 Shawnee Mission (66215) ***(G-11318)***
Drexel Technologies Inc (PA)...913 371-4430
10840 W 86th St Lenexa (66214) ***(G-5826)***
Dri Duck Traders Inc (PA)...913 648-8222
7007 College Blvd Ste 700 Overland Park (66211) ***(G-8661)***
Drive-In Facility, Seneca *Also called United Bank & Trust* ***(G-10885)***
Drs Alley and Brammer LC...316 265-0856
1601 N Willow Ln Wichita (67208) ***(G-14238)***
Drs Dobbins & Letourneau...785 843-5665
831 Vermont St Lawrence (66044) ***(G-4841)***
Drs Fisher & Yarrow PA, Wichita *Also called Fisher Ronald Od PA* ***(G-14378)***
Drs Price Young Odle Horsch PA...620 343-7120
512 Commercial St Emporia (66801) ***(G-1733)***
Drubers Donut Shop...316 283-1206
116 W 6th St Newton (67114) ***(G-7338)***
Drury Hotels Company LLC...316 267-1961
400 W Douglas Ave Wichita (67202) ***(G-14239)***
Drury Hotels Company LLC...913 345-1500
10963 Metcalf Ave Overland Park (66210) ***(G-8662)***
Drury Hotels Company LLC...913 236-9200
9009 Shawnee Mission Pkwy Shawnee Mission (66202) ***(G-11319)***
Drury Inn & Suites Overland Pk, Overland Park *Also called Drury Hotels Company LLC* ***(G-8662)***
Drury Inn Shawnee Mission, Shawnee Mission *Also called Drury Hotels Company LLC* ***(G-11319)***
Drury Place Apartments, Topeka *Also called Liberty Assisted Living Center* ***(G-12843)***
Drury Plaza Hotel Broadview, Wichita *Also called Drury Hotels Company LLC* ***(G-14239)***
Dry Clean City...785 776-1515
427 E Poyntz Ave Manhattan (66502) ***(G-6617)***
Dry Cleaning and Laundry Sups, Lenexa *Also called Fabriclean Supply Kansas Lc* ***(G-5845)***
Dry Creek Farms, Hesston *Also called L & J Wood Products Inc* ***(G-2996)***
Drywall Inc...620 662-3454
507 N Whiteside St Hutchinson (67501) ***(G-3269)***
Drywall Supply...316 269-3304
3420 N Ohio St Wichita (67219) ***(G-14240)***
Drywall Systems Inc (PA)...316 832-0233
3919 S West St Wichita (67217) ***(G-14241)***
Drywall Systems Inc...316 260-9411
3901 S West St Wichita (67217) ***(G-14242)***
Ds Bus Lines Inc...913 384-1190
313 E Front St Bonner Springs (66012) ***(G-551)***
DS&o Electric Cooperative...785 655-2011
201 Dakota Solomon (67480) ***(G-12050)***
Dsnwk, Hays *Also called Developmental Svcs NW Kans Inc* ***(G-2785)***
Dsnwk, Hays *Also called Developmental Svcs NW Kans Inc* ***(G-2786)***
Dti Machining, Olathe *Also called Daniel Todd Industries Inc* ***(G-7641)***
Dubs Dread Golf Course, Kansas City *Also called National Golf Properties LLC* ***(G-4281)***
Ducommun Aerostructures Inc...620 421-3401
3333 Main St Parsons (67357) ***(G-9682)***
Dudley Construction Co Inc...620 665-1166
7311 N Halstead St Ste B Hutchinson (67502) ***(G-3270)***
Dudley Williams and Assoc PA...316 263-7591
230 S Laura Ave Ste 206 Wichita (67211) ***(G-14243)***
Dudrey Cattle Co Inc...620 549-3234
802 E 1st Ave Saint John (67576) ***(G-10350)***
Duerksen Fine Arts Center, Wichita *Also called Wichita State University* ***(G-16034)***
Duffens Optical, Overland Park *Also called Essilor Laboratories Amer Inc* ***(G-8691)***
Duffens Opticals...785 234-3481
8140 Marshall Dr Overland Park (66214) ***(G-8663)***
Duffers Repair & Supply, Bern *Also called Flint Hills Powersports Inc* ***(G-522)***
Duffins-Langley Optical Co...913 492-5379
8140 Marshall Dr Shawnee Mission (66214) ***(G-11320)***
Duffy Construction Company Inc...913 381-1668
7211 W 98th Ter Ste 110 Shawnee Mission (66212) ***(G-11321)***
Dugan Truck Line LLC (PA)...316 946-5935
3520 S Hoover Rd Wichita (67215) ***(G-14244)***
Dugas, Council Grove *Also called Geo Bit Exploration Inc* ***(G-1168)***
Duggan Shadwick Doerr Kurlbaum...913 498-3536
9101 W 110th St Ste 200 Overland Park (66210) ***(G-8664)***
Duis Meat Processing Inc (PA)...785 243-7850
1991 E 6th St Concordia (66901) ***(G-1109)***
Duke Aerial Inc...785 494-8001
11080 Legion Dr Saint George (66535) ***(G-10346)***
Duke Drilling Co Inc...620 793-8366
5539 2nd St Great Bend (67530) ***(G-2556)***
Duke Energy Corporation...620 855-6830
8502 State Road 23 Cimarron (67835) ***(G-824)***

ALPHABETIC

Duke Realty Corporation 913 829-1453
27200 W 157th St New Century (66031) ***(G-7281)***
Dunami Inc 303 981-3303
7500 College Blvd Ste 450 Overland Park (66210) ***(G-8665)***
Duncans Movie Magic Inc 785 266-3010
108 Se 29th St Topeka (66605) ***(G-12562)***
Dunco Inc 785 594-7137
1729 Bullene Ave Lawrence (66044) ***(G-4842)***
Dunes Residential Services Inc 913 955-2900
4707 College Blvd Ste 203 Leawood (66211) ***(G-5380)***
Dunn Knives, Rossville *Also called Dunns Custom Knives Inc* ***(G-10251)***
Dunning Express Inc 785 806-3915
1910 Roseport Rd Elwood (66024) ***(G-1685)***
Dunns Custom Knives Inc 785 584-6856
5830 Nw Carlson Rd Rossville (66533) ***(G-10251)***
Dupont 913 327-3518
6363 College Blvd Ste 300 Overland Park (66211) ***(G-8666)***
Dupont Denisco Plant, New Century *Also called E I Du Pont De Nemours & Co* ***(G-7282)***
Duranotic Door Inc 913 764-3408
14901 W 117th St Olathe (66062) ***(G-7661)***
Durasafe Products Inc 316 942-3282
1380 S Bebe St Wichita (67209) ***(G-14245)***
Durham School Services, Louisburg *Also called National Express LLC* ***(G-6460)***
Durham School Services, Hutchinson *Also called National Express LLC* ***(G-3388)***
Durham School Services, Wellington *Also called National Express LLC* ***(G-13519)***
Durham School Services L P 913 755-3593
611 1/2 Parker Ave Osawatomie (66064) ***(G-8192)***
Durham School Services L P 620 331-7088
1125 E Main St Independence (67301) ***(G-3512)***
Durrie Vsion Cokingtin Eye Ctr, Overland Park *Also called Daniel S Durrie Cokingtin LLC* ***(G-8633)***
Dustrol Inc (HQ) 316 536-2262
1201 E Main Towanda (67144) ***(G-13264)***
Dusty Dahmer Construction, Overland Park *Also called Dahmer Contracting Group LLC* ***(G-8630)***
Dvack, Salina *Also called Domestic Vlnce Assn of Cntl Ka* ***(G-10480)***
DVC Training Specialists LLC 913 908-3393
814 E Main St Gardner (66030) ***(G-2340)***
Dvt LLC 913 636-3056
7325 W 161st St Overland Park (66085) ***(G-8667)***
Dw Industries LLC 913 782-7575
310 N Winchester St Ste A Olathe (66062) ***(G-7662)***
Dwayne's Photo Service, Parsons *Also called Steinle Inc* ***(G-9741)***
Dwight D Eisenhower Library, Abilene *Also called National Archives and Rec ADM* ***(G-47)***
Dxp Enterprises Inc 913 888-0108
11691 W 85th St Lenexa (66214) ***(G-5827)***
Dymax Inc 785 456-2705
402 Miller Dr Wamego (66547) ***(G-13415)***
Dynamarine Performance Boats, Topeka *Also called Scs Tech LLC* ***(G-13045)***
Dynamic Cmpt Sltons Topeka Inc 785 354-7000
2214 Sw 10th Ave Topeka (66604) ***(G-12563)***
Dynamic Control Systems Inc 316 262-2525
450 S Greenwood St Wichita (67211) ***(G-14246)***
Dynamic Discs LLC (PA) 620 208-3472
912 Commercial St Emporia (66801) ***(G-1734)***
Dynamic Drywall Inc 316 945-7087
3921 N Bridgeport Cir Wichita (67219) ***(G-14247)***
Dynamic Logistix LLC (PA) 913 274-3800
7220 W 98th Ter Bldg 9 Overland Park (66212) ***(G-8668)***
Dynamic Machine LLC 316 941-4005
202 W 11th St N Wichita (67203) ***(G-14248)***
Dynamic Management Solutions 785 456-1794
5566 Maefield Dr Ste B Wamego (66547) ***(G-13416)***
Dynamic N/C LLC 316 712-5028
16531 Sw 190th St Rose Hill (67133) ***(G-10237)***
Dynamold Corporation 785 667-4626
706 E Salemsborg Rd Assaria (67416) ***(G-201)***
Dynegy, Pawnee Rock *Also called Tri Resources Inc* ***(G-9755)***
Dynegy, Pratt *Also called Tri Resources Inc* ***(G-10162)***
E & J Rental & Leasing Inc 316 721-0442
8535 W Kellogg Dr Wichita (67209) ***(G-14249)***
E & M Plbg Htg & A Conditionin, Hutchinson *Also called E & M Plumbing Inc* ***(G-3271)***
E & M Plumbing Inc 620 662-1281
701 W 2nd Ave Hutchinson (67501) ***(G-3271)***
E & R Machine Inc 785 456-2373
315 Sandusky Ave Wamego (66547) ***(G-13417)***
E Architects PA 785 234-6664
1250 Sw Oakley Ave # 200 Topeka (66604) ***(G-12564)***
E Brent Nelson 316 789-9999
1120 N Rock Rd Ste 100 Derby (67037) ***(G-1241)***
E C I, Wichita *Also called Eci Electrical Contractors* ***(G-14257)***
E C Manufacturing 913 825-3077
23501 W 84th St Shawnee (66227) ***(G-10942)***
E C P, Olathe *Also called Earth Contact Products LLC* ***(G-7665)***
E C S, Kansas City *Also called Epoxy Coating Specialists Inc* ***(G-3993)***
E D Bishop Lumber Muncie Inc 913 441-2691
2300 S 138th St Bonner Springs (66012) ***(G-552)***
E F Hadel Realty Inc 913 681-1600
13246 Long St Shawnee Mission (66213) ***(G-11322)***
E G E, Minneola *Also called Emergent Green Energy Inc* ***(G-7124)***
E I Du Pont De Nemours & Co 302 774-1000
4 New Century Pkwy New Century (66031) ***(G-7282)***
E I Du Pont De Nemours & Co 913 764-8100
4 New Century Pkwy New Century (66031) ***(G-7283)***
E I F K C Landfill Gas, Shawnee *Also called Enpower Operations Corp* ***(G-10948)***
E M Specialist PA 913 676-2214
9100 W 74th St Shawnee Mission (66204) ***(G-11323)***
E S Wilson Transport Inc 785 263-9845
1120 S Buckeye Ave Abilene (67410) ***(G-25)***
E State Management LLC 785 312-9945
1311 George Ct Lawrence (66044) ***(G-4843)***
E T C Institute Inc 913 747-0646
725 W Frontier Ln Olathe (66061) ***(G-7663)***
E T I, Wichita *Also called Extreme Tanning Inc* ***(G-14325)***
E-Consultsusa LLC 913 696-1001
8900 State Line Rd Ste 50 Leawood (66206) ***(G-5381)***
E-Z Info Inc 913 367-5020
801 Atchison St Atchison (66002) ***(G-226)***
E-Z Salsa Inc 620 521-9097
1712 E Fulton Plz Garden City (67846) ***(G-2150)***
E-Z Shelving Systems Inc 913 384-1331
5538 Merriam Dr Shawnee Mission (66203) ***(G-11324)***
E-Z-Go Golf Cars, Park City *Also called Kansas Golf and Turf Inc* ***(G-9622)***
E. Wichita Claims Office, Wichita *Also called Farm Bureau Mutl Insur Co Inc* ***(G-14341)***
E3 Roofing Group Inc 913 782-3332
310 N Winchester St Ste C Olathe (66062) ***(G-7664)***
E4 Excavating Inc 785 379-5111
1452 E 1st Rd Berryton (66409) ***(G-526)***
EAC Audit Inc 785 594-6707
Rr 3 Baldwin City (66006) ***(G-359)***
Eagel Transit Inc 620 343-3444
4245 W Us Highway 50 Emporia (66801) ***(G-1735)***
Eagle Auto Salon Inc 785 272-2886
2110 Sw Chelsea Dr Topeka (66614) ***(G-12565)***
Eagle Auto Wash Dtailing Salon, Topeka *Also called Eagle Auto Salon Inc* ***(G-12565)***
Eagle Bar Ranch Inc 620 257-5106
1768 Avenue J Lyons (67554) ***(G-6482)***
Eagle Bend Golf Course, Lawrence *Also called City of Lawrence* ***(G-4790)***
Eagle Beverage Co Inc 620 231-7970
250 N Cayuga St Frontenac (66763) ***(G-2054)***
Eagle Bradband Investments LLC 785 625-5910
2703 Hall St Ste 15 Hays (67601) ***(G-2792)***
Eagle Care Inc 785 227-2304
840 N 2nd St Lindsborg (67456) ***(G-6397)***
Eagle Case Management LLC 913 334-9035
7345 Leavenworth Rd Kansas City (66109) ***(G-3978)***
Eagle Communications Inc (PA) 785 625-5910
2703 Hall St 15 Hays (67601) ***(G-2793)***
Eagle Communications Inc 620 792-3101
1200 Baker Ave Great Bend (67530) ***(G-2557)***
Eagle Communications Inc 785 726-3291
1007 W 27th St Hays (67601) ***(G-2794)***
Eagle Communications Inc 785 650-5349
2300 Hall St Hays (67601) ***(G-2795)***
Eagle Communications Inc 785 587-0103
301 S 4th St Ste 130 Manhattan (66502) ***(G-6618)***
Eagle Communications Inc 785 483-3244
336 E Wichita Ave Russell (67665) ***(G-10273)***
Eagle Communications Inc 620 662-4486
25 N Main St Hutchinson (67501) ***(G-3272)***
Eagle Communications Inc 785 825-4631
1825 S Ohio St Salina (67401) ***(G-10482)***
Eagle Environmental Svcs LLC 316 944-2445
5909 W Harry St Wichita (67209) ***(G-14250)***
Eagle Estates Inc 620 331-1662
1354 Taylor Rd Independence (67301) ***(G-3513)***
Eagle Med Inc 785 899-3810
217 E 10th St Goodland (67735) ***(G-2468)***
Eagle Products, Kansas City *Also called D Rockey Holdings Inc* ***(G-3950)***
Eagle Radio, Hays *Also called Eagle Communications Inc* ***(G-2793)***
Eagle Radio, Great Bend *Also called Eagle Communications Inc* ***(G-2557)***
Eagle Security Inc 913 721-1360
5340 N 109th St Kansas City (66109) ***(G-3979)***
Eagle Security Services 620 251-0085
2444 Cr 4500 Coffeyville (67337) ***(G-935)***
Eagle Software Inc 785 823-7257
124 Indiana Ave Salina (67401) ***(G-10483)***
Eagle Technologies, Salina *Also called Eagle Software Inc* ***(G-10483)***
Eagle Trailer Company Inc 785 841-3200
920 E 30th St Lawrence (66046) ***(G-4844)***
Eaglecrest Operations LLC 785 272-1535
3715 Sw 29th St Topeka (66614) ***(G-12566)***
Eaglecrest Retirement Cmnty 785 309-1501
1501 E Magnolia Rd # 239 Salina (67401) ***(G-10484)***
Eaglemed LLC (HQ) 316 613-4855
6601 W Pueblo Dr Wichita (67209) ***(G-14251)***

Eaglepicher Technologies LLC 620 232-3631
2919 N Rotary Ter Pittsburg (66762) ***(G-9854)***
EAR NOSE AND THROAT CLINIC, Kansas City *Also called Otolaryngic Head/Neck Surgry* ***(G-4301)***
Earl Barnes 620 662-6761
211 S Main St Hutchinson (67501) ***(G-3273)***
Earl Bryant Enterprises Inc 913 724-4100
15280 Briar Rd Basehor (66007) ***(G-374)***
Earl Resse Welding 620 624-6141
1441 General Welch Blvd Liberal (67901) ***(G-6306)***
Earl, Bryant Heating & AC, Basehor *Also called Earl Bryant Enterprises Inc* ***(G-374)***
Early Childhood Connections 785 623-2430
2501 E 13th St Ste 1 Hays (67601) ***(G-2796)***
Early Childhood Dev Ctr 620 544-4334
507 S Madison St Hugoton (67951) ***(G-3161)***
Early Chldhood Cnnection/Pre K 785 726-2413
100 E 13th St Ellis (67637) ***(G-1642)***
Early Education Center, Hutchinson *Also called Training & Evaluation Cente* ***(G-3468)***
Early Head Start, Wichita *Also called Child Start Inc* ***(G-14006)***
Early Head Start Clay County 877 688-5454
1021 4th St Clay Center (67432) ***(G-861)***
Early Headstart Cmnty Action 785 266-3152
2400 Se Highland Ave Topeka (66605) ***(G-12567)***
Early Learning Center 316 685-2059
9333 E Douglas Ave Wichita (67207) ***(G-14252)***
Earp Distribution, Edwardsville *Also called Earp Meat Company* ***(G-1497)***
Earp Meat Company 913 287-3311
2730 S 98th St Edwardsville (66111) ***(G-1497)***
Earth Care Products Inc 620 331-0090
800 N 21st St Independence (67301) ***(G-3514)***
Earth Contact Products LLC 913 393-0007
15612 S Keeler Ter Olathe (66062) ***(G-7665)***
Earth Designs Inc 913 791-2858
10101 W 156th St Shawnee Mission (66221) ***(G-11325)***
Earth Rising Inc 913 796-2141
25110 235th St Mc Louth (66054) ***(G-6926)***
Earthcare Services Landscape, Salina *Also called Waters Inc* ***(G-10760)***
Earthmovers Inc 785 325-2236
1802 Industrial Park Dr Washington (66968) ***(G-13463)***
Earthmovers International, Washington *Also called Earthmovers Inc* ***(G-13463)***
Eas, Wichita *Also called Emerald Aerospace Services LLC* ***(G-14275)***
East Branch, Wichita *Also called Ultra Modern Pool & Patio Inc* ***(G-15829)***
East Branch YMCA Preschool, Wichita *Also called Young Mens Christian Associat* ***(G-16096)***
East Central Kansas Economic (PA) 785 242-6413
1320 S Ash St Ottawa (66067) ***(G-8266)***
East Central Kansas Economic 913 294-4880
22795 W 255th St Paola (66071) ***(G-9554)***
East Cntl Kans Area Agcy On AG 785 242-7200
117 S Main St Ottawa (66067) ***(G-8267)***
East Garden Village, Garden City *Also called Martin Mobile Home Park Inc* ***(G-2228)***
East Heights United Methdst Ch 316 682-6518
4407 E Douglas Ave Wichita (67218) ***(G-14253)***
East High Sch Child Lrng Ctr, Wichita *Also called Unified School District 259* ***(G-15834)***
East Kansas Agri-Energy LLC 785 448-2888
1304 S Main St Garnett (66032) ***(G-2372)***
East Kansas Quartly Cnfrce Fre 785 272-1843
5864 Sw 26th St Topeka (66614) ***(G-12568)***
East Orlndo Hlth Rehab Ctr Inc 913 383-9866
6501 W 75th St Shawnee Mission (66204) ***(G-11326)***
East Ridge, Centralia *Also called Centrlia Cmmmity Hlth Care Svc* ***(G-697)***
East Wichita Dialysis Center, Wichita *Also called Renal Trtmnt Centers-West Inc* ***(G-15445)***
Easton Bus Service Inc 913 682-2244
1320 Ottawa St Leavenworth (66048) ***(G-5235)***
Eastside Barbershop & Salon 800 857-2906
2410 Se 6th Ave Topeka (66607) ***(G-12569)***
Eastside Mkt Westside Mkt LLC 785 532-8686
219 E Poyntz Ave Manhattan (66502) ***(G-6619)***
Eastwynn Theatres Inc (HQ) 913 213-2000
11500 Ash St Leawood (66211) ***(G-5382)***
Easy Cash Asap LLC 913 291-1134
8900 State Line Rd # 230 Leawood (66206) ***(G-5383)***
Easy Credit Auto Sales Inc 316 522-3279
3101 S Broadway Ave Wichita (67216) ***(G-14254)***
Easy Money Pawn Shop Inc 316 687-2727
2525 S Oliver St Wichita (67210) ***(G-14255)***
Eatherly Constructors Inc (PA) 620 276-6611
1810 Boots Rd Garden City (67846) ***(G-2151)***
Eatherly Constructors Inc 913 685-9026
4831 W 136th St Overland Park (66224) ***(G-8669)***
Eaton Corporation 620 663-5751
3401 E 4th Ave Hutchinson (67501) ***(G-3274)***
Eaton Corporation 913 451-6314
11305 Strang Line Rd Lenexa (66215) ***(G-5828)***
Eb Group 217 787-9000
13795 S Mur Len Rd Olathe (66062) ***(G-7666)***
Ebc, Salina *Also called K S A J Oldies* ***(G-10559)***
Ebco Construction Group LLC (PA) 866 297-2185
13795 S Mur Len Rd # 301 Olathe (66062) ***(G-7667)***
Ebe, Olathe *Also called R K Black Missouri LLC* ***(G-8017)***
Ebert Construction Co Inc 785 456-2455
103 E Valley St Wamego (66547) ***(G-13418)***
Ebi Construction Inc 785 456-7449
4745 N Highway 99 Wamego (66547) ***(G-13419)***
Eby Corporation (PA) 316 268-3500
2525 E 36th Cir N Wichita (67219) ***(G-14256)***
EBY Group Inc 913 782-3200
13795 S Mur Len Rd # 301 Olathe (66062) ***(G-7668)***
EBY Holdings, Olathe *Also called EBY Group Inc* ***(G-7668)***
EBY Realty Group LLC (HQ) 913 782-3200
13795 S Mur Len Rd # 301 Olathe (66062) ***(G-7669)***
EC Manufacturing LLC 913 825-3077
27508 Lone Star Rd Paola (66071) ***(G-9555)***
Ecdc, Hugoton *Also called Early Childhood Dev Ctr* ***(G-3161)***
Eci Electrical Contractors 316 722-0204
4009 W Saint Louis Ave Wichita (67212) ***(G-14257)***
Eci Systems, Wamego *Also called Electrical Concepts Inc* ***(G-13420)***
Eck & Eck Machine Company Inc 316 942-5924
4606 W Harry St Wichita (67209) ***(G-14258)***
Eck Agency Inc (PA) 620 254-7222
123 N Main St Attica (67009) ***(G-277)***
ECKAN, Ottawa *Also called East Central Kansas Economic* ***(G-8266)***
Eckan, Paola *Also called East Central Kansas Economic* ***(G-9554)***
Ecology and Environment Inc 913 339-9519
9300 W 110th St Ste 460 Overland Park (66210) ***(G-8670)***
Econo Lodge, Overland Park *Also called Tirupati Balaji LLC* ***(G-9412)***
Econo Lodge, Emporia *Also called Sady Vijay Inc* ***(G-1819)***
Econo Lodge 785 242-3400
2331 S Cedar St Ottawa (66067) ***(G-8268)***
Econo Lodge 785 625-4839
3503 Vine St Hays (67601) ***(G-2797)***
Econo-Larue Machine, Chanute *Also called Larue Machine Inc* ***(G-738)***
Economic & Empolyment Support 785 296-4276
915 Sw Harrison St 681w Topeka (66612) ***(G-12570)***
Economic Opprtunity Foundation (PA) 913 371-7800
950 Quindaro Blvd Kansas City (66101) ***(G-3980)***
Economy Mfg Co Inc 620 725-3520
833 State Highway 99 Sedan (67361) ***(G-10842)***
Economy Storage, Liberal *Also called Ronald Carlile* ***(G-6361)***
Economy Store, Sedan *Also called Economy Mfg Co Inc* ***(G-10842)***
Ecs Inc International 913 782-7787
15351 W 109th St Lenexa (66219) ***(G-5829)***
Eden West Inc 913 384-3800
10000 W 75tj St Ste 100 Tj Shawnee Mission (66204) ***(G-11327)***
Edge Enterprises Inc 785 749-1473
708 W 9th St Ste 107 Lawrence (66044) ***(G-4845)***
Edge Pest Control Kans Cy LLC 913 262-3343
6230 Merriam Dr Shawnee (66203) ***(G-10943)***
Edgemore Recreation Centers, Wichita *Also called City of Wichita* ***(G-14027)***
Edison Operating Company LLC 316 201-1744
1625 N Waterfront Pkwy Wichita (67206) ***(G-14259)***
Edmiston Oil Company Inc (PA) 316 265-5241
125 N Market St Ste 1420 Wichita (67202) ***(G-14260)***
Edmiston Oil Company Inc 620 792-6924
231 S Us Highway 281 Great Bend (67530) ***(G-2558)***
Edna Banking Center, Edna *Also called Community National Bank* ***(G-1492)***
Edoc Printing 913 469-0071
9401 Indian Creek Pkwy # 250 Shawnee Mission (66210) ***(G-11328)***
Edr Lawrence Ltd Partnership 785 842-0032
2511 W 31st St Lawrence (66047) ***(G-4846)***
EDS, Topeka *Also called Perspecta Entp Solutions LLC* ***(G-12970)***
Education Market Resources Inc 913 390-8110
804 N Meadowbrook Dr # 116 Olathe (66062) ***(G-7670)***
Educational Credit Union (PA) 785 271-6900
2808 Sw Arrowhead Rd Topeka (66614) ***(G-12571)***
Educational Credit Union 785 267-4900
3623 Se 29th St Topeka (66605) ***(G-12572)***
Educational Publishers, Manhattan *Also called Master Teacher Inc* ***(G-6733)***
Educational Resources Inc 913 262-0448
7500 W 160th St Stilwell (66085) ***(G-12146)***
Edward French Loy 785 825-4646
1100 Louise Ln Salina (67401) ***(G-10485)***
Edward J Lind II 316 788-6963
1101 N Rock Rd Ste 100 Derby (67037) ***(G-1242)***
Edward Rose & Sons LLC 316 202-3920
2925 N Boulder Dr Wichita (67226) ***(G-14261)***
Edwards & Wilson Periodontides 785 843-4076
4830 Quail Crest Pl Ste A Lawrence (66049) ***(G-4847)***
Edwards Chemicals Inc (PA) 913 365-5158
1504 Roseport Rd Elwood (66024) ***(G-1686)***
Edwards County Gas Company 316 682-3022
1710 N Waterfront Pkwy Wichita (67206) ***(G-14262)***
Edwards County Hospital 620 659-2732
620 W 8th St Kinsley (67547) ***(G-4616)***
Edwardslle Untd Mthdst Daycare 913 422-5384
302 N 4th St Edwardsville (66111) ***(G-1498)***

ALPHABETIC

Edwardsville United Methdst Ch, Edwardsville *Also called Edwardslle Untd Mthdst Daycare* ***(G-1498)***
Edwin Myers............316 799-2112
14566 Nw 110th St Whitewater (67154) ***(G-13570)***
EE Newcomer Enterprises Inc (PA)............816 221-0543
1901 E 119th St Olathe (66061) ***(G-7671)***
Efi Global Inc............913 648-5232
10323 Maple Dr Shawnee Mission (66207) ***(G-11329)***
Efreightship LLC............913 871-9309
6900 College Blvd Ste 470 Overland Park (66211) ***(G-8671)***
Egbert Oil Operations Inc............620 662-4533
500 N Monroe St Ste 1 Hutchinson (67501) ***(G-3275)***
Egos Salon & Day Spa Inc............785 272-1181
2120 Sw Brandywine Ln # 130 Topeka (66614) ***(G-12573)***
Ehersman Packing Co, Garden City *Also called Plankenhorn Inc* ***(G-2256)***
Ehlers Industries Inc............913 381-7884
10217 Howe Dr Leawood (66206) ***(G-5384)***
Ehresman Packing Co............620 276-3791
912 E Fulton St Garden City (67846) ***(G-2152)***
Eichhorn Holdings LLC............785 843-1426
3727 W 6th St Lawrence (66049) ***(G-4848)***
Eidson's Florist & Tuxedo, Kansas City *Also called Eidsons Florist* ***(G-3981)***
Eidsons Florist............913 721-2775
2420 N 131st St Kansas City (66109) ***(G-3981)***
Eighteen Capital Group............866 799-5157
11615 Rosewood St Ste 100 Leawood (66211) ***(G-5385)***
Eiko Global LLC............913 441-8500
8420 Hedge Ln Shawnee (66227) ***(G-10944)***
Eiko Global LLC (PA)............800 852-2217
23220 W 84th St Shawnee (66227) ***(G-10945)***
Eisenbarth Plumbing Inc............785 336-2361
13 N 2nd St Seneca (66538) ***(G-10865)***
Ejrex Inc............620 421-6200
1818 Broadway Ave Parsons (67357) ***(G-9683)***
EKA Consulting LLC............913 244-2980
5626 Brownridge Dr Shawnee (66218) ***(G-10946)***
El Centro Inc (PA)............913 677-0100
650 Minnesota Ave Fl 1 Kansas City (66101) ***(G-3982)***
El Centro Inc............913 677-1115
1330 S 30th St Kansas City (66106) ***(G-3983)***
El Dorado Animal Clinic, El Dorado *Also called Davy Harkins Dvm* ***(G-1555)***
El Dorado Banking Center, Newton *Also called Community National Bank & Tr* ***(G-7332)***
El Dorado Clinic PA............316 321-2010
700 W Central Ave Ste 205 El Dorado (67042) ***(G-1557)***
El Dorado Correctional Fcilty, El Dorado *Also called Corrections Kansas Department* ***(G-1551)***
El Dorado Intrnal Medicine LLC............316 321-2100
700 W Central Ave Ste 201 El Dorado (67042) ***(G-1558)***
El Dorado Livestock Auction............316 320-3212
2595 Se Us Highway 54 El Dorado (67042) ***(G-1559)***
El Dorado Sales Company, El Dorado *Also called El Dorado Livestock Auction* ***(G-1559)***
El Dorado Times, The, El Dorado *Also called Gatehuse Mdia Kans Hldings Inc* ***(G-1564)***
El Dorado YMCA, El Dorado *Also called Young Mens Christian Associa* ***(G-1616)***
El Paso Animal Clinic............316 788-1561
841 N Buckner St Derby (67037) ***(G-1243)***
El Taquito Inc............913 371-0452
640 Reynolds Ave Kansas City (66101) ***(G-3984)***
El Taquito Manufacturing Plant, Kansas City *Also called El Taquito Inc* ***(G-3984)***
El Zarape, Garden City *Also called E-Z Salsa Inc* ***(G-2150)***
Elanco Kc............816 442-4114
10850 Lakeview Ave Lenexa (66219) ***(G-5830)***
Elavon Inc............913 648-6444
9400 Antioch Rd Overland Park (66212) ***(G-8672)***
Elco Manufacturing Inc............620 896-7333
939 N State Road 14 Harper (67058) ***(G-2720)***
Elder & Disability Law Firm PA, Overland Park *Also called Elder & Disability Law Firm PA* ***(G-8673)***
Elder & Disability Law Firm PA (PA)............913 338-5713
9225 Indian Creek Pkwy # 1100 Overland Park (66210) ***(G-8673)***
Eldercare Inc............620 792-5942
1121 Washington St Ste A Great Bend (67530) ***(G-2559)***
Elderslie Farm, Valley Center *Also called Elderslie LLC* ***(G-13341)***
Elderslie LLC............316 680-2637
3501 E 101st St N Valley Center (67147) ***(G-13341)***
Eldorado National Kansas Inc (HQ)............785 827-1033
1655 Wall St Salina (67401) ***(G-10486)***
Eldredge Well Service LLC............620 649-2841
509 N Shoshone Ct Satanta (67870) ***(G-10784)***
Eldridge Holding LLC............785 749-5011
701 Massachusetts St Lawrence (66044) ***(G-4849)***
Eldridge House Invest Ltd Ptnr............785 749-5011
701 Massachusetts St Lawrence (66044) ***(G-4850)***
Elec-Tron Inc............316 522-3401
2050 E Northern St Wichita (67216) ***(G-14263)***
Elecsys Corporation (HQ)............913 647-0158
846 N Martway Ct Olathe (66061) ***(G-7672)***
Elecsys International Corp............913 647-0158
846 N Martway Ct Olathe (66061) ***(G-7673)***
Electrex Inc............620 662-4866
6 N Walnut St Hutchinson (67501) ***(G-3276)***
Electri Tech............316 683-2841
11828 E Lewis St Wichita (67207) ***(G-14264)***
Electric Dept Power Plant, Chanute *Also called City of Chanute* ***(G-716)***
Electric Operations, Kansas City *Also called Kansas City Bd Pub Utilities* ***(G-4138)***
Electrical Associates LLC............913 825-2537
308 W Elm St Olathe (66061) ***(G-7674)***
Electrical Concepts Inc............785 456-8896
4525 Horizon Trl Wamego (66547) ***(G-13420)***
Electrical Enterprises Inc............785 242-7971
414 W Wilson St Ottawa (66067) ***(G-8269)***
Electrical Systems Inc............316 263-2415
1815 S Pattie St Wichita (67211) ***(G-14265)***
Electromech Technologies LLC (HQ)............316 941-0400
2600 S Custer Ave Wichita (67217) ***(G-14266)***
Electromech Technologies LLC............316 941-0400
2600 S Custer Ave Wichita (67217) ***(G-14267)***
Electronic Contrls Assembly Co............913 780-0036
886 N Jan Mar Ct Olathe (66061) ***(G-7675)***
Electronic Funds Transfer Inc............913 831-2055
15301 W 87th St Ste 220 Lenexa (66219) ***(G-5831)***
Electronic Sensors Inc............316 267-2807
2063 S Edwards St Wichita (67213) ***(G-14268)***
Electronic Technology Inc............913 962-8083
5700 Merriam Dr Shawnee Mission (66203) ***(G-11330)***
Element Fitness............913 268-3633
7880 Quivira Rd Shawnee Mission (66216) ***(G-11331)***
Elevated Living LLC............316 619-7690
14909 W 90th Ter Lenexa (66215) ***(G-5832)***
Elias Animal Health LLC............913 492-2221
10900 S Clay Blair Blvd Olathe (66061) ***(G-7676)***
Elite Cementing Acidizing............620 583-5561
810 E 7th St Eureka (67045) ***(G-1884)***
Elite Cleaners............316 651-5997
6161 E 13th St N Wichita (67208) ***(G-14269)***
Elite Electric Inc............913 724-1645
2211 N 145th Ter Basehor (66007) ***(G-375)***
Elite Endeavors LLC............620 391-1577
2063 O Rd Plains (67869) ***(G-9974)***
Elite Fireplace Facings Inc............913 631-5443
6540 Pflumm Rd Shawnee Mission (66216) ***(G-11332)***
Elite Pipe Testing............785 726-4366
1305 Maple St Ellis (67637) ***(G-1643)***
Elite Transportation LLC............316 295-4829
200 W Douglas Ave Ste 520 Wichita (67202) ***(G-14270)***
Elitegear4ucom LLC............316 993-4398
3242 W 13th St N Ste 500 Wichita (67203) ***(G-14271)***
Elizabeth B Ballard Comm Ctr............785 842-0729
708 Elm St Lawrence (66044) ***(G-4851)***
Elizabeth Layton Center Inc............785 242-3780
2537 Eisenhower Rd Ottawa (66067) ***(G-8270)***
Elk County Development Corp............620 325-3333
1001 Wilson St Neodesha (66757) ***(G-7239)***
Elk's Lodge 1037, Junction City *Also called Benevolent/Protectv Order Elks* ***(G-3674)***
Elkhart Coop Equity Exchnge (PA)............620 697-2135
840 N Border Ave Elkhart (67950) ***(G-1619)***
Elkhart Telephone Company Inc............620 697-2111
610 S Cosmos St Elkhart (67950) ***(G-1620)***
Elkhorn Valley Packing............620 326-3443
1509 E 16th St Wellington (67152) ***(G-13498)***
Elkhorn Valley Packing Co............620 896-2300
101 Central St Harper (67058) ***(G-2721)***
Elks Club............785 263-1675
417 Nw 4th St Abilene (67410) ***(G-26)***
Elks Lodge Inc............620 672-2011
1103 W 5th St Pratt (67124) ***(G-10110)***
Ellinwood District Hospital, Ellinwood *Also called Great Plains Ellinwood Inc* ***(G-1634)***
Ellinwood Heights Apartments, Ellinwood *Also called Yarco Company Inc* ***(G-1640)***
Ellinwood Tank Service Inc (PA)............620 793-0246
601 E Santa Fe Blvd Ellinwood (67526) ***(G-1630)***
Elliott Insurance Inc (PA)............913 294-2110
278 Fairlane Dr Louisburg (66053) ***(G-6446)***
Elliott Mortuary Inc............620 663-3327
1219 N Main St Hutchinson (67501) ***(G-3277)***
Ellis Cable TV Co, Hays *Also called Eagle Communications Inc* ***(G-2794)***
Ellis County Concrete Co, Hays *Also called Concrete Service Co Inc* ***(G-2776)***
Ellis County Highway Dept, Hays *Also called County of Ellis* ***(G-2778)***
Ellis Grubb Martens Coml Group (PA)............316 262-0000
435 S Broadway Ave Wichita (67202) ***(G-14272)***
Ellis Kinney Swimming Pool............620 672-7724
201 S Haskell St Cullison (67124) ***(G-1185)***
Ellsworth Coop (PA)............785 472-3261
100 N Kansas Ave Ellsworth (67439) ***(G-1667)***
Ellsworth County Ambulance............785 472-3454
1107 Evans St Ellsworth (67439) ***(G-1668)***
Ellsworth County Highway Dept............785 472-4182
408 W 15th St Ellsworth (67439) ***(G-1669)***

Ellsworth County Medical Ctr.......785 472-3111
1604 Aylward Ave Ellsworth (67439) *(G-1670)*
Ellsworth Medical Clinic Inc.......785 472-3277
1604 Aylward Ave Ellsworth (67439) *(G-1671)*
Ellsworth Reporter Inc.......785 472-5085
304 N Douglas Ave Ellsworth (67439) *(G-1672)*
Ellswrth Knplis Chmber Cmmerce.......785 472-4071
114 N Douglas Ave Ellsworth (67439) *(G-1673)*
Elm Acres Youth & Family Svcs (PA).......620 231-9840
1102 S Rouse St Pittsburg (66762) *(G-9855)*
Elm Acres Youth & Family Svcs.......620 231-6129
503 N Walnut St Pittsburg (66762) *(G-9856)*
Elm Acres Youth Home, Pittsburg *Also called Elm Acres Youth & Family Svcs (G-9855)*
Elm Grove Esttes Rtrment Cmnty, Hutchinson *Also called Emeritus Corporation (G-3279)*
Elm Services LLC.......913 954-4414
9393 W 110th St Ste 500 Overland Park (66210) *(G-8674)*
Elmdale Community Center.......620 663-6170
400 E Avenue E Hutchinson (67501) *(G-3278)*
Elnicki Inc.......620 232-5800
3078 N Free King Hwy Pittsburg (66762) *(G-9857)*
Elrac LLC.......913 642-9669
10661 Metcalf Ave Overland Park (66212) *(G-8675)*
Em Sales LLC.......913 486-6762
1949 Foxridge Dr Kansas City (66106) *(G-3985)*
EMB Statistical Solutions LLC.......913 322-6555
9300 W 110th St Ste 550 Overland Park (66210) *(G-8676)*
Embassy Suites, Shawnee Mission *Also called Park Hotels & Resorts Inc (G-11716)*
Embassy Suites Olathe.......913 353-9280
10401 S Ridgeview Rd Olathe (66061) *(G-7677)*
Emberhope Inc (PA).......316 529-9100
900 W Broadway St Newton (67114) *(G-7339)*
Emberhope Inc.......316 529-9100
4505 E 47th St S Wichita (67210) *(G-14273)*
Emberhope Inc.......620 225-0276
11200 Lariat Way Dodge City (67801) *(G-1357)*
EMC Corporation.......913 530-0433
11225 College Blvd # 200 Overland Park (66210) *(G-8677)*
EMC Insurance Companies, Overland Park *Also called Employers Mutual Casualty Co (G-8679)*
EMC Insurance Companies, Wichita *Also called Employers Mutual Casualty Co (G-14279)*
EMC Shorts Guitars, Wichita *Also called Wichita Band Instrument Co (G-15979)*
Emco Specialty Products Inc.......913 281-4555
408 Miami Ave Kansas City (66105) *(G-3986)*
Emcor Services Fagan, Kansas City *Also called Fagan Company (G-4002)*
Emeditrack, Overland Park *Also called Soleran Inc (G-9324)*
Emerald Aerospace Holdings LLC.......316 440-6966
4174 S Oliver St Wichita (67210) *(G-14274)*
Emerald Aerospace Services LLC.......316 644-4284
4174 S Oliver St Wichita (67210) *(G-14275)*
Emerald City Gymnastics Inc.......913 438-4444
9063 Bond St Overland Park (66214) *(G-8678)*
Emerald Transformer Kansas LLC.......620 251-6380
2474 N Us Highway 169 Coffeyville (67337) *(G-936)*
Emerald Transformer Ppm LLC.......620 251-6380
2474 N Us Highway 169 Coffeyville (67337) *(G-937)*
Emergency Assistance Sites.......913 782-3640
420 E Santa Fe St Olathe (66061) *(G-7678)*
Emergency Dept Physicians.......913 469-1411
14400 College Blvd # 105 Shawnee Mission (66215) *(G-11333)*
Emergency Medical Care.......913 791-4357
20333 W 151st St Olathe (66061) *(G-7679)*
Emergency Medical Services, Wakeeney *Also called County of Trego (G-13385)*
Emergency Services of Kansas.......866 815-9776
301 N Main St Ste 300 Newton (67114) *(G-7340)*
Emergency Services PA.......316 962-2239
550 N Hillside St Wichita (67214) *(G-14276)*
Emergency Veterinary Clinic, Shawnee Mission *Also called Blueparl Vtrinary Partners LLC (G-11172)*
Emergent Care Plus LLC.......913 428-8000
4800 W 135th St Leawood (66224) *(G-5386)*
Emergent Green Energy Inc.......620 450-4320
450 County Rd Cll C Minneola (67865) *(G-7124)*
Emeritus Corporation.......620 663-9195
2416 Brentwood St Ofc Ofc Hutchinson (67502) *(G-3279)*
Emerson Construction Inc (PA).......785 235-0555
4149 Nw 25th St Topeka (66618) *(G-12574)*
Emerson Electric Co.......913 752-6000
10048 Industrial Blvd Shawnee Mission (66215) *(G-11334)*
Emily Kaemmer and Associates, Shawnee *Also called EKA Consulting LLC (G-10946)*
Emmanuel Church, Abilene *Also called Emmanuel United Methodist Ch (G-27)*
Emmanuel United Methodist Ch.......785 263-3342
1300 N Vine St Abilene (67410) *(G-27)*
Emmis Communications Corp.......620 793-7868
833 N Main St Wichita (67203) *(G-14277)*
Emotorpro (PA).......785 437-2046
27010 Highway 24 Saint Marys (66536) *(G-10362)*
Empac Inc.......316 265-9922
300 W Douglas Ave Ste 930 Wichita (67202) *(G-14278)*
Empire Candle Co LLC.......913 621-4555
2900 Fairfax Trfy Kansas City (66115) *(G-3987)*
Empire Candle Co LLC.......913 621-4555
3100 Fairfax Trfy Kansas City (66115) *(G-3988)*
Empire Candle Co LLC (PA).......913 621-4555
2925 Fairfax Trfy Kansas City (66115) *(G-3989)*
Empire Construction Group LLC.......913 375-8886
9128 W 91st Ter Shawnee Mission (66212) *(G-11335)*
Empire District Electric Co.......620 848-3456
7240 Se Highway 66 Riverton (66770) *(G-10212)*
Empire District Electric Co.......620 856-2121
905 Ottawa Ave Baxter Springs (66713) *(G-405)*
Empire Energy E&P LLC.......785 434-4900
904 W Mill St Plainville (67663) *(G-9987)*
Empirical Technology Inc.......620 277-2753
3105 N Ibp Rd Holcomb (67851) *(G-3074)*
Employers Mutual Casualty Co.......913 663-0119
7300 W 110th St Ste 300 Overland Park (66210) *(G-8679)*
Employers Mutual Casualty Co.......316 352-5700
245 N Waco St Ste 330 Wichita (67202) *(G-14279)*
Employers Reassurance Corp.......913 676-5200
5200 Metcalf Ave Shawnee Mission (66202) *(G-11336)*
Employment Edge, Overland Park *Also called Pivot Companies LLC (G-9170)*
Emporia Cold Storage Co.......620 343-8010
2601 W 6th Ave Emporia (66801) *(G-1736)*
Emporia Community Daycare Ctr (PA).......620 343-2888
802 Commercial St Emporia (66801) *(G-1737)*
Emporia Construction & Rmdlg.......620 341-3131
306 Market St Emporia (66801) *(G-1738)*
Emporia Country Club Inc.......620 342-0343
1801 Rural St Emporia (66801) *(G-1739)*
Emporia Dialysis, Emporia *Also called Total Renal Care Inc (G-1839)*
Emporia Fitness, Emporia *Also called Hoover Bachman & Assoc Inc (G-1774)*
Emporia Freight and Dlvry Svc.......785 862-1611
4631 Se Adams St Topeka (66609) *(G-12575)*
Emporia Gazette, Emporia *Also called White Corporation Inc (G-1851)*
Emporia Orthodontics.......620 343-7275
919 W 12th Ave Ste A Emporia (66801) *(G-1740)*
Emporia Parole Office, Emporia *Also called Corrections Kansas Department (G-1726)*
Emporia Pet Foods, Emporia *Also called Emporia Pet Products Inc (G-1741)*
Emporia Pet Products Inc.......620 342-1650
841 Graphic Arts Rd Emporia (66801) *(G-1741)*
Emporia Physical Therapy.......620 342-4100
1024 W 12th Ave Ste B Emporia (66801) *(G-1742)*
Emporia Prsbt Mnor of Mid Amer.......620 412-2019
2300 Industrial Rd Emporia (66801) *(G-1743)*
Emporia Public Works Dept, Emporia *Also called City of Emporia (G-1720)*
Emporia State Federal Cr Un.......620 342-2336
310 W 12th Ave Emporia (66801) *(G-1744)*
Emporia State Univ Fndtion Inc.......620 341-5440
1500 Highland St Emporia (66801) *(G-1745)*
Emporia Veterinary Hospital.......620 342-6515
710 Anderson St Emporia (66801) *(G-1746)*
Emporia Wholesale Coffee Co (PA).......620 343-7000
309 Merchant St Emporia (66801) *(G-1747)*
Emporia Winery LLC.......620 481-7129
627 Commercial St Emporia (66801) *(G-1748)*
Emporias Radio Stations Inc.......620 342-1400
1420 C Of E Dr Ste 200 Emporia (66801) *(G-1749)*
Emprise Bank (HQ).......316 383-4400
257 N Broadway Ave Wichita (67202) *(G-14280)*
Emprise Bank.......316 776-9584
1402 N Rose Hill Rd Rose Hill (67133) *(G-10238)*
Emprise Bank.......316 383-4301
2140 N Woodlawn St Wichita (67208) *(G-14281)*
Emprise Bank.......316 775-4233
1700 Ohio St Augusta (67010) *(G-318)*
Emprise Bank.......316 264-1569
2323 S Hydraulic St Wichita (67211) *(G-14282)*
Emprise Bank.......316 689-0717
11111 E Harry St Wichita (67207) *(G-14283)*
Emprise Bank.......316 794-2258
701 N Goddard Rd Goddard (67052) *(G-2437)*
Emprise Bank.......620 767-5128
20 S Mission St Council Grove (66846) *(G-1164)*
Emprise Bank.......620 241-7113
109 N Main St McPherson (67460) *(G-6958)*
Emprise Bank.......316 383-4498
8807 W Central Ave Wichita (67212) *(G-14284)*
Emprise Bank.......316 383-4131
2433 S Seneca St Wichita (67217) *(G-14285)*
Emprise Bank.......785 838-2001
1121 Wakarusa Dr Lawrence (66049) *(G-4852)*
Emprise Bank.......620 584-2201
201 E Ross St Clearwater (67026) *(G-891)*
Emprise Bank.......316 522-2222
330 N Main St Haysville (67060) *(G-2941)*
Emprise Bank National Assn (HQ).......785 625-6595
1011 W 27th St Hays (67601) *(G-2798)*

A L P H A B E T I C

Empyre Construction LLC...316 558-8186
6902 Martindale Rd Shawnee (66218) ***(G-10947)***
EMR-Pcg Construction Group...406 249-7730
2110 Delaware St Ste B Lawrence (66046) ***(G-4853)***
En Engineering LLC...913 901-4400
17775 W 106th St Ste 200 Olathe (66061) ***(G-7680)***
En- Tire Car Care Center, Lawrence *Also called Premium Ventures LLC* ***(G-5073)***
Enchanted Smiles Easthetic...785 246-6300
2949 Sw Wanamaker Dr # 1 Topeka (66614) ***(G-12576)***
Enco of Kansas Inc...316 788-4143
3701 E Haven Dr Derby (67037) ***(G-1244)***
Encobotics Inc...316 788-5656
3701 E Haven Dr Derby (67037) ***(G-1245)***
ENCOMPASS HEALTH, Wichita *Also called Wesley Rehabilitation Hospital* ***(G-15954)***
ENCOMPASS HEALTH, Topeka *Also called Kansas Rehabilitation Hospital* ***(G-12800)***
Encompass Health Corporation...913 649-3701
6509 W 103rd St Shawnee Mission (66212) ***(G-11337)***
Encompass Home Health, Hutchinson *Also called Advanced Homecare MGT Inc* ***(G-3193)***
Encompass Medical Group PA (PA)...913 495-2000
8550 Marshall Dr Ste 200 Lenexa (66214) ***(G-5833)***
Encore Receivable MGT Inc...913 782-3333
4600 W Kellogg Dr Ste 200 Wichita (67209) ***(G-14286)***
Encounters In Hair, Shawnee Mission *Also called Karen Tobin* ***(G-11520)***
Endacott Lighting Inc...785 776-4472
511 Fort Riley Blvd Manhattan (66502) ***(G-6620)***
Endless Ideas Inc...913 766-0680
15845 S Mahaffie St Olathe (66062) ***(G-7681)***
Endoscopic Associates LLC...913 492-0800
10200 W 105th St Ste 100 Overland Park (66212) ***(G-8680)***
Endoscopic Imaging Center, Overland Park *Also called Endoscopic Associates LLC* ***(G-8680)***
Endoscopic Services PA...316 687-0234
1431 S Bluffview Dr # 215 Wichita (67218) ***(G-14287)***
Endoscopy & Surgery Ctr Topeka...785 354-1254
2200 Sw 6th Ave Ste 103 Topeka (66606) ***(G-12577)***
Enel Green Power N Amer Inc...785 524-4900
223 N Highway 14 Lincoln (67455) ***(G-6381)***
Energy and Envmtl Systems Inc...913 845-3553
1204 Tonganoxie Rd Tonganoxie (66086) ***(G-12260)***
Energy Management & Ctrl Corp...785 233-0289
6600 Sw 10th Ave Ste B Topeka (66615) ***(G-12578)***
Energy Tech Unlimited LLC...913 837-4616
306 Broadmoor Dr Louisburg (66053) ***(G-6447)***
Enersys...785 625-3355
1 Enersys Rd Hays (67601) ***(G-2799)***
Enexaw, Wichita *Also called Waxene Products Company Inc* ***(G-15938)***
Engels Sales & Service Center (PA)...785 877-3391
209 W Lincoln St Norton (67654) ***(G-7444)***
Engie Services US Inc...913 225-7081
12980 Foster St Ste 400 Overland Park (66213) ***(G-8681)***
Engineered Air, De Soto *Also called Airtex Inc* ***(G-1191)***
Engineered Air, De Soto *Also called Airtex Manufacturing Lllp* ***(G-1192)***
Engineered Door Products Inc...316 267-1984
1040 S Santa Fe St Wichita (67211) ***(G-14288)***
Engineered Machine Tool Co...316 942-6147
2950 S All Hallows St Wichita (67217) ***(G-14289)***
Engineered Systems & Eqp Inc...620 879-5841
106 C Industrial Park Caney (67333) ***(G-667)***
Engineering Dept, Kansas City *Also called Wyandtte Cnty Unfied Gvernment* ***(G-4556)***
Engineering Technology Dept, Salina *Also called Kansas State University* ***(G-10567)***
Englewood Beach House LLC...913 385-5400
5100 W 95th St Prairie Village (66207) ***(G-10027)***
Engquist Tractor Service Inc...620 654-3651
1788 17th Ave McPherson (67460) ***(G-6959)***
Enhanced Home Care LLC...913 327-0000
10600 W 87th St Overland Park (66214) ***(G-8682)***
Enjet Aero LLC (PA)...913 717-7396
9401 Indian Creek Pkwy Overland Park (66210) ***(G-8683)***
Ennis Inc...620 223-6500
2920 Richards Rd Fort Scott (66701) ***(G-1965)***
Ennis Business Forms of Kansas...620 223-6500
2920 Richards Rd Fort Scott (66701) ***(G-1966)***
Enpower Operations Corp...913 441-3633
15941 W 65th St Shawnee (66217) ***(G-10948)***
Enserv LLC...316 283-5943
1021 S Spencer Rd Newton (67114) ***(G-7341)***
Ensignal Inc (PA)...316 265-8311
800 E 1st St N Ste 240 Wichita (67202) ***(G-14290)***
Ent Assctes Greater Kans Cy PC...816 478-4200
6815 Frontage Rd Merriam (66204) ***(G-7091)***
Entercom Communications Corp...316 685-2121
9111 E Douglas Ave # 130 Wichita (67207) ***(G-14291)***
Entercom Kansas City LLC...913 744-3600
7000 Squibb Rd Ste 200 Shawnee Mission (66202) ***(G-11338)***
Enterprise Bank (HQ)...913 663-5525
12695 Metcalf Ave Shawnee Mission (66213) ***(G-11339)***
Enterprise Bank & Trust...620 431-7070
17 S Lincoln Ave Chanute (66720) ***(G-725)***
Enterprise Bank & Trust...913 791-9950
15084 S Blackbob Rd Olathe (66062) ***(G-7682)***
Enterprise Bank & Trust...913 782-3211
110 N Clairborne Rd Olathe (66062) ***(G-7683)***
Enterprise Bank & Trust...913 791-9300
14670 S Harrison St Olathe (66061) ***(G-7684)***
Enterprise Bank & Trust...913 791-9100
444 E Santa Fe St Olathe (66061) ***(G-7685)***
Enterprise Banking N A, Shawnee Mission *Also called Enterprise Bank* ***(G-11339)***
Enterprise Bus Solutions LLC...913 529-4350
11320 W 79th St Lenexa (66214) ***(G-5834)***
Enterprise Cmnty Nursing Hm...785 263-8278
602 Crestview Dr Enterprise (67441) ***(G-1854)***
ENTERPRISE ESTATES NURSING CEN, Enterprise *Also called Enterprise Cmnty Nursing Hm* ***(G-1854)***
Enterprise Leasing Co KS LLC (HQ)...913 383-1515
5359 Merriam Dr Shawnee Mission (66203) ***(G-11340)***
Enterprise Leasing Co KS LLC...913 254-0012
1610 E Santa Fe St Olathe (66061) ***(G-7686)***
Enterprise Leasing Co KS LLC...913 782-6381
15500 W 117th St Olathe (66062) ***(G-7687)***
Enterprise Leasing Co KS LLC...913 631-7663
6000 Nieman Rd Shawnee Mission (66203) ***(G-11341)***
Enterprise Leasing Co KS LLC...913 402-1322
14873 Metcalf Ave Overland Park (66223) ***(G-8684)***
Enterprise Leasing Co KS LLC...913 262-8888
10000 Shwnee Mission Pkwy Shawnee Mission (66203) ***(G-11342)***
Enterprise Rent-A-Car, Overland Park *Also called Elrac LLC* ***(G-8675)***
Enterprise Rent-A-Car, Olathe *Also called Enterprise Leasing Co KS LLC* ***(G-7686)***
Enterprise Rent-A-Car, Olathe *Also called Enterprise Leasing Co KS LLC* ***(G-7687)***
Enterprise Rent-A-Car, Shawnee Mission *Also called Enterprise Leasing Co KS LLC* ***(G-11341)***
Enterprise Rent-A-Car, Overland Park *Also called Enterprise Leasing Co KS LLC* ***(G-8684)***
Entertainment Enterprises Inc...316 722-4201
905 N Stratford Ln Wichita (67206) ***(G-14292)***
Entertainment Specialties...620 342-3322
701 Graham St Emporia (66801) ***(G-1750)***
Entracare LLC...913 451-2234
11315 Strang Line Rd Shawnee Mission (66215) ***(G-11343)***
Enturia, Shawnee Mission *Also called Cardinal Health Inc* ***(G-11202)***
Envirnmntal Advisors Engineers...913 599-4326
19211 W 64th Ter Shawnee Mission (66218) ***(G-11344)***
Enviro-Health Corp...785 235-8300
1608 Sw Macvicar Ave Topeka (66604) ***(G-12579)***
Environmental Mech Contrs Inc...913 829-0100
14872 W 117th St Olathe (66062) ***(G-7688)***
Environmental Mfg Inc...785 587-0807
8887 Green Valley Dr Manhattan (66502) ***(G-6621)***
Environmental Protection Agcy...913 551-7118
11201 Renner Blvd Lenexa (66219) ***(G-5835)***
Environmental Systems Research...913 383-8235
8700 State Line Rd Leawood (66206) ***(G-5387)***
Environmental View Landscaping, Kansas City *Also called Environmental View LLC* ***(G-3990)***
Environmental View LLC...913 432-5011
1044 Merriam Ln Kansas City (66103) ***(G-3990)***
Envirotech Heating & Cooling, Shawnee *Also called Jim Jam Inc* ***(G-10979)***
Envision Inc...316 440-1600
610 N Main St Ste 400 Wichita (67203) ***(G-14293)***
Envision Inc...316 425-7123
2301 S Water St Wichita (67213) ***(G-14294)***
Envision Inc...316 267-2244
925 Sunshine Rd Kansas City (66115) ***(G-3991)***
Envision Inc...316 440-3737
2050 S Edwards St Ste B Wichita (67213) ***(G-14295)***
Envision Industries Inc...316 267-2244
2301 S Water St Wichita (67213) ***(G-14296)***
Envision Print, Wichita *Also called Envision Inc* ***(G-14294)***
Envision Technology Group LLC...913 390-5141
6985 W 153rd St Overland Park (66223) ***(G-8685)***
Ep Resorts Inc...970 586-5958
15954 S Mur Len Rd Olathe (66062) ***(G-7689)***
Epay North America, Leawood *Also called Payspot LLC* ***(G-5518)***
Epay North America...913 327-4200
3500 College Blvd Leawood (66211) ***(G-5388)***
Epi Holdings Inc...816 474-9423
87 Shawnee Ave Kansas City (66105) ***(G-3992)***
Epic Homes of Kansas Inc...785 537-3773
101 Waterbridge Rd Manhattan (66503) ***(G-6622)***
Epic Insulation Inc...316 500-1650
17600 W Highview Dr Goddard (67052) ***(G-2438)***
Epic Irrigation Inc...913 764-0178
15460 S Keeler St Olathe (66062) ***(G-7690)***
Epic Landscape, Olathe *Also called Epic Irrigation Inc* ***(G-7690)***
Epic Landscape Productions (PA)...913 897-3858
23933 W 175th St Gardner (66030) ***(G-2341)***
Epic Landscape Productions Lc...913 856-0113
23933 W 175th St Gardner (66030) ***(G-2342)***

Epic Sports......316 612-0150
9750 E 53rd St N Bel Aire (67226) ***(G-432)***
Episcopal Social Services Inc......316 269-4160
1010 N Main St Wichita (67203) ***(G-14297)***
Eplus Envrmental Solutions LLC......913 814-9860
4948 W 130th Ter Shawnee Mission (66209) ***(G-11345)***
Epoch Asssted Lving Ovrland Pk, Shawnee Mission *Also called Sunbrdge Asssted Lving Rsdnces* ***(G-11907)***
Epoxy Coating Specialists Inc......913 362-4141
3940 S Ferree St Kansas City (66103) ***(G-3993)***
Epro Services Inc (PA)......316 262-2513
1328 E Kellogg Dr Ste 1 Wichita (67211) ***(G-14298)***
Epsilon Sigma Alpha Intl......620 331-1063
3001 Terra Vista Dr Independence (67301) ***(G-3515)***
Eqh - Leavenworth LLC......913 651-8600
120 Delaware St Leavenworth (66048) ***(G-5236)***
Equilon Enterprises LLC......913 648-0535
9640 Nall Ave Shawnee Mission (66207) ***(G-11346)***
Equity Bank NA......731 989-2161
10314 Shawnee Msn 100 Shawnee (66203) ***(G-10949)***
Equity Bank NA......913 371-1242
650 Kansas Ave Kansas City (66105) ***(G-3994)***
Equity Bank NA......620 624-1971
1700 N Lincoln Ave Liberal (67901) ***(G-6307)***
Equity Bank NA (HQ)......316 612-6000
7701 E Kellogg Dr Ste 300 Wichita (67207) ***(G-14299)***
Erc/Resource & Referral Inc......785 357-5171
1100 Sw Wanamaker Rd # 101 Topeka (66604) ***(G-12580)***
Ergon Asphalt & Emulsions Inc......913 788-5300
10520 Wolcott Dr Kansas City (66109) ***(G-3995)***
Eri Solutions Inc......316 927-4290
125 N 1st St Colwich (67030) ***(G-1094)***
Eric Fisher Salon (PA)......316 729-0777
2441 N Maize Rd Ste 113 Wichita (67205) ***(G-14300)***
Eric K Johnson......785 267-2410
3649 Sw Burlingame Rd # 102 Topeka (66611) ***(G-12581)***
Erik J Peterson DDS......785 227-2299
101 N Harrison St Lindsborg (67456) ***(G-6398)***
Erin Is Hope Foundation Inc......316 681-3204
4921 E 21st St N Wichita (67208) ***(G-14301)***
Erise Ip......913 777-5600
7015 College Blvd Ste 700 Overland Park (66211) ***(G-8686)***
Erm-West Inc......913 661-0770
9225 Indian Creek Pkwy # 1050 Overland Park (66210) ***(G-8687)***
Erman Corporation Inc......913 287-4800
6600 Thorn Dr Kansas City (66106) ***(G-3996)***
Ermator Inc......813 684-7091
17400 W 119th St Olathe (66061) ***(G-7691)***
Ermc II LP......913 859-9621
11149 W 95th St Overland Park (66214) ***(G-8688)***
Ernest Spencer Custom Coatings, Ottawa *Also called Ernest-Spencer Metals Inc* ***(G-8271)***
Ernest-Spencer Inc (PA)......785 484-3165
3323 82nd St Meriden (66512) ***(G-7080)***
Ernest-Spencer Metals Inc......785 242-8538
1510 N Davis Ave Ottawa (66067) ***(G-8271)***
Ernst & Young LLP......316 636-4900
1625 N Waterfront Pkwy # 170 Wichita (67206) ***(G-14302)***
Ernsting's Radiator, Ellinwood *Also called Ernstings Incorporated* ***(G-1631)***
Ernstings Incorporated......620 564-2793
180a Se 100 Ave Ellinwood (67526) ***(G-1631)***
Ernstmann Machine Co Inc......316 943-5282
151 S Westfield St Wichita (67209) ***(G-14303)***
Erosion Control Inc......913 397-7324
31306 W 268th Ter Paola (66071) ***(G-9556)***
Errol E Engel Inc......785 625-3195
5500 N Vine St Hays (67601) ***(G-2800)***
Ervs Body Shop Inc......620 225-4015
1409 W Mcartor Rd Dodge City (67801) ***(G-1358)***
ESA P Prtfolio Oper Lessee LLC......316 652-8844
9450 E Corporate Hills Dr Wichita (67207) ***(G-14304)***
ESA P Prtfolio Oper Lessee LLC......913 661-9299
10750 Quivira Rd Overland Park (66210) ***(G-8689)***
ESA P Prtfolio Oper Lessee LLC......913 541-4000
9775 Lenexa Dr Lenexa (66215) ***(G-5836)***
ESA P Prtfolio Oper Lessee LLC......913 236-6006
6451 Frontage Rd Merriam (66202) ***(G-7092)***
Esb Financial (PA)......620 342-3454
801 Merchant St Emporia (66801) ***(G-1751)***
Esb Financial......785 539-3553
224 E Poyntz Ave Manhattan (66502) ***(G-6623)***
Escoute LLC......816 678-8398
18401 W 114th St Olathe (66061) ***(G-7692)***
Escoute Consulting, Olathe *Also called Escoute LLC* ***(G-7692)***
Eskridge Inc......913 782-1238
1900 E Kansas City Rd Olathe (66061) ***(G-7693)***
Eslinger Construction & Rdymx......620 659-2371
1321 90th Ave Kinsley (67547) ***(G-4617)***
Esolutions Inc (PA)......866 633-4726
8215 W 108th Ter Overland Park (66210) ***(G-8690)***
Espi LLC......785 777-2707
6030 Lincoln Ave Clay Center (67432) ***(G-862)***
Essex Group Inc......620 653-2191
75 E State Road 4 Hoisington (67544) ***(G-3063)***
Essilor Laboratories Amer Inc......800 397-2020
8140 Marshall Dr Overland Park (66214) ***(G-8691)***
Essilor Labs of America, Overland Park *Also called Duffens Opticals* ***(G-8663)***
Esslinger Manufacturing......620 431-4338
22165 Harper Rd Chanute (66720) ***(G-726)***
Estates Unlimited Inc......316 262-7600
310 S Ellis St Wichita (67211) ***(G-14305)***
Estes Express Lines......620 260-9580
284 N Industrial Dr Garden City (67846) ***(G-2153)***
Estes Express Lines Inc......316 554-0864
3838 S Gold St Wichita (67217) ***(G-14306)***
Estes Express Lines Inc......913 281-1723
4601 Speaker Rd Kansas City (66106) ***(G-3997)***
Esther V Rettig......620 245-0556
901 N Main St McPherson (67460) ***(G-6960)***
Etc Endure Energy LLC......913 956-4500
7400 W 129th St Ste 250 Overland Park (66213) ***(G-8692)***
Etco Specialty Products Inc......620 724-6463
621 W Saint John St Girard (66743) ***(G-2403)***
Etezazi Industries Inc......316 831-9937
2101 E 21st St N Wichita (67214) ***(G-14307)***
Ethanol Products LLC......316 303-1380
3939 N Webb Rd Wichita (67226) ***(G-14308)***
Etritionware, Wichita *Also called Superior School Supplies Inc* ***(G-15699)***
Eubanks Custom Woodworks......785 364-4377
310 New York Ave Holton (66436) ***(G-3088)***
Eudora Animal Hospital Inc......785 542-3265
1905 Elm St Eudora (66025) ***(G-1873)***
Eudora Lion Club Foundation......785 542-2315
1135 Locust St 31 Eudora (66025) ***(G-1874)***
Eureka Foundation......620 583-8630
416 E 5th St Eureka (67045) ***(G-1885)***
Eureka Greenhouses Inc......620 583-8676
420 N Pine St Eureka (67045) ***(G-1886)***
Eureka Technology LLC......913 557-9639
2 S Gold St Paola (66071) ***(G-9557)***
Eurodent Dental Lab Inc......913 685-9930
8303 W 126th St Ste D Shawnee Mission (66213) ***(G-11347)***
Euronet Worldwide Inc (PA)......913 327-4200
3500 College Blvd Leawood (66211) ***(G-5389)***
European Wax Center......316 425-0909
10096 E 13th St N Ste 122 Wichita (67206) ***(G-14309)***
Eurot Verti Fligh Solut LLC......785 331-2220
1040 Ocl Pkwy Eudora (66025) ***(G-1875)***
Eurotec Vfs, Eudora *Also called Eurot Verti Fligh Solut LLC* ***(G-1875)***
Eurotech Inc......913 549-1000
12721 Metcalf Ave Ste 102 Overland Park (66213) ***(G-8693)***
Evangelical Lthrn Good Smrtn (PA)......785 456-9482
2011 Grandview Dr Wamego (66547) ***(G-13421)***
Evangelical Lutheran......620 663-1189
810 E 30th Ave Hutchinson (67502) ***(G-3280)***
Evangelical Lutheran......785 475-2245
108 E Ash St Oberlin (67749) ***(G-7493)***
Evangelical Lutheran......785 626-9015
650 Lake Rd Atwood (67730) ***(G-284)***
Evangelical Lutheran......785 625-7331
2700 Canal Blvd Hays (67601) ***(G-2801)***
Evangelical Lutheran......620 624-3832
2160 Zinnia Ln Liberal (67901) ***(G-6308)***
Evangelical Lutheran......785 621-2499
2703 Hall St Ste 6 Hays (67601) ***(G-2802)***
Evangelical Lutheran......785 332-3588
217 Us Highway 36 Saint Francis (67756) ***(G-10341)***
Evangelical Lutheran......913 782-1372
20705 W 151st St Olathe (66061) ***(G-7694)***
Evangelical Lutheran......620 257-5163
1311 S Douglas Ave Lyons (67554) ***(G-6483)***
Evangelical Lutheran......785 726-3101
1101 Spruce St Ellis (67637) ***(G-1644)***
Evangelical Lutheran......785 890-7517
208 W 2nd St Goodland (67735) ***(G-2469)***
Evangelical Lutheran......785 456-9482
2011 Grandview Dr Wamego (66547) ***(G-13422)***
Evangelical Lutheran......785 472-3167
1156 Highway 14 Ellsworth (67439) ***(G-1674)***
Evangelical Lutheran......620 421-1110
709 Leawood Dr Parsons (67357) ***(G-9684)***
Evans & Mullinix PA......913 962-8700
7225 Renner Rd Ste 200 Shawnee Mission (66217) ***(G-11348)***
Evans Building Co Inc......316 524-0103
7700 W 53rd St N Maize (67101) ***(G-6513)***
Evans Ceramic Supply, Wichita *Also called Evans Industries Inc* ***(G-14310)***
Evans Industries Inc......316 262-2551
1518 S Washington Ave Wichita (67211) ***(G-14310)***
Evans Media Group......913 489-7364
15621 W 87th Street Pkwy # 223 Lenexa (66219) ***(G-5837)***

ALPHABETIC

Evaptech Inc 913 322-5165
2644 S 96th St Edwardsville (66111) ***(G-1499)***
Evco, Emporia *Also called Emporia Wholesale Coffee Co* ***(G-1747)***
Evcon Holdings Inc (HQ) 316 832-6300
3110 N Mead St Wichita (67219) ***(G-14311)***
Eveans Bash Klein Inc 913 345-7000
7500 College Blvd # 1212 Overland Park (66210) ***(G-8694)***
Eveland Bros Collision Repair, Shawnee Mission *Also called Eveland Brothers Body Shop* ***(G-11349)***
Eveland Brothers Body Shop 913 262-6050
7200 W Frontage Rd Shawnee Mission (66203) ***(G-11349)***
Even Temp of Wichita Inc 316 469-5321
216 S Commerce St Wichita (67202) ***(G-14312)***
Evening Telegram Company 417 624-0233
2950 Ne Hwy 69 Pittsburg (66762) ***(G-9858)***
Event Elements LLC 316 440-2829
230 S Topeka Ave Wichita (67202) ***(G-14313)***
Event Systems Inc 316 641-1848
811 E 10th St N Wichita (67214) ***(G-14314)***
Eventide Convalescent Center 785 233-8918
2015 Se 10th Ave Topeka (66607) ***(G-12582)***
Everbrite Electronics Inc 620 431-7383
720 W Cherry St Chanute (66720) ***(G-727)***
Everest Bancshares Inc 785 863-2267
518 Liberty St Oskaloosa (66066) ***(G-8225)***
Everetts Inc 785 263-4172
205 S Van Buren St Abilene (67410) ***(G-28)***
Evergance Partners LLC 913 825-1000
6900 College Blvd Ste 470 Shawnee Mission (66211) ***(G-11350)***
Evergreen Apartments 913 341-5572
7913 Grant St Overland Park (66204) ***(G-8695)***
Evergreen Community, Olathe *Also called County of Johnson* ***(G-7621)***
Evergreen Design Build LLC 620 342-6622
813 Graham St Emporia (66801) ***(G-1752)***
Evergreen Lving Innvations Inc 913 477-8227
11875 S Sunset Dr Ste 100 Olathe (66061) ***(G-7695)***
Evergreen Pallet LLC 316 821-9991
302 W 53rd St N Park City (67204) ***(G-9617)***
Evergy Kansas Central Inc (HQ) 785 575-6300
818 S Kansas Ave Topeka (66612) ***(G-12583)***
Evergy Kansas Central Inc 316 283-5521
300 W 1st St Newton (67114) ***(G-7342)***
Evergy Kansas Central Inc 785 587-2350
225 S Seth Child Rd Manhattan (66502) ***(G-6624)***
Evergy Kansas Central Inc 620 793-3515
1800 Kansas Ave Great Bend (67530) ***(G-2560)***
Evergy Kansas Central Inc 785 742-2185
1701 Oregon St Hiawatha (66434) ***(G-3007)***
Evergy Kansas Central Inc 316 299-7155
100 N Broadway Ave # 800 Wichita (67202) ***(G-14315)***
Evergy Kansas Central Inc 800 383-1183
700 N Star St El Dorado (67042) ***(G-1560)***
Evergy Kansas Central Inc 800 383-1183
1101 E Main St Independence (67301) ***(G-3516)***
Evergy Kansas Central Inc 913 667-5134
23505 W 86th St Shawnee (66227) ***(G-10950)***
Evergy Kansas Central Inc 800 794-6101
Rr 3 Pratt (67124) ***(G-10111)***
Evergy Kansas Central Inc 785 456-6125
25905 Jeffrey Rd Saint Marys (66536) ***(G-10363)***
Evergy Kansas Central Inc 620 820-8205
2605 Flynn Dr Parsons (67357) ***(G-9685)***
Evergy Kansas Central Inc 620 532-2782
990 Sw 70 Ave Kingman (67068) ***(G-4589)***
Evergy Kansas Central Inc 785 575-1352
4001 Nw 14th St Topeka (66618) ***(G-12584)***
Evergy Kansas Central Inc 785 263-2023
209 Olive St Abilene (67410) ***(G-29)***
Evergy Kansas Central Inc 785 331-4700
1250 N 1800 Rd Lawrence (66049) ***(G-4854)***
Evergy Kansas Central Inc 316 291-8626
6001 N 151st St W Colwich (67030) ***(G-1095)***
Evergy Kansas Central Inc 316 291-8612
6001 N 151st St W Colwich (67030) ***(G-1096)***
Evergy Kansas Central Inc 620 341-7020
210 E 2nd Ave Emporia (66801) ***(G-1753)***
Evergy Kansas South Inc 620 441-2427
3113 N Summit St Arkansas City (67005) ***(G-155)***
Evergy Metro Inc 913 757-4451
Rr 1 La Cygne (66040) ***(G-4640)***
Evergy Metro Inc 913 294-6200
101 W Ottawa St Paola (66071) ***(G-9558)***
Evergy Metro Inc 913 894-3000
16215 W 108th St Lenexa (66219) ***(G-5838)***
Evergy Missouri West Inc 620 793-1279
335 Nw 50 Ave Great Bend (67530) ***(G-2561)***
Everhance LLC 785 218-1406
9800 Metcalf Ave Ste 5 Overland Park (66212) ***(G-8696)***
Everidge LLC 316 733-1385
215 E 13th St Andover (67002) ***(G-91)***
Everseal Gasket Inc (PA) 913 441-9232
8309 Cole Pkwy Shawnee Mission (66227) ***(G-11351)***
Evologic LLC 913 599-5292
17501 W 98th St Spc 1859 Lenexa (66219) ***(G-5839)***
Evolv Solutions LLC (PA) 913 469-8900
9401 Indian Creek Pkwy # 250 Shawnee Mission (66210) ***(G-11352)***
Evolve Gran Natural Stone Inc 913 254-1800
1140 S Enterprise St Olathe (66061) ***(G-7696)***
Evolve Paleo Chef, Lenexa *Also called Cro Magnon Repast LLC* ***(G-5793)***
Evonik Corporation 316 529-9670
6601 S Ridge Rd Haysville (67060) ***(G-2942)***
Evoqua Water Technologies LLC 913 422-7600
7019 Mackey St Overland Park (66204) ***(G-8697)***
Ew & 7 Products LLC 316 440-7486
300 W Murdock St Wichita (67203) ***(G-14316)***
EW Scripps Company 316 436-1045
4200 N Old Lawrence Rd Wichita (67219) ***(G-14317)***
Ewell Construction Inc 913 499-7331
5324 Sw 53rd St Topeka (66610) ***(G-12585)***
Ewy Animal Hosp Inc 785 823-8428
545 E North St Salina (67401) ***(G-10487)***
Ewy, Kenneth L Dvm, Salina *Also called Ewy Animal Hosp Inc* ***(G-10487)***
Exacta Aerospace Inc 316 941-4200
4200 W Harry St Wichita (67209) ***(G-14318)***
Exaltia LLC 316 616-6200
8415 E 21st St N Ste 100 Wichita (67206) ***(G-14319)***
Examfx Inc 800 586-2253
11161 Overbrook Rd Leawood (66211) ***(G-5390)***
Examinetics Inc (PA) 913 748-2000
10561 Barkley St Ste 400 Overland Park (66212) ***(G-8698)***
Examone World Wide Inc (HQ) 913 888-1770
10101 Renner Blvd Lenexa (66219) ***(G-5840)***
Excalibur Production Co Inc (PA) 620 241-1265
1016 N Main St McPherson (67460) ***(G-6961)***
Excel Beef, Dodge City *Also called Cargill Meat Solutions Corp* ***(G-1317)***
Excel Constructors Inc 913 261-1000
8041 W 47th St Overland Park (66203) ***(G-8699)***
Excel Industries Inc 800 942-4911
605 Commerce Dr Hesston (67062) ***(G-2989)***
Excel Lighting LLC 816 461-4694
735 Southwest Blvd Ste B Kansas City (66103) ***(G-3998)***
Excel Linen Supply, Kansas City *Also called Whiteway Inc* ***(G-4541)***
Excel Linen Supply 816 842-6565
501 Funston Rd Kansas City (66115) ***(G-3999)***
Excel Mower Sales, Hesston *Also called Excel Industries Inc* ***(G-2989)***
Excel Personnel Services Inc (PA) 913 341-1150
9401 Indian Creek Pkwy # 40 Shawnee Mission (66210) ***(G-11353)***
Excel Sales Inc 620 327-4911
200 S Ridge Rd Hesston (67062) ***(G-2990)***
Excel Temporary Services, Overland Park *Also called Kleeb Services Inc* ***(G-8922)***
Excel Tool and Mfg Inc 913 894-6415
14344 W 96th Ter Lenexa (66215) ***(G-5841)***
Excel Wireline LLC 785 764-9557
457 Yucca Ln Pratt (67124) ***(G-10112)***
Excell Art Sign Products LLC 620 378-4477
1641 N 15th St Fredonia (66736) ***(G-2031)***
Excellart Sign Products LLC (PA) 913 764-2364
1654 S Lone Elm Rd Olathe (66061) ***(G-7697)***
Excellent Surgery Center, Topeka *Also called Stormont-Vail Healthcare Inc* ***(G-13108)***
Exchange Bank 785 762-4121
702 N Washington St Junction City (66441) ***(G-3688)***
Exchange National Bank & Tr Co (HQ) 913 367-6000
600 Commercial St Atchison (66002) ***(G-227)***
Exchange National Bank & Tr Co 913 833-5560
423 Main St Effingham (66023) ***(G-1523)***
Exchange National Bank & Tr Co (PA) 913 833-5560
600 Commercial St Atchison (66002) ***(G-228)***
Exchange National Bank Inc 620 273-6389
235 Broadway St Cottonwood Falls (66845) ***(G-1153)***
Execustay Oakwood Corp Hsing, Wichita *Also called Transitions Group Inc* ***(G-15791)***
Executive Airshare LLC (PA) 816 221-7200
8345 Lenexa Dr Ste 120 Lenexa (66214) ***(G-5842)***
Executive Beechcraft Inc 913 782-9003
280 Gardner Dr New Century (66031) ***(G-7284)***
Executive Flight Services, Lenexa *Also called Executive Airshare LLC* ***(G-5842)***
Executive Hills Family Dental 913 451-1606
8605 College Blvd Shawnee Mission (66210) ***(G-11354)***
Executive Hills Management 913 451-9000
5000 College Blvd Ste 400 Leawood (66211) ***(G-5391)***
Executive Hills Style Shop 913 451-1204
8660 College Blvd Shawnee Mission (66210) ***(G-11355)***
Executive Inn, Wichita *Also called Executives Inc* ***(G-14320)***
Executive Mnor Leavenworth Inc (PA) 785 234-5400
420 Se 6th Ave Ste A Topeka (66607) ***(G-12586)***
Executive Office of Kansas 785 272-8681
6425 Sw 6th Ave Topeka (66615) ***(G-12587)***
Executive Office of The St KS, Topeka *Also called Bank Commssnr Kansas Offce* ***(G-12363)***
Executives Inc 316 685-8131
250 N Rock Rd Ste 300 Wichita (67206) ***(G-14320)***

Exhibit Arts LLC.....316 264-2915
326 N Athenian Ave Wichita (67203) **(G-14321)**
Exide Technologies.....913 321-3561
3001 Fairfax Trfy Kansas City (66115) **(G-4000)**
Exide Technologies.....785 825-6276
413 E Berg Rd Salina (67401) **(G-10488)**
Exide Technologies.....913 321-4600
501 Kindleberger Rd Kansas City (66115) **(G-4001)**
Exline Inc (PA).....785 825-4683
3256 E Country Club Rd Salina (67401) **(G-10489)**
Exline Leasing Inc.....785 825-4683
3256 E Country Club Rd Salina (67401) **(G-10490)**
Exline Services, Salina *Also called Exline Inc* **(G-10489)**
Exltube, Manhattan *Also called Steel Ventures LLC* **(G-6810)**
Exon, Robert A, Topeka *Also called Webber Webber & Exon* **(G-13236)**
Experis Us Inc.....913 800-3027
7300 W 110th St Overland Park (66210) **(G-8700)**
Experitec Inc.....913 894-4044
7932 Nieman Rd Shawnee Mission (66214) **(G-11356)**
Expert Alteration.....913 322-2242
4759 Rainbow Blvd Ste B Westwood (66205) **(G-13553)**
Expert Auto Center.....316 440-6600
5230 E Central Ave Wichita (67208) **(G-14322)**
Expert Roofing LLC.....785 286-1999
2730 Ne Spring Creek Dr Topeka (66617) **(G-12588)**
Experts Exteriors, Wichita *Also called Pro Home Remodeling LLC* **(G-15352)**
Exploration Place Inc.....316 660-0600
300 N Mclean Blvd Wichita (67203) **(G-14323)**
Express Auto Service Inc (PA).....816 373-9995
11490 Strang Line Rd Lenexa (66215) **(G-5843)**
Express Auto Service & Tire, Lenexa *Also called Express Auto Service Inc* **(G-5843)**
Express Card and Label Co Inc.....785 233-0369
2012 Ne Meriden Rd Topeka (66608) **(G-12589)**
Express Personnel Services, Salina *Also called Express Services Inc* **(G-10492)**
Express Print and Signs LLC.....785 825-8434
248 S Santa Fe Ave Salina (67401) **(G-10491)**
Express Scale Parts Inc.....913 441-4787
14560 W 99th St Lenexa (66215) **(G-5844)**
Express Services Inc.....785 825-4545
2326 Planet Ave Salina (67401) **(G-10492)**
Express Well Service & Sup Inc.....785 735-9405
1110 Us Highway 40 Victoria (67671) **(G-13375)**
Express Yourself Digital.....620 724-8389
1706 Carline Rd Girard (66743) **(G-2404)**
Expressions Embroidery LLC.....913 764-7070
1794 E Kansas City Rd Olathe (66061) **(G-7698)**
Exsalonce LLC.....785 823-1724
2115 E Crawford St Salina (67401) **(G-10493)**
Extended Stay America, Overland Park *Also called ESA P Prtfolio Oper Lessee LLC* **(G-8689)**
Extended Stay America.....316 652-8844
9450 E Corporate Hills Dr Wichita (67207) **(G-14324)**
Extended Stay America, Inc., Wichita *Also called ESA P Prtfolio Oper Lessee LLC* **(G-14304)**
Extended Stay America, Inc., Lenexa *Also called ESA P Prtfolio Oper Lessee LLC* **(G-5836)**
Extended Stay America, Inc., Merriam *Also called ESA P Prtfolio Oper Lessee LLC* **(G-7092)**
Extension Agricultural Engrg, Manhattan *Also called Kansas State University* **(G-6690)**
Extra Inn Inc.....620 232-2800
4023 Parkview Dr Pittsburg (66762) **(G-9859)**
Extreme Detail Kc LLC.....913 568-4045
1356 E 155th St Olathe (66062) **(G-7699)**
Extreme Limousine LLC.....913 831-2039
9916 W 67th St Shawnee (66203) **(G-10951)**
Extreme Tanning Inc (PA).....316 712-0190
10646 W Central Ave # 110 Wichita (67212) **(G-14325)**
Extru-Tech Inc.....785 284-2153
100 Airport Rd Sabetha (66534) **(G-10309)**
Extrusions, Fort Scott *Also called Anodizing Inc* **(G-1955)**
Extrusions Inc (PA).....620 223-1111
2401 S Main St Fort Scott (66701) **(G-1967)**
Ey, Wichita *Also called Ernst & Young LLP* **(G-14302)**
Eye Associates, Olathe *Also called Vincent Pennipede Od* **(G-8141)**
Eye Associates of Olathe, Overland Park *Also called Eye Association Overland Park* **(G-8701)**
Eye Associates of Wichita.....316 943-0433
4600 W Kellogg Dr Ste 215 Wichita (67209) **(G-14326)**
Eye Association Overland Park (PA).....913 339-9090
10120 W 119th St Overland Park (66213) **(G-8701)**
Eye Care, Pittsburg *Also called Chris O D Jacquinot* **(G-9831)**
Eye Care PC.....816 478-4400
11500 Granada St Leawood (66211) **(G-5392)**
Eye Care Associates.....785 823-7403
900 Westchester Dr Salina (67401) **(G-10494)**
Eye Care Associates.....316 685-1898
321 S Hillside St Wichita (67211) **(G-14327)**
Eye Doctors, The, Junction City *Also called Price & Young & Odle* **(G-3739)**
Eye Doctors, The, Topeka *Also called The Eye Doctors* **(G-13157)**
Eye Doctors, The, Manhattan *Also called Price & Young & Odle* **(G-6779)**
Eye Doctors, The, Topeka *Also called Price & Young & Odle* **(G-12987)**
Eye Specialists.....785 628-8218
2214 Canterbury Dr # 312 Hays (67601) **(G-2803)**
Eye Surgery Center Wichita LLC.....316 681-2020
6100 E Central Ave Ste 5 Wichita (67208) **(G-14328)**
Ez2 Technologies Inc.....913 498-8872
6520 W 110th St Ste 205 Leawood (66211) **(G-5393)**
F & F Iron & Metal Co.....785 877-3830
514 W Washington St Norton (67654) **(G-7445)**
F & H Abatement Services Inc.....316 264-2208
5003 E 61st St N Kechi (67067) **(G-4567)**
F & L Enterprises Inc.....785 266-4933
4431 Se California Ave Topeka (66609) **(G-12590)**
F & R Swine Inc.....316 799-1983
13652 Nw Butler Rd Whitewater (67154) **(G-13571)**
F D I C, Wichita *Also called Federal Deposit Insurance Corp* **(G-14346)**
F G Holl Company LLC (PA).....316 684-8481
9431 E Central Ave # 100 Wichita (67206) **(G-14329)**
F G Holl Company LLC.....620 995-3171
Corner Of Hwy 15 And 9 Belpre (67519) **(G-505)**
F L I, Overland Park *Also called Fli Inc* **(G-8729)**
F T I Dental Lab, Wichita *Also called Ful Tech Dental Lab Inc* **(G-14430)**
F&F Productions Inc.....785 235-8300
1608 Sw Macvicar Ave Topeka (66604) **(G-12591)**
F/X Termite and Pest Control.....913 599-5990
13036 W 79th St Shawnee Mission (66215) **(G-11357)**
Fab Works LLC.....620 585-2626
800 E Center St Inman (67546) **(G-3581)**
Fabpro Oriented Polymers LLC.....620 532-5141
100 Fabpro Way Kingman (67068) **(G-4590)**
Fabriclean Supply Kansas Lc (HQ).....913 492-1743
14400 W 97th Ter Lenexa (66215) **(G-5845)**
Facc Solutions Inc.....316 425-4040
800 E 37th St N Wichita (67219) **(G-14330)**
Facial Expressions LLC.....316 390-0417
1025 S Stagecoach St Wichita (67230) **(G-14331)**
Facility Mgmt Svs Grp of Kc.....913 888-7600
14720 W 105th St Lenexa (66215) **(G-5846)**
Facility Solutions Group Inc.....913 422-8400
6435 Vista Dr Shawnee (66218) **(G-10952)**
Factory Authorized Video Svc, Shawnee Mission *Also called Overland TV Inc* **(G-11711)**
Factory Direct Appliance.....785 272-8800
1040 Sw Wanamaker Rd Topeka (66604) **(G-12592)**
Faerber Surgical Arts.....913 469-8895
4601 W 109th St Ste 118 Shawnee Mission (66211) **(G-11358)**
Fagan Company.....913 621-4444
3125 Brinkerhoff Rd Kansas City (66115) **(G-4002)**
Fagan Construction Co.....913 238-5903
4511 W 82nd Ter Prairie Village (66208) **(G-10028)**
Fagron Compounding Svcs LLC.....316 773-0405
8710 E 34th St N Wichita (67226) **(G-14332)**
Fagron Sterile Services, Wichita *Also called Fagron Compounding Svcs LLC* **(G-14332)**
Faimon Publications Inc.....620 364-5325
324 Hudson St Burlington (66839) **(G-634)**
Fain, Douglas W, Prairie Village *Also called Oral and Facial Associate* **(G-10055)**
Fairbank Equipment Inc (PA).....316 943-2247
3700 W Jewell St Wichita (67213) **(G-14333)**
Fairbanks Morse Pump Corp (HQ).....630 859-7000
P.O. Box 6999 Kansas City (66106) **(G-4003)**
Fairbanks Morse Pump Corp.....913 371-5000
3601 Fairbanks Ave Kansas City (66106) **(G-4004)**
Fairfax Terminal, Kansas City *Also called Jack Cooper Transport Co Inc* **(G-4116)**
Fairfeld Inn Suites Hutchinson.....620 259-8787
1111 N Lorraine St Hutchinson (67501) **(G-3281)**
Fairfield Inn, Overland Park *Also called Apple Eght Hospitality MGT Inc* **(G-8389)**
Fairfield Inn, Manhattan *Also called Riley Hotel Suites LLC* **(G-6793)**
Fairfield Inn, Hays *Also called Ferguson Properties Inc* **(G-2805)**
Fairfield Inn, Wichita *Also called Ruffin Hotel of Wichita LLC* **(G-15492)**
Fairfield Inn, Wichita *Also called Douglas Webb Co LP* **(G-14232)**
Fairfield Inn, Olathe *Also called Rhw Management Inc* **(G-8033)**
Fairfield Inn By Marriott.....913 768-7000
12245 S Strang Line Rd Olathe (66062) **(G-7700)**
Fairfield Inn By Marrtt Wichta.....316 685-3777
333 S Webb Rd Wichita (67207) **(G-14334)**
Fairlawn Burial Park Assn.....620 662-3431
2401 Carey Blvd Hutchinson (67501) **(G-3282)**
Fairlawn Burial Pk & Mausoleum, Hutchinson *Also called Fairlawn Burial Park Assn* **(G-3282)**
Fairleigh Corporation.....620 872-1111
207 E Bellevue Ave Scott City (67871) **(G-10809)**
Fairleigh Feed Yard, Scott City *Also called Fairleigh Ranch Corporation* **(G-10810)**
Fairleigh Ranch Corporation.....620 872-2111
7400 S Falcon Rd Scott City (67871) **(G-10810)**
Fairmount Technologies LLC.....316 978-3313
1845 Fairmount St 35 Wichita (67260) **(G-14335)**
Fairview Express, Seneca *Also called Fexp Inc* **(G-10867)**

A
L
P
H
A
B
E
T
I
C

Fairview Mills LLC (HQ) 785 336-2148
604 Nemaha St Seneca (66538) **(G-10866)**
Fairview Mills LLC 785 336-2148
217 S 7th St Elwood (66024) **(G-1687)**
Fairway Animal Hospital, Fairway *Also called Hires Gage Dvm* **(G-1910)**
Fairway Independent Mrtg Corp 785 841-4434
2701 W 6th St Lawrence (66049) **(G-4855)**
Fairways of Ironhorse 913 396-7931
5241 W 151st Ter Leawood (66224) **(G-5394)**
Faith Evangelical Lutheran Ch 316 788-1715
208 S Derby Ave Derby (67037) **(G-1246)**
Faith Lutheran School, Derby *Also called Faith Evangelical Lutheran Ch* **(G-1246)**
Faith Technologies Inc 913 541-4700
11086 Strang Line Rd Lenexa (66215) **(G-5847)**
Faith Technologies Inc 785 938-4499
1164 County Road 54 Gove (67736) **(G-2493)**
Faith Village II, Gardner *Also called Faith Village Inc* **(G-2343)**
Faith Village Inc 913 856-4607
123 E Colleen Dr Gardner (66030) **(G-2343)**
Faith Village Inc (HQ) 913 906-5000
14150 W 113th St Olathe (66215) **(G-7701)**
Faithlink LLC 913 904-1070
7180 W 107th St Ste 24 Overland Park (66212) **(G-8702)**
Falcon Design and Mfg 913 441-1074
23825 W 40th St Shawnee (66226) **(G-10953)**
Falcon Enterprises Inc 727 579-1233
1520 S Tyler Rd Wichita (67209) **(G-14336)**
Falcon Golf Management, Basehor *Also called Falcon Lakes Maintenance* **(G-377)**
Falcon Industries Inc 620 289-4290
100 W Main St Tyro (67364) **(G-13276)**
Falcon Lakes Golf LLC 913 724-4653
4605 Clubhouse Dr Basehor (66007) **(G-376)**
Falcon Lakes Maintenance 913 724-4460
14011 Hollingsworth Rd Basehor (66007) **(G-377)**
Falcon Ridge Golf Club 913 393-4653
20200 Prairie Star Pkwy Shawnee Mission (66220) **(G-11359)**
Falls Apartments, Shawnee Mission *Also called Nolan Real Estate Services Inc* **(G-11686)**
Fam Host, Wichita *Also called Servicetitan Inc* **(G-15568)**
Famhost, Wichita *Also called Mgmttv Inc* **(G-15062)**
Families Together Inc 620 276-6364
1518 Taylor Plz E Garden City (67846) **(G-2154)**
Family & Implant Dentistry, Manhattan *Also called Mark Hungerford MD* **(G-6731)**
Family Care Center 620 221-9500
1305 E 19th Ave Winfield (67156) **(G-16141)**
Family Center, Manhattan *Also called Kansas State University* **(G-6696)**
Family Center For Health Care 785 462-6184
310 E College Dr Colby (67701) **(G-1003)**
Family Conservancy Inc (PA) 913 342-1110
444 Minnesota Ave Ste 200 Kansas City (66101) **(G-4005)**
Family Conservancy Inc 913 287-1300
5424 State Ave Kansas City (66102) **(G-4006)**
Family Crisis Center Inc 620 793-9941
1924 Broadway Ave Great Bend (67530) **(G-2562)**
FAMILY CRISIS SERVICES, Garden City *Also called Heart Spport Group For Bttred* **(G-2193)**
Family Dentistry PA, Buhler *Also called Dalton L Hunt DDS* **(G-615)**
Family Eyecare Center, Leavenworth *Also called Norris & Kelly Drs* **(G-5277)**
Family First Center For Autism 913 250-5634
1719 Metropolitan Ave Leavenworth (66048) **(G-5237)**
Family First Child Care LLC 316 333-1481
215 N Meridian Rd Newton (67114) **(G-7343)**
Family Fitness Center, Paola *Also called Health Connection Inc* **(G-9565)**
Family Ftres Edtorial Synd Inc 913 722-0055
5825 Dearborn St Shawnee Mission (66202) **(G-11360)**
Family Health Center, Lakin *Also called County of Kearny* **(G-4649)**
Family Health Ctr Morris Cnty 620 767-5126
604 N Washington St Council Grove (66846) **(G-1165)**
Family Hlth Rhbltation Ctr LLC 316 425-5600
639 S Maize Ct Wichita (67209) **(G-14337)**
Family Life Services Emporia 620 342-2244
615 Congress St Emporia (66801) **(G-1754)**
Family Med Center, Iola *Also called Prefered Medical Associates* **(G-3626)**
Family Med Center Southeast, Wichita *Also called Physicians Medical Clinics* **(G-15296)**
Family Media Group Inc 913 815-6600
11936 W 119th St 335 Overland Park (66213) **(G-8703)**
Family Medical Care of Olathe, Olathe *Also called Olathe Medical Services Inc* **(G-7945)**
Family Medical Group PA 913 299-9200
8101 Parallel Pkwy # 100 Kansas City (66112) **(G-4007)**
Family Medicine Associates PA 785 830-0100
4921 W 18th St Lawrence (66047) **(G-4856)**
Family Medicine East Chartered 316 689-6630
1709 S Rock Rd Wichita (67207) **(G-14338)**
Family Physicians Kansas LLC 316 733-4500
524 N Andover Rd Andover (67002) **(G-92)**
Family Physicians Mgt Corp 620 365-3115
1408 East St Ste A Iola (66749) **(G-3599)**
Family Practice, Clyde *Also called Clay Center Fmly Physicians PA* **(G-905)**
Family Practice Associates, Holton *Also called Rural Hlth Rsurces Jackson Inc* **(G-3111)**
Family Practice Associates 620 241-7400
1000 Hospital Dr McPherson (67460) **(G-6962)**
Family Practice Associates (PA) 913 299-2100
1150 N 75th Pl Ste 200 Kansas City (66112) **(G-4008)**
Family Practice Associates 913 438-2226
8760 Monrovia St Lenexa (66215) **(G-5848)**
Family Practice Clinic, Hiawatha *Also called Hiawatha Hospital Association* **(G-3010)**
Family Practice Optometry, Wichita *Also called Lentz & Baker Eye Care* **(G-14955)**
Family Prctice Assoc Wstn Kans, Dodge City *Also called Merrill R Conant MD* **(G-1404)**
Family Resource Center Inc 620 235-3150
1600 N Walnut St Pittsburg (66762) **(G-9860)**
Family Svc Gdnce Ctr Tpeka Inc (PA) 785 232-5005
325 Sw Frazier Ave Topeka (66606) **(G-12593)**
Family Therapy Inst Midwest 785 830-8299
2619 W 6th St Ste B Lawrence (66049) **(G-4857)**
Family Tree Nursery, Kansas City *Also called Overland Park Garden Ctr Inc* **(G-4303)**
Family Video Movie Club Inc 620 342-4659
1012 Commercial St Emporia (66801) **(G-1755)**
Family Video Movie Club Inc 913 254-7219
12708 S Blackbob Rd Olathe (66062) **(G-7702)**
Family Video Movie Club Inc 785 263-3853
409 N Buckeye Ave Abilene (67410) **(G-30)**
Family Video Movie Club Inc 785 478-0606
6749 Sw 29th St Ste A Topeka (66614) **(G-12594)**
Family Video Movie Club Inc 785 762-2377
215 W 6th St Junction City (66441) **(G-3689)**
Fanchon Ballroom & Supper Club 785 628-8154
2350 Old Hwy 40 Hays (67601) **(G-2804)**
Fandhill Orthpd & Spt Medicine 620 275-8400
101 E Fulton St Garden City (67846) **(G-2155)**
Fanestil Meats, Emporia *Also called S&S Quality Meats LLC* **(G-1818)**
Fannect LLC 913 271-2346
16132 Birch St Overland Park (66085) **(G-8704)**
Fantastic Sams, Shawnee Mission *Also called C & W Operations Ltd* **(G-11196)**
Fantastic Sams, Kansas City *Also called C & W Operations Ltd* **(G-3884)**
Fantastic Sams, Shawnee Mission *Also called C & W Operations Ltd* **(G-11197)**
Farha Construction Inc 316 943-0000
303 S Broadway Ave # 100 Wichita (67202) **(G-14339)**
Farm & Ranch Realty Inc 785 462-3904
1420 W 4th St Colby (67701) **(G-1004)**
Farm and Family Insur Assoc 785 823-5071
2105 E Crawford Pl Salina (67401) **(G-10495)**
Farm Bur Property Cslty Insur 316 978-9950
300 W Douglas Ave Wichita (67202) **(G-14340)**
Farm Bureau Claims 620 275-9195
1707 E Maggie St Garden City (67846) **(G-2156)**
Farm Bureau Insurance, Manhattan *Also called Farm Bureau Mutl Insur Co Inc* **(G-6625)**
Farm Bureau Insurance, Wichita *Also called Farm Bur Property Cslty Insur* **(G-14340)**
Farm Bureau Mutl Insur Co Inc (PA) 785 587-6000
2627 Kfb Plz Manhattan (66503) **(G-6625)**
Farm Bureau Mutl Insur Co Inc 620 275-9195
1707 E Maggie St Garden City (67846) **(G-2157)**
Farm Bureau Mutl Insur Co Inc 316 652-1800
7421 E 21st St N Wichita (67206) **(G-14341)**
Farm Cr Grdn Cy P C A/F L C A, Garden City *Also called Garden City Production Cr Assn* **(G-2175)**
Farm Credit Ness City F L C A, Ness City *Also called Cobank Acb* **(G-7257)**
Farm Credit of Garden City, Hugoton *Also called Federal Land Bank Assoc* **(G-3162)**
Farm Credit of Western Kansas (PA) 785 462-6714
1190 S Range Ave Colby (67701) **(G-1005)**
Farm Credit of Western Kansas 785 462-6714
1055 S Range Ave Colby (67701) **(G-1006)**
Farm Credit Services, Emporia *Also called Cobank Acb* **(G-1722)**
Farm Credit Services, Chanute *Also called Cobank Acb* **(G-717)**
Farm Credit Wstn KS PCA/Ffca, Colby *Also called Farm Credit of Western Kansas* **(G-1005)**
Farm Management Services Inc 785 243-1854
310 Washington St Concordia (66901) **(G-1110)**
Farm Talk, Parsons *Also called Cnhi LLC* **(G-9673)**
Farmer Direct Foods Inc 785 823-8787
5641 E Mariposa Rd New Cambria (67470) **(G-7270)**
Farmer Union Co Op, Clay Center *Also called Farmers Union Coop Assn* **(G-863)**
Farmer's, Junction City *Also called Upu Industries Inc* **(G-3762)**
Farmers & Drovers Bank (PA) 620 767-2265
201 W Main St Council Grove (66846) **(G-1166)**
Farmers & Merchants Bank Colby 785 460-3321
240 W 4th St Colby (67701) **(G-1007)**
Farmers & Merchants Bank Hl Cy (PA) 785 421-2131
120 E Main St Hill City (67642) **(G-3034)**
Farmers Alliance Mutl Insur Co (PA) 620 241-2200
1122 N Main St McPherson (67460) **(G-6963)**
Farmers Bank & Trust (PA) 785 626-3233
101 S 4th St Atwood (67730) **(G-285)**
Farmers Bank & Trust (HQ) 620 792-2411
1017 Harrison St Great Bend (67530) **(G-2563)**
Farmers Bank & Trust 620 285-3177
102 W 6th St Larned (67550) **(G-4702)**

Farmers Bank & Trust 913 402-7257
14231 Metcalf Ave Ste 100 Overland Park (66223) ***(G-8705)***
Farmers Co-Op Crop Consulting, Nickerson *Also called Central Prairie Co-Op* ***(G-7431)***
Farmers Co-Operative Equity Co (PA) 620 739-4335
102 N Burr St Isabel (67065) ***(G-3639)***
Farmers Co-Operative Union 620 278-2141
225 S Broadway Ave Sterling (67579) ***(G-12116)***
Farmers Coop Grn Assn Inc (PA) 620 456-2222
524 E Parallel St Conway Springs (67031) ***(G-1141)***
Farmers Cooperative Assn 620 856-2365
10th & Railroad Baxter Springs (66713) ***(G-406)***
Farmers Cooperative Elev Assn (PA) 785 747-2236
401 Commercial St Greenleaf (66943) ***(G-2668)***
Farmers Cooperative Elev Co (PA) 316 835-2261
302 W 1st St Halstead (67056) ***(G-2699)***
Farmers Cooperative Elev Co 620 545-7138
7115 S 183rd St W Viola (67149) ***(G-13378)***
Farmers Cooperative Elev Inc (PA) 785 284-2185
204 N 9th St Sabetha (66534) ***(G-10310)***
Farmers Cooperative Grain (PA) 620 326-7496
9011 N A St Wellington (67152) ***(G-13499)***
Farmers Cooperative Grain Co 620 845-6441
102 N Arapahoe St Caldwell (67022) ***(G-658)***
Farmers Dream Inc 785 562-5588
1155 Pony Express Hwy Marysville (66508) ***(G-6888)***
Farmers Grain Cooperative 620 837-3313
E Hwy 50 Walton (67151) ***(G-13400)***
Farmers Group Inc 785 271-8088
5654 Sw 29th St Topeka (66614) ***(G-12595)***
Farmers Group Inc 785 267-4653
3646 Sw Plass Ave Topeka (66611) ***(G-12596)***
Farmers Group Inc 316 682-4500
12627 E Central Ave # 301 Wichita (67206) ***(G-14342)***
Farmers Group Inc 316 263-4927
7230 W 13th St N Ste 4 Wichita (67212) ***(G-14343)***
Farmers Group Inc 913 227-2000
10551 S Ridgeview Rd Olathe (66061) ***(G-7703)***
Farmers Group Inc 913 227-3200
17000 W 119th St Olathe (66061) ***(G-7704)***
FARMERS INSURANCE, Council Grove *Also called Farmers & Drovers Bank* ***(G-1166)***
Farmers Insurance, Topeka *Also called Farmers Group Inc* ***(G-12595)***
Farmers Insurance, Wichita *Also called Farmers Group Inc* ***(G-14342)***
Farmers Insurance, Wichita *Also called Farmers Group Inc* ***(G-14343)***
Farmers Insurance, Olathe *Also called Farmers Group Inc* ***(G-7703)***
Farmers Insurance, Olathe *Also called Farmers Group Inc* ***(G-7704)***
Farmers Nat Bnk of Canfield 785 346-2000
102 W Main St Osborne (67473) ***(G-8208)***
Farmers National Bank (PA) 785 543-6541
759 State St Phillipsburg (67661) ***(G-9785)***
FARMERS NATIONAL BANK OF STAFF, Stafford *Also called Prairie Bank of Kansas* ***(G-12107)***
Farmers Rnchers Livstock Cmnty 785 825-0211
1500 W Old Highway 40 Salina (67401) ***(G-10496)***
Farmers State Bank 785 989-4431
211 Saint Joseph St Wathena (66090) ***(G-13474)***
Farmers State Bank Blue Mound (PA) 913 756-2221
205 S 5th Blue Mound (66010) ***(G-532)***
Farmers State Bank of Bucklin 620 826-3231
111 N Main St Bucklin (67834) ***(G-592)***
Farmers State Bank of Oakley 785 672-3251
100 Center Ave Oakley (67748) ***(G-7474)***
Farmers State Bankshares Inc (PA) 785 924-3311
205 Lincoln St Circleville (66416) ***(G-838)***
Farmers State Bankshares Inc 785 364-4691
209 Montana Ave Holton (66436) ***(G-3089)***
Farmers State Bnk of Wstmrland (PA) 785 457-3316
307 Main St Westmoreland (66549) ***(G-13547)***
Farmers State Bnk of Wstmrland 785 889-4211
301 Leonard St Onaga (66521) ***(G-8176)***
Farmers Store & Deli, Healy *Also called Healy Cooperative Elevator Co* ***(G-2966)***
Farmers Union Coop Assn 785 632-5632
625 W Court St Clay Center (67432) ***(G-863)***
Farmobile Inc 844 337-2255
4001 W 114th St Ste 300 Leawood (66211) ***(G-5395)***
Farmway Cooperative Inc 785 439-6457
2332 Commercial Ave Scottsville (67420) ***(G-10838)***
Farmway Credit Union (PA) 785 738-2224
200 S Hersey Ave Beloit (67420) ***(G-483)***
Farney's Distributing, Haysville *Also called Farneys Inc* ***(G-2943)***
Farneys Inc 316 522-7248
280 Cain Dr Haysville (67060) ***(G-2943)***
Farrar Corporation (PA) 785 537-7733
142 W Burns Ave Norwich (67118) ***(G-7466)***
Farrar Corporation 620 478-2212
142 W Burns Ave Norwich (67118) ***(G-7467)***
Farrar Corporation 620 478-2212
129 S Somerset St Norwich (67118) ***(G-7468)***
Farrar Corporation 620 478-2212
218 Main Norwich (67118) ***(G-7469)***
Farris Burns Corp 913 262-0555
6210 Merriam Dr Shawnee Mission (66203) ***(G-11361)***
Farview Farms Meat Co 785 246-1154
6325 Nw Topeka Blvd Topeka (66617) ***(G-12597)***
Fas, Shawnee Mission *Also called Financial Advisory Service Inc* ***(G-11367)***
Fashion Inc 785 242-8111
1019 E North St Ottawa (66067) ***(G-8272)***
Fast Print 316 688-1242
7710 E Harry St Wichita (67207) ***(G-14344)***
Fast Print of Wichita, Wichita *Also called Fast Print* ***(G-14344)***
Fast Signs Inc 785 271-8899
5999 Sw 22nd Park Ste C Topeka (66614) ***(G-12598)***
Fastenair Corporation 316 684-2875
10800 E Central Ave Wichita (67206) ***(G-14345)***
Fastenal Company 316 283-2266
1605 W 1st St Newton (67114) ***(G-7344)***
Fastenal Company 316 320-2223
2502 W Central Ave El Dorado (67042) ***(G-1561)***
Fastfittingscom 913 709-4467
10561 Barkley St Ste 62 Overland Park (66212) ***(G-8706)***
Fastsigns, Topeka *Also called Fast Signs Inc* ***(G-12598)***
Fastsigns, Wichita *Also called Signs of Business Inc* ***(G-15593)***
Fastsigns Inc 913 649-3600
8844 W 95th St Overland Park (66212) ***(G-8707)***
Faulkner Grain Inc (PA) 620 597-2636
9904 Sw Falcon Ln Chetopa (67336) ***(G-817)***
Faulkner Real Estate 620 356-5808
112 S Main St Ulysses (67880) ***(G-13295)***
Favorite Hlthcare Staffing Inc (PA) 913 383-9733
7255 W 98th Ter Ste 150 Overland Park (66212) ***(G-8708)***
Favorite Hlthcare Staffing Inc 913 648-6563
8700 State Line Rd # 330 Leawood (66206) ***(G-5396)***
Fbd Consulting Inc (HQ) 913 319-8850
12017 Bluejacket St Overland Park (66213) ***(G-8709)***
Fbo Air - Garden City Inc (HQ) 620 275-5055
2117 S Air Service Dr Garden City (67846) ***(G-2158)***
Fcg Inc 620 545-8300
6315 S 151st St W Clearwater (67026) ***(G-892)***
Fcii, Lenexa *Also called Fire Cnslting Case Review Intl* ***(G-5853)***
Fcs Manufacturing 620 427-4200
3430 Ee Rd Gridley (66852) ***(G-2690)***
Feal Invesments, Olathe *Also called Dinosaur Den Child Dev Ctr* ***(G-7656)***
Federal Deposit Insurance Corp 316 729-0301
2118 N Tyler Rd Ste 100d Wichita (67212) ***(G-14346)***
Federal Express Corporation 800 463-3339
809m Levee Dr Manhattan (66502) ***(G-6626)***
Federal Express Corporation 800 463-3339
1850 Sw 42nd St Topeka (66609) ***(G-12599)***
Federal Express Corporation 316 941-4438
2073 S Air Cargo Rd Wichita (67209) ***(G-14347)***
Federal Express Corporation 800 463-3339
3450 Centennial Rd Salina (67401) ***(G-10497)***
Federal Home Loan Bank Topeka (PA) 785 233-0507
500 Sw Wanamaker Rd Topeka (66606) ***(G-12600)***
Federal Land Bank, Garden City *Also called Cobank Acb* ***(G-2128)***
Federal Land Bank Assoc 620 544-4006
600 S Monroe St Hugoton (67951) ***(G-3162)***
Federal Prison Industries 913 682-8700
1300 Metropolitan Ave Leavenworth (66048) ***(G-5238)***
Federated Mutual Insurance Co 913 906-9363
6900 College Blvd Ste 700 Leawood (66211) ***(G-5397)***
Federated Rural Elc Insur Exch (PA) 913 541-0150
7725 Renner Rd Shawnee (66217) ***(G-10954)***
Federated Rural Elc MGT Corp (HQ) 913 541-0150
7725 Renner Rd Lenexa (66217) ***(G-5849)***
Fedex, Manhattan *Also called Federal Express Corporation* ***(G-6626)***
Fedex, Topeka *Also called Federal Express Corporation* ***(G-12599)***
Fedex, Wichita *Also called Federal Express Corporation* ***(G-14347)***
Fedex, Salina *Also called Federal Express Corporation* ***(G-10497)***
Fedex Corporation 913 393-0953
15014 S Blackbob Rd Olathe (66062) ***(G-7705)***
Fedex Corporation 913 677-5005
5700 Broadmoor St Shawnee Mission (66202) ***(G-11362)***
Fedex Freight Corporation 888 880-1320
666 E 19th St Goodland (67735) ***(G-2470)***
Fedex Freight Corporation 800 872-7028
9140 Woodend Rd Edwardsville (66111) ***(G-1500)***
Fedex Freight Corporation 800 426-0104
3560 S Maize Rd Wichita (67215) ***(G-14348)***
Fedex Freight Corporation 800 752-0047
2115 Ne Meriden Rd Topeka (66608) ***(G-12601)***
Fedex Freight Corporation 800 752-0045
1017 N Liberty St Cherryvale (67335) ***(G-806)***
Fedex Freight Corporation 888 399-4737
301 10th St Great Bend (67530) ***(G-2564)***
Fedex Freight Corporation 800 541-2032
505 Graves Blvd Ste 4 Salina (67401) ***(G-10498)***
Fedex Ground Package Sys Inc 800 463-3339
3660 Scanlan Ave Salina (67401) ***(G-10499)***

ALPHABETIC

Fedex Ground Package Sys Inc 800 463-3339
22161 W 167th St Olathe (66062) *(G-7706)*
Fedex Ground Package Sys Inc 913 422-3161
8000 Cole Pkwy Shawnee Mission (66227) *(G-11363)*
Fedex Ground Package Sys Inc 800 463-3339
6700 Sw Topeka Blvd 820 Topeka (66620) *(G-12602)*
Fedex Ground Package Sys Inc 800 463-3339
5180 N Industry Dr Wichita (67226) *(G-14349)*
Fedex Office & Print Svcs Inc 913 239-9399
7340 W 135th St Overland Park (66223) *(G-8710)*
Fedex Office & Print Svcs Inc 913 894-2010
13450 W 87th Street Pkwy Lenexa (66215) *(G-5850)*
Fedex Office & Print Svcs Inc 316 636-5443
3605 N Rock Rd Ste 111 Wichita (67226) *(G-14350)*
Fedex Office & Print Svcs Inc 316 682-1327
7701 E Kellogg Dr Ste 200 Wichita (67207) *(G-14351)*
Fedex Office & Print Svcs Inc 785 537-7340
1329 Anderson Ave Manhattan (66502) *(G-6627)*
Fedex Office & Print Svcs Inc 316 941-9909
240 S West St Ste 10a Wichita (67213) *(G-14352)*
Fedex Office & Print Svcs Inc 913 661-0192
11026 Metcalf Ave Ste 7a Shawnee Mission (66210) *(G-11364)*
Fedex Office & Print Svcs Inc 913 677-4488
5437 Johnson Dr Shawnee Mission (66205) *(G-11365)*
Fedex Office & Print Svcs Inc 316 721-6529
2441 N Maize Rd Ste 2507 Wichita (67205) *(G-14353)*
Fedex Office & Print Svcs Inc 913 383-2178
8829 Metcalf Ave Overland Park (66212) *(G-8711)*
Fedex Office & Print Svcs Inc 785 272-2500
2201 Sw Wanamaker Rd # 102 Topeka (66614) *(G-12603)*
Fedex Office & Print Svcs Inc 913 393-0953
15014 S Blackbob Rd Olathe (66062) *(G-7707)*
Fedex Office & Print Svcs Inc 913 780-6010
2099 E Santa Fe St Olathe (66062) *(G-7708)*
Fee Insurance Group Inc 620 662-2381
1 N Main St Ste 700 Hutchinson (67501) *(G-3283)*
Feed Mercantile Transport Inc (PA) 620 275-4158
1513 E Fulton Ter Garden City (67846) *(G-2159)*
Feed-Lot Magazine Inc 620 397-2838
116 E Long St Dighton (67839) *(G-1285)*
Feed-Lot Magazine Main Ofc, Dighton *Also called Feed-Lot Magazine Inc (G-1285)*
Feedex Companies LLC 620 500-5016
1616 E Wasp Rd Hutchinson (67501) *(G-3284)*
Feet On Ground Marketing Inc 913 242-5558
1301 Louisiana St Lawrence (66044) *(G-4858)*
Femco Inc 620 241-3513
1132 W 1st St McPherson (67460) *(G-6964)*
Fenix Company Incorporated 316 945-4842
802 W 2nd St N Wichita (67203) *(G-14354)*
Fenix Heating & Cooling, Wichita *Also called Fenix Company Incorporated (G-14354)*
Ferco, Salina *Also called Frank Construction Company (G-10505)*
Ferco Inc 785 825-6380
264 S Broadway Blvd Salina (67401) *(G-10500)*
Ferco Rental, Salina *Also called Ferco Inc (G-10500)*
Ferguson 216, Wichita *Also called Ferguson Enterprises LLC (G-14355)*
Ferguson Dry Wall Company Inc 913 334-5658
224 N 72nd St Kansas City (66112) *(G-4009)*
Ferguson Drywall Co Inc, Kansas City *Also called Ferguson Dry Wall Company Inc (G-4009)*
Ferguson Enterprises LLC 316 262-0681
2222 W Harry St Wichita (67213) *(G-14355)*
Ferguson Enterprises LLC 785 354-4305
2220 Se Lakewood Blvd Topeka (66605) *(G-12604)*
Ferguson Enterprises LLC 913 752-5660
9301 Rosehill Rd Lenexa (66215) *(G-5851)*
Ferguson Paving Inc 316 942-3374
3600 W Esthner Ave Wichita (67213) *(G-14356)*
Ferguson Production Inc 620 241-2400
2130 Industrial Dr McPherson (67460) *(G-6965)*
Ferguson Properties Inc 785 625-3344
377 W Mopar Dr Hays (67601) *(G-2805)*
Ferguson Ranch 620 467-2265
9203 327th Rd Cambridge (67023) *(G-663)*
Ferguson Zy Farms Inc 785 476-2297
1062 120 Rd Kensington (66951) *(G-4575)*
Ferguson-Phillips Homeware, Wichita *Also called Ferguson-Phillips LLC (G-14357)*
Ferguson-Phillips LLC 316 612-4663
4801 E Douglas Ave Wichita (67218) *(G-14357)*
Ferree Bunn OGrady & Rundberg 913 381-8180
9300 Metcalf Ave Ste 300 Shawnee Mission (66212) *(G-11366)*
Ferrell Companies Inc (PA) 913 661-1500
7500 College Blvd # 1000 Overland Park (66210) *(G-8712)*
Ferrellgas Inc (HQ) 913 661-1500
7500 College Blvd # 1000 Overland Park (66210) *(G-8713)*
Ferrellgas Partners LP (PA) 913 661-1500
7500 College Blvd # 1000 Overland Park (66210) *(G-8714)*
Ferrill Conant MD, Smith Center *Also called Smith County Family Practice (G-12042)*
Ferroloy Inc 316 838-0897
515 E 29th St N Wichita (67219) *(G-14358)*
Festival Grogs Inc 913 721-2110
628 N 126th St Bonner Springs (66012) *(G-553)*
Fetal Well-Being LLC 316 644-8919
9300 E 29th St N Ste 102 Wichita (67226) *(G-14359)*
Feuerborn Fmly Fnrl Svc 620 365-2948
1883 Us Highway 54 Iola (66749) *(G-3600)*
Fexp Inc 785 336-2148
604 Nemaha St Seneca (66538) *(G-10867)*
Feyerherm Construction Inc 913 962-5888
7424 Constance St Shawnee (66216) *(G-10955)*
Fh Companies Inc 316 264-2208
5003 E 61st St N Kechi (67067) *(G-4568)*
FH Kaysing Company LLC (PA) 316 721-8980
1950 S Florence St Wichita (67209) *(G-14360)*
FHLBANK TOPEKA, Topeka *Also called Federal Home Loan Bank Topeka (G-12600)*
Fhr Biofuels & Ingredients LLC (HQ) 316 828-2400
4111 E 37th St N Wichita (67220) *(G-14361)*
Fiber Glass Systems LP 316 946-3900
2501 S West St Wichita (67217) *(G-14362)*
Fidelity Bank 316 265-2261
2251 N Maize Rd Ste 101 Wichita (67205) *(G-14363)*
Fidelity Bank 316 722-1460
8442 W 13th St N Wichita (67212) *(G-14364)*
Fidelity Investments Instituti 913 345-8079
5400 College Blvd Leawood (66211) *(G-5398)*
Fidelity Kansas Bankshares 785 295-2100
600 S Kansas Ave Topeka (66603) *(G-12605)*
Fidelity Management Corp (HQ) 316 291-5950
100 E English St Ste 500 Wichita (67202) *(G-14365)*
Fidelity Management Corp 785 266-8010
3201 Sw Randolph Ave Ofc Topeka (66611) *(G-12606)*
Fidelity National Fincl Inc 913 422-5122
6700 College Blvd Ste 300 Leawood (66211) *(G-5399)*
Fidelity State Bank & Trust, Topeka *Also called Fidelity Kansas Bankshares (G-12605)*
Fidelity State Bank and Tr Co (PA) 785 295-2100
600 S Kansas Ave Topeka (66603) *(G-12607)*
Fidelity State Bnk Tr Ddge Cy (HQ) 620 227-8586
510 N 2nd Ave Dodge City (67801) *(G-1359)*
Field & Stream Club Inc 785 233-4793
1901 Sw Collins Ave Topeka (66604) *(G-12608)*
Fifth Ave, Wichita *Also called Perfect Touch Inc (G-15281)*
Figeac Aero North America Inc 316 634-2500
9313 E 39th St N Wichita (67226) *(G-14366)*
File A Gem Inc 620 856-3800
120 W 11th St Baxter Springs (66713) *(G-407)*
Financial Advisory Service Inc 913 239-2300
4747 W 135th St Ste 100 Shawnee Mission (66224) *(G-11367)*
Financial Benefits of Kansas 913 385-7000
11350 Tomahawk Creek Pkwy # 200 Leawood (66211) *(G-5400)*
Financial Consultants America 316 943-7307
6700 W Central Ave # 110 Wichita (67212) *(G-14367)*
Financial Counselors Inc (PA) 816 329-1500
5901 College Blvd Ste 110 Leawood (66211) *(G-5401)*
Financial Designs Inc 913 451-4747
11225 College Blvd # 420 Overland Park (66210) *(G-8715)*
Financial Institution Tech Inc 785 273-5578
6301 Sw 9th St Topeka (66615) *(G-12609)*
Financial Institution Tech Inc 888 848-7349
6206 Sw 9th Ter B Topeka (66615) *(G-12610)*
Financial Insurance Corp 913 631-7441
8600 Farley St Ste 200 Overland Park (66212) *(G-8716)*
Financial Placements, Roeland Park *Also called Bank News Publications Inc (G-10217)*
Financial Printing Resource 913 599-6979
15009 W 101st Ter Lenexa (66215) *(G-5852)*
Finch Bayless Crane Sls & Svc, Kansas City *Also called Crane Sales & Service Co Inc (G-3944)*
Finch Hollow Senior Residences 316 721-9596
707 N Golden Hls Apt 101 Wichita (67212) *(G-14368)*
Finch Sign Company Inc 785 423-3213
1459 N 300th Rd Baldwin City (66006) *(G-360)*
Finch Theatres 785 524-4350
122 E Lincoln Ave Lincoln (67455) *(G-6382)*
Fincher Office, Topeka *Also called Roger Fincher (G-13024)*
Finchers Findings Inc 620 886-5952
900 W Central Medicine Lodge (67104) *(G-7060)*
Finest Beef, Dodge City *Also called Wilroads Feed Yard LLC (G-1457)*
Finishpro Tools LLC 913 631-0804
15785 S Keeler Ter Olathe (66062) *(G-7709)*
Finley Auto Spa, Atwood *Also called Finley Construction & Rdymx (G-286)*
Finley Construction & Rdymx 785 626-3282
N Hwy 25 Atwood (67730) *(G-286)*
Finney & Trnp SD Trnsprttn 785 235-2393
603 Sw Topeka Blvd # 401 Topeka (66603) *(G-12611)*
Finney Cnty Committee On Aging 620 272-3626
907 N 10th St Garden City (67846) *(G-2160)*
Finney County Attorneys Office 620 272-3568
409 N 9th St Garden City (67846) *(G-2161)*
Finney County Community Hlth 620 765-1185
310 E Walnut St Ste 202 Garden City (67846) *(G-2162)*

Finney County Emergency Med...620 272-3822
803 W Mary St Garden City (67846) *(G-2163)*
Finney County Ems, Garden City *Also called Finney County Emergency Med (G-2163)*
Finney County Feed Yard Inc...620 275-7163
4170 N Finney Feeders Rd Garden City (67846) *(G-2164)*
Finney County Feedyard, Garden City *Also called Finney County Feed Yard Inc (G-2164)*
Finucane Enterprises Inc...913 829-5665
32565 Lexington Ave Ste A De Soto (66018) *(G-1199)*
Fire Alarm Specialist Inc...785 743-5287
29073 S Rd Wakeeney (67672) *(G-13387)*
Fire Cnslting Case Review Intl...913 262-5200
13415 W 98th St Lenexa (66215) *(G-5853)*
Fire Protection Services Inc...316 262-2452
1117 N Santa Fe St Wichita (67214) *(G-14369)*
Fire Sprinkler Consultant, Overland Park *Also called S C F Inc (G-9267)*
Fire Station Headquarters, Shawnee Mission *Also called City of Shawnee (G-11233)*
Fireboard Labs LLC...816 945-2232
24260 W 112th Ter Olathe (66061) *(G-7710)*
Firefighters Bnfit Asn-Sedgwic...316 660-3473
7750 N Wild West Dr Park City (67147) *(G-9618)*
Firelake-Arrowhead...913 312-9540
14217 W 95th St Lenexa (66215) *(G-5854)*
Firelk-Diversified Joint Ventr...913 312-9540
14217 W 95th St Lenexa (66215) *(G-5855)*
Firemans Relief Assoc Inc...620 365-4972
408 N Washington Ave Iola (66749) *(G-3601)*
Firemon LLC (PA)...913 948-9570
8400 W 110th St Ste 500 Overland Park (66210) *(G-8717)*
Firestone, Olathe *Also called Bridgestone Ret Operations LLC (G-7561)*
Firestone, Kansas City *Also called Bridgestone Ret Operations LLC (G-3878)*
Firestone, Shawnee Mission *Also called Bridgestone Ret Operations LLC (G-11181)*
Firestone, Wichita *Also called Bridgestone Ret Operations LLC (G-13889)*
First American Title Company...316 554-2872
10100 W Maple St Wichita (67209) *(G-14370)*
First American Title Company (PA)...316 267-8371
727 N Waco Ave Ste 300 Wichita (67203) *(G-14371)*
First Assembly God Inc...316 524-4981
1100 E Grand Ave Haysville (67060) *(G-2944)*
First Bancshares Inc...913 371-1242
650 Kansas Ave Kansas City (66105) *(G-4010)*
First Bank (HQ)...620 278-2161
128 S Broadway Ave Sterling (67579) *(G-12117)*
First Bank Kansas (HQ)...785 825-2211
235 S Santa Fe Ave Salina (67401) *(G-10501)*
First Bank of Newton (PA)...316 283-2600
128 E Broadway St Newton (67114) *(G-7345)*
FIRST BANK OF STERLING, Sterling *Also called First Bank (G-12117)*
First Bank of Sterling, Sterling *Also called Coronado Inc (G-12115)*
First Baptist Church Olathe...913 764-7088
2024 E 151st St Olathe (66062) *(G-7711)*
First Biomedical Inc (HQ)...800 962-9656
11130 Strang Line Rd Lenexa (66215) *(G-5856)*
First Birth Women Center, Topeka *Also called Josie Norris MD (G-12749)*
First Business Bank (HQ)...913 681-2223
11300 Tomahwk Crk Pkwy # 100 Leawood (66211) *(G-5402)*
First Business Bank...913 681-2223
11300 Tomahawk Creek Pkwy # 100 Leawood (66211) *(G-5403)*
First Call...785 234-2881
1137 Sw Gage Blvd Topeka (66604) *(G-12612)*
First Call For Help Ellis Cnty...785 623-2800
607 E 13th St Hays (67601) *(G-2806)*
First Call Hospitality LLC...913 345-2661
5800 College Blvd Shawnee Mission (66211) *(G-11368)*
First Care Clinic Inc...785 621-4990
105 W 13th St Hays (67601) *(G-2807)*
First Choice Chiropractic PA...913 402-7444
11960 Quivira Rd Ste 200 Overland Park (66213) *(G-8718)*
First Choice Credit Union (PA)...316 425-5712
1401 N Maize Rd Wichita (67212) *(G-14372)*
First Choice Support Services...785 823-3555
115 N 7th St Salina (67401) *(G-10502)*
First Class Hair...316 721-2662
2260 N Ridge Rd Ste 220 Wichita (67205) *(G-14373)*
First Class Transportation...785 266-1331
2300 Sw 29th St Ste 125 Topeka (66611) *(G-12613)*
First Command Financial Plg, Manhattan *Also called First Command Fincl Plg Inc (G-6628)*
First Command Fincl Plg Inc...785 537-0497
1121 Hudson Ave Ste B Manhattan (66503) *(G-6628)*
First Command Fincl Plg Inc...913 651-6820
417 S 2nd St Leavenworth (66048) *(G-5239)*
First Commerce Bank...785 562-5558
902 Broadway Marysville (66508) *(G-6889)*
First Commerical, Chanute *Also called Enterprise Bank & Trust (G-725)*
First Con Incorporated...316 425-7690
3242 W 13th St N Ste 300 Wichita (67203) *(G-14374)*
First Construction LLC...785 749-0006
901 New Hampshire St Lawrence (66044) *(G-4859)*

First Dental...620 225-5154
2306 1st Ave Dodge City (67801) *(G-1360)*
First Edition Inc...620 232-6002
3411 Airport Rd Pittsburg (66762) *(G-9861)*
First Excess Reinsurance Corp...913 676-5524
6329 Glenwood St Ste 300 Shawnee Mission (66202) *(G-11369)*
FIRST FEDERAL, Independence *Also called First Independence Corporation (G-3517)*
First Federal Bank Kansas City...913 233-6100
711 Minnesota Ave Kansas City (66101) *(G-4011)*
First Federal Savings & Loan...785 743-5751
229 N Main St Wakeeney (67672) *(G-13388)*
First Financial Leasing Inc...913 236-8800
6300 Nall Ave Ste 200 Shawnee Mission (66202) *(G-11370)*
First Grade Excavating Inc...316 524-0900
430 E 63rd St S Wichita (67216) *(G-14375)*
First Heritage Bank (PA)...785 857-3341
620 4th St Centralia (66415) *(G-699)*
First Horizon Bank...913 339-5400
7500 College Blvd Ste 850 Shawnee Mission (66210) *(G-11371)*
First Horizon Bank...913 317-2000
7400 W 110th St Ste 520 Overland Park (66210) *(G-8719)*
First Horizon National Corp...913 339-5400
7500 College Blvd # 1170 Overland Park (66210) *(G-8720)*
First Impressions, Topeka *Also called Patterson Advertising Agency (G-12964)*
First Imprssons Crbscaping LLC...913 620-5164
18220 Windsor Dr Stilwell (66085) *(G-12147)*
First Independence Corporation (HQ)...620 331-1660
112 E Myrtle St Independence (67301) *(G-3517)*
First Independence Corporation (PA)...620 331-1660
112 E Myrtle St Independence (67301) *(G-3518)*
First Intermark Corporation...620 442-2460
400 S Summit St Arkansas City (67005) *(G-156)*
First Kansas Bank (PA)...620 653-4921
101 N Main St Hoisington (67544) *(G-3064)*
First Layer Communications (PA)...913 491-0062
14906 Benson St Shawnee Mission (66221) *(G-11372)*
First Management Inc...785 232-5555
1425 Sw Lane St Apt 205 Topeka (66604) *(G-12614)*
First Management Inc (PA)...785 749-0006
901 New Hampshire St # 201 Lawrence (66044) *(G-4860)*
First Manhattan Bancorporation (PA)...785 537-0200
701 Poyntz Ave Manhattan (66502) *(G-6629)*
First Med PA...785 865-5300
2323 Ridge Ct Lawrence (66046) *(G-4861)*
First Medical Walk-In, Lawrence *Also called First Med PA (G-4861)*
First Nat Bncshres of Fredonia...620 378-2151
730 Madison St Fredonia (66736) *(G-2032)*
First Nat Bnk of Hutchinson (HQ)...620 663-1521
1 N Main St Ste 320 Hutchinson (67501) *(G-3285)*
First Nat Bnk of Hutchinson...620 662-7858
2500 N Main St Ste H Hutchinson (67502) *(G-3286)*
First Nat Bnk of Hutchinson...620 465-2225
101 N Kansas St Haven (67543) *(G-2730)*
First Nat Bnk of Hutchinson...620 694-2304
2501 N Main St Hutchinson (67502) *(G-3287)*
First Nat Bnk of Hutchinson...620 663-1521
1 N Main St Hutchinson (67501) *(G-3288)*
First Nat Bnk Syracuse Inc (PA)...620 384-7441
11 N Main St Syracuse (67878) *(G-12224)*
First Nat Bnk Syracuse Inc...620 276-6971
2414 E Kansas Ave Garden City (67846) *(G-2165)*
First Nat Bnk Syracuse Inc...620 492-1754
509 N Main St Johnson (67855) *(G-3653)*
First Nat Bnkshares Beloit Inc...785 738-2251
101 E Main St Beloit (67420) *(G-484)*
First Nat Bnkshres of Scott Cy...620 872-2143
501 S Main St Scott City (67871) *(G-10811)*
FIRST NATIONAL BANK, Dighton *Also called 1st National Bank of Dighton (G-1282)*
FIRST NATIONAL BANK, Centralia *Also called First Heritage Bank (G-699)*
First National Bank, Pratt *Also called First Pratt Bankshares Inc (G-10114)*
First National Bank, Shawnee Mission *Also called Arvest Bank Operations Inc (G-11121)*
First National Bank, Salina *Also called Sunflower Bank National Assn (G-10724)*
First National Bank, Manhattan *Also called Sunflower Bank National Assn (G-6817)*
First National Bank, Hays *Also called Sunflower Bank National Assn (G-2914)*
First National Bank, Salina *Also called Sunflower Bank National Assn (G-10725)*
First National Bank, Junction City *Also called Sunflower Bank National Assn (G-3758)*
First National Bank, Manhattan *Also called Bank of Flint Hills (G-6552)*
First National Bank, Neodesha *Also called Community National Bank (G-7237)*
First National Bank (HQ)...785 890-2000
202 E 11th St Goodland (67735) *(G-2471)*
First National Bank (PA)...785 366-7225
112 N Main St Hope (67451) *(G-3121)*
First National Bank...785 852-2000
133 N Main St Sharon Springs (67758) *(G-10897)*
First National Bank (PA)...620 855-3416
121 N Main St Cimarron (67835) *(G-825)*
First National Bank & Trust (PA)...785 543-6511
225 State St Phillipsburg (67661) *(G-9786)*

ALPHABETIC

First National Bank & Trust Co...785 762-4121
1038 W 6th St Junction City (66441) ***(G-3690)***
First National Bank Clifton...785 437-6585
414 W Bertrand Ave Saint Marys (66536) ***(G-10364)***
First National Bank Elkhart (PA)...620 697-2777
601 Morton St Elkhart (67950) ***(G-1621)***
First National Bank In Pratt...620 672-6421
223 S Main St Pratt (67124) ***(G-10113)***
First National Bank Inc (HQ)...785 263-1090
401 N Spruce St Abilene (67410) ***(G-31)***
First National Bank Louisburg...913 766-6701
4200 W 83rd St Ste 100 Shawnee Mission (66208) ***(G-11373)***
First National Bank Louisburg (PA)...913 837-5191
1201 W Amity St Louisburg (66053) ***(G-6448)***
First National Bank NA (HQ)...620 326-3361
206 E Harvey Ave Wellington (67152) ***(G-13500)***
First National Bank of Girard...620 724-6111
205 S Summit St Girard (66743) ***(G-2405)***
First National Bank of Hutchin...316 661-2471
100 N Ohio St Mount Hope (67108) ***(G-7204)***
First National Bank of Kansas...785 733-2564
600 N 4th St Burlington (66839) ***(G-635)***
First National Bank of Omaha...913 768-1120
13518 S Alden St Olathe (66062) ***(G-7712)***
First National Bank of Omaha...913 451-5824
4650 College Blvd Overland Park (66211) ***(G-8721)***
First National Bank of Omaha...913 631-0016
6301 Pflumm Rd Shawnee (66216) ***(G-10956)***
First National Bnk of Scott Cy...620 872-2143
501 S Main St Scott City (67871) ***(G-10812)***
First National Bnk of Sedan KS...620 725-3106
101 W Main St Sedan (67361) ***(G-10843)***
First Natl Bank, Scott City *Also called First Nat Bnkshres of Scott Cy* ***(G-10811)***
First Neodesha Bank, Neodesha *Also called Southeast Bancshares Inc* ***(G-7249)***
First Neodesha Bank (HQ)...620 325-2632
524 Main St Neodesha (66757) ***(G-7240)***
FIRST OPTION BANK, Osawatomie *Also called Osawatomie Agency Inc* ***(G-8201)***
First Option Bank, Paola *Also called Osawatomie Agency Inc* ***(G-9577)***
First Option Bank and Trust (HQ)...913 294-3811
601 Main St Osawatomie (66064) ***(G-8193)***
First Place, The, Wichita *Also called D J Company* ***(G-14158)***
First Point Urgent Care Inc...913 856-1369
907 E Lincoln Ln Gardner (66030) ***(G-2344)***
First Pratt Bankshares Inc (PA)...620 672-6421
223 S Main St Pratt (67124) ***(G-10114)***
First Response...913 557-2187
21495 W 303rd St Paola (66071) ***(G-9559)***
First Response Emergency Train, Paola *Also called First Response* ***(G-9559)***
First Savings Bank, Manhattan *Also called First Manhattan Bancorporation* ***(G-6629)***
First Seacoast Bank...913 766-2500
10551 Barkley St Ste 308 Overland Park (66212) ***(G-8722)***
First Security Bank (PA)...785 665-7155
312 Maple St Overbrook (66524) ***(G-8324)***
First Security Bank & Trust Co (PA)...785 877-3313
201 E Main St Norton (67654) ***(G-7446)***
First Serve Tennis...785 749-3200
5200 Clinton Pkwy Lawrence (66047) ***(G-4862)***
First Start Rentl Sls Svc Inc...620 343-0983
2026 W 6th Ave Emporia (66801) ***(G-1756)***
First State Bank, Kansas City *Also called First Bancshares Inc* ***(G-4010)***
First State Bank...785 798-2212
206 N Pennsylvania Ave Ness City (67560) ***(G-7262)***
First State Bank (PA)...785 877-3341
105 W Main St Norton (67654) ***(G-7447)***
First State Bank...785 675-3241
801 Main St Hoxie (67740) ***(G-3137)***
First State Bank & Trust (HQ)...913 845-2500
400 S Bury St Tonganoxie (66086) ***(G-12261)***
First State Bank & Trust...785 749-0400
3901 W 6th St Lawrence (66049) ***(G-4863)***
First State Bank & Trust...785 597-5151
402 Plaza Dr Perry (66073) ***(G-9767)***
First State Bank & Trust...913 724-2121
15506 Pinehurst Dr Basehor (66007) ***(G-378)***
First State Bank (inc)...785 654-2421
115 S Topeka Ave Burlingame (66413) ***(G-623)***
First State Bank of Edna Inc...620 922-3294
100 N Delaware St Edna (67342) ***(G-1493)***
First State Bnk of St Charles...913 469-5400
6800 College Blvd Leawood (66211) ***(G-5404)***
First State Bnk Tr of Larned (HQ)...620 285-6931
116 W 6th St Larned (67550) ***(G-4703)***
First Step House, Lawrence *Also called Dccca Inc* ***(G-4829)***
First Steps Childcare and Lear...620 518-1532
4531 Prairie Rose Dr Great Bend (67530) ***(G-2565)***
First Student Inc...620 251-8441
204 N Central St Coffeyville (67337) ***(G-938)***
First Student Inc...913 422-8501
8020 Monticello Ter Lenexa (66227) ***(G-5857)***
First Student Inc...785 841-3594
1548 E 23rd St Ste C Lawrence (66046) ***(G-4864)***
First Student Inc...913 856-5650
19450 S Gardner Rd Gardner (66030) ***(G-2345)***
First Student Inc...913 782-1050
18950 W 157th Ter Olathe (66062) ***(G-7713)***
First Team Sports Inc...620 663-6080
902 Corey Rd Hutchinson (67501) ***(G-3289)***
First United Methodist Church...316 263-6244
330 N Broadway Ave Wichita (67202) ***(G-14376)***
First United Methodist Church...316 755-1112
560 N Park Ave Valley Center (67147) ***(G-13342)***
First Untd Methdst Pre-School, Wichita *Also called First United Methodist Church* ***(G-14376)***
First-Citizens Bank & Trust Co...913 312-5108
7950 College Blvd Ste A Overland Park (66210) ***(G-8723)***
Firstlight HM Care Overland Pk, Overland Park *Also called Teakwood Investments LLC* ***(G-9395)***
Firstlight Home Care, Wichita *Also called True Home Care LLC* ***(G-15808)***
Firstoak Bank (PA)...620 331-2265
113 N Penn Ave Independence (67301) ***(G-3519)***
Firstrust Mortgage Inc...913 312-2000
4400 Shawnee Mission Pkwy # 208 Fairway (66205) ***(G-1907)***
Firstsource Solutions USA Inc...620 223-8200
4500 Campbell Dr Fort Scott (66701) ***(G-1968)***
Fisch Bowl Inc...316 200-5200
524 S Commerce St Wichita (67202) ***(G-14377)***
Fischer Pipe Testing Inc...785 726-3411
1858 Ellis Ave Ellis (67637) ***(G-1645)***
Fischer Well Service Inc...785 628-3837
1316 Central St Hays (67601) ***(G-2808)***
Fisher Pttrson Syler Smith LLP (PA)...785 232-7761
3550 Sw 5th St Topeka (66606) ***(G-12615)***
Fisher Ronald Od PA...316 942-7496
2635 W Douglas Ave Wichita (67213) ***(G-14378)***
Fishing Lights Etc LLC (PA)...785 621-2646
2707 Vine St Ste 7 Hays (67601) ***(G-2809)***
Fishman and Co Realtors Inc...913 782-9000
7939 Floyd St Overland Park (66204) ***(G-8724)***
Fishnet Security...816 701-3315
6130 Sprint Pkwy Leawood (66211) ***(G-5405)***
Fit Physique...316 721-2230
2111 N Maize Rd Wichita (67212) ***(G-14379)***
Fitness Plus More LLC...913 383-2636
4500 W 107th St Overland Park (66207) ***(G-8725)***
Fittings Export LLC...620 364-2930
3916 4th St Burlington (66839) ***(G-636)***
Five Clothes LLC (PA)...913 713-6216
8251 Melrose Dr Overland Park (66214) ***(G-8726)***
Five Rivers Cattle Feeding LLC...620 356-4466
7597 W Rd 17 Ulysses (67880) ***(G-13296)***
Five Star Amoco, Hays *Also called Five Star Service Inc* ***(G-2810)***
Five Star Hotel Management...316 686-7331
411 S Webb Rd Wichita (67207) ***(G-14380)***
Five Star Masonry LLC...785 484-9737
7529 Lakeview Rd Meriden (66512) ***(G-7081)***
Five Star Mechanical Inc...316 943-7827
1707 S Hoover Rd Wichita (67209) ***(G-14381)***
Five Star Quality Care-Ks LLC...620 564-2337
510 W 7th St Ellinwood (67526) ***(G-1632)***
Five Star Senior Living Inc...913 648-4500
3501 W 95th St Leawood (66206) ***(G-5406)***
Five Star Service Inc...785 625-9400
1300 Vine St Hays (67601) ***(G-2810)***
Flame Engineering Inc...785 222-2873
230 Highway 4 La Crosse (67548) ***(G-4633)***
Flamings Plumbing Heating & AC (PA)...620 382-2181
113 S 2nd St Marion (66861) ***(G-6869)***
Flanner & Mc Bratney Mds PA...913 651-3111
1004 Progress Dr Ste 200 Lansing (66043) ***(G-4673)***
Flatland Food Distributors LLC...316 945-5171
3930 W 29th St S Ste 90 Wichita (67217) ***(G-14382)***
Flatlands Transportation Ict...316 250-1280
3151 N Den Hollow St Wichita (67205) ***(G-14383)***
Flca of Hays, Larned *Also called High Plains Farm Credit Flca* ***(G-4705)***
Fleeson Ging Coulson Kitch LLC...316 267-7361
301 N Main St Ste 1900 Wichita (67202) ***(G-14384)***
Fleeson.com, Wichita *Also called Fleeson Ging Coulson Kitch LLC* ***(G-14384)***
Fleet Auto Rent Inc...913 901-9900
9831 Outlook Dr Overland Park (66207) ***(G-8727)***
Fleet Early Learning Stn LLC...913 638-7178
13304 W 172nd St Overland Park (66221) ***(G-8728)***
Fleet Services Topeka...785 368-3735
210 Se 4th St Topeka (66603) ***(G-12616)***
Fleetpride Inc...785 862-1540
4812 Sw Topeka Blvd Topeka (66609) ***(G-12617)***
Fleetpride Inc...316 942-4227
4401 W Esthner Ave Wichita (67209) ***(G-14385)***
Fleetpride Inc...800 362-2600
4501 W Esthner Ave Wichita (67209) ***(G-14386)***

Fleming Feed & Grain Inc (PA) 316 742-3411
309 S Main St Leon (67074) ***(G-6247)***
Fleming Feed & Seed, Leon *Also called Fleming Feed & Grain Inc* ***(G-6247)***
Flesh Company 620 421-6120
2407 Jothi Ave Parsons (67357) ***(G-9686)***
Flesher, Jack D, Wichita *Also called Bever Dye Lc* ***(G-13843)***
Flex Build LLC 913 890-2500
5410 Antioch Dr Shawnee Mission (66202) ***(G-11374)***
Flex-N-Gate Missouri LLC 913 387-3857
900 S 68th St Kansas City (66111) ***(G-4012)***
Flexcon Company Inc 913 768-8669
1305 S Fountain Dr Olathe (66061) ***(G-7714)***
Flextronics Lighting Solution, Overland Park *Also called Lw Holding Lc* ***(G-8975)***
Fli Inc (PA) 913 851-2247
12980 Metcalf Ave Ste 240 Overland Park (66213) ***(G-8729)***
Flic Luminaries LLC 888 550-3542
719 N Brookfield St Wichita (67206) ***(G-14387)***
Flightsafety International 316 612-5300
9721 E Central Ave Wichita (67206) ***(G-14388)***
FLIGHTSAFETY INTERNATIONAL INC, Wichita *Also called Flightsafety International* ***(G-14388)***
Flightsafety International Inc 316 220-3200
1951 S Airport Rd Wichita (67209) ***(G-14389)***
Flint Hills Area Trnsp Agcy Bd 787 537-6345
5815 Marlatt Ave Manhattan (66503) ***(G-6630)***
Flint Hills Auto, Manhattan *Also called Flint Hills Ford Inc* ***(G-6632)***
Flint Hills Bank (PA) 785 449-2266
103 1/2 N Main St Eskridge (66423) ***(G-1866)***
Flint Hills Beverage LLC 785 776-2337
5900 Corporate Dr Manhattan (66503) ***(G-6631)***
Flint Hills Care Center 620 342-3280
1620 Wheeler St Emporia (66801) ***(G-1757)***
Flint Hills Clay Works Inc 620 382-3620
126 W Main St Marion (66861) ***(G-6870)***
Flint Hills Cmnty Hlth Ctr Inc 620 342-4864
420 W 15th Ave Emporia (66801) ***(G-1758)***
Flint Hills Ford Inc 785 776-4004
7920 E Us Highway 24 Manhattan (66502) ***(G-6632)***
Flint Hills Heart Vascular 785 320-5858
3905 Vanesta Dr Ste A Manhattan (66503) ***(G-6633)***
Flint Hills Hospitality LLC 785 320-7995
210 Blue Earth Pl Manhattan (66502) ***(G-6634)***
Flint Hills Industries Inc 620 947-3127
220 Industrial Rd Hillsboro (67063) ***(G-3048)***
Flint Hills Mall LLC 620 342-4631
1632 Industrial Rd Emporia (66801) ***(G-1759)***
Flint Hills National Golf Club 316 733-4131
12400 Sw Butler Rd Andover (67002) ***(G-93)***
Flint Hills Powersports Inc (PA) 785 336-3901
423 Main St Bern (66408) ***(G-522)***
Flint Hills Resources LLC (HQ) 316 828-5500
8415 E 21st St N Ste 200 Wichita (67206) ***(G-14390)***
Flint Hills Resources Central (HQ) 316 828-5500
4111 E 37th St N Wichita (67220) ***(G-14391)***
Flint Hills Resources Port (HQ) 316 828-5500
8415 E 21st St N Ste 200 Wichita (67206) ***(G-14392)***
Flint Hills Roof Service 785 238-8609
2206 Vane Rd Chapman (67431) ***(G-778)***
Flint Hlls Area Trnsp Agcy Inc 785 537-6345
5815 Marlatt Ave Manhattan (66503) ***(G-6635)***
Flint Hlls Rsrces Longview LLC (HQ) 316 828-5500
8415 E 21st St N Ste 200 Wichita (67206) ***(G-14393)***
Flint Hlls Rur Elc Coop Assn I (PA) 620 767-5144
1564 S 1000 Rd Council Grove (66846) ***(G-1167)***
Flint Oak, Fall River *Also called Flint Oak* ***(G-1927)***
Flint Oak 620 658-4401
2639 Quail Fall River (67047) ***(G-1927)***
Flint Telecom Group Inc (PA) 913 815-1570
7500 College Blvd Ste 500 Overland Park (66210) ***(G-8730)***
Flintells Eyecare 620 343-7120
512 Commercial St Emporia (66801) ***(G-1760)***
Flinthills Clay Works, Marion *Also called Flint Hills Clay Works Inc* ***(G-6870)***
Flinthills Construction Inc 785 379-5499
5221 Se Stanley Rd Tecumseh (66542) ***(G-12239)***
Flinthills Services Inc (PA) 316 321-2325
505 S Walnut Valley Dr El Dorado (67042) ***(G-1562)***
Flinthills Trading Company (PA) 785 392-3017
G L Huyett Expy Exit 49 Minneapolis (67467) ***(G-7117)***
Floors To Go, Topeka *Also called Kaw Valley Hardwood Inc* ***(G-12812)***
Florence Bob Contractor Inc 785 357-0341
1934 S Kansas Ave Topeka (66612) ***(G-12618)***
Florence Corporation Kansas (HQ) 785 323-4400
5935 Corporate Dr Manhattan (66503) ***(G-6636)***
Florence Crittenton Services 785 233-0516
2649 Sw Arrowhead Rd Topeka (66614) ***(G-12619)***
Florence Manufacturing Company, Manhattan *Also called Florence Corporation Kansas* ***(G-6636)***
Florence Rock Company LLC 620 878-4544
13707 Nw Diamond Rd Newton (67114) ***(G-7346)***
Florida Information Consortium 913 498-3468
25501 W Valley Pkwy # 300 Olathe (66061) ***(G-7715)***
Florists Review Entps Inc 785 266-0888
3300 Sw Van Buren St Topeka (66611) ***(G-12620)***
Flowers Baking Co Lenexa LLC 913 564-1100
8960 Marshall Dr Lenexa (66215) ***(G-5858)***
Flowmark Vacuum Trucks, Kansas City *Also called Skymark Refuelers LLC* ***(G-4424)***
Floyd Mechanical Corporation 316 262-3556
1635 E 37th St N Ste 4 Wichita (67219) ***(G-14394)***
Fluebrothers LLC 913 236-7141
1701 Southwest Blvd Kansas City (66103) ***(G-4013)***
Fluesbrothers Chimney Service, Kansas City *Also called Fluebrothers LLC* ***(G-4013)***
Fluidpro, Garden City *Also called Kanamak Hydraulics Inc* ***(G-2212)***
Fluidtech LLC (HQ) 913 492-3300
10940 Eicher Dr Lenexa (66219) ***(G-5859)***
Fluidtech LLC 913 492-3300
10940 Eicher Dr Lenexa (66219) ***(G-5860)***
Fluidtech LLC 913 492-3300
10940 Eicher Dr Lenexa (66219) ***(G-5861)***
Fluidtech 0079, Lenexa *Also called Fluidtech LLC* ***(G-5860)***
Flying Colors, Wichita *Also called Sands Enterprises Inc* ***(G-15518)***
Flyover Innovations Inc 913 827-2248
622 E Meadowlark Pl Gardner (66030) ***(G-2346)***
FMC Corporation 316 729-5321
750 N Socora St Ste 500 Wichita (67212) ***(G-14395)***
FMC Technologies Inc 913 214-4300
8040 Nieman Rd Lenexa (66214) ***(G-5862)***
Fmh Benefit Services Inc 913 685-4740
13160 Foster St Ste 190 Overland Park (66213) ***(G-8731)***
Fmh Bnfit Svcs A Div Cresource, Overland Park *Also called Fmh Benefit Services Inc* ***(G-8731)***
Fms Midwest Dialysis Ctrs LLC 316 634-6760
9341 E 21st St N Wichita (67206) ***(G-14396)***
Fms Midwest Dialysis Ctrs LLC 620 431-1239
703 S Plummer Ave Chanute (66720) ***(G-728)***
Fms Midwest Dialysis Ctrs LLC 316 729-5321
750 N Socora St Ste 500 Wichita (67212) ***(G-14397)***
Fmw Inc 316 943-4217
7016 W Pueblo Dr Ste A Wichita (67209) ***(G-14398)***
Focalpoint Imaging LLC 620 325-2298
3347 County Road 6400 Neodesha (66757) ***(G-7241)***
Foe 3650, Clay Center *Also called Fraternal Order Eagles Inc* ***(G-864)***
Fogelman Management Group LLC 913 345-2888
8401 W 123rd St Shawnee Mission (66213) ***(G-11375)***
Foil Stamping & Embossing Assn 785 271-5816
2150 Sw Westport Dr # 101 Topeka (66614) ***(G-12621)***
Foley Equipment Company 620 225-4121
1600 E Wyatt Earp Blvd Dodge City (67801) ***(G-1361)***
Foley Equipment Company 785 825-4661
2225 N Ohio St Salina (67401) ***(G-10503)***
Foley Equipment Company 913 393-0303
15854 S Us 169 Hwy Olathe (66062) ***(G-7716)***
Foley Equipment Company 316 943-4211
1601 E 77th St N Park City (67147) ***(G-9619)***
Foley Equipment Company 620 626-6555
1701 E 5th St Liberal (67901) ***(G-6309)***
Foley Equipment Company 785 266-5784
1637 Sw 42nd St Topeka (66609) ***(G-12622)***
Foley Equipment Company 620 792-5246
701 10th St Great Bend (67530) ***(G-2566)***
Foley Equipment Company 785 537-2101
5104 Skyway Dr Manhattan (66503) ***(G-6637)***
Foley Equipment Company 785 266-5770
1737 Sw 42nd St Topeka (66609) ***(G-12623)***
Foley Equiptment, Salina *Also called Foley Equipment Company* ***(G-10503)***
Foley Group Inc (PA) 913 342-3336
333 N 6th St Kansas City (66101) ***(G-4014)***
Foley Industries Inc (PA) 316 943-4211
1550 S West St Wichita (67213) ***(G-14399)***
Foley Supply LLC 316 944-7368
1210 S West St Wichita (67213) ***(G-14400)***
Foley Tractor, Wichita *Also called Foley Industries Inc* ***(G-14399)***
Folgers Gymnastics Inc 316 733-7525
241 N Lancaster Ct Wichita (67230) ***(G-14401)***
Follow Up Sales Systems, Arkansas City *Also called First Intermark Corporation* ***(G-156)***
Fontastik Inc 816 474-4366
1851 Merriam Ln Ste C Kansas City (66106) ***(G-4015)***
Food Industry Services, Westwood *Also called Retail Groc Assn Grter Kans Cy* ***(G-13558)***
Food Service Specialists Inc (PA) 913 648-6611
9290 Glenwood St Shawnee Mission (66212) ***(G-11376)***
Food Trends Inc 913 383-3600
5600 W 95th St Ste 212 Overland Park (66207) ***(G-8732)***
Foodbrands Sup Chain Svcs Inc 913 393-7000
20701 W 159th St Olathe (66062) ***(G-7717)***
Foot Specialist Kansas City (PA) 913 677-3600
8550 Marshall Dr Ste 120 Overland Park (66214) ***(G-8733)***
For Central Kansas Foundation (PA) 785 825-6224
617 E Elm St Salina (67401) ***(G-10504)***

ALPHABETIC

For Profit, Basehor *Also called Integrated Behavioral Tech Inc* ***(G-380)***

For Women Only Inc ... 913 541-9495
4550 W 109th St Ste 130 Leawood (66211) ***(G-5407)***

For Wyandot Center ... 913 362-0393
2205 W 36th Ave Kansas City (66103) ***(G-4016)***

For Wyandot Center ... 913 328-4600
7840 Washington Ave Kansas City (66112) ***(G-4017)***

Ford Cattle Company Inc ... 620 369-2252
12466 Us Highway 400 Ford (67842) ***(G-1931)***

Ford County Communications, Dodge City *Also called County of Ford* ***(G-1332)***

Ford County Equipment, Dodge City *Also called Kanequip Inc* ***(G-1384)***

Ford County Feed Yard Inc ... 620 369-2252
12466 Us Highway 400 Ford (67842) ***(G-1932)***

Ford Lincoln Mercury, Fort Scott *Also called Ray Shepherd Motors Inc* ***(G-2001)***

Ford Lincoln Mercury, Winfield *Also called Kline Motors Inc* ***(G-16153)***

Foresite Msp LLC ... 800 940-4699
7311 W 132nd St Ste 305 Overland Park (66213) ***(G-8734)***

Forest City Enterprises Inc ... 785 539-3500
100 Manhattan Town Ctr Manhattan (66502) ***(G-6638)***

Foresters Financial Svcs Inc ... 913 310-0435
6900 College Blvd Ste 800 Leawood (66211) ***(G-5408)***

Forget-Me-Not-farms, Cimarron *Also called Powerline Dairy LLC* ***(G-832)***

Form Systems Inc ... 316 522-9285
330 Cain Dr Haysville (67060) ***(G-2945)***

Formation Plastics Inc ... 785 754-3828
2025 Sheridan Ave Apt 9 Hoxie (67740) ***(G-3138)***

Forming Specialists Inc ... 620 488-3243
631 Industrial Park Rd Belle Plaine (67013) ***(G-446)***

Formufit Lc ... 913 782-0444
17501 W 98th St Spc 1843 Lenexa (66219) ***(G-5863)***

Forshee Painting Contractors ... 316 263-7777
7200 W 13th St N Ste 217 Wichita (67212) ***(G-14402)***

Fort Hays State University ... 785 628-4286
3000 Sternberg Dr Hays (67601) ***(G-2811)***

Fort Larned Nat Historic Site, Larned *Also called National Park Service* ***(G-4708)***

Fort Leavenworth Credit Union (PA) ... 913 651-6575
301 Kansas Ave Fort Leavenworth (66027) ***(G-1938)***

Fort Leavenworth Frontier ... 913 682-6300
220 Hancock Ave Fort Leavenworth (66027) ***(G-1939)***

Fort Leavenworth Nat Cmtry 887, Leavenworth *Also called National Cemetery ADM* ***(G-5274)***

Fort Riley Recycle Center, Fort Riley *Also called United States Dept of Army* ***(G-1951)***

Fort Scott Country Club Inc ... 620 223-5060
2414 Horton St Fort Scott (66701) ***(G-1969)***

Fort Scott Livestock Market ... 620 223-4600
Old Hwy 54 Fort Scott (66701) ***(G-1970)***

Fort Scott Presbyterian Vlg ... 620 223-5550
2401 Horton St Fort Scott (66701) ***(G-1971)***

Fort Scott Truck & Tractor ... 620 223-6506
2595 Quail Rd Fort Scott (66701) ***(G-1972)***

Forterra Concrete Products Inc ... 913 422-3634
23600 W 40th St Shawnee (66226) ***(G-10957)***

Forum At Overland Park, Leawood *Also called Five Star Senior Living Inc* ***(G-5406)***

Forum Energy Tecnhologies ... 620 437-2440
113 W Main St Madison (66860) ***(G-6500)***

Forum Health Care ... 913 648-4980
3509 W 95th St Shawnee Mission (66206) ***(G-11377)***

Fossil Creek Hotel & Suites ... 785 483-4200
1430 S Fossil St Russell (67665) ***(G-10274)***

Fossil Drilling Inc ... 620 672-5625
10213 Bluestem Blvd Pratt (67124) ***(G-10115)***

Foster Callanan Financial Svc ... 866 363-9595
2950 Sw Mcclure Rd Topeka (66614) ***(G-12624)***

Foster Design Inc ... 316 832-9700
200 W Douglas Ave Ste 110 Wichita (67202) ***(G-14403)***

Foster Unruh Inc ... 620 227-2165
11311 Us Highway 50 Dodge City (67801) ***(G-1362)***

Foulston Conlee Schmidt Emerso ... 316 264-3300
200 W Douglas Ave Ste 300 Wichita (67202) ***(G-14404)***

Foulston Siefkin LLP ... 316 291-9514
700 Bank Of America Cente Wichita (67202) ***(G-14405)***

Foulston Siefkin LLP (PA) ... 316 267-6371
1551 N Waterfront Pkwy # 100 Wichita (67206) ***(G-14406)***

Foulston Siefkin LLP ... 913 498-2100
9225 Indian Creek Pkwy # 600 Overland Park (66210) ***(G-8735)***

Foulston Siefkin LLP ... 785 233-3600
534 S Kansas Ave Ste 1400 Topeka (66603) ***(G-12625)***

Foundation For A Christian Civ ... 785 584-6251
426 Main St Rossville (66533) ***(G-10252)***

Foundation of Neosho Memorial ... 620 431-4000
629 S Plummer Ave Chanute (66720) ***(G-729)***

Fountain Glass Inc ... 913 764-6014
15815 W 110th St Lenexa (66219) ***(G-5864)***

Fountain Mortgage, Prairie Village *Also called M Squared Financial LLC* ***(G-10045)***

Fountain Villa Inc ... 620 365-6002
2620 N Kentucky St Iola (66749) ***(G-3602)***

Fountainview Nursing & ... 316 776-2194
601 N Rose Hill Rd Rose Hill (67133) ***(G-10239)***

Four Cnty Mental Hlth Ctr Inc (PA) ... 620 331-1748
3751 W Main St Independence (67301) ***(G-3520)***

Four Cnty Mental Hlth Ctr Inc ... 620 251-8180
813 Union St Coffeyville (67337) ***(G-939)***

Four Cnty Mental Hlth Ctr Inc ... 620 325-2141
101 S 8th St Neodesha (66757) ***(G-7242)***

Four Cnty Mental Hlth Ctr Inc ... 620 331-0057
220 E Chestnut St Independence (67301) ***(G-3521)***

Four Corners Construction LLC ... 620 662-8163
921 S Main St Hutchinson (67501) ***(G-3290)***

Four Oaks Golf Course, Pittsburg *Also called City of Pittsburg* ***(G-9832)***

Four of Wichita Inc ... 316 943-2373
6335 W Kellogg Dr Wichita (67209) ***(G-14407)***

Four of Wichita Inc (PA) ... 316 636-2022
3741 N Rock Rd Wichita (67226) ***(G-14408)***

Four of Wichita Inc ... 316 634-2303
7856 E 36th St N Wichita (67226) ***(G-14409)***

Four of Wichita Inc ... 316 858-3343
3343 E Central Ave Wichita (67208) ***(G-14410)***

Four Points By Sheraton ... 785 539-5311
530 Richards Dr Ste B Manhattan (66502) ***(G-6639)***

Four Seasons Cleaners, Wichita *Also called Parker Enterprises Inc* ***(G-15263)***

Four Seasons Rv Acres Inc ... 785 598-2221
2502 Mink Rd Abilene (67410) ***(G-32)***

Four Star Tool and Die Inc ... 316 264-2913
1612 S Mead St Wichita (67211) ***(G-14411)***

Four State Maintenance Sup Inc ... 620 251-7033
503 N Cline Rd Coffeyville (67337) ***(G-940)***

Fourth Judicial Dist Comnity C ... 785 229-3510
1418 S Main St Ste 3 Ottawa (66067) ***(G-8273)***

Fowler Feeders LLC ... 620 646-5269
5113 23 Rd Fowler (67844) ***(G-2019)***

Fowler Nursing Home ... 620 646-5215
401 E 6th Ave Fowler (67844) ***(G-2020)***

Fowlers LLC ... 785 475-3451
201 E Frontier Pkwy Oberlin (67749) ***(G-7494)***

Fox Business Systems, Manhattan *Also called Fox Computer Inc* ***(G-6640)***

Fox Ceramic Tile Inc ... 785 437-2792
916 E Jesuit Ln Saint Marys (66536) ***(G-10365)***

Fox Computer Inc ... 785 776-1452
531 Fort Riley Blvd Manhattan (66502) ***(G-6640)***

Fox Realty Inc ... 316 681-1313
9330 E Central Ave # 200 Wichita (67206) ***(G-14412)***

Fox Ridge Coop Townhouses Inc ... 785 273-0640
1209 Sw Glendale Dr Topeka (66604) ***(G-12626)***

Fox Run Apartments, Shawnee Mission *Also called J A Peterson Realty Co Inc* ***(G-11474)***

FP Supply LLC ... 316 284-6700
701 S Spencer Rd Newton (67114) ***(G-7347)***

Frameworks ... 316 636-4470
9103 E 37th St N Wichita (67226) ***(G-14413)***

Franchise Development Inc ... 620 662-3283
300 Hayes St Hutchinson (67501) ***(G-3291)***

Francis Casing Crews Inc (PA) ... 620 793-9630
5810 Anchor Way Great Bend (67530) ***(G-2567)***

Francis Casing Crews Inc ... 620 275-0443
Industrial Dr Garden City (67846) ***(G-2166)***

Frank Agency Inc ... 913 648-8333
10561 Barkley St Ste 200 Overland Park (66212) ***(G-8736)***

Frank Bills ... 620 736-2875
Hwy 99 Severy (67137) ***(G-10890)***

Frank Black Pipe & Supply Co ... 620 241-2582
1375 17th Ave McPherson (67460) ***(G-6966)***

Frank C Allison Jr ... 913 648-2080
8000 Foster St Shawnee Mission (66204) ***(G-11378)***

Frank Colladay Hardware Co ... 620 663-4477
2516 E 14th Ave Hutchinson (67501) ***(G-3292)***

Frank Communications Hays Inc ... 785 623-1500
1005 E 17th St Hays (67601) ***(G-2812)***

Frank Construction Company ... 785 825-4213
262 S Broadway Blvd Salina (67401) ***(G-10505)***

Frank E Seufert & Associates ... 785 456-2782
411 Lincoln Ave Ste B Wamego (66547) ***(G-13423)***

Frank Walker Museum, Stockton *Also called Rooks County Historical Museum* ***(G-12185)***

Frankenstein Trikes LLC ... 913 352-6788
9453 Trump Ter Pleasanton (66075) ***(G-9995)***

Frankfort Community Care Home ... 785 292-4442
510 N Walnut St Frankfort (66427) ***(G-2022)***

Franklin Cnty Cncer Foundation ... 785 242-6703
215 S Main St Ottawa (66067) ***(G-8274)***

Franklin County Ambulance Svc, Ottawa *Also called County of Franklin* ***(G-8260)***

Franklin Covey Co ... 800 819-1812
11006 Metcalf Ave Overland Park (66210) ***(G-8737)***

Franklin L Taylor PA ... 913 782-2350
7450 W 130th St Ste 140 Overland Park (66213) ***(G-8738)***

Fraternal Order Eagles Inc ... 785 632-3521
419 Lincoln Ave Clay Center (67432) ***(G-864)***

Fraternal Order of Police ... 620 694-2830
210 W 1st Ave Hutchinson (67501) ***(G-3293)***

Frax ... 888 987-3729
110 S Main St Ste 200 Wichita (67202) ***(G-14414)***

Frazier Brothers Plbg & Contg......785 452-9707
1408 Prospect Ave Salina (67401) ***(G-10506)***
Frazier Enterprises Inc (PA)......316 788-0263
444 S Baltimore Ave Derby (67037) ***(G-1247)***
Frechin Pest Control LLC......816 358-5776
6501 W 156th St Overland Park (66223) ***(G-8739)***
Fred Pflumm Plumbing Inc......913 441-6309
8329 Monticello Rd Ste E Shawnee Mission (66227) ***(G-11379)***
Fred Pryor Seminars, Shawnee Mission *Also called Pryor Learning Solutions Inc* ***(G-11760)***
Fred Spigarelli PA (PA)......620 231-1290
100 S Broadway St Ste 200 Pittsburg (66762) ***(G-9862)***
Freddie Wayne Long......316 263-8941
925 E Murdock St Wichita (67214) ***(G-14415)***
Freddy Van Inc......620 231-1127
2513 E 4th St Pittsburg (66762) ***(G-9863)***
Frederick Excavating Inc......913 772-0225
19406 High Prairie Rd Leavenworth (66048) ***(G-5240)***
Frederick Harvesting......620 534-2211
301 N Pioneer St Alden (67512) ***(G-58)***
Frederick Plumbing & Heating......316 262-3713
815 N Main St Wichita (67203) ***(G-14416)***
Fredonia Livestock Auction LLC......620 378-2212
360 W Madison St Fredonia (66736) ***(G-2033)***
Free State Brewing Co Inc......785 843-4555
636 Massachusetts St Lawrence (66044) ***(G-4865)***
Free State Security Svcs LLC......785 843-7073
P.O. Box 746 Baldwin City (66006) ***(G-11380)***
Freedom 1st Federal Credit Un......316 685-0205
57915 Leavenworth St Wichita (67221) ***(G-14417)***
Freedom Ready Mix Inc......620 224-2800
1740 Highway 54 Fort Scott (66701) ***(G-1973)***
Freeman Concrete Cnstr LLC......913 825-0744
8357 Monticello Rd # 100 Lenexa (66227) ***(G-5865)***
Freeman Holdings LLC......785 862-0950
740 Se Airport Dr Ste 10 Topeka (66619) ***(G-12627)***
Freeman Holdings LLC (PA)......913 951-5600
740 Se Airport Dr Ste 10 Topeka (66619) ***(G-12628)***
Freeman Srgcl Ctr Pttsbrg LLC......620 231-9072
100 N Pine St Pittsburg (66762) ***(G-9864)***
Freeman Supply Inc......620 662-2330
221 W 3rd Ave Hutchinson (67501) ***(G-3294)***
Freeport-Mcmoran Oil & Gas LLC......316 636-1801
9320 E Central Ave Wichita (67206) ***(G-14418)***
Freestate Advisors LLC......888 735-2724
10333 E 21st St N Wichita (67206) ***(G-14419)***
Freestate Electric Coop Inc......913 796-6111
507 N Union St Mc Louth (66054) ***(G-6927)***
Freestyle Sign Co Inc......316 267-5507
1925 N Broadway Ave Wichita (67214) ***(G-14420)***
Freight Brokers America LLC......913 438-4300
10460 Mastin St Ste 120 Overland Park (66212) ***(G-8740)***
Freight Logistics Inc......316 719-2074
3404 N Emporia St Wichita (67219) ***(G-14421)***
Freightliner Trucks, Salina *Also called Omaha Truck Center Inc* ***(G-10619)***
Fremont Industries Inc......913 962-7676
1358 S Enterprise St Olathe (66061) ***(G-7718)***
French Gerleman, Lenexa *Also called French-Gerleman Electric Co* ***(G-5866)***
French Quarter LLC......316 440-7004
2145 N Topeka St Wichita (67214) ***(G-14422)***
French-Gerleman Electric Co......314 569-3122
9735 Commerce Pkwy Lenexa (66219) ***(G-5866)***
Fresenius Kidney Care Topeka E, Topeka *Also called Bio-Mdcal Applcations Kans Inc* ***(G-12383)***
Fresenius Med Care W Wllow LLC......785 625-0033
2905 Canterbury Dr Hays (67601) ***(G-2813)***
Fresenius Med Care W Wllow LLC......913 491-6341
6751 W 119th St Overland Park (66209) ***(G-8741)***
Fresenius Medical Care Saline, Salina *Also called Bio-Mdcal Applcations Kans Inc* ***(G-10424)***
Fresenius Medical Service......316 264-3115
1007 N Emporia St Wichita (67214) ***(G-14423)***
Fresh Apprach Clg Prfessionals......913 707-5500
16030 W 80th St Shawnee Mission (66219) ***(G-11381)***
Fresh Kc Water Inc......913 745-0002
6917 Martindale Rd Shawnee (66218) ***(G-10958)***
Freund Construction, Hutchinson *Also called Freund Investment Inc* ***(G-3295)***
Freund Investment Inc......620 669-9649
1201 N Halstead St Hutchinson (67501) ***(G-3295)***
Friedman Group......310 590-1248
11065 Hauser St Overland Park (66210) ***(G-8742)***
Friend That Cooks LLC......913 660-0790
6100 Nieman Rd Ste 150b Shawnee (66203) ***(G-10959)***
Friendly Dentistry, Overland Park *Also called Le John Minh DDS* ***(G-8949)***
Friends Kansas Christn HM Inc......316 283-6600
1035 Se 3rd St Newton (67114) ***(G-7348)***
Friends of Montessori Assn......913 649-6160
3531 Somerset Dr Prairie Village (66208) ***(G-10029)***
Friends of The Department......620 694-2387
1 N Main St Ste 804 Hutchinson (67501) ***(G-3296)***
Friends of Yates Inc......913 321-1566
1418 Garfield Ave Kansas City (66104) ***(G-4018)***
Friends University......316 295-5638
2100 W University Ave Wichita (67213) ***(G-14424)***
FRIENDSHIP MEALS, Great Bend *Also called Eldercare Inc* ***(G-2559)***
Friesen Tool Co Inc......316 262-6808
233 N Ohio Ave Wichita (67214) ***(G-14425)***
Frigiquip International Inc......316 321-2400
3910 W Central Ave El Dorado (67042) ***(G-1563)***
Friona Cattle Feeders N 1 2, Satanta *Also called Friona Industries LP* ***(G-10785)***
Friona Cattle Feeders North 1, Sublette *Also called Friona Industries LP* ***(G-12201)***
Friona Industries LP......620 649-2235
922 Road 90 2 Sublette (67877) ***(G-12201)***
Friona Industries LP (HQ)......620 649-3700
1174 Empire Cir Satanta (67870) ***(G-10785)***
Frito-Lay North America Inc......785 267-2600
4236 Sw Kirklawn Ave Topeka (66609) ***(G-12629)***
Frito-Lay North America Inc......620 251-4367
2209 W 8th St Coffeyville (67337) ***(G-941)***
Frito-Lay North America Inc......785 625-6581
2000 Front St Hays (67601) ***(G-2814)***
Frito-Lay North America Inc......316 942-8764
3815 W 30th St S Wichita (67217) ***(G-14426)***
Frito-Lay North America Inc......913 261-4700
9600 Dice Ln Shawnee Mission (66215) ***(G-11382)***
Fritz's Superior Meat Co, Shawnee Mission *Also called Fritzs Mt Superior Sausage LLC* ***(G-11383)***
Fritzs Mt Superior Sausage LLC......913 381-4618
10326 State Line Rd Shawnee Mission (66206) ***(G-11383)***
Frontier Ag Inc......785 734-7011
1201 W Us Highway 24 Goodland (67735) ***(G-2472)***
Frontier Ag Inc......785 734-2331
W Hwy 36 Bird City (67731) ***(G-530)***
Frontier Ag Inc (PA)......785 462-2063
415 W 2nd St Oakley (67748) ***(G-7475)***
Frontier Ag Inc......785 694-2281
428 Kansas Ave Brewster (67732) ***(G-583)***
Frontier Ag Inc......785 824-3201
100 Railroad Ave Grinnell (67738) ***(G-2692)***
Frontier Dairy LLC......620 372-2156
11501 Sw Cr 31 Syracuse (67878) ***(G-12225)***
Frontier Developemental Center, Norton *Also called Developmental Svcs NW Kans Inc* ***(G-7443)***
Frontier Estates, Abilene *Also called Abilene Housing Inc* ***(G-5)***
Frontier Farm Credit......620 421-4030
2005 Harding Dr Parsons (67357) ***(G-9687)***
Frontier Farm Credit......785 594-2900
1270 N 300th Rd Baldwin City (66006) ***(G-361)***
Frontier Farm Credit Aca......785 776-6955
2009 Vanesta Pl Manhattan (66503) ***(G-6641)***
Frontier Farm Credit, Flca, Manhattan *Also called Frontier Farm Credit Aca* ***(G-6641)***
Frontier Lodging Concordia LLC......785 243-2700
2175 Lincoln St Concordia (66901) ***(G-1111)***
Frontier Lodging Liberal LLC......620 624-9700
1550 N Lincoln Ave Liberal (67901) ***(G-6310)***
Frontline Management......620 227-8551
510 W Frontview St Dodge City (67801) ***(G-1363)***
Frontr-Rrwhead Joint Ventr LLC......913 461-3804
14635 S Rene St Olathe (66062) ***(G-7719)***
Frugal Inc......785 776-9088
3625 Legion Ln Saint George (66535) ***(G-10347)***
Fruhauf Uniforms Inc......316 263-7500
800 E Gilbert St Wichita (67211) ***(G-14427)***
Fry Eye Associates (PA)......620 275-7248
502 College Dr Garden City (67846) ***(G-2167)***
Fry Eye Associates......620 276-7699
411 N Campus Dr Garden City (67846) ***(G-2168)***
Fry Eye Surgery Center LLC......620 276-7699
411 N Campus Dr Ste 101 Garden City (67846) ***(G-2169)***
Fry Orthodontics Prairie Vlg......913 387-2500
4026 W 83rd St Prairie Village (66208) ***(G-10030)***
Fry-Wagner Mid MO Mvg & Stor, Lenexa *Also called B C A /fry-wagner Inc* ***(G-5679)***
Fry-Wagner Systems Inc......913 438-2925
11550 Lakeview Dr Lenexa (66219) ***(G-5867)***
Fry-Wagner Systems Dist Ctr, Lenexa *Also called Fry-Wagner Systems Inc* ***(G-5867)***
Fryslie Inc......620 672-6407
1336 E 1st St Pratt (67124) ***(G-10116)***
Fsig LLC......785 784-2566
265 Stewart Ave Fort Riley (66442) ***(G-1948)***
Fss Psychiatric LLC......913 677-0500
10711 Barkley St Leawood (66211) ***(G-5409)***
Fsw Subtech Holdings LLC......816 795-9955
236 N 7th St Kansas City (66101) ***(G-4019)***
Fuchs Lubricants Co......913 422-4022
2140 S 88th St Kansas City (66111) ***(G-4020)***
Fugate Enterprises, Wichita *Also called Fugate Leasing Inc* ***(G-14429)***
Fugate Enterprises......316 722-5670
208 S Maize Rd Wichita (67209) ***(G-14428)***

ALPHABETIC

Fugate Leasing Inc (PA)....316 722-5670
208 S Maize Rd Wichita (67209) ***(G-14429)***
Fujifilm Graphic Systems, Kansas City *Also called Fujifilm North America Corp* ***(G-4021)***
Fujifilm North America Corp....816 914-5942
1101 W Cambridge Cir Dr Kansas City (66103) ***(G-4021)***
Fujifilm Sericol USA Inc....913 342-4060
1101 W Cambridge Dr Kansas City (66103) ***(G-4022)***
Fujitsu America Inc....913 327-2800
6900 College Blvd Ste 700 Shawnee Mission (66211) ***(G-11384)***
Ful Tech Dental Lab Inc....316 681-3546
522 N St Francis St Wichita (67214) ***(G-14430)***
Fulk's Chiropractic, Olathe *Also called Chiroserve Inc* ***(G-7594)***
Full Faith Church of Love....913 262-3145
2737 S 42nd St Kansas City (66106) ***(G-4023)***
Full Vision Inc....316 283-3344
3017 Full Vision Dr Newton (67114) ***(G-7349)***
Fuller Foundation Company Inc....913 764-8222
19125 W 151st Ter Ste A Olathe (66062) ***(G-7720)***
Fuller Industries LLC....620 792-1711
1 Fuller Way Great Bend (67530) ***(G-2568)***
Fullmer Cattle Co KS LLC....620 384-7499
3200 S Hwy 27 Syracuse (67878) ***(G-12226)***
Fulsom Brothers Inc....620 758-2828
980 Kansas Rd Cedar Vale (67024) ***(G-694)***
Fun Center 24 Bowl, Dodge City *Also called Spare Tyme LLC* ***(G-1433)***
Fun Services of Kansas City (PA)....913 631-3772
12119 Johnson Dr Shawnee Mission (66216) ***(G-11385)***
Fundamental Technologies LLC....785 840-0800
2411 Ponderosa Dr Ste A Lawrence (66046) ***(G-4866)***
Funzee Limited, Kansas City *Also called Midpoint National Inc* ***(G-4248)***
Fuqua Construction Inc....620 585-2270
118 S Main St Inman (67546) ***(G-3582)***
Fur Is Flying LLC....785 621-7300
700 E 8th St Hays (67601) ***(G-2815)***
Furniture Options, Lenexa *Also called Transitions Group Inc* ***(G-6190)***
Furniture Options, Wichita *Also called Transitions Group Inc* ***(G-15792)***
Furst In Tile Inc....913 962-4599
18320 W 66th Ter Shawnee Mission (66218) ***(G-11386)***
Fusion Global Solutions LLC....913 707-2866
7300 W 110th St Ste 743 Overland Park (66210) ***(G-8743)***
Fusion Telecom Intl Inc....913 262-4638
5700 Broadmoor St Shawnee Mission (66202) ***(G-11387)***
Future Electronics Corp....913 498-1531
8700 Indian Creek Pkwy # 200 Shawnee Mission (66210) ***(G-11388)***
Future Foam Inc....316 283-8600
520 S Payton Ave Newton (67114) ***(G-7350)***
Futures Unlimited Inc (PA)....620 326-8906
2410 N A St Wellington (67152) ***(G-13501)***
Fyrs Car Care....913 385-3600
9535 Nall Ave Overland Park (66207) ***(G-8744)***
G & D Metals Inc....316 303-9090
725 E Skinner St Wichita (67211) ***(G-14431)***
G & F Construction Co LLC....316 260-3313
118 E Harry St Wichita (67211) ***(G-14432)***
G & G Dozer, Caney *Also called Gary Gorby* ***(G-668)***
G & L Well Service Inc....620 278-3105
612 E Washington Ave Sterling (67579) ***(G-12118)***
G & N Cabinets, Wichita *Also called Guthridge/Nighswonger Corp* ***(G-14529)***
G & R Trucking Inc....620 356-4500
921 N Stubbs Rd Ulysses (67880) ***(G-13297)***
G & S Roustabout Service LLC....620 213-0172
902 N Walnut St Medicine Lodge (67104) ***(G-7061)***
G and S Mechanical USA Inc....316 946-9988
3409 W Harry St Wichita (67213) ***(G-14433)***
G Coopers Inc....785 267-4100
401 Sw 32nd Ter Topeka (66611) ***(G-12630)***
G E Reinsurance, Shawnee Mission *Also called First Excess Reinsurance Corp* ***(G-11369)***
G E V Investment Inc (PA)....913 677-5333
3241 N 7th Street Trfy Kansas City (66115) ***(G-4024)***
G F Enterprises....785 539-7113
1810 Poyntz Ave Manhattan (66502) ***(G-6642)***
G H C Associates Inc....785 243-1555
201 W 6th St Concordia (66901) ***(G-1112)***
G H K Farms....785 462-6440
1580 Highway K25 Colby (67701) ***(G-1008)***
G I P Inc (PA)....785 749-0005
3000 Four Wheel Dr Ste B Lawrence (66047) ***(G-4867)***
G K Smith & Sons Inc....913 294-5379
1700 Industrial Park Dr Paola (66071) ***(G-9560)***
G L Huyett, Minneapolis *Also called Flinthills Trading Company* ***(G-7117)***
G R Fiss and Company, Shawnee Mission *Also called Johnston Insurance Agency* ***(G-11501)***
G S Enterprises, Kansas City *Also called Greg Smith Enterprises Inc* ***(G-4052)***
G S Inc of Kansas....620 443-5121
562 Locust St Americus (66835) ***(G-76)***
G T Sales & Manufacturing Inc (PA)....316 943-2171
2202 S West St Wichita (67213) ***(G-14434)***
G W Inc (PA)....316 262-3403
4747 N Webb Rd Wichita (67226) ***(G-14435)***
G-B Construction LLC....913 837-5240
30790 Switzer Rd Louisburg (66053) ***(G-6449)***
G.V.g, Wichita *Also called Grene Vision Group LLC* ***(G-14515)***
Gabel Lease Service Inc....785 798-3122
319 W Sycamore St Ness City (67560) ***(G-7263)***
Gablers Nursery Inc....913 642-4164
8131 Metcalf Ave Shawnee Mission (66204) ***(G-11389)***
Gaeddert Farms Sweet Corn Inc....620 543-2473
13209 E 82nd Ave Buhler (67522) ***(G-616)***
Gaelic Management Inc....316 683-5150
400 N Woodlawn St Ste 210 Wichita (67208) ***(G-14436)***
Gage Bowls, Topeka *Also called Rekat Recreation Inc* ***(G-13007)***
Gage Center Bowl, Topeka *Also called Rekat Recreation Inc* ***(G-13008)***
Gage Center Dental Group PA....785 273-4770
1271 Suthwest Woodhull St Topeka (66604) ***(G-12631)***
Gaia Inc....785 539-2622
421 Poyntz Ave Manhattan (66502) ***(G-6643)***
Gaia Salon, Manhattan *Also called Gaia Inc* ***(G-6643)***
Galaxie Business Equipment Inc....620 221-3469
913 Main St Winfield (67156) ***(G-16142)***
Galaxy Audio Inc....316 263-2852
601 E Pawnee St Frnt Wichita (67211) ***(G-14437)***
Galaxy Technologies Inc....620 221-6262
1111 Industrial Blvd Winfield (67156) ***(G-16143)***
Galen Blenn Trucking....785 457-3995
308 N 4th St Westmoreland (66549) ***(G-13548)***
Galena Manor Nursing Center, Galena *Also called Rh Montgomery Properties Inc* ***(G-2083)***
Galena Medical Properties LLC....620 783-4616
444 Four States Dr Ste 1 Galena (66739) ***(G-2073)***
Galena Sentinel Times....620 783-5034
511 S Main St Galena (66739) ***(G-2074)***
Galichia Medical Group PA....316 684-3838
9415 E Harry St Ste 407 Wichita (67207) ***(G-14438)***
Galichia Medical Group Kans PA (PA)....316 684-3838
9415 E Harry St Ste 407 Wichita (67207) ***(G-14439)***
Galicia Heart Hospital, Wichita *Also called Westley Woodlawn Hosp Emrgncy* ***(G-15962)***
Gallery Xii Inc....316 267-5915
412 E Douglas Ave Ste A Wichita (67202) ***(G-14440)***
Galley Products Group, Lenexa *Also called B/E Aerospace Inc* ***(G-5681)***
Galt Ventures LLC (PA)....316 722-3801
3527 N Ridge Rd Wichita (67205) ***(G-14441)***
Galt Ventures LLC....316 942-2211
701 N West St Wichita (67203) ***(G-14442)***
Galyon Lumber Inc....620 897-6290
798 26th Rd Little River (67457) ***(G-6418)***
Gamoict Inc....316 262-2123
1008 S Washington Ave Wichita (67211) ***(G-14443)***
Gannett Co Inc....785 832-6319
609 New Hampshire St Lawrence (66044) ***(G-4868)***
Gansel House LLC....620 331-7422
3768 Cr 5250 Independence (67301) ***(G-3522)***
Gao Qizhi....316 691-8811
9235 E Harry St Ste 1a Wichita (67207) ***(G-14444)***
Garage Door Group Inc....757 253-0522
1010 Cottonwood St Junction City (66441) ***(G-3691)***
Garber Surveying Service PA....620 241-4441
115 E Marlin St Ste 102 McPherson (67460) ***(G-6967)***
Garber Surveying Service PA (PA)....620 665-7032
2908 N Plum St Ste B Hutchinson (67502) ***(G-3297)***
Garcia and Antosh LLP....620 225-7400
1401 Central Ave Dodge City (67801) ***(G-1364)***
Garda CL West Inc....316 942-9700
2018 S Kessler St Wichita (67213) ***(G-14445)***
Garden City Claims Office, Garden City *Also called Farm Bureau Mutl Insur Co Inc* ***(G-2157)***
Garden City Co-Op Inc (PA)....620 275-6161
106 N 6th St Garden City (67846) ***(G-2170)***
Garden City Co-Op Inc (PA)....620 356-1219
501 S Colorado St Ulysses (67880) ***(G-13298)***
Garden City Co-Op Inc....620 276-8903
1304 Massey Ferguson Rd Garden City (67846) ***(G-2171)***
Garden City Dialysis Center, Garden City *Also called Renal Trtmnt Centers-West Inc* ***(G-2266)***
Garden City Feed Yard LLC....620 275-4191
1805 W Annie Scheer Rd Garden City (67846) ***(G-2172)***
Garden City Hilton Inn, Garden City *Also called Minter-Wilson Drilling Co Inc* ***(G-2237)***
Garden City Iron & Metal....620 277-0227
3710 W Jones Ave Garden City (67846) ***(G-2173)***
Garden City Kansas Kennel Club....620 275-4739
3460 N Farmland Rd Garden City (67846) ***(G-2174)***
Garden City Plaza Inn, The, Garden City *Also called Minter-Wilson Drilling Co Inc* ***(G-2238)***
Garden City Production Cr Assn (PA)....620 275-4281
1606 E Kansas Ave Garden City (67846) ***(G-2175)***
Garden City Public Schools....620 275-0291
714 Ballinger St Garden City (67846) ***(G-2176)***
Garden City Telegram....620 275-8500
310 N 7th St Garden City (67846) ***(G-2177)***
Garden City Tire Center Inc (PA)....620 276-7652
611 E Fulton St Garden City (67846) ***(G-2178)***

Garden City Travel Plaza LLC..........620 275-4404
1265 Solar Ave Garden City (67846) *(G-2179)*
Garden City Water Department, Garden City *Also called City of Garden City (G-2126)*
Garden Cy Ammonia Program LLC..........620 271-0037
2405 E Fulton Plz Garden City (67846) *(G-2180)*
Garden Cy Area Chmber Commerce..........620 276-3264
1509 E Fulton Ter Garden City (67846) *(G-2181)*
Garden Medical Clinic Group, Garden City *Also called Garden Medical Clinic PA (G-2182)*
Garden Medical Clinic PA..........620 275-3702
311 E Spruce St Garden City (67846) *(G-2182)*
Garden Plain Bancshares Inc (PA)..........316 721-1500
10526 W Maple St Wichita (67209) *(G-14446)*
Garden Plain Service Center, Garden Plain *Also called Stuhlsatz Service Inc (G-2322)*
GARDEN PLAIN STATE BANK, Wichita *Also called Garden Plain Bancshares Inc (G-14446)*
Garden Plain State Bank (PA)..........316 721-1500
10526 W Maple St Wichita (67209) *(G-14447)*
Garden Surgical Assoc..........620 275-3740
311 E Spruce St Garden City (67846) *(G-2183)*
GARDEN VILLAS, Lenexa *Also called Delmar Gardens of Lenexa Inc (G-5809)*
Garden Villas Retirement Cmnty, Shawnee Mission *Also called Delmar Gardens of Lenexa Inc (G-11299)*
Garden Vly Retirement Vlg LLC..........620 275-9651
1505 E Spruce St Garden City (67846) *(G-2184)*
Gardeners Flooring America, Topeka *Also called Gardner Floor Covering Inc (G-12632)*
Gardiner Angus Ranch..........620 635-2932
2605 Cr 13 Ashland (67831) *(G-194)*
Gardn-Wise Distributors Inc (PA)..........316 838-6104
1515 E 29th St N Wichita (67219) *(G-14448)*
Gardner Animal Hospital PA..........913 856-6255
945 E Santa Fe St Gardner (66030) *(G-2347)*
Gardner Bancshares Inc (HQ)..........855 856-0233
13423 W 92nd St Lenexa (66215) *(G-5868)*
Gardner Dental Care..........913 856-7123
971 E Lincoln Ln Gardner (66030) *(G-2348)*
Gardner Floor Covering Inc (PA)..........785 266-6220
3401 S Kansas Ave Topeka (66611) *(G-12632)*
Gardner Hospitality LLC..........913 856-2100
151 S Cedar Niles Rd Gardner (66030) *(G-2349)*
Gardner News, Gardner *Also called Tri-County Newspapers Inc (G-2366)*
Gardner, James Dixon MD, Manhattan *Also called Primary Care Physcans Mnhattan (G-6780)*
Garmin International Inc..........913 440-8462
151 New Century Pkwy New Century (66031) *(G-7285)*
Garmin International Inc..........312 787-3221
1200 E 151st St Olathe (66062) *(G-7721)*
Garmin International Inc (HQ)..........913 397-8200
1200 E 151st St Olathe (66062) *(G-7722)*
Garnand Funeral Chapel, Garden City *Also called Garnand Funeral Home Inc (G-2185)*
Garnand Funeral Home Inc (PA)..........620 276-3219
412 N 7th St Garden City (67846) *(G-2185)*
Garnett Auto Supply Inc (PA)..........316 267-4393
801 E Zimmerly St Wichita (67211) *(G-14449)*
Garnett Publishing Inc..........785 448-3121
112 W 6th Ave Garnett (66032) *(G-2373)*
Garozzos III Inc..........913 491-8300
9950 College Blvd Shawnee Mission (66210) *(G-11390)*
Garrison Plumbing Inc..........913 768-1311
1375 N Winchester St Olathe (66061) *(G-7723)*
Garrison Transportation LLC..........785 404-6744
1630 Copper Ct Salina (67401) *(G-10507)*
Garsite Progress LLC (PA)..........913 342-5600
539 S 10th St Kansas City (66105) *(G-4025)*
Garver LLC..........913 696-9755
7301 W 129th St Ste 330 Overland Park (66213) *(G-8745)*
Garvey Industiral Park, Wichita *Also called Builders Inc (G-13910)*
Garvey Public Warehouse Inc..........316 522-4745
5755 S Hoover Rd Bldg 5 Wichita (67215) *(G-14450)*
Garwin Electric LLC..........913 780-1200
432 S Kansas Ave Olathe (66061) *(G-7724)*
Gary Bell..........785 233-6677
118 E 5th St Holton (66436) *(G-3090)*
Gary Community Hosp Rur Clinic, Junction City *Also called Geary Community Hospital (G-3692)*
Gary Dean Anderson..........785 475-2340
189 S Penn Ave Oberlin (67749) *(G-7495)*
Gary Gorby..........620 879-5243
Hwy 75 N Caney (67333) *(G-668)*
Gary J Newman DDS PA..........785 273-1544
5225 Sw 7th St Ste 1 Topeka (66606) *(G-12633)*
Gary L Harbin, Md, PA, Salina *Also called Salina Sports Med &ORth Clinic (G-10691)*
Gaskell Machine & Metal Inc..........785 486-2674
505 W 7th St Horton (66439) *(G-3123)*
Gaston, Jerry G Do, Wichita *Also called Surgical Specialists PA (G-15701)*
Gastrointestinal Associates PA..........913 495-9600
10116 W 105th St Overland Park (66212) *(G-8746)*
Gatehouse Media LLC..........913 682-0305
422 Seneca St Leavenworth (66048) *(G-5241)*
Gatehouse Media LLC..........620 326-3326
113 W Harvey Ave Wellington (67152) *(G-13502)*
Gatehouse Media LLC..........620 241-2422
116 S Main St McPherson (67460) *(G-6968)*
Gatehouse Media LLC..........620 672-5512
320 S Main St Pratt (67124) *(G-10117)*
Gatehouse Media LLC..........913 682-0305
422 Seneca St Leavenworth (66048) *(G-5242)*
Gatehouse Media Inc..........913 367-0583
308 Commercial St Atchison (66002) *(G-229)*
Gatehuse Mdia Kans Hldings Inc..........316 321-6136
114 N Vine St El Dorado (67042) *(G-1564)*
Gates Corporation..........620 365-4100
1450 Montana Rd Iola (66749) *(G-3603)*
Gates Shields Ferguson Swall H..........913 661-0222
10990 Quivira Rd Ste 200 Overland Park (66210) *(G-8747)*
Gateway Ethanol LLC..........620 933-2288
10333 Ne 30th St Pratt (67124) *(G-10118)*
Gateway Housing LP..........913 621-3840
1430 N 4th St Kansas City (66101) *(G-4026)*
Gateway Inn..........620 624-0242
720 E Pancake Blvd Liberal (67901) *(G-6311)*
Gateway Plaza Townhomes, Kansas City *Also called Gateway Housing LP (G-4026)*
Gateway Plaza West Ltd..........913 621-3840
1430 N 4th St Kansas City (66101) *(G-4027)*
Gateway Solutions Inc (PA)..........913 851-1055
12980 Metcalf Ave Ste 330 Overland Park (66213) *(G-8748)*
Gateway Wireless Services, Wichita *Also called Gateway Wreless Netwrk Svcs Lc (G-14452)*
Gateway Wireless Services LLC (PA)..........316 264-0037
121 S Lulu Ave Wichita (67211) *(G-14451)*
Gateway Wreless Netwrk Svcs Lc..........316 264-0037
121 S Lulu Ave Wichita (67211) *(G-14452)*
Gaughan Rebecca N M.D., Olathe *Also called Midwest Ear Nose Throat PA (G-7895)*
Gavilon Grain LLC..........316 226-7250
5755 S Hoover Rd Unit 2 Wichita (67215) *(G-14453)*
Gavilon Grain LLC..........785 263-7275
513 W 1st St Abilene (67410) *(G-33)*
GBA Architects Inc..........913 492-0400
9801 Renner Blvd Ste 300 Lenexa (66219) *(G-5869)*
GBA Builders Llc..........913 492-0400
9801 Renner Blvd Ste 300 Lenexa (66219) *(G-5870)*
Gbk Ventures LLC..........620 603-6565
3821 10th St Great Bend (67530) *(G-2569)*
Gbw Railcar Services LLC..........844 364-7403
1604 Spruce St Coffeyville (67337) *(G-942)*
Gbw Railcar Services LLC..........888 968-4364
10895 Grandview Dr # 350 Overland Park (66210) *(G-8749)*
Gbw Railcar Services LLC..........620 325-3001
701 Klayder Dr Neodesha (66757) *(G-7243)*
Gbw Railcar Services LLC..........866 785-4082
Hwy 59 W Atchison (66002) *(G-230)*
GC Labels Inc..........913 897-6966
6870 W 206th St Stilwell (66085) *(G-12148)*
Gcb Holdings LLC..........785 841-5185
643 Massachusetts St Lawrence (66044) *(G-4869)*
Gcsaa..........800 832-4410
1421 Research Park Dr Lawrence (66049) *(G-4870)*
Gdm Enterprises LLC..........816 753-2900
3505 Shawnee Mission Pkwy Fairway (66205) *(G-1908)*
GE Capital Montgomery Ward..........913 676-4100
9510 W 67th St Shawnee Mission (66203) *(G-11391)*
GE Engine Services LLC..........316 264-4741
7577 4th Ave Arkansas City (67005) *(G-157)*
GE Oil & Gas Compression..........785 823-9211
1648 W Magnolia Rd Salina (67401) *(G-10508)*
GE Steam Power Inc..........785 243-3300
1830 E 6th St Concordia (66901) *(G-1113)*
Gear For Sports, Lenexa *Also called Gfsi LLC (G-5875)*
Gear Headquarters Inc..........913 831-1700
3012 S 24th St Kansas City (66106) *(G-4028)*
Geary Community Hospital, Junction City *Also called Geary County Hospital (G-3694)*
Geary Community Hospital..........785 762-5437
1106 Saint Marys Rd # 310 Junction City (66441) *(G-3692)*
Geary Corrections Center..........785 762-4679
801 N Washington St Ste E Junction City (66441) *(G-3693)*
Geary County Hospital (PA)..........785 238-4131
1102 Saint Marys Rd Junction City (66441) *(G-3694)*
Geary County Public Works..........785 238-3612
310 E 8th St Junction City (66441) *(G-3695)*
Geary Rhabilitation Fitnes Ctr..........785 238-3747
104 S Washington St Junction City (66441) *(G-3696)*
Gecko Painting Inc..........913 782-7000
700 E Dennis Ave Olathe (66061) *(G-7725)*
Geesu Inc..........913 648-0087
6939 W 75th St Shawnee Mission (66204) *(G-11392)*
Geha, Daniel J, Leawood *Also called Daniel J Geha MD (G-5369)*
Geiger Ready-Mix Co Inc (PA)..........913 772-4010
1333 S 2nd St Leavenworth (66048) *(G-5243)*
Geiger Ready-Mix Co Inc..........913 281-0111
4303 Speaker Rd Kansas City (66106) *(G-4029)*

ALPHABETIC

Geisler Roofing Inc....785 243-7298
908 E 6th St Concordia (66901) **(G-1114)**
Gems Inc....785 731-2849
410 S Vermont Ave Ransom (67572) **(G-10192)**
Gemtech LLC....913 782-3080
15665 S Keeler St Olathe (66062) **(G-7726)**
Genco Manufacturing....785 448-2501
29128 N Highway 59 Garnett (66032) **(G-2374)**
Gene Oswald Company....316 263-7191
519 N Hydraulic St Wichita (67214) **(G-14454)**
General Automatic Sprinkler Fl....913 390-1105
10324 W 79th St Overland Park (66214) **(G-8750)**
General Delivery Inc....913 281-6580
1601 Fairfax Trfy Kansas City (66115) **(G-4030)**
General Distributors, Wichita *Also called Atlantic Dev Corp of PA* **(G-13762)**
General Distributors Inc (PA)....316 634-2133
1445 N Rock Rd Ste 200 Wichita (67206) **(G-14455)**
General Dynamics Info Tech Inc....913 684-5770
1100 N 2nd St Leavenworth (66048) **(G-5244)**
General Dynamics Info Tech Inc....785 832-0207
3833 Greenway Dr Lawrence (66046) **(G-4871)**
General Electric Company....785 320-2350
2627 Kfb Plz Ste 401e Manhattan (66503) **(G-6644)**
General Electric Company....785 229-3710
324 S Beech St Ottawa (66067) **(G-8275)**
General Electric Company....913 541-1839
10500 Lackman Rd Lenexa (66219) **(G-5871)**
General Electric Company....816 244-9672
7101 College Blvd Ste 800 Overland Park (66210) **(G-8751)**
General Electric Company....785 666-4244
19797 Winterset Ln Dorrance (67634) **(G-1464)**
General Finance Incorporated....785 243-1284
1716 Quail Rd Concordia (66901) **(G-1115)**
General Financial Services Inc....316 636-1070
8441 E 32nd St N Ste 200 Wichita (67226) **(G-14456)**
General Fire Sprinkler Co LLC....913 390-1105
10324 W 79th St Shawnee (66214) **(G-10960)**
General Grnd Chpter Estrn Star....620 326-3797
14 Shadybrook Dr Wellington (67152) **(G-13503)**
General Hays Inn, Hays *Also called H Schwaller & Sons Inc* **(G-2822)**
General Machinery & Sup Co Inc....620 231-1550
510 N Elm St Ste 12 Pittsburg (66762) **(G-9865)**
General Motors LLC....913 573-7981
3201 Fairfax Trfy Kansas City (66115) **(G-4031)**
General Pest Control LLC....620 855-7768
15609 State Rd 23 Cimarron (67835) **(G-826)**
General Repair & Supply Inc....620 365-5954
1008 N Industrial Rd Iola (66749) **(G-3604)**
General Tech A Svcs & Pdts Co....913 766-5566
2016 E Spruce Cir Olathe (66062) **(G-7727)**
Generations Bank....913 928-6181
7900 College Blvd Overland Park (66210) **(G-8752)**
Genesee & Wyoming Inc....785 899-2307
1801 Main Ave Goodland (67735) **(G-2473)**
Genesis 10, Shawnee Mission *Also called Genesis Corp* **(G-11393)**
Genesis Children Pre-School, Tonganoxie *Also called Genesis School Inc* **(G-12262)**
Genesis Corp....913 906-9991
6950 Squibb Rd Ste 430 Shawnee Mission (66202) **(G-11393)**
Genesis Family Health, Garden City *Also called United Methodist Western Kansa* **(G-2307)**
Genesis Health Club, Wichita *Also called Steven Enterprises LLC* **(G-15667)**
Genesis Health Club Inc....316 721-8938
854 N Socora St Ste B Wichita (67212) **(G-14457)**
Genesis Health Club Inc (PA)....316 945-8331
3725 W 13th St N Wichita (67203) **(G-14458)**
Genesis Health Club Inc....620 663-9090
412 E 30th Ave Hutchinson (67502) **(G-3298)**
Genesis Health Club Rock Road, Wichita *Also called Genesis Health Clubs MGT LLC* **(G-14459)**
Genesis Health Clubs MGT LLC....316 634-0094
1551 N Rock Rd Wichita (67206) **(G-14459)**
Genesis Healthcare Corporation....785 594-6492
1223 Orchard Ln Baldwin City (66006) **(G-362)**
Genesis Hlth Clubs Emporia LLC....620 343-6034
1007 Commercial St Emporia (66801) **(G-1761)**
Genesis School Inc....913 845-9498
204 E Washington St Tonganoxie (66086) **(G-12262)**
Genesis Solution LLC....785 317-5710
205 E 2nd St Chapman (67431) **(G-779)**
Geneva-Roth Ventures Inc....913 825-1200
6950 W 56th St Shawnee Mission (66202) **(G-11394)**
Genex Services LLC....913 310-0303
11900 W 87th Street Pkwy # 210 Lenexa (66215) **(G-5872)**
Genigraphics LLC....913 441-1410
5645 Lakecrest Dr Shawnee (66218) **(G-10961)**
Genoa Healthcare Kansas LLC....785 783-0209
330 Sw Oakley Ave Topeka (66606) **(G-12634)**
Genoa Healthcare Mass LLC....913 680-1652
500 Limit St Leavenworth (66048) **(G-5245)**
Genstler Eye Center, Topeka *Also called Arla Jean Genstler MD PA* **(G-12338)**
Genstler Eye Center, Topeka *Also called Topeka Surgery Center Inc* **(G-13186)**
Gentiva Health Services Inc....913 814-2800
12900 Foster St Ste 400 Overland Park (66213) **(G-8753)**
Gentiva Health Services Inc....913 906-0522
11880 Quivira Rd Ste 4a Overland Park (66210) **(G-8754)**
Gentle Care Animal Hospital....785 841-1919
601 Kasold Dr Ste D105 Lawrence (66049) **(G-4872)**
Gentle Dental Service Corp....913 248-8880
13100 W 87th Street Pkwy Lenexa (66215) **(G-5873)**
Gentry, Donald A, Kansas City *Also called Associated Podiatrist PA* **(G-3824)**
Genuine Parts Company....913 631-4329
6550 Nieman Rd Shawnee Mission (66203) **(G-11395)**
Genzada Pharmaceuticals LLC (PA)....620 204-7150
119 W Main St Sterling (67579) **(G-12119)**
Genzada Pharmaceuticals Usa....620 204-7150
101 S Broadway Ave Sterling (67579) **(G-12120)**
Geo Bit Exploration Inc....940 888-3134
100 Blue Heron Pt Council Grove (66846) **(G-1168)**
Geo Form Int'l, Olathe *Also called Geo Form International Inc* **(G-7728)**
Geo Form International Inc....913 782-1166
519 E Kansas City Rd Olathe (66061) **(G-7728)**
Geocore LLC....785 826-1616
2775 Arnold Ave Ste D Salina (67401) **(G-10509)**
Geoprobe Systems, Salina *Also called Kejr Inc* **(G-10573)**
George Eschbaugh Advg Inc....785 658-2105
3946 205th Rd Wilson (67490) **(G-16105)**
George G Kerasotes Corporation....913 213-2000
11500 Ash St Leawood (66211) **(G-5410)**
George Goracke Basement....785 388-9542
120 3200 Ave Solomon (67480) **(G-12051)**
George King Bio-Medical Inc....913 469-5464
11771 W 112th St Ste 100 Shawnee Mission (66210) **(G-11396)**
Georgetown Apartments, Shawnee Mission *Also called Malkin Properties LLC* **(G-11593)**
Georgetown Village Associates, Wichita *Also called Via Christi Health Inc* **(G-15890)**
Georgia Kenworth Inc (HQ)....816 483-6444
11120 Tomahawk Creek Pkwy Leawood (66211) **(G-5411)**
Georgia-Pacific LLC....785 363-7767
2127 Us Highway 77 Blue Rapids (66411) **(G-536)**
Geosource LLC....785 272-7200
1605 Sw 41st St Topeka (66609) **(G-12635)**
Geotechnology Inc....913 438-1900
5055 Antioch Rd Shawnee (66203) **(G-10962)**
Gerald A Wallace....620 275-2484
1803 Humphrey Rd Garden City (67846) **(G-2186)**
Gerard Tank & Steel Inc....785 243-3895
1540 E 11th St Concordia (66901) **(G-1116)**
Gerber Group Inc....316 945-7007
5617 W Kellogg Dr Wichita (67209) **(G-14460)**
Gerber Insurance Group....913 649-7800
5200 W 94th Ter Ste 110 Prairie Village (66207) **(G-10031)**
Geres....620 276-6179
3102 Vfw Rd Garden City (67846) **(G-2187)**
Gerken Rent-All Inc (PA)....913 294-3783
31600 Old Kc Rd Paola (66071) **(G-9561)**
Gerstberger Medical Clinic....620 356-2432
301 E Grant Ave Ulysses (67880) **(G-13299)**
Get A Move On, Wichita *Also called Gamoict Inc* **(G-14443)**
Get A Move On Inc....316 729-4897
1008 S Washington Ave Wichita (67211) **(G-14461)**
Get After It LLC....402 885-0964
1620 Fort Riley Blvd Manhattan (66502) **(G-6645)**
Gfe LLC....316 260-8433
519 N Hydraulic St Wichita (67214) **(G-14462)**
Gfg AG Services LLC....913 233-0001
501 S Coy St Kansas City (66105) **(G-4032)**
Gfsi Inc....913 693-3200
9700 Lackman Rd Lenexa (66219) **(G-5874)**
Gfsi LLC (HQ)....913 693-3200
9700 Commerce Pkwy Lenexa (66219) **(G-5875)**
Ggga Management Consultants, Overland Park *Also called Gorham Gold Greenwich & Assoc* **(G-8766)**
Ggnsc Holdings LLC....913 422-5832
750 Blake St Kansas City (66111) **(G-4033)**
Ggnsc Spring Hill LLC....913 592-3100
251 E Wilson St Spring Hill (66083) **(G-12084)**
Ggnsc Wellington LLC....620 326-7437
102 W Botkin St Wellington (67152) **(G-13504)**
Ghd Services Inc....785 783-8982
1502 Sw 41st St Topeka (66609) **(G-12636)**
Ghost Lake Corporation....816 809-9411
6500 W 194th St Stilwell (66085) **(G-12149)**
Ghumms Auto Center LLC....620 544-7800
531 S Jackson St Hugoton (67951) **(G-3163)**
Giant Communications Inc....785 362-9331
418 W 5th St Ste B Holton (66436) **(G-3091)**
Giant Kfn Holding Company LLC....785 362-2532
418 W 5th St Holton (66436) **(G-3092)**
Gibbs Technology Company....913 621-2424
1212 W Cambridge Cir Dr Kansas City (66103) **(G-4034)**

Gibraltar Mortgage, Overland Park *Also called Zillow Home Loans LLC* ***(G-9527)***
Gibson Electric Motor Shop, McPherson *Also called Gibson Industrial Controls Inc* ***(G-6969)***
Gibson Industrial Controls Inc (PA)....620 241-3551
525 N Baer St McPherson (67460) ***(G-6969)***
Gibson Products Co Salina Inc....785 827-4474
321 S Broadway Blvd Salina (67401) ***(G-10510)***
Gibson Wholesale Co Inc (PA)....316 945-3471
3104 W Central Ave Wichita (67203) ***(G-14463)***
Gibsons Ace Hardware....785 632-3147
728 W Crawford St Clay Center (67432) ***(G-865)***
Gift of Health, The, Wichita *Also called Ctr Imprvmnt Hmn Fnctnng Int* ***(G-14140)***
Gigot Agra Services Inc (PA)....620 276-8444
8105 S 295th St W Cheney (67025) ***(G-792)***
Gigstad Hay Company, Garnett *Also called Robert Gigstad* ***(G-2387)***
Gill Bebco LLC....816 942-3100
10800 Lackman Rd Lenexa (66219) ***(G-5876)***
Gillian & Hayes LLP....316 264-7321
301 N Main St Ste 1300 Wichita (67202) ***(G-14464)***
Gilliland & Hayes PA (PA)....620 662-0537
20 W 2nd Ave Ste 200 Hutchinson (67501) ***(G-3299)***
Gilliland & Hayes PA....913 317-5100
9225 Indian Creek Pkwy # 1070 Overland Park (66210) ***(G-8755)***
Gilliland & Hayes PA....316 264-7321
301 N Main St Ste 1300 Wichita (67202) ***(G-14465)***
Gilmore & Bell A Prof Corp....316 267-2091
100 N Main St Ste 800 Wichita (67202) ***(G-14466)***
Gilmore Shellenberger & Maxwel....620 624-5599
500 N Kansas Ave Liberal (67901) ***(G-6312)***
Gilmores Roustabout Service....620 624-0452
1540 N Fairview Ave Liberal (67901) ***(G-6313)***
Gina B Pinamonti DDS....620 231-6910
2602 S Rouse St Pittsburg (66762) ***(G-9866)***
Girard Animal Hospital PA....620 724-6068
207 E Southern Blvd Girard (66743) ***(G-2406)***
Girard Banking Center, Girard *Also called Community National Bank* ***(G-2398)***
Girard Medical Center, Girard *Also called Home Health Agency Hosp Dst* ***(G-2412)***
Girard Medical Center....620 724-7288
804 W Saint John St Girard (66743) ***(G-2407)***
Girard Medical Center (PA)....620 724-8291
302 N Hospital Dr Girard (66743) ***(G-2408)***
Girard National Bank (HQ)....620 724-8223
100 E Forest Ave Girard (66743) ***(G-2409)***
Girard National Bank....785 866-2920
314 2nd St Wetmore (66550) ***(G-13566)***
Girard National Bank....785 486-2124
110 E 8th St Horton (66439) ***(G-3124)***
Girard National Bank....785 742-7120
805 S 1st St Hiawatha (66434) ***(G-3008)***
Girard Tarps Inc....620 724-8909
411 W Saint John St Girard (66743) ***(G-2410)***
Girl Scouts Kans Heartland Inc (PA)....316 684-6531
360 Lexington Rd Wichita (67218) ***(G-14467)***
Girl Scts of Ne Kansas & NW MO (PA)....816 358-8750
2919 Sw Wanamaker Rd L Topeka (66614) ***(G-12637)***
Girton Propane Service Inc....785 632-6273
1156 Bridge St Clay Center (67432) ***(G-866)***
Givens Carpet Cleaning Service, Wichita *Also called Givens Cleaning Contractors* ***(G-14468)***
Givens Cleaning Contractors....316 265-1315
250 N Pennsylvania Ave Wichita (67214) ***(G-14468)***
Givens Investments LLC....620 662-1784
1300 N Grand St Hutchinson (67501) ***(G-3300)***
Gjo Inc....913 621-6611
5320 Speaker Rd Kansas City (66106) ***(G-4035)***
Gjo Holdings Inc....913 621-6611
5320 Speaker Rd Kansas City (66106) ***(G-4036)***
Gkc Michigan Theatres Inc....913 213-2000
11500 Ash St Leawood (66211) ***(G-5412)***
GKN Aerospace Precision Machin....620 326-5952
429 N West Rd Wellington (67152) ***(G-13505)***
GKN Armstrong Wheels Inc....316 943-3571
801 E Skinner St Wichita (67211) ***(G-14469)***
GKN Wichita, Wichita *Also called GKN Armstrong Wheels Inc* ***(G-14469)***
Glacier Petroleum Inc....620 342-1148
825 Commercial St Emporia (66801) ***(G-1762)***
Glaciers Edge Winery & Vinyrd....785 862-2298
1636 Se 85th St Wakarusa (66546) ***(G-13384)***
Glantz Holdings Inc....913 722-1000
1921 Foxridge Dr Kansas City (66106) ***(G-4037)***
Glantz, N & Son, Kansas City *Also called Glantz Holdings Inc* ***(G-4037)***
Glass King Manufacturing Co....620 793-7838
211 N Us Highway 281 Great Bend (67530) ***(G-2570)***
Glass Services Inc....785 823-5444
161 S Broadway Blvd Salina (67401) ***(G-10511)***
Glassman Bird Powell LLP....785 625-6919
200 W 13th St Hays (67601) ***(G-2816)***
Glassman Corporation....785 625-2115
900 Commerce Pkwy Hays (67601) ***(G-2817)***
Glaxosmithkline LLC....316 214-4811
518 N Bracken St Wichita (67206) ***(G-14470)***
Glazers Beer and Beverage LLC....620 227-8168
1409 W Wyatt Earp Blvd Dodge City (67801) ***(G-1365)***
Gleason & Son Signs Inc....785 823-8615
2440 N 9th St Salina (67401) ***(G-10512)***
Glen Shadow Golf Club (PA)....913 764-2299
26000 Shadow Glen Dr Olathe (66061) ***(G-7729)***
Glen Shadow Golf Club....913 764-6572
26577 College Blvd Olathe (66061) ***(G-7730)***
Glen Thurber....785 233-9541
2041 Sw Western Ave Topeka (66604) ***(G-12638)***
Glen-Gery Corporation....913 281-2800
336 S 42nd St Kansas City (66106) ***(G-4038)***
Glencare/Cherryvale CA Ltd Pt....620 336-2102
1001 W Main St Cherryvale (67335) ***(G-807)***
Glendo LLC....620 343-1084
900 Overlander Rd Emporia (66801) ***(G-1763)***
Glenn Pk Christn Ch Preschool....316 943-4283
2757 S Glenn Ave Wichita (67217) ***(G-14471)***
Glenn V Hemberger DDS....913 345-0331
8575 W 110th St Ste 310 Shawnee Mission (66210) ***(G-11397)***
Glenwood Arts Theater (PA)....913 642-1132
3859 W 95th St Overland Park (66206) ***(G-8756)***
Glenwood Estate Inc....620 331-2260
621 S 2nd St Independence (67301) ***(G-3523)***
Gli LLC (PA)....913 648-7858
7200 W 107th St Overland Park (66212) ***(G-8757)***
Gliem & Giddings, Overland Park *Also called L J Gliem & Associates LLC* ***(G-8935)***
Glmv Architecture Inc (PA)....316 265-9367
1525 E Douglas Ave Wichita (67211) ***(G-14472)***
Global Aviation Services LLC (PA)....913 780-0300
540 E Old Highway 56 Olathe (66061) ***(G-7731)***
Global Aviation Tech LLC....316 425-0999
6545 W Pueblo Ct Wichita (67209) ***(G-14473)***
Global Cnc Corporation....316 516-3400
1029 N Wichita St Ste 2 Wichita (67203) ***(G-14474)***
Global Connections Inc (PA)....913 498-0960
5360 College Blvd Ste 200 Leawood (66211) ***(G-5413)***
Global Engineering & Tech Inc....316 729-9232
1720 S 151st St W Goddard (67052) ***(G-2439)***
Global Engineering and Tech....620 664-6268
1200 N Halstead St Hutchinson (67501) ***(G-3301)***
Global Ground Support LLC....913 780-0300
540 E Old Highway 56 Olathe (66061) ***(G-7732)***
Global Industries Inc....913 310-9963
11617 W 81st St Overland Park (66214) ***(G-8758)***
Global Montessori Academy....816 561-4533
7457 Cherokee Dr Prairie Village (66208) ***(G-10032)***
Global Oilfield Services LLC....785 445-3525
24 S Lincoln St Russell (67665) ***(G-10275)***
Global Partner Solutions LLC....316 263-1288
100 S Market St Ste 2b Wichita (67202) ***(G-14475)***
Global Parts Inc (HQ)....316 733-9240
901 Industrial Rd Augusta (67010) ***(G-319)***
Global Parts Aero, Augusta *Also called Global Parts Inc* ***(G-319)***
Global Parts Aero Mfg....316 775-9292
901 Industrial Rd Augusta (67010) ***(G-320)***
Global Parts Group Inc (PA)....316 733-9240
901 Industrial Rd Augusta (67010) ***(G-321)***
Global Prairie Marketing LLC....913 722-7244
5527 E Mission Dr Mission Hills (66208) ***(G-7142)***
Global Procurement Corporation....913 458-2000
11401 Lamar Ave Overland Park (66211) ***(G-8759)***
Global Services Inc....913 451-0960
5360 College Blvd Ste 200 Leawood (66211) ***(G-5414)***
Global Soft Systems Inc....913 338-1400
10801 Mastin St Ste 510 Overland Park (66210) ***(G-8760)***
Global Stone LLC (PA)....913 310-9500
421 N Rawhide Dr Olathe (66061) ***(G-7733)***
Global Systems Incorporated....913 829-5900
13470 S Arapaho Dr # 130 Olathe (66062) ***(G-7734)***
Global Technical Services, Shawnee Mission *Also called Crawford & Company* ***(G-11277)***
Global Vacations, Leawood *Also called Global Connections Inc* ***(G-5413)***
Globalcom Solutions LLC....785 832-8101
850 N 1663 Rd Lawrence (66049) ***(G-4873)***
Globalink Inc....785 823-8284
2725 Arnold Ave Ste 528 Salina (67401) ***(G-10513)***
Globe Engineering Co Inc....316 943-1266
1539 S Saint Paul St Wichita (67213) ***(G-14476)***
Globl Adams Communications LLC....913 402-4499
9635 Widmer Rd Lenexa (66215) ***(G-5877)***
Gloden Corral, Topeka *Also called Capital City Corral Inc* ***(G-12425)***
Glover Inc....800 654-1511
878 N Jan Mar Ct Olathe (66061) ***(G-7735)***
Glow Golf....316 685-1040
7570 W 21st St N 1026c Wichita (67205) ***(G-14477)***
Glpt, Kingman *Also called Great Lakes Polymer Tech LLC* ***(G-4591)***
Gmed, Wichita *Also called Galichia Medical Group Kans PA* ***(G-14439)***
Gmls Industries Inc (PA)....620 983-2136
1658 Us Highway 50 Peabody (66866) ***(G-9759)***

ALPHABETIC

GNB Industrial, Kansas City *Also called Exide Technologies* ***(G-4001)***
Go Local LLC....913 231-3083
10975 Benson Dr Ste 250 Overland Park (66210) ***(G-8761)***
Go-Modern LLC....785 271-1445
2950 Sw Mcclure Rd Topeka (66614) ***(G-12639)***
Goddard Intermediate Lrng Ctr, Goddard *Also called Goddard Public Schools* ***(G-2440)***
Goddard Machine LLC....316 838-1381
1738 N Mosley Ave Wichita (67214) ***(G-14478)***
Goddard Manufacturing Inc....785 689-4341
107 S Mill St Logan (67646) ***(G-6424)***
Goddard Public Schools....316 794-2281
335 N Walnut St Goddard (67052) ***(G-2440)***
Goddard School....913 764-1331
15040 W 138th St Olathe (66062) ***(G-7736)***
Goddard School....913 451-1066
11060 Oakmont St Shawnee Mission (66210) ***(G-11398)***
Goddard Veterinary Clinic....316 794-8022
19912 W Kellogg Dr Goddard (67052) ***(G-2441)***
Godly Play Resources Inc....620 635-4018
122 W 8th Ave Ashland (67831) ***(G-195)***
Goentzel Construction Inc....316 264-6333
7570 W 21st St N 1050f Wichita (67205) ***(G-14479)***
Golconda Group LLC....913 579-4795
6878 Martindale Rd Shawnee (66218) ***(G-10963)***
Gold Insurance Agency, Seneca *Also called SBS Insurance* ***(G-10880)***
Gold Key Inc....316 942-1925
5212 N Saint Clair Ave Wichita (67204) ***(G-14480)***
Gold Key Realtors, Wichita *Also called Gold Key Inc* ***(G-14480)***
Gold Star Concrete Cnstr....785 478-4495
6021 Sw 29th St Topeka (66614) ***(G-12640)***
Gold Star Transportation Inc (PA)....913 341-0081
9424 Reeds Rd Ste 201 Overland Park (66207) ***(G-8762)***
Golden Acres Nursing Center, Onaga *Also called Deseret Hlth Rhab At Onaga LLC* ***(G-8174)***
Golden Acres Nursing Home, Leoti *Also called Wichita Cnty Long Term Rest Hm* ***(G-6262)***
Golden Belt Bank F S A, Hays *Also called Golden Belt Banking & Sav Assn* ***(G-2818)***
Golden Belt Banking & Sav Assn....785 625-7345
1101 E 27th St Hays (67601) ***(G-2818)***
Golden Belt Coop Assn Inc....785 726-3115
917 Monroe St Ellis (67637) ***(G-1646)***
Golden Belt Country Club Inc....620 792-4303
1438 24th St Great Bend (67530) ***(G-2571)***
Golden Belt Feeders Inc (PA)....620 549-3241
1149 Nw 10th Ave Saint John (67576) ***(G-10351)***
Golden Belt Feeders Inc....620 659-2111
1278 P Rd Kinsley (67547) ***(G-4618)***
Golden Belt Printing II LLC....620 793-6351
1125 Us Highway 281 Byp Great Bend (67530) ***(G-2572)***
Golden Belt Telephone Assn Inc (PA)....785 372-4236
103 Lincoln St Rush Center (67575) ***(G-10259)***
Golden Boomers Home....316 730-3110
9306 E Carson St Wichita (67210) ***(G-14481)***
Golden Boy Pies Inc....913 384-6460
4945 Hadley St Overland Park (66203) ***(G-8763)***
Golden Eagle Casino....785 486-6601
1121 Goldfinch Rd Horton (66439) ***(G-3125)***
Golden Fox Buildings, Peabody *Also called Gmls Industries Inc* ***(G-9759)***
Golden Heights Living Center, Garnett *Also called Manor of Garnett Inc* ***(G-2382)***
Golden Key Salon....316 744-0230
4023 Clarendon St Bel Aire (67220) ***(G-433)***
Golden Lc Edwardsvill....913 441-1900
751 Blake St Edwardsville (66111) ***(G-1501)***
Golden Living Center, Edwardsville *Also called Beaver Dam Health Care Center* ***(G-1495)***
Golden Living Center....913 727-1284
210 N Plaza Dr Lansing (66043) ***(G-4674)***
Golden Living Center Wichita....316 683-7588
4007 E Lincoln St Wichita (67218) ***(G-14482)***
Golden Living Centers, El Dorado *Also called Beaver Dam Health Care Center* ***(G-1535)***
Golden Living Centre, Cottonwood Falls *Also called Beaver Dam Health Care Center* ***(G-1151)***
Golden Livingcenter - Eskridge....785 449-2294
505 N Main St Eskridge (66423) ***(G-1867)***
Golden Livingcenter Room 132b....785 658-2505
611 31st St Wilson (67490) ***(G-16106)***
Golden Livingcenter Wellington....620 326-7437
102 W Botkin St Wellington (67152) ***(G-13506)***
Golden Livingcenter-Wellington, Wellington *Also called Ggnsc Wellington LLC* ***(G-13504)***
Golden Oaks Healthcare Inc....913 788-2100
8900 Parallel Pkwy Kansas City (66112) ***(G-4039)***
Golden Plains AG Tech....785 462-6753
650 E Pine St Colby (67701) ***(G-1009)***
Golden Plains Credit Union (PA)....620 275-8187
1714 E Kansas Ave Garden City (67846) ***(G-2188)***
Golden Plains Credit Union....620 624-8491
21 Medical Dr Liberal (67901) ***(G-6314)***
Golden Plains Credit Union....785 628-1007
2720 Broadway Ave Hays (67601) ***(G-2819)***
Golden Plains Motel, Colby *Also called Service Oil Company* ***(G-1040)***
Golden Plains Publishers Inc (PA)....620 855-3902
101 N Main Cimarron (67835) ***(G-827)***
Golden Plains Publishing, Cimarron *Also called Gray County Printers* ***(G-828)***
Golden Prairie Hunting Service....620 675-8490
607 W Gwinn Ct Sublette (67877) ***(G-12202)***
Golden Sea Graphics Inc....785 747-2822
704 Main St Greenleaf (66943) ***(G-2669)***
Golden Star Inc....913 874-2178
7712 Industrial Park Ln Atchison (66002) ***(G-231)***
Golden Valley Inc (PA)....620 527-4216
102 S Main Rozel (67574) ***(G-10258)***
Golden West Community Services, Goodland *Also called RES-Care Inc* ***(G-2482)***
Golden Wheat Inc (PA)....620 782-3341
106 W 1st St Udall (67146) ***(G-13277)***
Golden-Q, Hays *Also called Q Golden Billiards* ***(G-2893)***
Golds Gym, Shawnee Mission *Also called R & D Fitness Inc* ***(G-11770)***
Golf Club At Southwind LLC....620 275-2117
77 Grandview Dr Garden City (67846) ***(G-2189)***
Golf Crse Superintendents Amer....785 841-2240
1421 Research Park Dr Lawrence (66049) ***(G-4874)***
Golf Operations Management LLC....913 897-3809
12501 Quivira Rd Overland Park (66213) ***(G-8764)***
Gone Logo Screen Printing....785 625-3070
2717 Plaza Ave Hays (67601) ***(G-2820)***
Gonzales Cmmunications Inc GCI....913 685-4866
15145 Metcalf Ave Overland Park (66223) ***(G-8765)***
Good Life Snacks Inc....913 220-2117
9900 Pflumm Rd Ste 46 Lenexa (66215) ***(G-5878)***
Good News Publishing Co Inc....620 879-5460
124 N State St Caney (67333) ***(G-669)***
Good Riddance Corporation....620 633-5222
6983 200 Rd Fredonia (66736) ***(G-2034)***
Good Samaritan Center, Wamego *Also called Evangelical Lthrn Good Smrtn* ***(G-13421)***
Good Samaritan Cntral KS, Hays *Also called Evangelical Lutheran* ***(G-2802)***
Good Samaritan NW KS Home, Saint Francis *Also called Evangelical Lutheran* ***(G-10341)***
Good Samaritan Soc - Atwood, Atwood *Also called Evangelical Lutheran* ***(G-284)***
Good Samaritan Soc - Liberal, Liberal *Also called Evangelical Lutheran* ***(G-6308)***
Good Samaritan Soc - Olathe, Olathe *Also called Evangelical Lutheran* ***(G-7694)***
Good Samaritan Soc - Parsons, Parsons *Also called Evangelical Lutheran* ***(G-9684)***
Good Samaritan Soc - Vly Vista, Wamego *Also called Evangelical Lutheran* ***(G-13422)***
Good Samaritan Society....620 663-1189
810 E 30th Ave Hutchinson (67502) ***(G-3302)***
Good Samaritan Society - Ellis, Ellis *Also called Evangelical Lutheran* ***(G-1644)***
Good Samaritan Society - Hays, Hays *Also called Evangelical Lutheran* ***(G-2801)***
Good Samaritan Society - Lyons, Lyons *Also called Evangelical Lutheran* ***(G-6483)***
Good Shepherd Child Care Ctr....620 429-4611
128 W Elm St Columbus (66725) ***(G-1076)***
Good Shepherd Villages Inc....785 244-6418
613 3rd St Summerfield (66541) ***(G-12214)***
Good Smrtan Soc - Decatur Cnty, Oberlin *Also called Evangelical Lutheran* ***(G-7493)***
Good Smrtan Soc - Ellswrth Vlg, Ellsworth *Also called Evangelical Lutheran* ***(G-1674)***
Good Smrtan Soc - Htchnson Vlg, Hutchinson *Also called Evangelical Lutheran* ***(G-3280)***
Good Smrtan Soc - Sherman Cnty, Goodland *Also called Evangelical Lutheran* ***(G-2469)***
Goodart Consrtuction Inc....913 557-0044
26685 Waverly Rd Paola (66071) ***(G-9562)***
Goodart Construction, Paola *Also called Goodart Consrtuction Inc* ***(G-9562)***
Goodell Stratton Edmonds & P....785 233-0593
515 S Kansas Ave Ste 100 Topeka (66603) ***(G-12641)***
Goodell, Gerald L, Topeka *Also called Goodell Stratton Edmonds & P* ***(G-12641)***
Goodencoff & Malone Inc....785 483-6220
639 N Main St Russell (67665) ***(G-10276)***
Goodland Assisted Living, Goodland *Also called Heritage Healthcare Management* ***(G-2477)***
Goodland Machine & Auto LLC....785 899-6628
419 E 19th St Goodland (67735) ***(G-2474)***
Goodland Municipal Power Plant, Goodland *Also called City of Goodland* ***(G-2465)***
Goodland Regional Medical Ctr, Goodland *Also called County of Sherman* ***(G-2467)***
Goodland Star News, The, Goodland *Also called Haynes Publishing Co* ***(G-2475)***
Goodman Manufacturing Co LP....316 946-9145
1749 S Sabin St Wichita (67209) ***(G-14483)***
Goodrich....316 448-4282
P.O. Box 75157 Wichita (67275) ***(G-14484)***
Goodrich Corporation....316 943-3322
7016 W Pueblo Dr Ste B Wichita (67209) ***(G-14485)***
Goodrich Corporation....316 721-3100
1643 S Maize Rd Wichita (67209) ***(G-14486)***
Goodrich Quality Theaters Inc....620 232-2256
202 E Centennial Dr Pittsburg (66762) ***(G-9867)***
Goodwill Inds Easter Seals Soc, Garden City *Also called Goodwill Industries Ea* ***(G-2190)***
Goodwill Industries Ea....316 789-8804
1247 N Rainbow Dr Derby (67037) ***(G-1248)***
Goodwill Industries Ea....620 343-3564
904 E 12th Ave Emporia (66801) ***(G-1764)***
Goodwill Industries Ea....620 275-1007
2005 E Schulman Ave Garden City (67846) ***(G-2190)***
Goodwill Store 11, Topeka *Also called Goodwill Wstn MO & Eastrn Kans* ***(G-12642)***

Goodwill Store 12, Olathe *Also called Goodwill Wstn MO & Eastrn Kans* ***(G-7737)***
Goodwill Store 5, Lawrence *Also called Goodwill Wstn MO & Eastrn Kans* ***(G-4875)***
Goodwill Wstn MO & Eastrn Kans 785 331-3908
2200 W 31st St Lawrence (66047) ***(G-4875)***
Goodwill Wstn MO & Eastrn Kans 913 768-9540
16630 W 135th St Olathe (66062) ***(G-7737)***
Goodwill Wstn MO & Eastrn Kans 785 228-9774
5515 Sw 21st St Ste C Topeka (66604) ***(G-12642)***
Goodwin Industries Inc 620 726-5281
215 W Broadway St Burns (66840) ***(G-646)***
Goodwin Pro Turf Inc 913 685-1000
6945 W 152nd Ter Shawnee Mission (66223) ***(G-11399)***
Goodwin Proturf, Shawnee Mission *Also called Goodwin Pro Turf Inc* ***(G-11399)***
Goodwin Sporting Goods Inc 785 625-2419
109 W 11th St Hays (67601) ***(G-2821)***
Goody Tickets LLC 913 231-2674
7007 College Blvd Ste 100 Leawood (66211) ***(G-5415)***
Goodyear, Wichita *Also called Karls Tire & Auto Service Inc* ***(G-14833)***
Goodyear Tire & Rubber Company 785 266-3862
420 Sw Croix St Topeka (66611) ***(G-12643)***
Googols of Learning 785 856-6002
500 Rockledge Rd Lawrence (66049) ***(G-4876)***
Goppert State Service Bank (PA) 785 448-3111
106 E 5th Ave Garnett (66032) ***(G-2375)***
Gordon Lawn & Garden Co, Shawnee *Also called Pbi-Gordon Corporation* ***(G-11009)***
Gore Oil Company (PA) 316 263-3535
202 S Saint Francis Ave Wichita (67202) ***(G-14487)***
Gorges Dairy Inc 620 545-7297
6555 S 183rd St W Viola (67149) ***(G-13379)***
Gorges Motor Co, Eastborough *Also called Marc Gorges* ***(G-1476)***
Gorham Gold Greenwich & Assoc 913 981-4442
9150 Glenwood St Overland Park (66212) ***(G-8766)***
Gorydz Inc 913 486-1665
2636 N Early St Kansas City (66101) ***(G-4040)***
Gospel Publishers 620 345-2532
100 S Avenue C Moundridge (67107) ***(G-7183)***
Gospel Publishers Book Store, Moundridge *Also called Gospel Publishers* ***(G-7183)***
Gossen Livingston Associates 620 225-3300
100 Military Ave Ste 126 Dodge City (67801) ***(G-1366)***
Gottlob Lawn & Landscape LLC 620 222-8870
5001 E 9th Ave Winfield (67156) ***(G-16144)***
Gourmet Specialties Inc 913 432-5228
111 Southwest Blvd Kansas City (66103) ***(G-4041)***
Gove County Medical Center, Quinter *Also called County of Gove* ***(G-10181)***
GP Express Inc 620 223-1244
103 W 19th St Fort Scott (66701) ***(G-1974)***
GP Traps LLC 620 394-2341
2711 Se 190th St Atlanta (67008) ***(G-274)***
Gpha, Phillipsburg *Also called Great Plains Hlth Aliance Inc* ***(G-9787)***
GPS AFTER SCHOOL PROGRAM, Hoisington *Also called Gps Kids Club* ***(G-3065)***
Gps Kids Club 620 282-2288
352 W 12th St Hoisington (67544) ***(G-3065)***
Gpw & Associates LLC 785 865-2332
1001 New Hampshire St Lawrence (66044) ***(G-4877)***
Gq Inc 785 843-2138
511 W 9th St Lawrence (66044) ***(G-4878)***
Grabar Voice and Data Inc 701 258-3528
8555 E 32nd St N Wichita (67226) ***(G-14488)***
Grabill Plumbing Inc 913 432-9660
3121 Merriam Ln Ste G Kansas City (66106) ***(G-4042)***
Grace Agapes Inc 913 837-5885
2 S Mulberry St Louisburg (66053) ***(G-6450)***
Grace Angels Family Service 913 233-2944
1220 Troup Ave Ste B Kansas City (66104) ***(G-4043)***
Grace Construction & Assoc Inc 316 617-1729
102 Reyer St Derby (67037) ***(G-1249)***
Grace Dental 913 685-9111
12611 Antioch Rd Overland Park (66213) ***(G-8767)***
Grace Grdns Assistd Lvng Fclty 913 685-4800
5201 W 143rd St Leawood (66224) ***(G-5416)***
Grace Management Inc 913 367-2655
1301 N 4th St Atchison (66002) ***(G-232)***
Grace of Wichita Ks LLC 316 832-9009
6803 W Taft Ave Ste 305 Wichita (67209) ***(G-14489)***
Grace United Methodist Church, Olathe *Also called New Day Educare* ***(G-7917)***
Grace United Methodist Church 913 859-0111
11485 S Ridgeview Rd Olathe (66061) ***(G-7738)***
Gracemed Health Clinic Inc 316 440-7938
1905 S Laura Ave Wichita (67211) ***(G-14490)***
Gracemed Health Clinic Inc (PA) 316 866-2001
1122 N Topeka St Wichita (67214) ***(G-14491)***
Gracious Senior Living, Wichita *Also called Broadmoor One LLC* ***(G-13893)***
Graco Supply Company 316 943-4200
2056 S Edwards St Ste C Wichita (67213) ***(G-14492)***
Grady Bolding Corporation 620 564-2240
114 N Main St Ellinwood (67526) ***(G-1633)***
Graf & Associates Inc (PA) 316 686-2090
2445 S Glendale St Wichita (67210) ***(G-14493)***
Graf Electric, Wichita *Also called Graf & Associates Inc* ***(G-14493)***
Grafton Inc (PA) 913 498-0701
6801 W 121st St Ste 100 Overland Park (66209) ***(G-8768)***
Grafton Staffing Companies, Overland Park *Also called Grafton Inc* ***(G-8768)***
GRAHAM COUNTY HOSPITAL, Hill City *Also called Hospice of Graham County* ***(G-3035)***
Graham County Hospital, Hill City *Also called County of Graham* ***(G-3031)***
Graham Ship By Truck Co 913 621-7500
7916 Fontana St Prairie Village (66208) ***(G-10033)***
Graham Ship By Truck Company (PA) 913 621-7575
7916 Fontana St Prairie Village (66208) ***(G-10034)***
Grahem-Hrbers VFW Post No 3084 ....785 213-6232
405 Walnut St Valley Falls (66088) ***(G-13363)***
Grain Belt Supply Company Inc 785 827-4491
217 E Diamond Dr Salina (67401) ***(G-10514)***
Grain Craft Inc 316 267-7311
701 E 17th St N Wichita (67214) ***(G-14494)***
Grain Craft Inc 913 890-6300
4400 W 109th St Ste 200 Leawood (66211) ***(G-5417)***
Grain Craft Inc 913 262-1779
56 Silver Ave Kansas City (66103) ***(G-4044)***
Grain Craft Inc 620 241-2410
416 N Main St McPherson (67460) ***(G-6970)***
Grain Sorghum Hogs Inc 620 872-3866
1014 S Washington St Scott City (67871) ***(G-10813)***
Grainger 409, Lenexa *Also called WW Grainger Inc* ***(G-6237)***
Grainger 920, Wichita *Also called WW Grainger Inc* ***(G-16079)***
Gram Enterprises Inc (PA) 913 888-3689
13224 W 87th Street Pkwy Lenexa (66215) ***(G-5879)***
Gran Villa 620 583-7473
1820 E River St Eureka (67045) ***(G-1887)***
Gran Villas 785 528-5095
1403 Laing St Osage City (66523) ***(G-8184)***
Gran Villas of Hiawatha, Hiawatha *Also called Medicalodges Inc* ***(G-3017)***
Gran Villas of Holton Inc 785 364-5051
410 Juniper Dr Holton (66436) ***(G-3093)***
Gran Villas of Wamego 785 456-8997
1607 4th St Wamego (66547) ***(G-13424)***
Granada Theater 785 842-1390
1020 Massachusetts St Lawrence (66044) ***(G-4879)***
Grand Central Hotel & Grill, Cottonwood Falls *Also called Grand Central Hotel Corp* ***(G-1154)***
Grand Central Hotel Corp 620 273-6763
215 Broadway St Cottonwood Falls (66845) ***(G-1154)***
Grand Court of Overland Park, Overland Park *Also called Brookdale Senior Living Inc* ***(G-8488)***
Grand Mesa Operating Company 316 634-0699
1700 N Waterfront Pkwy # 600 Wichita (67206) ***(G-14495)***
Grand Prairie Ht & Convention 620 669-9311
1400 N Lorraine St Hutchinson (67501) ***(G-3303)***
Grand Villas, Neodesha *Also called Medical Lodges Inc* ***(G-7244)***
Grandma Hoerners Foods Inc 785 765-2300
31862 Thompson Rd Alma (66401) ***(G-63)***
Grandstand Glassware and AP, Lawrence *Also called Screen-It Grphics Lawrence Inc* ***(G-5107)***
Grandview Pdts Cherryville Div, Cherryvale *Also called Grandview Products Co* ***(G-808)***
Grandview Products Co 620 336-2309
200 N Galveston St Cherryvale (67335) ***(G-808)***
Grandview Products Co Inc (HQ) 620 421-6950
1601 Superior Dr Parsons (67357) ***(G-9688)***
Grandview Water Disposal Inc 785 335-2649
1390 70 Rd Scandia (66966) ***(G-10799)***
Granite City Food & Brewry Ltd 913 334-2255
1701 Village West Pkwy Kansas City (66111) ***(G-4045)***
Granite Transformation Kans Cy 913 492-7600
14125 Marshall Dr Lenexa (66215) ***(G-5880)***
Granite Trnsfrmtion Wchita LLC 316 681-1900
6254 E 37th St N Ste 130 Bel Aire (67220) ***(G-434)***
Grannies Homemade Mustard 620 947-3259
410 W 7th St Newton (67114) ***(G-7351)***
Grannys 913 837-5222
201 Crestview Cir Louisburg (66053) ***(G-6451)***
Grant County Bank 620 356-4142
201 S Main St Ulysses (67880) ***(G-13300)***
Grant County Feeders, Ulysses *Also called Five Rivers Cattle Feeding LLC* ***(G-13296)***
Grant County Recreation Comm, Ulysses *Also called County of Grant* ***(G-13292)***
Grant D Ringler DDS Inc 620 669-0835
3008 Garden Grove Pkwy Hutchinson (67502) ***(G-3304)***
Grant Phipps DDS 620 326-7983
119 E Lincoln Ave Wellington (67152) ***(G-13507)***
Grant Thornton LLP 316 265-3231
1617 N Waterfront Pkwy # 100 Wichita (67206) ***(G-14496)***
Grapevine Designs LLC (PA) 913 307-0225
8406 Melrose Dr Lenexa (66214) ***(G-5881)***
Graphic Images Inc 316 283-3776
407 W 10th St Newton (67114) ***(G-7352)***
Graphic Impressions, Wichita *Also called Frameworks* ***(G-14413)***

ALPHABETIC

Graphic Impressions Inc....620 663-5939
1101 N Halstead St Hutchinson (67501) ***(G-3305)***
Graphic Systems Division, Kansas City *Also called Fujifilm Sericol USA Inc* ***(G-4022)***
Graphics Four Inc....913 268-0564
7838 Oakview Ln Shawnee (66216) ***(G-10964)***
Graphics Systems Inc (HQ)....316 267-4171
313 S Ida St Wichita (67211) ***(G-14497)***
Grass & Grain, Manhattan *Also called AG Press Inc* ***(G-6536)***
Grass Hopper Company, Moundridge *Also called Moridge Manufacturing Inc* ***(G-7193)***
Grass Pad Inc (PA)....913 764-4100
425 N Rawhide Dr Olathe (66061) ***(G-7739)***
Grass Pad Inc....913 681-8948
8160 W 199th St Bucyrus (66013) ***(G-597)***
Grass Pad Warehouse, Bucyrus *Also called Grass Pad Inc* ***(G-597)***
Grassland Heritage Foundation....913 856-4784
26062 W 150th St Olathe (66061) ***(G-7740)***
Grasslands Estates, Wichita *Also called Harvest Facility Holdings LP* ***(G-14567)***
GRASSROOTS ART CENTER, Lucas *Also called Lucas Arts Hmnties Council Inc* ***(G-6473)***
Grathes and Draden, Topeka *Also called Kansas Consulting Engineers* ***(G-12767)***
Gravel & Concrete Inc....620 422-3249
7010 N Nickerson Rd Nickerson (67561) ***(G-7432)***
Gray & Company Inc....785 232-0913
625 Se Hancock St Topeka (66607) ***(G-12644)***
Gray Construction Inc....316 721-3000
204 N Woodchuck St Wichita (67212) ***(G-14498)***
Gray County Feed Yard, Cimarron *Also called Irsik & Doll Feed Services Inc* ***(G-831)***
Gray County Printers....620 855-2467
101 N Main St Cimarron (67835) ***(G-828)***
Gray Television Group Inc....316 838-1212
2815 E 37th St N Wichita (67219) ***(G-14499)***
Gray Television Group Inc....785 272-6397
631 Sw Commerce Pl Topeka (66615) ***(G-12645)***
Graybar Electric Company Inc....316 265-8964
3609 W Pawnee St Wichita (67213) ***(G-14500)***
Graybeal Construction Co Inc....785 232-1033
8700 Pine St Lenexa (66220) ***(G-5882)***
Grayco Over 50....620 855-3711
221 S Main St Cimarron (67835) ***(G-829)***
Grayling Inc....913 341-5444
10258 W 87th St Overland Park (66212) ***(G-8769)***
Great Amercn Hardwood Flrg Co....316 264-3660
157 S Washington Ave Wichita (67202) ***(G-14501)***
Great American Bank (HQ)....913 585-1131
33050 W 83rd St De Soto (66018) ***(G-1200)***
Great American Bank (HQ)....785 838-9704
888 New Hampshire St A Lawrence (66044) ***(G-4880)***
Great American Insurance Co....785 840-1100
4910 Corp Centre Dr # 200 Lawrence (66047) ***(G-4881)***
Great Bend Child Day Care Assn....620 792-2421
1802 22nd St Great Bend (67530) ***(G-2573)***
Great Bend Childrens Clinic PA....620 792-5437
1021 Eisenhower Ave Great Bend (67530) ***(G-2574)***
Great Bend Childrens Lrng Ctr, Great Bend *Also called Great Bend Child Day Care Assn* ***(G-2573)***
Great Bend Commission On Aging....620 792-3906
2005 Kansas Ave Great Bend (67530) ***(G-2575)***
Great Bend Coop, The, Great Bend *Also called City of Great Bend* ***(G-2543)***
Great Bend Cooperative Assn (PA)....620 793-3531
606 Main St Great Bend (67530) ***(G-2576)***
Great Bend Cooperative Assn....620 792-1281
2302 10th St Great Bend (67530) ***(G-2577)***
Great Bend Farm Equipment Inc....620 793-3509
3412 23rd St Great Bend (67530) ***(G-2578)***
Great Bend Feeding Inc....620 792-2508
355 Nw 30 Ave Great Bend (67530) ***(G-2579)***
Great Bend Foundation Inc....620 792-4217
3720 10th St Great Bend (67530) ***(G-2580)***
GREAT BEND HEALTH AND REHAB, Great Bend *Also called Great Bend Manor* ***(G-2583)***
Great Bend Industrial Fabrics, Great Bend *Also called USA Gym Supply* ***(G-2652)***
Great Bend Industries, Great Bend *Also called Hampton Hydraulics Llc* ***(G-2590)***
Great Bend Industries Inc....620 792-4368
8701 6th St Great Bend (67530) ***(G-2581)***
Great Bend Internists PA....620 793-8429
3515 Broadway Ave Ste 107 Great Bend (67530) ***(G-2582)***
Great Bend Manor....620 792-2448
1560 State Road 96 Great Bend (67530) ***(G-2583)***
Great Bend Parole Office, Great Bend *Also called Corrections Kansas Department* ***(G-2547)***
Great Bend Tribune, Great Bend *Also called Morris Newspaper Corp Kansas* ***(G-2613)***
Great Bend, City of, Great Bend *Also called City of Great Bend* ***(G-2541)***
Great Clips, Shawnee Mission *Also called Midland Clippers* ***(G-11630)***
Great Clips, Olathe *Also called Ruth Grimsley* ***(G-8048)***
Great Clips....913 727-1917
1110 Eisenhower Rd Leavenworth (66048) ***(G-5246)***
Great Clips For Hair....913 888-7447
14904 W 87th Street Pkwy Lenexa (66215) ***(G-5883)***
Great Clips For Hair (PA)....913 888-3400
11540 W 95th St Overland Park (66214) ***(G-8770)***
Great Clips For Hair....913 338-2580
10154 W 119th St Overland Park (66213) ***(G-8771)***
Great Lakes Polymer Tech, Kingman *Also called Great Lkes Plymers Hldngs Corp* ***(G-4594)***
Great Lakes Polymer Tech LLC (PA)....620 532-5141
701 E A Ave Kingman (67068) ***(G-4591)***
Great Lakes Polymer Tech LLC....507 320-7000
100 Fabpro Way Kingman (67068) ***(G-4592)***
Great Lakes Polymer Tech LLC....208 324-2120
100 Fabpro Way Kingman (67068) ***(G-4593)***
Great Lkes Plymers Hldngs Corp (HQ)....507 320-7000
100 Fabpro Way Kingman (67068) ***(G-4594)***
Great Northwest Railroad....620 231-2230
315 W 3rd St Pittsburg (66762) ***(G-9868)***
Great Outdoors, Atwood *Also called Beaver Valley Supply Co Inc* ***(G-281)***
Great Plains, Wichita *Also called Edwards County Gas Company* ***(G-14262)***
Great Plains Alfalfa Inc....620 672-9431
70036 Nw 30th St Pratt (67124) ***(G-10119)***
Great Plains Annuity Marketing....913 888-0488
10901 W 84th Ter Ste 125 Overland Park (66214) ***(G-8772)***
Great Plains Christian Radio....620 873-2991
909 W Carthage St Meade (67864) ***(G-7049)***
Great Plains Ellinwood Inc....620 564-2548
605 N Main St Ellinwood (67526) ***(G-1634)***
Great Plains Federal Cr Un....620 331-4060
123 E Main St Independence (67301) ***(G-3524)***
Great Plains Federal Cr Un....620 241-4181
720 N Main St McPherson (67460) ***(G-6971)***
Great Plains Federal Cr Un....785 823-9226
605 S Ohio St Salina (67401) ***(G-10515)***
Great Plains Financial Group....785 843-7070
3310 Mesa Way Ste 101 Lawrence (66049) ***(G-4882)***
Great Plains Funeral Service, Logan *Also called Logan Funeral Home* ***(G-6426)***
Great Plains Hlth Aliance Inc (PA)....785 543-2111
625 3rd St Phillipsburg (67661) ***(G-9787)***
Great Plains Hlth Aliance Inc....785 332-2104
210 W 1st St Saint Francis (67756) ***(G-10342)***
Great Plains Hlth Aliance Inc....785 284-2121
14th & Oregon St Sabetha (66534) ***(G-10311)***
Great Plains Hlth Aliance Inc....316 685-1523
250 N Rock Rd Ste 160 Wichita (67206) ***(G-14502)***
Great Plains Hlth Aliance Inc....620 723-3341
921 N Sycamore St Greensburg (67054) ***(G-2675)***
Great Plains Industries Inc....316 686-7361
5252 E 36th St N Wichita (67220) ***(G-14503)***
Great Plains Insptn & Lining....620 793-7090
5858 10th St Great Bend (67530) ***(G-2584)***
Great Plains International LLC (HQ)....785 823-3276
1525 E North St Salina (67401) ***(G-10516)***
Great Plains Investments Ltd....913 492-9880
11300 W 80th St Overland Park (66214) ***(G-8773)***
Great Plains Kiowa Co Inc (HQ)....620 723-3341
721 W Kansas Ave Greensburg (67054) ***(G-2676)***
Great Plains Laboratory Inc....913 341-8949
11813 W 77th St Overland Park (66214) ***(G-8774)***
Great Plains Locating Svc Inc....316 263-1200
1550 N Broadway Ave Wichita (67214) ***(G-14504)***
Great Plains Logistics Inc....785 823-2261
1935 E North St Salina (67401) ***(G-10517)***
Great Plains Manufacturing Inc (HQ)....785 823-3276
1525 E North St Salina (67401) ***(G-10518)***
Great Plains Manufacturing Inc....785 263-2486
1100 Nw 8th St Abilene (67410) ***(G-34)***
Great Plains Manufacturing Inc....785 825-1509
1733 Dewey St Salina (67401) ***(G-10519)***
Great Plains Manufacturing Inc....785 373-4145
607 Main Tipton (67485) ***(G-12248)***
Great Plains Manufacturing Inc....785 472-3508
1607 State St Ellsworth (67439) ***(G-1675)***
Great Plains Manufacturing Inc....785 823-2255
1935 E North St Salina (67401) ***(G-10520)***
Great Plains Manufacturing Inc....785 525-6128
240 S Greeley Ave Lucas (67648) ***(G-6471)***
Great Plains Mobile HM Movers....620 463-2420
209 N Burrton Ave Burrton (67020) ***(G-648)***
Great Plains Mutual Insur Co....785 825-5531
124 Iowa Ave Salina (67401) ***(G-10521)***
Great Plains of Kiowa County, Greensburg *Also called Great Plains Hlth Aliance Inc* ***(G-2675)***
Great Plains of Sabetha Inc....785 284-2121
14th And Oregon Sts Sabetha (66534) ***(G-10312)***
Great Plains Roofg Shtmtl Inc....913 677-4679
2820 Roe Ln Ste O Kansas City (66103) ***(G-4046)***
Great Plains Smith Co Inc....785 282-6845
921 E Highway 36 Smith Center (66967) ***(G-12034)***
Great Plains Spca....913 831-7722
5428 Antioch Dr Merriam (66202) ***(G-7093)***
Great Plains Supply Inc....913 492-1520
13891 W 101st St Shawnee Mission (66215) ***(G-11400)***
Great Plains Trucking, Salina *Also called Great Plains Manufacturing Inc* ***(G-10520)***

Great Plains Trucking Inc 785 823-2261
1621 Dewey St Salina (67401) ***(G-10522)***
Great Plains Trust Company 913 831-7999
7700 Shawnee Miksion Pkwy Overland Park (66202) ***(G-8775)***
Great Plains Ventures Inc (PA) 316 684-1540
3504 N Great Plains Dr # 100 Wichita (67220) ***(G-14505)***
Great Plins Gas Cmpression LLC 620 544-3578
210 E 1st St Hugoton (67951) ***(G-3164)***
Great Plins Trnspration Museum 316 263-0944
700 E Douglas Ave Wichita (67202) ***(G-14506)***
Great Point Health Alliance, Wichita *Also called Midwest Health Services Inc* ***(G-15095)***
Great Salt Plins Midstream LLC 316 262-2819
8301 E 21st St N Ste 370 Wichita (67206) ***(G-14507)***
Great Southern Bank 620 365-3101
119 E Madison Ave Iola (66749) ***(G-3605)***
Great Southern Bank 620 421-5700
1900 Main St Parsons (67357) ***(G-9689)***
Great Southern Bank 913 557-4311
1 S Pearl St Paola (66071) ***(G-9563)***
Great Western Bank 913 248-3300
10610 Shawnee Mission Pkw Shawnee Mission (66203) ***(G-11401)***
Great Western Dining Svc Inc 620 792-9224
245 Ne 30 Rd Great Bend (67530) ***(G-2585)***
Great Western Mfg Co Inc 913 682-2291
2017 S 4th St Leavenworth (66048) ***(G-5247)***
Great Western Pet Supply, Lawrence *Also called Lawrence Feed & Farm Sup Inc* ***(G-4966)***
Great Western Tire of Dodge Cy 620 225-1343
200 W Frontview St Dodge City (67801) ***(G-1367)***
Great Wolf Kansas City, Kansas City *Also called Great Wolf Kansas Spe LLC* ***(G-4047)***
Great Wolf Kansas Spe LLC 913 299-7001
10401 Cabela Dr Kansas City (66111) ***(G-4047)***
Great Wolf Lodge Kansas Cy LLC 913 299-7001
10401 Cabela Dr Kansas City (66111) ***(G-4048)***
Great-West Financial Retiremen 847 857-3000
11500 Outlook St Overland Park (66211) ***(G-8776)***
Greater Kansas Chapter, Overland Park *Also called March of Dimes Inc* ***(G-8988)***
Greater Kansas City Division, Shawnee Mission *Also called American Heart Association Ka* ***(G-11104)***
Greater Topeka Commerce 785 234-2644
719 S Kansas Ave 100 Topeka (66603) ***(G-12646)***
GREATER WICHITA CON & VISITORS, Wichita *Also called Wichita Convention Tourism Bur* ***(G-15991)***
Greater Wichita Partnr Inc 316 500-6650
501 E Douglas Ave Wichita (67202) ***(G-14508)***
Greater Wichita YMCA, Wichita *Also called Young Mens Christian Associa* ***(G-16093)***
Greatwhite Logistics, Hutchinson *Also called Brisk Transportation* ***(G-3225)***
Greeley Cnty Hosp & Long TRM C 785 852-4230
104 E 4th Sharon Springs (67758) ***(G-10898)***
Greeley Cnty Hosp & Long TRM C (PA) 620 376-4225
302 E Greeley Ave Tribune (67879) ***(G-13268)***
GREELEY COUNTY FAMILY PRACTICE, Tribune *Also called Greeley County Health Svcs Inc* ***(G-13270)***
Greeley County Family Practice 620 376-4251
321 E Harper St Tribune (67879) ***(G-13269)***
Greeley County Health Svcs Inc 620 376-4221
506 3rd St Tribune (67879) ***(G-13270)***
Greeley County Republican 620 376-4264
507 Broadway Ave Tribune (67879) ***(G-13271)***
Greeley Seed Co, Greeley *Also called Donohue Ranch* ***(G-2665)***
Green Clean Kc LLC 913 499-7106
8220 Travis St Ste 210 Overland Park (66204) ***(G-8777)***
Green DOT, Emporia *Also called DOT Green Bioplastics Inc* ***(G-1730)***
Green DOT, Onaga *Also called DOT Green Bioplastics LLC* ***(G-8175)***
Green Earth, Wichita *Also called Green Hills Inc* ***(G-14509)***
Green Energy Products LLC 316 416-4106
250 E Industrial Dr Sedgwick (67135) ***(G-10850)***
Green Environmental Services, Erie *Also called John F Hafner LLC* ***(G-1859)***
Green Expectations Ldscpg Inc 913 897-8076
1910 S 74th St Kansas City (66106) ***(G-4049)***
Green Hills Inc 316 686-7673
3623 E Harry St Bldg 1 Wichita (67218) ***(G-14509)***
Green Lantern Inc 316 721-9242
10510 W 21st St N Wichita (67205) ***(G-14510)***
Green Lawn Inc 913 393-2238
6906 Martindale Rd Shawnee (66218) ***(G-10965)***
Green Line Inc 620 896-7372
851 N State Road 14 Harper (67058) ***(G-2722)***
Green Meadows Lawn Landscaping 316 788-0282
7800 E Lyons Cir Derby (67037) ***(G-1250)***
Green Medical Group 316 691-3937
655 N Woodlawn St Wichita (67208) ***(G-14511)***
Green Plains Cattle Co LLC 620 624-6296
19016 Road I Kismet (67859) ***(G-4630)***
Green Plains Inc 620 375-2255
857 N Highway 25 Leoti (67861) ***(G-6252)***
Green Product Solutions LLC 913 633-1274
8310 Reeds Rd Overland Park (66207) ***(G-8778)***
Green Ready Mix of Missouri, Shawnee Mission *Also called Pennys Concrete Inc* ***(G-11724)***
Green Vision Group, Wichita *Also called Green Medical Group* ***(G-14511)***
Greenamyre Construction LLC 913 772-1776
2500 S 2nd St Leavenworth (66048) ***(G-5248)***
Greenamyre Rentals Inc 913 651-9717
2500 S 2nd St Leavenworth (66048) ***(G-5249)***
Greenbrier Companies Inc 866 722-7068
100 Ne Woodruff Ave Topeka (66616) ***(G-12647)***
Greenbrier Rail Services, Osawatomie *Also called Gunderson Rail Services LLC* ***(G-8194)***
Greenbrier Railcar LLC 913 342-0010
1109 S 12th St Kansas City (66105) ***(G-4050)***
Greenbrier Repair & Services, Topeka *Also called Greenbrier Companies Inc* ***(G-12647)***
Greenbush, Girard *Also called Southeast Kans Educatn Svc Ctr* ***(G-2418)***
Greenhouse Effect Inc 913 492-7407
7931 Darnell Ln Shawnee Mission (66215) ***(G-11402)***
Greenleaf & Brooks Smith 620 624-6266
400 N Washington Ave Liberal (67901) ***(G-6315)***
Greenpoint Cnstr Dem Proc Ctr 785 234-6000
1405 Se Madison St Topeka (66607) ***(G-12648)***
Greensburg Family Practice PA 620 723-2127
721 W Kansas Ave Greensburg (67054) ***(G-2677)***
Greensburg State Bank 620 723-2131
240 S Main St Greensburg (67054) ***(G-2678)***
Greentouch Lawn Service, Topeka *Also called Cut-N-Edge Inc* ***(G-12541)***
Greenwich Hotel LLC 316 925-5100
1236 N Greenwich Rd Wichita (67206) ***(G-14512)***
Greenwood Cnty Hosp Foundation 620 583-5909
100 W 16th St Eureka (67045) ***(G-1888)***
Greenwood Cnty Rur Wtr Dst 1 620 583-7181
106 E 3rd St Eureka (67045) ***(G-1889)***
Greenwood County Road & Bridge, Eureka *Also called County of Greenwood* ***(G-1882)***
Greer, Gregory G, Wichita *Also called South Wichita Family Medicine* ***(G-15620)***
Greg Bair Track Hoe Svc Inc 913 897-1243
15300 Broadmoor St Shawnee Mission (66223) ***(G-11403)***
Greg Cohen DDS 785 273-2350
1125 Sw Gage Blvd Ste A Topeka (66604) ***(G-12649)***
Greg E Ross Drywall 785 478-9557
7934 Sw 10th Ave Topeka (66615) ***(G-12650)***
Greg Ketzner 913 334-6770
7860 Washington Ave Kansas City (66112) ***(G-4051)***
Greg Orscheln Trnsp Co 913 371-1260
9220 Marshall Dr Lenexa (66215) ***(G-5884)***
Greg Smith Enterprises Inc 913 543-7614
2540 S 88th St Kansas City (66111) ***(G-4052)***
Gregg Tire Co Inc (PA) 785 233-4156
300 Sw 6th Ave Topeka (66603) ***(G-12651)***
Gregg Tire Co Inc 785 233-4156
300 Sw 6th Ave Topeka (66603) ***(G-12652)***
Greggpiercy Inc 913 469-9274
12400 Blue Valley Pkwy Overland Park (66213) ***(G-8779)***
Gregory A Scott Inc 913 677-0414
6320 Kansas Ave Kansas City (66111) ***(G-4053)***
Greif Inc 620 221-2330
7604 Railroad Ave Winfield (67156) ***(G-16145)***
Grene Vision Group, Wichita *Also called Donald B Scrafford* ***(G-14225)***
Grene Vision Group, Hutchinson *Also called Brian Strange* ***(G-3222)***
Grene Vision Group LLC 316 721-2701
3910 N Ridge Rd Wichita (67205) ***(G-14513)***
Grene Vision Group LLC 316 722-8883
834 1277 N Maize Rd Wichita (67212) ***(G-14514)***
Grene Vision Group LLC (PA) 316 691-4444
1851 N Webb Rd Wichita (67206) ***(G-14515)***
Grene Vision Group LLC 316 684-5158
655 N Woodlawn St Wichita (67208) ***(G-14516)***
Grenola Senior Citizens 620 358-3601
121 N Main St Grenola (67346) ***(G-2686)***
Gressel Oil Field Service LLC (PA) 316 524-1225
9801 S Meridian St Peck (67120) ***(G-9763)***
Greteman Group Inc 316 263-1004
1425 E Douglas Ave Fl 2 Wichita (67211) ***(G-14517)***
Grey Mountain Partners LLC 785 776-9482
1822 Fair Ln Manhattan (66502) ***(G-6646)***
Greyhound Hall of Fame 785 263-3000
407 S Buckeye Ave Abilene (67410) ***(G-35)***
Greyhound Lines Inc 785 827-9754
671 Westport Blvd Salina (67401) ***(G-10523)***
Griffin Wheel Company 913 299-2223
7111 Griffin Rd Kansas City (66111) ***(G-4054)***
Griffith Developement 316 686-1831
8909 E Harry St Wichita (67207) ***(G-14518)***
Griffith Lumber & Hardware, Manhattan *Also called Griffith Lumber Company Inc* ***(G-6647)***
Griffith Lumber Company Inc (PA) 785 776-4104
820 Levee Dr Manhattan (66502) ***(G-6647)***
Griffith Steel Erection Inc 316 941-4455
1355 S Anna St Wichita (67209) ***(G-14519)***
Grigsby, Keith M DDS, Leavenworth *Also called Heartland Dental Group PA* ***(G-5251)***
Grimmett Masonry Inc 620 342-6582
2026 W 6th Ave Emporia (66801) ***(G-1765)***

A L P H A B E T I C

Grimmett Scott Masonry, Emporia *Also called Grimmett Masonry Inc* ***(G-1765)***
Grin Eye Care, Olathe *Also called Milton B Grin MD PA* ***(G-7901)***
Grinnell Locker Plant Inc....785 824-3400
108 S Adams Grinnell (67738) ***(G-2693)***
Grisell Memorial Hospital Assn (PA)....785 731-2231
210 S Vermont Ave Ransom (67572) ***(G-10193)***
Grisell Memorial Hospital Assn....785 731-2231
210 S Vermont Ave Ransom (67572) ***(G-10194)***
Griswold Home Care, Overland Park *Also called Rooney Enterprises Corporation* ***(G-9257)***
Grizzly Bowl, El Dorado *Also called Aj Investors LLC* ***(G-1526)***
Groendyke Transport, Hutchinson *Also called V & M Transport Inc* ***(G-3478)***
Groendyke Transport Inc....316 755-1266
3350 N Ohio St Wichita (67219) ***(G-14520)***
Groendyke Transport Inc....913 621-2200
299 E Donovan Rd Kansas City (66115) ***(G-4055)***
Gross PHD Judith M S....913 645-2437
2737 N 68th St Kansas City (66109) ***(G-4056)***
Gross Real Estate, Fort Scott *Also called John C Gross III* ***(G-1976)***
Groupsource Gpo LLC (PA)....913 888-9191
1570 S Mahaffie Cir Olathe (66062) ***(G-7741)***
Growing Futures Early Educ....913 649-6057
8155 Santa Fe Dr Overland Park (66204) ***(G-8780)***
Grs, Emporia *Also called Glendo LLC* ***(G-1763)***
Grs, Atchison *Also called Gbw Railcar Services LLC* ***(G-230)***
Grubb Ellis/The Winbury Group, Lawrence *Also called Winbury Group of KC LLC* ***(G-5187)***
Grundfos CBS Inc....281 994-2830
11936 W 119th St Ste 232 Overland Park (66213) ***(G-8781)***
Gs Enterprises Inc....913 543-7614
51 Osage Ave Kansas City (66105) ***(G-4057)***
Gsi Engineering LLC....316 554-0725
4503 E 47th St S Wichita (67210) ***(G-14521)***
Gsi Engineering LLC....515 270-6542
4503 E 47th St S Wichita (67210) ***(G-14522)***
Gsi Engineering Nthrn Div LLC....316 554-0725
4503 E 47th St S Wichita (67210) ***(G-14523)***
Gsi-Flo, Olathe *Also called Global Systems Incorporated* ***(G-7734)***
GSM Sales LLC....816 674-1066
4110 W 47th Ter Roeland Park (66205) ***(G-10223)***
Gsr Construction Inc....785 749-1770
932 Msschsetts St Ste 304 Lawrence (66044) ***(G-4883)***
GSSB, Garnett *Also called Goppert State Service Bank* ***(G-2375)***
Gt Kansas LLC....913 266-1106
12321 Metcalf Ave Shawnee Mission (66213) ***(G-11404)***
Gt Mfg Inc....785 632-2151
324 5th St Clay Center (67432) ***(G-867)***
Guaranty State Bnk Tr Bloit Ka (HQ)....785 738-3501
201 S Mill St Beloit (67420) ***(G-485)***
Guardian Business Services....785 823-1635
141 S 4th St Salina (67401) ***(G-10524)***
Guardian Title & Trust Company....620 223-3330
8621 E 21st St N Ste 150 Wichita (67206) ***(G-14524)***
Guardsmark LLC....316 440-6646
144 N Oliver Ave Ste 301 Wichita (67208) ***(G-14525)***
Gudenkauf, Pam CPA, Russell *Also called Goodencoff & Malone Inc* ***(G-10276)***
Guerrilla Marketing Inc....800 946-9150
1027 Washington Rd Ste D Newton (67114) ***(G-7353)***
Guest Communications Corp....913 888-1217
15009 W 101st Ter Shawnee Mission (66215) ***(G-11405)***
Guest Home Estates (PA)....620 431-7115
1910 E Centennial Dr Pittsburg (66762) ***(G-9869)***
Guest Home Estates....620 879-5199
400 S Mcgee St Caney (67333) ***(G-670)***
Guest Home Estates VI....620 223-1620
737 Heylman St Fort Scott (66701) ***(G-1975)***
Guidance Center....913 367-1593
201 Main St Atchison (66002) ***(G-233)***
Guild Mortgage Company....316 749-2789
300 N Main St Ste 200 Wichita (67202) ***(G-14526)***
Guilfoyle Roofing....785 233-9315
3432 Nw Lwer Silver Lk Rd Topeka (66618) ***(G-12653)***
Gulfeagle Supply, Wichita *Also called Gulfside Supply Inc* ***(G-14527)***
Gulfside Supply Inc....913 384-9610
5660 Inland Dr Kansas City (66106) ***(G-4058)***
Gulfside Supply Inc....316 941-9322
2424 S Sheridan St Wichita (67217) ***(G-14527)***
Gulick Drilling....620 583-5804
910 E 7th St Eureka (67045) ***(G-1890)***
Gunderson Rail Services LLC....913 827-3536
610 Kelly Ave Osawatomie (66064) ***(G-8194)***
Gunter Construction Company....913 362-7844
520 Division St Kansas City (66103) ***(G-4059)***
Gunter Pest Management Inc....913 397-0220
13505 S Mur Len Rd Olathe (66062) ***(G-7742)***
Gunze Plas & Engrg Corp Amer....913 829-5577
1400 S Hamilton Cir Olathe (66061) ***(G-7743)***
Gupta Ganesh....913 451-0000
10730 Nall Ave Overland Park (66211) ***(G-8782)***
Guptons Pets & Supplies Inc....316 682-8111
2815 S George Wash Blvd Wichita (67210) ***(G-14528)***
Gurney, Lawrence M, Wichita *Also called Lee Wilson & Gurney* ***(G-14944)***
Gust Orothondtcs PA G Morrison....620 662-3255
1000 E 30th Ave Hutchinson (67502) ***(G-3306)***
Gust Orthodontics....316 283-1090
504 N Main St Newton (67114) ***(G-7354)***
Gustafson Concrete Inc....785 238-7747
7115 Davis Creek Rd Junction City (66441) ***(G-3697)***
Guthridge/Nighswonger Corp (PA)....316 264-7900
1702 S Laura Ave Wichita (67211) ***(G-14529)***
Guthrie, Richard A MD, Mount Hope *Also called Mid-America Diabetes Assoc PA* ***(G-7206)***
GVL Polymers Inc....320 693-8411
8515 N Hesston Rd Hesston (67062) ***(G-2991)***
Gwaltney Inc (PA)....620 225-2622
100 E Mcartor St Dodge City (67801) ***(G-1368)***
Gwaltney Inc....785 537-8008
9300 E Us Highway 24 Manhattan (66502) ***(G-6648)***
Gyp Hills Roustabout LLC....620 886-0931
318 W Kansas Ave Medicine Lodge (67104) ***(G-7062)***
H & B Cable Service Inc....785 252-4000
108 N Main St Holyrood (67450) ***(G-3114)***
H & B Communications Inc (PA)....620 562-3598
108 N Main St Holyrood (67450) ***(G-3115)***
H & B Video, Holyrood *Also called H & B Cable Service Inc* ***(G-3114)***
H & C Insulation Co Inc....316 522-0236
418 W 54th St S Wichita (67217) ***(G-14530)***
H & P Inc....785 263-4183
1101 Portland Ave Abilene (67410) ***(G-36)***
H & R Block, Wichita *Also called H&R Block Inc* ***(G-14535)***
H & R Block, Wichita *Also called H&R Block Inc* ***(G-14536)***
H & R Block, Emporia *Also called Shemar Inc* ***(G-1827)***
H & R Block, Ottawa *Also called H&R Block Inc* ***(G-8276)***
H & R Block, Salina *Also called H&R Block Inc* ***(G-10527)***
H & R Block, Wichita *Also called H&R Block Inc* ***(G-14537)***
H & R Block, Kansas City *Also called H&R Block Inc* ***(G-4060)***
H & R Block, Great Bend *Also called H&R Block Inc* ***(G-2587)***
H & R Block, Dodge City *Also called Dave Tarter* ***(G-1339)***
H & R Block, Manhattan *Also called H&R Block Inc* ***(G-6649)***
H & R Block, Baxter Springs *Also called Sharon Miller* ***(G-412)***
H & R Block, Hays *Also called J L D J Inc* ***(G-2855)***
H & R Block, Newton *Also called H&R Block Inc* ***(G-7355)***
H & R Block, Cherryvale *Also called H&R Block Inc* ***(G-809)***
H & R Block, Kansas City *Also called H&R Block Inc* ***(G-4061)***
H & R Block....316 321-6960
1430 W Central Ave El Dorado (67042) ***(G-1565)***
H & R Block....620 421-2850
1705 Parsons Plz Parsons (67357) ***(G-9690)***
H & R Block Inc....785 271-0706
2900 Sw Oakley Ave Ste I Topeka (66614) ***(G-12654)***
H & R Block Tax Services LLC....316 775-7331
299 W 7th Ave Augusta (67010) ***(G-322)***
H & R Block Tax Services LLC....913 648-1040
15254 W 119th St Olathe (66062) ***(G-7744)***
H & R Block Tax Services LLC....620 231-5563
101 W 29th St Ste H Pittsburg (66762) ***(G-9870)***
H & R Block Tax Services LLC....785 749-1649
2104 W 25th St Lawrence (66047) ***(G-4884)***
H & R Lawn & Landscape Inc....913 897-9705
6735 W 207th St Bucyrus (66013) ***(G-598)***
H & R Parts Co Inc....316 942-6984
3066 S Hoover Rd Wichita (67215) ***(G-14531)***
H & R Plumbing Inc....785 233-4427
1300 Se Monroe St Topeka (66612) ***(G-12655)***
H B J Farms Inc....785 595-3236
2467 Highway 7 White Cloud (66094) ***(G-13568)***
H B Landscaping & Septic Tanks....620 793-3985
323 N Washington Ave Great Bend (67530) ***(G-2586)***
H C Davis Sons Mfg Co....913 422-3000
416 E Front St Bonner Springs (66012) ***(G-554)***
H J Born Stone Inc (PA)....316 838-7788
30994 141st Rd Arkansas City (67005) ***(G-158)***
H K W Oil Company Inc....785 483-6185
Graves Blvd Salina (67401) ***(G-10525)***
H M Dunn Company Inc....316 522-5426
4201 S 119th St W Wichita (67215) ***(G-14532)***
H M Dunn Company Inc....314 535-6684
1804 W 2nd St N Wichita (67203) ***(G-14533)***
H M Dunn Company Inc....316 522-5426
4201 S 119th St W Wichita (67215) ***(G-14534)***
H P A, Wichita *Also called Historic Presrvtn Aliance of W* ***(G-14617)***
H Schwaller & Sons Inc....785 628-6162
1500 Vine St Hays (67601) ***(G-2822)***
H W Lochner Inc....785 827-3603
1823 S Ohio St Salina (67401) ***(G-10526)***
H W Lochner Inc....816 945-5840
16105 W 113th St Ste 107 Lenexa (66219) ***(G-5885)***

H&H Amusement, Wichita *Also called Roller City Inc* ***(G-15477)***
H&H Design & Manufacturing LLC 620 421-9800
304 S 53rd St Parsons (67357) ***(G-9691)***
H&R Block, Liberal *Also called Bob Thornton* ***(G-6285)***
H&R Block Inc 316 636-4009
1223 N Rock Rd Ste A100 Wichita (67206) ***(G-14535)***
H&R Block Inc 316 267-8257
2561 S Seneca St Ste 30 Wichita (67217) ***(G-14536)***
H&R Block Inc 913 837-5418
2334 S Princeton St Ottawa (66067) ***(G-8276)***
H&R Block Inc 785 827-4253
1219 W Crawford St Ste A Salina (67401) ***(G-10527)***
H&R Block Inc 316 683-4211
534 S Rock Rd Wichita (67207) ***(G-14537)***
H&R Block Inc 913 788-7779
5008 State Ave 5010 Kansas City (66102) ***(G-4060)***
H&R Block Inc 620 793-9361
2023 Lakin Ave Great Bend (67530) ***(G-2587)***
H&R Block Inc 785 776-7531
634 Tuttle Creek Blvd Manhattan (66502) ***(G-6649)***
H&R Block Inc 316 283-1495
105 E Broadway St Newton (67114) ***(G-7355)***
H&R Block Inc 620 336-2750
308c E Main St Cherryvale (67335) ***(G-809)***
H&R Block Inc 913 788-5222
7616 State Ave Kansas City (66112) ***(G-4061)***
H-40 Drilling Inc 316 773-3640
5735 Sw Walstead Medicine Lodge (67104) ***(G-7063)***
H2 Oil Field Services 620 792-7115
705 Harrison St Great Bend (67530) ***(G-2588)***
H2 Plains LLC 785 798-3995
10500 E Berkeley Square P Wichita (67206) ***(G-14538)***
Haag & Decker Oil, Topeka *Also called Haag Oil Co LLC* ***(G-12656)***
Haag Decker Oil Company, Topeka *Also called Haag Oil Company LLC* ***(G-12657)***
Haag Inc (PA) 785 256-2311
7233 Sw 85th St Auburn (66402) ***(G-295)***
Haag Oil Co LLC 785 357-0270
326 Se 15th St Topeka (66607) ***(G-12656)***
Haag Oil Company LLC 785 357-0270
326 Se 15th St Topeka (66607) ***(G-12657)***
Haarslev Inc 785 527-5641
537 28th St Belleville (66935) ***(G-457)***
Haas Wilkerson & Wohlberg Inc (PA) 913 432-4400
4300 Shawnee Mission Pkwy Fairway (66205) ***(G-1909)***
Haas & Wilkerson Ins Agency, Shawnee Mission *Also called W Ralph Wilkerson Jr Inc* ***(G-11986)***
Haas & Wilkerson Insurange, Fairway *Also called Haas Wilkerson & Wohlberg Inc* ***(G-1909)***
Haas Metal Engineering, Topeka *Also called M E H Inc* ***(G-12855)***
Habco Inc 785 823-0440
248 E Berg Rd Salina (67401) ***(G-10528)***
Habitat For Hmanity Ellis Cnty 785 623-4200
1316 Donald Dr Hays (67601) ***(G-2823)***
Hachmeister Service Center LLC 785 567-4818
22623 Road W6 Lenora (67645) ***(G-6243)***
Hackney & Sons, Independence *Also called VT Hackney Inc* ***(G-3571)***
Haddock Computer Center, Wichita *Also called Haddock Corporation* ***(G-14539)***
Haddock Corporation (PA) 316 558-3849
8625 E 37th St N Ste 104 Wichita (67226) ***(G-14539)***
HADLEY DAY CARE CENTER, Hutchinson *Also called Hadley Day Care Ctr Inc* ***(G-3307)***
Hadley Day Care Ctr Inc 620 663-9622
1010 E 5th Ave Hutchinson (67501) ***(G-3307)***
Hadley Transit LLC 620 726-5853
12287 Nw Boyer Rd Burns (66840) ***(G-647)***
Hahner Foreman & Harness LLC (PA) 316 264-0306
423 N Saint Francis Ave Wichita (67202) ***(G-14540)***
Hail Signature Tech LLC 913 620-4928
2720 W 161st Ter Stilwell (66085) ***(G-12150)***
Hair Affair'e Beauty Salon, Salina *Also called Hair Affaire* ***(G-10529)***
Hair Affaire 785 827-0445
808 E Crawford St Salina (67401) ***(G-10529)***
Hair Club For Men Ltd Inc 888 888-8986
7500 College Blvd Ste 600 Overland Park (66210) ***(G-8783)***
Hair Connection 316 685-7213
2424 N Woodlawn Blvd # 105 Wichita (67220) ***(G-14541)***
Hair Cutting Company 316 283-0532
526 N Main St Newton (67114) ***(G-7356)***
Hair Design Company 913 897-4776
7936 W 151st St Overland Park (66223) ***(G-8784)***
Hair E Clips Ltd 620 793-9050
1914 Main St Great Bend (67530) ***(G-2589)***
Hair Experts 785 776-4455
1323 Anderson Ave Manhattan (66502) ***(G-6650)***
Hair Experts Design Team, Manhattan *Also called Hair Experts* ***(G-6650)***
Hair Experts Design Team 785 841-6886
529 Sandpiper Dr Lawrence (66044) ***(G-4885)***
Hair Experts Salon & Spa, Lawrence *Also called Hair Experts Design Team* ***(G-4885)***
Hair Force 316 684-3361
1113 S Rock Rd Wichita (67207) ***(G-14542)***
Hair Loft 785 827-2306
1330 W Crawford St Salina (67401) ***(G-10530)***
Hair Loft Salon, Salina *Also called Hair Loft* ***(G-10530)***
Hair Productions Inc 785 273-2881
4002 Sw Huntoon St Topeka (66604) ***(G-12658)***
Hair Professionals, Shawnee Mission *Also called Jhon-Josephsons Salon* ***(G-11490)***
Hair Shop & Retailing Center, Olathe *Also called Hair Shop West Inc* ***(G-7746)***
Hair Shop & Retailing Center 913 397-9888
16140 W 135th St Olathe (66062) ***(G-7745)***
Hair Shop West Inc 913 829-4868
131 N Parker St Olathe (66061) ***(G-7746)***
Hair U Wear, Lenexa *Also called Hairuwear Inc* ***(G-5886)***
Hair Wear and Co 785 625-2875
2703 Hall St Ste A2 Hays (67601) ***(G-2824)***
Hairem of Olathe LLC 913 829-1260
12805 S Mur Len Rd Ste C5 Olathe (66062) ***(G-7747)***
Hairuwear Inc (PA) 954 835-2200
14865 W 105th St Lenexa (66215) ***(G-5886)***
Haivala Concrete Tools Inc 316 263-1683
1330 S Walnut St Wichita (67213) ***(G-14543)***
Hajoca Corporation 316 262-2471
711 N Hydraulic St Wichita (67214) ***(G-14544)***
Hajoca Corporation 785 825-1333
333 N Front St Salina (67401) ***(G-10531)***
Haldex Brake Products Corp 620 365-5275
2702 N State St Iola (66749) ***(G-3606)***
Haley & Aldrich Inc 913 693-1900
11020 King St Ste 450 Overland Park (66210) ***(G-8785)***
Half Price Bks Rec Mgzines Inc 913 829-9959
15309 W 119th St Olathe (66062) ***(G-7748)***
Halfpricebannerscom Inc 913 441-9299
8130 Monticello Ter Shawnee (66227) ***(G-10966)***
Haling's Greenhouse, Shawnee Mission *Also called Halings Florist* ***(G-11406)***
Halings Florist 913 642-5034
6303 W 75th St Shawnee Mission (66204) ***(G-11406)***
Hall Brothers Inc (PA) 785 562-2386
1196 Pony Express Hwy Marysville (66508) ***(G-6890)***
Hall Chiropractic Center 785 242-6444
10216 W 87th St Overland Park (66212) ***(G-8786)***
Hall Industrial Dev LLC 316 264-7268
1221 E Murdock St Ste D Wichita (67214) ***(G-14545)***
Hall Industrial Services Inc 316 945-4255
1221 E Murdock St Wichita (67214) ***(G-14546)***
Hall Publications Inc 785 232-8600
630 S Kansas Ave Lowr Topeka (66603) ***(G-12659)***
Hall Steel & Fabrication Inc 316 263-4222
1221 E Murdock St Wichita (67214) ***(G-14547)***
Hallauer Oil Co Inc 785 364-3140
19425 P Rd Holton (66436) ***(G-3094)***
Hallbrook Country Club 913 345-9292
11200 Overbrook Rd Leawood (66211) ***(G-5418)***
Hallcon Corporation (PA) 913 890-6105
14325 W 95th St Lenexa (66215) ***(G-5887)***
Hallcon Crew Transport, Lenexa *Also called Hallcon Corporation* ***(G-5887)***
Hallmark Cards Incorporated 785 843-9050
101 Mcdonald Dr Lawrence (66044) ***(G-4886)***
Hallowell Manufacturing LLC 620 597-2552
3600 Nw 74th St Columbus (66725) ***(G-1077)***
Halstd-Bntley Unfied Schl Dst (PA) 316 835-2641
521 W 6th St Halstead (67056) ***(G-2700)***
Halstead Hlth & Rehabilitation, Halstead *Also called Midwest Health Services Inc* ***(G-2703)***
Halstead Place Assisted Living, Halstead *Also called Halstead Place Inc* ***(G-2701)***
Halstead Place Inc 316 830-2424
715 W 6th St Halstead (67056) ***(G-2701)***
Halstead Sixty Plus Club, Halstead *Also called Senior Center* ***(G-2704)***
Halstontine Corp 913 780-2171
15425 Metcalf Ave Overland Park (66223) ***(G-8787)***
Hamilton & Wilson DDS (PA) 785 272-3722
2235 Sw Westport Dr Topeka (66614) ***(G-12660)***
Hamilton Bob Plumbing Htg & AC, Overland Park *Also called Robert J Hamilton Inc* ***(G-9250)***
Hamilton Cnty Hospital Extnded, Syracuse *Also called County of Hamilton* ***(G-12223)***
Hamilton County Hospital 620 384-7461
700 N Huser St Syracuse (67878) ***(G-12227)***
Hamilton Laughlin, Topeka *Also called Eric K Johnson* ***(G-12581)***
Hamm Inc (HQ) 785 597-5111
609 Perry Pl Perry (66073) ***(G-9768)***
Hamm Inc (HQ) 785 597-5111
609 Perry Pl Perry (66073) ***(G-9769)***
Hamm Inc 785 235-6568
2450 Nw Water Works Dr Topeka (66606) ***(G-12661)***
Hamm Inc 785 242-1045
745 N Locust St Ottawa (66067) ***(G-8277)***
Hamm Inc 785 233-7263
6721 Nw 17th St Topeka (66618) ***(G-12662)***
Hamm Asphalt, Perry *Also called Hamm Inc* ***(G-9768)***
Hamm Asphalt Inc 785 597-5421
Hwy 24 & 59 Jct Perry (66073) ***(G-9770)***

ALPHABETIC

Hamm Maintenance Shop, Perry *Also called Hamm Asphalt Inc* ***(G-9770)***
Hamm Sanitary Landfill, Lawrence *Also called N R Hamm Quarry Inc* ***(G-5035)***
Hammel Scale Co Inc (PA)....316 264-1358
1530 N Mosley Ave Wichita (67214) ***(G-14548)***
Hammel Scale Kansas City Inc (PA)....913 321-5428
612 Kansas Ave Kansas City (66105) ***(G-4062)***
Hammer Realty Group, Salina *Also called Kan Tex Hospitality Inc* ***(G-10561)***
Hammersmith Mfg & Sales Inc (PA)....785 486-2121
401 Central Ave Horton (66439) ***(G-3126)***
Hammersmith Mfg & Sales Inc....785 364-4140
1000 Vermont Ave Holton (66436) ***(G-3095)***
Hammersmith Mfg & Sales Inc....913 338-0754
10801 Mastin St Ste 1050 Overland Park (66210) ***(G-8788)***
Hamon Cooling Towers Division, Overland Park *Also called SPX Cooling Technologies Inc* ***(G-9345)***
Hampel Oil Inc....913 321-0139
2920 Fairfax Trfy Kansas City (66115) ***(G-4063)***
Hampel Oil Distributors Inc (PA)....316 529-1162
3727 S West St Wichita (67217) ***(G-14549)***
Hampel Oil Distributors Inc....800 530-5848
1245 N West St Wichita (67203) ***(G-14550)***
Hampton & Royce Lc....785 827-7251
119 W Iron Ave Ste 1000 Salina (67401) ***(G-10532)***
Hampton Hydraulics, Great Bend *Also called Great Bend Industries Inc* ***(G-2581)***
Hampton Hydraulics Llc....620 792-4368
8701 6th St Great Bend (67530) ***(G-2590)***
Hampton Inn, Shawnee Mission *Also called Shawnee Inn Inc* ***(G-11852)***
Hampton Inn, Olathe *Also called Chaudhrys Investment Group Inc* ***(G-7590)***
Hampton Inn, Shawnee Mission *Also called Rhw Management Inc* ***(G-11800)***
Hampton Inn, Wichita *Also called S & B Motels Inc* ***(G-15499)***
Hampton Inn, Merriam *Also called Kansas Global Hotel LLC* ***(G-7098)***
Hampton Inn, Hutchinson *Also called Maa Santoshi LLC* ***(G-3361)***
Hampton Inn, Topeka *Also called Shree-Guru Investments Inc* ***(G-13071)***
Hampton Inn, Lawrence *Also called Magers Lodgings Inc* ***(G-5006)***
Hampton Inn....316 636-5594
2433 N Greenwich Rd Wichita (67226) ***(G-14551)***
Hampton Inn....620 272-0454
2505 E Crestway Dr Garden City (67846) ***(G-2191)***
Hampton Inn....785 460-2333
1000 E Willow Ave Colby (67701) ***(G-1010)***
Hampton Inn....913 328-1400
1400 Village West Pkwy Kansas City (66111) ***(G-4064)***
Hampton Inn....785 228-0111
1515 Sw Arrowhead Rd Topeka (66604) ***(G-12663)***
Hampton Inn By Hlton Lvenworth, Leavenworth *Also called Crystal Hospitality LLC* ***(G-5229)***
Hampton Inn Derby, Derby *Also called Derby Hotel Inc* ***(G-1236)***
Hampton Inn Gdnr Cnference Ctr, Gardner *Also called Gardner Hospitality LLC* ***(G-2349)***
Hampton Inn Hays-North I-70....785 621-4444
4002 General Hays Rd Hays (67601) ***(G-2825)***
Hampton Inn Junction City....785 579-4633
1039 S Washington St Junction City (66441) ***(G-3698)***
Hampton Inn Kansas City Arprt, Overland Park *Also called Hit Portfolio I Hil Trs LLC* ***(G-8816)***
Hampton Inn Suites....620 604-0699
508 Hotel Dr Liberal (67901) ***(G-6316)***
Hampton Inn Wichita Northwest, Wichita *Also called HCW Wichita Hotel LLC* ***(G-14573)***
Hampton Inns LLC....785 823-9800
401 W Schilling Rd Salina (67401) ***(G-10533)***
Hams Pool Service LLC....913 927-0882
4400 W 97th St Overland Park (66207) ***(G-8789)***
Hand Center PA....316 688-5656
625 N Carriage Pkwy # 125 Wichita (67208) ***(G-14552)***
Hand Controls & Van Lifts, Wichita *Also called Easy Money Pawn Shop Inc* ***(G-14255)***
Hand In Hand & Hospice....620 340-6177
1201 W 12th Ave Emporia (66801) ***(G-1766)***
Handcrafted Wines LLC (PA)....913 829-4500
17501 W 98th St Spc 46-27 Lenexa (66219) ***(G-5888)***
Handcrafted Wines of Kansas, Lenexa *Also called Handcrafted Wines LLC* ***(G-5888)***
Hands 2 Help....785 832-2515
401 Cattleman Ct Lawrence (66049) ***(G-4887)***
Handy Mailing Service....316 944-6258
3839 W Dora St Wichita (67213) ***(G-14553)***
Handyman Services, Topeka *Also called Winston-Brown Construction Co* ***(G-13246)***
Hanger Inc....913 677-1488
9301 W 74th St Merriam (66204) ***(G-7094)***
Hanger Clinic, Wichita *Also called Hanger Prosthetics &* ***(G-14554)***
Hanger Clinic, Kansas City *Also called Hanger Prosthetics &* ***(G-4065)***
Hanger Clinic, Topeka *Also called Hanger Prosthetics &* ***(G-12664)***
Hanger Prosthetics &....913 341-8897
10777 Nall Ave Ste 300 Overland Park (66211) ***(G-8790)***
Hanger Prosthetics &....316 609-3000
410 N Hillside St Ste 100 Wichita (67214) ***(G-14554)***
Hanger Prosthetics &....913 498-1540
6600 College Blvd Ste 215 Shawnee Mission (66211) ***(G-11407)***
Hanger Prosthetics &....913 588-6548
3914 Rainbow Blvd Kansas City (66103) ***(G-4065)***
Hanger Prosthetics &....785 232-5382
830 Sw Lane St Ste B Topeka (66606) ***(G-12664)***
Hanger Prsthetcs & Ortho Inc....316 685-1268
410 N Hillside St Ste 100 Wichita (67214) ***(G-14555)***
Hanna Heating & AC (PA)....316 945-3481
220 N West St Wichita (67203) ***(G-14556)***
Hannah & Oltjen (PA)....913 829-2244
1441 E 151st St Olathe (66062) ***(G-7749)***
Hannah & Oltjen....620 343-3000
3021 Eaglecrest Dr Ste A Emporia (66801) ***(G-1767)***
Hannah & Oltjen....913 268-5559
7505 Quivira Rd Shawnee Mission (66216) ***(G-11408)***
Hannah J Joseph, Emporia *Also called Hannah & Oltjen* ***(G-1767)***
Hannebaum Grain Co Inc (PA)....785 825-8205
2130 S Ohio St Ste A Salina (67401) ***(G-10534)***
Hanneman & Hewitt CPA....316 269-4500
205 W 2nd St N Ste A Wichita (67202) ***(G-14557)***
Hanneman & Hewitt PA, Wichita *Also called Hanneman & Hewitt CPA* ***(G-14557)***
Hanover Electric Inc....785 337-2711
105 W Washington St Hanover (66945) ***(G-2711)***
Hanover Home Healthcare, Hanover *Also called Hanover Hospital & Clinic* ***(G-2712)***
Hanover Hospital & Clinic....785 337-2214
205 S Hanover St Hanover (66945) ***(G-2712)***
Hanover Rs Limited Partnership....913 851-4200
13340 Outlook St Overland Park (66209) ***(G-8791)***
Hans Rudolph Inc....913 422-7788
8325 Cole Pkwy Shawnee (66227) ***(G-10967)***
Hansen Water Treatment Plant, Kansas City *Also called Water Dst No1 Jhnson Cnty Kans* ***(G-4532)***
Hanson, Suzanne Sweetman, Wichita *Also called Grene Vision Group LLC* ***(G-14513)***
Hantover Inc (PA)....913 214-4800
5200 W 110th St Ste 200 Overland Park (66211) ***(G-8792)***
Happy Autos LLC....785 621-4100
801 Main St Hays (67601) ***(G-2826)***
Happy Food Co LLC....816 835-3600
11878 W 91st St Overland Park (66214) ***(G-8793)***
Happy Hearts Child Development....316 613-3550
5833 E 37th St N Wichita (67220) ***(G-14558)***
Happy Hearts Learning Ctr LLC....913 334-3331
1901 N 63rd Dr Kansas City (66102) ***(G-4066)***
Happy House Child Care Ctr 2, Olathe *Also called Happy House Day Care* ***(G-7751)***
Happy House Day Care (PA)....913 782-1115
825 E Sheridan St Olathe (66061) ***(G-7750)***
Happy House Day Care....913 782-1115
825 E Sheridan St Olathe (66061) ***(G-7751)***
Happy Shirt Printing Co LLC....785 371-1660
608 N 2nd St Lawrence (66044) ***(G-4888)***
Harbin Construction LLC....785 825-1651
2200 Centennial Rd Salina (67401) ***(G-10535)***
Harbison-Fischer Inc....620 624-9042
1470 General Welch Blvd Liberal (67901) ***(G-6317)***
Harbison-Fischer Sales, Liberal *Also called Harbison-Fischer Inc* ***(G-6317)***
Harbisonwalker Intl Inc....913 888-0425
9734 Pflumm Rd Lenexa (66215) ***(G-5889)***
Harbor Freight Tools Usa Inc....316 269-2779
2487 S Seneca St Wichita (67217) ***(G-14559)***
Harbor House, Wichita *Also called Catholic Charities of Wichita* ***(G-13962)***
Harbour Construction Inc....913 441-2555
2717 S 88th St Kansas City (66111) ***(G-4067)***
Harcros Chemicals Inc (PA)....913 321-3131
5200 Speaker Rd Kansas City (66106) ***(G-4068)***
Harcros Chemicals Inc....913 621-7721
5200 Speaker Rd Kansas City (66106) ***(G-4069)***
Hard Rock Lanes, Garden City *Also called Raymire Inc* ***(G-2263)***
Hardage Hotels I LLC....913 491-3333
6300 W 110th St Shawnee Mission (66211) ***(G-11409)***
Harder Family Practice PA....316 775-7500
2820 Ohio St Augusta (67010) ***(G-323)***
Hardister Painting & Dctg Svc, Lawrence *Also called Hardister Painting and Dctg* ***(G-4889)***
Hardister Painting and Dctg....785 842-2832
1081 E 1200 Rd Lawrence (66047) ***(G-4889)***
Hardman Wholesale LLC....785 346-2131
404 N 1st St Osborne (67473) ***(G-8209)***
Hardrock Sand & Gravel LLC....620 408-4030
11170 106 Rd Dodge City (67801) ***(G-1369)***
Hardwood Manufacturing LLC....620 463-2663
202 E Dean St Burrton (67020) ***(G-649)***
Haren & Laughlin Cnstr Co Inc....913 495-9558
8035 Nieman Rd Lenexa (66214) ***(G-5890)***
Haren Laughlin Construction, Lenexa *Also called Haren & Laughlin Cnstr Co Inc* ***(G-5890)***
Haren Laughlin Restoration Inc....913 495-9558
7700 Wedd St Ste 500 Overland Park (66204) ***(G-8794)***
HARENLAUGHLIN RESTORATION, Overland Park *Also called Haren Laughlin Restoration Inc* ***(G-8794)***
Harlan C Parker Insurance Agcy....913 782-3310
13095 S Mur Len Rd # 180 Olathe (66062) ***(G-7752)***
Harlan Hermanson....316 263-5958
1735 W Mccormick Ave Wichita (67213) ***(G-14560)***

Harlow Aerostructures LLC (PA)..........316 265-5268
1501 S Mclean Blvd Wichita (67213) *(G-14561)*
Harman Huffman Cnstr Group Inc (PA)..........316 744-2081
5615 Huffman Dr Kechi (67067) *(G-4569)*
Harmon & Miller, Garden City *Also called Bill Harmon (G-2110)*
Harmon Construction Inc..........913 962-5888
18989 W 158th St Olathe (66062) *(G-7753)*
Harp Well Pump Svc Corporated..........316 722-1411
215 S Tyler Rd Wichita (67209) *(G-14562)*
Harpenau Power & Process Inc..........913 451-2227
11370 Strang Line Rd Lenexa (66215) *(G-5891)*
Harper County Engineer, Anthony *Also called County of Harper (G-126)*
Harper Hospital District 5 (PA)..........620 896-7324
485 N Ks Hwy 2 Anthony (67003) *(G-127)*
Harper Industries Inc..........620 896-7381
151 E Us Highway 160 Harper (67058) *(G-2723)*
Harper Trucks Inc..........316 942-1381
1522 S Florence St Wichita (67209) *(G-14563)*
Harrahs North Kansas City LLC..........816 472-7777
9401 Reeds Rd Overland Park (66207) *(G-8795)*
Harrington Bros Htg & Coolg..........913 422-5444
8147 Cole Pkwy Shawnee Mission (66227) *(G-11410)*
Harrington Industrial Plas LLC..........816 400-9438
14401 W 100th St Lenexa (66215) *(G-5892)*
Harrington Pure Indus Plas, Lenexa *Also called Harrington Industrial Plas LLC (G-5892)*
Harris Bmo Bank National Assn..........913 441-7900
21900 Shwnee Mission Pkwy Shawnee Mission (66226) *(G-11411)*
Harris Bmo Bank National Assn..........620 231-2000
417 N Broadway St Pittsburg (66762) *(G-9871)*
Harris Bmo Bank National Assn..........913 307-0707
6860 W 115th St Overland Park (66211) *(G-8796)*
Harris Bmo Bank National Assn..........913 693-1600
8840 State Line Rd Leawood (66206) *(G-5419)*
Harris Bmo Bank National Assn..........913 254-6600
15203 W 119th St Olathe (66062) *(G-7754)*
Harris Bmo Bank National Assn..........620 235-7250
402 N Walnut St Pittsburg (66762) *(G-9872)*
Harris Bmo Bank National Assn..........913 962-1400
7225 Renner Rd Shawnee Mission (66217) *(G-11412)*
Harris Computer Systems..........785 843-8150
4911 Legends Dr Lawrence (66049) *(G-4890)*
Harris Enterprises Group..........785 827-6035
1118 W Cloud St Salina (67401) *(G-10536)*
Harris Healthcare LLC..........316 721-4828
5240 N Sullivan Rd Wichita (67204) *(G-14564)*
Harris Quality Inc..........402 332-5857
11623 S Iowa St Olathe (66061) *(G-7755)*
Harrison Machine Shop & Wldg..........913 764-0730
806 S Kansas Ave Olathe (66061) *(G-7756)*
Harrod's, Howard *Also called Harrods Blacksmith & Welding (G-3134)*
Harrods Blacksmith & Welding..........620 374-2323
436 W Washington St Howard (67349) *(G-3134)*
Harry B Rusk Company Inc..........316 263-4680
352 N New York Ave Wichita (67214) *(G-14565)*
HARRY B. DORST POST NO 24, McPherson *Also called American Legion (G-6933)*
HARRY HYNES MEMORIAL HOSPICE, Wichita *Also called Hospice Incorporated (G-14637)*
Harry Hynes Memorial Hospice, Newton *Also called Hospice Incorporated (G-7363)*
Harrys Machine Works Inc..........620 227-2201
407 W Mcartor Rd Dodge City (67801) *(G-1370)*
Harte-Hankes Direct Marketing, Shawnee Mission *Also called Harte-Hanks Inc (G-11413)*
Harte-Hanks Inc..........913 312-8100
7801 Nieman Rd Shawnee Mission (66214) *(G-11413)*
Hartfiel Automation Inc..........913 894-6545
8017 Flint St Overland Park (66214) *(G-8797)*
Hartford Fire Insurance Co..........913 693-8500
7300 W 110th St Ste 300 Shawnee Mission (66210) *(G-11414)*
Hartland Geriatric, Overland Park *Also called Charles I Davis MD PA (G-8541)*
Hartley Sheet Metal Co Inc..........620 251-4330
405 Walnut St Coffeyville (67337) *(G-943)*
Hartley, James M, Andover *Also called Family Physicians Kansas LLC (G-92)*
Hartley, Roy W MD, Norton *Also called Norton County Hospital (G-7458)*
Hartman Masonry LLC..........620 767-5286
204 N 8th St Council Grove (66846) *(G-1169)*
Hartwood Painting..........316 554-7510
3937 S Baehr St Wichita (67215) *(G-14566)*
Hartzler Lorenda..........785 749-2424
2330 Yale Rd Lawrence (66049) *(G-4891)*
Harvest AG Fabricating LLC..........620 345-8205
11528 Nw 96th St Moundridge (67107) *(G-7184)*
Harvest America Corporation (PA)..........913 342-2121
10000 W 75th St Ste 247 Overland Park (66204) *(G-8798)*
Harvest Brands Stockade..........620 231-6700
1057 S Highway 69 Pittsburg (66762) *(G-9873)*
Harvest Facility Holdings LP..........316 722-5100
10665 W 13th St N Wichita (67212) *(G-14567)*
Harvest Facility Holdings LP..........785 228-0555
2901 Sw Armstrong Ave # 215 Topeka (66614) *(G-12665)*
Harvest Fuel Inc..........785 486-2626
1505 4th Ave E Horton (66439) *(G-3127)*
Harvest Graphics LLC..........913 438-5556
14625 W 100th St Shawnee Mission (66215) *(G-11415)*
Harvest Meat Company Inc..........913 371-2333
1301 Argentine Blvd Kansas City (66105) *(G-4070)*
Harvey & Son Electric..........620 624-3688
E Hwy 54 Liberal (67901) *(G-6318)*
Harvey County Dv/SA Task Force..........316 284-6920
800 N Main St Ste 104 Newton (67114) *(G-7357)*
Harvey County Health Dept, Newton *Also called County of Harvey (G-7337)*
Harvey County Independent..........316 835-2235
220 Main St Halstead (67056) *(G-2702)*
Haskell Foundation..........785 749-8425
155 Indian Ave Lawrence (66046) *(G-4892)*
Haskin Incorporated Transfer, Kansas City *Also called Hit Inc (G-4082)*
Hastco Inc..........785 235-8718
2801 Nw Button Rd Topeka (66618) *(G-12666)*
Hastings Books Music & Video, Olathe *Also called Young Mens Christian Gr Kansas (G-8163)*
Hasty Awards Inc..........785 242-5297
1015 Enterprise St Ottawa (66067) *(G-8278)*
Hatcher Consultants Inc (PA)..........785 271-5557
2955 Sw Wanamaker Dr C Topeka (66614) *(G-12667)*
Hatcher Land & Cattle Company..........620 624-1186
1701 N Kansas Ave Ste 102 Liberal (67901) *(G-6319)*
Hauer Turf Farms Inc..........913 837-2400
15355 W 263rd St Paola (66071) *(G-9564)*
Haul4u, Wichita *Also called Robert Denton (G-15473)*
Haupt Construction Company..........913 686-4411
19951 W 207th St Spring Hill (66083) *(G-12085)*
Haus of Sytle, Hays *Also called Hair Wear and Co (G-2824)*
Have It Maid..........316 264-0110
737 S Washington Ave # 1 Wichita (67211) *(G-14568)*
Haven Commodities Inc (HQ)..........620 345-6328
307 W Cole St Moundridge (67107) *(G-7185)*
Haven Steel Products Inc..........620 465-2573
13206 S Willison Rd Haven (67543) *(G-2731)*
Haverkamp Brothers Inc..........785 858-4457
2964 L4 Rd Bern (66408) *(G-523)*
Haviland Bancshares Inc (PA)..........620 862-5222
209 N Main St Haviland (67059) *(G-2740)*
HAVILAND STATE BANK, Haviland *Also called Haviland Bancshares Inc (G-2740)*
Haviland Telephone Company Inc (HQ)..........620 862-5211
106 N Main St Haviland (67059) *(G-2741)*
Haw Ranch Feedlot 2 LLC..........620 752-3221
7800 Nw Piwakoni Rd Potwin (67123) *(G-10007)*
Hawk Wash Window Cleaning..........785 749-0244
2113 E 28th St Lawrence (66046) *(G-4893)*
Hawk Woodworking Tools, Bushton *Also called Bushton Manufacturing LLC (G-652)*
Hawker Beechcraft, Wichita *Also called Textron Aviation Inc (G-15736)*
Hawker Beechcraft Parts & Dist, Wichita *Also called Textron Aviation Inc (G-15734)*
Hawker Beechcraft Parts & Dist, Wichita *Also called Textron Aviation Inc (G-15753)*
Hawkins Inc..........785 448-1610
1202 E 2nd Ave Garnett (66032) *(G-2376)*
Hawks Besler, Rogers & Gerson, Shawnee Mission *Also called Hawks Bsler Rgers Optmtrist PA (G-11416)*
Hawks Bsler Rgers Optmtrist PA..........913 341-4508
5703 W 95th St Shawnee Mission (66207) *(G-11416)*
Hawks Funeral Home Inc (PA)..........620 442-0220
906 W Kansas Ave Arkansas City (67005) *(G-159)*
Hawks Interstate Pestmasters..........316 267-8331
814 N Main St Wichita (67203) *(G-14569)*
Hawthorn Suites, Wichita *Also called Five Star Hotel Management (G-14380)*
Hawthorn Suites, Overland Park *Also called Rockgate Management Company (G-9253)*
Hawthorn Suites, Wichita *Also called Wyndham International Inc (G-16081)*
Hawthorn Suites..........913 344-8100
11400 College Blvd Overland Park (66210) *(G-8799)*
Hawthorne Animal Hospital..........913 345-8147
11966 Roe Ave Shawnee Mission (66209) *(G-11417)*
Hay & Rice Assoc Chartered (PA)..........620 624-8471
21 Plaza Dr Ste 6 Liberal (67901) *(G-6320)*
Hay Medical Center, Hays *Also called Hays Family Practice Center (G-2829)*
Hayden Tower Service Inc..........785 232-1840
2836 Nw Us Highway 24 Topeka (66618) *(G-12668)*
Haydens Salon and Day Spa..........620 663-2179
13 E 2nd Ave Hutchinson (67501) *(G-3308)*
Hayes Bros Const Co Inc..........913 685-3636
20745 Foster Ct Bucyrus (66013) *(G-599)*
Hayes Company LLC (PA)..........316 838-8000
559 W Douglas Ave Wichita (67213) *(G-14570)*
Hayes Retail Services, Wichita *Also called Hayes Company LLC (G-14570)*
Hayes Tooling & Plastics Inc..........913 782-0046
640 S Rogers Rd Olathe (66062) *(G-7757)*
Hayesbrand Molding Inc..........913 238-0424
614 S Oak St Garnett (66032) *(G-2377)*
Hayford East..........316 267-6259
129 E 2nd St N Wichita (67202) *(G-14571)*

ALPHABETIC

Haynes Electric Inc....620 285-2242
321 W 14th St Larned (67550) ***(G-4704)***
Haynes Publishing Co....785 475-2206
204 Penn Ave Oberlin (67749) ***(G-7496)***
Haynes Publishing Co (PA)....785 475-2206
170 S Penn Ave Oberlin (67749) ***(G-7497)***
Haynes Publishing Co....785 899-2338
1205 Main Ave Goodland (67735) ***(G-2475)***
Haynes Publishing Co....785 462-3963
155 W 5th St Colby (67701) ***(G-1011)***
Haynes Salon and Supply Inc....785 539-5512
718 N Manhattan Ave Manhattan (66502) ***(G-6651)***
Hays Academy of Hair Design....785 628-6624
1214 E 27th St Hays (67601) ***(G-2827)***
Hays Area Children Center Inc....785 625-3257
94 Lewis Dr Hays (67601) ***(G-2828)***
Hays Daily News, Hays *Also called News Publishing Co Inc* ***(G-2877)***
Hays Family Practice Center....785 623-5095
2509 Canterbury Dr Hays (67601) ***(G-2829)***
Hays Feeder Holdings LLC....785 625-3415
1174 Feedlot Rd Hays (67601) ***(G-2830)***
HAYS HUMANE SOCIETY, Hays *Also called Humane Soc of High Plains* ***(G-2851)***
Hays Livestock Market Center....785 628-8206
Hwy 183 Hays (67601) ***(G-2831)***
Hays Mack Sales and Svc Inc....785 625-7343
451 240th Ave Hays (67601) ***(G-2832)***
Hays Medical Center Inc....785 623-5774
2220 Canterbury Dr Hays (67601) ***(G-2833)***
Hays Medical Center Inc (PA)....785 623-5000
2220 Canterbury Dr Hays (67601) ***(G-2834)***
Hays Medical Center Inc....785 623-6270
2500 Canterbury Dr # 204 Hays (67601) ***(G-2835)***
Hays Orthopedic Clinic PA....785 625-3012
2500 Canterbury Dr # 112 Hays (67601) ***(G-2836)***
Hays Pathology Laboratories PA (HQ)....785 650-2700
207 E 7th St A Hays (67601) ***(G-2837)***
Hays Planing Mill Inc....785 625-6507
1013 Elm St Hays (67601) ***(G-2838)***
Hays Veterinary Hosp Prof Assn....785 625-2719
1016 E 8th St Hays (67601) ***(G-2839)***
Hayse Management Services....620 548-2369
107 Northern Rd Mullinville (67109) ***(G-7209)***
Hayse, Richard F, Topeka *Also called Morris Laing Evans Brock* ***(G-12912)***
Haysmed, Hays *Also called Hays Medical Center Inc* ***(G-2834)***
Haysville Family Medcenter....316 858-4165
7107 S Meridian St Haysville (67060) ***(G-2946)***
Haysville Healthcare, Haysville *Also called National Healthcare Corp* ***(G-2952)***
Haysville Healthcare Center, Haysville *Also called Seniortrust of Haysville LLC* ***(G-2959)***
Hayward Baker Inc....913 390-0085
114 N Water St Olathe (66061) ***(G-7758)***
Haz-Mat Response Inc (PA)....913 782-5151
1203 S Parker St Ste C Olathe (66061) ***(G-7759)***
Hazen Construction Services....316 777-0206
10809 S Greenwich Rd Mulvane (67110) ***(G-7216)***
HBD Industries Inc....620 431-9100
201 N Allen Ave Chanute (66720) ***(G-730)***
HCA Holdings Inc....620 365-1330
826 E Madison Ave Iola (66749) ***(G-3607)***
HCA Hospital Svcs San Diego (HQ)....316 962-2000
550 N Hillside St Wichita (67214) ***(G-14572)***
HCA Inc....913 498-7409
12140 Nall Ave Ste 200 Overland Park (66209) ***(G-8800)***
HCA Inc....620 365-1000
3066 N Kentucky St Iola (66749) ***(G-3608)***
Hci Energy LLC....913 283-8855
7923 Nieman Rd Lenexa (66214) ***(G-5893)***
Hcm, Overland Park *Also called Hair Club For Men Ltd Inc* ***(G-8783)***
Hcr Manicure, Wichita *Also called Heartland HM Hlth & Hospice PA* ***(G-14584)***
HCW Wichita Hotel LLC....316 925-6600
10047 W 29th St N Wichita (67205) ***(G-14573)***
Hd Engineering & Design Inc....913 631-2222
11656 W 75th St Shawnee Mission (66214) ***(G-11418)***
Hd Supply Inc....816 283-3687
4600 Kansas Ave Kansas City (66106) ***(G-4071)***
Hdb Construction Inc....785 232-5444
2040 Ne Meriden Rd Topeka (66608) ***(G-12669)***
Hdb Construction Inc....785 232-5444
729 Se Wear Ave Ste A Topeka (66607) ***(G-12670)***
Head & Neck Surgery Kans Cy PA....913 599-4800
5370 College Blvd Ste 100 Leawood (66211) ***(G-5420)***
Head & Neck Surgical Assoc....913 663-5100
5701 W 119th St Ste 425 Leawood (66209) ***(G-5421)***
HEAD START, Clay Center *Also called Clay County Child Care Ctr Inc* ***(G-853)***
Head Start, Lawrence *Also called Community Childrens Center Inc* ***(G-4803)***
Head Start, Kansas City *Also called Project Eagle* ***(G-4345)***
Head Start, Liberal *Also called Kansas Childrens Service Leag* ***(G-6326)***
Head Start Child Dev Cncil Inc....316 267-1997
238 N Waco St Wichita (67202) ***(G-14574)***
Head Start Western Kansas, Garden City *Also called Kansas Childrens Service Leag* ***(G-2213)***
Headache & Pain Center PA....913 491-3999
8101 W 135th St Overland Park (66223) ***(G-8801)***
Headco Industries Inc....913 831-1444
3010 S 24th St Kansas City (66106) ***(G-4072)***
Headhaulcom LLC....913 905-5189
8500 W 110th St Ste 300 Overland Park (66210) ***(G-8802)***
Headstart Program....620 341-2260
19 Constitution St Emporia (66801) ***(G-1768)***
Health Adminisource LLC....913 384-5600
6640 Johnson Dr Shawnee Mission (66202) ***(G-11419)***
Health and Benefit Systems LLC....913 642-1666
6363 College Blvd Ste 500 Leawood (66211) ***(G-5422)***
Health and Envmt Kans Dept....620 231-8540
4033 Parkview Dr Frontenac (66763) ***(G-2055)***
Health and Envmt Kans Dept....620 272-3600
919 W Zerr Rd Garden City (67846) ***(G-2192)***
Health Care Inc (PA)....620 665-2000
1701 E 23rd Ave Hutchinson (67502) ***(G-3309)***
Health Care Stabilization Fund....785 291-3777
300 Sw 8th Ave Ste 200 Topeka (66603) ***(G-12671)***
Health Centl Bone & Joint Ctr, Pratt *Also called Ian S Kovach MD PHD* ***(G-10121)***
Health Connection Inc....913 294-1000
708 Baptiste Dr Paola (66071) ***(G-9565)***
Health Data Specialists LLC....785 242-3419
1720 Sand Creek Rd Pomona (66076) ***(G-10004)***
Health Department, Garden City *Also called County of Finney* ***(G-2134)***
Health Dpknsas Assn Lcal Depts....785 271-8391
300 Sw 8th Ave Fl 3 Topeka (66603) ***(G-12672)***
Health Facilities Group LLC (PA)....316 262-2500
142 N Mosley St Fl 3 Wichita (67202) ***(G-14575)***
Health In Sync Home Inc....316 295-4692
1107 S Glendale St # 224 Wichita (67218) ***(G-14576)***
Health Management of Kansas....620 431-7474
324 E Main St Ste A Chanute (66720) ***(G-731)***
Health Management of Kansas....620 251-1866
106 Tyler Blvd Coffeyville (67337) ***(G-944)***
Health Management of Kansas....620 429-3803
111 S Pennsylvania Ave Columbus (66725) ***(G-1078)***
Health Management of Kansas....620 251-5190
2921 W 1st St Coffeyville (67337) ***(G-945)***
Health Management of Kansas (PA)....620 251-6545
104 W 8th St Coffeyville (67337) ***(G-946)***
Health Management Strategies....785 233-1165
107 Sw 6th Ave Topeka (66603) ***(G-12673)***
Health Mart, Wichita *Also called Dandurand Drug Company Inc* ***(G-14165)***
Health Ministries Clinic Inc....316 283-6103
720 Medical Center Dr Newton (67114) ***(G-7358)***
Health Ministries Clinic Inc....620 727-1183
209 S Pine St Ste 200 Newton (67114) ***(G-7359)***
Health Options That Matter....913 722-3100
340 Southwest Blvd Kansas City (66103) ***(G-4073)***
Health Partnership Clinic Inc (PA)....913 433-7583
407 S Clairborne Rd # 104 Olathe (66062) ***(G-7760)***
Health Professionals Winfield....620 221-4000
1230 E 6th Ave Ste 1b Winfield (67156) ***(G-16146)***
Health- E-Quip, Hutchinson *Also called Hutchinson Hlth Care Svcs Inc* ***(G-3321)***
Healthback of Wichita....316 687-0340
1133 S Rock Rd Ste 7 Wichita (67207) ***(G-14577)***
Healthcare Administrative Svcs....816 763-5446
8717 W 110th St Ste 600 Overland Park (66210) ***(G-8803)***
Healthcare Alliance Group LLC....913 956-2080
10053 Lakeview Ave Lenexa (66219) ***(G-5894)***
Healthcare Prfmce Group Inc....316 796-0337
23419 W 215th St Spring Hill (66083) ***(G-12086)***
Healthcare Resort of Kansas Cy, Kansas City *Also called Golden Oaks Healthcare Inc* ***(G-4039)***
Healthcare Resort of Topeka, Topeka *Also called Top City Healthcare Inc* ***(G-13163)***
Healthcare Revenue Group LLC....913 717-4000
19800 Metcalf Ave # 414 Stilwell (66085) ***(G-12151)***
Healthcore Clinic Inc....316 691-0249
2707 E 21st St N Wichita (67214) ***(G-14578)***
Healthpeak Properties Inc....316 733-2645
8200 E Pawnee St Ofc Wichita (67207) ***(G-14579)***
Healthridge Fitness Center LLC....913 888-0656
23990 W 121st St Olathe (66061) ***(G-7761)***
HealthSouth, Shawnee Mission *Also called Encompass Health Corporation* ***(G-11337)***
Healthstaff Dental LLC....913 402-4334
14109 Overbrook Rd Ste E Leawood (66224) ***(G-5423)***
Healy Biodiesel Inc....620 545-7800
11130 W 47th St S Clearwater (67026) ***(G-893)***
Healy Cooperative Elevator Co....620 398-2211
225 S Dodge Rd Healy (67850) ***(G-2966)***
Heart America Eye Care PA....913 492-0021
10985 Cody St Ste 120 Overland Park (66210) ***(G-8804)***
Heart America Eye Care PA (PA)....913 362-3210
8800 W 75th St Ste 140 Overland Park (66204) ***(G-8805)***

Heart America Hospice Kans LLC 785 228-0400
3715 Sw 29th St Ste 100 Topeka (66614) ***(G-12674)***
Heart America Management LLC 913 397-0100
12070 S Strang Line Rd Olathe (66062) ***(G-7762)***
Heart America Surgery Center, Kansas City *Also called Heart America Surgery Ctr LLC* ***(G-4074)***
Heart America Surgery Ctr LLC 913 334-8935
8935 State Ave Kansas City (66112) ***(G-4074)***
Heart Ctr At Ovrland Pk Rgonal 913 541-5374
10500 Quivira Rd Overland Park (66215) ***(G-8806)***
Heart Living Centers Colo LLC 817 739-8529
2035 E Iron Ave Ste 224 Salina (67401) ***(G-10537)***
Heart of America Bone Marrow D (PA) 913 901-3131
8700 State Line Rd # 340 Shawnee Mission (66206) ***(G-11420)***
Heart of America Inn Inc 785 827-9315
632 Westport Blvd Ste 1 Salina (67401) ***(G-10538)***
Heart of America Police Supply, Kansas City *Also called Abraham Jacob Gorelick* ***(G-3779)***
Heart Spport Group For Bttred 620 275-5911
106 W Fulton St Garden City (67846) ***(G-2193)***
Heart To Heart Intl Inc (PA) 913 764-5200
11550 Renner Blvd Lenexa (66219) ***(G-5895)***
HEARTLAND, Overland Park *Also called Bank of Blue Valley* ***(G-8428)***
Heartland Adjustments Inc 785 823-5100
801 E Prescott Rd Salina (67401) ***(G-10539)***
Heartland Animal Clinic PA 913 648-1662
7821 Marty St Shawnee Mission (66204) ***(G-11421)***
Heartland Animal Hospital 316 744-8160
4100 N Woodlawn Blvd Bel Aire (67220) ***(G-435)***
Heartland Assisted Living 913 248-6600
16207 Midland Dr Apt 3 Shawnee (66217) ***(G-10968)***
Heartland At-Chlor Systems LLC 806 373-4277
1733 Southwest Blvd Wichita (67213) ***(G-14580)***
Heartland Building Maintenance 913 268-7132
7127 Oakview St Shawnee Mission (66216) ***(G-11422)***
Heartland Cardiology LLC 316 686-5300
3535 N Webb Rd Wichita (67226) ***(G-14581)***
Heartland Cement Company 620 331-0200
1765 Limestone Ln Independence (67301) ***(G-3525)***
Heartland Clinic 785 263-4131
511 Ne 10th St Abilene (67410) ***(G-37)***
Heartland Coca-Cola Btlg LLC 785 735-9498
1310 Cathedral Victoria (67671) ***(G-13376)***
Heartland Coca-Cola Btlg LLC 785 232-9372
435 Se 70th St Topeka (66619) ***(G-12675)***
Heartland Coca-Cola Btlg LLC 785 243-1071
439 Us Hwy 81 Concordia (66901) ***(G-1117)***
Heartland Coca-Cola Btlg LLC 913 599-9142
10001 Industrial Blvd Lenexa (66215) ***(G-5896)***
Heartland Coca-Cola Btlg LLC 620 276-3221
4645 E Commerce Dr Garden City (67846) ***(G-2194)***
Heartland Coca-Cola Btlg LLC 316 942-3838
3151 S West St Wichita (67217) ***(G-14582)***
Heartland Coffee & Packg Corp 785 232-0383
719 Se Hancock St Topeka (66607) ***(G-12676)***
Heartland Community Health Ctr, Lawrence *Also called Heartland Medical Clinic Inc* ***(G-4894)***
Heartland Credit Union (PA) 620 669-0177
900 E 23rd Ave Hutchinson (67502) ***(G-3310)***
Heartland Credit Union Assn (PA) 913 297-2480
6800 College Blvd Ste 300 Overland Park (66211) ***(G-8807)***
Heartland Credit Union Assn 316 942-7965
2544 N Maize Ct Ste 100 Wichita (67205) ***(G-14583)***
Heartland Cstmer Solutions LLC (HQ) 913 685-8855
14206 Overbrook Rd Leawood (66224) ***(G-5424)***
Heartland Deisel Repair 913 403-0208
2200 W 47th Pl Apt 216 Shawnee Mission (66205) ***(G-11423)***
Heartland Dental Care, Leavenworth *Also called Heartland Dental Group* ***(G-5250)***
Heartland Dental Group 913 682-1000
3507 S 4th St Leavenworth (66048) ***(G-5250)***
Heartland Dental Group PA 913 682-1000
3507 S 4th St Leavenworth (66048) ***(G-5251)***
Heartland Dermatology Center (PA) 785 628-3231
2707 Vine St Ste 10 Hays (67601) ***(G-2840)***
Heartland Early Childhood Ctr, Olathe *Also called Olathe Unified School Dst 233* ***(G-7953)***
Heartland Electric Inc 785 233-9546
1721 Sw Van Buren St Topeka (66612) ***(G-12677)***
Heartland Eye Care LLC 785 235-3322
619 Sw Corporate Vw Topeka (66615) ***(G-12678)***
Heartland Feeders Inc 620 872-0800
5503 E Road 210 Scott City (67871) ***(G-10814)***
Heartland Food Products Inc 866 571-0222
1900 W 47th Pl Shawnee Mission (66205) ***(G-11424)***
Heartland Foods, Shawnee Mission *Also called Heartland Food Products Inc* ***(G-11424)***
Heartland Golf Dev II LLC 913 856-7235
6431 Sagamore Rd Mission Hills (66208) ***(G-7143)***
Heartland Hay 785 525-6331
1237 N 13th Rd Lucas (67648) ***(G-6472)***
Heartland Hbtat For Hmnity Inc 913 342-3047
155 S 18th St Ste 120 Kansas City (66102) ***(G-4075)***
Heartland Health 785 985-2211
207 S Main St Troy (66087) ***(G-13274)***
Heartland Health Labs Inc (PA) 913 599-3636
10435 Lackman Rd Lenexa (66219) ***(G-5897)***
Heartland HM Hlth & Hospice PA 316 788-7626
2872 N Ridge Rd Ste 122 Wichita (67205) ***(G-14584)***
Heartland HM Hlth Care Hospice, Leawood *Also called Heartland Hospice Services LLC* ***(G-5425)***
Heartland HM Hlth Care Hospice, Topeka *Also called Heartland Hospice Services LLC* ***(G-12679)***
Heartland HM Hlth Care Hospice, Wichita *Also called Heartland Hospice Services LLC* ***(G-14585)***
Heartland Hospice Services LLC 913 362-0044
4601 College Blvd Ste 160 Leawood (66211) ***(G-5425)***
Heartland Hospice Services LLC 785 271-6500
2231 Sw Wanamaker Rd # 202 Topeka (66614) ***(G-12679)***
Heartland Hospice Services LLC 419 252-5743
2872 N Ridge Rd Ste 122 Wichita (67205) ***(G-14585)***
Heartland Imaging Companies 913 621-1211
1211 W Cambridge Cir Dr Kansas City (66103) ***(G-4076)***
Heartland Leasing Services Inc (PA) 913 268-0069
11222 Johnson Dr Shawnee (66203) ***(G-10969)***
Heartland Management Company 785 233-6655
520 Sw 27th St Topeka (66611) ***(G-12680)***
Heartland Medical Clinic Inc 785 841-7297
346 Maine St Ste 150 Lawrence (66044) ***(G-4894)***
Heartland Midwest LLC 913 397-9911
15795 S Mahaffie St # 100 Olathe (66062) ***(G-7763)***
Heartland Midwest LLC 913 471-4840
8270 Wood Rd Pleasanton (66075) ***(G-9996)***
Heartland Mill Inc 620 379-4472
904 E Highway 96 Modoc (67863) ***(G-7153)***
Heartland Moving & Storage 316 554-0224
2111 E Industrial St Wichita (67216) ***(G-14586)***
Heartland Multiple Ll 913 661-1600
11150 Overbrook Rd # 125 Leawood (66211) ***(G-5426)***
Heartland Payment Systems LLC 316 390-1988
3500 N Rock Rd Bldg 1300 Wichita (67226) ***(G-14587)***
Heartland Plant Innovations 785 320-4300
1990 Kimball Ave Manhattan (66502) ***(G-6652)***
Heartland Plastics Inc 316 775-2199
930 West St Augusta (67010) ***(G-324)***
Heartland Plumbing Inc 913 856-5846
800 Creekside Dr Gardner (66030) ***(G-2350)***
Heartland Pool & Spa Svc Inc 913 438-2909
14810 W 89th St Lenexa (66215) ***(G-5898)***
Heartland Precision Fas Inc 913 829-4447
301 Prairie Village Dr New Century (66031) ***(G-7286)***
Heartland Primary Care PA 913 299-3700
2040 Hutton Rd Ste 102 Kansas City (66109) ***(G-4077)***
HEARTLAND RADAC, Roeland Park *Also called Heartland Reg Alchl & Drug* ***(G-10224)***
Heartland Reg Alchl & Drug 913 789-0951
5500 Buena Vista St # 202 Roeland Park (66205) ***(G-10224)***
Heartland Research, Wichita *Also called Family Medicine East Chartered* ***(G-14338)***
Heartland Rural Elc Coop Inc (PA) 620 724-8251
110 Enterprise St Girard (66743) ***(G-2411)***
Heartland Seating, Shawnee *Also called Heartland Leasing Services Inc* ***(G-10969)***
Heartland Seating Inc 913 268-0069
11222 Johnson Dr Shawnee (66203) ***(G-10970)***
Heartland Services Inc 913 685-8855
14212 Overbrook Rd Leawood (66224) ***(G-5427)***
Heartland Services Inc (PA) 913 685-8855
14206 Overbrook Rd Leawood (66224) ***(G-5428)***
Heartland Surgical Care 913 647-3999
7201 W 110th St Ste 120 Overland Park (66210) ***(G-8808)***
Heartland Technologies Inc 316 932-8001
5200a E 35th St N Wichita (67220) ***(G-14588)***
Heartland Womens Group At Wes 316 962-7175
3243 E Murdock St Ste 401 Wichita (67208) ***(G-14589)***
Heartland Works Inc 785 234-0500
5020 Sw 28th St Ste 100 Topeka (66614) ***(G-12681)***
Heartman Publishing, Halstead *Also called Harvey County Independent* ***(G-2702)***
Heartspring Inc 316 634-8700
8700 E 29th St N Wichita (67226) ***(G-14590)***
Heartstone Inc 316 942-1135
1651 S Eisenhower St Wichita (67209) ***(G-14591)***
Heartstrings Cmnty Foundation (PA) 913 649-5700
7086 W 105th St Shawnee Mission (66212) ***(G-11425)***
Hearttraining LLC 913 402-6012
7300 W 110th St Ste 700 Overland Park (66210) ***(G-8809)***
Heath Family Dentistry 785 234-5410
2714 Nw Topeka Blvd # 101 Topeka (66617) ***(G-12682)***
Heating and Cooling Distrs Inc 913 262-5848
5150 W 175th St Stilwell (66085) ***(G-12152)***
Heatron Inc (HQ) 913 651-4420
3000 Wilson Ave Leavenworth (66048) ***(G-5252)***
Heatsource 1, Galesburg *Also called Cvr Manufacturing Inc* ***(G-2091)***
Heaven Engineering LLC 316 262-1244
340 S Pattie Ave Wichita (67211) ***(G-14592)***

ALPHABETIC

Hechler, Steven L, Overland Park *Also called Steven L Hechler DDS Ms* ***(G-9361)***
Heck, Brian W DDS, Lawrence *Also called Allen K Kelley DDS PA* ***(G-4728)***
Heckendorn Eqp Co of Kans....620 983-2186
122 W 2nd St Peabody (66866) ***(G-9760)***
Heckert Construction Co Inc....620 231-6090
746 E 520th Ave Pittsburg (66762) ***(G-9874)***
Hedges Neon Sales Inc....785 827-9341
616 Reynolds St Salina (67401) ***(G-10540)***
Hedlund Electric Inc....620 241-3757
1201 S Main St McPherson (67460) ***(G-6972)***
Hedrick Exotic Animal Farm....620 422-3245
7910 N Roy L Smith Rd Nickerson (67561) ***(G-7433)***
Hedricks Promotions Inc....620 422-3296
7910 N Roy L Smith Rd Nickerson (67561) ***(G-7434)***
Hefner Machine Inc....620 225-4999
1108 S 14th Ave Dodge City (67801) ***(G-1371)***
Heft & Sons LLC (PA)....620 723-2495
14081 I St Greensburg (67054) ***(G-2679)***
Heights of Learning Preschool, Tecumseh *Also called Shawnee Hts Untd Methdst Ch* ***(G-12243)***
Heilind Electronics, Olathe *Also called Ermator Inc* ***(G-7691)***
Heimen Ldscp & Irrigation LLC....913 432-5011
1044 Merriam Ln Kansas City (66103) ***(G-4078)***
Heineken Electric Co Inc (PA)....785 738-3831
3121b Us 24 Hwy Beloit (67420) ***(G-486)***
Heineken Electric Company Inc....785 404-3157
1627 Sunflower Rd Salina (67401) ***(G-10541)***
Heineken Electric Company Inc....785 539-7400
2151 Fort Riley Blvd F Manhattan (66502) ***(G-6653)***
Heinen Custom Operations Inc....785 945-6759
13424 Edwards Rd Valley Falls (66088) ***(G-13364)***
Heinen P-H-E Services Inc....785 945-6668
1808 Linn St Valley Falls (66088) ***(G-13365)***
Helen Frsman Spence Museum Art, Lawrence *Also called University of Kansas* ***(G-5165)***
Helen Jon, Overland Park *Also called Five Clothes LLC* ***(G-8726)***
Helena Agri-Enterprises LLC....620 275-9531
1004 N Anderson Rd Garden City (67846) ***(G-2195)***
Helena Agri-Enterprises LLC....785 899-2391
6409 Road 25 Goodland (67735) ***(G-2476)***
Helena Chemical Company....913 441-0676
8215 Hedge Lane Ter Shawnee (66227) ***(G-10971)***
Helena Chemical Company....620 375-2073
207 S Hwy 25 Leoti (67861) ***(G-6253)***
Helmwood Long Term Care, Tribune *Also called Greeley Cnty Hosp & Long TRM C* ***(G-13268)***
Help Housing Corporation....913 651-6810
700 N 3rd St Leavenworth (66048) ***(G-5253)***
Helpers Inc....913 322-7212
15540 S Pflumm Rd Olathe (66062) ***(G-7764)***
Helping Hands Humane Society....785 233-7325
5720 Sw 21st St Topeka (66604) ***(G-12683)***
Helping Hands Services-Kansas....417 438-6102
1001 Grant Ave Baxter Springs (66713) ***(G-408)***
Hemslojd Inc....785 227-2983
201 N Main St Lindsborg (67456) ***(G-6399)***
Hen House Supermarket 22, Prairie Village *Also called B Four Corp* ***(G-10012)***
Henderson Bldg Solutions LLC....913 894-9720
8345 Lenexa Dr Ste 110 Lenexa (66214) ***(G-5899)***
Henderson Engineers Inc....913 742-5000
8345 Lenexa Dr Ste 300 Overland Park (66214) ***(G-8810)***
Henderson Engineers Inc (PA)....913 742-5000
8345 Lenexa Dr Ste 300 Lenexa (66214) ***(G-5900)***
Henges Insulation Company, Olathe *Also called Jay Henges Enterprises Inc* ***(G-7808)***
Henke Manufacturing Corp (HQ)....913 682-9000
3070 Wilson Ave Leavenworth (66048) ***(G-5254)***
Henry J Kanarek....913 451-8555
4601 W 109th St Ste 350 Shawnee Mission (66211) ***(G-11426)***
Henry L Bumgardner Jr Od....316 264-4648
2205 S Seneca St Wichita (67213) ***(G-14593)***
Henry Schein Inc....913 894-8444
11135 W 79th St Shawnee Mission (66214) ***(G-11427)***
Henry Scherer Crop Insurance....785 847-6843
14225 318th Rd Atchison (66002) ***(G-234)***
Henry Steckman Plumbing....785 388-2782
3266 Dove Rd Manchester (67410) ***(G-6524)***
Henrys Ltd....785 388-2480
822 6th Rd Longford (67458) ***(G-6430)***
Henson Hutton Mudrick Gragson....785 232-2200
100 Se 9th St Fl 2 Topeka (66612) ***(G-12684)***
Henton Plumbing & AC, Manhattan *Also called Henton Plumbing & AC Inc* ***(G-6654)***
Henton Plumbing & AC Inc....785 776-5548
8838 Quail Ln Manhattan (66502) ***(G-6654)***
Hentzen, Page Ann MD, Hutchinson *Also called Womans Place PA* ***(G-3491)***
Herald and Banner Press....913 432-0331
7407 Metcalf Ave Overland Park (66204) ***(G-8811)***
Herald Sabetha Inc....785 284-3300
1024 Main St Sabetha (66534) ***(G-10313)***
Herbs & More Inc....785 865-4372
2108 W 27th St Ste D Lawrence (66047) ***(G-4895)***
Hereford House, The, Shawnee Mission *Also called B & C Restaurant Corporation* ***(G-11138)***
Herff Jones LLC....913 432-8100
2525 Midpoint Dr Edwardsville (66111) ***(G-1502)***
Herington Livestock Market....785 258-2205
502 E Lewerenz St Herington (67449) ***(G-2974)***
Herington Main Street Program, Herington *Also called Chamber of Commerce* ***(G-2972)***
Herington Opco LLC....785 789-4750
2 E Ash St Herington (67449) ***(G-2975)***
Heritage Builders Inc....785 776-6011
217 S 4th St Manhattan (66502) ***(G-6655)***
Heritage Cmpt Consulting Inc....913 529-4227
10104 W 105th St Overland Park (66212) ***(G-8812)***
Heritage Electric LLC....913 747-0528
841 N Martway Dr Olathe (66061) ***(G-7765)***
Heritage Feeders LP....620 275-4195
1506 Road 30 Sublette (67877) ***(G-12203)***
Heritage Group Lc....316 261-5301
7309 E 21st St N Ste 120 Wichita (67206) ***(G-14594)***
Heritage Healthcare Management....785 899-0100
707 Wheat Ridge Cir Ofc Goodland (67735) ***(G-2477)***
Heritage Home Works LLC....316 288-9033
5734 W Us Highway 50 Newton (67114) ***(G-7360)***
Heritage House, Chetopa *Also called Woodworth Enterprises Inc* ***(G-818)***
Heritage House Assisted Living....620 473-3456
615 Franklin St Humboldt (66748) ***(G-3184)***
Heritage Inn Wichita Opco LLC....316 686-2844
9525 E Corporate Hills Dr Wichita (67207) ***(G-14595)***
Heritage Management Corp (PA)....785 273-2995
5629 Sw Barrington Ct S Topeka (66614) ***(G-12685)***
Heritage Nursing Home, Girard *Also called T W G Nursing Home Inc* ***(G-2420)***
HERITAGE OF GERING, Liberal *Also called Park Wheatridge Care Center* ***(G-6355)***
Heritage Restaurant Inc....316 524-7495
4551 S Broadway Ave Wichita (67216) ***(G-14596)***
Heritage Ridge Apts, Manhattan *Also called Lee Construction Co* ***(G-6711)***
Heritage Sublette, Sublette *Also called Heritage Feeders LP* ***(G-12203)***
Heritage Tractor Inc....620 231-0950
1076 S Highway 69 Pittsburg (66762) ***(G-9875)***
Heritage Tractor Inc (PA)....785 594-6486
915 Industrial Park Rd Baldwin City (66006) ***(G-363)***
Heritage Tractor Inc....913 529-2376
19905 W 157th St Olathe (66062) ***(G-7766)***
Heritage Tractor Inc....785 235-5100
2701 Nw Us Highway 24 Topeka (66618) ***(G-12686)***
Heritage Village of Eskridge, Eskridge *Also called Beverly Enterprises-Kansas LLC* ***(G-1865)***
Herman Miller Inc....913 599-4700
10930 Lackman Rd Shawnee Mission (66219) ***(G-11428)***
Hermes Co Inc (PA)....913 888-2413
13030 W 87th Street Pkwy # 100 Lenexa (66215) ***(G-5901)***
Hermes Nursery Inc....913 441-2400
20000 W 47th St Shawnee Mission (66218) ***(G-11429)***
Hermey Landscaping, Lenexa *Also called Hermes Co Inc* ***(G-5901)***
Herod, Jeff J Dvm, Derby *Also called El Paso Animal Clinic* ***(G-1243)***
Herrmann Land & Cattle Co....620 369-2252
12466 Us Highway 400 Ford (67842) ***(G-1933)***
Herrmans Excavating Inc....785 233-4146
1459 Se Jefferson St Topeka (66607) ***(G-12687)***
Herron Inc....913 731-2507
1601 E Peoria St Paola (66071) ***(G-9566)***
Herrs Machine....785 325-2875
1745 Prospect Blvd Washington (66968) ***(G-13464)***
Hertel Bible Publishers, Wichita *Also called Devore & Sons Inc* ***(G-14205)***
Hertel Tank Service Inc....785 628-2445
704 E 12th St Hays (67601) ***(G-2841)***
Hertz, Salina *Also called Central Kansas Auto Rental* ***(G-10439)***
Hertz, Topeka *Also called Hobart Transportation Co Inc* ***(G-12696)***
Hertz Corporation....620 342-6322
602 State St Emporia (66801) ***(G-1769)***
Hertz Corporation....913 962-1226
6001 Nieman Rd Shawnee Mission (66203) ***(G-11430)***
Hertz Corporation....316 689-3773
550 N Webb Rd Ste D Wichita (67206) ***(G-14597)***
Hertz Corporation....913 341-1782
8130 Metcalf Ave Overland Park (66204) ***(G-8813)***
Hertz Corporation....316 946-4860
1590 S Airport Rd Wichita (67209) ***(G-14598)***
Hertz Corporation....316 946-4860
2010 S Airport Rd Wichita (67209) ***(G-14599)***
Hertz Corporation....316 946-4860
2121 S Hoover Rd Wichita (67209) ***(G-14600)***
Hertz Corporation....316 946-4860
1760 S Airport Rd Wichita (67209) ***(G-14601)***
Hertz Corporation....620 341-9656
3105 W 6th Ave Emporia (66801) ***(G-1770)***
Hertz Corporation....316 284-6084
810 N Oliver Newton Newton (67114) ***(G-7361)***

Hertz Corporation 913 696-0003
13750 W 108th St Lenexa (66215) ***(G-5902)***
Herzberg L J & Sons Roofing Co, Wichita *Also called L J Herzberg Roofing Co Inc* ***(G-14906)***
Hess & Son Salvage Inc 785 238-3382
1209 Perry St Junction City (66441) ***(G-3699)***
Hess Medical Services PA 785 628-7495
2201 Canterbury Dr Hays (67601) ***(G-2842)***
Hess Medical Services & Clinic, Hays *Also called Hess Medical Services PA* ***(G-2842)***
Hess Oil Company (PA) 620 241-4640
2080 E Kansas Ave McPherson (67460) ***(G-6973)***
Hess Services Inc 785 625-9295
2670 E 9th St Hays (67601) ***(G-2843)***
Hesston Golf Course, Hesston *Also called City of Hesston* ***(G-2987)***
Hesston Record 620 327-4831
347 N Old Us Highway 81 Hesston (67062) ***(G-2992)***
Hesston Unified School Dst 460 ....620 327-2989
200 N Ridge Rd Hesston (67062) ***(G-2993)***
Heston Recreation Commission, Hesston *Also called Hesston Unified School Dst 460* ***(G-2993)***
Hetlinger Dvlopmental Svcs Inc 620 342-1087
707 S Commercial St Emporia (66801) ***(G-1771)***
Hetrick Air Services Inc 785 842-0000
1930 N Airport Rd Lawrence (66044) ***(G-4896)***
Hett Construction 620 382-2236
1212 Pawnee Rd Marion (66861) ***(G-6871)***
Heubel Material Handling Inc 316 941-4115
1220 E Central Ave Wichita (67214) ***(G-14602)***
Hewitt USA, Wichita *Also called G T Sales & Manufacturing Inc* ***(G-14434)***
Hf Rubber Machinery Inc (HQ) 785 235-2336
1701 Nw Topeka Blvd Topeka (66608) ***(G-12688)***
Hl Hritg Inn Wchita Opco LLC 316 686-3576
9449 E Corporate Hills Dr Wichita (67207) ***(G-14603)***
Hl Plains Cooperative Assn (PA) 785 462-3351
405 E 4th St Colby (67701) ***(G-1012)***
Hl Plains Feed LLC 620 277-2886
1650 N Sherlock Rd Garden City (67846) ***(G-2196)***
Hl Tek Innovations, Fredonia *Also called Hightech Solutions Inc* ***(G-2035)***
Hi-Line Plastics Inc 913 782-3535
801 E Old Highway 56 Olathe (66061) ***(G-7767)***
Hi-Plains Co-Op, Colby *Also called Hl Plains Cooperative Assn* ***(G-1012)***
Hi-Plains Door Systems Inc 785 462-6352
1120 S Country Club Dr Colby (67701) ***(G-1013)***
Hi-Plains Motel & Restaurant 620 375-4438
312 E Broadway Leoti (67861) ***(G-6254)***
Hi-Tech Interiors Inc 785 742-1766
1651 Apache Ave Hiawatha (66434) ***(G-3009)***
Hi-Tech Interiors Inc (PA) 785 539-7266
5006 Skyway Dr Manhattan (66503) ***(G-6656)***
Hi-Tech Weld Overlay Group LLC 816 524-9010
14720 W 99th St Ste B Lenexa (66215) ***(G-5903)***
Hiawatha Hospital, Hiawatha *Also called Physical Rsprtory Therapy Svcs* ***(G-3021)***
Hiawatha Hospital Association 785 742-2161
300 Utah St Hiawatha (66434) ***(G-3010)***
Hickory Pointe 785 863-2108
700 Cherokee St Oskaloosa (66066) ***(G-8226)***
Hickory Pointe Care Rehab Ctr, Oskaloosa *Also called Hickory Pointe* ***(G-8226)***
Hidden Valley Homeowners Assn, Mound City *Also called Sugar Valley Lakes Homes Assn* ***(G-7175)***
Hieb & Associates LLC 620 663-9430
708 W 2nd Ave Hutchinson (67501) ***(G-3311)***
Higdon & Hale, Shawnee Mission *Also called Higdon and Hale Cpas P C* ***(G-11431)***
Higdon and Hale Cpas P C 913 831-7000
6310 Lamar Ave Ste 110 Shawnee Mission (66202) ***(G-11431)***
High Choice Feeders LLC (PA) 620 872-7271
553 W Road 40 Scott City (67871) ***(G-10815)***
High Choice Feeders LLC 620 872-5376
553 W Road 40 Scott City (67871) ***(G-10816)***
High Plains Daily Leader, Liberal *Also called Seward County Publishing LLC* ***(G-6367)***
High Plains Dairy LLC 620 563-9441
2042 V Rd Plains (67869) ***(G-9975)***
High Plains Distlery, Atchison *Also called High Plains Inc* ***(G-235)***
High Plains Educational Coop, Ulysses *Also called Unified School District 214* ***(G-13328)***
High Plains Farm Credit Flca (PA) 620 285-6978
605 Main St Larned (67550) ***(G-4705)***
High Plains Farm Credit Flca 785 625-2110
2905 Vine St Hays (67601) ***(G-2844)***
High Plains Hybrids, Hugoton *Also called Kramer Seed Farms* ***(G-3170)***
High Plains Inc 913 773-5780
1700 Rooks Rd Atchison (66002) ***(G-235)***
High Plains Journal, Dodge City *Also called High Plains Publishers Inc* ***(G-1372)***
High Plains Machine Works Inc 785 625-4672
208 E 7th St Hays (67601) ***(G-2845)***
High Plains Mental Health Care, Hays *Also called High Plains Mental Health Ctr* ***(G-2847)***
High Plains Mental Health Ctr (PA) 785 628-2871
208 E 7th St Hays (67601) ***(G-2846)***
High Plains Mental Health Ctr 785 543-5284
783 7th St Phillipsburg (67661) ***(G-9788)***
High Plains Mental Health Ctr 785 462-6774
750 S Range Ave Colby (67701) ***(G-1014)***
High Plains Mental Health Ctr 785 625-2400
1412 E 29th St Hays (67601) ***(G-2847)***
High Plains Printing 785 460-6350
680 N Riddle Ave Colby (67701) ***(G-1015)***
High Plains Publishers Inc (PA) 620 227-7171
1500 E Wyatt Earp Blvd Dodge City (67801) ***(G-1372)***
High Plains Ranch LLC 559 805-5636
12225 E Hwy 160 Satanta (67870) ***(G-10786)***
High Plains Retirement Village, Lakin *Also called Kearny County Home For Aged* ***(G-4652)***
High Quality Tech Inc 316 448-3559
2302 N Hood Ave Ste 200 Wichita (67204) ***(G-14604)***
High Reach Equipment LLC (PA) 316 942-5438
3624 W 30th St S Wichita (67217) ***(G-14605)***
High Touch Inc (PA) 316 462-4001
110 S Main St Ste 600 Wichita (67202) ***(G-14606)***
High Touch Tech Solutions, Wichita *Also called High Touch Inc* ***(G-14606)***
Higher Ground 316 262-2060
247 N Market St Wichita (67202) ***(G-14607)***
Highland Golf Country Club, Hutchinson *Also called Twb Inc* ***(G-3470)***
Highland Healthcare and 785 442-3217
402 S Avenue Highland (66035) ***(G-3029)***
Highland Lodging LLC (PA) 620 792-2431
3017 10th St Great Bend (67530) ***(G-2591)***
Highlands Golf Club, Hutchinson *Also called American Golf Corporation* ***(G-3198)***
Highlands Highpoint Village 913 381-0335
10020 W 80th St Overland Park (66204) ***(G-8814)***
Highlands North and South, The, Overland Park *Also called Highlands Highpoint Village* ***(G-8814)***
Highlawn Montessori School, Prairie Village *Also called Friends of Montessori Assn* ***(G-10029)***
Hightech Signs LLC 913 894-4422
2338 Merriam Ln Kansas City (66106) ***(G-4079)***
Hightech Solutions Inc 620 228-2216
705 Cement Plant Rd Fredonia (66736) ***(G-2035)***
Highway Dept, Belleville *Also called County of Republic* ***(G-456)***
Highway Dept, Abilene *Also called County of Dickinson* ***(G-21)***
Highway Dept, Russell *Also called County of Russell* ***(G-10270)***
Hiland Dairy, Topeka *Also called Roberts Dairy Company LLC* ***(G-13022)***
Hiland Dairy Foods Company LLC 620 225-4111
1103 E Trail St Dodge City (67801) ***(G-1373)***
Hiland Dairy Foods Company LLC 785 539-7541
2710 Amherst Ave Manhattan (66502) ***(G-6657)***
Hiland Dairy Foods Company LLC 316 267-4221
700 E Central Ave Wichita (67202) ***(G-14608)***
Hiland/Steffen Dairy Foods Co, Dodge City *Also called Hiland Dairy Foods Company LLC* ***(G-1373)***
Hill & Company Inc (PA) 785 235-5374
1424 Se Monroe St Topeka (66612) ***(G-12689)***
Hill Investment & Rental Co 785 537-9064
625 Pebblebrook Cir Manhattan (66503) ***(G-6658)***
Hill Top Center 316 686-9095
1329 S Terrace Dr Wichita (67218) ***(G-14609)***
Hill's Pet Products, Topeka *Also called Hills Pet Nutrition Inc* ***(G-12691)***
Hill's Tech Center, Topeka *Also called Hills Pet Nutrition Inc* ***(G-12692)***
Hillcrest Apartment Bldg Co 316 684-7204
115 S Rutan Ave Wichita (67218) ***(G-14610)***
Hillcrest Best Western Motel, Pratt *Also called Fryslie Inc* ***(G-10116)***
Hillcrest Chrstn Child Dev Ctr 913 663-1997
11411 Quivira Rd Shawnee Mission (66210) ***(G-11432)***
Hillcrest Covenant Church 913 901-2300
8801 Nall Ave Shawnee Mission (66207) ***(G-11433)***
Hillcrest Covenant Pre-School, Shawnee Mission *Also called Hillcrest Covenant Church* ***(G-11433)***
Hiller Inc 316 264-5231
630 N Washington Ave Wichita (67214) ***(G-14611)***
Hills Pet Nutrition Inc 620 340-6920
400 S Weaver St Emporia (66801) ***(G-1772)***
Hills Pet Nutrition Inc (HQ) 800 255-0449
400 Sw 8th Ave Ste 101 Topeka (66603) ***(G-12690)***
Hills Pet Nutrition Inc 785 231-2812
320 Ne Crane St Topeka (66603) ***(G-12691)***
Hills Pet Nutrition Inc 785 286-1451
1035 Ne 43rd St Topeka (66617) ***(G-12692)***
Hills Pet Nutrition Sales Inc (HQ) 785 354-8523
400 Sw 8th Ave Ste 101 Topeka (66603) ***(G-12693)***
Hillsboro Community Hospital, Hillsboro *Also called Cah Acquisition Company 5 LLC* ***(G-3043)***
Hillsboro Ford Inc 620 947-3134
202 S Main St Hillsboro (67063) ***(G-3049)***
Hillsboro Free Press, Hillsboro *Also called Print Source Direct LLC* ***(G-3056)***
Hillsboro Industries, Hillsboro *Also called Flint Hills Industries Inc* ***(G-3048)***
Hillsboro Star-Journal, Marion *Also called Hoch Publishing Co Inc* ***(G-6872)***
Hillsboro State Bank 620 947-3961
200 N Main St Hillsboro (67063) ***(G-3050)***

ALPHABETIC

Hillshire Brands Company......316 262-5443
427 S Washington Ave Wichita (67202) **(G-14612)**
Hillside Funeral Home, Wichita *Also called Alderwoods (kansas) Inc* **(G-13661)**
Hillside Medical Office......316 685-1381
855 N Hillside St Wichita (67214) **(G-14613)**
Hillside Nursery Inc......316 686-6414
2200 S Hillside St Wichita (67211) **(G-14614)**
Hillside Village LLC......913 583-1266
33600 W 85th St De Soto (66018) **(G-1201)**
Hillside Village of De Soto, De Soto *Also called Hillside Village LLC* **(G-1201)**
Hilltop Child Development Ctr......785 864-4940
1605 Irving Hill Rd Lawrence (66045) **(G-4897)**
Hilltop House, Bucklin *Also called Bucklin Hospital District Inc* **(G-590)**
Hilltop Lodge......785 738-2509
815 N Independence Ave Beloit (67420) **(G-487)**
Hilltop Manor Inc......620 298-2781
403 S Valley St Cunningham (67035) **(G-1187)**
Hilltop Manor Mutal Hsing Corp......316 684-5141
1411 S Oliver St Wichita (67218) **(G-14615)**
Hillview Christian Center, Kansas City *Also called Hillview Church of God Inc* **(G-4080)**
Hillview Church of God Inc......913 299-4406
701 N 78th St Kansas City (66112) **(G-4080)**
Hilton, Overland Park *Also called Si Overland Park LP* **(G-9310)**
Hilton Garden In, Lenexa *Also called Bartlesville SW Hotel Inc* **(G-5688)**
Hilton Garden Inn 23930......913 342-7900
520 Minnesota Ave Kansas City (66101) **(G-4081)**
Hilton Garden Inn Wichita, Wichita *Also called Bradley Hotel Wichita* **(G-13881)**
Hilton Grdn Inn Wichita Dwntwn, Wichita *Also called T M H Hotels Inc* **(G-15713)**
Hilton Hotels, Kansas City *Also called Hilton Garden Inn 23930* **(G-4081)**
Himalaya Mortgage Inc......913 649-9700
11881 W 112th St Shawnee Mission (66210) **(G-11434)**
Himoinsa Power Systems Inc......913 495-5557
16600 Theden St Olathe (66062) **(G-7768)**
Himoinsa USA, Olathe *Also called Himoinsa Power Systems Inc* **(G-7768)**
Hinkin, Douglas P MD, Manhattan *Also called Stonecreek Family Physicians* **(G-6813)**
Hinkle Law Firm LLC (PA)......316 267-2000
1617 N Waterfront Pkwy # 400 Wichita (67206) **(G-14616)**
Hinrichszenk + Pesavento......785 691-5407
7285 W 132nd St Ste 140 Overland Park (66213) **(G-8815)**
Hiper Technology Inc......785 749-6011
2920 Haskell Ave Ste 300 Lawrence (66046) **(G-4898)**
Hiperformance LLC......913 829-3400
402 New Century Pkwy New Century (66031) **(G-7287)**
Hiplains Farm Equipment Inc......620 225-0064
1509 S 2nd Ave Dodge City (67801) **(G-1374)**
Hippalus Technologies, Overland Park *Also called Kaliaperumal Mamalay* **(G-8885)**
Hires Gage Dvm......913 432-7611
6000 Mission Rd Fairway (66205) **(G-1910)**
His and Her Hairstyling Inc......785 232-9724
3311 Sw 6th Ave Topeka (66606) **(G-12694)**
Hisonic LLC......913 782-0012
310 N Marion St Olathe (66061) **(G-7769)**
Historic Harley Davidson, Topeka *Also called Big Twin Inc* **(G-12381)**
Historic Presrvtn Aliance of W......316 269-9432
230 N Market St Ste 201 Wichita (67202) **(G-14617)**
Historic Wichita Sedqwick Cnty......316 219-1871
1865 W Museum Blvd Wichita (67203) **(G-14618)**
Hit Inc......913 281-4040
29 Woodswether Rd Kansas City (66118) **(G-4082)**
Hit Portfolio I Hil Trs LLC......816 464-5454
10591 Metcalf Frontage Rd Overland Park (66212) **(G-8816)**
Hit Portfolio I Trs LLC......913 451-2553
6801 W 112th St Overland Park (66211) **(G-8817)**
Hitchin Post Steak Co......913 647-0543
808 N Meadowbrook Dr Olathe (66062) **(G-7770)**
Hite Collision Repair Ctr Inc......785 843-8991
3401 W 6th St Lawrence (66049) **(G-4899)**
Hite Fanning & Honeyman LLP......316 265-7741
100 N Broadway Ave # 950 Wichita (67202) **(G-14619)**
Hix Corporation......620 231-8568
1201 E 27th Ter Pittsburg (66762) **(G-9876)**
HMC Hays Psychological Assoc, Hays *Also called Hays Medical Center Inc* **(G-2835)**
HMC Medical Oncology Services, Hays *Also called Hays Medical Center Inc* **(G-2833)**
HMC Performance Coatings, Tonganoxie *Also called Hobby Monster Customs LLC* **(G-12263)**
HMK Concrete......913 262-1555
5713 Kessler Ln Ste 101 Shawnee Mission (66203) **(G-11435)**
Hmn Architects Inc (PA)......913 451-9075
7400 W 110th St Ste 200 Overland Park (66210) **(G-8818)**
Hmong Manufacturing Inc......913 371-2752
1900 Osage Ave Kansas City (66105) **(G-4083)**
HMS Holdings Corp......785 271-9300
2348 Sw Topeka Blvd # 101 Topeka (66611) **(G-12695)**
Hnb Corporation......620 442-4040
126 S Summit St Arkansas City (67005) **(G-160)**
Hnry Logistics Inc (HQ)......833 810-4679
5200 W 110th St Overland Park (66211) **(G-8819)**
Hntb Corporation......913 491-9333
7400 W 129th St Ste 100 Overland Park (66213) **(G-8820)**
Hobart Sales and Service Inc......913 469-9600
10631 Summit St Lenexa (66215) **(G-5904)**
Hobart Transportation Co Inc (PA)......785 267-4468
313 S Kansas Ave Topeka (66603) **(G-12696)**
Hobby Monster Customs LLC......913 417-7088
1625 Tonganoxie Rd Ste B Tonganoxie (66086) **(G-12263)**
Hoc Industries Inc......316 838-4663
3511 N Ohio St Wichita (67219) **(G-14620)**
Hoch Publishing Co Inc......620 382-2165
117 S 3rd St Marion (66861) **(G-6872)**
Hockenbergs Restaurant Supply......913 696-9773
14603 W 112th St Shawnee Mission (66215) **(G-11436)**
Hodes & Nauser Mds PA......913 491-6878
4840 College Blvd Overland Park (66211) **(G-8821)**
Hodgdon Powder Company Inc......785 258-3388
1347 S 2600 Rd Herington (67449) **(G-2976)**
Hodgeman County Health Center (PA)......620 357-8361
809 W Bramley St Jetmore (67854) **(G-3647)**
Hodges Farms & Dredging LLC......620 343-0513
501 N West St Lebo (66856) **(G-5606)**
Hoefer Custom Stained Glass, South Hutchinson *Also called Hoefer Enterprises Inc* **(G-12059)**
Hoefer Enterprises Inc......620 663-1778
910 S Main St South Hutchinson (67505) **(G-12059)**
Hoefer Wysocki Architects LLC (PA)......913 307-3700
11460 Tomahawk Creek Pkwy Leawood (66211) **(G-5429)**
Hoelker Tooling......316 744-7777
355 N Martinson St Wichita (67203) **(G-14621)**
Hoelscher Inc......620 562-3575
312 S Main St Bushton (67427) **(G-653)**
Hofer & Hofer & Associates Inc......620 473-3919
1201 N 10th St Humboldt (66748) **(G-3185)**
Hoffman Inc......316 942-8011
3703 W 30th St S Wichita (67217) **(G-14622)**
Hoffman Orthodontics, Shawnee Mission *Also called William E Hoffman DDS* **(G-12007)**
Hoffmann Fabricating LLC......316 262-6041
909 E Waterman St Wichita (67202) **(G-14623)**
Hoffmanns Green Industries......316 634-1500
1120 E 26th St Wichita (67206) **(G-14624)**
Hoffs Machine & Welding Inc......785 823-6215
925 E North St Salina (67401) **(G-10542)**
Hog Slat Incorporated......580 338-5003
1000 W Pancake Blvd Liberal (67901) **(G-6321)**
Hogoboom Oilfield Trckg Svcs, El Dorado *Also called Albert G Hogoboom* **(G-1527)**
Hogzilla Grinders, Sabetha *Also called C W Mill Equipment Co Inc* **(G-10308)**
Hoisington Homestead......620 653-4121
259 W 6th St Hoisington (67544) **(G-3066)**
Hokanson Lehman & Stevens......913 338-2525
3400 College Blvd Ste 100 Leawood (66211) **(G-5430)**
Holcomb Recreation Commission......620 277-2152
106 Wiley St Holcomb (67851) **(G-3075)**
Holderman Printing LLC......913 557-6848
11 W Wea St Paola (66071) **(G-9567)**
Holderman Printing LLC (PA)......913 557-6848
110 W 4th Ave Garnett (66032) **(G-2378)**
Holiday Cleaners......913 631-6181
7945 Frontage Rd Overland Park (66204) **(G-8822)**
Holiday Cleaning Center, Overland Park *Also called Holiday Cleaners* **(G-8822)**
Holiday Healthcare LLC......785 825-2201
2825 Resort Dr Salina (67401) **(G-10543)**
Holiday Healthcare LLC (PA)......620 343-9285
2700 W 30th Ave Emporia (66801) **(G-1773)**
Holiday Inn, Lenexa *Also called Kandarpam Hotels LLC* **(G-5935)**
Holiday Inn, Pittsburg *Also called Venture Hotels LLC* **(G-9954)**
Holiday Inn, Wichita *Also called Wichita East Hotel Associates* **(G-15996)**
Holiday Inn, Wichita *Also called Wichita Arprt Hospitality LLC* **(G-15977)**
Holiday Inn, Shawnee Mission *Also called Overland Park Hospitality LLC* **(G-11708)**
Holiday Inn, Great Bend *Also called Gbk Ventures LLC* **(G-2569)**
Holiday Inn, Atchison *Also called Atchison Hospitality Group LLC* **(G-210)**
Holiday Inn, Salina *Also called Six Continents Hotels Inc* **(G-10709)**
Holiday Inn, Great Bend *Also called Six Continents Hotels Inc* **(G-2636)**
Holiday Inn, Colby *Also called Six Continents Hotels Inc* **(G-1041)**
Holiday Inn, Topeka *Also called Tenth Street Ht Partners LLC* **(G-13151)**
Holiday Inn, Liberal *Also called Frontier Lodging Liberal LLC* **(G-6310)**
Holiday Inn, Wichita *Also called Kinseth Hospitality Co Inc* **(G-14864)**
Holiday Inn, Emporia *Also called Summit Hotel Properties LLC* **(G-1833)**
Holiday Inn, Lawrence *Also called Lilken Lllp* **(G-4997)**
Holiday Inn, Liberal *Also called C B H Consultants Inc* **(G-6289)**
Holiday Inn, Overland Park *Also called Overland Park Hotel Assoc Lc* **(G-9120)**
Holiday Inn, McPherson *Also called Wingate Inns International Inc* **(G-7043)**
Holiday Inn, Shawnee Mission *Also called I Samco Investments Ltd* **(G-11447)**
Holiday Inn, Dodge City *Also called Leisure Hotel Corporation* **(G-1398)**
Holiday Inn, Manhattan *Also called A Scampis Bar & Grill* **(G-6527)**

Holiday Inn, Lawrence *Also called Lodgian Inc* ***(G-5000)***
Holiday Inn, Overland Park *Also called Park-Rn Overland Park LLC* ***(G-9142)***
Holiday Inn, Garden City *Also called Leisure Hotel Corporation* ***(G-2224)***
Holiday Inn & Suites.......620 508-6350
1903 Pauline Pl Pratt (67124) ***(G-10120)***
Holiday Inn Ex Ht & Suites.......785 263-4049
110 E Lafayette Ave Abilene (67410) ***(G-38)***
Holiday Inn Ex Suites Topeka N.......785 861-7200
601 Nw Us Highway 24 Topeka (66608) ***(G-12697)***
Holiday Inn Express, Concordia *Also called Frontier Lodging Concordia LLC* ***(G-1111)***
Holiday Inn Express.......913 250-1000
120 Express Ln Lansing (66043) ***(G-4675)***
Holiday Inn Express.......785 625-8000
4650 Roth Ave Hays (67601) ***(G-2848)***
Holiday Inn Express.......785 890-9060
2631 Enterprise Rd Goodland (67735) ***(G-2478)***
Holiday Inn Express & Suites.......316 804-7040
1430 E Broadway Ct Newton (67114) ***(G-7362)***
Holiday Inn Express & Suites.......785 404-3300
755 W Diamond Dr Salina (67401) ***(G-10544)***
Holiday Inn Express & Suites.......620 431-0817
3401 Blue Comet Dr Chanute (66720) ***(G-732)***
Holiday Inn Express and Suites.......316 322-7275
3100 El Dorado Ave El Dorado (67042) ***(G-1566)***
Holiday Inn Express Village W.......913 328-1024
1931 Prairie Crossing St Kansas City (66111) ***(G-4084)***
Holiday Lanes, Pittsburg *Also called Lynco Rec Inc* ***(G-9896)***
Holiday Manor Motel, McPherson *Also called Sagar Inc* ***(G-7023)***
Holiday Rsort Adult Care Rehab, Salina *Also called Holiday Healthcare LLC* ***(G-10543)***
Holland Paving Inc.......316 722-7114
1255 S Tyler Rd Wichita (67209) ***(G-14625)***
Holliday Sand & Gravel, Pittsburg *Also called Central Plains Contracting Co* ***(G-9830)***
Holliday Sand & Gravel Co LLC.......913 492-5920
9660 Legler Rd Lenexa (66219) ***(G-5905)***
Hollyfrntier El Dorado Ref LLC.......316 321-2200
1401 Douglas Rd El Dorado (67042) ***(G-1567)***
Hollywood Casino, Kansas City *Also called Kansas Entertaiment LLC* ***(G-4154)***
Holman Hansen and Colvile PC (PA).......913 648-7272
6900 College Blvd Ste 700 Leawood (66211) ***(G-5431)***
Holmes Basement Construction.......785 823-6770
1950 Ridgelea Dr Salina (67401) ***(G-10545)***
Holst Machine Shop.......316 794-8477
18621 W 39th St S Goddard (67052) ***(G-2442)***
Holthaus Autohaus LLC.......785 467-3101
720 W Oak St Fairview (66425) ***(G-1904)***
HOLTON COMMUNITY HOSPITAL, Holton *Also called Rural Hlth Rsurces Jackson Inc* ***(G-3110)***
Holton Dental.......785 364-3038
1100 Columbine Dr Ste B Holton (66436) ***(G-3096)***
Holton Family Health Clinic, Holton *Also called Community Healthcare Sys Inc* ***(G-3086)***
HOLTON FARM & HOME, Holton *Also called Two-Bee Inc* ***(G-3113)***
Holton Livestock Exchange Inc.......785 364-4114
13788 Highway K16 Holton (66436) ***(G-3097)***
Holton National Bank (PA).......785 364-2166
100 E 5th St Holton (66436) ***(G-3098)***
Holton Recorder, Holton *Also called Powls Publishing Company Inc* ***(G-3108)***
Holy Family Medical Inc.......316 682-9900
144 S Hillside St Ste A Wichita (67211) ***(G-14626)***
Holy Family Medical Assoc LLP.......316 682-9900
144 S Hillside St Ste A Wichita (67211) ***(G-14627)***
Holy Name Catholic Church (PA).......785 232-7744
911 Sw Clay St Topeka (66606) ***(G-12698)***
Holy Name Church, Topeka *Also called Holy Name Catholic Church* ***(G-12698)***
Holy Name Church.......785 232-1603
911 Sw Clay St Topeka (66606) ***(G-12699)***
Holyrood Bancshares Inc.......785 252-3239
100 S Main St Holyrood (67450) ***(G-3116)***
Home Bank and Trust Company (PA).......620 583-5516
217 N Main St Eureka (67045) ***(G-1891)***
Home Center Construction Inc.......620 231-5607
420 W Atkinson Rd Pittsburg (66762) ***(G-9877)***
Home Cleaning Centers America, Overland Park *Also called Dalan Inc* ***(G-8631)***
Home Communications Inc.......620 654-3381
211 S Main St Galva (67443) ***(G-2093)***
Home Depot USA Inc.......913 310-0204
8805 Lenexa Dr Overland Park (66214) ***(G-8823)***
Home Depot USA Inc.......913 789-8899
5700 Antioch Rd Merriam (66202) ***(G-7095)***
Home Depot USA Inc.......785 217-2260
5200 Sw Wenger Dr Topeka (66609) ***(G-12700)***
Home Depot USA Inc.......316 681-0899
3350 N Woodlawn Blvd Wichita (67220) ***(G-14628)***
Home Depot USA Inc.......316 773-1988
8444 W Mccormick Ave Wichita (67209) ***(G-14629)***
Home Depot USA Inc.......785 749-2074
1910 W 31st St Lawrence (66046) ***(G-4900)***
Home Depot USA Inc.......620 275-5943
3110 E Kansas City Garden City (67846) ***(G-2197)***
Home Depot USA Inc.......913 871-1221
11940 Metcalf Ave Overland Park (66213) ***(G-8824)***
Home Depot USA Inc.......913 888-9090
9900 Pflumm Rd Ste 64 Shawnee Mission (66215) ***(G-11437)***
Home Depot USA Inc.......785 272-5949
5900 Sw Huntoon St Frnt Topeka (66604) ***(G-12701)***
Home Depot USA Inc.......913 648-7811
9600 Metcalf Ave Shawnee Mission (66212) ***(G-11438)***
Home Depot, The, Overland Park *Also called Home Depot USA Inc* ***(G-8823)***
Home Depot, The, Merriam *Also called Home Depot USA Inc* ***(G-7095)***
Home Depot, The, Topeka *Also called Home Depot USA Inc* ***(G-12700)***
Home Depot, The, Wichita *Also called Home Depot USA Inc* ***(G-14628)***
Home Depot, The, Wichita *Also called Home Depot USA Inc* ***(G-14629)***
Home Depot, The, Lawrence *Also called Home Depot USA Inc* ***(G-4900)***
Home Depot, The, Garden City *Also called Home Depot USA Inc* ***(G-2197)***
Home Depot, The, Overland Park *Also called Home Depot USA Inc* ***(G-8824)***
Home Depot, The, Topeka *Also called Home Depot USA Inc* ***(G-12701)***
Home Depot, The, Shawnee Mission *Also called Home Depot USA Inc* ***(G-11438)***
Home Equipment Co, Coffeyville *Also called Medicalodges Cnstr Co Inc* ***(G-961)***
Home Health Agency.......785 826-6600
125 W Elm St Salina (67401) ***(G-10546)***
Home Health Agency Hosp Dst.......620 724-8469
804 W Saint John St Girard (66743) ***(G-2412)***
Home Health of Kansas LLC.......316 684-5122
7607 E Harry St Wichita (67207) ***(G-14630)***
HOME HEATH BY WESLEY TOWERS, Hutchinson *Also called Wesley Towers Inc* ***(G-3485)***
Home Instead Senior Care.......316 612-7541
3062 N Cranberry St Wichita (67226) ***(G-14631)***
Home Instead Senior Care.......785 272-6101
2900 Sw Wanamaker Dr # 103 Topeka (66614) ***(G-12702)***
Home National Bank, Arkansas City *Also called Hnb Corporation* ***(G-160)***
Home Readers Inc.......913 893-6900
604 W Hulett St Edgerton (66021) ***(G-1484)***
Home Remodeling Specialist, Silver Lake *Also called Window Design Company* ***(G-12030)***
Home Rental Services Inc.......913 469-6633
6900 College Blvd Ste 990 Overland Park (66211) ***(G-8825)***
Home Resource, Summerfield *Also called Precision Truss Inc* ***(G-12215)***
Home Savings Bank.......620 431-1100
214 N Lincoln Ave Chanute (66720) ***(G-733)***
Home State Bank & Trust Co (PA).......620 241-3732
223 N Main St McPherson (67460) ***(G-6974)***
Home Stl Siding & Windows LLC.......785 625-8622
1390 E 8th St Ste B Hays (67601) ***(G-2849)***
Home Store (PA).......620 421-4272
1725 Main St Parsons (67357) ***(G-9692)***
Home Telephone Co Inc.......620 654-3381
211 N Main St Galva (67443) ***(G-2094)***
Home Town Real.......620 271-9500
1135 College Dr Ste A Garden City (67846) ***(G-2198)***
Home2 Suites By Hilton, Leavenworth *Also called Eqh - Leavenworth LLC* ***(G-5236)***
Homecare of Hutchinson, Hutchinson *Also called Hospice of Reno County Inc* ***(G-3314)***
Homeland Roofing and Cnstr LLC.......316 832-9901
1107 S West St Wichita (67213) ***(G-14632)***
Homeless & Housing Services, Wichita *Also called Humankind Mnstries Wichita Inc* ***(G-14653)***
Homer Cove, Pittsburg *Also called Senior Svcs of Southeast Kans* ***(G-9936)***
Homestead, Olathe *Also called Wyncroft Hill Apartments* ***(G-8162)***
Homestead Assisted Living, Garden City *Also called Midwest Health Services Inc* ***(G-2233)***
Homestead Assisted Living.......785 272-2200
5820 Sw Drury Ln Topeka (66604) ***(G-12703)***
Homestead Asssted Lving Rsdnce, Manhattan *Also called Midwest Health Services Inc* ***(G-6750)***
Homestead Country Club.......913 262-4100
4100 Homestead Ct Prairie Village (66208) ***(G-10035)***
Homestead Health Center Inc.......316 262-4473
2133 S Elizabeth St Wichita (67213) ***(G-14633)***
Homestead Inc.......785 325-2361
311 E 2nd St Washington (66968) ***(G-13465)***
Homestead Nursing Home, Washington *Also called Homestead Inc* ***(G-13465)***
Homestead of Augusta.......316 775-1000
1611 Fairway Dr Augusta (67010) ***(G-325)***
Homestead of Hays.......785 628-3200
2929 Sternberg Dr Hays (67601) ***(G-2850)***
Homestead of Olathe North.......913 829-1403
791 N Somerset Ter Olathe (66062) ***(G-7771)***
HOMESTEAD, THE, Prairie Village *Also called Homestead Country Club* ***(G-10035)***
Homette, Arkansas City *Also called Skyline Corporation* ***(G-180)***
Homewood Suites, Wichita *Also called Lighthouse Properties LLC* ***(G-14964)***
Honey Creek Disposal Service.......913 369-8999
26195 Linwood Rd Lawrence (66044) ***(G-4901)***
Honeywell Authorized Dealer, Leavenworth *Also called Jf Denney Inc* ***(G-5257)***
Honeywell Authorized Dealer, Winfield *Also called Winfield Plumbing & Heating* ***(G-16188)***
Honeywell Authorized Dealer, Gardner *Also called BCI Mechanical Inc* ***(G-2329)***
Honeywell Authorized Dealer, Salina *Also called Pestinger Heating & AC Inc* ***(G-10634)***

ALPHABETIC

Honeywell Authorized Dealer, Shawnee Mission *Also called McCarty Mechanical Inc* ***(G-11607)***
Honeywell Authorized Dealer, Topeka *Also called Lower Heating & AC Inc* ***(G-12851)***
Honeywell Authorized Dealer, Wichita *Also called Waldinger Corporation* ***(G-15916)***
HONEYWELL AUTHORIZED DEALER, Kansas City *Also called Design Mechanical Inc* ***(G-3970)***
Honeywell Authorized Dealer, Lenexa *Also called Atronic Alarms Inc* ***(G-5674)***
Honeywell Authorized Dealer, Kansas City *Also called Baxter Mechanical Contractors* ***(G-3849)***
Honeywell Authorized Dealer, Salina *Also called Callabresi Heating & Coolg Inc* ***(G-10435)***
Honeywell Authorized Dealer, Shawnee Mission *Also called Harrington Bros Htg & Coolg* ***(G-11410)***
Honeywell Authorized Dealer, Overland Park *Also called Overland Park Heating & Coolg* ***(G-9119)***
Honeywell International Inc....316 522-8172
7227 W Harry St Wichita (67209) ***(G-14634)***
Honeywell International Inc....913 782-0400
23500 W 105th St Olathe (66061) ***(G-7772)***
Honeywell International Inc....816 997-7149
23500 W 105th St Md300 Olathe (66061) ***(G-7773)***
Honeywell International Inc....316 204-5503
306 S Brook Forest Rd Derby (67037) ***(G-1251)***
Honeywell International Inc....913 712-6017
101 New Century Pkwy New Century (66031) ***(G-7288)***
Honeywell International Inc....913 712-3000
23500 W 105th St Olathe (66061) ***(G-7774)***
Honeywell International Inc....402 597-2279
23500 W 105th St Olathe (66061) ***(G-7775)***
Honeywell International Inc....913 712-0400
23500 W 105th St Olathe (66061) ***(G-7776)***
Honeywell International Inc....620 783-1343
U.S Route 69a Pittsburg (66762) ***(G-9878)***
Hongs Landscape & Nursery Inc....316 687-3492
8904 E 31st St S Wichita (67210) ***(G-14635)***
Hood Htg Air Plg Electric Inc....785 243-1489
2201 E 6th St Concordia (66901) ***(G-1118)***
Hooper Holmes Inc (HQ)....913 764-1045
560 N Rogers Rd Olathe (66062) ***(G-7777)***
Hoover Bachman & Assoc Inc....620 342-2348
2812 W 12th Ave Emporia (66801) ***(G-1774)***
Hoover Stores Inc....620 364-5444
314 Cross St Burlington (66839) ***(G-637)***
Hoovers, Burlington *Also called Hoover Stores Inc* ***(G-637)***
Hope Hlth Hspice Dckinson Cnty, Abilene *Also called Hospital District 1 of Dcknsn* ***(G-39)***
Hope Lutheran Church Shawnee....913 631-6940
6308 Quivira Rd Shawnee Mission (66216) ***(G-11439)***
Hope Lutheran School, Shawnee Mission *Also called Hope Lutheran Church Shawnee* ***(G-11439)***
Hope Planting Intl Inc....785 776-8523
3310 Germann Dr Manhattan (66503) ***(G-6659)***
Hopkins & Hopkins....620 275-5375
802 N Campus Dr Garden City (67846) ***(G-2199)***
Hopkins Manufacturing Corp (PA)....620 342-7320
428 Peyton St Emporia (66801) ***(G-1775)***
Hopkins, George A, Garden City *Also called Hopkins & Hopkins* ***(G-2199)***
Hoppers Glass Inc....316 262-0497
880 E Bayley St Wichita (67211) ***(G-14636)***
Horizon Pipe Testing Inc....785 726-3773
301 W 2nd Street Ter Ellis (67637) ***(G-1647)***
Horizonpsi Inc....785 842-1299
1101 Horizon Dr Lawrence (66046) ***(G-4902)***
Horizons Mental Health Ctr Inc....620 532-3895
760 W D Ave Ste 1 Kingman (67068) ***(G-4595)***
Horizons Mental Health Ctr Inc (PA)....620 663-7595
1600 N Lorraine St # 202 Hutchinson (67501) ***(G-3312)***
Hormel Foods Corp Svcs LLC....913 888-8744
8700 Monrovia St Ste 200 Shawnee Mission (66215) ***(G-11440)***
Hornet Cutting Systems LLC....316 755-3683
430 W Clay St Valley Center (67147) ***(G-13343)***
Horst Trrill Krst Archtects PA (PA)....785 266-5373
900 S Kansas Ave Ste 200 Topeka (66612) ***(G-12704)***
Horton Main Branch, Horton *Also called Girard National Bank* ***(G-3124)***
Hose Products Division, Manhattan *Also called Parker-Hannifin Corporation* ***(G-6768)***
Hospice Incorporated (PA)....316 265-9441
313 S Market St Wichita (67202) ***(G-14637)***
Hospice Incorporated....316 283-1103
606 N Main St Ste 202 Newton (67114) ***(G-7363)***
Hospice Incorporated....620 251-1640
2404 W 8th St Coffeyville (67337) ***(G-947)***
Hospice Incorporated....620 229-8398
206 E 9th Ave Ste 1 Winfield (67156) ***(G-16147)***
Hospice Advantage LLC....913 859-9582
10101 W 87th St Ste 200 Overland Park (66212) ***(G-8826)***
Hospice Care of Kansas (PA)....316 283-2116
117 E Euclid St McPherson (67460) ***(G-6975)***
Hospice Care of Kansas LLC (PA)....316 721-8803
2622 W Central Ave # 501 Wichita (67203) ***(G-14638)***
Hospice HM Hlth Olathe Med Ctr, Olathe *Also called Olathe Medical Center Inc* ***(G-7941)***
Hospice of Graham County....785 421-2121
304 W Prout St Hill City (67642) ***(G-3035)***
Hospice of Reno County Inc....620 669-3773
1523 E 20th Ave Hutchinson (67502) ***(G-3313)***
Hospice of Reno County Inc (PA)....620 665-2473
1600 N Lorraine St # 203 Hutchinson (67501) ***(G-3314)***
Hospice of Salina Inc....785 825-1717
730 Holly Ln Salina (67401) ***(G-10547)***
HOSPICE OF THE PRAIRIE AND HOM, Dodge City *Also called Hospice of The Prairie Inc* ***(G-1375)***
Hospice of The Prairie Inc....620 227-7209
200 4th Cir Dodge City (67801) ***(G-1375)***
Hospice Preferred Choice Inc....785 840-0820
411 N Iowa St Ste A Lawrence (66044) ***(G-4903)***
Hospice Services Inc....785 543-2900
424 8th St Phillipsburg (67661) ***(G-9789)***
Hospira Inc....620 241-6200
1776 Centennial Dr McPherson (67460) ***(G-6976)***
Hospital District 1....620 724-8291
302 N Hospital Dr Girard (66743) ***(G-2413)***
Hospital District 1 of Dcknsn....785 263-6630
1111 N Brady St Abilene (67410) ***(G-39)***
Hospital District 1 Rice Cnty....620 257-5173
619 S Clark Ave Lyons (67554) ***(G-6484)***
Hospital District 2 Rice Cnty....620 897-6266
440 State St Little River (67457) ***(G-6419)***
Hospital District 3 Clark Cnty (PA)....620 635-2241
625 S Kentucky Ashland Ashland (67831) ***(G-196)***
Hospital Dst 1 Crawford Cnty, Girard *Also called Girard Medical Center* ***(G-2408)***
Hospital Dst 1 Dcknson Cnty Ka (PA)....785 263-2100
511 Ne 10th St Abilene (67410) ***(G-40)***
Hospital Dst 1 Marion Cnty....620 382-2177
535 S Freeborn St Marion (66861) ***(G-6873)***
Hospital Dst 1 of Rice Cnty (PA)....620 257-5173
619 S Clark Ave Lyons (67554) ***(G-6485)***
Hospital Dst 1 of Rice Cnty....620 278-2123
239 N Broadway Ave Sterling (67579) ***(G-12121)***
Hospital Dst 6 Harper Cnty....620 914-1200
485 N Ks Hwy 2 Anthony (67003) ***(G-128)***
Hospital Linen Services Inc....913 621-2228
611 S 4th St Kansas City (66105) ***(G-4085)***
Hospital Management Corp....913 492-0159
12920 Metcalf Ave Overland Park (66213) ***(G-8827)***
Hospitality Management LLC....316 262-0000
435 S Broadway Ave Wichita (67202) ***(G-14639)***
Hospitality Management Systems (PA)....913 438-5040
8064 Reeder St Overland Park (66214) ***(G-8828)***
Hospitality Oakley Group LLC....785 671-1111
3768 E Hwy 40 Oakley (67748) ***(G-7476)***
Hoss and Brown Engineers Inc (PA)....785 832-1105
4910 Corporate Centre Dr # 177 Lawrence (66047) ***(G-4904)***
Hostess Brands LLC....620 342-6811
1525 Industrial Rd Emporia (66801) ***(G-1776)***
Hostetler & Associates, Overland Park *Also called Superior Crt Reporting Svc LLC* ***(G-9377)***
Hotel, Wichita *Also called Wyndham Garden* ***(G-16080)***
Hotel At Old Town Inc....316 267-4800
830 E 1st St N Wichita (67202) ***(G-14640)***
Hotel At Old Town Cnfrence Ctr, Wichita *Also called Latour Management Inc* ***(G-14932)***
Hotel Clubs Corp Woods Inc....913 451-6100
10100 College Blvd Overland Park (66210) ***(G-8829)***
Hotel MGT & Consulting Inc....913 602-8470
7200 W 132nd St Ste 220 Overland Park (66213) ***(G-8830)***
Hotel Wichita Greenwich....316 681-1800
1220 N Greenwich Rd Wichita (67206) ***(G-14641)***
House of Dance....913 839-1962
18833 W 158th St Olathe (66062) ***(G-7778)***
House of Rocks Inc....913 432-5990
1725 Merriam Ln Kansas City (66106) ***(G-4086)***
House of Schwan Inc....316 636-9100
3636 N Comotara St Wichita (67226) ***(G-14642)***
Housekeeping Unlimited....785 842-2444
1611 Saint Andrews Dr Lawrence (66047) ***(G-4905)***
Housing and Credit Counseling (PA)....785 234-0217
1195 Sw Buchanan St # 101 Topeka (66604) ***(G-12705)***
Hovey Williams LLP....913 647-9050
10801 Mastin St Ste 1000 Overland Park (66210) ***(G-8831)***
Howard & Helmer Architects PA, Wichita *Also called Alloy Architecture PA* ***(G-13677)***
Howard Electronic Instrs Inc....316 321-2800
974 Se Pioneer Rd El Dorado (67042) ***(G-1568)***
Howard Johnson Express Inn....316 943-8165
6575 W Kellogg Dr Wichita (67209) ***(G-14643)***
Howard Stultz Construction....785 842-4796
983 E 1700 Rd Baldwin City (66006) ***(G-364)***
Howe Landscape Inc (PA)....785 485-2857
12780 Madison Rd Ste A Riley (66531) ***(G-10206)***
Howell Construction Co Inc....816 474-7766
16687 Lamar Ave Stilwell (66085) ***(G-12153)***

Howell Country Feeders LLC 620 227-6612
10256 Us Highway 50 Dodge City (67801) ***(G-1376)***
Howell Matthew D Dr DDS PA 316 260-6220
1145 N Andover Rd Ste 101 Andover (67002) ***(G-94)***
Howell Mouldings LC 913 782-0500
201 Overland Park Pl New Century (66031) ***(G-7289)***
Howie's Trash Service, Manhattan *Also called Howies Enterprises LLC* ***(G-6660)***
Howies Enterprises LLC 785 776-8352
625 S 10th St Manhattan (66502) ***(G-6660)***
Howl-A-Dayz Inn LLC 785 539-7849
530 Mccall Rd Ste 150 Manhattan (66502) ***(G-6661)***
Howmedica Osteonics Corp 913 491-3505
6600 College Blvd Ste 100 Leawood (66211) ***(G-5432)***
Hoxie Implement Co Inc 785 675-3201
933 Oak Ave Hwy 23 & 24 Hoxie (67740) ***(G-3139)***
Hoyt Pallet Co 785 986-6785
11621 P4 Rd Hoyt (66440) ***(G-3145)***
Hoyt's Truck Center, Topeka *Also called Spencer & Company* ***(G-13090)***
Hpb Biodiesel Inc 800 262-7907
9000 W 67th St Ste 200 Shawnee Mission (66202) ***(G-11441)***
Hpt Trs Ihg 2 Inc 316 942-0400
570 S Julia St Wichita (67209) ***(G-14644)***
Hpt Trs Ihg-2 Inc 913 469-5557
11001 Oakmont St Shawnee Mission (66210) ***(G-11442)***
Hpt Trs Ihg-2 Inc 316 634-6070
3141 N Webb Rd Wichita (67226) ***(G-14645)***
Hre—Colorado Springs LLC 817 739-8529
2035 E Iron Ave Ste 224 Salina (67401) ***(G-10548)***
Hro Fort Stewart, Fort Leavenworth *Also called United States Dept of Army* ***(G-1942)***
Hsbc Finance Corporation 913 362-1400
5115 Roe Blvd Roeland Park (66205) ***(G-10225)***
Hss IT Management Inc (PA) 913 498-9988
6601 College Blvd Fl 6 Overland Park (66211) ***(G-8832)***
Hsu, C H, Topeka *Also called Topeka Urology Clinic PA* ***(G-13191)***
Htc Inc 865 689-2311
17400 W 119th St Olathe (66061) ***(G-7779)***
Htk Architects, Topeka *Also called Horst Trrill Krst Archtects PA* ***(G-12704)***
Hub Cap & Wheel Store Inc 913 432-0002
2810 S 44th St Kansas City (66106) ***(G-4087)***
Hub Chemical Storage, Sterling *Also called Central Prairie Co-Op* ***(G-12113)***
Hub Supply, Wichita *Also called Motion Industries Inc* ***(G-15133)***
Hubbard Feeds, Beloit *Also called Ridley USA Inc* ***(G-500)***
Hubco Inc 620 663-8301
215 S Poplar St Hutchinson (67501) ***(G-3315)***
Huber Inc 316 267-0289
117 N Handley St Wichita (67203) ***(G-14646)***
Huber Sand Company 620 275-7601
395 N Industrial Dr Garden City (67846) ***(G-2200)***
Hubergroup Usa Inc 913 262-2510
3008 S 44th St Kansas City (66106) ***(G-4088)***
Hubris Communications 316 858-3000
266 N Main St Ste 150 Wichita (67202) ***(G-14647)***
Hudson Crop Insurance Svcs Inc 866 450-1446
7300 W 110th St Ste 400 Overland Park (66210) ***(G-8833)***
Hudson Holding Inc 866 404-3300
14301 W Hardtner Ct Wichita (67235) ***(G-14648)***
Hudson Inc 620 232-1145
450 E 540th Ave Pittsburg (66762) ***(G-9879)***
Hufford House 620 225-0276
11200 Lariat Way Dodge City (67801) ***(G-1377)***
Hughes Development Company Inc (PA) 913 321-2262
1021 N 7th St Ste 106 Kansas City (66101) ***(G-4089)***
Hughes Drilling Co 785 883-2235
122 Main St Wellsville (66092) ***(G-13543)***
Hughes Machinery Company (HQ) 913 492-0355
14400 College Blvd Lenexa (66215) ***(G-5906)***
Hughes Machinery Company 316 612-0868
11021 E 28th St N Ste 1 Wichita (67226) ***(G-14649)***
Hughes, C W Dntst, Manhattan *Also called Dental Associates* ***(G-6612)***
Hugo's Mini Storage, Independence *Also called Hugos Industrial Supply Inc* ***(G-3526)***
Hugos Industrial Supply Inc 620 331-4846
2700 W Main St Independence (67301) ***(G-3526)***
Hugoton Jay Hawk Gas Plant, Satanta *Also called BP America Production Company* ***(G-10777)***
Hugoton Swimming Pool 620 544-2793
114 E 5th St Hugoton (67951) ***(G-3165)***
Huhtamaki Inc (HQ) 913 583-3025
9201 Packaging Dr De Soto (66018) ***(G-1202)***
Huhtamaki Americas Inc 913 583-3025
9201 Packaging Dr De Soto (66018) ***(G-1203)***
Huhtamaki Films Inc 913 583-3025
9201 Packaging Dr De Soto (66018) ***(G-1204)***
Hullings Jon G DDS Ms PA 316 636-1980
1700 N Waterfront Pkwy Wichita (67206) ***(G-14650)***
Hulsing Hotels Kansas Inc (PA) 785 841-7077
200 Mcdonald Dr Lawrence (66044) ***(G-4906)***
Hulsing Hotels Kansas Inc 785 539-5311
530 Richards Dr Ste B Manhattan (66502) ***(G-6662)***

Humana Inc 316 612-6820
601 S Greenwich Rd # 111 Wichita (67207) ***(G-14651)***
Humana Inc 913 217-3300
7311 W 132nd St Ste 200 Overland Park (66213) ***(G-8834)***
Humane Soc of High Plains 785 625-5252
2050 E Us Highway 40 Hays (67601) ***(G-2851)***
Humankind Mnstries Wichita Inc (PA) 316 264-9303
829 N Market St Wichita (67214) ***(G-14652)***
Humankind Mnstries Wichita Inc 316 264-8051
320 E Central Ave Wichita (67202) ***(G-14653)***
Humbert Envelope Machinery 785 845-6085
3742 Ne Kincaid Rd Topeka (66617) ***(G-12706)***
Hume Music Inc 816 474-1960
16010 Metcalf Ave Ste 200 Stilwell (66085) ***(G-12154)***
Humidor East 316 688-0112
2221 N Woodlawn Blvd Wichita (67220) ***(G-14654)***
Hummert International Inc 785 234-5652
1415 Nw Moundview Dr Topeka (66618) ***(G-12707)***
Hummon Corporation 620 930-2645
101 N Main St Medicine Lodge (67104) ***(G-7064)***
Humphrey Products Inc (PA) 316 267-2201
719 E Zimmerly St Wichita (67211) ***(G-14655)***
Hunkeler Eye Institute PA 913 338-4733
7950 College Blvd Ste B Shawnee Mission (66210) ***(G-11443)***
Hunn Leather Products Inc 316 775-6300
900 Industrial Rd Augusta (67010) ***(G-326)***
Hunter Health Clinic Inc (PA) 316 262-2415
2318 E Central Ave Wichita (67214) ***(G-14656)***
Hunters Ridge Branch, Topeka *Also called Corefirst Bank & Trust* ***(G-12510)***
Huntingdon Park Standard Svc 785 272-4499
3120 Sw Gage Blvd Topeka (66614) ***(G-12708)***
Hurricane Services Inc 620 437-2661
3613a Y Rd Madison (66860) ***(G-6501)***
Hurricane Services Inc (PA) 316 303-9515
250 N Water St Ste 200 Wichita (67202) ***(G-14657)***
Husky Hogs LLC 785 854-7666
1271 W Fox Rd Long Island (67647) ***(G-6427)***
Husky Liners Inc 620 221-2268
22425 D St Strother Fld Winfield (67156) ***(G-16148)***
Husqvarna Chain Saws & Pwr Eqp 785 263-7668
1701 W 1st St Abilene (67410) ***(G-41)***
Husqvarna US Holding Inc 913 928-1000
17400 W 119th St Olathe (66061) ***(G-7780)***
Husqvrna Cnstr Pdts N Amer Inc (HQ) 913 928-1000
17400 W 119th St Olathe (66061) ***(G-7781)***
Hussmann Corporation 816 373-1274
10542 Lackman Rd Lenexa (66219) ***(G-5907)***
Huston Contracting Inc 913 782-1333
614 S Kansas Ave Olathe (66061) ***(G-7782)***
Hutch Good Samaritan Village 620 663-1189
810 E 30th Ave Hutchinson (67502) ***(G-3316)***
Hutch Rec Comm, Hutchinson *Also called Elmdale Community Center* ***(G-3278)***
Hutch Sign 620 663-6108
1325 A Half N Halstead St Hutchinson (67501) ***(G-3317)***
Hutchens Corporation 785 252-3423
204 N County Rd Holyrood (67450) ***(G-3117)***
Hutchins & Associates 913 338-4455
11900 College Blvd # 310 Shawnee Mission (66210) ***(G-11444)***
Hutchinson Care Center LLC 620 662-0597
2301 N Severance St Hutchinson (67502) ***(G-3318)***
Hutchinson Clinic PA (PA) 620 669-2500
2101 N Waldron St Hutchinson (67502) ***(G-3319)***
Hutchinson Clinic PA 620 486-2985
609 E 1st Ave Saint John (67576) ***(G-10352)***
Hutchinson Community College 620 665-3500
1521 N Ford St Hutchinson (67501) ***(G-3320)***
Hutchinson Health Care, Hutchinson *Also called Deseret Health Group Llc* ***(G-3262)***
Hutchinson Hlth Care Svcs Inc (HQ) 620 665-0528
803 E 30th Ave Hutchinson (67502) ***(G-3321)***
Hutchinson Mall, Hutchinson *Also called Melvin Simon & Associates Inc* ***(G-3372)***
Hutchinson Mayrath, Clay Center *Also called AG Growth International Inc* ***(G-842)***
Hutchinson News, Hutchinson *Also called Hutchinson Publishing Co* ***(G-3322)***
Hutchinson Publishing Co 620 694-5700
300 W 2nd Ave Hutchinson (67501) ***(G-3322)***
Hutchinson Recreation Comm, Hutchinson *Also called Dillon Nature Center* ***(G-3265)***
Hutchinson Recreation Comm 620 663-6179
17 E 1st Ave Hutchinson (67501) ***(G-3323)***
Hutchinson Salt Company Inc 620 856-3332
136 W 12th St Baxter Springs (66713) ***(G-409)***
Hutchinson Salt Company Inc 620 662-3341
3300 Carey Blvd Hutchinson (67501) ***(G-3324)***
Hutchinson Symphony Assn 620 543-2511
10104 N Tobacco Rd Hutchinson (67502) ***(G-3325)***
Hutchinson Theatre Guild 620 662-9202
901 W 1st Ave Hutchinson (67501) ***(G-3326)***
Hutchinson Usd 308 ....620 615-5575
815 W 4th Ave Hutchinson (67501) ***(G-3327)***
Hutchinson Vending Company (PA) 620 662-6474
24 Prairie Dunes Dr Hutchinson (67502) ***(G-3328)***

ALPHABETIC

Hutchinson/Mayrath 785 632-2161
514 W Crawford St Clay Center (67432) ***(G-868)***
Hutchinson/Reno County Chamber 620 662-3391
117 N Walnut St Hutchinson (67501) ***(G-3329)***
Hutchnson Hosp Psychiatric Ctr 620 665-2364
1701 E 23rd Ave Hutchinson (67502) ***(G-3330)***
Hutchnson Regional Med Ctr Inc 620 665-2000
1701 E 23rd Ave Hutchinson (67502) ***(G-3331)***
Hutchnson Reno Cnty Legal Svcs, Hutchinson *Also called Kansas Legal Services Inc* ***(G-3346)***
Hutton & Hutton 316 688-1166
8100 E 22nd St N # 1200 Wichita (67226) ***(G-14658)***
Hutton & Hutton Law Firm 316 688-1166
8100 E 22nd St N # 1200 Wichita (67226) ***(G-14659)***
Hutton Construction Corp (PA) 316 942-8855
2229 S West St Wichita (67213) ***(G-14660)***
Huxtable & Associates Inc 785 843-2910
2151 Haskell Ave Blgd1 Lawrence (66046) ***(G-4907)***
Huyett Jones Partners 785 228-0900
3200 Sw Huntoon St Topeka (66604) ***(G-12709)***
Hwa Davis Cnstr & Sup Inc 316 283-0330
414 N Main St Ste 150 Newton (67114) ***(G-7364)***
Hy Plains Feedyard LLC 620 846-2226
Hwy 56 Montezuma (67867) ***(G-7156)***
Hy-Test Boots & Shoes, Lenexa *Also called Sid Bdeker Safety Shoe Svc Inc* ***(G-6134)***
Hyatt Corporation 316 293-1234
400 W Waterman St Wichita (67202) ***(G-14661)***
Hyatt Place, Topeka *Also called AHP H6 Topeka* ***(G-12302)***
Hyatt Place Kansas, Overland Park *Also called Hit Portfolio I Trs LLC* ***(G-8817)***
Hyatt Place KS Cty/Overlnd Pk, Overland Park *Also called Select Hotels Group LLC* ***(G-9289)***
Hyatt Place Lenexa City Center, Lenexa *Also called Lenexa City Center Hotel Corp* ***(G-5968)***
Hyatt Regency Wichita, Wichita *Also called Hyatt Corporation* ***(G-14661)***
Hybrid Turkeys LLC 620 951-4705
1418 Cow Palace Rd Newton (67114) ***(G-7365)***
Hydeman Company Inc 913 384-2620
3300 Rainbow Ext Kansas City (66103) ***(G-4090)***
Hydro Geologic, Shawnee Mission *Also called Hydrogeologic Inc* ***(G-11445)***
Hydro Rsrces - Mid Cntnent Inc 620 277-2389
3795 W Jones Ave Garden City (67846) ***(G-2201)***
Hydrochem LLC 316 321-7541
703 N Taylor St El Dorado (67042) ***(G-1569)***
Hydrochempsc, El Dorado *Also called Hydrochem LLC* ***(G-1569)***
Hydrogeologic Inc 913 317-8860
6340 Glenwood St Ste 200 Shawnee Mission (66202) ***(G-11445)***
Hygienic Dry Cleaners Inc (PA) 785 478-0066
2930 Sw Mcclure Rd Topeka (66614) ***(G-12710)***
Hyland Holdings LLC (HQ) 913 227-7000
8900 Renner Blvd Lenexa (66219) ***(G-5908)***
Hyland LLC (HQ) 440 788-5045
18103 W 106th St Ste 200 Olathe (66061) ***(G-7783)***
Hyper Pet, Wichita *Also called Kth Properties Corporation* ***(G-14897)***
Hyr Global Source Inc 913 815-2597
7304 W 130th St Ste 220 Overland Park (66213) ***(G-8835)***
Hyspeco Inc (PA) 316 943-0254
1729 S Sabin St Wichita (67209) ***(G-14662)***
I 70 Tax Services LLC 785 539-5240
100 Bluemont Ave Ste G Manhattan (66502) ***(G-6663)***
I A M A W District Lodge 70 316 522-1591
3830 S Meridian Ave Wichita (67217) ***(G-14663)***
I B P, Holcomb *Also called Tyson Fresh Meats Inc* ***(G-3082)***
I B S Industries Inc 913 281-0787
500 State Ave Rm 176 Kansas City (66101) ***(G-4091)***
I B T Reference Laboratory, Lenexa *Also called Progene Biomedical Inc* ***(G-6074)***
I C I, El Dorado *Also called Insurance Center Inc* ***(G-1571)***
I F C, Lenexa *Also called Industrial Fumigant Collc* ***(G-5913)***
I M S of Kansas City Inc 913 599-6007
11555 W 83rd Ter Shawnee Mission (66214) ***(G-11446)***
I N G, Lenexa *Also called Interntnal Mtr Coach Group Inc* ***(G-5920)***
I P E Co, Wichita *Also called Industrial Process Eqp Co* ***(G-14686)***
I P H F H A Inc 316 685-1200
7829 E Rockhill St # 201 Wichita (67206) ***(G-14664)***
I S C, Kansas City *Also called Kansas Speedway Corporation* ***(G-4157)***
I S G, Hutchinson *Also called Integrated Solutions Group Inc* ***(G-3334)***
I S L, Olathe *Also called Industrial Sling Lbrcation Inc* ***(G-7788)***
I Samco Investments Ltd (PA) 913 345-2111
10985 Cody St Ste 220 Shawnee Mission (66210) ***(G-11447)***
I T G Consulting Inc 785 228-1585
2207 Sw Alameda Ct Topeka (66614) ***(G-12711)***
I T Power LLC 913 384-5800
6811 Shawnee Mission Pkwy # 107 Shawnee Mission (66202) ***(G-11448)***
I X T, Kansas City *Also called International Ex Trckg Inc* ***(G-4106)***
I-70 Auto Auction, Topeka *Also called Carlson Auction Service Inc* ***(G-12451)***
I-70 Truck Repair, Hays *Also called Errol E Engel Inc* ***(G-2800)***
I-Machine, Goddard *Also called Landwehr Machine* ***(G-2445)***
I2 Asia LLC 913 422-1600
21983 W 83rd St Shawnee (66227) ***(G-10972)***
Iaa Inc 316 832-1101
270 W 53rd St N Park City (67204) ***(G-9620)***
Iaa Inc 913 422-9303
2663 S 88th St Kansas City (66111) ***(G-4092)***
Iaa 527, Kansas City *Also called Iaa Inc* ***(G-4092)***
Iaa 533, Park City *Also called Iaa Inc* ***(G-9620)***
IAC Systems Inc 913 384-5511
4800 Lamar Ave Ste 203 Shawnee Mission (66202) ***(G-11449)***
Ian F Yeats MD Chartered 620 624-0142
1411 W 15th St Ste 102 Liberal (67901) ***(G-6322)***
Ian S Kovach MD PHD 620 672-1002
203 Watson St Ste 300 Pratt (67124) ***(G-10121)***
Ibt Inc 913 428-4958
3003 Power Dr Kansas City (66106) ***(G-4093)***
Ibt Inc 913 677-3151
5420 England Shawnee Mission (66203) ***(G-11450)***
Ibt Aerospace, Kansas City *Also called Ibt Inc* ***(G-4093)***
Icare Usa Inc 919 624-9095
100 Abbie Ave Kansas City (66103) ***(G-4094)***
Ice Sports Kansas City LLC 913 441-3033
19900 Johnson Dr Shawnee Mission (66218) ***(G-11451)***
Ice Sports-Kansas City, Shawnee Mission *Also called Ice Sports Kansas City LLC* ***(G-11451)***
Ice-Masters Inc (HQ) 660 827-6900
6218 Melrose Ln Shawnee Mission (66203) ***(G-11452)***
Ice-Masters Inc 316 945-6900
2569 W Pawnee St Wichita (67213) ***(G-14665)***
Icg Inc 913 461-8759
11401 Linden St Leawood (66211) ***(G-5433)***
ICI Manufacturing, Topeka *Also called Industrial Chrome Inc* ***(G-12721)***
Iclean Prof Clg Svcs LLC 913 521-5995
12022 Blue Valley Pkwy # 1 Overland Park (66213) ***(G-8836)***
ICM, Topeka *Also called Industrial Cleaning and Maint* ***(G-12722)***
Icm Inc (PA) 316 796-0900
310 N 1st St Colwich (67030) ***(G-1097)***
Icon Industries Inc 785 738-3547
1600 W 8th St Beloit (67420) ***(G-488)***
Icon Integration & Design Inc 913 221-8801
9393 W 110th St Ste 500 Overland Park (66210) ***(G-8837)***
Icon Poker, Olathe *Also called Rutland Inc* ***(G-8049)***
Ics Inc 620 654-3020
210 N Elder St McPherson (67460) ***(G-6977)***
Ict Billet LLC 316 300-0833
1107 S West St Unit 2 Wichita (67213) ***(G-14666)***
Idea Center Inc 785 320-2400
301 S 4th St Ste 200 Manhattan (66502) ***(G-6664)***
Idealease of Mo-Kan Inc 785 235-8711
500 E Tenth St Topeka (66607) ***(G-12712)***
Idealease of Mo-Kan Inc 785 379-2300
346 N James St Kansas City (66118) ***(G-4095)***
Ideatek Telecom LLC 620 543-2580
111 Old Mill St Buhler (67522) ***(G-617)***
Identigen North America Inc 785 856-8800
2029 Becker Dr Lawrence (66047) ***(G-4908)***
Ideolity, Mission *Also called Twenty-First Century* ***(G-7139)***
Idexx Laboratories Inc 913 339-4550
11250 Strang Line Rd Lenexa (66215) ***(G-5909)***
Idle Hour Club, Frontenac *Also called Bartos Enterprises Inc* ***(G-2053)***
Iet, Wichita *Also called Integrated Electrical Tech LLC* ***(G-14701)***
If, Olathe *Also called Innovative Fluid Power* ***(G-7794)***
Ifft & Co PA 913 345-1120
11030 Granada Ln Ste 100 Overland Park (66211) ***(G-8838)***
IFR Systems Inc 316 522-4981
10200 W York St Wichita (67215) ***(G-14667)***
Igt Global Solutions Corp 785 861-7300
128 N Kansas Ave Fl 1 Topeka (66603) ***(G-12713)***
Iheartcommunications Inc 316 494-6600
9323 E 37th St N Wichita (67226) ***(G-14668)***
Iheartcommunications Inc 316 832-9600
2402 E 37th St N Wichita (67219) ***(G-14669)***
IICS, Overland Park *Also called International Inst Christian S* ***(G-8858)***
III Investments Inc (PA) 913 262-6500
11313 El Monte St Leawood (66211) ***(G-5434)***
Illinois Auto Electric Co 913 543-7600
9630 Woodend Rd Edwardsville (66111) ***(G-1503)***
Illinois Tool Works Inc 913 856-2546
147 Cherokee St Gardner (66030) ***(G-2351)***
Illinois Tool Works Inc 913 397-9889
805 E Old Highway 56 Olathe (66061) ***(G-7784)***
Illinois Tool Works Inc 800 262-7907
9000 W 67th St Shawnee Mission (66202) ***(G-11453)***
Ilm 1 Holding Inc 316 687-3741
2455 N Woodlawn Blvd Ofc Wichita (67220) ***(G-14670)***
Ils Farm Partnership 620 792-6166
551a Sw 30 Rd Great Bend (67530) ***(G-2592)***
Ils National LLC (PA) 913 888-9191
1570 S Mahaffie Cir Olathe (66062) ***(G-7785)***

Ilsn, Olathe *Also called Ils National LLC* ***(G-7785)***
Im Olathe LP 913 829-6700
12215 S Strang Line Rd Olathe (66062) ***(G-7786)***
Ima Inc 316 267-9221
8200 E 32nd St N Wichita (67226) ***(G-14671)***
Ima Financial Group Inc (PA) 316 267-9221
8200 E 32nd St N Wichita (67226) ***(G-14672)***
Ima Financial Group Inc 785 232-2202
2820 Sw Mission Woods Dr # 150 Topeka (66614) ***(G-12714)***
Ima of Kansas Inc 316 267-9221
8200 E 32nd St N Wichita (67226) ***(G-14673)***
Ima Select LLC (HQ) 316 266-6203
8200 E 32nd St N Wichita (67226) ***(G-14674)***
Ima Wealth Inc 316 266-6582
8200 E 32nd St N Ste 100 Wichita (67226) ***(G-14675)***
Image Flooring LLC 314 432-3000
14720 W 105th St Lenexa (66215) ***(G-5910)***
Image Quest Inc (HQ) 316 686-3200
11021 E 26th St N Wichita (67226) ***(G-14676)***
Images (PA) 785 827-0824
132 S 4th St Salina (67401) ***(G-10549)***
Images Hairstyling, Lawrence *Also called Gq Inc* ***(G-4878)***
Images Recycling, Salina *Also called Images* ***(G-10549)***
Images Salon & Day Spa 785 843-2138
511 W 9th St Lawrence (66044) ***(G-4909)***
Imaging Solutions Company 316 630-0440
201 N Mead St Wichita (67202) ***(G-14677)***
Imagintive Cnsulting Group Inc 913 481-1936
7111 W 151st St Ste 154 Overland Park (66223) ***(G-8839)***
IMI, Topeka *Also called Industrial Maint Topeka Inc* ***(G-12723)***
IMPACT BANK, Wellington *Also called Lena M Rush Scholarship Trust* ***(G-13511)***
Imperial American Oil Corp 316 721-0036
13906 W Onewood St Wichita (67235) ***(G-14678)***
Imperial Sleep Products Inc 620 465-2242
8819 E Industrial Rd Haven (67543) ***(G-2732)***
Impresa Aerospace LLC 316 942-9100
2232 S Custer Ave Wichita (67213) ***(G-14679)***
Imprints Wholesale, Kansas City *Also called Stardust Corporation* ***(G-4439)***
In Terminal Consolidation Co 913 671-7755
4010 Argentine Blvd Kansas City (66106) ***(G-4096)***
In-Terminal Services, Edgerton *Also called Intermodal Acquisition LLC* ***(G-1485)***
In2itive Bus Solutions LLC 913 344-7002
6330 Sprint Pkwy Ste 425 Leawood (66211) ***(G-5435)***
Incisive Consultants LLC 800 973-1743
13725 Metcalf Ave Ste 296 Overland Park (66223) ***(G-8840)***
Inclusion Technologies LLC 913 370-8070
1145 Main St Atchison (66002) ***(G-236)***
Incred-A-Bowl LLC 913 851-1700
16332 Larsen St Overland Park (66221) ***(G-8841)***
Indel Corporation 785 478-9719
2257 Sw Romar Rd Topeka (66614) ***(G-12715)***
Independence Inc 785 841-0333
2001 Haskell Ave Lawrence (66046) ***(G-4910)***
Independence Anesthesia Inc 913 707-5294
8725 Rosehill Rd Lenexa (66215) ***(G-5911)***
Independence Country Club 620 331-1270
2824 Country Club Cir Independence (67301) ***(G-3527)***
Independence Daily Reporter, Independence *Also called Montgomery County Media LLC* ***(G-3541)***
Independence Dialysis Center, Independence *Also called Renal Trtmnt Centers-West Inc* ***(G-3554)***
Independence Main Street Inc 620 331-2300
109 E Main St Independence (67301) ***(G-3528)***
Independence Ready Mix Inc 620 331-4150
915 N Penn Ave Independence (67301) ***(G-3529)***
Independent Digital Printing, Wichita *Also called Independent Oil & Gas Svc Inc* ***(G-14680)***
Independent Electric McHy Co (PA) 913 362-1155
4425 Oliver St Kansas City (66106) ***(G-4097)***
Independent Electric McHy Co 620 257-5375
456 Wabash Ave Lyons (67554) ***(G-6486)***
Independent Electric McHy Co 785 233-4282
2221 Nw Vail Ave Topeka (66608) ***(G-12716)***
Independent Oil & Gas Svc Inc 316 263-8281
226 N Emporia Ave Wichita (67202) ***(G-14680)***
Independent Order Oddfellows 785 456-9493
17165 Elm Slough Rd Wamego (66547) ***(G-13425)***
Independent Salt Company 785 472-4421
1126 20th Rd Kanopolis (67454) ***(G-3772)***
Indepndent Living Resource Ctr 316 942-6300
3033 W 2nd St N Ste 1 Wichita (67203) ***(G-14681)***
Indevco Inc 913 236-7222
6911 W 66th Ter Shawnee Mission (66202) ***(G-11454)***
Indian Creek, Overland Park *Also called Marc A Asher Md Comprehensi* ***(G-8986)***
Indian Creek Racquet Club, Shawnee Mission *Also called Tennis Corporation of America* ***(G-11926)***
Indian Hills Animal Clinic 316 942-3900
3223 W 13th St N Wichita (67203) ***(G-14682)***
Indian Hills Country Club 913 362-6200
6847 Tomahawk Rd Mission Hills (66208) ***(G-7144)***
Indian Hills Hardware Inc 785 841-1479
4309 Quail Pointe Rd Lawrence (66047) ***(G-4911)***
Indian Hills Meat and Plty Inc 316 264-1644
1200 N Mosley Ave Wichita (67214) ***(G-14683)***
Indigents Defense Svcs Kans Bd 785 296-1833
701 Sw Jackson St Topeka (66603) ***(G-12717)***
Indigents Defense Svcs Kans Bd (HQ) 785 296-6631
700 Sw Jackson St Topeka (66603) ***(G-12718)***
Indigents Defense Svcs Kans Bd 785 296-5484
700 Sw Jackson St Ste 900 Topeka (66603) ***(G-12719)***
Indigents Defense Svcs Kans Bd 316 264-8700
604 N Main St Ste D Wichita (67203) ***(G-14684)***
Individual Support Systems Inc 785 228-9443
3500 Sw 10th Ave Topeka (66604) ***(G-12720)***
Induction Dynamics LLC (PA) 913 663-5600
10661 Rene St Lenexa (66215) ***(G-5912)***
Industrial Accessories Company (PA) 913 384-5511
4800 Lamar Ave Ste 203 Shawnee Mission (66202) ***(G-11455)***
Industrial Battery Pdts Inc 913 236-6500
5360 Merriam Dr Merriam (66203) ***(G-7096)***
Industrial Chrome Inc (PA) 785 235-3463
834 Ne Madison St Topeka (66608) ***(G-12721)***
Industrial Cleaning and Maint 785 246-9262
4330 Nw Westgate Rd Topeka (66618) ***(G-12722)***
Industrial Coatings Inc 913 321-2116
200 S 5th St Kansas City (66101) ***(G-4098)***
Industrial Crating Inc 620 449-2003
413 N Front St Saint Paul (66771) ***(G-10381)***
Industrial Fumigant Collc (HQ) 913 782-7600
13420 W 99th St Lenexa (66215) ***(G-5913)***
Industrial Insulation Svcs Inc 316 321-5358
2200 W 6th Ave El Dorado (67042) ***(G-1570)***
Industrial Maint Topeka Inc 785 842-6252
4501 Nw Us Highway 24 Topeka (66618) ***(G-12723)***
Industrial Maintenance Inc 316 267-7933
708 E 18th St N Wichita (67214) ***(G-14685)***
Industrial Mfg & Repair Svc, Garden City *Also called Industrial Mfg & Repr Svc* ***(G-2202)***
Industrial Mfg & Repr Svc 620 275-0481
2805 W Mary St Garden City (67846) ***(G-2202)***
Industrial Mtal Fbrication Inc 316 283-3303
1401 S Spencer Rd Newton (67114) ***(G-7366)***
Industrial Process Eqp Co 316 722-7800
8974 W Monroe Cir Wichita (67209) ***(G-14686)***
Industrial Roofg Met Works Inc 316 262-4758
2209 W Harry St Wichita (67213) ***(G-14687)***
Industrial Sales Company Inc (PA) 913 829-3500
1150 W Marley Rd Olathe (66061) ***(G-7787)***
Industrial Sling Lbrcation Inc 913 294-3001
15430 S Keeler St Olathe (66062) ***(G-7788)***
Industrial State Bank (HQ) 913 831-2000
3201 Strong Ave Kansas City (66106) ***(G-4099)***
Industrial Uniform Company LLC 316 264-2871
3550 N Comotara St Wichita (67226) ***(G-14688)***
Industrial Ventures Inc (PA) 316 634-6699
731 S Industrial Ct Rose Hill (67133) ***(G-10240)***
Ineeda Cleaners, Hutchinson *Also called Ineeda Laundry & Dry Cleaners* ***(G-3332)***
Ineeda Laundry & Dry Cleaners (PA) 620 662-6450
1224 N Main St Hutchinson (67501) ***(G-3332)***
Ineeda Laundry and Drycleaners 620 663-5688
1 Compound Dr 8 Hutchinson (67502) ***(G-3333)***
Infant Tddler Svcs Jhnson Cnty 913 432-2900
6400 Glenwood St Ste 205 Shawnee Mission (66202) ***(G-11456)***
Infectious Disease Cons PA (PA) 316 264-3505
1100 N St Francis St # 130 Wichita (67214) ***(G-14689)***
Infectious Disease Consultants 316 264-3505
1100 N St Francis St # 130 Wichita (67214) ***(G-14690)***
Inficon Edc Inc 913 888-1750
9075 Cody St Overland Park (66214) ***(G-8842)***
Infinia At Wichita Inc 316 691-9999
1600 S Woodlawn Blvd Wichita (67218) ***(G-14691)***
Infinite Fitness 913 469-8850
3617 W 133rd St Overland Park (66209) ***(G-8843)***
Infinitech Surface Finishing, Wichita *Also called Isf LLC* ***(G-14730)***
Infinity Fasteners Inc (PA) 913 438-8547
11028 Strang Line Rd Lenexa (66215) ***(G-5914)***
Infinity Insur Solutions LLC 913 338-3200
10707 Barkley St Ste B Leawood (66211) ***(G-5436)***
Infinity Roofing, Olathe *Also called E3 Roofing Group Inc* ***(G-7664)***
Infinity Tents Inc 913 820-3700
5050 Kansas Ave Kansas City (66106) ***(G-4100)***
Informa Business Media Inc 913 341-1300
17300 W 119th St Olathe (66061) ***(G-7789)***
Information Tech Intl Inc 913 579-8079
3800 Post Rd Hays (67601) ***(G-2852)***
Information Technical Dept, Topeka *Also called Topeka Unified School Dst 501* ***(G-13190)***
Informtion Cmmunications Group 913 469-6767
4701 College Blvd Ste 110 Leawood (66211) ***(G-5437)***

ALPHABETIC

Infosync Services Llc 316 685-1622
1938 N Woodlawn St # 110 Wichita (67208) ***(G-14692)***

Infusion Design Incorporated (PA) 913 422-0317
110 W 3rd St Bonner Springs (66012) ***(G-555)***

Infusion LLC 316 686-1610
1909 E Central Ave Wichita (67214) ***(G-14693)***

Infutor Data Solutions LLC 913 782-8544
1533 E Spruce St Olathe (66061) ***(G-7790)***

Ingalls Feed Yard 620 335-5174
10505 Us Highway 50 Ingalls (67853) ***(G-3576)***

Ingenium Solutions Inc 913 239-0050
10801 Mastin St Ste 550 Overland Park (66210) ***(G-8844)***

Ingstad Broadcasting Inc 620 276-2366
1402 E Kansas Ave Garden City (67846) ***(G-2203)***

Inityaero Inc 316 265-0603
1935 W Walker St Wichita (67213) ***(G-14694)***

Inkcycle Inc 913 894-8387
10601 W 79th St Shawnee (66214) ***(G-10973)***

Inland Associates Inc (PA) 913 764-7977
18965 W 158th St Olathe (66062) ***(G-7791)***

Inland Corporation 620 478-2450
15243 Se 150 St Norwich (67118) ***(G-7470)***

Inland Industries Inc (PA) 913 492-9050
19841 Benson St Bucyrus (66013) ***(G-600)***

Inland Newspaper Mchy Corp 913 492-9050
14500 W 105th St Shawnee Mission (66215) ***(G-11457)***

Inland Truck Parts Company 913 492-7559
1370 S Hamilton Cir Olathe (66061) ***(G-7792)***

Inn At Tallgrass, The, Wichita *Also called Inntel Corporation of America* ***(G-14696)***

Inn Hampton and Suites 620 225-0000
4002 W Comanche St Dodge City (67801) ***(G-1378)***

Innara Health Inc 913 742-7770
10900 S Clay Blair Blvd # 900 Olathe (66061) ***(G-7793)***

Innco Hospitality Inc (PA) 913 451-1300
7300 W 110th St Ste 990 Shawnee Mission (66210) ***(G-11458)***

Innotech LLC 913 888-4646
9600 Dice Ln Ste 214 Lenexa (66215) ***(G-5915)***

Innova Consulting LLC 913 210-2002
13220 Metcalf Ave Ste 310 Overland Park (66213) ***(G-8845)***

Innovative Adhesives Company (PA) 913 371-8555
450 Funston Rd Kansas City (66115) ***(G-4101)***

Innovative Broadcasting Corp 620 232-5993
412 N Locust St Pittsburg (66762) ***(G-9880)***

Innovative Cnstr Svcs Inc 316 260-1644
1725 E Wassall St Wichita (67216) ***(G-14695)***

Innovative Fluid Power 913 768-7008
19000 W 158th St Ste A Olathe (66062) ***(G-7794)***

Innovative Livestock Svcs Inc (PA) 620 793-9200
2006 Broadway Ave Ste 2c Great Bend (67530) ***(G-2593)***

Innovative Service Solutions 913 851-7745
16021 King St Overland Park (66221) ***(G-8846)***

Innovative Technology Services 785 271-2070
5924 Sw Cherokee Ct Topeka (66614) ***(G-12724)***

Innovision Corporation 913 438-3200
12022 Blue Valley Pkwy Overland Park (66213) ***(G-8847)***

Innovtive Cinema Solutions LLC 855 401-4567
13610 W 107th St Lenexa (66215) ***(G-5916)***

Inntel Corporation of America 316 684-3466
2280 N Tara Cir Wichita (67226) ***(G-14696)***

Innworks Inc 620 342-7567
2913 W Us Highway 50 Emporia (66801) ***(G-1777)***

Insco Environmental Inc 912 422-8001
6902 Martindale Rd Shawnee (66218) ***(G-10974)***

Insco Industries Inc (PA) 913 422-8001
6902 Martindale Rd Shawnee Mission (66218) ***(G-11459)***

Inscyt LLC 913 579-7335
7285 W 132nd St Ste 100 Overland Park (66213) ***(G-8848)***

Inside Sports and Fitness LLC (PA) 913 888-9247
11301 W 88th St Overland Park (66214) ***(G-8849)***

Inside Sports and Fitness LLC 913 894-4752
9111 Flint St Overland Park (66214) ***(G-8850)***

Insideresponse LLC 855 969-0812
9800 Metcalf Ave Overland Park (66212) ***(G-8851)***

Insight 2 Design LLC 913 937-9386
8681 W 137th St Overland Park (66223) ***(G-8852)***

Insight Financial Services LLC 913 402-2020
7101 College Blvd # 1501 Overland Park (66210) ***(G-8853)***

Inspire Hospice LLC 913 521-2727
11827 W 112th St Ste 100 Overland Park (66210) ***(G-8854)***

Installation and Svc Tech Inc 913 652-7000
8340 Mission Rd Ste B4 Leawood (66206) ***(G-5438)***

Institute For Professional Dev 913 491-4432
8001 College Blvd Shawnee Mission (66210) ***(G-11460)***

Instruments and Flight Res Inc 316 684-5177
2716 S George Wash Blvd Wichita (67210) ***(G-14697)***

Insulation Drywall Contrs Inc 785 862-0554
510 Sw 49th St Topeka (66609) ***(G-12725)***

Insulite Glass Co Inc (PA) 800 452-7721
780 W Frontier Ln Olathe (66061) ***(G-7795)***

Insurance Center Inc (PA) 316 321-5600
120 W Central Ave El Dorado (67042) ***(G-1571)***

Insurance Designer Kansas City 913 451-3960
9401 Indian Creek Pkwy # 150 Shawnee Mission (66210) ***(G-11461)***

Insurance Designers, Shawnee Mission *Also called Insurance Designer Kansas City* ***(G-11461)***

Insurance Guys LLC 316 775-0606
416 State St Augusta (67010) ***(G-327)***

Insurance Planning Inc (PA) 785 625-5605
3006 Broadway Ave Hays (67601) ***(G-2853)***

Insurance Services, Beloit *Also called Mitchell County Farm Bur Assn* ***(G-494)***

Insysiv LLC 816 694-9397
9850 Meek Rd Kansas City (66109) ***(G-4102)***

Integra Holdings Inc (PA) 316 630-6805
3450 N Rock Rd Ste 100 Wichita (67226) ***(G-14698)***

Integra Realty Resources (PA) 913 236-4700
1901 W 47th Pl Ste 300 Shawnee Mission (66205) ***(G-11462)***

Integra Technologies LLC (HQ) 316 630-6800
3450 N Rock Rd Ste 100 Wichita (67226) ***(G-14699)***

Integral Care Provider Inc 913 384-2273
6811 Shawnee Mission Pkwy # 115 Shawnee Mission (66202) ***(G-11463)***

Integrated Behavioral Tech Inc 913 662-7071
1106 N 155th St Ste B Basehor (66007) ***(G-379)***

Integrated Behavioral Tech Inc 913 662-7071
1106 N 155th St Basehor (66007) ***(G-380)***

Integrated Components Inc 316 942-6600
2525 S Leonine Rd Wichita (67217) ***(G-14700)***

Integrated Controls Inc 913 782-9600
15707 S Mahaffie St Olathe (66062) ***(G-7796)***

Integrated Electrical Tech LLC 316 684-0193
2406 W Timbercreek Cir Wichita (67204) ***(G-14701)***

Integrated Facilities Group 316 262-1417
125 S Washington Ave # 200 Wichita (67202) ***(G-14702)***

Integrated Health Systems LLC 913 647-9020
7520 W 160th St Ste 101 Stilwell (66085) ***(G-12155)***

Integrated Media Group LLC 316 425-8333
1300 E Central Ave Wichita (67214) ***(G-14703)***

Integrated Nuclear Enterprises, Topeka *Also called Med Care of Kansas Inc* ***(G-12877)***

Integrated Solutions Inc (PA) 316 264-7050
215 S Laura Ave Wichita (67211) ***(G-14704)***

Integrated Solutions Group, Topeka *Also called Computech Service of Kansas* ***(G-12497)***

Integrated Solutions Group, Topeka *Also called Isg Technology LLC* ***(G-12728)***

Integrated Solutions Group, Wichita *Also called Isg Technology LLC* ***(G-14731)***

Integrated Solutions Group Inc (HQ) 620 662-5796
1632 E 23rd Ave Hutchinson (67502) ***(G-3334)***

Integrated Stadium Seating Inc 316 494-6514
7330 W 33rd St N Ste 112 Wichita (67205) ***(G-14705)***

Integrity Home Care Inc 913 685-1616
8826 Santa Fe Dr Ste 209 Overland Park (66212) ***(G-8855)***

Integrity Locating Svcs LLC 913 530-6315
18993 W 158th St Olathe Olathe (66062) ***(G-7797)***

Integrity Siding & Window Co 316 993-6426
2538 N Lake Ridge Ct Wichita (67205) ***(G-14706)***

Integrted Cnslting Engners Inc 316 264-3588
349 S Hydraulic St Wichita (67211) ***(G-14707)***

Integrted Hlthcare Systems Inc 316 689-9111
3311 E Murdock St Wichita (67208) ***(G-14708)***

Intellectual Growth Engrg 913 210-8570
19300 W 64th Ter Shawnee (66218) ***(G-10975)***

Inter-Americas Insurance Corp (PA) 316 794-2200
1035 S 183rd St W Goddard (67052) ***(G-2443)***

Inter-State Studio & Pubg Co 913 745-6700
144 N Nettleton Ave Bonner Springs (66012) ***(G-556)***

Interactive Technologies Inc 913 254-0887
15655 S Mahaffie St Olathe (66062) ***(G-7798)***

Intercity Direct LLC 913 647-7550
13202 W 98th St Lenexa (66215) ***(G-5917)***

Interdent Inc 913 248-8880
13100 W 87th Street Pkwy Lenexa (66215) ***(G-5918)***

Interim Health Care Services, Leawood *Also called Interim Healthcare Kansas City* ***(G-5439)***

Interim Healthcare Inc 785 272-1616
1251 Sw Arrowhead Rd Topeka (66604) ***(G-12726)***

Interim Healthcare Inc 620 663-2423
525 N Main St Hutchinson (67501) ***(G-3335)***

Interim Healthcare Kansas City 913 381-3100
10977 Granada Ln Ste 205 Leawood (66211) ***(G-5439)***

Interim Healthcare of Topeka, Topeka *Also called Interim Healthcare Inc* ***(G-12726)***

Interior Surface Entps LLC 913 397-8100
19940 W 161st St Olathe (66062) ***(G-7799)***

Intermarc Signs, Wichita *Also called Barton Industries Inc* ***(G-13815)***

Intermediate Adult Care Fcilty, Stafford *Also called Leisure Homestead Association* ***(G-12106)***

Intermodal Acquisition LLC 708 225-2400
32880 W 191st St Edgerton (66021) ***(G-1485)***

Internal Medicine 316 321-2100
700 W Central Ave Ste 201 El Dorado (67042) ***(G-1572)***

Internal Medicine Associates 620 342-2521
1301 W 12th Ave Ste 202 Emporia (66801) ***(G-1778)***

Internal Medicine Foundation, Kansas City *Also called University of Kansas* ***(G-4505)***

Internal Medicine Group, Lawrence *Also called Richard F Sosinski* ***(G-5096)***

Internal Medicine Group PA..........785 843-5160
4525 W 6th St Ste 100 Lawrence (66049) ***(G-4912)***
International Assn Lions Clubs..........620 673-8081
3121 Junction Rd Havana (67347) ***(G-2728)***
International Assn Lions Clubs..........785 388-2764
623 3300 Ave Abilene (67410) ***(G-42)***
International Assn Lions Clubs..........785 694-2278
320 Illinois Ave Brewster (67732) ***(G-584)***
International Assn Plas Dist (PA)..........913 345-1005
6734 W 121st St Overland Park (66209) ***(G-8856)***
International Association..........785 760-5005
218 Arizona St Lawrence (66049) ***(G-4913)***
International Association of..........785 842-8847
1005 N 1116 Rd Lawrence (66047) ***(G-4914)***
International Association of..........620 327-4271
421 N Streeter Ave Hesston (67062) ***(G-2994)***
International Association of..........785 283-4746
148 N 90th Rd Tescott (67484) ***(G-12245)***
INTERNATIONAL ASSOCIATION OF M, Wichita *Also called I A M A W District Lodge 70* ***(G-14663)***
International Brotherhood (PA)..........913 371-2640
753 State Ave Ste 570 Kansas City (66101) ***(G-4103)***
International Brotherhood..........913 281-5036
753 State Ave Ste 800 Kansas City (66101) ***(G-4104)***
International Brotherhood of..........913 371-2640
753 State Ave Ste 565 Kansas City (66101) ***(G-4105)***
International Code Council Inc..........913 888-0304
11711 W 85th St Shawnee Mission (66214) ***(G-11464)***
International Design Guild, Leawood *Also called Madden-Mcfarland Interiors Ltd* ***(G-5462)***
International Electric Inc..........913 451-8458
21973 W 83rd St Lenexa (66227) ***(G-5919)***
International Ex Trckg Inc (HQ)..........913 621-1525
3359 Brinkerhoff Rd Kansas City (66115) ***(G-4106)***
International Fincl Svcs Inc..........620 665-7708
327 W 4th Ave Hutchinson (67501) ***(G-3336)***
International Food Group, Kansas City *Also called International Food Pdts Corp* ***(G-4107)***
International Food Pdts Corp..........913 788-7720
6721 Griffin Rd Kansas City (66111) ***(G-4107)***
International Forest Pdts LLC..........913 451-6945
9393 W 110th St Ste 500 Overland Park (66210) ***(G-8857)***
International Inst Christian S..........913 962-4422
10100 W 87th St Ste 303 Overland Park (66212) ***(G-8858)***
International Paper, Topeka *Also called Veritiv Operating Company* ***(G-13219)***
International Paper Company..........620 272-8318
2502 E Us Highway 50 Garden City (67846) ***(G-2204)***
International Paper Company..........316 943-1033
4300 W 29th St S Wichita (67215) ***(G-14709)***
International Pizza Hut Franch, Wichita *Also called I P H F H A Inc* ***(G-14664)***
International Trans Logis Inc..........913 621-2750
701 S 38th St Kansas City (66106) ***(G-4108)***
International Trnsp Svcs, Kansas City *Also called Reconserve of Kansas Inc* ***(G-4364)***
International Union United Au..........913 342-7330
500 Kindleberger Rd Kansas City (66115) ***(G-4109)***
International Union United Au..........620 251-2022
900 Hall St Ste 107 Coffeyville (67337) ***(G-948)***
Internet Svc Prvders Ntwrk Inc..........913 859-9500
14303 W 95th St Shawnee Mission (66215) ***(G-11465)***
Interntional Forest Friendship..........913 367-1419
913 Main St Atchison (66002) ***(G-237)***
Interntional Wheat Gluten Assn..........913 381-8180
9300 Metcalf Ave Overland Park (66212) ***(G-8859)***
Interntnal Mtr Coach Group Inc..........913 906-0111
12351 W 96th Ter Ste 101 Lenexa (66215) ***(G-5920)***
Interntnal Pnck Day Lberal Inc..........620 624-6423
318 N Lincoln Ave Liberal (67901) ***(G-6323)***
Interntnal Rscue Committee Inc..........316 201-1804
245 N Waco St Ste 500 Wichita (67202) ***(G-14710)***
Interntnal Sclpture Foundation..........785 864-2599
14246 W 124th Ter Olathe (66062) ***(G-7800)***
Interskate 77..........620 229-7655
515 Main St Winfield (67156) ***(G-16149)***
Interstate Cleaning Corp..........314 428-0566
20700 W 151st St Olathe (66061) ***(G-7801)***
Interstate Elec Cnstr Inc..........620 421-5510
1715 Us Highway 59 Parsons (67357) ***(G-9693)***
Interstate Elevator Inc..........785 234-2817
2406 Nw Clay St Topeka (66618) ***(G-12727)***
Interstate Flooring LLC (PA)..........913 573-0600
5100 Kansas Ave Kansas City (66106) ***(G-4110)***
Interstate Flooring LLC..........913 541-9700
9801 Commerce Pkwy Lenexa (66219) ***(G-5921)***
Interstate Jayhawk Glass Co, Junction City *Also called Manko Window Systems Inc* ***(G-3724)***
Interstate Publishers Inc..........913 341-4445
8014 State Line Rd # 208 Prairie Village (66208) ***(G-10036)***
Interstate Supply Company..........316 265-6653
2140 W Harry St Wichita (67213) ***(G-14711)***
Interstate Wrecker Service..........316 269-1133
1026 N Mosley St Ste 1028 Wichita (67214) ***(G-14712)***
Intertech PSI, Kansas City *Also called Professional Service Inds Inc* ***(G-4343)***
Intouch Group LLC (PA)..........913 317-9700
7045 College Blvd Ste 300 Overland Park (66211) ***(G-8860)***
Intra Care, Wichita *Also called Exaltia LLC* ***(G-14319)***
Intrust Bank NA..........316 440-9000
500 E Waterman St Wichita (67202) ***(G-14713)***
Intrust Bank NA..........785 761-2265
121 N Washington St Junction City (66441) ***(G-3700)***
Intrust Bank NA..........316 383-3350
308 W Central Ave Andover (67002) ***(G-95)***
Intrust Bank NA..........316 383-3340
112 W 7th Ave Augusta (67010) ***(G-328)***
Intrust Bank NA..........316 383-1767
1501 N Rock Rd Derby (67037) ***(G-1252)***
Intrust Bank NA..........316 321-1640
100 S Main St El Dorado (67042) ***(G-1573)***
Intrust Bank NA..........785 565-5400
630 Humboldt St Manhattan (66502) ***(G-6665)***
Intrust Bank NA..........316 755-1225
142 N Ash Ave Valley Center (67147) ***(G-13344)***
Intrust Bank NA..........316 383-1731
1435 N Waco Ave Wichita (67203) ***(G-14714)***
Intrust Bank NA..........316 383-1816
2005 W 21st St N Wichita (67203) ***(G-14715)***
Intrust Bank NA..........316 383-1563
8202 E 21st St N Wichita (67206) ***(G-14716)***
Intrust Bank NA..........316 383-1342
2244 N Rock Rd Wichita (67226) ***(G-14717)***
Intrust Bank NA..........316 383-1549
3801 N Rock Rd Wichita (67226) ***(G-14718)***
Intrust Bank NA..........316 383-1096
4747 S Broadway Ave Wichita (67216) ***(G-14719)***
Intrust Bank NA..........316 383-1194
10515 W Central Ave Wichita (67212) ***(G-14720)***
Intrust Bank NA..........316 383-1960
3433 E Central Ave Wichita (67208) ***(G-14721)***
Intrust Bank NA..........316 383-1505
1544 S Webb Rd Wichita (67207) ***(G-14722)***
Intrust Bank National Assn (HQ)..........316 383-1111
105 N Main St Wichita (67202) ***(G-14723)***
Intrust Bank National Assn..........913 385-8200
4000 Somerset Dr Shawnee Mission (66208) ***(G-11466)***
Intrust Bank National Assn..........785 238-1121
121 N Washington St Junction City (66441) ***(G-3701)***
Intrust Bank National Assn..........913 385-8330
18225 W 106th St Olathe (66061) ***(G-7802)***
Intrust Bank National Assn..........316 383-1339
7800 E Central Ave Wichita (67206) ***(G-14724)***
Intrust Bank National Assn..........316 383-1040
123 N Main St Wichita (67202) ***(G-14725)***
Intrust Bank National Assn..........316 383-1234
3932 W 13th St N Wichita (67203) ***(G-14726)***
Intrust Bank National Assn..........785 830-2600
901 Vermont St Lawrence (66044) ***(G-4915)***
Intrust Bank National Assn..........316 524-3251
107 S Wayne Ave Haysville (67060) ***(G-2947)***
Intrust Financial Corporation (PA)..........316 383-1111
105 N Main St Wichita (67202) ***(G-14727)***
Invena Corporation..........620 583-8630
416 E 5th St Eureka (67045) ***(G-1892)***
Inventory Sales Co..........913 371-7002
2949 Chrysler Rd Kansas City (66115) ***(G-4111)***
Invista Equities LLC (HQ)..........770 792-4221
4111 E 37th St N Wichita (67220) ***(G-14728)***
INX International Ink Co..........913 441-0057
2647 S 96th St Edwardsville (66111) ***(G-1504)***
Iola Broadcasting Inc..........620 365-3151
2221 S State St Iola (66749) ***(G-3609)***
Iola Community Support Office, Iola *Also called Tri-Valley Developmental Svcs* ***(G-3637)***
Iola Head Start, Iola *Also called Southeast Kansas Community* ***(G-3634)***
Iola Madison Banking Center, Iola *Also called Community National Bank & Tr* ***(G-3595)***
Iola Pre Schl For Excptnl Chld..........620 365-6730
819 Kansas Dr Iola (66749) ***(G-3610)***
Iola Register Inc..........620 365-2111
302 S Washington Ave Iola (66749) ***(G-3611)***
Iowa Kenworth Inc (HQ)..........816 483-6444
11120 Tomahawk Creek Pkwy Leawood (66211) ***(G-5440)***
Iowa Tribe Kansas & Nebraska..........785 595-3430
5 Miles Nw Of White Cloud White Cloud (66094) ***(G-13569)***
Ipeco Wichita Inc..........316 722-7800
8974 W Monroe Cir Wichita (67209) ***(G-14729)***
Ipi Financial Services, Hays *Also called Insurance Planning Inc* ***(G-2853)***
Iq Group Inc..........913 722-6700
9641 Inspiration St Lenexa (66227) ***(G-5922)***
Iqvia Phase One Services LLC..........913 708-6000
6700 W 115th St Overland Park (66211) ***(G-8861)***
Iqvua RDS Inc..........913 894-5533
11250 Corporate Ave Shawnee Mission (66219) ***(G-11467)***
Iqvua RDS Inc..........913 708-6000
6700 W 115th St Overland Park (66211) ***(G-8862)***

ALPHABETIC

Irc Kansas Office For Refugees, Wichita *Also called Interntnal Rscue Committee Inc* ***(G-14710)***
Iresq, Olathe *Also called Resq Systems LLC* ***(G-8027)***
Iris Data Services Inc (HQ)....913 937-0590
501 Kansas Ave Kansas City (66105) ***(G-4112)***
Iris Strgc Mktg Support Inc....913 232-4825
10801 Lakeview Ave Lenexa (66219) ***(G-5923)***
Irish Express Inc....785 765-2500
32750 Wabaunsee Rd Alma (66401) ***(G-64)***
Iron Horse Golf Club, Shawnee Mission *Also called City of Leawood* ***(G-11228)***
Ironhorse Golf Club Maint....913 897-8181
15300 Mission Rd Shawnee Mission (66224) ***(G-11468)***
Iroquois Ctr For Humn Dev Inc....620 723-2272
610 E Grant Ave Greensburg (67054) ***(G-2680)***
Irrigation & Turf Equipment....620 365-2121
2725 N State St Iola (66749) ***(G-3612)***
Irsik & Doll Feed Services Inc (PA)....620 855-3747
104 W Ave A Cimarron (67835) ***(G-830)***
Irsik & Doll Feed Services Inc....620 872-5371
11060 N Falcon Rd Scott City (67871) ***(G-10817)***
Irsik & Doll Feed Services Inc....620 855-3486
23405 State Road 23 Cimarron (67835) ***(G-831)***
Irsik & Doll Feed Services Inc....620 275-7131
8220 E Us Highway 50 Garden City (67846) ***(G-2205)***
Irsik & Doll Feed Yard, Garden City *Also called Irsik & Doll Feed Services Inc* ***(G-2205)***
Irsik Equities LP....620 335-5454
3705 F Rd Ste Fm Garden City (67846) ***(G-2206)***
Irsik Family Partnership....620 335-5363
5405 6 Rd Ingalls (67853) ***(G-3577)***
Irwin Army Community Hospital, Fort Riley *Also called United States Dept of Army* ***(G-1953)***
ISC Surfaces, Kansas City *Also called Interstate Flooring LLC* ***(G-4110)***
Isf LLC....316 945-4040
4420 W 29th Cir S Wichita (67215) ***(G-14730)***
Isg Technology LLC (PA)....785 823-1555
3030 Cortland Cir 300 Salina (67401) ***(G-10550)***
Isg Technology LLC....785 266-2585
3301 S Kansas Ave Ste B Topeka (66611) ***(G-12728)***
Isg Technology LLC....316 636-5655
8201 E 34th Cir N Ste 807 Wichita (67226) ***(G-14731)***
ISI Environmental Services, Wichita *Also called Integrated Solutions Inc* ***(G-14704)***
Isigma Consulting LLC....620 757-6363
4745 W 136th St Ste 48 Overland Park (66224) ***(G-8863)***
Island Financial Printing, Lenexa *Also called Financial Printing Resource* ***(G-5852)***
Island Hospitality MGT LLC....316 631-3773
9444 E 29th St N Wichita (67226) ***(G-14732)***
Isodyne Inc....316 682-5634
7706 E Osie St Wichita (67207) ***(G-14733)***
Isp Technologies Inc (PA)....785 760-1572
4225 Wimbledon Dr Lawrence (66047) ***(G-4916)***
Ispn, Shawnee Mission *Also called Internet Svc Prvders Ntwrk Inc* ***(G-11465)***
Issd, Lenexa *Also called Performance Contracting Inc* ***(G-6051)***
Ist, Leawood *Also called Installation and Svc Tech Inc* ***(G-5438)***
It21 Inc....913 393-4821
11955 W 153rd St Overland Park (66221) ***(G-8864)***
Italk Telecontracting Inc....816 436-8080
6950 Squibb Rd Ste 200 Mission (66202) ***(G-7131)***
Itc Great Plains LLC....785 783-2226
3500 Sw Fairlawn Rd # 101 Topeka (66614) ***(G-12729)***
Itedium Inc....913 499-4850
6717 Shawnee Mission Pkwy C Overland Park (66202) ***(G-8865)***
Itgs Shipping....316 322-3000
420 N Industrial Rd El Dorado (67042) ***(G-1574)***
Itransport & Logistics Inc....316 665-7653
422 N Baughman Ave Haysville (67060) ***(G-2948)***
Its Greek To Me Inc (HQ)....800 336-4486
520 Mccall Rd Manhattan (66502) ***(G-6666)***
ITW Dymon....913 397-9889
805 E Old 56 Hwy Olathe (66061) ***(G-7803)***
ITW Labels, Gardner *Also called Illinois Tool Works Inc* ***(G-2351)***
ITW Pro Brands, Olathe *Also called Illinois Tool Works Inc* ***(G-7784)***
Iuka Coop Farm Supply, Iuka *Also called Kanza Cooperative Association* ***(G-3641)***
Ivy Animal Health Inc (HQ)....913 310-7900
10850 Lakeview Ave Lenexa (66219) ***(G-5924)***
Ivy Animal Health Inc....913 888-2192
10850 Lakeview Ave Lenexa (66219) ***(G-5925)***
Ivy Funds Distributor Inc (HQ)....913 261-2800
6300 Lamar Ave Shawnee Mission (66202) ***(G-11469)***
Ivy Funds VIP Small Cap Growth....800 777-6472
6300 Lamar Ave Overland Park (66202) ***(G-8866)***
Ivy League Learning Center....913 338-4060
7260 W 121st St Overland Park (66213) ***(G-8867)***
Ivy League Learning Ctr & Nurs, Overland Park *Also called Ivy League Learning Center* ***(G-8867)***
Iway, Olivia N MD, Elkhart *Also called Morton County Hospital* ***(G-1624)***
Iwp LLC....316 308-8507
234 S Sheridan Ct Valley Center (67147) ***(G-13345)***
J & A Rentals Inc (PA)....316 788-4540
1600 E Patriot Ave Derby (67037) ***(G-1253)***
J & B Inc....816 590-1174
11552 Carter St Shawnee Mission (66210) ***(G-11470)***
J & D Equipment Inc....913 342-1450
3250 Harvester Rd Kansas City (66115) ***(G-4113)***
J & H Transportation Inc (PA)....316 733-8200
1534 N Main St Andover (67002) ***(G-96)***
J & J Contractors Inc (PA)....620 365-5500
1646 1600th St Iola (66749) ***(G-3613)***
J & J Drainage Products Co....620 663-1575
110 N Pershing St Hutchinson (67501) ***(G-3337)***
J & J Fence, Wichita *Also called A L C Enterprises Inc* ***(G-13587)***
J & J Martin Trucking....620 544-7976
101 N Jackson St Hugoton (67951) ***(G-3166)***
J & J Powerline Contractors....620 227-2467
2716 Butter And Egg Rd Dodge City (67801) ***(G-1379)***
J & K Contracting Lc....785 238-3298
801 W 6th St Ste B Junction City (66441) ***(G-3702)***
J & L Smith Farms Inc....620 356-1070
9170 E Road 2 Ulysses (67880) ***(G-13301)***
J & M Contracting Inc....913 397-0272
1712 E 123rd St Olathe (66061) ***(G-7804)***
J & M Industries Inc....913 362-8994
8800 Rosewood Dr Prairie Village (66207) ***(G-10037)***
J & S Tool and Fastener Inc....913 677-2000
3040 S 44th St Kansas City (66106) ***(G-4114)***
J & W Equipment Inc....620 365-2341
2795 N State St Iola (66749) ***(G-3614)***
J A G II Construction, Dodge City *Also called J-A-G Construction Company* ***(G-1381)***
J A G II Inc....620 276-8409
615 N Industrial Dr Garden City (67846) ***(G-2207)***
J A Lyden Construction Co....785 286-1427
3825 Nw Button Rd Topeka (66618) ***(G-12730)***
J A Peterson Enterprises Inc (PA)....913 384-3800
10000 W 75th St Ste 100 Shawnee Mission (66204) ***(G-11471)***
J A Peterson Enterprises Inc....913 642-9020
9130 Riggs Ln Shawnee Mission (66212) ***(G-11472)***
J A Peterson Realty Co Inc (HQ)....913 384-3800
10000 W 75th St Ste 100 Shawnee Mission (66204) ***(G-11473)***
J A Peterson Realty Co Inc....913 631-2332
7650 Goddard St Shawnee Mission (66214) ***(G-11474)***
J A Peterson Realty Co Inc....785 842-1455
2401 W 25th St Apt 9a3 Lawrence (66047) ***(G-4917)***
J A Peterson Realty Co Inc....913 432-5050
7350 Kings Cove Dr Shawnee Mission (66203) ***(G-11475)***
J and J Plastics....620 660-9048
P.O. Box 6 Rosalia (67132) ***(G-10234)***
J and S Trucking Inc....785 973-2768
1276 W Mohawk Rd Prairie View (67664) ***(G-10011)***
J B D, Sedan *Also called Jones & Buck Development Oil* ***(G-10844)***
J B Hinz....913 492-5566
9818 W 100th Ter Shawnee Mission (66212) ***(G-11476)***
J B L Inc (PA)....316 529-3100
4911 S Meridian Ave Wichita (67217) ***(G-14734)***
J B Pearl Sales & Svc Inc (PA)....785 437-2772
27425 Highway 24 Saint Marys (66536) ***(G-10366)***
J B Turner Son Roofg & Shtmtl, Topeka *Also called T R Management Inc* ***(G-13130)***
J B Turner Sons....785 233-9603
620 W Main St Herington (67449) ***(G-2977)***
J C Nichols Residential, Lawrence *Also called Joe Barns* ***(G-4924)***
J Corp....785 628-8101
1707 E 10th St Hays (67601) ***(G-2854)***
J D Reece Realtors, Leawood *Also called Reece & Nichols Realtors Inc* ***(G-5535)***
J D Skiles Inc....785 626-9338
101 Grant St Atwood (67730) ***(G-287)***
J Diamond Inc....316 264-9505
2020 W Harry St Wichita (67213) ***(G-14735)***
J F Beaver Advertising, Scott City *Also called Joseph F Beaver* ***(G-10818)***
J F McGivern Inc....785 354-1787
3333 Se 21st St Topeka (66607) ***(G-12731)***
J Graham Construction Inc....620 252-2395
1306 Elm St Coffeyville (67337) ***(G-949)***
J Hawk Plant, Galena *Also called Pbi-Gordon Corporation* ***(G-2080)***
J Huston Howery....316 945-0023
3900 W Rita St Wichita (67213) ***(G-14736)***
J Huston Howery (PA)....316 945-0023
3900 W Rita St Wichita (67213) ***(G-14737)***
J J Martiny Concrete Co....913 268-7775
7350 Douglas Ave Kansas City (66106) ***(G-4115)***
J L D J Inc....785 625-6316
2707 Vine St Ste 12 Hays (67601) ***(G-2855)***
J M O'Connor Co, Wichita *Also called OConnor Company Inc* ***(G-15208)***
J M OConnor Inc....913 438-7867
14925 W 99th St Shawnee Mission (66215) ***(G-11477)***
J Marquez Trucking....620 335-5872
13909 M Rd Ingalls (67853) ***(G-3578)***
J P Weigand & Sons Inc (PA)....316 686-3773
150 N Market St Wichita (67202) ***(G-14738)***

J P Weigand & Sons Inc...316 722-6182
2872 N Ridge Rd Ste 112 Wichita (67205) *(G-14739)*
J P Weigand & Sons Inc...316 788-5581
1121 N College Park St # 700 Derby (67037) *(G-1254)*
J P Weigand and Sons Inc...620 663-4458
1009 N Main St Hutchinson (67501) *(G-3338)*
J P Weigand and Sons Inc (PA)...316 292-3991
150 N Market St Wichita (67202) *(G-14740)*
J P Weigand and Sons Inc...316 283-1330
400 S Main St Ste 101 Newton (67114) *(G-7367)*
J R Galley Inc...785 938-8024
1175 S Range Ave Colby (67701) *(G-1016)*
J S Transportation LLC...816 651-1827
21306 W 82nd St Lenexa (66220) *(G-5926)*
J Schmid & Assoc Inc...913 236-8988
5800 Foxridge Dr Ste 200 Shawnee Mission (66202) *(G-11478)*
J T Lardner Cut Stone Inc...785 234-8634
128 Nw Van Buren St Topeka (66603) *(G-12732)*
J W Power Co, Liberal *Also called J-W Operating Company (G-6324)*
J W Trucking, Emporia *Also called Waechter LLC (G-1848)*
J&J Driveaway Systems LLC...913 387-0158
7270 W 162nd St Overland Park (66085) *(G-8868)*
J&M Tools LLC...785 608-3343
5241 Nw Arroyo Ct Topeka (66618) *(G-12733)*
J-A-G Construction Company (PA)...620 225-0061
11257 109 Rd Dodge City (67801) *(G-1380)*
J-A-G Construction Company...620 225-0061
108 N 14th Ave Ste E Dodge City (67801) *(G-1381)*
J-Con Reprographics Inc...913 859-0800
14324 W 96th Ter Lenexa (66215) *(G-5927)*
J-DOT Inc...785 272-1633
3365 Sw Gage Blvd Topeka (66614) *(G-12734)*
J-Six Enterprises LLC (PA)...785 336-2149
604 Nemaha St Seneca (66538) *(G-10868)*
J-Six Farms LLC...785 336-2148
604 Nemaha St Seneca (66538) *(G-10869)*
J-W Operating Company...620 626-7243
1480 General Welch Blvd Liberal (67901) *(G-6324)*
J2 Design Solutions LLC...316 303-9460
120 E 1st St N Ste 270 Wichita (67202) *(G-14741)*
Jaafar Inc...913 269-5113
15968 S Clairborne St Olathe (66062) *(G-7805)*
Jacam Carriers 2013 LLC...620 278-3355
205 S Broadway Ave Sterling (67579) *(G-12122)*
Jacam Chemicals 2013 LLC (PA)...620 278-3355
205 S Broadway Ave Sterling (67579) *(G-12123)*
Jacam Chemicals LLC...620 275-1500
2725 N Ray Rd Garden City (67846) *(G-2208)*
Jack B Kelley Inc...620 792-8205
Us Hwy 281 S Great Bend (67530) *(G-2594)*
Jack Cooper Transport Co Inc...913 321-8500
200 E Marley Rd Kansas City (66115) *(G-4116)*
Jack Foster Co Erectors...316 263-2901
1119 S Santa Fe St Wichita (67211) *(G-14742)*
Jack Henry & Associates Inc...913 422-3233
23001 W 81st St Shawnee Mission (66227) *(G-11479)*
Jack Henry & Associates Inc...913 341-3434
10910 W 87th St Shawnee Mission (66214) *(G-11480)*
Jack Jill Prschl-Extended Care...913 682-1222
130 N 6th St Leavenworth (66048) *(G-5255)*
Jack Jones Inc...620 342-4221
1620 Road 210 Emporia (66801) *(G-1779)*
Jack M Schwartz (PA)...785 823-3035
111 S 5th St Salina (67401) *(G-10551)*
Jack Wilson & Associates Inc...785 856-4546
901 Kentucky St Ste 106 Lawrence (66044) *(G-4918)*
Jacks Food Market...785 348-5411
303 5th St Linn (66953) *(G-6407)*
Jacks Genuine Mfg Inc...620 948-3000
1629 Cr 3700 Coffeyville (67337) *(G-950)*
Jackson & Baalman...316 722-6452
982 N Tyler Rd Ste A Wichita (67212) *(G-14743)*
Jackson Agrobuilders LLC...913 909-6391
26000 W 69th Ter Shawnee (66226) *(G-10976)*
Jackson County Ems, Holton *Also called Techs Inc (G-3112)*
Jackson County Head Start, Holton *Also called Nek Cap Inc (G-3107)*
Jackson County Nursing Home...785 364-3164
1121 W 7th St Holton (66436) *(G-3099)*
Jackson Farmers Inc (PA)...785 364-3161
509 Lowell Ave Holton (66436) *(G-3100)*
Jackson Lewis PC...913 982-5747
7101 College Blvd # 1150 Overland Park (66210) *(G-8869)*
Jackson Meats, Hutchinson *Also called Jacksons Frozen Food Center (G-3339)*
Jacksonian Newspaper, Cimarron *Also called Golden Plains Publishers Inc (G-827)*
Jacksons Frozen Food Center...620 662-4465
13 W 6th Ave Hutchinson (67501) *(G-3339)*
Jacksons Greenhouse & Grdn Ctr...785 232-3416
1933 Nw Lwer Silver Lk Rd Topeka (66608) *(G-12735)*
Jaco General Contractor Inc...316 252-8200
420 S Emporia Ave Ste 200 Wichita (67202) *(G-14744)*
Jade Dental Lab Inc...913 469-9500
13720 W 108th St Shawnee Mission (66215) *(G-11481)*
Jade Millwrights Inc...785 544-7771
2583 Prairie Rd Hiawatha (66434) *(G-3011)*
Jade Travel Center Inc (PA)...785 273-1226
2655 Sw Wanamaker Rd E Topeka (66614) *(G-12736)*
Jahnke & Sons Construction Inc...800 351-2525
9130 Flint St Overland Park (66214) *(G-8870)*
Jajo Inc...316 267-6700
131 N Rock Island St Wichita (67202) *(G-14745)*
Jak 3 Inc (PA)...785 336-2148
604 Nemaha St Seneca (66538) *(G-10870)*
Jakes Fireworks Inc (PA)...620 231-2264
1500 E 27th Ter Pittsburg (66762) *(G-9881)*
Jakobe Furniture LLC...913 371-8900
450 S 55th St Kansas City (66106) *(G-4117)*
Jakubs Ladder Inc...316 214-8932
330 N Valley Stream Dr Derby (67037) *(G-1255)*
James & Son Farms...620 262-1512
581 Road 24 Hugoton (67951) *(G-3167)*
James Avery Craftsman Inc...913 307-0419
11149 W 95th St Overland Park (66214) *(G-8871)*
James B Stddard Trnsf Stor Inc...913 727-3627
201 Commercial St Leavenworth (66048) *(G-5256)*
James Gruver Construction Inc...620 663-7982
105 N Main St Hutchinson (67501) *(G-3340)*
James L Ruhlen MD PA...913 829-4001
20805 W 151st St 224 Olathe (66061) *(G-7806)*
James Mason Enterprises Inc...316 838-7399
3810 N Bridgeport Cir Wichita (67219) *(G-14746)*
James Mirabile...913 888-7546
4550 W 109th St Ste 130 Overland Park (66211) *(G-8872)*
James P Gertken DDS...620 669-0411
2901 N Lorraine St Ste A Hutchinson (67502) *(G-3341)*
James R Barber...785 349-2801
422 S 6th St White City (66872) *(G-13567)*
James R Kiene Jr DDS PA LLC...913 825-9373
11005 W 60th St Ste 240 Shawnee Mission (66203) *(G-11482)*
James S Willard...785 267-0040
3301 Sw Van Buren St B Topeka (66611) *(G-12737)*
James Spencer, Manhattan *Also called Manhattan Martin Luther King J (G-6723)*
James Voegeli Construction...316 721-6800
9325 W 53rd St N Maize (67101) *(G-6514)*
Jamestown State Bank (PA)...785 439-6224
422 Walnut St Jamestown (66948) *(G-3643)*
Jani-King, Lenexa *Also called Majestic Franchising Inc (G-5983)*
Janki Inc...620 225-7373
2400 W Wyatt Earp Blvd Dodge City (67801) *(G-1382)*
Janssen Glass & Door, Shawnee *Also called Janssen Glass & Mirror Inc (G-10977)*
Janssen Glass & Mirror Inc...913 677-5727
4949 Hadley St Shawnee (66203) *(G-10977)*
Jantz Inc...620 345-2783
2175 Cheyenne Rd Moundridge (67107) *(G-7186)*
Jantz Trucking, Moundridge *Also called Jantz Inc (G-7186)*
Jaray Software Inc...316 267-5758
245 N Waco St Ste 230 Wichita (67202) *(G-14747)*
Jarden Branded Consumable...913 856-1177
17150 Mercury St Olathe (66061) *(G-7807)*
Jarden Corp Outdoor Solutions...316 832-2441
2111 E 37th St N Wichita (67219) *(G-14748)*
Jarden Corporation...316 390-1343
3600 N Hydraulic St Wichita (67219) *(G-14749)*
Jarit Manufacturing Inc...785 448-2501
29128 N Highway 59 Garnett (66032) *(G-2379)*
Jasper Investments Inc...913 599-0899
11944 W 95th St Lenexa (66215) *(G-5928)*
Jay E Suddreth & Associates...913 451-5820
2127 W 116th St Leawood (66211) *(G-5441)*
Jay Hatfield Mobility LLC...785 452-9888
11922 E Kellogg Dr Wichita (67207) *(G-14750)*
Jay Hatfield Mobility LLC (PA)...620 429-2636
200 S East Ave Columbus (66725) *(G-1079)*
Jay Hawk Area Agency On Aging...785 235-1367
2910 Sw Topeka Blvd Topeka (66611) *(G-12738)*
Jay Henges Enterprises Inc...913 764-4600
15640 S Keeler St Olathe (66062) *(G-7808)*
Jay Maa Ambe LLC...785 554-1044
10401 France Family Dr Kansas City (66111) *(G-4118)*
Jay McConnell Construction Inc...913 492-9300
5721 Georgia Ave Kansas City (66104) *(G-4119)*
Jayhawk Area Cncl Bsa Cncl (PA)...785 354-0291
1020 Se Monroe St Topeka (66612) *(G-12739)*
Jayhawk Auto Incorporated...785 354-1758
910 Sw 6th Ave Topeka (66606) *(G-12740)*
Jayhawk Beverage Inc...785 234-8611
4435 Nw Us Highway 24 Topeka (66618) *(G-12741)*
Jayhawk Body, Topeka *Also called Jayhawk Auto Incorporated (G-12740)*
Jayhawk Bowling Sup & Eqp Inc...785 842-3237
355 N Iowa St Lawrence (66044) *(G-4919)*

ALPHABETIC

Jayhawk Fine Chemicals Corp..........620 783-1321
8545 Jayhawk Dr Galena (66739) *(G-2075)*
Jayhawk Fire Sprinkler Co Inc..........913 422-3770
12030 S Hedge Lane Ter Olathe (66061) *(G-7809)*
Jayhawk Guttering, Lawrence *Also called Nieder Contracting Inc (G-5040)*
Jayhawk Millwright Erectors Inc..........913 371-5212
811 S Coy St Kansas City (66105) *(G-4120)*
Jayhawk Pipeline LLC (HQ)..........620 241-9270
2000 S Main St McPherson (67460) *(G-6978)*
Jayhawk Pipeline LLC..........620 938-2971
1390 10th Rd Chase (67524) *(G-783)*
Jayhawk Plumbing Inc..........785 865-5225
3009 Four Wheel Dr Ste A Lawrence (66047) *(G-4920)*
Jayhawk Primary Care Inc (PA)..........913 588-9000
2330 Shawnee Mission Pkwy Westwood (66205) *(G-13554)*
Jayhawk Roofing & Supply Co..........785 825-5466
917 W North St Salina (67401) *(G-10552)*
Jayhawk Software..........620 365-8065
1000 W Miller Rd Iola (66749) *(G-3615)*
Jayhawk Trophy Company Inc..........785 843-3900
3341 W 6th St Lawrence (66049) *(G-4921)*
JBN Telephone Company Inc..........785 362-3323
418 W 5th St Ste A Holton (66436) *(G-3101)*
JC Auto..........785 266-1300
1645 Se 77th St Berryton (66409) *(G-527)*
JC Nchols Dnton Rbrts Rltors..........913 299-1600
2100 Hutton Rd Kansas City (66109) *(G-4121)*
JC Nichols Denton & Roberts, Kansas City *Also called JC Nchols Dnton Rbrts Rltors (G-4121)*
Jc.net/Cromwell/Builders, Carlton *Also called Cromwell Builders Mfg (G-686)*
Jci Industries Inc..........316 942-6200
1335 S Young St Wichita (67209) *(G-14751)*
Jcor Inc..........913 461-8804
10510 W 142nd Ter Overland Park (66221) *(G-8873)*
Jcs, Stilwell *Also called Johnson Cmmunications Svcs Inc (G-12159)*
Jdamc Inc..........913 310-8100
10789 S Ridgeview Rd Olathe (66061) *(G-7810)*
Jdb Enterprises Inc..........316 263-2411
111 S Main St Wichita (67202) *(G-14752)*
JED Installation LLC..........913 724-4600
2722 N 155th St Basehor (66007) *(G-381)*
Jeff Goldman..........785 842-0351
1420 N 3rd St Lawrence (66044) *(G-4922)*
Jeff Hoge Concrete LLC..........913 239-0903
6884 W 183rd St Stilwell (66085) *(G-12156)*
Jeff L Krehbiel..........316 267-8233
1300 E Lewis St Wichita (67211) *(G-14753)*
Jeff L Krehbiel Associates, Wichita *Also called Jeff L Krehbiel (G-14753)*
Jefferson Cnty Svc Orgnization..........785 863-2637
610 Delaware St Oskaloosa (66066) *(G-8227)*
JEFFERSON CO SERV ORGANIZATION, Oskaloosa *Also called Jefferson Cnty Svc Orgnization (G-8227)*
Jefferson County Geriatric Ctr, Winchester *Also called Jefferson County Mem Hosp Inc (G-16110)*
Jefferson County Health Dept, Oskaloosa *Also called County of Jefferson (G-8222)*
Jefferson County Mem Hosp Inc..........913 774-4340
408 Delaware St Winchester (66097) *(G-16110)*
Jefferson Pointe Apartments..........913 906-9100
11810 Farley St Shawnee Mission (66210) *(G-11483)*
Jefferson St Ht Partners LLC..........785 234-5400
420 Se 6th Ave Ste A Topeka (66607) *(G-12742)*
Jeffrey A Harris..........785 823-8760
2231d Centennial Rd Ste 1 Salina (67401) *(G-10553)*
Jeffrey Energy..........785 456-2035
25905 Jeffrey Rd Saint Marys (66536) *(G-10367)*
Jem Industries Inc..........913 837-3202
208 S 1st St Louisburg (66053) *(G-6452)*
Jem International Inc (PA)..........913 441-4788
6873 Martindale Rd Shawnee (66218) *(G-10978)*
Jenkins & Leblanc PA (PA)..........913 378-9610
8226 Mission Rd Prairie Village (66208) *(G-10038)*
Jenkins Building Maintenance..........316 529-1263
7030 S Plaza Dr Haysville (67060) *(G-2949)*
Jennifer Brunetti..........620 235-0100
214 E Mckay St Frontenac (66763) *(G-2056)*
Jens House & Coml Clg LLC..........785 286-2463
4149 Ne State Road K4 Topeka (66617) *(G-12743)*
Jensen Design Inc..........316 943-7900
933 S West St Wichita (67213) *(G-14754)*
Jensen, Mark S DDS PA, Shawnee Mission *Also called Mark S Jensen DDS PA (G-11598)*
Jerry Boresow..........913 441-1111
5695 Clare Rd Shawnee Mission (66226) *(G-11484)*
Jerry R Lundgrin DDS..........785 825-5473
909 E Wayne Ave Salina (67401) *(G-10554)*
Jerry Wray..........785 255-4644
1183 Stafford Rd Pomona (66076) *(G-10005)*
Jerrys Nursery and Ldscpg Inc..........913 721-1444
5319 N 139th St Kansas City (66109) *(G-4122)*
Jeserich, Gerald N, Kansas City *Also called Williamson & Cubbison (G-4545)*
Jesse Inc..........913 342-4282
940 Miami Ave Kansas City (66105) *(G-4123)*
Jesse Latham & Sons Inc..........785 361-4281
417 Main St Republic (66964) *(G-10200)*
Jessee Trucking Incorporated..........620 389-2546
6878 Se Highway 160 Columbus (66725) *(G-1080)*
Jet Airwerks LLC..........620 442-3625
3015 N Summit St Arkansas City (67005) *(G-161)*
Jet Digital Printing & Copies..........316 685-2679
6410 E Central Ave Wichita (67206) *(G-14755)*
Jet Stream Guttering Corp..........913 262-2913
5023 Antioch Rd Shawnee Mission (66203) *(G-11485)*
Jetz Service Co Inc (PA)..........785 354-7588
901 Ne River Rd Ste 3 Topeka (66616) *(G-12744)*
Jevons, Robert E, Kansas City *Also called Associates Family Medicine PA (G-3827)*
Jewell County Ems..........785 378-3069
510 E North St Mankato (66956) *(G-6858)*
Jewell County Hospital..........785 378-3137
100 Crestvue Ave Mankato (66956) *(G-6859)*
Jewell Implement Company Inc..........785 428-3261
105 S Custer St Jewell (66949) *(G-3650)*
Jewish Cmnty Ctr Grter Kans Cy..........913 327-8000
5801 W 115th St Ste 101 Shawnee Mission (66211) *(G-11486)*
Jewish Community Campus..........913 327-8200
5801 W 115th St Ste 100 Shawnee Mission (66211) *(G-11487)*
Jewish Family and Chld Svc..........913 327-8250
5801 W 115th St Ste 103 Shawnee Mission (66211) *(G-11488)*
Jewish Family Services..........913 327-8250
5801 W 115th St Ste 103 Overland Park (66211) *(G-8874)*
Jewish Fdrtion Greater Kans Cy..........913 327-8100
5801 W 115th St Ste 201 Shawnee Mission (66211) *(G-11489)*
Jewish Heritage Fndtn Greater..........913 981-8866
5801 W 115th St Ste 104 Leawood (66211) *(G-5442)*
Jf Denney Inc..........913 772-8994
76 Ash St Leavenworth (66048) *(G-5257)*
Jfaonlinecom LLc..........316 554-1222
5550 S West St Wichita (67217) *(G-14756)*
Jgs Auto Wrecking..........913 321-2716
1128 Pawnee Ave Kansas City (66105) *(G-4124)*
Jgs Auto Wrecking & Tow, Kansas City *Also called Jgs Auto Wrecking (G-4124)*
Jhon-Josephsons Salon..........913 338-4443
4324 W 119th St Shawnee Mission (66209) *(G-11490)*
Jies LLC..........620 668-5585
2134 70th Rd Copeland (67837) *(G-1149)*
Jiffy Lube, Kansas City *Also called Team Car Care LLC (G-4461)*
Jiffy Lube, Topeka *Also called Team Car Care LLC (G-13147)*
Jiffy Lube, Topeka *Also called Team Car Care LLC (G-13148)*
Jiffy Lube, Shawnee Mission *Also called Team Car Care LLC (G-11922)*
Jiffy Lube, Lawrence *Also called Team Car Care LLC (G-5132)*
Jiffy Lube, Leawood *Also called Team Car Care LLC (G-5570)*
Jiffy Lube International Inc..........913 682-7020
3120 S 4th St Leavenworth (66048) *(G-5258)*
Jills Helping Hands Inc..........785 622-4254
27438 Us Highway 283 Lenora (67645) *(G-6244)*
Jim Bishop & Associates..........620 231-4370
904 S Broadway St Pittsburg (66762) *(G-9882)*
Jim Haas Builders Inc..........913 897-9721
7230 W 162nd St Ste C Stilwell (66085) *(G-12157)*
Jim Jam Inc..........913 268-6700
11003 W 59th Ter Shawnee (66203) *(G-10979)*
Jim Mitten Trucking Inc..........785 672-3279
3660 Us 40 Oakley (67748) *(G-7477)*
Jim Ogrady Trucking..........620 624-5343
720 W 2nd St Liberal (67901) *(G-6325)*
Jim Starkey Music Center Inc..........316 262-2351
1318 W 18th St N Wichita (67203) *(G-14757)*
Jim Woods Marketing Inc..........620 856-3554
2308 Sunset Ave Baxter Springs (66713) *(G-410)*
Jims Electric Inc..........785 460-2844
210 E 2nd St Colby (67701) *(G-1017)*
Jims Formal Wear LLC..........785 825-1529
2118 Planet Ave Salina (67401) *(G-10555)*
JM Tran-Sport LLC..........785 545-3756
2275 200 Rd Glen Elder (67446) *(G-2426)*
Jmar Construction Inc..........620 922-3690
627 7000 Rd Edna (67342) *(G-1494)*
Jmh Cleaning Service..........785 819-0725
P.O. Box 2985 Salina (67402) *(G-10556)*
Jmt Industries Inc..........316 267-1221
8310 E Oak Knoll St Wichita (67207) *(G-14758)*
Jmz Corporation..........620 365-7782
800 W Miller Rd Iola (66749) *(G-3616)*
Jnn LLC..........785 843-9100
2309 Iowa St Lawrence (66046) *(G-4923)*
Job Board Network LLC..........913 238-1181
5211 W 156th St Overland Park (66224) *(G-8875)*
Jobbers Automotive Whse Inc (PA)..........316 267-4393
801 E Zimmerly St Wichita (67211) *(G-14759)*

Jockey International Globl Inc 913 334-4455
1811 Village West Pkwy Kansas City (66111) ***(G-4125)***
Joco Barking Club 913 558-2625
15109 Rosewood Dr Overland Park (66224) ***(G-8876)***
Jody Phillips Dance Company 913 897-9888
14840 Metcalf Ave Overland Park (66223) ***(G-8877)***
Joe Barns 785 842-2772
1127 Iowa St Lawrence (66044) ***(G-4924)***
Joe Bob Outfitters LLC 785 639-7121
4850 General Hays Rd Hays (67601) ***(G-2856)***
Joe Rosenberg DDS 620 285-3886
205 N Santa Fe St Saint John (67576) ***(G-10353)***
Joe Self Chevrolet Inc (PA) 316 689-4390
8801 E Kellogg Dr Wichita (67207) ***(G-14760)***
Joe Smith Company 620 231-3610
902 E Jefferson St Pittsburg (66762) ***(G-9883)***
Joe Thoele Foundation 913 685-2282
16012 Metcalf Ave Stilwell (66085) ***(G-12158)***
Joe's Carpet, Lenexa *Also called Weber Carpet Inc* ***(G-6224)***
Joe's Express Lube & Oil, Wichita *Also called Joes Seat Cover Car Wash Ctr* ***(G-14761)***
Joel Fritzel Construction Co (PA) 785 843-0566
1616 New Hampshire St Lawrence (66044) ***(G-4925)***
Joes Seat Cover Car Wash Ctr 316 262-2486
206 N Seneca St Wichita (67203) ***(G-14761)***
John A Marshall Company (PA) 913 599-4700
10930 Lackman Rd Lenexa (66219) ***(G-5929)***
John B Baker 316 263-2820
447 S Greenwood St Wichita (67211) ***(G-14762)***
John C Gross III (PA) 620 223-2550
18 S National Ave Fort Scott (66701) ***(G-1976)***
John C Patton DDS 620 342-0673
1507 W 12th Ave Emporia (66801) ***(G-1780)***
John D Ebeling MD 785 232-3555
634 Sw Mulvane St Ste 202 Topeka (66606) ***(G-12745)***
John D Meschke DDS PA (PA) 620 662-6667
2 Compound Dr Hutchinson (67502) ***(G-3342)***
John Deere, Olathe *Also called Deere & Company* ***(G-7646)***
John Deere AG Center, Olathe *Also called Deere & Company* ***(G-7645)***
John Deere Authorized Dealer, Baldwin City *Also called Heritage Tractor Inc* ***(G-363)***
John Deere Authorized Dealer, Kingman *Also called Plp Inc* ***(G-4610)***
John Deere Authorized Dealer, Anthony *Also called Plp Inc* ***(G-132)***
John Deere Authorized Dealer, Marion *Also called Plp Inc* ***(G-6875)***
John Deere Authorized Dealer, Ulysses *Also called American Implement Main Office* ***(G-13282)***
John Deere Authorized Dealer, Emporia *Also called Plp Inc* ***(G-1812)***
John Deere Authorized Dealer, Beloit *Also called Carrico Implement Co Inc* ***(G-480)***
John Deere Authorized Dealer, Bucklin *Also called Bucklin Tractor & Impt Co Inc* ***(G-591)***
John Deere Authorized Dealer, Great Bend *Also called Great Bend Farm Equipment Inc* ***(G-2578)***
John Deere Authorized Dealer, Liberal *Also called Keating Tractor & Eqp Inc* ***(G-6327)***
John Deere Authorized Dealer, Hutchinson *Also called Plp Inc* ***(G-3408)***
John Deere Authorized Dealer, Elkhart *Also called American Implement Inc* ***(G-1617)***
John Deere Authorized Dealer, Seneca *Also called Todd Tractor Co Inc* ***(G-10884)***
John Deere Authorized Dealer, Garden City *Also called American Implement Inc* ***(G-2098)***
John Deere Authorized Dealer, Ellsworth *Also called Carrico Implement Co Inc* ***(G-1658)***
John Deere Authorized Dealer, Dodge City *Also called Murphy Tractor & Eqp Co Inc* ***(G-1408)***
John Deere Authorized Dealer, Great Bend *Also called Murphy Tractor & Eqp Co Inc* ***(G-2614)***
John Deere Authorized Dealer, Park City *Also called Murphy Tractor & Eqp Co Inc* ***(G-9638)***
John Deere Authorized Dealer, Topeka *Also called Murphy Tractor & Eqp Co Inc* ***(G-12919)***
John Deere Authorized Dealer, Wichita *Also called Plp Inc* ***(G-15307)***
John Deere Authorized Dealer, Olathe *Also called Heritage Tractor Inc* ***(G-7766)***
John Deere Authorized Dealer, Hugoton *Also called American Implement Inc* ***(G-3147)***
John Deere Authorized Dealer, Olathe *Also called Palmer Johnson Pwr Systems LLC* ***(G-7972)***
John Deere Authorized Dealer, Olathe *Also called Van-Wall Equipment Inc* ***(G-8138)***
John Deere Authorized Dealer, Ness City *Also called Bti Ness City* ***(G-7253)***
John Deere Authorized Dealer, Dodge City *Also called Foster Unruh Inc* ***(G-1362)***
John Deere Authorized Dealer, Abilene *Also called Concordia Tractor Inc* ***(G-20)***
John Deere Authorized Dealer, Marysville *Also called Oregon Trail Equipment LLC* ***(G-6905)***
John Deere Authorized Dealer, Topeka *Also called Heritage Tractor Inc* ***(G-12686)***
John Deere Authorized Dealer, Hays *Also called Carrico Implement Co Inc* ***(G-2765)***
John Deere Authorized Dealer, Scott City *Also called American Implement Inc* ***(G-10803)***
John Deere Authorized Dealer, Coffeyville *Also called Darwin Industries Inc* ***(G-932)***
John Deere Implmnt Co, Hutchinson *Also called Pankratz Implement Co* ***(G-3399)***
John Deere Tractors, Pittsburg *Also called Heritage Tractor Inc* ***(G-9875)***
John Dere Cffeyville Works Inc 620 251-3400
2624 N Us Highway 169 Coffeyville (67337) ***(G-951)***
John E Jones Oil Co Inc 785 425-6746
1016 S Cedar St Stockton (67669) ***(G-12182)***
John F Dahm Dr 620 665-5582
2411 N Main St Hutchinson (67502) ***(G-3343)***
John F Hafner LLC 620 244-5393
608 E 2nd St Erie (66733) ***(G-1859)***
John Fales Dr 913 782-2207
13496 S Arapaho Dr Olathe (66062) ***(G-7811)***
John G Levin (PA) 785 234-5551
115 Nw Van Buren St Topeka (66603) ***(G-12746)***
John H Hay DDS 785 749-2525
10 E 9th St Ste D Lawrence (66044) ***(G-4926)***
John H Moffitt & Co Inc (PA) 913 491-6800
5300 College Blvd Shawnee Mission (66211) ***(G-11491)***
John Jaco Inc 620 792-2541
820 Main St Great Bend (67530) ***(G-2595)***
John K Burch Company 800 365-1988
5775 Foxridge Dr Shawnee Mission (66202) ***(G-11492)***
John Knox Village 913 403-8343
6600 College Blvd Ste 300 Leawood (66211) ***(G-5443)***
John Knox Village HM Hlth Agcy, Leawood *Also called John Knox Village* ***(G-5443)***
John O Farmer Inc 785 483-3144
370 W Wichita Ave Russell (67665) ***(G-10277)***
John P Gravino Do 785 842-5070
3510 Clinton Pl Ste 200 Lawrence (66047) ***(G-4927)***
John Rohrer Contracting Co Inc (PA) 913 236-5005
2820 Roe Ln Kansas City (66103) ***(G-4126)***
JOHN RORHER CONTRACTING, Kansas City *Also called John Rohrer Contracting Co Inc* ***(G-4126)***
John Schmidt & Sons Inc (PA) 316 445-2103
12903 E Silver Lake Rd Mount Hope (67108) ***(G-7205)***
John Schmidt & Sons Inc 620 221-0300
2303 W 9th Ave Winfield (67156) ***(G-16150)***
John T Arnold Associates Inc 316 263-7242
100 S Main St Ste 100 # 100 Wichita (67202) ***(G-14763)***
John Zink Company LLC 316 828-7380
4111 E 37th St N Wichita (67220) ***(G-14764)***
John's Market, Topeka *Also called Pauline Food Center* ***(G-12965)***
Johnny Schwindt Inc 620 275-0633
201 E Kansas Ave Garden City (67846) ***(G-2209)***
Johns Body Shop Inc 620 225-2213
110 W Beeson Rd Dodge City (67801) ***(G-1383)***
Johns Farm, Wichita *Also called Schueller John* ***(G-15534)***
Johns Manville Corporation 620 241-6260
1465 17th Ave McPherson (67460) ***(G-6979)***
Johnson & White Sales Company 913 390-9808
1710 E 123rd Ter Olathe (66061) ***(G-7812)***
Johnson Bowser Funeral Chapel 785 233-3039
723 Sw 6th Ave Topeka (66603) ***(G-12747)***
Johnson Bros Auto Supply, Wichita *Also called Poorman Auto Supply Inc* ***(G-15315)***
Johnson Business Cards, Shawnee *Also called Metal Arts Engravers Inc* ***(G-10994)***
Johnson Cmmunications Svcs Inc 913 681-5505
16144 Foster St Stilwell (66085) ***(G-12159)***
Johnson Cntrls SEC Sltions LLC 316 634-1792
3450 N Rock Rd Ste 509 Wichita (67226) ***(G-14765)***
Johnson Cnty Dept Hlth & Envmt 913 826-1200
11875 S Sunset Dr Ste 300 Olathe (66061) ***(G-7813)***
Johnson Cnty Grls Athc Complex 913 422-7837
20200 Johnson Dr Shawnee Mission (66218) ***(G-11493)***
Johnson Cnty Ob-Gyn Chartered 913 236-6455
7440 W Frontage Rd Shawnee Mission (66203) ***(G-11494)***
Johnson Cnty Pk Recreation Dst 913 438-7275
7900 Renner Rd Shawnee Mission (66219) ***(G-11495)***
Johnson Contrls Authorized Dlr, Wichita *Also called Washer Specialties Company* ***(G-15930)***
Johnson Controls, Shawnee Mission *Also called Clarios* ***(G-11237)***
Johnson Controls, Wichita *Also called Wichita Wholesale Supply Inc* ***(G-16044)***
Johnson Controls, Wichita *Also called Clarios* ***(G-14034)***
Johnson Controls, Topeka *Also called Clarios* ***(G-12478)***
Johnson Controls, Wichita *Also called Clarios* ***(G-14035)***
Johnson Controls, Wichita *Also called Clarios* ***(G-14036)***
Johnson Controls, Salina *Also called Clarios* ***(G-10454)***
Johnson Controls 913 894-0010
11019 Strang Line Rd Lenexa (66215) ***(G-5930)***
Johnson Controls 316 686-6363
625 N Carriage Pkwy # 140 Wichita (67208) ***(G-14766)***
Johnson Controls Fire 785 267-9675
4024 Sw Topeka Blvd Topeka (66609) ***(G-12748)***
Johnson Cooperative Grn Co Inc (PA) 620 492-6210
304 E Highland Johnson (67855) ***(G-3654)***
Johnson Cooperative Grn Co Inc 620 492-2297
104 W Highland Rd Johnson (67855) ***(G-3655)***
Johnson County Aggregates 913 764-2127
23555 W 151st St Olathe (66061) ***(G-7814)***
Johnson County Aggregiates, Olathe *Also called Johnson County Aggregates* ***(G-7814)***
Johnson County Animal Clinic 913 642-2714
9425 W 75th St Shawnee Mission (66204) ***(G-11496)***
Johnson County Answering Svc, Olathe *Also called Johnson County Communications* ***(G-7815)***

Johnson County Automotive LLC...913 432-1721
5829 Kessler Ln Shawnee Mission (66203) ***(G-11497)***
Johnson County Communications...913 764-2876
407 S Clairborne Rd # 208 Olathe (66062) ***(G-7815)***
Johnson County Dermatology...913 764-1125
153 W 151st St Ste 100 Olathe (66061) ***(G-7816)***
Johnson County Dev Support (PA)...913 826-2626
10501 Lackman Rd Lenexa (66219) ***(G-5931)***
Johnson County Imaging Ctr PA...913 469-8998
11717 W 112th St Overland Park (66210) ***(G-8878)***
Johnson County Investors Inc...913 631-0000
11501 Shwnee Mission Pkwy Shawnee Mission (66203) ***(G-11498)***
Johnson County Kansas Heritage...913 481-3137
1200 E Kansas City Rd Olathe (66061) ***(G-7817)***
Johnson County Landfill...913 631-8181
17955 Holiday Dr Shawnee Mission (66217) ***(G-11499)***
Johnson County Med-Act...913 715-1950
11811 S Sunset Dr # 1100 Olathe (66061) ***(G-7818)***
Johnson County Pediatrics...913 384-5500
8800 W 75th St Ste 220 Merriam (66204) ***(G-7097)***
Johnson County Pntg, Fairway *Also called Johnson County Pntg & Hm Repr* ***(G-1911)***
Johnson County Pntg & Hm Repr (PA)...913 631-5252
5839 Mission Rd Fairway (66205) ***(G-1911)***
Johnson County Surgery Center, Shawnee Mission *Also called Surgicenter Johnson County Ltd* ***(G-11914)***
Johnson County Unified Wstwtr (PA)...913 715-8500
11811 S Sunset Dr # 2500 Olathe (66061) ***(G-7819)***
Johnson Duncan & Hollowell CPA...316 267-3402
535 S Emporia Ave Ste 103 Wichita (67202) ***(G-14767)***
Johnson Food Equipment Inc...913 621-3366
2955 Fairfax Trfy Kansas City (66115) ***(G-4127)***
Johnson Gage & Inspection Inc...316 943-7532
5920 W 21st St N Wichita (67205) ***(G-14768)***
Johnson Monument & Trigard, Belleville *Also called Los Primos Inc* ***(G-460)***
Johnson Mortuary Inc...620 431-1220
101 N Highland Ave Chanute (66720) ***(G-734)***
Johnson State Bank (PA)...620 492-6200
202 S Main St Johnson (67855) ***(G-3656)***
Johnson State Bankshares Inc...620 492-6200
202 S Main St Johnson (67855) ***(G-3657)***
Johnson Wilson Embers...913 438-9095
8207 Melrose Dr Ste 145 Shawnee Mission (66214) ***(G-11500)***
Johnson, Douglas D, Wichita *Also called Kennedy & Willis* ***(G-14849)***
Johnson, Pamela J, Wichita *Also called Johnson Duncan & Hollowell CPA* ***(G-14767)***
Johnsons Garden Center Inc (PA)...316 942-3751
2707 W 13th St N Wichita (67203) ***(G-14769)***
Johnsonville LLC...785 364-3126
619 E 4th St Holton (66436) ***(G-3102)***
Johnston Insurance Agency...913 396-0800
5225 W 75th St Ste 200 Shawnee Mission (66208) ***(G-11501)***
Jojacs Landscape & Mowing...316 945-3525
205 Cain Dr Haysville (67060) ***(G-2950)***
Joma Bowling, Wichita *Also called Boulevard One Inc* ***(G-13873)***
Jomax Construction Company Inc (HQ)...620 792-3686
238 Se 10 Ave Great Bend (67530) ***(G-2596)***
Jones & Buck Development Oil...620 725-3636
7777 Hwy 99 Sedan (67361) ***(G-10844)***
Jones & Jones Development LLC...913 422-9477
2527 S 142nd St Bonner Springs (66012) ***(G-557)***
Jones Construction, Leoti *Also called Mark C Jones* ***(G-6256)***
Jones Foundation...620 342-1714
2501 W 18th Ave Ste D Emporia (66801) ***(G-1781)***
Jones Janitorial Service...316 722-5520
1124 N Emerson Ave Wichita (67212) ***(G-14770)***
Jones Lang Lasalle Inc...816 531-2323
7500 College Blvd Ste 920 Overland Park (66210) ***(G-8879)***
Jones-Seel-Huyett, Topeka *Also called Huyett Jones Partners* ***(G-12709)***
Jorban-Riscoe Associates Inc (PA)...913 438-1244
9808 Alden St Lenexa (66215) ***(G-5932)***
Jordan Companies Inc...316 943-6222
1133 S Gordon St Wichita (67213) ***(G-14771)***
Jordan Spray Insulation, Wichita *Also called Jordan Companies Inc* ***(G-14771)***
Joseph & Hollander PA (PA)...316 262-9400
500 N Market St Wichita (67214) ***(G-14772)***
Joseph F Beaver...620 872-2395
514 S Main St Scott City (67871) ***(G-10818)***
Joseph P Steven DDS PA...316 262-5273
232 N Seneca St Wichita (67203) ***(G-14773)***
Joseph Stowers Painting Inc...913 722-2534
6839 Nall Ave Shawnee Mission (66208) ***(G-11502)***
Joseph T Ryerson & Son Inc...316 942-6061
1874 S Florence Ct Wichita (67209) ***(G-14774)***
Joseph Wommack DDS...620 421-0980
1701 Washington Ave Parsons (67357) ***(G-9694)***
Joshua's Pest Control, Lenexa *Also called Moxie Services LLC* ***(G-6013)***
Josie Norris MD...785 232-6950
1109 Sw Topeka Blvd Topeka (66612) ***(G-12749)***
Jouras, Peter A Jr, Fairway *Also called Law Office of Pter A Jouras Jr* ***(G-1912)***
Joyful Noise Academy...316 688-5060
2900 N Rock Rd Wichita (67226) ***(G-14775)***
JP Murray Company Inc...913 451-1279
7400 College Blvd Ste 210 Overland Park (66210) ***(G-8880)***
JP Weigand, Hutchinson *Also called J P Weigand and Sons Inc* ***(G-3338)***
JR Custom Metal Products Inc...316 263-1318
2237 S West Street Ct Wichita (67213) ***(G-14776)***
Jri Investments LLC...785 404-2210
2313 N Zoo Park Cir Wichita (67205) ***(G-14777)***
Jrko LLC...913 648-7858
7200 W 107th St Shawnee Mission (66212) ***(G-11503)***
Jrm Enterprises Inc...785 404-1328
2010 Rogers Ct Salina (67401) ***(G-10557)***
Js Sign & Awning LLC...785 776-8860
2726 Amherst Ave Ste A Manhattan (66502) ***(G-6667)***
Js Westhoff & Company Inc...913 663-9900
14006 W 107th St Lenexa (66215) ***(G-5933)***
Jt Maintenance Inc...913 642-5656
5750 W 95th St Ste 200 Overland Park (66207) ***(G-8881)***
Jt2 Inc...913 323-4915
9393 W 110th St Ste 533 Overland Park (66210) ***(G-8882)***
Jts Transports Inc...316 554-0706
7426 S Broadway Ave Haysville (67060) ***(G-2951)***
Jtweigand, Wichita *Also called KB Properties of Kansas LLC* ***(G-14836)***
Judiciary Court of The State...785 296-6290
220 Se 6th Ave Topeka (66603) ***(G-12750)***
Judiciary Court of The State...785 233-8200
200 Se 7th St Ste 209 Topeka (66603) ***(G-12751)***
Julie K Samuelson...785 852-4900
126 N Main St Sharon Springs (67758) ***(G-10899)***
Julius Kaaz Cnstr Co Inc...913 682-3550
716 Cherokee St Leavenworth (66048) ***(G-5259)***
Junction City Bowl Inc...785 238-6813
835 S Washington St Junction City (66441) ***(G-3703)***
Junction City Daily Union, Junction City *Also called Montgomery Communications Inc* ***(G-3727)***
Junction City Family YMCA, Junction City *Also called Armed Services YMCA of USA* ***(G-3668)***
Junction City Family YMCA Inc (PA)...785 762-4780
1703 Mcfarland Rd Junction City (66441) ***(G-3704)***
Junction City Lodging LLC...785 579-5787
221 E Ash St Junction City (66441) ***(G-3705)***
Junction City Transportation, Junction City *Also called Junction CT-Ft Rly Mht Trnsinc* ***(G-3707)***
Junction City Wire Harness LLC...785 762-4400
1002 Perry St Junction City (66441) ***(G-3706)***
Junction CT Geary Cnty Hlth De, Junction City *Also called County of Geary* ***(G-3684)***
Junction CT-Ft Rly Mht Trnsinc...785 762-2219
301 E 4th St Junction City (66441) ***(G-3707)***
Juniper Gardens Childrens Prj...913 321-3143
444 Minnesota Ave Fl 3 Kansas City (66101) ***(G-4128)***
Juniper Payments LLC...316 267-3200
9440 E Boston St Ste 150 Wichita (67207) ***(G-14778)***
Jupiter Esources LLC (HQ)...405 488-3886
501 Kansas Ave Kansas City (66105) ***(G-4129)***
Jury & Associates Inc...913 642-5656
5750 W 95th St Ste 200 Shawnee Mission (66207) ***(G-11504)***
Jurysync LLC...913 338-4301
25255 W 102nd Ter Ste A Olathe (66061) ***(G-7820)***
Just For Kids Express...785 238-8555
2722 Gateway Ct Junction City (66441) ***(G-3708)***
Just In Time Adult Câre...913 371-3391
3227 Georgia Ave Kansas City (66104) ***(G-4130)***
Just Our Laundry Inc...913 649-8364
8730 Santa Fe Dr Shawnee Mission (66212) ***(G-11505)***
Justis Law Firm LLC...913 955-3710
10955 Lowell Ave Ste 520 Overland Park (66210) ***(G-8883)***
Juvenile Residential Facility, Wichita *Also called County of Sedgwick* ***(G-14110)***
Jvf Enterprises Inc...913 888-9111
14827 W 95th St Lenexa (66215) ***(G-5934)***
Jwavideo, Lawrence *Also called Jack Wilson & Associates Inc* ***(G-4918)***
K & D Ferguson Partnership...785 476-2657
2051 120 Rd Kensington (66951) ***(G-4576)***
K & F Distributors Inc...316 213-2030
1303 E Kechi Rd Ste C Kechi (67067) ***(G-4570)***
K & K Industries Inc...906 293-5242
9170 Clarks Creek Rd Junction City (66441) ***(G-3709)***
K & K Motors, Colby *Also called K Young Inc* ***(G-1019)***
K & K Water Wells LLC...620 675-2222
806 W La Lande Ave Sublette (67877) ***(G-12204)***
K & L Tank Truck Service Inc...620 277-0101
4940 E Us Highway 50 Garden City (67846) ***(G-2210)***
K & N Motorcycles Corporation...316 945-8221
2537 Sunnydale Ct Valley Center (67147) ***(G-13346)***
K & S LLC...620 275-7471
1911 E Kansas Ave Garden City (67846) ***(G-2211)***
K & S Eastside Amoco Inc...620 342-3565
1102 Whittier St Emporia (66801) ***(G-1782)***

K & W Underground Incorporated 913 782-7387
15608 S Keeler Ter Olathe (66062) **(G-7821)**
K and C Technical Service LLC 316 650-4464
11341 W 325th St Reading (66868) **(G-10199)**
K B, Lenexa *Also called Kocher + Beck USA LP* **(G-5955)**
K B Machine Shop Inc 913 829-3100
15325 S Keeler St Olathe (66062) **(G-7822)**
K B S, Shawnee Mission *Also called Kansas Builders Supply Co Inc* **(G-11508)**
K C Abrasive Co LLC 913 342-2900
3140 Dodge Rd Kansas City (66115) **(G-4131)**
K C Abrasive Company, Kansas City *Also called K C Abrasive Co LLC* **(G-4131)**
K C Construction Inc 913 724-1474
1211 158th St Basehor (66007) **(G-382)**
K C D Inc 785 827-0445
808 E Crawford St Salina (67401) **(G-10558)**
K C Feeders, Scott City *Also called High Choice Feeders LLC* **(G-10816)**
K C Freightliner Body Shop 913 342-4269
11 N James St Kansas City (66118) **(G-4132)**
K C I Roadrunner Express Inc 785 238-6161
1002 N Washington St Junction City (66441) **(G-3710)**
K C K Animal Control 913 321-1445
3301 Park Dr Kansas City (66102) **(G-4133)**
K C Kansas Housing Authority, Kansas City *Also called Wyandtte Cnty Unfied Gvernment* **(G-4555)**
K C P, Kingman *Also called Klaver Construction Pdts LLC* **(G-4604)**
K C Pork Inc 785 455-3410
451 3rd Rd Clifton (66937) **(G-901)**
K C R International Trucking, Topeka *Also called Idealease of Mo-Kan Inc* **(G-12712)**
K C Sign Express Inc 913 432-2500
5033 Mackey St Shawnee Mission (66203) **(G-11506)**
K C Wood Products 913 422-3320
10651 Kaw Dr Ste 700 Edwardsville (66111) **(G-1505)**
K C X, Emporia *Also called Kansas Continental Express Inc* **(G-1786)**
K Construction Inc 785 499-5296
515 Main St Alta Vista (66834) **(G-70)**
K Craig Place MD 913 385-9009
9009 Roe Ave Prairie Village (66207) **(G-10039)**
K D Sullivan Investments LLC 785 460-0170
1979 W 4th St Colby (67701) **(G-1018)**
K E Y N FM, Wichita *Also called Entercom Communications Corp* **(G-14291)**
K G Moats & Sons LLC 785 437-2021
27010 Highway 24 Saint Marys (66536) **(G-10368)**
K H A Z FM Radio, Hays *Also called Eagle Communications Inc* **(G-2795)**
K H U T F M Country Music 620 662-4486
1700 W 17th Ave Hutchinson (67501) **(G-3344)**
K J H K 907 FM 785 864-4745
1301 Jayhawk Blvd 4274f Lawrence (66045) **(G-4928)**
K K O W AM FM, Pittsburg *Also called American Media Investments Inc* **(G-9808)**
K N Z A Inc (PA) 785 547-3461
5 Onehalf Mi S Hiawatha H Hiawatha (66434) **(G-3012)**
K P L Gas Service, Colwich *Also called Evergy Kansas Central Inc* **(G-1096)**
K P L Gas Service, Emporia *Also called Evergy Kansas Central Inc* **(G-1753)**
K R Johnson, Lenexa *Also called Kenneth R Johnson Inc* **(G-5945)**
K S A J Oldies 785 823-1111
131 N Santa Fe Ave Fl 3 Salina (67401) **(G-10559)**
K State Rabies Laboratory 785 532-4472
2005 Research Park Cir Manhattan (66502) **(G-6668)**
K T I, Overland Park *Also called Kruger Technologies Inc* **(G-8929)**
K U Endowment Association (PA) 785 830-7600
1891 Constant Ave Lawrence (66047) **(G-4929)**
K V O E FM, Emporia *Also called Emporias Radio Stations Inc* **(G-1749)**
K W Brock Directories Inc (PA) 620 231-4000
1225 E Centennial Dr Pittsburg (66762) **(G-9884)**
K X B Z-104.7 F M, Manhattan *Also called Kxbz B 104 7 FM* **(G-6706)**
K X X, Dodge City *Also called M Rocking Radio Inc* **(G-1400)**
K Young Inc 785 475-3888
105 W Horton Ave Colby (67701) **(G-1019)**
K&J Outdoor Products LLC 816 769-6060
5306 Cr 6200 Cherryvale (67335) **(G-810)**
K-Rock, Manhattan *Also called Manhattan Broadcasting Co Inc* **(G-6718)**
K-State Alumni Association, Manhattan *Also called Kansas State Univ Alumni Assn* **(G-6677)**
K-State Diagnostic & Analyticl 785 532-3294
1800 Denison Ave Manhattan (66506) **(G-6669)**
K-State Hrtclture Ntral Rsrces 785 532-6170
1712 Claflin Rd Manhattan (66506) **(G-6670)**
K-State Student Union, Manhattan *Also called K-State Union Corporation* **(G-6671)**
K-State Union Corporation 785 532-6575
918 N 17th St Manhattan (66506) **(G-6671)**
K-STATE UNIVERSITY FERDERAL CR, Manhattan *Also called Kansas State Univ Federal Cr* **(G-6678)**
K-W Manufacturing LLC 785 548-7454
404 Locust St Everest (66424) **(G-1900)**
K. C. L. Y. FM, Clay Center *Also called Taylor Communications Inc* **(G-883)**
K2b Incorporated (PA) 913 663-3311
7500 College Blvd # 1213 Shawnee Mission (66210) **(G-11507)**
K5 Painting Inc 316 283-9612
204 W 6th St Newton (67114) **(G-7368)**
Ka-Comm Inc (PA) 785 827-8555
326 S Clark St Salina (67401) **(G-10560)**
Ka-Comm Inc 785 776-8177
2321 Skyvue Ln Ste A Manhattan (66502) **(G-6672)**
Kaeser Compressors Inc 913 599-5100
8334 Melrose Dr Overland Park (66214) **(G-8884)**
Kahn Culvert, Paola *Also called Contech Engnered Solutions LLC* **(G-9549)**
Kahrs Nelson Fanning Hite Kllg 316 265-7741
100 N Broadway Ave # 950 Wichita (67202) **(G-14779)**
Kai Total Pavement Management, Bucyrus *Also called Kansas Asphalt Inc* **(G-601)**
Kalhd, Topeka *Also called Health Dpknsas Assn Lcal Depts* **(G-12672)**
Kaliaperumal Mamalay 816 210-1248
10901 W 144th St Overland Park (66221) **(G-8885)**
Kalmar Solutions LLC (HQ) 785 242-2200
415 E Dundee St Ottawa (66067) **(G-8279)**
Kalos Inc 785 232-3606
3518 Se 21st St Ste B Topeka (66607) **(G-12752)**
Kalvesta Implement Co Inc 620 855-3567
32730 E State Road 156 Kalvesta (67835) **(G-3771)**
Kaman Composites - Wichita 316 942-1241
1650 S Mccomas St Wichita (67213) **(G-14780)**
Kammco, Topeka *Also called Kansas Medical Mutual Insur Co* **(G-12790)**
Kammco Health Solutions Inc 800 435-2104
623 Sw 10th Ave Topeka (66612) **(G-12753)**
Kammerer Auto Body & Paint 316 265-0211
307 S Washington Ave Wichita (67202) **(G-14781)**
Kan Colo Credit Union 620 653-4415
216 N Maple St Hoisington (67544) **(G-3067)**
Kan Fab Inc 620 342-5669
623 Graham St Emporia (66801) **(G-1783)**
Kan Pak LLC (HQ) 620 442-6820
151 S Whittier Rd Wichita (67207) **(G-14782)**
Kan Pak International Inc 316 201-4210
151 S Whittier Rd Wichita (67207) **(G-14783)**
Kan Tex Hospitality Inc 785 404-1870
222 E Diamond Dr Salina (67401) **(G-10561)**
Kan-AM Products Inc (PA) 316 943-8806
1830 W Harry St Wichita (67213) **(G-14784)**
Kan-Seal, Burlington *Also called Menard Incorporated* **(G-640)**
Kana Software Inc 913 802-6756
7400 W 129th St Ste 200 Overland Park (66213) **(G-8886)**
Kanamak Hydraulics Inc 800 473-5843
2218 W Mary St Garden City (67846) **(G-2212)**
Kanas Cattlemens Associate 785 238-1483
725 N Washington St Ste B Junction City (66441) **(G-3711)**
Kanawha River Railroad LLC 620 231-2030
315 W 3rd St Pittsburg (66762) **(G-9885)**
Kanbrews LLC (PA) 913 499-6495
9100 Bond St Overland Park (66214) **(G-8887)**
Kandarpam Hotels LLC 785 762-4200
25900 W 96th St Lenexa (66227) **(G-5935)**
Kaneb Pipe Line, Wichita *Also called Nustar Pipeline Oper Partnr LP* **(G-15200)**
Kaneb Services, El Dorado *Also called Nustar Pipeline Oper Partnr LP* **(G-1586)**
Kanequip Inc 785 267-9200
2901 Nw Us Highway 24 Topeka (66618) **(G-12754)**
Kanequip Inc 785 472-3114
704 Kunkle Dr Ellsworth (67439) **(G-1676)**
Kanequip Inc 785 632-3441
615 W Court St Clay Center (67432) **(G-869)**
Kanequip Inc (PA) 785 456-2041
18035 E Us Highway 24 Wamego (66547) **(G-13426)**
Kanequip Inc 620 225-0016
1451 S 2nd Ave Dodge City (67801) **(G-1384)**
Kanequip Inc 785 562-2377
1152 Pony Express Hwy Marysville (66508) **(G-6891)**
Kanequip Inc 785 562-2377
1152 Pony Express Hwy Marysville (66508) **(G-6892)**
Kangolf Inc 785 539-7529
800 Anneberg Cir Manhattan (66503) **(G-6673)**
Kannarr Eye Care LLC 620 235-1737
2521 N Broadway St Pittsburg (66762) **(G-9886)**
Kanokla Communications LLC (HQ) 620 845-5682
100 Kanokla Ave Caldwell (67022) **(G-659)**
Kanokla Networks, Caldwell *Also called Kanokla Communications LLC* **(G-659)**
Kanokla Networks, Caldwell *Also called Kanokla Telephone Association* **(G-660)**
Kanokla Telephone Association (PA) 620 845-5682
100 Kanokla Ave Caldwell (67022) **(G-660)**
Kans Dept Health and Envmt 785 296-0461
1000 Sw Jackson St # 200 Topeka (66612) **(G-12755)**
Kansas & Oklahoma Railroad, Wichita *Also called Watco Companies LLC* **(G-15935)**
Kansas & Oklahoma Railroad LLC (HQ) 620 231-2230
315 W 3rd St Pittsburg (66762) **(G-9887)**
Kansas 10th Judicial District, Olathe *Also called County of Johnson* **(G-7622)**
Kansas 4-H Foundation Inc 785 257-3221
1168 K157 Hwy Junction City (66441) **(G-3712)**
Kansas Acid Inc 785 625-5599
2140 E 8th St Hays (67601) **(G-2857)**

Kansas Affordable Housing Corp (PA)....316 942-4848
2145 N Topeka St Wichita (67214) ***(G-14785)***
Kansas AFL, Topeka *Also called American Federation* ***(G-12315)***
Kansas African American Aff....785 296-4874
900 Sw Jackson St Rm 100 Topeka (66612) ***(G-12756)***
Kansas Air Center Inc (PA)....785 776-1991
1705 S Airport Rd Manhattan (66503) ***(G-6674)***
Kansas Air Center Topeka Inc....785 234-2602
3600 Ne Sardou Ave Ste 4a Topeka (66616) ***(G-12757)***
Kansas American Tooling Inc....620 241-4200
1101 W 1st St McPherson (67460) ***(G-6980)***
Kansas Asphalt Inc (PA)....877 384-2280
7000 W 206th St Bucyrus (66013) ***(G-601)***
Kansas Assc Home For Aged Inc....785 233-7443
217 Se 8th Ave Topeka (66603) ***(G-12758)***
Kansas Asset Recovery Inc....316 303-1000
921 E Douglas Ave Wichita (67202) ***(G-14786)***
Kansas Assistive Tech Corp (PA)....620 341-9002
215 W 6th Ave Ste 205 Emporia (66801) ***(G-1784)***
Kansas Assn For Conserv & Envr....785 889-4384
22900 Independence Rd Onaga (66521) ***(G-8177)***
Kansas Assn of Insur Agents....785 232-0561
815 Sw Topeka Blvd Ste 1 Topeka (66612) ***(G-12759)***
Kansas Assn of Pub Employees....785 233-1956
1300 Sw Topeka Blvd Topeka (66612) ***(G-12760)***
Kansas Assn of Schl Boards....785 273-3600
1420 Sw Arrowhead Rd Topeka (66604) ***(G-12761)***
Kansas Assoc, Topeka *Also called Berkshire Hthway Frst Realtors* ***(G-12371)***
Kansas Association of Child....785 823-3343
1508 E Iron Ave Salina (67401) ***(G-10562)***
Kansas Athletics Incorporated....785 864-7050
1651 Naismith Dr Lawrence (66045) ***(G-4930)***
Kansas Auto Auction Inc (PA)....913 365-0460
1507 Roseport Rd Elwood (66024) ***(G-1688)***
Kansas AVI Independence LLC....620 331-7716
401 Freedom Dr Independence (67301) ***(G-3530)***
Kansas Aviation Independence, Independence *Also called Kansas AVI Independence LLC* ***(G-3530)***
Kansas Bankers Association....785 232-3444
610 Sw Corporate Vw Topeka (66615) ***(G-12762)***
Kansas Bankers Services, Topeka *Also called Kansas Bankers Association* ***(G-12762)***
Kansas Bar Association....785 234-5696
1200 Sw Harrison St Topeka (66612) ***(G-12763)***
KANSAS BEEF COUNCIL, Topeka *Also called Kansas Livestock Association* ***(G-12785)***
Kansas Big Bros Big Ssters Inc....620 231-1145
310 N Pine St Ste B Pittsburg (66762) ***(G-9888)***
Kansas Big Bros Big Ssters Inc (PA)....316 263-3300
310 E 2nd St N Wichita (67202) ***(G-14787)***
Kansas Big Bros Big Ssters Inc....785 843-7359
536 Fireside Ct Ste B Lawrence (66049) ***(G-4931)***
Kansas Big Bros Big Ssters Inc....620 421-0472
120 N 22nd St Parsons (67357) ***(G-9695)***
Kansas Biological Survey, Lawrence *Also called University of Kansas* ***(G-5161)***
Kansas Biological Survey....785 864-1505
2101 Constant Ave Lawrence (66047) ***(G-4932)***
Kansas Biomanufacturing Fcilty, Junction City *Also called Ventria Bioscience Inc* ***(G-3764)***
Kansas Body Works Inc....316 263-5506
1137 N Mosley Ave Wichita (67214) ***(G-14788)***
Kansas Brick & Tile, Hoisington *Also called Kansas Brick and Tile Co Inc* ***(G-3068)***
Kansas Brick and Tile Co Inc....620 653-2157
767 N Us Highway 281 Hoisington (67544) ***(G-3068)***
Kansas Broadband Internet....785 825-0199
Charles W Jameson Ste 601 Salina (67401) ***(G-10563)***
Kansas Builders Supply Co Inc....913 831-1511
5723 Kessler Ln Shawnee Mission (66203) ***(G-11508)***
Kansas Building Products, Salina *Also called Salina Concrete Products Inc* ***(G-10668)***
Kansas Building Supply, Shawnee Mission *Also called Vos Window & Door Inc* ***(G-11984)***
Kansas Building Supply Co Inc....913 962-5227
7600 Wedd St Overland Park (66204) ***(G-8888)***
Kansas Business Forms LLC....620 724-5234
300 N Summit St Girard (66743) ***(G-2414)***
Kansas Cancer Institute, Kansas City *Also called University of Kansas* ***(G-4498)***
Kansas Candy & Tobacco Inc....316 942-9081
4430 W 29th Cir S Wichita (67215) ***(G-14789)***
Kansas Cardiovascular Assoc....913 682-6950
712 1st Ter Ste C Lansing (66043) ***(G-4676)***
Kansas Carpet & Tile Inc....316 942-2111
2411 S Leonine Rd Wichita (67217) ***(G-14790)***
Kansas Center Entreprnrshp....316 425-8808
550 N 159th St E Ste 208 Wichita (67230) ***(G-14791)***
Kansas Chapter, Topeka *Also called The Nature Conservancy* ***(G-13158)***
Kansas Childrens Service Leag....620 340-0408
402 Commercial St Emporia (66801) ***(G-1785)***
Kansas Childrens Service Leag (PA)....316 942-4261
1365 N Custer St Wichita (67203) ***(G-14792)***
Kansas Childrens Service Leag....785 274-3100
3545 Sw 5th St Topeka (66606) ***(G-12764)***
Kansas Childrens Service Leag....785 274-3800
3545 Sw 5th St Topeka (66606) ***(G-12765)***
Kansas Childrens Service Leag....620 276-3232
2111 E Labrador Blvd Garden City (67846) ***(G-2213)***
Kansas Childrens Service Leag....620 626-5339
150 Plaza Dr Ste B Liberal (67901) ***(G-6326)***
Kansas City Aviation Ctr Inc....913 782-0530
15325 S Pflumm Rd Olathe (66062) ***(G-7823)***
Kansas City Bd Pub Utilities (PA)....913 573-9000
540 Minnesota Ave Kansas City (66101) ***(G-4134)***
Kansas City Bd Pub Utilities....913 573-9280
4301 Brenner Dr Kansas City (66104) ***(G-4135)***
Kansas City Bd Pub Utilities....913 573-9000
540 Minnesota Ave Kansas City (66101) ***(G-4136)***
Kansas City Bd Pub Utilities....913 573-9300
3601 N 12th St Kansas City (66104) ***(G-4137)***
Kansas City Bd Pub Utilities....913 573-9556
6742 Riverview Ave Kansas City (66102) ***(G-4138)***
Kansas City Bd Pub Utilities....913 573-9675
380 S 11th St Kansas City (66102) ***(G-4139)***
Kansas City Bd Pub Utilities....913 573-9700
4240 N 55th St Kansas City (66104) ***(G-4140)***
Kansas City Bd Pub Utilities....913 573-9143
540 Minnesota Ave Kansas City (66101) ***(G-4141)***
Kansas City Bd Pub Utilities....913 573-6810
312 N 65th St Kansas City (66102) ***(G-4142)***
Kansas City Blues Society Inc....913 660-4692
13624 S Sycamore St Olathe (66062) ***(G-7824)***
Kansas City Bone & Joint Clini....913 381-5225
10701 Nall Ave Ste 200 Overland Park (66211) ***(G-8889)***
Kansas City Brokerage Inc....913 384-4994
6700 Antioch Rd Ste 420 Overland Park (66204) ***(G-8890)***
Kansas City Cancer Center LLC....913 788-8883
8919 Parallel Pkwy # 326 Kansas City (66112) ***(G-4143)***
Kansas City Cancer Center LLC (PA)....913 541-4600
9200 Indian Creek Pkwy # 300 Overland Park (66210) ***(G-8891)***
Kansas City Cash Register, Overland Park *Also called Data Systems Inc* ***(G-8637)***
Kansas City Christian School....913 648-5227
4801 W 79th St Prairie Village (66208) ***(G-10040)***
Kansas City Coml Whsng Co....913 287-3800
1021 Pacific Ave Kansas City (66102) ***(G-4144)***
Kansas City Compensation & Ben....913 381-4458
8826 Santa Fe Dr Ste 208 Overland Park (66212) ***(G-8892)***
Kansas City Country Club....913 236-2100
6200 Indian Ln Mission Hills (66208) ***(G-7145)***
Kansas City Ctr For Anxty Trmt....913 649-8820
10555 Marty St Ste 100 Overland Park (66212) ***(G-8893)***
Kansas City Deaerator Inc....913 312-5800
6731 W 121st St Overland Park (66209) ***(G-8894)***
Kansas City Electrical Sup Co (PA)....913 563-7002
14851 W 99th St Lenexa (66215) ***(G-5936)***
Kansas City Eye Clinic PA....913 341-3100
7504 Antioch Rd Shawnee Mission (66204) ***(G-11509)***
Kansas City Financial Group....913 649-7447
4801 W 110th St Ste 200 Overland Park (66211) ***(G-8895)***
Kansas City Heater Company, Overland Park *Also called Kansas City Deaerator Inc* ***(G-8894)***
Kansas City Hospice Inc....816 363-2600
10100 W 87th St Ste 100 Overland Park (66212) ***(G-8896)***
Kansas City Hydraulics Inc....913 371-6151
944 Osage Ave Kansas City (66105) ***(G-4145)***
Kansas City Imaging Center....913 667-5600
11011 Haskell Ave Kansas City (66109) ***(G-4146)***
Kansas City Mechanical Inc....913 334-1101
6822 Kansas Ave Kansas City (66111) ***(G-4147)***
Kansas City Millwork Company....913 768-0068
1120 W 149th St Olathe (66061) ***(G-7825)***
Kansas City Millwork Company....913 768-0068
1120 W 149th St Olathe (66061) ***(G-7826)***
Kansas City Office, Overland Park *Also called McCarthy Bldg Companies Inc* ***(G-9000)***
Kansas City Orthoped....913 338-4100
3651 College Blvd Ste 210 Leawood (66211) ***(G-5444)***
Kansas City Peterbilt Inc (PA)....913 441-2888
8915 Woodend Rd Kansas City (66111) ***(G-4148)***
Kansas City Piggy Back, Kansas City *Also called In Terminal Consolidation Co* ***(G-4096)***
Kansas City Power Products Inc....913 321-7040
80 S James St Kansas City (66118) ***(G-4149)***
Kansas City Presbyterian Manor, Kansas City *Also called Presbyterian Manors Inc* ***(G-4333)***
Kansas City Racquet Club....913 789-8000
6501 Frontage Rd Shawnee Mission (66202) ***(G-11510)***
Kansas City Railcar Svc Inc (PA)....913 621-0326
1147 S 14th St Kansas City (66105) ***(G-4150)***
Kansas City Regional....913 661-1600
11150 Overbrook Rd # 100 Leawood (66211) ***(G-5445)***
Kansas City Renaissance, Bonner Springs *Also called Festival Grogs Inc* ***(G-553)***
Kansas City SC LLC....913 575-1278
15009 W 150th Ter Olathe (66062) ***(G-7827)***
Kansas City Staffing, Overland Park *Also called Maxim Healthcare Services Inc* ***(G-8998)***

Kansas City Strings Violin Sp 913 677-0400
5842 Merriam Dr Shawnee Mission (66203) ***(G-11511)***
Kansas City T-Bones, Kansas City *Also called T-Bones Baseball Club LLC* ***(G-4455)***
Kansas City Transcription Inc 913 469-1000
4550 W 109th St Ste 303 Shawnee Mission (66211) ***(G-11512)***
Kansas City Tree Care LLC 913 722-4048
5217 Walmer St Shawnee Mission (66202) ***(G-11513)***
Kansas City Tstg & Engrg LLC 913 321-8100
1308 Adams St Kansas City (66103) ***(G-4151)***
Kansas City Urology Care 913 831-1003
1314 S 8th St Humboldt (66748) ***(G-3186)***
Kansas City Urology Care 913 338-5585
10701 Nall Ave Ste 100 Overland Park (66211) ***(G-8897)***
Kansas City Urology Care PA 913 341-7985
10701 Nall Ave Ste 100 Overland Park (66211) ***(G-8898)***
Kansas City Urology Care PA, Humboldt *Also called Kansas City Urology Care* ***(G-3186)***
Kansas City Winnelson Co 913 262-6868
1529 Lake Ave Kansas City (66103) ***(G-4152)***
Kansas City Womens Clinic PA (PA) 913 894-8500
10600 Quivira Rd Ste 320 Shawnee Mission (66215) ***(G-11514)***
Kansas Cnty Dst Attys Associat 785 232-5822
4601 State Ave Unit 58 Kansas City (66102) ***(G-4153)***
Kansas Coachworks Ltd 913 888-0991
9116 Marshall Dr Shawnee Mission (66215) ***(G-11515)***
Kansas Coalittion Against 785 232-9784
634 Sw Harrison St Topeka (66603) ***(G-12766)***
Kansas Coil Spring, Wichita *Also called Wkcsc Inc* ***(G-16060)***
Kansas Coliseum Inc 316 440-0888
1229 E 85th St N Park City (67147) ***(G-9621)***
Kansas Communications Inc 913 402-2200
14641 W 95th St Lenexa (66215) ***(G-5937)***
Kansas Consulting Engineers 785 357-1824
825 S Kansas Ave Ste 500 Topeka (66612) ***(G-12767)***
Kansas Continental Express Inc 620 343-7100
709 Industrial Rd Emporia (66801) ***(G-1786)***
Kansas Corporate Credit Union 316 721-2600
8615 W Frazier Ln Ste 1 Wichita (67212) ***(G-14793)***
Kansas Counselors Inc 316 942-8335
1421 N Saint Paul St Wichita (67203) ***(G-14794)***
Kansas Counselors Kans Cy Inc 913 541-9704
8725 Rosehill Rd Ste 411 Lenexa (66215) ***(G-5938)***
Kansas Credit Union Assn (PA) 316 942-7965
2544 N Maize Ct Ste 100 Wichita (67205) ***(G-14795)***
Kansas Crop Improvement Assn 785 532-6118
2000 Kimball Ave Manhattan (66502) ***(G-6675)***
Kansas Cutting Concrete, Wichita *Also called KC Coring & Cutng Cnstr Inc* ***(G-14837)***
Kansas Cy Freightliner Sls Inc 913 780-6606
15580 S Highway 169 Olathe (66062) ***(G-7828)***
Kansas Cy Gen Vscular Surgeons 913 754-2800
10730 Nall Ave Ste 101 Overland Park (66211) ***(G-8899)***
Kansas Cy Internal Medicine PA 913 451-8500
12140 Nall Ave Ste 100 Overland Park (66209) ***(G-8900)***
Kansas Cy Ob Gyn Pysicians PC 913 648-1840
10339 Alhambra St Overland Park (66207) ***(G-8901)***
Kansas Cy Physcl Therapy Group, Shawnee Mission *Also called Health Adminisource LLC* ***(G-11419)***
Kansas Cy Renaissance Festival 913 721-2110
628 N 126th St Bonner Springs (66012) ***(G-558)***
Kansas Dairy Ingredients, Leawood *Also called KDI Operating Company LLC* ***(G-5448)***
Kansas Dairy Ingredients Plant, Hugoton *Also called KDI Operating Company LLC* ***(G-3168)***
Kansas Department Commerce 785 296-5298
1000 Sw Jackson St # 100 Topeka (66612) ***(G-12768)***
Kansas Department of Labor 913 680-2200
515 Limit St Ste 200 Leavenworth (66048) ***(G-5260)***
Kansas Department Trnsp 785 527-2520
1652 Us Highway 81 Belleville (66935) ***(G-458)***
Kansas Department Trnsp 785 672-3113
3501 Highway 40 Oakley (67748) ***(G-7478)***
Kansas Department Trnsp 316 321-3370
205 Oil Hill Rd El Dorado (67042) ***(G-1575)***
Kansas Department Trnsp 785 823-3754
1006 N 3rd St Salina (67401) ***(G-10564)***
Kansas Department Trnsp 785 486-2142
1686 1st Ave E Horton (66439) ***(G-3128)***
Kansas Department Trnsp 620 583-5661
1308 E 7th St Eureka (67045) ***(G-1893)***
Kansas Department Trnsp 316 744-1271
3200 E 45th St N Bldg 2 Wichita (67220) ***(G-14796)***
Kansas Dept For Aging & Disabi 620 285-2131
1301 Ks Highway 264 Larned (67550) ***(G-4706)***
Kansas Dept For Aging & Disabi 913 755-7000
500 State Hospital Dr Osawatomie (66064) ***(G-8195)***
Kansas Dept For Aging & Disabi 785 296-5389
3107 Sw 21st St Topeka (66604) ***(G-12769)***
Kansas Dept For Aging & Disabi (HQ) 785 296-2917
503 S Kansas Ave Topeka (66603) ***(G-12770)***
Kansas Dept For Chldren Fmlies 913 651-6200
515 Limit St Ste 100 Leavenworth (66048) ***(G-5261)***
Kansas Dept For Chldren Fmlies 785 296-1368
500 Sw Van Buren St Topeka (66603) ***(G-12771)***
Kansas Dept For Chldren Fmlies 913 755-7000
500 State Hospital Dr Osawatomie (66064) ***(G-8196)***
Kansas Dept For Chldren Fmlies 620 421-4500
300 N 17th St Parsons (67357) ***(G-9696)***
Kansas Dept For Chldren Fmlies 785 296-3237
915 Sw Harrison St Fl 8 Topeka (66612) ***(G-12772)***
Kansas Dept For Chldren Fmlies 785 462-6769
180 W 5th St Colby (67701) ***(G-1020)***
Kansas Dept For Chldren Fmlies 913 755-2162
616 Brown Ave Osawatomie (66064) ***(G-8197)***
Kansas Dept For Chldren Fmlies 620 241-3802
115 E Euclid St Ste 1 McPherson (67460) ***(G-6981)***
Kansas Dept Humn Resources, Topeka *Also called Ui Benefit Overpayments* ***(G-13202)***
Kansas Development Fin Auth 785 357-4445
534 S Kansas Ave Ste 800 Topeka (66603) ***(G-12773)***
Kansas Dialysis Services LLC 785 234-2277
634 Sw Mulvane St Ste 300 Topeka (66606) ***(G-12774)***
Kansas Div, Parsons *Also called Day and Zimmermann Inc* ***(G-9680)***
Kansas Door Inc 620 793-7600
3708 17th St Great Bend (67530) ***(G-2597)***
Kansas East Conference United 913 631-2280
10700 Johnson Dr Shawnee Mission (66203) ***(G-11516)***
Kansas East Conference United 913 383-9146
8412 W 95th St Shawnee Mission (66212) ***(G-11517)***
Kansas Electric Cooperatives 785 478-4554
7332 Sw 21st St Topeka (66615) ***(G-12775)***
Kansas Electric Inc 316 283-4750
1420 Nw 36th St Newton (67114) ***(G-7369)***
Kansas Electric Power Coop Inc 785 273-7010
600 Sw Corporate Vw Topeka (66615) ***(G-12776)***
Kansas Elks Training (PA) 316 383-8700
1006 E Waterman St Wichita (67211) ***(G-14797)***
Kansas Entertaiment LLC 913 288-9300
777 Hollywood Casino Blvd Kansas City (66111) ***(G-4154)***
Kansas Ethanol LLC 620 257-2300
1630 Avenue Q Lyons (67554) ***(G-6487)***
Kansas Expocentre, Topeka *Also called Smg Holdings Inc* ***(G-13078)***
Kansas Farm Mgt Assoc SC (PA) 620 662-7868
1722 N Plum St Hutchinson (67502) ***(G-3345)***
Kansas Fast Lube Inc 620 241-5656
201 W Kansas Ave McPherson (67460) ***(G-6982)***
Kansas Feeds Inc (PA) 620 225-3500
1110 E Trail St Dodge City (67801) ***(G-1385)***
Kansas Fiber Network LLC 316 712-6030
8201 E 34th Street Cir N # 1500 Wichita (67226) ***(G-14798)***
Kansas Firefighters Museum 316 264-5990
1300 S Broadway Ave Wichita (67211) ***(G-14799)***
Kansas Fmly Advsory Netwrk Inc 316 264-2400
333 E English St Ste 215 Wichita (67202) ***(G-14800)***
Kansas Fmly Mdicine Foundation 913 588-1900
3901 Rainbow Blvd # 4010 Kansas City (66160) ***(G-4155)***
Kansas Fndtion For Med Care In 785 273-2552
800 Sw Jackson St Ste 700 Topeka (66612) ***(G-12777)***
Kansas Food Bank Warehouse Inc (PA) 316 265-3663
1919 E Douglas Ave Wichita (67211) ***(G-14801)***
Kansas Forklift Inc (PA) 316 262-1426
1750 W Harry St Wichita (67213) ***(G-14802)***
Kansas Freightlines & Sales, Kansas City *Also called K C Freightliner Body Shop* ***(G-4132)***
Kansas Gas Service, Kansas City *Also called Oneok Inc* ***(G-4295)***
Kansas Gas Service, Emporia *Also called Oneok Inc* ***(G-1810)***
Kansas Gas Service, Topeka *Also called Oneok Inc* ***(G-12947)***
Kansas Gas Service, Topeka *Also called Oneok Inc* ***(G-12948)***
Kansas Gas Service, Beloit *Also called Oneok Inc* ***(G-499)***
Kansas Gas Service, Pratt *Also called Oneok Inc* ***(G-10127)***
Kansas Gas Service, Wichita *Also called Oneok Inc* ***(G-15220)***
Kansas Gas Service 800 794-4780
11401 W 89th St Overland Park (66214) ***(G-8902)***
Kansas Genealogical Socie 620 225-1951
2601 Central Ave Ste 17b Dodge City (67801) ***(G-1386)***
Kansas General Appraisal Svc, Salina *Also called Realty Associates Inc* ***(G-10651)***
Kansas Global Hotel LLC 913 722-0800
7400 W Frontage Rd Merriam (66203) ***(G-7098)***
Kansas Golf and Turf Inc 316 267-9111
5701 N Chuzy Dr Park City (67219) ***(G-9622)***
Kansas Grain Inspection Svc 785 827-3671
1700 E Iron Ave Ste A Salina (67401) ***(G-10565)***
Kansas Grain Inspection Svc (PA) 785 233-7063
3800 Nw 14th St Topeka (66618) ***(G-12778)***
Kansas Granite Industries, Ellis *Also called Wolf Memorial Co Inc* ***(G-1655)***
Kansas Graphics Inc 620 273-6111
418 N Walnut St Cottonwood Falls (66845) ***(G-1155)***
Kansas Gun Drilling Inc 316 943-4241
2204 W Harry Ct Wichita (67213) ***(G-14803)***
Kansas Guttering, Wichita *Also called Midwest Roofing Services Inc* ***(G-15099)***
Kansas Guttering, Wichita *Also called Industrial Roofg Met Works Inc* ***(G-14687)***

Kansas Gymnastics & Dance Ctr.....913 764-8282
1702 E 123rd Ter Olathe (66061) ***(G-7829)***
Kansas Gymnastics Dance Cheer, Olathe *Also called Kansas Gymnastics & Dance Ctr* ***(G-7829)***
Kansas Hardwoods Inc.....785 456-8141
22620 Highway 24 Belvue (66407) ***(G-506)***
Kansas Health Foundation.....316 262-7676
309 E Douglas Ave Wichita (67202) ***(G-14804)***
Kansas Health Institute.....785 233-5443
212 Sw 8th Ave Ste 300 Topeka (66603) ***(G-12779)***
Kansas Health Solutions Inc.....785 575-9393
2121 Sw Chelsea Dr Topeka (66614) ***(G-12780)***
Kansas Healthcare, Topeka *Also called Health Care Stabilization Fund* ***(G-12671)***
Kansas Heart Hospital LLC.....800 574-3278
3601 N Webb Rd Wichita (67226) ***(G-14805)***
Kansas Heavy Construction LLC.....913 845-2121
19425 State Ave Tonganoxie (66086) ***(G-12264)***
Kansas Hospital Association (PA).....785 233-7436
215 Se 8th Ave Topeka (66603) ***(G-12781)***
Kansas Housing Resources Corp.....785 217-2001
611 S Kansas Ave Fl 3 Topeka (66603) ***(G-12782)***
Kansas Humane Soc Wichita Kans.....316 524-9196
3313 N Hillside Ave Wichita (67219) ***(G-14806)***
Kansas Imaging Consultants.....316 268-5000
929 N St Francis St Wichita (67214) ***(G-14807)***
Kansas Imaging Consultants PA.....316 689-5043
3600 E Harry St Wichita (67218) ***(G-14808)***
Kansas Info Consortium LLC.....785 296-5059
534 S Kansas Ave Ste 1210 Topeka (66603) ***(G-12783)***
Kansas Inn Limited Partnership.....316 269-9999
1011 N Topeka St Wichita (67214) ***(G-14809)***
Kansas Inn, The, Wichita *Also called Kansas Inn Limited Partnership* ***(G-14809)***
Kansas Intrschlstc Athltc Admn.....316 655-8929
2301 E Douglas Ave Wichita (67211) ***(G-14810)***
Kansas Investigative Services.....316 267-1357
250 S Laura Ave Wichita (67211) ***(G-14811)***
Kansas Investment Corporation.....785 843-6611
2903 W 6th St Lawrence (66049) ***(G-4933)***
Kansas Kenworth Inc.....785 823-9700
2301 N Ohio St Salina (67401) ***(G-10566)***
Kansas Kids Daycare Preschool.....785 762-4338
110 N Eisenhower Dr Junction City (66441) ***(G-3713)***
Kansas Laleche League Inc.....785 865-5919
807 W 28th Ter Lawrence (66046) ***(G-4934)***
Kansas Legal Services Inc.....620 227-7349
701 E Comanche Ln Ste F Dodge City (67801) ***(G-1387)***
Kansas Legal Services Inc.....620 694-2955
206 W 1st Ave Hutchinson (67501) ***(G-3346)***
Kansas Legal Services Inc (PA).....785 354-8531
712 S Kansas Ave Ste 200 Topeka (66603) ***(G-12784)***
Kansas Legal Services Inc.....316 265-9681
340 S Broadway Ave Wichita (67202) ***(G-14812)***
Kansas Legal Services Inc.....913 621-0200
400 State Ave Ste 1015 Kansas City (66101) ***(G-4156)***
Kansas Livestock Association.....785 273-5115
6031 Sw 37th St Topeka (66614) ***(G-12785)***
Kansas Long Term Care Phys.....316 315-0145
1131 S Clifton Ave Ste B Wichita (67218) ***(G-14813)***
Kansas Ltd Liability Company.....888 222-6359
7240 W 98th Ter Overland Park (66212) ***(G-8903)***
Kansas Maid Inc.....620 437-2958
2369 Ks 58 Hwy Madison (66860) ***(G-6502)***
Kansas Manufacturing Company.....785 843-2892
201 Perry St Lawrence (66044) ***(G-4935)***
KANSAS MANUFACTURING SOLUTIONS, Overland Park *Also called Mid-America Mfg Tech Ctr Inc* ***(G-9025)***
Kansas Masonic Home.....316 269-7500
401 S Seneca St Wichita (67213) ***(G-14814)***
Kansas Medical Assoc Inc.....316 733-4747
943 N Andover Rd Andover (67002) ***(G-97)***
Kansas Medical Clinic PA.....785 233-3553
2860 Sw Mission Woods Dr C Topeka (66614) ***(G-12786)***
Kansas Medical Clinic PA.....785 233-3555
2200 Sw 6th Ave Ste 105 Topeka (66606) ***(G-12787)***
Kansas Medical Clinic PA (PA).....785 233-3555
2200 Sw 6th Ave Ste 104 Topeka (66606) ***(G-12788)***
Kansas Medical Insur Svcs Corp.....785 232-2224
W 10th Ave Ste 200 Topeka (66612) ***(G-12789)***
Kansas Medical Mutual Insur Co.....316 681-8119
3020 N Cypress St Ste 100 Wichita (67226) ***(G-14815)***
Kansas Medical Mutual Insur Co (PA).....785 232-2224
623 Sw 10th Ave Fl 2 Topeka (66612) ***(G-12790)***
Kansas Medical Society.....785 235-2383
623 Sw 10th Ave Topeka (66612) ***(G-12791)***
Kansas Municipal Energy Agency.....913 677-2884
6300 W 95th St Overland Park (66212) ***(G-8904)***
Kansas Museum of Mltry Histry.....316 775-1425
135 N Walnut St Augusta (67010) ***(G-329)***
Kansas Mutual Insurance Co.....785 354-1076
1435 Sw Topeka Blvd Topeka (66612) ***(G-12792)***
Kansas National Education Assn.....913 268-4005
11015 W 75th Ter Shawnee Mission (66214) ***(G-11518)***
Kansas National Education Assn (PA).....785 232-8271
715 Sw 10th Ave Ste B Topeka (66612) ***(G-12793)***
Kansas Neurological Institute, Topeka *Also called Kansas Dept For Aging & Disabi* ***(G-12769)***
Kansas Newspaper Foundation.....785 271-5304
5423 Sw 7th St Topeka (66606) ***(G-12794)***
Kansas Nphrology Physicians PA.....316 263-7285
1035 N Emporia St Ste 105 Wichita (67214) ***(G-14816)***
Kansas Operation Lifesaver.....785 806-8801
800 Sw Jackson St Ste 808 Topeka (66612) ***(G-12795)***
Kansas Orthopedic Center PA.....316 838-2020
7550 W Village Cir Ste 1 Wichita (67205) ***(G-14817)***
Kansas Pathology Cons PA.....316 681-2741
8201 E 34th Cir N # 1301 Wichita (67226) ***(G-14818)***
Kansas Paving, Park City *Also called Conspec Inc* ***(G-9612)***
Kansas Personnel Services Inc.....785 272-9999
5840 Sw Huntoon St Ste C Topeka (66604) ***(G-12796)***
Kansas Plastics, Wellington *Also called Tramec Sloan LLC* ***(G-13537)***
Kansas Powertrain & Eqp LLC.....785 861-7034
1534 Nw Tyler St Topeka (66608) ***(G-12797)***
Kansas Prferred Providers Assn, Wichita *Also called Wppa Inc* ***(G-16074)***
Kansas Prffsnl Anesthesia.....316 618-1515
1515 S Clifton Ave # 200 Wichita (67218) ***(G-14819)***
Kansas Prof Anesthesia Pain Mg, Wichita *Also called Kansas Prffsnl Anesthesia* ***(G-14819)***
Kansas Pub Emplyee Rtrment Sys.....785 296-1019
611 S Kansas Ave Fl 2 Topeka (66603) ***(G-12798)***
Kansas Public Telecom Svc Inc.....316 838-3090
320 W 21st St N Wichita (67203) ***(G-14820)***
Kansas Ready Mix LLC.....316 832-0828
4850 N Broadway Ave Park City (67219) ***(G-9623)***
Kansas Real Estate Commission.....785 296-3411
3 Townsite Plz Ste 200 Topeka (66603) ***(G-12799)***
Kansas Regional Assn Realtors.....913 498-1100
11150 Overbrook Rd # 100 Shawnee Mission (66211) ***(G-11519)***
Kansas Rehabilitation Hospital.....785 235-6600
1504 Sw 8th Ave Topeka (66606) ***(G-12800)***
Kansas Rental Inc.....785 272-1232
5966 Sw 29th St Topeka (66614) ***(G-12801)***
Kansas Rest Hospitality Assn.....316 267-8383
3500 N Rock Rd Bldg 1300 Wichita (67226) ***(G-14821)***
Kansas Rgnrtive Mdcine Ctr LLC.....785 320-4700
4809 Vue Du Lac Pl Manhattan (66503) ***(G-6676)***
Kansas Rural Housing Service.....785 862-4877
7204 Sw Timberway Dr Topeka (66619) ***(G-12802)***
KANSAS RUSH SOCCER CLUB, Olathe *Also called Olathe Soccer Club* ***(G-7949)***
Kansas Sand and Concrete Inc.....785 235-6284
531 Nw Tyler St Topeka (66608) ***(G-12803)***
Kansas Schl For Effective Lrng.....316 263-9620
1650 N Fairview Ave Wichita (67203) ***(G-14822)***
Kansas Scholastic Press Assoc.....785 864-7612
2063 Dale Ctr Lawrence (66045) ***(G-4936)***
Kansas Secured Title (HQ).....316 320-2410
220 W Central Ave El Dorado (67042) ***(G-1576)***
Kansas Secured Title Sedgwick (PA).....316 262-8261
232 N Mead St Wichita (67202) ***(G-14823)***
Kansas Secured Ttle Inc.....785 232-9349
3497 Sw Fairlawn Rd Topeka (66614) ***(G-12804)***
Kansas Specialty Services Inc.....620 221-6040
814 Main St Winfield (67156) ***(G-16151)***
Kansas Speedway Corporation.....913 328-3300
400 Speedway Blvd Kansas City (66111) ***(G-4157)***
Kansas Spine Spcialty Hosp LLC.....316 462-5000
3333 N Webb Rd Wichita (67226) ***(G-14824)***
Kansas Srgery Recovery Ctr LLC.....316 634-0090
2770 N Webb Rd Wichita (67226) ***(G-14825)***
Kansas St of Scl & Rehab Srvc, Colby *Also called Kansas Dept For Chldren Fmlies* ***(G-1020)***
Kansas Starbase Inc.....785 861-4709
5920 Sw Coyote Dr Topeka (66619) ***(G-12805)***
Kansas State Bank (HQ).....785 364-2166
100 E 5th St Holton (66436) ***(G-3103)***
Kansas State Bank (PA).....785 242-1011
236 N Main St Ottawa (66067) ***(G-8280)***
Kansas State Bank (PA).....785 665-7121
400 Maple St Overbrook (66524) ***(G-8325)***
Kansas State Council of Fire.....620 662-1808
817 W 19th Ave Hutchinson (67502) ***(G-3347)***
Kansas State High Schl Actvtie.....785 273-5329
601 Sw Commerce Pl Topeka (66615) ***(G-12806)***
Kansas State Historical Soc (PA).....785 272-8681
6425 Sw 6th Ave Topeka (66615) ***(G-12807)***
Kansas State Univ Alumni Assn.....785 532-6260
1720 Anderson Ave Manhattan (66506) ***(G-6677)***
Kansas State Univ Federal Cr (PA).....785 776-3003
2600 Anderson Ave Manhattan (66502) ***(G-6678)***
Kansas State Univ Foundation.....785 532-6266
1800 Kimball Ave Ste 200 Manhattan (66502) ***(G-6679)***

Kansas State University...785 532-7718
701 Beach Ln Manhattan (66506) ***(G-6680)***
Kansas State University...785 826-2646
2310 Centennial Rd Tc100a Salina (67401) ***(G-10567)***
Kansas State University...620 275-9164
4500 E Mary St Garden City (67846) ***(G-2214)***
Kansas State University...785 532-6376
104 Pittman Building Manhattan (66506) ***(G-6681)***
Kansas State University...785 539-4971
1800 College Ave Manhattan (66502) ***(G-6682)***
Kansas State University...785 532-5961
302 Seaton Hall Manhattan (66506) ***(G-6683)***
Kansas State University...620 421-4826
N 32nd And Pefley Parsons (67357) ***(G-9697)***
Kansas State University...785 564-7459
1320 Research Park Dr Manhattan (66502) ***(G-6684)***
Kansas State University...785 532-6980
101 Recreation Complex Manhattan (66506) ***(G-6685)***
Kansas State University...785 532-6011
116 Cardwell Hall Manhattan (66506) ***(G-6686)***
Kansas State University...785 532-7600
1800 College Ave Manhattan (66502) ***(G-6687)***
Kansas State University...785 625-3425
1232 240th Ave Hays (67601) ***(G-2858)***
Kansas State University...785 532-5650
1800 Denison Ave Manhattan (66506) ***(G-6688)***
Kansas State University...785 532-5640
1600 Denison Ave Ste 103 Manhattan (66506) ***(G-6689)***
Kansas State University...785 532-5813
237 Seaton Hall Manhattan (66506) ***(G-6690)***
Kansas State University...785 532-6412
108 Edwards Hall Manhattan (66506) ***(G-6691)***
Kansas State University...785 532-6506
100 Holtz Hall Manhattan (66506) ***(G-6692)***
Kansas State University...785 532-5654
139 Call Hall Manhattan (66506) ***(G-6693)***
Kansas State University...785 532-3900
2005 Research Park Cir Manhattan (66502) ***(G-6694)***
Kansas State University...785 532-6804
2 Fairchild Hall Manhattan (66506) ***(G-6695)***
Kansas State University...785 532-6984
100 Justin Hall Manhattan (66506) ***(G-6696)***
Kansas State University Golf C...785 776-6475
5200 Colbert Hills Dr Manhattan (66503) ***(G-6697)***
Kansas Statewide Homeless...785 354-4990
2001 Haskell Ave Ste 207 Lawrence (66046) ***(G-4937)***
Kansas Surgical Consultants (PA)...316 685-6222
3243 E Murdock St Ste 404 Wichita (67208) ***(G-14826)***
Kansas Surgical Consultants...316 219-9360
9300 E 29th St N Ste 203 Wichita (67226) ***(G-14827)***
Kansas Teachers Cmnty Cr Un (PA)...620 231-5719
416 N Broadway St Pittsburg (66762) ***(G-9889)***
Kansas Teachers Cmnty Cr Un...620 223-1475
24 S National Ave Fort Scott (66701) ***(G-1977)***
Kansas Tire & Wheel Co LLC...620 421-0005
1530 Flynn Dr Parsons (67357) ***(G-9698)***
Kansas Training Center, Salina *Also called Nickell Barracks Training Ctr* ***(G-10613)***
Kansas Trane Sales Company, Wichita *Also called Knipp Equipment Inc* ***(G-14871)***
Kansas Trapshooters Assn Inc...316 755-2933
3432 E 117th N Valley Center (67147) ***(G-13347)***
Kansas Truck Center, Salina *Also called Omaha Truck Center Inc* ***(G-10620)***
Kansas Truck Equipment Co Inc...316 722-4291
1521 S Tyler Rd Wichita (67209) ***(G-14828)***
Kansas Trucking LLC...913 586-5911
9620 Lexington Ave De Soto (66018) ***(G-1205)***
Kansas Turnpike Authority...620 326-5044
850 E 10th Ave Wellington (67152) ***(G-13508)***
Kansas Turnpike Authority...785 266-9414
3939 Sw Topeka Blvd Topeka (66609) ***(G-12808)***
Kansas Turnpike Authority (PA)...316 682-4537
9401 E Kellogg Dr Wichita (67207) ***(G-14829)***
Kansas Turnpike Authority...316 321-0631
Rr 4 El Dorado (67042) ***(G-1577)***
Kansas Univ Physicians Inc...913 742-7611
7420 Switzer St Shawnee (66203) ***(G-10980)***
Kansas Univ Physicians Inc (PA)...913 362-2128
3901 Rainbow Blvd Kansas City (66160) ***(G-4158)***
Kansas University Physicians, Kansas City *Also called Ku Womens Hlth Specialty Ctrs* ***(G-4183)***
Kansas Van & Stor Criqui Corp...785 266-6992
1650 Sw 41st St Topeka (66609) ***(G-12809)***
Kansas-Smith Farms LLC...620 417-6765
23179 5 Rd Plains (67869) ***(G-9976)***
Kansasland Bank (PA)...785 754-2500
314 Main St Quinter (67752) ***(G-10182)***
Kansasland Tire Inc (HQ)...316 522-5434
2904 S Spruce St Wichita (67216) ***(G-14830)***
Kansasland Tire Inc...785 243-2706
1721 Lincoln St Concordia (66901) ***(G-1119)***
Kansasland Tire Inc...620 231-7210
901 N Broadway St Pittsburg (66762) ***(G-9890)***
Kansasland Tire Inc...316 744-0401
5941 N Air Cap Dr Park City (67219) ***(G-9624)***
Kansasland Tr/Cmmrical Svc Ctr, Park City *Also called Kansasland Tire Inc* ***(G-9624)***
KANSEL, Wichita *Also called Kansas Schl For Effective Lrng* ***(G-14822)***
Kansota Transport Inc...620 792-9100
1910 Broadway Ave Great Bend (67530) ***(G-2598)***
Kansys Inc (PA)...913 780-5291
910 W Frontier Ln Olathe (66061) ***(G-7830)***
Kanza Bank (PA)...620 532-5821
151 N Main St Kingman (67068) ***(G-4596)***
Kanza Bank...316 636-5821
2233 N Greenwich Rd Wichita (67226) ***(G-14831)***
Kanza Bank...316 773-7007
13605 W Maple St Ste 101 Wichita (67235) ***(G-14832)***
Kanza Cooperative Association...620 234-5252
700 S Main St Stafford (67578) ***(G-12104)***
Kanza Cooperative Association (PA)...620 546-2231
102 N Main St Iuka (67066) ***(G-3640)***
Kanza Cooperative Association...316 444-2141
220 N Main St Andale (67001) ***(G-78)***
Kanza Cooperative Association...620 234-5252
611 S Buckeye St Stafford (67578) ***(G-12105)***
Kanza Cooperative Association...620 672-6761
916 S Main St Pratt (67124) ***(G-10122)***
Kanza Cooperative Association...620 546-2593
109 N Main St Iuka (67066) ***(G-3641)***
Kanzou Explorations Inc...913 294-2125
16205 W 287th St Paola (66071) ***(G-9568)***
KAPE, Topeka *Also called Kansas Assn of Pub Employees* ***(G-12760)***
Karcher Investments Inc...785 452-2850
4820 N Dorman Dr Salina (67401) ***(G-10568)***
Karen Tobin...913 341-1976
11156 Antioch Rd Shawnee Mission (66210) ***(G-11520)***
Karg Art Glass...316 744-2442
111 N Oliver St Kechi (67067) ***(G-4571)***
Karis Inc...620 260-9931
1515 E Fulton Ter Garden City (67846) ***(G-2215)***
Karls Tire & Auto Service Inc...316 685-5338
401 S Market St Wichita (67202) ***(G-14833)***
Kasa Companies Inc...785 825-5612
304 E Avenue B Salina (67401) ***(G-10569)***
Kasa Companies Inc (PA)...785 825-7181
418 E Avenue B Salina (67401) ***(G-10570)***
Kasa Companies Inc...785 825-5612
41 E Ave B Salina (67401) ***(G-10571)***
Kasa Fab, Salina *Also called Kasa Companies Inc* ***(G-10570)***
Kasa Fab, Salina *Also called Kasa Companies Inc* ***(G-10571)***
Kasa Fabrication, Salina *Also called Kasa Companies Inc* ***(G-10569)***
KASB, Topeka *Also called Kansas Assn of Schl Boards* ***(G-12761)***
Kastl Plumbing Inc...785 841-2112
4920 Legends Dr Ste 100 Lawrence (66049) ***(G-4938)***
Katco, Emporia *Also called Kansas Assistive Tech Corp* ***(G-1784)***
Kauffman Museum Association...316 283-1612
2801 N Main St North Newton (67117) ***(G-7436)***
Kauffman Seeds Inc...620 465-2245
9218 S Halstead St Hutchinson (67501) ***(G-3348)***
Kauffman Seeds Inc...877 664-3526
7508 S Mayfield Rd Haven (67543) ***(G-2733)***
Kaw Valley Bank (HQ)...785 232-2700
1110 N Kansas Ave Topeka (66608) ***(G-12810)***
Kaw Valley Bank...785 272-8100
4848 Sw 21st St Ste 102 Topeka (66604) ***(G-12811)***
KAW VALLEY CENTER, Olathe *Also called Kvc Behavioral Healthcare Inc* ***(G-7844)***
Kaw Valley Center...913 334-0294
4300 Brenner Dr Kansas City (66104) ***(G-4159)***
Kaw Valley Companies Inc (PA)...913 281-9950
5600 Kansas Ave Kansas City (66106) ***(G-4160)***
Kaw Valley Companies Inc...913 596-9752
5622 Kansas Ave Kansas City (66106) ***(G-4161)***
Kaw Valley Engineering Inc...316 440-4304
200 N Emporia Ave Wichita (67202) ***(G-14834)***
Kaw Valley Engineering Inc (PA)...785 762-5040
2319 N Jackson St Junction City (66441) ***(G-3714)***
Kaw Valley Engineering Inc...913 894-5150
14700 W 114th Ter Shawnee Mission (66215) ***(G-11521)***
Kaw Valley Exterminator...785 456-7357
411 Lincoln Ave Wamego (66547) ***(G-13427)***
Kaw Valley Hardwood Inc...785 925-0142
1131 Sw Winding Rd Topeka (66615) ***(G-12812)***
Kaw Valley Industrial Inc...785 841-9751
2218 N 1400th Rd Eudora (66025) ***(G-1876)***
Kaw Valley Printing, Topeka *Also called Copy Shoppe* ***(G-12508)***
Kaw Valley Rabbit Club...913 764-1531
32320 W 363 Olathe (66061) ***(G-7831)***
Kaw Valley Sand & Gravel, Kansas City *Also called Kaw Valley Companies Inc* ***(G-4160)***
Kaw Valley Sand and Gravel Inc (HQ)...913 281-9950
5600 Kansas Ave Kansas City (66106) ***(G-4162)***

A L P H A B E T I C

Kaw Valley State Bank 785 542-4200
739 Main St Eudora (66025) *(G-1877)*
Kaw Valley State Bank & Tr Co 785 437-6585
414 W Bertrand Ave Saint Marys (66536) *(G-10369)*
Kaw Valley State Bank & Tr Co (PA) 785 456-2025
1015 Kaw Valley Park Cir Wamego (66547) *(G-13428)*
Kaylor Dental Laboratory Inc 316 943-3226
619 N Florence St Wichita (67212) *(G-14835)*
KB Complete Inc 913 722-6835
5621 Foxridge Dr Shawnee Mission (66202) *(G-11522)*
KB Properties of Kansas LLC 316 292-3924
150 N Market St Wichita (67202) *(G-14836)*
KBK Industries LLC (PA) 785 372-4331
1914 Highway 183 Rush Center (67575) *(G-10260)*
Kbs, Wichita *Also called Koch Business Solutions LP (G-14874)*
Kbs Constructors Inc (PA) 785 266-4222
1701 Sw 41st St Topeka (66609) *(G-12813)*
Kbuf/Kkjq, Garden City *Also called Ingstad Broadcasting Inc (G-2203)*
Kc Blind All-Stars Foundation 913 281-3308
1100 State Ave Kansas City (66102) *(G-4163)*
Kc Bowl Inc 913 299-1110
8201 State Ave Kansas City (66112) *(G-4164)*
Kc Brokerage, Overland Park *Also called Kansas City Brokerage Inc (G-8890)*
Kc Cabinetwright Inc 913 825-6555
9837 Lackman Rd Lenexa (66219) *(G-5939)*
Kc Cleaning Solutions 913 236-0040
9290 Bond St Ste 112 Overland Park (66214) *(G-8905)*
Kc Colors Auto Body Ltd 913 491-0696
2007 W 103rd Ter Shawnee Mission (66206) *(G-11523)*
Kc Commercial Realty Group 913 232-5100
5000 W 95th St Ste 200 Prairie Village (66207) *(G-10041)*
KC Coring & Cutng Cnstr Inc 316 832-1580
3410 N Ohio St Wichita (67219) *(G-14837)*
Kc Digical 913 541-2688
15504 College Blvd Lenexa (66219) *(G-5940)*
Kc Granite & Cabinetry LLC 913 888-0003
10045 Lackman Rd Lenexa (66219) *(G-5941)*
KC Hopps Ltd (PA) 913 322-2440
9401 Reeds Rd Ste 101 Overland Park (66207) *(G-8906)*
Kc House of Hope 913 262-8885
7044 Antioch Rd Overland Park (66204) *(G-8907)*
Kc Irrigation Specialist 913 406-0670
3315 W 92nd St Leawood (66206) *(G-5446)*
Kc Pain Centers, Overland Park *Also called Anesthesia Assoc Kans Cy PC (G-8385)*
Kc Parent, Overland Park *Also called Family Media Group Inc (G-8703)*
Kc Presort 913 432-0866
2820 Roe Ln Ste U Kansas City (66103) *(G-4165)*
Kc Restoration LLC 913 766-2200
1465 N Winchester St Olathe (66061) *(G-7832)*
Kc Smile PA 913 491-6874
12850 Metcalf Ave 200 Overland Park (66213) *(G-8908)*
Kc Solar LLC 913 444-9593
8101 College Blvd Ste 100 Overland Park (66210) *(G-8909)*
Kc Strings, Shawnee Mission *Also called Kansas City Strings Violin Sp (G-11511)*
Kc Tool LLC 913 440-9766
1280 N Winchester St Olathe (66061) *(G-7833)*
Kc Window Film, Merriam *Also called A Glass & Tint Shop Kc Inc (G-7085)*
Kc Wine Co 913 908-3039
13875 S Gardner Rd Olathe (66061) *(G-7834)*
Kca Internet 913 735-7206
5580 W 201st St Stilwell (66085) *(G-12160)*
Kcai LP 913 596-6000
701 Village West Pkwy Kansas City (66111) *(G-4166)*
Kcas LLC 913 248-3000
12400 Shawnee Mission Pkwy Shawnee Mission (66216) *(G-11524)*
Kcas Bio Anlytcal Bmarker Svcs, Shawnee Mission *Also called Kcas LLC (G-11524)*
Kcc Conservation District II 316 630-4000
3450 N Rock Rd Ste 601 Wichita (67226) *(G-14838)*
KCCBA, Overland Park *Also called Kansas City Compensation & Ben (G-8892)*
Kccm, Wichita *Also called Gao Qizhi (G-14444)*
Kccv, Shawnee Mission *Also called Bott Communications Inc (G-11176)*
Kccv Am 760 ....913 642-7600
10550 Barkley St Ste 100 Shawnee Mission (66212) *(G-11525)*
Kcg Inc (PA) 913 438-4142
15720 W 108th St Ste 100 Lenexa (66219) *(G-5942)*
Kcg Inc 913 888-0882
15740 W 108th St Lenexa (66219) *(G-5943)*
Kcg Inc 913 236-4909
1136 Southwest Blvd Kansas City (66103) *(G-4167)*
Kci Kansas Counselors Inc 913 541-9704
8725 Rosehill Rd Ste 415 Shawnee Mission (66215) *(G-11526)*
Kcic, Kansas City *Also called Kansas City Imaging Center (G-4146)*
Kcoe Isom LLP 785 825-1561
3030 Cortland Cir Salina (67401) *(G-10572)*
Kcoe Isom LLP 316 685-0222
1605 N Waterfront Pkwy # 200 Wichita (67206) *(G-14839)*
Kcoe Isom LLP 785 899-3676
520 Main Ave Ste 1 Goodland (67735) *(G-2479)*
Kcoe Isom LLP 913 643-5000
8801 Renner Ave Ste 100 Lenexa (66219) *(G-5944)*
Kcoe Isom LLP 620 672-7476
816 N Campus Dr Ste 100 Garden City (67846) *(G-2216)*
KCR International, Topeka *Also called Diamond Intl Trcks Inc (G-12555)*
Kcsc, Olathe *Also called Kansas City SC LLC (G-7827)*
Kcsc Space Works Inc 620 662-2305
1100 N Plum St Hutchinson (67501) *(G-3349)*
KCSDV, Topeka *Also called Kansas Coalittion Against (G-12766)*
Kctv5, Fairway *Also called Meredith Corporation (G-1914)*
Kcwc, Shawnee Mission *Also called Kansas City Womens Clinic PA (G-11514)*
Kd Christian Construction Co 913 451-0466
7387 W 162nd St Stilwell (66085) *(G-12161)*
Kdads, Topeka *Also called Kansas Dept For Aging & Disabi (G-12770)*
Kdc Construction Inc 913 677-1920
12205 Buena Vista St Leawood (66209) *(G-5447)*
Kdck/Channel 21, Bunker Hill *Also called Smoky Hills Public TV Corp (G-620)*
Kdhe Ber Attn R Avila 785 291-3121
1000 Sw Jackson St # 410 Topeka (66612) *(G-12814)*
KDI Operating Company LLC 620 544-4114
1010 E 10th St Hugoton (67951) *(G-3168)*
KDI Operating Company LLC (PA) 620 453-1034
11050 Roe Ave Ste 211 Leawood (66211) *(G-5448)*
Kdjm Consulting Inc (PA) 913 362-0600
6405 Metcalf Ave Ste 108 Shawnee Mission (66202) *(G-11527)*
Kdoll Koatings Inc 620 456-2588
751 E Spring Ave Conway Springs (67031) *(G-1142)*
Kea Advisors 913 832-6099
3320 Mesa Way Ste D Lawrence (66049) *(G-4939)*
Kearney Construction Inc 913 367-1200
6199 Osage Rd Atchison (66002) *(G-238)*
Kearney Equipment LLC (PA) 316 722-8710
5820 N 119th St W Maize (67101) *(G-6515)*
Kearney Regional Med Ctr LLC 316 682-6770
200 W Douglas Ave Ste 950 Wichita (67202) *(G-14840)*
KEARNY COUNTY BANK, Lakin *Also called Lakin Bancshares Inc (G-4654)*
Kearny County Bank 620 355-6222
221 N Main St Lakin (67860) *(G-4650)*
Kearny County Feeders LLC 620 355-6630
1544 Rd 180 Lakin (67860) *(G-4651)*
Kearny County Home For Aged 620 355-7836
607 Court Pl Lakin (67860) *(G-4652)*
Kearny County Hospital (PA) 620 355-7111
500 E Thorpe St Lakin (67860) *(G-4653)*
Keating & Associates Inc (PA) 785 537-0366
1011 Poyntz Ave Manhattan (66502) *(G-6698)*
Keating Tractor & Eqp Inc 620 624-1668
1900 W 2nd St Liberal (67901) *(G-6327)*
Keebler Company 913 342-2300
801 Sunshine Rd Kansas City (66115) *(G-4168)*
Keen Wealth Advisors, Overland Park *Also called Kwmg LLC (G-8933)*
Keesecker Agri Business Inc 785 325-3134
2069 Prairie Rd Washington (66968) *(G-13466)*
Keil Vtrnary Ophthalmology LLC 785 331-4600
11519 W 83rd Ter Overland Park (66214) *(G-8910)*
Keim T S, Sabetha *Also called T S Keim Inc (G-10333)*
Keimig Body Shop 913 367-0184
300 Main St Atchison (66002) *(G-239)*
Keith and Assoc Dentistry LLC 913 384-0044
6299 Nall Ave Ste 300 Mission (66202) *(G-7132)*
Keith Baker Construction, Leavenworth *Also called Baker Construction Inc (G-5206)*
Keith Connell Inc (PA) 913 681-5585
7500 W 151st St Stilwell (66085) *(G-12162)*
Keith Shaw 316 262-7297
220 W Douglas Ave Ste 155 Wichita (67202) *(G-14841)*
Kejr Inc (PA) 785 825-1842
1835 Wall St Salina (67401) *(G-10573)*
Keller & Associates, Lawrence *Also called Tjk Inc (G-5139)*
Keller & Miller Cpas LLP 620 275-6883
401 N Campus Dr Garden City (67846) *(G-2217)*
Keller & Owens LLC 913 338-3500
10955 Lowell Ave Ste 800 Overland Park (66210) *(G-8911)*
Keller Bros Harvesting & Trckg 785 726-3555
Rr 2 Box 107a Ellis (67637) *(G-1648)*
Keller Fire & Safety Inc (HQ) 913 371-8494
1129 Scott Ave Kansas City (66105) *(G-4169)*
Keller Leisure Arts Center, Hutchinson *Also called Hutchinson Recreation Comm (G-3323)*
Keller Leopold Insurance LLC (PA) 620 276-7671
302 Fleming St Ste 1 Garden City (67846) *(G-2218)*
Keller RE & Insur Agcy 620 792-2128
1101 Williams St Great Bend (67530) *(G-2599)*
Keller Williams Dave Neal 316 681-3600
1635 N Waterfront Pkwy # 150 Wichita (67206) *(G-14842)*
Keller Williams Realtors, Wichita *Also called Keller Williams Dave Neal (G-14842)*
Keller Williams Realtors, Olathe *Also called Diamond Partners Jnc (G-7653)*
Kelley Construction Co Inc 785 235-6040
2548 Nw Button Rd Topeka (66618) *(G-12815)*

Kelley Instruments Inc..........316 945-7171
4131 W May St Wichita (67209) *(G-14843)*
Kelley York & Associates Ltd..........316 267-8200
515 S Main St Ste 105 Wichita (67202) *(G-14844)*
Kellogg Hospitality LLC..........316 942-5600
6815 W Kellogg Dr Wichita (67209) *(G-14845)*
Kelly B Deeter DDS Chartered..........785 267-6120
2300 Sw 29th St Ste 223 Topeka (66611) *(G-12816)*
Kelly Enterprise Inc (PA)..........913 685-1800
13224 Craig St Overland Park (66213) *(G-8912)*
Kelly House II, Topeka *Also called Contemprary Hsing Altrntves of (G-12505)*
Kelly Maclaskey..........316 321-9011
105 N Industrial Rd El Dorado (67042) *(G-1578)*
Kelly Manufacturing Company..........316 265-4271
55 S Topeka Independence (67301) *(G-3531)*
Kelly Manufacturing Company..........620 358-3826
311 N Cana St Grenola (67346) *(G-2687)*
Kelly Manufacturing Company (PA)..........316 265-6868
555 S Topeka Ave Wichita (67202) *(G-14846)*
Kelly S Henrichs DDS..........620 225-6555
100 W Ross Blvd Ste 2c Dodge City (67801) *(G-1388)*
Kelly Services Inc..........913 451-1400
9200 Indian Creek Pkwy Overland Park (66210) *(G-8913)*
Kellys Corporate Apparel..........316 263-5858
355 Pattie St Wichita (67211) *(G-14847)*
Kelsey Construction Inc..........913 894-0330
14308 W 96th Ter Shawnee Mission (66215) *(G-11528)*
Keltech Solutions LLC..........785 841-4611
4920 Legends Dr Ste 200 Lawrence (66049) *(G-4940)*
Kemira Chemicals Inc..........785 434-2474
1733 W Rd Plainville (67663) *(G-9988)*
Kemira Water Solutions Inc..........785 842-7424
3211 Clinton Parkway Ct # 1 Lawrence (66047) *(G-4941)*
Kemiron Customer Service Ctr, Lawrence *Also called Kemira Water Solutions Inc (G-4941)*
Kemlee Manufacturing Inc (PA)..........620 783-5035
1404 Industrial Prk Rd Galena (66739) *(G-2076)*
Kemp Construction Company, Derby *Also called Tommy J Kemp (G-1276)*
Kemper Auction Group..........913 287-3207
5629 Pawnee Ave Kansas City (66106) *(G-4170)*
Kemper Insurance, Prairie Village *Also called Gerber Insurance Group (G-10031)*
Kemper Insurance, Attica *Also called Eck Agency Inc (G-277)*
Ken Babcock Sales Inc..........785 544-6592
105 S 1st St Hiawatha (66434) *(G-3013)*
Ken OKelly..........816 868-6028
1912 W 74th St Prairie Village (66208) *(G-10042)*
Kenai Dialysis LLC..........913 649-2671
10787 Nall Ave Ste 130 Overland Park (66211) *(G-8914)*
Kenai Drilling Limited..........805 937-7871
2007 W 7th St Liberal (67901) *(G-6328)*
Kenco Trucking Inc (PA)..........316 943-4881
1405 N Shefford St Wichita (67212) *(G-14848)*
Kendall Construction Inc..........785 246-1207
2551 Nw Button Rd Topeka (66618) *(G-12817)*
Kendall Packaging Corporation..........620 231-9804
1901 E 27th Ter Pittsburg (66762) *(G-9891)*
Kendall State Bank (PA)..........785 945-3231
406 Broadway St Valley Falls (66088) *(G-13366)*
Kennedy & Willis..........316 263-4921
727 N Waco Ave Ste 585 Wichita (67203) *(G-14849)*
Kennedy Academy, Topeka *Also called Books & Blocks Academy Inc (G-12397)*
Kennedy Brkley Yrnvich Wllmson (PA)..........785 825-4674
119 W Iron Ave Ste 710 Salina (67401) *(G-10574)*
Kennedy Glass Inc..........785 843-4416
730 New Jersey St Lawrence (66044) *(G-4942)*
Kennedy Mc Kee and Company LLP..........620 227-3135
1100 W Frontview St Dodge City (67801) *(G-1389)*
Kennel Creek..........913 498-9900
10750 El Monte St Overland Park (66211) *(G-8915)*
Kenneth R Johnson Inc..........913 599-1133
13851 W 101st St Lenexa (66215) *(G-5945)*
Kenny Livingston Trucking Inc..........785 598-2493
1375 Highway 18 Abilene (67410) *(G-43)*
Kennys Electrical Co Inc..........620 662-2359
1035 W 4th Ave Hutchinson (67501) *(G-3350)*
Kens Auto Tow..........316 941-4300
3760 S Broadway Ave Wichita (67216) *(G-14850)*
Kens Garage Inc..........913 651-2433
108 Shawnee St Leavenworth (66048) *(G-5262)*
Kens' Road & Field Service, Leavenworth *Also called Kens Garage Inc (G-5262)*
Kensington Lockers Inc..........785 476-2834
218 W Highway 36 Kensington (66951) *(G-4577)*
Kensington Senior Cmnty Ctr..........785 476-2224
102 E Pne Kensington (66951) *(G-4578)*
Kent Audio Visual, Wichita *Also called Kent Business Systems Corp (G-14851)*
Kent Business Systems Corp..........316 262-4487
1131 E 1st St N Wichita (67214) *(G-14851)*
Kent Hall HCC Girls Dormitory, Hutchinson *Also called Hutchinson Community College (G-3320)*
Kent W Haverkamp MD..........785 267-0744
2909 Se Walnut Dr Topeka (66605) *(G-12818)*
Kenwood Plaza Inc..........620 549-6133
607 E 1st Ave Saint John (67576) *(G-10354)*
KEPCO, Topeka *Also called Kansas Electric Power Coop Inc (G-12776)*
Kepley Well Service LLC..........620 431-9212
19245 Ford Rd Chanute (66720) *(G-735)*
Kermit Cottrell Allstate Agcy..........785 843-2532
2233 Louisiana St Ste H2 Lawrence (66046) *(G-4943)*
Kerry Inc..........913 780-1212
400 Prairie Village Dr New Century (66031) *(G-7290)*
Kessinger/Hunter & Company Lc..........816 842-2690
11020 King St Shawnee Mission (66210) *(G-11529)*
Kesters Mdsg Display Intl..........913 281-4200
400 Funston Rd Kansas City (66115) *(G-4171)*
KETCH, Wichita *Also called Kansas Elks Training (G-14797)*
Keurig Dr Pepper Inc..........913 894-6777
9960 Lakeview Ave Lenexa (66219) *(G-5946)*
Keurig Dr Pepper Inc..........620 223-6166
425 Marble Rd Fort Scott (66701) *(G-1978)*
Kevin J Stuever MD..........785 843-5160
4525 W 6th St Ste 100 Lawrence (66049) *(G-4944)*
Kevin Mosier MD..........620 421-0881
S Hwy 59 Bldg D Parsons (67357) *(G-9699)*
Kevin R McDonald..........785 628-6014
2214 Canterbury Dr # 308 Hays (67601) *(G-2859)*
Key Construction Inc (PA)..........316 263-9515
741 W 2nd St N Wichita (67203) *(G-14852)*
Key Construction Missouri LLC..........816 221-7171
741 W 2nd St N Wichita (67203) *(G-14853)*
Key Energy Services Inc..........620 649-2368
P.O. Box 747 Satanta (67870) *(G-10787)*
Key Energy Services Inc..........620 353-1002
2444 W Oklahoma Ave Ulysses (67880) *(G-13302)*
Key Energy Services Inc..........620 353-1002
713 S Simpson St Ulysses (67880) *(G-13303)*
Key Equipment & Supply Co..........913 788-2546
6716 Berger Ave Kansas City (66111) *(G-4172)*
Key Impact Sales & Systems Inc..........913 648-6611
831 N Martway Dr Olathe (66061) *(G-7835)*
Key Industries Inc..........620 223-2000
400 Marble Rd Fort Scott (66701) *(G-1979)*
Key Office Products Inc (PA)..........620 227-2101
108 W Plaza Ave Dodge City (67801) *(G-1390)*
Key Rehabilitation Inc..........620 231-3887
2614 N Joplin St Pittsburg (66762) *(G-9892)*
Key Staffing, Topeka *Also called Kansas Personnel Services Inc (G-12796)*
Keybank Real Estate..........216 813-4756
11501 Outlook St Leawood (66211) *(G-5449)*
Keycentrix Inc..........316 262-2231
2420 N Woodlawn Blvd 100a Wichita (67220) *(G-14854)*
Keypath Education, Lenexa *Also called Thruline Marketing Inc (G-6180)*
Keys For Networking Inc..........785 233-8732
900 S Kansas Ave Ste 301 Topeka (66612) *(G-12819)*
Keystone Auto Holdings Inc..........913 371-3249
90 Shawnee Ave Kansas City (66105) *(G-4173)*
Keystone Automotive Inds Inc..........785 235-1920
5725 Sw Topeka Blvd Topeka (66619) *(G-12820)*
Keystone Automotive Inds Inc..........316 262-0500
3002 W Pawnee St Ste 100 Wichita (67213) *(G-14855)*
Keystone Automotive Inds Inc..........816 921-8929
555 River Park Dr Kansas City (66105) *(G-4174)*
Keystone Construction Inc..........316 778-1566
1250 N Main St Benton (67017) *(G-516)*
Keystone Financial LLC..........620 757-3593
1250 N Main St Benton (67017) *(G-517)*
Keystone Learning Services, Ozawkie *Also called Northeast Kans Educatn Svc Ctr (G-9536)*
Keystone Solid Surfaces, Benton *Also called Keystone Construction Inc (G-516)*
Keywest Technology Inc..........913 492-4666
14563 W 96th Ter Lenexa (66215) *(G-5947)*
Kfdi FM, Wichita *Also called EW Scripps Company (G-14317)*
KFMC, Topeka *Also called Kansas Fndtion For Med Care In (G-12777)*
Kfn, Wichita *Also called Kansas Fiber Network LLC (G-14798)*
Kforce Inc..........913 890-5000
7101 College Blvd Ste 750 Overland Park (66210) *(G-8916)*
Kgcr Radio, Brewster *Also called Praise Network Inc (G-585)*
Kggf AM 690, Coffeyville *Also called Kggf K U S N Broadcasting Stn (G-952)*
Kggf K U S N Broadcasting Stn (PA)..........620 251-3800
306 W 8th St Coffeyville (67337) *(G-952)*
Kgj Quarter Horses..........316 775-0954
4278 Sw 100th St Augusta (67010) *(G-330)*
Kgno-Am/Kols-fm, Dodge City *Also called Waitt Media Inc (G-1448)*
Kgp Products Inc..........800 755-1950
600 New Century Pkwy New Century (66031) *(G-7291)*
Kgp Telecommunications Inc..........800 755-1950
600 New Century Pkwy New Century (66031) *(G-7292)*
Khaos Apparel LLC..........316 804-4900
601 Se 36th St Ste 121 Newton (67114) *(G-7370)*

ALPHABETIC

Khut & Kwbw, Hutchinson *Also called Eagle Communications Inc* ***(G-3272)***
Kice Industries Inc (PA) 316 744-7148
5500 N Mill Heights Dr Park City (67219) ***(G-9625)***
Kickapoo Nation Health Center 785 486-2154
1117 Goldfinch Rd Horton (66439) ***(G-3129)***
Kickapoo Tribe In Kansas Inc (PA) 785 486-2131
824 111th Dr Horton (66439) ***(G-3130)***
Kid Stop LLC 913 422-9999
5542 Hedge Lane Ter Shawnee (66226) ***(G-10981)***
Kid Stuff Marketing Inc 785 862-3707
1401 Nw Moundview Dr C Topeka (66618) ***(G-12821)***
Kidcare Connection Inc 316 944-6434
3059 W 13th St N Wichita (67203) ***(G-14856)***
Kiddi Kollege 3, Kansas City *Also called Kiddi Kollege Inc* ***(G-4175)***
Kiddi Kollege Inc 913 814-7770
15020 Antioch Rd Overland Park (66221) ***(G-8917)***
Kiddi Kollege Inc (PA) 913 764-4423
340 N Lindenwood Dr Olathe (66062) ***(G-7836)***
Kiddi Kollege Inc 913 788-7060
7502 Nebraska Ave Kansas City (66112) ***(G-4175)***
Kiddi Kollege Inc 913 649-4747
9921 W 86th St Shawnee Mission (66212) ***(G-11530)***
Kiddi Kollege Inc 913 780-0246
1000 E Harold St Olathe (66061) ***(G-7837)***
Kiddicat Child Care Center 785 272-2001
4640 Sw 35th St Topeka (66614) ***(G-12822)***
Kiddie Kollege, Haysville *Also called First Assembly God Inc* ***(G-2944)***
Kiddie Kollege 6, Shawnee Mission *Also called Kiddi Kollege Inc* ***(G-11530)***
Kids At Heart Childcare, Overland Park *Also called Kids At Heart Inc* ***(G-8918)***
Kids At Heart Inc 913 648-8577
7401 W 97th St Overland Park (66212) ***(G-8918)***
Kids First Day Care Preschool 620 231-4994
102 S Cayuga St Frontenac (66763) ***(G-2057)***
Kids Kampus 620 241-8499
1381 S Main St Mcpherson (67460) ***(G-6983)***
Kids R Kids 913 390-0234
1585 S Mahaffie Cir Olathe (66062) ***(G-7838)***
Kids R Kids 1 Kansas, Olathe *Also called Kids R Kids* ***(G-7838)***
Kids R Kids International, Overland Park *Also called Peanut Co LLC* ***(G-9150)***
Kidsay, Olathe *Also called Education Market Resources Inc* ***(G-7670)***
Kidspark, Olathe *Also called Swan Corporation* ***(G-8090)***
Kidstlc Inc 913 764-2887
480 S Rogers Rd Olathe (66062) ***(G-7839)***
Kiefs Cds & Tapes 785 842-1544
2429 Iowa St Ste D Lawrence (66046) ***(G-4945)***
Kiene, Pete, Shawnee Mission *Also called James R Kiene Jr DDS PA LLC* ***(G-11482)***
Kier Enterprises Inc (PA) 785 325-2150
126 E 2nd St Washington (66968) ***(G-13467)***
Kier's Thriftway, Washington *Also called Kier Enterprises Inc* ***(G-13467)***
Kiewit Corporation 913 928-7000
9401 Renner Blvd Lenexa (66219) ***(G-5948)***
Kiewit Engineering Group Inc (HQ) 402 943-1465
9401 Renner Blvd Lenexa (66219) ***(G-5949)***
Kiewit Power Constructors Co (HQ) 913 928-7800
9401 Renner Blvd Lenexa (66219) ***(G-5950)***
Kiewit Power Group Inc 913 227-3600
9401 Renner Blvd Lenexa (66219) ***(G-5951)***
Kiewit Power Nuclear Co 913 928-7800
9401 Renner Blvd Lenexa (66219) ***(G-5952)***
Kilian Electrical Service Inc (PA) 316 942-4600
4107 W Harry St Wichita (67209) ***(G-14857)***
Killough Construction Inc 785 242-1500
3633 Highway 59 Ottawa (66067) ***(G-8281)***
Kimberly A Allman LLC 316 733-3003
524 N Andover Rd Andover (67002) ***(G-98)***
Kimple Inc 620 564-2300
113 N Main St Ellinwood (67526) ***(G-1635)***
Kimple Furniture & Gifts, Ellinwood *Also called Kimple Inc* ***(G-1635)***
Kina, Salina *Also called Eagle Communications Inc* ***(G-10482)***
Kincaid Coach Lines Inc (PA) 913 441-6200
9207 Woodend Rd Edwardsville (66111) ***(G-1506)***
Kincaid, Paul D D S, Lawrence *Also called Associates In Dentistry* ***(G-4740)***
Kincheloe Inc 620 672-6401
10517 N Us Highway 281 Pratt (67124) ***(G-10123)***
Kinder Morgan Kansas Inc 620 384-7830
Hc Box 83 Syracuse (67878) ***(G-12228)***
Kinder Mrgan Enrgy Partners LP 785 543-6602
105 E Quail Rd Phillipsburg (67661) ***(G-9790)***
Kinder Mrgan Enrgy Partners LP 620 834-2211
420 Us Highway 56 Windom (67491) ***(G-16112)***
Kindercare Center 729, Wichita *Also called Kindercare Learning Ctrs LLC* ***(G-14860)***
Kindercare Child Care Network, Lansing *Also called Kindercare Learning Ctrs LLC* ***(G-4677)***
Kindercare Child Care Network, Derby *Also called Kindercare Learning Ctrs LLC* ***(G-1256)***
Kindercare Child Care Network, Manhattan *Also called Kindercare Learning Ctrs LLC* ***(G-6699)***
Kindercare Education LLC 913 631-6910
6350 Long Ave Shawnee Mission (66216) ***(G-11531)***
Kindercare Education LLC 913 441-9202
5416 Martindale Rd Shawnee (66218) ***(G-10982)***
Kindercare Education LLC 316 721-0168
805 N Socora St Wichita (67212) ***(G-14858)***
Kindercare Education LLC 316 733-2066
836 N Andover Rd Andover (67002) ***(G-99)***
Kindercare Education LLC 316 684-4574
9500 E Boston St Wichita (67207) ***(G-14859)***
Kindercare Education LLC 316 775-7503
1300 State St Augusta (67010) ***(G-331)***
Kindercare Learning Center, Shawnee Mission *Also called Kindercare Education LLC* ***(G-11531)***
Kindercare Learning Ctr 1300, Shawnee Mission *Also called Kindercare Learning Ctrs LLC* ***(G-11534)***
Kindercare Learning Ctr 760, Shawnee Mission *Also called Kindercare Learning Ctrs LLC* ***(G-11533)***
Kindercare Learning Ctrs LLC 316 733-2066
836 N Andover Rd Andover (67002) ***(G-100)***
Kindercare Learning Ctrs LLC 913 402-1024
7600 W 150th St Shawnee Mission (66223) ***(G-11532)***
Kindercare Learning Ctrs LLC 913 727-6267
100 E Mary St Lansing (66043) ***(G-4677)***
Kindercare Learning Ctrs LLC 316 721-0168
8722 W Thurman St Wichita (67212) ***(G-14860)***
Kindercare Learning Ctrs LLC 316 788-5925
1720 E Walnut Grove Rd Derby (67037) ***(G-1256)***
Kindercare Learning Ctrs LLC 913 492-3221
10456 Mastin St Shawnee Mission (66212) ***(G-11533)***
Kindercare Learning Ctrs LLC 785 539-7540
1205 Hylton Heights Rd Manhattan (66502) ***(G-6699)***
Kindercare Learning Ctrs LLC 913 451-6066
11842 W 112th St Shawnee Mission (66210) ***(G-11534)***
Kindred Healthcare Oper LLC 913 906-0522
11880 College Blvd Ste 4a Overland Park (66210) ***(G-8919)***
Kindsvater Inc 620 227-6191
2301 E Trail St Dodge City (67801) ***(G-1391)***
Kindsvater Truck Lines, Dodge City *Also called Kindsvater Inc* ***(G-1391)***
King Bancshares Inc (PA) 620 532-5162
300 N Main St Kingman (67068) ***(G-4597)***
King Cabinets Inc 913 422-7554
20201 W 55th St Shawnee Mission (66218) ***(G-11535)***
King Construction Company Inc 620 327-4251
301 N Lancaster Ave Hesston (67062) ***(G-2995)***
King Enterprises Inc 620 624-3332
1924 W 2nd St Liberal (67901) ***(G-6329)***
King Excavating, Liberal *Also called King Enterprises Inc* ***(G-6329)***
King Industries Inc 785 823-1785
1368 W Grand Ave Salina (67401) ***(G-10575)***
King Louie, Leawood *Also called King Louie America Lc* ***(G-5450)***
King Louie America Lc (PA) 913 338-5212
6740 W 121st St Ste 100 Leawood (66209) ***(G-5450)***
King Luminaire Company Inc 913 255-3112
14503 Wallick Rd Atchison (66002) ***(G-240)***
King of Freight LLC 316 409-4024
651 S Quentin St Wichita (67218) ***(G-14861)***
King of Freight LLC (PA) 316 440-4661
110 S Main St Ste 300 Wichita (67202) ***(G-14862)***
King Street III, Shawnee Mission *Also called Kessinger/Hunter & Company Lc* ***(G-11529)***
King Wood Products Inc 913 837-5300
609 S Metcalf Rd Louisburg (66053) ***(G-6453)***
King's Avionics Inc, New Century *Also called Butler Avionics Inc* ***(G-7271)***
King's Court Association, Olathe *Also called Kings Court Investors* ***(G-7840)***
King's North Amercn Van Lines, Junction City *Also called Kings Moving & Storage Inc* ***(G-3715)***
King's Window Coverings, Salina *Also called King Industries Inc* ***(G-10575)***
Kingdom Cartridge, Hutchinson *Also called Warren Consulting Inc* ***(G-3481)***
Kingman Cnty Ecnmic Dev Cncil 620 532-3694
324 N Main St Kingman (67068) ***(G-4598)***
Kingman County Highway Dept, Kingman *Also called County of Kingman* ***(G-4588)***
Kingman County Retirement Assn 620 532-5801
750 W Washington Ave Kingman (67068) ***(G-4599)***
Kingman Drug Inc (PA) 620 532-5113
211 N Main St Kingman (67068) ***(G-4600)***
Kingman Emergency Medical Svcs 620 532-5624
332 N Main St Kingman (67068) ***(G-4601)***
Kingman Leader Courier 620 532-3151
140 N Main St Kingman (67068) ***(G-4602)***
Kingman Pharmacy, Kingman *Also called Kingman Drug Inc* ***(G-4600)***
Kings Alcohol & Drug 620 221-6252
2720 E 12th Ave Winfield (67156) ***(G-16152)***
Kings Camp & Retreat Center 316 794-2913
24401 W 39th St S Goddard (67052) ***(G-2444)***
Kings Construction Co Inc 785 863-2534
205 Walnut St Oskaloosa (66066) ***(G-8228)***
Kings Court Investors 913 764-7500
2300 E Willow Dr Olathe (66062) ***(G-7840)***
Kings Cove Apts, Shawnee Mission *Also called J A Peterson Realty Co Inc* ***(G-11475)***

Kings Moving & Storage Inc (PA)....316 247-6528
2111 E Industrial St Wichita (67216) ***(G-14863)***
Kings Moving & Storage Inc....785 238-7341
906 Perry St Junction City (66441) ***(G-3715)***
Kings North American, Wichita *Also called Kings Moving & Storage Inc* ***(G-14863)***
Kingston Printing & Design Inc....785 690-7222
1030 Ocl Pkwy Eudora (66025) ***(G-1878)***
Kinney Plumbing Co Inc....913 782-2840
15755 S Keeler Ter Olathe (66062) ***(G-7841)***
Kinney's Plumbing Co, Olathe *Also called Kinney Plumbing Co Inc* ***(G-7841)***
Kinseth Hospitality Co Inc....316 686-7131
549 S Rock Rd Wichita (67207) ***(G-14864)***
Kiowa County Ems....620 723-3112
721 W Kansas Ave Greensburg (67054) ***(G-2681)***
Kiowa County Highway Dept, Greensburg *Also called County of Kiowa* ***(G-2673)***
Kiowa County Memorial Hospital, Greensburg *Also called Great Plains Kiowa Co Inc* ***(G-2676)***
Kiowa County Memorial Hospital, Greensburg *Also called County of Kiowa* ***(G-2674)***
Kiowa District Hospital....620 825-4117
1020 Main St Kiowa (67070) ***(G-4624)***
Kiowa District Hospital (PA)....620 825-4131
1002 S 4th St Kiowa (67070) ***(G-4625)***
Kiowa Hospital District Manor, Kiowa *Also called Kiowa District Hospital* ***(G-4624)***
Kiowa Locker System LLC....620 825-4538
128 S 6th St Kiowa (67070) ***(G-4626)***
Kiowa Service Co Inc....316 636-1070
8441 E 32nd St N Ste 200 Wichita (67226) ***(G-14865)***
Kirby Meat Co Inc....620 225-0031
2501 E Wyatt Earp Blvd Dodge City (67801) ***(G-1392)***
Kirk & Cobb Realty....785 272-5555
2810 Sw Gage Blvd Ste 1 Topeka (66614) ***(G-12823)***
Kirkpatrick Sprecker & Co....316 685-1411
311 S Hillside St Wichita (67211) ***(G-14866)***
Kisco, Wichita *Also called Steven Joseph Jr DDS* ***(G-15670)***
Kiser AG Service LLC (PA)....785 689-4292
305 S Douglas St Logan (67646) ***(G-6425)***
Kiser Manufacturing Co Inc....620 435-6981
601 E Us Highway 160 Argonia (67004) ***(G-138)***
Kissner Group Holdings LP (PA)....913 713-0600
10955 Lowell Ave Ste 500 Overland Park (66210) ***(G-8920)***
Kistler Service Inc (PA)....620 782-3611
301 Highway K15 Udall (67146) ***(G-13278)***
Kitchens Inc....620 225-0208
2301 W Frontview St Dodge City (67801) ***(G-1393)***
Kiwanis Club, Smith Center *Also called Kiwanis International Inc* ***(G-12035)***
Kiwanis Club of Iola, Iola *Also called Kiwanis International Inc* ***(G-3617)***
Kiwanis International Inc....620 672-6257
106 S Oak St Pratt (67124) ***(G-10124)***
Kiwanis International Inc....316 733-4984
722 S Daisy Ln Andover (67002) ***(G-101)***
Kiwanis International Inc....785 742-2596
100 S 2nd St Hiawatha (66434) ***(G-3014)***
Kiwanis International Inc....913 724-1120
3707 N 155th St Basehor (66007) ***(G-383)***
Kiwanis International Inc....913 727-1039
203 Emile St Lansing (66043) ***(G-4678)***
Kiwanis International Inc....620 365-3925
P.O. Box 503 Iola (66749) ***(G-3617)***
Kiwanis International Inc....620 544-8445
Hc 1 Box 29 Hugoton (67951) ***(G-3169)***
Kiwanis International Inc....785 238-4521
1407 Mcfarland Rd Junction City (66441) ***(G-3716)***
Kiwanis International Inc....785 462-6007
1025 Villa Vista Dr Colby (67701) ***(G-1021)***
Kiwanis International Inc....785 282-6680
205 S Main St Smith Center (66967) ***(G-12035)***
Kizzar Well Servicing Inc....620 938-2555
320 Frontage Rd Chase (67524) ***(G-784)***
Kjck AM, Junction City *Also called Q 1035* ***(G-3743)***
KJIL, Meade *Also called Great Plains Christian Radio* ***(G-7049)***
Kjww Corp....913 952-6636
7381 W 133rd St Ste 201 Overland Park (66213) ***(G-8921)***
Kkrd, Wichita *Also called Iheartcommunications Inc* ***(G-14669)***
KLA Environmental Services....785 823-0097
1700 E Iron Ave Salina (67401) ***(G-10576)***
Klaus Masonry LLC....785 650-3854
1908 E 25th St Hays (67601) ***(G-2860)***
Klaver Construction Co Inc....620 532-3183
701 E Ave D Kingman (67068) ***(G-4603)***
Klaver Construction Pdts LLC (PA)....620 532-3661
245 E Sherman Ave Kingman (67068) ***(G-4604)***
Kleeb Services Inc (PA)....913 253-7000
10901 W 84th Ter Ste 100 Overland Park (66214) ***(G-8922)***
Klein Construction Inc....316 262-3313
919 E 53rd St N Park City (67219) ***(G-9626)***
Kleinfelder Inc....913 962-0909
11529 W 79th St Overland Park (66214) ***(G-8923)***
Kleinfelder Inc....913 962-0909
11529 W 79th St Bldg 21 Lenexa (66214) ***(G-5953)***
Klemp Electric Machinery Co....913 371-4330
739 Central Ave Kansas City (66101) ***(G-4176)***
Klenda Austerman LLC....316 267-0331
301 N Main St Ste 1600 Wichita (67202) ***(G-14867)***
Kline Motors Inc....620 221-2040
1721 Main St Winfield (67156) ***(G-16153)***
Klm Exploration Co Inc....913 796-6763
600 E Lake St Mc Louth (66054) ***(G-6928)***
Kls Industries LLC....877 952-2548
3439 Merriam Dr Shawnee (66203) ***(G-10983)***
Klwn-AM Radio, Lawrence *Also called Zimmer Radio Group* ***(G-5194)***
Kmaj, Topeka *Also called CM Wind Down Topco Inc* ***(G-12481)***
Kmi Inc....316 777-0146
101 Industrial Dr Mulvane (67110) ***(G-7217)***
Kmi Metals, Galena *Also called Kemlee Manufacturing Inc* ***(G-2076)***
Kmis, Topeka *Also called Kansas Medical Insur Svcs Corp* ***(G-12789)***
Kms Inc....316 264-8833
811 E Waterman St Ste 1 Wichita (67202) ***(G-14868)***
Kmuw-FM 89.1 Public Radio, Wichita *Also called Wichita State University* ***(G-16033)***
Kmw Ltd (PA)....620 278-3641
535 W Garfield Ave Sterling (67579) ***(G-12124)***
Knck Inc....785 243-1414
1391 W 11th St Concordia (66901) ***(G-1120)***
Kneisley Manufacturing Company....620 365-6628
900 W Miller Rd Iola (66749) ***(G-3618)***
Knickerbocker Properties Inc....913 451-4466
8717 W 110th St Ste 240 Shawnee Mission (66210) ***(G-11536)***
Knight Enterprises Ltd....785 843-5511
4840 Bob Billings Pkwy # 1000 Lawrence (66049) ***(G-4946)***
Knight Farms Inc....620 257-5106
2648 Ave J Lyons (67554) ***(G-6488)***
Knight Trenching & Excvtg Inc....913 599-6999
14168 Santa Fe Trail Dr Lenexa (66215) ***(G-5954)***
Knight Trucking LLC....620 256-6525
2424 Fauna Rd Lebo (66856) ***(G-5607)***
Knight-Swift Trnsp Hldings Inc....913 535-5155
9000 Woodend Rd Kansas City (66111) ***(G-4177)***
Knighton Bus Solutions LLC....913 747-2818
9120 Nieman Rd Overland Park (66214) ***(G-8924)***
Knighton Oil Co Inc....316 630-9905
1700 N Wtrfrnt Pkwy 100a Wichita (67206) ***(G-14869)***
Knights Inn, Lenexa *Also called Shri Ram Corp* ***(G-6133)***
Knights Inn....316 942-1341
6125 E Kellogg Dr Wichita (67218) ***(G-14870)***
Knights of Columbus....785 636-5453
22800 Newbury Rd Paxico (66526) ***(G-9756)***
Knights of Columbus....620 825-4378
1218 Main St Kiowa (67070) ***(G-4627)***
Knights of Columbus....620 251-2891
1723 Main St Parsons (67357) ***(G-9700)***
Knights of Columbus....620 442-7264
29731 41st Rd Arkansas City (67005) ***(G-162)***
Knights of Kentucky, Lawrence *Also called Douglas County Bank* ***(G-4837)***
Knipp Equipment Inc....316 265-9655
120 S Ida St Wichita (67211) ***(G-14871)***
Knit-Rite Inc (PA)....913 279-6310
120 Osage Ave Kansas City (66105) ***(G-4178)***
Knk Telecom Llc....913 768-8000
1010 W Santa Fe St Olathe (66061) ***(G-7842)***
Knology Inc....785 841-2100
1 Riverfront Plz Lawrence (66044) ***(G-4947)***
Knopke Company LLC....816 231-1001
2804 W 132nd St Leawood (66209) ***(G-5451)***
Knopke Contracting Services, Leawood *Also called Knopke Company LLC* ***(G-5451)***
Knork Flatware, Newton *Also called Phantom Enterprises Inc* ***(G-7405)***
Knowledge Learning, Wichita *Also called Kindercare Education LLC* ***(G-14858)***
Knox Electronic Ltd....316 321-2400
3910 W Central Ave El Dorado (67042) ***(G-1579)***
Knox Presbt Ch Child Dev Ctr....913 888-0089
9595 W 95th St Overland Park (66212) ***(G-8925)***
Knudsen Monroe & Company LLC....316 283-5366
512 N Main St Newton (67114) ***(G-7371)***
Knudsen, John III MD, Hutchinson *Also called Midwest Pain Management* ***(G-3380)***
Knwa, Pittsburg *Also called Kanawha River Railroad LLC* ***(G-9885)***
Koam-TV, Pittsburg *Also called Evening Telegram Company* ***(G-9858)***
Kobler Center, Hill City *Also called Developmental Svcs NW Kans Inc* ***(G-3033)***
Koch & Co Inc (PA)....785 336-6022
1809 North St Seneca (66538) ***(G-10871)***
Koch AG & Energy Solutions LLC (HQ)....316 828-5500
4111 E 37th St N Wichita (67220) ***(G-14872)***
Koch Asphalt Solutions-Sw, Wichita *Also called Nk Asphalt Partners* ***(G-15182)***
Koch Business Holdings LLC....316 828-8943
4111 E 37th St N Wichita (67220) ***(G-14873)***
Koch Business Solutions LP (HQ)....316 828-5500
4111 E 37th St N Wichita (67220) ***(G-14874)***
KOCH CABINETS, Seneca *Also called Koch & Co Inc* ***(G-10871)***

ALPHABETIC

Koch Carbon LLC (HQ) 316 828-5500
4111 E 37th St N Wichita (67220) *(G-14875)*
Koch Companies Pub Sector LLC 316 828-5500
4111 E 37th St N Wichita (67220) *(G-14876)*
Koch Energy Inc 316 828-5500
4111 E 37th St N Wichita (67220) *(G-14877)*
Koch Exploration Company (HQ) 316 828-5508
4111 E 37th St N Wichita (67220) *(G-14878)*
Koch Exploration Company LLC (HQ) 316 828-5508
4111 E 37th St N Wichita (67220) *(G-14879)*
Koch Fertilizer LLC 620 227-8631
11559 Us Highway 50 Dodge City (67801) *(G-1394)*
Koch Fertilizer LLC (HQ) 316 828-5010
4111 E 37th St N Wichita (67220) *(G-14880)*
Koch Hydrcrbon LPG Stge Fac, McPherson *Also called Magellan Midstream Partners LP (G-6987)*
Koch Hydrocarbon Southwes 620 662-6691
1910 S Broadacres Rd Hutchinson (67501) *(G-3351)*
Koch Industries Inc (PA) 316 828-5500
4111 E 37th St N Wichita (67220) *(G-14881)*
Koch Industries Inc 620 227-8631
11559 Us Highway 50 Dodge City (67801) *(G-1395)*
Koch Industries Inc 316 321-6380
35 Se 20th St El Dorado (67042) *(G-1580)*
Koch Industries Inc 620 834-2204
462 Hwy 56 McPherson (67460) *(G-6984)*
Koch Industries Inc 620 662-6691
1910 S Broadacres Rd Hutchinson (67501) *(G-3352)*
Koch Industries Inc 316 828-8737
1760 S Airport Rd Wichita (67209) *(G-14882)*
Koch Materials LLC 316 828-5500
4111 E 37th St N Wichita (67220) *(G-14883)*
Koch Mineral Services LLC (HQ) 316 828-5500
4111 E 37th St N Wichita (67220) *(G-14884)*
Koch Nitrogen Company, Wichita *Also called Koch Pipeline Company LP (G-14885)*
Koch Pavement Solutions, Wichita *Also called Koch Materials LLC (G-14883)*
Koch Pipeline Company LP 620 834-2309
1299 8th Ave Conway (67460) *(G-1134)*
Koch Pipeline Company LP (HQ) 316 828-5511
4111 E 37th St N Wichita (67220) *(G-14885)*
Koch Rail LLC 316 828-5500
4111 E 37th St N Wichita (67220) *(G-14886)*
Koch Residential Services, Wichita *Also called Koch Business Holdings LLC (G-14873)*
Koch Resources LLC (HQ) 316 828-5500
4111 E 37th St N Wichita (67220) *(G-14887)*
Koch Siedhoff Hand & Dunn LLP 316 943-0286
3580 W 13th St N Wichita (67203) *(G-14888)*
Koch Sulfur Products Co LLC 316 828-5500
4111 E 37th St N Wichita (67220) *(G-14889)*
Koch Supply & Trading, Wichita *Also called KS&t International Holdings LP (G-14896)*
Koch Supply & Trading LP (HQ) 316 828-5500
4111 E 37th St N Wichita (67220) *(G-14890)*
Koch Supply and Trading, Wichita *Also called Koch Supply & Trading LP (G-14890)*
Koch-Glitsch LP (HQ) 316 828-5000
4111 E 37th St N Wichita (67220) *(G-14891)*
Kocher + Beck USA LP (PA) 913 529-4336
15850 W 99th St Lenexa (66219) *(G-5955)*
Kocher + Beck USA LP 913 529-4336
15850 W 99th St Lenexa (66219) *(G-5956)*
Koehler Bortnick Team LLC 913 239-2069
5000 W 136th Leawood (66209) *(G-5452)*
Koehn Construction 620 345-6457
720 S Christian Ave Moundridge (67107) *(G-7187)*
Koehn Construction Svcs LLC 620 378-3002
1111 N 2nd St Fredonia (66736) *(G-2036)*
Koehn Customs 316 304-7979
107 W Texcoco St Montezuma (67867) *(G-7157)*
Koehn Machine Inc 316 282-2298
315 W 16th St Newton (67114) *(G-7372)*
Koehn Painting Co LLC 316 283-9612
204 W 6th St Newton (67114) *(G-7373)*
Koers-Turgeon Consulting Svc 620 272-9131
2018 N Henderson Dr Garden City (67846) *(G-2219)*
Koesten Hirschmann & Crabtree 913 345-1881
10000 College Blvd # 260 Shawnee Mission (66210) *(G-11537)*
Kohlman Systems Research Inc 785 843-4099
5916 Longleaf Dr Lawrence (66049) *(G-4948)*
Koken Manufacturing Co Inc 316 942-7600
2080 S Edwards St Wichita (67213) *(G-14892)*
Kolde Construction Inc 785 437-3730
28630 Highway 24 Saint Marys (66536) *(G-10370)*
Koller Enterprises Inc 913 422-2027
14601 W 99th St Lenexa (66215) *(G-5957)*
Kolterman & Hammel DDS, Clay Center *Also called Clay Center Family Dentistry (G-850)*
Kone Inc 316 942-1201
3450 N Rock Rd Ste 507 Wichita (67226) *(G-14893)*
Konica Minolta Business Soluti 913 563-1800
14300 W 105th St Lenexa (66215) *(G-5958)*
Konradys Lawn & Ldscpg Inc 913 722-1163
15705 S Pflumm Rd Olathe (66062) *(G-7843)*
Konradys Ldscp Winter Svc Inc 913 647-0286
4512 Speaker Rd Kansas City (66106) *(G-4179)*
Konza Constr Co Inc 785 762-2995
3107 N Highway K57 Junction City (66441) *(G-3717)*
Konza Construction & Sand, Junction City *Also called Konza Constr Co Inc (G-3717)*
Konza Prairie Cmnty Hlth Ctr 785 238-4711
361 Grant Ave Junction City (66441) *(G-3718)*
Kopco Inc (PA) 620 879-2117
Hwy 166 E Caney (67333) *(G-671)*
Koppers Recovery Resources LLC 913 213-6127
9401 Indian Creek Pkwy Overland Park (66210) *(G-8926)*
Korte Trucking Inc 620 276-8873
2180 N Anderson Rd Garden City (67846) *(G-2220)*
Kpers, Topeka *Also called Kansas Pub Emplyee Rtrment Sys (G-12798)*
Kpl Gas Service, Pratt *Also called Evergy Kansas Central Inc (G-10111)*
Kpl Gas Service, Saint Marys *Also called Evergy Kansas Central Inc (G-10363)*
Kpl Gas Service, Lawrence *Also called Evergy Kansas Central Inc (G-4854)*
Kpl South Texas LLC 316 828-5500
4111 E 37th St N Wichita (67220) *(G-14894)*
KPTS, Wichita *Also called Kansas Public Telecom Svc Inc (G-14820)*
Kraft Leasing LLC (PA) 913 601-6999
320 Kindleberger Rd Kansas City (66115) *(G-4180)*
Kraft Tool Company (PA) 913 422-4848
8325 Hedge Lane Ter Shawnee Mission (66227) *(G-11538)*
Kramer & Associates Cpas LLC 913 680-1690
2050 Spruce St Leavenworth (66048) *(G-5263)*
Kramer Seed Farms 620 544-4330
1114 S Monroe St Hugoton (67951) *(G-3170)*
Kratzer Industries 620 824-6405
603 10th St Geneseo (67444) *(G-2393)*
Krdq-FM, Colby *Also called M Rocking Radio Inc (G-1027)*
Kreamer Kincaid Taylor 913 782-2350
7450 W 130th St Ste 140 Overland Park (66213) *(G-8927)*
Krehbiels Specialty Meats Inc 620 241-0103
1636 Mohawk Rd McPherson (67460) *(G-6985)*
Kreider Rehab South, Lawrence *Also called Lawrence Memorial Hospital End (G-4976)*
Krha, Wichita *Also called Kansas Rest Hospitality Assn (G-14821)*
Kriers Auto Parts Inc 785 738-3526
223 N Mill St Beloit (67420) *(G-489)*
Krina Corporation 620 251-1034
1215 E 3rd St 166169n Coffeyville (67337) *(G-953)*
Kristie Winters 913 648-8946
201 W 4th St Park (67751) *(G-9597)*
Kriz-Daviz Whlesle Electl Sups, Salina *Also called Border States Industries Inc (G-10430)*
Krizman Hairdressing Salon, Prairie Village *Also called Krizmans Beauty Salons Inc (G-10043)*
Krizmans Beauty Salons Inc 913 648-6080
5215 W 94th Ter Prairie Village (66207) *(G-10043)*
Krucial Staffing LLC 913 802-2560
7240 W 98th Ter Overland Park (66212) *(G-8928)*
Kruger Technologies Inc (PA) 913 498-1114
8271 Melrose Dr Overland Park (66214) *(G-8929)*
Kruse Corporation 785 320-7990
8971 Green Valley Dr # 1 Manhattan (66502) *(G-6700)*
Kruse Corporation (PA) 316 838-7885
3636 N Topeka St Wichita (67219) *(G-14895)*
KS City Marriott Overland Park 913 338-8627
10800 Metcalf Ave Overland Park (66210) *(G-8930)*
KS Commercial RE Svcs Inc 785 272-2525
435 S Kansas Ave Ste 200 Topeka (66603) *(G-12824)*
KS Dept Trnsp Dist 5 Area 2, El Dorado *Also called Kansas Department Trnsp (G-1575)*
KS OL, Topeka *Also called Kansas Operation Lifesaver (G-12795)*
KS St U Dept of Housing D, Manhattan *Also called Kansas State University (G-6681)*
KS Statebank 785 587-4000
8803 E Us Highway 24 Manhattan (66502) *(G-6701)*
KS Statebank 785 762-5050
539 W 6th St Junction City (66441) *(G-3719)*
KS Statebank 785 587-4000
555 Poyntz Ave Manhattan (66502) *(G-6702)*
KS Transit Inc 281 841-6078
3716 W 154th St Overland Park (66224) *(G-8931)*
KS&t International Holdings LP 316 828-5500
4111 E 37th St N Wichita (67220) *(G-14896)*
Ksal-FM, Salina *Also called Alpha Media LLC (G-10400)*
Kscb-Am-Fm Radio Station, Liberal *Also called Seward County Broadcasting Co (G-6364)*
Ksds Inc 785 325-2256
120 W 7th St Washington (66968) *(G-13468)*
KSHSAA, Topeka *Also called Kansas State High Schl Actvtie (G-12806)*
Ksi Conveyor Inc (PA) 785 284-0600
2345 U Rd Sabetha (66534) *(G-10314)*
Ksku-FM Knzs-FM Kxk-FM Kwhk-FM, Hutchinson *Also called Ad Astra Per Aspera Broadcasti (G-3190)*
Ksnc-Tv2, Wichita *Also called Emmis Communications Corp (G-14277)*
Ksnt, Topeka *Also called Nexstar Broadcasting Inc (G-12931)*

Ksnw, Wichita *Also called Nexstar Broadcasting Inc* ***(G-15173)***
Ksnw Channel 3, Wichita *Also called Channel News Department* ***(G-13999)***
Ksnw-TV, Wichita *Also called Nvt Wichita LLC* ***(G-15201)***
Ksu Animal Science, Manhattan *Also called Kansas State University* ***(G-6693)***
Ksu Dprtment of Clncal Science....785 532-5690
1800 Denison Ave Manhattan (66506) ***(G-6703)***
Ksu Football Operation....785 532-6832
2201 Kimball Ave Manhattan (66502) ***(G-6704)***
Ksu Foundation, Manhattan *Also called Kansas State Univ Foundation* ***(G-6679)***
Ksu National Gas Machinery Lab....785 532-2617
245 Levee Dr Manhattan (66502) ***(G-6705)***
Ksu/Land Arch/ Reg Co, Manhattan *Also called Kansas State University* ***(G-6683)***
Ksugcmrf, Manhattan *Also called Kansas State University Golf C* ***(G-6697)***
Kth Properties Corporation (PA)....316 941-1100
3100 S Meridian Ave Wichita (67217) ***(G-14897)***
Ktpk-FM, Topeka *Also called Alpha Media LLC* ***(G-12310)***
Ktwu Channel 11 Pbs, Topeka *Also called Washburn University of Topeka* ***(G-13233)***
KU ALUMNI ASSOCIATION, Lawrence *Also called University Kansas Alumni Assn* ***(G-5155)***
KU Childrens Ctr Foundation (PA)....913 588-6301
3901 39th And Rnbow 2026 Kansas City (66160) ***(G-4181)***
Ku Credit Union, Lawrence *Also called Truity Credit Union* ***(G-5147)***
Ku Eye Center - Miller Clinic, Kansas City *Also called University of Kansas Hospital* ***(G-4507)***
Ku Medcal Cntr/Dept Opthmology, Shawnee Mission *Also called University of Kansas* ***(G-11967)***
Ku Medical Occupational Health, Kansas City *Also called Wyandtte Occpational Hlth Svcs* ***(G-4557)***
Ku Medwest Primary Care, Shawnee Mission *Also called University of Kansas Hospital* ***(G-11968)***
KU MEMORIAL UNIONS, Lawrence *Also called University Kansas Mem Corp* ***(G-5156)***
Ku Midwest Ambulatory Svc Ctr....913 588-8452
7405 Renner Rd Shawnee Mission (66217) ***(G-11539)***
Ku Midwest Surgery Center, Shawnee Mission *Also called Ku Midwest Ambulatory Svc Ctr* ***(G-11539)***
Ku Natural History Museum, Lawrence *Also called University of Kansas* ***(G-5167)***
Ku Physicians Inc....913 588-3243
3901 Rainb Blvd Mails 401 Kansas City (66160) ***(G-4182)***
Ku Womens Hlth Specialty Ctrs (PA)....913 588-6200
3901 Rainbow Blvd Kansas City (66160) ***(G-4183)***
Ku Workgroup For Community Hea....785 864-0533
1000 Sunnysde Av R4082 Fl Lawrence (66045) ***(G-4949)***
Kubota Authorized Dealer, Wichita *Also called Price Bros Equipment Co* ***(G-15340)***
Kubota Authorized Dealer, Louisburg *Also called Romans Outdoor Power Inc* ***(G-6466)***
Kubota Authorized Dealer, Hoxie *Also called Hoxie Implement Co Inc* ***(G-3139)***
Kubota Authorized Dealer, Iola *Also called Storrer Implement Inc* ***(G-3636)***
Kubota Authorized Dealer, Lawrence *Also called McConnell Machinery Co Inc* ***(G-5016)***
Kubota Authorized Dealer, Salina *Also called Sellers Equipment Inc* ***(G-10703)***
Kubota Authorized Dealer, Whitewater *Also called Ravenscraft Implement Inc* ***(G-13572)***
Kubota Authorized Dealer, Independence *Also called Romans Outdoor Power Inc* ***(G-3556)***
Kubota Authorized Dealer, Russell *Also called Radke Implement Inc* ***(G-10286)***
Kubota Authorized Dealer, Marysville *Also called Kanequip Inc* ***(G-6892)***
Kubota Authorized Dealer, Wamego *Also called Kanequip Inc* ***(G-13426)***
Kubota Authorized Dealer, Colby *Also called Colby A G Center LLC* ***(G-995)***
Kubota Tractor Corporation....913 215-5298
30901 W 191st St Edgerton (66030) ***(G-1486)***
Kuderx LLC....785 760-2298
302 E 13th St Concordia (66901) ***(G-1121)***
Kugler Oil Company....620 356-4347
795 S Road H Ulysses (67880) ***(G-13304)***
Kuglers Vineyard....785 843-8516
1235 N 1100 Rd Lawrence (66047) ***(G-4950)***
Kuhlman and Majors DDS....316 652-0000
1831 N Rock Road Ct # 101 Wichita (67206) ***(G-14898)***
Kuhlmann Installations LLC....316 634-6531
4465 N Webb Rd Wichita (67226) ***(G-14899)***
Kuhlmann Roberts & Janasek....316 681-0991
8150 E Douglas Ave Ste 50 Wichita (67206) ***(G-14900)***
Kuhn & Wittenborn Advertising, Overland Park *Also called Kuhn and Wittenborn Inc* ***(G-8932)***
Kuhn and Wittenborn Inc....816 471-7888
9325 Linden Reserve Dr Overland Park (66207) ***(G-8932)***
Kuhn Co LLC (PA)....316 788-6500
4640 E 63rd St S Derby (67037) ***(G-1257)***
Kuhn Mechanical Inc....620 441-9339
1001 E Kansas Ave Arkansas City (67005) ***(G-163)***
Kuhns H Richard Jr Md El....316 320-1917
700 W Central Ave Ste 201 El Dorado (67042) ***(G-1581)***
KUMC RESEARCH INTITUTE, Fairway *Also called University of KS Medcl* ***(G-1925)***
Kunshek Chat & Coal Inc....620 231-8270
304 Memorial Dr Pittsburg (66762) ***(G-9893)***
Kupi Rprdctive Endcrnology Lab....913 588-6377
3901 Rainbow Blvd Kansas City (66160) ***(G-4184)***
Kushs Painting....913 888-0230
1401 Minnesota Ave Kansas City (66102) ***(G-4185)***
Kustom Karriers LLC....316 283-1060
1450 S Spencer Rd Newton (67114) ***(G-7374)***
Kustom Signals Inc....620 431-2700
1010 W Chestnut St Chanute (66720) ***(G-736)***
Kustom Warehousing, Newton *Also called Kustom Karriers LLC* ***(G-7374)***
Kutak Rock LLP....316 609-7900
1605 N Waterfront Pkwy # 150 Wichita (67206) ***(G-14901)***
Kvc Behavioral Healthcare Inc....620 820-7680
2410 Main St Parsons (67357) ***(G-9701)***
Kvc Behavioral Healthcare Inc (HQ)....913 322-4900
21350 W 153rd St Olathe (66061) ***(G-7844)***
Kvc Health Systems Inc....913 621-5753
4300 Brenner Dr Kansas City (66104) ***(G-4186)***
Kvc Health Systems Inc....316 796-5503
1507 W 21st St N Wichita (67203) ***(G-14902)***
Kvc Health Systems Inc (PA)....913 322-4900
21350 W 153rd St Olathe (66061) ***(G-7845)***
Kvc Hospitals Inc (HQ)....913 322-4900
21350 W 153rd St Olathe (66061) ***(G-7846)***
Kvco....785 243-4444
2221 Campus Dr Concordia (66901) ***(G-1122)***
Kw Trucking Inc....785 346-5881
1123 W Us Highway 24 Osborne (67473) ***(G-8210)***
Kwch, Wichita *Also called Gray Television Group Inc* ***(G-14499)***
Kwch TV, Wichita *Also called Sunflower Broadcasting Inc* ***(G-15687)***
Kwch-CBS TV, Wichita *Also called Schurz Communications Inc* ***(G-15535)***
Kwik Staff LLC....785 430-5806
2600 Sw 17th St Topeka (66604) ***(G-12825)***
Kwikom Communications, Iola *Also called Jmz Corporation* ***(G-3616)***
Kwmg LLC....913 624-1841
6201 Cllege Pk Blvd 325 Overland Park (66211) ***(G-8933)***
Kwxd, Pittsburg *Also called Innovative Broadcasting Corp* ***(G-9880)***
Kxbz B 104 7 FM....785 539-1047
2414 Casement Rd Manhattan (66502) ***(G-6706)***
Kxxx Kqls, Colby *Also called Waitt Media Inc* ***(G-1047)***
Kye, Win, Dodge City *Also called Medical Heights Medical Center* ***(G-1403)***
Kyle Railroad Company, Phillipsburg *Also called Railamerica Inc* ***(G-9796)***
Kyle Tipton MD LLC....316 321-2100
700 W Central Ave Ste 201 El Dorado (67042) ***(G-1582)***
Kyys-Knbc-Kudl-wdaf-kcmo, Shawnee Mission *Also called Entercom Kansas City LLC* ***(G-11338)***
L & C Home Health Agency Inc....785 465-7444
1175 S Range Ave Ste 1 Colby (67701) ***(G-1022)***
L & D Oilfield Service Inc....620 624-3329
11130 Hwy 54 Liberal (67901) ***(G-6330)***
L & J Wood Products Inc....620 327-2183
9015 N Emma Creek Rd Hesston (67062) ***(G-2996)***
L & L Farms, Hugoton *Also called Lewis Wheeler Lee Wheeler Ptr* ***(G-3171)***
L & L Floor Covering Inc....620 275-0499
112 N Main St Garden City (67846) ***(G-2221)***
L & L Manufacturing Inc....816 257-8411
3130 Brinkerhoff Rd Kansas City (66115) ***(G-4187)***
L & M Contractors Inc....620 793-8137
1405 State Road 96 Great Bend (67530) ***(G-2600)***
L & M Oil Company (PA)....913 856-8502
20315 S Gardner Rd Gardner (66030) ***(G-2352)***
L & M Oil Company....913 893-9789
20315 S Gardner Rd Gardner (66030) ***(G-2353)***
L & M Steel & Mfg....785 462-8216
1130 Plains Ave Colby (67701) ***(G-1023)***
L & S Scott Inc....785 643-1488
511 N Santa Fe Ave Salina (67401) ***(G-10577)***
L & T Machining Inc....316 946-9744
1827 S Leonine St Wichita (67213) ***(G-14903)***
L & W Supply Corporation....913 782-1777
15660 S Keeler Ter Olathe (66062) ***(G-7847)***
L B Supply Company, Coffeyville *Also called Liebert Brothers Electric Co* ***(G-956)***
L B White Trucking Inc....620 326-8921
510 E Hillside St Wellington (67152) ***(G-13509)***
L Blixt Construction Inc....785 922-6180
2646 Sage Rd Chapman (67431) ***(G-780)***
L C Crossfaith....620 723-2626
22259 183 Hwy Greensburg (67054) ***(G-2682)***
L C Enterprises (PA)....316 682-3300
8100 E 22nd St N Bldg 900 Wichita (67226) ***(G-14904)***
L C Epoch Group....855 753-7624
10740 Nall Ave Ste 100 Overland Park (66211) ***(G-8934)***
L C McClain Inc (PA)....785 584-6151
203 Perry St Rossville (66533) ***(G-10253)***
L D Drilling Inc....620 793-3051
7 Sw 26 Ave Great Bend (67530) ***(G-2601)***
L D F Company....316 636-5575
10610 E 26th Cir N Wichita (67226) ***(G-14905)***
L G Barcus and Sons Inc (PA)....913 621-1100
1430 State Ave Kansas City (66102) ***(G-4188)***
L G Everist Incorporated....913 302-5394
2101 S 86th St Kansas City (66111) ***(G-4189)***

ALPHABETIC

L G Pike Shtmtl Mar Fbrication, Arkansas City *Also called LG Pike Construction Co Inc* ***(G-164)***
L J Gliem & Associates LLC 913 557-9402
9120 W 135th St Ste 203 Overland Park (66221) ***(G-8935)***
L J Herzberg Roofing Co Inc 316 529-2222
15223 E Zimmerly Ct Wichita (67230) ***(G-14906)***
L Kcp 913 894-3009
16215 W 108th St Lenexa (66219) ***(G-5959)***
L L C Fun Services of K C 913 441-9200
7803 Meadow View Dr Shawnee (66227) ***(G-10984)***
L L C Oasis of Hutchinson 620 663-4800
1818 E 23rd Ave Hutchinson (67502) ***(G-3353)***
L L L Transport Inc 913 777-5400
6950 Squibb Rd Ste 520 Shawnee Mission (66202) ***(G-11540)***
L M C C Inc 913 371-1070
54 N 10th St Kansas City (66102) ***(G-4190)***
L M H, Lawrence *Also called Lawrence Memorial Hospital* ***(G-4973)***
L M S, Shawnee Mission *Also called LMS Company LLC* ***(G-11576)***
L P E, Lawrence *Also called Landplan Engineering PA* ***(G-4954)***
L S Industries Inc 316 265-7997
710 E 17th St N Wichita (67214) ***(G-14907)***
L T Huxtable Service Inc 785 235-5331
2150a S Kansas Ave Topeka (66611) ***(G-12826)***
L T I, Shawnee *Also called Legacy Technologies Inc* ***(G-10986)***
L V S Inc (PA) 316 636-5005
3411 N Rock Rd Ste 100 Wichita (67226) ***(G-14908)***
L-K Acid, Hays *Also called L-K Wireline Inc* ***(G-2861)***
L-K Wireline Inc 785 625-6877
2480 E 8th St Hays (67601) ***(G-2861)***
La Crosse Livestock Market 785 222-2586
P.O. Box 657 La Crosse (67548) ***(G-4634)***
La Cygne Station, La Cygne *Also called Evergy Metro Inc* ***(G-4640)***
La Dow & Spohn Inc 620 378-2541
433 Madison St Fredonia (66736) ***(G-2037)***
La Mesa Mexican Restaurant 913 837-3455
116 Harvest Dr Louisburg (66053) ***(G-6454)***
La Nena Tortilleria Rostiseria 913 281-8993
1200 Minnesota Ave Kansas City (66102) ***(G-4191)***
La Palm Products, Wichita *Also called Millenia Productions LLC* ***(G-15108)***
La Petite Academy Inc 913 685-2800
15012 Newton Dr Shawnee Mission (66223) ***(G-11541)***
La Petite Academy Inc 913 441-5100
22211 W 66th St Shawnee Mission (66226) ***(G-11542)***
La Petite Academy Inc 785 843-5703
3211 W 6th St Lawrence (66049) ***(G-4951)***
La Petite Academy Inc 316 684-5916
7431 E 21st St N Wichita (67206) ***(G-14909)***
La Petite Academy Inc 785 273-9393
3325 Sw Gage Blvd Topeka (66614) ***(G-12827)***
La Petite Academy Inc 913 432-5053
6410 Antioch Rd Shawnee Mission (66202) ***(G-11543)***
La Petite Academy Inc 913 764-2345
1810 S Scarborough St Olathe (66062) ***(G-7848)***
La Petite Academy Inc 913 492-4183
15039 W 86th St Lenexa (66215) ***(G-5960)***
La Petite Academy Inc 913 649-5773
8621 W 96th St Overland Park (66212) ***(G-8936)***
La Petite Academy Inc 785 843-6445
3200 Clinton Parkway Ct Lawrence (66047) ***(G-4952)***
La Petite Academy Inc 913 780-2318
1825 N Ridgeview Rd Olathe (66061) ***(G-7849)***
La Petite Academy Inc 913 469-1006
11114 Antioch Rd Overland Park (66210) ***(G-8937)***
La Quinta, Dodge City *Also called Janki Inc* ***(G-1382)***
La Quinta Inn, Wichita *Also called Tgc Greenwich Hotel LLC* ***(G-15754)***
La Quinta Inn, Lenexa *Also called Lq Management LLC* ***(G-5980)***
La Siesta Foods, Topeka *Also called Resers Fine Foods Inc* ***(G-13009)***
La Superior Food Products Inc 913 362-6611
4307 Merriam Dr Shawnee Mission (66203) ***(G-11544)***
Lab Animal Resources, Kansas City *Also called University of Kansas* ***(G-4503)***
Labconco Corporation 620 223-5700
2500 Liberty Bell Rd Fort Scott (66701) ***(G-1980)***
Label Express/Excel Brand, Saint Marys *Also called Roll Products Inc* ***(G-10374)***
Labette Avenue 620 795-2550
711 4th St Oswego (67356) ***(G-8234)***
Labette Center For Mental Inc 620 421-9402
906 S 13th St Parsons (67357) ***(G-9702)***
Labette County Highway Dept, Altamont *Also called County of Labette* ***(G-72)***
Labette County Medical Center 620 421-4880
1902 S Us Highway 59 D Parsons (67357) ***(G-9703)***
Labette Ctr For Mntal Hlth Svc 620 421-3770
1730 Belmont Ave Parsons (67357) ***(G-9704)***
Labette Health Foundation Inc (PA) 620 421-4881
1902 S Us Highway 59 Parsons (67357) ***(G-9705)***
Labette Health Foundation Inc 620 922-3838
575 2000 Rd Coffeyville (67337) ***(G-954)***
Labone Inc 913 577-1643
11000 Renner Rd Shawnee Mission (66201) ***(G-11545)***
Labone Inc (HQ) 913 888-1770
10101 Renner Blvd Lenexa (66219) ***(G-5961)***
Labor On Demand, Kansas City *Also called On Demand Employment Svcs LLC* ***(G-4294)***
Labor Source LLC (PA) 913 764-5333
235 S Kansas Ave Olathe (66061) ***(G-7850)***
Laboratory Corporation America 785 539-2537
1133 College Ave Bldg E Manhattan (66502) ***(G-6707)***
Laboratory Corporation America 913 338-4070
7800 W 110th St Overland Park (66210) ***(G-8938)***
Laboratory Corporation America 316 636-2300
9120 E 37th St N Wichita (67226) ***(G-14910)***
Lacey, Phillip, Wichita *Also called Gilmore & Bell A Prof Corp* ***(G-14466)***
Lacrosse Furniture Co 785 222-2541
1215 Oak St La Crosse (67548) ***(G-4635)***
Lacy Rv Ranch Inc 620 245-9608
2475 E Kansas Ave McPherson (67460) ***(G-6986)***
LAd Global Enterprises Inc 913 768-0888
25000 College Blvd Olathe (66061) ***(G-7851)***
Ladiwalla Hospitality LLC 316 773-1700
7515 W Taft St Wichita (67209) ***(G-14911)***
Lady Lords Rehabilitaion Hosp, Wichita *Also called Ascension Via Christi Hospital* ***(G-13751)***
Lafarge North America Inc 620 378-4458
1400 S Cement Rd Fredonia (66736) ***(G-2038)***
Lafarge North America Inc 620 455-3720
1438 122nd Rd Oxford (67119) ***(G-9533)***
Lafarge North America Inc 316 943-3500
3500 N West St Wichita (67205) ***(G-14912)***
Lafarge North America Inc 316 613-5100
3600 N West St Ste 100 Wichita (67205) ***(G-14913)***
Lafarge North America Inc 913 780-6809
1245 W 149th St Olathe (66061) ***(G-7852)***
Lafarge North America Inc 816 365-9143
317 S 3rd St Kansas City (66118) ***(G-4192)***
Lafayette Life Plan Inc 785 742-7465
302 E Iowa St Hiawatha (66434) ***(G-3015)***
Lafe T Williams & Assoc Inc 316 262-0479
1509 S Washington Ave Wichita (67211) ***(G-14914)***
Laforge & Budd, Parsons *Also called Laforge and Budd Cnstr Co Inc* ***(G-9706)***
Laforge and Budd Cnstr Co Inc 620 421-4470
2020 N 21st St Parsons (67357) ***(G-9706)***
Laird Noler Ford Body Shop, Topeka *Also called Laird Noller Ford Inc* ***(G-12830)***
Laird Noller Ford Inc (PA) 785 235-9211
2245 Sw Topeka Blvd Topeka (66611) ***(G-12828)***
Laird Noller Ford Inc 785 264-2800
2946 S Kansas Ave Topeka (66611) ***(G-12829)***
Laird Noller Ford Inc 785 232-8347
2310 S Kansas Ave Topeka (66611) ***(G-12830)***
Laird Noller Tlmh, Topeka *Also called Laird Noller Ford Inc* ***(G-12829)***
Lake Garnett Sporting Club 785 448-5803
432 E 1st Ave Garnett (66032) ***(G-2380)***
Lake Perry Yacht & Marina LLC 785 783-4927
10770 Perry Park Dr Perry (66073) ***(G-9771)***
Lake Point Nursing & Rehab, El Dorado *Also called Butler County Health Services* ***(G-1540)***
LAKE POINT NURSING CENTER, Augusta *Also called Augusta L Lakepoint L C* ***(G-307)***
Lake Pointe Hotel Co LLC 913 451-1222
6704 W 121st St Shawnee Mission (66209) ***(G-11546)***
Lake Region RC&d, Ottawa *Also called Lake Region Resource Conservat* ***(G-8282)***
Lake Region Resource Conservat 785 242-2073
113 N Oak St Ottawa (66067) ***(G-8282)***
Lakemary Center Inc 913 768-6831
15145 S Keeler St Ste A Olathe (66062) ***(G-7853)***
Lakemary Center Homes Inc 913 557-4000
100 Lakemary Dr Paola (66071) ***(G-9569)***
Lakepint Nrsing Rhbltation Ctr 316 776-2194
601 N Rose Hill Rd Rose Hill (67133) ***(G-10241)***
Lakepoint Corporate 316 990-6792
2101 Dearborn St Augusta (67010) ***(G-332)***
Lakepoint Family Physicians 316 636-2662
8020 E Central Ave # 200 Wichita (67206) ***(G-14915)***
Lakepoint Family Physicians PA, Wichita *Also called Lakepoint Family Physicians* ***(G-14915)***
Lakeshore Learning Center Svcs 785 271-9146
5525 Sw 17th St Topeka (66604) ***(G-12831)***
Lakeside Camp of The United 620 872-2021
300 E Scott Lake Dr Scott City (67871) ***(G-10819)***
Lakeside Terrace 785 284-0005
1100 Harrison St Sabetha (66534) ***(G-10315)***
Lakeview Funeral Home, Wichita *Also called D W Newcomers Sons Inc* ***(G-14160)***
Lakeview Village Inc 913 888-1900
9100 Park St Lenexa (66215) ***(G-5962)***
Lakeview Vlg Retirement Cmnty, Lenexa *Also called Lakeview Village Inc* ***(G-5962)***
Lakewood Middle School Pto 913 239-5800
6601 Edgewater Dr Overland Park (66223) ***(G-8939)***
Lakewood Senior Living Seville, Wichita *Also called Survey Companies LLC* ***(G-15703)***
Lakhani Commercial Corp (PA) 913 677-1100
6828 Kaw Dr Kansas City (66111) ***(G-4193)***
Lakin Bancshares Inc (PA) 620 355-6222
221 N Main St Lakin (67860) ***(G-4654)***

Lakin Dairy 620 355-6640
771 Road R Lakin (67860) *(G-4655)*
Lamar Advertising Company 785 234-0501
2501 Ne Meriden Rd Topeka (66617) *(G-12832)*
Lamar Advertising Company 913 438-4048
9088 Bond St Overland Park (66214) *(G-8940)*
Lamar Court 913 906-9696
11909 Lamar Ave Overland Park (66209) *(G-8941)*
Lamb-Roberts-Heise Funeral HM, Ottawa *Also called Carriage Services Inc (G-8253)*
Lambda CHI Alpha Frternity Inc 785 843-1172
2005 Stewart Ave Lawrence (66046) *(G-4953)*
Lambert Vet Supply LLC 785 527-2209
814 K St Belleville (66935) *(G-459)*
Lambriar Kennels, Mahaska *Also called Lambriars Inc (G-6505)*
Lambriars Inc 785 245-3231
113 N Pine St Mahaska (66955) *(G-6505)*
Lambrier Vet Supply, Belleville *Also called Lambert Vet Supply LLC (G-459)*
Laminage Products Inc 316 267-5233
970 N Santa Fe St Wichita (67214) *(G-14916)*
Laminate Works Inc 913 281-7474
1200 S 5th St Kansas City (66105) *(G-4194)*
Laminate Works Inc (PA) 913 800-8263
15900 College Blvd # 200 Lenexa (66219) *(G-5963)*
Laminate Works Kansas City LLC 913 281-7474
1200 S 5th St Kansas City (66105) *(G-4195)*
Lamont Hill Resort Inc 785 828-3131
22975 Highway 368 Vassar (66543) *(G-13371)*
Lampton Welding Supply Co Inc (PA) 316 263-3293
601 N Washington Ave Wichita (67214) *(G-14917)*
Lamunyon Clg & Restoration 785 632-1259
1541 18th Rd Clay Center (67432) *(G-870)*
Lamunyon Restoration, Clay Center *Also called Cleaning By Lamunyon Inc (G-855)*
Lance Anderson DDS 316 687-2104
9415 E Harry St Ste 101 Wichita (67207) *(G-14918)*
Land Acquisitions Inc 847 749-0675
6308 E Ironhorse St Wichita (67220) *(G-14919)*
Land Air Express Inc 316 942-0191
3215 W Pawnee St Wichita (67213) *(G-14920)*
Land Fill, Hutchinson *Also called County of Reno (G-3248)*
Land Institute 785 823-5376
2440 E Water Well Rd Salina (67401) *(G-10578)*
Land of Paws LLC (PA) 913 341-1011
4021 Somerset Dr Shawnee Mission (66208) *(G-11547)*
Land OLakes Inc 785 445-4030
1068 E 15th St Russell (67665) *(G-10278)*
Land Pride, Salina *Also called Great Plains Manufacturing Inc (G-10518)*
Land Surveyor, Wichita *Also called Savoy Rgls BHN Engnrng Lnd Sur (G-15523)*
Land Title Services Inc 785 823-7223
136 N 7th St Salina (67401) *(G-10579)*
Landgenuity LLC 913 594-1845
1001 N 2nd St E Louisburg (66053) *(G-6455)*
Landis+gyr Inc 913 312-4710
11146 Thompson Ave Lenexa (66219) *(G-5964)*
Landmark Bancorp Inc (PA) 785 565-2000
701 Poyntz Ave Manhattan (66502) *(G-6708)*
Landmark Implement Inc 785 282-6601
910 W Highway 36 Smith Center (66967) *(G-12036)*
Landmark Inn Hstrc Bnk Oberlin, Oberlin *Also called Gary Dean Anderson (G-7495)*
Landmark Landscape LLC 785 608-6907
1330 Nw 86th St Topeka (66618) *(G-12833)*
Landmark National Bank 913 239-2719
8101 W 135th St Overland Park (66223) *(G-8942)*
Landmark National Bank 785 883-2145
112 W 6th St Wellsville (66092) *(G-13544)*
Landmark National Bank (HQ) 620 225-1745
701 Poyntz Ave Manhattan (66502) *(G-6709)*
Landmasters Landscape 913 667-3382
718 W Wabash St Olathe (66061) *(G-7854)*
Landoll Corporation (PA) 785 562-5381
1900 North St Marysville (66508) *(G-6893)*
Landoll Corporation 785 562-4780
1104 Pony Express Hwy Marysville (66508) *(G-6894)*
Landoll Corporation 785 738-6613
1600 W 8th St Beloit (67420) *(G-490)*
Landplan Engineering PA (PA) 785 843-7530
1310 Wakarusa Dr Ste 100 Lawrence (66049) *(G-4954)*
Landpride, Lucas *Also called Great Plains Manufacturing Inc (G-6471)*
Landscape Management Services, Salina *Also called Karcher Investments Inc (G-10568)*
Landscape Outfitters LLC 620 221-1108
20480 81st Rd Winfield (67156) *(G-16154)*
Landscapes Inc 316 262-7557
1100 S West St Wichita (67213) *(G-14921)*
Landvest Corporation (PA) 316 634-6510
9103 E 37th St N Wichita (67226) *(G-14922)*
Landwehr Machine 316 794-3390
2100 S 231st St W Goddard (67052) *(G-2445)*
Landwehr Manufacturing Company 316 942-1719
1332 S Anna St Wichita (67209) *(G-14923)*
Landworks Inc 913 422-9300
9317 Woodend Rd Edwardsville (66111) *(G-1507)*
Lane County Feeders Inc 620 397-5341
16 W Road 230 Dighton (67839) *(G-1286)*
Lane County Hospital (PA) 620 397-5321
235 W Vine St Dighton (67839) *(G-1287)*
Lane Myers Company Inc 620 622-4310
415 N Broadway Protection (67127) *(G-10175)*
Lanesfield Schl Historic Site 913 893-6645
18745 Dillie Rd Edgerton (66021) *(G-1487)*
Lang Builders LLC 620 331-5850
2067 N 21st St Independence (67301) *(G-3532)*
Lang Diesel Inc 785 462-2412
1280 S Country Club Dr Colby (67701) *(G-1024)*
Lang Diesel Inc 620 947-3182
603 N Ash St Hillsboro (67063) *(G-3051)*
Lang Diesel Inc 620 431-6700
201 35th Pkwy Chanute (66720) *(G-737)*
Lang Diesel Inc 785 284-3401
15 N Old 75 Hwy Sabetha (66534) *(G-10316)*
Lange Company LLC 620 456-2996
205 S Highland St Conway Springs (67031) *(G-1143)*
Lange Homes, Wichita *Also called J B L Inc (G-14734)*
Langley Muehlberger Con Cnstr, Kansas City *Also called L M C C Inc (G-4190)*
Langley, Jay D, Ellsworth *Also called Clubine & Rettele (G-1662)*
Langley/Empire Candle, Kansas City *Also called Empire Candle Co LLC (G-3989)*
Lano Company, The, Fairway *Also called Gdm Enterprises LLC (G-1908)*
Lansing Care Rhbltion Ctr LLC 913 727-1284
210 N Plaza Dr Lansing (66043) *(G-4679)*
Lansing Correctional Facility, Lansing *Also called Corrections Kansas Department (G-4672)*
Lansing Ethanol Services LLC 913 748-3000
10975 Benson Dr Ste 400 Overland Park (66210) *(G-8943)*
Lansing Grain Company LLC 913 748-4320
10975 Benson Dr Ste 400 Overland Park (66210) *(G-8944)*
Lansing Kiwanis Club, Lansing *Also called Kiwanis International Inc (G-4678)*
Lansing Lvnworth Fmly Hlth Ctr, Lansing *Also called Peter J Cristiano Dr (G-4690)*
Lansing Trade Group LLC (HQ) 913 748-3000
10975 Benson Dr Ste 400 Overland Park (66210) *(G-8945)*
Lansing Unified Schl Dst 469 ....913 250-0749
1102 Industrial St Lansing (66043) *(G-4680)*
Lantern Park Manor, Colby *Also called Beverly Enterprises-Kansas LLC (G-990)*
Laquinta Inn and Suites 913 648-5555
10610 Marty St Overland Park (66212) *(G-8946)*
Larc Dvs, Liberal *Also called Liberal Area Rape Crisis (G-6331)*
Lario Oil & Gas Company (HQ) 316 265-5611
301 S Market St Wichita (67202) *(G-14924)*
Lario Oil & Gas Company 785 625-5023
2501 280th Ave Hays (67601) *(G-2862)*
Larkin Excavating, Inc. 913 727-3772
13575 Gilman Rd Leavenworth (66048) *(G-5264)*
LARKSFIELD PLACE, Wichita *Also called Wesley Retirement Community (G-15955)*
Larksfield Place 316 636-1000
7373 E 29th St N Ofc Wichita (67226) *(G-14925)*
Larned Healthcare & Living Ctr, Larned *Also called National Healthcare Corp (G-4707)*
Larned State Hospital, Larned *Also called Kansas Dept For Aging & Disabi (G-4706)*
Larrison-Forsyth Fnrl HM LLC 620 886-5641
120 E Lincoln Ave Medicine Lodge (67104) *(G-7065)*
Larry Bair Excavating Inc 913 947-7222
2785 W 247th St Louisburg (66053) *(G-6456)*
Larry Booze Roofing Co Inc 316 263-7796
13926 W Westport Ct Wichita (67235) *(G-14926)*
Larry D Sheldon DDS 913 782-7580
125 E Park St Olathe (66061) *(G-7855)*
Larry Lawrenz Construction 785 258-2056
220 W Walnut St Ste 1 Herington (67449) *(G-2978)*
Larry Theurer 620 326-2715
802 E 16th St Wellington (67152) *(G-13510)*
Larrys Trailer Sales & Svc LLC 316 838-1491
4153 N Broadway Ave Wichita (67219) *(G-14927)*
Larsen & Associates Inc 785 841-8707
1311 E 25th St Ste B Lawrence (66046) *(G-4955)*
Larson & Company PA 316 263-8030
200 W Douglas Ave # 1000 Wichita (67202) *(G-14928)*
Larson Construction Inc 785 537-0160
2616 Eureka Ter Manhattan (66503) *(G-6710)*
Larue Machine Inc 620 431-3303
220 W 14th St Chanute (66720) *(G-738)*
Las Tarascas 316 941-5511
5701 E Lincoln St Wichita (67218) *(G-14929)*
Las Villas Del Norte (PA) 760 741-1046
416 W Spruce St Junction City (66441) *(G-3720)*
Las Villas Del Norte Hlth Ctr, Junction City *Also called Las Villas Del Norte (G-3720)*
Laser Recycling Company 785 865-4075
4724 Killarney Cir Lawrence (66047) *(G-4956)*
Laser Specialists Inc (PA) 913 780-9990
19879 W 156th St Olathe (66062) *(G-7856)*
Laserequipment, Overland Park *Also called Perfect Output LLC (G-9154)*

ALPHABETIC

Lash Company LLC...316 265-5527
207 N Emporia Ave Wichita (67202) ***(G-14930)***
Last Chance Graphics Inc...785 263-4470
201 N Broadway St Abilene (67410) ***(G-44)***
Lathem Water Service, Ulysses *Also called Wal-Mac Inc* ***(G-13331)***
Lathrom Manufacturing Inc...316 522-0001
315 E 55th St S Wichita (67216) ***(G-14931)***
Lathrop & Gage LLP...913 451-5100
10851 Mastin St Ste 1000 Shawnee Mission (66210) ***(G-11548)***
Latimer Sommers & Associates, Topeka *Also called Latimer Sommers and Assoc PA* ***(G-12834)***
Latimer Sommers and Assoc PA...785 233-3232
3639 Sw Smmrfeld Dr Ste A Topeka (66614) ***(G-12834)***
Latour At Terradyne, Andover *Also called Latour Management Inc* ***(G-102)***
Latour Management Inc...316 262-7300
210 N Mosley St Wichita (67202) ***(G-14932)***
Latour Management Inc (PA)...316 524-2290
2949 N Rock Rd Ste 100 Wichita (67226) ***(G-14933)***
Latour Management Inc...316 733-1922
1400 Terradyne Dr Andover (67002) ***(G-102)***
Latta Whitlow By Stryker, Topeka *Also called Stryker Services Inc* ***(G-13115)***
Laurence Volbrecht and Assoc, Wichita *Also called Estates Unlimited Inc* ***(G-14305)***
Laurie D Fisher MD...913 345-3650
5701 W 119th St Ste 410 Overland Park (66209) ***(G-8947)***
Laurie's Kitchen, Overland Park *Also called Old World Spices Seasoning Inc* ***(G-9098)***
Lauries Kitchen Inc...316 777-9198
113 W Main St Mulvane (67110) ***(G-7218)***
Law Company Inc (PA)...316 268-0200
345 N Rverview St Ste 300 Wichita (67203) ***(G-14934)***
Law Department, Overland Park *Also called City of Overland Park* ***(G-8554)***
Law Kingdon, Wichita *Also called Lk Architecture Inc* ***(G-14969)***
Law Office of Pter A Jouras Jr...913 677-1999
4330 Shawnee Mission Pkwy # 205 Fairway (66205) ***(G-1912)***
Law Offices of M Steven Wagle...316 264-4878
301 N Market St Wichita (67202) ***(G-14935)***
Lawing Financial Group Inc (PA)...913 491-6226
6201 College Blvd Fl 7 Overland Park (66211) ***(G-8948)***
Lawn Magic, Shawnee Mission *Also called J B Hinz* ***(G-11476)***
Lawns By Beck Inc...913 631-8873
14404 W 74th St Shawnee Mission (66216) ***(G-11549)***
Lawnworks Inc...316 838-3500
3621 N Santa Fe St Wichita (67219) ***(G-14936)***
Lawrenc-Douglas Cnty Hlth Dept...785 843-3060
200 Maine St Ste B Lawrence (66044) ***(G-4957)***
Lawrence Anaesthesia PA...785 842-7026
613 N 2nd St Lawrence (66044) ***(G-4958)***
Lawrence Cancer Center...785 749-3600
330 Arkansas St Ste 120 Lawrence (66044) ***(G-4959)***
Lawrence City Vehicle Maint...785 832-3020
1141 Haskell Ave Lawrence (66044) ***(G-4960)***
Lawrence Cllsion Spcalists LLC...785 841-3672
800 E 23rd St Lawrence (66046) ***(G-4961)***
Lawrence Community Shelter...785 832-8864
3701 Franklin Park Cir Lawrence (66046) ***(G-4962)***
Lawrence Country Club...785 842-0592
400 Country Club Ter Lawrence (66049) ***(G-4963)***
LAWRENCE COUNTRY CLUB POOL, Lawrence *Also called Lawrence Country Club* ***(G-4963)***
Lawrence Dialysis, Lawrence *Also called Total Renal Care Inc* ***(G-5144)***
Lawrence Distribution Center, Lawrence *Also called Standard Beverage Corporation* ***(G-5117)***
Lawrence Eye Care Optical, Lawrence *Also called Lawrence Eyecare Associates* ***(G-4964)***
Lawrence Eyecare Associates...785 841-2280
1112 W 6th St Ste 214 Lawrence (66044) ***(G-4964)***
Lawrence Family Practice Ctr...785 841-6540
4951 W 18th St Lawrence (66047) ***(G-4965)***
Lawrence Feed & Farm Sup Inc...785 843-4311
545 Wisconsin St Lawrence (66044) ***(G-4966)***
Lawrence Funeral Chapel Inc...785 841-3822
3821 W 6th St Lawrence (66049) ***(G-4967)***
Lawrence Glass & Mirror Co...913 631-5533
12215 Johnson Dr Shawnee Mission (66216) ***(G-11550)***
Lawrence Gymnastics Academy...785 865-0856
4930 Legends Dr Lawrence (66049) ***(G-4968)***
Lawrence Home Builders Assn...785 748-0612
604 N 600th Rd Lawrence (66047) ***(G-4969)***
Lawrence Home Training, Lawrence *Also called Total Renal Care Inc* ***(G-5143)***
Lawrence Internal Medicine PA...785 842-7200
1440 Wakarusa Dr Ste 300 Lawrence (66049) ***(G-4970)***
Lawrence Landscape...785 749-7554
608 Lincoln Ct Lawrence (66044) ***(G-4971)***
Lawrence Landscape Inc...785 843-4370
600 Lincoln St Lawrence (66044) ***(G-4972)***
Lawrence Lions Club, Lawrence *Also called International Association of* ***(G-4914)***
Lawrence Mem Occupational Hlth, Lawrence *Also called Lawrence Memorial Hospital End* ***(G-4975)***
Lawrence Memorial Hospital (PA)...785 505-5000
325 Maine St Lawrence (66044) ***(G-4973)***
Lawrence Memorial Hospital End (HQ)...785 505-3315
330 Arkansas St Ste 201 Lawrence (66044) ***(G-4974)***
Lawrence Memorial Hospital End...785 840-3114
325 Maine St Lawrence (66044) ***(G-4975)***
Lawrence Memorial Hospital End...785 505-3780
3500 Clinton Pkwy Lawrence (66047) ***(G-4976)***
Lawrence Municipal Airport-Lwc...785 842-0000
1930 N Airport Rd Lawrence (66044) ***(G-4977)***
Lawrence Occpational Hlth Svcs...785 838-1500
3511 Clinton Pl Ste B Lawrence (66047) ***(G-4978)***
Lawrence Oral Maxillofacial Sg, Lawrence *Also called Lawrence Oral Surgery* ***(G-4979)***
Lawrence Oral Surgery...785 843-5490
308 Maine St Lawrence (66044) ***(G-4979)***
Lawrence Orthopedic Surgery, Lawrence *Also called Lawrence Orthpaedic Surgery PA* ***(G-4980)***
Lawrence Orthpaedic Surgery PA...785 843-9125
1112 W 6th St Ste 124 Lawrence (66044) ***(G-4980)***
Lawrence Otlryngology Assoc PA (PA)...620 343-6600
1112 W 6th St Ste 216 Lawrence (66044) ***(G-4981)***
Lawrence Paper Company (PA)...785 843-8111
2801 Lakeview Rd Lawrence (66049) ***(G-4982)***
Lawrence Pediatrics PA...785 856-9090
3310 Clinton Parkway Ct Lawrence (66047) ***(G-4983)***
Lawrence Photo-Graphic, Kansas City *Also called Heartland Imaging Companies* ***(G-4076)***
Lawrence Presbyterian Manor, Lawrence *Also called Presbyterian Manors Inc* ***(G-5074)***
Lawrence Printing and Design...785 843-4600
2317 Ponderosa Dr Lawrence (66046) ***(G-4984)***
Lawrence Prompt Care, Lawrence *Also called Lawrence Occpational Hlth Svcs* ***(G-4978)***
Lawrence Public Lib Foundation, Lawrence *Also called Lawrence Public Lib Foundation* ***(G-4985)***
Lawrence Public Lib Foundation...785 843-3833
707 Vermont St Lawrence (66044) ***(G-4985)***
Lawrence Ready Mix, Lawrence *Also called Lrm Industries Inc* ***(G-5001)***
Lawrence Realty Associates...785 841-2727
4321 W 6th St Lawrence (66049) ***(G-4986)***
Lawrence Surgery Center LLC...785 832-0588
1112 W 6th St Ste 220 Lawrence (66044) ***(G-4987)***
Lawrence Theatre Inc...785 843-7469
4660 Bauer Farm Dr Lawrence (66049) ***(G-4988)***
Lawrence Transit System, Lawrence *Also called Mv Transportation Inc* ***(G-5034)***
Lawrence Wmens Trnstnal Cre S...785 865-3956
2518 Ridge Ct Lawrence (66046) ***(G-4989)***
Lawrenz Masonry LLC...785 366-0866
220 W Walnut St Herington (67449) ***(G-2979)***
Lawyers Title of Kansas Inc (PA)...785 271-9500
5715 Sw 21st St Topeka (66604) ***(G-12835)***
Laxminarayan Lodging Llc...785 462-3933
1950 S Range Ave Colby (67701) ***(G-1025)***
Layne Christensen Company...316 264-5365
1011 W Harry St Wichita (67213) ***(G-14937)***
Layne Christensen Company...913 321-5000
620 S 38th St Kansas City (66106) ***(G-4196)***
Layne Christensen Company...913 321-5000
620 S 38th St Kansas City (66106) ***(G-4197)***
Layne-Western, Wichita *Also called Layne Christensen Company* ***(G-14937)***
Layne-Western, Kansas City *Also called Layne Christensen Company* ***(G-4196)***
Lazer Spot Inc...913 839-2654
815 S Clairborne Rd 275c Olathe (66062) ***(G-7857)***
Lb Steel LLC...785 862-1071
5600 Sw Topeka Blvd Topeka (66609) ***(G-12836)***
Lba Air Cndtoning Htg Plbg Inc...816 454-5515
6850 W 47th Ter Shawnee Mission (66203) ***(G-11551)***
Lbubs 2003-C5 Nismith Hall LLC...785 832-8676
1800 Naismith Dr Lawrence (66045) ***(G-4990)***
Lc Enterprises, Wichita *Also called L C Enterprises* ***(G-14904)***
Lcd Unlimited Inc...316 721-4803
1229 S Byron Rd Wichita (67209) ***(G-14938)***
Lcrc...913 383-2085
8101 Mission Rd Prairie Village (66208) ***(G-10044)***
LDB Inc...620 532-2236
1040 E Us Highway 54 Kingman (67068) ***(G-4605)***
Le John Minh DDS...913 888-9399
10616 W 87th St Overland Park (66214) ***(G-8949)***
Leader One Financial Corp (PA)...913 747-4000
7500 College Blvd # 1150 Overland Park (66210) ***(G-8950)***
Leading Edge Aerospace LLC...316 942-1301
1360 S Anna St Wichita (67209) ***(G-14939)***
League Kansas Municipalities...785 354-9565
300 Sw 8th Ave Ste 100 Topeka (66603) ***(G-12837)***
Leander Health Tech Inc...785 856-7474
315 Ne Industrial Ln A Lawrence (66044) ***(G-4991)***
Learjet Inc (HQ)...316 946-2000
1 Learjet Way Wichita (67209) ***(G-14940)***
Learjet Inc...316 946-3001
1 Learjet Way Wichita (67209) ***(G-14941)***
Learjet Inc...316 946-2000
7761 W Kellogg Dr Bldg 11 Wichita (67209) ***(G-14942)***

Learn & Grow Childcare Center 316 777-0355
1020 N 2nd Ave Mulvane (67110) ***(G-7219)***
LEARN & GROW CHILDCARE CTR, Mulvane *Also called Learn & Grow Childcare Center* ***(G-7219)***
Learning Care Group Inc 913 851-7800
11100 W 135th St Shawnee Mission (66221) ***(G-11552)***
Leavcon II Inc 913 351-1430
108 American Ave Lansing (66043) ***(G-4681)***
Leavenworth Country Club 913 727-6600
455 W Eisenhower Rd Lansing (66043) ***(G-4682)***
Leavenworth County Co-Op, Lansing *Also called Leavenworth County Coop Assn* ***(G-4683)***
Leavenworth County Coop Assn (PA) 913 727-1900
1101 Industrial St Lansing (66043) ***(G-4683)***
Leavenworth County Headstart, Leavenworth *Also called Nek Cap Inc* ***(G-5276)***
Leavenworth County Hwy Dept, Leavenworth *Also called County of Leavenworth* ***(G-5228)***
Leavenworth Detention Center, Leavenworth *Also called Corecivic Inc* ***(G-5225)***
Leavenworth Excvtg Eqp Co Inc 913 727-1234
5037 S 4th St Leavenworth (66048) ***(G-5265)***
Leavenworth Family Health Ctr 913 682-5588
720 1st Ter Lansing (66043) ***(G-4684)***
Leavenworth Floral, Leavenworth *Also called William O Broeker Enterprises* ***(G-5306)***
Leavenworth Job Service Center, Leavenworth *Also called Kansas Department of Labor* ***(G-5260)***
Leavenworth Maintenance Dept, Leavenworth *Also called City of Leavenworth* ***(G-5219)***
Leavenworth National Cmtry 897, Leavenworth *Also called National Cemetery ADM* ***(G-5273)***
Leavenworth Technical Services 913 351-3344
4501 Commercial Pl Leavenworth (66048) ***(G-5266)***
Leavenwrth Rverfront Cmnty Ctr, Leavenworth *Also called City of Leavenworth* ***(G-5220)***
Leavenwrth Tms/Chrncle Shopper, Leavenworth *Also called Gatehouse Media LLC* ***(G-5241)***
Leavenwrth-Knsas Cy Imaging PA 913 651-6066
10800 Farley St Ste 265 Overland Park (66210) ***(G-8951)***
Leawood Branch, Leawood *Also called Arvest Bank* ***(G-5330)***
Leawood Branch, Leawood *Also called Wells Fargo Bank National Assn* ***(G-5596)***
Leawood Ctr For Dntl Excllence 913 491-4466
11201 Nall Ave Ste 120 Shawnee Mission (66211) ***(G-11553)***
Leawood Family Care PA 913 338-4515
11301 Ash St Leawood (66211) ***(G-5453)***
Leawood Family Physicians 913 451-4443
7020 W 121st St Shawnee Mission (66209) ***(G-11554)***
Leawood Pediatrics LLC 913 825-3627
5401 College Blvd Ste 101 Leawood (66211) ***(G-5454)***
Leawood South Country Club 913 491-1313
12700 Overbrook Rd Shawnee Mission (66209) ***(G-11555)***
Lecompton Historical Soc Inc 785 887-6260
640 E Woodson Ave Lecompton (66050) ***(G-5611)***
Led Direct LLC 913 912-3760
735 Southwest Blvd Ste B Kansas City (66103) ***(G-4198)***
Led2 Lighting Inc (PA) 816 912-2180
600 Minnesota Ave Kansas City (66101) ***(G-4199)***
Ledic Management Group LLC 316 685-8768
1945 N Rock Rd Wichita (67206) ***(G-14943)***
Lee Wilson & Gurney 316 685-2245
1861 N Rock Rd Ste 320 Wichita (67206) ***(G-14944)***
Lee & Associates Kansas Cy LLC 913 890-2000
8700 State Line Rd Leawood (66206) ***(G-5455)***
Lee & Devlin DDS 316 685-2309
387 N Woodlawn St Wichita (67208) ***(G-14945)***
Lee Aerospace Inc 316 636-9200
9323 E 34th St N Wichita (67226) ***(G-14946)***
Lee Air Inc 316 524-4622
3000 S Hydraulic Wichita Wichita (67216) ***(G-14947)***
Lee Ann Britian Infant Dev Ctr 913 676-2253
9100 W 74th St Shawnee Mission (66204) ***(G-11556)***
Lee Apparel Company Inc (HQ) 913 789-0330
1 Lee Dr Shawnee Mission (66202) ***(G-11557)***
Lee Apparel Company Inc 913 384-4000
9001 W 67th St Shawnee Mission (66202) ***(G-11558)***
Lee Construction Inc 620 276-6811
1711 Eaman Rd Garden City (67846) ***(G-2222)***
Lee Construction Co 785 539-7961
3108 Heritage Ct Apt 45 Manhattan (66503) ***(G-6711)***
Lee Dental Laboratory 913 599-3888
24202 W 68th St Shawnee (66226) ***(G-10985)***
Lee Enterprises Incorporated 620 276-2311
204 E Fulton Ter Garden City (67846) ***(G-2223)***
Lee Haworth Construction Co 785 823-7168
348 E Avenue A Salina (67401) ***(G-10580)***
Lee Jeans Co, Shawnee Mission *Also called Lee Apparel Company Inc* ***(G-11558)***
Lee Jeans Company Inc (HQ) 913 384-4000
9001 W 67th St Merriam (66202) ***(G-7099)***
Lee Phillips Oil Company 316 681-4470
151 S Whittier Rd # 1400 Wichita (67207) ***(G-14948)***
Lee Reed Engraving Inc 316 943-9700
3417 W Central Ave Wichita (67203) ***(G-14949)***
Lee Richardson Zoo, Garden City *Also called City of Garden City* ***(G-2125)***

Lee Shafer Ricky 620 252-9126
1272 Cr 4500 Coffeyville (67337) ***(G-955)***
Leech Products, Hutchinson *Also called Barker B&C Investments LLC* ***(G-3215)***
Lees Energy Connection 913 682-3782
211 N 5th St Leavenworth (66048) ***(G-5267)***
Lees Printing Company Inc 913 371-0569
804 Central Ave Kansas City (66101) ***(G-4200)***
Legacy Bank, Colwich *Also called Colwich Financial Corp* ***(G-1092)***
Legacy Bank (HQ) 316 796-1221
3711 N Ridge Rd Wichita (67205) ***(G-14950)***
Legacy Bank 316 260-3755
7555 W 21st St N Wichita (67205) ***(G-14951)***
Legacy Bank 316 260-3711
3711 N Ridge Rd Wichita (67205) ***(G-14952)***
Legacy Community Foundation 620 221-7224
1216 Main St Winfield (67156) ***(G-16155)***
Legacy Financial Strategy LLC 913 403-0600
11300 Tomahawk Creek Pkwy # 190 Leawood (66211) ***(G-5456)***
Legacy Foods, Hutchinson *Also called CHS Inc* ***(G-3238)***
Legacy Home Inspections 913 484-4157
15301 W 87th St Ste 220 Lenexa (66219) ***(G-5965)***
LEGACY ON 10TH AVENUE, THE, Topeka *Also called Legacy On 10th Opco LLC* ***(G-12838)***
Legacy On 10th Opco LLC 785 233-8918
2015 Se 10th Ave Topeka (66607) ***(G-12838)***
Legacy Rgonal Cmnty Foundation, Winfield *Also called Legacy Community Foundation* ***(G-16155)***
Legacy Technologies Inc 913 432-2487
6700 W 47th Ter Shawnee (66203) ***(G-10986)***
Legacy Technologies LLC 913 432-2020
6700 W 47th Ter Shawnee Mission (66203) ***(G-11559)***
Legal Printing Company Inc 913 369-1623
15591 Cedar Ln Bonner Springs (66012) ***(G-559)***
Legend Senior Living LLC 316 337-5450
10604 E 13th St N Wichita (67206) ***(G-14953)***
Legend Senior Living LLC (PA) 316 616-6288
8415 E 21st St N Ste 100 Wichita (67206) ***(G-14954)***
Legends Drive Dental Ctr LLC 785 841-5590
4900 Legends Dr Lawrence (66049) ***(G-4992)***
Legends Printing & Graphics 620 225-0020
901 N 2nd Ave Dodge City (67801) ***(G-1396)***
Leidos Inc 913 317-5120
7015 College Blvd Shawnee Mission (66211) ***(G-11560)***
Leiker Propane, Claflin *Also called Brackeen Line Cleaning Inc* ***(G-839)***
Leiker Well Service Inc 620 793-2336
1200 Main St Great Bend (67530) ***(G-2602)***
Leiser Construction LLC 620 437-2747
1927 365th St Madison (66860) ***(G-6503)***
Leisure Homestead Association 620 234-5208
405 Grand Ave Stafford (67578) ***(G-12106)***
Leisure Homestead At St John 620 549-3541
402 N Santa Fe St Saint John (67576) ***(G-10355)***
LEISURE HOMESTEAD AT STAFFORD, Saint John *Also called Leisure Homestead At St John* ***(G-10355)***
Leisure Hotel Corporation 913 250-1000
120 Express Ln Lansing (66043) ***(G-4685)***
Leisure Hotel Corporation (PA) 913 905-1460
8725 Rosehill Rd Ste 300 Lenexa (66215) ***(G-5966)***
Leisure Hotel Corporation 316 832-9387
915 E 53rd St N Park City (67219) ***(G-9627)***
Leisure Hotel Corporation 620 225-3924
1708 W Wyatt Earp Blvd Dodge City (67801) ***(G-1397)***
Leisure Hotel Corporation 620 227-5000
2320 W Wyatt Earp Blvd Dodge City (67801) ***(G-1398)***
Leisure Hotel Corporation 620 275-5900
2502 E Kansas Ave Garden City (67846) ***(G-2224)***
Leisure Hotel Group Companies, Lenexa *Also called Leisure Hotel Corporation* ***(G-5966)***
Leisure Hotels LLC 913 905-1460
8725 Rosehill Rd Ste 300 Lenexa (66215) ***(G-5967)***
Leisure Operations LLC 718 327-5762
5211 W 103rd St Overland Park (66207) ***(G-8952)***
Leisure Time Products 620 308-5224
3305 Airport Dr Pittsburg (66762) ***(G-9894)***
Leisure-Lift, Kansas City *Also called Burke Inc* ***(G-3880)***
Leisureterrace LLC 773 945-1000
5211 W 103rd St Overland Park (66207) ***(G-8953)***
Leiszler Oil Co Inc (PA) 785 632-5648
8228 Southport Dr Manhattan (66502) ***(G-6712)***
Lena M Rush Scholarship Trust 620 326-3361
P.O. Box 398 Wellington (67152) ***(G-13511)***
Lenere LLC 785 320-0208
1213 N Pawnee Dr Saint Marys (66536) ***(G-10371)***
Lenexa Automotive Inc 913 492-8250
13311 Walnut St Shawnee Mission (66215) ***(G-11561)***
Lenexa Candlewood Suites, Lenexa *Also called Dab of Lenexa KS I LLC* ***(G-5799)***
Lenexa Chamber of Commerce 913 888-1414
11180 Lackman Rd Shawnee Mission (66219) ***(G-11562)***
Lenexa City Center Hotel Corp (PA) 913 742-7777
8741 Ryckert St Lenexa (66219) ***(G-5968)***

ALPHABETIC

Lenexa Community Center, Lenexa *Also called City of Lenexa* ***(G-5755)***
Lenexa Dental Group Chartered 913 888-8008
9430 Gillette St Ste 100 Shawnee Mission (66215) ***(G-11563)***
Lenexa Family Practice, Shawnee Mission *Also called Shawnee Mission Med Ctr Inc* ***(G-11860)***
Lenexa FDA Oc LLC 913 894-9735
11510 W 80th St Lenexa (66214) ***(G-5969)***
Lenexa Holiday Inn Express, Lenexa *Also called Dab of Lenexa KS II LLC* ***(G-5800)***
Lenexa Hotel LP (PA) 785 841-3100
730 New Hampshire St # 206 Lawrence (66044) ***(G-4993)***
Lenexa Hotel LP 913 217-1000
12601 W 95th St Lenexa (66215) ***(G-5970)***
Lenexa Services Inc 913 541-0150
7725 Renner Rd Shawnee (66217) ***(G-10987)***
Lenexa-Records Management, Shawnee Mission *Also called Meritex Enterprises Inc* ***(G-11617)***
Lennox Industries Inc 913 339-9993
11350 Strang Line Rd Shawnee Mission (66215) ***(G-11564)***
Lentz & Baker Eye Care (PA) 316 634-2020
1223 N Rock Rd Bldg C Wichita (67206) ***(G-14955)***
Leo J Debrabander Foundation 913 780-1600
21035 College Blvd Olathe (66061) ***(G-7858)***
Leo Nia's Crescent Limousines, Topeka *Also called Crescent Limousines* ***(G-12530)***
Leonard's Metal, Wichita *Also called LMI Aerospace Inc* ***(G-14972)***
Leonardville Nursing Home Inc 785 468-3661
409 W Barton Rd Leonardville (66449) ***(G-6249)***
Leons Welding & Fabrication 785 625-5736
1027 E Us Highway 40 Byp Hays (67601) ***(G-2863)***
Leoti Greentech Incorporated 620 375-2621
232 Kansas 96 Leoti (67861) ***(G-6255)***
Leroy Cook 316 321-0844
121 W Ash Ave El Dorado (67042) ***(G-1583)***
Leroy Cooperative Assn Inc (PA) 620 964-2225
505 E 6th St Le Roy (66857) ***(G-5196)***
Leslie Company Inc 913 764-6660
15290 S Keeler St Olathe (66062) ***(G-7859)***
Leslie D Boeckner 785 741-1036
710 N 1st St Hiawatha (66434) ***(G-3016)***
Lets Grow Preschool 913 262-2261
8718 W 62nd Ter Shawnee Mission (66202) ***(G-11565)***
Lets Help Inc 785 234-6208
200 S Kansas Ave Topeka (66603) ***(G-12839)***
Letts Vankirk and Associates, Kansas City *Also called Mid-America Pump LLC* ***(G-4244)***
Leukemia & Lymphoma Soc Inc 913 262-1515
6811 W 63rd St Ste 202 Shawnee Mission (66202) ***(G-11566)***
Leukemia Soc of Amrca, MD Amrc, Shawnee Mission *Also called Leukemia & Lymphoma Soc Inc* ***(G-11566)***
Level Devil, Wichita *Also called Electronic Sensors Inc* ***(G-14268)***
Level Five Solutions Inc 913 400-2014
7525 W 160th St Stilwell (66085) ***(G-12163)***
Lewer Agency Inc 816 753-4390
9900 W 109th St Ste 200 Overland Park (66210) ***(G-8954)***
Lewis & Ellis Inc 913 491-3388
11225 College Blvd # 320 Overland Park (66210) ***(G-8955)***
Lewis Auto & Truck Parts, Topeka *Also called Lewis Auto Salvage LLC* ***(G-12841)***
Lewis Auto Plaza Inc 785 266-8850
3206 Sw Topeka Blvd Topeka (66611) ***(G-12840)***
Lewis Auto Salvage LLC 785 233-0561
229 Ne Burgess St Topeka (66608) ***(G-12841)***
Lewis Brsbois Bsgard Smith LLP 316 609-7900
1605 N Waterfront Pkwy Wichita (67206) ***(G-14956)***
Lewis Collision Center, Topeka *Also called Lewis Auto Plaza Inc* ***(G-12840)***
Lewis Hoooper & Dick, Garden City *Also called Lewis Hooper & Dick LLC* ***(G-2225)***
Lewis Hooper & Dick LLC (PA) 620 275-9267
405 N 6th St Garden City (67846) ***(G-2225)***
Lewis Legal News Inc 913 780-5790
1701 E Cedar St Ste 111 Olathe (66062) ***(G-7860)***
Lewis Wheeler Lee Wheeler Ptr 620 544-8289
2044 Road H Hugoton (67951) ***(G-3171)***
Lewis-Goetz and Company Inc 316 265-4623
2113 S West St Ste 200 Wichita (67213) ***(G-14957)***
Lewonowski, Kris MD, Wichita *Also called Kansas Orthopedic Center PA* ***(G-14817)***
Lexinet Corporation 620 767-6346
701 N Union St Council Grove (66846) ***(G-1170)***
Lexington Farms, Overland Park *Also called Amli Management Company* ***(G-8383)***
Lexington Prk Nrsng Ctr, Topeka *Also called Midwest Health Services Inc* ***(G-12899)***
Lextron Animal Health, Garden City *Also called Animal Health Intl Inc* ***(G-2101)***
Lg Elctrnics Mbilecomm USA Inc 913 234-3701
6363 College Blvd Ste 220 Leawood (66211) ***(G-5457)***
LG Pike Construction Co Inc 620 442-9150
815 W Madison Ave Arkansas City (67005) ***(G-164)***
Libel & Ripple Dvm 620 227-2751
1007 E Trail St Dodge City (67801) ***(G-1399)***
Liberal Academy of Hair Design, Hays *Also called Hays Academy of Hair Design* ***(G-2827)***
Liberal Area Rape Crisis 620 624-3079
111 E 2nd St Liberal (67901) ***(G-6331)***
Liberal Country Club Assn 620 624-3992
339 W 18th St Liberal (67901) ***(G-6332)***
Liberal Gasket Mfg Co 620 624-4921
15 W 5th St Liberal (67901) ***(G-6333)***
Liberal Inn, Liberal *Also called Branding Iron Restaurant & CLB* ***(G-6286)***
Liberal Office Machines Co 620 624-5653
1015 N Kansas Ave Liberal (67901) ***(G-6334)***
Liberal School District 620 604-2400
624 N Grant Ave Liberal (67901) ***(G-6335)***
Liberal Street & Alley, Liberal *Also called City of Liberal* ***(G-6292)***
Liberal Super 8 Motel 620 624-8880
747 E Pancake Blvd Liberal (67901) ***(G-6336)***
Liberty Assisted Living Center 785 273-0886
5015 Sw 28th St Topeka (66614) ***(G-12842)***
Liberty Assisted Living Center 785 273-6847
4200 Sw Drury Ln Ofc Topeka (66604) ***(G-12843)***
Liberty Bank and Trust Company 913 321-7200
1314 N 5th St Kansas City (66101) ***(G-4201)***
Liberty Fruit Company Inc 913 281-5200
1247 Argentine Blvd Kansas City (66105) ***(G-4202)***
Liberty Hall Inc 785 749-1972
642 Massachusetts St Lawrence (66044) ***(G-4994)***
Liberty Hall Inc 785 749-1972
644 Massachusetts St Lawrence (66044) ***(G-4995)***
Liberty Hall Video, Lawrence *Also called Liberty Hall Inc* ***(G-4994)***
Liberty Healthcare of Oklahoma 785 823-7107
1007 Johnstown Ave Salina (67401) ***(G-10581)***
Liberty Inc (PA) 785 770-8788
8872 Green Valley Dr Manhattan (66502) ***(G-6713)***
Liberty Labels LLC 620 223-2208
2146 Native Rd Fort Scott (66701) ***(G-1981)***
Liberty Mutual Insurance Co 913 648-5900
10561 Barkley St Ste 400 Shawnee Mission (66212) ***(G-11567)***
Liberty Tax, Manhattan *Also called I 70 Tax Services LLC* ***(G-6663)***
Liberty Tax 913 384-1040
4994 Roe Blvd Roeland Park (66205) ***(G-10226)***
Liberty Tax Service 316 219-4829
1361 N West St Wichita (67203) ***(G-14958)***
Liberty Terrace Care Center 816 792-2211
10540 Barkley St Ste 280 Overland Park (66212) ***(G-8956)***
Licausi-Styers Company, Shawnee Mission *Also called Ls Construction Services Inc* ***(G-11580)***
Licausi-Styers Company 913 681-5888
8301 W 125th St Ste 210 Shawnee Mission (66213) ***(G-11568)***
Liebert Brothers Electric Co (PA) 620 251-0299
313 W 8th St 315 Coffeyville (67337) ***(G-956)***
Lies Trash Service LLC 316 522-1699
4631 S Palisade Ave Wichita (67217) ***(G-14959)***
Lif Inc 316 260-6092
2440 N Fountain St Wichita (67220) ***(G-14960)***
Life Care Center Burlington 620 364-2117
601 Cross St Burlington (66839) ***(G-638)***
Life Care Center of Andover, Andover *Also called Life Care Centers America Inc* ***(G-103)***
Life Care Center of Osawatomie, Osawatomie *Also called Life Care Centers America Inc* ***(G-8198)***
Life Care Center of Seneca, Seneca *Also called Life Care Centers America Inc* ***(G-10872)***
Life Care Center of Wichita, Wichita *Also called Life Care Centers America Inc* ***(G-14961)***
Life Care Centers America Inc 316 733-5376
621 W 21st St Andover (67002) ***(G-103)***
Life Care Centers America Inc 423 472-9585
7541 Switzer St Overland Park (66214) ***(G-8957)***
Life Care Centers America Inc 620 364-2117
601 Cross St Burlington (66839) ***(G-639)***
Life Care Centers America Inc 316 686-5100
622 N Edgemoor St Wichita (67208) ***(G-14961)***
Life Care Centers America Inc 913 755-4165
1615 Parker Ave Osawatomie (66064) ***(G-8198)***
Life Care Centers America Inc 785 336-3528
512 Community Dr Seneca (66538) ***(G-10872)***
Life Care Centers America Inc 913 631-2273
7541 Switzer St Shawnee Mission (66214) ***(G-11569)***
Life Care Ctr Shawnee Mission, Shawnee Mission *Also called Life Care Centers America Inc* ***(G-11569)***
Life Care Services LLC 785 762-2162
1417 W Ash St Junction City (66441) ***(G-3721)***
Life Span Institute, Lawrence *Also called University of Kansas* ***(G-5163)***
Life Star, Topeka *Also called Topeka Air Ambulance Inc* ***(G-13165)***
Life Time Fitness Inc 913 492-4781
16851 W 90th St Lenexa (66219) ***(G-5971)***
Life Time Fitness Inc 913 239-9000
6800 W 138th St Overland Park (66223) ***(G-8958)***
Life Touch Ems Inc 785 825-5115
901 E Crawford St Ste 300 Salina (67401) ***(G-10582)***
Lifeboat Creative, Wichita *Also called J2 Design Solutions LLC* ***(G-14741)***
Lifeline 800 635-6156
1500 Sw 10th Ave Topeka (66604) ***(G-12844)***
Lifesave, Wichita *Also called Airmd LLC* ***(G-13654)***

Lifesource Inc 913 660-9275
10606 Widmer Rd Lenexa (66215) *(G-5972)*
Lifespace Communities Inc 913 383-2085
8101 Mission Rd Apt 322 Shawnee Mission (66208) *(G-11570)*
Lifetouch Inc 316 262-6611
1803 S Eisenhower St Wichita (67209) *(G-14962)*
Lifeworks Chiropractic 913 441-2293
22742 Midland Dr Shawnee (66226) *(G-10988)*
Lift Inc 913 287-4343
5525 Kaw Dr Kansas City (66102) *(G-4203)*
Lift Truck Center Inc (HQ) 316 942-7465
4000 W 33rd St S Wichita (67215) *(G-14963)*
Ligand Pharmaceuticals Inc 785 856-2346
2029 Becker Dr Lawrence (66047) *(G-4996)*
Light Bulbs Etc Inc 913 894-9030
14821 W 99th St Shawnee Mission (66215) *(G-11571)*
Lighthouse Properties LLC (PA) 785 825-2221
500 Graves Blvd Salina (67401) *(G-10583)*
Lighthouse Properties LLC 316 260-8844
1550 N Waterfront Pkwy Wichita (67206) *(G-14964)*
Lightning Aerospace LLC 316 295-4670
6650 N Broadway Ave Park City (67219) *(G-9628)*
Lightning Creek, Caney *Also called Guest Home Estates (G-670)*
Lightning Grounds Services Inc (PA) 913 441-3900
8315 Monticello Rd Shawnee Mission (66227) *(G-11572)*
Lightning Ldscp & Irrigation, Shawnee Mission *Also called Lightning Grounds Services Inc (G-11572)*
Lightwild Inc 913 851-3000
7320 W 162nd St Overland Park (66085) *(G-8959)*
LIL CUB CHILDCARE, Sterling *Also called Child Care Services Strlng Inc (G-12114)*
Lil Sprouts Playcare LLC 785 343-7529
1250 E Commercial Rd Ottawa (66067) *(G-8283)*
Lil Toledo Lodge LLC 620 244-5668
10600 170th Rd Chanute (66720) *(G-739)*
Lil' Toledo Lodge, Chanute *Also called Lil Toledo Lodge LLC (G-739)*
Lilken Lllp 785 749-7555
3411 S Iowa St Lawrence (66046) *(G-4997)*
Limestone Feeders LLC 402 770-4118
3575 Jazmine Trl Beloit (67420) *(G-491)*
Linaweaver Construction Inc (PA) 913 351-3474
719 E Gilman Rd Lansing (66043) *(G-4686)*
Lincare Inc 316 684-4689
7777 E Osie St Ste 301 Wichita (67207) *(G-14965)*
Lincare Inc 913 438-8200
14333 W 95th St Lenexa (66215) *(G-5973)*
Lincoln Center Ob/Gyn, Topeka *Also called Lincoln Ctr Obstrcs/Gynclgy PA (G-12845)*
Lincoln County Hospital 785 524-4403
624 N 2nd St Lincoln (67455) *(G-6383)*
Lincoln Ctr Obstrcs/Gynclgy PA (PA) 785 273-4010
800 Sw Lincoln St Topeka (66606) *(G-12845)*
Lincoln Ctr Obstrcs/Gynclgy PA 785 273-4010
2830 Sw Urish Rd Topeka (66614) *(G-12846)*
Lincoln East Nursing Home, Wichita *Also called Beverly Enterprises-Kansas LLC (G-13844)*
Lincoln Fincl Advisors Corp 913 451-1505
10851 Mastin St Ste 950 Shawnee Mission (66210) *(G-11573)*
Lincoln Medical Clinic, Lincoln *Also called County of Lincoln (G-6380)*
Lincoln Sentinel Republican 785 524-4200
141 W Lincoln Ave Lincoln (67455) *(G-6384)*
Lindan Auto Mechanical & Body 913 722-4243
9200 W 57th St Shawnee Mission (66203) *(G-11574)*
Lindburg Vogel Pierc Faris Ch (PA) 620 669-0461
2301 N Halstead St Hutchinson (67502) *(G-3354)*
Linde Gas North America LLC 785 387-2281
W Hwy 4 Otis (67565) *(G-8240)*
Linder & Associates Inc 316 265-1616
840 N Main St Wichita (67203) *(G-14966)*
Linders Welding Inc 913 681-2394
19490 Metcalf Ave Stilwell (66085) *(G-12164)*
Lindsborg Community Hosp Assn 785 227-3308
605 W Lincoln St Lindsborg (67456) *(G-6400)*
Lindsborg Family Dental Care, Lindsborg *Also called Erik J Peterson DDS (G-6398)*
Lindsborg House, Lindsborg *Also called Multi Community Diversfd Svcs (G-6405)*
Lindsborg House 2 .... 785 227-3652
127 W Mcpherson St Lindsborg (67456) *(G-6401)*
Lindsborg II House, Lindsborg *Also called Lindsborg House 2 (G-6401)*
Lindsey Management Co Inc 316 788-3070
2600 N Triple Creek Dr Derby (67037) *(G-1258)*
Lindsey Masonry Co Inc 913 721-2458
4623 N 123rd Ter Kansas City (66109) *(G-4204)*
Lindweld, Topeka *Also called Matheson Tri-Gas Inc (G-12864)*
Lindyspring Systems,, Topeka *Also called John G Levin (G-12746)*
Line Central, Saint Marys *Also called Emotorpro (G-10362)*
Line Construction Company 913 341-1212
9119 Barton St Shawnee Mission (66214) *(G-11575)*
Line Medical Inc 316 262-3444
825 N Waco Ave Wichita (67203) *(G-14967)*
Lineage, Overland Park *Also called Avcorp Business Systems LLC (G-8415)*
Lineage, Overland Park *Also called Step Two Investments LLC (G-9357)*
Link Inc 785 625-6942
2401 E 13th St Hays (67601) *(G-2864)*
Linn Community Nursing Home 785 348-5551
612 3rd St Linn (66953) *(G-6408)*
Linn County Congregate Meals, Mound City *Also called Linn County Nutrition Project (G-7172)*
Linn County News, Pleasanton *Also called Linn County Publishing Inc (G-9997)*
Linn County Nutrition Project (PA) 913 795-2279
306 Main St Mound City (66056) *(G-7172)*
Linn County Printing, Pleasanton *Also called Walker Publishing Inc (G-10003)*
Linn County Publishing Inc 913 352-6235
808 Main St Pleasanton (66075) *(G-9997)*
Linn Energy Inc 620 657-8310
10565 E Road 20 Ulysses (67880) *(G-13305)*
Linn Post & Pipe Inc (PA) 785 348-5526
711 Horizon Cir Linn (66953) *(G-6409)*
Linn Valley Lake Property Assn 913 757-4591
9 Linn Valley Ave Linn Valley (66040) *(G-6414)*
Linn Wood Place Incorporated 785 945-3634
1509 Linn St Valley Falls (66088) *(G-13367)*
Linnwood Place, Valley Falls *Also called Linn Wood Place Incorporated (G-13367)*
Linsco Priovate Ledger, Salina *Also called Jack M Schwartz (G-10551)*
Linux New Media Usa LLC 785 856-3080
2721 W 6th St Ste D Lawrence (66049) *(G-4998)*
Linweld, Manhattan *Also called Matheson Tri-Gas Inc (G-6734)*
Linweld, Wichita *Also called Matheson Tri-Gas Inc (G-15019)*
Linweld, Salina *Also called Matheson Tri-Gas Inc (G-10594)*
Lion Nathan Usa Inc 913 338-4433
8717 W 110th St Ste 430 Overland Park (66210) *(G-8960)*
Lionsgate Pet Hospital 913 402-8300
14327 Metcalf Ave Overland Park (66223) *(G-8961)*
Lionshare Marketing Inc 913 631-8400
7830 Barton St Lenexa (66214) *(G-5974)*
Lippert Components Inc 785 282-6366
20090 Highway 281 Smith Center (66967) *(G-12037)*
Lippert Components Mfg Inc 323 663-1261
600 W 24th St North Newton (67117) *(G-7437)*
Lippert Components Mfg Inc 316 283-0627
600 W 24th St North Newton (67117) *(G-7438)*
Liquidynamics Inc 316 943-5477
2311 S Edwards St Wichita (67213) *(G-14968)*
Lisa R Gonzales DDS P C 913 299-3999
7503 Park St Shawnee (66216) *(G-10989)*
Lithko Contracting LLC 913 281-2700
10800 Lakeview Ave Lenexa (66219) *(G-5975)*
Litigation Insights Inc (PA) 913 339-9885
9393 W 110th St Ste 400 Overland Park (66210) *(G-8962)*
Little & Miller Chartered Inc 785 841-6245
645 Country Club Ter Lawrence (66049) *(G-4999)*
LITTLE ANGEL CHRISTIAN CENTER, Basehor *Also called Angel Little Learning Ctr Inc (G-372)*
Little Apple Brewing Company 785 539-5500
1110 Westloop Pl Manhattan (66502) *(G-6714)*
Little Apple Lanes 785 539-0371
515 Richards Dr Manhattan (66502) *(G-6715)*
Little Bldg Blocks Daycare LLC 913 856-5633
813 E Lincoln Ln Gardner (66030) *(G-2354)*
Little Creek Dairy 785 348-5576
1510 10th Rd Linn (66953) *(G-6410)*
Little Creek Trucking Inc 316 778-1873
13457 Sw 20th St Benton (67017) *(G-518)*
Little Giant Fittings Company 620 793-5399
11 Ne 50 Ave Great Bend (67530) *(G-2603)*
Little Hse On Prrie Museum Inc 559 202-8147
2507 Cr 3000 Independence (67301) *(G-3533)*
Little Joes Asphalt Inc 913 721-3261
610 N 134th St Bonner Springs (66012) *(G-560)*
Little Laundrymat, Shawnee Mission *Also called Bubble Rm Coin Ldry Dry Clean (G-11188)*
Little Learners, Bonner Springs *Also called A Step Above Academy-Wyandotte (G-538)*
Little Learners Early Childho 913 254-1818
26121 W Valley Pkwy Olathe (66061) *(G-7861)*
Little Soldier 785 845-1987
14187 N1 Rd Mayetta (66509) *(G-6915)*
Little Tots Montessori Corp (PA) 913 602-7923
3001 N 115th St Kansas City (66109) *(G-4205)*
Little Wnders Christn Day Care 913 393-3035
651 N Somerset Ter Ste C Olathe (66062) *(G-7862)*
Livengood Jl Farms Inc 785 399-2251
6020 Road 3 Kanorado (67741) *(G-3773)*
Livestock Exchange, Potwin *Also called Haw Ranch Feedlot 2 LLC (G-10007)*
Livestock Marketing Assn (PA) 816 891-0502
11501 Outlook St Ste 250 Leawood (66211) *(G-5458)*
Livestock Nutrition Center LLC 913 725-0300
11225 College Blvd # 220 Overland Park (66210) *(G-8963)*
Livewatch Security LLC 785 844-2130
522 W Bertrand Ave Saint Marys (66536) *(G-10372)*
Livewell Northwest Kansas Inc 785 460-8177
460 N Garfield Ave Colby (67701) *(G-1026)*

ALPHABETIC

Living Center Inc 620 665-2170
1701 E 23rd Ave Hutchinson (67502) ***(G-3355)***
Livingston Enterprises Inc 402 247-3323
56265 702nd Rd Mahaska (66955) ***(G-6506)***
Liz Gonzalez Examinetics Inc 913 748-2042
8900 Indian Creek Pkwy # 500 Overland Park (66210) ***(G-8964)***
Lk Architecture Inc (HQ) 316 268-0230
345 N Rverview St Ste 200 Wichita (67203) ***(G-14969)***
Lk Architecture/Mead & Hunt 316 268-0230
345 N Riverview St # 200 Wichita (67203) ***(G-14970)***
Lkq Corporation 785 862-0000
5725 Sw Topeka Blvd Topeka (66619) ***(G-12847)***
Lkq Keystone, Kansas City *Also called Keystone Automotive Inds Inc* ***(G-4174)***
Lkq Mid-America Auto Parts, Topeka *Also called Lkq Corporation* ***(G-12847)***
LLC Black Stone 816 519-5650
4759 Rainbow Blvd Ste A Westwood (66205) ***(G-13555)***
LLP Moss Adams 913 599-3236
7285 W 132nd St Ste 220 Overland Park (66213) ***(G-8965)***
Lmh, Lawrence *Also called Lawrence Memorial Hospital End* ***(G-4974)***
LMI Aerospace Inc 913 469-6400
11064 Strang Line Rd Lenexa (66215) ***(G-5976)***
LMI Aerospace Inc 620 378-4441
1075 Fillmore St Fredonia (66736) ***(G-2039)***
LMI Aerospace Inc 316 944-4143
2853 S Hillside St Wichita (67216) ***(G-14971)***
LMI Aerospace Inc 316 943-6059
2853 S Hillside St Wichita (67216) ***(G-14972)***
LMI Aerospace - Lenexa, Shawnee Mission *Also called Valent Arstrctres - Lenexa LLC* ***(G-11972)***
LMI Lenexa 913 491-6975
11064 Strang Line Rd Lenexa (66215) ***(G-5977)***
LMS Company LLC 913 648-4123
10005 Howe Dr Shawnee Mission (66206) ***(G-11576)***
Lo Mar Bowling Supply, Russell *Also called Lo-Mar Bowling Supply Inc* ***(G-10279)***
Lo-Mar Bowling Supply Inc 785 483-2222
341 S Fossil St Russell (67665) ***(G-10279)***
Local Gvernment Online Ind LLC 913 498-3468
25501 W Valley Pkwy # 300 Olathe (66061) ***(G-7863)***
Locamp LLC 913 287-4400
1333 Meadowlark Ln # 103 Kansas City (66102) ***(G-4206)***
Locke Equipment Sales Co 913 782-8500
15705 S Us 169 Hwy Olathe (66062) ***(G-7864)***
Lockhart Geophysical Company 785 625-9175
1846 250th Ave Hays (67601) ***(G-2865)***
Lockhart Geophysical Kans Inc 620 277-7771
2802 W Jones Ave Garden City (67846) ***(G-2226)***
Locknclimb LLC 620 331-8247
2500 W Laurel St Independence (67301) ***(G-3534)***
Lockpath Inc 913 601-4800
6240 Sprint Pkwy Ste 100 Overland Park (66211) ***(G-8966)***
Locks & Pulls Inc 913 381-1335
10333 Metcalf Ave Overland Park (66212) ***(G-8967)***
Lockton Affinity LLC 913 652-7500
10895 Lowell Ave Ste 300 Overland Park (66210) ***(G-8968)***
Lockwood Business Forms, Atchison *Also called Lockwood Company Inc* ***(G-241)***
Lockwood Company Inc (PA) 913 367-0110
8191 Pratt Rd Atchison (66002) ***(G-241)***
Lodge 785 594-0574
502 Ames St Baldwin City (66006) ***(G-365)***
LODGE 124, Hutchinson *Also called Masonic Lodge* ***(G-3366)***
Lodge of Overland Park LLC 913 648-8000
7575 W 106th St Overland Park (66212) ***(G-8969)***
Lodgeworks LP (PA) 316 681-5100
8100 E 22nd St N Bldg 500 Wichita (67226) ***(G-14973)***
Lodgeworks Partners LP 316 681-5100
8100 E 22nd St N Bldg 500 Wichita (67226) ***(G-14974)***
Lodgian Inc 785 841-7077
200 Mcdonald Dr Lawrence (66044) ***(G-5000)***
Lodging Enterprises Inc 620 326-8191
1177 E 16th St Wellington (67152) ***(G-13512)***
Lodging Enterprises LLC 785 852-4664
109 E Commerce St Sharon Springs (67758) ***(G-10900)***
Lodging Enterprises LLC (HQ) 316 630-6300
8080 E Central Ave # 180 Wichita (67206) ***(G-14975)***
Log-Tech Inc 785 625-3858
1011 240th Ave Hays (67601) ***(G-2866)***
Logan Business Machines Inc (PA) 785 233-1102
417b Ne Us Highway 24 Topeka (66608) ***(G-12848)***
Logan Contractors Supply Inc 913 768-1551
1325 S Enterprise St Olathe (66061) ***(G-7865)***
Logan County Health Services, Oakley *Also called Logan County Manor* ***(G-7480)***
Logan County Hospital 785 672-3211
211 Cherry Ave Oakley (67748) ***(G-7479)***
Logan County Manor 785 672-8109
615 Price Ave Oakley (67748) ***(G-7480)***
Logan Farms Inc 785 256-6334
20849 Massasoit Rd Eskridge (66423) ***(G-1868)***
Logan Funeral Home 785 689-4211
102 E Church St Logan (67646) ***(G-6426)***
Logan Manor Nursing Home, Logan *Also called City of Logan* ***(G-6422)***
Logan Street Finewood Products 316 266-4948
1824 E Douglas Ave Wichita (67214) ***(G-14976)***
Logic Extension Resources, Olathe *Also called PSI Services Inc* ***(G-8010)***
Logicsafari, Morland *Also called Applied Content RES Tech LLC* ***(G-7166)***
Logo Depot, Wichita *Also called Industrial Uniform Company LLC* ***(G-14688)***
Logo Indiana, Olathe *Also called Local Gvernment Online Ind LLC* ***(G-7863)***
Loma Vista Garden Center Inc 913 897-7010
1107 E 23rd St Ottawa (66067) ***(G-8284)***
Lone Pine AG Services Inc 785 887-6559
1557 E 100 Rd Lecompton (66050) ***(G-5612)***
Lone Star Industries Inc 913 422-1050
12200 Kaw Dr Bonner Springs (66012) ***(G-561)***
Lone Star Services LLC 620 626-7100
6116 Old Hwy 54 Liberal (67901) ***(G-6337)***
Lone Tree Retirement Center, Meade *Also called Meade Hospital District* ***(G-7052)***
Long Island Grain Co Inc 785 854-7431
Hwy 383 N Of Town Long Island (67647) ***(G-6428)***
Long Motor Corporation (PA) 913 541-1525
14600 W 107th St Lenexa (66215) ***(G-5978)***
Long Motor Corporation 913 541-1525
15450 W 108th St Lenexa (66219) ***(G-5979)***
Long Shot Enterprises LLC 785 493-0171
824 N 8th & 9th St # 9 Salina (67401) ***(G-10584)***
Long Shots Bar, Junction City *Also called Junction City Bowl Inc* ***(G-3703)***
Long Term Care Specialists LLC 620 326-0251
22 Sunset Rd Wellington (67152) ***(G-13513)***
Longfellow Foundation Inc (PA) 620 662-1228
909 Corey Rd Hutchinson (67501) ***(G-3356)***
Longfellow Foundations Nic, Hutchinson *Also called Longfellow Foundation Inc* ***(G-3356)***
Longford Rodeo LLC 785 388-2330
Rodeo Grounds Longford (67458) ***(G-6431)***
Longford Water Company LLC 785 388-2233
108 Main St Longford (67458) ***(G-6432)***
Loomis Armored Us LLC 316 267-0269
419 Wabash St Wichita (67214) ***(G-14977)***
Loper C-I Electric 316 263-1291
819 E Indianapolis St Wichita (67211) ***(G-14978)***
Loquient Inc 913 221-0430
2016 W 72nd Ter Shawnee Mission (66208) ***(G-11577)***
Loqvient Technology Services, Shawnee Mission *Also called Loquient Inc* ***(G-11577)***
Lorac Company Inc 316 263-2565
624 E Harry St Wichita (67211) ***(G-14979)***
Lord of Life Lutheran Church 913 681-5167
3105 W 135th St Leawood (66224) ***(G-5459)***
Lord of Life Pre School, Leawood *Also called Lord of Life Lutheran Church* ***(G-5459)***
Lords Diner 316 295-2122
2825 S Hillside St Wichita (67216) ***(G-14980)***
Lorenzetti, Lisa A, Leavenworth *Also called Womens Clinic Assoc PA* ***(G-5307)***
Los Primos Inc (PA) 785 527-5535
630 M St Belleville (66935) ***(G-460)***
Loud & Clear, Kansas City *Also called Mobile Fx Inc* ***(G-4266)***
Louis Dengel & Son Mortuary 785 242-2323
235 S Hickory St Ottawa (66067) ***(G-8285)***
Louisberg Square Apartments 913 381-4997
9301 Santa Fe Ln Overland Park (66212) ***(G-8970)***
Louisburg Chamber of Commerce 913 837-2826
16 S Broadway St Louisburg (66053) ***(G-6457)***
Louisburg Herald 913 837-4321
121 S Pearl St Paola (66071) ***(G-9570)***
Louisburg Residential Care Ctr, Louisburg *Also called Rh Montgomery Properties Inc* ***(G-6465)***
Louisburg Square Apartments, Shawnee Mission *Also called Price Brothers Realty Inc* ***(G-11751)***
Louisiana Southern Railroad 620 235-7360
4746 Quitman Hwy Pittsburg (66762) ***(G-9895)***
Loves Enterprise Inc 785 235-0479
916 Se 4th St Topeka (66607) ***(G-12849)***
Loves Travel Stops 785 263-3390
2322 Fair Rd Abilene (67410) ***(G-45)***
Loves Travel Stops 785 726-2561
200 Washington St Ellis (67637) ***(G-1649)***
Loves Travel Stops 620 872-5727
1720 S Main St Scott City (67871) ***(G-10820)***
Lovetts L P Gas & Fuel Service, Junction City *Also called Propane Central* ***(G-3742)***
Lovewell Marina & Grill Inc 785 753-4351
2400 250 Rd Webber (66970) ***(G-13484)***
Loving Arms Child Care Center 316 722-1912
1241 N Ridge Rd Wichita (67212) ***(G-14981)***
Loving Arms Chldcare Preschool, Junction City *Also called Loving Arms Daycare Ctrs Inc* ***(G-3722)***
Loving Arms Daycare Ctrs Inc 785 238-2767
1531 Saint Marys Rd Ste A Junction City (66441) ***(G-3722)***
Loving Heart 785 783-7200
4300 Sw Drury Ln Topeka (66604) ***(G-12850)***
Loving Touch Home Healthcare, Wichita *Also called Diversified Family Svcs LLC* ***(G-14215)***
Lovinggood, Thomas A, Olathe *Also called Orthosynetics Inc* ***(G-7965)***

Lowe Fryldnhoven Mds Chartered.....913 677-2508
8901 W 74th St Ste 356 Shawnee Mission (66204) ***(G-11578)***
Lowe-North Construction Inc.....913 592-4025
800 S A Line Dr Spring Hill (66083) ***(G-12087)***
Lowen Corporation.....620 663-2161
1501 N Halstead St Hutchinson (67501) ***(G-3357)***
Lowen Corporation (PA).....620 663-2161
1111 Airport Rd Hutchinson (67501) ***(G-3358)***
Lowen Sign Company, Hutchinson *Also called Lowen Corporation* ***(G-3358)***
Lower Heating & AC Inc.....785 357-5123
501 Se 17th St Topeka (66607) ***(G-12851)***
Lowes Home Centers LLC.....913 631-3003
16300 W 65th St Shawnee Mission (66217) ***(G-11579)***
Lowes Home Centers LLC.....316 773-1800
333 S Ridge Rd Wichita (67209) ***(G-14982)***
Lowes Home Centers LLC.....785 452-9303
3035 S 9th St Salina (67401) ***(G-10585)***
Lowes Home Centers LLC.....620 513-2000
1930 E 17th Ave Hutchinson (67501) ***(G-3359)***
Lowes Home Centers LLC.....316 684-3117
11959 E Kellogg Dr Wichita (67207) ***(G-14983)***
Lowes Home Centers LLC.....913 397-7070
13750 S Blackbob Rd Olathe (66062) ***(G-7866)***
Lowes Home Centers LLC.....785 273-0888
1621 Sw Arvonia Pl Topeka (66615) ***(G-12852)***
Lowes Home Centers LLC.....316 206-0000
424 W Patriot Ave Derby (67037) ***(G-1259)***
Lowes Home Centers LLC.....913 328-7170
6920 State Ave Kansas City (66102) ***(G-4207)***
Lowes Home Centers LLC.....913 261-1040
4960 Roe Blvd Roeland Park (66205) ***(G-10227)***
Lowes Home Centers LLC.....316 206-1030
2626 N Maize Rd Wichita (67205) ***(G-14984)***
Lowry Electric Co Inc.....316 838-4363
1524 W 29th St N Wichita (67204) ***(G-14985)***
Loyalty Properties LLC.....913 323-6850
9393 W 110th St Ste 500 Overland Park (66210) ***(G-8971)***
Loyd Builders Inc.....785 242-1213
2126 S Elm St Ottawa (66067) ***(G-8286)***
LP Technologies Inc.....316 831-9696
7330 W 13th St N Wichita (67212) ***(G-14986)***
LPI Information Systems.....913 381-9118
10020 Fontana Ln Overland Park (66207) ***(G-8972)***
Lpl Financial.....913 345-2908
6800 College Blvd Ste 200 Leawood (66211) ***(G-5460)***
Lq Management LLC.....913 492-5500
9461 Lenexa Dr Lenexa (66215) ***(G-5980)***
Lr Energy.....620 627-2499
211 W Myrtle St Independence (67301) ***(G-3535)***
Lrico Services LLC.....316 847-4800
2416 E 37th St N Wichita (67219) ***(G-14987)***
Lrm Industries Inc (PA).....785 843-1688
4705 Cherry Hills Ct Lawrence (66047) ***(G-5001)***
Lrs Financial, Overland Park *Also called Berkshire Risk Services LLC* ***(G-8441)***
Lrw Partnership, Syracuse *Also called R & H Implement Company Inc* ***(G-12230)***
Ls Construction Services Inc (PA).....913 681-5888
8301 W 125th St Ste 210 Shawnee Mission (66213) ***(G-11580)***
LSI Corporation.....316 201-2000
8200 E 34th Cir N # 2000 Wichita (67226) ***(G-14988)***
LSI International Inc.....913 894-4493
640 Miami Ave Kansas City (66105) ***(G-4208)***
LSI Logic, Wichita *Also called LSI Corporation* ***(G-14988)***
Lsl of Derby Ks LLC.....316 788-3739
445 N Westview Dr Derby (67037) ***(G-1260)***
Lsl of Kansas LLC.....785 527-5636
2626 Wesleyan Dr Belleville (66935) ***(G-461)***
Ltkansas, Topeka *Also called Lawyers Title of Kansas Inc* ***(G-12835)***
Lubrication Engineers Inc (PA).....800 537-7683
1919 E Tulsa St Wichita (67216) ***(G-14989)***
Lubrication Engineers Inc.....316 529-2112
1919 E Tulsa St Wichita (67216) ***(G-14990)***
Lucas Arts Hmnties Council Inc.....785 525-6118
213 S Main St Lucas (67648) ***(G-6473)***
Luce Press Clippings Inc.....785 232-0201
715 Sw Harrison St Topeka (66603) ***(G-12853)***
Lucity Inc.....800 492-2468
10561 Barkley St Ste 100 Overland Park (66212) ***(G-8973)***
Luco Manufacturing Co Inc.....620 273-6723
705 N Cottonwood St Strong City (66869) ***(G-12193)***
Ludwig Truck Line Inc.....620 878-4243
1164 Hwy 77 Florence (66851) ***(G-1929)***
Ludwikoski & Associates Inc.....913 879-2224
1920 143rd St Ste 140 Overland Park (66224) ***(G-8974)***
Luka Irrigation Systems Inc.....913 248-0400
7015 Martindale Rd Shawnee (66218) ***(G-10990)***
Luke Kushs Painting.....913 888-0230
9218 Metcalf Ave Ste 396 Shawnee Mission (66212) ***(G-11581)***
Lulu Mimi Hsclners Extrrdnaire.....913 649-6022
7620 Metcalf Ave Ste P Shawnee Mission (66204) ***(G-11582)***
Lulu Salon & Spa.....913 648-3658
4480 W 107th St Shawnee Mission (66207) ***(G-11583)***
Lumber One LLC.....913 583-9889
9800 Sunflower Rd De Soto (66018) ***(G-1206)***
Luminous Neon Inc (PA).....620 662-2363
1429 W 4th Ave Hutchinson (67501) ***(G-3360)***
Luminous Neon Inc.....785 842-4930
801 E 23rd St Lawrence (66046) ***(G-5002)***
Luminous Neon Inc.....785 823-1789
1500 W Schilling Rd Salina (67401) ***(G-10586)***
Luminous Neon Inc.....913 780-3330
1255 N Winchester St Olathe (66061) ***(G-7867)***
Luminous Neon Art Sign Systems, Hutchinson *Also called Luminous Neon Inc* ***(G-3360)***
Luminous Neon Art Sign Systems, Lawrence *Also called Luminous Neon Inc* ***(G-5002)***
Luminous Neon Art Sign Systems, Salina *Also called Luminous Neon Inc* ***(G-10586)***
Lungrin Dntl Assctes Chartered, Salina *Also called Jerry R Lundgrin DDS* ***(G-10554)***
Lusker Masonry.....620 231-9899
452 S 210th St Frontenac (66763) ***(G-2058)***
Lustercraft Plastics LLC.....316 942-8451
1818 S Meridian Ave Wichita (67213) ***(G-14991)***
Lutes, David W, Topeka *Also called Cardivsclar Thrcic Surgeons PA* ***(G-12445)***
Lutheran Home WA Keeney.....785 743-5787
320 South Ave Wakeeney (67672) ***(G-13389)***
Luthers Jerky USA, Le Roy *Also called Luthers Smokehouse Inc* ***(G-5197)***
Luthers Smokehouse Inc.....620 964-2222
98 W 6th St Le Roy (66857) ***(G-5197)***
Lutz Daily & Brain Llc.....913 831-0833
6400 Glenwood St Ste 200 Shawnee Mission (66202) ***(G-11584)***
Luxury Lawn & Landscape Inc.....785 233-5296
2015 Nw Brickyard Rd Topeka (66618) ***(G-12854)***
Lvt Trucking Inc.....913 233-2111
1401 Fairfax Traffic Way Kansas City (66115) ***(G-4209)***
Lw Holding Lc.....913 851-3000
7320 W 162nd St Overland Park (66085) ***(G-8975)***
Lybarger Oil Inc (PA).....785 448-5512
704 N Maple St Garnett (66032) ***(G-2381)***
Lyddon Aero Center Inc.....620 624-1646
757 Terminal Rd Liberal (67901) ***(G-6338)***
Lyerla Associates.....913 888-9247
11301 W 88th St Shawnee Mission (66214) ***(G-11585)***
Lyle Law LLC (PA).....913 225-6463
7270 W 98th Ter Ste 100 Overland Park (66212) ***(G-8976)***
Lynco Rec Inc.....620 231-2222
2406 N Broadway St Pittsburg (66762) ***(G-9896)***
Lyndon State Bank (PA).....785 828-4411
817 Topeka Ave Lyndon (66451) ***(G-6477)***
Lynk Inc.....913 492-9202
8241 Melrose Dr 43 Shawnee Mission (66214) ***(G-11586)***
Lynn Care LLC.....913 707-4639
6335 W 110th St Overland Park (66211) ***(G-8977)***
Lynn Care LLC.....913 491-3562
6600 College Blvd Ste 300 Overland Park (66211) ***(G-8978)***
Lynn Elc & Communications Inc.....785 843-5079
725 N 2nd St Ste K Lawrence (66044) ***(G-5003)***
Lynn Peavey Company, Lenexa *Also called Peavey Corporation* ***(G-6047)***
Lynn Tape & Label.....913 422-0484
11551 Kaw Dr Kansas City (66111) ***(G-4210)***
Lynn W ONeal.....785 841-2280
1112 W 6th St Ste 214 Lawrence (66044) ***(G-5004)***
Lynne M Schopper DDS PA.....913 451-2929
11313 Ash St Leawood (66211) ***(G-5461)***
Lynns Heavy Hauling LLC.....913 393-3863
22780 College Blvd Olathe (66061) ***(G-7868)***
Lyntec, Shawnee Mission *Also called R D C Inc* ***(G-11771)***
Lyntec Inc.....913 529-2233
8401 Melrose Dr Shawnee Mission (66214) ***(G-11587)***
Lyon County State Bank (PA).....620 342-3523
902 Merchant St Emporia (66801) ***(G-1787)***
Lyon County State Bank.....620 343-4444
527 Commercial St Emporia (66801) ***(G-1788)***
LYON'S FEDERAL SAVINGS, Lyons *Also called Lyons Federal Savings Assn* ***(G-6490)***
Lyons Daily News.....620 257-2368
210 W Commercial St Lyons (67554) ***(G-6489)***
Lyons Federal Savings Assn (PA).....620 257-2316
200 East Ave S Lyons (67554) ***(G-6490)***
Lyons Hospital, Lyons *Also called Hospital Dst 1 of Rice Cnty* ***(G-6485)***
Lyons Manufacturing Co Inc.....620 257-2331
711 E Main St Lyons (67554) ***(G-6491)***
Lyons Medical Center, Hutchinson *Also called Hutchinson Clinic PA* ***(G-3319)***
Lyons Salt Company.....620 257-5626
1660 Avenue N Lyons (67554) ***(G-6492)***
Lyons State Bank.....620 257-3775
101 E Main St Lyons (67554) ***(G-6493)***
M & A Barnett Trucking Inc.....785 673-4700
218 Main St Grainfield (67737) ***(G-2495)***
M & A Construction, Kansas City *Also called Paredes Construction Inc* ***(G-4312)***
M & D Excavating Inc.....785 628-3169
1116 E 8th St Hays (67601) ***(G-2867)***

M & D of Hays Incorporated 785 628-3169
1116 E 8th St Hays (67601) *(G-2868)*
M & J Electric Wichita LLC (PA) 316 831-9879
1444 S Saint Clair Ave D Wichita (67213) *(G-14992)*
M & K Daylight Donuts 913 495-2529
8736 Lackman Rd Shawnee Mission (66219) *(G-11588)*
M & S Trucks Inc 620 842-3764
632 S Jennings Ave Anthony (67003) *(G-129)*
M & W Mfg Inc 620 365-7456
129 N Kentucky St Iola (66749) *(G-3619)*
M A M, Le Roy *Also called Mid-American Machine & Eqp Inc (G-5199)*
M C M Restoration Company Inc (PA) 620 223-6602
2 N Main St Fort Scott (66701) *(G-1982)*
M D I, Cheney *Also called Manufacturing Development Inc (G-793)*
M E H Inc 785 235-1524
2828 Nw Button Rd Topeka (66618) *(G-12855)*
M H C Sterling, Leawood *Also called Southwest Sterling Inc (G-5555)*
M H P Management Services 913 441-0194
10011 Woodend Rd Edwardsville (66111) *(G-1508)*
M I F Inc (PA) 316 838-3970
5615 N Broadway Ave Park City (67219) *(G-9629)*
M I I Managing Group, Overland Park *Also called Mutualaid Exchange (G-9065)*
M I S, Wichita *Also called Martin Interconnect Svcs Inc (G-15011)*
M L K Child Development Center 785 827-3841
1215 N Santa Fe Ave Salina (67401) *(G-10587)*
M Motel, The, Stockton *Also called Rooks County Holdings LLC (G-12186)*
M P I, Kansas City *Also called Metal Panels Inc (G-4236)*
M P M, Wichita *Also called Machining Programming Mfg Inc (G-14998)*
M P M Services Inc 785 841-5797
600 Lawrence Ave Ste 2d Lawrence (66049) *(G-5005)*
M R I of Rock Creek 913 351-4674
712 1st Ter Ste B Lansing (66043) *(G-4687)*
M R Imaging Center LP 316 268-6742
928 N St Francis St Wichita (67214) *(G-14993)*
M Rocking Radio Inc (PA) 785 565-0406
1707 Thomas Cir Ste A Manhattan (66502) *(G-6716)*
M Rocking Radio Inc 620 225-8080
2601 Central Ave Ste C Dodge City (67801) *(G-1400)*
M Rocking Radio Inc 785 460-3306
1065 S Range Ave Colby (67701) *(G-1027)*
M Squared Financial LLC 913 745-7000
8340 Mission Rd Ste 240 Prairie Village (66206) *(G-10045)*
M T A A, Topeka *Also called Metropolitan Topeka Arprt Auth (G-12885)*
M W C Inc 316 267-7676
806 E Skinner St Wichita (67211) *(G-14994)*
M-Act, Marysville *Also called Marysvlle Area Cmnty Thtre Inc (G-6903)*
M-C Fabrication Inc 913 764-5454
15612 S Keeler Ter Olathe (66062) *(G-7869)*
M.A. Energy Resources, LLC, Overland Park *Also called Koppers Recovery Resources LLC (G-8926)*
M.E. Group, Overland Park *Also called Branchpattern Inc (G-8480)*
M6 Concrete Accessories Co Inc (PA) 316 263-7251
1040 S West St Wichita (67213) *(G-14995)*
M6 Concrete Accessories Co Inc 316 452-5466
933 Oil Hill Rd El Dorado (67042) *(G-1584)*
Maa Santoshi LLC 620 665-9800
1401 E 11th Ave Hutchinson (67501) *(G-3361)*
Maaco Auto Painting, Shawnee Mission *Also called A D L M LLC (G-11062)*
Maas Paint and Paper LLC 785 643-4790
4616 E 69th Ave Hutchinson (67502) *(G-3362)*
Mac Adams Recreation Center 316 265-6111
1329 E 16th St N Wichita (67214) *(G-14996)*
Mac Equipment Inc 785 284-2191
810 S Old 75 Hwy Sabetha (66534) *(G-10317)*
Mac Fasteners Inc 785 242-2538
1110 Enterprise St Ottawa (66067) *(G-8287)*
Mac Process, Sabetha *Also called Mac Equipment Inc (G-10317)*
Mac-Tech Inc (HQ) 620 326-5952
429 N West Rd Wellington (67152) *(G-13514)*
Maccallum Char RE Group 913 782-8857
1819 S Ridgeview Rd Olathe (66062) *(G-7870)*
Macconnell Enterprises LLC 785 885-8081
102 N Main St Natoma (67651) *(G-7231)*
Macfarlane Group LLC 913 825-1200
6950 W 56th St Shawnee Mission (66202) *(G-11589)*
Mach V 0082, Lenexa *Also called Fluidtech LLC (G-5861)*
Machine Design Services Inc 620 663-4949
225 N Main St South Hutchinson (67505) *(G-12060)*
Machine Works Inc (PA) 316 265-7997
710 E 17th St N Wichita (67214) *(G-14997)*
Machining Programming Mfg Inc 316 945-1227
2100 S West St Wichita (67213) *(G-14998)*
Mack McClain & Associates Inc (PA) 913 339-6677
15090 W 116th St Olathe (66062) *(G-7871)*
Mack Pickens General Cont 316 778-1131
207 N Main St Benton (67017) *(G-519)*
Mackie Clemens Fuel Company (PA) 785 242-2177
2526 Hwy 59 Ottawa (66067) *(G-8288)*
Macquarie Infrastructure 620 638-4339
1150 E 700th Ave Arcadia (66711) *(G-137)*
Macs Fence Inc 913 287-6173
6037 Speaker Rd Kansas City (66111) *(G-4211)*
Mad Dog Metal Inc 620 275-9685
3005 W Mary St Garden City (67846) *(G-2227)*
Madden-Mcfarland Interiors Ltd (PA) 913 681-2821
1903 W 135th St Leawood (66224) *(G-5462)*
Maderak Construction Co Inc 913 299-3929
220 S 74th St Kansas City (66111) *(G-4212)*
Maderak, J A Construction Co, Kansas City *Also called Maderak Construction Co Inc (G-4212)*
Madill Carbide Inc 316 263-9285
1504 E Waterman St Wichita (67211) *(G-14999)*
Madison Brothers Concrete Inc 620 224-6098
2461 Quail Rd Fort Scott (66701) *(G-1983)*
Madison Square Clubhouse, Fredonia *Also called City of Fredonia (G-2029)*
Madrigal & Associates Inc (PA) 316 265-5680
431 Lulu St Wichita (67211) *(G-15000)*
Magellan Midstream Partners LP 620 834-2205
1299 8th Ave McPherson (67460) *(G-6987)*
Magellan Pipeline Company LP 913 647-8400
401 E Donovan Rd Kansas City (66115) *(G-4213)*
Magellan Pipeline Company LP 913 647-8504
1090a Sunshine Rd Kansas City (66115) *(G-4214)*
Magellan Pipeline Company LP 913 310-7710
13424 W 98th St Shawnee Mission (66215) *(G-11590)*
Magellan Pipeline Company LP 316 321-3730
1309 Sunset Rd El Dorado (67042) *(G-1585)*
Magers Lodgings Inc 785 841-4994
2300 W 6th St Lawrence (66049) *(G-5006)*
Magic Distributors/Rms, Olathe *Also called McAfee Enterprises LLC (G-7880)*
Magna Infotech Ltd 203 748-7680
9300 W 110th St Ste 650 Overland Park (66210) *(G-8979)*
Magna Tech Inc 620 431-3490
4331 S Johnson Rd Chanute (66720) *(G-740)*
Magna Transportation, Chanute *Also called Magna Tech Inc (G-740)*
Magna-Plus, Kansas City *Also called Stouse LLC (G-4441)*
Magnatec Enginineer, Tonganoxie *Also called Energy and Envmtl Systems Inc (G-12260)*
Magnatech Engineering Inc 913 845-3553
1204 Tonganoxie Rd Tonganoxie (66086) *(G-12265)*
Magnum 913 783-4600
209 Central St Hillsdale (66036) *(G-3059)*
Magnum Systems Inc (PA) 620 421-5550
2205 Jothi Ave Parsons (67357) *(G-9707)*
Magnus Inc 620 793-9222
800 Washington St Great Bend (67530) *(G-2604)*
Magtek Inc 913 451-1151
9913 Pflumm Rd Lenexa (66215) *(G-5981)*
Mahaney Group Inc 316 262-4768
2822 N Mead St Wichita (67219) *(G-15001)*
MAI Excavating Inc 785 483-3387
906 W Witt Ave Russell (67665) *(G-10280)*
MAI Sky Systems Inc 785 825-9151
234 E Avenue A Salina (67401) *(G-10588)*
Maice, Maize *Also called Kearney Equipment LLC (G-6515)*
Maico Industries Inc 785 472-5390
936 Highway 14 Ellsworth (67439) *(G-1677)*
Maid Services Inc 785 537-6243
2049 Fort Riley Ln Manhattan (66502) *(G-6717)*
Maids, Wichita *Also called Residential Services Inc (G-15449)*
Mail Contractors of America 913 287-9811
250 S 59th Ln Kansas City (66111) *(G-4215)*
Mail Right, Wichita *Also called Copy Shop Inc (G-14100)*
Main Street Chanute Inc 620 431-0056
4 E Elm St Chanute (66720) *(G-741)*
Main Street Media Inc 785 483-2116
958 E Wichita Ave Russell (67665) *(G-10281)*
Main Street Salon and Spa, Garden City *Also called Design Court (G-2145)*
Maine Flame LLC 913 208-9484
20775 W 227th St Spring Hill (66083) *(G-12088)*
Mainline Hollowgraphic, Topeka *Also called Mainline Printing Inc (G-12856)*
Mainline Printing Inc 785 233-2338
3500 Sw Topeka Blvd Topeka (66611) *(G-12856)*
Mainstreet Credit Union 785 856-5200
901 Iowa St Ste A Lawrence (66044) *(G-5007)*
Mainstreet Federal Credit Un 785 856-5200
901 Iowa St Lawrence (66044) *(G-5008)*
Mainstreet Federal Credit Un (PA) 913 599-1010
13001 W 95th St Lenexa (66215) *(G-5982)*
Mainstreet Federal Credit Un 785 842-5657
1001 E 23rd St Lawrence (66046) *(G-5009)*
Mainstreet Federal Credit Un 913 754-3926
6025 Lamar Ave Shawnee Mission (66202) *(G-11591)*
Maintaince Shop, Shawnee Mission *Also called City of Overland Park (G-11230)*
Maintanence Shop, Andover *Also called Flint Hills National Golf Club (G-93)*
Maintenance Department, Manhattan *Also called Usd 383 Mnhttan Ogden Schl Dst (G-6839)*
Maintenance Dept, Wichita *Also called Rolling Hills Country Club (G-15479)*

Maison De Naissance Foundation 913 402-6800
5000 W 134th St Leawood (66209) *(G-5463)*
Majestic Franchising Inc 913 385-1440
14821 W 95th St Lenexa (66215) *(G-5983)*
Major Inc 316 265-7000
1449 S Osage St Wichita (67213) *(G-15002)*
Major Video of Kansas Inc 913 649-7137
6979 W 75th St Overland Park (66204) *(G-8980)*
Making The Mark Inc 913 402-8000
12120 State Line Rd 376 Shawnee Mission (66209) *(G-11592)*
Maksa, Leawood *Also called Mid-Amrca Kdny Stn Assctn LLC (G-5480)*
Malkin Properties LLC 913 262-2666
7200 Eby Ave Shawnee Mission (66204) *(G-11593)*
Mallery Clinic LLC 785 825-9024
655 S Santa Fe Ave Salina (67401) *(G-10589)*
Mallon Family LLC 620 342-6622
813 Graham St Emporia (66801) *(G-1789)*
Malm Construction Co 785 227-3190
530 E State St Ste 269 Lindsborg (67456) *(G-6402)*
Malone Finkle Echardt & Clns 913 322-1400
7780 W 119th St Overland Park (66213) *(G-8981)*
Mama Lupe's Tortilla Products, Moundridge *Also called Tortilla King Inc (G-7199)*
Mama Socorros 913 541-1074
8879 Lenexa Dr Overland Park (66214) *(G-8982)*
Mame Inc 620 964-2156
815 E 6th St Le Roy (66857) *(G-5198)*
Manchester Inc 913 262-0440
10573 Riley St Overland Park (66212) *(G-8983)*
Mane Event 785 827-1999
1529 W Crawford St Salina (67401) *(G-10590)*
Mane Thing 785 762-2397
902 W 7th St Junction City (66441) *(G-3723)*
Manhattan Broadcasting Co Inc 785 776-1350
2414 Casement Rd Manhattan (66502) *(G-6718)*
Manhattan Chamber of Commerce 785 776-8829
501 Poyntz Ave Manhattan (66502) *(G-6719)*
MANHATTAN COMMUNITY FOUNDATION, Manhattan *Also called Manhattan-City (G-6729)*
Manhattan Country Club Inc 785 539-7501
1531 N 10th St Manhattan (66502) *(G-6720)*
Manhattan Day Care & Lrng Ctr (PA) 785 776-5071
612 Poyntz Ave Manhattan (66502) *(G-6721)*
Manhattan Day Care Association, Manhattan *Also called Manhattan Day Care & Lrng Ctr (G-6721)*
Manhattan Emrgncy Shelter Inc 785 537-3113
416 S 4th St Manhattan (66502) *(G-6722)*
Manhattan Hampton Inn, Manhattan *Also called Rhw Management Inc (G-6792)*
Manhattan Martin Luther King J 785 410-4599
3418 Treesmill Cir Manhattan (66503) *(G-6723)*
Manhattan Medical Center Inc 785 537-2651
1133 College Ave Manhattan (66502) *(G-6724)*
Manhattan Mercury, Manhattan *Also called Seaton Publishing Co Inc (G-6798)*
Manhattan Oral Surgery & 785 477-4038
4201 Anderson Ave Ste E Manhattan (66503) *(G-6725)*
Manhattan Radiology LLP 785 539-7641
1133 College Ave Ste C143 Manhattan (66502) *(G-6726)*
Manhattan Rtrment Fndation Inc 785 537-4610
2121 Meadowlark Rd Manhattan (66502) *(G-6727)*
Manhattan Surgical Center, Manhattan *Also called Nueterra Holdings LLC (G-6763)*
Manhattan Town Center, Manhattan *Also called Mtc Development LLC (G-6755)*
Manhattan Trenching Inc 785 537-2330
805 Willard Pl Manhattan (66502) *(G-6728)*
MANHATTAN VISITORS BUREAU, Manhattan *Also called Manhattan Chamber of Commerce (G-6719)*
Manhattan Warehouse, Manhattan *Also called Unified School District 383 (G-6837)*
Manhattan-City 785 587-8995
555 Poyntz Ave Ste 269 Manhattan (66502) *(G-6729)*
Manildra Milling Corporation (HQ) 913 362-0777
4501 College Blvd Ste 310 Leawood (66211) *(G-5464)*
Mankato Livestock Comm Co, Mankato *Also called Mankato Livestock Inc (G-6860)*
Mankato Livestock Inc 785 378-3283
810 N Commercial St Mankato (66956) *(G-6860)*
Manko Corporation 785 825-1301
410 N Front St Salina (67401) *(G-10591)*
Manko Window Systems Inc 785 238-3188
2005 N Jackson St Junction City (66441) *(G-3724)*
Manko Window Systems Inc (PA) 785 776-9643
800 Hayes Dr Manhattan (66502) *(G-6730)*
Mann & Co Architects/Engineers 620 662-4493
1703 Landon St Hutchinson (67502) *(G-3363)*
Mann Fence Company Inc 913 782-2332
15415 S Us 169 Hwy Olathe (66062) *(G-7872)*
Manna Pro Products LLC 913 621-2355
3158 N 7th Street Trfy Kansas City (66115) *(G-4216)*
Manning Construction Co Inc 913 390-1007
1708 E 123rd St Olathe (66061) *(G-7873)*
Manning Music Inc 785 272-1740
3400 Sw 6th Ave Topeka (66606) *(G-12857)*
Manor At Grace Gardens, The, Shawnee Mission *Also called Baptist Senior Ministries (G-11150)*
Manor Care of Kansas Inc 316 684-8018
7101 E 21st St N Wichita (67206) *(G-15003)*
Manor Care of Kansas Inc 785 271-6808
2515 Sw Wanamaker Rd Topeka (66614) *(G-12858)*
Manor Care of Kansas Inc 913 383-2569
5211 W 103rd St Overland Park (66207) *(G-8984)*
Manor Care of Wichita Ks LLC 316 684-8018
7101 E 21st St N Wichita (67206) *(G-15004)*
Manor of Garnett Inc 785 448-2434
101 N Pine St Garnett (66032) *(G-2382)*
Manor of Liberal Inc 620 624-0130
1501 S Holly Dr Liberal (67901) *(G-6339)*
Manor of The Plains, Dodge City *Also called Presbyterian Manors Inc (G-1421)*
Manorcare Health Svcs Topeka, Topeka *Also called Manor Care of Kansas Inc (G-12858)*
Manorcare Health Svcs Wichita, Wichita *Also called Manor Care of Kansas Inc (G-15003)*
Manorcare Hlth Svcs Ovrland Pk, Overland Park *Also called Manor Care of Kansas Inc (G-8984)*
Manpower, Lawrence *Also called Topeka Services Inc (G-5141)*
Manpower, Lawrence *Also called Temporary Employment Corp (G-5134)*
Manpowergroup Inc 316 946-0088
800 E Douglas Ave Wichita (67202) *(G-15005)*
Mansfeild Agency, Hanover *Also called Blue Valley Insurance Agencies (G-2710)*
Manson Ward Legion/Sjcf, Wichita *Also called Schaefer Johnson Cox Frey (G-15526)*
Manufacture Precst-Prestrssed, Kansas City *Also called Omega Concrete Systems Inc (G-4293)*
Manufacturing, Dodge City *Also called Curtis Machine Company Inc (G-1338)*
Manufacturing Development Inc 316 542-0182
37515 W 15th St S Cheney (67025) *(G-793)*
Manufacturing Services Inc 316 267-4111
2239 S Mead St Wichita (67211) *(G-15006)*
Manufacturing Solutions Inc 316 282-0556
2320 N Oliver Rd Newton (67114) *(G-7375)*
Manweiler Chevrolet Co Inc 620 653-2121
271 S Main St Hoisington (67544) *(G-3069)*
Mapes & Miller CPA 785 877-5833
418 E Holme St Norton (67654) *(G-7448)*
Maple Gardens Apartments, Wichita *Also called Maple Gardens Assoc Ltd Partnr (G-15007)*
Maple Gardens Assoc Ltd Partnr 316 722-7960
10200 W Maple St Apt B109 Wichita (67209) *(G-15007)*
Maple Hills Healthcare Inc 913 383-2001
7600 Antioch Rd Overland Park (66204) *(G-8985)*
Maple Hts Nrsing Rhabilitation, Hiawatha *Also called Lafayette Life Plan Inc (G-3015)*
Maps Inc 913 599-0500
11630 W 85th St Lenexa (66214) *(G-5984)*
Mar Lan Construction LC 785 749-2647
1008 Nh St Ste 200 Lawrence (66044) *(G-5010)*
Mar-Beck Appliance Svc Co Inc (PA) 913 322-4022
17501 W 98th St Spc 17-56 Lenexa (66219) *(G-5985)*
Marais Des Cygnes Chapter Daug 913 898-3088
5630 W 2200 Rd Parker (66072) *(G-9658)*
Maranatha Kinderprep, Kansas City *Also called Full Faith Church of Love (G-4023)*
Marathon Reprographics Inc 816 221-7881
901 N 8th St Kansas City (66101) *(G-4217)*
Marble Products, Wichita *Also called Koken Manufacturing Co Inc (G-14892)*
Marc A Asher Md Comprehensi 913 945-9800
10730 Nall Ave Ste 200 Overland Park (66211) *(G-8986)*
Marc Gorges 316 630-0689
15 N High Dr Eastborough (67206) *(G-1476)*
March Inc 913 449-7640
101 S Kansas Ave Overland Park (66223) *(G-8987)*
March of Dimes Inc 913 469-3611
4400 College Blvd Ste 180 Overland Park (66211) *(G-8988)*
Marche Associates Inc 785 749-2925
123 W 8th St Ste 200 Lawrence (66044) *(G-5011)*
Marcus Mllchap RE Inv Svcs Inc 816 410-1010
7400 College Blvd Ste 105 Overland Park (66210) *(G-8989)*
Marel Inc (HQ) 913 888-9110
8145 Flint St Lenexa (66214) *(G-5986)*
Maria Court, Mulvane *Also called Maria Villa Inc (G-7221)*
Maria Villa Inc (PA) 316 777-1129
116 S Central Ave Mulvane (67110) *(G-7220)*
Maria Villa Inc 316 777-9917
633 E Main St Mulvane (67110) *(G-7221)*
Marian Clinic Inc 785 233-2800
3164 Se 6th Ave Topeka (66607) *(G-12859)*
MARIAN DENTAL CLINIC, Topeka *Also called Marian Clinic Inc (G-12859)*
Marianna Kstler Bch Museum Art, Manhattan *Also called Kansas State University (G-6680)*
Marick Inc 316 941-9575
13915 W 53rd St N Colwich (67030) *(G-1098)*
Marietta Kellogg & Price 785 825-5403
148 S 7th St Salina (67401) *(G-10592)*
Marietta Martin Materials Inc 620 736-2962
1900 Us Highway 400 St Severy (67137) *(G-10891)*
Marillac Center Inc (PA) 816 508-3300
8000 W 127th St Overland Park (66213) *(G-8990)*

ALPHABETIC

Marilyn M Wilder....316 283-8746
301 N Main St Ste 400 Newton (67114) *(G-7376)*
Marilynn's Place, Osage City *Also called Brown Management Inc (G-8181)*
Mariner LLC (PA)....913 647-9700
5700 W 112th St Ste 200 Leawood (66211) *(G-5465)*
Mariner Wealth Advisors, Leawood *Also called Mariner LLC (G-5465)*
Mariner Wealth Advisors LLC (PA)....913 904-5700
5700 W 112th St Ste 500 Overland Park (66211) *(G-8991)*
Marino & Associates Inc....816 478-1122
11221 Roe Ave Leawood (66211) *(G-5466)*
MARION COUNTY HOME CARE, Marion *Also called Hospital Dst 1 Marion Cnty (G-6873)*
Marion Die & Fixture, Marion *Also called Bradbury Co Inc (G-6866)*
Marion Manufacturing Inc....620 382-3751
201 S Coble St Marion (66861) *(G-6874)*
Mark 8 Inn Lc....316 265-4679
1130 N Broadway Ave Wichita (67214) *(G-15008)*
Mark A McCune....913 541-3230
10600 Quivira Rd 430450 Shawnee Mission (66215) *(G-11594)*
Mark Arts....316 634-2787
1307 N Rock Rd Wichita (67206) *(G-15009)*
Mark Boose....785 234-4808
623 S Kansas Ave Topeka (66603) *(G-12860)*
Mark Borecky Construction....620 259-6655
201 N Van Buren St Hutchinson (67501) *(G-3364)*
Mark C Jones....620 375-2357
612 E Orange St Leoti (67861) *(G-6256)*
Mark Debrabander Foundation Co....913 856-4044
31715 W 115th St Olathe (66061) *(G-7874)*
Mark G Romain, Olathe *Also called Olathe Animal Hospital Inc (G-7927)*
Mark H Armfield DDS....316 775-5451
2814 Ohio St Augusta (67010) *(G-333)*
Mark Hall DDS, Topeka *Also called Gary J Newman DDS PA (G-12633)*
Mark Hungerford MD....785 539-5949
1305 Westloop Pl Manhattan (66502) *(G-6731)*
Mark IV Associates LLC....913 345-2120
10965 Granada Ln Ste 300 Shawnee Mission (66211) *(G-11595)*
Mark Molos....913 962-2122
7230 Renner Rd Shawnee Mission (66217) *(G-11596)*
Mark R Davis DDS....316 684-8261
5805 E Central Ave Wichita (67208) *(G-15010)*
Mark Randolf....620 431-7788
3502 S Santa Fe Ave Chanute (66720) *(G-742)*
Mark S Humphrey MD....913 541-8897
10600 Quivira Rd Ste 130 Shawnee Mission (66215) *(G-11597)*
Mark S Jensen DDS PA....913 384-0600
8901 W 74th St Ste 245 Shawnee Mission (66204) *(G-11598)*
Mark Troilo DDS PA....316 776-2144
106 E Yeager St Rose Hill (67133) *(G-10242)*
Market, The, Topeka *Also called Ridge Auto Center (G-13018)*
Marketing Concepts....785 364-4611
2007 Frontage Rd Holton (66436) *(G-3104)*
Marketing Services of Kansas (PA)....913 888-4555
9903 Pflumm Rd Shawnee Mission (66215) *(G-11599)*
Marketing Technologies Inc....913 342-9111
550 Stanley Rd Kansas City (66115) *(G-4218)*
Marketsphere Consulting LLC....913 608-3648
9393 W 110th St Ste 430 Overland Park (66210) *(G-8992)*
Marketsphere Unclmed Prprty Sp, Overland Park *Also called Marketsphere Consulting LLC (G-8992)*
Marlatt Construction Co Inc....913 367-3342
17588 274th Rd Atchison (66002) *(G-242)*
Marlen Research Corp....913 888-3333
9202 Barton St Lenexa (66214) *(G-5987)*
Marlene Schoenberger....785 625-8189
106 W 10th St Ellis (67637) *(G-1650)*
Marley Cooling Tower Co Inc....913 664-7400
P.O. Box 25948 Overland Park (66225) *(G-8993)*
Marquee Event Rentals, Kansas City *Also called All Seasons Party Rental Inc (G-3798)*
Marquis Place Concordia LLc....785 243-2255
205 W 21st St Concordia (66901) *(G-1123)*
Marriott, Overland Park *Also called Woods of Cherry Creek Inc (G-9504)*
Marriott International Inc....913 451-8000
10800 Metcalf Ave Shawnee Mission (66210) *(G-11600)*
Marrones Inc....620 231-6610
800 E 14th St Pittsburg (66762) *(G-9897)*
Marroquin Express Inc....316 295-0595
6045 N Maize Rd Maize (67101) *(G-6516)*
Mars Chocolate North Amer LLC....785 861-1800
100 Mars Blvd Topeka (66619) *(G-12861)*
Marsh & McLennan Agency LLC....913 451-3900
4300 W 133rd St Leawood (66209) *(G-5467)*
Marshall County Agcy On Aging....785 562-5522
111 S 8th St Marysville (66508) *(G-6895)*
MARSHALL COUNTY BANK OF BEATTIE, Olathe *Also called Bank of Prairie (G-7548)*
Marshall Publishing Inc....620 278-2114
107 N Broadway Ave Sterling (67579) *(G-12125)*
Martech, Kansas City *Also called Marketing Technologies Inc (G-4218)*
Marten Transport Ltd....913 535-5255
2519 S 88th St Kansas City (66111) *(G-4219)*
Marten Transport Ltd....913 535-5259
10020 Woodend Rd Kansas City (66111) *(G-4220)*
Marten's Company, The, Wichita *Also called Hospitality Management LLC (G-14639)*
Martens Enterprises Inc....913 851-2772
2111 E Santa Fe St Stilwell (66085) *(G-12165)*
Martin & Son Logging, Lucas *Also called Martin James (G-6474)*
Martin Dysart Enterprises Inc....785 776-6731
1668 Hayes Dr Manhattan (66502) *(G-6732)*
Martin Interconnect Svcs Inc....316 616-1001
3001 E Harry St Wichita (67211) *(G-15011)*
Martin James....785 525-7761
354 W 290th Dr Lucas (67648) *(G-6474)*
Martin K EBY Cnstr Co Inc (HQ)....316 268-3500
2525 E 36th Cir N Wichita (67219) *(G-15012)*
Martin Luther Homes Kansas Inc....620 229-8702
2120 E 9th Ave Winfield (67156) *(G-16156)*
Martin Luther King Jr Child De....785 827-3841
1215 N Santa Fe Ave Salina (67401) *(G-10593)*
Martin Marietta Aggregates, Severy *Also called Marietta Martin Materials Inc (G-10891)*
Martin Marietta Aggregates, Ottawa *Also called Martin Marietta Materials Inc (G-8289)*
Martin Marietta Materials Inc....913 390-8396
14670 S Harrison St Olathe (66061) *(G-7875)*
Martin Marietta Materials Inc....785 242-3232
2807 Sand Creek Rd Ottawa (66067) *(G-8289)*
Martin Marietta Materials Inc....316 775-5458
7160 Sw Diamond Rd Augusta (67010) *(G-334)*
Martin Marietta Materials Inc....913 583-3311
34135 W 95th St De Soto (66018) *(G-1207)*
Martin Mobile Home Park Inc....620 275-4722
4101 E Us Highway 50 Ofc Garden City (67846) *(G-2228)*
Martin Peck Bea Anmal Shlter I....785 248-3454
3173 Highway K 68 Ottawa (66067) *(G-8290)*
Martin Pringle Oliver Wallace, Wichita *Also called Martin Pringle Olivr Wallace (G-15013)*
Martin Pringle Olivr Wallace (PA)....316 265-9311
100 N Broadway Ave # 500 Wichita (67202) *(G-15013)*
Martin Roofing Company Inc....316 524-3293
102 E Patterson St Wichita (67216) *(G-15014)*
Martin Southwest Trucking, Hugoton *Also called Southwest Express Inc (G-3176)*
Martin Trucking Inc....620 544-4920
1015 W City Limits St Hugoton (67951) *(G-3172)*
Martin Welding....620 545-7311
16401 W 55th St S Clearwater (67026) *(G-894)*
Martin-Logan Ltd....785 749-0133
2001 Delaware St Lawrence (66046) *(G-5012)*
Martindell Swearer Shaffer....620 662-3331
20 Compound Dr Hutchinson (67502) *(G-3365)*
Martinek & Flynn Wholesale Inc....785 233-6666
118 Sw Roby Pl Topeka (66612) *(G-12862)*
Martinez Inc....316 587-7814
5247 N Arkansas Ave Wichita (67204) *(G-15015)*
Martinous Produce Company Inc....620 231-5840
3510 Lone Star Pittsburg (66762) *(G-9898)*
Marvins Tow Service Inc (PA)....913 764-7630
15607 S Keeler St Olathe (66062) *(G-7876)*
Mary Carr....913 207-0900
2531 S 53rd St Kansas City (66106) *(G-4221)*
Mary Elizabeth Maternity Home....785 625-6800
204 W 7th St Hays (67601) *(G-2869)*
Mary Kate & Company LLC....316 721-4101
8112 W Central Ave Wichita (67212) *(G-15016)*
Marys Lake Lodge, Olathe *Also called Ep Resorts Inc (G-7689)*
Marysville Advocate, Marysville *Also called Advocate Publishing Co Inc (G-6878)*
Marysville Ambulance Service, Marysville *Also called Marysville Chamber Commerce (G-6896)*
Marysville Chamber Commerce....785 562-2359
410 N 6th St Marysville (66508) *(G-6896)*
Marysville Chamber Commerce (PA)....785 562-3101
101 N 10th St Marysville (66508) *(G-6897)*
Marysville Clinic....785 562-2744
1902 May St Marysville (66508) *(G-6898)*
Marysville Health Corporation....785 562-2424
1100 N 16th St Marysville (66508) *(G-6899)*
Marysville High, Marysville *Also called Marysville School District (G-6902)*
Marysville Livestock Inc....785 562-1015
1180 Us Highway 77 Marysville (66508) *(G-6900)*
Marysville Mutual Insurance Co....785 562-2379
1001 Broadway Marysville (66508) *(G-6901)*
Marysville School District....785 562-5386
1011 Walnut St Marysville (66508) *(G-6902)*
Marysville Super 8, Marysville *Also called Farmers Dream Inc (G-6888)*
Marysvlle Area Cmnty Thtre Inc....785 268-0420
2401 North St Marysville (66508) *(G-6903)*
Mas Cow Dairy LLC....620 626-7151
1699 Rd 20 Liberal (67901) *(G-6340)*
Mas Manufacturing, Overland Park *Also called Mid-America Fittings LLC (G-9024)*

Mason Stone Inc 316 744-3884
540 E 17th St N Wichita (67214) *(G-15017)*
Masonic Lodge 620 662-7012
1800 E 23rd Ave Hutchinson (67502) *(G-3366)*
Masonic Order 785 625-3127
107 W 11th St Fl 2 Hays (67601) *(G-2870)*
Masonic Temple, Hays *Also called Masonic Order (G-2870)*
Masonic Temple 620 342-3913
424 Merchant St Emporia (66801) *(G-1790)*
Masonite International Corp 620 231-8200
911 E Jefferson St Pittsburg (66762) *(G-9899)*
Masonry & Glass Systems Inc 913 748-6142
9024 Cody St Shawnee Mission (66214) *(G-11601)*
Mass Medical Storage LLC 913 438-8835
7848 Barton St Lenexa (66214) *(G-5988)*
Massachusetts Mutl Lf Insur Co 913 234-0300
10975 Benson Dr Ste 350 Overland Park (66210) *(G-8994)*
Massage Envy, Lenexa *Also called Gram Enterprises Inc (G-5879)*
Massman Construction Co (PA) 913 291-2600
4400 W 109th St Ste 300 Leawood (66211) *(G-5468)*
Massmutual, Overland Park *Also called Massachusetts Mutl Lf Insur Co (G-8994)*
Mast Trucking Inc 620 668-5121
31800 2 Rd Copeland (67837) *(G-1150)*
Master Maintance Services, Paola *Also called B J F Inc (G-9540)*
Master Paint Indus Coating, Newton *Also called Master Pnt Indus Coating Corp (G-7377)*
Master Pnt Indus Coating Corp 316 283-3999
1701 Se 9th St Newton (67114) *(G-7377)*
Master Teacher Inc (PA) 785 539-0555
2600 Leadership Ln Manhattan (66502) *(G-6733)*
Mastercraft Agency, Lawrence *Also called Mastercraft Corporation (G-5013)*
Mastercraft Corporation 785 842-4455
2601 Dover Sq Lawrence (66049) *(G-5013)*
Mastercraft Pattern Inc 620 231-3530
765 E 520th Ave Pittsburg (66762) *(G-9900)*
Masterhand Milling, Plains *Also called Elite Endeavors LLC (G-9974)*
Masterpiece Engineering LLC 928 771-2040
17400 W 119th St Olathe (66061) *(G-7877)*
Masthead International Inc (HQ) 913 888-8600
11145 Thompson Ave Lenexa (66219) *(G-5989)*
Matcalf Ridge Golf Club, Louisburg *Also called Ann N Hogan LLC (G-6438)*
Matcor Metal Fabrication, Independence *Also called Matsu Manufacturing Inc (G-3536)*
Materdei Childhood Center, Topeka *Also called Holy Name Church (G-12699)*
Material Control Systems, Shawnee Mission *Also called Control Systems Intl Inc (G-11264)*
Material Management Inc 620 221-9060
2016 Country Club Rd Winfield (67156) *(G-16157)*
Material Management Solutions, Salina *Also called MAI Sky Systems Inc (G-10588)*
Materials Transport Company 913 345-2030
11011 Cody St Shawnee Mission (66210) *(G-11602)*
Maternal Fetal Medicine Inc 316 962-7188
551 N Hillside St Ste 330 Wichita (67214) *(G-15018)*
Mather Flare Rental Inc (PA) 785 478-9696
7537 Sw Robinhood Ct Topeka (66614) *(G-12863)*
Mathes Early Learning Center, Topeka *Also called Seaman Unified School Dst 345 (G-13048)*
Matheson Tri-Gas Inc 785 537-0395
511 E Poyntz Ave Manhattan (66502) *(G-6734)*
Matheson Tri-Gas Inc 316 554-9353
1844 S Florence Ct Wichita (67209) *(G-15019)*
Matheson Tri-Gas Inc 785 234-3424
100 Se Madison St Topeka (66607) *(G-12864)*
Matheson Tri-Gas Inc 785 493-8200
100b E Avenue A Salina (67401) *(G-10594)*
Matrix Capital Group, Wichita *Also called Advisors Asset Management Inc (G-13631)*
Matsu Manufacturing Inc 620 331-8737
2400 W Laurel Independence (67301) *(G-3536)*
Maupin Truck Parts Inc 620 225-4433
Hwy 283 Dodge City (67801) *(G-1401)*
Maupin Western Star, Dodge City *Also called Maupin Truck Parts Inc (G-1401)*
Maurices 411, Garden City *Also called Maurices Incorporated (G-2229)*
Maurices Incorporated 620 275-1210
2206 E Kansas Ave Ste 9 Garden City (67846) *(G-2229)*
Maverick Floor Management, Shawnee *Also called Sam Carlini (G-11024)*
Mavicor LLC 888 387-1620
4425 Indian Creek Pkwy Overland Park (66207) *(G-8995)*
Max Jantz Excavating Inc 620 846-2634
26503 11 Rd Montezuma (67867) *(G-7158)*
Max Papay LLC 620 873-5350
14010 17th Rd Meade (67864) *(G-7050)*
Max RE Professional Inc 620 227-3629
1206 W Frontview St # 202 Dodge City (67801) *(G-1402)*
Max Rieke & Brothers Inc (PA) 913 631-7111
15400 Midland Dr Shawnee (66217) *(G-10991)*
Max Share Fund Inc 913 338-1100
4400 College Blvd Ste 250 Overland Park (66211) *(G-8996)*
Maxidize Production Svcs LLC 620 222-1235
12885 132nd Rd Winfield (67156) *(G-16158)*
Maxim Healthcare Services Inc 913 381-8233
10881 Lowell Ave Ste 100 Overland Park (66210) *(G-8997)*
Maxim Healthcare Services Inc 913 383-2220
10881 Lowell Ave Ste 100 Overland Park (66210) *(G-8998)*
Maxima Precision Inc 316 832-2211
3616 N Topeka St Wichita (67219) *(G-15020)*
Maximus Fitness and Wellness 785 267-2132
2061 Se 29th St Topeka (66605) *(G-12865)*
Maximus Fitness and Wellness (PA) 785 266-8000
2909 Sw 37th St Topeka (66614) *(G-12866)*
Maximus Fitness and Wellness 785 232-3133
2020 Nw Topeka Blvd # 200 Topeka (66608) *(G-12867)*
Maximus Fitness Wellness, Topeka *Also called Maximus Fitness and Wellness (G-12865)*
Maxines Inc 620 669-8189
2627 E 4th Ave Hutchinson (67501) *(G-3367)*
Mayberrys Inc 620 793-9400
3101 Washington St Great Bend (67530) *(G-2605)*
Mayhew Envmtl Training Assoc 800 444-6382
2200 W 25th St Lawrence (66047) *(G-5014)*
Maynard Early Childhood Center, Emporia *Also called Headstart Program (G-1768)*
Mazuma Credit Union (PA) 913 574-5000
7260 W 135th St Overland Park (66223) *(G-8999)*
MB Health Specialist Inc 913 438-6337
12345 W 95th St Ste 215 Shawnee Mission (66215) *(G-11603)*
MBB Advertising, Leawood *Also called MBB Inc (G-5469)*
MBB Inc 816 531-1992
5250 W 116th Pl Ste 200 Leawood (66211) *(G-5469)*
MBC Well Logging & Leasing 620 873-2953
21156 22 Rd Meade (67864) *(G-7051)*
Mbs Inc 913 393-2525
601 N Mur Len Rd Ste 16 Olathe (66062) *(G-7878)*
Mc Call Pattern Co, Manhattan *Also called McCall Pattern Company (G-6735)*
Mc Coy Company Inc 913 342-1653
3130 Brinkerhoff Rd Kansas City (66115) *(G-4222)*
Mc Coy Sales, Kansas City *Also called Mc Coy Company Inc (G-4222)*
Mc Dowell Rice Smith Buchanan 913 338-5400
7101 College Blvd Ste 200 Shawnee Mission (66210) *(G-11604)*
Mc Electric 913 721-2988
2701 S 96th St Kansas City (66111) *(G-4223)*
Mc Flooring, Shawnee *Also called Mo-Can Flooring Inc (G-10999)*
Mc Grew Realestate Inc (PA) 785 843-2055
1501 Kasold Dr Lawrence (66047) *(G-5015)*
Mc Intire Welding Inc 785 823-5454
1630 Copper Ct Salina (67401) *(G-10595)*
Mc Janitorial LLC 913 780-0731
118 N Emma St Olathe (66061) *(G-7879)*
Mc Kinnes Iron & Metal Inc 620 257-3821
316 N State St Lyons (67554) *(G-6494)*
Mc Pherson Area Solid Wast 620 585-2321
1431 17th Ave McPherson (67460) *(G-6988)*
Mc Pherson County Food Bank 620 241-8050
707 S Main St McPherson (67460) *(G-6989)*
Mc Pherson Eye Care LLP 620 241-2262
1323 E 1st St McPherson (67460) *(G-6990)*
Mc Pherson Wrecking Inc (PA) 785 246-3012
2333 Barton Rd Grantville (66429) *(G-2497)*
Mc Real Estate Service Inc 913 451-4466
8717 W 110th St Ste 240 Shawnee Mission (66210) *(G-11605)*
McAfee Enterprises LLC 913 839-3328
902 N Canyon Dr Olathe (66061) *(G-7880)*
McAfee Henderson Solutions Inc (PA) 913 888-4647
15700 College Blvd # 202 Lenexa (66219) *(G-5990)*
McAfee Henderson Solutions Inc 913 888-4647
15700 College Blvd # 202 Lenexa (66219) *(G-5991)*
McAlister Transportation LLC 620 326-2491
312 N Washington Ave Wellington (67152) *(G-13515)*
McAnany Construction Inc 913 631-5440
15320 Midland Dr Shawnee Mission (66217) *(G-11606)*
McAnany Van Cleave & Phillips 913 371-3838
10 E Cambridge Circle Dr # 300 Kansas City (66103) *(G-4224)*
McAnany Van Cleave Phillips PA (PA) 913 371-3838
10 E Cambridge Circle Dr # 300 Kansas City (66103) *(G-4225)*
McBride Construction Inc 620 544-7146
613 E 11th St Hugoton (67951) *(G-3173)*
McBride Electric, Wichita *Also called Critical Elc Systems Group LLC (G-14132)*
McC, Olathe *Also called Midcontinental Chemical Co Inc (G-7893)*
McCall Manor, Salina *Also called Windsor Estates Inc (G-10770)*
McCall Pattern Company 785 776-4041
615 Mccall Rd Manhattan (66502) *(G-6735)*
McCann Plumbing & Heating Inc 913 727-6225
4500 Brewer Pl Leavenworth (66048) *(G-5268)*
McCarthy Auto Grp, Olathe *Also called McCarthy Collision Center (G-7881)*
McCarthy Bldg Companies Inc 913 202-7002
7930 Santa Fe Dr Ste 200 Overland Park (66204) *(G-9000)*
McCarthy Collision Center 913 324-7300
1610 E Prairie St Olathe (66061) *(G-7881)*
McCarty Dairy LLC (PA) 785 465-9002
2231 County Road 31 Rexford (67753) *(G-10201)*
McCarty Family Farms LLC 785 465-9006
2231 County Road 31 Rexford (67753) *(G-10202)*

ALPHABETIC

McCarty Farms Scott City LLC...620 872-5661
6650 N Highway 83 Scott City (67871) ***(G-10821)***
McCarty Mechanical Inc...913 432-5100
5100 Merriam Dr Ste B Shawnee Mission (66203) ***(G-11607)***
McCarty Office Machines Inc (PA)...620 421-5530
1715 Main St Parsons (67357) ***(G-9708)***
McCartys...620 251-6169
214 W 9th St Coffeyville (67337) ***(G-957)***
McCartys Office Machines, Coffeyville *Also called McCartys* ***(G-957)***
McClain Medical Clinic, Ransom *Also called Grisell Memorial Hospital Assn* ***(G-10194)***
McClatchy Newspapers Inc...816 234-4636
8455 College Blvd Shawnee Mission (66210) ***(G-11608)***
McClelland Sound Inc...316 265-8686
345 N Ohio Ave Wichita (67214) ***(G-15021)***
MCCOLM POST 5, Emporia *Also called Ball-Mccolm Post No 5 Inc* ***(G-1701)***
McConnell Machinery Co Inc (PA)...785 843-2676
1111 E 23rd St Lawrence (66046) ***(G-5016)***
McCormick-Armstrong Co Inc (PA)...316 264-1363
1501 E Douglas Ave Wichita (67211) ***(G-15022)***
McCown Marketing LLC...913 284-5584
20924 Floyd St Bucyrus (66013) ***(G-602)***
McCoy Petroleum Corporation (PA)...316 636-2737
9342 E Central Ave Wichita (67206) ***(G-15023)***
McCray Lumber & Millwork, Olathe *Also called McCray Lumber Company* ***(G-7882)***
McCray Lumber Company...913 780-0060
15295 S Highway 169 Olathe (66062) ***(G-7882)***
McCray Lumber Company...913 321-8840
3200 Mccormick Rd Kansas City (66115) ***(G-4226)***
MCCRITE PLAZA RETIREMENT CENTE, Topeka *Also called McCrite Retirement Association* ***(G-12868)***
McCrite Retirement Association...785 267-2960
1608 Sw 37th St 1610 Topeka (66611) ***(G-12868)***
McCullough Developement Inc...785 776-3010
2700 Amherst Ave Manhattan (66502) ***(G-6736)***
McCullough Development Inc (PA)...888 776-3010
210 N 4th St Ste C Manhattan (66502) ***(G-6737)***
McCullough Enterprises Inc (PA)...316 942-8118
1750 S West St Wichita (67213) ***(G-15024)***
McCullough Excavation Inc...316 634-2199
9210 E 34th St N Wichita (67226) ***(G-15025)***
McCullough Property Management, Manhattan *Also called McCullough Development Inc* ***(G-6737)***
McCullough Wareheim & Labunker...785 233-2323
1507 Sw Topeka Blvd Topeka (66612) ***(G-12869)***
McCune Farmers Union Coop...620 632-4226
708 Main St Mc Cune (66753) ***(G-6920)***
McCurdy Auction LLC...316 683-0612
12041 E 13th St N Wichita (67206) ***(G-15026)***
McDaniel Co Inc...316 942-8325
4301 W Harry St Wichita (67209) ***(G-15027)***
McDaniel Kntson Fincl Partners, Lawrence *Also called McDaniel Knutson Inc* ***(G-5017)***
McDaniel Knutson Inc...785 841-4664
2500 W 31st St Ste B Lawrence (66047) ***(G-5017)***
McDonald Tinker Skaer Quinn...316 440-4882
300 W Douglas Ave Ste 500 Wichita (67202) ***(G-15028)***
McDonald Tank and Eqp Co Inc...620 793-3555
620 Morton St Great Bend (67530) ***(G-2606)***
McDonald Tank II...620 792-3661
470 C Ave Great Bend (67530) ***(G-2607)***
McDonalds Plaza LLC...913 362-1999
6310 Lamar Ave Ste 220 Overland Park (66202) ***(G-9001)***
McDs Clubhouse 5...620 504-6044
935 Clubhouse Dr McPherson (67460) ***(G-6991)***
McElroy Electric Inc...785 266-7111
3300 Sw Topeka Blvd Ste 1 Topeka (66611) ***(G-12870)***
McElroys Inc...785 266-4870
3310 Sw Topeka Blvd Topeka (66611) ***(G-12871)***
McFarlane Aviation Inc...785 594-2741
696 E 1700 Rd Baldwin City (66006) ***(G-366)***
McFarlane Aviation Products, Baldwin City *Also called McFarlane Aviation Inc* ***(G-366)***
McGhee and Associates LLC...785 341-2550
417 Firethorn Dr Manhattan (66503) ***(G-6738)***
McGinleys Crpt Pro Jantr Svcs...785 825-2627
2141 Centennial Rd Salina (67401) ***(G-10596)***
McGrath Publishing Company...785 738-2424
221 S Mill St Beloit (67420) ***(G-492)***
Mclcv Courtyard By Marriott...913 317-8500
11001 Woodson Ave Overland Park (66211) ***(G-9002)***
McInnes Group Inc (PA)...913 831-0999
4300 Shawnee Mission Pkwy # 100 Fairway (66205) ***(G-1913)***
McIntire Welding Service, Salina *Also called Mc Intire Welding Inc* ***(G-10595)***
McKee Pool & Landscaping Inc...785 843-9119
600 Lincoln St Lawrence (66044) ***(G-5018)***
McKee, Richard W CPA, Dodge City *Also called Kennedy Mc Kee and Company LLP* ***(G-1389)***
McKenzie Paint & Body Inc...620 662-3721
45 Kansas Ave South Hutchinson (67505) ***(G-12061)***
McKissick Enterprises LLC (PA)...316 687-0272
5520 E Central Ave Wichita (67208) ***(G-15029)***
McLa, Paola *Also called Paola Lifestock Auction Inc* ***(G-9581)***
McLane Company Inc...913 492-7090
16945 W 116th St Shawnee Mission (66219) ***(G-11609)***
McLane Foodservice Inc...913 422-6100
8200 Monticello Rd Lenexa (66227) ***(G-5992)***
McLaughlin Equipment, Cheney *Also called McLaughlin Leasing Inc* ***(G-794)***
McLaughlin Leasing Inc...316 542-0303
15775 Se 20 St Cheney (67025) ***(G-794)***
McLaughlin Roofing LLC...785 764-9582
3514 Elton Pkwy Ste 426a Oskaloosa (66066) ***(G-8229)***
McLiney Lumber and Supply LLC...913 766-7102
4200 W 83rd St Ste 200 Prairie Village (66208) ***(G-10046)***
McM, WA Keeney *Also called Midwest Contracting & Mfg* ***(G-13383)***
McM Manufacturing Inc (PA)...785 235-1015
2001 Nw Us Highway 24 Topeka (66618) ***(G-12872)***
McMc LLC...913 341-8811
9300 W 110th St Ste 520 Overland Park (66210) ***(G-9003)***
MCN Shawnee LLC...913 631-2100
7530 Cody St Shawnee (66214) ***(G-10992)***
McNish Foundations Inc...785 865-2413
1643 N 1300 Rd Lawrence (66046) ***(G-5019)***
McOn LLC...785 989-4550
1004 Vernon Rd Wathena (66090) ***(G-13475)***
McPherson & Mcvey Law Offices...620 793-3420
2109 12th St Great Bend (67530) ***(G-2608)***
McPherson Bd of Pub Utilities...620 245-2515
401 W Kansas Ave McPherson (67460) ***(G-6992)***
McPherson Branch, McPherson *Also called Emprise Bank* ***(G-6958)***
McPherson Care Center LLC...620 241-5360
1601 N Main St McPherson (67460) ***(G-6993)***
McPherson Con Stor Systems Inc (PA)...620 241-4362
116 N Augustus St McPherson (67460) ***(G-6994)***
McPherson Concrete Pdts Inc...620 241-1678
116 N Augustus St McPherson (67460) ***(G-6995)***
McPherson Contractors Inc...785 273-3880
3501 Sw Fairlawn Rd # 100 Topeka (66614) ***(G-12873)***
McPherson Country Club Inc...620 241-3541
1396 Pioneer Rd Mcpherson (67460) ***(G-6996)***
McPherson Custom Products, McPherson *Also called Chemstar Products Company* ***(G-6947)***
McPherson Daily Sentinel, McPherson *Also called Gatehouse Media LLC* ***(G-6968)***
McPherson Dairy Queen, McPherson *Also called R & K Horn LLC* ***(G-7021)***
McPherson Dental Care LLC (PA)...620 241-5000
700 N Maple St McPherson (67460) ***(G-6997)***
McPherson Development Co Inc...785 272-9521
3501 Sw Fairlawn Rd # 100 Topeka (66614) ***(G-12874)***
McPherson Ems, McPherson *Also called McPherson Hospital Inc* ***(G-7000)***
McPherson Family Clinic...785 861-8800
322 N Main St Ste 101 McPherson (67460) ***(G-6998)***
McPherson Family Ymca Inc...620 241-0363
220 N Walnut St McPherson (67460) ***(G-6999)***
McPherson Hospital Inc...620 241-0917
1000 Hospital Dr McPherson (67460) ***(G-7000)***
McPherson Opera House Company...620 241-1952
219 S Main St McPherson (67460) ***(G-7001)***
McPu Polymer Engineering LLC...620 231-4239
826 E 4th St Pittsburg (66762) ***(G-9901)***
McQuaid Brothers Rmdlg Co Inc...913 894-9128
7927 Bond St Shawnee Mission (66214) ***(G-11610)***
McQueeny Group Inc...913 396-4700
8820 Bond St Overland Park (66214) ***(G-9004)***
McShares Inc (PA)...785 825-2181
1835 E North St Salina (67401) ***(G-10597)***
McShares Inc...785 825-2181
1835 E North St Salina (67401) ***(G-10598)***
MD Associates 3 Inc...913 831-2996
5201 Johnson Dr Ste 450 Shawnee Mission (66205) ***(G-11611)***
MD Associates 4 Inc...913 831-2996
5201 Johnson Dr Ste 411 Shawnee Mission (66205) ***(G-11612)***
MD Management, Shawnee Mission *Also called MD Associates 4 Inc* ***(G-11612)***
MD Management, Shawnee Mission *Also called MD Associates 3 Inc* ***(G-11611)***
Mdc Drywall, Wichita *Also called Midwest Drywall Co Inc* ***(G-15092)***
Mdf Industries Inc...785 827-4450
1012 N Marymount Rd Salina (67401) ***(G-10599)***
Mead Lumber, Pratt *Also called Mead Rental Center* ***(G-10125)***
Mead Rental Center...620 672-7718
1502 E 1st St Pratt (67124) ***(G-10125)***
Meade Hospital District...620 873-2146
801 E Grant St Meade (67864) ***(G-7052)***
Meade Rural Health Clinic (PA)...620 873-2112
119 N Hart St Meade (67864) ***(G-7053)***
Meadowbrook Apartments...785 842-4200
2601 Dover Sq Lawrence (66049) ***(G-5020)***
Meadowlark Adult Care Home...316 773-2277
254 S Robin Rd Wichita (67209) ***(G-15030)***

Meadowlark Dairy Nutrition LLC 620 765-7700
330 S Us Highway 83 Garden City (67846) *(G-2230)*
Meadowlark Hill Apts, Shawnee Mission *Also called Nfi Management Co Inc (G-11684)*
Meadowlark Hills, Manhattan *Also called Manhattan Rtrment Fndation Inc (G-6727)*
Meadows Const Co Inc 913 369-3335
1014 Front St Tonganoxie (66086) *(G-12266)*
Meadows, The, Burlington *Also called Coffey County Hospital (G-629)*
Meals On Wheels, Wichita *Also called Senior Services Inc Wichita (G-15560)*
Meals On Whls of Shwnee & Jeff 785 354-5420
2701 Sw East Circle Dr S # 2 Topeka (66606) *(G-12875)*
MEALS-ON-WHEELS PROGRAM, Wichita *Also called Senior Services Inc Wichita (G-15559)*
Meara Welch Browne PC 816 561-1400
2020 W 89th St Ste 300 Leawood (66206) *(G-5470)*
Mechanical Engineering Tech, Shawnee Mission *Also called Spencer Reed Group LLC (G-11884)*
Mechanical Systems, Wichita *Also called Mechanics Inc (G-15032)*
Mechanical Systems Inc (PA) 316 262-2021
625 E 13th St N Wichita (67214) *(G-15031)*
Mechanics Inc 316 262-2021
625 E 13th St N Wichita (67214) *(G-15032)*
Med Care of Kansas Inc 785 295-8548
1505 Sw 6th Ave Topeka (66606) *(G-12876)*
Med Care of Kansas Inc (HQ) 785 295-8548
1700 Sw 7th St Topeka (66606) *(G-12877)*
Med James Inc (PA) 913 663-5500
8595 College Blvd Ste 200 Overland Park (66210) *(G-9005)*
Medallion Dental Lab Inc 913 642-0039
4650 W 90th Ter Prairie Village (66207) *(G-10047)*
Medart Inc 636 282-2300
9630 Woodend Rd Kansas City (66111) *(G-4227)*
Medart Engines Division, Kansas City *Also called Medart Inc (G-4227)*
Medevac Midamerica Inc 785 233-2400
401 Sw Jackson St Topeka (66603) *(G-12878)*
Medforce Technologies Inc 845 426-0459
2348 Sw Topeka Blvd # 103 Topeka (66611) *(G-12879)*
Medi Coach LLC 913 825-1945
12510 W 62nd Ter Ste 103 Shawnee (66216) *(G-10993)*
Medi-Weightloss Clinics LLC 316 733-8505
1145 N Andover Rd Ste 109 Andover (67002) *(G-104)*
Media Partners Inc 316 652-2210
15 E Douglas Ave Eastborough (67207) *(G-1477)*
Mediacorp LLC 913 317-8900
8712 W 151st St Overland Park (66221) *(G-9006)*
Mediacorp Marketing & Dist, Overland Park *Also called Mediacorp LLC (G-9006)*
Medica Lodges, Wamego *Also called Gran Villas of Wamego (G-13424)*
Medical ADM Svcs Ku Med Ctr, Westwood *Also called University of Kansas Med Ctr (G-13562)*
Medical Administrative K U Med 913 588-8400
3901 Rainbow Blvd Kansas City (66160) *(G-4228)*
Medical Arts Clinic-Emporia, Emporia *Also called Stormont-Vail Healthcare Inc (G-1830)*
Medical Arts Clnic A Prof Assn 620 343-2900
1301 W 12th Ave Ste 401 Emporia (66801) *(G-1791)*
Medical Assistance Progra 785 842-0726
303 W 11th St Lawrence (66044) *(G-5021)*
Medical Assoc Manhattan PA 785 537-2651
1133 College Ave Ste E110 Manhattan (66502) *(G-6739)*
Medical Associates Manhattan, Manhattan *Also called Stormont-Vail Healthcare Inc (G-6814)*
Medical Associates Manhattan, Manhattan *Also called Medical Assoc Manhattan PA (G-6739)*
Medical Center, Hutchinson *Also called William Unsderfer MD (G-3490)*
Medical Center P A (PA) 620 669-6690
104 Crescent Blvd Hutchinson (67502) *(G-3368)*
Medical Center P A 620 669-9657
104 Crescent Blvd Hutchinson (67502) *(G-3369)*
Medical Center West, Hutchinson *Also called Medical Center P A (G-3369)*
Medical Design Systems, Lenexa *Also called Mass Medical Storage LLC (G-5988)*
Medical Eqp Solutions Inc 816 241-3334
14116 Fontana St Leawood (66224) *(G-5471)*
Medical Equipment Exchange 913 451-2888
14170 W 107th St Shawnee Mission (66215) *(G-11613)*
Medical Heights Dental Center, Dodge City *Also called Kelly S Henrichs DDS (G-1388)*
Medical Heights Medical Center 620 227-3141
100 W Ross Blvd Ste 2a Dodge City (67801) *(G-1403)*
Medical Lodge Adult Care, Leavenworth *Also called Medicalodges Inc (G-5269)*
Medical Lodges, Holton *Also called Gran Villas of Holton Inc (G-3093)*
Medical Lodges Inc 620 325-2244
400 Fir St Neodesha (66757) *(G-7244)*
Medical Plaza Consultants P C 913 945-6900
10787 Nall Ave Ste 310 Overland Park (66211) *(G-9007)*
Medical Positioning Inc 816 474-1555
1146 Booth St Kansas City (66103) *(G-4229)*
Medical Society Sedgwick Cnty 316 683-7557
1102 S Hillside St Wichita (67211) *(G-15033)*
Medical Specialist 785 623-2312
2214 Canterbury Dr # 202 Hays (67601) *(G-2871)*
Medical-Surgical Eye Care PA 913 299-8800
8919 Parallel Pkwy # 226 Kansas City (66112) *(G-4230)*
Medicalodge Clay Center, Clay Center *Also called Medicalodges Inc (G-871)*
Medicalodge Construction Div, Coffeyville *Also called Medicalodges Inc (G-960)*
Medicalodge of Fort Scott, Fort Scott *Also called Medicalodges Inc (G-1985)*
Medicalodge of Goddard, Goddard *Also called Medicalodges Inc (G-2446)*
Medicalodge South, Pittsburg *Also called Medicalodges Inc (G-9902)*
Medicalodges Inc 620 223-5085
120 E Wall St Fort Scott (66701) *(G-1984)*
Medicalodges Inc 913 367-2077
1635 Riley St Atchison (66002) *(G-243)*
Medicalodges Inc 913 772-1844
1503 Ohio St Leavenworth (66048) *(G-5269)*
Medicalodges Inc 620 429-4317
101 Lee Ave Columbus (66725) *(G-1081)*
Medicalodges Inc 620 223-0210
915 Horton St Fort Scott (66701) *(G-1985)*
Medicalodges Inc (PA) 620 251-6700
201 W 8th St Coffeyville (67337) *(G-958)*
Medicalodges Inc 620 231-0300
2520 S Rouse St Pittsburg (66762) *(G-9902)*
Medicalodges Inc 620 429-2134
101 Lee Ave Columbus (66725) *(G-1082)*
Medicalodges Inc 785 742-4566
400 Kansas Ave Hiawatha (66434) *(G-3017)*
Medicalodges Inc 620 442-9300
203 E Osage Ave Arkansas City (67005) *(G-165)*
Medicalodges Inc 620 659-2156
620 Winchester Ave Kinsley (67547) *(G-4619)*
Medicalodges Inc 316 794-8635
501 Easy St Goddard (67052) *(G-2446)*
Medicalodges Inc 785 632-5696
715 Liberty St Clay Center (67432) *(G-871)*
Medicalodges Inc 620 583-7418
1020 N School St Eureka (67045) *(G-1894)*
Medicalodges Inc 620 251-3705
720 W 1st St Coffeyville (67337) *(G-959)*
Medicalodges Inc 913 367-6066
1637 Riley St Atchison (66002) *(G-244)*
Medicalodges Inc 620 251-6700
201 W 8th St Coffeyville (67337) *(G-960)*
Medicalodges Inc 316 755-1288
821 W 3rd St Valley Center (67147) *(G-13348)*
Medicalodges Arkansas City, Arkansas City *Also called Medicalodges Inc (G-165)*
Medicalodges Cnstr Co Inc 620 251-6700
201 W 8th St Coffeyville (67337) *(G-961)*
Medicalodges Frontenac 620 231-0322
206 S Dittman St Frontenac (66763) *(G-2059)*
Medicalodges of Coffeyville, Coffeyville *Also called Medicalodges Inc (G-959)*
Medicalodges of Columbus, Columbus *Also called Medicalodges Inc (G-1082)*
Medicalodges of Eureka, Eureka *Also called Medicalodges Inc (G-1894)*
Medicalodges of Kansas City 913 334-0200
6500 Greeley Ave Kansas City (66104) *(G-4231)*
Medicalodges of Kinsley, Kinsley *Also called Medicalodges Inc (G-4619)*
Medicalodges Post Center, Kansas City *Also called Medicalodges of Kansas City (G-4231)*
Medicap Pharmacy, Winfield *Also called 3c Healthcare Inc (G-16113)*
Medicare Advisors 365 LLC 866 956-0745
8523 Caenen Lake Ct Lenexa (66215) *(G-5993)*
Medicine Lodge Indian & Peace 620 886-9815
103 E Washington Ave Medicine Lodge (67104) *(G-7066)*
Medicine Lodge Memorial Hosp 620 886-3771
710 N Walnut St Medicine Lodge (67104) *(G-7067)*
Medina Logistics LLC 785 506-4002
3831 Sw Munson Ave Topeka (66604) *(G-12880)*
Mednax Inc 913 599-1396
12200 W 106th St Ste 110 Shawnee Mission (66215) *(G-11614)*
Medova Hlthcare Fncl Group LLC (PA) 316 616-6160
345 N Rverview St Ste 600 Wichita (67203) *(G-15034)*
Medplans Partners Inc 620 223-8200
3601 W 133rd St Shawnee Mission (66209) *(G-11615)*
Medtrak Services LLC 913 262-2187
7101 College Blvd # 1000 Overland Park (66210) *(G-9008)*
Medventures International Inc 785 862-2300
929 Sw University Blvd E2 Topeka (66619) *(G-12881)*
Meeker, Larry K, Wichita *Also called Stinson Leonard Street LLP (G-15674)*
Meemaws Country Kitchen 913 352-6297
602 Main St Pleasanton (66075) *(G-9998)*
Mega Manufacturing Inc (PA) 620 663-1127
1 N Main St Ste 604 Hutchinson (67501) *(G-3370)*
Mega Manufacturing Inc 620 663-1127
3310 E 4th Ave Hutchinson (67501) *(G-3371)*
Megaforce LLC (PA) 913 402-0800
4200 W 115th St Ste 300 Leawood (66211) *(G-5472)*
Meico Lamp Parts Company 913 469-5888
13840 W 108th St Shawnee Mission (66215) *(G-11616)*
Meiers Ready Mix Inc (PA) 785 233-9900
2013 Nw Lwer Silver Lk Rd Topeka (66618) *(G-12882)*
Meineke Car Care, Wichita *Also called R&B Services LLC (G-15407)*

Meitler Consulting Inc....913 422-9339
16979 Chieftain Rd Tonganoxie (66086) ***(G-12267)***
Mel Hambelton Ford Inc (PA)....316 462-3673
11771 W Kellogg St Wichita (67209) ***(G-15035)***
Mel Rick Inc....785 284-3577
P.O. Box 33 Sabetha (66534) ***(G-10318)***
Mel Stevenson & Associates Inc (PA)....913 262-0505
2840 Roe Ln Kansas City (66103) ***(G-4232)***
Mel Stevenson & Associates Inc....913 262-0505
2840 Roe Ln Kansas City (66103) ***(G-4233)***
Mel Stevenson & Associates Inc....316 262-5959
925 W Harry St Wichita (67213) ***(G-15036)***
Melissa Wilbert....316 361-2787
7907 W Birdie Lane Cir Wichita (67205) ***(G-15037)***
Mellies Products Inc....785 926-4331
307 Allen Ave Morganville (67468) ***(G-7165)***
Mels Pump & Plumbing....785 632-3392
208 S 6th St Clay Center (67432) ***(G-872)***
Mels Tire LLC....620 342-8473
915 Graham St Emporia (66801) ***(G-1792)***
Melvin Simon & Associates Inc....620 665-5307
1500 E 11th Ave Ste 400 Hutchinson (67501) ***(G-3372)***
Melvin Winger....620 492-6214
507 N Main Johnson (67855) ***(G-3658)***
Mem Industrial LLC (PA)....316 944-4400
2939 W Pawnee St Wichita (67213) ***(G-15038)***
Members Mortgage Services LLC....620 665-7713
200 E 1st Ave Hutchinson (67501) ***(G-3373)***
Memorial Adtrium Cnvention Ctr, Pittsburg *Also called City of Pittsburg* ***(G-9833)***
Memorial Health System, Abilene *Also called Hospital Dst 1 Dcknson Cnty Ka* ***(G-40)***
Memorial Hospital Fitness Ctr....785 263-3888
418 N Broadway St Abilene (67410) ***(G-46)***
Memorial Union Corp Emporia....620 341-5901
1200 Coml St Pmb 4066 4066 Pmb Emporia (66801) ***(G-1793)***
Memory and Music Inc....913 449-4473
11936 W 119th St Overland Park (66213) ***(G-9009)***
Memory Foam Liquidators, Topeka *Also called Mfl Inc* ***(G-12886)***
Men's Shelter, Wichita *Also called Union Rescue Mission Inc* ***(G-15839)***
Menard Incorporated....620 364-3600
1905 Us Highway 75 Burlington (66839) ***(G-640)***
Mennonite Bethesda Society....620 367-2291
408 E Main St Goessel (67053) ***(G-2458)***
Mennonite Church USA (PA)....316 283-5100
718 N Main St Newton (67114) ***(G-7378)***
Mennonite Frndship Communities (PA)....620 663-7175
600 W Blanchard Ave South Hutchinson (67505) ***(G-12062)***
Mennonite Frndship Communities....620 663-7175
606 Centre Ct Hutchinson (67505) ***(G-3374)***
Mennonite Gen Cnfrnce Cntl Off, Newton *Also called Mennonite Church USA* ***(G-7378)***
MENNONITE HOUSING, Wichita *Also called Kansas Affordable Housing Corp* ***(G-14785)***
Mennonite Media, Newton *Also called Mennonite Mission Network* ***(G-7379)***
Mennonite Mission Network....540 434-6701
718 N Main St Newton (67114) ***(G-7379)***
Mennonite Press Inc....316 283-3060
532 N Oliver Rd Newton (67114) ***(G-7380)***
Mennonite Union Aid....620 846-2286
102 E Parks Ave Montezuma (67867) ***(G-7159)***
Mennonite Weekly Review Inc....316 283-3670
129 W 6th St Newton (67114) ***(G-7381)***
Menorah Medical Ctr Cancer Ctr, Overland Park *Also called HCA Inc* ***(G-8800)***
Mental Health Amr, Kansas City *Also called Mental Health Association* ***(G-4234)***
Mental Health Association....913 281-2221
739 Minnesota Ave Kansas City (66101) ***(G-4234)***
Mental Health Association of (PA)....316 685-1821
555 N Woodlawn St # 3105 Wichita (67208) ***(G-15039)***
Mental Health Association of....316 651-5368
2332 N Pinecrest St Ofc Wichita (67220) ***(G-15040)***
Mental Hlth Ctr of Est-Cntral (PA)....620 343-2211
1000 Lincoln St Emporia (66801) ***(G-1794)***
Menufycom LLC (PA)....913 738-9399
6900 College Blvd Ste 500 Leawood (66211) ***(G-5473)***
Mer Sea, Lenexa *Also called Mer-Sea & Co LLC* ***(G-5994)***
Mer-Sea & Co LLC....816 974-3115
14832 W 107th St Lenexa (66215) ***(G-5994)***
Mercer Bus Service....785 836-7174
1252 W 141st St Carbondale (66414) ***(G-684)***
Mercer-Zimmerman Inc (PA)....913 438-4546
8981 Bond St Overland Park (66214) ***(G-9010)***
Merchants Automotive Group Inc....913 901-9900
6300 College Blvd Leawood (66211) ***(G-5474)***
Merchants First Pymnt Systems, Wellsville *Also called Q Solutions LLC* ***(G-13545)***
Merck Sharp & Dohme Corp....913 422-6001
35500 W 91st St De Soto (66018) ***(G-1208)***
Mercury Wireless Kansas LLC....800 354-4915
3301 S Kansas Ave Ste B Topeka (66611) ***(G-12883)***
Mercury Wireline....785 625-1182
1023 Reservation Rd Hays (67601) ***(G-2872)***
Mercy & Truth Med Missions Inc (PA)....913 248-9965
721 N 31st St Kansas City (66102) ***(G-4235)***
Mercy Clinic Glenn County, Pleasanton *Also called Mercy Kansas Communities Inc* ***(G-9999)***
Mercy Health....620 223-2200
401 Woodland Hills Blvd Fort Scott (66701) ***(G-1986)***
Mercy Hlth Fndtion Sthstern PA....620 223-2200
710 W 8th St Fort Scott (66701) ***(G-1987)***
Mercy Home Health....620 223-8090
901 Horton St Fort Scott (66701) ***(G-1988)***
Mercy Hosp Fdn of Independence....620 331-2200
800 W Myrtle St Independence (67301) ***(G-3537)***
Mercy Hospital, Fort Scott *Also called Mercy Kansas Communities Inc* ***(G-1989)***
Mercy Hospital, Independence *Also called Woodich John* ***(G-3574)***
Mercy Hospital, Independence *Also called Mercy Kansas Communities Inc* ***(G-3539)***
Mercy Hospital Inc....620 345-6391
218 E Pack St Moundridge (67107) ***(G-7188)***
MERCY HOSPITAL & SKILLED NURSI, Moundridge *Also called Mercy Hospital Inc* ***(G-7188)***
Mercy Hospital Columbus....620 429-2545
220 N Pennsylvania Ave Columbus (66725) ***(G-1083)***
Mercy Kansas Communities Inc (HQ)....620 223-7075
401 Woodland Hills Blvd Fort Scott (66701) ***(G-1989)***
Mercy Kansas Communities Inc....620 332-3215
422 W Main St Independence (67301) ***(G-3538)***
Mercy Kansas Communities Inc....620 332-3264
800 W Myrtle St Independence (67301) ***(G-3539)***
Mercy Kansas Communities Inc....913 352-8379
11155 Tucker Rd Pleasanton (66075) ***(G-9999)***
Mercy Physicans Group, Fort Scott *Also called Mercy Hlth Fndtion Sthstern PA* ***(G-1987)***
Mercy Physicians Group, Fort Scott *Also called Parris R David MD* ***(G-1997)***
Meredith Corporation....913 677-5555
4500 Shawnee Mission Pkwy Fairway (66205) ***(G-1914)***
Meriden Animal Hospital, Meriden *Also called Van Petten Animal Health Inc* ***(G-7083)***
Meridian Analytical Labs LLC....620 328-3222
111 E 5th St Mound Valley (67354) ***(G-7177)***
Meridian Chemicals LLC (HQ)....913 253-2220
10955 Lowell Ave Ste 600 Overland Park (66210) ***(G-9011)***
Meridian Nursing Center Inc....316 942-8471
1555 N Meridian Ave Wichita (67203) ***(G-15041)***
Meridianpro Inc....620 421-1107
3207 Grand Ave Parsons (67357) ***(G-9709)***
Merit Energy Company LLC....620 356-3032
446 S Road M Ulysses (67880) ***(G-13306)***
Merit Energy Company LLC....620 675-8372
703 W La Lande Ave Sublette (67877) ***(G-12205)***
Merit Energy Company LLC....620 629-4200
1900 W 2nd St Liberal (67901) ***(G-6341)***
Merit General Contractors....913 747-7400
16400 W 118th Ter Olathe (66061) ***(G-7883)***
Meritage Portfolio Management, Overland Park *Also called Eveans Bash Klein Inc* ***(G-8694)***
Meritex Enterprises Inc....913 888-0601
17501 W 98th St Spc 2632 Shawnee Mission (66219) ***(G-11617)***
Meritrust Credit Union....785 579-5700
343 E Chestnut St Junction City (66441) ***(G-3725)***
Meritrust Credit Union....785 320-7222
104 Mccall Rd Manhattan (66502) ***(G-6740)***
Meritrust Credit Union (PA)....316 683-1199
8710 E 32nd St N Wichita (67226) ***(G-15042)***
Meritrust Credit Union....316 219-7614
1257 N Buckner St Derby (67037) ***(G-1261)***
Meritrust Credit Union....316 683-1199
8015 E 22nd St N Wichita (67226) ***(G-15043)***
Meritrust Credit Union....316 761-4645
1322 W Pawnee St Wichita (67213) ***(G-15044)***
Meritrust Credit Union....316 761-4645
2900 S Oliver St Wichita (67210) ***(G-15045)***
Meritrust Credit Union....785 856-7878
650 Congressional Dr A Lawrence (66049) ***(G-5022)***
Merriam Office, Merriam *Also called Ent Assctes Greater Kans Cy PC* ***(G-7091)***
Merrifield Hotel Associates LP (HQ)....316 681-5100
8100 E 22nd St N Bldg 500 Wichita (67226) ***(G-15046)***
Merrill Lynch Pierce Fenner....316 631-3500
2959 N Rock Rd Ste 200 Wichita (67226) ***(G-15047)***
Merrill Lynch Pierce Fenner....913 906-5200
3401 College Blvd Leawood (66211) ***(G-5475)***
Merrill R Conant MD....620 227-6550
120 W Ross Blvd Dodge City (67801) ***(G-1404)***
Merry Maids, Salina *Also called Cs Cleaners Inc* ***(G-10469)***
Merry Maids, Wichita *Also called Grace of Wichita Ks LLC* ***(G-14489)***
Merry Maids, Manhattan *Also called Maid Services Inc* ***(G-6717)***
Merry Maids 391....785 273-3422
211 Sw 33rd St Topeka (66611) ***(G-12884)***
Merry Maids Ltd Partnership....913 403-0813
7959 Frontage Rd Overland Park (66204) ***(G-9012)***
Merry Maids Ltd Partnership....785 842-2410
2201 W 25th St Ste D Lawrence (66047) ***(G-5023)***
Merry X-Ray Chemical Corp....858 565-4472
11621 W 83rd Ter Overland Park (66214) ***(G-9013)***
Mersoft Corporation....913 871-6200
7007 College Blvd Ste 450 Leawood (66211) ***(G-5476)***

Meschke, John D, Hutchinson *Also called John D Meschke DDS PA* ***(G-3342)***
Mesler Roofing Co, Lawrence *Also called Scott Mesler* ***(G-5106)***
Messenger Lawn and Ldscpg LLC (PA)..........913 681-6165
19160 Metcalf Ave Stilwell (66085) ***(G-12166)***
Messenger Lawn and Ldscpg LLC..........913 681-6165
7360 W 162nd St Stilwell (66085) ***(G-12167)***
Messenger Petroleum Inc..........620 532-5400
525 S Main St Kingman (67068) ***(G-4606)***
Messer LLC..........785 387-2281
3805 Highway 4 Otis (67565) ***(G-8241)***
Messer LLC..........620 251-9190
210 Cedar St Coffeyville (67337) ***(G-962)***
Meta, Lawrence *Also called Mayhew Envmtl Training Assoc* ***(G-5014)***
Metal Arts LLC..........316 942-7958
3629 W 30th St S Wichita (67217) ***(G-15048)***
Metal Arts Engravers Inc..........913 262-1979
22615 W 46th Ter Shawnee (66226) ***(G-10994)***
Metal Arts Machine Co LLC..........316 425-2579
3921 N Bridgeport Cir Wichita (67219) ***(G-15049)***
Metal Cut To Length..........913 829-8600
700 S Rogers Rd Ste B Olathe (66062) ***(G-7884)***
Metal Finishing Co Inc (PA)..........316 267-7289
1423 S Mclean Blvd Wichita (67213) ***(G-15050)***
Metal Finishing Co Inc..........316 267-7289
1329 S Mclean Blvd Wichita (67213) ***(G-15051)***
Metal Finishing Company Inc..........316 267-7289
721 E Murdock St Wichita (67214) ***(G-15052)***
Metal Finishing Company Inc (PA)..........316 267-7289
1423 S Mclean Blvd Wichita (67213) ***(G-15053)***
Metal Finishing Company Inc..........620 326-7655
27 Clark Ave Wellington (67152) ***(G-13516)***
Metal Forming Incorporated..........620 488-3930
305 S Farmer St Belle Plaine (67013) ***(G-447)***
Metal Improvement Company LLC..........620 326-5509
440 N West Rd Wellington (67152) ***(G-13517)***
Metal Panels Inc..........913 766-7200
8341 Ruby Ave Kansas City (66111) ***(G-4236)***
Metal Pros LLC..........316 942-2238
4323 W Bounous St Wichita (67209) ***(G-15054)***
Metal-Fab Inc (PA)..........316 943-2351
3025 W May St Wichita (67213) ***(G-15055)***
Metal-Fab Inc..........316 943-2351
2013 S West St Wichita (67213) ***(G-15056)***
Metal-Fab Inc..........316 946-5875
2009 S West St Wichita (67213) ***(G-15057)***
Metalform Industries Inc..........316 945-6700
1721 S Eisenhower St Wichita (67209) ***(G-15058)***
Metalwest LLC..........913 829-8585
201 Leawood Dr New Century (66031) ***(G-7293)***
Metcalf 107 Animal Clinic Inc..........913 642-1077
6881 W 107th St Overland Park (66212) ***(G-9014)***
Metcalf Bank (HQ)..........913 648-4540
7840 Metcalf Ave Shawnee Mission (66204) ***(G-11618)***
Metcalf Bank..........913 685-3801
15100 Metcalf St Shawnee Mission (66204) ***(G-11619)***
Metcalf Bank..........913 782-6522
13446 S Blackbob Rd Olathe (66062) ***(G-7885)***
Metcalf Bank..........913 451-1199
7800 College Blvd Shawnee Mission (66210) ***(G-11620)***
Meter Engineers Inc..........316 721-4214
1600 E Tigua St Kechi (67067) ***(G-4572)***
Metland Group, The, Wichita *Also called Western Professional Assoc* ***(G-15961)***
MetLife, Overland Park *Also called Metropolitan Life Insur Co* ***(G-9016)***
MetLife, Shawnee Mission *Also called Metropolitan Life Insur Co* ***(G-11621)***
MetLife, Wichita *Also called Metropolitan Life Insur Co* ***(G-15061)***
Metro Air Conditioning Co..........913 888-3991
8151 Mccoy St Lenexa (66227) ***(G-5995)***
Metro Collision Repair Inc..........913 839-1044
2202 N Rogers Rd Olathe (66062) ***(G-7886)***
Metro Companies Inc..........316 838-3345
3518 N Ohio St Wichita (67219) ***(G-15059)***
Metro Park Warehouses Inc..........913 621-3116
251 S 55th St Kansas City (66106) ***(G-4237)***
Metro Park Warehouses Inc..........913 342-8141
4141 Fairbanks Ave Kansas City (66106) ***(G-4238)***
Metro Park Warehouses Inc..........913 287-7366
5020 Swartz Rd Kansas City (66106) ***(G-4239)***
Metro Tile Contractors Inc..........913 381-7770
10577 Widmer Rd Lenexa (66215) ***(G-5996)***
Metro Title Services LLC..........913 236-9923
8033 Flint St Lenexa (66214) ***(G-5997)***
METRO XPRESS, Wichita *Also called Metro Companies Inc* ***(G-15059)***
Metrocall..........316 634-1430
2260 N Ridge Rd Ste 100 Wichita (67205) ***(G-15060)***
Metropolitan Area Plannin, Wichita *Also called City of Wichita* ***(G-14024)***
Metropolitan Court Reporters..........913 317-8800
1880 College Blvd Ste 405 Overland Park (66210) ***(G-9015)***
Metropolitan Life Insur Co..........913 234-4800
10801 Mastin St Ste 550 Overland Park (66210) ***(G-9016)***
Metropolitan Life Insur Co..........913 451-8282
8717 W 110th St Ste 700 Shawnee Mission (66210) ***(G-11621)***
Metropolitan Life Insur Co..........316 688-5600
1938 N Woodlawn St # 304 Wichita (67208) ***(G-15061)***
Metropolitan Mortgage Corp..........913 642-8300
7381 W 133rd St Ste 200 Overland Park (66213) ***(G-9017)***
Metropolitan Spine Rehab PA..........913 387-2800
10777 Nall Ave Overland Park (66211) ***(G-9018)***
Metropolitan Topeka Arprt Auth..........785 862-2362
6510 Se Forbes Ave Topeka (66619) ***(G-12885)***
Meyer Truck Center Inc..........913 764-2000
19930 W 159th St Olathe (66062) ***(G-7887)***
Meyer Veterinary Hospital..........913 682-6000
3525 S 4th St Leavenworth (66048) ***(G-5270)***
Meyers Brothers Cnstr Co..........913 681-2667
19055 Metcalf Ave Stilwell (66085) ***(G-12168)***
Meyers Turf Farms Inc..........913 533-2456
12390 W 215th St Bucyrus (66013) ***(G-603)***
MFA Enterprises Inc..........620 237-4668
203 N Locust St Moran (66755) ***(G-7162)***
Mfg Solutions, Newton *Also called Manufacturing Solutions Inc* ***(G-7375)***
Mfl Inc..........785 862-2767
7215 Sw Topeka Blvd 5a Topeka (66619) ***(G-12886)***
Mgc, Olathe *Also called Minick Gambrell Contrs LLC* ***(G-7902)***
Mges LLC..........913 334-6333
640 Southwest Blvd Kansas City (66103) ***(G-4240)***
MGM Marketing Inc..........913 451-0023
12732 S Pflumm Rd Olathe (66062) ***(G-7888)***
Mgmttv Inc..........316 262-4678
245 N Waco St Ste 230 Wichita (67202) ***(G-15062)***
Mgp Ingredients Inc (PA)..........913 367-1480
100 Commercial St Atchison (66002) ***(G-245)***
Mgp Ingredients Inc..........913 367-1480
1300 Main St Atchison (66002) ***(G-246)***
Mgpi Processing Inc (HQ)..........913 367-1480
100 Commercial St Atchison (66002) ***(G-247)***
Mgpi Processing Inc..........913 367-1480
1300 Main St Atchison (66002) ***(G-248)***
Mha Residential Care Inc..........316 685-1821
555 N Woodlawn St Ste 120 Wichita (67208) ***(G-15063)***
Mhc Kenworth - Savannah, Leawood *Also called Georgia Kenworth Inc* ***(G-5411)***
Mhc Kenworth- Durham, Leawood *Also called North Carolina Kenworth Inc* ***(G-5503)***
Mhc Truck Leasing Inc (HQ)..........816 483-0604
11120 Tomahawk Creek Pkwy Leawood (66211) ***(G-5477)***
MHS Home Health LLC..........913 663-9930
8600 W 110th St Ste 210 Overland Park (66210) ***(G-9019)***
Ml Rancho Tequila Usa Inc..........913 530-7260
11005 Northridge Dr Kansas City (66109) ***(G-4241)***
Miami County Ambulance, Paola *Also called Miami County Emergency Med Svc* ***(G-9571)***
Miami County Emergency Med Svc..........913 294-5010
32765 Clover Dr Paola (66071) ***(G-9571)***
Miami County Medical Center..........913 791-4940
20375 W 151st St Ste 351 Olathe (66061) ***(G-7889)***
Miami County Medical Ctr Inc..........913 294-2327
2100 Baptiste Dr Paola (66071) ***(G-9572)***
Miami County Publishing Co, Paola *Also called Louisburg Herald* ***(G-9570)***
Miami County Publishing Co..........913 294-2311
121 S Pearl St Paola (66071) ***(G-9573)***
Miami County Republic, The, Paola *Also called Miami County Publishing Co* ***(G-9573)***
Miami Lumber Inc..........913 294-2041
1014 N Pearl St Paola (66071) ***(G-9574)***
Mias Bridal & Tailoring LLC..........913 764-9114
2235 E Kansas City Rd Olathe (66061) ***(G-7890)***
Michael A Dold DDS..........316 721-2024
7570 W 21st St N 1050b Wichita (67205) ***(G-15064)***
Michael Barber, Prairie Village *Also called Oral & Facial Surgery Assoc* ***(G-10054)***
Michael Bennett Trucking Inc..........785 336-2942
Hwy 36 W Seneca (66538) ***(G-10873)***
Michael Downey..........316 540-6166
4958 N Maize Rd Maize (67101) ***(G-6517)***
Michael E Evans CPA..........620 669-0461
2301 N Halstead St Hutchinson (67502) ***(G-3375)***
Michael E Fromholtz..........913 492-8290
13311 Walnut St Shawnee Mission (66215) ***(G-11622)***
Michael F Cassidy DDS..........785 233-0582
600 Sw Governor Vw Topeka (66606) ***(G-12887)***
Michael J Randall..........913 498-3636
4601 W 109th St Ste 250 Leawood (66211) ***(G-5478)***
Michael J Unrein Atty..........785 354-1100
100 Se 9th St Ofc Topeka (66612) ***(G-12888)***
Michael Kirkham & Assoc Inc..........785 472-3163
217 N Douglas Ave Ellsworth (67439) ***(G-1678)***
Michael L Sebes..........620 324-5509
1975 Us Highway 50 Lewis (67552) ***(G-6269)***
Michael P Harris Inc..........620 276-7623
218 E Fulton Ter Garden City (67846) ***(G-2231)***
Michael R Magee..........913 339-6551
123 Metcalf Ste 320 Shawnee Mission (66209) ***(G-11623)***

ALPHABETIC

Michael S Hundley Cnstr Inc 913 367-7059
1900 Main St Atchison (66002) ***(G-249)***
Michael S Klein DDS 913 829-4466
975 N Mur Len Rd Ste C Olathe (66062) ***(G-7891)***
Michael W Ryan Atty 785 632-5666
509 Court St Clay Center (67432) ***(G-873)***
Michael Yowell DDS PA 620 241-0842
1540 N Main St McPherson (67460) ***(G-7002)***
Michel Drywall LLC 316 260-6458
1913 N Ohio Ave Wichita (67214) ***(G-15065)***
Micro Air, Wichita *Also called Metal-Fab Inc* ***(G-15057)***
MICRO AIR - DIVISION OF METAL-, Wichita *Also called Metal-Fab Inc* ***(G-15055)***
Micro Center, Shawnee Mission *Also called Micro Electronics Inc* ***(G-11624)***
Micro Electronics Inc 913 341-4297
9294 Metcalf Ave Shawnee Mission (66212) ***(G-11624)***
Micro-Lite LLc 620 537-7025
Micro Lite St Buffalo (66717) ***(G-613)***
Microline Products, Norton *Also called Miltech Machine Corporation* ***(G-7450)***
Micros of Kansas City, Overland Park *Also called Hospitality Management Systems* ***(G-8828)***
Microsoft Corporation 913 323-1200
10801 Mastin St Ste 620 Overland Park (66210) ***(G-9020)***
Microtech Computers Inc 785 841-9513
4921 Legends Dr Lawrence (66049) ***(G-5024)***
Microtel Inn & Suites 620 331-0088
2917 W Main St Independence (67301) ***(G-3540)***
Microtool Inc 913 492-1588
14430 W 100th St Shawnee Mission (66215) ***(G-11625)***
Mid America Assc Computer Ed 785 273-3680
1301 Sw Ward Pkwy Topeka (66604) ***(G-12889)***
Mid America Cabling Comm, Kansas City *Also called Schultz Brothers Elc Co Inc* ***(G-4406)***
Mid America Cardiology, Leavenworth *Also called University of Kansas Hospital* ***(G-5303)***
Mid America Cardiology 913 588-9549
2330 Shawnee Mission Pkwy Westwood (66205) ***(G-13556)***
Mid America Crdiolgy Assoc PC 913 588-9600
2330 Shawnee Mission Pkwy Westwood (66205) ***(G-13557)***
Mid America Crdiolgy Assoc PC 913 588-9554
5799 Broadmoor St Shawnee Mission (66202) ***(G-11626)***
Mid America Crdiolgy Assoc PC (PA) 913 588-9600
3901 Rainbow Blvd G600 Kansas City (66160) ***(G-4242)***
Mid America Crdiolgy Assoc PC 913 588-9400
10787 Nall Ave Ste 300 Overland Park (66211) ***(G-9021)***
Mid America Credit Bureau LLC 913 307-0551
13021 W 95th St Ste A Lenexa (66215) ***(G-5998)***
Mid America Exteriors LLC 316 265-5444
1900 E Douglas Ave # 200 Wichita (67214) ***(G-15066)***
Mid America Eye Center Inc (PA) 913 384-1441
3830 W 75th St Prairie Village (66208) ***(G-10048)***
Mid America Graphics, Wichita *Also called Graphics Systems Inc* ***(G-14497)***
Mid America Ils Inc 620 792-1378
251 Nw 10 Ave Lot 4 Great Bend (67530) ***(G-2609)***
Mid America Pathology Lab LLC 913 341-6275
7301 College Blvd Ste 110 Overland Park (66210) ***(G-9022)***
Mid America Peripheral Support, Lenexa *Also called Maps Inc* ***(G-5984)***
Mid America Physicians Charter 913 422-2020
6815 Hilltop Rd Ste 100 Shawnee Mission (66226) ***(G-11627)***
Mid America Pipe Fabg Sup LLC 620 827-6121
2674 Nw Highway 102 Scammon (66773) ***(G-10796)***
Mid America Polyclinic PA 913 599-2440
7100 College Blvd Overland Park (66210) ***(G-9023)***
Mid America Power Sports, Valley Center *Also called K & N Motorcycles Corporation* ***(G-13346)***
Mid America Printed 913 432-2700
5401 Hayes St Merriam (66203) ***(G-7100)***
Mid America Products Inc 913 856-6550
800 N Center St Gardner (66030) ***(G-2355)***
Mid America Truss, Shawnee Mission *Also called Indevco Inc* ***(G-11454)***
Mid America Urology PC (PA) 913 948-8365
6740 W 121st St Ste 300 Leawood (66209) ***(G-5479)***
Mid American Credit Union (PA) 316 779-0052
8404 W Kellogg Dr Wichita (67209) ***(G-15067)***
Mid Amrica Prpts Pittsburg LLC 620 232-1678
1035 N Highway 69 Frontenac (66763) ***(G-2060)***
Mid Central Contract Svcs Inc 620 231-1166
450 E 540th Ave Pittsburg (66762) ***(G-9903)***
Mid Continent Anesthesiology 316 789-8444
3450 N Rock Rd Ste 208 Wichita (67226) ***(G-15068)***
Mid Continent Cabinetry, Newton *Also called Norcraft Companies LP* ***(G-7397)***
Mid Continent Controls Inc 316 789-0088
901 N River St Derby (67037) ***(G-1262)***
Mid Continent Farms 785 325-2089
400 E College St Washington (66968) ***(G-13469)***
Mid Continent Mfg., Wichita *Also called J Huston Howery* ***(G-14737)***
Mid Continent Transportation (PA) 620 793-3573
3711 Main St Great Bend (67530) ***(G-2610)***
Mid Family Practice PA, Hesston *Also called Mid Kansas Family Practice* ***(G-2997)***
Mid Kansas Cable Services Inc 620 345-2832
109 N Christian Ave Moundridge (67107) ***(G-7189)***
Mid Kansas Family Practice 620 327-2440
705 E Randall St Hesston (67062) ***(G-2997)***
Mid Kansas Machine Inc 620 241-2959
801 N Us Highway 81 Byp McPherson (67460) ***(G-7003)***
Mid Kansas Marine & Rv Inc (PA) 620 665-0396
517 E 4th Ave Hutchinson (67501) ***(G-3376)***
Mid Kansas Pediatric Assoc PA 316 773-3100
6837 W 37th St N Wichita (67205) ***(G-15069)***
Mid Kansas Pediatric Assoc PA (PA) 316 634-0057
9825 E Shannon Woods Cir Wichita (67226) ***(G-15070)***
Mid Kansas Tool & Electric Inc (PA) 785 825-9521
314 W Cloud St Salina (67401) ***(G-10600)***
Mid Kansas Tool and Electric, Salina *Also called Mid Kansas Tool & Electric Inc* ***(G-10600)***
Mid Knsas Drmtology Clinic P A 316 612-1833
1861 N Rock Rd Ste 310 Wichita (67206) ***(G-15071)***
Mid Land Seed, Haven *Also called Kauffman Seeds Inc* ***(G-2733)***
Mid Star Lab Inc (PA) 913 369-8734
1701 Commerce Rd Tonganoxie (66086) ***(G-12268)***
Mid States Fitness Equipment, Wichita *Also called Mid States Health Products* ***(G-15072)***
Mid States Hay Inc 620 355-7976
River Rd Lakin (67860) ***(G-4656)***
Mid States Health Products 316 681-3611
235 S Topeka Ave Wichita (67202) ***(G-15072)***
Mid West Color Graphics Inc 620 429-1088
500 S Railroad Ave Columbus (66725) ***(G-1084)***
Mid West Elc Transformers Inc 316 283-7500
1324 N Oliver Rd Newton (67114) ***(G-7382)***
Mid West Pnsion Administrators 913 663-2777
15641 S Mahafie St Shawnee Mission (66215) ***(G-11628)***
Mid West Ready Mix & Bldg Sups (PA) 785 284-2911
926 Grant St Sabetha (66534) ***(G-10319)***
Mid West Ready Mix & Bldg Sups 785 742-3678
1456 230th St Hiawatha (66434) ***(G-3018)***
Mid-AM Building Supply Inc 913 592-4313
20301 W 207th St Spring Hill (66083) ***(G-12089)***
Mid-AM Building Supply Inc 316 942-0389
601 S Anna St Wichita (67209) ***(G-15073)***
Mid-America AG Network Inc 316 721-8484
1632 S Maize Rd Ste 200 Wichita (67209) ***(G-15074)***
Mid-America Auto Auction Inc 316 500-7700
5817 E Kellogg Dr Wichita (67218) ***(G-15075)***
Mid-America Diabetes Assoc PA 316 687-3100
22015 W 101st St N Mount Hope (67108) ***(G-7206)***
Mid-America Fittings LLC 913 962-7277
7604 Wedd St Overland Park (66204) ***(G-9024)***
Mid-America Maintenance Kansas 620 365-3872
117 N Stanley St Gas (66742) ***(G-2391)***
Mid-America Mfg Tech Ctr Inc 913 649-4333
10550 Barkley St Ste 116 Overland Park (66212) ***(G-9025)***
Mid-America Millwright Svc Inc 620 275-6796
2720 N 11th St Garden City (67846) ***(G-2232)***
Mid-America Mnfct Hsng Cmmnts 913 441-0194
10011 Woodend Rd Kansas City (66111) ***(G-4243)***
Mid-America Nutrition Program (PA) 785 242-8341
117 S Main St Ottawa (66067) ***(G-8291)***
Mid-America Orthopedics PA (PA) 316 262-4886
1923 N Webb Rd Wichita (67206) ***(G-15076)***
Mid-America Orthopedics PA 316 440-1100
12112 W Us Highway 54 Wichita (67235) ***(G-15077)***
Mid-America Pump LLC 913 287-3900
5600 Inland Dr Kansas City (66106) ***(G-4244)***
Mid-America Redi-Mix Inc (PA) 620 663-1559
2510 W Blanchard Ave Hutchinson (67501) ***(G-3377)***
Mid-America Surgery Institute 913 906-0855
5525 W 119th St Ste 100 Overland Park (66209) ***(G-9026)***
Mid-America Toxicology Course, Leawood *Also called Curtis Klaassen* ***(G-5366)***
Mid-American Machine & Eqp Inc (PA) 620 964-2156
815 E 6th St Le Roy (66857) ***(G-5199)***
Mid-American Water & Plbg Inc 785 537-1072
5009 Murray Rd Manhattan (66503) ***(G-6741)***
Mid-Amrca Kdny Stn Assctn LLC 913 766-1860
10983 Granada Ln 110 Leawood (66211) ***(G-5480)***
Mid-Amrcan Dstrbtrs/Jyhawk RAD 913 321-9664
8022 Leavenworth Rd Kansas City (66109) ***(G-4245)***
Mid-Amrica Rhumatology Cons PA (PA) 913 661-9980
5701 W 119th St Ste 209 Overland Park (66209) ***(G-9027)***
Mid-Amrica Yuth Basketball Inc 316 284-0354
2309 S Kansas Rd Newton (67114) ***(G-7383)***
Mid-Cntinental Restoration Inc (PA) 620 223-3700
401 E Hudson St Fort Scott (66701) ***(G-1990)***
Mid-Continent AVI Svcs Inc 316 927-4204
1640 S Airport Rd Wichita (67209) ***(G-15078)***
Mid-Continent Harley-Davidson 316 440-5700
5427 N Chuzy Dr Park City (67219) ***(G-9630)***
Mid-Continent Industries Inc 316 283-9648
1801 Se 9th St Newton (67114) ***(G-7384)***
Mid-Continent Mfg & Sales, Wichita *Also called J Huston Howery* ***(G-14736)***
Mid-Continent Thermal-Guard 316 838-4044
1516 W 29th St N Wichita (67204) ***(G-15079)***
Mid-Kansas Cooperative Assn, Moundridge *Also called Haven Commodities Inc* ***(G-7185)***

Mid-Kansas Cooperative Assn (PA).....620 345-6328
307 W Cole St Moundridge (67107) ***(G-7190)***
Mid-Kansas Cooperative Assn.....785 776-9467
3384 Excel Rd Manhattan (66502) ***(G-6742)***
Mid-Kansas Cooperative Assn.....620 837-3313
100 Main St Walton (67151) ***(G-13401)***
Mid-Kansas Cooperative Assn.....785 227-3361
320 E Grant St Lindsborg (67456) ***(G-6403)***
Mid-Kansas Cooperative Assn.....785 227-3343
321 E Lincoln St Lindsborg (67456) ***(G-6404)***
Mid-Kansas Cooperative Assn.....620 465-2292
112 W 2nd St Haven (67543) ***(G-2734)***
Mid-Kansas Cooperative Assn.....620 345-6361
117 N Edwards Ave Moundridge (67107) ***(G-7191)***
Mid-Kansas Credit Union (PA).....620 543-2662
104 S Avenue B Moundridge (67107) ***(G-7192)***
Mid-Kansas Cylinder Head Inc.....620 241-6800
1308 1/2 N Us Hwy 81 Byp McPherson (67460) ***(G-7004)***
Mid-Kansas Machine & Tool.....316 777-1189
1057 E 147th Ave N Mulvane (67110) ***(G-7222)***
Mid-Kansas Womens Center PA.....316 685-3081
9300 E 29th St N Ste 201 Wichita (67226) ***(G-15080)***
Mid-Land Management Inc (PA).....785 272-1398
3501 Sw Fairlawn Rd Topeka (66614) ***(G-12890)***
Mid-South Milling Company Inc.....913 621-5442
213 Central Ave Kansas City (66118) ***(G-4246)***
Mid-State Aerospace Inc (PA).....913 764-3600
710 N Lindenwood Dr Olathe (66062) ***(G-7892)***
Mid-State Farmers Co-Op Inc (PA).....785 372-4239
819 W Un Rush Center (67575) ***(G-10261)***
Mid-States Energy Works Inc.....785 827-3631
618 N Santa Fe Ave Salina (67401) ***(G-10601)***
Mid-States Laboratories Inc (PA).....316 264-6758
216 E 1st St N Wichita (67202) ***(G-15081)***
Mid-States Laboratories Inc.....316 262-7013
600 N St Francis St Wichita (67214) ***(G-15082)***
Mid-States Materials LLC.....785 887-6038
18486 S Berryton Rd Scranton (66537) ***(G-10839)***
Mid-States Millwork Inc.....913 492-6300
9111 Cody St Overland Park (66214) ***(G-9028)***
Mid-West Conveyor Company.....734 288-4400
2601 S 90th St Kansas City (66111) ***(G-4247)***
Mid-West Electrical Supply Inc.....316 265-0562
925 N Mosley St Wichita (67214) ***(G-15083)***
Mid-West Fertilizer Inc.....620 431-3430
1971 S Country Club Rd Chanute (66720) ***(G-743)***
Mid-West Oilfield Service.....620 930-2051
1990 Se Us Highway 160 Medicine Lodge (67104) ***(G-7068)***
Midamerica Appraisals Inc.....620 231-0939
1800 E 4th St Pittsburg (66762) ***(G-9904)***
Midamerica Meter.....913 441-0790
6922 Martindale Rd Shawnee (66218) ***(G-10995)***
Midamerica Rehabilitation Ctr.....913 491-2432
5701 W 110th St Shawnee Mission (66211) ***(G-11629)***
MidAmerican Bank & Trust Co, Leavenworth *Also called Country Club Bank* ***(G-5226)***
MidAmerican Sales Group.....913 689-8505
2645 W 139th Ter Overland Park (66224) ***(G-9029)***
Midas Auto Repair, Leawood *Also called Midwest Dynamics Inc* ***(G-5483)***
Midas Auto Systems Experts.....316 636-9299
3330 N Rock Rd Wichita (67226) ***(G-15084)***
Midas Lenexa LLC.....913 225-9955
17190 W 87th St Lenexa (66219) ***(G-5999)***
Midas Muffler, Wichita *Also called Midas Auto Systems Experts* ***(G-15084)***
Midas Touch Golden Tans.....620 340-1011
2918 W Us Highway 50 F Emporia (66801) ***(G-1795)***
Midco Holdings LLC (HQ).....316 522-0900
8225 E 35th St N Wichita (67226) ***(G-15085)***
Midco Plastics Inc.....785 263-8999
801 S Bluff St Enterprise (67441) ***(G-1855)***
Midcontinent Communications.....785 841-2100
1 Riverfront Plz Lawrence (66044) ***(G-5025)***
Midcontinent Credit Svcs Inc.....316 721-6467
3161 N Rock Rd Wichita (67226) ***(G-15086)***
Midcontinental Chemical Co Inc.....913 390-5556
1802 E 123rd Ter Olathe (66061) ***(G-7893)***
Midian Shriners (PA).....316 265-9676
130 N Topeka Ave Wichita (67202) ***(G-15087)***
Midkansas Ear Nose Throat Assn, Wichita *Also called Wichita Srgical Specialists PA* ***(G-16024)***
Midland Care.....785 232-2044
200 Sw Frazier Cir Topeka (66606) ***(G-12891)***
Midland Care Connection Inc (PA).....785 232-2044
200 Sw Frazier Cir Topeka (66606) ***(G-12892)***
Midland Clippers.....913 962-7070
11906 Shwnee Mission Pkwy Shawnee Mission (66216) ***(G-11630)***
Midland Exteriors LLC (PA).....785 537-5130
8226 Southport Dr Manhattan (66502) ***(G-6743)***
Midland Genetics, Ottawa *Also called Sylvester Ranch Inc* ***(G-8315)***
Midland Group The, Lawrence *Also called Midland Professional Services* ***(G-5026)***
Midland Industrial Group, Caney *Also called Agra Axe International Inc* ***(G-664)***
Midland National Bank.....316 283-1700
1212 Washington Rd Newton (67114) ***(G-7385)***
Midland National Bank (PA).....316 283-1700
527 N Main St Newton (67114) ***(G-7386)***
Midland Professional Services (PA).....785 840-9676
1310 Wakarusa Dr Ste A Lawrence (66049) ***(G-5026)***
Midland Properties Inc (PA).....913 677-5300
2001 Shawnee Mission Pkwy Mission Woods (66205) ***(G-7151)***
Midland Property Management (HQ).....913 677-5300
2001 Shawnee Mission Pkwy Mission Woods (66205) ***(G-7152)***
Midland Restoration Company.....620 223-6855
2159 Indian Rd Fort Scott (66701) ***(G-1991)***
Midland Steel Company (PA).....785 989-4442
202 Boeh Ln Wathena (66090) ***(G-13476)***
Midland Theater Foundation Inc.....901 501-6832
214 W 8th St Coffeyville (67337) ***(G-963)***
Midpoint National Inc.....913 362-7400
1263 Southwest Blvd Kansas City (66103) ***(G-4248)***
Midstate Mechanical Inc.....785 537-4343
230 Levee Dr Manhattan (66502) ***(G-6744)***
Midtown Signs LLC.....816 561-7446
2416 S 8th St Kansas City (66103) ***(G-4249)***
Midway Co-Op Association.....785 346-5401
411 N 1st St Osborne (67473) ***(G-8211)***
Midway Co-Op Association.....785 346-5451
403 N 1st St Osborne (67473) ***(G-8212)***
Midway Manufacturing Inc.....620 659-3631
400 Winchester Ave Kinsley (67547) ***(G-4620)***
Midway Motors Inc.....620 241-7737
2045 E Kansas Ave McPherson (67460) ***(G-7005)***
Midway Sales & Distrg Inc (PA).....785 233-7406
218 Se Branner St Topeka (66607) ***(G-12893)***
Midway Sales & Distrg Inc.....785 537-4665
603 Pecan Cir Manhattan (66502) ***(G-6745)***
Midway Wholesale, Topeka *Also called Midway Sales & Distrg Inc* ***(G-12893)***
Midwest A Traffic Ctrl Svc Inc.....913 782-7082
7300 W 129th St Overland Park (66213) ***(G-9030)***
Midwest Anesthesia Assoc PA.....913 642-4900
6720 W 121st St 103 Leawood (66209) ***(G-5481)***
Midwest B R D Inc.....785 256-6240
11731 Sw 49th St Topeka (66610) ***(G-12894)***
Midwest Bioscience RES Pk LLC.....913 319-0300
5901 College Blvd Ste 100 Leawood (66211) ***(G-5482)***
Midwest Bulk Inc.....316 831-9700
3404 N Emporia St Wichita (67219) ***(G-15088)***
Midwest Bus Sales Inc (PA).....913 422-1000
313 E Front St Bonner Springs (66012) ***(G-562)***
Midwest Business Service, Emporia *Also called Rps Inc* ***(G-1817)***
Midwest Car Corporation.....316 946-4851
1300 S Airport Rd Wichita (67209) ***(G-15089)***
Midwest Cardiology Associates.....913 894-9015
12200 W 106th St Ste 320 Lenexa (66215) ***(G-6000)***
Midwest Cardiology Associates (PA).....913 253-3045
5701 W 119th St Ste 430 Shawnee Mission (66209) ***(G-11631)***
Midwest Carrier Transicold, Kansas City *Also called Murphy-Hoffman Company* ***(G-4274)***
Midwest Cast Stone Kansas Inc.....913 371-3300
1610 State Ave Kansas City (66102) ***(G-4250)***
Midwest Coating Inc.....785 232-4276
3830 Nw 16th St Topeka (66618) ***(G-12895)***
Midwest Color Graphics, Columbus *Also called Mid West Color Graphics Inc* ***(G-1084)***
Midwest Combustn Solutions Inc.....316 425-0929
4601 S Palisade Ave Wichita (67217) ***(G-15090)***
Midwest Concrete Materials Inc.....785 776-8811
701 S 4th St Manhattan (66502) ***(G-6746)***
Midwest Consulting Group Inc (PA).....913 693-8200
11880 College Blvd # 400 Overland Park (66210) ***(G-9031)***
Midwest Contracting & Mfg.....785 743-2026
2 Rte 2 WA Keeney (67672) ***(G-13383)***
Midwest Contractors Inc.....785 877-3565
912 N State St Norton (67654) ***(G-7449)***
Midwest Corporate Aviation Inc.....316 636-9700
3512 N Webb Rd Wichita (67226) ***(G-15091)***
Midwest Crane and Rigging LLC.....913 747-5100
15520 S Mahaffie St Olathe (66062) ***(G-7894)***
Midwest Cypress Siding, Perry *Also called Wood Haven Inc* ***(G-9775)***
Midwest Dairy Association.....913 345-2225
8645 College Blvd Ste 250 Overland Park (66210) ***(G-9032)***
Midwest Dairy Council, Overland Park *Also called Midwest Dairy Association* ***(G-9032)***
Midwest Digital, Lawrence *Also called Overfield Corporation* ***(G-5052)***
Midwest Distribution Center, Olathe *Also called Flexcon Company Inc* ***(G-7714)***
Midwest Distributors Co Inc.....913 287-2020
6501 Kansas Ave Kansas City (66111) ***(G-4251)***
Midwest Division - Oprmc LLC.....913 541-5000
10500 Quivira Rd Shawnee Mission (66215) ***(G-11632)***
Midwest Drywall Co Inc (PA).....316 722-9559
1351 S Reca Ct Ste 101 Wichita (67209) ***(G-15092)***
Midwest Drywall Co Inc.....316 722-9559
1351 S Reca Ct Ste 101 Wichita (67209) ***(G-15093)***

ALPHABETIC

Midwest Duct Cleaning Services 913 648-5300
9111 W 51st Ter Shawnee Mission (66203) ***(G-11633)***
Midwest Dynamics Inc (PA) 913 383-9320
10342 Dateline Leawood (66206) ***(G-5483)***
Midwest Ear Nose Throat PA 913 764-2737
20375 W 151st St Ste 106 Olathe (66061) ***(G-7895)***
Midwest Educational Center 785 776-1234
1006 Leavenworth St Manhattan (66502) ***(G-6747)***
Midwest Electric Service Inc 620 241-8655
621 N Hickory St McPherson (67460) ***(G-7006)***
Midwest Electrical Cnstr Inc 785 215-8902
4601 Se Adams St Topeka (66609) ***(G-12896)***
Midwest Energy Inc 620 792-1301
1025 Patton Rd Great Bend (67530) ***(G-2611)***
Midwest Energy Inc (PA) 785 625-3437
1330 Canterbury Dr Hays (67601) ***(G-2873)***
Midwest Energy Inc 785 462-8251
1125 S Range Ave Colby (67701) ***(G-1028)***
Midwest Energy Inc 620 872-2179
1301 S Main St Scott City (67871) ***(G-10822)***
Midwest Engine Warehouse, Edwardsville *Also called Illinois Auto Electric Co* ***(G-1503)***
Midwest Engraving Inc 913 294-5348
9 E Piankishaw St Paola (66071) ***(G-9575)***
Midwest Express Corporation (PA) 913 573-1400
9220 Marshall Dr Lenexa (66215) ***(G-6001)***
Midwest Feeders Inc 620 335-5790
5013 13 Rd Ingalls (67853) ***(G-3579)***
Midwest Fuels LLC 913 299-3331
300 N 78th St Kansas City (66112) ***(G-4252)***
Midwest Glass & Glazing LLC 913 768-6778
3909 Mission Rd Kansas City (66103) ***(G-4253)***
Midwest Health Services Inc 785 440-0399
1021 Sw Fleming Ct Topeka (66604) ***(G-12897)***
Midwest Health Services Inc 913 829-4663
751 N Somerset Ter Olathe (66062) ***(G-7896)***
Midwest Health Services Inc 913 894-0014
8740 Caenen Lake Rd Lenexa (66215) ***(G-6002)***
Midwest Health Services Inc 913 663-3351
12720 State Line Rd Leawood (66209) ***(G-5484)***
Midwest Health Services Inc 785 537-1065
2029 Little Kitten Ave Manhattan (66503) ***(G-6748)***
Midwest Health Services Inc 316 835-4810
915 Mcnair St Halstead (67056) ***(G-2703)***
Midwest Health Services Inc 785 272-2200
5820 Sw Drury Ln Topeka (66604) ***(G-12898)***
Midwest Health Services Inc 785 765-3318
234 Manor Cir Alma (66401) ***(G-65)***
Midwest Health Services Inc 785 945-3832
400 12th St Valley Falls (66088) ***(G-13368)***
Midwest Health Services Inc 913 727-6100
657 W Eisenhower Rd Lansing (66043) ***(G-4688)***
Midwest Health Services Inc 785 440-0500
1031 Sw Fleming Ct Topeka (66604) ***(G-12899)***
Midwest Health Services Inc 785 776-0065
2025 Little Kitten Ave Manhattan (66503) ***(G-6749)***
Midwest Health Services Inc 785 233-0544
440 Se Woodland Ave Topeka (66607) ***(G-12900)***
Midwest Health Services Inc 316 729-2400
12221 W Maple St Ofc Ofc Wichita (67235) ***(G-15094)***
Midwest Health Services Inc 620 272-9800
2414 N Henderson Dr Garden City (67846) ***(G-2233)***
Midwest Health Services Inc 620 276-7643
2308 N 3rd St Garden City (67846) ***(G-2234)***
Midwest Health Services Inc 785 776-1772
1923 Little Kitten Ave Manhattan (66503) ***(G-6750)***
Midwest Health Services Inc 316 685-1587
250 N Rock Rd Ste 160 Wichita (67206) ***(G-15095)***
Midwest Health Services Inc 785 665-7124
700 W 7th St Overbrook (66524) ***(G-8326)***
Midwest Heritage Inn 785 273-6800
1530 Sw Westport Dr Topeka (66604) ***(G-12901)***
Midwest Historical & Genealogi, Wichita *Also called Midwest Hstrcal Gnalogical Soc* ***(G-15096)***
Midwest Holiday Creations, Olathe *Also called Aspen Lawn Landscaping Inc* ***(G-7535)***
Midwest Homestead of Topeka, Topeka *Also called Midwest Health Services Inc* ***(G-12898)***
Midwest Hstrcal Gnalogical Soc 316 264-3611
1203 N Main St Wichita (67203) ***(G-15096)***
Midwest Industries & Dev Ltd 620 241-5996
1125 W 1st St McPherson (67460) ***(G-7007)***
Midwest Iron & Metal Co Inc (PA) 620 662-5663
700 S Main St Hutchinson (67501) ***(G-3378)***
Midwest Kenworth, Salina *Also called Kansas Kenworth Inc* ***(G-10566)***
Midwest Legacy LLC 316 518-9350
1411 E Ashford St Park City (67219) ***(G-9631)***
Midwest Lens Inc 913 894-1030
14304 W 100th St Shawnee Mission (66215) ***(G-11634)***
Midwest Machining Inc 620 896-5050
1100 W Main St Harper (67058) ***(G-2724)***
Midwest Malibu Center Inc 620 728-1356
1180 Airport Rd Hutchinson (67501) ***(G-3379)***
Midwest Masonry Construction 785 861-7500
5606 Sw Topekablvd Ste C Topeka (66609) ***(G-12902)***
Midwest Materials By Mueller (PA) 785 337-2252
203 W North St Hanover (66945) ***(G-2713)***
Midwest Merchandising Inc 913 428-8430
3701 W 95th St Overland Park (66206) ***(G-9033)***
Midwest Merchandising Inc 913 451-1515
11500 W 135th St Shawnee Mission (66221) ***(G-11635)***
Midwest Mill Modernization 620 583-6883
1206 E River St Eureka (67045) ***(G-1895)***
Midwest Mixer Service LLC 620 872-7251
40 E Road 160 Scott City (67871) ***(G-10823)***
Midwest Mixer Service LLC 620 225-7150
1501 S 2nd Ave Dodge City (67801) ***(G-1405)***
Midwest Motorsports Inc 913 334-0477
6285 State Ave Kansas City (66102) ***(G-4254)***
Midwest Office Technologies (PA) 785 272-7704
1502 Sw 41st St Topeka (66609) ***(G-12903)***
Midwest Office Technology, Overland Park *Also called Sta-Mot-Ks LLC* ***(G-9349)***
Midwest Office Technology 913 894-9600
11316 W 80th St Overland Park (66214) ***(G-9034)***
Midwest Orthodontics Inc 316 942-8703
4318 W Central Ave Wichita (67212) ***(G-15097)***
Midwest Orthopedics PA 913 362-8317
8800 W 75th St Ste 350 Shawnee Mission (66204) ***(G-11636)***
Midwest Pain Management 620 664-6724
1708 E 23rd Ave Hutchinson (67502) ***(G-3380)***
Midwest Painting, Wichita *Also called OFlynn Contracting Inc* ***(G-15211)***
Midwest Pallet, Kansas City *Also called Mrg Holdings Inc* ***(G-4269)***
Midwest Pathology Assoc LLC 913 341-6275
7301 College Blvd Overland Park (66210) ***(G-9035)***
Midwest Perinatal Associates, Shawnee Mission *Also called Mednax Inc* ***(G-11614)***
Midwest Pest Control LLC 316 681-3417
2308 E Mount Vernon St Wichita (67211) ***(G-15098)***
Midwest PMS LLC 620 872-2189
810 E 1st St Scott City (67871) ***(G-10824)***
Midwest PMS LLC 620 276-0970
985 N Anderson Rd Garden City (67846) ***(G-2235)***
Midwest Precision Inc 913 307-0211
9900 Pflumm Rd U1112 Lenexa (66215) ***(G-6003)***
Midwest Property Management, Lawrence *Also called T & J Holdings Inc* ***(G-5131)***
Midwest Ready Mix & Bldg Sup, Sabetha *Also called Mid West Ready Mix & Bldg Sups* ***(G-10319)***
Midwest Refrigerated Svcs LLC 913 621-1111
1601 Fairfax Trfy Kansas City (66115) ***(G-4255)***
Midwest Regional Credit Union (PA) 913 755-2127
7240 State Ave Kansas City (66112) ***(G-4256)***
Midwest Reproductive Center PA 913 780-4300
20375 W 151st St Ste 403 Olathe (66061) ***(G-7897)***
Midwest Roofing Services Inc (PA) 316 262-4758
2209 W Harry St Wichita (67213) ***(G-15099)***
Midwest Sales, Kansas City *Also called Gregory A Scott Inc* ***(G-4053)***
Midwest Service Bureau Inc 316 263-1051
625 W Maple St Wichita (67213) ***(G-15100)***
Midwest Services, Park City *Also called Midwest Legacy LLC* ***(G-9631)***
Midwest Services & Towing Inc 913 281-1003
400 Kansas Ave Kansas City (66105) ***(G-4257)***
Midwest Sewing & Vacuum Center 316 722-9737
111 S Pattie Ave Wichita (67211) ***(G-15101)***
Midwest Siding Incorporated (PA) 785 825-5576
1550 S Broadway Blvd Salina (67401) ***(G-10602)***
Midwest Siding Inc 785 825-0606
1504 W State St Salina (67401) ***(G-10603)***
Midwest Sign Company LLC 913 568-7552
550 Stanley Rd Kansas City (66115) ***(G-4258)***
Midwest Single Source Inc (PA) 316 267-6333
1501 E 1st St N Wichita (67214) ***(G-15102)***
Midwest Sports Productions LLC 913 543-6116
21967 W 83rd St Lenexa (66227) ***(G-6004)***
Midwest Star Equities LLC 620 225-3000
2523 E Wyatt Earp Blvd Dodge City (67801) ***(G-1406)***
Midwest Steel Fab LLC 316 832-9669
3690 N Old Lawrence Rd Wichita (67219) ***(G-15103)***
Midwest Surgery Center Lc 316 683-3937
825 N Hillside St Ste 100 Wichita (67214) ***(G-15104)***
Midwest Surgical 316 687-1090
1431 S Bluffview Dr # 210 Wichita (67218) ***(G-15105)***
Midwest Surveys Inc 913 755-2128
35750 Plum Creek Rd Osawatomie (66064) ***(G-8199)***
Midwest Tinting Inc (PA) 913 384-2665
7755 Shawnee Mission Pkwy Overland Park (66202) ***(G-9036)***
Midwest Title Co Inc 913 393-2511
124 E Park St Olathe (66061) ***(G-7898)***
Midwest Tow Service, Kansas City *Also called Midwest Services & Towing Inc* ***(G-4257)***
Midwest Trailer Supply Inc 316 744-1515
5929 N Broadway Ave Park City (67219) ***(G-9632)***
Midwest Transplant Network Inc (PA) 913 262-1668
1900 W 47th Pl Ste 400 Shawnee Mission (66205) ***(G-11637)***

Midwest Trnspt Specialists Inc 913 281-1003
400 Kansas Ave Kansas City (66105) *(G-4259)*
Midwest Truck Equipment Inc 316 744-2889
200 W 61st St N Park City (67204) *(G-9633)*
MIDWEST TRUST, Leawood *Also called Midwest Bioscience RES Pk LLC (G-5482)*
Midwest Trust Company (PA) 913 319-0300
5901 College Blvd Ste 100 Shawnee Mission (66211) *(G-11638)*
Midwest Turf, El Dorado *Also called William Barnes (G-1614)*
Midwest Turf & Landscape LLC 785 383-7839
9748 Sw Hoch Rd Auburn (66402) *(G-296)*
Midwestern Financial Group, Overland Park *Also called W S Griffith Inc (G-9476)*
Midwestern Litho 620 378-2912
321 N 6th St Fredonia (66736) *(G-2040)*
Midwestern Metals Inc (PA) 785 232-1582
1105 Nw Lower Silver Topeka (66608) *(G-12904)*
Midwestern Oilfield Svcs LLC 620 309-7027
2461 Lilac Dr Liberal (67901) *(G-6342)*
Midwestern Well Service Inc 620 624-8203
341 S Country Estates Rd Liberal (67901) *(G-6343)*
Mies & Sons Trucking Inc 316 796-0186
19620 W 85th St N Colwich (67030) *(G-1099)*
Mies Construction Inc 316 945-7227
1919 Southwest Blvd Wichita (67213) *(G-15106)*
Mll Management Group Inc 620 947-3608
207 S Lincoln St Hillsboro (67063) *(G-3052)*
Mike Grbic Team Realtors Inc 316 684-0000
7309 E 21st St N Ste 200 Wichita (67206) *(G-15107)*
Mike Groves Oil Inc 620 442-0480
801 E Madison Ave Arkansas City (67005) *(G-166)*
Mike Keimig Harvesting 620 278-2334
7317 N Andre Rd Sterling (67579) *(G-12126)*
Mikes Equipment Company 620 543-2535
9716 E 82nd Ave Buhler (67522) *(G-618)*
Mikes Heating & Cooling LLC 913 441-7807
1711 E 123rd Ter Olathe (66061) *(G-7899)*
Mikes Pipe Inspection Inc 620 624-9245
417 E Oak St Liberal (67901) *(G-6344)*
Mikes Testing & Salvage Inc 620 938-2943
1125 S Main St Chase (67524) *(G-785)*
Mil-Spec Security Group LLC 785 832-1351
520 E 22nd Ter Ste A Lawrence (66046) *(G-5027)*
Milacron Marketing Company LLC 620 241-1624
2085 E 1st St McPherson (67460) *(G-7008)*
Milburn Country Club, Shawnee Mission *Also called Milburn Golf and Country Club (G-11639)*
Milburn Golf and Country Club 913 432-0490
7501 W 69th St Shawnee Mission (66204) *(G-11639)*
Miles Automotive Inc 785 843-7700
3400 Iowa St Lawrence (66046) *(G-5028)*
Miles Excavating Inc 913 724-1934
15063 State Ave Basehor (66007) *(G-384)*
Milk Palace Dairy LLC 620 372-2021
12701 Sw County Road 32 Coolidge (67836) *(G-1146)*
Mill Creek LLC 785 364-2328
19035 Us Highway 75 Holton (66436) *(G-3105)*
Mill Creek Animal Clinic PA 913 268-0900
13428 W 62nd Ter Shawnee Mission (66216) *(G-11640)*
Mill Valley Construction Inc 913 764-6539
16510 W 119th St Olathe (66061) *(G-7900)*
Mill-Tel Inc (PA) 316 262-7171
5550 N Hydraulic St Park City (67219) *(G-9634)*
Millenia Productions LLC 316 425-2500
3819 N Toben St Wichita (67226) *(G-15108)*
Millennium Bancshares Inc 785 761-2265
121 N Washington St Junction City (66441) *(G-3726)*
Millennium Bank, Junction City *Also called Millennium Bancshares Inc (G-3726)*
Millennium Concepts Inc 316 977-8870
8955 W Monroe Cir Ste 300 Wichita (67209) *(G-15109)*
Millennium Concepts Inc 316 821-9300
9050 W Monroe Cir Wichita (67209) *(G-15110)*
Millennium Machine & Tool Inc 316 282-0884
900 W 1st St Newton (67114) *(G-7387)*
Millennium Marketing, Shawnee Mission *Also called Subscription Ink Co (G-11905)*
Millennium Rail Inc (HQ) 620 231-2230
315 W 3rd St Pittsburg (66762) *(G-9905)*
Miller & Midyett Realtor Inc 785 843-8566
1045 E 23rd St Lawrence (66046) *(G-5029)*
Miller & Newberg Inc 913 393-2522
8717 W 110th St Ste 530 Overland Park (66210) *(G-9037)*
Miller - Stauch Cnstr Co Inc 913 599-1040
32 N 6th St Kansas City (66101) *(G-4260)*
Miller Building Services Inc 913 649-5599
10312 W 79th St Shawnee (66214) *(G-10996)*
Miller Construction 785 448-6788
19324 Nw Highway 31 Garnett (66032) *(G-2383)*
Miller Group 816 333-3000
6363 College Blvd Ste 400 Leawood (66211) *(G-5485)*
Miller Homebuilders Inc 620 662-1687
301 Hemlock St Hutchinson (67502) *(G-3381)*
Miller Paving & Cnstr LLC 913 334-5579
7150 Kaw Dr Kansas City (66111) *(G-4261)*
Miller Plumbing Co Inc 913 851-1333
20625 Metcalf Ave Bucyrus (66013) *(G-604)*
Miller Sign Shoppe, Bonner Springs *Also called Millers Sign Shoppe LLC (G-563)*
Miller Stauch Construction, Kansas City *Also called Miller - Stauch Cnstr Co Inc (G-4260)*
Miller Sullivan & Assoc DDS PA 913 492-5052
12136 W 87th Street Pkwy Shawnee Mission (66215) *(G-11641)*
Miller Trucking Ltd 785 222-3170
1st & Peace St La Crosse (67548) *(G-4636)*
Miller Veterinary Services PA 913 592-2770
602 N Webster St Spring Hill (66083) *(G-12090)*
Miller Welding Inc 785 454-3425
354 W Highway 24 Downs (67437) *(G-1472)*
Miller, Chris, Lawrence *Also called Little & Miller Chartered Inc (G-4999)*
Miller-Marley Schl Dance Voice, Shawnee Mission *Also called Shirley Marley Enterprises (G-11865)*
Millers Inc (PA) 620 231-8050
610 E Jefferson St Pittsburg (66762) *(G-9906)*
Millers Sign Shoppe LLC 913 441-6883
15146 174th St Bonner Springs (66012) *(G-563)*
Millett Industries (PA) 913 752-3572
9200 Cody St Overland Park (66214) *(G-9038)*
Millett Sights, Overland Park *Also called Millett Industries (G-9038)*
Million Air, Topeka *Also called Freeman Holdings LLC (G-12628)*
Million Air Topeka, Topeka *Also called Freeman Holdings LLC (G-12627)*
Million Packaging Inc 913 402-0055
14508 Ballentine St Overland Park (66221) *(G-9039)*
Miltech Machine Corporation 785 877-5381
15277 Washington Rd Norton (67654) *(G-7450)*
Milton B Grin MD PA 913 829-5511
21020 W 151st St Olathe (66061) *(G-7901)*
MINANITE SUNSET MANOR, Pretty Prairie *Also called Prairie Sunset Home Inc (G-10168)*
Minds Matter LLC 866 429-6757
7819 Conser Pl Overland Park (66204) *(G-9040)*
Miner Technologies, Shawnee Mission *Also called Sanden North America Inc (G-11826)*
Mineral-Right Inc 785 543-6571
10 W Quail Rd Phillipsburg (67661) *(G-9791)*
Mingo Custom Woods 785 462-2200
1965 W 4th St Colby (67701) *(G-1029)*
Mini Adventures 913 334-6008
545 S 94th St Kansas City (66111) *(G-4262)*
Mini Bus Service Inc 620 272-3626
907 N 10th St Garden City (67846) *(G-2236)*
Mini Maid Joco Incorporated 913 894-2200
13100 W 95th St Ste 4c Lenexa (66215) *(G-6005)*
Mini Masters Lrng Academy LLC 785 862-0772
3909b Sw Burlingame Rd Topeka (66609) *(G-12905)*
Mini Warehouse Limited II 785 273-4004
4101 Sw Twilight Dr Topeka (66614) *(G-12906)*
Mini-Mac Inc 316 733-0661
1703 Southwest Blvd Ste 1 Wichita (67213) *(G-15111)*
Mini-Train Gage Park 785 273-6108
Gage Park Topeka (66604) *(G-12907)*
Miniature Plastic Molding LLC 316 264-2827
1111 N Washington Ave Wichita (67214) *(G-15112)*
Minick Gambrell Contrs LLC 913 538-5391
405 S Clairborne Rd Ste 6 Olathe (66062) *(G-7902)*
Minneapolis Messenger Pubg Co 785 392-2129
401 W 2nd St Minneapolis (67467) *(G-7118)*
Minneola Co-Op Inc 620 885-4361
500 W Front St Minneola (67865) *(G-7125)*
Minneola Community Clinic, Bloom *Also called Minneola Hospital District 2 (G-531)*
Minneola Hospital District 2 .... 620 885-4202
222 Main St Bloom (67865) *(G-531)*
Minneola Hospital District 2 .... 620 885-4238
207 S Chestnut St Minneola (67865) *(G-7126)*
Minneola Long Term Unit, Minneola *Also called Minneola Hospital District 2 (G-7126)*
Minnesota Pipe Line Co LLC (HQ) 316 828-5500
4111 E 37th St N Wichita (67220) *(G-15113)*
Minter-Wilson Drilling Co Inc (PA) 620 276-8269
2007 W Jones Ave Garden City (67846) *(G-2237)*
Minter-Wilson Drilling Co Inc 620 275-7471
1911 E Kansas Ave Garden City (67846) *(G-2238)*
Minuteman Press, Lawrence *Also called Bisel Inc (G-4758)*
Minuteman Press 913 829-0300
924 E Park St Olathe (66061) *(G-7903)*
Miq Logistics LLC (HQ) 913 696-7100
11501 Outlook St Ste 500 Overland Park (66211) *(G-9041)*
Mirabile MD Hlth Buty Wellness, Overland Park *Also called James Mirabile (G-8872)*
Miracles Inc 316 303-9520
1015 E 2nd St N Wichita (67214) *(G-15114)*
Miracles House 316 264-5900
1250 N Market St Wichita (67214) *(G-15115)*
Miracorp Inc 913 322-8000
15317 W 95th St Lenexa (66219) *(G-6006)*
Mires Machine Co Inc 316 942-6547
4224 W Esthner Ave Wichita (67209) *(G-15116)*

ALPHABETIC

Mirror Inc 316 634-3954
3820 N Toben St Wichita (67226) *(G-15117)*
Mirror Inc 913 248-1943
6221 Richards Dr Shawnee Mission (66216) *(G-11642)*
Mirror Inc 620 326-8822
1014 W 8th St Wellington (67152) *(G-13518)*
Mirror Inc 316 283-7829
1309 N Duncan St Newton (67114) *(G-7388)*
Mirror Inc (PA) 316 283-6743
130 E 5th St Newton (67114) *(G-7389)*
Miss Mrias Acrbat Dance Studio 913 888-0060
10370 S Ridgeview Rd Olathe (66061) *(G-7904)*
Mission Animal Clinic PA 913 432-3341
5915 Broadmoor St Shawnee Mission (66202) *(G-11643)*
Mission Bowl, Olathe *Also called Mission Recreation Inc (G-7906)*
Mission Bowl N Olathe 913 782-0279
1020 S Weaver St Olathe (66061) *(G-7905)*
Mission Car Wash LLC 913 236-6886
5960 Barkley St Shawnee Mission (66202) *(G-11644)*
Mission Heating and AC 913 631-6506
11012 W 58th St Shawnee Mission (66203) *(G-11645)*
Mission Hills Country Club Inc 913 722-5400
5400 Mission Dr Mission Hills (66208) *(G-7146)*
Mission Medvet 913 722-5566
5914 Johnson Dr Shawnee Mission (66202) *(G-11646)*
Mission Mortgage LLC 913 469-1999
40 Corporate Woods 9401 Overland Park (66210) *(G-9042)*
Mission Place Ltd LP 620 662-8731
3101 N Plum St Hutchinson (67502) *(G-3382)*
Mission Project Inc 913 777-6722
5960 Dearborn St Ste 201 Shawnee Mission (66202) *(G-11647)*
Mission Recreation Inc 913 782-0279
1020 S Weaver St Olathe (66061) *(G-7906)*
Mission Road Animal Clinic 913 649-0552
9420 Mission Rd Leawood (66206) *(G-5486)*
Mission Village Living Ctr Inc 785 486-2697
1890 Euclid Ave Unit Frnt Horton (66439) *(G-3131)*
Missouri Hospice Holdings LLC 913 905-0255
13002 State Line Rd Leawood (66209) *(G-5487)*
Missouri Livestock Mktg Assn (PA) 816 891-0502
11501 Outlook St 250 Leawood (66211) *(G-5488)*
Missouri Vly Tennis Foundation 913 322-4800
6400 W 95th St Ste 102 Overland Park (66212) *(G-9043)*
Missouri-Kansas Supply Co Inc 816 842-6513
1202 Adams St Kansas City (66103) *(G-4263)*
Mister K'S Food Town, Plainville *Also called R & O Partnership (G-9991)*
Misty Glenn Apts, Topeka *Also called Fidelity Management Corp (G-12606)*
Mitchell Capital Management Co 913 428-3222
11460 Tomahawk Creek Pkwy Leawood (66211) *(G-5489)*
Mitchell Count Hospi Healt Sys 785 738-2266
400 W 8th St Beloit (67420) *(G-493)*
Mitchell County Farm Bur Assn 785 738-2551
1674 Kansas 14 Hwy Beloit (67420) *(G-494)*
Mitchell County Hospital, Beloit *Also called County of Mitchell (G-482)*
Mitchell County Rur Wtr Dst 2 ....785 545-3341
109 E Kansas St Glen Elder (67446) *(G-2427)*
Mitchell Farms 580 696-4568
Hwy 95 S Elkhart (67950) *(G-1622)*
Mitchell-Markowitz Cnstr 620 343-6840
414 Graham St Emporia (66801) *(G-1796)*
Mitel (delaware) Inc 913 752-9100
16201 W 95th St Ste 210 Lenexa (66219) *(G-6007)*
Mitel Technologies Inc 913 752-9100
16201 W 95th St Ste 210 Lenexa (66219) *(G-6008)*
Mitre Corporation 913 946-1900
401 Delaware St Leavenworth (66048) *(G-5271)*
Mittelmans Furniture Co Inc 913 897-5505
3704 W 141st St Overland Park (66224) *(G-9044)*
Mitten Inc 785 672-3062
1001 Highway 40 Oakley (67748) *(G-7481)*
Mitten Truck Stop, Oakley *Also called Mitten Inc (G-7481)*
Mixology, Wichita *Also called Kan Pak LLC (G-14782)*
Mixon-Hill Inc 913 239-8400
12980 Metcalf Ave Ste 470 Shawnee Mission (66213) *(G-11648)*
Mixture LLC 913 944-2441
9325 W 53rd St Shawnee (66203) *(G-10997)*
Mize & Co Inc 620 532-3191
2020 N Koch Industrial St Kingman (67068) *(G-4607)*
Mize Elementary Pto 913 441-0880
7301 Mize Rd Shawnee (66227) *(G-10998)*
Mize Houser & Company PA 913 451-1882
7101 College Blvd Ste 900 Shawnee Mission (66210) *(G-11649)*
Mize Houser & Company PA (PA) 785 233-0536
534 S Kansas Ave Ste 700 Topeka (66603) *(G-12908)*
Mize Houser & Company PA 785 842-8844
211 E 8th St Ste A Lawrence (66044) *(G-5030)*
Mize Wire Products, Kingman *Also called Mize & Co Inc (G-4607)*
Mize, John W, Salina *Also called Clark Mize Linville Chartered (G-10456)*

Mj Transportation Inc 316 832-1321
601 E 49th St N Park City (67219) *(G-9635)*
Mjv Holdings LLC 913 432-5348
5924 Broadmoor St Shawnee Mission (66202) *(G-11650)*
Mk Minerals Inc 785 989-4566
1025 Vernon Rd Wathena (66090) *(G-13477)*
Mkc, Moundridge *Also called Mid-Kansas Cooperative Assn (G-7190)*
Mkc Golf 3 LLC 913 526-3312
8409 Nieman Rd Lenexa (66214) *(G-6009)*
Mkec Engineering Inc (PA) 316 684-9600
411 N Webb Rd Wichita (67206) *(G-15118)*
Mkec Engineering Cons Inc 913 317-9390
11827 W 112th St Ste 200 Overland Park (66210) *(G-9045)*
Mkl Acquisitions LLC 620 704-5228
1014 E 580th Ave Pittsburg (66762) *(G-9907)*
Mks Pipe & Valve, Kansas City *Also called Missouri-Kansas Supply Co Inc (G-4263)*
Mkt Community Development Inc 913 596-7310
2100 N 57th St Kansas City (66104) *(G-4264)*
ML Nevius Builders Inc 620 662-7767
1915 W 82nd Ave Hutchinson (67502) *(G-3383)*
Mlr Welding LLC 785 203-1020
2409 280th Ave Hays (67601) *(G-2874)*
Mm Companyies, Kansas City *Also called Mm Property MGT & Rmdlg LLC (G-4265)*
Mm Distribution LLC 800 689-2098
519 E 1st St Douglass (67039) *(G-1467)*
Mm Property MGT & Rmdlg LLC 913 871-6867
912 Minnesota Ave Kansas City (66101) *(G-4265)*
MMC Corp (PA) 913 469-0101
10955 Lowell Ave Ste 350 Overland Park (66210) *(G-9046)*
Mnvc Financial Services LLC 816 589-4336
7701 College Blvd Overland Park (66210) *(G-9047)*
Mo-Can Flooring Inc 913 362-0711
6800 W 47th Ter Shawnee (66203) *(G-10999)*
Mo-Kan Transit Mix Inc 913 367-1332
1503 Highway 59 Atchison (66002) *(G-250)*
Mobile Addiction LLC (PA) 316 773-3463
8918 W 21st St N Wichita (67205) *(G-15119)*
Mobile Fx Inc 913 287-1556
5237 State Ave Kansas City (66102) *(G-4266)*
Mobile Health Clinics LLC 913 383-0991
6227 W 126th Ter Leawood (66209) *(G-5490)*
Mobile Mini Inc 316 838-2663
250 W 53rd St N Park City (67204) *(G-9636)*
Mobile Products Inc 903 759-0610
15 Compound Dr Hutchinson (67502) *(G-3384)*
Mobile Radio Service Inc 620 793-3231
156 S Us Highway 281 Great Bend (67530) *(G-2612)*
Mobile Reasoning Inc 913 888-2600
15737 W 100th Ter Lenexa (66219) *(G-6010)*
Mobilecal, Wichita *Also called Alltite Inc (G-13678)*
Mobilecare 2u LLC 913 362-1112
8500 W 110th St Ste 450 Overland Park (66210) *(G-9048)*
Mockry & Sons Machine Co Inc 316 788-7878
621 N River St Derby (67037) *(G-1263)*
Mod-Co Garage Door and Sup Div, Salina *Also called Delbert Chopp Co Inc (G-10472)*
Modern Air Conditioning Inc 620 342-7577
106 Commercial St Emporia (66801) *(G-1797)*
Modern Maintenance Inc 913 345-9777
14400 W 96th Ter Shawnee Mission (66215) *(G-11651)*
Modern Methods 316 686-6391
439 N Estelle Ave Wichita (67214) *(G-15120)*
Modern Office, Topeka *Also called Midwest Office Technologies (G-12903)*
Modern Paving Systems Inc 913 962-7208
14001 W 56th Ter Shawnee Mission (66216) *(G-11652)*
Modus Group LLC 785 584-6057
555 Nishnabe Trl Rossville (66533) *(G-10254)*
Moeller Dermatology, Wichita *Also called Christopher Moeller (G-14016)*
Mohan Construction Inc 785 233-1615
125 S Kansas Ave Topeka (66603) *(G-12909)*
Mojack Distributors LLC 877 466-5225
3535 N Rock Rd Ste 300 Wichita (67226) *(G-15121)*
Mokan Dial Inc 913 837-2219
112 S Broadway St Louisburg (66053) *(G-6458)*
Mokan Hospitality LLC 913 541-9999
10360 S Ridgeview Rd Olathe (66061) *(G-7907)*
Molex LLC 630 969-4550
4111 E 37th St N Wichita (67220) *(G-15122)*
Moly Manufacturing Inc 785 472-3388
2435 10th Rd Lorraine (67459) *(G-6433)*
Monaco & Associates Inc 785 272-5501
1243 Sw Topeka Blvd Ste B Topeka (66612) *(G-12910)*
Monarch Cement Company (PA) 620 473-2222
449 1200th St Humboldt (66748) *(G-3187)*
Monarch Inventories Services 913 541-0645
9716 Rosehill Rd Lenexa (66215) *(G-6011)*
Monarch Molding Inc 620 767-5115
120 Liberty St Council Grove (66846) *(G-1171)*
Monarch Plastic Surgery 913 663-3838
4801 W 135th St Overland Park (66224) *(G-9049)*

Monarch Skin Care 913 317-9386
5401 College Blvd # 203204 Shawnee Mission (66211) **(G-11653)**
Monarch Skin Rejuvenation Ctr, Shawnee Mission *Also called Monarch Skin Care* **(G-11653)**
Monnat & Spurrier Chartered 316 264-2800
200 W Douglas Ave Ste 830 Wichita (67202) **(G-15123)**
Monoflo International Inc 785 242-2928
1550 N Davis Ave Ottawa (66067) **(G-8292)**
Monster Pump Operations Inc 785 623-4488
1515 Commerce Pkwy Hays (67601) **(G-2875)**
Montana Mike's Steakhouse, Hutchinson *Also called Stockade Companies LLC* **(G-3448)**
Montara LLC 785 862-1030
7105 Sw Montara Pkwy Topeka (66619) **(G-12911)**
Monterey Way House, Lawrence *Also called Community Lving Opprtnties Inc* **(G-4805)**
Montes De Areia LLC 620 663-5301
922 Crazy Horse Rd Hutchinson (67502) **(G-3385)**
Montessori Unlimited, Shawnee Mission *Also called Learning Care Group Inc* **(G-11552)**
Montgomery Communications Inc (PA) 785 762-5000
222 W 6th St Junction City (66441) **(G-3727)**
Montgomery County Chronicle 620 879-2156
202 W 4th Ave Caney (67333) **(G-672)**
Montgomery County Media LLC 620 331-3550
320 N 6th St Independence (67301) **(G-3541)**
Moon Abstract Company 620 342-1917
7300 W 110th St Ste 700 Overland Park (66210) **(G-9050)**
Moon Marble Company, Bonner Springs *Also called Bruces Woodworks LLC* **(G-543)**
Moonlite Trucking Inc 620 767-5499
1126 Old Us Highway 56 Council Grove (66846) **(G-1172)**
Moonshot Innovations LLC 913 815-6611
7220 W 98th Ter Ste 150 Overland Park (66212) **(G-9051)**
Moonwalks For Fun Inc 316 522-2224
8545 W Irving St Wichita (67209) **(G-15124)**
Moore Buick Chevrolet Pontiac 785 346-5972
120 S 2nd St Osborne (67473) **(G-8213)**
Moore Enterprises Inc 913 451-5900
8000 W 110th St Ste 115 Overland Park (66210) **(G-9052)**
Moore Jeff PHD Audiologist 316 686-6608
9350 E Central Ave Wichita (67206) **(G-15125)**
Moore Rubber Co Inc 913 422-5679
20151 W 55th St Shawnee Mission (66218) **(G-11654)**
Moore, John B IV, Olathe *Also called Premier Plastic Surgery* **(G-8003)**
Moorekc Enterprises LLC 316 347-0121
13418 W 77th Ter Shawnee (66216) **(G-11000)**
Moores Lnny Collision Repr LLC 316 744-1151
201 W 61st St N Park City (67204) **(G-9637)**
Moran Manor Nursing Center, Moran *Also called Rh Montgomery Properties Inc* **(G-7164)**
Moran Meat Locker 620 237-4331
209 S Cedar St Moran (66755) **(G-7163)**
More Floods Inc 913 469-9464
14804 W 114th Ter Lenexa (66215) **(G-6012)**
Morgan Advanced Materials, Emporia *Also called Thermal Ceramics Inc* **(G-1837)**
Morgan Chance Inc 316 945-6555
4219 W Irving St Wichita (67209) **(G-15126)**
Morgan Concrete Services Inc 785 842-1686
1201 E 24th St Lawrence (66046) **(G-5031)**
Morgan Hunter Corporation 913 491-3434
7600 W 110th St Ste 100 Overland Park (66210) **(G-9053)**
Morgan Stanley 913 402-5200
11161 Overbrook Rd # 225 Leawood (66211) **(G-5491)**
Morgan Stanley & Co LLC 316 383-8300
1617 N Wtrfrnt Pkwy # 200 Wichita (67206) **(G-15127)**
Morgan Stanley & Co LLC 785 749-1111
1429 Oread West St # 100 Lawrence (66049) **(G-5032)**
Morgan Stanley Smith Barney, Wichita *Also called Citigroup Global Markets Inc* **(G-14022)**
Morgan, David L, Olathe *Also called Rhulen & Morgan Prof Assn* **(G-8032)**
Moridge Manufacturing Inc 620 345-6301
105 Old Us Highway 81 Moundridge (67107) **(G-7193)**
Morley Bancshares Corporation 620 488-2211
502 N Merchant St Belle Plaine (67013) **(G-448)**
Morningstar Communications Co 913 660-9630
12307 Flint St Overland Park (66213) **(G-9054)**
Morningstar Family Dental PA 913 344-9990
7000 W 121st St Ste 200 Overland Park (66209) **(G-9055)**
Morrill Hay Company Inc 620 285-6941
24021 Eagle Ct Paola (66071) **(G-9576)**
Morris Laing Evans Brock (PA) 316 838-1084
300 N Mead St Ste 200 Wichita (67202) **(G-15128)**
Morris Laing Evans Brock 785 232-2662
800 Sw Jackson St # 1310 Topeka (66612) **(G-12912)**
Morris Communications Co LLC 620 442-4200
200 E 5th Ave Arkansas City (67005) **(G-167)**
Morris Communications Co LLC 785 823-1111
131 N Santa Fe Ave Fl 3 Salina (67401) **(G-10604)**
Morris Communications Co LLC 316 283-1500
121 W 6th St Newton (67114) **(G-7390)**
Morris Communications Co LLC 620 231-2600
701 N Locust St Pittsburg (66762) **(G-9908)**
Morris Communications Co LLC 785 272-3456
1210 Sw Executive Dr Topeka (66615) **(G-12913)**
Morris Communications Co LLC 620 225-4151
705 N 2nd Ave Dodge City (67801) **(G-1407)**
Morris Communications Co LLC 785 295-1111
616 Se Jefferson St Topeka (66607) **(G-12914)**
Morris Newspaper Corp Kansas 620 792-1211
2012 Forest Ave Great Bend (67530) **(G-2613)**
Morrison Optometric Assoc PA (PA) 785 462-8231
1005 S Range Ave Ste 100 Colby (67701) **(G-1030)**
Morrow & Company LLC 316 263-2223
421 E 3rd St N Wichita (67202) **(G-15129)**
Morrow Engineering Inc 316 942-0402
405 S Holland St Ste 100 Wichita (67209) **(G-15130)**
Morse Early Childhood Center, Kansas City *Also called Board of Edcatn of Kans Cy Ks* **(G-3870)**
Mortgage Company 785 825-8100
155 N 7th St Salina (67401) **(G-10605)**
Mortgage Lenders America, Leawood *Also called Zillow Group Inc* **(G-5604)**
Morton Buildings Inc 785 364-4177
2006 Frontage Rd Holton (66436) **(G-3106)**
Morton Buildings Inc 785 823-6359
711 W Diamond Dr Salina (67401) **(G-10606)**
Morton Buildings Inc 620 221-4180
7748 7th Ave Winfield (67156) **(G-16159)**
Morton Buildings Inc 620 275-4105
4255 E Us Highway 50 Garden City (67846) **(G-2239)**
Morton Buildings Inc 620 221-3265
7866 7th Ave Winfield (67156) **(G-16160)**
Morton County Health System, Elkhart *Also called Morton County Hospital* **(G-1623)**
Morton County Hospital (PA) 620 697-2141
445 Hilltop Ave Elkhart (67950) **(G-1623)**
Morton County Hospital 620 697-2175
411 Sunset St Elkhart (67950) **(G-1624)**
Morton Salt Inc 620 669-0401
1000 Morton Dr South Hutchinson (67505) **(G-12063)**
Mosaic, Winfield *Also called Martin Luther Homes Kansas Inc* **(G-16156)**
Mosaic 620 624-3817
441 Industrial Park Ave Liberal (67901) **(G-6345)**
Mosaic 620 231-5590
2807 N Broadway St Pittsburg (66762) **(G-9909)**
Mosaic 913 788-8400
8047 Parallel Pkwy Ste 9 Kansas City (66112) **(G-4267)**
Mosaic 620 276-7972
2708 N 11th St Garden City (67846) **(G-2240)**
Mosaic 785 472-4081
117 N Douglas Ave Ellsworth (67439) **(G-1679)**
Mosaic 620 229-8702
2120 E 9th Ave Winfield (67156) **(G-16161)**
Mosier Mosier Fmly Physicians, Manhattan *Also called Mosier Mosier Fmly Physicians* **(G-6751)**
Mosier Mosier Fmly Physicians 785 539-8700
2900 Amherst Ave Ste A Manhattan (66503) **(G-6751)**
Mosley Street Melodrama, Wichita *Also called Actors LLC* **(G-13610)**
Moss Enterprises Inc 620 277-2646
3255 W Jones Ave Garden City (67846) **(G-2241)**
Moss Printing, Shawnee Mission *Also called Sky Printing and Pubg Inc* **(G-11873)**
Motel 6, Olathe *Also called Rhw Management Inc* **(G-8034)**
Motel 6, Park City *Also called C & I LLC* **(G-9607)**
Motel 6 ....316 684-6363
465 S Webb Rd Wichita (67207) **(G-15131)**
Motel 6 Operating LP 316 945-8440
5736 W Kellogg Dr Wichita (67209) **(G-15132)**
Motel 6 Operating LP 785 827-8397
635 W Diamond Dr Salina (67401) **(G-10607)**
Motel 6 Operating LP 913 541-8558
9725 Lenexa Dr Shawnee Mission (66215) **(G-11655)**
Motel 6 Operating LP 785 537-1022
510 Tuttle Creek Blvd Manhattan (66502) **(G-6752)**
Motel 6 Operating LP 785 273-2896
1224 Sw Wanamaker Rd Topeka (66604) **(G-12915)**
Motel 6 Operating LP 785 272-8283
709 Sw Fairlawn Rd Topeka (66606) **(G-12916)**
Motel 6 Operating LP 620 343-1240
2630 W 18th Ave Emporia (66801) **(G-1798)**
Mother Earth News, Topeka *Also called Ogden Publications Inc* **(G-12943)**
Mothers Day Out, Shawnee Mission *Also called Lets Grow Preschool* **(G-11565)**
Motion Industries Inc 316 265-9608
2546 N Lonaine St Wichita (67219) **(G-15133)**
Motivated RE Solutions LLC 785 842-3530
3227 Huntington Rd Lawrence (66049) **(G-5033)**
Motivational Tubing LLC 316 283-7301
2610 Nw 12th St Newton (67114) **(G-7391)**
Motivtion Thrugh Incntives Inc 913 438-2600
10400 W 103rd St Ste 10 Overland Park (66214) **(G-9056)**
Motor Mouth Wireless LLC (PA) 316 260-4660
247 S Holyoke St Wichita (67218) **(G-15134)**
Motorola Solutions Inc 913 317-3020
7500 College Blvd Ste 500 Overland Park (66210) **(G-9057)**
Motorsports of Kansas City, Kansas City *Also called Midwest Motorsports Inc* **(G-4254)**

ALPHABETIC

Moufarrij Nazih....316 263-0296
818 N Emporia St Ste 200 Wichita (67214) *(G-15135)*
Mound City Vault Co Inc....913 795-2529
414 S 4th St Mound City (66056) *(G-7173)*
Moundridge Telcom, Moundridge *Also called Moundridge Telephone Company (G-7194)*
Moundridge Telephone Company....620 345-2831
109 N Christian Ave Moundridge (67107) *(G-7194)*
Mount Carmel Home Health Svcs, Pittsburg *Also called Ascension Via Christi (G-9812)*
Mount Crmel Rgional Cancer Ctr, Pittsburg *Also called Cancer Center (G-9828)*
Mount Crmel Rhabilitation Svcs, Pittsburg *Also called Ascension Via Christi (G-9814)*
Mount Hope Cemetery Company....785 272-1122
4700 Sw 17th St Topeka (66604) *(G-12917)*
Mount St Mary's Convent, Wichita *Also called Sisters St Joseph Wichita KS (G-15598)*
MOUNT ST MARY'S CONVENT, Manhattan *Also called Via Christi Vlg Manhattan Inc (G-6842)*
Mount St Scholastica Inc....913 906-8990
2220 Central Ave Kansas City (66102) *(G-4268)*
Mount Vernon Lodge, Beloit *Also called Ancient Free & Accptd Masons (G-473)*
Moving Kings LLC....913 882-2121
9393 W 110th St Overland Park (66210) *(G-9058)*
Mowery Clinic LLC....785 827-7261
737 E Crawford St Salina (67401) *(G-10608)*
Moxie Services LLC....913 416-1205
14635 W 101st Ter Lenexa (66215) *(G-6013)*
Moxley &WAgle Dr....316 685-2731
825 S Hillside St Wichita (67211) *(G-15136)*
Mpi, Morganville *Also called Mellies Products Inc (G-7165)*
Mpp Co Inc....913 895-0269
8500 Shawnee Mission Pkwy # 200 Shawnee Mission (66202) *(G-11656)*
Mpressions....913 897-4401
16230 Metcalf Ave Stilwell (66085) *(G-12169)*
Mr Goodcents Franchise Systems....913 583-8400
8997 Commerce Dr De Soto (66018) *(G-1209)*
Mr Penguin, Salina *Also called Jims Formal Wear LLC (G-10555)*
Mr PS Party Outlet Inc (PA)....785 537-1804
3039 Conrow Dr Manhattan (66503) *(G-6753)*
Mr PS Truckn Inc....785 372-4371
102 E Florence Rush Center (67575) *(G-10262)*
Mrg Holdings Inc....913 371-3555
1161 S 12th St Kansas City (66105) *(G-4269)*
Mriglobal - Kansas LLC....816 753-7600
2005 Research Park Cir Manhattan (66502) *(G-6754)*
Mrv Holding Company....785 272-1398
3501 Sw Fairlawn Rd # 200 Topeka (66614) *(G-12918)*
Ms Biotec LLC....785 456-1388
1300 Kaw Valley Rd Wamego (66547) *(G-13429)*
Ms Electronics LLC....913 233-8518
10661 Rene St Lenexa (66215) *(G-6014)*
Ms Electronics LLC (PA)....866 663-9770
10661 Rene St Lenexa (66215) *(G-6015)*
Msaver Resources LlC....913 663-4672
7400 W 110th St Ste 520 Overland Park (66210) *(G-9059)*
MSE Audio, Lenexa *Also called Ms Electronics LLC (G-6014)*
MSE Audio, Lenexa *Also called Induction Dynamics LLC (G-5912)*
MSI, Shawnee Mission *Also called Multi Systems Installation Inc (G-11658)*
MSI....316 262-2021
625 E 13th St N Wichita (67214) *(G-15137)*
MSI Automation Inc....316 681-3566
4065 N Woodlawn Ct Ste 4 Bel Aire (67220) *(G-436)*
Msip-Sscc Holdings LLC....620 657-4166
12725 E Us Highway 160 Satanta (67870) *(G-10788)*
Mss Transport Inc....785 825-7291
200 E Avenue B Salina (67401) *(G-10609)*
Mt 3 Corporation....785 843-3433
1556 Lecompton Rd Perry (66073) *(G-9772)*
Mt Carmel Redevelopment Corp (PA)....913 621-4111
1130 Troup Ave Kansas City (66104) *(G-4270)*
Mt Hope Community Development (PA)....316 667-2431
704 E Main St Mount Hope (67108) *(G-7207)*
MT HOPE NURSING CENTER, Mount Hope *Also called Mt Hope Community Development (G-7207)*
Mt Pleasant News Inc (HQ)....913 492-9050
14500 W 105th St Shawnee Mission (66215) *(G-11657)*
Mt Pleasant News, The, Shawnee Mission *Also called Mt Pleasant News Inc (G-11657)*
Mt. Carmel Apartments, Kansas City *Also called Yarco Company Inc (G-4563)*
Mtc Development LLC....785 539-3500
100 Manhattan Town Ctr # 480 Manhattan (66502) *(G-6755)*
Mtc Holding Corporation....913 319-0300
5901 College Blvd Ste 100 Overland Park (66211) *(G-9060)*
MTI Events, Overland Park *Also called Motivtion Thrugh Incntives Inc (G-9056)*
MTS Quanta LLC....913 383-0800
10551 Barkley St Ste 200 Overland Park (66212) *(G-9061)*
Mtsqh, Wichita *Also called McDonald Tinker Skaer Quinn (G-15028)*
Muckenthaler Incorporated (PA)....620 342-5653
308 Commercial St Emporia (66801) *(G-1799)*
Mud-Co/Service Mud Inc....620 672-2957
279 Ne 70th Ave Ste 3 Pratt (67124) *(G-10126)*
Mueller Sand & Gravel, Hanover *Also called Midwest Materials By Mueller (G-2713)*
Mueller-Yurgae Associates Inc....913 362-7777
10500 Barkley St Ste 102 Overland Park (66212) *(G-9062)*
Mulberry Limestone Quarry Co....620 764-3337
325 N 260th St Mulberry (66756) *(G-7208)*
Mull Drilling Company Inc (PA)....316 264-6366
1700 N Wtrfrnt Pkwy # 1200 Wichita (67206) *(G-15138)*
Mull Family Farms Oper Partnr....620 982-4336
553 R Rd Pawnee Rock (67567) *(G-9753)*
Mull Investments LP....620 982-4336
553 R Rd Pawnee Rock (67567) *(G-9754)*
Muller Construction Inc....620 251-1110
204 N Central St Coffeyville (67337) *(G-964)*
Multi Community Diversfd Svcs (PA)....620 241-6693
2107 Industrial Dr McPherson (67460) *(G-7009)*
Multi Community Diversfd Svcs....785 227-2712
218 N Mckinley St Lindsborg (67456) *(G-6405)*
Multi Svc Tech Solutions Inc (HQ)....800 239-1064
8650 College Blvd Overland Park (66210) *(G-9063)*
Multi Systems Installation Inc (PA)....913 422-8282
20101 W 55th St Shawnee Mission (66218) *(G-11658)*
Multi-Media International LLC (PA)....913 469-6800
13915 W 107th St Shawnee Mission (66215) *(G-11659)*
Multimedia Cablevision....620 251-6610
102 W 11th St Coffeyville (67337) *(G-965)*
MULTIPLE LISTING SERVICE, Wichita *Also called Wichita Area Assn of Realtors (G-15974)*
Multiprens Usa Inc (PA)....913 371-6999
20 Ohio Ave Kansas City (66118) *(G-4271)*
Multispecialty Kanza Group PA....913 788-7099
8919 Parallel Pkwy # 555 Kansas City (66112) *(G-4272)*
Mulvane Cooperative Union Inc (PA)....316 777-1121
220 Poplar St Mulvane (67110) *(G-7223)*
Mulvane Family Medcenter....316 777-0176
1004 Se Louis Dr Mulvane (67110) *(G-7224)*
Mulvane News and Bandwagon....316 777-4233
204 W Main St Mulvane (67110) *(G-7225)*
Munchkin Village....620 577-2440
500 S 9th St Independence (67301) *(G-3542)*
Munson Army Health Center, Fort Leavenworth *Also called United States Dept of Army (G-1943)*
Murdock Companies Inc (PA)....316 262-4476
1111 E 1st St N Wichita (67214) *(G-15139)*
Murdock Electric & Supply, Wichita *Also called Murdock Companies Inc (G-15139)*
Murfin Drilling Company Inc (HQ)....316 267-3241
250 N Water St Ste 300 Wichita (67202) *(G-15140)*
Murfin Drilling Company Inc....785 483-5371
400 S Van Houten St Russell (67665) *(G-10282)*
Murfin Drilling Company Inc....785 421-2101
E Hwy 24 Hill City (67642) *(G-3036)*
Murfin Drilling Company Inc....785 462-7541
675 E College Dr Colby (67701) *(G-1031)*
Murphey, Robert L, Salina *Also called Eye Care Associates (G-10494)*
Murphy & Sons Roofing (PA)....913 287-2116
1010 N 54th St Kansas City (66102) *(G-4273)*
Murphy Tractor & Eqp Co Inc....620 227-3139
10893 112 Rd Dodge City (67801) *(G-1408)*
Murphy Tractor & Eqp Co Inc....620 792-2748
325 S Us Highway 281 Great Bend (67530) *(G-2614)*
Murphy Tractor & Eqp Co Inc (HQ)....855 246-9124
5375 N Deere Rd Park City (67219) *(G-9638)*
Murphy Tractor & Eqp Co Inc....785 233-0556
1621 Nw Gage Blvd Topeka (66618) *(G-12919)*
Murphy USA Inc....620 664-9479
1903 E 17th Ave Hutchinson (67501) *(G-3386)*
Murphy USA Inc....620 227-5607
1907 N 14th Ave Dodge City (67801) *(G-1409)*
Murphy-Hoffman Company....913 441-6300
2700 S 88th St Kansas City (66111) *(G-4274)*
Murphy-Hoffman Company (PA)....816 483-6444
11120 Tomahawk Creek Pkwy Leawood (66211) *(G-5492)*
Murray and Sons Cnstr Co Inc....785 267-1961
3641 Sw Plass Ave Ste C Topeka (66611) *(G-12920)*
Murray Clary Anita C DDS....785 272-6060
6231 Sw 29th St Ste 100 Topeka (66614) *(G-12921)*
Murray Gill Energy Center, Colwich *Also called Evergy Kansas Central Inc (G-1095)*
Museum of Anthropology, Lawrence *Also called University of Kansas (G-5164)*
Museum of Kansas Nat Guard, Topeka *Also called Adjutant Generals Dept Kans (G-12288)*
Mustang Softball....316 260-9770
2250 N Hoover Rd Wichita (67205) *(G-15141)*
Mustang Softball Academy, Wichita *Also called Mustang Softball (G-15141)*
Mutual Fund Store Inc....913 338-2323
11095 Metcalf Ave Shawnee Mission (66210) *(G-11660)*
Mutual Fund Store LLC (HQ)....913 319-8181
10950 Grandview Dr # 500 Overland Park (66210) *(G-9064)*
Mutual Savings Association....913 441-5555
229 Oak St Bonner Springs (66012) *(G-564)*
Mutual Savings Association (PA)....913 682-3491
100 S 4th St Leavenworth (66048) *(G-5272)*

Mutualaid Exchange (PA)....913 338-1100
4400 College Blvd Ste 250 Overland Park (66211) ***(G-9065)***
Muve Health LLC....303 862-9215
11221 Roe Ave Ste 210 Leawood (66211) ***(G-5493)***
Mv Partners LLC....316 267-3241
250 N Water St Ste 300 Wichita (67202) ***(G-15142)***
Mv Purchasing LLC (PA)....316 262-2819
8301 E 21st St N Ste 370 Wichita (67206) ***(G-15143)***
Mv Transportation Inc....785 312-7054
1260 Timberedge Rd Lawrence (66049) ***(G-5034)***
Mvp Electric Llc....913 322-0868
21514 W 51st Ter Shawnee (66226) ***(G-11001)***
Mvp Electric Heating & Cooling, Shawnee *Also called Mvp Electric Llc* ***(G-11001)***
Mvp Electric LLC....913 322-0868
21514 W 51st Ter Shawnee Mission (66226) ***(G-11661)***
Mw Builders Inc (HQ)....913 469-0101
13725 W 109th St Lenexa (66215) ***(G-6016)***
Mw Lawn & Landscape....913 829-4949
19003 W 157th Ter Olathe (66062) ***(G-7908)***
MWH Global Inc....913 383-2086
11835 Roe Ave Ste 242 Leawood (66211) ***(G-5494)***
Mwi Veterinary Supply Co....913 422-3900
2450 Midpoint Dr Edwardsville (66111) ***(G-1509)***
MWM Group Inc....913 469-0101
11100 Ash St Ste 100 Shawnee Mission (66211) ***(G-11662)***
MWM Oil Co Inc....316 265-1992
821 High St Towanda (67144) ***(G-13265)***
Mwv Calmar Plant, Winfield *Also called Westrock Dspensing Systems Inc* ***(G-16182)***
My Child Advocate PA....913 829-8838
201 E Loula St Ste 109 Olathe (66061) ***(G-7909)***
My Contracting LLC....913 747-9015
2013 E Prairie Cir Ste A Olathe (66062) ***(G-7910)***
My Laundry, Shawnee Mission *Also called Just Our Laundry Inc* ***(G-11505)***
My Oread Family Practice, Lawrence *Also called John P Gravino Do* ***(G-4927)***
My1stop LLC....316 554-9700
3200 Liberty Bell Rd Fort Scott (66701) ***(G-1992)***
My1stop.com, Fort Scott *Also called My1stop LLC* ***(G-1992)***
Myers and Stauffer Lc....785 228-6700
1131 Sw Winding Rd Ste C Topeka (66615) ***(G-12922)***
Myers Ice Company, Garden City *Also called Arctic Glacier Inc* ***(G-2102)***
Myfreightworld Carrier MGT Inc....877 549-9438
7007 College Blvd Ste 150 Overland Park (66211) ***(G-9066)***
Myfreightworld Tech Inc (PA)....913 677-6691
7007 College Blvd Ste 150 Leawood (66211) ***(G-5495)***
Myriad Machine Co....620 624-2962
5 S Cntry Estates Rd Liberal (67901) ***(G-6346)***
Myron International Inc....913 281-5552
200 N 6th St Kansas City (66101) ***(G-4275)***
Myrons Dental Laboratories (PA)....800 359-7111
200 N 6th St Kansas City (66101) ***(G-4276)***
Mysmartplans, Kansas City *Also called Marathon Reprographics Inc* ***(G-4217)***
Mystik Lubricants, Kansas City *Also called City Oil Company Inc* ***(G-3912)***
N & B Enterprises Inc....620 431-6424
1302 S Henry St Chanute (66720) ***(G-744)***
N A C M Credit Services Inc....913 383-9300
10670 Barkley St Shawnee Mission (66212) ***(G-11663)***
N C K Commercial Laundry Inc....785 243-4432
217 W 3rd St Concordia (66901) ***(G-1124)***
N C R A, McPherson *Also called Jayhawk Pipeline LLC* ***(G-6978)***
N C R A, Phillipsburg *Also called Chc McPherson Refinery Inc* ***(G-9779)***
N C R A, McPherson *Also called CHS McPherson Refinery Inc* ***(G-6949)***
N C R A, Hill City *Also called CHS McPherson Refinery Inc* ***(G-3030)***
N C R A, Great Bend *Also called Chc McPherson Refinery Inc* ***(G-2536)***
N Central KS Reg Juven Deten....785 238-4549
820 N Monroe St Junction City (66441) ***(G-3728)***
N J Investors Inc....316 652-0616
7701 E Kellogg Dr Ste 895 Wichita (67207) ***(G-15144)***
N P C, Valley Center *Also called National Plastics Color Inc* ***(G-13349)***
N P L, Topeka *Also called Npl Construction Co* ***(G-12940)***
N R Hamm Contractor Inc....785 597-5111
609 Perry Pl Perry (66073) ***(G-9773)***
N R Hamm Quarry Inc....785 842-3236
16984 3rd St Lawrence (66044) ***(G-5035)***
N T C, Kansas City *Also called Nebraska Transport Co Inc* ***(G-4284)***
N T S LLC....913 281-5353
801 Armourdale Pkwy Kansas City (66105) ***(G-4277)***
N-Zone Sportswear, Manhattan *Also called Acres Inc* ***(G-6532)***
N2 Kids Enterprises Inc....913 648-5457
9215 Slater St Shawnee Mission (66212) ***(G-11664)***
Naab Electric Inc....620 276-8101
2013 W Jones Ave Garden City (67846) ***(G-2242)***
Nabholz Construction Corp....913 393-6500
17300 W 116th St Lenexa (66219) ***(G-6017)***
Nacada The Glbl Comm For Acdm....785 532-3398
2323 Anderson Ave Ste 225 Manhattan (66502) ***(G-6756)***
Nachlas, Michael J, Shawnee Mission *Also called Podiatry Associates PA* ***(G-11741)***
Nadia Inc....316 686-6190
2250 N Rock Rd Ste 118 Wichita (67226) ***(G-15145)***
Nai Heartland Co....913 362-1000
4400 College Blvd Ste 170 Leawood (66211) ***(G-5496)***
Nail Perfection LLC....913 722-0799
5110 Johnson Dr Roeland Park (66205) ***(G-10228)***
Nail Pro....913 402-0882
12086 W 135th St Shawnee Mission (66221) ***(G-11665)***
Nailery....913 599-2225
11655 W 95th St Ste 120 Overland Park (66214) ***(G-9067)***
Nailery Too....913 599-3331
11373 W 95th St Ste 37 Shawnee Mission (66214) ***(G-11666)***
Nalco Champion, Liberal *Also called Nalco Company* ***(G-6347)***
Nalco Champion, Hays *Also called Nalco Company LLC* ***(G-2876)***
Nalco Company....620 624-1594
1541 W Beckett St Liberal (67901) ***(G-6347)***
Nalco Company LLC....785 885-4161
419 6th St Natoma (67651) ***(G-7232)***
Nalco Company LLC....785 625-3822
1019 Reservation Rd Hays (67601) ***(G-2876)***
Nall Ave Baptist Church....913 432-4141
6701 Nall Ave Prairie Village (66208) ***(G-10049)***
Nall Avenue Child Dev Center, Prairie Village *Also called Nall Ave Baptist Church* ***(G-10049)***
Nall Dialysis, Overland Park *Also called Kenai Dialysis LLC* ***(G-8914)***
Nall Hills Animal Hospital....913 341-8836
9610 Nall Ave Shawnee Mission (66207) ***(G-11667)***
Nallwood Heights Corporation....913 341-4880
10770 El Monte St Shawnee Mission (66211) ***(G-11668)***
Names and Numbers, Pittsburg *Also called K W Brock Directories Inc* ***(G-9884)***
Namsco Inc....913 344-9100
8300 College Blvd Ste 300 Shawnee Mission (66210) ***(G-11669)***
Nance Manufacturing Inc (PA)....316 942-8671
2005 S West St Wichita (67213) ***(G-15146)***
Nance Manufacturing Inc....620 842-3761
396 W Highway 2 Anthony (67003) ***(G-130)***
NAPA Auto Parts, Emporia *Also called Cline Auto Supply Inc* ***(G-1721)***
NAPA Auto Parts, Shawnee Mission *Also called Genuine Parts Company* ***(G-11395)***
Nasb Financial Inc....913 327-2000
10950 El Monte St Leawood (66211) ***(G-5497)***
Nate Apple Concrete Inc....913 837-3022
7840 W 255th St Louisburg (66053) ***(G-6459)***
Nathan Weiner & Associates (PA)....913 390-0508
1450 S Lone Elm Rd Olathe (66061) ***(G-7911)***
Natio Assoc For The Advan of....913 334-0366
7103 Waverly Ave Kansas City (66109) ***(G-4278)***
Natio Assoc For The Advan of....913 362-2272
6505 Frontage Rd Ste 3 Shawnee Mission (66202) ***(G-11670)***
Nation-Wide Repr Holdg Co Inc....913 248-1722
16151 Foster St Stilwell (66085) ***(G-12170)***
National Advisors Holdings Inc....913 234-8200
8717 W 110th St Ste 700 Overland Park (66210) ***(G-9068)***
National AG Ctr & Hall Fame....913 721-1075
630 N 126th St Bonner Springs (66012) ***(G-565)***
National Almnm-Brass Fndry Inc....816 833-4500
12509 Juniper St Leawood (66209) ***(G-5498)***
National Archives and Rec ADM....785 263-6700
200 Se 4th St Abilene (67410) ***(G-47)***
National Assn Ltr Carriers....620 378-3263
602 N 6th St Coyville (66736) ***(G-1183)***
National Assn Ltr Carriers....620 257-3934
513 S Bell Ave Lyons (67554) ***(G-6495)***
National Assn Ltr Carriers....785 232-6835
1949 Nw Topeka Blvd Topeka (66608) ***(G-12923)***
National Auctioneers Assn....913 541-8084
8880 Ballentine St Shawnee Mission (66214) ***(G-11671)***
National Bd For Rspratory Care....913 895-4900
10801 Mastin St Ste 300 Overland Park (66210) ***(G-9069)***
National Beef Packing Co LLC....800 449-2333
1501 E 8th St Liberal (67901) ***(G-6348)***
National Beef Packing Co LLC....620 624-1851
1501 E 8th St Liberal (67901) ***(G-6349)***
National Beef Packing Co LLC....620 227-7135
2000 E Trail St Dodge City (67801) ***(G-1410)***
National Builders Inc....316 729-7445
7570 W 21st St N 1006e Wichita (67205) ***(G-15147)***
National Car Rental, Wichita *Also called Midwest Car Corporation* ***(G-15089)***
National Cemetery ADM....913 758-4105
150 Muncie Rd Leavenworth (66048) ***(G-5273)***
National Cemetery ADM....913 758-4105
150 Muncie Rd Leavenworth (66048) ***(G-5274)***
National Center For Competency....913 498-1000
7007 College Blvd Ste 250 Shawnee Mission (66211) ***(G-11672)***
National Christian Charita, Overland Park *Also called Servant Foundation* ***(G-9297)***
National Cold Storage Inc....913 422-4050
12755 Loring Dr Bonner Springs (66012) ***(G-566)***
National Cold Storage Kc Inc....913 422-4050
12755 Loring Dr Bonner Springs (66012) ***(G-567)***
National Commercial Bldrs Inc....913 599-0200
10555 Rene St Lenexa (66215) ***(G-6018)***

ALPHABETIC

National Contractors Inc...316 722-8484
621 N Birkdale Dr Wichita (67230) ***(G-15148)***
National Credit Adjusters LLC...888 768-0674
327 W 4th Ave Hutchinson (67501) ***(G-3387)***
National Crop Insur Svcs Inc...913 685-2767
8900 Indian Creek Pkwy Overland Park (66210) ***(G-9070)***
National Ctstrphe Rstrtion Inc...913 663-4111
8065 Flint St Shawnee Mission (66214) ***(G-11673)***
National Ctstrphe Rstrtion Inc (PA)...316 636-5700
8447 E 35th St N Wichita (67226) ***(G-15149)***
National Ctstrphe Rstrtion Inc...913 663-4111
8065 Flint St Overland Park (66214) ***(G-9071)***
National Engraving...785 776-5757
1712 Westbank Way Manhattan (66503) ***(G-6757)***
National Express LLC...913 837-4470
7420 W 68 Hwy Louisburg (66053) ***(G-6460)***
National Express LLC...620 662-1299
1401 W 4th Ave Hutchinson (67501) ***(G-3388)***
National Express LLC...620 326-3318
14 Industrial Ave Wellington (67152) ***(G-13519)***
National Fabric Co Inc...913 281-1833
901 S 7th St Kansas City (66105) ***(G-4279)***
National Fiber Supply Co, Kansas City *Also called National Fiber Supply LLC* ***(G-4280)***
National Fiber Supply LLC...913 321-0066
3210 N 7th Street Trfy Kansas City (66115) ***(G-4280)***
National Fire Suppression, Kansas City *Also called Western States Fire Protection* ***(G-4537)***
National Gibson Company, Medicine Lodge *Also called New Ngc Inc* ***(G-7069)***
National Golf Properties LLC...913 721-1333
12601 Hollingsworth Rd Kansas City (66109) ***(G-4281)***
National Greyhound Association...785 263-4660
729 Old 40 Abilene (67410) ***(G-48)***
National Gympson...620 248-3247
20672 Nw White Sands Rd Sun City (67143) ***(G-12217)***
National Healthcare Corp...620 767-5172
400 Sunset Dr Council Grove (66846) ***(G-1173)***
National Healthcare Corp...316 524-3211
215 N Lamar Ave Haysville (67060) ***(G-2952)***
National Healthcare Corp...620 285-6914
1114 W 11th St Larned (67550) ***(G-4707)***
National Healthcare Corp...316 772-5185
712 N Monroe Ave Sedgwick (67135) ***(G-10851)***
National Healthcare Corp...620 431-4940
530 W 14th St Chanute (66720) ***(G-745)***
National Healthcareer Assn...800 499-9092
11161 Overbrook Rd Leawood (66211) ***(G-5499)***
National Home Buyers Alliance, Shawnee Mission *Also called Quest Capital Management Inc* ***(G-11766)***
National Metal Finishing, Wichita *Also called Figeac Aero North America Inc* ***(G-14366)***
National Opinion Research Ctr...316 221-5800
2021 N Amidon Ave # 1300 Wichita (67203) ***(G-15150)***
National Park Service...620 285-6911
1767 Ks Highway 156 Larned (67550) ***(G-4708)***
National Plastics Color Inc...316 755-1273
100 W Industrial St Valley Center (67147) ***(G-13349)***
National Publishers Group Inc...316 788-6271
1326 E 79th St S Haysville (67060) ***(G-2953)***
National Rent A Car, Wichita *Also called National Rental (us) Inc* ***(G-15151)***
National Rental (us) Inc...316 946-4851
1300 S Airport Rd Wichita (67209) ***(G-15151)***
National Rgstred Agents Inc NJ...913 754-0637
11600 College Blvd # 210 Overland Park (66210) ***(G-9072)***
National Rural Health Assn...913 220-2997
4501 College Blvd Ste 225 Leawood (66211) ***(G-5500)***
National Screening Bureau LLC...316 263-4400
515 N Ridge Rd Ste 202 Wichita (67212) ***(G-15152)***
National Sign Company Inc...785 242-4111
1415 N Industrial Ave Ottawa (66067) ***(G-8293)***
National Soc Tole/Dec Pntr Inc (PA)...316 269-9300
393 N Mclean Blvd Wichita (67203) ***(G-15153)***
National Society Daughters Rev...785 448-5959
417 W 6th Ave Garnett (66032) ***(G-2384)***
National Socty of The Daughtrs...620 356-2570
1675 W Patterson Ave Ulysses (67880) ***(G-13307)***
National Tire Wholesale, Kansas City *Also called Carrolls LLC* ***(G-3893)***
National Veterinary Associates...913 782-0173
457 N K 7 Hwy Olathe (66061) ***(G-7912)***
National Weather Service...785 899-2360
920 Armory Rd Goodland (67735) ***(G-2480)***
National Weather Service...785 234-2592
1116 Ne Strait Ave Topeka (66616) ***(G-12924)***
National Weather Service...620 225-6514
104 Airport Rd Dodge City (67801) ***(G-1411)***
National-Spencer Inc (PA)...316 265-5601
9021 W Kellogg Dr Wichita (67209) ***(G-15154)***
NationaLease, Kansas City *Also called Success Truck Leasing Inc* ***(G-4445)***
Nationl Soc Daught AMR Rev...620 457-8747
1074 S 160th St Pittsburg (66762) ***(G-9910)***
Nations Holding Company (PA)...913 383-8185
5370 W 95th St Prairie Village (66207) ***(G-10050)***
Nations Lending Services, Prairie Village *Also called Nations Title Agency* ***(G-10051)***
Nations Mailing Systems, Shawnee Mission *Also called I M S of Kansas City Inc* ***(G-11446)***
Nations Title Agency (HQ)...913 341-2705
5370 W 95th St Prairie Village (66207) ***(G-10051)***
Nationwide, Overland Park *Also called Boulevard Insurance LLC* ***(G-8476)***
Nationwide, Olathe *Also called C & T Enterprises Inc* ***(G-7572)***
Nationwide, Winfield *Also called Risk Counselors Inc* ***(G-16169)***
Nationwide, Leawood *Also called Livestock Marketing Assn* ***(G-5458)***
Nationwide, Salina *Also called Assurance Partners LLC* ***(G-10411)***
Nationwide, Hutchinson *Also called Provalue Cooperative Inc* ***(G-3416)***
Nationwide, Great Bend *Also called John Jaco Inc* ***(G-2595)***
Nationwide, Burlington *Also called Trustpoint Services Inc* ***(G-644)***
Nationwide, Leawood *Also called Robert E Miller Insurance Agcy* ***(G-5540)***
Nationwide, Wellington *Also called Renn & Company Inc* ***(G-13523)***
Nationwide, Lawrence *Also called Calvin Eddy & Kappelman Inc* ***(G-4774)***
Nationwide, Overland Park *Also called Cobbs Allen & Hall Inc* ***(G-8571)***
Nationwide, Great Bend *Also called Keller RE & Insur Agcy* ***(G-2599)***
Nationwide, Topeka *Also called Agency Services Corp Kansas* ***(G-12301)***
Nationwide, Independence *Also called Newkirk Dennis & Buckles* ***(G-3543)***
Nationwide, Prairie Village *Also called T S A Inc* ***(G-10072)***
Nationwide, Overland Park *Also called Lockton Affinity LLC* ***(G-8968)***
Nationwide, Leavenworth *Also called Armed Forces Insurance Exhange* ***(G-5204)***
Nationwide, Overland Park *Also called Willis North America Inc* ***(G-9495)***
Nationwide, Wichita *Also called USI Insurance Services LLC* ***(G-15864)***
Nationwide, Topeka *Also called Peoples/Commercial Insur LLC* ***(G-12968)***
Nationwide Learning LLC...785 862-2292
1345 Sw 42nd St Topeka (66609) ***(G-12925)***
Nationwide Transportation and...913 888-1685
5940 Nieman Rd Shawnee (66203) ***(G-11002)***
Natoma Corporation...785 877-3529
16596 Us Highway 36 Norton (67654) ***(G-7451)***
Natoma Leasing LLC...785 877-3529
16596 Us Highway 36 Norton (67654) ***(G-7452)***
Natoma Manufacturing Corp...785 877-3529
16596 Us Highway 36 Norton (67654) ***(G-7453)***
Natoma Realty LLC...785 877-3529
16596 Us Highway 36 Norton (67654) ***(G-7454)***
Natrional Assoc Advncmnt Color, Kansas City *Also called Natio Assoc For The Advan of* ***(G-4278)***
Natural Breeze Remodeling, Lawrence *Also called Nb Remodeling LLC* ***(G-5036)***
Natural Creations Inc...913 390-8058
995 N Marion St Olathe (66061) ***(G-7913)***
Natural Gas Pipeline Amer LLC...620 885-4505
12653 114 Rd Minneola (67865) ***(G-7127)***
Natural Gas Pipeline Amer LLC...620 793-7118
846 Nw 40 Rd Great Bend (67530) ***(G-2615)***
Natural Gas Pipeline Amer LLC...785 568-2231
687 Deer Rd Glasco (67445) ***(G-2422)***
Natural Life Pet Products, Frontenac *Also called Arthur Dogswell LLC* ***(G-2052)***
Natural Rsource Protection Inc...316 303-0505
9131 E 37th St N Wichita (67226) ***(G-15155)***
Natural Way Chiropractic...913 385-1999
9150 Glenwood St Shawnee Mission (66212) ***(G-11674)***
Natures Way Inc...785 486-3302
1374 Horned Owl Rd Horton (66439) ***(G-3132)***
Navrats Inc (PA)...620 342-2092
728 Mechanic St Emporia (66801) ***(G-1800)***
Navy Federal Credit Union...888 842-6328
301 Cheyenne St Leavenworth (66048) ***(G-5275)***
Nazdar Company (HQ)...913 422-1888
8501 Hedge Lane Ter Shawnee (66227) ***(G-11003)***
Nazdar Company...913 422-1888
8420 Hedge Ln Shawnee (66227) ***(G-11004)***
Nazdar Source One, Shawnee *Also called Nazdar Company* ***(G-11003)***
Nb Remodeling LLC...785 749-1855
1440 Wakarusa Dr Ste 800 Lawrence (66049) ***(G-5036)***
Nbh Bank...785 842-4300
4831 W 6th St Lawrence (66049) ***(G-5037)***
Nbh Bank...785 242-2900
434 S Main St Ottawa (66067) ***(G-8294)***
Nbh Bank...913 782-5400
2002 E Santa Fe St Olathe (66062) ***(G-7914)***
Nbh Bank...913 831-4184
4600 Shawnee Dr Kansas City (66106) ***(G-4282)***
Nbh Bank...913 441-6800
110 S 4th St Edwardsville (66111) ***(G-1510)***
Nbh Bank...913 299-9700
7804 State Ave Kansas City (66112) ***(G-4283)***
Nbrc, Overland Park *Also called National Bd For Rspratory Care* ***(G-9069)***
NCADD, Topeka *Also called Shawnee Regl Prevention An* ***(G-13064)***
Ncct, Shawnee Mission *Also called National Center For Competency* ***(G-11672)***
Nck Wellness Center Inc...785 738-3995
3033 Us 24 Hwy Beloit (67420) ***(G-495)***
Ncri, Wichita *Also called National Ctstrphe Rstrtion Inc* ***(G-15149)***

Ncs Healthcare of Kansas LLC 316 522-3449
8200 E 34th Cir N Wichita (67226) **(G-15156)**
Ncs Precision Manufacturing, Shawnee Mission *Also called Numerical Control Support Inc* **(G-11690)**
Nctc, Sabetha *Also called Nemaha County Training Center* **(G-10321)**
Ne KS Community Action Program, Hiawatha *Also called Nek Cap Inc* **(G-3019)**
Ne Wichita Dialysis Cntr, Wichita *Also called Renal Trtmnt Centers-West Inc* **(G-15444)**
Neal John E, Hutchinson *Also called Ineeda Laundry and Drycleaners* **(G-3333)**
Neals Foundations Inc 316 744-0064
5515 Huffman Dr Kechi (67067) **(G-4573)**
Nearing Staats Prelogar 913 831-1415
3515 W 75th St Ste 201 Prairie Village (66208) **(G-10052)**
Nearman Creek Power Plant, Kansas City *Also called Kansas City Bd Pub Utilities* **(G-4140)**
Nearman Water Plant, Kansas City *Also called Kansas City Bd Pub Utilities* **(G-4135)**
Nebco Inc (PA) 785 462-3943
723 Osage Ave Salina (67401) **(G-10610)**
Nebraska Transport Co Inc 913 281-9991
6125 Speaker Rd Kansas City (66111) **(G-4284)**
Needham & Associates Inc (PA) 913 385-5300
15950 College Blvd Lenexa (66219) **(G-6019)**
Neff Packaging Systems, Kansas City *Also called Neff Sales Co Inc* **(G-4285)**
Neff Sales Co Inc 913 371-0777
555 Sunshine Rd Kansas City (66115) **(G-4285)**
Neighborhood Connection 316 267-0197
200 S Walnut St Wichita (67213) **(G-15157)**
Neighborhood Group Inc 913 362-0000
8826 Santa Fe Dr Ste 190 Shawnee Mission (66212) **(G-11675)**
Neighborhood Learning Ctr LLC 785 238-2321
227 W 7th St Junction City (66441) **(G-3729)**
Neighborhood Network LLC 913 341-9316
11627 W 79th St Lenexa (66214) **(G-6020)**
Neighbors & Associates Inc 620 423-3010
1801 S 21st St Parsons (67357) **(G-9710)**
Neighbors Construction Co Inc (PA) 913 422-5555
15226 W 87th Street Pkwy Lenexa (66219) **(G-6021)**
Nek Cap Inc 785 364-4798
130 S Iowa Ave Holton (66436) **(G-3107)**
Nek Cap Inc (PA) 785 742-2222
1260 220th St Hiawatha (66434) **(G-3019)**
Nek Cap Inc 913 367-7848
751 S 8th St Rm 101 Atchison (66002) **(G-251)**
Nek Cap Inc 913 651-5692
2940 Ralph Bunch Dr Leavenworth (66048) **(G-5276)**
Nek Cap Inc 785 456-9165
714 Plum St Wamego (66547) **(G-13430)**
Nek-Cap Headstart, Wamego *Also called Nek Cap Inc* **(G-13430)**
Nelson Electric Inc 316 794-8025
1200 N 199th St W Goddard (67052) **(G-2447)**
Nelson Harmon Kapln WMS MD 913 599-3800
10550 Quivira Rd Ste 335 Lenexa (66215) **(G-6022)**
Nelson Poultry Farms Inc (PA) 785 587-0399
8530 E Us Highway 24 Manhattan (66502) **(G-6758)**
Nelson Quarries Inc 620 496-2211
1307 2000 St Gas (66742) **(G-2392)**
Nelson, John B, Lenexa *Also called Nelson Harmon Kapln WMS MD* **(G-6022)**
Nemaha County Assisted Living, Seneca *Also called Country Place Senior Living* **(G-10860)**
Nemaha County Community Hlth 785 284-2152
1004 Main St Sabetha (66534) **(G-10320)**
Nemaha County Cooperative Assn (PA) 785 336-6153
223 E Main St Seneca (66538) **(G-10874)**
Nemaha County Cooperative Assn 785 456-6924
305 Noble Ave Belvue (66407) **(G-507)**
Nemaha County Training Center (PA) 785 336-6116
12 S 11th St Seneca (66538) **(G-10875)**
Nemaha County Training Center 785 300-1306
329 N 11th St Sabetha (66534) **(G-10321)**
Nemaha Valley Community Hosp (PA) 785 336-6181
1600 Community Dr Seneca (66538) **(G-10876)**
Nemaha Valley Community Hosp 785 336-6107
1600 Community Dr Seneca (66538) **(G-10877)**
Nemaha-Marshall Electric 785 736-2345
402 Prairie St Axtell (66403) **(G-351)**
Nendels Inn, Dodge City *Also called Midwest Star Equities LLC* **(G-1406)**
Neodesha Fire Department, Neodesha *Also called City of Neodesha* **(G-7235)**
Neodesha Plastics Inc (PA) 620 325-3096
1206 Worley Dr Twin Twin Rivers Neodesha (66757) **(G-7245)**
Neodesha Plastics Inc 620 325-3096
1000 Reece St Neodesha (66757) **(G-7246)**
Neosho County Fair Assn Inc 620 433-0446
600 W Canville St Erie (66733) **(G-1860)**
Neosho County Road and Bridge 620 244-3855
515 E 4th St Erie (66733) **(G-1861)**
Neosho Gardens LLC 620 767-6920
601 N Union St Council Grove (66846) **(G-1174)**
Neosho Small Parts LLC 620 244-3263
301 S Broadway St Erie (66733) **(G-1862)**
Nephrology Associates Inc 913 381-0622
1295 E 151st St Ste 7 Olathe (66062) **(G-7915)**

Nesco Holdings Inc 913 287-0001
5320 Kansas Ave Kansas City (66106) **(G-4286)**
Nesika Energy LLC 785 335-2054
1020 70 Rd Scandia (66966) **(G-10800)**
Ness City Farm and Feed, Ness City *Also called D E Bondurant Grain Co Inc* **(G-7260)**
Ness County Engineers Office 785 798-3350
12330 Us Highway 283 Ness City (67560) **(G-7264)**
Ness County Hospital Dst No 2 ....785 798-2107
312 Custer St Ness City (67560) **(G-7265)**
Nestegg Consulting Inc 316 383-1064
100 N Main St Fl 10 Wichita (67202) **(G-15158)**
Net Systems LLC 316 691-9400
2709 E Boulevard Plz Wichita (67211) **(G-15159)**
Net-Ability LLC 316 691-4527
2420 N Woodlawn Blvd 100a Wichita (67220) **(G-15160)**
Netapp Inc 316 636-8000
3718 N Rock Rd Wichita (67226) **(G-15161)**
Netapp Inc 913 451-6718
9393 W 110th St Ste 200 Overland Park (66210) **(G-9073)**
Netchemia LLC (HQ) 913 789-0996
7801 Nieman Rd Ste 200 Overland Park (66214) **(G-9074)**
Netco Construction Co Inc 316 942-2062
1650 S Meridian Ave Ste 7 Wichita (67213) **(G-15162)**
Netco Home Improvement Center, Wichita *Also called Netco Construction Co Inc* **(G-15162)**
Netsmart LLC (PA) 913 327-7444
4950 College Blvd Overland Park (66211) **(G-9075)**
Netsmart Technologies Inc (HQ) 913 327-7444
4950 College Blvd Overland Park (66211) **(G-9076)**
Netstandard Inc (PA) 913 428-4200
10300 W 103rd St Ste 100 Overland Park (66214) **(G-9077)**
Network Computer Solutions, Saint George *Also called Frugal Inc* **(G-10347)**
Network Consulting Inc 913 893-4150
20265 Peppertree Rd Edgerton (66021) **(G-1488)**
Network Kansas, Wichita *Also called Kansas Center Entreprnrshp* **(G-14791)**
Network Management Group Inc 620 665-3611
324 E 4th Ave Hutchinson (67501) **(G-3389)**
Networks International Corp 913 685-3400
15237 Broadmoor St Overland Park (66223) **(G-9078)**
Networks Plus, Manhattan *Also called Civicplus LLC* **(G-6589)**
Networks Plus 785 825-0400
753 N 12th St Salina (67401) **(G-10611)**
Networks Plus (PA) 785 825-0400
2627 Kfb Plz Ste 206w Manhattan (66503) **(G-6759)**
Netzer Sales Inc (PA) 913 599-6464
12625 W 92nd St Shawnee Mission (66215) **(G-11676)**
Neu Consulting Group, Overland Park *Also called Neufinancial Inc* **(G-9079)**
Neufinancial Inc 913 825-0000
8417 Santa Fe Dr Ste 200 Overland Park (66212) **(G-9079)**
Neural Technologies Inc 913 831-0273
6340 Glenwood St Ste 110 Shawnee Mission (66202) **(G-11677)**
Neurological Associates Kansas, Wichita *Also called Neurology Associates Kans LLC* **(G-15163)**
Neurology Associates Kans LLC 316 682-5544
3243 E Murdock St Ste 104 Wichita (67208) **(G-15163)**
Neurology Center of Wichita 316 686-6866
220 S Hillside St Ste A Wichita (67211) **(G-15164)**
Neurology Cons Chartered 913 632-9810
8800 W 75th St Ste 100 Shawnee Mission (66204) **(G-11678)**
Neurology Consultants Kans LLC 316 261-3220
2135 N Collective Ln Wichita (67206) **(G-15165)**
Neurosurgery Kansas City PA 913 299-9507
12200 W 106th St Ste 400e Lenexa (66215) **(G-6023)**
Neville Cstm Bilt Smi-Trailers, Kingman *Also called Neville Welding Inc* **(G-4608)**
Neville Welding Inc 620 532-3487
5581 Sw 50 St Kingman (67068) **(G-4608)**
Nevin K Waters DDS PA 913 782-1330
751 N Mur Len Rd Ste B Olathe (66062) **(G-7916)**
Nevius, M L, Hutchinson *Also called ML Nevius Builders Inc* **(G-3383)**
New Age Industrial Corp Inc 785 877-5121
16788 Us Highway 36 Norton (67654) **(G-7455)**
NEW BEGINING ENTERPRISES, Neodesha *Also called Elk County Development Corp* **(G-7239)**
New Beginnings Enterprise 620 583-6835
219 N Main St Eureka (67045) **(G-1896)**
New Beginnings Inc 620 966-0274
100 E 2nd Ave Hutchinson (67501) **(G-3390)**
New Boston Creative Group LLC 785 587-8185
315 Houston St Ste E Manhattan (66502) **(G-6760)**
New Century Air 913 768-9400
2 Aero Plz New Century (66031) **(G-7294)**
New Chance Inc (PA) 620 225-0476
2500 E Wyatt Earp Blvd Dodge City (67801) **(G-1412)**
NEW CHANGE, Dodge City *Also called New Chance Inc* **(G-1412)**
New Choices Program, Hutchinson *Also called Hutchnson Hosp Psychiatric Ctr* **(G-3330)**
New Cingular Wireless Svcs Inc 785 832-2700
520 W 23rd St Ste H Lawrence (66046) **(G-5038)**
New Cingular Wireless Svcs Inc 913 344-2845
10895 Lowell Ave Ste 100 Shawnee Mission (66210) **(G-11679)**

ALPHABETIC

New Day Educare.....913 764-1353
520 S Harrison St Olathe (66061) ***(G-7917)***
New Dimension Pdts Emporia Inc.....620 342-6412
1015 Scott St Emporia (66801) ***(G-1801)***
New Directions Emrgncy Shelter.....785 223-0500
1115 W 14th St Junction City (66441) ***(G-3730)***
New Drctons Bhavioral Hlth LLC (HQ).....816 237-2300
6100 Sprint Pkwy Ste 200 Overland Park (66211) ***(G-9080)***
New England Life Insurance Co.....620 754-3725
391 3800th St Elsmore (66732) ***(G-1683)***
New Frontier Lawn & Tree Care, Wichita *Also called New Frontier Lawn Care Inc* ***(G-15166)***
New Frontier Lawn Care Inc (PA).....316 838-0778
2533 E 36th Cir N Wichita (67219) ***(G-15166)***
New Frontiers.....785 672-3261
212 Maple Ave Oakley (67748) ***(G-7482)***
New Frontiers Health Services, Oakley *Also called New Frontiers* ***(G-7482)***
New Generation.....620 223-1506
1502 Scott Ave Fort Scott (66701) ***(G-1993)***
New Hope Services.....620 231-9895
2614 N Joplin St Pittsburg (66762) ***(G-9911)***
New Horizons Dental Care (PA).....785 376-0250
1920 S Ohio St Salina (67401) ***(G-10612)***
New Horizons of Valley Center, Valley Center *Also called Medicalodges Inc* ***(G-13348)***
New Horizons Rv Corp.....785 238-7575
2401 Lacy Dr Junction City (66441) ***(G-3731)***
New Image Concrete Design LLC.....913 489-1699
5300 Hedge Lane Ter Shawnee (66226) ***(G-11005)***
New Image Roofing LLC.....316 201-1180
114 N Wabash Ave Wichita (67214) ***(G-15167)***
New Market Health Care LLC.....316 773-1212
2131 N Ridge Rd Ste 101 Wichita (67212) ***(G-15168)***
New Media Samurai LLC.....785 856-6673
123 W 8th St Ste 302 Lawrence (66044) ***(G-5039)***
New Mountain Capital I LLC.....913 451-3222
10975 Grandview Dr # 400 Shawnee Mission (66210) ***(G-11680)***
New Ngc Inc.....620 886-5613
1218 Sw Mill Rd Medicine Lodge (67104) ***(G-7069)***
New Paradigm Solutions Inc.....785 313-0946
4130 Taneil Dr Manhattan (66502) ***(G-6761)***
New Song Academy Inc.....316 688-1911
6868 E 32nd St N Wichita (67226) ***(G-15169)***
New Song Academy Preshool, Wichita *Also called New Song Academy Inc* ***(G-15169)***
New Theatre Company.....913 649-7469
9229 Foster St Shawnee Mission (66212) ***(G-11681)***
New Theatre Restaurant, Shawnee Mission *Also called New Theatre Company* ***(G-11681)***
New Wave Enterprises Inc.....913 287-7671
6320 Kansas Ave Kansas City (66111) ***(G-4287)***
New Windows For America LLC.....316 263-0711
3949 N Bridgeport Cir Wichita (67219) ***(G-15170)***
New York Blood Center Inc.....785 233-0195
6220 Sw 29th St Ste 100 Topeka (66614) ***(G-12926)***
New York Life Insurance Co.....913 451-9100
7500 College Blvd Ste 800 Overland Park (66210) ***(G-9081)***
New York Life Insurance Co.....913 906-4000
11400 Tomahwk Crk Pkwy # 540 Leawood (66211) ***(G-5501)***
New York Life Insurance Co.....316 262-0671
125 N Market St Ste 1600 Wichita (67202) ***(G-15171)***
Newberry Ungerer & Heckert LLP.....785 273-5250
2231 Sw Wanamaker Rd # 101 Topeka (66614) ***(G-12927)***
Newcomer Funeral Home-Casper, Topeka *Also called Heartland Management Company* ***(G-12680)***
Newcomer Funeral Svc Group Inc (PA).....785 233-6655
520 Sw 27th St Topeka (66611) ***(G-12928)***
Newcomer Funeral Svc Group Inc.....785 354-8558
1321 Sw 10th Ave Topeka (66604) ***(G-12929)***
Newell & Associates.....913 592-4421
17935 W 183rd St Olathe (66062) ***(G-7918)***
Newkirk Dennis & Buckles (PA).....620 331-3700
304 N Penn Ave Independence (67301) ***(G-3543)***
Newman Home Health, Emporia *Also called Newman Mem Hosp Foundation* ***(G-1805)***
Newman Mem Hosp Foundation.....620 342-2521
1301 W 12th Ave Ste 301 Emporia (66801) ***(G-1802)***
Newman Mem Hosp Foundation (PA).....620 343-6800
1201 W 12th Ave Emporia (66801) ***(G-1803)***
Newman Mem Hosp Foundation.....620 343-1800
1015 Industrial Rd Emporia (66801) ***(G-1804)***
Newman Mem Hosp Foundation.....620 340-6161
1201 W 12th Ave Emporia (66801) ***(G-1805)***
Newman Regional Health, Emporia *Also called Newman Mem Hosp Foundation* ***(G-1803)***
News Publishing Co Inc.....785 628-1081
507 Main St Hays (67601) ***(G-2877)***
Newton Animal Hospital, Newton *Also called Shane Paul LLC* ***(G-7418)***
Newton Animal Hospital, Newton *Also called Shane Paul Inc* ***(G-7417)***
Newton City Parks Dept, Newton *Also called City of Newton* ***(G-7329)***
Newton Cmnty Child Care Ctr.....316 284-6525
207 Se 9th St Newton (67114) ***(G-7392)***
Newton Healthcare Corporation.....316 283-2700
600 Medical Center Dr Newton (67114) ***(G-7393)***
Newton Kansan, Newton *Also called Morris Communications Co LLC* ***(G-7390)***
Newton Medical Center, Newton *Also called Newton Healthcare Corporation* ***(G-7393)***
Newton Medical Ctr Child Care.....316 804-6094
805 Medical Center Dr Newton (67114) ***(G-7394)***
Newton Presbyterian Manor, Newton *Also called Presbyterian Manors Inc* ***(G-7408)***
Newton Recreation Commission.....316 283-7330
415 N Poplar St Newton (67114) ***(G-7395)***
Newton Surgery Ctr.....316 283-9977
800 Medical Center Dr # 240 Newton (67114) ***(G-7396)***
Newton Wellness Center, Newton *Also called Newton Recreation Commission* ***(G-7395)***
Newton William Memorial Hosp.....620 221-2916
1305 E 5th Ave Winfield (67156) ***(G-16162)***
Newton William Memorial Hosp (PA).....620 221-2300
1300 E 5th Ave Winfield (67156) ***(G-16163)***
Newtons Inc.....620 336-2276
116 W Main St Cherryvale (67335) ***(G-811)***
Nex-Tech, Lenora *Also called Rural Telephone Service Co Inc* ***(G-6245)***
Nex-Tech LLC.....785 421-4197
118 W Main St Hill City (67642) ***(G-3037)***
Nex-Tech LLC (HQ).....785 625-7070
2418 Vine St Hays (67601) ***(G-2878)***
Nex-Tech Wireless LLC (HQ).....785 567-4281
3001 New Way Hays (67601) ***(G-2879)***
Nexeo Solutions Kansas City, Kansas City *Also called Univar Solutions USA Inc* ***(G-4493)***
Nexlearn LLC.....316 265-2170
100 S Main St Ste 416 Wichita (67202) ***(G-15172)***
Nexlynx.....785 232-5969
123 Sw 6th Ave 100 Topeka (66603) ***(G-12930)***
Nexstar Broadcasting Inc.....785 582-4000
6835 Nw Us Highway 24 Topeka (66618) ***(G-12931)***
Nexstar Broadcasting Inc.....316 265-3333
833 N Main St Wichita (67203) ***(G-15173)***
Next Led Signs LLC.....888 263-6530
3526 N Comotara St Wichita (67226) ***(G-15174)***
Next To Nature Landscape LLC.....913 963-8180
11785 S Conley St Olathe (66061) ***(G-7919)***
Nextaff LLC (PA).....913 562-5620
11225 College Blvd # 250 Overland Park (66210) ***(G-9082)***
Nextel of California Inc (HQ).....866 505-2385
6200 Sprint Pkwy Overland Park (66251) ***(G-9083)***
Nextel Partners Operating Corp (HQ).....800 829-0965
6200 Sprint Pkwy Overland Park (66251) ***(G-9084)***
Nexus It Group Inc.....913 815-1750
7512 W 80th St Overland Park (66204) ***(G-9085)***
Nexus Medical LLC.....913 451-2234
11315 Strang Line Rd Shawnee Mission (66215) ***(G-11682)***
Nfi Management Co Inc (PA).....913 341-4411
7031 W 97th Ter Shawnee Mission (66212) ***(G-11683)***
Nfi Management Co Inc.....913 642-3700
9152 Foster St Shawnee Mission (66212) ***(G-11684)***
Ngc Industries LLC.....620 248-3248
20672 Nw White Sands Rd Sun City (67143) ***(G-12218)***
Nguyen, Colleen A DDS, Kansas City *Also called Ann Barber* ***(G-3813)***
Nhi of Chanute LLC.....620 431-4940
530 W 14th St Chanute (66720) ***(G-746)***
Nibarger Tool Service Inc.....316 262-6152
1765 N Emporia St Wichita (67214) ***(G-15175)***
Nic Inc (PA).....877 234-3468
25501 W Valley Pkwy # 300 Olathe (66061) ***(G-7920)***
Nic Solutions LLC.....913 498-3468
25501 W Valley Pkwy # 300 Olathe (66061) ***(G-7921)***
Nicholas Water Service LLC.....620 930-7511
1201 Sw Mill Rd Medicine Lodge (67104) ***(G-7070)***
Nichols Enterprises Inc.....913 706-4581
4500 W 139th St Leawood (66224) ***(G-5502)***
Nichols Fluid Service, Liberal *Also called Nichols Water Svc An Okla Corp* ***(G-6350)***
Nichols Lawn Service Inc.....316 688-0431
2516 E 13th St N Wichita (67214) ***(G-15176)***
Nichols Water Svc An Okla Corp.....620 624-5582
316 Industrial Park Ave Liberal (67901) ***(G-6350)***
Nicholson Ventures.....620 225-4637
11089 Whirlwind Rd Dodge City (67801) ***(G-1413)***
Nickell Barracks Training Ctr.....785 822-1198
2930 Scanlan Ave Salina (67401) ***(G-10613)***
Nicklaus Golf CLB At Lionsgate, Overland Park *Also called Nicklaus Golf Club LP* ***(G-9086)***
Nicklaus Golf Club LP.....913 402-1000
14225 Dearborn St Overland Park (66223) ***(G-9086)***
Nicklaus Golf Club Maintenance.....913 897-1624
14220 Nall Ave Shawnee Mission (66223) ***(G-11685)***
Nicol Home Inc.....785 568-2251
303 E Buffalo St Glasco (67445) ***(G-2423)***
Nicusa Inc (HQ).....913 498-3468
25501 W Valley Pkwy # 300 Olathe (66061) ***(G-7922)***
Niece Products of Kansas Inc.....620 223-0340
3904 Liberty Bell Rd Fort Scott (66701) ***(G-1994)***
Nieder Contracting Inc.....785 842-0094
692 N 1610 Rd Lawrence (66049) ***(G-5040)***
Niehoff Dunco Heating & Coolg, Lawrence *Also called Niehoff Heating & Air Inc* ***(G-5041)***

Niehoff Heating & Air Inc 785 594-7137
1729 Bullene Ave Unit D Lawrence (66044) ***(G-5041)***
Nies Construction Inc 316 684-0161
10333 E 21st St N Ste 303 Wichita (67206) ***(G-15177)***
Nies Homes Inc 316 684-0161
10333 E 21st St N Ste 303 Wichita (67206) ***(G-15178)***
Nies Investments LP 316 684-0161
10333 E 21st St N Ste 303 Wichita (67206) ***(G-15179)***
Nies Properties, Wichita *Also called Nies Investments LP* ***(G-15179)***
Nies Remodeling, Wichita *Also called Nies Construction Inc* ***(G-15177)***
Nifast Corporation 913 888-9344
9733 Lackman Rd Lenexa (66219) ***(G-6024)***
Niffie Printing Inc 913 592-3040
111 W Johnson St Spring Hill (66083) ***(G-12091)***
Nifty Nut House LLC 316 265-0571
537 N St Francis St Wichita (67214) ***(G-15180)***
Nilk Brothers Sporting Goods, Kansas City *Also called Nill Brothers Silkscreen Inc* ***(G-4288)***
Nill Bros Sporting Goods Inc (PA) 913 345-8655
2814 S 44th St Overland Park (66213) ***(G-9087)***
Nill Bros Sports, Overland Park *Also called Nill Bros Sporting Goods Inc* ***(G-9087)***
Nill Brothers Silkscreen Inc 913 384-4242
2814 S 44th St Kansas City (66106) ***(G-4288)***
Ninnescah Sailing Association 316 729-5757
9415 E Harry St Ste 107 Wichita (67207) ***(G-15181)***
NINNESCAH YACHT CLUB, Wichita *Also called Ninnescah Sailing Association* ***(G-15181)***
Nips LLC 913 592-2365
20150 W 191st St Spring Hill (66083) ***(G-12092)***
Nisly Brothers Inc 620 662-6561
5212 S Herren Rd Hutchinson (67501) ***(G-3391)***
Nisly Brothers Trash Service, Hutchinson *Also called Nisly Brothers Inc* ***(G-3391)***
NISTAC, Manhattan *Also called Kansas State University* ***(G-6694)***
Nixon, Dan A, Hays *Also called R P Nixon Operations Inc* ***(G-2896)***
Nk Asphalt Partners (PA) 316 828-5500
4111 E 37th St N Wichita (67220) ***(G-15182)***
NL Wilson Moving Inc 913 652-9488
15360 S Mahaffie St Olathe (66062) ***(G-7923)***
Nmrmc Ems 620 244-3522
515 Power Dr Erie (66733) ***(G-1863)***
Nms3, Lawrence *Also called New Media Samurai LLC* ***(G-5039)***
Nn8 LLC 913 948-1107
9300 W 110th St Ste 235 Overland Park (66210) ***(G-9088)***
No Spill Inc 913 888-9200
9808 Pflumm Rd Lenexa (66215) ***(G-6025)***
Noa Group LLC 316 821-9700
3629 N Hydraulic St Wichita (67219) ***(G-15183)***
Noah's Ark, Olathe *Also called First Baptist Church Olathe* ***(G-7711)***
NOAHS ARK CACFP, Chanute *Also called Noahs Ark Christian Day Care* ***(G-747)***
Noahs Ark Christian Day Care 620 431-1832
208 N Lincoln Ave Chanute (66720) ***(G-747)***
Noahs Arkademy 620 331-7791
2246 S 10th St Unit D Independence (67301) ***(G-3544)***
Noatum Logistics Usa LLC (HQ) 913 696-7100
11501 Outlook St Ste 500 Overland Park (66211) ***(G-9089)***
Noble House Jewelry Ltd (PA) 913 491-4861
11620 Metcalf Ave Overland Park (66210) ***(G-9090)***
Nogales Hotel Company LLC 785 238-1454
100 Hammons Dr Junction City (66441) ***(G-3732)***
Nokia of America Corporation 316 636-4800
3450 N Rock Rd Ste 100 Wichita (67226) ***(G-15184)***
Nolan Company 913 888-3500
8900 Indian Creek Pkwy # 200 Overland Park (66210) ***(G-9091)***
Nolan Real Estate Services Inc 913 362-1920
6565 Foxridge Dr Ofc Shawnee Mission (66202) ***(G-11686)***
Noland, Edsel, Chanute *Also called N & B Enterprises Inc* ***(G-744)***
Noller Lincoln-Mercury Inc 785 267-2800
2946 S Kansas Ave Topeka (66611) ***(G-12932)***
NON PROFIT, Basehor *Also called Integrated Behavioral Tech Inc* ***(G-379)***
Non-Emergency Medical Trnspt, Shawnee *Also called Medi Coach LLC* ***(G-10993)***
None, Viola *Also called Youngers and Sons Mfg Co Inc* ***(G-13381)***
Nonprofit Solutions Inc 620 343-6111
618 Commercial St Ste B Emporia (66801) ***(G-1806)***
Noonshine Window Cleaning Svc 913 381-3780
8100 Marty St Ste 105 Overland Park (66204) ***(G-9092)***
Noonshine Window Cleaning Svc 913 381-9666
9180 W 92nd St Shawnee Mission (66212) ***(G-11687)***
Nor West Newspaper Inc 785 332-3162
310 W Washington St Saint Francis (67756) ***(G-10343)***
Norag LLC (PA) 913 851-7200
20710 Foster Ct Bucyrus Bucyrus (66013) ***(G-605)***
Norbrook Inc 913 802-5050
9401 Indian Creek Pkwy # 80 Overland Park (66210) ***(G-9093)***
Norbrook Inc 913 599-5777
9733 Loiret Blvd Lenexa (66219) ***(G-6026)***
Norcraft Companies LP 316 283-8804
810 S Columbus Ave Newton (67114) ***(G-7397)***
Norcraft Companies LP 316 283-2859
900 S Meridian Rd Newton (67114) ***(G-7398)***
Norder Supply Inc 620 805-5972
809 W Mary St Garden City (67846) ***(G-2243)***
Norder Supply Inc 620 872-3058
250 N Pawnee Rd Scott City (67871) ***(G-10825)***
Nordic Foods Inc 913 281-1167
4747 Speaker Rd Kansas City (66106) ***(G-4289)***
Norfolk Iron & Metal Co 620 342-9202
1701 E South Ave Emporia (66801) ***(G-1807)***
Norris & Kelly Drs 913 682-2929
2301 10th Ave Leavenworth (66048) ***(G-5277)***
Norris Collision Center LLC 316 794-1161
19918 W Kellogg Dr Goddard (67052) ***(G-2448)***
Norris Quarries LLC 641 682-3427
P.O. Box 16507 Wichita (67216) ***(G-15185)***
Norse LLC 620 225-0778
1009 E Trail St Dodge City (67801) ***(G-1414)***
North Amdon Fmly Physicians PA 316 838-8585
3443 N Amidon Ave Wichita (67204) ***(G-15186)***
North American Aviation Inc 316 744-6450
7330 N Broadway Ave Park City (67219) ***(G-9639)***
North American Buildings Inc 316 821-9590
9139 E 37th St N Wichita (67226) ***(G-15187)***
North Amrcn Specialty Pdts LLC 620 241-5511
500 W 1st St McPherson (67460) ***(G-7010)***
North Carolina Kenworth Inc (HQ) 816 483-6444
11120 Tomahawk Creek Pkwy Leawood (66211) ***(G-5503)***
North Centl Kans Hm Hlth Agcy 785 738-5175
310 W 8th St Beloit (67420) ***(G-496)***
North Central Flint Hills Area (PA) 785 323-4300
401 Houston St Manhattan (66502) ***(G-6762)***
North Central Region, Wichita *Also called Securitas SEC Svcs USA Inc* ***(G-15540)***
North East Medical Home Health, Prairie Village *Also called Cryo Management Inc* ***(G-10023)***
North Enterprises LLC 913 592-4025
800 S A Line Dr Spring Hill (66083) ***(G-12093)***
North Face Logistics, Shawnee Mission *Also called Vf Outdoor Inc* ***(G-11976)***
North Lindenwood Support Ctr, Olathe *Also called Olathe Unified School Dst 233* ***(G-7950)***
North Rock Hosp For Animals PC 316 636-1200
8338 E 29th St N Wichita (67226) ***(G-15188)***
North Shawnee Community Center 785 286-0676
300 Ne 43rd St Topeka (66617) ***(G-12933)***
North Shore Marina MGT LLC 785 453-2240
200 N Shore Marina Dr Quenemo (66528) ***(G-10178)***
North Star Gifts, Leawood *Also called Ehlers Industries Inc* ***(G-5384)***
North Topeka Fabrication LLC 785 233-4430
3801 Nw 14th St Topeka (66618) ***(G-12934)***
Northast Kans Area Agcy On Agi 785 742-7152
1803 Oregon St Hiawatha (66434) ***(G-3020)***
Northast Kans Chpter 13 Trstee 785 234-1551
509 Sw Jackson St Topeka (66603) ***(G-12935)***
Northeast Family Physicians, Wichita *Also called Physicians Medical Clinics* ***(G-15295)***
Northeast Kans Educatn Svc Ctr 913 538-7250
500 Sunflower Blvd Ozawkie (66070) ***(G-9536)***
Northeast Kansas Hydraulics 785 235-0405
1531 Nw Eugene St Topeka (66608) ***(G-12936)***
Northeast Optimist Club, Wichita *Also called Optimist International* ***(G-15228)***
Northend Disposal Service, Dodge City *Also called Waste Connections Us Inc* ***(G-1449)***
Northern Lights Oil Co L L C 316 733-1515
450 N County Line Rd Wichita (67230) ***(G-15189)***
Northern Natural Gas Company 620 675-2239
Rr 1 Box 17 Kismet (67859) ***(G-4631)***
Northern Natural Gas Company 785 455-3311
2930 Gas City Rd Clifton (66937) ***(G-902)***
Northern Natural Gas Company 620 723-2151
14049 17th Ave Mullinville (67109) ***(G-7210)***
Northern Natural Gas Company 620 277-2364
P.O. Box 37 Holcomb (67851) ***(G-3076)***
Northern Natural Gas Company 620 298-5111
20307 Ne 150th Ave Cunningham (67035) ***(G-1188)***
Northern Pipeline Construction 785 232-0034
1120 Nw Us Highway 24 Topeka (66608) ***(G-12937)***
Northern Tool & Eqp Co Inc 316 854-9422
6610 W Kellogg Dr Wichita (67209) ***(G-15190)***
Northon Disposal Callecia, Wichita *Also called Waste Connections Kansas Inc* ***(G-15934)***
Northrdge Plycare Boarding LLC 316 677-8107
7351 W 33rd St N Wichita (67205) ***(G-15191)***
Northridge Family Dev Ctr 785 284-2401
316 Lincoln St Sabetha (66534) ***(G-10322)***
Northrock Lanes Inc 316 636-5444
3232 N Rock Rd Wichita (67226) ***(G-15192)***
Northrock Suites, Wichita *Also called Four of Wichita Inc* ***(G-14409)***
Northrock Suites, Wichita *Also called P & A Investments* ***(G-15246)***
Northrop Grumman Systems Corp 785 861-3375
Forbes Indus Pk Bldg 8 Topeka (66624) ***(G-12938)***
Northrop Grumman Systems Corp 913 651-8311
530 Organ Ave Bldg 222 Fort Leavenworth (66027) ***(G-1940)***
Northrop Grumman Systems Corp 785 861-3398
7215 Sw Topeka Blvd Topeka (66619) ***(G-12939)***

ALPHABETIC

Northstar Automotive Glass Inc (PA)....316 686-3648
2326 S Southeast Blvd Wichita (67211) ***(G-15193)***
Northstar Property Management....316 689-8577
203 N Mathewson Ave Wichita (67214) ***(G-15194)***
Northview Development Services....316 281-3213
300 S Spencer Rd Newton (67114) ***(G-7399)***
Northview Developmental Svcs (PA)....316 283-5170
700 E 14th St Newton (67114) ***(G-7400)***
Northwest Abuse, Colby *Also called Livewell Northwest Kansas Inc* ***(G-1026)***
Northwest Awards & Signs....785 621-2116
131 W 8th St Hays (67601) ***(G-2880)***
Northwest Centre LLC....316 262-3331
8111 E 32nd St N Ste 101 Wichita (67226) ***(G-15195)***
Northwest Cot Growers Coop Inc....620 598-2008
3 And A Half Mile Sw Moscow (67952) ***(G-7168)***
Northwest Freight Handlers Inc....509 869-7678
2531 S Kessler St Wichita (67217) ***(G-15196)***
Northwest Hardwoods Inc....913 894-9790
15720 W 108th St Lenexa (66219) ***(G-6027)***
Northwest Kansas Juvenile Svcs, Oberlin *Also called County of Decatur* ***(G-7489)***
Northwest YMCA, Wichita *Also called Young Mens Christian Associa* ***(G-16094)***
Northwestern Mutual....316 265-8139
10500 E Berkeley Square P Wichita (67206) ***(G-15197)***
Northwestern Printers Inc....785 625-1110
114 W 9th St Hays (67601) ***(G-2881)***
Northwind Merchant Company....785 856-1183
1705 Haskell Ave Ste A Lawrence (66044) ***(G-5042)***
Northwind Technical Svcs LLC....785 284-0080
2751 Antelope Rd Sabetha (66534) ***(G-10323)***
Norton County Co-Op Assn Inc (PA)....785 877-5900
314 W North St Norton (67654) ***(G-7456)***
Norton County Cooperative Assn, Norton *Also called Norton County Co-Op Assn Inc* ***(G-7456)***
Norton County Ems/Ambulance, Norton *Also called County of Norton* ***(G-7442)***
Norton County Health Dept, Norton *Also called Norton County Hospital* ***(G-7459)***
Norton County Hospital (PA)....785 877-3351
102 E Holme St Norton (67654) ***(G-7457)***
Norton County Hospital....785 877-3305
711 N Norton Ave Norton (67654) ***(G-7458)***
Norton County Hospital....785 877-5745
801 N Norton Ave Norton (67654) ***(G-7459)***
Norton Enterprises....620 221-1987
3221 Central Ave Winfield (67156) ***(G-16164)***
Norton Retirement and Assisted....785 874-4314
200 Whispering Pines St Norton (67654) ***(G-7460)***
Norton Wssrman Jones Kelly LLC....785 827-3646
213 S Santa Fe Ave Salina (67401) ***(G-10614)***
Nortonlifelock Inc....913 451-6710
9393 W 110th St Ste 500 Shawnee Mission (66210) ***(G-11688)***
Norvell Company Inc....620 223-3110
4002 Liberty Bell Rd Fort Scott (66701) ***(G-1995)***
Norvell Company Inc....785 825-6663
468 Upper Mill Heights Dr Salina (67401) ***(G-10615)***
Notes To Self LLC....913 730-0037
5442 Martway St Mission (66205) ***(G-7133)***
Novasource, Overland Park *Also called Centrinex LLC* ***(G-8539)***
Novatech LLC....913 451-1880
13555 W 107th St Lenexa (66215) ***(G-6028)***
Novation Iq LLC....913 492-6000
9806 Lackman Rd Lenexa (66219) ***(G-6029)***
Nowak Construction Co Inc....316 794-8898
200 S Goddard Rd Goddard (67052) ***(G-2449)***
Nowak Pipe Reaming Inc....316 794-8898
200 S Goddard Rd Goddard (67052) ***(G-2450)***
Noxious Weeds, Lawrence *Also called County of Douglas* ***(G-4813)***
Npc Quality Burgers Inc (HQ)....913 327-5555
7300 W 129th St Overland Park (66213) ***(G-9094)***
Npi Property Management Corp....913 648-4339
8000 Perry St Shawnee Mission (66204) ***(G-11689)***
Npl Construction Co....785 232-0034
1120 Nw Us Highway 24 Topeka (66608) ***(G-12940)***
NPS Sales Inc....913 406-1454
1701 E Cedar St Ste 111 Olathe (66062) ***(G-7924)***
Nra-Ukmc Kansas LLC....913 299-1044
6401 Parallel Pkwy Kansas City (66102) ***(G-4290)***
NSA Rv Products Inc....620 365-7714
445 W Lincoln Rd Iola (66749) ***(G-3620)***
NTS LLC....913 321-3838
51 Osage Ave Kansas City (66105) ***(G-4291)***
NTS Technical Systems....316 832-1600
7447 W 33rd St N Wichita (67205) ***(G-15198)***
Nu-Line Company Inc (PA)....316 942-0990
3310 W Central Ave Wichita (67203) ***(G-15199)***
Nu-WA Industries Inc (PA)....620 431-2088
3939 S Ross Ln Chanute (66720) ***(G-748)***
Nuehealth Management Svcs LLC (HQ)....913 387-0510
11221 Roe Ave Ste 300 Leawood (66211) ***(G-5504)***
Nuesynergy Inc....913 396-0884
4601 College Blvd Ste 280 Leawood (66211) ***(G-5505)***
Nueterra DC Holdings LLC (PA)....913 387-0689
11221 Roe Ave Ste 1a Leawood (66211) ***(G-5506)***
Nueterra Healthcare, Leawood *Also called Nueterra DC Holdings LLC* ***(G-5506)***
Nueterra Healthcare MGT LLC, Leawood *Also called Nuehealth Management Svcs LLC* ***(G-5504)***
Nueterra Holdings LLC....785 776-5100
1829 College Ave Manhattan (66502) ***(G-6763)***
Nulook Custom Finishes....913 385-2574
16406 W 156th Ter Olathe (66062) ***(G-7925)***
Number 7 Software, Overland Park *Also called Daniel Zimmerman* ***(G-8634)***
Numerical Control Support Inc....913 441-3500
21945 W 83rd St Shawnee Mission (66227) ***(G-11690)***
Nunik Engineering....913 384-0010
9301 W 53rd St Shawnee Mission (66203) ***(G-11691)***
Nursing By Numbers LLC....913 788-0566
2364 W Elizabeth St Olathe (66061) ***(G-7926)***
Nursing Home Legacy At Pk View....620 356-3331
510 E San Jacinto Ave Ulysses (67880) ***(G-13308)***
Nusser Oil Company Inc....620 697-4624
570 Border Ave Elkhart (67950) ***(G-1625)***
Nustar Pipeline Oper Partnr LP....316 321-3500
1624 Sunset Rd El Dorado (67042) ***(G-1586)***
Nustar Pipeline Oper Partnr LP....316 773-9000
7340 W 21st St N Ste 200 Wichita (67205) ***(G-15200)***
Nutrien AG Solutions Inc....316 794-2231
530 Industrial Rd Goddard (67052) ***(G-2451)***
Nutrien AG Solutions Inc....620 872-2174
181 N Front St Scott City (67871) ***(G-10826)***
Nutrien AG Solutions Inc....620 275-4271
S Star Rte Garden City (67846) ***(G-2244)***
Nutritional Services, Kansas City *Also called Board of Edcatn of Kans Cy Ks* ***(G-3871)***
Nuvidia, Lenexa *Also called Twa LLC* ***(G-6195)***
Nuvidia LLC....913 599-5200
10575 Widmer Rd Lenexa (66215) ***(G-6030)***
NV Fitness Co, Wichita *Also called Wichita State University* ***(G-16032)***
Nvt Wichita LLC (HQ)....316 265-3333
833 N Main St Wichita (67203) ***(G-15201)***
O D T, Overland Park *Also called On Demand Technologies LLC* ***(G-9102)***
O H Gerry Optical Company (PA)....913 362-8822
8857 W 75th St Overland Park (66204) ***(G-9095)***
O I C Inc (PA)....816 471-5400
125 N Main St Hesston (67062) ***(G-2998)***
O K Coop Grn & Merc Co (PA)....620 825-4212
130 Main St Kiowa (67070) ***(G-4628)***
O K Electric Work Inc....620 251-2270
10 E North St Coffeyville (67337) ***(G-966)***
O K Thompsons Tire Inc (PA)....785 738-2283
1015 N Independence Ave Beloit (67420) ***(G-497)***
O K Tire of Dodge City Inc....620 225-0204
1808 W Wyatt Earp Blvd Dodge City (67801) ***(G-1415)***
O P I, Great Bend *Also called Office Products Inc* ***(G-2616)***
O Reilly Auto Parts 133, Shawnee Mission *Also called OReilly Automotive Stores Inc* ***(G-11702)***
O Ring Sales and Service Inc....913 310-0001
15019 W 95th St Lenexa (66215) ***(G-6031)***
O S S Inc....620 343-8799
25 W 5th Ave Emporia (66801) ***(G-1808)***
O T M, Shawnee *Also called Overland Tool & Machinery Inc* ***(G-11007)***
O'Brien Ready Mix, Parsons *Also called OBrien Rock Company Inc* ***(G-9711)***
O'Connor Company, Shawnee Mission *Also called J M OConnor Inc* ***(G-11477)***
O'Neal Electric Service, Kansas City *Also called Winavie LLC* ***(G-4547)***
O'Reilly Auto Parts, El Dorado *Also called OReilly Automotive Stores Inc* ***(G-1588)***
O'Reilly Auto Parts, Hutchinson *Also called OReilly Automotive Stores Inc* ***(G-3396)***
O'Reilly Auto Parts, Parsons *Also called OReilly Automotive Stores Inc* ***(G-9714)***
O'Reilly Auto Parts, Lawrence *Also called OReilly Automotive Stores Inc* ***(G-5048)***
O'Reilly Auto Parts, Kansas City *Also called OReilly Automotive Stores Inc* ***(G-4296)***
O'Reilly Auto Parts, Overland Park *Also called OReilly Automotive Stores Inc* ***(G-9111)***
O'Reilly Auto Parts, Olathe *Also called OReilly Automotive Stores Inc* ***(G-7962)***
O'Reilly Auto Parts, Topeka *Also called OReilly Automotive Stores Inc* ***(G-12951)***
O'Reilly Auto Parts, Coffeyville *Also called OReilly Automotive Stores Inc* ***(G-967)***
O'Reilly Auto Parts, Independence *Also called OReilly Automotive Stores Inc* ***(G-3545)***
O'Reilly Auto Parts, Wichita *Also called OReilly Automotive Stores Inc* ***(G-15233)***
O'Reilly Auto Parts, Wichita *Also called OReilly Automotive Stores Inc* ***(G-15234)***
O'Reilly Auto Parts, Topeka *Also called OReilly Automotive Stores Inc* ***(G-12952)***
O'Reilly Auto Parts, Topeka *Also called OReilly Automotive Stores Inc* ***(G-12953)***
O'Reilly Auto Parts, Topeka *Also called OReilly Automotive Stores Inc* ***(G-12954)***
O'Reilly Auto Parts, Lawrence *Also called OReilly Automotive Stores Inc* ***(G-5049)***
O'Reilly Auto Parts, Atchison *Also called OReilly Automotive Stores Inc* ***(G-253)***
O'Reilly Auto Parts, Wichita *Also called OReilly Automotive Stores Inc* ***(G-15235)***
O'Reilly Auto Parts, Wichita *Also called OReilly Automotive Stores Inc* ***(G-15236)***
O'Reilly Auto Parts 170, Kansas City *Also called OReilly Automotive Stores Inc* ***(G-4297)***
O'Reilly Auto Parts 196, Olathe *Also called OReilly Automotive Stores Inc* ***(G-7963)***
O2 Corporation....316 634-1240
235 N Washington Ave Wichita (67202) ***(G-15202)***

Oak Park Cleaners Inc......913 599-3040
12230 W 95th St Shawnee Mission (66215) ***(G-11692)***
Oak Park Dental Group, Lenexa *Also called Steven G Mitchell DDS* ***(G-6154)***
Oak Park Mall......913 888-4400
11149 W 95th St Overland Park (66214) ***(G-9096)***
Oak Park Merchants, Overland Park *Also called Oak Park Mall* ***(G-9096)***
Oak Park Village......913 888-1500
9670 Halsey St Lenexa (66215) ***(G-6032)***
Oak Ridge Youth Dev Corp......913 788-5657
9301 Parallel Pkwy Kansas City (66112) ***(G-4292)***
Oak Tree and Pennys Diner......785 562-1234
1127 Pony Ex Hwy Ste A Marysville (66508) ***(G-6904)***
Oak Tree Inn, Wichita *Also called Lodging Enterprises LLC* ***(G-14975)***
Oak Tree Inn, Marysville *Also called Oak Tree and Pennys Diner* ***(G-6904)***
Oak Tree Inn, The, Wellington *Also called Lodging Enterprises Inc* ***(G-13512)***
Oakbrook Animal Hospital Inc......913 884-8778
500 W Main St Gardner (66030) ***(G-2356)***
Oakland Avenue Craftsmen Co......316 685-3955
29 N Cypress Dr Wichita (67206) ***(G-15203)***
Oakley Area Chamber Commerce......785 672-4862
222 Center Ave 1 Oakley (67748) ***(G-7483)***
Oakley Manor, Oakley *Also called Beverly Enterprises-Kansas LLC* ***(G-7472)***
Oakley Motors Inc (PA)......785 672-3238
611 S Freeman Ave Oakley (67748) ***(G-7484)***
Oakley Sleep Inn and Suites, Oakley *Also called Hospitality Oakley Group LLC* ***(G-7476)***
Oard's Auto & Truck Repair Svc, Salina *Also called Oards Auto & Truck Repr Svcs* ***(G-10616)***
Oards Auto & Truck Repr Svcs......785 823-9732
2259 Centennial Rd Ste A Salina (67401) ***(G-10616)***
Oasis Car Wash Systems Inc......620 783-1355
1909 E 12th St Galena (66739) ***(G-2077)***
Oasis Productions......316 210-4488
8351 E 35th St N Wichita (67226) ***(G-15204)***
Ob-Gyn Office, Manhattan *Also called Womens Health Group PA* ***(G-6856)***
Oberlin Harrold News, Oberlin *Also called Haynes Publishing Co* ***(G-7496)***
Oberlin Herald, Oberlin *Also called Haynes Publishing Co* ***(G-7497)***
Oberlin Livestock Auction Inc......785 475-2323
Hwy 83 Oberlin (67749) ***(G-7498)***
Object Tech Solutions Inc (PA)......913 345-9080
6363 College Blvd Ste 230 Leawood (66211) ***(G-5507)***
Obrian Pharmacy, Shawnee Mission *Also called OBrien Pharmacy* ***(G-11693)***
OBrien Pharmacy......913 322-0001
5453 W 61st Pl Shawnee Mission (66205) ***(G-11693)***
OBrien Rock Company Inc (PA)......620 449-2257
712 Central St Saint Paul (66771) ***(G-10382)***
OBrien Rock Company Inc......620 231-4940
791 E 590th Ave Frontenac (66763) ***(G-2061)***
OBrien Rock Company Inc......620 421-5127
N Blvd Parsons (67357) ***(G-9711)***
Oc Services......316 655-3952
2126 N Shadybrook Wichita (67214) ***(G-15205)***
Occidental Chemical Corp......316 524-4211
6200 S Ridge Rd Wichita (67215) ***(G-15206)***
Occk Inc......785 243-1977
1502 Lincoln St Concordia (66901) ***(G-1125)***
Occk Inc......785 738-3490
501 W 7th St Beloit (67420) ***(G-498)***
Occk Inc (PA)......785 827-9383
1710 W Schilling Rd Salina (67401) ***(G-10617)***
Occupational Hlth Partners LLC......785 823-8381
1101 E Republic Ave Salina (67401) ***(G-10618)***
Och Regional Office......913 599-6137
8235 Melrose Dr Shawnee Mission (66214) ***(G-11694)***
Ochsner Eye Center, Wichita *Also called Bruce Ochsner MD* ***(G-13901)***
OConnor Company Inc......316 263-3187
5200 E 35th St N Ste B Wichita (67220) ***(G-15207)***
OConnor Company Inc (HQ)......913 894-8788
16910 W 116th St Lenexa (66219) ***(G-6033)***
OConnor Company Inc......316 267-2246
811 E Bayley St Wichita (67211) ***(G-15208)***
OConnor Company Inc......316 263-3187
5200 E 35th St N Wichita (67220) ***(G-15209)***
ODonnell-Way Cnstr Co Inc......913 498-3355
7321 High Dr Prairie Village (66208) ***(G-10053)***
Oetinger-Lloyd Construction......785 632-2106
1819 Meadowlark Rd Clay Center (67432) ***(G-874)***
Ofc of US Trustee......316 269-6607
301 N Main St Ste 1150 Wichita (67202) ***(G-15210)***
Offerle Coop Grn & Sup Co (PA)......620 659-2165
222 E Santa Fe Offerle (67563) ***(G-7500)***
Office Installation Company, Hesston *Also called O I C Inc* ***(G-2998)***
Office of Long-Term Care, Topeka *Also called Administration Kansas Dept* ***(G-12291)***
OFFICE OUTFITTERS, Liberal *Also called Liberal Office Machines Co* ***(G-6334)***
Office Plus of Kansas, Park City *Also called Daniksco Office Interiors LLC* ***(G-9616)***
Office Products, Emporia *Also called Navrats Inc* ***(G-1800)***
Office Products Inc (PA)......620 793-8180
1204 Main St Great Bend (67530) ***(G-2616)***
Office Works LLC......785 462-2222
960 S Range Ave Colby (67701) ***(G-1032)***
OfficeMax Incorporated......913 667-5300
2401 Midpoint Dr Edwardsville (66111) ***(G-1511)***
Ofg Financial Services Inc (PA)......785 233-4071
120 Se 6th Ave Ste 105 Topeka (66603) ***(G-12941)***
OFlynn Contracting Inc......316 524-2500
120 N Westfield St Wichita (67212) ***(G-15211)***
Ogden Check Approval Network......785 228-5600
3615 Sw 29th St Bsmt 101 Topeka (66614) ***(G-12942)***
Ogden Publications Inc......785 274-4300
1503 Sw 42nd St Topeka (66609) ***(G-12943)***
Ohldes Dairy Inc......785 348-5697
1814 9th Rd Linn (66953) ***(G-6411)***
Ohlsen Right of Way and Maint......785 336-6112
892 Us Highway 36 Seneca (66538) ***(G-10878)***
Oil Field Shelters, Wichita *Also called Durasafe Products Inc* ***(G-14245)***
Oil Patch Pump and Supply Inc (PA)......620 431-1890
3290 S Plummer Ave Chanute (66720) ***(G-749)***
Oil Producers Inc of Kansas......316 681-0231
1710 N Waterfront Pkwy Wichita (67206) ***(G-15212)***
Oilfield Cementing, Russell *Also called Global Oilfield Services LLC* ***(G-10275)***
Oilpure Technologies Inc......913 906-0400
13104 Falmouth St Leawood (66209) ***(G-5508)***
OK Tank Line, Park City *Also called United Petro Transports Inc* ***(G-9651)***
Okonite Company......913 441-4465
2631 S 96th St Edwardsville (66111) ***(G-1512)***
Olathe Animal Hospital Inc......913 764-1415
13800 W 135th St Olathe (66062) ***(G-7927)***
Olathe Billiards Inc (PA)......913 780-5740
810 W Old Highway 56 Olathe (66061) ***(G-7928)***
Olathe Branch, Olathe *Also called Intrust Bank National Assn* ***(G-7802)***
Olathe Branch, Olathe *Also called Umb Bank National Association* ***(G-8131)***
Olathe Chamber of Commerce......913 764-1050
18103 W 106th St 100 Olathe (66061) ***(G-7929)***
Olathe Dental Care Center......913 782-1420
234 S Cherry St Olathe (66061) ***(G-7930)***
Olathe Endodontics......913 829-0060
16093 W 135th St Ste A Olathe (66062) ***(G-7931)***
Olathe Family Dentistry PA......913 829-1438
450 S Parker St Olathe (66061) ***(G-7932)***
Olathe Family Physicians, Olathe *Also called Olathe Medical Services Inc* ***(G-7944)***
Olathe Family Practice PA......913 782-3322
1750 S Mahaffie Pl Olathe (66062) ***(G-7933)***
Olathe Family Vision (PA)......913 782-5993
13839 S Mur Len Rd Ste A Olathe (66062) ***(G-7934)***
Olathe Family Vision......913 254-0200
740 W Cedar St Olathe (66061) ***(G-7935)***
Olathe Family YMCA, Olathe *Also called Young Mens Christian Gr Kansas* ***(G-8164)***
Olathe Ford Lincoln, Olathe *Also called Olathe Ford Sales Inc* ***(G-7936)***
Olathe Ford Outlet, Olathe *Also called Olathe Ford Sales Inc* ***(G-7937)***
Olathe Ford R V Sales, Gardner *Also called Olathe Ford Sales Inc* ***(G-2357)***
Olathe Ford Sales Inc (PA)......913 782-0881
1845 E Santa Fe St Olathe (66062) ***(G-7936)***
Olathe Ford Sales Inc......913 856-8145
19310 S Gardner Rd Gardner (66030) ***(G-2357)***
Olathe Ford Sales Inc......913 829-1957
205 S Fir St Olathe (66061) ***(G-7937)***
Olathe Glass & Framed Prints, Olathe *Also called Olathe Glass Company Inc* ***(G-7938)***
Olathe Glass Company Inc......913 782-7444
510 E Santa Fe St Olathe (66061) ***(G-7938)***
Olathe Hotels LLC......913 829-6700
12215 S Strang Line Rd Olathe (66062) ***(G-7939)***
Olathe Lanes East, Olathe *Also called Boyd & Boyd Inc* ***(G-7558)***
OLATHE MEDICAL CENTER, Paola *Also called Miami County Medical Ctr Inc* ***(G-9572)***
Olathe Medical Center Inc (HQ)......913 791-4200
20333 W 151st St Olathe (66061) ***(G-7940)***
Olathe Medical Center Inc......913 791-4315
20333 W 151st St St301 Olathe (66061) ***(G-7941)***
Olathe Medical Services Inc......913 780-4900
20805 W 51st 400dtrs Olathe (66061) ***(G-7942)***
Olathe Medical Services Inc......913 782-3798
14425 College Blvd # 100 Lenexa (66215) ***(G-6034)***
Olathe Medical Services Inc......913 755-3044
100 E Main St Osawatomie (66064) ***(G-8200)***
Olathe Medical Services Inc (PA)......913 782-7515
15435 W 134th Pl Olathe (66062) ***(G-7943)***
Olathe Medical Services Inc......913 782-8487
20375 W 151st St Ste 105 Olathe (66061) ***(G-7944)***
Olathe Medical Services Inc......913 764-0036
1701 E Cedar St Ste 111 Olathe (66062) ***(G-7945)***
Olathe Medical Services Inc......913 782-1610
18695 W 151st St Olathe (66062) ***(G-7946)***
Olathe Millwork LLC......913 738-8074
15785 S Keeler Ter # 100 Olathe (66062) ***(G-7947)***
Olathe Millwork Company (PA)......913 894-5010
16002 W 110th St Lenexa (66219) ***(G-6035)***
Olathe Parole Office, Olathe *Also called Department Corrections Kansas* ***(G-7649)***

ALPHABETIC

Olathe Regional Oncology Ctr 913 768-7200
20375 W 151st St Ste 180 Olathe (66061) ***(G-7948)***
Olathe Service Center, Olathe *Also called Olathe Unified School Dst 233* ***(G-7951)***
Olathe Soccer Club 913 764-4111
1570 S Mahaffie Cir Olathe (66062) ***(G-7949)***
Olathe Unified School Dst 233 ....913 780-7002
315 N Lindenwood Dr Olathe (66062) ***(G-7950)***
Olathe Unified School Dst 233 ....913 780-7011
1500 W 56th Hwy Olathe (66061) ***(G-7951)***
Olathe Unified School Dst 233 ....913 780-7880
311 E Park St Olathe (66061) ***(G-7952)***
Olathe Unified School Dst 233 ....913 780-7410
1700 W Sheridan St Olathe (66061) ***(G-7953)***
Olathe Womens Center Inc 913 780-3388
20375 W 151st St Ste 250 Olathe (66061) ***(G-7954)***
Olathe Youth Baseball Inc 913 393-9891
885 S Parker St Olathe (66061) ***(G-7955)***
Old Castle Precast Inc 785 232-2982
5230 Nw 17th St Topeka (66618) ***(G-12944)***
OLD COWTOWN MUSEUM, Wichita *Also called Historic Wichita Sedqwick Cnty* ***(G-14618)***
Old Creek Senior Living 785 272-2601
3224 Sw 29th St Topeka (66614) ***(G-12945)***
Old Depot Museum, Ottawa *Also called County of Franklin* ***(G-8261)***
Old Dominion Freight Line Inc 316 522-3562
4520 S Santa Fe St Wichita (67216) ***(G-15213)***
Old Dominion Freight Line Inc 785 354-7336
3508 Se 21st St Topeka (66607) ***(G-12946)***
Old Dominion Freight Line Inc 620 421-4121
2600 Flynn Dr Parsons (67357) ***(G-9712)***
Old Dominion Freight Line Inc 620 792-2006
71 Sw 40 Ave Great Bend (67530) ***(G-2617)***
Old Fort Genealgcl Socty SE KS 620 223-3300
3rd And National Ave Fort Scott (66701) ***(G-1996)***
Old Mission Mortuary 316 686-7311
3424 E 21st St N Wichita (67208) ***(G-15214)***
Old Mission United Methdist Ch, Fairway *Also called Old Mission United Methdst Ch* ***(G-1915)***
Old Mission United Methdst Ch 913 262-1040
5519 State Park Rd Fairway (66205) ***(G-1915)***
Old Ppp Inc (HQ) 620 421-3400
3333 Main St Parsons (67357) ***(G-9713)***
Old United Casualty Company 913 432-6400
8500 Shwnee Mksn Pkwy 2 Shawnee Mission (66202) ***(G-11695)***
Old World Balloonery LLC 913 338-2628
12600 W 142nd St Overland Park (66221) ***(G-9097)***
Old World Cabinets Inc 913 723-3740
322 Main St Linwood (66052) ***(G-6417)***
Old World Spices Seasoning Inc 816 861-0400
5320 College Blvd Overland Park (66211) ***(G-9098)***
Oldcastle Apg Midwest Inc 913 667-1792
P.O. Box 8 Bonner Springs (66012) ***(G-568)***
Oldcastle Infrastructure Inc 620 662-3307
1600 N Lorraine St Ste 1 Hutchinson (67501) ***(G-3392)***
Oldham Sales Inc 785 625-2547
815 E 11th St Hays (67601) ***(G-2882)***
Oliver Electric Cnstr Inc 785 748-0777
3104 Haskell Ave Ste A Lawrence (66046) ***(G-5043)***
Oliver Insurance Agency Inc 913 341-1900
10955 Lowell Ave Ste 1010 Overland Park (66210) ***(G-9099)***
Oliver P Steinnagel Inc 913 338-2266
7512 W 119th St Shawnee Mission (66213) ***(G-11696)***
Oliver's Salon, Shawnee Mission *Also called Oliver P Steinnagel Inc* ***(G-11696)***
Olpe Locker 620 475-3375
1530 Williby Ave Emporia (66801) ***(G-1809)***
Olpe State Bank Inc 620 475-3213
202 Westphalia St Olpe (66865) ***(G-8166)***
Olsson Inc 785 539-6900
302 S 4th St Ste 110 Manhattan (66502) ***(G-6764)***
Olsson Inc 913 381-1170
7301 W 133rd St Ste 200 Overland Park (66213) ***(G-9100)***
Olsson Inc 913 829-0078
1700 E 123rd St Olathe (66061) ***(G-7956)***
Oltjen, Jay M, Shawnee Mission *Also called Hannah & Oltjen* ***(G-11408)***
Olu, Topeka *Also called World Publishing Inc* ***(G-13252)***
Omaha Truck Center Inc 785 823-2204
2552 N 9th St Salina (67401) ***(G-10619)***
Omaha Truck Center Inc 785 823-2204
2552 N 9th St Salina (67401) ***(G-10620)***
OMalley Beverage of Kansas 785 843-8816
2050 Packer Ct Lawrence (66044) ***(G-5044)***
Omc Distribution Center 913 791-3592
1660 S Lone Elm Rd Olathe (66061) ***(G-7957)***
Omega Concrete Systems Inc 913 287-4343
5525 Kaw Dr Kansas City (66102) ***(G-4293)***
Omega Senior Living LLC 316 260-9494
333 S Broadway Ave # 105 Wichita (67202) ***(G-15215)***
Omni Aerospace Inc 316 529-8998
3130 W Pawnee St Wichita (67213) ***(G-15216)***

Omni Center II 316 689-4256
111 S Whittier St Wichita (67207) ***(G-15217)***
Omni Center LP (PA) 316 268-9108
111 S Whittier Rd Wichita (67207) ***(G-15218)***
Omni Employment MGT Svc LLC 913 341-2119
8700 Indian Creek Pkwy # 250 Overland Park (66210) ***(G-9101)***
Omni Secretarial, Wichita *Also called Omni Center LP* ***(G-15218)***
Omni Secretarial Service, Wichita *Also called Omni Center II* ***(G-15217)***
Omnicare of Wichita, Wichita *Also called Ncs Healthcare of Kansas LLC* ***(G-15156)***
On Call Mobile Therapies LLC 913 449-1679
15621 W 87th Street Pkwy # 356 Lenexa (66219) ***(G-6036)***
On Demand Employment Svcs LLC 913 371-3212
1718 Central Ave B Kansas City (66102) ***(G-4294)***
On Demand Technologies LLC (PA) 913 438-1800
9291 Cody St Overland Park (66214) ***(G-9102)***
ON MY OWN, Shawnee Mission *Also called Heartstrings Cmnty Foundation* ***(G-11425)***
On-Line Communications Inc 316 831-0500
7370 E 37th St N Ste 100 Wichita (67226) ***(G-15219)***
Onaga Historical Society 785 889-7104
310 E 2nd St Onaga (66521) ***(G-8178)***
Oncimmune, De Soto *Also called Biodesix Inc* ***(G-1195)***
One Fleet Source, Overland Park *Also called Fleet Auto Rent Inc* ***(G-8727)***
One Gas Inc 913 319-8617
7421 W 129th St Overland Park (66213) ***(G-9103)***
One Hope United - Northern Reg 785 827-1756
2026 Starlight Dr Salina (67401) ***(G-10621)***
One Oak, McPherson *Also called Koch Industries Inc* ***(G-6984)***
One of Kind Progressive Chld C 785 830-9040
4640 W 27th St Lawrence (66047) ***(G-5045)***
One Power LLC 913 219-5061
9770 Legler Rd Shawnee Mission (66219) ***(G-11697)***
One Source Staffing, Olathe *Also called Labor Source LLC* ***(G-7850)***
Oneal Lynn W, Lawrence *Also called Lynn W ONeal* ***(G-5004)***
Oneok Inc 913 319-8600
7421 W 129th St Ste 100 Overland Park (66213) ***(G-9104)***
Oneok Inc 620 562-4205
777 Avenue Y Bushton (67427) ***(G-654)***
Oneok Inc 800 794-4780
1421 N 3rd St Kansas City (66101) ***(G-4295)***
Oneok Inc 785 483-2501
450 S Front St Russell (67665) ***(G-10283)***
Oneok Inc 620 341-7054
220 Mechanic St Emporia (66801) ***(G-1810)***
Oneok Inc 913 599-8936
1300 E Logan St Ottawa (66067) ***(G-8295)***
Oneok Inc 785 431-4201
200 E 1st Ave Topeka (66603) ***(G-12947)***
Oneok Inc 785 575-8554
501 Sw Gage Blvd Topeka (66606) ***(G-12948)***
Oneok Inc 785 738-9700
701 W 8th St Beloit (67420) ***(G-499)***
Oneok Inc 620 792-0603
1800 Kansas Ave Great Bend (67530) ***(G-2618)***
Oneok Inc 620 728-4303
110 W 2nd Ave Hutchinson (67501) ***(G-3393)***
Oneok Inc 620 669-2300
4817 N Dean Rd Hutchinson (67502) ***(G-3394)***
Oneok Inc 785 223-5408
1118 S Madison St Junction City (66441) ***(G-3733)***
Oneok Inc 620 241-0837
1644 W Kansas Ave McPherson (67460) ***(G-7011)***
Oneok Inc 620 672-6706
40135 N Us Highway 281 Pratt (67124) ***(G-10127)***
Oneok Inc 785 822-3522
1001 Edison Pl Salina (67401) ***(G-10622)***
Oneok Inc 316 322-8131
700 N Star St El Dorado (67042) ***(G-1587)***
Oneok Inc 316 821-2722
1021 E 26th St N Wichita (67219) ***(G-15220)***
Oneok Energy Marketing, Topeka *Also called Oneok Energy Services Co II* ***(G-12949)***
Oneok Energy Services Co II (HQ) 785 274-4900
3706 Sw Topeka Blvd # 100 Topeka (66609) ***(G-12949)***
Oneok Field Services, Bushton *Also called Oneok Inc* ***(G-654)***
Oneok Field Services Co LLC 620 544-2179
114 W 2nd St Hugoton (67951) ***(G-3174)***
Oneok Field Services Co LLC 620 248-3258
30317 N Us Highway 281 Pratt (67124) ***(G-10128)***
Oneok Field Services Co LLC 620 356-2231
1407 E Oklahoma Ave Ulysses (67880) ***(G-13309)***
Oneok Hydrocarbon LP (HQ) 620 669-3759
1910 S Broadacres Rd Hutchinson (67501) ***(G-3395)***
Oneok Hydrocarbon LP 620 834-2204
462 Hwy 56 Conway (67460) ***(G-1135)***
Online Vend Mch Sls & Svc Inc 913 492-1097
14408 W 90th Ter Lenexa (66215) ***(G-6037)***
Onpoint Specialty Products, Kansas City *Also called Terrell Publishing Co* ***(G-4464)***
Onsite Solutions LLC 913 912-7384
6950 Squibb Rd Ste 320 Shawnee Mission (66202) ***(G-11698)***

Onspring Technologies LLC 913 601-4900
10801 Mastin St Ste 400 Overland Park (66210) *(G-9105)*
Onyx Collection Inc 785 456-8604
202 Broadway St Belvue (66407) *(G-508)*
Onyx Meetings Inc 913 381-1123
7200 W 75th St Overland Park (66204) *(G-9106)*
Onyx Meetings and Events, Overland Park *Also called Onyx Meetings Inc (G-9106)*
Open Arms Lthran Child Dev Ctr 316 721-5675
12885 W Maple St Wichita (67235) *(G-15221)*
Open Arms Lthran Child Dev Ctr 913 856-4250
306 E Madison St Gardner (66030) *(G-2358)*
Open Minds Child Dev Ctr LLC 913 703-6736
1778 E Harold St Olathe (66061) *(G-7958)*
Open Road Brands LLC 316 337-7550
1425 E Douglas Ave # 300 Wichita (67211) *(G-15222)*
Operations Management Intl Inc 913 367-5563
515 Kansas Ave Atchison (66002) *(G-252)*
Ophthalmic Services PA 913 498-2015
9950 W 151st St Overland Park (66221) *(G-9107)*
Oppliger Banking Systems Inc 913 829-6300
1355 N Winchester St Olathe (66061) *(G-7959)*
Opportunity Project Lrng Ctr 316 522-8677
4600 S Clifton Ave Wichita (67216) *(G-15223)*
OPPORTUNITY PROJECT, THE, Wichita *Also called Wichita Top Childrens Fund (G-16041)*
Oprc Inc 913 642-6880
6800 W 91st St Overland Park (66212) *(G-9108)*
Opti-Life East Wichita LLC 316 927-5959
9758 E 21st St N Wichita (67206) *(G-15224)*
Opti-Life Services LLC 316 518-8757
7200 W 13th St N Ste 5 Wichita (67212) *(G-15225)*
Optic Fuel Clean Inc 913 712-8373
15503 W 147th Dr Olathe (66062) *(G-7960)*
Optical Industries, Shawnee Mission *Also called Donegan Optical Company Inc (G-11314)*
Optileaf Incorporated 855 678-4532
924 N Main St Wichita (67203) *(G-15226)*
Optimal Performance LLC 316 440-4440
11444 E Central Ave Wichita (67206) *(G-15227)*
Optimation Holographics Inc 785 233-6000
3500 Sw Topeka Blvd Topeka (66611) *(G-12950)*
Optimist International 316 744-0849
6215 Clairedon Wichita (67220) *(G-15228)*
Optimized Process Furnaces Inc 620 431-1260
3995 S Santa Fe Ave Chanute (66720) *(G-750)*
Optimum Health Family Practice, Topeka *Also called Rick R Tague MD MPH (G-13015)*
Optimus Industries LLC 620 431-3100
1700 S Washington Ave Chanute (66720) *(G-751)*
Optimuz Manufacturing Inc 316 519-1354
2331 S Mead St Wichita (67211) *(G-15229)*
Option Care Enterprises Inc 913 599-3745
8940 Nieman Rd Overland Park (66214) *(G-9109)*
Options, Wichita *Also called Dccca Inc (G-14179)*
Options Dom & Sexual Violenc 785 625-4202
2716 Plaza Ave Hays (67601) *(G-2883)*
Options For Animals, Wellsville *Also called Animal Chiropractic Center (G-13540)*
Optiv Security Inc 816 421-6611
6130 Sprint Pkwy Ste 400 Overland Park (66211) *(G-9110)*
Oracle Systems Corporation 913 663-3400
9200 Indian Creek Pkwy # 560 Shawnee Mission (66210) *(G-11699)*
Oral & Facial Surgery Assoc (PA) 913 381-5194
3700 W 83rd St Ste 103 Prairie Village (66208) *(G-10054)*
Oral & Facial Surgery Assoc 913 782-1529
1441 E 151st St Ste 4 Olathe (66062) *(G-7961)*
Oral & Facial Surgery Assoc 913 541-1888
12208 W 87th Street Pkwy # 150 Shawnee Mission (66215) *(G-11700)*
Oral and Facial Associate 913 381-5194
3700 W 83rd St Ste 103 Prairie Village (66208) *(G-10055)*
Oral and Maxilla Facial Assoc 316 634-1414
1919 N Webb Rd Wichita (67206) *(G-15230)*
Oral Mxilo Ofcial Srgery Assoc 913 268-9500
11005 W 60th St Ste 150 Shawnee Mission (66203) *(G-11701)*
Orange Industries LLC 816 694-1919
5806 Walmer St Mission (66202) *(G-7134)*
Orangetheory Fitness 316 440-4640
1423 N Webb Rd Ste 159 Wichita (67206) *(G-15231)*
Orazem & Scalora Engrg PA 785 537-2553
2312 Anderson Ave Manhattan (66502) *(G-6765)*
Orbis Corporation 785 528-4875
515 S 4th St Osage City (66523) *(G-8185)*
Orchard Grdns Hlth Rhblitation, Wichita *Also called Woodlawn Care and Rehab LLC (G-16067)*
Order of The Eastern Star, Wellington *Also called General Grnd Chpter Estrn Star (G-13503)*
Oread Hotel 785 843-1200
1200 Oread Ave Lawrence (66044) *(G-5046)*
Oread Orthodontics 785 856-2483
1425 Wakarusa Dr Lawrence (66049) *(G-5047)*
Oregon Trail Equipment LLC 785 562-2346
553 Pony Express Hwy Marysville (66508) *(G-6905)*
OReilly Automotive Stores Inc 316 321-4371
1816 W Central Ave El Dorado (67042) *(G-1588)*
OReilly Automotive Stores Inc 620 664-6800
1101 E 30th Ave Hutchinson (67502) *(G-3396)*
OReilly Automotive Stores Inc 620 421-6070
2424 Main St Parsons (67357) *(G-9714)*
OReilly Automotive Stores Inc 316 685-7900
3109 E Pawnee St Wichita (67211) *(G-15232)*
OReilly Automotive Stores Inc 913 268-6001
6136 Nieman Rd Shawnee Mission (66203) *(G-11702)*
OReilly Automotive Stores Inc 785 842-9800
1008 W 23rd St Lawrence (66046) *(G-5048)*
OReilly Automotive Stores Inc 913 287-2409
4700 Parallel Pkwy Kansas City (66104) *(G-4296)*
OReilly Automotive Stores Inc 913 381-0451
6725 W 75th St Overland Park (66204) *(G-9111)*
OReilly Automotive Stores Inc 913 764-8685
913 E Santa Fe St Olathe (66061) *(G-7962)*
OReilly Automotive Stores Inc 785 235-9241
1701 S Kansas Ave Topeka (66612) *(G-12951)*
OReilly Automotive Stores Inc 620 251-5280
611 W 11th St Coffeyville (67337) *(G-967)*
OReilly Automotive Stores Inc 620 331-1018
224 W Main St Independence (67301) *(G-3545)*
OReilly Automotive Stores Inc 913 829-6188
1115 W Dennis Ave Olathe (66061) *(G-7963)*
OReilly Automotive Stores Inc 316 729-7311
544 N Tyler Rd Wichita (67212) *(G-15233)*
OReilly Automotive Stores Inc 316 686-5536
4850 E 13th St N Wichita (67208) *(G-15234)*
OReilly Automotive Stores Inc 785 235-5658
1726 Nw Topeka Blvd Topeka (66608) *(G-12952)*
OReilly Automotive Stores Inc 785 862-4749
4710 Sw Topeka Blvd Topeka (66609) *(G-12953)*
OReilly Automotive Stores Inc 785 266-3688
2950 Se California Ave Topeka (66605) *(G-12954)*
OReilly Automotive Stores Inc 913 621-6939
2901 State Ave Kansas City (66102) *(G-4297)*
OReilly Automotive Stores Inc 785 832-0408
906 N 2nd St Lawrence (66044) *(G-5049)*
OReilly Automotive Stores Inc 913 367-4138
819 Main St Atchison (66002) *(G-253)*
OReilly Automotive Stores Inc 316 264-6422
2219 S Seneca St Wichita (67213) *(G-15235)*
OReilly Automotive Stores Inc 316 831-9112
714 W 21st St N Wichita (67203) *(G-15236)*
Original Juan Specialty Foods, Kansas City *Also called Spicin Foods Inc (G-4435)*
Orion Communications Inc 913 538-7110
10650 Roe Ave Overland Park (66207) *(G-9112)*
Orion Education and Training, Clearwater *Also called South Centl KS Educatn Svc Ctr (G-897)*
Orion Information Systems LLC 913 825-3272
12302 W 129th Ter Overland Park (66213) *(G-9113)*
Orion Security Inc 913 385-5657
5600 W 95th St Ste 315 Overland Park (66207) *(G-9114)*
Orion Utility Automation, Lenexa *Also called Novatech LLC (G-6028)*
Orizon Arostructures - Nkc LLC 620 431-4037
615 W Cherry St Chanute (66720) *(G-752)*
Orizon Arostructures - Nkc LLC (HQ) 816 788-7800
801 W Old Highway 56 Olathe (66061) *(G-7964)*
Orizon Arstrctres - Chnute Inc 816 788-7800
2522 W 21st St Chanute (66720) *(G-753)*
Orizon Arstructures - Proc Inc 620 305-2402
2526 W 21st St Chanute (66720) *(G-754)*
Orkin LLC 785 827-0314
1207 Holiday St Salina (67401) *(G-10623)*
Orkin LLC 913 492-4029
8605 Quivira Rd Lenexa (66215) *(G-6038)*
Orkin Pest Control 791, Lenexa *Also called Orkin LLC (G-6038)*
Orkin Pest Control 792, Salina *Also called Orkin LLC (G-10623)*
Orrick Trailer Services LLC 913 321-0400
600 Sunshine Rd Kansas City (66115) *(G-4298)*
Orschelin Farm and Home 127, Concordia *Also called Orscheln Farm and Home LLC (G-1126)*
Orschelin Farm and Home 21, Parsons *Also called Orscheln Farm and Home LLC (G-9715)*
Orschelin Farm and Home 31, Great Bend *Also called Orscheln Farm and Home LLC (G-2619)*
Orschelin Farm and Home 34, Dodge City *Also called Orscheln Farm and Home LLC (G-1416)*
Orschelin Farm and Home 36, Coffeyville *Also called Orscheln Farm and Home LLC (G-968)*
Orschelin Farm and Home 37, Topeka *Also called Orscheln Farm and Home LLC (G-12955)*
Orschelin Farm and Home 39, Manhattan *Also called Orscheln Farm and Home LLC (G-6766)*
Orschelin Farm and Home 40, Arkansas City *Also called Orscheln Farm and Home LLC (G-168)*
Orschelin Farm and Home 48, Lawrence *Also called Orscheln Farm and Home LLC (G-5050)*
Orschelin Farm and Home 52, Ottawa *Also called Orscheln Farm and Home LLC (G-8296)*
Orschelin Farm and Home 57, Salina *Also called Orscheln Farm and Home LLC (G-10624)*

A L P H A B E T I C

Orschelin Farm and Home 58, Hutchinson *Also called Orscheln Farm and Home LLC* ***(G-3397)***
Orschelin Farm and Home 58, Hays *Also called Orscheln Farm and Home LLC* ***(G-2884)***
Orschelin Farm and Home 60, McPherson *Also called Orscheln Farm and Home LLC* ***(G-7012)***
Orschelin Farm and Home 69, El Dorado *Also called Orscheln Farm and Home LLC* ***(G-1589)***
Orschelin Farm and Home 71, Junction City *Also called Orscheln Farm and Home LLC* ***(G-3734)***
Orschelin Farm and Home 80, Atchison *Also called Orscheln Farm and Home LLC* ***(G-254)***
Orschelin Farm and Home 97, Smith Center *Also called Orscheln Farm and Home LLC* ***(G-12038)***
Orscheln Farm & Home, Medicine Lodge *Also called Orscheln Farm and Home LLC* ***(G-7071)***
Orscheln Farm & Home 98, Marysville *Also called Orscheln Farm and Home LLC* ***(G-6906)***
Orscheln Farm and Home LLC....620 241-0707
2204 E Kansas Ave McPherson (67460) ***(G-7012)***
Orscheln Farm and Home LLC....620 331-2551
2900 W Main St Independence (67301) ***(G-3546)***
Orscheln Farm and Home LLC....785 825-1681
360 N Ohio St Salina (67401) ***(G-10624)***
Orscheln Farm and Home LLC....620 583-5043
501 Us Highway 54 Eureka (67045) ***(G-1897)***
Orscheln Farm and Home LLC....620 442-5760
2715 N Summit St Arkansas City (67005) ***(G-168)***
Orscheln Farm and Home LLC....620 930-3276
300 S Iliff St Medicine Lodge (67104) ***(G-7071)***
Orscheln Farm and Home LLC....913 728-2014
15256 Wolfcreek Pkwy Basehor (66007) ***(G-385)***
Orscheln Farm and Home LLC....785 562-2459
1095 Pony Express Hwy Marysville (66508) ***(G-6906)***
Orscheln Farm and Home LLC....785 762-4411
1023 S Washington St Junction City (66441) ***(G-3734)***
Orscheln Farm and Home LLC....913 367-2261
605 S 10th St Atchison (66002) ***(G-254)***
Orscheln Farm and Home LLC....620 421-0555
211 Main St Parsons (67357) ***(G-9715)***
Orscheln Farm and Home LLC....785 282-3272
122 W Highway 36 Smith Center (66967) ***(G-12038)***
Orscheln Farm and Home LLC....785 243-6071
1620 Lincoln St Concordia (66901) ***(G-1126)***
Orscheln Farm and Home LLC....620 662-8867
1500 E 11th Ave Hutchinson (67501) ***(G-3397)***
Orscheln Farm and Home LLC....620 251-2950
1702 W 11th St Coffeyville (67337) ***(G-968)***
Orscheln Farm and Home LLC....785 838-3184
1541 E 23rd St Lawrence (66046) ***(G-5050)***
Orscheln Farm and Home LLC....620 227-8700
1701 N 14th Ave Ste D Dodge City (67801) ***(G-1416)***
Orscheln Farm and Home LLC....620 792-5480
5320 10th St Great Bend (67530) ***(G-2619)***
Orscheln Farm and Home LLC....316 283-2969
321 Windward Dr Newton (67114) ***(G-7401)***
Orscheln Farm and Home LLC....785 776-1476
530 Mccall Rd Manhattan (66502) ***(G-6766)***
Orscheln Farm and Home LLC....785 460-1551
1915 S Range Ave Colby (67701) ***(G-1033)***
Orscheln Farm and Home LLC....785 899-7132
2021 Enterprise Rd Goodland (67735) ***(G-2481)***
Orscheln Farm and Home LLC....620 326-2804
1201 W 8th St Wellington (67152) ***(G-13520)***
Orscheln Farm and Home LLC....620 365-7695
1918 N State St Iola (66749) ***(G-3621)***
Orscheln Farm and Home LLC....316 321-4004
2354 W Central Ave El Dorado (67042) ***(G-1589)***
Orscheln Farm and Home LLC....785 625-7316
2900 Broadway Ave Hays (67601) ***(G-2884)***
Orscheln Farm and Home LLC....785 242-3133
2008 Princeton Rd Ottawa (66067) ***(G-8296)***
Orscheln Farm and Home LLC....785 228-9688
1133 Sw Wanamaker Rd # 100 Topeka (66604) ***(G-12955)***
Orscheln Farm Home, Basehor *Also called Orscheln Farm and Home LLC* ***(G-385)***
Orschenlin Farm & Home 73, Independence *Also called Orscheln Farm and Home LLC* ***(G-3546)***
Orthman Mfg....785 754-9985
2550 County Road 74 Quinter (67752) ***(G-10183)***
Ortho 4-States Real Estate LLC....417 206-7846
444 Four States Dr Ste 1 Galena (66739) ***(G-2078)***
Ortho Innovations LLC....913 449-8376
13401 W 125th St Overland Park (66213) ***(G-9115)***
Orthodonics Thompson PC (PA)....913 681-8300
4851 W 134th St Ste A Leawood (66209) ***(G-5509)***
Orthodontics P A Young....913 592-2900
22438 S Harrison St Spring Hill (66083) ***(G-12094)***
Orthokansas PA....785 843-9125
1112 W 6th St Lawrence (66044) ***(G-5051)***
Orthopaedic MGT Svcs LLC....913 319-7500
3651 College Blvd 100a Shawnee Mission (66211) ***(G-11703)***
Orthopdic Spcalists Four State....620 783-4441
444 Four States Dr Ste 1 Galena (66739) ***(G-2079)***
Orthopdic Spt Mdicine Cons LLC....913 319-7534
3651 College Blvd 100b Leawood (66211) ***(G-5510)***
Orthopdic Spt Medicine Ctr LLP....785 537-4200
1600 Charles Pl Manhattan (66502) ***(G-6767)***
Orthopedic & Spo....913 319-7546
3651 College Blvd 100a Leawood (66211) ***(G-5511)***
Orthopedic & Sports Medicine....316 219-8299
10100 E Shannon Woods St # 1 Wichita (67226) ***(G-15237)***
Orthopedic Professional Assn (PA)....913 788-7111
8919 Parallel Pkwy # 270 Kansas City (66112) ***(G-4299)***
Orthopedic Sports Med Clinic O, Topeka *Also called Tall Grass Prarie Surg Spclsts* ***(G-13132)***
Orthopedics & Sports Medicine, Topeka *Also called Tallgrass Prairie Surgical* ***(G-13136)***
Orthosynetics Inc....913 782-1663
1295 E 151st St Ste 1 Olathe (66062) ***(G-7965)***
OS Companies Inc (PA)....316 265-5611
301 S Market St Wichita (67202) ***(G-15238)***
Osage Cnty Ecnmic Dev Corp Inc....785 828-3242
P.O. Box 226 Lyndon (66451) ***(G-6478)***
Osage Co Hwy Dept, Lyndon *Also called County of Osage* ***(G-6476)***
Osage County Clinic, Carbondale *Also called Stormont-Vail Healthcare Inc* ***(G-685)***
Osage County Herald....785 528-3511
527 Market St Osage City (66523) ***(G-8186)***
Osage Graphics....785 654-3939
223 W Hall Ave Burlingame (66413) ***(G-624)***
Osage Hills Inc....620 449-2713
8520 Wallace Rd Saint Paul (66771) ***(G-10383)***
Osage Nursing Center, Osage City *Also called Rh Montgomery Properties Inc* ***(G-8188)***
Osawatomie Agency Inc....913 592-3811
21101 W 223rd St Spring Hill (66083) ***(G-12095)***
Osawatomie Agency Inc (PA)....913 755-3811
601 Main St Osawatomie (66064) ***(G-8201)***
Osawatomie Agency Inc....913 294-3811
702 Baptiste Dr Paola (66071) ***(G-9577)***
Osawatomie State Hospital, Osawatomie *Also called Kansas Dept For Aging & Disabi* ***(G-8195)***
Osborne County Ambulance, Osborne *Also called County of Osborne* ***(G-8207)***
Osborne County Memorial Hosp....785 346-2121
424 W New Hampshire St Osborne (67473) ***(G-8214)***
Osborne Development Company....785 346-2114
811 N 1st St Osborne (67473) ***(G-8215)***
Osborne Industries Inc....785 346-2192
120 N Industrial Ave Osborne (67473) ***(G-8216)***
Osborne Investment Inc....785 346-2147
102 W Main St Osborne (67473) ***(G-8217)***
OSI....316 688-5011
4316 E Lewis St Wichita (67218) ***(G-15239)***
Oskaloosa Independent, Valley Falls *Also called Davis Publications Inc* ***(G-13362)***
Osmckc, Leawood *Also called Orthopedic & Spo* ***(G-5511)***
Oswald Manufacturing Co Inc....785 258-2877
450 S 5th St Herington (67449) ***(G-2980)***
Oswalt Arnold Oswald & Henry....620 662-5489
330 W 1st Ave Hutchinson (67501) ***(G-3398)***
Oswego Medical Center LLC....620 795-2386
800 Barker Dr Ste A Oswego (67356) ***(G-8235)***
Otis Elevator Company....316 682-6886
3979 N Woodlawn Ct Ste 1 Bel Aire (67220) ***(G-437)***
Otis Elevator Company....913 621-8800
1100 W Cambridg Cir Kansas City (66103) ***(G-4300)***
Otl Logistics Inc....816 918-7688
14500 Parallel Rd Ste A Basehor (66007) ***(G-386)***
Otolaryngic Head/Neck Surgry....913 588-6700
3901 Rainbow Blvd Kansas City (66160) ***(G-4301)***
Ott Electric Inc....785 562-2641
810 Broadway Marysville (66508) ***(G-6907)***
Ottawa Bus Service Inc....913 829-6644
1320 W 149th St Olathe (66061) ***(G-7966)***
Ottawa County Health Center....785 392-2044
215 E 8th St Minneapolis (67467) ***(G-7119)***
Ottawa County Health Plg Comm, Minneapolis *Also called Ottawa County Health Center* ***(G-7119)***
Ottawa Fmly Physcans Chartered....785 242-1620
1418 S Main St Ste 5 Ottawa (66067) ***(G-8297)***
Ottawa Herald Inc....785 242-4700
214 S Hickory St Ottawa (66067) ***(G-8298)***
Ottawa Recreation Commission....785 242-1939
705 W 15th St Ottawa (66067) ***(G-8299)***
Ottawa Retirement Plaza Inc....785 242-1127
1042 W 15th St Ofc Ottawa (66067) ***(G-8300)***
Ottawa Retirement Vlg Complex, Ottawa *Also called Ottawa Retirement Plaza Inc* ***(G-8300)***
Ottawa Rtirement Vlg Vlg Manor, Ottawa *Also called Deaconess Long Term Care of MI* ***(G-8264)***
Ottawa Rtrment Vlg Vlg Med Svc, Ottawa *Also called Deaconess Long Term Care of MI* ***(G-8265)***

Ottawa Sanitation Service ...785 242-3227
211 W Wilson St Ottawa (66067) ***(G-8301)***
Ottawa Truck Inc ...785 242-2200
415 E Dundee St Ottawa (66067) ***(G-8302)***
Ottaway Amusement Co Inc ...316 529-0086
19650 Straight Creek Rd Onaga (66521) ***(G-8179)***
Our Ladys Montessori School ...913 403-9550
3020 S 7th St Kansas City (66103) ***(G-4302)***
Outdoor Custom Sportswear LLC ...866 288-5070
7007 College Blvd Ste 200 Overland Park (66211) ***(G-9116)***
Outdoor Lighting Services LP ...913 422-8400
6435 Vista Dr Shawnee (66218) ***(G-11006)***
Outlaws Group LLC ...913 381-5565
4587 Indian Creek Pkwy Shawnee Mission (66207) ***(G-11704)***
Ovation Cabinetry Inc ...785 452-9000
1750 Wall St Salina (67401) ***(G-10625)***
Over Cat Products LLC ...913 256-2126
607 Kelly Ave Osawatomie (66064) ***(G-8202)***
Overand Park Turf Care Center, Overland Park *Also called City of Overland Park* ***(G-8557)***
Overbrook Livestock Comm Co ...785 665-7181
507 Sunset Ln Overbrook (66524) ***(G-8327)***
Overbudget Productions ...913 254-1186
1528 W Forest Dr Olathe (66061) ***(G-7967)***
Overfield Corporation ...785 843-3434
1915 W 24th St Lawrence (66046) ***(G-5052)***
Overhead Door Co Kansas City, Olathe *Also called D H Pace Company Inc* ***(G-7638)***
Overhead Door Co of Topeka, Topeka *Also called Ray Anderson Co Inc* ***(G-13000)***
Overhead Door Company ...316 265-4634
6215 E Kellogg Dr Wichita (67218) ***(G-15240)***
Overhead Door Company Kans Cy, Olathe *Also called D H Pace Company Inc* ***(G-7636)***
Overhead Door Company NW Kans, Goodland *Also called Weathercraft Company N Platte* ***(G-2490)***
Overhead Door N Centl Kans Inc ...785 823-3786
425 E Avenue A Salina (67401) ***(G-10626)***
Overhead Door South Centl Kans, Wichita *Also called D H Pace Company Inc* ***(G-14157)***
Overland Cabinet Company Inc ...913 441-1985
13933 Leavenworth St Bonner Springs (66012) ***(G-569)***
Overland Charters Inc ...316 652-9463
3333 N Hillside Ave Wichita (67219) ***(G-15241)***
Overland Concrete Cnstr Inc ...913 393-4200
1401 W Ott St Olathe (66061) ***(G-7968)***
Overland Limousine Service, Leawood *Also called Wheatland Enterprises Inc* ***(G-5598)***
Overland Park Appliance, Olathe *Also called Regarding Kitchens Inc* ***(G-8023)***
Overland Park Arboretm & Btncl ...913 685-3604
8909 W 179th St Bucyrus (66013) ***(G-606)***
Overland Park Chamber Commerce ...913 491-3600
9001 W 110th St Ste 150 Shawnee Mission (66210) ***(G-11705)***
Overland Park Commercial Off, Lenexa *Also called Evergy Metro Inc* ***(G-5838)***
Overland Park Convention Ctr, Overland Park *Also called City of Overland Park* ***(G-8555)***
Overland Park Dental ...913 383-2343
9601 Antioch Rd Shawnee Mission (66212) ***(G-11706)***
Overland Park Dentistry PA ...913 647-8700
8700 W 151st St Shawnee Mission (66221) ***(G-11707)***
Overland Park Development Corp (PA) ...913 234-2100
6100 College Blvd Overland Park (66211) ***(G-9117)***
Overland Park Fmly Hlth Prtnr ...913 894-6500
5405 W 151st St Overland Park (66224) ***(G-9118)***
Overland Park Garden Ctr Inc (PA) ...913 788-7974
5430 N 97th St Kansas City (66109) ***(G-4303)***
Overland Park Heating & Coolg ...913 649-0303
16172 Metcalf Ave Overland Park (66085) ***(G-9119)***
Overland Park Hospitality LLC ...913 312-0900
10920 Nall Ave Shawnee Mission (66211) ***(G-11708)***
Overland Park Hotel Assoc Lc ...913 888-8440
8787 Reeder St Overland Park (66214) ***(G-9120)***
Overland Park Manor, Shawnee Mission *Also called Shawnee Mission Health Care* ***(G-11856)***
Overland Park Manor, Shawnee Mission *Also called East Orlndo Hlth Rehab Ctr Inc* ***(G-11326)***
Overland Park Police Dept, Shawnee Mission *Also called City of Overland Park* ***(G-11231)***
Overland Park Public Works, Overland Park *Also called City of Overland Park* ***(G-8556)***
Overland Park Racquet Club, Overland Park *Also called Oprc Inc* ***(G-9108)***
Overland Park Reg Med Staff Df ...913 541-5000
10500 Quivira Rd Ste 40 Shawnee Mission (66215) ***(G-11709)***
Overland Park Regional Hosp ...913 541-5406
10500 Quivira Rd Overland Park (66215) ***(G-9121)***
Overland Park Regional Med Ctr, Shawnee Mission *Also called Midwest Division - Oprmc LLC* ***(G-11632)***
Overland Park Senior Living ...913 912-7800
10101 W 127th St Overland Park (66213) ***(G-9122)***
Overland Park Seniorcare LLC ...913 491-1144
11000 Oakmont St Shawnee Mission (66210) ***(G-11710)***
Overland Park Smiles ...913 851-8400
6700 W 121st St Ste 104 Leawood (66209) ***(G-5512)***
Overland Park South Kindercare, Shawnee Mission *Also called Kindercare Learning Ctrs LLC* ***(G-11532)***
Overland Park Super-Sport Club, Overland Park *Also called 24 Hour Fitness Usa Inc* ***(G-8329)***
Overland Park Surgery Ctr LLC ...913 894-7260
10601 Quivira Rd Ste 100 Overland Park (66215) ***(G-9123)***
Overland Park Veterinary Ctr ...913 642-9371
8120 Santa Fe Dr Overland Park (66204) ***(G-9124)***
Overland Pk Nursing Rehab Ctr ...913 383-9866
6501 W 75th St Overland Park (66204) ***(G-9125)***
Overland Pk Rgonal Med Ctr Inc ...913 541-0000
10500 Quivira Rd Overland Park (66215) ***(G-9126)***
Overland Solutions Inc (HQ) ...913 451-3222
10975 Grandview Dr # 400 Overland Park (66210) ***(G-9127)***
Overland Tool & Machinery Inc ...913 599-4044
7431 Monrovia St Shawnee (66216) ***(G-11007)***
Overland Tow Service Inc (PA) ...913 722-3505
3505 Merriam Dr Overland Park (66203) ***(G-9128)***
Overland TV Inc ...913 648-2222
7135 W 80th St Shawnee Mission (66204) ***(G-11711)***
Overlnd Prk Cnvntn & Vstrs Bre ...913 491-0123
9001 W 110th St Ste 100 Overland Park (66210) ***(G-9129)***
Oversize Warning Products Inc ...620 792-5266
258 Se 20 Rd Great Bend (67530) ***(G-2620)***
Owens Bonding Inc ...316 283-3983
600 N Main St Ste 200 Wichita (67203) ***(G-15242)***
Owens Corning Sales LLC ...913 281-9495
3201 Mccormick Rd Kansas City (66115) ***(G-4304)***
Owens Corning Sales LLC ...419 248-8000
300 Sunshine Rd Kansas City (66115) ***(G-4305)***
Oxford Animal Hospital P A ...913 681-2600
13433 Switzer Rd Overland Park (66213) ***(G-9130)***
Oxford Grand Assisted Living ...316 927-2007
3051 N Park Pl Wichita (67204) ***(G-15243)***
Oxford Management Group LLC (PA) ...316 201-3210
125 N Market St Ste 1230 Wichita (67202) ***(G-15244)***
Oxford Senior Living, Wichita *Also called Oxford Management Group LLC* ***(G-15244)***
Oxwell Inc ...620 326-7481
600 E 16th St Wellington (67152) ***(G-13521)***
OXY Inc ...620 629-4200
1701 N Kansas Ave Liberal (67901) ***(G-6351)***
Oz Accommodations Inc ...913 894-8400
7925 Bond St Overland Park (66214) ***(G-9131)***
Oz Winery ...785 456-7417
417 Lincoln Ave Ste A Wamego (66547) ***(G-13431)***
Ozanam Pathways ...316 682-4000
315 N Hillside St Wichita (67214) ***(G-15245)***
Ozark Country Home, Chanute *Also called Caney Guest Home Inc* ***(G-709)***
P & A Investments ...316 634-2303
7856 E 36th St N Wichita (67226) ***(G-15246)***
P & B Trucking Inc ...316 283-6868
1307 Cow Palace Rd Newton (67114) ***(G-7402)***
P & D Inc (PA) ...913 782-2247
300 W Park St Olathe (66061) ***(G-7969)***
P & F Services Inc ...785 456-9401
16375 6th Street Rd Wamego (66547) ***(G-13432)***
P & R Supply Co, Dodge City *Also called Beck Sales Company* ***(G-1305)***
P & S Elc & Roustabout Svc Inc ...620 792-7426
255 W Barton County Rd Great Bend (67530) ***(G-2621)***
P & W Incorporated ...316 267-4277
801 E Mount Vernon St Wichita (67211) ***(G-15247)***
P 1, Wichita *Also called P1 Group Inc* ***(G-15252)***
P A Comcare ...785 392-2144
311 N Mill St Ste 1 Minneapolis (67467) ***(G-7120)***
P A Comcare (PA) ...785 825-8221
2090 S Ohio St Salina (67401) ***(G-10627)***
P A Comcare ...785 827-6453
1001 S Ohio St Salina (67401) ***(G-10628)***
P A Family Medcenters ...316 771-9999
1101 N Rock Rd Stop 1 Derby (67037) ***(G-1264)***
P A Heartland Cardiology ...316 773-5300
8710 W 13th St N Ste 102 Wichita (67212) ***(G-15248)***
P A Heartland Cardiology (PA) ...316 686-5300
3535 N Webb Rd Wichita (67226) ***(G-15249)***
P A Med Assist ...785 272-2161
4011 Sw 29th St Topeka (66614) ***(G-12956)***
P A S, Lenexa *Also called Performance Abatement Svcs Inc* ***(G-6050)***
P A Select Healthcare ...913 948-6400
12140 Nall Ave Ste 305 Leawood (66209) ***(G-5513)***
P A Therapyworks Inc ...785 749-1300
1311 Wakarusa Dr Ste 1000 Lawrence (66049) ***(G-5053)***
P A Treanorhl ...785 235-0012
719 Sw Van Buren St Ste 2 Topeka (66603) ***(G-12957)***
P B Hoidale Co Inc ...913 438-1500
6909 Martindale Rd Shawnee (66218) ***(G-11008)***
P B Hoidale Co Inc ...316 942-1361
3737 W Harry St Wichita (67213) ***(G-15250)***
P B P, Wichita *Also called Pbp Management Group Inc* ***(G-15274)***
P C I, Topeka *Also called Piping Contractors Kansas Inc* ***(G-12977)***
P C Southlaw (PA) ...913 663-7600
13160 Foster St Ste 100 Overland Park (66213) ***(G-9132)***

ALPHABETIC

P D Q Sales and Service, Prairie Village *Also called T W Lacy & Associates Inc* ***(G-10073)***
P F S Group Limited....316 722-0001
1835 N Tony Ln Wichita (67212) ***(G-15251)***
P G I Oriented Polymer Div, Kingman *Also called Polymer Group Inc* ***(G-4611)***
P G I Oriented Polymers Div, Kingman *Also called Polymer Group Inc* ***(G-4612)***
P I L R, Hutchinson *Also called Prairie Ind Lving Resource Ctr* ***(G-3411)***
P K C Realty Company LLC....913 491-1550
8300 College Blvd Ste 100 Overland Park (66210) ***(G-9133)***
P K M Steel Service Inc....785 827-3638
228 E Avenue A Salina (67401) ***(G-10629)***
P P T, Kansas City *Also called Plastic Packaging Tech LLC* ***(G-4325)***
P Q, Kansas City *Also called PQ Corporation* ***(G-4329)***
P&S Electric, Great Bend *Also called P & S Elc & Roustabout Svc Inc* ***(G-2621)***
P-Americas LLC....913 791-3000
1775 E Kansas City Rd Olathe (66061) ***(G-7970)***
P-Ayr Products....913 651-5543
719 Delaware St Leavenworth (66048) ***(G-5278)***
P/Strada LLC....816 256-4577
12401 W 82nd Ter Lenexa (66215) ***(G-6039)***
P1 Group, Lenexa *Also called A D J-Hux Service Inc* ***(G-5616)***
P1 Group Inc (PA)....913 529-5000
13605 W 96th Ter Lenexa (66215) ***(G-6040)***
P1 Group Inc....316 267-3256
2333 S West St Ste 319 Wichita (67213) ***(G-15252)***
P1 Group Inc....785 235-5331
2150a S Kansas Ave Topeka (66611) ***(G-12958)***
P1 Group Inc....785 843-2910
2151 Haskell Ave Bldg 1 Lawrence (66046) ***(G-5054)***
P1 Group International Inc....913 529-5000
13605 W 96th Ter Lenexa (66215) ***(G-6041)***
P1 Transportation LLC....913 249-1505
7360 W 162nd St Ste 108 Overland Park (66085) ***(G-9134)***
PA Acquisition Corp....913 498-3700
11635 Metcalf Ave Shawnee Mission (66210) ***(G-11712)***
PA Hays Anesthesiologist Assoc....785 628-8300
2220 Canterbury Dr Antonino (67601) ***(G-136)***
Pac Mig Inc....316 269-3040
1002 Se Louis Dr Mulvane (67110) ***(G-7226)***
Paccar Leasing Corporation....913 829-1444
1301 S Hamilton Cir Olathe (66061) ***(G-7971)***
Pace Analytical Services Inc....913 599-5665
9608 Loiret Blvd Lenexa (66219) ***(G-6042)***
Paces Wyandot Ctr Youth Svcs....913 956-3420
1620 S 37th St Kansas City (66106) ***(G-4306)***
Pacific 1 Mortgage, Wichita *Also called Financial Consultants America* ***(G-14367)***
Pacific Dental Services LLC....913 299-8860
10818 Parallel Pkwy Kansas City (66109) ***(G-4307)***
Pacific Investment Inc....785 827-1271
2760 S 9th St Salina (67401) ***(G-10630)***
Packerware LLC....785 331-4236
2330 Packer Rd Lawrence (66049) ***(G-5055)***
PacLease, Olathe *Also called Paccar Leasing Corporation* ***(G-7971)***
Paco Designs Inc....913 541-1708
14306 W 99th St Shawnee Mission (66215) ***(G-11713)***
Padgett-Thompson Division, Shawnee Mission *Also called American Management Assn Intl* ***(G-11105)***
Page Corporation....316 262-7200
6333 Sw Santa Fe Lake Rd Augusta (67010) ***(G-335)***
Page Enterprise LLC....913 898-4722
21368 Earnest Rd Parker (66072) ***(G-9659)***
Paige Technologies LLC....913 381-0600
7171 W 95th St Ste 500 Overland Park (66212) ***(G-9135)***
Paincare PA....913 901-8880
10501 Metcalf Ave Overland Park (66212) ***(G-9136)***
Paint Glaze & Fire....913 661-2529
12683 Metcalf Ave Overland Park (66213) ***(G-9137)***
Paint Glaze and Fire Ceramics, Overland Park *Also called Paint Glaze & Fire* ***(G-9137)***
Paint Masters Inc....316 683-5203
2801 E Kellogg Dr Wichita (67211) ***(G-15253)***
Paint Pro Inc....913 685-4089
6930 W 152nd Ter Overland Park (66223) ***(G-9138)***
Palacio, Camilo H, Derby *Also called Via Christi Clinic PA* ***(G-1280)***
Palenske Ranch Inc....620 279-4467
2274a Old Highway 50 Strong City (66869) ***(G-12194)***
Paleteria Tarahumara....620 805-6509
1101 N Taylor Ave Garden City (67846) ***(G-2245)***
Palleton of Kansas Inc (PA)....620 257-3571
103 Industrial Dr Lyons (67554) ***(G-6496)***
Pallucca & Sons Super Market, Frontenac *Also called Pallucca and Sons* ***(G-2062)***
Pallucca and Sons....620 231-7700
207 E Mckay St Frontenac (66763) ***(G-2062)***
Palmer DDS, Haysville *Also called Palmer Family Dentistry* ***(G-2954)***
Palmer Family Dentistry....316 453-6918
1425 W Grand Ave Ste 101 Haysville (67060) ***(G-2954)***
Palmer Grain Fert & Chem Plant, Palmer *Also called Palmer Grain Inc* ***(G-9538)***
Palmer Grain Inc....785 692-4212
208 N Nadeau Ave Palmer (66962) ***(G-9538)***
Palmer Johnson Pwr Systems LLC....913 268-2941
15360 S Mahaffie St Olathe (66062) ***(G-7972)***
Palmer Leatherman & White LLP....785 233-1836
2348 Sw Topeka Blvd # 100 Topeka (66611) ***(G-12959)***
Palmer Oil Inc....620 275-2963
3118 Cummings Rd Garden City (67846) ***(G-2246)***
Palmer Square Capital MGT LLC....816 994-3201
2000 Shawnee Mission Pkwy # 300 Shawnee Mission (66205) ***(G-11714)***
Palmer Webber Macy....785 823-7201
338 N Front St Salina (67401) ***(G-10631)***
Pandarama Prschool Toddler Ctr (PA)....913 342-9692
1118 N 7th St Kansas City (66101) ***(G-4308)***
Panel Systems Plus Inc....913 321-0111
3255 Harvester Rd Kansas City (66115) ***(G-4309)***
Panhandle Eastern Pipeline, Haven *Also called Panhandle Eastrn Pipe Line LP* ***(G-2735)***
Panhandle Eastern Pipeline, Liberal *Also called Panhandle Eastrn Pipe Line LP* ***(G-6352)***
Panhandle Eastrn Pipe Line LP....620 465-2201
12610 S Kent Rd Haven (67543) ***(G-2735)***
Panhandle Eastrn Pipe Line LP....620 624-8661
2330 N Kansas Ave Liberal (67901) ***(G-6352)***
Panhandle Eastrn Pipe Line LP....620 723-2185
1 Mile W 3/4 N On Hwy 183 Greensburg (67054) ***(G-2683)***
Panhandle Eastrn Pipe Line LP....913 906-1500
7500 College Blvd Ste 300 Overland Park (66210) ***(G-9139)***
Panhandle Eastrn Pipe Line LP....620 624-7241
610 W 2nd St Liberal (67901) ***(G-6353)***
Panhandle Eastrn Pipe Line LP....620 624-8661
13 1/2 E Us Highway 54 Liberal (67901) ***(G-6354)***
Panhandle Eastrn Pipe Line LP....620 475-3226
985 Road 90 Olpe (66865) ***(G-8167)***
Panhandle Eastrn Pipe Line LP....913 837-5163
29115 Metcalf Rd Louisburg (66053) ***(G-6461)***
Panhandle Energy, Overland Park *Also called Panhandle Eastrn Pipe Line LP* ***(G-9139)***
Panhandle Federal Credit Union....620 326-2285
403 N Washington Ave Wellington (67152) ***(G-13522)***
Panhandle Steel Erectors Inc....620 271-9878
6800 E Us Highway 50 Garden City (67846) ***(G-2247)***
Pankratz Implement Co....620 662-8681
1800 S Lorraine St Hutchinson (67501) ***(G-3399)***
Pantry, Hutchinson *Also called T & E Oil Company Inc 1* ***(G-3460)***
Pantry Shelf Company....620 662-9342
401 S Adams St Hutchinson (67501) ***(G-3400)***
Paola Assembly of God Inc....913 294-5198
1016 N Pearl St Paola (66071) ***(G-9578)***
Paola Christian Academy, Paola *Also called Paola Assembly of God Inc* ***(G-9578)***
Paola Commercial Office, Paola *Also called Evergy Metro Inc* ***(G-9558)***
Paola Country Club Inc....913 294-2910
29651 Old Kansas City Rd Paola (66071) ***(G-9579)***
Paola Dialysis, Paola *Also called Windcreek Dialysis LLC* ***(G-9596)***
Paola Fire Department, Paola *Also called City of Paola* ***(G-9547)***
Paola Inn and Suites....913 294-3700
1600 E Hedge Lane Ct Paola (66071) ***(G-9580)***
Paola Lifestock Auction Inc....913 294-3335
26701 Eagle Dr Paola (66071) ***(G-9581)***
Papa John's, Lenexa *Also called Devlin Partners LLC* ***(G-5814)***
Papa Murphys Take N Bake....913 897-0008
13473 Switzer Rd Unit G Overland Park (66213) ***(G-9140)***
Paper Graphics Inc....620 276-7641
2006 E Schulman Ave Garden City (67846) ***(G-2248)***
Paper Supply, Prairie Village *Also called Ken OKelly* ***(G-10042)***
Pappas Concrete Inc (PA)....620 277-2127
2104 Road 140 Lakin (67860) ***(G-4657)***
Par Exsalonce (PA)....913 469-9532
11849 College Blvd Shawnee Mission (66210) ***(G-11715)***
Par Forms Corporation....620 421-0970
1716 Corning Ave Parsons (67357) ***(G-9716)***
Par Forms Printing, Parsons *Also called Par Forms Corporation* ***(G-9716)***
Paracom Technologies Inc....316 293-2900
3020 N Cypress St 200b Wichita (67226) ***(G-15254)***
Paradigm Alliance Inc (PA)....316 554-9225
222 S Ridge Rd Wichita (67209) ***(G-15255)***
Paradigm Liaison Services LLC....316 554-9225
222 S Ridge Rd Wichita (67209) ***(G-15256)***
Paragon Aerospace Services....316 945-5285
1015 S West St Wichita (67213) ***(G-15257)***
Paragon Geophysical Svcs Inc....316 636-5552
3500 N Rock Rd Bldg 800b Wichita (67226) ***(G-15258)***
Paragon Holdings Lc....620 343-0920
3700 Oakes Dr Emporia (66801) ***(G-1811)***
Paragon Laser Systems, Emporia *Also called Paragon Holdings Lc* ***(G-1811)***
Paragon N D T & Finishes Inc....316 945-5285
1015 S West St Wichita (67213) ***(G-15259)***
Paragon Ndt LLC....316 927-4283
2210 S Edwards St Wichita (67213) ***(G-15260)***
Paragon Services, Wichita *Also called Paragon Aerospace Services* ***(G-15257)***
Parallel Pkwy Emrgncy Physcans....913 596-4000
8929 Parallel Pkwy Kansas City (66112) ***(G-4310)***

Paramount Landscape Inc ...913 375-1697
7756 Holliday Dr Kansas City (66106) ***(G-4311)***
Paramount Management Corp (PA) ...316 269-4477
3413 W 13th St N Wichita (67203) ***(G-15261)***
Paredes Construction Inc ...913 334-9662
1407 N 79th St Kansas City (66112) ***(G-4312)***
Park & Recreation- Maint Sp, Shawnee Mission *Also called County of Johnson* ***(G-11271)***
Park Aerospace Tech Corp ...316 283-6500
486 N Oliver Rd Bldg Z Newton (67114) ***(G-7403)***
Park Hill Lanes ...620 842-5571
Hwy 14 Anthony (67003) ***(G-131)***
Park Hills Country Club, Pratt *Also called Park Hills Golf & Supper Club* ***(G-10129)***
Park Hills Golf & Supper Club ...620 672-7541
337 Lake Rd Pratt (67124) ***(G-10129)***
Park Hotels & Resorts Inc ...913 649-7060
10601 Metcalf Ave Shawnee Mission (66212) ***(G-11716)***
Park Lanes Family Fun Center, Shawnee Mission *Also called Bobec Inc* ***(G-11175)***
Park Meadows Senior Living LLC ...913 901-8200
5901 W 107th St Overland Park (66207) ***(G-9141)***
Park Pl Healthcare & Rehab Ctr, Chanute *Also called National Healthcare Corp* ***(G-745)***
Park Twenty-Five Apartments, Lawrence *Also called J A Peterson Realty Co Inc* ***(G-4917)***
Park View ...620 424-2000
750 N Missouri St Ulysses (67880) ***(G-13310)***
PARK VILLA NURSING HOME, Clyde *Also called Clyde Development Inc* ***(G-906)***
Park West Plaza LLC ...316 729-4114
505 N Maize Rd Ofc Wichita (67212) ***(G-15262)***
Park Wheatridge Care Center ...620 624-0130
1501 S Holly Dr Liberal (67901) ***(G-6355)***
Park-Rn Overland Park LLC ...913 850-5400
7580 W 135th St Overland Park (66223) ***(G-9142)***
Parkdale Pre-School Center ...785 235-7240
2331 Sw Topeka Blvd Topeka (66611) ***(G-12960)***
Parker & Hay LLP ...785 266-3044
2887 Sw Macvicar Ave # 4 Topeka (66611) ***(G-12961)***
Parker ATI, Ottawa *Also called Clarcor Air Filtration Pdts* ***(G-8256)***
Parker Enterprises Inc ...316 682-4543
858 S Hillside St Wichita (67211) ***(G-15263)***
Parker Hafkins Insurance Inc ...620 225-2888
1712 Central Ave Dodge City (67801) ***(G-1417)***
Parker Oil Co Inc (PA) ...316 529-4343
4343 S West St Wichita (67217) ***(G-15264)***
Parker Oil Co Inc ...316 529-4343
6601 Kansas Ave Kansas City (66111) ***(G-4313)***
Parker Oil Company Inc ...913 596-6247
6601 Kansas Ave Kansas City (66111) ***(G-4314)***
Parker Pest Control Inc ...316 524-4311
1002 Wirth St Augusta (67010) ***(G-336)***
Parker Truss & Stuff ...913 898-2775
19825 County Road 1077 Parker (66072) ***(G-9660)***
Parker-Hannifin Corporation ...785 537-4181
1501 Hayes Dr Manhattan (66502) ***(G-6768)***
Parking Systems Inc ...913 345-9272
12452 Granada Dr Shawnee Mission (66209) ***(G-11717)***
Parkinsons Exercise and ...913 276-4665
3665 W 95th St Leawood (66206) ***(G-5514)***
Parklane AA ...316 682-9960
1060 S Oliver St Wichita (67218) ***(G-15265)***
Parklane Shopping Center, Wichita *Also called Builders Commercials Inc* ***(G-13912)***
Parklane Towers Inc ...316 684-7247
5051 E Lincoln St Ofc Ofc Wichita (67218) ***(G-15266)***
Parks & Recreation Department, Olathe *Also called County of Johnson* ***(G-7623)***
Parks & Recreation Dept, Shawnee Mission *Also called County of Johnson* ***(G-11272)***
Parks & Recreation Dept, Manhattan *Also called City of Manhattan* ***(G-6587)***
Parks & Recrection Dept, Shawnee Mission *Also called County of Johnson* ***(G-11273)***
Parkside Homes Inc ...620 947-2301
200 Willow Rd Ofc Hillsboro (67063) ***(G-3053)***
PARKVIEW CARE CENTER, Osborne *Also called Osborne Development Company* ***(G-8215)***
Parkview Joint Venture ...785 267-3410
2887 Sw Macvicar Ave Topeka (66611) ***(G-12962)***
Parkview Partnership, Topeka *Also called Parkview Joint Venture* ***(G-12962)***
Parkview Villa, Spearville *Also called Spearville District Hospital* ***(G-12071)***
Parkway 4000 LP ...785 749-2555
4001 Parkway Cir Lawrence (66047) ***(G-5056)***
Parkway Center, Shawnee *Also called Equity Bank NA* ***(G-10949)***
Parkway Insurance Agency Inc ...913 385-5000
5750 W 95th St Ste 105 Shawnee Mission (66207) ***(G-11718)***
Parkwood Inn and Suites, Manhattan *Also called 17th Street Properties LLC* ***(G-6525)***
Parkwood Village ...620 672-5541
401 Rochester St Apt 102 Pratt (67124) ***(G-10130)***
Parkwood Village Pratt, Pratt *Also called Parkwood Village* ***(G-10130)***
Parmac LLC ...620 251-5000
201 E 12th St Coffeyville (67337) ***(G-969)***
Parman Tnner Soule Jackson CPA (PA) ...620 442-3700
110 S 1st St Arkansas City (67005) ***(G-169)***
Parnell Corporate Svcs US Inc ...913 274-2100
7015 College Blvd Ste 600 Leawood (66211) ***(G-5515)***
Paronto Mall Construction Inc ...785 632-2484
223 6th St Clay Center (67432) ***(G-875)***
Parris R David MD ...620 223-8045
403 Woodland Hills Blvd Fort Scott (66701) ***(G-1997)***
Parrish, David L, Olathe *Also called Pediatric Dental Specialist PA* ***(G-7978)***
Parrot-Fa-Nalia, Wichita *Also called United Distributors Inc* ***(G-15842)***
Pars Consulting Engineers Inc (PA) ...913 432-0107
14109 Cambridge Leawood (66224) ***(G-5516)***
Parsons Aaron Painting LLC ...620 532-1076
1113 S High St Kingman (67068) ***(G-4609)***
Parsons Area SRS, Parsons *Also called Kansas Dept For Chldren Fmlies* ***(G-9696)***
Parsons Banking Center, Parsons *Also called Community National Bank* ***(G-9677)***
Parsons Brnckrhoff Hldings Inc ...913 310-9943
16201 W 95th St Lenexa (66219) ***(G-6043)***
Parsons Clinic, Parsons *Also called Veterans Health Administration* ***(G-9748)***
Parsons Corporation ...913 233-3100
104 Greystone Ave Kansas City (66103) ***(G-4315)***
Parsons Dialysis Center, Parsons *Also called Renal Trtmnt Centers-West Inc* ***(G-9730)***
Parsons Eye Clinic PA ...620 421-5900
220 N 32nd St Parsons (67357) ***(G-9717)***
Parsons Golf Club Restaurant ...620 421-5290
1808 24000 Rd Parsons (67357) ***(G-9718)***
Parsons Livestock Auction LLC ...620 421-2900
25012 Us Highway 59 Parsons (67357) ***(G-9719)***
Parsons Livestock Market Inc ...620 421-2900
N Hwy 59 Parsons (67357) ***(G-9720)***
Parsons Publishing Company LLC ...620 421-2000
220 S 18th St Parsons (67357) ***(G-9721)***
Parsons State Child Care Ctr, Parsons *Also called Community Child Care Center* ***(G-9676)***
Parsons State Hosp Trining Ctr ...620 421-6550
2601 Gabriel Ave Parsons (67357) ***(G-9722)***
Parsons Sun, Parsons *Also called Parsons Publishing Company LLC* ***(G-9721)***
Parsons Theatre, Parsons *Also called Acme Cinema Inc* ***(G-9663)***
Parsons Transfer Station, Parsons *Also called Waste Corporation Kansas LLC* ***(G-9749)***
Partners Family Practice LLC (PA) ...620 345-6322
200 E Pack St Moundridge (67107) ***(G-7195)***
Partners In Family Care, Moundridge *Also called Partners Family Practice LLC* ***(G-7195)***
Partners In Pediatrics PA ...785 234-4624
631 Sw Horne St Ste 340 Topeka (66606) ***(G-12963)***
Partners In Primary Care ...913 335-6986
7527 State Ave Kansas City (66112) ***(G-4316)***
Partners In Primary Care ...913 815-5508
16575 W 119th St Olathe (66061) ***(G-7973)***
Partners In Promotion, Olathe *Also called Partners N Promotion Inc* ***(G-7974)***
Partners Inc (PA) ...913 906-5400
11005 Metcalf Ave Overland Park (66210) ***(G-9143)***
Partners Kan-Verting LLC ...913 894-2700
17501 W 98th St Unit 1439 Lenexa (66219) ***(G-6044)***
Partners N Promotion Inc (PA) ...913 397-9500
1465 N Winchester St Olathe (66061) ***(G-7974)***
Party Bnce Monwalk Rentals LLC ...316 519-5174
4323 W 31st St S Wichita (67215) ***(G-15267)***
Party City, Wichita *Also called L V S Inc* ***(G-14908)***
Party City, Shawnee Mission *Also called PA Acquisition Corp* ***(G-11712)***
Passmore Bros Inc ...620 544-2189
E Hwy 51 Hugoton (67951) ***(G-3175)***
Passport Incentives Meetings, Overland Park *Also called Shorts Travel Management Inc* ***(G-9308)***
Pastimes Catering, Olathe *Also called Overbudget Productions* ***(G-7967)***
Pastorserve Inc ...877 918-4746
6804 W 107th St Ste 100 Overland Park (66212) ***(G-9144)***
Patc's, Newton *Also called Park Aerospace Tech Corp* ***(G-7403)***
Patchen Electric & Indus Sup ...785 843-4522
602 E 9th St Lawrence (66044) ***(G-5057)***
Patient Resource Pubg LLC ...913 725-1000
8455 Lenexa Dr Overland Park (66214) ***(G-9145)***
Patrick A Blanchard MD ...785 456-8778
711 Genn Dr Wamego (66547) ***(G-13433)***
Patrick Friess LLP ...620 227-3135
1100 W Frontview St Dodge City (67801) ***(G-1418)***
Patrick J Pirrote Od PA ...316 721-8877
746 N Maize Rd Ste 100 Wichita (67212) ***(G-15268)***
Patrick Properties Services ...913 262-6824
11755 W 86th Ter Overland Park (66214) ***(G-9146)***
Patrick S Kearney ...913 367-3161
16083 262nd Rd Atchison (66002) ***(G-255)***
Patriot Abatement Services LLC ...913 397-6181
19021 W 160th Ct Olathe (66062) ***(G-7975)***
Patriot Pawn & Firearms, Wichita *Also called Owens Bonding Inc* ***(G-15242)***
Patterson Advertising Agency ...785 232-0533
305 Se 17th St Ste C Topeka (66607) ***(G-12964)***
Patterson Dental 230, Lenexa *Also called Patterson Dental Supply Inc* ***(G-6045)***
Patterson Dental 360, Wichita *Also called Patterson Dental Supply Inc* ***(G-15269)***
Patterson Dental Supply Inc ...913 492-6100
11280 Renner Blvd Lenexa (66219) ***(G-6045)***
Patterson Dental Supply Inc ...316 315-1800
8201 E 34th Cir N # 1307 Wichita (67226) ***(G-15269)***

Patterson Health Center, Anthony *Also called Hospital Dst 6 Harper Cnty* ***(G-128)***
Patterson Racing Inc.....316 775-7771
920 Industrial Rd Augusta (67010) ***(G-337)***
Patton Cramer & Laprod Charter.....620 672-5533
113 E 3rd St Pratt (67124) ***(G-10131)***
Patton Termite & Pest Ctrl Inc.....316 773-3825
7920 W Kellogg Dr Ste 100 Wichita (67209) ***(G-15270)***
Paul Davis Restoratio of Great.....785 842-0351
1420 N 3rd St Lawrence (66044) ***(G-5058)***
Paul Henson Family YMCA Inc.....913 642-6800
4200 W 79th St Prairie Village (66208) ***(G-10056)***
Paul W Murphy MD.....316 686-6303
1855 N Webb Rd Wichita (67206) ***(G-15271)***
Paul-Wertenberger Cnstr Inc.....785 625-8220
1102 E 8th St Hays (67601) ***(G-2885)***
Pauline Food Center.....785 862-2774
5812 S Topeka St Topeka (66619) ***(G-12965)***
Pauls Valley Third Additon.....316 733-1648
14752 Sw Anemone Rd Rose Hill (67133) ***(G-10243)***
Pavers Inc.....785 825-6771
505 Francis Ave Salina (67401) ***(G-10632)***
Paving Construction Inc (PA).....316 684-6161
212 N Market St Ste 315 Wichita (67202) ***(G-15272)***
Paw Prints Animal Hospital.....785 267-1918
4144 Se 45th St Berryton (66409) ***(G-528)***
Pawnee Avenue Church of God.....316 683-5648
2611 E Pawnee St Wichita (67211) ***(G-15273)***
Pawnee County Highway Dept, Larned *Also called County of Pawnee* ***(G-4700)***
Pawnee County Humane Soc Inc.....620 285-8510
1406 M5 Rd Larned (67550) ***(G-4709)***
Pawnee Mental Health Svcs Inc (PA).....785 762-5250
2001 Claflin Rd Manhattan (66502) ***(G-6769)***
Pawnee Mental Health Svcs Inc.....785 762-5250
814 Caroline Ave Junction City (66441) ***(G-3735)***
Pawnee Mental Health Svcs Inc.....785 587-4344
425 Houston St Manhattan (66502) ***(G-6770)***
Pawnee Rock State Hstoric Site, Topeka *Also called Executive Office of Kansas* ***(G-12587)***
Pawnee Valley, Hanston *Also called Winter Livestock Inc* ***(G-2715)***
Pawrnee Valley Scouts Inc.....620 285-6427
109 E 15th St Larned (67550) ***(G-4710)***
Pawsh Wash.....785 856-7297
1520 Wakarusa Dr Ste C Lawrence (66047) ***(G-5059)***
Payal Hotels LLC.....785 579-5787
221 E Ash St Junction City (66441) ***(G-3736)***
Paychex Inc.....913 814-7776
5901 College Blvd Ste 400 Leawood (66211) ***(G-5517)***
Paycor Inc.....913 262-9484
8050 Marshall Dr Ste 100 Shawnee Mission (66214) ***(G-11719)***
Paydia, Lenexa *Also called Core Cashless LLC* ***(G-5788)***
Payless Concrete Products Inc.....620 365-5588
802 N Industrial Rd Iola (66749) ***(G-3622)***
Payne & Brockway P A.....913 782-4800
426 S Kansas Ave Olathe (66061) ***(G-7976)***
Payne and Jones Chartered.....913 469-4100
100 King Overland Park (66225) ***(G-9147)***
Payne and Jones Chartered (PA).....816 960-3600
11000 King St Ste 200 Shawnee Mission (66210) ***(G-11720)***
Payne's Truck Parts, Frontenac *Also called Paynes Inc* ***(G-2063)***
Paynes Inc.....620 231-3170
806 W Mckay St Frontenac (66763) ***(G-2063)***
Payroll Partners Plus, Overland Park *Also called Keller & Owens LLC* ***(G-8911)***
Payroll Plus.....620 846-2658
8505 Dd Rd Montezuma (67867) ***(G-7160)***
Payspot LLC.....913 327-4200
3500 College Blvd Leawood (66211) ***(G-5518)***
PB&j.....913 648-6033
10220 W 87th St Overland Park (66212) ***(G-9148)***
Pbi-Gordon Corporation (PA).....816 421-4070
22701 W 68th Ter Shawnee (66226) ***(G-11009)***
Pbi-Gordon Corporation.....816 421-4070
300 S 3rd St Kansas City (66118) ***(G-4317)***
Pbi-Gordon Corporation.....620 848-3849
7530 Se Boston Mills Rd Galena (66739) ***(G-2080)***
Pbi-Gordon Corporation.....620 848-3849
69 Alternate Hwy Crestline (66728) ***(G-1184)***
Pbp Management Group Inc.....316 262-2900
4029 N Sweet Bay Ct Wichita (67226) ***(G-15274)***
Pcdisposalcom LLC.....913 980-4750
400 New Century Pkwy New Century (66031) ***(G-7295)***
PCI Knsas Cy Pntg Coating Svcs, Lenexa *Also called Performance Contracting Inc* ***(G-6053)***
Pcs Incorporated.....913 981-1100
1948 E Santa Fe St Olathe (66062) ***(G-7977)***
Pda of Kansas City Inc.....913 631-0711
6400 Glenwood St Ste 313 Overland Park (66202) ***(G-9149)***
PDQ Auto Reconditioning, Shawnee Mission *Also called PDQ Tools and Equipment Inc* ***(G-11721)***
PDQ Construction Inc.....785 842-6844
531 Nw Tyler Ct Ste A Topeka (66608) ***(G-12966)***
PDQ Tools and Equipment Inc.....913 492-5800
9018 Rosehill Rd Shawnee Mission (66215) ***(G-11721)***
Peabody State Bancorp Inc (PA).....620 983-2810
589 Quail Crk Peabody (66866) ***(G-9761)***
Peabody State Bank (HQ).....620 983-2181
201 N Walnut St Peabody (66866) ***(G-9762)***
Peace of Mind.....316 260-7046
400 E School St Rose Hill (67133) ***(G-10244)***
Peachwave.....620 624-2045
1033 N Kansas Ave Liberal (67901) ***(G-6356)***
Peanut Co LLC.....913 647-2240
7489 W 161st St Overland Park (66085) ***(G-9150)***
Pearce Keller American Legion.....785 776-4556
114 Mccall Rd Manhattan (66502) ***(G-6771)***
Pearson Construction LLC.....316 263-3100
3450 N Rock Rd Ste 300 Wichita (67226) ***(G-15275)***
Pearson Excavating Inc.....316 263-3100
821 E 25th St N Wichita (67219) ***(G-15276)***
Pearson Kent McKinley Raaf Eng (PA).....913 492-2400
13300 W 98th St Lenexa (66215) ***(G-6046)***
Peavey Corporation.....913 888-0600
11042 Strang Line Rd Lenexa (66215) ***(G-6047)***
PEC, Wichita *Also called Professional Engrg Cons PA* ***(G-15359)***
PEC, Pittsburg *Also called Professional Engrg Cons PA* ***(G-9924)***
PEC, Topeka *Also called Professional Engrg Cons PA* ***(G-12990)***
Peckham Gyton Albers Viets Inc.....913 362-6500
1900 W 47th Pl Ste 300 Shawnee Mission (66205) ***(G-11722)***
Pediatric Assoc of Kansan City, Overland Park *Also called Gupta Ganesh* ***(G-8782)***
Pediatric Cardiology Dept, Kansas City *Also called University of Kansas Med Ctr* ***(G-4508)***
Pediatric Care, Topeka *Also called Stormont Vale Hospital* ***(G-13102)***
Pediatric Care Specialist PA.....913 906-0900
12541 Foster St Ste 260 Overland Park (66213) ***(G-9151)***
Pediatric Dental Specialist PA.....913 829-0981
975 N Mur Len Rd Ste A Olathe (66062) ***(G-7978)***
Pediatric Dentistry, Hutchinson *Also called Roger D Gausman DDS* ***(G-3429)***
Pediatric Eye Care, Olathe *Also called Trudi R Grin* ***(G-8122)***
Pediatric Orthopedic Surgery.....913 451-0000
5250 W 94th Ter Prairie Village (66207) ***(G-10057)***
Pediatric Partners.....913 888-4567
7301 W 133rd St Ste 102 Overland Park (66213) ***(G-9152)***
Pediatric Professional Assn.....913 541-3300
10600 Quivira Rd Ste 210 Shawnee Mission (66215) ***(G-11723)***
Pediatriccare, Topeka *Also called Stormont-Vail Healthcare Inc* ***(G-13109)***
Pediatrics Associates.....785 235-0335
3500 Sw 6th Ave Ste 200 Topeka (66606) ***(G-12967)***
Pedro Lopez Co Inc.....785 220-1509
2775 Us Highway 75 Lebo (66856) ***(G-5608)***
Peerless Conveyor and Mfg Corp.....913 342-2240
201 E Quindaro Blvd Kansas City (66115) ***(G-4318)***
Peerless Products Inc.....620 223-4610
2403 S Main St Fort Scott (66701) ***(G-1998)***
Pegasus Communication Solution.....913 937-8552
12181 Craig St Overland Park (66213) ***(G-9153)***
Pella Products Kansas City Inc (PA).....913 492-7927
11333 Strang Line Rd Lenexa (66215) ***(G-6048)***
Pelton Painting Inc.....785 242-7363
109 S Main St Ottawa (66067) ***(G-8303)***
Pemco Inc (PA).....913 294-2361
401 W Wea St Paola (66071) ***(G-9582)***
Pendello Solutions.....913 677-6744
7301 Mission Rd Ste 100 Prairie Village (66208) ***(G-10058)***
Peninsula Overhead Doors, Junction City *Also called Garage Door Group Inc* ***(G-3691)***
Penn Enterprises Inc.....785 762-3600
1116 Grant Ave Junction City (66441) ***(G-3737)***
Penn Manor Apartments, Independence *Also called Southeast Kansas Lutherans Inc* ***(G-3561)***
Penn Mutual Life Insurance Co.....316 685-9296
5940 E Central Ave Wichita (67208) ***(G-15277)***
Penn Mutual Life Insurance Co.....913 322-9177
4000 W 114th St Ste 180 Leawood (66211) ***(G-5519)***
Penner Feed & Supply Inc.....620 585-6612
778 Cherokee Rd Inman (67546) ***(G-3583)***
Penner Trucking Inc.....620 353-8475
1808 Road Pp Sublette (67877) ***(G-12206)***
Pennington Co Fundraising LLC.....785 843-1661
501 Gateway Dr Ste A Lawrence (66049) ***(G-5060)***
Pennsylvania Place, Holton *Also called 4-B Properties LLC* ***(G-3083)***
Pennys Concrete Inc (PA).....913 441-8781
23400 W 82nd St Shawnee Mission (66227) ***(G-11724)***
Pennys Concrete Inc.....913 441-8781
30078 Lone Star Rd Paola (66071) ***(G-9583)***
Pennys Concrete Inc.....913 441-8781
7905 W 247th St Louisburg (66053) ***(G-6462)***
Pennys Concrete & Rdymx LLC.....785 242-1045
745 N Locust St Ottawa (66067) ***(G-8304)***
Pennzoil 10 Minute Lube Center, McPherson *Also called Kansas Fast Lube Inc* ***(G-6982)***
Penske Truck Leasing Co LP.....316 943-8500
1440 S Hoover Rd Wichita (67209) ***(G-15278)***

Penske Truck Leasing Co LP 785 776-3139
1927 Fort Riley Ln Manhattan (66502) *(G-6772)*
Pentair Flow Technologies LLC 913 371-5000
3601 Fairbanks Ave Kansas City (66106) *(G-4319)*
Penwell Gabel Funeral Home, Chanute *Also called Johnson Mortuary Inc (G-734)*
Penwell Gabel Midtwn Funrl Hme, Topeka *Also called Newcomer Funeral Svc Group Inc (G-12929)*
Penwell Gbl Frl Wlf Brns Chpl 620 251-3100
2405 Woodland Ave Coffeyville (67337) *(G-970)*
Peoples Bank (PA) 620 672-5611
222 S Main St Pratt (67124) *(G-10132)*
Peoples Bank 620 582-2166
101 E Main St Coldwater (67029) *(G-1056)*
Peoples Bank 785 282-6682
136 S Main St Smith Center (66967) *(G-12039)*
Peoples Bank & Trust Co (PA) 620 241-2100
101 S Main St McPherson (67460) *(G-7013)*
Peoples Bank & Trust Co 620 662-6502
6300 W Morgan Ave Hutchinson (67501) *(G-3401)*
Peoples Bank & Trust Co 620 669-0234
601 E 30th Ave Hutchinson (67502) *(G-3402)*
Peoples Bank & Trust Co 620 585-2265
215 S Main St Inman (67546) *(G-3584)*
Peoples Bank & Trust Co 620 241-6908
1320 1/2 N Main St McPherson (67460) *(G-7014)*
Peoples Bank & Trust Co 620 241-7664
719 N Main St McPherson (67460) *(G-7015)*
Peoples Bank & Trust Co 620 663-4000
1020 N Main St Ste 1 Hutchinson (67501) *(G-3403)*
Peoples Telecommunications LLC 913 757-2500
208 N Broadway St La Cygne (66040) *(G-4641)*
Peoples/Commercial Insur LLC 785 271-8097
1414 Sw Ashworth Pl # 10 Topeka (66604) *(G-12968)*
Peppermint Pttys Mntssori Schl 913 631-9376
11010 W 56th Ter Shawnee Mission (66203) *(G-11725)*
Pepsi Beverages Company 316 522-3131
101 W 48th St S Wichita (67217) *(G-15279)*
Pepsi Cola Btlg Co of Salina (HQ) 785 827-7297
604 N 9th St Salina (67401) *(G-10633)*
Pepsi-Cola, Salina *Also called Pepsi Cola Btlg Co of Salina (G-10633)*
Pepsi-Cola Btlg Co Topeka Inc 785 232-9389
2625 Nw Topeka Blvd Topeka (66617) *(G-12969)*
Pepsi-Cola Btlg Marysville Inc 785 537-4730
703 Levee Dr Manhattan (66502) *(G-6773)*
Pepsi-Cola Btlg of Pittsburg 620 231-3800
1211 N Broadway St Pittsburg (66762) *(G-9912)*
Pepsi-Cola Metro Btlg Co Inc 620 251-2890
2406 N 169 Coffeyville (67337) *(G-971)*
Pepsi-Cola Metro Btlg Co Inc 620 227-8123
811 E Wyatt Earp Blvd Dodge City (67801) *(G-1419)*
Pepsi-Cola Metro Btlg Co Inc 620 624-0287
212 S Virginia Ave Liberal (67901) *(G-6357)*
Pepsi-Cola Metro Btlg Co Inc 316 529-9840
101 W 48th St S Wichita (67217) *(G-15280)*
Pepsi-Cola Metro Btlg Co Inc 785 628-3024
2000 Front St Hays (67601) *(G-2886)*
Pepsico, Topeka *Also called Pepsi-Cola Btlg Co Topeka Inc (G-12969)*
Pepsico, Manhattan *Also called Pepsi-Cola Btlg Marysville Inc (G-6773)*
Pepsico, Hays *Also called Pepsi-Cola Metro Btlg Co Inc (G-2886)*
Pepsico Inc 620 275-5312
355 Industrial Park Garden City (67846) *(G-2249)*
Percision Mfg 913 362-9244
5734 Barton Dr Shawnee (66203) *(G-11010)*
Perfect Details Inc 913 592-5022
516 N Webster St Spring Hill (66083) *(G-12096)*
Perfect Output LLC (PA) 913 317-8400
9200 Indian Creek Pkwy Overland Park (66210) *(G-9154)*
Perfect Smiles Dental Care PA 913 631-2677
8650 Candlelight Ln Ste 1 Lenexa (66215) *(G-6049)*
Perfect Touch Inc 316 522-9205
535 W Douglas Ave Ste 120 Wichita (67213) *(G-15281)*
Perfection II Masonry Inc 785 499-6307
223 S 1000 Rd Alta Vista (66834) *(G-71)*
Perfection Strl Components LLC 316 942-8361
1666 S Saint Clair Ave Wichita (67213) *(G-15282)*
Perfekta Inc (HQ) 316 263-2056
480 E 21st St N Wichita (67214) *(G-15283)*
Perfekta Aerospace, Wichita *Also called Perfekta Inc (G-15283)*
Performance Abatement Svcs Inc (HQ) 913 888-8600
11145 Thompson Ave Lenexa (66219) *(G-6050)*
Performance Contg Intl Inc 913 888-8600
16400 College Blvd Shawnee Mission (66219) *(G-11726)*
Performance Contracting Inc (HQ) 913 888-8600
11145 Thompson Ave Lenexa (66219) *(G-6051)*
Performance Contracting Inc 913 928-2832
16407 110th Lenexa (66219) *(G-6052)*
Performance Contracting Inc 913 928-2850
16047 W 110th St Lenexa (66219) *(G-6053)*
Performance Contracting Inc 913 928-2800
16047 W 110th St Lenexa (66219) *(G-6054)*
Performance Electric LLC 785 242-5748
206 N Oak St Ottawa (66067) *(G-8305)*
Performance Enhancement Center 620 421-2125
2100 Commerce Dr Parsons (67357) *(G-9723)*
Performance Glass Inc 913 441-1290
15955 Linwood Rd Bonner Springs (66012) *(G-570)*
Performance Packg Group LLC 913 438-2012
17501 W 98th St 32 Shawnee Mission (66219) *(G-11727)*
Performance Rehab LLC 913 681-9909
11408 W 135th St Overland Park (66221) *(G-9155)*
Performance Tire & Wheel Group, Topeka *Also called Super Oil Co Inc (G-13125)*
Performix High Plains LLC 620 225-0080
1650 N Sherlock Rd Garden City (67846) *(G-2250)*
Performix Nutrition Systems 620 277-2886
1650 N Sherlock Rd Garden City (67846) *(G-2251)*
Perimeter Solutions LP 785 749-8100
440 N 9th St Lawrence (66044) *(G-5061)*
Perinatal Consultants PA 785 354-5952
15315 W Hendryx St Goddard (67052) *(G-2452)*
Periodontist PA 913 451-6158
10870 Benson Dr Ste 2100 Overland Park (66210) *(G-9156)*
Perkinelmer Inc 316 773-0055
3108 N Tee Time Wichita (67205) *(G-15284)*
Perkins Smart & Boyd Inc (PA) 800 344-1621
4330 Shawnee Mission Pkwy # 204 Fairway (66205) *(G-1916)*
Perl Auto Center Inc 620 251-4050
806 W 8th St Coffeyville (67337) *(G-972)*
Permanent Paving Inc 913 451-7834
11011 Cody St Ste 300 Overland Park (66210) *(G-9157)*
Pernod Ricard Usa LLC 913 393-2015
14235 W 124th St Olathe (66062) *(G-7979)*
Perrys Inc 620 662-2375
615 N Main St Hutchinson (67501) *(G-3404)*
Perserve At Overland Park 913 685-3700
12401 W 120th St Overland Park (66213) *(G-9158)*
Personal Marketing Company Inc 913 492-0377
11511 W 83rd Ter Overland Park (66214) *(G-9159)*
Personal Membership 785 979-7812
617 E 1450 Rd Lawrence (66046) *(G-5062)*
Personal Savings Network, Leawood *Also called Global Services Inc (G-5414)*
Personalized Lawn Care Inc 913 727-3977
1410 Corey Ln Lansing (66043) *(G-4689)*
Personnel Services, Fort Leavenworth *Also called United States Dept of Army (G-1944)*
Perspecta Entp Solutions LLC 785 274-4200
6511 Se Forbes Ave Topeka (66619) *(G-12970)*
Pest Services, Wichita *Also called Schendel Services Inc (G-15530)*
Pestinger Heating & AC Inc (PA) 785 827-6361
125 E Avenue A Salina (67401) *(G-10634)*
Pet Clinic At Webb Village, Wichita *Also called Animal Clinic Wichita PA (G-13711)*
Pet Haven LLC 316 942-2151
2524 W 13th St N Wichita (67203) *(G-15285)*
Pete & Macs Recreational Reso 913 888-8889
8809 Monrovia St Lenexa (66215) *(G-6055)*
Peter J Cristiano Dr 913 682-5588
720 1st Ter Lansing (66043) *(G-4690)*
Peterbilt of Garden City, Garden City *Also called Moss Enterprises Inc (G-2241)*
Peters-Howell Lujeana 785 415-2125
1116 Main St Stockton (67669) *(G-12183)*
Petersen Development Corp 785 228-9494
1111 Sw Gage Blvd Ste 100 Topeka (66604) *(G-12971)*
Petersen Printing Inc 620 275-7331
1002 N 4th St Garden City (67846) *(G-2252)*
Peterson Companies, Overland Park *Also called Cambridgen Inc (G-8507)*
Peterson Companies 316 682-4903
505 N Rock Rd Ste 200 Wichita (67206) *(G-15286)*
PETERSON COMPANIES, THE, Shawnee Mission *Also called J A Peterson Realty Co Inc (G-11473)*
Peterson Companies, The, Shawnee Mission *Also called J A Peterson Enterprises Inc (G-11471)*
Peterson Laboratory Svcs PA 785 539-5363
1133 College Ave Bldg B Manhattan (66502) *(G-6774)*
Peterson Mch Tl Acqisition Inc 316 634-6699
731 S Industrial Ct Rose Hill (67133) *(G-10245)*
Peterson Publications Inc 785 271-5801
2150 Sw Westport Dr # 101 Topeka (66614) *(G-12972)*
Petl Management Corp Inc 620 792-1717
919 Adams St Great Bend (67530) *(G-2622)*
Petnet Solutions Inc 913 310-9270
9012 Cody St Overland Park (66214) *(G-9160)*
Petrakis, Patricia M, Salina *Also called Compcare (G-10458)*
Petro Chem Ref Pipeline Indust, El Dorado *Also called CD&h Inc (G-1544)*
Petroleum Property Services 316 265-3351
125 N Market St Ste 1251 Wichita (67202) *(G-15287)*
Petronomics Mfg Group Inc 620 663-8559
208 E 2nd Ave Hutchinson (67501) *(G-3405)*

ALPHABETIC

Petropower LLC......316 361-0222
3003 E 37th St N Ste 100 Wichita (67219) *(G-15288)*
Petrosantander (usa) Inc......620 272-7187
11130 E 7 Mile Rd Garden City (67846) *(G-2253)*
Petsmart Inc......913 393-4111
15255 W 119th St Olathe (66062) *(G-7980)*
Petsmart Inc......913 338-5544
11501 Metcalf Ave Shawnee Mission (66210) *(G-11728)*
Petsmart Inc......785 272-3323
2020 Sw Westport Dr # 200 Topeka (66604) *(G-12973)*
Petsmart Inc......913 384-4445
5810 Antioch Rd Shawnee Mission (66202) *(G-11729)*
Petty Products Inc......913 782-0028
224 N Monroe St Olathe (66061) *(G-7981)*
Petworks Inc......913 381-3131
9232 Metcalf Ave Shawnee Mission (66212) *(G-11730)*
Petworks Vtrnary Hosp Pet Sups, Shawnee Mission *Also called Petworks Inc (G-11730)*
Pexco Company Llc......913 907-5022
6731 W 121st St 216 Leawood (66209) *(G-5520)*
Pfaltzgraff Co......316 283-7754
601 Se 36th St Newton (67114) *(G-7404)*
Pfefferkorn Engrg & Envmtl LLC......913 490-3967
19957 W 162nd St Olathe (66062) *(G-7982)*
Pfizer Inc......913 897-3054
12744 Granada Ln Leawood (66209) *(G-5521)*
Pgw Auto Glass LLC......913 927-2753
555 River Park Dr Kansas City (66105) *(G-4320)*
Pgw Autoglass, Kansas City *Also called Pgw Auto Glass LLC (G-4320)*
PH Enterprises Inc......620 232-1900
200 E Centennial Dr 10a Pittsburg (66762) *(G-9913)*
Phantom Enterprises Inc......316 264-7070
101 S Evans St Newton (67114) *(G-7405)*
Phares Petroleum Inc......316 682-3349
207 N Burr Oak Rd Wichita (67206) *(G-15289)*
Pharmacy Dist Partners LLC......903 357-3391
6416 Ensley Ln Mission Hills (66208) *(G-7147)*
Pharmacy Express, Olathe *Also called Miami County Medical Center (G-7889)*
Pharmcare Hlth Specialists LLC......316 681-2181
2740 N Regency Park Wichita (67226) *(G-15290)*
Pharmion Corporation......913 266-0300
9900 W 109th St Ste 300 Overland Park (66210) *(G-9161)*
Phelps Engineering Inc......913 393-1155
1270 N Winchester St Olathe (66061) *(G-7983)*
Phenix Label Company Inc......913 327-7000
11610 S Alden St Olathe (66062) *(G-7984)*
PHI Kappa Theta......785 539-7491
1965 College Heights Rd Manhattan (66502) *(G-6775)*
Philip Morris USA Inc......913 339-9317
4000 W 114th St Ste 110 Shawnee Mission (66211) *(G-11731)*
Phillip G Ruffin (PA)......316 942-7940
1522 S Florence St Wichita (67209) *(G-15291)*
Phillips 66......316 821-2250
2400 E 37th St N Wichita (67219) *(G-15292)*
Phillips and Associates Inc......913 706-7625
8001 Granada Rd Prairie Village (66208) *(G-10059)*
Phillips County Health Systems, Phillipsburg *Also called Phillips County Hospital (G-9792)*
Phillips County Hospital......785 543-5226
1150 State St Phillipsburg (67661) *(G-9792)*
Phillips County Retirement Ctr......785 543-2131
1300 State St Phillipsburg (67661) *(G-9793)*
Phillips Resource Network Inc......913 236-7777
8041 W 47th St Shawnee Mission (66203) *(G-11732)*
Phillips Southern Elc Co Inc......316 265-4186
650 E Gilbert St Wichita (67211) *(G-15293)*
Phillips Well Service Inc......316 321-6650
315 N Industrial Rd El Dorado (67042) *(G-1590)*
Phoenix Corporation......913 321-5200
201 E Donovan Rd Kansas City (66115) *(G-4321)*
Phoenix Medical Research Inc......913 381-7180
7301 Mission Rd Ste 135 Prairie Village (66208) *(G-10060)*
Phoenix Metals, Kansas City *Also called Phoenix Corporation (G-4321)*
Phoenix Restoration Service......620 276-6994
1612 Terminal Ave Garden City (67846) *(G-2254)*
Phoenix Rnvtion Rstoration Inc......913 599-0055
16250 Foster St Stilwell (66085) *(G-12171)*
Phoenix Supply Inc (PA)......316 262-7241
1826 S Pattie St Wichita (67211) *(G-15294)*
Phone Connection of Kansas, Manhattan *Also called Tpcks Inc (G-6828)*
Phone Tech Communications Inc......913 859-9150
6004 W 146th St Overland Park (66223) *(G-9162)*
Physical Rsprtory Therapy Svcs......785 742-2131
300 Utah St Hiawatha (66434) *(G-3021)*
Physical Rsprtory Therapy Svcs......785 742-7606
700 Oregon St Hiawatha (66434) *(G-3022)*
Physician Office Partners LLC......913 754-0467
6050 Sprint Pkwy Ste 300 Overland Park (66211) *(G-9163)*
Physicians Business Netwrk Inc, Overland Park *Also called Physicians Business Netwrk LLC (G-9164)*
Physicians Business Netwrk LLC (HQ)......913 381-5200
8900 Indian Creek Pkwy # 500 Overland Park (66210) *(G-9164)*
Physicians Medical Clinics......316 683-4334
3009 N Cypress St Wichita (67226) *(G-15295)*
Physicians Medical Clinics......316 687-2651
7150 E Harry St Wichita (67207) *(G-15296)*
Physicians Medical Clinics......316 261-3130
848 N St Francis St Wichita (67214) *(G-15297)*
Physicians Medical Clinics......316 721-4910
8200 W Central Ave Ste 1 Wichita (67212) *(G-15298)*
Physicians Optical......913 829-5511
21020 W 151st St Olathe (66061) *(G-7985)*
Physicians Surgery Center......913 384-9600
3840 W 75th St Shawnee Mission (66208) *(G-11733)*
Phytotech Labs Inc......913 341-5343
14610 W 106th St Lenexa (66215) *(G-6056)*
Phytotechnology Labs LLC......913 341-5343
14610 W 106th St Lenexa (66215) *(G-6057)*
PI Arm......913 661-1662
8717 W 110th St Ste 300 Overland Park (66210) *(G-9165)*
PI Beta PHI House Inc......785 539-1818
1819 Todd Rd Manhattan (66502) *(G-6776)*
PI Kappa PHI House Mother......785 856-1400
1537 Tennessee St Lawrence (66044) *(G-5063)*
PI Timberline LLC......913 674-0438
8826 Santa Fe Dr Ste 300 Overland Park (66212) *(G-9166)*
Piat Inc......913 782-4693
15365 S Keeler St Olathe (66062) *(G-7986)*
Pickel Gear, Kansas City *Also called Em Sales LLC (G-3985)*
Pickrell Drilling Co Inc (PA)......316 262-8427
100 S Main St Ste 505 Wichita (67202) *(G-15299)*
Pickrell Drilling Co Inc......620 793-5742
Railroad Ave Great Bend (67530) *(G-2623)*
Picture & Frame Industries Inc......913 384-3751
35 Southwest Blvd Kansas City (66103) *(G-4322)*
Picture Perfect, Wichita *Also called McKissick Enterprises LLC (G-15029)*
Picture Perfect Interiors LLC......913 829-3365
11922 College Blvd Overland Park (66210) *(G-9167)*
Pihl Repair & Fabrication LLC......785 668-2014
8625 S Lightville Rd Falun (67442) *(G-1928)*
Piland Auto Dismantling......620 275-5506
803 W Lake Ave Garden City (67846) *(G-2255)*
Pilgrims Pride Corporation......620 597-2820
6410 Sw Hallowell Rd Columbus (66725) *(G-1085)*
Pillar Hotels and Resorts LLC......785 271-6165
2033 Sw Wanamaker Rd Topeka (66604) *(G-12974)*
Pine Decals, Olathe *Also called Pps Inc (G-7996)*
Pine Howard Grdn Ctr & Grnhse......785 749-0302
1320 N 3rd St Lawrence (66044) *(G-5064)*
Pine Village......620 345-2901
86 22nd Ave Moundridge (67107) *(G-7196)*
Pines International Inc......800 697-4637
1992 E 1400 Rd Lawrence (66044) *(G-5065)*
Ping Apparel, Overland Park *Also called Custom Branded Sportswear Inc (G-8625)*
Pinkerton Pain Therapy LLC......417 649-6406
10680 S Cedar Niles Blvd Olathe (66061) *(G-7987)*
Pinnacle Consulting Group LLC......913 254-3030
11225 College Blvd # 150 Overland Park (66210) *(G-9168)*
Pinnacle Hlth Fclties Xviii LP......913 441-2515
520 E Morse Ave Bonner Springs (66012) *(G-571)*
Pinnacle Lawn Care Inc......913 851-0423
15315 Kenneth Rd Shawnee Mission (66224) *(G-11734)*
Pinnacle Plotting and Sup Lc......913 766-1822
9339 W 53rd St Shawnee (66203) *(G-11011)*
Pinnacle Plus Financial, Overland Park *Also called Pinnacle Consulting Group LLC (G-9168)*
Pinnacle Regional Hospital Inc......913 541-0230
12850 Metcalf Ave Overland Park (66213) *(G-9169)*
Pinnacle Technology Inc......785 832-8866
2721 Oregon St Lawrence (66046) *(G-5066)*
Pintail Petroleum Ltd......316 263-2243
225 N Market St Ste 300 Wichita (67202) *(G-15300)*
Pioneer - Ram Incorporated......316 685-2266
5000 E 29th St N Wichita (67220) *(G-15301)*
Pioneer Automation Technology......316 322-0123
1220 N Haverhill Rd El Dorado (67042) *(G-1591)*
Pioneer Balloon Company, El Dorado *Also called Continental American Corp (G-1550)*
Pioneer Communications, Ulysses *Also called Pioneer Telephone Assn Inc (G-13312)*
Pioneer Community Care Inc......620 582-2123
300 W 3rd St Coldwater (67029) *(G-1057)*
Pioneer Electric Coop Inc (PA)......620 356-1211
1850 W Oklahoma Ave Ulysses (67880) *(G-13311)*
Pioneer Feedyard LLC......785 672-3257
1021 County Road Cc Oakley (67748) *(G-7485)*
Pioneer Hi-Bred Intl Inc......785 776-1335
3400 Wood Green Ct Manhattan (66503) *(G-6777)*
Pioneer Industries Intl Inc......913 233-1368
305 Sunshine Rd Kansas City (66115) *(G-4323)*
Pioneer Janitorial LLC......785 379-5101
103 Sw 32nd Ter Topeka (66611) *(G-12975)*

Pioneer Lan Assistance, Ulysses *Also called Pioneer Telephone Assn Inc* ***(G-13313)***
Pioneer Lodge, Coldwater *Also called Pioneer Community Care Inc* ***(G-1057)***
Pioneer Manor, Hugoton *Also called County of Stevens* ***(G-3155)***
PIONEER MOBILE HOME VILLAGE, Council Grove *Also called Hartman Masonry LLC* ***(G-1169)***
Pioneer Pre School LLC...913 338-4282
11100 College Blvd Shawnee Mission (66210) ***(G-11735)***
Pioneer Ridge Ind Living...785 749-6785
650 Congressional Dr D Lawrence (66049) ***(G-5067)***
Pioneer Ridge Retirement Cmnty...785 344-1100
4851 Harvard Rd Lawrence (66049) ***(G-5068)***
Pioneer Tank & Steel Inc...620 672-2153
40190 Runway Blvd Pratt (67124) ***(G-10133)***
Pioneer Telephone Assn Inc (PA)...620 356-3211
120 W Kansas Ave Ulysses (67880) ***(G-13312)***
Pioneer Telephone Assn Inc...620 356-1985
120 W Kansas Ave Ulysses (67880) ***(G-13313)***
Pioneer Toy Company, Natoma *Also called Macconnell Enterprises LLC* ***(G-7231)***
Pioneer Wood Products, Kansas City *Also called McCray Lumber Company* ***(G-4226)***
Pipeline Tstg Consortium Inc...620 669-8800
9 Compound Dr Hutchinson (67502) ***(G-3406)***
Piper, The, Kansas City *Also called Ala Operations LLC* ***(G-3795)***
Piping & Equipment Company Inc...316 838-7511
1111 E 37th St N Wichita (67219) ***(G-15302)***
Piping Alloys Inc (PA)...913 677-3833
13899 W 101st St Lenexa (66215) ***(G-6058)***
Piping Contractors Kansas Inc...785 233-4321
4141 Nw 25th St Topeka (66618) ***(G-12976)***
Piping Contractors Kansas Inc (PA)...785 233-2010
115 Sw Jackson St Topeka (66603) ***(G-12977)***
Piping Technology Co...620 241-3592
1331 N Us Highway 81 Byp McPherson (67460) ***(G-7016)***
Piqua Farmers Coop Assn Incthe...620 468-2535
201 S Washington St Piqua (66761) ***(G-9801)***
Piqua Petro Inc...620 468-2681
1331 Xylan Rd Piqua (66761) ***(G-9802)***
Piranha Fabrication Equipment, Hutchinson *Also called Mega Manufacturing Inc* ***(G-3370)***
Pishny Real Estate Services...913 227-0251
12202 W 88th St Lenexa (66215) ***(G-6059)***
Pishny Restoration Services, Lenexa *Also called Pishny Real Estate Services* ***(G-6059)***
Pitney Bowes Inc...913 681-5579
7908 W 140th St Shawnee Mission (66223) ***(G-11736)***
Pitney Bowes Inc...785 266-6750
3320 Sw Harrison St Ste 8 Topeka (66611) ***(G-12978)***
Pitsco Inc (PA)...620 231-0000
915 E Jefferson St Pittsburg (66762) ***(G-9914)***
Pitsco Inc...800 835-0686
1003 E Adams St Pittsburg (66762) ***(G-9915)***
Pitsco Inc...620 231-2424
1002 E Adams St Pittsburg (66762) ***(G-9916)***
Pitsco Inc...620 231-0010
1002 E Adams St Pittsburg (66762) ***(G-9917)***
Pitt Plastics Inc (HQ)...620 231-4030
1400 E Atkinson Ave Pittsburg (66762) ***(G-9918)***
Pitt Steel LLC (PA)...620 231-8100
748 E 520th Ave Pittsburg (66762) ***(G-9919)***
Pittcraft Printing Inc (PA)...620 231-6200
112 E Rose St Pittsburg (66762) ***(G-9920)***
Pittsburg 8 Theater, Pittsburg *Also called Goodrich Quality Theaters Inc* ***(G-9867)***
Pittsburg Internal Medcine PA...620 231-1650
2401 S Tucker Ave Ste 1 Pittsburg (66762) ***(G-9921)***
Pittsburg Morning Sun, Pittsburg *Also called Morris Communications Co LLC* ***(G-9908)***
Pittsburg Police Dept, Pittsburg *Also called City of Pittsburg* ***(G-9834)***
Pittsburg State Univ Foundatio...620 235-4764
401 E Ford St Pittsburg (66762) ***(G-9922)***
Pittsburg Steel & Mfg Co Inc...620 231-8100
10511 Mission Rd Unit 207 Leawood (66206) ***(G-5522)***
Pivot Companies LLC...800 581-6398
11225 College Blvd Overland Park (66210) ***(G-9170)***
Pivot International Inc (PA)...913 312-6900
11030 Strang Line Rd Lenexa (66215) ***(G-6060)***
Pivot-Digittron Inc...913 441-0221
23875 W 83rd Ter Shawnee (66227) ***(G-11012)***
Pix Printing, Wichita *Also called Printing Inc* ***(G-15350)***
Pixius Communications LLC (PA)...316 219-8500
301 N Saint Francis Ave Wichita (67202) ***(G-15303)***
Pizza Ranch...620 662-2066
1805 E 17th Ave Hutchinson (67501) ***(G-3407)***
Pk Industrial Pk Industries, Augusta *Also called Pro-Kleen Inc* ***(G-339)***
Pk Safety Services Inc...316 260-4141
5351 Sw 100th St Augusta (67010) ***(G-338)***
Pk Technology LLC...316 866-2955
10811 E Harry St Wichita (67207) ***(G-15304)***
Pkc Construction Co...913 782-4646
7802 Barton St Lenexa (66214) ***(G-6061)***
Pkhls Architecture PA...316 321-4774
101 S Star St El Dorado (67042) ***(G-1592)***
Pkmr Engineers, Lenexa *Also called Pearson Kent McKinley Raaf Eng* ***(G-6046)***
Plain Jan's, Scott City *Also called Plainjans Feedlot Service* ***(G-10827)***
Plainjans Feedlot Service...620 872-5777
511 Monroe St Scott City (67871) ***(G-10827)***
Plains Equity Exch & Coop Un (PA)...620 563-9566
206 E Indiana St Plains (67869) ***(G-9977)***
Plains Marketing LP...620 365-3208
Old Hwy 169 Iola (66749) ***(G-3623)***
Plains Marketing LP...785 483-3171
2559 Hwy 40 Russell (67665) ***(G-10284)***
Plains Marketing LP...620 365-3208
1170 Mississippi Rd Iola (66749) ***(G-3624)***
Plainville Ambulance Service...785 434-2530
1111 Sw 8th St Plainville (67663) ***(G-9989)***
Plainville Rural Hospital...785 434-2622
1210 N Washington St Plainville (67663) ***(G-9990)***
Plankenhorn Inc...620 276-3791
912 E Fulton St Garden City (67846) ***(G-2256)***
Planned Parenthood of Kansas (PA)...316 263-7575
2226 E Central Ave Wichita (67214) ***(G-15305)***
Planned Prenthood Great Plains (PA)...913 312-5100
4401 W 109th St Ste 200 Overland Park (66211) ***(G-9171)***
Plans Professional Inc...785 357-7777
112 Sw 6th Ave Ste 400 Topeka (66603) ***(G-12979)***
Plant Kingdom Garden Center, Wichita *Also called Campbells Phoenix Greenhouse* ***(G-13931)***
Plastic Omnium Auto Inergy...913 370-6081
220 Kindleberger Rd Kansas City (66115) ***(G-4324)***
Plastic Packaging Tech LLC (HQ)...913 287-3383
750 S 65th St Kansas City (66111) ***(G-4325)***
Plastikon Healthcare LLC...785 330-7100
3780 Greenway Cir Lawrence (66046) ***(G-5069)***
Plastikon Industries Inc...785 749-1630
3780 Greenway Cir Lawrence (66046) ***(G-5070)***
Platform Advertising...913 254-6000
500 N Rogers Rd Olathe (66062) ***(G-7988)***
Platform Technologies LLC...816 285-3874
4220 Shawnee Mission Pkwy Fairway (66205) ***(G-1917)***
Platinum Contracting LLC...913 210-2003
4800 Lamar Ave 101 Shawnee Mission (66202) ***(G-11737)***
Platinum Inc...316 773-9700
10248 W 13th St N Wichita (67212) ***(G-15306)***
Platinum Salon and Spa, Wichita *Also called Platinum Inc* ***(G-15306)***
Players Choice Mounds, Baxter Springs *Also called Brock Maggard* ***(G-401)***
Plaza Astle Realty, Hutchinson *Also called Astle Realty Inc* ***(G-3208)***
Plaza Belmont MGT Group II LLC (PA)...913 381-7177
8016 State Line Rd Shawnee Mission (66208) ***(G-11738)***
Plaza Inn, Topeka *Also called Shamir Corp* ***(G-13062)***
Plaza Limousine, Leawood *Also called Wheatland Enterprises Inc* ***(G-5599)***
Plaza Mortgage...913 671-1865
2000 Shawnee Mission Pkwy # 225 Shawnee Mission (66205) ***(G-11739)***
Plaza Theatre, Ottawa *Also called B & B Cinemas* ***(G-8247)***
Plaza West Care Center Inc...785 271-6700
1570 Sw Westport Dr Topeka (66604) ***(G-12980)***
PLAZA WEST REGIONAL HEALTH CEN, Topeka *Also called Plaza West Care Center Inc* ***(G-12980)***
Pleasant Valley Nursing LLC...620 725-3154
613 E Elm St Sedan (67361) ***(G-10845)***
Pleasant Vly Nursing Rehab Ctr, Sedan *Also called Rh Montgomery Properties Inc* ***(G-10846)***
Plex Plus...913 888-6223
6370 College Blvd Leawood (66211) ***(G-5523)***
Plp Inc...620 532-3106
1202 E Us Highway 54 Kingman (67068) ***(G-4610)***
Plp Inc...620 842-5137
501 W Main St Anthony (67003) ***(G-132)***
Plp Inc...620 382-3794
902 N Cedar St Marion (66861) ***(G-6875)***
Plp Inc...620 342-5000
1744 Road F Emporia (66801) ***(G-1812)***
Plp Inc (PA)...620 664-5860
811 E 30th Ave Ste F Hutchinson (67502) ***(G-3408)***
Plp Inc...316 943-4261
2218 S West St Wichita (67213) ***(G-15307)***
Plumbing & Hvac, Manchester *Also called Henry Steckman Plumbing* ***(G-6524)***
Plumbing By Carlson Inc...785 232-0515
1820 Sw Van Buren St Topeka (66612) ***(G-12981)***
Plumbing Specialists Inc...316 945-8383
1838 S Anna St Wichita (67209) ***(G-15308)***
Plus It View Home Improvement, Hutchinson *Also called Reno Fabricating & Sls Co Inc* ***(G-3426)***
Plymouth Preschool Lrng Ctr...316 684-0222
202 N Clifton Ave Wichita (67208) ***(G-15309)***
Pma, Wichita *Also called Physicians Medical Clinics* ***(G-15297)***
Pma Andover...316 733-1331
308 E Central Ave Andover (67002) ***(G-105)***
PMa Medical Associates PA (PA)...316 261-3100
848 N St Francis St Wichita (67214) ***(G-15310)***

ALPHABETIC

Pma Twin Lakes Medical Off P A......316 832-0465
1900 N Amidon Ave Ste 100 Wichita (67203) ***(G-15311)***
Pmhm, Wichita *Also called Preferred Mental Health Mgt* ***(G-15328)***
Pmhs, Junction City *Also called Pawnee Mental Health Svcs Inc* ***(G-3735)***
PMMA, Wichita *Also called Presbytrian Mnors of Md-Merica* ***(G-15336)***
PMMA, Wichita *Also called Aberdeen Village Inc* ***(G-13597)***
Pmti Inc......913 432-7500
5425 Antioch Dr Shawnee Mission (66202) ***(G-11740)***
PNC Bank National Association......913 253-9490
10851 Mastin St Ste 300 Overland Park (66210) ***(G-9172)***
PNS, Leawood *Also called Squadbuilders Inc* ***(G-5559)***
Podiatry Associates PA......913 432-5052
8901 W 74th St Ste 200 Shawnee Mission (66204) ***(G-11741)***
Poe & Associates Inc......316 685-4114
5940 E Central Ave # 201 Wichita (67208) ***(G-15312)***
Poe & Associates of Kansas......316 685-4114
5940 E Central Ave # 200 Wichita (67208) ***(G-15313)***
Poe Well Service Inc (PA)......785 475-3422
215 S York Ave Oberlin (67749) ***(G-7499)***
Poet Ethanol Products, Wichita *Also called Ethanol Products LLC* ***(G-14308)***
Point Inc......913 928-2720
16900 W 118th Ter Olathe (66061) ***(G-7989)***
Pointe Royal Town Houses, Shawnee Mission *Also called Fogelman Management Group LLC* ***(G-11375)***
Pokorny, John C MD, Hays *Also called Eye Specialists* ***(G-2803)***
Poky Feeders Inc......620 872-7046
600 E Road 30 Scott City (67871) ***(G-10828)***
Poky Pig, Scott City *Also called Poky Feeders Inc* ***(G-10828)***
Polansky Seed Inc......785 527-2271
2729 M St Belleville (66935) ***(G-462)***
Polaris Electronics Corp......913 764-5210
630 S Rogers Rd Olathe (66062) ***(G-7990)***
Polestar AC & Plbg Htg......913 432-3342
1900 E 123rd St Olathe (66061) ***(G-7991)***
Pollard Licklider Clinic, Wichita *Also called Erin Is Hope Foundation Inc* ***(G-14301)***
Pollen Inc......877 465-4045
2020 W 89th St Ste 200 Leawood (66206) ***(G-5524)***
Polsinelli PC......913 451-8788
6201 College Blvd Ste 500 Shawnee Mission (66211) ***(G-11742)***
Polymer Group Inc......620 532-5141
701 E A Ave Kingman (67068) ***(G-4611)***
Polymer Group Inc......620 532-4000
100 Fabpro Way Kingman (67068) ***(G-4612)***
Polynova (usa) LLC......913 309-6977
9810 Pflumm Rd Lenexa (66215) ***(G-6062)***
Polyplastics, Park City *Also called Buckley Industries Inc* ***(G-9606)***
Pomps Tire Service Inc......913 621-5200
401 S 42nd St Kansas City (66106) ***(G-4326)***
Ponca Products Inc......316 262-4051
1910 E Northern St Wichita (67216) ***(G-15314)***
Ponton Construction Inc......785 823-9584
1325 Armory Rd Salina (67401) ***(G-10635)***
Pontons Construction, Salina *Also called Ponton Construction Inc* ***(G-10635)***
Ponzeryoungquist PA......913 782-0541
227 E Dennis Ave Olathe (66061) ***(G-7992)***
Poodle & Steve's Auto Auction, Elwood *Also called Kansas Auto Auction Inc* ***(G-1688)***
Pool & Patio Inc (PA)......913 888-2226
11409 W 89th St Shawnee Mission (66214) ***(G-11743)***
Pool & Patio Supply Inc......913 888-2226
11409 W 89th St Shawnee Mission (66214) ***(G-11744)***
Poole Fire Protection Inc......913 747-2044
19910 W 161st St Olathe (66062) ***(G-7993)***
Pools Plus......785 823-7665
2501 Market Pl Ste I Salina (67401) ***(G-10636)***
Poorman Auto Supply Inc (PA)......316 265-6284
1400 E Douglas Ave Wichita (67214) ***(G-15315)***
Pop-A-Shot Enterprise LLC......785 827-6229
200 N 3rd St Salina (67401) ***(G-10637)***
Popup Industries Inc......620 431-9196
220 W 14th St Chanute (66720) ***(G-755)***
Popup Towing Products, Chanute *Also called Youngs Products LLC* ***(G-774)***
Porta-Ad, Wichita *Also called T V Hephner and Elec Inc* ***(G-15715)***
Portfolio Recovery Assoc LLC......620 662-2800
500 W 1st Ave Hutchinson (67501) ***(G-3409)***
Pos-T-Vac LLC......800 279-7434
2111 W Wyatt Earp Blvd Dodge City (67801) ***(G-1420)***
Pos-T-Vac Medical, Dodge City *Also called Pos-T-Vac LLC* ***(G-1420)***
Positive Bright Start, Lawrence *Also called Douglas County Child Dev Assn* ***(G-4838)***
Post & Mastin Well Service......620 276-3442
3210 W Jones Ave Garden City (67846) ***(G-2257)***
Post Rock Rual Water District, Ellsworth *Also called County of Ellsworth* ***(G-1665)***
Post-Secondary Education, Arkansas City *Also called Cowley College & Area* ***(G-150)***
Postal Presort Inc......316 262-3333
820 W 2nd St N Wichita (67203) ***(G-15316)***
Postrock Energy Corporation......620 432-4200
4402 S Johnson Rd Chanute (66720) ***(G-756)***
Pottawatomie Cnty Emrgncy Svcs......785 456-0911
514 Plum St Wamego (66547) ***(G-13434)***
Pottawtmie Cnty Ambulance Svcs, Wamego *Also called Pottawatomie Cnty Emrgncy Svcs* ***(G-13434)***
Pottberg Gssman Hffman Chrtred (PA)......785 238-5166
816 N Washington St Junction City (66441) ***(G-3738)***
Potts Law Firm LLP......816 931-2230
1901 W 47th Pl Ste 210 Shawnee Mission (66205) ***(G-11745)***
Potwin Lions Club......620 752-3644
7400 Nw Ayr Rd Potwin (67123) ***(G-10008)***
Powdertech Llc......316 832-9210
810 E 37th St N Wichita (67219) ***(G-15317)***
Powell Electrical Systems Inc......785 856-5863
4218 Tamarisk Ct Lawrence (66047) ***(G-5071)***
Power Ad Company Inc......785 823-9483
3344 Scanlan Ave Salina (67401) ***(G-10638)***
Power Admin LLC......800 401-2339
12710 S Pflumm Rd Ste 206 Olathe (66062) ***(G-7994)***
Power Chemicals Inc......316 524-7899
2901 S Kansas Ave Wichita (67216) ***(G-15318)***
Power Control Devices Inc......913 829-1900
821 N Martway Dr Olathe (66061) ***(G-7995)***
Power Drive, Wichita *Also called Fleetpride Inc* ***(G-14385)***
Power Equipment Sales Co......913 384-3848
1507 Lake Ave Kansas City (66103) ***(G-4327)***
Power Flame Incorporated......620 421-0480
2001 S 21st St Parsons (67357) ***(G-9724)***
Power Group, Shawnee Mission *Also called Rx Power* ***(G-11817)***
Power Lift Found Repair......316 685-0888
9918 E Harry St Wichita (67207) ***(G-15319)***
Power Plant, Winfield *Also called City of Winfield* ***(G-16120)***
Power Sales and Advertising (PA)......913 324-4900
9909 Lakeview Ave Lenexa (66219) ***(G-6063)***
Power Tech Electric Motors LLC......913 888-4488
9054 Cody St Overland Park (66214) ***(G-9173)***
Power Technologies, Overland Park *Also called ABB Enterprise Software Inc* ***(G-8337)***
Power Vac Inc......785 826-8220
508 Graves Blvd Salina (67401) ***(G-10639)***
Power Washers Unlimited......316 262-9274
1802 W Mccormick Ave Wichita (67213) ***(G-15320)***
Powerhouse Electric Inc......913 856-4141
123 W Warren St Gardner (66030) ***(G-2359)***
Powerhouse Graphics, Bonner Springs *Also called Legal Printing Company Inc* ***(G-559)***
Powerline Dairy LLC......620 855-2844
22502 R Rd Cimarron (67835) ***(G-832)***
Powerline Machine Works Inc......620 824-6204
791 5th Rd Chase (67524) ***(G-786)***
Powls Publishing Company Inc......785 364-3141
109 W 4th St Holton (66436) ***(G-3108)***
Powwwer Net, El Dorado *Also called Regional Media Corporation Inc* ***(G-1598)***
PPG 4622, Overland Park *Also called PPG Industries Inc* ***(G-9174)***
PPG 4631, Bel Aire *Also called PPG Industries Inc* ***(G-438)***
PPG Industries Inc......316 262-2456
6334 Crestmark St Bel Aire (67220) ***(G-438)***
PPG Industries Inc......913 681-5573
7960 W 151st St Overland Park (66223) ***(G-9174)***
Ppm Information Solutions, Overland Park *Also called Preferred Physicians Mdcl Rrg* ***(G-9179)***
Ppm Services Inc......913 262-2585
11880 College Blvd # 300 Overland Park (66210) ***(G-9175)***
Pps Inc......913 791-0164
14824 W 117th St Olathe (66062) ***(G-7996)***
Ppt Holdings LLC (HQ)......913 287-3383
750 S 65th St Kansas City (66111) ***(G-4328)***
PQ Corporation......913 371-3020
1700 Kansas Ave Kansas City (66105) ***(G-4329)***
PQ Corporation......913 744-2056
15200 Santa Fe Dr Lenexa (66219) ***(G-6064)***
PQ Corporation......913 227-0561
15200 Santa Fe Trail Dr # 101 Lenexa (66219) ***(G-6065)***
PRA International......913 410-2000
9755 Ridge Dr Lenexa (66219) ***(G-6066)***
PRA International LLC......913 345-5754
10836 Strang Line Rd Lenexa (66215) ***(G-6067)***
PRA Intrntional Operations Inc......913 410-2000
9755 Ridge Dr Shawnee Mission (66219) ***(G-11746)***
Prairie Band LLC (PA)......785 364-2463
19035 Us Highway 75 Holton (66436) ***(G-3109)***
Prairie Band Casino and Resort......785 966-7777
12305 150th Rd Mayetta (66509) ***(G-6916)***
Prairie Band Potawatomi Bingo......785 966-4000
16277 Q Rd Mayetta (66509) ***(G-6917)***
Prairie Bank of Kansas (PA)......620 234-5226
200 S Main St Stafford (67578) ***(G-12107)***
Prairie Belting Inc......620 842-5147
396 W State Road 2 Anthony (67003) ***(G-133)***
Prairie Bend Potawamtomi Early, Mayetta *Also called Prairie Bend Ptwtomi Childcare* ***(G-6918)***

Prairie Bend Ptwtomi Childcare 785 966-2707
15380 K Rd Mayetta (66509) *(G-6918)*
Prairie Cleaning Service 785 539-4997
532 Pillsbury Dr Manhattan (66502) *(G-6778)*
Prairie Ctr Christn Childcare 913 390-0230
105 S Montclaire Dr Olathe (66061) *(G-7997)*
Prairie Dental Care, Prairie Village *Also called Ziegenhorn & Linneman DDS (G-10089)*
Prairie Developmental Center, Atwood *Also called Developmental Svcs NW Kans Inc (G-283)*
Prairie Dog Golf Club, Norton *Also called Robin White Hills Inc (G-7462)*
Prairie Dog Press 785 669-2009
523 Main St Almena (67622) *(G-68)*
Prairie Early Childhood Center, Shawnee Mission *Also called American Baptist Church (G-11102)*
Prairie Elder Care, Overland Park *Also called Prairie Elder Homes LLC (G-9176)*
Prairie Elder Homes LLC 913 257-5425
15354 Quivira Rd Overland Park (66221) *(G-9176)*
Prairie Fire Winery LLC 785 636-5533
20250 Hudson Ranch Rd Paxico (66526) *(G-9757)*
Prairie Haven 785 476-2623
117 W 1st St Smith Center (66967) *(G-12040)*
Prairie Hills Nursery Inc 620 665-5500
2999 E 30th Ave Hutchinson (67502) *(G-3410)*
Prairie Hills Tree Nurs Ldscpg, Hutchinson *Also called Prairie Hills Nursery Inc (G-3410)*
PRAIRIE HOMESTEAD, Wichita *Also called American Baptist Estates Inc (G-13683)*
Prairie Horzn Agri-Energy LLC 785 543-6719
1664 E 100 Rd Phillipsburg (67661) *(G-9794)*
Prairie Ind Lving Resource Ctr (PA) 620 663-3989
17 S Main St Hutchinson (67501) *(G-3411)*
Prairie Inn Inc 316 283-3330
105 Manchester Ave Newton (67114) *(G-7406)*
Prairie Land Electric Coop Inc 785 877-3323
14935 Us Highway 36 Norton (67654) *(G-7461)*
Prairie Landworks Inc 620 504-5049
905 N Vngard St Mcpherson Mcpherson (67460) *(G-7017)*
Prairie Lf Ctr of Overland Pk 913 764-5444
13655 S Alden St Olathe (66062) *(G-7998)*
Prairie Lf Ctr of Overland Pk (PA) 913 648-8077
10351 Barkley St Overland Park (66212) *(G-9177)*
Prairie Mission Retirement Vlg, Saint Paul *Also called Prairie Mission Retirement Vlg (G-10384)*
Prairie Mission Retirement Vlg 620 449-2400
242 Carroll St Saint Paul (66771) *(G-10384)*
PRAIRIE MOON WALDORF SCHOOL, Lawrence *Also called Waldorf Association Lawrence (G-5177)*
Prairie Patches Inc 785 749-4565
1327 Covington Ct Lawrence (66049) *(G-5072)*
Prairie Paws Animal Shelter, Ottawa *Also called Martin Peck Bea Anmal Shlter I (G-8290)*
Prairie Pipe Line, Belpre *Also called F G Holl Company LLC (G-505)*
Prairie Point 913 322-1222
12116 W 95th St Lenexa (66215) *(G-6068)*
Prairie Print Inc 316 267-1950
3748 N Ohio St Wichita (67219) *(G-15321)*
Prairie Products 620 947-3922
111 Commerce St Hillsboro (67063) *(G-3054)*
Prairie Senior Living Complex, Colby *Also called Rural Health Development Inc (G-1037)*
Prairie Sports Inc 785 625-2916
2400 Vine St Hays (67601) *(G-2887)*
Prairie Sunset Home Inc 620 459-6822
601 E Main St Pretty Prairie (67570) *(G-10168)*
Prairie Trails Golf Cntry CLB 316 321-4114
1100 Country Club Ln El Dorado (67042) *(G-1593)*
Prairie View Inc (PA) 316 284-6400
1901 E 1st St Newton (67114) *(G-7407)*
Prairie View Inc 620 245-5000
1102 Hospital Dr McPherson (67460) *(G-7018)*
Prairie View Inc 620 947-3200
508 S Ash St Hillsboro (67063) *(G-3055)*
Prairie Village Animal Hosp PA 913 642-7060
4045 Somerset Dr Prairie Village (66208) *(G-10061)*
Prairie Village Phillips 66, Mission Hills *Also called Ronco Inc (G-7148)*
Prairie Village Swimming Pool, Shawnee Mission *Also called City of Prairie Village (G-11232)*
Prairie Vista Dental LLC 620 424-4311
209 W Central Ave Ulysses (67880) *(G-13314)*
Prairie Wind Villa Assstant 785 543-6180
1302 State St Phillipsburg (67661) *(G-9795)*
Prairiebrooke Arts Inc 913 341-0333
7900 Santa Fe Dr Overland Park (66204) *(G-9178)*
Prairieland Partners LLC 620 664-6552
811 E 30th Ave Ste F Hutchinson (67502) *(G-3412)*
Prairiestar Health Center Inc 620 663-8484
2700 E 30th Ave Hutchinson (67502) *(G-3413)*
Prairiewood, Manhattan *Also called Capstone MGT & Dev Group Inc (G-6576)*
Praise Network Inc 785 694-2877
3410 Road 66 Brewster (67732) *(G-585)*
Prater Oil Gas Operations Inc 620 672-7600
10356 Bluestem Blvd Pratt (67124) *(G-10134)*
Pratt & Whitney Eng Svcs Inc 316 945-9763
1955 Midfield Rd Wichita (67209) *(G-15322)*
Pratt County Achievement Place 620 672-6610
104 N Oak St Pratt (67124) *(G-10135)*
Pratt County Ems, Pratt *Also called County of Pratt (G-10103)*
Pratt Cy Municpl Pwr Plant 1, Pratt *Also called City of Pratt (G-10101)*
Pratt Energy LLC 620 933-2288
10333 Ne 30th St Pratt (67124) *(G-10136)*
Pratt Family Practice 620 672-7422
203 Watson St Ste 200 Pratt (67124) *(G-10137)*
Pratt Feeders LLC (PA) 620 672-3401
40010 Nw 20th Ave Pratt (67124) *(G-10138)*
Pratt Feeders LLC 620 635-2213
2590 County Rd L Ashland (67831) *(G-197)*
Pratt Glass Inc 620 672-6463
210 S Jackson St Pratt (67124) *(G-10139)*
Pratt Health and Rehab 620 672-6541
1221 Larimer St Pratt (67124) *(G-10140)*
Pratt Industries USA Inc 316 838-0851
3600 N Santa Fe St Wichita (67219) *(G-15323)*
Pratt Industries USA Inc 316 838-0851
700 E 37th St N Wichita (67219) *(G-15324)*
Pratt Intrnal Mdicine Group PA 620 672-7417
420 Country Club Rd # 100 Pratt (67124) *(G-10141)*
Pratt Livestock Inc (PA) 620 672-5961
111 S Broadway Ave Sterling (67579) *(G-12127)*
Pratt Livestock Inc 620 672-5961
30274 E Us Highway 54 Pratt (67124) *(G-10142)*
Pratt Regional Med Ctr Corp 620 672-3424
227 S Howard St Pratt (67124) *(G-10143)*
Pratt Regional Med Ctr Corp (PA) 620 672-7451
200 Commodore St Pratt (67124) *(G-10144)*
Pratt Swimming Pool, Cullison *Also called Ellis Kinney Swimming Pool (G-1185)*
Pratt Unified 12th Dist Transp 620 672-4590
1007 W 5th St Pratt (67124) *(G-10145)*
Praxair Inc 620 657-2711
Ste Dd Rr 1 Box 14 Satanta (67870) *(G-10789)*
Praxair Inc 620 225-1368
11547 Us Highway 50 Wright (67882) *(G-16193)*
Praxair Inc 620 562-4500
2486 8th Rd Lorraine (67459) *(G-6434)*
Praxair Distribution Inc 913 492-1551
9725 Alden St Lenexa (66215) *(G-6069)*
Pray Building Stone Inc 620 221-7422
1000 Industrial Blvd Winfield (67156) *(G-16165)*
Pray Stone, Winfield *Also called Pray Building Stone Inc (G-16165)*
Pre-Awards Services, Manhattan *Also called Kansas State University (G-6695)*
Pre-Mac, Wellington *Also called Mac-Tech Inc (G-13514)*
Precise Racing, Wichita *Also called Chris Archer Group Inc (G-14014)*
Precision Aviation Controls 620 331-8180
101 Freedom Dr Independence (67301) *(G-3547)*
Precision Boring Tech Inc 913 735-4728
14713 S Saint Andrews Ave Olathe (66061) *(G-7999)*
Precision Craft Inc 913 780-9077
19919 W 162nd St Olathe (66062) *(G-8000)*
Precision Cut Inc 913 422-0777
23410 W 79th St Shawnee Mission (66227) *(G-11747)*
Precision Elec Contrs LLC 785 309-0094
668 N Ohio Ct Salina (67401) *(G-10640)*
Precision Industries Inc (PA) 620 241-5010
533 N Baer St McPherson (67460) *(G-7019)*
Precision International 620 365-7255
25 W Miller Rd Iola (66749) *(G-3625)*
Precision Machine & Welding, Salina *Also called Jeffrey A Harris (G-10553)*
Precision Manifold Systems Inc 913 829-1221
700 W Frontier Ln Olathe (66061) *(G-8001)*
Precision Pallet 620 221-4066
15665 Us Highway 77 Winfield (67156) *(G-16166)*
Precision Pipe Cover Inc 785 233-2000
2700 Nw Button Rd Ste C Topeka (66618) *(G-12982)*
Precision Printing, Shawnee Mission *Also called Professional Graphics Inc (G-11755)*
Precision Products 316 943-0477
2524 N Lorraine Ave Wichita (67219) *(G-15325)*
Precision Railway Eqp Co LLC (PA) 817 737-5885
825 S 19th St Independence (67301) *(G-3548)*
Precision Truss Inc 785 244-6456
2537 Eagle Rd Summerfield (66541) *(G-12215)*
Prefered Medical Associates 620 365-6933
401 S Washington Ave Iola (66749) *(G-3626)*
Preferred AG Services Inc 620 271-7366
535 E Us Highway 50 Byp Garden City (67846) *(G-2258)*
Preferred Cartage Service Inc (PA) 620 276-8080
1401 W Joe Mcgraw St Garden City (67846) *(G-2259)*
Preferred Contg Systems Co 913 341-0111
2012 W 104th St Leawood (66206) *(G-5525)*
Preferred Diagnostic Services, Wichita *Also called Ascension Via Christi Hospital (G-13748)*
Preferred Family Healthcare, Wichita *Also called Adolescent Adult Fmly Recovery (G-13614)*
Preferred Fmly Healthcare Inc 620 221-6252
2720 E 12th Ave Winfield (67156) *(G-16167)*

ALPHABETIC

Preferred Land Company Inc.....316 634-1313
3500 N Rock Rd Bldg 100 Wichita (67226) **(G-15326)**
Preferred Lawn Service.....785 379-8873
4000 Se Shawnee Hts Rd Tecumseh (66542) **(G-12240)**
Preferred Lawn Service.....785 887-9900
1895 E 56th Rd Lecompton (66050) **(G-5613)**
Preferred Medical Associates, Wichita *Also called Ascension Via Christi Hospital* **(G-13749)**
Preferred Medical Associates.....316 268-8080
1100 N St Francis St # 400 Wichita (67214) **(G-15327)**
Preferred Medical Associates.....316 733-1331
308 E Central Ave Andover (67002) **(G-106)**
Preferred Mental Health Mgt.....316 262-0444
401 E Douglas Ave Ste 300 Wichita (67202) **(G-15328)**
Preferred Mortuary Svcs LLC.....316 522-7300
210 Cain Dr Haysville (67060) **(G-2955)**
Preferred Pediatrics PA.....913 764-7060
824 W Frontier Ln Olathe (66061) **(G-8002)**
Preferred Physicians Mdcl Rrg.....913 262-2585
11880 College Blvd # 300 Overland Park (66210) **(G-9179)**
Preferred Registry of Nurses.....785 456-8628
1010 Lincoln Ave Wamego (66547) **(G-13435)**
Preferred Seamless Guttering.....620 663-7600
11017 S Osage Rd Hutchinson (67501) **(G-3414)**
Pregnancy Crises Center, Wichita *Also called Pregnncy Crisis Ctr of Wichita* **(G-15329)**
Pregnncy Crisis Ctr of Wichita.....316 945-9400
1040 N West St Wichita (67203) **(G-15329)**
Premier, New Century *Also called Kgp Products Inc* **(G-7291)**
Premier Bank (HQ).....913 888-8490
15301 W 87th Street Pkwy # 100 Shawnee Mission (66219) **(G-11748)**
Premier Bank.....913 541-6180
11830 W 135th St Shawnee Mission (66221) **(G-11749)**
Premier Casting & Machine Svc.....620 241-2040
2118 Industrial Dr McPherson (67460) **(G-7020)**
Premier Cattle Co LLC (PA).....620 384-5711
State Lake Rd Syracuse (67878) **(G-12229)**
Premier Cattle Co LLC.....620 855-3162
13745 16 Rd Cimarron (67835) **(G-833)**
Premier Contracting Inc.....913 362-4141
3940 S Ferree St Kansas City (66103) **(G-4330)**
Premier Custom Foods LLC.....913 225-9505
756 Pawnee Ave Kansas City (66105) **(G-4331)**
Premier Dermatologic.....913 327-1117
14404 Outlook St Overland Park (66223) **(G-9180)**
Premier Employment Solutions, Topeka *Also called Premier Personnel Inc* **(G-12983)**
Premier Equipment, Kansas City *Also called Premier Contracting Inc* **(G-4330)**
Premier Food Service Inc.....316 269-2447
8225 W Irving St Wichita (67209) **(G-15330)**
Premier Homes, Holcomb *Also called Premier Housing Inc* **(G-3077)**
Premier Housing Inc.....620 277-0707
7845 W Us Highway 50 Holcomb (67851) **(G-3077)**
Premier Landscape, Andover *Also called Premier Landscaping Inc* **(G-107)**
Premier Landscaping Inc.....316 733-4773
12739 Sw Butler Rd Andover (67002) **(G-107)**
Premier Living By Warden LLC.....316 945-2028
234 S Anna St Wichita (67209) **(G-15331)**
Premier Mechanical Pdts LLC.....913 271-5002
3016 S 24th St Kansas City (66106) **(G-4332)**
Premier One Data Systems, Topeka *Also called Dave McDermott* **(G-12546)**
Premier Open Mri Inc (HQ).....316 262-1103
500 S Main St Ste 100 Wichita (67202) **(G-15332)**
Premier Painting Co LLC.....913 897-7000
8109 W 129th St Overland Park (66213) **(G-9181)**
Premier Pediatrics PA.....913 384-5500
8675 College Blvd Ste 100 Overland Park (66210) **(G-9182)**
Premier Personnel Inc.....785 273-9944
2813 Sw Wanamaker Rd Topeka (66614) **(G-12983)**
Premier Plastic Surgery.....913 782-0707
20375 W 151st St Ste 370 Olathe (66061) **(G-8003)**
Premier Processing.....316 425-3565
3002 W Pawnee St Ste 104 Wichita (67213) **(G-15333)**
Premier Realty LLC.....316 773-2707
2243 N Ridge Rd 105 Wichita (67205) **(G-15334)**
Premier Tillage Inc (PA).....785 754-2381
301 Park St Quinter (67752) **(G-10184)**
Premiere Marketing Group Inc (PA).....913 362-9100
10561 Barkley St Overland Park (66212) **(G-9183)**
Premiere Pork Inc.....620 872-7073
440 N Eagle Rd Scott City (67871) **(G-10829)**
Premium Feeders Inc.....785 335-2221
705 Hwy 36 Scandia (66966) **(G-10801)**
Premium Heating & Cooling Inc.....913 780-5639
11860 S Conley St Olathe (66061) **(G-8004)**
Premium Nutritional Pdts Inc.....913 962-8887
10504 W 79th St Shawnee Mission (66214) **(G-11750)**
Premium Source Ag LLC.....620 277-2009
3495 S Holcomb Ln Holcomb (67851) **(G-3078)**
Premium Ventures LLC (PA).....785 842-5500
1801 W 31st St Lawrence (66046) **(G-5073)**
Presbyterian Manor Arkansas Cy, Arkansas City *Also called Presbyterian Manors Inc* **(G-170)**
Presbyterian Manors Inc.....913 334-3666
7850 Freeman Ave Kansas City (66112) **(G-4333)**
Presbyterian Manors Inc.....785 825-1366
2601 E Crawford St Ofc Salina (67401) **(G-10641)**
Presbyterian Manors Inc.....785 632-5646
924 8th St Clay Center (67432) **(G-876)**
Presbyterian Manors Inc.....316 942-7456
4700 W 13th St N Ofc Wichita (67212) **(G-15335)**
Presbyterian Manors Inc.....785 841-4262
1429 Kasold Dr Lawrence (66049) **(G-5074)**
Presbyterian Manors Inc.....620 278-3651
204 W Washington Ave Sterling (67579) **(G-12128)**
Presbyterian Manors Inc.....316 283-5400
1200 E 7th St Newton (67114) **(G-7408)**
Presbyterian Manors Inc.....620 421-1450
3501 Dirr Ave Parsons (67357) **(G-9725)**
Presbyterian Manors Inc.....620 442-8700
1711 N 4th St Arkansas City (67005) **(G-170)**
Presbyterian Manors Inc.....620 225-4474
200 Campus Dr Ofc Ofc Dodge City (67801) **(G-1421)**
Presbyterian Manors Inc.....785 272-6510
4712 Sw 6th Ave Topeka (66606) **(G-12984)**
Presbytrian Mnors of Md-Merica (PA).....316 685-1100
2414 N Woodlawn Blvd Wichita (67220) **(G-15336)**
Presbytrian Mnors of MD-Merica.....620 223-5550
2401 Horton St Apt 121 Fort Scott (66701) **(G-1999)**
Presbytrian Village, Fort Scott *Also called Presbytrian Mnors of MD-Merica* **(G-1999)**
Prescott State Bnk Holdg Inc.....913 471-4321
283 Main St Prescott (66767) **(G-10167)**
Prescription Centre.....620 364-5523
312 Cross St Burlington (66839) **(G-641)**
Prescriptive Payroll Inc.....316 247-3166
501 S Robin Rd Wichita (67209) **(G-15337)**
Presig Holdings LLC.....913 706-1315
12318 Beverly St Overland Park (66209) **(G-9184)**
Prestige Bus Charters, Wichita *Also called Prestige Trnsp Systems* **(G-15339)**
Prestige Graphics Inc.....316 262-3480
500 N Birkdale Cir Wichita (67230) **(G-15338)**
Prestige Home Care of Kansas.....913 680-0493
109 Delaware St Leavenworth (66048) **(G-5279)**
Prestige Masonry LLC.....785 925-3090
2510 Sw Valley Glen Ct Topeka (66614) **(G-12985)**
Prestige Property Co.....800 730-1249
2410 Se 6th Ave Topeka (66607) **(G-12986)**
Prestige Real Estate.....785 242-1167
406 S Main St Ottawa (66067) **(G-8306)**
Prestige Trnsp Systems (PA).....316 263-9141
8620 W 21st St N Wichita (67205) **(G-15339)**
Preston Pharmacy, Wichita *Also called Hudson Holding Inc* **(G-14648)**
Pretech Corporation.....913 441-4600
8934 Woodend Rd Kansas City (66111) **(G-4334)**
Prevail Innvtive Wlth Strtgies, Leawood *Also called Prevail Strategies LLC* **(G-5526)**
Prevail Strategies LLC.....913 295-9500
4745 W 136th St Leawood (66224) **(G-5526)**
Prevention Services, Topeka *Also called Kansas Childrens Service Leag* **(G-12764)**
Prias Prairie View LLC.....816 437-9636
11415 W 87th Ter Overland Park (66214) **(G-9185)**
Price & Young & Odle.....785 223-5777
1025 W 6th St Junction City (66441) **(G-3739)**
Price & Young & Odle.....913 780-3200
15311 W 119th St Olathe (66062) **(G-8005)**
Price & Young & Odle (PA).....785 537-1118
3012 Anderson Ave Manhattan (66503) **(G-6779)**
Price & Young & Odle.....785 272-0707
2800 Sw Wanamaker Rd # 192 Topeka (66614) **(G-12987)**
Price Bros Equipment Co (PA).....316 265-9577
619 S Washington Ave Wichita (67211) **(G-15340)**
Price Brothers Realty Inc (PA).....913 381-2280
12721 Metcalf Ave Ste 200 Shawnee Mission (66213) **(G-11751)**
Price Chopper, Emporia *Also called Reeble Inc* **(G-1816)**
Price Truck Line Inc (PA).....316 945-6915
4931 S Victoria St Wichita (67216) **(G-15341)**
Price Truck Line Inc.....913 596-9779
5510 Kansas Ave Kansas City (66106) **(G-4335)**
Price Truck Line Inc.....785 232-1183
2000 Se Rice Rd Topeka (66607) **(G-12988)**
Price Truck Line Inc.....785 625-2603
1198 280th Ave Hays (67601) **(G-2888)**
Price Truck Line Inc.....620 365-6626
1421 S Washington Ave Iola (66749) **(G-3627)**
Priceless.....785 625-7664
2719 Plaza Ave Hays (67601) **(G-2889)**
Pride AG Resources, Dodge City *Also called Dodge City Cooperative Exch* **(G-1344)**
Pride AG Resources.....620 227-8671
708 W Trail St Dodge City (67801) **(G-1422)**
Pride Amusements LLC.....417 529-3810
1202 W 12th St Baxter Springs (66713) **(G-411)**

Pride Cleaners 31081, Shawnee Mission *Also called Mjv Holdings LLC* ***(G-11650)***
Pride of Prairie Orchestra Inc....785 460-5518
1255 S Range Ave Colby (67701) ***(G-1034)***
Pride-International Assn Black, Kansas City *Also called Pride/Chapter Intl Assoc* ***(G-4336)***
Pride/Chapter Intl Assoc....913 321-2733
1726 Quindaro Blvd Kansas City (66104) ***(G-4336)***
Prim and Polished LLC....316 516-2537
1030 E Splitwood Way St Derby (67037) ***(G-1265)***
Primary Care Associates LLC....316 684-2851
7111 E 21st St N Ste A Wichita (67206) ***(G-15342)***
Primary Care Landscape Inc....913 768-8880
15739 W 150th St Olathe (66062) ***(G-8006)***
Primary Care Physcans Mnhattan....785 537-4940
1133 College Ave Ste D200 Manhattan (66502) ***(G-6780)***
Prime Communications LP....785 371-4990
4821 W 6th St Ste M Lawrence (66049) ***(G-5075)***
Prime Concepts Group Inc....316 942-1111
7570 W 21st St N 1038a Wichita (67205) ***(G-15343)***
Prime Development Company....316 634-0643
8916 E Windwood St Wichita (67226) ***(G-15344)***
Prime Feeders LLC....620 492-6674
4256 N Rd L Johnson (67855) ***(G-3659)***
Prime Health Servi-Saint John....913 680-6000
3500 S 4th St Leavenworth (66048) ***(G-5280)***
Prime Healthcare Services Inc....913 596-4000
8929 Parallel Pkwy Kansas City (66112) ***(G-4337)***
Prime Healthcare Services Inc....913 651-3542
3500 S 4th St Leavenworth (66048) ***(G-5281)***
Prime Lending....913 327-5507
7101 College Blvd Ste 520 Leawood (66211) ***(G-5527)***
Prime Place LLC....785 317-5265
1532 College Ave Apt F19 Manhattan (66502) ***(G-6781)***
Prime SEC Svcs Borrower LLC....630 410-0662
1035 N 3rd St Ste 101 Lawrence (66044) ***(G-5076)***
Primrose School....316 807-8622
2072 S 127th St E Wichita (67207) ***(G-15345)***
Primrose School of Leawood, Leawood *Also called Sas Childcare Inc* ***(G-5548)***
Primus International Inc....316 425-8105
4330 W May St Wichita (67209) ***(G-15346)***
Primus Sterilizer Company LLC....620 793-7177
175 N Us Highway 281 Great Bend (67530) ***(G-2624)***
Princeton Childrens Center Wl....316 618-0275
3590 N Woodlawn Blvd Wichita (67220) ***(G-15347)***
Principal Landscape Group LLC....913 362-0089
3065 Merriam Ln Kansas City (66106) ***(G-4338)***
Pringle Auto Body & Sales Inc....913 432-6361
2720 S 34th St Kansas City (66106) ***(G-4339)***
Print Source Inc....316 945-7052
404 S Tracy St Wichita (67209) ***(G-15348)***
Print Source Inc (PA)....316 945-7052
404 S Tracy St Wichita (67209) ***(G-15349)***
Print Source Direct LLC....620 947-5702
116 S Main St Hillsboro (67063) ***(G-3056)***
Print Tech Inc....913 894-6644
11696 W 177th Ter Olathe (66062) ***(G-8007)***
Print Time Inc....913 345-8900
6700 W 121st St Ste 300 Leawood (66209) ***(G-5528)***
Print-Docs, Topeka *Also called Tmi Corp* ***(G-13161)***
Printed Media Center, Pittsburg *Also called Pitsco Inc* ***(G-9916)***
Printery Inc (PA)....785 632-5501
411 Court St Clay Center (67432) ***(G-877)***
Printery Inc....785 762-5112
221 N Washington St Junction City (66441) ***(G-3740)***
Printery, The, Junction City *Also called Printery Inc* ***(G-3740)***
Printing Inc....316 265-1201
627 E 3rd St N Wichita (67202) ***(G-15350)***
Printing Dynamics Inc....816 524-0444
12645 S Parker Ter Olathe (66061) ***(G-8008)***
Printing Services Inc....913 492-1500
13309 W 98th St Lenexa (66215) ***(G-6070)***
Printing Solutions Kansas Inc....785 841-8336
725 N 2nd St Ste W Lawrence (66044) ***(G-5077)***
Printingplus Inc....316 269-3010
231 N Saint Francis Ave Wichita (67202) ***(G-15351)***
Prior Productions Incorporated....816 654-5473
15513 W 152nd St Olathe (66062) ***(G-8009)***
Priority Envelope Inc....913 859-9710
17501 W 98th St Spc 1742 Lenexa (66219) ***(G-6071)***
Priority Logistics Inc....913 991-7281
6900 College Blvd Ste 470 Overland Park (66211) ***(G-9186)***
Prism Real Estate Services LLC....913 674-0438
8826 Santa Fe Dr Ste 300 Overland Park (66212) ***(G-9187)***
Private Business Data Systems, Ellinwood *Also called A R Systems Inc* ***(G-1626)***
Prizm Incorporated....785 456-1831
1304 Kaw Valley Rd Wamego (66547) ***(G-13436)***
Prn Home Health Hospice, Wamego *Also called Preferred Registry of Nurses* ***(G-13435)***
Pro Advantage, Lawrence *Also called Hiper Technology Inc* ***(G-4898)***
Pro AG Marketing....785 476-2211
228 S Main St Kensington (66951) ***(G-4579)***
Pro Carpet Building Svcs LLC....620 331-4304
919 W Oak St Independence (67301) ***(G-3549)***
Pro Carpet Plus, Independence *Also called Pro Carpet Building Svcs LLC* ***(G-3549)***
Pro Carwash Systems Inc....316 788-9933
3019 N Oliver St Derby (67037) ***(G-1266)***
Pro Electric LC....913 621-6611
5320 Speaker Rd Kansas City (66106) ***(G-4340)***
Pro Home Remodeling LLC....316 821-9818
616 E 34th St N Wichita (67219) ***(G-15352)***
Pro Ice, Baxter Springs *Also called Diversified Sports Tech LLC* ***(G-404)***
Pro Partners MD Holbrook....913 451-4776
4501 College Blvd Ste 300 Leawood (66211) ***(G-5529)***
Pro Pay LLC....913 826-6300
1217 Shoreline Dr W Salina (67401) ***(G-10642)***
Pro R Sales and Service Inc....316 773-3400
4267 S Boyd St Wichita (67215) ***(G-15353)***
Pro Securtiy, Wichita *Also called Garda CL West Inc* ***(G-14445)***
Pro Shop, Topeka *Also called City of Topeka* ***(G-12469)***
Pro Staff, Overland Park *Also called Atterro Inc* ***(G-8412)***
Pro Tech Spraying Service Inc....620 855-7793
E Hwy 50 Cimarron (67835) ***(G-834)***
Pro X Property Solutions LLC....620 249-5767
107 E Rose St Pittsburg (66762) ***(G-9923)***
Pro-Bound Sports LLC....785 666-4207
428 Hwy 40 Dorrance (67634) ***(G-1465)***
Pro-Dig LLC....785 856-2661
1604 Roseport Rd Elwood (66024) ***(G-1689)***
Pro-Kleen Inc (PA)....316 775-6898
5351 Sw 100th St Augusta (67010) ***(G-339)***
Pro-Kleen Inc....316 253-7556
10886 Sw Ohio Street Rd Augusta (67010) ***(G-340)***
Pro-Tow LLC....913 262-3300
11410 W 89th St Shawnee Mission (66214) ***(G-11752)***
Pro-Weld LLC....316 648-6316
2133 W Rio Vista Dr Wichita (67204) ***(G-15354)***
Proactive Home Care Inc....316 688-5511
3450 N Rock Rd Ste 213 Wichita (67226) ***(G-15355)***
Proactive Solutions Inc (PA)....913 948-8000
5625 Foxridge Dr Shawnee Mission (66202) ***(G-11753)***
Probation Satellite Office, Kansas City *Also called United States Courts ADM* ***(G-4489)***
Probation Services, Great Bend *Also called County of Barton* ***(G-2548)***
Probuild Company LLC....785 827-2644
707 N Broadway Blvd Salina (67401) ***(G-10643)***
Procharger, Lenexa *Also called Accessible Technologies Inc* ***(G-5621)***
Prochaska Howell Prochaska LLC....316 683-9080
8415 E 21st St N Ste 230 Wichita (67206) ***(G-15356)***
Prockish Trucking & Excavating....785 456-7320
409 E Hickory St Louisville (66547) ***(G-6470)***
Procter & Gamble Mfg Co....913 573-0200
1900 Kansas Ave Kansas City (66105) ***(G-4341)***
Prodrivers, Wichita *Also called Professional Drivers GA Inc* ***(G-15358)***
Producers Coop Assn Girard (PA)....620 724-8241
300 E Buffalo St Girard (66743) ***(G-2415)***
Product Dev & Designers....913 783-4364
21565 W 255th St Paola (66071) ***(G-9584)***
Product Manufacturing, Wichita *Also called Atlas Aerospace LLC* ***(G-13763)***
Profab....785 392-3442
1110 Limestone Rd Bldg C Minneapolis (67467) ***(G-7121)***
Professional Bank Forms....620 455-2205
605 W Main St Oxford (67119) ***(G-9534)***
Professional Benefit Cons....913 268-0515
11014 W 50th Ter Shawnee Mission (66203) ***(G-11754)***
Professional Cargo Svcs Inc (PA)....316 522-2224
3735 S West St Wichita (67217) ***(G-15357)***
Professional Cargo Svcs Inc....785 625-2249
724 E 7th St Hays (67601) ***(G-2890)***
Professional Data Services (HQ)....620 663-5282
1632 E 23rd Ave Hutchinson (67502) ***(G-3415)***
Professional Drivers GA Inc....316 945-9700
303 N West St Ste 275 Wichita (67203) ***(G-15358)***
Professional Engrg Cons PA (PA)....316 262-2691
303 S Topeka Ave Wichita (67202) ***(G-15359)***
Professional Engrg Cons PA....620 235-0195
104 S Pine St Pittsburg (66762) ***(G-9924)***
Professional Engrg Cons PA....785 290-0550
1161 Sw Mulvane St Topeka (66604) ***(G-12989)***
Professional Engrg Cons PA....316 262-6457
350 S Washington Ave Wichita (67202) ***(G-15360)***
Professional Engrg Cons PA....785 233-8300
400 S Kansas Ave Ste 200 Topeka (66603) ***(G-12990)***
Professional Express Inc....913 722-6060
835 S Saint Paul St Kansas City (66105) ***(G-4342)***
Professional Fleet Svcs LLC....316 524-6000
2650 S Custer Ave Wichita (67217) ***(G-15361)***
Professional Glass Installers, Lawrence *Also called G I P Inc* ***(G-4867)***
Professional Graphics Inc....913 663-3330
15025 W 114th Ter Shawnee Mission (66215) ***(G-11755)***
Professional Group....785 762-5855
2101 N Jackson St Junction City (66441) ***(G-3741)***

ALPHABETIC

Professional Hairstyling.....913 888-3536
12243 W 87th Pkwy Lenexa (66215) ***(G-6072)***
Professional Home Health Svcs.....785 625-0055
1307 Lawrence Dr Hays (67601) ***(G-2891)***
Professional Insurance Mgt.....316 942-0699
4906 N Portwest Cir Wichita (67204) ***(G-15362)***
Professional Ldscpg Svcs LLC.....316 832-0061
1347 S Washington Ave Wichita (67211) ***(G-15363)***
Professional Machine & Tool.....316 755-1271
510 E 5th St Valley Center (67147) ***(G-13350)***
Professional Mech Contrs Inc.....316 684-1927
4053 E Navajo Ln Wichita (67210) ***(G-15364)***
Professional Moving & Storage.....785 842-1115
431 N Iowa St Lawrence (66044) ***(G-5078)***
Professional Orthc & Prosthtc.....785 375-7458
260 Johnson Rd Unit A Manhattan (66502) ***(G-6782)***
Professional Pharmacy, Wichita *Also called Rx Plus Pharmacies Inc* ***(G-15495)***
Professional Printing Kans Inc.....620 343-7125
315 Constitution St Emporia (66801) ***(G-1813)***
Professional Products of Kans.....316 522-9300
4456 S Clifton Ave Wichita (67216) ***(G-15365)***
Professional Pulling Svc LLC.....785 625-8928
1835 Nunjor Rd Hays (67601) ***(G-2892)***
Professional Renewal Center PA.....785 842-9772
1421 Res Pk Dr Ste 3b Lawrence (66049) ***(G-5079)***
Professional Roofing Systems.....785 392-0603
615 N Rothsay Ave Minneapolis (67467) ***(G-7122)***
Professional Sales Svcs Inc.....316 941-4542
410 N Industrial Rd El Dorado (67042) ***(G-1594)***
Professional Service Inds Inc.....913 310-1600
1211 W Cambridge Cir Dr Kansas City (66103) ***(G-4343)***
Professional Software Inc.....316 269-4264
12401 W Jayson Ct Wichita (67235) ***(G-15366)***
Professionals Business MGT Inc.....913 888-1444
6703 W 91st St Overland Park (66212) ***(G-9188)***
Professnal Toxicology Svcs Inc.....913 599-3535
7917 Bond St Overland Park (66214) ***(G-9189)***
Professnal Turf Pdts Ltd Prtnr.....913 599-1449
10935 Eicher Dr Lenexa (66219) ***(G-6073)***
Professnal Wtrprfing Insul LLC.....316 264-3101
8401 E Oak Knoll St Wichita (67207) ***(G-15367)***
Professors of Peace LLC.....316 213-7233
150 Stewart Ave Haysville (67060) ***(G-2956)***
Proffitt, John, Olathe *Also called Johnson County Dermatology* ***(G-7816)***
Profiles Inc.....316 636-1214
2939 N Rock Rd Ste 100 Wichita (67226) ***(G-15368)***
Profillment LLC.....316 260-7910
1930 S Hoover Rd Ste 200 Wichita (67209) ***(G-15369)***
Profit Builders Inc.....316 721-3370
2872 N Ridge Rd Ste 201 Wichita (67205) ***(G-15370)***
Profit Plus Bus Solutions LLC.....913 583-8440
8997 Commerce Dr De Soto (66018) ***(G-1210)***
Profitt Builders and Supply.....620 278-3667
2470 18th Rd Sterling (67579) ***(G-12129)***
Proforma, Hutchinson *Also called Graphic Impressions Inc* ***(G-3305)***
Proforma Marketing.....913 685-9098
8220 Nieman Rd Overland Park (66214) ***(G-9190)***
Progene Biomedical Inc.....913 492-2224
11274 Renner Blvd Lenexa (66219) ***(G-6074)***
Progreen Window Cleaning Inc.....913 387-3210
8215 Melrose Dr Ste 100 Lenexa (66214) ***(G-6075)***
Progress Rail Services.....256 593-1260
2604 Indul Rd Atchison (66002) ***(G-256)***
Progress Rail Services Corp.....913 345-4807
8400 W 110th St Ste 300 Overland Park (66210) ***(G-9191)***
Progress Rail Services Corp.....913 352-6613
1710 Laurel St Pleasanton (66075) ***(G-10000)***
Progressive AG Coop Assn.....620 962-5238
420 Ryan Ave Danville (67036) ***(G-1190)***
Progressive Care Prof Hm Care.....785 984-2290
513 Mill St Alton (67623) ***(G-74)***
Progressive Casualty Insur Co.....913 202-6600
1930 S 45th St Ste 150 Kansas City (66106) ***(G-4344)***
Progressive Contractors Inc.....785 235-3032
3333 Se 21st St Topeka (66607) ***(G-12991)***
Progressive HM Hlth & Hospice, Wichita *Also called Progressive Home Health Care* ***(G-15371)***
Progressive Home Health Care (PA).....316 691-5050
3500 N Rock Rd Bldg 400 Wichita (67226) ***(G-15371)***
Progressive Insurance, Kansas City *Also called Progressive Casualty Insur Co* ***(G-4344)***
Progressive Manufacturing Co.....913 383-2239
9217 Lee Blvd Leawood (66206) ***(G-5530)***
Progressive Products Inc.....620 235-1712
3305 Airport Cir Pittsburg (66762) ***(G-9925)***
Progrssive Tech Intgrators LLC.....913 663-0870
5901 College Blvd Ste 200 Overland Park (66211) ***(G-9192)***
Prohoe Mfg LLC.....785 987-5450
204 Munden Ave Munden (66959) ***(G-7229)***
Prohome International LLc (PA).....316 687-6776
550 N 159th St E Ste 2000 Wichita (67230) ***(G-15372)***
Project Concern Inc.....913 367-4655
504 Kansas Ave Atchison (66002) ***(G-257)***
Project Eagle.....913 281-2648
444 Minnesota Ave Ste 100 Kansas City (66101) ***(G-4345)***
Promise Hosp Overland Pk Inc.....913 275-5092
6509 W 103rd St Overland Park (66212) ***(G-9193)***
Promise Regional Medical Ctr, Hutchinson *Also called Health Care Inc* ***(G-3309)***
Promotional Headwear Intl Inc.....913 541-0901
17740 College Blvd Lenexa (66219) ***(G-6076)***
Pronto Print.....785 823-2285
627 E Crawford St Salina (67401) ***(G-10644)***
Propak Logistics Inc.....913 213-3896
4600 Kansas Ave Kansas City (66106) ***(G-4346)***
Propane Central.....785 762-5160
2618 Central Dr Junction City (66441) ***(G-3742)***
Propane Resources LLC (PA).....913 262-8345
6950 Squibb Rd Ste 306 Shawnee Mission (66202) ***(G-11756)***
Propane Resources Trnsp Inc.....913 262-8345
6950 Squibb Rd Ste 306 Shawnee Mission (66202) ***(G-11757)***
Property Damage Appraisers, Overland Park *Also called Pda of Kansas City Inc* ***(G-9149)***
Property Tax Advisory Group.....913 897-4744
11300 Tomahawk Creek Pkwy Overland Park (66211) ***(G-9194)***
Property Valuation Services, Overland Park *Also called Complex Property Advisers Corp* ***(G-8591)***
Propharma Group LLC (HQ).....888 242-0559
8717 W 110th St Ste 300 Overland Park (66210) ***(G-9195)***
Propio Language Services, Overland Park *Also called Propio Ls LLC* ***(G-9196)***
Propio Ls LLC.....913 381-3143
11020 King St Ste 420 Overland Park (66210) ***(G-9196)***
Proprint Incorporated (PA).....785 272-0070
1033 Sw Gage Blvd Ste 200 Topeka (66604) ***(G-12992)***
Proprint Incorporated.....785 842-3610
4931 W 6th St Ste 104 Lawrence (66049) ***(G-5080)***
Proscape Inc.....785 263-7104
955 2440 Ln Abilene (67410) ***(G-49)***
Proshred Security, Kansas City *Also called T2 Holdings LLC* ***(G-4456)***
Prosoco, Lawrence *Also called Boyer Industries Corporation* ***(G-4762)***
Prosoco Inc (HQ).....785 865-4200
3741 Greenway Cir Lawrence (66046) ***(G-5081)***
Prosperity Netwrk Advisors LLC (PA).....913 451-4501
100955 Lowell Ste 900 Overland Park (66210) ***(G-9197)***
Prosser Wilbert Cnstr Inc.....913 906-0104
13730 W 108th St Lenexa (66215) ***(G-6077)***
Protec Construction & Sup LLC.....913 441-2121
108 S 9th St Edwardsville (66111) ***(G-1513)***
Protection One, Wichita *Also called ADT LLC* ***(G-13618)***
Protection One Alarm Mnitoring, Lawrence *Also called ADT LLC* ***(G-4720)***
Protection Valley Manor Inc.....620 622-4261
600 S Broadway Protection (67127) ***(G-10176)***
Protective Equipment Testing, Great Bend *Also called Petl Management Corp Inc* ***(G-2622)***
Protiviti Inc.....913 685-6200
9401 Indian Creek Pkwy # 730 Overland Park (66210) ***(G-9198)***
Proud Anmal Lovers Shelter Inc.....620 421-0445
P.O. Box 48 Parsons (67357) ***(G-9726)***
Provalue Cooperative Inc (PA).....620 662-5406
1515 E 30th Ave Hutchinson (67502) ***(G-3416)***
Provalue Insurance LLC.....620 662-5406
1515 E 30th Ave Hutchinson (67502) ***(G-3417)***
Provant Health, Olathe *Also called Hooper Holmes Inc* ***(G-7777)***
Providence, Kansas City *Also called Sisters of Charity of Leavenwo* ***(G-4422)***
Providence Living Center Inc.....785 233-0588
1112 Se Republican Ave Topeka (66607) ***(G-12993)***
Providence Medical Center, Kansas City *Also called Prime Healthcare Services Inc* ***(G-4337)***
Providence Medical Center (HQ).....913 596-4870
8929 Parallel Pkwy Kansas City (66112) ***(G-4347)***
Providence Place Inc.....913 596-4200
8909 Parallel Pkwy Kansas City (66112) ***(G-4348)***
Providence Project, The, Whitewater *Also called Edwin Myers* ***(G-13570)***
PROVIDENCE-MEDICAL CENTER GIFT SHOP, Kansas City *Also called Providence Medical Center* ***(G-4347)***
Provident Payroll, Olathe *Also called Tax 911com Incorporated* ***(G-8102)***
Provimi North America Inc.....620 327-2280
300 N Main St Hesston (67062) ***(G-2999)***
Prs Inc.....844 679-2273
13160 Foster St Ste 100 Overland Park (66213) ***(G-9199)***
Prts, Hiawatha *Also called Physical Rsprtory Therapy Svcs* ***(G-3022)***
Prudential, Overland Park *Also called P K C Realty Company LLC* ***(G-9133)***
Prudential, Winfield *Also called Albright Investment Company* ***(G-16114)***
Prudential, Wichita *Also called Dinning Beard Inc* ***(G-14212)***
Prudential Dinning Beard, Augusta *Also called Chuck Krte Rlty Est Auctn Svcs* ***(G-313)***
Prudential Henry & Burrows.....913 345-3000
11150 Overbrook Rd # 150 Shawnee Mission (66211) ***(G-11758)***
Prudential Insur Co of Amer.....913 327-1060
10801 Mastin St Ste 200 Shawnee Mission (66210) ***(G-11759)***
Prudential Kansas City Realty.....913 491-1550
8101 College Blvd Ste 210 Overland Park (66210) ***(G-9200)***

Pryor Autmtc Fire Sprnklr Inc...620 792-6400
694c Harrison St Great Bend (67530) *(G-2625)*
Pryor Learning Solutions Inc (PA)...913 967-8300
5700 Broadmoor St Ste 300 Shawnee Mission (66202) *(G-11760)*
PS Holdings LLC...913 599-1600
10881 Lowell Ave Ste 250 Overland Park (66210) *(G-9201)*
PSC Group LLC...847 517-7200
10561 Barkley St Overland Park (66212) *(G-9202)*
PSI Services Inc...843 520-2992
18000 W 105th St Olathe (66061) *(G-8010)*
PSI Services Inc (HQ)...913 895-4600
18000 W 105th St Olathe (66061) *(G-8011)*
PSI Transport LLC...785 675-3881
742 Us 24 Hoxie (67740) *(G-3140)*
Pssk LLC...620 277-7100
2412 E Kansas Ave Garden City (67846) *(G-2260)*
Psychiatric Associates...913 438-8221
4601 W 109th St Ste 208 Shawnee Mission (66211) *(G-11761)*
Psychiatric Associates Billing, Shawnee Mission *Also called Psychiatric Associates (G-11761)*
Psychiatry Assoc Kans Cy PC...913 385-7252
8900 State Line Rd # 380 Shawnee Mission (66206) *(G-11762)*
Psychiatry Associates Kans Cy, Shawnee Mission *Also called Psychiatry Assoc Kans Cy PC (G-11762)*
Pt Integrators, Overland Park *Also called Progrssive Tech Intgrators LLC (G-9192)*
Pt Kansas LLC...620 791-7082
4110 Quail Creek Dr Great Bend (67530) *(G-2626)*
Pt Solutions Group, Overland Park *Also called Paige Technologies LLC (G-9135)*
Pta Kansas Congress Oxford...913 897-1719
12500 Switzer Rd Overland Park (66213) *(G-9203)*
Ptmw Inc...785 232-7792
5040 Nw Us Highway 24 Topeka (66618) *(G-12994)*
Public Storage...316 522-1162
206 E Macarthur Rd Wichita (67216) *(G-15373)*
Public Whl Wtr Sup Dst No 13...913 795-2503
318 Montgomery Ct Mound City (66056) *(G-7174)*
Public Work Dept, Lawrence *Also called County of Douglas (G-4814)*
Public Works, Wichita *Also called County of Sedgwick (G-14112)*
Public Works Department, Parsons *Also called City of Parsons (G-9671)*
Public Works Dept, Olathe *Also called County of Johnson (G-7619)*
Public Works Dept, Kansas City *Also called Wyandtte Cnty Unfied Gvernment (G-4554)*
Publishers Delivery Solut...913 894-1299
10973 Eicher Dr Lenexa (66219) *(G-6078)*
Puckett Construction, Fredonia *Also called R Puckett Farms Inc (G-2043)*
Puddle Jumpers Dive Shop, Russell *Also called Russell Block Company Inc (G-10294)*
Pulmonary Sleep Consultant...316 440-1010
3009 N Cypress St Wichita (67226) *(G-15374)*
Pulse Design Group Inc...913 438-9095
8207 Melrose Dr Ste 145 Lenexa (66214) *(G-6079)*
Pulse Needlefree Systems Inc...913 599-1590
8210 Marshall Dr Lenexa (66214) *(G-6080)*
Pulse Systems Inc (HQ)...316 636-5900
3020 N Cypress St Ste 200 Wichita (67226) *(G-15375)*
Pump & Power Equipment, Lenexa *Also called Dxp Enterprises Inc (G-5827)*
Pumphrey Machine Co Inc...316 832-1841
3758 N Old Lawrence Rd Wichita (67219) *(G-15376)*
Punch Boxing Plus Fitness...816 589-2690
5421 Martindale Rd Shawnee (66218) *(G-11013)*
Pur-O-Zone Inc...785 843-0771
345 N Iowa St Lawrence (66044) *(G-5082)*
Purac America Inc (HQ)...913 890-5500
8250 Flint St Lenexa (66214) *(G-6081)*
Purdum Inc...913 766-0835
7301 W 133rd St Ste 100 Overland Park (66213) *(G-9204)*
Purdum Construction, Overland Park *Also called Purdum Inc (G-9204)*
Purifan Inc...316 932-8001
5200 E 35th St N Wichita (67220) *(G-15377)*
Purina Animal Nutrition LLC...316 265-0624
414 E 18th St N Wichita (67214) *(G-15378)*
Purina Mills LLC...316 265-0624
414 E 18th St N Wichita (67214) *(G-15379)*
Purple Wave Auction...785 537-5057
825 Levee Dr Manhattan (66502) *(G-6783)*
Purplefrogintl...816 510-0871
14407 W 65th Ter Shawnee (66216) *(G-11014)*
Purpose Productions...913 620-3508
1804 N 78th Pl Kansas City (66112) *(G-4349)*
Pwd Inc...316 283-0335
1214 Cow Palace Rd Newton (67114) *(G-7409)*
Pwi Inc (PA)...316 942-2811
109 S Knight St Wichita (67213) *(G-15380)*
Pwi Inc...316 942-2811
3407 W Douglas Ave Wichita (67213) *(G-15381)*
Pyramid Contractors Inc...913 764-6225
795 W Ironwood St Olathe (66061) *(G-8012)*
Pyrodex Division, Herington *Also called Hodgdon Powder Company Inc (G-2976)*
Pyxis Inc...316 682-8092
334 N Topeka Ave Wichita (67202) *(G-15382)*

Q 1035 (PA)...785 762-5525
1030 Southwind Ct Junction City (66441) *(G-3743)*
Q Consldated Oil Well Svcs LLC (HQ)...620 431-9210
1322 S Grant Ave Chanute (66720) *(G-757)*
Q Golden Billiards...785 625-6913
809 Ash St Hays (67601) *(G-2893)*
Q S Nurses Kansas LLC...620 793-7262
1117 Washington St Great Bend (67530) *(G-2627)*
Q Solutions LLC...913 948-5931
406 E 4th St Wellsville (66092) *(G-13545)*
Q4 Industries LLC...913 894-6240
8261 Melrose Dr Overland Park (66214) *(G-9205)*
Qae Acquisition Company LLC...913 814-9988
12851 Foster St Overland Park (66213) *(G-9206)*
Qc Financial Services Inc (HQ)...913 439-1100
9401 Indian Creek Pkwy # 1500 Shawnee Mission (66210) *(G-11763)*
Qc Holdings Inc (PA)...866 660-2243
8208 Melrose Dr Lenexa (66214) *(G-6082)*
Qes Pressure Pumping LLC (HQ)...620 431-9210
1322 S Grant Ave Chanute (66720) *(G-758)*
Qes Pressure Pumping LLC...785 242-4044
2631 S Eisenhower Ave Ottawa (66067) *(G-8307)*
Qes Pressure Pumping LLC...785 672-8822
226 Prospect Ave Oakley (67748) *(G-7486)*
Qins International Inc...913 342-4488
844 S 14th St Kansas City (66105) *(G-4350)*
Qmc, Quinter *Also called Quinter Mfg & Cnstr Inc (G-10186)*
Qspec Solutions Inc...877 467-7732
7949 Bond St Overland Park (66214) *(G-9207)*
Qti Inc...913 579-3131
15880 S Cherry Ct Olathe (66062) *(G-8013)*
Qts Finance Corporation...913 814-9988
12851 Foster St Overland Park (66213) *(G-9208)*
Qts Invstmnt Props Carpathia...913 814-9988
12851 Foster St Overland Park (66213) *(G-9209)*
Qts Realty Trust Inc (PA)...913 814-9988
12851 Foster St Overland Park (66213) *(G-9210)*
Quad/Graphics Inc...816 936-8536
14900 W 99th St Lenexa (66215) *(G-6083)*
Quail Ridge Homes Assoc Inc...913 381-2042
10764 Walmer St Shawnee Mission (66211) *(G-11764)*
Quality Care...785 228-1118
1136 Sw Wanamaker Rd Topeka (66604) *(G-12995)*
Quality Carriers Inc...913 281-0901
20 Central Ave Kansas City (66118) *(G-4351)*
Quality Connectionz Inc...620 380-6262
449 W Lincoln Rd Iola (66749) *(G-3628)*
Quality Elc Douglas Cnty Inc...785 843-9211
1011 E 31st St Lawrence (66046) *(G-5083)*
Quality Granite & Marble Inc...316 946-0530
1123 S West St Wichita (67213) *(G-15383)*
Quality Group Companies LLC (PA)...913 814-9988
12851 Foster St Ste 205 Overland Park (66213) *(G-9211)*
Quality Health Care Inc (PA)...316 263-8880
1527 Madison St Fl 2 Fredonia (66736) *(G-2041)*
Quality Homes Inc...402 248-6218
N State Line Summerfield (66541) *(G-12216)*
Quality Industries, Parsons *Also called Class Ltd (G-9672)*
Quality Inn, Colby *Also called Sunflower Partners Inc (G-1042)*
Quality Inn, Wichita *Also called Quality Suites Airport (G-15385)*
Quality Inn...785 784-5106
305 E Chestnut St Junction City (66441) *(G-3744)*
Quality Inn...785 770-8000
150 E Poyntz Ave Manhattan (66502) *(G-6784)*
Quality Inn...620 663-4444
11 Des Moines Ave South Hutchinson (67505) *(G-12064)*
Quality Intrcnnect Systems Inc (PA)...620 783-5087
1009 W 11th St Galena (66739) *(G-2081)*
Quality Inv Prpts Land Co LLC...913 312-5500
12851 Foster St Ste 100 Overland Park (66213) *(G-9212)*
Quality Inventory Services (PA)...913 888-7700
6231 Ikea Way Merriam (66202) *(G-7101)*
Quality Investment Properties...913 814-9988
12851 Foster St Ste 205 Overland Park (66213) *(G-9213)*
Quality Litho Inc...913 262-5341
4627 Mission Rd Kansas City (66103) *(G-4352)*
Quality Milling LLC...620 724-4900
309 E Saint John St Girard (66743) *(G-2416)*
Quality Movers Express of Kans, Shawnee Mission *Also called Coleman American Mvg Svcs Inc (G-11246)*
Quality Oilwell Cementing Inc...785 483-1071
740 W Wichita Ave Russell (67665) *(G-10285)*
Quality Power Products Inc...785 263-0060
427 Old 40 Hwy Solomon (67480) *(G-12052)*
Quality Printing, Wichita *Also called D P Enterprises Inc (G-14159)*
Quality Printing & Gift Shop...620 654-3487
1307 21st Ave Galva (67443) *(G-2095)*
Quality Printing and Off Sups, Lenexa *Also called Quality Printing and Off Sups (G-6084)*

ALPHABETIC

Quality Printing and Off Sups 913 491-6366
13610 W 107th St Lenexa (66215) ***(G-6084)***
Quality Printing Inc 620 421-0630
124 Ricewick Rd Parsons (67357) ***(G-9727)***
Quality Profile Services Inc 620 767-6757
701 Donnon St Council Grove (66846) ***(G-1175)***
Quality Record Pressings 785 820-2931
543 N 10th St Salina (67401) ***(G-10645)***
Quality Remodeler 785 823-7665
2501 Market Pl Ste I Salina (67401) ***(G-10646)***
Quality Roofg Installation LLC 316 946-1068
1218 S Washington Ave Wichita (67211) ***(G-15384)***
Quality Solutions, Inc., Colwich *Also called Cushman Wkefield Solutions LLC* ***(G-1093)***
Quality Steel & Wire Pdts Co 913 888-2929
9802 Widmer Rd Lenexa (66215) ***(G-6085)***
Quality Structures Inc (PA) 785 835-6100
167 Highway 59 Richmond (66080) ***(G-10203)***
Quality Suites Airport 316 945-2600
658 S Westdale Dr Wichita (67209) ***(G-15385)***
Quality Tech Metals 316 945-4781
2518 W May St Wichita (67213) ***(G-15386)***
Quality Tech Svcs Frt Worth II 913 814-9988
12851 Foster St Overland Park (66213) ***(G-9214)***
Quality Tech Svcs Lenexa LLC 913 814-9988
12851 Foster St Overland Park (66213) ***(G-9215)***
Quality Tech Svcs Nrtheast LLC 913 814-9988
12851 Foster St Overland Park (66213) ***(G-9216)***
Quality Technology Svcs LLC (HQ) 913 814-9988
12851 Foster St Overland Park (66213) ***(G-9217)***
Quality Technology Svcs NJ LLC 913 814-9988
12851 Foster St Overland Park (66213) ***(G-9218)***
Quality Tool Service Inc 316 265-0048
1501 S Handley St Wichita (67213) ***(G-15387)***
Quality Trust Inc 785 375-6372
1906 Mcfarland Rd Junction City (66441) ***(G-3745)***
Quality Water Inc 785 825-4912
658 E North St Salina (67401) ***(G-10647)***
Qualitytech LP (HQ) 877 787-3282
12851 Foster St Overland Park (66213) ***(G-9219)***
Quantum Credit Union (PA) 316 263-5756
6300 W 21st St N Wichita (67205) ***(G-15388)***
Quantum Credit Union 316 263-5756
6300 W 21st St N Wichita (67205) ***(G-15389)***
Quantum Health Professionals 913 894-1910
6901 Shawnee Mission Pkwy # 207 Mission (66202) ***(G-7135)***
Quark Studios LLC 913 871-5154
12595 S Race St Olathe (66061) ***(G-8014)***
Quarters At Cambridge LP 316 636-1277
9911 E 21st St N Ofc Wichita (67206) ***(G-15390)***
Queen Foods, Kansas City *Also called Qins International Inc* ***(G-4350)***
Queen-Morris Ventures LLC 913 383-2563
8686 Antioch Rd Shawnee Mission (66212) ***(G-11765)***
Queens Price Shopper, Shawnee Mission *Also called Queen-Morris Ventures LLC* ***(G-11765)***
Quentin Mc Kee & Son Ldscpg 785 827-5155
21 Red Fox Ln Salina (67401) ***(G-10648)***
Quentin, McKee & Son, Salina *Also called Quentin Mc Kee & Son Ldscpg* ***(G-10648)***
Quest Capital Management Inc (PA) 913 599-6422
15482 College Blvd Shawnee Mission (66219) ***(G-11766)***
Quest Credit Union, Topeka *Also called Educational Credit Union* ***(G-12572)***
Quest Diagnostics, Lenexa *Also called Labone Inc* ***(G-5961)***
Quest Diagnostics Incorporated 785 621-4300
2501 Canterbury Dr Ste 1 Hays (67601) ***(G-2894)***
Quest Diagnostics Incorporated 913 768-1959
20920 W 151st St Olathe (66061) ***(G-8015)***
Quest Diagnostics Incorporated 913 299-8538
10940 Parallel Pkwy Kansas City (66109) ***(G-4353)***
Quest Diagnostics Incorporated 913 982-2900
10101 Renner Blvd Shawnee Mission (66219) ***(G-11767)***
Quest Diagnostics Incorporated 316 634-1946
3100 E Central Ave Ste A Wichita (67214) ***(G-15391)***
Quest Drilling Services LLC 316 260-2196
607 N Armour St Wichita (67206) ***(G-15392)***
Quest Research & Development 316 267-1216
1042 N Waco Ave Wichita (67203) ***(G-15393)***
Quest Services Inc 620 208-6180
2608 W 12th Ave Emporia (66801) ***(G-1814)***
Quickertek Inc 316 691-1585
777 E Osie St Ste 304a Wichita (67207) ***(G-15394)***
Quicksilver Ex Courier of MO 913 321-5959
1126 Adams St Kansas City (66103) ***(G-4354)***
Quik Cash, Shawnee Mission *Also called Qc Financial Services Inc* ***(G-11763)***
Quik Print, Topeka *Also called Tarrant Enterprises Inc* ***(G-13142)***
Quik Print, Wichita *Also called Tarrant Inc* ***(G-15717)***
Quik Tek Machining LLC 316 260-9980
1901 Southwest Blvd Wichita (67213) ***(G-15395)***
Quikrete Companies Inc 913 441-6525
2424 S 88th St Kansas City (66111) ***(G-4355)***
Quikrete Companies LLC 316 721-3900
2806 N Ridge Rd Wichita (67205) ***(G-15396)***
Quikrete of Kansas City, Kansas City *Also called Quikrete Companies Inc* ***(G-4355)***
Quikrete of Wichita, Wichita *Also called Quikrete Companies LLC* ***(G-15396)***
Quindaro Power Station, Kansas City *Also called Kansas City Bd Pub Utilities* ***(G-4137)***
Quinn Plastic Surgery Ctr LLC 913 492-3443
6920 W 121st St Ste 102 Leawood (66209) ***(G-5531)***
Quinter Ambulance Service Inc 785 754-3734
412 Main St Quinter (67752) ***(G-10185)***
Quinter Mfg & Cnstr Inc 785 754-3310
2520 Castle Rock Rd Quinter (67752) ***(G-10186)***
Quivira Athletic Club L C 913 268-3633
7880 Quivira Rd Lenexa (66216) ***(G-6086)***
Quivira Cncil Boy Scuts Amer I (PA) 316 264-4466
3247 N Oliver St Wichita (67220) ***(G-15397)***
Quivira Country Club Inc 913 631-4820
100 Crescent Blvd Kansas City (66106) ***(G-4356)***
Quivira Falls Community Assn 913 469-5463
10990 Westgate Rd Shawnee Mission (66210) ***(G-11768)***
Quivira Internal Medicine 913 541-3340
10601 Quivira Rd Ste 200 Shawnee Mission (66215) ***(G-11769)***
Quivira Sports Clubs, Lenexa *Also called Quivira Athletic Club L C* ***(G-6086)***
Quivira Sports Clubs, Shawnee Mission *Also called Element Fitness* ***(G-11331)***
Qwest Corporation 913 851-9024
15440 Long St Overland Park (66221) ***(G-9220)***
Qxt, Overland Park *Also called Airtech Engineering Inc* ***(G-8363)***
R & B Oil & Gas Inc 620 254-7251
111 N Blaine St Attica (67009) ***(G-278)***
R & D Fitness Inc 913 722-2001
6501 Frontage Rd Shawnee Mission (66202) ***(G-11770)***
R & D Transports, Lakin *Also called Ramon E Guardiola* ***(G-4658)***
R & F Farm Supply Inc 620 244-3275
10200 Highway 59 Erie (66733) ***(G-1864)***
R & H Concrete Inc 785 286-0335
1887 E 1450 Rd Lawrence (66044) ***(G-5084)***
R & H Implement Company Inc 620 384-7421
1100 W Hwy 50 Syracuse (67878) ***(G-12230)***
R & J Salina Tax Service Inc 785 827-1304
318 W Cloud St Salina (67401) ***(G-10649)***
R & K Horn LLC 620 241-5083
1514 Sunflower Dr McPherson (67460) ***(G-7021)***
R & L Carriers Inc 316 529-1222
4949 S Victoria St Wichita (67216) ***(G-15398)***
R & O Partnership 785 434-4534
109 S Jefferson St Plainville (67663) ***(G-9991)***
R & R Aerospace, Wichita *Also called R & R Holdings Inc* ***(G-15399)***
R & R Builders Inc 913 682-1234
608 Delaware St Leavenworth (66048) ***(G-5282)***
R & R Developers Inc 785 762-2255
217 N Washington St Junction City (66441) ***(G-3746)***
R & R Equipment Inc 620 223-2450
2355 Locust Rd Fort Scott (66701) ***(G-2000)***
R & R Holdings Inc 316 942-6699
2615 W Esthner Ct Wichita (67213) ***(G-15399)***
R & R Industries Inc 620 672-7463
30340 Runway Blvd Pratt (67124) ***(G-10146)***
R & R Manufacturing, Pratt *Also called R & R Industries Inc* ***(G-10146)***
R & R Manufacturing Inc 620 672-7461
30340 Runway Blvd Pratt (67124) ***(G-10147)***
R & R Plumbing & Heating, Lincoln *Also called R & R Street Plbg Htg & Elec* ***(G-6385)***
R & R Precision Machine Inc 316 942-6699
2615 W Esthner Ct Wichita (67213) ***(G-15400)***
R & R Street Plbg Htg & Elec 785 524-4551
2009 E Highway 18 Lincoln (67455) ***(G-6385)***
R & S Construction Inc 620 325-2130
221 S 11th St Neodesha (66757) ***(G-7247)***
R & S Digital Services Inc (PA) 620 792-6171
1920 A 24th St Great Bend (67530) ***(G-2628)***
R & S Pipe Supply 620 365-8114
503 W Lincoln Rd Iola (66749) ***(G-3629)***
R & S Pipe Supply LLC 785 448-5401
210 S Catalpa St Garnett (66032) ***(G-2385)***
R & T Specialty Cnstr Lc 316 942-8141
3108 W Maple St Wichita (67213) ***(G-15401)***
R A Ruud & Son Inc 316 788-5000
7760 S Hydraulic St Haysville (67060) ***(G-2957)***
R and P Calf Ranch LLC 620 855-2550
17502 19th Rd Cimarron (67835) ***(G-835)***
R B Manufacturing Company 913 829-3233
1301 W Dennis Ave Olathe (66061) ***(G-8016)***
R B P Inc 316 303-9606
1004 E Murdock St Wichita (67214) ***(G-15402)***
R C A, Wright *Also called Right Cooperative Association* ***(G-16194)***
R C Kennels 785 238-7000
12344 Kennel Dr Junction City (66441) ***(G-3747)***
R C Kennels Boarding Grooming, Junction City *Also called R C Kennels* ***(G-3747)***
R D C Inc 913 529-2233
8385 Melrose Dr Shawnee Mission (66214) ***(G-11771)***
R D H Electric Inc 785 625-3833
800 E 12th St Hays (67601) ***(G-2895)***

R D Johnson Excavating Co Inc 785 842-9100
1705 N 1399 Rd Lawrence (66046) ***(G-5085)***
R D K Machine LLC 316 267-6678
625 E Pawnee St Ste A Wichita (67211) ***(G-15403)***
R E B Inc 620 365-5701
900 W Miller Rd Iola (66749) ***(G-3630)***
R F Fisher Holdings Inc (PA) 913 384-1500
1707 W 39th Ave Kansas City (66103) ***(G-4357)***
R K Black Missouri LLC (PA) 913 577-8100
15080 W 116th St Ste 100 Olathe (66062) ***(G-8017)***
R L C Inc 913 352-8744
1511 Ash St Pleasanton (66075) ***(G-10001)***
R L Dial Co Inc 316 721-0108
513 N Covington Ct Wichita (67212) ***(G-15404)***
R M Baril General Contr Inc 785 537-2190
1600 Fair Ln Manhattan (66502) ***(G-6785)***
R M I Golf Carts, Olathe *Also called Rogers Manufacturing Inc* ***(G-8040)***
R Messner Construction Co 316 634-2381
3122 N Cypress St Ste 500 Wichita (67226) ***(G-15405)***
R Miller Sales Co Inc 913 341-3727
9215 Cherokee Ln Ste 230 Shawnee Mission (66206) ***(G-11772)***
R O K K Concrete Inc 785 286-0662
5139 Nw Rochester Rd Topeka (66617) ***(G-12996)***
R O Terex Corporation 913 782-1200
550 E Old Highway 56 Olathe (66061) ***(G-8018)***
R P 3 Inc 620 827-6136
8519 Nw 50th St Mc Cune (66753) ***(G-6921)***
R P M Smith Corporation 913 888-0695
15019 W 95th St Lenexa (66215) ***(G-6087)***
R P Nixon Operations Inc 785 628-3834
207 W 12th St Hays (67601) ***(G-2896)***
R P Products Inc 913 492-6380
13611 W 109th St Shawnee Mission (66215) ***(G-11773)***
R Puckett Farms Inc 620 378-3565
314 N 14th St Fredonia (66736) ***(G-2042)***
R Puckett Farms Inc 620 378-3342
1020 N 2nd St Fredonia (66736) ***(G-2043)***
R R A Inc (PA) 316 262-3411
100 S Main St Ste 510 Wichita (67202) ***(G-15406)***
R S Bickford & Co Inc 913 451-1480
8600 W 110th St Ste 110 Shawnee Mission (66210) ***(G-11774)***
R S I, Independence *Also called Remediation Services Inc* ***(G-3553)***
R T Sporting Goods Inc 620 275-5507
1135 College Dr Ste E Garden City (67846) ***(G-2261)***
R V Products Div, Wichita *Also called Airxcel Inc* ***(G-13656)***
R W H Farms, Wamego *Also called R W Milling Company Inc* ***(G-13437)***
R W Milling Company Inc 785 456-7866
18124 Military Trail Rd Wamego (66547) ***(G-13437)***
R Wilson Co, Overland Park *Also called Robert Wilson Co Inc* ***(G-9251)***
R&B Services LLC 316 265-7859
2344 S Seneca St Wichita (67213) ***(G-15407)***
R&R Pallet Garden City Inc 620 275-2394
2008 W Mary St Garden City (67846) ***(G-2262)***
R-Tech Tool & Machine Inc 785 456-9541
403 Miller Dr Wamego (66547) ***(G-13438)***
R.I.C. Construction, Coffeyville *Also called Lee Shafer Ricky* ***(G-955)***
R.T.C.A., Everest *Also called Rainbow Telecom Assn Inc* ***(G-1902)***
R2 Center For Assisting LLC (PA) 316 749-2097
13121 E 21st St N Ste 107 Wichita (67230) ***(G-15408)***
RA Knapp Construction Inc 913 287-8700
12209 W 88th St Lenexa (66215) ***(G-6088)***
Raab Sales Inc 913 227-0814
14521 W 96th Ter Shawnee Mission (66215) ***(G-11775)***
Rabbit Creek Products Inc 913 837-3073
903 N Broadway St Louisburg (66053) ***(G-6463)***
Radiant Electric Cooperative (PA) 620 378-2161
100 N 15th St Fredonia (66736) ***(G-2044)***
Radiation Oncology 913 588-3600
3901 Rainbow Blvd Kansas City (66160) ***(G-4358)***
Radiator Express, Kansas City *Also called 1-800 Radiator & A/C* ***(G-3774)***
Radio Kansas 620 662-6646
815 N Walnut St Ste 300 Hutchinson (67501) ***(G-3418)***
Radio Shop Inc 316 265-1851
1211 E 1st St N Wichita (67214) ***(G-15409)***
Radio Station Kiks-AM, Iola *Also called Iola Broadcasting Inc* ***(G-3609)***
Radiofrquency Saftey Intl Corp 620 825-4600
543 Main St Kiowa (67070) ***(G-4629)***
Radiologic Prof Svcs PA 785 841-3211
1112 W 6th St Ste 10 Lawrence (66044) ***(G-5086)***
Radiological Wichita Group PA (PA) 316 685-1367
551 N Hillside St Ste 320 Wichita (67214) ***(G-15410)***
Radiological Wichita Group PA 316 681-1827
9300 E 29th St N Ste 202 Wichita (67226) ***(G-15411)***
Radiologix, Topeka *Also called Radiology Nuclear Medicine LLC* ***(G-12997)***
Radiology Department, Kansas City *Also called University of Kansas Med Ctr* ***(G-4509)***
Radiology Nuclear Medicine LLC (PA) 785 234-3454
2200 Sw 10th Ave Topeka (66604) ***(G-12997)***
Radish Patch Catering, Ottawa *Also called Mid-America Nutrition Program* ***(G-8291)***
Radke Implement Inc (PA) 620 935-4310
3099 182nd St Russell (67665) ***(G-10286)***
Raeanns Fancy Footwork 316 788-4499
949 N K 15 Hwy Derby (67037) ***(G-1267)***
Ragland Specialty Printing 785 542-3058
1499 E 2300 Rd Eudora (66025) ***(G-1879)***
Ragland Specialty Prtg & Mfg, Eudora *Also called Ragland Specialty Printing* ***(G-1879)***
Railamerica Inc 785 543-6527
38 Railroad Ave Phillipsburg (67661) ***(G-9796)***
Railcrew Xpress LLC 913 928-5000
9867 Widmer Rd Lenexa (66215) ***(G-6089)***
Railroad Group 913 375-1157
2131 S 74th St Kansas City (66106) ***(G-4359)***
Railserve Inc 316 321-3816
304 E 12th Ave El Dorado (67042) ***(G-1595)***
Railway Construction 620 663-9233
1816 Tracy Ln Hutchinson (67501) ***(G-3419)***
Rain Pro Irrigation, Wichita *Also called Stans Sprinkler Service Inc* ***(G-15654)***
Rainbo Bread, Garden City *Also called Bimbo Bakeries Usa Inc* ***(G-2111)***
Rainbow Car Wash Inc 913 432-1116
4604 Rainbow Blvd Kansas City (66103) ***(G-4360)***
Rainbow Communications LLC 785 548-7511
608 Main St Everest (66424) ***(G-1901)***
Rainbow Organic Farms Co 620 939-4933
1976 55th St Bronson (66716) ***(G-587)***
Rainbow Telecom Assn Inc 785 548-7511
608 Main St Everest (66424) ***(G-1902)***
Rainbow Village Management 913 677-3060
501 Southwest Blvd Kansas City (66103) ***(G-4361)***
Rainbows United Inc 316 684-7060
2901a W Taft St Wichita (67213) ***(G-15412)***
Raintree Inc 913 262-7013
10700 State Line Rd Shawnee Mission (66211) ***(G-11776)***
Rakies Oil LLC 620 442-2210
302 N Summit St Arkansas City (67005) ***(G-171)***
Ral Contractors 913 888-8128
8305 Rosehill Rd Shawnee Mission (66215) ***(G-11777)***
Ralph Bharati MD PA 316 686-7884
8911 E Orme St Ste A Wichita (67207) ***(G-15413)***
Ralph S Passman & Associates 913 642-5432
12218 Ash St Overland Park (66209) ***(G-9221)***
Ram Metal Products Inc 913 422-0099
6 S 59th Ln Leawood (66206) ***(G-5532)***
Rama Operating Co Inc 620 234-6034
101 S Main St Stafford (67578) ***(G-12108)***
Ramada Conference Center Salin 785 823-1739
1616 W Crawford St Salina (67401) ***(G-10650)***
Ramada Inn, Wichita *Also called Wichita Hsptlity Holdings LLC* ***(G-16006)***
Ramada Inn, Topeka *Also called Jefferson St Ht Partners LLC* ***(G-12742)***
Ramada Inn, Overland Park *Also called 7240 Shawnee Mission Hospitali* ***(G-8331)***
Ramada Inn Downtown Hotel Conv, Topeka *Also called Executive Mnor Leavenworth Inc* ***(G-12586)***
Ramboll Environ US Corporation 816 891-8228
7500 College Blvd Ste 920 Overland Park (66210) ***(G-9222)***
Ramchandani Medical Clinic, Ulysses *Also called Gerstberger Medical Clinic* ***(G-13299)***
Ramco Building Maintenance, Wichita *Also called Tee Time Investments Inc* ***(G-15727)***
Ramon E Guardiola 620 355-4266
1007 Kendall Ave Lakin (67860) ***(G-4658)***
Ramsey Oil, Hutchinson *Also called Crossfaith Ventures Lc* ***(G-3251)***
Ranch Mart Inc 913 649-0123
3705 W 95th St Overland Park (66206) ***(G-9223)***
Ranch West Bowling Center, Kansas City *Also called B & E Inc* ***(G-3833)***
Ranch-Aid Inc 620 583-5585
304 E 9th St Eureka (67045) ***(G-1898)***
Rand Graphics Inc 316 942-1125
2820 S Hoover Rd Wichita (67215) ***(G-15414)***
Randal J Steiner 785 539-4155
5281 Tuttle Creek Blvd Manhattan (66502) ***(G-6786)***
Randall Farmers Coop Un Inc (PA) 785 739-2312
101 Walnut St Randall (66963) ***(G-10190)***
Randall G Ford LLC 316 945-1500
534 N Ridge Rd Ste B Wichita (67212) ***(G-15415)***
Randel Solutions LLC 703 459-7672
7300 W 110th St Ste 700 Overland Park (66210) ***(G-9224)***
Randolf Carter Trucking, Louisburg *Also called Randolph Carter Entps Inc* ***(G-6464)***
Randolph Carter Entps Inc 913 837-3955
5 S Peoria St Ste 213 Louisburg (66053) ***(G-6464)***
Randstad Technologies LLC 913 696-0808
9200 Indian Creek Pkwy # 670 Overland Park (66210) ***(G-9225)***
Randy Johnson 316 775-6786
10426 Sw Eagle Rd Augusta (67010) ***(G-341)***
Randy Schwindt 785 391-2277
1 S Hwy 4 Utica (67584) ***(G-13335)***
Rane Management 620 663-3341
21007 S Whiteside Rd Pretty Prairie (67570) ***(G-10169)***
Range 54 LLC 316 440-2854
5725 E Kellogg Dr Wichita (67218) ***(G-15416)***

ALPHABETIC

Rangeland Cooperatives Inc (PA).....785 543-2114
250 W F St Phillipsburg (67661) *(G-9797)*
Ranginenі, Raj MD, Atchison *Also called Saint Joseph Oncology Inc (G-260)*
Ranieri Camera & Video Inc.....785 336-3719
413 Main St Seneca (66538) *(G-10879)*
Ranieri Prof One Hr Photo, Seneca *Also called Ranieri Camera & Video Inc (G-10879)*
RANSOM MEMORIAL HOME HEALTH AG, Ottawa *Also called Ransom Memorial Hospital Chari (G-8309)*
Ransom Memorial Hospital Chari.....785 229-8200
901 S Main St Ottawa (66067) *(G-8308)*
Ransom Memorial Hospital Chari (PA).....785 229-8200
1301 S Main St Ottawa (66067) *(G-8309)*
Rapco Inc.....785 524-4232
365 N Highway 14 Lincoln (67455) *(G-6386)*
Rapid Processing Solutions Inc.....316 265-2001
1367 S Anna St Wichita (67209) *(G-15417)*
Rapid Rubble Removal.....785 862-8875
2730 Sw 57th St Ste W1 Topeka (66609) *(G-12998)*
Raptor Manufacturing Lc.....316 201-1772
2252 S Hoover Rd Wichita (67209) *(G-15418)*
Rare Moon Media.....913 951-8360
4551 W 107th St Ste 250 Overland Park (66207) *(G-9226)*
Ratzlaff Craig D Ratzlaff DDS.....316 722-7100
7570 W 21st St N 1020a Wichita (67205) *(G-15419)*
Rau Construction Company.....913 642-6000
9101 W 110th St Ste 150 Overland Park (66210) *(G-9227)*
Raudin McCormick Inc.....913 928-5000
15729 College Blvd Lenexa (66219) *(G-6090)*
Raven Lining Systems Inc.....918 615-0020
686 S Adams St Kansas City (66105) *(G-4362)*
Ravenscraft Implement Inc.....316 799-2141
223 S Main St Whitewater (67154) *(G-13572)*
Ravenwood Hunting Preserve Inc.....785 256-6444
10147 Sw 61st St Topeka (66610) *(G-12999)*
Ravenwood Lodge, Topeka *Also called Ravenwood Hunting Preserve Inc (G-12999)*
Ravin Printing LLC.....620 431-5830
1526 S Santa Fe Ave Chanute (66720) *(G-759)*
Rawhide Portable Corral Inc.....785 263-3436
900 N Washington St Abilene (67410) *(G-50)*
Rawhide Well Service LLC.....620 624-2902
1661 W 7th St Liberal (67901) *(G-6358)*
RAWLINS BANCSHARES, Atwood *Also called Farmers Bank & Trust (G-285)*
Rawlins Cnty Dntl Clinic Fund.....785 626-8290
515 State St Atwood (67730) *(G-288)*
Rawlins County Health Center.....785 626-3211
707 Grant St Atwood (67730) *(G-289)*
Rawlins County Sq Deal Pubg.....785 626-3600
114 S 4th St Atwood (67730) *(G-290)*
Ray A Cheely Chartered.....620 793-8436
809 S Patton Rd Great Bend (67530) *(G-2629)*
Ray Anderson Co Inc (PA).....785 233-7454
2322 Sw 6th Ave Topeka (66606) *(G-13000)*
Ray Bechard Inc.....785 864-5077
275 Parrott Athletic Ctr Lawrence (66045) *(G-5087)*
Ray Hodge & Associates LLC.....316 269-1414
8558 W 21st St N Ste 300 Wichita (67205) *(G-15420)*
Ray Lindsey Co.....913 339-6666
17221 Bel Ray Pl Olathe (66062) *(G-8019)*
Ray Omo Inc.....620 227-3101
19204 W 98th Ter Lenexa (66220) *(G-6091)*
Ray Products Inc.....620 421-1510
1212 Corporate Dr Parsons (67357) *(G-9728)*
Ray Shepherd Motors Inc.....620 644-2625
1819 S Main St Fort Scott (66701) *(G-2001)*
Rayers Bearden Stained GL Sup.....316 942-2929
6205 W Kellogg Dr Wichita (67209) *(G-15421)*
Rayes Inc (PA).....785 726-4885
204 W 2nd St Ellis (67637) *(G-1651)*
Rayes Inc.....785 726-4885
500 Commerce Pkwy Hays (67601) *(G-2897)*
Raymarr Inc.....913 648-3480
11615 W 108th Ct Shawnee Mission (66210) *(G-11778)*
Raymire Inc.....620 275-4061
1612 E Laurel St Garden City (67846) *(G-2263)*
Raymond Baugher.....620 421-1253
20100 Kiowa Rd Parsons (67357) *(G-9729)*
Raymond Development, Wichita *Also called Raymond Oil Company Inc (G-15422)*
Raymond James, Hays *Also called David M King & Associates (G-2782)*
Raymond James Fincl Svcs Inc.....785 383-1893
711 Wakarusa Dr Lawrence (66049) *(G-5088)*
Raymond James Fincl Svcs Inc.....620 442-1198
118 W Chestnut Ave Arkansas City (67005) *(G-172)*
Raymond James Fincl Svcs Inc.....785 537-0366
1011 Poyntz Ave Manhattan (66502) *(G-6787)*
Raymond Oil Company Inc (PA).....316 267-4214
155 N Market St Ste 800 Wichita (67202) *(G-15422)*
Raynor Gar Door Co Inc Kans Cy.....913 422-0441
8235 Mccoy St Shawnee Mission (66227) *(G-11779)*
Rays Electric Inc.....316 838-8231
1524 W 29th St N Wichita (67204) *(G-15423)*
Rba Associates Inc.....816 444-4270
6299 Nall Ave Ste 300 Mission (66202) *(G-7136)*
Rbc Capital Markets LLC.....913 451-3500
4001 W 114th St Ste 200 Leawood (66211) *(G-5533)*
Rbc Medical Innovations, Shawnee Mission *Also called Revolutionary Bus Concepts Inc (G-11793)*
RC Geven Farms LLC.....620 372-2021
12701 Sw Counrty Rd 32 Syracuse (67878) *(G-12231)*
RC Sports Inc (PA).....913 894-5177
17501 W 98th St Spc 1851 Lenexa (66219) *(G-6092)*
Rcat, Hutchinson *Also called Reno County Abstract & Title (G-3423)*
Rcb Bank.....620 860-7797
1330 E 17th Ave Hutchinson (67501) *(G-3420)*
Rcb Bank Service Inc.....620 442-4040
601 N Summit St Arkansas City (67005) *(G-173)*
Rci, Lenexa *Also called Research Concepts Inc (G-6106)*
Rci, Horton *Also called Regulatory Consultants Inc (G-3133)*
RD Henry & Company LLC.....316 529-3431
3738 S Norman St Wichita (67215) *(G-15424)*
Rd Mann, Kansas City *Also called Carpet Factory Outlet Inc (G-3892)*
Rd Thomann Contracting.....913 268-5580
12810 W 70th St Shawnee Mission (66216) *(G-11780)*
Rd2rx LLC.....816 754-8047
16825 W 116th St Lenexa (66219) *(G-6093)*
Rdcs Inc.....913 238-5377
14304 W 99th St Lenexa (66215) *(G-6094)*
Rdr Excavating Inc.....785 582-4645
2222 Nw Huxman Rd Topeka (66618) *(G-13001)*
RE Max Professionals L L C.....785 843-9393
545 Columbia Dr Lawrence (66049) *(G-5089)*
RE Pedrotti Company Inc (PA).....913 677-7754
5855 Beverly Ave Ste A Shawnee Mission (66202) *(G-11781)*
Re/Max, Overland Park *Also called David W Head (G-8642)*
Re/Max, Topeka *Also called Capstan AG Systems Inc (G-12442)*
Re/Max, Wichita *Also called Preferred Land Company Inc (G-15326)*
Re/Max, Wichita *Also called P F S Group Limited (G-15251)*
Re/Max, Lawrence *Also called RE Max Professionals L L C (G-5089)*
Re/Max Excel.....785 856-8484
1420 Wakarusa Dr Ste 203 Lawrence (66049) *(G-5090)*
Re/Max Premier, Wichita *Also called Premier Realty LLC (G-15334)*
Real Estate Corporation Inc.....913 642-5134
8014 State Line Rd # 210 Prairie Village (66208) *(G-10062)*
Real Estate Ctr Indpndence LLC.....620 331-7550
533 N Penn Ave Independence (67301) *(G-3550)*
Real Media LLC.....913 894-8989
9101 Barton St Overland Park (66214) *(G-9228)*
Reality Executives Center.....316 686-4111
8100 E 22nd St N 2100-4 Wichita (67226) *(G-15425)*
Realm Brands LLC.....316 821-9700
3629 N Hydraulic St Wichita (67219) *(G-15426)*
Realty Associates Inc.....785 827-0331
2103 S Ohio St Salina (67401) *(G-10651)*
Realty Executives, El Dorado *Also called Trail Wood Company Inc (G-1610)*
Realty Professionals LLC.....785 271-8400
2900 Sw Wanamaker Dr # 200 Topeka (66614) *(G-13002)*
Realty World Alliance LLC.....316 688-0077
6100 E Central Ave # 215 Wichita (67208) *(G-15427)*
Reardon Pallet Company Inc.....816 221-3300
100 Funston Rd Kansas City (66115) *(G-4363)*
Rebel Staffing LLC.....888 372-3302
205 F St Ste 230 Phillipsburg (67661) *(G-9798)*
Rebound Physical Therapy.....785 271-5533
5220 Sw 17th St Ste 130 Topeka (66604) *(G-13003)*
Rebuild Homes, Overland Park *Also called Redmon Housing LLC (G-9229)*
Rebuilding Together Shawnee/Jo.....913 558-5079
5802 Lackman Rd Shawnee (66217) *(G-11015)*
Recall S D S Lenexa Fcilty 23, Shawnee Mission *Also called Recall Secure Destruction Serv (G-11782)*
Recall Secure Destruction Serv.....913 310-0811
8059 Flint St Shawnee Mission (66214) *(G-11782)*
Reconserve of Kansas Inc.....913 621-5619
41 N James St Kansas City (66118) *(G-4364)*
Record Center of Wichita, Hutchinson *Also called Underground Vaults & Stor Inc (G-3472)*
Record Center of Wichita, Wichita *Also called Underground Vaults & Stor Inc (G-15831)*
Record Newspaper, Kansas City *Also called Record Publications (G-4365)*
Record Publications.....913 362-1988
3414 Strong Ave Kansas City (66106) *(G-4365)*
Recovery For All Foundation.....316 322-7057
226 W Central Ave El Dorado (67042) *(G-1596)*
Recovery Unlimited Inc.....316 941-9948
3835 W Douglas Ave Wichita (67213) *(G-15428)*
Recreation Commission.....620 223-0386
735 Scott Ave Fort Scott (66701) *(G-2002)*
Recreational Service Ksu, Manhattan *Also called Kansas State University (G-6685)*

Recreational Vehicle Products 316 832-3400
3050 N Saint Francis St Wichita (67219) *(G-15429)*
Recycling Enterprises Inc (PA) 316 536-2262
1200 Main St Towanda (67144) *(G-13266)*
Red Coach Inn 316 321-6900
2525 W Central Ave El Dorado (67042) *(G-1597)*
Red Hills Resources Inc 620 669-9996
1304 W 24th Ave Hutchinson (67502) *(G-3421)*
Red Line Inc 620 343-1000
2805 Bel Aire Dr Emporia (66801) *(G-1815)*
Red River Commodities Inc 785 462-3911
1320 E College Dr Colby (67701) *(G-1035)*
Red Rock Auto Center Inc 620 663-9822
200 N Main St South Hutchinson (67505) *(G-12065)*
Red Roof Wichita, Wichita *Also called Vchp Wichita LLC (G-15872)*
Red Tail Mfg, Olathe *Also called Endless Ideas Inc (G-7681)*
Red Wheel Fundraising, Shawnee *Also called Chavey Ventures Inc (G-10926)*
Red Wing Bus Advantage Account, Overland Park *Also called Multi Svc Tech Solutions Inc (G-9063)*
Redbud E&P Inc 620 331-7870
211 W Myrtle St Independence (67301) *(G-3551)*
Redbud Pediatrics LLC 316 201-1202
8725 E 32nd St N Wichita (67226) *(G-15430)*
Redbud Village 785 425-6312
115 N Walnut St Stockton (67669) *(G-12184)*
Reddi Services Inc (PA) 913 287-5005
4011 Bonner Industrial Dr Shawnee Mission (66226) *(G-11783)*
Reddy Electric Systems Inc 913 764-0840
15385 S Us 169 Hwy Ste 4 Olathe (66062) *(G-8020)*
Redemption Plus LLC 913 563-4331
9829 Commerce Pkwy Lenexa (66219) *(G-6095)*
Redguard LLC (PA) 316 554-9000
4340 S West St Wichita (67217) *(G-15431)*
Redi Systems Inc 785 587-9100
1601 Tuttle Creek Blvd Manhattan (66502) *(G-6788)*
Redivus Health 816 582-5428
22201 W Innovation Dr Olathe (66061) *(G-8021)*
Redmon Michael Law Office 913 342-5917
831 Armstrong Ave Kansas City (66101) *(G-4366)*
Redmon Housing LLC 913 432-4945
10200 W 75th St Ste 100 Overland Park (66204) *(G-9229)*
Redneck Inc 316 263-6090
10606 E 26th Cir N Wichita (67226) *(G-15432)*
Redneck Street Rods, Atchison *Also called Keimig Body Shop (G-239)*
Redneck Trailer Supplies, Wichita *Also called Redneck Inc (G-15432)*
Redstone Logistics LLC (PA) 913 998-7905
8500 W 110th St Ste 260 Overland Park (66210) *(G-9230)*
Redtreestudios.com, Prairie Village *Also called DCI Studios (G-10026)*
Redwood Group LLC (HQ) 816 979-1786
5920 Nall Ave Ste 400 Mission (66202) *(G-7137)*
Reeble Inc (PA) 620 342-0404
1020 Merchant St Emporia (66801) *(G-1816)*
Reece & Nichols Alliance Inc 913 262-7755
7455 Mission Rd Prairie Village (66208) *(G-10063)*
Reece & Nichols Alliance Inc 913 451-4415
11100 Antioch Rd Shawnee Mission (66210) *(G-11784)*
Reece & Nichols Alliance Inc (HQ) 913 782-8822
2140 E Santa Fe St Olathe (66062) *(G-8022)*
Reece & Nichols Premier Realty, Basehor *Also called Reece & Nichols Realtors Inc (G-387)*
Reece & Nichols Realtors Inc 913 851-8082
15133 Rosewood Dr Leawood (66224) *(G-5534)*
Reece & Nichols Realtors Inc 913 620-3419
8410 W 128th St Overland Park (66213) *(G-9231)*
Reece & Nichols Realtors Inc 913 351-5600
15510 State Ave Ste 7 Basehor (66007) *(G-387)*
Reece & Nichols Realtors Inc 913 247-3064
104 E Cedar St Spring Hill (66083) *(G-12097)*
Reece & Nichols Realtors Inc (HQ) 913 491-1001
11601 Granada St Leawood (66211) *(G-5535)*
Reece & Nichols Realtors Inc 913 307-4000
7070 Renner Rd Shawnee (66217) *(G-11016)*
Reece & Nichols Realtors Inc 913 339-6800
11901 W 119th St Shawnee Mission (66213) *(G-11785)*
Reece and Nchls The Koehlr BRT, Leawood *Also called Koehler Bortnick Team LLC (G-5452)*
Reece and Nichols Realtors Inc 913 945-3704
11601 Granada St Fl 2 Leawood (66211) *(G-5536)*
Reed Company LLC 785 456-7333
4455 N Highway 99 Wamego (66547) *(G-13439)*
Reed Dillon & Associates 785 832-0083
1213 E 24th St Lawrence (66046) *(G-5091)*
Reed Mineral Division 913 757-4561
18730 E 2150 Rd La Cygne (66040) *(G-4642)*
Reedy Ford, Arkansas City *Also called Reedy Ford Inc (G-174)*
Reedy Ford Inc 620 442-4800
3319 N Summit St Arkansas City (67005) *(G-174)*
Rees Contract Service Inc (PA) 913 888-0590
10111 W 105th St Shawnee Mission (66212) *(G-11786)*
Rees Msilionis Turley Arch LLC 816 842-1292
2000 Shawnee Mission Pkwy Shawnee Mission (66205) *(G-11787)*
Reese & Novelly Cpa's PA, Wamego *Also called Reese & Novelly PA (G-13440)*
Reese & Novelly PA (PA) 785 456-2000
514 Lincoln Ave Wamego (66547) *(G-13440)*
Reese Group Inc 913 383-8260
6200 Mastin St Merriam (66203) *(G-7102)*
Reeve Agri-Energy Inc 620 275-7541
5665 S Us Old Hwy 83 Garden City (67846) *(G-2264)*
Reeve Cattle Co Inc 620 275-0234
7 Mi South Of Town Garden City (67846) *(G-2265)*
Reflection Ridge Golf Corp 316 721-0500
2300 N Tyler Rd Wichita (67205) *(G-15433)*
Reflection Ridge Maintenance 316 721-9483
7414 W 21st St N Wichita (67205) *(G-15434)*
Refresh Medical Spa LLC 913 681-6200
13453 Switzer Rd Overland Park (66213) *(G-9232)*
Refrigerated Express Delivery, Emporia *Also called Red Line Inc (G-1815)*
Refrigeration Technologies 316 542-0397
38121 W 55th St S Cheney (67025) *(G-795)*
Regal Audio Video 785 628-2700
124 W 9th St Hays (67601) *(G-2898)*
Regal Cinemas Inc 925 757-0466
11500 Ash St Leawood (66211) *(G-5537)*
Regal Distributing Co (PA) 913 894-8787
17201 W 113th St Lenexa (66219) *(G-6096)*
Regal Estate 305 751-4257
1000 Mulberry St Independence (67301) *(G-3552)*
Regal Inn, Coffeyville *Also called Krina Corporation (G-953)*
Regan Marketing Inc (PA) 816 531-5111
10934 Strang Line Rd Lenexa (66215) *(G-6097)*
Regarding Kitchens Inc 913 642-6184
1736 E Harold St Olathe (66061) *(G-8023)*
Regasa Aerospace Inc 316 425-0079
4327 W May St Wichita (67209) *(G-15435)*
Regency Gas Services LLC 620 355-7905
1473 Us Highway 50 Lakin (67860) *(G-4659)*
Regency Midwest Ventures Limit 785 273-8888
924 Sw Henderson Rd Topeka (66615) *(G-13004)*
Regent Financial Group Inc 316 462-1341
10209 W Central Ave Ste 1 Wichita (67212) *(G-15436)*
Regent Pk Rhblttion Healthcare, Wichita *Also called Legend Senior Living LLC (G-14953)*
Regents Flooring, Lenexa *Also called Db Flooring LLC (G-5806)*
Regents Flooring Co Inc 913 663-9922
10035 Lakeview Ave Lenexa (66219) *(G-6098)*
Regents Walk, Shawnee Mission *Also called J A Peterson Enterprises Inc (G-11472)*
Reger Rental Sales & Service, Hutchinson *Also called Perrys Inc (G-3404)*
Regier Carr & Monroe LLP CPA (PA) 316 264-2335
300 W Douglas Ave Ste 900 Wichita (67202) *(G-15437)*
Regional Insurance Service Co 316 686-6553
2400 N Woodlawn Blvd # 110 Wichita (67220) *(G-15438)*
Regional Legal Counsel, Topeka *Also called Kansas Dept For Chldren Fmlies (G-12771)*
Regional Media Corporation Inc 316 320-1120
216 S Vine St El Dorado (67042) *(G-1598)*
Regional Prvntion Ctr Wyndotte 913 288-7685
7250 State Ave Ste 33-31 Kansas City (66112) *(G-4367)*
Regis Corporation 316 685-5333
7700 E Kellogg Dr Ste L02 Wichita (67207) *(G-15439)*
Regis Corporation 785 273-2992
1490 E Wanamaker Rd Topeka (66604) *(G-13005)*
Regis Corporation 785 628-2111
2938 Vine St Hays (67601) *(G-2899)*
Regis Salon, Wichita *Also called Regis Corporation (G-15439)*
Regis Salon, Hays *Also called Regis Corporation (G-2899)*
Regis Salon Corp 785 273-2992
1801 Sw Wanamaker Rd Topeka (66604) *(G-13006)*
Registered Graphics Inc 913 681-4907
8070 W 172nd Ter Stilwell (66085) *(G-12172)*
Regnier Properties, Overland Park *Also called Vic Regnier Builders Inc (G-9463)*
Regulatory Consultants Inc 785 486-2882
140 W 8th St Horton (66439) *(G-3133)*
Rehabilitation Services, Topeka *Also called Stormont-Vail Healthcare Inc (G-13110)*
Rehrig Pacific Company 913 585-1175
8875 Commerce Dr De Soto (66018) *(G-1211)*
Rehrig Penn Logistics Inc 620 624-5171
1620 W Pancake Blvd Liberal (67901) *(G-6359)*
Reib Inc 620 662-0583
201 E 2nd Ave Ste A Hutchinson (67501) *(G-3422)*
Reid Plumbing Heating & AC Inc 785 537-2869
8964 Green Valley Dr Manhattan (66502) *(G-6789)*
Reifenhauser Incorporated 316 260-2122
12260 W 53rd St N Maize (67101) *(G-6518)*
Reifschneider Eye Center PC 913 682-2900
1001 6th Ave Ste 100 Leavenworth (66048) *(G-5283)*
Reilly Company LLC 913 682-1234
608 Delaware St Leavenworth (66048) *(G-5284)*
Reimer, Paul E, Emporia *Also called Flintells Eyecare (G-1760)*
Reimers Furniture Mfg Inc 913 727-5100
1213 136th St Lansing (66043) *(G-4691)*

ALPHABETIC

Reinhardt Services Inc.....785 483-2556
14th E Laray & S 281 Hwy Russell (67665) ***(G-10287)***
Reinke Manufacturing Co Inc.....785 527-8024
1207 H St Belleville (66935) ***(G-463)***
Reintjes & Hiter Co Inc.....913 371-1872
101 Sunshine Rd Kansas City (66115) ***(G-4368)***
Reit Management & Research.....913 492-4375
15737 College Blvd Lenexa (66219) ***(G-6099)***
Rejuvene Day Spa, Lawrence *Also called Herbs & More Inc* ***(G-4895)***
Rekat Recreation Inc.....785 272-1881
4200 Sw Huntoon St Ste A Topeka (66604) ***(G-13007)***
Rekat Recreation Inc (PA).....785 272-1881
4200 Sw Huntoon St Ste A Topeka (66604) ***(G-13008)***
Relation Insurance Services.....800 955-1991
9225 Indian Creek Pkwy Overland Park (66210) ***(G-9233)***
Relation Insurance Services.....800 955-1991
9225 Indian Creek Pkwy # 700 Overland Park (66210) ***(G-9234)***
Relax Investments Inc.....785 838-4242
740 Iowa St Lawrence (66044) ***(G-5092)***
Relevium Labs Inc.....614 568-7000
500 Park St Dodge City (67801) ***(G-1423)***
Reliable Caps LLC.....913 764-2277
1001 W Old Highway 56 Olathe (66061) ***(G-8024)***
Reliable Concrete Products.....913 321-8108
615 Scott Ave Kansas City (66105) ***(G-4369)***
Reliable Construction Svcs Inc (PA).....913 764-7274
13505 S Mur Len Rd Olathe (66062) ***(G-8025)***
Reliable Power Products Group, Winfield *Also called Zeeco Inc* ***(G-16192)***
Reliable Transfer & Storage (PA).....785 776-4887
1600 S 16th St Manhattan (66502) ***(G-6790)***
Reliance Label Solutions Inc.....913 294-1600
205 N Gold St Paola (66071) ***(G-9585)***
Reliance Steel & Aluminum Co.....316 636-4500
3900 Comotara Dr Wichita (67226) ***(G-15440)***
Reliance Steel & Aluminum Co.....316 838-9351
2750 S Rock Rd Wichita (67210) ***(G-15441)***
Rellec Apparel Graphics LLC.....913 707-5249
10618 Summit St Lenexa (66215) ***(G-6100)***
Reload Express Inc (HQ).....620 231-2230
315 W 3rd St Pittsburg (66762) ***(G-9926)***
Remediation Contractors Inc.....316 269-1549
319 N Mathewson Ave Wichita (67214) ***(G-15442)***
Remediation Services Inc.....800 335-1201
2735 S 10th St Independence (67301) ***(G-3553)***
Remel.....913 895-4362
17501 W 98th St Spc 3060 Lenexa (66219) ***(G-6101)***
Remel Inc (HQ).....800 255-6730
12076 Santa Fe Trail Dr Lenexa (66215) ***(G-6102)***
Remington Apts, Wichita *Also called Summer Stone Duplexes* ***(G-15681)***
Renal Care Group Chanute, Chanute *Also called Fms Midwest Dialysis Ctrs LLC* ***(G-728)***
Renal Care Group Wichita East, Wichita *Also called Fms Midwest Dialysis Ctrs LLC* ***(G-14396)***
Renal Care Group Wichita West, Wichita *Also called Fms Midwest Dialysis Ctrs LLC* ***(G-14397)***
Renal Treatment Ctrs - Derby, Derby *Also called Renal Trtmnt Centers-West Inc* ***(G-1268)***
Renal Trtmnt Centers-West Inc.....316 788-2899
250 W Red Powell Dr Derby (67037) ***(G-1268)***
Renal Trtmnt Centers-West Inc.....620 421-1081
1902 S Us Highway 59 B Parsons (67357) ***(G-9730)***
Renal Trtmnt Centers-West Inc.....316 263-9090
909 N Topeka St Wichita (67214) ***(G-15443)***
Renal Trtmnt Centers-West Inc.....316 636-5719
2630 N Webb Rd Ste 100 Wichita (67226) ***(G-15444)***
Renal Trtmnt Centers-West Inc.....620 331-6117
801 W Myrtle St Independence (67301) ***(G-3554)***
Renal Trtmnt Centers-West Inc.....316 684-3200
320 N Hillside St Wichita (67214) ***(G-15445)***
Renal Trtmnt Centers-West Inc.....620 260-9852
2308 E Kansas Ave Garden City (67846) ***(G-2266)***
Renew.....913 768-6606
11695 S Blackbob Rd Ste B Olathe (66062) ***(G-8026)***
Renew Counseling Center, Olathe *Also called Renew* ***(G-8026)***
Renewal By Andersen, Great Bend *Also called Southard Corporation* ***(G-2637)***
Renn & Company Inc (PA).....620 326-2271
209 S Washington Ave Wellington (67152) ***(G-13523)***
Reno County Abstract & Title.....620 662-5455
408 N Main St Hutchinson (67501) ***(G-3423)***
Reno County Ambulance Service.....620 665-2120
1701 E 23rd Ave Hutchinson (67502) ***(G-3424)***
Reno County Cmnty Corrections, Hutchinson *Also called County of Reno* ***(G-3249)***
Reno County Youth Services.....620 694-2500
219 W 2nd Ave Hutchinson (67501) ***(G-3425)***
Reno Fabricating & Sls Co Inc.....620 663-1269
6401 W Morgan Ave Hutchinson (67501) ***(G-3426)***
Rensen House of Lights Inc.....913 888-0888
9212 Marshall Dr Lenexa (66215) ***(G-6103)***
Rent A Center, Wichita *Also called Ctmd LLC* ***(G-14139)***
Rental Station LLC.....620 431-7368
2029 S Santa Fe Ave Chanute (66720) ***(G-760)***
Renzenberger Inc (HQ).....913 631-0450
14325 W 95th St Lenexa (66215) ***(G-6104)***
Rep Profit Management Systems, Overland Park *Also called Rpms LLC* ***(G-9261)***
Repair Shack Inc.....913 732-0514
14021 W 95th St Lenexa (66215) ***(G-6105)***
Repairs Unlimited Inc (PA).....913 262-6937
1940 Merriam Ln Kansas City (66106) ***(G-4370)***
Reporting Services Company.....913 385-2699
8001 Conser St Ste 200 Overland Park (66204) ***(G-9235)***
Reproductive Rsrce Ctr of Grtr.....913 894-2323
12200 W 106th St Ste 120 Shawnee Mission (66215) ***(G-11788)***
Republic Bancshares Inc (PA).....785 483-2300
436 N Main St Russell (67665) ***(G-10288)***
Republic County Ems.....785 527-7149
2405 F St Belleville (66935) ***(G-464)***
Republic County Family.....785 527-2237
2337 G St Ste 100 Belleville (66935) ***(G-465)***
Republic Services Inc.....620 336-3678
4237 Cr 5300 Cherryvale (67335) ***(G-812)***
Republic Services Inc.....620 783-5841
1715 E Front St Galena (66739) ***(G-2082)***
Republican Valley Irrigation, Clay Center *Also called Callaway Electric* ***(G-847)***
RES Care, Kansas City *Also called RES-Care Kansas Inc* ***(G-4372)***
RES-Care Inc.....913 281-1161
132 S 17th St Kansas City (66102) ***(G-4371)***
RES-Care Inc.....620 421-2454
1772 24000 Rd Parsons (67357) ***(G-9731)***
RES-Care Inc.....620 793-8501
2317 Washington St Great Bend (67530) ***(G-2630)***
RES-Care Inc.....620 271-0176
2102 E Spruce St Garden City (67846) ***(G-2267)***
RES-Care Inc.....785 899-2322
1080 Aspen Rd Goodland (67735) ***(G-2482)***
RES-Care Inc.....620 624-5117
418 S Washington Ave Liberal (67901) ***(G-6360)***
RES-Care Inc.....316 283-5170
700 E 14th St Newton (67114) ***(G-7410)***
RES-Care Inc.....620 221-4112
317 N Viking Blvd Winfield (67156) ***(G-16168)***
RES-Care Kansas Inc (HQ).....913 342-9426
5031 Matney Ave Kansas City (66106) ***(G-4372)***
RES-Care Kansas Inc.....785 728-7198
108 Aspen Rd Goodland (67735) ***(G-2483)***
RES-Care Kansas Inc.....620 793-8501
2317 Washington St Great Bend (67530) ***(G-2631)***
Rescare Kansas Wichita.....316 651-2585
5112 E 36th St N Ste 100 Wichita (67220) ***(G-15446)***
Research Concepts Inc.....913 422-0210
9501 Dice Ln Lenexa (66215) ***(G-6106)***
Research Partnership Inc.....316 263-6433
125 N Market St Ste 1810 Wichita (67202) ***(G-15447)***
Resellers Edge LLC.....620 364-3398
615 N 4th St Burlington (66839) ***(G-642)***
Resers Fine Foods Inc.....785 233-6431
3728 Se 6th St Topeka (66607) ***(G-13009)***
Reserve On West 31st St, The, Lawrence *Also called Edr Lawrence Ltd Partnership* ***(G-4846)***
Residence Inn By Marriott, Olathe *Also called Im Olathe LP* ***(G-7786)***
Residence Inn By Marriott LLC.....316 686-7331
411 S Webb Rd Wichita (67207) ***(G-15448)***
Residence Inn Olathe, Olathe *Also called Olathe Hotels LLC* ***(G-7939)***
Residence Inn Overland Park, Overland Park *Also called Apple Eght Svcs Ovrland Pk Inc* ***(G-8390)***
Residential Appraisal Services.....913 492-0226
13830 Santa Fe Trail Dr # 100 Shawnee Mission (66215) ***(G-11789)***
Residential Services Inc.....316 832-9058
1525 W 29th St N Wichita (67204) ***(G-15449)***
Residential Treatment Service.....620 421-1155
1407 Broadway Ave Parsons (67357) ***(G-9732)***
Residentialsoultion LLC.....913 268-2967
12684 Shwnee Mission Pkwy Shawnee (66216) ***(G-11017)***
Residnce Inn Kans Cy At Lgends, Kansas City *Also called Rl Heritage Inn of Kc LLC* ***(G-4377)***
Resnick Associates.....913 681-5454
8500 W 110th St Shawnee Mission (66210) ***(G-11790)***
Resolution Services LLC.....785 843-1638
900 Msschsetts St Ste 380 Lawrence (66044) ***(G-5093)***
Resonate Relationship Clinic.....913 647-8092
7381 W 133rd St Overland Park (66213) ***(G-9236)***
Resource Center For Ind Living.....785 267-1717
1507 Sw 21st St Ste 203 Topeka (66604) ***(G-13010)***
Resource Center For Ind Living (PA).....785 528-3105
1137 Laing St Osage City (66523) ***(G-8187)***
Resource Management Co Inc.....785 398-2240
25656 160 Rd Brownell (67521) ***(G-589)***
Resource Residential, Lenexa *Also called Oak Park Village* ***(G-6032)***
Resource Service Solutions LLC.....913 338-5050
16309 W 108th Cir Lenexa (66219) ***(G-6107)***

Resources Inv Advisors Inc....913 338-5300
4860 College Blvd Ste 100 Leawood (66211) *(G-5538)*
Resq Systems LLC....913 390-1030
15346 S Keeler St Olathe (66062) *(G-8027)*
Rest Easy LLC....913 684-4091
214 Grant Ave Bldg 695 Fort Leavenworth (66027) *(G-1941)*
Rest Haven Mortuary, Wichita *Also called Resthaven Gardens of Memory (G-15450)*
Restaurant Purchasing Svcs LLC....800 548-2292
12101 W 110th St Ste 300 Overland Park (66210) *(G-9237)*
Restaurantlink, Overland Park *Also called Restaurant Purchasing Svcs LLC (G-9237)*
Resthaven Gardens of Memory....316 722-2100
11800 W Kellogg St Wichita (67209) *(G-15450)*
Resthaven Mortuary Inc....316 722-2100
11800 W Kellogg St Wichita (67209) *(G-15451)*
Restonic & Imperial Sleep Pdts, Haven *Also called Imperial Sleep Products Inc (G-2732)*
Restorative Justice Authority....620 235-7118
665 S Highway 69 Pittsburg (66762) *(G-9927)*
Restore It Systems LLC (PA)....620 331-3997
1817 W Main St Independence (67301) *(G-3555)*
Restortion Wtr Proofing Contrs....913 321-6226
901 Scott Ave Kansas City (66105) *(G-4373)*
Restortion Wtrprfing Cntrs Inc (PA)....316 942-6602
2222 S Hoover Rd Wichita (67209) *(G-15452)*
Restortion Wtrprfing Cntrs Inc....785 478-9538
1416 Sw Auburn Rd Topeka (66615) *(G-13011)*
Results Technology Inc (PA)....913 928-8300
10333 W 84th Ter Overland Park (66214) *(G-9238)*
Resurrection Hospital Physn CL....785 483-3333
222 S Kansas St Ste E Russell (67665) *(G-10289)*
Retail Groc Assn Grter Kans Cy (PA)....913 384-3830
2809 W 47th St Westwood (66205) *(G-13558)*
Retail Services Wis Corp....913 831-6400
10200 W 75th St Ste 115 Shawnee Mission (66204) *(G-11791)*
Retail Services Wis Corp....316 683-3289
4065 N Woodlawn Ct Ste 1 Bel Aire (67220) *(G-439)*
Retel Brokerage Services Inc....678 292-5723
7701 E Kellogg Dr Ste 670 Wichita (67207) *(G-15453)*
Retirement Planning Group Inc....913 498-8898
4811 W 136th St Overland Park (66224) *(G-9239)*
Retreat of Shawnee Apartments....913 624-1326
11128 W 76th Ter Shawnee Mission (66214) *(G-11792)*
Retrochem Inc....913 422-8810
4923 Lakecrest Dr Shawnee (66218) *(G-11018)*
Return Products Management Inc (PA)....913 768-1747
2111 E Crossroads Ln # 201 Olathe (66062) *(G-8028)*
Reuter Organ Co Inc....785 843-2622
1220 Timberedge Rd Lawrence (66049) *(G-5094)*
Revest LLC....316 262-8460
2002 S Hydraulic St Wichita (67211) *(G-15454)*
Revhoney Inc....785 778-2006
1104 Main St Haddam (66944) *(G-2695)*
Revisor of Statutes....785 296-2321
Capitol Federal Bldg Sw10th Topeka (66603) *(G-13012)*
Revocable Trust....785 210-1500
310 Hammons Dr Junction City (66441) *(G-3748)*
Revolutionary Bus Concepts Inc (PA)....913 385-5700
13715 W 109th St Ste 100 Shawnee Mission (66215) *(G-11793)*
Rew Acoustical Products, Kansas City *Also called Rew Materials Inc (G-4374)*
Rew Materials, Lenexa *Also called Kcg Inc (G-5942)*
Rew Materials Inc....913 236-4909
1136 Southwest Blvd Kansas City (66103) *(G-4374)*
Rew Materials Inc....785 233-3651
730 Ne Us Highway 24 Topeka (66608) *(G-13013)*
Rex Materials of Kansas Inc....620 767-5119
1000 N Union St Council Grove (66846) *(G-1176)*
Rex Roto, Council Grove *Also called Rex Materials of Kansas Inc (G-1176)*
Reyes Media Group Inc....913 287-1480
1701 S 55th St Kansas City (66106) *(G-4375)*
Reynold Fork Berkl Suter Rose....620 663-7131
129 W 2nd Ave Ste 200 Hutchinson (67501) *(G-3427)*
Reynolds Construction Inc....913 780-6624
11793 S Clare Rd Olathe (66061) *(G-8029)*
Rezac Sales Barn....785 437-2785
27425 W Drew Rd Saint Marys (66536) *(G-10373)*
Rf Benchmark, Manhattan *Also called Rf Construction Inc (G-6791)*
Rf Construction Inc....785 776-8855
4361 S Dam Rd Manhattan (66502) *(G-6791)*
RFB Construction Co Inc....620 232-2900
565 E 520th Ave Pittsburg (66762) *(G-9928)*
Rfc Logo Inc....913 319-3100
7500 W 110th St Shawnee Mission (66210) *(G-11794)*
Rfm Preferred Seating, Lansing *Also called Reimers Furniture Mfg Inc (G-4691)*
Rfp360, Leawood *Also called Upg Solutions LLC (G-5591)*
RFS Associates LLC....913 871-0456
2107 W 49th Ter Westwood Hills (66205) *(G-13565)*
RGI Publications Inc....913 829-8723
14258 W 131st St Olathe (66062) *(G-8030)*
Rgis LLC....316 685-6233
7777 E Osie St Ste 308 Wichita (67207) *(G-15455)*
Rgs Industries Inc....913 780-9033
15612 S Keeler St Olathe (66062) *(G-8031)*
Rh Montgomery Properties Inc....620 783-1383
1220 E 8th St Galena (66739) *(G-2083)*
Rh Montgomery Properties Inc....913 294-4308
908 N Pearl St Paola (66071) *(G-9586)*
Rh Montgomery Properties Inc....785 445-3732
320 S Lincoln St Russell (67665) *(G-10290)*
Rh Montgomery Properties Inc....620 237-4300
3940 Us Highway 54 Moran (66755) *(G-7164)*
Rh Montgomery Properties Inc....913 837-2916
1200 S Broadway St Louisburg (66053) *(G-6465)*
Rh Montgomery Properties Inc....620 725-3154
613 E Elm St Sedan (67361) *(G-10846)*
Rh Montgomery Properties Inc....785 284-3411
1441 Oregon St Sabetha (66534) *(G-10324)*
Rh Montgomery Properties Inc....785 528-3138
1017 Main St Osage City (66523) *(G-8188)*
Rh Montgomery Properties Inc....785 284-3418
913 Dakota St Sabetha (66534) *(G-10325)*
Rheuark FSI Sales Inc (PA)....913 432-9500
5809 Reeds Rd Shawnee Mission (66202) *(G-11795)*
Rheumatology Cons Chartered....913 661-9990
12330 Metcalf Ave Ste 570 Shawnee Mission (66213) *(G-11796)*
Rhino Builders Inc....913 722-4353
1040 Merriam Ln Kansas City (66103) *(G-4376)*
Rhs Inc....785 742-2949
2021 Iowa St Hiawatha (66434) *(G-3023)*
Rhulen & Morgan Prof Assn....913 782-8300
20805 W 151st St Olathe (66061) *(G-8032)*
Rhum Wee Rockets Pre School....316 776-9330
109 S Main St Rose Hill (67133) *(G-10246)*
Rhw Construction Inc....913 451-1222
6704 W 100 121st St Shawnee Mission (66209) *(G-11797)*
Rhw Hotel Holdings Company LLC (PA)....913 451-1222
6704 W 121st St Shawnee Mission (66209) *(G-11798)*
Rhw Management Inc....785 776-8829
501 E Poyntz Ave Manhattan (66502) *(G-6792)*
Rhw Management Inc (PA)....913 451-1222
6704 W 121st St Shawnee Mission (66209) *(G-11799)*
Rhw Management Inc....913 768-7000
12245 S Strang Line Rd Olathe (66062) *(G-8033)*
Rhw Management Inc....913 631-8800
17250 Midland Dr Shawnee (66217) *(G-11019)*
Rhw Management Inc....913 722-0800
7400 W Frontage Rd Shawnee Mission (66203) *(G-11800)*
Rhw Management Inc....913 397-9455
1501 S Hamilton Cir Olathe (66061) *(G-8034)*
Rhycom Advertising....913 451-9102
10975 Grandview Dr Overland Park (66210) *(G-9240)*
Rhythm Engineering LLC....913 227-0603
11228 Thompson Ave Lenexa (66219) *(G-6108)*
Rl Heritage Inn of Kc LLC....913 788-5650
1875 Village West Pkwy Kansas City (66111) *(G-4377)*
Rice Community Healthcare, Lyons *Also called Hospital District 1 Rice Cnty (G-6484)*
Rice Precision Mfg Inc....785 594-2670
401 E High St Baldwin City (66006) *(G-367)*
Richard A Orchards MD....785 841-2280
1112 W 6th St Ste 214 Lawrence (66044) *(G-5095)*
Richard Allen Cultural Center....913 682-8772
412 Kiowa St Leavenworth (66048) *(G-5285)*
Richard E Crowder DDS....316 684-5184
7015 E Central Ave Uppr Wichita (67206) *(G-15456)*
Richard F Sosinski....785 843-5160
4525 W 6th St Ste 100 Lawrence (66049) *(G-5096)*
Richard Hoffman Trucking, Wichita *Also called Hoffman Inc (G-14622)*
Richard L Pride....785 485-2900
7714 Jenkins Rd Riley (66531) *(G-10207)*
Richard Nachbar Plumbing Inc....913 268-9488
9053 Cottonwood Canyon Pl Lenexa (66219) *(G-6109)*
Richard Winburn....913 492-5180
10351 Mastin St Shawnee Mission (66212) *(G-11801)*
Richeson Anderson Byrd....785 242-1234
216 S Hickory St Ottawa (66067) *(G-8310)*
Richman Helstrom Trucking Inc....785 478-3186
6017 Sw 46th St Topeka (66610) *(G-13014)*
Richmond Electric Inc....316 264-2344
246 S Morningside St Wichita (67218) *(G-15457)*
Richmond Healthcare....785 835-6135
340 E South St Richmond (66080) *(G-10204)*
Richs Roustabout Service Inc....785 798-3323
1020 N Pennsylvania Ness City (67560) *(G-7266)*
Rick R Tague MD MPH....785 228-2277
2840 Sw Urish Rd Topeka (66614) *(G-13015)*
Rick Sauceda Trucking LLC....913 231-8584
3348 W 1200 Ln Centerville (66014) *(G-696)*
Rick Wayland & Associates....316 524-0079
4801 S Cedardale Ave Wichita (67216) *(G-15458)*
Rickerson Pipe Lining LLC....785 448-5401
210 S Catalpa St Garnett (66032) *(G-2386)*

ALPHABETIC

Rickman Machine Co Inc 316 263-0841
922 N Santa Fe St Wichita (67214) ***(G-15459)***
Ricks Appliance Service Inc 316 265-2866
1617 W Harry St Wichita (67213) ***(G-15460)***
Ricks Auto Restoration 620 326-5635
Hwy 81 Rr 1 Rt 1 Wellington (67152) ***(G-13524)***
Ricks Barbr Sp & Natural Hair 913 268-3944
6423 Quivira Rd Shawnee (66216) ***(G-11020)***
Ricks Concrete Sawing Inc 785 862-5400
4739 Se Adams St Topeka (66609) ***(G-13016)***
Ricoh Usa Inc 316 262-7172
8200 E 34th Cir N # 1406 Wichita (67226) ***(G-15461)***
Ricoh Usa Inc 316 558-5488
209 W Main St Ste D Valley Center (67147) ***(G-13351)***
Ricoh Usa Inc 913 890-5100
8050 Marshall Dr Ste 150 Shawnee Mission (66214) ***(G-11802)***
Ricoh Usa Inc 785 272-0248
2655 Sw Wanamaker Rd Topeka (66614) ***(G-13017)***
Riddles Group Inc 620 371-6284
2601 Central Ave Ste 8 Dodge City (67801) ***(G-1424)***
Riden Plumbing, Overland Park *Also called Riden Service Company Inc* ***(G-9241)***
Riden Service Company Inc 913 432-8495
11306 W 89th St Overland Park (66214) ***(G-9241)***
Ridge Auto Center 785 286-1498
4431 Nw Green Hills Rd Topeka (66618) ***(G-13018)***
Ridge Enterprises LLC 620 491-2141
2120 N Koch Industrial St Kingman (67068) ***(G-4613)***
Ridgeview Animal Hospital 913 780-0078
816 N Ridgeview Rd Olathe (66061) ***(G-8035)***
Ridgewood Surgery and End 316 768-4197
4013 N Ridge Rd Ste 100 Wichita (67205) ***(G-15462)***
Ridley Block Operations, Pittsburg *Also called Ridley USA Inc* ***(G-9929)***
Ridley USA Inc 620 231-6700
1057 S Highway 69 Pittsburg (66762) ***(G-9929)***
Ridley USA Inc 785 738-2215
3154 Us Highway 24 Beloit (67420) ***(G-500)***
Riedel Garden Center 785 628-2877
1358 Us Highway 40 Hays (67601) ***(G-2900)***
Riedl First Securities of Kans 316 265-9341
1841 N Rock Road Ct # 400 Wichita (67206) ***(G-15463)***
Rieke Concrete Systems Inc 913 492-0270
9014 Parkhill St Shawnee Mission (66215) ***(G-11803)***
Rieke Grading Inc 913 441-2669
8200 Hedge Lane Ter Shawnee Mission (66227) ***(G-11804)***
Rig 6 Drilling Inc 620 365-6294
Rr 3 Bronson (66716) ***(G-588)***
Rigdon Carpet & Flooring, Kansas City *Also called Rigdon Floor Coverings Inc* ***(G-4378)***
Rigdon Floor Coverings Inc 913 362-9829
3015 Merriam Ln Kansas City (66106) ***(G-4378)***
Rigdon Inc 913 322-9274
13827 Mackey St Overland Park (66223) ***(G-9242)***
Right At Home, Wichita *Also called There Is No Place Like Home* ***(G-15758)***
Right Cooperative Association 620 227-8611
10881 Main St Wright (67882) ***(G-16194)***
Right Golf At Western Hills, Topeka *Also called Western Hills Golf Club Inc* ***(G-13241)***
Right Management Consultants, Shawnee Mission *Also called S T Carter Inc* ***(G-11821)***
Right Management Inc 913 451-1100
7300 W 110th St Ste 800 Shawnee Mission (66210) ***(G-11805)***
Right Stuff Co 913 722-4002
7105 Mission Rd Apt 313 Prairie Village (66208) ***(G-10064)***
Riley Communities LLC 785 717-2210
211 Custer Ave Fort Riley (66442) ***(G-1949)***
Riley County Appraisers, Manhattan *Also called County of Riley* ***(G-6604)***
Riley County Emrgncy Med Svcs, Manhattan *Also called County of Riley* ***(G-6603)***
Riley County Senior Svc Ctr, Manhattan *Also called County of Riley* ***(G-6602)***
Riley Food Services, Fort Riley *Also called Fsig LLC* ***(G-1948)***
Riley Ford Mercury Co 620 356-1206
715 E Oklahoma Ave Ulysses (67880) ***(G-13315)***
Riley Hotel Suites LLC 785 539-2400
300 Colorado St Manhattan (66502) ***(G-6793)***
Riley State Bank of Riley Kans (PA) 785 485-2811
201 S Broadway St Riley (66531) ***(G-10208)***
Rimpull Corporation (PA) 913 782-4000
15600 S Us 169 Hwy Olathe (66062) ***(G-8036)***
Ringneck Ranch Incorporated 785 373-4835
655 Solomon Ln Tipton (67485) ***(G-12249)***
Rings and Cages Inc 816 945-7772
315 Main St Bucyrus (66013) ***(G-607)***
Ringside, Lenexa *Also called Combat Brands LLC* ***(G-5770)***
Riordan Bio-Center Laboratory, Wichita *Also called Riordan Clinic Inc* ***(G-15464)***
Riordan Clinic Inc 316 682-3100
3100 N Hillside Ave Wichita (67219) ***(G-15464)***
Rippels Inc 620 674-1944
6694 Ne Belleview Rd Scammon (66773) ***(G-10797)***
Rise Vision USA Inc 866 770-1150
216 N Mosley St Ste 120 Wichita (67202) ***(G-15465)***
Risenow LLC 913 948-7405
4901 W 136th St Ste 101 Leawood (66224) ***(G-5539)***
Risk Counselors Inc 620 221-1760
808 Millington St Winfield (67156) ***(G-16169)***
Riskanalytics, Overland Park *Also called Inscyt LLC* ***(G-8848)***
Riskanalytics LLC 913 685-6526
6700 Antioch Rd Ste 100 Overland Park (66204) ***(G-9243)***
Rita Oplotnik DO 913 764-0036
801 N Mur Len Rd Olathe (66062) ***(G-8037)***
Ritchey Motors LLC 785 380-0222
1818 Sw Topeka Blvd Topeka (66612) ***(G-13019)***
Ritchie Associates, Wichita *Also called Ritchie Building Co Inc* ***(G-15467)***
Ritchie Associates Inc (PA) 316 684-7300
8100 E 22nd St N # 1000 Wichita (67226) ***(G-15466)***
Ritchie Building Co Inc 316 684-7300
8100 E 22nd St N # 1000 Wichita (67226) ***(G-15467)***
Ritchie Building Company, Wichita *Also called Ritchie Associates Inc* ***(G-15466)***
Ritchie Exploration Inc 316 691-9500
8100 E 22nd St N Bldg 700 Wichita (67226) ***(G-15468)***
Rite-Made Paper Converters LLC 913 621-5000
2600 Bi State Dr Kansas City (66103) ***(G-4379)***
Ritz, Charles O P, Overland Park *Also called Charles Ritz Inc* ***(G-8542)***
River Bend Feed Yard Inc 620 356-4100
17 Mi S & 5 Mi W Ulysses (67880) ***(G-13316)***
River City Brewery Inc 316 263-2739
150 N Mosley St Wichita (67202) ***(G-15469)***
River City Digital, Wichita *Also called Choose Networks Inc* ***(G-14013)***
River City Elevator LLC 316 773-3161
428 S Socora St Wichita (67209) ***(G-15470)***
River City Mechanical Inc 316 682-2672
312 N Indiana Ave Wichita (67214) ***(G-15471)***
River Oak Mechanical 573 338-7203
7800 Nieman Rd Overland Park (66214) ***(G-9244)***
Riverbend Rgnal Hlthcare Fndti 913 367-2131
800 Ravenhill Dr Atchison (66002) ***(G-258)***
Riverchase, Manhattan *Also called American Rsdntial Cmmnties LLC* ***(G-6542)***
Riverfront Community Center 913 651-2132
123 N Esplanade St Leavenworth (66048) ***(G-5286)***
Riverfront Park Campground, Leavenworth *Also called Riverfront Community Center* ***(G-5286)***
Riverpark Plaza Apartments, Wichita *Also called Sentinel Real Estate Corp* ***(G-15562)***
Riverpoint Group Illinois LLC 913 663-2002
8700 Indian Creek Pkwy Overland Park (66210) ***(G-9245)***
Rivers Edge Scrap Management, Kansas City *Also called Scrap Management LLC* ***(G-4408)***
Riverside Industries LLC 316 788-4428
3701 E Haven Dr Derby (67037) ***(G-1269)***
Riverside Recreation Assn 785 332-3401
W Hwy 36 Saint Francis (67756) ***(G-10344)***
Riverside Resources Inc 913 651-6810
700 N 3rd St Leavenworth (66048) ***(G-5287)***
Riverside Transport Inc (PA) 913 233-5500
5400 Kansas Ave Kansas City (66106) ***(G-4380)***
Riverside Village Senior Livin 316 942-7000
777 N Mclean Blvd Ofc Wichita (67203) ***(G-15472)***
Riverview Estates Inc 785 546-2211
202 S Washington St Marquette (67464) ***(G-6877)***
Riverview Manor & Village, Oxford *Also called Riverview Manor Inc* ***(G-9535)***
Riverview Manor Inc 620 455-2214
200 S Ohio Oxford (67119) ***(G-9535)***
RJ Crman Derailment Svcs LLC 913 371-1537
5380 Speaker Rd Kansas City (66106) ***(G-4381)***
Rj's Auction Service, Topeka *Also called Rjs Discount Sales Inc* ***(G-13020)***
Rjs Discount Sales Inc 785 267-7476
3737 Sw South Park Ave Topeka (66609) ***(G-13020)***
RL Duncan Cnstr Co Inc 913 583-1160
9560 Lexington Ave De Soto (66018) ***(G-1212)***
Rmvk Enterprises Inc 913 321-1915
30 Osage Ave Kansas City (66105) ***(G-4382)***
Rnn Enterprises LLC 913 499-1230
15520 Windsor St Overland Park (66224) ***(G-9246)***
Rnw Transit LLC 785 285-0083
2436 168th Rd Sabetha (66534) ***(G-10326)***
Roach Building Co Inc 785 233-9606
1321 Sw 21st St Topeka (66604) ***(G-13021)***
Roach Hardware, Topeka *Also called Roach Building Co Inc* ***(G-13021)***
Road & Bridge, Sedan *Also called County of Chautauqua* ***(G-10841)***
Road and Bridge Department, Coldwater *Also called Comanche County* ***(G-1054)***
Road Builders McHy & Sup Co 913 371-3822
1103 S Mill St Kansas City (66105) ***(G-4383)***
Road Builders Mchy & Sup Co (PA) 913 371-3822
1001 S 7th St Kansas City (66105) ***(G-4384)***
Road Dept, Elkhart *Also called County of Morton* ***(G-1618)***
Roadruner Manufacturing LLC 785 586-2228
1130 County Road R Levant (67743) ***(G-6265)***
Roadsafe Traffic Systems Inc 316 778-2112
1224 W 6th Ave El Dorado (67042) ***(G-1599)***
Roadsafe Traffic Systems Inc 316 322-3070
2504 Enterprise Ave El Dorado (67042) ***(G-1600)***
Roadway Express, Kansas City *Also called Yrc Inc* ***(G-4565)***

Roady Trucking.......785 562-1221
1203 8th Rd Marysville (66508) *(G-6908)*
Roark & Associates PA.......785 842-3431
3504 Westridge Dr Lawrence (66049) *(G-5097)*
Roat Bud Standard Service, Wichita *Also called Bud Roat Inc (G-13906)*
Rob Caroll Sandblasting & Pntg, Arkansas City *Also called Sign Solutions (G-179)*
Rob Carolls Sndblst & Pntg.......620 442-1361
12046 292nd Rd Arkansas City (67005) *(G-175)*
Robbie Flexibles, Lenexa *Also called Robbie Transcontinental Inc (G-6110)*
Robbie Transcontinental Inc.......913 492-3400
10810 Mid America Dr Lenexa (66219) *(G-6110)*
Robert A Kumin PC.......913 432-1826
6901 Shawnee Mission Pkwy # 250 Shawnee Mission (66202) *(G-11806)*
Robert Brogden Auto Plaza, Olathe *Also called Robert Brogden Buick Gmc Inc (G-8038)*
Robert Brogden Buick Gmc Inc.......913 782-1500
1500 E Santa Fe St Olathe (66061) *(G-8038)*
Robert Denton.......316 691-7046
2019 E 2nd St N Wichita (67214) *(G-15473)*
Robert E Miller Insurance Agcy (PA).......816 333-3000
6363 College Blvd Ste 400 Leawood (66211) *(G-5540)*
Robert G Smith DDS Chartered.......913 649-5600
3700 W 83rd St Ste 103 Shawnee Mission (66208) *(G-11807)*
Robert Gigstad.......785 448-6923
27718 Nw Indiana Rd Garnett (66032) *(G-2387)*
Robert Half International Inc.......913 451-7600
7400 College Blvd Ste 200 Overland Park (66210) *(G-9247)*
Robert Half International Inc.......816 421-6623
10851 Mastin St Overland Park (66210) *(G-9248)*
Robert Half International Inc.......913 339-9849
7400 College Blvd Ste 200 Shawnee Mission (66210) *(G-11808)*
Robert Half International Inc.......913 451-1014
7400 College Blvd Ste 200 Overland Park (66210) *(G-9249)*
Robert J Dole V A Medical Ctr, Wichita *Also called Veterans Health Administration (G-15878)*
Robert J Hamilton Inc.......913 888-4262
7899 Frontage Rd Overland Park (66204) *(G-9250)*
Robert Nelson Od, Wichita *Also called Wichita Fmly Vision Clinic PA (G-16002)*
Robert Smith Dental Clinic, Shawnee Mission *Also called Robert G Smith DDS Chartered (G-11807)*
Robert Vanlerberg Foundations.......913 441-6823
24630 W 79th St Shawnee Mission (66227) *(G-11809)*
Robert Wilson Co Inc.......913 642-1500
10530 Marty St Overland Park (66212) *(G-9251)*
Roberts Blue Barnett, Emporia *Also called Turnbull Corporation (G-1841)*
Roberts Dairy Company LLC.......785 232-1274
7215 Sw Topeka Blvd Topeka (66619) *(G-13022)*
Roberts Group Inc (PA).......913 381-3930
10076 Hemlock Dr Overland Park (66212) *(G-9252)*
Roberts Hutch-Line Inc.......620 662-3356
413 E 3rd Ave Hutchinson (67501) *(G-3428)*
Roberts Products Inc.......913 780-1702
10415 S Millbrook Ln Olathe (66061) *(G-8039)*
Roberts Truck Ctr Holdg Co LLC.......316 262-8413
5549 N Chuzy Dr Park City (67219) *(G-9640)*
Robin Chiropractic & Acupnctur.......913 962-7408
7410 Switzer St Shawnee Mission (66203) *(G-11810)*
Robin White Hills Inc.......785 877-3399
P.O. Box 159 Norton (67654) *(G-7462)*
Robinson Js Construction Inc.......913 441-2988
8325 Monticello Rd Ste D Shawnee Mission (66227) *(G-11811)*
Robinson Oil Co Inc.......620 275-4237
710 N Vfw Rd Garden City (67846) *(G-2268)*
Robinson Supply LLC.......620 251-0490
2804 Walnut St Coffeyville (67337) *(G-973)*
Robinsons Delivery Service.......913 281-4952
1 Shawnee Ave Kansas City (66105) *(G-4385)*
Robotzone LLC.......620 221-7071
3850 E 12th Ave Winfield (67156) *(G-16170)*
Robson Oil Co Inc.......785 263-2470
1302 Portland Ave Abilene (67410) *(G-51)*
Rock Creek Open M R I, Lansing *Also called M R I of Rock Creek (G-4687)*
Rock Creek Technologies LLC.......620 364-1400
117 Osage St New Strawn (66839) *(G-7304)*
Rock Pre-K Center.......785 266-2285
3819 Sw Burlingame Rd Topeka (66609) *(G-13023)*
Rock Ridge Steel Company LLC.......913 365-5200
901 Woodsdale Rd Elwood (66024) *(G-1690)*
Rock Study Boxing Kansas City, Leawood *Also called Parkinsons Exercise and (G-5514)*
Rockgate Management Company.......402 331-0101
10990 Quivira Rd Ste 200 Overland Park (66210) *(G-9253)*
Rockhill Womens Care Inc.......816 942-3339
5701 W 119th St Ste 225 Leawood (66209) *(G-5541)*
Rockhurst University Continuin.......913 432-7755
6901 W 63rd St Fl 3 Flr 3 Shawnee Mission (66202) *(G-11812)*
Rockies Express Pipeline LLC.......913 928-6060
4200 W 115th St Ste 350 Leawood (66211) *(G-5542)*
Rockwell Automation Inc.......913 577-2500
8047 Bond St Lenexa (66214) *(G-6111)*
Rockwell Collins Inc.......316 677-4808
2051 S Airport Rd Wichita (67209) *(G-15474)*
Rockwell Security LLC.......913 362-3300
11201 W 59th Ter Shawnee (66203) *(G-11021)*
Rocky Top Counter Top LLC.......316 262-0497
1336 S Mosley Ave Wichita (67211) *(G-15475)*
Rod's Thriftway, Concordia *Also called Rods Food Stores Inc (G-1127)*
Rodney Lyles MD.......913 894-2323
12200 W 106th St Ste 120 Shawnee Mission (66215) *(G-11813)*
Rodriguez Mech Contrs Inc.......913 281-1814
541 S 11th St Kansas City (66105) *(G-4386)*
Rodrock & Associates Inc.......913 533-9980
12643 Hemlock St Overland Park (66213) *(G-9254)*
Rodrock Development, Overland Park *Also called Rodrock & Associates Inc (G-9254)*
Rodrock Homes LLC.......913 851-0347
9550 Dice Ln Lenexa (66215) *(G-6112)*
Rods Food Stores Inc.......785 243-2035
307 W 6th St Concordia (66901) *(G-1127)*
Roeland Park Community Center.......913 722-0310
4850 Rosewood Dr Roeland Park (66205) *(G-10229)*
Roeland Park Multi Service Ctr, Roeland Park *Also called Roeland Park Community Center (G-10229)*
Roeser Homes LLC.......913 220-7477
P.O. Box 24165 Overland Park (66283) *(G-9255)*
Roger A Riedmiller.......316 448-1028
532 N Market St Wichita (67214) *(G-15476)*
Roger D Gausman DDS.......620 663-5044
1311 Wheatland Dr Hutchinson (67502) *(G-3429)*
Roger Fincher.......785 430-5770
1263 Sw Topeka Blvd Topeka (66612) *(G-13024)*
Roger L Johnson.......785 233-4226
534 S Kansas Ave Ste 1500 Topeka (66603) *(G-13025)*
Roger L Stevens Dentist.......785 539-2314
1110 Westport Dr Manhattan (66502) *(G-6794)*
Rogers & Son Concrete, Fort Scott *Also called Madison Brothers Concrete Inc (G-1983)*
Rogers Contracting.......316 613-2002
1912 E Diedrich St Ste A Haysville (67060) *(G-2958)*
Rogers Duncan Dillehay DDS PA (PA).......316 683-6518
1821 E Madison Ave Derby (67037) *(G-1270)*
Rogers Manufacturing Inc (PA).......843 423-4680
19882 W 156th St Olathe (66062) *(G-8040)*
Rohrer Custom and Fabrication.......620 359-1707
161 S Hillside Rd Wellington (67152) *(G-13525)*
Rok-Hard Ready-Mix, Lakin *Also called Pappas Concrete Inc (G-4657)*
Rokenn Enterprises Inc.......785 523-4251
137 N 110th Rd Delphos (67436) *(G-1217)*
Rolf Perrin & Associates PC.......913 671-8600
4210 Shawnee Mission Pkwy 202a Fairway (66205) *(G-1918)*
Roll Out Inc.......620 347-4753
232 N 230th St Arma (66712) *(G-190)*
Roll Products Inc.......785 437-6000
511 W Palmer St Saint Marys (66536) *(G-10374)*
Roller City Inc.......316 942-4555
3234 S Meridian Ave Wichita (67217) *(G-15477)*
Rollers, Emporia *Also called Entertainment Specialties (G-1750)*
Rolling Hills Country Club (PA).......316 722-4273
223 S Westlink St Wichita (67209) *(G-15478)*
Rolling Hills Country Club.......316 721-6780
330 N Maize Rd Wichita (67212) *(G-15479)*
Rolling Hills Electric Coop (PA).......785 534-1601
3075b Us Highway 24 Beloit (67420) *(G-501)*
Rolling Hills Electric Coop.......785 472-4021
208 W 1st St Ellsworth (67439) *(G-1680)*
Rolling Hills Health and Rehab.......316 722-6916
1319 S Seville Ave Wichita (67209) *(G-15480)*
Rolling Hills Health Center (PA).......785 273-5001
2400 Sw Urish Rd Topeka (66614) *(G-13026)*
Rolling Hills Health Center.......785 273-2202
2410 Sw Urish Rd Topeka (66614) *(G-13027)*
Rolling Hills Zoo Foundation.......785 827-9488
625 N Hedville Rd Salina (67401) *(G-10652)*
Rolling Meadows Golf Club, Milford *Also called City of Junction City (G-7111)*
Rolling Meadows Landscape.......913 839-0229
901 N 10th St Kansas City (66101) *(G-4387)*
Rollsource, Pittsburg *Also called Veritiv Operating Company (G-9955)*
Romans Outdoor Power Inc.......913 837-5225
203 Crestview Cir Louisburg (66053) *(G-6466)*
Romans Outdoor Power Inc (PA).......620 331-2970
3011 W Main St Independence (67301) *(G-3556)*
Rome Corporation (PA).......785 625-1182
1023 Reservation Rd Hays (67601) *(G-2901)*
Romero Custom.......913 548-3852
126 Circle Dr Gardner (66030) *(G-2360)*
Ron D Hansen Od Inc.......620 662-2355
3120 N Plum St Hutchinson (67502) *(G-3430)*
Ron J Marek Do PA.......316 462-1050
1901 N Maize Rd Wichita (67212) *(G-15481)*
Ron Stierly Floor Services.......913 724-4822
14428 Parallel Rd Basehor (66007) *(G-388)*
Ron Weers Construction Inc.......913 681-5575
20765 Foster Ct Bucyrus (66013) *(G-608)*

ALPHABETIC

Ron's Tire Service, Oberlin *Also called Fowlers LLC* ***(G-7494)***
Ronald Carlile 620 624-2632
2240w Pine St Liberal (67901) ***(G-6361)***
Ronald G Higgins 620 584-2223
136 N Gorin St Clearwater (67026) ***(G-895)***
Ronald J Burgmeier DDS PA 913 764-1169
13025 S Mur Len Rd # 250 Olathe (66062) ***(G-8041)***
Ronald McDnald Hse Chrties Nrt 785 235-6852
825 Sw Buchanan St Topeka (66606) ***(G-13028)***
Ronans Roofing Inc 913 384-0901
14122 W 107th St Lenexa (66215) ***(G-6113)***
Ronco Inc 913 362-7200
2201 W 70th St Mission Hills (66208) ***(G-7148)***
Ronnie Diehl Construction Inc 785 823-7800
521 Bishop St Salina (67401) ***(G-10653)***
Rons Market 620 277-2073
106 N Jones Ave Holcomb (67851) ***(G-3079)***
Rons Sign Co Inc 316 267-8914
1329 S Handley St Wichita (67213) ***(G-15482)***
Rons Welding & Pipeline Svcs 620 935-4275
18542 I 70 Rd Russell (67665) ***(G-10291)***
Roof-Techs International, Augusta *Also called Page Corporation* ***(G-335)***
Roofing Services Unlimited 316 284-9900
202 E 4th St Newton (67114) ***(G-7411)***
Roofing Solutions Inc 913 897-1840
6728 W 153rd St Overland Park (66223) ***(G-9256)***
Roofing Sup Grup-Kansas Cy LLC 913 281-4300
200 S 42nd St Kansas City (66106) ***(G-4388)***
Roofmasters Roofing Co Inc 785 462-6642
425 E Hill St Colby (67701) ***(G-1036)***
ROOKS COUNTY HEALTH CENTER, Plainville *Also called Plainville Rural Hospital* ***(G-9990)***
Rooks County Historical Museum 785 425-7217
Hwy S 183 Stockton (67669) ***(G-12185)***
Rooks County Holdings LLC 785 261-0455
1401 Main St Stockton (67669) ***(G-12186)***
Rooks County Sheriff S Dept, Stockton *Also called Redbud Village* ***(G-12184)***
Rooks County Trailer Sales, Stockton *Also called Peters-Howell Lujeana* ***(G-12183)***
Rooney Enterprises Corporation 913 325-4770
3861 W 95th St Overland Park (66206) ***(G-9257)***
Root Laboratory Inc 913 491-3555
5201 College Blvd Ste 290 Leawood (66211) ***(G-5543)***
Rosas Drywall Co 620 665-6959
1519 Linwood Dr Hutchinson (67502) ***(G-3431)***
Rosas Ezra, Hutchinson *Also called Rosas Drywall Co* ***(G-3431)***
Rose Companies Inc (PA) 913 782-0777
863 N Martway Dr Olathe (66061) ***(G-8042)***
Rose Construction, Olathe *Also called Rose Companies Inc* ***(G-8042)***
Rose Construction Co Inc 913 782-0777
863 N Martway Dr Olathe (66061) ***(G-8043)***
Rose Hill Bank (HQ) 316 776-2131
107 N Rose Hill Rd Rose Hill (67133) ***(G-10247)***
Rose Hill Unified School Dst 316 776-3340
104 N Rose Hill Rd Rose Hill (67133) ***(G-10248)***
Rose Hill United Youth Center, Rose Hill *Also called Rhum Wee Rockets Pre School* ***(G-10246)***
Rose Hl Prmry Schl/Kndergarten, Rose Hill *Also called Rose Hill Unified School Dst* ***(G-10248)***
Rose Motor Supply Inc 620 662-1254
109 E Sherman St Hutchinson (67501) ***(G-3432)***
Rose Villa Inc (PA) 785 232-0671
2075 Sw Fillmore St Topeka (66604) ***(G-13029)***
Rose, Tom MD, Great Bend *Also called Central Kans Fmly Practice PA* ***(G-2527)***
Rosedale Development Assn Inc 913 677-5097
1403 Southwest Blvd Kansas City (66103) ***(G-4389)***
Rosenberg, Joe O, Saint John *Also called Joe Rosenberg DDS* ***(G-10353)***
Rosencrantz Bemis Enterprises (PA) 620 792-2488
1105 Us Highway 281 Byp Great Bend (67530) ***(G-2632)***
Rosewood Services Inc 620 793-5888
384 N Washington Ave Great Bend (67530) ***(G-2633)***
Ross Consultants Inc 213 926-2090
6230 W 137th St Apt 104 Overland Park (66223) ***(G-9258)***
Ross Manufacturing Inc 785 332-3012
301 W Washington St Saint Francis (67756) ***(G-10345)***
Rossville Healthcare 785 584-6104
600 Perry St Rossville (66533) ***(G-10255)***
ROSSVILLE STATE BANK, Saint Marys *Also called St Marys State Bank* ***(G-10377)***
Rota-Carrus, Kansas City *Also called Bennet Rogers Pipe Coating* ***(G-3853)***
Rotary International 785 626-9444
305 S 4th St Atwood (67730) ***(G-291)***
Rotary International 913 299-0466
7938 Greeley Ave Kansas City (66109) ***(G-4390)***
Rotek Services Inc 316 263-3131
955 N Mosley St Wichita (67214) ***(G-15483)***
Roth Equipment, Great Bend *Also called Straub International Inc* ***(G-2641)***
Roth Farm 785 944-3329
1924 Valleyview Rd Green (67447) ***(G-2666)***
Roth Heating & AC 316 942-4141
4141 W Maple St Wichita (67209) ***(G-15484)***
Roth K Christopherson 316 269-2494
719 S Saint Francis St Wichita (67211) ***(G-15485)***
Rothfuss Motels (PA) 785 632-2148
905 Crawford St Clay Center (67432) ***(G-878)***
Rothfuss Motels 785 632-5611
1136 Crawford St Clay Center (67432) ***(G-879)***
Rothwell Landscape Inc 785 238-2647
1607 Fair Ln Manhattan (66502) ***(G-6795)***
Roto-Mix LLC (PA) 620 225-1142
2205 E Wyatt Earp Blvd Dodge City (67801) ***(G-1425)***
Roto-Mix LLC 620 872-1100
1451 S Highway 83 Scott City (67871) ***(G-10830)***
Roto-Mix LLC 620 653-7323
558 S Main St Hoisington (67544) ***(G-3070)***
Roto-Rooter, Wichita *Also called P & W Incorporated* ***(G-15247)***
Rotor Quality LLC 316 425-0418
7804 E Funston St Ste 222 Wichita (67207) ***(G-15486)***
Round Hill Bath &TEnnis Club 913 381-2603
8932 Maple Cir Shawnee Mission (66207) ***(G-11814)***
Rouse Frets White Goss Gentile 913 387-1600
5250 W 116th Pl Ste 400 Overland Park (66211) ***(G-9259)***
Royal Beef, Scott City *Also called Irsik & Doll Feed Services Inc* ***(G-10817)***
Royal Caribbean Cruises Ltd 316 554-5000
4729 Palisade St Wichita (67217) ***(G-15487)***
Royal Crest Lanes, Lawrence *Also called Tins Inc* ***(G-5137)***
Royal Drilling Inc 785 483-6446
719 W Witt Ave Russell (67665) ***(G-10292)***
Royal Farms Dairy LLC 620 335-5704
3705 F Rd Garden City (67846) ***(G-2269)***
Royal Flush Plumbing LLC 316 794-2656
5500 S 231st St W Goddard (67052) ***(G-2453)***
Royal Mechanical Services Inc 913 897-3436
19175 Metcalf Ave Overland Park (66085) ***(G-9260)***
Royal Metal Industries Inc (PA) 913 829-3000
1000 W Ironwood St Olathe (66061) ***(G-8044)***
Royal Prestige, Shawnee Mission *Also called R P Products Inc* ***(G-11773)***
Royal Spa 316 681-0002
7700 E Kellogg Dr Q02a Wichita (67207) ***(G-15488)***
Royal Ter Nrsing Rhbltion Ctr, Olathe *Also called Centennial Healthcare Corp* ***(G-7584)***
Royal Terrace Healthcare LLC 913 829-2273
201 E Flaming Rd Olathe (66061) ***(G-8045)***
Royal Tractor Company Inc 913 782-2598
109 Overland Park Pl New Century (66031) ***(G-7296)***
Royer Brothers Tree Svc LLC 620 899-7621
2401 S Lorraine St Hutchinson (67501) ***(G-3433)***
Roys Custom Cabinets 785 625-6724
821 E 11th St Hays (67601) ***(G-2902)***
RPM Motorsports LLC 316 259-4576
10817 W Kellogg St Wichita (67209) ***(G-15489)***
Rpms LLC 800 776-7435
11771 W 112th St Ste 200 Overland Park (66210) ***(G-9261)***
Rppg Inc 620 705-5100
1409 W Madison Ave Arkansas City (67005) ***(G-176)***
Rps Inc 620 342-3026
1224 Frontier Way Emporia (66801) ***(G-1817)***
Rs Electronics, Overland Park *Also called Carlton-Bates Company* ***(G-8518)***
Rs Used Oil Services Inc (HQ) 866 778-7336
2932 N Ohio St Wichita (67219) ***(G-15490)***
Rsvp Medspa LLC 913 387-1104
13300 Metcalf Ave Overland Park (66213) ***(G-9262)***
Rsvp of Northeast Kansas Inc 785 562-2154
813 Broadway Marysville (66508) ***(G-6909)***
Rt Painting Inc 913 390-6650
1330 S Hamilton Cir Olathe (66061) ***(G-8046)***
RTS Financial Service Inc 877 642-8553
9300 Metcalf Ave Overland Park (66212) ***(G-9263)***
Ruan Trnsp MGT Systems Inc 785 274-6672
1100 Sw 57th St Topeka (66609) ***(G-13030)***
Rubber Belting & Hose Sup Inc 316 269-1151
1850 N Ohio Ave Wichita (67214) ***(G-15491)***
Rubenstein Real Estate Co LLC 913 362-1999
6310 Lamar Ave Ste 220 Shawnee Mission (66202) ***(G-11815)***
Rubin, Robert, Shawnee Mission *Also called Parking Systems Inc* ***(G-11717)***
Rueschhoff Communications 785 841-0111
3727 W 6th St Ste A Lawrence (66049) ***(G-5098)***
Rueschhoff Locksmith, Lawrence *Also called Rueschhoff Communications* ***(G-5098)***
Rueschhoff Lsmith SEC Systems, Lawrence *Also called Eichhorn Holdings LLC* ***(G-4848)***
Ruf Strategic Solution, Olathe *Also called Infutor Data Solutions LLC* ***(G-7790)***
Ruffin Hotel of Wichita LLC 316 685-3777
417 S Webb Rd Wichita (67207) ***(G-15492)***
Ruffin Oil Co, Wichita *Also called Town and Country Food Mkts Inc* ***(G-15779)***
Ruffin Properties, Wichita *Also called Phillip G Ruffin* ***(G-15291)***
Ruffin Riverfront Hotel LLC 316 293-1234
400 W Waterman St Wichita (67202) ***(G-15493)***
Rui Contracting, Kansas City *Also called Repairs Unlimited Inc* ***(G-4370)***
Rule Properties LLC 785 621-8000
1708 Copper Creek Ct Hays (67601) ***(G-2903)***
Rumsey-Yost Fnrl HM Crematory, Lawrence *Also called Rumsey-Yost Funeral Inc* ***(G-5099)***

Rumsey-Yost Funeral Inc 785 843-5111
601 Indiana St Lawrence (66044) ***(G-5099)***
Run-R-Way Express Co Inc 785 346-2900
20031 300 Rd Portis (67474) ***(G-10006)***
Rural Health Clinic, Ellsworth *Also called Ellsworth Medical Clinic Inc* ***(G-1671)***
Rural Health Development Inc 785 462-8295
1625 S Franklin Ave Colby (67701) ***(G-1037)***
Rural Hlth Rsurces Jackson Inc (PA) 785 364-2116
1110 Columbine Dr Holton (66436) ***(G-3110)***
Rural Hlth Rsurces Jackson Inc 785 364-2126
1100 Columbine Dr Ste D Holton (66436) ***(G-3111)***
Rural Telephone, Hill City *Also called Nex-Tech LLC* ***(G-3037)***
Rural Telephone Service Co Inc (PA) 785 567-4281
145 N Main St Lenora (67645) ***(G-6245)***
Rural Telephone Service Co Inc 785 483-5555
238 E Wichita Ave Russell (67665) ***(G-10293)***
Rural Water Dist 5 Sumner Cnty 620 456-2350
202 W Spring Ave Conway Springs (67031) ***(G-1144)***
Rural Water Distribution 3 ....913 755-4503
35680 Plum Creek Rd Osawatomie (66064) ***(G-8203)***
Rural Water Dst 3 Cowley Cnty 620 442-7131
10972 286th Rd Arkansas City (67005) ***(G-177)***
Rural Water Dst 7 Osage Cnty 785 528-5090
104 N 9th St Osage City (66523) ***(G-8189)***
Rush County Memorial Hospital 785 222-2545
801 Locust St La Crosse (67548) ***(G-4637)***
Rush County Nursing Home Soc 785 222-2574
701 W 6th St La Crosse (67548) ***(G-4638)***
Rush Truck Center, Kansas City, Olathe *Also called Rush Truck Centers Kansas Inc* ***(G-8047)***
Rush Truck Centers Kansas Inc 913 764-6000
11525 S Rogers Rd Olathe (66062) ***(G-8047)***
Ruskin Company 620 421-6090
1700 N 21st St Parsons (67357) ***(G-9733)***
Russel County Ems, Russell *Also called County of Russell* ***(G-10269)***
Russell & Russell LLC 785 827-4878
1100 W Grand Ave Ste H Salina (67401) ***(G-10654)***
Russell Block Company Inc 785 483-6271
2123 Us Highway 40 Russell (67665) ***(G-10294)***
Russell Cable TV, Russell *Also called Eagle Communications Inc* ***(G-10273)***
Russell Child Dev Ctr Inc (PA) 620 275-0291
2735 N Jennie Barker Rd Garden City (67846) ***(G-2270)***
Russell County News, Russell *Also called Main Street Media Inc* ***(G-10281)***
Russell Family Medical Care, Hoisington *Also called Clara Barton Hospital* ***(G-3061)***
Russell Livestock Commission 785 483-2961
51 S Fossil St Russell (67665) ***(G-10295)***
Russell Livestock LLC 785 483-2961
720 S Fossil St Russell (67665) ***(G-10296)***
Russell Publishing Co (PA) 785 483-2116
802 N Maple St Russell (67665) ***(G-10297)***
Russell Regional Hospital, Russell *Also called West Central Kansas Assn Inc* ***(G-10303)***
Russell Steel Products Inc (PA) 913 831-4600
2221 Metropolitan Ave Kansas City (66106) ***(G-4391)***
Russell Stover 109, Abilene *Also called Russell Stover Chocolates LLC* ***(G-52)***
Russell Stover Chocolates LLC 785 263-0463
1993 Caramel Blvd Abilene (67410) ***(G-52)***
Russell-Hampton Co, New Century *Also called Diligence Inc* ***(G-7279)***
Russells America Inn LLC 785 483-4200
1430 S Fossil St Russell (67665) ***(G-10298)***
Rusty S Baits & Lures 620 842-5301
213 E Main St Anthony (67003) ***(G-134)***
Rusty's Channel Cat Baits, Anthony *Also called Rusty S Baits & Lures* ***(G-134)***
Ruth Burke & Associates, Mission *Also called Rba Associates Inc* ***(G-7136)***
Ruth Grimsley 913 393-1711
13538 S Alden St Olathe (66062) ***(G-8048)***
Ruther & Associates LLC 913 894-8877
8877 Bourgade St Ste B Shawnee Mission (66219) ***(G-11816)***
Rutland Inc 913 782-8862
15610 S Keeler St Olathe (66062) ***(G-8049)***
Rutter Cline Associates Inc 620 276-8274
110 W Chestnut St Garden City (67846) ***(G-2271)***
Rv Products (HQ) 316 832-3400
3050 N Saint Francis St Wichita (67219) ***(G-15494)***
RVB Trucking Inc 620 365-6823
28 Davis St Iola (66749) ***(G-3631)***
Rvc Enterprises Inc 785 937-4386
202 Main St Princeton (66078) ***(G-10170)***
Rx Plus Pharmacies Inc 316 263-5218
744 N Waco Ave Wichita (67203) ***(G-15495)***
Rx Power 913 696-0691
10800 Farley St Shawnee Mission (66210) ***(G-11817)***
Rx Savings LLC 913 815-3139
11225 College Blvd # 400 Overland Park (66210) ***(G-9264)***
Rx Savings Solutions, Overland Park *Also called Rx Savings LLC* ***(G-9264)***
Ryan Condray and Wenger LLC 785 632-5666
509 Court St Clay Center (67432) ***(G-880)***
Ryan and Mullin, Clay Center *Also called Michael W Ryan Atty* ***(G-873)***
Ryan D&M Inc 620 231-4559
1005 Canterbury Rd Pittsburg (66762) ***(G-9930)***
Ryan Development Company LLC (PA) 316 630-9223
8301 E 21st St N Wichita (67206) ***(G-15496)***
Ryan Farms Inc 785 263-1613
2231 Deer Rd Abilene (67410) ***(G-53)***
Ryan Lawn & Tree Inc (PA) 913 381-1505
9120 Barton St Overland Park (66214) ***(G-9265)***
Ryan Mortuary & Crematory, Salina *Also called Ryan Mortuary Inc* ***(G-10655)***
Ryan Mortuary Inc 785 825-4242
137 N 8th St Salina (67401) ***(G-10655)***
Ryan Transportation Svc Inc (HQ) 800 860-7926
9350 Metcalf Ave Overland Park (66212) ***(G-9266)***
Ryans Comet Cleaner 620 231-4559
1005 Canterbury Rd Pittsburg (66762) ***(G-9931)***
Ryder Truck Rental Inc 316 945-8484
3525 N Hydraulic St Wichita (67219) ***(G-15497)***
Ryder Truck Rental Inc 913 573-2119
5500 State Ave Kansas City (66102) ***(G-4392)***
Ryder Truck Rental Inc 913 621-3300
37 S James St Kansas City (66118) ***(G-4393)***
Ryder Truck Rental Inc 913 888-5040
10000 Darnell St Shawnee Mission (66215) ***(G-11818)***
Ryder Truck Rental Inc 913 492-4420
10003 Lackman Rd Lenexa (66219) ***(G-6114)***
Rydex Fund Services Inc 301 296-5100
1 Sw Security Benefit Pl Topeka (66636) ***(G-13031)***
Rydex Funds, Topeka *Also called Rydex Fund Services Inc* ***(G-13031)***
Ryko Solutions Inc 913 451-3719
14058 W 107th St Lenexa (66215) ***(G-6115)***
Rylie Equipment & Contg Co 913 621-2725
913 S Boeke St Kansas City (66105) ***(G-4394)***
S & A Construction Inc 316 558-8422
1600 S Topeka Ave Wichita (67211) ***(G-15498)***
S & B Motels Inc 785 899-7181
2519 Enterprise Rd Goodland (67735) ***(G-2484)***
S & B Motels Inc (PA) 316 522-3864
400 N Woodlawn St Ste 205 Wichita (67208) ***(G-15499)***
S & B Motels Inc 785 823-8808
120 E Diamond Dr Salina (67401) ***(G-10656)***
S & G Water Service Inc 620 246-5212
10286 Sw 170 Ave Nashville (67112) ***(G-7230)***
S & H Inc 620 251-4422
204 W 1st St Coffeyville (67337) ***(G-974)***
S & S Auto Body 785 524-4641
229 W Lincoln Ave Lincoln (67455) ***(G-6387)***
S & S Equipment Co Inc 316 267-7471
1901 N Broadway Ave Wichita (67214) ***(G-15500)***
S & S Manufacturing Inc 316 946-5755
2661 W Esthner Ave Wichita (67213) ***(G-15501)***
S & S Underground LLC 620 704-1397
1623 E 20th St Pittsburg (66762) ***(G-9932)***
S & T Telephone Coop Assn (PA) 785 694-2256
320 Kansas Ave Brewster (67732) ***(G-586)***
S & T Telephone Coop Assn 785 460-7300
755 Davis Ave Colby (67701) ***(G-1038)***
S & T Telephone Coop Assn 785 890-7400
1318 Main Ave Goodland (67735) ***(G-2485)***
S & W Supply Company Inc (HQ) 785 625-7363
300 E 8th St Hays (67601) ***(G-2904)***
S and Y Industries Inc 620 221-4001
606 Industrial Blvd Winfield (67156) ***(G-16171)***
S C F Inc 913 722-3473
9225 Indian Creek Pkwy Overland Park (66210) ***(G-9267)***
S C O R E, Topeka *Also called Service Corps Retired Execs* ***(G-13060)***
S C O R E 0673, Great Bend *Also called Service Corps Retired Execs* ***(G-2635)***
S C O R E 143, Wichita *Also called Service Corps Retired Execs* ***(G-15567)***
S Central Mental Health, El Dorado *Also called Counseling Ctr For Butlr Cnty* ***(G-1552)***
S D M Die Cutting Equipment 913 782-3737
9320 W 54th St Shawnee (66203) ***(G-11022)***
S E K Otolaryngology PA 620 232-7500
107 N Pine St Ste B Pittsburg (66762) ***(G-9933)***
S F B Plastics Inc 800 343-8133
1819 W Harry St Wichita (67213) ***(G-15502)***
S F P, Leawood *Also called Specialty Fertilizer Pdts LLC* ***(G-5556)***
S J Investments Inc of Topeka 785 233-1568
3637 Se 6th St Lh Topeka (66607) ***(G-13032)***
S Jackson Service Center Inc 913 422-7438
10635 Kaw Dr Edwardsville (66111) ***(G-1514)***
S K Design Group Inc 913 451-1818
4600 College Blvd Ste 100 Shawnee Mission (66211) ***(G-11819)***
S N C Inc 620 665-6651
10021 Paganica Ct Hutchinson (67502) ***(G-3434)***
S Noble Trucking Inc 620 704-0886
113 Main St Mc Cune (66753) ***(G-6922)***
S P D Transfer Service Lc 913 321-0333
7015 Richards Dr Shawnee Mission (66216) ***(G-11820)***
S S & C Business & Tax Svcs, Lawrence *Also called Summers & Spencer Company* ***(G-5126)***
S S of Kansas Inc 620 663-5951
1526 E 17th Ave Hutchinson (67501) ***(G-3435)***

ALPHABETIC

S S of Kansas Inc 785 823-2787
2351 S 9th St Fl 1 Salina (67401) *(G-10657)*
S T Carter Inc (PA) 913 451-1100
7300 W 110th St Ste 800 Shawnee Mission (66210) *(G-11821)*
S T G, Wichita *Also called Siemens Industry Inc (G-15585)*
S W Agro Center 620 563-7264
303 Main St Kismet (67859) *(G-4632)*
S&K 913 634-2234
13030 W 105th St Overland Park (66215) *(G-9268)*
S&K Fuels LLC 785 454-6219
605 Wisconsin St Cawker City (67430) *(G-689)*
S&S Limousine LLC 316 794-3340
24401 W 39th St S Goddard (67052) *(G-2454)*
S&S Quality Meats LLC 620 342-6354
1542 S Highway 99 Emporia (66801) *(G-1818)*
S-Kmac Investments LLC (PA) 316 990-5095
3804 W Douglas Ave Wichita (67203) *(G-15503)*
S.E.k Academy, Independence *Also called Four Cnty Mental Hlth Ctr Inc (G-3521)*
SA Consumer Products Inc (PA) 888 792-4264
3305 W 132nd St Leawood (66209) *(G-5544)*
SA Imprints Inc 620 421-6380
1730 Main St Parsons (67357) *(G-9734)*
Sabates Eye Centers PC (PA) 913 261-2020
11261 Nall Ave Ste 100 Shawnee Mission (66211) *(G-11822)*
Sabates Eye Centers PC 913 261-2020
11261 Nall Ave Leawood (66211) *(G-5545)*
Sabates Eye Centers PC 913 469-8806
11213 Nall Ave Ste 100 Shawnee Mission (66211) *(G-11823)*
Sabetha Community Hospital, Sabetha *Also called Great Plains of Sabetha Inc (G-10312)*
Sabetha Country Inn Inc 785 284-2300
1473 S 75 Hwy Sabetha (66534) *(G-10327)*
Sabetha Golf Club Inc 785 284-2023
2551 X Rd Sabetha (66534) *(G-10328)*
Sabetha Manor Incorporated 785 284-3411
1441 Oregon St Sabetha (66534) *(G-10329)*
Sabetha Manor Nursing Rehabili, Sabetha *Also called Rh Montgomery Properties Inc (G-10324)*
SABETHA NURSING & REHAB CENTER, Sabetha *Also called Sabetha Manor Incorporated (G-10329)*
Sabetha Residential Care Ctr, Sabetha *Also called Rh Montgomery Properties Inc (G-10325)*
Sac & Fox Casino, Powhattan *Also called Sac & Fox Ntion MO In Kans Neb (G-10010)*
Sac & Fox Gaming Commission 785 467-8070
1324 Us Highway 75 Powhattan (66527) *(G-10009)*
Sac & Fox Ntion MO In Kans Neb 785 467-8000
1322 Us Highway 75 Powhattan (66527) *(G-10010)*
Sacred Heart Home Care 913 299-4515
13021 Meadow Ln Kansas City (66109) *(G-4395)*
Sady Vijay Inc 620 343-7750
2511 W 18th Ave Emporia (66801) *(G-1819)*
Safarik Tool Co Inc 316 755-4800
400 W Clay St Valley Center (67147) *(G-13352)*
Safc Biosciences Inc (HQ) 913 469-5580
13804 W 107th St Lenexa (66215) *(G-6116)*
Safc Biosciences Lenexa, Lenexa *Also called Safc Biosciences Inc (G-6116)*
Safe Home Inc 913 432-9300
P.O. Box 4563 Overland Park (66204) *(G-9269)*
Safehouse Crisis Center Inc 620 231-8692
409 N Walnut St Ste 1 Pittsburg (66762) *(G-9934)*
SAFEHOUSE FOR BATTERED SPOUSES, Pittsburg *Also called Safehouse Crisis Center Inc (G-9934)*
Safehouse Inc 620 251-0030
1317 W 8th St Coffeyville (67337) *(G-975)*
Safehouse Satellite Ofc, Coffeyville *Also called Safehouse Inc (G-975)*
Safelink Security Systems Inc 913 338-3888
103 W 4th St Tonganoxie (66086) *(G-12269)*
Safelite Autoglass 6270, Shawnee *Also called Safelite Fulfillment Inc (G-11023)*
Safelite Fulfillment Inc 913 236-5888
10306 Shwnee Mission Pkwy Shawnee (66203) *(G-11023)*
Safely Delicious LLC 913 963-5140
13029 Flint St Overland Park (66213) *(G-9270)*
Safety-Kleen (wt) Inc 316 269-7400
2549 N New York Ave Wichita (67219) *(G-15504)*
Safety-Kleen Systems Inc 316 942-5001
4801 W Irving St Wichita (67209) *(G-15505)*
Safety-Kleen Systems Inc 913 829-6677
19930 W 157th St Olathe (66062) *(G-8050)*
Sagar Inc 620 241-5566
2302 E Kansas Ave McPherson (67460) *(G-7022)*
Sagar Inc (PA) 620 241-5343
2211 E Kansas Ave McPherson (67460) *(G-7023)*
Sagar Inc 620 241-5343
2211 E Kansas Ave McPherson (67460) *(G-7024)*
Sage Restoration LLC 913 905-0500
6520 W 110th St Ste 201b Overland Park (66211) *(G-9271)*
Saia Motor Freight Line LLC 316 522-1786
4525 S Palisade Ave Wichita (67217) *(G-15506)*
Saicon Consultants Inc (PA) 913 451-1178
9300 W 110th St Ste 650 Overland Park (66210) *(G-9272)*
Saint Ann Child Care Center 913 362-4660
7225 Mission Rd Shawnee Mission (66208) *(G-11824)*
Saint Catherine Home Care Svc, Garden City *Also called St Catherine Hospital (G-2289)*
Saint Francis Academy, Colby *Also called Saint Francis Cmnty Svcs Inc (G-1039)*
Saint Francis Academy Newton 316 284-2477
516 N Main St Newton (67114) *(G-7412)*
Saint Francis Acdmy Inc Atchsn 785 625-6651
105 W 13th St Hays (67601) *(G-2905)*
Saint Francis Acdmy Inc Atchsn (PA) 913 367-5005
19137 258th Rd Atchison (66002) *(G-259)*
Saint Francis At Salina, Salina *Also called St Francis Academy Inc (G-10714)*
Saint Francis Cmnty Svcs Inc 620 326-6373
1421 W 8th St Wellington (67152) *(G-13526)*
Saint Francis Cmnty Svcs Inc 785 587-8818
222 Southwind Pl Manhattan (66503) *(G-6796)*
Saint Francis Cmnty Svcs Inc 785 210-1000
1013 W 8th St Ste A Junction City (66441) *(G-3749)*
Saint Francis Cmnty Svcs Inc 785 476-3234
129 S Main St Kensington (66951) *(G-4580)*
Saint Francis Cmnty Svcs Inc 785 825-0541
1646b N 9th St Salina (67401) *(G-10658)*
Saint Francis Cmnty Svcs Inc 620 276-4482
1110 J C St Garden City (67846) *(G-2272)*
Saint Francis Cmnty Svcs Inc (PA) 785 825-0541
509 E Elm St Salina (67401) *(G-10659)*
Saint Francis Cmnty Svcs Inc 785 452-9653
509 E Elm St Salina (67401) *(G-10660)*
Saint Francis Cmnty Svcs Inc 785 462-6679
180 W 5th St Colby (67701) *(G-1039)*
Saint Francis Cmnty Svcs Inc 316 831-0330
1999 N Amidon Ave 100b Wichita (67203) *(G-15507)*
Saint Francis Cmnty Svcs Inc 785 243-4215
904 Broadway Concordia (66901) *(G-1128)*
Saint Francis Community 785 825-0541
509 E Elm St Salina (67401) *(G-10661)*
Saint Francis Community and RE 785 825-0541
509 E Elm St Salina (67401) *(G-10662)*
Saint Francs Acdmy Bldng Fmls, Hays *Also called Saint Francis Acdmy Inc Atchsn (G-2905)*
Saint Frncis Acdemy Great Bend 620 793-7454
1508 Main St Great Bend (67530) *(G-2634)*
Saint Frncis Acdemy Hutchinson 620 669-3734
501 N Monroe St Hutchinson (67501) *(G-3436)*
Saint Frncis Acdemy Wellington, Wellington *Also called Saint Francis Cmnty Svcs Inc (G-13526)*
Saint Frncis Cmnty Svcs In Ill 785 825-0541
509 E Elm St Salina (67401) *(G-10663)*
Saint Frncis Radiation Therapy 316 268-5927
817 N Emporia St Wichita (67214) *(G-15508)*
Saint Jhns Vctria Nrsing Fclty, Hays *Also called St Johns Rest Home Inc (G-2910)*
Saint John Home Health Center, Leavenworth *Also called Prime Healthcare Services Inc (G-5281)*
Saint Johns Regional Hlth Ctr, Salina *Also called Salina Regional Health Ctr Inc (G-10688)*
Saint Joseph Early Educatn Ctr, Shawnee Mission *Also called Archdiocese Kansas Cy In Kans (G-11117)*
Saint Joseph Oncology Inc 913 367-9175
104 N 6th St Ste 15 Atchison (66002) *(G-260)*
Saint Jude Hospice 785 742-3823
708 Oregon St Hiawatha (66434) *(G-3024)*
Saint Lkes Med Group - Lansing, Lansing *Also called St Lukes Health Corporation (G-4693)*
Saint Lkes S Srgery Centre LLC 913 317-3200
12541 Foster St Ste 120 Overland Park (66213) *(G-9273)*
Saint Lukes Cushing Hospital (PA) 913 684-1100
711 Marshall St Leavenworth (66048) *(G-5288)*
Saint Lukes Hosp Garnett Inc (PA) 785 448-3131
421 S Maple St Garnett (66032) *(G-2388)*
Saint Lukes Primary Care At 913 317-7990
4061 Indian Creek Pkwy # 200 Overland Park (66207) *(G-9274)*
Saint Lukes South Hospital Inc (PA) 913 317-7000
12300 Metcalf Ave Shawnee Mission (66213) *(G-11825)*
Saint Lukes South Hospital Inc 913 317-7514
12300 Metcalf Ave Kansas City (66103) *(G-4396)*
Saint Lukes South Hospital Inc 913 317-7990
12541 Foster St Ste 300 Overland Park (66213) *(G-9275)*
Saint Marys Manor, Saint Marys *Also called Community Healthcare Sys Inc (G-10361)*
Saint Raphael Home Care Inc 316 269-5400
903 W 18th St N Wichita (67203) *(G-15509)*
Saint Vincent Depaul Society 620 421-8004
1122 Main St Parsons (67357) *(G-9735)*
Saker Aviation Services, Garden City *Also called Fbo Air - Garden City Inc (G-2158)*
SAKW, Robinson *Also called State Assn of Kans Watersheds (G-10215)*
SALEM HOME, Hillsboro *Also called Salem Hospital Inc (G-3057)*
Salem Hospital Inc 620 947-2272
704 S Ash St Hillsboro (67063) *(G-3057)*
Salina Airport Authority 785 827-3914
3237 Arnold Ave Salina (67401) *(G-10664)*
Salina Ambassador Hotel, Salina *Also called Andrea Investments LLC (G-10402)*

Salina Area Chmber Cmmerce Inc......785 827-9301
120 W Ash St Salina (67401) ***(G-10665)***
Salina Blueprint, Salina *Also called Salina Microfilm* ***(G-10680)***
Salina Building Systems Inc......785 823-6812
4329 E Cntry Estates Cir Salina (67401) ***(G-10666)***
Salina Child Care Association......785 827-6431
155 N Oakdale Ave Ste 100 Salina (67401) ***(G-10667)***
Salina Clinic, Salina *Also called Veterans Health Administration* ***(G-10752)***
Salina Concrete Products Inc (HQ)......785 827-7281
1100 W Ash St Salina (67401) ***(G-10668)***
Salina Concrete Products Inc......316 943-3241
1600 S Hoover Rd Wichita (67209) ***(G-15510)***
Salina Country Club......785 827-0388
2101 E Country Club Rd Salina (67401) ***(G-10669)***
Salina County Dialysis, Salina *Also called Salina County Medical Supply* ***(G-10670)***
Salina County Medical Supply (PA)......785 823-6416
700 E Iron Ave Salina (67401) ***(G-10670)***
Salina Dental Arts......785 823-2472
1829 S Ohio St Salina (67401) ***(G-10671)***
Salina Dental Associates PA......785 827-4401
950 Elmhurst Blvd Salina (67401) ***(G-10672)***
Salina Economic Dev Corp......785 827-9301
120 W Ash St Salina (67401) ***(G-10673)***
SALINA FAMILY HEALTHCARE AND D, Salina *Also called Salina Hlth Educatn Foundation* ***(G-10674)***
Salina Fire Department, Salina *Also called City of Salina* ***(G-10451)***
Salina Hlth Educatn Foundation......785 825-7251
651 E Prescott Rd Salina (67401) ***(G-10674)***
Salina Homes......785 820-5900
300 S 9th St Ste 101 Salina (67401) ***(G-10675)***
Salina Housing Authority......785 827-0441
469 S 5th St Salina (67401) ***(G-10676)***
Salina Iron & Metal Company......785 826-9838
312 N 5th St Salina (67401) ***(G-10677)***
Salina Journal Inc......785 823-6363
333 S 4th St Salina (67401) ***(G-10678)***
Salina Journal, The, Salina *Also called Salina Journal Inc* ***(G-10678)***
Salina KS Lodging LLC......785 827-1271
2760 S 9th St Salina (67401) ***(G-10679)***
Salina Microfilm......785 827-6648
212 S 5th St Salina (67401) ***(G-10680)***
Salina Pediatric Care......785 825-2273
501 S Santa Fe Ave # 100 Salina (67401) ***(G-10681)***
Salina Physical Therapy Clinic......785 825-1361
1101 E Republic Ave Salina (67401) ***(G-10682)***
Salina Planing Mill Inc......785 825-0588
1100 W Crawford St Salina (67401) ***(G-10683)***
Salina Presbyterian Manor, Salina *Also called Presbyterian Manors Inc* ***(G-10641)***
Salina Red Coach Inn......785 825-2111
2110 W Crawford St Salina (67401) ***(G-10684)***
Salina Regional Health Ctr Inc......785 823-1032
501 S Santa Fe Ave # 300 Salina (67401) ***(G-10685)***
Salina Regional Health Ctr Inc (PA)......785 452-7000
400 S Santa Fe Ave Salina (67401) ***(G-10686)***
Salina Regional Health Ctr Inc......785 452-4850
511 S Santa Fe Ave Salina (67401) ***(G-10687)***
Salina Regional Health Ctr Inc......785 452-7000
139 N Penn Ave Salina (67401) ***(G-10688)***
Salina Rescue Mission Inc......785 823-3317
1716 Summers Rd Salina (67401) ***(G-10689)***
Salina Scale Sales & Service (PA)......785 827-4441
415 N 9th St Salina (67401) ***(G-10690)***
Salina Sports Med &ORth Clinic......785 823-7213
523 S Santa Fe Ave Salina (67401) ***(G-10691)***
Salina Steel Supply Inc......785 825-2138
234 E Avenue A Salina (67401) ***(G-10692)***
Salina Supply Company......785 823-2221
302 N Santa Fe Ave Salina (67401) ***(G-10693)***
Salina Surgical Center LLC......785 827-0610
401 S Santa Fe Ave Salina (67401) ***(G-10694)***
SALINA SURGICAL HOSPITAL, Salina *Also called Salina Surgical Center LLC* ***(G-10694)***
Salina Urology Associates PA......785 827-9635
501 S Santa Fe Ave # 380 Salina (67401) ***(G-10695)***
Salina Vortex Corp......785 825-7177
1725 Vortex Ave Salina (67401) ***(G-10696)***
Salina Waste Systems, Salina *Also called Waste Connections Kansas Inc* ***(G-10759)***
Saline County Comm On Aging......785 823-6666
245 N 9th St Salina (67401) ***(G-10697)***
Saline County Health, Salina *Also called County of Saline* ***(G-10465)***
Saline Valley Farm Inc......785 524-4562
2019 E Lark Dr Lincoln (67455) ***(G-6388)***
Sallee Inc......620 227-3320
1201 E Trail St Dodge City (67801) ***(G-1426)***
Salon 103......913 383-9040
10344 Metcalf Ave Overland Park (66212) ***(G-9276)***
Salon Avanti......913 829-2424
115 S Clairborne Rd Ste B Olathe (66062) ***(G-8051)***
Salon Brands......785 301-2984
4325 Vine St Ste 30 Hays (67601) ***(G-2906)***
Salon Dimarco and Day Spa......785 843-0044
733 Massachusetts St Lawrence (66044) ***(G-5100)***
Salon Knotty......316 636-4400
1445 N Rock Rd Ste 175 Wichita (67206) ***(G-15511)***
Salon Mission & Day Spa, Overland Park *Also called Salon Mission Inc* ***(G-9277)***
Salon Mission Inc......913 642-8333
3791 W 95th St Overland Park (66206) ***(G-9277)***
Salon One 19 & Spa......913 451-7119
4581 W 119th St Leawood (66209) ***(G-5546)***
Salon Progressions & Day Spa......316 729-1980
2360 N Maize Rd Ste 100 Wichita (67205) ***(G-15512)***
Salon Ten O Seven......785 628-6000
1007 Main St Hays (67601) ***(G-2907)***
Salon X......620 343-8634
518 Commercial St Emporia (66801) ***(G-1820)***
Saltcreek Fitness & Rehab......785 528-1123
104 W Market St Ste B&C Osage City (66523) ***(G-8190)***
Salvation Army, Olathe *Also called Emergency Assistance Sites* ***(G-7678)***
Salvation Army, Pittsburg *Also called Womens Chldren Shelter Linwood* ***(G-9971)***
Salvation Army......316 685-8699
1739 S Elpyco St Wichita (67218) ***(G-15513)***
Salvation Army......620 343-3166
520 Constitution St Emporia (66801) ***(G-1821)***
Salvation Army......913 782-3640
420 E Santa Fe St Olathe (66061) ***(G-8052)***
Salvation Army......620 276-4027
216 N 9th St Garden City (67846) ***(G-2273)***
Salvation Army......316 283-3190
208 W 6th St Newton (67114) ***(G-7413)***
Salvation Army......316 263-2769
350 N Market St Wichita (67202) ***(G-15514)***
Salvation Army......620 663-3353
700 N Walnut St Hutchinson (67501) ***(G-3437)***
Salvation Army......620 225-4871
1100 Avenue E Dodge City (67801) ***(G-1427)***
Salvation Army......620 276-6622
203 N 8th St Garden City (67846) ***(G-2274)***
Salvation Army......785 843-1716
946 New Hampshire St Lawrence (66044) ***(G-5101)***
Salvation Army......913 782-3640
420 E Santa Fe St Olathe (66061) ***(G-8053)***
Salvation Army......785 233-9648
1320 Se 6th Ave Topeka (66607) ***(G-13033)***
Salvation Army......913 232-5400
6711 State Ave Kansas City (66102) ***(G-4397)***
Salvation Army......785 233-9648
1320 Se 6th Ave Topeka (66607) ***(G-13034)***
Salvation Army......913 232-5400
7623 State Ave Kansas City (66112) ***(G-4398)***
Salvation Army National Corp......316 943-9893
1910 S Everett St Wichita (67213) ***(G-15515)***
Salvation Army National Corp......913 299-4822
1331 N 75th Pl Kansas City (66112) ***(G-4399)***
Salvation Army The, Newton *Also called Salvation Army* ***(G-7413)***
Salvation Army Thrift Store, Garden City *Also called Salvation Army* ***(G-2273)***
Sam Carlini......913 416-1280
6936 Martindale Rd Shawnee (66218) ***(G-11024)***
Samco Inc......785 234-4000
3840 Nw 14th St Ste C Topeka (66618) ***(G-13035)***
Samco Drywall Company......620 864-2289
273 M Rd Severy (67137) ***(G-10892)***
Sampson Homes, Severy *Also called Samco Drywall Company* ***(G-10892)***
Sams Fantastic......913 856-4247
315 N Moonlight Rd Gardner (66030) ***(G-2361)***
Samuel Heck, Wichita *Also called Via Christi Health Inc* ***(G-15888)***
Sana Hospitality Corp......620 342-7567
2913 W Us Highway 50 Emporia (66801) ***(G-1822)***
Sanctuary Unit The, Fredonia *Also called Quality Health Care Inc* ***(G-2041)***
Sand and Sage Farm and Ranch......620 723-3052
22035 183 Hwy Greensburg (67054) ***(G-2684)***
Sand Creek Station Golf Course......316 284-6161
920 Meadowbrook Dr Newton (67114) ***(G-7414)***
Sand Dollar Hospitality 2 LLC......913 299-4700
1805 N 110th St Kansas City (66111) ***(G-4400)***
Sanden North America Inc......913 888-6667
9900 Pflumm Rd Ste 22 Shawnee Mission (66215) ***(G-11826)***
Sanders Warren & Russell LLP......913 234-6100
40 Corporate Woods Ste Overland Park (66210) ***(G-9278)***
Sandhill Orthopaedic......620 624-7400
2132 N Kansas Ave Ste B Liberal (67901) ***(G-6362)***
Sandhill Orthpdic Spt Medicine, Garden City *Also called Fandhill Orthpd & Spt Medicine* ***(G-2155)***
Sandifer Engrg & Contrls Inc......316 794-8880
229 S Ellis St Wichita (67211) ***(G-15516)***
Sandmeyer Henthorn and Company......913 951-2010
6500 W 110th St Ste 102 Leawood (66211) ***(G-5547)***
Sandpiper Healthcare and......316 945-3606
5808 W 8th St N Wichita (67212) ***(G-15517)***

Sands Enterprises Inc 316 942-8686
240 S West St Ste 40 Wichita (67213) ***(G-15518)***
Sands Level & Tool Div, Neodesha *Also called Sands Level and Tool Company* ***(G-7248)***
Sands Level and Tool Company 620 325-2687
1250 Tank Ave Neodesha (66757) ***(G-7248)***
Sands Level and Tool Company 989 428-4141
8325 Hedge Lane Ter Lenexa (66227) ***(G-6117)***
Sands Motor Inn 620 356-1404
622 W Oklahoma Ave Ulysses (67880) ***(G-13317)***
Sandstone Inc 913 422-0794
4025 Bonner Industrial Dr Shawnee Mission (66226) ***(G-11827)***
Sandstone Creek Apartments 913 402-8282
7450 W 139th Ter Shawnee Mission (66223) ***(G-11828)***
Sandstone Heights Nursing Home, Little River *Also called Hospital District 2 Rice Cnty* ***(G-6419)***
Sani Wax Inc 913 383-9703
4500 W 90th Ter Ste 206 Prairie Village (66207) ***(G-10065)***
Sanibel Investments Inc 913 422-7949
6447 Vista Dr Shawnee Mission (66218) ***(G-11829)***
Santa Fe AC & Rfrgn Inc 913 856-5801
1100 E Santa Fe St Gardner (66030) ***(G-2362)***
Santa Fe Body Inc 913 894-6090
8717 Lenexa Dr Shawnee Mission (66214) ***(G-11830)***
Santa Fe Distributing Inc 913 492-8288
9640 Legler Rd Shawnee Mission (66219) ***(G-11831)***
Santa Fe Law Building 913 648-3220
8000 Foster St Shawnee Mission (66204) ***(G-11832)***
Santa Fe Law Office, Shawnee Mission *Also called Santa Fe Law Building* ***(G-11832)***
Santa Fe Market Inc 785 594-7466
309 Ames St Baldwin City (66006) ***(G-368)***
Santa Fe Medical Building, Shawnee Mission *Also called Shawnee Mission Med Ctr Inc* ***(G-11857)***
Santa Fe Products LLC 913 362-6611
4307 Merriam Dr Overland Park (66203) ***(G-9279)***
Santa Fe Tow Service Inc (PA) 417 553-3676
9125 Rosehill Rd Shawnee Mission (66215) ***(G-11833)***
Santa Fe Trail Association 620 285-2054
1349 K156 Hwy Larned (67550) ***(G-4711)***
Santa Fe Trails Plumbing Inc 913 441-1441
8325 Monticello Rd Ste E Shawnee Mission (66227) ***(G-11834)***
Santa Marta Retirement Cmnty 913 906-0990
13800 W 116th St Olathe (66062) ***(G-8054)***
Sara It Solutions Inc 913 269-6980
9393 W 110th St Overland Park (66210) ***(G-9280)***
Sara Lee Corp 913 233-3200
4612 Speaker Rd Kansas City (66106) ***(G-4401)***
Sara Software Systems LLC 913 370-4197
804 N Meadowbrook Dr # 114 Olathe (66062) ***(G-8055)***
Saragenes Short Stop 620 235-1141
4002 N Broadway St Pittsburg (66762) ***(G-9935)***
Sarahlee Coffee and Tea Corp 316 262-0398
427 S Washington Ave Wichita (67202) ***(G-15519)***
Saratoga Capital Inc 316 838-1972
1915 N Porter Ave Apt 162 Wichita (67203) ***(G-15520)***
Sarik LLC 785 379-1235
1517 Sw Medford Ave Topeka (66604) ***(G-13036)***
Sarin Energy Inc 913 912-3235
9209 Quivira Rd Overland Park (66215) ***(G-9281)***
Sarin Energy Solutions, Overland Park *Also called Sarin Energy Inc* ***(G-9281)***
Sarto Countertops 785 437-3344
930 E Jesuit Ln Saint Marys (66536) ***(G-10375)***
Sas Childcare Inc 913 897-8900
4820 W 137th St Leawood (66224) ***(G-5548)***
Sasnak Management Corporation (PA) 316 683-2611
1877 N Rock Rd Wichita (67206) ***(G-15521)***
Satanta District Hosp & Long T 620 649-2761
401 Cheyenne Ste 401 # 401 Satanta (67870) ***(G-10790)***
Satanta Gas Plant, Ulysses *Also called Linn Energy Inc* ***(G-13305)***
Satchell Creek Express Inc 316 775-1300
508 State St Augusta (67010) ***(G-342)***
Satellite Engrg Group Inc 913 324-6000
10814 W 78th St Overland Park (66214) ***(G-9282)***
Sauder Custom Fabrication Inc 620 342-2550
220 Weaver St Emporia (66801) ***(G-1823)***
Sauer Brands Inc 913 324-3700
101 Prairie Village Dr New Century (66031) ***(G-7297)***
Sauerwein Construction Co Inc 316 942-0028
2055 S Edwards St Wichita (67213) ***(G-15522)***
Savage Holdings Inc 913 583-1007
11364 Strang Line Rd Lenexa (66215) ***(G-6118)***
Save, Manhattan *Also called Servicmmber AG Vcation Educatn* ***(G-6799)***
Savoy Rgls BHN Engnrng Lnd Sur 316 264-8008
924 N Main St Wichita (67203) ***(G-15523)***
Sb Manufacturing Inc 316 941-9591
3707 W Mccormick St Wichita (67213) ***(G-15524)***
SBC Funding LLC 785 438-3000
1 Sw Security Benefit Pl Topeka (66636) ***(G-13037)***
SBS Insurance 785 336-2821
305 Main St Seneca (66538) ***(G-10880)***
SC Hall Industrial Svcs Inc 316 945-4255
1221 E Murdock St Wichita (67214) ***(G-15525)***
Sca Construction Inc 620 331-8247
2500 W Laurel St Independence (67301) ***(G-3557)***
Scandinavian Gifts, Lindsborg *Also called Hemslojd Inc* ***(G-6399)***
Scanneddocs.com, Lenexa *Also called Casey Associates Inc* ***(G-5731)***
Scanning America Inc (PA) 785 749-7471
1440 N 3rd St Lawrence (66044) ***(G-5102)***
Scart, Wichita *Also called Sedgwick Country Animal Respon* ***(G-15546)***
Scavuzzos Inc 816 231-1517
6550 Kansas Ave Kansas City (66111) ***(G-4402)***
SCCA, Topeka *Also called Sports Car Club America Inc* ***(G-13091)***
Schaben Industries Inc 316 283-4444
7000 Schaben Ct Newton (67114) ***(G-7415)***
Schaefer Johnson Cox Frey (PA) 316 684-0171
257 N Broadway Ave Wichita (67202) ***(G-15526)***
Schaefer Johnson Cox Frey Arch 316 684-0171
257 N Broadway Ave Wichita (67202) ***(G-15527)***
Schammerhorn Inc 316 265-8659
124 S Seneca St Wichita (67213) ***(G-15528)***
Schankie Well Service Inc 620 437-2595
1006 Sw Blvd Madison (66860) ***(G-6504)***
Scheer Dentistry PA 316 636-1222
7707 E 29th St N Wichita (67226) ***(G-15529)***
Schell Electronics Inc 620 431-2350
120 N Lincoln Ave Chanute (66720) ***(G-761)***
Schellers Inc 620 342-3990
401 S Prairie St Emporia (66801) ***(G-1824)***
Schenck Accurate Inc 262 473-2441
P.O. Box 205 Sabetha (66534) ***(G-10330)***
Schenck Process LLC 785 284-2191
810 S Us Old 75 Hwy Sabetha (66534) ***(G-10331)***
Schendel Lawn & Landscape, Topeka *Also called Creative Landscaping Inc* ***(G-12527)***
Schendel Pest Control, Olathe *Also called Schendel Services Inc* ***(G-8056)***
Schendel Services Inc 913 498-1811
215 S Kansas Ave Olathe (66061) ***(G-8056)***
Schendel Services Inc 316 320-6422
1545 S Broadway Ave Wichita (67211) ***(G-15530)***
Schenker Inc 316 260-6367
3801 S Oliver St Wichita (67210) ***(G-15531)***
Schenker Inc 316 942-0146
1659 S Sabin St Wichita (67209) ***(G-15532)***
Scheopners Water Cond LLC 620 275-5121
2203 E Fulton Plz Garden City (67846) ***(G-2275)***
Schermoly, Martin J, Olathe *Also called James L Ruhlen MD PA* ***(G-7806)***
Schimmels, Alan D Dvm, Wichita *Also called North Rock Hosp For Animals PC* ***(G-15188)***
Schippers Oil Field Svcs LLC 785 675-9991
1255 E Us Highway 24 Hoxie (67740) ***(G-3141)***
Schlage Lock Company LLC 888 805-9837
2119 E Kansas City Rd Olathe (66061) ***(G-8057)***
Schlagel & Associates PA 913 492-5158
14920 W 107th St Shawnee Mission (66215) ***(G-11835)***
Schlagel Kinzer LLC 913 782-5885
100 E Park St Ste 8 Olathe (66061) ***(G-8058)***
Schlosser Inc 785 899-6535
1301 W 25th Goodland (67735) ***(G-2486)***
Schlosser Ready Mix, Goodland *Also called Schlosser Inc* ***(G-2486)***
Schlotterbeck Machine Shop 620 678-3210
2599 W Rd N Hamilton (66853) ***(G-2708)***
Schlumberger Technology Corp 785 841-5610
2400 Packer Rd Lawrence (66049) ***(G-5103)***
Schmidt Haven Ford Sales Inc 620 465-2252
121 S Kansas St Haven (67543) ***(G-2736)***
Schmidt Vending Inc 785 354-7397
1911 Nw Lower Silver Lk Topeka (66608) ***(G-13038)***
Schmidtlein Electric Inc 785 357-4572
305 Ne Croco Rd Topeka (66616) ***(G-13039)***
Schmitz King & Associates Inc 913 397-6080
10501 W 70th Ter Apt 101 Shawnee (66203) ***(G-11025)***
Schmuhl Brothers Inc 913 422-1111
1134 S 12th St Kansas City (66105) ***(G-4403)***
Schneider Pallets, Natoma *Also called Tasler Inc* ***(G-7233)***
Schnell & Pestinger Inc 785 738-3624
108 S Mill St Beloit (67420) ***(G-502)***
Schoenberger Nursing Agency, Ellis *Also called Marlene Schoenberger* ***(G-1650)***
Scholastic Book Fairs Inc 913 599-5700
14710 W 105th St Shawnee Mission (66215) ***(G-11836)***
Scholastic Photography Inc 913 384-9126
5808 Maple St Shawnee Mission (66202) ***(G-11837)***
Scholfield Body Shop Inc (PA) 316 688-6550
11516 E Kellogg Dr Wichita (67207) ***(G-15533)***
School of Medicine, Wichita *Also called University of Kansas* ***(G-15856)***
School of Medicine, Wichita *Also called University of Kansas* ***(G-15857)***
School of Nursing, Topeka *Also called Trustees of The Baker Univ* ***(G-13199)***
School of The Magdalen, Wichita *Also called Church of Magdalen* ***(G-14019)***
Schopper, Lynne M, Leawood *Also called Lynne M Schopper DDS PA* ***(G-5461)***
Schowalter Villa 620 327-0400
200 W Cedar St Hesston (67062) ***(G-3000)***

Schraad & Associates.....913 661-2404
10100 W 119th St Ste 102 Overland Park (66213) *(G-9283)*
Schreiner M & Sons Cnstr.....785 246-1130
7731 Ne Indian Creek Rd Topeka (66617) *(G-13040)*
Schroeder's, Dodge City *Also called Shoroeders Jim Sftwr & Video (G-1430)*
Schroer Manufacturing Company (PA).....913 281-1500
511 Osage Ave Kansas City (66105) *(G-4404)*
Schroff Development Corp.....913 262-2664
6800 Squibb Rd Shawnee Mission (66202) *(G-11838)*
Schueller John.....316 371-7761
1230 N Broadway Ave # 125 Wichita (67214) *(G-15534)*
Schueman Transfer.....785 378-3114
10 Frontase St Mankato (66956) *(G-6861)*
Schuff Steel Company.....913 677-2485
6701 W 64th St Overland Park (66202) *(G-9284)*
Schuff Steel Midwest, Overland Park *Also called Schuff Steel Company (G-9284)*
Schuler Heating and Cooling.....913 262-2969
3400 Shawnee Dr Kansas City (66106) *(G-4405)*
Schult Homes, Plainville *Also called Clayton Homes Inc (G-9981)*
Schultz Brothers Elc Co Inc.....913 321-8338
3030 S 24th St Ste A Kansas City (66106) *(G-4406)*
Schulz Oil & Gas, Canton *Also called Schulz Welding Service Inc (G-681)*
Schulz Welding Service Inc.....620 628-4431
114 S Main St Canton (67428) *(G-681)*
Schurle Signs Inc.....785 832-9897
1837 E 1450 Rd Lawrence (66044) *(G-5104)*
Schurle Signs Inc (PA).....785 485-2885
7555 Falcon Rd Riley (66531) *(G-10209)*
Schurz Communications Inc.....316 838-1212
2815 E 37th St N Wichita (67219) *(G-15535)*
Schwab-Eaton PA (PA).....785 539-4687
4361 S Dam Rd Manhattan (66502) *(G-6797)*
Schwabs Tinker Shop Intl Inc (PA).....620 624-7611
430 Rollie Rd Liberal (67901) *(G-6363)*
Schwabs Tinker Shop Intl Inc.....620 564-2547
110 W D St Ellinwood (67526) *(G-1636)*
Schwan's Food Manufacturing, Salina *Also called Sfc Global Supply Chain Inc (G-10705)*
Schwartz Inc.....620 275-5800
1335 Hineman Dr Garden City (67846) *(G-2276)*
Schwerdt Design Group Inc (PA).....785 273-7540
2231 Sw Wanamaker Rd # 303 Topeka (66614) *(G-13041)*
Schwieterman Inc (PA).....620 275-4100
1616 E Kansas Ave Garden City (67846) *(G-2277)*
SCI, Wichita *Also called Service Corp International (G-15565)*
SCI, Kansas City *Also called Service Corp International (G-4418)*
SCI, Olathe *Also called Service Corp International (G-8059)*
SCI, Shawnee *Also called Surface Center Interiors LLC (G-11037)*
SCI, Wichita *Also called Service Corp International (G-15566)*
Scientific Engineering Inc.....785 827-7071
2782 Arnold Ave Salina (67401) *(G-10698)*
Scientific Plastics Co Inc.....913 432-0322
1016 Southwest Blvd Kansas City (66103) *(G-4407)*
Sckats Inc.....620 662-2368
1722 N Plum St Hutchinson (67502) *(G-3438)*
Sckedd, Bel Aire *Also called South Central Kansas (G-440)*
SCKEDD/TAG, Wichita *Also called South Central KS Econ Dev Dist (G-15617)*
Scooters LLC.....785 284-2978
1008 Main St Sabetha (66534) *(G-10332)*
Scope Inc.....316 393-7414
425 S Greenwood St Ste 1 Wichita (67211) *(G-15536)*
Scor Globl Lf USA Reinsurance (HQ).....913 901-4600
11625 Rosewood St Ste 300 Leawood (66211) *(G-5549)*
Scotch Fabric Care Services, Lawrence *Also called Scotch Industries Inc (G-5105)*
Scotch Industries Inc.....785 235-3401
134 Se Quincy St Topeka (66603) *(G-13042)*
Scotch Industries Inc.....785 843-8585
611 Florida St Lawrence (66044) *(G-5105)*
Scotsman Inn West LLC.....316 943-3800
5922 W Kellogg Dr Wichita (67209) *(G-15537)*
Scott Cooperative Association.....620 872-5823
4993 N Venison Rd Scott City (67871) *(G-10831)*
Scott County Hospital.....620 872-2187
204 S College St Scott City (67871) *(G-10832)*
Scott County Hospital Inc (PA).....620 872-5811
201 Albert Ave Scott City (67871) *(G-10833)*
Scott Erickson.....316 942-0146
1659 S Sabin St Wichita (67209) *(G-15538)*
Scott Heller Trucking.....816 591-1638
17210 W 84th St Lenexa (66219) *(G-6119)*
Scott Masonry Inc.....785 286-3513
6001 Nw 35th St Topeka (66618) *(G-13043)*
Scott Mesler.....785 749-0462
1628 Highway 40 Lawrence (66044) *(G-5106)*
Scott Qinlan Willard Barns LLC.....785 267-0040
1613 Sw 37th St Topeka (66611) *(G-13044)*
Scott Quilan & Heck Partnr, Topeka *Also called James S Willard (G-12737)*
Scott Specialties Inc (PA).....785 527-5627
512 M St Belleville (66935) *(G-466)*
Scott Specialties Inc.....785 632-3161
1827 Meadowlark Rd Clay Center (67432) *(G-881)*
Scott Specialties Inc.....785 243-2594
1820 E 7th St Concordia (66901) *(G-1129)*
Scott-Pro, Scott City *Also called Midwest PMS LLC (G-10824)*
Scotts Powerline Construction.....316 440-8290
9911 E 21st St N Apt 803 Wichita (67206) *(G-15539)*
Scotts Well Service Inc.....785 254-7828
110 N Memory Ln Roxbury (67476) *(G-10257)*
Scotwood Industries Inc.....913 851-3500
12980 Metcalf Ave Ste 240 Overland Park (66213) *(G-9285)*
Scoular Company.....785 823-6301
2880 E Country Club Rd Salina (67401) *(G-10699)*
Scoular Company.....785 392-9024
524 W 2nd St Minneapolis (67467) *(G-7123)*
Scoular Company.....620 372-8611
12501 W Hwy 50 Coolidge (67836) *(G-1147)*
Scoular Elevator, Salina *Also called Scoular Company (G-10699)*
Scp Distributors LLC.....913 660-0061
14792 W 99th St Lenexa (66215) *(G-6120)*
Scp Specialty Infusion LLC.....913 747-3700
9801 Renner Blvd Ste 275 Lenexa (66219) *(G-6121)*
Scrap Management LLC.....913 573-1000
836 S 26th St Kansas City (66106) *(G-4408)*
Scrap Management Kansas Inc.....316 832-1198
850 E 45th St N Park City (67219) *(G-9641)*
Screen Machine LLC.....785 762-3081
115 E 7th St Junction City (66441) *(G-3750)*
Screen Machine Sports, Junction City *Also called Screen Machine LLC (G-3750)*
Screen-It Grphics Lawrence Inc.....785 843-8888
3840 Greenway Cir Lawrence (66046) *(G-5107)*
Scriptpro LLC.....913 403-5260
10911 Georgia Ave Kansas City (66109) *(G-4409)*
Scriptpro LLC (PA).....913 384-1008
5828 Reeds Rd Shawnee Mission (66202) *(G-11839)*
Scriptpro USA Inc.....913 384-1008
5828 Reeds Rd Shawnee Mission (66202) *(G-11840)*
Scrommel Resource Management.....785 825-7771
2775 Arnold Ave Ste E Salina (67401) *(G-10700)*
Scs Aquaterra, Overland Park *Also called Stearns Conrad and Schmidt (G-9356)*
Scs Tech LLC.....785 424-4478
2529 Nw Topeka Blvd Topeka (66617) *(G-13045)*
Sctelcom, Medicine Lodge *Also called South Central Tele Assn Inc (G-7074)*
Sctelcom, Medicine Lodge *Also called South Central Wireless Inc (G-7075)*
SD & S Trucking LLC.....316 744-2318
300 W 61st St N Park City (67204) *(G-9642)*
SD Engineering LLC.....785 233-8880
3649 Nw 25th St Topeka (66618) *(G-13046)*
SDC Publications, Shawnee Mission *Also called Schroff Development Corp (G-11838)*
Sdk Laboratories Inc.....620 665-5661
1000 Corey Rd Hutchinson (67501) *(G-3439)*
Sdr, Lawrence *Also called Spatial Data Research Inc (G-5114)*
Sdsi, Great Bend *Also called Southwest Developmental Svcs (G-2638)*
SE Kansas, Oswego *Also called Southeast Kansas Community (G-8236)*
SE Kansas Nture Ctr Schrmrhorn.....620 783-5207
3511 S Main St Galena (66739) *(G-2084)*
SE Kansas Orthopedic Clinic.....620 421-0881
1902 S Us Highway 59 Parsons (67357) *(G-9736)*
Se2 LLC.....800 747-3940
5801 Sw 6th Ave Topeka (66636) *(G-13047)*
Sea Coast Disposal Inc.....785 784-5308
2325 N Jackson St Junction City (66441) *(G-3751)*
Seaboard Corporation (HQ).....913 676-8800
9000 W 67th St Merriam (66202) *(G-7103)*
Seaboard Energy Oklahoma LLC (HQ).....913 261-2620
9000 W 67th St Ste 200 Shawnee Mission (66202) *(G-11841)*
Seaboard Feed Mill.....620 375-3300
132 N County Road 14 Leoti (67861) *(G-6257)*
Seaboard Foods LLC.....620 375-4523
211 N 4th St Leoti (67861) *(G-6258)*
Seaboard Foods LLC (HQ).....913 261-2600
9000 W 67th St Ste 200 Shawnee Mission (66202) *(G-11842)*
Seaboard Foods LLC.....620 375-4431
108 E Broadway Leoti (67861) *(G-6259)*
Seaboard Foods LLC.....620 593-4353
Dermont Rd Rolla (67954) *(G-10233)*
Seaboard Logistics, Shawnee Mission *Also called Illinois Tool Works Inc (G-11453)*
Seaboard Transport LLC.....913 676-8800
9000 W 67th St Ste 200 Shawnee Mission (66202) *(G-11843)*
Seal Tite Div, Independence *Also called Werner Pipe Service Inc (G-3572)*
Seals Inc.....913 438-1212
9900 Pflumm Rd Ste 67 Shawnee Mission (66215) *(G-11844)*
Sealy Inc.....913 321-3677
435 River Park Dr Kansas City (66105) *(G-4410)*
Sealy Mattress Co Kans Cy Inc.....913 321-3677
435 River Park Dr Kansas City (66105) *(G-4411)*
Seaman Unified School Dst 345.....785 286-7103
2032 N Kansas Ave Topeka (66608) *(G-13048)*

ALPHABETIC

Searles Valley Minerals Inc (HQ) 913 344-9500
9401 Indian Creek Pkwy # 1000 Overland Park (66210) *(G-9286)*
Sears Roebuck and Co 785 271-4200
1781 Sw Wanamater Rd Topeka (66609) *(G-13049)*
Sears Roebuck and Co 785 826-4378
2259 S 9th St Ste 7200 Salina (67401) *(G-10701)*
Sears Auto Center, Topeka *Also called Sears Roebuck and Co (G-13049)*
Sears Home Imprv Pdts Inc 913 438-5911
8246 Nieman Rd Shawnee Mission (66214) *(G-11845)*
Seasonal Solutions LLC 913 685-4222
6920 W 153rd St Ste A Overland Park (66223) *(G-9287)*
Seat King LLC (PA) 620 665-5464
6 N Walnut St Hutchinson (67501) *(G-3440)*
Seaton Publishing Co Inc (PA) 785 776-2200
318 N 5th St Manhattan (66502) *(G-6798)*
Seats Incorporated 913 686-3137
701 N Lincoln St Spring Hill (66083) *(G-12098)*
Sebes Hay LLC 620 285-6941
1175 Morris Ave Larned (67550) *(G-4712)*
Sebring & Co 913 888-8141
9261 Cody St Overland Park (66214) *(G-9288)*
Second Hand Enterprises Inc 316 775-7627
P.O. Box 780688 Wichita (67278) *(G-343)*
Secureaire Ltd Liability Co 813 766-0400
14900 W 107th St Lenexa (66215) *(G-6122)*
Securitas SEC Svcs USA Inc 316 838-2900
225 N Market St Ste 310 Wichita (67202) *(G-15540)*
Securities Commissioner Kansas (HQ) 785 296-3307
109 Sw 9th St Ste 600 Topeka (66612) *(G-13050)*
Security 1st Title LLC 620 442-7029
111 N Summit St Arkansas City (67005) *(G-178)*
Security 1st Title LLC 620 842-3333
110 N Jennings Ave Anthony (67003) *(G-135)*
Security 1st Title LLC 316 322-8164
114 E Central Ave El Dorado (67042) *(G-1601)*
Security 1st Title LLC 316 722-2463
2872 N Ridge Rd Wichita (67205) *(G-15541)*
Security 1st Title LLC 620 326-7460
116 E Harvey Ave Wellington (67152) *(G-13527)*
Security 1st Title LLC 316 260-5634
703 State St Augusta (67010) *(G-344)*
Security 1st Title LLC (PA) 316 267-8371
727 N Waco Ave Ste 300 Wichita (67203) *(G-15542)*
Security Bank of Kansas City (HQ) 913 281-3165
701 Minnesota Ave Kansas City (66101) *(G-4412)*
Security Bank of Kansas City 913 621-8423
8155 Parallel Pkwy Kansas City (66112) *(G-4413)*
Security Bank of Kansas City 913 621-8465
1901 Central Ave Kansas City (66102) *(G-4414)*
Security Bank of Kansas City 913 621-8462
7364 State Ave Kansas City (66112) *(G-4415)*
Security Bank of Kansas City 913 299-6200
1300 N 78th St Ste 100 Kansas City (66112) *(G-4416)*
Security Bank of Kansas City 913 621-8430
5800 Foxridge Dr Ste 400 Shawnee Mission (66202) *(G-11846)*
Security Bank of Kansas City 913 384-3300
2701 Shawnee Mission Pkwy Fairway (66205) *(G-1919)*
Security Benefit Academy Inc 785 438-3000
1 Sw Security Benefit Pl Topeka (66636) *(G-13051)*
Security Benefit Corporation (HQ) 785 438-3000
1 Sw Security Benefit Pl Topeka (66636) *(G-13052)*
Security Benefit Group Inc 785 438-3000
1 Sw Security Benefit Pl Topeka (66636) *(G-13053)*
Security Benefit Life Insur Co (HQ) 785 438-3000
1 Sw Security Benefit Pl Topeka (66636) *(G-13054)*
Security Bneft Group Companies, Topeka *Also called Security Benefit Group Inc (G-13053)*
Security Farms Inc (PA) 620 275-4200
911 N Main St Garden City (67846) *(G-2278)*
Security Management Co LLC 785 438-3000
1 Sw Security Benefit Pl Topeka (66636) *(G-13055)*
Security National Fincl Corp 620 241-3400
822 N Main St McPherson (67460) *(G-7025)*
Security Portfolio X LP 316 634-1115
1223 N Rock Rd Ste E200 Wichita (67206) *(G-15543)*
Security State Bank (HQ) 620 872-7224
506 S Main St Scott City (67871) *(G-10834)*
Security State Bank 620 326-7417
101 N Washington Ave Wellington (67152) *(G-13528)*
Security Storage Prpts LLC 316 634-6510
9103 E 37th St N Wichita (67226) *(G-15544)*
Security Transport Service 785 267-3030
1643 Sw 41st St Topeka (66609) *(G-13056)*
Sedan AR Egy Mdl Sv Dt 2 Inc 620 725-5670
120 S Chautauqua St Sedan (67361) *(G-10847)*
Sedan City Hospital 620 725-3115
300 W North St Sedan (67361) *(G-10848)*
Sedgwick Cnty Dvlpmntl Dsablty 316 660-7630
615 N Main St Wichita (67203) *(G-15545)*
Sedgwick Country Animal Respon 316 619-1723
6505 E Central Ave Wichita (67206) *(G-15546)*
Sedgwick County Accounting 316 383-7184
4035 E Harry St Wichita (67218) *(G-15547)*
Sedgwick County Elc Coop Assn 316 542-3131
1355 S 383rd St W Cheney (67025) *(G-796)*
Sedgwick County EXT Council, Wichita *Also called County of Sedgwick (G-14111)*
Sedgwick County Regional, Wichita *Also called County of Sedgwick (G-14109)*
Sedgwick County Transportation 316 660-7070
1015 W Stillwell St Fl 2 Wichita (67213) *(G-15548)*
Sedgwick County Zoological Soc 316 660-9453
5555 W Zoo Blvd Wichita (67212) *(G-15549)*
Sedgwick Healthcare Center, Sedgwick *Also called National Healthcare Corp (G-10851)*
Sedgwick Juvenile Field Svcs 316 660-5380
3803 E Harry St Ste 125 Wichita (67218) *(G-15550)*
Sedgwick Plz Rtrment Residence, Wichita *Also called Ilm 1 Holding Inc (G-14670)*
Seeber Thermoforming & Mfg, Augusta *Also called Stm Inc (G-348)*
Seeders Inc 316 722-8345
4111 S Broad St Wichita (67215) *(G-15551)*
Seen Merchandising LLC 913 233-1981
5024 Hadley St Shawnee (66203) *(G-11026)*
Segebrecht, Stephen L MD, Lawrence *Also called Lawrence Otlryngology Assoc PA (G-4981)*
Sek Ready Mix Inc 620 252-8699
2453 N Us Highway 169 Coffeyville (67337) *(G-976)*
SEK-CAP, Girard *Also called Southeast Kansas Community (G-2419)*
Sekan Occasion Shops, Fort Scott *Also called Sekan Printing Company Inc (G-2003)*
Sekan Printing Company Inc 620 223-5190
2210 S Main St Fort Scott (66701) *(G-2003)*
Sekisui-Xenotech, Kansas City *Also called Xenotech LLC (G-4559)*
Sektam of Independence Inc 620 331-5480
120 S 24th St Independence (67301) *(G-3558)*
Select Brands Inc (PA) 913 663-4500
10817 Renner Blvd Lenexa (66219) *(G-6123)*
Select Hotels Group LLC 913 491-9002
5001 W 110th St Overland Park (66211) *(G-9289)*
Select Medical Corporation 316 687-4581
3243 E Murdock St Ste 101 Wichita (67208) *(G-15552)*
Select Medical Corporation 316 261-8303
929 N St Francis St Sw Wichita (67214) *(G-15553)*
Select Medical Corporation 913 239-9539
11330 W 135th St Overland Park (66221) *(G-9290)*
Select Medical Corporation 316 687-9227
2434 N Woodlawn Blvd # 370 Wichita (67220) *(G-15554)*
Select Medical Corporation 913 385-0075
10730 Nall Ave Ste 204 Overland Park (66211) *(G-9291)*
Select Physical Therapy, Overland Park *Also called Select Medical Corporation (G-9291)*
Selective Site Consultants Inc (PA) 913 438-7700
7171 W 95th St Ste 600 Overland Park (66212) *(G-9292)*
Selex Es Inc (HQ) 913 945-2600
11300 W 89th St Overland Park (66214) *(G-9293)*
Selfs Inc (HQ) 316 267-1295
721 E Mount Vernon St Wichita (67211) *(G-15555)*
Selfs Inc 913 962-7353
5340 Merriam Dr Shawnee Mission (66203) *(G-11847)*
Sellers Companies Inc (PA) 785 823-6378
400 N Chicago St Salina (67401) *(G-10702)*
Sellers Equipment Inc (HQ) 785 823-6378
400 N Chicago St Salina (67401) *(G-10703)*
Sellers Equipment Inc 316 943-9311
1645 S West St Wichita (67213) *(G-15556)*
Sellers Farms Inc 620 257-5144
1420 Avenue N Lyons (67554) *(G-6497)*
Sellers Feedlot, Lyons *Also called Sellers Farms Inc (G-6497)*
Semcrude LP 620 234-5532
598 Arthur Ave Stafford (67578) *(G-12109)*
Semmaterials LP 785 825-1535
1100 W Grand Ave Ste M Salina (67401) *(G-10704)*
Senate United States 620 227-2244
100 Military Ave Ste 203 Dodge City (67801) *(G-1428)*
Senate Luxury Suites Inc 785 233-5050
900 Sw Tyler St Topeka (66612) *(G-13057)*
Senate Management, Topeka *Also called Senate Luxury Suites Inc (G-13057)*
Seneca Family Practice, Seneca *Also called Nemaha Valley Community Hosp (G-10877)*
Seneca Ready Mix Concrete Inc 785 336-3511
1201 Baltimore St Seneca (66538) *(G-10881)*
Seneca Wholesale Company Inc 785 336-2118
36 S 8th St Seneca (66538) *(G-10882)*
Seneca Wholesale Dr Pepper, Seneca *Also called Seneca Wholesale Company Inc (G-10882)*
Senihcam Inc 316 524-4561
460 E 46th St S Wichita (67216) *(G-15557)*
Senio Livin Retir Commu LLC 913 534-8872
13800 Metcalf Ave Overland Park (66223) *(G-9294)*
Senior Aerospace Composites, Wichita *Also called Senior Operations LLC (G-15558)*
Senior Center, Garden City *Also called Finney Cnty Committee On Aging (G-2160)*
Senior Center 316 835-2283
523 Poplar St Halstead (67056) *(G-2704)*
SENIOR CITIZENS CENTER, Liberal *Also called Seward County Council On Aging (G-6365)*
Senior Helpers of East Kansas, Overland Park *Also called C&L Management LLC (G-8504)*

Senior Operations LLC 316 942-3208
2700 S Custer Ave Wichita (67217) *(G-15558)*
Senior Rsrce Ctr For Dglas CNT 785 842-0543
745 Vermont St Lawrence (66044) *(G-5108)*
SENIOR SERVICES, Lawrence *Also called Senior Rsrce Ctr For Dglas CNT (G-5108)*
Senior Services Inc Wichita (PA) 316 267-0302
200 S Walnut St Wichita (67213) *(G-15559)*
Senior Services Inc Wichita 316 267-0122
200 S Walnut St Wichita (67213) *(G-15560)*
Senior Svcs of Southeast Kans 620 232-7443
3003 N Joplin St Pittsburg (66762) *(G-9936)*
Seniorcare Homes LLC 913 236-0036
5200 W 94th Ter Prairie Village (66207) *(G-10066)*
Seniortrust of Haysville LLC 316 524-3211
215 N Lamar Ave Haysville (67060) *(G-2959)*
Senne and Company Inc 785 235-1015
2001 Nw Us Highway 24 Topeka (66618) *(G-13058)*
Sensor-1, Princeton *Also called Wildcat Connectors Inc (G-10171)*
Sentage Corporation 785 235-9293
2820 Sw Fairlawn Rd # 200 Topeka (66614) *(G-13059)*
Sentage Corporation 316 263-0284
201 N Emporia Ave Wichita (67202) *(G-15561)*
Sentinel Real Estate Corp 913 451-8976
7171 W 115th St Overland Park (66210) *(G-9295)*
Sentinel Real Estate Corp 316 265-9471
400 W Central Ave Ofc Wichita (67203) *(G-15562)*
Ser Corporation (PA) 316 264-5372
1020 N Main St Ste D Wichita (67203) *(G-15563)*
Sera Inc 913 541-1307
9900 Pflumm Rd Ste 61 Shawnee Mission (66215) *(G-11848)*
Serenty Rehab Nrsng Ovrlnd Prk, Overland Park *Also called Leisure Operations LLC (G-8952)*
Sergeants Pet Care Pdts Inc 913 627-1245
16 Kansas Ave Kansas City (66105) *(G-4417)*
Servant Chrstn Cmnty Fundation 913 310-0279
7171 W 95th St Ste 501 Overland Park (66212) *(G-9296)*
Servant Foundation 913 310-0279
7171 W 95th St Ste 501 Overland Park (66212) *(G-9297)*
Servants of Mary Ministers, Kansas City *Also called Sisters Servants of Mary (G-4423)*
Servervault LLC 913 814-9988
12851 Foster St Overland Park (66213) *(G-9298)*
Servi Tech Inc (PA) 620 227-7509
1816 E Wyatt Earp Blvd Dodge City (67801) *(G-1429)*
Servi-Tech Laboratories, Dodge City *Also called Servi Tech Inc (G-1429)*
Service Auto Glass Inc (PA) 630 628-0398
1580 W Ogden Ave Unit 140 Mc Louth (66054) *(G-6929)*
Service Body Shop 316 260-5300
2550 W Pawnee St Wichita (67213) *(G-15564)*
Service Corp International 316 722-2100
11800 W Highway 54 Wichita (67209) *(G-15565)*
Service Corp International 913 334-3366
701 N 94th St Kansas City (66112) *(G-4418)*
Service Corp International 913 782-0582
105 E Loula St Olathe (66061) *(G-8059)*
Service Corp International 316 263-0244
201 S Hydraulic St Wichita (67211) *(G-15566)*
Service Corps Retired Execs 316 269-6273
220 W Douglas Ave Ste 450 Wichita (67202) *(G-15567)*
Service Corps Retired Execs 620 793-3420
1400 Main St Ste 107 Great Bend (67530) *(G-2635)*
Service Corps Retired Execs 785 234-3049
120 Se 6th Ave Ste 110 Topeka (66603) *(G-13060)*
Service Oil Company (HQ) 785 462-3441
285 E 4th St Colby (67701) *(G-1040)*
Service Pak Inc 913 438-3500
17501 W 98th St Spc 1761 Lenexa (66219) *(G-6124)*
Service Pak Group, Lenexa *Also called Service Pak Inc (G-6124)*
Service Technologies Midwest 913 671-3340
6800 W 64th St Ste 101 Overland Park (66202) *(G-9299)*
Service USA Inc 913 543-3844
4745 W 136th St Ste 77 Leawood (66224) *(G-5550)*
ServiceMaster, Hutchinson *Also called Burkhart Enterprises Inc (G-3226)*
ServiceMaster, Wichita *Also called Circle Enterprises Inc (G-14021)*
ServiceMaster, El Dorado *Also called Best Corporation Inc (G-1536)*
ServiceMaster, Wichita *Also called Best Corporation Inc (G-13837)*
ServiceMaster, Hays *Also called C & P Enterprises Inc (G-2762)*
ServiceMaster, Hutchinson *Also called Franchise Development Inc (G-3291)*
ServiceMaster AAA, Topeka *Also called Alert Enterprises Inc (G-12304)*
ServiceMaster Cleansweep Jantr, Lawrence *Also called Cleansweep Janitorial Inc (G-4792)*
ServiceMaster Company LLC 620 260-9994
3020 E Kansas Ave Garden City (67846) *(G-2279)*
ServiceMaster Consumer Service 316 283-5404
2216 N Anderson Ave Newton (67114) *(G-7416)*
ServiceMaster North Centl Kans 785 243-1965
610 Industrial Rd Concordia (66901) *(G-1130)*
Services Offering Safety 620 343-8799
25 W 5th Ave Emporia (66801) *(G-1825)*
Servicetitan Inc 316 267-5758
245 N Waco St Ste 230 Wichita (67202) *(G-15568)*
Servicmmber AG Vcation Educatn 785 537-7493
212 S 4th St Ste 130 Manhattan (66502) *(G-6799)*
Servimster Prof Rstoration Clg 785 832-0055
18730 174th St Bonner Springs (66012) *(G-572)*
SERVPRO, Leavenworth *Also called Thorman Enterprises LLC (G-5297)*
SERVPRO, Olathe *Also called Piat Inc (G-7986)*
SERVPRO, Wichita *Also called Butler & Mcllvain Inc (G-13921)*
Sesc, Wichita *Also called Spray Equipment & Svc Ctr LLC (G-15647)*
Settle Inn 913 381-5700
4401 W 107th St Overland Park (66207) *(G-9300)*
Severy Cooperative Association 620 736-2211
210 N Kansas Ave Severy (67137) *(G-10893)*
Sevo Systems Inc 913 677-1112
14335 W 97th Ter Lenexa (66215) *(G-6125)*
Sew Easy Sewing Center Inc 913 341-1122
9840 W 87th St Overland Park (66212) *(G-9301)*
Seward & Wilson Rentals, Pittsburg *Also called Seward and Wilson Electric (G-9937)*
Seward and Wilson Electric 620 232-1696
1202 E 4th St Pittsburg (66762) *(G-9937)*
Seward County Broadcasting Co 620 624-3891
1410 N Western Ave Liberal (67901) *(G-6364)*
Seward County Council On Aging 620 624-2511
701 N Grant Ave Liberal (67901) *(G-6365)*
Seward County Emrgncy Med Svc, Liberal *Also called County of Seward (G-6299)*
Seward County Historical Soc 620 624-7624
567 E Cedar St Liberal (67901) *(G-6366)*
Seward County Landfill, Liberal *Also called County of Seward (G-6298)*
Seward County Publishing LLC 620 626-0840
16 S Kansas Ave Liberal (67901) *(G-6367)*
Sewing Workshop 785 357-6231
301 S Kansas Ave Apt A Topeka (66603) *(G-13061)*
SF Hotel Company LP 316 681-5100
8100 E 22nd St N Bldg 500 Wichita (67226) *(G-15569)*
SF Trucking, Topeka *Also called Speculative Funding LLC (G-13089)*
Sfc Global Supply Chain Inc 785 825-1671
3019 Scanlan Ave Salina (67401) *(G-10705)*
Sgl LLC (HQ) 800 835-0588
1818 Broadway Ave Parsons (67357) *(G-9737)*
Sgws of KS, Edwardsville *Also called Southern Glazer SPI KS (G-1515)*
Shackelford Machine Inc 620 584-2436
116 S Tracy St Clearwater (67026) *(G-896)*
Shadmea Ministries Inc 912 332-0563
2610 Strauss Blvd # 1106 Junction City (66441) *(G-3752)*
Shadow 7 LLC 316 687-5777
1223 N Rock Rd 200 Wichita (67206) *(G-15570)*
Shady Creek Sales Inc 316 321-0943
1000 Ne Marina Rd El Dorado (67042) *(G-1602)*
Shafer Kline & Warren Inc (PA) 913 888-7800
11250 Corporate Ave Lenexa (66219) *(G-6126)*
Shahrokhi Inc 913 764-5775
525 N Lindenwood Dr Ste A Olathe (66062) *(G-8060)*
Shamburg Unlimited LLC 785 379-0760
3244 Se Stanley Rd Tecumseh (66542) *(G-12241)*
Shamir Corp 785 266-8880
3802 Sw Topeka Blvd Topeka (66609) *(G-13062)*
Shamrock Resources Inc 316 636-9557
4502 N Spyglass Cir Wichita (67226) *(G-15571)*
Shamrock Tire & Auto Service (PA) 316 522-2297
3001 S Broadway Ave Wichita (67216) *(G-15572)*
Shamrock Trading Corporation (PA) 877 642-8553
9300 Metcalf Ave Overland Park (66212) *(G-9302)*
Shane Paul Inc 316 283-1650
3700 S Kansas Rd Newton (67114) *(G-7417)*
Shane Paul LLC 316 283-1650
3700 S Kansas Rd Newton (67114) *(G-7418)*
Shaner Appraisals Inc 913 451-1451
10990 Quivira Rd Ste 100 Overland Park (66210) *(G-9303)*
Shank & Hamilton PC 816 471-0909
1968 Shawnee Mission Pkwy # 100 Shawnee Mission (66205) *(G-11849)*
Shannahan Crane & Hoist Inc 816 746-9822
10901 Kaw Dr Kansas City (66111) *(G-4419)*
Shark's Surf Shop, Lawrence *Also called Sharks Investment Inc (G-5109)*
Sharks Investment Inc 785 841-8289
813 Massachusetts St Lawrence (66044) *(G-5109)*
Sharon Baptist Church 316 684-5156
2221 S Oliver Ave Wichita (67218) *(G-15573)*
SHARON LANE NURSING HOME, Shawnee Mission *Also called C & H Health LLC (G-11193)*
Sharon Lee Family Health Care 913 722-3100
340 Southwest Blvd Kansas City (66103) *(G-4420)*
Sharon Miller 620 856-3377
2321 Military Ave Baxter Springs (66713) *(G-412)*
Sharon Sigma Realtors LLC 913 381-6794
5267 W 95th St Overland Park (66207) *(G-9304)*
Sharp McQueen Mckinley Mora 620 624-2548
419 N Kansas Ave Liberal (67901) *(G-6368)*
Sharp Bros Seed Company (PA) 620 398-2231
1005 S Sycamore Healy (67850) *(G-2967)*

ALPHABETIC

Sharp Construction Company...316 943-9511
505 W Clay St Valley Center (67147) *(G-13353)*
Sharp Farms, Healy *Also called Sharp Bros Seed Company (G-2967)*
Sharp Manufacturing LLC...785 363-7336
608 Main St Blue Rapids (66411) *(G-537)*
Sharpe Printing Co Inc...316 262-4041
345 N Waco St Wichita (67202) *(G-15574)*
Sharpening Specialists LLC...316 945-0593
2124 S Edwards St Wichita (67213) *(G-15575)*
Sharper Images Company LLC...620 331-7646
3345 W Main St Independence (67301) *(G-3559)*
Sharpline Converting Inc...316 722-9080
1520 S Tyler Rd Wichita (67209) *(G-15576)*
Sharps Auto Bdy Collision Inc...620 231-6011
202 N Elm St Pittsburg (66762) *(G-9938)*
Shasta Beverages Inc...913 888-6777
9901 Widmer Rd Lenexa (66215) *(G-6127)*
Shasta Midwest, Lenexa *Also called Shasta Beverages Inc (G-6127)*
Shasta Midwest Inc...913 888-6777
9901 Widmer Rd Lenexa (66215) *(G-6128)*
Shaughnessy Paper, Lenexa *Also called Shaughnsy-Knp-Hw-ppr Co St (G-6129)*
Shaughnsy-Knp-Hw-ppr Co St...913 541-0080
14449 W 100th St Lenexa (66215) *(G-6129)*
Shaw Feedyard Inc...620 635-2670
2428 Cr 15 Ashland (67831) *(G-198)*
Shaw Group Inc...316 220-8020
7330 W 33rd St N Ste 106 Wichita (67205) *(G-15577)*
Shaw Motor Co Inc...785 673-4228
Hwy Jct I 70 & K 23 Grainfield (67737) *(G-2496)*
Shawmar Oil & Gas Co Inc (PA)...620 382-2932
1116 E Main St Marion (66861) *(G-6876)*
Shawnee Biscuit Inc (PA)...913 441-7306
13851 W 101st St Lenexa (66215) *(G-6130)*
Shawnee Church of Nazarene...913 631-5555
5539 Quivira Rd Shawnee Mission (66216) *(G-11850)*
Shawnee Club, Shawnee Mission *Also called 24 Hour Fitness Usa Inc (G-11058)*
Shawnee Copy Center Inc...913 268-4343
12211 Shwnee Mission Pkwy Shawnee Mission (66216) *(G-11851)*
Shawnee Country Club...785 233-2373
913 Se 29th St Topeka (66605) *(G-13063)*
Shawnee County Health Agency, Topeka *Also called County of Shawnee (G-12522)*
Shawnee County Public Works, Topeka *Also called County of Shawnee (G-12521)*
Shawnee County Solid Waste, Topeka *Also called County of Shawnee (G-12517)*
Shawnee Courtyard, Shawnee *Also called Rhw Management Inc (G-11019)*
Shawnee Cycle Plaza, Shawnee Mission *Also called Clevlun Enterprises Inc (G-11239)*
Shawnee Gardens Health...913 631-2146
6416 Long Ave Shawnee (66216) *(G-11027)*
Shawnee Goodyear, Shawnee Mission *Also called Action Tire & Service Inc (G-11072)*
Shawnee Heating and Cooling...913 492-0824
10666 Widmer Rd Lenexa (66215) *(G-6131)*
Shawnee Hills Sr Living, Shawnee Mission *Also called Spectrum Retirement Shawnee KS (G-11882)*
Shawnee Hts Booster CLB Pto...785 379-5880
4201 Se Shawnee Hts Rd Tecumseh (66542) *(G-12242)*
Shawnee Hts Untd Methdst Ch...785 379-5492
6020 Se 44th St Tecumseh (66542) *(G-12243)*
Shawnee Inn Inc...913 248-1900
16555 Midland Dr Shawnee Mission (66217) *(G-11852)*
Shawnee Mission Bch Volleyball...913 422-4070
19800 Johnson Dr Shawnee Mission (66218) *(G-11853)*
Shawnee Mission Builders LLC...913 631-7020
10662 Widmer Rd Shawnee Mission (66215) *(G-11854)*
Shawnee Mission Corp Care LLC...913 492-9675
11140 Thompson Ave Shawnee Mission (66219) *(G-11855)*
Shawnee Mission Fmly Practice, Shawnee Mission *Also called Shawnee Mission Med Ctr Inc (G-11859)*
Shawnee Mission Health Care...913 676-2000
9100 W 74th St Shawnee Mission (66204) *(G-11856)*
Shawnee Mission Home Hlth Care, Shawnee Mission *Also called Adventist Health System/Sunbel (G-11081)*
Shawnee Mission Med Ctr Inc...913 632-9800
9301 W 74th St Ste 300 Shawnee Mission (66204) *(G-11857)*
Shawnee Mission Med Ctr Inc (HQ)...913 676-2000
9100 W 74th St Shawnee Mission (66204) *(G-11858)*
Shawnee Mission Med Ctr Inc...913 422-2020
6815 Hilltop Rd Shawnee (66226) *(G-11028)*
Shawnee Mission Med Ctr Inc...913 789-1980
9119 W 74th St Ste 150 Shawnee Mission (66204) *(G-11859)*
Shawnee Mission Med Ctr Inc...913 676-8400
8700 Bourgade St Ste 2 Shawnee Mission (66219) *(G-11860)*
Shawnee Mission Pediatrics PA...913 362-1660
7450 Kessler Ln Ste 105 Overland Park (66204) *(G-9305)*
Shawnee Mission Tree Svc Inc (PA)...913 441-8888
8250 Cole Pkwy Shawnee (66227) *(G-11029)*
Shawnee Mission Tree Svc Inc...316 838-3111
3428 N Emporia St Wichita (67219) *(G-15578)*
Shawnee Mission Wound Care Ctr, Shawnee Mission *Also called Critical Care Systems Intl Inc (G-11281)*
Shawnee Mssion Plmnary Cons PA...913 362-0300
8901 W 74th St Ste 390 Shawnee Mission (66204) *(G-11861)*
Shawnee Mssion Plmonary Conslt, Shawnee Mission *Also called Shawnee Mssion Plmnary Cons PA (G-11861)*
Shawnee Presby Preschool, Shawnee Mission *Also called Shawnee Presbyterian Church (G-11862)*
Shawnee Presbyterian Church...913 631-6689
6837 Nieman Rd Shawnee Mission (66203) *(G-11862)*
Shawnee Regl Prevention An...785 266-8666
2209 Sw 29th St Topeka (66611) *(G-13064)*
Shawnee Rock Company, Olathe *Also called Deffenbaugh Industries Inc (G-7647)*
Shawnee Steel & Welding Inc (PA)...913 432-8046
6124 Merriam Dr Shawnee Mission (66203) *(G-11863)*
Shawnee Storm Water Hardware, Shawnee Mission *Also called Ceo Enterprises Inc (G-11214)*
Shawnee Terminal Elevator, Topeka *Also called White Cloud Grain Company Inc (G-13242)*
Shawnee United Methodist Ch, Shawnee Mission *Also called Kansas East Conference United (G-11516)*
Shawnee Well Service Inc...620 254-7893
Miles N Of Hwy 160 Attica (67009) *(G-279)*
Shawnee Woodwork Inc...785 354-1163
112 Sw Harrison St Topeka (66603) *(G-13065)*
Shawns Foundations...316 214-1070
762 Us Highway 56 Garfield (67529) *(G-2367)*
Shc Holdings LLC...620 273-6900
200 N Walnut St Cottonwood Falls (66845) *(G-1156)*
Shc Services Inc...913 652-9229
6700 Antioch Rd Ste 120 Overland Park (66204) *(G-9306)*
Shea Vision Associates...316 686-6071
2251 N Woodlawn Blvd Wichita (67220) *(G-15579)*
Shear Designers...620 342-5393
2607 W 18th Ave Emporia (66801) *(G-1826)*
Shears Shop...785 823-6201
1329 W North St Salina (67401) *(G-10706)*
Sheet Metal Contractors Inc...913 397-9130
15655 S Keeler Ter Olathe (66062) *(G-8061)*
Sheets Adams Realtors Inc...620 241-3648
1605 N Main St McPherson (67460) *(G-7026)*
Sheila M Burdett Agency LLC...785 762-2451
517 Wheatland Dr Junction City (66441) *(G-3753)*
Sheldon C Clayton...913 927-9248
3685 Reno Rd Ottawa (66067) *(G-8311)*
Shell Oil Products U S, Shawnee Mission *Also called Equilon Enterprises LLC (G-11346)*
Shell Topco LP (HQ)...316 942-7266
2533 S West St Wichita (67217) *(G-15580)*
Shelley Electric Inc...785 862-0507
5331 Sw Randolph Ave Topeka (66609) *(G-13066)*
Shelter Insurance...785 272-7181
2701 Sw Wanamaker Rd Topeka (66614) *(G-13067)*
Sheltered Living Inc (PA)...785 233-2566
3401 Sw Harrison St Topeka (66611) *(G-13068)*
Sheltered Living Inc...785 266-8686
2126 Sw 36th St Topeka (66611) *(G-13069)*
Shelton Body Shop, Derby *Also called Shelton Collision Repair Inc (G-1271)*
Shelton Collision Repair Inc...316 788-1528
325 W Patriot Ave Derby (67037) *(G-1271)*
Shemar Inc...620 342-5787
729 W 6th Ave Emporia (66801) *(G-1827)*
SHEPHERD CENTER, Cimarron *Also called Shepherd of Plains Foundation (G-836)*
Shepherd of Plains Foundation...620 855-3498
101 E Cedar Ridge Dr Cimarron (67835) *(G-836)*
Shepherds Truck & Tractor...620 331-2970
3720 W Main St Independence (67301) *(G-3560)*
Sheraton Overland Park Hotel, Overland Park *Also called Overland Park Development Corp (G-9117)*
Sheridan County Health Complex, Hoxie *Also called County of Sheridan (G-3136)*
Sherow Cattle Co...620 596-2813
22703 W Castleton Rd Langdon (67583) *(G-4664)*
Sherwin-Williams Company...913 782-0126
1209 E Santa Fe St Olathe (66061) *(G-8062)*
Sherwood Construction Co Inc (PA)...316 943-0211
3219 W May St Wichita (67213) *(G-15581)*
Sherwood Lake Club Inc...785 478-3305
6910 Sw Fountaindale Rd Topeka (66614) *(G-13070)*
Shi International Corp...512 226-3984
12980 Foster St Overland Park (66213) *(G-9307)*
Shield Agricultural Equipment, Hutchinson *Also called Shield Industries Inc (G-3441)*
Shield Industries Inc...620 662-7221
950 Scott Blvd Hutchinson (67505) *(G-3441)*
Shields Oil Producers Inc...785 483-3141
326 N Main St Russell (67665) *(G-10299)*
Shilling Construction Co Inc...785 776-5077
9620 E Us Highway 24 Manhattan (66502) *(G-6800)*
Shimadzu Scientific Instrs Inc...913 888-9449
8052 Reeder St Shawnee Mission (66214) *(G-11864)*

Shining Stars Daycare Center 913 829-5000
16310 W 159th Ter Olathe (66062) **(G-8063)**
Shirconn Investments Inc 913 390-9500
20662 W 151st St Olathe (66061) **(G-8064)**
Shire Graphics, Park City *Also called Shire Signs LLC* **(G-9643)**
Shire Signs LLC 316 838-1362
225 W 59th St N Ste A Park City (67204) **(G-9643)**
Shirley Alexander 316 651-3621
5500 E Kellogg Dr Bldg 5b Wichita (67218) **(G-15582)**
Shirley Marley Enterprises 913 492-0004
10448 Mastin St Shawnee Mission (66212) **(G-11865)**
Shirts Plus Inc 316 788-1550
703 N Buckner St Derby (67037) **(G-1272)**
Shooters, Olathe *Also called Olathe Billiards Inc* **(G-7928)**
Shop Carts, Topeka *Also called Adapa Incorporated* **(G-12286)**
Shor-Line, Kansas City *Also called Schroer Manufacturing Company* **(G-4404)**
Shore Tire Co Inc 913 541-9300
9300 Marshall Dr Lenexa (66215) **(G-6132)**
Shorman & Associates Inc 913 341-8811
7299 W 98th Ter Ste 100 Shawnee Mission (66212) **(G-11866)**
Shoroeders Jim Sftwr & Video 620 227-7628
1410 Circle Lake Dr Dodge City (67801) **(G-1430)**
Short Creek Construction 620 783-2896
815 W 7th St Galena (66739) **(G-2085)**
Short Go Inc 620 223-2866
400 N National Ave Fort Scott (66701) **(G-2004)**
Short Stop, Manhattan *Also called Leiszler Oil Co Inc* **(G-6712)**
Shorts Travel Management Inc (PA) 319 234-5577
7815 Floyd St Overland Park (66204) **(G-9308)**
Shostak Iron and Metal Co Inc 913 321-9210
6517 W 106th St Overland Park (66212) **(G-9309)**
Show Engraving, Lane *Also called Snow Inc* **(G-4663)**
Show ME Birds Hunting Resort 620 674-8863
2400 Quaker Rd Baxter Springs (66713) **(G-413)**
Shred It Kansas City, Lenexa *Also called Boyer-Kansas Inc* **(G-5710)**
Shred-It Kansas City, Lenexa *Also called Stericycle Inc* **(G-6153)**
Shree Ram Investments of Pltte 913 948-9000
15475 S Rogers Rd Olathe (66062) **(G-8065)**
Shree-Guru Investments Inc 785 273-0003
1401 Sw Ashworth Pl Topeka (66604) **(G-13071)**
Shreeji Investments Inc 785 838-4242
740 Iowa St Lawrence (66044) **(G-5110)**
Shri Ram Corp 248 477-3200
8601 Candlelight Ln Lenexa (66215) **(G-6133)**
Shriji Inc 785 242-9898
2335 S Oak St Ottawa (66067) **(G-8312)**
Shuttle Aerospace Inc 316 832-0210
12550 W 53rd St N Maize (67101) **(G-6519)**
Shuttle Bus General Pub Trnsp 620 326-3953
2410 N A St Wellington (67152) **(G-13529)**
Si Funeral Services, Overland Park *Also called Suhor Industries Inc* **(G-9371)**
Si Overland Park LP 913 345-2661
5800 College Blvd Overland Park (66211) **(G-9310)**
Sid Bdeker Safety Shoe Svc Inc 913 599-6463
14501 W 101st Ter # 1104 Lenexa (66215) **(G-6134)**
Side Pockets Inc 913 888-7665
13320 W 87th Street Pkwy Shawnee Mission (66215) **(G-11867)**
Sids Corrugating & Machinery 316 744-0061
5844 N Broadway Ave Park City (67219) **(G-9644)**
Siemens Energy Inc 316 315-4534
1090 E 37th St N Wichita (67219) **(G-15583)**
Siemens Industry Inc 913 683-9787
1001 N 8th St Lansing (66043) **(G-4692)**
Siemens Industry Inc 316 267-5814
618 E Douglas Ave Wichita (67202) **(G-15584)**
Siemens Industry Inc 316 946-4190
2219b S Air Cargo Rd Wichita (67209) **(G-15585)**
Siemens Industry Inc 316 260-4340
740 N Gilda St Wichita (67212) **(G-15586)**
Siemens Industry Inc 620 252-4223
400 N Linden St Coffeyville (67337) **(G-977)**
Siemens Industry Inc 785 762-7814
3200 Industrial St Junction City (66441) **(G-3754)**
Sierra Gypsum, Lenexa *Also called Kcg Inc* **(G-5943)**
Sierra Hills Exec Golf CLB, Wichita *Also called Sierra Hills Golf Club* **(G-15587)**
Sierra Hills Golf Club 316 733-9333
13420 E Pawnee St Wichita (67230) **(G-15587)**
Sigma Distributing Company Inc (PA) 316 943-4499
901 S Sabin St Wichita (67209) **(G-15588)**
Sigma Tek Inc (PA) 316 775-6373
1001 Industrial Rd Augusta (67010) **(G-345)**
Sign Here Inc 913 856-0148
558 W Main St Gardner (66030) **(G-2363)**
Sign House Inc 785 827-2729
3110 Enterprise Dr Salina (67401) **(G-10707)**
Sign Solutions 620 442-5649
12046 292nd Rd Arkansas City (67005) **(G-179)**
Sign Systems, Olathe *Also called Luminous Neon Inc* **(G-7867)**
Signal 88 Security, Wichita *Also called Total Security Solutions LLC* **(G-15776)**
Signal Kit LLC 866 297-7585
15023 Ash St Leawood (66224) **(G-5551)**
Signal Theory Inc (PA) 316 263-0124
255 N Mead St Wichita (67202) **(G-15589)**
Signature Cleaning, Lawrence *Also called Jeff Goldman* **(G-4922)**
Signature Flight Support Corp 316 522-2010
1980 S Airport Rd Wichita (67209) **(G-15590)**
Signature Landscape LLC 913 829-8181
15705 S Pflumm Rd Olathe (66062) **(G-8066)**
Signature Logo Embroidery Inc 913 671-8548
5855 Beverly Ave Ste C Shawnee Mission (66202) **(G-11868)**
Signature Manufacturing 913 766-0680
9825 W 67th St Merriam (66203) **(G-7104)**
Signature Select LLC, Wichita *Also called Ima Select LLC* **(G-14674)**
Signature Sportswear Inc 620 421-1871
519 N Turnberry Cir Wichita (67230) **(G-15591)**
Signify North America Corp 785 826-5218
3861 S 9th St Salina (67401) **(G-10708)**
Signs & Design LLC 316 264-7446
4545 W Central Ave Wichita (67212) **(G-15592)**
Signs By Shire Inc 316 838-1362
225 W 59th St N Ste A Park City (67204) **(G-9645)**
Signs of Business Inc (PA) 316 683-5700
150 S Rock Rd Wichita (67207) **(G-15593)**
Silencer, Lorraine *Also called Moly Manufacturing Inc* **(G-6433)**
Silva Security Service 316 942-7872
2042 N Gow St Wichita (67203) **(G-15594)**
Silver City Cmnty Resource Ctr 913 362-3367
2332 Birch Dr Kansas City (66106) **(G-4421)**
Silver Crest At Deercreek 913 681-1101
13060 Metcalf Ave Shawnee Mission (66213) **(G-11869)**
Silver Lake Bank (PA) 785 232-0102
201 Nw Us Highway 24 # 201 Topeka (66608) **(G-13072)**
Silvercrest At College View Sr 913 915-6041
13600 W 110th Ter Apt 214 Lenexa (66215) **(G-6135)**
Simmons Manufacturing, Shawnee Mission *Also called Ssb Manufacturing Company* **(G-11889)**
Simmons Pet Food Inc 620 342-1323
1400 E Logan Ave Emporia (66801) **(G-1828)**
Simmons Prepared Foods Inc 479 524-8151
417 Warren Way Emporia (66801) **(G-1829)**
Simon & Simon Inc 913 888-9889
7806 W 100th Ter Overland Park (66212) **(G-9311)**
Simplex Time Recorder 472, Wichita *Also called Simplex Time Recorder LLC* **(G-15595)**
Simplex Time Recorder LLC 316 686-6363
625 N Carriage Pkwy # 140 Wichita (67208) **(G-15595)**
Simply Fuel LLC 913 269-1889
14330 Juniper St Overland Park (66224) **(G-9312)**
Simpson Construction Svcs Inc 316 942-3206
567 W Douglas Ave Wichita (67213) **(G-15596)**
Simpson Farm Enterprises Inc (PA) 785 731-2700
20333 N Ness Cnty Line Rd Ransom (67572) **(G-10195)**
Simpson Lgback Lynch Norris PA (PA) 913 342-2500
7400 W 110th St Ste 600 Overland Park (66210) **(G-9313)**
Sims Fertilizer and Chem Co 785 346-5681
1006 Industrial Ave Osborne (67473) **(G-8218)**
Sims Insurance Services I 316 722-9977
4621 N Maize Rd Maize (67101) **(G-6520)**
Sinclair & Sons Custom Welding 316 263-3500
1023 S Santa Fe St Wichita (67211) **(G-15597)**
Sinclair Companies 785 799-3116
402 3rd St Home (66438) **(G-3120)**
Single Tree Inn 620 356-1500
2033 W Oklahoma Ave Ulysses (67880) **(G-13318)**
Sink Gordon & Associates LLP 785 537-0190
727 Poyntz Ave Ste 601 Manhattan (66502) **(G-6801)**
Sir Speedy, Manhattan *Also called Martin Dysart Enterprises Inc* **(G-6732)**
Sirius Computer Solutions Inc 913 469-7900
10801 Mastin St Ste 900 Overland Park (66210) **(G-9314)**
Sirloin Stockade, Hutchinson *Also called S S of Kansas Inc* **(G-3435)**
Sirloin Stockade, Salina *Also called S S of Kansas Inc* **(G-10657)**
Sisters of Charity of Leavenwo 785 295-7800
1700 Sw 7th St Topeka (66606) **(G-13073)**
Sisters of Charity of Leavenwo 913 825-0500
8919 Parallel Pkwy # 118 Kansas City (66112) **(G-4422)**
Sisters of Charity of Leavenwo 785 295-5310
600 Sw Jewell Ave Topeka (66606) **(G-13074)**
Sisters Servants of Mary 913 371-3423
800 N 18th St Kansas City (66102) **(G-4423)**
Sisters St Joseph Wichita KS (HQ) 316 686-7171
3700 E Lincoln St Wichita (67218) **(G-15598)**
Site 393, Galena *Also called Allied Services LLC* **(G-2068)**
Six Continents Hotels Inc 785 827-9000
201 E Diamond Dr Salina (67401) **(G-10709)**
Six Continents Hotels Inc 620 792-2431
3017 10th St Great Bend (67530) **(G-2636)**
Six Continents Hotels Inc 785 462-8787
645 W Willow Ave Colby (67701) **(G-1041)**

ALPHABETIC

Sizewise Rentals LLC...800 814-9389
204 W 2nd St Ellis (67637) ***(G-1652)***
Sizewise Rentals LLC...785 726-4371
210 Jefferson St Ellis (67637) ***(G-1653)***
Sjcf Architecture, Wichita *Also called Schaefer Johnson Cox Frey Arch* ***(G-15527)***
Sjh Family Corp...785 856-5296
2400 Franklin Rd Ste A Lawrence (66046) ***(G-5111)***
Sjn Banc Co...620 549-3225
116 E 3rd Ave Saint John (67576) ***(G-10356)***
Sjn Bank of Kansas (PA)...620 549-3225
116 E 3rd Ave Saint John (67576) ***(G-10357)***
Sk8away Inc...785 272-0303
815 Sw Fairlawn Rd Topeka (66606) ***(G-13075)***
Skaer Veterinary Clinic P A...316 683-4641
404 S Edgemoor St Ste 100 Wichita (67218) ***(G-15599)***
Skaggs Inc...620 672-5312
107 S Main St Pratt (67124) ***(G-10148)***
Skate South Inc...316 524-7261
1900 E Macarthur Rd Wichita (67216) ***(G-15600)***
Skc Communication Products LLC (PA)...913 422-4222
8320 Hedge Lane Ter Shawnee Mission (66227) ***(G-11870)***
Skc Corporation...800 882-7779
8320 Hedge Lane Ter Shawnee Mission (66227) ***(G-11871)***
Skeeters Body Shop Inc...620 275-7255
3104 W Jones Ave Garden City (67846) ***(G-2280)***
Skiles Industries, Atwood *Also called J D Skiles Inc* ***(G-287)***
Skilled Saws Inc...785 249-5084
8617 Nw 66th St Silver Lake (66539) ***(G-12028)***
Skillett & Sons Incorporated...785 222-3611
2309 Highway 183 La Crosse (67548) ***(G-4639)***
Skillman Construction LLC...620 364-2505
345 N Main St New Strawn (66839) ***(G-7305)***
Skillpath Seminars Inc (HQ)...913 362-3900
6900 Squibb Rd Shawnee Mission (66202) ***(G-11872)***
Skin Renewal...913 722-5551
8490 College Blvd Overland Park (66210) ***(G-9315)***
Skit, Clearwater *Also called Clearwater Cable Vision Inc* ***(G-888)***
Skookum Contract Services, Fort Riley *Also called Skookum Educational Programs* ***(G-1950)***
Skookum Educational Programs...785 307-8180
315 Marshall Ave Fort Riley (66442) ***(G-1950)***
Skutouch Solutions LLC...913 538-5165
8226 Nieman Rd Lenexa (66214) ***(G-6136)***
Sky Blue Inc...785 842-9013
2110 Delaware St Ste B Lawrence (66046) ***(G-5112)***
Sky Printing and Pubg Inc...913 362-9292
5406 Johnson Dr Shawnee Mission (66205) ***(G-11873)***
Skycom Inc...785 273-1000
1020 Sw Wanamaker Rd Topeka (66604) ***(G-13076)***
Skyland Grain LLC...620 672-3961
100 Cairo Main St Cunningham (67035) ***(G-1189)***
Skyland Grain LLC (PA)...620 492-2126
304 E Highland Johnson (67855) ***(G-3660)***
Skyler Ridge Apartments, Overland Park *Also called Sentinel Real Estate Corp* ***(G-9295)***
Skyline Construction Company...913 642-7100
9120 Flint St Overland Park (66214) ***(G-9316)***
Skyline Corporation...620 442-9060
315 W Skyline Rd Arkansas City (67005) ***(G-180)***
Skyline E3 Inc...913 599-4787
9511 Legler Rd Lenexa (66219) ***(G-6137)***
Skyline Motel...620 431-1500
1216 W Main St Chanute (66720) ***(G-762)***
Skymark Refuelers LLC (PA)...913 653-8100
610 S Adams St Kansas City (66105) ***(G-4424)***
Skyton Lawn & Landscape LLC...913 302-9056
11202 W 163rd Ter Olathe (66062) ***(G-8067)***
Skyward Credit Union...316 517-6578
4 Cessna Blvd Wichita (67215) ***(G-15601)***
Slape and Howard Chartered...316 262-3445
1009 S Broadway Ave Wichita (67211) ***(G-15602)***
Slape, Dale V, Wichita *Also called Slape and Howard Chartered* ***(G-15602)***
Slappy's Electric Paradise, Salina *Also called Web Creations & Consulting LLC* ***(G-10762)***
Slawson Co, Wichita *Also called Canyon Oil & Gas Co* ***(G-13935)***
Slawson Exploration Co Inc (PA)...316 263-3201
727 N Waco Ave Ste 400 Wichita (67203) ***(G-15603)***
Slawson Investment Corporation (PA)...316 263-3201
727 N Waco Ave Ste 400 Wichita (67203) ***(G-15604)***
Sleep Haven Inc...620 465-2242
8819 E Industrial Dr Haven (67543) ***(G-2737)***
Sleep Inn, Topeka *Also called Swami Inc* ***(G-13128)***
Sleep Inn, Olathe *Also called Shirconn Investments Inc* ***(G-8064)***
Sleep Inn & Suites...620 223-2555
302 E Wall St Fort Scott (66701) ***(G-2005)***
Sleep Inn & Suites Parsons...620 421-6126
1807 Harding Dr Parsons (67357) ***(G-9738)***
Sleep Inn and Suite...620 688-6400
202 E 11th St Coffeyville (67337) ***(G-978)***
Sleep Inn and Suites 07...620 805-6535
1931 E Kansas Ave Garden City (67846) ***(G-2281)***
Sleep Inn Inn & Suites...785 625-2700
1011 E 41st St Hays (67601) ***(G-2908)***
Sleep Inn Suite...316 425-6077
651 E 71st St S Haysville (67060) ***(G-2960)***
Sleep One Inc (PA)...913 859-0001
5737 W 146th St Overland Park (66223) ***(G-9317)***
Sleepcair Inc...913 438-8200
14333 W 95th St Lenexa (66215) ***(G-6138)***
Sleepcair Pharmacy, Lenexa *Also called Sleepcair Inc* ***(G-6138)***
Sleepright, Lenexa *Also called Splintek Inc* ***(G-6148)***
Sloan Eisenbarth Glassman (PA)...785 357-6311
534 S Kansas Ave Ste 1000 Topeka (66603) ***(G-13077)***
Small Beginnings...913 851-2223
15801 Metcalf Ave Shawnee Mission (66223) ***(G-11874)***
Small Business Bank (PA)...913 856-7199
13423 W 92nd St Lenexa (66215) ***(G-6139)***
Smallwood Lock Supply Inc (PA)...913 371-5678
1008 N 18th St Kansas City (66102) ***(G-4425)***
Smallwood Locksmiths, Kansas City *Also called Smallwood Lock Supply Inc* ***(G-4425)***
Smart Beverage Inc (PA)...785 656-2166
16113 W 130th Ter Olathe (66062) ***(G-8068)***
Smart Home Innovations LLC...913 339-8641
1136 Adams St Kansas City (66103) ***(G-4426)***
Smart Money Concepts Inc...913 962-9806
7300 W 110th St Fl 7 Overland Park (66210) ***(G-9318)***
Smart Security Solutions Inc...913 568-2573
11539 Hadley St Overland Park (66210) ***(G-9319)***
Smart Start of Kansas LLC...620 345-6000
141 S Christian Ave Moundridge (67107) ***(G-7197)***
Smart Truck Line Inc...785 353-2411
511 Hamilton St Beattie (66406) ***(G-419)***
Smart Warehousing LLC (PA)...913 888-3222
18905 Kill Creek Rd Edgerton (66021) ***(G-1489)***
Smart Way...913 764-3071
540 E 126th Ter Olathe (66061) ***(G-8069)***
Smartway Transportation Inc...877 537-2681
10901 Granada Ln Overland Park (66211) ***(G-9320)***
SMC Concrete and Cnstr LLC...785 545-5186
1417 Locust St Cawker City (67430) ***(G-690)***
Smg Holdings Inc...316 440-9016
500 E Waterman St Wichita (67202) ***(G-15605)***
Smg Holdings Inc...785 235-1986
1 Expocentre Dr Topeka (66612) ***(G-13078)***
SMH Consultants PA...785 776-0541
2017 Vanesta Pl Ste 110 Manhattan (66503) ***(G-6802)***
Smile Centre...913 651-9800
309 S 2nd St Leavenworth (66048) ***(G-5289)***
Smile Junction, Wichita *Also called Stephen P Moore DDS* ***(G-15662)***
Smiles, Wichita *Also called Richard E Crowder DDS* ***(G-15456)***
Smith Ned E Jr DDS Ms Charter...913 383-3233
10325 Mohawk Rd Leawood (66206) ***(G-5552)***
Smith & Boucher Inc (PA)...913 345-2127
25501 W Valley Pkwy # 200 Olathe (66061) ***(G-8070)***
Smith & Smith Aircraft Intl...316 945-0204
3738 W 29th St S Wichita (67217) ***(G-15606)***
Smith and Loveless Inc (PA)...913 888-5201
14040 Santa Fe Trail Dr Shawnee Mission (66215) ***(G-11875)***
Smith Audio Visual Inc...785 235-3481
5233 Sw 25th St Topeka (66614) ***(G-13079)***
Smith Auto & Truck Parts Inc...620 275-9145
402 E Burnside Dr Garden City (67846) ***(G-2282)***
Smith Brothers Inc...620 754-3958
21585 Victory Rd Stark (66775) ***(G-12112)***
Smith Center Chamber Commerce...785 282-3895
219 S Main St Smith Center (66967) ***(G-12041)***
Smith Cnty Pionr Newsppr Agcy, Smith Center *Also called Smith County Pioneer* ***(G-12043)***
Smith Construction Company Inc...316 942-7989
4620 W Esthner Ave Wichita (67209) ***(G-15607)***
Smith County Ems, Smith Center *Also called County of Smith* ***(G-12033)***
Smith County Family Practice...785 282-6834
119 E Parliament St Smith Center (66967) ***(G-12042)***
Smith County Memorial Hospital, Smith Center *Also called Great Plains Smith Co Inc* ***(G-12034)***
Smith County Pioneer...785 282-3371
201 S Main St Smith Center (66967) ***(G-12043)***
Smith Monuments Inc...785 425-6762
110 S Cedar St Stockton (67669) ***(G-12187)***
Smith Pressroom Products, Lenexa *Also called R P M Smith Corporation* ***(G-6087)***
Smith Shay Farmer & Wetta LLC...316 267-5293
200 W Douglas Ave Ste 350 Wichita (67202) ***(G-15608)***
Smith Transportation Inc...913 543-7614
2540 S 88th St Kansas City (66111) ***(G-4427)***
Smith's Market, Hutchinson *Also called Earl Barnes* ***(G-3273)***
Smithcon LLC...316 744-3406
3030 N Ohio St Wichita (67219) ***(G-15609)***
Smithcon Construction, Wichita *Also called Smithcon LLC* ***(G-15609)***
Smithfield Direct LLC...785 762-3306
1920 Lacy Dr Junction City (66441) ***(G-3755)***

Smithfield Foods Inc 785 762-3306
1920 Lacy Dr Junction City (66441) *(G-3756)*
Smithfield Packaged Meats Corp 316 942-8461
2323 S Sheridan St Wichita (67213) *(G-15610)*
Smiths Connectors, Kansas City *Also called Smiths Intrcnnect Americas Inc (G-4428)*
Smiths Intrcnnect Americas Inc 913 342-5544
5101 Richland Ave Kansas City (66106) *(G-4428)*
Smiths Intrcnnect Americas Inc (HQ) 913 342-5544
5101 Richland Ave Kansas City (66106) *(G-4429)*
Smithyman & Zakoura Chartered 913 661-9800
7400 W 110th St Ste 750 Shawnee Mission (66210) *(G-11876)*
Smittys Lawn & Grdn Equiptment, Olathe *Also called Century Partners LLC (G-7586)*
Smokey Hill Meat Processing 785 735-2278
108 Ball Park Rd Victoria (67671) *(G-13377)*
Smoky Hill LLC 785 825-0810
645 E Crawford St Unit E8 Salina (67401) *(G-10710)*
Smoky Hill Country Club Inc 785 625-4021
3303 N Hall St Hays (67601) *(G-2909)*
Smoky Hill Museum, Salina *Also called City of Salina (G-10450)*
SMOKY HILL PRO SHOP, Hays *Also called Smoky Hill Country Club Inc (G-2909)*
Smoky Hill Ranch, Gove *Also called Faith Technologies Inc (G-2493)*
Smoky Hill Rehabilitation Ctr, Salina *Also called Liberty Healthcare of Oklahoma (G-10581)*
Smoky Hills Public TV Corp 785 483-6990
604 Elm St Bunker Hill (67626) *(G-620)*
Smoky Valley Concrete Inc 785 820-8113
1700 W State St Salina (67401) *(G-10711)*
SMS, Hamilton *Also called Schlotterbeck Machine Shop (G-2708)*
Smyth Oil and Gas Services 620 356-4091
2398 W Rd 10 Ulysses (67880) *(G-13319)*
SNC Alarm Service 620 665-6651
2611 E 17th Ave Hutchinson (67501) *(G-3442)*
Snell Harvesting Inc 620 564-3312
509 W 6th St Ellinwood (67526) *(G-1637)*
Snodgrass & Sons Cnstr Co Inc 316 687-3110
2700 S George Wash Blvd Wichita (67210) *(G-15611)*
Snodgrass Dunlap & Company PA (PA) 620 365-3125
16 W Jackson Ave Iola (66749) *(G-3632)*
Snow Inc 785 869-2021
703 6th St Lane (66042) *(G-4663)*
Snyder Law Firm LLC 913 685-3900
13401 Mission Rd Leawood (66209) *(G-5553)*
Social and Rehabilitation Serv 620 272-5800
1710 Palace Dr Garden City (67846) *(G-2283)*
SOCIAL AND REHABILITATION SERVICES, KANSAS DEPT OF, Garden City *Also called Social and Rehabilitation Serv (G-2283)*
Social Security Administration, Manhattan *Also called Social Security Employees (G-6803)*
Social Security Employees 877 840-5741
1121a Hudson Ave Ste A Manhattan (66503) *(G-6803)*
Society of Tchers Fmly Mdicine 913 906-6000
11400 Thawk Ck Pkwy 540 Shawnee Mission (66211) *(G-11877)*
Society of Teachers of Family 913 906-6000
11400 Tomahawk Creek Pkwy Shawnee Mission (66211) *(G-11878)*
Sod Shop Inc 913 814-0044
1783 E 1500 Rd Ste B Lawrence (66044) *(G-5113)*
Sod Shop Inc 913 814-0044
4855 W 231st St Bucyrus (66013) *(G-609)*
Soft Armor, Overland Park *Also called Rnn Enterprises LLC (G-9246)*
Softek Illuminate Inc 913 981-5300
7299 W 98th Ter Ste 130 Overland Park (66212) *(G-9321)*
Softek Solutions Inc (PA) 913 649-1024
4500 W 89th St Ste 100 Prairie Village (66207) *(G-10067)*
Softwarfare LLC 202 854-9268
7301 Mission Rd Ste 141 Prairie Village (66208) *(G-10068)*
Sogeti USA LLC 913 451-9600
7101 College Blvd # 1150 Overland Park (66210) *(G-9322)*
Sohum Systems LLC 913 221-7204
7900 College Blvd Ste 135 Overland Park (66210) *(G-9323)*
Soil Conservation Service USDA 785 823-4500
760 S Broadway Blvd Salina (67401) *(G-10712)*
Sokkia Corporation (HQ) 816 322-0939
16900 W 118th Ter Olathe (66061) *(G-8071)*
Sokolov Dental Laboratory Inc 913 262-5444
8056 Reeder St Shawnee Mission (66214) *(G-11879)*
Soleo Health, Lenexa *Also called Biomed Kansas Inc (G-5705)*
Soleran Inc 913 647-5900
7400 W 132nd St Ste 140 Overland Park (66213) *(G-9324)*
Solid State Sonics & Elec 785 232-0497
4137 Nw Lwer Silver Lk Rd Topeka (66618) *(G-13080)*
Solida John & Sons Tree Svc 785 543-2810
95 E Santa Fe Rd Phillipsburg (67661) *(G-9799)*
Solomon Electric Company, Solomon *Also called Solomon Transformers LLC (G-12054)*
Solomon State Bank (PA) 785 655-2941
126 W Main St Solomon (67480) *(G-12053)*
Solomon Transformers LLC (PA) 785 655-2191
103 W Main St Solomon (67480) *(G-12054)*
Solomon Valley Feeders LLC 785 738-2263
3575 Jazmine Trl Beloit (67420) *(G-503)*
Solomon Valley Manor, Stockton *Also called City of Stockton (G-12181)*

Solutions North Bank (PA) 785 425-6721
123 N Cedar St Stockton (67669) *(G-12188)*
Solutions North Bank 785 743-2104
134 N Main St Wakeeney (67672) *(G-13390)*
Solutions Now Inc 913 327-5805
6400 Glenwood St Ste 314 Overland Park (66202) *(G-9325)*
Solvenet Solutions, Leawood *Also called Custom Rdo Communications Ltd (G-5367)*
Soma By Chicos LLC 913 317-8566
5032 W 119th St Leawood (66209) *(G-5554)*
Something Different Inc (PA) 785 537-1171
1008 Kaw Valley Park Cir # 501 Wamego (66547) *(G-13441)*
Something Different Media Prod 913 764-9500
13401 S Mur Len Rd # 100 Olathe (66062) *(G-8072)*
Sommerset Ridge Vineyard 913 491-0038
29725 Somerset Rd Paola (66071) *(G-9587)*
Somnicare Inc 913 498-1331
10590 Barkley St Overland Park (66212) *(G-9326)*
Somnitech Inc (HQ) 913 498-8120
10590 Barkley St Overland Park (66212) *(G-9327)*
Somnograph Inc 316 925-4624
7111 E 21st St N Ste G Wichita (67206) *(G-15612)*
Sonar Sangam Inc 316 529-4911
4510 S Broadway Ave Wichita (67216) *(G-15613)*
Sonic Equipment Co, Iola *Also called R E B Inc (G-3630)*
Sonnys Inc 316 942-2390
1030 S West St Wichita (67213) *(G-15614)*
Sonoco Products Company 620 662-2331
100 N Halstead St Hutchinson (67501) *(G-3443)*
Sonodora Inc 316 494-2218
4601 E Douglas Ave Wichita (67218) *(G-15615)*
Sooner Oil LLC 785 340-5602
1626 Rivendell St Junction City (66441) *(G-3757)*
Sorella Group Inc 913 390-9544
14844 W 107th St Lenexa (66215) *(G-6140)*
Soroptimist International 316 321-0433
737 Harvard Ave El Dorado (67042) *(G-1603)*
SOS Metals Midwest LLC 316 522-0101
9800 W York St Wichita (67215) *(G-15616)*
Sound Products Inc 913 599-3666
1365 N Winchester St Olathe (66061) *(G-8073)*
Soundtube Entertainment Inc 913 233-8520
13720 W 109th St Lenexa (66215) *(G-6141)*
Soundtube Entertainment Inc (PA) 435 647-9555
8005 W 110th St Ste 208 Overland Park (66210) *(G-9328)*
Source Incorporated Missouri 913 663-2700
6840 Silverheel St Shawnee (66226) *(G-11030)*
Source Building Services Inc 913 341-7500
7211 W 98th Ter Ste 100 Overland Park (66212) *(G-9329)*
Source Inc., Shawnee *Also called Source Incorporated Missouri (G-11030)*
Source One Distributors Inc 620 221-8919
511 Industrial Blvd Winfield (67156) *(G-16172)*
Sourdough Express Incorporated 907 452-1181
219 S Main St Medicine Lodge (67104) *(G-7072)*
South Centl Communications Inc 620 930-1000
215 S Iliff St Medicine Lodge (67104) *(G-7073)*
South Centl KS Educatn Svc Ctr (PA) 620 584-3300
13939 W Diagonal Rd Clearwater (67026) *(G-897)*
South Central Kansas 316 262-7035
9730 E 50th St N Bel Aire (67226) *(G-440)*
South Central Kansas Med Ctr, Arkansas City *Also called South Cntl Kans Rgonal Med Ctr (G-181)*
South Central KS Econ Dev Dist 316 262-7035
9730 E 50th St N Wichita (67226) *(G-15617)*
South Central Mntl Hlth CN 316 775-5491
520 E Augusta Ave Augusta (67010) *(G-346)*
South Central Pathology Lab PA 316 689-5668
3600 E Harry St Wichita (67218) *(G-15618)*
South Central Pool 20, Lenexa *Also called Scp Distributors LLC (G-6120)*
South Central Pub Defender Off, Wichita *Also called Indigents Defense Svcs Kans Bd (G-14684)*
South Central Tele Assn Inc (PA) 620 930-1000
215 S Iliff St Medicine Lodge (67104) *(G-7074)*
South Central Tele Assn Inc 620 933-1000
214 S Main St Pratt (67124) *(G-10149)*
South Central Telephone Assn, Medicine Lodge *Also called South Centl Communications Inc (G-7073)*
South Central Wireless Inc 620 930-1000
215 S Iliff St Medicine Lodge (67104) *(G-7075)*
South Cntl Kans Bone Joint Ctr 620 672-1002
203 Watson St Ste 300 Pratt (67124) *(G-10150)*
South Cntl Kans Rgonal Med Ctr 620 442-2500
6401 Patterson Pkwy Arkansas City (67005) *(G-181)*
South Cntl Mntal Hlth Cnseling 316 733-5047
217 W Ira Ct Andover (67002) *(G-108)*
South Cntl Mntal Hlth Cnsling (PA) 316 321-6036
524 N Main St El Dorado (67042) *(G-1604)*
South Drive In, Dodge City *Also called Cooper Enterprises (G-1331)*
South Kans Cy Surgical Ctr Lc 913 901-9000
10730 Nall Ave Ste 100 Overland Park (66211) *(G-9330)*

A L P H A B E T I C

South Kansas and Okla RR Inc.....620 336-2291
123 N Depot St Cherryvale (67335) ***(G-813)***
South Kansas and Okla RR Inc (HQ).....620 231-2230
315 W 3rd St Pittsburg (66762) ***(G-9939)***
South Kansas and Okla RR Inc.....620 221-3470
314 E 6th Ave Winfield (67156) ***(G-16173)***
South Rock Billiard LLC.....316 651-0444
2020 S Rock Rd Ste 20 Wichita (67207) ***(G-15619)***
South Star Chrysler Inc.....785 242-5600
440 E 11th St Ottawa (66067) ***(G-8313)***
South West Butler Quarry LLC.....316 775-1737
9423 Sw 165th St Augusta (67010) ***(G-347)***
South Wichita Family Medicine.....316 524-4338
3133 S Seneca St Wichita (67217) ***(G-15620)***
South YMCA, Wichita *Also called Young Mens Christian Associa* ***(G-16095)***
Southard Corporation (PA).....620 793-5434
1222 10th St Great Bend (67530) ***(G-2637)***
Southast Kans Ind Lving Rsrce (PA).....620 421-5502
1801 Main St Parsons (67357) ***(G-9739)***
Southast Kans Rgnal Jvnile Dtn.....620 724-4174
270 Enterprise St Girard (66743) ***(G-2417)***
Southborough Partners.....316 529-3200
4911 S Meridian Ave Wichita (67217) ***(G-15621)***
Southcreek Viii Associates, Overland Park *Also called D D I Realty Services Inc* ***(G-8627)***
Southeast Bancshares Inc.....620 325-2632
524 Main St Neodesha (66757) ***(G-7249)***
Southeast Bancshares Inc (PA).....620 431-1400
101 W Main St Chanute (66720) ***(G-763)***
SOUTHEAST CHECK PRINTING, Chanute *Also called Bank of Commerce* ***(G-705)***
SOUTHEAST CHECK PRINTING, Neodesha *Also called First Neodesha Bank* ***(G-7240)***
Southeast Check Printing, Chanute *Also called Southeast Bancshares Inc* ***(G-763)***
Southeast Family Healthcare.....316 612-1332
863 N Stagecoach St Wichita (67230) ***(G-15622)***
Southeast Kans Educatn Svc Ctr (PA).....620 724-6281
947 W 47 Hwy Girard (66743) ***(G-2418)***
Southeast Kans Experiment Stn, Parsons *Also called Kansas State University* ***(G-9697)***
Southeast Kans Mental Hlth Ctr (PA).....620 473-2241
1106 S 9th St Humboldt (66748) ***(G-3188)***
Southeast Kans Mental Hlth Ctr.....913 352-8214
505 W 15th St Pleasanton (66075) ***(G-10002)***
Southeast Kans Mental Hlth Ctr.....620 223-5030
212 State St Fort Scott (66701) ***(G-2006)***
Southeast Kans Mental Hlth Ctr.....785 448-6806
519 S Elm St Garnett (66032) ***(G-2389)***
Southeast Kans Mental Hlth Ctr.....620 431-7890
402 S Kansas Ave Chanute (66720) ***(G-764)***
Southeast Kans Mental Hlth Ctr.....620 365-5717
304 N Jefferson Ave Iola (66749) ***(G-3633)***
Southeast Kansas Community (PA).....620 724-8204
401 N Sinnett St Girard (66743) ***(G-2419)***
Southeast Kansas Community.....620 365-7189
223 S Sycamore St Iola (66749) ***(G-3634)***
Southeast Kansas Community.....620 795-2102
207 Commercial St Oswego (67356) ***(G-8236)***
Southeast Kansas Lutherans Inc.....620 331-8010
601 S Penn Ave Independence (67301) ***(G-3561)***
Southeast Kansas Orthpd Clinic.....620 421-0881
1902 S Us Highway 59 Parsons (67357) ***(G-9740)***
Southeast KS AR AG Aging.....620 431-2980
1 W Ash St Chanute (66720) ***(G-765)***
Southeastern Kansas, Fort Scott *Also called Old Fort Genealgcl Socty SE KS* ***(G-1996)***
Southern Care Inc.....913 906-9497
5375 Sw 7th St Ste 500 Topeka (66606) ***(G-13081)***
Southern Fastening Systems, Kansas City *Also called J & S Tool and Fastener Inc* ***(G-4114)***
Southern Foods Group LLC.....316 264-5011
240 N Handley St Wichita (67203) ***(G-15623)***
Southern Glazer SPI KS.....913 745-2900
1100 Blake St Edwardsville (66111) ***(G-1515)***
Southern Glazers Wine and Sp.....913 396-4900
5200 Metcalf Ave Overland Park (66202) ***(G-9331)***
Southern Glazers Wine and Sp.....316 264-1354
4626 S Palisade Ave Wichita (67217) ***(G-15624)***
Southern Kansas Cotton Growers.....620 221-1370
19493 51st Rd Winfield (67156) ***(G-16174)***
Southern Kansas Tele Co Inc (PA).....620 584-2255
112 S Lee St Clearwater (67026) ***(G-898)***
Southern Kansas Tele Co Inc.....620 584-2255
128 N Gorin St Clearwater (67026) ***(G-899)***
Southern Pioneer Electric Co (HQ).....620 356-3370
1850 W Oklahoma Ave Ulysses (67880) ***(G-13320)***
Southern Plains Co-Op At Lewis (PA).....620 324-5536
100 N Main St Lewis (67552) ***(G-6270)***
Southern Star Central Gas Pipe.....913 422-6304
8195 Cole Pkwy Lenexa (66227) ***(G-6142)***
Southern Star Central Gas Pipe.....785 448-4800
19209 Sw Maryland Rd Welda (66091) ***(G-13487)***
Southern Star Central Gas Pipe.....620 657-2130
13 Mils Nw Stnt Hwy 160 Satanta (67870) ***(G-10791)***
Southern Star Central Gas Pipe.....620 257-7800
455 Wabash Ave Lyons (67554) ***(G-6498)***
Southerncare Lawrence, Topeka *Also called Southern Care Inc* ***(G-13081)***
Southerncarlson Inc.....316 942-1392
4245 W 31st St S Wichita (67215) ***(G-15625)***
Southside Homes Inc.....316 522-7100
3020 S Broadway Ave Wichita (67216) ***(G-15626)***
Southside Pet Hospital.....913 782-0173
457 N K 7 Hwy Olathe (66061) ***(G-8074)***
Southview Homecare (PA).....913 837-5121
107 S Broadway St Ste D Louisburg (66053) ***(G-6467)***
Southwest and Associates Inc.....620 463-5631
100 N Reno Ave Burrton (67020) ***(G-650)***
Southwest Bowl.....785 272-1324
5265 Sw 28th Ct Ste A Topeka (66614) ***(G-13082)***
Southwest Dairy Quality Svc.....620 384-6953
200 E Hwy 50 Syracuse (67878) ***(G-12232)***
Southwest Developmental Svcs.....620 793-7604
1105 Main St Ste D Great Bend (67530) ***(G-2638)***
Southwest Express Inc.....620 544-7500
1015 W City Limits St Hugoton (67951) ***(G-3176)***
Southwest Glass & Door Inc.....620 626-7400
115 W 2nd St Ste 1 Liberal (67901) ***(G-6369)***
Southwest Guidance Center.....620 624-8171
333 W 15th St Liberal (67901) ***(G-6370)***
Southwest Guidance Ctr.....620 624-0280
21 Plaza Dr Ste 5 Liberal (67901) ***(G-6371)***
Southwest Holding Corporation (PA).....785 233-5662
4000 Se Adams St Topeka (66609) ***(G-13083)***
Southwest Kansas Coop Svcs LLC.....620 492-2126
304 W Highland St Johnson (67855) ***(G-3661)***
Southwest KS Agency On Aging (PA).....620 225-8230
236 San Jose Dodge City (67801) ***(G-1431)***
Southwest KS Coord Trans Counc.....620 227-8803
1100 E Wyatt Earp Blvd Dodge City (67801) ***(G-1432)***
Southwest Market Area, Wichita *Also called Veritiv Operating Company* ***(G-15874)***
Southwest Medical Center (PA).....620 624-1651
315 W 15th St Liberal (67901) ***(G-6372)***
Southwest National Bank (HQ).....316 291-5299
400 E Douglas Ave Wichita (67202) ***(G-15627)***
Southwest National Bank.....316 942-4004
454 S Tracy St Wichita (67209) ***(G-15628)***
Southwest National Bank.....316 941-1335
2700 W 13th St N Wichita (67203) ***(G-15629)***
Southwest National Bank.....316 838-5741
2150 N Woodrow Ave Wichita (67203) ***(G-15630)***
Southwest Pallets.....620 275-4343
50 S Farmland Rd Garden City (67846) ***(G-2284)***
Southwest Pallets & Warehouse, Garden City *Also called Southwest Pallets* ***(G-2284)***
Southwest Paper Company Inc (PA).....316 838-7755
3930 N Bridgeport Cir Wichita (67219) ***(G-15631)***
Southwest Plains Dairy LLC.....620 384-6813
12701 Sw Cr 32 Syracuse (67878) ***(G-12233)***
Southwest Plins Rgonal Svc Ctr.....620 675-2241
W Hwy 56 Lark Ave Sublette (67877) ***(G-12207)***
Southwest Pubg & Mailing Corp (HQ).....785 233-5662
4000 Se Adams St Ste 1 Topeka (66609) ***(G-13084)***
Southwest Publishing, Topeka *Also called Southwest Holding Corporation* ***(G-13083)***
Southwest Research EXT Ctr, Garden City *Also called Kansas State University* ***(G-2214)***
Southwest Salt Company LLC.....913 755-1955
4 S Silver St Paola (66071) ***(G-9588)***
Southwest Steel Fabricators, Bonner Springs *Also called Southwest Stl Fabrication LLC* ***(G-573)***
Southwest Sterling Inc (HQ).....816 483-6444
11120 Tomahawk Creek Pkwy Leawood (66211) ***(G-5555)***
Southwest Stl Fabrication LLC.....913 422-5500
2520 Scheidt Ln Bonner Springs (66012) ***(G-573)***
Southwest Stl Fabricators Inc (PA).....913 422-5500
2520 Scheidt Ln Bonner Springs (66012) ***(G-574)***
Southwest Truck Parts Inc (PA).....620 672-5686
1630 E 1st St Pratt (67124) ***(G-10151)***
Southwestern Bell Telephone Co.....785 862-5538
823 Se Quincy St Ste 1043 Topeka (66612) ***(G-13085)***
Southwestern Electrical Co Inc.....316 263-1264
1638 E 1st St N Wichita (67214) ***(G-15632)***
Southwestern Remodeling Contrs.....316 263-1239
134 N Elizabeth St Wichita (67203) ***(G-15633)***
Southwestern Roofing & Siding, Wichita *Also called Southwestern Remodeling Contrs* ***(G-15633)***
Southwind Development Co.....620 275-2117
50 Grandview Dr Garden City (67846) ***(G-2285)***
Southwind Drilling Inc.....620 564-3800
8 N Main St Ellinwood (67526) ***(G-1638)***
Southwind Eyecare.....620 662-2355
3120 N Plum St Hutchinson (67502) ***(G-3444)***
Southwind Hospice Inc (PA).....620 672-7553
496 Yucca Ln Pratt (67124) ***(G-10152)***
Southwind Residential Services, Winfield *Also called RES-Care Inc* ***(G-16168)***

Sowards Glass Inc...785 233-4466
2600 Nw Topeka Blvd C Topeka (66617) ***(G-13086)***
Sp Foundry, Coffeyville *Also called Star Pipe Usa LLC* ***(G-980)***
Sp Foundy, Coffeyville *Also called Star Pipe Usa LLC* ***(G-979)***
Spaces Inc (PA)...913 894-8900
14950 W 86th St Lenexa (66215) ***(G-6143)***
Spangenberg Phillips Inc...316 267-4002
121 N Mead St Ste 201 Wichita (67202) ***(G-15634)***
Spangler Graphics LLC...913 722-4500
8345 Lenexa Dr Ste 275 Overland Park (66214) ***(G-9332)***
Spanish Gardens Food Mfg Co...913 831-4242
2301 Metropolitan Ave Kansas City (66106) ***(G-4430)***
Spanos, The, Overland Park *Also called A G Spanos Development Inc* ***(G-8335)***
Spare Tyme LLC...620 225-2695
11150 Kliesen St Dodge City (67801) ***(G-1433)***
Sparhawk Laboratories Inc (PA)...913 888-7500
12340 Santa Fe Trail Dr Lenexa (66215) ***(G-6144)***
Sparker Industries Inc...913 963-5261
8802 W 193rd Ter Bucyrus (66013) ***(G-610)***
Sparkle Auto LLC...620 272-9559
163 N Campus Dr Garden City (67846) ***(G-2286)***
Sparkleauto.com, Garden City *Also called Sparkle Auto LLC* ***(G-2286)***
Sparks Music Co...620 442-5030
315 S Summit St Arkansas City (67005) ***(G-182)***
Spartan Foundation Repair, Lenexa *Also called Spartan Installation Repr LLC* ***(G-6145)***
Spartan Installation Repr LLC...816 237-0017
9010 Rosehill Rd Lenexa (66215) ***(G-6145)***
Spatial Data Research Inc...314 705-0772
1220 Timberedge Rd Lawrence (66049) ***(G-5114)***
Spc Telequip, Shawnee *Also called Special Product Company* ***(G-11031)***
Spears Caney Inc...620 879-2131
1609 Cr 1900 Caney (67333) ***(G-673)***
Spears Manufacturing, Caney *Also called Spears Caney Inc* ***(G-673)***
Spears Manufacturing Co...620 879-2131
Hwy 166 Caney (67333) ***(G-674)***
Spearville District Hospital...620 385-2632
202 Park St Spearville (67876) ***(G-12071)***
Spearville Senior Living Inc...785 506-6003
6025 Sw 39th Ct Topeka (66610) ***(G-13087)***
Spec Personnel LLC...913 534-8430
6750 Antioch Rd Ste 201 Overland Park (66204) ***(G-9333)***
Spec Roofers Wholeseller, Kansas City *Also called Mel Stevenson & Associates Inc* ***(G-4233)***
Spec Roofing Contractors Sup, Kansas City *Also called Mel Stevenson & Associates Inc* ***(G-4232)***
Spec Roofing Contractors Suppl, Wichita *Also called Mel Stevenson & Associates Inc* ***(G-15036)***
Specchem LLC...913 371-8705
444b Richmond Ave Kansas City (66101) ***(G-4431)***
Specchem LLC...816 968-5600
444 Richmond Ave Kansas City (66101) ***(G-4432)***
Special Beginnings Inc (PA)...913 894-0131
10216 Pflumm Rd Shawnee Mission (66215) ***(G-11880)***
Special Beginnings Inc...913 393-2223
14169 S Mur Len Rd Olathe (66062) ***(G-8075)***
Special Ed Coop, Iola *Also called Iola Pre Schl For Excptnl Chld* ***(G-3610)***
Special Olympics Kansas Inc (PA)...913 236-9290
5280 Foxridge Dr Shawnee Mission (66202) ***(G-11881)***
Special Product Company...972 208-1460
8540 Hedge Lane Ter Lenexa (66227) ***(G-6146)***
Special Product Company (PA)...913 491-8088
8540 Hedge Lane Ter Shawnee (66227) ***(G-11031)***
Special Tee Graphics...620 227-8160
503 N 2nd Ave Dodge City (67801) ***(G-1434)***
Specialists Group LLC (PA)...316 267-7375
105 S Broadway Ave # 200 Wichita (67202) ***(G-15635)***
Speciality Services, Overland Park *Also called Cardinal Health 127 Inc* ***(G-8513)***
Specialty Fabrication Inc...316 264-0603
1517 N Santa Fe St Wichita (67214) ***(G-15636)***
Specialty Fertilizer Pdts LLC (HQ)...913 956-7500
11550 Ash St Ste 220 Leawood (66211) ***(G-5556)***
Specialty Home Healthcare, Winfield *Also called Kansas Specialty Services Inc* ***(G-16151)***
Specialty Patterns Inc...316 945-8131
1300 S Bebe St Wichita (67209) ***(G-15637)***
Specialty Projects Corp Inc...620 429-1086
500 S Railroad Ave Columbus (66725) ***(G-1086)***
Specialty Technology Inc...620 241-6307
618 N Mulberry St McPherson (67460) ***(G-7027)***
Specpro Environmental Svcs LLC...913 583-3000
35425 W 103rd St De Soto (66018) ***(G-1213)***
Spectragraphics Inc...913 888-6828
14701 W 106th St Lenexa (66215) ***(G-6147)***
Spectrum Brands Inc...949 279-4099
31100 W 196th St Edgerton (66021) ***(G-1490)***
Spectrum Construction Co...785 232-3407
2400 Nw Water Works Dr Topeka (66606) ***(G-13088)***
Spectrum Elite Corp...913 579-7037
16644 W 147th St Olathe (66062) ***(G-8076)***
Spectrum Elite Wireless, Olathe *Also called Spectrum Elite Corp* ***(G-8076)***
Spectrum Health Foundation Inc...913 831-2979
2915 Strong Ave Kansas City (66106) ***(G-4433)***
SPECTRUM HOME HEALTH AGENCY, Kansas City *Also called Spectrum Health Foundation Inc* ***(G-4433)***
Spectrum Medical Equipment Inc...913 831-2979
2915 Strong Ave Kansas City (66106) ***(G-4434)***
Spectrum MGT Holdg Co LLC...913 682-2113
541 Mcdonald Rd Leavenworth (66048) ***(G-5290)***
Spectrum Private Care Services...913 299-7100
7740 Hedge Lane Ter Shawnee (66227) ***(G-11032)***
Spectrum Promotional Pdts Inc...316 262-1199
9212 E 37th St N Wichita (67226) ***(G-15638)***
Spectrum Retirement, Overland Park *Also called Park Meadows Senior Living LLC* ***(G-9141)***
Spectrum Retirement Shawnee KS...913 631-0058
6335 Maurer Rd Shawnee Mission (66217) ***(G-11882)***
Speculative Funding LLC...785 267-1996
5375 Sw 7th St Ste 400 Topeka (66606) ***(G-13089)***
Speedway Service Corporation...913 488-6695
15217 W 121st Ter Olathe (66062) ***(G-8077)***
Speedy and Rapid Cash, Wichita *Also called Curo Management LLC* ***(G-14145)***
Speedy Cash, Wichita *Also called Galt Ventures LLC* ***(G-14441)***
Speedy Cash, Wichita *Also called Galt Ventures LLC* ***(G-14442)***
Speedy Cash, Wichita *Also called Curo Financial Tech Corp* ***(G-14141)***
Speedy Falcon Carwash, Shawnee Mission *Also called Speedy Falcon LLC* ***(G-11883)***
Speedy Falcon LLC (PA)...913 451-2100
11401 Strang Line Rd Shawnee Mission (66215) ***(G-11883)***
Spencer & Company...785 235-3131
4425 Nw Us Highway 24 Topeka (66618) ***(G-13090)***
Spencer Fane Britt Browne LLP...913 345-8100
9401 Indian Creek Pkwy # 700 Overland Park (66210) ***(G-9334)***
Spencer Reed Group LLC...913 722-7860
5800 Foxridge Dr Ste 100 Shawnee Mission (66202) ***(G-11884)***
Spencer Reed Group LLC (PA)...913 663-4400
5700 W 112th St Ste 100 Leawood (66211) ***(G-5557)***
Spice Merchant & Co...316 263-4121
1300 E Douglas Ave Wichita (67214) ***(G-15639)***
Spicin Foods Inc...913 432-5228
111 Southwest Blvd Kansas City (66103) ***(G-4435)***
Spideroak Inc...847 564-8900
5920 Nall Ave Ste 200 Mission (66202) ***(G-7138)***
Spikes Spider, El Dorado *Also called Frigiquip International Inc* ***(G-1563)***
Spinal Simplicity LLC...913 451-4414
6600 College Blvd Ste 220 Leawood (66211) ***(G-5558)***
Spirit Aerosystems Inc...316 523-2995
3800 S Turnpike Dr Wichita (67210) ***(G-15640)***
Spirit Aerosystems Inc (HQ)...316 526-9000
3801 S Oliver St Wichita (67210) ***(G-15641)***
Spirit Aerosystems Innovative (HQ)...316 526-9000
4200 W Macarthur Rd Wichita (67215) ***(G-15642)***
Spirit Arosystems Holdings Inc...316 523-3950
4555 E Macarthur Rd Wichita (67210) ***(G-15643)***
Spirit Arosystems Holdings Inc (PA)...316 526-9000
3801 S Oliver St Wichita (67210) ***(G-15644)***
Spirit Industries Inc...913 749-5858
1021 E 31st St Lawrence (66046) ***(G-5115)***
Spirit/Boeing Employees Assn (PA)...316 522-2996
4226 S Gold St Wichita (67217) ***(G-15645)***
Spivey Oil Field Service LLC...620 532-5178
115 S Main St Spivey (67142) ***(G-12073)***
Splashtacular LLC...800 844-5334
102 W Kaskaskia St # 201 Paola (66071) ***(G-9589)***
Splashtacular Entertainment, Paola *Also called Splashtacular Inc* ***(G-9590)***
Splashtacular Inc...800 844-5334
102 W Kaskaskia St # 201 Paola (66071) ***(G-9590)***
Splintek Inc...816 531-1900
15555 W 108th St Lenexa (66219) ***(G-6148)***
Spoon Creek Holdings LLC...913 375-2275
12700 S Spoon Creek Rd Olathe (66061) ***(G-8078)***
Sporer Land Development Inc...785 672-4319
431 Us Highway 83 Oakley (67748) ***(G-7487)***
Sport Aid, Rebound, Scott, Belleville *Also called Scott Specialties Inc* ***(G-466)***
Sports Car Club America Inc (PA)...785 357-7222
6620 Se Dwight St Topeka (66619) ***(G-13091)***
Sports Center Inc...785 272-5522
6545 Sw 10th Ave Topeka (66615) ***(G-13092)***
Sports Nutz of Kansas Inc...913 400-7733
1803 Vlg West Pkwy M137 Kansas City (66111) ***(G-4436)***
Sports Radio 1510, Shawnee Mission *Also called Union Broadcasting Inc* ***(G-11961)***
Sports Rehab/Physl Thrpy Assoc (PA)...913 663-2555
10701 Nall Ave Overland Park (66211) ***(G-9335)***
Sports Rhbltion Physcl Thrapy, Overland Park *Also called Sports Rehab/Physl Thrpy Assoc* ***(G-9335)***
Sportsgear Outdoor Products...913 888-0379
14308 W 96th Ter Lenexa (66215) ***(G-6149)***
Sportsman Cap, Lenexa *Also called Promotional Headwear Intl Inc* ***(G-6076)***
Spotless Janitorial Services...316 682-2070
1460 N Hillside St Wichita (67214) ***(G-15646)***

ALPHABETIC

Spray Equipment & Svc Ctr LLC (PA)....316 264-4349
311 Pattie St Wichita (67211) ***(G-15647)***
Spriggs Concrete Inc....620 795-4841
611 Kansas St Oswego (67356) ***(G-8237)***
Spring Hill Chamber Commerce....913 592-3893
613 S Race St Spring Hill (66083) ***(G-12099)***
Spring Hill Veterinary Clinic, Spring Hill *Also called Miller Veterinary Services PA* ***(G-12090)***
Spring Rver Mntal Hlth Wllness (PA)....620 848-2300
6610 Se Quakervale Rd Riverton (66770) ***(G-10213)***
Spring Valley Woodworks Inc....620 345-8330
2592 Chisholm Rd Canton (67428) ***(G-682)***
Spring View Manor Inc....620 456-2285
412 S 8th St Conway Springs (67031) ***(G-1145)***
Springhill Suites, Lenexa *Also called Midas Lenexa LLC* ***(G-5999)***
Springhill Suites....316 260-4404
6633 W Kellogg Dr Wichita (67209) ***(G-15648)***
Springhill Suites Overland Pk, Shawnee Mission *Also called Apple Eght Hospitality MGT Inc* ***(G-11113)***
Sprint, Overland Park *Also called Nextel of California Inc* ***(G-9083)***
Sprint....703 433-4000
6391 Sprint Pkwy Overland Park (66251) ***(G-9336)***
Sprint Communications Inc (HQ)....855 848-3280
6200 Sprint Pkwy Overland Park (66251) ***(G-9337)***
Sprint Communications Co LP (HQ)....800 829-0965
6391 Sprint Pkwy Overland Park (66251) ***(G-9338)***
Sprint Communications NH Inc (HQ)....800 829-0965
6200 Sprint Pkwy Overland Park (66251) ***(G-9339)***
Sprint Corporation (HQ)....877 564-3166
6200 Sprint Pkwy Overland Park (66251) ***(G-9340)***
Sprint International Inc (HQ)....800 259-3755
2330 Shawnee Mission Pkwy Westwood (66205) ***(G-13559)***
Sprint Solutions Inc....800 829-0965
Ksopht0101-Z4300 6391 Overland Park (66251) ***(G-9341)***
Sprint Spectrum Holding Co LP....800 829-0965
6160 Sprint Pkwy Shawnee Mission (66251) ***(G-11885)***
Sprint Spectrum LP....785 537-3500
707 Commons Pl Manhattan (66503) ***(G-6804)***
Sprint Spectrum LP....913 962-7777
15150 Shawnee Mission Pkw Shawnee Mission (66217) ***(G-11886)***
Sprint Spectrum LP....316 634-4900
3101 N Rock Rd Ste 175 Wichita (67226) ***(G-15649)***
Sprint Spectrum LP....913 671-7007
5640 Antioch Rd Merriam (66202) ***(G-7105)***
Sprint Spectrum LP....913 894-1375
11788 W 95th St Overland Park (66214) ***(G-9342)***
Sprint Spectrum LP (HQ)....703 433-4000
6800 Sprint Pkwy Overland Park (66251) ***(G-9343)***
Sprint Spectrum LP....913 323-5000
4901 Town Center Dr Shawnee Mission (66211) ***(G-11887)***
Spsi Inc....913 541-8304
7943 Flint St Lenexa (66214) ***(G-6150)***
Spt Distribution Center....785 862-5226
7215 Sw Topeka Blvd Topeka (66624) ***(G-13093)***
SPX Cooling Technologies Inc....913 782-1600
1200 W Marley Rd Olathe (66061) ***(G-8079)***
SPX Cooling Technologies Inc (HQ)....913 664-7400
7401 W 129th St Overland Park (66213) ***(G-9344)***
SPX Cooling Technologies Inc....913 722-3600
7401 W 129th St Overland Park (66213) ***(G-9345)***
SPX Dry Cooling Usa LLC....913 685-0009
7450 W 130th St Ste 310 Overland Park (66213) ***(G-9346)***
Squad It Services LLC....785 844-3114
1100 N Broadway Apt 119 Herington (67449) ***(G-2981)***
Squadbuilders Inc....913 649-4401
10310 State Line Rd # 100 Leawood (66206) ***(G-5559)***
Square Deal Newspaper, Atwood *Also called Rawlins County Sq Deal Pubg* ***(G-290)***
Squaretwo Financial Commercial....913 888-8300
10865 Grandview Dr Overland Park (66210) ***(G-9347)***
Squires Corporation....316 944-0040
3414 W 29th St S Wichita (67217) ***(G-15650)***
Sr Food and Beverage Co Inc....913 299-9797
9700 Leavenworth Rd Kansas City (66109) ***(G-4437)***
Sra Benefits....913 236-3090
5201 Johnson Dr Ste 500 Shawnee Mission (66205) ***(G-11888)***
Srd Environmental Services....620 665-5590
315 W Blanchard Ave Hutchinson (67505) ***(G-3445)***
Srg III LLC....913 663-4400
5700 W 112th St Ste 100 Overland Park (66211) ***(G-9348)***
Srh Mechanical Contractors Inc....785 842-0301
12612 246th St Lawrence (66044) ***(G-5116)***
SRS Strategic Development....785 296-4327
555 S Kansas Ave Ste 100 Topeka (66603) ***(G-13094)***
SS&c Business & Tax Services, Topeka *Also called Summers & Spencer Company* ***(G-13116)***
SS&c Wealth MGT Group LLC....785 825-5479
218 S Santa Fe Ave Salina (67401) ***(G-10713)***
Ssb Manufacturing Company....913 422-8000
7910 Hedge Lane Ter Shawnee Mission (66227) ***(G-11889)***
Ssi Inc....316 722-9631
12011 W 34th St S Wichita (67227) ***(G-15651)***
Ssi Sprinkler Systems, Wichita *Also called Ssi Inc* ***(G-15651)***
St Agnes Montessori Pre School....913 262-2400
5149 Mission Rd Westwood (66205) ***(G-13560)***
St Catherine Hospital....620 272-2660
601 N Main St Ste B Garden City (67846) ***(G-2287)***
St Catherine Hospital (HQ)....620 272-2222
401 E Spruce St Garden City (67846) ***(G-2288)***
St Catherine Hospital....620 272-2519
602 N 6th St Garden City (67846) ***(G-2289)***
St Cathrine Hosp Dev Fundation....620 272-2222
401 E Spruce St Garden City (67846) ***(G-2290)***
St Francis Academy Inc....785 825-0563
5097 W Cloud St Salina (67401) ***(G-10714)***
St Francis Herald, Saint Francis *Also called Nor West Newspaper Inc* ***(G-10343)***
St Francis Hospital....785 945-3263
403 Sycamore St Valley Falls (66088) ***(G-13369)***
St Francis Medical Clinic....785 232-4248
6001 Sw 6th Ave Ste 320 Topeka (66615) ***(G-13095)***
St Francis Medical Practice, Topeka *Also called Sisters of Charity of Leavenwo* ***(G-13074)***
St Francis Publications, Wichita *Also called Ascension Via Christi Hospital* ***(G-13750)***
St Jhns Maude Norton Mem Hosp....620 429-2545
220 N Pennsylvania Ave Columbus (66725) ***(G-1087)***
St Joe Concrete Products (PA)....913 365-7281
1807 Roseport Rd Elwood (66024) ***(G-1691)***
St John Clinic, Saint John *Also called Hutchinson Clinic PA* ***(G-10352)***
St Johns Child Dev Ctr LLC....620 564-2044
512 N Wilhelm Ave Ellinwood (67526) ***(G-1639)***
St Johns of Hays, Hays *Also called St Johns Rest Home Inc* ***(G-2911)***
St Johns Rest Home Inc (PA)....785 735-2208
2225 Canterbury Dr Hays (67601) ***(G-2910)***
St Johns Rest Home Inc....785 628-3241
2401 Canterbury Dr Hays (67601) ***(G-2911)***
St Joseph Truss Company Inc (PA)....785 989-4496
2257 169th Rd Wathena (66090) ***(G-13478)***
St Lukes Health Corporation....913 250-1244
1004 Progress Dr Ste 220 Lansing (66043) ***(G-4693)***
St Lukes Hospital Inc....620 326-7451
1323 N A St Ste 2 Wellington (67152) ***(G-13530)***
St Marys Hosp of Blue Sprng....816 523-4525
101 S 1st St Iola (66749) ***(G-3635)***
St Marys Literary Club....785 437-6418
101 E Lasley St Saint Marys (66536) ***(G-10376)***
St Marys State Bank (HQ)....785 437-2271
905 E Bertrand Ave Saint Marys (66536) ***(G-10377)***
St Michaels Day School Inc....913 432-1174
6630 Nall Ave Shawnee Mission (66202) ***(G-11890)***
St Paul Fire and Mar Insur Co....913 469-2720
15829 Maple St Shawnee Mission (66223) ***(G-11891)***
St Rose Campus, Great Bend *Also called Central Kansas Medical Center* ***(G-2529)***
St. Francis Community Svc, Junction City *Also called Saint Francis Cmnty Svcs Inc* ***(G-3749)***
St. Joseph Surgery, Wichita *Also called Ascension Arizona* ***(G-13745)***
Sta-Mot-Ks LLC (PA)....913 894-9600
11316 W 80th St Overland Park (66214) ***(G-9349)***
Stackify LLC....816 888-5055
8900 State Line Rd # 100 Leawood (66206) ***(G-5560)***
Stadium Chair Company LLC....432 682-4682
9824 Pflumm Rd Lenexa (66215) ***(G-6151)***
Staffbridge LLC....913 381-4044
7240 W 98th Ter Bldg 8 Overland Park (66212) ***(G-9350)***
Stafford County Flour Mills Co (PA)....620 458-4121
108 S Church St Hudson (67545) ***(G-3146)***
Stafford County Flour Mills Co....620 486-2493
118 N Main St Sylvia (67581) ***(G-12221)***
Stafford County Historical....620 234-5664
100 N Main St Stafford (67578) ***(G-12110)***
Stafford District Hospital 4....620 234-5221
502 S Buckeye St Stafford (67578) ***(G-12111)***
STAFFORD DISTRICT HOSPITAL HOM, Stafford *Also called Stafford District Hospital 4* ***(G-12111)***
Stag Hill Golf Club Inc....785 539-1041
4441 Riley Blvd Manhattan (66502) ***(G-6805)***
Stagg Hill Golf Club, Manhattan *Also called Stag Hill Golf Club Inc* ***(G-6805)***
Stagg Hill Golf Club Inc....785 539-1041
4441 Fort Riley Blvd Manhattan (66502) ***(G-6806)***
Stainless Systems Inc....620 663-4346
300 E 4th Ave South Hutchinson (67505) ***(G-12066)***
Stallard Technologies Inc....913 851-2260
16041 Marty Cir Overland Park (66085) ***(G-9351)***
Stampede Feeders, Scott City *Also called Heartland Feeders Inc* ***(G-10814)***
Standard Beverage Corporation (PA)....316 838-7707
2526 E 36th Cir N Wichita (67219) ***(G-15652)***
Standard Beverage Corporation....800 999-8797
2300 Lakeview Rd Lawrence (66049) ***(G-5117)***
Standard Beverage Corporation....913 888-7200
14415 W 106th St Lenexa (66215) ***(G-6152)***

Standard Electric Co Inc.....913 782-5409
2006 E Prairie Cir Olathe (66062) **(G-8080)**
Standard Emplyee Bnefits Insur, Overland Park *Also called Standard Insurance Company* **(G-9352)**
Standard Insurance Company.....913 661-9241
7500 College Blvd Ste 750 Overland Park (66210) **(G-9352)**
Standard Motor Products Inc.....620 331-1000
1300 W Oak St Independence (67301) **(G-3562)**
Standard Motor Products Inc.....913 441-6500
845 S 9th St Edwardsville (66111) **(G-1516)**
Standard Plumbing Inc.....785 776-5012
609 Pecan Cir Manhattan (66502) **(G-6807)**
Standard Style In Baldwin, Leawood *Also called Baldwin LLC* **(G-5338)**
Standees Pv LLC.....913 601-5250
3935 W 69th Ter Prairie Village (66208) **(G-10069)**
Standees-Entertaining Eatery, Prairie Village *Also called Standees Pv LLC* **(G-10069)**
Standridge Color Corporation.....316 283-5061
1011 Industrial Dr Newton (67114) **(G-7419)**
Stanion Whl Elc Co Str 6, Manhattan *Also called Stanion Wholesale Elc Co Inc* **(G-6808)**
Stanion Wholesale Elc Co Inc.....316 616-9200
2710 W Pawnee St Wichita (67213) **(G-15653)**
Stanion Wholesale Elc Co Inc (PA).....620 672-5678
812 S Main St Pratt (67124) **(G-10153)**
Stanion Wholesale Elc Co Inc.....785 841-8420
2958 Four Wheel Dr Lawrence (66047) **(G-5118)**
Stanion Wholesale Elc Co Inc.....913 829-8111
1370 N Winchester St Olathe (66061) **(G-8081)**
Stanion Wholesale Elc Co Inc.....785 823-2323
1061 E North St Salina (67401) **(G-10715)**
Stanion Wholesale Elc Co Inc.....785 537-4600
2305 Skyvue Ln Manhattan (66502) **(G-6808)**
Stanion Wholesale Elc Co Inc.....913 342-1177
2040 S 45th St Kansas City (66106) **(G-4438)**
Stanley Bank (PA).....913 681-8800
7835 W 151st St Overland Park (66223) **(G-9353)**
STANLEY BANK COLUMBUS, Overland Park *Also called Stanley Bank* **(G-9353)**
Stanley Dairy Queen.....913 851-1850
7580 W 151st St Shawnee Mission (66223) **(G-11892)**
Stanley Steemer, Wichita *Also called Clk Inc* **(G-14043)**
Stanley Steemer Carpet Cleaner, Lawrence *Also called Bluestreak Enterprises Inc* **(G-4761)**
Stanley Veterinary Clinic, Shawnee Mission *Also called Stannley Veterinary Clinic* **(G-11894)**
Stanley Wood Products Inc.....913 681-2804
15248 Broadmoor St Shawnee Mission (66223) **(G-11893)**
Stannley Veterinary Clinic.....913 897-2080
8695 W 151st St Shawnee Mission (66223) **(G-11894)**
Stans Sprinkler Service Inc.....800 570-5932
3656 S West St Wichita (67217) **(G-15654)**
Stantec Consulting Svcs Inc.....913 202-6867
6800 College Blvd Ste 750 Overland Park (66211) **(G-9354)**
Stanton County Hosp Aux Inc.....620 492-6250
404 N Chestnut St Johnson (67855) **(G-3662)**
Star Communication, Lyons *Also called Lyons Daily News* **(G-6489)**
Star Communication Corporation.....620 285-3111
115 W 5th St Larned (67550) **(G-4713)**
STAR FLOORING AND DECORATING, Wichita *Also called Perfection Strl Components LLC* **(G-15282)**
Star Fuel Center, Overland Park *Also called Star Transport LLC* **(G-9355)**
Star Fuel Centers Inc (PA).....913 652-9400
11161 Overbrook Rd # 150 Leawood (66211) **(G-5561)**
Star Innovations II LLC.....913 764-7738
100 Mission Woods Dr New Century (66031) **(G-7298)**
Star Lube Auto Ex Care Inc.....620 856-4281
1510 Military Ave Baxter Springs (66713) **(G-414)**
Star Motors Ltd.....913 432-7800
5400 Antioch Dr Shawnee Mission (66202) **(G-11895)**
Star Pipe Usa LLC.....281 558-3000
1004 W 14th St Coffeyville (67337) **(G-979)**
Star Pipe Usa LLC (HQ).....620 251-5700
1004 W 14th St Coffeyville (67337) **(G-980)**
Star Seed Inc (PA).....800 782-7311
101 N Industrial Ave Osborne (67473) **(G-8219)**
Star Signs LLC.....785 842-4892
801 E 9th St Lawrence (66044) **(G-5119)**
Star Signs & Graphics Inc (PA).....785 842-2881
801 E 9th St Lawrence (66044) **(G-5120)**
Star Tool Service Inc.....316 943-1942
1920 S Florence St Wichita (67209) **(G-15655)**
Star Transport LLC.....913 396-5070
7415 W 130th St Ste 100 Overland Park (66213) **(G-9355)**
Star-Kist, Topeka *Also called Big Heart Pet Brands* **(G-12380)**
Stardust Corporation.....913 894-1966
9525 Woodend Rd Kansas City (66111) **(G-4439)**
Starfire Enterprises Inc.....785 842-1111
2029 Becker Dr Lawrence (66047) **(G-5121)**
Starflite Manufacturing Co.....316 267-7297
1438 S Washington Ave Wichita (67211) **(G-15656)**
Starkey Inc (PA).....316 942-4221
4500 W Maple St Wichita (67209) **(G-15657)**
Starlite Mold Co.....316 262-3350
1518 S Washington Ave Wichita (67211) **(G-15658)**
Starlite Skate Center South.....785 862-2241
301 Se 45th St Topeka (66609) **(G-13096)**
Starlite Skate Center West, Topeka *Also called Starlite Skate Center South* **(G-13096)**
Starstruck Prfrmg Arts Ctr LLC.....913 492-3186
11650 W 85th St Shawnee Mission (66214) **(G-11896)**
Start To Finish Celebration.....785 364-2257
3736 South St Grantville (66429) **(G-2498)**
Starwood Htls & Rsrts Wrldwde.....888 625-4988
4301 E Harry St Wichita (67209) **(G-15659)**
Statcare Family Medical Clinic, Salina *Also called P A Comcare* **(G-10628)**
State Assn of Kans Watersheds.....785 544-6686
121 Parsons St Robinson (66532) **(G-10215)**
State Bank, Oskaloosa *Also called Everest Bancshares Inc* **(G-8225)**
State Bank, Bern *Also called Bern Bancshares Inc* **(G-520)**
State Bank (PA).....785 675-3261
745 Main St Hoxie (67740) **(G-3142)**
State Bank of Canton.....620 628-4425
103 S Main St Canton (67428) **(G-683)**
State Bank of Kansas (PA).....620 378-2114
501 Madison St Fredonia (66736) **(G-2045)**
State Bank of Spring Hill.....913 592-3326
201 S Webster St Spring Hill (66083) **(G-12100)**
State Beauty Supply, Shawnee Mission *Also called Netzer Sales Inc* **(G-11676)**
State Line Animal Hospital.....913 381-3272
2009 W 104th St Leawood (66206) **(G-5562)**
State Line Swine, Mahaska *Also called Livingston Enterprises Inc* **(G-6506)**
State of Kansas.....620 225-4804
100 Military Ave Ste 220 Dodge City (67801) **(G-1435)**
State Theatre.....620 285-3535
617 Broadway St Larned (67550) **(G-4714)**
State Tractor Trucking Inc.....913 287-3322
4101 Powell Dr Shawnee (66226) **(G-11033)**
Stateline Surgery Center LLC.....620 783-4072
444 Four States Dr Ste 2 Galena (66739) **(G-2086)**
Stationery Now, Overland Park *Also called Z3 Graphix Inc* **(G-9525)**
Statland Clinic Ltd PA.....913 345-8500
5701 W 119th St Ste 240 Shawnee Mission (66209) **(G-11897)**
Stauffer Lawn and Ldscp LLC.....785 256-7300
1150 Washington St Auburn (66402) **(G-297)**
Staybridge Suites, Wichita *Also called Brandon Hospitality LLC* **(G-13885)**
STC Aerospace, Valley Center *Also called Safarik Tool Co Inc* **(G-13352)**
Stealth Technologies LLC.....913 228-2214
15752 S Mahaffie St Olathe (66062) **(G-8082)**
Steam Action Restoration.....620 276-0622
2116 W Mary St Garden City (67846) **(G-2291)**
Steam Way Carpet Restorations (PA).....620 331-9553
1817 W Main St Independence (67301) **(G-3563)**
Steam Way Restorations, Independence *Also called Restore It Systems LLC* **(G-3555)**
Steamatic, Wichita *Also called D & D Roland Enterprises Llc* **(G-14154)**
Steamboat Pilot/Today, The, Lawrence *Also called Worldwest Ltd Liability Co* **(G-5192)**
Stearman Aircraft, Valley Center *Also called Professional Machine & Tool* **(G-13350)**
Stearman Aircraft Pdts Corp.....316 755-1271
510 E 5th St Valley Center (67147) **(G-13354)**
Stearns Conrad and Schmidt.....913 681-0030
7311 W 130th St Ste 100 Overland Park (66213) **(G-9356)**
Stecklein Enterprises LLC.....785 625-2529
2505 Canterbury Dr Hays (67601) **(G-2912)**
Steckline Communications, Wichita *Also called Mid-America AG Network Inc* **(G-15074)**
Steel and Pipe Supply Co Inc (HQ).....785 587-5100
555 Poyntz Ave Ste 122 Manhattan (66502) **(G-6809)**
Steel and Pipe Supply Co Inc.....913 768-4333
401 New Century Pkwy New Century (66031) **(G-7299)**
Steel Building Sales LLC.....316 733-5380
13323 Sw Butler Rd Rose Hill (67133) **(G-10249)**
Steel Fabrications Inc.....785 625-3075
1640 E Us Highway 40 Byp Hays (67601) **(G-2913)**
Steel Ventures LLC.....785 587-5100
555 Poyntz Ave Ste 122 Manhattan (66502) **(G-6810)**
Steeltec, Ottawa *Also called Fashion Inc* **(G-8272)**
Steinle Inc.....620 421-3940
415 S 32nd St Parsons (67357) **(G-9741)**
Steinlite Corporation.....913 367-3945
121 N 4th St Atchison (66002) **(G-261)**
Steinlite Corporation.....913 367-3945
1015 Main St Atchison (66002) **(G-262)**
Stelbar Oil Corporation Inc (PA).....316 264-8378
1625 Nw Fr Pkwy Wichita (67206) **(G-15660)**
Stelbar Production Company, Wichita *Also called Stelbar Oil Corporation Inc* **(G-15660)**
Stem 2 LLC.....913 236-9368
5660 Antioch Rd Merriam (66202) **(G-7106)**
Stem Hair & Body Salon, Merriam *Also called Stem 2 LLC* **(G-7106)**
Stenner Sales Company.....913 768-4114
401 Prairie Village Dr New Century (66031) **(G-7300)**
Step Two Investments LLC.....913 888-9000
11551 W 83rd Ter Overland Park (66214) **(G-9357)**

ALPHABETIC

Step2 Discovery LLC (PA) 620 232-2400
3001 N Rouse St Pittsburg (66762) ***(G-9940)***
Stephanie Wilson 913 563-1240
209 N Silver St Paola (66071) ***(G-9591)***
Stephen Commercial, Lawrence *Also called Stephens Realestate Inc* ***(G-5122)***
Stephen Jr & Kay Irsik 620 335-5363
5405 6 Rd Ingalls (67853) ***(G-3580)***
Stephen M Criser 316 685-1040
9415 E Harry St Ste 603 Wichita (67207) ***(G-15661)***
Stephen P Moore DDS 316 681-3228
2143 N Collective Ln B Wichita (67206) ***(G-15662)***
Stephen Rohner Doctor Office 316 687-0006
1148 S Hillside St # 104 Wichita (67211) ***(G-15663)***
Stephens & Associates Advg Inc 913 661-0910
14720 Metcalf Ave Overland Park (66223) ***(G-9358)***
Stephens Realestate Inc (PA) 785 841-4500
2701 W 6th St Lawrence (66049) ***(G-5122)***
Stephenson Edward B & Co CPA 620 221-9320
1002 Main St Winfield (67156) ***(G-16175)***
Stepp and Rothwell 913 345-4800
7300 College Blvd Ste 100 Overland Park (66210) ***(G-9359)***
STEPPING STONES DAY CARE CENTE, Lawrence *Also called Stepping Stones Inc* ***(G-5123)***
Stepping Stones Day Care Ctr 913 724-7700
15515 Elm St Basehor (66007) ***(G-389)***
Stepping Stones Inc 785 843-5919
1100 Wakarusa Dr Lawrence (66049) ***(G-5123)***
Stericycle Inc 913 307-9400
10000 Lackman Rd Lenexa (66219) ***(G-6153)***
Stericycle Inc 913 321-3928
3140 N 7th St Kansas City (66115) ***(G-4440)***
Sterling, Olathe *Also called Nathan Weiner & Associates* ***(G-7911)***
Sterling Bulletin, Sterling *Also called Marshall Publishing Inc* ***(G-12125)***
Sterling Centrecorp Inc 785 841-6500
730 Iowa St Ste 200 Lawrence (66044) ***(G-5124)***
Sterling Centrecorp Inc 913 651-6000
3211 S 4th St Ste 200 Leavenworth (66048) ***(G-5291)***
Sterling Centrecorp Inc 785 242-7000
2209 S Princeton St Ottawa (66067) ***(G-8314)***
Sterling Country Club Inc 620 278-9956
2225 13th Rd Sterling (67579) ***(G-12130)***
Sterling Drilling Company 620 672-9508
573 Yucca Ln Pratt (67124) ***(G-10154)***
Sterling Energy Resources Inc 913 469-9072
10551 Barkley St Ste 108 Overland Park (66212) ***(G-9360)***
Sterling Food Mart Inc 620 278-3371
114 Kisiwa Pkwy Hutchinson (67502) ***(G-3446)***
Sterling House Asbury Village, Coffeyville *Also called Brookdale Senior Living Commun* ***(G-914)***
Sterling House Junction City, Junction City *Also called Brookdale Senior Living Commun* ***(G-3675)***
Sterling House of Abilene I, Abilene *Also called Brookdale Senior Living Commun* ***(G-17)***
Sterling House of Abilene II, Abilene *Also called Brookdale Snior Lving Cmmnties* ***(G-18)***
Sterling House of Dodge City, Dodge City *Also called Brookdale Senior Living Commun* ***(G-1313)***
Sterling House of Emporia, Emporia *Also called Brookdale Senior Living Commun* ***(G-1708)***
Sterling House of Great Bend, Great Bend *Also called Brookdale Senior Living Commun* ***(G-2522)***
Sterling House of Hays, Hays *Also called Brookdale Senior Living Commun* ***(G-2761)***
Sterling House of Lawrence, Lawrence *Also called Brookdale Snior Lving Cmmnties* ***(G-4769)***
Sterling House of McPherson, Conway *Also called Brookdale Senior Living Commun* ***(G-1133)***
Sterling House of Wellington, Wellington *Also called Brookdale Senior Living Commun* ***(G-13492)***
Sterling House of Wichita, Wichita *Also called Brookdale Senior Living Commun* ***(G-13897)***
Sterling House Salina, Salina *Also called Brookdale Senior Living Commun* ***(G-10432)***
Sterling Manufacturing Co Inc 620 783-5234
1220 W 7th St Galena (66739) ***(G-2087)***
Sterling Medical Center, Sterling *Also called Hospital Dst 1 of Rice Cnty* ***(G-12121)***
Sterling Readiness Rounds LLC 785 542-1405
112 E 10th St Eudora (66025) ***(G-1880)***
Sterling Sand & Gravel, Hutchinson *Also called Mid-America Redi-Mix Inc* ***(G-3377)***
Sterling Screen Printing Inc 913 441-4411
23825 W 40th St Shawnee (66226) ***(G-11034)***
Sterling Trucking Inc 620 534-2461
9 Pioneer St Alden (67512) ***(G-59)***
Sterlingmeadow, Parsons *Also called Parsons Golf Club Restaurant* ***(G-9718)***
Sternberg Mseum Ntural History, Hays *Also called Fort Hays State University* ***(G-2811)***
Steve Hilker Trucking Inc 620 855-3257
602 E Ave A Cimarron (67835) ***(G-837)***
Steve Hnsens Prcision Dntl Lab (PA) 913 432-6951
5755 Foxridge Dr Shawnee Mission (66202) ***(G-11898)***
Steve Johnson Companies 316 722-2660
1555 S Tyler Rd Wichita (67209) ***(G-15664)***
Steve Kemp Concrete Cnstr 316 263-8902
315 N Seneca St Wichita (67203) ***(G-15665)***
Steve Priddle 785 776-1400
1620 Charles Pl Manhattan (66502) ***(G-6811)***
Steven Bradon Auto Center 316 634-0427
1633 N Rock Rd Wichita (67206) ***(G-15666)***
Steven D Braun 620 662-1212
1701 E 23rd Ave Hutchinson (67502) ***(G-3447)***
Steven Donnenwerth 620 672-7422
203 Watson St Ste 200 Pratt (67124) ***(G-10155)***
Steven Enterprises LLC 316 681-3010
6100 E Central Ave Ste 3 Wichita (67208) ***(G-15667)***
Steven F Twietmeyer DDS 316 942-3113
3920 W 31st St S Wichita (67217) ***(G-15668)***
Steven G Mitchell DDS 913 492-9660
12148 W 95th St Lenexa (66215) ***(G-6154)***
Steven Import Group Inc 316 652-2135
650 S Webb Rd Wichita (67207) ***(G-15669)***
Steven J Pierce DDS PA 913 888-2882
8615 Rosehill Rd Ste 101 Shawnee Mission (66215) ***(G-11899)***
Steven Joseph Jr DDS 316 262-5273
232 N Seneca St Wichita (67203) ***(G-15670)***
Steven L Hechler DDS Ms 913 345-0541
12800 Metcalf Ave Ste 2 Overland Park (66213) ***(G-9361)***
Steven L Thomas DDS 913 451-7680
12800 Metcalf Ave Ste 2 Shawnee Mission (66213) ***(G-11900)***
Steven Motors Full Line Collis, Wichita *Also called Steven Import Group Inc* ***(G-15669)***
Stevens & Brand LLP (PA) 785 843-0811
Us Bank Tower Ste 500900 Lawrence (66044) ***(G-5125)***
Stevens County Clinic, Hugoton *Also called Stevens County Hospital* ***(G-3177)***
Stevens County Hospital 620 544-8511
1006 S Jackson St Hugoton (67951) ***(G-3177)***
Stevenson Company Inc 785 233-0691
818 Nw Jackson St Topeka (66608) ***(G-13097)***
Stevenson Company Inc (PA) 785 233-1303
116 Nw Norris St Topeka (66608) ***(G-13098)***
Steves Electric Roustabout Co 785 434-7590
1695 Y Rd Plainville (67663) ***(G-9992)***
Steves Mobile Maintenance Svc, Kansas City *Also called Rmvk Enterprises Inc* ***(G-4382)***
Steves Quick Lube 785 742-3500
97 Sioux Ave Hiawatha (66434) ***(G-3025)***
Stewart Enterprises Inc 316 686-2766
12100 E 13th St N Wichita (67206) ***(G-15671)***
Stewart Realty Co Inc 620 223-6700
1707 S National Ave Fort Scott (66701) ***(G-2007)***
Stewart Truck Leasing Inc 785 827-0336
1944a N 9th St Salina (67401) ***(G-10716)***
Stewarts Sports & Awards 620 241-5990
117 N Main St McPherson (67460) ***(G-7028)***
STI, Overland Park *Also called Stallard Technologies Inc* ***(G-9351)***
STI, McPherson *Also called Specialty Technology Inc* ***(G-7027)***
Stickels Inc 785 539-5722
714 N 12th St Manhattan (66502) ***(G-6812)***
Stifel Nicolaus & Company Inc 316 264-6321
301 N Main St Ste 800 Wichita (67202) ***(G-15672)***
Stifel Nicolaus & Company Inc 785 271-1300
2445 Sw Wanamaker Rd # 100 Topeka (66614) ***(G-13099)***
Stifel Nicolaus & Company Inc 913 345-4200
9401 Indian Creek Pkwy # 1100 Overland Park (66210) ***(G-9362)***
Stiles Glaucoma Cons P A 913 897-9299
7200 W 129th St Overland Park (66213) ***(G-9363)***
Still Builders Inc 913 780-0702
15740 S Mahaffie St Olathe (66062) ***(G-8083)***
Stilwell Venturing Crew 913 306-2419
19950 Broadmoor Ln Stilwell (66085) ***(G-12173)***
Stinger By Axe 620 767-7555
1040 N Union St Council Grove (66846) ***(G-1177)***
Stinger Ltd 620 465-2683
302 E Dean St Burrton (67020) ***(G-651)***
Stinnett Timbers LLC 620 363-4757
30213 Se Highway 31 Kincaid (66039) ***(G-4581)***
Stinson Lasswell & Wilson LLC 316 264-9137
200 W Douglas Ave Ste 100 Wichita (67202) ***(G-15673)***
Stinson Leonard Street LLP 913 451-8600
9200 Indian Creek Pkwy Shawnee Mission (66210) ***(G-11901)***
Stinson Leonard Street LLP 316 265-8800
1625 N Wtrfrnt Pkwy # 300 Wichita (67206) ***(G-15674)***
Stith Bob Heating Coolg & Plbg, Wichita *Also called Bob Stith Heating and Cooling* ***(G-13861)***
Stjosephs Via Christy Med Ctr, Wichita *Also called South Central Pathology Lab PA* ***(G-15618)***
Stm Inc 316 775-2223
1000 Industrial Rd Augusta (67010) ***(G-348)***
Stock Exchange Bank 620 442-2400
103 S Main St Caldwell (67022) ***(G-661)***
Stockade Brands Incorporated 620 231-6700
1057 S Highway 69 Pittsburg (66762) ***(G-9941)***
Stockade Companies LLC (PA) 620 669-9372
2908 N Plum St Ste A Hutchinson (67502) ***(G-3448)***

Stockgrowers State Bank (HQ) ...800 772-2265
622 Main St Ashland (67831) (G-199)
Stockgrowers State Bank (PA) ...785 256-4241
225 Main St Maple Hill (66507) (G-6864)
Stockgrowers State Bank ...620 873-2123
203 N Fowler St Meade (67864) (G-7054)
Stockton Burial Vault Company, Mound City Also called Mound City Vault Co Inc (G-7173)
Stockton National Bank (PA) ...785 425-6721
123 N Cedar St Stockton (67669) (G-12189)
Stoltz Management Company, Overland Park Also called Stoltz Realty Delaware Inc (G-9364)
Stoltz Realty Delaware Inc ...913 451-4466
8717 W 110th St Ste 240 Overland Park (66210) (G-9364)
Stone Croft Ministries Inc ...816 763-7800
10561 Barkley St Ste 500 Overland Park (66212) (G-9365)
Stone House Animal Hospital ...785 228-9411
1010 Sw Fairlawn Rd Topeka (66604) (G-13100)
Stone Investment Inc ...913 367-0276
216 S 10th St Atchison (66002) (G-263)
Stone Lock Global Inc ...800 970-6168
101 N Church St Ste A Olathe (66061) (G-8084)
Stone Post Dairy LLC ...620 357-8634
33002 Se K Rd Jetmore (67854) (G-3648)
Stone Sand Co Inc ...620 793-7864
421 S Washington Ave Great Bend (67530) (G-2639)
Stonecreek Family Physicians ...785 587-4101
4101 Anderson Ave Manhattan (66503) (G-6813)
Stonelock Global ...800 970-6168
12635 Hemlock St Ste A Overland Park (66213) (G-9366)
Stoner Door & Dock Corporation ...785 478-3074
1410 Sw Auburn Rd Topeka (66615) (G-13101)
Stoneridge, Great Bend Also called Golden Belt Country Club Inc (G-2571)
Stoneworth Building Products, Shawnee Mission Also called Sandstone Inc (G-11827)
Stoney Pointe Apartment, Wichita Also called Edward Rose & Sons LLC (G-14261)
Stoneybrook Assisted Living, Manhattan Also called Midwest Health Services Inc (G-6748)
Stoneybrook Retirement Cmnty, Manhattan Also called Midwest Health Services Inc (G-6749)
Stoppel Dirt Inc ...620 675-2653
910 W Edelle Ave Sublette (67877) (G-12208)
Storm Sheltors Plus, Wichita Also called Southborough Partners (G-15621)
Stormont Vail Health, Topeka Also called Stormont-Vail Healthcare Inc (G-13104)
Stormont Vail West, Topeka Also called Stormont-Vail Healthcare Inc (G-13103)
Stormont Vale Hospital (PA) ...785 273-8224
4100 Sw 15th St Topeka (66604) (G-13102)
Stormont-Vail Cotton O'Nei, Topeka Also called Thomas E Moskow MD (G-13159)
Stormont-Vail Healthcare Inc ...785 270-4600
3707 Sw 6th Ave Topeka (66606) (G-13103)
Stormont-Vail Healthcare Inc (PA) ...785 354-6000
1500 Sw 10th Ave Topeka (66604) (G-13104)
Stormont-Vail Healthcare Inc ...785 584-6705
423 Main St Rossville (66533) (G-10256)
Stormont-Vail Healthcare Inc ...785 270-4820
720 Sw Lane St Topeka (66606) (G-13105)
Stormont-Vail Healthcare Inc ...785 270-8625
830 Sw Mulvane St Topeka (66606) (G-13106)
Stormont-Vail Healthcare Inc ...785 863-3417
209 W Jefferson St Oskaloosa (66066) (G-8230)
Stormont-Vail Healthcare Inc ...785 354-9591
3520 Sw 6th Ave Topeka (66606) (G-13107)
Stormont-Vail Healthcare Inc ...785 231-1800
920 Sw Lane St Topeka (66606) (G-13108)
Stormont-Vail Healthcare Inc ...620 343-2900
1301 W 12th Ave Emporia (66801) (G-1830)
Stormont-Vail Healthcare Inc ...785 537-2651
1133 College Ave Ste E110 Manhattan (66502) (G-6814)
Stormont-Vail Healthcare Inc ...785 273-8224
4100 Sw 15th St Topeka (66604) (G-13109)
Stormont-Vail Healthcare Inc ...785 354-6116
4019 Sw 10th Ave Topeka (66604) (G-13110)
Stormont-Vail Healthcare Inc ...785 354-5545
731 Sw Mulvane St Topeka (66606) (G-13111)
Stormont-Vail Healthcare Inc ...785 270-8605
1504 Sw 8th Ave Topeka (66606) (G-13112)
Stormont-Vail Healthcare Inc ...785 354-5225
6725 Sw 29th St Topeka (66614) (G-13113)
Stormont-Vail Healthcare Inc ...785 836-7111
211 Main St Carbondale (66414) (G-685)
Stormont-Vail Healthcare Inc ...785 456-2207
1704 Commercial Cir Wamego (66547) (G-13442)
Stormont-Vail Healthcare, Inc., Topeka Also called Cotton-Neil Clnic Revocable Tr (G-12513)
Stormont-Vail Mri Center Kans, Topeka Also called Stormont-Vail Healthcare Inc (G-13111)
Stormont-Vail Workcare, Topeka Also called Stormont-Vail Healthcare Inc (G-13112)
Storrer Implement Inc ...620 365-5692
1801 East St Iola (66749) (G-3636)
Stouse LLC (PA) ...913 764-5757
300 New Century Pkwy New Century (66031) (G-7301)
Stouse LLC ...913 384-0014
2828 S 44th St Kansas City (66106) (G-4441)
Stovers Restoration Inc ...316 686-5005
112 E Albert St Maize (67101) (G-6521)
Straight Upp, Manhattan Also called Dell Ann Upp (G-6611)
Straightline Hdd Inc ...620 802-0200
1816 E Wasp Rd Hutchinson (67501) (G-3449)
Strands ...620 663-6397
2520 N Main St Hutchinson (67502) (G-3450)
Strasburg-Children, Shawnee Mission Also called Strasburg-Jarvis Inc (G-11902)
Strasburg-Jarvis Inc ...913 888-1115
9810 Industrial Blvd Shawnee Mission (66215) (G-11902)
Strata Drilling Inc ...620 793-7971
5286 Timber Creek Rd Great Bend (67530) (G-2640)
Strate Construction Inc ...620 659-2251
220 W 10th St Kinsley (67547) (G-4621)
Strategic Global Services LLC ...316 655-2761
1910 E Norton Wichita (67216) (G-15675)
Strategic Value Media ...913 214-5203
8700 Indian Creek Pkwy # 300 Overland Park (66210) (G-9367)
Stratford Commons, Shawnee Mission Also called Tutera Group Inc (G-11951)
Stratgic Knwldge Solutions Inc ...913 682-2002
2524 Kensington Pl Leavenworth (66048) (G-5292)
Strathman Sales Company Inc ...785 354-8537
2127 Se Lakewood Blvd Topeka (66605) (G-13114)
Straub International Inc ...620 672-2998
10134 Ne State Road 61 Pratt (67124) (G-10156)
Straub International Inc (PA) ...620 792-5256
200 S Patton Rd Great Bend (67530) (G-2641)
Straub International Inc ...620 662-0211
1100 Wilbeck Dr Hutchinson (67505) (G-3451)
Straub International Inc ...785 825-1300
3637 S 9th St Salina (67401) (G-10717)
Strawberry Hill Povitica Co, Merriam Also called Strawberry Hill Povitica Inc (G-7107)
Strawberry Hill Povitica Inc ...800 631-1002
7226 W Frontage Rd Merriam (66203) (G-7107)
Strawder Security Service ...620 343-8392
926 Dove Run Emporia (66801) (G-1831)
Streamline Benefits Group LLC ...913 744-2900
10053 Lakeview Ave Lenexa (66219) (G-6155)
Streamline Insurance Group, Lenexa Also called Streamline Benefits Group LLC (G-6155)
Strecker Machine Inc ...620 793-7128
610 Bend Ave Heizer (67530) (G-2968)
Street and Highway Dept, Hugoton Also called County of Stevens (G-3154)
Street Maintenance Division, Topeka Also called City of Topeka (G-12474)
Streeter Concessions, Manhattan Also called Streeter Enterprises LLC (G-6815)
Streeter Enterprises LLC ...785 537-0100
1911 Tuttle Creek Blvd Manhattan (66502) (G-6815)
Stress Panel Manufacturers ...620 347-8200
104 S Industrial Dr Arma (66712) (G-191)
Stresscrete Inc ...913 255-3112
14503 Wallick Rd Atchison (66002) (G-264)
Stretch It Limousine Service ...913 269-1955
11800 Shwnee Mission Pkwy Shawnee Mission (66203) (G-11903)
Strickland Construction Co ...913 764-7000
720 S Rogers Rd Ste B Olathe (66062) (G-8085)
Strickland Properties, Olathe Also called Attic Management Group LLC (G-7541)
Stroberg Equipment Co Inc ...620 662-7650
602 Urban Dr Hutchinson (67501) (G-3452)
Stromgren Supports, Hays Also called Arveda Llc (G-2750)
Strong City Elevator ...620 273-6483
P.O. Box 210 Strong City (66869) (G-12195)
Stroot Locker Inc ...316 777-4421
115 N 1st Ave Mulvane (67110) (G-7227)
Structral Intgrity Systems LLC ...316 634-1396
10302 E Bronco St Wichita (67206) (G-15676)
Structura ...913 390-8787
19922 W 162nd St Olathe (66062) (G-8086)
Structural Integrity Group LLC ...316 633-9403
118 Circle Dr Wichita (67218) (G-15677)
Stryker Services Inc ...785 357-1281
1440 Sw 41st St Topeka (66609) (G-13115)
Studdard Group, Leavenworth Also called Studdard Moving & Storage Inc (G-5293)
Studdard Moving & Storage Inc (PA) ...913 341-4600
201 Commercial St Leavenworth (66048) (G-5293)
Studdard Relocation Svcs LLC ...816 524-2772
201 Commercial St Leavenworth (66048) (G-5294)
Student Health Center Psu ...620 235-4452
1701 S Broadway St Pittsburg (66762) (G-9942)
Student In Free Enterpris ...620 235-4574
1701 S Broadway St Pittsburg (66762) (G-9943)
Studentreasures Publishing, Topeka Also called Nationwide Learning LLC (G-12925)
Studer Truck Line Inc ...785 353-2241
309 Center St Beattie (66406) (G-420)
Studio 13 Inc ...913 948-1284
6731 W 121st St Overland Park (66209) (G-9368)
Stueder Contractors Inc ...620 792-6044
3410 10th St Great Bend (67530) (G-2642)
Stuhlsatz Service Inc (PA) ...316 531-2282
29622 W Harry St Garden Plain (67050) (G-2322)

STURDI-BILT DOOR CO (DIV), Hutchinson *Also called Sturdi-Bilt Storage Barns Inc* ***(G-3453)***
Sturdi-Bilt Storage Barns Inc.......620 663-5998
3909 Stacy Rd Hutchinson (67501) ***(G-3453)***
Sturgis Materials Inc.......913 371-7757
550 S Packard St 552 Kansas City (66105) ***(G-4442)***
Stutzman Greenhouse Inc.......620 662-0559
6709 W State Road 61 Hutchinson (67501) ***(G-3454)***
Stutzman Grnhse Grdn Ctr Gift, Hutchinson *Also called Stutzman Greenhouse Inc* ***(G-3454)***
Styers Equipment Company.......913 681-5225
8301 W 125th St Ste 100 Overland Park (66213) ***(G-9369)***
Style Crest Inc.......316 832-6303
811 E 33rd St N Wichita (67219) ***(G-15678)***
Stylecraft Auto Upholstery.......316 262-0449
1148 N Mosley Ave Wichita (67214) ***(G-15679)***
Styling Studios.......913 685-8800
12661 Antioch Rd Shawnee Mission (66213) ***(G-11904)***
Sub-Technologies Inc (PA).......816 795-9955
236 N 7th St Kansas City (66101) ***(G-4443)***
Sublette Cooperative Inc (PA).......620 675-2297
500 W Lalande Ave Sublette (67877) ***(G-12209)***
Sublette Enterprises Inc.......620 668-5501
6 Mi E 1 Mi N On Hwy 56 Sublette (67877) ***(G-12210)***
Sublette Feeders, Sublette *Also called Sublette Enterprises Inc* ***(G-12210)***
Sublette Recreation Commission.......620 675-8211
406 Wallace St Sublette (67877) ***(G-12211)***
Sublette Recreational Center, Sublette *Also called Sublette Recreation Commission* ***(G-12211)***
Subscription Ink Co.......913 248-1800
10406 Shawnee Mission Pkwy Shawnee Mission (66203) ***(G-11905)***
Substance Abuse Center Kansas.......316 267-3825
940 N Waco Ave Wichita (67203) ***(G-15680)***
Substance Abuse Cntr E Kansas (PA).......913 362-0045
2005 Washington Blvd Kansas City (66102) ***(G-4444)***
Substance Abuse Recovery Prog, Topeka *Also called Valeo Behavioral Health Care* ***(G-13215)***
Subtech USA, Kansas City *Also called Sub-Technologies Inc* ***(G-4443)***
Suburban Landscape Management, Wichita *Also called Biehler Companies Inc* ***(G-13847)***
Suburban Lawn & Garden Inc.......913 649-8700
10501 Roe Ave Shawnee Mission (66207) ***(G-11906)***
Success Truck Leasing Inc (PA).......913 321-1716
77 S James St Kansas City (66118) ***(G-4445)***
Suddenlink Communications, Fort Scott *Also called Cequel Communications LLC* ***(G-1958)***
Sugar Creek Packing Co.......620 232-2700
1600 W Mc Ky Frontenac (66763) ***(G-2064)***
Sugar Hills Golf Club Inc.......785 899-2785
6450 Road 16 Goodland (67735) ***(G-2487)***
Sugar Rush Inc.......913 839-2158
13778 S Blackbob Rd Olathe (66062) ***(G-8087)***
Sugar Scholl Magee Carriker (PA).......913 384-4990
9301 W 74th St Ste 325 Overland Park (66204) ***(G-9370)***
Sugar Valley Lakes Homes Assn.......913 795-2120
53 Fairway Dr Mound City (66056) ***(G-7175)***
Sugarcat Hospitality Inc.......620 275-5800
1335 Hineman Dr Garden City (67846) ***(G-2292)***
Suhor Industries Inc.......620 421-4434
10965 Granada Ln Ste 300 Overland Park (66211) ***(G-9371)***
Suicide Prvntion For Btlr Cnty, Andover *Also called South Cntl Mntal Hlth Cnseling* ***(G-108)***
Sullivan Schein Dental, Shawnee Mission *Also called Henry Schein Inc* ***(G-11427)***
Summer Snow LLC.......785 706-1003
700 Pecan Cir Manhattan (66502) ***(G-6816)***
Summer Stone Duplexes.......316 636-9000
7272 E 37th St N Ofc Wichita (67226) ***(G-15681)***
Summerfield Hotel Co, Wichita *Also called SF Hotel Company LP* ***(G-15569)***
Summerfield Suites Mgt Co L P.......316 681-5100
8100 E 22nd St N Bldg 500 Wichita (67226) ***(G-15682)***
Summers & Spencer Company (PA).......785 272-4484
5825 Sw 29th St Ste 101 Topeka (66614) ***(G-13116)***
Summers & Spencer Company.......785 838-4484
3320 Clinton Parkway Ct # 220 Lawrence (66047) ***(G-5126)***
Summit Care Inc.......913 239-8777
6830 W 121st Ct Leawood (66209) ***(G-5563)***
Summit Drilling Co Inc.......620 343-3278
825 Commercial St Emporia (66801) ***(G-1832)***
Summit Group of Salina KS LP.......785 826-1711
1820 W Crawford St Salina (67401) ***(G-10718)***
Summit Hospitality LLC.......970 765-5690
2760 S 9th St Salina (67401) ***(G-10719)***
Summit Hotel Properties Inc.......785 826-1711
1820 W Crawford St Salina (67401) ***(G-10720)***
Summit Hotel Properties LLC.......620 341-9393
2921 W 18th Ave Emporia (66801) ***(G-1833)***
Summit Producers Company Inc.......785 827-9331
1700 E Iron Ave Ste A Salina (67401) ***(G-10721)***
Summit Roofing & Contg LLC.......417 873-9191
1035 N Highway 69 Frontenac (66763) ***(G-2065)***
Summit Surgical LLC.......620 663-4800
1818 E 23rd Ave Hutchinson (67502) ***(G-3455)***
Summit, The, Hutchinson *Also called L L C Oasis of Hutchinson* ***(G-3353)***
SUMMIT, THE, Hutchinson *Also called Summit Surgical LLC* ***(G-3455)***
Summitt Drilling, Emporia *Also called Summit Drilling Co Inc* ***(G-1832)***
Summitt Rest Care LLC.......620 624-5117
2281 N Grant Ave Liberal (67901) ***(G-6373)***
Sumner Cable Tv Inc.......620 326-8989
117 W Harvey Ave Wellington (67152) ***(G-13531)***
Sumner County Appraiser.......620 326-8986
500 N Wash Ave Ste 102 Wellington (67152) ***(G-13532)***
Sumner County Family Care Ctr (PA).......620 326-3301
507 E 16th St Ste 1 Wellington (67152) ***(G-13533)***
Sumner County Home Health Agcy, Wellington *Also called County of Sumner* ***(G-13496)***
Sumner County Hospital Dst 1.......620 845-6492
601 S Osage St Caldwell (67022) ***(G-662)***
Sumner Mental Health Center (PA).......620 326-7448
1601 W 16th St Wellington (67152) ***(G-13534)***
Sumner Regional Medical Center, Wellington *Also called St Lukes Hospital Inc* ***(G-13530)***
Sun Creations Inc.......785 830-0403
2000 Delaware St Lawrence (66046) ***(G-5127)***
Sun Marble LLC.......913 438-3366
9600 Dice Ln Lenexa (66215) ***(G-6156)***
Sun Microsystems Inc.......913 327-7820
9200 Indian Creek Pkwy # 560 Overland Park (66210) ***(G-9372)***
Sun Valley Inc.......620 662-0101
1601 E Blanchard Ave Hutchinson (67501) ***(G-3456)***
Sunbelt Business Advisors.......316 684-9040
9920 E Harry St Ste 150 Wichita (67207) ***(G-15683)***
Sunbelt Business Brokers.......913 383-2671
7101 College Blvd # 1600 Overland Park (66210) ***(G-9373)***
Sunbelt Chemicals Inc.......972 296-3920
P.O. Box 860665 Shawnee (66286) ***(G-11035)***
Sunbelt Rentals Inc.......316 789-7000
3410 W 30th St S Wichita (67217) ***(G-15684)***
Sunbrdge Asssted Lving Rsdnces.......913 385-2052
9201 Foster St Shawnee Mission (66212) ***(G-11907)***
Sunburst Properties Inc.......913 393-4747
16120 Foster St Stilwell (66085) ***(G-12174)***
Sunburst Systems Inc.......913 383-9309
807 Armourdale Pkwy Kansas City (66105) ***(G-4446)***
Sundance Apartments, Wichita *Also called Ledic Management Group LLC* ***(G-14943)***
Sunfield LLC.......785 338-0314
4601 E Douglas Ave # 150 Wichita (67218) ***(G-15685)***
Sunflower Adult Day Services, Salina *Also called Saline County Comm On Aging* ***(G-10697)***
Sunflower Adult Day Services.......785 823-6666
401 W Iron Ave Salina (67401) ***(G-10722)***
Sunflower Auto Auction LLC.......785 862-2900
545 Se Engle St Bldg 131 Topeka (66619) ***(G-13117)***
Sunflower Bank.......785 827-5564
3025 Cortland Cir Salina (67401) ***(G-10723)***
Sunflower Bank Inc.......620 225-0086
2408 1st Ave Dodge City (67801) ***(G-1436)***
Sunflower Bank NA, McPherson *Also called Sunflower Holdings Inc* ***(G-7029)***
Sunflower Bank National Assn.......785 312-7274
4831 Quail Crest Pl Lawrence (66049) ***(G-5128)***
Sunflower Bank National Assn.......316 652-1279
2073 N Webb Rd Wichita (67206) ***(G-15686)***
Sunflower Bank National Assn.......785 827-5564
2450 S 9th St Salina (67401) ***(G-10724)***
Sunflower Bank National Assn.......785 537-0550
2710 Anderson Ave Manhattan (66502) ***(G-6817)***
Sunflower Bank National Assn.......785 625-8888
1010 E 27th St Hays (67601) ***(G-2914)***
Sunflower Bank National Assn.......785 825-6900
176 N Santa Fe Ave Salina (67401) ***(G-10725)***
Sunflower Bank National Assn.......785 238-3177
510 N Jefferson St Ste 1 Junction City (66441) ***(G-3758)***
Sunflower Bank National Assn.......620 624-2063
711 N Kansas Ave Liberal (67901) ***(G-6374)***
Sunflower Broadband, Lawrence *Also called Knology Inc* ***(G-4947)***
Sunflower Broadcasting Inc.......316 838-1212
2815 E 37th St N Wichita (67219) ***(G-15687)***
Sunflower Chapter of Ahsgr, Hays *Also called Sunflower Chapter of The Ameri* ***(G-2915)***
Sunflower Chapter of The Ameri.......785 656-0329
2301 Canal Blvd Hays (67601) ***(G-2915)***
Sunflower Concrete, Lawrence *Also called Sunflower Paving Inc* ***(G-5129)***
Sunflower Dental Studio Inc.......785 354-1981
1527 Nw Tyler St Topeka (66608) ***(G-13118)***
Sunflower Diversified Svcs Inc (PA).......620 792-1321
8823 4th St Great Bend (67530) ***(G-2643)***
Sunflower Diversified Svcs Inc.......620 792-4087
1312 Patton Rd Great Bend (67530) ***(G-2644)***
Sunflower Diversified Svcs Inc.......620 792-1325
1521 State Road 96 Great Bend (67530) ***(G-2645)***
Sunflower Early Education Ctr, Great Bend *Also called Sunflower Diversified Svcs Inc* ***(G-2645)***
Sunflower Elec Systems LLC.......913 894-1442
17501 W 98th St Lenexa (66219) ***(G-6157)***
Sunflower Electric Power Corp.......620 277-2590
2440 S Holcomb Ln Holcomb (67851) ***(G-3080)***

Sunflower Electric Power Corp (HQ) 785 628-2845
301 W 13th St Hays (67601) *(G-2916)*
Sunflower Electric Power Corp 620 275-0161
2075 Saint John St Garden City (67846) *(G-2293)*
Sunflower Electric Power Corp 620 657-4400
14255 E Hwy 160 Satanta (67870) *(G-10792)*
Sunflower Food Company, Lenexa *Also called Sunflower Hills Inc (G-6158)*
Sunflower Hills Golf Course 913 721-2727
122 Riverview Rd Bonner Springs (66012) *(G-575)*
Sunflower Hills Inc 913 894-2233
14612 W 106th St Lenexa (66215) *(G-6158)*
Sunflower Holdings Inc 620 241-1220
120 W Kansas Ave Ste A McPherson (67460) *(G-7029)*
Sunflower House 913 631-5800
15440 W 65th St Shawnee Mission (66217) *(G-11908)*
Sunflower Medical LLC 785 726-2486
206 Jefferson St Ellis (67637) *(G-1654)*
Sunflower Medical Group 913 432-2080
5555 W 58th St Shawnee Mission (66202) *(G-11909)*
Sunflower Medical Group PA 913 261-5800
8800 W 75th St Ste 300 Shawnee Mission (66204) *(G-11910)*
Sunflower Medical Group PA 913 722-4240
5555 W 58th St Shawnee Mission (66202) *(G-11911)*
Sunflower Partners Inc 785 462-3933
1950 S Range Ave Colby (67701) *(G-1042)*
Sunflower Paving Inc 785 856-4590
1457 N 1823 Rd Lawrence (66044) *(G-5129)*
Sunflower Prompt Care 785 246-3733
3405 Nw Hunters Ridge Ter # 100 Topeka (66618) *(G-13119)*
Sunflower Quarry, De Soto *Also called Martin Marietta Materials Inc (G-1207)*
Sunflower Rental, Topeka *Also called Sunflower Rents Inc (G-13120)*
Sunflower Rents Inc (PA) 785 233-9489
221 Sw Hampton St Topeka (66612) *(G-13120)*
Sunflower Restaurant Sup Inc (PA) 785 823-6394
1647 Sunflower Rd Salina (67401) *(G-10726)*
Sunflower Soccer Assn 785 233-9700
4829 Nw 17th St Topeka (66618) *(G-13121)*
Sunflower State Hlth Plan Inc 877 644-4623
8325 Lenexa Dr Overland Park (66214) *(G-9374)*
Sunflower Supply Company Inc 620 783-5473
1001 W 7th St Galena (66739) *(G-2088)*
Sunflower Supports Company 785 267-3093
2521 Sw 37th St Topeka (66611) *(G-13122)*
Sunflower Taxi Courier Svc LLC 785 826-1881
752 Duvall Ave Salina (67401) *(G-10727)*
Sunflower Travel Corporation (PA) 316 634-1700
1223 N Rock Rd Ste G200 Wichita (67206) *(G-15688)*
Sunflower Vegetable Oil Inc 913 541-8882
9880 Widmer Rd Lenexa (66215) *(G-6159)*
Sunflwer Child Spport Svcs LLC 785 623-4516
205 E 7th St Ste 400a Hays (67601) *(G-2917)*
Sunflwer Elc Sup Htchinson Inc (PA) 620 662-0531
100 W 2nd Ave Hutchinson (67501) *(G-3457)*
Sunflwer Pcemakers Quilt Guild 913 727-1870
18502 Tonganoxie Dr Leavenworth (66048) *(G-5295)*
Sunflwer Wchita State Unvrstys, Wichita *Also called Wichita State Sunflower Inc (G-16030)*
Sunglo Feeds, Hesston *Also called Provimi North America Inc (G-2999)*
Sunlite Science & Technology 785 832-8818
4811 Quail Crest Pl Lawrence (66049) *(G-5130)*
Sunporch of Smith Center 785 506-6003
614 S Main St Smith Center (66967) *(G-12044)*
Sunrise Motel, Clay Center *Also called Rothfuss Motels (G-879)*
Sunrise of Leawood, Leawood *Also called Sunrise Senior Living LLC (G-5564)*
Sunrise of Lenexa, Lenexa *Also called Sunrise Senior Living Inc (G-6160)*
Sunrise of Overland Park, Overland Park *Also called Sunrise Senior Living LLC (G-9376)*
Sunrise Point Elementary Pto 913 239-7500
15800 Roe Blvd Overland Park (66224) *(G-9375)*
Sunrise Senior Living Inc 913 262-1611
7105 Mission Rd Prairie Village (66208) *(G-10070)*
Sunrise Senior Living Inc 913 307-0665
15055 W 87th Street Pkwy Lenexa (66215) *(G-6160)*
Sunrise Senior Living LLC 913 685-3340
12500 W 135th St Overland Park (66221) *(G-9376)*
Sunrise Senior Living LLC 913 906-0200
11661 Granada St Leawood (66211) *(G-5564)*
Sunrise Senior Living Svcs Inc 913 262-1611
7105 Mission Rd Prairie Village (66208) *(G-10071)*
Sunset Home Inc 785 243-2720
620 2nd Ave Concordia (66901) *(G-1131)*
Sunset Inn 316 321-9172
1901 W Central Ave El Dorado (67042) *(G-1605)*
Sunset Manor Inc 620 231-7340
206 S Dittman St Frontenac (66763) *(G-2066)*
Sunset Manor Nursing Home, Frontenac *Also called Sunset Manor Inc (G-2066)*
Sunset Nursing Home, Waverly *Also called Coffey County Hospital (G-13481)*
Sunset Zoological Pk Wildlife 785 587-2737
2333 Oak St Manhattan (66502) *(G-6818)*
Sunshine Connections Inc 785 625-2093
2517 Indian Trl Apt B Hays (67601) *(G-2918)*
Sunshine Day Care LLC 620 221-1177
19789 81st Rd Winfield (67156) *(G-16176)*
Sunshine Horizons 620 276-1787
2718 Cummings Rd Ste W Garden City (67846) *(G-2294)*
SUNSHINE MEADOWS RETIREMENT CO, Buhler *Also called Buhler Sunshine Home Inc (G-614)*
Sunshine Nursing Agency Inc 620 276-8868
2718 Cummings Rd Ste E Garden City (67846) *(G-2295)*
Sunshine Rooms Inc 316 838-0033
3333 N Mead St Ste B Wichita (67219) *(G-15689)*
Sunshine's Nursing Horizons, Garden City *Also called Sunshine Nursing Agency Inc (G-2295)*
Sunstar Wichita Inc 316 943-2181
5500 W Kellogg Dr Wichita (67209) *(G-15690)*
Suntell, Topeka *Also called Financial Institution Tech Inc (G-12610)*
Super 8 Forbes Landing 785 862-2222
5922 Sw Topeka Blvd Topeka (66619) *(G-13123)*
Super 8 Gardner, Gardner *Also called Chaudhrys Investment Group (G-2332)*
Super 8 Hotel In Colby Kansas 785 462-8248
1040 Zelfer Ave 223-224 Colby (67701) *(G-1043)*
Super 8 Motel, Emporia *Also called Sana Hospitality Corp (G-1822)*
Super 8 Motel, Independence *Also called V & R Motel LLC (G-3570)*
Super 8 Motel, Goodland *Also called Americal Inc (G-2461)*
Super 8 Motel, Iola *Also called Allen County Lodging LLC (G-3586)*
Super 8 Motel, Chanute *Also called Mark Randolf (G-742)*
Super 8 Motel, Shawnee Mission *Also called True North Hotel Group Inc (G-11944)*
Super 8 Motel, Winfield *Also called Darlene Coffey (G-16139)*
Super 8 Motel, Abilene *Also called Abilene Super Eight (G-9)*
Super 8 Motel, Emporia *Also called Innworks Inc (G-1777)*
Super 8 Motel, Dodge City *Also called Leisure Hotel Corporation (G-1397)*
Super 8 Motel, Colby *Also called Super 8 Hotel In Colby Kansas (G-1043)*
Super 8 Motel, Pittsburg *Also called Condor Hospitality Trust Inc (G-9843)*
Super 8 Motel, Salina *Also called S & B Motels Inc (G-10656)*
Super 8 Motel 913 721-3877
13041 Ridge Dr Bonner Springs (66012) *(G-576)*
Super 8 Motel 785 743-6442
709 S 13th St Wakeeney (67672) *(G-13391)*
Super 8 Motel 316 945-5261
6245 W Kellogg Dr Wichita (67209) *(G-15691)*
Super 8 Motel 620 421-8000
229 Main St Parsons (67357) *(G-9742)*
Super 8 Motel of Beloit 785 738-4300
3018 Us 24 Hwy Beloit (67420) *(G-504)*
Super 8 Motel of Concordia 785 243-4200
1320 Lincoln St Concordia (66901) *(G-1132)*
Super 8 Motel of Pratt Inc 620 672-5945
1906 E 1st St Pratt (67124) *(G-10157)*
Super Chief Inc 785 272-7277
2120 Sw Belle Ave Topeka (66614) *(G-13124)*
Super Floral Retailing Magazin, Topeka *Also called Florists Review Entps Inc (G-12620)*
Super Oil Co Inc (PA) 785 354-1410
1735 N Kansas Ave Topeka (66608) *(G-13125)*
Super Speed Printing Inc 316 283-5828
3200 Witmarsum Dr North Newton (67117) *(G-7439)*
Supercar Life, Leawood *Also called Anthem Motorsports Inc (G-5328)*
Supercuts, Shawnee Mission *Also called Geesu Inc (G-11392)*
Supercuts Inc 316 218-1400
229 N Andover Rd Ste 500 Andover (67002) *(G-109)*
Superior Building Maintenance 316 943-2347
2007 S West St Wichita (67213) *(G-15692)*
Superior Car Care Center LLC 620 492-6856
608 S Main St Johnson (67855) *(G-3663)*
Superior Computer Supply Inc 316 942-5577
2355 S Edwards St Ste A Wichita (67213) *(G-15693)*
Superior Crt Reporting Svc LLC 913 262-0100
8001 Conser St Ste 200 Overland Park (66204) *(G-9377)*
Superior Disposal Service Inc (PA) 913 938-4552
447 N Cherry St Gardner (66030) *(G-2364)*
Superior Disposal Service Inc 913 406-9460
2114 N 1300th Rd Eudora (66025) *(G-1881)*
Superior Door Service Inc 913 381-1767
106 Greystone Ave Kansas City (66103) *(G-4447)*
Superior Essex Inc 620 653-2191
75 E State Road 4 Hoisington (67544) *(G-3071)*
Superior Excavating LLC 316 260-1829
10401 N Woodlawn St Valley Center (67147) *(G-13355)*
Superior Hardwood Floors LLC 316 554-9663
P.O. Box 16628 Wichita (67216) *(G-15694)*
Superior Holding Inc (PA) 620 662-6693
3524 E 4th Ave Hutchinson (67501) *(G-3458)*
Superior Home Improvements LLC 620 225-3560
11164 Kliesen St Dodge City (67801) *(G-1437)*
Superior Installation Services, Topeka *Also called B A Designs LLC (G-12356)*
Superior Masonry & Stucco LLC 316 928-2365
1008 S Santa Fe St Wichita (67211) *(G-15695)*

ALPHABETIC

Superior Mobile Wash Inc....913 915-9642
1839 N 10th St Kansas City (66104) ***(G-4448)***
Superior Office, Wichita *Also called Superior Computer Supply Inc* ***(G-15693)***
Superior Plumbing & Heating Co....785 827-5611
1645 Copper Ct Salina (67401) ***(G-10728)***
Superior Plumbing of Wichita....316 684-8349
6837 E Harry St Wichita (67207) ***(G-15696)***
Superior Pools....316 838-4968
4811 N Alexander St Wichita (67204) ***(G-15697)***
Superior Printing Co....913 682-3313
602 Grand Ave Leavenworth (66048) ***(G-5296)***
Superior Products Intl II Inc....913 962-4848
10835 W 78th St Shawnee Mission (66214) ***(G-11912)***
Superior Rbr Stamp & Seal Inc....316 682-5511
2725 E Douglas Ave Wichita (67211) ***(G-15698)***
Superior Refrigeration and Htg, Lawrence *Also called Srh Mechanical Contractors Inc* ***(G-5116)***
Superior School Supplies Inc (PA)....316 265-7683
1818 W 2nd St N Wichita (67203) ***(G-15699)***
Superior School Supplies Inc....620 421-3190
1410 Corporate Dr Parsons (67357) ***(G-9743)***
Superior Sheet Metal Co Inc....913 831-9900
3940 S Ferree St Kansas City (66103) ***(G-4449)***
Superior Signals Inc....913 780-1440
16355 S Lone Elm Rd Olathe (66062) ***(G-8088)***
Superior Tool Service Inc....316 945-8488
722 E Zimmerly St Wichita (67211) ***(G-15700)***
Supernova Painting LLC....785 850-0158
1419 Santa Fe St Atchison (66002) ***(G-265)***
Supervan Service Co Inc....913 281-4044
511 Miami Ave Kansas City (66105) ***(G-4450)***
Supply Technologies LLC....913 982-4016
14621 W 112th St Lenexa (66215) ***(G-6161)***
Supported Employment Services....620 431-1805
222 W Main St Ste C Chanute (66720) ***(G-766)***
Supreme Cattle Feeders Div, Kismet *Also called Green Plains Cattle Co LLC* ***(G-4630)***
Supreme Court United States....785 295-2790
444 Se Quincy St Ste 375 Topeka (66683) ***(G-13126)***
Sur-Tec Inc....913 647-7720
6840 Silverheel St Shawnee (66226) ***(G-11036)***
Sure Check Brokerage Inc (PA)....785 823-1334
141 S 4th St Salina (67401) ***(G-10729)***
Sure Crop Liquid Fertilizers, Seneca *Also called AG Connection Sales Inc* ***(G-10856)***
Surefire AG Systems Inc (PA)....785 626-3670
9904 Highway 25 Atwood (67730) ***(G-292)***
Surewest Communications....913 825-2882
14859 W 95th St Lenexa (66215) ***(G-6162)***
Surewest Kans Connections LLC (HQ)....913 890-4483
14859 W 95th St Lenexa (66215) ***(G-6163)***
Surface Center Interiors LLC....913 422-0500
12800 Shwnee Mission Pkwy Shawnee (66216) ***(G-11037)***
Surface Mining Section, Frontenac *Also called Health and Envmt Kans Dept* ***(G-2055)***
Surface Protection Svcs LLC....316 322-5135
2012 W 6th Ave El Dorado (67042) ***(G-1606)***
Surface Solutions Intl Inc....913 742-7744
14400 Maple St Overland Park (66223) ***(G-9378)***
Surgery Center of Kansas, Wichita *Also called Wichita Orthopaedic Assoc LLC* ***(G-16015)***
Surgery Center of Leawood LLC....913 661-9977
11413 Ash St Ste 100 Shawnee Mission (66211) ***(G-11913)***
Surgery Center Olathe LLC....913 829-4001
20375 W 151st St Ste 351 Olathe (66061) ***(G-8089)***
Surgery Center S Centl Kans, Hutchinson *Also called Surgery Ctr S Centl Kans LLC* ***(G-3459)***
Surgery Ctr S Centl Kans LLC....620 663-7187
1708 E 23rd St Ave Hutchinson (67502) ***(G-3459)***
Surgical Specialists PA....316 945-7309
4013 N Ridge Rd Ste 210 Wichita (67205) ***(G-15701)***
Surgical Weight Loss Center, Overland Park *Also called Heartland Surgical Care* ***(G-8808)***
Surgicare of Wichita Inc....316 685-2207
2818 N Greenwich Rd Wichita (67226) ***(G-15702)***
Surgicenter Johnson County Ltd....913 894-4050
8800 Ballentine St Shawnee Mission (66214) ***(G-11914)***
Survey Companies LLC....620 862-5291
200 Main St Haviland (67059) ***(G-2742)***
Survey Companies LLC....316 722-6916
1319 S Seville Ave Wichita (67209) ***(G-15703)***
Surveying and Mapping LLC....913 344-9933
9393 W 110th St Overland Park (66210) ***(G-9379)***
Surveys Inc....785 472-4456
111 W North Main St Ellsworth (67439) ***(G-1681)***
Susan B Allen Memorial Hosp (PA)....316 322-4510
720 W Central Ave El Dorado (67042) ***(G-1607)***
Susan Pool....316 266-6574
8200 E 32nd St N Ste 100 Wichita (67226) ***(G-15704)***
Suther Building Supply Inc....785 336-2255
103 N 1st St Seneca (66538) ***(G-10883)***
Suther Feeds Inc (PA)....785 292-4414
105 S Kansas Ave Frankfort (66427) ***(G-2023)***
Suther Feeds Inc....785 292-4415
105 S Kansas Ave Frankfort (66427) ***(G-2024)***
Sutherland Builders Inc....316 529-2620
6053 S Seneca St Wichita (67217) ***(G-15705)***
Suthers, Frankfort *Also called Suther Feeds Inc* ***(G-2024)***
Suture Express Inc....913 384-2220
11020 King St Ste 400 Overland Park (66210) ***(G-9380)***
Suzanna Wesley Child Care....785 478-3703
7433 Sw 29th St Topeka (66614) ***(G-13127)***
Svetas Body Therapy LLC....316 630-0400
2141 N Bradley Fair Pkwy Wichita (67206) ***(G-15706)***
SW Agro Center, Kismet *Also called S W Agro Center* ***(G-4632)***
Swaim Funeral Home Inc....620 227-2136
1901 6th Ave Dodge City (67801) ***(G-1438)***
Swami Inc....785 228-2500
1024 Sw Wanamaker Rd Topeka (66604) ***(G-13128)***
Swami Investment Inc....913 788-9929
10920 Parallel Pkwy Kansas City (66109) ***(G-4451)***
Swan Corporation....913 390-1411
15296 W 119th St Olathe (66062) ***(G-8090)***
Swan Engineering & Sup Co Inc....913 371-7425
1132 Adams St Kansas City (66103) ***(G-4452)***
Swank-Standley Motors, Osborne *Also called Moore Buick Chevrolet Pontiac* ***(G-8213)***
Swansons Streamway Dog P....913 422-8242
6241 Woodland Rd Shawnee Mission (66218) ***(G-11915)***
Swarovski North America Ltd....913 599-3791
11559 W 95th St Overland Park (66214) ***(G-9381)***
Swartz Veterinary Hospital....785 460-1078
1775 W 4th St Colby (67701) ***(G-1044)***
Swedish Country Inn....785 227-2985
112 W Lincoln St Lindsborg (67456) ***(G-6406)***
Sweet Adelines Intrntnl Chorus....316 733-4467
14105 E Lakeview Ct Wichita (67230) ***(G-15707)***
Sweet Art Company, Lenexa *Also called Altura Incorporated* ***(G-5643)***
Sweet Life At Rosehill....913 962-7600
12605 W 132nd St Overland Park (66213) ***(G-9382)***
Sweet Life At Shawnee, Shawnee Mission *Also called American Retirement Corp* ***(G-11108)***
Sweetpro Feeds, Horton *Also called Harvest Fuel Inc* ***(G-3127)***
Swift Bullet Co....785 754-2374
201 Main St Quinter (67752) ***(G-10187)***
Swift Services Inc....785 798-2380
100 S Pennsylvania Ave Ness City (67560) ***(G-7267)***
Swimtime, Sterling *Also called United Industries Inc* ***(G-12131)***
Swindoll Janzen Hawk Lloyd LLC (PA)....620 241-1826
123 S Main St McPherson (67460) ***(G-7030)***
Swindoll Janzen Hawk Lloyd LLC....316 265-5600
220 W Douglas Ave Ste 300 Wichita (67202) ***(G-15708)***
Swiss Burger Brand Meat Co....316 838-7514
3763 N Emporia St Wichita (67219) ***(G-15709)***
Swiss Made Inc....913 341-6400
7251 W 97th St Overland Park (66212) ***(G-9383)***
Swiss RE America Holding Corp (HQ)....913 676-5200
5200 Metcalf Ave Overland Park (66202) ***(G-9384)***
Swiss RE Management US Corp....913 676-5200
5200 Metcalf Ave Overland Park (66202) ***(G-9385)***
Swiss RE Solutions Holdg Corp (HQ)....913 676-5200
5200 Metcalf Ave Overland Park (66202) ***(G-9386)***
Swiss Reinsurance America Corp....913 676-5200
5200 Metcalf Ave Overland Park (66202) ***(G-9387)***
Swmc, Liberal *Also called Southwest Medical Center* ***(G-6372)***
Swope Health Services....816 922-7600
21 N 12th St Ste 400 Kansas City (66102) ***(G-4453)***
Sylvan Sales Commission LLC....785 526-7123
400 E 1st St Sylvan Grove (67481) ***(G-12220)***
Sylvester Powell Jr Cmnty Ctr, Shawnee Mission *Also called City of Mission* ***(G-11229)***
Sylvester Ranch Inc....785 242-3598
1906 Kingman Rd Ottawa (66067) ***(G-8315)***
Symantec, Shawnee Mission *Also called Nortonlifelock Inc* ***(G-11688)***
Syndeo Outsourcing LLC....316 630-9107
3504 N Great Plains Dr # 200 Wichita (67220) ***(G-15710)***
Synergetix, Kansas City *Also called Smiths Intrcnnect Americas Inc* ***(G-4429)***
Synexis LLC (PA)....816 399-0895
8905 Lenexa Dr Overland Park (66214) ***(G-9388)***
Syngenta Seeds Inc....785 210-0218
11783 Ascher Rd Junction City (66441) ***(G-3759)***
Syntech Research Lab Svcs LLC....913 378-0998
17745 Metcalf Ave Stilwell (66085) ***(G-12175)***
Syracuse Dairy II LLC....620 492-2525
751 S Suuny Rd 36 Syracuse (67878) ***(G-12234)***
Syracuse Feed Yard, Syracuse *Also called Cactus Feeders Inc* ***(G-12222)***
Sysco Corporation....913 829-5555
1915 E Kansas City Rd Olathe (66061) ***(G-8091)***
Sysco Kansas City Inc (HQ)....913 829-5555
1915 E Kansas City Rd Olathe (66061) ***(G-8092)***
Sysco Kansas City Inc....316 942-4205
1001 S Young St Wichita (67209) ***(G-15711)***
Systech Environmental Corp....620 378-4451
1420 S Cement Plant Rd Fredonia (66736) ***(G-2046)***

System Air, Lenexa *Also called Systemair Mfg Inc* ***(G-6164)***
System Building Services, Lenexa *Also called Systems Building Services LLC* ***(G-6165)***
Systemair Mfg Inc....913 752-6000
10048 Indl Blvd Lenexa (66215) ***(G-6164)***
Systems 4 Inc....785 823-9119
430 N Santa Fe Ave Salina (67401) ***(G-10730)***
Systems Building Services LLC....913 385-1496
15950 College Blvd Lenexa (66219) ***(G-6165)***
Systronics Inc....913 829-9229
14902 W 117th St Olathe (66062) ***(G-8093)***
T & C Mfg & Operating Inc....620 793-5483
1020 Hoover St Great Bend (67530) ***(G-2646)***
T & C Tank Rental & Anchor Svc....806 592-3286
7400 W 130th St Ste 270 Overland Park (66213) ***(G-9389)***
T & C Tank Rentals Anchr Serv, Overland Park *Also called T & C Tank Rental & Anchor Svc* ***(G-9389)***
T & E Oil Company Inc 1 (PA)....620 663-3777
911 N Halstead St Hutchinson (67501) ***(G-3460)***
T & J Holdings Inc....785 841-4935
1203 Iowa St Lawrence (66044) ***(G-5131)***
T & M Contracting Inc....913 393-1087
17498 W 158th Pl Olathe (66062) ***(G-8094)***
T & M Electronics....785 537-1455
3360 Excel Rd Manhattan (66502) ***(G-6819)***
T & M Financial Inc....785 266-8333
3706 Sw Topeka Blvd # 400 Topeka (66609) ***(G-13129)***
T & T Flatworks Inc....620 794-0619
32015 S Wanamaker Rd Lebo (66856) ***(G-5609)***
T & W Tire LLC....316 683-8364
2280 S Sheridan St Wichita (67213) ***(G-15712)***
T and C Aviation Enterprises (PA)....913 764-4800
12901 W 151st St Ste B Olathe (66062) ***(G-8095)***
T and M Financials, Topeka *Also called T & M Financial Inc* ***(G-13129)***
T C K Financial Advisors, Wichita *Also called Tck- The Trust Company Kansas* ***(G-15718)***
T D C Ltd....913 780-9631
11860 S Conley St Olathe (66061) ***(G-8096)***
T F I Family Services, Emporia *Also called Tfi Family Services Inc* ***(G-1835)***
T G S, Lenexa *Also called Technology Group Solutions LLC* ***(G-6172)***
T H Rogers Lumber Company....620 231-0900
1701 N Broadway St Pittsburg (66762) ***(G-9944)***
T K H L Architects, El Dorado *Also called Pkhls Architecture PA* ***(G-1592)***
T Kennel Systems Inc....816 668-8995
415 Osage Ave Kansas City (66105) ***(G-4454)***
T L C Professional LLC....785 823-7444
747 Manchester Rd Salina (67401) ***(G-10731)***
T L C Trucking LLC....620 277-0140
3830 N Big Lowe Rd Holcomb (67851) ***(G-3081)***
T M H Hotels Inc....316 669-6175
401 E Douglas Ave Wichita (67202) ***(G-15713)***
T Mobile 8631, Olathe *Also called T-Mobile Usa Inc* ***(G-8098)***
T N T Machine Inc....316 440-6004
1300 S Bebe St Wichita (67209) ***(G-15714)***
T O Haas LLC....620 662-0261
16 W Avenue A Hutchinson (67501) ***(G-3461)***
T O P Learning Center, Wichita *Also called Opportunity Project Lrng Ctr* ***(G-15223)***
T R Management Inc....785 233-9603
6840 Se Johnston St Topeka (66619) ***(G-13130)***
T R Service & Rental....620 672-9100
470 Yucca Ln Pratt (67124) ***(G-10158)***
T R'S Sportswear, Hays *Also called CP Partnerships Inc* ***(G-2779)***
T S A Inc....913 322-2800
7400 State Line Rd Ste 20 Prairie Village (66208) ***(G-10072)***
T S Keim Inc (PA)....785 284-2147
1249 N Ninth St Sabetha (66534) ***(G-10333)***
T T Companies Inc....913 599-6886
10841 S Ridgeview Rd Olathe (66061) ***(G-8097)***
T V Hephner and Elec Inc....316 264-3284
737 S Washington Ave # 3 Wichita (67211) ***(G-15715)***
T W G Nursing Home Inc....620 724-8288
511 N Western Ave Girard (66743) ***(G-2420)***
T W Lacy & Associates Inc (PA)....913 706-7625
8001 Granada Rd Prairie Village (66208) ***(G-10073)***
T-143 Inc....913 681-8313
14337 Metcalf Ave Overland Park (66223) ***(G-9390)***
T-Bone Feeders Inc....785 899-6551
1751 Road 65 Goodland (67735) ***(G-2488)***
T-Bones Baseball Club LLC....913 328-2255
1800 Village West Pkwy Kansas City (66111) ***(G-4455)***
T-Kennels Systems, Kansas City *Also called T Kennel Systems Inc* ***(G-4454)***
T-L Irrigation Co....620 675-2253
1893 Us Highway 83 Sublette (67877) ***(G-12212)***
T-Mobile 8618, Topeka *Also called T-Mobile Usa Inc* ***(G-13131)***
T-Mobile Usa Inc....913 402-6500
12980 Foster St Ste 200 Shawnee Mission (66213) ***(G-11916)***
T-Mobile Usa Inc....316 201-6120
1918 W 21st St N Wichita (67203) ***(G-15716)***
T-Mobile Usa Inc....913 268-4414
15610 Shwnee Mission Pkwy Shawnee (66217) ***(G-11038)***
T-Mobile Usa Inc....913 262-2789
5303 Johnson Dr Shawnee Mission (66205) ***(G-11917)***
T-Mobile Usa Inc....785 273-5021
2040 Sw Wanamaker Rd # 102 Topeka (66604) ***(G-13131)***
T-Mobile Usa Inc....913 254-1674
14953 W 119th St Olathe (66062) ***(G-8098)***
T.F.I., Derby *Also called Twin Fiddle Investment Co LLC* ***(G-1277)***
T2 Holdings LLC....913 327-8889
3052 S 24th St Kansas City (66106) ***(G-4456)***
T2 Wireless Inc....785 537-8034
711 Commons Pl Manhattan (66503) ***(G-6820)***
Ta Millwork LLC....316 744-3440
6024 N Broadway Ave Park City (67219) ***(G-9646)***
Tabco Incorporated....913 287-3333
1323 S 59th St Kansas City (66106) ***(G-4457)***
Taben Group LLC....913 649-0468
10875 Benson Dr Ste 130 Shawnee Mission (66210) ***(G-11918)***
Tafs Inc....877 898-9797
15910 S Us 169 Hwy Olathe (66062) ***(G-8099)***
Takako America Co Inc....620 663-1790
715 Corey Rd Hutchinson (67501) ***(G-3462)***
Talent On Parade....316 522-4836
137 Pirner Ste 5 Haysville (67060) ***(G-2961)***
Tall Grass Prairie Surg Spclsts....785 233-7491
631 Sw Horne St Ste 200 Topeka (66606) ***(G-13132)***
Tall Oaks Conf Ctr, Linwood *Also called Christian Ch of Grater Kans Cy* ***(G-6416)***
Talley Inc....913 390-8484
19935 W 157th St Olathe (66062) ***(G-8100)***
Tallgrass, Wichita *Also called Somnograph Inc* ***(G-15612)***
Tallgrass Brewing Company....785 537-1131
5960 Dry Hop Cir Manhattan (66503) ***(G-6821)***
Tallgrass Commodities LLC....855 494-8484
420 Lincoln Ave Wamego (66547) ***(G-13443)***
Tallgrass Country Club, Wichita *Also called American Golf Corporation* ***(G-13692)***
Tallgrass Development LP (PA)....513 941-0500
4200 W 115th St Ste 350 Leawood (66211) ***(G-5565)***
Tallgrass Energy LP (PA)....913 928-6060
4200 W 115th St Ste 350 Leawood (66211) ***(G-5566)***
Tallgrass Energy Partners, Leawood *Also called Tallgrass Operations LLC* ***(G-5569)***
Tallgrass Energy Partners LP....620 355-7122
2089 Road 130 Lakin (67860) ***(G-4660)***
Tallgrass Energy Partners LP (HQ)....913 928-6060
4200 W 115th St Ste 350 Leawood (66211) ***(G-5567)***
Tallgrass Immediate Care LLC....785 234-0880
601 Sw Corp Vw Ste 200 Topeka (66615) ***(G-13133)***
Tallgrass Interstate Gas Trans....913 928-6060
4200 W 115th St Ste 350 Leawood (66211) ***(G-5568)***
Tallgrass Operations LLC (HQ)....913 928-6060
4200 W 115th St Ste 350 Leawood (66211) ***(G-5569)***
Tallgrass Orthpdics Spt Mdcine....785 228-9999
6730 Sw Mission View Dr Topeka (66614) ***(G-13134)***
Tallgrass Orthpdics Spt Mdcine (PA)....785 228-4700
6001 Sw 6th Ave Ste 200 Topeka (66615) ***(G-13135)***
Tallgrass Prairie Surgical (PA)....785 234-9830
6001 Sw 6th Ave Ste 220 Topeka (66615) ***(G-13136)***
Tallgrass Prairie Surgical....785 295-4500
601 Sw Corp Vw Ste 200 Topeka (66615) ***(G-13137)***
Tallgrass Surgical Center LLC....785 272-8807
6001 Sw 6th Ave Ste 100 Topeka (66615) ***(G-13138)***
Tamko Building Products Inc....785 543-2144
1598 Highway 183 Phillipsburg (67661) ***(G-9800)***
Tamko Building Products Inc....620 429-1800
600 Ne Bethlehem Rd Columbus (66725) ***(G-1088)***
Tandem Truck Service Inc....913 782-5454
19944 W 157th St Olathe (66062) ***(G-8101)***
Tangent Rail Energy Inc....913 948-9478
15700 College Blvd # 300 Lenexa (66219) ***(G-6166)***
Tanglewood Family Dentistry, Derby *Also called Dennis C McAllister DDS PA* ***(G-1234)***
Tanglewood Family Med Ctr PA....316 788-3787
606 N Mulberry Rd Derby (67037) ***(G-1273)***
Tanglewood Family Medical Ctr....316 788-3787
606 N Mulberry Rd Derby (67037) ***(G-1274)***
Tanglewood Hlth Rehabilitation....785 273-0886
5015 Sw 28th St Topeka (66614) ***(G-13139)***
Tanglewood Lk Owners Assn Inc....913 795-2286
610 Sw Lakeside Dr La Cygne (66040) ***(G-4643)***
Tank Connection LLC (PA)....620 423-0251
3609 N 16th St Parsons (67357) ***(G-9744)***
Tank Wind-Down Corp....620 421-0200
2101 S 21st St Parsons (67357) ***(G-9745)***
Tann Electric Inc....913 236-7337
13216 W 99th St Lenexa (66215) ***(G-6167)***
Tanners, Overland Park *Also called T-143 Inc* ***(G-9390)***
Tantillo Financial Group LLC....913 649-3200
10777 Barkley St Ste 200 Shawnee Mission (66211) ***(G-11919)***
Tapco Mat Rental, Shawnee Mission *Also called Tapco Products Co* ***(G-11920)***
Tapco Products Co....913 492-2777
15553 W 110th St Shawnee Mission (66219) ***(G-11920)***

ALPHABETIC

Tarbet Construction Co Inc (PA)...620 356-2110
303 S Road I Ulysses (67880) ***(G-13321)***
Tarbet Construction Co Inc...785 462-7432
1055 Plains Ave Colby (67701) ***(G-1045)***
Tarbet Ready Mix, Colby *Also called Tarbet Construction Co Inc* ***(G-1045)***
Tarbet Ready-Mix, Ulysses *Also called Tarbet Construction Co Inc* ***(G-13321)***
Tarc Inc...785 266-2323
1800 Sw 42nd St Topeka (66609) ***(G-13140)***
Tarc Industries, Topeka *Also called Tarc Inc* ***(G-13140)***
Target Corporation...785 274-6500
5400 Wenger St Topeka (66609) ***(G-13141)***
Target DC 3803, Topeka *Also called Target Corporation* ***(G-13141)***
Target Felker Brilliant Truco, Olathe *Also called D B Investments Inc* ***(G-7635)***
Target Insurance Services LLC...913 384-6300
11020 Oakmont St Overland Park (66210) ***(G-9391)***
Tarps Unlimited/Wilkens Mfg, Stockton *Also called Wilkens Manufacturing Inc* ***(G-12190)***
Tarrant Enterprises Inc...785 273-8503
6300 Sw 9th Ter Topeka (66615) ***(G-13142)***
Tarrant Inc...316 942-2208
217 N Pennsylvania Ave Wichita (67214) ***(G-15717)***
Tartan Manufacturing Inc...913 432-7100
800 Southwest Blvd Kansas City (66103) ***(G-4458)***
Tarwater Farm Supply, Topeka *Also called Tarwaters Inc* ***(G-13143)***
Tarwaters Inc (PA)...785 286-2390
4107 Nw Topeka Blvd Topeka (66617) ***(G-13143)***
Tasler Inc...785 885-4533
2716 W 210th Dr Natoma (67651) ***(G-7233)***
Tasty Pastry Bakery...785 632-2335
511 Court St Clay Center (67432) ***(G-882)***
Tatge Manufacturing Inc (PA)...785 965-7213
607 N D St Ramona (67475) ***(G-10189)***
Tatro Plumbing Co Inc (PA)...620 277-2167
1285 Acraway St Ste 300 Garden City (67846) ***(G-2296)***
Tatro Plumbing Co Inc...620 356-5319
1325 E Oklahoma Ave Ulysses (67880) ***(G-13322)***
Tax 911com Incorporated...913 712-8539
501 N Mur Len Rd Ste B Olathe (66062) ***(G-8102)***
Tax Favored Benefits Inc...913 648-5526
4801 W 110th St Ste 200 Overland Park (66211) ***(G-9392)***
Taylor Mih Womens Clinic...620 431-0340
1409 W 7th St Chanute (66720) ***(G-767)***
Taylor Communications Inc...785 632-5661
1815 Meadowlark Rd Clay Center (67432) ***(G-883)***
Taylor Crane & Rigging Inc (PA)...620 251-1530
1211 W 12th St Coffeyville (67337) ***(G-981)***
Taylor Forge Engineered (PA)...785 867-2590
208 N Iron St Paola (66071) ***(G-9592)***
Taylor Forge Engineered...785 448-6803
1312 S Maple St Garnett (66032) ***(G-2390)***
Taylor Implement Co Inc...785 675-3272
451 W Highway 24 Hoxie (67740) ***(G-3143)***
Taylor Made Visions LLC...913 210-0699
4101 S Minnie St Kansas City (66103) ***(G-4459)***
Taylor Printing Inc...620 672-3656
405 S Main St Pratt (67124) ***(G-10159)***
Taylor Products & Smoot Co, Parsons *Also called Magnum Systems Inc* ***(G-9707)***
Taylor Products Co Inc (HQ)...620 421-5550
2205 Jothi Ave Parsons (67357) ***(G-9746)***
Taylor Seed Farms, White Cloud *Also called H B J Farms Inc* ***(G-13568)***
Taylormade Proformance...620 326-3537
2710 N A St Wellington (67152) ***(G-13535)***
Tbc Software, Topeka *Also called Tbcsoft Inc* ***(G-13144)***
Tbcsoft Inc...785 272-5993
3410 Sw Van Buren St # 202 Topeka (66611) ***(G-13144)***
Tc Industries Inc...913 371-7922
101 Central Ave Kansas City (66118) ***(G-4460)***
TCI FABRICATION, Fredonia *Also called Tindle Construction Inc* ***(G-2047)***
Tck- The Trust Company Kansas (PA)...316 264-6010
245 N Waco St Ste 120 Wichita (67202) ***(G-15718)***
Tcv Publishing Inc...316 681-1155
2918 E Douglas Ave Wichita (67214) ***(G-15719)***
Td Auto Finance LLC...913 663-6300
6800 College Blvd Ste 700 Shawnee Mission (66211) ***(G-11921)***
Td Electric Services LLC...913 722-5560
8843 Bond St Overland Park (66214) ***(G-9393)***
Tdb Communications Inc...913 327-7400
10901 W 84th Ter Ste 105 Lenexa (66214) ***(G-6168)***
Tdc Filter Manufacturing Inc...630 410-6200
11501 Outlook St Ste 100 Overland Park (66211) ***(G-9394)***
Tdc Learning Centers Inc...785 234-2273
817 Sw Harrison St Topeka (66612) ***(G-13145)***
Tdi Global Solutions Inc...877 834-6750
6736 Grace Edmond Dr Meriden (66512) ***(G-7082)***
Tdn Farms...620 324-5296
1566 210th Ave Lewis (67552) ***(G-6271)***
TDS Allocation Co...800 857-2906
2410 Se 6th Ave Ste D Topeka (66607) ***(G-13146)***
Teaching Parents Assn Inc...316 347-9900
1526 N Caddy Ct Wichita (67212) ***(G-15720)***
Teague Electric Cnstr Inc (PA)...913 529-4600
12425 W 92nd St Lenexa (66215) ***(G-6169)***
Teague Electric Company Inc...913 529-4600
12425 W 92nd St Lenexa (66215) ***(G-6170)***
Teakwood Investments LLC...913 203-7444
8101 College Blvd Ste 100 Overland Park (66210) ***(G-9395)***
Team Car Care LLC...913 334-5950
1010 N 78th St Kansas City (66112) ***(G-4461)***
Team Car Care LLC...785 266-7696
3301 Sw Topeka Blvd Topeka (66611) ***(G-13147)***
Team Car Care LLC...785 228-1824
1830 Sw Wanamaker Rd Topeka (66604) ***(G-13148)***
Team Car Care LLC...913 362-3349
5850 Broadmoor St Shawnee Mission (66202) ***(G-11922)***
Team Car Care LLC...785 749-1599
914 W 23rd St Lawrence (66046) ***(G-5132)***
Team Car Care LLC...913 381-1005
10300 State Line Rd Leawood (66206) ***(G-5570)***
Team Construction LLC...913 469-9990
6920 W 82nd St Overland Park (66204) ***(G-9396)***
Team Drive-Away Inc...913 825-4776
401 W Frontier Ln Ste 100 Olathe (66061) ***(G-8103)***
Team International Inc...913 681-0740
3906 W 141st Dr Overland Park (66224) ***(G-9397)***
Team Ko LLC...913 897-1300
12066 W 135th St Overland Park (66221) ***(G-9398)***
Team Marketing Alliance LLC (PA)...620 345-3560
307 W Cole St Moundridge (67107) ***(G-7198)***
Team Threads...620 429-4402
119 W Maple St Columbus (66725) ***(G-1089)***
Team Vision Surgery Center, Wichita *Also called Eye Surgery Center Wichita LLC* ***(G-14328)***
Team Vision Surgery Center...316 729-6000
834 N Socora St Ste A Wichita (67212) ***(G-15721)***
Teamsters Union Local 795...316 683-2651
4921 E Cessna Dr Wichita (67210) ***(G-15722)***
TEC Engineering Inc (PA)...316 259-8881
2233 S West Street Ct Wichita (67213) ***(G-15723)***
TEC Fab Parts Inc...913 369-0882
1015 E 1st St Tonganoxie (66086) ***(G-12270)***
TECH, Hutchinson *Also called Training & Evaluation Cente* ***(G-3467)***
Tech Electronics Kansas LLC...785 379-0300
6431 Se Bleckley St Topeka (66619) ***(G-13149)***
Tech Gurus LLC...913 299-8700
5434 Webster Ave Kansas City (66104) ***(G-4462)***
Tech Inc (PA)...913 492-6440
10601 Lackman Rd Lenexa (66219) ***(G-6171)***
Tech Investments III LLC...816 674-9993
5900 Overhill Rd Mission Hills (66208) ***(G-7149)***
Tech Supply, Lenexa *Also called Tech Inc* ***(G-6171)***
Tech-Air Inc (PA)...913 677-5777
10200 W 75th St Ste 102 Shawnee Mission (66204) ***(G-11923)***
Tech-Air Inc...913 677-5777
E Mill St Osawatomie (66064) ***(G-8204)***
Tech-Aire Instruments Inc...316 262-4020
1326 S Walnut St Wichita (67213) ***(G-15724)***
Techmer Pm LLC...316 943-1520
7015 W Pueblo Dr Wichita (67209) ***(G-15725)***
Techncal Trning Prfssonals LLC...865 312-4189
9401 Indian Creek Pkwy Overland Park (66210) ***(G-9399)***
Technical Mfg Concepts Inc...913 764-1011
19000 W 158th St Ste B Olathe (66062) ***(G-8104)***
Technical Services LLC...785 825-1250
3125 Enterprise Dr Salina (67401) ***(G-10732)***
Technique Manufacturing Inc...620 663-6360
614 E 1st Ave Hutchinson (67501) ***(G-3463)***
Technisource, Overland Park *Also called Randstad Technologies LLC* ***(G-9225)***
Technological Literacy Group, Pittsburg *Also called Pitsco Inc* ***(G-9914)***
Technology Group Solutions LLC...913 451-9900
8551 Quivira Rd Lenexa (66215) ***(G-6172)***
Techs Inc...785 364-1911
300 W 4th St Holton (66436) ***(G-3112)***
Tecnet International Inc...913 859-9515
11535 W 83rd Ter Lenexa (66214) ***(G-6173)***
Tect Aerospace LLC (HQ)...316 425-3638
300 W Douglas Ave Ste 100 Wichita (67202) ***(G-15726)***
Tect Aerospace Wellington Inc (HQ)...620 359-5000
1515 N A St Wellington (67152) ***(G-13536)***
Tect Hypervelocity Inc...316 529-5000
5545 N Mill Heights Dr Park City (67219) ***(G-9647)***
Tect Hypervelocity Inc (HQ)...316 529-5000
5545 N Mill Heights Dr Park City (67219) ***(G-9648)***
Tect Power, Wichita *Also called Turbine Eng Comp Tech Turning* ***(G-15815)***
Ted Mfg Corporation...913 631-6211
11415 Johnson Dr Shawnee Mission (66203) ***(G-11924)***
Ted Row Inc...816 223-9666
7745 W 183rd St Stilwell (66085) ***(G-12176)***
Ted Systems LLC...913 677-5771
9745 Widmer Rd Lenexa (66215) ***(G-6174)***
Teds Plumbing LLC...620 356-5319
1325 E Oklahoma Ave Ste 1 Ulysses (67880) ***(G-13323)***

Tee & Bee Electric Company....913 782-8161
1401 N Woodland St Olathe (66061) ***(G-8105)***
Tee Time Investments Inc....316 262-7900
410 N Saint Francis Ave Wichita (67202) ***(G-15727)***
Teeter Irrigation Inc (PA)....620 353-1111
2729 W Oklahoma Ave Ulysses (67880) ***(G-13324)***
Teeter Irrigation Inc....620 276-8257
2707 W Jones Ave Garden City (67846) ***(G-2297)***
Tehan Maintenance, Leawood *Also called Tiehen Group* ***(G-5575)***
Teksystems Inc....316 448-4500
727 N Waco Ave Ste 140 Wichita (67203) ***(G-15728)***
Telcon Associates Inc....855 864-1571
10500 Barkley St Ste 100 Overland Park (66212) ***(G-9400)***
Telecommunication Systems Inc....913 593-9489
7300 W 110th St Fl 7 Overland Park (66210) ***(G-9401)***
Teledata Communications LLC....913 663-2010
10620 Widmer Rd Lenexa (66215) ***(G-6175)***
Telephone Cooperative, Russell *Also called Rural Telephone Service Co Inc* ***(G-10293)***
Telesales Group, Overland Park *Also called Annan Marketing Services Inc* ***(G-8387)***
Telescope Inc....785 527-2244
1805 N St Belleville (66935) ***(G-467)***
Tell Industries LLC....316 260-3297
6255 N Hydraulic St Park City (67219) ***(G-9649)***
Tellers....785 843-4111
746 Massachusetts St Lawrence (66044) ***(G-5133)***
Temp Con, Olathe *Also called Temp-Con Inc* ***(G-8106)***
Temp-Con Inc....913 768-4888
15670 S Keeler St Olathe (66062) ***(G-8106)***
Temporary Employment Corp (PA)....785 749-2800
3300 Bob Billings Pkwy # 4 Lawrence (66049) ***(G-5134)***
Temps Disposal Service Inc....785 562-5360
783 Jayhawk Rd Marysville (66508) ***(G-6910)***
Temps Waste Systems, Marysville *Also called Temps Disposal Service Inc* ***(G-6910)***
Tender Hearts Inc....913 962-2200
11740 W 77th St Shawnee Mission (66214) ***(G-11925)***
Tender Hearts Child Care Ctr....785 754-3937
504 Castle Rock St Quinter (67752) ***(G-10188)***
Tender Hearts Inc....913 788-2273
2035 N 82nd St Kansas City (66109) ***(G-4463)***
Tender Hrts Preschool Day Care, Shawnee Mission *Also called Tender Hearts Inc* ***(G-11925)***
Tendercare Lawn and Landscape....316 788-5416
219 S Water St Derby (67037) ***(G-1275)***
Tengasco Inc....785 625-6374
1327 Noose Rd Hays (67601) ***(G-2919)***
Tennessee Info Consortium LLC....913 498-3468
25501 W Valley Pkwy # 300 Olathe (66061) ***(G-8107)***
Tennessee Kenworth Inc (HQ)....816 483-6444
11120 Tomahawk Creek Pkwy Leawood (66211) ***(G-5571)***
Tennis Corporation of America....913 491-4116
6700 W 110th St Shawnee Mission (66211) ***(G-11926)***
Tennison Brothers Inc....316 263-7581
1021 S Washington Ave Wichita (67211) ***(G-15729)***
Tension Envelope Corporation....785 562-2307
1601 Spring St Marysville (66508) ***(G-6911)***
Tenth Street Ht Partners LLC (PA)....785 233-5411
700 Sw Jackson St Topeka (66603) ***(G-13150)***
Tenth Street Ht Partners LLC....785 228-9500
901 Sw Robinson Ave Topeka (66606) ***(G-13151)***
Teracrunch LLC....214 405-7158
2913 W 112th St Leawood (66211) ***(G-5572)***
Terex Cranes, Olathe *Also called R O Terex Corporation* ***(G-8018)***
Terminal 18, Great Bend *Also called Jack B Kelley Inc* ***(G-2594)***
Terminix Intl Co Ltd Partnr....913 696-0351
10623 Rene St Lenexa (66215) ***(G-6176)***
Terminix Intl Co Ltd Partnr....785 266-2600
5604 Sw Topeka Blvd Ste A Topeka (66609) ***(G-13152)***
Terminix Intl Co Ltd Partnr....913 696-0351
9214 Bond St Overland Park (66214) ***(G-9402)***
Terrace House, Lawrence *Also called Community Lving Opprtnties Inc* ***(G-4806)***
Terracon Consultants Inc....316 262-0171
1815 S Eisenhower St Wichita (67209) ***(G-15730)***
Terracon Consultants Inc....785 267-3310
3113 Sw Van Buren St # 131 Topeka (66611) ***(G-13153)***
Terracon Consultants Inc....785 539-9099
1120 Hostetler Dr Manhattan (66502) ***(G-6822)***
Terracon Consultants Inc....913 492-7777
13910 W 96th Ter Lenexa (66215) ***(G-6177)***
Terracon Consultants 1, Wichita *Also called Terracon Consultants Inc* ***(G-15730)***
Terracon Consultants 14, Topeka *Also called Terracon Consultants Inc* ***(G-13153)***
Terracon Consultants 2, Lenexa *Also called Terracon Consultants Inc* ***(G-6177)***
Terracon Consultants C6, Manhattan *Also called Terracon Consultants Inc* ***(G-6822)***
Terradatum....888 212-4793
14221 Metcalf Ave Ste 150 Overland Park (66223) ***(G-9403)***
Terradyne Country Club LLC....316 733-2582
1400 Terradyne Dr Andover (67002) ***(G-110)***
Terrell Publishing Co....913 948-8226
1310 Adams St Kansas City (66103) ***(G-4464)***
Terry Koehn, Montezuma *Also called Payroll Plus* ***(G-7160)***
Terry Lake Project Office, Perry *Also called U S Army Corps of Engineers* ***(G-9774)***
Terry Trucking & Wrecking LLC....913 281-3854
3645 N 85th St Kansas City (66109) ***(G-4465)***
Tescott Lions CLB 1055007136, Tescott *Also called International Association of* ***(G-12245)***
Tessenderlo Kerley Inc....620 251-3111
515 N Laurel St Coffeyville (67337) ***(G-982)***
Tessenderlo Kerley Inc....620 241-1727
1360 Iron Horse Rd McPherson (67460) ***(G-7031)***
Test and Measurement Inc....913 233-2724
1304 Adams St Kansas City (66103) ***(G-4466)***
Tetra Management Inc....316 685-6221
8100 E 22nd St N Bldg 200 Wichita (67226) ***(G-15731)***
Teva Neuroscience Inc (HQ)....913 777-3000
11100 Nall Ave Leawood (66211) ***(G-5573)***
Teva Pharmaceuticals....610 727-6055
11100 Nall Ave Leawood (66211) ***(G-5574)***
Tevis Architectural Group....913 599-3003
10820 Shawnee Msn Shawnee (66203) ***(G-11039)***
Tex Cnslver Mniciple Golf Crse, Wichita *Also called City of Wichita* ***(G-14030)***
Tex-Ok-Kan Oil Field Svcs LLC....620 271-7310
2005 N Taylor Ave Garden City (67846) ***(G-2298)***
Textron Airland LLC....541 390-8888
5800 E Pawnee Ave Bldg 88 Wichita (67218) ***(G-15732)***
Textron Aviation Defense LLC....316 676-2508
201 S Greenwich Rd Wichita (67207) ***(G-15733)***
Textron Aviation Inc....316 676-7111
2656 Scanlan Ave Salina (67401) ***(G-10733)***
Textron Aviation Inc....888 727-4344
9709 E Central Ave Wichita (67206) ***(G-15734)***
Textron Aviation Inc....316 517-8270
6263 W 34th St S Wichita (67215) ***(G-15735)***
Textron Aviation Inc....316 517-8270
1980 S Airport Rd Wichita (67209) ***(G-15736)***
Textron Aviation Inc (HQ)....316 517-6000
1 Cessna Blvd Wichita (67215) ***(G-15737)***
Textron Aviation Inc....316 517-1375
2 Cessna Blvd Ste P35 Wichita (67215) ***(G-15738)***
Textron Aviation Inc....888 727-4344
9709 E Central Ave Wichita (67206) ***(G-15739)***
Textron Aviation Inc....316 517-6000
1 Cessna Blvd Wichita (67215) ***(G-15740)***
Textron Aviation Inc....316 676-7111
10511 E Central Ave Wichita (67206) ***(G-15741)***
Textron Aviation Inc....316 831-4021
7751 E Pawnee St Wichita (67207) ***(G-15742)***
Textron Aviation Inc....316 293-9703
2125 S Hoover Rd Wichita (67209) ***(G-15743)***
Textron Aviation Inc....316 676-7111
9709 E Central Ave Wichita (67206) ***(G-15744)***
Textron Aviation Inc....316 517-6000
2617 S Hoover Rd Wichita (67215) ***(G-15745)***
Textron Aviation Inc....316 517-6081
2625 S Hoover Rd Wichita (67215) ***(G-15746)***
Textron Aviation Inc....316 517-6000
5800 E Pawnee Ave Wichita (67218) ***(G-15747)***
Textron Aviation Inc....800 835-4090
7121 Southwest Blvd Wichita (67215) ***(G-15748)***
Textron Aviation Inc....316 831-2000
7603 E Pawnee St Wichita (67207) ***(G-15749)***
Textron Aviation Inc....316 517-6000
5 Cessna Blvd Wichita (67215) ***(G-15750)***
Textron Aviation Inc....620 332-0228
1 Cessna Blvd Independence (67301) ***(G-3564)***
Textron Aviation Inc....316 721-3100
1643 S Maize Rd Wichita (67209) ***(G-15751)***
Textron Aviation Inc....316 676-7111
10511 E Central Ave Wichita (67206) ***(G-15752)***
Textron Aviation Inc....316 676-5373
515 N Goebel St Wichita (67201) ***(G-15753)***
Tfi LLC....785 235-1524
300 Sw Jackson St Topeka (66603) ***(G-13154)***
Tfi Family Services Inc (PA)....620 342-2239
618 Commercial St Ste C Emporia (66801) ***(G-1834)***
Tfi Family Services Inc....913 894-2985
8300 College Blvd Ste 301 Overland Park (66210) ***(G-9404)***
Tfi Family Services Inc....620 231-0443
105 W 7th St Pittsburg (66762) ***(G-9945)***
Tfi Family Services Inc....620 342-2239
618 Commercial St Ste A Emporia (66801) ***(G-1835)***
Tfi Family Services Inc....620 431-0312
424 W 14th St Chanute (66720) ***(G-768)***
Tfi Family Services Inc....785 232-1019
217 Se 4th St Fl 2 Topeka (66603) ***(G-13155)***
Tfi Family Services Inc....620 342-2239
618 Commercial St Emporia (66801) ***(G-1836)***
Tfmcomm Inc (PA)....785 233-2343
125 Sw Jackson St Topeka (66603) ***(G-13156)***
Tfmcomm Inc....785 841-2924
910 E 28th St Lawrence (66046) ***(G-5135)***

ALPHABETIC

TFT Global Inc...519 842-4540
5300 Kansas Ave Kansas City (66106) **(G-4467)**
Tfwilson LLC (PA)...913 327-0200
7400 College Blvd Ste 100 Shawnee Mission (66210) **(G-11927)**
Tgc Greenwich Hotel LLC...316 500-2660
2660 N Greenwich Ct Wichita (67226) **(G-15754)**
Thai Binh Supermarket...316 838-8882
1530 W 21st St N Wichita (67203) **(G-15755)**
Thai Noodle...785 320-2899
1126 Laramie St Manhattan (66502) **(G-6823)**
Thairapy Salon...316 321-6263
625 N Washington St El Dorado (67042) **(G-1608)**
Thats A Wrap LLC...913 390-0035
665 N Lindenwood Dr Olathe (66062) **(G-8108)**
Thayer Aerospace Plating Inc...316 522-5426
4201 S 119th St W Wichita (67215) **(G-15756)**
The Arnold Group, Wichita *Also called Arnold & Associates of Wichita* **(G-13735)**
The Eye Doctors...785 272-3322
2800 Sw Wanamaker Rd # 192 Topeka (66614) **(G-13157)**
THE FIRST NATIONAL BANK OF HUTCHINSON INVESTMENT COMPANY, INC, Mount Hope *Also called First National Bank of Hutchin* **(G-7204)**
The Hairem, Olathe *Also called Hairem of Olathe LLC* **(G-7747)**
The Ledger, McPherson *Also called Davies Communications Inc* **(G-6956)**
The Nature Conservancy...785 233-4400
2420 Nw Button Rd Topeka (66618) **(G-13158)**
The Nature Conservancy...316 689-4237
151 S Whittier Rd Wichita (67207) **(G-15757)**
The Wichita Clinic, Wichita *Also called Via Christi Clinic PA* **(G-15886)**
Therafirm, Kansas City *Also called Knit-Rite Inc* **(G-4178)**
Therapyworks Wellness Center, Lawrence *Also called P A Therapyworks Inc* **(G-5053)**
There Is No Place Like Home...316 721-6001
7348 W 21st St N Ste 101 Wichita (67205) **(G-15758)**
Therien & Company Inc (PA)...415 956-8850
308 W Mill St Plainville (67663) **(G-9993)**
Therien Studios, Plainville *Also called Therien & Company Inc* **(G-9993)**
Thermal Ceramics Inc...620 343-2308
221 Weaver St Emporia (66801) **(G-1837)**
Thermal Comfort Air Inc (PA)...785 537-2436
705 Pecan Cir Manhattan (66502) **(G-6824)**
Thermal King Windows Inc...913 451-2300
14368 W 96th Ter Shawnee Mission (66215) **(G-11928)**
Thermo Fisher Scientific Inc...800 255-6730
12076 Santa Fe Dr Lenexa (66215) **(G-6178)**
Thermo Fsher Scntfic Rmel Pdts, Lenexa *Also called Thermo Fisher Scientific Inc* **(G-6178)**
Thermo Fsher Scntfic Rmel Pdts, Lenexa *Also called Remel Inc* **(G-6102)**
Thermoformed Plastic Products...316 214-9623
2148 S Hoover Rd Ste 2 Wichita (67209) **(G-15759)**
Thermovac Inc...620 431-3270
1120 W Beech St Chanute (66720) **(G-769)**
Theurer Auction & Realty, Wellington *Also called Larry Theurer* **(G-13510)**
Thi of Kans At Spclty Hosp LLC...913 649-3701
6509 W 103rd St Overland Park (66212) **(G-9405)**
Thi of Kansas Indian Meadows...913 649-5110
6505 W 103rd St Overland Park (66212) **(G-9406)**
Thoele Foundations LLC...913 757-2317
23319 Querry Rd La Cygne (66040) **(G-4644)**
Thomas and Sons Trucking LLC...785 454-3839
240 Morgan Ave Downs (67437) **(G-1473)**
Thomas C Klein MD...316 682-7411
1709 S Rock Rd Wichita (67207) **(G-15760)**
Thomas County Feeders Inc...785 462-3947
1762 Us Highway 83 Colby (67701) **(G-1046)**
Thomas E Moskow MD...785 273-8224
4100 Sw 15th St Topeka (66604) **(G-13159)**
Thomas G Geha & Associates...913 563-6707
8012 State Line Rd # 200 Prairie Village (66208) **(G-10074)**
Thomas Manufacturing Inc...620 724-6220
414 S Cherokee St Girard (66743) **(G-2421)**
Thomas Mfg, Girard *Also called Advanced Machine Solutions LLC* **(G-2394)**
Thomas Outdoor Advertising Inc...785 537-2010
902 Fair Ln Manhattan (66502) **(G-6825)**
Thomas P Eyen...913 663-5100
5520 College Blvd Shawnee Mission (66211) **(G-11929)**
Thomas Property Management, Emporia *Also called Double T Enterprises* **(G-1731)**
Thomas Transfer & Stor Co Inc (PA)...620 342-2321
906 E 6th Ave Emporia (66801) **(G-1838)**
Thomas Transfer & Stor Co Inc...800 835-3300
7701 E Osie St Wichita (67207) **(G-15761)**
Thompson Bros Eqp & Wldg Sups, Coffeyville *Also called Thompson Bros Supplies Inc* **(G-983)**
Thompson Bros Supplies Inc (PA)...620 251-1740
2319 W 8th St Coffeyville (67337) **(G-983)**
Thompson Dehydrating Co Inc...785 272-7722
2953 Sw Wanamaker Dr Topeka (66614) **(G-13160)**
Thompson Dryers, Topeka *Also called Thompson Dehydrating Co Inc* **(G-13160)**
Thompson Pump Co...913 788-2583
504 S 70th St Kansas City (66111) **(G-4468)**
Thompson Ramsdell Qualseth PA...785 841-4554
333 W 9th St Lawrence (66044) **(G-5136)**
Thompson Tax & Associates LLC...916 346-7829
406 Kelly St Waverly (66871) **(G-13482)**
Thomspon R Wayne DDS Inc (PA)...913 631-0110
11005 W 60th St Ste 180 Shawnee Mission (66203) **(G-11930)**
Thorman Enterprises LLC...913 772-1818
629 Delaware St Leavenworth (66048) **(G-5297)**
Thornes Tree Service Inc...913 845-2387
15170 234th St Tonganoxie (66086) **(G-12271)**
Thornton Air Rotary LLC...620 879-2073
2186 Us Highway 166 Caney (67333) **(G-675)**
Thornton Place, Topeka *Also called Harvest Facility Holdings LP* **(G-12665)**
Thoughtful Care Inc...816 256-8200
8340 Mission Rd Ste 118b Prairie Village (66206) **(G-10075)**
Thrash Floor Maintenance, Wichita *Also called Thrash Inc* **(G-15762)**
Thrash Inc...316 265-5331
116 N Martinson St Wichita (67203) **(G-15762)**
Thrasher Bsmnt Foundation Repr (PA)...316 320-1853
804 N Haverhill Rd El Dorado (67042) **(G-1609)**
Threadwear, Topeka *Also called Sewing Workshop* **(G-13061)**
Three Click Ventres Inc DBA AV...913 955-3700
10975 Grandview Dr Overland Park (66210) **(G-9407)**
Three Rivers Inc (PA)...785 456-9915
504 Miller Dr Wamego (66547) **(G-13444)**
THREE RIVERS INDEPENDENT LIVIN, Wamego *Also called Three Rivers Inc* **(G-13444)**
Three Way Pattern Inc...316 942-7421
1623 S Mccomas St Wichita (67213) **(G-15763)**
Thresher Artisan Wheat, Leawood *Also called Agspring Idaho LLC* **(G-5315)**
Thrift Marketing Inc...913 236-7474
5960 Dearborn St Ste 204 Shawnee Mission (66202) **(G-11931)**
Thrivent Financial For Luthera...620 364-2177
1020 Osborne St Burlington (66839) **(G-643)**
Thriver Services LLC...913 955-2555
11320 W 79th St Lenexa (66214) **(G-6179)**
Thruline Marketing Inc (PA)...913 254-6000
15500 W 113th St Ste 200 Lenexa (66219) **(G-6180)**
Thunder Hill Speedway LLC...785 313-2922
11995 142nd Rd Mayetta (66509) **(G-6919)**
Thunder Struck Inc...785 200-6680
401 Cottage Ave Abilene (67410) **(G-54)**
Thunderhead Engrg Cons Inc...785 770-8511
403 Poyntz Ave Ste B Manhattan (66502) **(G-6826)**
Thunderhills Speedway, Mayetta *Also called B & H Motor Sports* **(G-6914)**
Thyssenkrupp Elevator Corp...913 888-8046
11314 W 80th St Overland Park (66214) **(G-9408)**
Thyssenkrupp Elevator Corp...316 529-2233
4939 S Lulu Ct Ste 20 Wichita (67216) **(G-15764)**
Thyssenkrupp Materials NA Inc...620 802-0900
3001 E 11th Ave Hutchinson (67501) **(G-3464)**
Tic International Corporation...913 236-5490
6405 Metcalf Ave Ste 200 Overland Park (66202) **(G-9409)**
Ticket Solutions LLC (PA)...913 384-4751
10000 College Blvd # 130 Shawnee Mission (66210) **(G-11932)**
Tidy Up Angels LLC...913 642-2006
6600 W 95th St Ste 103 Overland Park (66212) **(G-9410)**
Tiehen Group...913 648-1188
3401 College Blvd Ste 250 Leawood (66211) **(G-5575)**
Tiehen Group Inc...913 648-1188
3401 College Blvd Ste 250 Leawood (66211) **(G-5576)**
Tiger Cool Express LLC (PA)...913 305-3510
5750 W 95th St Ste 250 Overland Park (66207) **(G-9411)**
Tiger Tow & Transport Inc...913 422-7300
2914 Loring Dr Bonner Springs (66012) **(G-577)**
Tile Shop LLC...913 631-8453
6400 Nieman Rd Shawnee (66203) **(G-11040)**
Tiller & Toiler Newspaper, Larned *Also called Star Communication Corporation* **(G-4713)**
TILRC, Topeka *Also called Topeka Ind Lving Rsrce Ctr Inc* **(G-13179)**
Tim R Schwab Inc...316 772-9055
101 E Industrial Dr Sedgwick (67135) **(G-10852)**
Tim Razumovsky, Olathe *Also called Time Inc* **(G-8109)**
Timber Creek Paper Inc (PA)...316 264-3232
520 S Saint Francis Ave Wichita (67202) **(G-15765)**
Timber Products Inc...316 941-9381
2286 S Custer Ave Wichita (67213) **(G-15766)**
Timber Roots...316 755-3114
131 W Industrial St Valley Center (67147) **(G-13356)**
Timberline Cabinetry Mllwk LLC...785 323-0206
3475 Crown C Cir Manhattan (66502) **(G-6827)**
Timberview Farm...785 336-2399
1732 208th Rd Bern (66408) **(G-524)**
Time Inc...816 288-5394
15585 S Keeler St Olathe (66062) **(G-8109)**
Time Line Dairy LLC...620 492-3232
2000 E Rd 2 Syracuse (67878) **(G-12235)**
Time Warner American Cablvsn, Leavenworth *Also called Spectrum MGT Holdg Co LLC* **(G-5290)**
Time-Sentinel, The, Cheney *Also called Times Sentinel Newspapers* **(G-797)**

Times Sentinel Newspapers 316 540-0500
125 N Main St Cheney (67025) *(G-797)*
Timken Company 913 492-4848
14871 W 99th St Lenexa (66215) *(G-6181)*
Timken Smo LLC 620 223-0080
4505 Campbell Dr Fort Scott (66701) *(G-2008)*
Timothy D White 620 331-7060
411 N Penn Ave Independence (67301) *(G-3565)*
Timothy M Koehler MD 316 462-6220
2020 N Tyler Rd Wichita (67212) *(G-15767)*
Timothy R Keenan 620 793-7811
5260 Timber Creek Rd Great Bend (67530) *(G-2647)*
Tindle Construction Inc 620 378-2046
933 Fillmore St Fredonia (66736) *(G-2047)*
Tins Inc 785 842-1234
933 Iowa St Lawrence (66044) *(G-5137)*
Tioga Territory Ltd 620 431-2479
502 E Main St Chanute (66720) *(G-770)*
Tire Dealers Warehouse, Wichita *Also called Shamrock Tire & Auto Service (G-15572)*
Tire Town Inc (PA) 913 682-3201
1825 S 4th St Leavenworth (66048) *(G-5298)*
Tires Plus Total Car Care, Shawnee Mission *Also called Bridgestone Ret Operations LLC (G-11180)*
Tires Plus Total Car Care, Wichita *Also called Bridgestone Ret Operations LLC (G-13887)*
Tires Plus Total Car Care, Wichita *Also called Bridgestone Ret Operations LLC (G-13888)*
Tires Plus Total Car Care, Overland Park *Also called Bridgestone Ret Operations LLC (G-8485)*
Tires Plus Total Car Care, Kansas City *Also called Bridgestone Ret Operations LLC (G-3877)*
Tires Plus Total Car Care, Olathe *Also called Bridgestone Ret Operations LLC (G-7560)*
Tirupati Balaji LLC 913 262-9600
7508 Shawnee Mission Pkwy Overland Park (66202) *(G-9412)*
Tischlerei-Fine Wdwkg LLC 785 404-3322
2656 Scanlan Ave Salina (67401) *(G-10734)*
Titan Built LLC 913 782-6700
8207 Melrose Dr Ste 200 Overland Park (66214) *(G-9413)*
Titan Cnstr Organization Inc 913 782-6700
11865 S Conley St Olathe (66061) *(G-8110)*
Titan Construction Inc 913 782-6700
11865 S Conley St Olathe (66061) *(G-8111)*
Titan Monitoring Inc 913 441-0911
9350 Metcalf Ave Ste 110 Overland Park (66212) *(G-9414)*
Titan West Inc 785 348-5660
203 5th St Linn (66953) *(G-6412)*
Title Boxing LLC 913 438-4427
14711 W 112th St Lenexa (66215) *(G-6182)*
Title Boxing Club, Lenexa *Also called Title Boxing LLC (G-6182)*
Title Boxing Club 785 856-2696
1520 Wakarusa Dr Ste J Lawrence (66047) *(G-5138)*
Title Boxing Club LLC 913 991-8285
5360 College Blvd Ste 120 Overland Park (66211) *(G-9415)*
Title Midwest Inc (HQ) 785 232-9110
4400 Shawnee Mission Pkwy # 208 Fairway (66205) *(G-1920)*
Tivol Plaza Inc 913 345-0200
4721 W 119th St Overland Park (66209) *(G-9416)*
Tiyosaye Inc Higher Ground 316 262-2060
247 N Market St Wichita (67202) *(G-15768)*
TIYOSPAYE PUEBLO PROGRAM, Wichita *Also called Tiyosaye Inc Higher Ground (G-15768)*
Tjaden, Bruce L Do, Wichita *Also called Center For Rprductive Medicine (G-13972)*
Tjk Inc (PA) 785 841-0110
120 E 9th St Ste 201 Lawrence (66044) *(G-5139)*
Tk & Company Inc of Kansas 785 472-3226
312 Kunkle Dr Ellsworth (67439) *(G-1682)*
Tk Metals Inc 913 667-3055
8115 Monticello Ter Lenexa (66227) *(G-6183)*
Tkfast Inc 316 260-2500
437 S Hydraulic St Wichita (67211) *(G-15769)*
Tl Enterprises Inc 785 448-7100
923 S Doreen St Wichita (67207) *(G-15770)*
TLC Lawn Care Inc 913 780-5296
19600 W 159th St Olathe (66062) *(G-8112)*
Tlm Enterprises Inc 316 265-3833
406 S Market St Wichita (67202) *(G-15771)*
Tm Holdings Inc (PA) 785 232-9110
4400 Shawnee Mission Pkwy Fairway (66205) *(G-1921)*
Tmd Telecom Inc 316 462-0400
3534 W 29th St S Wichita (67217) *(G-15772)*
Tmfs Management LLC 913 319-8100
10950 Grandview Dr # 500 Overland Park (66210) *(G-9417)*
Tmhc, Topeka *Also called Consortium Inc (G-12503)*
Tmi Corp 785 232-8705
127 Se 29th St Topeka (66605) *(G-13161)*
Tno LLC 913 278-1911
2405 Merriam Ln Kansas City (66106) *(G-4469)*
Tobys Carnival Inc 620 235-6667
503 N West St Arma (66712) *(G-192)*
Todays Dentistry 785 267-5010
5310 Sw 37th St Topeka (66614) *(G-13162)*
Todays Tomorrows Lrng Ctr LLC 888 602-1815
1639 N Timbers Edge Ct Mulvane (67110) *(G-7228)*
Todd Tractor Co Inc 785 336-2138
2004 State Highway 63 Seneca (66538) *(G-10884)*
Todds Clothiers & Tailor Shop 913 681-8633
7052 W 135th St Overland Park (66223) *(G-9418)*
Toll Free 1 877 841 7323, Edgerton *Also called Home Readers Inc (G-1484)*
Tom Burge Fence & Iron Inc 913 681-7600
6770 W 152nd Ter Shawnee Mission (66223) *(G-11933)*
Tom Jones Real Estate Company 913 341-7777
9036 W 95th St Ste 5 Shawnee Mission (66212) *(G-11934)*
Tom Jones Realtors, Shawnee Mission *Also called Tom Jones Real Estate Company (G-11934)*
Tommy J Kemp 316 522-7255
612 N Mulberry Rd Derby (67037) *(G-1276)*
Tompkins Industries Inc (PA) 913 764-8088
1912 E 123rd St Olathe (66061) *(G-8113)*
Tompkins Manufacturing, Olathe *Also called Tompkins Industries Inc (G-8113)*
Toms Ditching & Backhoe Inc 620 879-2215
1876 Us Highway 75 Caney (67333) *(G-676)*
Toms Machine & Welding Svc 785 434-2800
510 S Washington St Plainville (67663) *(G-9994)*
Tonercycle, Shawnee *Also called Inkcycle Inc (G-10973)*
Tonys Pizza 620 275-4626
220 Air Links Rd Garden City (67846) *(G-2299)*
Too Cute Totes 775 423-5907
8339 Monticello Rd Lenexa (66227) *(G-6184)*
Top City Healthcare Inc 785 272-2124
6300 Sw 6th Ave Topeka (66615) *(G-13163)*
Top Flight Kids Learning Ctr 913 768-4661
300 S Rogers Rd Olathe (66062) *(G-8114)*
Top It 620 431-1866
401 W Cherry Ave Chanute (66720) *(G-771)*
Top Notch Inc 913 441-8900
23754 W 82nd Ter Lenexa (66227) *(G-6185)*
Topcon Positioning Systems, Olathe *Also called Sokkia Corporation (G-8071)*
Topeka Adult Care Center 785 233-7397
3314 Sw Front St Topeka (66606) *(G-13164)*
Topeka Air Ambulance Inc 785 862-5433
1500 Sw 10th Ave Topeka (66604) *(G-13165)*
Topeka Allrgy Asthma Clinic PA 785 273-9999
1123 Sw Gage Blvd Topeka (66604) *(G-13166)*
Topeka Ansthsia Pain Trtmnt PA 785 295-8000
1700 Sw 7th St Topeka (66606) *(G-13167)*
Topeka Attorneys 785 267-2410
3649 Sw Burlingame Rd Topeka (66611) *(G-13168)*
Topeka Blue Print & Sup Co Inc 785 232-7209
608 Sw Jackson St Topeka (66603) *(G-13169)*
Topeka Blueprint, Topeka *Also called Topeka Blue Print & Sup Co Inc (G-13169)*
Topeka Capital Journal 785 295-1111
100 Se 9th St Ste 200 Topeka (66612) *(G-13170)*
Topeka Cemetery Association 785 233-4132
1601 Se 10th Ave Ste 1 Topeka (66607) *(G-13171)*
Topeka Civic Theatre & Academy 785 357-5211
3028 Sw 8th Ave Topeka (66606) *(G-13172)*
Topeka Country Club 785 232-2090
2700 Sw Buchanan St Topeka (66611) *(G-13173)*
Topeka Day Care Inc 785 272-5051
2200 Sw Gage Blvd Topeka (66622) *(G-13174)*
Topeka Dialysis, Topeka *Also called Total Renal Care Inc (G-13194)*
Topeka Ear Nose & Throat (PA) 620 340-0168
920 Sw Lane St Ste 200 Topeka (66606) *(G-13175)*
Topeka Engineering Division, Topeka *Also called City of Topeka (G-12471)*
Topeka Ent, Topeka *Also called Topeka Ear Nose & Throat (G-13175)*
Topeka Fairfield Inn, Topeka *Also called Midwest Heritage Inn (G-12901)*
Topeka Foundry and Ir Works Co 785 232-8212
300 Sw Jackson St Topeka (66603) *(G-13176)*
Topeka Home Buyers Guide, Topeka *Also called Hall Publications Inc (G-12659)*
Topeka Hospital LLC (HQ) 785 295-8000
1700 Sw 7th St Ste 840 Topeka (66606) *(G-13177)*
Topeka Income Tax Service Inc 785 478-2833
213 Sw 6th Ave Topeka (66603) *(G-13178)*
Topeka Ind Lving Rsrce Ctr Inc 785 233-4572
501 Sw Jackson St Ste 100 Topeka (66603) *(G-13179)*
Topeka Landscape Inc 785 232-8873
3220 Sw Auburn Rd Topeka (66614) *(G-13180)*
Topeka Lutheran Schl Cntr For 785 272-1704
1732 Sw Gage Blvd Ste 3a9 Lawrence (66044) *(G-5140)*
Topeka Mechanical Shops, Topeka *Also called Burlington Nthrn Santa Fe LLC (G-12415)*
Topeka Metal Specialties, Topeka *Also called Lb Steel LLC (G-12836)*
Topeka Metal Specialties 785 862-1071
02 Div Of Lb Steel Llc Topeka (66609) *(G-13181)*
Topeka Metro News, The, Olathe *Also called NPS Sales Inc (G-7924)*
Topeka Metropolitan Trnst Auth (PA) 785 233-2011
201 N Kansas Ave Topeka (66603) *(G-13182)*
Topeka Pathology Group PA 785 354-6031
1500 Se 10th Ave Topeka (66604) *(G-13183)*

ALPHABETIC

Topeka Performing Arts Center..........785 234-2787
214 Se 8th Ave Frnt Ste Topeka (66603) **(G-13184)**
Topeka Presbyterian Manor, Topeka *Also called Presbyterian Manors Inc* **(G-12984)**
Topeka Round Up Club Inc..........785 478-4431
7843 Sw 37th St Topeka (66614) **(G-13185)**
Topeka Services Inc (PA)..........785 228-7800
3300 Bob Billings Pkwy # 4 Lawrence (66049) **(G-5141)**
Topeka Sprinkler Supply, Topeka *Also called Blackburn Nursery Inc* **(G-12387)**
Topeka Surgery Center Inc..........785 273-8282
3630 Sw Fairlawn Rd Topeka (66614) **(G-13186)**
Topeka Swim Association, Topeka *Also called Topeka Unified School Dst 501* **(G-13189)**
Topeka Trailer Repair Inc..........785 862-6010
929 Sw University Blvd Topeka (66619) **(G-13187)**
Topeka Trailer Storage, Topeka *Also called Mather Flare Rental Inc* **(G-12863)**
Topeka Transit, Topeka *Also called Topeka Metropolitan Trnst Auth* **(G-13182)**
Topeka Transmission Service..........785 234-2597
1824 Sw Harrison St Topeka (66612) **(G-13188)**
Topeka Unified School Dst 501..........785 295-3750
2751 Sw East Circle Dr S # 1 Topeka (66606) **(G-13189)**
Topeka Unified School Dst 501..........785 438-4750
1900 Sw Hope St Topeka (66604) **(G-13190)**
Topeka Urology Clinic PA..........785 232-1005
1516 Sw 6th Ave Ste 1 Topeka (66606) **(G-13191)**
Topeka Water Pollution Control, Topeka *Also called City of Topeka* **(G-12470)**
Topeka Zoological Park, Topeka *Also called City of Topeka* **(G-12468)**
Topps Products Inc (PA)..........913 685-2500
20105 Metcalf Ave Bucyrus (66013) **(G-611)**
Torch Research LLC..........913 955-2738
4303 W 119th St Leawood (66209) **(G-5577)**
Torgeson Electric Company..........785 233-3060
3545 Sw 6th Ave Ste 2 Topeka (66606) **(G-13192)**
Torgeson Trenching Inc..........785 233-3060
3545 Sw 6th Ave Topeka (66606) **(G-13193)**
Torgeson Trenching Service, Topeka *Also called Torgeson Trenching Inc* **(G-13193)**
Torotel Inc (PA)..........913 747-6111
520 N Rogers Rd Olathe (66062) **(G-8115)**
Torotel Products Inc..........913 747-6111
550 N Rogers Rd Olathe (66062) **(G-8116)**
Torrey, David P Od, Garden City *Also called Bealmear Bowl Trrey Hoch Reves* **(G-2105)**
Tortilla King Inc..........620 345-2674
249 23rd Ave Moundridge (67107) **(G-7199)**
Tortilleria La Tradicion..........316 264-3148
1701 N Broadway Ave Wichita (67214) **(G-15773)**
Tortillria Los III Prtllos LLC..........316 831-0811
318 W 29th St N Wichita (67204) **(G-15774)**
Tortoise Capital Advisors, Leawood *Also called Tortoise Energy Independenc* **(G-5580)**
Tortoise Capital Advisors LLC..........913 981-1020
11550 Ash St Ste 300 Leawood (66211) **(G-5578)**
Tortoise Energy Capital Corp..........913 981-1020
11550 Ash St Ste 300 Leawood (66211) **(G-5579)**
Tortoise Energy Independenc..........913 981-1020
11550 Ash St Ste 300 Leawood (66211) **(G-5580)**
Toshiba Amer Bus Solutions Inc..........785 242-4942
711 W 23rd St Lawrence (66046) **(G-5142)**
Total 4164, Shawnee Mission *Also called Tpi Petroleum Inc* **(G-11938)**
Total Courier, Westwood *Also called Total Distribution System Inc* **(G-13561)**
Total Distribution System Inc (PA)..........913 677-2292
2803 W 47th St Westwood (66205) **(G-13561)**
Total Elctrnic Dsgned Slutions, Lenexa *Also called Ted Systems LLC* **(G-6174)**
Total Electric Inc..........316 524-2642
1857 N Mosley St Wichita (67214) **(G-15775)**
Total Electric Construction Co..........913 441-0192
109 S 4th St Edwardsville (66111) **(G-1517)**
Total Electric Contractors..........913 441-0192
9247 Woodend Rd Edwardsville (66111) **(G-1518)**
Total Installation Management..........316 267-0584
3919 N Hillcrest St Ste 2 Bel Aire (67220) **(G-441)**
Total Lease Service Inc (PA)..........785 735-9520
1309 Toulon Ave Hays (67601) **(G-2920)**
Total Renal Care Inc..........785 235-1094
634 Sw Mulvane St Ste 300 Topeka (66606) **(G-13194)**
Total Renal Care Inc..........785 841-0490
3510 Clinton Pkwy Ste 110 Lawrence (66047) **(G-5143)**
Total Renal Care Inc..........620 340-8043
1616 Industrial Rd # 2004 Emporia (66801) **(G-1839)**
Total Renal Care Inc..........785 273-1824
3711 Sw Wanamaker Rd Topeka (66610) **(G-13195)**
Total Renal Care Inc..........785 843-2000
330 Arkansas St Ste 100 Lawrence (66044) **(G-5144)**
Total Renal Care Inc..........913 287-5724
5001 State Ave Kansas City (66102) **(G-4470)**
Total Renovation Group Inc..........913 491-5000
10680 Widmer Rd Lenexa (66215) **(G-6186)**
Total Security Solutions LLC..........316 209-0436
934 N Sagebrush Ct Wichita (67230) **(G-15776)**
Total Tool Supply Inc..........913 722-7879
275 Southwest Blvd Kansas City (66103) **(G-4471)**
Total Turfcare Inc..........785 827-6983
827 York Ave Salina (67401) **(G-10735)**
Total/One Stop, Newton *Also called Wenger Oil Inc* **(G-7427)**
Touch Enterprises LLC (PA)..........913 638-2130
117 N Cooper St Olathe (66061) **(G-8117)**
Touchnet Info Systems Inc..........913 599-6699
15520 College Blvd Lenexa (66219) **(G-6187)**
Touchpoint Dashboard LLC..........512 585-5975
8918 W 21st St N Pmb 211 Pmb211 Wichita (67205) **(G-15777)**
Touchton Alarms, Pittsburg *Also called Touchton Electric Inc* **(G-9946)**
Touchton Electric Inc..........620 232-9294
111 N Broadway St Pittsburg (66762) **(G-9946)**
Tow All of Kansas City LLC..........913 208-0327
4839 Merriam Dr Overland Park (66203) **(G-9419)**
Tow Service Inc..........316 522-8908
3760 S Broadway Ave Wichita (67216) **(G-15778)**
Tower Metal Products LP..........620 215-2622
301 N Hill St Fort Scott (66701) **(G-2009)**
Tower Metal Works Inc..........785 256-4281
29273 Windy Hill Rd Maple Hill (66507) **(G-6865)**
Town & Country Animal Clinic (PA)..........316 283-1650
504 N Meridian Rd Newton (67114) **(G-7420)**
Town & Country Animal Hospital..........785 823-2217
1001 Schippel Dr Salina (67401) **(G-10736)**
Town & Country Guttering Inc..........913 441-0003
6423 Vista Dr Shawnee Mission (66218) **(G-11935)**
Town & Country Landscaping (PA)..........816 358-4511
12741 Grandview St Overland Park (66213) **(G-9420)**
Town & Country Racquet Club..........620 792-1366
3806 Broadway Ave Ste 1 Great Bend (67530) **(G-2648)**
Town & Country Sheetmetal Inc..........913 441-1208
6423 Vista Dr Shawnee (66218) **(G-11041)**
Town & Country Super Market..........620 653-2330
818 N Elm St Hoisington (67544) **(G-3072)**
Town and Country Food Mkts Inc..........316 942-7940
1522 S Florence St Wichita (67209) **(G-15779)**
Town Center Plaza LLC..........913 498-1111
5000 W 119th St Leawood (66209) **(G-5581)**
Town Drilling & Production, Paola *Also called Town Oil Company* **(G-9593)**
Town Oil Company..........913 294-2125
16205 W 287th St Paola (66071) **(G-9593)**
Town Village Leawood LLC..........913 491-3681
4400 W 115th St Apt 145 Shawnee Mission (66211) **(G-11936)**
Towne East Square..........316 686-9672
7700 E Kellogg Dr Ste 799 Wichita (67207) **(G-15780)**
Towne Place Suites Leavenworth, Leavenworth *Also called Tps Leavenworth Lp* **(G-5299)**
Towne West Square, Wichita *Also called Washington Prime Group Inc* **(G-15931)**
TownePlace Suites, Wichita *Also called Island Hospitality MGT LLC* **(G-14732)**
Tox-Eol Pest Management Inc..........785 825-5143
417 S Clark St Salina (67401) **(G-10737)**
Toyota Motor Credit Corp..........913 661-6800
10851 Mastin St Ste 220 Shawnee Mission (66210) **(G-11937)**
Toys-4-Trux, Hays *Also called Vernies Trux-N-Equip Inc* **(G-2923)**
Tpa, Wichita *Also called Teaching Parents Assn Inc* **(G-15720)**
Tpac, Topeka *Also called Topeka Performing Arts Center* **(G-13184)**
Tpcks Inc..........785 776-4429
322 Houston St Ste 110 Manhattan (66502) **(G-6828)**
Tpi Petroleum Inc..........913 831-3145
6501 Johnson Dr Shawnee Mission (66202) **(G-11938)**
Tpp Acquisition Inc..........913 317-5591
12055 Metcalf Ave Overland Park (66213) **(G-9421)**
Tpp Crtfied Pub Accntants LLC..........913 498-2200
7300 College Blvd Ste 400 Overland Park (66210) **(G-9422)**
Tpp Rtirement Plan Specialists, Overland Park *Also called Tpp Crtfied Pub Accntants LLC* **(G-9422)**
Tps Leavenworth Lp..........913 297-5400
1001 N 4th St Leavenworth (66048) **(G-5299)**
Tr Sales & Distribution Inc..........800 478-5468
15352 S Keeler St Ste A Olathe (66062) **(G-8118)**
Tr Services Inc..........785 623-1066
271 Lake Rd Pratt (67124) **(G-10160)**
Trac Staffing Service Inc (PA)..........913 341-1150
10901 W 84th Ter Shawnee Mission (66214) **(G-11939)**
Tracker Door Systems LLC..........913 585-3100
35000 W 95th St De Soto (66018) **(G-1214)**
Tractor Supply 1179, Manhattan *Also called Tractor Supply Company* **(G-6829)**
Tractor Supply 1277, Fort Scott *Also called Tractor Supply Company* **(G-2010)**
Tractor Supply Company..........620 408-9119
2612 Central Ave Dodge City (67801) **(G-1439)**
Tractor Supply Company..........785 827-3300
3120 Riffel Dr Salina (67401) **(G-10738)**
Tractor Supply Company..........620 672-1102
1727 E 1st St Pratt (67124) **(G-10161)**
Tractor Supply Company..........620 663-7607
1203 N Lorraine St Hutchinson (67501) **(G-3465)**
Tractor Supply Company..........785 587-8949
8110 Southport Rd Manhattan (66502) **(G-6829)**

Tractor Supply Company 620 223-4900
2420 S Main St Fort Scott (66701) ***(G-2010)***
Tracy Electric Inc 316 522-8408
8025 S Broadway St Haysville (67060) ***(G-2962)***
Tracy Pedigo 316 945-3414
3804 W Maple St Wichita (67213) ***(G-15781)***
Tracy's Automotive, Wichita *Also called Tracy Pedigo* ***(G-15781)***
Trade Finders, Shawnee Mission *Also called Discovery Concepts Inc* ***(G-11309)***
Trade Home Shoes Stores, Manhattan *Also called Tradehome Shoe Stores Inc* ***(G-6830)***
Tradehome Shoe Stores Inc 785 539-4003
100 Manhattan Town Ctr # 670 Manhattan (66502) ***(G-6830)***
Trademark Incorporated 316 264-8310
7540 W Northwind St # 100 Wichita (67205) ***(G-15782)***
Tradenet Publishing Inc 913 856-4070
1200 Energy Center Dr Gardner (66030) ***(G-2365)***
Tradesmen International LLC 316 688-0291
1117 S Rock Rd Ste 4b Wichita (67207) ***(G-15783)***
Tradewind Energy Inc (HQ) 913 888-9463
16105 W 113th St Ste 105 Lenexa (66219) ***(G-6188)***
Traditional Trucking Corp 785 456-8604
202 Broadway St Belvue (66407) ***(G-509)***
Traf-O-Teria System, El Dorado *Also called Leroy Cook* ***(G-1583)***
Traffic Control Services Inc 316 448-0402
405 N Cleveland Ave Wichita (67214) ***(G-15784)***
Traffic Tech Inc 888 592-2009
22418 S Harrison St Spring Hill (66083) ***(G-12101)***
Traftec Inc 913 621-2919
1428 Kansas Ave Kansas City (66105) ***(G-4472)***
Trail West Hardware & Feed, Gardner *Also called Alternative Building Tech* ***(G-2325)***
Trail Wood Company Inc 316 321-6500
615 N Main St El Dorado (67042) ***(G-1610)***
Trail Worthy Inc 316 337-5311
312 E 1st St Halstead (67056) ***(G-2705)***
Trailblazer Pipeline Co LLC 913 928-6060
4200 W 115th St Ste 350 Leawood (66211) ***(G-5582)***
Trailers and More, Wichita *Also called Trailers n More LLC* ***(G-15785)***
Trailers n More LLC 316 945-8900
433 N Maize Rd Wichita (67212) ***(G-15785)***
Train Wreck Promotion, Fort Scott *Also called Trainwreck Tees LLC* ***(G-2011)***
Training & Educational Service 913 498-1914
7007 College Blvd Ste 385 Overland Park (66211) ***(G-9423)***
Training & Evaluation Cente 620 663-2216
3000 E Avenue B Hutchinson (67501) ***(G-3466)***
Training & Evaluation Cente (PA) 620 663-1596
10 E 1st Ave Hutchinson (67501) ***(G-3467)***
Training & Evaluation Cente 620 615-5850
303 E Bigger St Hutchinson (67501) ***(G-3468)***
Training Department, Wichita *Also called Saint Francis Cmnty Svcs Inc* ***(G-15507)***
Training Tech & Support Inc 913 682-7048
1931 Woodridge Dr Leavenworth (66048) ***(G-5300)***
Trainwreck Tees LLC 620 224-2480
108 Scott Ave Fort Scott (66701) ***(G-2011)***
Tramec Sloan LLC 620 326-5007
32 Clark Ave Wellington (67152) ***(G-13537)***
Trammell Crow Company 913 722-1155
6810 Roe Ave Prairie Village (66208) ***(G-10076)***
Tran Majher and Shaw Od PA (PA) 316 686-6063
2251 N Woodlawn Blvd Wichita (67220) ***(G-15786)***
Tran Aerospace Inc 316 260-8808
7709 E Harry St Wichita (67207) ***(G-15787)***
Trane US Inc 785 272-3224
2200 Sw Gage Blvd Topeka (66622) ***(G-13196)***
Trane US Inc 316 265-9655
120 S Ida St Wichita (67211) ***(G-15788)***
Trane US Inc 417 863-2110
11211 Lakeview Ave Lenexa (66219) ***(G-6189)***
Trans Continental Cold Storage, Emporia *Also called Tyson Fresh Meats Inc* ***(G-1844)***
Trans Pacific Oil, Wichita *Also called Trans Pacific Properties LLC* ***(G-15790)***
Trans Pacific Oil Corporation 316 262-3596
100 S Main St Ste 200 Wichita (67202) ***(G-15789)***
Trans Pacific Properties LLC 316 262-3596
100 S Main St Ste 200 Wichita (67202) ***(G-15790)***
Trans Services Inc 913 592-3878
702 N Lincoln St Spring Hill (66083) ***(G-12102)***
Trans-Pak Inc (PA) 620 275-1758
4555 N Jennie Barker Rd Garden City (67846) ***(G-2300)***
Transam Trucking Inc (PA) 913 782-5300
15910 S Us 169 Hwy Olathe (66062) ***(G-8119)***
Transatlantic Reinsurance Co 913 319-2510
7500 College Blvd # 1100 Overland Park (66210) ***(G-9424)***
Transcare of Ks LLC 620 431-6300
113 W 2nd St Chanute (66720) ***(G-772)***
Transcription Unlimited Inc 816 350-3800
11013 W 48th Ter Shawnee (66203) ***(G-11042)***
Transerve Inc 620 231-2230
315 W 3rd St Pittsburg (66762) ***(G-9947)***
Transervice Logistics Inc 785 493-4295
413 E Berg Rd Salina (67401) ***(G-10739)***
Transit Services, Olathe *Also called County of Johnson* ***(G-7620)***
Transitions Group Inc 913 327-0700
10900 Pflumm Rd Lenexa (66215) ***(G-6190)***
Transitions Group Inc (PA) 316 262-9100
116 N Cleveland Ave Wichita (67214) ***(G-15791)***
Transitions Group Inc 316 263-5750
1336 E Douglas Ave Wichita (67214) ***(G-15792)***
Transport Funding LLC 913 319-7400
8717 W 110th St Ste 700 Overland Park (66210) ***(G-9425)***
Transportation Inc 785 242-3660
2643 Kingman Rd Ottawa (66067) ***(G-8316)***
Transtecs Corporation (PA) 316 651-0389
2102 E 21st St N Wichita (67214) ***(G-15793)***
Transweb Llc 856 205-1313
11501 Outlook St Ste 100 Leawood (66211) ***(G-5583)***
Transwood Inc 620 331-5924
4158 County Rd 4200 Independence (67301) ***(G-3566)***
Transwood Inc 620 331-5699
810 Cement St Independence (67301) ***(G-3567)***
Transwood Edwardsville66 ....913 745-1773
8907 Woodend Rd Kansas City (66111) ***(G-4473)***
Transwood Inc Mechanic, Independence *Also called Transwood Inc* ***(G-3566)***
Transystems Corporation 316 303-3000
245 N Waco St Ste 222 Wichita (67202) ***(G-15794)***
Transystems Corporation 620 331-3999
115 S 6th St Ste B Independence (67301) ***(G-3568)***
Traq-It Inc 913 498-1221
7300 W 110th St Ste 920 Overland Park (66210) ***(G-9426)***
Traq-It Software, Overland Park *Also called Traq-It Inc* ***(G-9426)***
Trash Mountain Project Inc 785 246-6845
1555 Nw Gage Blvd Topeka (66618) ***(G-13197)***
Travel Lodge, Dodge City *Also called Dodge Enteprise Inc* ***(G-1356)***
Treanorhl Inc (PA) 785 842-4858
1040 Vermont St Lawrence (66044) ***(G-5145)***
Treasurer Kansas State (HQ) 785 296-3171
900 Sw Jackson St Rm 201 Topeka (66612) ***(G-13198)***
Treat America Limited (PA) 913 384-4900
8500 Shawnee Mission Pkwy # 100 Shawnee Mission (66202) ***(G-11940)***
Treatco Inc 316 265-7900
9242 E Lakepoint Dr Wichita (67226) ***(G-15795)***
Treb Construction Inc 785 373-4935
609 Iowa Tipton (67485) ***(G-12250)***
Treco Inc 620 544-2606
823 E 11th St Hugoton (67951) ***(G-3178)***
Treco Inc (PA) 620 356-4785
2871 W Oklahoma Ulysses (67880) ***(G-13325)***
Tree House Learning Center 316 773-3335
449 N Maize Rd Wichita (67212) ***(G-15796)***
Tree Top Nursery and Landscape 316 686-7491
5910 E 37th St N Wichita (67220) ***(G-15797)***
Tree-Rific Landscaping Inc 316 733-0900
13594 Sw Us Highway 54 Andover (67002) ***(G-111)***
Treescape Inc 316 733-6388
1202 N Andover Rd Andover (67002) ***(G-112)***
Treescapes, Andover *Also called Treescape Inc* ***(G-112)***
Treger Texas, Plainville *Also called Crawford Supply Co* ***(G-9984)***
Trego Hospital Endowment Fndtn 785 743-2182
320 N 13th St Wakeeney (67672) ***(G-13392)***
Trek Trucking, Garden City *Also called Preferred Cartage Service Inc* ***(G-2259)***
Trendstone LLC 913 599-5492
10821 Lakeview Ave Lenexa (66219) ***(G-6191)***
Trenton Agri Products LLC (PA) 316 265-3311
2020 N Bramblewood St Wichita (67206) ***(G-15798)***
Tresko Inc (PA) 913 631-6900
6218 Melrose Ln Shawnee Mission (66203) ***(G-11941)***
Tresses Family Hair Salon, Hutchinson *Also called Tresses Hair Salon* ***(G-3469)***
Tresses Hair Salon 620 662-2299
2901 N Lorraine St Ste B Hutchinson (67502) ***(G-3469)***
Tri City Assisted Living LLC (PA) 913 782-3200
13795 S Mur Len Rd # 301 Olathe (66062) ***(G-8120)***
Tri Resources Inc 620 982-4568
Great Bend At Patton 10th Pawnee Rock (67567) ***(G-9755)***
Tri Resources Inc 620 672-9425
30317 N Us Highway 281 Pratt (67124) ***(G-10162)***
Tri Star Utilities Inc 620 331-7159
2109 W Maple St Independence (67301) ***(G-3569)***
Tri State Construction Inc 620 231-5260
816 E Jefferson St Pittsburg (66762) ***(G-9948)***
Tri-Com Technical Services LLC 913 652-0600
11115 Ash St Leawood (66211) ***(G-5584)***
Tri-County Concrete Inc 913 764-7700
15520 S Us 169 Hwy Olathe (66062) ***(G-8121)***
Tri-County Newspapers Inc 913 856-7615
936 E Santa Fe St Gardner (66030) ***(G-2366)***
Tri-County Telephone Assn Inc 785 366-7000
1568 S 1000 Rd Council Grove (66846) ***(G-1178)***
Tri-County Title & Abstract Co 913 682-8911
360 Santa Fe St Leavenworth (66048) ***(G-5301)***
Tri-Dim Filter Corporation 316 425-0462
1659 S Sabin St Wichita (67209) ***(G-15799)***

ALPHABETIC

Tri-Ko Inc (PA)...913 755-3025
301 1st St Osawatomie (66064) ***(G-8205)***
Tri-Rotor Spray & Chemical, Ulysses *Also called J & L Smith Farms Inc* ***(G-13301)***
Tri-Star Seed, Spring Hill *Also called Beachner Seed Co Inc* ***(G-12078)***
Tri-Valley Developmental Svcs...620 365-3307
405 N Jefferson Ave Iola (66749) ***(G-3637)***
Tri-Valley Developmental Svcs...620 223-3990
4305 Campbell Dr Fort Scott (66701) ***(G-2012)***
Tria Health LLC...888 799-8742
7101 College Blvd Ste 600 Overland Park (66210) ***(G-9427)***
Triad Capital Advisors Inc (PA)...816 561-7000
4400 Shawnee Mission Pkwy # 209 Fairway (66205) ***(G-1922)***
Triad Manufacturing Inc...785 825-6050
1100 W Grand Ave Ste K Salina (67401) ***(G-10740)***
Triad Mortgage, Fairway *Also called Triad Capital Advisors Inc* ***(G-1922)***
Triangle H...620 276-4004
1955 W Plymell Rd Garden City (67846) ***(G-2301)***
Triangle H Grain & Cattle Co...620 276-4004
1955 W Plymell Rd Garden City (67846) ***(G-2302)***
Triangle Sales Inc (PA)...913 541-1800
15300 W 110th St Shawnee Mission (66219) ***(G-11942)***
Triangle Trucking Inc...785 827-5500
2250 Hein Ave Salina (67401) ***(G-10741)***
Tribe Construction LLC...913 850-0211
13358 Leasure Rd Mound City (66056) ***(G-7176)***
Tribine Harvester LLC...316 282-8011
1010 Industrial Dr Newton (67114) ***(G-7421)***
Tricentury Bank (PA)...913 648-8010
33485 Lexington Ave De Soto (66018) ***(G-1215)***
Trideum Corporation...913 364-5900
1000 S 4th St Ste C Leavenworth (66048) ***(G-5302)***
Trieb Sheet Metal Co...913 831-1166
1642 S 45th St Kansas City (66106) ***(G-4474)***
Trigard Vaults (PA)...785 527-5595
630 M St Belleville (66935) ***(G-468)***
Trilobite Testing Inc (PA)...785 625-4778
1515 Commerce Pkwy Hays (67601) ***(G-2921)***
Trimac Industrial Systems LLC...913 441-0043
12601 Kaw Dr Ste C Bonner Springs (66012) ***(G-578)***
Trimark Signworks Inc...316 263-2224
318 S Osage St Wichita (67213) ***(G-15800)***
Trimble & Maclaskey Oil LLC...620 836-2000
110 South St Gridley (66852) ***(G-2691)***
Trinity Animation Inc...816 525-0103
9200 Indian Creek Pkwy # 650 Overland Park (66210) ***(G-9428)***
Trinity Daycare & Preschool...316 838-0909
2402 N Arkansas Ave Wichita (67204) ***(G-15801)***
Trinity Feedyard LLC...620 275-4191
1805 W Annie Scheer Rd Garden City (67846) ***(G-2303)***
Trinity In-Home Care Inc...785 842-3159
2201 W 25th St Ste Q Lawrence (66047) ***(G-5146)***
Trinity Manor, Dodge City *Also called Frontline Management* ***(G-1363)***
Trinity Nursing & Rehab Center...913 671-7376
9700 W 62nd St Shawnee Mission (66203) ***(G-11943)***
Trinity Precision Inc...316 265-0603
1935 W Walker St Wichita (67213) ***(G-15802)***
Trinity Property Group LLC...620 342-8723
1105 Scott St Emporia (66801) ***(G-1840)***
Trinity Sales LLC...316 942-5555
2225 S West St Wichita (67213) ***(G-15803)***
Trinity Steel and Pipe Inc...620 396-8900
204 S Madison Ave Weir (66781) ***(G-13486)***
Triple B Investments Inc...913 681-2500
3401 W 159th St Overland Park (66224) ***(G-9429)***
Triple C Manufacturing Inc...785 284-3674
902 Hwy K 246 Sabetha (66534) ***(G-10334)***
Triple J Machining LLC...316 214-2414
204 E 5th Ave Ste C Augusta (67010) ***(G-349)***
Triple T Farms...620 355-6707
101 N Main St Lakin (67860) ***(G-4661)***
Triple T Pallets...316 772-9155
11500 N Broadway St Valley Center (67147) ***(G-13357)***
Triple-I Corporation...913 563-7227
4200 W 115th St Ste 300 Leawood (66211) ***(G-5585)***
Triplett Inc (PA)...785 823-7839
429 N Ohio St Salina (67401) ***(G-10742)***
Triplett Woolf & Garretson LLC...316 630-8100
2959 N Rock Rd Ste 300 Wichita (67226) ***(G-15804)***
Tristar Publishing Inc...913 491-4200
7285 W 132nd St Ste 300 Overland Park (66213) ***(G-9430)***
Tritats LLC...913 219-5949
10819 W 157th Ter Overland Park (66221) ***(G-9431)***
Triumph Accessory Services, Wellington *Also called Triumph Group Operations Inc* ***(G-13538)***
Triumph Group Operations Inc...620 326-5761
411 N West Rd Wellington (67152) ***(G-13538)***
Triumph Strctres - Kans Cy Inc (HQ)...913 882-7200
31800 W 196th St Edgerton (66021) ***(G-1491)***
Triumph Strctres - Wichita Inc (HQ)...316 942-0432
3258 S Hoover Rd Wichita (67215) ***(G-15805)***
Troostwood Garage & Body Shop...816 444-3800
1516 N 13th St Kansas City (66102) ***(G-4475)***
Tropical Designs, Wichita *Also called Hoffmanns Green Industries* ***(G-14624)***
Tropicana Products Inc...316 838-1000
214 W 21st St N Ste 200 Wichita (67203) ***(G-15806)***
Trs Logistics, Sedgwick *Also called Tim R Schwab Inc* ***(G-10852)***
Tru Green-Chemlawn, Wichita *Also called Trugreen Limited Partnership* ***(G-15812)***
Tru Green-Chemlawn, Lenexa *Also called Trugreen Limited Partnership* ***(G-6193)***
Tru Home Solutions LLC...913 219-7547
9601 Legler Rd Lenexa (66219) ***(G-6192)***
Tru Wichita Northeast, Wichita *Also called Greenwich Hotel LLC* ***(G-14512)***
Tru8 Solutions LLC (PA)...678 451-0264
1107 N 5th St Manhattan (66502) ***(G-6831)***
Truck Insurance Mart Inc (PA)...913 441-0349
10027 Woodend Rd Edwardsville (66111) ***(G-1519)***
Truck Insurance Mart Inc...620 654-3921
245 W Highway 56 Galva (67443) ***(G-2096)***
Truck Parts & Equipment, Wichita *Also called Fleetpride Inc* ***(G-14386)***
Truck Sales Inc...620 225-4155
1305 Rath Ave Dodge City (67801) ***(G-1440)***
Truck Stuff Inc...316 264-1908
427 N Washington Ave Wichita (67202) ***(G-15807)***
Truck Utilities Kansas City, Kansas City *Also called Nesco Holdings Inc* ***(G-4286)***
Trucking By George Inc...620 879-2117
Ind Pk Hwy 166 E Caney (67333) ***(G-677)***
Trudi R Grin...913 888-1888
11735 W 144th Ter Olathe (66062) ***(G-8122)***
True Home Care LLC...316 776-4685
12828 E 13th St N Ste 6 Wichita (67230) ***(G-15808)***
True North Hotel Group Inc...913 341-4440
10750 Barkley St Shawnee Mission (66211) ***(G-11944)***
True North Inc (PA)...316 266-6574
8200 E 32nd St N Ste 100 Wichita (67226) ***(G-15809)***
True North Outdoor LLC...913 322-1340
3909 Mission Rd Kansas City (66103) ***(G-4476)***
True North Services LLC (PA)...888 478-9470
5400 Johnson Dr Shawnee Mission (66205) ***(G-11945)***
True Spec Finishes LLC...620 254-7733
121 N Harper St Attica (67009) ***(G-280)***
True Value, Beloit *Also called Ackerman Supply Inc* ***(G-469)***
True Value, Valley Center *Also called Bartels Inc* ***(G-13336)***
True Value, Emporia *Also called Waters Inc* ***(G-1849)***
True Value, Manhattan *Also called Waters Inc* ***(G-6847)***
True Value, Junction City *Also called Waters Inc* ***(G-3767)***
True Value, Dodge City *Also called Waters Inc* ***(G-1451)***
True Value Hardware, Cherryvale *Also called Newtons Inc* ***(G-811)***
Truecare Nursing Services LLC...626 818-2420
4601 E Douglas Ave # 201 Wichita (67218) ***(G-15810)***
Truenorth Companies Lc...913 307-0838
9290 Bond St Ste 205 Overland Park (66214) ***(G-9432)***
Truett & Osborn Cycle Inc...316 682-4781
3345 E 31st St S Wichita (67216) ***(G-15811)***
Trugreen Limited Partnership...316 448-6253
1652 S West St Wichita (67213) ***(G-15812)***
Trugreen Limited Partnership...785 267-4121
8420 Cole Pkwy Lenexa (66227) ***(G-6193)***
Truist Bank...913 491-6700
4501 College Blvd Ste 320 Leawood (66211) ***(G-5586)***
Truity Credit Union...785 749-2224
3400 W 6th St Lawrence (66049) ***(G-5147)***
Trujillo Jan & Crpt Clg Svc...316 263-8204
339 S Laura St Wichita (67211) ***(G-15813)***
Trumove Physical Therapy PA...913 642-7746
7279 W 105th St Overland Park (66212) ***(G-9433)***
Trumpet Behavioral Health LLC...816 802-6969
7001 W 79th St Overland Park (66204) ***(G-9434)***
Trust Company of Manhattan...785 537-7200
800 Poyntz Ave Manhattan (66502) ***(G-6832)***
Trust Sourcing Solutions LLC...913 319-0300
5901 College Blvd Ste 100 Shawnee Mission (66211) ***(G-11946)***
Trustees Indiana University...913 499-6661
5755 Windsor Dr Fairway (66205) ***(G-1923)***
Trustees of The Baker Univ...785 354-5850
1500 Sw 10th Ave Fl 2 Topeka (66604) ***(G-13199)***
Trustpoint Services Inc...620 364-5665
800 N 4th St Ste 101 Burlington (66839) ***(G-644)***
Tsi, Spring Hill *Also called Trans Services Inc* ***(G-12102)***
Tsi Kansas Inc...785 632-5183
612 W Court St Clay Center (67432) ***(G-884)***
Tsr LLC...316 946-1527
325 S West St Wichita (67213) ***(G-15814)***
Tsunami Surf Riders LLC...913 498-3468
25501 W Valley Pkwy # 300 Olathe (66061) ***(G-8123)***
Tsvc Inc (PA)...913 599-6886
10841 S Ridgeview Rd Olathe (66061) ***(G-8124)***
Tuckers Bar & Grill...785 235-3172
3435 Se 39th Ter Topeka (66609) ***(G-13200)***

Tucson Hotels LP 785 431-7200
1717 Sw Topeka Blvd Topeka (66612) ***(G-13201)***
Tucson Hotels LP 785 210-1500
310 Hammons Dr Junction City (66441) ***(G-3760)***
Tucson Transformer & Appa 620 227-5100
11075 Quaker Rd Dodge City (67801) ***(G-1441)***
Tuff Shed Inc 913 541-8833
8811 Lenexa Dr Shawnee Mission (66214) ***(G-11947)***
Tuff Turf Inc 913 362-4545
5948 Merriam Dr Shawnee Mission (66203) ***(G-11948)***
Tuls Dairy Farms LLC 620 624-6455
12541 Road C Liberal (67901) ***(G-6375)***
Tumbleweed Festival Inc 620 275-9141
1719 E Texas St Garden City (67846) ***(G-2304)***
Turbine Eng Comp Tech Turning 316 925-4020
2019 Southwest Blvd Wichita (67213) ***(G-15815)***
Turf Design Inc (PA) 913 764-6531
23770 W 81st Ter Lenexa (66227) ***(G-6194)***
Turf Management LLC 785 410-0394
1012 Sedam Ave Manhattan (66502) ***(G-6833)***
Turkey Creek Golf Course 620 241-8530
1000 Fox Run Rd McPherson (67460) ***(G-7032)***
Turkey Creek Golf Course & Dev, McPherson *Also called Turkey Creek Golf Course* ***(G-7032)***
Turnbull Corporation (PA) 620 342-2134
605 State St Emporia (66801) ***(G-1841)***
Turner Ceramic Tile Inc 913 441-6161
11535 Kaw Dr Kansas City (66111) ***(G-4477)***
Turner Farms Partnership, Great Bend *Also called Turner Trust Partnership* ***(G-2649)***
Turner House Clinic Inc 913 342-2552
21 N 12th St Ste 300 Kansas City (66102) ***(G-4478)***
Turner Recreation Commission 913 287-2111
831 S 55th St Kansas City (66106) ***(G-4479)***
Turner Trust Partnership (PA) 620 792-6144
551a Sw 30 Rd Great Bend (67530) ***(G-2649)***
Turnpike Investments Inc 316 524-4400
4875 S Laura St Wichita (67216) ***(G-15816)***
Turntine Oclar Prosthetics Inc 913 962-6299
6342 Long Ave Ste H Shawnee Mission (66216) ***(G-11949)***
Turon Welding and Fabrication 620 388-4458
308 E Chicago St Turon (67583) ***(G-13275)***
Turtle Wax Auto Appearance Ctr, Shawnee Mission *Also called Turtle Wax Inc* ***(G-11950)***
Turtle Wax Inc 913 236-6886
5960 Barkley St Shawnee Mission (66202) ***(G-11950)***
Tusar Inc 316 522-1800
4849 S Laura St Wichita (67216) ***(G-15817)***
Tutera Group Inc 913 851-0215
12340 Quivira Rd Shawnee Mission (66213) ***(G-11951)***
Tutera Group Inc 913 381-6000
7300 W 107th St Ofc Shawnee Mission (66212) ***(G-11952)***
Tutor Time Lrng Systems Inc 316 721-0848
10710 W Maple St Wichita (67209) ***(G-15818)***
Tutor Time Lrng Systems Inc 316 721-0464
7026 W 21st St N Wichita (67205) ***(G-15819)***
Tux Shop, The, Towanda *Also called Dcm Wichita Inc* ***(G-13263)***
Tvh Parts Co (PA) 913 829-1000
16355 S Lone Elm Rd Olathe (66062) ***(G-8125)***
TW Metals Inc 316 744-5000
1200 E Blake Dr Park City (67219) ***(G-9650)***
Twa LLC 913 599-5200
10575 Widmer Rd Lenexa (66215) ***(G-6195)***
Twb Inc 620 663-8396
922 Crazy Horse Rd Hutchinson (67502) ***(G-3470)***
TWC Services Inc 316 265-7831
1840 S West St Wichita (67213) ***(G-15820)***
Twenty-First Century 913 713-2121
5800 Foxridge Dr Ste 102 Mission (66202) ***(G-7139)***
Twice As Nice Barbershop 319 201-4542
6249 E 21st St N Ste 110 Wichita (67208) ***(G-15821)***
Twietmeyer, Rebecca L, Wichita *Also called Steven F Twietmeyer DDS* ***(G-15668)***
Twin Fiddle Investment Co LLC 316 788-2855
6020 S Greenwich Rd Derby (67037) ***(G-1277)***
Twin Fitness, Park *Also called Kristie Winters* ***(G-9597)***
Twin Lake Apartments, Wichita *Also called Saratoga Capital Inc* ***(G-15520)***
Twin Oaks Industries Inc 785 827-4839
2001 W Grand Ave Salina (67401) ***(G-10743)***
Twin Rivers Developmental Supp 620 402-6395
22179 D St Arkansas City (67005) ***(G-183)***
Twin Rvers Dvlpmental Supports 620 442-3575
4th St Arkansas City (67005) ***(G-184)***
Twin Rvers Wine Gourmet Shoppe, Emporia *Also called Emporia Winery LLC* ***(G-1748)***
Twin Traffic Marking Corp 913 428-2575
626 N 47th St Kansas City (66102) ***(G-4480)***
Twin Valley Communications, Miltonvale *Also called Twin Valley Telephone Inc* ***(G-7112)***
Twin Valley Dev Srvs, Beattie *Also called Twin Vly Dvelopmental Svcs Inc* ***(G-422)***
Twin Valley Electric Coop 620 784-5500
501 S Huston St Altamont (67330) ***(G-73)***
Twin Valley Laundry, Greenleaf *Also called Twin Vly Dvelopmental Svcs Inc* ***(G-2670)***
Twin Valley Telephone Inc (PA) 785 427-2211
22 W Spruce Ave Miltonvale (67466) ***(G-7112)***
Twin Vly Dvelopmental Svcs Inc (PA) 785 747-2611
413 Commercial St Greenleaf (66943) ***(G-2670)***
Twin Vly Dvelopmental Svcs Inc 785 353-2347
307 Whiting St Beattie (66406) ***(G-421)***
Twin Vly Dvelopmental Svcs Inc 785 353-2347
811 Oak St Beattie (66406) ***(G-422)***
Twin Vly Dvelopmental Svcs Inc 785 353-2226
1109 Main St Beattie (66406) ***(G-423)***
Twinmounds.com, Fredonia *Also called Midwestern Litho* ***(G-2040)***
Twisted Cow LLC 316 804-4949
1400 S Kansas Ave # 1400 Newton (67114) ***(G-7422)***
Twister Trailer Manufacturing, Fort Scott *Also called Short Go Inc* ***(G-2004)***
Two Guys & A Grill 913 393-4745
109 N Chester St Olathe (66061) ***(G-8126)***
Two Rivers Consumers Coop Assn (PA) 620 442-2360
210 S D St Arkansas City (67005) ***(G-185)***
Two Trees Technologies, Wichita *Also called Woodard Tech & Investments LLC* ***(G-16064)***
Two-Bee Inc 785 364-2162
925 W 6th St Holton (66436) ***(G-3113)***
Twotrees Technologies LLC 800 364-5700
200 N Emporia Ave Ste 300 Wichita (67202) ***(G-15822)***
Tyler Physicians PA 316 729-9100
10202 W 13th St N Wichita (67212) ***(G-15823)***
Tyr Energy Inc (HQ) 913 754-5800
7500 College Blvd Ste 400 Overland Park (66210) ***(G-9435)***
Tyson Foods Inc 913 393-7000
20701 W 159th St Olathe (66062) ***(G-8127)***
Tyson Foods Inc 620 663-6141
9 N Washington St South Hutchinson (67505) ***(G-12067)***
Tyson Foods Inc 620 669-8761
521 S Main St Hutchinson (67501) ***(G-3471)***
Tyson Foods Inc 620 343-3640
2101 W 6th Ave Emporia (66801) ***(G-1842)***
Tyson Fresh Meats Inc 620 277-2614
3105 N Ibp Rd Holcomb (67851) ***(G-3082)***
Tyson Fresh Meats Inc 620 343-3640
2101 W 6th Ave Emporia (66801) ***(G-1843)***
Tyson Fresh Meats Inc 620 343-8010
2601 W 6th Ave Emporia (66801) ***(G-1844)***
Tytan International LLC (PA) 913 492-3222
16240 W 110th St Lenexa (66219) ***(G-6196)***
U A W Local 31, Kansas City *Also called International Union United Au* ***(G-4109)***
U Bathe Pets 913 829-3275
100 S Parker St Olathe (66061) ***(G-8128)***
U Haul Co Independent Dealers 316 722-0216
4160 N Maize Rd Maize (67101) ***(G-6522)***
U Inc 913 814-7708
9200 Glenwood St Ste 102 Overland Park (66212) ***(G-9436)***
U P S Stores 913 829-3750
13505 S Mur Len Rd # 105 Olathe (66062) ***(G-8129)***
U Priority Inc 913 712-8524
14111 W 95th St Lenexa (66215) ***(G-6197)***
U S A Today, Lawrence *Also called Gannett Co Inc* ***(G-4868)***
U S Army Corps of Engineers 785 537-7392
5040 Tuttle Creek Blvd Manhattan (66502) ***(G-6834)***
U S Army Corps of Engineers 785 597-5144
10419 Perry Park Dr Perry (66073) ***(G-9774)***
U S Army Corps of Engineers 785 453-2201
5260 Pomona Dam Rd Vassar (66543) ***(G-13372)***
U S Automation Inc 913 894-2410
8803 Long St Shawnee Mission (66215) ***(G-11953)***
U S Central Credit Union (PA) 913 227-6000
9701 Renner Blvd Lenexa (66219) ***(G-6198)***
U S Custom Harvester, Hutchinson *Also called United States Cstm Harvesters* ***(G-3477)***
U S Logo Inc 316 264-1321
520 N West St Wichita (67203) ***(G-15824)***
U S Road Freight Express Inc (PA) 316 942-9944
3655 S Maize Rd Wichita (67215) ***(G-15825)***
U S S A Inc (PA) 316 686-1653
1208 S Rock Rd Wichita (67207) ***(G-15826)***
U S Stone Industries LLC 913 529-4154
2561 Q Ave Herington (67449) ***(G-2982)***
U S Toy Co Inc 913 642-8247
2008 W 103rd Ter Leawood (66206) ***(G-5587)***
U S Weatherford L P 620 624-9324
1401 E Pine St Liberal (67901) ***(G-6376)***
U S Weatherford L P 620 624-6273
1500 General Welch Blvd Liberal (67901) ***(G-6377)***
U S X-Ray LLC 913 652-0550
11201 Strang Line Rd Lenexa (66215) ***(G-6199)***
U-Haul, Arkansas City *Also called Mike Groves Oil Inc* ***(G-166)***
U-Haul, Maize *Also called U Haul Co Independent Dealers* ***(G-6522)***
U-Haul Co of Kansas Inc (HQ) 913 287-1327
5200 State Ave Kansas City (66102) ***(G-4481)***
U-Haul Co of Oregon 913 780-4494
12540 S Rogers Rd Olathe (66062) ***(G-8130)***
U-Save Pharmacy, Hays *Also called Stecklein Enterprises LLC* ***(G-2912)***

ALPHABETIC

U-Tek Cnc Solutions LLC 888 317-6503
1322 260th St Hiawatha (66434) **(G-3026)**
Ube Services LLC 316 616-3500
2868 N Ridge Rd Wichita (67205) **(G-15827)**
Ubiquitel Inc (HQ) 913 315-5800
6391 Sprint Pkwy Overland Park (66251) **(G-9437)**
UBS Financial Services Inc 913 345-3200
11150 Overbrook Rd # 300 Shawnee Mission (66211) **(G-11954)**
UBS Financial Services Inc 316 612-6500
121 S Whittier Rd Wichita (67207) **(G-15828)**
UBS Securities LLC 913 345-3200
11150 Overbrook Rd Leawood (66211) **(G-5588)**
Ucc, Kansas City *Also called Universal Construction Co Inc* **(G-4494)**
UCI, Wichita *Also called Utility Contractors Inc* **(G-15866)**
Ufcw District Union Local 2 (PA) 816 842-4086
3951 N Woodlawn Ct Bel Aire (67220) **(G-442)**
Ui Benefit Overpayments 785 296-5000
401 Sw Topeka Blvd Topeka (66603) **(G-13202)**
Ukhs Great Bend LLC 620 792-8833
514 Cleveland St Great Bend (67530) **(G-2650)**
UKSM-W MEDICAL PRACTICE ASSOCI, Wichita *Also called University of Kansas School of* **(G-15858)**
Ultimate Escape Day Spa LLC 913 851-3385
11674 W 135th St Overland Park (66221) **(G-9438)**
Ultimate Group LLP 816 813-8182
8014 State Line Rd # 206 Prairie Village (66208) **(G-10077)**
Ultimate Tan 785 842-4949
2449 Iowa St Ste O Lawrence (66046) **(G-5148)**
Ultra Electronics Ice Inc 785 776-6423
2700 Amherst Ave Manhattan (66502) **(G-6835)**
Ultra Modern Pool & Patio Inc 316 681-3011
5620 E Kellogg Dr Wichita (67218) **(G-15829)**
Ultra-Chem Inc (PA) 913 492-2929
8043 Flint St Shawnee Mission (66214) **(G-11955)**
Ultra-Tech Aerospace Inc 913 262-7009
3000 Power Dr Kansas City (66106) **(G-4482)**
Ultrafab Inc 620 245-0781
811 W 1st St McPherson (67460) **(G-7033)**
Ultrasound For Women LLC (PA) 785 331-4160
4500 Woodland Dr Lawrence (66049) **(G-5149)**
Ulysis Feed Yard, Ulysses *Also called Cactus Feeders Inc* **(G-13286)**
Ulysses Family Physicians 620 356-1261
505 N Main St Ulysses (67880) **(G-13326)**
Ulysses Standard Supply Inc 620 356-4171
502 S Colorado St Ulysses (67880) **(G-13327)**
Umb Bank National Association 785 263-1130
400 N Broadway St Abilene (67410) **(G-55)**
Umb Bank National Association 620 223-1255
324 S National Ave Fort Scott (66701) **(G-2013)**
Umb Bank National Association 785 838-2500
1441 Wakarusa Dr Lawrence (66049) **(G-5150)**
Umb Bank National Association 785 776-9400
529 Humboldt St Ste 1 Manhattan (66502) **(G-6836)**
Umb Bank National Association 785 483-6800
507 N Main St Russell (67665) **(G-10300)**
Umb Bank National Association 913 234-2070
7109 W 80th St Shawnee Mission (66204) **(G-11956)**
Umb Bank National Association 913 791-6600
18261 W 119th St Olathe (66061) **(G-8131)**
Umb Bank National Association 913 360-6060
320 Commercial St Atchison (66002) **(G-266)**
Umb Bank National Association 913 236-0300
6900 Mission Rd Prairie Village (66208) **(G-10078)**
Umb Bank National Association 913 402-3600
6960 W 135th St Shawnee Mission (66223) **(G-11957)**
Umb Bank National Association 913 667-5400
22320 W 66th St Shawnee Mission (66226) **(G-11958)**
Umb Bank National Association 913 621-8002
909 N 6th St Kansas City (66101) **(G-4483)**
Umb Bank National Association 913 894-4088
11101 W 87th St Shawnee Mission (66214) **(G-11959)**
Umb Bank National Association 316 267-1191
130 N Market St Wichita (67202) **(G-15830)**
Umb Financial Corporation 785 826-4000
2375 S 9th St Salina (67401) **(G-10744)**
Umcprint, Shawnee *Also called Universal Manufacturing Co* **(G-11044)**
Unbound (PA) 913 384-6500
1 Elmwood Ave Kansas City (66103) **(G-4484)**
Under Axe Equipment, Council Grove *Also called Stinger By Axe* **(G-1177)**
Underground Specialists Inc 620 276-3344
520 Airlinks Dr Garden City (67846) **(G-2305)**
Underground Vaults & Stor Inc (PA) 620 662-6769
906 N Halstead St Hutchinson (67501) **(G-3472)**
Underground Vaults & Stor Inc 316 838-2121
3333 N Mead St Ste B Wichita (67219) **(G-15831)**
Underground Vaults & Stor Inc 620 663-5434
3500 E Avenue G Hutchinson (67501) **(G-3473)**
Undergrund Cvern Stblztion LLC (PA) 620 662-6367
1020 Hoover St Great Bend (67530) **(G-2651)**
Undergrund Cvern Stblztion LLC 620 617-0302
7513 S K 14 Hwy Hutchinson (67501) **(G-3474)**
Underhill Finish Carpentry LLC 316 253-7129
14350 W Hardtner Ct Wichita (67235) **(G-15832)**
Unell Manufacturing Co, Lenexa *Also called Sands Level and Tool Company* **(G-6117)**
UNI Computers, Lawrence *Also called Keltech Solutions LLC* **(G-4940)**
UNI Floor Inc 913 238-4633
6711 W 157th Ter Overland Park (66223) **(G-9439)**
Unified Gvrnment Cmnty Corectn 913 573-4180
812 N 7th St Fl 3 Kansas City (66101) **(G-4485)**
Unified Life Insur Co Texas 913 685-2233
7201 W 129th St Ste 300 Shawnee Mission (66213) **(G-11960)**
Unified School District 214 620 356-4577
207 N Main St Ulysses (67880) **(G-13328)**
Unified School District 259 (PA) 316 973-4000
903 S Edgemoor St Wichita (67218) **(G-15833)**
Unified School District 259 316 973-7292
2301 E Douglas Ave Wichita (67211) **(G-15834)**
Unified School District 259 316 683-3315
2418 E 9th St N Wichita (67214) **(G-15835)**
Unified School District 259 316 973-4200
201 N Water St Wichita (67202) **(G-15836)**
Unified School District 383 785 587-2850
1112 Hayes Dr Manhattan (66502) **(G-6837)**
Unified School District 383 785 587-2190
1120 Hayes Dr Manhattan (66502) **(G-6838)**
Unifirst Corporation 785 233-1550
1309 Nw Western Ave Topeka (66608) **(G-13203)**
Unifirst Corporation 316 264-2342
1707 N Mosley St Wichita (67214) **(G-15837)**
Unifirst Corporation 785 825-8766
1924 Jumper Rd Salina (67401) **(G-10745)**
Unifirst Corporation 620 275-0231
903 W Prospect Ave Garden City (67846) **(G-2306)**
Uniformed Services Beneft Assn 913 327-5500
7301 W 129th St Ste 200 Overland Park (66213) **(G-9440)**
Unimed II Inc (PA) 913 533-2202
6785 W 193rd St Stilwell (66085) **(G-12177)**
Union Bank and Trust Company 913 491-0909
11460 Tomahawk Creek Pkwy # 120 Leawood (66211) **(G-5589)**
Union Broadcasting Inc 913 344-1500
6721 W 121st St Ste 200 Shawnee Mission (66209) **(G-11961)**
Union Horse Distilling Co LLC 913 492-3275
11740 W 86th Ter Lenexa (66214) **(G-6200)**
Union Machine & Tool Works Inc 913 342-6000
1141 S 12th St Kansas City (66105) **(G-4486)**
Union Pacific Railroad Company 316 250-0260
1399 Oakmont St McPherson (67460) **(G-7034)**
Union Pacific Railroad Company 316 268-9446
2646 New York Ave Wichita (67219) **(G-15838)**
Union Pacific Railroad Company 785 232-7814
901 Nw Norris St Topeka (66608) **(G-13204)**
Union Pacific Railroad Company 209 642-1032
727 N Main St Pratt (67124) **(G-10163)**
Union Rescue Mission Inc 316 687-4673
2800 N Hillside Ave Wichita (67219) **(G-15839)**
Union State Bancshares Inc (PA) 620 756-4305
204 Sherman St Uniontown (66779) **(G-13333)**
Union State Bank (HQ) 620 442-5200
127 S Summit St Arkansas City (67005) **(G-186)**
Union State Bank 620 221-3040
823 Main St Winfield (67156) **(G-16177)**
Union State Bank (PA) 785 632-3122
701 5th St Clay Center (67432) **(G-885)**
Union State Bank Inc (PA) 785 468-3341
204 E Highway 16 Olsburg (66520) **(G-8169)**
Union State Bank Inc 785 293-5516
201 S Front St Randolph (66554) **(G-10191)**
Union State Bank of Everest (HQ) 785 548-7521
545 Main St Everest (66424) **(G-1903)**
Union State Bank of Everest 913 367-2700
701 Kansas Ave Atchison (66002) **(G-267)**
Union Valley Pto 620 662-4891
2501 E 30th Ave Hutchinson (67502) **(G-3475)**
Unique Design Inc 785 272-6044
1920 Sw Westport Dr # 100 Topeka (66604) **(G-13205)**
Unique Metal Fabrication Inc 620 232-3060
2888 N Rotary Ter Pittsburg (66762) **(G-9949)**
Unitas Global LLC 913 339-2300
9900 W 109th St Ste 400 Overland Park (66210) **(G-9441)**
United AG Service Inc 785 525-6455
300 W S Harvest St Lucas (67648) **(G-6475)**
United Agency Inc 620 442-0400
726 N Summit St Arkansas City (67005) **(G-187)**
United Auto Parts Inc 316 721-6868
14801 W Us Highway 54 Wichita (67235) **(G-15840)**
United Bank & Trust 785 284-2187
511 Paramount St Sabetha (66534) **(G-10335)**
United Bank & Trust 785 336-2123
602 North St Seneca (66538) **(G-10885)**

United Bank & Trust (PA)....785 562-4330
2333 Broadway Marysville (66508) ***(G-6912)***
United Bio Energy, Wichita *Also called Ube Services LLC* ***(G-15827)***
United Biosource LLC....913 339-7000
12900 Foster St Overland Park (66213) ***(G-9442)***
United Communications Assn Inc....620 227-8645
1107 W Mcartor Rd Dodge City (67801) ***(G-1442)***
United Disaster Response LLC....913 963-8403
5217 Walmer St Shawnee Mission (66202) ***(G-11962)***
United Distributors Inc (PA)....316 712-2174
420 S Seneca St Wichita (67213) ***(G-15841)***
United Distributors Inc....316 263-6181
420 S Seneca St Wichita (67213) ***(G-15842)***
United Engine Specialists, Wichita *Also called United Auto Parts Inc* ***(G-15840)***
United Healthcare Services Inc....888 340-9716
10895 Grandview Dr # 200 Overland Park (66210) ***(G-9443)***
United Industries Inc....620 278-3160
202 E Cleveland Ave Sterling (67579) ***(G-12131)***
United Machine Company Inc....316 264-3367
602 N Hydraulic St Wichita (67214) ***(G-15843)***
United Manufacturing Inc....913 780-0056
301 Overland Park Pl New Century (66031) ***(G-7302)***
United Medical Group LLC....913 287-7800
5701 State Ave Ste 100 Kansas City (66102) ***(G-4487)***
United Methodist Homes Inc....785 478-9440
7220 Sw Asbury Dr Topeka (66614) ***(G-13206)***
United Methodist Open Door....316 265-9371
402 E 2nd St N 220 Wichita (67202) ***(G-15844)***
UNITED METHODIST PRE SCHOOL, Topeka *Also called Countryside United Methdst Ch* ***(G-12516)***
United Methodist Western Kansa (PA)....620 275-1766
712 Saint John St Garden City (67846) ***(G-2307)***
United National Bank....785 483-2146
436 N Main St Russell (67665) ***(G-10301)***
United Office Products Inc....913 782-4441
601 W Dennis Ave Olathe (66061) ***(G-8132)***
United Omaha Life Insurance Co....913 402-1191
7200 W 132nd St Ste 270 Shawnee Mission (66213) ***(G-11963)***
United Parcel Service Inc....620 421-1346
1901 S 21st St Parsons (67357) ***(G-9747)***
United Parcel Service Inc....785 354-1111
126 Ne Madison St Topeka (66607) ***(G-13207)***
United Parcel Service Inc....785 628-3253
1101 General Custer Rd Hays (67601) ***(G-2922)***
United Parcel Service Inc....620 662-5961
2518 E 14th Ave Hutchinson (67501) ***(G-3476)***
United Parcel Service Inc....785 843-6530
331 Ne Industrial Ln Lawrence (66044) ***(G-5151)***
United Parcel Service Inc....316 946-4074
1935 S Air Cargo Rd Wichita (67209) ***(G-15845)***
United Parcel Service Inc....913 541-3700
14650 Santa Fe Trail Dr Lenexa (66215) ***(G-6201)***
United Parcel Service Inc....800 742-5877
1502 W North St Salina (67401) ***(G-10746)***
United Parcel Service Inc....316 941-2010
3003 S West St Wichita (67217) ***(G-15846)***
United Parcel Service Inc....913 599-0899
11944 W 95th St Shawnee Mission (66215) ***(G-11964)***
United Parcel Service Inc....913 573-4701
233 N James St Kansas City (66118) ***(G-4488)***
United Parcel Service Inc....913 894-0255
16200 W 110th St Lenexa (66219) ***(G-6202)***
United Parcel Service Inc....620 235-1220
2106 W 4th St Pittsburg (66762) ***(G-9950)***
United Petro Transports Inc....316 263-6868
6021 N Broadway Ave Park City (67219) ***(G-9651)***
United Pipe & Supply....785 357-0612
5111 Nw Us Highway 24 Topeka (66618) ***(G-13208)***
United Plains AG (PA)....785 852-4241
102 N Front St Sharon Springs (67758) ***(G-10901)***
United Prairie Ag LLC....620 356-2212
7119 E Highway 160 Ulysses (67880) ***(G-13329)***
United Prairie Ag LLC (PA)....620 356-1241
1125 W Oklahoma Ave Ulysses (67880) ***(G-13330)***
United Prarie AG....620 544-2017
509 Northwest Ave Hugoton (67951) ***(G-3179)***
United Ptriot Abtment Svcs LLC....785 856-1349
4000 W 6th St Ste B341 Lawrence (66049) ***(G-5152)***
United Rdlgy Group Chartered, Salina *Also called United Rdlgy Group Chartered* ***(G-10747)***
United Rdlgy Group Chartered....785 827-9526
148 S Santa Fe Ave Salina (67401) ***(G-10747)***
United Rentals North Amer Inc....785 272-6006
5830 Sw 19th Ter Topeka (66604) ***(G-13209)***
United Rentals North Amer Inc....785 838-4110
930 E 30th St Lawrence (66046) ***(G-5153)***
United Rentals North Amer Inc....316 722-7368
9127 W Kellogg Dr Wichita (67209) ***(G-15847)***
United Rentals North Amer Inc....620 245-0550
1101 W Woodside St McPherson (67460) ***(G-7035)***
United Rentals North Amer Inc....316 682-7368
9127 W Kellogg Dr Wichita (67209) ***(G-15848)***
United Rentals North Amer Inc....913 696-5628
11615 S Rogers Rd Olathe (66062) ***(G-8133)***
United Rotary Brush Corp (PA)....913 888-8450
15607 W 100th Ter Lenexa (66219) ***(G-6203)***
United Services Auto Assn....913 451-6100
10100 College Blvd Shawnee Mission (66210) ***(G-11965)***
United Sports of America, Salina *Also called USA Inc* ***(G-10748)***
United States Aviation Underwr....316 267-1325
301 N Main St Ste 1450 Wichita (67202) ***(G-15849)***
United States Awards Inc....620 231-8470
603 E Washington St Pittsburg (66762) ***(G-9951)***
United States Cellular Corp....620 231-2444
2597 S Broadway St Pittsburg (66762) ***(G-9952)***
United States Courts ADM....913 735-2242
500 State Ave Rm M35 Kansas City (66101) ***(G-4489)***
United States Cstm Harvesters....620 664-6297
119 W Sherman St Hutchinson (67501) ***(G-3477)***
United States Dept of Army....913 684-2747
821 Mcclellan Ave Fort Leavenworth (66027) ***(G-1942)***
United States Dept of Army....785 239-2385
407 Pershing Ct Fort Riley (66442) ***(G-1951)***
United States Dept of Army....913 684-6000
550 Pope Ave Fort Leavenworth (66027) ***(G-1943)***
United States Dept of Army....785 240-0308
7920 Apennines Dr Fort Riley (66442) ***(G-1952)***
United States Dept of Army....913 684-2151
821 Mcclellan Ave Fort Leavenworth (66027) ***(G-1944)***
United States Dept of Army....785 239-7000
650 Huebner Rd Fort Riley (66442) ***(G-1953)***
United States Systems Inc....913 281-1010
1028 Scott Ave Kansas City (66105) ***(G-4490)***
United States Tennis....913 322-4823
6400 W 95th St Ste 102 Overland Park (66212) ***(G-9444)***
United Steel Wrkrs of America....785 234-5688
1603 Nw Taylor St Topeka (66608) ***(G-13210)***
United Steelworkers....913 674-5067
625 Commercial St Ste 2 Atchison (66002) ***(G-268)***
United Sttes Bowl Congress Inc....913 631-7209
12210 Johnson Dr Shawnee (66216) ***(G-11043)***
United Tech Arospc Systems....316 721-3100
1643 S Maize Rd Wichita (67209) ***(G-15850)***
United Telephone Assn Inc (PA)....620 227-8641
1107 W Mcartor Rd Dodge City (67801) ***(G-1443)***
United Van Lines, Emporia *Also called Thomas Transfer & Stor Co Inc* ***(G-1838)***
United Van Lines, Wichita *Also called Thomas Transfer & Stor Co Inc* ***(G-15761)***
United Warehouse Company (PA)....316 712-1000
901 E 45th St N Park City (67219) ***(G-9652)***
United Water Works Co....913 287-1280
6636 Berger Ave Kansas City (66111) ***(G-4491)***
United Way of Greater Topeka....785 228-5110
1315 Sw Arrowhead Rd B Topeka (66604) ***(G-13211)***
United Way of McPherson County....620 241-5152
306 N Main St McPherson (67460) ***(G-7036)***
United Way of Wyandotte County....913 371-3674
434 Minnesota Ave Kansas City (66101) ***(G-4492)***
United West Community Cr Un (PA)....620 227-7181
1200 W Frontview St Dodge City (67801) ***(G-1444)***
United Wireless Communications, Dodge City *Also called United Telephone Assn Inc* ***(G-1443)***
United Wrless Cmmnications Inc....620 227-8127
1107 W Mcartor Rd Dodge City (67801) ***(G-1445)***
United Wrlss Arina Mgrk Conf C....620 371-7390
4100 W Comanche St Dodge City (67801) ***(G-1446)***
Unitedhealth Group Inc....952 936-1300
6860 W 115th St Overland Park (66211) ***(G-9445)***
Unitedlex Corporation (PA)....913 685-8900
6130 Sprint Pkwy Ste 300 Overland Park (66211) ***(G-9446)***
Unity Church of Overland Park....913 649-1750
10300 Antioch Rd Shawnee Mission (66212) ***(G-11966)***
Univar Solutions USA Inc....913 621-7494
5420 Speaker Rd Kansas City (66106) ***(G-4493)***
Univar Solutions USA Inc....316 267-1002
2041 N Mosley Ave Wichita (67214) ***(G-15851)***
Universal Avonics Systems Corp....316 524-9500
3815 Midco St Wichita (67215) ***(G-15852)***
Universal Cable Services Inc....913 481-7839
18900 W 158th St Ste F Olathe (66062) ***(G-8134)***
Universal Comfort Systems, Leawood *Also called Universal Mechanical LLC* ***(G-5590)***
Universal Communications LLC....913 839-1634
19915 W 161st St Ste E Olathe (66062) ***(G-8135)***
Universal Construction Co Inc (PA)....913 342-1150
1615 Argentine Blvd Kansas City (66105) ***(G-4494)***
Universal Construction Pdts....316 946-5885
3348 S Hoover Rd Wichita (67215) ***(G-15853)***
Universal Consulting & Svcs, Sabetha *Also called Usc LLC* ***(G-10336)***
Universal Electric Inc....913 238-3024
19947 W 162nd St Ste 103 Olathe (66062) ***(G-8136)***

ALPHABETIC

Universal Engraving Inc (PA)..........913 599-0600
9090 Nieman Rd Overland Park (66214) ***(G-9447)***
Universal Lubricants, Wichita *Also called Clean Harbors Wichita LLC* ***(G-14039)***
Universal Machining Shtmtl Inc..........316 425-7610
116 S Lulu Ave Wichita (67211) ***(G-15854)***
Universal Management Inc (PA)..........913 321-3521
1021 N 7th St Ste 106 Kansas City (66101) ***(G-4495)***
Universal Manufacturing Co..........816 231-2771
5030 Mackey St Shawnee (66203) ***(G-11044)***
Universal Mechanical LLC..........573 636-8373
2804 W 132nd St Leawood (66209) ***(G-5590)***
Universal Money Center, Lenexa *Also called Electronic Funds Transfer Inc* ***(G-5831)***
Universal Money Centers Inc (PA)..........913 831-2055
15301 W 87th Street Pkwy Lenexa (66219) ***(G-6204)***
Universal Motor Fuels Inc..........316 832-0151
2824 N Ohio St Wichita (67219) ***(G-15855)***
Universal Oil, Kansas City *Also called Clean Harbors Wichita LLC* ***(G-3919)***
Universal Products Inc..........316 794-8601
521 Industrial Rd Goddard (67052) ***(G-2455)***
Universal Sign & Display LLC..........785 242-8111
1535 N Industrial Ave Ottawa (66067) ***(G-8317)***
University Daily Kansan..........785 864-4358
120 Stauffer Flint Hall Lawrence (66045) ***(G-5154)***
University Kans Med Ctr Police, Kansas City *Also called University of Kansas* ***(G-4499)***
University Kansas Alumni Assn..........785 864-4760
1266 Oread Ave Lawrence (66045) ***(G-5155)***
University Kansas Health Sys, Kansas City *Also called University of Kansas Hosp Auth* ***(G-4506)***
University Kansas Mem Corp (PA)..........785 864-4651
1301 Jayhawk Blvd Lawrence (66045) ***(G-5156)***
University Nat Bnk of Lawrence..........785 841-1988
1400 Kasold Dr Lawrence (66049) ***(G-5157)***
University of Kansas, Kansas City *Also called Kansas Univ Physicians Inc* ***(G-4158)***
University of Kansas..........785 864-2277
2100 Watkins Health Ctr Lawrence (66045) ***(G-5158)***
University of Kansas..........785 864-9520
1200 Schwegler Dr Lawrence (66045) ***(G-5159)***
University of Kansas..........913 677-1590
4350 Shawnee Mission Pkwy Fairway (66205) ***(G-1924)***
University of Kansas..........785 864-8885
1425 Jayhawk Blvd Rm 210s Lawrence (66045) ***(G-5160)***
University of Kansas..........913 588-5238
3901 Rainbow Blvd Shawnee Mission (66213) ***(G-11967)***
University of Kansas..........913 588-6798
3901 Rainbow Blvd Kansas City (66160) ***(G-4496)***
University of Kansas..........785 864-1500
Constant Ave Lawrence (66047) ***(G-5161)***
University of Kansas..........913 588-5900
3901 Rainbow Blvd Kansas City (66160) ***(G-4497)***
University of Kansas..........913 588-4718
3901 Rainbow Blvd Kansas City (66160) ***(G-4498)***
University of Kansas..........913 588-5133
115 Support Services Bldg Kansas City (66106) ***(G-4499)***
University of Kansas..........785 864-4780
1122 W Campus Rd Lawrence (66045) ***(G-5162)***
University of Kansas..........913 588-5000
3901 Rainbow Blvd Kansas City (66160) ***(G-4500)***
University of Kansas..........316 293-2607
1010 N Kansas St Ste 3007 Wichita (67214) ***(G-15856)***
University of Kansas..........913 588-1443
3901 Rainbow Blvd Kansas City (66160) ***(G-4501)***
University of Kansas..........913 588-5436
3901 Rainbow Blvd Kansas City (66160) ***(G-4502)***
University of Kansas..........785 864-2700
1000 Sunnyside Ave Lawrence (66045) ***(G-5163)***
University of Kansas..........785 864-2451
Spooner Hall 1430 Jy Hawk Lawrence (66045) ***(G-5164)***
University of Kansas..........785 864-4710
1301 Mississippi St Lawrence (66045) ***(G-5165)***
University of Kansas..........785 864-4154
2502 Westbrooke Cir Lawrence (66045) ***(G-5166)***
University of Kansas..........316 293-2620
1010 N Kansas St Wichita (67214) ***(G-15857)***
University of Kansas..........913 588-7015
2010 W 39th Ave Kansas City (66103) ***(G-4503)***
University of Kansas..........913 588-2720
4004 Robinson Hall Mail Kansas City (66160) ***(G-4504)***
University of Kansas..........785 864-4540
1345 Jayhawk Blvd Lawrence (66045) ***(G-5167)***
University of Kansas..........913 588-6000
3901 Rainbow Blvd Kansas City (66160) ***(G-4505)***
University of Kansas Hosp Auth (PA)..........913 588-5000
4000 Cambridge St Kansas City (66160) ***(G-4506)***
University of Kansas Hospital..........913 682-6950
3601 S 4th St Ste 1 Leavenworth (66048) ***(G-5303)***
University of Kansas Hospital..........913 588-5000
3901 Rainbow Blvd Kansas City (66160) ***(G-4507)***
University of Kansas Hospital..........913 588-8400
7405 Renner Rd Shawnee Mission (66217) ***(G-11968)***
University of Kansas Mdcl Ctr, Kansas City *Also called University of Kansas* ***(G-4502)***
University of Kansas Med Ctr..........913 945-5598
2330 Shawnee Mission Pkwy Westwood (66205) ***(G-13562)***
University of Kansas Med Ctr..........913 588-6311
3901 Rainbow Blvd # 4004 Kansas City (66160) ***(G-4508)***
University of Kansas Med Ctr..........913 588-6805
3901 Rainbow Blvd Kansas City (66160) ***(G-4509)***
UNIVERSITY OF KANSAS MEDICAL C, Great Bend *Also called Ukhs Great Bend LLC* ***(G-2650)***
University of Kansas School of..........316 293-3432
1010 N Kansas St Rm 3049 Wichita (67214) ***(G-15858)***
University of KS Medcl (HQ)..........913 588-1261
4330 Shawnee Mission Pkwy Fairway (66205) ***(G-1925)***
University Physcans Dlysis Ctr, Kansas City *Also called Nra-Ukmc Kansas LLC* ***(G-4290)***
University Press, Lawrence *Also called University of Kansas* ***(G-5166)***
University Press of Kansas..........785 864-4155
2502 Westbrooke Cir Lawrence (66045) ***(G-5168)***
Unlimited Logistics LLC..........913 851-4900
7500 W 161st St Stilwell (66085) ***(G-12178)***
Unlimited Service Options LLC..........316 522-1503
1920 E Northern St Wichita (67216) ***(G-15859)***
Unrein, Eric I, Topeka *Also called Michael J Unrein Atty* ***(G-12888)***
Unruh Excavating LLC..........620 345-3344
10028 N Hertzler Rd Moundridge (67107) ***(G-7200)***
Unruh Fab Inc (PA)..........316 772-5400
100 Indl Dr Sedgwick (67135) ***(G-10853)***
Unruh Fire Inc (HQ)..........316 772-5400
100 E Industrial Dr Sedgwick (67135) ***(G-10854)***
Unruh Sand & Gravel..........620 582-2774
P.O. Box 462 Coldwater (67029) ***(G-1058)***
Unruh-Foster Inc (PA)..........620 846-2215
501 E Texcoco St Montezuma (67867) ***(G-7161)***
Unxmed-Immediate Medical Care..........316 440-2565
4722 W Kellogg Dr Wichita (67209) ***(G-15860)***
Upg Solutions LLC..........844 737-0365
8700 State Line Rd 250 Leawood (66206) ***(G-5591)***
Upland Mutual Insurance Inc..........785 762-4324
2220 Lacy Dr Junction City (66441) ***(G-3761)***
Upper Lake Processing Services..........855 418-9500
7201 W 110th St Ste 225 Overland Park (66210) ***(G-9448)***
UPS, Parsons *Also called United Parcel Service Inc* ***(G-9747)***
UPS, Wichita *Also called Nadia Inc* ***(G-15145)***
UPS, Topeka *Also called United Parcel Service Inc* ***(G-13207)***
UPS, Hays *Also called United Parcel Service Inc* ***(G-2922)***
UPS, Hutchinson *Also called United Parcel Service Inc* ***(G-3476)***
UPS, Lawrence *Also called United Parcel Service Inc* ***(G-5151)***
UPS, Wichita *Also called United Parcel Service Inc* ***(G-15845)***
UPS, Lenexa *Also called United Parcel Service Inc* ***(G-6201)***
UPS, Salina *Also called United Parcel Service Inc* ***(G-10746)***
UPS, Wichita *Also called United Parcel Service Inc* ***(G-15846)***
UPS, Shawnee Mission *Also called United Parcel Service Inc* ***(G-11964)***
UPS, Kansas City *Also called United Parcel Service Inc* ***(G-4488)***
UPS, Lenexa *Also called United Parcel Service Inc* ***(G-6202)***
UPS, Pittsburg *Also called United Parcel Service Inc* ***(G-9950)***
UPS Express Critical, Overland Park *Also called UPS Supply Chain Solutions Inc* ***(G-9450)***
UPS Ground Freight Inc..........913 281-0055
3800 Kansas Ave Kansas City (66106) ***(G-4510)***
UPS Srvice Parts Logistics Inc..........800 451-4550
10881 Lowell Ave Ste 220 Overland Park (66210) ***(G-9449)***
UPS Store 4657, Lenexa *Also called Jasper Investments Inc* ***(G-5928)***
UPS Store, The, Shawnee Mission *Also called Waisner Inc* ***(G-11989)***
UPS Supply Chain Solutions Inc..........800 714-8779
10881 Lowell Ave Overland Park (66210) ***(G-9450)***
Upsilon Chapter Alpha PHI Intl..........785 233-7466
1839 Sw Jewell Ave Topeka (66621) ***(G-13212)***
Upu Industries Inc..........785 238-6990
3002 Indl St Junction City (66441) ***(G-3762)***
Urban League of Kansas Inc..........316 440-9217
2418 E 9th St N Wichita (67214) ***(G-15861)***
Urban League of Mid Plains, Wichita *Also called Unified School District 259* ***(G-15835)***
Urban Ministries Institute, Wichita *Also called World Impact Inc* ***(G-16073)***
Urban Outfitters Inc..........785 331-2885
1013 Massachusetts St Lawrence (66044) ***(G-5169)***
Uriolgist Center of Olthe, Leawood *Also called Mid America Urology PC* ***(G-5479)***
Urologic Surgery Associates PA (PA)..........913 438-3833
10550 Quivira Rd Ste 105 Shawnee Mission (66215) ***(G-11969)***
Urology Associates Topeka PA..........785 233-4256
823 Sw Mulvane St Ste 275 Topeka (66606) ***(G-13213)***
US Attorneys Office - Dst Kans..........316 269-6481
301 N Main St Ste 1200 Wichita (67202) ***(G-15862)***
US Bank, Lawrence *Also called US Bank National Association* ***(G-5170)***
US Bank, Lawrence *Also called US Bank National Association* ***(G-5171)***
US Bank, Overland Park *Also called US Bank National Association* ***(G-9451)***
US Bank, Prairie Village *Also called US Bank National Association* ***(G-10079)***
US Bank, Overland Park *Also called US Bank National Association* ***(G-9452)***

US Bank, Overland Park *Also called US Bank National Association* ***(G-9453)***
US Bank, Pittsburg *Also called US Bank National Association* ***(G-9953)***
US Bank, Overland Park *Also called US Bank National Association* ***(G-9454)***
US Bank, Leawood *Also called US Bank National Association* ***(G-5592)***
US Bank, Shawnee *Also called US Bank National Association* ***(G-11045)***
US Bank, Overland Park *Also called US Bank National Association* ***(G-9455)***
US Bank, Lawrence *Also called US Bank National Association* ***(G-5172)***
US Bank, Merriam *Also called US Bank National Association* ***(G-7108)***
US Bank, Overland Park *Also called US Bank National Association* ***(G-9456)***
US Bank, Roeland Park *Also called US Bank National Association* ***(G-10230)***
US Bank, Topeka *Also called US Bank National Association* ***(G-13214)***
US Bank National Association 785 312-5280
2701 Iowa St Lawrence (66046) ***(G-5170)***
US Bank National Association 785 312-5060
3500 W 6th St Lawrence (66049) ***(G-5171)***
US Bank National Association 913 432-9633
7000 W 75th St Overland Park (66204) ***(G-9451)***
US Bank National Association 913 261-5663
6940 Mission Rd Prairie Village (66208) ***(G-10079)***
US Bank National Association 913 323-5314
10100 W 119th St Overland Park (66213) ***(G-9452)***
US Bank National Association 913 338-0646
6450 Sprint Pkwy Overland Park (66251) ***(G-9453)***
US Bank National Association 620 231-4040
306 N Broadway St Ste 100 Pittsburg (66762) ***(G-9953)***
US Bank National Association 913 725-7000
12800 Foster St Overland Park (66213) ***(G-9454)***
US Bank National Association 913 383-2126
3700 W 95th St Leawood (66206) ***(G-5592)***
US Bank National Association 913 248-1001
12010 W 63rd St Shawnee (66216) ***(G-11045)***
US Bank National Association 913 402-6919
6900 W 135th St Overland Park (66223) ***(G-9455)***
US Bank National Association 785 312-6880
1807 W 23rd St Lawrence (66046) ***(G-5172)***
US Bank National Association 913 671-2723
8600 Shwn Mssn Pkwy A Merriam (66202) ***(G-7108)***
US Bank National Association 913 239-8204
8401 W 135th St Overland Park (66223) ***(G-9456)***
US Bank National Association 913 261-5401
4970 Roe Blvd Roeland Park (66205) ***(G-10230)***
US Bank National Association 785 276-6300
719 S Kansas Ave Topeka (66603) ***(G-13214)***
US Boatworks Inc 913 342-0011
930 Osage Ave Kansas City (66105) ***(G-4511)***
US Filter, Overland Park *Also called Evoqua Water Technologies LLC* ***(G-8697)***
US Foods Inc 316 942-9679
3409 W 29th St S Wichita (67217) ***(G-15863)***
US Foods Inc 913 894-6161
16805 College Blvd Lenexa (66219) ***(G-6205)***
US Healthworks Medical Group 913 495-9905
15319 W 95th St Lenexa (66219) ***(G-6206)***
US Minerals Inc 219 798-5472
911 Linnco Dr La Cygne (66040) ***(G-4645)***
US Pipe Fabrication LLC 785 242-6284
1534 N Industrial Ave Ottawa (66067) ***(G-8318)***
US Probation & Parole Office, Topeka *Also called Supreme Court United States* ***(G-13126)***
US Road Freight, Wichita *Also called U S Road Freight Express Inc* ***(G-15825)***
US Textiles LLC (PA) 913 660-0995
9540 W 62nd St Shawnee Mission (66203) ***(G-11970)***
US Tower Corp (PA) 785 524-9966
702 E North St Lincoln (67455) ***(G-6389)***
USA Gym Supply 620 792-2800
1721 4th St Great Bend (67530) ***(G-2652)***
USA Gym Supply Inc (PA) 620 792-2209
319 Mckinley St Great Bend (67530) ***(G-2653)***
USA Inc (PA) 785 825-6247
122 S Santa Fe Ave Salina (67401) ***(G-10748)***
USA Missions Church of God 620 345-2532
100 S Avenue C Moundridge (67107) ***(G-7201)***
USAA, Shawnee Mission *Also called United Services Auto Assn* ***(G-11965)***
Usaig, Wichita *Also called United States Aviation Underwr* ***(G-15849)***
Usc LLC 785 431-7900
2320 124th Rd Sabetha (66534) ***(G-10336)***
Usd 383 Mnhttan Ogden Schl Dst 785 587-2180
2031 Casement Rd Manhattan (66502) ***(G-6839)***
Usd 443, Dodge City *Also called Dodge Cy Unified Schl Dst 443* ***(G-1354)***
USF Holland LLC 913 287-1770
9711 State Ave Kansas City (66111) ***(G-4512)***
USFreightways, Kansas City *Also called USF Holland LLC* ***(G-4512)***
USI Insurance Services LLC 316 263-3211
245 N Waco St Ste 412 Wichita (67202) ***(G-15864)***
Usoc, Wichita *Also called Unlimited Service Options LLC* ***(G-15859)***
USP Technical Services 310 517-1800
7311 E 58th St S Derby (67037) ***(G-1278)***
Uspa, Leavenworth *Also called First Command Fincl Plg Inc* ***(G-5239)***
USTA, Overland Park *Also called United States Tennis* ***(G-9444)***
Uswa, Atchison *Also called United Steelworkers* ***(G-268)***
Utah Machine & Mill Supply 801 364-2812
5844 N Broadway Ave Park City (67219) ***(G-9653)***
UTC Aerospace Systems, Wichita *Also called United Tech Arospc Systems* ***(G-15850)***
Utilities Plus Inc 316 946-9416
3505 W 30th St S Wichita (67217) ***(G-15865)***
Utility Contractors Inc (PA) 316 942-1253
1930 S Hoover Rd Ste 100 Wichita (67209) ***(G-15866)***
Utility Maintenance Contrs LLC 316 945-8833
4151 N Seneca St Wichita (67204) ***(G-15867)***
V & M Transport Inc 620 662-7281
301 N Kirby St Hutchinson (67501) ***(G-3478)***
V & R Motel LLC 620 331-8288
2800 W Main St Independence (67301) ***(G-3570)***
V & V Electric Company Inc 785 539-1975
629 Pecan Cir Manhattan (66502) ***(G-6840)***
V & V Electric Inc 785 468-3364
7860 Greene Rd Olsburg (66520) ***(G-8170)***
V G Electracon Inc 913 780-9995
1812 E 123rd St Olathe (66061) ***(G-8137)***
V H C Van Hoecke Htg & Coolg, Lenexa *Also called Vhc Van Hoecke Contracting Inc* ***(G-6212)***
V Mach Inc 913 894-2001
10936 Eicher Dr Shawnee Mission (66219) ***(G-11971)***
V W C Inc 316 262-4422
1411 N Broadway Ave Wichita (67214) ***(G-15868)***
V Wealth Advisors LLC 913 827-4600
6800 College Blvd Ste 630 Overland Park (66211) ***(G-9457)***
V Wealth Management, Overland Park *Also called V Wealth Advisors LLC* ***(G-9457)***
VA Hospital, Topeka *Also called Veterans Health Administration* ***(G-13222)***
Vail Products, Horton *Also called Hammersmith Mfg & Sales Inc* ***(G-3126)***
Val Energy Inc 316 263-6688
125 N Market St Ste 1710 Wichita (67202) ***(G-15869)***
Val Pak of Kansas City, Shawnee Mission *Also called Adkins Systems Inc* ***(G-11076)***
Valent Aerostructures LLC 316 682-4551
2853 S Hillside St Wichita (67216) ***(G-15870)***
Valent Aerostructures LLC (HQ) 816 423-5600
11064 Strang Line Rd Lenexa (66215) ***(G-6207)***
Valent Aerostructures LLC 620 378-4441
1075 Fillmore St Fredonia (66736) ***(G-2048)***
Valent Arstrctres - Lenexa LLC 913 469-6400
11064 Strang Line Rd Shawnee Mission (66215) ***(G-11972)***
Valeo Behavioral Health Care 785 233-1730
330 Sw Oakley Ave Topeka (66606) ***(G-13215)***
Valeo Behavioral Hlth Care Inc (PA) 785 273-2252
5401 Sw 7th St Topeka (66606) ***(G-13216)***
Valeo Behavioral Hlth Care Inc 785 233-1730
400 Sw Oakley Ave Topeka (66606) ***(G-13217)***
Valiant Global Def Svcs Inc 913 651-9782
426 Delaware St Ste C3 Leavenworth (66048) ***(G-5304)***
Validity Screening Solutions, Overland Park *Also called 1138 Inc* ***(G-8328)***
Valley Center City Yard 316 755-7320
545 W Clay St Valley Center (67147) ***(G-13358)***
Valley Center Pre School, Valley Center *Also called First United Methodist Church* ***(G-13342)***
Valley Falls Medical Clinic, Valley Falls *Also called St Francis Hospital* ***(G-13369)***
Valley Feed & Supply Co., Bonner Springs *Also called Vfs Acquisition Corp* ***(G-579)***
Valley Feeds Inc 785 854-7611
2 1/2 Mile W Long Island (67647) ***(G-6429)***
Valley Floral Company LLC (PA) 316 838-3355
4619 N Arkansas Ave Wichita (67204) ***(G-15871)***
Valley Health Care Center, Valley Falls *Also called Midwest Health Services Inc* ***(G-13368)***
Valley Hope Association (PA) 785 877-2421
103 S Wabash Ave Norton (67654) ***(G-7463)***
Valley Hope Association 785 877-5101
709 W Holme St Norton (67654) ***(G-7464)***
Valley Hope Association 913 367-1618
1816 N 2nd St Atchison (66002) ***(G-269)***
Valley Hope Treatment Center, Norton *Also called Valley Hope Association* ***(G-7463)***
Valley Hope Treatment Center, Norton *Also called Valley Hope Association* ***(G-7464)***
Valley Machinery Inc 316 755-1911
11402 N Broadway St Valley Center (67147) ***(G-13359)***
Valley Moving, Wamego *Also called Wamego Lumber Co Inc* ***(G-13453)***
Valley Moving Company LLC 785 456-2400
18162 Hwy 24 Ste 1 Wamego (66547) ***(G-13445)***
Valley Offset Printing Inc 316 755-0061
160 S Sheridan Ave Valley Center (67147) ***(G-13360)***
Valley Property, Olathe *Also called Still Builders Inc* ***(G-8083)***
Valley Realtors Inc (PA) 785 233-4222
600 Sw Van Buren St Topeka (66603) ***(G-13218)***
Valley Springs 785 256-7100
280 Valley Springs Dr Auburn (66402) ***(G-298)***
Valley State Bank 620 488-2211
502 N Merchant St Belle Plaine (67013) ***(G-449)***
Valley State Bank (HQ) 620 384-7451
110 W Ave B Syracuse (67878) ***(G-12236)***
Valley State Bank The, Belle Plaine *Also called Morley Bancshares Corporation* ***(G-448)***
VALLEY STATE BANK THE, Belle Plaine *Also called Valley State Bank* ***(G-449)***

ALPHABETIC

Valley Trucking Trailer....785 945-3554
1401 K4 Hwy Valley Falls (66088) ***(G-13370)***
Valley View Greenhouse LLC....785 549-3621
31272 S Croco Rd Melvern (66510) ***(G-7077)***
Valley View Milling....785 858-4777
2875 State Highway 63 Seneca (66538) ***(G-10886)***
Valley View Milling LLC....785 858-4777
2875 State Highway 63 Seneca (66538) ***(G-10887)***
Valley View Mothers Day Out, Shawnee Mission *Also called Kansas East Conference United* ***(G-11517)***
Valley View Senior Life LLC....316 733-1144
1417 W Ash St Junction City (66441) ***(G-3763)***
Valley View State Bank (HQ)....913 381-3311
7500 W 95th St Shawnee Mission (66212) ***(G-11973)***
Valley View State Bank....913 381-3311
10300 Mastin St Overland Park (66212) ***(G-9458)***
Valley View State Bank....913 381-3311
11813 Roe Ave Shawnee Mission (66211) ***(G-11974)***
Valley Vista, Junction City *Also called Life Care Services LLC* ***(G-3721)***
Valmont Ctngs Slina Glvanizing, Salina *Also called Valmont Industries Inc* ***(G-10749)***
Valmont Industries Inc....316 321-1201
955 N Haverhill Rd El Dorado (67042) ***(G-1611)***
Valmont Industries Inc....785 452-9630
1100 N Ohio St Salina (67401) ***(G-10749)***
Valu Merchandisers Company....620 223-1313
4805 Campbell Dr Fort Scott (66701) ***(G-2014)***
Valu Merchandisers Company (HQ)....913 319-8500
5000 Kansas Ave Kansas City (66106) ***(G-4513)***
Value Place Hotel....913 831-1417
6950 Foxridge Dr Shawnee Mission (66202) ***(G-11975)***
Value Place Topeka....785 271-8862
7200 W 132nd St Ste 220 Overland Park (66213) ***(G-9459)***
Van Booven Lawn & Landscaping....913 722-3275
10021 Woodend Rd Edwardsville (66111) ***(G-1520)***
Van Lerberg Robert Foundations, Shawnee Mission *Also called Robert Vanlerberg Foundations* ***(G-11809)***
Van Petten Animal Health Inc....785 484-3358
7146 K4 Hwy Meriden (66512) ***(G-7083)***
Van-Wall Equipment Inc....913 397-6009
1362 S Enterprise St Olathe (66061) ***(G-8138)***
Vanberg Specialized Coatings....913 948-9825
10705 Cottonwood St Lenexa (66215) ***(G-6208)***
Vanguard Industries Inc (PA)....620 241-6369
831 N Vanguard St McPherson (67460) ***(G-7037)***
Vanguard Piping Systems Inc (HQ)....620 241-6369
2211 Viega Ave McPherson (67460) ***(G-7038)***
Vanguard Plastics Inc....620 241-6369
901 N Vanguard St McPherson (67460) ***(G-7039)***
Vanguard Shrink Films Inc....913 599-1111
16945 W 116th St Lenexa (66219) ***(G-6209)***
Vannahmen Construction Inc....785 494-2354
3541 Vineyard Rd Saint George (66535) ***(G-10348)***
Varney & Associates Cpas LLC (PA)....785 537-2202
120 N Juliette Ave Manhattan (66502) ***(G-6841)***
Vascular Surgery Associates PA (PA)....913 262-9201
7420 Switzer St Shawnee (66203) ***(G-11046)***
Vbc Enterprises LLC....316 789-0114
1300 N Nelson Dr Derby (67037) ***(G-1279)***
Vchp Wichita LLC....316 685-1281
7335 E Kellogg Dr Wichita (67207) ***(G-15872)***
Vector Technologies Inc....620 262-2700
22245 C St Winfield (67156) ***(G-16178)***
Vector Tooling Technologies, Winfield *Also called Vector Technologies Inc* ***(G-16178)***
Vee Village Parts Inc (PA)....816 421-6441
15145 Sweetbriar Dr Basehor (66007) ***(G-390)***
Vegetation Management Supply, Kansas City *Also called Chem-Trol Inc* ***(G-3909)***
Vektek LLC (PA)....620 342-7637
1334 E 6th Ave Emporia (66801) ***(G-1845)***
Vello Kass MD....316 283-3600
720 Medical Center Dr Newton (67114) ***(G-7423)***
Velociti Inc....913 233-7230
120 Kansas Ave Kansas City (66105) ***(G-4514)***
Velocity Manufacturing Co LLC....620 223-1277
523 E Wall St Fort Scott (66701) ***(G-2015)***
Velocity Staff Inc....913 693-4626
5251 W 116th Pl Ste 200 Overland Park (66211) ***(G-9460)***
Vend-Tech Enterprise LLC....316 689-6850
250 N Rock Rd Ste 360 Wichita (67206) ***(G-15873)***
Ventra Kansas LLC....913 334-0614
900 S 68th St Kansas City (66111) ***(G-4515)***
Ventria Bioscience Inc....785 238-1101
2718 Industrial St Junction City (66441) ***(G-3764)***
Ventura Hotel Corp....785 841-3100
730 New Hampshire St # 206 Lawrence (66044) ***(G-5173)***
Venture Construction Company....913 642-2972
7010 W 107th St Ste 220 Overland Park (66212) ***(G-9461)***
Venture Corporation....620 792-5921
214 S Us Highway 281 Great Bend (67530) ***(G-2654)***
Venture Hotels LLC....620 231-1177
4011 Parkview Dr Pittsburg (66762) ***(G-9954)***
Veolia Water North America Ope....785 762-5855
2101 N Jackson St Junction City (66441) ***(G-3765)***
Veracity Consulting Inc....913 945-1912
8100 Newton St Overland Park (66204) ***(G-9462)***
Verde Oil Company....620 754-3800
3345 Arizona Rd Savonburg (66772) ***(G-10793)***
Veridian Behavorial Health....785 452-4930
501 S Santa Fe Ave # 300 Salina (67401) ***(G-10750)***
Veriprime Inc....620 873-7175
806 E Washington St Meade (67864) ***(G-7055)***
Veritiv Operating Company....913 667-1500
2552 S 98th St Kansas City (66111) ***(G-4516)***
Veritiv Operating Company....913 492-5050
10960 Lakeview Ave Kansas City (66101) ***(G-4517)***
Veritiv Operating Company....785 862-2233
3721 Sw South Park Ave Topeka (66609) ***(G-13219)***
Veritiv Operating Company....316 522-3494
4700 S Palisade Ave Wichita (67217) ***(G-15874)***
Veritiv Operating Company....620 231-2508
3004 N Rotary Ter Pittsburg (66762) ***(G-9955)***
Verizon, Wichita *Also called Cellco Partnership* ***(G-13970)***
Verizon Wireless, Overland Park *Also called Cellco Partnership* ***(G-8535)***
Verizon Wireless, Garden City *Also called Cellco Partnership* ***(G-2122)***
Verizon Wireless, Derby *Also called Cellco Partnership* ***(G-1228)***
Verizon Wireless, Manhattan *Also called Cellco Partnership* ***(G-6580)***
Verizon Wireless, Wichita *Also called Cellco Partnership* ***(G-13971)***
Verizon Wireless, Overland Park *Also called Cellco Partnership* ***(G-8536)***
Verizon Wreless Authorized Ret, Pratt *Also called ABC Phones North Carolina Inc* ***(G-10091)***
Vermeer Equipment, Olathe *Also called Vermeer Great Plains Inc* ***(G-8139)***
Vermeer Great Plains Inc (PA)....913 782-3655
15505 S Us 169 Hwy Olathe (66062) ***(G-8139)***
Vermillion Incorporated....316 524-3100
4754 S Palisade St Wichita (67217) ***(G-15875)***
Vernies Trux-N-Equip Inc....785 625-5087
655 E 41st St Hays (67601) ***(G-2923)***
Vernon D Rowe, MD, Shawnee Mission *Also called Consultants In Neurology PA* ***(G-11262)***
Vernon Enterprises....620 343-9111
700 Overlander Rd Emporia (66801) ***(G-1846)***
Vernon Jewelers of Salina Inc....785 825-0531
123 N Santa Fe Ave Salina (67401) ***(G-10751)***
Vernon L Goedecke Company Inc....913 621-1284
1413 Osage Ave Kansas City (66105) ***(G-4518)***
Versacourt Multi Sport Game Co, Wichita *Also called Versasport of Kansas Inc* ***(G-15876)***
Versaflex Inc (PA)....913 321-9000
686 S Adams St Kansas City (66105) ***(G-4519)***
Versasport of Kansas Inc....316 393-0487
6801 N Meridian Ave Wichita (67204) ***(G-15876)***
Vertical 1 Inc....913 829-8100
19906 W 99th St Lenexa (66220) ***(G-6210)***
Vess Oil Corporation....316 682-1537
1700 N Waterfront Pkwy # 500 Wichita (67206) ***(G-15877)***
Vesta Lee Lumber Company, Bonner Springs *Also called E D Bishop Lumber Muncie Inc* ***(G-552)***
Vet Medical Surgery....785 267-6060
1515 Sw 29th St Topeka (66611) ***(G-13220)***
Veteran Fdsrvice Solutions LLC....913 307-9922
8811 Long St Lenexa (66215) ***(G-6211)***
Veterans Affairs Kans Comm On....785 350-4489
2200 Sw Gage Blvd Topeka (66622) ***(G-13221)***
Veterans Fgn Wars Post 9076....785 625-9940
2106 Vine St Hays (67601) ***(G-2924)***
Veterans Health Administration....316 685-2221
5500 E Kellogg Dr Wichita (67218) ***(G-15878)***
Veterans Health Administration....785 350-3111
2200 Sw Gage Blvd Topeka (66622) ***(G-13222)***
Veterans Health Administration....785 826-1580
1410 E Iron Ave Ste 1 Salina (67401) ***(G-10752)***
Veterans Health Administration....620 423-3858
1401 Main St Parsons (67357) ***(G-9748)***
Veterinary Clinic....785 242-4780
3633 Highway 59 Ottawa (66067) ***(G-8319)***
VETERINARY DIAGNOSTIC LABORATO, Manhattan *Also called K-State Diagnostic & Analyticl* ***(G-6669)***
Veterinary Hospital, Dodge City *Also called Libel & Ripple Dvm* ***(G-1399)***
Veterinary Research and Cnslt....785 324-9200
4413 Larned Cir Hays (67601) ***(G-2925)***
Veternary Emrgncy Clnic Wchita, Wichita *Also called Wichita Emrgncy Veterinary LLC* ***(G-15997)***
Vetlife, Lenexa *Also called Ivy Animal Health Inc* ***(G-5924)***
Vets First Choice, Manhattan *Also called Direct Vet Marketing Inc* ***(G-6614)***
Vf Outdoor Inc....913 384-4000
16910 W 116th St Shawnee Mission (66219) ***(G-11976)***
Vfs Acquisition Corp....913 422-4088
600 W 2nd St Bonner Springs (66012) ***(G-579)***

Vhc Van Hoecke Contracting Inc 913 888-0036
14150 Santa Fe Trail Dr Lenexa (66215) ***(G-6212)***
Via Christi 316 613-4931
1947 N Founders Cir Wichita (67206) ***(G-15879)***
Via Christi Clinic PA 316 613-4680
1947 N Founders Cir Wichita (67206) ***(G-15880)***
Via Christi Clinic PA 316 789-8222
1720 E Osage Rd Derby (67037) ***(G-1280)***
Via Christi Clinic PA (HQ) 316 689-9111
3311 E Murdock St Wichita (67208) ***(G-15881)***
Via Christi Clinic PA 316 945-5400
14700 W Saint Teresa St Wichita (67235) ***(G-15882)***
Via Christi Clinic PA 316 609-4440
9211 E 21st St N Ste 100 Wichita (67206) ***(G-15883)***
Via Christi Clinic PA 316 689-9111
3311 E Murdock St Wichita (67208) ***(G-15884)***
Via Christi Clinic PA 316 689-9111
3243 E Murdock St Ste 300 Wichita (67208) ***(G-15885)***
Via Christi Clinic PA 316 651-2252
818 N Carriage Pkwy Ste 2 Wichita (67208) ***(G-15886)***
Via Christi Clinic PA 316 733-6618
612 N Andover Rd Andover (67002) ***(G-113)***
Via Christi Foundation Inc 316 239-3520
8200 E Thorn Dr Ste 200 Wichita (67226) ***(G-15887)***
VIA CHRISTI HEALTH, Pittsburg *Also called Via Christi Vlg Pittsburg Inc* ***(G-9956)***
Via Christi Health Inc 785 456-6288
711 Genn Dr Wamego (66547) ***(G-13446)***
Via Christi Health Inc 316 773-4500
13610 W Maple St Wichita (67235) ***(G-15888)***
Via Christi Health Inc 316 268-7000
14800 W Saint Teresa St Wichita (67235) ***(G-15889)***
Via Christi Health Inc 316 685-0400
1655 S Georgetown St Ofc Wichita (67218) ***(G-15890)***
Via Christi Health Inc (HQ) 316 858-4900
2622 W Central Ave # 102 Wichita (67203) ***(G-15891)***
Via Christi Hlth Partners Inc (HQ) 316 719-3240
8200 E Thorn Dr Ste 300 Wichita (67226) ***(G-15892)***
Via Christi Hope Inc 316 858-1111
2622 W Central Ave # 101 Wichita (67203) ***(G-15893)***
Via Christi Hospital, Wichita *Also called Via Chrsti Rhbltation Hosp Inc* ***(G-15902)***
Via Christi Hospital 316 796-7000
14800 W Saint Teresa St Wichita (67235) ***(G-15894)***
Via Christi Medical Management 316 268-8123
1100 N St Francis St # 200 Wichita (67214) ***(G-15895)***
Via Christi Rehabilitation Ctr 316 634-3400
1151 N Rock Rd Wichita (67206) ***(G-15896)***
Via Christi Research 316 291-4774
1035 N Emporia St Ste 230 Wichita (67214) ***(G-15897)***
Via Christi Village Hays Inc 785 628-3241
2225 Canterbury Dr Hays (67601) ***(G-2926)***
Via Christi Villages Inc (HQ) 316 946-5200
2622 W Central Ave # 100 Wichita (67203) ***(G-15898)***
Via Christi Vlg Manhattan Inc 785 539-7671
2800 Willow Grove Rd Manhattan (66502) ***(G-6842)***
Via Christi Vlg Pittsburg Inc 620 235-0020
1502 E Centennial Dr Pittsburg (66762) ***(G-9956)***
Via Christy St Francis 316 613-6511
929 N St Francis St Wichita (67214) ***(G-15899)***
Via Chrsti HM Hlth Wichita Inc 316 268-8588
1035 N Emporia St Ste 230 Wichita (67214) ***(G-15900)***
Via Chrsti Hsptals Wichita Inc, Wichita *Also called Ascension Via Christi Hospital* ***(G-13747)***
Via Chrsti Rehabilitation Hosp (HQ) 316 268-5000
8200 E Thorn Dr Wichita (67226) ***(G-15901)***
Via Chrsti Rhbltation Hosp Inc 316 268-8040
929 N St Francis St Wichita (67214) ***(G-15902)***
Via Chrsti Rhbltation Hosp Inc 316 946-1790
750 N Socora St Ste 100 Wichita (67212) ***(G-15903)***
Via Chrsti Rvrside Med Ctr Inc 316 689-5335
3600 E Harry St Wichita (67218) ***(G-15904)***
Via Express Delivery Systems 913 341-8101
11235 Mastin St Ste 103 Shawnee Mission (66210) ***(G-11977)***
Viavi Solutions Avcomm, Wichita *Also called Viavi Solutions LLC* ***(G-15905)***
Viavi Solutions LLC (HQ) 316 522-4981
10200 W York St Wichita (67215) ***(G-15905)***
Viavi Solutions LLC 913 764-2452
14408 W 105th St Lenexa (66215) ***(G-6213)***
Vibrant Health, Kansas City *Also called Turner House Clinic Inc* ***(G-4478)***
Vic Regnier Builders Inc (PA) 913 649-0123
3705 W 95th St Overland Park (66206) ***(G-9463)***
Victor L Phillips Company 316 854-1118
3250 N Hydraulic St Wichita (67219) ***(G-15906)***
Victor L Phillips Company 785 380-0678
1305 Sw 42nd St Topeka (66609) ***(G-13223)***
Victor Ritter 785 678-2423
Hc 1 Jennings (67643) ***(G-3644)***
Victoria British, Lenexa *Also called Long Motor Corporation* ***(G-5978)***
Victoria Flls Sklld Cre & Rhab 316 733-0654
224 E Central Ave Andover (67002) ***(G-114)***
Victorian Glass, Beloit *Also called Bell Memorials LLC* ***(G-474)***
Victorian Paper Company (PA) 913 438-3995
15600 W 99th St Lenexa (66219) ***(G-6214)***
Victorian Trading Company, Lenexa *Also called Victorian Paper Company* ***(G-6214)***
Victory Elc Cooperative Mkec, Dodge City *Also called Victory Electric Coop Assn Inc* ***(G-1447)***
Victory Electric Coop Assn Inc 620 227-2139
3230 N 14th Ave Dodge City (67801) ***(G-1447)***
Victory Hill Retirement Cmnty 913 299-1166
1900 N 70th St Ofc Kansas City (66102) ***(G-4520)***
Vidricksen Distributing Co 785 827-2386
1825 Bailey Rd Salina (67401) ***(G-10753)***
Vidtronix LLC 913 441-9777
6607 Martindale Rd Shawnee (66218) ***(G-11047)***
Viega LLC 678 447-1882
2211 Viega Ave McPherson (67460) ***(G-7040)***
Vielhauer Plumbing Inc 913 268-9385
12107 Johnson Dr Shawnee Mission (66216) ***(G-11978)***
Vigiias Telehealth, Wichita *Also called Vigilias LLC* ***(G-15907)***
Vigilias LLC 800 924-8140
4704 E Oakland Wichita (67218) ***(G-15907)***
Viking Blast and Wash Systems, Rose Hill *Also called Viking Corporation* ***(G-10250)***
Viking Corporation 316 634-6699
731 S Industrial Ct Rose Hill (67133) ***(G-10250)***
Viking Industries Inc (PA) 620 795-2143
12057 Us Highway 59 Oswego (67356) ***(G-8238)***
Viking Peterson, Rose Hill *Also called Industrial Ventures Inc* ***(G-10240)***
Vilela Rndy Auto Bdy Repr Pntg 620 231-6350
103 S Elm St Pittsburg (66762) ***(G-9957)***
Vilela, Randy Auto Salvage, Pittsburg *Also called Vilela Rndy Auto Bdy Repr Pntg* ***(G-9957)***
Villa Saint Joseph, Shawnee Mission *Also called Benedictine Health System* ***(G-11160)***
Villa St Francis Inc 913 254-3264
16600 W 126th St Olathe (66062) ***(G-8140)***
Villa St Joseph, Overland Park *Also called Carondelet Health* ***(G-8520)***
Village Cleaners, Topeka *Also called Band Box Corporation* ***(G-12361)***
Village Elementary School Pto 620 341-2282
2302 W 15th Ave Emporia (66801) ***(G-1847)***
Village Pediatrics LLC 913 642-2100
8340 Mission Rd Ste 100 Prairie Village (66206) ***(G-10080)***
Village Shalom Inc 913 317-2600
5500 W 123rd St Shawnee Mission (66209) ***(G-11979)***
Village Villa Inc 913 886-6400
412 E Walnut St Nortonville (66060) ***(G-7465)***
Villages Inc (PA) 785 267-5900
7240 Sw 10th Ave Topeka (66615) ***(G-13224)***
Vince & Assoc Clinical RES, Overland Park *Also called Altasciences Clinical Kans Inc* ***(G-8373)***
Vincent Pennipede Od 913 825-2600
10120 W 119th St Overland Park (66213) ***(G-9464)***
Vincent Pennipede Od (PA) 913 780-9696
15257 W 135th St Olathe (66062) ***(G-8141)***
Vincent Roofing Inc 785 233-9603
340 Se 15th St Topeka (66607) ***(G-13225)***
Vinland Aerodrome Inc 785 594-2741
696 E 1700 Rd Baldwin City (66006) ***(G-369)***
Vinsolutions (HQ) 913 825-6124
5700 Broadmoor St Ste 901 Shawnee Mission (66202) ***(G-11980)***
Vintage Companies, Saint John *Also called Kenwood Plaza Inc* ***(G-10354)***
Vintage Greenmark Cnstr Inc 785 843-2700
790 N 2nd St Lawrence (66044) ***(G-5174)***
Vintage Group Inc 316 321-7777
1650 E 12th Ave El Dorado (67042) ***(G-1612)***
Vintage Group Inc 785 483-5882
1070 E Wichita Ave Russell (67665) ***(G-10302)***
Vintage Park, Shawnee Mission *Also called Brookdale Senior Living Commun* ***(G-11183)***
Vintage Park Assisted Living 785 456-8997
1607 4th St Wamego (66547) ***(G-13447)***
Vintage Park At Hiawatha LLC 785 742-4566
400 Kansas Ave Hiawatha (66434) ***(G-3027)***
Vintage Park At Osawatomie LLC 913 755-2167
1520 Parker Ave Osawatomie (66064) ***(G-8206)***
Vintage Park At Ottawa LLC 785 242-3715
2250 S Elm St Ottawa (66067) ***(G-8320)***
Vintage Park At Tonganoxie LLC 913 845-2204
120 W 8th St Tonganoxie (66086) ***(G-12272)***
Vintage Park of Lenexa LLC 913 894-6979
8710 Caenen Lake Rd Shawnee Mission (66215) ***(G-11981)***
Vintage Park of Paola 913 557-0202
601 N East St Paola (66071) ***(G-9594)***
Vintage Place Assistant Living, El Dorado *Also called Vintage Group Inc* ***(G-1612)***
Vintage Place Assistant Living, Russell *Also called Vintage Group Inc* ***(G-10302)***
Vintage Place Assisted Living, Pittsburg *Also called Vintage Place of Pittsburg* ***(G-9958)***
Vintage Place of Pittsburg 620 231-4554
1004 E Centennial Dr Pittsburg (66762) ***(G-9958)***
Vintage Prk Assistd Lvng Rsdnc 913 837-5133
202 S Rogers Rd Louisburg (66053) ***(G-6468)***
Vinyl Building Prod Div, McPherson *Also called Certainteed LLC* ***(G-6946)***

Vinylplex Inc....620 231-8290
1800 E Atkinson Ave Pittsburg (66762) *(G-9959)*
Viobin U.S.A., Salina *Also called McShares Inc (G-10597)*
Viralnova LLC....913 706-9710
12722 Flint Ln Overland Park (66213) *(G-9465)*
Virginia Inn Motel, Lawrence *Also called Kansas Investment Corporation (G-4933)*
Virtus Insurance, Overland Park *Also called Virtus LLC (G-9466)*
Virtus LLC....816 919-2323
9800 Metcalf Ave Ste 500 Overland Park (66212) *(G-9466)*
Vision Bank (HQ)....785 357-4669
3031 Sw Wanamaker Rd Topeka (66614) *(G-13226)*
Vision Communications Ks Inc....316 634-6747
1235 S Mead St Wichita (67211) *(G-15908)*
Vision Green Group....620 663-7187
1708 E 23rd Ave Hutchinson (67502) *(G-3479)*
Vision Source of Colby, Colby *Also called Morrison Optometric Assoc PA (G-1030)*
Vision Today Inc....913 397-9111
12120 S Strang Line Rd Olathe (66062) *(G-8142)*
Vision Woodworks LLC....620 336-2158
111 E Main St Cherryvale (67335) *(G-814)*
Visiting Nurses Association....785 843-3738
200 Maine St Ste C Lawrence (66044) *(G-5175)*
Vista Drive Inn, Manhattan *Also called Vista Franchise Inc (G-6843)*
Vista Franchise Inc....785 537-0100
1911 Tuttle Creek Blvd Manhattan (66502) *(G-6843)*
Vista Manufacturing Company....913 342-4939
1307 Central Ave Kansas City (66102) *(G-4521)*
Vista Outdoor Inc....913 752-3400
9200 Cody St Overland Park (66214) *(G-9467)*
Vista Outdoor Sales, Olathe *Also called Bushnell Holdings Inc (G-7570)*
Vita Craft Corporation....913 631-6265
11100 W 58th St Shawnee Mission (66203) *(G-11982)*
Vital Sign Center....913 262-4447
3410 Gibbs Rd Kansas City (66106) *(G-4522)*
Vitalcore Hlth Strategies LLC....785 246-6840
719 Sw Van Buren St # 100 Topeka (66603) *(G-13227)*
Vitalograph Inc....913 888-4221
13310 W 99th St Lenexa (66215) *(G-6215)*
Vitas Healthcare Corp Midwest (HQ)....913 722-1631
8527 Bluejacket St Overland Park (66214) *(G-9468)*
Vitas Healthcare Corporation....913 722-1631
8527 Bluejacket St Lenexa (66214) *(G-6216)*
Vitre-Retinal Cons Surgeons PA....316 683-5611
530 N Lorraine Ave # 100 Wichita (67214) *(G-15909)*
Viva International....913 859-0438
8357 Melrose Dr Shawnee Mission (66214) *(G-11983)*
Vizion Interactive....888 484-9466
7500 W 151 St Overland Park (66213) *(G-9469)*
Vizworx Inc (HQ)....316 691-4589
2420 N Woodlawn Blvd # 500 Wichita (67220) *(G-15910)*
Voegeli Concrete Construction, Maize *Also called James Voegeli Construction (G-6514)*
Voestalpine Nortrak Inc....316 284-0088
405 W 1st St Newton (67114) *(G-7424)*
Vogts-Parga Construction LLC....316 284-2801
717 N Main St Newton (67114) *(G-7425)*
Voica, Roxana I MD, Topeka *Also called Topeka Allrgy Asthma Clinic PA (G-13166)*
Voice Products Inc....316 616-1111
8555 E 32nd St N Wichita (67226) *(G-15911)*
Vold & Morris LLC....913 696-0001
9225 Indian Creek Pkwy # 1100 Overland Park (66210) *(G-9470)*
Volga-Canal Housing Inc....785 625-5678
2703 Hall St Ste 10 Hays (67601) *(G-2927)*
Volley Ball Inc....913 422-4070
4925 Widmer Rd Shawnee (66216) *(G-11048)*
Volt Management Corp....913 906-9568
7300 W 110th St Ste 140 Overland Park (66210) *(G-9471)*
Volt Workforce Solutions, Overland Park *Also called Volt Management Corp (G-9471)*
Volunteers With Heart Inc....913 563-5100
800 W Frontier Ln Olathe (66061) *(G-8143)*
Volz Oil Company - Kinsley Inc....620 659-2979
1001 E Kansas Ave Greensburg (67054) *(G-2685)*
Vornado Air LLC....316 733-0035
415 E 13th St Andover (67002) *(G-115)*
Vorona LLC....913 888-4646
9600 Dice Ln Ste 213 Lenexa (66215) *(G-6217)*
Vortex Valves, Salina *Also called Salina Vortex Corp (G-10696)*
Vos Design Inc....913 825-6556
13731 W 108th St Lenexa (66215) *(G-6218)*
Vos Window & Door Inc....913 962-5227
7600 Wedd St Shawnee Mission (66204) *(G-11984)*
VT Hackney Inc....620 331-6600
300 N Hackney Ave Independence (67301) *(G-3571)*
Vulcan Machine & Repair....620 796-2190
247 E Us Highway 56 Great Bend (67530) *(G-2655)*
Vvf Intervest LLC (HQ)....913 281-7444
1705 Kansas Ave Kansas City (66105) *(G-4523)*
Vvf Kansas LLC....913 281-7444
1705 Kansas Ave Kansas City (66105) *(G-4524)*
Vvf Kansas Services LLC....913 529-2292
1705 Kansas Ave Kansas City (66105) *(G-4525)*
W & R Corporate LLC....913 236-2000
6300 Lamar Ave Overland Park (66202) *(G-9472)*
W + D Machinery Co Inc....913 492-9880
11300 W 80th St Overland Park (66214) *(G-9473)*
W + D North America Inc....913 492-9880
11300 W 80th St Overland Park (66214) *(G-9474)*
W B Carter Construction Co....316 942-4214
2550 S Hoover Rd Wichita (67215) *(G-15912)*
W C Imaging Center, Wichita *Also called Via Christi Clinic PA (G-15884)*
W Carter & Assoc Glazing LLC....913 543-2600
1938 Foxridge Dr Kansas City (66106) *(G-4526)*
W Carter and Glass, Kansas City *Also called W Carter & Assoc Glazing LLC (G-4526)*
W Carter Orvil Inc (PA)....620 251-4700
105 W 11th St Unit 111 Coffeyville (67337) *(G-984)*
W D Mavchinery, Overland Park *Also called Great Plains Investments Ltd (G-8773)*
W F E, Salina *Also called Weis Fire Safety Equip Co Inc (G-10765)*
W F Leonard Co Inc....785 484-3342
111 W Main St Meriden (66512) *(G-7084)*
W G Fertilizer-Chanute, Chanute *Also called Mid-West Fertilizer Inc (G-743)*
W H Debrick Co Inc....913 294-3281
610 W Shawnee St Paola (66071) *(G-9595)*
W J E Healthcare Architects, Shawnee Mission *Also called Johnson Wilson Embers (G-11500)*
W N H, Winfield *Also called Newton William Memorial Hosp (G-16163)*
W O K, Ellis *Also called Rayes Inc (G-1651)*
W R Grace & Co - Conn....913 764-8040
701 S Kansas Ave Olathe (66061) *(G-8144)*
W R Grace Construction Pdts, Olathe *Also called W R Grace & Co - Conn (G-8144)*
W R King Contracting Inc....913 238-7496
7915 W 51st St Shawnee Mission (66202) *(G-11985)*
W Ralph Wilkerson Jr Inc....913 432-4400
4300 Shwn Miksn Pkwy 10 Shawnee Mission (66205) *(G-11986)*
W Ross Greenlaw DMD....207 374-5538
8001 Conser St Ste 200 Overland Park (66204) *(G-9475)*
W S Griffith Inc....913 451-1855
9401 Indian Creek Pkwy # 475 Overland Park (66210) *(G-9476)*
W W Drilling LLC....785 743-6774
675 S 13th St Wakeeney (67672) *(G-13393)*
W W Mails Inc....316 943-0703
7106 W Pueblo Dr Wichita (67209) *(G-15913)*
W-W Production Co....620 431-4137
1150 Highway 39 Chanute (66720) *(G-773)*
W/K Holding Company Inc (PA)....620 223-5500
2401 Cooper St Fort Scott (66701) *(G-2016)*
W/K-Short Run Division, Fort Scott *Also called Ward-Kraft Inc (G-2018)*
W2005/Fargo Hotels (pool C)....785 271-6165
2033 Sw Wanamaker Rd Topeka (66604) *(G-13228)*
Wab Co Road & Bridge....785 765-3432
215 Kansas Ave Alma (66401) *(G-66)*
Wabash National Corporation....913 621-7298
539 S 10th St Kansas City (66105) *(G-4527)*
Wachter Inc (PA)....913 541-2500
16001 W 99th St Lenexa (66219) *(G-6219)*
Wachter Tech Solutions Inc (HQ)....856 222-0643
16001 W 99th St Lenexa (66219) *(G-6220)*
Wachter, Bill, Pittsburg *Also called Wilbert & Towner PA (G-9969)*
Wachter, John H, Topeka *Also called Wright Henson Clark & Bakr LLP (G-13253)*
Waconda Trader, Beloit *Also called McGrath Publishing Company (G-492)*
Waddell & Reed Inc (HQ)....913 236-2000
6300 Lamar Ave Shawnee Mission (66202) *(G-11987)*
Waddell & Reed Inc....913 491-9202
4000 W 114th St Ste 310 Leawood (66211) *(G-5593)*
Waddell & Reed Inc....316 942-9010
1861 N Rock Rd Ste 100 Wichita (67206) *(G-15914)*
Waddell & Reed Inc....785 827-3606
2036 S Ohio St Salina (67401) *(G-10754)*
Waddell & Reed Inc....785 263-7496
203 Nw 15th St Abilene (67410) *(G-56)*
Waddell & Reed Inc....785 537-4505
555 Poyntz Ave Ste 280 Manhattan (66502) *(G-6844)*
Waddell & Reed Financial Inc (PA)....913 236-2000
6300 Lamar Ave Overland Park (66202) *(G-9477)*
Waddell & Reed Fincl Svcs Inc (HQ)....913 236-2000
6300 Lamar Ave Overland Park (66202) *(G-9478)*
Waddell & Reed Inc (PA)....785 233-6400
534 S Kansas Ave Ste 1300 Topeka (66603) *(G-13229)*
Waddell & Reed Inv MGT Co....913 491-9202
4000 W 114th St Ste 310 Leawood (66211) *(G-5594)*
Waddell & Reed Inv Mgt Co (HQ)....913 236-2000
6300 Lamar Ave Shawnee Mission (66202) *(G-11988)*
Waddles Heating & Cooling....785 827-2621
346 N 9th St Salina (67401) *(G-10755)*
Waddles Manufacturing & Mch Co....785 825-6166
2816 Centennial Rd Salina (67401) *(G-10756)*
Wade Agricultural Products Inc (PA)....913 757-2255
23096 E 2400 Rd La Cygne (66040) *(G-4646)*

Wade Quarries, La Cygne *Also called Wade Agricultural Products Inc* ***(G-4646)***
Waechter LLC 620 342-1080
1761 Road G Emporia (66801) ***(G-1848)***
Waggoner Enterprises Inc 620 465-3807
3509 E Switzer Rd Yoder (67585) ***(G-16196)***
Waggoners Inc 620 662-0181
9316 S Halstead St Hutchinson (67501) ***(G-3480)***
Wagle Painting 316 682-2531
342 N Bluff Ave Wichita (67208) ***(G-15915)***
Wagner Auto Body & Sales Inc 913 422-1955
741 E Front St Bonner Springs (66012) ***(G-580)***
Wagner Interior Systems Inc 913 647-6622
3411 Brinkerhoff Rd Kansas City (66115) ***(G-4528)***
Wagner Intr Sup Kans Cy Inc (PA) 913 647-6622
3411 Brinkerhoff Rd Kansas City (66115) ***(G-4529)***
Wagner's Auto Body & Sales, Bonner Springs *Also called Wagner Auto Body & Sales Inc* ***(G-580)***
Wagoner Bankruptcy Group PC 913 422-0909
15095 W 116th St Olathe (66062) ***(G-8145)***
Waisner Inc (PA) 913 345-2663
11184 Antioch Rd Shawnee Mission (66210) ***(G-11989)***
Waitt Media Inc 785 462-3305
1065 S Range Ave Colby (67701) ***(G-1047)***
Waitt Media Inc 620 225-8080
2601 Central Ave Ste C Dodge City (67801) ***(G-1448)***
Wakarusa Veterinary Hospital 785 843-5577
1825 Wakarusa Dr Lawrence (66047) ***(G-5176)***
Wakeeney Truck Line Inc 785 743-6778
324 N 4th St Wakeeney (67672) ***(G-13394)***
Wakefield Rehabilitation Ctr, Wakefield *Also called Beverly Enterprises-Kansas LLC* ***(G-13398)***
Wal-Mac Inc 620 356-3422
902 S Colorado St Ulysses (67880) ***(G-13331)***
Waldeck Matteuzzi & Sloan 913 253-2500
10111 W 105th St Overland Park (66212) ***(G-9479)***
Waldinger Corporation 316 942-7722
1630 S Baehr St Wichita (67209) ***(G-15916)***
Waldorf Association Lawrence 785 841-8800
1853 E 1600 Rd Lawrence (66044) ***(G-5177)***
Waldorf-Riley, Arkansas City *Also called Comfort Management Inc* ***(G-149)***
Walgreen Co 913 393-2757
545 E Santa Fe St Olathe (66061) ***(G-8146)***
Walgreen Co 785 628-1767
2600 Vine St Hays (67601) ***(G-2928)***
Walgreen Co 316 652-9147
1625 S Webb Rd Wichita (67207) ***(G-15917)***
Walgreen Co 316 689-0866
5505 E Harry St Wichita (67218) ***(G-15918)***
Walgreen Co 316 729-6171
555 N Maize Rd Wichita (67212) ***(G-15919)***
Walgreen Co 316 943-2299
710 N West St Wichita (67203) ***(G-15920)***
Walgreen Co 913 814-7977
8450 W 151st St Overland Park (66223) ***(G-9480)***
Walgreen Co 913 829-3176
13450 S Blackbob Rd Olathe (66062) ***(G-8147)***
Walgreen Co 913 789-9275
8701 Johnson Dr Merriam (66202) ***(G-7109)***
Walgreen Co 316 218-0819
440 N Andover Rd Andover (67002) ***(G-116)***
Walgreen Co 913 341-1725
7500 Metcalf Ave Overland Park (66204) ***(G-9481)***
Walgreen Co 316 684-2828
1330 N Woodlawn St Wichita (67208) ***(G-15921)***
Walgreen Co 785 841-9000
3421 W 6th St Lawrence (66049) ***(G-5178)***
Walgreen Co 785 832-8388
400 W 23rd St Lawrence (66046) ***(G-5179)***
Walgreens, Olathe *Also called Walgreen Co* ***(G-8146)***
Walgreens, Hays *Also called Walgreen Co* ***(G-2928)***
Walgreens, Wichita *Also called Walgreen Co* ***(G-15917)***
Walgreens, Wichita *Also called Walgreen Co* ***(G-15918)***
Walgreens, Wichita *Also called Walgreen Co* ***(G-15919)***
Walgreens, Wichita *Also called Walgreen Co* ***(G-15920)***
Walgreens, Overland Park *Also called Walgreen Co* ***(G-9480)***
Walgreens, Olathe *Also called Walgreen Co* ***(G-8147)***
Walgreens, Merriam *Also called Walgreen Co* ***(G-7109)***
Walgreens, Andover *Also called Walgreen Co* ***(G-116)***
Walgreens, Overland Park *Also called Walgreen Co* ***(G-9481)***
Walgreens, Wichita *Also called Walgreen Co* ***(G-15921)***
Walgreens, Lawrence *Also called Walgreen Co* ***(G-5178)***
Walgreens, Lawrence *Also called Walgreen Co* ***(G-5179)***
Walk In Health Care, Lenexa *Also called Olathe Medical Services Inc* ***(G-6034)***
Walker Centrifuge Services LLC 785 826-8265
516 Graves Blvd Apt B Salina (67401) ***(G-10757)***
Walker Products Company Inc (PA) 785 524-4107
414 S 6th St Lincoln (67455) ***(G-6390)***
Walker Publishing Inc 913 352-6700
808 Main St Pleasanton (66075) ***(G-10003)***
Wall-Ties & Forms Inc 913 441-0073
4000 Bonner Industrial Dr Shawnee (66226) ***(G-11049)***
Wallaby's Grill and Pub, Lenexa *Also called Wallabys Inc* ***(G-6221)***
Wallabys Inc 913 541-9255
9562 Lackman Rd Lenexa (66219) ***(G-6221)***
Wallace County Family Practice, Sharon Springs *Also called Greeley Cnty Hosp & Long TRM C* ***(G-10898)***
Wallace Electric, Garden City *Also called Gerald A Wallace* ***(G-2186)***
Wallace Saunders Chartered (PA) 913 888-1000
10111 W 87th St Overland Park (66212) ***(G-9482)***
Wallace Saunders Chartered 316 269-2100
200 W Douglas Ave Ste 400 Wichita (67202) ***(G-15922)***
Wallace Saunders Chartered 913 888-1000
10111 W 87th St Shawnee Mission (66212) ***(G-11990)***
Wallboard Specialties Inc 913 422-5023
23759 W 81st Ter Shawnee Mission (66227) ***(G-11991)***
Wallis Lubricant, Kansas City *Also called Wallis Oil Company* ***(G-4530)***
Wallis Oil Company 913 621-6521
445 Sunshine Rd Kansas City (66115) ***(G-4530)***
Walmart Inc 785 899-2111
2160 Commerce Rd Goodland (67735) ***(G-2489)***
Walmart Inc 316 347-2092
18631 W Kellogg Dr Goddard (67052) ***(G-2456)***
Walmart Inc 620 275-0775
3101 E Kansas Ave Ste 7 Garden City (67846) ***(G-2308)***
Walmart Inc 620 232-1593
2710 N Broadway St Pittsburg (66762) ***(G-9960)***
Walmart Inc 316 945-2800
6110 W Kellogg Dr Stop 1 Wichita (67209) ***(G-15923)***
Walmart Inc 316 636-5384
3030 N Rock Rd Wichita (67226) ***(G-15924)***
Walnut Bowl, Great Bend *Also called Mayberrys Inc* ***(G-2605)***
Walnut Manufacturing, Kansas City *Also called Airfixture LLC* ***(G-3794)***
Walnut Ridge Group Inc 620 232-3359
304 W 11th St Pittsburg (66762) ***(G-9961)***
Walnut Valley Packing LLC 866 421-3595
1000 S Main St El Dorado (67042) ***(G-1613)***
Walson Ink Inc 785 537-7370
610 S Delaware Ave Manhattan (66502) ***(G-6845)***
Walsworth Publishing Co Inc 800 265-6795
7300 W 110th St Ste 600 Overland Park (66210) ***(G-9483)***
Walt Carstar Auto Inc 785 273-7701
5926 Sw 19th Ter Topeka (66604) ***(G-13230)***
Walters-Morgan Cnstr Inc 785 539-7513
2616 Tuttle Creek Blvd Manhattan (66502) ***(G-6846)***
Walton Plumbing & Heating Inc 620 278-3462
112 N Broadway Ave Sterling (67579) ***(G-12132)***
Walton Swathing 620 492-6827
6501 E Road 10 Johnson (67855) ***(G-3664)***
Waltons Inc (PA) 316 262-0651
3639 N Comotara St Wichita (67226) ***(G-15925)***
Walz Tetrick Advertising Inc (PA) 913 789-8778
5201 Johnson Dr Ste 500 Mission (66205) ***(G-7140)***
Wamego Chmber Cmmrce Minstreet 785 456-7849
529 Lincoln Ave Wamego (66547) ***(G-13448)***
Wamego City Hospital, Wamego *Also called City of Wamego* ***(G-13413)***
Wamego Country Club Inc 785 456-2649
1900 Country Club Dr Wamego (66547) ***(G-13449)***
Wamego Dental Center Inc 785 456-2330
1519 W Us Highway 24 Wamego (66547) ***(G-13450)***
WAMEGO HEALTH CENTER, Wamego *Also called Wamego Hospital Association* ***(G-13451)***
Wamego Hospital Association 785 456-2295
711 Genn Dr Wamego (66547) ***(G-13451)***
Wamego Inn and Suites 785 458-8888
1300 Lilac Ln Wamego (66547) ***(G-13452)***
Wamego Lodge No 80, Wamego *Also called Independent Order Oddfellows* ***(G-13425)***
Wamego Lumber Co Inc 785 456-2400
18612 E Highway 24 Ste 1 Wamego (66547) ***(G-13453)***
Wamego Recreation Dept 785 456-8810
430 Lincoln Ave Wamego (66547) ***(G-13454)***
Wamego Recycling LLC 785 456-2439
18070 E Us Highway 24 Wamego (66547) ***(G-13455)***
Wamego Telecom Comapny, Wamego *Also called Wamego Telephone Company Inc* ***(G-13456)***
Wamego Telephone Company Inc (PA) 785 456-1001
1009 Lincoln Ave Wamego (66547) ***(G-13456)***
Wanamaker Dialysis, Topeka *Also called Total Renal Care Inc* ***(G-13195)***
Wanda America Inv Holdg Co Ltd 913 213-2000
11500 Ash St Leawood (66211) ***(G-5595)***
Ward Feed Yard Inc 620 285-2183
1190 100th Ave Larned (67550) ***(G-4715)***
Ward Parkway Health Services, Shawnee Mission *Also called Ward Parkway Medical Group* ***(G-11992)***
Ward Parkway Medical Group 913 383-9099
8800 State Line Rd Shawnee Mission (66206) ***(G-11992)***

ALPHABETIC

Ward-Kraft Inc (HQ)...800 821-4021
2401 Cooper St Fort Scott (66701) ***(G-2017)***
Ward-Kraft Inc...620 223-1104
2400 Liberty Bell Rd Fort Scott (66701) ***(G-2018)***
Wardcraft Homes Inc...785 632-5664
614 Maple St Clay Center (67432) ***(G-886)***
Warden Triplett Grier LLP...816 877-8100
3515 W 75th St Ste 102 Prairie Village (66208) ***(G-10081)***
Wardrobe Cleaners, Dodge City *Also called Al Morris* ***(G-1291)***
Warkentin House Museum, Newton *Also called City of Newton* ***(G-7330)***
Warmack and Company LLC...785 825-0122
2259 S 9th St Salina (67401) ***(G-10758)***
Warren Clinic...785 337-2214
205 S Hanover St Hanover (66945) ***(G-2714)***
Warren Consulting Inc...620 727-2468
2005 N Adams St Hutchinson (67502) ***(G-3481)***
Warren Davidson Trucking...785 625-5126
200 W 38th St Hays (67601) ***(G-2929)***
Warren McElwain Mortuary LLC...785 843-1120
120 W 13th St Lawrence (66044) ***(G-5180)***
Warren Moore Painting LLC...913 558-8549
9600 W 104th St Shawnee Mission (66212) ***(G-11993)***
Warren Old Town Theatre Grill...316 262-7123
353 N Mead St Wichita (67202) ***(G-15926)***
Warren Theatres LLC...316 612-0469
11611 E 13th St N Wichita (67206) ***(G-15927)***
Warren Theatres LLC...316 722-7060
9150 W 21st St N Wichita (67205) ***(G-15928)***
Warren Travel Inc...316 685-1118
6903 E Aberdeen St Wichita (67206) ***(G-15929)***
Warrick, David A MD, Topeka *Also called St Francis Medical Clinic* ***(G-13095)***
Washburn Endowment Association...785 670-4483
1729 Sw Macvicar Ave Topeka (66604) ***(G-13231)***
Washburn University Foundation...785 670-4483
1729 Sw Macvicar Ave Topeka (66604) ***(G-13232)***
Washburn University of Topeka...785 670-1111
1700 Sw College Ave Topeka (66621) ***(G-13233)***
Washer Specialties Company...316 263-8179
224 N Indiana Ave Wichita (67214) ***(G-15930)***
Washington 1st Banco Inc (PA)...785 325-2221
101 C St Washington (66968) ***(G-13470)***
Washington Companies Inc (PA)...620 792-2430
828 10th St Great Bend (67530) ***(G-2656)***
Washington FNB...785 325-2221
101 C St Washington (66968) ***(G-13471)***
Washington Gradeschool, Ellis *Also called Early Chldhood Cnnection/Pre K* ***(G-1642)***
Washington Prime Group Inc...316 945-9374
4600 W Kellogg Dr Ofc Wichita (67209) ***(G-15931)***
Washington Road Branch, Newton *Also called Midland National Bank* ***(G-7385)***
Wasi Inc...620 782-3337
4425 W May St Bldg B Wichita (67209) ***(G-15932)***
Wasi, Inc., Wichita *Also called Atlas Aerospace LLC* ***(G-13764)***
Waste Connections, Garden City *Also called County of Finney* ***(G-2136)***
Waste Connections Inc...316 941-4320
4300 W 37th St N Wichita (67205) ***(G-15933)***
Waste Connections Kansas Inc...785 827-3939
1848 Summers Rd Salina (67401) ***(G-10759)***
Waste Connections Kansas Inc (HQ)...316 838-4920
2745 N Ohio St Wichita (67219) ***(G-15934)***
Waste Connections Us Inc...620 227-3371
1108 E Trail St Dodge City (67801) ***(G-1449)***
Waste Corporation Kansas LLC...713 292-2400
21075 Us Highway 59 Parsons (67357) ***(G-9749)***
Waste Management, Kansas City *Also called Deffenbaugh Industries Inc* ***(G-3965)***
Waste Management of Kansas (HQ)...785 233-3541
3611 Nw 16th St Topeka (66618) ***(G-13234)***
Waste Management of Kansas...913 631-3300
2601 Midwest Dr Kansas City (66111) ***(G-4531)***
Waste Management of Kansas...785 246-0413
7351 Nw Us Highway 75 Topeka (66618) ***(G-13235)***
Waste Management of Kansas...785 238-3293
2300 Elmdale Ave Junction City (66441) ***(G-3766)***
Wastewater Treatment, Manhattan *Also called City of Manhattan* ***(G-6588)***
Wastewater Treatment Facility, Lawrence *Also called City of Lawrence* ***(G-4791)***
Waswick, William A MD, Wichita *Also called Kansas Surgical Consultants* ***(G-14826)***
Watco Inc (HQ)...208 734-4644
315 W 3rd St Pittsburg (66762) ***(G-9962)***
Watco Co, Winfield *Also called South Kansas and Okla RR Inc* ***(G-16173)***
Watco Companies, Pittsburg *Also called Transerve Inc* ***(G-9947)***
Watco Companies LLC (PA)...575 745-2329
315 W 3rd St Pittsburg (66762) ***(G-9963)***
Watco Companies LLC...316 263-3113
1825 W Harry St Wichita (67213) ***(G-15935)***
Watco Companies LLC...620 336-2291
123 N Depot St Cherryvale (67335) ***(G-815)***
Watco Railroad Co Holdings (PA)...620 231-2230
315 W 3rd St Pittsburg (66762) ***(G-9964)***
Watco Sek Railroad, Pittsburg *Also called Watco Switching Inc* ***(G-9965)***
Watco Supply Chain Svcs LLC...479 502-3658
9047 6th St Great Bend (67530) ***(G-2657)***
Watco Switching Inc...620 231-2230
315 W 3rd St Pittsburg (66762) ***(G-9965)***
Watco Transloading LLC (HQ)...620 231-2230
315 W 3rd St Pittsburg (66762) ***(G-9966)***
Watco Transportation Svcs LLC (HQ)...620 231-2230
315 W 3rd St Pittsburg (66762) ***(G-9967)***
Water Department, Dodge City *Also called City of Dodge City* ***(G-1322)***
Water Department, Leavenworth *Also called City of Leavenworth* ***(G-5222)***
Water Department, Liberal *Also called City of Liberal* ***(G-6293)***
Water Depot Inc...913 782-7277
15605 S Keeler Ter Ste B Olathe (66062) ***(G-8148)***
Water Dst No1 Jhnson Cnty Kans (PA)...913 895-5500
10747 Renner Blvd Lenexa (66219) ***(G-6222)***
Water Dst No1 Jhnson Cnty Kans...913 895-5800
7601 Holliday Dr Kansas City (66106) ***(G-4532)***
Water Pollution Control Dept, Great Bend *Also called City of Great Bend* ***(G-2542)***
Water Pollution Control Div, Leavenworth *Also called City of Leavenworth* ***(G-5221)***
Water Spt Rcreation Campground...620 225-9003
500 Cherry St Ofc Dodge City (67801) ***(G-1450)***
Water Systems Engineering Inc...785 242-5853
3201 Labette Ter Ottawa (66067) ***(G-8321)***
Water Technology Investments, Wichita *Also called Twotrees Technologies LLC* ***(G-15822)***
Water Treatment Plant, Topeka *Also called City of Topeka* ***(G-12472)***
Water's Edge Aquatic Design, Shawnee Mission *Also called Waters Edge Aquatic Design LLC* ***(G-11994)***
Waterfront Assisted Living...316 945-3344
900 N Bayshore Dr Ofc Wichita (67212) ***(G-15936)***
Waterman Group Inc...913 685-4900
7415 W 130th St Overland Park (66213) ***(G-9484)***
WATERONE, Lenexa *Also called Water Dst No1 Jhnson Cnty Kans* ***(G-6222)***
Waters Inc...785 822-6540
3213 Arnold Ave Salina (67401) ***(G-10760)***
Waters Inc...620 343-2800
2727 W Us Highway 50 Emporia (66801) ***(G-1849)***
Waters Inc...785 537-1340
338 N Seth Child Rd Ste A Manhattan (66502) ***(G-6847)***
Waters Inc...785 238-3114
129 E 6th St Junction City (66441) ***(G-3767)***
Waters Inc...620 227-2900
310 W Frontview St Dodge City (67801) ***(G-1451)***
Waters Edge Aquatic Design LLC...913 438-4338
11205 W 79th St Shawnee Mission (66214) ***(G-11994)***
Waters, Nevin K, Olathe *Also called Nevin K Waters DDS PA* ***(G-7916)***
Watersource Technologies Inc...316 927-2100
952 E Grand Ave Haysville (67060) ***(G-2963)***
Waterville Fire Department, Waterville *Also called City of Waterville* ***(G-13473)***
Waterwalk Apartments, Wichita *Also called Waterwalk Wichita LLC* ***(G-15937)***
Waterwalk Overland Park, Leawood *Also called Ww Kc Metcalf LLC* ***(G-5602)***
Waterwalk Wichita LLC...316 201-1899
411 W Maple St Wichita (67213) ***(G-15937)***
Waterway Gas & Wash 32, Shawnee Mission *Also called Waterway Gas & Wash Company* ***(G-11996)***
Waterway Gas & Wash Company...913 897-3111
8110 W 135th St Overland Park (66223) ***(G-9485)***
Waterway Gas & Wash Company...913 339-9542
12100 College Blvd Shawnee Mission (66210) ***(G-11995)***
Waterway Gas & Wash Company...913 339-9964
4200 W 119th St Ste 32 Shawnee Mission (66209) ***(G-11996)***
Wathena Healthcare...785 989-3141
2112 Highway 36 Wathena (66090) ***(G-13479)***
Wathena Heights Apartments...417 883-7887
509 N 3rd St Wathena (66090) ***(G-13480)***
Watkins Calcara Rondeau Friede...620 792-8231
1321 Main St Ste 300 Great Bend (67530) ***(G-2658)***
WATKINS COMMUNITY MUSEUM OF HI, Lawrence *Also called Douglas County Historical Soc* ***(G-4840)***
Watkins Memorial Health Center, Lawrence *Also called University of Kansas* ***(G-5159)***
Watson Electric Inc...785 827-2924
318 N 8th St Salina (67401) ***(G-10761)***
Watson Library Acquisitions, Lawrence *Also called University of Kansas* ***(G-5160)***
Waugh-Yokum & Friskel Memorial, Iola *Also called Feuerborn Fmly Fnrl Svc* ***(G-3600)***
Wave Review Salon...913 345-9252
12010 College Blvd Shawnee Mission (66210) ***(G-11997)***
Waxene Products Company Inc...316 263-8523
2023 N Broadway Ave Wichita (67214) ***(G-15938)***
Waxman Candles Inc (PA)...785 843-8593
609 Massachusetts St Lawrence (66044) ***(G-5181)***
Wayne Holmes Basements, Salina *Also called Holmes Basement Construction* ***(G-10545)***
Wayne R Ward & Associates...785 263-7272
2205 N Buckeye Ave Ste C Abilene (67410) ***(G-57)***
Waynes Printing & Copying...620 662-4655
26 S Main St Hutchinson (67501) ***(G-3482)***
Wc Construction LLC...816 741-4810
5410 Antioch Rd Merriam (66202) ***(G-7110)***

Wcnoc, Burlington *Also called Wolf Creek Nuclear Oper Corp* ***(G-645)***
Wdm Architects PA....316 262-4700
105 N Washington Ave Wichita (67202) ***(G-15939)***
Wds Inc....913 894-1881
15007 W 95th St Lenexa (66215) ***(G-6223)***
We Land & Cattle Co Inc....620 675-2747
2108 Us Highway 83 Sublette (67877) ***(G-12213)***
We R Kids LLC....316 729-0172
10221 W 13th St N Wichita (67212) ***(G-15940)***
We-Mac Manufacturing Co....913 367-3778
11016 Us Highway 59 Atchison (66002) ***(G-270)***
We-Mac Manufacturing Co....620 879-2187
Industrial Park Caney (67333) ***(G-678)***
Weary Davis LLC (PA)....785 762-2210
819 N Washington St Junction City (66441) ***(G-3768)***
Weary Law Firm, Junction City *Also called Weary Davis LLC* ***(G-3768)***
Weather Metrics Inc....913 438-7666
11100 W 91st St Overland Park (66214) ***(G-9486)***
Weathercraft Company N Platte....785 899-3064
716 W Hwy 24 Goodland (67735) ***(G-2490)***
Weaver's Auto Center, Shawnee *Also called Weavers Auto Body Inc* ***(G-11050)***
Weavers Auto Body Inc....913 441-0001
6502 Vista Dr Shawnee (66218) ***(G-11050)***
Web & Rodrick Funeral Home, Topeka *Also called Newcomer Funeral Svc Group Inc* ***(G-12928)***
Web Creations & Consulting LLC....785 823-7630
119 W Iron Ave Fl 3 Salina (67401) ***(G-10762)***
Webber Webber & Exon....785 232-7707
1919 Sw 10th Ave Ste 102 Topeka (66604) ***(G-13236)***
Webco Air Craft....316 283-7929
1134 N Oliver Rd Newton (67114) ***(G-7426)***
Webco Aircraft & Engine Svc, Newton *Also called Webco Air Craft* ***(G-7426)***
Webco Manufacturing Inc....913 764-7111
20570 W 162nd St Olathe (66062) ***(G-8149)***
Webcon, Hutchinson *Also called Maxines Inc* ***(G-3367)***
Weber Carpet Inc (PA)....913 469-5430
11400 Rogers Rd Lenexa (66215) ***(G-6224)***
Weber Manufacturing LLC....620 251-9800
1300 E 3rd St Coffeyville (67337) ***(G-985)***
Weber Palmer & Macy Chartered (PA)....785 823-7201
338 N Front St Salina (67401) ***(G-10763)***
Weber Refrigeration & Htg Inc....580 338-7338
711 N Main St Garden City (67846) ***(G-2309)***
Weber Refrigeration & Htg Inc (PA)....620 225-7700
11154 Kliesen St Dodge City (67801) ***(G-1452)***
Webster Combustion Tech LLC....620 221-7464
619 Industrial Blvd Winfield (67156) ***(G-16179)***
Webster Conference Center Inc....785 827-6565
2601 N Ohio St Salina (67401) ***(G-10764)***
Weddle and Sons Inc (PA)....785 532-8347
2601 Anderson Ave 200a Manhattan (66502) ***(G-6848)***
Wedgewood Golf Course....316 835-2991
9007 W 1st St Halstead (67056) ***(G-2706)***
Wee Workshop Inc....913 681-2191
7305 W 162nd St Stilwell (66085) ***(G-12179)***
Weed Department, Oskaloosa *Also called County of Jefferson* ***(G-8221)***
Weigand-Omega Associates Inc (PA)....316 925-6341
333 S Broadway Ave # 105 Wichita (67202) ***(G-15941)***
Weigand-Omega Management Inc (PA)....316 925-6341
333 S Broadway Ave # 105 Wichita (67202) ***(G-15942)***
Weigel Construction Inc....913 780-1274
19015 Madison St Ste A Spring Hill (66083) ***(G-12103)***
Weight Watchers, Overland Park *Also called Ww North America Holdings Inc* ***(G-9507)***
Weight Watchers, Overland Park *Also called Ww North America Holdings Inc* ***(G-9508)***
Weis Fire & Safety Eqp LLC....303 421-2001
6720 Mccormick Dr Shawnee (66226) ***(G-11051)***
Weis Fire Safety Equip Co Inc....785 825-9527
111 E Pacific Ave Salina (67401) ***(G-10765)***
Weisbender Contracting Inc....785 776-5034
1812 Fair Ln Manhattan (66502) ***(G-6849)***
Weishaar Adaptation....913 367-6299
7237 Elm Dr Atchison (66002) ***(G-271)***
Welborn Animal Hospital....913 334-6770
7860 Washington Ave Kansas City (66112) ***(G-4533)***
Welborn Pet Hospital, Kansas City *Also called Welborn Animal Hospital* ***(G-4533)***
Welborn Sales Inc....785 823-2394
3288 S Avenue C Salina (67401) ***(G-10766)***
Welch Machine Inc....620 896-2764
870 N State Road 14 Harper (67058) ***(G-2725)***
Welch Sign Co Inc....913 831-4499
9410 W 61st St Shawnee Mission (66203) ***(G-11998)***
Welco Services Inc....620 241-3000
1426 13th Ave McPherson (67460) ***(G-7041)***
Welco Technologies....316 941-0400
2600 S Custer Ave Wichita (67217) ***(G-15943)***
Welker Heating and Cooling....913 669-7555
St 6830 152 Ter Overland Park (66223) ***(G-9487)***
Well Refined Drilling Co Inc....620 763-2619
4270 Gray Rd Thayer (66776) ***(G-12246)***
Well Servicing & Completions, Sterling *Also called G & L Well Service Inc* ***(G-12118)***
Well Watch LLC....785 798-0020
804 E Cedar St Ness City (67560) ***(G-7268)***
Weller Tractor Salvage Inc....620 792-5243
200 Sw 40 Ave Great Bend (67530) ***(G-2659)***
Wellhead Systems, Hill City *Also called Wsi Holdings LLC* ***(G-3038)***
WELLINGTON CABLE TV, Wellington *Also called Sumner Cable Tv Inc* ***(G-13531)***
Wellington Daily News, Wellington *Also called Gatehouse Media LLC* ***(G-13502)***
Wellington Experience Inc (PA)....913 897-9229
7304 W 130th St Ste 370 Shawnee Mission (66213) ***(G-11999)***
Wellington Fmly Pract Clinc....620 399-1222
399 S Seneca Rd Wellington (67152) ***(G-13539)***
Wellington Promotions, Shawnee Mission *Also called Wellington Experience Inc* ***(G-11999)***
Wellness Services Inc....913 438-8779
9724 Legler Rd Shawnee Mission (66219) ***(G-12000)***
Wellness Services Inc (HQ)....913 894-6600
9724 Legler Rd Lenexa (66219) ***(G-6225)***
Wellnitz Tree Care Inc....620 340-2484
310 Congress St Emporia (66801) ***(G-1850)***
Wells Aircraft Inc....620 663-1546
800 Airport Rd Hutchinson (67501) ***(G-3483)***
Wells Fargo & Company....913 782-9603
2137 E Santa Fe St Ste A Olathe (66062) ***(G-8150)***
Wells Fargo Advisors, Topeka *Also called Wells Fargo Clearing Svcs LLC* ***(G-13238)***
Wells Fargo Advisors, Wichita *Also called Wells Fargo Clearing Svcs LLC* ***(G-15946)***
Wells Fargo Advisors, Shawnee Mission *Also called Wells Fargo Clearing Svcs LLC* ***(G-12002)***
Wells Fargo Advisors, Salina *Also called Wells Fargo Clearing Svcs LLC* ***(G-10767)***
Wells Fargo Advisors, Hutchinson *Also called Wells Fargo Clearing Svcs LLC* ***(G-3484)***
Wells Fargo Advisors, Wichita *Also called Wells Fargo Clearing Svcs LLC* ***(G-15947)***
Wells Fargo Advisors, Overland Park *Also called Wells Fargo Clearing Svcs LLC* ***(G-9489)***
Wells Fargo Bank NA....913 631-6600
11809 Shwnee Mission Pkwy Shawnee (66203) ***(G-11052)***
Wells Fargo Bank National Assn....816 234-2929
7500 College Blvd Ste 250 Overland Park (66210) ***(G-9488)***
Wells Fargo Bank National Assn....316 685-5495
6321 E Central Ave Wichita (67208) ***(G-15944)***
Wells Fargo Bank National Assn....913 341-4774
2000 W 103rd St Leawood (66206) ***(G-5596)***
Wells Fargo Bank National Assn....316 943-3159
455 S West St Wichita (67213) ***(G-15945)***
Wells Fargo Bank National Assn....785 271-2492
6342 Sw 21st St Topeka (66615) ***(G-13237)***
Wells Fargo Bank National Assn....913 663-6040
7500 College Blvd Shawnee Mission (66210) ***(G-12001)***
Wells Fargo Clearing Svcs LLC....785 271-2492
6342 Sw 21st St Topeka (66615) ***(G-13238)***
Wells Fargo Clearing Svcs LLC....316 267-0300
300 S Main St Wichita (67202) ***(G-15946)***
Wells Fargo Clearing Svcs LLC....913 267-7200
1900 Shawnee Mission Pkwy # 210 Shawnee Mission (66205) ***(G-12002)***
Wells Fargo Clearing Svcs LLC....785 825-4636
118 W Iron Ave Salina (67401) ***(G-10767)***
Wells Fargo Clearing Svcs LLC....620 665-0659
1 N Main St Ste 402 Hutchinson (67501) ***(G-3484)***
Wells Fargo Clearing Svcs LLC....316 634-6690
8301 E 21st St N Ste 320 Wichita (67206) ***(G-15947)***
Wells Fargo Clearing Svcs LLC....913 402-5100
7400 W 130th St Ste 200 Overland Park (66213) ***(G-9489)***
Wells Fargo Home Mortgage Inc....785 565-2900
2601 Anderson Ave Ste 202 Manhattan (66502) ***(G-6850)***
Wells Fargo Home Mortgage Inc....913 319-7900
7127 W 110th St Shawnee Mission (66210) ***(G-12003)***
Wells Fargo Home Mortgage Inc....405 475-2880
10616 W Maple St Ste 100 Wichita (67209) ***(G-15948)***
Wellsky Corporation (PA)....913 307-1000
11300 Switzer St Overland Park (66210) ***(G-9490)***
Welstone....913 788-6045
6050 Broadmoor St Shawnee Mission (66202) ***(G-12004)***
Wenger Manufacturing Inc (PA)....785 284-2133
15 Commerce Dr Sabetha (66534) ***(G-10337)***
Wenger Oil Inc (PA)....316 283-8795
2701 N Anderson Ave Newton (67114) ***(G-7427)***
Werner Pipe Service Inc....620 331-7384
4307 E Us Highway 160 Independence (67301) ***(G-3572)***
Werth Htg Plbg Airconditioning....785 628-8088
516 E 8th St Hays (67601) ***(G-2930)***
Wes Material Handling Inc (PA)....913 369-9375
23659 Parallel Rd Tonganoxie (66086) ***(G-12273)***
Wesbanco Inc....785 539-3553
224 E Poyntz Ave Manhattan (66502) ***(G-6851)***
Wesco Aircraft Hardware Corp....316 315-1200
3851 N Webb Rd Wichita (67226) ***(G-15949)***
Wescon Controls LLC....316 942-7266
2533 S West St Wichita (67217) ***(G-15950)***
Wescon Plastics LLC....855 731-6055
2810 S West St Wichita (67217) ***(G-15951)***

ALPHABETIC

Wescorp Ltd (PA)....913 281-1833
901 S 7th St Kansas City (66105) ***(G-4534)***
Wesley Inn, Wichita *Also called Four of Wichita Inc* ***(G-14410)***
Wesley Management Inc....913 682-6844
823 Miami St Leavenworth (66048) ***(G-5305)***
Wesley Medical Center LLC (HQ)....316 962-2000
550 N Hillside St Wichita (67214) ***(G-15952)***
Wesley Medical Center LLC....316 858-2610
2610 N Woodlawn Blvd Wichita (67220) ***(G-15953)***
Wesley Property Management, Leavenworth *Also called Wesley Management Inc* ***(G-5305)***
Wesley Rehabilitation Hospital....316 729-9999
8338 W 13th St N Wichita (67212) ***(G-15954)***
Wesley Retirement Community....316 636-1000
7373 E 29th St N Apt W118 Wichita (67226) ***(G-15955)***
Wesley Towers Inc....620 663-9175
700 Monterey Pl Ofc Hutchinson (67502) ***(G-3485)***
Wessel Iron & Supply Inc....620 225-0568
803 E Trail St Dodge City (67801) ***(G-1453)***
West Acres Bowl, Wichita *Also called Boulevard One Inc* ***(G-13874)***
West Central Kansas Assn Inc (PA)....785 483-3131
200 S Main St Russell (67665) ***(G-10303)***
West Coast Equipment Inc....623 842-0978
15607 W 100th Ter Lenexa (66219) ***(G-6226)***
West Glenn Gstrintestinal Cons, Shawnee Mission *Also called Mark Molos* ***(G-11596)***
West Plains Transport Inc....620 563-7665
1402 Superior St Plains (67869) ***(G-9978)***
West Ridge Lanes Fmly Fun Ctr....785 273-3333
1935 Sw Westport Dr Topeka (66604) ***(G-13239)***
West Side Dairy, Syracuse *Also called Syracuse Dairy II LLC* ***(G-12234)***
West Side Good Neighbor Center....316 942-7349
3500 W 13th St N Wichita (67203) ***(G-15956)***
West Side Kids Day Out Program....913 764-0813
1700 W Santa Fe St Olathe (66061) ***(G-8151)***
West Side Mechanical Inc....913 788-1800
424 Stone Grove Dr Manhattan (66503) ***(G-6852)***
West Texas Gas Hugoton, Hugoton *Also called Wtg Hugoton LP* ***(G-3180)***
West Wchita Asssted Living LLC....316 361-2500
629 S Maize Ct Wichita (67209) ***(G-15957)***
West Wichita Family Physicians, Wichita *Also called Physicians Medical Clinics* ***(G-15298)***
West Wichita Fmly Optometrist (PA)....316 262-3716
1202 W Maple St Wichita (67213) ***(G-15958)***
West Wichita Gas Gathering LLC....970 764-6653
13521 Ne 10 St Cheney (67025) ***(G-798)***
West Wichita Pet Clinic....316 722-0100
8615 W 21st St N Wichita (67205) ***(G-15959)***
West Wind Energy LLC....785 387-2623
405 N Main St Otis (67565) ***(G-8242)***
Westar Energy Inc....316 261-6575
1900 E Central Ave Wichita (67214) ***(G-15960)***
Westar Industries Inc (HQ)....785 575-6507
818 S Kansas Ave Topeka (66612) ***(G-13240)***
Westdale Asset Management Ltd....913 307-5900
8730 Bourgade St Lenexa (66219) ***(G-6227)***
Western AG Enterprises Inc....620 793-8355
120 S Patton Rd Great Bend (67530) ***(G-2660)***
Western Air Maps, Overland Park *Also called Wilson Inc Engneers Architects* ***(G-9496)***
Western Aluminum & Glass Co....785 625-2418
1507 E 27th St Hays (67601) ***(G-2931)***
Western Beverage Inc....620 227-7641
301 E Wyatt Earp Blvd Dodge City (67801) ***(G-1454)***
Western Beverage-Hays....785 625-3712
2100 E Us Hwy 40 Byp Hays (67601) ***(G-2932)***
Western Chandelier Company....913 685-2000
14975 Metcalf Ave Overland Park (66223) ***(G-9491)***
Western Chemical Pumps Inc....913 829-1888
603 S Kansas Ave Olathe (66061) ***(G-8152)***
Western Contracting Corp....620 449-2286
6th And Central Saint Paul (66771) ***(G-10385)***
Western Cooperative Elc Assn....785 743-5561
635 S 13th St Wakeeney (67672) ***(G-13395)***
Western Enterprise Inc....913 342-0505
956 Osage Ave Kansas City (66105) ***(G-4535)***
Western Extralite Company....913 438-1777
14903 W 99th St Shawnee Mission (66215) ***(G-12005)***
Western Feed Mills Inc....620 758-2283
403 Sale Barn Rd Cedar Vale (67024) ***(G-695)***
Western Feed Yard Inc....620 492-6256
548 S Road I Johnson (67855) ***(G-3665)***
Western First Aid & Safety LLC (HQ)....316 263-0687
5360 College Blvd Ste 200 Leawood (66211) ***(G-5597)***
Western Hills Golf Club Inc....785 478-4000
8533 Sw 21st St Ste A Topeka (66615) ***(G-13241)***
Western Hydro LLC....620 277-2132
3585c N Williams Rd Garden City (67846) ***(G-2310)***
Western Inds Plastic Pdts LLC....620 221-9464
7727 1st Ave Winfield (67156) ***(G-16180)***
Western Industries Inc....620 221-9464
1st & B Sts Winfield (67156) ***(G-16181)***
Western International Inc....785 856-1840
701 E 22nd St Lawrence (66046) ***(G-5182)***
Western Irrigation Inc....620 275-4033
2990 Morton Rd Garden City (67846) ***(G-2311)***
Western Kansas and Supply....620 792-4731
80 E Tents St Great Bend (67530) ***(G-2661)***
Western Kansas Child Advocacy....620 872-3706
212 E 5th St Scott City (67871) ***(G-10835)***
Western Kansas Valley Inc....785 852-4606
W Hwy 40 Sharon Springs (67758) ***(G-10902)***
Western Kansas World Inc....785 743-2155
205 N Main St Wakeeney (67672) ***(G-13396)***
Western Metal Company Inc (PA)....913 681-8787
1202 S Metcalf Rd Louisburg (66053) ***(G-6469)***
Western Plains Energy LLC (PA)....785 672-8810
3022 County Road 18 Oakley (67748) ***(G-7488)***
Western Plains Home Health Ctr, Dodge City *Also called Western Plins Rgional Hosp LLC* ***(G-1455)***
Western Plains Medical Complex, Dodge City *Also called Dodge Cy Healthcare Group LLC* ***(G-1353)***
Western Plains Medical Complex, Dodge City *Also called Western Plins Rgional Hosp LLC* ***(G-1456)***
Western Plins Rgional Hosp LLC....620 225-8700
3001 A Ave 334 Dodge City (67801) ***(G-1455)***
Western Plins Rgional Hosp LLC (HQ)....620 225-8400
3001 Avenue A Dodge City (67801) ***(G-1456)***
Western Professional Assoc....316 264-5628
727 N Waco Ave Ste 280 Wichita (67203) ***(G-15961)***
Western Roofing Co Services....816 931-1075
2820 Roe Ln Ste O Kansas City (66103) ***(G-4536)***
Western Sky Industries, Wichita *Also called Welco Technologies* ***(G-15943)***
Western Sprinklers Inc (PA)....785 462-6755
1100 S Range Ave Colby (67701) ***(G-1048)***
Western State Bank....785 899-2393
815 Center Ave Goodland (67735) ***(G-2491)***
Western States Fire Protection....913 321-9208
501 Sunshine Rd Kansas City (66115) ***(G-4537)***
Western Supply Co Inc (PA)....620 663-9082
2514 E 14th Ave Hutchinson (67501) ***(G-3486)***
Western Times, The, Sharon Springs *Also called Julie K Samuelson* ***(G-10899)***
Western Trailer Service Inc....913 281-2226
3550 Fairbanks Ave Kansas City (66106) ***(G-4538)***
Western Transport....620 271-0540
100 N 7th St Garden City (67846) ***(G-2312)***
Western Truck Equipment Co....620 793-8464
1310 10th St Great Bend (67530) ***(G-2662)***
Western Union....800 325-6000
615 Niles Ave Kinsley (67547) ***(G-4622)***
Western Well Service, Hays *Also called Rome Corporation* ***(G-2901)***
Westfall Newco LLC....844 663-5939
1101 N Halstead St Hutchinson (67501) ***(G-3487)***
Westglen Endoscopy Center LLC....913 248-8800
16663 Midland Dr Ste 200 Shawnee Mission (66217) ***(G-12006)***
Westheffer Company Inc....785 843-1633
921 N 1st St Lawrence (66044) ***(G-5183)***
Westhoff Interiors Inc....620 449-2900
14006 Wast 107th St Saint Paul (66771) ***(G-10386)***
Westirland Industries Inc....620 795-4421
1108 6th St Oswego (67356) ***(G-8239)***
Westley Woodlawn Hosp Emrgncy....316 962-2000
2610 N Woodlawn Blvd Wichita (67220) ***(G-15962)***
Westlink Branch, Wichita *Also called Emprise Bank* ***(G-14284)***
Westmore Drilling Company Inc....785 749-3712
4801 Innsbrook Dr Lawrence (66047) ***(G-5184)***
Weston Point Apartment, Overland Park *Also called Hanover Rs Limited Partnership* ***(G-8791)***
Westport Insurance Corporation (HQ)....913 676-5270
5200 Metcalf Ave Overland Park (66202) ***(G-9492)***
Westpro Construction Solutions (PA)....816 561-7667
2850 Fairfax Trfy Kansas City (66115) ***(G-4539)***
Westridge Apartments, Girard *Also called Crawford Cnty Assistd Lvng Com* ***(G-2400)***
Westrock Cp LLC....816 746-0403
5050 Kansas Ave Kansas City (66106) ***(G-4540)***
Westrock Dspensing Systems Inc....620 229-5000
3719 E 12th Ave Winfield (67156) ***(G-16182)***
Westside Vet Clnic Mnhattan PA....785 539-7922
3130 Anderson Ave Manhattan (66503) ***(G-6853)***
Westside Veterinary Clinic, Manhattan *Also called Westside Vet Clnic Mnhattan PA* ***(G-6853)***
WESTVIEW MANOR, Derby *Also called Lsl of Derby Ks LLC* ***(G-1260)***
Westview Mnor Healthcare Assoc....316 788-3739
445 N Westview Dr Derby (67037) ***(G-1281)***
Westview of Derby, Derby *Also called Westview Mnor Healthcare Assoc* ***(G-1281)***
Westwood Animal Hospital....913 362-2512
4820 Rainbow Blvd Westwood (66205) ***(G-13563)***
Westwood Manor, Topeka *Also called Liberty Assisted Living Center* ***(G-12842)***
Westy Community Care Home Inc....785 457-2806
105 N Highway 99 Westmoreland (66549) ***(G-13549)***

Weyerhaeuser Company...316 284-6700
701 S Spencer Rd Newton (67114) *(G-7428)*
Whale Ventures LLC...913 814-9988
12851 Foster St Overland Park (66213) *(G-9493)*
Whartons For Every...620 276-6000
906 N 10th St Garden City (67846) *(G-2313)*
What A Wonder Christian Daycre, Olathe *Also called Little Wnders Christn Day Care* *(G-7862)*
Wheat State, Udall *Also called Golden Wheat Inc* *(G-13277)*
Wheat State Manor Inc...316 799-2181
601 S Main St Whitewater (67154) *(G-13573)*
Wheat State Technologies, Udall *Also called Wheat State Telephone Inc* *(G-13279)*
Wheat State Telephone Inc (HQ)...620 782-3341
106 W 1st St Udall (67146) *(G-13279)*
Wheatbelt Inc...620 947-2323
300 Industrial Rd Hillsboro (67063) *(G-3058)*
Wheatland Broadband Services...620 872-0006
101 N Main St Scott City (67871) *(G-10836)*
Wheatland Contracting LLC...913 833-2304
6204 246th Rd Effingham (66023) *(G-1524)*
Wheatland Electric Coop Inc...620 275-0261
2005 W Fulton St Garden City (67846) *(G-2314)*
Wheatland Electric Coop Inc...620 793-4223
2300 Broadway Ave Great Bend (67530) *(G-2663)*
Wheatland Enterprises Inc (PA)...913 381-3504
2017 W 104th St Leawood (66206) *(G-5598)*
Wheatland Enterprises Inc...816 756-1700
2017 W 104th St Leawood (66206) *(G-5599)*
Wheatland Investments Inc...620 465-2225
101 N Kansas St Haven (67543) *(G-2738)*
Wheatland Medical Clinic PA...316 524-9400
5735 W Macarthur Rd Wichita (67215) *(G-15963)*
Wheatland Nursing Center, Russell *Also called Rh Montgomery Properties Inc* *(G-10290)*
Wheatland Vaults, Great Bend *Also called Concrete Vaults Inc* *(G-2546)*
Wheatland Waters Inc...785 267-0512
19625 W Old 56th Hwy Olathe (66061) *(G-8153)*
WHEATLANDS HEALTH CARE CENTER,, Kingman *Also called Kingman County Retirement Assn* *(G-4599)*
Wheelchairs of Kansas, Hays *Also called Rayes Inc* *(G-2897)*
Wheeler & Mitchelson Chartered...620 231-4650
319 N Broadway St Pittsburg (66762) *(G-9968)*
Wheeler Consolidated Inc...785 733-2848
1959 Old Highway 50 Waverly (66871) *(G-13483)*
Wheeler Lumber, Waverly *Also called Wheeler Consolidated Inc* *(G-13483)*
Wheeler, Sean MD, Belleville *Also called Belleville Medical Clinic P A* *(G-451)*
Whichita Thunder, Wichita *Also called Wichita Thnder Prof Hckey Team* *(G-16039)*
Whispering Pines Retirement HM, Norton *Also called Norton Retirement and Assisted* *(G-7460)*
Whistle Stop Carwash, Pittsburg *Also called Saragenes Short Stop* *(G-9935)*
Whitco Petroleum, Leoti *Also called Whitham Frank E Trust 2* *(G-6261)*
White & Ellis Drilling Inc (PA)...316 263-1102
10500 E Berkeley Sq Pk210 Wichita (67206) *(G-15964)*
White Chapel Memorial Corp...316 684-1612
1806 N Oliver Ave Wichita (67208) *(G-15965)*
White Cloud Grain Company Inc...785 235-5381
2300 Nw Menoken Rd Topeka (66618) *(G-13242)*
White Corporation Inc...620 342-4800
517 Merchant St Frnt Emporia (66801) *(G-1851)*
White Lawn and Landscape LLC...913 709-1472
10953 Kaw Dr Edwardsville (66111) *(G-1521)*
White Paladin Group Inc...913 722-4688
5500 W 69th St Prairie Village (66208) *(G-10082)*
White Star Machinery & Sup Co, Topeka *Also called Berry Companies Inc* *(G-12375)*
White William & Sons Cnstr Co...913 375-9161
15427 Stoneridge Dr Basehor (66007) *(G-391)*
Whiteley's Pallet & Blocking, Topeka *Also called Whiteleys Inc* *(G-13243)*
Whiteleys Inc...785 233-3801
310 Nw Norris St Topeka (66608) *(G-13243)*
Whiteway Inc...816 842-6565
501 Funston Rd Kansas City (66115) *(G-4541)*
Whitham Farms Feedyard Inc...620 375-4684
902 Broadway Plz Leoti (67861) *(G-6260)*
Whitham Frank E Trust 2...620 375-2229
2nd & Broadway Leoti (67861) *(G-6261)*
Whitichata Clinic, Newton *Also called Vello Kass MD* *(G-7423)*
Whiting House Group LLC...816 272-4496
16820 W 89th St Lenexa (66219) *(G-6228)*
Whole Child Development Center, Lenexa *Also called Crazy Girls LLC* *(G-5791)*
Wholesale AR, Le Roy *Also called Arnolds Greenhouse Inc* *(G-5195)*
Wholesale Batteries Inc (PA)...913 342-0113
605 Kansas Ave Kansas City (66105) *(G-4542)*
Wholesale Beauty Club Inc (PA)...316 687-9890
7732 E Central Ave # 102 Wichita (67206) *(G-15966)*
Wholesale Beauty Club Inc...316 941-9500
4800 W Maple St Ste 106 Wichita (67209) *(G-15967)*
Wholesale Feed Co, Salina *Also called Diamond Transfer & Dist Co* *(G-10476)*
Wholesale Sheet Metal, Kansas City *Also called Tartan Manufacturing Inc* *(G-4458)*
Wholesale Sheet Metal Inc (PA)...913 432-7100
800 Southwest Blvd Kansas City (66103) *(G-4543)*
Wholmoor Amrcn Lgion Post 237...785 348-5370
100 5th St Linn (66953) *(G-6413)*
Whp Training Towers, Overland Park *Also called Jahnke & Sons Construction Inc* *(G-8870)*
Wibw TV 13, Topeka *Also called Gray Television Group Inc* *(G-12645)*
Wichita Air Services Inc (PA)...316 631-1332
3324 N Jabara Rd Wichita (67226) *(G-15968)*
Wichita Airport Authority (PA)...316 946-4700
2173 S Air Cargo Rd Wichita (67209) *(G-15969)*
Wichita Airport Authority...316 636-9700
3512 N Webb Rd Wichita (67226) *(G-15970)*
Wichita Airport Hilton, Wichita *Also called Wichita Airport Ht Assoc L P* *(G-15971)*
Wichita Airport Ht Assoc L P...316 945-5272
2098 S Airport Rd Wichita (67209) *(G-15971)*
Wichita Aloft...316 744-1100
3642 N Oliver St Wichita (67220) *(G-15972)*
Wichita Ansthsiology Chartered...316 686-1564
8080 E Central Ave # 250 Wichita (67206) *(G-15973)*
Wichita Area Assn of Realtors...316 263-3167
170 W Dewey St Wichita (67202) *(G-15974)*
Wichita Area Chamber Commerce...316 265-7771
350 W Douglas Ave Wichita (67202) *(G-15975)*
Wichita Area Sxual Assault Ctr...316 263-0185
355 N Waco St Ste 100 Wichita (67202) *(G-15976)*
Wichita Arprt Hospitality LLC...316 522-0008
1236 S Dugan Rd Wichita (67209) *(G-15977)*
Wichita Awning Co Inc...316 838-4432
357 N Wabash Ave Wichita (67214) *(G-15978)*
Wichita Band Instrument Co...316 684-0291
2525 E Douglas Ave Wichita (67211) *(G-15979)*
Wichita Bar Association...316 263-2251
225 N Market St Ste 200 Wichita (67202) *(G-15980)*
WICHITA BAR FOUNDATION, Wichita *Also called Wichita Bar Association* *(G-15980)*
Wichita Bindery Inc...316 262-3473
622 S Commerce St Wichita (67202) *(G-15981)*
Wichita Body & Equipment Co...316 522-1080
6701 S Broadway Ave Haysville (67060) *(G-2964)*
Wichita Brass and Alum Fndry...316 838-4286
412 E 29th St N Wichita (67219) *(G-15982)*
Wichita Business Journal Inc...316 267-6406
121 N Mead St Ste 100 Wichita (67202) *(G-15983)*
Wichita Cabinet Company...316 617-0176
6859 31st Rd Udall (67146) *(G-13280)*
Wichita Canteen Company Inc (PA)...316 524-2254
4430 W 29th Cir S Wichita (67215) *(G-15984)*
Wichita Center For The Arts...316 315-0151
9112 E Central Ave Wichita (67206) *(G-15985)*
Wichita Chapter of Links Inc...316 744-7873
4819 N Harding St Bel Aire (67220) *(G-443)*
Wichita Child Guidance Center...316 686-6671
1365 N Custer St Wichita (67203) *(G-15986)*
Wichita Childrens Home...316 684-6581
7271 E 37th St N Wichita (67226) *(G-15987)*
Wichita Clinic, Wichita *Also called Via Christi Clinic PA* *(G-15883)*
Wichita Clinic Pharmacy, Wichita *Also called Via Christi Clinic PA* *(G-15881)*
Wichita Cntry CLB Maintennance...316 634-2882
8501 E 13th St N Ste 1022 Wichita (67206) *(G-15988)*
Wichita Cnty Long Term Rest Hm...620 375-4600
211 E Earl St Leoti (67861) *(G-6262)*
Wichita Comfort Inn, Wichita *Also called Heritage Inn Wichita Opco LLC* *(G-14595)*
Wichita Concrete Pipe Inc...316 838-8651
221 W 37th St N Wichita (67204) *(G-15989)*
Wichita Consulting Company LP...316 681-5102
8100 E 22nd St N Bldg 500 Wichita (67226) *(G-15990)*
Wichita Convention Tourism Bur...316 265-2800
515 S Main St Ste 115 Wichita (67202) *(G-15991)*
Wichita County Health Center...620 375-2233
211 E Earl St Leoti (67861) *(G-6263)*
Wichita County Health Center...620 375-2233
211 E Earl St Leoti (67861) *(G-6264)*
Wichita Crime Stoppers Program...316 267-2111
455 N Main St Fl 12 Wichita (67202) *(G-15992)*
Wichita Dialysis Center, Wichita *Also called Renal Trtmnt Centers-West Inc* *(G-15443)*
Wichita Division, Wichita *Also called Lewis-Goetz and Company Inc* *(G-14957)*
Wichita Drywall Acoustics LLC...316 773-7826
740 N Gilda St Wichita (67212) *(G-15993)*
Wichita Eagle Beacon Pubg Inc (HQ)...316 268-6000
330 N Mead St Wichita (67202) *(G-15994)*
Wichita Ear Clinic PA...316 686-6608
9350 E Central Ave Wichita (67206) *(G-15995)*
Wichita East Hotel Associates...316 686-7131
549 S Rock Rd Wichita (67207) *(G-15996)*
Wichita Emrgncy Veterinary LLC...316 262-5321
727 S Washington Ave Wichita (67211) *(G-15997)*
Wichita Family Crisis Ctr Inc...316 263-7501
1111 N Saint Francis Ave Wichita (67214) *(G-15998)*

ALPHABETIC

Wichita Family Medicine Specia 316 858-5800
800 N Carriage Pkwy Wichita (67208) *(G-15999)*
Wichita Federal Credit Union 316 941-0600
3730 W 13th St N Wichita (67203) *(G-16000)*
Wichita Fence Co Inc 316 838-1342
4901 N Broadway Ave Park City (67219) *(G-9654)*
Wichita Festivals Inc 316 267-2817
444 E William St Wichita (67202) *(G-16001)*
Wichita Fmly Vision Clinic PA 316 722-1001
437 N Tyler Rd Wichita (67212) *(G-16002)*
Wichita Gymnastics Club Inc 316 634-1900
9400 E 37th St N Wichita (67226) *(G-16003)*
Wichita Habitat For Humanity 316 269-0755
130 E Murdock St Ste 102 Wichita (67214) *(G-16004)*
Wichita Hampton Inn, Wichita *Also called HI Hritg Inn Wchita Opco LLC (G-14603)*
Wichita Home Health Care Group 316 219-0095
505 S Broadway Ave # 209 Wichita (67202) *(G-16005)*
Wichita Hoops LLC 316 440-4990
5260 N Toler Dr Bel Aire (67226) *(G-444)*
Wichita Hspttlity Holdings LLC 316 685-1281
400 W Douglas Ave Wichita (67202) *(G-16006)*
Wichita Ind Neighborhoods Inc 316 260-8000
2755 E 19th St N Wichita (67214) *(G-16007)*
Wichita Inn Suites Inc 316 685-2233
5211 E Kellogg Dr Wichita (67218) *(G-16008)*
Wichita Inn-North, Wichita *Also called Four of Wichita Inc (G-14408)*
Wichita Inn-West, Wichita *Also called Four of Wichita Inc (G-14407)*
Wichita Iron & Metals Corp Inc 316 267-3291
922 W Merton St Wichita (67213) *(G-16009)*
Wichita Kenworth Inc (PA) 316 838-0867
5115 N Broadway Ave Park City (67219) *(G-9655)*
Wichita Kinesiology Group PA, Wichita *Also called Chiro Plus Inc (G-14012)*
Wichita Lawyers Care, Wichita *Also called Kansas Legal Services Inc (G-14812)*
Wichita Machine Products Inc 316 522-7401
2930 S Old Lawrence Rd Wichita (67217) *(G-16010)*
Wichita Market Research, Wichita *Also called Research Partnership Inc (G-15447)*
Wichita Marriott, Wichita *Also called Corporate Hills LLC (G-14104)*
Wichita Material Recovery LLC 316 303-9303
624 E Morris St Wichita (67211) *(G-16011)*
Wichita Montessori School 316 686-7265
8311 E Douglas Ave Wichita (67207) *(G-16012)*
Wichita Nephrology Group PA 316 263-5891
818 N Emporia St Ste 310 Wichita (67214) *(G-16013)*
Wichita Northeast Branch, Wichita *Also called Sunflower Bank National Assn (G-15686)*
Wichita Ob Gyn Associates PA 316 685-0559
551 N Hillside St Ste 510 Wichita (67214) *(G-16014)*
Wichita Orthopaedic Assoc LLC 316 838-2020
7550 W Village Cir Ste 2 Wichita (67205) *(G-16015)*
Wichita Park Cmtry & Mausoleum 316 686-5594
3424 E 21st St N Wichita (67208) *(G-16016)*
Wichita Physical Medicine P A 316 729-1030
8338 W 13th St N Wichita (67212) *(G-16017)*
Wichita Presbyterian Manor, Wichita *Also called Presbyterian Manors Inc (G-15335)*
Wichita Press Inc 316 945-5651
4401 W Irving St Wichita (67209) *(G-16018)*
WICHITA PUBLIC SCHOOLS, Wichita *Also called Unified School District 259 (G-15833)*
Wichita Pump & Supply Company 316 264-8308
1010 E 14th St N Wichita (67214) *(G-16019)*
Wichita Residence Assoc LP 316 263-1061
711 S Main St Wichita (67213) *(G-16020)*
Wichita Roofing and Rmdlg Inc 316 943-0600
3821 W Bounous St Wichita (67213) *(G-16021)*
Wichita Rugby Foundation Inc 316 262-6800
727 N Waco Ave Ste 200 Wichita (67203) *(G-16022)*
Wichita Service Center, Wichita *Also called Pratt & Whitney Eng Svcs Inc (G-15322)*
Wichita Southeast Kansas Trnst 620 421-2272
2600 Flynn Dr Parsons (67357) *(G-9750)*
Wichita Sports Forum 316 201-1414
2668 N Greenwich Ct Wichita (67226) *(G-16023)*
Wichita Srgical Specialists PA 316 722-5814
982 N Tyler Rd Ste D Wichita (67212) *(G-16024)*
Wichita Srgical Specialists PA (PA) 316 263-0296
818 N Emporia St Ste 200 Wichita (67214) *(G-16025)*
Wichita Srgical Specialists PA 316 631-1600
2778 N Webb Rd Wichita (67226) *(G-16026)*
Wichita Srgical Specialists PA 316 688-7500
1861 N Webb Rd Wichita (67206) *(G-16027)*
Wichita Srgical Specialists PA 316 684-2838
310 S Hillside St Wichita (67211) *(G-16028)*
Wichita Stamp and Seal Inc 316 263-4223
807 N Main St Wichita (67203) *(G-16029)*
Wichita State Sunflower Inc 316 978-6917
1845 Fairmount St Wichita (67260) *(G-16030)*
Wichita State Univ Inter Cllga 316 978-3250
1845 Fairmount St Wichita (67260) *(G-16031)*
Wichita State University 316 978-3584
1845 Fairmount St Wichita (67260) *(G-16032)*
Wichita State University 316 978-6789
121 N Mead St Ste 200 Wichita (67202) *(G-16033)*
Wichita State University 316 978-3581
Duerksen Arts Cntr 1845 Wichita (67260) *(G-16034)*
Wichita State Unvsity Almni As 316 978-3290
1845 Fairmount St Wichita (67260) *(G-16035)*
Wichita Suites Hotel, Wichita *Also called Wichita Inn Suites Inc (G-16008)*
Wichita Swim Club 316 683-1491
8323 E Douglas Ave Wichita (67207) *(G-16036)*
Wichita Symphony Society 316 267-7658
225 W Douglas Ave Ste 207 Wichita (67202) *(G-16037)*
Wichita Terminal Association 316 262-0441
2649 N New York Ave Wichita (67219) *(G-16038)*
Wichita Thnder Prof Hckey Team 316 264-4625
505 W Maple St Wichita (67213) *(G-16039)*
Wichita Tobacco & Candy Co 316 264-2412
924 W 2nd St N Wichita (67203) *(G-16040)*
Wichita Top Childrens Fund 316 260-9479
1625 N Waterfront Pkwy Wichita (67206) *(G-16041)*
Wichita Tractor Company, Wichita *Also called McCullough Enterprises Inc (G-15024)*
Wichita Transit, Wichita *Also called City of Wichita (G-14031)*
Wichita Urology Group, Wichita *Also called Ayham J Farha MD (G-13783)*
Wichita Water Conditioning Inc (PA) 316 267-5287
10821 E 26th St N Wichita (67226) *(G-16042)*
Wichita Welding Supply Inc (PA) 316 838-8671
3001 N Broadway Ave Wichita (67219) *(G-16043)*
Wichita Wholesale Supply Inc 316 267-3629
1320 E 2nd St N Wichita (67214) *(G-16044)*
Wichita Wilbert Vault, Wichita *Also called Wilbert Funeral Services Inc (G-16046)*
Wickham Glass Co, Wichita *Also called G W Inc (G-14435)*
Widgets Family Fun Center 785 320-5099
8232 Southport Dr Manhattan (66502) *(G-6854)*
Wiebe Tire & Automotive 316 283-4242
1107 Washington Rd Newton (67114) *(G-7429)*
Wieneke Construction Co Inc 620 632-4529
954 S 87th St Mc Cune (66753) *(G-6923)*
Wiens & Company Construction 620 665-1155
219 N Whiteside St Hutchinson (67501) *(G-3488)*
Wiese Material Handling, Wichita *Also called Wiese Usa Inc (G-16045)*
Wiese Usa Inc 316 942-1600
1446 S Florence St Wichita (67209) *(G-16045)*
Wifco Steel Products Inc 620 543-2827
8003 Medora Rd Hutchinson (67502) *(G-3489)*
Wilbert & Towner PA (PA) 620 231-5620
506 N Pine St Pittsburg (66762) *(G-9969)*
Wilbert Funeral Services Inc 316 832-1114
2532 N Washington Ave Wichita (67219) *(G-16046)*
Wilbert Funeral Services Inc (PA) 913 345-2120
10965 Granada Ln Ste 300 Overland Park (66211) *(G-9494)*
Wilbert Manufacturers Assn, Overland Park *Also called Wilbert Funeral Services Inc (G-9494)*
Wilbert Screen Printing Inc 620 231-1730
1012 N Broadway St Pittsburg (66762) *(G-9970)*
Wilbur Inc 913 207-6535
12285 S Nelson Rd Olathe (66061) *(G-8154)*
Wilbur-Ellis Company LLC 785 582-4052
2620 Nw Huxman Rd Silver Lake (66539) *(G-12029)*
Wilbur-Ellis Company LLC 785 359-6569
1299 Ash Point Rd Leona (66532) *(G-6248)*
Wilco Inc 316 943-9379
3502 W Harry St Wichita (67213) *(G-16047)*
Wilcox Advanced Physical 316 942-5448
2243 S Meridian Ave # 100 Wichita (67213) *(G-16048)*
Wild Wild West Inc 785 827-8938
1035 N 3rd St Salina (67401) *(G-10768)*
Wildcat Concrete Services Inc 785 478-9000
2244 Nw Brickyard Rd Topeka (66618) *(G-13244)*
Wildcat Connectors Inc 785 937-4385
202 Main St Princeton (66078) *(G-10171)*
Wildcat Construction 316 945-9408
2244 Nw Brickyard Rd Topeka (66618) *(G-13245)*
Wildcat Construction Co Inc (PA) 316 945-9408
3219 W May St Wichita (67213) *(G-16049)*
Wildcat Creek Sports Center, Manhattan *Also called Kangolf Inc (G-6673)*
Wildcat Gttering Exteriors Inc 785 485-2194
6116 Summit Dr Manhattan (66503) *(G-6855)*
Wildcat Inns A Gen Partnerhip, Manhattan *Also called McCullough Developement Inc (G-6736)*
Wildcat Painting Inc 316 263-8076
4500 W Harry St Wichita (67209) *(G-16050)*
Wildcat Services Inc 785 922-6466
2175 Old Hwy 40 Chapman (67431) *(G-781)*
Wilde Tool Co Inc (PA) 785 742-7171
1210 Pottawatomie St Hiawatha (66434) *(G-3028)*
Wildflower Internet LLC 620 543-2580
102 N Main St Buhler (67522) *(G-619)*
Wilke International, Lenexa *Also called Wilke Resources Inc (G-6229)*
Wilke Resources Inc (PA) 913 438-5544
14321 W 96th Ter Lenexa (66215) *(G-6229)*

Wilkens Manufacturing Inc (PA)..........785 425-7070
1480 Highway 183 Stockton (67669) **(G-12190)**
Wilkerson Anderson & Anderson..........785 843-6060
831 Vermont St Ste 1 Lawrence (66044) **(G-5185)**
Wilkerson Crane Rental Inc..........913 238-7030
9131 Noland Rd Lenexa (66215) **(G-6230)**
Willgrattten Publications LLC..........785 762-5000
222 W 6th St Junction City (66441) **(G-3769)**
William Barnes..........316 321-3094
1975 Jamaica St El Dorado (67042) **(G-1614)**
William E Hoffman DDS..........913 663-2992
11213 Nall Ave Ste 130 Shawnee Mission (66211) **(G-12007)**
William F Frey Inc..........913 541-1000
11184 Antioch Rd Shawnee Mission (66210) **(G-12008)**
William G Woods..........620 285-6971
1041 K19 Hwy S Larned (67550) **(G-4716)**
William H Griffin..........913 677-1311
5115 Roe Blvd Ste 200 Roeland Park (66205) **(G-10231)**
William H Griffin Trustee, Roeland Park *Also called William H Griffin* **(G-10231)**
William Hoffman..........913 649-8890
3700 W 83rd St Ste 206 Shawnee Mission (66208) **(G-12009)**
William O Broeker Enterprises..........913 682-2022
701 Delaware St Leavenworth (66048) **(G-5306)**
William R Harris Trucking..........913 422-5551
20501 W 67th St Ste A Shawnee Mission (66218) **(G-12010)**
William Sonoma Store Inc..........316 636-5990
2000 N Rock Rd Ste 152 Wichita (67206) **(G-16051)**
William Unsderfer MD..........620 669-6690
104 Crescent Blvd Hutchinson (67502) **(G-3490)**
Williams Automotive Inc..........620 343-0086
3105 W 6th Ave Emporia (66801) **(G-1852)**
Williams Company Inc..........785 873-3260
137 S Whiting St Whiting (66552) **(G-13575)**
Williams Construction Co Inc..........316 264-1964
2008 W Harry Ct Wichita (67213) **(G-16052)**
Williams Diversified Mtls Inc..........620 679-9810
2903 Military Ave Baxter Springs (66713) **(G-415)**
Williams Farms & Trucking, Leon *Also called Clinton L Williams* **(G-6246)**
Williams Foods Inc (HQ)..........913 888-4343
13301 W 99th St Lenexa (66215) **(G-6231)**
Williams Investigation & SEC..........620 275-1134
4245 Chambers Dr Garden City (67846) **(G-2315)**
Williams Janitor Supplies, Wichita *Also called Lafe T Williams & Assoc Inc* **(G-14914)**
Williams Machine and Tl Co Inc..........620 783-5184
1009 Schermerhorn Rd Galena (66739) **(G-2089)**
Williams Natural Gas Company..........913 422-4496
8195 Cole Pkwy Shawnee Mission (66227) **(G-12011)**
Williams Security, Garden City *Also called Williams Investigation & SEC* **(G-2315)**
Williams Service Inc..........620 878-4225
1101 Main St Florence (66851) **(G-1930)**
Williams-Carver Company Inc..........913 236-4949
4001 Mission Rd Kansas City (66103) **(G-4544)**
Williams-Sonoma Store, Wichita *Also called William Sonoma Store Inc* **(G-16051)**
Williamson & Cubbison..........913 371-1930
748 Ann Ave Kansas City (66101) **(G-4545)**
Willis North America Inc..........913 339-0800
12980 Metcalf Ave Ste 500 Overland Park (66213) **(G-9495)**
Willlowtree Supports Inc..........913 353-1970
23733 W 83rd Ter Shawnee (66227) **(G-11053)**
Willowridge Landscape Inc..........785 842-7022
1453 E 800th Rd Lawrence (66049) **(G-5186)**
Wilroads Feed Yard LLC..........620 225-3960
11449 Lariat Way Dodge City (67801) **(G-1457)**
Wilson Ielah..........913 954-9798
2503 N 91st St Kansas City (66109) **(G-4546)**
Wilson Building Maintenance..........316 264-0699
624 E 1st St N Wichita (67202) **(G-16053)**
Wilson Communication Co Inc..........785 658-2111
2504 Avenue D Wilson (67490) **(G-16107)**
Wilson Concrete Batch Plant, Kansas City *Also called Cemex Materials LLC* **(G-3900)**
Wilson County Citizen Inc..........620 378-4415
406 N 7th St Fredonia (66736) **(G-2049)**
Wilson County Hospital (PA)..........620 325-2611
2600 Ottawa Rd Neodesha (66757) **(G-7250)**
Wilson Inc Engneers Architects..........913 652-9911
9401 Reeds Rd Overland Park (66207) **(G-9496)**
Wilson Inc Engneers Architects..........785 827-0433
1700 E Iron Ave Salina (67401) **(G-10769)**
WILSON MEDICAL CENTER, Neodesha *Also called Wilson County Hospital* **(G-7250)**
Wilson Nursing Home, Wilson *Also called Beverly Enterprises-Kansas LLC* **(G-16104)**
Wilson State Bank (PA)..........785 658-3441
422 26th St Wilson (67490) **(G-16108)**
Wilson State Bank..........620 653-4113
201 N Main St Hoisington (67544) **(G-3073)**
Wilson Telephone Company Inc (PA)..........785 658-2111
2504 Avenue D Wilson (67490) **(G-16109)**
Wilson Trailer Sales Kans Inc..........620 225-6220
2730 E Trail St Dodge City (67801) **(G-1458)**
Wilson Transportation Inc..........913 851-7900
16226 Foster St Overland Park (66085) **(G-9497)**
Wilson, Angela DDS Ms, Lawrence *Also called Edwards & Wilson Periodontides* **(G-4847)**
Wimase International Inc..........620 783-1361
8500 Se Jayhawk Dr Riverton (66770) **(G-10214)**
WIN, Wichita *Also called Wichita Ind Neighborhoods Inc* **(G-16007)**
Winavie LLC..........913 789-8169
3073 Merriam Ln Kansas City (66106) **(G-4547)**
Winburn, Richard L, Shawnee Mission *Also called Richard Winburn* **(G-11801)**
Winbury Group of KC LLC..........785 865-5100
805 New Hampshire St C Lawrence (66044) **(G-5187)**
Wince Family Dental..........620 241-0266
1325 E 1st St McPherson (67460) **(G-7042)**
Winchester Meat Processing..........913 774-2860
203 Winchester St Winchester (66097) **(G-16111)**
Winchester Place Pet Care Ctr..........913 451-2827
15070 W 116th St Olathe (66062) **(G-8155)**
Winco Fireworks Intl LLC (PA)..........913 649-2071
5200 W 94th Ter Ste 114 Prairie Village (66207) **(G-10083)**
Windcreek Dialysis LLC..........913 294-8417
1605 E Peoria St Paola (66071) **(G-9596)**
Winding Specialists Co Inc..........316 265-9358
1225 N Wellington Pl Wichita (67203) **(G-16054)**
Windjammer Cables, Overland Park *Also called Windjammer Communications LLC* **(G-9498)**
Windjammer Communications LLC..........913 563-5450
8500 W 110th St Ste 600 Overland Park (66210) **(G-9498)**
Windmill Inn Inc..........785 336-3696
603 N 4th St Seneca (66538) **(G-10888)**
Window Design Company..........785 582-2888
9939 Nw Us Highway 24 # 1 Silver Lake (66539) **(G-12030)**
Window Flair Draperies..........913 722-6070
11810 W 62nd Pl Shawnee (66203) **(G-11054)**
Windriver Grain LLC..........620 275-2101
2810 E Us Highway 50 Garden City (67846) **(G-2316)**
Windsor Estates, Salina *Also called Windsor Nursing Home Assoc* **(G-10771)**
Windsor Estates Inc..........785 825-8183
626 S 3rd St Salina (67401) **(G-10770)**
Windsor Home Care, Chanute *Also called Health Management of Kansas* **(G-731)**
Windsor Nursing Home Assoc..........785 825-6757
623 S 3rd St Salina (67401) **(G-10771)**
Windsor of Lawrence..........785 832-9900
3220 Peterson Rd Lawrence (66049) **(G-5188)**
Windsor Place, Coffeyville *Also called Health Management of Kansas* **(G-945)**
Windsor Place, Coffeyville *Also called Health Management of Kansas* **(G-946)**
Windsor Place..........620 251-6545
600 E Garfield St Iola (66749) **(G-3638)**
WINDSOR PLACE AT IOLA, Iola *Also called Windsor Place* **(G-3638)**
Windsor Place At-Home Care..........620 331-3388
201 N Penn Ave Ste 104 Independence (67301) **(G-3573)**
Windsor Place Home Care Div, Coffeyville *Also called Health Management of Kansas* **(G-944)**
Windstream Nuvox Kansas LLC..........913 747-7000
7957 Bond St Shawnee Mission (66214) **(G-12012)**
Windtrax Inc..........913 789-9100
6800 Foxridge Dr Shawnee Mission (66202) **(G-12013)**
Winfield Area E M S..........620 221-2300
1300 E 5th Ave Winfield (67156) **(G-16183)**
Winfield Area Hbtat For Hmnity..........620 221-7298
1004 Clyde Winfield (67156) **(G-16184)**
Winfield Country Club..........620 221-1570
2916 Country Club Rd Winfield (67156) **(G-16185)**
Winfield Daily Courier, Winfield *Also called Winfield Publishing Co Inc* **(G-16189)**
Winfield Medical Arts PA..........620 221-6100
3625 Quail Ridge Rd Winfield (67156) **(G-16186)**
Winfield Motor Company Inc (PA)..........620 221-2840
1901 Main St Winfield (67156) **(G-16187)**
Winfield Plumbing & Heating..........620 221-2210
1910 Wheat Rd Winfield (67156) **(G-16188)**
Winfield Publishing Co Inc..........620 221-1100
201 E 9th Ave Winfield (67156) **(G-16189)**
Winfield Rest Haven Inc..........620 221-9290
1611 Ritchie St Winfield (67156) **(G-16190)**
Winfield Solutions LLC..........620 277-2231
4460 Jones Ave Ste B Garden City (67846) **(G-2317)**
Winfield Walnut KS LLC..........216 520-1250
1201 Menor St Winfield (67156) **(G-16191)**
Wingate Inns International Inc..........620 241-5566
2302 E Kansas Ave McPherson (67460) **(G-7043)**
Wingate Inns International Inc..........316 733-8833
600 S Allen St Andover (67002) **(G-117)**
Winger Cattle Co Inc..........620 492-6214
507 N Main St Johnson (67855) **(G-3666)**
Winger Seed, Johnson *Also called Winger Cattle Co Inc* **(G-3666)**
Wingert Animal Hospital..........316 524-3257
4419 S Seneca St Wichita (67217) **(G-16055)**
Winkel Manufacturing Co..........785 545-3297
2225a 200 Rd Glen Elder (67446) **(G-2428)**
Winn Enterprise, Wichita *Also called Landscapes Inc* **(G-14921)**

ALPHABETIC

Winner Cir Feedyard Dodge LLC 620 227-2246
11995 Quaker Rd Dodge City (67801) ***(G-1459)***
Winning Spirit Inc 316 684-0855
934 S Oliver St Wichita (67218) ***(G-16056)***
Winning Streak Sports LLC 913 768-8868
9821 Widmer Rd Lenexa (66215) ***(G-6232)***
Winona Van Norman Inc 316 219-3500
710 E 17th St N Wichita (67214) ***(G-16057)***
Winston-Brown Construction Co (PA) 785 271-1661
5600 Sw 29th St Ste A Topeka (66614) ***(G-13246)***
Winter Architects Inc 316 267-7142
1024 E 1st St N Wichita (67214) ***(G-16058)***
Winter Feed Yard Inc 620 225-4128
Ft Dodge Rd Dodge City (67801) ***(G-1460)***
Winter Livestock Inc 620 525-6271
4 Mi East & 3 Mi St Mi Ea Hanston (67849) ***(G-2715)***
Winter Livestock Inc 620 225-4159
1414 E Trail St Dodge City (67801) ***(G-1461)***
Winters Excelsior, Hutchinson *Also called Delmarva Pad Co* ***(G-3261)***
Wireco Worldgroup Inc 816 270-4700
2400 W 75th St Prairie Village (66208) ***(G-10084)***
Wireco Worldgroup Inc (HQ) 816 270-4700
2400 75th Prairie Village (66208) ***(G-10085)***
Wireco Wrldgroup US Hldngs Inc (PA) 816 270-4700
2400 W 75th St Prairie Village (66208) ***(G-10086)***
Wireless Lifestyle LLC (PA) 913 962-0002
11200 W 93rd St Overland Park (66214) ***(G-9499)***
Wirths & Sons Inc 316 838-0509
109 E 37th St N Wichita (67219) ***(G-16059)***
Wise & Breymer 620 241-0554
120 W Kansas Ave Ste B McPherson (67460) ***(G-7044)***
Wise Connect 913 276-4100
7501 College Blvd Ste 100 Overland Park (66210) ***(G-9500)***
Wise Construction Inc 785 781-4383
604 Wisconsin St Cawker City (67430) ***(G-691)***
Wiseman Discount Tire Inc 620 231-5291
4078 Parkview Dr Frontenac (66763) ***(G-2067)***
Wiston Property Management (PA) 913 383-8100
8826 Santa Fe Dr Ste 310 Shawnee Mission (66212) ***(G-12014)***
Witchita Clinic Inc 620 583-7436
100 W 16th St Eureka (67045) ***(G-1899)***
Witchita Public School Mngt In, Wichita *Also called Unified School District 259* ***(G-15836)***
Witzkes Screen Printing 913 839-8270
1165 W Dennis Ave Olathe (66061) ***(G-8156)***
Wkcsc Inc 316 652-7113
4310 S Southeast Blvd Wichita (67210) ***(G-16060)***
Wki Operations Inc 316 838-0867
1301 Minneola Rd Dodge City (67801) ***(G-1462)***
Wm F Hurst Co LLC 800 741-0543
21981 W 83rd St Shawnee (66227) ***(G-11055)***
Wm Law, Olathe *Also called Wagoner Bankruptcy Group PC* ***(G-8145)***
Wolf & Hatfield Inc 620 227-3071
2520 N 14th Ave Dodge City (67801) ***(G-1463)***
Wolf 100.5 The, Wichita *Also called Connoisseur Media LLC* ***(G-14089)***
Wolf Construction Inc (PA) 785 862-2474
5630 Sw Randolph Ave Topeka (66609) ***(G-13247)***
Wolf Creek Golf Links Inc 913 592-3329
18695 S Lackman Rd Olathe (66062) ***(G-8157)***
Wolf Creek Nuclear Oper Corp 620 364-4141
1550 Oxen Ln Burlington (66839) ***(G-645)***
Wolf Memorial Co Inc 785 726-4430
205 W 9th St Ellis (67637) ***(G-1655)***
Wolfe Electric Inc 316 943-2751
7761 W Kellogg Dr Wichita (67209) ***(G-16061)***
Wolfe Machine, Mulvane *Also called Kmi Inc* ***(G-7217)***
Wolfert Landscape Co LLC 913 592-4189
17140 S Us 169 Hwy Olathe (66062) ***(G-8158)***
Wolfes Camera Shops Inc 785 235-1386
635 S Kansas Ave Topeka (66603) ***(G-13248)***
Wolfes Cmras Cmcrders Cmputers, Topeka *Also called Wolfes Camera Shops Inc* ***(G-13248)***
Wolfgang Construction LLC 785 456-8729
17755 High St Wamego (66547) ***(G-13457)***
Wolski & Associates 913 281-3233
753 State Ave Ste 370 Kansas City (66101) ***(G-4548)***
Wolters Kluwer Health Inc 316 612-5000
9111 E Douglas Ave Wichita (67207) ***(G-16062)***
Wolters Kluwer/Cch, Wichita *Also called Wolters Kluwer Health Inc* ***(G-16062)***
Woman's Choice A, Shawnee Mission *Also called Center For Woman Health* ***(G-11210)***
Womans Place PA 620 662-2229
1818 E 23rd Ave Hutchinson (67502) ***(G-3491)***
Women In Trnstion Together Inc 785 424-7516
1307 W 27th St Lawrence (66046) ***(G-5189)***
Women of Divine Wisdom, Leavenworth *Also called Andrea Clark* ***(G-5203)***
Women's Health Associates PA, Shawnee Mission *Also called Womens Health Associates Inc* ***(G-12015)***
Women's Healthcare Group The, Lenexa *Also called Womens Health Care Group* ***(G-6233)***
Womens Care, Overland Park *Also called Sugar Scholl Magee Carriker* ***(G-9370)***
Womens Care (PA) 913 384-4990
9301 W 74th St Ste 325 Overland Park (66204) ***(G-9501)***
Womens Chldren Shelter Linwood 620 231-0415
307 E 5th St Pittsburg (66762) ***(G-9971)***
Womens Clinic Assoc PA 913 788-9797
3550 S 4th St Ste 150 Leavenworth (66048) ***(G-5307)***
Womens Clinic Johnson County (PA) 913 491-4020
5525 W 119th St Leawood (66209) ***(G-5600)***
Womens Clinic Johnson County 913 491-4020
9119 W 74th St Ste 268 Overland Park (66204) ***(G-9502)***
Womens Community Y 913 682-6404
520 S Broadway St Leavenworth (66048) ***(G-5308)***
Womens Health Associates Inc (PA) 913 677-3113
9119 W 74th St Ste 300 Shawnee Mission (66204) ***(G-12015)***
Womens Health Care Group 816 589-2121
3510 Clinton Pl Ste 310 Lawrence (66047) ***(G-5190)***
Womens Health Care Group (PA) 913 438-0018
10600 Quivira Rd Ste 200 Lenexa (66215) ***(G-6233)***
Womens Health Group PA 785 776-1400
1133 College Ave Bldg E Manhattan (66502) ***(G-6856)***
Womens Health Svcs Kans Cy PC 816 941-2700
2104 W 119th Ter Leawood (66209) ***(G-5601)***
WONDER WORKSHOP, Manhattan *Also called Midwest Educational Center* ***(G-6747)***
Woner Glenn Reder Grant Riordn (PA) 785 235-5371
5611 Sw Berrington Topeka (66614) ***(G-13249)***
Wood Ribble & Twyman Inc 913 396-4400
7301 W 129th St Ste 110 Overland Park (66213) ***(G-9503)***
Wood Haven Inc 785 597-5618
401 W Bridge St Perry (66073) ***(G-9775)***
Wood RE New Joco Inc 913 661-9663
11507 S Strang Line Rd A Olathe (66062) ***(G-8159)***
Wood Rot Pro 913 638-5732
15126 W 157th Ter Olathe (66062) ***(G-8160)***
Wood Valley Racquet Club Inc 785 506-8928
2909 Sw 37th St Topeka (66614) ***(G-13250)***
Wood View Apartments LLC 913 262-8733
3124 Woodview Ridge Dr Kansas City (66103) ***(G-4549)***
Wood Vly Rcquet CLB Fitnes Ctr, Topeka *Also called Wood Valley Racquet Club Inc* ***(G-13250)***
Woodard Hernandez Roth Day LLC 316 263-4958
245 N Waco St Ste 260 Wichita (67202) ***(G-16063)***
Woodard Tech & Investments LLC 316 636-2122
200 N Emporia Ave Ste 300 Wichita (67202) ***(G-16064)***
Woodcraft Supply LLC 913 599-2800
8645 Bluejacket St Shawnee Mission (66214) ***(G-12016)***
Wooden Stuff Cabinets Inc 785 887-6003
515 E Woodson Ave Lecompton (66050) ***(G-5614)***
Woodhaven Care Center, Ellinwood *Also called Five Star Quality Care-Ks LLC* ***(G-1632)***
Woodich John 620 332-3280
800 W Laurel St Independence (67301) ***(G-3574)***
Woodland Health Care Center, Topeka *Also called Midwest Health Services Inc* ***(G-12900)***
Woodland Hlth Ctr Oprtions LLC 785 234-6147
440 Se Woodland Ave Topeka (66607) ***(G-13251)***
Woodland Lakes Community Churc 316 682-9522
770 S Greenwich Rd Wichita (67207) ***(G-16065)***
Woodland United Methodist Ch 316 265-6669
1100 W 15th St N Wichita (67203) ***(G-16066)***
Woodland Untd Mthdst Pr-School, Wichita *Also called Woodland United Methodist Ch* ***(G-16066)***
Woodlands, Kansas City *Also called Sr Food and Beverage Co Inc* ***(G-4437)***
Woodlawn Care and Rehab LLC 316 691-9999
1600 S Woodlawn Blvd Wichita (67218) ***(G-16067)***
Woodridge Estates LLC 620 421-2431
329 Kay Ln Parsons (67357) ***(G-9751)***
Woods & Durham LLC (PA) 785 825-5494
1619 E Iron Ave Salina (67401) ***(G-10772)***
Woods Alfalfa 620 376-4999
1705 Road F Tribune (67879) ***(G-13272)***
Woods and Durham Chartered, Salina *Also called Woods & Durham LLC* ***(G-10772)***
Woods of Cherry Creek Inc 913 491-3030
12321 Metcalf Ave Overland Park (66213) ***(G-9504)***
Woods Painting Co Inc 913 897-3741
3505 W 194th St Stilwell (66085) ***(G-12180)***
Woods, Gregory A MD, Hays *Also called Hays Orthopedic Clinic PA* ***(G-2836)***
Woodside Tennis & Health Club 913 831-0034
2000 W 47th Pl Shawnee Mission (66205) ***(G-12017)***
Woodstone Homes, Shawnee Mission *Also called Woodstone Inc* ***(G-12018)***
Woodstone Inc 913 685-2282
14300 Kenneth Rd Shawnee Mission (66224) ***(G-12018)***
Woodwork Mfg & Sup Inc 620 663-3393
403 S Adams St Hutchinson (67501) ***(G-3492)***
Woodworth Enterprises Inc 620 236-7248
814 Walnut St Chetopa (67336) ***(G-818)***
Woodworth International Inc 620 236-7248
814 Walnut St Chetopa (67336) ***(G-819)***
Woodys Automotive Svc & Sls 316 838-8011
2600 N Amidon Ave Wichita (67204) ***(G-16068)***
Woofs Play & Stay Inc 913 768-9663
585 N Central St Olathe (66061) ***(G-8161)***

Woofter Cnstr & Irrigation, Colby *Also called Woofter Cnstr & Irrigation Inc (G-1049)*
Woofter Cnstr & Irrigation Inc (PA).......785 462-8653
1965 Thielen Ave Colby (67701) **(G-1049)**
Woofter Pump & Well Inc.......785 675-3991
1024 Oak Ave Hoxie (67740) **(G-3144)**
Woofter Woofter Stupka Inc.......785 460-6683
1110 Plains Ave Ste 1 Colby (67701) **(G-1050)**
Woolsey Petroleum Corporation (PA).......316 267-4379
125 N Market St Ste 1000 Wichita (67202) **(G-16069)**
Woolsey Petroleum Corporation.......620 886-5606
1966 Se Rodeo Dr Medicine Lodge (67104) **(G-7076)**
Wooten Enterprises LLC.......316 830-2328
312 E 1st St Halstead (67056) **(G-2707)**
Wooten Printing Co Inc.......316 265-8575
239 N Handley St Wichita (67203) **(G-16070)**
Word of Life Preschool.......316 838-5683
3811 N Meridian Cir Wichita (67204) **(G-16071)**
Word Park Services, Shawnee Mission *Also called Christopher B Geha (G-11223)*
Word-Tech Inc.......913 722-3334
5625 Foxridge Dr Ste 110 Shawnee Mission (66202) **(G-12019)**
Word-Tech Business Systems, Shawnee Mission *Also called Word-Tech Inc (G-12019)*
Work Comp Specialty Associates.......785 841-7751
4840 Bob Billings Pkwy # 1000 Lawrence (66049) **(G-5191)**
Workforce Alliance of South.......316 771-6600
300 W Douglas Ave Ste 850 Wichita (67202) **(G-16072)**
Workman Printing Co, Clay Center *Also called Printery Inc (G-877)*
World Fuel Services Inc.......913 643-2300
6000 Metcalf Ave Ste 200 Overland Park (66202) **(G-9505)**
World Fuel Services Corp.......913 451-2400
8650 College Blvd Overland Park (66210) **(G-9506)**
World Impact Inc.......316 687-9398
3701 E 13th St N Ofc Ofc Wichita (67208) **(G-16073)**
World Office, Wakeeney *Also called Western Kansas World Inc (G-13396)*
World Pest Control, Sylvan Grove *Also called Bats Inc (G-12219)*
World Publishing Inc.......785 221-8174
1622 Sw Knollwood Dr Topeka (66611) **(G-13252)**
Worldwest Ltd Liability Co (PA).......785 843-1000
609 New Hampshire St Lawrence (66044) **(G-5192)**
Worldwide Energy Inc.......913 310-0705
10413 W 84th Ter Lenexa (66214) **(G-6234)**
Worldwide Windows.......785 826-1701
736 N 9th St Salina (67401) **(G-10773)**
Worship Woodworks Inc.......620 622-4568
207 W Walnut St Protection (67127) **(G-10177)**
Worship Woodworks.com, Protection *Also called Worship Woodworks Inc (G-10177)*
Worthington Cylinder Corp.......316 529-6950
5605 N 119th St W Maize (67101) **(G-6523)**
Worthington Cylinder Corp.......620 275-7461
2814 W Jones Ave Garden City (67846) **(G-2318)**
Wow, Lawrence *Also called Midcontinent Communications (G-5025)*
Wpm, Salina *Also called Weber Palmer & Macy Chartered (G-10763)*
Wppa Inc.......316 683-4111
1102 S Hillside St Wichita (67211) **(G-16074)**
Wrap Factory.......913 667-3010
10933 Kaw Dr Edwardsville (66111) **(G-1522)**
Wray & Sons Roofing Inc.......620 663-7107
229 E 3rd Ave Hutchinson (67501) **(G-3493)**
Wray Roofing Inc.......316 283-6840
1521 Nw 36th St Newton (67117) **(G-7430)**
Wray's Woodworking, Pomona *Also called Jerry Wray (G-10005)*
Wrg, Wichita *Also called Radiological Wichita Group PA (G-15410)*
Wright Henson Clark & Bakr LLP.......785 232-2200
100 Se 9th St Fl 2 Topeka (66612) **(G-13253)**
Wright Intl Studnt Svcs.......913 677-1142
6405 Metcalf Ave Ste 504 Shawnee Mission (66202) **(G-12020)**
Wright Landscaping LLC.......816 225-1050
8113 Parkhill St Lenexa (66215) **(G-6235)**
Wright Redden & Associates LLC.......620 251-6204
109 W 7th St Coffeyville (67337) **(G-986)**
Wright, Larry CPA, Coffeyville *Also called Wright Redden & Associates LLC (G-986)*
WSC Services Inc.......913 660-0454
7534 Windsor St Prairie Village (66208) **(G-10087)**
Wsi Holdings LLC.......785 421-2255
710 W Mcvey St Hill City (67642) **(G-3038)**
Wskt, Parsons *Also called Wichita Southeast Kansas Trnst (G-9750)*
Wsm Industries Inc (HQ).......316 942-9412
1601 S Sheridan St Wichita (67213) **(G-16075)**
Wsm Industries Inc.......913 492-9299
9755 Lackman Rd Lenexa (66219) **(G-6236)**
Wsm Investments Inc (PA).......316 942-9412
1601 S Sheridan St Wichita (67213) **(G-16076)**
Wsu Sunflower Newspaper.......316 978-6900
1845 Fairmount St 134 Wichita (67260) **(G-16077)**
WSU-ICAA, Wichita *Also called Wichita State Univ Inter Cllga (G-16031)*
Wt Contractors.......620 356-4801
2214 W Rd 10 Ulysses (67880) **(G-13332)**
Wtc Communications Inc.......785 456-1000
1009 Lincoln Ave Wamego (66547) **(G-13458)**
WTCS, Lawrence *Also called Lawrence Wmens Trnstnal Cre S (G-4989)*
Wtg Hugoton LP.......620 544-4381
2272 Road Q Hugoton (67951) **(G-3180)**
Wurst, Wendel W, Garden City *Also called Calihan Brwn Burgrdt Wurst (G-2120)*
Wurth/Service Supply Inc.......316 869-2159
3144 N Ohio St Ste A Wichita (67219) **(G-16078)**
WW Grainger Inc.......316 945-5101
1920 S West St Wichita (67213) **(G-16079)**
WW Grainger Inc.......913 492-8550
14790 W 99th St Lenexa (66215) **(G-6237)**
Ww Kc Metcalf LLC.......913 956-0234
11200 Glenwood St Leawood (66211) **(G-5602)**
Ww North America Holdings Inc.......913 227-0152
11752 W 95th St Overland Park (66214) **(G-9507)**
Ww North America Holdings Inc.......913 495-1400
7171 W 95th St Ste 400 Overland Park (66212) **(G-9508)**
Www.4thgenerationinc.com, Olathe *Also called 4th Gneration Promotional Pdts (G-7502)*
WWW.ELCENTROINC.COM, Kansas City *Also called El Centro Inc (G-3982)*
Www.frozendrinkrus.biz, Olathe *Also called Smart Beverage Inc (G-8068)*
Www.kbp.com, Wichita *Also called ARC Document Solutions (G-13727)*
Www.oversizewarningproductscom, Great Bend *Also called Oversize Warning Products Inc (G-2620)*
Wyandot Center For Community B (PA).......913 233-3300
757 Armstrong Ave Kansas City (66101) **(G-4550)**
Wyandot Inc.......913 233-3300
757 Armstrong Ave Kansas City (66101) **(G-4551)**
Wyandotte Central Dialysis LLC.......913 233-0536
3737 State Ave Kansas City (66102) **(G-4552)**
Wyandotte County Dialysis, Kansas City *Also called Total Renal Care Inc (G-4470)*
Wyandotte County Sports Assn.......913 299-9197
10100 Leavenworth Rd Kansas City (66109) **(G-4553)**
Wyandtt-Leavenworth Legal Svcs, Kansas City *Also called Kansas Legal Services Inc (G-4156)*
Wyandtte Cnty Unfied Gvernment.......913 573-8300
5033 State Ave Kansas City (66102) **(G-4554)**
Wyandtte Cnty Unfied Gvernment.......913 281-3300
1124 N 9th St Kansas City (66101) **(G-4555)**
Wyandtte Cnty Unfied Gvernment.......913 573-5700
701 N 7th St Kansas City (66101) **(G-4556)**
Wyandtte Occpational Hlth Svcs.......913 945-9740
4810 State Ave Kansas City (66102) **(G-4557)**
Wyatt-Harris, Patricia G MD, Wichita *Also called College Hill Ob/Gyn Inc (G-14056)*
Wyldewood Cellars Inc (PA).......316 554-9463
951 E 119th St S Peck (67120) **(G-9764)**
Wyncroft Hill Apartments.......913 829-1404
12235 S Blackbob Rd Olathe (66062) **(G-8162)**
Wyndham Garden.......316 269-2090
221 E Kellogg St Wichita (67202) **(G-16080)**
Wyndham International Inc.......913 383-2550
7000 W 108th St Overland Park (66211) **(G-9509)**
Wyndham International Inc.......316 729-5700
2405 N Ridge Rd Wichita (67205) **(G-16081)**
Wynne Transport Service Inc.......316 321-3900
805 N Haverhill Rd El Dorado (67042) **(G-1615)**
Wynnewood Refining Company LLC.......913 982-0500
10 E Cambridge Circle Dr Kansas City (66103) **(G-4558)**
Wyoming Casing Service Inc.......620 793-9630
386 Sw 20 Ave Great Bend (67530) **(G-2664)**
X F Enterprises Inc.......620 672-5616
211 Pedigo Dr Pratt (67124) **(G-10164)**
X TEC Repair Inc.......913 829-3773
10602 Lackman Rd Lenexa (66219) **(G-6238)**
X Tech Midwest Inc.......316 777-6648
2423 E 13th St N Wichita (67214) **(G-16082)**
X-Pert Service Tools Inc.......785 421-5600
310 Plum St Hill City (67642) **(G-3039)**
X-Press Signs and Graphics LLC.......316 613-2360
5830 W Hendryx Ave Wichita (67209) **(G-16083)**
Xact, Shawnee Mission *Also called Xcellence Inc (G-12021)*
XCEL Erectors Inc (HQ).......913 664-7400
7401 W 129th St Overland Park (66213) **(G-9510)**
XCEL NDT LLC.......785 455-2027
104 Avon St Clifton (66937) **(G-903)**
Xcellence Inc (PA).......913 362-8662
5800 Foxridge Dr Ste 406 Shawnee Mission (66202) **(G-12021)**
Xec Inc.......913 563-4260
11200 W 79th St Overland Park (66214) **(G-9511)**
Xelocity Inc.......913 647-8660
9300 W 110th St Ste 620 Overland Park (66210) **(G-9512)**
Xenometrics, Stilwell *Also called Citoxlab Usa LLC (G-12141)*
Xenotech LLC.......913 438-7450
1101 W Cambridge Cir Dr Kansas City (66103) **(G-4559)**
Xiphium Hair Salon.......913 696-1616
10589 Mission Rd Leawood (66206) **(G-5603)**
Xit Ranch, Maple Hill *Also called Adams Cattle Company (G-6862)*
Xk Solutions Inc.......877 954-9656
6709 W 119th St Ste 242 Overland Park (66209) **(G-9513)**
Xpedx, Kansas City *Also called Veritiv Operating Company (G-4516)*

ALPHABETIC

Xpo Logistics Freight Inc....913 281-3535
234 E Donovan Rd Kansas City (66115) ***(G-4560)***
Xpo Logistics Freight Inc....785 823-3926
358 E Berg Rd Salina (67401) ***(G-10774)***
Xpo Logistics Freight Inc....316 942-0498
4330 W 29th St S Wichita (67215) ***(G-16084)***
Xpo Stacktrain LLC....913 422-6400
2663 S 88th St Kansas City (66111) ***(G-4561)***
Xpressotech Solutions LLC....316 993-9397
18500 W 2nd Cir N Goddard (67052) ***(G-2457)***
Xsis Electronics Inc....913 631-0448
12620 Shawnee Mission Pkw Shawnee (66216) ***(G-11056)***
Xtec, Lenexa *Also called X TEC Repair Inc* ***(G-6238)***
Xto Energy Inc....620 355-7838
805 Highway 25 S Lakin (67860) ***(G-4662)***
Xtreme Clean 88 LLC....913 451-9274
11872 W 91st St Overland Park (66214) ***(G-9514)***
Xxtra Clean....785 210-5255
10937 Clarks Creek Rd Junction City (66441) ***(G-3770)***
Y & M Business Services LLC....620 331-4600
208 E Laurel St Independence (67301) ***(G-3575)***
Y M C A, Hutchinson *Also called YMCA of Hutchinson Reno Cnty* ***(G-3494)***
Y M C A, Atchison *Also called Young Mens Christian Assoc At* ***(G-272)***
Y M C A Fitness Center, Shawnee Mission *Also called Young Mens Christian Gr Kansas* ***(G-12024)***
Yaco Productions....913 669-7380
2900 S 63rd St Kansas City (66106) ***(G-4562)***
Yaeger Architecture Inc....913 742-8000
8655 Penrose Ln Ste 300 Lenexa (66219) ***(G-6239)***
Yaeger-Acuity Solutions....913 742-8000
7780 W 119th St Overland Park (66213) ***(G-9515)***
Yarco Company Inc....913 225-8733
1130 Troup Ave Kansas City (66104) ***(G-4563)***
Yarco Company Inc....620 564-2180
511 S Bismark Ave 515 Ellinwood (67526) ***(G-1640)***
Yard, The, Wichita *Also called Bachus & Son Inc* ***(G-13789)***
Yellow Cab Taxi Tpeka Kans LLC....785 357-4444
1012 Sw 17th St Topeka (66604) ***(G-13254)***
Yellow Customer Solutions Inc....913 696-6100
10990 Roe Ave Shawnee Mission (66211) ***(G-12022)***
Yellow Frt Sys Employees CLB....913 344-3000
10990 Roe Ave Overland Park (66211) ***(G-9516)***
Yellow Roadway Receivables Fun....913 491-6363
10990 Roe Ave Overland Park (66211) ***(G-9517)***
Yellow Transportation, Baxter Springs *Also called Yrc Inc* ***(G-416)***
Yellowfin Transportation Inc....913 645-4834
5817 Constance St Shawnee (66216) ***(G-11057)***
Yeretsky & Maher Law Firm, Shawnee Mission *Also called Yeretsky & Maher LLC* ***(G-12023)***
Yeretsky & Maher LLC....913 897-5813
7200 W 132nd St Ste 330 Shawnee Mission (66213) ***(G-12023)***
Yesco, Leavenworth *Also called Young Hoins Service Group LLC* ***(G-5309)***
Yingling Aircraft Inc....316 943-3246
2010 S Airport Rd Wichita (67209) ***(G-16085)***
Yingling Auto Electric Inc....785 232-0484
2525 Nw Topeka Blvd Topeka (66617) ***(G-13255)***
Yingling Aviation, Wichita *Also called Yingling Aircraft Inc* ***(G-16085)***
YMCA, Wichita *Also called Young Mens Christian Associa* ***(G-16091)***
YMCA, Pittsburg *Also called Young MNS Chrstn Assn Pttsburg* ***(G-9972)***
YMCA Child Care Sites, Prairie Village *Also called Young Mens Christian Gr Kansas* ***(G-10088)***
YMCA Farha Sport Centers, Wichita *Also called Young Mens Christian Associa* ***(G-16092)***
YMCA of Greater Kansas City, Kansas City *Also called Young Mens Christian Associa* ***(G-4564)***
YMCA of Hutchinson Reno Cnty....620 662-1203
716 E 13th Ave Hutchinson (67501) ***(G-3494)***
YMCA of Salina Kansas, The, Salina *Also called Young MNS Chrstn Assn Slina Ka* ***(G-10775)***
YMCA OF TOPEKA, Topeka *Also called Young MNS Chrstn Assn of Tpeka* ***(G-13259)***
YMCA of Topeka, Topeka *Also called Young Mens Christian* ***(G-13258)***
YMCA Topeaka Downtown Branch, Topeka *Also called YMCA Topeaka Downtown Branch* ***(G-13256)***
YMCA Topeaka Downtown Branch....785 354-8591
3635 Sw Chelsea Dr Topeka (66614) ***(G-13256)***
Yoder Builders Inc....620 669-8542
1718 W Blanchard Ave South Hutchinson (67505) ***(G-12068)***
Yoder Meats, Yoder *Also called Waggoner Enterprises Inc* ***(G-16196)***
Yoder Smokers Inc....620 802-0201
1816 E Wasp Rd Hutchinson (67501) ***(G-3495)***
Yoh Services LLC....913 648-4004
10740 Nall Ave Ste 330 Overland Park (66211) ***(G-9518)***
Yorgensen-Meloan Inc....785 539-7481
1616 Poyntz Ave Manhattan (66502) ***(G-6857)***
Yorgensn-Mloan-Londeen Fnrl HM, Manhattan *Also called Yorgensen-Meloan Inc* ***(G-6857)***
York International Corporation....316 832-6400
811 E 33rd St N Wichita (67219) ***(G-16086)***
York International Corporation....316 832-6300
3110 N Mead St Wichita (67219) ***(G-16087)***
Yorke, Craig H MD, Topeka *Also called John D Ebeling MD* ***(G-12745)***
Yost Auto Service....316 264-8482
1818 E 2nd St N Wichita (67214) ***(G-16088)***
Yost Electric Inc....785 637-5454
4212 176th St Gorham (67640) ***(G-2492)***
Young Bogle McCausland Wells....316 265-7841
100 N Main St Ste 1001 Wichita (67202) ***(G-16089)***
Young Electric Inc....316 681-8118
3046 E 31st St S Wichita (67216) ***(G-16090)***
Young Hoins Service Group LLC....913 772-0708
326 Choctaw St Leavenworth (66048) ***(G-5309)***
Young Kansas Christian....785 233-1750
225 Sw 12th St Topeka (66612) ***(G-13257)***
Young Management Corporation (PA)....913 947-3134
22602 State Line Rd Bucyrus (66013) ***(G-612)***
Young Management Corporation....913 341-3113
8580 Farley St Overland Park (66212) ***(G-9519)***
Young Management Group Inc....913 213-3827
10660 Barkley St Ste 300 Overland Park (66212) ***(G-9520)***
Young Mens Christian....785 233-9815
1936 Nw Tyler St Fl 1 Topeka (66608) ***(G-13258)***
Young Mens Christian Assn....620 275-1199
1224 Center St Garden City (67846) ***(G-2319)***
Young Mens Christian Assoc At....913 367-4948
321 Commercial St Atchison (66002) ***(G-272)***
Young Mens Christian Associa....316 733-9622
1115 E Us Highway 54 Andover (67002) ***(G-118)***
Young Mens Christian Associa....316 942-2271
6940 W Newell St Wichita (67212) ***(G-16091)***
Young Mens Christian Associa....316 945-2255
3405 S Meridian Ave Wichita (67217) ***(G-16092)***
Young Mens Christian Associa (PA)....316 219-9622
402 N Market St Wichita (67202) ***(G-16093)***
Young Mens Christian Associa....316 320-9622
300 N Main St El Dorado (67042) ***(G-1616)***
Young Mens Christian Associa (PA)....913 321-9622
900 N 8th St Kansas City (66101) ***(G-4564)***
Young Mens Christian Associa....316 260-9622
13838 W 21st St N Wichita (67235) ***(G-16094)***
Young Mens Christian Associa....316 942-5511
3405 S Meridian Ave Wichita (67217) ***(G-16095)***
Young Mens Christian Associat....316 685-2251
9333 E Douglas Ave Wichita (67207) ***(G-16096)***
Young Mens Christian Associat....620 545-7290
26201 W 71st St S Viola (67149) ***(G-13380)***
Young Mens Christian Gr Kansas....913 642-6800
4200 W 79th St Shawnee Mission (66208) ***(G-12024)***
Young Mens Christian Gr Kansas....913 362-3489
7230 Belinder Ave Prairie Village (66208) ***(G-10088)***
Young Mens Christian Gr Kansas....913 393-9622
21400 W 153rd St Olathe (66061) ***(G-8163)***
Young Mens Christian Gr Kansas....913 782-7707
1700 E Pawnee Dr Olathe (66062) ***(G-8164)***
Young MNS Chrstn Assn of Sthwe....620 275-1199
1224 Center St Garden City (67846) ***(G-2320)***
Young MNS Chrstn Assn of Tpeka (PA)....785 354-8591
3635 Sw Chelsea Dr Topeka (66614) ***(G-13259)***
Young MNS Chrstn Assn Pttsburg....620 231-1100
1100 N Miles St Pittsburg (66762) ***(G-9972)***
Young MNS Chrstn Assn Slina Ka (PA)....785 825-2151
570 Ymca Dr Salina (67401) ***(G-10775)***
Young Sign Co Inc....913 651-5432
326 Choctaw St Leavenworth (66048) ***(G-5310)***
Young Welders, Wichita *Also called Wichita Welding Supply Inc* ***(G-16043)***
Younger Energy Company....316 681-2542
9415 E Harry St Ste 403 Wichita (67207) ***(G-16097)***
Youngers and Sons Mfg Co Inc....620 545-7133
19223 W State Road 42 Viola (67149) ***(G-13381)***
Youngs Products LLC....620 431-2199
4330 S Johnson Rd Chanute (66720) ***(G-774)***
Younie Lawnscapes....620 672-3301
10093 Ne 10th St Pratt (67124) ***(G-10165)***
Youth Aftercare Program, Wichita *Also called County of Sedgwick* ***(G-14113)***
Youth Crisis Shelter Inc....620 421-6941
1915 Crawford Ave Parsons (67357) ***(G-9752)***
Youthfront Inc (PA)....913 262-3900
4715 Rainbow Blvd Westwood (66205) ***(G-13564)***
YOUTHFRONT ASSOCIATION, Westwood *Also called Youthfront Inc* ***(G-13564)***
YOUTHVILLE, Newton *Also called Emberhope Inc* ***(G-7339)***
Youthville, Wichita *Also called Emberhope Inc* ***(G-14273)***
Youthville Family Cnsltn Svc....316 264-8317
560 N Exposition St Wichita (67203) ***(G-16098)***
Yoxall Antrim & Yoxall....620 624-8444
101 W 4th St Liberal (67901) ***(G-6378)***
Yrc Enterprise Services Inc....913 696-6100
10990 Roe Ave Overland Park (66211) ***(G-9521)***
Yrc Freight, Overland Park *Also called Yrc Inc* ***(G-9523)***
Yrc Global....913 696-6100
10990 Roe Ave Overland Park (66211) ***(G-9522)***

Yrc Inc (HQ)....913 696-6100
10990 Roe Ave Overland Park (66211) ***(G-9523)***
Yrc Inc....620 856-2161
2600 Powell Rd Baxter Springs (66713) ***(G-416)***
Yrc Inc....913 696-6100
233 S 42nd St Kansas City (66106) ***(G-4565)***
Yrc Worldwide Inc (PA)....913 696-6100
10990 Roe Ave Overland Park (66211) ***(G-9524)***
Yrc Worldwide Technologies Inc....913 344-3000
10990 Roe Ave Shawnee Mission (66211) ***(G-12025)***
Ysidro Trucking Inc....316 522-3716
3760 S Broadway Ave Wichita (67216) ***(G-16099)***
Yusen Logistics Americas Inc....913 768-4484
16500 Indian Creek Pkwy # 108 Olathe (66062) ***(G-8165)***
YWCA OF TOPEKA, Topeka *Also called Young Kansas Christian* ***(G-13257)***
Z Bottling Corp....620 872-0100
907 W 5th St Scott City (67871) ***(G-10837)***
Z Wireless, Salina *Also called Aka Wireless Inc* ***(G-10399)***
Z Wireless, Concordia *Also called ABC Phones North Carolina Inc* ***(G-1100)***
Z3 Graphix Inc (PA)....913 599-3355
8455 Lenexa Dr Overland Park (66214) ***(G-9525)***
Zack Group, Overland Park *Also called Lynn Care LLC* ***(G-8977)***
Zack Group, Overland Park *Also called Lynn Care LLC* ***(G-8978)***
Zack Taylor Contracting Inc....785 235-8704
711 Se Adams St Topeka (66607) ***(G-13260)***
Zamani Davis and Associate....913 851-0092
12912 Lucille St Shawnee Mission (66213) ***(G-12026)***
Zda, Shawnee Mission *Also called Zamani Davis and Associate* ***(G-12026)***
Zeeco Inc....620 705-5100
22695 D St Strother Fld Winfield (67156) ***(G-16192)***
Zeeline, Wichita *Also called National-Spencer Inc* ***(G-15154)***
Zeitlow Distributing Co Inc (PA)....620 241-4279
2060 E South Front St McPherson (67460) ***(G-7045)***
Zell-Metall Usa Inc....913 327-0300
10908 Strang Line Rd Lenexa (66215) ***(G-6240)***
Zenith Drilling Corporation (PA)....316 684-9777
1223 N Rock Rd Ste A200 Wichita (67206) ***(G-16100)***
Zenor Electric Company Inc....620 662-4694
1203 W 4th Ave Hutchinson (67501) ***(G-3496)***
Zepick Cardiology....316 616-2020
630 S Hillside St Wichita (67211) ***(G-16101)***
Zernco....316 775-9991
2400 S Greenwich Rd Wichita (67210) ***(G-16102)***
Zeroburn LLC....877 207-7100
7700 Wedd St Ste 200 Overland Park (66204) ***(G-9526)***
Zeroburn Fire Prevention Sys, Overland Park *Also called Zeroburn LLC* ***(G-9526)***
Ziegenhorn & Linneman DDS....913 649-7500
7515 Nall Ave Prairie Village (66208) ***(G-10089)***
Ziegler Corporation....785 841-4250
1513 Brink Ct Lawrence (66047) ***(G-5193)***
Ziegler Electric Service Inc....316 262-2842
1602 E 2nd St N Wichita (67214) ***(G-16103)***
Zieson Construction Co LLC (PA)....785 783-8335
5853 Se 29th St Topeka (66614) ***(G-13261)***
Zillner Mktg Cmmunications Inc....913 599-3230
8725 Rosehill Rd Lenexa (66215) ***(G-6241)***
Zillow Group Inc....913 491-4299
10975 El Monte St Leawood (66211) ***(G-5604)***
Zillow Home Loans LLC....913 491-4299
10975 El Monte St Overland Park (66211) ***(G-9527)***
Zimmer Inc....913 888-1024
9545 Alden St Lenexa (66215) ***(G-6242)***
Zimmer Radio Group....785 843-1320
3125 W 6th St Lawrence (66049) ***(G-5194)***
Zimmer Titus Associates, Lenexa *Also called C A Titus Inc* ***(G-5724)***
Zimmer Titus Associates, Lenexa *Also called Zimmer Inc* ***(G-6242)***
Zimmerman Construction Company....913 685-2255
12509 Hemlock St Overland Park (66213) ***(G-9528)***
Zimmerman Electric Service....620 431-2260
1202 W Beech St Chanute (66720) ***(G-775)***
Ziwi USA Incorporated....913 291-0189
10985 Cody St Ste 110 Overland Park (66210) ***(G-9529)***
Ziwipeak USA Inc., Overland Park *Also called Ziwi USA Incorporated* ***(G-9529)***
ZMC Inc....913 599-3230
8725 Rosehill Rd Ste 209 Shawnee Mission (66215) ***(G-12027)***
Zodiac Industries Inc....620 783-5041
724 W 7th St Galena (66739) ***(G-2090)***
Zoltenko Farms Inc....785 278-5405
2980 Cedar Rd Courtland (66939) ***(G-1181)***
Zook Construction....785 388-2183
1454 3600 Ave Wakefield (67487) ***(G-13399)***
Zu Preem, Shawnee Mission *Also called Premium Nutritional Pdts Inc* ***(G-11750)***
Zurich Agency Services Inc (HQ)....913 339-1000
7045 College Blvd Overland Park (66211) ***(G-9530)***
Zurich American Insurance Co....913 339-1000
7045 College Blvd Overland Park (66211) ***(G-9531)***
Zurich Direct Markets, Overland Park *Also called Zurich Agency Services Inc* ***(G-9530)***

ALPHABETIC

PRODUCT INDEX

• **Product categories are listed in alphabetical order.**

A

C

D

E

F

INDEX

M

INDEX

N

O

P

Q

R

T

U

V

W

X

Y

Z

PRODUCT & SERVICES SECTION

Product category — **BOXES: Folding**
Edgar & Son Paperboard ... G ... 999 999-9999
Yourtown *(G-11480)*
Ready Box Co ... E ... 999 999-9999
City — Anytown *(G-7097)*

Indicates approximate employment figure
A = Over 500 employees, B = 251-500
C = 101-250, D = 51-100, E = 20-50
F = 10-19, G = 5-9

Business phone

Geographic Section entry number where full company information appears.

See footnotes for symbols and codes identification.

- Refer to the Industrial Product Index preceding this section to locate product headings.

ABRASIVES

Husqvrna Cnstr Pdts N Amer Inc ... A ... 913 928-1000
Olathe *(G-7781)*
US Minerals Inc ... G ... 219 798-5472
La Cygne *(G-4645)*

ABRASIVES: Aluminum Oxide Fused

K C Abrasive Co LLC ... E ... 913 342-2900
Kansas City *(G-4131)*

ACADEMIC TUTORING SVCS

Kansas Schl For Effective Lrng ... E ... 316 263-9620
Wichita *(G-14822)*
Tutor Time Lrng Systems Inc ... E ... 316 721-0464
Wichita *(G-15819)*

ACADEMY

Saint Francis Cmnty Svcs Inc ... E ... 785 825-0541
Salina *(G-10658)*

ACCELERATION INDICATORS & SYSTEM COMPONENTS: Aerospace

Orizon Arstructures - Proc Inc ... E ... 620 305-2402
Chanute *(G-754)*

ACCOUNTING SVCS, NEC

Agler and Gaeddert Chartered ... E ... 620 342-7641
Emporia *(G-1693)*
B C C Business Services Inc ... F ... 913 682-4548
Leavenworth *(G-5205)*
Bruce Oil Co LLC ... G ... 620 241-2938
McPherson *(G-6939)*
Byron G Bird Assoc Chartered ... F ... 620 624-1994
Liberal *(G-6288)*
City of Wichita ... E ... 316 268-4651
Wichita *(G-14026)*
Goodencoff & Malone Inc ... F ... 785 483-6220
Russell *(G-10276)*
Heritage Group Lc ... F ... 316 261-5301
Wichita *(G-14594)*
Johnson Duncan & Hollowell CPA ... F ... 316 267-3402
Wichita *(G-14767)*
Jri Investments LLC ... A ... 785 404-2210
Wichita *(G-14777)*
Kirkpatrick Sprecker & Co ... F ... 316 685-1411
Wichita *(G-14866)*
Kramer & Associates Cpas LLC ... F ... 913 680-1690
Leavenworth *(G-5263)*
Larson & Company PA ... F ... 316 263-8030
Wichita *(G-14928)*
Lindburg Vogel Pierc Faris Ch ... E ... 620 669-0461
Hutchinson *(G-3354)*
Parman Tnner Soule Jackson CPA ... F ... 620 442-3700
Arkansas City *(G-169)*
Patton Cramer & Laprod Charter ... F ... 620 672-5533
Pratt *(G-10131)*
SS&c Wealth MGT Group LLC ... E ... 785 825-5479
Salina *(G-10713)*
Summers & Spencer Company ... E ... 785 272-4484
Topeka *(G-13116)*
Swindoll Janzen Hawk Lloyd LLC ... E ... 620 241-1826
McPherson *(G-7030)*
Woods & Durham LLC ... E ... 785 825-5494
Salina *(G-10772)*
Wright Redden & Associates LLC ... F ... 620 251-6204
Coffeyville *(G-986)*

ACCOUNTING SVCS: Certified Public

Adams Brown Bran Ball Chrtered ... F ... 316 683-2067
Wichita *(G-13612)*
Adams Brown Bran Ball Chrtered ... F ... 620 549-3271
Great Bend *(G-2500)*
Adams Brown Bran Ball Chrtered ... F ... 620 663-5659
Hutchinson *(G-3191)*
Adams Brown Bran Ball Chrtered ... E ... 785 628-3046
Hays *(G-2744)*
Adams Brown Bran Ball Chrtered ... F ... 620 241-2090
McPherson *(G-6931)*
Allen Gibbs & Houlik Llc ... C ... 316 267-7231
Wichita *(G-13667)*
Bkd LLP ... D ... 316 265-2811
Wichita *(G-13852)*
Boan Connealy & Houlehan LLC ... F ... 913 491-9178
Overland Park *(G-8472)*
Chance Purinton and Mills LLC ... F ... 913 491-8200
Shawnee Mission *(G-11216)*
Cliftonlarsonallen LLP ... F ... 913 491-6655
Overland Park *(G-8567)*
Clubine & Rettele ... E ... 785 472-3915
Ellsworth *(G-1662)*
Cochran Head Vick & Co PA ... F ... 913 378-1100
Overland Park *(G-8572)*
Cummins Coffman & ... F ... 785 267-2030
Topeka *(G-12534)*
Dana F Cole & Company LLP ... F ... 913 341-8200
Overland Park *(G-8632)*
Demaranville & Assoc Cpas LLC ... F ... 913 682-4548
Leavenworth *(G-5232)*
Diehl Banwart Bolton Jarred ... E ... 620 223-4300
Fort Scott *(G-1964)*
Ernst & Young LLP ... C ... 316 636-4900
Wichita *(G-14302)*
Grant Thornton LLP ... D ... 316 265-3231
Wichita *(G-14496)*
Hanneman & Hewitt CPA ... F ... 316 269-4500
Wichita *(G-14557)*
Hay & Rice Assoc Chartered ... F ... 620 624-8471
Liberal *(G-6320)*
Higdon and Hale Cpas P C ... F ... 913 831-7000
Shawnee Mission *(G-11431)*
Hinrichszenk + Pesavento ... F ... 785 691-5407
Overland Park *(G-8815)*
Hutchins & Associates ... F ... 913 338-4455
Shawnee Mission *(G-11444)*
Ifft & Co PA ... F ... 913 345-1120
Overland Park *(G-8838)*
Kcoe Isom LLP ... E ... 316 685-0222
Wichita *(G-14839)*
Kcoe Isom LLP ... F ... 785 899-3676
Goodland *(G-2479)*
Kcoe Isom LLP ... F ... 913 643-5000
Lenexa *(G-5944)*
Kcoe Isom LLP ... F ... 620 672-7476
Garden City *(G-2216)*
Keller & Miller Cpas LLP ... F ... 620 275-6883
Garden City *(G-2217)*
Keller & Owens LLC ... E ... 913 338-3500
Overland Park *(G-8911)*
Knudsen Monroe & Company LLC ... F ... 316 283-5366
Newton *(G-7371)*
Koch Siedhoff Hand & Dunn LLP ... E ... 316 943-0286
Wichita *(G-14888)*
Lewis Hooper & Dick LLC ... E ... 620 275-9267
Garden City *(G-2225)*
LLP Moss Adams ... F ... 913 599-3236
Overland Park *(G-8965)*
Mapes & Miller CPA ... F ... 785 877-5833
Norton *(G-7448)*
Meara Welch Browne PC ... E ... 816 561-1400
Leawood *(G-5470)*
Michael E Evans CPA ... E ... 620 669-0461
Hutchinson *(G-3375)*
Morrow & Company LLC ... F ... 316 263-2223
Wichita *(G-15129)*
Patrick Friess LLP ... F ... 620 227-3135
Dodge City *(G-1418)*
Pottberg Gssman Hffman Chrtred ... F ... 785 238-5166
Junction City *(G-3738)*
Property Tax Advisory Group ... F ... 913 897-4744
Overland Park *(G-9194)*
Randall G Ford LLC ... F ... 316 945-1500
Wichita *(G-15415)*
Ray A Cheely Chartered ... F ... 620 793-8436
Great Bend *(G-2629)*
Reese & Novelly PA ... F ... 785 456-2000
Wamego *(G-13440)*
Regier Carr & Monroe LLP CPA ... F ... 316 264-2335
Wichita *(G-15437)*
Roark & Associates PA ... F ... 785 842-3431
Lawrence *(G-5097)*
Robert E Miller Insurance Agcy ... E ... 816 333-3000
Leawood *(G-5540)*
Roger L Johnson ... E ... 785 233-4226
Topeka *(G-13025)*
Rolf Perrin & Associates PC ... F ... 913 671-8600
Fairway *(G-1918)*
Sink Gordon & Associates LLP ... E ... 785 537-0190
Manhattan *(G-6801)*
Snodgrass Dunlap & Company PA ... E ... 620 365-3125
Iola *(G-3632)*
Stephen M Criser ... E ... 316 685-1040
Wichita *(G-15661)*
Stephenson Edward B & Co CPA ... F ... 620 221-9320
Winfield *(G-16175)*
Summers & Spencer Company ... F ... 785 838-4484
Lawrence *(G-5126)*
Swindoll Janzen Hawk Lloyd LLC ... F ... 316 265-5600
Wichita *(G-15708)*
Tpp Crtfied Pub Accntants LLC ... E ... 913 498-2200
Overland Park *(G-9422)*
Varney & Associates Cpas LLC ... E ... 785 537-2202
Manhattan *(G-6841)*
Wolski & Associates ... F ... 913 281-3233
Kansas City *(G-4548)*

ACIDS: Sulfuric, Oleum

Chemtrade Refinery Svcs Inc ... D ... 785 843-2290
Lawrence *(G-4785)*
Meridian Chemicals LLC ... G ... 913 253-2220
Overland Park *(G-9011)*

ACUPUNCTURISTS' OFFICES

Advanced Chiropractic Svcs PA ... F ... 785 842-4181
Lawrence *(G-4721)*
Gao Qizhi ... F ... 316 691-8811
Wichita *(G-14444)*
Svetas Body Therapy LLC ... F ... 316 630-0400
Wichita *(G-15706)*

ADHESIVES

Barker B&C Investments LLC ... F ... 620 669-0145
Hutchinson *(G-3215)*
Certanteed Gyps Fnshg Pdts Inc ... F ... 785 762-2994
Junction City *(G-3680)*

ADHESIVES & SEALANTS

Evonik Corporation ... A ... 316 529-9670
Haysville *(G-2942)*

Prosoco Inc ....D.... 785 865-4200
Lawrence *(G-5081)*
Specchem LLC ....F.... 913 371-8705
Kansas City *(G-4431)*

ADJUSTMENT BUREAU, EXC INSURANCE

Ad Astra Recover Service ....F.... 316 941-5448
Wichita *(G-13611)*
Credit Bureau Services ....E.... 620 276-7631
Garden City *(G-2139)*
Golden Plains Credit Union ....E.... 620 275-8187
Garden City *(G-2188)*

ADOPTION SVCS

American Adoptions Inc ....E.... 913 492-2229
Overland Park *(G-8374)*
Archdiocese Kansas Cy In Kans ....E.... 913 621-5090
Kansas City *(G-3816)*
Caring Hands Humane Society ....F.... 316 284-0487
Newton *(G-7326)*
Catholic Charities of Southwes ....F.... 620 227-1562
Dodge City *(G-1319)*
Kansas Childrens Service Leag ....F.... 620 340-0408
Emporia *(G-1785)*
Kansas Childrens Service Leag ....D.... 316 942-4261
Wichita *(G-14792)*
Kansas Childrens Service Leag ....F.... 785 274-3800
Topeka *(G-12765)*
Sedgwick Country Animal Respon ....F.... 316 619-1723
Wichita *(G-15546)*

ADULT DAYCARE CENTERS

Adult Health Services Inc ....C.... 913 788-9896
Kansas City *(G-3786)*
Catholic Charities Adult Svcs ....E.... 316 942-2008
Wichita *(G-13961)*
Fort Scott Presbyterian Vlg ....E.... 620 223-5550
Fort Scott *(G-1971)*
Lakemary Center Inc ....E.... 913 768-6831
Olathe *(G-7853)*
Loving Heart ....D.... 785 783-7200
Topeka *(G-12850)*
Medicalodges Inc ....E.... 620 659-2156
Kinsley *(G-4619)*
Midland Care Connection Inc ....C.... 785 232-2044
Topeka *(G-12892)*
Mount St Scholastica Inc ....C.... 913 906-8990
Kansas City *(G-4268)*
Sunflower Adult Day Services ....F.... 785 823-6666
Salina *(G-10722)*
Topeka Adult Care Center ....F.... 785 233-7397
Topeka *(G-13164)*

ADVERTISING AGENCIES

Anthem Media LLC ....E.... 913 894-6923
Leawood *(G-5327)*
Callahan Creek Inc ....D.... 785 838-4774
Lawrence *(G-4772)*
Greteman Group Inc ....F.... 316 263-1004
Wichita *(G-14517)*
Hss IT Management Inc ....C.... 913 498-9988
Overland Park *(G-8832)*
Insideresponse LLC ....E.... 855 969-0812
Overland Park *(G-8851)*
Jajo Inc ....E.... 316 267-6700
Wichita *(G-14745)*
Kuhn and Wittenborn Inc ....E.... 816 471-7888
Overland Park *(G-8932)*
Making The Mark Inc ....G.... 913 402-8000
Shawnee Mission *(G-11592)*
MBB Inc ....E.... 816 531-1992
Leawood *(G-5469)*
Montgomery County Media LLC ....E.... 620 331-3550
Independence *(G-3541)*
Patterson Advertising Agency ....G.... 785 232-0533
Topeka *(G-12964)*
Platform Advertising ....E.... 913 254-6000
Olathe *(G-7988)*
Rba Associates Inc ....F.... 816 444-4270
Mission *(G-7136)*
Security Benefit Group Inc ....B.... 785 438-3000
Topeka *(G-13053)*
ZMC Inc ....E.... 913 599-3230
Shawnee Mission *(G-12027)*

ADVERTISING AGENCIES: Consultants

Armstrong Creative Services ....F.... 316 522-3000
Haysville *(G-2937)*
Associated Intergrated Mktg ....E.... 316 683-4691
Wichita *(G-13755)*
Biehler Companies Inc ....D.... 316 529-0002
Wichita *(G-13847)*
Brush Art Corporation ....E.... 785 454-3415
Downs *(G-1469)*
Frank Agency Inc ....D.... 913 648-8333
Overland Park *(G-8736)*
Huyett Jones Partners ....F.... 785 228-0900
Topeka *(G-12709)*
Media Partners Inc ....F.... 316 652-2210
Eastborough *(G-1477)*
Rhycom Advertising ....F.... 913 451-9102
Overland Park *(G-9240)*
Signal Theory Inc ....E.... 316 263-0124
Wichita *(G-15589)*
Stephens & Associates Advg Inc ....E.... 913 661-0910
Overland Park *(G-9358)*
Walz Tetrick Advertising Inc ....E.... 913 789-8778
Mission *(G-7140)*

ADVERTISING MATERIAL DISTRIBUTION

AP Roofing Specialty Codings ....F.... 620 532-1076
Kingman *(G-4582)*
Beauty Brands LLC ....F.... 913 227-0797
Shawnee Mission *(G-11156)*
Trainwreck Tees LLC ....G.... 620 224-2480
Fort Scott *(G-2011)*

ADVERTISING REPRESENTATIVES: Electronic Media

Answer Media LLC ....F.... 816 984-8853
Leawood *(G-5326)*
Viralnova LLC ....E.... 913 706-9710
Overland Park *(G-9465)*

ADVERTISING REPRESENTATIVES: Media

Eagle Communications Inc ....D.... 785 650-5349
Hays *(G-2795)*

ADVERTISING REPRESENTATIVES: Newspaper

Morris Communications Co LLC ....E.... 316 283-1500
Newton *(G-7390)*
Wichita Business Journal Inc ....F.... 316 267-6406
Wichita *(G-15983)*

ADVERTISING REPRESENTATIVES: Printed Media

Printing Services Inc ....G.... 913 492-1500
Lenexa *(G-6070)*

ADVERTISING REPRESENTATIVES: Radio

Eagle Communications Inc ....F.... 785 587-0103
Manhattan *(G-6618)*
Eagle Communications Inc ....F.... 785 825-4631
Salina *(G-10482)*
EW Scripps Company ....E.... 316 436-1045
Wichita *(G-14317)*
Great Plains Christian Radio ....F.... 620 873-2991
Meade *(G-7049)*
Innovative Broadcasting Corp ....F.... 620 232-5993
Pittsburg *(G-9880)*
K S A J Oldies ....D.... 785 823-1111
Salina *(G-10559)*
Praise Network Inc ....F.... 785 694-2877
Brewster *(G-585)*
Waitt Media Inc ....F.... 620 225-8080
Dodge City *(G-1448)*

ADVERTISING REPRESENTATIVES: Television & Radio Time Sales

Eagle Communications Inc ....F.... 785 726-3291
Hays *(G-2794)*
Eagle Communications Inc ....E.... 785 483-3244
Russell *(G-10273)*
Nvt Wichita LLC ....E.... 316 265-3333
Wichita *(G-15201)*

ADVERTISING SPECIALTIES, WHOLESALE

4th Gneration Promotional Pdts ....G.... 913 393-0837
Olathe *(G-7502)*
Creative Consumer Concepts Inc ....E.... 913 491-6444
Overland Park *(G-8610)*
Diligence Inc ....E.... 913 254-0500
New Century *(G-7279)*
Finchers Findings Inc ....G.... 620 886-5952
Medicine Lodge *(G-7060)*
Iris Strgc Mktg Support Inc ....E.... 913 232-4825
Lenexa *(G-5923)*
John B Baker ....G.... 316 263-2820
Wichita *(G-14762)*
Joseph F Beaver ....F.... 620 872-2395
Scott City *(G-10818)*
Kid Stuff Marketing Inc ....E.... 785 862-3707
Topeka *(G-12821)*
Midwest Single Source Inc ....E.... 316 267-6333
Wichita *(G-15102)*
Peavey Corporation ....D.... 913 888-0600
Lenexa *(G-6047)*
Power Sales and Advertising ....D.... 913 324-4900
Lenexa *(G-6063)*
Rfc Logo Inc ....A.... 913 319-3100
Shawnee Mission *(G-11794)*
United States Awards Inc ....E.... 620 231-8470
Pittsburg *(G-9951)*
Wds Inc ....D.... 913 894-1881
Lenexa *(G-6223)*

ADVERTISING SVCS, NEC

Feet On Ground Marketing Inc ....F.... 913 242-5558
Lawrence *(G-4858)*
New Media Samurai LLC ....F.... 785 856-6673
Lawrence *(G-5039)*
Proforma Marketing ....F.... 913 685-9098
Overland Park *(G-9190)*

ADVERTISING SVCS: Billboards

Lamar Advertising Company ....F.... 785 234-0501
Topeka *(G-12832)*

ADVERTISING SVCS: Direct Mail

Adkins Systems Inc ....F.... 913 438-8440
Shawnee Mission *(G-11076)*
Cahill Business Services LLC ....F.... 913 515-8398
Shawnee Mission *(G-11199)*
Direct Mail Printers Inc ....F.... 316 263-1855
Wichita *(G-14213)*
Knight Enterprises Ltd ....E.... 785 843-5511
Lawrence *(G-4946)*
Marketing Technologies Inc ....D.... 913 342-9111
Kansas City *(G-4218)*
Occk Inc ....E.... 785 243-1977
Concordia *(G-1125)*
Personal Marketing Company Inc ....E.... 913 492-0377
Overland Park *(G-9159)*
Professional Printing Kans Inc ....F.... 620 343-7125
Emporia *(G-1813)*
Southwest Holding Corporation ....E.... 785 233-5662
Topeka *(G-13083)*

ADVERTISING SVCS: Outdoor

Boyles Portable Sign Rent ....F.... 785 266-5401
Topeka *(G-12399)*
Iheartcommunications Inc ....D.... 316 494-6600
Wichita *(G-14668)*
Lamar Advertising Company ....F.... 913 438-4048
Overland Park *(G-8940)*
Partners N Promotion Inc ....F.... 913 397-9500
Olathe *(G-7974)*

ADVERTISING: Aerial

Old World Balloonery LLC ....F.... 913 338-2628
Overland Park *(G-9097)*

ADVOCACY GROUP

Harvey County Dv/SA Task Force ....F.... 316 284-6920
Newton *(G-7357)*
Willlowtree Supports Inc ....E.... 913 353-1970
Shawnee *(G-11053)*

AERIAL WORK PLATFORMS

R O Terex Corporation ....D.... 913 782-1200
Olathe *(G-8018)*

AEROBIC DANCE & EXERCISE CLASSES

City of Wamego ....E.... 785 456-2295
Wamego *(G-13413)*
Dermatology & Skin Cancer Ctr ....F.... 913 451-7546
Shawnee Mission *(G-11302)*

Folgers Gymnastics Inc ....F 316 733-7525
Wichita ***(G-14401)***
Health Connection Inc ....F 913 294-1000
Paola ***(G-9565)***
Maximus Fitness and Wellness ....F 785 266-8000
Topeka ***(G-12866)***
P A Therapyworks Inc ....E 785 749-1300
Lawrence ***(G-5053)***
Performance Enhancement Center ....F 620 421-2125
Parsons ***(G-9723)***
Young Mens Christian Gr Kansas ....D 913 642-6800
Shawnee Mission ***(G-12024)***
Young MNS Chrstn Assn Slina Ka ....D 785 825-2151
Salina ***(G-10775)***

AGENTS & MANAGERS: Entertainers

Talent On Parade ....F 316 522-4836
Haysville ***(G-2961)***

AGENTS, BROKERS & BUREAUS: Personal Service

Benchmark Rehabilitation Partn ....D 913 384-5810
Shawnee Mission ***(G-11159)***
Boyer-Kansas Inc ....E 913 307-9400
Lenexa ***(G-5710)***
Business Technology Career ....F 316 688-1888
Wichita ***(G-13920)***
City of Paola ....D 913 259-3600
Paola ***(G-9547)***
Consortium Inc ....D 785 232-1196
Topeka ***(G-12503)***
Elecsys International Corp ....C 913 647-0158
Olathe ***(G-7673)***
Epay North America ....F 913 327-4200
Leawood ***(G-5388)***
Evergance Partners LLC ....E 913 825-1000
Shawnee Mission ***(G-11350)***
Financial Benefits of Kansas ....F 913 385-7000
Leawood ***(G-5400)***
Heartland Payment Systems LLC ....D 316 390-1988
Wichita ***(G-14587)***
Lauries Kitchen Inc ....F 316 777-9198
Mulvane ***(G-7218)***
McDonalds Plaza LLC ....E 913 362-1999
Overland Park ***(G-9001)***
National Center For Competency ....E 913 498-1000
Shawnee Mission ***(G-11672)***
Osborne Investment Inc ....F 785 346-2147
Osborne ***(G-8217)***
P A Select Healthcare ....F 913 948-6400
Leawood ***(G-5513)***
Pioneer Industries Intl Inc ....E 913 233-1368
Kansas City ***(G-4323)***
Tarrant Inc ....E 316 942-2208
Wichita ***(G-15717)***
Tevis Architectural Group ....F 913 599-3003
Shawnee ***(G-11039)***
Turner Recreation Commission ....D 913 287-2111
Kansas City ***(G-4479)***

AGENTS: Loan

Citizens Bank of Kansas NA ....F 620 886-5686
Medicine Lodge ***(G-7058)***
Kansas Assistive Tech Corp ....E 620 341-9002
Emporia ***(G-1784)***

AGRICULTURAL CREDIT INSTITUTIONS

Cobank Acb ....E 620 275-4281
Garden City ***(G-2128)***
Cobank Acb ....F 785 798-2278
Ness City ***(G-7257)***
Commercial Bank ....F 620 431-3200
Chanute ***(G-719)***
Farm Credit of Western Kansas ....E 785 462-6714
Colby ***(G-1005)***
Frontier Farm Credit Aca ....C 785 776-6955
Manhattan ***(G-6641)***
Garden City Production Cr Assn ....E 620 275-4281
Garden City ***(G-2175)***

AGRICULTURAL EQPT: BARN, SILO, POULTRY, DAIRY/LIVESTOCK MACH

Beck Sales Company ....G 620 225-1770
Dodge City ***(G-1305)***

AGRICULTURAL EQPT: Dusters, Mechanical

Rhs Inc ....E 785 742-2949
Hiawatha ***(G-3023)***

AGRICULTURAL EQPT: Elevators, Farm

Central Plains Coop ....G 785 282-6813
Smith Center ***(G-12032)***

AGRICULTURAL EQPT: Fertilizing Machinery

Golden Plains AG Tech ....G 785 462-6753
Colby ***(G-1009)***
J D Skiles Inc ....F 785 626-9338
Atwood ***(G-287)***
Oswald Manufacturing Co Inc ....G 785 258-2877
Herington ***(G-2980)***
R & R Industries Inc ....F 620 672-7463
Pratt ***(G-10146)***

AGRICULTURAL EQPT: Harvesters, Fruit, Vegetable, Tobacco

United States Cstm Harvesters ....G 620 664-6297
Hutchinson ***(G-3477)***

AGRICULTURAL EQPT: Haying Mach, Mowers, Rakes, Stackers, Etc

AGCO Corporation ....C 620 327-6413
Hesston ***(G-2984)***
Harper Industries Inc ....D 620 896-7381
Harper ***(G-2723)***
Hoelscher Inc ....F 620 562-3575
Bushton ***(G-653)***

AGRICULTURAL EQPT: Loaders, Manure & General Utility

Gt Mfg Inc ....E 785 632-2151
Clay Center ***(G-867)***
Kmw Ltd ....C 620 278-3641
Sterling ***(G-12124)***

AGRICULTURAL EQPT: Soil Preparation Mach, Exc Turf & Grounds

LDB Inc ....G 620 532-2236
Kingman ***(G-4605)***

AGRICULTURAL EQPT: Soil Sampling Machines

Kejr Inc ....C 785 825-1842
Salina ***(G-10573)***

AGRICULTURAL EQPT: Stackers, Grain

Tribine Harvester LLC ....G 316 282-8011
Newton ***(G-7421)***

AGRICULTURAL EQPT: Tractors, Farm

Agsynergy LLC ....G 785 336-6333
Seneca ***(G-10857)***

AGRICULTURAL EQPT: Trailers & Wagons, Farm

Donahue Manufacturing LLC ....F 620 732-2665
Durham ***(G-1475)***
Liberty Inc ....D 785 770-8788
Manhattan ***(G-6713)***
Neville Welding Inc ....E 620 532-3487
Kingman ***(G-4608)***
Peters-Howell Lujeana ....G 785 415-2125
Stockton ***(G-12183)***
Wilkens Manufacturing Inc ....D 785 425-7070
Stockton ***(G-12190)***

AGRICULTURAL EQPT: Turf & Grounds Eqpt

Heckendorn Eqp Co of Kans ....G 620 983-2186
Peabody ***(G-9760)***

AGRICULTURAL EQPT: Turf Eqpt, Commercial

Excel Industries Inc ....F 800 942-4911
Hesston ***(G-2989)***

Irrigation & Turf Equipment ....G 620 365-2121
Iola ***(G-3612)***

AGRICULTURAL INSURANCE

Amtrust AG Insurance Svcs LLC ....D 844 350-2767
Leawood ***(G-5325)***

AGRICULTURAL MACHINERY & EQPT REPAIR

Bruna Brothers Implement LLC ....F 785 562-5304
Marysville ***(G-6881)***
Bruna Brothers Implement LLC ....F 785 742-2261
Hiawatha ***(G-3005)***
Bruna Brothers Implement LLC ....F 785 336-2111
Seneca ***(G-10858)***
Bruna Brothers Implement LLC ....E 785 325-2232
Washington ***(G-13461)***
Colby A G Center LLC ....F 785 462-6132
Colby ***(G-995)***
Dauer Implement Company Inc ....F 785 825-2141
Salina ***(G-10470)***
Jies LLC ....F 620 668-5585
Copeland ***(G-1149)***
Kanequip Inc ....F 785 562-2377
Marysville ***(G-6891)***
Ravenscraft Implement Inc ....F 316 799-2141
Whitewater ***(G-13572)***
Storrer Implement Inc ....F 620 365-5692
Iola ***(G-3636)***
Straub International Inc ....F 620 662-0211
Hutchinson ***(G-3451)***
Teeter Irrigation Inc ....D 620 353-1111
Ulysses ***(G-13324)***

AGRICULTURAL MACHINERY & EQPT: Wholesalers

AG Power Equipment Co ....F 785 899-3432
Goodland ***(G-2460)***
American Implement Inc ....E 620 872-7244
Scott City ***(G-10803)***
American Implement Main Office ....F 620 356-3460
Ulysses ***(G-13282)***
B & D Equipment Co Inc ....F 913 367-1744
Atchison ***(G-211)***
Bekemeyer Enterprises Inc ....F 785 325-2274
Washington ***(G-13459)***
Berry Companies Inc ....F 620 277-2290
Garden City ***(G-2109)***
Bretz Inc ....F 620 397-5329
Dighton ***(G-1283)***
Bruna Brothers Implement LLC ....F 785 632-5621
Clay Center ***(G-845)***
Bruna Brothers Implement LLC ....F 785 742-2261
Hiawatha ***(G-3005)***
Bruna Brothers Implement LLC ....F 785 336-2111
Seneca ***(G-10858)***
Concordia Tractor Inc ....F 785 263-3051
Abilene ***(G-20)***
Conrady Western Inc ....E 620 842-5137
Anthony ***(G-124)***
Conrady Western Inc ....E 316 943-4261
Wichita ***(G-14090)***
Dauer Implement Company Inc ....F 785 825-2141
Salina ***(G-10470)***
Delaney Implement Co Inc ....F 620 525-6221
Burdett ***(G-621)***
Fairbank Equipment Inc ....E 316 943-2247
Wichita ***(G-14333)***
Fort Scott Truck & Tractor ....F 620 223-6506
Fort Scott ***(G-1972)***
Hiplains Farm Equipment Inc ....F 620 225-0064
Dodge City ***(G-1374)***
John Schmidt & Sons Inc ....F 620 221-0300
Winfield ***(G-16150)***
Kiowa Service Co Inc ....F 316 636-1070
Wichita ***(G-14865)***
Lang Diesel Inc ....F 620 947-3182
Hillsboro ***(G-3051)***
Lang Diesel Inc ....F 620 431-6700
Chanute ***(G-737)***
Lang Diesel Inc ....F 785 284-3401
Sabetha ***(G-10316)***
Midwest Mixer Service LLC ....E 620 872-7251
Scott City ***(G-10823)***
Prairieland Partners LLC ....D 620 664-6552
Hutchinson ***(G-3412)***
Price Bros Equipment Co ....E 316 265-9577
Wichita ***(G-15340)***

Ravenscraft Implement Inc ... F ... 316 799-2141
Whitewater *(G-13572)*
Shaw Motor Co Inc ... F ... 785 673-4228
Grainfield *(G-2496)*
Straub International Inc ... F ... 620 672-2998
Pratt *(G-10156)*
Straub International Inc ... E ... 620 792-5256
Great Bend *(G-2641)*
Straub International Inc ... F ... 785 825-1300
Salina *(G-10717)*
Taylor Implement Co Inc ... E ... 785 675-3272
Hoxie *(G-3143)*
Todd Tractor Co Inc ... F ... 785 336-2138
Seneca *(G-10884)*
Ulysses Standard Supply Inc ... F ... 620 356-4171
Ulysses *(G-13327)*

AGRICULTURAL PROG REG OFFICES, GOVT: Extension Svcs

County of Sedgwick ... E ... 316 660-0100
Wichita *(G-14111)*

AIR CLEANING SYSTEMS

Kice Industries Inc ... C ... 316 744-7148
Park City *(G-9625)*
Metal-Fab Inc ... C ... 316 943-2351
Wichita *(G-15055)*
Metal-Fab Inc ... G ... 316 946-5875
Wichita *(G-15057)*
Purifan Inc ... G ... 316 932-8001
Wichita *(G-15377)*

AIR CONDITIONERS, AUTOMOTIVE: Wholesalers

Frigiquip International Inc ... G ... 316 321-2400
El Dorado *(G-1563)*

AIR CONDITIONERS: Motor Vehicle

Recreational Vehicle Products ... C ... 316 832-3400
Wichita *(G-15429)*

AIR CONDITIONING & VENTILATION EQPT & SPLYS: Wholesales

Aggreko LLC ... F ... 913 281-9782
Shawnee Mission *(G-11085)*
Airtex Manufacturing Lllp ... C ... 913 583-3181
De Soto *(G-1192)*
Automated Control Systems Corp ... D ... 913 766-2336
Leawood *(G-5337)*
Even Temp of Wichita Inc ... F ... 316 469-5321
Wichita *(G-14312)*
Hajoca Corporation ... F ... 785 825-1333
Salina *(G-10531)*
Lba Air Cndtoning Htg Plbg Inc ... E ... 816 454-5515
Shawnee Mission *(G-11551)*
McQueeny Group Inc ... F ... 913 396-4700
Overland Park *(G-9004)*
OConnor Company Inc ... F ... 316 263-3187
Wichita *(G-15207)*
OConnor Company Inc ... E ... 913 894-8788
Lenexa *(G-6033)*
OConnor Company Inc ... E ... 316 263-3187
Wichita *(G-15209)*
Weber Refrigeration & Htg Inc ... E ... 580 338-7338
Garden City *(G-2309)*
Wichita Wholesale Supply Inc ... F ... 316 267-3629
Wichita *(G-16044)*

AIR CONDITIONING EQPT

Rv Products ... E ... 316 832-3400
Wichita *(G-15494)*

AIR CONDITIONING EQPT, WHOLE HOUSE: Wholesalers

Hajoca Corporation ... E ... 316 262-2471
Wichita *(G-14544)*

AIR CONDITIONING REPAIR SVCS

Air Power Consultants Inc ... F ... 913 894-0044
Olathe *(G-7514)*
Auman Co Inc ... F ... 785 628-2833
Hays *(G-2752)*
CMS Mechanical Services LLC ... E ... 321 473-0488
Lenexa *(G-5767)*
Lba Air Cndtoning Htg Plbg Inc ... E ... 816 454-5515
Shawnee Mission *(G-11551)*
R & R Street Plbg Htg & Elec ... F ... 785 524-4551
Lincoln *(G-6385)*
Thermal Comfort Air Inc ... E ... 785 537-2436
Manhattan *(G-6824)*
Vhc Van Hoecke Contracting Inc ... E ... 913 888-0036
Lenexa *(G-6212)*

AIR CONDITIONING UNITS: Complete, Domestic Or Indl

Airtex Manufacturing Lllp ... C ... 913 583-3181
De Soto *(G-1192)*

AIR DUCT CLEANING SVCS

Lamunyon Clg & Restoration ... F ... 785 632-1259
Clay Center *(G-870)*
Phoenix Restoration Service ... E ... 620 276-6994
Garden City *(G-2254)*
Steam Way Carpet Restorations ... F ... 620 331-9553
Independence *(G-3563)*
Stovers Restoration Inc ... F ... 316 686-5005
Maize *(G-6521)*

AIR POLLUTION CONTROL EQPT & SPLYS WHOLESALERS

IAC Systems Inc ... E ... 913 384-5511
Shawnee Mission *(G-11449)*
Industrial Accessories Company ... D ... 913 384-5511
Shawnee Mission *(G-11455)*
Weis Fire Safety Equip Co Inc ... F ... 785 825-9527
Salina *(G-10765)*

AIR POLLUTION MEASURING SVCS

Phoenix Restoration Service ... E ... 620 276-6994
Garden City *(G-2254)*

AIR PURIFICATION EQPT

Bha Altair LLC ... C ... 816 356-8400
Overland Park *(G-8445)*
Eplus Envrmental Solutions LLC ... E ... 913 814-9860
Shawnee Mission *(G-11345)*
Heartland Technologies Inc ... G ... 316 932-8001
Wichita *(G-14588)*
Tech-Air Inc ... G ... 913 677-5777
Shawnee Mission *(G-11923)*
Tech-Air Inc ... F ... 913 677-5777
Osawatomie *(G-8204)*

AIR TRAFFIC CONTROL SVCS

Midwest A Traffic Ctrl Svc Inc ... F ... 913 782-7082
Overland Park *(G-9030)*

AIR, WATER & SOLID WASTE PROGRAMS ADMINISTRATION SVCS

County of Johnson ... D ... 913 782-2640
Olathe *(G-7619)*

AIRCRAFT & AEROSPACE FLIGHT INSTRUMENTS & GUIDANCE SYSTEMS

J Diamond Inc ... E ... 316 264-9505
Wichita *(G-14735)*

AIRCRAFT & HEAVY EQPT REPAIR SVCS

Apph Wichita Inc ... E ... 316 943-5752
Wichita *(G-13720)*
Executive Beechcraft Inc ... E ... 913 782-9003
New Century *(G-7284)*
Garsite Progress LLC ... D ... 913 342-5600
Kansas City *(G-4025)*
GE Engine Services LLC ... A ... 316 264-4741
Arkansas City *(G-157)*
Global Aviation Services LLC ... D ... 913 780-0300
Olathe *(G-7731)*
Kcsc Space Works Inc ... E ... 620 662-2305
Hutchinson *(G-3349)*
T and C Aviation Enterprises ... E ... 913 764-4800
Olathe *(G-8095)*
Textron Aviation Inc ... A ... 316 676-7111
Wichita *(G-15741)*
Wilkerson Crane Rental Inc ... E ... 913 238-7030
Lenexa *(G-6230)*

AIRCRAFT ASSEMBLY PLANTS

Air Capital Interiors Inc ... F ... 316 633-4790
Wichita *(G-13648)*
Airbus Americas Inc ... C ... 316 264-0552
Wichita *(G-13650)*
Avcon Industries Inc ... E ... 913 780-9595
Newton *(G-7313)*
Boeing Company ... F ... 480 509-5449
Wichita *(G-13865)*
Boeing Company ... F ... 312 544-2000
Wichita *(G-13866)*
Butler National Corporation ... E ... 913 780-9595
Olathe *(G-7571)*
Emerald Aerospace Holdings LLC ... D ... 316 440-6966
Wichita *(G-14274)*
Learjet Inc ... A ... 316 946-2000
Wichita *(G-14940)*
Learjet Inc ... E ... 316 946-3001
Wichita *(G-14941)*
Learjet Inc ... A ... 316 946-2000
Wichita *(G-14942)*
Textron Airland LLC ... G ... 541 390-8888
Wichita *(G-15732)*
Textron Aviation Inc ... A ... 888 727-4344
Wichita *(G-15734)*
Textron Aviation Inc ... C ... 316 517-8270
Wichita *(G-15736)*
Textron Aviation Inc ... D ... 316 517-6000
Wichita *(G-15745)*
Textron Aviation Inc ... B ... 316 517-6081
Wichita *(G-15746)*
Textron Aviation Inc ... C ... 316 517-6000
Wichita *(G-15750)*
Textron Aviation Inc ... A ... 316 676-7111
Wichita *(G-15752)*

AIRCRAFT CLEANING & JANITORIAL SVCS

Alliance Jantr Advisors Inc ... F ... 913 815-8807
Olathe *(G-7520)*
Cessna Aircraft Company ... F ... 316 686-3961
Wichita *(G-13993)*

AIRCRAFT CONTROL SYSTEMS:

Kelly Manufacturing Company ... D ... 316 265-4271
Independence *(G-3531)*
Kelly Manufacturing Company ... D ... 316 265-6868
Wichita *(G-14846)*

AIRCRAFT DEALERS

Kansas City Aviation Ctr Inc ... D ... 913 782-0530
Olathe *(G-7823)*
T and C Aviation Enterprises ... E ... 913 764-4800
Olathe *(G-8095)*
Yingling Aircraft Inc ... D ... 316 943-3246
Wichita *(G-16085)*

AIRCRAFT ELECTRICAL EQPT REPAIR SVCS

Aircraft Instr & Rdo Co Inc ... E ... 316 945-9820
Wichita *(G-13651)*
Alltite Inc ... E ... 316 686-3010
Wichita *(G-13678)*
Tech-Aire Instruments Inc ... F ... 316 262-4020
Wichita *(G-15724)*

AIRCRAFT ENGINES & ENGINE PARTS: Mount Parts

Specialty Patterns Inc ... F ... 316 945-8131
Wichita *(G-15637)*
Spirit Arosystems Holdings Inc ... E ... 316 526-9000
Wichita *(G-15644)*

AIRCRAFT ENGINES & ENGINE PARTS: Research & Development, Mfr

Emerald Aerospace Services LLC ... E ... 316 644-4284
Wichita *(G-14275)*

AIRCRAFT ENGINES & PARTS

Dcs Inc ... G ... 316 806-4899
Derby *(G-1233)*
Eurot Verti Fligh Solut LLC ... G ... 785 331-2220
Eudora *(G-1875)*
Facc Solutions Inc ... G ... 316 425-4040
Wichita *(G-14330)*

Garsite Progress LLC ... D ... 913 342-5600
Kansas City *(G-4025)*
GE Engine Services LLC ... A ... 316 264-4741
Arkansas City *(G-157)*
Global Cnc Corporation ... G ... 316 516-3400
Wichita *(G-14474)*
Honeywell International Inc ... C ... 316 522-8172
Wichita *(G-14634)*
Honeywell International Inc ... A ... 816 997-7149
Olathe *(G-7773)*
Honeywell International Inc ... A ... 316 204-5503
Derby *(G-1251)*
Honeywell International Inc ... E ... 913 712-6017
New Century *(G-7288)*
Honeywell International Inc ... D ... 913 712-3000
Olathe *(G-7774)*
Honeywell International Inc ... D ... 620 783-1343
Pittsburg *(G-9878)*
Kansas AVI Independence LLC ... D ... 620 331-7716
Independence *(G-3530)*
Maxima Precision Inc ... E ... 316 832-2211
Wichita *(G-15020)*
Pratt & Whitney Eng Svcs Inc ... G ... 316 945-9763
Wichita *(G-15322)*
Smith & Smith Aircraft Intl ... F ... 316 945-0204
Wichita *(G-15606)*
Triumph Group Operations Inc ... D ... 620 326-5761
Wellington *(G-13538)*
Triumph Strctres - Kans Cy Inc ... D ... 913 882-7200
Edgerton *(G-1491)*
Turbine Eng Comp Tech Turning ... E ... 316 925-4020
Wichita *(G-15815)*

AIRCRAFT EQPT & SPLYS WHOLESALERS

Aircraft Instr & Rdo Co Inc ... E ... 316 945-9820
Wichita *(G-13651)*
Boeing Distribution Svcs Inc ... E ... 316 630-4900
Wichita *(G-13867)*
Cav Ice Protection Inc ... E ... 913 738-5391
New Century *(G-7272)*
Graco Supply Company ... F ... 316 943-4200
Wichita *(G-14492)*
Honeywell International Inc ... E ... 913 712-0400
Olathe *(G-7776)*
Kelley Instruments Inc ... F ... 316 945-7171
Wichita *(G-14843)*
Omni Aerospace Inc ... E ... 316 529-8998
Wichita *(G-15216)*
Tech-Aire Instruments Inc ... F ... 316 262-4020
Wichita *(G-15724)*
Wm F Hurst Co LLC ... F ... 800 741-0543
Shawnee *(G-11055)*

AIRCRAFT FLIGHT INSTRUMENT REPAIR SVCS

Aircraft Instrument & Rdo Svcs ... F ... 316 945-9820
Wichita *(G-13652)*
Ametek Arcft Parts & ACC Inc ... E ... 316 264-2397
Wichita *(G-13699)*
Butler Avionics Inc ... F ... 913 829-4606
New Century *(G-7271)*
Century Instrument Corp ... F ... 316 683-7571
Wichita *(G-13991)*
Kelley Instruments Inc ... F ... 316 945-7171
Wichita *(G-14843)*
Paragon N D T & Finishes Inc ... E ... 316 945-5285
Wichita *(G-15259)*

AIRCRAFT FUELING SVCS

Executive Beechcraft Inc ... E ... 913 782-9003
New Century *(G-7284)*
Fbo Air - Garden City Inc ... F ... 620 275-5055
Garden City *(G-2158)*
Jrm Enterprises Inc ... E ... 785 404-1328
Salina *(G-10557)*
Lyddon Aero Center Inc ... F ... 620 624-1646
Liberal *(G-6338)*
Yingling Aircraft Inc ... D ... 316 943-3246
Wichita *(G-16085)*

AIRCRAFT LIGHTING

Airfixture LLC ... E ... 913 312-1100
Kansas City *(G-3794)*
B/E Aerospace Inc ... G ... 316 609-4300
Wichita *(G-13788)*
Instruments and Flight Res Inc ... G ... 316 684-5177
Wichita *(G-14697)*

AIRCRAFT MAINTENANCE & REPAIR SVCS

Air Plains Services Corp ... F ... 620 326-8581
Wellington *(G-13488)*
Figeac Aero North America Inc ... D ... 316 634-2500
Wichita *(G-14366)*
Freeman Holdings LLC ... F ... 913 951-5600
Topeka *(G-12628)*
General Electric Company ... D ... 785 320-2350
Manhattan *(G-6644)*
Global Aviation Tech LLC ... F ... 316 425-0999
Wichita *(G-14473)*
Global Engineering and Tech ... E ... 620 664-6268
Hutchinson *(G-3301)*
Global Parts Aero Mfg ... E ... 316 775-9292
Augusta *(G-320)*
Global Parts Group Inc ... D ... 316 733-9240
Augusta *(G-321)*
Honeywell International Inc ... E ... 913 712-0400
Olathe *(G-7776)*
Jet Airwerks LLC ... E ... 620 442-3625
Arkansas City *(G-161)*
Kansas City Aviation Ctr Inc ... D ... 913 782-0530
Olathe *(G-7823)*
Mid-Continent AVI Svcs Inc ... F ... 316 927-4204
Wichita *(G-15078)*
Midwest Malibu Center Inc ... F ... 620 728-1356
Hutchinson *(G-3379)*
Webco Air Craft ... G ... 316 283-7929
Newton *(G-7426)*
Wichita Air Services Inc ... F ... 316 631-1332
Wichita *(G-15968)*
Yingling Aircraft Inc ... D ... 316 943-3246
Wichita *(G-16085)*

AIRCRAFT PARTS & AUX EQPT: Panel Assy/Hydro Prop Test Stands

Air Capitol Dial Inc ... F ... 316 264-2483
Wichita *(G-13649)*

AIRCRAFT PARTS & AUXILIARY EQPT: Assemblies, Fuselage

Orizon Arstrctres - Chnute Inc ... D ... 816 788-7800
Chanute *(G-753)*

AIRCRAFT PARTS & AUXILIARY EQPT: Assys, Subassemblies/Parts

Advanced Welding Tech LLC ... E ... 316 295-2333
Wichita *(G-13627)*
Apex Engineering Intl LLC ... C ... 316 262-1494
Wichita *(G-13718)*
Atlas Aerospace LLC ... G ... 316 977-7398
Wichita *(G-13763)*
Capps Manufacturing Inc ... D ... 316 942-9351
Wichita *(G-13940)*
Capps Manufacturing Inc ... D ... 316 942-9351
Wichita *(G-13941)*
Clearwater Engineering Inc ... E ... 316 425-0202
Derby *(G-1230)*
D-J Engineering Inc ... C ... 316 775-1212
Augusta *(G-316)*
Eck & Eck Machine Company Inc ... E ... 316 942-5924
Wichita *(G-14258)*
Etezazi Industries Inc ... E ... 316 831-9937
Wichita *(G-14307)*
Forming Specialists Inc ... G ... 620 488-3243
Belle Plaine *(G-446)*
Hisonic LLC ... E ... 913 782-0012
Olathe *(G-7769)*
Jmt Industries Inc ... G ... 316 267-1221
Wichita *(G-14758)*
Lathrom Manufacturing Inc ... F ... 316 522-0001
Wichita *(G-14931)*
LMI Aerospace Inc ... C ... 316 943-6059
Wichita *(G-14972)*
Lyons Manufacturing Co Inc ... E ... 620 257-2331
Lyons *(G-6491)*
M I F Inc ... D ... 316 838-3970
Park City *(G-9629)*
Manufacturing Development Inc ... E ... 316 542-0182
Cheney *(G-793)*
Old Ppp Inc ... D ... 620 421-3400
Parsons *(G-9713)*
Orizon Arostructures - Nkc LLC ... E ... 620 431-4037
Chanute *(G-752)*
Orizon Arostructures - Nkc LLC ... F ... 816 788-7800
Olathe *(G-7964)*
Quality Tech Metals ... E ... 316 945-4781
Wichita *(G-15386)*
Tect Aerospace Wellington Inc ... C ... 620 359-5000
Wellington *(G-13536)*
Universal Avonics Systems Corp ... G ... 316 524-9500
Wichita *(G-15852)*
Winding Specialists Co Inc ... F ... 316 265-9358
Wichita *(G-16054)*

AIRCRAFT PARTS & AUXILIARY EQPT: Bodies

Metal Forming Incorporated ... F ... 620 488-3930
Belle Plaine *(G-447)*

AIRCRAFT PARTS & AUXILIARY EQPT: Body & Wing Assys & Parts

H & R Parts Co Inc ... E ... 316 942-6984
Wichita *(G-14531)*
Primus International Inc ... C ... 316 425-8105
Wichita *(G-15346)*
Triumph Strctres - Wichita Inc ... D ... 316 942-0432
Wichita *(G-15805)*

AIRCRAFT PARTS & AUXILIARY EQPT: Body Assemblies & Parts

Figeac Aero North America Inc ... D ... 316 634-2500
Wichita *(G-14366)*
Globe Engineering Co Inc ... C ... 316 943-1266
Wichita *(G-14476)*
Lee Aerospace Inc ... C ... 316 636-9200
Wichita *(G-14946)*
Spirit Arosystems Holdings Inc ... E ... 316 526-9000
Wichita *(G-15644)*
Wasi Inc ... E ... 620 782-3337
Wichita *(G-15932)*

AIRCRAFT PARTS & AUXILIARY EQPT: Deicing Eqpt

Global Ground Support LLC ... D ... 913 780-0300
Olathe *(G-7732)*
Landoll Corporation ... B ... 785 562-5381
Marysville *(G-6893)*
R O Terex Corporation ... D ... 913 782-1200
Olathe *(G-8018)*

AIRCRAFT PARTS & AUXILIARY EQPT: Empennage/Tail Assy/Parts

Trinity Precision Inc ... D ... 316 265-0603
Wichita *(G-15802)*

AIRCRAFT PARTS & AUXILIARY EQPT: Oxygen Systems

B/E Aerospace Inc ... C ... 913 338-7292
Shawnee Mission *(G-11142)*

AIRCRAFT PARTS & AUXILIARY EQPT: Research & Development, Mfr

Archein Aerospace LLC ... E ... 682 499-2150
Wichita *(G-13730)*
Ultra Electronics Ice Inc ... D ... 785 776-6423
Manhattan *(G-6835)*
Universal Machining Shtmtl Inc ... E ... 316 425-7610
Wichita *(G-15854)*

AIRCRAFT PARTS & AUXILIARY EQPT: Wing Assemblies & Parts

Dynamic N/C LLC ... D ... 316 712-5028
Rose Hill *(G-10237)*

AIRCRAFT PARTS & EQPT, NEC

AAA Air Support Mfg LLC ... G ... 316 946-9299
Haysville *(G-2934)*
Accurus Aerospace Wichita LLC ... E ... 316 683-0266
Wichita *(G-13604)*
Aei Investment Holdings Inc ... D ... 817 283-3722
Wichita *(G-13633)*
Aero Metal Forms Inc ... E ... 316 942-0909
Wichita *(G-13634)*
Aero Space Controls Corp ... E ... 316 264-2875
Wichita *(G-13635)*
Aero Space Manufacturing Corp ... F ... 620 378-4441
Fredonia *(G-2026)*

Aero-Mach Laboratories Inc ....C....... 316 682-7707
Wichita *(G-13636)*
Aero-Tech Engineering Inc ....D....... 316 942-8604
Maize *(G-6507)*
Aerospace Systems Cmpnents Inc ....D....... 316 686-7392
Wichita *(G-13638)*
Aerospace Turbine Rotables Inc ....D....... 316 943-6100
Wichita *(G-13639)*
Apph Wichita Inc ....E....... 316 943-5752
Wichita *(G-13720)*
Atlas Aerospace LLC ....F....... 316 219-5862
Wichita *(G-13764)*
Avcon Industries Inc ....E....... 913 780-9595
Newton *(G-7313)*
B/E Aerospace Inc ....D....... 316 609-3360
Wichita *(G-13787)*
B/E Aerospace Inc ....D....... 913 338-9800
Lenexa *(G-5681)*
B/E Aerospace Inc ....G....... 316 609-4300
Wichita *(G-13788)*
Beechcraft Holdings LLC ....E....... 316 676-7111
Wichita *(G-13826)*
Beechcraft Intl Svc Co ....G....... 316 676-7111
Wichita *(G-13827)*
Burnham Cmpsite Structures Inc ....E....... 316 946-5900
Wichita *(G-13917)*
Butler National Corporation ....E....... 913 780-9595
Olathe *(G-7571)*
Ceco Inc ....E....... 316 942-7431
Wichita *(G-13969)*
Center Industries Corporation ....C....... 316 942-8255
Wichita *(G-13976)*
Charles Engineering Inc ....E....... 620 584-2381
Clearwater *(G-887)*
Cheyenne Mfg Inc ....E....... 316 942-7665
Wichita *(G-14002)*
Cmj Manufacturing Inc ....F....... 316 777-9692
Mulvane *(G-7214)*
Cox Machine Inc ....D....... 316 943-1342
Wichita *(G-14121)*
Cox Machine Inc ....D....... 316 943-1342
Harper *(G-2718)*
D & S Manufacturing Inc ....G....... 316 685-5337
Wichita *(G-14156)*
D-J Engineering Inc ....G....... 620 456-3211
Conway Springs *(G-1138)*
Ducommun Aerostructures Inc ....E....... 620 421-3401
Parsons *(G-9682)*
Dynamic Machine LLC ....F....... 316 941-4005
Wichita *(G-14248)*
Enjet Aero LLC ....F....... 913 717-7396
Overland Park *(G-8683)*
Exacta Aerospace Inc ....C....... 316 941-4200
Wichita *(G-14318)*
Fastenair Corporation ....E....... 316 684-2875
Wichita *(G-14345)*
Flame Engineering Inc ....E....... 785 222-2873
La Crosse *(G-4633)*
Fmw Inc ....F....... 316 943-4217
Wichita *(G-14398)*
Freddie Wayne Long ....F....... 316 263-8941
Wichita *(G-14415)*
Global Aviation Tech LLC ....F....... 316 425-0999
Wichita *(G-14473)*
Global Engineering & Tech Inc ....C....... 316 729-9232
Goddard *(G-2439)*
Goodrich Corporation ....F....... 316 943-3322
Wichita *(G-14485)*
Goodrich Corporation ....A....... 316 721-3100
Wichita *(G-14486)*
H M Dunn Company Inc ....C....... 316 522-5426
Wichita *(G-14532)*
H M Dunn Company Inc ....C....... 314 535-6684
Wichita *(G-14533)*
Harlow Aerostructures LLC ....C....... 316 265-5268
Wichita *(G-14561)*
Hiller Inc ....E....... 316 264-5231
Wichita *(G-14611)*
Impresa Aerospace LLC ....D....... 316 942-9100
Wichita *(G-14679)*
Industrial Process Eqp Co ....G....... 316 722-7800
Wichita *(G-14686)*
Inityaero Inc ....E....... 316 265-0603
Wichita *(G-14694)*
Kelly Manufacturing Company ....F....... 620 358-3826
Grenola *(G-2687)*
Kmi Inc ....E....... 316 777-0146
Mulvane *(G-7217)*
Lee Air Inc ....E....... 316 524-4622
Wichita *(G-14947)*
LMI Aerospace Inc ....F....... 913 469-6400
Lenexa *(G-5976)*
LMI Aerospace Inc ....F....... 620 378-4441
Fredonia *(G-2039)*
LMI Aerospace Inc ....G....... 316 944-4143
Wichita *(G-14971)*
LMI Lenexa ....G....... 913 491-6975
Lenexa *(G-5977)*
Machining Programming Mfg Inc ....E....... 316 945-1227
Wichita *(G-14998)*
Maxima Precision Inc ....E....... 316 832-2211
Wichita *(G-15020)*
McFarlane Aviation Inc ....D....... 785 594-2741
Baldwin City *(G-366)*
Mid Continent Controls Inc ....E....... 316 789-0088
Derby *(G-1262)*
Millennium Concepts Inc ....D....... 316 977-8870
Wichita *(G-15109)*
Mini-Mac Inc ....G....... 316 733-0661
Wichita *(G-15111)*
Mockry & Sons Machine Co Inc ....E....... 316 788-7878
Derby *(G-1263)*
Nance Manufacturing Inc ....E....... 620 842-3761
Anthony *(G-130)*
Nance Manufacturing Inc ....E....... 316 942-8671
Wichita *(G-15146)*
Omni Aerospace Inc ....E....... 316 529-8998
Wichita *(G-15216)*
Optimuz Manufacturing Inc ....E....... 316 519-1354
Wichita *(G-15229)*
Oxwell Inc ....D....... 620 326-7481
Wellington *(G-13521)*
Park Aerospace Tech Corp ....D....... 316 283-6500
Newton *(G-7403)*
Precision Aviation Controls ....D....... 620 331-8180
Independence *(G-3547)*
Precision Products ....G....... 316 943-0477
Wichita *(G-15325)*
Professional Machine & Tool ....F....... 316 755-1271
Valley Center *(G-13350)*
R & R Holdings Inc ....E....... 316 942-6699
Wichita *(G-15399)*
R & R Precision Machine Inc ....E....... 316 942-6699
Wichita *(G-15400)*
Rickman Machine Co Inc ....E....... 316 263-0841
Wichita *(G-15459)*
Senior Operations LLC ....C....... 316 942-3208
Wichita *(G-15558)*
Sigma Tek Inc ....E....... 316 775-6373
Augusta *(G-345)*
Spirit Aerosystems Inc ....E....... 316 523-2995
Wichita *(G-15640)*
Spirit Aerosystems Inc ....C....... 316 526-9000
Wichita *(G-15641)*
Spirit Aerosystems Innovative ....D....... 316 526-9000
Wichita *(G-15642)*
Spirit Arosystems Holdings Inc ....F....... 316 523-3950
Wichita *(G-15643)*
Tect Aerospace LLC ....C....... 316 425-3638
Wichita *(G-15726)*
Tect Hypervelocity Inc ....D....... 316 529-5000
Park City *(G-9647)*
Tect Hypervelocity Inc ....D....... 316 529-5000
Park City *(G-9648)*
Textron Aviation Inc ....G....... 316 517-1375
Wichita *(G-15738)*
Textron Aviation Inc ....C....... 316 517-6000
Wichita *(G-15747)*
Textron Aviation Inc ....B....... 316 721-3100
Wichita *(G-15751)*
Textron Aviation Inc ....A....... 316 676-7111
Salina *(G-10733)*
Textron Aviation Inc ....A....... 316 676-7111
Wichita *(G-15744)*
Textron Aviation Inc ....A....... 316 676-5373
Wichita *(G-15753)*
Torotel Products Inc ....C....... 913 747-6111
Olathe *(G-8116)*
Triumph Group Operations Inc ....D....... 620 326-5761
Wellington *(G-13538)*
Turbine Eng Comp Tech Turning ....E....... 316 925-4020
Wichita *(G-15815)*
United Tech Arospc Systems ....F....... 316 721-3100
Wichita *(G-15850)*
Valent Aerostructures LLC ....D....... 316 682-4551
Wichita *(G-15870)*
Valent Aerostructures LLC ....E....... 816 423-5600
Lenexa *(G-6207)*
Valent Aerostructures LLC ....G....... 620 378-4441
Fredonia *(G-2048)*
Vinland Aerodrome Inc ....G....... 785 594-2741
Baldwin City *(G-369)*
Webco Air Craft ....G....... 316 283-7929
Newton *(G-7426)*

AIRCRAFT PARTS WHOLESALERS

Ametek Arcft Parts & ACC Inc ....E....... 316 264-2397
Wichita *(G-13699)*
Century Instrument Corp ....F....... 316 683-7571
Wichita *(G-13991)*
Dodson International Parts Inc ....D....... 785 878-8000
Rantoul *(G-10196)*
Dodson Investments Inc ....D....... 785 878-4000
Rantoul *(G-10197)*
Global Ground Support LLC ....D....... 913 780-0300
Olathe *(G-7732)*
Global Parts Inc ....D....... 316 733-9240
Augusta *(G-319)*
Ipeco Wichita Inc ....E....... 316 722-7800
Wichita *(G-14729)*
Mid-State Aerospace Inc ....F....... 913 764-3600
Olathe *(G-7892)*
Midwest Corporate Aviation Inc ....E....... 316 636-9700
Wichita *(G-15091)*

AIRCRAFT RADIO EQPT REPAIR SVCS

Bevan-Rabell Inc ....E....... 316 946-4870
Wichita *(G-13842)*

AIRCRAFT SEATS

B/E Aerospace Inc ....G....... 316 609-4300
Wichita *(G-13788)*

AIRCRAFT SERVICING & REPAIRING

Aero Interior Maintenance Inc ....F....... 316 990-5088
Cheney *(G-787)*
Cav Ice Protection Inc ....E....... 913 738-5391
New Century *(G-7272)*
Hetrick Air Services Inc ....F....... 785 842-0000
Lawrence *(G-4896)*
IFR Systems Inc ....B....... 316 522-4981
Wichita *(G-14667)*
Jrm Enterprises Inc ....E....... 785 404-1328
Salina *(G-10557)*
Kansas Air Center Inc ....F....... 785 776-1991
Manhattan *(G-6674)*
Lyddon Aero Center Inc ....F....... 620 624-1646
Liberal *(G-6338)*
Pratt & Whitney Eng Svcs Inc ....G....... 316 945-9763
Wichita *(G-15322)*
Signature Flight Support Corp ....D....... 316 522-2010
Wichita *(G-15590)*
T and C Aviation Enterprises ....E....... 913 764-4800
Olathe *(G-8095)*

AIRCRAFT STORAGE SVCS

Executive Beechcraft Inc ....E....... 913 782-9003
New Century *(G-7284)*

AIRCRAFT: Airplanes, Fixed Or Rotary Wing

Beechcraft Holdings LLC ....E....... 316 676-7111
Wichita *(G-13826)*
Boeing Company ....A....... 316 523-7084
Wichita *(G-13864)*
Textron Aviation Inc ....A....... 316 676-7111
Salina *(G-10733)*
Textron Aviation Inc ....A....... 316 517-6000
Wichita *(G-15740)*
Textron Aviation Inc ....A....... 316 676-7111
Wichita *(G-15744)*
Textron Aviation Inc ....C....... 800 835-4090
Wichita *(G-15748)*
Textron Aviation Inc ....C....... 316 831-2000
Wichita *(G-15749)*
Textron Aviation Inc ....C....... 620 332-0228
Independence *(G-3564)*
Textron Aviation Inc ....A....... 316 676-5373
Wichita *(G-15753)*
Textron Aviation Inc ....G....... 316 517-1375
Wichita *(G-15738)*

AIRCRAFT: Motorized

Lathrom Manufacturing Inc ....F....... 316 522-0001
Wichita *(G-14931)*

AIRCRAFT: Research & Development, Manufacturer

Smith & Smith Aircraft Intl ....F 316 945-0204
Wichita *(G-15606)*

AIRPORT

Flightsafety International Inc ....F 316 220-3200
Wichita *(G-14389)*
Lawrence Municipal Airport-Lwc ....F 785 842-0000
Lawrence *(G-4977)*
Metropolitan Topeka Arprt Auth ....E 785 862-2362
Topeka *(G-12885)*
Midwest Corporate Aviation Inc ....E 316 636-9700
Wichita *(G-15091)*
Salina Airport Authority ....F 785 827-3914
Salina *(G-10664)*
Wichita Airport Authority ....F 316 946-4700
Wichita *(G-15969)*
Wichita Airport Authority ....E 316 636-9700
Wichita *(G-15970)*

AIRPORT TERMINAL SVCS

Crotts Aircraft Service Inc ....F 620 227-3553
Dodge City *(G-1336)*

AIRPORTS, FLYING FIELDS & SVCS

AvFlight Salina Corporation ....F 734 663-6466
Salina *(G-10415)*
Brp US Inc ....B 316 946-2000
Wichita *(G-13899)*
Freeman Holdings LLC ....F 785 862-0950
Topeka *(G-12627)*
New Century Air ....F 913 768-9400
New Century *(G-7294)*
Textron Aviation Inc ....D 316 517-8270
Wichita *(G-15735)*
Textron Aviation Inc ....C 316 517-6000
Wichita *(G-15737)*
Textron Aviation Inc ....F 888 727-4344
Wichita *(G-15739)*
Textron Aviation Inc ....D 316 293-9703
Wichita *(G-15743)*
Textron Aviation Inc ....C 316 517-8270
Wichita *(G-15736)*
Triumph Group Operations Inc ....D 620 326-5761
Wellington *(G-13538)*

ALARM SYSTEMS WHOLESALERS

American Sentry Security Sys ....E 785 232-1525
Topeka *(G-12323)*

ALARMS: Burglar

Honeywell International Inc ....E 402 597-2279
Olathe *(G-7775)*

ALARMS: Fire

Certified Life Safety LLC ....G 913 837-5319
Louisburg *(G-6442)*
Fire Alarm Specialist Inc ....F 785 743-5287
Wakeeney *(G-13387)*

ALCOHOL TREATMENT CLINIC, OUTPATIENT

Dccca Inc ....F 620 670-2803
Pittsburg *(G-9851)*
Dccca Inc ....F 620 672-7546
Pratt *(G-10107)*
Dccca Inc ....F 620 670-2814
Winfield *(G-16140)*
Dccca Inc ....F 785 830-8238
Lawrence *(G-4828)*
Dccca Inc ....E 785 843-9262
Lawrence *(G-4829)*
Dccca Inc ....E 316 265-6011
Wichita *(G-14179)*
Heartland Reg Alchl & Drug ....E 913 789-0951
Roeland Park *(G-10224)*
Kings Alcohol & Drug ....E 620 221-6252
Winfield *(G-16152)*
Southeast Kans Mental Hlth Ctr ....E 620 365-5717
Iola *(G-3633)*
Valley Hope Association ....E 785 877-5101
Norton *(G-7464)*
Valley Hope Association ....E 913 367-1618
Atchison *(G-269)*
Valley Hope Association ....E 785 877-2421
Norton *(G-7463)*

ALCOHOL: Ethyl & Ethanol

Arkalon Energy LLC ....E 620 624-2901
Liberal *(G-6279)*
Bonanza Bioenergy LLC ....E 620 276-4741
Garden City *(G-2115)*
East Kansas Agri-Energy LLC ....E 785 448-2888
Garnett *(G-2372)*
Gateway Ethanol LLC ....E 620 933-2288
Pratt *(G-10118)*
Kansas Ethanol LLC ....D 620 257-2300
Lyons *(G-6487)*
Lansing Trade Group LLC ....C 913 748-3000
Overland Park *(G-8945)*
Nesika Energy LLC ....G 785 335-2054
Scandia *(G-10800)*
Pratt Energy LLC ....E 620 933-2288
Pratt *(G-10136)*
Reeve Agri-Energy Inc ....F 620 275-7541
Garden City *(G-2264)*
Trenton Agri Products LLC ....G 316 265-3311
Wichita *(G-15798)*
Ube Services LLC ....E 316 616-3500
Wichita *(G-15827)*
Western Plains Energy LLC ....E 785 672-8810
Oakley *(G-7488)*

ALCOHOLISM COUNSELING, NONTREATMENT

Alcoholics Anonymous ....E 620 793-3962
Great Bend *(G-2502)*
Miracles House ....F 316 264-5900
Wichita *(G-15115)*
Parklane AA ....F 316 682-9960
Wichita *(G-15265)*

ALTERNATORS: Automotive

Clare Generator Service Inc ....F 785 827-3321
Salina *(G-10453)*
Dels Alternator & Starter Svc ....G 785 825-4466
Salina *(G-10473)*

ALUMINUM PRDTS

Aero Space Manufacturing Corp ....F 620 378-4441
Fredonia *(G-2026)*
Anodizing Inc ....D 620 223-1111
Fort Scott *(G-1955)*
Bmg of Kansas Inc ....D 620 327-4038
Hesston *(G-2985)*
D-J Extruding LLC ....E 620 456-3211
Conway Springs *(G-1139)*
Extrusions Inc ....D 620 223-1111
Fort Scott *(G-1967)*
Reno Fabricating & Sls Co Inc ....E 620 663-1269
Hutchinson *(G-3426)*

AMBULANCE SVCS

9 Line Medical Solutions LLC ....F 402 470-1696
Manhattan *(G-6526)*
Airmd LLC ....E 316 932-1440
Wichita *(G-13654)*
American Medical Response Inc ....C 913 227-0911
Kansas City *(G-3805)*
Bennington Ambulance Service ....F 785 488-3768
Bennington *(G-512)*
Chase County Ems ....F 620 273-6590
Cottonwood Falls *(G-1152)*
Cherokee Cnty Ambulance & Assn ....E 620 429-3018
Columbus *(G-1065)*
Cherokee County Ambulance ....F 620 856-2561
Baxter Springs *(G-402)*
City of Galena ....F 620 783-5065
Galena *(G-2071)*
City of Salina ....D 785 826-7340
Salina *(G-10451)*
Claflin Ambulance Service Assn ....E 620 587-3498
Claflin *(G-840)*
County of Clay ....E 785 632-2166
Clay Center *(G-858)*
County of Ford ....F 620 227-4556
Dodge City *(G-1332)*
County of Franklin ....F 785 229-7300
Ottawa *(G-8260)*
County of Norton ....E 785 877-5784
Norton *(G-7442)*
County of Osborne ....F 785 346-2379
Osborne *(G-8207)*
County of Pratt ....E 620 672-4130
Pratt *(G-10103)*
County of Russell ....E 785 445-3720
Russell *(G-10269)*
County of Stevens ....E 620 544-2562
Hugoton *(G-3156)*
County of Thomas ....E 785 460-4585
Colby *(G-1001)*
County of Trego ....F 785 743-5337
Wakeeney *(G-13385)*
Critical Care Transfer Inc ....F 620 353-4145
Ulysses *(G-13293)*
Ellsworth County Ambulance ....E 785 472-3454
Ellsworth *(G-1668)*
Finney County Emergency Med ....E 620 272-3822
Garden City *(G-2163)*
Jewell County Ems ....E 785 378-3069
Mankato *(G-6858)*
Kingman Emergency Medical Svcs ....E 620 532-5624
Kingman *(G-4601)*
Kiowa County Ems ....F 620 723-3112
Greensburg *(G-2681)*
Life Touch Ems Inc ....F 785 825-5115
Salina *(G-10582)*
Marysville Chamber Commerce ....F 785 562-2359
Marysville *(G-6896)*
Medevac Midamerica Inc ....C 785 233-2400
Topeka *(G-12878)*
Miami County Emergency Med Svc ....E 913 294-5010
Paola *(G-9571)*
Nmrmc Ems ....E 620 244-3522
Erie *(G-1863)*
Plainville Ambulance Service ....F 785 434-2530
Plainville *(G-9989)*
Pottawatomie Cnty Emrgncy Svcs ....E 785 456-0911
Wamego *(G-13434)*
Quinter Ambulance Service Inc ....E 785 754-3734
Quinter *(G-10185)*
Reno County Ambulance Service ....E 620 665-2120
Hutchinson *(G-3424)*
Republic County Ems ....F 785 527-7149
Belleville *(G-464)*
Saint Lukes Hosp Garnett Inc ....C 785 448-3131
Garnett *(G-2388)*
Sedan AR Egy Mdl Sv Dt 2 Inc ....E 620 725-5670
Sedan *(G-10847)*
Techs Inc ....D 785 364-1911
Holton *(G-3112)*
Transcare of Ks LLC ....E 620 431-6300
Chanute *(G-772)*

AMBULANCE SVCS: Air

Collins Industries Inc ....E 620 663-5551
Hutchinson *(G-3243)*
Eagle Med Inc ....F 785 899-3810
Goodland *(G-2468)*
Eaglemed LLC ....E 316 613-4855
Wichita *(G-14251)*
Topeka Air Ambulance Inc ....E 785 862-5433
Topeka *(G-13165)*

AMBULATORY SURGICAL CENTERS

Endoscopic Services PA ....F 316 687-0234
Wichita *(G-14287)*
Lawrence Surgery Center LLC ....E 785 832-0588
Lawrence *(G-4987)*
Mid-America Surgery Institute ....E 913 906-0855
Overland Park *(G-9026)*
Midwest Surgical ....F 316 687-1090
Wichita *(G-15105)*
Ridgewood Surgery and End ....F 316 768-4197
Wichita *(G-15462)*
Saint Lkes S Srgery Centre LLC ....F 913 317-3200
Overland Park *(G-9273)*
Surgery Ctr S Centl Kans LLC ....F 620 663-7187
Hutchinson *(G-3459)*
Surgicenter Johnson County Ltd ....E 913 894-4050
Shawnee Mission *(G-11914)*
Tallgrass Surgical Center LLC ....E 785 272-8807
Topeka *(G-13138)*

AMMONIUM NITRATE OR AMMONIUM SULFATE

Coffeyvlle Rsrces Ref Mktg LLC ....D 620 251-4000
Coffeyville *(G-925)*

AMMUNITION

Day and Zimmermann Inc ....C....... 620 421-7400
Parsons *(G-9680)*
Endless Ideas Inc ....F....... 913 766-0680
Olathe *(G-7681)*
Vista Outdoor Inc ....C....... 913 752-3400
Overland Park *(G-9467)*

AMMUNITION: Small Arms

Swift Bullet Co ....F....... 785 754-2374
Quinter *(G-10187)*
Velocity Manufacturing Co LLC ....F....... 620 223-1277
Fort Scott *(G-2015)*

AMUSEMENT & REC SVCS: Attractions, Concessions & Rides

AMF Bowling Centers Inc ....E....... 913 451-6400
Overland Park *(G-8382)*
County of Johnson ....F....... 913 631-5208
Shawnee Mission *(G-11271)*
Great Wolf Kansas Spe LLC ....B....... 913 299-7001
Kansas City *(G-4047)*
Incred-A-Bowl LLC ....D....... 913 851-1700
Overland Park *(G-8841)*
Kansas Cy Renaissance Festival ....F....... 913 721-2110
Bonner Springs *(G-558)*
Moonwalks For Fun Inc ....E....... 316 522-2224
Wichita *(G-15124)*

AMUSEMENT & REC SVCS: Baseball Club, Exc Pro & Semi-Pro

Mustang Softball ....F....... 316 260-9770
Wichita *(G-15141)*
Olathe Youth Baseball Inc ....F....... 913 393-9891
Olathe *(G-7955)*

AMUSEMENT & RECREATION SVCS: Amusement Mach Rental, Coin-Op

Memorial Union Corp Emporia ....D....... 620 341-5901
Emporia *(G-1793)*

AMUSEMENT & RECREATION SVCS: Amusement Ride

Morgan Chance Inc ....E....... 316 945-6555
Wichita *(G-15126)*
Pride Amusements LLC ....E....... 417 529-3810
Baxter Springs *(G-411)*

AMUSEMENT & RECREATION SVCS: Arcades

Kangolf Inc ....F....... 785 539-7529
Manhattan *(G-6673)*

AMUSEMENT & RECREATION SVCS: Art Gallery, Commercial

Chanute Art Gallery ....F....... 620 431-7807
Chanute *(G-711)*

AMUSEMENT & RECREATION SVCS: Baseball Batting Cage

Kangolf Inc ....F....... 785 539-7529
Manhattan *(G-6673)*

AMUSEMENT & RECREATION SVCS: Card & Game Svcs

Core Cashless LLC ....E....... 913 529-8200
Lenexa *(G-5788)*

AMUSEMENT & RECREATION SVCS: Carnival Operation

Creative Carnivals Events LLC ....F....... 913 642-0900
Overland Park *(G-8609)*
Tobys Carnival Inc ....E....... 620 235-6667
Arma *(G-192)*

AMUSEMENT & RECREATION SVCS: Concession Operator

Wichita Canteen Company Inc ....E....... 316 524-2254
Wichita *(G-15984)*

AMUSEMENT & RECREATION SVCS: Festival Operation

Festival Grogs Inc ....F....... 913 721-2110
Bonner Springs *(G-553)*
Independence Main Street Inc ....F....... 620 331-2300
Independence *(G-3528)*
Kansas City Blues Society Inc ....F....... 913 660-4692
Olathe *(G-7824)*
Tumbleweed Festival Inc ....F....... 620 275-9141
Garden City *(G-2304)*
Wichita Festivals Inc ....F....... 316 267-2817
Wichita *(G-16001)*

AMUSEMENT & RECREATION SVCS: Gambling & Lottery Svcs

Bhcmc LLC ....B....... 620 682-7777
Dodge City *(G-1308)*

AMUSEMENT & RECREATION SVCS: Game Parlor

Executive Mnor Leavenworth Inc ....F....... 785 234-5400
Topeka *(G-12586)*

AMUSEMENT & RECREATION SVCS: Golf Club, Membership

American Golf Corporation ....D....... 316 684-4110
Wichita *(G-13692)*
American Golf Corporation ....E....... 620 663-5301
Hutchinson *(G-3198)*
American Golf Corporation ....E....... 913 681-3100
Shawnee Mission *(G-11103)*
Ann N Hogan LLC ....E....... 913 271-7440
Louisburg *(G-6438)*
Barton County Club Inc ....F....... 620 653-4255
Great Bend *(G-2516)*
Flint Hills National Golf Club ....D....... 316 733-4131
Andover *(G-93)*
Glen Shadow Golf Club ....D....... 913 764-2299
Olathe *(G-7729)*
Glen Shadow Golf Club ....E....... 913 764-6572
Olathe *(G-7730)*
Golf Club At Southwind LLC ....E....... 620 275-2117
Garden City *(G-2189)*
Kansas City Country Club ....C....... 913 236-2100
Mission Hills *(G-7145)*
Lindsey Management Co Inc ....F....... 316 788-3070
Derby *(G-1258)*
Montes De Areia LLC ....E....... 620 663-5301
Hutchinson *(G-3385)*
National Golf Properties LLC ....E....... 913 721-1333
Kansas City *(G-4281)*
Nicklaus Golf Club Maintenance ....F....... 913 897-1624
Shawnee Mission *(G-11685)*
Osage Hills Inc ....F....... 620 449-2713
Saint Paul *(G-10383)*
Park Hills Golf & Supper Club ....F....... 620 672-7541
Pratt *(G-10129)*
Reflection Ridge Maintenance ....F....... 316 721-9483
Wichita *(G-15434)*
Sabetha Golf Club Inc ....F....... 785 284-2023
Sabetha *(G-10328)*
Shawnee Mission Bch Volleyball ....E....... 913 422-4070
Shawnee Mission *(G-11853)*
Stagg Hill Golf Club Inc ....F....... 785 539-1041
Manhattan *(G-6806)*
Sterling Country Club Inc ....F....... 620 278-9956
Sterling *(G-12130)*
Turkey Creek Golf Course ....F....... 620 241-8530
McPherson *(G-7032)*
Wolf Creek Golf Links Inc ....E....... 913 592-3329
Olathe *(G-8157)*

AMUSEMENT & RECREATION SVCS: Golf Professionals

Dynamic Discs LLC ....F....... 620 208-3472
Emporia *(G-1734)*

AMUSEMENT & RECREATION SVCS: Golf Svcs & Professionals

City of Leawood ....D....... 913 685-4550
Shawnee Mission *(G-11228)*
Falcon Ridge Golf Club ....F....... 913 393-4653
Shawnee Mission *(G-11359)*
Golf Operations Management LLC ....E....... 913 897-3809
Overland Park *(G-8764)*

AMUSEMENT & RECREATION SVCS: Hot Air Balloon Rides

Old World Balloonery LLC ....F....... 913 338-2628
Overland Park *(G-9097)*

AMUSEMENT & RECREATION SVCS: Hunting Club, Membership

Lil Toledo Lodge LLC ....E....... 620 244-5668
Chanute *(G-739)*
Ravenwood Hunting Preserve Inc ....F....... 785 256-6444
Topeka *(G-12999)*

AMUSEMENT & RECREATION SVCS: Hunting Guides

Golden Prairie Hunting Service ....F....... 620 675-8490
Sublette *(G-12202)*

AMUSEMENT & RECREATION SVCS: Instruction Schools, Camps

Challenger Sports Corp ....E....... 913 599-4884
Lenexa *(G-5749)*
Kansas Starbase Inc ....F....... 785 861-4709
Topeka *(G-12805)*

AMUSEMENT & RECREATION SVCS: Lawn Bowling Club, Membership

J R Galley Inc ....F....... 785 938-8024
Colby *(G-1016)*

AMUSEMENT & RECREATION SVCS: Lottery Tickets, Sales

Cervs Conoco & Convenience ....F....... 785 625-7777
Hays *(G-2767)*
Heritage Restaurant Inc ....E....... 316 524-7495
Wichita *(G-14596)*

AMUSEMENT & RECREATION SVCS: Recreation Center

Boys Grls CLB Lwrnce Lwrnce K ....D....... 785 841-5672
Lawrence *(G-4763)*
Chanute Recreation Commission ....D....... 620 431-4199
Chanute *(G-713)*
City of Leavenworth ....E....... 913 651-2132
Leavenworth *(G-5220)*
City of Topeka Employees ....F....... 785 272-5503
Topeka *(G-12476)*
City of Wichita ....E....... 316 744-9719
Wichita *(G-14027)*
Coffeyvlle Unfied Schl Dst 445 ....E....... 620 251-5910
Coffeyville *(G-927)*
County of Grant ....F....... 620 356-4233
Ulysses *(G-13292)*
Dillon Nature Center ....E....... 620 663-7411
Hutchinson *(G-3265)*
Hesston Unified School Dst 460 ....E....... 620 327-2989
Hesston *(G-2993)*
Holcomb Recreation Commission ....D....... 620 277-2152
Holcomb *(G-3075)*
Hutchinson Recreation Comm ....F....... 620 663-6179
Hutchinson *(G-3323)*
K-State Union Corporation ....C....... 785 532-6575
Manhattan *(G-6671)*
Mac Adams Recreation Center ....F....... 316 265-6111
Wichita *(G-14996)*
Mini-Train Gage Park ....F....... 785 273-6108
Topeka *(G-12907)*
Newton Recreation Commission ....E....... 316 283-7330
Newton *(G-7395)*
Q Golden Billiards ....F....... 785 625-6913
Hays *(G-2893)*
Riverfront Community Center ....E....... 913 651-2132
Leavenworth *(G-5286)*
Wamego Recreation Dept ....E....... 785 456-8810
Wamego *(G-13454)*
Wyandotte County Sports Assn ....F....... 913 299-9197
Kansas City *(G-4553)*

AMUSEMENT & RECREATION SVCS: Recreation SVCS

Blue Valley Recreation Comm .... E 913 685-6030
Shawnee Mission (G-11171)
County of Johnson .... C 913 888-4713
Shawnee Mission (G-11272)
Derby Recreation Comm Usd 260 .... D 316 788-3781
Derby (G-1238)
Elmdale Community Center .... F 620 663-6170
Hutchinson (G-3278)
Ottawa Recreation Commission .... C 785 242-1939
Ottawa (G-8299)

AMUSEMENT & RECREATION SVCS: Rodeo Operation

Longford Rodeo LLC .... D 785 388-2330
Longford (G-6431)

AMUSEMENT & RECREATION SVCS: School, Baseball Instruction

Between Lnes Elite Spt Academy .... F 913 422-1221
Lenexa (G-5700)

AMUSEMENT & RECREATION SVCS: School, Hockey Instruction

Wichita Thnder Prof Hckey Team .... F 316 264-4625
Wichita (G-16039)

AMUSEMENT & RECREATION SVCS: Shooting Range

Capital City Gun Club Inc .... F 785 478-4682
Topeka (G-12426)
Flint Oak .... E 620 658-4401
Fall River (G-1927)
Range 54 LLC .... F 316 440-2854
Wichita (G-15416)

AMUSEMENT & RECREATION SVCS: Skating Rink Operation

Canlan Ice Spt Ctr Wichita LLC .... D 316 337-9199
Wichita (G-13934)
Ice Sports Kansas City LLC .... E 913 441-3033
Shawnee Mission (G-11451)
Interskate 77 .... F 620 229-7655
Winfield (G-16149)

AMUSEMENT & RECREATION SVCS: Soccer Club, Exc Pro/Semi-Pro

Kansas City SC LLC .... F 913 575-1278
Olathe (G-7827)

AMUSEMENT & RECREATION SVCS: Swimming Club, Membership

Coffeyville Country Club .... E 620 251-5236
Coffeyville (G-918)
McPherson Family Ymca Inc .... D 620 241-0363
McPherson (G-6999)
Round Hill Bath &TEnnis Club .... F 913 381-2603
Shawnee Mission (G-11814)
Wichita Swim Club .... E 316 683-1491
Wichita (G-16036)
YMCA of Hutchinson Reno Cnty .... D 620 662-1203
Hutchinson (G-3494)

AMUSEMENT & RECREATION SVCS: Swimming Pool, Non-Membership

City of Prairie Village .... F 913 642-6010
Shawnee Mission (G-11232)
Ellis Kinney Swimming Pool .... E 620 672-7724
Cullison (G-1185)
Hugoton Swimming Pool .... E 620 544-2793
Hugoton (G-3165)

AMUSEMENT & RECREATION SVCS: Tennis & Professionals

Genesis Health Club Inc .... E 316 945-8331
Wichita (G-14458)
Tennis Corporation of America .... E 913 491-4116
Shawnee Mission (G-11926)
United States Tennis .... F 913 322-4823
Overland Park (G-9444)

AMUSEMENT & RECREATION SVCS: Tennis Club, Membership

First Serve Tennis .... D 785 749-3200
Lawrence (G-4862)
Genesis Health Clubs MGT LLC .... E 316 634-0094
Wichita (G-14459)
Missouri Vly Tennis Foundation .... F 913 322-4800
Overland Park (G-9043)
Oprc Inc .... E 913 642-6880
Overland Park (G-9108)
Woodside Tennis & Health Club .... C 913 831-0034
Shawnee Mission (G-12017)

AMUSEMENT & RECREATION SVCS: Tennis Courts, Non-Member

Bishop Rink Holdings LLC .... E 913 268-2625
Shawnee (G-10918)
Lamont Hill Resort Inc .... E 785 828-3131
Vassar (G-13371)

AMUSEMENT & RECREATION SVCS: Theme Park

Dillon Nature Center .... E 620 663-7411
Hutchinson (G-3265)
RPM Motorsports LLC .... F 316 259-4576
Wichita (G-15489)
Splashtacular Inc .... F 800 844-5334
Paola (G-9590)

AMUSEMENT & RECREATION SVCS: Zoological Garden, Commercial

City of Manhattan .... E 785 587-2737
Manhattan (G-6587)
Hedrick Exotic Animal Farm .... E 620 422-3245
Nickerson (G-7433)
Sunset Zoological Pk Wildlife .... E 785 587-2737
Manhattan (G-6818)

AMUSEMENT ARCADES

B & E Inc .... F 913 299-1110
Kansas City (G-3833)
Bird Music & Amusement Svcs .... E 785 537-2930
Manhattan (G-6561)
Coin Machine Distributors Inc .... F 316 652-0361
Wichita (G-14052)
Hutchinson Vending Company .... F 620 662-6474
Hutchinson (G-3328)
United Distributors Inc .... F 316 712-2174
Wichita (G-15841)

AMUSEMENT MACHINES: Coin Operated

Pop-A-Shot Enterprise LLC .... G 785 827-6229
Salina (G-10637)

AMUSEMENT PARK DEVICES & RIDES

Chance Rides Manufacturing Inc .... C 316 945-6555
Wichita (G-13997)

AMUSEMENT PARKS

1010 N Webb Road LLC .... E 316 722-7529
Wichita (G-13576)
Sedgwick County Zoological Soc .... C 316 660-9453
Wichita (G-15549)
Widgets Family Fun Center .... F 785 320-5099
Manhattan (G-6854)

AMUSEMENT/REC SVCS: Ticket Sales, Sporting Events, Contract

Goody Tickets LLC .... F 913 231-2674
Leawood (G-5415)
Ticket Solutions LLC .... E 913 384-4751
Shawnee Mission (G-11932)

ANALYZERS: Network

Firemon LLC .... E 913 948-9570
Overland Park (G-8717)
Frugal Inc .... G 785 776-9088
Saint George (G-10347)
Wppa Inc .... F 316 683-4111
Wichita (G-16074)

ANALYZERS: Respiratory

Lifesource Inc .... G 913 660-9275
Lenexa (G-5972)

ANIMAL & REPTILE EXHIBIT

Hedricks Promotions Inc .... E 620 422-3296
Nickerson (G-7434)

ANIMAL BASED MEDICINAL CHEMICAL PRDTS

Ivy Animal Health Inc .... F 913 888-2192
Lenexa (G-5925)
Suther Feeds Inc .... F 785 292-4414
Frankfort (G-2023)

ANIMAL FEED & SUPPLEMENTS: Livestock & Poultry

APC Inc .... E 620 675-8691
Sublette (G-12197)
Archer-Daniels-Midland Company .... E 785 263-2260
Abilene (G-12)
Cargill Incorporated .... F 620 241-5120
McPherson (G-6940)
Cargill Incorporated .... E 620 277-2558
Garden City (G-2121)
Cargill Incorporated .... F 316 291-1939
Wichita (G-13947)
Darling Ingredients Inc .... D 316 264-6951
Wichita (G-14169)
HI Plains Feed LLC .... G 620 277-2886
Garden City (G-2196)
Hills Pet Nutrition Inc .... B 800 255-0449
Topeka (G-12690)
Hills Pet Nutrition Inc .... C 785 231-2812
Topeka (G-12691)
Hills Pet Nutrition Inc .... C 785 286-1451
Topeka (G-12692)
Natures Way Inc .... G 785 486-3302
Horton (G-3132)
Purina Animal Nutrition LLC .... E 316 265-0624
Wichita (G-15378)
Quality Milling LLC .... F 620 724-4900
Girard (G-2416)
Ranch-Aid Inc .... F 620 583-5585
Eureka (G-1898)
Ridley USA Inc .... E 785 738-2215
Beloit (G-500)
Suther Feeds Inc .... F 785 292-4414
Frankfort (G-2023)
Western Feed Mills Inc .... E 620 758-2283
Cedar Vale (G-695)

ANIMAL FEED: Wholesalers

American Midwest Distrs LLC .... F 816 842-1905
Overland Park (G-8379)
Bert and Wetta Sales Inc .... E 785 263-2258
Abilene (G-14)
Bluestem Farm and Rnch Sup Inc .... D 620 342-5502
Emporia (G-1705)
Cargill Incorporated .... E 620 277-2558
Garden City (G-2121)
Cargill Animal Nutrition .... E 620 342-1650
Emporia (G-1717)
Chisholm Trail Country Str LLC .... F 316 283-3276
Newton (G-7328)
CSC Gold Inc .... F 913 664-8100
Shawnee Mission (G-11284)
Darling Ingredients Inc .... G 913 371-7083
Kansas City (G-3957)
Farmers Cooperative Elev Co .... F 620 545-7138
Viola (G-13378)
Manna Pro Products LLC .... E 913 621-2355
Kansas City (G-4216)
Provimi North America Inc .... E 620 327-2280
Hesston (G-2999)
Purina Mills LLC .... E 316 265-0624
Wichita (G-15379)

ANIMAL FOOD & SUPPLEMENTS: Alfalfa Or Alfalfa Meal

Alfalfa Inc .... G 620 675-8686
Sublette (G-12196)

Bert & Wetta Larned Inc .... E 620 285-7777
Larned *(G-4695)*
Bert and Wetta Sales Inc .... E 620 285-7777
Larned *(G-4696)*
Bert and Wetta Sales Inc .... E 785 263-2258
Abilene *(G-14)*
Cross Brand Feed & Alfalfa Inc .... E 620 324-5571
Lewis *(G-6266)*
Cross Brand Office Inc .... E 620 324-5571
Lewis *(G-6267)*

ANIMAL FOOD & SUPPLEMENTS: Cat

Big Heart Pet Brands .... C 785 312-3662
Lawrence *(G-4757)*

ANIMAL FOOD & SUPPLEMENTS: Chicken Feeds, Prepared

Kansas Feeds Inc .... F 620 225-3500
Dodge City *(G-1385)*

ANIMAL FOOD & SUPPLEMENTS: Dog

Big Heart Pet Brands .... C 785 338-9240
Topeka *(G-12380)*
Emporia Pet Products Inc .... E 620 342-1650
Emporia *(G-1741)*
Treatco Inc .... D 316 265-7900
Wichita *(G-15795)*

ANIMAL FOOD & SUPPLEMENTS: Dog & Cat

Ainsworth Pet Nutrition LLC .... C 620 231-7779
Frontenac *(G-2051)*
Cargill Incorporated .... E 913 299-2326
Kansas City *(G-3890)*
Darling Ingredients Inc .... E 620 276-7618
Garden City *(G-2142)*
Darling Ingredients Inc .... D 316 264-6951
Wichita *(G-14169)*
Hills Pet Nutrition Inc .... C 785 231-2812
Topeka *(G-12691)*
Hills Pet Nutrition Inc .... B 800 255-0449
Topeka *(G-12690)*
Simmons Pet Food Inc .... C 620 342-1323
Emporia *(G-1828)*
Ziwi USA Incorporated .... F 913 291-0189
Overland Park *(G-9529)*

ANIMAL FOOD & SUPPLEMENTS: Feed Premixes

Mid-South Milling Company Inc .... E 913 621-5442
Kansas City *(G-4246)*
Purina Mills LLC .... E 316 265-0624
Wichita *(G-15379)*

ANIMAL FOOD & SUPPLEMENTS: Feed Supplements

Micro-Lite LLc .... F 620 537-7025
Buffalo *(G-613)*
Performix High Plains LLC .... E 620 225-0080
Garden City *(G-2250)*
Performix Nutrition Systems .... E 620 277-2886
Garden City *(G-2251)*

ANIMAL FOOD & SUPPLEMENTS: Livestock

Alternative Building Tech .... F 913 856-4536
Gardner *(G-2325)*
Ashland Feed & Seed Co .... G 620 635-2856
Ashland *(G-193)*
Blair Milling & Elev Co Inc .... E 913 367-2310
Atchison *(G-216)*
Elite Endeavors LLC .... F 620 391-1577
Plains *(G-9974)*
Elnicki Inc .... F 620 232-5800
Pittsburg *(G-9857)*
Fairleigh Ranch Corporation .... F 620 872-2111
Scott City *(G-10810)*
Provimi North America Inc .... E 620 327-2280
Hesston *(G-2999)*
R W Milling Company Inc .... G 785 456-7866
Wamego *(G-13437)*
Reeve Agri-Energy Inc .... F 620 275-7541
Garden City *(G-2264)*
Ridley USA Inc .... E 620 231-6700
Pittsburg *(G-9929)*
Stockade Brands Incorporated .... E 620 231-6700
Pittsburg *(G-9941)*

ANIMAL FOOD & SUPPLEMENTS: Meat Meal & Tankage

Bern Meat Plant Incorporated .... F 785 336-2165
Bern *(G-521)*

ANIMAL FOOD & SUPPLEMENTS: Mineral feed supplements

X F Enterprises Inc .... F 620 672-5616
Pratt *(G-10164)*

ANIMAL FOOD & SUPPLEMENTS: Pet, Exc Dog & Cat, Canned

Ceva Animal Health LLC .... D 800 999-0297
Lenexa *(G-5744)*
Hills Pet Nutrition Inc .... D 620 340-6920
Emporia *(G-1772)*

ANIMAL FOOD & SUPPLEMENTS: Pet, Exc Dog & Cat, Dry

Ceva USA Inc .... E 800 999-0297
Lenexa *(G-5748)*
Jak 3 Inc .... G 785 336-2148
Seneca *(G-10870)*

ANIMAL FOOD & SUPPLEMENTS: Specialty, Mice & Other Pets

Manna Pro Products LLC .... E 913 621-2355
Kansas City *(G-4216)*

ANIMAL FOOD & SUPPLEMENTS: Stock Feeds, Dry

Feedex Companies LLC .... F 620 500-5016
Hutchinson *(G-3284)*
Midwest PMS LLC .... E 620 872-2189
Scott City *(G-10824)*
Midwest PMS LLC .... G 620 276-0970
Garden City *(G-2235)*

ANTENNAS: Receiving

Molex LLC .... G 630 969-4550
Wichita *(G-15122)*

ANTIQUE & CLASSIC AUTOMOBILE RESTORATION

Ricks Auto Restoration .... E 620 326-5635
Wellington *(G-13524)*

ANTIQUE AUTOMOBILE DEALERS

Briggs Auto Group Inc .... C 785 537-8330
Manhattan *(G-6570)*

ANTIQUE REPAIR & RESTORATION SVCS, EXC FURNITURE & AUTOS

Kiowa Service Co Inc .... F 316 636-1070
Wichita *(G-14865)*

ANTIQUE SHOPS

Box Central Inc .... F 316 689-8484
Wichita *(G-13875)*
D J Company .... F 316 685-3241
Wichita *(G-14158)*
Therien & Company Inc .... F 415 956-8850
Plainville *(G-9993)*

ANTIQUES, WHOLESALE

Therien & Company Inc .... F 415 956-8850
Plainville *(G-9993)*

APARTMENT LOCATING SVCS

Chase Manhattan Apartment .... F 785 776-3663
Manhattan *(G-6586)*
M P M Services Inc .... F 785 841-5797
Lawrence *(G-5005)*
T & J Holdings Inc .... F 785 841-4935
Lawrence *(G-5131)*

APPAREL ACCESS STORES

Urban Outfitters Inc .... E 785 331-2885
Lawrence *(G-5169)*

APPAREL DESIGNERS: Commercial

Rellec Apparel Graphics LLC .... G 913 707-5249
Lenexa *(G-6100)*

APPAREL FILLING MATERIALS: Cotton Waste, Kapok/Related Matl

Precision Cut Inc .... E 913 422-0777
Shawnee Mission *(G-11747)*

APPLIANCES: Small, Electric

B/E Aerospace Inc .... C 913 338-7292
Shawnee Mission *(G-11142)*

APPLICATIONS SOFTWARE PROGRAMMING

Agelix Consulting LLC .... E 913 708-8145
Overland Park *(G-8357)*
Apex Innovations Inc .... F 913 254-0250
Olathe *(G-7531)*
Firemon LLC .... E 913 948-9570
Overland Park *(G-8717)*
Juniper Payments LLC .... E 316 267-3200
Wichita *(G-14778)*
Mobile Reasoning Inc .... G 913 888-2600
Lenexa *(G-6010)*
Networks Plus .... E 785 825-0400
Manhattan *(G-6759)*
Sara It Solutions Inc .... F 913 269-6980
Overland Park *(G-9280)*
Spatial Data Research Inc .... F 314 705-0772
Lawrence *(G-5114)*

APPRAISAL SVCS, EXC REAL ESTATE

Claim Solution Inc .... E 913 322-2300
Shawnee Mission *(G-11236)*
County of Cowley .... F 620 221-5430
Winfield *(G-16128)*
Pda of Kansas City Inc .... F 913 631-0711
Overland Park *(G-9149)*

ARCHITECTURAL SVCS

B G Consultants Inc .... E 785 537-7448
Manhattan *(G-6551)*
Black Veatch-Altan Joint Ventr .... B 913 458-4300
Overland Park *(G-8461)*
E Architects PA .... F 785 234-6664
Topeka *(G-12564)*
Gossen Livingston Associates .... D 620 225-3300
Dodge City *(G-1366)*
Gpw & Associates LLC .... F 785 865-2332
Lawrence *(G-4877)*
H W Lochner Inc .... D 816 945-5840
Lenexa *(G-5885)*
Innovative Cnstr Svcs Inc .... F 316 260-1644
Wichita *(G-14695)*
Johnson Wilson Embers .... E 913 438-9095
Shawnee Mission *(G-11500)*
Kiewit Engineering Group Inc .... C 402 943-1465
Lenexa *(G-5949)*
Monarch Plastic Surgery .... E 913 663-3838
Overland Park *(G-9049)*
Oldcastle Apg Midwest Inc .... E 913 667-1792
Bonner Springs *(G-568)*
R Messner Construction Co .... E 316 634-2381
Wichita *(G-15405)*
Schaefer Johnson Cox Frey Arch .... E 316 684-0171
Wichita *(G-15527)*
Shafer Kline & Warren Inc .... E 913 888-7800
Lenexa *(G-6126)*
Wilson Inc Engineers Architects .... D 785 827-0433
Salina *(G-10769)*
Yaeger Architecture Inc .... E 913 742-8000
Lenexa *(G-6239)*

ARCHITECTURAL SVCS: Engineering

Associates Gould-Evens .... E 785 842-3800
Lawrence *(G-4739)*
Brr Architecture Inc .... C 913 262-9095
Overland Park *(G-8489)*
Dlr Group Inc .... D 913 897-7811
Overland Park *(G-8659)*

GBA Architects Inc ....E.... 913 492-0400
Lenexa *(G-5869)*
Lk Architecture/Mead & Hunt ....D.... 316 268-0230
Wichita *(G-14970)*

ARCHITECTURAL SVCS: Engineering

Alloy Architecture PA ....E.... 316 634-1111
Wichita *(G-13677)*
Bell/Knott and Associates C ....E.... 913 378-1600
Leawood *(G-5339)*
Davidson & Associates Inc ....E.... 913 271-6859
Leawood *(G-5372)*
Davidson Architure and Engr ....F.... 913 451-9390
Shawnee Mission *(G-11292)*
Glmv Architecture Inc ....E.... 316 265-9367
Wichita *(G-14472)*
Health Facilities Group LLC ....F.... 316 262-2500
Wichita *(G-14575)*
Hmn Architects Inc ....D.... 913 451-9075
Overland Park *(G-8818)*
Hoefer Wysocki Architects LLC ....D.... 913 307-3700
Leawood *(G-5429)*
Horst Trrill Krst Archtects PA ....E.... 785 266-5373
Topeka *(G-12704)*
Jeff L Krehbiel ....F.... 316 267-8233
Wichita *(G-14753)*
Lk Architecture Inc ....D.... 316 268-0230
Wichita *(G-14969)*
Mann & Co Architects/Engineers ....F.... 620 662-4493
Hutchinson *(G-3363)*
Michael Kirkham & Assoc Inc ....E.... 785 472-3163
Ellsworth *(G-1678)*
Nearing Staats Prelogar ....E.... 913 831-1415
Prairie Village *(G-10052)*
P A Treanorhl ....F.... 785 235-0012
Topeka *(G-12957)*
Peckham Gyton Albers Viets Inc ....E.... 913 362-6500
Shawnee Mission *(G-11722)*
Pkhls Architecture PA ....F.... 316 321-4774
El Dorado *(G-1592)*
Rees Msilionis Turley Arch LLC ....E.... 816 842-1292
Shawnee Mission *(G-11787)*
Schaefer Johnson Cox Frey ....D.... 316 684-0171
Wichita *(G-15526)*
Schwerdt Design Group Inc ....E.... 785 273-7540
Topeka *(G-13041)*
Scientific Engineering Inc ....F.... 785 827-7071
Salina *(G-10698)*
Spangenberg Phillips Inc ....F.... 316 267-4002
Wichita *(G-15634)*
Tevis Architectural Group ....F.... 913 599-3003
Shawnee *(G-11039)*
Treanorhl Inc ....E.... 785 842-4858
Lawrence *(G-5145)*
Wdm Architects PA ....E.... 316 262-4700
Wichita *(G-15939)*
Winter Architects Inc ....F.... 316 267-7142
Wichita *(G-16058)*
Yaeger-Acuity Solutions ....E.... 913 742-8000
Overland Park *(G-9515)*

ARCHITECTURAL SVCS: House Designer

R S Bickford & Co Inc ....F.... 913 451-1480
Shawnee Mission *(G-11774)*

ARMATURE REPAIRING & REWINDING SVC

Atkinson Industries Inc ....D.... 620 231-6900
Pittsburg *(G-9816)*
Yost Electric Inc ....G.... 785 637-5454
Gorham *(G-2492)*

ARMORED CAR SVCS

Brinks Incorporated ....F.... 316 945-0244
Wichita *(G-13891)*
Garda CL West Inc ....C.... 316 942-9700
Wichita *(G-14445)*
Loomis Armored Us LLC ....F.... 316 267-0269
Wichita *(G-14977)*

ART & ORNAMENTAL WARE: Pottery

Flint Hills Clay Works Inc ....F.... 620 382-3620
Marion *(G-6870)*

ART DEALERS & GALLERIES

Chanute Art Gallery ....F.... 620 431-7807
Chanute *(G-711)*
Deans Designs Inc ....F.... 316 686-6674
Wichita *(G-14181)*
Gallery Xii Inc ....E.... 316 267-5915
Wichita *(G-14440)*
Prairiebrooke Arts Inc ....F.... 913 341-0333
Overland Park *(G-9178)*

ART DESIGN SVCS

MBB Inc ....E.... 816 531-1992
Leawood *(G-5469)*

ART GALLERIES

Mark Arts ....F.... 316 634-2787
Wichita *(G-15009)*

ART GALLERY, NONCOMMERCIAL

Wichita Center For The Arts ....F.... 316 315-0151
Wichita *(G-15985)*

ART GOODS & SPLYS WHOLESALERS

Fittings Export LLC ....G.... 620 364-2930
Burlington *(G-636)*
Humidor East ....E.... 316 688-0112
Wichita *(G-14654)*

ART SPLY STORES

Nazdar Company ....F.... 913 422-1888
Shawnee *(G-11004)*

ARTISTS' AGENTS & BROKERS

National Rgstred Agents Inc NJ ....F.... 913 754-0637
Overland Park *(G-9072)*

ARTISTS' MATERIALS, WHOLESALE

Nazdar Company ....F.... 913 422-1888
Shawnee *(G-11004)*

ARTISTS' MATERIALS: Paints, Gold Or Bronze

Company Business Intl Sarl ....G.... 913 286-9771
Olathe *(G-7606)*

ARTS & CRAFTS SCHOOL

Lansing Unified Schl Dst 469 ....E.... 913 250-0749
Lansing *(G-4680)*
Munchkin Village ....F.... 620 577-2440
Independence *(G-3542)*

ARTS OR SCIENCES CENTER

Lucas Arts Hmnties Council Inc ....F.... 785 525-6118
Lucas *(G-6473)*

ASBESTOS PRDTS: Pipe Covering, Heat Insulatng Matl, Exc Felt

Precision Pipe Cover Inc ....E.... 785 233-2000
Topeka *(G-12982)*

ASBESTOS PRODUCTS

Patriot Abatement Services LLC ....F.... 913 397-6181
Olathe *(G-7975)*

ASPHALT & ASPHALT PRDTS

Asphalt Sales Company ....E.... 913 788-8806
Olathe *(G-7536)*
Koch Materials LLC ....C.... 316 828-5500
Wichita *(G-14883)*

ASPHALT COATINGS & SEALERS

Cutting Edge Tile & Grout ....G.... 316 648-5516
Wichita *(G-14149)*
Mm Distribution LLC ....G.... 800 689-2098
Douglass *(G-1467)*

ASPHALT PLANTS INCLUDING GRAVEL MIX TYPE

Andrews Asphalt & Cnstr Inc ....G.... 785 232-0188
Topeka *(G-12326)*

ASSEMBLING SVC: Plumbing Fixture Fittings, Plastic

Daves Service & Repair Inc ....G.... 620 662-8285
Hutchinson *(G-3257)*

ASSOCIATION FOR THE HANDICAPPED

ARC of Sedgwick County Inc ....E.... 316 943-1191
Wichita *(G-13729)*
Cerebral Palsy Research Fo ....D.... 316 688-5314
Wichita *(G-13992)*
Home Readers Inc ....F.... 913 893-6900
Edgerton *(G-1484)*
Indepndent Living Resource Ctr ....E.... 316 942-6300
Wichita *(G-14681)*
Southast Kans Ind Lving Rsrce ....E.... 620 421-5502
Parsons *(G-9739)*
Special Olympics Kansas Inc ....F.... 913 236-9290
Shawnee Mission *(G-11881)*
Training & Evaluation Cente ....E.... 620 663-2216
Hutchinson *(G-3466)*
Training & Evaluation Cente ....E.... 620 663-1596
Hutchinson *(G-3467)*
Training & Evaluation Cente ....E.... 620 615-5850
Hutchinson *(G-3468)*

ASSOCIATIONS: Alumni

Alpha CHI Omega ....F.... 785 843-7600
Lawrence *(G-4731)*
Cherryvale Alumni Commnty/Educ ....F.... 620 336-3198
Cherryvale *(G-802)*
Emporia State Univ Fndtion Inc ....F.... 620 341-5440
Emporia *(G-1745)*
Kansas State Univ Alumni Assn ....E.... 785 532-6260
Manhattan *(G-6677)*
University Kansas Alumni Assn ....E.... 785 864-4760
Lawrence *(G-5155)*

ASSOCIATIONS: Bar

Henson Hutton Mudrick Gragson ....F.... 785 232-2200
Topeka *(G-12684)*
Kansas Bar Association ....E.... 785 234-5696
Topeka *(G-12763)*
Wichita Bar Association ....F.... 316 263-2251
Wichita *(G-15980)*

ASSOCIATIONS: Business

Abwa Management LLC ....E.... 913 732-5100
Overland Park *(G-8338)*
City of Great Bend ....E.... 620 793-4111
Great Bend *(G-2540)*
City of Halstead ....E.... 316 835-2286
Halstead *(G-2697)*
City of Overland Park ....C.... 913 895-6000
Shawnee Mission *(G-11231)*
City of Pittsburg ....D.... 620 308-6916
Pittsburg *(G-9834)*
Department of Kansas Disabled ....E.... 316 681-1948
Wichita *(G-14195)*
Diecks Inc ....E.... 785 632-5550
Clay Center *(G-860)*
Garden City Co-Op Inc ....F.... 620 276-8903
Garden City *(G-2171)*
K U Endowment Association ....F.... 785 830-7600
Lawrence *(G-4929)*
Kansas Assn of Insur Agents ....F.... 785 232-0561
Topeka *(G-12759)*
Kansas Credit Union Assn ....E.... 316 942-7965
Wichita *(G-14795)*
Midwest Energy Inc ....D.... 785 625-3437
Hays *(G-2873)*
National Publishers Group Inc ....F.... 316 788-6271
Haysville *(G-2953)*
PSI Services Inc ....C.... 913 895-4600
Olathe *(G-8011)*
Redbud Village ....F.... 785 425-6312
Stockton *(G-12184)*
Service Corps Retired Execs ....F.... 316 269-6273
Wichita *(G-15567)*
Service Corps Retired Execs ....F.... 620 793-3420
Great Bend *(G-2635)*
Service Corps Retired Execs ....F.... 785 234-3049
Topeka *(G-13060)*
State Assn of Kans Watersheds ....F.... 785 544-6686
Robinson *(G-10215)*
Treasurer Kansas State ....E.... 785 296-3171
Topeka *(G-13198)*

Weishaar Adaptation ....E.... 913 367-6299
Atchison *(G-271)*
Workforce Alliance of South ....D.... 316 771-6600
Wichita *(G-16072)*

ASSOCIATIONS: Dentists'

Dental Associates ....F.... 620 276-7681
Garden City *(G-2144)*

ASSOCIATIONS: Fraternal

Ancient Free & Accepted M ....E.... 785 284-3169
Sabetha *(G-10304)*
Ancient Free & Accptd Masons ....D.... 785 738-5095
Beloit *(G-473)*
Benevolent/Protectv Order Elks ....F.... 785 762-2922
Junction City *(G-3674)*
Beta Theta PHI ....D.... 785 843-4711
Leavenworth *(G-5209)*
Elks Lodge Inc ....E.... 620 672-2011
Pratt *(G-10110)*
Fraternal Order Eagles Inc ....E.... 785 632-3521
Clay Center *(G-864)*
Fraternal Order of Police ....D.... 620 694-2830
Hutchinson *(G-3293)*
Knights of Columbus ....E.... 785 636-5453
Paxico *(G-9756)*
Knights of Columbus ....F.... 620 825-4378
Kiowa *(G-4627)*
Knights of Columbus ....F.... 620 251-2891
Parsons *(G-9700)*
Knights of Columbus ....F.... 620 442-7264
Arkansas City *(G-162)*
Masonic Order ....E.... 785 625-3127
Hays *(G-2870)*
Masonic Temple ....F.... 620 342-3913
Emporia *(G-1790)*
PHI Kappa Theta ....F.... 785 539-7491
Manhattan *(G-6775)*
Pride/Chapter Intl Assoc ....E.... 913 321-2733
Kansas City *(G-4336)*
Rotary International ....F.... 785 626-9444
Atwood *(G-291)*

ASSOCIATIONS: Homeowners

Deer Lk Esttes Homeowners Assn ....D.... 316 640-6592
Wichita *(G-14185)*
Pauls Valley Third Additon ....F.... 316 733-1648
Rose Hill *(G-10243)*
Quail Ridge Homes Assoc Inc ....E.... 913 381-2042
Shawnee Mission *(G-11764)*
Quivira Falls Community Assn ....E.... 913 469-5463
Shawnee Mission *(G-11768)*
Sugar Valley Lakes Homes Assn ....E.... 913 795-2120
Mound City *(G-7175)*
Tanglewood Lk Owners Assn Inc ....F.... 913 795-2286
La Cygne *(G-4643)*

ASSOCIATIONS: Parent Teacher

Blue River Elementary Pto Inc ....E.... 913 239-6000
Overland Park *(G-8467)*
Lakewood Middle School Pto ....D.... 913 239-5800
Overland Park *(G-8939)*
Mize Elementary Pto ....F.... 913 441-0880
Shawnee *(G-10998)*
Pta Kansas Congress Oxford ....F.... 913 897-1719
Overland Park *(G-9203)*
Shawnee Hts Booster CLB Pto ....F.... 785 379-5880
Tecumseh *(G-12242)*
Sunrise Point Elementary Pto ....F.... 913 239-7500
Overland Park *(G-9375)*
Union Valley Pto ....F.... 620 662-4891
Hutchinson *(G-3475)*
Village Elementary School Pto ....D.... 620 341-2282
Emporia *(G-1847)*

ASSOCIATIONS: Real Estate Management

American Rsdntial Cmmnties LLC ....F.... 785 776-4440
Manhattan *(G-6542)*
Amli Management Company ....F.... 913 851-3200
Overland Park *(G-8383)*
Amli Management Company ....F.... 913 685-3700
Shawnee Mission *(G-11110)*
Anderson Management Company ....F.... 316 681-1711
Wichita *(G-13706)*
Archon Residential MGT LP ....F.... 913 631-2100
Shawnee Mission *(G-11118)*
Associated Management Services ....F.... 785 228-9494
Topeka *(G-12344)*
Barnds Brothers Inc ....E.... 913 897-2340
Shawnee Mission *(G-11152)*
Canlan Ice Spt Ctr Wichita LLC ....D.... 316 337-9199
Wichita *(G-13934)*
Cohen-Esrey LLC ....E.... 913 671-3300
Overland Park *(G-8573)*
Cohen-Esrey Communities LLC ....D.... 913 671-3300
Overland Park *(G-8574)*
Commercial Management Company ....F.... 785 234-2882
Topeka *(G-12489)*
Dunes Residential Services Inc ....E.... 913 955-2900
Leawood *(G-5380)*
Eden West Inc ....E.... 913 384-3800
Shawnee Mission *(G-11327)*
Ellis Grubb Martens Coml Group ....E.... 316 262-0000
Wichita *(G-14272)*
Gt Kansas LLC ....E.... 913 266-1106
Shawnee Mission *(G-11404)*
Heritage Management Corp ....F.... 785 273-2995
Topeka *(G-12685)*
Hilltop Manor Mutal Hsing Corp ....F.... 316 684-5141
Wichita *(G-14615)*
Home Rental Services Inc ....F.... 913 469-6633
Overland Park *(G-8825)*
Hughes Development Company Inc ....F.... 913 321-2262
Kansas City *(G-4089)*
Jones Lang Lasalle Inc ....F.... 816 531-2323
Overland Park *(G-8879)*
Kelly Enterprise Inc ....F.... 913 685-1800
Overland Park *(G-8912)*
Landvest Corporation ....E.... 316 634-6510
Wichita *(G-14922)*
Ls Construction Services Inc ....E.... 913 681-5888
Shawnee Mission *(G-11580)*
M H P Management Services ....E.... 913 441-0194
Edwardsville *(G-1508)*
Mastercraft Corporation ....E.... 785 842-4455
Lawrence *(G-5013)*
Mid-Land Management Inc ....D.... 785 272-1398
Topeka *(G-12890)*
Midland Properties Inc ....F.... 913 677-5300
Mission Woods *(G-7151)*
Midland Property Management ....F.... 913 677-5300
Mission Woods *(G-7152)*
Neighborhood Group Inc ....E.... 913 362-0000
Shawnee Mission *(G-11675)*
Northstar Property Management ....F.... 316 689-8577
Wichita *(G-15194)*
Paramount Management Corp ....E.... 316 269-4477
Wichita *(G-15261)*
Pro X Property Solutions LLC ....F.... 620 249-5767
Pittsburg *(G-9923)*
Retel Brokerage Services Inc ....E.... 678 292-5723
Wichita *(G-15453)*
Summerfield Suites Mgt Co L P ....D.... 316 681-5100
Wichita *(G-15682)*
Sunburst Properties Inc ....F.... 913 393-4747
Stilwell *(G-12174)*
T & J Holdings Inc ....F.... 785 841-4935
Lawrence *(G-5131)*
Trinity Property Group LLC ....E.... 620 342-8723
Emporia *(G-1840)*
Tutera Group Inc ....E.... 913 851-0215
Shawnee Mission *(G-11951)*
Universal Management Inc ....E.... 913 321-3521
Kansas City *(G-4495)*
Waddell & Reed Fincl Svcs Inc ....B.... 913 236-2000
Overland Park *(G-9478)*
Wesley Management Inc ....F.... 913 682-6844
Leavenworth *(G-5305)*

ASSOCIATIONS: Trade

Bluetooth Sig Inc ....F.... 913 317-4700
Overland Park *(G-8470)*
Coopertive Cpon Rdemption Assn ....F.... 913 384-3830
Westwood *(G-13552)*
Gcsaa ....F.... 800 832-4410
Lawrence *(G-4870)*
Heartland Credit Union Assn ....F.... 913 297-2480
Overland Park *(G-8807)*
Heartland Credit Union Assn ....F.... 316 942-7965
Wichita *(G-14583)*
International Assn Plas Dist ....F.... 913 345-1005
Overland Park *(G-8856)*
Kansas Bankers Association ....E.... 785 232-3444
Topeka *(G-12762)*
Kansas Consulting Engineers ....F.... 785 357-1824
Topeka *(G-12767)*
Kansas Livestock Association ....E.... 785 273-5115
Topeka *(G-12785)*
Kansas Regional Assn Realtors ....E.... 913 498-1100
Shawnee Mission *(G-11519)*
Kansas Rest Hospitality Assn ....F.... 316 267-8383
Wichita *(G-14821)*
League Kansas Municipalities ....F.... 785 354-9565
Topeka *(G-12837)*
Missouri Livestock Mktg Assn ....E.... 816 891-0502
Leawood *(G-5488)*
National Auctioneers Assn ....F.... 913 541-8084
Shawnee Mission *(G-11671)*

ATHLETIC CLUB & GYMNASIUMS, MEMBERSHIP

Infinite Fitness ....F.... 913 469-8850
Overland Park *(G-8843)*
Lyerla Associates ....E.... 913 888-9247
Shawnee Mission *(G-11585)*
Opti-Life Services LLC ....E.... 316 518-8757
Wichita *(G-15225)*
Punch Boxing Plus Fitness ....E.... 816 589-2690
Shawnee *(G-11013)*

ATHLETIC ORGANIZATION

Bartlett Cooperative Assn ....E.... 620 236-7143
Chetopa *(G-816)*
Johnson Cnty Grls Athc Complex ....D.... 913 422-7837
Shawnee Mission *(G-11493)*
Kansas Athletics Incorporated ....B.... 785 864-7050
Lawrence *(G-4930)*
Kansas State University ....A.... 785 539-4971
Manhattan *(G-6682)*
Kansas Trapshooters Assn Inc ....F.... 316 755-2933
Valley Center *(G-13347)*
Mize Houser & Company PA ....E.... 913 451-1882
Shawnee Mission *(G-11649)*
Mize Houser & Company PA ....F.... 785 842-8844
Lawrence *(G-5030)*
Social Security Employees ....F.... 877 840-5741
Manhattan *(G-6803)*
United Sttes Bowl Congress Inc ....D.... 913 631-7209
Shawnee *(G-11043)*
Wichita State Univ Inter Cllga ....D.... 316 978-3250
Wichita *(G-16031)*
Wichita Thnder Prof Hckey Team ....F.... 316 264-4625
Wichita *(G-16039)*

ATOMIZERS

Crosswind Industries Inc ....G.... 785 380-8668
Topeka *(G-12532)*

AUCTION SVCS: Livestock

Anthony Livestock Sales Co ....F.... 620 842-3757
Anthony *(G-120)*
Atchison County Auction Co ....E.... 913 367-5278
Atchison *(G-208)*
Colby Livestock Auction ....F.... 785 460-3231
Colby *(G-998)*
El Dorado Livestock Auction ....E.... 316 320-3212
El Dorado *(G-1559)*
Farmers Rnchers Livstock Cmnty ....D.... 785 825-0211
Salina *(G-10496)*
Fort Scott Livestock Market ....E.... 620 223-4600
Fort Scott *(G-1970)*
Fredonia Livestock Auction LLC ....E.... 620 378-2212
Fredonia *(G-2033)*
Hays Livestock Market Center ....E.... 785 628-8206
Hays *(G-2831)*
Herington Livestock Market ....E.... 785 258-2205
Herington *(G-2974)*
Holton Livestock Exchange Inc ....E.... 785 364-4114
Holton *(G-3097)*
La Crosse Livestock Market ....E.... 785 222-2586
La Crosse *(G-4634)*
Mankato Livestock Inc ....E.... 785 378-3283
Mankato *(G-6860)*
Marysville Livestock Inc ....F.... 785 562-1015
Marysville *(G-6900)*
Oberlin Livestock Auction Inc ....F.... 785 475-2323
Oberlin *(G-7498)*
Overbrook Livestock Comm Co ....E.... 785 665-7181
Overbrook *(G-8327)*
Pratt Livestock Inc ....E.... 620 672-5961
Sterling *(G-12127)*
Pratt Livestock Inc ....E.... 620 672-5961
Pratt *(G-10142)*
R and P Calf Ranch LLC ....F.... 620 855-2550
Cimarron *(G-835)*

Rezac Sales Barn.........E....... 785 437-2785
Saint Marys *(G-10373)*
Russell Livestock Commission.........E....... 785 483-2961
Russell *(G-10295)*
Russell Livestock LLC.........E....... 785 483-2961
Russell *(G-10296)*
Sylvan Sales Commission LLC.........E....... 785 526-7123
Sylvan Grove *(G-12220)*
Winter Livestock Inc.........E....... 620 525-6271
Hanston *(G-2715)*
Winter Livestock Inc.........F....... 620 225-4159
Dodge City *(G-1461)*

AUCTION SVCS: Motor Vehicle

Copart of Kansas Inc.........F....... 913 287-6200
Kansas City *(G-3939)*
Iaa Inc.........F....... 316 832-1101
Park City *(G-9620)*
Iaa Inc.........F....... 913 422-9303
Kansas City *(G-4092)*
Kansas Auto Auction Inc.........E....... 913 365-0460
Elwood *(G-1688)*
Mid-America Auto Auction Inc.........C....... 316 500-7700
Wichita *(G-15075)*
Sunflower Auto Auction LLC.........E....... 785 862-2900
Topeka *(G-13117)*

AUCTIONEERS: Fee Basis

Bud Palmer Auction.........E....... 316 838-4141
Wichita *(G-13905)*
Carlson Auction Service Inc.........E....... 785 478-4250
Topeka *(G-12451)*
Carr Auction & Realestate.........E....... 620 285-3148
Larned *(G-4697)*
Larry Theurer.........F....... 620 326-2715
Wellington *(G-13510)*
McCurdy Auction LLC.........E....... 316 683-0612
Wichita *(G-15026)*
Paola Lifestock Auction Inc.........E....... 913 294-3335
Paola *(G-9581)*
Purple Wave Auction.........D....... 785 537-5057
Manhattan *(G-6783)*

AUDIO & VIDEO EQPT, EXC COMMERCIAL

Flyover Innovations Inc.........G....... 913 827-2248
Gardner *(G-2346)*
Marketing Services of Kansas.........G....... 913 888-4555
Shawnee Mission *(G-11599)*

AUDIO ELECTRONIC SYSTEMS

Lyntec Inc.........G....... 913 529-2233
Shawnee Mission *(G-11587)*
R D C Inc.........G....... 913 529-2233
Shawnee Mission *(G-11771)*

AUDIO-VISUAL PROGRAM PRODUCTION SVCS

AVI Systems Inc.........E....... 913 495-9494
Lenexa *(G-5677)*
Digital Sound Systems Inc.........E....... 913 492-5775
Lenexa *(G-5819)*
Retail Groc Assn Grter Kans Cy.........F....... 913 384-3830
Westwood *(G-13558)*

AUDIOLOGISTS' OFFICES

Associated Audiologists Inc.........E....... 913 403-0018
Shawnee Mission *(G-11125)*
Audiology Consultants Inc.........F....... 785 823-3761
Salina *(G-10412)*
Heartspring Inc.........B....... 316 634-8700
Wichita *(G-14590)*
Lawrence Otlryngology Assoc PA.........F....... 620 343-6600
Lawrence *(G-4981)*
Moore Jeff PHD Audiologist.........F....... 316 686-6608
Wichita *(G-15125)*

AUDITING SVCS

Protiviti Inc.........F....... 913 685-6200
Overland Park *(G-9198)*
R & J Salina Tax Service Inc.........E....... 785 827-1304
Salina *(G-10649)*

AUTHOR

Baker Sr Marcellus.........F....... 316 670-6329
Wichita *(G-13795)*

AUTHORS' AGENTS & BROKERS

Midwest Mixer Service LLC.........E....... 620 872-7251
Scott City *(G-10823)*

AUTO & HOME SUPPLY STORES: Auto & Truck Eqpt & Parts

Built-So-Well.........G....... 785 537-5166
Manhattan *(G-6571)*
Cline Auto Supply Inc.........E....... 620 343-6000
Emporia *(G-1721)*
Dodge City International Inc.........E....... 620 225-4177
Dodge City *(G-1348)*
Genuine Parts Company.........F....... 913 631-4329
Shawnee Mission *(G-11395)*
John Dere Cffeyville Works Inc.........B....... 620 251-3400
Coffeyville *(G-951)*
Omaha Truck Center Inc.........E....... 785 823-2204
Salina *(G-10620)*

AUTO & HOME SUPPLY STORES: Auto Air Cond Eqpt, Sell/Install

Lenexa Automotive Inc.........F....... 913 492-8250
Shawnee Mission *(G-11561)*
Mid-Amrcan Dstrbtrs/Jyhawk RAD.........F....... 913 321-9664
Kansas City *(G-4245)*

AUTO & HOME SUPPLY STORES: Automotive Access

OReilly Automotive Stores Inc.........F....... 316 831-9112
Wichita *(G-15236)*

AUTO & HOME SUPPLY STORES: Automotive parts

A & A Auto Salvage.........F....... 785 286-2728
Topeka *(G-12276)*
A D L M LLC.........F....... 913 888-0770
Shawnee Mission *(G-11062)*
A-One Auto Salvage of Wichita.........F....... 316 524-3273
Haysville *(G-2933)*
Accessible Technologies Inc.........D....... 913 338-2886
Lenexa *(G-5621)*
Advance Stores Company Inc.........C....... 785 826-2400
Salina *(G-10396)*
Automotive Supply Inc.........E....... 316 942-8285
Wichita *(G-13775)*
Autozone Inc.........F....... 785 452-9790
Salina *(G-10414)*
Blaylock Diesel Service Inc.........F....... 620 856-5227
Baxter Springs *(G-399)*
Central Marketing Inc.........F....... 316 613-2404
Wichita *(G-13980)*
Frontier Ag Inc.........E....... 785 462-2063
Oakley *(G-7475)*
Garnett Auto Supply Inc.........E....... 316 267-4393
Wichita *(G-14449)*
Gfe LLC.........F....... 316 260-8433
Wichita *(G-14462)*
Joe Self Chevrolet Inc.........C....... 316 689-4390
Wichita *(G-14760)*
Kriers Auto Parts Inc.........G....... 785 738-3526
Beloit *(G-489)*
L C McClain Inc.........F....... 785 584-6151
Rossville *(G-10253)*
Laird Noller Ford Inc.........C....... 785 235-9211
Topeka *(G-12828)*
Laird Noller Ford Inc.........E....... 785 264-2800
Topeka *(G-12829)*
Lewis Auto Salvage LLC.........F....... 785 233-0561
Topeka *(G-12841)*
Midway Motors Inc.........D....... 620 241-7737
McPherson *(G-7005)*
Noller Lincoln-Mercury Inc.........E....... 785 267-2800
Topeka *(G-12932)*
OReilly Automotive Stores Inc.........F....... 316 321-4371
El Dorado *(G-1588)*
OReilly Automotive Stores Inc.........F....... 316 685-7900
Wichita *(G-15232)*
OReilly Automotive Stores Inc.........F....... 785 842-9800
Lawrence *(G-5048)*
OReilly Automotive Stores Inc.........F....... 913 381-0451
Overland Park *(G-9111)*
OReilly Automotive Stores Inc.........E....... 913 764-8685
Olathe *(G-7962)*
OReilly Automotive Stores Inc.........F....... 620 331-1018
Independence *(G-3545)*
OReilly Automotive Stores Inc.........F....... 620 664-6800
Hutchinson *(G-3396)*
OReilly Automotive Stores Inc.........F....... 913 268-6001
Shawnee Mission *(G-11702)*
OReilly Automotive Stores Inc.........F....... 785 235-9241
Topeka *(G-12951)*
OReilly Automotive Stores Inc.........F....... 620 251-5280
Coffeyville *(G-967)*
OReilly Automotive Stores Inc.........F....... 913 829-6188
Olathe *(G-7963)*
OReilly Automotive Stores Inc.........F....... 316 686-5536
Wichita *(G-15234)*
OReilly Automotive Stores Inc.........F....... 785 235-5658
Topeka *(G-12952)*
OReilly Automotive Stores Inc.........F....... 785 862-4749
Topeka *(G-12953)*
OReilly Automotive Stores Inc.........F....... 785 266-3688
Topeka *(G-12954)*
OReilly Automotive Stores Inc.........F....... 785 832-0408
Lawrence *(G-5049)*
OReilly Automotive Stores Inc.........F....... 913 367-4138
Atchison *(G-253)*
OReilly Automotive Stores Inc.........E....... 316 264-6422
Wichita *(G-15235)*
Riley Ford Mercury Co.........F....... 620 356-1206
Ulysses *(G-13315)*
Rose Motor Supply Inc.........F....... 620 662-1254
Hutchinson *(G-3432)*
S & W Supply Company Inc.........E....... 785 625-7363
Hays *(G-2904)*
Smith Auto & Truck Parts Inc.........F....... 620 275-9145
Garden City *(G-2282)*
Taylor Implement Co Inc.........E....... 785 675-3272
Hoxie *(G-3143)*
Vee Village Parts Inc.........F....... 816 421-6441
Basehor *(G-390)*
W Carter Orvil Inc.........E....... 620 251-4700
Coffeyville *(G-984)*

AUTO & HOME SUPPLY STORES: Batteries, Automotive & Truck

Wholesale Batteries Inc.........F....... 913 342-0113
Kansas City *(G-4542)*

AUTO & HOME SUPPLY STORES: Speed Shops, Incl Race Car Splys

Midwest Motorsports Inc.........E....... 913 334-0477
Kansas City *(G-4254)*

AUTO & HOME SUPPLY STORES: Trailer Hitches, Automotive

B & W Custom Truck Beds Inc.........C....... 800 810-4918
Humboldt *(G-3181)*
Redneck Inc.........E....... 316 263-6090
Wichita *(G-15432)*

AUTO & HOME SUPPLY STORES: Truck Eqpt & Parts

Central Pwr Systems & Svcs LLC.........E....... 620 792-1361
Great Bend *(G-2534)*
Fleetpride Inc.........F....... 316 942-4227
Wichita *(G-14385)*
Fleetpride Inc.........D....... 800 362-2600
Wichita *(G-14386)*
Georgia Kenworth Inc.........E....... 816 483-6444
Leawood *(G-5411)*
Maupin Truck Parts Inc.........E....... 620 225-4433
Dodge City *(G-1401)*
Midwest Truck Equipment Inc.........F....... 316 744-2889
Park City *(G-9633)*
Paynes Inc.........F....... 620 231-3170
Frontenac *(G-2063)*
Southwest Sterling Inc.........E....... 816 483-6444
Leawood *(G-5555)*
Southwest Truck Parts Inc.........D....... 620 672-5686
Pratt *(G-10151)*
Straub International Inc.........E....... 620 792-5256
Great Bend *(G-2641)*
Tractor Supply Company.........F....... 785 827-3300
Salina *(G-10738)*
Tractor Supply Company.........F....... 620 663-7607
Hutchinson *(G-3465)*
Truck Stuff Inc.........F....... 316 264-1908
Wichita *(G-15807)*
Western Truck Equipment Co.........F....... 620 793-8464
Great Bend *(G-2662)*

Williams Service Inc ....E 620 878-4225
Florence (G-1930)

AUTOMATED TELLER MACHINE NETWORK

Electronic Funds Transfer Inc ....E 913 831-2055
Lenexa (G-5831)
Euronet Worldwide Inc ....D 913 327-4200
Leawood (G-5389)
Residential Treatment Service ....E 620 421-1155
Parsons (G-9732)

AUTOMATIC REGULATING CNTRLS: Flame Safety, Furnaces & Boiler

Midwest Combustn Solutions Inc ....G 316 425-0929
Wichita (G-15090)

AUTOMATIC REGULATING CONTROLS: AC & Refrigeration

Ademco Inc ....G 913 438-1111
Lenexa (G-5629)
Honeywell International Inc ....E 402 597-2279
Olathe (G-7775)
Siemens Industry Inc ....D 316 260-4340
Wichita (G-15586)

AUTOMATIC REGULATING CONTROLS: Hardware, Environmental Reg

Clean Air Management Co Inc ....E 913 831-0740
Lenexa (G-5760)

AUTOMATIC REGULATING CONTROLS: Oil & Hydronic, Combination

Power Flame Incorporated ....C 620 421-0480
Parsons (G-9724)

AUTOMATIC TELLER MACHINES

1-Stop LLC ....G 913 898-6211
Parker (G-9656)

AUTOMOBILE FABRICS, WHOLESALE

National Fabric Co Inc ....F 913 281-1833
Kansas City (G-4279)

AUTOMOBILE RECOVERY SVCS

Clinical Reference Lab Inc ....F 913 492-3652
Lenexa (G-5764)
Flint Hills Ford Inc ....E 785 776-4004
Manhattan (G-6632)
J-Six Enterprises LLC ....F 785 336-2149
Seneca (G-10868)

AUTOMOBILES & OTHER MOTOR VEHICLES WHOLESALERS

Briggs Auto Group Inc ....C 785 776-7799
Manhattan (G-6568)
Briggs Auto Group Inc ....C 785 537-8330
Manhattan (G-6570)
Fleetpride Inc ....F 785 862-1540
Topeka (G-12617)
Kansas Cy Freightliner Sls Inc ....E 913 780-6606
Olathe (G-7828)
Midwest Truck Equipment Inc ....F 316 744-2889
Park City (G-9633)

AUTOMOBILES: Off-Road, Exc Recreational Vehicles

Motivational Tubing LLC ....G 316 283-7301
Newton (G-7391)

AUTOMOBILES: Wholesalers

Briggs Auto Group Inc ....E 785 776-3677
Manhattan (G-6569)
Coyson Transportation LLC ....E 620 336-2846
Cherryvale (G-805)
Easy Credit Auto Sales Inc ....E 316 522-3279
Wichita (G-14254)

AUTOMOTIVE & TRUCK GENERAL REPAIR SVC

A-Plus Logistics LLC ....E 316 945-5757
Park City (G-9598)
Action Tire & Service Inc ....F 913 631-9600
Shawnee Mission (G-11072)
Advance Auto Parts Inc ....F 913 782-0076
Olathe (G-7511)
All American Automotive Inc ....F 316 721-3600
Wichita (G-13662)
Allen Samuels Waco D C J Inc ....E 620 860-1869
Hutchinson (G-3196)
Auto Masters LLC ....F 316 789-8540
Derby (G-1219)
Auto Service Ctr Shawnee LLC ....F 913 422-5388
Shawnee (G-10912)
Autobody of Lawrence ....E 785 843-3055
Lawrence (G-4744)
B & B Redimix Inc ....F 785 543-5133
Phillipsburg (G-9777)
Berning Tire Inc ....F 913 422-3033
Bonner Springs (G-541)
Bme Inc ....E 785 274-5116
Topeka (G-12391)
Bob Allen Ford Inc ....D 913 381-3000
Overland Park (G-8473)
Boss Motors Inc ....F 785 562-3696
Marysville (G-6880)
Brets Autoworks Corp ....F 913 764-8677
Olathe (G-7559)
Browns Super Service Inc ....F 785 267-1080
Topeka (G-12409)
Calverts Auto Express ....E 913 631-9995
Lenexa (G-5725)
Calverts Express Auto S ....E 913 631-9995
Lenexa (G-5726)
Central Pwr Systems & Svcs LLC ....E 620 792-1361
Great Bend (G-2534)
Central Pwr Systems & Svcs LLC ....E 316 943-1231
Wichita (G-13984)
City of Hutchinson ....D 620 694-1970
Hutchinson (G-3241)
City of Salina ....F 785 309-5752
Salina (G-10452)
Complete Automotive LLC ....E 620 245-0600
McPherson (G-6951)
Conklin Fangman Investment Co ....C 620 662-4467
Hutchinson (G-3245)
Cooperative Elevator & Sup Co ....F 620 873-2376
Meade (G-7048)
Credit Motors Inc ....F 913 621-1206
Kansas City (G-3945)
Cstk Inc ....F 316 744-2061
Park City (G-9614)
Dept Lincoln Service ....E 316 928-7331
Wichita (G-14197)
Dick Edwards Ford Lincoln Merc ....D 785 320-4499
Junction City (G-3687)
Dodge City Cooperative Exch ....E 620 225-4193
Dodge City (G-1344)
Don Hattan Derby Inc ....E 316 744-1275
Derby (G-1240)
Done With Care Auto Repair LLC ....F 913 722-3466
Shawnee (G-10941)
Dons Body Shop Inc ....F 913 782-9255
Olathe (G-7660)
Doug Reh Chevrolet Inc ....E 620 672-5633
Pratt (G-10109)
Engels Sales & Service Center ....F 785 877-3391
Norton (G-7444)
Errol E Engel Inc ....E 785 625-3195
Hays (G-2800)
Expert Auto Center ....F 316 440-6600
Wichita (G-14322)
Express Auto Service Inc ....E 816 373-9995
Lenexa (G-5843)
Fyrs Car Care ....F 913 385-3600
Overland Park (G-8744)
Georgia Kenworth Inc ....E 816 483-6444
Leawood (G-5411)
Ghumms Auto Center LLC ....F 620 544-7800
Hugoton (G-3163)
Great Western Tire of Dodge Cy ....F 620 225-1343
Dodge City (G-1367)
Gregg Tire Co Inc ....F 785 233-4156
Topeka (G-12651)
Hachmeister Service Center LLC ....F 785 567-4818
Lenora (G-6243)
Hertel Tank Service Inc ....G 785 628-2445
Hays (G-2841)
Huntingdon Park Standard Svc ....F 785 272-4499
Topeka (G-12708)
JC Auto ....F 785 266-1300
Berryton (G-527)
Joe Self Chevrolet Inc ....C 316 689-4390
Wichita (G-14760)
Johnson County Investors Inc ....C 913 631-0000
Shawnee Mission (G-11498)
K C Freightliner Body Shop ....F 913 342-4269
Kansas City (G-4132)
Kansas Cy Freightliner Sls Inc ....E 913 780-6606
Olathe (G-7828)
Kansas Tire & Wheel Co LLC ....F 620 421-0005
Parsons (G-9698)
Kansasland Tire Inc ....C 316 522-5434
Wichita (G-14830)
Kansasland Tire Inc ....F 785 243-2706
Concordia (G-1119)
Kansasland Tire Inc ....F 620 231-7210
Pittsburg (G-9890)
Kansasland Tire Inc ....F 316 744-0401
Park City (G-9624)
Karls Tire & Auto Service Inc ....F 316 685-5338
Wichita (G-14833)
Kens Garage Inc ....F 913 651-2433
Leavenworth (G-5262)
Kistler Service Inc ....E 620 782-3611
Udall (G-13278)
Kline Motors Inc ....F 620 221-2040
Winfield (G-16153)
Laird Noller Ford Inc ....C 785 235-9211
Topeka (G-12828)
Laird Noller Ford Inc ....E 785 264-2800
Topeka (G-12829)
Lenexa Automotive Inc ....F 913 492-8250
Shawnee Mission (G-11561)
Manweiler Chevrolet Co Inc ....F 620 653-2121
Hoisington (G-3069)
McKenzie Paint & Body Inc ....F 620 662-3721
South Hutchinson (G-12061)
Mel Hambelton Ford Inc ....C 316 462-3673
Wichita (G-15035)
Metro Collision Repair Inc ....F 913 839-1044
Olathe (G-7886)
Midway Motors Inc ....D 620 241-7737
McPherson (G-7005)
Miles Automotive Inc ....D 785 843-7700
Lawrence (G-5028)
Mitten Inc ....E 785 672-3062
Oakley (G-7481)
Noller Lincoln-Mercury Inc ....E 785 267-2800
Topeka (G-12932)
O K Tire of Dodge City Inc ....F 620 225-0204
Dodge City (G-1415)
Oakley Motors Inc ....E 785 672-3238
Oakley (G-7484)
Omaha Truck Center Inc ....E 785 823-2204
Salina (G-10619)
Perl Auto Center Inc ....F 620 251-4050
Coffeyville (G-972)
Plastic Omnium Auto Inergy ....F 913 370-6081
Kansas City (G-4324)
Premium Ventures LLC ....F 785 842-5500
Lawrence (G-5073)
Quality Care ....F 785 228-1118
Topeka (G-12995)
Red Rock Auto Center Inc ....F 620 663-9822
South Hutchinson (G-12065)
Reedy Ford Inc ....E 620 442-4800
Arkansas City (G-174)
Riley Ford Mercury Co ....F 620 356-1206
Ulysses (G-13315)
Robert Brogden Buick Gmc Inc ....E 913 782-1500
Olathe (G-8038)
Rohrer Custom and Fabrication ....G 620 359-1707
Wellington (G-13525)
Ronco Inc ....F 913 362-7200
Mission Hills (G-7148)
S Jackson Service Center Inc ....F 913 422-7438
Edwardsville (G-1514)
Schmidt Haven Ford Sales Inc ....F 620 465-2252
Haven (G-2736)
South Star Chrysler Inc ....F 785 242-5600
Ottawa (G-8313)
Star Lube Auto Ex Care Inc ....F 620 856-4281
Baxter Springs (G-414)
Steven Bradon Auto Center ....F 316 634-0427
Wichita (G-15666)
Steves Quick Lube ....F 785 742-3500
Hiawatha (G-3025)

Transwood Inc ... E ... 620 331-5924
Independence *(G-3566)*
Troostwood Garage & Body Shop ... E ... 816 444-3800
Kansas City *(G-4475)*
Vee Village Parts Inc ... F ... 816 421-6441
Basehor *(G-390)*
Watco Companies LLC ... C ... 575 745-2329
Pittsburg *(G-9963)*
Wiebe Tire & Automotive ... F ... 316 283-4242
Newton *(G-7429)*
Williams Automotive Inc ... F ... 620 343-0086
Emporia *(G-1852)*
Winfield Motor Company Inc ... E ... 620 221-2840
Winfield *(G-16187)*
Wiseman Discount Tire Inc ... F ... 620 231-5291
Frontenac *(G-2067)*
Yingling Auto Electric Inc ... F ... 785 232-0484
Topeka *(G-13255)*

AUTOMOTIVE BATTERIES WHOLESALERS

Wholesale Batteries Inc ... F ... 913 342-0113
Kansas City *(G-4542)*

AUTOMOTIVE BODY SHOP

Alan Clark Body Shop Inc ... F ... 785 776-5333
Manhattan *(G-6538)*
Allied Body Shop Incorporated ... F ... 785 841-3672
Lawrence *(G-4730)*
Auto Techs Frame & Body Repair ... F ... 620 221-6616
Winfield *(G-16115)*
Auto-Craft Inc ... E ... 316 265-6828
Wichita *(G-13770)*
Auto-Craft Inc ... F ... 316 630-9494
Wichita *(G-13771)*
Automotive Specialists Inc ... F ... 316 321-5130
El Dorado *(G-1532)*
Autotech Collision & Service ... F ... 316 942-0707
Wichita *(G-13778)*
Briggs Auto Group Inc ... E ... 785 776-3677
Manhattan *(G-6569)*
Butler Enterprises Inc ... F ... 913 262-9109
Shawnee Mission *(G-11192)*
Car Star Inc ... F ... 785 232-2084
Topeka *(G-12443)*
Car Star Spc ... E ... 201 444-0601
Overland Park *(G-8512)*
Carstar Inc ... F ... 316 652-7821
Wichita *(G-13955)*
Carstar Inc ... F ... 913 685-2886
Stilwell *(G-12139)*
College Body Shop ... F ... 785 235-5628
Topeka *(G-12487)*
Collision Works LLC ... E ... 316 265-6828
Wichita *(G-14058)*
Dons Body Shop Inc ... F ... 913 782-9255
Olathe *(G-7660)*
Dons Car Care & Body Shop Inc ... F ... 620 669-8178
Hutchinson *(G-3268)*
Ervs Body Shop Inc ... F ... 620 225-4015
Dodge City *(G-1358)*
Eveland Brothers Body Shop ... E ... 913 262-6050
Shawnee Mission *(G-11349)*
Hillsboro Ford Inc ... E ... 620 947-3134
Hillsboro *(G-3049)*
Hite Collision Repair Ctr Inc ... F ... 785 843-8991
Lawrence *(G-4899)*
Jayhawk Auto Incorporated ... F ... 785 354-1758
Topeka *(G-12740)*
Johns Body Shop Inc ... F ... 620 225-2213
Dodge City *(G-1383)*
K C Freightliner Body Shop ... F ... 913 342-4269
Kansas City *(G-4132)*
Kammerer Auto Body & Paint ... F ... 316 265-0211
Wichita *(G-14781)*
Kansas Body Works Inc ... F ... 316 263-5506
Wichita *(G-14788)*
Kansas Coachworks Ltd ... F ... 913 888-0991
Shawnee Mission *(G-11515)*
Keimig Body Shop ... F ... 913 367-0184
Atchison *(G-239)*
Lawrence Cllsion Spcalists LLC ... F ... 785 841-3672
Lawrence *(G-4961)*
Lewis Auto Plaza Inc ... F ... 785 266-8850
Topeka *(G-12840)*
Lindan Auto Mechanical & Body ... E ... 913 722-4243
Shawnee Mission *(G-11574)*
Manweiler Chevrolet Co Inc ... F ... 620 653-2121
Hoisington *(G-3069)*
McKenzie Paint & Body Inc ... F ... 620 662-3721
South Hutchinson *(G-12061)*
Metro Collision Repair Inc ... F ... 913 839-1044
Olathe *(G-7886)*
Moore Buick Chevrolet Pontiac ... F ... 785 346-5972
Osborne *(G-8213)*
Moores Lnny Collision Repr LLC ... F ... 316 744-1151
Park City *(G-9637)*
Olathe Ford Sales Inc ... E ... 913 829-1957
Olathe *(G-7937)*
P & D Inc ... F ... 913 782-2247
Olathe *(G-7969)*
PDQ Tools and Equipment Inc ... G ... 913 492-5800
Shawnee Mission *(G-11721)*
Pringle Auto Body & Sales Inc ... F ... 913 432-6361
Kansas City *(G-4339)*
Quality Trust Inc ... E ... 785 375-6372
Junction City *(G-3745)*
S & S Auto Body ... F ... 785 524-4641
Lincoln *(G-6387)*
Santa Fe Body Inc ... F ... 913 894-6090
Shawnee Mission *(G-11830)*
Santa Fe Tow Service Inc ... D ... 417 553-3676
Shawnee Mission *(G-11833)*
Scholfield Body Shop Inc ... E ... 316 688-6550
Wichita *(G-15533)*
Sharps Auto Bdy Collision Inc ... F ... 620 231-6011
Pittsburg *(G-9938)*
Shelton Collision Repair Inc ... F ... 316 788-1528
Derby *(G-1271)*
Skeeters Body Shop Inc ... F ... 620 275-7255
Garden City *(G-2280)*
Sonnys Inc ... F ... 316 942-2390
Wichita *(G-15614)*
Steven Import Group Inc ... F ... 316 652-2135
Wichita *(G-15669)*
Vernies Trux-N-Equip Inc ... G ... 785 625-5087
Hays *(G-2923)*
Vilela Rndy Auto Bdy Repr Pntg ... F ... 620 231-6350
Pittsburg *(G-9957)*
Wagner Auto Body & Sales Inc ... F ... 913 422-1955
Bonner Springs *(G-580)*
Walt Carstar Auto Inc ... E ... 785 273-7701
Topeka *(G-13230)*
Weavers Auto Body Inc ... F ... 913 441-0001
Shawnee *(G-11050)*
Wiseman Discount Tire Inc ... F ... 620 231-5291
Frontenac *(G-2067)*

AUTOMOTIVE BODY, PAINT & INTERIOR REPAIR & MAINTENANCE SVC

Dacus LLC ... F ... 620 241-6054
McPherson *(G-6955)*
Dick Edwards Ford Lincoln Merc ... D ... 785 320-4499
Junction City *(G-3687)*
G I P Inc ... F ... 785 749-0005
Lawrence *(G-4867)*
Joe Self Chevrolet Inc ... C ... 316 689-4390
Wichita *(G-14760)*
Laird Noller Ford Inc ... E ... 785 232-8347
Topeka *(G-12830)*

AUTOMOTIVE BRAKE REPAIR SHOPS

Bridgestone Ret Operations LLC ... F ... 913 782-1833
Olathe *(G-7561)*
Bridgestone Ret Operations LLC ... E ... 913 334-1555
Kansas City *(G-3878)*
Bridgestone Ret Operations LLC ... F ... 913 492-8160
Shawnee Mission *(G-11181)*
Mels Tire LLC ... F ... 620 342-8473
Emporia *(G-1792)*
Vee Village Parts Inc ... F ... 816 421-6441
Basehor *(G-390)*

AUTOMOTIVE COLLISION SHOPS

Classic Collision Center ... F ... 913 287-9410
Kansas City *(G-3918)*
Collision Works LLC ... E ... 316 788-5722
Derby *(G-1231)*
Gerber Group Inc ... E ... 316 945-7007
Wichita *(G-14460)*

AUTOMOTIVE EXHAUST REPAIR SVC

Auto Masters LLC ... F ... 316 789-8540
Derby *(G-1219)*
Gregg Tire Co Inc ... F ... 785 233-4156
Topeka *(G-12652)*

AUTOMOTIVE EXTERIOR REPAIR SVCS

Tlm Enterprises Inc ... F ... 316 265-3833
Wichita *(G-15771)*
Williams Automotive Inc ... F ... 620 343-0086
Emporia *(G-1852)*

AUTOMOTIVE GLASS REPLACEMENT SHOPS

A Glass & Tint Shop Kc Inc ... F ... 913 491-8468
Merriam *(G-7085)*
Alan Clark Body Shop Inc ... F ... 785 776-5333
Manhattan *(G-6538)*
Dons Car Care & Body Shop Inc ... F ... 620 669-8178
Hutchinson *(G-3268)*
G I P Inc ... F ... 785 749-0005
Lawrence *(G-4867)*
Kennedy Glass Inc ... E ... 785 843-4416
Lawrence *(G-4942)*
Norris Collision Center LLC ... F ... 316 794-1161
Goddard *(G-2448)*
Safelite Fulfillment Inc ... F ... 913 236-5888
Shawnee *(G-11023)*
Service Auto Glass Inc ... F ... 630 628-0398
Mc Louth *(G-6929)*
Southwest Glass & Door Inc ... F ... 620 626-7400
Liberal *(G-6369)*

AUTOMOTIVE PAINT SHOP

A D L M LLC ... F ... 913 888-0770
Shawnee Mission *(G-11062)*
Auto-Craft Inc ... E ... 785 579-5997
Junction City *(G-3669)*
Brenneman & Bremmeman Inc ... F ... 316 282-8834
Newton *(G-7321)*
Kc Colors Auto Body Ltd ... F ... 913 491-0696
Shawnee Mission *(G-11523)*
Norris Collision Center LLC ... F ... 316 794-1161
Goddard *(G-2448)*
Service Body Shop ... F ... 316 260-5300
Wichita *(G-15564)*
Troostwood Garage & Body Shop ... E ... 816 444-3800
Kansas City *(G-4475)*

AUTOMOTIVE PARTS, ACCESS & SPLYS

Abilene Machine LLC ... C ... 785 655-9455
Solomon *(G-12046)*
Accessible Technologies Inc ... D ... 913 338-2886
Lenexa *(G-5621)*
Blaylock Diesel Service Inc ... F ... 620 856-5227
Baxter Springs *(G-399)*
Cross Manufacturing Inc ... C ... 620 324-5525
Lewis *(G-6268)*
Frankenstein Trikes LLC ... G ... 913 352-6788
Pleasanton *(G-9995)*
Frigiquip International Inc ... G ... 316 321-2400
El Dorado *(G-1563)*
Hampton Hydraulics Llc ... D ... 620 792-4368
Great Bend *(G-2590)*
Hopkins Manufacturing Corp ... B ... 620 342-7320
Emporia *(G-1775)*
Husky Liners Inc ... D ... 620 221-2268
Winfield *(G-16148)*
Ict Billet LLC ... G ... 316 300-0833
Wichita *(G-14666)*
Industrial Chrome Inc ... D ... 785 235-3463
Topeka *(G-12721)*
Inityaero Inc ... E ... 316 265-0603
Wichita *(G-14694)*
Kasa Companies Inc ... C ... 785 825-7181
Salina *(G-10570)*
Kasa Companies Inc ... D ... 785 825-5612
Salina *(G-10571)*
Kasa Companies Inc ... D ... 785 825-5612
Salina *(G-10569)*
Roll Out Inc ... G ... 620 347-4753
Arma *(G-190)*
Rv Products ... E ... 316 832-3400
Wichita *(G-15494)*
Standard Motor Products Inc ... B ... 620 331-1000
Independence *(G-3562)*
Standard Motor Products Inc ... B ... 913 441-6500
Edwardsville *(G-1516)*
Truett & Osborn Cycle Inc ... G ... 316 682-4781
Wichita *(G-15811)*

AUTOMOTIVE PARTS: Plastic

Ventra Kansas LLC ....D 913 334-0614
Kansas City (G-4515)

AUTOMOTIVE RADIATOR REPAIR SHOPS

Ernstings Incorporated ....G....... 620 564-2793
Ellinwood (G-1631)
Mid-Amrcan Dstrbtrs/Jyhawk RAD ....F 913 321-9664
Kansas City (G-4245)

AUTOMOTIVE REPAIR SHOPS: Auto Front End Repair

Tracy Pedigo........F 316 945-3414
Wichita (G-15781)

AUTOMOTIVE REPAIR SHOPS: Axle Straightening

Bosleys Tire Service Co Inc........E 316 524-8511
Wichita (G-13871)
Brierton Engineering Inc........E 785 263-7711
Abilene (G-16)

AUTOMOTIVE REPAIR SHOPS: Brake Repair

Fowlers LLC........F 785 475-3451
Oberlin (G-7494)
Midwest Dynamics Inc........F 913 383-9320
Leawood (G-5483)

AUTOMOTIVE REPAIR SHOPS: Diesel Engine Repair

Automotive Associates........E 620 231-6350
Pittsburg (G-9818)
Central Pwr Systems & Svcs LLC........F 785 825-8291
Salina (G-10444)
Cummins Central Power LLC........F 785 462-3945
Colby (G-1002)
Engquist Tractor Service Inc........E 620 654-3651
McPherson (G-6959)
Foley Equipment Company........C 785 266-5770
Topeka (G-12623)
Macconnell Enterprises LLC........E 785 885-8081
Natoma (G-7231)
Spencer & Company........F 785 235-3131
Topeka (G-13090)

AUTOMOTIVE REPAIR SHOPS: Electrical Svcs

Welco Services Inc........E 620 241-3000
McPherson (G-7041)

AUTOMOTIVE REPAIR SHOPS: Engine Rebuilding

Goodland Machine & Auto LLC........G....... 785 899-6628
Goodland (G-2474)
Harrys Machine Works Inc........G....... 620 227-2201
Dodge City (G-1370)

AUTOMOTIVE REPAIR SHOPS: Engine Repair, Exc Diesel

Oards Auto & Truck Repr Svcs........F 785 823-9732
Salina (G-10616)

AUTOMOTIVE REPAIR SHOPS: Frame Repair Shops

Randy Schwindt........F 785 391-2277
Utica (G-13335)
Wichita Body & Equipment Co........G....... 316 522-1080
Haysville (G-2964)

AUTOMOTIVE REPAIR SHOPS: Machine Shop

GKN Aerospace Precision Machin........B 620 326-5952
Wellington (G-13505)
Herrs Machine........G....... 785 325-2875
Washington (G-13464)
T N T Machine Inc........F 316 440-6004
Wichita (G-15714)
Ultrafab Inc........E 620 245-0781
McPherson (G-7033)

AUTOMOTIVE REPAIR SHOPS: Muffler Shop, Sale/Rpr/Installation

Midas Auto Systems Experts........F 316 636-9299
Wichita (G-15084)
Midwest Dynamics Inc........F 913 383-9320
Leawood (G-5483)

AUTOMOTIVE REPAIR SHOPS: Rebuilding & Retreading Tires

Blizzard Energy Inc........F 620 796-2396
Great Bend (G-2521)
Bridgestone Ret Operations LLC........E 913 334-1555
Kansas City (G-3878)
Bridgestone Ret Operations LLC........F 913 492-8160
Shawnee Mission (G-11181)
Bridgestone Ret Operations LLC........F 316 684-2682
Wichita (G-13889)
Midwest Trailer Supply Inc........E 316 744-1515
Park City (G-9632)

AUTOMOTIVE REPAIR SHOPS: Sound System Svc & Installation

Mobile Fx Inc........F 913 287-1556
Kansas City (G-4266)

AUTOMOTIVE REPAIR SHOPS: Springs, Rebuilding & Repair

Atlas Spring & Axle Co Inc........F 316 943-2386
Wichita (G-13767)

AUTOMOTIVE REPAIR SHOPS: Tire Recapping

O K Thompsons Tire Inc........E 785 738-2283
Beloit (G-497)

AUTOMOTIVE REPAIR SHOPS: Tire Repair Shop

Goodyear Tire & Rubber Company........F 785 266-3862
Topeka (G-12643)
Superior Car Care Center LLC........F 620 492-6856
Johnson (G-3663)

AUTOMOTIVE REPAIR SHOPS: Trailer Repair

Contract Trailer Service Inc........F 913 281-2589
Kansas City (G-3936)
Eagle Trailer Company Inc........G....... 785 841-3200
Lawrence (G-4844)
Landoll Corporation........E 785 738-6613
Beloit (G-490)
Larrys Trailer Sales & Svc LLC........F 316 838-1491
Wichita (G-14927)
Miller Welding Inc........F 785 454-3425
Downs (G-1472)
Orrick Trailer Services LLC........F 913 321-0400
Kansas City (G-4298)
Rmvk Enterprises Inc........E 913 321-1915
Kansas City (G-4382)
Topeka Trailer Repair Inc........F 785 862-6010
Topeka (G-13187)
Western Trailer Service Inc........E 913 281-2226
Kansas City (G-4538)

AUTOMOTIVE REPAIR SHOPS: Truck Engine Repair, Exc Indl

Garden City Travel Plaza LLC........E 620 275-4404
Garden City (G-2179)
Meyer Truck Center Inc........F 913 764-2000
Olathe (G-7887)
Southwest Truck Parts Inc........D 620 672-5686
Pratt (G-10151)

AUTOMOTIVE REPAIR SHOPS: Wheel Alignment

A-Plus Logistics LLC........E 316 945-5757
Park City (G-9598)
Allied Body Shop Incorporated........F 785 841-3672
Lawrence (G-4730)
Auto Masters LLC........F 316 789-8540
Derby (G-1219)
Auto Masters LLC........E 316 789-8540
Derby (G-1220)
Axle & Wheel Aligning Co Inc........F 316 263-0213
Wichita (G-13782)
Great Bend Cooperative Assn........F 620 792-1281
Great Bend (G-2577)
Pomps Tire Service Inc........F 913 621-5200
Kansas City (G-4326)
Super Oil Co Inc........F 785 354-1410
Topeka (G-13125)
Weavers Auto Body Inc........F 913 441-0001
Shawnee (G-11050)

AUTOMOTIVE REPAIR SVC

Blue Valley Goodyear Service........F 913 345-1380
Shawnee Mission (G-11170)
Bridgestone Ret Operations LLC........F 913 393-2212
Olathe (G-7560)
Briggs Auto Group Inc........E 785 776-3677
Manhattan (G-6569)
Calverts Express Auto S........E 913 631-9995
Lenexa (G-5726)
Car Star Spc........E 201 444-0601
Overland Park (G-8512)
City of Ellinwood........F 620 564-3046
Ellinwood (G-1628)
Express Auto Service Inc........E 816 373-9995
Lenexa (G-5843)
Five Star Service Inc........E 785 625-9400
Hays (G-2810)
G F Enterprises........G....... 785 539-7113
Manhattan (G-6642)
Iowa Kenworth Inc........E 816 483-6444
Leawood (G-5440)
Johnson County Automotive LLC........F 913 432-1721
Shawnee Mission (G-11497)
Michael E Fromholtz........F 913 492-8290
Shawnee Mission (G-11622)
O K Electric Work Inc........G....... 620 251-2270
Coffeyville (G-966)
OReilly Automotive Stores Inc........F 913 287-2409
Kansas City (G-4296)
Star Motors Ltd........E 913 432-7800
Shawnee Mission (G-11895)
Truck Sales Inc........F 620 225-4155
Dodge City (G-1440)
Wilkens Manufacturing Inc........D....... 785 425-7070
Stockton (G-12190)
Woodys Automotive Svc & Sls........F....... 316 838-8011
Wichita (G-16068)
Yost Auto Service........F 316 264-8482
Wichita (G-16088)

AUTOMOTIVE SPLYS & PARTS, NEW, WHOL: Auto Servicing Eqpt

Central Marketing Inc........F 316 613-2404
Wichita (G-13980)
LAd Global Enterprises Inc........F 913 768-0888
Olathe (G-7851)
Magna Tech Inc........E 620 431-3490
Chanute (G-740)
PDQ Tools and Equipment Inc........G....... 913 492-5800
Shawnee Mission (G-11721)
Popup Industries Inc........E 620 431-9196
Chanute (G-755)

AUTOMOTIVE SPLYS & PARTS, NEW, WHOLESALE: Alternators

Automotive Associates........E 620 231-6350
Pittsburg (G-9818)

AUTOMOTIVE SPLYS & PARTS, NEW, WHOLESALE: Engines/Eng Parts

Automotive Equipment Services........E 913 254-2600
Olathe (G-7543)
Boettcher Supply Inc........E 785 738-5781
Beloit (G-479)

AUTOMOTIVE SPLYS & PARTS, NEW, WHOLESALE: Radiators

1-800 Radiator & A/C........E 913 677-1799
Kansas City (G-3774)
Mid-Amrcan Dstrbtrs/Jyhawk RAD........F 913 321-9664
Kansas City (G-4245)
Williams Automotive Inc........F 620 343-0086
Emporia (G-1852)

AUTOMOTIVE SPLYS & PARTS, NEW, WHOLESALE: Seat Belts

Clancey Co ... F ... 913 894-4444
Overland Park (G-8559)

AUTOMOTIVE SPLYS & PARTS, NEW, WHOLESALE: Splys

Farneys Inc ... F ... 316 522-7248
Haysville (G-2943)
Jobbers Automotive Whse Inc ... D ... 316 267-4393
Wichita (G-14759)
OReilly Automotive Stores Inc ... F ... 620 421-6070
Parsons (G-9714)
W Carter Orvil Inc ... E ... 620 251-4700
Coffeyville (G-984)

AUTOMOTIVE SPLYS & PARTS, NEW, WHOLESALE: Trailer Parts

Redneck Inc ... E ... 316 263-6090
Wichita (G-15432)
Trailers n More LLC ... E ... 316 945-8900
Wichita (G-15785)

AUTOMOTIVE SPLYS & PARTS, NEW, WHOLESALE: Wheels

Hiper Technology Inc ... F ... 785 749-6011
Lawrence (G-4898)

AUTOMOTIVE SPLYS & PARTS, USED, WHOLESALE

A & A Auto Salvage ... F ... 785 286-2728
Topeka (G-12276)
Diamond Coach Corporation ... D ... 620 795-2191
Oswego (G-8233)
Griffin Wheel Company ... E ... 913 299-2223
Kansas City (G-4054)
Lkq Corporation ... E ... 785 862-0000
Topeka (G-12847)
Piland Auto Dismantling ... F ... 620 275-5506
Garden City (G-2255)
Vilela Rndy Auto Bdy Repr Pntg ... F ... 620 231-6350
Pittsburg (G-9957)

AUTOMOTIVE SPLYS & PARTS, USED, WHOLESALE: Hardware

LAd Global Enterprises Inc ... F ... 913 768-0888
Olathe (G-7851)

AUTOMOTIVE SPLYS & PARTS, USED, WHOLESALE: Servicing Eqpt

Liquidynamics Inc ... F ... 316 943-5477
Wichita (G-14968)

AUTOMOTIVE SPLYS & PARTS, WHOLESALE, NEC

A-One Auto Salvage of Wichita ... F ... 316 524-3273
Haysville (G-2933)
Automotive Supply Inc ... E ... 316 942-8285
Wichita (G-13775)
Automotive Supply Inc ... E ... 316 942-8287
Wichita (G-13776)
Automotive Warehouse Company ... E ... 316 942-8285
Wichita (G-13777)
Blackjack Tire Supplies Inc ... F ... 816 872-1158
Kansas City (G-3865)
Burnett Automotive Inc ... F ... 785 539-8970
Manhattan (G-6572)
Burnett Automotive Inc ... F ... 913 681-8824
Overland Park (G-8494)
Clare Generator Service Inc ... F ... 785 827-3321
Salina (G-10453)
Cline Auto Supply Inc ... E ... 620 343-6000
Emporia (G-1721)
Cross Manufacturing Inc ... C ... 620 324-5525
Lewis (G-6268)
Garnett Auto Supply Inc ... E ... 316 267-4393
Wichita (G-14449)
Genuine Parts Company ... F ... 913 631-4329
Shawnee Mission (G-11395)
Hub Cap & Wheel Store Inc ... F ... 913 432-0002
Kansas City (G-4087)
Keystone Auto Holdings Inc ... F ... 913 371-3249
Kansas City (G-4173)
Keystone Automotive Inds Inc ... F ... 785 235-1920
Topeka (G-12820)
Keystone Automotive Inds Inc ... F ... 316 262-0500
Wichita (G-14855)
Keystone Automotive Inds Inc ... E ... 816 921-8929
Kansas City (G-4174)
Lewis Auto Salvage LLC ... F ... 785 233-0561
Topeka (G-12841)
Long Motor Corporation ... C ... 913 541-1525
Lenexa (G-5978)
Medart Inc ... F ... 636 282-2300
Kansas City (G-4227)
Oldham Sales Inc ... F ... 785 625-2547
Hays (G-2882)
OReilly Automotive Stores Inc ... F ... 620 664-6800
Hutchinson (G-3396)
OReilly Automotive Stores Inc ... F ... 913 268-6001
Shawnee Mission (G-11702)
OReilly Automotive Stores Inc ... F ... 785 235-9241
Topeka (G-12951)
OReilly Automotive Stores Inc ... F ... 620 251-5280
Coffeyville (G-967)
OReilly Automotive Stores Inc ... F ... 913 829-6188
Olathe (G-7963)
OReilly Automotive Stores Inc ... F ... 785 235-5658
Topeka (G-12952)
OReilly Automotive Stores Inc ... F ... 785 862-4749
Topeka (G-12953)
OReilly Automotive Stores Inc ... F ... 785 266-3688
Topeka (G-12954)
OReilly Automotive Stores Inc ... F ... 913 621-6939
Kansas City (G-4297)
OReilly Automotive Stores Inc ... F ... 785 832-0408
Lawrence (G-5049)
OReilly Automotive Stores Inc ... F ... 913 367-4138
Atchison (G-253)
OReilly Automotive Stores Inc ... E ... 316 264-6422
Wichita (G-15235)
OReilly Automotive Stores Inc ... F ... 316 685-7900
Wichita (G-15232)
OReilly Automotive Stores Inc ... F ... 785 842-9800
Lawrence (G-5048)
OReilly Automotive Stores Inc ... F ... 620 331-1018
Independence (G-3545)
Patterson Racing Inc ... F ... 316 775-7771
Augusta (G-337)
Pgw Auto Glass LLC ... F ... 913 927-2753
Kansas City (G-4320)
Poorman Auto Supply Inc ... E ... 316 265-6284
Wichita (G-15315)
Rose Motor Supply Inc ... F ... 620 662-1254
Hutchinson (G-3432)
Smith Auto & Truck Parts Inc ... F ... 620 275-9145
Garden City (G-2282)
Sparkle Auto LLC ... F ... 620 272-9559
Garden City (G-2286)
Standard Motor Products Inc ... B ... 913 441-6500
Edwardsville (G-1516)
Two-Bee Inc ... F ... 785 364-2162
Holton (G-3113)
United Auto Parts Inc ... E ... 316 721-6868
Wichita (G-15840)
Vee Village Parts Inc ... F ... 816 421-6441
Basehor (G-390)
Wescorp Ltd ... F ... 913 281-1833
Kansas City (G-4534)

AUTOMOTIVE SPLYS, USED, WHOLESALE & RETAIL

Hess & Son Salvage Inc ... F ... 785 238-3382
Junction City (G-3699)
Smith Auto & Truck Parts Inc ... F ... 620 275-9145
Garden City (G-2282)

AUTOMOTIVE SPLYS/PARTS, NEW, WHOL: Body Rpr/Paint Shop Splys

Commercial Fltr Svc Knsas Cty ... G ... 913 384-5858
Kansas City (G-3929)

AUTOMOTIVE SVCS

Car Clinic Auto Salon ... F ... 913 208-5478
Kansas City (G-3889)
McCarthy Collision Center ... E ... 913 324-7300
Olathe (G-7881)
Ridge Auto Center ... F ... 785 286-1498
Topeka (G-13018)

AUTOMOTIVE SVCS, EXC REPAIR & CARWASHES: Customizing

Chris Carlson Hot Rods LLC ... F ... 316 777-4774
Mulvane (G-7212)

AUTOMOTIVE SVCS, EXC REPAIR & CARWASHES: Glass Tinting

A Glass & Tint Shop Kc Inc ... F ... 913 491-8468
Merriam (G-7085)
Andrade Auto Sales Inc ... F ... 620 624-2400
Liberal (G-6278)
Midwest Tinting Inc ... F ... 913 384-2665
Overland Park (G-9036)

AUTOMOTIVE SVCS, EXC REPAIR & CARWASHES: Lubrication

Jiffy Lube International Inc ... F ... 913 682-7020
Leavenworth (G-5258)
Joes Seat Cover Car Wash Ctr ... E ... 316 262-2486
Wichita (G-14761)
Kansas Fast Lube Inc ... F ... 620 241-5656
McPherson (G-6982)
Team Car Care LLC ... F ... 913 334-5950
Kansas City (G-4461)
Team Car Care LLC ... F ... 785 266-7696
Topeka (G-13147)
Team Car Care LLC ... F ... 785 228-1824
Topeka (G-13148)
Team Car Care LLC ... F ... 913 362-3349
Shawnee Mission (G-11922)
Team Car Care LLC ... F ... 785 749-1599
Lawrence (G-5132)
Team Car Care LLC ... F ... 913 381-1005
Leawood (G-5570)

AUTOMOTIVE SVCS, EXC REPAIR & CARWASHES: Maintenance

Automotive Specialists Inc ... F ... 316 321-5130
El Dorado (G-1532)
Happy Autos LLC ... F ... 785 621-4100
Hays (G-2826)
Lawrence City Vehicle Maint ... F ... 785 832-3020
Lawrence (G-4960)
Midwest Dynamics Inc ... F ... 913 383-9320
Leawood (G-5483)
R&B Services LLC ... E ... 316 265-7859
Wichita (G-15407)
Ritchey Motors LLC ... F ... 785 380-0222
Topeka (G-13019)
Sears Roebuck and Co ... F ... 785 271-4200
Topeka (G-13049)
T & W Tire LLC ... E ... 316 683-8364
Wichita (G-15712)

AUTOMOTIVE SVCS, EXC REPAIR & CARWASHES: Road Svc

Asurion LLC ... A ... 816 237-3000
Leawood (G-5336)

AUTOMOTIVE SVCS, EXC REPAIR: Carwash, Automatic

Rainbow Car Wash Inc ... F ... 913 432-1116
Kansas City (G-4360)
Ronco Inc ... F ... 913 362-7200
Mission Hills (G-7148)
Saragenes Short Stop ... F ... 620 235-1141
Pittsburg (G-9935)

AUTOMOTIVE SVCS, EXC REPAIR: Carwash, Self-Service

Extreme Detail Kc LLC ... F ... 913 568-4045
Olathe (G-7699)
L & M Oil Company ... F ... 913 856-8502
Gardner (G-2352)
Rakies Oil LLC ... F ... 620 442-2210
Arkansas City (G-171)

AUTOMOTIVE SVCS, EXC REPAIR: Truck Wash

Blue Beacon LP II ... B ... 785 825-2221
Salina (G-10427)

PRDT & SVC

Blue Beacon USA LP............A....... 785 825-2221
Salina *(G-10428)*
Blue Beacon USA LP II............E....... 785 672-3328
Oakley *(G-7473)*
Superior Mobile Wash Inc............F....... 913 915-9642
Kansas City *(G-4448)*

AUTOMOTIVE SVCS, EXC REPAIR: Washing & Polishing

Auto Masters LLC............E....... 316 789-8540
Derby *(G-1220)*
Car Clinic Auto Salon............F....... 913 208-5478
Kansas City *(G-3889)*
Car Star Spc............E....... 201 444-0601
Overland Park *(G-8512)*
Car Wash Center of Mission Inc............F....... 913 236-6886
Shawnee Mission *(G-11201)*
Eagle Auto Salon Inc............E....... 785 272-2886
Topeka *(G-12565)*
Finley Construction & Rdymx............G....... 785 626-3282
Atwood *(G-286)*
Green Lantern Inc............E....... 316 721-9242
Wichita *(G-14510)*
Joes Seat Cover Car Wash Ctr............E....... 316 262-2486
Wichita *(G-14761)*
Mission Car Wash LLC............E....... 913 236-6886
Shawnee Mission *(G-11644)*
Speedy Falcon LLC............F....... 913 451-2100
Shawnee Mission *(G-11883)*
Waterway Gas & Wash Company............E....... 913 897-3111
Overland Park *(G-9485)*
Waterway Gas & Wash Company............E....... 913 339-9542
Shawnee Mission *(G-11995)*
Waterway Gas & Wash Company............D....... 913 339-9964
Shawnee Mission *(G-11996)*

AUTOMOTIVE SVCS, EXC RPR/CARWASHES: High Perf Auto Rpr/Svc

Auto Masters LLC............E....... 316 789-8540
Derby *(G-1220)*

AUTOMOTIVE TOWING & WRECKING SVC

Almighty Tow Service LLC............F....... 913 362-8697
Overland Park *(G-8372)*
Brenneman & Bremmeman Inc............F....... 316 282-8834
Newton *(G-7321)*
Dales Tow Service Inc............F....... 913 782-2289
Olathe *(G-7640)*
Jgs Auto Wrecking............F....... 913 321-2716
Kansas City *(G-4124)*
Santa Fe Tow Service Inc............D....... 417 553-3676
Shawnee Mission *(G-11833)*

AUTOMOTIVE TOWING SVCS

A & M Towing & Recovery Inc............F....... 785 331-3100
Lawrence *(G-4717)*
Alan Clark Body Shop Inc............F....... 785 776-5333
Manhattan *(G-6538)*
All City Tow Service............F....... 913 371-1000
Kansas City *(G-3796)*
Arrow Wrecker Service Inc............E....... 316 267-6621
Wichita *(G-13737)*
Auto House Inc............F....... 785 825-6644
Salina *(G-10413)*
Browns Super Service Inc............F....... 785 267-1080
Topeka *(G-12409)*
Bud Roat Inc............F....... 316 683-9072
Wichita *(G-13906)*
Dons Car Care & Body Shop Inc............F....... 620 669-8178
Hutchinson *(G-3268)*
Ervs Body Shop Inc............F....... 620 225-4015
Dodge City *(G-1358)*
Interstate Wrecker Service............F....... 316 269-1133
Wichita *(G-14712)*
Kens Auto Tow............F....... 316 941-4300
Wichita *(G-14850)*
Marvins Tow Service Inc............F....... 913 764-7630
Olathe *(G-7876)*
Midwest Services & Towing Inc............E....... 913 281-1003
Kansas City *(G-4257)*
Overland Tow Service Inc............F....... 913 722-3505
Overland Park *(G-9128)*
Pro-Tow LLC............F....... 913 262-3300
Shawnee Mission *(G-11752)*
Tiger Tow & Transport Inc............F....... 913 422-7300
Bonner Springs *(G-577)*
Tow All of Kansas City LLC............E....... 913 208-0327
Overland Park *(G-9419)*
Tow Service Inc............E....... 316 522-8908
Wichita *(G-15778)*
Williams Automotive Inc............F....... 620 343-0086
Emporia *(G-1852)*

AUTOMOTIVE TRANSMISSION REPAIR SVC

Auto Masters LLC............F....... 316 789-8540
Derby *(G-1219)*
Auto Masters LLC............E....... 316 789-8540
Derby *(G-1220)*
Central Pwr Systems & Svcs LLC............E....... 316 943-1231
Wichita *(G-13984)*
Chance Transmissions Inc............F....... 316 529-1883
Wichita *(G-13998)*
Haag Inc............D....... 785 256-2311
Auburn *(G-295)*
Topeka Transmission Service............F....... 785 234-2597
Topeka *(G-13188)*

AUTOMOTIVE UPHOLSTERY SHOPS

Joes Seat Cover Car Wash Ctr............E....... 316 262-2486
Wichita *(G-14761)*
Stylecraft Auto Upholstery............F....... 316 262-0449
Wichita *(G-15679)*

AUTOMOTIVE WELDING SVCS

Kan Fab Inc............G....... 620 342-5669
Emporia *(G-1783)*
Pihl Repair & Fabrication LLC............G....... 785 668-2014
Falun *(G-1928)*
Vernies Trux-N-Equip Inc............G....... 785 625-5087
Hays *(G-2923)*

AUTOMOTIVE: Seating

Clarios............G....... 316 634-1309
Wichita *(G-14036)*
Clarios............E....... 785 827-6829
Salina *(G-10454)*
Seat King LLC............E....... 620 665-5464
Hutchinson *(G-3440)*

AWNINGS & CANOPIES

Wichita Awning Co Inc............G....... 316 838-4432
Wichita *(G-15978)*

AWNINGS & CANOPIES: Awnings, Fabric, From Purchased Matls

Rons Sign Co Inc............E....... 316 267-8914
Wichita *(G-15482)*

AWNINGS & CANOPIES: Fabric

Home Stl Siding & Windows LLC............F....... 785 625-8622
Hays *(G-2849)*
Midwest Siding Inc............E....... 785 825-0606
Salina *(G-10603)*

AWNINGS: Metal

Arko Manufacturing Co Inc............G....... 316 838-7162
Wichita *(G-13733)*
Champion Window Co Kans Cy Inc............E....... 913 541-8282
Lenexa *(G-5751)*
Western Aluminum & Glass Co............F....... 785 625-2418
Hays *(G-2931)*

AXLES

Brierton Engineering Inc............E....... 785 263-7711
Abilene *(G-16)*
Cromwell Builders Mfg............F....... 785 949-2433
Carlton *(G-686)*

BABYSITTING BUREAU

T L C Professional LLC............E....... 785 823-7444
Salina *(G-10731)*

BACKHOES

Full Vision Inc............D....... 316 283-3344
Newton *(G-7349)*

BADGES, WHOLESALE

Heritage Cmpt Consulting Inc............F....... 913 529-4227
Overland Park *(G-8812)*
Lee Reed Engraving Inc............G....... 316 943-9700
Wichita *(G-14949)*

BAGS: Garment & Wardrobe, Plastic Film

Kendall Packaging Corporation............E....... 620 231-9804
Pittsburg *(G-9891)*

BAGS: Paper

Tdc Filter Manufacturing Inc............C....... 630 410-6200
Overland Park *(G-9394)*

BAGS: Paper, Made From Purchased Materials

Bagcraftpapercon I LLC............C....... 620 856-4615
Baxter Springs *(G-395)*

BAGS: Plastic

Bagcraftpapercon I LLC............C....... 620 856-4615
Baxter Springs *(G-395)*
Plastic Packaging Tech LLC............C....... 913 287-3383
Kansas City *(G-4325)*
Ppt Holdings LLC............G....... 913 287-3383
Kansas City *(G-4328)*

BAGS: Plastic, Made From Purchased Materials

Deelliotte Company Inc............D....... 913 764-0606
New Century *(G-7278)*
Envision Inc............F....... 316 425-7123
Wichita *(G-14294)*
Envision Inc............E....... 316 267-2244
Kansas City *(G-3991)*
Envision Industries Inc............D....... 316 267-2244
Wichita *(G-14296)*
Midco Plastics Inc............E....... 785 263-8999
Enterprise *(G-1855)*
Pitt Plastics Inc............B....... 620 231-4030
Pittsburg *(G-9918)*

BAGS: Textile

Central Bag Company............E....... 913 250-0325
Leavenworth *(G-5215)*
Hubco Inc............E....... 620 663-8301
Hutchinson *(G-3315)*
Tdc Filter Manufacturing Inc............C....... 630 410-6200
Overland Park *(G-9394)*

BAGS: Wardrobe, Closet Access, Made From Purchased Materials

Nichols Enterprises Inc............F....... 913 706-4581
Leawood *(G-5502)*

BAIL BONDING SVCS

Owens Bonding Inc............E....... 316 283-3983
Wichita *(G-15242)*

BAKERIES, COMMERCIAL: On Premises Baking Only

B Four Corp............C....... 913 648-1441
Prairie Village *(G-10012)*
B Four Corp............C....... 913 432-1107
Shawnee Mission *(G-11140)*
Bakery Projects Inc............G....... 316 831-9434
Wichita *(G-13796)*
Bernices Foods Inc............G....... 913 334-8283
Olathe *(G-7550)*
Bimbo Bakeries Usa Inc............G....... 913 328-1234
Kansas City *(G-3862)*
Bimbo Bakeries Usa Inc............G....... 620 276-6308
Garden City *(G-2111)*
Bobs Super Saver Inc............D....... 620 251-6820
Coffeyville *(G-913)*
Dillon Companies Inc............C....... 620 663-4464
Hutchinson *(G-3263)*
Dillon Companies Inc............C....... 785 272-0661
Topeka *(G-12557)*
Dillon Companies Inc............D....... 785 823-9403
Salina *(G-10478)*
Kansas Maid Inc............G....... 620 437-2958
Madison *(G-6502)*
Queen-Morris Ventures LLC............C....... 913 383-2563
Shawnee Mission *(G-11765)*

Walmart Inc.....B..... 316 636-5384
Wichita *(G-15924)*
Williams Foods Inc.....C..... 913 888-4343
Lenexa *(G-6231)*

BAKERIES: On Premises Baking & Consumption

Bobs Super Saver Inc.....D..... 620 251-6820
Coffeyville *(G-913)*
Dillon Companies Inc.....C..... 620 225-6130
Dodge City *(G-1341)*
Tasty Pastry Bakery.....E..... 785 632-2335
Clay Center *(G-882)*

BAKERY MACHINERY

Altura Incorporated.....G..... 913 492-3701
Lenexa *(G-5643)*

BAKERY PRDTS: Biscuits, Baked, Baking Powder & Raised

Keebler Company.....D..... 913 342-2300
Kansas City *(G-4168)*

BAKERY PRDTS: Bread, All Types, Fresh Or Frozen

Bagatelle Inc.....E..... 316 684-5662
Wichita *(G-13793)*
Bimbo Bakeries Usa Inc.....C..... 620 218-2365
Wichita *(G-13849)*

BAKERY PRDTS: Buns, Bread Type, Fresh Or Frozen

Best Harvest LLC.....D..... 913 287-6300
Kansas City *(G-3856)*
Flowers Baking Co Lenexa LLC.....C..... 913 564-1100
Lenexa *(G-5858)*

BAKERY PRDTS: Cakes, Bakery, Exc Frozen

Las Tarascas.....G..... 316 941-5511
Wichita *(G-14929)*

BAKERY PRDTS: Cakes, Bakery, Frozen

Sugar Rush Inc.....G..... 913 839-2158
Olathe *(G-8087)*

BAKERY PRDTS: Cookies & crackers

Bagatelle Inc.....E..... 316 684-5662
Wichita *(G-13793)*
Keebler Company.....D..... 913 342-2300
Kansas City *(G-4168)*

BAKERY PRDTS: Doughnuts, Exc Frozen

Donut X-Press.....G..... 620 544-4700
Hugoton *(G-3160)*
Drubers Donut Shop.....G..... 316 283-1206
Newton *(G-7338)*
Johnny Schwindt Inc.....G..... 620 275-0633
Garden City *(G-2209)*
M & K Daylight Donuts.....G..... 913 495-2529
Shawnee Mission *(G-11588)*

BAKERY PRDTS: Frozen

Custom Foods Inc.....E..... 913 585-1900
De Soto *(G-1198)*
Kansas Maid Inc.....G..... 620 437-2958
Madison *(G-6502)*

BAKERY PRDTS: Pies, Exc Frozen

Golden Boy Pies Inc.....E..... 913 384-6460
Overland Park *(G-8763)*

BAKERY PRDTS: Pretzels

Dots Pretzels LLC.....D..... 913 274-1705
Lenexa *(G-5823)*

BAKERY PRDTS: Wholesalers

Bagel Works Cafe Inc.....F..... 913 789-7333
Kansas City *(G-3838)*
CSM Bakery Solutions LLC.....C..... 913 441-7216
Bonner Springs *(G-546)*

Tasty Pastry Bakery.....E..... 785 632-2335
Clay Center *(G-882)*

BAKERY: Wholesale Or Wholesale & Retail Combined

Cereal Ingredients Inc.....D..... 913 727-3434
Leavenworth *(G-5217)*
Hostess Brands LLC.....G..... 620 342-6811
Emporia *(G-1776)*
Sara Lee Corp.....G..... 913 233-3200
Kansas City *(G-4401)*

BALANCES EXC LABORATORY WHOLESALERS

Arrow Fork Lift Parts Inc.....G..... 816 231-4410
Lenexa *(G-5663)*

BALLOONS: Novelty & Toy

Mr PS Party Outlet Inc.....F..... 785 537-1804
Manhattan *(G-6753)*
PA Acquisition Corp.....F..... 913 498-3700
Shawnee Mission *(G-11712)*

BALLOONS: Toy & Advertising, Rubber

Continental American Corp.....C..... 316 321-4551
El Dorado *(G-1550)*

BANKRUPTCY REFEREE

Northast Kans Chpter 13 Trstee.....F..... 785 234-1551
Topeka *(G-12935)*

BANKS: Commercial, NEC

Country Club Bank.....F..... 913 438-5660
Lenexa *(G-5790)*
Country Club Bank.....F..... 816 751-4270
Kansas City *(G-3943)*
Country Club Bank.....F..... 816 931-4060
Shawnee Mission *(G-11268)*
Country Club Bank.....F..... 816 931-4060
Leawood *(G-5360)*
Country Club Bank.....F..... 913 441-2444
Shawnee *(G-10936)*
Dewaay Financial Network LLC.....F..... 316 303-1985
Wichita *(G-14206)*
Exchange National Bank & Tr Co.....F..... 913 833-5560
Effingham *(G-1523)*
Farm Credit of Western Kansas.....E..... 785 462-6714
Colby *(G-1006)*
Farmers Bank & Trust.....F..... 913 402-7257
Overland Park *(G-8705)*
Fidelity Bank.....F..... 316 722-1460
Wichita *(G-14364)*
Kanza Bank.....F..... 316 773-7007
Wichita *(G-14832)*
Osawatomie Agency Inc.....E..... 913 592-3811
Spring Hill *(G-12095)*
Osawatomie Agency Inc.....F..... 913 294-3811
Paola *(G-9577)*
Sunflower Bank.....A..... 785 827-5564
Salina *(G-10723)*
Sunflower Bank National Assn.....F..... 785 827-5564
Salina *(G-10724)*
Wells Fargo Bank National Assn.....F..... 816 234-2929
Overland Park *(G-9488)*

BANKS: Mortgage & Loan

A Divis of P Midla Loan Servi.....B..... 913 253-9000
Overland Park *(G-8334)*
Affinity Mortgage LLC.....F..... 913 469-0777
Lenexa *(G-5637)*
Arvest Bank Operations Inc.....E..... 913 261-2265
Shawnee Mission *(G-11121)*
Ballyhoo Banners.....G..... 913 385-5050
Lenexa *(G-5684)*
BNC National Bank.....E..... 913 647-7000
Overland Park *(G-8471)*
Bok Financial Corporation.....D..... 913 234-6632
Overland Park *(G-8474)*
Citizens Bank of Kansas NA.....F..... 620 886-5686
Medicine Lodge *(G-7058)*
Citywide Mortgage Associates.....F..... 913 498-8822
Overland Park *(G-8558)*
Cornerstone Home Lending Inc.....F..... 913 317-5626
Overland Park *(G-8600)*

Emprise Bank.....F..... 785 838-2001
Lawrence *(G-4852)*
Fairway Independent Mrtg Corp.....F..... 785 841-4434
Lawrence *(G-4855)*
First Nat Bncshres of Fredonia.....F..... 620 378-2151
Fredonia *(G-2032)*
First Seacoast Bank.....F..... 913 766-2500
Overland Park *(G-8722)*
Firstrust Mortgage Inc.....E..... 913 312-2000
Fairway *(G-1907)*
Guild Mortgage Company.....F..... 316 749-2789
Wichita *(G-14526)*
High Plains Farm Credit Flca.....E..... 620 285-6978
Larned *(G-4705)*
High Plains Farm Credit Flca.....F..... 785 625-2110
Hays *(G-2844)*
Metropolitan Mortgage Corp.....F..... 913 642-8300
Overland Park *(G-9017)*
Prime Lending.....E..... 913 327-5507
Leawood *(G-5527)*
Western State Bank.....F..... 785 899-2393
Goodland *(G-2491)*

BANKS: National Commercial

1st National Bank of Dighton.....F..... 620 397-5324
Dighton *(G-1282)*
Armed Forces Bank Nat Assn.....B..... 913 682-9090
Fort Leavenworth *(G-1934)*
Armed Forces Bank Nat Assn.....F..... 913 651-2992
Fort Leavenworth *(G-1935)*
Armed Forces Bank Nat Assn.....F..... 785 238-2241
Junction City *(G-3667)*
Arvest Bank Operations Inc.....E..... 913 261-2265
Shawnee Mission *(G-11121)*
Banccentral National Assn.....F..... 620 842-1000
Anthony *(G-121)*
Bank America National Assn.....F..... 316 788-2811
Derby *(G-1222)*
Bank America National Assn.....F..... 785 625-3413
Hays *(G-2755)*
Bank America National Assn.....F..... 913 768-1340
Olathe *(G-7546)*
Bank America National Assn.....F..... 316 261-4242
Dodge City *(G-1302)*
Bank America National Assn.....F..... 816 979-8482
Prairie Village *(G-10013)*
Bank America National Assn.....F..... 316 261-4242
Liberal *(G-6281)*
Bank America National Assn.....F..... 816 979-8561
Olathe *(G-7547)*
Bank America National Assn.....F..... 785 235-1532
Topeka *(G-12362)*
Bank America National Assn.....F..... 316 261-2025
Wichita *(G-13800)*
Bank America National Assn.....F..... 816 979-8215
Kansas City *(G-3839)*
Bank America National Assn.....F..... 785 842-1000
Lawrence *(G-4749)*
Bank America National Assn.....F..... 785 227-3344
Lindsborg *(G-6391)*
Bank America National Assn.....F..... 316 261-2274
Wichita *(G-13801)*
Bank America National Assn.....F..... 785 238-8012
Junction City *(G-3671)*
Bank America National Assn.....E..... 816 979-4592
Overland Park *(G-8425)*
Bank America National Assn.....E..... 316 261-4359
Wichita *(G-13802)*
Bank America National Assn.....E..... 620 331-4800
Independence *(G-3498)*
Bank America National Assn.....F..... 816 979-8200
Overland Park *(G-8426)*
Bank America National Assn.....F..... 316 261-4242
Liberal *(G-6282)*
Bank America National Assn.....E..... 785 235-1532
Lawrence *(G-4750)*
Bank America National Assn.....F..... 816 979-8608
Shawnee Mission *(G-11146)*
Bank America National Assn.....F..... 816 979-8257
Kansas City *(G-3840)*
Bank America National Assn.....F..... 316 529-6730
Andover *(G-84)*
Bank America National Assn.....F..... 816 979-8219
Lenexa *(G-5685)*
Bank America National Assn.....F..... 913 897-1470
Overland Park *(G-8427)*
Bank America National Assn.....F..... 316 261-4216
Wichita *(G-13803)*
Bank America National Assn.....D..... 620 694-4395
Hutchinson *(G-3212)*

PRDT & SVC

Bank America National Assn ....F 316 261-2210
Wichita ***(G-13804)***
Bank America National Assn ....F 316 261-4040
Wichita ***(G-13805)***
Bank America National Assn ....F 316 261-2143
Wichita ***(G-13806)***
Bank America National Assn ....F 913 441-1067
Shawnee ***(G-10913)***
Bank of Blue Valley ....F 913 888-7852
Shawnee Mission ***(G-11147)***
Bank of Flint Hills ....F 785 765-2220
Alma ***(G-62)***
Bank of Tescott ....E 785 825-1621
Salina ***(G-10418)***
Bank Snb ....F 316 315-1600
Wichita ***(G-13810)***
Bank Snb ....F 620 728-3000
Hutchinson ***(G-3214)***
Bankers Bank of Kansas NA ....E 316 681-2265
Wichita ***(G-13811)***
Bok Financial Corporation ....E 785 273-9993
Topeka ***(G-12396)***
Cbi-Kansas Inc ....E 785 625-6542
Hays ***(G-2766)***
Centera Bank ....F 620 227-6370
Dodge City ***(G-1320)***
Central National Bank ....E 785 238-4114
Junction City ***(G-3676)***
Central National Bank ....F 620 382-2129
Marion ***(G-6868)***
Central National Bank ....F 785 838-1960
Lawrence ***(G-4779)***
Central National Bank ....F 785 238-4114
Junction City ***(G-3677)***
Central National Bank ....F 785 838-1893
Lawrence ***(G-4780)***
Central National Bank ....F 785 234-2265
Topeka ***(G-12456)***
Central of Kansas Inc ....D 785 238-4114
Junction City ***(G-3678)***
Citizens Bank NA ....F 913 239-2700
Overland Park ***(G-8553)***
Citizens Bank NA ....E 620 223-1200
Fort Scott ***(G-1959)***
Citizens Bank of Kansas NA ....F 316 788-1111
Derby ***(G-1229)***
Citizens Bank of Kansas NA ....F 620 886-5686
Medicine Lodge ***(G-7058)***
Citizens National Bank ....D 785 747-2261
Greenleaf ***(G-2667)***
Citizens National Bank ....F 913 727-3266
Lansing ***(G-4671)***
Citizens State Bank ....E 316 518-6621
Hugoton ***(G-3152)***
Commerce Bank ....F 816 234-2000
Kansas City ***(G-3927)***
Commerce Bank ....E 620 276-5600
Garden City ***(G-2129)***
Commerce Bank ....E 316 261-4795
Wichita ***(G-14064)***
Commerce Bank ....F 785 865-4799
Lawrence ***(G-4799)***
Commerce Bank ....D 316 261-4700
Wichita ***(G-14066)***
Commerce Bank ....F 785 532-3500
Manhattan ***(G-6596)***
Commerce Bank ....F 316 261-5590
Wichita ***(G-14067)***
Commerce Bank ....F 816 234-2000
Olathe ***(G-7603)***
Commerce Bank ....F 816 234-2000
Lawrence ***(G-4801)***
Commerce Bank ....E 785 537-1234
Manhattan ***(G-6598)***
Community National Bank ....F 913 369-0100
Tonganoxie ***(G-12256)***
Community National Bank ....F 620 423-0314
Parsons ***(G-9677)***
Community National Bank ....F 316 775-6068
Augusta ***(G-314)***
Community National Bank ....F 913 724-9901
Basehor ***(G-373)***
Community National Bank ....F 620 922-3294
Edna ***(G-1492)***
Community National Bank ....E 620 235-1345
Pittsburg ***(G-9842)***
Community National Bank & Tr ....F 620 365-6000
Iola ***(G-3595)***
Community National Bank & Tr ....F 316 283-0059
Newton ***(G-7332)***
Community National Bank & Tr ....F 620 336-2145
Cherryvale ***(G-803)***
Conway Bank ....E 620 456-2255
Conway Springs ***(G-1137)***
Conway Bank N A ....F 316 263-6767
Wichita ***(G-14096)***
Corefirst Bank & Trust ....F 913 248-7000
Shawnee ***(G-10934)***
Country Club Bank ....E 913 682-0001
Leavenworth ***(G-5226)***
Country Club Bank ....F 913 682-2300
Leavenworth ***(G-5227)***
Enterprise Bank & Trust ....F 913 791-9950
Olathe ***(G-7682)***
Equity Bank NA ....F 731 989-2161
Shawnee ***(G-10949)***
Equity Bank NA ....D 620 624-1971
Liberal ***(G-6307)***
Equity Bank NA ....F 316 612-6000
Wichita ***(G-14299)***
Exchange National Bank & Tr Co ....F 913 833-5560
Effingham ***(G-1523)***
Exchange National Bank Inc ....F 620 273-6389
Cottonwood Falls ***(G-1153)***
Farmers & Merchants Bank Colby ....E 785 460-3321
Colby ***(G-1007)***
Farmers Bank & Trust ....F 913 402-7257
Overland Park ***(G-8705)***
Farmers National Bank ....F 785 543-6541
Phillipsburg ***(G-9785)***
First Bank of Newton ....E 316 283-2600
Newton ***(G-7345)***
First Heritage Bank ....F 785 857-3341
Centralia ***(G-699)***
First Horizon Bank ....E 913 317-2000
Overland Park ***(G-8719)***
First Nat Bnk of Hutchinson ....D 620 663-1521
Hutchinson ***(G-3285)***
First Nat Bnk of Hutchinson ....E 620 662-7858
Hutchinson ***(G-3286)***
First Nat Bnk of Hutchinson ....E 620 465-2225
Haven ***(G-2730)***
First Nat Bnk of Hutchinson ....F 620 694-2304
Hutchinson ***(G-3287)***
First Nat Bnk of Hutchinson ....E 620 663-1521
Hutchinson ***(G-3288)***
First Nat Bnk Syracuse Inc ....F 620 384-7441
Syracuse ***(G-12224)***
First Nat Bnk Syracuse Inc ....F 620 276-6971
Garden City ***(G-2165)***
First Nat Bnk Syracuse Inc ....F 620 492-1754
Johnson ***(G-3653)***
First Nat Bnkshares Beloit Inc ....F 785 738-2251
Beloit ***(G-484)***
First Nat Bnkshres of Scott Cy ....E 620 872-2143
Scott City ***(G-10811)***
First National Bank ....D 785 890-2000
Goodland ***(G-2471)***
First National Bank ....F 785 852-2000
Sharon Springs ***(G-10897)***
First National Bank ....E 620 855-3416
Cimarron ***(G-825)***
First National Bank & Trust ....E 785 543-6511
Phillipsburg ***(G-9786)***
First National Bank Clifton ....F 785 437-6585
Saint Marys ***(G-10364)***
First National Bank Louisburg ....F 913 766-6701
Shawnee Mission ***(G-11373)***
First National Bank Louisburg ....F 913 837-5191
Louisburg ***(G-6448)***
First National Bank of Girard ....F 620 724-6111
Girard ***(G-2405)***
First National Bank of Hutchin ....E 316 661-2471
Mount Hope ***(G-7204)***
First National Bank of Kansas ....F 785 733-2564
Burlington ***(G-635)***
First National Bank of Omaha ....D 913 768-1120
Olathe ***(G-7712)***
First National Bank of Omaha ....D 913 451-5824
Overland Park ***(G-8721)***
First National Bank of Omaha ....D 913 631-0016
Shawnee ***(G-10956)***
First National Bnk of Scott Cy ....E 620 872-2143
Scott City ***(G-10812)***
First National Bnk of Sedan KS ....F 620 725-3106
Sedan ***(G-10843)***
First Pratt Bankshares Inc ....E 620 672-6421
Pratt ***(G-10114)***
First Security Bank & Trust Co ....E 785 877-3313
Norton ***(G-7446)***
Firstoak Bank ....F 620 331-2265
Independence ***(G-3519)***
Gardner Bancshares Inc ....E 855 856-0233
Lenexa ***(G-5868)***
Generations Bank ....F 913 928-6181
Overland Park ***(G-8752)***
Girard National Bank ....F 620 724-8223
Girard ***(G-2409)***
Girard National Bank ....F 785 866-2920
Wetmore ***(G-13566)***
Girard National Bank ....F 785 486-2124
Horton ***(G-3124)***
Girard National Bank ....F 785 742-7120
Hiawatha ***(G-3008)***
Intrust Bank NA ....F 316 440-9000
Wichita ***(G-14713)***
Intrust Bank NA ....F 316 383-1767
Derby ***(G-1252)***
Intrust Bank NA ....F 316 755-1225
Valley Center ***(G-13344)***
Intrust Bank National Assn ....B 316 383-1111
Wichita ***(G-14723)***
Intrust Bank National Assn ....D 913 385-8200
Shawnee Mission ***(G-11466)***
Intrust Bank National Assn ....E 316 383-1339
Wichita ***(G-14724)***
Intrust Bank National Assn ....F 316 383-1040
Wichita ***(G-14725)***
Intrust Bank National Assn ....F 785 830-2600
Lawrence ***(G-4915)***
Landmark Bancorp Inc ....F 785 565-2000
Manhattan ***(G-6708)***
Landmark National Bank ....F 913 239-2719
Overland Park ***(G-8942)***
Landmark National Bank ....D 620 225-1745
Manhattan ***(G-6709)***
Lena M Rush Scholarship Trust ....E 620 326-3361
Wellington ***(G-13511)***
Midland National Bank ....F 316 283-1700
Newton ***(G-7386)***
Millennium Bancshares Inc ....F 785 761-2265
Junction City ***(G-3726)***
Peoples Bank & Trust Co ....E 620 585-2265
Inman ***(G-3584)***
Small Business Bank ....E 913 856-7199
Lenexa ***(G-6139)***
Southwest National Bank ....F 316 942-4004
Wichita ***(G-15628)***
Stanley Bank ....F 913 681-8800
Overland Park ***(G-9353)***
Stock Exchange Bank ....F 620 442-2400
Caldwell ***(G-661)***
Stockton National Bank ....E 785 425-6721
Stockton ***(G-12189)***
Sunflower Bank Inc ....E 620 225-0086
Dodge City ***(G-1436)***
Sunflower Bank National Assn ....E 785 625-8888
Hays ***(G-2914)***
Tricentury Bank ....F 913 648-8010
De Soto ***(G-1215)***
Truist Bank ....E 913 491-6700
Leawood ***(G-5586)***
Umb Bank National Association ....F 785 263-1130
Abilene ***(G-55)***
Umb Bank National Association ....F 620 223-1255
Fort Scott ***(G-2013)***
Umb Bank National Association ....F 785 838-2500
Lawrence ***(G-5150)***
Umb Bank National Association ....E 785 776-9400
Manhattan ***(G-6836)***
Umb Bank National Association ....F 785 483-6800
Russell ***(G-10300)***
Umb Bank National Association ....E 913 234-2070
Shawnee Mission ***(G-11956)***
Umb Bank National Association ....F 913 791-6600
Olathe ***(G-8131)***
Umb Bank National Association ....F 913 360-6060
Atchison ***(G-266)***
Umb Bank National Association ....F 913 236-0300
Prairie Village ***(G-10078)***
Umb Bank National Association ....F 913 402-3600
Shawnee Mission ***(G-11957)***
Umb Bank National Association ....F 913 667-5400
Shawnee Mission ***(G-11958)***
Umb Bank National Association ....F 913 621-8002
Kansas City ***(G-4483)***
Umb Bank National Association ....F 913 894-4088
Shawnee Mission ***(G-11959)***
Umb Bank National Association ....F 316 267-1191
Wichita ***(G-15830)***

Umb Financial Corporation F 785 826-4000
Salina *(G-10744)*
United National Bank F 785 483-2146
Russell *(G-10301)*
University Nat Bnk of Lawrence E 785 841-1988
Lawrence *(G-5157)*
US Bank National Association F 785 312-5280
Lawrence *(G-5170)*
US Bank National Association F 785 312-5060
Lawrence *(G-5171)*
US Bank National Association F 913 432-9633
Overland Park *(G-9451)*
US Bank National Association E 913 261-5663
Prairie Village *(G-10079)*
US Bank National Association F 913 323-5314
Overland Park *(G-9452)*
US Bank National Association F 913 338-0646
Overland Park *(G-9453)*
US Bank National Association F 620 231-4040
Pittsburg *(G-9953)*
US Bank National Association F 913 725-7000
Overland Park *(G-9454)*
US Bank National Association F 913 383-2126
Leawood *(G-5592)*
US Bank National Association F 913 248-1001
Shawnee *(G-11045)*
US Bank National Association F 913 402-6919
Overland Park *(G-9455)*
US Bank National Association F 785 312-6880
Lawrence *(G-5172)*
US Bank National Association F 913 671-2723
Merriam *(G-7108)*
US Bank National Association F 913 239-8204
Overland Park *(G-9456)*
US Bank National Association F 913 261-5401
Roeland Park *(G-10230)*
US Bank National Association F 785 276-6300
Topeka *(G-13214)*
Wells Fargo & Company F 913 782-9603
Olathe *(G-8150)*
Wells Fargo Bank NA F 913 631-6600
Shawnee *(G-11052)*
Wells Fargo Bank National Assn F 816 234-2929
Overland Park *(G-9488)*
Wells Fargo Bank National Assn F 316 685-5495
Wichita *(G-15944)*
Wells Fargo Bank National Assn F 913 341-4774
Leawood *(G-5596)*
Wells Fargo Bank National Assn F 316 943-3159
Wichita *(G-15945)*
Wells Fargo Bank National Assn E 785 271-2492
Topeka *(G-13237)*
Wells Fargo Bank National Assn E 913 663-6040
Shawnee Mission *(G-12001)*
Wells Fargo Home Mortgage Inc E 785 565-2900
Manhattan *(G-6850)*
Wilson State Bank F 620 653-4113
Hoisington *(G-3073)*

BANKS: Other Activities, NEC

Crossfirst Bank C 913 312-6800
Leawood *(G-5364)*
Western Union F 800 325-6000
Kinsley *(G-4622)*

BANKS: State Commercial

Alliant Bank F 316 772-5111
Wichita *(G-13671)*
Alta Vista State Bank F 785 499-6304
Alta Vista *(G-69)*
American Bank Baxter Springs F 620 856-2301
Baxter Springs *(G-393)*
American State Bank & Trust Co F 620 793-5900
Great Bend *(G-2506)*
American State Bank & Trust Co F 620 271-0123
Garden City *(G-2099)*
American State Bank & Trust Co F 620 549-3244
Saint John *(G-10349)*
Andover State Bank F 316 219-1600
Wichita *(G-13707)*
Arvest Bank F 785 229-3950
Ottawa *(G-8245)*
Astra Bank E 785 335-2243
Scandia *(G-10798)*
Baldwin State Bank E 785 594-6421
Baldwin City *(G-355)*
Bank 7 F 620 846-2221
Montezuma *(G-7155)*
Bank of Blue Valley E 785 742-2121
Hiawatha *(G-3002)*
Bank of Flint Hills E 785 456-2221
Wamego *(G-13404)*
Bank of Flint Hills F 785 539-8322
Manhattan *(G-6552)*
Bank of Labor F 913 321-4242
Overland Park *(G-8429)*
Bank of Prairie F 785 353-2298
Olathe *(G-7548)*
Bank of Prairie Village F 913 713-0300
Prairie Village *(G-10014)*
Bank of West F 316 283-7310
Newton *(G-7317)*
Bank of West F 913 642-5212
Shawnee Mission *(G-11149)*
Bankwest of Kansas E 785 899-2342
Goodland *(G-2463)*
Baxter State Bank F 620 856-2323
Baxter Springs *(G-397)*
Bennington State Bank F 785 488-3344
Bennington *(G-513)*
Bern Bancshares Inc F 785 336-6121
Bern *(G-520)*
Busey Bank E 913 338-4300
Overland Park *(G-8495)*
Cbi-Kansas Inc F 620 341-7420
Emporia *(G-1718)*
Centera Bank F 620 649-2220
Satanta *(G-10780)*
Central Bank of Midwest F 913 268-3202
Shawnee *(G-10925)*
Central Bank of Midwest D 913 893-6049
Edgerton *(G-1481)*
Central Bank of Midwest D 913 791-9988
Overland Park *(G-8537)*
Chisholm Trail State Bank E 316 744-1293
Park City *(G-9610)*
Citizens Bank of Kansas E 620 532-5162
Kingman *(G-4586)*
Citizens Bank of Kansas NA F 620 886-5686
Medicine Lodge *(G-7058)*
Citizens State Bank F 316 542-3142
Cheney *(G-791)*
Citizens State Bank E 785 562-2186
Marysville *(G-6882)*
Citizens State Bank F 620 327-4941
Hesston *(G-2986)*
Colt Investments Inc E 913 385-5010
Prairie Village *(G-10020)*
Commerce Bank F 620 429-2515
Columbus *(G-1068)*
Commerce Bank E 913 381-2386
Overland Park *(G-8578)*
Commerce Bank F 816 234-2000
Shawnee Mission *(G-11252)*
Commerce Bank E 316 321-1250
El Dorado *(G-1546)*
Commerce Bank F 316 261-4927
Wichita *(G-14065)*
Commerce Bank F 785 625-6542
Hays *(G-2773)*
Commerce Bank F 913 682-8282
Leavenworth *(G-5224)*
Commerce Bank F 913 888-0700
Lenexa *(G-5773)*
Commerce Bank F 816 234-2000
Lawrence *(G-4800)*
Commerce Bank F 816 234-2000
Leawood *(G-5355)*
Commerce Bank F 785 587-1696
Manhattan *(G-6597)*
Commerce Bank F 816 234-2000
Olathe *(G-7604)*
Commerce Bank F 816 234-2000
Overland Park *(G-8579)*
Commerce Bank F 816 234-2000
Shawnee *(G-10931)*
Commerce Bank E 816 234-2000
Shawnee *(G-10932)*
Commerce Bank F 816 234-2000
Shawnee Mission *(G-11253)*
Commerce Bank F 620 231-8400
Pittsburg *(G-9839)*
Commerce Bank F 816 234-2000
Kansas City *(G-3928)*
Commercial Bank E 620 423-0770
Parsons *(G-9675)*
Commercial Bank F 620 431-3200
Chanute *(G-719)*
Community Bank E 785 440-4400
Topeka *(G-12491)*
Community Bank Wichita Inc F 316 634-1600
Wichita *(G-14078)*
Community First National Bank E 785 323-1111
Manhattan *(G-6599)*
Community National Bank E 785 336-6143
Seneca *(G-10859)*
Community National Bank F 620 724-4446
Girard *(G-2398)*
Community National Bank F 620 325-2900
Neodesha *(G-7237)*
Community National Bank F 620 221-1400
Winfield *(G-16126)*
Community National Bank & Tr E 620 431-2265
Chanute *(G-721)*
Corefirst Bank & Trust F 785 286-5100
Topeka *(G-12510)*
Cornerstone Bank D 913 239-8100
Overland Park *(G-8599)*
Crossfirst Bank E 316 494-4844
Wichita *(G-14134)*
Crossfirst Bank D 913 327-1212
Overland Park *(G-8617)*
Douglas County Bank E 785 865-1022
Lawrence *(G-4837)*
Emprise Bank F 316 264-1569
Wichita *(G-14282)*
Emprise Bank F 316 689-0717
Wichita *(G-14283)*
Emprise Bank F 620 767-5128
Council Grove *(G-1164)*
Emprise Bank F 620 241-7113
McPherson *(G-6958)*
Emprise Bank F 316 383-4131
Wichita *(G-14285)*
Emprise Bank F 620 584-2201
Clearwater *(G-891)*
Emprise Bank F 316 522-2222
Haysville *(G-2941)*
Emprise Bank National Assn E 785 625-6595
Hays *(G-2798)*
Enterprise Bank E 913 663-5525
Shawnee Mission *(G-11339)*
Enterprise Bank & Trust E 913 782-3211
Olathe *(G-7683)*
Enterprise Bank & Trust F 913 791-9300
Olathe *(G-7684)*
Enterprise Bank & Trust F 913 791-9100
Olathe *(G-7685)*
Equity Bank NA E 913 371-1242
Kansas City *(G-3994)*
Exchange National Bank & Tr Co D 913 833-5560
Atchison *(G-228)*
Exchange National Bank & Tr Co F 913 833-5560
Effingham *(G-1523)*
Farmers & Merchants Bank Colby E 785 460-3321
Colby *(G-1007)*
Farmers & Merchants Bank Hl Cy F 785 421-2131
Hill City *(G-3034)*
Farmers Bank & Trust E 620 792-2411
Great Bend *(G-2563)*
Farmers Bank & Trust F 620 285-3177
Larned *(G-4702)*
Farmers Nat Bnk of Canfield F 785 346-2000
Osborne *(G-8208)*
Farmers State Bank Blue Mound E 913 756-2221
Blue Mound *(G-532)*
Farmers State Bankshares Inc E 785 364-4691
Holton *(G-3089)*
Fidelity Bank F 316 265-2261
Wichita *(G-14363)*
Fidelity Kansas Bankshares E 785 295-2100
Topeka *(G-12605)*
Fidelity State Bnk Tr Ddge Cy E 620 227-8586
Dodge City *(G-1359)*
First Bank Kansas D 785 825-2211
Salina *(G-10501)*
First Business Bank F 913 681-2223
Leawood *(G-5403)*
First Federal Savings & Loan F 785 743-5751
Wakeeney *(G-13388)*
First National Bank & Trust Co F 785 762-4121
Junction City *(G-3690)*
First National Bank Elkhart F 620 697-2777
Elkhart *(G-1621)*
First National Bank Inc E 785 263-1090
Abilene *(G-31)*
First National Bank NA E 620 326-3361
Wellington *(G-13500)*
First Security Bank F 785 665-7155
Overbrook *(G-8324)*

Employee Codes: A=Over 500 employees, B=251-500
C=101-250, D=51-100, E=20-50, F=10-19, G=5-9

First State Bank....E....785 877-3341
Norton (G-7447)
First-Citizens Bank & Trust Co....F....913 312-5108
Overland Park (G-8723)
Flint Hills Bank....E....785 449-2266
Eskridge (G-1866)
Garden Plain Bancshares Inc....E....316 721-1500
Wichita (G-14446)
Garden Plain State Bank....E....316 721-1500
Wichita (G-14447)
Grant County Bank....E....620 356-4142
Ulysses (G-13300)
Great American Bank....F....785 838-9704
Lawrence (G-4880)
Great Southern Bank....F....620 365-3101
Iola (G-3605)
Great Southern Bank....E....620 421-5700
Parsons (G-9689)
Great Southern Bank....C....913 557-4311
Paola (G-9563)
Great Western Bank....F....913 248-3300
Shawnee Mission (G-11401)
Greensburg State Bank....F....620 723-2131
Greensburg (G-2678)
Harris Bmo Bank National Assn....E....913 307-0707
Overland Park (G-8796)
Harris Bmo Bank National Assn....E....913 962-1400
Shawnee Mission (G-11412)
Haviland Bancshares Inc....F....620 862-5222
Haviland (G-2740)
Hillsboro State Bank....F....620 947-3961
Hillsboro (G-3050)
Home Savings Bank....F....620 431-1100
Chanute (G-733)
Intrust Bank NA....F....785 761-2265
Junction City (G-3700)
Intrust Bank National Assn....F....785 238-1121
Junction City (G-3701)
Intrust Bank National Assn....F....913 385-8330
Olathe (G-7802)
Intrust Bank National Assn....F....316 383-1234
Wichita (G-14726)
Intrust Bank National Assn....E....316 524-3251
Haysville (G-2947)
Intrust Financial Corporation....E....316 383-1111
Wichita (G-14727)
Kansasland Bank....F....785 754-2500
Quinter (G-10182)
Kaw Valley State Bank & Tr Co....F....785 437-6585
Saint Marys (G-10369)
Kearny County Bank....E....620 355-6222
Lakin (G-4650)
King Bancshares Inc....E....620 532-5162
Kingman (G-4597)
KS Statebank....E....785 587-4000
Manhattan (G-6701)
Lakin Bancshares Inc....E....620 355-6222
Lakin (G-4654)
Liberty Bank and Trust Company....F....913 321-7200
Kansas City (G-4201)
Lyon County State Bank....F....620 343-4444
Emporia (G-1788)
Metcalf Bank....E....913 648-4540
Shawnee Mission (G-11618)
Metcalf Bank....F....913 685-3801
Shawnee Mission (G-11619)
Metcalf Bank....F....913 782-6522
Olathe (G-7885)
Metcalf Bank....F....913 451-1199
Shawnee Mission (G-11620)
Midland National Bank....E....316 283-1700
Newton (G-7385)
Morley Bancshares Corporation....D....620 488-2211
Belle Plaine (G-448)
Nbh Bank....F....785 842-4300
Lawrence (G-5037)
Nbh Bank....E....785 242-2900
Ottawa (G-8294)
Nbh Bank....F....913 782-5400
Olathe (G-7914)
Nbh Bank....F....913 831-4184
Kansas City (G-4282)
Nbh Bank....F....913 441-6800
Edwardsville (G-1510)
Nbh Bank....F....913 299-9700
Kansas City (G-4283)
Osawatomie Agency Inc....D....913 755-3811
Osawatomie (G-8201)
Peoples Bank & Trust Co....D....620 662-6502
Hutchinson (G-3401)
Peoples Bank & Trust Co....E....620 669-0234
Hutchinson (G-3402)
Peoples Bank & Trust Co....E....620 241-6908
McPherson (G-7014)
Peoples Bank & Trust Co....E....620 241-7664
McPherson (G-7015)
Peoples Bank & Trust Co....F....620 663-4000
Hutchinson (G-3403)
PNC Bank National Association....F....913 253-9490
Overland Park (G-9172)
Prairie Bank of Kansas....E....620 234-5226
Stafford (G-12107)
Premier Bank....E....913 888-8490
Shawnee Mission (G-11748)
Premier Bank....F....913 541-6180
Shawnee Mission (G-11749)
Prescott State Bnk Holdg Inc....F....913 471-4321
Prescott (G-10167)
Security State Bank....F....620 326-7417
Wellington (G-13528)
Silver Lake Bank....E....785 232-0102
Topeka (G-13072)
Sjn Banc Co....F....620 549-3225
Saint John (G-10356)
Sjn Bank of Kansas....F....620 549-3225
Saint John (G-10357)
Solomon State Bank....F....785 655-2941
Solomon (G-12053)
Solutions North Bank....E....785 425-6721
Stockton (G-12188)
Solutions North Bank....E....785 743-2104
Wakeeney (G-13390)
Southeast Bancshares Inc....F....620 325-2632
Neodesha (G-7249)
Southeast Bancshares Inc....E....620 431-1400
Chanute (G-763)
St Marys State Bank....E....785 437-2271
Saint Marys (G-10377)
State Bank....F....785 675-3261
Hoxie (G-3142)
Union Bank and Trust Company....D....913 491-0909
Leawood (G-5589)
Union State Bancshares Inc....E....620 756-4305
Uniontown (G-13333)
Union State Bank....F....620 221-3040
Winfield (G-16177)
Union State Bank....E....785 632-3122
Clay Center (G-885)
Union State Bank Inc....F....785 293-5516
Randolph (G-10191)
Union State Bank of Everest....E....913 367-2700
Atchison (G-267)
United Bank & Trust....F....785 284-2187
Sabetha (G-10335)
United Bank & Trust....F....785 336-2123
Seneca (G-10885)
Valley State Bank....F....620 384-7451
Syracuse (G-12236)
Valley View State Bank....F....913 381-3311
Overland Park (G-9458)
Vision Bank....F....785 357-4669
Topeka (G-13226)
Washington 1st Banco Inc....F....785 325-2221
Washington (G-13470)
Washington FNB....F....785 325-2221
Washington (G-13471)

BANNERS: Fabric

George Eschbaugh Advg Inc....E....785 658-2105
Wilson (G-16105)

BANQUET HALL FACILITIES

B & C Restaurant Corporation....C....913 327-0800
Shawnee Mission (G-11138)
Bobby TS Bar & Grill Inc....F....785 537-8383
Manhattan (G-6564)
Bockers Two Catering Inc....F....785 539-9431
Manhattan (G-6566)
Brown Management Inc....F....785 528-3769
Osage City (G-8181)
Charles Ritz Inc....F....913 685-2600
Overland Park (G-8542)
China Palace....F....620 365-3723
Iola (G-3592)
City of Leawood....D....913 685-4550
Shawnee Mission (G-11228)
City of Salina....E....785 826-7200
Salina (G-10449)
Eldridge House Invest Ltd Ptnr....E....785 749-5011
Lawrence (G-4850)
Falcon Ridge Golf Club....F....913 393-4653
Shawnee Mission (G-11359)
Free State Brewing Co Inc....D....785 843-4555
Lawrence (G-4865)
Garozzos III Inc....D....913 491-8300
Shawnee Mission (G-11390)
Heart America Management LLC....E....913 397-0100
Olathe (G-7762)
Hedricks Promotions Inc....E....620 422-3296
Nickerson (G-7434)
Hulsing Hotels Kansas Inc....D....785 539-5311
Manhattan (G-6662)
Hyatt Corporation....C....316 293-1234
Wichita (G-14661)
La Mesa Mexican Restaurant....F....913 837-3455
Louisburg (G-6454)
Latour Management Inc....F....316 262-7300
Wichita (G-14932)
Leisure Hotel Corporation....E....620 227-5000
Dodge City (G-1398)
Leisure Hotel Corporation....E....620 275-5900
Garden City (G-2224)
Liberty Hall Inc....F....785 749-1972
Lawrence (G-4994)
Little Apple Brewing Company....C....785 539-5500
Manhattan (G-6714)
Northrock Lanes Inc....E....316 636-5444
Wichita (G-15192)
Overland Park Hotel Assoc Lc....C....913 888-8440
Overland Park (G-9120)
River City Brewery Inc....D....316 263-2739
Wichita (G-15469)
S S of Kansas Inc....E....620 663-5951
Hutchinson (G-3435)
S S of Kansas Inc....D....785 823-2787
Salina (G-10657)
Salina Red Coach Inn....F....785 825-2111
Salina (G-10684)
Tellers....D....785 843-4111
Lawrence (G-5133)
Wichita Airport Ht Assoc L P....C....316 945-5272
Wichita (G-15971)
Windmill Inn Inc....F....785 336-3696
Seneca (G-10888)

BAR

Black Stag Brewery LLC....D....785 764-1628
Lawrence (G-4760)
Blind Pig....F....785 827-7449
Salina (G-10426)
Coffeyville Country Club....E....620 251-5236
Coffeyville (G-918)
Little Apple Brewing Company....C....785 539-5500
Manhattan (G-6714)
Olathe Billiards Inc....F....913 780-5740
Olathe (G-7928)
River City Brewery Inc....D....316 263-2739
Wichita (G-15469)
Side Pockets Inc....F....913 888-7665
Shawnee Mission (G-11867)
T-143 Inc....E....913 681-8313
Overland Park (G-9390)

BAR JOISTS & CONCRETE REINFORCING BARS: Fabricated

AMBS and Associates Inc....G....913 599-5939
Lenexa (G-5644)
Femco Inc....D....620 241-3513
McPherson (G-6964)

BARBECUE EQPT

Yoder Smokers Inc....D....620 802-0201
Hutchinson (G-3495)

BARBER SHOPS

Crisp Cuts & Styles Etcllc....F....816 916-1841
Shawnee Mission (G-11280)
Hair Experts Design Team....F....785 841-6886
Lawrence (G-4885)
Professional Hairstyling....F....913 888-3536
Lenexa (G-6072)
Ricks Barbr Sp & Natural Hair....F....913 268-3944
Shawnee (G-11020)
Salon 103....F....913 383-9040
Overland Park (G-9276)
Twice As Nice Barbershop....F....319 201-4542
Wichita (G-15821)

BARS: Cargo, Stabilizing, Metal

Multiprens Usa Inc .... E 913 371-6999
Kansas City *(G-4271)*

BARS: Concrete Reinforcing, Fabricated Steel

Southwest Stl Fabrication LLC .... E 913 422-5500
Bonner Springs *(G-573)*
Structura .... F 913 390-8787
Olathe *(G-8086)*

BATHING SUIT STORES

Wichita Swim Club .... E 316 683-1491
Wichita *(G-16036)*

BATTERIES, EXC AUTOMOTIVE: Wholesalers

Industrial Battery Pdts Inc .... F 913 236-6500
Merriam *(G-7096)*

BATTERIES: Lead Acid, Storage

Enersys .... C 785 625-3355
Hays *(G-2799)*

BATTERIES: Storage

Exide Technologies .... C 913 321-3561
Kansas City *(G-4000)*
Exide Technologies .... D 785 825-6276
Salina *(G-10488)*

BATTERIES: Wet

Exide Technologies .... C 913 321-3561
Kansas City *(G-4000)*
Spectrum Brands Inc .... G 949 279-4099
Edgerton *(G-1490)*

BATTERY CHARGERS

Espi LLC .... F 785 777-2707
Clay Center *(G-862)*
Exide Technologies .... G 913 321-4600
Kansas City *(G-4001)*
Exide Technologies .... C 913 321-3561
Kansas City *(G-4000)*
Exide Technologies .... D 785 825-6276
Salina *(G-10488)*

BEARINGS & PARTS Ball

Manko Corporation .... F 785 825-1301
Salina *(G-10591)*

BEARINGS: Plastic

Westirland Industries Inc .... G 620 795-4421
Oswego *(G-8239)*

BEAUTY & BARBER SHOP EQPT

Fremont Industries Inc .... G 913 962-7676
Olathe *(G-7718)*
Mkc Golf 3 LLC .... G 913 526-3312
Lenexa *(G-6009)*
Oneok Hydrocarbon LP .... G 620 834-2204
Conway *(G-1135)*
Signature Manufacturing .... F 913 766-0680
Merriam *(G-7104)*

BEAUTY & BARBER SHOP EQPT & SPLYS WHOLESALERS

Gaia Inc .... F 785 539-2622
Manhattan *(G-6643)*

BEAUTY CULTURE SCHOOL

Hays Academy of Hair Design .... F 785 628-6624
Hays *(G-2827)*

BEAUTY SALONS

Beauty Brands LLC .... E 816 505-2800
Kansas City *(G-3850)*
Beauty Brands LLC .... E 913 492-7900
Lenexa *(G-5694)*
Beauty Brands LLC .... E 913 393-4800
Olathe *(G-7549)*
Beauty Brands LLC .... E 785 228-9778
Topeka *(G-12369)*
Bella Vita Salon & Day Spa Inc .... E 913 651-6161
Leavenworth *(G-5207)*
Courtland Day Spa .... F 620 223-0098
Fort Scott *(G-1962)*
Design Court .... F 620 276-3019
Garden City *(G-2145)*
Diane Londene .... F 785 233-1991
Topeka *(G-12556)*
Dream Waves LLC .... F 316 942-9283
Wichita *(G-14237)*
European Wax Center .... F 316 425-0909
Wichita *(G-14309)*
Exsalonce LLC .... F 785 823-1724
Salina *(G-10493)*
Extreme Tanning Inc .... F 316 712-0190
Wichita *(G-14325)*
Gq Inc .... F 785 843-2138
Lawrence *(G-4878)*
Hair Design Company .... F 913 897-4776
Overland Park *(G-8784)*
Hair Experts Design Team .... F 785 841-6886
Lawrence *(G-4885)*
Haydens Salon and Day Spa .... F 620 663-2179
Hutchinson *(G-3308)*
K C D Inc .... F 785 827-0445
Salina *(G-10558)*
Kansas State University .... D 785 826-2646
Salina *(G-10567)*
Platinum Inc .... F 316 773-9700
Wichita *(G-15306)*
Profiles Inc .... F 316 636-1214
Wichita *(G-15368)*
Regis Corporation .... F 785 273-2992
Topeka *(G-13005)*
Regis Corporation .... F 785 628-2111
Hays *(G-2899)*
Salon 103 .... F 913 383-9040
Overland Park *(G-9276)*
Salon Knotty .... F 316 636-4400
Wichita *(G-15511)*
Salon X .... F 620 343-8634
Emporia *(G-1820)*
Thairapy Salon .... F 316 321-6263
El Dorado *(G-1608)*
Tresses Hair Salon .... F 620 662-2299
Hutchinson *(G-3469)*

BED & BREAKFAST INNS

Englewood Beach House LLC .... F 913 385-5400
Prairie Village *(G-10027)*
Gary Dean Anderson .... E 785 475-2340
Oberlin *(G-7495)*

BEDS: Hospital

Caregiver Company LLC .... F 316 247-4005
Andover *(G-85)*

BEER & ALE WHOLESALERS

Seneca Wholesale Company Inc .... F 785 336-2118
Seneca *(G-10882)*

BEER & ALE, WHOLESALE: Beer & Other Fermented Malt Liquors

Ark Valley Distributing Inc .... F 620 221-6500
Arkansas City *(G-145)*
Best Beverage Sales Inc .... F 620 331-7100
Independence *(G-3500)*
Big Sky Distributors Kans LLC .... C 913 897-4488
Shawnee Mission *(G-11164)*
City Beverage Co Inc .... E 620 662-6271
Hutchinson *(G-3239)*
Demo Sales Inc .... F 316 320-6670
El Dorado *(G-1556)*
Eagle Beverage Co Inc .... F 620 231-7970
Frontenac *(G-2054)*
Flint Hills Beverage LLC .... F 785 776-2337
Manhattan *(G-6631)*
Glazers Beer and Beverage LLC .... E 620 227-8168
Dodge City *(G-1365)*
House of Schwan Inc .... D 316 636-9100
Wichita *(G-14642)*
Jayhawk Beverage Inc .... E 785 234-8611
Topeka *(G-12741)*
Midwest Distributors Co Inc .... D 913 287-2020
Kansas City *(G-4251)*
OMalley Beverage of Kansas .... E 785 843-8816
Lawrence *(G-5044)*
Pepsi Beverages Company .... D 316 522-3131
Wichita *(G-15279)*
Southern Glazer SPI KS .... C 913 745-2900
Edwardsville *(G-1515)*
Standard Beverage Corporation .... F 316 838-7707
Wichita *(G-15652)*
Strathman Sales Company Inc .... E 785 354-8537
Topeka *(G-13114)*
Vidricksen Distributing Co .... F 785 827-2386
Salina *(G-10753)*
Western Beverage Inc .... E 620 227-7641
Dodge City *(G-1454)*
Western Beverage-Hays .... F 785 625-3712
Hays *(G-2932)*

BEER, WINE & LIQUOR STORES: Hard Liquor

Blacks Retail Liquor LLC .... F 913 281-1551
Kansas City *(G-3866)*

BEER, WINE & LIQUOR STORES: Wine

Wyldewood Cellars Inc .... F 316 554-9463
Peck *(G-9764)*

BEER, WINE & LIQUOR STORES: Wine & Beer

Egbert Oil Operations Inc .... F 620 662-4533
Hutchinson *(G-3275)*

BELTING: Rubber

Prairie Belting Inc .... E 620 842-5147
Anthony *(G-133)*

BELTS: Conveyor, Made From Purchased Wire

Colby Supply & Mfg Co .... F 785 462-3981
Colby *(G-999)*

BEVERAGE STORES

Hillshire Brands Company .... E 316 262-5443
Wichita *(G-14612)*

BEVERAGES, ALCOHOLIC: Beer

Dodge City Brewing Co LLC .... G 620 338-7247
Dodge City *(G-1342)*
Free State Brewing Co Inc .... D 785 843-4555
Lawrence *(G-4865)*
Granite City Food & Brewry Ltd .... D 913 334-2255
Kansas City *(G-4045)*
Tallgrass Brewing Company .... E 785 537-1131
Manhattan *(G-6821)*

BEVERAGES, ALCOHOLIC: Beer & Ale

Bishop Brew .... G 785 242-8920
Ottawa *(G-8249)*
Brew Lab .... G 913 400-2343
Overland Park *(G-8484)*
Little Apple Brewing Company .... C 785 539-5500
Manhattan *(G-6714)*
River City Brewery Inc .... D 316 263-2739
Wichita *(G-15469)*

BEVERAGES, ALCOHOLIC: Distilled Liquors

High Plains Inc .... G 913 773-5780
Atchison *(G-235)*
Mgpi Processing Inc .... E 913 367-1480
Atchison *(G-247)*
Mgpi Processing Inc .... G 913 367-1480
Atchison *(G-248)*
Pernod Ricard Usa LLC .... D 913 393-2015
Olathe *(G-7979)*

BEVERAGES, ALCOHOLIC: Wines

Ad Astra Selections LLC .... G 913 307-0272
Lenexa *(G-5627)*
Bluejcket Crssing Vnyrd Winery .... G 785 542-1764
Eudora *(G-1871)*
Glaciers Edge Winery & Vinyrd .... G 785 862-2298
Wakarusa *(G-13384)*
Kc Wine Co .... G 913 908-3039
Olathe *(G-7834)*

Kuglers Vineyard ....G.... 785 843-8516
Lawrence *(G-4950)*
Oz Winery ....F.... 785 456-7417
Wamego *(G-13431)*
Prairie Fire Winery LLC ....G.... 785 636-5533
Paxico *(G-9757)*
Sommerset Ridge Vineyard ....F.... 913 491-0038
Paola *(G-9587)*
Wyldewood Cellars Inc ....F.... 316 554-9463
Peck *(G-9764)*

BEVERAGES, NONALCOHOLIC: Bottled & canned soft drinks

American Bottling Company ....E.... 785 233-7471
Topeka *(G-12314)*
American Bottling Company ....D.... 785 625-4488
Hays *(G-2746)*
American Bottling Company ....C.... 913 894-6777
Lenexa *(G-5645)*
Coca Cola Bottling Co Mid Amer ....E.... 785 243-1071
Topeka *(G-12483)*
Coca-Cola Bottling Emporia Inc ....E.... 239 444-1746
Emporia *(G-1723)*
Coca-Cola Btlg of Wnfield Kans ....F.... 620 221-2710
Winfield *(G-16121)*
Coca-Cola Company ....F.... 913 492-8100
Lenexa *(G-5768)*
Coca-Cola Refreshments USA Inc ....B.... 913 492-8100
Shawnee Mission *(G-11243)*
Revhoney Inc ....F.... 785 778-2006
Haddam *(G-2695)*
Shasta Midwest Inc ....E.... 913 888-6777
Lenexa *(G-6128)*
Z Bottling Corp ....G.... 620 872-0100
Scott City *(G-10837)*

BEVERAGES, NONALCOHOLIC: Carbonated

P-Americas LLC ....B.... 913 791-3000
Olathe *(G-7970)*
Pepsi Beverages Company ....D.... 316 522-3131
Wichita *(G-15279)*
Pepsi-Cola Btlg Co Topeka Inc ....D.... 785 232-9389
Topeka *(G-12969)*
Pepsi-Cola Btlg Marysville Inc ....E.... 785 537-4730
Manhattan *(G-6773)*
Pepsi-Cola Metro Btlg Co Inc ....E.... 620 251-2890
Coffeyville *(G-971)*

BEVERAGES, NONALCOHOLIC: Carbonated, Canned & Bottled, Etc

Heartland Coca-Cola Btlg LLC ....A.... 785 735-9498
Victoria *(G-13376)*
Heartland Coca-Cola Btlg LLC ....A.... 785 232-9372
Topeka *(G-12675)*
Heartland Coca-Cola Btlg LLC ....A.... 785 243-1071
Concordia *(G-1117)*
Heartland Coca-Cola Btlg LLC ....A.... 913 599-9142
Lenexa *(G-5896)*
Heartland Coca-Cola Btlg LLC ....A.... 620 276-3221
Garden City *(G-2194)*
Heartland Coca-Cola Btlg LLC ....A.... 316 942-3838
Wichita *(G-14582)*

BEVERAGES, NONALCOHOLIC: Flavoring extracts & syrups, nec

Cereal Ingredients Inc ....D.... 913 727-3434
Leavenworth *(G-5217)*

BEVERAGES, NONALCOHOLIC: Soft Drinks, Canned & Bottled, Etc

American Bottling Company ....D.... 316 529-3777
Wichita *(G-13686)*
American Bottling Company ....E.... 785 537-2100
Manhattan *(G-6540)*
Keurig Dr Pepper Inc ....D.... 913 894-6777
Lenexa *(G-5946)*
Keurig Dr Pepper Inc ....D.... 620 223-6166
Fort Scott *(G-1978)*
Pepsi-Cola Btlg of Pittsburg ....E.... 620 231-3800
Pittsburg *(G-9912)*
Pepsi-Cola Metro Btlg Co Inc ....C.... 316 529-9840
Wichita *(G-15280)*
Seneca Wholesale Company Inc ....F.... 785 336-2118
Seneca *(G-10882)*
Shasta Beverages Inc ....D.... 913 888-6777
Lenexa *(G-6127)*

BEVERAGES, WINE & DISTILLED ALCOHOLIC, WHOLESALE: Liquor

Southern Glazers Wine and Sp ....D.... 913 396-4900
Overland Park *(G-9331)*
Standard Beverage Corporation ....F.... 316 838-7707
Wichita *(G-15652)*
Standard Beverage Corporation ....C.... 800 999-8797
Lawrence *(G-5117)*
Standard Beverage Corporation ....E.... 913 888-7200
Lenexa *(G-6152)*

BEVERAGES, WINE & DISTILLED ALCOHOLIC, WHOLESALE: Wine

Handcrafted Wines LLC ....F.... 913 829-4500
Lenexa *(G-5888)*
Lion Nathan Usa Inc ....E.... 913 338-4433
Overland Park *(G-8960)*
Southern Glazers Wine and Sp ....F.... 316 264-1354
Wichita *(G-15624)*

BIBLE CAMPS

Association of Kansas Nebraska ....F.... 785 468-3638
Olsburg *(G-8168)*
Lakeside Camp of The United ....F.... 620 872-2021
Scott City *(G-10819)*

BICYCLE REPAIR SHOP

Midwest Merchandising Inc ....F.... 913 451-1515
Shawnee Mission *(G-11635)*

BICYCLE SHOPS

Midwest Merchandising Inc ....F.... 913 451-1515
Shawnee Mission *(G-11635)*

BILLIARD & POOL PARLORS

Olathe Billiards Inc ....F.... 913 780-5740
Olathe *(G-7928)*
Rekat Recreation Inc ....E.... 785 272-1881
Topeka *(G-13007)*
Side Pockets Inc ....F.... 913 888-7665
Shawnee Mission *(G-11867)*
South Rock Billiard LLC ....F.... 316 651-0444
Wichita *(G-15619)*

BILLIARD EQPT & SPLYS WHOLESALERS

Olathe Billiards Inc ....F.... 913 780-5740
Olathe *(G-7928)*
Pools Plus ....F.... 785 823-7665
Salina *(G-10636)*

BILLING & BOOKKEEPING SVCS

Anesthesia Billing Inc ....E.... 316 281-3700
Newton *(G-7309)*
Berberich Trahan & Co PA ....E.... 785 234-3427
Topeka *(G-12370)*
Bhr Inc ....F.... 913 469-1599
Overland Park *(G-8446)*
Cbiz Med MGT Professionals Inc ....F.... 913 652-1899
Shawnee Mission *(G-11208)*
Cbiz Med MGT Professionals Inc ....E.... 316 686-7327
Wichita *(G-13965)*
In2itive Bus Solutions LLC ....E.... 913 344-7002
Leawood *(G-5435)*
L L C Oasis of Hutchinson ....E.... 620 663-4800
Hutchinson *(G-3353)*
Professionals Business MGT Inc ....F.... 913 888-1444
Overland Park *(G-9188)*

BINDING SVC: Books & Manuals

Administration Kansas Dept ....D.... 785 296-3631
Topeka *(G-12289)*
Adr Inc ....D.... 316 522-5599
Wichita *(G-13616)*
Bindery Express Inc ....G.... 316 944-8163
Wichita *(G-13850)*
Cookbook Publishers Inc ....E.... 913 689-3038
Overland Park *(G-8598)*
Copy Center of Topeka Inc ....E.... 785 233-6677
Topeka *(G-12507)*
Davis Publications Inc ....F.... 785 945-6170
Valley Falls *(G-13362)*
Deluxe Corporation ....C.... 913 888-3801
Lenexa *(G-5810)*
Documart Inc ....F.... 913 649-3800
Shawnee Mission *(G-11312)*
Ejrex Inc ....D.... 620 421-6200
Parsons *(G-9683)*
Fedex Office & Print Svcs Inc ....F.... 316 941-9909
Wichita *(G-14352)*
Gary Bell ....G.... 785 233-6677
Holton *(G-3090)*
Graphic Images Inc ....F.... 316 283-3776
Newton *(G-7352)*
J-Con Reprographics Inc ....F.... 913 859-0800
Lenexa *(G-5927)*
Kelsey Construction Inc ....G.... 913 894-0330
Shawnee Mission *(G-11528)*
Kopco Inc ....D.... 620 879-2117
Caney *(G-671)*
Mennonite Press Inc ....E.... 316 283-3060
Newton *(G-7380)*
Midwestern Litho ....G.... 620 378-2912
Fredonia *(G-2040)*
Navrats Inc ....F.... 620 342-2092
Emporia *(G-1800)*
On Demand Technologies LLC ....F.... 913 438-1800
Overland Park *(G-9102)*
Pittcraft Printing Inc ....E.... 620 231-6200
Pittsburg *(G-9920)*
Print Time Inc ....E.... 913 345-8900
Leawood *(G-5528)*
Printery Inc ....F.... 785 632-5501
Clay Center *(G-877)*
Printing Inc ....E.... 316 265-1201
Wichita *(G-15350)*
Proprint Incorporated ....E.... 785 842-3610
Lawrence *(G-5080)*
Quality Litho Inc ....E.... 913 262-5341
Kansas City *(G-4352)*
Quality Printing Inc ....G.... 620 421-0630
Parsons *(G-9727)*
RGI Publications Inc ....E.... 913 829-8723
Olathe *(G-8030)*
Taylor Printing Inc ....G.... 620 672-3656
Pratt *(G-10159)*
Valley Offset Printing Inc ....E.... 316 755-0061
Valley Center *(G-13360)*

BINGO HALL

Iowa Tribe Kansas & Nebraska ....F.... 785 595-3430
White Cloud *(G-13569)*
Prairie Band Potawatomi Bingo ....E.... 785 966-4000
Mayetta *(G-6917)*

BINOCULARS

Bushnell Inc ....C.... 913 752-3400
Overland Park *(G-8499)*

BINS: Prefabricated, Sheet Metal

Gmls Industries Inc ....G.... 620 983-2136
Peabody *(G-9759)*

BIOFEEDBACK CENTERS

Elm Acres Youth & Family Svcs ....C.... 620 231-9840
Pittsburg *(G-9855)*

BIOLOGICAL PRDTS: Blood Derivatives

Csl Plasma Inc ....E.... 785 749-5750
Lawrence *(G-4819)*
Csl Plasma Inc ....F.... 785 776-9177
Manhattan *(G-6607)*

BIOLOGICAL PRDTS: Exc Diagnostic

Alpha Biosystems Inc ....G.... 316 265-7929
Wichita *(G-13680)*
Bio-Next Inc ....G.... 316 260-1540
Wichita *(G-13851)*
Ceva Biomune ....E.... 913 894-0230
Lenexa *(G-5746)*
Ms Biotec LLC ....E.... 785 456-1388
Wamego *(G-13429)*
Xenotech LLC ....C.... 913 438-7450
Kansas City *(G-4559)*

BIOLOGICAL PRDTS: Vaccines

Biomune Company ....F.... 913 894-0230
Lenexa *(G-5706)*
Biomune Company ....D.... 913 894-0230
Lenexa *(G-5707)*

BIOLOGICAL PRDTS: Veterinary

Aratana Therapeutics Inc ....D 913 353-1000
Leawood *(G-5329)*
Central Biomedia Inc ....E 913 541-0090
Shawnee Mission *(G-11212)*

BIRTH CONTROL CLINIC

Planned Prenthood Great Plains ....E 913 312-5100
Overland Park *(G-9171)*

BLACKSMITH SHOP

Harrods Blacksmith & Welding ....G 620 374-2323
Howard *(G-3134)*

BLINDS : Window

King Industries Inc ....E 785 823-1785
Salina *(G-10575)*
Schammerhorn Inc ....G 316 265-8659
Wichita *(G-15528)*

BLOCKS & BRICKS: Concrete

Ash Grove Cement Company ....C 913 451-8900
Overland Park *(G-8403)*
Big Block Inc ....F 913 927-2135
Lenexa *(G-5702)*
Cemex Materials LLC ....D 913 287-5725
Kansas City *(G-3900)*
Midwest Concrete Materials Inc ....C 785 776-8811
Manhattan *(G-6746)*
Salina Concrete Products Inc ....E 785 827-7281
Salina *(G-10668)*

BLOCKS: Insulating, Concrete

Form Systems Inc ....F 316 522-9285
Haysville *(G-2945)*

BLOCKS: Standard, Concrete Or Cinder

Capitol Concrete Pdts Co Inc ....F 785 233-3271
Topeka *(G-12436)*

BLOOD BANK

Csl Plasma Inc ....D 316 264-6973
Wichita *(G-14137)*
New York Blood Center Inc ....E 785 233-0195
Topeka *(G-12926)*

BLOOD RELATED HEALTH SVCS

Animal Care Center of Top ....F 785 232-2205
Topeka *(G-12329)*
Central Care PA ....E 620 272-2579
Garden City *(G-2123)*
Childrens Hospital Association ....E 913 262-1436
Overland Park *(G-8547)*
Community Memorial Healthcare ....E 785 562-4062
Marysville *(G-6883)*
Emergency Medical Care ....F 913 791-4357
Olathe *(G-7679)*
Forum Health Care ....C 913 648-4980
Shawnee Mission *(G-11377)*
Fresenius Med Care W Wllow LLC ....F 913 491-6341
Overland Park *(G-8741)*
Health Care Stabilization Fund ....F 785 291-3777
Topeka *(G-12671)*
Johnson County Med-Act ....F 913 715-1950
Olathe *(G-7818)*
Kearney Regional Med Ctr LLC ....E 316 682-6770
Wichita *(G-14840)*
Miami County Medical Center ....F 913 791-4940
Olathe *(G-7889)*
Preferred Medical Associates ....F 316 268-8080
Wichita *(G-15327)*
Quality Health Care Inc ....F 316 263-8880
Fredonia *(G-2041)*
Ransom Memorial Hospital Chari ....B 785 229-8200
Ottawa *(G-8309)*

BLOWERS & FANS

Aerospace Systems Cmpnents Inc ....D 316 686-7392
Wichita *(G-13638)*
Airtex Manufacturing Lllp ....C 913 583-3181
De Soto *(G-1192)*
Ruskin Company ....E 620 421-6090
Parsons *(G-9733)*
Vornado Air LLC ....D 316 733-0035
Andover *(G-115)*

BLUEPRINTING SVCS

Copy Co Corporation ....G 785 832-2679
Lawrence *(G-4811)*
Copy Co Corporation ....E 785 823-2679
Salina *(G-10463)*
Marathon Reprographics Inc ....F 816 221-7881
Kansas City *(G-4217)*
Topeka Blue Print & Sup Co Inc ....G 785 232-7209
Topeka *(G-13169)*

BOAT BUILDING & REPAIR

Accessible Technologies Inc ....D 913 338-2886
Lenexa *(G-5621)*
Scs Tech LLC ....G 785 424-4478
Topeka *(G-13045)*

BOAT BUILDING & REPAIRING: Fiberglass

Cobalt Boats LLC ....B 620 325-2653
Neodesha *(G-7236)*

BOAT DEALERS

Shady Creek Sales Inc ....F 316 321-0943
El Dorado *(G-1602)*

BOAT DEALERS: Jet Skis

K & N Motorcycles Corporation ....E 316 945-8221
Valley Center *(G-13346)*

BOAT DEALERS: Motor

Mid Kansas Marine & Rv Inc ....F 620 665-0396
Hutchinson *(G-3376)*

BOAT REPAIR SVCS

Mid Kansas Marine & Rv Inc ....F 620 665-0396
Hutchinson *(G-3376)*
Shady Creek Sales Inc ....F 316 321-0943
El Dorado *(G-1602)*
US Boatworks Inc ....F 913 342-0011
Kansas City *(G-4511)*

BOAT YARD: Boat yards, storage & incidental repair

Clinton Marina Inc ....E 785 749-3222
Lawrence *(G-4793)*
Lake Perry Yacht & Marina LLC ....F 785 783-4927
Perry *(G-9771)*

BOATS: Plastic, Nonrigid

Charloma Inc ....E 620 364-2701
Burlington *(G-626)*

BODIES: Truck & Bus

Diamond Acquisition LLC ....E 620 795-2191
Oswego *(G-8232)*
Frigiquip International Inc ....G 316 321-2400
El Dorado *(G-1563)*
Full Vision Inc ....D 316 283-3344
Newton *(G-7349)*
Kalmar Solutions LLC ....B 785 242-2200
Ottawa *(G-8279)*
Skymark Refuelers LLC ....D 913 653-8100
Kansas City *(G-4424)*
Vernies Trux-N-Equip Inc ....G 785 625-5087
Hays *(G-2923)*

BODY PARTS: Automobile, Stamped Metal

Alan Grove Components Inc ....G 913 837-4368
Louisburg *(G-6437)*
Amphenol Adronics Inc ....D 785 625-3000
Hays *(G-2747)*
Rotor Quality LLC ....G 316 425-0418
Wichita *(G-15486)*
Taylormade Proformance ....G 620 326-3537
Wellington *(G-13535)*

BOILER & HEATING REPAIR SVCS

R & R Street Plbg Htg & Elec ....F 785 524-4551
Lincoln *(G-6385)*

BOILER REPAIR SHOP

Lba Air Cndtoning Htg Plbg Inc ....E 816 454-5515
Shawnee Mission *(G-11551)*
MSI ....E 316 262-2021
Wichita *(G-15137)*

BOILERS & BOILER SHOP WORK

Midwest Combustn Solutions Inc ....G 316 425-0929
Wichita *(G-15090)*
Superior Holding Inc ....F 620 662-6693
Hutchinson *(G-3458)*

BOLTS: Metal

Gaskell Machine & Metal Inc ....F 785 486-2674
Horton *(G-3123)*

BOND & MORTGAGE COMPANIES

Wells Fargo Home Mortgage Inc ....E 913 319-7900
Shawnee Mission *(G-12003)*

BOND DEALERS & BROKERS

First Horizon Bank ....F 913 339-5400
Shawnee Mission *(G-11371)*
Kansas Development Fin Auth ....F 785 357-4445
Topeka *(G-12773)*

BONDS, RAIL: Electric, Propulsion & Signal Circuit Uses

Amsted Rail Company Inc ....F 800 621-8442
Atchison *(G-205)*

BONDSPERSON

A1 Bonding ....D 785 539-3950
Manhattan *(G-6528)*

BOOK STORES

Claflin Books & Copies ....F 785 776-3771
Manhattan *(G-6591)*
Hillcrest Covenant Church ....E 913 901-2300
Shawnee Mission *(G-11433)*

BOOK STORES: College

K-State Union Corporation ....C 785 532-6575
Manhattan *(G-6671)*
University Kansas Mem Corp ....D 785 864-4651
Lawrence *(G-5156)*

BOOK STORES: Religious

Gospel Publishers ....G 620 345-2532
Moundridge *(G-7183)*
Mennonite Weekly Review Inc ....G 316 283-3670
Newton *(G-7381)*

BOOKS, WHOLESALE

Design Analysis and RES Corp ....F 785 832-0434
Lawrence *(G-4833)*
Scholastic Book Fairs Inc ....F 913 599-5700
Shawnee Mission *(G-11836)*
Western International Inc ....F 785 856-1840
Lawrence *(G-5182)*

BOTANICAL GARDENS

Botanica Inc ....F 316 264-0448
Wichita *(G-13872)*
Overland Park Arboretm & Btncl ....E 913 685-3604
Bucyrus *(G-606)*
Pine Howard Grdn Ctr & Grnhse ....E 785 749-0302
Lawrence *(G-5064)*

BOTTLE CAPS & RESEALERS: Plastic

Berry Global Inc ....C 800 777-3080
Lawrence *(G-4754)*
Reliable Caps LLC ....E 913 764-2277
Olathe *(G-8024)*

BOTTLED GAS DEALERS: Butane

Geo Bit Exploration Inc ....F 940 888-3134
Council Grove *(G-1168)*

BOTTLED GAS DEALERS: Liquefied Petro, Dlvrd To Customers

Consumer Oil Company Inc ....F....... 785 988-4459
Bendena *(G-511)*
Kanza Cooperative Association ....E....... 316 444-2141
Andale *(G-78)*
Propane Central ....F....... 785 762-5160
Junction City *(G-3742)*

BOTTLED GAS DEALERS: Propane

Garden City Co-Op Inc ....F....... 620 276-8903
Garden City *(G-2171)*
L C McClain Inc ....F....... 785 584-6151
Rossville *(G-10253)*
Nusser Oil Company Inc ....E....... 620 697-4624
Elkhart *(G-1625)*
Rolling Hills Electric Coop ....F....... 785 534-1601
Beloit *(G-501)*

BOTTLED WATER DELIVERY

John G Levin ....E....... 785 234-5551
Topeka *(G-12746)*
Z Bottling Corp ....G....... 620 872-0100
Scott City *(G-10837)*

BOTTLES: Plastic

Container Services Inc ....D....... 620 947-2664
Hillsboro *(G-3046)*
Pepsi-Cola Btlg of Pittsburg ....E....... 620 231-3800
Pittsburg *(G-9912)*

BOUTIQUE STORES

Perfect Touch Inc ....F....... 316 522-9205
Wichita *(G-15281)*

BOWLING CENTERS

Cheney Lanes Inc ....F....... 316 542-3126
Cheney *(G-790)*
Hutchinson Vending Company ....F....... 620 662-6474
Hutchinson *(G-3328)*
Little Apple Lanes ....F....... 785 539-0371
Manhattan *(G-6715)*
Mission Bowl N Olathe ....E....... 913 782-0279
Olathe *(G-7905)*
Park Hill Lanes ....F....... 620 842-5571
Anthony *(G-131)*

BOWLING EQPT & SPLY STORES

Lynco Rec Inc ....F....... 620 231-2222
Pittsburg *(G-9896)*
Rekat Recreation Inc ....E....... 785 272-1881
Topeka *(G-13007)*

BOWLING EQPT & SPLYS

Jayhawk Bowling Sup & Eqp Inc ....F....... 785 842-3237
Lawrence *(G-4919)*

BOXES & CRATES: Rectangular, Wood

Cratetech Incorporated ....E....... 316 682-6223
Wichita *(G-14126)*
United Manufacturing Inc ....E....... 913 780-0056
New Century *(G-7302)*

BOXES & SHOOK: Nailed Wood

Cratetech Incorporated ....E....... 316 682-6223
Wichita *(G-14126)*
Industrial Crating Inc ....E....... 620 449-2003
Saint Paul *(G-10381)*
United Manufacturing Inc ....E....... 913 780-0056
New Century *(G-7302)*

BOXES: Corrugated

American Box & Tape Co ....E....... 913 384-0992
Shawnee *(G-10909)*
International Paper Company ....D....... 620 272-8318
Garden City *(G-2204)*
Pratt Industries USA Inc ....D....... 316 838-0851
Wichita *(G-15323)*
Westrock Cp LLC ....C....... 816 746-0403
Kansas City *(G-4540)*

BOXES: Paperboard, Folding

Russell Stover Chocolates LLC ....E....... 785 263-0463
Abilene *(G-52)*

BOXES: Paperboard, Set-Up

Ray Products Inc ....E....... 620 421-1510
Parsons *(G-9728)*

BOYS' TOWNS

Lif Inc ....F....... 316 260-6092
Wichita *(G-14960)*

BRASS & BRONZE PRDTS: Die-casted

Dempsey Inc ....G....... 913 371-3107
Kansas City *(G-3968)*
National Almnm-Brass Fndry Inc ....E....... 816 833-4500
Leawood *(G-5498)*

BRASS GOODS, WHOLESALE

Amsted Rail Company Inc ....F....... 913 299-2223
Kansas City *(G-3808)*
Norder Supply Inc ....E....... 620 805-5972
Garden City *(G-2243)*

BRIC-A-BRAC

D J Inc ....F....... 785 667-4651
Assaria *(G-200)*

BRICK, STONE & RELATED PRDTS WHOLESALERS

Apac-Kansas Inc ....E....... 785 625-3459
Hutchinson *(G-3201)*
J T Lardner Cut Stone Inc ....F....... 785 234-8634
Topeka *(G-12732)*
Quikrete Companies Inc ....E....... 913 441-6525
Kansas City *(G-4355)*
Salina Concrete Products Inc ....E....... 785 827-7281
Salina *(G-10668)*
Stone Sand Co Inc ....E....... 620 793-7864
Great Bend *(G-2639)*

BRICKS & BLOCKS: Structural

General Finance Incorporated ....D....... 785 243-1284
Concordia *(G-1115)*

BRICKS : Ceramic Glazed, Clay

Paint Glaze & Fire ....G....... 913 661-2529
Overland Park *(G-9137)*

BRICKS: Clay

Kansas Brick and Tile Co Inc ....E....... 620 653-2157
Hoisington *(G-3068)*

BRIDAL SHOPS

Green Hills Inc ....F....... 316 686-7673
Wichita *(G-14509)*
Mias Bridal & Tailoring LLC ....F....... 913 764-9114
Olathe *(G-7890)*
Sekan Printing Company Inc ....E....... 620 223-5190
Fort Scott *(G-2003)*

BROADCASTING & COMMS EQPT: Rcvr-Transmitter Unt, Transceiver

Schell Electronics Inc ....G....... 620 431-2350
Chanute *(G-761)*

BROADCASTING STATIONS, RADIO: Educational

Training & Educational Service ....E....... 913 498-1914
Overland Park *(G-9423)*

BROADCASTING STATIONS, RADIO: Music Format

Ad Astra Per Aspera Broadcasti ....E....... 620 665-5758
Hutchinson *(G-3190)*
Connoisseur Media LLC ....F....... 316 558-8800
Wichita *(G-14089)*
Entercom Communications Corp ....D....... 316 685-2121
Wichita *(G-14291)*
Great Plains Christian Radio ....F....... 620 873-2991
Meade *(G-7049)*
Ingstad Broadcasting Inc ....E....... 620 276-2366
Garden City *(G-2203)*
Taylor Communications Inc ....E....... 785 632-5661
Clay Center *(G-883)*
Union Broadcasting Inc ....E....... 913 344-1500
Shawnee Mission *(G-11961)*
Zimmer Radio Group ....E....... 785 843-1320
Lawrence *(G-5194)*

BROADCASTING STATIONS, RADIO: News

K N Z A Inc ....F....... 785 547-3461
Hiawatha *(G-3012)*
Mid-America AG Network Inc ....E....... 316 721-8484
Wichita *(G-15074)*

BROADCASTING STATIONS, RADIO: Religious Music

Bott Radio Network Inc ....D....... 913 642-7770
Overland Park *(G-8475)*

BROKERS & DEALERS: Mortgages, Buying & Selling

Members Mortgage Services LLC ....E....... 620 665-7713
Hutchinson *(G-3373)*

BROKERS & DEALERS: Securities

Advisors Asset Management Inc ....F....... 316 858-1766
Wichita *(G-13631)*
Bats Trading Inc ....D....... 913 815-7000
Lenexa *(G-5690)*
Client One Securities LLC ....F....... 913 814-6097
Leawood *(G-5354)*
Cornerstone Financial LLC ....F....... 316 630-0670
Wichita *(G-14102)*
Hokanson Lehman & Stevens ....F....... 913 338-2525
Leawood *(G-5430)*
Securities Commissioner Kansas ....E....... 785 296-3307
Topeka *(G-13050)*
Stifel Nicolaus & Company Inc ....F....... 785 271-1300
Topeka *(G-13099)*
UBS Financial Services Inc ....E....... 913 345-3200
Shawnee Mission *(G-11954)*
W & R Corporate LLC ....E....... 913 236-2000
Overland Park *(G-9472)*
Waddell & Reed Fincl Svcs Inc ....B....... 913 236-2000
Overland Park *(G-9478)*
Wells Fargo Clearing Svcs LLC ....E....... 785 271-2492
Topeka *(G-13238)*

BROKERS & DEALERS: Security

CU Capital Mkt Solutions LLC ....F....... 913 402-2627
Overland Park *(G-8622)*
Kansas City Brokerage Inc ....E....... 913 384-4994
Overland Park *(G-8890)*
Merrill Lynch Pierce Fenner ....D....... 913 906-5200
Leawood *(G-5475)*
Morgan Stanley ....F....... 913 402-5200
Leawood *(G-5491)*
Ofg Financial Services Inc ....F....... 785 233-4071
Topeka *(G-12941)*
Riedl First Securities of Kans ....F....... 316 265-9341
Wichita *(G-15463)*
Security Benefit Group Inc ....B....... 785 438-3000
Topeka *(G-13053)*
Waddell & Reed Financial Inc ....D....... 913 236-2000
Overland Park *(G-9477)*
Wells Fargo Clearing Svcs LLC ....E....... 316 634-6690
Wichita *(G-15947)*

BROKERS & DEALERS: Stock

Cooper Malone McClain Inc ....E....... 316 685-5777
Wichita *(G-14098)*
Merrill Lynch Pierce Fenner ....E....... 316 631-3500
Wichita *(G-15047)*
Perkins Smart & Boyd Inc ....F....... 800 344-1621
Fairway *(G-1916)*
Stifel Nicolaus & Company Inc ....F....... 913 345-4200
Overland Park *(G-9362)*
Wells Fargo Clearing Svcs LLC ....D....... 913 267-7200
Shawnee Mission *(G-12002)*
Wells Fargo Clearing Svcs LLC ....D....... 913 402-5100
Overland Park *(G-9489)*

BROKERS' SVCS

Citigroup Global Markets Inc .... E 316 630-4400
Wichita *(G-14022)*
Colt Tech LLC .... G 913 839-8198
Olathe *(G-7600)*
Sunbelt Business Brokers .... F 913 383-2671
Overland Park *(G-9373)*

BROKERS, MARINE TRANSPORTATION

AG Source Inc .... F 785 841-1315
Lawrence *(G-4724)*
Central Trnsp Svcs Inc .... D 316 263-3333
Wichita *(G-13990)*
Fli Inc .... E 913 851-2247
Overland Park *(G-8729)*
Great Plains Logistics Inc .... D 785 823-2261
Salina *(G-10517)*
Headhaulcom LLC .... E 913 905-5189
Overland Park *(G-8802)*
Jasper Investments Inc .... F 913 599-0899
Lenexa *(G-5928)*
Traffic Tech Inc .... C 888 592-2009
Spring Hill *(G-12101)*

BROKERS: Business

Humbert Envelope Machinery .... F 785 845-6085
Topeka *(G-12706)*
J P Weigand and Sons Inc .... E 316 292-3991
Wichita *(G-14740)*
Kingman Cnty Ecnmic Dev Cncil .... A 620 532-3694
Kingman *(G-4598)*
Sunbelt Business Advisors .... E 316 684-9040
Wichita *(G-15683)*

BROKERS: Commodity Contracts

Baxter Cmmdts-Dntity Grins LLC .... F 620 492-4040
Johnson *(G-3651)*
Schwieterman Inc .... F 620 275-4100
Garden City *(G-2277)*
Southern Plains Co-Op At Lewis .... E 620 324-5536
Lewis *(G-6270)*
Wells Fargo Clearing Svcs LLC .... F 620 665-0659
Hutchinson *(G-3484)*

BROKERS: Contract Basis

Textron Aviation Defense LLC .... E 316 676-2508
Wichita *(G-15733)*

BROKERS: Food

Acosta Inc .... D 913 227-1000
Shawnee Mission *(G-11068)*
Acosta Sales Co Inc .... E 316 733-0248
Wichita *(G-13607)*
Advantage Sales & Mktg LLC .... F 913 696-1700
Overland Park *(G-8351)*
Crossmark Inc .... E 913 338-1133
Lenexa *(G-5794)*
CSC Gold Inc .... F 913 664-8100
Shawnee Mission *(G-11284)*
Emporia Wholesale Coffee Co .... C 620 343-7000
Emporia *(G-1747)*
Food Service Specialists Inc .... F 913 648-6611
Shawnee Mission *(G-11376)*
Food Trends Inc .... G 913 383-3600
Overland Park *(G-8732)*
Key Impact Sales & Systems Inc .... E 913 648-6611
Olathe *(G-7835)*
Marrones Inc .... E 620 231-6610
Pittsburg *(G-9897)*
Mueller-Yurgae Associates Inc .... F 913 362-7777
Overland Park *(G-9062)*
Reese Group Inc .... F 913 383-8260
Merriam *(G-7102)*
Regan Marketing Inc .... F 816 531-5111
Lenexa *(G-6097)*
Rheuark FSI Sales Inc .... F 913 432-9500
Shawnee Mission *(G-11795)*
Schraad & Associates .... F 913 661-2404
Overland Park *(G-9283)*
Trans-Pak Inc .... F 620 275-1758
Garden City *(G-2300)*
US Foods Inc .... C 316 942-9679
Wichita *(G-15863)*
US Foods Inc .... C 913 894-6161
Lenexa *(G-6205)*

BROKERS: Loan

Affinity Mortgage LLC .... F 913 469-0777
Lenexa *(G-5637)*
Bank Commssnr Kansas Offce .... D 785 296-2266
Topeka *(G-12363)*
Communityamerica Credit Union .... C 913 905-7000
Lenexa *(G-5778)*
Curo Group Holdings Corp .... F 316 772-3801
Wichita *(G-14142)*
Meritrust Credit Union .... D 316 683-1199
Wichita *(G-15042)*
Meritrust Credit Union .... F 316 219-7614
Derby *(G-1261)*
Meritrust Credit Union .... F 316 761-4645
Wichita *(G-15044)*
Meritrust Credit Union .... F 316 761-4645
Wichita *(G-15045)*
Metcalf Bank .... F 913 685-3801
Shawnee Mission *(G-11619)*
Metcalf Bank .... F 913 782-6522
Olathe *(G-7885)*
Midland National Bank .... F 316 283-1700
Newton *(G-7386)*
Panhandle Federal Credit Union .... F 620 326-2285
Wellington *(G-13522)*
Quantum Credit Union .... F 316 263-5756
Wichita *(G-15389)*
Wichita Inn Suites Inc .... E 316 685-2233
Wichita *(G-16008)*

BROKERS: Mortgage, Arranging For Loans

Advantage Commercial Lending .... F 316 215-0115
Sedgwick *(G-10849)*
Agape Mortgage Partners Corp .... F 913 871-7377
Louisburg *(G-6436)*
Baystone Financial Group .... F 785 587-4050
Manhattan *(G-6554)*
Cobank Acb .... F 316 290-2000
Wichita *(G-14048)*
Himalaya Mortgage Inc .... F 913 649-9700
Shawnee Mission *(G-11434)*
Mission Mortgage LLC .... F 913 469-1999
Overland Park *(G-9042)*
Plaza Mortgage .... F 913 671-1865
Shawnee Mission *(G-11739)*
Regent Financial Group Inc .... F 316 462-1341
Wichita *(G-15436)*
Sunbelt Business Brokers .... F 913 383-2671
Overland Park *(G-9373)*
Zillow Group Inc .... E 913 491-4299
Leawood *(G-5604)*
Zillow Home Loans LLC .... E 913 491-4299
Overland Park *(G-9527)*

BROKERS: Note

Qts Finance Corporation .... F 913 814-9988
Overland Park *(G-9208)*

BROKERS: Printing

Barker Printing and Copy Svcs .... G 785 233-5533
Topeka *(G-12365)*
Print Source Direct LLC .... E 620 947-5702
Hillsboro *(G-3056)*

BROKERS: Security

David M King & Associates .... F 785 841-9517
Lawrence *(G-4827)*
David M King & Associates .... F 319 377-4636
Hays *(G-2782)*
Great Plains Financial Group .... F 785 843-7070
Lawrence *(G-4882)*
Jack M Schwartz .... F 785 823-3035
Salina *(G-10551)*
Raymond James Fincl Svcs Inc .... F 785 383-1893
Lawrence *(G-5088)*
Raymond James Fincl Svcs Inc .... F 620 442-1198
Arkansas City *(G-172)*
Raymond James Fincl Svcs Inc .... E 785 537-0366
Manhattan *(G-6787)*
Rbc Capital Markets LLC .... F 913 451-3500
Leawood *(G-5533)*
Security Benefit Life Insur Co .... B 785 438-3000
Topeka *(G-13054)*
Stifel Nicolaus & Company Inc .... F 316 264-6321
Wichita *(G-15672)*
UBS Securities LLC .... E 913 345-3200
Leawood *(G-5588)*

Wells Fargo Clearing Svcs LLC .... F 785 825-4636
Salina *(G-10767)*
Wells Fargo Clearing Svcs LLC .... F 620 665-0659
Hutchinson *(G-3484)*

BRONZE FOUNDRY, NEC

Smith Monuments Inc .... G 785 425-6762
Stockton *(G-12187)*

BROOMS & BRUSHES: Household Or Indl

United Rotary Brush Corp .... D 913 888-8450
Lenexa *(G-6203)*
West Coast Equipment Inc .... F 623 842-0978
Lenexa *(G-6226)*

BROOMS & BRUSHES: Street Sweeping, Hand Or Machine

Mobile Products Inc .... C 903 759-0610
Hutchinson *(G-3384)*

BUFFING FOR THE TRADE

Cardinal Buffing Co Inc .... G 316 263-8475
Wichita *(G-13943)*

BUILDING & OFFICE CLEANING SVCS

Alliance Jantr Advisors Inc .... F 913 815-8807
Olathe *(G-7520)*
American Superclean .... F 913 815-3257
Olathe *(G-7528)*
Lenere LLC .... F 785 320-0208
Saint Marys *(G-10371)*
Resource Service Solutions LLC .... E 913 338-5050
Lenexa *(G-6107)*
Valley Center City Yard .... F 316 755-7320
Valley Center *(G-13358)*

BUILDING & STRUCTURAL WOOD MBRS: Timbers, Struct, Lam Lumber

International Forest Pdts LLC .... D 913 451-6945
Overland Park *(G-8857)*

BUILDING & STRUCTURAL WOOD MEMBERS

Weisbender Contracting Inc .... G 785 776-5034
Manhattan *(G-6849)*

BUILDING BOARD: Gypsum

New Ngc Inc .... C 620 886-5613
Medicine Lodge *(G-7069)*

BUILDING CLEANING & MAINTENANCE SVCS

Alert Enterprises Inc .... F 785 862-9800
Topeka *(G-12304)*
Best Corporation Inc .... E 316 687-1895
El Dorado *(G-1536)*
Best Corporation Inc .... E 316 687-1895
Wichita *(G-13837)*
Burkhart Enterprises Inc .... E 620 662-8678
Hutchinson *(G-3226)*
Butler & Mcllvain Inc .... F 316 684-6700
Wichita *(G-13921)*
C & P Enterprises Inc .... E 785 628-6712
Hays *(G-2762)*
Central Plains Maintenance .... D 316 945-4774
Wichita *(G-13983)*
Chavez Restoration & Cleaning .... F 785 232-3779
Topeka *(G-12463)*
Circle Enterprises Inc .... F 316 943-9834
Wichita *(G-14021)*
City of Halstead .... E 316 835-3492
Halstead *(G-2698)*
City of Leavenworth .... F 913 684-1560
Leavenworth *(G-5219)*
City Wide Franchise Co Inc .... E 913 888-5700
Lenexa *(G-5756)*
Cleansweep Janitorial Inc .... F 785 856-8617
Lawrence *(G-4792)*
Consociates Group LLC .... F 316 321-7500
El Dorado *(G-1549)*
Contract Services Inc .... D 785 239-9069
Fort Riley *(G-1946)*

Coverall North America Inc....F....913 888-5009
Leawood *(G-5362)*
D & D Roland Enterprises Llc....E....316 942-6474
Wichita *(G-14154)*
Dalan Inc....E....913 384-5662
Overland Park *(G-8631)*
DCS Sanitation Management Inc....C....620 624-5533
Liberal *(G-6302)*
Development Inc....F....913 651-9717
Leavenworth *(G-5233)*
Franchise Development Inc....E....620 662-3283
Hutchinson *(G-3291)*
Givens Cleaning Contractors....F....316 265-1315
Wichita *(G-14468)*
Hospitality Management LLC....E....316 262-0000
Wichita *(G-14639)*
Icg Inc....E....913 461-8759
Leawood *(G-5433)*
Jt Maintenance Inc....F....913 642-5656
Overland Park *(G-8881)*
Lulu Mimi Hsclners Extrrdnaire....F....913 649-6022
Shawnee Mission *(G-11582)*
Maid Services Inc....E....785 537-6243
Manhattan *(G-6717)*
Mid Central Contract Svcs Inc....E....620 231-1166
Pittsburg *(G-9903)*
Olathe Unified School Dst 233....D....913 780-7011
Olathe *(G-7951)*
Piat Inc....F....913 782-4693
Olathe *(G-7986)*
S & H Inc....F....620 251-4422
Coffeyville *(G-974)*
Sage Restoration LLC....F....913 905-0500
Overland Park *(G-9271)*
Sentinel Real Estate Corp....F....316 265-9471
Wichita *(G-15562)*
ServiceMaster Company LLC....F....620 260-9994
Garden City *(G-2279)*
ServiceMaster Consumer Service....F....316 283-5404
Newton *(G-7416)*
ServiceMaster North Centl Kans....F....785 243-1965
Concordia *(G-1130)*
Servimster Prof Rstoration Clg....F....785 832-0055
Bonner Springs *(G-572)*
Thorman Enterprises LLC....F....913 772-1818
Leavenworth *(G-5297)*
Trujillo Jan & Crpt Clg Svc....F....316 263-8204
Wichita *(G-15813)*
Wyandtte Cnty Unfied Gvernment....C....913 281-3300
Kansas City *(G-4555)*
Xxtra Clean....F....785 210-5255
Junction City *(G-3770)*

BUILDING COMPONENTS: Structural Steel

Advantage Building Systems LLC....F....785 233-1393
Topeka *(G-12296)*
Doherty Steel Inc....C....913 557-9200
Paola *(G-9553)*
Lippert Components Inc....G....785 282-6366
Smith Center *(G-12037)*
MAI Sky Systems Inc....G....785 825-9151
Salina *(G-10588)*
Mdf Industries Inc....F....785 827-4450
Salina *(G-10599)*
Metal Pros LLC....E....316 942-2238
Wichita *(G-15054)*
Midland Steel Company....D....785 989-4442
Wathena *(G-13476)*
Midwest Steel Fab LLC....F....316 832-9669
Wichita *(G-15103)*
Ptmw Inc....C....785 232-7792
Topeka *(G-12994)*
Schuff Steel Company....F....913 677-2485
Overland Park *(G-9284)*
Unique Metal Fabrication Inc....E....620 232-3060
Pittsburg *(G-9949)*
Viking Industries Inc....F....620 795-2143
Oswego *(G-8238)*

BUILDING EXTERIOR CLEANING SVCS

Rigdon Inc....F....913 322-9274
Overland Park *(G-9242)*

BUILDING INSPECTION SVCS

Barrier Compliance Svcs LLC....F....913 905-2695
Overland Park *(G-8434)*
City Goodland Inspection Dept....D....785 890-4500
Goodland *(G-2464)*

City of Lawrence....F....785 832-7700
Lawrence *(G-4789)*

BUILDING MAINTENANCE SVCS, EXC REPAIRS

B A Barnes Electric Inc....E....913 764-4455
Olathe *(G-7544)*
Best Value Services LLC....D....316 440-1048
Wichita *(G-13839)*
Clean Tech Inc....C....316 729-8100
Wichita *(G-14040)*
LMS Company LLC....F....913 648-4123
Shawnee Mission *(G-11576)*

BUILDING PRDTS & MATERIALS DEALERS

Champion Window Co Kans Cy Inc....E....913 541-8282
Lenexa *(G-5751)*
Griffith Lumber Company Inc....E....785 776-4104
Manhattan *(G-6647)*
Healy Cooperative Elevator Co....E....620 398-2211
Healy *(G-2966)*
Juniper Payments LLC....E....316 267-3200
Wichita *(G-14778)*
Kansas City Millwork Company....E....913 768-0068
Olathe *(G-7825)*
Kansas City Millwork Company....E....913 768-0068
Olathe *(G-7826)*
Quality Homes Inc....E....402 248-6218
Summerfield *(G-12216)*
Rew Materials Inc....D....913 236-4909
Kansas City *(G-4374)*
Salina Concrete Products Inc....E....785 827-7281
Salina *(G-10668)*
Suther Building Supply Inc....F....785 336-2255
Seneca *(G-10883)*
T H Rogers Lumber Company....F....620 231-0900
Pittsburg *(G-9944)*
Victor L Phillips Company....F....316 854-1118
Wichita *(G-15906)*

BUILDING PRDTS: Concrete

Vogts-Parga Construction LLC....F....316 284-2801
Newton *(G-7425)*

BUILDINGS & COMPONENTS: Prefabricated Metal

Ciac LLC....G....316 262-0953
Wichita *(G-14020)*
Jahnke & Sons Construction Inc....F....800 351-2525
Overland Park *(G-8870)*

BUILDINGS: Farm & Utility

Morton Buildings Inc....E....785 364-4177
Holton *(G-3106)*

BUILDINGS: Portable

Mobile Mini Inc....F....316 838-2663
Park City *(G-9636)*
Morton Buildings Inc....D....620 221-4180
Winfield *(G-16159)*
Morton Buildings Inc....F....620 221-3265
Winfield *(G-16160)*

BUILDINGS: Prefabricated, Metal

Gmls Industries Inc....G....620 983-2136
Peabody *(G-9759)*

BUILDINGS: Prefabricated, Wood

Advanced Systems Homes Inc....E....620 431-3320
Chanute *(G-702)*
Clayton Homes Inc....C....785 434-4617
Plainville *(G-9981)*
Tuff Shed Inc....F....913 541-8833
Shawnee Mission *(G-11947)*
Wardcraft Homes Inc....D....785 632-5664
Clay Center *(G-886)*

BURGLAR ALARM MAINTENANCE & MONITORING SVCS

ADT LLC....A....785 856-5500
Lawrence *(G-4720)*
ADT LLC....E....316 858-4300
Wichita *(G-13618)*

ADT Security Corporation....E....612 721-3690
Wichita *(G-13619)*
Johnson Cntrls SEC Sltions LLC....E....316 634-1792
Wichita *(G-14765)*
Optiv Security Inc....F....816 421-6611
Overland Park *(G-9110)*
Safelink Security Systems Inc....E....913 338-3888
Tonganoxie *(G-12269)*

BURGLARY PROTECTION SVCS

WSC Services Inc....F....913 660-0454
Prairie Village *(G-10087)*

BURIAL VAULTS: Concrete Or Precast Terrazzo

Concrete Vaults Inc....F....316 283-3790
Newton *(G-7333)*
Concrete Vaults Inc....G....620 792-6687
Great Bend *(G-2546)*
Fairlawn Burial Park Assn....F....620 662-3431
Hutchinson *(G-3282)*
Los Primos Inc....G....785 527-5535
Belleville *(G-460)*
Mound City Vault Co Inc....G....913 795-2529
Mound City *(G-7173)*
Suhor Industries Inc....A....620 421-4434
Overland Park *(G-9371)*
Wilbert Funeral Services Inc....E....316 832-1114
Wichita *(G-16046)*
Wilbert Funeral Services Inc....B....913 345-2120
Overland Park *(G-9494)*

BURIAL VAULTS: Stone

Melissa Wilbert....G....316 361-2787
Wichita *(G-15037)*

BURNERS: Gas-Oil, Combination

Power Flame Incorporated....C....620 421-0480
Parsons *(G-9724)*

BUS CHARTER SVC: Local

Agenda Usa Inc....E....913 268-4466
Shawnee Mission *(G-11084)*
Just For Kids Express....F....785 238-8555
Junction City *(G-3708)*
Mercer Bus Service....F....785 836-7174
Carbondale *(G-684)*
National Express LLC....E....913 837-4470
Louisburg *(G-6460)*
National Express LLC....E....620 662-1299
Hutchinson *(G-3388)*
National Express LLC....F....620 326-3318
Wellington *(G-13519)*

BUS CHARTER SVC: Long-Distance

Busco Inc....F....816 453-8727
Manhattan *(G-6573)*
Durham School Services L P....E....620 331-7088
Independence *(G-3512)*
First Student Inc....E....620 251-8441
Coffeyville *(G-938)*
Just For Kids Express....F....785 238-8555
Junction City *(G-3708)*
Ottawa Bus Service Inc....E....913 829-6644
Olathe *(G-7966)*
Overland Charters Inc....E....316 652-9463
Wichita *(G-15241)*
Prestige Trnsp Systems....E....316 263-9141
Wichita *(G-15339)*

BUS TERMINALS & SVC FACILITIES

Reload Express Inc....F....620 231-2230
Pittsburg *(G-9926)*

BUSES: Wholesalers

Kansas Truck Equipment Co Inc....E....316 722-4291
Wichita *(G-14828)*
Midwest Bus Sales Inc....E....913 422-1000
Bonner Springs *(G-562)*

BUSINESS ACTIVITIES: Non-Commercial Site

A Plus Construction LLC....E....620 212-4029
Saint Paul *(G-10378)*

A+ Decor LLC ....F 816 699-6817
Pittsburg (G-9803)
African Americans Renewing Int ....E 316 312-0183
Wichita (G-13642)
American Comm & Residentl Svcs ....F 316 633-5866
Wichita (G-13690)
Andrews Asphalt & Cnstr Inc ....G 785 232-0188
Topeka (G-12326)
Black & Veatch - Er JV ....A 913 458-6650
Overland Park (G-8453)
Brock Maggard ....F 417 793-7790
Baxter Springs (G-401)
Carson Mobile HM Pk Sewer Dst ....D 785 537-6330
Manhattan (G-6577)
Commercial Rofg Spcialists LLC ....F 316 304-1423
Wichita (G-14072)
Container Services Inc ....D 620 947-2664
Hillsboro (G-3046)
CPM Technologies Inc ....F 256 777-9869
Wichita (G-14124)
EKA Consulting LLC ....F 913 244-2980
Shawnee (G-10946)
Empire Construction Group LLC ....F 913 375-8886
Shawnee Mission (G-11335)
EMR-Pcg Construction Group ....E 406 249-7730
Lawrence (G-4853)
Epic Insulation Inc ....F 316 500-1650
Goddard (G-2438)
Fcg Inc ....F 620 545-8300
Clearwater (G-892)
Fischer Well Service Inc ....G 785 628-3837
Hays (G-2808)
Flic Luminaries LLC ....F 888 550-3542
Wichita (G-14387)
Grace Agapes Inc ....E 913 837-5885
Louisburg (G-6450)
Gross PHD Judith M S ....F 913 645-2437
Kansas City (G-4056)
Holy Family Medical Inc ....E 316 682-9900
Wichita (G-14626)
Icg Inc ....E 913 461-8759
Leawood (G-5433)
Insysiv LLC ....F 816 694-9397
Kansas City (G-4102)
J-Six Farms LLC ....F 785 336-2148
Seneca (G-10869)
Jies LLC ....F 620 668-5585
Copeland (G-1149)
Kaliaperumal Mamalay ....G 816 210-1248
Overland Park (G-8885)
Lee Shafer Ricky ....E 620 252-9126
Coffeyville (G-955)
Little Soldier ....F 785 845-1987
Mayetta (G-6915)
Motivated RE Solutions LLC ....D 785 842-3530
Lawrence (G-5033)
Patriot Abatement Services LLC ....F 913 397-6181
Olathe (G-7975)
Petropower LLC ....G 316 361-0222
Wichita (G-15288)
Pharmacy Dist Partners LLC ....F 903 357-3391
Mission Hills (G-7147)
Presig Holdings LLC ....F 913 706-1315
Overland Park (G-9184)
Primary Care Landscape Inc ....F 913 768-8880
Olathe (G-8006)
Pt Kansas LLC ....E 620 791-7082
Great Bend (G-2626)
Richman Helstrom Trucking Inc ....F 785 478-3186
Topeka (G-13014)
Robert Denton ....F 316 691-7046
Wichita (G-15473)
Roberts Group Inc ....G 913 381-3930
Overland Park (G-9252)
Saline Valley Farm Inc ....F 785 524-4562
Lincoln (G-6388)
Shadmea Ministries Inc ....E 912 332-0563
Junction City (G-3752)
Sooner Oil LLC ....F 785 340-5602
Junction City (G-3757)
Structural Integrity Group LLC ....E 316 633-9403
Wichita (G-15677)
Superior Masonry & Stucco LLC ....E 316 928-2365
Wichita (G-15695)
Teracrunch LLC ....F 214 405-7158
Leawood (G-5572)
Tk & Company Inc of Kansas ....F 785 472-3226
Ellsworth (G-1682)
University Kansas Mem Corp ....D 785 864-4651
Lawrence (G-5156)
USA Missions Church of God ....E 620 345-2532
Moundridge (G-7201)
Versasport of Kansas Inc ....E 316 393-0487
Wichita (G-15876)
Western Feed Mills Inc ....E 620 758-2283
Cedar Vale (G-695)
Women In Trnstion Together Inc ....F 785 424-7516
Lawrence (G-5189)

BUSINESS FORMS WHOLESALERS

Ennis Inc ....D 620 223-6500
Fort Scott (G-1965)
Ennis Business Forms of Kansas ....D 620 223-6500
Fort Scott (G-1966)
Kalos Inc ....E 785 232-3606
Topeka (G-12752)
Midwest Single Source Inc ....E 316 267-6333
Wichita (G-15102)
Navrats Inc ....F 620 342-2092
Emporia (G-1800)
Professional Bank Forms ....G 620 455-2205
Oxford (G-9534)

BUSINESS FORMS: Printed, Continuous

Calibrated Forms ....C 620 429-1120
Columbus (G-1064)
General Dynamics Info Tech Inc ....E 785 832-0207
Lawrence (G-4871)

BUSINESS FORMS: Printed, Manifold

Ace Forms of Kansas Inc ....D 620 232-9290
Pittsburg (G-9805)
Ennis Inc ....D 620 223-6500
Fort Scott (G-1965)
Ennis Business Forms of Kansas ....D 620 223-6500
Fort Scott (G-1966)
Federal Prison Industries ....D 913 682-8700
Leavenworth (G-5238)
Ward-Kraft Inc ....B 800 821-4021
Fort Scott (G-2017)

BUSINESS MACHINE REPAIR, ELECTRIC

Century Business Systems Inc ....F 785 776-0495
Manhattan (G-6583)
Heartland Services Inc ....E 913 685-8855
Leawood (G-5427)
Heartland Services Inc ....E 913 685-8855
Leawood (G-5428)
McCarty Office Machines Inc ....F 620 421-5530
Parsons (G-9708)
Midwest Office Technologies ....E 785 272-7704
Topeka (G-12903)
Midwest Office Technology ....E 913 894-9600
Overland Park (G-9034)
Office Products Inc ....E 620 793-8180
Great Bend (G-2616)
Sta-Mot-Ks LLC ....E 913 894-9600
Overland Park (G-9349)

BUSINESS SUPPORT SVCS

Csd7 Social Medal ....D 620 203-0477
Burlington (G-633)
Dion A Daniel Inc ....F 816 287-1452
Mission (G-7130)
Goodrich ....F 316 448-4282
Wichita (G-14484)
Hyr Global Source Inc ....F 913 815-2597
Overland Park (G-8835)
Kansas Fmly Advsory Netwrk Inc ....F 316 264-2400
Wichita (G-14800)
Lil Sprouts Playcare LLC ....F 785 343-7529
Ottawa (G-8283)
Nn8 LLC ....F 913 948-1107
Overland Park (G-9088)
Sjh Family Corp ....F 785 856-5296
Lawrence (G-5111)

BUSINESS TRAINING SVCS

American Management Assn Intl ....C 913 451-2700
Shawnee Mission (G-11105)
Nexlearn LLC ....E 316 265-2170
Wichita (G-15172)
Service Corps Retired Execs ....F 316 269-6273
Wichita (G-15567)

CABINETS: Bathroom Vanities, Wood

Crown Tl Inc ....G 785 263-7061
Abilene (G-23)
Eubanks Custom Woodworks ....G 785 364-4377
Holton (G-3088)

CABINETS: Entertainment

Cabinet Shopof Basehor Inc ....E 913 845-2182
Tonganoxie (G-12255)
Stanley Wood Products Inc ....E 913 681-2804
Shawnee Mission (G-11893)

CABINETS: Filing, Office, Wood

Ovation Cabinetry Inc ....D 785 452-9000
Salina (G-10625)

CABINETS: Kitchen, Metal

Cabinet Shopof Basehor Inc ....E 913 845-2182
Tonganoxie (G-12255)

CABINETS: Kitchen, Wood

Cabinet Shopof Basehor Inc ....E 913 845-2182
Tonganoxie (G-12255)
Cambridge Cabinetry ....G 816 795-5082
Stilwell (G-12137)
Century Wood Products Inc ....G 913 839-8725
Olathe (G-7587)
Creative Hardwoods ....G 620 249-4160
Scammon (G-10795)
Crestwood Inc ....C 785 823-1532
Salina (G-10467)
Crestwood Inc ....G 785 827-0317
Salina (G-10468)
Crooks Floor Covering ....G 785 242-4153
Ottawa (G-8262)
Custom Cbnets By Lwrence Cnstr ....F 913 208-9797
Kansas City (G-3948)
Global Engineering & Tech Inc ....C 316 729-9232
Goddard (G-2439)
Grandview Products Co ....D 620 336-2309
Cherryvale (G-808)
Grandview Products Co Inc ....C 620 421-6950
Parsons (G-9688)
Hays Planing Mill Inc ....G 785 625-6507
Hays (G-2838)
Jay Henges Enterprises Inc ....E 913 764-4600
Olathe (G-7808)
Jerry Wray ....G 785 255-4644
Pomona (G-10005)
Kitchens Inc ....F 620 225-0208
Dodge City (G-1393)
Koch & Co Inc ....B 785 336-6022
Seneca (G-10871)
Mingo Custom Woods ....G 785 462-2200
Colby (G-1029)
Norcraft Companies LP ....F 316 283-8804
Newton (G-7397)
Norcraft Companies LP ....B 316 283-2859
Newton (G-7398)
Old World Cabinets Inc ....G 913 723-3740
Linwood (G-6417)
Ovation Cabinetry Inc ....D 785 452-9000
Salina (G-10625)
Overland Cabinet Company Inc ....F 913 441-1985
Bonner Springs (G-569)
RD Henry & Company LLC ....C 316 529-3431
Wichita (G-15424)
Scope Inc ....G 316 393-7414
Wichita (G-15536)
Stanley Wood Products Inc ....E 913 681-2804
Shawnee Mission (G-11893)
Technical Services LLC ....G 785 825-1250
Salina (G-10732)
Technique Manufacturing Inc ....F 620 663-6360
Hutchinson (G-3463)
Timberline Cabinetry Mllwk LLC ....G 785 323-0206
Manhattan (G-6827)
Vision Woodworks LLC ....F 620 336-2158
Cherryvale (G-814)
Wichita Cabinet Company ....G 316 617-0176
Udall (G-13280)
Wooden Stuff Cabinets Inc ....F 785 887-6003
Lecompton (G-5614)

CABINETS: Office, Metal

Griffith Lumber Company Inc ....E 785 776-4104
Manhattan (G-6647)

CABINETS: Office, Wood

Cabinetry & Mllwk Concepts Inc .... F 785 232-1234
Topeka *(G-12417)*
Old World Cabinets Inc .... G 913 723-3740
Linwood *(G-6417)*
Precision Craft Inc .... F 913 780-9077
Olathe *(G-8000)*

CABLE & OTHER PAY TELEVISION DISTRIBUTION

Cox Enterprises Inc .... E 913 825-6124
Overland Park *(G-8607)*
Eagle Communications Inc .... F 785 726-3291
Hays *(G-2794)*
Eagle Communications Inc .... E 785 483-3244
Russell *(G-10273)*
Globl Adams Communications LLC .... E 913 402-4499
Lenexa *(G-5877)*
Multimedia Cablevision .... F 620 251-6610
Coffeyville *(G-965)*
S & T Telephone Coop Assn .... F 785 460-7300
Colby *(G-1038)*
Windjammer Communications LLC .... C 913 563-5450
Overland Park *(G-9498)*

CABLE & PAY TELEVISION SVCS: Direct Broadcast Satellite

Directv Group Inc .... C 620 235-0743
Pittsburg *(G-9853)*
Directv Group Inc .... C 620 663-8132
Hutchinson *(G-3266)*
Dish Network Corporation .... D 816 256-5622
Kansas City *(G-3973)*
Skycom Inc .... F 785 273-1000
Topeka *(G-13076)*

CABLE TELEVISION

Cequel Communications LLC .... E 620 223-1804
Fort Scott *(G-1958)*
Clearwater Cable Vision Inc .... E 620 584-2077
Clearwater *(G-888)*
Comcast Corporation .... C 800 934-6489
Olathe *(G-7602)*
Cox Communications .... F 620 474-4318
Hutchinson *(G-3250)*
Cox Communications Inc .... D 316 260-7392
Wichita *(G-14119)*
Cox Communications Inc .... F 620 227-3361
Dodge City *(G-1333)*
Cox Communications Inc .... C 316 219-5000
Wichita *(G-14120)*
Cox Communications Inc .... F 620 275-5552
Garden City *(G-2137)*
Cox Communications Inc .... D 785 238-6165
Junction City *(G-3686)*
Cox Communications Inc .... E 785 368-1000
Topeka *(G-12524)*
Eagle Communications Inc .... F 785 625-5910
Hays *(G-2793)*
Golden Wheat Inc .... E 620 782-3341
Udall *(G-13277)*
H & B Cable Service Inc .... E 785 252-4000
Holyrood *(G-3114)*
Pioneer Telephone Assn Inc .... C 620 356-3211
Ulysses *(G-13312)*
Rainbow Communications LLC .... E 785 548-7511
Everest *(G-1901)*
S & T Telephone Coop Assn .... E 785 694-2256
Brewster *(G-586)*
Spectrum MGT Holdg Co LLC .... F 913 682-2113
Leavenworth *(G-5290)*
Sumner Cable Tv Inc .... F 620 326-8989
Wellington *(G-13531)*
United Communications Assn Inc .... E 620 227-8645
Dodge City *(G-1442)*
Universal Cable Services Inc .... F 913 481-7839
Olathe *(G-8134)*

CABLE WIRING SETS: Battery, Internal Combustion Engines

Cmt Inc .... C 785 762-4400
Junction City *(G-3683)*
Junction City Wire Harness LLC .... D 785 762-4400
Junction City *(G-3706)*

CABLE: Noninsulated

Wireco Worldgroup Inc .... B 816 270-4700
Prairie Village *(G-10085)*

CABS: Indl Trucks & Tractors

Full Vision Inc .... D 316 283-3344
Newton *(G-7349)*

CAFES

Bagel Works Cafe Inc .... F 913 789-7333
Kansas City *(G-3838)*
Garozzos III Inc .... D 913 491-8300
Shawnee Mission *(G-11390)*
Pauline Food Center .... F 785 862-2774
Topeka *(G-12965)*

CAFETERIAS

University Kansas Mem Corp .... D 785 864-4651
Lawrence *(G-5156)*

CALIBRATING SVCS, NEC

Johnson Gage & Inspection Inc .... F 316 943-7532
Wichita *(G-14768)*

CALIPERS & DIVIDERS

MSI Automation Inc .... F 316 681-3566
Bel Aire *(G-436)*

CAMERA & PHOTOGRAPHIC SPLYS STORES

Wolfes Camera Shops Inc .... E 785 235-1386
Topeka *(G-13248)*

CAMERA & PHOTOGRAPHIC SPLYS STORES: Cameras

Ranieri Camera & Video Inc .... F 785 336-3719
Seneca *(G-10879)*

CAMERA REPAIR SHOP

Heartland Cstmer Solutions LLC .... C 913 685-8855
Leawood *(G-5424)*

CAMPGROUNDS

Association of Kansas Nebraska .... E 785 478-4726
Topeka *(G-12345)*
Four Seasons Rv Acres Inc .... E 785 598-2221
Abilene *(G-32)*
Kansas 4-H Foundation Inc .... F 785 257-3221
Junction City *(G-3712)*
North Shore Marina MGT LLC .... G 785 453-2240
Quenemo *(G-10178)*
Water Spt Rcreation Campground .... F 620 225-9003
Dodge City *(G-1450)*

CAMPSITES

Saint Francis Acdmy Inc Atchsn .... E 913 367-5005
Atchison *(G-259)*

CANDLE SHOPS

Waxman Candles Inc .... G 785 843-8593
Lawrence *(G-5181)*

CANDLES

Empire Candle Co LLC .... G 913 621-4555
Kansas City *(G-3987)*
Empire Candle Co LLC .... F 913 621-4555
Kansas City *(G-3988)*
Empire Candle Co LLC .... C 913 621-4555
Kansas City *(G-3989)*
Waxman Candles Inc .... G 785 843-8593
Lawrence *(G-5181)*

CANDY, NUT & CONFECTIONERY STORES: Candy

Russell Stover Chocolates LLC .... E 785 263-0463
Abilene *(G-52)*

CANOPIES: Sheet Metal

Fashion Inc .... E 785 242-8111
Ottawa *(G-8272)*

CANS: Metal

Mid-West Conveyor Company .... C 734 288-4400
Kansas City *(G-4247)*

CANS: Oil, Metal

No Spill Inc .... G 913 888-9200
Lenexa *(G-6025)*

CANS: Tin

Jacks Food Market .... G 785 348-5411
Linn *(G-6407)*

CANVAS PRDTS

Ponca Products Inc .... E 316 262-4051
Wichita *(G-15314)*

CAPACITORS: NEC

Regal Audio Video .... G 785 628-2700
Hays *(G-2898)*

CAR LOADING SVCS

L L L Transport Inc .... F 913 777-5400
Shawnee Mission *(G-11540)*

CAR WASH EQPT

Dewald Enterprises .... G 316 655-1155
Andover *(G-90)*
Power Vac Inc .... E 785 826-8220
Salina *(G-10639)*
Windtrax Inc .... E 913 789-9100
Shawnee Mission *(G-12013)*

CAR WASH EQPT & SPLYS WHOLESALERS

Pro Carwash Systems Inc .... F 316 788-9933
Derby *(G-1266)*
Ryko Solutions Inc .... F 913 451-3719
Lenexa *(G-6115)*
Windtrax Inc .... E 913 789-9100
Shawnee Mission *(G-12013)*

CAR WASHES

Auto-Craft Inc .... E 785 579-5997
Junction City *(G-3669)*
Greggpiercy Inc .... F 913 469-9274
Overland Park *(G-8779)*
Lakhani Commercial Corp .... D 913 677-1100
Kansas City *(G-4193)*
Profab .... E 785 392-3442
Minneapolis *(G-7121)*
Star Fuel Centers Inc .... E 913 652-9400
Leawood *(G-5561)*
Turtle Wax Inc .... E 913 236-6886
Shawnee Mission *(G-11950)*

CARBON & GRAPHITE PRDTS, NEC

Birla Carbon USA Inc .... E 620 356-3151
Ulysses *(G-13283)*
Hiper Technology Inc .... F 785 749-6011
Lawrence *(G-4898)*

CARBON BLACK

Birla Carbon USA Inc .... E 620 356-3151
Ulysses *(G-13283)*

CARDS: Greeting

Hallmark Cards Incorporated .... E 785 843-9050
Lawrence *(G-4886)*
World Publishing Inc .... E 785 221-8174
Topeka *(G-13252)*

CARNIVAL SPLYS, WHOLESALE

U S Toy Co Inc .... E 913 642-8247
Leawood *(G-5587)*

CARPET & RUG CLEANING & REPAIRING PLANTS

First Response .... F 913 557-2187
Paola *(G-9559)*

CARPET & UPHOLSTERY CLEANING SVCS

All-Pro Services Inc.....F..... 785 842-1402
Lawrence *(G-4727)*
Design Source Flooring LLC.....E..... 913 387-5858
Lenexa *(G-5813)*
Givens Cleaning Contractors.....F..... 316 265-1315
Wichita *(G-14468)*
McGinleys Crpt Pro Jantr Svcs.....E..... 785 825-2627
Salina *(G-10596)*
Mid-America Maintenance Kansas.....F..... 620 365-3872
Gas *(G-2391)*
Phoenix Restoration Service.....E..... 620 276-6994
Garden City *(G-2254)*
Pro Carpet Building Svcs LLC.....E..... 620 331-4304
Independence *(G-3549)*
Resource Service Solutions LLC.....E..... 913 338-5050
Lenexa *(G-6107)*

CARPET & UPHOLSTERY CLEANING SVCS: Carpet/Furniture, On Loc

Alliance Jantr Advisors Inc.....F..... 913 815-8807
Olathe *(G-7520)*
Bluestreak Enterprises Inc.....F..... 785 550-8179
Lawrence *(G-4761)*
Clean-Rite LLC.....F..... 785 628-1945
Hays *(G-2771)*
Clk Inc.....F..... 316 686-3238
Wichita *(G-14043)*
Steam Action Restoration.....F..... 620 276-0622
Garden City *(G-2291)*
Steam Way Carpet Restorations.....F..... 620 331-9553
Independence *(G-3563)*

CARPET & UPHOLSTERY CLEANING SVCS: On Customer Premises

Dalan Inc.....E..... 913 384-5662
Overland Park *(G-8631)*
ServiceMaster North Centl Kans.....F..... 785 243-1965
Concordia *(G-1130)*
Stovers Restoration Inc.....F..... 316 686-5005
Maize *(G-6521)*

CARPETS, RUGS & FLOOR COVERING

Golden Star Inc.....D..... 913 874-2178
Atchison *(G-231)*
More Floods Inc.....G..... 913 469-9464
Lenexa *(G-6012)*
Selfs Inc.....E..... 913 962-7353
Shawnee Mission *(G-11847)*

CASES: Plastic

Plex Plus.....G..... 913 888-6223
Leawood *(G-5523)*

CASES: Shipping, Nailed Or Lock Corner, Wood

L & J Wood Products Inc.....G..... 620 327-2183
Hesston *(G-2996)*

CASH REGISTERS WHOLESALERS

Data Systems Inc.....F..... 913 281-1333
Overland Park *(G-8637)*

CASINO HOTELS & MOTELS

7th Street Casino.....E..... 913 371-3500
Kansas City *(G-3775)*
Bhcmc LLC.....B..... 620 682-7777
Dodge City *(G-1308)*
Golden Eagle Casino.....B..... 785 486-6601
Horton *(G-3125)*
Kansas Entertaiment LLC.....E..... 913 288-9300
Kansas City *(G-4154)*
Kickapoo Tribe In Kansas Inc.....C..... 785 486-2131
Horton *(G-3130)*
Prairie Band Casino and Resort.....A..... 785 966-7777
Mayetta *(G-6916)*

CASKETS WHOLESALERS

Artco Casket Co Inc.....E..... 913 438-2655
Lenexa *(G-5665)*

CASTINGS: Aerospace, Aluminum

S & S Manufacturing Inc.....G..... 316 946-5755
Wichita *(G-15501)*

CASTINGS: Aluminum

Denco Aluminum Inc.....F..... 620 724-6325
Girard *(G-2402)*
Wichita Brass and Alum Fndry.....F..... 316 838-4286
Wichita *(G-15982)*

CASTINGS: Die, Aluminum

Dempsey Inc.....G..... 913 371-3107
Kansas City *(G-3968)*

CASTINGS: Gray Iron

Acme Foundry Inc.....B..... 620 251-6800
Coffeyville *(G-907)*
Ferroloy Inc.....E..... 316 838-0897
Wichita *(G-14358)*

CASTINGS: Magnesium

Wichita Brass and Alum Fndry.....F..... 316 838-4286
Wichita *(G-15982)*

CATALOG & MAIL-ORDER HOUSES

Long Motor Corporation.....C..... 913 541-1525
Lenexa *(G-5979)*

CATALOG SHOWROOMS

Ferguson Enterprises LLC.....D..... 913 752-5660
Lenexa *(G-5851)*

CATERERS

Bockers Two Catering Inc.....F..... 785 539-9431
Manhattan *(G-6566)*
Cro Magnon Repast LLC.....F..... 913 747-5559
Lenexa *(G-5793)*
Eldridge House Invest Ltd Ptnr.....E..... 785 749-5011
Lawrence *(G-4850)*
Hulsing Hotels Kansas Inc.....D..... 785 539-5311
Manhattan *(G-6662)*
Hyatt Corporation.....C..... 316 293-1234
Wichita *(G-14661)*
Meemaws Country Kitchen.....F..... 913 352-6297
Pleasanton *(G-9998)*
Pedro Lopez Co Inc.....F..... 785 220-1509
Lebo *(G-5608)*
Wichita Canteen Company Inc.....E..... 316 524-2254
Wichita *(G-15984)*

CATS, WHOLESALE

Lambriars Inc.....D..... 785 245-3231
Mahaska *(G-6505)*

CATTLE WHOLESALERS

Michael L Sebes.....F..... 620 324-5509
Lewis *(G-6269)*
Mid Continent Farms.....F..... 785 325-2089
Washington *(G-13469)*

CEMENT ROCK: Crushed & Broken

L G Everist Incorporated.....F..... 913 302-5394
Kansas City *(G-4189)*

CEMENT: Heat Resistant

Rex Materials of Kansas Inc.....D..... 620 767-5119
Council Grove *(G-1176)*

CEMENT: Hydraulic

Ash Grove Cement Company.....E..... 620 433-3500
Chanute *(G-703)*
Lafarge North America Inc.....D..... 620 378-4458
Fredonia *(G-2038)*
Lafarge North America Inc.....E..... 620 455-3720
Oxford *(G-9533)*
Lafarge North America Inc.....E..... 316 943-3500
Wichita *(G-14912)*
Lafarge North America Inc.....E..... 316 613-5100
Wichita *(G-14913)*
Lafarge North America Inc.....E..... 816 365-9143
Kansas City *(G-4192)*

CEMENT: Masonry

Ash Grove Cement Company.....E..... 913 422-2523
Kansas City *(G-3821)*
Ash Grove Cement Company.....E..... 785 267-1996
Topeka *(G-12339)*
Heartland Cement Company.....F..... 620 331-0200
Independence *(G-3525)*

CEMENT: Portland

Ash Grove Cement Company.....C..... 913 451-8900
Overland Park *(G-8403)*
Lone Star Industries Inc.....F..... 913 422-1050
Bonner Springs *(G-561)*
Monarch Cement Company.....C..... 620 473-2222
Humboldt *(G-3187)*

CEMETERIES

National Cemetery ADM.....F..... 913 758-4105
Leavenworth *(G-5273)*
National Cemetery ADM.....F..... 913 758-4105
Leavenworth *(G-5274)*
White Chapel Memorial Corp.....E..... 316 684-1612
Wichita *(G-15965)*

CEMETERIES: Real Estate Operation

Catholic Cemteries Inc.....E..... 913 371-4040
Kansas City *(G-3894)*
Fairlawn Burial Park Assn.....F..... 620 662-3431
Hutchinson *(G-3282)*
Hawks Funeral Home Inc.....F..... 620 442-0220
Arkansas City *(G-159)*
Mount Hope Cemetery Company.....F..... 785 272-1122
Topeka *(G-12917)*
Resthaven Gardens of Memory.....E..... 316 722-2100
Wichita *(G-15450)*
Service Corp International.....E..... 913 334-3366
Kansas City *(G-4418)*

CEMETERY ASSOCIATION

Topeka Cemetery Association.....F..... 785 233-4132
Topeka *(G-13171)*

CEMETERY MEMORIAL DEALERS

Kimple Inc.....F..... 620 564-2300
Ellinwood *(G-1635)*
Rumsey-Yost Funeral Inc.....F..... 785 843-5111
Lawrence *(G-5099)*

CERAMIC FLOOR & WALL TILE WHOLESALERS

Interstate Flooring LLC.....C..... 913 573-0600
Kansas City *(G-4110)*

CHAMBERS OF COMMERCE

Asian Amrcn Chmber of Commerce.....F..... 913 338-0774
Shawnee Mission *(G-11124)*
Atchison Area Chamber Commerce.....F..... 913 367-2427
Atchison *(G-206)*
Caldwell Area Chambe.....F..... 620 845-6914
Caldwell *(G-655)*
Chamber of Commerce.....F..... 785 258-2115
Herington *(G-2972)*
Ellswrth Knplis Chmber Cmmerce.....F..... 785 472-4071
Ellsworth *(G-1673)*
Garden Cy Area Chmber Commerce.....F..... 620 276-3264
Garden City *(G-2181)*
Greater Topeka Commerce.....E..... 785 234-2644
Topeka *(G-12646)*
Hutchinson/Reno County Chamber.....F..... 620 662-3391
Hutchinson *(G-3329)*
Lenexa Chamber of Commerce.....F..... 913 888-1414
Shawnee Mission *(G-11562)*
Louisburg Chamber of Commerce.....F..... 913 837-2826
Louisburg *(G-6457)*
Manhattan Chamber of Commerce.....F..... 785 776-8829
Manhattan *(G-6719)*
Marysville Chamber Commerce.....F..... 785 562-3101
Marysville *(G-6897)*
Oakley Area Chamber Commerce.....F..... 785 672-4862
Oakley *(G-7483)*
Olathe Chamber of Commerce.....F..... 913 764-1050
Olathe *(G-7929)*
Overland Park Chamber Commerce.....F..... 913 491-3600
Shawnee Mission *(G-11705)*

Salina Area Chmber Cmmerce Inc ....F 785 827-9301
Salina *(G-10665)*
Salina Economic Dev Corp ....F 785 827-9301
Salina *(G-10673)*
Smith Center Chamber Commerce ....F 785 282-3895
Smith Center *(G-12041)*
Spring Hill Chamber Commerce............F 913 592-3893
Spring Hill *(G-12099)*
Wamego Chmber Cmmrce Minstreet ....F 785 456-7849
Wamego *(G-13448)*
Wichita Area Chamber Commerce ....E 316 265-7771
Wichita *(G-15975)*

CHANGE MAKING MACHINES

Cummins - Allison Corp ....G....... 913 894-2266
Lenexa *(G-5797)*

CHARGE ACCOUNT SVCS

Charge It LLC ....E 913 341-8772
Paola *(G-9546)*

CHASSIS: Motor Vehicle

P-Ayr Products..F 913 651-5543
Leavenworth *(G-5278)*
Reinke Manufacturing Co Inc ....G....... 785 527-8024
Belleville *(G-463)*

CHECK CASHING SVCS

Curo Financial Tech Corp ....E 316 722-3801
Wichita *(G-14141)*
Curo Management LLC..........................D 316 683-2274
Wichita *(G-14144)*
Galt Ventures LLC..................................F........ 316 942-2211
Wichita *(G-14442)*
Qc Financial Services Inc......................D 913 439-1100
Shawnee Mission *(G-11763)*

CHECK CLEARING SVCS

Bankers Life & Casualty Co...................F 913 894-6553
Overland Park *(G-8430)*
United Ptriot Abtment Svcs LLC ....F 785 856-1349
Lawrence *(G-5152)*

CHECK VALIDATION SVCS

Ogden Check Approval Network ....E 785 228-5600
Topeka *(G-12942)*

CHEESE WHOLESALERS

Bern Meat Plant Incorporated................F 785 336-2165
Bern *(G-521)*

CHEMICAL CLEANING SVCS

Hydrochem LLC ....E 316 321-7541
El Dorado *(G-1569)*

CHEMICAL SPLYS FOR FOUNDRIES

Jacam Chemicals LLC.............................F 620 275-1500
Garden City *(G-2208)*

CHEMICAL: Sodm Compnds/Salts, Inorg, Exc Rfnd Sodm Chloride

Compass Minerals Group Inc ....C....... 913 344-9100
Overland Park *(G-8588)*

CHEMICALS & ALLIED PRDTS WHOLESALERS, NEC

Air Products and Chemicals Inc............E 620 624-8151
Liberal *(G-6273)*
Airgas Usa LLC ....E 785 823-8100
Salina *(G-10398)*
Blue Valley Chemical LLC......................F 816 984-2125
Overland Park *(G-8469)*
Bobs Janitorial Service & Sup...............C....... 785 271-6600
Topeka *(G-12395)*
Fujifilm North America Corp..................F 816 914-5942
Kansas City *(G-4021)*
Helena Chemical Company....................F 913 441-0676
Shawnee *(G-10971)*
Koch Fertilizer LLC ....E 620 227-8631
Dodge City *(G-1394)*
Koch Fertilizer LLC ....E 316 828-5010
Wichita *(G-14880)*
Koch Industries Inc................................A....... 316 828-5500
Wichita *(G-14881)*
Lyons Salt Company ....D 620 257-5626
Lyons *(G-6492)*
Nalco Company LLC..............................E 785 625-3822
Hays *(G-2876)*
Prosoco Inc ....D 785 865-4200
Lawrence *(G-5081)*

CHEMICALS & ALLIED PRDTS, WHOL: Food Additives/Preservatives

Danisco USA Inc ....C....... 913 764-8100
New Century *(G-7277)*
E I Du Pont De Nemours & Co ....C....... 913 764-8100
New Century *(G-7283)*
Wilke Resources Inc...............................F 913 438-5544
Lenexa *(G-6229)*

CHEMICALS & ALLIED PRDTS, WHOL: Gases, Compressed/Liquefied

Wichita Welding Supply Inc ....F 316 838-8671
Wichita *(G-16043)*

CHEMICALS & ALLIED PRDTS, WHOLESALE: Acids

Meridian Chemicals LLC ....G....... 913 253-2220
Overland Park *(G-9011)*

CHEMICALS & ALLIED PRDTS, WHOLESALE: Aerosols

Airosol Co Inc...E 620 325-2666
Neodesha *(G-7234)*

CHEMICALS & ALLIED PRDTS, WHOLESALE: Alcohols

Ethanol Products LLC ....C....... 316 303-1380
Wichita *(G-14308)*

CHEMICALS & ALLIED PRDTS, WHOLESALE: Anti-Freeze Compounds

Clean Harbors Wichita LLC....................C....... 316 832-0151
Wichita *(G-14039)*

CHEMICALS & ALLIED PRDTS, WHOLESALE: Chemical Additives

Chemstation of Kansas Inc....................F 316 201-1851
Wichita *(G-14001)*
Midcontinental Chemical Co Inc............E 913 390-5556
Olathe *(G-7893)*

CHEMICALS & ALLIED PRDTS, WHOLESALE: Chemicals, Indl

American Chem Systems II LLC.............E 316 263-4448
Wichita *(G-13689)*
Barton Solvents Inc ....F 316 321-1540
El Dorado *(G-1534)*
Barton Solvents Inc ....F 913 287-5500
Kansas City *(G-3847)*
Chemical Services Inc............................F 620 792-6886
Great Bend *(G-2537)*
Edwards Chemicals Inc..........................F 913 365-5158
Elwood *(G-1686)*
Flint Hills Resources LLC ....B 316 828-5500
Wichita *(G-14390)*
Scotwood Industries Inc ....E 913 851-3500
Overland Park *(G-9285)*
Ultra-Chem Inc ....C....... 913 492-2929
Shawnee Mission *(G-11955)*
Univar Solutions USA Inc.......................F 913 621-7494
Kansas City *(G-4493)*
Univar Solutions USA Inc.......................F 316 267-1002
Wichita *(G-15851)*
Wilbur-Ellis Company LLC.....................F 785 582-4052
Silver Lake *(G-12029)*
Wilbur-Ellis Company LLC.....................F 785 359-6569
Leona *(G-6248)*

CHEMICALS & ALLIED PRDTS, WHOLESALE: Detergent/Soap

Power Vac Inc...E 785 826-8220
Salina *(G-10639)*

CHEMICALS & ALLIED PRDTS, WHOLESALE: Drilling Mud

Mud-Co/Service Mud Inc ....F 620 672-2957
Pratt *(G-10126)*

CHEMICALS & ALLIED PRDTS, WHOLESALE: Indl Gases

Harcros Chemicals Inc ....C....... 913 321-3131
Kansas City *(G-4068)*

CHEMICALS & ALLIED PRDTS, WHOLESALE: Oil Additives

Baker Petrolite LLC.................................D 620 793-3546
Great Bend *(G-2514)*

CHEMICALS & ALLIED PRDTS, WHOLESALE: Oxygen

Broadway Home Medical Inc ....F 316 264-8600
Wichita *(G-13895)*
Denison Inc...F 620 378-4148
Fredonia *(G-2030)*

CHEMICALS & ALLIED PRDTS, WHOLESALE: Plastics Materials, NEC

Bagcraftpapercon I LLC ....C....... 620 856-4615
Baxter Springs *(G-395)*

CHEMICALS & ALLIED PRDTS, WHOLESALE: Plastics Prdts, NEC

Koller Enterprises Inc............................D 913 422-2027
Lenexa *(G-5957)*

CHEMICALS & ALLIED PRDTS, WHOLESALE: Plastics Sheets & Rods

Lustercraft Plastics LLC.........................F 316 942-8451
Wichita *(G-14991)*

CHEMICALS & ALLIED PRDTS, WHOLESALE: Polyurethane Prdts

Buckley Industries Inc...........................D 316 744-7587
Park City *(G-9606)*
Crown Packaging Corp ....E 913 888-1951
Shawnee Mission *(G-11283)*

CHEMICALS & ALLIED PRDTS, WHOLESALE: Resin, Synthetic Rubber

General Tech A Svcs & Pdts Co ....G....... 913 766-5566
Olathe *(G-7727)*

CHEMICALS & ALLIED PRDTS, WHOLESALE: Spec Clean/Sanitation

Cleaning By Lamunyon Inc....................F 785 632-1259
Clay Center *(G-855)*
Pur-O-Zone Inc ....E 785 843-0771
Lawrence *(G-5082)*
Q4 Industries LLC..................................F 913 894-6240
Overland Park *(G-9205)*

CHEMICALS & OTHER PRDTS DERIVED FROM COKING

Koch Energy Inc......................................F 316 828-5500
Wichita *(G-14877)*

CHEMICALS, AGRICULTURE: Wholesalers

Archer-Daniels-Midland Company ....F 620 872-2174
Scott City *(G-10804)*
Fleming Feed & Grain Inc......................E 316 742-3411
Leon *(G-6247)*
General Tech A Svcs & Pdts Co ....G....... 913 766-5566
Olathe *(G-7727)*
J B Pearl Sales & Svc Inc ....E 785 437-2772
Saint Marys *(G-10366)*
Wilbur-Ellis Company LLC.....................F 785 582-4052
Silver Lake *(G-12029)*
Wilbur-Ellis Company LLC.....................F 785 359-6569
Leona *(G-6248)*
Winfield Solutions LLC...........................F 620 277-2231
Garden City *(G-2317)*

CHEMICALS: Agricultural

Dupont ....F 913 327-3518
Overland Park *(G-8666)*
FMC Corporation ....D 316 729-5321
Wichita *(G-14395)*
Jayhawk Fine Chemicals Corp ....C 620 783-1321
Galena *(G-2075)*
Specialty Fertilizer Pdts LLC ....F 913 956-7500
Leawood *(G-5556)*

CHEMICALS: Fire Retardant

Akrofire Inc ....E 913 888-7172
Shawnee Mission *(G-11090)*

CHEMICALS: Fuel Tank Or Engine Cleaning

Optic Fuel Clean Inc ....G 913 712-8373
Olathe *(G-7960)*

CHEMICALS: High Purity, Refined From Technical Grade

Helena Chemical Company ....G 620 375-2073
Leoti *(G-6253)*

CHEMICALS: Inorganic, NEC

American Phoenix Inc ....E 785 862-7722
Topeka *(G-12320)*
Ce Water Management Inc ....G 913 621-7047
Kansas City *(G-3899)*
Compass Minerals America Inc ....C 620 257-2324
Lyons *(G-6480)*
Conspec Marketing and Mfg Co ....A 913 287-1700
Kansas City *(G-3933)*
Corbion America Holdings Inc ....D 913 890-5500
Lenexa *(G-5787)*
Event Elements LLC ....G 316 440-2829
Wichita *(G-14313)*
Harcros Chemicals Inc ....C 913 621-7721
Kansas City *(G-4069)*
Kemira Chemicals Inc ....G 785 434-2474
Plainville *(G-9988)*
Koch Mineral Services LLC ....E 316 828-5500
Wichita *(G-14884)*
Koch Sulfur Products Co LLC ....E 316 828-5500
Wichita *(G-14889)*
Mineral-Right Inc ....F 785 543-6571
Phillipsburg *(G-9791)*
Nalco Company ....G 620 624-1594
Liberal *(G-6347)*
Occidental Chemical Corp ....E 316 524-4211
Wichita *(G-15206)*
Perimeter Solutions LP ....C 785 749-8100
Lawrence *(G-5061)*
PQ Corporation ....D 913 371-3020
Kansas City *(G-4329)*

CHEMICALS: NEC

Bg Products Incorporated ....E 316 265-2686
Wichita *(G-13845)*
British Salt Holdings LLC ....C 913 253-2203
Overland Park *(G-8486)*
Chemtrade Phosphorous Spc LLC ....E 785 843-2290
Lawrence *(G-4784)*
Dayton Superior Corporation ....D 913 596-9784
Kansas City *(G-3960)*
E I Du Pont De Nemours & Co ....F 302 774-1000
New Century *(G-7282)*
Jayhawk Fine Chemicals Corp ....C 620 783-1321
Galena *(G-2075)*
Koch Industries Inc ....F 620 662-6691
Hutchinson *(G-3352)*
Maxidize Production Svcs LLC ....G 620 222-1235
Winfield *(G-16158)*
Pbi-Gordon Corporation ....E 816 421-4070
Kansas City *(G-4317)*
Peavey Corporation ....D 913 888-0600
Lenexa *(G-6047)*
PQ Corporation ....D 913 371-3020
Kansas City *(G-4329)*

CHEMICALS: Organic, NEC

Abengoa Bnergy Hybrid Kans LLC ....F 316 796-1234
Colwich *(G-1091)*
Corbion America Holdings Inc ....D 913 890-5500
Lenexa *(G-5787)*
Flint Hills Resources Port ....D 316 828-5500
Wichita *(G-14392)*
FMC Corporation ....D 316 729-5321
Wichita *(G-14395)*
Harcros Chemicals Inc ....C 913 321-3131
Kansas City *(G-4068)*
Kemira Chemicals Inc ....G 785 434-2474
Plainville *(G-9988)*
Koch Industries Inc ....G 620 834-2204
McPherson *(G-6984)*
Koch Industries Inc ....F 620 662-6691
Hutchinson *(G-3352)*
Pbi-Gordon Corporation ....E 816 421-4070
Kansas City *(G-4317)*
Purac America Inc ....E 913 890-5500
Lenexa *(G-6081)*

CHEMICALS: Potassium Compound/Salt, Exc Hydroxide/Carbonate

Compass Minerals Intl Inc ....C 913 344-9200
Overland Park *(G-8589)*

CHEMICALS: Soda Ash

FMC Corporation ....D 316 729-5321
Wichita *(G-14395)*

CHEMICALS: Sodium Silicate

PQ Corporation ....F 913 227-0561
Lenexa *(G-6065)*

CHEMICALS: Water Treatment

Enviro-Health Corp ....F 785 235-8300
Topeka *(G-12579)*
Meridian Chemicals LLC ....G 913 253-2220
Overland Park *(G-9011)*
Mineral-Right Inc ....F 785 543-6571
Phillipsburg *(G-9791)*

CHICKEN SLAUGHTERING & PROCESSING

Hitchin Post Steak Co ....D 913 647-0543
Olathe *(G-7770)*
Tyson Foods Inc ....E 620 343-3640
Emporia *(G-1842)*

CHILD & YOUTH SVCS, NEC

Avenue of Life Inc ....E 816 519-8419
Kansas City *(G-3830)*
Casa Jhnson Wyndtte Cnties Inc ....F 913 715-4040
Mission *(G-7128)*
Child Advcacy Ctr Sdgwick Cnty ....F 316 660-9494
Wichita *(G-14005)*
Child Support Enforcement ....F 620 331-7231
Independence *(G-3502)*
County of Finney ....F 620 271-6120
Garden City *(G-2133)*
Family First Center For Autism ....E 913 250-5634
Leavenworth *(G-5237)*
Infant Tddler Svcs Jhnson Cnty ....F 913 432-2900
Shawnee Mission *(G-11456)*
Kansas Childrens Service Leag ....E 785 274-3100
Topeka *(G-12764)*
Kansas Dept For Chldren Fmlies ....E 785 296-3237
Topeka *(G-12772)*
Kansas Dept For Chldren Fmlies ....E 785 462-6769
Colby *(G-1020)*
Paces Wyandot Ctr Youth Svcs ....E 913 956-3420
Kansas City *(G-4306)*
Saint Francis Community and RE ....D 785 825-0541
Salina *(G-10662)*
Saint Frncis Acdemy Great Bend ....E 620 793-7454
Great Bend *(G-2634)*
Saint Frncis Cmnty Svcs In Ill ....E 785 825-0541
Salina *(G-10663)*
Southwest Guidance Ctr ....F 620 624-0280
Liberal *(G-6371)*
Sunflower House ....E 913 631-5800
Shawnee Mission *(G-11908)*
Sunshine Connections Inc ....F 785 625-2093
Hays *(G-2918)*
Wichita Child Guidance Center ....D 316 686-6671
Wichita *(G-15986)*

CHILD DAY CARE SVCS

A Step Above Academy-Wyandotte ....F 913 721-3770
Bonner Springs *(G-538)*
Abilene Unified Schl Dst 435 ....F 785 825-9185
Salina *(G-10389)*
Aldersgate Untd Meth Pre Schl ....E 913 764-2407
Olathe *(G-7516)*
American Baptist Church ....F 913 236-7067
Shawnee Mission *(G-11102)*
Ancilla Center For Children ....F 913 758-6113
Leavenworth *(G-5202)*
Angel Wings Learning Ctr LLC ....F 316 249-4818
Wichita *(G-13709)*
Angels Little Playgrnd Daycare ....F 785 823-1448
Salina *(G-10404)*
Archdiocese Kansas Cy In Kans ....E 913 631-0004
Shawnee Mission *(G-11117)*
Assoction Christn Schools Intl ....D 785 232-3878
Topeka *(G-12347)*
Bccc Child Development Center ....E 620 786-1131
Great Bend *(G-2518)*
Bonner Springs Head Start ....F 913 441-2828
Bonner Springs *(G-542)*
Boys Girls Clubs Huthinson Inc ....D 620 665-7171
Hutchinson *(G-3220)*
Brookridge Day School ....E 913 649-2228
Shawnee Mission *(G-11185)*
BS Family Development LLC ....E 913 961-6579
Olathe *(G-7563)*
Building Blocks of Topeka Inc ....E 785 232-0441
Topeka *(G-12413)*
Caring Connections ....F 620 544-2050
Hugoton *(G-3150)*
Child Care Services Strlng Inc ....F 620 904-4231
Sterling *(G-12114)*
Childhood Memories Toddler ....F 316 554-1646
Wichita *(G-14009)*
Childrens Learning Center Inc ....E 785 841-2185
Lawrence *(G-4786)*
Christ King Early Educatn Ctr ....E 785 272-2999
Topeka *(G-12466)*
Christian Rainbow Knowledge ....F 316 686-2169
Wichita *(G-14015)*
Creme De La Creme Kansas Inc ....E 913 451-0858
Shawnee Mission *(G-11279)*
Early Childhood Connections ....E 785 623-2430
Hays *(G-2796)*
East Heights United Methdst Ch ....E 316 682-6518
Wichita *(G-14253)*
Edwardslle Untd Mthdst Daycare ....F 913 422-5384
Edwardsville *(G-1498)*
Elizabeth B Ballard Comm Ctr ....F 785 842-0729
Lawrence *(G-4851)*
Faith Evangelical Lutheran Ch ....E 316 788-1715
Derby *(G-1246)*
Family First Child Care LLC ....F 316 333-1481
Newton *(G-7343)*
Family Resource Center Inc ....D 620 235-3150
Pittsburg *(G-9860)*
First Assembly God Inc ....E 316 524-4981
Haysville *(G-2944)*
First Steps Childcare and Lear ....F 620 518-1532
Great Bend *(G-2565)*
First United Methodist Church ....E 316 263-6244
Wichita *(G-14376)*
Fleet Early Learning Stn LLC ....E 913 638-7178
Overland Park *(G-8728)*
Full Faith Church of Love ....F 913 262-3145
Kansas City *(G-4023)*
Garden City Public Schools ....E 620 275-0291
Garden City *(G-2176)*
Goddard Public Schools ....E 316 794-2281
Goddard *(G-2440)*
Grace Angels Family Service ....F 913 233-2944
Kansas City *(G-4043)*
Halstd-Bntley Unfied Schl Dst ....C 316 835-2641
Halstead *(G-2700)*
Happy Hearts Child Development ....F 316 613-3550
Wichita *(G-14558)*
Happy Hearts Learning Ctr LLC ....F 913 334-3331
Kansas City *(G-4066)*
Happy House Day Care ....F 913 782-1115
Olathe *(G-7750)*
Head Start Child Dev Cncil Inc ....F 316 267-1997
Wichita *(G-14574)*
Helpers Inc ....F 913 322-7212
Olathe *(G-7764)*
Hill Top Center ....F 316 686-9095
Wichita *(G-14609)*
Integrated Behavioral Tech Inc ....D 913 662-7071
Basehor *(G-379)*
Jewish Cmnty Ctr Grter Kans Cy ....B 913 327-8000
Shawnee Mission *(G-11486)*
Junction City Family YMCA Inc ....E 785 762-4780
Junction City *(G-3704)*

Kansas Childrens Service Leag ....D....... 620 276-3232
Garden City *(G-2213)*
Kansas City Christian School ....D....... 913 648-5227
Prairie Village *(G-10040)*
Kansas East Conference United ....E....... 913 631-2280
Shawnee Mission *(G-11516)*
Kansas East Conference United ....F....... 913 383-9146
Shawnee Mission *(G-11517)*
Kiddicat Child Care Center ....F....... 785 272-2001
Topeka *(G-12822)*
Kindercare Education LLC ....F....... 913 441-9202
Shawnee *(G-10982)*
Lakeshore Learning Center Svcs ....E....... 785 271-9146
Topeka *(G-12831)*
M L K Child Development Center ....E....... 785 827-3841
Salina *(G-10587)*
Martin Luther King Jr Child De ....E....... 785 827-3841
Salina *(G-10593)*
Marysville School District ....D....... 785 562-5386
Marysville *(G-6902)*
My Child Advocate PA ....F....... 913 829-8838
Olathe *(G-7909)*
N2 Kids Enterprises Inc ....E....... 913 648-5457
Shawnee Mission *(G-11664)*
Nall Ave Baptist Church ....E....... 913 432-4141
Prairie Village *(G-10049)*
New Generation ....F....... 620 223-1506
Fort Scott *(G-1993)*
Newton Cmnty Child Care Ctr ....E....... 316 284-6525
Newton *(G-7392)*
Newton Medical Ctr Child Care ....F....... 316 804-6094
Newton *(G-7394)*
Noahs Arkademy ....F....... 620 331-7791
Independence *(G-3544)*
Northridge Family Dev Ctr ....E....... 785 284-2401
Sabetha *(G-10322)*
Paola Assembly of God Inc ....F....... 913 294-5198
Paola *(G-9578)*
Pawnee Avenue Church of God ....E....... 316 683-5648
Wichita *(G-15273)*
Prairie Bend Ptwtomi Childcare ....E....... 785 966-2707
Mayetta *(G-6918)*
Prairie Ctr Christn Childcare ....E....... 913 390-0230
Olathe *(G-7997)*
Rose Hill Unified School Dst ....E....... 316 776-3340
Rose Hill *(G-10248)*
Saint Ann Child Care Center ....F....... 913 362-4660
Shawnee Mission *(G-11824)*
Sas Childcare Inc ....E....... 913 897-8900
Leawood *(G-5548)*
Security Benefit Academy Inc ....E....... 785 438-3000
Topeka *(G-13051)*
Shawnee Church of Nazarene ....F....... 913 631-5555
Shawnee Mission *(G-11850)*
Shawnee Presbyterian Church ....E....... 913 631-6689
Shawnee Mission *(G-11862)*
Small Beginnings ....E....... 913 851-2223
Shawnee Mission *(G-11874)*
Smart Start of Kansas LLC ....F....... 620 345-6000
Moundridge *(G-7197)*
St Johns Child Dev Ctr LLC ....F....... 620 564-2044
Ellinwood *(G-1639)*
Start To Finish Celebration ....F....... 785 364-2257
Grantville *(G-2498)*
Stepping Stones Day Care Ctr ....F....... 913 724-7700
Basehor *(G-389)*
Sunset Zoological Pk Wildlife ....E....... 785 587-2737
Manhattan *(G-6818)*
Suzanna Wesley Child Care ....F....... 785 478-3703
Topeka *(G-13127)*
Swan Corporation ....F....... 913 390-1411
Olathe *(G-8090)*
Tdc Learning Centers Inc ....F....... 785 234-2273
Topeka *(G-13145)*
Tender Hearts Child Care Ctr ....F....... 785 754-3937
Quinter *(G-10188)*
Topeka Day Care Inc ....F....... 785 272-5051
Topeka *(G-13174)*
Training & Evaluation Cente ....E....... 620 615-5850
Hutchinson *(G-3468)*
Tutor Time Lrng Systems Inc ....E....... 316 721-0464
Wichita *(G-15819)*
Unified School District 259 ....B....... 316 973-7292
Wichita *(G-15834)*
Victoria Flls Sklld Cre & Rhab ....F....... 316 733-0654
Andover *(G-114)*
Wichita Top Childrens Fund ....D....... 316 260-9479
Wichita *(G-16041)*
YMCA of Hutchinson Reno Cnty ....D....... 620 662-1203
Hutchinson *(G-3494)*
YMCA Topeaka Downtown Branch ....E....... 785 354-8591
Topeka *(G-13256)*
Young Mens Christian ....F....... 785 233-9815
Topeka *(G-13258)*
Young Mens Christian Assn ....E....... 620 275-1199
Garden City *(G-2319)*
Young Mens Christian Associa ....D....... 316 320-9622
El Dorado *(G-1616)*
Young Mens Christian Associa ....C....... 316 219-9622
Wichita *(G-16093)*
Young Mens Christian Associa ....D....... 316 260-9622
Wichita *(G-16094)*
Young Mens Christian Associa ....C....... 316 942-5511
Wichita *(G-16095)*
Young Mens Christian Associat ....C....... 620 545-7290
Viola *(G-13380)*
Young Mens Christian Gr Kansas ....D....... 913 362-3489
Prairie Village *(G-10088)*
Young Mens Christian Gr Kansas ....C....... 913 393-9622
Olathe *(G-8163)*
Young Mens Christian Gr Kansas ....D....... 913 782-7707
Olathe *(G-8164)*
Young MNS Chrstn Assn of Tpeka ....C....... 785 354-8591
Topeka *(G-13259)*
Young MNS Chrstn Assn Pttsburg ....D....... 620 231-1100
Pittsburg *(G-9972)*

CHILD GUIDANCE SVCS

Childrens Therapy Group ....F....... 913 383-9014
Mission *(G-7129)*
Hays Area Children Center Inc ....E....... 785 625-3257
Hays *(G-2828)*

CHILDBIRTH PREPARATION CLINIC

Preferred Fmly Healthcare Inc ....F....... 620 221-6252
Winfield *(G-16167)*
Trumpet Behavioral Health LLC ....F....... 816 802-6969
Overland Park *(G-9434)*

CHILDREN'S AID SOCIETY

Douglas County Child Dev Assn ....F....... 785 842-9679
Lawrence *(G-4838)*
Noahs Ark Christian Day Care ....F....... 620 431-1832
Chanute *(G-747)*
Western Kansas Child Advocacy ....F....... 620 872-3706
Scott City *(G-10835)*

CHILDREN'S DANCING SCHOOL

Shirley Marley Enterprises ....F....... 913 492-0004
Shawnee Mission *(G-11865)*

CHILDREN'S HOME

Elm Acres Youth & Family Svcs ....C....... 620 231-9840
Pittsburg *(G-9855)*
Elm Acres Youth & Family Svcs ....E....... 620 231-6129
Pittsburg *(G-9856)*
Kidstlc Inc ....C....... 913 764-2887
Olathe *(G-7839)*
One Hope United - Northern Reg ....E....... 785 827-1756
Salina *(G-10621)*
Villages Inc ....F....... 785 267-5900
Topeka *(G-13224)*
Wichita Childrens Home ....D....... 316 684-6581
Wichita *(G-15987)*

CHIMNEY CLEANING SVCS

Fluebrothers LLC ....F....... 913 236-7141
Kansas City *(G-4013)*

CHIMNEYS & FITTINGS

Salina Concrete Products Inc ....F....... 316 943-3241
Wichita *(G-15510)*

CHINA: Decorated

Discovery Concepts Inc ....G....... 913 814-7100
Shawnee Mission *(G-11309)*

CHIROPRACTORS' OFFICES

Advanced Chiropractic Svcs PA ....F....... 785 842-4181
Lawrence *(G-4721)*
Advantage Medical Group ....F....... 785 749-0130
Lawrence *(G-4722)*
Animal Chiropractic Center ....E....... 309 658-2920
Wellsville *(G-13540)*
Chiro Plus Inc ....F....... 316 684-0550
Wichita *(G-14012)*
Chiroserve Inc ....E....... 913 764-6237
Olathe *(G-7594)*
Cleveland University - Kans Cy ....D....... 913 234-0600
Overland Park *(G-8565)*
Cohoon Chiropractic ....F....... 316 612-0600
Wichita *(G-14051)*
Counslman Wade Chrprctic Clnic ....F....... 785 234-0521
Topeka *(G-12514)*
First Choice Chiropractic PA ....F....... 913 402-7444
Overland Park *(G-8718)*
Hall Chiropractic Center ....F....... 785 242-6444
Overland Park *(G-8786)*
Lifeworks Chiropractic ....F....... 913 441-2293
Shawnee *(G-10988)*
Natural Way Chiropractic ....F....... 913 385-1999
Shawnee Mission *(G-11674)*
Robin Chiropractic & Acupnctur ....F....... 913 962-7408
Shawnee Mission *(G-11810)*
Saint Lukes South Hospital Inc ....F....... 913 317-7990
Overland Park *(G-9275)*
Walmart Inc ....B....... 620 232-1593
Pittsburg *(G-9960)*

CHLORINE

Clorox Company ....F....... 913 664-9000
Overland Park *(G-8568)*

CHOCOLATE, EXC CANDY FROM BEANS: Chips, Powder, Block, Syrup

Mars Chocolate North Amer LLC ....G....... 785 861-1800
Topeka *(G-12861)*
Russell Stover Chocolates LLC ....E....... 785 263-0463
Abilene *(G-52)*

CHOCOLATE, EXC CANDY FROM PURCH CHOC: Chips, Powder, Block

Chocolate Specialty Corp ....D....... 816 941-3088
Stilwell *(G-12140)*

CHRISTMAS NOVELTIES, WHOLESALE

Nathan Weiner & Associates ....F....... 913 390-0508
Olathe *(G-7911)*

CHRISTMAS TREES WHOLESALERS

Treescape Inc ....E....... 316 733-6388
Andover *(G-112)*

CHURCHES

First Assembly God Inc ....E....... 316 524-4981
Haysville *(G-2944)*
Paola Assembly of God Inc ....F....... 913 294-5198
Paola *(G-9578)*
Salvation Army ....E....... 316 685-8699
Wichita *(G-15513)*
Salvation Army National Corp ....E....... 316 943-9893
Wichita *(G-15515)*
Unity Church of Overland Park ....E....... 913 649-1750
Shawnee Mission *(G-11966)*

CIRCUIT BOARD REPAIR SVCS

Nation-Wide Repr Holdg Co Inc ....E....... 913 248-1722
Stilwell *(G-12170)*

CIRCUITS: Electronic

B & C Specialty Products Inc ....F....... 316 283-8000
Newton *(G-7315)*
Control Vision Corporation ....E....... 620 231-5816
Pittsburg *(G-9845)*
Elecsys Corporation ....C....... 913 647-0158
Olathe *(G-7672)*
Marche Associates Inc ....F....... 785 749-2925
Lawrence *(G-5011)*
Pivot International Inc ....E....... 913 312-6900
Lenexa *(G-6060)*
Regasa Aerospace Inc ....G....... 316 425-0079
Wichita *(G-15435)*
Schell Electronics Inc ....G....... 620 431-2350
Chanute *(G-761)*
Tecnet International Inc ....F....... 913 859-9515
Lenexa *(G-6173)*

CLAIMS ADJUSTING SVCS

Crawford & Company ....F 913 909-4552
Shawnee Mission *(G-11277)*
Crawford & Company ....F 913 323-0300
Great Bend *(G-2550)*

CLEANING & DESCALING SVC: Metal Prdts

101st Earthborn Envmtl Tech LP ....G 785 691-8918
Colby *(G-987)*

CLEANING & DYEING PLANTS, EXC RUGS

Band Box Corporation ....E 785 272-6646
Topeka *(G-12361)*
Bayless Dry Cleaning Inc ....F 620 793-3576
Great Bend *(G-2517)*
Elite Cleaners ....F 316 651-5997
Wichita *(G-14269)*
Hygienic Dry Cleaners Inc ....E 785 478-0066
Topeka *(G-12710)*
Mjv Holdings LLC ....F 913 432-5348
Shawnee Mission *(G-11650)*

CLEANING COMPOUNDS: Rifle Bore

Sportsgear Outdoor Products ....G 913 888-0379
Lenexa *(G-6149)*

CLEANING EQPT: Blast, Dustless

Abrasive Blast Systems Inc ....E 785 263-3786
Abilene *(G-10)*

CLEANING EQPT: Commercial

Fuller Industries LLC ....C 620 792-1711
Great Bend *(G-2568)*
Peterson Mch Tl Acqisition Inc ....F 316 634-6699
Rose Hill *(G-10245)*

CLEANING EQPT: Floor Washing & Polishing, Commercial

City Wide Window Washing Inc ....F 913 888-5700
Lenexa *(G-5759)*

CLEANING OR POLISHING PREPARATIONS, NEC

Illinois Tool Works Inc ....D 913 397-9889
Olathe *(G-7784)*
Sani Wax Inc ....G 913 383-9703
Prairie Village *(G-10065)*

CLEANING PRDTS: Degreasing Solvent

W F Leonard Co Inc ....G 785 484-3342
Meriden *(G-7084)*

CLEANING PRDTS: Deodorants, Nonpersonal

Product Dev & Designers ....F 913 783-4364
Paola *(G-9584)*

CLEANING PRDTS: Disinfectants, Household Or Indl Plant

Clorox Products Mfg Co ....G 913 620-1777
Overland Park *(G-8569)*

CLEANING PRDTS: Drain Pipe Solvents Or Cleaners

Thrift Marketing Inc ....G 913 236-7474
Shawnee Mission *(G-11931)*

CLEANING PRDTS: Laundry Preparations

Clorox Company ....F 913 664-9000
Overland Park *(G-8568)*
Heartland At-Chlor Systems LLC ....F 806 373-4277
Wichita *(G-14580)*

CLEANING PRDTS: Sanitation Preparations

Pur-O-Zone Inc ....E 785 843-0771
Lawrence *(G-5082)*

CLEANING PRDTS: Specialty

Rehrig Penn Logistics Inc ....G 620 624-5171
Liberal *(G-6359)*
Ultra-Chem Inc ....C 913 492-2929
Shawnee Mission *(G-11955)*

CLEANING SVCS

Allen Commercial Clg Svcs LLC ....E 913 322-2900
Lenexa *(G-5641)*
Cottagecare Inc ....F 913 469-8778
Overland Park *(G-8603)*
Daka Inc ....E 913 768-1803
Prairie Village *(G-10025)*
Fresh Apprach Clg Prfessionals ....F 913 707-5500
Shawnee Mission *(G-11381)*
Green Clean Kc LLC ....F 913 499-7106
Overland Park *(G-8777)*
Iclean Prof Clg Svcs LLC ....F 913 521-5995
Overland Park *(G-8836)*
Interstate Cleaning Corp ....C 314 428-0566
Olathe *(G-7801)*
Jens House & Coml Clg LLC ....F 785 286-2463
Topeka *(G-12743)*
Jmh Cleaning Service ....F 785 819-0725
Salina *(G-10556)*
Landscapes Inc ....E 316 262-7557
Wichita *(G-14921)*
Midwest Duct Cleaning Services ....F 913 648-5300
Shawnee Mission *(G-11633)*
Noonshine Window Cleaning Svc ....F 913 381-3780
Overland Park *(G-9092)*
Ryans Comet Cleaner ....F 620 231-4559
Pittsburg *(G-9931)*

CLEANING SVCS: Industrial Or Commercial

Cogen Cleaning Technology Inc ....E 281 339-5751
Stilwell *(G-12142)*
Eagle Environmental Svcs LLC ....E 316 944-2445
Wichita *(G-14250)*
Helping Hands Services-Kansas ....E 417 438-6102
Baxter Springs *(G-408)*
Jeff Goldman ....F 785 842-0351
Lawrence *(G-4922)*
Restore It Systems LLC ....F 620 331-3997
Independence *(G-3555)*

CLIPS & FASTENERS, MADE FROM PURCHASED WIRE

Farris Burns Corp ....G 913 262-0555
Shawnee Mission *(G-11361)*

CLOTHING & ACCESS, WOMEN, CHILD & INFANT, WHSLE: Sportswear

Branded Custom Sportswear Inc ....E 913 663-6800
Overland Park *(G-8481)*

CLOTHING & ACCESS, WOMEN, CHILDREN/INFANT, WHOL: Swimsuits

Five Clothes LLC ....F 913 713-6216
Overland Park *(G-8726)*

CLOTHING & APPAREL STORES: Custom

Epic Sports ....C 316 612-0150
Bel Aire *(G-432)*

CLOTHING & FURNISHINGS, MEN & BOY, WHOLESALE: Suits/Trousers

Dcm Wichita Inc ....F 800 662-9573
Towanda *(G-13263)*

CLOTHING & FURNISHINGS, MEN'S & BOYS', WHOLESALE: Caps

Design Resources Inc ....D 913 652-6522
Overland Park *(G-8651)*
Finchers Findings Inc ....G 620 886-5952
Medicine Lodge *(G-7060)*
Promotional Headwear Intl Inc ....F 913 541-0901
Lenexa *(G-6076)*

CLOTHING & FURNISHINGS, MEN'S & BOYS', WHOLESALE: Outerwear

Key Industries Inc ....E 620 223-2000
Fort Scott *(G-1979)*

CLOTHING & FURNISHINGS, MENS & BOYS, WHOL: Sportswear/Work

Branded Custom Sportswear Inc ....E 913 663-6800
Overland Park *(G-8481)*

CLOTHING STORES, NEC

United Distributors Inc ....F 316 263-6181
Wichita *(G-15842)*

CLOTHING STORES: Lingerie, Outerwear

Salon X ....F 620 343-8634
Emporia *(G-1820)*

CLOTHING STORES: T-Shirts, Printed, Custom

Golden Sea Graphics Inc ....G 785 747-2822
Greenleaf *(G-2669)*
Sands Enterprises Inc ....G 316 942-8686
Wichita *(G-15518)*
Super Speed Printing Inc ....F 316 283-5828
North Newton *(G-7439)*
Team Threads ....G 620 429-4402
Columbus *(G-1089)*

CLOTHING STORES: Uniforms & Work

Kellys Corporate Apparel ....G 316 263-5858
Wichita *(G-14847)*

CLOTHING STORES: Work

Orscheln Farm and Home LLC ....F 620 241-0707
McPherson *(G-7012)*
Orscheln Farm and Home LLC ....F 620 331-2551
Independence *(G-3546)*
Orscheln Farm and Home LLC ....F 785 825-1681
Salina *(G-10624)*
Orscheln Farm and Home LLC ....F 620 442-5760
Arkansas City *(G-168)*
Orscheln Farm and Home LLC ....F 785 762-4411
Junction City *(G-3734)*
Orscheln Farm and Home LLC ....F 913 367-2261
Atchison *(G-254)*
Orscheln Farm and Home LLC ....E 620 421-0555
Parsons *(G-9715)*
Orscheln Farm and Home LLC ....F 620 662-8867
Hutchinson *(G-3397)*
Orscheln Farm and Home LLC ....F 620 251-2950
Coffeyville *(G-968)*
Orscheln Farm and Home LLC ....F 785 838-3184
Lawrence *(G-5050)*
Orscheln Farm and Home LLC ....E 785 776-1476
Manhattan *(G-6766)*
Orscheln Farm and Home LLC ....F 316 321-4004
El Dorado *(G-1589)*
Orscheln Farm and Home LLC ....F 785 625-7316
Hays *(G-2884)*
Orscheln Farm and Home LLC ....E 785 242-3133
Ottawa *(G-8296)*
Orscheln Farm and Home LLC ....F 785 228-9688
Topeka *(G-12955)*
Tractor Supply Company ....F 785 827-3300
Salina *(G-10738)*
Tractor Supply Company ....F 620 663-7607
Hutchinson *(G-3465)*

CLOTHING: Athletic & Sportswear, Men's & Boys'

Action Custom Sportswear LLC ....G 913 433-9900
Overland Park *(G-8344)*
CC Products LLC ....B 913 693-3200
Lenexa *(G-5737)*
Gfsi Inc ....F 913 693-3200
Lenexa *(G-5874)*
Gfsi LLC ....B 913 693-3200
Lenexa *(G-5875)*
Lee Apparel Company Inc ....C 913 384-4000
Shawnee Mission *(G-11558)*
Outdoor Custom Sportswear LLC ....E 866 288-5070
Overland Park *(G-9116)*

PRDT & SVC

CLOTHING: Athletic & Sportswear, Women's & Girls'

CC Products LLC ....B 913 693-3200
Lenexa *(G-5737)*
Outdoor Custom Sportswear LLC ....E 866 288-5070
Overland Park *(G-9116)*

CLOTHING: Children's, Girls'

Lee Apparel Company Inc ....C 913 384-4000
Shawnee Mission *(G-11558)*

CLOTHING: Coats, Hunting & Vests, Men's

Noa Group LLC ....F 316 821-9700
Wichita *(G-15183)*

CLOTHING: Outerwear, Women's & Misses' NEC

Lee Apparel Company Inc ....C 913 384-4000
Shawnee Mission *(G-11558)*

CLOTHING: Shirts

Rfc Logo Inc ....A 913 319-3100
Shawnee Mission *(G-11794)*

CLOTHING: Socks

Notes To Self LLC ....G 913 730-0037
Mission *(G-7133)*
Tradehome Shoe Stores Inc ....G 785 539-4003
Manhattan *(G-6830)*

CLOTHING: Sportswear, Women's

Gfsi Inc ....F 913 693-3200
Lenexa *(G-5874)*
Gfsi LLC ....B 913 693-3200
Lenexa *(G-5875)*

CLOTHING: Tailored Suits & Formal Jackets

Todds Clothiers & Tailor Shop ....G 913 681-8633
Overland Park *(G-9418)*

CLOTHING: Uniforms, Ex Athletic, Women's, Misses' & Juniors'

Deyno LLC ....F 785 551-8949
Lawrence *(G-4835)*
Fruhauf Uniforms Inc ....C 316 263-7500
Wichita *(G-14427)*

CLOTHING: Uniforms, Men's & Boys'

Fruhauf Uniforms Inc ....C 316 263-7500
Wichita *(G-14427)*

CLOTHING: Uniforms, Team Athletic

Challenger Sports Teamwear LLC ....E 913 599-4884
Lenexa *(G-5750)*

CLOTHING: Uniforms, Work

Deyno LLC ....F 785 551-8949
Lawrence *(G-4835)*

COAL & OTHER MINERALS & ORES WHOLESALERS

Koch Carbon LLC ....E 316 828-5500
Wichita *(G-14875)*

COAL MINING EXPLORATION & TEST BORING SVC

Continental Coal Inc ....E 913 491-1717
Shawnee Mission *(G-11263)*

COAL MINING: Bituminous Coal & Lignite-Surface Mining

Harbour Construction Inc ....F 913 441-2555
Kansas City *(G-4067)*

COAL MINING: Lignite, Surface, NEC

Health and Envmt Kans Dept ....F 620 231-8540
Frontenac *(G-2055)*

COAL, MINERALS & ORES, WHOLESALE: Coal

Pride AG Resources ....F 620 227-8671
Dodge City *(G-1422)*

COAL, MINERALS & ORES, WHOLESALE: Sulfur

Tessenderlo Kerley Inc ....F 620 251-3111
Coffeyville *(G-982)*

COATING SVC: Hot Dip, Metals Or Formed Prdts

Landoll Corporation ....E 785 738-6613
Beloit *(G-490)*

COATING SVC: Metals & Formed Prdts

Bob Eisel Powder Coatings ....E 316 942-8870
Wichita *(G-13860)*
Hobby Monster Customs LLC ....G 913 417-7088
Tonganoxie *(G-12263)*
Powdertech Llc ....E 316 832-9210
Wichita *(G-15317)*

COATINGS: Epoxy

Raven Lining Systems Inc ....F 918 615-0020
Kansas City *(G-4362)*

COATINGS: Polyurethane

Versaflex Inc ....E 913 321-9000
Kansas City *(G-4519)*

COCKTAIL LOUNGE

Bartos Enterprises Inc ....F 620 232-9813
Frontenac *(G-2053)*

COFFEE SVCS

Coffee Time Inc ....D 316 267-3771
Wichita *(G-14050)*
Rule Properties LLC ....F 785 621-8000
Hays *(G-2903)*
Sarahlee Coffee and Tea Corp ....E 316 262-0398
Wichita *(G-15519)*

COILS & TRANSFORMERS

Kneisley Manufacturing Company ....F 620 365-6628
Iola *(G-3618)*
Networks International Corp ....E 913 685-3400
Overland Park *(G-9078)*
Pwi Inc ....E 316 942-2811
Wichita *(G-15380)*

COIN-OPERATED EQUIPMENT WHOLESALERS

United Distributors Inc ....F 316 712-2174
Wichita *(G-15841)*

COIN-OPERATED LAUNDRY

Bubble Rm Coin Ldry Dry Clean ....F 913 962-4046
Shawnee Mission *(G-11188)*
Just Our Laundry Inc ....F 913 649-8364
Shawnee Mission *(G-11505)*
Lamont Hill Resort Inc ....E 785 828-3131
Vassar *(G-13371)*

COKE OVEN PRDTS: Beehive

Brown Honey Farms ....G 785 778-2002
Haddam *(G-2694)*

COKE: Petroleum, Not From Refineries

Koch Carbon LLC ....E 316 828-5500
Wichita *(G-14875)*
Koch Mineral Services LLC ....E 316 828-5500
Wichita *(G-14884)*
Koch Sulfur Products Co LLC ....E 316 828-5500
Wichita *(G-14889)*

COLD STORAGE MACHINERY WHOLESALERS

Tyson Foods Inc ....F 913 393-7000
Olathe *(G-8127)*

COLLECTION AGENCIES

A/R Allegiance Group LLC ....F 913 338-4790
Leawood *(G-5311)*
Encore Receivable MGT Inc ....A 913 782-3333
Wichita *(G-14286)*
International Fincl Svcs Inc ....E 620 665-7708
Hutchinson *(G-3336)*
Kansas Counselors Kans Cy Inc ....E 913 541-9704
Lenexa *(G-5938)*
Ui Benefit Overpayments ....F 785 296-5000
Topeka *(G-13202)*

COLLECTION AGENCY, EXC REAL ESTATE

Account Rcvery Specialists Inc ....E 620 227-8510
Wichita *(G-13603)*
Account Rcvery Specialists Inc ....F 620 227-8510
Dodge City *(G-1288)*
Affiliated Management Svcs Inc ....F 913 677-9470
Shawnee Mission *(G-11083)*
Aih Receivable Management Svcs ....F 800 666-4606
Shawnee Mission *(G-11086)*
Berlin-Wheeler Inc ....C 785 271-1000
Topeka *(G-12372)*
C B C S Inc ....F 620 343-6220
Emporia *(G-1714)*
Central States Recovery Inc ....E 620 663-8811
Hutchinson *(G-3234)*
Collection Bureau Kansas Inc ....E 785 228-3636
Topeka *(G-12486)*
Credit World Services Inc ....E 913 362-3950
Shawnee Mission *(G-11278)*
Creditors Service Bureau Inc ....F 785 266-3223
Topeka *(G-12529)*
Kansas Counselors Inc ....D 316 942-8335
Wichita *(G-14794)*
Mid America Credit Bureau LLC ....E 913 307-0551
Lenexa *(G-5998)*
Midcontinent Credit Svcs Inc ....F 316 721-6467
Wichita *(G-15086)*
Midwest Service Bureau Inc ....E 316 263-1051
Wichita *(G-15100)*
National Credit Adjusters LLC ....C 888 768-0674
Hutchinson *(G-3387)*
Portfolio Recovery Assoc LLC ....C 620 662-2800
Hutchinson *(G-3409)*
Sure Check Brokerage Inc ....F 785 823-1334
Salina *(G-10729)*
Yellow Roadway Receivables Fun ....F 913 491-6363
Overland Park *(G-9517)*

COLLEGE, EXC JUNIOR

Bethany College ....D 785 227-3380
Lindsborg *(G-6393)*

COLLEGES, UNIVERSITIES & PROFESSIONAL SCHOOLS

Gross PHD Judith M S ....F 913 645-2437
Kansas City *(G-4056)*
Idea Center Inc ....F 785 320-2400
Manhattan *(G-6664)*
Institute For Professional Dev ....E 913 491-4432
Shawnee Mission *(G-11460)*
Kansas State University ....D 785 532-6011
Manhattan *(G-6686)*
Rockhurst University Continuin ....D 913 432-7755
Shawnee Mission *(G-11812)*
University of Kansas ....A 913 588-4718
Kansas City *(G-4498)*
University of Kansas ....E 913 588-5133
Kansas City *(G-4499)*

COLOR PIGMENTS

Standridge Color Corporation ....F 316 283-5061
Newton *(G-7419)*

COLOR SEPARATION: Photographic & Movie Film

Graphics Four Inc ....G 913 268-0564
Shawnee *(G-10964)*

COLORS: Pigments, Organic

Standridge Color Corporation .... F 316 283-5061
Newton *(G-7419)*

COMBINATION UTILITIES, NEC

Campus Electric Power Company .... E 785 271-4824
Topeka *(G-12420)*
City of Iola .... C 620 365-4900
Iola *(G-3593)*
City of Ottawa .... F 785 229-3750
Ottawa *(G-8254)*
City of Ottawa .... E 785 229-3710
Ottawa *(G-8255)*
Heartland Midwest LLC .... C 913 397-9911
Olathe *(G-7763)*

COMBINED ELEMENTARY & SECONDARY SCHOOLS, PRIVATE

Kansas City Christian School .... D 913 648-5227
Prairie Village *(G-10040)*
Paola Assembly of God Inc .... F 913 294-5198
Paola *(G-9578)*

COMMERCIAL & INDL SHELVING WHOLESALERS

Custom Cabinet & Rack Inc .... E 785 862-2271
Topeka *(G-12537)*

COMMERCIAL & OFFICE BUILDINGS RENOVATION & REPAIR

Action Plumbing of Lawrence .... F 785 843-5670
Lawrence *(G-4718)*
Chambless Roofing Inc .... F 620 275-8410
Scott City *(G-10807)*
Coal Creek Construction Co .... F 785 256-7171
Auburn *(G-294)*
Damage Ctrl & Restoration Inc .... E 913 722-0228
Kansas City *(G-3954)*
Duffy Construction Company Inc .... F 913 381-1668
Shawnee Mission *(G-11321)*
Flinthills Construction Inc .... F 785 379-5499
Tecumseh *(G-12239)*
Guthridge/Nighswonger Corp .... F 316 264-7900
Wichita *(G-14529)*
Heinen Custom Operations Inc .... F 785 945-6759
Valley Falls *(G-13364)*
Howell Construction Co Inc .... E 816 474-7766
Stilwell *(G-12153)*
Hudson Inc .... E 620 232-1145
Pittsburg *(G-9879)*
Jay McConnell Construction Inc .... F 913 492-9300
Kansas City *(G-4119)*
Jayhawk Plumbing Inc .... F 785 865-5225
Lawrence *(G-4920)*
Kearney Construction Inc .... F 913 367-1200
Atchison *(G-238)*
Kendall Construction Inc .... E 785 246-1207
Topeka *(G-12817)*
Keystone Construction Inc .... F 316 778-1566
Benton *(G-516)*
Klein Construction Inc .... F 316 262-3313
Park City *(G-9626)*
Line Construction Company .... F 913 341-1212
Shawnee Mission *(G-11575)*
Main Street Chanute Inc .... F 620 431-0056
Chanute *(G-741)*
Midland Restoration Company .... F 620 223-6855
Fort Scott *(G-1991)*
Mohan Construction Inc .... E 785 233-1615
Topeka *(G-12909)*
National Ctstrphe Rstrtion Inc .... D 316 636-5700
Wichita *(G-15149)*
Netco Construction Co Inc .... E 316 942-2062
Wichita *(G-15162)*
Nieder Contracting Inc .... E 785 842-0094
Lawrence *(G-5040)*
Paint Masters Inc .... F 316 683-5203
Wichita *(G-15253)*
Paul-Wertenberger Cnstr Inc .... E 785 625-8220
Hays *(G-2885)*
PDQ Construction Inc .... F 785 842-6844
Topeka *(G-12966)*
Ponton Construction Inc .... F 785 823-9584
Salina *(G-10635)*
Prosser Wilbert Cnstr Inc .... F 913 906-0104
Lenexa *(G-6077)*
R D H Electric Inc .... E 785 625-3833
Hays *(G-2895)*
Redmon Housing LLC .... F 913 432-4945
Overland Park *(G-9229)*
Regarding Kitchens Inc .... F 913 642-6184
Olathe *(G-8023)*
Retrochem Inc .... F 913 422-8810
Shawnee *(G-11018)*
Rhino Builders Inc .... F 913 722-4353
Kansas City *(G-4376)*
Rose Companies Inc .... F 913 782-0777
Olathe *(G-8042)*
Shamburg Unlimited LLC .... F 785 379-0760
Tecumseh *(G-12241)*
Snodgrass & Sons Cnstr Co Inc .... D 316 687-3110
Wichita *(G-15611)*
Southwestern Remodeling Contrs .... E 316 263-1239
Wichita *(G-15633)*
Winston-Brown Construction Co .... E 785 271-1661
Topeka *(G-13246)*
Wood RE New Joco Inc .... G 913 661-9663
Olathe *(G-8159)*

COMMERCIAL ART & GRAPHIC DESIGN SVCS

Astronomical Society Kansas Cy .... F 913 631-8413
Shawnee Mission *(G-11127)*
Custom Design Inc .... F 913 764-6511
Olathe *(G-7630)*
Davinci Reprographics .... F 913 371-0014
Kansas City *(G-3958)*
Jack Jones Inc .... F 620 342-4221
Emporia *(G-1779)*
Kca Internet .... F 913 735-7206
Stilwell *(G-12160)*
Sgl LLC .... E 800 835-0588
Parsons *(G-9737)*

COMMERCIAL EQPT WHOLESALERS, NEC

Bar Code Systems .... F 913 894-6368
Shawnee Mission *(G-11151)*
Kanequip Inc .... C 785 562-2377
Marysville *(G-6892)*
Kansas Powertrain & Eqp LLC .... F 785 861-7034
Topeka *(G-12797)*
Norvell Company Inc .... E 785 825-6663
Salina *(G-10615)*
Pitsco Inc .... F 620 231-0010
Pittsburg *(G-9917)*
Sunflower Medical LLC .... F 785 726-2486
Ellis *(G-1654)*

COMMERCIAL EQPT, WHOLESALE: Comm Cooking & Food Svc Eqpt

Ice-Masters Inc .... F 316 945-6900
Wichita *(G-14665)*
Marel Inc .... E 913 888-9110
Lenexa *(G-5986)*
Stevenson Company Inc .... F 785 233-1303
Topeka *(G-13098)*
Veteran Fdsrvice Solutions LLC .... F 913 307-9922
Lenexa *(G-6211)*

COMMERCIAL EQPT, WHOLESALE: Restaurant, NEC

AAA Restaurant Supply LLC .... F 316 265-4365
Wichita *(G-13592)*
American Fun Food Company Inc .... F 316 838-9329
Park City *(G-9600)*
B & J Food Service Eqp Inc .... E 913 621-6165
Kansas City *(G-3835)*
Dee Jays Enterprises .... F 620 227-3126
Dodge City *(G-1340)*
Fsw Subtech Holdings LLC .... F 816 795-9955
Kansas City *(G-4019)*
Heartland Food Products Inc .... F 866 571-0222
Shawnee Mission *(G-11424)*
Hobart Sales and Service Inc .... E 913 469-9600
Lenexa *(G-5904)*
Hockenbergs Restaurant Supply .... F 913 696-9773
Shawnee Mission *(G-11436)*
Muckenthaler Incorporated .... F 620 342-5653
Emporia *(G-1799)*
Sub-Technologies Inc .... E 816 795-9955
Kansas City *(G-4443)*
Sunflower Restaurant Sup Inc .... F 785 823-6394
Salina *(G-10726)*

COMMERCIAL EQPT, WHOLESALE: Scales, Exc Laboratory

Express Scale Parts Inc .... E 913 441-4787
Lenexa *(G-5844)*
Hammel Scale Co Inc .... E 316 264-1358
Wichita *(G-14548)*
Hammel Scale Kansas City Inc .... F 913 321-5428
Kansas City *(G-4062)*
Salina Scale Sales & Service .... F 785 827-4441
Salina *(G-10690)*

COMMERCIAL EQPT, WHOLESALE: Store Eqpt

Concepts For Business LLC .... F 913 888-8686
Shawnee Mission *(G-11258)*

COMMERCIAL PRINTING & NEWSPAPER PUBLISHING COMBINED

Advocate Publishing Co Inc .... E 785 562-2317
Marysville *(G-6878)*
Blade Empire Publishing Co .... E 785 243-2424
Concordia *(G-1103)*
Clay Center Publishing Co Inc .... G 785 632-2127
Clay Center *(G-852)*
Ellsworth Reporter Inc .... G 785 472-5085
Ellsworth *(G-1672)*
Envision Inc .... E 316 440-3737
Wichita *(G-14295)*
Garden City Telegram .... E 620 275-8500
Garden City *(G-2177)*
Gatehouse Media LLC .... E 620 672-5512
Pratt *(G-10117)*
Golden Plains Publishers Inc .... G 620 855-3902
Cimarron *(G-827)*
Haynes Publishing Co .... G 785 475-2206
Oberlin *(G-7497)*
Herald Sabetha Inc .... G 785 284-3300
Sabetha *(G-10313)*
Hesston Record .... G 620 327-4831
Hesston *(G-2992)*
Hutchinson Publishing Co .... C 620 694-5700
Hutchinson *(G-3322)*
Julie K Samuelson .... G 785 852-4900
Sharon Springs *(G-10899)*
Kingman Leader Courier .... G 620 532-3151
Kingman *(G-4602)*
Linn County Publishing Inc .... F 913 352-6235
Pleasanton *(G-9997)*
News Publishing Co Inc .... D 785 628-1081
Hays *(G-2877)*
Osage County Herald .... G 785 528-3511
Osage City *(G-8186)*
Seaton Publishing Co Inc .... D 785 776-2200
Manhattan *(G-6798)*
Seward County Publishing LLC .... E 620 626-0840
Liberal *(G-6367)*
Star Communication Corporation .... F 620 285-3111
Larned *(G-4713)*
Topeka Capital Journal .... E 785 295-1111
Topeka *(G-13170)*
Worldwest Ltd Liability Co .... C 785 843-1000
Lawrence *(G-5192)*

COMMERCIAL SECTOR REGULATION, LICENSING/INSP, GOVT: Banking

Bank Commssnr Kansas Offce .... D 785 296-2266
Topeka *(G-12363)*

COMMODITY CONTRACT TRADING COMPANIES

Cassian Energy LLC .... F 913 948-1107
Overland Park *(G-8525)*

COMMODITY CONTRACTS BROKERS, DEALERS

Gavilon Grain LLC .... F 785 263-7275
Abilene *(G-33)*
Lansing Ethanol Services LLC .... E 913 748-3000
Overland Park *(G-8943)*

COMMODITY INSPECTION SVCS

Kansas Grain Inspection Svc .... D 785 233-7063
Topeka *(G-12778)*

COMMON SAND MINING

Stone Sand Co Inc .... E 620 793-7864
Great Bend *(G-2639)*

COMMUNICATIONS CARRIER: Wired

Wise Connect .... C 913 276-4100
Overland Park *(G-9500)*

COMMUNICATIONS EQPT REPAIR & MAINTENANCE

All Systems Inc .... E 913 281-5100
Kansas City *(G-3799)*
AVI Systems Inc .... E 913 495-9494
Lenexa *(G-5677)*
Communications Tech Assoc .... E 316 267-5016
Wichita *(G-14076)*
G E V Investment Inc .... E 913 677-5333
Kansas City *(G-4024)*
Ka-Comm Inc .... G 785 776-8177
Manhattan *(G-6672)*
Teledata Communications LLC .... E 913 663-2010
Lenexa *(G-6175)*
Tfmcomm Inc .... E 785 233-2343
Topeka *(G-13156)*

COMMUNICATIONS EQPT WHOLESALERS

Adams Cable Equipment Inc .... E 913 888-5100
Lenexa *(G-5628)*
All Systems Inc .... E 913 281-5100
Kansas City *(G-3799)*
Bevan-Rabell Inc .... E 316 946-4870
Wichita *(G-13842)*
Communications Tech Assoc .... E 316 267-5016
Wichita *(G-14076)*
G E V Investment Inc .... E 913 677-5333
Kansas City *(G-4024)*
Ka-Comm Inc .... F 785 827-8555
Salina *(G-10560)*
McClelland Sound Inc .... F 316 265-8686
Wichita *(G-15021)*
Skc Communication Products LLC .... C 913 422-4222
Shawnee Mission *(G-11870)*
Southern Kansas Tele Co Inc .... E 620 584-2255
Clearwater *(G-899)*
Southern Kansas Tele Co Inc .... E 620 584-2255
Clearwater *(G-898)*
Talley Inc .... F 913 390-8484
Olathe *(G-8100)*

COMMUNICATIONS SVCS

Home Communications Inc .... F 620 654-3381
Galva *(G-2093)*
Mitel (delaware) Inc .... F 913 752-9100
Lenexa *(G-6007)*
Retel Brokerage Services Inc .... E 678 292-5723
Wichita *(G-15453)*

COMMUNICATIONS SVCS, NEC

Evans Media Group .... F 913 489-7364
Lenexa *(G-5837)*
Rare Moon Media .... F 913 951-8360
Overland Park *(G-9226)*
Zillner Mktg Cmmunications Inc .... E 913 599-3230
Lenexa *(G-6241)*

COMMUNICATIONS SVCS: Cellular

ABC Phones North Carolina Inc .... E 785 243-4099
Concordia *(G-1100)*
ABC Phones North Carolina Inc .... E 785 263-3553
Manhattan *(G-6530)*
ABC Phones North Carolina Inc .... E 620 508-6167
Pratt *(G-10091)*
Aka Wireless Inc .... D 785 823-6605
Salina *(G-10399)*
Answer Topeka Inc .... E 785 234-4444
Topeka *(G-12331)*
AT&T Corp .... D 620 272-0383
Garden City *(G-2103)*
AT&T Corp .... E 785 272-4002
Topeka *(G-12349)*
AT&T Corp .... D 913 383-4943
Overland Park *(G-8407)*
AT&T Corp .... F 913 894-0800
Overland Park *(G-8408)*
AT&T Corp .... E 785 832-2700
Lawrence *(G-4742)*
AT&T Corp .... F 913 254-0303
Olathe *(G-7538)*
AT&T Corp .... B 913 676-1261
Shawnee Mission *(G-11128)*
AT&T Corp .... F 913 334-9615
Kansas City *(G-3829)*
AT&T Corp .... F 620 421-7612
Parsons *(G-9668)*
AT&T Corp .... D 620 626-5168
Liberal *(G-6280)*
AT&T Inc .... F 913 676-1136
Lenexa *(G-5673)*
AT&T Mobility LLC .... E 913 254-0303
Olathe *(G-7539)*
Cellco Partnership .... D 316 636-5155
Wichita *(G-13970)*
Cellco Partnership .... D 620 276-6776
Garden City *(G-2122)*
Cellco Partnership .... D 785 820-6311
Salina *(G-10438)*
Cellco Partnership .... D 316 722-4532
Wichita *(G-13971)*
Cellco Partnership .... D 913 631-0677
Overland Park *(G-8536)*
Cellco Partnership .... F 913 897-5022
Overland Park *(G-8535)*
Cellco Partnership .... F 316 789-9911
Derby *(G-1228)*
Cellco Partnership .... F 785 537-6159
Manhattan *(G-6580)*
Clearwire LLC .... F 202 628-3544
Overland Park *(G-8564)*
Cricket Communications LLC .... F 316 636-6387
Wichita *(G-14130)*
Cricket Communications LLC .... F 913 999-0163
Roeland Park *(G-10222)*
Discount Tobacco & Cellular .... F 913 281-3067
Kansas City *(G-3972)*
Ensignal Inc .... E 316 265-8311
Wichita *(G-14290)*
Flint Telecom Group Inc .... F 913 815-1570
Overland Park *(G-8730)*
Gateway Wreless Netwrk Svcs Lc .... F 316 264-0037
Wichita *(G-14452)*
Hightech Solutions Inc .... C 620 228-2216
Fredonia *(G-2035)*
Ka-Comm Inc .... G 785 776-8177
Manhattan *(G-6672)*
Motor Mouth Wireless LLC .... F 316 260-4660
Wichita *(G-15134)*
New Cingular Wireless Svcs Inc .... F 785 832-2700
Lawrence *(G-5038)*
New Cingular Wireless Svcs Inc .... B 913 344-2845
Shawnee Mission *(G-11679)*
Nex-Tech Wireless LLC .... D 785 567-4281
Hays *(G-2879)*
Nextel of California Inc .... E 866 505-2385
Overland Park *(G-9083)*
Nextel Partners Operating Corp .... C 800 829-0965
Overland Park *(G-9084)*
Overfield Corporation .... F 785 843-3434
Lawrence *(G-5052)*
Sprint Communications NH Inc .... E 800 829-0965
Overland Park *(G-9339)*
Sprint Corporation .... C 877 564-3166
Overland Park *(G-9340)*
Sprint Spectrum LP .... F 785 537-3500
Manhattan *(G-6804)*
T-Mobile Usa Inc .... D 913 402-6500
Shawnee Mission *(G-11916)*
T-Mobile Usa Inc .... F 316 201-6120
Wichita *(G-15716)*
T-Mobile Usa Inc .... F 913 268-4414
Shawnee *(G-11038)*
T-Mobile Usa Inc .... F 913 262-2789
Shawnee Mission *(G-11917)*
T-Mobile Usa Inc .... F 785 273-5021
Topeka *(G-13131)*
T-Mobile Usa Inc .... F 913 254-1674
Olathe *(G-8098)*
T2 Wireless Inc .... F 785 537-8034
Manhattan *(G-6820)*
Ubiquitel Inc .... D 913 315-5800
Overland Park *(G-9437)*
United States Cellular Corp .... F 620 231-2444
Pittsburg *(G-9952)*
United Wrless Cmmnications Inc .... E 620 227-8127
Dodge City *(G-1445)*
United Wrlss Arina Mgrk Conf C .... F 620 371-7390
Dodge City *(G-1446)*

COMMUNICATIONS SVCS: Data

Alltech Communications Inc .... F 785 267-0316
Topeka *(G-12309)*
Bear Communications LLC .... C 785 856-3333
Lawrence *(G-4753)*
Cox Media LLC .... A 785 215-8880
Topeka *(G-12525)*
Cox Media LLC .... E 623 322-2000
Wichita *(G-14122)*
Envision Technology Group LLC .... E 913 390-5141
Overland Park *(G-8685)*
Jmz Corporation .... E 620 365-7782
Iola *(G-3616)*

COMMUNICATIONS SVCS: Electronic Mail

1&1 Internet Inc .... F 816 621-4795
Lenexa *(G-5615)*
Em Sales LLC .... F 913 486-6762
Kansas City *(G-3985)*

COMMUNICATIONS SVCS: Internet Connectivity Svcs

Allegiant Networks LLC .... E 913 599-6900
Leawood *(G-5316)*
Eagle Bradband Investments LLC .... F 785 625-5910
Hays *(G-2792)*
Exaltia LLC .... F 316 616-6200
Wichita *(G-14319)*
Hubris Communications .... F 316 858-3000
Wichita *(G-14647)*
Ideatek Telecom LLC .... E 620 543-2580
Buhler *(G-617)*
Kansas Broadband Internet .... F 785 825-0199
Salina *(G-10563)*
Mavicor LLC .... E 888 387-1620
Overland Park *(G-8995)*
Mercury Wireless Kansas LLC .... F 800 354-4915
Topeka *(G-12883)*
Midcontinent Communications .... C 785 841-2100
Lawrence *(G-5025)*
Pixius Communications LLC .... D 316 219-8500
Wichita *(G-15303)*
S & T Telephone Coop Assn .... E 785 694-2256
Brewster *(G-586)*
United Communications Assn Inc .... E 620 227-8645
Dodge City *(G-1442)*
Wheatland Broadband Services .... F 620 872-0006
Scott City *(G-10836)*
Wildflower Internet LLC .... E 620 543-2580
Buhler *(G-619)*

COMMUNICATIONS SVCS: Internet Host Svcs

1&1 Internet Inc .... F 816 621-4795
Lenexa *(G-5615)*
Clearwire Corporation .... E 425 216-7600
Overland Park *(G-8563)*
Connex International Inc .... C 785 749-9500
Lawrence *(G-4810)*
Extreme Tanning Inc .... F 316 712-0190
Wichita *(G-14325)*
Internet Svc Prvders Ntwrk Inc .... E 913 859-9500
Shawnee Mission *(G-11465)*
Iq Group Inc .... F 913 722-6700
Lenexa *(G-5922)*
Kca Internet .... F 913 735-7206
Stilwell *(G-12160)*
Nexlynx .... F 785 232-5969
Topeka *(G-12930)*

COMMUNICATIONS SVCS: Online Svc Providers

Civicplus LLC .... F 785 267-6800
Manhattan *(G-6589)*
Eagle Communications Inc .... F 785 726-3291
Hays *(G-2794)*
Eagle Communications Inc .... E 785 483-3244
Russell *(G-10273)*
Iris Data Services Inc .... D 913 937-0590
Kansas City *(G-4112)*
It21 Inc .... F 913 393-4821
Overland Park *(G-8864)*
Papa Murphys Take N Bake .... F 913 897-0008
Overland Park *(G-9140)*
Pcs Incorporated .... F 913 981-1100
Olathe *(G-7977)*

Regional Media Corporation Inc............F........ 316 320-1120
El Dorado (G-1598)
Viralnova LLC..E....... 913 706-9710
Overland Park (G-9465)

COMMUNICATIONS SVCS: Phone Cable, Svcs, Land Or Submarine

AT&T Corp ....E....... 785 625-0120
Hays (G-2751)

COMMUNICATIONS SVCS: Proprietary Online Svcs Networks

Twotrees Technologies LLC ....F 800 364-5700
Wichita (G-15822)

COMMUNICATIONS SVCS: Satellite Earth Stations

Capps Manufacturing Inc........................D....... 316 942-9351
Wichita (G-13941)

COMMUNICATIONS SVCS: Telephone, Broker

Euronet Worldwide Inc ....D....... 913 327-4200
Leawood (G-5389)

COMMUNICATIONS SVCS: Telephone, Data

Teledata Communications LLC ....E....... 913 663-2010
Lenexa (G-6175)

COMMUNICATIONS SVCS: Telephone, Local

American Telephone Inc.........................F 913 780-3166
Gardner (G-2326)
AT&T Corp ....B....... 785 276-8201
Topeka (G-12348)
AT&T Corp ....F 800 403-3022
Topeka (G-12352)
Blue Vly Tl-Communications Inc..........D....... 785 799-3311
Home (G-3119)
Columbus Telephone Company ....F 620 429-3132
Columbus (G-1067)
Craw-Kan Telephone Coop Inc ....D....... 620 724-8235
Girard (G-2399)
Cunningham Telephone Company.........F 785 545-3215
Glen Elder (G-2425)
Elkhart Telephone Company Inc ....E....... 620 697-2111
Elkhart (G-1620)
Giant Communications Inc ....E....... 785 362-9331
Holton (G-3091)
Golden Belt Telephone Assn Inc ....E....... 785 372-4236
Rush Center (G-10259)
H & B Communications Inc....................F 620 562-3598
Holyrood (G-3115)
Haviland Telephone Company Inc.........F....... 620 862-5211
Haviland (G-2741)
JBN Telephone Company Inc ....F 785 362-3323
Holton (G-3101)
Kansas Fiber Network LLC ....E....... 316 712-6030
Wichita (G-14798)
Moundridge Telephone Company ....F 620 345-2831
Moundridge (G-7194)
Nex-Tech LLC ....F 785 421-4197
Hill City (G-3037)
Peoples Telecommunications LLC.........F 913 757-2500
La Cygne (G-4641)
Pioneer Telephone Assn Inc ....C....... 620 356-3211
Ulysses (G-13312)
Pioneer Telephone Assn Inc ....F 620 356-1985
Ulysses (G-13313)
Rural Telephone Service Co Inc ....F 785 483-5555
Russell (G-10293)
Southern Kansas Tele Co Inc ....E....... 620 584-2255
Clearwater (G-898)
Southwestern Bell Telephone Co ....E....... 785 862-5538
Topeka (G-13085)
Tri-County Telephone Assn Inc ....D....... 785 366-7000
Council Grove (G-1178)
Wamego Telephone Company Inc.........E....... 785 456-1001
Wamego (G-13456)
Wheat State Telephone Inc ....F 620 782-3341
Udall (G-13279)
Wilson Telephone Company Inc............E....... 785 658-2111
Wilson (G-16109)
Wtc Communications Inc ....F 785 456-1000
Wamego (G-13458)

COMMUNICATIONS SVCS: Telephone, Local & Long Distance

AT&T Corp ....E....... 913 676-1000
Shawnee Mission (G-11129)
AT&T Corp ....C....... 913 676-1000
Shawnee Mission (G-11130)
AT&T Corp ....E....... 785 749-7155
Lawrence (G-4743)
Centurylink Inc ....E....... 913 791-4971
New Century (G-7273)
Cunningham Communications Inc.........F 785 545-3215
Glen Elder (G-2424)
Golden Wheat Inc....................................E....... 620 782-3341
Udall (G-13277)
Home Telephone Co Inc ....F 620 654-3381
Galva (G-2094)
Kanokla Communications LLC..............D....... 620 845-5682
Caldwell (G-659)
Mokan Dial Inc...F 913 837-2219
Louisburg (G-6458)
Prime Communications LP ....F 785 371-4990
Lawrence (G-5075)
Rural Telephone Service Co Inc ....D....... 785 567-4281
Lenora (G-6245)
Sprint...E....... 703 433-4000
Overland Park (G-9336)
Sprint Communications Inc ....A....... 855 848-3280
Overland Park (G-9337)
Sprint Spectrum LP ....E....... 913 962-7777
Shawnee Mission (G-11886)
Sprint Spectrum LP ....E....... 316 634-4900
Wichita (G-15649)
Sprint Spectrum LP ....F 913 894-1375
Overland Park (G-9342)
Sprint Spectrum LP ....C....... 703 433-4000
Overland Park (G-9343)
Sprint Spectrum LP ....E....... 913 323-5000
Shawnee Mission (G-11887)
Surewest Kans Connections LLC ....D....... 913 890-4483
Lenexa (G-6163)
Twin Valley Telephone Inc ....E....... 785 427-2211
Miltonvale (G-7112)

COMMUNICATIONS SVCS: Telephone, Long Distance

Cellco Partnership ....F 785 537-6159
Manhattan (G-6580)
Sprint Communications Co LP ....A....... 800 829-0965
Overland Park (G-9338)
Sprint Corporation ....C....... 877 564-3166
Overland Park (G-9340)
Sprint International Inc..........................C....... 800 259-3755
Westwood (G-13559)

COMMUNICATIONS SVCS: Telephone, Voice

Direct Communications Inc ....F 913 599-5577
Overland Park (G-8657)
Kanokla Telephone Association ....E....... 620 845-5682
Caldwell (G-660)
South Central Tele Assn Inc...................E....... 620 933-1000
Pratt (G-10149)

COMMUNITY ACTION AGENCY

Shawnee Regl Prevention An ....F 785 266-8666
Topeka (G-13064)
Southeast Kansas Community ....E....... 620 724-8204
Girard (G-2419)

COMMUNITY CENTER

Alliance Equities Corporation................F 913 428-8278
Overland Park (G-8370)
City of Lenexa ....D....... 913 541-0209
Lenexa (G-5755)
City of Mission ....D....... 913 722-8200
Shawnee Mission (G-11229)
Coalition For Independence....................E....... 913 321-5140
Kansas City (G-3921)
Compass Behavioral Health ....E....... 620 276-6470
Garden City (G-2131)
Jewish Community Campus ....E....... 913 327-8200
Shawnee Mission (G-11487)
North Shawnee Community Center.......F ....°785 286-0676
Topeka (G-12933)
Project Eagle ....E....... 913 281-2648
Kansas City (G-4345)
Silver City Cmnty Resource Ctr.............F 913 362-3367
Kansas City (G-4421)

Southwest Developmental Svcs ....F 620 793-7604
Great Bend (G-2638)
Webster Conference Center Inc ....E....... 785 827-6565
Salina (G-10764)

COMMUNITY CENTERS: Adult

Cawker City Senior Center.....................F 785 781-4763
Cawker City (G-688)
City of Great Bend ....F 620 792-3906
Great Bend (G-2541)
Cowley County Council On Aging.........F 620 221-7020
Winfield (G-16130)
Daughters & Company Inc ....E....... 913 341-2500
Overland Park (G-8639)
Downs Senior Citizens Inc.....................F 785 454-6228
Downs (G-1471)
East Cntl Kans Area Agcy On AG..........E....... 785 242-7200
Ottawa (G-8267)
El Centro Inc ....F 913 677-0100
Kansas City (G-3982)
Eldercare Inc ....C....... 620 792-5942
Great Bend (G-2559)
Finch Hollow Senior Residences ....D....... 316 721-9596
Wichita (G-14368)
Grayco Over 50 ....F....... 620 855-3711
Cimarron (G-829)
Great Bend Commission On Aging.......F 620 792-3906
Great Bend (G-2575)
Grenola Senior Citizens ....F 620 358-3601
Grenola (G-2686)
Jay Hawk Area Agency On Aging..........E....... 785 235-1367
Topeka (G-12738)
Jefferson Cnty Svc Orgnization ....E....... 785 863-2637
Oskaloosa (G-8227)
Kensington Senior Cmnty Ctr................F 785 476-2224
Kensington (G-4578)
Linn Wood Place Incorporated ....E....... 785 945-3634
Valley Falls (G-13367)
Mini Bus Service Inc...............................F 620 272-3626
Garden City (G-2236)
Neighborhood Connection.....................E....... 316 267-0197
Wichita (G-15157)
Northast Kans Area Agcy On Agi ....F 785 742-7152
Hiawatha (G-3020)
Saline County Comm On Aging.............E....... 785 823-6666
Salina (G-10697)
Salvation Army National Corp ....F 913 299-4822
Kansas City (G-4399)
Senior Rsrce Ctr For Dglas CNT............F 785 842-0543
Lawrence (G-5108)
Senior Services Inc Wichita ....D....... 316 267-0122
Wichita (G-15560)
Senior Svcs of Southeast Kans..............F 620 232-7443
Pittsburg (G-9936)
Seniorcare Homes LLC ....F 913 236-0036
Prairie Village (G-10066)
Seward County Council On Aging ....E....... 620 624-2511
Liberal (G-6365)
Southwest KS Agency On Aging............F 620 225-8230
Dodge City (G-1431)
Spectrum Retirement Shawnee KS........E....... 913 631-0058
Shawnee Mission (G-11882)
Via Christi Villages Inc ....E....... 316 946-5200
Wichita (G-15898)

COMMUNITY CENTERS: Youth

Boys & Girls Club of S Central ....E....... 316 687-5437
Wichita (G-13877)
Boys Girls Clubs Huthinson Inc.............D....... 620 665-7171
Hutchinson (G-3220)
Boys Grls CLB Lwrnce Lwrnce K..........D....... 785 841-5672
Lawrence (G-4763)
Catacombs Youth Ministry ....E....... 316 689-8410
Wichita (G-13958)
Central Knss Cncil of Grl Sct.................F 785 827-3679
Salina (G-10442)
Cherry Street Youth Center....................F 620 431-0818
Chanute (G-715)
County of Sedgwick.................................E....... 316 660-0100
Wichita (G-14111)
Emberhope Inc...D....... 620 225-0276
Dodge City (G-1357)
Emmanuel United Methodist Ch............F 785 263-3342
Abilene (G-27)
Kansas Big Bros Big Ssters Inc..............F 620 231-1145
Pittsburg (G-9888)
Mid-Amrica Yuth Basketball Inc ....F 316 284-0354
Newton (G-7383)
Reno County Youth Services..................E....... 620 694-2500
Hutchinson (G-3425)

PRDT & SVC

World Impact Inc....E.... 316 687-9398
Wichita *(G-16073)*
Young Mens Christian Associa....D.... 316 945-2255
Wichita *(G-16092)*
Young Mens Christian Associat....C.... 316 685-2251
Wichita *(G-16096)*
Young MNS Chrstn Assn Slina Ka....D.... 785 825-2151
Salina *(G-10775)*

COMMUNITY DEVELOPMENT GROUPS

Ku Workgroup For Community Hea....E.... 785 864-0533
Lawrence *(G-4949)*
Mt Carmel Redevelopment Corp....F.... 913 621-4111
Kansas City *(G-4270)*
Rebuilding Together Shawnee/Jo....F.... 913 558-5079
Shawnee *(G-11015)*
Residential Treatment Service....E.... 620 421-1155
Parsons *(G-9732)*
Rosewood Services Inc....E.... 620 793-5888
Great Bend *(G-2633)*
Rsvp of Northeast Kansas Inc....C.... 785 562-2154
Marysville *(G-6909)*
Saint Francis Cmnty Svcs Inc....D.... 785 243-4215
Concordia *(G-1128)*
Salvation Army....F.... 620 343-3166
Emporia *(G-1821)*
Trash Mountain Project Inc....F.... 785 246-6845
Topeka *(G-13197)*
Urban League of Kansas Inc....F.... 316 440-9217
Wichita *(G-15861)*
Young Kansas Christian....C.... 785 233-1750
Topeka *(G-13257)*

COMMUNITY SVCS EMPLOYMENT TRAINING PROGRAM

Empac Inc....F.... 316 265-9922
Wichita *(G-14278)*
Optimal Performance LLC....F.... 316 440-4440
Wichita *(G-15227)*
Pyxis Inc....C.... 316 682-8092
Wichita *(G-15382)*
Ser Corporation....E.... 316 264-5372
Wichita *(G-15563)*

COMMUNITY THEATER PRODUCTION SVCS

City of Pittsburg....F.... 620 231-7827
Pittsburg *(G-9833)*

COMPACT DISCS OR CD'S, WHOLESALE

Kiefs Cds & Tapes....E.... 785 842-1544
Lawrence *(G-4945)*

COMPACTORS: Trash & Garbage, Residential

Howies Enterprises LLC....F.... 785 776-8352
Manhattan *(G-6660)*

COMPRESSORS: Air & Gas

Exline Inc....C.... 785 825-4683
Salina *(G-10489)*
Westheffer Company Inc....E.... 785 843-1633
Lawrence *(G-5183)*

COMPRESSORS: Refrigeration & Air Conditioning Eqpt

York International Corporation....D.... 316 832-6400
Wichita *(G-16086)*

COMPRESSORS: Repairing

Mid Kansas Tool & Electric Inc....F.... 785 825-9521
Salina *(G-10600)*
S & S Equipment Co Inc....F.... 316 267-7471
Wichita *(G-15500)*

COMPRESSORS: Wholesalers

Exline Leasing Inc....C.... 785 825-4683
Salina *(G-10490)*
Kaeser Compressors Inc....F.... 913 599-5100
Overland Park *(G-8884)*
S & S Equipment Co Inc....F.... 316 267-7471
Wichita *(G-15500)*

COMPUTER & COMPUTER SOFTWARE STORES

Dataco Derex Inc....F.... 913 438-2444
Leawood *(G-5370)*
Network Management Group Inc....E.... 620 665-3611
Hutchinson *(G-3389)*
S & T Telephone Coop Assn....F.... 785 460-7300
Colby *(G-1038)*
Wolfes Camera Shops Inc....E.... 785 235-1386
Topeka *(G-13248)*

COMPUTER & COMPUTER SOFTWARE STORES: Peripheral Eqpt

Eagle Software Inc....E.... 785 823-7257
Salina *(G-10483)*
Fox Computer Inc....E.... 785 776-1452
Manhattan *(G-6640)*
Rural Telephone Service Co Inc....D.... 785 567-4281
Lenora *(G-6245)*

COMPUTER & COMPUTER SOFTWARE STORES: Personal Computers

Haddock Corporation....E.... 316 558-3849
Wichita *(G-14539)*
Hightech Solutions Inc....C.... 620 228-2216
Fredonia *(G-2035)*
Keltech Solutions LLC....F.... 785 841-4611
Lawrence *(G-4940)*

COMPUTER & COMPUTER SOFTWARE STORES: Printers & Plotters

Drexel Technologies Inc....E.... 913 371-4430
Lenexa *(G-5826)*

COMPUTER & COMPUTER SOFTWARE STORES: Software & Access

Computer Distribution Corp....E.... 785 354-1086
Topeka *(G-12498)*
Images....G.... 785 827-0824
Salina *(G-10549)*
Networks Plus....E.... 785 825-0400
Manhattan *(G-6759)*

COMPUTER & COMPUTER SOFTWARE STORES: Software, Bus/Non-Game

Casey Associates Inc....F.... 913 276-3200
Lenexa *(G-5731)*

COMPUTER & DATA PROCESSING EQPT REPAIR & MAINTENANCE

Iris Data Services Inc....D.... 913 937-0590
Kansas City *(G-4112)*
Word-Tech Inc....E.... 913 722-3334
Shawnee Mission *(G-12019)*

COMPUTER & OFFICE MACHINE MAINTENANCE & REPAIR

Alliance Technologies Inc....F.... 913 262-7977
Overland Park *(G-8371)*
Computech Service of Kansas....E.... 785 266-2585
Topeka *(G-12497)*
Dataco Derex Inc....F.... 913 438-2444
Leawood *(G-5370)*
Fox Computer Inc....E.... 785 776-1452
Manhattan *(G-6640)*
Haddock Corporation....E.... 316 558-3849
Wichita *(G-14539)*
Heritage Cmpt Consulting Inc....F.... 913 529-4227
Overland Park *(G-8812)*
Installation and Svc Tech Inc....C.... 913 652-7000
Leawood *(G-5438)*
Isigma Consulting LLC....F.... 620 757-6363
Overland Park *(G-8863)*
Jack Henry & Associates Inc....C.... 913 422-3233
Shawnee Mission *(G-11479)*
Loquient Inc....F.... 913 221-0430
Shawnee Mission *(G-11577)*
Maps Inc....E.... 913 599-0500
Lenexa *(G-5984)*
Network Management Group Inc....E.... 620 665-3611
Hutchinson *(G-3389)*
Niffie Printing Inc....F.... 913 592-3040
Spring Hill *(G-12091)*
Repair Shack Inc....E.... 913 732-0514
Lenexa *(G-6105)*
Resq Systems LLC....F.... 913 390-1030
Olathe *(G-8027)*
Ricoh Usa Inc....C.... 913 890-5100
Shawnee Mission *(G-11802)*
Tech Gurus LLC....F.... 913 299-8700
Kansas City *(G-4462)*
Wolfes Camera Shops Inc....E.... 785 235-1386
Topeka *(G-13248)*

COMPUTER & SFTWR STORE: Modem, Monitor, Terminal/Disk Drive

Galaxie Business Equipment Inc....E.... 620 221-3469
Winfield *(G-16142)*
Stallard Technologies Inc....E.... 913 851-2260
Overland Park *(G-9351)*

COMPUTER CALCULATING SVCS

American Gvrnment Slutions LLC....F.... 913 428-2550
Leawood *(G-5320)*

COMPUTER DISKETTES WHOLESALERS

Optiv Security Inc....F.... 816 421-6611
Overland Park *(G-9110)*

COMPUTER FACILITIES MANAGEMENT SVCS

Computer Sciences Corporation....C.... 913 469-8700
Overland Park *(G-8593)*
Convergeone Inc....C.... 913 307-2300
Overland Park *(G-8597)*
Quality Tech Svcs Frt Worth II....F.... 913 814-9988
Overland Park *(G-9214)*
Quality Tech Svcs Nrtheast LLC....F.... 913 814-9988
Overland Park *(G-9216)*
Quality Technology Svcs LLC....D.... 913 814-9988
Overland Park *(G-9217)*
Sara Software Systems LLC....E.... 913 370-4197
Olathe *(G-8055)*
Topeka Unified School Dst 501....E.... 785 438-4750
Topeka *(G-13190)*

COMPUTER FORMS

Flesh Company....D.... 620 421-6120
Parsons *(G-9686)*
Kansas Business Forms LLC....E.... 620 724-5234
Girard *(G-2414)*

COMPUTER GRAPHICS SVCS

1&1 Internet Inc....F.... 816 621-4795
Lenexa *(G-5615)*
Capital Graphics Inc....E.... 785 233-6677
Topeka *(G-12431)*
Civicplus LLC....C.... 888 228-2233
Manhattan *(G-6590)*
Digital Evolution Group LLC....C.... 913 498-9988
Overland Park *(G-8655)*
Digital Lagoon Inc....F.... 913 648-6900
Overland Park *(G-8656)*
Florida Information Consortium....F.... 913 498-3468
Olathe *(G-7715)*
Iq Group Inc....F.... 913 722-6700
Lenexa *(G-5922)*
Mgmttv Inc....F.... 316 262-4678
Wichita *(G-15062)*
Nic Solutions LLC....F.... 913 498-3468
Olathe *(G-7921)*
R & S Digital Services Inc....F.... 620 792-6171
Great Bend *(G-2628)*
Trinity Animation Inc....F.... 816 525-0103
Overland Park *(G-9428)*
Tsunami Surf Riders LLC....F.... 913 498-3468
Olathe *(G-8123)*
Web Creations & Consulting LLC....G.... 785 823-7630
Salina *(G-10762)*

COMPUTER PERIPHERAL EQPT REPAIR & MAINTENANCE

ADI Systems Inc....F.... 785 825-5975
Salina *(G-10394)*
Kanokla Telephone Association....E.... 620 845-5682
Caldwell *(G-660)*

Keltech Solutions LLC..........F....... 785 841-4611
Lawrence *(G-4940)*

COMPUTER PERIPHERAL EQPT, NEC

Cisco Systems Inc..........D....... 913 344-6100
Shawnee Mission *(G-11227)*
Computerwise Inc..........F....... 408 389-8241
Olathe *(G-7609)*
Convergeone Inc..........C....... 913 307-2300
Overland Park *(G-8597)*
K G Moats & Sons LLC..........E....... 785 437-2021
Saint Marys *(G-10368)*
Knox Electronic Ltd..........F....... 316 321-2400
El Dorado *(G-1579)*
Leavenworth Technical Services..........G....... 913 351-3344
Leavenworth *(G-5266)*

COMPUTER PERIPHERAL EQPT, WHOLESALE

Arrow Electronics Inc..........E....... 913 242-3012
Overland Park *(G-8396)*
Cloud Storage Corporation..........F....... 785 621-4350
Hays *(G-2772)*
Communication Cable Company..........D....... 610 644-5155
Leawood *(G-5356)*
Control Systems Intl Inc..........D....... 913 599-5010
Shawnee Mission *(G-11264)*
Convergeone Inc..........C....... 913 307-2300
Overland Park *(G-8597)*
Inland Associates Inc..........F....... 913 764-7977
Olathe *(G-7791)*
Microtech Computers Inc..........E....... 785 841-9513
Lawrence *(G-5024)*
Shi International Corp..........F....... 512 226-3984
Overland Park *(G-9307)*

COMPUTER PROCESSING SVCS

Covansys Corporation..........C....... 913 469-8700
Shawnee Mission *(G-11275)*
Insysiv LLC..........F....... 816 694-9397
Kansas City *(G-4102)*
Universal Money Centers Inc..........E....... 913 831-2055
Lenexa *(G-6204)*

COMPUTER PROGRAMMING SVCS

AT&T Corp..........E....... 785 276-5553
Topeka *(G-12351)*
Builder Designs Inc..........F....... 913 393-3367
Olathe *(G-7566)*
Clarus Group LLC..........E....... 913 599-5255
Overland Park *(G-8560)*
Computerwise Inc..........F....... 408 389-8241
Olathe *(G-7609)*
Control Vision Corporation..........E....... 620 231-5816
Pittsburg *(G-9845)*
Creative Capsule LLC..........D....... 816 421-1714
Overland Park *(G-8608)*
Cybertron International Inc..........D....... 316 303-1022
Wichita *(G-14150)*
Datateam Systems Inc..........E....... 785 843-8150
Lawrence *(G-4826)*
Digital Evolution Group LLC..........C....... 913 498-9988
Overland Park *(G-8655)*
I T Power LLC..........E....... 913 384-5800
Shawnee Mission *(G-11448)*
Innova Consulting LLC..........F....... 913 210-2002
Overland Park *(G-8845)*
Innovative Technology Services..........E....... 785 271-2070
Topeka *(G-12724)*
J & M Industries Inc..........E....... 913 362-8994
Prairie Village *(G-10037)*
Jaray Software Inc..........G....... 316 267-5758
Wichita *(G-14747)*
Nic Inc..........B....... 877 234-3468
Olathe *(G-7920)*
Rhythm Engineering LLC..........E....... 913 227-0603
Lenexa *(G-6108)*
Servicetitan Inc..........G....... 316 267-5758
Wichita *(G-15568)*
Sohum Systems LLC..........E....... 913 221-7204
Overland Park *(G-9323)*
Solutions Now Inc..........E....... 913 327-5805
Overland Park *(G-9325)*
Veracity Consulting Inc..........D....... 913 945-1912
Overland Park *(G-9462)*

COMPUTER PROGRAMMING SVCS: Custom

Advantage Computer Entps Inc..........E....... 620 365-5156
Iola *(G-3585)*
Chelsoft Solutions Co..........D....... 913 579-1399
Olathe *(G-7591)*
Kaliaperumal Mamalay..........G....... 816 210-1248
Overland Park *(G-8885)*
Moonshot Innovations LLC..........E....... 913 815-6611
Overland Park *(G-9051)*
Netsmart Technologies Inc..........C....... 913 327-7444
Overland Park *(G-9076)*

COMPUTER RELATED MAINTENANCE SVCS

Eagle Software Inc..........E....... 785 823-7257
Salina *(G-10483)*
General Dynamics Info Tech Inc..........D....... 913 684-5770
Leavenworth *(G-5244)*
Heartland Cstmer Solutions LLC..........C....... 913 685-8855
Leawood *(G-5424)*
Isg Technology LLC..........C....... 785 823-1555
Salina *(G-10550)*
Net Systems LLC..........F....... 316 691-9400
Wichita *(G-15159)*
Veracity Consulting Inc..........D....... 913 945-1912
Overland Park *(G-9462)*

COMPUTER RELATED SVCS, NEC

Sun Microsystems Inc..........F....... 913 327-7820
Overland Park *(G-9372)*

COMPUTER SOFTWARE DEVELOPMENT

911 Datamaster Inc..........E....... 913 469-6401
Overland Park *(G-8333)*
Ad Astra Info Systems LLC..........E....... 913 652-4100
Shawnee Mission *(G-11073)*
All of E Solutions LLC..........E....... 785 832-2900
Lawrence *(G-4725)*
Atonix Digital LLC..........E....... 913 458-2000
Overland Park *(G-8411)*
Bowman Systems LLC..........D....... 318 213-8780
Overland Park *(G-8478)*
Cactus Software LLC..........D....... 913 677-0092
Overland Park *(G-8506)*
CCH Incorporated..........B....... 316 612-5000
Wichita *(G-13966)*
Centralized Showing Svc Inc..........D....... 913 851-8405
Overland Park *(G-8538)*
Certtech LLC..........E....... 913 814-9770
Lenexa *(G-5743)*
Command Alkon Incorporated..........E....... 913 384-0880
Lenexa *(G-5772)*
Computer Instruments Inc..........E....... 913 307-8850
Lenexa *(G-5782)*
Distributorcentral LLC..........F....... 888 516-7401
Gardner *(G-2338)*
E-Consultsusa LLC..........F....... 913 696-1001
Leawood *(G-5381)*
Fannect LLC..........F....... 913 271-2346
Overland Park *(G-8704)*
Fusion Global Solutions LLC..........E....... 913 707-2866
Overland Park *(G-8743)*
Global Soft Systems Inc..........E....... 913 338-1400
Overland Park *(G-8760)*
Information Tech Intl Inc..........F....... 913 579-8079
Hays *(G-2852)*
Innovision Corporation..........E....... 913 438-3200
Overland Park *(G-8847)*
Iq Group Inc..........F....... 913 722-6700
Lenexa *(G-5922)*
Jack Henry & Associates Inc..........C....... 913 422-3233
Shawnee Mission *(G-11479)*
Jupiter Esources LLC..........F....... 405 488-3886
Kansas City *(G-4129)*
K2b Incorporated..........E....... 913 663-3311
Shawnee Mission *(G-11507)*
Kalos Inc..........E....... 785 232-3606
Topeka *(G-12752)*
Kansys Inc..........E....... 913 780-5291
Olathe *(G-7830)*
Keycentrix Inc..........E....... 316 262-2231
Wichita *(G-14854)*
Leidos Inc..........G....... 913 317-5120
Shawnee Mission *(G-11560)*
Lexinet Corporation..........E....... 620 767-6346
Council Grove *(G-1170)*
Lockpath Inc..........D....... 913 601-4800
Overland Park *(G-8966)*
Marathon Reprographics Inc..........F....... 816 221-7881
Kansas City *(G-4217)*
Netsmart LLC..........E....... 913 327-7444
Overland Park *(G-9075)*
Neural Technologies Inc..........C....... 913 831-0273
Shawnee Mission *(G-11677)*
On Demand Technologies LLC..........F....... 913 438-1800
Overland Park *(G-9102)*
Onspring Technologies LLC..........F....... 913 601-4900
Overland Park *(G-9105)*
Orion Information Systems LLC..........F....... 913 825-3272
Overland Park *(G-9113)*
Presig Holdings LLC..........F....... 913 706-1315
Overland Park *(G-9184)*
Sara Software Systems LLC..........E....... 913 370-4197
Olathe *(G-8055)*
Signal Kit LLC..........F....... 866 297-7585
Leawood *(G-5551)*
Stackify LLC..........F....... 816 888-5055
Leawood *(G-5560)*
Tennessee Info Consortium LLC..........E....... 913 498-3468
Olathe *(G-8107)*
Traq-It Inc..........F....... 913 498-1221
Overland Park *(G-9426)*
Upg Solutions LLC..........F....... 844 737-0365
Leawood *(G-5591)*
Vigilias LLC..........E....... 800 924-8140
Wichita *(G-15907)*
Vinsolutions..........C....... 913 825-6124
Shawnee Mission *(G-11980)*
Vos Design Inc..........F....... 913 825-6556
Lenexa *(G-6218)*
Xpressotech Solutions LLC..........F....... 316 993-9397
Goddard *(G-2457)*

COMPUTER SOFTWARE DEVELOPMENT & APPLICATIONS

Actuarial Resources Corp Kans..........E....... 913 451-0044
Overland Park *(G-8345)*
Applied Content RES Tech LLC..........F....... 785 422-4980
Morland *(G-7166)*
Bardavon Hlth Innovations LLC..........E....... 913 236-1020
Overland Park *(G-8433)*
Bungii LLC..........E....... 913 353-6683
Overland Park *(G-8491)*
Catapult International LLC..........E....... 913 232-2389
Lenexa *(G-5733)*
Chocolatey Software Inc..........F....... 785 783-4720
Topeka *(G-12465)*
Cowley College & Area..........B....... 620 442-0430
Arkansas City *(G-150)*
Ddsports Inc..........G....... 913 636-0432
Merriam *(G-7090)*
Dunami Inc..........E....... 303 981-3303
Overland Park *(G-8665)*
Faithlink LLC..........F....... 913 904-1070
Overland Park *(G-8702)*
Gorydz Inc..........F....... 913 486-1665
Kansas City *(G-4040)*
Inscyt LLC..........A....... 913 579-7335
Overland Park *(G-8848)*
Itedium Inc..........E....... 913 499-4850
Overland Park *(G-8865)*
Myfreightworld Carrier MGT Inc..........E....... 877 549-9438
Overland Park *(G-9066)*
Nicusa Inc..........C....... 913 498-3468
Olathe *(G-7922)*
Object Tech Solutions Inc..........D....... 913 345-9080
Leawood *(G-5507)*
Platform Technologies LLC..........E....... 816 285-3874
Fairway *(G-1917)*
Prs Inc..........F....... 844 679-2273
Overland Park *(G-9199)*
PS Holdings LLC..........E....... 913 599-1600
Overland Park *(G-9201)*
R & O Partnership..........E....... 785 434-4534
Plainville *(G-9991)*
Softek Illuminate Inc..........F....... 913 981-5300
Overland Park *(G-9321)*
Solutions North Bank..........E....... 785 425-6721
Stockton *(G-12188)*
Staffbridge LLC..........F....... 913 381-4044
Overland Park *(G-9350)*
Stonelock Global..........F....... 800 970-6168
Overland Park *(G-9366)*
Terradatum..........D....... 888 212-4793
Overland Park *(G-9403)*
Torch Research LLC..........E....... 913 955-2738
Leawood *(G-5577)*

Tri-Com Technical Services LLC ....C....... 913 652-0600
Leawood *(G-5584)*
United States Dept of Army ....D....... 785 240-0308
Fort Riley *(G-1952)*
Washington FNB ....F....... 785 325-2221
Washington *(G-13471)*

COMPUTER SOFTWARE SYSTEMS ANALYSIS & DESIGN: Custom

Aceware Systems Inc ....F....... 785 537-2937
Manhattan *(G-6531)*
Adventuretech Group Inc ....F....... 913 402-9600
Overland Park *(G-8354)*
American Gvrnment Slutions LLC ....F....... 913 428-2550
Leawood *(G-5320)*
Aquent LLC ....E....... 913 345-9119
Shawnee Mission *(G-11115)*
CSS Group Inc ....F....... 316 269-9090
Wichita *(G-14138)*
Dg Business Solutions Inc ....F....... 913 766-0163
Lenexa *(G-5815)*
Esolutions Inc ....D....... 866 633-4726
Overland Park *(G-8690)*
Fujitsu America Inc ....E....... 913 327-2800
Shawnee Mission *(G-11384)*
Fundamental Technologies LLC ....F....... 785 840-0800
Lawrence *(G-4866)*
Galaxie Business Equipment Inc ....E....... 620 221-3469
Winfield *(G-16142)*
Healthcare Prfmce Group Inc ....D....... 316 796-0337
Spring Hill *(G-12086)*
Heritage Cmpt Consulting Inc ....F....... 913 529-4227
Overland Park *(G-8812)*
LPI Information Systems ....G....... 913 381-9118
Overland Park *(G-8972)*
Lucity Inc ....E....... 800 492-2468
Overland Park *(G-8973)*
Paige Technologies LLC ....E....... 913 381-0600
Overland Park *(G-9135)*
Pegasus Communication Solution ....F....... 913 937-8552
Overland Park *(G-9153)*
PSC Group LLC ....E....... 847 517-7200
Overland Park *(G-9202)*
Quest Research & Development ....F....... 316 267-1216
Wichita *(G-15393)*
Softek Solutions Inc ....E....... 913 649-1024
Prairie Village *(G-10067)*
Sur-Tec Inc ....G....... 913 647-7720
Shawnee *(G-11036)*
Valiant Global Def Svcs Inc ....D....... 913 651-9782
Leavenworth *(G-5304)*

COMPUTER STORAGE DEVICES, NEC

Data Locker Inc ....G....... 913 310-9088
Overland Park *(G-8636)*
EMC Corporation ....D....... 913 530-0433
Overland Park *(G-8677)*
Sur-Tec Inc ....G....... 913 647-7720
Shawnee *(G-11036)*

COMPUTER SYSTEM SELLING SVCS

Air Power Consultants Inc ....F....... 913 894-0044
Olathe *(G-7514)*
Orion Information Systems LLC ....F....... 913 825-3272
Overland Park *(G-9113)*

COMPUTER SYSTEMS ANALYSIS & DESIGN

Clarus Group LLC ....E....... 913 599-5255
Overland Park *(G-8560)*
Design Analysis and RES Corp ....F....... 785 832-0434
Lawrence *(G-4833)*
Innova Consulting LLC ....F....... 913 210-2002
Overland Park *(G-8845)*
Saicon Consultants Inc ....F....... 913 451-1178
Overland Park *(G-9272)*

COMPUTER TERMINALS

Computerwise Inc ....F....... 408 389-8241
Olathe *(G-7609)*
Elec-Tron Inc ....D....... 316 522-3401
Wichita *(G-14263)*
Hydeman Company Inc ....G....... 913 384-2620
Kansas City *(G-4090)*
Igt Global Solutions Corp ....E....... 785 861-7300
Topeka *(G-12713)*

COMPUTER TIME-SHARING

Infutor Data Solutions LLC ....F....... 913 782-8544
Olathe *(G-7790)*

COMPUTER TRAINING SCHOOLS

S & T Telephone Coop Assn ....F....... 785 460-7300
Colby *(G-1038)*

COMPUTER-AIDED ENGINEERING SYSTEMS SVCS

Depco LLC ....E....... 620 231-0019
Pittsburg *(G-9852)*

COMPUTERS, NEC

Aegis Business Solutions LLC ....G....... 913 307-9922
Olathe *(G-7512)*
Cybertron International Inc ....D....... 316 303-1022
Wichita *(G-14150)*
Data Max of Kansas City ....E....... 913 752-2200
Lenexa *(G-5803)*
Elecsys International Corp ....C....... 913 647-0158
Olathe *(G-7673)*
High Quality Tech Inc ....G....... 316 448-3559
Wichita *(G-14604)*
Net-Ability LLC ....F....... 316 691-4527
Wichita *(G-15160)*
Stallard Technologies Inc ....E....... 913 851-2260
Overland Park *(G-9351)*

COMPUTERS, NEC, WHOLESALE

Copy Products Inc ....D....... 620 365-7611
Iola *(G-3596)*
Digital Simplistics Inc ....E....... 913 643-2445
Lenexa *(G-5818)*
Direct Communications Inc ....F....... 913 599-5577
Overland Park *(G-8657)*
Jack Henry & Associates Inc ....C....... 913 422-3233
Shawnee Mission *(G-11479)*
Kanokla Telephone Association ....E....... 620 845-5682
Caldwell *(G-660)*
Keltech Solutions LLC ....F....... 785 841-4611
Lawrence *(G-4940)*
On Demand Technologies LLC ....F....... 913 438-1800
Overland Park *(G-9102)*
Word-Tech Inc ....E....... 913 722-3334
Shawnee Mission *(G-12019)*

COMPUTERS, PERIPH & SOFTWARE, WHLSE: Acctg Machs, Readable

Optiv Security Inc ....F....... 816 421-6611
Overland Park *(G-9110)*

COMPUTERS, PERIPH & SOFTWARE, WHLSE: Personal & Home Entrtn

Integrated Health Systems LLC ....F....... 913 647-9020
Stilwell *(G-12155)*

COMPUTERS, PERIPHERALS & SOFTWARE, WHOLESALE: Disk Drives

Asi Computer Technologies Inc ....E....... 913 888-8843
Lenexa *(G-5667)*

COMPUTERS, PERIPHERALS & SOFTWARE, WHOLESALE: Printers

Data Max of Kansas City ....E....... 913 752-2200
Lenexa *(G-5803)*
Dataco Derex Inc ....F....... 913 438-2444
Leawood *(G-5370)*

COMPUTERS, PERIPHERALS & SOFTWARE, WHOLESALE: Software

Cobalt Iron Inc ....E....... 888 584-4766
Lawrence *(G-4796)*
Environmental Systems Research ....D....... 913 383-8235
Leawood *(G-5387)*
Gateway Solutions Inc ....F....... 913 851-1055
Overland Park *(G-8748)*
Iris Strgc Mktg Support Inc ....E....... 913 232-4825
Lenexa *(G-5923)*
J & M Industries Inc ....E....... 913 362-8994
Prairie Village *(G-10037)*

Shoroeders Jim Sftwr & Video ....F....... 620 227-7628
Dodge City *(G-1430)*
Voice Products Inc ....E....... 316 616-1111
Wichita *(G-15911)*

COMPUTERS: Personal

Apple Central LLC Applebe ....G....... 203 987-6162
Wichita *(G-13721)*

CONCERT MANAGEMENT SVCS

Kansas City Blues Society Inc ....F....... 913 660-4692
Olathe *(G-7824)*
Liberty Hall Inc ....E....... 785 749-1972
Lawrence *(G-4995)*

CONCRETE BUILDING PRDTS WHOLESALERS

Carter-Waters LLC ....F....... 316 942-6712
Wichita *(G-13956)*
Coleman Materials LLC ....F....... 316 267-9812
Wichita *(G-14054)*

CONCRETE CURING & HARDENING COMPOUNDS

W R Grace & Co - Conn ....G....... 913 764-8040
Olathe *(G-8144)*

CONCRETE PLANTS

Lafarge North America Inc ....B....... 913 780-6809
Olathe *(G-7852)*

CONCRETE PRDTS

Ash Grove Materials Corp ....D....... 913 345-2030
Overland Park *(G-8404)*
Canyon Stone Inc ....E....... 913 254-9300
Olathe *(G-7575)*
Cemex Materials LLC ....D....... 913 287-5725
Kansas City *(G-3900)*
Chemsystems Kansas Inc ....G....... 913 422-4443
Shawnee *(G-10927)*
Coreslab Structures Kansas Inc ....D....... 913 287-5725
Kansas City *(G-3942)*
Cretex Concrete Products Inc ....F....... 785 863-3300
Oskaloosa *(G-8224)*
Dayton Superior Corporation ....D....... 913 596-9784
Kansas City *(G-3960)*
King Luminaire Company Inc ....G....... 913 255-3112
Atchison *(G-240)*
M6 Concrete Accessories Co Inc ....G....... 316 452-5466
El Dorado *(G-1584)*
Permanent Paving Inc ....F....... 913 451-7834
Overland Park *(G-9157)*
Quikrete Companies Inc ....E....... 913 441-6525
Kansas City *(G-4355)*
Quikrete Companies LLC ....E....... 316 721-3900
Wichita *(G-15396)*
Rayers Bearden Stained GL Sup ....F....... 316 942-2929
Wichita *(G-15421)*
Russell Block Company Inc ....F....... 785 483-6271
Russell *(G-10294)*
Stresscrete Inc ....F....... 913 255-3112
Atchison *(G-264)*

CONCRETE PRDTS, PRECAST, NEC

Finley Construction & Rdymx ....G....... 785 626-3282
Atwood *(G-286)*
Glen-Gery Corporation ....G....... 913 281-2800
Kansas City *(G-4038)*
Old Castle Precast Inc ....E....... 785 232-2982
Topeka *(G-12944)*
Omega Concrete Systems Inc ....E....... 913 287-4343
Kansas City *(G-4293)*
Reliable Concrete Products ....G....... 913 321-8108
Kansas City *(G-4369)*
St Joe Concrete Products ....E....... 913 365-7281
Elwood *(G-1691)*

CONCRETE REINFORCING MATERIAL

Dayton Superior Corporation ....C....... 937 866-0711
Parsons *(G-9681)*

CONCRETE: Ready-Mixed

Alsop Sand Co Inc ....E....... 785 243-4249
Concordia *(G-1101)*

American Concrete Co Inc ....G....... 620 231-1520
Pittsburg *(G-9807)*
Andale Construction Inc ....D....... 316 832-0063
Wichita *(G-13703)*
Andale Ready Mix Central Inc ....D....... 316 832-0063
Wichita *(G-13704)*
Andale Ready Mix Central Inc ....F....... 316 832-0063
Andale *(G-77)*
Ash Grove Cement Company ....C....... 913 451-8900
Overland Park *(G-8403)*
Ash Grove Materials Corp ....D....... 913 345-2030
Overland Park *(G-8404)*
B & B Redimix Inc ....G....... 785 543-5133
Phillipsburg *(G-9776)*
B & B Redimix Inc ....F....... 785 543-5133
Phillipsburg *(G-9777)*
B&B Redi Mix ....F....... 785 543-5133
Phillipsburg *(G-9778)*
Beloit Ready Mix Incorporated ....G....... 785 738-4683
Beloit *(G-478)*
Builders Concrete & Supply ....F....... 316 283-4540
Newton *(G-7324)*
Century Concrete Inc ....E....... 913 451-8900
Shawnee Mission *(G-11213)*
Century Concrete Inc ....F....... 913 764-4264
Olathe *(G-7585)*
Concrete Enterprises Inc ....F....... 620 662-1219
Hutchinson *(G-3244)*
Concrete Enterprises Inc ....E....... 620 532-1165
Kingman *(G-4587)*
Concrete Express Inc ....F....... 805 643-2992
Olathe *(G-7610)*
Concrete Products Co Inc ....F....... 620 947-5921
Hillsboro *(G-3045)*
Concrete Service Co Inc ....E....... 620 792-2558
Great Bend *(G-2545)*
Concrete Service Co Inc ....G....... 785 628-2100
Hays *(G-2776)*
Cornejo & Sons LLC ....G....... 620 251-1690
Coffeyville *(G-931)*
Dodge City Concrete Inc ....F....... 620 227-3041
Dodge City *(G-1343)*
Eslinger Construction & Rdymx ....F....... 620 659-2371
Kinsley *(G-4617)*
Finley Construction & Rdymx ....G....... 785 626-3282
Atwood *(G-286)*
Freedom Ready Mix Inc ....G....... 620 224-2800
Fort Scott *(G-1973)*
Geiger Ready-Mix Co Inc ....E....... 913 772-4010
Leavenworth *(G-5243)*
Geiger Ready-Mix Co Inc ....E....... 913 281-0111
Kansas City *(G-4029)*
Gravel & Concrete Inc ....G....... 620 422-3249
Nickerson *(G-7432)*
H & P Inc ....G....... 785 263-4183
Abilene *(G-36)*
Hamm Inc ....E....... 785 235-6568
Topeka *(G-12661)*
Hamm Inc ....G....... 785 233-7263
Topeka *(G-12662)*
Heft & Sons LLC ....E....... 620 723-2495
Greensburg *(G-2679)*
Independence Ready Mix Inc ....G....... 620 331-4150
Independence *(G-3529)*
J-A-G Construction Company ....C....... 620 225-0061
Dodge City *(G-1380)*
J-A-G Construction Company ....E....... 620 225-0061
Dodge City *(G-1381)*
Kansas Ready Mix LLC ....E....... 316 832-0828
Park City *(G-9623)*
Kansas Sand and Concrete Inc ....E....... 785 235-6284
Topeka *(G-12803)*
Klaver Construction Pdts LLC ....E....... 620 532-3661
Kingman *(G-4604)*
Lafarge North America Inc ....E....... 816 365-9143
Kansas City *(G-4192)*
Lrm Industries Inc ....E....... 785 843-1688
Lawrence *(G-5001)*
McPherson Concrete Pdts Inc ....D....... 620 241-1678
McPherson *(G-6995)*
Meiers Ready Mix Inc ....E....... 785 233-9900
Topeka *(G-12882)*
Mid West Ready Mix & Bldg Sups ....G....... 785 284-2911
Sabetha *(G-10319)*
Mid West Ready Mix & Bldg Sups ....G....... 785 742-3678
Hiawatha *(G-3018)*
Mid-America Redi-Mix Inc ....F....... 620 663-1559
Hutchinson *(G-3377)*
Midwest Concrete Materials Inc ....C....... 785 776-8811
Manhattan *(G-6746)*
Midwest Materials By Mueller ....F....... 785 337-2252
Hanover *(G-2713)*
Mo-Kan Transit Mix Inc ....G....... 913 367-1332
Atchison *(G-250)*
Monarch Cement Company ....C....... 620 473-2222
Humboldt *(G-3187)*
OBrien Rock Company Inc ....D....... 620 449-2257
Saint Paul *(G-10382)*
OBrien Rock Company Inc ....G....... 620 231-4940
Frontenac *(G-2061)*
OBrien Rock Company Inc ....G....... 620 421-5127
Parsons *(G-9711)*
Pappas Concrete Inc ....E....... 620 277-2127
Lakin *(G-4657)*
Payless Concrete Products Inc ....F....... 620 365-5588
Iola *(G-3622)*
Pennys Concrete Inc ....E....... 913 441-8781
Shawnee Mission *(G-11724)*
Pennys Concrete Inc ....F....... 913 441-8781
Paola *(G-9583)*
Pennys Concrete Inc ....E....... 913 441-8781
Louisburg *(G-6462)*
Pennys Concrete & Rdymx LLC ....F....... 785 242-1045
Ottawa *(G-8304)*
Quikrete Companies Inc ....E....... 913 441-6525
Kansas City *(G-4355)*
R A Ruud & Son Inc ....F....... 316 788-5000
Haysville *(G-2957)*
Salina Concrete Products Inc ....E....... 785 827-7281
Salina *(G-10668)*
Schlosser Inc ....G....... 785 899-6535
Goodland *(G-2486)*
Sek Ready Mix Inc ....E....... 620 252-8699
Coffeyville *(G-976)*
Seneca Ready Mix Concrete Inc ....F....... 785 336-3511
Seneca *(G-10881)*
Sherwood Construction Co Inc ....C....... 316 943-0211
Wichita *(G-15581)*
Smoky Valley Concrete Inc ....G....... 785 820-8113
Salina *(G-10711)*
Tarbet Construction Co Inc ....F....... 620 356-2110
Ulysses *(G-13321)*
Tarbet Construction Co Inc ....G....... 785 462-7432
Colby *(G-1045)*
Tri-County Concrete Inc ....E....... 913 764-7700
Olathe *(G-8121)*
Walker Products Company Inc ....F....... 785 524-4107
Lincoln *(G-6390)*

CONFECTIONS & CANDY

Cereal Ingredients Inc ....D....... 913 727-3434
Leavenworth *(G-5217)*
Mars Chocolate North Amer LLC ....G....... 785 861-1800
Topeka *(G-12861)*
Sunflower Hills Inc ....F....... 913 894-2233
Lenexa *(G-6158)*

CONFINEMENT SURVEILLANCE SYS MAINTENANCE & MONITORING SVCS

Titan Monitoring Inc ....E....... 913 441-0911
Overland Park *(G-9414)*

CONNECTORS & TERMINALS: Electrical Device Uses

Molex LLC ....G....... 630 969-4550
Wichita *(G-15122)*
Ted Mfg Corporation ....E....... 913 631-6211
Shawnee Mission *(G-11924)*

CONNECTORS: Electrical

Sunflower Elec Systems LLC ....G....... 913 894-1442
Lenexa *(G-6157)*

CONNECTORS: Electronic

Dme Electronics ....G....... 316 529-2441
Haysville *(G-2940)*
Wildcat Connectors Inc ....G....... 785 937-4385
Princeton *(G-10171)*

CONSERVATION PROGRAMS ADMINISTRATION SVCS

County of Johnson ....F....... 913 631-5208
Shawnee Mission *(G-11271)*

CONSTRUCTION & MINING MACHINERY WHOLESALERS

B&B Redi Mix ....F....... 785 543-5133
Phillipsburg *(G-9778)*
Bti Ness City ....E....... 785 798-2251
Ness City *(G-7253)*
Concordia Tractor Inc ....E....... 785 632-3181
Clay Center *(G-856)*
Crawford Supply Co ....F....... 785 434-4631
Plainville *(G-9984)*
Ferco Inc ....E....... 785 825-6380
Salina *(G-10500)*
Foley Equipment Company ....D....... 913 393-0303
Olathe *(G-7716)*
Foley Equipment Company ....F....... 316 943-4211
Park City *(G-9619)*
Foley Equipment Company ....D....... 620 626-6555
Liberal *(G-6309)*
Foley Equipment Company ....D....... 785 266-5784
Topeka *(G-12622)*
Foley Supply LLC ....E....... 316 944-7368
Wichita *(G-14400)*
Heritage Tractor Inc ....E....... 785 235-5100
Topeka *(G-12686)*
Htc Inc ....E....... 865 689-2311
Olathe *(G-7779)*
Laser Specialists Inc ....E....... 913 780-9990
Olathe *(G-7856)*
Mather Flare Rental Inc ....F....... 785 478-9696
Topeka *(G-12863)*
Plp Inc ....E....... 620 842-5137
Anthony *(G-132)*
Plp Inc ....E....... 620 382-3794
Marion *(G-6875)*
Plp Inc ....E....... 620 342-5000
Emporia *(G-1812)*
Plp Inc ....C....... 620 664-5860
Hutchinson *(G-3408)*
Plp Inc ....E....... 316 943-4261
Wichita *(G-15307)*

CONSTRUCTION & ROAD MAINTENANCE EQPT: Drags, Road

Haivala Concrete Tools Inc ....G....... 316 263-1683
Wichita *(G-14543)*

CONSTRUCTION EQPT REPAIR SVCS

Central Plains Contracting Co ....F....... 620 231-2660
Pittsburg *(G-9830)*
Laser Specialists Inc ....E....... 913 780-9990
Olathe *(G-7856)*
McCullough Enterprises Inc ....F....... 316 942-8118
Wichita *(G-15024)*
Road Builders Mchy & Sup Co ....D....... 913 371-3822
Kansas City *(G-4384)*
Weller Tractor Salvage Inc ....F....... 620 792-5243
Great Bend *(G-2659)*

CONSTRUCTION EQPT: Attachments

Caterpillar Work Tools Inc ....B....... 785 456-2224
Wamego *(G-13410)*
Caterpillar Work Tools Inc ....F....... 785 456-2224
Wamego *(G-13411)*
Coneqtec Corp ....E....... 316 943-8889
Wichita *(G-14088)*

CONSTRUCTION EQPT: Backhoes, Tractors, Cranes & Similar Eqpt

Crane Sales & Service Co Inc ....F....... 913 621-7040
Kansas City *(G-3944)*
Nesco Holdings Inc ....G....... 913 287-0001
Kansas City *(G-4286)*
Shannahan Crane & Hoist Inc ....F....... 816 746-9822
Kansas City *(G-4419)*

CONSTRUCTION EQPT: Blade, Grader, Scraper, Dozer/Snow Plow

Icon Industries Inc ....E....... 785 738-3547
Beloit *(G-488)*
Weller Tractor Salvage Inc ....F....... 620 792-5243
Great Bend *(G-2659)*

CONSTRUCTION EQPT: Cranes

Broderson Manufacturing Corp............D....... 913 888-0606
Lenexa *(G-5718)*

CONSTRUCTION EQPT: Entrenching Machines

Cnh Industrial America LLC..................D....... 316 945-0111
Wichita *(G-14046)*

CONSTRUCTION EQPT: Roofing Eqpt

Bainter Construction Co Inc.................E....... 785 675-3297
Hoxie *(G-3135)*

CONSTRUCTION EQPT: Spreaders, Aggregates

Broce Manufacturing Co Inc................G....... 620 227-8811
Dodge City *(G-1312)*

CONSTRUCTION MATERIALS, WHOL: Concrete/Cinder Bldg Prdts

AMBS and Associates Inc......................G....... 913 599-5939
Lenexa *(G-5644)*

CONSTRUCTION MATERIALS, WHOLESALE: Aggregate

Huber Sand Company..........................F....... 620 275-7601
Garden City *(G-2200)*

CONSTRUCTION MATERIALS, WHOLESALE: Architectural Metalwork

Topeka Foundry and Ir Works Co..........D....... 785 232-8212
Topeka *(G-13176)*

CONSTRUCTION MATERIALS, WHOLESALE: Awnings

Wichita Awning Co Inc.........................G....... 316 838-4432
Wichita *(G-15978)*

CONSTRUCTION MATERIALS, WHOLESALE: Brick, Exc Refractory

Capitol Concrete Pdts Co Inc...............F....... 785 233-3271
Topeka *(G-12436)*
Glen-Gery Corporation..........................G....... 913 281-2800
Kansas City *(G-4038)*
Salina Concrete Products Inc...............F....... 316 943-3241
Wichita *(G-15510)*

CONSTRUCTION MATERIALS, WHOLESALE: Building Stone

Pray Building Stone Inc.........................F....... 620 221-7422
Winfield *(G-16165)*

CONSTRUCTION MATERIALS, WHOLESALE: Building Stone, Granite

Bedrock International LLC...................E....... 913 438-7625
Lenexa *(G-5697)*
Braco Sales Inc....................................E....... 816 471-5005
Kansas City *(G-3874)*
Direct Source Gran & Stone Imp..........F....... 913 766-9200
Overland Park *(G-8658)*
Emotorpro..F....... 785 437-2046
Saint Marys *(G-10362)*
Global Stone LLC..................................G....... 913 310-9500
Olathe *(G-7733)*

CONSTRUCTION MATERIALS, WHOLESALE: Building Stone, Marble

Sun Marble LLC....................................F....... 913 438-3366
Lenexa *(G-6156)*

CONSTRUCTION MATERIALS, WHOLESALE: Building, Exterior

American Bldrs Contrs Sup Inc............D....... 913 722-4747
Kansas City *(G-3803)*
American Wholesale Corporation.........F....... 785 364-4901
Holton *(G-3084)*
Carter-Waters LLC................................F....... 316 942-6712
Wichita *(G-13956)*
Confederated Builders Supply.............E....... 316 788-3913
Derby *(G-1232)*
Hardman Wholesale LLC......................E....... 785 346-2131
Osborne *(G-8209)*
Hd Supply Inc......................................E....... 816 283-3687
Kansas City *(G-4071)*
Kan-AM Products Inc...........................F....... 316 943-8806
Wichita *(G-14784)*
Kansas Building Supply Co Inc............D....... 913 962-5227
Overland Park *(G-8888)*
Lowes Home Centers LLC....................C....... 913 631-3003
Shawnee Mission *(G-11579)*
Lowes Home Centers LLC....................C....... 316 773-1800
Wichita *(G-14982)*
Lowes Home Centers LLC....................C....... 785 452-9303
Salina *(G-10585)*
Lowes Home Centers LLC....................C....... 620 513-2000
Hutchinson *(G-3359)*
Lowes Home Centers LLC....................C....... 316 684-3117
Wichita *(G-14983)*
Lowes Home Centers LLC....................C....... 913 397-7070
Olathe *(G-7866)*
Lowes Home Centers LLC....................C....... 785 273-0888
Topeka *(G-12852)*
Lowes Home Centers LLC....................C....... 316 206-0000
Derby *(G-1259)*
Lowes Home Centers LLC....................C....... 913 328-7170
Kansas City *(G-4207)*
Lowes Home Centers LLC....................C....... 913 261-1040
Roeland Park *(G-10227)*
Lowes Home Centers LLC....................C....... 316 206-1030
Wichita *(G-14984)*
Mid-AM Building Supply Inc................D....... 913 592-4313
Spring Hill *(G-12089)*
Mid-AM Building Supply Inc................F....... 316 942-0389
Wichita *(G-15073)*

CONSTRUCTION MATERIALS, WHOLESALE: Building, Interior

Midway Sales & Distrg Inc...................D....... 785 233-7406
Topeka *(G-12893)*
Midway Sales & Distrg Inc...................F....... 785 537-4665
Manhattan *(G-6745)*

CONSTRUCTION MATERIALS, WHOLESALE: Ceiling Systems & Prdts

Wagner Intr Sup Kans Cy Inc................F....... 913 647-6622
Kansas City *(G-4529)*

CONSTRUCTION MATERIALS, WHOLESALE: Cement

Ash Grove Cement Company.................E....... 620 433-3500
Chanute *(G-703)*
OBrien Rock Company Inc....................G....... 620 421-5127
Parsons *(G-9711)*

CONSTRUCTION MATERIALS, WHOLESALE: Ceramic, Exc Refractory

Interstate Supply Company..................E....... 316 265-6653
Wichita *(G-14711)*

CONSTRUCTION MATERIALS, WHOLESALE: Doors, Garage

Kansas Door Inc....................................F....... 620 793-7600
Great Bend *(G-2597)*
Superior Door Service Inc....................F....... 913 381-1767
Kansas City *(G-4447)*

CONSTRUCTION MATERIALS, WHOLESALE: Drywall Materials

Drywall Supply......................................F....... 316 269-3304
Wichita *(G-14240)*
Kcg Inc..E....... 913 438-4142
Lenexa *(G-5942)*
Kcg Inc..G....... 913 888-0882
Lenexa *(G-5943)*
Kcg Inc..E....... 913 236-4909
Kansas City *(G-4167)*
L & W Supply Corporation....................E....... 913 782-1777
Olathe *(G-7847)*
Rew Materials Inc.................................D....... 913 236-4909
Kansas City *(G-4374)*

CONSTRUCTION MATERIALS, WHOLESALE: Glass

Adelhardt Enterprises Inc.....................F....... 620 672-6463
Pratt *(G-10093)*
Binswanger Enterprises LLC................F....... 785 267-4090
Topeka *(G-12382)*
City Glass and Mirror Inc.....................F....... 785 233-5650
Topeka *(G-12467)*
Insulite Glass Co Inc............................D....... 800 452-7721
Olathe *(G-7795)*
Lippert Components Mfg Inc................D....... 316 283-0627
North Newton *(G-7438)*
Manko Window Systems Inc.................B....... 785 776-9643
Manhattan *(G-6730)*
Masonry & Glass Systems Inc..............G....... 913 748-6142
Shawnee Mission *(G-11601)*
Olathe Glass Company Inc...................E....... 913 782-7444
Olathe *(G-7938)*

CONSTRUCTION MATERIALS, WHOLESALE: Insulation, Thermal

Buckley Industries Inc..........................D....... 316 744-7587
Park City *(G-9606)*

CONSTRUCTION MATERIALS, WHOLESALE: Joists

Mdf Industries Inc.................................F....... 785 827-4450
Salina *(G-10599)*

CONSTRUCTION MATERIALS, WHOLESALE: Limestone

U S Stone Industries LLC.......................C....... 913 529-4154
Herington *(G-2982)*

CONSTRUCTION MATERIALS, WHOLESALE: Metal Buildings

Weigel Construction Inc........................F....... 913 780-1274
Spring Hill *(G-12103)*
Western Metal Company Inc.................F....... 913 681-8787
Louisburg *(G-6469)*

CONSTRUCTION MATERIALS, WHOLESALE: Millwork

Olathe Millwork Company.....................E....... 913 894-5010
Lenexa *(G-6035)*
Woodwork Mfg & Sup Inc.....................E....... 620 663-3393
Hutchinson *(G-3492)*

CONSTRUCTION MATERIALS, WHOLESALE: Paving Materials

Apac-Kansas Inc....................................D....... 316 522-4881
Wichita *(G-13715)*

CONSTRUCTION MATERIALS, WHOLESALE: Prefabricated Structures

Dayton Superior Corporation................E....... 913 279-4800
Kansas City *(G-3959)*
Interstate Supply Company..................E....... 316 265-6653
Wichita *(G-14711)*
Morton Buildings Inc............................F....... 785 823-6359
Salina *(G-10606)*
Morton Buildings Inc............................D....... 620 221-4180
Winfield *(G-16159)*
Morton Buildings Inc............................F....... 620 275-4105
Garden City *(G-2239)*
Pro-Dig LLC..F....... 785 856-2661
Elwood *(G-1689)*
Tuff Shed Inc..F....... 913 541-8833
Shawnee Mission *(G-11947)*

CONSTRUCTION MATERIALS, WHOLESALE: Roof, Asphalt/Sheet Metal

Arrow Renovation & Cnstr LLC.............E....... 913 703-3000
Olathe *(G-7534)*
Gulfside Supply Inc...............................F....... 913 384-9610
Kansas City *(G-4058)*
Mel Stevenson & Associates Inc..........D....... 913 262-0505
Kansas City *(G-4232)*
Protec Construction & Sup LLC...........E....... 913 441-2121
Edwardsville *(G-1513)*

CONSTRUCTION MATERIALS, WHOLESALE: Roofing & Siding Material

American Bldrs Contrs Sup Inc ....F 785 354-7398
Topeka *(G-12313)*
American Bldrs Contrs Sup Inc ....E 316 265-8276
Wichita *(G-13684)*
American Wholesale Corporation ....F 785 364-4901
Holton *(G-3084)*
Associated Materials LLC ....F 888 544-9774
Wichita *(G-13757)*
Associated Materials LLC ....F 316 944-0800
Wichita *(G-13758)*
Beacon Sales Acquisition Inc ....D 913 262-7663
Shawnee Mission *(G-11155)*
Beacon Sales Acquisition Inc ....F 785 234-8406
Topeka *(G-12368)*
Discount Siding Supply LP ....F 785 625-4619
Hays *(G-2788)*
Gulfside Supply Inc ....F 316 941-9322
Wichita *(G-14527)*
Mel Stevenson & Associates Inc ....F 316 262-5959
Wichita *(G-15036)*
Mid-AM Building Supply Inc ....D 913 592-4313
Spring Hill *(G-12089)*
Midway Sales & Distrg Inc ....D 785 233-7406
Topeka *(G-12893)*
Midway Sales & Distrg Inc ....F 785 537-4665
Manhattan *(G-6745)*

CONSTRUCTION MATERIALS, WHOLESALE: Sand

Kansas Sand and Concrete Inc ....E 785 235-6284
Topeka *(G-12803)*
Kaw Valley Companies Inc ....C 913 281-9950
Kansas City *(G-4160)*
Kaw Valley Sand and Gravel Inc ....E 913 281-9950
Kansas City *(G-4162)*
Kunshek Chat & Coal Inc ....E 620 231-8270
Pittsburg *(G-9893)*
R A Ruud & Son Inc ....F 316 788-5000
Haysville *(G-2957)*
Sturgis Materials Inc ....E 913 371-7757
Kansas City *(G-4442)*
Williams Diversified Mtls Inc ....E 620 679-9810
Baxter Springs *(G-415)*

CONSTRUCTION MATERIALS, WHOLESALE: Septic Tanks

We-Mac Manufacturing Co ....F 913 367-3778
Atchison *(G-270)*

CONSTRUCTION MATERIALS, WHOLESALE: Stone, Crushed Or Broken

Apac-Kansas Inc ....E 620 662-3307
Hutchinson *(G-3200)*
Deffenbaugh Industries Inc ....E 913 208-1000
Olathe *(G-7647)*
Florence Rock Company LLC ....G 620 878-4544
Newton *(G-7346)*
House of Rocks Inc ....E 913 432-5990
Kansas City *(G-4086)*
South West Butler Quarry LLC ....F 316 775-1737
Augusta *(G-347)*

CONSTRUCTION MATERIALS, WHOLESALE: Stucco

Air Capital Stucco L L C ....E 316 650-2450
Newton *(G-7308)*

CONSTRUCTION MATERIALS, WHOLESALE: Tile & Clay Prdts

Classic Floors & Design Center ....E 913 780-2171
Overland Park *(G-8561)*
Flint Hills Clay Works Inc ....F 620 382-3620
Marion *(G-6870)*

CONSTRUCTION MATERIALS, WHOLESALE: Wallboard

Dahmer Contracting Group LLC ....D 816 795-3332
Overland Park *(G-8630)*

CONSTRUCTION MATERIALS, WHOLESALE: Windows

American Bldrs Contrs Sup Inc ....F 785 354-7398
Topeka *(G-12313)*
American Bldrs Contrs Sup Inc ....E 316 265-8276
Wichita *(G-13684)*
Lorac Company Inc ....F 316 263-2565
Wichita *(G-14979)*
Mid-States Millwork Inc ....F 913 492-6300
Overland Park *(G-9028)*
New Windows For America LLC ....F 316 263-0711
Wichita *(G-15170)*
Pella Products Kansas City Inc ....E 913 492-7927
Lenexa *(G-6048)*
Roberts Products Inc ....F 913 780-1702
Olathe *(G-8039)*
Southard Corporation ....E 620 793-5434
Great Bend *(G-2637)*

CONSTRUCTION MATLS, WHOL: Lumber, Rough, Dressed/Finished

Century Building Solutions Inc ....F 913 422-5555
Lenexa *(G-5740)*
Galyon Lumber Inc ....F 620 897-6290
Little River *(G-6418)*
Georgia-Pacific LLC ....C 785 363-7767
Blue Rapids *(G-536)*
Griffith Lumber Company Inc ....E 785 776-4104
Manhattan *(G-6647)*
L & J Wood Products Inc ....G 620 327-2183
Hesston *(G-2996)*
McCray Lumber Company ....E 913 780-0060
Olathe *(G-7882)*
Miami Lumber Inc ....F 913 294-2041
Paola *(G-9574)*
Northwest Hardwoods Inc ....E 913 894-9790
Lenexa *(G-6027)*
T H Rogers Lumber Company ....F 620 231-0900
Pittsburg *(G-9944)*
Weyerhaeuser Company ....E 316 284-6700
Newton *(G-7428)*

CONSTRUCTION MATLS, WHOLESALE: Soil Erosion Cntrl Fabrics

Erosion Control Inc ....F 913 397-7324
Paola *(G-9556)*

CONSTRUCTION MATLS, WHOLESALE: Struct Assy, Prefab, NonWood

Tennison Brothers Inc ....F 316 263-7581
Wichita *(G-15729)*

CONSTRUCTION MTRLS, WHOL: Exterior Flat Glass, Plate/Window

Curb Appeal of Kansas Inc ....E 620 488-5214
Belle Plaine *(G-445)*

CONSTRUCTION SAND MINING

Alsop Sand Co Inc ....E 785 243-4249
Concordia *(G-1101)*
Heft & Sons LLC ....E 620 723-2495
Greensburg *(G-2679)*
Midwest Materials By Mueller ....F 785 337-2252
Hanover *(G-2713)*

CONSTRUCTION SITE PREPARATION SVCS

Barnharts Excavation LLC ....F 620 431-0959
Chanute *(G-706)*
CS Carey LLC ....F 913 432-4877
Kansas City *(G-3947)*
Doctors Inc ....E 913 681-8041
Stilwell *(G-12145)*

CONSTRUCTION: Agricultural Building

Bolivar Contracting Inc ....E 913 533-2240
Bucyrus *(G-594)*
Ken Babcock Sales Inc ....F 785 544-6592
Hiawatha *(G-3013)*

CONSTRUCTION: Apartment Building

CK Contracting LLC ....F 316 267-1996
Wichita *(G-14033)*
Nfi Management Co Inc ....F 913 642-3700
Shawnee Mission *(G-11684)*
Titan Construction Inc ....C 913 782-6700
Olathe *(G-8111)*

CONSTRUCTION: Athletic & Recreation Facilities

Pishny Real Estate Services ....F 913 227-0251
Lenexa *(G-6059)*

CONSTRUCTION: Bank

Service Technologies Midwest ....E 913 671-3340
Overland Park *(G-9299)*

CONSTRUCTION: Bridge

American Bridge Company ....F 913 948-5800
Overland Park *(G-8375)*
BRB Contractors Inc ....C 785 232-1245
Topeka *(G-12403)*
Bridges Inc ....E 316 283-9350
Newton *(G-7322)*
Bryan-Ohlmeier Construction ....E 913 557-9972
Paola *(G-9543)*
County of Ellis ....D 785 628-9455
Hays *(G-2778)*
County of Greenwood ....E 620 583-8112
Eureka *(G-1882)*
Crossland Heavy Contrs Inc ....D 620 429-1410
Columbus *(G-1072)*
Dondlinger & Sons Cnstr Co Inc ....C 316 945-0555
Wichita *(G-14226)*
Eby Corporation ....F 316 268-3500
Wichita *(G-14256)*
J & J Contractors Inc ....F 620 365-5500
Iola *(G-3613)*
King Construction Company Inc ....D 620 327-4251
Hesston *(G-2995)*
Klaver Construction Co Inc ....D 620 532-3183
Kingman *(G-4603)*
L & M Contractors Inc ....D 620 793-8137
Great Bend *(G-2600)*
L G Barcus and Sons Inc ....D 913 621-1100
Kansas City *(G-4188)*
Massman Construction Co ....E 913 291-2600
Leawood *(G-5468)*
Wildcat Construction Co Inc ....C 316 945-9408
Wichita *(G-16049)*

CONSTRUCTION: Cable Television Line

Chase Contractors Inc ....G 620 431-2142
Chanute *(G-714)*
K & W Underground Incorporated ....D 913 782-7387
Olathe *(G-7821)*

CONSTRUCTION: Chemical Facility

Blackburn Construction Inc ....C 316 321-5358
El Dorado *(G-1538)*
Utility Contractors Inc ....E 316 942-1253
Wichita *(G-15866)*

CONSTRUCTION: Co-op

Central Gc Construction Inc ....F 913 484-2400
Spring Hill *(G-12081)*

CONSTRUCTION: Commercial & Institutional Building

American Construction Svcs LLC ....F 913 754-3777
Lenexa *(G-5647)*
Benchmark Enterprises ....F 785 537-4447
Manhattan *(G-6555)*
D & R Construction Inc ....E 785 776-1087
Manhattan *(G-6608)*
Ebco Construction Group LLC ....F 866 297-2185
Olathe *(G-7667)*
Frazier Brothers Plbg & Contg ....F 785 452-9707
Salina *(G-10506)*
Frontr-Rrwhead Joint Ventr LLC ....E 913 461-3804
Olathe *(G-7719)*
Hahner Foreman & Harness LLC ....E 316 264-0306
Wichita *(G-14540)*
Homeland Roofing and Cnstr LLC ....F 316 832-9901
Wichita *(G-14632)*
J-A-G Construction Company ....E 620 225-0061
Dodge City *(G-1381)*

Jahnke & Sons Construction Inc .... F 800 351-2525
Overland Park *(G-8870)*
James Gruver Construction Inc .... E 620 663-7982
Hutchinson *(G-3340)*
Kbs Constructors Inc .... E 785 266-4222
Topeka *(G-12813)*
Leavcon II Inc .... E 913 351-1430
Lansing *(G-4681)*
Michael S Hundley Cnstr Inc .... F 913 367-7059
Atchison *(G-249)*
Murray and Sons Cnstr Co Inc .... E 785 267-1961
Topeka *(G-12920)*
National Contractors Inc .... E 316 722-8484
Wichita *(G-15148)*
Prairie Landworks Inc .... F 620 504-5049
Mcpherson *(G-7017)*
Quality Structures Inc .... E 785 835-6100
Richmond *(G-10203)*
Rf Construction Inc .... E 785 776-8855
Manhattan *(G-6791)*
Rylie Equipment & Contg Co .... D 913 621-2725
Kansas City *(G-4394)*
Tommy J Kemp .... E 316 522-7255
Derby *(G-1276)*
Wildcat Services Inc .... F 785 922-6466
Chapman *(G-781)*

CONSTRUCTION: Commercial & Office Building, New

2point Construction Co LLC .... E 913 749-1855
Shawnee *(G-10903)*
A G Spanos Development Inc .... F 913 663-2400
Overland Park *(G-8335)*
A L Huber Inc .... E 913 341-4880
Shawnee Mission *(G-11064)*
Accel Construction LLC .... E 316 866-2885
Bel Aire *(G-425)*
AL Huber Construction Inc .... E 913 341-4880
Shawnee Mission *(G-11091)*
Allied Retail Concepts LLC .... F 913 492-8008
Shawnee *(G-10908)*
Altmar Inc .... E 785 233-0053
Topeka *(G-12311)*
Appliance Doctor Inc .... E 316 263-0005
Wichita *(G-13723)*
Arrowhead Contracting Inc .... D 913 814-9994
Lenexa *(G-5664)*
B A Green Construction Co Inc .... E 785 843-5277
Lawrence *(G-4747)*
Bhs Construction Inc .... E 785 537-2068
Manhattan *(G-6557)*
Bowden Contracting Company Inc .... F 913 342-5112
Kansas City *(G-3872)*
Bratton Bros Contracting Inc .... F 913 422-7771
Shawnee *(G-10920)*
Building Erection Svcs Co Inc .... E 913 764-5560
Olathe *(G-7568)*
Carrothers Construction Co Inc .... E 913 294-2361
Paola *(G-9544)*
Commerce Construction Svcs Inc .... E 316 262-0547
Wichita *(G-14068)*
Commercial Builders Inc .... D 785 625-6272
Hays *(G-2774)*
Conco Inc .... C 316 943-7111
Wichita *(G-14085)*
Confederated Builders Supply .... E 316 788-3913
Derby *(G-1232)*
Construction Svcs Bryant Inc .... F 316 262-1010
Wichita *(G-14093)*
Coonrod & Assoc Cnstr Co Inc .... C 316 942-8430
Wichita *(G-14097)*
Cornejo & Sons LLC .... C 316 522-5100
Wichita *(G-14101)*
Crookham Construction LLC .... E 913 369-3341
Tonganoxie *(G-12259)*
Crossland Construction Co Inc .... C 620 429-1414
Columbus *(G-1071)*
Czarnieckis Construction Inc .... F 316 946-9991
Wichita *(G-14153)*
Davidson & Associates Inc .... E 913 271-6859
Leawood *(G-5372)*
Decker Construction Inc .... E 620 251-7693
Coffeyville *(G-933)*
Designbuild Construction Inc .... E 316 722-8180
Wichita *(G-14201)*
Dick Construction Inc .... F 620 275-1806
Garden City *(G-2147)*
Diggs Construction Company .... E 316 691-1255
Wichita *(G-14210)*
Eby Corporation .... F 316 268-3500
Wichita *(G-14256)*
Emporia Construction & Rmdlg .... E 620 341-3131
Emporia *(G-1738)*
EMR-Pcg Construction Group .... E 406 249-7730
Lawrence *(G-4853)*
Epic Homes of Kansas Inc .... E 785 537-3773
Manhattan *(G-6622)*
Evans Building Co Inc .... E 316 524-0103
Maize *(G-6513)*
Excel Constructors Inc .... D 913 261-1000
Overland Park *(G-8699)*
Fagan Construction Co .... F 913 238-5903
Prairie Village *(G-10028)*
Feyerherm Construction Inc .... F 913 962-5888
Shawnee *(G-10955)*
Finley Construction & Rdymx .... G 785 626-3282
Atwood *(G-286)*
First Construction LLC .... E 785 749-0006
Lawrence *(G-4859)*
Golconda Group LLC .... F 913 579-4795
Shawnee *(G-10963)*
Grayling Inc .... F 913 341-5444
Overland Park *(G-8769)*
Harbin Construction LLC .... E 785 825-1651
Salina *(G-10535)*
Haren & Laughlin Cnstr Co Inc .... E 913 495-9558
Lenexa *(G-5890)*
Haren Laughlin Restoration Inc .... E 913 495-9558
Overland Park *(G-8794)*
Harman Huffman Cnstr Group Inc .... E 316 744-2081
Kechi *(G-4569)*
Harmon Construction Inc .... E 913 962-5888
Olathe *(G-7753)*
Hastco Inc .... E 785 235-8718
Topeka *(G-12666)*
Hieb & Associates LLC .... F 620 663-9430
Hutchinson *(G-3311)*
Hofer & Hofer & Associates Inc .... E 620 473-3919
Humboldt *(G-3185)*
Home Center Construction Inc .... E 620 231-5607
Pittsburg *(G-9877)*
Hutton Construction Corp .... C 316 942-8855
Wichita *(G-14660)*
J & M Contracting Inc .... F 913 397-0272
Olathe *(G-7804)*
J A G II Inc .... E 620 276-8409
Garden City *(G-2207)*
J A Lyden Construction Co .... F 785 286-1427
Topeka *(G-12730)*
J-A-G Construction Company .... C 620 225-0061
Dodge City *(G-1380)*
Jaco General Contractor Inc .... E 316 252-8200
Wichita *(G-14744)*
Joel Fritzel Construction Co .... E 785 843-0566
Lawrence *(G-4925)*
JP Murray Company Inc .... F 913 451-1279
Overland Park *(G-8880)*
Julius Kaaz Cnstr Co Inc .... E 913 682-3550
Leavenworth *(G-5259)*
K Construction Inc .... F 785 499-5296
Alta Vista *(G-70)*
Kdc Construction Inc .... F 913 677-1920
Leawood *(G-5447)*
Kelley Construction Co Inc .... E 785 235-6040
Topeka *(G-12815)*
Key Construction Inc .... C 316 263-9515
Wichita *(G-14852)*
Laforge and Budd Cnstr Co Inc .... D 620 421-4470
Parsons *(G-9706)*
Law Company Inc .... C 316 268-0200
Wichita *(G-14934)*
Lee Haworth Construction Co .... F 785 823-7168
Salina *(G-10580)*
Loyd Builders Inc .... F 785 242-1213
Ottawa *(G-8286)*
Ls Construction Services Inc .... E 913 681-5888
Shawnee Mission *(G-11580)*
Manning Construction Co Inc .... E 913 390-1007
Olathe *(G-7873)*
Mar Lan Construction LC .... F 785 749-2647
Lawrence *(G-5010)*
Martin K EBY Cnstr Co Inc .... C 316 268-3500
Wichita *(G-15012)*
Mastercraft Corporation .... E 785 842-4455
Lawrence *(G-5013)*
McBride Construction Inc .... F 620 544-7146
Hugoton *(G-3173)*
McCullough Development Inc .... E 888 776-3010
Manhattan *(G-6737)*
McPherson Contractors Inc .... D 785 273-3880
Topeka *(G-12873)*
McPherson Development Co Inc .... F 785 272-9521
Topeka *(G-12874)*
Merit General Contractors .... F 913 747-7400
Olathe *(G-7883)*
Midwest Masonry Construction .... E 785 861-7500
Topeka *(G-12902)*
Miller - Stauch Cnstr Co Inc .... E 913 599-1040
Kansas City *(G-4260)*
Miller Construction .... F 785 448-6788
Garnett *(G-2383)*
Mitchell-Markowitz Cnstr .... E 620 343-6840
Emporia *(G-1796)*
Nabholz Construction Corp .... D 913 393-6500
Lenexa *(G-6017)*
National Commercial Bldrs Inc .... F 913 599-0200
Lenexa *(G-6018)*
North American Buildings Inc .... F 316 821-9590
Wichita *(G-15187)*
Oetinger-Lloyd Construction .... F 785 632-2106
Clay Center *(G-874)*
Page Corporation .... F 316 262-7200
Augusta *(G-335)*
Pkc Construction Co .... E 913 782-4646
Lenexa *(G-6061)*
Purdum Inc .... E 913 766-0835
Overland Park *(G-9204)*
Quinter Mfg & Cnstr Inc .... F 785 754-3310
Quinter *(G-10186)*
R M Baril General Contr Inc .... E 785 537-2190
Manhattan *(G-6785)*
Rau Construction Company .... E 913 642-6000
Overland Park *(G-9227)*
Rhw Construction Inc .... F 913 451-1222
Shawnee Mission *(G-11797)*
Rose Construction Co Inc .... F 913 782-0777
Olathe *(G-8043)*
Sauerwein Construction Co Inc .... F 316 942-0028
Wichita *(G-15522)*
Sca Construction Inc .... E 620 331-8247
Independence *(G-3557)*
Senne and Company Inc .... E 785 235-1015
Topeka *(G-13058)*
Skyline Construction Company .... D 913 642-7100
Overland Park *(G-9316)*
Smith Construction Company Inc .... E 316 942-7989
Wichita *(G-15607)*
Spartan Installation Repr LLC .... F 816 237-0017
Lenexa *(G-6145)*
Strate Construction Inc .... F 620 659-2251
Kinsley *(G-4621)*
Strickland Construction Co .... E 913 764-7000
Olathe *(G-8085)*
Sutherland Builders Inc .... F 316 529-2620
Wichita *(G-15705)*
Titan Built LLC .... E 913 782-6700
Overland Park *(G-9413)*
Titan Cnstr Organization Inc .... F 913 782-6700
Olathe *(G-8110)*
Titan Construction Inc .... C 913 782-6700
Olathe *(G-8111)*
Venture Construction Company .... E 913 642-2972
Overland Park *(G-9461)*
Wc Construction LLC .... E 816 741-4810
Merriam *(G-7110)*
Wiens & Company Construction .... E 620 665-1155
Hutchinson *(G-3488)*
Williams Construction Co Inc .... F 316 264-1964
Wichita *(G-16052)*
Woofter Cnstr & Irrigation Inc .... E 785 462-8653
Colby *(G-1049)*
Zernco .... D 316 775-9991
Wichita *(G-16102)*
Zieson Construction Co LLC .... F 785 783-8335
Topeka *(G-13261)*

CONSTRUCTION: Commercial & Office Buildings, Prefabricated

D J Carpenter Building Systems .... F 785 537-9789
Manhattan *(G-6609)*
Wise Construction Inc .... F 785 781-4383
Cawker City *(G-691)*

CONSTRUCTION: Curb

Scott Heller Trucking .... E 816 591-1638
Lenexa *(G-6119)*

CONSTRUCTION: Dam

Eby Corporation ....F 316 268-3500
Wichita *(G-14256)*
Massman Construction Co ....E 913 291-2600
Leawood *(G-5468)*
Sporer Land Development Inc ....E 785 672-4319
Oakley *(G-7487)*

CONSTRUCTION: Dams, Waterways, Docks & Other Marine

CD&h Inc ....F 316 320-7187
El Dorado *(G-1544)*
Max Rieke & Brothers Inc ....D 913 631-7111
Shawnee *(G-10991)*

CONSTRUCTION: Drainage System

Lightning Grounds Services Inc ....E 913 441-3900
Shawnee Mission *(G-11572)*

CONSTRUCTION: Electric Power Line

Coxmontgomery Inc ....F 620 508-6260
Pratt *(G-10104)*
Dobson-Davis Co ....F 913 894-4922
Shawnee Mission *(G-11311)*
J & J Powerline Contractors ....E 620 227-2467
Dodge City *(G-1379)*
Phillips Southern Elc Co Inc ....E 316 265-4186
Wichita *(G-15293)*

CONSTRUCTION: Farm Building

96 Agri Sales Inc ....F 316 661-2281
Mount Hope *(G-7202)*
Hog Slat Incorporated ....F 580 338-5003
Liberal *(G-6321)*
McPherson Con Stor Systems Inc ....F 620 241-4362
McPherson *(G-6994)*
Profitt Builders and Supply ....F 620 278-3667
Sterling *(G-12129)*
Treb Construction Inc ....F 785 373-4935
Tipton *(G-12250)*

CONSTRUCTION: Foundation & Retaining Wall

Berkel & Company Contrs Inc ....D 913 422-5125
Bonner Springs *(G-540)*

CONSTRUCTION: Garage

Sturdi-Bilt Storage Barns Inc ....E 620 663-5998
Hutchinson *(G-3453)*

CONSTRUCTION: Gas Main

Shawnee Mission Tree Svc Inc ....D 913 441-8888
Shawnee *(G-11029)*

CONSTRUCTION: Golf Course

Wildcat Construction Co Inc ....C 316 945-9408
Wichita *(G-16049)*

CONSTRUCTION: Grain Elevator

Black Hawk Inc ....E 785 539-8240
Manhattan *(G-6562)*
Ernest-Spencer Inc ....E 785 484-3165
Meriden *(G-7080)*
Industrial Maintenance Inc ....E 316 267-7933
Wichita *(G-14685)*
Midwest Mill Modernization ....F 620 583-6883
Eureka *(G-1895)*

CONSTRUCTION: Greenhouse

Jackson Agrobuilders LLC ....F 913 909-6391
Shawnee *(G-10976)*

CONSTRUCTION: Guardrails, Highway

J & J Contractors Inc ....F 620 365-5500
Iola *(G-3613)*

CONSTRUCTION: Heavy Highway & Street

Apac-Kansas Inc ....E 620 342-2047
Emporia *(G-1695)*
Apac-Kansas Inc ....E 316 775-7639
Augusta *(G-300)*
Banzet Concrete Inc ....F 316 776-9961
Rose Hill *(G-10236)*
City of Junction City ....E 785 238-7142
Junction City *(G-3682)*
City of Parsons ....E 620 421-7025
Parsons *(G-9671)*
County of Leavenworth ....D 913 727-1800
Leavenworth *(G-5228)*
County of Pawnee ....E 620 285-6141
Larned *(G-4700)*
County of Reno ....D 620 694-2976
South Hutchinson *(G-12058)*
County of Shawnee ....D 785 862-2071
Topeka *(G-12520)*
County of Shawnee ....D 785 233-7702
Topeka *(G-12521)*
Fulsom Brothers Inc ....F 620 758-2828
Cedar Vale *(G-694)*
Goodart Consrtuction Inc ....F 913 557-0044
Paola *(G-9562)*
Hamm Inc ....G 785 597-5111
Perry *(G-9769)*
Kansas Department Trnsp ....E 785 486-2142
Horton *(G-3128)*
Kaw Valley Companies Inc ....C 913 281-9950
Kansas City *(G-4160)*
Kiewit Power Constructors Co ....C 913 928-7800
Lenexa *(G-5950)*
Laforge and Budd Cnstr Co Inc ....D 620 421-4470
Parsons *(G-9706)*
Max Rieke & Brothers Inc ....D 913 631-7111
Shawnee *(G-10991)*
R D Johnson Excavating Co Inc ....E 785 842-9100
Lawrence *(G-5085)*
Sherwood Construction Co Inc ....C 316 943-0211
Wichita *(G-15581)*

CONSTRUCTION: Hospital

Tutera Group Inc ....E 913 851-0215
Shawnee Mission *(G-11951)*
Universal Construction Co Inc ....E 913 342-1150
Kansas City *(G-4494)*

CONSTRUCTION: Hotel & Motel, New

Econo Lodge ....F 785 625-4839
Hays *(G-2797)*

CONSTRUCTION: Indl Building & Warehouse

Arrowhead Contracting Inc ....D 913 814-9994
Lenexa *(G-5664)*
Berry Holdings LP ....B 620 251-4400
Coffeyville *(G-911)*
Bhs Construction Inc ....E 785 537-2068
Manhattan *(G-6557)*
Coonrod & Assoc Cnstr Co Inc ....C 316 942-8430
Wichita *(G-14097)*
Decker Construction Inc ....E 620 251-7693
Coffeyville *(G-933)*
Evergreen Design Build LLC ....E 620 342-6622
Emporia *(G-1752)*
Hahner Foreman & Harness LLC ....E 316 264-0306
Wichita *(G-14540)*
Haren & Laughlin Cnstr Co Inc ....E 913 495-9558
Lenexa *(G-5890)*
Julius Kaaz Cnstr Co Inc ....E 913 682-3550
Leavenworth *(G-5259)*
Laforge and Budd Cnstr Co Inc ....D 620 421-4470
Parsons *(G-9706)*
Leavcon II Inc ....E 913 351-1430
Lansing *(G-4681)*
Lee Construction Inc ....E 620 276-6811
Garden City *(G-2222)*
Lee Shafer Ricky ....E 620 252-9126
Coffeyville *(G-955)*
Manning Construction Co Inc ....E 913 390-1007
Olathe *(G-7873)*
Merit General Contractors ....F 913 747-7400
Olathe *(G-7883)*
R M Baril General Contr Inc ....E 785 537-2190
Manhattan *(G-6785)*
Rylie Equipment & Contg Co ....D 913 621-2725
Kansas City *(G-4394)*
Sauerwein Construction Co Inc ....F 316 942-0028
Wichita *(G-15522)*
Strickland Construction Co ....E 913 764-7000
Olathe *(G-8085)*
Team Construction LLC ....F 913 469-9990
Overland Park *(G-9396)*
Universal Construction Co Inc ....E 913 342-1150
Kansas City *(G-4494)*
Wds Inc ....D 913 894-1881
Lenexa *(G-6223)*

CONSTRUCTION: Indl Building, Prefabricated

Qti Inc ....F 913 579-3131
Olathe *(G-8013)*
Salina Building Systems Inc ....E 785 823-6812
Salina *(G-10666)*
Weigel Construction Inc ....F 913 780-1274
Spring Hill *(G-12103)*

CONSTRUCTION: Indl Buildings, New, NEC

BKM Construction LLC ....F 913 297-0049
Leavenworth *(G-5212)*
Building Erection Svcs Co Inc ....E 913 764-5560
Olathe *(G-7568)*
Busboom & Rauh Construction Co ....E 785 825-4664
Salina *(G-10434)*
Conco Inc ....C 316 943-7111
Wichita *(G-14085)*
Diggs Construction Company ....E 316 691-1255
Wichita *(G-14210)*
Dondlinger & Sons Cnstr Co Inc ....C 316 945-0555
Wichita *(G-14226)*
Eby Corporation ....F 316 268-3500
Wichita *(G-14256)*
Excel Constructors Inc ....D 913 261-1000
Overland Park *(G-8699)*
Feyerherm Construction Inc ....F 913 962-5888
Shawnee *(G-10955)*
GBA Builders Llc ....E 913 492-0400
Lenexa *(G-5870)*
Gsr Construction Inc ....F 785 749-1770
Lawrence *(G-4883)*
Harbin Construction LLC ....E 785 825-1651
Salina *(G-10535)*
Hastco Inc ....E 785 235-8718
Topeka *(G-12666)*
Ken Babcock Sales Inc ....F 785 544-6592
Hiawatha *(G-3013)*
Key Construction Inc ....C 316 263-9515
Wichita *(G-14852)*
Loyd Builders Inc ....F 785 242-1213
Ottawa *(G-8286)*
Miller - Stauch Cnstr Co Inc ....E 913 599-1040
Kansas City *(G-4260)*
Mohan Construction Inc ....E 785 233-1615
Topeka *(G-12909)*
Morton Buildings Inc ....F 620 275-4105
Garden City *(G-2239)*
National Builders Inc ....F 316 729-7445
Wichita *(G-15147)*
North Enterprises LLC ....F 913 592-4025
Spring Hill *(G-12093)*
Rose Companies Inc ....F 913 782-0777
Olathe *(G-8042)*
Rose Construction Co Inc ....F 913 782-0777
Olathe *(G-8043)*
Simpson Construction Svcs Inc ....E 316 942-3206
Wichita *(G-15596)*
Snodgrass & Sons Cnstr Co Inc ....D 316 687-3110
Wichita *(G-15611)*
Titan Cnstr Organization Inc ....F 913 782-6700
Olathe *(G-8110)*
Wolf Construction Inc ....D 785 862-2474
Topeka *(G-13247)*

CONSTRUCTION: Indl Plant

CDI Industrial Mech Contrs Inc ....C 913 287-0334
Kansas City *(G-3898)*
Tindle Construction Inc ....D 620 378-2046
Fredonia *(G-2047)*

CONSTRUCTION: Indoor Athletic Court

Versasport of Kansas Inc ....E 316 393-0487
Wichita *(G-15876)*

CONSTRUCTION: Institutional Building

McCarthy Bldg Companies Inc ....E 913 202-7002
Overland Park *(G-9000)*
Sky Blue Inc ....D 785 842-9013
Lawrence *(G-5112)*

CONSTRUCTION: Irrigation System

Lawns By Beck Inc .... F 913 631-8873
Shawnee Mission *(G-11549)*
Luka Irrigation Systems Inc .... E 913 248-0400
Shawnee *(G-10990)*
Luxury Lawn & Landscape Inc .... F 785 233-5296
Topeka *(G-12854)*
Rosencrantz Bemis Enterprises .... E 620 792-2488
Great Bend *(G-2632)*
Western Irrigation Inc .... E 620 275-4033
Garden City *(G-2311)*

CONSTRUCTION: Multi-Family Housing

City Wide Holding Company Inc .... C 913 888-5700
Lenexa *(G-5757)*
DF Osborne Construction Inc .... F 785 862-0333
Topeka *(G-12554)*
Law Company Inc .... C 316 268-0200
Wichita *(G-14934)*
Mastercraft Corporation .... E 785 842-4455
Lawrence *(G-5013)*
MCN Shawnee LLC .... D 913 631-2100
Shawnee *(G-10992)*
R & R Developers Inc .... F 785 762-2255
Junction City *(G-3746)*

CONSTRUCTION: Multi-family Dwellings, New

Jakubs Ladder Inc .... G 316 214-8932
Derby *(G-1255)*
McPherson Development Co Inc .... F 785 272-9521
Topeka *(G-12874)*
Mitchell-Markowitz Cnstr .... E 620 343-6840
Emporia *(G-1796)*
Prairie Landworks Inc .... F 620 504-5049
Mcpherson *(G-7017)*
Tommy J Kemp .... E 316 522-7255
Derby *(G-1276)*

CONSTRUCTION: Oil & Gas Line & Compressor Station

Prairie Landworks Inc .... F 620 504-5049
Mcpherson *(G-7017)*

CONSTRUCTION: Oil & Gas Pipeline Construction

Jomax Construction Company Inc .... F 620 792-3686
Great Bend *(G-2596)*
MAI Excavating Inc .... G 785 483-3387
Russell *(G-10280)*
Npl Construction Co .... D 785 232-0034
Topeka *(G-12940)*
Total Lease Service Inc .... G 785 735-9520
Hays *(G-2920)*

CONSTRUCTION: Parking Lot

Max Rieke & Brothers Inc .... D 913 631-7111
Shawnee *(G-10991)*
Paving Construction Inc .... F 316 684-6161
Wichita *(G-15272)*
Prairie Landworks Inc .... F 620 504-5049
Mcpherson *(G-7017)*

CONSTRUCTION: Pipeline, NEC

Ace Construction Corporation .... E 316 536-2202
Towanda *(G-13262)*
American Energies Gas Svc LLC .... F 620 628-4424
Canton *(G-679)*
ANR Pipeline Company .... F 785 479-5814
Enterprise *(G-1853)*
Coffeyville Resources LLC .... F 620 221-2107
Winfield *(G-16122)*
Eatherly Constructors Inc .... F 620 276-6611
Garden City *(G-2151)*
Northern Pipeline Construction .... F 785 232-0034
Topeka *(G-12937)*
Piping & Equipment Company Inc .... C 316 838-7511
Wichita *(G-15302)*
Toms Ditching & Backhoe Inc .... F 620 879-2215
Caney *(G-676)*

CONSTRUCTION: Power & Communication Transmission Tower

D L Smith Electrical Cnstr .... C 785 267-4920
Topeka *(G-12543)*
Teledata Communications LLC .... E 913 663-2010
Lenexa *(G-6175)*

CONSTRUCTION: Power Plant

Black & Veatch Cnstr Inc .... E 913 458-2000
Overland Park *(G-8454)*
Enpower Operations Corp .... F 913 441-3633
Shawnee *(G-10948)*
Kiewit Power Group Inc .... F 913 227-3600
Lenexa *(G-5951)*

CONSTRUCTION: Pumping Station

Harp Well Pump Svc Corporated .... F 316 722-1411
Wichita *(G-14562)*

CONSTRUCTION: Railroad & Subway

Tangent Rail Energy Inc .... D 913 948-9478
Lenexa *(G-6166)*

CONSTRUCTION: Railway Roadbed

Amsted Rail Company Inc .... F 913 299-2223
Kansas City *(G-3808)*
Railway Construction .... F 620 663-9233
Hutchinson *(G-3419)*
Ronnie Diehl Construction Inc .... E 785 823-7800
Salina *(G-10653)*

CONSTRUCTION: Refineries

C-Tech Industrial Group Inc .... F 316 321-5358
El Dorado *(G-1542)*

CONSTRUCTION: Religious Building

DF Osborne Construction Inc .... F 785 862-0333
Topeka *(G-12554)*
Fuqua Construction Inc .... F 620 585-2270
Inman *(G-3582)*

CONSTRUCTION: Residential, Nec

Baronda Supplies & Service .... F 785 466-2501
Herington *(G-2971)*
BKM Construction LLC .... F 913 297-0049
Leavenworth *(G-5212)*
Building Solutions LLC .... F 620 225-1199
Dodge City *(G-1314)*
CU - Once Joint Venture LLC .... F 913 707-2165
Stilwell *(G-12143)*
Dondlinger & Sons Cnstr Co Inc .... F 316 943-9393
Wichita *(G-14227)*
Ebco Construction Group LLC .... F 866 297-2185
Olathe *(G-7667)*
Epic Homes of Kansas Inc .... E 785 537-3773
Manhattan *(G-6622)*
G & F Construction Co LLC .... E 316 260-3313
Wichita *(G-14432)*
Heartland Hbtat For Hmnity Inc .... F 913 342-3047
Kansas City *(G-4075)*
Iqvia Phase One Services LLC .... D 913 708-6000
Overland Park *(G-8861)*
Kdc Construction Inc .... F 913 677-1920
Leawood *(G-5447)*
Lang Builders LLC .... F 620 331-5850
Independence *(G-3532)*
National Builders Inc .... F 316 729-7445
Wichita *(G-15147)*
Neals Foundations Inc .... E 316 744-0064
Kechi *(G-4573)*
Neighbors Construction Co Inc .... E 913 422-5555
Lenexa *(G-6021)*
P & F Services Inc .... F 785 456-9401
Wamego *(G-13432)*
Patrick S Kearney .... F 913 367-3161
Atchison *(G-255)*
Quality Structures Inc .... E 785 835-6100
Richmond *(G-10203)*
Rd Thomann Contracting .... F 913 268-5580
Shawnee Mission *(G-11780)*
Spartan Installation Repr LLC .... F 816 237-0017
Lenexa *(G-6145)*
Wieneke Construction Co Inc .... F 620 632-4529
Mc Cune *(G-6923)*
Wildcat Services Inc .... F 785 922-6466
Chapman *(G-781)*

CONSTRUCTION: Retaining Wall

Konradys Lawn & Ldscpg Inc .... E 913 722-1163
Olathe *(G-7843)*

CONSTRUCTION: Roads, Gravel or Dirt

J Corp .... F 785 628-8101
Hays *(G-2854)*
R Puckett Farms Inc .... E 620 378-3565
Fredonia *(G-2042)*
Skillman Construction LLC .... D 620 364-2505
New Strawn *(G-7305)*

CONSTRUCTION: School Building

B & G Construction .... F 620 431-0849
Chanute *(G-704)*
Pemco Inc .... F 913 294-2361
Paola *(G-9582)*

CONSTRUCTION: Sewer Line

BRB Contractors Inc .... C 785 232-1245
Topeka *(G-12403)*
Eby Corporation .... F 316 268-3500
Wichita *(G-14256)*
Emerson Construction Inc .... F 785 235-0555
Topeka *(G-12574)*
McCullough Excavation Inc .... E 316 634-2199
Wichita *(G-15025)*
Meadows Const Co Inc .... E 913 369-3335
Tonganoxie *(G-12266)*
Pearson Construction LLC .... C 316 263-3100
Wichita *(G-15275)*
Ron Weers Construction Inc .... E 913 681-5575
Bucyrus *(G-608)*
Utility Maintenance Contrs LLC .... F 316 945-8833
Wichita *(G-15867)*

CONSTRUCTION: Silo, Agricultural

Borton Lc .... E 620 669-8211
South Hutchinson *(G-12057)*

CONSTRUCTION: Single-Family Housing

A Lert Corp .... F 620 378-4153
Coyville *(G-1182)*
AMZ Construction Inc .... F 913 915-7867
Olathe *(G-7529)*
Antes Concrete Inc .... F 913 856-4535
Olathe *(G-7530)*
Apex Construction Inc .... E 913 341-3688
Lenexa *(G-5657)*
Bartec Construction LLC .... E 913 208-0015
Tonganoxie *(G-12252)*
Benchmark Construction LLC .... F 785 862-0340
Eudora *(G-1870)*
BKM Construction LLC .... F 913 297-0049
Leavenworth *(G-5212)*
Budreau Construction Inc .... F 785 446-3665
Clyde *(G-904)*
Caro Construction Co Inc .... E 316 267-7505
Wichita *(G-13952)*
Cdh Enterprises .... F 316 320-7187
El Dorado *(G-1545)*
Compton Construction Svcs LLC .... E 316 262-8885
Wichita *(G-14083)*
Construction Systems Inc .... F 913 208-6401
Shawnee Mission *(G-11260)*
Construction Technologies LLC .... F 913 671-3440
Shawnee Mission *(G-11261)*
Coonrod & Assoc Cnstr Co Inc .... C 316 942-8430
Wichita *(G-14097)*
Cornerstone Cnstr Svcs LLC .... F 913 207-1751
Olathe *(G-7616)*
Coyote Investment & Networking .... E 785 550-6028
Lawrence *(G-4815)*
Crossland Construction Co Inc .... E 316 942-9090
Wichita *(G-14135)*
Darrell Bybee Construction LLC .... F 316 409-4186
Wichita *(G-14171)*
Dennis R Sumner Construction .... F 785 478-1701
Topeka *(G-12552)*
Double K Cnstr of Mound Cy .... F 913 795-3147
Mound City *(G-7171)*
Empire Construction Group LLC .... F 913 375-8886
Shawnee Mission *(G-11335)*

Farha Construction Inc..........E....... 316 943-0000
Wichita *(G-14339)*
G-B Construction LLC..........E....... 913 837-5240
Louisburg *(G-6449)*
Gray Construction Inc..........E....... 316 721-3000
Wichita *(G-14498)*
Great Western Dining Svc Inc..........F....... 620 792-9224
Great Bend *(G-2585)*
Greenamyre Construction LLC..........F....... 913 772-1776
Leavenworth *(G-5248)*
Heartland Midwest LLC..........E....... 913 471-4840
Pleasanton *(G-9996)*
Heritage Home Works LLC..........F....... 316 288-9033
Newton *(G-7360)*
Jakubs Ladder Inc..........G....... 316 214-8932
Derby *(G-1255)*
Kansas Heavy Construction LLC..........E....... 913 845-2121
Tonganoxie *(G-12264)*
Mark C Jones..........F....... 620 375-2357
Leoti *(G-6256)*
McPherson Development Co Inc..........F....... 785 272-9521
Topeka *(G-12874)*
Michael S Hundley Cnstr Inc..........F....... 913 367-7059
Atchison *(G-249)*
Miller Building Services Inc..........E....... 913 649-5599
Shawnee *(G-10996)*
National Builders Inc..........F....... 316 729-7445
Wichita *(G-15147)*
Page Corporation..........F....... 316 262-7200
Augusta *(G-335)*
Prime Place LLC..........F....... 785 317-5265
Manhattan *(G-6781)*
Quality Homes Inc..........E....... 402 248-6218
Summerfield *(G-12216)*
Rdcs Inc..........F....... 913 238-5377
Lenexa *(G-6094)*
Reliable Construction Svcs Inc..........F....... 913 764-7274
Olathe *(G-8025)*
Rf Construction Inc..........E....... 785 776-8855
Manhattan *(G-6791)*
Riley Communities LLC..........D....... 785 717-2210
Fort Riley *(G-1949)*
Short Creek Construction..........F....... 620 783-2896
Galena *(G-2085)*
Suther Building Supply Inc..........F....... 785 336-2255
Seneca *(G-10883)*
Tommy J Kemp..........E....... 316 522-7255
Derby *(G-1276)*
Tribe Construction LLC..........F....... 913 850-0211
Mound City *(G-7176)*
Wichita Habitat For Humanity..........F....... 316 269-0755
Wichita *(G-16004)*
Wolfgang Construction LLC..........F....... 785 456-8729
Wamego *(G-13457)*

CONSTRUCTION: Single-family Housing, New

Acklin Construction..........F....... 316 321-6648
El Dorado *(G-1525)*
B L Rieke & Associates Inc..........F....... 913 599-3393
Shawnee Mission *(G-11141)*
Blecha Enterprises LLC..........F....... 785 539-6640
Manhattan *(G-6563)*
Clark Dargal Builders Inc..........F....... 785 478-4811
Topeka *(G-12479)*
D & R Construction Inc..........E....... 785 776-1087
Manhattan *(G-6608)*
Don Julian Builders Inc..........E....... 913 894-6300
Lenexa *(G-5822)*
Don Klausmeyer Cnstr LLC..........E....... 316 554-0001
Wichita *(G-14224)*
Freund Investment Inc..........F....... 620 669-9649
Hutchinson *(G-3295)*
Goentzel Construction Inc..........F....... 316 264-6333
Wichita *(G-14479)*
Heinen Custom Operations Inc..........F....... 785 945-6759
Valley Falls *(G-13364)*
Heritage Builders Inc..........F....... 785 776-6011
Manhattan *(G-6655)*
Indel Corporation..........F....... 785 478-9719
Topeka *(G-12715)*
J Graham Construction Inc..........E....... 620 252-2395
Coffeyville *(G-949)*
Jim Haas Builders Inc..........F....... 913 897-9721
Stilwell *(G-12157)*
Joel Fritzel Construction Co..........E....... 785 843-0566
Lawrence *(G-4925)*
Key Construction Missouri LLC..........F....... 816 221-7171
Wichita *(G-14853)*
Koehn Construction..........F....... 620 345-6457
Moundridge *(G-7187)*
Lee Haworth Construction Co..........F....... 785 823-7168
Salina *(G-10580)*
Martens Enterprises Inc..........F....... 913 851-2772
Stilwell *(G-12165)*
McBride Construction Inc..........F....... 620 544-7146
Hugoton *(G-3173)*
McCullough Development Inc..........E....... 888 776-3010
Manhattan *(G-6737)*
Miller Construction..........F....... 785 448-6788
Garnett *(G-2383)*
Miller Homebuilders Inc..........E....... 620 662-1687
Hutchinson *(G-3381)*
Oakland Avenue Craftsmen Co..........F....... 316 685-3955
Wichita *(G-15203)*
Oetinger-Lloyd Construction..........F....... 785 632-2106
Clay Center *(G-874)*
Paul-Wertenberger Cnstr Inc..........E....... 785 625-8220
Hays *(G-2885)*
Premier Housing Inc..........E....... 620 277-0707
Holcomb *(G-3077)*
Quality Trust Inc..........E....... 785 375-6372
Junction City *(G-3745)*
R & R Builders Inc..........D....... 913 682-1234
Leavenworth *(G-5282)*
R & R Developers Inc..........F....... 785 762-2255
Junction City *(G-3746)*
Ritchie Associates Inc..........E....... 316 684-7300
Wichita *(G-15466)*
Ritchie Building Co Inc..........E....... 316 684-7300
Wichita *(G-15467)*
Robinson Js Construction Inc..........E....... 913 441-2988
Shawnee Mission *(G-11811)*
Rodrock Homes LLC..........F....... 913 851-0347
Lenexa *(G-6112)*
Roeser Homes LLC..........F....... 913 220-7477
Overland Park *(G-9255)*
Still Builders Inc..........F....... 913 780-0702
Olathe *(G-8083)*
Strate Construction Inc..........F....... 620 659-2251
Kinsley *(G-4621)*
Wamego Lumber Co Inc..........F....... 785 456-2400
Wamego *(G-13453)*
Wardcraft Homes Inc..........D....... 785 632-5664
Clay Center *(G-886)*
Yoder Builders Inc..........E....... 620 669-8542
South Hutchinson *(G-12068)*

CONSTRUCTION: Single-family Housing, Prefabricated

Advanced Systems Homes Inc..........E....... 620 431-3320
Chanute *(G-702)*

CONSTRUCTION: Stadium

Kuhlmann Installations LLC..........F....... 316 634-6531
Wichita *(G-14899)*

CONSTRUCTION: Steel Buildings

All-Steel Building Systems LLC..........F....... 785 271-5559
Topeka *(G-12306)*
BJ Koetting Inc..........F....... 785 823-8580
Salina *(G-10425)*
Ewell Construction Inc..........F....... 913 499-7331
Topeka *(G-12585)*
Roofmasters Roofing Co Inc..........E....... 785 462-6642
Colby *(G-1036)*
Treb Construction Inc..........F....... 785 373-4935
Tipton *(G-12250)*

CONSTRUCTION: Street Surfacing & Paving

Apac-Kansas Inc..........E....... 620 662-2112
Hutchinson *(G-3202)*
Apac-Kansas Inc..........D....... 316 524-5200
Wichita *(G-13716)*
Ballou Pavement Solutions Inc..........C....... 785 827-4439
Salina *(G-10416)*
Barkley Construction..........F....... 316 945-6500
Wichita *(G-13812)*
Central Paving Inc..........E....... 316 778-1194
Benton *(G-514)*
Circle C Paving and Cnstr LLC..........E....... 316 794-5070
Goddard *(G-2432)*
Cornejo & Sons LLC..........C....... 316 522-5100
Wichita *(G-14101)*
Heartstone Inc..........F....... 316 942-1135
Wichita *(G-14591)*
Holland Paving Inc..........E....... 316 722-7114
Wichita *(G-14625)*
ODonnell-Way Cnstr Co Inc..........F....... 913 498-3355
Prairie Village *(G-10053)*
Pavers Inc..........E....... 785 825-6771
Salina *(G-10632)*
Sunflower Paving Inc..........D....... 785 856-4590
Lawrence *(G-5129)*
T & T Flatworks Inc..........E....... 620 794-0619
Lebo *(G-5609)*
W R King Contracting Inc..........E....... 913 238-7496
Shawnee Mission *(G-11985)*

CONSTRUCTION: Swimming Pools

Banks Swimming Pool Company..........E....... 913 897-9290
Overland Park *(G-8431)*
Continental Pools Inc..........F....... 913 856-2841
Gardner *(G-2334)*
Green Meadows Lawn Landscaping..........F....... 316 788-0282
Derby *(G-1250)*
McKee Pool & Landscaping Inc..........F....... 785 843-9119
Lawrence *(G-5018)*
Merit General Contractors..........F....... 913 747-7400
Olathe *(G-7883)*
Pool & Patio Supply Inc..........F....... 913 888-2226
Shawnee Mission *(G-11744)*
Pools Plus..........F....... 785 823-7665
Salina *(G-10636)*
Superior Pools..........F....... 316 838-4968
Wichita *(G-15697)*

CONSTRUCTION: Telephone & Communication Line

Cronister & Company Inc..........E....... 785 862-5003
Topeka *(G-12531)*
Dreiling Construction LLC..........F....... 620 275-9433
Garden City *(G-2149)*
Midwest Contractors Inc..........E....... 785 877-3565
Norton *(G-7449)*
Zook Construction..........F....... 785 388-2183
Wakefield *(G-13399)*

CONSTRUCTION: Tennis Court

Versasport of Kansas Inc..........E....... 316 393-0487
Wichita *(G-15876)*

CONSTRUCTION: Transmitting Tower, Telecommunication

Alea Communications LLC..........F....... 913 439-7391
Gardner *(G-2323)*
Hayden Tower Service Inc..........D....... 785 232-1840
Topeka *(G-12668)*
Legacy Technologies LLC..........E....... 913 432-2020
Shawnee Mission *(G-11559)*
Lowe-North Construction Inc..........E....... 913 592-4025
Spring Hill *(G-12087)*

CONSTRUCTION: Utility Line

Becker Construction Inc..........F....... 316 744-6800
Park City *(G-9603)*
Bennett Rgers Pipe Coating Inc..........E....... 913 371-3880
Kansas City *(G-3854)*
Bsj Power Services Inc..........F....... 417 850-1707
Cherokee *(G-799)*
Carrothers Construction Co LLC..........E....... 913 294-8120
Paola *(G-9545)*
City of Waterville..........E....... 785 363-2367
Waterville *(G-13473)*
Gerard Tank & Steel Inc..........E....... 785 243-3895
Concordia *(G-1116)*
Lrm Industries Inc..........E....... 785 843-1688
Lawrence *(G-5001)*
R D Johnson Excavating Co Inc..........E....... 785 842-9100
Lawrence *(G-5085)*
Scotts Powerline Construction..........F....... 316 440-8290
Wichita *(G-15539)*
Tl Enterprises Inc..........F....... 785 448-7100
Wichita *(G-15770)*
W B Carter Construction Co..........E....... 316 942-4214
Wichita *(G-15912)*

CONSTRUCTION: Warehouse

Jaco General Contractor Inc..........E....... 316 252-8200
Wichita *(G-14744)*

CONSTRUCTION: Waste Water & Sewage Treatment Plant

BRB Contractors Inc..............C....... 785 232-1245
Topeka *(G-12403)*
City of Liberal..............F....... 620 626-0138
Liberal *(G-6293)*
Walters-Morgan Cnstr Inc..............D....... 785 539-7513
Manhattan *(G-6846)*

CONSTRUCTION: Water & Sewer Line

Bayer Construction Company Inc..............C....... 785 776-8839
Manhattan *(G-6553)*
Diamond Engineering Company..............E....... 316 943-5701
Wichita *(G-14208)*
J Corp..............F....... 785 628-8101
Hays *(G-2854)*
Linaweaver Construction Inc..............F....... 913 351-3474
Lansing *(G-4686)*
Max Rieke & Brothers Inc..............D....... 913 631-7111
Shawnee *(G-10991)*
Mels Pump & Plumbing..............F....... 785 632-3392
Clay Center *(G-872)*
Ohlsen Right of Way and Maint..............F....... 785 336-6112
Seneca *(G-10878)*
Smoky Hill LLC..............D....... 785 825-0810
Salina *(G-10710)*
Utility Contractors Inc..............E....... 316 942-1253
Wichita *(G-15866)*

CONSTRUCTION: Water Main

Layne Christensen Company..............E....... 316 264-5365
Wichita *(G-14937)*
Nowak Construction Co Inc..............D....... 316 794-8898
Goddard *(G-2449)*
RA Knapp Construction Inc..............E....... 913 287-8700
Lenexa *(G-6088)*
Rodriguez Mech Contrs Inc..............D....... 913 281-1814
Kansas City *(G-4386)*

CONSTRUCTION: Waterway

Bernard D Ohlsen Cnstr Co..............F....... 785 873-3462
Whiting *(G-13574)*

CONSULTING SVC: Actuarial

Actuarial Resources Corp Kans..............E....... 913 451-0044
Overland Park *(G-8345)*
Ad Astra Recover Service..............F....... 316 941-5448
Wichita *(G-13611)*
Lewis & Ellis Inc..............E....... 913 491-3388
Overland Park *(G-8955)*
Miller & Newberg Inc..............F....... 913 393-2522
Overland Park *(G-9037)*

CONSULTING SVC: Business, NEC

360 Document Solutions LLC..............F....... 316 630-8334
Wichita *(G-13580)*
Adams-Gabbert & Associates LLC..............F....... 913 735-4390
Overland Park *(G-8346)*
Advanced Manufacturing Inst..............E....... 785 532-7044
Manhattan *(G-6534)*
Advantage Tech Inc..............D....... 913 888-5050
Overland Park *(G-8352)*
Anthem Media LLC..............E....... 913 894-6923
Leawood *(G-5327)*
Archein Aerospace LLC..............E....... 682 499-2150
Wichita *(G-13730)*
Auditing For Cmpliance Educatn..............F....... 913 648-8572
Shawnee Mission *(G-11133)*
Baxter Vault Company Inc..............F....... 620 856-3441
Baxter Springs *(G-398)*
BE Smith Inc..............B....... 913 341-9116
Lenexa *(G-5691)*
Blue Infotech Inc..............F....... 816 945-2583
Leawood *(G-5341)*
Cardinal Health 127 Inc..............D....... 913 451-3955
Overland Park *(G-8513)*
Cbiz Inc..............F....... 913 345-0500
Overland Park *(G-8528)*
Clarence M Kelley & Assoc of K..............D....... 913 647-7700
Shawnee *(G-10929)*
Convergeone Inc..............C....... 913 307-2300
Overland Park *(G-8597)*
Design Analysis and RES Corp..............F....... 785 832-0434
Lawrence *(G-4833)*
Elm Services LLC..............D....... 913 954-4414
Overland Park *(G-8674)*
EMB Statistical Solutions LLC..............F....... 913 322-6555
Overland Park *(G-8676)*
F & L Enterprises Inc..............F....... 785 266-4933
Topeka *(G-12590)*
Foster Design Inc..............C....... 316 832-9700
Wichita *(G-14403)*
Friedman Group..............E....... 310 590-1248
Overland Park *(G-8742)*
Garcia and Antosh LLP..............F....... 620 225-7400
Dodge City *(G-1364)*
Gateway Plaza West Ltd..............F....... 913 621-3840
Kansas City *(G-4027)*
Groupsource Gpo LLC..............F....... 913 888-9191
Olathe *(G-7741)*
Hotel MGT & Consulting Inc..............F....... 913 602-8470
Overland Park *(G-8830)*
Housing and Credit Counseling..............E....... 785 234-0217
Topeka *(G-12705)*
Innova Consulting LLC..............F....... 913 210-2002
Overland Park *(G-8845)*
It21 Inc..............F....... 913 393-4821
Overland Park *(G-8864)*
Jarden Corp Outdoor Solutions..............F....... 316 832-2441
Wichita *(G-14748)*
Jvf Enterprises Inc..............F....... 913 888-9111
Lenexa *(G-5934)*
Kansas Center Entreprnrshp..............E....... 316 425-8808
Wichita *(G-14791)*
Kansas Secured Title..............F....... 316 320-2410
El Dorado *(G-1576)*
Kansas State University..............F....... 785 532-6804
Manhattan *(G-6695)*
Koch Business Solutions LP..............C....... 316 828-5500
Wichita *(G-14874)*
Lakepoint Corporate..............F....... 316 990-6792
Augusta *(G-332)*
Land Acquisitions Inc..............E....... 847 749-0675
Wichita *(G-14919)*
Led2 Lighting Inc..............G....... 816 912-2180
Kansas City *(G-4199)*
Litigation Insights Inc..............E....... 913 339-9885
Overland Park *(G-8962)*
Marketsphere Consulting LLC..............D....... 913 608-3648
Overland Park *(G-8992)*
Needham & Associates Inc..............G....... 913 385-5300
Lenexa *(G-6019)*
P/Strada LLC..............F....... 816 256-4577
Lenexa *(G-6039)*
Pendello Solutions..............F....... 913 677-6744
Prairie Village *(G-10058)*
Perinatal Consultants PA..............F....... 785 354-5952
Goddard *(G-2452)*
Pl Arm..............C....... 913 661-1662
Overland Park *(G-9165)*
Professors of Peace LLC..............F....... 316 213-7233
Haysville *(G-2956)*
Progress Rail Services..............F....... 256 593-1260
Atchison *(G-256)*
Propharma Group LLC..............D....... 888 242-0559
Overland Park *(G-9195)*
Provalue Cooperative Inc..............E....... 620 662-5406
Hutchinson *(G-3416)*
Qspec Solutions Inc..............F....... 877 467-7732
Overland Park *(G-9207)*
Regency Gas Services LLC..............F....... 620 355-7905
Lakin *(G-4659)*
Resolution Services LLC..............E....... 785 843-1638
Lawrence *(G-5093)*
S C F Inc..............E....... 913 722-3473
Overland Park *(G-9267)*
Security Benefit Life Insur Co..............B....... 785 438-3000
Topeka *(G-13054)*
Security Management Co LLC..............E....... 785 438-3000
Topeka *(G-13055)*
Service Corps Retired Execs..............F....... 316 269-6273
Wichita *(G-15567)*
Something Different Media Prod..............F....... 913 764-9500
Olathe *(G-8072)*
Southeast Kans Educatn Svc Ctr..............C....... 620 724-6281
Girard *(G-2418)*
Southwest Plins Rgonal Svc Ctr..............D....... 620 675-2241
Sublette *(G-12207)*
Stratgic Knwldge Solutions Inc..............F....... 913 682-2002
Leavenworth *(G-5292)*
Techncal Trning Prfssonals LLC..............F....... 865 312-4189
Overland Park *(G-9399)*
Veracity Consulting Inc..............D....... 913 945-1912
Overland Park *(G-9462)*
Wachter Inc..............C....... 913 541-2500
Lenexa *(G-6219)*
Wachter Tech Solutions Inc..............D....... 856 222-0643
Lenexa *(G-6220)*
Wichita Consulting Company LP..............E....... 316 681-5102
Wichita *(G-15990)*

CONSULTING SVC: Chemical

Hawkins Inc..............E....... 785 448-1610
Garnett *(G-2376)*

CONSULTING SVC: Computer

Acceligent Inc..............F....... 972 504-6660
Overland Park *(G-8339)*
Advisors Tech LLC..............F....... 844 671-6071
Topeka *(G-12299)*
Agelix Consulting LLC..............E....... 913 708-8145
Overland Park *(G-8357)*
Agvantis Inc..............D....... 316 266-5400
Wichita *(G-13644)*
ASK Associates Inc..............E....... 785 841-8194
Lawrence *(G-4738)*
Avazpour Networking Svcs Inc..............E....... 913 323-1411
Overland Park *(G-8414)*
Cgf Investments Inc..............E....... 316 691-4500
Wichita *(G-13994)*
Choose Networks Inc..............F....... 316 773-0920
Wichita *(G-14013)*
Clarus Group LLC..............E....... 913 599-5255
Overland Park *(G-8560)*
Communication Cable Company..............D....... 610 644-5155
Leawood *(G-5356)*
Computer Sciences Corporation..............C....... 913 469-8700
Overland Park *(G-8593)*
Comtrsys Inc..............F....... 316 265-1585
Wichita *(G-14084)*
Dave McDermott..............F....... 785 354-8233
Topeka *(G-12546)*
Digital Printing Services Inc..............F....... 913 492-1500
Lenexa *(G-5817)*
Dunami Inc..............E....... 303 981-3303
Overland Park *(G-8665)*
Electronic Technology Inc..............F....... 913 962-8083
Shawnee Mission *(G-11330)*
Escoute LLC..............F....... 816 678-8398
Olathe *(G-7692)*
Genesis Corp..............C....... 913 906-9991
Shawnee Mission *(G-11393)*
Health Data Specialists LLC..............E....... 785 242-3419
Pomona *(G-10004)*
Hyr Global Source Inc..............F....... 913 815-2597
Overland Park *(G-8835)*
I T G Consulting Inc..............F....... 785 228-1585
Topeka *(G-12711)*
Imagintive Cnsulting Group Inc..............F....... 913 481-1936
Overland Park *(G-8839)*
Integrated Solutions Group Inc..............E....... 620 662-5796
Hutchinson *(G-3334)*
Isg Technology LLC..............F....... 785 266-2585
Topeka *(G-12728)*
Isg Technology LLC..............E....... 316 636-5655
Wichita *(G-14731)*
Isigma Consulting LLC..............F....... 620 757-6363
Overland Park *(G-8863)*
Kanokla Telephone Association..............E....... 620 845-5682
Caldwell *(G-660)*
Loquient Inc..............F....... 913 221-0430
Shawnee Mission *(G-11577)*
LP Technologies Inc..............F....... 316 831-9696
Wichita *(G-14986)*
Magna Infotech Ltd..............D....... 203 748-7680
Overland Park *(G-8979)*
Mize Houser & Company PA..............D....... 785 233-0536
Topeka *(G-12908)*
PSC Group LLC..............E....... 847 517-7200
Overland Park *(G-9202)*
Quark Studios LLC..............F....... 913 871-5154
Olathe *(G-8014)*
Randel Solutions LLC..............F....... 703 459-7672
Overland Park *(G-9224)*
Risenow LLC..............F....... 913 948-7405
Leawood *(G-5539)*
Rx Savings LLC..............F....... 913 815-3139
Overland Park *(G-9264)*
Saicon Consultants Inc..............F....... 913 451-1178
Overland Park *(G-9272)*
Teksystems Inc..............E....... 316 448-4500
Wichita *(G-15728)*
Tkfast Inc..............E....... 316 260-2500
Wichita *(G-15769)*
Twenty-First Century..............F....... 913 713-2121
Mission *(G-7139)*

White Paladin Group Inc ....E 913 722-4688
Prairie Village *(G-10082)*
Whiting House Group LLC ....F 816 272-4496
Lenexa *(G-6228)*
Word-Tech Inc ....E 913 722-3334
Shawnee Mission *(G-12019)*

CONSULTING SVC: Data Processing

A R Systems Inc ....E 620 564-3790
Ellinwood *(G-1626)*
Gateway Solutions Inc ....F 913 851-1055
Overland Park *(G-8748)*
Globalink Inc ....D 785 823-8284
Salina *(G-10513)*
Network Management Group Inc ....E 620 665-3611
Hutchinson *(G-3389)*
Shoroeders Jim Sftwr & Video ....F 620 227-7628
Dodge City *(G-1430)*

CONSULTING SVC: Educational

Educational Resources Inc ....D 913 262-0448
Stilwell *(G-12146)*
El Centro Inc ....F 913 677-1115
Kansas City *(G-3983)*
Kansas State University ....F 785 532-5813
Manhattan *(G-6690)*

CONSULTING SVC: Engineering

3 S Engineering LLC ....F 316 260-2258
Wichita *(G-13579)*
Abrasive Blast Systems Inc ....E 785 263-3786
Abilene *(G-10)*
Affinis Corp ....E 913 239-1100
Overland Park *(G-8356)*
Agelix Consulting LLC ....E 913 708-8145
Overland Park *(G-8357)*
Alfred Benesch & Company ....F 785 539-2202
Manhattan *(G-6539)*
Allied Environmental Cons Inc ....F 316 262-5698
Wichita *(G-13672)*
Alph Omega Geotech Inc ....E 913 371-0000
Kansas City *(G-3801)*
Argus Consulting Inc ....E 816 228-7500
Overland Park *(G-8395)*
Aviation Cnslting Engrg Sltons ....G 316 265-8335
Maize *(G-6508)*
B G Consultants Inc ....F 785 749-4474
Lawrence *(G-4748)*
B&V-Baker Guam JV ....A 913 458-4300
Overland Park *(G-8424)*
Bgr Consulting Engineers Inc ....F 816 842-2800
Overland Park *(G-8444)*
Black & Veatch Corporation ....A 913 458-2000
Overland Park *(G-8455)*
Black & Veatch Corporation ....E 913 458-2000
Overland Park *(G-8456)*
Black & Veatch Holding Company ....D 913 458-2000
Overland Park *(G-8457)*
Black & Veatch-Olsson JV ....E 913 458-6650
Overland Park *(G-8459)*
Black Veatch-Altan Joint Ventr ....B 913 458-4300
Overland Park *(G-8461)*
Black Vtch Spcial Prjects Corp ....B 913 458-2000
Overland Park *(G-8463)*
Blot Engineering Inc ....F 913 441-1636
Shawnee *(G-10919)*
Brack/Asscts Cnsltng Engnrs PA ....F 785 271-6644
Topeka *(G-12401)*
Branchpattern Inc ....F 913 951-8311
Overland Park *(G-8480)*
Bse Structural Engineers LLC ....E 913 492-7400
Lenexa *(G-5720)*
Continental Consulting Inc ....E 913 642-6642
Leawood *(G-5358)*
Delich Roth & Goodwillie PA ....F 913 441-1100
Bonner Springs *(G-548)*
Delich Roth & Goodwillie PA ....F 913 441-1100
Bonner Springs *(G-549)*
Efi Global Inc ....F 913 648-5232
Shawnee Mission *(G-11329)*
En Engineering LLC ....D 913 901-4400
Olathe *(G-7680)*
Erm-West Inc ....F 913 661-0770
Overland Park *(G-8687)*
Garver LLC ....E 913 696-9755
Overland Park *(G-8745)*
Geotechnology Inc ....E 913 438-1900
Shawnee *(G-10962)*
Global Procurement Corporation ....F 913 458-2000
Overland Park *(G-8759)*
H W Lochner Inc ....E 785 827-3603
Salina *(G-10526)*
H W Lochner Inc ....D 816 945-5840
Lenexa *(G-5885)*
Hntb Corporation ....D 913 491-9333
Overland Park *(G-8820)*
Icm Inc ....C 316 796-0900
Colwich *(G-1097)*
Integrted Cnslting Engners Inc ....F 316 264-3588
Wichita *(G-14707)*
Kiewit Engineering Group Inc ....C 402 943-1465
Lenexa *(G-5949)*
KLA Environmental Services ....F 785 823-0097
Salina *(G-10576)*
Kleinfelder Inc ....E 913 962-0909
Overland Park *(G-8923)*
Latimer Sommers and Assoc PA ....E 785 233-3232
Topeka *(G-12834)*
Lutz Daily & Brain Llc ....E 913 831-0833
Shawnee Mission *(G-11584)*
Michael Kirkham & Assoc Inc ....E 785 472-3163
Ellsworth *(G-1678)*
Mid-America Mfg Tech Ctr Inc ....F 913 649-4333
Overland Park *(G-9025)*
Northwind Technical Svcs LLC ....F 785 284-0080
Sabetha *(G-10323)*
Olsson Inc ....F 785 539-6900
Manhattan *(G-6764)*
Olsson Inc ....C 913 381-1170
Overland Park *(G-9100)*
Olsson Inc ....E 913 829-0078
Olathe *(G-7956)*
Orazem & Scalora Engrg PA ....F 785 537-2553
Manhattan *(G-6765)*
Parsons Corporation ....F 913 233-3100
Kansas City *(G-4315)*
Pearson Kent McKinley Raaf Eng ....E 913 492-2400
Lenexa *(G-6046)*
Pinnacle Technology Inc ....E 785 832-8866
Lawrence *(G-5066)*
Professional Engrg Cons PA ....C 316 262-2691
Wichita *(G-15359)*
Professional Engrg Cons PA ....F 620 235-0195
Pittsburg *(G-9924)*
Professional Engrg Cons PA ....E 785 290-0550
Topeka *(G-12989)*
Professional Engrg Cons PA ....E 316 262-6457
Wichita *(G-15360)*
Professional Engrg Cons PA ....E 785 233-8300
Topeka *(G-12990)*
Rice Precision Mfg Inc ....E 785 594-2670
Baldwin City *(G-367)*
Rock Creek Technologies LLC ....E 620 364-1400
New Strawn *(G-7304)*
Schlagel & Associates PA ....E 913 492-5158
Shawnee Mission *(G-11835)*
SMH Consultants PA ....F 785 776-0541
Manhattan *(G-6802)*
Smith & Boucher Inc ....E 913 345-2127
Olathe *(G-8070)*
Stearns Conrad and Schmidt ....D 913 681-0030
Overland Park *(G-9356)*
Summers & Spencer Company ....E 785 272-4484
Topeka *(G-13116)*
Summers & Spencer Company ....F 785 838-4484
Lawrence *(G-5126)*
TEC Engineering Inc ....E 316 259-8881
Wichita *(G-15723)*
Terracon Consultants Inc ....E 785 539-9099
Manhattan *(G-6822)*
Terracon Consultants Inc ....C 913 492-7777
Lenexa *(G-6177)*
Thunderhead Engrg Cons Inc ....F 785 770-8511
Manhattan *(G-6826)*
Transystems Corporation ....F 316 303-3000
Wichita *(G-15794)*
Transystems Corporation ....E 620 331-3999
Independence *(G-3568)*
U S Army Corps of Engineers ....D 785 537-7392
Manhattan *(G-6834)*
Wilson Inc Engineers Architects ....D 785 827-0433
Salina *(G-10769)*

CONSULTING SVC: Executive Placement & Search

A1 Staffing ....F 913 652-0005
Overland Park *(G-8336)*
Ace Personnel Inc ....F 913 384-1100
Shawnee Mission *(G-11067)*
Aquent LLC ....E 913 345-9119
Shawnee Mission *(G-11115)*
Bartunek Group Inc ....E 913 327-8800
Overland Park *(G-8435)*
Bradford and Galt Incorporated ....E 913 663-1264
Shawnee Mission *(G-11177)*
Chase Group Inc ....F 913 696-6300
Overland Park *(G-8543)*
Experis Us Inc ....F 913 800-3027
Overland Park *(G-8700)*
Grafton Inc ....A 913 498-0701
Overland Park *(G-8768)*
Ingenium Solutions Inc ....E 913 239-0050
Overland Park *(G-8844)*
Kforce Inc ....E 913 890-5000
Overland Park *(G-8916)*
Morgan Hunter Corporation ....E 913 491-3434
Overland Park *(G-9053)*
Premier Personnel Inc ....D 785 273-9944
Topeka *(G-12983)*
Quantum Health Professionals ....D 913 894-1910
Mission *(G-7135)*
Specialists Group LLC ....F 316 267-7375
Wichita *(G-15635)*
Spencer Reed Group LLC ....C 913 663-4400
Leawood *(G-5557)*
Srg III LLC ....F 913 663-4400
Overland Park *(G-9348)*
Velocity Staff Inc ....E 913 693-4626
Overland Park *(G-9460)*

CONSULTING SVC: Financial Management

Accountable Finance Inc ....F 913 381-4077
Overland Park *(G-8341)*
AIG ....C 503 323-2500
Overland Park *(G-8361)*
American Gen Lf Insur Co Del ....E 913 402-5000
Overland Park *(G-8377)*
Ameriprise Financial Inc ....E 913 239-8140
Leawood *(G-5323)*
Ameriprise Financial Svcs Inc ....E 913 451-2811
Shawnee Mission *(G-11109)*
Axa Financial Inc ....E 913 345-2800
Overland Park *(G-8419)*
Barber Financial Group Inc ....F 913 393-1000
Lenexa *(G-5686)*
Bok Financial Corporation ....E 785 273-9993
Topeka *(G-12396)*
Capital Financial Group ....F 785 228-1234
Topeka *(G-12430)*
Collateral Services Inc ....F 913 680-1015
Leavenworth *(G-5223)*
Design Benefits ....F 316 729-7676
Wichita *(G-14200)*
Eveans Bash Klein Inc ....F 913 345-7000
Overland Park *(G-8694)*
Financial Advisory Service Inc ....F 913 239-2300
Shawnee Mission *(G-11367)*
Grant Thornton LLP ....D 316 265-3231
Wichita *(G-14496)*
Kansas City Financial Group ....E 913 649-7447
Overland Park *(G-8895)*
Koesten Hirschmann & Crabtree ....F 913 345-1881
Shawnee Mission *(G-11537)*
Lpl Financial ....F 913 345-2908
Leawood *(G-5460)*
McDaniel Knutson Inc ....F 785 841-4664
Lawrence *(G-5017)*
Miller Group ....F 816 333-3000
Leawood *(G-5485)*
Revest LLC ....E 316 262-8460
Wichita *(G-15454)*
T & M Financial Inc ....F 785 266-8333
Topeka *(G-13129)*
Tantillo Financial Group LLC ....F 913 649-3200
Shawnee Mission *(G-11919)*
Tck- The Trust Company Kansas ....E 316 264-6010
Wichita *(G-15718)*
Thomas G Geha & Associates ....F 913 563-6707
Prairie Village *(G-10074)*
Trust Company of Manhattan ....F 785 537-7200
Manhattan *(G-6832)*
V Wealth Advisors LLC ....E 913 827-4600
Overland Park *(G-9457)*
Varney & Associates Cpas LLC ....E 785 537-2202
Manhattan *(G-6841)*
W S Griffith Inc ....E 913 451-1855
Overland Park *(G-9476)*

Waddell & Reed Inc...F ... 913 491-9202
Leawood *(G-5593)*
Waddell & Reed Inc...E ... 785 537-4505
Manhattan *(G-6844)*
Waddell & Reed Inc...F ... 785 233-6400
Topeka *(G-13229)*
Waddell & Reed Inv MGT Co...E ... 913 491-9202
Leawood *(G-5594)*
Wells Fargo Clearing Svcs LLC...F ... 785 825-4636
Salina *(G-10767)*

CONSULTING SVC: Human Resource

Grafton Inc...A ... 913 498-0701
Overland Park *(G-8768)*
Hyr Global Source Inc...F ... 913 815-2597
Overland Park *(G-8835)*
Omni Employment MGT Svc LLC...E ... 913 341-2119
Overland Park *(G-9101)*
Right Management Inc...E ... 913 451-1100
Shawnee Mission *(G-11805)*
S T Carter Inc...E ... 913 451-1100
Shawnee Mission *(G-11821)*
State of Kansas...B ... 620 225-4804
Dodge City *(G-1435)*
Syndeo Outsourcing LLC...E ... 316 630-9107
Wichita *(G-15710)*

CONSULTING SVC: Management

Adams-Gabbert & Associates LLC...F ... 913 735-4390
Overland Park *(G-8346)*
Agelix Consulting LLC...E ... 913 708-8145
Overland Park *(G-8357)*
Ally Servicing LLC...C ... 316 652-6301
Wichita *(G-13679)*
Arrowhead Intermodal Svcs LLC...F ... 816 509-0746
Edgerton *(G-1479)*
Ascend Learning LLC...B ... 855 856-7705
Leawood *(G-5331)*
Asset MGT Analis Group LLC...E ... 803 270-0996
Leawood *(G-5335)*
Asset Services Inc...F ... 913 383-2738
Overland Park *(G-8405)*
Beshenich Muir & Assoc LLC...F ... 913 904-1880
Leavenworth *(G-5208)*
Black Vatch MGT Consulting LLC...B ... 913 458-2000
Overland Park *(G-8460)*
Booz Allen Hamilton Inc...D ... 913 682-5300
Leavenworth *(G-5213)*
Century Health Solutions Inc...F ... 785 233-1816
Topeka *(G-12459)*
Commercial RE Women Netwrk...F ... 785 832-1808
Lawrence *(G-4802)*
Control Systems Intl Inc...D ... 913 599-5010
Shawnee Mission *(G-11264)*
Copy Co Corporation...G ... 785 832-2679
Lawrence *(G-4811)*
Corporate Enterprise SEC Inc...F ... 913 422-0410
Lenexa *(G-5789)*
Cpg Communications Group LLC...G ... 913 317-2888
Shawnee Mission *(G-11276)*
CPM Technologies Inc...F ... 256 777-9869
Wichita *(G-14124)*
Creative Capsule LLC...D ... 816 421-1714
Overland Park *(G-8608)*
Deere & Company...E ... 913 310-8100
Olathe *(G-7645)*
Dg Business Solutions Inc...F ... 913 766-0163
Lenexa *(G-5815)*
E T C Institute Inc...E ... 913 747-0646
Olathe *(G-7663)*
Electronic Sensors Inc...F ... 316 267-2807
Wichita *(G-14268)*
Exhibit Arts LLC...E ... 316 264-2915
Wichita *(G-14321)*
First Management Inc...D ... 785 749-0006
Lawrence *(G-4860)*
Fujitsu America Inc...E ... 913 327-2800
Shawnee Mission *(G-11384)*
Genesis Corp...C ... 913 906-9991
Shawnee Mission *(G-11393)*
Ghd Services Inc...E ... 785 783-8982
Topeka *(G-12636)*
Glover Inc...E ... 800 654-1511
Olathe *(G-7735)*
Hayse Management Services...F ... 620 548-2369
Mullinville *(G-7209)*
Ill Investments Inc...D ... 913 262-6500
Leawood *(G-5434)*
Kansas Medical Society...F ... 785 235-2383
Topeka *(G-12791)*
KC Hopps Ltd...E ... 913 322-2440
Overland Park *(G-8906)*
Latour Management Inc...E ... 316 524-2290
Wichita *(G-14933)*
McCullough Development Inc...E ... 888 776-3010
Manhattan *(G-6737)*
Midcontinental Chemical Co Inc...E ... 913 390-5556
Olathe *(G-7893)*
New Paradigm Solutions Inc...F ... 785 313-0946
Manhattan *(G-6761)*
Object Tech Solutions Inc...D ... 913 345-9080
Leawood *(G-5507)*
Phillips and Associates Inc...D ... 913 706-7625
Prairie Village *(G-10059)*
Propane Resources LLC...E ... 913 262-8345
Shawnee Mission *(G-11756)*
Regan Marketing Inc...F ... 816 531-5111
Lenexa *(G-6097)*
RFS Associates LLC...E ... 913 871-0456
Westwood Hills *(G-13565)*
Shamrock Trading Corporation...B ... 877 642-8553
Overland Park *(G-9302)*
Transerve Inc...D ... 620 231-2230
Pittsburg *(G-9947)*
U Inc...F ... 913 814-7708
Overland Park *(G-9436)*
Veracity Consulting Inc...D ... 913 945-1912
Overland Park *(G-9462)*
Veterinary Research and Cnslt...F ... 785 324-9200
Hays *(G-2925)*
Xelocity Inc...F ... 913 647-8660
Overland Park *(G-9512)*
Yellow Customer Solutions Inc...F ... 913 696-6100
Shawnee Mission *(G-12022)*
Young Management Corporation...F ... 913 947-3134
Bucyrus *(G-612)*

CONSULTING SVC: Marketing Management

360directories LLC...E ... 316 269-6920
Wichita *(G-13581)*
Advantage Sales & Mktg LLC...F ... 913 890-0900
Lenexa *(G-5634)*
Advantage Sales & Mktg LLC...F ... 316 721-7727
Wichita *(G-13628)*
Annan Marketing Services Inc...E ... 913 254-0050
Overland Park *(G-8387)*
Archein Aerospace LLC...E ... 682 499-2150
Wichita *(G-13730)*
Bajillion Agency...E ... 785 408-5927
Topeka *(G-12359)*
Bankonip...F ... 913 928-6297
Stilwell *(G-12135)*
Central States Mktg & Mfg Inc...E ... 620 245-9955
McPherson *(G-6944)*
Daymon Worldwide Inc...F ... 620 669-4200
Hutchinson *(G-3258)*
Feet On Ground Marketing Inc...F ... 913 242-5558
Lawrence *(G-4858)*
Greteman Group Inc...F ... 316 263-1004
Wichita *(G-14517)*
Guerrilla Marketing Inc...G ... 800 946-9150
Newton *(G-7353)*
Harte-Hanks Inc...B ... 913 312-8100
Shawnee Mission *(G-11413)*
Hss IT Management Inc...C ... 913 498-9988
Overland Park *(G-8832)*
Intouch Group LLC...C ... 913 317-9700
Overland Park *(G-8860)*
Iris Strgc Mktg Support Inc...E ... 913 232-4825
Lenexa *(G-5923)*
J Schmid & Assoc Inc...F ... 913 236-8988
Shawnee Mission *(G-11478)*
Lionshare Marketing Inc...F ... 913 631-8400
Lenexa *(G-5974)*
Macfarlane Group LLC...E ... 913 825-1200
Shawnee Mission *(G-11589)*
MGM Marketing Inc...F ... 913 451-0023
Olathe *(G-7888)*
Morningstar Communications Co...F ... 913 660-9630
Overland Park *(G-9054)*
Motivtion Thrugh Incntives Inc...E ... 913 438-2600
Overland Park *(G-9056)*
New Boston Creative Group LLC...F ... 785 587-8185
Manhattan *(G-6760)*
Pro AG Marketing...F ... 785 476-2211
Kensington *(G-4579)*
Research Partnership Inc...E ... 316 263-6433
Wichita *(G-15447)*
Shc Holdings LLC...F ... 620 273-6900
Cottonwood Falls *(G-1156)*
Three Click Ventres Inc DBA AV...F ... 913 955-3700
Overland Park *(G-9407)*
Thruline Marketing Inc...C ... 913 254-6000
Lenexa *(G-6180)*
Zamani Davis and Associate...E ... 913 851-0092
Shawnee Mission *(G-12026)*

CONSULTING SVC: New Business Start Up

American Gvrnment Slutions LLC...F ... 913 428-2550
Leawood *(G-5320)*

CONSULTING SVC: Online Technology

Buchanan Technologies Inc...E ... 316 219-0124
Wichita *(G-13903)*
It21 Inc...F ... 913 393-4821
Overland Park *(G-8864)*
Local Gvernment Online Ind LLC...E ... 913 498-3468
Olathe *(G-7863)*
Menufycom LLC...E ... 913 738-9399
Leawood *(G-5473)*
Riverpoint Group Illinois LLC...F ... 913 663-2002
Overland Park *(G-9245)*
Smart Security Solutions Inc...E ... 913 568-2573
Overland Park *(G-9319)*
Softwarfare LLC...F ... 202 854-9268
Prairie Village *(G-10068)*
Sogeti USA LLC...E ... 913 451-9600
Overland Park *(G-9322)*
Technology Group Solutions LLC...D ... 913 451-9900
Lenexa *(G-6172)*
Vizion Interactive...F ... 888 484-9466
Overland Park *(G-9469)*
Wood Ribble & Twyman Inc...D ... 913 396-4400
Overland Park *(G-9503)*

CONSULTING SVC: Productivity Improvement

Great Plains Hlth Aliance Inc...F ... 785 543-2111
Phillipsburg *(G-9787)*
Great Plains Hlth Aliance Inc...F ... 316 685-1523
Wichita *(G-14502)*
Great Plains Hlth Aliance Inc...D ... 620 723-3341
Greensburg *(G-2675)*

CONSULTING SVC: Sales Management

Big Creek Investment Corp Inc...G ... 620 431-3445
Chanute *(G-707)*
Kemira Water Solutions Inc...F ... 785 842-7424
Lawrence *(G-4941)*
Menufycom LLC...E ... 913 738-9399
Leawood *(G-5473)*

CONSULTING SVC: Telecommunications

Alea Communications LLC...F ... 913 439-7391
Gardner *(G-2323)*
Centrinex LLC...B ... 913 744-3410
Overland Park *(G-8539)*
Darren Miller...F ... 620 276-4515
Garden City *(G-2143)*
Innovative Service Solutions...F ... 913 851-7745
Overland Park *(G-8846)*
Johnson Cmmunications Svcs Inc...F ... 913 681-5505
Stilwell *(G-12159)*
Kansys Inc...E ... 913 780-5291
Olathe *(G-7830)*
Knk Telecom Llc...E ... 913 768-8000
Olathe *(G-7842)*
Network Consulting Inc...F ... 913 893-4150
Edgerton *(G-1488)*
Phone Tech Communications Inc...F ... 913 859-9150
Overland Park *(G-9162)*
Schultz Brothers Elc Co Inc...E ... 913 321-8338
Kansas City *(G-4406)*
Skc Corporation...E ... 800 882-7779
Shawnee Mission *(G-11871)*
Spectrum Elite Corp...G ... 913 579-7037
Olathe *(G-8076)*
Studio 13 Inc...F ... 913 948-1284
Overland Park *(G-9368)*

CONSULTING SVCS, BUSINESS: Agricultural

A G 1 Source LLC...E ... 620 327-2205
Hesston *(G-2983)*
Agspring LLC...E ... 913 333-3035
Leawood *(G-5314)*
Central Prairie Co-Op...F ... 620 422-3221
Nickerson *(G-7431)*

Crop Quest Inc.....F.....620 225-2233
Dodge City *(G-1335)*
K & D Ferguson Partnership.....F.....785 476-2657
Kensington *(G-4576)*
Kcoe Isom LLP.....F.....620 672-7476
Garden City *(G-2216)*
Koers-Turgeon Consulting Svc.....F.....620 272-9131
Garden City *(G-2219)*
Servi Tech Inc.....C.....620 227-7509
Dodge City *(G-1429)*
Veterinary Research and Cnslt.....F.....785 324-9200
Hays *(G-2925)*

CONSULTING SVCS, BUSINESS: City Planning

City of Wichita.....E.....316 268-4421
Wichita *(G-14024)*

CONSULTING SVCS, BUSINESS: Communications

Allied Business Solutions Inc.....F.....913 856-2323
Gardner *(G-2324)*
Cox Communications Inc.....F.....620 227-3361
Dodge City *(G-1333)*
Jurysync LLC.....F.....913 338-4301
Olathe *(G-7820)*
Selective Site Consultants Inc.....E.....913 438-7700
Overland Park *(G-9292)*

CONSULTING SVCS, BUSINESS: Economic

Greater Wichita Partnr Inc.....F.....316 500-6650
Wichita *(G-14508)*
Kansas Housing Resources Corp.....E.....785 217-2001
Topeka *(G-12782)*
South Central Kansas.....E.....316 262-7035
Bel Aire *(G-440)*

CONSULTING SVCS, BUSINESS: Employee Programs Administration

Century Health Solutions Inc.....F.....785 233-1816
Topeka *(G-12459)*
Keating & Associates Inc.....E.....785 537-0366
Manhattan *(G-6698)*

CONSULTING SVCS, BUSINESS: Energy Conservation

Icm Inc.....C.....316 796-0900
Colwich *(G-1097)*
Jay Henges Enterprises Inc.....E.....913 764-4600
Olathe *(G-7808)*
Mid-States Energy Works Inc.....F.....785 827-3631
Salina *(G-10601)*
Worldwide Energy Inc.....F.....913 310-0705
Lenexa *(G-6234)*

CONSULTING SVCS, BUSINESS: Environmental

Air & Waste Management Assn.....F.....913 940-0081
Overland Park *(G-8362)*
Airsource Technologies Inc.....F.....913 422-9001
Shawnee Mission *(G-11089)*
Allied Environmental Cons Inc.....F.....316 262-5698
Wichita *(G-13672)*
Applied Ecological Svcs Inc.....F.....785 594-2245
Baldwin City *(G-354)*
Arcadis US Inc.....E.....913 492-4156
Lenexa *(G-5659)*
Associated Environmental Inc.....F.....785 776-7755
Manhattan *(G-6547)*
CB&i Envmtl Infrastructure Inc.....E.....913 451-1224
Lenexa *(G-5735)*
Dpra Incorporated.....F.....785 539-3565
Manhattan *(G-6616)*
EAC Audit Inc.....F.....785 594-6707
Baldwin City *(G-359)*
Ecology and Environment Inc.....F.....913 339-9519
Overland Park *(G-8670)*
Envirnmntal Advisors Engineers.....E.....913 599-4326
Shawnee Mission *(G-11344)*
Erm-West Inc.....F.....913 661-0770
Overland Park *(G-8687)*
Fire Cnslting Case Review Intl.....F.....913 262-5200
Lenexa *(G-5853)*
Geocore LLC.....E.....785 826-1616
Salina *(G-10509)*
Haley & Aldrich Inc.....F.....913 693-1900
Overland Park *(G-8785)*
Integrated Solutions Inc.....D.....316 264-7050
Wichita *(G-14704)*
KLA Environmental Services.....F.....785 823-0097
Salina *(G-10576)*
Kleinfelder Inc.....D.....913 962-0909
Lenexa *(G-5953)*
Larsen & Associates Inc.....F.....785 841-8707
Lawrence *(G-4955)*
Meitler Consulting Inc.....F.....913 422-9339
Tonganoxie *(G-12267)*
Professional Service Inds Inc.....E.....913 310-1600
Kansas City *(G-4343)*
Ramboll Environ US Corporation.....E.....816 891-8228
Overland Park *(G-9222)*
Regulatory Consultants Inc.....E.....785 486-2882
Horton *(G-3133)*
Safety-Kleen (wt) Inc.....E.....316 269-7400
Wichita *(G-15504)*
SE Kansas Nture Ctr Schrmrhorn.....E.....620 783-5207
Galena *(G-2084)*
Specpro Environmental Svcs LLC.....F.....913 583-3000
De Soto *(G-1213)*
Srd Environmental Services.....E.....620 665-5590
Hutchinson *(G-3445)*
Stantec Consulting Svcs Inc.....E.....913 202-6867
Overland Park *(G-9354)*
Systech Environmental Corp.....E.....620 378-4451
Fredonia *(G-2046)*
T & C Mfg & Operating Inc.....E.....620 793-5483
Great Bend *(G-2646)*
Terracon Consultants Inc.....F.....785 267-3310
Topeka *(G-13153)*

CONSULTING SVCS, BUSINESS: Lighting

Green Expectations Ldscpg Inc.....F.....913 897-8076
Kansas City *(G-4049)*

CONSULTING SVCS, BUSINESS: Publishing

Montgomery County Media LLC.....E.....620 331-3550
Independence *(G-3541)*

CONSULTING SVCS, BUSINESS: Safety Training Svcs

Kansas Operation Lifesaver.....F.....785 806-8801
Topeka *(G-12795)*
SRS Strategic Development.....F.....785 296-4327
Topeka *(G-13094)*

CONSULTING SVCS, BUSINESS: Sys Engnrg, Exc Computer/Prof

Billy Murphy & Associates LLC.....F.....913 306-0381
Leavenworth *(G-5210)*
Choice Solutions LLC.....E.....913 338-4950
Overland Park *(G-8550)*
Kansas Department Commerce.....E.....785 296-5298
Topeka *(G-12768)*
Netstandard Inc.....D.....913 428-4200
Overland Park *(G-9077)*
Quest Research & Development.....F.....316 267-1216
Wichita *(G-15393)*
Structral Intgrity Systems LLC.....F.....316 634-1396
Wichita *(G-15676)*

CONSULTING SVCS, BUSINESS: Systems Analysis & Engineering

Corporate Enterprise SEC Inc.....F.....913 422-0410
Lenexa *(G-5789)*
Eri Solutions Inc.....E.....316 927-4290
Colwich *(G-1094)*
Midwest Consulting Group Inc.....C.....913 693-8200
Overland Park *(G-9031)*
Rhythm Engineering LLC.....E.....913 227-0603
Lenexa *(G-6108)*

CONSULTING SVCS, BUSINESS: Test Development & Evaluation

Purplefrogintl.....G.....816 510-0871
Shawnee *(G-11014)*

CONSULTING SVCS, BUSINESS: Testing, Educational Or Personnel

Assessment Tech Inst LLC.....B.....800 667-7531
Leawood *(G-5334)*
Computrzed Assssments Lrng LLC.....F.....785 856-1034
Lawrence *(G-4807)*
Nexlearn LLC.....E.....316 265-2170
Wichita *(G-15172)*
Student In Free Enterpris.....E.....620 235-4574
Pittsburg *(G-9943)*

CONSULTING SVCS, BUSINESS: Traffic

Cellint Usa Inc.....F.....913 871-6500
Olathe *(G-7582)*

CONSULTING SVCS, BUSINESS: Urban Planning & Consulting

Community Foundation of Ellis.....F.....785 726-2660
Ellis *(G-1641)*
Community Hsing Wyandotte Cnty.....F.....913 342-7580
Kansas City *(G-3931)*
Eureka Foundation.....F.....620 583-8630
Eureka *(G-1885)*
Kansas State University.....F.....785 532-3900
Manhattan *(G-6694)*

CONSULTING SVCS: Oil

Crown Consulting Inc.....F.....620 624-0156
Liberal *(G-6300)*
Tr Services Inc.....G.....785 623-1066
Pratt *(G-10160)*
Trans Pacific Properties LLC.....G.....316 262-3596
Wichita *(G-15790)*

CONSULTING SVCS: Scientific

EKA Consulting LLC.....F.....913 244-2980
Shawnee *(G-10946)*
Veterinary Research and Cnslt.....F.....785 324-9200
Hays *(G-2925)*

CONSUMER CREDIT REPORTING BUREAU

1138 Inc.....E.....913 322-5900
Overland Park *(G-8328)*
C B C S Inc.....F.....620 343-6220
Emporia *(G-1714)*
Collection of Lawrence Inc.....E.....785 843-4210
Lawrence *(G-4797)*
Credit Bureau Services.....E.....620 276-7631
Garden City *(G-2139)*
N A C M Credit Services Inc.....E.....913 383-9300
Shawnee Mission *(G-11663)*

CONTACT LENSES

Donegan Optical Company Inc.....E.....913 492-2500
Shawnee Mission *(G-11314)*

CONTAINERS: Cargo, Wood

Containercraft Inc.....F.....620 663-1168
Hutchinson *(G-3246)*

CONTAINERS: Glass

Jarden Branded Consumable.....G.....913 856-1177
Olathe *(G-7807)*

CONTAINERS: Ice Cream, Made From Purchased Materials

Huhtamaki Inc.....B.....913 583-3025
De Soto *(G-1202)*

CONTAINERS: Metal

Bmg of Kansas Inc.....D.....620 327-4038
Hesston *(G-2985)*
United Manufacturing Inc.....E.....913 780-0056
New Century *(G-7302)*

CONTAINERS: Plastic

B P E Inc.....G.....620 343-3783
Emporia *(G-1700)*
Consolidated Container Co LP.....C.....913 888-9494
Shawnee Mission *(G-11259)*
Huhtamaki Americas Inc.....B.....913 583-3025
De Soto *(G-1203)*

Huhtamaki Films Inc ....A....... 913 583-3025
De Soto *(G-1204)*
Jarden Corporation ....D....... 316 390-1343
Wichita *(G-14749)*
S F B Plastics Inc ....D....... 800 343-8133
Wichita *(G-15502)*
Westrock Dspensing Systems Inc ....C....... 620 229-5000
Winfield *(G-16182)*

CONTAINERS: Wood

Asset Lifecycle LLC ....F....... 785 861-3100
Topeka *(G-12341)*

CONTRACTOR: Framing

Advantage Framing Systems Inc ....E....... 913 592-4150
Spring Hill *(G-12075)*
Delbert Chopp Co Inc ....F....... 785 825-8530
Salina *(G-10472)*
Wichita Drywall Acoustics LLC ....E....... 316 773-7826
Wichita *(G-15993)*

CONTRACTORS: Access Control System Eqpt

Atronic Alarms Inc ....E....... 913 432-4545
Lenexa *(G-5674)*

CONTRACTORS: Acoustical & Ceiling Work

Acoustical Stretched Fabric ....G....... 913 345-1520
Shawnee Mission *(G-11069)*
Delbert Chopp Co Inc ....F....... 785 825-8530
Salina *(G-10472)*

CONTRACTORS: Acoustical & Insulation Work

Cleaning By Lamunyon Inc ....F....... 785 632-1259
Clay Center *(G-855)*
D and D Insulation Inc ....E....... 913 492-1346
Shawnee Mission *(G-11289)*

CONTRACTORS: Antenna Installation

Hayden Tower Service Inc ....D....... 785 232-1840
Topeka *(G-12668)*

CONTRACTORS: Asbestos Removal & Encapsulation

Acm Removal LLC ....F....... 316 684-1800
Wichita *(G-13606)*
Arrowhead Contracting Inc ....D....... 913 814-9994
Lenexa *(G-5664)*
Associated Insulation Inc ....D....... 785 776-0145
Manhattan *(G-6548)*
B & R Insulation Inc ....E....... 913 492-1346
Shawnee Mission *(G-11139)*
D & D Services Inc ....D....... 913 492-1346
Shawnee Mission *(G-11288)*
F & H Abatement Services Inc ....C....... 316 264-2208
Kechi *(G-4567)*
Performance Abatement Svcs Inc ....D....... 913 888-8600
Lenexa *(G-6050)*
Remediation Contractors Inc ....F....... 316 269-1549
Wichita *(G-15442)*
Remediation Services Inc ....E....... 800 335-1201
Independence *(G-3553)*

CONTRACTORS: Asphalt

Andrews Asphalt & Cnstr Inc ....G....... 785 232-0188
Topeka *(G-12326)*
Apac-Kansas Inc ....F....... 785 823-8944
Salina *(G-10405)*
Barkley Construction ....F....... 316 945-6500
Wichita *(G-13812)*
Hamm Inc ....G....... 785 597-5111
Perry *(G-9769)*
L M C C Inc ....E....... 913 371-1070
Kansas City *(G-4190)*
Little Joes Asphalt Inc ....F....... 913 721-3261
Bonner Springs *(G-560)*
Meadows Const Co Inc ....E....... 913 369-3335
Tonganoxie *(G-12266)*
Modern Paving Systems Inc ....F....... 913 962-7208
Shawnee Mission *(G-11652)*

CONTRACTORS: Awning Installation

Wildcat Gttering Exteriors Inc ....F....... 785 485-2194
Manhattan *(G-6855)*

CONTRACTORS: Blasting, Exc Building Demolition

Freddy Van Inc ....G....... 620 231-1127
Pittsburg *(G-9863)*
Pexco Company Llc ....E....... 913 907-5022
Leawood *(G-5520)*

CONTRACTORS: Boiler & Furnace

Waddles Heating & Cooling ....E....... 785 827-2621
Salina *(G-10755)*

CONTRACTORS: Boiler Maintenance Contractor

Clarios ....E....... 785 827-6829
Salina *(G-10454)*
Locke Equipment Sales Co ....E....... 913 782-8500
Olathe *(G-7864)*

CONTRACTORS: Boring, Building Construction

Rdr Excavating Inc ....F....... 785 582-4645
Topeka *(G-13001)*

CONTRACTORS: Bricklaying

Cleland Masonry Inc ....F....... 620 347-8546
Arma *(G-189)*
Lindsey Masonry Co Inc ....F....... 913 721-2458
Kansas City *(G-4204)*
Perfection II Masonry Inc ....F....... 785 499-6307
Alta Vista *(G-71)*

CONTRACTORS: Building Board-up

Janssen Glass & Mirror Inc ....F....... 913 677-5727
Shawnee *(G-10977)*

CONTRACTORS: Building Eqpt & Machinery Installation

Belger Cartage Service Inc ....E....... 913 541-9100
Shawnee Mission *(G-11158)*
Bl Brooks & Sons Inc ....G....... 913 829-5494
Olathe *(G-7553)*
CDI Industrial Mech Contrs Inc ....C....... 913 287-0334
Kansas City *(G-3898)*
Hall Industrial Services Inc ....E....... 316 945-4255
Wichita *(G-14546)*
Temp-Con Inc ....D....... 913 768-4888
Olathe *(G-8106)*

CONTRACTORS: Building Movers

Valley Moving Company LLC ....F....... 785 456-2400
Wamego *(G-13445)*

CONTRACTORS: Building Sign Installation & Mntnce

Coffelt Sign Co Inc ....G....... 620 343-6411
Emporia *(G-1724)*
Finch Sign Company Inc ....G....... 785 423-3213
Baldwin City *(G-360)*
Freestyle Sign Co Inc ....G....... 316 267-5507
Wichita *(G-14420)*
Gleason & Son Signs Inc ....G....... 785 823-8615
Salina *(G-10512)*
Luminous Neon Inc ....G....... 785 842-4930
Lawrence *(G-5002)*
Luminous Neon Inc ....G....... 785 823-1789
Salina *(G-10586)*
Luminous Neon Inc ....E....... 913 780-3330
Olathe *(G-7867)*
Star Signs LLC ....E....... 785 842-4892
Lawrence *(G-5119)*

CONTRACTORS: Building Site Preparation

Hayward Baker Inc ....D....... 913 390-0085
Olathe *(G-7758)*
Marlatt Construction Co Inc ....F....... 913 367-3342
Atchison *(G-242)*

Spectrum Construction Co ....F....... 785 232-3407
Topeka *(G-13088)*

CONTRACTORS: Cable TV Installation

Mid Kansas Cable Services Inc ....F....... 620 345-2832
Moundridge *(G-7189)*
Mill-Tel Inc ....E....... 316 262-7171
Park City *(G-9634)*

CONTRACTORS: Carpentry Work

Apac-Kansas Inc ....E....... 316 321-3221
El Dorado *(G-1528)*
Dade Construction LLC ....F....... 913 208-1968
Kansas City *(G-3951)*
Dahmer Contracting Group LLC ....D....... 816 795-3332
Overland Park *(G-8630)*
Douglas A Firebaugh Cnstr ....C....... 913 451-8599
Overland Park *(G-8660)*
Overhead Door Company ....E....... 316 265-4634
Wichita *(G-15240)*
Wood RE New Joco Inc ....G....... 913 661-9663
Olathe *(G-8159)*

CONTRACTORS: Carpentry, Cabinet & Finish Work

Barnes Millworks Inc ....F....... 620 232-8746
Pittsburg *(G-9822)*
Cabinet Shopof Basehor Inc ....E....... 913 845-2182
Tonganoxie *(G-12255)*
CCM Countertop & Cab Mfg LLC ....F....... 316 554-0113
Wichita *(G-13967)*
Doubrava Woodworking Inc ....G....... 785 472-4204
Ellsworth *(G-1666)*
Guthridge/Nighswonger Corp ....F....... 316 264-7900
Wichita *(G-14529)*
Norcraft Companies LP ....B....... 316 283-2859
Newton *(G-7398)*
Ovation Cabinetry Inc ....D....... 785 452-9000
Salina *(G-10625)*

CONTRACTORS: Carpentry, Cabinet Building & Installation

Bhjllc Inc ....E....... 785 272-8800
Topeka *(G-12379)*
Byrne Custom Wood Products Inc ....F....... 913 894-4777
Lenexa *(G-5722)*
Four Corners Construction LLC ....G....... 620 662-8163
Hutchinson *(G-3290)*
Halstontine Corp ....F....... 913 780-2171
Overland Park *(G-8787)*
Hays Planing Mill Inc ....G....... 785 625-6507
Hays *(G-2838)*
K C Wood Products ....F....... 913 422-3320
Edwardsville *(G-1505)*
King Wood Products Inc ....F....... 913 837-5300
Louisburg *(G-6453)*
Roys Custom Cabinets ....G....... 785 625-6724
Hays *(G-2902)*

CONTRACTORS: Carpentry, Finish & Trim Work

Ben Kitchens Painting Co Inc ....F....... 785 375-3288
Junction City *(G-3673)*

CONTRACTORS: Carpet Laying

Austin Tile Inc ....F....... 913 829-6607
Olathe *(G-7542)*
Bills Floor Covering Inc ....F....... 913 492-1964
Shawnee Mission *(G-11166)*
Custom Renovation ....F....... 620 544-2653
Hugoton *(G-3158)*
Db Flooring LLC ....E....... 913 663-9922
Lenexa *(G-5806)*
Delta Homes Inc ....E....... 316 777-0009
Mulvane *(G-7215)*
Interior Surface Entps LLC ....F....... 913 397-8100
Olathe *(G-7799)*
L & L Floor Covering Inc ....F....... 620 275-0499
Garden City *(G-2221)*
Mo-Can Flooring Inc ....E....... 913 362-0711
Shawnee *(G-10999)*

CONTRACTORS: Ceramic Floor Tile Installation

Furst In Tile Inc ....F 913 962-4599
Shawnee Mission *(G-11386)*

CONTRACTORS: Coating, Caulking & Weather, Water & Fire

Desco Coatings LLC ....D 913 782-3330
Olathe *(G-7650)*

CONTRACTORS: Commercial & Office Building

Baker Construction Inc ....E 913 682-6302
Leavenworth *(G-5206)*
Benchmark Construction LLC ....F 785 862-0340
Eudora *(G-1870)*
Busboom & Rauh Construction Co ....E 785 825-4664
Salina *(G-10434)*
Caro Construction Co Inc ....E 316 267-7505
Wichita *(G-13952)*
Cmg Construction Inc ....E 913 384-2883
Paola *(G-9548)*
Coast To Coast Builders Inc ....F 316 265-2515
Wichita *(G-14047)*
Compton Construction Svcs LLC ....E 316 262-8885
Wichita *(G-14083)*
Davis Construction LLC ....F 620 674-3100
Columbus *(G-1074)*
Dondlinger & Sons Cnstr Co Inc ....C 316 945-0555
Wichita *(G-14226)*
Firelake-Arrowhead ....D 913 312-9540
Lenexa *(G-5854)*
Firelk-Diversified Joint Ventr ....E 913 312-9540
Lenexa *(G-5855)*
First Con Incorporated ....F 316 425-7690
Wichita *(G-14374)*
Flex Build LLC ....F 913 890-2500
Shawnee Mission *(G-11374)*
Fox Ceramic Tile Inc ....E 785 437-2792
Saint Marys *(G-10365)*
G & F Construction Co LLC ....E 316 260-3313
Wichita *(G-14432)*
Grace Construction & Assoc Inc ....F 316 617-1729
Derby *(G-1249)*
Kiewit Corporation ....D 913 928-7000
Lenexa *(G-5948)*
Koehn Construction Svcs LLC ....E 620 378-3002
Fredonia *(G-2036)*
Lee Construction Inc ....E 620 276-6811
Garden City *(G-2222)*
McOn LLC ....F 785 989-4550
Wathena *(G-13475)*
Mill Creek LLC ....F 785 364-2328
Holton *(G-3105)*
Miller Homebuilders Inc ....E 620 662-1687
Hutchinson *(G-3381)*
Minick Gambrell Contrs LLC ....F 913 538-5391
Olathe *(G-7902)*
Mm Property MGT & Rmdlg LLC ....F 913 871-6867
Kansas City *(G-4265)*
MMC Corp ....E 913 469-0101
Overland Park *(G-9046)*
Mw Builders Inc ....C 913 469-0101
Lenexa *(G-6016)*
Preferred Contg Systems Co ....F 913 341-0111
Leawood *(G-5525)*
Sharp Construction Company ....E 316 943-9511
Valley Center *(G-13353)*
Simpson Construction Svcs Inc ....E 316 942-3206
Wichita *(G-15596)*
Starflite Manufacturing Co ....G 316 267-7297
Wichita *(G-15656)*
Xec Inc ....E 913 563-4260
Overland Park *(G-9511)*
Zimmerman Construction Company ....F 913 685-2255
Overland Park *(G-9528)*

CONTRACTORS: Communications Svcs

Communications Tech Assoc ....E 316 267-5016
Wichita *(G-14076)*
G E V Investment Inc ....E 913 677-5333
Kansas City *(G-4024)*
Kanokla Telephone Association ....E 620 845-5682
Caldwell *(G-660)*
M & J Electric Wichita LLC ....E 316 831-9879
Wichita *(G-14992)*

CONTRACTORS: Computer Installation

Alliance Technologies Inc ....F 913 262-7977
Overland Park *(G-8371)*
Industrial Battery Pdts Inc ....F 913 236-6500
Merriam *(G-7096)*
Net Systems LLC ....F 316 691-9400
Wichita *(G-15159)*
Networks Plus ....E 785 825-0400
Salina *(G-10611)*
Networks Plus ....E 785 825-0400
Manhattan *(G-6759)*

CONTRACTORS: Concrete

B & B Redimix Inc ....F 785 543-5133
Phillipsburg *(G-9777)*
Banzet Concrete Inc ....F 316 776-9961
Rose Hill *(G-10236)*
Beran Concrete Inc ....C 316 425-7600
Wichita *(G-13830)*
Beran Concrete Inc ....D 316 618-6089
Wichita *(G-13831)*
Beran Icf Solutions LLC ....F 316 944-2131
Wichita *(G-13832)*
Better Concrete Construction ....F 913 390-8500
Olathe *(G-7552)*
Brad Murray Inc ....F 316 943-2516
Wichita *(G-13879)*
Brak-Hard Concrete Cnstr Co ....F 620 225-1957
Dodge City *(G-1311)*
Bruce Davis Construction LLC ....E 620 342-5001
Emporia *(G-1710)*
Brulez Foundation Inc ....E 913 422-3355
Olathe *(G-7562)*
Bryant and Bryant Cnstr Inc ....E 316 835-3322
Halstead *(G-2696)*
Carl Harris Co Inc ....E 316 267-8700
Wichita *(G-13950)*
Ceco Concrete Cnstr Del LLC ....F 913 362-1855
Olathe *(G-7581)*
Chad Eakin Concrete ....F 620 285-2097
Larned *(G-4698)*
Chance Rides Manufacturing Inc ....C 316 945-6555
Wichita *(G-13997)*
Concrete Inc ....F 785 594-4838
Lawrence *(G-4808)*
Concrete Unlimited Inc ....D 785 232-8636
Topeka *(G-12500)*
Custom Flatwork Inc ....F 316 794-8282
Goddard *(G-2435)*
CW Concrete Inc ....E 913 780-2316
Olathe *(G-7632)*
D JS Foundation & Flatwork ....F 913 441-1909
Bonner Springs *(G-547)*
Designer Construction Inc ....D 785 776-9878
Manhattan *(G-6613)*
Dinkel Construction Inc ....F 785 232-3377
Topeka *(G-12558)*
Emerson Construction Inc ....F 785 235-0555
Topeka *(G-12574)*
Emporia Construction & Rmdlg ....E 620 341-3131
Emporia *(G-1738)*
Finley Construction & Rdymx ....G 785 626-3282
Atwood *(G-286)*
First Grade Excavating Inc ....F 316 524-0900
Wichita *(G-14375)*
Freeman Concrete Cnstr LLC ....E 913 825-0744
Lenexa *(G-5865)*
Gold Star Concrete Cnstr ....E 785 478-4495
Topeka *(G-12640)*
Graybeal Construction Co Inc ....E 785 232-1033
Lenexa *(G-5882)*
Gustafson Concrete Inc ....F 785 238-7747
Junction City *(G-3697)*
Hamm Inc ....F 785 242-1045
Ottawa *(G-8277)*
Hett Construction ....F 620 382-2236
Marion *(G-6871)*
HMK Concrete ....F 913 262-1555
Shawnee Mission *(G-11435)*
Holmes Basement Construction ....F 785 823-6770
Salina *(G-10545)*
Industrial Cleaning and Maint ....E 785 246-9262
Topeka *(G-12722)*
Iwp LLC ....F 316 308-8507
Valley Center *(G-13345)*
J Corp ....F 785 628-8101
Hays *(G-2854)*
James Voegeli Construction ....E 316 721-6800
Maize *(G-6514)*

Jeff Hoge Concrete LLC ....E 913 239-0903
Stilwell *(G-12156)*
Klaver Construction Co Inc ....D 620 532-3183
Kingman *(G-4603)*
Koehn Painting Co LLC ....E 316 283-9612
Newton *(G-7373)*
Kolde Construction Inc ....E 785 437-3730
Saint Marys *(G-10370)*
Leavcon II Inc ....E 913 351-1430
Lansing *(G-4681)*
Leslie D Boeckner ....F 785 741-1036
Hiawatha *(G-3016)*
Major Inc ....E 316 265-7000
Wichita *(G-15002)*
Miles Excavating Inc ....C 913 724-1934
Basehor *(G-384)*
Morgan Concrete Services Inc ....E 785 842-1686
Lawrence *(G-5031)*
Pfefferkorn Engrg & Envmtl LLC ....F 913 490-3967
Olathe *(G-7982)*
Restortion Wtrprfing Cntrs Inc ....F 785 478-9538
Topeka *(G-13011)*
Schreiner M & Sons Cnstr ....F 785 246-1130
Topeka *(G-13040)*
SMC Concrete and Cnstr LLC ....F 785 545-5186
Cawker City *(G-690)*
Smithcon LLC ....E 316 744-3406
Wichita *(G-15609)*
Smoky Hill LLC ....D 785 825-0810
Salina *(G-10710)*
Specchem LLC ....E 816 968-5600
Kansas City *(G-4432)*
Spriggs Concrete Inc ....E 620 795-4841
Oswego *(G-8237)*
Steve Kemp Concrete Cnstr ....F 316 263-8902
Wichita *(G-15665)*
Superior Excavating LLC ....F 316 260-1829
Valley Center *(G-13355)*
Surface Protection Svcs LLC ....F 316 322-5135
El Dorado *(G-1606)*
T & T Flatworks Inc ....E 620 794-0619
Lebo *(G-5609)*
Tarbet Construction Co Inc ....F 620 356-2110
Ulysses *(G-13321)*
Tarbet Construction Co Inc ....G 785 462-7432
Colby *(G-1045)*
Ted Row Inc ....F 816 223-9666
Stilwell *(G-12176)*
Thoele Foundations LLC ....E 913 757-2317
La Cygne *(G-4644)*
Vannahmen Construction Inc ....E 785 494-2354
Saint George *(G-10348)*
Vintage Greenmark Cnstr Inc ....F 785 843-2700
Lawrence *(G-5174)*
White William & Sons Cnstr Co ....D 913 375-9161
Basehor *(G-391)*
Wildcat Concrete Services Inc ....E 785 478-9000
Topeka *(G-13244)*
Wildcat Construction Co Inc ....C 316 945-9408
Wichita *(G-16049)*
Wise Construction Inc ....F 785 781-4383
Cawker City *(G-691)*
Wt Contractors ....E 620 356-4801
Ulysses *(G-13332)*

CONTRACTORS: Concrete Block Masonry Laying

Hartman Masonry LLC ....E 620 767-5286
Council Grove *(G-1169)*
Superior Masonry & Stucco LLC ....E 316 928-2365
Wichita *(G-15695)*

CONTRACTORS: Concrete Breaking, Street & Highway

Automotive Associates ....E 620 231-6350
Pittsburg *(G-9818)*
Gunter Construction Company ....F 913 362-7844
Kansas City *(G-4059)*
Ricks Concrete Sawing Inc ....F 785 862-5400
Topeka *(G-13016)*

CONTRACTORS: Concrete Pumping

Aci Cncrete Placement Kans LLC ....E 913 281-3700
Lenexa *(G-5623)*
Brundage-Bone Con Pmpg Inc ....E 785 823-7706
Salina *(G-10433)*
Concrete Pumping Service Inc ....F 316 612-8515
Wichita *(G-14087)*

Eslinger Construction & Rdymx............F....... 620 659-2371
Kinsley *(G-4617)*
Madison Brothers Concrete Inc............F....... 620 224-6098
Fort Scott *(G-1983)*
R & S Construction Inc............F....... 620 325-2130
Neodesha *(G-7247)*
R O K K Concrete Inc............F....... 785 286-0662
Topeka *(G-12996)*
Rieke Concrete Systems Inc............F....... 913 492-0270
Shawnee Mission *(G-11803)*

CONTRACTORS: Concrete Repair

John Rohrer Contracting Co Inc............E....... 913 236-5005
Kansas City *(G-4126)*

CONTRACTORS: Construction Site Cleanup

Eagle Environmental Svcs LLC............E....... 316 944-2445
Wichita *(G-14250)*
Mc Janitorial LLC............F....... 913 780-0731
Olathe *(G-7879)*
Noonshine Window Cleaning Svc............F....... 913 381-3780
Overland Park *(G-9092)*
Resource Service Solutions LLC............E....... 913 338-5050
Lenexa *(G-6107)*

CONTRACTORS: Construction Site Metal Structure Coating

C2i Inc............E....... 620 259-6610
Hutchinson *(G-3227)*

CONTRACTORS: Core Drilling & Cutting

Discovery Drilling Shop............E....... 785 650-0029
Hays *(G-2790)*
KC Coring & Cutng Cnstr Inc............F....... 316 832-1580
Wichita *(G-14837)*

CONTRACTORS: Countertop Installation

CCM Countertop & Cab Mfg LLC............F....... 316 554-0113
Wichita *(G-13967)*
Dimensional Stonework LLC............F....... 913 851-9390
Shawnee Mission *(G-11307)*
Granite Transformation Kans Cy............F....... 913 492-7600
Lenexa *(G-5880)*
Granite Trnsfrmtion Wchita LLC............F....... 316 681-1900
Bel Aire *(G-434)*
Kc Granite & Cabinetry LLC............E....... 913 888-0003
Lenexa *(G-5941)*
Quality Granite & Marble Inc............E....... 316 946-0530
Wichita *(G-15383)*
Surface Solutions Intl Inc............E....... 913 742-7744
Overland Park *(G-9378)*

CONTRACTORS: Curb & Sidewalk

Gunter Construction Company............F....... 913 362-7844
Kansas City *(G-4059)*
Nate Apple Concrete Inc............E....... 913 837-3022
Louisburg *(G-6459)*

CONTRACTORS: Demolition, Building & Other Structures

B-3 Construction Inc............F....... 620 479-2323
Columbus *(G-1060)*
Bradburn Wrecking Company............E....... 316 686-1959
Wichita *(G-13880)*
Cornejo & Sons LLC............C....... 316 522-5100
Wichita *(G-14101)*
Kaw Valley Companies Inc............C....... 913 281-9950
Kansas City *(G-4160)*
L Blixt Construction Inc............F....... 785 922-6180
Chapman *(G-780)*
Marlatt Construction Co Inc............F....... 913 367-3342
Atchison *(G-242)*
Mc Pherson Wrecking Inc............F....... 785 246-3012
Grantville *(G-2497)*
Pearson Construction LLC............C....... 316 263-3100
Wichita *(G-15275)*
Scott Heller Trucking............E....... 816 591-1638
Lenexa *(G-6119)*

CONTRACTORS: Demountable Partition Installation

R & T Specialty Cnstr Lc............G....... 316 942-8141
Wichita *(G-15401)*

CONTRACTORS: Directional Oil & Gas Well Drilling Svc

Hughes Drilling Co............G....... 785 883-2235
Wellsville *(G-13543)*
Murfin Drilling Company Inc............F....... 785 462-7541
Colby *(G-1031)*
Pickrell Drilling Co Inc............F....... 316 262-8427
Wichita *(G-15299)*
Southwind Drilling Inc............D....... 620 564-3800
Ellinwood *(G-1638)*
Trans Pacific Properties LLC............G....... 316 262-3596
Wichita *(G-15790)*

CONTRACTORS: Dock Eqpt Installation, Indl

Stoner Door & Dock Corporation............F....... 785 478-3074
Topeka *(G-13101)*

CONTRACTORS: Driveway

Wieneke Construction Co Inc............F....... 620 632-4529
Mc Cune *(G-6923)*

CONTRACTORS: Drywall

Allied Construction Svcs Inc............F....... 913 321-3170
Roeland Park *(G-10216)*
Danny Satterfield Drywall Corp............E....... 316 942-5155
Wichita *(G-14167)*
Douglas A Firebaugh Cnstr............C....... 913 451-8599
Overland Park *(G-8660)*
Drewco Inc............E....... 913 384-6226
Shawnee Mission *(G-11318)*
Drywall Inc............F....... 620 662-3454
Hutchinson *(G-3269)*
Drywall Supply............F....... 316 269-3304
Wichita *(G-14240)*
Drywall Systems Inc............D....... 316 832-0233
Wichita *(G-14241)*
Dynamic Drywall Inc............D....... 316 945-7087
Wichita *(G-14247)*
Ferguson Dry Wall Company Inc............E....... 913 334-5658
Kansas City *(G-4009)*
Greg E Ross Drywall............F....... 785 478-9557
Topeka *(G-12650)*
Hi-Tech Interiors Inc............D....... 785 742-1766
Hiawatha *(G-3009)*
Hi-Tech Interiors Inc............E....... 785 539-7266
Manhattan *(G-6656)*
Howard Stultz Construction............F....... 785 842-4796
Baldwin City *(G-364)*
Michel Drywall LLC............E....... 316 260-6458
Wichita *(G-15065)*
Midwest Drywall Co Inc............C....... 316 722-9559
Wichita *(G-15092)*
Midwest Drywall Co Inc............D....... 316 722-9559
Wichita *(G-15093)*
Randy Johnson............F....... 316 775-6786
Augusta *(G-341)*
Rew Materials Inc............F....... 785 233-3651
Topeka *(G-13013)*
Rosas Drywall Co............F....... 620 665-6959
Hutchinson *(G-3431)*
Samco Drywall Company............F....... 620 864-2289
Severy *(G-10892)*
Wallboard Specialties Inc............E....... 913 422-5023
Shawnee Mission *(G-11991)*
Wichita Drywall Acoustics LLC............E....... 316 773-7826
Wichita *(G-15993)*

CONTRACTORS: Earthmoving

Bob Bergkamp Cnstr Co Inc............D....... 316 522-3471
Wichita *(G-13859)*
Earthmovers Inc............F....... 785 325-2236
Washington *(G-13463)*
Hdb Construction Inc............E....... 785 232-5444
Topeka *(G-12670)*
Kings Construction Co Inc............D....... 785 863-2534
Oskaloosa *(G-8228)*
L Blixt Construction Inc............F....... 785 922-6180
Chapman *(G-780)*
Lrm Industries Inc............E....... 785 843-1688
Lawrence *(G-5001)*
Mies Construction Inc............D....... 316 945-7227
Wichita *(G-15106)*
Pearson Construction LLC............C....... 316 263-3100
Wichita *(G-15275)*

CONTRACTORS: Electric Power Systems

Nelson Electric Inc............F....... 316 794-8025
Goddard *(G-2447)*
Universal Electric Inc............E....... 913 238-3024
Olathe *(G-8136)*

CONTRACTORS: Electrical

A D J-Hux Service Inc............D....... 913 529-5200
Lenexa *(G-5616)*
Adams Electric & Plumbing LLC............E....... 620 672-7279
Pratt *(G-10092)*
Barone Electric Inc............F....... 316 263-9579
Wichita *(G-13813)*
Callaway Electric............G....... 785 632-5588
Clay Center *(G-847)*
City of Mulvane............D....... 316 777-0191
Mulvane *(G-7213)*
Clarios............D....... 913 307-4200
Shawnee Mission *(G-11237)*
Convergeone Inc............C....... 913 307-2300
Overland Park *(G-8597)*
Electronic Technology Inc............F....... 913 962-8083
Shawnee Mission *(G-11330)*
Facility Solutions Group Inc............E....... 913 422-8400
Shawnee *(G-10952)*
G Coopers Inc............F....... 785 267-4100
Topeka *(G-12630)*
G K Smith & Sons Inc............F....... 913 294-5379
Paola *(G-9560)*
General Electric Company............E....... 785 229-3710
Ottawa *(G-8275)*
General Electric Company............D....... 913 541-1839
Lenexa *(G-5871)*
Heinen P-H-E Services Inc............F....... 785 945-6668
Valley Falls *(G-13365)*
Hood Htg Air Plg Electric Inc............F....... 785 243-1489
Concordia *(G-1118)*
International Electric Inc............D....... 913 451-8458
Lenexa *(G-5919)*
K & K Industries Inc............E....... 906 293-5242
Junction City *(G-3709)*
Kiewit Power Group Inc............F....... 913 227-3600
Lenexa *(G-5951)*
Mvp Electric Llc............F....... 913 322-0868
Shawnee *(G-11001)*
Mvp Electric LLC............E....... 913 322-0868
Shawnee Mission *(G-11661)*
Newtons Inc............F....... 620 336-2276
Cherryvale *(G-811)*
Nokia of America Corporation............D....... 316 636-4800
Wichita *(G-15184)*
P1 Group Inc............B....... 913 529-5000
Lenexa *(G-6040)*
P1 Group Inc............F....... 785 235-5331
Topeka *(G-12958)*
P1 Group Inc............D....... 785 843-2910
Lawrence *(G-5054)*
Pestinger Heating & AC Inc............E....... 785 827-6361
Salina *(G-10634)*
Precision Elec Contrs LLC............E....... 785 309-0094
Salina *(G-10640)*
Schultz Brothers Elc Co Inc............E....... 913 321-8338
Kansas City *(G-4406)*
Stueder Contractors Inc............E....... 620 792-6044
Great Bend *(G-2642)*
Tann Electric Inc............F....... 913 236-7337
Lenexa *(G-6167)*
Total Electric Contractors............F....... 913 441-0192
Edwardsville *(G-1518)*
V & V Electric Inc............F....... 785 468-3364
Olsburg *(G-8170)*
Winavie LLC............E....... 913 789-8169
Kansas City *(G-4547)*

CONTRACTORS: Electronic Controls Installation

Bear Communications LLC............E....... 913 441-3355
Lenexa *(G-5693)*
Modus Group LLC............E....... 785 584-6057
Rossville *(G-10254)*
Redi Systems Inc............F....... 785 587-9100
Manhattan *(G-6788)*

CONTRACTORS: Energy Management Control

Mid-States Energy Works Inc............F....... 785 827-3631
Salina *(G-10601)*

CONTRACTORS: Epoxy Application

Epoxy Coating Specialists Inc...............E....... 913 362-4141
Kansas City *(G-3993)*

CONTRACTORS: Erection & Dismantling, Poured Concrete Forms

Ceco Concrete Cnstr Del LLC...............F....... 913 362-1855
Olathe *(G-7581)*

CONTRACTORS: Excavating

Apac-Kansas Inc...............E....... 620 227-6908
Dodge City *(G-1293)*
Apex Trucking Inc...............E....... 316 943-0774
Park City *(G-9601)*
Barnharts Excavation LLC...............F....... 620 431-0959
Chanute *(G-706)*
Bayer Construction Company Inc.........C....... 785 776-8839
Manhattan *(G-6553)*
Betzen Trenching Inc...............E....... 316 269-9331
Wichita *(G-13841)*
Bradburn Wrecking Company...............E....... 316 686-1959
Wichita *(G-13880)*
Bratton Bros Contracting Inc...............F....... 913 422-7771
Shawnee *(G-10920)*
Breason Excavating & Trucking...............F....... 785 597-5596
Perry *(G-9766)*
Buck Construction Co...............F....... 913 796-6510
Mc Louth *(G-6925)*
D B Excavating Inc...............E....... 913 208-7100
Spring Hill *(G-12083)*
Diversified Contracting LLC...............F....... 913 898-4722
Parker *(G-9657)*
E4 Excavating Inc...............F....... 785 379-5111
Berryton *(G-526)*
Emerson Construction Inc...............F....... 785 235-0555
Topeka *(G-12574)*
Ferco Inc...............E....... 785 825-6380
Salina *(G-10500)*
Freddy Van Inc...............G....... 620 231-1127
Pittsburg *(G-9863)*
Frederick Excavating Inc...............F....... 913 772-0225
Leavenworth *(G-5240)*
Gary Gorby...............E....... 620 879-5243
Caney *(G-668)*
Greg Bair Track Hoe Svc Inc...............F....... 913 897-1243
Shawnee Mission *(G-11403)*
Hayes Bros Const Co Inc...............F....... 913 685-3636
Bucyrus *(G-599)*
Hoffman Inc...............F....... 316 942-8011
Wichita *(G-14622)*
James R Barber...............F....... 785 349-2801
White City *(G-13567)*
Jims Electric Inc...............F....... 785 460-2844
Colby *(G-1017)*
Kaw Valley Companies Inc...............C....... 913 281-9950
Kansas City *(G-4160)*
Killough Construction Inc...............F....... 785 242-1500
Ottawa *(G-8281)*
King Enterprises Inc...............F....... 620 624-3332
Liberal *(G-6329)*
Larkin Excavating, Inc................D....... 913 727-3772
Leavenworth *(G-5264)*
M & D Excavating Inc...............F....... 785 628-3169
Hays *(G-2867)*
M & D of Hays Incorporated...............E....... 785 628-3169
Hays *(G-2868)*
Manhattan Trenching Inc...............E....... 785 537-2330
Manhattan *(G-6728)*
Midwest Concrete Materials Inc...............C....... 785 776-8811
Manhattan *(G-6746)*
Muller Construction Inc...............E....... 620 251-1110
Coffeyville *(G-964)*
Pearson Construction LLC...............C....... 316 263-3100
Wichita *(G-15275)*
R Puckett Farms Inc...............F....... 620 378-3342
Fredonia *(G-2043)*
Rippels Inc...............F....... 620 674-1944
Scammon *(G-10797)*
RL Duncan Cnstr Co Inc...............D....... 913 583-1160
De Soto *(G-1212)*
Ted Row Inc...............F....... 816 223-9666
Stilwell *(G-12176)*
Total Lease Service Inc...............G....... 785 735-9520
Hays *(G-2920)*
Vilela Rndy Auto Bdy Repr Pntg...............F....... 620 231-6350
Pittsburg *(G-9957)*

CONTRACTORS: Excavating Slush Pits & Cellars Svcs

Ysidro Trucking Inc...............F....... 316 522-3716
Wichita *(G-16099)*

CONTRACTORS: Exterior Concrete Stucco

Lithko Contracting LLC...............F....... 913 281-2700
Lenexa *(G-5975)*
New Image Concrete Design LLC.........F....... 913 489-1699
Shawnee *(G-11005)*
Superior Masonry & Stucco LLC...............E....... 316 928-2365
Wichita *(G-15695)*

CONTRACTORS: Exterior Insulation & Finish Application

Superior Masonry & Stucco LLC...............E....... 316 928-2365
Wichita *(G-15695)*

CONTRACTORS: Exterior Painting

Paint Masters Inc...............F....... 316 683-5203
Wichita *(G-15253)*
Parsons Aaron Painting LLC...............G....... 620 532-1076
Kingman *(G-4609)*

CONTRACTORS: Exterior Wall System Installation

Fh Companies Inc...............C....... 316 264-2208
Kechi *(G-4568)*

CONTRACTORS: Fence Construction

A L C Enterprises Inc...............F....... 316 943-6500
Wichita *(G-13587)*
American Fence and SEC Co Inc...............G....... 316 945-5001
Wichita *(G-13691)*
American Fence Company LLC...............E....... 913 307-0306
Overland Park *(G-8376)*
Browing Gayla...............E....... 620 343-2274
Emporia *(G-1709)*
Challenger Fence Co Inc...............F....... 913 432-3535
Shawnee Mission *(G-11215)*
Discount Siding Supply LP...............F....... 785 625-4619
Hays *(G-2788)*
Mann Fence Company Inc...............F....... 913 782-2332
Olathe *(G-7872)*
Tom Burge Fence & Iron Inc...............E....... 913 681-7600
Shawnee Mission *(G-11933)*
Tractor Supply Company...............F....... 620 663-7607
Hutchinson *(G-3465)*
Western Kansas and Supply...............F....... 620 792-4731
Great Bend *(G-2661)*
Wichita Fence Co Inc...............F....... 316 838-1342
Park City *(G-9654)*

CONTRACTORS: Fiber Optic Cable Installation

Cablecom Inc...............F....... 316 267-4777
Wichita *(G-13926)*
Cimarron Underground Inc...............E....... 913 438-2981
Overland Park *(G-8552)*
Cnc Underground LLC...............F....... 913 744-0485
Gardner *(G-2333)*
Gateway Wreless Netwrk Svcs Lc.........F....... 316 264-0037
Wichita *(G-14452)*
Qti Inc...............F....... 913 579-3131
Olathe *(G-8013)*
Toms Ditching & Backhoe Inc...............F....... 620 879-2215
Caney *(G-676)*
Universal Communications LLC...............E....... 913 839-1634
Olathe *(G-8135)*
Vision Communications Ks Inc...............F....... 316 634-6747
Wichita *(G-15908)*

CONTRACTORS: Fire Detection & Burglar Alarm Systems

All Systems Dsgned Sltions Inc...............E....... 913 281-5100
Kansas City *(G-3800)*
Clarios...............E....... 316 721-2777
Wichita *(G-14034)*
Johnson Controls...............E....... 316 686-6363
Wichita *(G-14766)*
Johnson Controls Fire...............G....... 785 267-9675
Topeka *(G-12748)*
Overfield Corporation...............F....... 785 843-3434
Lawrence *(G-5052)*
Touchton Electric Inc...............E....... 620 232-9294
Pittsburg *(G-9946)*

CONTRACTORS: Fire Sprinkler System Installation Svcs

American Fire Sprinkler Corp...............F....... 620 792-1909
Great Bend *(G-2505)*
Bamford Fire Sprinkler Co Inc...............E....... 785 825-7710
Salina *(G-10417)*
Bamford Fire Sprinkler Co Inc...............E....... 913 432-6688
Shawnee Mission *(G-11145)*
Fire Protection Services Inc...............E....... 316 262-2452
Wichita *(G-14369)*
General Automatic Sprinkler Fl...............E....... 913 390-1105
Overland Park *(G-8750)*
General Fire Sprinkler Co LLC...............F....... 913 390-1105
Shawnee *(G-10960)*
Jayhawk Fire Sprinkler Co Inc...............E....... 913 422-3770
Olathe *(G-7809)*
Johnson Controls...............E....... 316 686-6363
Wichita *(G-14766)*
McDaniel Co Inc...............E....... 316 942-8325
Wichita *(G-15027)*
Pryor Autmtc Fire Sprnklr Inc...............F....... 620 792-6400
Great Bend *(G-2625)*
R P 3 Inc...............F....... 620 827-6136
Mc Cune *(G-6921)*
Western States Fire Protection...............D....... 913 321-9208
Kansas City *(G-4537)*

CONTRACTORS: Floor Laying & Other Floor Work

Aegis Business Solutions LLC...............G....... 913 307-9922
Olathe *(G-7512)*
Better Life Technology LLC...............E....... 620 343-2212
Emporia *(G-1703)*
Classic Floors & Design Center...............E....... 913 780-2171
Overland Park *(G-8561)*
Commercial Floors...............E....... 913 583-3525
De Soto *(G-1197)*
Corporate Flooring Inc...............F....... 913 859-9180
Shawnee Mission *(G-11266)*
Design Source Flooring LLC...............E....... 913 387-5858
Lenexa *(G-5813)*
Great Amercn Hardwood Flrg Co...............F....... 316 264-3660
Wichita *(G-14501)*
Halstontine Corp...............F....... 913 780-2171
Overland Park *(G-8787)*
Kaw Valley Hardwood Inc...............E....... 785 925-0142
Topeka *(G-12812)*
Regents Flooring Co Inc...............F....... 913 663-9922
Lenexa *(G-6098)*
Sam Carlini...............F....... 913 416-1280
Shawnee *(G-11024)*
Superior Hardwood Floors LLC...............G....... 316 554-9663
Wichita *(G-15694)*
UNI Floor Inc...............F....... 913 238-4633
Overland Park *(G-9439)*
Zack Taylor Contracting Inc...............F....... 785 235-8704
Topeka *(G-13260)*

CONTRACTORS: Flooring

Fox Ceramic Tile Inc...............E....... 785 437-2792
Saint Marys *(G-10365)*
Gray & Company Inc...............E....... 785 232-0913
Topeka *(G-12644)*
Interstate Flooring LLC...............F....... 913 541-9700
Lenexa *(G-5921)*
Superior Hardwood Floors LLC...............G....... 316 554-9663
Wichita *(G-15694)*
Unlimited Service Options LLC...............F....... 316 522-1503
Wichita *(G-15859)*

CONTRACTORS: Food Concessions

American Multi-Cinema Inc...............C....... 913 213-2000
Leawood *(G-5322)*

CONTRACTORS: Foundation & Footing

ATM Concrete Inc...............F....... 785 484-2013
Meriden *(G-7078)*
B & H Construction Company...............F....... 620 231-0326
Pittsburg *(G-9820)*
Berkel & Company Contrs Inc...............D....... 913 422-5125
Bonner Springs *(G-540)*

Bottorff Construction Inc........D....... 913 874-5681
Atchison *(G-219)*
Calvin Opp Concrete Inc........D....... 316 944-4600
Wichita *(G-13928)*
Carpenter Construction Company........F....... 620 386-4155
Moundridge *(G-7179)*
Concrete Unlimited Cnstr Inc........E....... 785 232-8636
Topeka *(G-12499)*
Creten Basement Contractors........F....... 913 441-3333
Olathe *(G-7626)*
Creten John G Basement Contr........F....... 913 441-3333
Olathe *(G-7627)*
Ebi Construction Inc........F....... 785 456-7449
Wamego *(G-13419)*
George Goracke Basement........F....... 785 388-9542
Solomon *(G-12051)*
Leo J Debrabander Foundation........F....... 913 780-1600
Olathe *(G-7858)*
Longfellow Foundation Inc........F....... 620 662-1228
Hutchinson *(G-3356)*
Mark Debrabander Foundation Co........F....... 913 856-4044
Olathe *(G-7874)*
McNish Foundations Inc........F....... 785 865-2413
Lawrence *(G-5019)*
Overland Concrete Cnstr Inc........F....... 913 393-4200
Olathe *(G-7968)*
Power Lift Found Repair........E....... 316 685-0888
Wichita *(G-15319)*
R & H Concrete Inc........E....... 785 286-0335
Lawrence *(G-5084)*
Robert Vanlerberg Foundations........E....... 913 441-6823
Shawnee Mission *(G-11809)*
Thrasher Bsmnt Foundation Repr........D....... 316 320-1853
El Dorado *(G-1609)*

CONTRACTORS: Foundation Building

ATM Concrete Inc........F....... 785 484-2013
Meriden *(G-7078)*
B W Foundations Company Inc........F....... 913 764-8222
Olathe *(G-7545)*
Fuller Foundation Company Inc........E....... 913 764-8222
Olathe *(G-7720)*
Midwest Siding Inc........E....... 785 825-0606
Salina *(G-10603)*
Power Lift Found Repair........E....... 316 685-0888
Wichita *(G-15319)*
Robert Vanlerberg Foundations........E....... 913 441-6823
Shawnee Mission *(G-11809)*

CONTRACTORS: Garage Doors

D H Pace Company Inc........A....... 816 221-0543
Olathe *(G-7637)*
EE Newcomer Enterprises Inc........B....... 816 221-0543
Olathe *(G-7671)*
Garage Door Group Inc........F....... 757 253-0522
Junction City *(G-3691)*
Overhead Door N Centl Kans Inc........F....... 785 823-3786
Salina *(G-10626)*
Ray Anderson Co Inc........E....... 785 233-7454
Topeka *(G-13000)*
Tuff Shed Inc........F....... 913 541-8833
Shawnee Mission *(G-11947)*

CONTRACTORS: Gasoline Condensation Removal Svcs

Excel Wireline LLC........G....... 785 764-9557
Pratt *(G-10112)*

CONTRACTORS: General Electric

4 Rivers Electric Coop Inc........E....... 620 364-2116
Lebo *(G-5605)*
A & H Electric Inc........D....... 316 838-3003
Wichita *(G-13583)*
Accurate Electric Inc........G....... 785 825-4010
Salina *(G-10391)*
Ace Electric-Jones Company Inc........E....... 785 862-8200
Topeka *(G-12284)*
Advance Electric Inc........E....... 316 263-1300
Wichita *(G-13621)*
Alan Bitter........F....... 620 353-7407
Ulysses *(G-13281)*
Apple Electric Inc........F....... 913 837-5285
Louisburg *(G-6439)*
Atlas Electric LLC........D....... 316 858-1560
Wichita *(G-13765)*
B & W Electric Inc........F....... 785 337-2598
Hanover *(G-2709)*
B A Barnes Electric Inc........E....... 913 764-4455
Olathe *(G-7544)*
Baldridge Electric Inc........E....... 316 267-0058
Wichita *(G-13799)*
Belford Electric Inc........E....... 316 267-7060
Wichita *(G-13828)*
Brunner Electric Inc........F....... 913 268-5463
Shawnee Mission *(G-11187)*
Capital Electric Cnstr Co Inc........E....... 816 472-9500
Kansas City *(G-3888)*
Carlisle Heating & AC........F....... 316 321-6230
El Dorado *(G-1543)*
CDL Electric Company Inc........C....... 620 232-1242
Pittsburg *(G-9829)*
Central States Electric Inc........E....... 316 942-6640
Wichita *(G-13987)*
Citywide Electric Inc........E....... 913 631-1189
Shawnee Mission *(G-11234)*
Comfort Contractors Inc........E....... 620 431-4780
Chanute *(G-718)*
Commercl-Ndstrial Ele Cont Inc........E....... 316 263-1291
Wichita *(G-14074)*
Cox-Kent & Associates Inc........F....... 316 946-5596
Wichita *(G-14123)*
Creek Electric Incorporated........E....... 316 943-5888
Wichita *(G-14129)*
Critical Elc Systems Group LLC........E....... 316 684-0193
Wichita *(G-14132)*
Current Electrical Co Inc........E....... 785 267-2108
Topeka *(G-12535)*
D L Smith Electrical Cnstr........C....... 785 267-4920
Topeka *(G-12543)*
Darrell Bybee Construction LLC........F....... 316 409-4186
Wichita *(G-14171)*
Davin Electric Inc........E....... 785 234-2350
Topeka *(G-12548)*
Decker Electric Inc........D....... 316 265-8182
Wichita *(G-14183)*
Delta Electric Co Inc........E....... 316 267-2869
Wichita *(G-14189)*
Diversified Contracting LLC........F....... 913 898-4722
Parker *(G-9657)*
Eci Electrical Contractors........F....... 316 722-0204
Wichita *(G-14257)*
Electri Tech........F....... 316 683-2841
Wichita *(G-14264)*
Electrical Associates LLC........E....... 913 825-2537
Olathe *(G-7674)*
Electrical Concepts Inc........F....... 785 456-8896
Wamego *(G-13420)*
Electrical Enterprises Inc........E....... 785 242-7971
Ottawa *(G-8269)*
Electrical Systems Inc........F....... 316 263-2415
Wichita *(G-14265)*
Elite Electric Inc........E....... 913 724-1645
Basehor *(G-375)*
Faith Technologies Inc........D....... 913 541-4700
Lenexa *(G-5847)*
Faith Technologies Inc........B....... 785 938-4499
Gove *(G-2493)*
Garwin Electric LLC........F....... 913 780-1200
Olathe *(G-7724)*
Gjo Inc........E....... 913 621-6611
Kansas City *(G-4035)*
Graf & Associates Inc........F....... 316 686-2090
Wichita *(G-14493)*
Hanover Electric Inc........F....... 785 337-2711
Hanover *(G-2711)*
Harvey & Son Electric........F....... 620 624-3688
Liberal *(G-6318)*
Haynes Electric Inc........E....... 620 285-2242
Larned *(G-4704)*
Heartland Electric Inc........E....... 785 233-9546
Topeka *(G-12677)*
Hedlund Electric Inc........E....... 620 241-3757
McPherson *(G-6972)*
Heineken Electric Co Inc........E....... 785 738-3831
Beloit *(G-486)*
Heineken Electric Company Inc........F....... 785 404-3157
Salina *(G-10541)*
Heineken Electric Company Inc........F....... 785 539-7400
Manhattan *(G-6653)*
Heritage Electric LLC........E....... 913 747-0528
Olathe *(G-7765)*
Huxtable & Associates Inc........C....... 785 843-2910
Lawrence *(G-4907)*
Integrated Electrical Tech LLC........F....... 316 684-0193
Wichita *(G-14701)*
Interstate Elec Cnstr Inc........E....... 620 421-5510
Parsons *(G-9693)*
Jims Electric Inc........F....... 785 460-2844
Colby *(G-1017)*
Kansas Electric Inc........D....... 316 283-4750
Newton *(G-7369)*
Kennys Electrical Co Inc........F....... 620 662-2359
Hutchinson *(G-3350)*
Kilian Electrical Service Inc........E....... 316 942-4600
Wichita *(G-14857)*
King Enterprises Inc........F....... 620 624-3332
Liberal *(G-6329)*
L T Huxtable Service Inc........E....... 785 235-5331
Topeka *(G-12826)*
Liebert Brothers Electric Co........F....... 620 251-0299
Coffeyville *(G-956)*
Linder & Associates Inc........C....... 316 265-1616
Wichita *(G-14966)*
Loper C-I Electric........E....... 316 263-1291
Wichita *(G-14978)*
Lowry Electric Co Inc........F....... 316 838-4363
Wichita *(G-14985)*
Lynn Elc & Communications Inc........E....... 785 843-5079
Lawrence *(G-5003)*
Mc Electric........E....... 913 721-2988
Kansas City *(G-4223)*
McElroy Electric Inc........E....... 785 266-7111
Topeka *(G-12870)*
Midwest Electric Service Inc........F....... 620 241-8655
McPherson *(G-7006)*
Midwest Electrical Cnstr Inc........F....... 785 215-8902
Topeka *(G-12896)*
Norse LLC........E....... 620 225-0778
Dodge City *(G-1414)*
Oliver Electric Cnstr Inc........E....... 785 748-0777
Lawrence *(G-5043)*
Outdoor Lighting Services LP........F....... 913 422-8400
Shawnee *(G-11006)*
P & S Elc & Roustabout Svc Inc........F....... 620 792-7426
Great Bend *(G-2621)*
Performance Electric LLC........F....... 785 242-5748
Ottawa *(G-8305)*
Pro Electric LC........C....... 913 621-6611
Kansas City *(G-4340)*
Quality Elc Douglas Cnty Inc........E....... 785 843-9211
Lawrence *(G-5083)*
R D H Electric Inc........E....... 785 625-3833
Hays *(G-2895)*
R F Fisher Holdings Inc........C....... 913 384-1500
Kansas City *(G-4357)*
Rays Electric Inc........E....... 316 838-8231
Wichita *(G-15423)*
Reddy Electric Systems Inc........F....... 913 764-0840
Olathe *(G-8020)*
Schmidtlein Electric Inc........E....... 785 357-4572
Topeka *(G-13039)*
Seward and Wilson Electric........F....... 620 232-1696
Pittsburg *(G-9937)*
Shelley Electric Inc........E....... 785 862-0507
Topeka *(G-13066)*
Southern Pioneer Electric Co........F....... 620 356-3370
Ulysses *(G-13320)*
Southwestern Electrical Co Inc........C....... 316 263-1264
Wichita *(G-15632)*
Teague Electric Cnstr Inc........C....... 913 529-4600
Lenexa *(G-6169)*
Teague Electric Company Inc........D....... 913 529-4600
Lenexa *(G-6170)*
Tee & Bee Electric Company........F....... 913 782-8161
Olathe *(G-8105)*
Torgeson Electric Company........C....... 785 233-3060
Topeka *(G-13192)*
Total Electric Inc........G....... 316 524-2642
Wichita *(G-15775)*
Total Electric Construction Co........F....... 913 441-0192
Edwardsville *(G-1517)*
Tracy Electric Inc........E....... 316 522-8408
Haysville *(G-2962)*
V & V Electric Company Inc........E....... 785 539-1975
Manhattan *(G-6840)*
Wachter Inc........C....... 913 541-2500
Lenexa *(G-6219)*
Watson Electric Inc........F....... 785 827-2924
Salina *(G-10761)*
Wolfe Electric Inc........D....... 316 943-2751
Wichita *(G-16061)*
Yost Electric Inc........G....... 785 637-5454
Gorham *(G-2492)*
Young Electric Inc........E....... 316 681-8118
Wichita *(G-16090)*
Zenor Electric Company Inc........E....... 620 662-4694
Hutchinson *(G-3496)*

Ziegler Electric Service Inc .... F 316 262-2842
Wichita *(G-16103)*
Zimmerman Electric Service .... G 620 431-2260
Chanute *(G-775)*

CONTRACTORS: Geothermal Drilling

Rosencrantz Bemis Enterprises .... E 620 792-2488
Great Bend *(G-2632)*

CONTRACTORS: Glass Tinting, Architectural & Automotive

Manko Window Systems Inc .... F 785 238-3188
Junction City *(G-3724)*
Manko Window Systems Inc .... B 785 776-9643
Manhattan *(G-6730)*
Midwest Tinting Inc .... F 913 384-2665
Overland Park *(G-9036)*
Noonshine Window Cleaning Svc .... F 913 381-9666
Shawnee Mission *(G-11687)*

CONTRACTORS: Glass, Glazing & Tinting

A Glass & Tint Shop Kc Inc .... F 913 491-8468
Merriam *(G-7085)*
Byers Glass & Mirror Inc .... E 913 441-8717
Bonner Springs *(G-544)*
City Glass and Mirror Inc .... F 785 233-5650
Topeka *(G-12467)*
Drywall Systems Inc .... C 316 260-9411
Wichita *(G-14242)*
Fountain Glass Inc .... E 913 764-6014
Lenexa *(G-5864)*
G W Inc .... E 316 262-3403
Wichita *(G-14435)*
Grey Mountain Partners LLC .... E 785 776-9482
Manhattan *(G-6646)*
Hoppers Glass Inc .... E 316 262-0497
Wichita *(G-14636)*
Janssen Glass & Mirror Inc .... F 913 677-5727
Shawnee *(G-10977)*
Kennedy Glass Inc .... E 785 843-4416
Lawrence *(G-4942)*
Lawrence Glass & Mirror Co .... F 913 631-5533
Shawnee Mission *(G-11550)*
Masonry & Glass Systems Inc .... G 913 748-6142
Shawnee Mission *(G-11601)*
Midwest Glass & Glazing LLC .... E 913 768-6778
Kansas City *(G-4253)*
Performance Glass Inc .... F 913 441-1290
Bonner Springs *(G-570)*
Pratt Glass Inc .... F 620 672-6463
Pratt *(G-10139)*
Southwest Glass & Door Inc .... F 620 626-7400
Liberal *(G-6369)*
Sowards Glass Inc .... F 785 233-4466
Topeka *(G-13086)*
W Carter & Assoc Glazing LLC .... E 913 543-2600
Kansas City *(G-4526)*

CONTRACTORS: Grave Excavation

Suhor Industries Inc .... A 620 421-4434
Overland Park *(G-9371)*

CONTRACTORS: Gutters & Downspouts

Home Stl Siding & Windows LLC .... F 785 625-8622
Hays *(G-2849)*
Jet Stream Guttering Corp .... F 913 262-2913
Shawnee Mission *(G-11485)*
Nieder Contracting Inc .... E 785 842-0094
Lawrence *(G-5040)*
Town & Country Guttering Inc .... F 913 441-0003
Shawnee Mission *(G-11935)*

CONTRACTORS: Heating & Air Conditioning

Building Control Solutions LLC .... G 816 439-6046
Merriam *(G-7087)*
C & C Group of Companies .... D 913 492-8414
Lenexa *(G-5723)*
Clarios .... E 316 655-7578
Wichita *(G-14035)*
Clarios .... E 316 721-2777
Wichita *(G-14034)*
Comfort Management Inc .... F 620 442-5610
Arkansas City *(G-149)*
Even Temp of Wichita Inc .... F 316 469-5321
Wichita *(G-14312)*
Lower Heating & AC Inc .... E 785 357-5123
Topeka *(G-12851)*
Midwest Energy Inc .... E 785 462-8251
Colby *(G-1028)*
Premium Heating & Cooling Inc .... F 913 780-5639
Olathe *(G-8004)*
Reid Plumbing Heating & AC Inc .... F 785 537-2869
Manhattan *(G-6789)*
Stryker Services Inc .... E 785 357-1281
Topeka *(G-13115)*
Weber Refrigeration & Htg Inc .... E 580 338-7338
Garden City *(G-2309)*

CONTRACTORS: Heating Systems Repair & Maintenance Svc

Budget Plumbing & Heating .... F 620 231-5232
Pittsburg *(G-9826)*
Dans Heating & Cooling Inc .... E 316 522-0372
Wichita *(G-14168)*
Thermal Comfort Air Inc .... E 785 537-2436
Manhattan *(G-6824)*

CONTRACTORS: Highway & Street Construction, General

Amino Bros Co Inc .... C 913 334-2330
Kansas City *(G-3807)*
Apac-Kansas Inc .... E 620 662-3307
Hutchinson *(G-3200)*
B & B Bridges Company LLC .... F 620 449-2286
Saint Paul *(G-10379)*
County of Douglas .... E 785 832-5293
Lawrence *(G-4814)*
Diversified Contracting LLC .... F 913 898-4722
Parker *(G-9657)*
Dudley Construction Co Inc .... F 620 665-1166
Hutchinson *(G-3270)*
Ebert Construction Co Inc .... E 785 456-2455
Wamego *(G-13418)*
Hall Brothers Inc .... F 785 562-2386
Marysville *(G-6890)*
Heckert Construction Co Inc .... F 620 231-6090
Pittsburg *(G-9874)*
Hwa Davis Cnstr & Sup Inc .... F 316 283-0330
Newton *(G-7364)*
Jcor Inc .... F 913 461-8804
Overland Park *(G-8873)*
Kansas Department Trnsp .... E 316 321-3370
El Dorado *(G-1575)*
King Construction Company Inc .... D 620 327-4251
Hesston *(G-2995)*
Konza Constr Co Inc .... D 785 762-2995
Junction City *(G-3717)*
Lee Shafer Ricky .... E 620 252-9126
Coffeyville *(G-955)*
Miles Excavating Inc .... C 913 724-1934
Basehor *(G-384)*
N R Hamm Contractor Inc .... D 785 597-5111
Perry *(G-9773)*
Page Enterprise LLC .... F 913 898-4722
Parker *(G-9659)*
Pyramid Contractors Inc .... E 913 764-6225
Olathe *(G-8012)*
RFB Construction Co Inc .... E 620 232-2900
Pittsburg *(G-9928)*
Sporer Land Development Inc .... E 785 672-4319
Oakley *(G-7487)*
Tri State Construction Inc .... E 620 231-5260
Pittsburg *(G-9948)*
Western Contracting Corp .... D 620 449-2286
Saint Paul *(G-10385)*

CONTRACTORS: Highway & Street Paving

Apac-Kansas Inc .... D 785 625-3459
Hays *(G-2749)*
Apac-Kansas Inc .... E 785 823-5537
Salina *(G-10406)*
B & H Paving Inc .... F 620 872-3146
Scott City *(G-10805)*
Bettis Asphalt & Cnstr Inc .... E 785 235-8444
Topeka *(G-12377)*
Conspec Inc .... D 316 832-0828
Park City *(G-9612)*
Hamm Asphalt Inc .... F 785 597-5421
Perry *(G-9770)*
Harbour Construction Inc .... F 913 441-2555
Kansas City *(G-4067)*
Inland Corporation .... F 620 478-2450
Norwich *(G-7470)*
Kansas Asphalt Inc .... D 877 384-2280
Bucyrus *(G-601)*
Killough Construction Inc .... F 785 242-1500
Ottawa *(G-8281)*
Lrm Industries Inc .... E 785 843-1688
Lawrence *(G-5001)*
McAnany Construction Inc .... D 913 631-5440
Shawnee Mission *(G-11606)*
Oldcastle Infrastructure Inc .... F 620 662-3307
Hutchinson *(G-3392)*
Shilling Construction Co Inc .... E 785 776-5077
Manhattan *(G-6800)*
Venture Corporation .... D 620 792-5921
Great Bend *(G-2654)*

CONTRACTORS: Highway & Street Resurfacing

Cutler Repaving Inc .... D 785 843-1524
Lawrence *(G-4821)*
Julius Kaaz Cnstr Co Inc .... E 913 682-3550
Leavenworth *(G-5259)*
Paving Construction Inc .... F 316 684-6161
Wichita *(G-15272)*
Wade Agricultural Products Inc .... G 913 757-2255
La Cygne *(G-4646)*

CONTRACTORS: Indl Building Renovation, Remodeling & Repair

Awad Nicola .... E 913 381-6969
Overland Park *(G-8417)*
Hudson Inc .... E 620 232-1145
Pittsburg *(G-9879)*
National Ctstrphe Rstrtion Inc .... D 316 636-5700
Wichita *(G-15149)*
Overland Park Heating & Coolg .... E 913 649-0303
Overland Park *(G-9119)*
Paronto Mall Construction Inc .... F 785 632-2484
Clay Center *(G-875)*
Paul Davis Restoratio of Great .... E 785 842-0351
Lawrence *(G-5058)*
Sharper Images Company LLC .... F 620 331-7646
Independence *(G-3559)*

CONTRACTORS: Insulation Installation, Building

Associated Insulation Inc .... D 785 776-0145
Manhattan *(G-6548)*
Black Gold Inc .... E 785 354-4000
Topeka *(G-12386)*
Capital Insulation Inc .... E 785 246-1775
Topeka *(G-12432)*
D V Douglass Roofing Inc .... E 620 276-7474
Garden City *(G-2141)*
Epic Insulation Inc .... F 316 500-1650
Goddard *(G-2438)*
F & H Abatement Services Inc .... C 316 264-2208
Kechi *(G-4567)*
Fh Companies Inc .... C 316 264-2208
Kechi *(G-4568)*
H & C Insulation Co Inc .... F 316 522-0236
Wichita *(G-14530)*
Home Stl Siding & Windows LLC .... F 785 625-8622
Hays *(G-2849)*
Insco Industries Inc .... E 913 422-8001
Shawnee Mission *(G-11459)*
Insulation Drywall Contrs Inc .... E 785 862-0554
Topeka *(G-12725)*
Jay Henges Enterprises Inc .... E 913 764-4600
Olathe *(G-7808)*
Jordan Companies Inc .... E 316 943-6222
Wichita *(G-14771)*
Performance Contracting Inc .... A 913 888-8600
Lenexa *(G-6051)*
Pro R Sales and Service Inc .... F 316 773-3400
Wichita *(G-15353)*
Washington Companies Inc .... F 620 792-2430
Great Bend *(G-2656)*
Wray Roofing Inc .... D 316 283-6840
Newton *(G-7430)*

CONTRACTORS: Kitchen & Bathroom Remodeling

Mm Property MGT & Rmdlg LLC .... F 913 871-6867
Kansas City *(G-4265)*
Rhino Builders Inc .... F 913 722-4353
Kansas City *(G-4376)*
Window Design Company .... G 785 582-2888
Silver Lake *(G-12030)*

CONTRACTORS: Land Reclamation

Ballou Pavement Solutions Inc ....C....... 785 827-4439
Salina *(G-10416)*

CONTRACTORS: Lead Burning

Professional Service Inds Inc ....E....... 913 310-1600
Kansas City *(G-4343)*

CONTRACTORS: Lighting Syst

Phillips Southern Elc Co Inc ....E....... 316 265-4186
Wichita *(G-15293)*
Td Electric Services LLC ....F....... 913 722-5560
Overland Park *(G-9393)*

CONTRACTORS: Lightweight Steel Framing Installation

Danny Satterfield Drywall Corp ....E....... 316 942-5155
Wichita *(G-14167)*
Sarin Energy Inc ....F....... 913 912-3235
Overland Park *(G-9281)*

CONTRACTORS: Machine Rigging & Moving

Taylor Crane & Rigging Inc ....D....... 620 251-1530
Coffeyville *(G-981)*

CONTRACTORS: Machinery Dismantling

Alltite Inc ....E....... 316 686-3010
Wichita *(G-13678)*

CONTRACTORS: Machinery Installation

Adelphi Construction Lc ....D....... 913 384-5511
Shawnee Mission *(G-11075)*
Bear Communications LLC ....E....... 913 441-3355
Lenexa *(G-5693)*
Masthead International Inc ....E....... 913 888-8600
Lenexa *(G-5989)*
P1 Group Inc ....B....... 913 529-5000
Lenexa *(G-6040)*
Performance Contg Intl Inc ....D....... 913 888-8600
Shawnee Mission *(G-11726)*
Pioneer Automation Technology ....F....... 316 322-0123
El Dorado *(G-1591)*

CONTRACTORS: Masonry & Stonework

Alonge Stone Masonry ....F....... 785 832-1438
Tonganoxie *(G-12251)*
Boan Masonry Company Inc ....F....... 913 592-5369
Spring Hill *(G-12080)*
BPW Masonry Inc ....E....... 785 485-2840
Riley *(G-10205)*
Builders Stone & Masonry Inc ....D....... 913 764-4446
Olathe *(G-7567)*
Edward Rose & Sons LLC ....F....... 316 202-3920
Wichita *(G-14261)*
Grimmett Masonry Inc ....F....... 620 342-6582
Emporia *(G-1765)*
Hudson Inc ....E....... 620 232-1145
Pittsburg *(G-9879)*
Klaus Masonry LLC ....F....... 785 650-3854
Hays *(G-2860)*
Larry Lawrenz Construction ....F....... 785 258-2056
Herington *(G-2978)*
Lawrenz Masonry LLC ....E....... 785 366-0866
Herington *(G-2979)*
Maderak Construction Co Inc ....F....... 913 299-3929
Kansas City *(G-4212)*
ML Nevius Builders Inc ....F....... 620 662-7767
Hutchinson *(G-3383)*
Newell & Associates ....F....... 913 592-4421
Olathe *(G-7918)*
Prestige Masonry LLC ....F....... 785 925-3090
Topeka *(G-12985)*
S&K ....E....... 913 634-2234
Overland Park *(G-9268)*
Scott Masonry Inc ....F....... 785 286-3513
Topeka *(G-13043)*

CONTRACTORS: Mechanical

A D J-Hux Service Inc ....D....... 913 529-5200
Lenexa *(G-5616)*
B&C Mechanical Services LLC ....F....... 913 681-0088
Paola *(G-9541)*
Barnds Brothers Inc ....E....... 913 897-2340
Shawnee Mission *(G-11152)*
Baxter Mechanical Contractors ....F....... 913 281-6303
Kansas City *(G-3849)*
BCI Mechanical Inc ....F....... 913 856-6747
Gardner *(G-2329)*
Central Mech Cnstr Co Inc ....C....... 785 537-2437
Manhattan *(G-6581)*
Central Mechanical Wichita LLC ....D....... 316 267-7676
Wichita *(G-13981)*
Central States Contg Svcs Inc ....F....... 913 788-1100
Kansas City *(G-3903)*
Central States Mechanical Inc ....F....... 620 353-1797
Ulysses *(G-13287)*
City Wide Sheet Metal Inc ....F....... 913 871-7464
Kansas City *(G-3914)*
CJ Industries LLC ....F....... 913 788-1104
Kansas City *(G-3915)*
Commercial Mechanical Inc Kans ....D....... 316 262-1230
Wichita *(G-14070)*
Dean E Norris Inc ....D....... 316 688-1901
Wichita *(G-14180)*
Den Management Co Inc ....C....... 316 686-1964
Wichita *(G-14191)*
Design Mechanical Inc ....C....... 913 281-7200
Kansas City *(G-3970)*
Environmental Mech Contrs Inc ....D....... 913 829-0100
Olathe *(G-7688)*
Five Star Mechanical Inc ....F....... 316 943-7827
Wichita *(G-14381)*
Huxtable & Associates Inc ....C....... 785 843-2910
Lawrence *(G-4907)*
Interstate Elec Cnstr Inc ....E....... 620 421-5510
Parsons *(G-9693)*
Knopke Company LLC ....E....... 816 231-1001
Leawood *(G-5451)*
Kuhn Mechanical Inc ....F....... 620 441-9339
Arkansas City *(G-163)*
L T Huxtable Service Inc ....E....... 785 235-5331
Topeka *(G-12826)*
M W C Inc ....D....... 316 267-7676
Wichita *(G-14994)*
McElroys Inc ....C....... 785 266-4870
Topeka *(G-12871)*
Mechanical Systems Inc ....D....... 316 262-2021
Wichita *(G-15031)*
Mechanics Inc ....E....... 316 262-2021
Wichita *(G-15032)*
MMC Corp ....E....... 913 469-0101
Overland Park *(G-9046)*
P1 Group Inc ....F....... 785 235-5331
Topeka *(G-12958)*
P1 Group Inc ....D....... 785 843-2910
Lawrence *(G-5054)*
P1 Group International Inc ....C....... 913 529-5000
Lenexa *(G-6041)*
Piping Contractors Kansas Inc ....E....... 785 233-2010
Topeka *(G-12977)*
Professional Mech Contrs Inc ....E....... 316 684-1927
Wichita *(G-15364)*
Samco Inc ....E....... 785 234-4000
Topeka *(G-13035)*
Shell Topco LP ....F....... 316 942-7266
Wichita *(G-15580)*
TWC Services Inc ....E....... 316 265-7831
Wichita *(G-15820)*
West Side Mechanical Inc ....F....... 913 788-1800
Manhattan *(G-6852)*

CONTRACTORS: Millwrights

Borton Lc ....E....... 620 669-8211
South Hutchinson *(G-12057)*
Burns Boys Co Inc ....F....... 913 788-8654
Kansas City *(G-3881)*
Centurion Industries Inc ....B....... 620 378-4401
Fredonia *(G-2028)*
Habco Inc ....E....... 785 823-0440
Salina *(G-10528)*
Jade Millwrights Inc ....E....... 785 544-7771
Hiawatha *(G-3011)*
Jayhawk Mllwright Erectors Inc ....E....... 913 371-5212
Kansas City *(G-4120)*
Mid-America Millwright Svc Inc ....E....... 620 275-6796
Garden City *(G-2232)*
Senne and Company Inc ....E....... 785 235-1015
Topeka *(G-13058)*
Welco Services Inc ....E....... 620 241-3000
McPherson *(G-7041)*

CONTRACTORS: Multi-Family Home Remodeling

Arrow Renovation & Cnstr LLC ....E....... 913 703-3000
Olathe *(G-7534)*
Best Home Guys Holding Co ....F....... 316 681-2639
Wichita *(G-13838)*
Mill Valley Construction Inc ....F....... 913 764-6539
Olathe *(G-7900)*
Mm Property MGT & Rmdlg LLC ....F....... 913 871-6867
Kansas City *(G-4265)*

CONTRACTORS: Nonresidential Building Design & Construction

R Messner Construction Co ....E....... 316 634-2381
Wichita *(G-15405)*

CONTRACTORS: Nuclear Power Refueling

Kiewit Power Nuclear Co ....F....... 913 928-7800
Lenexa *(G-5952)*

CONTRACTORS: Office Furniture Installation

Evologic LLC ....E....... 913 599-5292
Lenexa *(G-5839)*
JED Installation LLC ....E....... 913 724-4600
Basehor *(G-381)*
Multi Systems Installation Inc ....D....... 913 422-8282
Shawnee Mission *(G-11658)*
O I C Inc ....E....... 816 471-5400
Hesston *(G-2998)*
Panel Systems Plus Inc ....E....... 913 321-0111
Kansas City *(G-4309)*
Total Installation Management ....F....... 316 267-0584
Bel Aire *(G-441)*

CONTRACTORS: Oil & Gas Aerial Geophysical Exploration Svcs

White & Ellis Drilling Inc ....G....... 316 263-1102
Wichita *(G-15964)*

CONTRACTORS: Oil & Gas Building, Repairing & Dismantling Svc

Dillco Fluid Service Inc ....E....... 620 544-2929
Hugoton *(G-3159)*
Eldredge Well Service LLC ....E....... 620 649-2841
Satanta *(G-10784)*
Phillips Well Service Inc ....G....... 316 321-6650
El Dorado *(G-1590)*
Schulz Welding Service Inc ....F....... 620 628-4431
Canton *(G-681)*

CONTRACTORS: Oil & Gas Field Geophysical Exploration Svcs

Edmiston Oil Company Inc ....G....... 620 792-6924
Great Bend *(G-2558)*
Paragon Geophysical Svcs Inc ....E....... 316 636-5552
Wichita *(G-15258)*

CONTRACTORS: Oil & Gas Field Salt Water Impound/Storing Svc

Grandview Water Disposal Inc ....G....... 785 335-2649
Scandia *(G-10799)*

CONTRACTORS: Oil & Gas Field Tools Fishing Svcs

Key Energy Services Inc ....G....... 620 649-2368
Satanta *(G-10787)*

CONTRACTORS: Oil & Gas Well Casing Cement Svcs

Allied of Kansas Inc ....F....... 785 483-2627
Russell *(G-10265)*
Allied of Kansas Inc ....G....... 620 793-5861
Great Bend *(G-2503)*
Allied Ofs LLC ....F....... 785 483-2627
Russell *(G-10266)*
Eatherly Constructors Inc ....F....... 913 685-9026
Overland Park *(G-8669)*
Global Oilfield Services LLC ....F....... 785 445-3525
Russell *(G-10275)*
Quality Oilwell Cementing Inc ....F....... 785 483-1071
Russell *(G-10285)*

CONTRACTORS: Oil & Gas Well Drilling Svc

Associated Environmental Inc ....F 785 776-7755
Manhattan (G-6547)
Bruce Oil Co LLC ....G....... 620 241-2938
McPherson (G-6939)
Canary Resources Inc ....G....... 913 239-8960
Stilwell (G-12138)
Crown Consulting Inc ....F 620 624-0156
Liberal (G-6300)
Discovery Drilling Co Inc ....E 785 623-2920
Hays (G-2789)
Duke Drilling Co Inc ....D....... 620 793-8366
Great Bend (G-2556)
Empire Energy E&P LLC ....G....... 785 434-4900
Plainville (G-9987)
Fossil Drilling Inc ....F 620 672-5625
Pratt (G-10115)
H-40 Drilling Inc ....F 316 773-3640
Medicine Lodge (G-7063)
Imperial American Oil Corp ....G....... 316 721-0036
Wichita (G-14678)
Jones & Buck Development Oil ....F 620 725-3636
Sedan (G-10844)
L D Drilling Inc ....E 620 793-3051
Great Bend (G-2601)
Mull Drilling Company Inc ....F 316 264-6366
Wichita (G-15138)
Murfin Drilling Company Inc ....E 785 483-5371
Russell (G-10282)
Murfin Drilling Company Inc ....E 316 267-3241
Wichita (G-15140)
Murfin Drilling Company Inc ....E 785 421-2101
Hill City (G-3036)
Mv Partners LLC ....G....... 316 267-3241
Wichita (G-15142)
Quest Drilling Services LLC ....E 316 260-2196
Wichita (G-15392)
R & B Oil & Gas Inc ....F 620 254-7251
Attica (G-278)
Rig 6 Drilling Inc ....G....... 620 365-6294
Bronson (G-588)
Shields Oil Producers Inc ....E 785 483-3141
Russell (G-10299)
Sterling Drilling Company ....D....... 620 672-9508
Pratt (G-10154)
Town Oil Company ....F 913 294-2125
Paola (G-9593)
Trans Pacific Oil Corporation ....F 316 262-3596
Wichita (G-15789)
Val Energy Inc ....G....... 316 263-6688
Wichita (G-15869)
W-W Production Co ....G....... 620 431-4137
Chanute (G-773)
Well Refined Drilling Co Inc ....F 620 763-2619
Thayer (G-12246)
Zenith Drilling Corporation ....G....... 316 684-9777
Wichita (G-16100)

CONTRACTORS: Oil & Gas Well On-Site Foundation Building Svcs

Bakken Well Service Inc ....F 620 276-3442
Garden City (G-2104)

CONTRACTORS: Oil & Gas Well Plugging & Abandoning Svcs

Kepley Well Service LLC ....F 620 431-9212
Chanute (G-735)

CONTRACTORS: Oil & Gas Well reworking

Hurricane Services Inc ....E 620 437-2661
Madison (G-6501)
Kepley Well Service LLC ....F 620 431-9212
Chanute (G-735)

CONTRACTORS: Oil & Gas Wells Svcs

American Well Service LLC ....G....... 620 672-5625
Pratt (G-10096)
C & R Well Service ....G....... 785 448-8792
Garnett (G-2371)
Cheyenne Well Service Inc ....F 785 798-2282
Ness City (G-7256)
Cyclone Well Service Inc ....G....... 620 628-4428
Canton (G-680)
Dreiling Oil Inc ....G....... 785 625-8327
Hays (G-2791)
G & L Well Service Inc ....G....... 620 278-3105
Sterling (G-12118)
Glacier Petroleum Inc ....F....... 620 342-1148
Emporia (G-1762)
Gressel Oil Field Service LLC ....G....... 316 524-1225
Peck (G-9763)
Kelly Maclaskey ....E 316 321-9011
El Dorado (G-1578)
Key Energy Services Inc ....E 620 353-1002
Ulysses (G-13302)
Key Energy Services Inc ....D....... 620 353-1002
Ulysses (G-13303)
Leiker Well Service Inc ....G....... 620 793-2336
Great Bend (G-2602)
Mikes Testing & Salvage Inc ....F 620 938-2943
Chase (G-785)
Post & Mastin Well Service ....F 620 276-3442
Garden City (G-2257)
Rawhide Well Service LLC ....E 620 624-2902
Liberal (G-6358)
Rome Corporation ....E 785 625-1182
Hays (G-2901)
Schippers Oil Field Svcs LLC ....G....... 785 675-9991
Hoxie (G-3141)
Schlumberger Technology Corp ....C....... 785 841-5610
Lawrence (G-5103)
Scotts Well Service Inc ....G....... 785 254-7828
Roxbury (G-10257)

CONTRACTORS: Oil Field Haulage Svcs

Alliance Inc ....G....... 785 445-3701
Russell (G-10264)
Nicholas Water Service LLC ....F....... 620 930-7511
Medicine Lodge (G-7070)
Sterling Trucking Inc ....F 620 534-2461
Alden (G-59)
Wyoming Casing Service Inc ....F 620 793-9630
Great Bend (G-2664)

CONTRACTORS: Oil Field Mud Drilling Svcs

Thornton Air Rotary LLC ....G....... 620 879-2073
Caney (G-675)

CONTRACTORS: Oil Field Pipe Testing Svcs

Damm Pipe Testing LLC ....G....... 620 617-8990
Great Bend (G-2552)
Horizon Pipe Testing Inc ....G....... 785 726-3773
Ellis (G-1647)
Midwestern Oilfield Svcs LLC ....G....... 620 309-7027
Liberal (G-6342)
Werner Pipe Service Inc ....F 620 331-7384
Independence (G-3572)

CONTRACTORS: Oil/Gas Field Casing,Tube/Rod Running,Cut/Pull

Francis Casing Crews Inc ....G....... 620 793-9630
Great Bend (G-2567)
Francis Casing Crews Inc ....E 620 275-0443
Garden City (G-2166)
Kizzar Well Servicing Inc ....F 620 938-2555
Chase (G-784)

CONTRACTORS: Oil/Gas Well Construction, Rpr/Dismantling Svcs

Allied of Kansas Inc ....F 620 624-5937
Liberal (G-6276)
Basic Energy Services Inc ....E 316 262-3699
Wichita (G-13819)
Jakubs Ladder Inc ....G....... 316 214-8932
Derby (G-1255)
Merit Energy Company LLC ....E 620 356-3032
Ulysses (G-13306)
Merit Energy Company LLC ....E 620 629-4200
Liberal (G-6341)
MTS Quanta LLC ....E 913 383-0800
Overland Park (G-9061)

CONTRACTORS: On-Site Mobile Home Repair Svcs

Southborough Partners ....F 316 529-3200
Wichita (G-15621)

CONTRACTORS: On-Site Welding

Cliffs Welding Shop Inc ....G....... 785 543-5895
Phillipsburg (G-9780)
Earl Resse Welding ....G....... 620 624-6141
Liberal (G-6306)
Industrial Mfg & Repr Svc ....G....... 620 275-0481
Garden City (G-2202)
Jeffrey A Harris ....E 785 823-8760
Salina (G-10553)
K B Machine Shop Inc ....F 913 829-3100
Olathe (G-7822)
Leons Welding & Fabrication ....F 785 625-5736
Hays (G-2863)
Martin Welding ....G....... 620 545-7311
Clearwater (G-894)
Miller Welding Inc ....F 785 454-3425
Downs (G-1472)
Pihl Repair & Fabrication LLC ....G....... 785 668-2014
Falun (G-1928)
Premier Tillage Inc ....E 785 754-2381
Quinter (G-10184)
R L C Inc ....F 913 352-8744
Pleasanton (G-10001)
Rice Precision Mfg Inc ....E 785 594-2670
Baldwin City (G-367)
Specialty Fabrication Inc ....F 316 264-0603
Wichita (G-15636)
Wilkerson Crane Rental Inc ....E 913 238-7030
Lenexa (G-6230)

CONTRACTORS: Painting & Wall Covering

1st Nation Painting Inc ....F 785 966-2935
Mayetta (G-6913)
Columbia Construction Inc ....E 913 247-3114
Olathe (G-7601)
D&K Painting Inc ....F 785 537-4779
Manhattan (G-6610)
DA Painting Inc ....E 913 829-2075
Olathe (G-7639)
Genesis Solution LLC ....F 785 317-5710
Chapman (G-779)
K5 Painting Inc ....F 316 283-9612
Newton (G-7368)
Kdoll Koatings Inc ....G....... 620 456-2588
Conway Springs (G-1142)
Kushs Painting ....F 913 888-0230
Kansas City (G-4185)
Pelton Painting Inc ....F 785 242-7363
Ottawa (G-8303)
Pishny Real Estate Services ....F 913 227-0251
Lenexa (G-6059)
Rt Painting Inc ....F 913 390-6650
Olathe (G-8046)
Supernova Painting LLC ....F 785 850-0158
Atchison (G-265)
Total Renovation Group Inc ....F 913 491-5000
Lenexa (G-6186)
Unlimited Service Options LLC ....F 316 522-1503
Wichita (G-15859)
Woods Painting Co Inc ....F 913 897-3741
Stilwell (G-12180)

CONTRACTORS: Painting, Aircraft

Figeac Aero North America Inc ....D....... 316 634-2500
Wichita (G-14366)

CONTRACTORS: Painting, Commercial

Aaron & Page Painting Inc ....F 316 267-2224
Wichita (G-13593)
Birch Contracting Group LLC ....F 913 400-3975
Overland Park (G-8452)
Design Source Flooring LLC ....E 913 387-5858
Lenexa (G-5813)
Forshee Painting Contractors ....D....... 316 263-7777
Wichita (G-14402)
Gray & Company Inc ....E 785 232-0913
Topeka (G-12644)
J F McGivern Inc ....E 785 354-1787
Topeka (G-12731)
Joseph Stowers Painting Inc ....E 913 722-2534
Shawnee Mission (G-11502)
Koehn Painting Co LLC ....E 316 283-9612
Newton (G-7373)
Maas Paint and Paper LLC ....F 785 643-4790
Hutchinson (G-3362)
OFlynn Contracting Inc ....F 316 524-2500
Wichita (G-15211)
Warren Moore Painting LLC ....F 913 558-8549
Shawnee Mission (G-11993)
Wildcat Painting Inc ....F 316 263-8076
Wichita (G-16050)
Zack Taylor Contracting Inc ....F 785 235-8704
Topeka (G-13260)

CONTRACTORS: Painting, Commercial, Exterior

Hardister Painting and Dctg..................F....... 785 842-2832
Lawrence *(G-4889)*
Ral Contractors.......................................F....... 913 888-8128
Shawnee Mission *(G-11777)*

CONTRACTORS: Painting, Commercial, Interior

Window Design Company......................G....... 785 582-2888
Silver Lake *(G-12030)*

CONTRACTORS: Painting, Indl

Albers Finshg & Solutions LLC.............F....... 316 542-0405
Cheney *(G-788)*
Hartwood Painting..................................E....... 316 554-7510
Wichita *(G-14566)*
Performance Contracting Inc................E....... 913 928-2850
Lenexa *(G-6053)*
Pro-Kleen Inc...E....... 316 775-6898
Augusta *(G-339)*
Rob Carrolls Sndblst & Pntg..................E....... 620 442-1361
Arkansas City *(G-175)*

CONTRACTORS: Painting, Residential

AP Roofing Specialty Codings..............F....... 620 532-1076
Kingman *(G-4582)*
Atlas Painting...E....... 316 686-1546
Wichita *(G-13766)*
Ben Kitchens Painting Co Inc................F....... 785 375-3288
Junction City *(G-3673)*
Citywide Painting & Rmdlg LLC.............F....... 913 238-9749
Leawood *(G-5352)*
Gecko Painting Inc..................................E....... 913 782-7000
Olathe *(G-7725)*
Johnson County Pntg & Hm Repr.........E....... 913 631-5252
Fairway *(G-1911)*
Luke Kushs Painting..............................F....... 913 888-0230
Shawnee Mission *(G-11581)*
Paint Pro Inc...F....... 913 685-4089
Overland Park *(G-9138)*
Premier Painting Co LLC.......................F....... 913 897-7000
Overland Park *(G-9181)*
R B P Inc...F....... 316 303-9606
Wichita *(G-15402)*
Wagle Painting..F....... 316 682-2531
Wichita *(G-15915)*

CONTRACTORS: Parking Facility Eqpt Installation

National Park Service.............................F....... 620 285-6911
Larned *(G-4708)*

CONTRACTORS: Parking Lot Maintenance

Apac-Kansas Inc......................................D....... 316 522-4881
Wichita *(G-13715)*
Apac-Kansas Inc......................................D....... 316 524-5200
Wichita *(G-13716)*
Icg Inc..E....... 913 461-8759
Leawood *(G-5433)*
Schellers Inc..F....... 620 342-3990
Emporia *(G-1824)*
Summer Snow LLC...................................E....... 785 706-1003
Manhattan *(G-6816)*

CONTRACTORS: Patio & Deck Construction & Repair

Champion Opco LLC...............................F....... 316 636-4200
Wichita *(G-13996)*
Discount Siding Supply LP....................F....... 785 625-4619
Hays *(G-2788)*
Mid America Exteriors LLC....................F....... 316 265-5444
Wichita *(G-15066)*
Mid-Continent Thermal-Guard...............E....... 316 838-4044
Wichita *(G-15079)*
Midwest Siding Inc...................................E....... 785 825-0606
Salina *(G-10603)*
Pools Plus..F....... 785 823-7665
Salina *(G-10636)*
Window Design Company......................G....... 785 582-2888
Silver Lake *(G-12030)*
Wood RE New Joco Inc..........................G....... 913 661-9663
Olathe *(G-8159)*

CONTRACTORS: Pavement Marking

C-Hawkk Construction Inc.....................F....... 785 542-1800
Eudora *(G-1872)*
Nu-Line Company Inc.............................F....... 316 942-0990
Wichita *(G-15199)*
Roadsafe Traffic Systems Inc...............E....... 316 322-3070
El Dorado *(G-1600)*
Traffic Control Services Inc..................F....... 316 448-0402
Wichita *(G-15784)*
Twin Traffic Marking Corp.....................E....... 913 428-2575
Kansas City *(G-4480)*

CONTRACTORS: Petroleum Storage Tanks, Pumping & Draining

Utility Contractors Inc.............................E....... 316 942-1253
Wichita *(G-15866)*

CONTRACTORS: Pile Driving

L G Barcus and Sons Inc.......................D....... 913 621-1100
Kansas City *(G-4188)*

CONTRACTORS: Pipe & Boiler Insulating

Accurate Construction Inc.....................F....... 620 275-0429
Garden City *(G-2097)*
Brace Integrated Services Inc...............E....... 316 832-0292
Wichita *(G-13878)*
Industrial Insulation Svcs Inc................D....... 316 321-5358
El Dorado *(G-1570)*

CONTRACTORS: Plastering, Plain or Ornamental

Florence Bob Contractor Inc..................D....... 785 357-0341
Topeka *(G-12618)*
Kd Christian Construction Co...............E....... 913 451-0466
Stilwell *(G-12161)*

CONTRACTORS: Plastic Wall Tile Installation

Designplast Inc...E....... 785 825-7714
Salina *(G-10475)*

CONTRACTORS: Plumbing

A M Plumbing Inc......................................E....... 316 945-8326
Wichita *(G-13589)*
Action Plumbing Inc.................................F....... 913 631-1188
Shawnee Mission *(G-11071)*
Action Plumbing of Lawrence................F....... 785 843-5670
Lawrence *(G-4718)*
American Mechanical Inc........................E....... 316 262-1100
Andover *(G-79)*
Armstrong Plumbing Inc.........................F....... 316 942-9535
Wichita *(G-13734)*
B & B Plumbing Heating & AC................F....... 785 472-5239
Ellsworth *(G-1657)*
B & W Electric Inc.....................................F....... 785 337-2598
Hanover *(G-2709)*
Beavers Plumbing L L C.........................F....... 316 619-6119
Augusta *(G-311)*
Bills Plumbing Service LLC...................F....... 913 829-8213
Olathe *(G-7555)*
Bobs Plumbing & Heating Inc................F....... 785 539-4155
Manhattan *(G-6565)*
Brand Plumbing Inc..................................F....... 316 942-2306
Wichita *(G-13884)*
Burnap Bros Inc..F....... 620 342-2645
Emporia *(G-1712)*
Butler Plumbing & Heating.....................F....... 785 456-8345
Wamego *(G-13407)*
Central Consolidated Inc........................C....... 316 945-0797
Wichita *(G-13978)*
Central Mech Svcs Mnhattan Inc...........F....... 785 776-9206
Manhattan *(G-6582)*
City of Hutchinson....................................B....... 620 694-2632
Hutchinson *(G-3240)*
Commercial Trade Services LLC...........F....... 316 721-5432
Wichita *(G-14073)*
Conklin Plumbing LLC............................F....... 785 806-5827
Osage City *(G-8182)*
Custom Sheet Metal & Roofg Inc...........E....... 785 357-6200
Topeka *(G-12539)*
DAgostino Mech Contrs Inc....................D....... 913 384-5170
Kansas City *(G-3952)*
Daves Service & Repair Inc....................G....... 620 662-8285
Hutchinson *(G-3257)*
David Cobler...F....... 785 234-3384
Topeka *(G-12547)*
David Lies Plumbing Inc.........................F....... 316 945-0117
Wichita *(G-14174)*
E & M Plumbing Inc.................................F....... 620 662-1281
Hutchinson *(G-3271)*
Eisenbarth Plumbing Inc........................F....... 785 336-2361
Seneca *(G-10865)*
Floyd Mechanical Corporation...............F....... 316 262-3556
Wichita *(G-14394)*
Fred Pflumm Plumbing Inc....................E....... 913 441-6309
Shawnee Mission *(G-11379)*
Frederick Plumbing & Heating...............F....... 316 262-3713
Wichita *(G-14416)*
G Coopers Inc...F....... 785 267-4100
Topeka *(G-12630)*
Garrison Plumbing Inc............................F....... 913 768-1311
Olathe *(G-7723)*
Glassman Corporation............................D....... 785 625-2115
Hays *(G-2817)*
Grabill Plumbing Inc................................E....... 913 432-9660
Kansas City *(G-4042)*
H & R Plumbing Inc..................................F....... 785 233-4427
Topeka *(G-12655)*
Heartland Plumbing Inc..........................F....... 913 856-5846
Gardner *(G-2350)*
Heinen P-H-E Services Inc....................F....... 785 945-6668
Valley Falls *(G-13365)*
Jayhawk Plumbing Inc............................F....... 785 865-5225
Lawrence *(G-4920)*
Jf Denney Inc..E....... 913 772-8994
Leavenworth *(G-5257)*
K & K Industries Inc.................................E....... 906 293-5242
Junction City *(G-3709)*
Kastl Plumbing Inc...................................E....... 785 841-2112
Lawrence *(G-4938)*
KB Complete Inc.......................................F....... 913 722-6835
Shawnee Mission *(G-11522)*
King Enterprises Inc.................................F....... 620 624-3332
Liberal *(G-6329)*
Kinney Plumbing Co Inc..........................E....... 913 782-2840
Olathe *(G-7841)*
McCann Plumbing & Heating Inc............E....... 913 727-6225
Leavenworth *(G-5268)*
Mels Pump & Plumbing...........................F....... 785 632-3392
Clay Center *(G-872)*
Mid-American Water & Plbg Inc..............E....... 785 537-1072
Manhattan *(G-6741)*
Midstate Mechanical Inc..........................F....... 785 537-4343
Manhattan *(G-6744)*
Miller Plumbing Co Inc............................F....... 913 851-1333
Bucyrus *(G-604)*
P & W Incorporated..................................E....... 316 267-4277
Wichita *(G-15247)*
Plumbing By Carlson Inc.........................E....... 785 232-0515
Topeka *(G-12981)*
Plumbing Specialists Inc.........................E....... 316 945-8383
Wichita *(G-15308)*
Polestar AC & Plbg Htg...........................F....... 913 432-3342
Olathe *(G-7991)*
R & R Street Plbg Htg & Elec..................F....... 785 524-4551
Lincoln *(G-6385)*
Randal J Steiner.......................................F....... 785 539-4155
Manhattan *(G-6786)*
Reddi Services Inc...................................D....... 913 287-5005
Shawnee Mission *(G-11783)*
Richard Nachbar Plumbing Inc...............F....... 913 268-9488
Lenexa *(G-6109)*
Riden Service Company Inc....................F....... 913 432-8495
Overland Park *(G-9241)*
River City Mechanical Inc........................F....... 316 682-2672
Wichita *(G-15471)*
Robert J Hamilton Inc...............................E....... 913 888-4262
Overland Park *(G-9250)*
Rodriguez Mech Contrs Inc......................D....... 913 281-1814
Kansas City *(G-4386)*
Royal Flush Plumbing LLC......................F....... 316 794-2656
Goddard *(G-2453)*
Santa Fe Trails Plumbing Inc..................F....... 913 441-1441
Shawnee Mission *(G-11834)*
Standard Plumbing Inc.............................F....... 785 776-5012
Manhattan *(G-6807)*
Superior Plumbing & Heating Co............E....... 785 827-5611
Salina *(G-10728)*
Superior Plumbing of Wichita..................F....... 316 684-8349
Wichita *(G-15696)*
Systems 4 Inc...E....... 785 823-9119
Salina *(G-10730)*
Tatro Plumbing Co Inc.............................F....... 620 277-2167
Garden City *(G-2296)*
Tatro Plumbing Co Inc.............................E....... 620 356-5319
Ulysses *(G-13322)*

Teds Plumbing LLC ....F 620 356-5319
Ulysses *(G-13323)*
Tl Enterprises Inc ....F 785 448-7100
Wichita *(G-15770)*
Vielhauer Plumbing Inc ....F 913 268-9385
Shawnee Mission *(G-11978)*
W H Debrick Co Inc ....F 913 294-3281
Paola *(G-9595)*
Walton Plumbing & Heating Inc ....F 620 278-3462
Sterling *(G-12132)*
Western Enterprise Inc ....F 913 342-0505
Kansas City *(G-4535)*
Wheatland Contracting LLC ....F 913 833-2304
Effingham *(G-1524)*
Winfield Plumbing & Heating ....F 620 221-2210
Winfield *(G-16188)*

CONTRACTORS: Post Disaster Renovations

Belfor USA Group Inc ....E 316 260-4087
Park City *(G-9604)*
Cleaning By Lamunyon Inc ....F 785 632-1259
Clay Center *(G-855)*
Damage Ctrl & Restoration Inc ....E 913 722-0228
Kansas City *(G-3954)*
Givens Cleaning Contractors ....F 316 265-1315
Wichita *(G-14468)*
Lamunyon Clg & Restoration ....F 785 632-1259
Clay Center *(G-870)*
Phoenix Restoration Service ....E 620 276-6994
Garden City *(G-2254)*
Phoenix Rnvtion Rstoration Inc ....E 913 599-0055
Stilwell *(G-12171)*
Preferred Contg Systems Co ....F 913 341-0111
Leawood *(G-5525)*
Repairs Unlimited Inc ....F 913 262-6937
Kansas City *(G-4370)*
Stovers Restoration Inc ....F 316 686-5005
Maize *(G-6521)*

CONTRACTORS: Precast Concrete Struct Framing & Panel Placing

Crossland Prefab LLC ....E 620 429-1414
Columbus *(G-1073)*
Wichita Concrete Pipe Inc ....E 316 838-8651
Wichita *(G-15989)*

CONTRACTORS: Prefabricated Window & Door Installation

Alenco Inc ....E 913 438-1902
Lenexa *(G-5638)*
All Wther Win Doors Siding Inc ....F 913 262-4380
Overland Park *(G-8367)*
Champion Opco LLC ....F 316 636-4200
Wichita *(G-13996)*
Columbia Industries Inc ....E 785 227-3351
Lindsborg *(G-6396)*
Discount Siding Supply LP ....F 785 625-4619
Hays *(G-2788)*
Home Stl Siding & Windows LLC ....F 785 625-8622
Hays *(G-2849)*
Mid America Exteriors LLC ....F 316 265-5444
Wichita *(G-15066)*
Mid-AM Building Supply Inc ....D 913 592-4313
Spring Hill *(G-12089)*
Mid-Continent Thermal-Guard ....E 316 838-4044
Wichita *(G-15079)*
Midway Sales & Distrg Inc ....F 785 537-4665
Manhattan *(G-6745)*
Midwest Siding Incorporated ....E 785 825-5576
Salina *(G-10602)*
Midwest Siding Inc ....E 785 825-0606
Salina *(G-10603)*
Pratt Glass Inc ....F 620 672-6463
Pratt *(G-10139)*
Worldwide Windows ....F 785 826-1701
Salina *(G-10773)*

CONTRACTORS: Process Piping

Piping Technology Co ....D 620 241-3592
McPherson *(G-7016)*

CONTRACTORS: Refrigeration

Liebert Brothers Electric Co ....F 620 251-0299
Coffeyville *(G-956)*
Marick Inc ....E 316 941-9575
Colwich *(G-1098)*
Srh Mechanical Contractors Inc ....F 785 842-0301
Lawrence *(G-5116)*
Weber Refrigeration & Htg Inc ....F 620 225-7700
Dodge City *(G-1452)*
Williams-Carver Company Inc ....E 913 236-4949
Kansas City *(G-4544)*

CONTRACTORS: Renovation, Aircraft Interiors

Emerald Aerospace Holdings LLC ....D 316 440-6966
Wichita *(G-14274)*
Emerald Aerospace Services LLC ....E 316 644-4284
Wichita *(G-14275)*

CONTRACTORS: Roof Repair

Chambless Roofing Inc ....F 620 275-8410
Scott City *(G-10807)*
E3 Roofing Group Inc ....F 913 782-3332
Olathe *(G-7664)*

CONTRACTORS: Roofing

A/R Roofing LLC ....F 620 672-2999
Pratt *(G-10090)*
Allstate Roofing Inc ....F 913 782-2000
Olathe *(G-7521)*
American Roofing Inc ....E 913 772-1776
Leavenworth *(G-5201)*
AR Commercial Roofing LLC ....F 620 672-3332
Pratt *(G-10098)*
Arch Design Builders LLC ....E 913 599-5565
Overland Park *(G-8392)*
Arr Roofing LLC ....D 913 829-0447
Olathe *(G-7533)*
Beck Roofing & Construction ....F 316 684-7663
Derby *(G-1223)*
Bill Davis Roofing ....F 913 764-4449
Olathe *(G-7554)*
Blackburns All Star Roofing ....E 913 321-3456
Kansas City *(G-3863)*
Borens Roofing Inc ....F 620 365-7663
Iola *(G-3588)*
Brad H Allen Roofing Inc ....F 785 423-3861
Lawrence *(G-4764)*
Buckley Roofing Company Inc ....D 316 838-9321
Wichita *(G-13904)*
Canadian West Inc ....E 913 422-0099
Kansas City *(G-3887)*
Centurion Industries Inc ....B 620 378-4401
Fredonia *(G-2028)*
Commercial Rofg Spcialists LLC ....F 316 304-1423
Wichita *(G-14072)*
D V Douglass Roofing Inc ....E 620 276-7474
Garden City *(G-2141)*
Davinci Roofscapes LLC ....E 913 599-0766
Lenexa *(G-5804)*
Delta Innovative Services Inc ....D 913 371-7100
Kansas City *(G-3967)*
Dm Roofing ....F 620 515-0015
Coffeyville *(G-934)*
Expert Roofing LLC ....F 785 286-1999
Topeka *(G-12588)*
Flint Hills Roof Service ....F 785 238-8609
Chapman *(G-778)*
Geisler Roofing Inc ....F 785 243-7298
Concordia *(G-1114)*
Great Plains Roofg Shtmtl Inc ....D 913 677-4679
Kansas City *(G-4046)*
Guilfoyle Roofing ....F 785 233-9315
Topeka *(G-12653)*
Gwaltney Inc ....D 620 225-2622
Dodge City *(G-1368)*
Gwaltney Inc ....E 785 537-8008
Manhattan *(G-6648)*
Homeland Roofing and Cnstr LLC ....F 316 832-9901
Wichita *(G-14632)*
Industrial Roofg Met Works Inc ....F 316 262-4758
Wichita *(G-14687)*
J B Turner Sons ....E 785 233-9603
Herington *(G-2977)*
Jayhawk Roofing & Supply Co ....E 785 825-5466
Salina *(G-10552)*
L J Herzberg Roofing Co Inc ....F 316 529-2222
Wichita *(G-14906)*
Larry Booze Roofing Co Inc ....F 316 263-7796
Wichita *(G-14926)*
Luminous Neon Inc ....E 913 780-3330
Olathe *(G-7867)*
Mahaney Group Inc ....D 316 262-4768
Wichita *(G-15001)*
Martin Roofing Company Inc ....E 316 524-3293
Wichita *(G-15014)*
Maxines Inc ....F 620 669-8189
Hutchinson *(G-3367)*
McLaughlin Roofing LLC ....F 785 764-9582
Oskaloosa *(G-8229)*
Midwest Coating Inc ....E 785 232-4276
Topeka *(G-12895)*
Midwest Roofing Services Inc ....E 316 262-4758
Wichita *(G-15099)*
Mt 3 Corporation ....E 785 843-3433
Perry *(G-9772)*
Murphy & Sons Roofing ....F 913 287-2116
Kansas City *(G-4273)*
New Image Roofing LLC ....E 316 201-1180
Wichita *(G-15167)*
Ponton Construction Inc ....F 785 823-9584
Salina *(G-10635)*
Premier Contracting Inc ....D 913 362-4141
Kansas City *(G-4330)*
Professional Roofing Systems ....E 785 392-0603
Minneapolis *(G-7122)*
Protec Construction & Sup LLC ....E 913 441-2121
Edwardsville *(G-1513)*
Ronans Roofing Inc ....E 913 384-0901
Lenexa *(G-6113)*
Roofing Services Unlimited ....F 316 284-9900
Newton *(G-7411)*
Roofing Solutions Inc ....F 913 897-1840
Overland Park *(G-9256)*
Roofmasters Roofing Co Inc ....E 785 462-6642
Colby *(G-1036)*
Scott Mesler ....F 785 749-0462
Lawrence *(G-5106)*
Summit Roofing & Contg LLC ....F 417 873-9191
Frontenac *(G-2065)*
T R Management Inc ....E 785 233-9603
Topeka *(G-13130)*
Total Renovation Group Inc ....F 913 491-5000
Lenexa *(G-6186)*
Vincent Roofing Inc ....E 785 233-9603
Topeka *(G-13225)*
Washington Companies Inc ....F 620 792-2430
Great Bend *(G-2656)*
Weddle and Sons Inc ....E 785 532-8347
Manhattan *(G-6848)*
Western Roofing Co Services ....E 816 931-1075
Kansas City *(G-4536)*
Wichita Roofing and Rmdlg Inc ....F 316 943-0600
Wichita *(G-16021)*
Wray & Sons Roofing Inc ....F 620 663-7107
Hutchinson *(G-3493)*
Wray Roofing Inc ....D 316 283-6840
Newton *(G-7430)*

CONTRACTORS: Roustabout Svcs

Ally Servicing LLC ....C 316 652-6301
Wichita *(G-13679)*
Bojack Roustabout LLC ....G 785 798-3504
Ness City *(G-7252)*
G & S Roustabout Service LLC ....G 620 213-0172
Medicine Lodge *(G-7061)*
Gilmores Roustabout Service ....F 620 624-0452
Liberal *(G-6313)*
Gyp Hills Roustabout LLC ....G 620 886-0931
Medicine Lodge *(G-7062)*
Passmore Bros Inc ....E 620 544-2189
Hugoton *(G-3175)*
Richs Roustabout Service Inc ....G 785 798-3323
Ness City *(G-7266)*
Total Lease Service Inc ....G 785 735-9520
Hays *(G-2920)*
Treco Inc ....E 620 544-2606
Hugoton *(G-3178)*

CONTRACTORS: Safety & Security Eqpt

4pc LLC ....G 316 833-6906
Augusta *(G-299)*
AG Services LLC ....F 620 662-5406
Hutchinson *(G-3194)*
Midwest Tinting Inc ....F 913 384-2665
Overland Park *(G-9036)*
Simplex Time Recorder LLC ....E 316 686-6363
Wichita *(G-15595)*
Westar Industries Inc ....C 785 575-6507
Topeka *(G-13240)*

CONTRACTORS: Sandblasting Svc, Building Exteriors

Cunningham Sndblst Pntg Co Inc.........F 620 848-3030
Riverton *(G-10211)*
Kdoll Koatings Inc.........G....... 620 456-2588
Conway Springs *(G-1142)*
Koehn Painting Co LLC.........E 316 283-9612
Newton *(G-7373)*
Pro-Kleen Inc.........E 316 775-6898
Augusta *(G-339)*
Pro-Kleen Inc.........F 316 253-7556
Augusta *(G-340)*
Rob Carrolls Sndblst & Pntg.........E 620 442-1361
Arkansas City *(G-175)*

CONTRACTORS: Septic System

Hertel Tank Service Inc.........G....... 785 628-2445
Hays *(G-2841)*
Paronto Mall Construction Inc.........F 785 632-2484
Clay Center *(G-875)*
Piping Contractors Kansas Inc.........F 785 233-4321
Topeka *(G-12976)*
Salina Concrete Products Inc.........F 316 943-3241
Wichita *(G-15510)*
Trigard Vaults.........F 785 527-5595
Belleville *(G-468)*

CONTRACTORS: Sheet Metal Work, NEC

API Americas Inc.........D....... 732 382-6800
Lawrence *(G-4737)*
Barnes & Dodge Inc.........E 913 321-6444
Lenexa *(G-5687)*
CD Custom Enterprises LLC.........F 316 804-4520
Newton *(G-7327)*
Custom Sheet Metal & Roofg Inc.........E 785 357-6200
Topeka *(G-12539)*
Debackers Inc.........E 785 232-6999
Topeka *(G-12550)*
Givens Investments LLC.........F 620 662-1784
Hutchinson *(G-3300)*
Hartley Sheet Metal Co Inc.........F 620 251-4330
Coffeyville *(G-943)*
Modern Air Conditioning Inc.........E 620 342-7577
Emporia *(G-1797)*
Pestinger Heating & AC Inc.........E 785 827-6361
Salina *(G-10634)*
Ray Omo Inc.........E 620 227-3101
Lenexa *(G-6091)*
Sheet Metal Contractors Inc.........E 913 397-9130
Olathe *(G-8061)*
Stevenson Company Inc.........F 785 233-0691
Topeka *(G-13097)*
Stevenson Company Inc.........F 785 233-1303
Topeka *(G-13098)*
Systems 4 Inc.........E 785 823-9119
Salina *(G-10730)*
TWC Services Inc.........E 316 265-7831
Wichita *(G-15820)*
Waddles Heating & Cooling.........E 785 827-2621
Salina *(G-10755)*
Wsm Industries Inc.........C....... 316 942-9412
Wichita *(G-16075)*
Wsm Investments Inc.........C....... 316 942-9412
Wichita *(G-16076)*

CONTRACTORS: Sheet metal Work, Architectural

Rice Precision Mfg Inc.........E 785 594-2670
Baldwin City *(G-367)*

CONTRACTORS: Sidewalk

Paronto Mall Construction Inc.........F 785 632-2484
Clay Center *(G-875)*

CONTRACTORS: Siding

Alenco Inc.........E 913 438-1902
Lenexa *(G-5638)*
All States Windows Siding LLC.........E 913 800-5211
Overland Park *(G-8366)*
All States Windows Siding LLC.........E 316 444-1220
Wichita *(G-13666)*
Champion Opco LLC.........F 316 636-4200
Wichita *(G-13996)*
Discount Siding Supply LP.........F 785 625-4619
Hays *(G-2788)*
Jordan Companies Inc.........E 316 943-6222
Wichita *(G-14771)*
Martinek & Flynn Wholesale Inc.........E 785 233-6666
Topeka *(G-12862)*
Mid-Continent Thermal-Guard.........E 316 838-4044
Wichita *(G-15079)*
Midwest Siding Incorporated.........E 785 825-5576
Salina *(G-10602)*
Midwest Siding Inc.........E 785 825-0606
Salina *(G-10603)*
Paint Masters Inc.........F 316 683-5203
Wichita *(G-15253)*
Paint Pro Inc.........F 913 685-4089
Overland Park *(G-9138)*
Reno Fabricating & Sls Co Inc.........E 620 663-1269
Hutchinson *(G-3426)*
Rhino Builders Inc.........F 913 722-4353
Kansas City *(G-4376)*
Western Aluminum & Glass Co.........F 785 625-2418
Hays *(G-2931)*
Wildcat Gttering Exteriors Inc.........F 785 485-2194
Manhattan *(G-6855)*
Wood Haven Inc.........G....... 785 597-5618
Perry *(G-9775)*

CONTRACTORS: Single-Family Home Fire Damage Repair

Birch Contracting Group LLC.........F 913 400-3975
Overland Park *(G-8452)*
C & P Enterprises Inc.........E 785 628-6712
Hays *(G-2762)*
Hudson Inc.........E 620 232-1145
Pittsburg *(G-9879)*
National Ctstrphe Rstrtion Inc.........F 913 663-4111
Shawnee Mission *(G-11673)*
National Ctstrphe Rstrtion Inc.........D....... 316 636-5700
Wichita *(G-15149)*
Paul Davis Restoratio of Great.........E 785 842-0351
Lawrence *(G-5058)*
Repairs Unlimited Inc.........F 913 262-6937
Kansas City *(G-4370)*

CONTRACTORS: Single-family Home General Remodeling

Alenco Inc.........E 913 438-1902
Lenexa *(G-5638)*
Appletech Design & Cnstr Inc.........F 785 776-3530
Manhattan *(G-6543)*
Augustine Home Improvement Co.........E 913 362-4707
Shawnee Mission *(G-11134)*
Borton Corporation.........D....... 620 669-8211
South Hutchinson *(G-12056)*
Carley Construction Co Inc.........F 785 456-2882
Wamego *(G-13408)*
Custom Renovation.........F 620 544-2653
Hugoton *(G-3158)*
Dade Construction LLC.........F 913 208-1968
Kansas City *(G-3951)*
Damage Ctrl & Restoration Inc.........E 913 722-0228
Kansas City *(G-3954)*
Emporia Construction & Rmdlg.........E 620 341-3131
Emporia *(G-1738)*
Fuqua Construction Inc.........F 620 585-2270
Inman *(G-3582)*
Genesis Solution LLC.........F 785 317-5710
Chapman *(G-779)*
Grace Construction & Assoc Inc.........F 316 617-1729
Derby *(G-1249)*
Green Hills Inc.........F 316 686-7673
Wichita *(G-14509)*
Guthridge/Nighswonger Corp.........F 316 264-7900
Wichita *(G-14529)*
Home Center Construction Inc.........E 620 231-5607
Pittsburg *(G-9877)*
Integrity Siding & Window Co.........F 316 993-6426
Wichita *(G-14706)*
James Gruver Construction Inc.........E 620 663-7982
Hutchinson *(G-3340)*
Jmar Construction Inc.........F 620 922-3690
Edna *(G-1494)*
Kansas Affordable Housing Corp.........E 316 942-4848
Wichita *(G-14785)*
Klein Construction Inc.........F 316 262-3313
Park City *(G-9626)*
Line Construction Company.........F 913 341-1212
Shawnee Mission *(G-11575)*
Mack Pickens General Cont.........E 316 778-1131
Benton *(G-519)*
Mark Borecky Construction.........F 620 259-6655
Hutchinson *(G-3364)*
McQuaid Brothers Rmdlg Co Inc.........E 913 894-9128
Shawnee Mission *(G-11610)*
Midland Exteriors LLC.........F 785 537-5130
Manhattan *(G-6743)*
Mill Valley Construction Inc.........F 913 764-6539
Olathe *(G-7900)*
Mitchell-Markowitz Cnstr.........E 620 343-6840
Emporia *(G-1796)*
Mm Property MGT & Rmdlg LLC.........F 913 871-6867
Kansas City *(G-4265)*
My Contracting LLC.........F 913 747-9015
Olathe *(G-7910)*
Nb Remodeling LLC.........F 785 749-1855
Lawrence *(G-5036)*
Netco Construction Co Inc.........E 316 942-2062
Wichita *(G-15162)*
New Dimension Pdts Emporia Inc.........E 620 342-6412
Emporia *(G-1801)*
Paint Masters Inc.........F 316 683-5203
Wichita *(G-15253)*
Paint Pro Inc.........F 913 685-4089
Overland Park *(G-9138)*
Ponton Construction Inc.........F 785 823-9584
Salina *(G-10635)*
Preferred Contg Systems Co.........F 913 341-0111
Leawood *(G-5525)*
Pro Home Remodeling LLC.........F 316 821-9818
Wichita *(G-15352)*
Quality Remodeler.........F 785 823-7665
Salina *(G-10646)*
Rhino Builders Inc.........F 913 722-4353
Kansas City *(G-4376)*
S & A Construction Inc.........F 316 558-8422
Wichita *(G-15498)*
Sears Home Imprv Pdts Inc.........E 913 438-5911
Shawnee Mission *(G-11845)*
Shawnee Mission Builders LLC.........G....... 913 631-7020
Shawnee Mission *(G-11854)*
Smart Home Innovations LLC.........F 913 339-8641
Kansas City *(G-4426)*
Southwestern Remodeling Contrs.........E 316 263-1239
Wichita *(G-15633)*
Total Renovation Group Inc.........F 913 491-5000
Lenexa *(G-6186)*
Weisbender Contracting Inc.........G....... 785 776-5034
Manhattan *(G-6849)*
Winston-Brown Construction Co.........E 785 271-1661
Topeka *(G-13246)*

CONTRACTORS: Skylight Installation

Strategic Global Services LLC.........F 316 655-2761
Wichita *(G-15675)*

CONTRACTORS: Solar Energy Eqpt

Brite Energy Solar Inc.........E 785 856-9936
Lawrence *(G-4768)*
Kc Solar LLC.........F 913 444-9593
Overland Park *(G-8909)*

CONTRACTORS: Solar Reflecting Insulation Film Installation

Wagner Interior Systems Inc.........E 913 647-6622
Kansas City *(G-4528)*

CONTRACTORS: Sound Eqpt Installation

Entertainment Specialties.........F 620 342-3322
Emporia *(G-1750)*
Gonzales Cmmunications Inc GCI.........E 913 685-4866
Overland Park *(G-8765)*
McClelland Sound Inc.........F 316 265-8686
Wichita *(G-15021)*

CONTRACTORS: Special Trades, NEC

Arg Contracting LLC.........F 913 441-1992
Lenexa *(G-5660)*
Hutchinson Theatre Guild.........F 620 662-9202
Hutchinson *(G-3326)*
Insco Environmental Inc.........F 912 422-8001
Shawnee *(G-10974)*
Platinum Contracting LLC.........F 913 210-2003
Shawnee Mission *(G-11737)*
Progressive Contractors Inc.........D....... 785 235-3032
Topeka *(G-12991)*

CONTRACTORS: Specialized Public Building

Quality Trust Inc .... E 785 375-6372
Junction City *(G-3745)*

CONTRACTORS: Sprinkler System

Karcher Investments Inc .... F 785 452-2850
Salina *(G-10568)*
Stans Sprinkler Service Inc .... E 800 570-5932
Wichita *(G-15654)*

CONTRACTORS: Stone Masonry

Lusker Masonry .... F 620 231-9899
Frontenac *(G-2058)*
Mason Stone Inc .... F 316 744-3884
Wichita *(G-15017)*
Richard L Pride .... F 785 485-2900
Riley *(G-10207)*

CONTRACTORS: Storage Tank Erection, Metal

Southwest and Associates Inc .... D 620 463-5631
Burrton *(G-650)*

CONTRACTORS: Structural Iron Work, Structural

Carl Harris Co Inc .... E 316 267-8700
Wichita *(G-13950)*

CONTRACTORS: Structural Steel Erection

Building Erection Svcs Co Inc .... E 913 764-5560
Olathe *(G-7568)*
Building Solutions LLC .... F 620 225-1199
Dodge City *(G-1314)*
CDI Industrial Mech Contrs Inc .... C 913 287-0334
Kansas City *(G-3898)*
Ceo Enterprises Inc .... F 913 432-8046
Shawnee Mission *(G-11214)*
Confab Inc .... E 316 321-5358
El Dorado *(G-1548)*
Energy and Envmtl Systems Inc .... E 913 845-3553
Tonganoxie *(G-12260)*
Frank Construction Company .... E 785 825-4213
Salina *(G-10505)*
Gerard Tank & Steel Inc .... E 785 243-3895
Concordia *(G-1116)*
Griffith Steel Erection Inc .... E 316 941-4455
Wichita *(G-14519)*
Jack Foster Co Erectors .... E 316 263-2901
Wichita *(G-14742)*
Leiser Construction LLC .... F 620 437-2747
Madison *(G-6503)*
Lift Inc .... F 913 287-4343
Kansas City *(G-4203)*
Panhandle Steel Erectors Inc .... F 620 271-9878
Garden City *(G-2247)*
Schuff Steel Company .... F 913 677-2485
Overland Park *(G-9284)*
Welco Services Inc .... E 620 241-3000
McPherson *(G-7041)*
XCEL Erectors Inc .... F 913 664-7400
Overland Park *(G-9510)*

CONTRACTORS: Stucco, Interior

Custom Stucco LLC .... F 913 294-3100
Paola *(G-9550)*
Reynolds Construction Inc .... E 913 780-6624
Olathe *(G-8029)*

CONTRACTORS: Svc Station Eqpt Installation, Maint & Repair

Broyles Inc .... F 620 473-3835
Humboldt *(G-3182)*
Pro Carwash Systems Inc .... F 316 788-9933
Derby *(G-1266)*

CONTRACTORS: Svc Well Drilling Svcs

Chase Contractors Inc .... G 620 431-2142
Chanute *(G-714)*
Cheyenne Well Service Inc .... F 785 798-2282
Ness City *(G-7256)*
Shawnee Well Service Inc .... F 620 254-7893
Attica *(G-279)*
Whitham Frank E Trust 2 .... F 620 375-2229
Leoti *(G-6261)*

CONTRACTORS: Terrazzo Work

Kc Restoration LLC .... F 913 766-2200
Olathe *(G-7832)*

CONTRACTORS: Tile Installation, Ceramic

Austin Tile Inc .... F 913 829-6607
Olathe *(G-7542)*
Carpet Factory Outlet Inc .... E 913 261-6800
Kansas City *(G-3892)*
Metro Tile Contractors Inc .... E 913 381-7770
Lenexa *(G-5996)*
Turner Ceramic Tile Inc .... F 913 441-6161
Kansas City *(G-4477)*

CONTRACTORS: Trenching

Allen Trenching Inc .... F 316 721-6300
Wichita *(G-13669)*
Callaway Electric .... G 785 632-5588
Clay Center *(G-847)*
Crystal Trenching Inc .... F 913 677-1233
Shawnee *(G-10937)*
Jmar Construction Inc .... F 620 922-3690
Edna *(G-1494)*
M & D Excavating Inc .... F 785 628-3169
Hays *(G-2867)*
Rdr Excavating Inc .... F 785 582-4645
Topeka *(G-13001)*
Toms Ditching & Backhoe Inc .... F 620 879-2215
Caney *(G-676)*
Torgeson Trenching Inc .... E 785 233-3060
Topeka *(G-13193)*
Western Kansas Valley Inc .... F 785 852-4606
Sharon Springs *(G-10902)*

CONTRACTORS: Tuck Pointing & Restoration

Five Star Masonry LLC .... E 785 484-9737
Meriden *(G-7081)*
Mid-Cntinental Restoration Inc .... C 620 223-3700
Fort Scott *(G-1990)*
Restortion Wtrprfing Cntrs Inc .... E 316 942-6602
Wichita *(G-15452)*
Retrochem Inc .... F 913 422-8810
Shawnee *(G-11018)*

CONTRACTORS: Underground Utilities

Amerine Utilities Construction .... E 620 792-1223
Great Bend *(G-2508)*
Bob Hull Inc .... E 785 292-4790
Frankfort *(G-2021)*
Cimarron Underground Inc .... E 913 438-2981
Overland Park *(G-8552)*
Great Plains Locating Svc Inc .... E 316 263-1200
Wichita *(G-14504)*
Herrmans Excavating Inc .... E 785 233-4146
Topeka *(G-12687)*
Huston Contracting Inc .... F 913 782-1333
Olathe *(G-7782)*
Integrity Locating Svcs LLC .... E 913 530-6315
Olathe *(G-7797)*
K C Construction Inc .... F 913 724-1474
Basehor *(G-382)*
Larson Construction Inc .... E 785 537-0160
Manhattan *(G-6710)*
Mies Construction Inc .... D 316 945-7227
Wichita *(G-15106)*
Miller Paving & Cnstr LLC .... C 913 334-5579
Kansas City *(G-4261)*
Precision Boring Tech Inc .... F 913 735-4728
Olathe *(G-7999)*
Rylie Equipment & Contg Co .... D 913 621-2725
Kansas City *(G-4394)*
Tri Star Utilities Inc .... F 620 331-7159
Independence *(G-3569)*
Utilities Plus Inc .... E 316 946-9416
Wichita *(G-15865)*
Wildcat Construction .... E 316 945-9408
Topeka *(G-13245)*
Wildcat Construction Co Inc .... C 316 945-9408
Wichita *(G-16049)*

CONTRACTORS: Ventilation & Duct Work

Adamson Brothers Sheet Metal .... F 785 242-9273
Ottawa *(G-8243)*

CONTRACTORS: Warm Air Heating & Air Conditioning

A & H AC & Htg Inc .... F 785 594-3357
Baldwin City *(G-352)*
A M Mechanical Service Co .... F 913 829-5885
Kansas City *(G-3778)*
A-1 Electric Inc .... F 620 431-7500
Chanute *(G-701)*
A1air Heating & Cooling LLC .... F 620 235-0600
Frontenac *(G-2050)*
AC Professional LLC .... E 816 668-4760
Olathe *(G-7508)*
Air Care Heating & Cooling Co .... F 913 362-5274
Shawnee Mission *(G-11087)*
Airtech Engineering Inc .... F 913 888-5900
Overland Park *(G-8363)*
Anthony Inc .... E 913 384-4440
Lenexa *(G-5656)*
Auman Co Inc .... F 785 628-2833
Hays *(G-2752)*
Barnes & Dodge Inc .... E 913 321-6444
Lenexa *(G-5687)*
Bbh LLC .... D 316 945-8208
Wichita *(G-13822)*
Becker Bros Inc .... F 316 531-2264
Garden Plain *(G-2321)*
Beebe Heating & AC Inc .... F 913 541-1222
Overland Park *(G-8438)*
Bob Stith Heating and Cooling .... F 316 262-1802
Wichita *(G-13861)*
Bryans Heating & AC .... F 316 755-2447
Valley Center *(G-13338)*
Callabresi Heating & Coolg Inc .... E 785 825-2599
Salina *(G-10435)*
Carlisle Heating & AC .... F 316 321-6230
El Dorado *(G-1543)*
Cates Heating & AC Svc Co .... E 913 888-4470
Lenexa *(G-5734)*
Chad Briney .... F 785 462-2445
Colby *(G-993)*
City Plumbing Heating & AC Inc .... F 785 472-3001
Ellsworth *(G-1661)*
City Wide Service Inc .... F 913 927-6124
Kansas City *(G-3913)*
Clouds Heating and AC .... E 785 842-2258
Lawrence *(G-4795)*
Comfort Contractors Inc .... E 620 431-4780
Chanute *(G-718)*
Debackers Inc .... E 785 232-6999
Topeka *(G-12550)*
Dennys Heating & Cooling .... F 316 283-1598
North Newton *(G-7435)*
Earl Bryant Enterprises Inc .... F 913 724-4100
Basehor *(G-374)*
Fagan Company .... C 913 621-4444
Kansas City *(G-4002)*
Fenix Company Incorporated .... E 316 945-4842
Wichita *(G-14354)*
Flamings Plumbing Heating & AC .... F 620 382-2181
Marion *(G-6869)*
G K Smith & Sons Inc .... F 913 294-5379
Paola *(G-9560)*
Hanna Heating & AC .... E 316 945-3481
Wichita *(G-14556)*
Hanover Electric Inc .... F 785 337-2711
Hanover *(G-2711)*
Harrington Bros Htg & Coolg .... F 913 422-5444
Shawnee Mission *(G-11410)*
Hartley Sheet Metal Co Inc .... F 620 251-4330
Coffeyville *(G-943)*
Henton Plumbing & AC Inc .... F 785 776-5548
Manhattan *(G-6654)*
Hood Htg Air Plg Electric Inc .... F 785 243-1489
Concordia *(G-1118)*
Jim Jam Inc .... F 913 268-6700
Shawnee *(G-10979)*
Kansas City Mechanical Inc .... E 913 334-1101
Kansas City *(G-4147)*
Knipp Equipment Inc .... E 316 265-9655
Wichita *(G-14871)*
Kruse Corporation .... E 785 320-7990
Manhattan *(G-6700)*
Kruse Corporation .... D 316 838-7885
Wichita *(G-14895)*
Lba Air Cndtoning Htg Plbg Inc .... E 816 454-5515
Shawnee Mission *(G-11551)*
McCarty Mechanical Inc .... F 913 432-5100
Shawnee Mission *(G-11607)*
Metro Air Conditioning Co .... D 913 888-3991
Lenexa *(G-5995)*

Mikes Heating & Cooling LLC ....E.... 913 441-7807
Olathe *(G-7899)*
Mission Heating and AC ....F.... 913 631-6506
Shawnee Mission *(G-11645)*
Modern Air Conditioning Inc ....E.... 620 342-7577
Emporia *(G-1797)*
MSI ....E.... 316 262-2021
Wichita *(G-15137)*
Niehoff Heating & Air Inc ....E.... 785 594-7137
Lawrence *(G-5041)*
Overland Park Heating & Coolg ....E.... 913 649-0303
Overland Park *(G-9119)*
P1 Group Inc ....E.... 316 267-3256
Wichita *(G-15252)*
Pestinger Heating & AC Inc ....E.... 785 827-6361
Salina *(G-10634)*
Ray Omo Inc ....E.... 620 227-3101
Lenexa *(G-6091)*
Resource Service Solutions LLC ....E.... 913 338-5050
Lenexa *(G-6107)*
Roth Heating & AC ....E.... 316 942-4141
Wichita *(G-15484)*
Santa Fe AC & Rfrgn Inc ....F.... 913 856-5801
Gardner *(G-2362)*
Schnell & Pestinger Inc ....F.... 785 738-3624
Beloit *(G-502)*
Schuler Heating and Cooling ....F.... 913 262-2969
Kansas City *(G-4405)*
Shawnee Heating and Cooling ....F.... 913 492-0824
Lenexa *(G-6131)*
Stueder Contractors Inc ....E.... 620 792-6044
Great Bend *(G-2642)*
Top Notch Inc ....F.... 913 441-8900
Lenexa *(G-6185)*
Vhc Van Hoecke Contracting Inc ....E.... 913 888-0036
Lenexa *(G-6212)*
Waldinger Corporation ....E.... 316 942-7722
Wichita *(G-15916)*
Welker Heating and Cooling ....F.... 913 669-7555
Overland Park *(G-9487)*

CONTRACTORS: Water Intake Well Drilling Svc

Freddy Van Inc ....G.... 620 231-1127
Pittsburg *(G-9863)*

CONTRACTORS: Water Well Drilling

Geocore LLC ....E.... 785 826-1616
Salina *(G-10509)*
Gulick Drilling ....F.... 620 583-5804
Eureka *(G-1890)*
Hydro Rsrces - Mid Cntnent Inc ....D.... 620 277-2389
Garden City *(G-2201)*
K & K Water Wells LLC ....F.... 620 675-2222
Sublette *(G-12204)*
Kenai Drilling Limited ....C.... 805 937-7871
Liberal *(G-6328)*
Layne Christensen Company ....E.... 913 321-5000
Kansas City *(G-4196)*
Minter-Wilson Drilling Co Inc ....F.... 620 276-8269
Garden City *(G-2237)*
Patchen Electric & Indus Sup ....G.... 785 843-4522
Lawrence *(G-5057)*
Pickrell Drilling Co Inc ....E.... 620 793-5742
Great Bend *(G-2623)*
Royal Drilling Inc ....E.... 785 483-6446
Russell *(G-10292)*
W W Drilling LLC ....D.... 785 743-6774
Wakeeney *(G-13393)*
Woofter Pump & Well Inc ....F.... 785 675-3991
Hoxie *(G-3144)*

CONTRACTORS: Water Well Servicing

Harp Well Pump Svc Corporated ....F.... 316 722-1411
Wichita *(G-14562)*
Layne Christensen Company ....F.... 913 321-5000
Kansas City *(G-4197)*

CONTRACTORS: Waterproofing

Iwp LLC ....F.... 316 308-8507
Valley Center *(G-13345)*
M C M Restoration Company Inc ....E.... 620 223-6602
Fort Scott *(G-1982)*
Michael Downey ....F.... 316 540-6166
Maize *(G-6517)*
Midland Restoration Company ....F.... 620 223-6855
Fort Scott *(G-1991)*
Professnal Wtrprfing Insul LLC ....F.... 316 264-3101
Wichita *(G-15367)*
Restortion Wtr Proofing Contrs ....E.... 913 321-6226
Kansas City *(G-4373)*
Restortion Wtrprfing Cntrs Inc ....E.... 316 942-6602
Wichita *(G-15452)*
Restortion Wtrprfing Cntrs Inc ....F.... 785 478-9538
Topeka *(G-13011)*

CONTRACTORS: Well Acidizing Svcs

Chaosland Services LLC ....G.... 620 356-1259
Ulysses *(G-13288)*
Elite Cementing Acidizing ....G.... 620 583-5561
Eureka *(G-1884)*
Maxidize Production Svcs LLC ....G.... 620 222-1235
Winfield *(G-16158)*

CONTRACTORS: Well Chemical Treating Svcs

Bachman Production Specialties ....F.... 620 792-2549
Great Bend *(G-2513)*

CONTRACTORS: Well Cleaning Svcs

Midwestern Well Service Inc ....E.... 620 624-8203
Liberal *(G-6343)*

CONTRACTORS: Well Logging Svcs

Consolidated Oil Well Ser ....F.... 620 431-9217
Chanute *(G-722)*
Midwest Surveys Inc ....G.... 913 755-2128
Osawatomie *(G-8199)*

CONTRACTORS: Well Swabbing Svcs

Walton Swathing ....G.... 620 492-6827
Johnson *(G-3664)*

CONTRACTORS: Window Treatment Installation

Unique Design Inc ....F.... 785 272-6044
Topeka *(G-13205)*

CONTRACTORS: Windows & Doors

Andersen Corporation ....F.... 913 385-1300
Lenexa *(G-5654)*
Glass Services Inc ....F.... 785 823-5444
Salina *(G-10511)*
Hi-Plains Door Systems Inc ....F.... 785 462-6352
Colby *(G-1013)*

CONTRACTORS: Wood Floor Installation & Refinishing

Acme Floor Company Inc ....D.... 913 888-3200
Lenexa *(G-5624)*
Kansas Carpet & Tile Inc ....E.... 316 942-2111
Wichita *(G-14790)*
Ron Stierly Floor Services ....F.... 913 724-4822
Basehor *(G-388)*

CONTRACTORS: Wrecking & Demolition

Greg Bair Track Hoe Svc Inc ....F.... 913 897-1243
Shawnee Mission *(G-11403)*
Ted Row Inc ....F.... 816 223-9666
Stilwell *(G-12176)*
Vilela Rndy Auto Bdy Repr Pntg ....F.... 620 231-6350
Pittsburg *(G-9957)*

CONTROL EQPT: Electric

Shell Topco LP ....F.... 316 942-7266
Wichita *(G-15580)*
Ultra Electronics Ice Inc ....D.... 785 776-6423
Manhattan *(G-6835)*

CONTROL PANELS: Electrical

Cmt Inc ....C.... 785 762-4400
Junction City *(G-3683)*
Custom Control Mfr Kans Inc ....E.... 913 722-0343
Shawnee Mission *(G-11286)*
G and S Mechanical USA Inc ....F.... 316 946-9988
Wichita *(G-14433)*
Integrated Controls Inc ....F.... 913 782-9600
Olathe *(G-7796)*
Junction City Wire Harness LLC ....D.... 785 762-4400
Junction City *(G-3706)*
K G Moats & Sons LLC ....E.... 785 437-2021
Saint Marys *(G-10368)*
Kasa Companies Inc ....D.... 785 825-5612
Salina *(G-10569)*
Kasa Companies Inc ....C.... 785 825-7181
Salina *(G-10570)*
Kasa Companies Inc ....D.... 785 825-5612
Salina *(G-10571)*
R & T Specialty Cnstr Lc ....G.... 316 942-8141
Wichita *(G-15401)*
U S Automation Inc ....G.... 913 894-2410
Shawnee Mission *(G-11953)*

CONTROLS & ACCESS: Indl, Electric

Elecsys International Corp ....C.... 913 647-0158
Olathe *(G-7673)*
Powerhouse Electric Inc ....G.... 913 856-4141
Gardner *(G-2359)*

CONTROLS & ACCESS: Motor

Castle Creations Inc ....D.... 913 390-6939
Olathe *(G-7580)*

CONTROLS: Access, Motor

K G Moats & Sons LLC ....E.... 785 437-2021
Saint Marys *(G-10368)*

CONTROLS: Electric Motor

Accurate Electric Inc ....G.... 785 825-4010
Salina *(G-10391)*

CONTROLS: Environmental

Bingham Canyon Corporation ....G.... 913 353-4560
Lenexa *(G-5703)*
Building Control Solutions LLC ....G.... 816 439-6046
Merriam *(G-7087)*
Dynamic Control Systems Inc ....F.... 316 262-2525
Wichita *(G-14246)*
John Zink Company LLC ....F.... 316 828-7380
Wichita *(G-14764)*

CONTROLS: Relay & Ind

Control Systems Intl Inc ....D.... 913 599-5010
Shawnee Mission *(G-11264)*
Kasa Companies Inc ....C.... 785 825-7181
Salina *(G-10570)*
Kasa Companies Inc ....D.... 785 825-5612
Salina *(G-10571)*
Rockwell Automation Inc ....F.... 913 577-2500
Lenexa *(G-6111)*
Smiths Intrcnnect Americas Inc ....C.... 913 342-5544
Kansas City *(G-4429)*
Wescon Controls LLC ....C.... 316 942-7266
Wichita *(G-15950)*

CONTROLS: Truck, Indl Battery

Exide Technologies ....G.... 913 321-4600
Kansas City *(G-4001)*

CONVALESCENT HOME

Cedars Inc ....C.... 620 241-0919
McPherson *(G-6942)*
Homestead Inc ....D.... 785 325-2361
Washington *(G-13465)*
Pinnacle Hlth Fclties Xviii LP ....D.... 913 441-2515
Bonner Springs *(G-571)*
St Francis Academy Inc ....E.... 785 825-0563
Salina *(G-10714)*
Thi of Kansas Indian Meadows ....E.... 913 649-5110
Overland Park *(G-9406)*
Top City Healthcare Inc ....D.... 785 272-2124
Topeka *(G-13163)*
Trustees of The Baker Univ ....E.... 785 354-5850
Topeka *(G-13199)*
Via Christi Village Hays Inc ....C.... 785 628-3241
Hays *(G-2926)*
Volga-Canal Housing Inc ....E.... 785 625-5678
Hays *(G-2927)*
Woodworth International Inc ....E.... 620 236-7248
Chetopa *(G-819)*

CONVALESCENT HOMES

Aberdeen Village Inc............E....... 316 685-1100
Wichita *(G-13597)*
Augusta L Lakepoint L C............D....... 316 775-6333
Augusta *(G-307)*
Augusta L Lakepoint L C............E....... 316 320-4140
El Dorado *(G-1531)*
Bethany Home Cottage Complex............F....... 785 227-2721
Lindsborg *(G-6395)*
Beverly Enterprises-Kansas LLC............E....... 316 683-7588
Wichita *(G-13844)*
Beverly Enterprises-Kansas LLC............E....... 913 351-1284
Lansing *(G-4669)*
Beverly Enterprises-Kansas LLC............D....... 785 263-1431
Abilene *(G-15)*
Beverly Enterprises-Kansas LLC............D....... 620 273-6369
Tonganoxie *(G-12253)*
Beverly Enterprises-Kansas LLC............E....... 785 449-2294
Eskridge *(G-1865)*
Beverly Enterprises-Kansas LLC............E....... 785 658-2505
Wilson *(G-16104)*
Beverly Enterprises-Kansas LLC............E....... 913 422-5832
Edwardsville *(G-1496)*
Beverly Enterprises-Kansas LLC............D....... 620 231-1120
Pittsburg *(G-9825)*
Beverly Enterprises-Kansas LLC............E....... 785 462-6721
Colby *(G-990)*
Blue Valley Health Care............E....... 785 363-7777
Blue Rapids *(G-534)*
Butler County Health Services............D....... 316 320-4140
El Dorado *(G-1540)*
C & H Health LLC............D....... 913 631-8200
Shawnee Mission *(G-11193)*
Catholic Care Center Inc............B....... 316 744-8651
Bel Aire *(G-428)*
Catholic Diocese of Wichita............B....... 316 744-2020
Bel Aire *(G-429)*
Chapman Adult Care Homes Inc............D....... 785 922-6525
Chapman *(G-777)*
City of Logan............E....... 785 689-4201
Logan *(G-6422)*
Crestview Operation Inc............D....... 785 336-2156
Seneca *(G-10862)*
Deseret Hlth Rhab At Yates LLC............E....... 620 625-2111
Yates Center *(G-16195)*
Emporia Prsbt Mnor of Mid Amer............D....... 620 412-2019
Emporia *(G-1743)*
Evangelical Lthrn Good Smrtn............D....... 785 456-9482
Wamego *(G-13421)*
Evangelical Lutheran............C....... 785 621-2499
Hays *(G-2802)*
Evangelical Lutheran............C....... 785 332-3588
Saint Francis *(G-10341)*
Family Hlth Rhbltation Ctr LLC............D....... 316 425-5600
Wichita *(G-14337)*
Golden Living Center Wichita............F....... 316 683-7588
Wichita *(G-14482)*
Golden Livingcenter - Eskridge............F....... 785 449-2294
Eskridge *(G-1867)*
Gran Villas............F....... 785 528-5095
Osage City *(G-8184)*
Gran Villas of Holton Inc............F....... 785 364-5051
Holton *(G-3093)*
Hickory Pointe............F....... 785 863-2108
Oskaloosa *(G-8226)*
Hillside Village LLC............D....... 913 583-1266
De Soto *(G-1201)*
Hilltop Lodge............C....... 785 738-2509
Beloit *(G-487)*
Hodgeman County Health Center............C....... 620 357-8361
Jetmore *(G-3647)*
Holiday Healthcare LLC............D....... 785 825-2201
Salina *(G-10543)*
Jackson County Nursing Home............D....... 785 364-3164
Holton *(G-3099)*
John Knox Village............F....... 913 403-8343
Leawood *(G-5443)*
Kingman County Retirement Assn............D....... 620 532-5801
Kingman *(G-4599)*
Kiowa District Hospital............E....... 620 825-4117
Kiowa *(G-4624)*
Lakepint Nrsing Rhbltation Ctr............E....... 316 776-2194
Rose Hill *(G-10241)*
Legacy On 10th Opco LLC............D....... 785 233-8918
Topeka *(G-12838)*
Legend Senior Living LLC............C....... 316 337-5450
Wichita *(G-14953)*
Life Care Centers America Inc............E....... 316 733-5376
Andover *(G-103)*
Life Care Centers America Inc............D....... 620 364-2117
Burlington *(G-639)*
Life Care Centers America Inc............C....... 316 686-5100
Wichita *(G-14961)*
Life Care Centers America Inc............C....... 913 755-4165
Osawatomie *(G-8198)*
Lincoln County Hospital............D....... 785 524-4403
Lincoln *(G-6383)*
Manor Care of Kansas Inc............C....... 316 684-8018
Wichita *(G-15003)*
Manor Care of Kansas Inc............D....... 785 271-6808
Topeka *(G-12858)*
Manor Care of Kansas Inc............C....... 913 383-2569
Overland Park *(G-8984)*
Manor of Garnett Inc............D....... 785 448-2434
Garnett *(G-2382)*
Medicalodges Inc............C....... 620 223-5085
Fort Scott *(G-1984)*
Medicalodges Inc............D....... 913 772-1844
Leavenworth *(G-5269)*
Medicalodges Inc............D....... 620 251-6700
Coffeyville *(G-958)*
Medicalodges Inc............F....... 785 742-4566
Hiawatha *(G-3017)*
Medicalodges Inc............D....... 620 442-9300
Arkansas City *(G-165)*
Medicalodges Inc............E....... 620 659-2156
Kinsley *(G-4619)*
Medicalodges Inc............D....... 316 794-8635
Goddard *(G-2446)*
Medicalodges Inc............D....... 785 632-5696
Clay Center *(G-871)*
Medicalodges Inc............E....... 620 251-3705
Coffeyville *(G-959)*
Medicalodges Inc............C....... 913 367-6066
Atchison *(G-244)*
Medicalodges Inc............D....... 620 251-6700
Coffeyville *(G-960)*
Medicalodges Frontenac............F....... 620 231-0322
Frontenac *(G-2059)*
Medicalodges of Kansas City............E....... 913 334-0200
Kansas City *(G-4231)*
Midwest Health Services Inc............E....... 316 835-4810
Halstead *(G-2703)*
Midwest Health Services Inc............E....... 785 945-3832
Valley Falls *(G-13368)*
Midwest Health Services Inc............B....... 913 727-6100
Lansing *(G-4688)*
Mt Hope Community Development............D....... 316 667-2431
Mount Hope *(G-7207)*
National Healthcare Corp............D....... 620 767-5172
Council Grove *(G-1173)*
National Healthcare Corp............C....... 316 524-3211
Haysville *(G-2952)*
National Healthcare Corp............D....... 620 285-6914
Larned *(G-4707)*
National Healthcare Corp............D....... 316 772-5185
Sedgwick *(G-10851)*
National Healthcare Corp............D....... 620 431-4940
Chanute *(G-745)*
Phillips County Retirement Ctr............D....... 785 543-2131
Phillipsburg *(G-9793)*
Plaza West Care Center Inc............C....... 785 271-6700
Topeka *(G-12980)*
Prairie Haven............F....... 785 476-2623
Smith Center *(G-12040)*
Pratt Regional Med Ctr Corp............E....... 620 672-3424
Pratt *(G-10143)*
Presbyterian Manors Inc............D....... 785 841-4262
Lawrence *(G-5074)*
Presbyterian Manors Inc............D....... 620 278-3651
Sterling *(G-12128)*
Presbyterian Manors Inc............D....... 316 283-5400
Newton *(G-7408)*
Presbyterian Manors Inc............D....... 620 442-8700
Arkansas City *(G-170)*
Presbyterian Manors Inc............D....... 785 272-6510
Topeka *(G-12984)*
Rh Montgomery Properties Inc............E....... 620 237-4300
Moran *(G-7164)*
Riverside Village Senior Livin............D....... 316 942-7000
Wichita *(G-15472)*
Riverview Manor Inc............E....... 620 455-2214
Oxford *(G-9535)*
Rolling Hills Health Center............C....... 785 273-5001
Topeka *(G-13026)*
Rossville Healthcare............D....... 785 584-6104
Rossville *(G-10255)*
Shawnee Mission Health Care............D....... 913 676-2000
Shawnee Mission *(G-11856)*
T W G Nursing Home Inc............D....... 620 724-8288
Girard *(G-2420)*
Trinity Nursing & Rehab Center............E....... 913 671-7376
Shawnee Mission *(G-11943)*
Via Christi Vlg Manhattan Inc............C....... 785 539-7671
Manhattan *(G-6842)*
Village Villa Inc............E....... 913 886-6400
Nortonville *(G-7465)*
Windsor Nursing Home Assoc............D....... 785 825-6757
Salina *(G-10771)*
Windsor of Lawrence............E....... 785 832-9900
Lawrence *(G-5188)*
Windsor Place............D....... 620 251-6545
Iola *(G-3638)*

CONVENIENCE STORES

Cervs Conoco & Convenience............F....... 785 625-7777
Hays *(G-2767)*
Farmers Cooperative Elev Inc............F....... 785 284-2185
Sabetha *(G-10310)*
Hallauer Oil Co Inc............F....... 785 364-3140
Holton *(G-3094)*
Murphy USA Inc............F....... 620 227-5607
Dodge City *(G-1409)*
Santa Fe Market Inc............F....... 785 594-7466
Baldwin City *(G-368)*
Saragenes Short Stop............F....... 620 235-1141
Pittsburg *(G-9935)*
Star Fuel Centers Inc............E....... 913 652-9400
Leawood *(G-5561)*
Sterling Food Mart Inc............G....... 620 278-3371
Hutchinson *(G-3446)*
Town and Country Food Mkts Inc............E....... 316 942-7940
Wichita *(G-15779)*

CONVENTION & TRADE SHOW SVCS

All Seasons Party Rental Inc............C....... 816 765-1444
Kansas City *(G-3798)*
Christian Ch of Grater Kans Cy............F....... 913 301-3004
Linwood *(G-6416)*
City of Overland Park............E....... 913 339-3000
Overland Park *(G-8555)*
City of Salina............E....... 785 826-7200
Salina *(G-10449)*
Colby Convention Center............E....... 785 460-0131
Colby *(G-997)*
Crosswind Conference Center............E....... 620 327-2700
Hesston *(G-2988)*
Digital Sound Systems Inc............E....... 913 492-5775
Lenexa *(G-5819)*
Leisure Hotel Corporation............E....... 620 227-5000
Dodge City *(G-1398)*
Overlnd Prk Cnvntn & Vstrs Bre............F....... 913 491-0123
Overland Park *(G-9129)*
Salina Red Coach Inn............F....... 785 825-2111
Salina *(G-10684)*
Spt Distribution Center............E....... 785 862-5226
Topeka *(G-13093)*

CONVEYOR SYSTEMS

Advanced Machine Solutions LLC............F....... 620 724-6220
Girard *(G-2394)*
Cargotec USA Inc............G....... 785 229-7111
Ottawa *(G-8252)*

CONVEYOR SYSTEMS: Bucket Type

R & R Industries Inc............F....... 620 672-7463
Pratt *(G-10146)*

CONVEYOR SYSTEMS: Bulk Handling

Custom Metal Fabricators Inc............E....... 785 258-3744
Herington *(G-2973)*
Mid-West Conveyor Company............C....... 734 288-4400
Kansas City *(G-4247)*

CONVEYOR SYSTEMS: Pneumatic Tube

Coperion K-Tron Salina Inc............C....... 785 825-1611
Salina *(G-10462)*
Horizonpsi Inc............D....... 785 842-1299
Lawrence *(G-4902)*
Schenck Process LLC............C....... 785 284-2191
Sabetha *(G-10331)*
United States Systems Inc............F....... 913 281-1010
Kansas City *(G-4490)*

PRDT & SVC

CONVEYORS & CONVEYING EQPT

Adapa Incorporated .... F 785 862-2060
Topeka *(G-12286)*
Bl Brooks & Sons Inc .... G 913 829-5494
Olathe *(G-7553)*
Bulk Conveyors Inc .... E 316 201-3158
Wichita *(G-13914)*
Clean Air Management Co Inc .... E 913 831-0740
Lenexa *(G-5760)*
Dearborn Mid West Conveyor Co .... G 913 261-2428
Overland Park *(G-8644)*
Express Scale Parts Inc .... E 913 441-4787
Lenexa *(G-5844)*
Grain Belt Supply Company Inc .... C 785 827-4491
Salina *(G-10514)*
JR Custom Metal Products Inc .... C 316 263-1318
Wichita *(G-14776)*
Mac Equipment Inc .... F 785 284-2191
Sabetha *(G-10317)*
Magnatech Engineering Inc .... G 913 845-3553
Tonganoxie *(G-12265)*
Peerless Conveyor and Mfg Corp .... F 913 342-2240
Kansas City *(G-4318)*
Rhs Inc .... E 785 742-2949
Hiawatha *(G-3023)*
Schenck Accurate Inc .... G 262 473-2441
Sabetha *(G-10330)*
Tech-Air Inc .... G 913 677-5777
Shawnee Mission *(G-11923)*
Thomas Manufacturing Inc .... F 620 724-6220
Girard *(G-2421)*

COOKING & FOOD WARMING EQPT: Commercial

Hi-Tech Weld Overlay Group LLC .... E 816 524-9010
Lenexa *(G-5903)*

COOKING SCHOOL

American Institute of Baking .... D 785 537-4750
Manhattan *(G-6541)*

COOKWARE, STONEWARE: Coarse Earthenware & Pottery

Pfaltzgraff Co .... F 316 283-7754
Newton *(G-7404)*

COOLERS & ICE CHESTS: Polystyrene Foam

Coleman Company Inc .... D 316 832-3015
Olathe *(G-7597)*
Coleman Company Inc .... G 800 835-3278
Wichita *(G-14053)*

COOLING TOWERS: Metal

Evaptech Inc .... D 913 322-5165
Edwardsville *(G-1499)*
SPX Cooling Technologies Inc .... G 913 722-3600
Overland Park *(G-9345)*

COPY MACHINES WHOLESALERS

Canon Solutions America Inc .... G 913 323-5010
Overland Park *(G-8508)*
Canon Solutions America Inc .... F 785 232-8222
Topeka *(G-12421)*
Copy Products Inc .... E 316 315-0102
Wichita *(G-14099)*
Evolv Solutions LLC .... E 913 469-8900
Shawnee Mission *(G-11352)*
Key Office Products Inc .... G 620 227-2101
Dodge City *(G-1390)*
R K Black Missouri LLC .... F 913 577-8100
Olathe *(G-8017)*
Toshiba Amer Bus Solutions Inc .... E 785 242-4942
Lawrence *(G-5142)*

CORD & TWINE

Custom Rope A Div Williams .... E 620 825-4196
Kiowa *(G-4623)*
Great Lakes Polymer Tech LLC .... C 507 320-7000
Kingman *(G-4592)*
Polymer Group Inc .... C 620 532-4000
Kingman *(G-4612)*

CORD & TWINE: Fiber, Hard

Great Lkes Plymers Hldngs Corp .... F 507 320-7000
Kingman *(G-4594)*

CORRECTIONAL FACILITY OPERATIONS

Corecivic Inc .... C 913 727-3246
Leavenworth *(G-5225)*
Corrections Kansas Department .... D 913 727-3235
Lansing *(G-4672)*
Corrections Kansas Department .... D 316 321-7284
El Dorado *(G-1551)*
N Central KS Reg Juven Deten .... F 785 238-4549
Junction City *(G-3728)*
Southeast Kans Rgnal Jvnile Dtn .... E 620 724-4174
Girard *(G-2417)*
Unified Gvrnment Cmnty Corectn .... E 913 573-4180
Kansas City *(G-4485)*

CORRECTIONAL INSTITUTIONS

Corrections Kansas Department .... C 620 285-0300
Larned *(G-4699)*
Corrections Kansas Department .... F 620 792-3549
Great Bend *(G-2547)*
Corrections Kansas Department .... E 620 341-3294
Emporia *(G-1726)*
Department Corrections Kansas .... F 913 829-6207
Olathe *(G-7649)*
Federal Prison Industries .... D 913 682-8700
Leavenworth *(G-5238)*

CORRECTIONAL INSTITUTIONS, GOVERNMENT: County

County of Reno .... E 620 665-7042
Hutchinson *(G-3249)*

CORRECTIONAL INSTITUTIONS, GOVERNMENT: State

Corrections Kansas Department .... D 913 727-3235
Lansing *(G-4672)*
Corrections Kansas Department .... D 316 321-7284
El Dorado *(G-1551)*

CORRUGATED PRDTS: Boxes, Partition, Display Items, Sheet/Pad

Pratt Industries USA Inc .... D 316 838-0851
Wichita *(G-15324)*

COSMETICS & TOILETRIES

Conopco Inc .... C 913 782-7171
New Century *(G-7274)*
Millenia Productions LLC .... F 316 425-2500
Wichita *(G-15108)*

COSMETICS WHOLESALERS

Gdm Enterprises LLC .... F 816 753-2900
Fairway *(G-1908)*

COSMETOLOGIST

Beauty Escntuals Salon Day Spa .... E 913 851-4644
Overland Park *(G-8437)*
Mary Kate & Company LLC .... F 316 721-4101
Wichita *(G-15016)*
Shear Designers .... F 620 342-5393
Emporia *(G-1826)*

COSMETOLOGY & PERSONAL HYGIENE SALONS

Bath & Body Works LLC .... F 785 749-0214
Lawrence *(G-4751)*
His and Her Hairstyling Inc .... F 785 232-9724
Topeka *(G-12694)*
Lash Company LLC .... F 316 265-5527
Wichita *(G-14930)*
Par Exsalonce .... E 913 469-9532
Shawnee Mission *(G-11715)*
Salon One 19 & Spa .... F 913 451-7119
Leawood *(G-5546)*

COSMETOLOGY SCHOOL

S-Kmac Investments LLC .... E 316 990-5095
Wichita *(G-15503)*

COTTON SAMPLING & INSPECTION SVCS

Return Products Management Inc .... F 913 768-1747
Olathe *(G-8028)*

COUNCIL FOR SOCIAL AGENCY

Cross-Lines Cmnty Outreach Inc .... F 913 281-3388
Kansas City *(G-3946)*
Kansas Food Bank Warehouse Inc .... E 316 265-3663
Wichita *(G-14801)*
Project Concern Inc .... F 913 367-4655
Atchison *(G-257)*
Purplefrogintl .... G 816 510-0871
Shawnee *(G-11014)*

COUNTER & SINK TOPS

Home Store .... F 620 421-4272
Parsons *(G-9692)*
Keystone Construction Inc .... F 316 778-1566
Benton *(G-516)*
Keystone Financial LLC .... F 620 757-3593
Benton *(G-517)*
Nulook Custom Finishes .... G 913 385-2574
Olathe *(G-7925)*
Top It .... G 620 431-1866
Chanute *(G-771)*

COUNTERS & COUNTING DEVICES

Omni Aerospace Inc .... E 316 529-8998
Wichita *(G-15216)*

COUNTING DEVICES: Production

BP America Production Company .... E 620 657-4300
Satanta *(G-10777)*

COUNTING DEVICES: Speed Indicators & Recorders, Vehicle

Digital Ally Inc .... D 913 814-7774
Lenexa *(G-5816)*

COUNTRY CLUBS

Abilene Country Club .... E 785 263-3811
Abilene *(G-3)*
Alvamar Inc .... E 785 842-2929
Lawrence *(G-4732)*
Augusta Country Club .... E 316 775-7281
Augusta *(G-301)*
Bellevue Golf and Country Club .... E 913 367-3022
Atchison *(G-213)*
Beloit Country Club Inc .... E 785 738-3163
Beloit *(G-476)*
Brookridge Golf & Country Club .... F 913 648-1600
Shawnee Mission *(G-11186)*
Crestwood Country Club Inc .... E 620 231-9697
Pittsburg *(G-9850)*
Dodge City Country Club .... E 620 225-5231
Dodge City *(G-1346)*
Emporia Country Club Inc .... E 620 342-0343
Emporia *(G-1739)*
Fort Scott Country Club Inc .... F 620 223-5060
Fort Scott *(G-1969)*
Golden Belt Country Club Inc .... E 620 792-4303
Great Bend *(G-2571)*
Hallbrook Country Club .... D 913 345-9292
Leawood *(G-5418)*
Homestead Country Club .... D 913 262-4100
Prairie Village *(G-10035)*
Independence Country Club .... E 620 331-1270
Independence *(G-3527)*
Indian Hills Country Club .... D 913 362-6200
Mission Hills *(G-7144)*
Ironhorse Golf Club Maint .... F 913 897-8181
Shawnee Mission *(G-11468)*
Lawrence Country Club .... D 785 842-0592
Lawrence *(G-4963)*
Leavenworth Country Club .... E 913 727-6600
Lansing *(G-4682)*
Leawood South Country Club .... E 913 491-1313
Shawnee Mission *(G-11555)*
Liberal Country Club Assn .... E 620 624-3992
Liberal *(G-6332)*
Manhattan Country Club Inc .... D 785 539-7501
Manhattan *(G-6720)*
McPherson Country Club Inc .... F 620 241-3541
Mcpherson *(G-6996)*
Milburn Golf and Country Club .... E 913 432-0490
Shawnee Mission *(G-11639)*

Mission Hills Country Club Inc ....D 913 722-5400
Mission Hills *(G-7146)*
Nicklaus Golf Club LP ....D 913 402-1000
Overland Park *(G-9086)*
Paola Country Club Inc ....F 913 294-2910
Paola *(G-9579)*
Parsons Golf Club Restaurant ....F 620 421-5290
Parsons *(G-9718)*
Prairie Trails Golf Cntry CLB ....E 316 321-4114
El Dorado *(G-1593)*
Quivira Country Club Inc ....E 913 631-4820
Kansas City *(G-4356)*
Riverside Recreation Assn ....F 785 332-3401
Saint Francis *(G-10344)*
Rolling Hills Country Club ....D 316 722-4273
Wichita *(G-15478)*
Rolling Hills Country Club ....E 316 721-6780
Wichita *(G-15479)*
Salina Country Club ....D 785 827-0388
Salina *(G-10669)*
Shawnee Country Club ....E 785 233-2373
Topeka *(G-13063)*
Slawson Investment Corporation ....E 316 263-3201
Wichita *(G-15604)*
Smoky Hill Country Club Inc ....E 785 625-4021
Hays *(G-2909)*
Sugar Hills Golf Club Inc ....E 785 899-2785
Goodland *(G-2487)*
Terradyne Country Club LLC ....E 316 733-2582
Andover *(G-110)*
Topeka Country Club ....D 785 232-2090
Topeka *(G-13173)*
Twb Inc ....E 620 663-8396
Hutchinson *(G-3470)*
Wamego Country Club Inc ....E 785 456-2649
Wamego *(G-13449)*
Wichita Cntry CLB Maintennance ....F 316 634-2882
Wichita *(G-15988)*
Winfield Country Club ....E 620 221-1570
Winfield *(G-16185)*

COUPLINGS: Hose & Tube, Hydraulic Or Pneumatic

Swan Engineering & Sup Co Inc ....F 913 371-7425
Kansas City *(G-4452)*

COURIER OR MESSENGER SVCS

Fedex Corporation ....F 913 393-0953
Olathe *(G-7705)*
Fedex Corporation ....F 913 677-5005
Shawnee Mission *(G-11362)*
Line Medical Inc ....E 316 262-3444
Wichita *(G-14967)*
Professional Express Inc ....F 913 722-6060
Kansas City *(G-4342)*
Publishers Delivery Solut ....F 913 894-1299
Lenexa *(G-6078)*
Quicksilver Ex Courier of MO ....D 913 321-5959
Kansas City *(G-4354)*
Via Express Delivery Systems ....F 913 341-8101
Shawnee Mission *(G-11977)*

COURIER SVCS, AIR: Letter Delivery, Private

Federal Express Corporation ....C 800 463-3339
Salina *(G-10497)*

COURIER SVCS, AIR: Package Delivery, Private

Federal Express Corporation ....F 800 463-3339
Topeka *(G-12599)*

COURIER SVCS: Air

Dhl Express (usa) Inc ....F 316 943-7683
Wichita *(G-14207)*
Land Air Express Inc ....E 316 942-0191
Wichita *(G-14920)*
Noatum Logistics Usa LLC ....E 913 696-7100
Overland Park *(G-9089)*
UPS Srvice Parts Logistics Inc ....A 800 451-4550
Overland Park *(G-9449)*

COURIER SVCS: Ground

Fedex Freight Corporation ....D 800 426-0104
Wichita *(G-14348)*
Fedex Ground Package Sys Inc ....D 800 463-3339
Wichita *(G-14349)*

Step Two Investments LLC ....E 913 888-9000
Overland Park *(G-9357)*
Total Distribution System Inc ....D 913 677-2292
Westwood *(G-13561)*

COURIER SVCS: Package By Vehicle

Fedex Ground Package Sys Inc ....E 800 463-3339
Salina *(G-10499)*
United Parcel Service Inc ....C 316 946-4074
Wichita *(G-15845)*
United Parcel Service Inc ....B 316 941-2010
Wichita *(G-15846)*

COURIER SVCS: Parcel By Vehicle

Boyd Delivery Systems Inc ....D 913 677-6700
Westwood *(G-13551)*
United Parcel Service Inc ....D 620 421-1346
Parsons *(G-9747)*
United Parcel Service Inc ....C 785 354-1111
Topeka *(G-13207)*
United Parcel Service Inc ....C 785 628-3253
Hays *(G-2922)*
United Parcel Service Inc ....D 620 662-5961
Hutchinson *(G-3476)*
United Parcel Service Inc ....D 785 843-6530
Lawrence *(G-5151)*
United Parcel Service Inc ....C 913 599-0899
Shawnee Mission *(G-11964)*
United Parcel Service Inc ....C 913 573-4701
Kansas City *(G-4488)*
United Parcel Service Inc ....D 913 894-0255
Lenexa *(G-6202)*
United Parcel Service Inc ....E 620 235-1220
Pittsburg *(G-9950)*

COURT REPORTING SVCS

Appino Biggs Reporting Svc Inc ....F 785 273-3063
Topeka *(G-12333)*
ARS Reporting LLC ....E 913 422-5198
Shawnee *(G-10911)*
Court Reporting Service Inc ....F 800 794-8798
Wichita *(G-14115)*
Jay E Suddreth & Associates ....E 913 451-5820
Leawood *(G-5441)*
Kelley York & Associates Ltd ....F 316 267-8200
Wichita *(G-14844)*
Metropolitan Court Reporters ....E 913 317-8800
Overland Park *(G-9015)*
Reporting Services Company ....E 913 385-2699
Overland Park *(G-9235)*
Superior Crt Reporting Svc LLC ....F 913 262-0100
Overland Park *(G-9377)*

COURTS

Kansas Cnty Dst Attys Associat ....D 785 232-5822
Kansas City *(G-4153)*
Supreme Court United States ....E 785 295-2790
Topeka *(G-13126)*

COURTS OF LAW: State

Judiciary Court of The State ....D 785 233-8200
Topeka *(G-12751)*

CRACKED CASTING REPAIR SVCS

Schulz Welding Service Inc ....F 620 628-4431
Canton *(G-681)*

CRANE & AERIAL LIFT SVCS

Belger Cartage Service Inc ....E 316 943-0101
Wichita *(G-13829)*
Catalyst Artificial Lift LLC ....E 620 365-7150
Iola *(G-3590)*
Crane Sales & Service Co Inc ....F 913 621-7040
Kansas City *(G-3944)*
Panhandle Steel Erectors Inc ....F 620 271-9878
Garden City *(G-2247)*
Shannahan Crane & Hoist Inc ....F 816 746-9822
Kansas City *(G-4419)*

CRANES: Indl Plant

Wilkerson Crane Rental Inc ....E 913 238-7030
Lenexa *(G-6230)*

CRANES: Overhead

Mid-West Conveyor Company ....C 734 288-4400
Kansas City *(G-4247)*

CRANKSHAFTS & CAMSHAFTS: Machining

Kan Fab Inc ....G 620 342-5669
Emporia *(G-1783)*
Quality Power Products Inc ....G 785 263-0060
Solomon *(G-12052)*

CREDIT & OTHER FINANCIAL RESPONSIBILITY INSURANCE

Progressive Casualty Insur Co ....F 913 202-6600
Kansas City *(G-4344)*

CREDIT AGENCIES: Export-Import Bank

Jaafar Inc ....F 913 269-5113
Olathe *(G-7805)*

CREDIT AGENCIES: Federal & Federally Sponsored

Community Nat Bnk of El Dorado ....F 316 320-2265
El Dorado *(G-1547)*
Federal Home Loan Bank Topeka ....D 785 233-0507
Topeka *(G-12600)*
Federal Land Bank Assoc ....F 620 544-4006
Hugoton *(G-3162)*

CREDIT AGENCIES: Federal Land Banks

Cobank Acb ....F 620 342-0138
Emporia *(G-1722)*
Cobank Acb ....E 316 721-1100
Wichita *(G-14049)*
Cobank Acb ....F 620 431-0240
Chanute *(G-717)*

CREDIT BUREAUS

Computer Sciences Corporation ....C 913 469-8700
Overland Park *(G-8593)*
Credit Restart LLC ....F 888 670-7709
Lenexa *(G-5792)*
Shamrock Trading Corporation ....B 877 642-8553
Overland Park *(G-9302)*

CREDIT CARD PROCESSING SVCS

Alliance Data Systems Corp ....C 214 494-3000
Shawnee Mission *(G-11097)*

CREDIT CARD SVCS

Basys Processing Inc ....E 800 386-0711
Lenexa *(G-5689)*
Multi Svc Tech Solutions Inc ....B 800 239-1064
Overland Park *(G-9063)*
Q Solutions LLC ....F 913 948-5931
Wellsville *(G-13545)*
World Fuel Services Corp ....B 913 451-2400
Overland Park *(G-9506)*

CREDIT INST, SHORT-TERM BUSINESS: Accts Receiv & Coml Paper

Medova Hlthcare Fncl Group LLC ....E 316 616-6160
Wichita *(G-15034)*

CREDIT INST, SHORT-TERM BUSINESS: Financing Dealers

Td Auto Finance LLC ....E 913 663-6300
Shawnee Mission *(G-11921)*

CREDIT INSTITUTIONS, SHORT-TERM BUS: Wrkg Capital Finance

Capital Resources LLC ....F 913 469-1630
Overland Park *(G-8511)*
Pollen Inc ....D 877 465-4045
Leawood *(G-5524)*
Speculative Funding LLC ....F 785 267-1996
Topeka *(G-13089)*
Squaretwo Financial Commercial ....F 913 888-8300
Overland Park *(G-9347)*
Transport Funding LLC ....E 913 319-7400
Overland Park *(G-9425)*

CREDIT INSTITUTIONS, SHORT-TERM BUSINESS: Factoring Svcs

Tafs Inc E 877 898-9797
Olathe (G-8099)

CREDIT INSTITUTIONS: Personal

Bank of Tescott E 785 825-1621
Salina (G-10418)

Claro Financiero LLC F 913 608-5444
Mission Hills (G-7141)

Community National Bank E 620 235-1345
Pittsburg (G-9842)

Community National Bank F 620 431-2265
Chanute (G-720)

Easy Cash Asap LLC E 913 291-1134
Leawood (G-5383)

Galt Ventures LLC F 316 722-3801
Wichita (G-14441)

Kansas Teachers Cmnty Cr Un E 620 231-5719
Pittsburg (G-9889)

Kansas Teachers Cmnty Cr Un F 620 223-1475
Fort Scott (G-1977)

Union State Bank of Everest E 913 367-2700
Atchison (G-267)

CREDIT INSTITUTIONS: Short-Term Business

Bankwest of Kansas F 785 462-7557
Colby (G-989)

Caterpillar Inc D 309 675-1000
Wamego (G-13409)

RTS Financial Service Inc C 877 642-8553
Overland Park (G-9263)

Shamrock Trading Corporation B 877 642-8553
Overland Park (G-9302)

CREDIT INVESTIGATION SVCS

ACS Data Search LLC F 913 649-1771
Shawnee Mission (G-11070)

CREDIT UNIONS: Federally Chartered

Augusta White Eagle Credit Un E 316 775-5747
Augusta (G-309)

Azura Credit Union E 785 233-5556
Topeka (G-12354)

Catholic Family Federal Cr Un F 316 264-9163
Wichita (G-13964)

Central Kansas Credit Union F 620 663-1566
Hutchinson (G-3232)

Country Club Bank F 816 751-4251
Leawood (G-5361)

Credit Union of America D 316 265-3272
Wichita (G-14128)

Educational Credit Union E 785 271-6900
Topeka (G-12571)

Emporia State Federal Cr Un E 620 342-2336
Emporia (G-1744)

Farmway Credit Union E 785 738-2224
Beloit (G-483)

Freedom 1st Federal Credit Un F 316 685-0205
Wichita (G-14417)

Great Plains Federal Cr Un F 620 331-4060
Independence (G-3524)

Great Plains Federal Cr Un F 620 241-4181
McPherson (G-6971)

Great Plains Federal Cr Un F 785 823-9226
Salina (G-10515)

Heartland Credit Union E 620 669-0177
Hutchinson (G-3310)

Kansas State Univ Federal Cr F 785 776-3003
Manhattan (G-6678)

Kansas Teachers Cmnty Cr Un F 620 223-1475
Fort Scott (G-1977)

Mainstreet Credit Union F 785 856-5200
Lawrence (G-5007)

Mainstreet Federal Credit Un E 785 856-5200
Lawrence (G-5008)

Mainstreet Federal Credit Un D 913 599-1010
Lenexa (G-5982)

Mainstreet Federal Credit Un F 785 842-5657
Lawrence (G-5009)

Mainstreet Federal Credit Un E 913 754-3926
Shawnee Mission (G-11591)

Mazuma Credit Union C 913 574-5000
Overland Park (G-8999)

Meritrust Credit Union F 785 856-7878
Lawrence (G-5022)

Mid-Kansas Credit Union F 620 543-2662
Moundridge (G-7192)

Navy Federal Credit Union C 888 842-6328
Leavenworth (G-5275)

Panhandle Federal Credit Union F 620 326-2285
Wellington (G-13522)

Quantum Credit Union F 316 263-5756
Wichita (G-15388)

Truity Credit Union F 785 749-2224
Lawrence (G-5147)

United West Community Cr Un F 620 227-7181
Dodge City (G-1444)

Wichita Federal Credit Union E 316 941-0600
Wichita (G-16000)

CREDIT UNIONS: State Chartered

Central Star Credit Union E 316 685-9555
Wichita (G-13985)

Great Plains Federal Cr Un F 620 331-4060
Independence (G-3524)

Kan Colo Credit Union F 620 653-4415
Hoisington (G-3067)

Kansas Corporate Credit Union F 316 721-2600
Wichita (G-14793)

Meritrust Credit Union F 785 320-7222
Manhattan (G-6740)

Truity Credit Union F 785 749-2224
Lawrence (G-5147)

CREMATORIES

Hays Veterinary Hosp Prof Assn F 785 625-2719
Hays (G-2839)

Resthaven Mortuary Inc F 316 722-2100
Wichita (G-15451)

Service Corp International F 913 782-0582
Olathe (G-8059)

Service Corp International E 913 334-3366
Kansas City (G-4418)

Suhor Industries Inc A 620 421-4434
Overland Park (G-9371)

CRISIS CENTER

Birthright Inc E 913 682-2700
Leavenworth (G-5211)

Brighthouse Inc E 620 665-3630
Hutchinson (G-3223)

Crisis Center Inc E 785 539-7935
Manhattan (G-6606)

Kansas Coalittion Against E 785 232-9784
Topeka (G-12766)

Safehouse Inc F 620 251-0030
Coffeyville (G-975)

Valeo Behavioral Hlth Care Inc E 785 233-1730
Topeka (G-13217)

Wichita Area Sxual Assault Ctr E 316 263-0185
Wichita (G-15976)

CRISIS INTERVENTION CENTERS

Catholic Charities of Wichita F 316 263-6000
Wichita (G-13962)

Comcare of Sedgwick County C 316 660-7700
Wichita (G-14062)

Comcare of Sedgwick County B 316 660-7600
Wichita (G-14061)

Compass Behavioral Health E 620 227-8566
Dodge City (G-1329)

Crisis Center of Dodge City F 620 225-6987
Dodge City (G-1334)

For Wyandot Center D 913 362-0393
Kansas City (G-4016)

Friends of Yates Inc E 913 321-1566
Kansas City (G-4018)

Liberal Area Rape Crisis F 620 624-3079
Liberal (G-6331)

New Directions Emrgncy Shelter E 785 223-0500
Junction City (G-3730)

Safehouse Crisis Center Inc E 620 231-8692
Pittsburg (G-9934)

CRUDE PETROLEUM & NATURAL GAS PRODUCTION

Castle Resources Inc E 785 625-5155
Schoenchen (G-10802)

Daystar Petroleum Inc G 316 755-3492
Valley Center (G-13340)

Ferrell Companies Inc D 913 661-1500
Overland Park (G-8712)

Messenger Petroleum Inc G 620 532-5400
Kingman (G-4606)

Petroleum Property Services G 316 265-3351
Wichita (G-15287)

Tengasco Inc E 785 625-6374
Hays (G-2919)

Younger Energy Company G 316 681-2542
Wichita (G-16097)

CRUDE PETROLEUM & NATURAL GAS PRODUCTION

Crown Consulting Inc F 620 624-0156
Liberal (G-6300)

Freeport-Mcmoran Oil & Gas LLC E 316 636-1801
Wichita (G-14418)

N & B Enterprises Inc G 620 431-6424
Chanute (G-744)

Natural Gas Pipeline Amer LLC G 785 568-2231
Glasco (G-2422)

Oneok Inc E 620 562-4205
Bushton (G-654)

R & S Pipe Supply G 620 365-8114
Iola (G-3629)

R R A Inc G 316 262-3411
Wichita (G-15406)

Summit Drilling Co Inc F 620 343-3278
Emporia (G-1832)

Town & Country Super Market E 620 653-2330
Hoisington (G-3072)

Tri Resources Inc F 620 672-9425
Pratt (G-10162)

Xto Energy Inc D 620 355-7838
Lakin (G-4662)

CRUDE PETROLEUM PRODUCTION

Aladdin Petroleum Corporation G 316 265-9602
Wichita (G-13657)

Allmetal Recycling LLC D 316 838-9381
Wichita (G-13676)

Anadarko Petroleum Corporation E 620 544-4344
Hugoton (G-3148)

Apollo Energies Inc F 620 672-5071
Pratt (G-10097)

Baird Oil Co Inc G 785 689-7456
Logan (G-6420)

Berexco Incorporated G 620 582-2575
Coldwater (G-1051)

Berexco LLC F 785 628-6101
Hays (G-2757)

Black Diamond Oil Inc G 785 625-5891
Hays (G-2759)

Bobcat Oil Field Service Inc F 913 980-3858
Louisburg (G-6441)

Buckeye Corporation G 316 321-1060
El Dorado (G-1539)

Buckeye Corporation G 785 483-3111
Russell (G-10267)

Butterfly Supply Inc F 620 793-7156
Great Bend (G-2525)

Canyon Oil & Gas Co G 316 263-3201
Wichita (G-13935)

CHS Inc D 620 241-4247
McPherson (G-6948)

Damar Resources Inc G 785 625-0020
Hays (G-2781)

Daystar Petroleum Inc G 620 583-5527
Eureka (G-1883)

Dreiling Oil Inc G 785 625-8327
Hays (G-2791)

Edmiston Oil Company Inc F 316 265-5241
Wichita (G-14260)

Egbert Oil Operations Inc F 620 662-4533
Hutchinson (G-3275)

Excalibur Production Co Inc G 620 241-1265
McPherson (G-6961)

F G Holl Company LLC G 316 684-8481
Wichita (G-14329)

F G Holl Company LLC F 620 995-3171
Belpre (G-505)

Glacier Petroleum Inc F 620 342-1148
Emporia (G-1762)

Gore Oil Company G 316 263-3535
Wichita (G-14487)

Grady Bolding Corporation G 620 564-2240
Ellinwood (G-1633)

Grand Mesa Operating Company F 316 634-0699
Wichita (G-14495)

H K W Oil Company Inc G 785 483-6185
Salina (G-10525)

Hess Oil Company ... E ... 620 241-4640
McPherson *(G-6973)*
Hughes Drilling Co ... G ... 785 883-2235
Wellsville *(G-13543)*
Hummon Corporation ... G ... 620 930-2645
Medicine Lodge *(G-7064)*
J-W Operating Company ... F ... 620 626-7243
Liberal *(G-6324)*
John O Farmer Inc ... F ... 785 483-3144
Russell *(G-10277)*
Kanzou Explorations Inc ... E ... 913 294-2125
Paola *(G-9568)*
Kinder Morgan Kansas Inc ... G ... 620 384-7830
Syracuse *(G-12228)*
Knighton Oil Co Inc ... G ... 316 630-9905
Wichita *(G-14869)*
Koch Exploration Company ... F ... 316 828-5508
Wichita *(G-14878)*
L D Drilling Inc ... E ... 620 793-3051
Great Bend *(G-2601)*
L-K Wireline Inc ... G ... 785 625-6877
Hays *(G-2861)*
Lario Oil & Gas Company ... E ... 316 265-5611
Wichita *(G-14924)*
Lario Oil & Gas Company ... F ... 785 625-5023
Hays *(G-2862)*
Lee Phillips Oil Company ... G ... 316 681-4470
Wichita *(G-14948)*
Linn Energy Inc ... E ... 620 657-8310
Ulysses *(G-13305)*
Merit Energy Company LLC ... G ... 620 675-8372
Sublette *(G-12205)*
Mull Drilling Company Inc ... F ... 316 264-6366
Wichita *(G-15138)*
Murfin Drilling Company Inc ... E ... 316 267-3241
Wichita *(G-15140)*
Murfin Drilling Company Inc ... E ... 785 421-2101
Hill City *(G-3036)*
Murfin Drilling Company Inc ... E ... 785 483-5371
Russell *(G-10282)*
Murfin Drilling Company Inc ... F ... 785 462-7541
Colby *(G-1031)*
Northern Lights Oil Co L L C ... G ... 316 733-1515
Wichita *(G-15189)*
Oil Producers Inc of Kansas ... F ... 316 681-0231
Wichita *(G-15212)*
OS Companies Inc ... E ... 316 265-5611
Wichita *(G-15238)*
OXY Inc ... F ... 620 629-4200
Liberal *(G-6351)*
Petrosantander (usa) Inc ... F ... 620 272-7187
Garden City *(G-2253)*
Pickrell Drilling Co Inc ... F ... 316 262-8427
Wichita *(G-15299)*
Pintail Petroleum Ltd ... G ... 316 263-2243
Wichita *(G-15300)*
Prater Oil Gas Operations Inc ... G ... 620 672-7600
Pratt *(G-10134)*
R P Nixon Operations Inc ... G ... 785 628-3834
Hays *(G-2896)*
Rama Operating Co Inc ... G ... 620 234-6034
Stafford *(G-12108)*
Raymond Oil Company Inc ... F ... 316 267-4214
Wichita *(G-15422)*
Shawmar Oil & Gas Co Inc ... E ... 620 382-2932
Marion *(G-6876)*
Shields Oil Producers Inc ... E ... 785 483-3141
Russell *(G-10299)*
Stelbar Oil Corporation Inc ... F ... 316 264-8378
Wichita *(G-15660)*
Sterling Drilling Company ... D ... 620 672-9508
Pratt *(G-10154)*
Strata Drilling Inc ... E ... 620 793-7971
Great Bend *(G-2640)*
Town Oil Company ... F ... 913 294-2125
Paola *(G-9593)*
Trans Pacific Oil Corporation ... F ... 316 262-3596
Wichita *(G-15789)*
Val Energy Inc ... G ... 316 263-6688
Wichita *(G-15869)*
Verde Oil Company ... G ... 620 754-3800
Savonburg *(G-10793)*
Vess Oil Corporation ... F ... 316 682-1537
Wichita *(G-15877)*
W-W Production Co ... G ... 620 431-4137
Chanute *(G-773)*
Westmore Drilling Company Inc ... G ... 785 749-3712
Lawrence *(G-5184)*
Woolsey Petroleum Corporation ... F ... 316 267-4379
Wichita *(G-16069)*
Zenith Drilling Corporation ... G ... 316 684-9777
Wichita *(G-16100)*

CRYSTALS

Legacy Technologies Inc ... D ... 913 432-2487
Shawnee *(G-10986)*
Networks International Corp ... E ... 913 685-3400
Overland Park *(G-9078)*

CULTURE MEDIA

Phytotech Labs Inc ... F ... 913 341-5343
Lenexa *(G-6056)*
Phytotechnology Labs LLC ... F ... 913 341-5343
Lenexa *(G-6057)*
Remel Inc ... A ... 800 255-6730
Lenexa *(G-6102)*
Safc Biosciences Inc ... E ... 913 469-5580
Lenexa *(G-6116)*

CULVERTS: Sheet Metal

J & J Drainage Products Co ... E ... 620 663-1575
Hutchinson *(G-3337)*

CUPS: Plastic Exc Polystyrene Foam

Pioneer - Ram Incorporated ... A ... 316 685-2266
Wichita *(G-15301)*

CURBING: Granite Or Stone

Global Stone LLC ... G ... 913 310-9500
Olathe *(G-7733)*

CURTAIN & DRAPERY FIXTURES: Poles, Rods & Rollers

Ew & 7 Products LLC ... F ... 316 440-7486
Wichita *(G-14316)*

CUSHIONS & PILLOWS

Splintek Inc ... E ... 816 531-1900
Lenexa *(G-6148)*

CUSTOM COMPOUNDING OF RUBBER MATERIALS

American Phoenix Inc ... E ... 785 862-7722
Topeka *(G-12320)*

CUSTOMHOUSE BROKERS

FH Kaysing Company LLC ... E ... 316 721-8980
Wichita *(G-14360)*

CUSTOMS CLEARANCE OF FREIGHT

Scott Erickson ... F ... 316 942-0146
Wichita *(G-15538)*

CUT STONE & STONE PRODUCTS

Continental Cast Stone LLC ... E ... 800 989-7866
Shawnee *(G-10933)*
H J Born Stone Inc ... F ... 316 838-7788
Arkansas City *(G-158)*
J T Lardner Cut Stone Inc ... F ... 785 234-8634
Topeka *(G-12732)*
Koken Manufacturing Co Inc ... E ... 316 942-7600
Wichita *(G-14892)*
Los Primos Inc ... G ... 785 527-5535
Belleville *(G-460)*
Sandstone Inc ... F ... 913 422-0794
Shawnee Mission *(G-11827)*

CUTLERY

Ary Inc ... F ... 913 214-4813
Overland Park *(G-8398)*

CUTLERY WHOLESALERS

Ary Inc ... F ... 913 214-4813
Overland Park *(G-8398)*

CYLINDER & ACTUATORS: Fluid Power

Cross Manufacturing Inc ... D ... 785 625-2585
Hays *(G-2780)*
Hampton Hydraulics Llc ... D ... 620 792-4368
Great Bend *(G-2590)*
Squires Corporation ... F ... 316 944-0040
Wichita *(G-15650)*
Vektek LLC ... C ... 620 342-7637
Emporia *(G-1845)*

CYLINDERS: Pressure

Worthington Cylinder Corp ... C ... 316 529-6950
Maize *(G-6523)*
Worthington Cylinder Corp ... C ... 620 275-7461
Garden City *(G-2318)*

CYLINDERS: Pump

Squires Corporation ... F ... 316 944-0040
Wichita *(G-15650)*

Convents

Sisters St Joseph Wichita KS ... E ... 316 686-7171
Wichita *(G-15598)*

DAIRY PRDTS STORE: Cheese

Bern Meat Plant Incorporated ... F ... 785 336-2165
Bern *(G-521)*
Eastside Mkt Westside Mkt LLC ... G ... 785 532-8686
Manhattan *(G-6619)*

DAIRY PRDTS WHOLESALERS: Fresh

Anderson Erickson Dairy Co ... D ... 913 621-4801
Kansas City *(G-3810)*
Associated Wholesale Groc Inc ... A ... 913 288-1000
Kansas City *(G-3825)*
Hiland Dairy Foods Company LLC ... F ... 620 225-4111
Dodge City *(G-1373)*
Hiland Dairy Foods Company LLC ... F ... 785 539-7541
Manhattan *(G-6657)*
KDI Operating Company LLC ... E ... 620 453-1034
Leawood *(G-5448)*
Roberts Dairy Company LLC ... F ... 785 232-1274
Topeka *(G-13022)*
Southwest Dairy Quality Svc ... F ... 620 384-6953
Syracuse *(G-12232)*

DAIRY PRDTS: Butter

Dairy Farmers America Inc ... B ... 816 801-6455
Kansas City *(G-3953)*

DAIRY PRDTS: Condensed Milk

Dairy Farmers America Inc ... B ... 816 801-6455
Kansas City *(G-3953)*

DAIRY PRDTS: Custard, Frozen

Culvers Frozen Custard ... E ... 913 402-9777
Overland Park *(G-8623)*

DAIRY PRDTS: Dietary Supplements, Dairy & Non-Dairy Based

Ancient Formulas Inc ... F ... 316 838-5600
Wichita *(G-13702)*
Cardiotabs Inc ... G ... 816 753-4298
Overland Park *(G-8514)*

DAIRY PRDTS: Frozen Desserts & Novelties

Braumss ... G ... 620 340-8169
Emporia *(G-1707)*
Kan Pak LLC ... D ... 620 442-6820
Wichita *(G-14782)*
Paleteria Tarahumara ... G ... 620 805-6509
Garden City *(G-2245)*

DAIRY PRDTS: Ice Cream & Ice Milk

Dairy Farmers America Inc ... B ... 816 801-6455
Kansas City *(G-3953)*

DAIRY PRDTS: Ice Cream, Bulk

Peachwave ... G ... 620 624-2045
Liberal *(G-6356)*
Twisted Cow LLC ... G ... 316 804-4949
Newton *(G-7422)*

DAIRY PRDTS: Milk, Condensed & Evaporated

Hiland Dairy Foods Company LLC ... C ... 316 267-4221
Wichita *(G-14608)*

Kerry Inc .... C 913 780-1212
New Century *(G-7290)*

DAIRY PRDTS: Milk, Fluid

Kerry Inc .... C 913 780-1212
New Century *(G-7290)*
Southern Foods Group LLC .... G 316 264-5011
Wichita *(G-15623)*

DAIRY PRDTS: Milk, Processed, Pasteurized, Homogenized/Btld

Dairy Farmers America Inc .... B 816 801-6455
Kansas City *(G-3953)*
Hiland Dairy Foods Company LLC .... C 316 267-4221
Wichita *(G-14608)*

DAIRY PRDTS: Natural Cheese

Dairy Farmers America Inc .... B 816 801-6455
Kansas City *(G-3953)*
Elderslie LLC .... F 316 680-2637
Valley Center *(G-13341)*

DAMAGED MERCHANDISE SALVAGING, SVCS ONLY

National Ctstrphe Rstrtion Inc .... F 913 663-4111
Overland Park *(G-9071)*

DANCE HALL OR BALLROOM OPERATION

Entertainment Enterprises Inc .... E 316 722-4201
Wichita *(G-14292)*
Fanchon Ballroom & Supper Club .... F 785 628-8154
Hays *(G-2804)*

DANCE INSTRUCTOR

Barbaras Conservatory Dance .... F 785 272-5991
Topeka *(G-12364)*

DANCE INSTRUCTOR & SCHOOL

Ballet Midwest Inc .... F 785 272-5991
Topeka *(G-12360)*
Beller Dance Studio Inc .... E 913 648-2626
Overland Park *(G-8439)*
Byrds Dance & Gymnastics Inc .... E 913 788-9792
Kansas City *(G-3883)*
Dance Factory Inc .... F 785 272-4548
Topeka *(G-12545)*
House of Dance .... F 913 839-1962
Olathe *(G-7778)*
Raeanns Fancy Footwork .... F 316 788-4499
Derby *(G-1267)*
Starstruck Prfrmg Arts Ctr LLC .... F 913 492-3186
Shawnee Mission *(G-11896)*

DANCE INSTRUCTOR & SCHOOL SVCS

Academy of Arts LLC .... F 913 441-7300
Shawnee Mission *(G-11065)*
Acrobatic Acadmy Ftns/Educ Ctr .... E 316 721-2230
Wichita *(G-13608)*
Dance Gallery .... F 785 838-9100
Lawrence *(G-4825)*
Jody Phillips Dance Company .... E 913 897-9888
Overland Park *(G-8877)*
Miss Mrias Acrbat Dance Studio .... E 913 888-0060
Olathe *(G-7904)*
Wichita State University .... E 316 978-3581
Wichita *(G-16034)*

DATA PROCESSING & PREPARATION SVCS

Accenture LLP .... C 913 319-1000
Overland Park *(G-8340)*
Aegis Processing Solutions Inc .... D 785 232-0061
Topeka *(G-12300)*
American Design Inc .... F 785 766-0409
Baldwin City *(G-353)*
Computer Sciences Corporation .... C 913 469-8700
Overland Park *(G-8593)*
Dimension X Design LLC .... F 913 908-3824
Olathe *(G-7655)*
Mize Houser & Company PA .... D 785 233-0536
Topeka *(G-12908)*
Neufinancial Inc .... E 913 825-0000
Overland Park *(G-9079)*
Northrop Grumman Systems Corp .... B 913 651-8311
Fort Leavenworth *(G-1940)*
Qualitytech LP .... E 877 787-3282
Overland Park *(G-9219)*
Servervault LLC .... F 913 814-9988
Overland Park *(G-9298)*
Teracrunch LLC .... F 214 405-7158
Leawood *(G-5572)*
Whale Ventures LLC .... C 913 814-9988
Overland Park *(G-9493)*

DATA PROCESSING SVCS

Automatic Data Processing Inc .... F 913 492-4200
Lenexa *(G-5675)*
Automatic Data Processing Inc .... C 515 875-3160
Wichita *(G-13773)*
Bradford and Galt Incorporated .... E 913 663-1264
Shawnee Mission *(G-11177)*
Casey Associates Inc .... F 913 276-3200
Lenexa *(G-5731)*
Central of Kansas Inc .... D 785 238-4114
Junction City *(G-3678)*
Convergys Corporation .... E 913 782-3333
Olathe *(G-7614)*
Convergys Corporation .... B 316 681-4800
Wichita *(G-14095)*
Data Center Inc .... C 620 694-6800
Hutchinson *(G-3255)*
Data Center Inc .... F 913 492-2468
Lenexa *(G-5802)*
Data Center Inc .... E 620 694-6800
Hutchinson *(G-3256)*
Farmobile Inc .... F 844 337-2255
Leawood *(G-5395)*
Iris Data Services Inc .... D 913 937-0590
Kansas City *(G-4112)*
Jack Henry & Associates Inc .... E 913 341-3434
Shawnee Mission *(G-11480)*
Jupiter Esources LLC .... F 405 488-3886
Kansas City *(G-4129)*
Megaforce LLC .... D 913 402-0800
Leawood *(G-5472)*
Northrop Grumman Systems Corp .... C 785 861-3375
Topeka *(G-12938)*
Perspecta Entp Solutions LLC .... F 785 274-4200
Topeka *(G-12970)*
Physicians Business Netwrk LLC .... E 913 381-5200
Overland Park *(G-9164)*
Postal Presort Inc .... D 316 262-3333
Wichita *(G-15316)*
Qts Realty Trust Inc .... E 913 814-9988
Overland Park *(G-9210)*
Systronics Inc .... F 913 829-9229
Olathe *(G-8093)*
Xcellence Inc .... D 913 362-8662
Shawnee Mission *(G-12021)*

DATABASE INFORMATION RETRIEVAL SVCS

Infutor Data Solutions LLC .... F 913 782-8544
Olathe *(G-7790)*
Qts Realty Trust Inc .... E 913 814-9988
Overland Park *(G-9210)*

DECORATIVE WOOD & WOODWORK

Country Accents Inc .... G 316 440-1343
Andover *(G-87)*
Country Crafts .... G 620 232-1818
Opolis *(G-8180)*
Godly Play Resources Inc .... G 620 635-4018
Ashland *(G-195)*
Hemslojd Inc .... G 785 227-2983
Lindsborg *(G-6399)*
Logan Street Finewood Products .... G 316 266-4948
Wichita *(G-14976)*
Precision Craft Inc .... F 913 780-9077
Olathe *(G-8000)*
Roys Custom Cabinets .... G 785 625-6724
Hays *(G-2902)*
Underhill Finish Carpentry LLC .... F 316 253-7129
Wichita *(G-15832)*
Wood Haven Inc .... G 785 597-5618
Perry *(G-9775)*
Worship Woodworks Inc .... G 620 622-4568
Protection *(G-10177)*

DEFENSE SYSTEMS & EQPT

Emerald Aerospace Holdings LLC .... D 316 440-6966
Wichita *(G-14274)*

DEGREASING MACHINES

L S Industries Inc .... E 316 265-7997
Wichita *(G-14907)*
Machine Works Inc .... E 316 265-7997
Wichita *(G-14997)*
Superior Mobile Wash Inc .... F 913 915-9642
Kansas City *(G-4448)*

DELIVERY SVCS, BY VEHICLE

ABC Taxi Cab Company Inc .... F 316 264-4222
Wichita *(G-13596)*
Allied Courier Systems Inc .... F 913 383-8666
Stilwell *(G-12134)*
Apartment Movers Inc .... E 316 267-5300
Wichita *(G-13717)*
B & B Delivery Enterprise LLC .... F 913 541-9090
Kansas City *(G-3832)*
Fedex Ground Package Sys Inc .... B 913 422-3161
Shawnee Mission *(G-11363)*
Fedex Ground Package Sys Inc .... E 800 463-3339
Topeka *(G-12602)*
J & B Inc .... F 816 590-1174
Shawnee Mission *(G-11470)*
Jim Mitten Trucking Inc .... F 785 672-3279
Oakley *(G-7477)*
Meemaws Country Kitchen .... F 913 352-6297
Pleasanton *(G-9998)*
N T S LLC .... E 913 281-5353
Kansas City *(G-4277)*
Quicksilver Ex Courier of MO .... D 913 321-5959
Kansas City *(G-4354)*
Randolph Carter Entps Inc .... F 913 837-3955
Louisburg *(G-6464)*
Robinsons Delivery Service .... E 913 281-4952
Kansas City *(G-4385)*
Sunflower Taxi Courier Svc LLC .... F 785 826-1881
Salina *(G-10727)*
Supervan Service Co Inc .... E 913 281-4044
Kansas City *(G-4450)*

DENTAL EQPT

Beyond 21st Century Inc .... G 913 631-4790
Shawnee *(G-10916)*

DENTAL EQPT & SPLYS

Henry Schein Inc .... F 913 894-8444
Shawnee Mission *(G-11427)*

DENTAL EQPT & SPLYS WHOLESALERS

Henry Schein Inc .... F 913 894-8444
Shawnee Mission *(G-11427)*
Patterson Dental Supply Inc .... E 913 492-6100
Lenexa *(G-6045)*
Patterson Dental Supply Inc .... F 316 315-1800
Wichita *(G-15269)*

DENTAL EQPT & SPLYS: Dental Materials

Myrons Dental Laboratories .... E 800 359-7111
Kansas City *(G-4276)*
Splintek Inc .... E 816 531-1900
Lenexa *(G-6148)*

DENTAL EQPT & SPLYS: Denture Materials

Chameleon Dental Products .... E 913 281-5552
Kansas City *(G-3908)*

DENTAL EQPT & SPLYS: Hand Pieces & Parts

Scope Inc .... G 316 393-7414
Wichita *(G-15536)*

DENTAL EQPT & SPLYS: Orthodontic Appliances

Midwest Orthodontics Inc .... F 316 942-8703
Wichita *(G-15097)*

DENTISTS' OFFICES & CLINICS

Gracemed Health Clinic Inc .... F 316 440-7938
Wichita *(G-14490)*
Gracemed Health Clinic Inc .... D 316 866-2001
Wichita *(G-14491)*
John F Dahm Dr .... F 620 665-5582
Hutchinson *(G-3343)*

John H Hay DDS....F....785 749-2525
Lawrence (G-4926)
Kaylor Dental Laboratory Inc....D....316 943-3226
Wichita (G-14835)
Keith and Assoc Dentistry LLC....E....913 384-0044
Mission (G-7132)
Mark R Davis DDS....F....316 684-8261
Wichita (G-15010)
Medallion Dental Lab Inc....F....913 642-0039
Prairie Village (G-10047)
Richard Winburn....F....913 492-5180
Shawnee Mission (G-11801)
Smile Centre....F....913 651-9800
Leavenworth (G-5289)
Wamego Dental Center Inc....F....785 456-2330
Wamego (G-13450)
William Hoffman....F....913 649-8890
Shawnee Mission (G-12009)

DEPARTMENT STORES: Country General

Crazy House Inc....F....620 275-2153
Garden City (G-2138)

DEPARTMENT STORES: Non-Discount

Sears Roebuck and Co....C....785 826-4378
Salina (G-10701)

DEPARTMENT STORES: Surplus & Salvage

Bachus & Son Inc....E....316 265-4673
Wichita (G-13789)

DEPOSIT INSURANCE

Ameritrust Group Inc....F....913 339-5000
Overland Park (G-8381)
Farmers Group Inc....E....913 227-3200
Olathe (G-7704)
Livestock Marketing Assn....E....816 891-0502
Leawood (G-5458)
Uniformed Services Beneft Assn....F....913 327-5500
Overland Park (G-9440)

DESIGN SVCS, NEC

Aat Aero Inc....F....316 832-1412
Wichita (G-13594)
C3i....F....913 327-2255
Overland Park (G-8505)
Global Engineering & Tech Inc....C....316 729-9232
Goddard (G-2439)
Icon Integration & Design Inc....F....913 221-8801
Overland Park (G-8837)
Insight 2 Design LLC....F....913 937-9386
Overland Park (G-8852)
Millennium Concepts Inc....F....316 821-9300
Wichita (G-15110)
Moorekc Enterprises LLC....F....316 347-0121
Shawnee (G-11000)
Profillment LLC....F....316 260-7910
Wichita (G-15369)
Pulse Design Group Inc....E....913 438-9095
Lenexa (G-6079)

DESIGN SVCS: Commercial & Indl

B A Designs LLC....E....785 267-8110
Topeka (G-12356)
Infusion Design Incorporated....E....913 422-0317
Bonner Springs (G-555)
U S Automation Inc....G....913 894-2410
Shawnee Mission (G-11953)
Winter Architects Inc....F....316 267-7142
Wichita (G-16058)

DESIGN SVCS: Computer Integrated Systems

Advantage Computer Entps Inc....E....620 365-5156
Iola (G-3585)
Aegis Business Solutions LLC....G....913 307-9922
Olathe (G-7512)
American Gvrnment Slutions LLC....F....913 428-2550
Leawood (G-5320)
Bartunek Group Inc....E....913 327-8800
Overland Park (G-8435)
Cerner Government Services Inc....E....816 201-2273
Kansas City (G-3905)
Control Systems Intl Inc....D....913 599-5010
Shawnee Mission (G-11264)
Financial Institution Tech Inc....E....888 848-7349
Topeka (G-12610)
GSM Sales LLC....F....816 674-1066
Roeland Park (G-10223)
Isigma Consulting LLC....F....620 757-6363
Overland Park (G-8863)
K G Moats & Sons LLC....E....785 437-2021
Saint Marys (G-10368)
Kaliaperumal Mamalay....G....816 210-1248
Overland Park (G-8885)
Mersoft Corporation....E....913 871-6200
Leawood (G-5476)
Netapp Inc....E....316 636-8000
Wichita (G-15161)
Netapp Inc....C....913 451-6718
Overland Park (G-9073)
Netstandard Inc....D....913 428-4200
Overland Park (G-9077)
Nokia of America Corporation....D....316 636-4800
Wichita (G-15184)
Northrop Grumman Systems Corp....E....785 861-3398
Topeka (G-12939)
Paracom Technologies Inc....E....316 293-2900
Wichita (G-15254)
Rhythm Engineering LLC....E....913 227-0603
Lenexa (G-6108)
Sirius Computer Solutions Inc....F....913 469-7900
Overland Park (G-9314)
Source Incorporated Missouri....F....913 663-2700
Shawnee (G-11030)
Stallard Technologies Inc....E....913 851-2260
Overland Park (G-9351)
Thunderhead Engrg Cons Inc....F....785 770-8511
Manhattan (G-6826)
Wachter Tech Solutions Inc....D....856 222-0643
Lenexa (G-6220)

DETECTIVE & ARMORED CAR SERVICES

Prime SEC Svcs Borrower LLC....F....630 410-0662
Lawrence (G-5076)

DETECTIVE SVCS

1138 Inc....E....913 322-5900
Overland Park (G-8328)
Owens Bonding Inc....E....316 283-3983
Wichita (G-15242)

DIAGNOSTIC SUBSTANCES

Abaxis Inc....E....913 787-7400
Olathe (G-7506)
Plastikon Healthcare LLC....E....785 330-7100
Lawrence (G-5069)
Progene Biomedical Inc....F....913 492-2224
Lenexa (G-6074)
Remel....G....913 895-4362
Lenexa (G-6101)

DIAGNOSTIC SUBSTANCES OR AGENTS: In Vitro

George King Bio-Medical Inc....F....913 469-5464
Shawnee Mission (G-11396)

DIAGNOSTIC SUBSTANCES OR AGENTS: Radioactive

Petnet Solutions Inc....G....913 310-9270
Overland Park (G-9160)

DIAGNOSTIC SUBSTANCES OR AGENTS: Veterinary

K State Rabies Laboratory....F....785 532-4472
Manhattan (G-6668)

DIAMONDS: Cutting & Polishing

Diamond Ethanol LLC....G....620 626-2026
Liberal (G-6304)

DIES & TOOLS: Special

Brittain Machine Inc....E....316 942-8223
Wichita (G-13892)
Ceco Inc....E....316 942-7431
Wichita (G-13969)
De Hoff Tool & Mfg Co Inc....F....913 342-2212
Kansas City (G-3963)
Excel Tool and Mfg Inc....E....913 894-6415
Lenexa (G-5841)
Four Star Tool and Die Inc....G....316 264-2913
Wichita (G-14411)
Friesen Tool Co Inc....G....316 262-6808
Wichita (G-14425)
Hoelker Tooling....G....316 744-7777
Wichita (G-14621)
Kocher + Beck USA LP....D....913 529-4336
Lenexa (G-5955)
Kocher + Beck USA LP....E....913 529-4336
Lenexa (G-5956)
Leading Edge Aerospace LLC....E....316 942-1301
Wichita (G-14939)
Metal Arts Engravers Inc....F....913 262-1979
Shawnee (G-10994)
Raptor Manufacturing Lc....E....316 201-1772
Wichita (G-15418)
Three Way Pattern Inc....F....316 942-7421
Wichita (G-15763)
Vector Technologies Inc....E....620 262-2700
Winfield (G-16178)

DIES: Plastic Forming

Hayes Tooling & Plastics Inc....F....913 782-0046
Olathe (G-7757)

DIET & WEIGHT REDUCING CENTERS

Ww North America Holdings Inc....E....913 227-0152
Overland Park (G-9507)
Ww North America Holdings Inc....E....913 495-1400
Overland Park (G-9508)

DIETICIANS' OFFICES

Board of Edcatn of Kans Cy Ks....E....913 627-3913
Kansas City (G-3871)
Hodes & Nauser Mds PA....F....913 491-6878
Overland Park (G-8821)
Quivira Athletic Club L C....D....913 268-3633
Lenexa (G-6086)

DIMENSION STONE: Buildings

Surface Center Interiors LLC....F....913 422-0500
Shawnee (G-11037)

DINNER THEATERS

Actors LLC....E....316 263-0222
Wichita (G-13610)
New Theatre Company....C....913 649-7469
Shawnee Mission (G-11681)

DIRECT SELLING ESTABLISHMENTS: Food Svcs

Danisco USA Inc....C....913 764-8100
New Century (G-7277)
Huhtamaki Films Inc....A....913 583-3025
De Soto (G-1204)

DISASTER SVCS

Advance Catastrophe Tech Inc....E....316 262-9992
Bel Aire (G-426)
Clean Tech Inc....C....316 729-8100
Wichita (G-14040)
Continuity Operation Plg LLC....F....913 227-0660
Lenexa (G-5785)
Lamunyon Clg & Restoration....F....785 632-1259
Clay Center (G-870)
Mc Pherson County Food Bank....F....620 241-8050
McPherson (G-6989)
United Disaster Response LLC....E....913 963-8403
Shawnee Mission (G-11962)

DISC JOCKEYS

Complete Music Inc....E....913 432-1111
Leawood (G-5357)

DISCOUNT DEPARTMENT STORES

McLane Company Inc....E....913 492-7090
Shawnee Mission (G-11609)
Walmart Inc....C....785 899-2111
Goodland (G-2489)
Walmart Inc....B....316 347-2092
Goddard (G-2456)
Walmart Inc....B....620 275-0775
Garden City (G-2308)

Walmart Inc....B....620 232-1593
Pittsburg *(G-9960)*
Walmart Inc....C....316 945-2800
Wichita *(G-15923)*
Walmart Inc....B....316 636-5384
Wichita *(G-15924)*

DISHWASHING EQPT: Commercial

Jesse Inc....F....913 342-4282
Kansas City *(G-4123)*

DISKETTE DUPLICATING SVCS

Optiv Security Inc....F....816 421-6611
Overland Park *(G-9110)*
Progrssive Tech Intgrators LLC....F....913 663-0870
Overland Park *(G-9192)*

DISPENSERS: Soap

Brightwell Dispensers Inc....G....913 956-4909
Lenexa *(G-5715)*

DISTILLERS DRIED GRAIN & SOLUBLES

Dark Horse Distillery LLC....F....913 492-3275
Lenexa *(G-5801)*
Lansing Trade Group LLC....C....913 748-3000
Overland Park *(G-8945)*
Mgp Ingredients Inc....C....913 367-1480
Atchison *(G-245)*
MI Rancho Tequila Usa Inc....G....913 530-7260
Kansas City *(G-4241)*
Union Horse Distilling Co LLC....F....913 492-3275
Lenexa *(G-6200)*

DOCUMENT DESTRUCTION SVC

Mosaic....C....620 276-7972
Garden City *(G-2240)*
Stericycle Inc....E....913 307-9400
Lenexa *(G-6153)*
T2 Holdings LLC....F....913 327-8889
Kansas City *(G-4456)*

DOCUMENT STORAGE SVCS

Document Resources Inc....F....316 683-1444
Wichita *(G-14219)*

DOLL & ACCESSORY REPAIR SVCS

Doll Cradle....F....913 631-1900
Shawnee Mission *(G-11313)*

DOMESTIC HELP SVCS

Dirty Work....F....316 652-9104
Wichita *(G-14214)*
Have It Maid....F....316 264-0110
Wichita *(G-14568)*
Housekeeping Unlimited....E....785 842-2444
Lawrence *(G-4905)*
Lulu Mimi Hsclners Extrrdnaire....F....913 649-6022
Shawnee Mission *(G-11582)*
Merry Maids Ltd Partnership....F....785 842-2410
Lawrence *(G-5023)*
Residential Services Inc....E....316 832-9058
Wichita *(G-15449)*
Vintage Place of Pittsburg....E....620 231-4554
Pittsburg *(G-9958)*

DOOR & WINDOW REPAIR SVCS

Cheney Door Co Inc....F....620 669-9306
Hutchinson *(G-3236)*
D H Pace Company Inc....C....816 221-0072
Olathe *(G-7636)*
D H Pace Company Inc....A....816 221-0543
Olathe *(G-7637)*
D H Pace Company Inc....E....316 944-3667
Wichita *(G-14157)*
D H Pace Company Inc....B....816 480-2600
Olathe *(G-7638)*
EE Newcomer Enterprises Inc....B....816 221-0543
Olathe *(G-7671)*
Glass Services Inc....F....785 823-5444
Salina *(G-10511)*
Janssen Glass & Mirror Inc....F....913 677-5727
Shawnee *(G-10977)*
Overhead Door Company....E....316 265-4634
Wichita *(G-15240)*

DOOR OPERATING SYSTEMS: Electric

Cheney Door Co Inc....F....620 669-9306
Hutchinson *(G-3236)*
Overhead Door Company....E....316 265-4634
Wichita *(G-15240)*
Raynor Gar Door Co Inc Kans Cy....F....913 422-0441
Shawnee Mission *(G-11779)*
Weathercraft Company N Platte....G....785 899-3064
Goodland *(G-2490)*

DOORS & WINDOWS WHOLESALERS: All Materials

American Drect Procurement Inc....C....913 677-5588
Lenexa *(G-5648)*
Home Stl Siding & Windows LLC....F....785 625-8622
Hays *(G-2849)*
Midwest Siding Inc....E....785 825-0606
Salina *(G-10603)*
Pratt Glass Inc....F....620 672-6463
Pratt *(G-10139)*
Window Design Company....G....785 582-2888
Silver Lake *(G-12030)*

DOORS & WINDOWS: Storm, Metal

Champion Window Co Kans Cy Inc....E....913 541-8282
Lenexa *(G-5751)*
Columbia Industries Inc....E....785 227-3351
Lindsborg *(G-6396)*
Columbia Metal Products Co....E....620 365-3166
Iola *(G-3594)*
Reno Fabricating & Sls Co Inc....E....620 663-1269
Hutchinson *(G-3426)*
Western Aluminum & Glass Co....F....785 625-2418
Hays *(G-2931)*

DOORS: Fiberglass

Masonite International Corp....E....620 231-8200
Pittsburg *(G-9899)*

DOORS: Folding, Plastic Or Plastic Coated Fabric

Classic Shower Door Inc....G....913 492-9670
Overland Park *(G-8562)*

DOORS: Garage, Overhead, Wood

Tracker Door Systems LLC....G....913 585-3100
De Soto *(G-1214)*

DOORS: Safe & Vault, Metal

Carlson Products LLC....D....316 722-0265
Maize *(G-6509)*

DOORS: Wooden

Koch & Co Inc....B....785 336-6022
Seneca *(G-10871)*
Technique Manufacturing Inc....F....620 663-6360
Hutchinson *(G-3463)*

DRAFTING SPLYS WHOLESALERS

Drafting Room Inc....G....316 267-2291
Wichita *(G-14236)*

DRAFTING SVCS

Rapco Inc....F....785 524-4232
Lincoln *(G-6386)*
Young Electric Inc....E....316 681-8118
Wichita *(G-16090)*

DRAPERIES & CURTAINS

Alderman Acres Mfg Inc....F....620 251-4095
Coffeyville *(G-909)*
Andrews and Abbey Riley LLC....F....913 262-2212
Kansas City *(G-3811)*
Long Shot Enterprises LLC....F....785 493-0171
Salina *(G-10584)*
Window Flair Draperies....G....913 722-6070
Shawnee *(G-11054)*

DRAPERY & UPHOLSTERY STORES: Draperies

Madden-Mcfarland Interiors Ltd....E....913 681-2821
Leawood *(G-5462)*

Schammerhorn Inc....G....316 265-8659
Wichita *(G-15528)*
Sewing Workshop....F....785 357-6231
Topeka *(G-13061)*

DRILLING MACHINERY & EQPT: Oil & Gas

Conrad Machine Inc....E....620 231-9458
Pittsburg *(G-9844)*

DRILLING MACHINERY & EQPT: Water Well

BYIS Manufacturing LLC....F....620 221-4603
Winfield *(G-16119)*

DRILLING MUD COMPOUNDS, CONDITIONERS & ADDITIVES

Undergrund Cvern Stblztion LLC....G....620 617-0302
Hutchinson *(G-3474)*

DRINKING PLACES: Alcoholic Beverages

B & C Restaurant Corporation....C....913 327-0800
Shawnee Mission *(G-11138)*
Corporate Hills LLC....C....316 651-0333
Wichita *(G-14104)*
Golden Eagle Casino....B....785 486-6601
Horton *(G-3125)*
Hulsing Hotels Kansas Inc....D....785 539-5311
Manhattan *(G-6662)*
Incred-A-Bowl LLC....D....913 851-1700
Overland Park *(G-8841)*
Lenexa Hotel LP....D....913 217-1000
Lenexa *(G-5970)*
Lodgian Inc....E....785 841-7077
Lawrence *(G-5000)*
New Theatre Company....C....913 649-7469
Shawnee Mission *(G-11681)*
Park Hotels & Resorts Inc....D....913 649-7060
Shawnee Mission *(G-11716)*
Quality Inn....D....620 663-4444
South Hutchinson *(G-12064)*
Sac & Fox Ntion MO In Kans Neb....B....785 467-8000
Powhattan *(G-10010)*
Sagar Inc....E....620 241-5343
McPherson *(G-7024)*
Shamir Corp....E....785 266-8880
Topeka *(G-13062)*
Tellers....D....785 843-4111
Lawrence *(G-5133)*
Wichita Airport Ht Assoc L P....C....316 945-5272
Wichita *(G-15971)*

DRINKING PLACES: Bars & Lounges

Elks Lodge Inc....E....620 672-2011
Pratt *(G-10110)*
Executive Mnor Leavenworth Inc....F....785 234-5400
Topeka *(G-12586)*

DRINKING PLACES: Night Clubs

Dodge Enteprise Inc....E....620 227-2125
Dodge City *(G-1356)*

DRINKING PLACES: Tavern

B & B Backyard....F....785 246-6348
Topeka *(G-12355)*
Stickels Inc....E....785 539-5722
Manhattan *(G-6812)*

DRUG CLINIC, OUTPATIENT

County of Crawford....E....620 231-5130
Pittsburg *(G-9848)*
County of Crawford....C....620 231-5141
Pittsburg *(G-9849)*
Mirror Inc....F....316 634-3954
Wichita *(G-15117)*
Mirror Inc....E....316 283-6743
Newton *(G-7389)*
Occupational Hlth Partners LLC....E....785 823-8381
Salina *(G-10618)*
Pipeline Tstg Consortium Inc....E....620 669-8800
Hutchinson *(G-3406)*

DRUG STORES

3c Healthcare Inc....F....620 221-7850
Winfield *(G-16113)*
Arbuthnots Inc....E....785 527-2146
Belleville *(G-450)*

CVS Pharmacy Inc ....E.... 913 651-2323
Leavenworth *(G-5230)*
CVS Pharmacy Inc ....F.... 913 722-3711
Shawnee Mission *(G-11287)*
Dandurand Drug Company Inc ....E.... 316 685-2353
Wichita *(G-14165)*
Dillon Companies Inc ....C.... 620 663-4464
Hutchinson *(G-3263)*
Dillon Companies Inc ....D.... 620 275-0151
Garden City *(G-2148)*
Dillon Companies Inc ....C.... 785 272-0661
Topeka *(G-12557)*
Gibson Wholesale Co Inc ....F.... 316 945-3471
Wichita *(G-14463)*
Kingman Drug Inc ....F.... 620 532-5113
Kingman *(G-4600)*
Rx Plus Pharmacies Inc ....F.... 316 263-5218
Wichita *(G-15495)*
Walgreen Co ....E.... 913 393-2757
Olathe *(G-8146)*
Walgreen Co ....E.... 785 628-1767
Hays *(G-2928)*
Walgreen Co ....E.... 316 652-9147
Wichita *(G-15917)*
Walgreen Co ....E.... 316 689-0866
Wichita *(G-15918)*
Walgreen Co ....E.... 316 729-6171
Wichita *(G-15919)*
Walgreen Co ....E.... 316 943-2299
Wichita *(G-15920)*
Walgreen Co ....E.... 913 814-7977
Overland Park *(G-9480)*
Walgreen Co ....E.... 913 829-3176
Olathe *(G-8147)*
Walgreen Co ....E.... 913 789-9275
Merriam *(G-7109)*
Walgreen Co ....E.... 316 218-0819
Andover *(G-116)*
Walgreen Co ....E.... 913 341-1725
Overland Park *(G-9481)*
Walgreen Co ....E.... 316 684-2828
Wichita *(G-15921)*
Walgreen Co ....E.... 785 841-9000
Lawrence *(G-5178)*
Walgreen Co ....E.... 785 832-8388
Lawrence *(G-5179)*

DRUGS & DRUG PROPRIETARIES, WHOLESALE: Animal Medicines

Bill Barr & Company ....F.... 913 599-6668
Overland Park *(G-8448)*
Sera Inc ....F.... 913 541-1307
Shawnee Mission *(G-11848)*

DRUGS & DRUG PROPRIETARIES, WHOLESALE: Druggists' Sundries

Wichita Tobacco & Candy Co ....F.... 316 264-2412
Wichita *(G-16040)*

DRUGS & DRUG PROPRIETARIES, WHOLESALE: Pharmaceuticals

Briovarx Infusion Svcs 305 LLC ....D.... 913 747-3700
Lenexa *(G-5717)*
Cardinal Health Inc ....D.... 316 264-6275
Wichita *(G-13944)*
Genzada Pharmaceuticals Usa ....F.... 620 204-7150
Sterling *(G-12120)*
Hudson Holding Inc ....D.... 866 404-3300
Wichita *(G-14648)*
Rx Plus Pharmacies Inc ....F.... 316 263-5218
Wichita *(G-15495)*
Stecklein Enterprises LLC ....F.... 785 625-2529
Hays *(G-2912)*

DRUGS ACTING ON THE CENTRAL NERVOUS SYSTEM & SENSE ORGANS

Teva Neuroscience Inc ....D.... 913 777-3000
Leawood *(G-5573)*

DRUMS: Shipping, Metal

Mobile Mini Inc ....F.... 316 838-2663
Park City *(G-9636)*

DRYCLEANING & LAUNDRY SVCS: Commercial & Family

Cintas Corporation No 2 ....C.... 913 782-8333
Olathe *(G-7596)*
Just Our Laundry Inc ....F.... 913 649-8364
Shawnee Mission *(G-11505)*
Penn Enterprises Inc ....E.... 785 762-3600
Junction City *(G-3737)*
Scotch Industries Inc ....E.... 785 843-8585
Lawrence *(G-5105)*

DRYCLEANING PLANTS

College Hill Cleaners Inc ....F.... 316 683-3331
Wichita *(G-14055)*
Comet 1 H R Cleaners Inc ....F.... 620 626-8100
Liberal *(G-6295)*
Dry Clean City ....F.... 785 776-1515
Manhattan *(G-6617)*
Ineeda Laundry & Dry Cleaners ....D.... 620 662-6450
Hutchinson *(G-3332)*
Ineeda Laundry and Drycleaners ....E.... 620 663-5688
Hutchinson *(G-3333)*
Just Our Laundry Inc ....F.... 913 649-8364
Shawnee Mission *(G-11505)*
Oak Park Cleaners Inc ....F.... 913 599-3040
Shawnee Mission *(G-11692)*
Parker Enterprises Inc ....E.... 316 682-4543
Wichita *(G-15263)*

DRYCLEANING SVC: Collecting & Distributing Agency

Al Morris ....F.... 620 225-5611
Dodge City *(G-1291)*
Heartland At-Chlor Systems LLC ....F.... 806 373-4277
Wichita *(G-14580)*
Holiday Cleaners ....F.... 913 631-6181
Overland Park *(G-8822)*
Scotch Industries Inc ....E.... 785 235-3401
Topeka *(G-13042)*

DRYCLEANING SVC: Drapery & Curtain

Scotch Industries Inc ....E.... 785 843-8585
Lawrence *(G-5105)*
Stickels Inc ....E.... 785 539-5722
Manhattan *(G-6812)*
Stovers Restoration Inc ....F.... 316 686-5005
Maize *(G-6521)*

DUCTING: Metal Plate

HBD Industries Inc ....D.... 620 431-9100
Chanute *(G-730)*

DUCTS: Sheet Metal

Sheet Metal Contractors Inc ....E.... 913 397-9130
Olathe *(G-8061)*

DUST OR FUME COLLECTING EQPT: Indl

Schenck Process LLC ....C.... 785 284-2191
Sabetha *(G-10331)*

EARTH SCIENCE SVCS

Gsi Engineering Nthrn Div LLC ....F.... 316 554-0725
Wichita *(G-14523)*

EATING PLACES

A Scampis Bar & Grill ....E.... 785 539-5311
Manhattan *(G-6527)*
Alvamar Inc ....E.... 785 842-2929
Lawrence *(G-4732)*
Angus Inn Best Western Motel ....D.... 620 792-3541
Great Bend *(G-2509)*
Bobby TS Bar & Grill Inc ....F.... 785 537-8383
Manhattan *(G-6564)*
Corporate Hills LLC ....C.... 316 651-0333
Wichita *(G-14104)*
Falcon Lakes Golf LLC ....E.... 913 724-4653
Basehor *(G-376)*
Free State Brewing Co Inc ....D.... 785 843-4555
Lawrence *(G-4865)*
Gary Dean Anderson ....E.... 785 475-2340
Oberlin *(G-7495)*
Golden Eagle Casino ....B.... 785 486-6601
Horton *(G-3125)*
Golf Operations Management LLC ....E.... 913 897-3809
Overland Park *(G-8764)*
Grand Central Hotel Corp ....E.... 620 273-6763
Cottonwood Falls *(G-1154)*
Hi-Plains Motel & Restaurant ....F.... 620 375-4438
Leoti *(G-6254)*
Hotel Clubs Corp Woods Inc ....D.... 913 451-6100
Overland Park *(G-8829)*
Incred-A-Bowl LLC ....D.... 913 851-1700
Overland Park *(G-8841)*
Kickapoo Tribe In Kansas Inc ....C.... 785 486-2131
Horton *(G-3130)*
Lamont Hill Resort Inc ....E.... 785 828-3131
Vassar *(G-13371)*
Latour Management Inc ....F.... 316 733-1922
Andover *(G-102)*
Lenexa Hotel LP ....D.... 913 217-1000
Lenexa *(G-5970)*
Lodgian Inc ....E.... 785 841-7077
Lawrence *(G-5000)*
Mission Recreation Inc ....E.... 913 782-0279
Olathe *(G-7906)*
Park Hotels & Resorts Inc ....D.... 913 649-7060
Shawnee Mission *(G-11716)*
Red Coach Inn ....E.... 316 321-6900
El Dorado *(G-1597)*
Rekat Recreation Inc ....E.... 785 272-1881
Topeka *(G-13007)*
River City Brewery Inc ....D.... 316 263-2739
Wichita *(G-15469)*
Robin White Hills Inc ....F.... 785 877-3399
Norton *(G-7462)*
Sac & Fox Ntion MO In Kans Neb ....B.... 785 467-8000
Powhattan *(G-10010)*
Sagar Inc ....E.... 620 241-5343
McPherson *(G-7024)*
Salina Red Coach Inn ....F.... 785 825-2111
Salina *(G-10684)*
Shamir Corp ....E.... 785 266-8880
Topeka *(G-13062)*
Topeka Country Club ....D.... 785 232-2090
Topeka *(G-13173)*
Walmart Inc ....B.... 620 275-0775
Garden City *(G-2308)*
Warren Theatres LLC ....D.... 316 722-7060
Wichita *(G-15928)*
Wichita Airport Ht Assoc L P ....C.... 316 945-5272
Wichita *(G-15971)*
Woodside Tennis & Health Club ....C.... 913 831-0034
Shawnee Mission *(G-12017)*

ECONOMIC PROGRAMS ADMINISTRATION SVCS, NEC

National Weather Service ....E.... 785 899-2360
Goodland *(G-2480)*
National Weather Service ....E.... 785 234-2592
Topeka *(G-12924)*
National Weather Service ....E.... 620 225-6514
Dodge City *(G-1411)*

EDUCATIONAL SVCS

Abwa Management LLC ....E.... 913 732-5100
Overland Park *(G-8338)*
International Inst Christian S ....E.... 913 962-4422
Overland Park *(G-8858)*
Medevac Midamerica Inc ....C.... 785 233-2400
Topeka *(G-12878)*
Olathe Unified School Dst 233 ....D.... 913 780-7011
Olathe *(G-7951)*
Southwest Plins Rgonal Svc Ctr ....D.... 620 675-2241
Sublette *(G-12207)*

EDUCATIONAL SVCS, NONDEGREE GRANTING: Continuing Education

Franklin Covey Co ....G.... 800 819-1812
Overland Park *(G-8737)*
Southeast Kans Educatn Svc Ctr ....C.... 620 724-6281
Girard *(G-2418)*

ELECTRIC & OTHER SERVICES COMBINED

City of Clay Center ....E.... 785 632-2139
Clay Center *(G-849)*
City of Wamego ....E.... 785 456-9598
Wamego *(G-13412)*
Duke Energy Corporation ....F.... 620 855-6830
Cimarron *(G-824)*

Kansas City Bd Pub Utilities........C....... 913 573-9000
Kansas City *(G-4134)*
Kansas City Bd Pub Utilities........C....... 913 573-9000
Kansas City *(G-4136)*
Kansas City Bd Pub Utilities........D....... 913 573-9300
Kansas City *(G-4137)*
Kansas City Bd Pub Utilities........C....... 913 573-9556
Kansas City *(G-4138)*
Kansas City Bd Pub Utilities........A....... 913 573-9143
Kansas City *(G-4141)*
Web Creations & Consulting LLC........G....... 785 823-7630
Salina *(G-10762)*

ELECTRIC MOTOR REPAIR SVCS

Gems Inc........G....... 785 731-2849
Ransom *(G-10192)*
Gibson Industrial Controls Inc........G....... 620 241-3551
McPherson *(G-6969)*
Independent Electric McHy Co........G....... 620 257-5375
Lyons *(G-6486)*
Independent Electric McHy Co........G....... 785 233-4282
Topeka *(G-12716)*
Klemp Electric Machinery Co........F....... 913 371-4330
Kansas City *(G-4176)*
Kriers Auto Parts Inc........G....... 785 738-3526
Beloit *(G-489)*
Naab Electric Inc........F....... 620 276-8101
Garden City *(G-2242)*
O K Electric Work Inc........G....... 620 251-2270
Coffeyville *(G-966)*
Patchen Electric & Indus Sup........G....... 785 843-4522
Lawrence *(G-5057)*
Rotek Services Inc........E....... 316 263-3131
Wichita *(G-15483)*

ELECTRIC POWER DISTRIBUTION TO CONSUMERS

Ark Valley Electric Coop Assn........F....... 620 662-6661
South Hutchinson *(G-12055)*
Bluestem Electric Coop Inc........F....... 785 456-2212
Wamego *(G-13406)*
Bluestem Electric Cooperative........E....... 785 632-3111
Clay Center *(G-844)*
Brown-Atchinson Elc Coop Assn........F....... 785 486-2117
Horton *(G-3122)*
Butler Rural Elc Coop Assn Inc........E....... 316 321-9600
El Dorado *(G-1541)*
Caney Valley Elc Coop Assn........F....... 620 758-2262
Cedar Vale *(G-692)*
City of Coffeyville........F....... 620 252-6180
Coffeyville *(G-915)*
DS&o Electric Cooperative........E....... 785 655-2011
Solomon *(G-12050)*
Empire District Electric Co........F....... 620 856-2121
Baxter Springs *(G-405)*
Evergy Kansas Central Inc........F....... 800 383-1183
El Dorado *(G-1560)*
Evergy Kansas Central Inc........E....... 800 383-1183
Independence *(G-3516)*
Evergy Kansas Central Inc........F....... 620 532-2782
Kingman *(G-4589)*
Evergy Kansas Central Inc........D....... 785 575-1352
Topeka *(G-12584)*
Evergy Kansas Central Inc........F....... 785 263-2023
Abilene *(G-29)*
Evergy Kansas Central Inc........E....... 316 291-8612
Colwich *(G-1096)*
Flint Hils Rur Elc Coop Assn I........E....... 620 767-5144
Council Grove *(G-1167)*
Heartland Rural Elc Coop Inc........E....... 620 724-8251
Girard *(G-2411)*
Itc Great Plains LLC........F....... 785 783-2226
Topeka *(G-12729)*
Jeffrey Energy........F....... 785 456-2035
Saint Marys *(G-10367)*
Kansas City Bd Pub Utilities........E....... 913 573-6810
Kansas City *(G-4142)*
Kansas Electric Power Coop Inc........E....... 785 273-7010
Topeka *(G-12776)*
Midwest Energy Inc........E....... 620 792-1301
Great Bend *(G-2611)*
Midwest Energy Inc........E....... 785 462-8251
Colby *(G-1028)*
Nemaha-Marshall Electric........F....... 785 736-2345
Axtell *(G-351)*
Prairie Land Electric Coop Inc........D....... 785 877-3323
Norton *(G-7461)*
Radiant Electric Cooperative........F....... 620 378-2161
Fredonia *(G-2044)*
Rolling Hills Electric Coop........F....... 785 534-1601
Beloit *(G-501)*
Rolling Hills Electric Coop........E....... 785 472-4021
Ellsworth *(G-1680)*
Sedgwick County Elc Coop Assn........F....... 316 542-3131
Cheney *(G-796)*
Twin Valley Electric Coop........F....... 620 784-5500
Altamont *(G-73)*
Victory Electric Coop Assn Inc........D....... 620 227-2139
Dodge City *(G-1447)*
Westar Energy Inc........F....... 316 261-6575
Wichita *(G-15960)*
Western Cooperative Elc Assn........E....... 785 743-5561
Wakeeney *(G-13395)*
Wheatland Electric Coop Inc........E....... 620 275-0261
Garden City *(G-2314)*
Wheatland Electric Coop Inc........F....... 620 793-4223
Great Bend *(G-2663)*

ELECTRIC POWER GENERATION: Fossil Fuel

City of Chanute........F....... 620 431-5270
Chanute *(G-716)*
Empire District Electric Co........D....... 620 848-3456
Riverton *(G-10212)*
Sunflower Electric Power Corp........C....... 620 277-2590
Holcomb *(G-3080)*

ELECTRIC POWER, COGENERATED

Biostar Renewables LLC........E....... 913 369-4100
Overland Park *(G-8450)*

ELECTRIC SERVICES

City of Goodland........F....... 785 890-4555
Goodland *(G-2465)*
City of Pratt........F....... 620 672-3831
Pratt *(G-10101)*
Cowley County Crime Stoppers........F....... 620 221-7777
Winfield *(G-16132)*
Duke Energy Corporation........F....... 620 855-6830
Cimarron *(G-824)*
Evergy Kansas Central Inc........F....... 620 793-3515
Great Bend *(G-2560)*
Evergy Kansas Central Inc........F....... 316 299-7155
Wichita *(G-14315)*
Evergy Kansas Central Inc........F....... 800 794-6101
Pratt *(G-10111)*
Evergy Kansas Central Inc........C....... 785 331-4700
Lawrence *(G-4854)*
Evergy Kansas Central Inc........D....... 620 341-7020
Emporia *(G-1753)*
Evergy Kansas Central Inc........D....... 316 283-5521
Newton *(G-7342)*
Federated Rural Elc MGT Corp........E....... 913 541-0150
Lenexa *(G-5849)*
Freestate Electric Coop Inc........E....... 913 796-6111
Mc Louth *(G-6927)*
Kansas City Bd Pub Utilities........C....... 913 573-9675
Kansas City *(G-4139)*
Kansas City Bd Pub Utilities........C....... 913 573-9556
Kansas City *(G-4138)*
Kansas City Bd Pub Utilities........A....... 913 573-9143
Kansas City *(G-4141)*
Kansas Gas Service........F....... 800 794-4780
Overland Park *(G-8902)*
L Kcp........F....... 913 894-3009
Lenexa *(G-5959)*
Merit Energy Company LLC........E....... 620 629-4200
Liberal *(G-6341)*
Personal Membership........F....... 785 979-7812
Lawrence *(G-5062)*
Powell Electrical Systems Inc........F....... 785 856-5863
Lawrence *(G-5071)*

ELECTRIC SVCS, NEC: Power Generation

Augusta Electric Plant 2........F....... 316 775-4527
Augusta *(G-303)*
Bradley R Lewis........F....... 816 453-7198
Overland Park *(G-8479)*
City of Winfield........F....... 620 221-5630
Winfield *(G-16120)*
Enel Green Power N Amer Inc........F....... 785 524-4900
Lincoln *(G-6381)*
Etc Endure Energy LLC........E....... 913 956-4500
Overland Park *(G-8692)*
Evergy Kansas Central Inc........A....... 785 575-6300
Topeka *(G-12583)*
Evergy Kansas Central Inc........D....... 785 587-2350
Manhattan *(G-6624)*
Evergy Kansas Central Inc........E....... 785 742-2185
Hiawatha *(G-3007)*
Evergy Kansas Central Inc........E....... 913 667-5134
Shawnee *(G-10950)*
Evergy Kansas Central Inc........B....... 785 456-6125
Saint Marys *(G-10363)*
Evergy Kansas Central Inc........F....... 620 820-8205
Parsons *(G-9685)*
Evergy Kansas Central Inc........E....... 316 291-8626
Colwich *(G-1095)*
Evergy Kansas South Inc........E....... 620 441-2427
Arkansas City *(G-155)*
Evergy Metro Inc........C....... 913 757-4451
La Cygne *(G-4640)*
Evergy Metro Inc........E....... 913 294-6200
Paola *(G-9558)*
Evergy Metro Inc........D....... 913 894-3000
Lenexa *(G-5838)*
Evergy Missouri West Inc........F....... 620 793-1279
Great Bend *(G-2561)*
Kansas Municipal Energy Agency........F....... 913 677-2884
Overland Park *(G-8904)*
Midwest Energy Inc........D....... 785 625-3437
Hays *(G-2873)*
Pioneer Electric Coop Inc........D....... 620 356-1211
Ulysses *(G-13311)*
Sunflower Electric Power Corp........E....... 785 628-2845
Hays *(G-2916)*
Sunflower Electric Power Corp........E....... 620 275-0161
Garden City *(G-2293)*
Sunflower Electric Power Corp........F....... 620 657-4400
Satanta *(G-10792)*

ELECTRIC TOOL REPAIR SVCS

Mid Kansas Tool & Electric Inc........F....... 785 825-9521
Salina *(G-10600)*
Richmond Electric Inc........G....... 316 264-2344
Wichita *(G-15457)*

ELECTRIC WATER HEATERS WHOLESALERS

Hajoca Corporation........F....... 785 825-1333
Salina *(G-10531)*

ELECTRICAL APPARATUS & EQPT WHOLESALERS

A-1 Electric Inc........F....... 620 431-7500
Chanute *(G-701)*
Ademco Inc........G....... 913 438-1111
Lenexa *(G-5629)*
Anixter Inc........F....... 620 365-7161
Iola *(G-3587)*
Eaton Corporation........E....... 913 451-6314
Lenexa *(G-5828)*
Farris Burns Corp........G....... 913 262-0555
Shawnee Mission *(G-11361)*
French-Gerleman Electric Co........E....... 314 569-3122
Lenexa *(G-5866)*
Gene Oswald Company........F....... 316 263-7191
Wichita *(G-14454)*
Independent Electric McHy Co........E....... 913 362-1155
Kansas City *(G-4097)*
Meter Engineers Inc........F....... 316 721-4214
Kechi *(G-4572)*
Source One Distributors Inc........F....... 620 221-8919
Winfield *(G-16172)*
Standard Electric Co Inc........F....... 913 782-5409
Olathe *(G-8080)*

ELECTRICAL APPLIANCES, TELEVISIONS & RADIOS WHOLESALERS

Blackmore and Glunt Inc........F....... 913 469-5715
Shawnee Mission *(G-11168)*
Clark Enterprises 2000 Inc........E....... 785 825-7172
Salina *(G-10455)*
Jetz Service Co Inc........F....... 785 354-7588
Topeka *(G-12744)*
Lowes Home Centers LLC........C....... 913 631-3003
Shawnee Mission *(G-11579)*
Lowes Home Centers LLC........C....... 316 773-1800
Wichita *(G-14982)*
Lowes Home Centers LLC........C....... 785 452-9303
Salina *(G-10585)*
Lowes Home Centers LLC........C....... 620 513-2000
Hutchinson *(G-3359)*

Lowes Home Centers LLC ....C 316 684-3117
Wichita (G-14983)
Lowes Home Centers LLC ....C 913 397-7070
Olathe (G-7866)
Lowes Home Centers LLC ....C 785 273-0888
Topeka (G-12852)
Lowes Home Centers LLC ....C 316 206-0000
Derby (G-1259)
Lowes Home Centers LLC ....C 913 328-7170
Kansas City (G-4207)
Lowes Home Centers LLC ....C 913 261-1040
Roeland Park (G-10227)
Lowes Home Centers LLC ....C 316 206-1030
Wichita (G-14984)
Mobile Addiction LLC ....F 316 773-3463
Wichita (G-15119)
Profillment LLC ....F 316 260-7910
Wichita (G-15369)
Wichita Wholesale Supply Inc ....F 316 267-3629
Wichita (G-16044)

ELECTRICAL CURRENT CARRYING WIRING DEVICES

Elec-Tron Inc ....D 316 522-3401
Wichita (G-14263)
Etco Specialty Products Inc ....E 620 724-6463
Girard (G-2403)
Falcon Design and Mfg ....E 913 441-1074
Shawnee (G-10953)
Kalmar Solutions LLC ....B 785 242-2200
Ottawa (G-8279)
Martin Interconnect Svcs Inc ....D 316 616-1001
Wichita (G-15011)
Mize & Co Inc ....E 620 532-3191
Kingman (G-4607)
National Almnm-Brass Fndry Inc ....E 816 833-4500
Leawood (G-5498)
Smiths Intrcnnect Americas Inc ....C 913 342-5544
Kansas City (G-4429)

ELECTRICAL EQPT & SPLYS

Azz Inc ....E 620 231-6900
Pittsburg (G-9819)
Colt Tech LLC ....G 913 839-8198
Olathe (G-7600)
Corrpro Companies Inc ....E 620 544-4411
Hugoton (G-3153)
Electronic Sensors Inc ....F 316 267-2807
Wichita (G-14268)
Occk Inc ....C 785 827-9383
Salina (G-10617)
Omni Aerospace Inc ....E 316 529-8998
Wichita (G-15216)
SNC Alarm Service ....E 620 665-6651
Hutchinson (G-3442)
United Manufacturing Inc ....E 913 780-0056
New Century (G-7302)
Valiant Global Def Svcs Inc ....D 913 651-9782
Leavenworth (G-5304)

ELECTRICAL EQPT FOR ENGINES

Electrex Inc ....C 620 662-4866
Hutchinson (G-3276)
Vermillion Incorporated ....D 316 524-3100
Wichita (G-15875)

ELECTRICAL EQPT REPAIR & MAINTENANCE

Abilene Machine LLC ....C 785 655-9455
Solomon (G-12046)
B & H Appliance ....F 620 364-8700
New Strawn (G-7303)
G F Enterprises ....G 785 539-7113
Manhattan (G-6642)
Oswald Manufacturing Co Inc ....G 785 258-2877
Herington (G-2980)
S D M Die Cutting Equipment ....G 913 782-3737
Shawnee (G-11022)
SC Hall Industrial Svcs Inc ....E 316 945-4255
Wichita (G-15525)
T V Hephner and Elec Inc ....F 316 264-3284
Wichita (G-15715)

ELECTRICAL EQPT REPAIR SVCS

Accurate Electric Inc ....G 785 825-4010
Salina (G-10391)
Broyles Petroleum Equipment Co ....E 417 863-6800
Humboldt (G-3183)
Elecsys International Corp ....C 913 647-0158
Olathe (G-7673)
Independent Electric McHy Co ....E 913 362-1155
Kansas City (G-4097)

ELECTRICAL EQPT REPAIR SVCS: High Voltage

Mid West Elc Transformers Inc ....F 316 283-7500
Newton (G-7382)

ELECTRICAL EQPT: Automotive, NEC

Standard Motor Products Inc ....B 913 441-6500
Edwardsville (G-1516)

ELECTRICAL EQPT: Household

Direct Voltage ....F 713 485-9999
Pratt (G-10108)

ELECTRICAL GOODS, WHOL: Antennas, Receiving/Satellite Dishes

Satellite Engrg Group Inc ....E 913 324-6000
Overland Park (G-9282)

ELECTRICAL GOODS, WHOLESALE: Alarms & Signaling Eqpt

Atronic Alarms Inc ....E 913 432-4545
Lenexa (G-5674)
Bhjllc Inc ....D 913 888-8028
Lenexa (G-5701)
Bhjllc Inc ....E 785 272-8800
Topeka (G-12379)
Williams Investigation & SEC ....E 620 275-1134
Garden City (G-2315)

ELECTRICAL GOODS, WHOLESALE: Batteries, Storage, Indl

Autozone Inc ....F 785 452-9790
Salina (G-10414)
Enersys ....C 785 625-3355
Hays (G-2799)
Exide Technologies ....D 785 825-6276
Salina (G-10488)
OReilly Automotive Stores Inc ....F 316 321-4371
El Dorado (G-1588)
OReilly Automotive Stores Inc ....F 316 831-9112
Wichita (G-15236)
OReilly Automotive Stores Inc ....F 316 729-7311
Wichita (G-15233)
OReilly Automotive Stores Inc ....F 316 686-5536
Wichita (G-15234)
OReilly Automotive Stores Inc ....E 316 264-6422
Wichita (G-15235)

ELECTRICAL GOODS, WHOLESALE: Burglar Alarm Systems

D H Pace Company Inc ....C 816 221-0072
Olathe (G-7636)
D H Pace Company Inc ....E 316 944-3667
Wichita (G-14157)
D H Pace Company Inc ....B 816 480-2600
Olathe (G-7638)
Overfield Corporation ....F 785 843-3434
Lawrence (G-5052)

ELECTRICAL GOODS, WHOLESALE: Citizens Band Radios

Santa Fe Distributing Inc ....E 913 492-8288
Shawnee Mission (G-11831)

ELECTRICAL GOODS, WHOLESALE: Electrical Appliances, Major

Bhjllc Inc ....D 913 888-8028
Lenexa (G-5701)

ELECTRICAL GOODS, WHOLESALE: Electronic Parts

Arrow Electronics Inc ....E 913 242-3012
Overland Park (G-8396)
Carlton-Bates Company ....F 913 375-1160
Overland Park (G-8518)
Future Electronics Corp ....F 913 498-1531
Shawnee Mission (G-11388)
Honeywell International Inc ....C 913 782-0400
Olathe (G-7772)
Isodyne Inc ....F 316 682-5634
Wichita (G-14733)
Satellite Engrg Group Inc ....E 913 324-6000
Overland Park (G-9282)
Wesco Aircraft Hardware Corp ....C 316 315-1200
Wichita (G-15949)

ELECTRICAL GOODS, WHOLESALE: Facsimile Or Fax Eqpt

Ricoh Usa Inc ....C 913 890-5100
Shawnee Mission (G-11802)

ELECTRICAL GOODS, WHOLESALE: Fans, Household

Rensen House of Lights Inc ....E 913 888-0888
Lenexa (G-6103)
Robert Wilson Co Inc ....E 913 642-1500
Overland Park (G-9251)
Vornado Air LLC ....D 316 733-0035
Andover (G-115)

ELECTRICAL GOODS, WHOLESALE: Fire Alarm Systems

Tech Electronics Kansas LLC ....E 785 379-0300
Topeka (G-13149)
Ted Systems LLC ....E 913 677-5771
Lenexa (G-6174)

ELECTRICAL GOODS, WHOLESALE: Generators

Aggreko LLC ....F 913 281-9782
Shawnee Mission (G-11085)
Central Pwr Systems & Svcs LLC ....E 316 943-1231
Wichita (G-13984)
Himoinsa Power Systems Inc ....E 913 495-5557
Olathe (G-7768)
Velociti Inc ....E 913 233-7230
Kansas City (G-4514)

ELECTRICAL GOODS, WHOLESALE: Household Appliances, NEC

Washer Specialties Company ....E 316 263-8179
Wichita (G-15930)

ELECTRICAL GOODS, WHOLESALE: Light Bulbs & Related Splys

Eiko Global LLC ....F 913 441-8500
Shawnee (G-10944)
Eiko Global LLC ....E 800 852-2217
Shawnee (G-10945)
Light Bulbs Etc Inc ....F 913 894-9030
Shawnee Mission (G-11571)

ELECTRICAL GOODS, WHOLESALE: Lighting Fittings & Access

Meico Lamp Parts Company ....F 913 469-5888
Shawnee Mission (G-11616)

ELECTRICAL GOODS, WHOLESALE: Lighting Fixtures, Comm & Indl

Endacott Lighting Inc ....F 785 776-4472
Manhattan (G-6620)
Facility Solutions Group Inc ....E 913 422-8400
Shawnee (G-10952)
Led2 Lighting Inc ....G 816 912-2180
Kansas City (G-4199)
Mercer-Zimmerman Inc ....F 913 438-4546
Overland Park (G-9010)

ELECTRICAL GOODS, WHOLESALE: Mobile telephone Eqpt

Lg Elctrnics Mbilecomm USA Inc ....E 913 234-3701
Leawood (G-5457)
Wireless Lifestyle LLC ....D 913 962-0002
Overland Park (G-9499)

ELECTRICAL GOODS, WHOLESALE: Motor Ctrls, Starters & Relays

Barr-Thorp Electric Company................E....... 913 789-8840
Merriam *(G-7086)*
RE Pedrotti Company Inc......................F....... 913 677-7754
Shawnee Mission *(G-11781)*

ELECTRICAL GOODS, WHOLESALE: Motors

ABB Motors and Mechanical Inc...........F....... 816 587-0272
Lenexa *(G-5618)*
B&B Electric Motor Co..........................F....... 316 267-1238
Wichita *(G-13786)*
Emotorpro..F....... 785 437-2046
Saint Marys *(G-10362)*
Flex-N-Gate Missouri LLC.....................D....... 913 387-3857
Kansas City *(G-4012)*
Gibson Industrial Controls Inc..............G....... 620 241-3551
McPherson *(G-6969)*
Klemp Electric Machinery Co................F....... 913 371-4330
Kansas City *(G-4176)*
Mid Kansas Tool & Electric Inc..............F....... 785 825-9521
Salina *(G-10600)*
Naab Electric Inc....................................F....... 620 276-8101
Garden City *(G-2242)*
WW Grainger Inc....................................E....... 913 492-8550
Lenexa *(G-6237)*
WW Grainger Inc....................................E....... 316 945-5101
Wichita *(G-16079)*

ELECTRICAL GOODS, WHOLESALE: Paging & Signaling Eqpt

Metrocall..F....... 316 634-1430
Wichita *(G-15060)*
Williams Investigation & SEC................E....... 620 275-1134
Garden City *(G-2315)*

ELECTRICAL GOODS, WHOLESALE: Panelboards

Company Business Intl Sarl..................G....... 913 286-9771
Olathe *(G-7606)*

ELECTRICAL GOODS, WHOLESALE: Radio Parts & Access, NEC

Aircraft Instr & Rdo Co Inc....................E....... 316 945-9820
Wichita *(G-13651)*

ELECTRICAL GOODS, WHOLESALE: Security Control Eqpt & Systems

Sandifer Engrg & Contrls Inc.................E....... 316 794-8880
Wichita *(G-15516)*
Sound Products Inc...............................F....... 913 599-3666
Olathe *(G-8073)*

ELECTRICAL GOODS, WHOLESALE: Signaling, Eqpt

Superior Signals Inc...............................E....... 913 780-1440
Olathe *(G-8088)*

ELECTRICAL GOODS, WHOLESALE: Sound Eqpt

Ms Electronics LLC................................F....... 913 233-8518
Lenexa *(G-6014)*
Radio Shop Inc.......................................F....... 316 265-1851
Wichita *(G-15409)*

ELECTRICAL GOODS, WHOLESALE: Telephone & Telegraphic Eqpt

Answernet Inc...F....... 785 301-2810
Hays *(G-2748)*
Cellco Partnership..................................F....... 913 897-5022
Overland Park *(G-8535)*
Cellco Partnership..................................F....... 785 537-6159
Manhattan *(G-6580)*
Cellco Partnership..................................F....... 316 789-9911
Derby *(G-1228)*
Kanokla Telephone Association...........E....... 620 845-5682
Caldwell *(G-660)*
South Centl Communications Inc.........E....... 620 930-1000
Medicine Lodge *(G-7073)*

ELECTRICAL GOODS, WHOLESALE: Telephone Eqpt

Direct Communications Inc...................F....... 913 599-5577
Overland Park *(G-8657)*
Kgp Telecommunications Inc...............D....... 800 755-1950
New Century *(G-7292)*
S N C Inc..E....... 620 665-6651
Hutchinson *(G-3434)*
Special Product Company.....................F....... 913 491-8088
Shawnee *(G-11031)*
Teledata Communications LLC.............E....... 913 663-2010
Lenexa *(G-6175)*

ELECTRICAL GOODS, WHOLESALE: Vacuum Cleaners, Household

Ermator Inc...F....... 813 684-7091
Olathe *(G-7691)*

ELECTRICAL GOODS, WHOLESALE: Video Eqpt

AVI Systems Inc.....................................E....... 913 495-9494
Lenexa *(G-5677)*
Cytek Media Systems Inc.......................E....... 785 295-4200
Topeka *(G-12542)*
Smith Audio Visual Inc...........................E....... 785 235-3481
Topeka *(G-13079)*

ELECTRICAL GOODS, WHOLESALE: Wire & Cable

Anixter Power Solutions Inc..................F....... 913 202-6945
Kansas City *(G-3812)*
Okonite Company...................................F....... 913 441-4465
Edwardsville *(G-1512)*
Quality Steel & Wire Pdts Co................G....... 913 888-2929
Lenexa *(G-6085)*

ELECTRICAL GOODS, WHOLESALE: Wire & Cable, Electronic

Anixter Inc...F....... 913 492-2622
Overland Park *(G-8386)*

ELECTRICAL GOODS, WHOLESALE: Wire/Cable, Telephone/Telegraph

Spectrum Elite Corp...............................G....... 913 579-7037
Olathe *(G-8076)*

ELECTRICAL HOUSEHOLD APPLIANCE REPAIR

Factory Direct Appliance........................F....... 785 272-8800
Topeka *(G-12592)*
Mar-Beck Appliance Svc Co Inc.............E....... 913 322-4022
Lenexa *(G-5985)*
Ott Electric Inc..F....... 785 562-2641
Marysville *(G-6907)*
Repair Shack Inc......................................E....... 913 732-0514
Lenexa *(G-6105)*
Ricks Appliance Service Inc....................F....... 316 265-2866
Wichita *(G-15460)*
Royal Flush Plumbing LLC......................F....... 316 794-2656
Goddard *(G-2453)*
Skaggs Inc...E....... 620 672-5312
Pratt *(G-10148)*

ELECTRICAL MEASURING INSTRUMENT REPAIR & CALIBRATION SVCS

Test and Measurement Inc......................F....... 913 233-2724
Kansas City *(G-4466)*

ELECTRICAL SPLYS

Boettcher Supply Inc...............................E....... 785 738-5781
Beloit *(G-479)*
Border States Industries Inc....................F....... 785 827-4497
Salina *(G-10430)*
Border States Industries Inc....................E....... 785 354-9532
Topeka *(G-12398)*
Border States Industries Inc....................F....... 316 945-1313
Wichita *(G-13870)*
C & O Elec Sales Co Inc..........................F....... 913 981-0008
Shawnee Mission *(G-11194)*
Calkins Electric Supply Co Inc................F....... 913 631-6363
Shawnee *(G-10923)*
Consolidated Elec Distrs Inc...................F....... 785 823-7161
Salina *(G-10459)*
Consolidated Elec Distrs Inc...................E....... 316 267-5311
Wichita *(G-14091)*
Consolidated Elec Distrs Inc...................E....... 316 262-3541
Wichita *(G-14092)*
Foley Group Inc.......................................F....... 913 342-3336
Kansas City *(G-4014)*
Graybar Electric Company Inc................F....... 316 265-8964
Wichita *(G-14500)*
Hill & Company Inc..................................F....... 785 235-5374
Topeka *(G-12689)*
Kansas City Electrical Sup Co................E....... 913 563-7002
Lenexa *(G-5936)*
Liebert Brothers Electric Co...................F....... 620 251-0299
Coffeyville *(G-956)*
Mid-West Electrical Supply Inc...............F....... 316 265-0562
Wichita *(G-15083)*
Power Equipment Sales Co.....................F....... 913 384-3848
Kansas City *(G-4327)*
Stanion Wholesale Elc Co Inc.................E....... 316 616-9200
Wichita *(G-15653)*
Stanion Wholesale Elc Co Inc.................E....... 620 672-5678
Pratt *(G-10153)*
Stanion Wholesale Elc Co Inc.................F....... 785 841-8420
Lawrence *(G-5118)*
Stanion Wholesale Elc Co Inc.................F....... 913 829-8111
Olathe *(G-8081)*
Stanion Wholesale Elc Co Inc.................F....... 785 823-2323
Salina *(G-10715)*
Stanion Wholesale Elc Co Inc.................F....... 785 537-4600
Manhattan *(G-6808)*
Stanion Wholesale Elc Co Inc.................F....... 913 342-1177
Kansas City *(G-4438)*
Sunflwer Elc Sup Htchinson Inc.............E....... 620 662-0531
Hutchinson *(G-3457)*
Welco Technologies................................G....... 316 941-0400
Wichita *(G-15943)*
Western Extralite Company....................F....... 913 438-1777
Shawnee Mission *(G-12005)*

ELECTROLYSIS & EPILATORY SVCS

Wichita Srgical Specialists PA................E....... 316 688-7500
Wichita *(G-16027)*

ELECTROMEDICAL EQPT

Care 4 All Home Medical Eqp................G....... 620 223-4141
Fort Scott *(G-1957)*
LSI International Inc...............................E....... 913 894-4493
Kansas City *(G-4208)*
Revolutionary Bus Concepts Inc............D....... 913 385-5700
Shawnee Mission *(G-11793)*
Vigilias LLC...E....... 800 924-8140
Wichita *(G-15907)*

ELECTROMEDICAL EQPT WHOLESALERS

Relevium Labs Inc...................................F....... 614 568-7000
Dodge City *(G-1423)*

ELECTRONIC EQPT REPAIR SVCS

B&B Electric Motor Co............................F....... 316 267-1238
Wichita *(G-13786)*
Honeywell International Inc....................C....... 913 782-0400
Olathe *(G-7772)*
Naab Electric Inc.....................................F....... 620 276-8101
Garden City *(G-2242)*
X TEC Repair Inc.....................................E....... 913 829-3773
Lenexa *(G-6238)*

ELECTRONIC LOADS & POWER SPLYS

EC Manufacturing LLC............................C....... 913 825-3077
Paola *(G-9555)*

ELECTRONIC PARTS & EQPT WHOLESALERS

Accu-Tech Corporation............................F....... 913 894-0444
Shawnee Mission *(G-11066)*
Asset Lifecycle LLC................................F....... 785 861-3100
Topeka *(G-12341)*
Border States Industries Inc...................E....... 785 354-9532
Topeka *(G-12398)*
Caliber Electronics Inc............................E....... 913 782-7787
Olathe *(G-7573)*
Cooper Electronics Inc............................E....... 913 782-0012
Olathe *(G-7615)*
Data Locker Inc.......................................G....... 913 310-9088
Overland Park *(G-8636)*

Decker Electric Inc....D.... 316 265-8182
Wichita *(G-14183)*
K and C Technical Service LLC....F.... 316 650-4464
Reading *(G-10199)*
Mitel Technologies Inc....E.... 913 752-9100
Lenexa *(G-6008)*
Tecnet International Inc....F.... 913 859-9515
Lenexa *(G-6173)*
Tfmcomm Inc....E.... 785 233-2343
Topeka *(G-13156)*

ELECTRONIC SECRETARIES

X Tech Midwest Inc....G.... 316 777-6648
Wichita *(G-16082)*

ELEMENTARY & SECONDARY PRIVATE DENOMINATIONAL SCHOOLS

Holy Name Catholic Church....C.... 785 232-7744
Topeka *(G-12698)*

ELEMENTARY & SECONDARY SCHOOLS, PRIVATE NEC

Association of Kansas Nebraska....E.... 785 478-4726
Topeka *(G-12345)*

ELEMENTARY & SECONDARY SCHOOLS, PUBLIC

Abilene Unified Schl Dst 435....F.... 785 825-9185
Salina *(G-10389)*
Coffeyvlle Unfied Schl Dst 445....E.... 620 251-5910
Coffeyville *(G-927)*
Dodge Cy Unified Schl Dst 443....D.... 620 227-7771
Dodge City *(G-1355)*
Goddard Public Schools....E.... 316 794-2281
Goddard *(G-2440)*
Halstd-Bntley Unfied Schl Dst....C.... 316 835-2641
Halstead *(G-2700)*
Kansas National Education Assn....F.... 913 268-4005
Shawnee Mission *(G-11518)*
Liberal School District....E.... 620 604-2400
Liberal *(G-6335)*
Marysville School District....D.... 785 562-5386
Marysville *(G-6902)*
Topeka Unified School Dst 501....E.... 785 438-4750
Topeka *(G-13190)*
Unified School District 259....C.... 316 973-4000
Wichita *(G-15833)*
Unified School District 383....D.... 785 587-2850
Manhattan *(G-6837)*

ELEMENTARY & SECONDARY SCHOOLS, SPECIAL EDUCATION

Northeast Kans Educatn Svc Ctr....C.... 913 538-7250
Ozawkie *(G-9536)*
Unified School District 214....D.... 620 356-4577
Ulysses *(G-13328)*

ELEMENTARY SCHOOLS, CATHOLIC

Church of Magdalen....E.... 316 634-1572
Wichita *(G-14019)*

ELEMENTARY SCHOOLS, NEC

Parkdale Pre-School Center....E.... 785 235-7240
Topeka *(G-12960)*

ELEMENTARY SCHOOLS, PRIVATE

Brookridge Day School....E.... 913 649-2228
Shawnee Mission *(G-11185)*
Century School Inc....E.... 785 832-0101
Lawrence *(G-4782)*
Friends of Montessori Assn....F.... 913 649-6160
Prairie Village *(G-10029)*
Wichita Montessori School....F.... 316 686-7265
Wichita *(G-16012)*

ELEMENTARY SCHOOLS, PUBLIC

Board of Edcatn of Kans Cy Ks....E.... 913 627-6550
Kansas City *(G-3870)*
Rose Hill Unified School Dst....E.... 316 776-3340
Rose Hill *(G-10248)*

ELEVATOR, STORAGE ONLY

CHS McPherson Refinery Inc....F.... 785 421-2157
Hill City *(G-3030)*

ELEVATOR: Grain, Storage Only

ADM Milling Co....D.... 620 442-6200
Arkansas City *(G-139)*
Agco Inc....F.... 785 483-2128
Russell *(G-10263)*
Agri Trails Coop Inc....F.... 785 258-2286
Herington *(G-2969)*
Alliance AG and Grain LLC....F.... 785 798-3775
Ness City *(G-7251)*
Anthony Frmrs Coop Elev Cmpnys....F.... 620 842-5181
Anthony *(G-119)*
Archer-Daniels-Midland Company....E.... 785 263-2260
Abilene *(G-13)*
Beachner Grain Inc....F.... 620 244-3277
Erie *(G-1856)*
Beaver Grain Corporation Inc....F.... 620 587-3417
Beaver *(G-424)*
Cargill Incorporated....E.... 785 825-8128
Salina *(G-10436)*
Cargill Incorporated....F.... 913 367-3579
Cummings *(G-1186)*
Cropland Co-Op Inc....F.... 620 356-1241
Ulysses *(G-13294)*
D E Bondurant Grain Co Inc....E.... 785 798-3322
Ness City *(G-7260)*
Dodge City Cooperative Exch....E.... 620 225-4193
Dodge City *(G-1344)*
Ellsworth Coop....F.... 785 472-3261
Ellsworth *(G-1667)*
Farmers Co-Operative Union....D.... 620 278-2141
Sterling *(G-12116)*
Farmers Coop Grn Assn Inc....F.... 620 456-2222
Conway Springs *(G-1141)*
Farmers Cooperative Grain....F.... 620 326-7496
Wellington *(G-13499)*
Golden Valley Inc....E.... 620 527-4216
Rozel *(G-10258)*
Great Bend Cooperative Assn....E.... 620 793-3531
Great Bend *(G-2576)*
Irsik & Doll Feed Services Inc....F.... 620 855-3747
Cimarron *(G-830)*
Kanza Cooperative Association....F.... 620 546-2231
Iuka *(G-3640)*
Kanza Cooperative Association....E.... 316 444-2141
Andale *(G-78)*
Nemaha County Cooperative Assn....F.... 785 456-6924
Belvue *(G-507)*
Norag LLC....D.... 913 851-7200
Bucyrus *(G-605)*
O K Coop Grn & Merc Co....F.... 620 825-4212
Kiowa *(G-4628)*
Piqua Farmers Coop Assn Incthe....F.... 620 468-2535
Piqua *(G-9801)*
Randall Farmers Coop Un Inc....F.... 785 739-2312
Randall *(G-10190)*
Skyland Grain LLC....F.... 620 492-2126
Johnson *(G-3660)*
Strong City Elevator....F.... 620 273-6483
Strong City *(G-12195)*
United Prarie AG....F.... 620 544-2017
Hugoton *(G-3179)*

ELEVATORS & EQPT

Interstate Elevator Inc....F.... 785 234-2817
Topeka *(G-12727)*

ELEVATORS WHOLESALERS

Columbia Elev Solutions Inc....E.... 620 442-2510
Winfield *(G-16123)*
Otis Elevator Company....F.... 316 682-6886
Bel Aire *(G-437)*
Otis Elevator Company....E.... 913 621-8800
Kansas City *(G-4300)*
River City Elevator LLC....F.... 316 773-3161
Wichita *(G-15470)*
Thyssenkrupp Elevator Corp....F.... 913 888-8046
Overland Park *(G-9408)*
Thyssenkrupp Elevator Corp....F.... 316 529-2233
Wichita *(G-15764)*

ELEVATORS: Installation & Conversion

Beachner Grain Inc....F.... 620 244-3277
Erie *(G-1856)*
Otis Elevator Company....F.... 316 682-6886
Bel Aire *(G-437)*
Southwest and Associates Inc....D.... 620 463-5631
Burrton *(G-650)*
Thyssenkrupp Elevator Corp....F.... 913 888-8046
Overland Park *(G-9408)*

EMBLEMS: Embroidered

David Camp Inc....C.... 913 648-0573
Overland Park *(G-8641)*

EMBOSSING SVC: Paper

Mainline Printing Inc....D.... 785 233-2338
Topeka *(G-12856)*

EMBROIDERING & ART NEEDLEWORK FOR THE TRADE

CP Partnerships Inc....F.... 785 625-7388
Hays *(G-2779)*
D Rockey Holdings Inc....E.... 816 474-9423
Kansas City *(G-3950)*
Expert Alteration....G.... 913 322-2242
Westwood *(G-13553)*
Gregory A Scott Inc....E.... 913 677-0414
Kansas City *(G-4053)*
Industrial Uniform Company LLC....F.... 316 264-2871
Wichita *(G-14688)*
Prairie Patches Inc....G.... 785 749-4565
Lawrence *(G-5072)*
SA Imprints Inc....F.... 620 421-6380
Parsons *(G-9734)*
Something Different Inc....G.... 785 537-1171
Wamego *(G-13441)*

EMBROIDERING SVC

4th Gneration Promotional Pdts....G.... 913 393-0837
Olathe *(G-7502)*
Expressions Embroidery LLC....F.... 913 764-7070
Olathe *(G-7698)*
Kellys Corporate Apparel....G.... 316 263-5858
Wichita *(G-14847)*
Plainjans Feedlot Service....F.... 620 872-5777
Scott City *(G-10827)*
Sands Enterprises Inc....G.... 316 942-8686
Wichita *(G-15518)*
Shirts Plus Inc....F.... 316 788-1550
Derby *(G-1272)*
Signature Logo Embroidery Inc....G.... 913 671-8548
Shawnee Mission *(G-11868)*
Stewarts Sports & Awards....G.... 620 241-5990
McPherson *(G-7028)*
Tioga Territory Ltd....F.... 620 431-2479
Chanute *(G-770)*
U S Logo Inc....F.... 316 264-1321
Wichita *(G-15824)*
U S S A Inc....G.... 316 686-1653
Wichita *(G-15826)*
Walson Ink Inc....G.... 785 537-7370
Manhattan *(G-6845)*
Winning Spirit Inc....E.... 316 684-0855
Wichita *(G-16056)*

EMBROIDERING SVC: Schiffli Machine

John B Baker....G.... 316 263-2820
Wichita *(G-14762)*
Sun Creations Inc....E.... 785 830-0403
Lawrence *(G-5127)*

EMBROIDERY ADVERTISING SVCS

Khaos Apparel LLC....F.... 316 804-4900
Newton *(G-7370)*
U S Logo Inc....F.... 316 264-1321
Wichita *(G-15824)*

EMERGENCY & RELIEF SVCS

American National Red Cross....E.... 785 309-0263
Salina *(G-10401)*
American National Red Cross....E.... 913 245-3565
Lenexa *(G-5652)*
City of Neodesha....F.... 620 325-2642
Neodesha *(G-7235)*
Family Crisis Center Inc....F.... 620 793-9941
Great Bend *(G-2562)*
Salvation Army....F.... 620 276-4027
Garden City *(G-2273)*

Services Offering Safety ....E.... 620 343-8799
Emporia *(G-1825)*
South Cntl Mntal Hlth Cnseling ....F.... 316 733-5047
Andover *(G-108)*
Youth Crisis Shelter Inc ....E.... 620 421-6941
Parsons *(G-9752)*

EMERGENCY ALARMS

Ademco Inc ....G.... 913 438-1111
Lenexa *(G-5629)*
Howard Electronic Instrs Inc ....G.... 316 321-2800
El Dorado *(G-1568)*
Johnson Controls ....G.... 913 894-0010
Lenexa *(G-5930)*
Johnson Controls ....E.... 316 686-6363
Wichita *(G-14766)*
Johnson Controls Fire ....G.... 785 267-9675
Topeka *(G-12748)*
Lifeline ....G.... 800 635-6156
Topeka *(G-12844)*

EMERGENCY SHELTERS

Ashby House Ltd ....F.... 785 826-4935
Salina *(G-10410)*
Lawrence Community Shelter ....F.... 785 832-8864
Lawrence *(G-4962)*
O S S Inc ....E.... 620 343-8799
Emporia *(G-1808)*
Safe Home Inc ....E.... 913 432-9300
Overland Park *(G-9269)*
Salvation Army ....F.... 316 263-2769
Wichita *(G-15514)*
Salvation Army ....F.... 913 232-5400
Kansas City *(G-4397)*

EMPLOYEE LEASING SVCS

Cbiz M&S Consulting Svcs LLC ....E.... 785 228-6700
Topeka *(G-12454)*

EMPLOYMENT AGENCY SVCS

Advantage Tech Inc ....D.... 913 888-5050
Overland Park *(G-8352)*
Excel Personnel Services Inc ....E.... 913 341-1150
Shawnee Mission *(G-11353)*
Express Services Inc ....D.... 785 825-4545
Salina *(G-10492)*
Global Partner Solutions LLC ....C.... 316 263-1288
Wichita *(G-14475)*
Jt2 Inc ....F.... 913 323-4915
Overland Park *(G-8882)*
Kansas Department of Labor ....F.... 913 680-2200
Leavenworth *(G-5260)*
Kansas State University ....E.... 785 532-6506
Manhattan *(G-6692)*
Krucial Staffing LLC ....F.... 913 802-2560
Overland Park *(G-8928)*
Labor Source LLC ....F.... 913 764-5333
Olathe *(G-7850)*
Lynn Care LLC ....E.... 913 707-4639
Overland Park *(G-8977)*
Lynn Care LLC ....C.... 913 491-3562
Overland Park *(G-8978)*
Macfarlane Group LLC ....E.... 913 825-1200
Shawnee Mission *(G-11589)*
McGhee and Associates LLC ....E.... 785 341-2550
Manhattan *(G-6738)*
Midwest Consulting Group Inc ....C.... 913 693-8200
Overland Park *(G-9031)*
Nextaff LLC ....E.... 913 562-5620
Overland Park *(G-9082)*
Pivot Companies LLC ....F.... 800 581-6398
Overland Park *(G-9170)*
Randstad Technologies LLC ....F.... 913 696-0808
Overland Park *(G-9225)*
Robert Half International Inc ....E.... 913 339-9849
Shawnee Mission *(G-11808)*
Robert Half International Inc ....F.... 913 451-1014
Overland Park *(G-9249)*
Shc Services Inc ....C.... 913 652-9229
Overland Park *(G-9306)*
Spec Personnel LLC ....D.... 913 534-8430
Overland Park *(G-9333)*
Supported Employment Services ....F.... 620 431-1805
Chanute *(G-766)*
Tdb Communications Inc ....C.... 913 327-7400
Lenexa *(G-6168)*
Ultimate Group LLP ....F.... 816 813-8182
Prairie Village *(G-10077)*

Waterman Group Inc ....F.... 913 685-4900
Overland Park *(G-9484)*

EMPLOYMENT SVCS: Labor Contractors

Kansas Ltd Liability Company ....F.... 888 222-6359
Overland Park *(G-8903)*
Onsite Solutions LLC ....C.... 913 912-7384
Shawnee Mission *(G-11698)*
Tradesmen International LLC ....E.... 316 688-0291
Wichita *(G-15783)*
Transerve Inc ....D.... 620 231-2230
Pittsburg *(G-9947)*

EMPLOYMENT SVCS: Nurses' Registry

Q S Nurses Kansas LLC ....D.... 620 793-7262
Great Bend *(G-2627)*
Squadbuilders Inc ....D.... 913 649-4401
Leawood *(G-5559)*

EMPLOYMENT SVCS: Registries

Amazing Grace Staffing Inc ....E.... 785 432-2920
Hays *(G-2745)*
National Greyhound Association ....F.... 785 263-4660
Abilene *(G-48)*

ENCODERS: Digital

Brg Precision Products Inc ....E.... 316 788-2000
Derby *(G-1225)*

ENGINE REBUILDING: Diesel

Detroit Diesel Remanufacturing ....C.... 620 343-3790
Emporia *(G-1729)*
Engquist Tractor Service Inc ....E.... 620 654-3651
McPherson *(G-6959)*
Herrs Machine ....G.... 785 325-2875
Washington *(G-13464)*

ENGINE REBUILDING: Gas

United Auto Parts Inc ....E.... 316 721-6868
Wichita *(G-15840)*

ENGINEERING HELP SVCS

USP Technical Services ....F.... 310 517-1800
Derby *(G-1278)*

ENGINEERING SVCS

Advanced Environmental Svcs ....F.... 785 231-9324
Topeka *(G-12295)*
Advanced Manufacturing Inst ....E.... 785 532-7044
Manhattan *(G-6534)*
Amec Fster Wheler E C Svcs Inc ....E.... 785 272-6830
Topeka *(G-12312)*
Archer-Daniels-Midland Company ....D.... 785 825-1541
Salina *(G-10407)*
Asset MGT Analis Group LLC ....E.... 803 270-0996
Leawood *(G-5335)*
Attica Engineering LLC ....F.... 620 254-7070
Attica *(G-275)*
Avatar Engineering Inc ....F.... 913 897-6757
Lenexa *(G-5676)*
Axius Group LLC ....F.... 316 285-0858
Wichita *(G-13781)*
B&V E&E JV ....D.... 913 458-4300
Overland Park *(G-8423)*
Black & Veatch-GEC Joint Ventr ....B.... 913 458-4300
Overland Park *(G-8458)*
Black Vtch - Gsyntec Jint Vntr ....D.... 913 458-4300
Overland Park *(G-8462)*
Bvspc - Envirocon JV ....D.... 913 458-6665
Overland Park *(G-8501)*
Carney Daniel M Rehab Engineer ....F.... 316 651-5200
Wichita *(G-13951)*
Cogen Cleaning Technology Inc ....E.... 281 339-5751
Stilwell *(G-12142)*
Colt Tech LLC ....G.... 913 839-8198
Olathe *(G-7600)*
Corps of Engineers Fall River ....F.... 620 658-4445
Fall River *(G-1926)*
County of Grant ....E.... 620 356-4837
Ulysses *(G-13291)*
County of Harper ....E.... 620 842-5240
Anthony *(G-126)*
County of Johnson ....D.... 913 782-2640
Olathe *(G-7619)*
CP Engners Land Srveyors Inc ....F.... 785 267-5071
Topeka *(G-12526)*

Davidson & Associates Inc ....E.... 913 271-6859
Leawood *(G-5372)*
Davidson Arch Engrg LLC ....F.... 913 451-9390
Overland Park *(G-8643)*
Den Management Co Inc ....C.... 316 686-1964
Wichita *(G-14191)*
Design Analysis and RES Corp ....F.... 785 832-0434
Lawrence *(G-4833)*
Dlr Group Inc ....D.... 913 897-7811
Overland Park *(G-8659)*
Energy Management & Ctrl Corp ....F.... 785 233-0289
Topeka *(G-12578)*
Envirnmntal Advisors Engineers ....E.... 913 599-4326
Shawnee Mission *(G-11344)*
First Layer Communications ....F.... 913 491-0062
Shawnee Mission *(G-11372)*
Foster Design Inc ....C.... 316 832-9700
Wichita *(G-14403)*
GBA Builders Llc ....E.... 913 492-0400
Lenexa *(G-5870)*
Global Aviation Tech LLC ....F.... 316 425-0999
Wichita *(G-14473)*
Global Partner Solutions LLC ....C.... 316 263-1288
Wichita *(G-14475)*
Gpw & Associates LLC ....F.... 785 865-2332
Lawrence *(G-4877)*
Green Product Solutions LLC ....G.... 913 633-1274
Overland Park *(G-8778)*
Gsi Engineering LLC ....D.... 515 270-6542
Wichita *(G-14522)*
Gsi Engineering Nthrn Div LLC ....F.... 316 554-0725
Wichita *(G-14523)*
Interactive Technologies Inc ....F.... 913 254-0887
Olathe *(G-7798)*
Kansas Department Trnsp ....F.... 785 527-2520
Belleville *(G-458)*
Kjww Corp ....E.... 913 952-6636
Overland Park *(G-8921)*
Marche Associates Inc ....F.... 785 749-2925
Lawrence *(G-5011)*
McPu Polymer Engineering LLC ....G.... 620 231-4239
Pittsburg *(G-9901)*
Miniature Plastic Molding LLC ....G.... 316 264-2827
Wichita *(G-15112)*
MTS Quanta LLC ....E.... 913 383-0800
Overland Park *(G-9061)*
MWH Global Inc ....F.... 913 383-2086
Leawood *(G-5494)*
Northrop Grumman Systems Corp ....C.... 785 861-3375
Topeka *(G-12938)*
Northrop Grumman Systems Corp ....B.... 913 651-8311
Fort Leavenworth *(G-1940)*
Nunik Engineering ....F.... 913 384-0010
Shawnee Mission *(G-11691)*
Optimus Industries LLC ....C.... 620 431-3100
Chanute *(G-751)*
Professional Group ....F.... 785 762-5855
Junction City *(G-3741)*
Progress Rail Services Corp ....E.... 913 345-4807
Overland Park *(G-9191)*
Schaefer Johnson Cox Frey ....D.... 316 684-0171
Wichita *(G-15526)*
SD Engineering LLC ....F.... 785 233-8880
Topeka *(G-13046)*
Sky Blue Inc ....D.... 785 842-9013
Lawrence *(G-5112)*
Splashtacular LLC ....F.... 800 844-5334
Paola *(G-9589)*
T & C Mfg & Operating Inc ....E.... 620 793-5483
Great Bend *(G-2646)*
T T Companies Inc ....A.... 913 599-6886
Olathe *(G-8097)*
Terracon Consultants Inc ....E.... 316 262-0171
Wichita *(G-15730)*
Textron Aviation Inc ....F.... 316 831-4021
Wichita *(G-15742)*
Transtecs Corporation ....D.... 316 651-0389
Wichita *(G-15793)*
Trideum Corporation ....E.... 913 364-5900
Leavenworth *(G-5302)*
Wyandtte Cnty Unfied Gvernment ....F.... 913 573-5700
Kansas City *(G-4556)*

ENGINEERING SVCS: Acoustical

Gsi Engineering LLC ....E.... 316 554-0725
Wichita *(G-14521)*
Jvf Enterprises Inc ....F.... 913 888-9111
Lenexa *(G-5934)*

(G-0000) Company's Geographic Section entry number

ENGINEERING SVCS: Aviation Or Aeronautical

Archein Aerospace LLC ....E....... 682 499-2150
Wichita *(G-13730)*
Emerald Aerospace Services LLC ....E....... 316 644-4284
Wichita *(G-14275)*

ENGINEERING SVCS: Building Construction

Bain Millwrights Inc ....F....... 785 945-3778
Valley Falls *(G-13361)*
Complete LLC ....F....... 913 238-0206
Overland Park *(G-8590)*
Construction Design Inc ....C....... 913 287-0334
Kansas City *(G-3935)*
Jaco General Contractor Inc ....E....... 316 252-8200
Wichita *(G-14744)*
Kleinfelder Inc ....D....... 913 962-0909
Lenexa *(G-5953)*
Performance Contracting Inc ....A....... 913 888-8600
Lenexa *(G-6051)*
Trademark Incorporated ....F....... 316 264-8310
Wichita *(G-15782)*
U S Army Corps of Engineers ....F....... 785 597-5144
Perry *(G-9774)*
U S Army Corps of Engineers ....F....... 785 453-2201
Vassar *(G-13372)*

ENGINEERING SVCS: Civil

Allenbrand-Drews and Assoc ....E....... 913 764-1076
Olathe *(G-7519)*
Asm Engineering Cons LLC ....F....... 316 260-5895
Andover *(G-83)*
B G Consultants Inc ....E....... 785 537-7448
Manhattan *(G-6551)*
Bartlett & West Inc ....C....... 785 272-2252
Topeka *(G-12366)*
Baughman Co PA ....E....... 316 262-7271
Wichita *(G-13820)*
Bird Engineering Company PA ....F....... 913 631-2222
Shawnee *(G-10917)*
Brungardt Honomichl & Co PA ....D....... 913 663-1900
Overland Park *(G-8490)*
City of Topeka ....E....... 785 295-3842
Topeka *(G-12471)*
Finney & Trnp SD Trnsprttn ....F....... 785 235-2393
Topeka *(G-12611)*
Geary County Public Works ....E....... 785 238-3612
Junction City *(G-3695)*
Hd Engineering & Design Inc ....F....... 913 631-2222
Shawnee Mission *(G-11418)*
Henderson Engineers Inc ....D....... 913 742-5000
Overland Park *(G-8810)*
Kaw Valley Engineering Inc ....E....... 785 762-5040
Junction City *(G-3714)*
Kaw Valley Engineering Inc ....E....... 913 894-5150
Shawnee Mission *(G-11521)*
Kruger Technologies Inc ....E....... 913 498-1114
Overland Park *(G-8929)*
McAfee Henderson Solutions Inc ....F....... 913 888-4647
Lenexa *(G-5990)*
McAfee Henderson Solutions Inc ....F....... 913 888-4647
Lenexa *(G-5991)*
Mkec Engineering Inc ....C....... 316 684-9600
Wichita *(G-15118)*
Pfefferkorn Engrg & Envmtl LLC ....F....... 913 490-3967
Olathe *(G-7982)*
Phelps Engineering Inc ....E....... 913 393-1155
Olathe *(G-7983)*
Poe & Associates Inc ....E....... 316 685-4114
Wichita *(G-15312)*
Poe & Associates of Kansas ....F....... 316 685-4114
Wichita *(G-15313)*
Ponzeryoungquist PA ....F....... 913 782-0541
Olathe *(G-7992)*
S K Design Group Inc ....E....... 913 451-1818
Shawnee Mission *(G-11819)*
Waters Edge Aquatic Design LLC ....F....... 913 438-4338
Shawnee Mission *(G-11994)*

ENGINEERING SVCS: Construction & Civil

Advatech LLC ....D....... 913 344-1000
Overland Park *(G-8353)*
Benchmark Construction LLC ....F....... 785 862-0340
Eudora *(G-1870)*
Camcorp Inc ....F....... 913 831-0740
Lenexa *(G-5727)*
County of Republic ....E....... 785 527-2235
Belleville *(G-456)*
Kansas City Tstg & Engrg LLC ....E....... 913 321-8100
Kansas City *(G-4151)*
Kaw Valley Engineering Inc ....F....... 316 440-4304
Wichita *(G-14834)*
Loves Enterprise Inc ....F....... 785 235-0479
Topeka *(G-12849)*
TI Enterprises Inc ....F....... 785 448-7100
Wichita *(G-15770)*

ENGINEERING SVCS: Electrical Or Electronic

Malone Finkle Echardt & Clns ....E....... 913 322-1400
Overland Park *(G-8981)*
Morrow Engineering Inc ....F....... 316 942-0402
Wichita *(G-15130)*
Research Concepts Inc ....F....... 913 422-0210
Lenexa *(G-6106)*
Shafer Kline & Warren Inc ....E....... 913 888-7800
Lenexa *(G-6126)*
Telecommunication Systems Inc ....E....... 913 593-9489
Overland Park *(G-9401)*
Young Electric Inc ....E....... 316 681-8118
Wichita *(G-16090)*

ENGINEERING SVCS: Energy conservation

Engie Services US Inc ....E....... 913 225-7081
Overland Park *(G-8681)*
Mid-States Energy Works Inc ....F....... 785 827-3631
Salina *(G-10601)*

ENGINEERING SVCS: Fire Protection

Poole Fire Protection Inc ....F....... 913 747-2044
Olathe *(G-7993)*
S C F Inc ....E....... 913 722-3473
Overland Park *(G-9267)*

ENGINEERING SVCS: Heating & Ventilation

Air Care Systems Hvac Inc ....F....... 360 403-9939
Berryton *(G-525)*
Thompson Dehydrating Co Inc ....F....... 785 272-7722
Topeka *(G-13160)*

ENGINEERING SVCS: Industrial

Charles Engineering Inc ....E....... 620 584-2381
Clearwater *(G-887)*
Control Systems Intl Inc ....D....... 913 599-5010
Shawnee Mission *(G-11264)*
Industrial Accessories Company ....D....... 913 384-5511
Shawnee Mission *(G-11455)*
Pars Consulting Engineers Inc ....E....... 913 432-0107
Leawood *(G-5516)*

ENGINEERING SVCS: Machine Tool Design

Performance Contracting Inc ....E....... 913 928-2832
Lenexa *(G-6052)*

ENGINEERING SVCS: Mechanical

GBA Architects Inc ....E....... 913 492-0400
Lenexa *(G-5869)*
Gfe LLC ....F....... 316 260-8433
Wichita *(G-14462)*
Hoss and Brown Engineers Inc ....E....... 785 832-1105
Lawrence *(G-4904)*
Locke Equipment Sales Co ....E....... 913 782-8500
Olathe *(G-7864)*
River Oak Mechanical ....F....... 573 338-7203
Overland Park *(G-9244)*
Sandmeyer Henthorn and Company ....F....... 913 951-2010
Leawood *(G-5547)*

ENGINEERING SVCS: Petroleum

Rapco Inc ....F....... 785 524-4232
Lincoln *(G-6386)*

ENGINEERING SVCS: Professional

Bredson and Associates Inc ....E....... 913 663-0100
Overland Park *(G-8482)*
Ecology and Environment Inc ....F....... 913 339-9519
Overland Park *(G-8670)*
Geosource LLC ....F....... 785 272-7200
Topeka *(G-12635)*
Henderson Engineers Inc ....B....... 913 742-5000
Lenexa *(G-5900)*
Js Westhoff & Company Inc ....F....... 913 663-9900
Lenexa *(G-5933)*
Mkec Engineering Cons Inc ....E....... 913 317-9390
Overland Park *(G-9045)*
Professional Service Inds Inc ....E....... 913 310-1600
Kansas City *(G-4343)*
Selective Site Consultants Inc ....E....... 913 438-7700
Overland Park *(G-9292)*
Spencer Reed Group LLC ....E....... 913 722-7860
Shawnee Mission *(G-11884)*

ENGINEERING SVCS: Sanitary

Landplan Engineering PA ....D....... 785 843-7530
Lawrence *(G-4954)*

ENGINEERING SVCS: Structural

Constructive Engrg Design ....F....... 913 341-3300
Overland Park *(G-8595)*
Dudley Williams and Assoc PA ....F....... 316 263-7591
Wichita *(G-14243)*
Needham & Associates Inc ....G....... 913 385-5300
Lenexa *(G-6019)*

ENGINES: Internal Combustion, NEC

Caterpillar Inc ....D....... 309 675-1000
Wamego *(G-13409)*
Cummins - Allison Corp ....G....... 913 894-2266
Lenexa *(G-5797)*
Cummins Central Power LLC ....F....... 785 462-3945
Colby *(G-1002)*

ENGRAVING SVC, NEC

Lee Reed Engraving Inc ....G....... 316 943-9700
Wichita *(G-14949)*
National Engraving ....E....... 785 776-5757
Manhattan *(G-6757)*
Northwest Awards & Signs ....G....... 785 621-2116
Hays *(G-2880)*

ENGRAVING SVC: Jewelry & Personal Goods

Jayhawk Trophy Company Inc ....G....... 785 843-3900
Lawrence *(G-4921)*

ENGRAVING SVCS

Fastsigns Inc ....G....... 913 649-3600
Overland Park *(G-8707)*
Lee Reed Engraving Inc ....G....... 316 943-9700
Wichita *(G-14949)*
Midwest Engraving Inc ....F....... 913 294-5348
Paola *(G-9575)*
Wichita Stamp and Seal Inc ....G....... 316 263-4223
Wichita *(G-16029)*

ENGRAVINGS: Plastic

Stealth Technologies LLC ....F....... 913 228-2214
Olathe *(G-8082)*

ENTERTAINERS & ENTERTAINMENT GROUPS

Little Soldier ....F....... 785 845-1987
Mayetta *(G-6915)*
Topeka Performing Arts Center ....F....... 785 234-2787
Topeka *(G-13184)*

ENTERTAINMENT PROMOTION SVCS

Liberty Hall Inc ....F....... 785 749-1972
Lawrence *(G-4994)*

ENTERTAINMENT SVCS

Glow Golf ....F....... 316 685-1040
Wichita *(G-14477)*
Hightech Solutions Inc ....C....... 620 228-2216
Fredonia *(G-2035)*
Smg Holdings Inc ....F....... 316 440-9016
Wichita *(G-15605)*
Wild Wild West Inc ....F....... 785 827-8938
Salina *(G-10768)*

ENVELOPES

Tension Envelope Corporation ....D....... 785 562-2307
Marysville *(G-6911)*

ENVELOPES WHOLESALERS

Food Trends Inc ....G....... 913 383-3600
Overland Park *(G-8732)*

Tension Envelope Corporation..............D....... 785 562-2307
Marysville *(G-6911)*

ENVIRON QUALITY PROGS ADMIN, GOVT: Water Control & Quality

City of Manhattan..................................F....... 785 587-4555
Manhattan *(G-6588)*

ENVIRONMENTAL QUALITY PROGS ADMIN, GOVT: Recreational

City of Manhattan..................................E....... 785 587-2737
Manhattan *(G-6587)*
County of Johnson................................C....... 913 888-4713
Shawnee Mission *(G-11272)*
County of Johnson................................E....... 913 829-4653
Olathe *(G-7623)*
County of Johnson................................C....... 913 403-8069
Shawnee Mission *(G-11273)*

ENVIRONMENTAL QUALITY PROGS ADMIN, GOVT: Waste Mgmt

City of Emporia....................................E....... 620 340-6339
Emporia *(G-1720)*
City of Lawrence..................................E....... 785 832-7840
Lawrence *(G-4791)*

ENZYMES

Natures Way Inc..................................G....... 785 486-3302
Horton *(G-3132)*

EQUIPMENT & VEHICLE FINANCE LEASING COMPANIES

Clune & Company Lc............................E....... 913 498-3000
Shawnee Mission *(G-11241)*

EQUIPMENT: Rental & Leasing, NEC

Aggreko LLC..F....... 913 281-9782
Shawnee Mission *(G-11085)*
Bartels Inc..F....... 316 755-1853
Valley Center *(G-13336)*
Building Erection Svcs Co Inc..............E....... 913 764-5560
Olathe *(G-7568)*
Capital City Pallet Inc..........................F....... 785 379-5099
Topeka *(G-12429)*
Clune & Company Lc............................F....... 913 498-3000
Shawnee Mission *(G-11242)*
Commercial Capital Company LLC......E....... 913 341-0053
Lenexa *(G-5774)*
Devlin Enterprises Inc..........................F....... 316 634-1800
Wichita *(G-14203)*
First Financial Leasing Inc..................E....... 913 236-8800
Shawnee Mission *(G-11370)*
Ice-Masters Inc......................................F....... 660 827-6900
Shawnee Mission *(G-11452)*
Ice-Masters Inc......................................F....... 316 945-6900
Wichita *(G-14665)*
Integrted Hlthcare Systems Inc............A....... 316 689-9111
Wichita *(G-14708)*
J & A Rentals Inc..................................F....... 316 788-4540
Derby *(G-1253)*
Kraft Leasing LLC................................E....... 913 601-6999
Kansas City *(G-4180)*
L C Enterprises....................................F....... 316 682-3300
Wichita *(G-14904)*
Laser Specialists Inc............................E....... 913 780-9990
Olathe *(G-7856)*
Lift Truck Center Inc............................E....... 316 942-7465
Wichita *(G-14963)*
Marc Gorges..E....... 316 630-0689
Eastborough *(G-1476)*
North American Buildings Inc..............F....... 316 821-9590
Wichita *(G-15187)*
Panhandle Steel Erectors Inc..............F....... 620 271-9878
Garden City *(G-2247)*
Party Bnce Monwalk Rentals LLC.........F....... 316 519-5174
Wichita *(G-15267)*
Perrys Inc..F....... 620 662-2375
Hutchinson *(G-3404)*
Safety-Kleen Systems Inc....................F....... 316 942-5001
Wichita *(G-15505)*
SC Hall Industrial Svcs Inc..................E....... 316 945-4255
Wichita *(G-15525)*
Sizewise Rentals LLC..........................F....... 800 814-9389
Ellis *(G-1652)*
Traftec Inc..F....... 913 621-2919
Kansas City *(G-4472)*
Tresko Inc..E....... 913 631-6900
Shawnee Mission *(G-11941)*
U S Weatherford L P............................D....... 620 624-6273
Liberal *(G-6377)*
U-Haul Co of Kansas Inc......................D....... 913 287-1327
Kansas City *(G-4481)*
United Rentals North Amer Inc............F....... 785 272-6006
Topeka *(G-13209)*
United Rentals North Amer Inc............E....... 620 245-0550
McPherson *(G-7035)*
United Rentals North Amer Inc............F....... 913 696-5628
Olathe *(G-8133)*
Wheatland Waters Inc..........................D....... 785 267-0512
Olathe *(G-8153)*

ESCROW INSTITUTIONS: Other Than Real Estate

Fidelity National Fincl Inc....................F....... 913 422-5122
Leawood *(G-5399)*

ETCHING & ENGRAVING SVC

R Miller Sales Co Inc............................E....... 913 341-3727
Shawnee Mission *(G-11772)*

ETHANOLAMINES

Fhr Biofuels & Ingredients LLC............G....... 316 828-2400
Wichita *(G-14361)*
Prairie Horzn Agri-Energy LLC............E....... 785 543-6719
Phillipsburg *(G-9794)*

EXCAVATING MACHINERY & EQPT WHOLESALERS

Valley Machinery Inc............................F....... 316 755-1911
Valley Center *(G-13359)*

EXECUTIVE OFFICES: Federal, State & Local

Administration Kansas Dept..................D....... 785 296-3631
Topeka *(G-12289)*
City of Salina..F....... 785 309-5752
Salina *(G-10452)*
City of Shawnee....................................F....... 913 631-1080
Shawnee Mission *(G-11233)*
Securities Commissioner Kansas.........E....... 785 296-3307
Topeka *(G-13050)*

EXERCISE EQPT STORES

Mid States Health Products..................F....... 316 681-3611
Wichita *(G-15072)*

EXERCISE SALON

Curves Ahead LLC................................F....... 785 221-9652
Topeka *(G-12536)*

EXHAUST HOOD OR FAN CLEANING SVCS

Rigdon Inc..F....... 913 322-9274
Overland Park *(G-9242)*
Sanibel Investments Inc......................E....... 913 422-7949
Shawnee Mission *(G-11829)*

EXHIBITORS, ITINERANT, MOTION PICTURE

AMC Entertainment Inc........................F....... 913 213-2000
Leawood *(G-5318)*
American Multi-Cinema Inc..................D....... 913 498-8696
Leawood *(G-5321)*
Astro 3 Theatre......................................F....... 785 562-3715
Marysville *(G-6879)*
B & B Cinemas......................................F....... 785 242-0777
Ottawa *(G-8247)*
Carmike Cinemas LLC..........................F....... 913 213-2000
Leawood *(G-5348)*
Carmike Reviews Holdings LLC............F....... 913 213-2000
Leawood *(G-5349)*
George G Kerasotes Corporation..........A....... 913 213-2000
Leawood *(G-5410)*
Warren Theatres LLC............................D....... 316 612-0469
Wichita *(G-15927)*
Warren Theatres LLC............................D....... 316 722-7060
Wichita *(G-15928)*

EXPLOSIVES

Detacorp Inc LLC..................................E....... 620 597-2552
Columbus *(G-1075)*
Hodgdon Powder Company Inc............D....... 785 258-3388
Herington *(G-2976)*
Wimase International Inc......................G....... 620 783-1361
Riverton *(G-10214)*

EXTENDED CARE FACILITY

Andover Health Care Center................C....... 316 448-4041
Andover *(G-80)*
Beaver Dam Health Care Center..........E....... 913 592-3100
Spring Hill *(G-12079)*
Beverly Enterprises-Kansas LLC..........E....... 785 672-3115
Oakley *(G-7472)*
Brookdale Snior Lving Cmmnties.........E....... 316 630-0788
Wichita *(G-13898)*
Brookdale Snior Lving Cmmnties.........D....... 913 491-1144
Shawnee Mission *(G-11184)*
Ggnsc Wellington LLC..........................E....... 620 326-7437
Wellington *(G-13504)*
Hospital Management Corp..................F....... 913 492-0159
Overland Park *(G-8827)*
Midwest Health Services Inc................E....... 785 537-1065
Manhattan *(G-6748)*
Midwest Health Services Inc................F....... 785 272-2200
Topeka *(G-12898)*
Midwest Health Services Inc................E....... 785 765-3318
Alma *(G-65)*
Midwest Health Services Inc................C....... 785 440-0500
Topeka *(G-12899)*
Midwest Health Services Inc................F....... 316 685-1587
Wichita *(G-15095)*
Rh Montgomery Properties Inc............E....... 620 783-1383
Galena *(G-2083)*
Rh Montgomery Properties Inc............D....... 913 294-4308
Paola *(G-9586)*

EXTERMINATING & FUMIGATING SVCS

Bats Inc..F....... 785 526-7185
Sylvan Grove *(G-12219)*
F/X Termite and Pest Control..............F....... 913 599-5990
Shawnee Mission *(G-11357)*
Frechin Pest Control LLC....................F....... 816 358-5776
Overland Park *(G-8739)*
Industrial Fumigant Collc....................E....... 913 782-7600
Lenexa *(G-5913)*
Kaw Valley Exterminator......................E....... 785 456-7357
Wamego *(G-13427)*
Tox-Eol Pest Management Inc..............F....... 785 825-5143
Salina *(G-10737)*

EYEGLASSES

Bushnell Group Holdings Inc................B....... 913 894-4224
Overland Park *(G-8496)*
Midwest Lens Inc..................................F....... 913 894-1030
Shawnee Mission *(G-11634)*

FABRIC STORES

Prairie Point..E....... 913 322-1222
Lenexa *(G-6068)*

FABRICATED METAL PRODUCTS, NEC

A & R Cstm Frms Fbrcations LLC..........E....... 620 423-0401
Parsons *(G-9661)*
Rohrer Custom and Fabrication............G....... 620 359-1707
Wellington *(G-13525)*

FABRICS & CLOTH: Quilted

Sunflwer Pcemakers Quilt Guild..........D....... 913 727-1870
Leavenworth *(G-5295)*

FABRICS: Apparel & Outerwear, Cotton

King Louie America Lc..........................F....... 913 338-5212
Leawood *(G-5450)*

FABRICS: Broadwoven, Cotton

Classic Cloth Inc....................................F....... 785 434-7200
Plainville *(G-9980)*

FABRICS: Chemically Coated & Treated

Invista Equities LLC..............................F....... 770 792-4221
Wichita *(G-14728)*

FABRICS: Coated Or Treated

HBD Industries Inc................................D....... 620 431-9100
Chanute *(G-730)*

FABRICS: Metallized

Zeeco Inc ....E 620 705-5100
Winfield *(G-16192)*

FABRICS: Nonwoven

Polymer Group Inc ....C 620 532-5141
Kingman *(G-4611)*

FABRICS: Stretch, Cotton

Acoustical Stretched Fabric ....G 913 345-1520
Shawnee Mission *(G-11069)*

FABRICS: Trimmings

Falcon Design and Mfg ....E 913 441-1074
Shawnee *(G-10953)*
Gfsi LLC ....B 913 693-3200
Lenexa *(G-5875)*
Graphic Impressions Inc ....E 620 663-5939
Hutchinson *(G-3305)*
Hasty Awards Inc ....D 785 242-5297
Ottawa *(G-8278)*
John B Baker ....G 316 263-2820
Wichita *(G-14762)*
Kansas Graphics Inc ....G 620 273-6111
Cottonwood Falls *(G-1155)*
Koller Enterprises Inc ....D 913 422-2027
Lenexa *(G-5957)*
Navrats Inc ....F 620 342-2092
Emporia *(G-1800)*
Prairie Print Inc ....G 316 267-1950
Wichita *(G-15321)*
Ragland Specialty Printing ....E 785 542-3058
Eudora *(G-1879)*
Shirts Plus Inc ....F 316 788-1550
Derby *(G-1272)*
Stouse LLC ....C 913 764-5757
New Century *(G-7301)*
Sunflwer Pcemakers Quilt Guild ....D 913 727-1870
Leavenworth *(G-5295)*
Winning Spirit Inc ....E 316 684-0855
Wichita *(G-16056)*

FABRICS: Underwear, Cotton

Jockey International Globl Inc ....G 913 334-4455
Kansas City *(G-4125)*

FACIAL SALONS

Bath & Body Works LLC ....F 620 338-8409
Dodge City *(G-1304)*
Facial Expressions LLC ....F 316 390-0417
Wichita *(G-14331)*
Gram Enterprises Inc ....E 913 888-3689
Lenexa *(G-5879)*
Green Medical Group ....E 316 691-3937
Wichita *(G-14511)*
Hair Loft ....F 785 827-2306
Salina *(G-10530)*
Monarch Skin Care ....E 913 317-9386
Shawnee Mission *(G-11653)*
Svetas Body Therapy LLC ....F 316 630-0400
Wichita *(G-15706)*
Ultimate Escape Day Spa LLC ....E 913 851-3385
Overland Park *(G-9438)*

FACILITIES SUPPORT SVCS

BKM Construction LLC ....F 913 297-0049
Leavenworth *(G-5212)*
Contract Services Inc ....D 785 239-9069
Fort Riley *(G-1946)*
Court Trustee Dept ....F 785 762-2583
Junction City *(G-3685)*
Envirnmntal Advisors Engineers ....E 913 599-4326
Shawnee Mission *(G-11344)*
Exhibit Arts LLC ....E 316 264-2915
Wichita *(G-14321)*
Landscapes Inc ....E 316 262-7557
Wichita *(G-14921)*
Oc Services ....F 316 655-3952
Wichita *(G-15205)*
Transtecs Corporation ....D 316 651-0389
Wichita *(G-15793)*
US Attorneys Office - Dst Kans ....D 316 269-6481
Wichita *(G-15862)*

FACILITIES: Inspection & fixed

International Trans Logis Inc ....F 913 621-2750
Kansas City *(G-4108)*

FACILITY RENTAL & PARTY PLANNING SVCS

Round Hill Bath &TEnnis Club ....F 913 381-2603
Shawnee Mission *(G-11814)*

FAMILY COUNSELING SVCS

Archdiocese of Miami Inc ....E 785 233-6300
Topeka *(G-12336)*
Christian Psychological Svcs ....F 785 843-2429
Lawrence *(G-4788)*
Counseling Inc ....F 785 472-4300
Ellsworth *(G-1664)*
County of Crawford ....E 620 231-5130
Pittsburg *(G-9848)*
County of Crawford ....C 620 231-5141
Pittsburg *(G-9849)*
Family Therapy Inst Midwest ....F 785 830-8299
Lawrence *(G-4857)*
Friends University ....F 316 295-5638
Wichita *(G-14424)*
Hays Medical Center Inc ....A 785 623-6270
Hays *(G-2835)*
High Plains Mental Health Ctr ....F 785 543-5284
Phillipsburg *(G-9788)*
High Plains Mental Health Ctr ....E 785 462-6774
Colby *(G-1014)*
Horizons Mental Health Ctr Inc ....F 620 532-3895
Kingman *(G-4595)*
Kansas State University ....E 785 532-6984
Manhattan *(G-6696)*

FAMILY OR MARRIAGE COUNSELING

Adult Child & Fmly Counseling ....F 316 945-5200
Wichita *(G-13620)*
Family Conservancy Inc ....D 913 342-1110
Kansas City *(G-4005)*
Family Conservancy Inc ....F 913 287-1300
Kansas City *(G-4006)*
Resonate Relationship Clinic ....F 913 647-8092
Overland Park *(G-9236)*
Youthville Family Cnsltn Svc ....E 316 264-8317
Wichita *(G-16098)*

FAMILY PLANNING CENTERS

Center For Rprductive Medicine ....E 316 687-2112
Wichita *(G-13972)*
Lawrenc-Douglas Cnty Hlth Dept ....E 785 843-3060
Lawrence *(G-4957)*

FAMILY PLANNING CLINIC

Birthright Inc ....E 913 682-2700
Leavenworth *(G-5211)*
Planned Parenthood of Kansas ....E 316 263-7575
Wichita *(G-15305)*

FAMILY SVCS AGENCY

Antioch Church ....F 785 232-1937
Topeka *(G-12332)*
Catholic Charities Inc ....C 316 264-8344
Wichita *(G-13959)*
Catholic Charities Inc ....F 316 264-7233
Wichita *(G-13960)*
Court Trustee Dept ....F 785 762-2583
Junction City *(G-3685)*
Jewish Family and Chld Svc ....F 913 327-8250
Shawnee Mission *(G-11488)*
Keys For Networking Inc ....E 785 233-8732
Topeka *(G-12819)*

FARM & GARDEN MACHINERY WHOLESALERS

Baker Abilene Machine Inc ....E 785 565-9455
Solomon *(G-12048)*
Deer Trail Implement Inc ....E 620 342-5000
Emporia *(G-1728)*
Deere & Company ....E 309 765-4826
Olathe *(G-7644)*
Deere & Company ....F 913 310-8344
Olathe *(G-7646)*
Deere & Company ....E 800 665-4620
Hutchinson *(G-3260)*
Deere & Company ....E 316 945-0501
Wichita *(G-14186)*
Great Plains Manufacturing Inc ....C 785 823-3276
Salina *(G-10518)*
Heritage Tractor Inc ....E 620 231-0950
Pittsburg *(G-9875)*
Heritage Tractor Inc ....D 785 594-6486
Baldwin City *(G-363)*
Heritage Tractor Inc ....E 913 529-2376
Olathe *(G-7766)*
Jdamc Inc ....A 913 310-8100
Olathe *(G-7810)*
Kanequip Inc ....E 785 472-3114
Ellsworth *(G-1676)*
Kanequip Inc ....F 785 267-9200
Topeka *(G-12754)*
Kanequip Inc ....E 785 456-2041
Wamego *(G-13426)*
Kanequip Inc ....C 785 562-2377
Marysville *(G-6892)*
Landmark Implement Inc ....E 785 282-6601
Smith Center *(G-12036)*
Magnum ....E 913 783-4600
Hillsdale *(G-3059)*
Murphy Tractor & Eqp Co Inc ....F 785 233-0556
Topeka *(G-12919)*
Norvell Company Inc ....E 785 825-6663
Salina *(G-10615)*
Oakley Motors Inc ....E 785 672-3238
Oakley *(G-7484)*
Orscheln Farm and Home LLC ....F 620 930-3276
Medicine Lodge *(G-7071)*
Radke Implement Inc ....F 620 935-4310
Russell *(G-10286)*
Romans Outdoor Power Inc ....F 620 331-2970
Independence *(G-3556)*

FARM MACHINERY REPAIR SVCS

B & D Equipment Co Inc ....F 913 367-1744
Atchison *(G-211)*
D & S Machine and Welding Inc ....G 785 798-3359
Ness City *(G-7259)*
Fort Scott Truck & Tractor ....F 620 223-6506
Fort Scott *(G-1972)*
Oswald Manufacturing Co Inc ....G 785 258-2877
Herington *(G-2980)*
Taylor Implement Co Inc ....E 785 675-3272
Hoxie *(G-3143)*
Todd Tractor Co Inc ....F 785 336-2138
Seneca *(G-10884)*
Unruh-Foster Inc ....E 620 846-2215
Montezuma *(G-7161)*
Van-Wall Equipment Inc ....E 913 397-6009
Olathe *(G-8138)*

FARM PRDTS, RAW MATERIALS, WHOLESALE: Bristles

Cargill Incorporated ....E 913 752-1200
Lenexa *(G-5730)*

FARM PRDTS, RAW MATERIALS, WHOLESALE: Farm Animals

Redwood Group LLC ....D 816 979-1786
Mission *(G-7137)*

FARM SPLY STORES

Agco Inc ....F 785 483-2128
Russell *(G-10263)*
Anthony Frmrs Coop Elev Cmpnys ....F 620 842-5181
Anthony *(G-119)*
Bartlett Cattle Company LP ....E 620 675-2244
Sublette *(G-12199)*
Countryside Feed LLC ....E 620 947-3111
Hillsboro *(G-3047)*
Countryside Feed LLC ....F 785 336-6777
Seneca *(G-10861)*
Cross Brand Office Inc ....E 620 324-5571
Lewis *(G-6267)*
Elkhart Coop Equity Exchnge ....E 620 697-2135
Elkhart *(G-1619)*
Farmers Cooperative Elev Co ....F 316 835-2261
Halstead *(G-2699)*
Frontier Ag Inc ....F 785 694-2281
Brewster *(G-583)*
Lawrence Feed & Farm Sup Inc ....F 785 843-4311
Lawrence *(G-4966)*

Orscheln Farm and Home LLC ... F ... 620 930-3276
Medicine Lodge *(G-7071)*
Orscheln Farm and Home LLC ... F ... 785 228-9688
Topeka *(G-12955)*
Piqua Farmers Coop Assn Incthe ... F ... 620 468-2535
Piqua *(G-9801)*
Plp Inc ... E ... 620 532-3106
Kingman *(G-4610)*
Producers Coop Assn Girard ... E ... 620 724-8241
Girard *(G-2415)*
Tractor Supply Company ... F ... 620 663-7607
Hutchinson *(G-3465)*
Wilbur-Ellis Company LLC ... F ... 785 582-4052
Silver Lake *(G-12029)*
Wilbur-Ellis Company LLC ... F ... 785 359-6569
Leona *(G-6248)*

FARM SPLYS WHOLESALERS

Ackerman Supply Inc ... F ... 785 738-5733
Beloit *(G-469)*
Atwood Distributing LP ... E ... 316 789-1800
Derby *(G-1218)*
Atwood Distributing LP ... F ... 316 744-8888
Park City *(G-9602)*
Bartlett Cooperative Assn ... E ... 620 226-3311
Bartlett *(G-371)*
Beattie Farmers Un Coop Assn ... E ... 785 353-2237
Beattie *(G-418)*
Beaver Valley Supply Co Inc ... E ... 800 982-1280
Atwood *(G-281)*
Bruna Brothers Implement LLC ... F ... 785 632-5621
Clay Center *(G-845)*
Bruna Brothers Implement LLC ... E ... 785 325-2232
Washington *(G-13461)*
Central Prairie Co-Op ... F ... 620 278-2470
Sterling *(G-12113)*
Central Valley AG Cooperative ... C ... 785 738-2241
Beloit *(G-481)*
CHS Inc ... F ... 785 754-3318
Quinter *(G-10180)*
CHS Inc ... D ... 620 663-5711
Hutchinson *(G-3238)*
Crazy House Inc ... F ... 620 275-2153
Garden City *(G-2138)*
Cropland Co-Op Inc ... F ... 620 356-1241
Ulysses *(G-13294)*
Darling Ingredients Inc ... D ... 316 264-6951
Wichita *(G-14169)*
Decatur Cooperative Assn ... F ... 785 475-2234
Oberlin *(G-7490)*
Dodge City Cooperative Exch ... F ... 620 227-8671
Dodge City *(G-1345)*
Ellsworth Coop ... F ... 785 472-3261
Ellsworth *(G-1667)*
Farmers Co-Operative Union ... D ... 620 278-2141
Sterling *(G-12116)*
Farmers Coop Grn Assn Inc ... F ... 620 456-2222
Conway Springs *(G-1141)*
Faulkner Grain Inc ... F ... 620 597-2636
Chetopa *(G-817)*
Frontier Ag Inc ... E ... 785 462-2063
Oakley *(G-7475)*
Garden City Co-Op Inc ... F ... 620 356-1219
Ulysses *(G-13298)*
Golden Belt Coop Assn Inc ... F ... 785 726-3115
Ellis *(G-1646)*
Golden Valley Inc ... E ... 620 527-4216
Rozel *(G-10258)*
Johnson Cooperative Grn Co Inc ... F ... 620 492-6210
Johnson *(G-3654)*
Kanza Cooperative Association ... F ... 620 546-2231
Iuka *(G-3640)*
Lawrence Feed & Farm Sup Inc ... F ... 785 843-4311
Lawrence *(G-4966)*
Leroy Cooperative Assn Inc ... E ... 620 964-2225
Le Roy *(G-5196)*
Mid-Kansas Cooperative Assn ... E ... 620 345-6328
Moundridge *(G-7190)*
Mid-Kansas Cooperative Assn ... F ... 785 776-9467
Manhattan *(G-6742)*
Mid-Kansas Cooperative Assn ... F ... 620 837-3313
Walton *(G-13401)*
Norder Supply Inc ... E ... 620 872-3058
Scott City *(G-10825)*
Nutrien AG Solutions Inc ... F ... 620 872-2174
Scott City *(G-10826)*
Orscheln Farm and Home LLC ... F ... 785 825-1681
Salina *(G-10624)*
Orscheln Farm and Home LLC ... F ... 620 442-5760
Arkansas City *(G-168)*
Orscheln Farm and Home LLC ... E ... 913 728-2014
Basehor *(G-385)*
Orscheln Farm and Home LLC ... F ... 785 762-4411
Junction City *(G-3734)*
Orscheln Farm and Home LLC ... F ... 913 367-2261
Atchison *(G-254)*
Orscheln Farm and Home LLC ... E ... 620 421-0555
Parsons *(G-9715)*
Orscheln Farm and Home LLC ... F ... 785 282-3272
Smith Center *(G-12038)*
Orscheln Farm and Home LLC ... F ... 785 243-6071
Concordia *(G-1126)*
Orscheln Farm and Home LLC ... F ... 620 251-2950
Coffeyville *(G-968)*
Orscheln Farm and Home LLC ... F ... 785 838-3184
Lawrence *(G-5050)*
Orscheln Farm and Home LLC ... F ... 620 227-8700
Dodge City *(G-1416)*
Orscheln Farm and Home LLC ... F ... 620 792-5480
Great Bend *(G-2619)*
Orscheln Farm and Home LLC ... F ... 316 283-2969
Newton *(G-7401)*
Orscheln Farm and Home LLC ... E ... 785 776-1476
Manhattan *(G-6766)*
Orscheln Farm and Home LLC ... F ... 785 460-1551
Colby *(G-1033)*
Orscheln Farm and Home LLC ... F ... 785 899-7132
Goodland *(G-2481)*
Orscheln Farm and Home LLC ... F ... 620 326-2804
Wellington *(G-13520)*
Orscheln Farm and Home LLC ... F ... 620 365-7695
Iola *(G-3621)*
Orscheln Farm and Home LLC ... F ... 316 321-4004
El Dorado *(G-1589)*
Orscheln Farm and Home LLC ... F ... 785 625-7316
Hays *(G-2884)*
Orscheln Farm and Home LLC ... E ... 785 242-3133
Ottawa *(G-8296)*
Orscheln Farm and Home LLC ... F ... 785 228-9688
Topeka *(G-12955)*
Orscheln Farm and Home LLC ... F ... 620 930-3276
Medicine Lodge *(G-7071)*
Palmer Grain Inc ... F ... 785 692-4212
Palmer *(G-9538)*
R & F Farm Supply Inc ... F ... 620 244-3275
Erie *(G-1864)*
Simpson Farm Enterprises Inc ... F ... 785 731-2700
Ransom *(G-10195)*
Sims Fertilizer and Chem Co ... F ... 785 346-5681
Osborne *(G-8218)*
Southern Plains Co-Op At Lewis ... E ... 620 324-5536
Lewis *(G-6270)*
Tarwaters Inc ... E ... 785 286-2390
Topeka *(G-13143)*
Tractor Supply Company ... F ... 620 408-9119
Dodge City *(G-1439)*
Tractor Supply Company ... F ... 620 672-1102
Pratt *(G-10161)*
Tractor Supply Company ... F ... 785 587-8949
Manhattan *(G-6829)*
Tractor Supply Company ... F ... 620 223-4900
Fort Scott *(G-2010)*
Western AG Enterprises Inc ... E ... 620 793-8355
Great Bend *(G-2660)*

FARM SPLYS, WHOLESALE: Alfalfa

Alfalfa Inc ... G ... 620 675-8686
Sublette *(G-12196)*
Bestifor Hay Co ... F ... 785 527-2450
Belleville *(G-454)*

FARM SPLYS, WHOLESALE: Equestrian Eqpt

Hunn Leather Products Inc ... F ... 316 775-6300
Augusta *(G-326)*

FARM SPLYS, WHOLESALE: Feed

Agco Inc ... F ... 785 483-2128
Russell *(G-10263)*
Agri Trails Coop Inc ... F ... 785 258-2286
Herington *(G-2969)*
Archer-Daniels-Midland Company ... G ... 620 375-4811
Leoti *(G-6250)*
Archer-Daniels-Midland Company ... G ... 620 357-8733
Jetmore *(G-3645)*
Bekemeyer Enterprises Inc ... F ... 785 325-2274
Washington *(G-13459)*
Central Planes Coop ... F ... 785 695-2216
Athol *(G-273)*
CHS Inc ... E ... 785 852-4241
Sharon Springs *(G-10895)*
Cooperative Elevator & Sup Co ... E ... 620 873-2161
Meade *(G-7047)*
Countryside Feed LLC ... E ... 620 947-3111
Hillsboro *(G-3047)*
Countryside Feed LLC ... F ... 785 336-6777
Seneca *(G-10861)*
Delphos Cooperative Assn ... E ... 785 523-4213
Delphos *(G-1216)*
Farmers Co-Operative Equity Co ... F ... 620 739-4335
Isabel *(G-3639)*
Farmers Cooperative Elev Assn ... F ... 785 747-2236
Greenleaf *(G-2668)*
Farmers Cooperative Elev Inc ... F ... 785 284-2185
Sabetha *(G-10310)*
Farmers Cooperative Grain ... F ... 620 326-7496
Wellington *(G-13499)*
Farmers Cooperative Grain Co ... F ... 620 845-6441
Caldwell *(G-658)*
Farmers Grain Cooperative ... E ... 620 837-3313
Walton *(G-13400)*
Frontier Ag Inc ... F ... 785 694-2281
Brewster *(G-583)*
Frontier Ag Inc ... E ... 785 824-3201
Grinnell *(G-2692)*
Garden City Co-Op Inc ... F ... 620 275-6161
Garden City *(G-2170)*
Great Bend Cooperative Assn ... E ... 620 793-3531
Great Bend *(G-2576)*
Hl Plains Cooperative Assn ... F ... 785 462-3351
Colby *(G-1012)*
Jackson Farmers Inc ... F ... 785 364-3161
Holton *(G-3100)*
Kanza Cooperative Association ... E ... 316 444-2141
Andale *(G-78)*
Land OLakes Inc ... E ... 785 445-4030
Russell *(G-10278)*
Leavenworth County Coop Assn ... F ... 913 727-1900
Lansing *(G-4683)*
Minneola Co-Op Inc ... F ... 620 885-4361
Minneola *(G-7125)*
Mulvane Cooperative Union Inc ... F ... 316 777-1121
Mulvane *(G-7223)*
Nemaha County Cooperative Assn ... D ... 785 336-6153
Seneca *(G-10874)*
Norton County Co-Op Assn Inc ... F ... 785 877-5900
Norton *(G-7456)*
O K Coop Grn & Merc Co ... F ... 620 825-4212
Kiowa *(G-4628)*
Orscheln Farm and Home LLC ... F ... 620 241-0707
McPherson *(G-7012)*
Orscheln Farm and Home LLC ... F ... 620 331-2551
Independence *(G-3546)*
Orscheln Farm and Home LLC ... F ... 785 562-2459
Marysville *(G-6906)*
Plains Equity Exch & Coop Un ... E ... 620 563-9566
Plains *(G-9977)*
Prime Feeders LLC ... F ... 620 492-6674
Johnson *(G-3659)*
Randall Farmers Coop Un Inc ... F ... 785 739-2312
Randall *(G-10190)*
Rangeland Cooperatives Inc ... E ... 785 543-2114
Phillipsburg *(G-9797)*
Seaboard Feed Mill ... E ... 620 375-3300
Leoti *(G-6257)*
Severy Cooperative Association ... F ... 620 736-2211
Severy *(G-10893)*
Stafford County Flour Mills Co ... E ... 620 458-4121
Hudson *(G-3146)*
Two Rivers Consumers Coop Assn ... E ... 620 442-2360
Arkansas City *(G-185)*
Two-Bee Inc ... F ... 785 364-2162
Holton *(G-3113)*
United Plains AG ... E ... 785 852-4241
Sharon Springs *(G-10901)*
William G Woods ... F ... 620 285-6971
Larned *(G-4716)*

FARM SPLYS, WHOLESALE: Fertilizers & Agricultural Chemicals

Archer-Daniels-Midland Company ... G ... 785 694-2286
Brewster *(G-582)*
City of Great Bend ... D ... 620 793-5031
Great Bend *(G-2543)*
Farmers Cooperative Elev Co ... F ... 316 835-2261
Halstead *(G-2699)*
Helena Agri-Enterprises LLC ... F ... 785 899-2391
Goodland *(G-2476)*

(G-0000) Company's Geographic Section entry number

Helena Agri-Enterprises LLC ....E 620 275-9531
Garden City (G-2195)
Helena Chemical Company ....G 620 375-2073
Leoti (G-6253)
Koch AG & Energy Solutions LLC ....E 316 828-5500
Wichita (G-14872)
Koch Companies Pub Sector LLC ....G 316 828-5500
Wichita (G-14876)
Koch Industries Inc ....E 620 227-8631
Dodge City (G-1395)
Lange Company LLC ....F 620 456-2996
Conway Springs (G-1143)
Mid-West Fertilizer Inc ....G 620 431-3430
Chanute (G-743)
Progressive AG Coop Assn ....F 620 962-5238
Danville (G-1190)
Scotwood Industries Inc ....E 913 851-3500
Overland Park (G-9285)

FARM SPLYS, WHOLESALE: Garden Splys

Gardn-Wise Distributors Inc ....F 316 838-6104
Wichita (G-14448)

FARM SPLYS, WHOLESALE: Greenhouse Eqpt & Splys

Orscheln Farm and Home LLC ....F 620 662-8867
Hutchinson (G-3397)

FARM SPLYS, WHOLESALE: Hay

Carl Leatherwood Inc ....E 620 855-3850
Cimarron (G-820)
Heartland Hay ....F 785 525-6331
Lucas (G-6472)
Morrill Hay Company Inc ....F 620 285-6941
Paola (G-9576)
R Puckett Farms Inc ....F 620 378-3342
Fredonia (G-2043)

FASTENERS WHOLESALERS

Clancey Co ....F 913 894-4444
Overland Park (G-8559)
J & S Tool and Fastener Inc ....F 913 677-2000
Kansas City (G-4114)

FASTENERS: Notions, NEC

Domestic Fastener & Forge Inc ....F 913 888-9447
New Century (G-7280)

FEDERAL CROP INSURANCE CORP

CGB Enterprises Inc ....E 913 367-5450
Atchison (G-222)
Hudson Crop Insurance Svcs Inc ....C 866 450-1446
Overland Park (G-8833)

FEDERAL DEPOSIT INSURANCE CORPORATION

Federal Deposit Insurance Corp ....E 316 729-0301
Wichita (G-14346)

FEDERAL SAVINGS & LOAN ASSOCIATIONS

Argentine Savings and Ln Assn ....F 913 831-2004
Kansas City (G-3818)
Capitol Federal Savings Bank ....E 785 235-1341
Topeka (G-12438)
Capitol Federal Savings Bank ....C 785 235-1341
Topeka (G-12439)
Capitol Federal Savings Bank ....E 316 689-3104
Wichita (G-13938)
Capitol Federal Savings Bank ....F 913 782-5100
Olathe (G-7577)
Capitol Federal Savings Bank ....F 785 749-9100
Lawrence (G-4775)
Citizens Savings & Loan Assn ....E 913 727-1040
Leavenworth (G-5218)
First Federal Bank Kansas City ....F 913 233-6100
Kansas City (G-4011)
Golden Belt Banking & Sav Assn ....E 785 625-7345
Hays (G-2818)
Landmark National Bank ....F 785 883-2145
Wellsville (G-13544)
Lyons Federal Savings Assn ....F 620 257-2316
Lyons (G-6490)
Mutual Savings Association ....F 913 441-5555
Bonner Springs (G-564)
Mutual Savings Association ....D 913 682-3491
Leavenworth (G-5272)

FEDERAL SAVINGS BANKS

A Divis of P Midla Loan Servi ....B 913 253-9000
Overland Park (G-8334)
Capitol Federal Financial Inc ....D 785 235-1341
Topeka (G-12437)
Capitol Federal Savings Bank ....F 316 689-0200
Wichita (G-13937)
Capitol Federal Savings Bank ....F 620 342-0125
Emporia (G-1716)
Capitol Federal Savings Bank ....F 785 539-9976
Manhattan (G-6575)
Capitol Federal Savings Bank ....F 316 689-0200
Wichita (G-13939)
First Manhattan Bancorporation ....E 785 537-0200
Manhattan (G-6629)
First Seacoast Bank ....F 913 766-2500
Overland Park (G-8722)

FENCING DEALERS

A L C Enterprises Inc ....F 316 943-6500
Wichita (G-13587)
Macs Fence Inc ....E 913 287-6173
Kansas City (G-4211)
Wichita Fence Co Inc ....F 316 838-1342
Park City (G-9654)

FERTILIZER, AGRICULTURAL: Wholesalers

AG Connection Sales Inc ....F 785 336-2121
Seneca (G-10856)
Ag-Service Inc ....F 620 947-3166
Hillsboro (G-3040)
Agri Trails Coop Inc ....D 785 479-5870
Chapman (G-776)
Alliance AG and Grain LLC ....F 620 723-3351
Greensburg (G-2671)
Archer-Daniels-Midland Company ....F 785 671-3171
Oakley (G-7471)
Beaver Grain Corporation Inc ....F 620 587-3417
Beaver (G-424)
Cropland Co-Op Inc ....F 620 649-2230
Satanta (G-10782)
Kugler Oil Company ....G 620 356-4347
Ulysses (G-13304)
Long Island Grain Co Inc ....F 785 854-7431
Long Island (G-6428)
McCune Farmers Union Coop ....F 620 632-4226
Mc Cune (G-6920)
MFA Enterprises Inc ....F 620 237-4668
Moran (G-7162)
Nutrien AG Solutions Inc ....F 316 794-2231
Goddard (G-2451)
Nutrien AG Solutions Inc ....E 620 275-4271
Garden City (G-2244)
Offerle Coop Grn & Sup Co ....F 620 659-2165
Offerle (G-7500)
Preferred AG Services Inc ....F 620 271-7366
Garden City (G-2258)
Ranch-Aid Inc ....F 620 583-5585
Eureka (G-1898)
Skyland Grain LLC ....F 620 492-2126
Johnson (G-3660)
Skyland Grain LLC ....F 620 672-3961
Cunningham (G-1189)
Specialty Fertilizer Pdts LLC ....F 913 956-7500
Leawood (G-5556)
Sublette Cooperative Inc ....E 620 675-2297
Sublette (G-12209)

FERTILIZERS: NEC

Archer-Daniels-Midland Company ....G 620 675-2226
Sublette (G-12198)
Cropland Co-Op Inc ....F 620 649-2230
Satanta (G-10782)
Farmers Union Coop Assn ....F 785 632-5632
Clay Center (G-863)
Helena Agri-Enterprises LLC ....E 620 275-9531
Garden City (G-2195)
Kugler Oil Company ....G 620 356-4347
Ulysses (G-13304)
Leroy Cooperative Assn Inc ....E 620 964-2225
Le Roy (G-5196)
Pbi-Gordon Corporation ....E 620 848-3849
Crestline (G-1184)
Pbi-Gordon Corporation ....E 816 421-4070
Kansas City (G-4317)
R & R Manufacturing Inc ....F 620 672-7461
Pratt (G-10147)
Right Cooperative Association ....E 620 227-8611
Wright (G-16194)

FERTILIZERS: Nitrogenous

Coffeyville Acquisition LLC ....E 913 982-0500
Kansas City (G-3922)
Coffeyville Resources LLC ....E 913 982-0500
Kansas City (G-3923)
Coffeyvlle Ntrgn Frtlizers Inc ....C 913 982-0500
Kansas City (G-3924)
Koch Fertilizer LLC ....E 620 227-8631
Dodge City (G-1394)
Koch Fertilizer LLC ....E 316 828-5010
Wichita (G-14880)
Koch Industries Inc ....E 620 227-8631
Dodge City (G-1395)
Koch Mineral Services LLC ....E 316 828-5500
Wichita (G-14884)
Tessenderlo Kerley Inc ....F 620 241-1727
McPherson (G-7031)
United Prairie Ag LLC ....D 620 356-2212
Ulysses (G-13329)

FERTILIZERS: Phosphatic

Blicks Phsphate Cnversions LLC ....G 800 932-5425
Garden City (G-2113)
Mid-West Fertilizer Inc ....G 620 431-3430
Chanute (G-743)

FIGURES, WAX

Emco Specialty Products Inc ....G 913 281-4555
Kansas City (G-3986)

FILM & SHEET: Unsuppported Plastic

Berry Global Inc ....C 800 777-3080
Lawrence (G-4754)
Lustercraft Plastics LLC ....F 316 942-8451
Wichita (G-14991)
Midco Plastics Inc ....E 785 263-8999
Enterprise (G-1855)
Vanguard Shrink Films Inc ....F 913 599-1111
Lenexa (G-6209)

FILM DEVELOPING & PRINTING SVCS

Millers Inc ....B 620 231-8050
Pittsburg (G-9906)

FILTER CLEANING SVCS

Air Filter Plus Inc ....E 785 542-3700
Eudora (G-1869)

FILTERS

Clarcor Air Filtration Pdts ....E 785 242-1811
Ottawa (G-8256)

FILTERS & SOFTENERS: Water, Household

Green Product Solutions LLC ....G 913 633-1274
Overland Park (G-8778)
Watersource Technologies Inc ....G 316 927-2100
Haysville (G-2963)

FILTERS: Air

Air Filter Plus Inc ....E 785 542-3700
Eudora (G-1869)
Clarcor Air Filtration Pdts ....E 785 242-1811
Ottawa (G-8256)
Commercial Fltr Svc Knsas Cty ....G 913 384-5858
Kansas City (G-3929)
Transweb Llc ....E 856 205-1313
Leawood (G-5583)
Tri-Dim Filter Corporation ....G 316 425-0462
Wichita (G-15799)

FILTERS: Air Intake, Internal Combustion Engine, Exc Auto

Arrow Fork Lift Parts Inc ....G 816 231-4410
Lenexa (G-5663)

FILTERS: Motor Vehicle

Aeromotive Inc ....F 913 647-7300
Shawnee Mission (G-11082)

FILTRATION DEVICES: Electronic

Cooper Electronics Inc..........E....... 913 782-0012
Olathe *(G-7615)*

FINANCIAL INVEST ACTS: Mineral, Oil & Gas Leasing & Royalty

Daystar Petroleum Inc..........G....... 316 755-3492
Valley Center *(G-13340)*

FINANCIAL INVESTMENT ACTIVITIES, NEC: Financial Reporting

True North Inc..........F....... 316 266-6574
Wichita *(G-15809)*

FINANCIAL INVESTMENT ACTIVITIES, NEC: Security Transfer

Waddell & Reed Inc..........A....... 913 236-2000
Shawnee Mission *(G-11987)*

FINANCIAL INVESTMENT ADVICE

Ameriprise Financial Inc..........E....... 316 858-1506
Wichita *(G-13697)*
Ameriprise Fincl Ameriprise..........F....... 913 451-2811
Leawood *(G-5324)*
Compass Fincl Resources LLC..........F....... 913 747-2000
Olathe *(G-7607)*
Demarche Associates Inc..........D....... 913 384-4994
Overland Park *(G-8648)*
Esb Financial..........F....... 785 539-3553
Manhattan *(G-6623)*
Financial Institution Tech Inc..........F....... 785 273-5578
Topeka *(G-12609)*
First Command Fincl Plg Inc..........F....... 785 537-0497
Manhattan *(G-6628)*
First Command Fincl Plg Inc..........F....... 913 651-6820
Leavenworth *(G-5239)*
Ima Wealth Inc..........E....... 316 266-6582
Wichita *(G-14675)*
Lawing Financial Group Inc..........D....... 913 491-6226
Overland Park *(G-8948)*
Legacy Financial Strategy LLC..........F....... 913 403-0600
Leawood *(G-5456)*
Lincoln Fincl Advisors Corp..........E....... 913 451-1505
Shawnee Mission *(G-11573)*
Midwest Trust Company..........F....... 913 319-0300
Shawnee Mission *(G-11638)*
Nasb Financial Inc..........E....... 913 327-2000
Leawood *(G-5497)*
New England Life Insurance Co..........E....... 620 754-3725
Elsmore *(G-1683)*
Pacific Investment Inc..........F....... 785 827-1271
Salina *(G-10630)*
Umb Bank National Association..........E....... 785 776-9400
Manhattan *(G-6836)*
Umb Bank National Association..........F....... 785 483-6800
Russell *(G-10300)*
Umb Bank National Association..........E....... 913 234-2070
Shawnee Mission *(G-11956)*
Waddell & Reed Inc..........E....... 785 827-3606
Salina *(G-10754)*
Waddell & Reed Financial Inc..........D....... 913 236-2000
Overland Park *(G-9477)*
Wesbanco Inc..........D....... 785 539-3553
Manhattan *(G-6851)*

FINANCIAL SVCS

Best Value Services LLC..........D....... 316 440-1048
Wichita *(G-13839)*
Deborah John & Associates..........E....... 316 777-0903
Wichita *(G-14182)*
Financial Consultants America..........E....... 316 943-7307
Wichita *(G-14367)*
First Horizon Bank..........E....... 913 317-2000
Overland Park *(G-8719)*
International Fincl Svcs Inc..........E....... 620 665-7708
Hutchinson *(G-3336)*
Mnvc Financial Services LLC..........E....... 816 589-4336
Overland Park *(G-9047)*
Morris Laing Evans Brock..........D....... 316 838-1084
Wichita *(G-15128)*
Plans Professional Inc..........F....... 785 357-7777
Topeka *(G-12979)*
Qc Holdings Inc..........C....... 866 660-2243
Lenexa *(G-6082)*
Retirement Planning Group Inc..........F....... 913 498-8898
Overland Park *(G-9239)*
Super Chief Inc..........F....... 785 272-7277
Topeka *(G-13124)*
Tantillo Financial Group LLC..........F....... 913 649-3200
Shawnee Mission *(G-11919)*
Upper Lake Processing Services..........F....... 855 418-9500
Overland Park *(G-9448)*

FINDINGS & TRIMMINGS: Fabric

Sharpline Converting Inc..........B....... 316 722-9080
Wichita *(G-15576)*

FINGERPRINT EQPT

Peavey Corporation..........D....... 913 888-0600
Lenexa *(G-6047)*

FINISHING SVCS

Country Club Bank..........F....... 816 751-4251
Leawood *(G-5361)*
Metal Finishing Company Inc..........F....... 316 267-7289
Wichita *(G-15053)*

FIRE ARMS, SMALL: Guns Or Gun Parts, 30 mm & Below

Carlsons Choke Tube/NW Arms..........F....... 785 626-3078
Atwood *(G-282)*
Cz-USA..........D....... 913 321-1811
Kansas City *(G-3949)*
Endless Ideas Inc..........F....... 913 766-0680
Olathe *(G-7681)*
Joe Bob Outfitters LLC..........F....... 785 639-7121
Hays *(G-2856)*

FIRE ARMS, SMALL: Pistols Or Pistol Parts, 30 mm & below

Millett Industries..........G....... 913 752-3572
Overland Park *(G-9038)*

FIRE CONTROL OR BOMBING EQPT: Electronic

City of Shawnee..........F....... 913 631-1080
Shawnee Mission *(G-11233)*

FIRE EXTINGUISHERS, WHOLESALE

Keller Fire & Safety Inc..........D....... 913 371-8494
Kansas City *(G-4169)*
Sevo Systems Inc..........E....... 913 677-1112
Lenexa *(G-6125)*

FIRE EXTINGUISHERS: Portable

Weis Fire Safety Equip Co Inc..........F....... 785 825-9527
Salina *(G-10765)*

FIRE OR BURGLARY RESISTIVE PRDTS

Best West Fabrication LLC..........G....... 785 527-2450
Belleville *(G-453)*
DI Machine LLC..........G....... 913 557-2000
Paola *(G-9552)*
Kan Fab Inc..........G....... 620 342-5669
Emporia *(G-1783)*
Mad Dog Metal Inc..........G....... 620 275-9685
Garden City *(G-2227)*
R Miller Sales Co Inc..........E....... 913 341-3727
Shawnee Mission *(G-11772)*

FIRE PROTECTION EQPT

Weis Fire Safety Equip Co Inc..........F....... 785 825-9527
Salina *(G-10765)*

FIRE PROTECTION SVCS: Contracted

1st Due Er Response Solutns LL..........F....... 620 226-3566
Bartlett *(G-370)*
Central Consolidated Inc..........C....... 316 945-0797
Wichita *(G-13978)*
S C F Inc..........E....... 913 722-3473
Overland Park *(G-9267)*

FIRE PROTECTION, EXC CONTRACT

ADT 24 7 Alarm and Security..........D....... 620 860-0229
Pratt *(G-10094)*

FIRE PROTECTION, GOVERNMENT: Local

City of Neodesha..........F....... 620 325-2642
Neodesha *(G-7235)*

FIREARMS & AMMUNITION, EXC SPORTING, WHOLESALE

FP Supply LLC..........F....... 316 284-6700
Newton *(G-7347)*
R Miller Sales Co Inc..........E....... 913 341-3727
Shawnee Mission *(G-11772)*

FIREARMS: Large, Greater Than 30mm

B 5 Inc..........G....... 316 721-3222
Wichita *(G-13785)*

FIREARMS: Small, 30mm or Less

Bell and Carlson Incorporated..........E....... 620 225-6688
Dodge City *(G-1306)*

FIREFIGHTING APPARATUS

Ruskin Company..........E....... 620 421-6090
Parsons *(G-9733)*

FIREPLACE EQPT & ACCESS

Elite Fireplace Facings Inc..........G....... 913 631-5443
Shawnee Mission *(G-11332)*

FIREWOOD, WHOLESALE

Martin James..........G....... 785 525-7761
Lucas *(G-6474)*

FIREWORKS SHOPS

Jakes Fireworks Inc..........F....... 620 231-2264
Pittsburg *(G-9881)*
Winco Fireworks Intl LLC..........E....... 913 649-2071
Prairie Village *(G-10083)*

FIREWORKS: Wholesalers

Jakes Fireworks Inc..........F....... 620 231-2264
Pittsburg *(G-9881)*
Winco Fireworks Intl LLC..........E....... 913 649-2071
Prairie Village *(G-10083)*

FIRST AID SVCS

Western First Aid & Safety LLC..........F....... 316 263-0687
Leawood *(G-5597)*

FITTINGS & ASSEMBLIES: Hose & Tube, Hydraulic Or Pneumatic

Austin A-7 Ltd..........F....... 316 945-8892
Wichita *(G-13769)*

FITTINGS: Pipe

Arrow Valve Co Inc..........G....... 620 879-2126
Caney *(G-665)*
Rickerson Pipe Lining LLC..........F....... 785 448-5401
Garnett *(G-2386)*

FITTINGS: Pipe, Fabricated

Callaway Electric..........G....... 785 632-5588
Clay Center *(G-847)*

FIXED BASE OPERATOR

Wells Aircraft Inc..........E....... 620 663-1546
Hutchinson *(G-3483)*

FLAT GLASS: Tempered

Lippert Components Mfg Inc..........D....... 316 283-0627
North Newton *(G-7438)*

FLEA MARKET

Disabled American Veterens Str..........F....... 785 827-6477
Salina *(G-10479)*

FLIGHT TRAINING SCHOOLS

Kansas Air Center Inc..........F....... 785 776-1991
Manhattan *(G-6674)*
Kansas City Aviation Ctr Inc..........D....... 913 782-0530
Olathe *(G-7823)*

Lyddon Aero Center Inc ....F 620 624-1646
Liberal *(G-6338)*
T and C Aviation Enterprises ....E 913 764-4800
Olathe *(G-8095)*

FLOOR COVERING STORES

Acme Floor Company Inc ....D 913 888-3200
Lenexa *(G-5624)*
Big Bobs Outlets Kansas Cy Inc ....F 913 362-2627
Shawnee Mission *(G-11163)*
Country Carpet Inc ....F 785 256-4800
Maple Hill *(G-6863)*
Crooks Floor Covering ....G 785 242-4153
Ottawa *(G-8262)*
Custom Renovation ....F 620 544-2653
Hugoton *(G-3158)*
Kimple Inc ....F 620 564-2300
Ellinwood *(G-1635)*
Madden-Mcfarland Interiors Ltd ....E 913 681-2821
Leawood *(G-5462)*
Sewing Workshop ....F 785 357-6231
Topeka *(G-13061)*
Sherwin-Williams Company ....F 913 782-0126
Olathe *(G-8062)*
UNI Floor Inc ....F 913 238-4633
Overland Park *(G-9439)*
Unique Design Inc ....F 785 272-6044
Topeka *(G-13205)*
Weber Carpet Inc ....C 913 469-5430
Lenexa *(G-6224)*

FLOOR COVERING STORES: Carpets

Cap Carpet Inc ....E 316 262-3496
Wichita *(G-13936)*
Cap Carpet Inc ....F 785 273-1402
Topeka *(G-12422)*
Carpet Factory Outlet Inc ....E 913 261-6800
Kansas City *(G-3892)*
Gardner Floor Covering Inc ....E 785 266-6220
Topeka *(G-12632)*
Great Amercn Hardwood Flrg Co ....F 316 264-3660
Wichita *(G-14501)*
Kansas Carpet & Tile Inc ....E 316 942-2111
Wichita *(G-14790)*
L & L Floor Covering Inc ....F 620 275-0499
Garden City *(G-2221)*
Mo-Can Flooring Inc ....E 913 362-0711
Shawnee *(G-10999)*
Rigdon Floor Coverings Inc ....E 913 362-9829
Kansas City *(G-4378)*
Schammerhorn Inc ....G 316 265-8659
Wichita *(G-15528)*

FLOOR COVERING STORES: Floor Tile

Tile Shop LLC ....F 913 631-8453
Shawnee *(G-11040)*

FLOOR COVERINGS WHOLESALERS

Design Materials Inc ....E 913 342-9796
Kansas City *(G-3969)*
General Distributors Inc ....E 316 634-2133
Wichita *(G-14455)*
Selfs Inc ....F 316 267-1295
Wichita *(G-15555)*
Tapco Products Co ....E 913 492-2777
Shawnee Mission *(G-11920)*
Weber Carpet Inc ....C 913 469-5430
Lenexa *(G-6224)*

FLOOR TRADERS: Security

Mil-Spec Security Group LLC ....F 785 832-1351
Lawrence *(G-5027)*

FLOOR WAXING SVCS

Thrash Inc ....E 316 265-5331
Wichita *(G-15762)*

FLOORING: Hardwood

Superior Hardwood Floors LLC ....G 316 554-9663
Wichita *(G-15694)*

FLORIST: Flowers, Fresh

Deans Designs Inc ....F 316 686-6674
Wichita *(G-14181)*
Eidsons Florist ....F 913 721-2775
Kansas City *(G-3981)*
Eureka Greenhouses Inc ....F 620 583-8676
Eureka *(G-1886)*
Whartons For Every ....E 620 276-6000
Garden City *(G-2313)*
William O Broeker Enterprises ....E 913 682-2022
Leavenworth *(G-5306)*

FLORIST: Plants, Potted

Arnolds Greenhouse Inc ....F 620 964-2463
Le Roy *(G-5195)*
Hoffmanns Green Industries ....E 316 634-1500
Wichita *(G-14624)*

FLORISTS

Blue Rapids Greenhouse Inc ....E 785 363-7300
Blue Rapids *(G-533)*
Dillon Companies Inc ....C 785 272-0661
Topeka *(G-12557)*
Dillon Companies Inc ....D 785 823-9403
Salina *(G-10478)*
Dillon Companies Inc ....C 620 225-6130
Dodge City *(G-1341)*
Queen-Morris Ventures LLC ....C 913 383-2563
Shawnee Mission *(G-11765)*
Valley Floral Company LLC ....E 316 838-3355
Wichita *(G-15871)*

FLORISTS' SPLYS, WHOLESALE

Baisch & Skinner Inc ....F 785 267-6931
Topeka *(G-12358)*
Baisch & Skinner Inc ....F 316 945-0074
Wichita *(G-13794)*

FLOWER ARRANGEMENTS: Artificial

Evans Industries Inc ....G 316 262-2551
Wichita *(G-14310)*

FLOWERS & NURSERY STOCK, WHOLESALE

Campbells Phoenix Greenhouse ....F 316 524-5311
Wichita *(G-13931)*

FLOWERS, ARTIFICIAL, WHOLESALE

Evans Industries Inc ....G 316 262-2551
Wichita *(G-14310)*

FLOWERS, FRESH, WHOLESALE

Absolutely Flowers ....F 620 728-0266
Hutchinson *(G-3189)*
Eureka Greenhouses Inc ....F 620 583-8676
Eureka *(G-1886)*
Overland Park Garden Ctr Inc ....E 913 788-7974
Kansas City *(G-4303)*
Valley Floral Company LLC ....E 316 838-3355
Wichita *(G-15871)*
William O Broeker Enterprises ....E 913 682-2022
Leavenworth *(G-5306)*

FLUES & PIPES: Stove Or Furnace

Metal-Fab Inc ....C 316 943-2351
Wichita *(G-15055)*
Metal-Fab Inc ....D 316 943-2351
Wichita *(G-15056)*
Metal-Fab Inc ....G 316 946-5875
Wichita *(G-15057)*

FLUID METERS & COUNTING DEVICES

Tank Wind-Down Corp ....C 620 421-0200
Parsons *(G-9745)*

FLUID POWER PUMPS & MOTORS

Apph Wichita Inc ....E 316 943-5752
Wichita *(G-13720)*
Broderson Manufacturing Corp ....D 913 888-0606
Lenexa *(G-5718)*
Cross Manufacturing Inc ....D 785 625-2585
Hays *(G-2780)*
Harper Industries Inc ....D 620 896-7381
Harper *(G-2723)*

FLUID POWER VALVES & HOSE FITTINGS

Cross Manufacturing Inc ....D 785 625-2585
Hays *(G-2780)*
Experitec Inc ....F 913 894-4044
Shawnee Mission *(G-11356)*
V Mach Inc ....E 913 894-2001
Shawnee Mission *(G-11971)*

FOAM RUBBER, WHOLESALE

Novation Iq LLC ....E 913 492-6000
Lenexa *(G-6029)*

FOAMS & RUBBER, WHOLESALE

Mfl Inc ....E 785 862-2767
Topeka *(G-12886)*

FOIL & LEAF: Metal

API Americas Inc ....D 732 382-6800
Lawrence *(G-4737)*

FOOD PRDTS, CANNED: Applesauce

Grandma Hoerners Foods Inc ....E 785 765-2300
Alma *(G-63)*

FOOD PRDTS, CANNED: Ethnic

Spanish Gardens Food Mfg Co ....F 913 831-4242
Kansas City *(G-4430)*

FOOD PRDTS, CANNED: Fruit Juices, Concentrated

Smart Beverage Inc ....F 785 656-2166
Olathe *(G-8068)*

FOOD PRDTS, CANNED: Fruits

Tropicana Products Inc ....D 316 838-1000
Wichita *(G-15806)*

FOOD PRDTS, CANNED: Jams, Jellies & Preserves

Eastside Mkt Westside Mkt LLC ....G 785 532-8686
Manhattan *(G-6619)*
Wyldewood Cellars Inc ....F 316 554-9463
Peck *(G-9764)*

FOOD PRDTS, CANNED: Mexican, NEC

E-Z Salsa Inc ....G 620 521-9097
Garden City *(G-2150)*
La Superior Food Products Inc ....E 913 362-6611
Shawnee Mission *(G-11544)*
Mama Socorros ....G 913 541-1074
Overland Park *(G-8982)*
Pedro Lopez Co Inc ....F 785 220-1509
Lebo *(G-5608)*

FOOD PRDTS, CANNED: Tomatoes

Spicin Foods Inc ....D 913 432-5228
Kansas City *(G-4435)*

FOOD PRDTS, CANNED: Tortillas

Resers Fine Foods Inc ....B 785 233-6431
Topeka *(G-13009)*

FOOD PRDTS, CONFECTIONERY, WHOLESALE: Candy

Joe Smith Company ....E 620 231-3610
Pittsburg *(G-9883)*
Kansas Candy & Tobacco Inc ....F 316 942-9081
Wichita *(G-14789)*
Nifty Nut House LLC ....F 316 265-0571
Wichita *(G-15180)*
Schmidt Vending Inc ....F 785 354-7397
Topeka *(G-13038)*
Seneca Wholesale Company Inc ....F 785 336-2118
Seneca *(G-10882)*
Shawnee Biscuit Inc ....E 913 441-7306
Lenexa *(G-6130)*
Wichita Tobacco & Candy Co ....F 316 264-2412
Wichita *(G-16040)*

FOOD PRDTS, CONFECTIONERY, WHOLESALE: Potato Chips

Frito-Lay North America Inc ....E 620 251-4367
Coffeyville *(G-941)*

FOOD PRDTS, CONFECTIONERY, WHOLESALE: Snack Foods

Frito-Lay North America Inc ... F ... 785 625-6581
Hays (G-2814)
Frito-Lay North America Inc ... E ... 316 942-8764
Wichita (G-14426)
Frito-Lay North America Inc ... D ... 913 261-4700
Shawnee Mission (G-11382)
Happy Food Co LLC ... F ... 816 835-3600
Overland Park (G-8793)

FOOD PRDTS, FISH & SEAFOOD, WHOLESALE: Fresh

Associated Wholesale Groc Inc ... A ... 913 288-1000
Kansas City (G-3825)

FOOD PRDTS, FISH & SEAFOOD, WHOLESALE: Seafood

Qins International Inc ... E ... 913 342-4488
Kansas City (G-4350)
Sysco Kansas City Inc ... E ... 316 942-4205
Wichita (G-15711)

FOOD PRDTS, FISH & SEAFOOD: Fish, Canned, Jarred, Etc

Culver Fish Farm Inc ... G ... 620 241-5200
McPherson (G-6954)

FOOD PRDTS, FROZEN: Ethnic Foods, NEC

Kan Pak International Inc ... E ... 316 201-4210
Wichita (G-14783)

FOOD PRDTS, FROZEN: NEC

Custom Foods Inc ... E ... 913 585-1900
De Soto (G-1198)
Dew - Drink Eat Well LLC ... E ... 785 856-3399
Lawrence (G-4834)

FOOD PRDTS, FROZEN: Pizza

Sfc Global Supply Chain Inc ... B ... 785 825-1671
Salina (G-10705)

FOOD PRDTS, FRUITS & VEGETABLES, FRESH, WHOLESALE

Earl Barnes ... F ... 620 662-6761
Hutchinson (G-3273)
Keith Connell Inc ... F ... 913 681-5585
Stilwell (G-12162)
Liberty Fruit Company Inc ... B ... 913 281-5200
Kansas City (G-4202)
Martinous Produce Company Inc ... E ... 620 231-5840
Pittsburg (G-9898)
Sysco Kansas City Inc ... E ... 316 942-4205
Wichita (G-15711)

FOOD PRDTS, FRUITS & VEGETABLES, FRESH, WHOLESALE: Vegetable

Chlorofields LLC ... F ... 785 304-3226
Overbrook (G-8323)

FOOD PRDTS, MEAT & MEAT PRDTS, WHOLESALE: Fresh

Bern Meat Plant Incorporated ... F ... 785 336-2165
Bern (G-521)
Bichelmeyer Meats A Corp ... F ... 913 342-5945
Kansas City (G-3859)
Duis Meat Processing Inc ... F ... 785 243-7850
Concordia (G-1109)
Harvest Meat Company Inc ... F ... 913 371-2333
Kansas City (G-4070)
Indian Hills Meat and Plty Inc ... E ... 316 264-1644
Wichita (G-14683)
Jacksons Frozen Food Center ... G ... 620 662-4465
Hutchinson (G-3339)
Kiowa Locker System LLC ... F ... 620 825-4538
Kiowa (G-4626)
Krehbiels Specialty Meats Inc ... E ... 620 241-0103
McPherson (G-6985)
Plankenhorn Inc ... F ... 620 276-3791
Garden City (G-2256)
Rons Market ... F ... 620 277-2073
Holcomb (G-3079)
Smithfield Direct LLC ... E ... 785 762-3306
Junction City (G-3755)

FOOD PRDTS, POULTRY, WHOLESALE: Poultry Prdts, NEC

Nelson Poultry Farms Inc ... F ... 785 587-0399
Manhattan (G-6758)

FOOD PRDTS, WHOL: Canned Goods, Fruit, Veg, Seafood/Meats

Sysco Kansas City Inc ... A ... 913 829-5555
Olathe (G-8092)

FOOD PRDTS, WHOLESALE: Barley

Bunge North America Inc ... D ... 620 342-7270
Emporia (G-1711)

FOOD PRDTS, WHOLESALE: Beverage Concentrates

Shasta Midwest Inc ... E ... 913 888-6777
Lenexa (G-6128)

FOOD PRDTS, WHOLESALE: Beverages, Exc Coffee & Tea

Heartland Coca-Cola Btlg LLC ... A ... 785 735-9498
Victoria (G-13376)
Heartland Coca-Cola Btlg LLC ... A ... 785 232-9372
Topeka (G-12675)
Heartland Coca-Cola Btlg LLC ... A ... 785 243-1071
Concordia (G-1117)
Heartland Coca-Cola Btlg LLC ... A ... 913 599-9142
Lenexa (G-5896)
Heartland Coca-Cola Btlg LLC ... A ... 620 276-3221
Garden City (G-2194)
Heartland Coca-Cola Btlg LLC ... A ... 316 942-3838
Wichita (G-14582)
John G Levin ... E ... 785 234-5551
Topeka (G-12746)

FOOD PRDTS, WHOLESALE: Chocolate

Kerry Inc ... C ... 913 780-1212
New Century (G-7290)

FOOD PRDTS, WHOLESALE: Coffee & Tea

Hillshire Brands Company ... E ... 316 262-5443
Wichita (G-14612)
Spice Merchant & Co ... F ... 316 263-4121
Wichita (G-15639)

FOOD PRDTS, WHOLESALE: Coffee, Green Or Roasted

Cardona Coffee LLP ... G ... 785 554-6060
Topeka (G-12446)

FOOD PRDTS, WHOLESALE: Cookies

Shawnee Biscuit Inc ... E ... 913 441-7306
Lenexa (G-6130)

FOOD PRDTS, WHOLESALE: Flour

ADM Milling Co ... D ... 785 825-1541
Salina (G-10395)
Grain Craft Inc ... E ... 316 267-7311
Wichita (G-14494)

FOOD PRDTS, WHOLESALE: Grain Elevators

ADM Milling Co ... E ... 620 227-8101
Dodge City (G-1289)
ADM Milling Co ... E ... 785 263-1631
Abilene (G-11)
ADM Milling Co ... D ... 785 825-1541
Salina (G-10395)
AG Valley Coop Non-Stock ... F ... 785 877-5131
Norton (G-7440)
Agmark LLC ... F ... 785 738-9641
Beloit (G-471)
Agri Trails Coop Inc ... F ... 785 258-2286
Herington (G-2969)
Agspring Idaho LLC ... F ... 952 956-6720
Leawood (G-5315)
Archer-Daniels-Midland Company ... F ... 620 675-8520
Copeland (G-1148)
Archer-Daniels-Midland Company ... E ... 620 663-7957
Hutchinson (G-3204)
Archer-Daniels-Midland Company ... G ... 785 737-4135
Palco (G-9537)
Bartlett Cooperative Assn ... E ... 620 226-3311
Bartlett (G-371)
Cargill Incorporated ... E ... 785 357-1989
Topeka (G-12448)
Cargill Incorporated ... F ... 785 235-3003
Topeka (G-12449)
Cargill Incorporated ... F ... 806 659-3554
Shawnee Mission (G-11204)
Cargill Incorporated ... E ... 785 825-8128
Salina (G-10436)
Cargill Incorporated ... F ... 913 367-3579
Cummings (G-1186)
Central Planes Coop ... F ... 785 695-2216
Athol (G-273)
Central Valley AG Cooperative ... C ... 785 738-2241
Beloit (G-481)
CHS Inc ... E ... 785 852-4241
Sharon Springs (G-10895)
Cooperative Elevator & Sup Co ... E ... 620 873-2161
Meade (G-7047)
Cropland Co-Op Inc ... F ... 620 649-2230
Satanta (G-10782)
Decatur Cooperative Assn ... F ... 785 475-2234
Oberlin (G-7490)
Delphos Cooperative Assn ... E ... 785 523-4213
Delphos (G-1216)
Dm & M Farms Inc ... E ... 620 855-3934
Cimarron (G-823)
Elkhart Coop Equity Exchnge ... E ... 620 697-2135
Elkhart (G-1619)
Farmers Cooperative Assn ... F ... 620 856-2365
Baxter Springs (G-406)
Farmers Cooperative Elev Co ... F ... 620 545-7138
Viola (G-13378)
Farmers Cooperative Grain Co ... F ... 620 845-6441
Caldwell (G-658)
Farmers Union Coop Assn ... F ... 785 632-5632
Clay Center (G-863)
Faulkner Grain Inc ... F ... 620 597-2636
Chetopa (G-817)
Frontier Ag Inc ... E ... 785 734-7011
Goodland (G-2472)
Frontier Ag Inc ... F ... 785 734-2331
Bird City (G-530)
Frontier Ag Inc ... E ... 785 824-3201
Grinnell (G-2692)
Garden City Co-Op Inc ... F ... 620 356-1219
Ulysses (G-13298)
Golden Belt Coop Assn Inc ... F ... 785 726-3115
Ellis (G-1646)
HI Plains Cooperative Assn ... F ... 785 462-3351
Colby (G-1012)
Johnson Cooperative Grn Co Inc ... F ... 620 492-6210
Johnson (G-3654)
Johnson Cooperative Grn Co Inc ... F ... 620 492-2297
Johnson (G-3655)
Kanza Cooperative Association ... F ... 620 234-5252
Stafford (G-12104)
Kanza Cooperative Association ... F ... 620 234-5252
Stafford (G-12105)
Kanza Cooperative Association ... F ... 620 672-6761
Pratt (G-10122)
Leroy Cooperative Assn Inc ... E ... 620 964-2225
Le Roy (G-5196)
Long Island Grain Co Inc ... F ... 785 854-7431
Long Island (G-6428)
McCune Farmers Union Coop ... F ... 620 632-4226
Mc Cune (G-6920)
Mid-Kansas Cooperative Assn ... E ... 620 345-6328
Moundridge (G-7190)
Mid-Kansas Cooperative Assn ... F ... 785 776-9467
Manhattan (G-6742)
Mid-Kansas Cooperative Assn ... F ... 620 837-3313
Walton (G-13401)
Mid-Kansas Cooperative Assn ... F ... 620 345-6361
Moundridge (G-7191)
Minneola Co-Op Inc ... F ... 620 885-4361
Minneola (G-7125)
Palmer Grain Inc ... F ... 785 692-4212
Palmer (G-9538)
Plains Equity Exch & Coop Un ... E ... 620 563-9566
Plains (G-9977)
Pride AG Resources ... F ... 620 227-8671
Dodge City (G-1422)

Rangeland Cooperatives Inc..........E....... 785 543-2114
Phillipsburg *(G-9797)*
Severy Cooperative Association..........F....... 620 736-2211
Severy *(G-10893)*
Southern Plains Co-Op At Lewis..........E....... 620 324-5536
Lewis *(G-6270)*
Stafford County Flour Mills Co..........E....... 620 458-4121
Hudson *(G-3146)*
Sublette Cooperative Inc..........E....... 620 675-2297
Sublette *(G-12209)*
Sublette Enterprises Inc..........D....... 620 668-5501
Sublette *(G-12210)*
Team Marketing Alliance LLC..........F....... 620 345-3560
Moundridge *(G-7198)*
United AG Service Inc..........F....... 785 525-6455
Lucas *(G-6475)*
United Plains AG..........E....... 785 852-4241
Sharon Springs *(G-10901)*
Walker Products Company Inc..........F....... 785 524-4107
Lincoln *(G-6390)*
White Cloud Grain Company Inc..........F....... 785 235-5381
Topeka *(G-13242)*
Windriver Grain LLC..........E....... 620 275-2101
Garden City *(G-2316)*

FOOD PRDTS, WHOLESALE: Grains

ADM Grain River System Inc..........F....... 913 788-7226
Kansas City *(G-3785)*
AG Partners Cooperative Inc..........E....... 785 742-2196
Hiawatha *(G-3001)*
Agco Inc..........F....... 785 483-2128
Russell *(G-10263)*
Agrex Inc..........E....... 913 851-6300
Overland Park *(G-8358)*
Alliance AG and Grain LLC..........F....... 785 798-3775
Ness City *(G-7251)*
Alliance AG and Grain LLC..........C....... 620 385-2898
Spearville *(G-12069)*
Alliance AG and Grain LLC..........F....... 620 723-3351
Greensburg *(G-2671)*
Alliance AG and Grain LLC..........F....... 620 622-4511
Protection *(G-10172)*
Anthony Frmrs Coop Elev Cmpnys..........F....... 620 842-5181
Anthony *(G-119)*
Archer-Daniels-Midland Company..........F....... 620 846-2218
Montezuma *(G-7154)*
Archer-Daniels-Midland Company..........C....... 913 491-9400
Overland Park *(G-8393)*
Archer-Daniels-Midland Company..........F....... 620 659-2099
Kinsley *(G-4614)*
Bartlett Grain Company LP..........F....... 316 838-7421
Wichita *(G-13814)*
Bartlett Grain Company LP..........F....... 913 321-0900
Kansas City *(G-3845)*
Bartlett Grain Company LP..........F....... 913 321-1696
Kansas City *(G-3846)*
Beachner Grain Inc..........E....... 620 820-8600
Parsons *(G-9669)*
Beattie Farmers Un Coop Assn..........E....... 785 353-2237
Beattie *(G-418)*
Bunge Milling Inc..........C....... 913 367-3251
Atchison *(G-221)*
Cargill Incorporated..........E....... 620 663-4401
Hutchinson *(G-3230)*
Cargill Incorporated..........E....... 785 743-2288
WA Keeney *(G-13382)*
Central Prairie Co-Op..........F....... 620 278-2470
Sterling *(G-12113)*
CGB Diversified Services Inc..........F....... 785 235-5566
Topeka *(G-12462)*
CHS Inc..........F....... 785 386-4546
Selden *(G-10855)*
Cornerstone Ag LLC..........F....... 785 462-3354
Colby *(G-1000)*
Cropland Co-Op Inc..........F....... 620 356-1241
Ulysses *(G-13294)*
D E Bondurant Grain Co Inc..........E....... 785 798-3322
Ness City *(G-7260)*
Dodge City Cooperative Exch..........E....... 620 225-4193
Dodge City *(G-1344)*
Ellsworth Coop..........F....... 785 472-3261
Ellsworth *(G-1667)*
Farmers Co-Operative Equity Co..........F....... 620 739-4335
Isabel *(G-3639)*
Farmers Co-Operative Union..........D....... 620 278-2141
Sterling *(G-12116)*
Farmers Coop Grn Assn Inc..........F....... 620 456-2222
Conway Springs *(G-1141)*
Farmers Cooperative Elev Assn..........F....... 785 747-2236
Greenleaf *(G-2668)*
Farmers Cooperative Elev Inc..........F....... 785 284-2185
Sabetha *(G-10310)*
Farmers Cooperative Grain..........F....... 620 326-7496
Wellington *(G-13499)*
Farmers Grain Cooperative..........E....... 620 837-3313
Walton *(G-13400)*
Farmway Cooperative Inc..........E....... 785 439-6457
Scottsville *(G-10838)*
Fleming Feed & Grain Inc..........E....... 316 742-3411
Leon *(G-6247)*
Gavilon Grain LLC..........E....... 316 226-7250
Wichita *(G-14453)*
Gfg AG Services LLC..........F....... 913 233-0001
Kansas City *(G-4032)*
Great Bend Cooperative Assn..........E....... 620 793-3531
Great Bend *(G-2576)*
Hannebaum Grain Co Inc..........F....... 785 825-8205
Salina *(G-10534)*
Haven Commodities Inc..........E....... 620 345-6328
Moundridge *(G-7185)*
Healy Cooperative Elevator Co..........E....... 620 398-2211
Healy *(G-2966)*
Irsik & Doll Feed Services Inc..........F....... 620 855-3747
Cimarron *(G-830)*
Jackson Farmers Inc..........F....... 785 364-3161
Holton *(G-3100)*
Kanza Cooperative Association..........F....... 620 546-2231
Iuka *(G-3640)*
Kanza Cooperative Association..........E....... 316 444-2141
Andale *(G-78)*
Kanza Cooperative Association..........D....... 620 546-2593
Iuka *(G-3641)*
Lansing Grain Company LLC..........F....... 913 748-4320
Overland Park *(G-8944)*
Mid Continent Farms..........F....... 785 325-2089
Washington *(G-13469)*
Mid-Kansas Cooperative Assn..........F....... 620 465-2292
Haven *(G-2734)*
Mulvane Cooperative Union Inc..........F....... 316 777-1121
Mulvane *(G-7223)*
Nemaha County Cooperative Assn..........D....... 785 336-6153
Seneca *(G-10874)*
Norton County Co-Op Assn Inc..........F....... 785 877-5900
Norton *(G-7456)*
O K Coop Grn & Merc Co..........F....... 620 825-4212
Kiowa *(G-4628)*
Offerle Coop Grn & Sup Co..........F....... 620 659-2165
Offerle *(G-7500)*
Producers Coop Assn Girard..........E....... 620 724-8241
Girard *(G-2415)*
Randall Farmers Coop Un Inc..........F....... 785 739-2312
Randall *(G-10190)*
Right Cooperative Association..........E....... 620 227-8611
Wright *(G-16194)*
Scott Cooperative Association..........E....... 620 872-5823
Scott City *(G-10831)*
Scoular Company..........E....... 785 823-6301
Salina *(G-10699)*
Scoular Company..........F....... 785 392-9024
Minneapolis *(G-7123)*
Skyland Grain LLC..........F....... 620 672-3961
Cunningham *(G-1189)*
Two Rivers Consumers Coop Assn..........E....... 620 442-2360
Arkansas City *(G-185)*

FOOD PRDTS, WHOLESALE: Honey

Eastside Mkt Westside Mkt LLC..........G....... 785 532-8686
Manhattan *(G-6619)*

FOOD PRDTS, WHOLESALE: Salt, Edible

Cargill Incorporated..........D....... 620 663-2141
Hutchinson *(G-3229)*
Hutchinson Salt Company Inc..........E....... 620 662-3341
Hutchinson *(G-3324)*

FOOD PRDTS, WHOLESALE: Sauces

Grandma Hoerners Foods Inc..........E....... 785 765-2300
Alma *(G-63)*

FOOD PRDTS, WHOLESALE: Specialty

Country Fresh Foods..........E....... 316 283-4414
Newton *(G-7336)*

FOOD PRDTS, WHOLESALE: Spices & Seasonings

Blend Tech Inc..........F....... 316 941-9660
Wichita *(G-13857)*

FOOD PRDTS, WHOLESALE: Sugar, Refined

International Food Pdts Corp..........F....... 913 788-7720
Kansas City *(G-4107)*

FOOD PRDTS, WHOLESALE: Water, Distilled

Quality Water Inc..........F....... 785 825-4912
Salina *(G-10647)*

FOOD PRDTS, WHOLESALE: Water, Mineral Or Spring, Bottled

Wheatland Waters Inc..........D....... 785 267-0512
Olathe *(G-8153)*

FOOD PRDTS, WHOLESALE: Wheat

Lansing Trade Group LLC..........C....... 913 748-3000
Overland Park *(G-8945)*
Scoular Company..........F....... 620 372-8611
Coolidge *(G-1147)*

FOOD PRDTS: Animal & marine fats & oils

Darling Ingredients Inc..........E....... 913 321-9328
Kansas City *(G-3956)*
Darling Ingredients Inc..........D....... 316 264-6951
Wichita *(G-14169)*
Darling Ingredients Inc..........F....... 785 336-2535
Seneca *(G-10864)*

FOOD PRDTS: Cheese Curls & Puffs

Frito-Lay North America Inc..........A....... 785 267-2600
Topeka *(G-12629)*

FOOD PRDTS: Chicken, Slaughtered & Dressed

Pilgrims Pride Corporation..........E....... 620 597-2820
Columbus *(G-1085)*

FOOD PRDTS: Chocolate, Baking

Kerry Inc..........C....... 913 780-1212
New Century *(G-7290)*

FOOD PRDTS: Coffee Roasting, Exc Wholesale Grocers

Heartland Coffee & Packg Corp..........G....... 785 232-0383
Topeka *(G-12676)*

FOOD PRDTS: Coffee Substitutes

Inclusion Technologies LLC..........F....... 913 370-8070
Atchison *(G-236)*

FOOD PRDTS: Corn & other vegetable starches

Sergeants Pet Care Pdts Inc..........G....... 913 627-1245
Kansas City *(G-4417)*

FOOD PRDTS: Corn Chips & Other Corn-Based Snacks

La Superior Food Products Inc..........E....... 913 362-6611
Shawnee Mission *(G-11544)*

FOOD PRDTS: Corn Oil, Meal

Cargill Incorporated..........E....... 785 743-2288
WA Keeney *(G-13382)*

FOOD PRDTS: Corn Oil, Refined

Cargill Incorporated..........F....... 316 291-1939
Wichita *(G-13947)*

FOOD PRDTS: Dough, Pizza, Prepared

Custom Foods Inc..........E....... 913 585-1900
De Soto *(G-1198)*

FOOD PRDTS: Edible fats & oils

Kerry Inc..........C....... 913 780-1212
New Century *(G-7290)*

FOOD PRDTS: Emulsifiers

Danisco USA Inc..........C....... 913 764-8100
New Century *(G-7276)*

FOOD PRDTS: Flour

Heartland Mill Inc .... E 620 379-4472
Modoc *(G-7153)*
McShares Inc .... E 785 825-2181
Salina *(G-10597)*
Stafford County Flour Mills Co .... F 620 486-2493
Sylvia *(G-12221)*

FOOD PRDTS: Flour & Other Grain Mill Products

Archer-Daniels-Midland Company .... D 785 825-1541
Salina *(G-10407)*
Archer-Daniels-Midland Company .... G 620 375-4811
Leoti *(G-6250)*
Archer-Daniels-Midland Company .... F 620 872-2174
Scott City *(G-10804)*
Archer-Daniels-Midland Company .... E 785 820-8019
Salina *(G-10408)*
Archer-Daniels-Midland Company .... G 913 321-1696
Kansas City *(G-3817)*
Archer-Daniels-Midland Company .... G 620 357-8733
Jetmore *(G-3645)*
Archer-Daniels-Midland Company .... G 620 675-2226
Sublette *(G-12198)*
Archer-Daniels-Midland Company .... F 620 657-3411
Satanta *(G-10776)*
Archer-Daniels-Midland Company .... E 913 491-9400
Overland Park *(G-8394)*
Archer-Daniels-Midland Company .... E 620 663-7957
Hutchinson *(G-3204)*
Archer-Daniels-Midland Company .... F 620 663-7278
Hutchinson *(G-3205)*
Archer-Daniels-Midland Company .... F 785 671-3171
Oakley *(G-7471)*
Archer-Daniels-Midland Company .... G 785 694-2286
Brewster *(G-582)*
Archer-Daniels-Midland Company .... G 785 820-8831
New Cambria *(G-7269)*
Archer-Daniels-Midland Company .... G 785 737-4135
Palco *(G-9537)*
Archer-Daniels-Midland Company .... E 785 899-3700
Goodland *(G-2462)*
Archer-Daniels-Midland Company .... E 785 263-2260
Abilene *(G-13)*
Farmers Union Coop Assn .... F 785 632-5632
Clay Center *(G-863)*
Grain Craft Inc .... E 620 241-2410
McPherson *(G-6970)*
Long Island Grain Co Inc .... F 785 854-7431
Long Island *(G-6428)*
Mgp Ingredients Inc .... F 913 367-1480
Atchison *(G-246)*
Mgp Ingredients Inc .... C 913 367-1480
Atchison *(G-245)*
Mgpi Processing Inc .... E 913 367-1480
Atchison *(G-247)*
Morrill Hay Company Inc .... F 620 285-6941
Paola *(G-9576)*
Purina Mills LLC .... E 316 265-0624
Wichita *(G-15379)*
Stafford County Flour Mills Co .... E 620 458-4121
Hudson *(G-3146)*

FOOD PRDTS: Flour Mixes & Doughs

Kansas Maid Inc .... G 620 437-2958
Madison *(G-6502)*

FOOD PRDTS: Flours & Flour Mixes, From Purchased Flour

Pantry Shelf Company .... G 620 662-9342
Hutchinson *(G-3400)*

FOOD PRDTS: Fruits, Dehydrated Or Dried

Good Life Snacks Inc .... G 913 220-2117
Lenexa *(G-5878)*

FOOD PRDTS: Honey

Barkman Honey LLC .... D 620 947-3173
Hillsboro *(G-3042)*
Brown Honey Farms .... G 785 778-2002
Haddam *(G-2694)*

FOOD PRDTS: Instant Coffee

Cardona Coffee LLP .... G 785 554-6060
Topeka *(G-12446)*

FOOD PRDTS: Macaroni, Noodles, Spaghetti, Pasta, Etc

Resers Fine Foods Inc .... B 785 233-6431
Topeka *(G-13009)*

FOOD PRDTS: Margarine, Including Imitation

Sauer Brands Inc .... C 913 324-3700
New Century *(G-7297)*

FOOD PRDTS: Mixes, Flour

Corbion America Holdings Inc .... D 913 890-5500
Lenexa *(G-5787)*

FOOD PRDTS: Mixes, Seasonings, Dry

Williams Foods Inc .... C 913 888-4343
Lenexa *(G-6231)*

FOOD PRDTS: Mustard, Prepared

Grannies Homemade Mustard .... G 620 947-3259
Newton *(G-7351)*

FOOD PRDTS: Nuts & Seeds

Red River Commodities Inc .... E 785 462-3911
Colby *(G-1035)*

FOOD PRDTS: Potato & Corn Chips & Similar Prdts

Sunflower Hills Inc .... F 913 894-2233
Lenexa *(G-6158)*

FOOD PRDTS: Potatoes, Dried

General Financial Services Inc .... G 316 636-1070
Wichita *(G-14456)*

FOOD PRDTS: Poultry, Processed, NEC

Tyson Foods Inc .... C 620 669-8761
Hutchinson *(G-3471)*

FOOD PRDTS: Preparations

Advanced Food Services Inc .... E 913 888-8088
Lenexa *(G-5632)*
City of Fredonia .... F 620 378-2802
Fredonia *(G-2029)*
Country Fresh Foods .... E 316 283-4414
Newton *(G-7336)*
Danisco Ingredients Usa Inc .... F 913 764-8100
New Century *(G-7275)*
Frito-Lay North America Inc .... A 785 267-2600
Topeka *(G-12629)*
Heartland Food Products Inc .... F 866 571-0222
Shawnee Mission *(G-11424)*
Kerry Inc .... C 913 780-1212
New Century *(G-7290)*
Old World Spices Seasoning Inc .... E 816 861-0400
Overland Park *(G-9098)*
Resers Fine Foods Inc .... B 785 233-6431
Topeka *(G-13009)*
Safely Delicious LLC .... F 913 963-5140
Overland Park *(G-9270)*
Sfc Global Supply Chain Inc .... B 785 825-1671
Salina *(G-10705)*

FOOD PRDTS: Sandwiches

Premier Custom Foods LLC .... D 913 225-9505
Kansas City *(G-4331)*

FOOD PRDTS: Seasonings & Spices

Rabbit Creek Products Inc .... F 913 837-3073
Louisburg *(G-6463)*

FOOD PRDTS: Semolina Flour

CHS Inc .... D 620 241-4247
McPherson *(G-6948)*

FOOD PRDTS: Soup Mixes, Dried

Rabbit Creek Products Inc .... F 913 837-3073
Louisburg *(G-6463)*

FOOD PRDTS: Soybean Oil, Refined, Exc Made In Mills

Cargill Incorporated .... D 316 292-2380
Wichita *(G-13946)*

FOOD PRDTS: Starch, Corn

ADM Grain River System Inc .... F 913 788-7226
Kansas City *(G-3785)*

FOOD PRDTS: Starch, Indl

Chemstar Products Company .... E 620 241-2611
McPherson *(G-6947)*

FOOD PRDTS: Stearin, Animal, Inedible

Darling Ingredients Inc .... G 913 371-7083
Kansas City *(G-3957)*

FOOD PRDTS: Syrups

Wyldewood Cellars Inc .... F 316 554-9463
Peck *(G-9764)*

FOOD PRDTS: Tofu, Exc Frozen Desserts

Central Soyfoods .... F 785 312-8638
Lawrence *(G-4781)*

FOOD PRDTS: Tortillas

Arts Mexican Products Inc .... F 913 371-2163
Kansas City *(G-3820)*
El Taquito Inc .... G 913 371-0452
Kansas City *(G-3984)*
La Nena Tortilleria Rostiseria .... G 913 281-8993
Kansas City *(G-4191)*
La Superior Food Products Inc .... E 913 362-6611
Shawnee Mission *(G-11544)*
Tortilla King Inc .... C 620 345-2674
Moundridge *(G-7199)*
Tortilleria La Tradicion .... G 316 264-3148
Wichita *(G-15773)*
Tortillria Los III Prtllos LLC .... G 316 831-0811
Wichita *(G-15774)*

FOOD PRDTS: Vegetable Oil Mills, NEC

Cargill Incorporated .... E 620 663-4401
Hutchinson *(G-3230)*

FOOD PRDTS: Vegetable Oil, Refined, Exc Corn

Sunflower Vegetable Oil Inc .... G 913 541-8882
Lenexa *(G-6159)*

FOOD PRDTS: Vegetables, Dried or Dehydrated Exc Freeze-Dried

Pines International Inc .... E 800 697-4637
Lawrence *(G-5065)*

FOOD PRDTS: Wheat Flour

Bartlett Milling Company LP .... E 620 251-4650
Coffeyville *(G-910)*
Farmer Direct Foods Inc .... F 785 823-8787
New Cambria *(G-7270)*

FOOD PRODUCTS MACHINERY

ADM Milling Co .... D 785 825-1541
Salina *(G-10395)*
AG Growth International Inc .... C 785 632-2161
Clay Center *(G-842)*
Archer-Daniels-Midland Company .... D 785 825-1541
Salina *(G-10407)*
Baader North America Corp .... F 913 621-3366
Kansas City *(G-3837)*
Extru-Tech Inc .... D 785 284-2153
Sabetha *(G-10309)*
Johnson Food Equipment Inc .... E 913 621-3366
Kansas City *(G-4127)*
Kemlee Manufacturing Inc .... D 620 783-5035
Galena *(G-2076)*
Kice Industries Inc .... C 316 744-7148
Park City *(G-9625)*
New Age Industrial Corp Inc .... C 785 877-5121
Norton *(G-7455)*
Numerical Control Support Inc .... E 913 441-3500
Shawnee Mission *(G-11690)*

Stainless Systems Inc ....E 620 663-4346
South Hutchinson *(G-12066)*
Wenger Manufacturing Inc ....C 785 284-2133
Sabetha *(G-10337)*
Williams-Carver Company Inc ....E 913 236-4949
Kansas City *(G-4544)*

FOOD STORES: Convenience, Independent

Egbert Oil Operations Inc ....F 620 662-4533
Hutchinson *(G-3275)*
Four Seasons Rv Acres Inc ....E 785 598-2221
Abilene *(G-32)*
K & S Eastside Amoco Inc ....F 620 342-3565
Emporia *(G-1782)*
L & M Oil Company ....F 913 856-8502
Gardner *(G-2352)*
Parker Oil Co Inc ....F 316 529-4343
Wichita *(G-15264)*
S Jackson Service Center Inc ....F 913 422-7438
Edwardsville *(G-1514)*

FOOD STORES: Cooperative

Two Rivers Consumers Coop Assn ....E 620 442-2360
Arkansas City *(G-185)*

FOOD STORES: Grocery, Independent

Dicks Thriftway ....E 785 456-2525
Wamego *(G-13414)*
Hoover Stores Inc ....D 620 364-5444
Burlington *(G-637)*
Kier Enterprises Inc ....E 785 325-2150
Washington *(G-13467)*
Pallucca and Sons ....F 620 231-7700
Frontenac *(G-2062)*
Pauline Food Center ....F 785 862-2774
Topeka *(G-12965)*
R & O Partnership ....E 785 434-4534
Plainville *(G-9991)*
Rods Food Stores Inc ....E 785 243-2035
Concordia *(G-1127)*
Rons Market ....F 620 277-2073
Holcomb *(G-3079)*
Town & Country Super Market ....E 620 653-2330
Hoisington *(G-3072)*

FOOD STORES: Supermarket, More Than 100K Sq Ft, Hypermrkt

Walmart Inc ....C 785 899-2111
Goodland *(G-2489)*
Walmart Inc ....B 620 275-0775
Garden City *(G-2308)*
Walmart Inc ....B 620 232-1593
Pittsburg *(G-9960)*
Walmart Inc ....B 316 636-5384
Wichita *(G-15924)*
Walmart Inc ....C 316 945-2800
Wichita *(G-15923)*

FOOD STORES: Supermarkets

B Four Corp ....C 913 648-1441
Prairie Village *(G-10012)*
Jacks Food Market ....G 785 348-5411
Linn *(G-6407)*

FOOD STORES: Supermarkets, Chain

B Four Corp ....C 913 432-1107
Shawnee Mission *(G-11140)*
Bobs Super Saver Inc ....D 620 251-6820
Coffeyville *(G-913)*
Dillon Companies Inc ....C 620 225-6130
Dodge City *(G-1341)*
Dillon Companies Inc ....C 620 663-4464
Hutchinson *(G-3263)*
Dillon Companies Inc ....C 785 272-0661
Topeka *(G-12557)*
Dillon Companies Inc ....D 785 823-9403
Salina *(G-10478)*
Dillon Companies Inc ....D 620 275-0151
Garden City *(G-2148)*

FORGINGS

Brierton Engineering Inc ....E 785 263-7711
Abilene *(G-16)*
Griffin Wheel Company ....E 913 299-2223
Kansas City *(G-4054)*

FORGINGS: Iron & Steel

Perfekta Inc ....G 316 263-2056
Wichita *(G-15283)*

FORMS: Concrete, Sheet Metal

Contractors Engineer Inc ....F 620 568-2391
Neodesha *(G-7238)*
Wall-Ties & Forms Inc ....C 913 441-0073
Shawnee *(G-11049)*

FOUNDRIES: Aluminum

National Almnm-Brass Fndry Inc ....E 816 833-4500
Leawood *(G-5498)*

FOUNDRIES: Brass, Bronze & Copper

National Almnm-Brass Fndry Inc ....E 816 833-4500
Leawood *(G-5498)*

FOUNDRIES: Gray & Ductile Iron

Acme Foundry Inc ....E 620 251-4920
Coffeyville *(G-908)*
Bradken Inc ....D 913 367-2121
Atchison *(G-220)*
Farrar Corporation ....E 620 478-2212
Norwich *(G-7468)*
Farrar Corporation ....B 785 537-7733
Norwich *(G-7466)*
Kice Industries Inc ....C 316 744-7148
Park City *(G-9625)*
Star Pipe Usa LLC ....C 281 558-3000
Coffeyville *(G-979)*
Star Pipe Usa LLC ....D 620 251-5700
Coffeyville *(G-980)*

FOUNDRIES: Iron

Farrar Corporation ....B 785 537-7733
Norwich *(G-7466)*

FOUNDRIES: Nonferrous

National Almnm-Brass Fndry Inc ....E 816 833-4500
Leawood *(G-5498)*
Tc Industries Inc ....F 913 371-7922
Kansas City *(G-4460)*

FOUNDRIES: Steel

Bradken Inc ....D 913 367-2121
Atchison *(G-220)*
Hampton Hydraulics Llc ....D 620 792-4368
Great Bend *(G-2590)*

FOUNDRIES: Steel Investment

Buffco Engineering Inc ....E 316 558-5390
Mulvane *(G-7211)*

FOUNDRY MACHINERY & EQPT

Industrial Ventures Inc ....D 316 634-6699
Rose Hill *(G-10240)*
Viking Corporation ....E 316 634-6699
Rose Hill *(G-10250)*

FRACTIONATION PRDTS OF CRUDE PETROLEUM, HYDROCARBONS, NEC

Coffeyville Acquisition LLC ....E 913 982-0500
Kansas City *(G-3922)*
Koch Hydrocarbon Southwes ....G 620 662-6691
Hutchinson *(G-3351)*

FRAMES & FRAMING WHOLESALE

Frameworks ....F 316 636-4470
Wichita *(G-14413)*
Picture & Frame Industries Inc ....E 913 384-3751
Kansas City *(G-4322)*

FRANCHISES, SELLING OR LICENSING

Big Bobs Outlets Kansas Cy Inc ....F 913 362-2627
Shawnee Mission *(G-11163)*
Capital City Corral Inc ....D 785 273-5354
Topeka *(G-12425)*
Coverall North America Inc ....F 913 888-5009
Leawood *(G-5362)*
Doc Grens Gourmet Salads Grill ....F 316 636-8997
Wichita *(G-14216)*
Majestic Franchising Inc ....F 913 385-1440
Lenexa *(G-5983)*
Mr Goodcents Franchise Systems ....E 913 583-8400
De Soto *(G-1209)*
Npc Quality Burgers Inc ....F 913 327-5555
Overland Park *(G-9094)*
Prohome International LLc ....E 316 687-6776
Wichita *(G-15372)*
Stanley Dairy Queen ....E 913 851-1850
Shawnee Mission *(G-11892)*
Stockade Companies LLC ....D 620 669-9372
Hutchinson *(G-3448)*
Title Boxing Club LLC ....E 913 991-8285
Overland Park *(G-9415)*
Vista Franchise Inc ....E 785 537-0100
Manhattan *(G-6843)*

FREIGHT CAR LOADING & UNLOADING SVCS

Ash Grove Resources LLC ....F 785 267-1996
Topeka *(G-12340)*
Fedex Freight Corporation ....F 888 880-1320
Goodland *(G-2470)*

FREIGHT CONSOLIDATION SVCS

In Terminal Consolidation Co ....E 913 671-7755
Kansas City *(G-4096)*

FREIGHT FORWARDING ARRANGEMENTS

Alliance Shippers Inc ....E 913 262-7060
Shawnee Mission *(G-11098)*
Box Central Inc ....F 316 689-8484
Wichita *(G-13875)*
CH Robinson Company Inc ....E 316 267-3300
Wichita *(G-13995)*
Elite Transportation LLC ....E 316 295-4829
Wichita *(G-14270)*
King of Freight LLC ....E 316 409-4024
Wichita *(G-14861)*
King of Freight LLC ....E 316 440-4661
Wichita *(G-14862)*
Miq Logistics LLC ....C 913 696-7100
Overland Park *(G-9041)*
Nicholas Water Service LLC ....F 620 930-7511
Medicine Lodge *(G-7070)*
Northwest Freight Handlers Inc ....F 509 869-7678
Wichita *(G-15196)*
Priority Logistics Inc ....E 913 991-7281
Overland Park *(G-9186)*

FREIGHT FORWARDING ARRANGEMENTS: Domestic

Waechter LLC ....E 620 342-1080
Emporia *(G-1848)*

FREIGHT FORWARDING ARRANGEMENTS: Foreign

212 Logistics LLC ....E 620 563-7656
Plains *(G-9973)*
Schenker Inc ....E 316 942-0146
Wichita *(G-15532)*

FREIGHT RATE INFORMATION SVCS

Data2logistics LLC ....C 816 483-9000
Shawnee Mission *(G-11291)*

FREIGHT TRANSPORTATION ARRANGEMENTS

Affton Trucking Company Inc ....F 913 871-1315
Kansas City *(G-3791)*
Burlington Nthrn Santa Fe LLC ....F 785 435-5065
Topeka *(G-12415)*
Catapult International LLC ....E 913 232-2389
Lenexa *(G-5733)*
Coldpoint Logistics LLC ....E 816 888-7380
Edgerton *(G-1483)*
Efreightship LLC ....F 913 871-9309
Overland Park *(G-8671)*
Itransport & Logistics Inc ....E 316 665-7653
Haysville *(G-2948)*
Jts Transports Inc ....E 316 554-0706
Haysville *(G-2951)*
Koch Carbon LLC ....E 316 828-5500
Wichita *(G-14875)*

Koch Mineral Services LLC ....E 316 828-5500
Wichita *(G-14884)*
Land Air Express Inc ....E 316 942-0191
Wichita *(G-14920)*
Nadia Inc ....F 316 686-6190
Wichita *(G-15145)*
Noatum Logistics Usa LLC ....E 913 696-7100
Overland Park *(G-9089)*
Professional Cargo Svcs Inc ....E 785 625-2249
Hays *(G-2890)*
Redstone Logistics LLC ....E 913 998-7905
Overland Park *(G-9230)*
Return Products Management Inc ....F 913 768-1747
Olathe *(G-8028)*
Schenker Inc ....E 316 260-6367
Wichita *(G-15531)*
Shamrock Trading Corporation ....B 877 642-8553
Overland Park *(G-9302)*
Smartway Transportation Inc ....F 877 537-2681
Overland Park *(G-9320)*
UPS Supply Chain Solutions Inc ....B 800 714-8779
Overland Park *(G-9450)*
Xpo Stacktrain LLC ....F 913 422-6400
Kansas City *(G-4561)*

FRUIT & VEGETABLE MARKETS

Depot Market ....F 785 374-4255
Courtland *(G-1180)*
Elderslie LLC ....F 316 680-2637
Valley Center *(G-13341)*

FRUIT STANDS OR MARKETS

Earl Barnes ....F 620 662-6761
Hutchinson *(G-3273)*
Eastside Mkt Westside Mkt LLC ....G 785 532-8686
Manhattan *(G-6619)*
Kier Enterprises Inc ....E 785 325-2150
Washington *(G-13467)*

FRUITS & VEGETABLES WHOLESALERS: Fresh

Associated Wholesale Groc Inc ....A 913 288-1000
Kansas City *(G-3825)*
Depot Market ....F 785 374-4255
Courtland *(G-1180)*

FUEL ADDITIVES

Bg Products Incorporated ....D 316 265-2686
Wichita *(G-13846)*
Bg Products Incorporated ....E 316 265-2686
Wichita *(G-13845)*
Midcontinental Chemical Co Inc ....E 913 390-5556
Olathe *(G-7893)*

FUEL OIL DEALERS

Crossfaith Ventures Lc ....E 620 662-8365
Hutchinson *(G-3251)*
Emerald Transformer Ppm LLC ....E 620 251-6380
Coffeyville *(G-937)*
Farmers Cooperative Elev Co ....F 316 835-2261
Halstead *(G-2699)*
Oil Patch Pump and Supply Inc ....F 620 431-1890
Chanute *(G-749)*

FUELS: Diesel

Hpb Biodiesel Inc ....F 800 262-7907
Shawnee Mission *(G-11441)*

FUELS: Ethanol

Emergent Green Energy Inc ....F 620 450-4320
Minneola *(G-7124)*
Energy Tech Unlimited LLC ....G 913 837-4616
Louisburg *(G-6447)*
Midwest Fuels LLC ....G 913 299-3331
Kansas City *(G-4252)*
S&K Fuels LLC ....G 785 454-6219
Cawker City *(G-689)*
Simply Fuel LLC ....G 913 269-1889
Overland Park *(G-9312)*

FUELS: Oil

Green Energy Products LLC ....G 316 416-4106
Sedgwick *(G-10850)*
Southwest Kansas Coop Svcs LLC ....E 620 492-2126
Johnson *(G-3661)*

FUND RAISING ORGANIZATION, NON-FEE BASIS

Als Assction Md-Merica Chapter ....F 913 648-2062
Shawnee Mission *(G-11099)*
City of Topeka Employees ....A 785 368-3749
Topeka *(G-12475)*
Cowley County United Way Inc ....F 620 221-9683
Winfield *(G-16134)*
Jewish Fdrtion Greater Kans Cy ....E 913 327-8100
Shawnee Mission *(G-11489)*
March of Dimes Inc ....F 913 469-3611
Overland Park *(G-8988)*
United Way of Greater Topeka ....F 785 228-5110
Topeka *(G-13211)*
United Way of Wyandotte County ....E 913 371-3674
Kansas City *(G-4492)*

FUNDRAISING SVCS

Casa of The Thirty-First Judic ....E 620 365-1448
Iola *(G-3589)*
Chavey Ventures Inc ....F 913 888-5108
Shawnee *(G-10926)*
Habitat For Hmanity Ellis Cnty ....F 785 623-4200
Hays *(G-2823)*
Haskell Foundation ....F 785 749-8425
Lawrence *(G-4892)*
Kansas State Univ Foundation ....D 785 532-6266
Manhattan *(G-6679)*
Kc Blind All-Stars Foundation ....F 913 281-3308
Kansas City *(G-4163)*
L L C Fun Services of K C ....F 913 441-9200
Shawnee *(G-10984)*
Pennington Co Fundraising LLC ....E 785 843-1661
Lawrence *(G-5060)*
Pittsburg State Univ Foundatio ....E 620 235-4764
Pittsburg *(G-9922)*
Via Christi Foundation Inc ....F 316 239-3520
Wichita *(G-15887)*

FUNERAL DIRECTOR

Day Funeral Home Inc ....F 620 326-5100
Wellington *(G-13497)*
Feuerborn Fmly Fnrl Svc ....F 620 365-2948
Iola *(G-3600)*
Preferred Mortuary Svcs LLC ....E 316 522-7300
Haysville *(G-2955)*
Rumsey-Yost Funeral Inc ....F 785 843-5111
Lawrence *(G-5099)*
Service Corp International ....E 316 722-2100
Wichita *(G-15565)*

FUNERAL HOME

Alderwoods (kansas) Inc ....F 316 682-5575
Wichita *(G-13661)*
Amos Family Inc ....E 913 631-7314
Shawnee Mission *(G-11111)*
Bath-Naylor Inc ....F 620 231-4700
Pittsburg *(G-9823)*
Broadway Mortuary Inc ....F 316 262-3435
Wichita *(G-13896)*
Bryant-Funeral Home ....F 620 793-3525
Great Bend *(G-2523)*
Carriage Services Inc ....F 785 242-3550
Ottawa *(G-8253)*
Carriage Services Inc ....F 913 682-2820
Leavenworth *(G-5214)*
Charter Funerals Kansas LLC ....F 913 671-7222
Merriam *(G-7088)*
D W Newcomers Sons Inc ....F 913 451-1860
Overland Park *(G-8629)*
D W Newcomers Sons Inc ....E 316 684-8200
Wichita *(G-14160)*
Downing & Lahey Inc ....F 316 733-2740
Wichita *(G-14234)*
Elliott Mortuary Inc ....F 620 663-3327
Hutchinson *(G-3277)*
Garnand Funeral Home Inc ....F 620 276-3219
Garden City *(G-2185)*
Johnson Bowser Funeral Chapel ....F 785 233-3039
Topeka *(G-12747)*
Johnson Mortuary Inc ....F 620 431-1220
Chanute *(G-734)*
Larrison-Forsyth Fnrl HM LLC ....F 620 886-5641
Medicine Lodge *(G-7065)*
Lawrence Funeral Chapel Inc ....F 785 841-3822
Lawrence *(G-4967)*
Logan Funeral Home ....F 785 689-4211
Logan *(G-6426)*
Louis Dengel & Son Mortuary ....F 785 242-2323
Ottawa *(G-8285)*
Newcomer Funeral Svc Group Inc ....F 785 233-6655
Topeka *(G-12928)*
Newcomer Funeral Svc Group Inc ....F 785 354-8558
Topeka *(G-12929)*
Old Mission Mortuary ....E 316 686-7311
Wichita *(G-15214)*
Penwell Gbl Frl Wlf Brns Chpl ....F 620 251-3100
Coffeyville *(G-970)*
Resthaven Gardens of Memory ....E 316 722-2100
Wichita *(G-15450)*
Ryan Mortuary Inc ....F 785 825-4242
Salina *(G-10655)*
Service Corp International ....F 316 263-0244
Wichita *(G-15566)*
Stewart Enterprises Inc ....F 316 686-2766
Wichita *(G-15671)*
Swaim Funeral Home Inc ....F 620 227-2136
Dodge City *(G-1438)*
Turnbull Corporation ....F 620 342-2134
Emporia *(G-1841)*
V W C Inc ....F 316 262-4422
Wichita *(G-15868)*
Warren McElwain Mortuary LLC ....F 785 843-1120
Lawrence *(G-5180)*
Yorgensen-Meloan Inc ....F 785 539-7481
Manhattan *(G-6857)*

FUNERAL HOMES & SVCS

First Call ....F 785 234-2881
Topeka *(G-12612)*
Hospice Incorporated ....D 316 265-9441
Wichita *(G-14637)*
Kimple Inc ....F 620 564-2300
Ellinwood *(G-1635)*
Morris Newspaper Corp Kansas ....E 620 792-1211
Great Bend *(G-2613)*

FUNGICIDES OR HERBICIDES

Pbi-Gordon Corporation ....E 620 848-3849
Crestline *(G-1184)*

FURNACES & OVENS: Indl

G S Inc of Kansas ....G 620 443-5121
Americus *(G-76)*
Hix Corporation ....D 620 231-8568
Pittsburg *(G-9876)*
Optimized Process Furnaces Inc ....F 620 431-1260
Chanute *(G-750)*
Trimac Industrial Systems LLC ....E 913 441-0043
Bonner Springs *(G-578)*

FURNITURE & CABINET STORES: Cabinets, Custom Work

Becker Cabinet Shop ....G 620 327-4448
Newton *(G-7318)*
Guthridge/Nighswonger Corp ....F 316 264-7900
Wichita *(G-14529)*

FURNITURE & CABINET STORES: Custom

Desert Steel Corporation ....F 316 282-2244
Wichita *(G-14199)*

FURNITURE REPAIR & MAINTENANCE SVCS

Big Lkes Developmental Ctr Inc ....E 785 632-5357
Clay Center *(G-843)*

FURNITURE STOCK & PARTS: Hardwood

R Miller Sales Co Inc ....E 913 341-3727
Shawnee Mission *(G-11772)*

FURNITURE STOCK & PARTS: Turnings, Wood

Eubanks Custom Woodworks ....G 785 364-4377
Holton *(G-3088)*
Hays Planing Mill Inc ....G 785 625-6507
Hays *(G-2838)*

FURNITURE STORES

Big Sur Waterbeds Inc ....F 316 944-6225
Wichita *(G-13848)*
Bud Palmer Auction ....E 316 838-4141
Wichita *(G-13905)*

De Leon Furniture Inc ....F 913 342-9446
Kansas City *(G-3964)*
Dinkels Custom Wood Products ....F 785 735-2461
Victoria *(G-13374)*
Ferguson-Phillips LLC ....F 316 612-4663
Wichita *(G-14357)*
Galaxie Business Equipment Inc ....E 620 221-3469
Winfield *(G-16142)*
K D Sullivan Investments LLC ....F 785 460-0170
Colby *(G-1018)*
Kimple Inc ....F 620 564-2300
Ellinwood *(G-1635)*
Schnell & Pestinger Inc ....F 785 738-3624
Beloit *(G-502)*
Sewing Workshop ....F 785 357-6231
Topeka *(G-13061)*
Spring Valley Woodworks Inc ....G 620 345-8330
Canton *(G-682)*
Transitions Group Inc ....F 913 327-0700
Lenexa *(G-6190)*
Walnut Ridge Group Inc ....F 620 232-3359
Pittsburg *(G-9961)*

FURNITURE STORES: Cabinets, Kitchen, Exc Custom Made

Crown Tl Inc ....G 785 263-7061
Abilene *(G-23)*

FURNITURE STORES: Custom Made, Exc Cabinets

Jensen Design Inc ....G 316 943-7900
Wichita *(G-14754)*

FURNITURE STORES: Office

Cort Business Services Corp ....E 913 888-0100
Overland Park *(G-8601)*
Design Central Inc ....F 785 825-4131
Salina *(G-10474)*
I M S of Kansas City Inc ....F 913 599-6007
Shawnee Mission *(G-11446)*
John A Marshall Company ....C 913 599-4700
Lenexa *(G-5929)*
Liberal Office Machines Co ....G 620 624-5653
Liberal *(G-6334)*
Office Products Inc ....E 620 793-8180
Great Bend *(G-2616)*
Ricoh Usa Inc ....C 913 890-5100
Shawnee Mission *(G-11802)*
Spaces Inc ....E 913 894-8900
Lenexa *(G-6143)*
Transitions Group Inc ....F 316 263-5750
Wichita *(G-15792)*

FURNITURE STORES: Outdoor & Garden

Pool & Patio Inc ....F 913 888-2226
Shawnee Mission *(G-11743)*
Pool & Patio Supply Inc ....F 913 888-2226
Shawnee Mission *(G-11744)*

FURNITURE WHOLESALERS

Aegis Business Solutions LLC ....G 913 307-9922
Olathe *(G-7512)*
Cross Creek Furniture LLC ....E 316 943-0286
Wichita *(G-14133)*
Designers Library Inc ....F 913 227-0010
Shawnee Mission *(G-11303)*
Ferguson-Phillips LLC ....F 316 612-4663
Wichita *(G-14357)*
Jakobe Furniture LLC ....D 913 371-8900
Kansas City *(G-4117)*
Midwest Single Source Inc ....E 316 267-6333
Wichita *(G-15102)*

FURNITURE, HOUSEHOLD: Wholesalers

Mittelmans Furniture Co Inc ....E 913 897-5505
Overland Park *(G-9044)*

FURNITURE, MATTRESSES: Wholesalers

Mfl Inc ....E 785 862-2767
Topeka *(G-12886)*
Sleep One Inc ....F 913 859-0001
Overland Park *(G-9317)*
Ssb Manufacturing Company ....C 913 422-8000
Shawnee Mission *(G-11889)*

FURNITURE, OFFICE: Wholesalers

Avcorp Business Systems LLC ....E 913 888-0333
Overland Park *(G-8415)*
Bolen Office Supply Inc ....F 620 672-7535
Pratt *(G-10100)*
Design Central Inc ....F 785 825-4131
Salina *(G-10474)*
Designed Bus Intrors Tpeka Inc ....F 785 233-2078
Topeka *(G-12553)*
Global Industries Inc ....F 913 310-9963
Overland Park *(G-8758)*
Integrated Facilities Group ....F 316 262-1417
Wichita *(G-14702)*
McCartys ....G 620 251-6169
Coffeyville *(G-957)*
Navrats Inc ....F 620 342-2092
Emporia *(G-1800)*
Office Works LLC ....F 785 462-2222
Colby *(G-1032)*
Roberts Hutch-Line Inc ....E 620 662-3356
Hutchinson *(G-3428)*
Spaces Inc ....E 913 894-8900
Lenexa *(G-6143)*
United Office Products Inc ....E 913 782-4441
Olathe *(G-8132)*

FURNITURE, WHOLESALE: Church Pews

R Messner Construction Co ....E 316 634-2381
Wichita *(G-15405)*

FURNITURE, WHOLESALE: Racks

Custom Cabinet & Rack Inc ....E 785 862-2271
Topeka *(G-12537)*
Unruh Fab Inc ....E 316 772-5400
Sedgwick *(G-10853)*

FURNITURE, WHOLESALE: School Desks

Superior School Supplies Inc ....E 316 265-7683
Wichita *(G-15699)*

FURNITURE: Altars, Cut Stone

Braco Sales Inc ....E 816 471-5005
Kansas City *(G-3874)*

FURNITURE: Box Springs, Assembled

Ssb Manufacturing Company ....C 913 422-8000
Shawnee Mission *(G-11889)*

FURNITURE: Chairs, Folding

Stadium Chair Company LLC ....E 432 682-4682
Lenexa *(G-6151)*

FURNITURE: Chairs, Office Wood

Triad Manufacturing Inc ....E 785 825-6050
Salina *(G-10740)*

FURNITURE: Church

Waggoners Inc ....E 620 662-0181
Hutchinson *(G-3480)*

FURNITURE: Couches, Sofa/Davenport, Upholstered Wood Frames

Lacrosse Furniture Co ....D 785 222-2541
La Crosse *(G-4635)*

FURNITURE: Desks & Tables, Office, Exc Wood

Leander Health Tech Inc ....F 785 856-7474
Lawrence *(G-4991)*

FURNITURE: Desks & Tables, Office, Wood

Sunfield LLC ....G 785 338-0314
Wichita *(G-15685)*

FURNITURE: Foundations & Platforms

Joe Thoele Foundation ....G 913 685-2282
Stilwell *(G-12158)*

FURNITURE: Household, Metal

Corbin Bronze Limited ....G 913 766-4012
Kansas City *(G-3940)*

FURNITURE: Household, Wood

Becker Cabinet Shop ....G 620 327-4448
Newton *(G-7318)*
Corbin Bronze Limited ....G 913 766-4012
Kansas City *(G-3940)*
Country Traditions Inc ....G 620 231-5382
Pittsburg *(G-9847)*
Four Corners Construction LLC ....G 620 662-8163
Hutchinson *(G-3290)*
Hays Planing Mill Inc ....G 785 625-6507
Hays *(G-2838)*
Jensen Design Inc ....G 316 943-7900
Wichita *(G-14754)*
King Cabinets Inc ....F 913 422-7554
Shawnee Mission *(G-11535)*
Mingo Custom Woods ....G 785 462-2200
Colby *(G-1029)*
Spring Valley Woodworks Inc ....G 620 345-8330
Canton *(G-682)*
Triad Manufacturing Inc ....E 785 825-6050
Salina *(G-10740)*

FURNITURE: Institutional, Exc Wood

Federal Prison Industries ....D 913 682-8700
Leavenworth *(G-5238)*
Triad Manufacturing Inc ....E 785 825-6050
Salina *(G-10740)*

FURNITURE: Mattresses, Box & Bedsprings

Hays Planing Mill Inc ....G 785 625-6507
Hays *(G-2838)*
Sleep Haven Inc ....F 620 465-2242
Haven *(G-2737)*

FURNITURE: Mattresses, Innerspring Or Box Spring

Imperial Sleep Products Inc ....E 620 465-2242
Haven *(G-2732)*
Sealy Inc ....C 913 321-3677
Kansas City *(G-4410)*

FURNITURE: Office, Exc Wood

Aegis Business Solutions LLC ....G 913 307-9922
Olathe *(G-7512)*
Triad Manufacturing Inc ....E 785 825-6050
Salina *(G-10740)*

FURNITURE: Office, Wood

Herman Miller Inc ....G 913 599-4700
Shawnee Mission *(G-11428)*
Reimers Furniture Mfg Inc ....G 913 727-5100
Lansing *(G-4691)*

FURNITURE: Table Tops, Marble

Evolve Gran Natural Stone Inc ....F 913 254-1800
Olathe *(G-7696)*

FURNITURE: Tables & Table Tops, Wood

Dinkels Custom Wood Products ....F 785 735-2461
Victoria *(G-13374)*

FURNITURE: Upholstered

Andrews and Abbey Riley LLC ....F 913 262-2212
Kansas City *(G-3811)*
Dessin Fournir Inc ....E 785 434-2777
Plainville *(G-9985)*
Dfc Holdings Inc ....F 785 434-2777
Plainville *(G-9986)*
Reimers Furniture Mfg Inc ....G 913 727-5100
Lansing *(G-4691)*
Triad Manufacturing Inc ....E 785 825-6050
Salina *(G-10740)*

FURRIERS

Alaskan Fur Company Inc ....E 913 649-4000
Overland Park *(G-8365)*

FUSE CLIPS & BLOCKS: Electric

Elec-Tron Inc ....D 316 522-3401
Wichita *(G-14263)*

Furs

Fur Is Flying LLC..................................G....... 785 621-7300
Hays *(G-2815)*

GAMBLING, NEC

Golden Eagle Casino..................................B....... 785 486-6601
Horton *(G-3125)*
Harrahs North Kansas City LLC............A....... 816 472-7777
Overland Park *(G-8795)*
Sac & Fox Ntion MO In Kans Neb..........B....... 785 467-8000
Powhattan *(G-10010)*

GAMBLING: Lotteries

Igt Global Solutions Corp..........................E....... 785 861-7300
Topeka *(G-12713)*

GAME MACHINES, COIN-OPERATED, WHOLESALE

Pop-A-Shot Enterprise LLC.......................G....... 785 827-6229
Salina *(G-10637)*

GAMES & TOYS: Board Games, Children's & Adults'

World Publishing Inc..............................E....... 785 221-8174
Topeka *(G-13252)*

GAMES & TOYS: Engines, Miniature

Advanced Engine Machine Inc.............G....... 785 825-6684
Salina *(G-10397)*

GAMES & TOYS: Marbles

Bruces Woodworks LLC..........................F....... 913 441-1432
Bonner Springs *(G-543)*

GAMES & TOYS: Tricycles

Midwest Contracting & Mfg....................G....... 785 743-2026
WA Keeney *(G-13383)*

GARAGE DOOR REPAIR SVCS

Delbert Chopp Co Inc...............................F....... 785 825-8530
Salina *(G-10472)*

GARBAGE CONTAINERS: Plastic

Good Riddance Corporation....................G....... 620 633-5222
Fredonia *(G-2034)*

GAS & OIL FIELD EXPLORATION SVCS

Allied Ofs LLC...F....... 785 483-2627
Russell *(G-10266)*
Baird Oil Co Inc.......................................G....... 785 689-7456
Logan *(G-6420)*
Berexco LLC...F....... 620 275-0320
Garden City *(G-2108)*
Bow Creek Oil Company LLC................G....... 785 650-1738
Hays *(G-2760)*
Castle Resources Inc..............................E....... 785 625-5155
Schoenchen *(G-10802)*
Cmx Inc..G....... 316 269-9052
Wichita *(G-14045)*
Colt Energy Inc..G....... 913 236-0016
Shawnee Mission *(G-11251)*
CST Oil & Gas Corporation....................G....... 620 829-5307
Fort Scott *(G-1963)*
D E Exploration Inc..................................F....... 785 883-4057
Wellsville *(G-13542)*
Damar Resources Inc..............................G....... 785 625-0020
Hays *(G-2781)*
Darrah Oil Company LLC.......................G....... 316 219-3390
Wichita *(G-14170)*
Dart Cherokee Basin Oper LLC.............G....... 620 331-7870
Independence *(G-3509)*
Edison Operating Company LLC.........G....... 316 201-1744
Wichita *(G-14259)*
Freeport-Mcmoran Oil & Gas LLC.........E....... 316 636-1801
Wichita *(G-14418)*
H2 Plains LLC..F....... 785 798-3995
Wichita *(G-14538)*
Hurricane Services Inc............................E....... 316 303-9515
Wichita *(G-14657)*
Independent Oil & Gas Svc Inc..............G....... 316 263-8281
Wichita *(G-14680)*
Kanzou Explorations Inc.........................E....... 913 294-2125
Paola *(G-9568)*
Klm Exploration Co Inc...........................F....... 913 796-6763
Mc Louth *(G-6928)*
Koch Exploration Company.....................F....... 316 828-5508
Wichita *(G-14878)*
Koch Exploration Company LLC..........G....... 316 828-5508
Wichita *(G-14879)*
Koch Mineral Services LLC....................E....... 316 828-5500
Wichita *(G-14884)*
Lario Oil & Gas Company.......................E....... 316 265-5611
Wichita *(G-14924)*
Lockhart Geophysical Company...........F....... 785 625-9175
Hays *(G-2865)*
Lockhart Geophysical Kans Inc............G....... 620 277-7771
Garden City *(G-2226)*
Lr Energy...G....... 620 627-2499
Independence *(G-3535)*
McCoy Petroleum Corporation..............F....... 316 636-2737
Wichita *(G-15023)*
Murfin Drilling Company Inc................E....... 316 267-3241
Wichita *(G-15140)*
MWM Oil Co Inc......................................G....... 316 265-1992
Towanda *(G-13265)*
OS Companies Inc...................................E....... 316 265-5611
Wichita *(G-15238)*
Postrock Energy Corporation...............F....... 620 432-4200
Chanute *(G-756)*
Redbud E&P Inc.......................................E....... 620 331-7870
Independence *(G-3551)*
Ritchie Exploration Inc..........................F....... 316 691-9500
Wichita *(G-15468)*
Shamrock Resources Inc........................G....... 316 636-9557
Wichita *(G-15571)*
Slawson Exploration Co Inc...................E....... 316 263-3201
Wichita *(G-15603)*
Smyth Oil and Gas Services..................E....... 620 356-4091
Ulysses *(G-13319)*
Stelbar Oil Corporation Inc...................F....... 316 264-8378
Wichita *(G-15660)*
Tengasco Inc...E....... 785 625-6374
Hays *(G-2919)*
Viva International...................................G....... 913 859-0438
Shawnee Mission *(G-11983)*
Woolsey Petroleum Corporation...........F....... 316 267-4379
Wichita *(G-16069)*
Woolsey Petroleum Corporation...........G....... 620 886-5606
Medicine Lodge *(G-7076)*

GAS & OIL FIELD SVCS, NEC

Clinton Enterprises LLC........................G....... 316 636-1801
Wichita *(G-14042)*
Shamrock Resources Inc........................G....... 316 636-9557
Wichita *(G-15571)*

GAS & OTHER COMBINED SVCS

Chips Inc..F....... 785 842-6921
Lawrence *(G-4787)*
Msip-Sscc Holdings LLC........................F....... 620 657-4166
Satanta *(G-10788)*
MTS Quanta LLC.....................................E....... 913 383-0800
Overland Park *(G-9061)*

GAS PROCESSING SVC

Panhandle Eastrn Pipe Line LP..............E....... 620 624-8661
Liberal *(G-6354)*
Sterling Food Mart Inc............................G....... 620 278-3371
Hutchinson *(G-3446)*

GAS PRODUCTION & DISTRIBUTION

American Energies Gas Svc LLC...........F....... 620 628-4424
Canton *(G-679)*
Dcp Operating Company LP...................E....... 620 626-1201
Liberal *(G-6301)*
Evergy Kansas Central Inc.....................D....... 316 283-5521
Newton *(G-7342)*

GAS STATIONS

Anthony Frmrs Coop Elev Cmpnys......F....... 620 842-5181
Anthony *(G-119)*
Bartlett Cooperative Assn.......................E....... 620 226-3311
Bartlett *(G-371)*
Burnett Automotive Inc..........................F....... 913 681-8824
Overland Park *(G-8494)*
Central Valley AG Cooperative.............C....... 785 738-2241
Beloit *(G-481)*
Great Bend Cooperative Assn...............F....... 620 792-1281
Great Bend *(G-2577)*
Iowa Tribe Kansas & Nebraska.............F....... 785 595-3430
White Cloud *(G-13569)*
Jim Woods Marketing Inc.......................F....... 620 856-3554
Baxter Springs *(G-410)*
L C McClain Inc.......................................F....... 785 584-6151
Rossville *(G-10253)*
Lakhani Commercial Corp......................D....... 913 677-1100
Kansas City *(G-4193)*
Leiszler Oil Co Inc..................................E....... 785 632-5648
Manhattan *(G-6712)*
Leroy Cooperative Assn Inc..................E....... 620 964-2225
Le Roy *(G-5196)*
Murphy USA Inc......................................F....... 620 664-9479
Hutchinson *(G-3386)*
Murphy USA Inc......................................F....... 620 227-5607
Dodge City *(G-1409)*
Nusser Oil Company Inc........................E....... 620 697-4624
Elkhart *(G-1625)*
Offerle Coop Grn & Sup Co...................F....... 620 659-2165
Offerle *(G-7500)*
Pauline Food Center................................F....... 785 862-2774
Topeka *(G-12965)*
Red Rock Auto Center Inc......................F....... 620 663-9822
South Hutchinson *(G-12065)*
Shaw Motor Co Inc..................................F....... 785 673-4228
Grainfield *(G-2496)*

GAS: Refinery

CHS Inc..D....... 620 241-4247
McPherson *(G-6948)*
CHS McPherson Refinery Inc................B....... 620 241-2340
McPherson *(G-6949)*
Coffeyville Resources LLC....................F....... 620 252-4781
Coffeyville *(G-921)*
Coffeyvlle Rsrces Ref Mktg LLC..........G....... 913 982-0500
Kansas City *(G-3925)*

GASES & LIQUIFIED PETROLEUM GASES

Flint Hills Resources Central..................G....... 316 828-5500
Wichita *(G-14391)*

GASES: Carbon Dioxide

Praxair Inc..G....... 620 225-1368
Wright *(G-16193)*

GASES: Helium

Air Products and Chemicals Inc...........F....... 620 626-7062
Liberal *(G-6274)*
Linde Gas North America LLC..............G....... 785 387-2281
Otis *(G-8240)*

GASES: Indl

Air Products and Chemicals Inc...........E....... 316 522-8181
Haysville *(G-2935)*
Air Products and Chemicals Inc...........D....... 620 626-5700
Liberal *(G-6275)*
Koch Fertilizer LLC................................E....... 620 227-8631
Dodge City *(G-1394)*
Koch Fertilizer LLC................................E....... 316 828-5010
Wichita *(G-14880)*
Praxair Inc..E....... 620 562-4500
Lorraine *(G-6434)*
Praxair Distribution Inc..........................E....... 913 492-1551
Lenexa *(G-6069)*

GASES: Nitrogen

Messer LLC...G....... 620 251-9190
Coffeyville *(G-962)*

GASES: Oxygen

Messer LLC...E....... 785 387-2281
Otis *(G-8241)*

GASKETS

Everseal Gasket Inc.................................E....... 913 441-9232
Shawnee Mission *(G-11351)*
G T Sales & Manufacturing Inc..............D....... 316 943-2171
Wichita *(G-14434)*
Liberal Gasket Mfg Co.............................G....... 620 624-4921
Liberal *(G-6333)*

GASOLINE FILLING STATIONS

Agco Inc..F....... 785 483-2128
Russell *(G-10263)*
Archer-Daniels-Midland Company........G....... 620 357-8733
Jetmore *(G-3645)*

Bennington Oil Co Inc ....F 785 392-3031
Minneapolis *(G-7113)*
Brecheisens Stop 2 Shop Inc ....E 620 392-5577
Hartford *(G-2727)*
Cervs Conoco & Convenience ....F 785 625-7777
Hays *(G-2767)*
Cropland Co-Op Inc ....F 620 356-1241
Ulysses *(G-13294)*
Dodge City Cooperative Exch ....E 620 225-4193
Dodge City *(G-1344)*
Ellsworth Coop ....F 785 472-3261
Ellsworth *(G-1667)*
Equilon Enterprises LLC ....F 913 648-0535
Shawnee Mission *(G-11346)*
Fairleigh Ranch Corporation ....F 620 872-2111
Scott City *(G-10810)*
Farmers Co-Operative Equity Co ....F 620 739-4335
Isabel *(G-3639)*
Farmers Co-Operative Union ....D 620 278-2141
Sterling *(G-12116)*
Farmers Grain Cooperative ....E 620 837-3313
Walton *(G-13400)*
Golden Belt Coop Assn Inc ....F 785 726-3115
Ellis *(G-1646)*
Golden Valley Inc ....E 620 527-4216
Rozel *(G-10258)*
Healy Cooperative Elevator Co ....E 620 398-2211
Healy *(G-2966)*
Huntingdon Park Standard Svc ....F 785 272-4499
Topeka *(G-12708)*
Jackson Farmers Inc ....F 785 364-3161
Holton *(G-3100)*
K & S Eastside Amoco Inc ....F 620 342-3565
Emporia *(G-1782)*
Kanza Cooperative Association ....F 620 546-2231
Iuka *(G-3640)*
Kier Enterprises Inc ....E 785 325-2150
Washington *(G-13467)*
Kistler Service Inc ....E 620 782-3611
Udall *(G-13278)*
L & M Oil Company ....F 913 856-8502
Gardner *(G-2352)*
Leavenworth County Coop Assn ....F 913 727-1900
Lansing *(G-4683)*
Mid-Kansas Cooperative Assn ....F 785 227-3361
Lindsborg *(G-6403)*
Nemaha County Cooperative Assn ....D 785 336-6153
Seneca *(G-10874)*
Phillips 66 ....F 316 821-2250
Wichita *(G-15292)*
Rainbow Car Wash Inc ....F 913 432-1116
Kansas City *(G-4360)*
Rakies Oil LLC ....F 620 442-2210
Arkansas City *(G-171)*
Right Cooperative Association ....E 620 227-8611
Wright *(G-16194)*
Robinson Oil Co Inc ....F 620 275-4237
Garden City *(G-2268)*
Robson Oil Co Inc ....F 785 263-2470
Abilene *(G-51)*
Ronco Inc ....F 913 362-7200
Mission Hills *(G-7148)*
Rons Market ....F 620 277-2073
Holcomb *(G-3079)*
S Jackson Service Center Inc ....F 913 422-7438
Edwardsville *(G-1514)*
Sharp Bros Seed Company ....E 620 398-2231
Healy *(G-2967)*
Skyland Grain LLC ....F 620 672-3961
Cunningham *(G-1189)*
Star Fuel Centers Inc ....E 913 652-9400
Leawood *(G-5561)*
Stuhlsatz Service Inc ....F 316 531-2282
Garden Plain *(G-2322)*
T & E Oil Company Inc 1 ....E 620 663-3777
Hutchinson *(G-3460)*
Town and Country Food Mkts Inc ....E 316 942-7940
Wichita *(G-15779)*
Universal Motor Fuels Inc ....F 316 832-0151
Wichita *(G-15855)*
Waterway Gas & Wash Company ....D 913 339-9964
Shawnee Mission *(G-11996)*

GASOLINE WHOLESALERS

Ethanol Products LLC ....C 316 303-1380
Wichita *(G-14308)*
Fleming Feed & Grain Inc ....E 316 742-3411
Leon *(G-6247)*
L & M Oil Company ....F 913 856-8502
Gardner *(G-2352)*
L & M Oil Company ....F 913 893-9789
Gardner *(G-2353)*
Mid-Kansas Cooperative Assn ....F 785 227-3343
Lindsborg *(G-6404)*

GEARS

Gear Headquarters Inc ....F 913 831-1700
Kansas City *(G-4028)*
Pro-Dig LLC ....F 785 856-2661
Elwood *(G-1689)*

GEARS: Power Transmission, Exc Auto

Curtis Machine Company Inc ....D 620 227-7164
Dodge City *(G-1338)*

GENEALOGICAL INVESTIGATION SVCS

Midwest Hstrcal Gnalogical Soc ....E 316 264-3611
Wichita *(G-15096)*
Old Fort Genealgcl Socty SE KS ....F 620 223-3300
Fort Scott *(G-1996)*

GENERAL COUNSELING SVCS

Adolescent Adult Fmly Recovery ....F 316 943-2051
Wichita *(G-13614)*
Center For Counseling & Cnsltn ....E 620 792-2544
Great Bend *(G-2526)*
Cfcc & Associates ....E 785 272-0778
Topeka *(G-12461)*
Dccca Inc ....E 316 267-2030
Wichita *(G-14178)*
Kansas Dept For Chldren Fmlies ....C 913 651-6200
Leavenworth *(G-5261)*
Pregnncy Crisis Ctr of Wichita ....F 316 945-9400
Wichita *(G-15329)*
Sumner Mental Health Center ....D 620 326-7448
Wellington *(G-13534)*
Wright Intl Studnt Svcs ....D 913 677-1142
Shawnee Mission *(G-12020)*

GENERAL ECONOMIC PROGRAM ADMINISTRATION, GOVERNMENT: State

Kansas Department Commerce ....E 785 296-5298
Topeka *(G-12768)*

GENERAL MERCHANDISE, NONDURABLE, WHOLESALE

Bachus & Son Inc ....E 316 265-4673
Wichita *(G-13789)*
Computer Distribution Corp ....E 785 354-1086
Topeka *(G-12498)*
Kms Inc ....E 316 264-8833
Wichita *(G-14868)*
Mediacorp LLC ....E 913 317-8900
Overland Park *(G-9006)*
Redemption Plus LLC ....D 913 563-4331
Lenexa *(G-6095)*
Regal Distributing Co ....E 913 894-8787
Lenexa *(G-6096)*
Rjs Discount Sales Inc ....F 785 267-7476
Topeka *(G-13020)*
Valu Merchandisers Company ....F 620 223-1313
Fort Scott *(G-2014)*
Valu Merchandisers Company ....E 913 319-8500
Kansas City *(G-4513)*

GENERATING APPARATUS & PARTS: Electrical

Hci Energy LLC ....F 913 283-8855
Lenexa *(G-5893)*

GENERATION EQPT: Electronic

Clore Automotive LLC ....E 913 310-1050
Lenexa *(G-5766)*
USP Technical Services ....F 310 517-1800
Derby *(G-1278)*

GENERATORS: Electrochemical, Fuel Cell

Earth Care Products Inc ....F 620 331-0090
Independence *(G-3514)*

GERIATRIC RESIDENTIAL CARE FACILITY

Country Place Senior Living ....F 785 336-6868
Seneca *(G-10860)*
Eldercare Inc ....C 620 792-5942
Great Bend *(G-2559)*
Gansel House LLC ....F 620 331-7422
Independence *(G-3522)*
Guest Home Estates VI ....E 620 223-1620
Fort Scott *(G-1975)*
Homestead of Olathe North ....C 913 829-1403
Olathe *(G-7771)*
Hospital Dst 1 of Rice Cnty ....D 620 257-5173
Lyons *(G-6485)*
Las Villas Del Norte ....D 760 741-1046
Junction City *(G-3720)*
Reflection Ridge Golf Corp ....E 316 721-0500
Wichita *(G-15433)*
Spearville Senior Living Inc ....E 785 506-6003
Topeka *(G-13087)*
Via Christi Health Inc ....D 316 685-0400
Wichita *(G-15890)*
Village Shalom Inc ....C 913 317-2600
Shawnee Mission *(G-11979)*

GERIATRIC SOCIAL SVCS

Home Instead Senior Care ....E 316 612-7541
Wichita *(G-14631)*
Kansas Dept For Aging & Disabi ....D 785 296-2917
Topeka *(G-12770)*
Oxford Management Group LLC ....E 316 201-3210
Wichita *(G-15244)*

GIFT SHOP

Arbuthnots Inc ....E 785 527-2146
Belleville *(G-450)*
Bruces Woodworks LLC ....F 913 441-1432
Bonner Springs *(G-543)*
Central Office Svc & Sup Inc ....F 785 632-2177
Clay Center *(G-848)*
Cottage House Hotel and Motel ....F 620 767-6828
Council Grove *(G-1159)*
D J Company ....F 316 685-3241
Wichita *(G-14158)*
Deans Designs Inc ....F 316 686-6674
Wichita *(G-14181)*
Doll Cradle ....F 913 631-1900
Shawnee Mission *(G-11313)*
Garden City Travel Plaza LLC ....E 620 275-4404
Garden City *(G-2179)*
Green Hills Inc ....F 316 686-7673
Wichita *(G-14509)*
Hemslojd Inc ....G 785 227-2983
Lindsborg *(G-6399)*
Hoffmanns Green Industries ....E 316 634-1500
Wichita *(G-14624)*
Its Greek To Me Inc ....C 800 336-4486
Manhattan *(G-6666)*
Kingman Drug Inc ....F 620 532-5113
Kingman *(G-4600)*
Land of Paws LLC ....F 913 341-1011
Shawnee Mission *(G-11547)*
Paint Glaze & Fire ....G 913 661-2529
Overland Park *(G-9137)*
Prairie Patches Inc ....G 785 749-4565
Lawrence *(G-5072)*
Quality Printing & Gift Shop ....G 620 654-3487
Galva *(G-2095)*
Sunset Zoological Pk Wildlife ....E 785 587-2737
Manhattan *(G-6818)*
Swedish Country Inn ....F 785 227-2985
Lindsborg *(G-6406)*
Whartons For Every ....E 620 276-6000
Garden City *(G-2313)*
William O Broeker Enterprises ....E 913 682-2022
Leavenworth *(G-5306)*

GIFT, NOVELTY & SOUVENIR STORES: Gifts & Novelties

Gary Dean Anderson ....E 785 475-2340
Oberlin *(G-7495)*
L V S Inc ....E 316 636-5005
Wichita *(G-14908)*
Mr PS Party Outlet Inc ....F 785 537-1804
Manhattan *(G-6753)*
U S Toy Co Inc ....E 913 642-8247
Leawood *(G-5587)*

GIFT, NOVELTY & SOUVENIR STORES: Party Favors

AAA Party Rental Inc...F ... 816 333-1767
Lenexa *(G-5617)*
Fun Services of Kansas City...E ... 913 631-3772
Shawnee Mission *(G-11385)*
PA Acquisition Corp...F ... 913 498-3700
Shawnee Mission *(G-11712)*

GIFTS & NOVELTIES: Wholesalers

Dd Traders Inc...B ... 913 402-6800
Leawood *(G-5376)*
Glover Inc...E ... 800 654-1511
Olathe *(G-7735)*
Hills Pet Nutrition Inc...C ... 785 286-1451
Topeka *(G-12692)*
Mer-Sea & Co LLC...E ... 816 974-3115
Lenexa *(G-5994)*
Prairie Patches Inc...G ... 785 749-4565
Lawrence *(G-5072)*
Prizm Incorporated...F ... 785 456-1831
Wamego *(G-13436)*
Victorian Paper Company...D ... 913 438-3995
Lenexa *(G-6214)*

GLASS FABRICATORS

Champion Window Co Kans Cy Inc...E ... 913 541-8282
Lenexa *(G-5751)*
Lippert Components Mfg Inc...D ... 316 283-0627
North Newton *(G-7438)*
Masonry & Glass Systems Inc...G ... 913 748-6142
Shawnee Mission *(G-11601)*
Petty Products Inc...G ... 913 782-0028
Olathe *(G-7981)*
PQ Corporation...F ... 913 227-0561
Lenexa *(G-6065)*
Rellec Apparel Graphics LLC...G ... 913 707-5249
Lenexa *(G-6100)*

GLASS PRDTS, PRESSED OR BLOWN: Glassware, Art Or Decorative

Karg Art Glass...E ... 316 744-2442
Kechi *(G-4571)*

GLASS PRDTS, PRESSED OR BLOWN: Level Instrument Vials

B P E Inc...G ... 620 343-3783
Emporia *(G-1700)*

GLASS STORE: Leaded Or Stained

Rayers Bearden Stained GL Sup...F ... 316 942-2929
Wichita *(G-15421)*

GLASS STORES

Auto-Craft Inc...E ... 785 579-5997
Junction City *(G-3669)*
Bell Memorials LLC...F ... 785 738-2257
Beloit *(G-474)*
Binswanger Enterprises LLC...F ... 785 267-4090
Topeka *(G-12382)*
G W Inc...E ... 316 262-3403
Wichita *(G-14435)*
Janssen Glass & Mirror Inc...F ... 913 677-5727
Shawnee *(G-10977)*
Kennedy Glass Inc...E ... 785 843-4416
Lawrence *(G-4942)*
Performance Glass Inc...F ... 913 441-1290
Bonner Springs *(G-570)*
Pratt Glass Inc...F ... 620 672-6463
Pratt *(G-10139)*

GLASS, AUTOMOTIVE: Wholesalers

Manko Window Systems Inc...F ... 785 238-3188
Junction City *(G-3724)*
Northstar Automotive Glass Inc...F ... 316 686-3648
Wichita *(G-15193)*
Sigma Distributing Company Inc...E ... 316 943-4499
Wichita *(G-15588)*

GLASS: Fiber

Hutchens Corporation...G ... 785 252-3423
Holyrood *(G-3117)*

GLASS: Flat

AGC Flat Glass North Amer Inc...B ... 913 592-6100
Spring Hill *(G-12076)*

GLASS: Insulating

G W Inc...E ... 316 262-3403
Wichita *(G-14435)*
Insulite Glass Co Inc...D ... 800 452-7721
Olathe *(G-7795)*

GLASS: Pressed & Blown, NEC

Pioneer - Ram Incorporated...A ... 316 685-2266
Wichita *(G-15301)*

GLASS: Stained

Hoefer Enterprises Inc...G ... 620 663-1778
South Hutchinson *(G-12059)*

GLASSWARE STORES

Hemslojd Inc...G ... 785 227-2983
Lindsborg *(G-6399)*

GLYCERIN

Seaboard Energy Oklahoma LLC...E ... 913 261-2620
Shawnee Mission *(G-11841)*

GOLF CARTS: Wholesalers

Kansas Golf and Turf Inc...F ... 316 267-9111
Park City *(G-9622)*

GOLF CLUB & EQPT REPAIR SVCS

City of Topeka...F ... 785 273-0811
Topeka *(G-12473)*

GOLF COURSES: Public

Alvamar Inc...E ... 785 842-2929
Lawrence *(G-4732)*
American Golf Corporation...E ... 913 681-3100
Shawnee Mission *(G-11103)*
Augusta Country Club...E ... 316 775-7281
Augusta *(G-301)*
Capital Frsght Golf Fitnes LLC...E ... 913 648-1600
Overland Park *(G-8509)*
City of Hesston...F ... 620 327-2331
Hesston *(G-2987)*
City of Junction City...F ... 785 238-4303
Milford *(G-7111)*
City of Lawrence...F ... 785 748-0600
Lawrence *(G-4790)*
City of Leawood...D ... 913 685-4550
Shawnee Mission *(G-11228)*
City of Overland Park...F ... 913 897-3806
Shawnee Mission *(G-11230)*
City of Overland Park...F ... 913 897-3805
Overland Park *(G-8557)*
City of Pittsburg...F ... 620 231-8070
Pittsburg *(G-9832)*
City of Topeka...F ... 785 291-2670
Topeka *(G-12469)*
City of Wichita...E ... 316 688-9341
Wichita *(G-14029)*
City of Wichita...F ... 316 337-9494
Wichita *(G-14030)*
County of Johnson...E ... 913 829-4653
Olathe *(G-7623)*
Falcon Lakes Golf LLC...E ... 913 724-4653
Basehor *(G-376)*
Falcon Lakes Maintenance...E ... 913 724-4460
Basehor *(G-377)*
Falcon Ridge Golf Club...F ... 913 393-4653
Shawnee Mission *(G-11359)*
Flint Hills National Golf Club...D ... 316 733-4131
Andover *(G-93)*
Golf Operations Management LLC...E ... 913 897-3809
Overland Park *(G-8764)*
Kangolf Inc...F ... 785 539-7529
Manhattan *(G-6673)*
Kansas State University Golf C...E ... 785 776-6475
Manhattan *(G-6697)*
Lamont Hill Resort Inc...E ... 785 828-3131
Vassar *(G-13371)*
Mayberrys Inc...F ... 620 793-9400
Great Bend *(G-2605)*
National Golf Properties LLC...E ... 913 721-1333
Kansas City *(G-4281)*
Robin White Hills Inc...F ... 785 877-3399
Norton *(G-7462)*
Sand Creek Station Golf Course...E ... 316 284-6161
Newton *(G-7414)*
Shawnee Country Club...E ... 785 233-2373
Topeka *(G-13063)*
Sierra Hills Golf Club...F ... 316 733-9333
Wichita *(G-15587)*
Stag Hill Golf Club Inc...F ... 785 539-1041
Manhattan *(G-6805)*
Sugar Hills Golf Club Inc...E ... 785 899-2785
Goodland *(G-2487)*
Sunflower Hills Golf Course...F ... 913 721-2727
Bonner Springs *(G-575)*
Twin Fiddle Investment Co LLC...E ... 316 788-2855
Derby *(G-1277)*
Wedgewood Golf Course...D ... 316 835-2991
Halstead *(G-2706)*
Western Hills Golf Club Inc...E ... 785 478-4000
Topeka *(G-13241)*

GOLF DRIVING RANGES

Sports Center Inc...E ... 785 272-5522
Topeka *(G-13092)*
Twin Fiddle Investment Co LLC...E ... 316 788-2855
Derby *(G-1277)*

GOLF GOODS & EQPT

Alvamar Inc...E ... 785 842-2929
Lawrence *(G-4732)*
Dynamic Discs LLC...F ... 620 208-3472
Emporia *(G-1734)*
Golf Operations Management LLC...E ... 913 897-3809
Overland Park *(G-8764)*
National Golf Properties LLC...E ... 913 721-1333
Kansas City *(G-4281)*
Reflection Ridge Maintenance...F ... 316 721-9483
Wichita *(G-15434)*
Twin Fiddle Investment Co LLC...E ... 316 788-2855
Derby *(G-1277)*

GOURMET FOOD STORES

La Mesa Mexican Restaurant...F ... 913 837-3455
Louisburg *(G-6454)*

GOVERNMENT LEGAL COUNSEL & PROSECUTION

Indigents Defense Svcs Kans Bd...F ... 785 296-1833
Topeka *(G-12717)*
Indigents Defense Svcs Kans Bd...E ... 785 296-5484
Topeka *(G-12719)*
Indigents Defense Svcs Kans Bd...E ... 316 264-8700
Wichita *(G-14684)*

GOVERNMENT, EXECUTIVE OFFICES: City & Town Managers' Offices

City of Halstead...E ... 316 835-2286
Halstead *(G-2697)*
City of Sedan...E ... 620 725-3193
Sedan *(G-10840)*

GOVERNMENT, EXECUTIVE OFFICES: County Supervisor/Exec Office

Comcare of Sedgwick County...F ... 316 660-7550
Wichita *(G-14060)*
County of Clay...E ... 785 632-3193
Clay Center *(G-859)*
County of Ellis...D ... 785 628-9455
Hays *(G-2778)*
County of Ellsworth...F ... 785 472-4486
Ellsworth *(G-1665)*
County of Finney...D ... 620 272-3564
Garden City *(G-2135)*
County of Grant...E ... 620 356-4837
Ulysses *(G-13291)*
County of Grant...F ... 620 356-4233
Ulysses *(G-13292)*
County of Harvey...F ... 316 283-1637
Newton *(G-7337)*
County of Jefferson...F ... 785 863-2581
Oskaloosa *(G-8221)*
County of Jefferson...E ... 785 863-2447
Oskaloosa *(G-8222)*
County of Morton...E ... 620 593-4288
Elkhart *(G-1618)*

County of Norton ....E.... 785 877-5784
Norton *(G-7442)*
County of Osage ....F.... 785 828-4444
Lyndon *(G-6476)*
County of Pawnee ....E.... 620 285-6141
Larned *(G-4700)*
County of Russell ....E.... 785 483-4032
Russell *(G-10270)*
County of Saline ....F.... 785 826-6606
Salina *(G-10465)*
County of Sedgwick ....E.... 316 660-4800
Wichita *(G-14109)*
County of Sedgwick ....E.... 316 660-9775
Wichita *(G-14110)*
County of Sedgwick ....E.... 316 660-7060
Wichita *(G-14114)*
County of Seward ....F.... 620 626-3266
Liberal *(G-6298)*
County of Shawnee ....D.... 785 233-4774
Topeka *(G-12517)*
County of Shawnee ....D.... 785 862-2071
Topeka *(G-12520)*
County of Shawnee ....D.... 785 233-7702
Topeka *(G-12521)*
County of Shawnee ....C.... 785 368-2000
Topeka *(G-12522)*
County of Smith ....E.... 785 282-6924
Smith Center *(G-12033)*
County of Stevens ....E.... 620 544-8782
Hugoton *(G-3154)*
County of Stevens ....E.... 620 544-2562
Hugoton *(G-3156)*
County of Thomas ....E.... 785 460-4585
Colby *(G-1001)*
County of Trego ....E.... 785 743-6441
Wakeeney *(G-13386)*
Guidance Center ....E.... 913 367-1593
Atchison *(G-233)*
Norton County Hospital ....F.... 785 877-5745
Norton *(G-7459)*
Smg Holdings Inc ....E.... 785 235-1986
Topeka *(G-13078)*

GOVERNMENT, EXECUTIVE OFFICES: Local

City of Great Bend ....E.... 620 793-4111
Great Bend *(G-2540)*
City of Wichita ....E.... 316 268-4651
Wichita *(G-14026)*
City of Wichita ....E.... 316 268-8351
Wichita *(G-14028)*

GOVERNMENT, EXECUTIVE OFFICES: Mayors'

City of Ellinwood ....F.... 620 564-3046
Ellinwood *(G-1628)*
City of Great Bend ....F.... 620 792-3906
Great Bend *(G-2541)*
City of Great Bend ....F.... 620 793-4170
Great Bend *(G-2542)*
City of Leawood ....D.... 913 685-4550
Shawnee Mission *(G-11228)*
City of Lenexa ....D.... 913 541-0209
Lenexa *(G-5755)*
City of Salina ....E.... 785 826-7305
Salina *(G-10448)*
City of Salina ....E.... 785 826-7200
Salina *(G-10449)*
City of Salina ....F.... 785 309-5775
Salina *(G-10450)*
City of Topeka ....E.... 785 368-9180
Topeka *(G-12468)*
City of Topeka ....F.... 785 291-2670
Topeka *(G-12469)*
City of Topeka ....D.... 785 368-3851
Topeka *(G-12470)*
City of Topeka ....E.... 785 295-3842
Topeka *(G-12471)*
City of Topeka ....E.... 785 368-3860
Topeka *(G-12472)*
City of Topeka ....D.... 785 295-3803
Topeka *(G-12474)*
City of Topeka Employees ....F.... 785 272-5503
Topeka *(G-12476)*
City of Wichita ....F.... 316 337-9494
Wichita *(G-14030)*
City of Wichita ....C.... 316 265-7221
Wichita *(G-14031)*

GOVERNMENT, EXECUTIVE OFFICES: State

Administration Kansas Dept ....C.... 785 296-3001
Topeka *(G-12290)*

GOVERNMENT, GENERAL: Administration

City of Parsons ....E.... 620 421-7025
Parsons *(G-9671)*
City of Waterville ....E.... 785 363-2367
Waterville *(G-13473)*
County of Johnson ....F.... 913 715-2550
Overland Park *(G-8605)*

GOVERNMENT, GENERAL: Administration, County

City of Overland Park ....E.... 913 895-6040
Overland Park *(G-8556)*
County of Finney ....F.... 620 275-4421
Garden City *(G-2136)*

GOVERNMENT, GENERAL: Administration, Federal

Senate United States ....F.... 620 227-2244
Dodge City *(G-1428)*

GOVERNMENT, GENERAL: Administration, Level Of Government

City of Lawrence ....F.... 785 832-7700
Lawrence *(G-4789)*
County of Trego ....F.... 785 743-5337
Wakeeney *(G-13385)*

GOVERNMENT, GENERAL: Administration, Local

City of Spring Hill ....F.... 913 592-3781
Spring Hill *(G-12082)*

GOVERNMENT, GENERAL: Administration, State

Executive Office of Kansas ....F.... 785 272-8681
Topeka *(G-12587)*
Judiciary Court of The State ....E.... 785 296-6290
Topeka *(G-12750)*
Securities Commissioner Kansas ....E.... 785 296-3307
Topeka *(G-13050)*
Veterans Affairs Kans Comm On ....F.... 785 350-4489
Topeka *(G-13221)*

GOVERNMENT, LEGISLATIVE BODIES: County

County of Douglas ....E.... 785 832-5293
Lawrence *(G-4814)*

GOVERNMENT, LEGISLATIVE BODIES: Local

City of Waterville ....E.... 785 363-2367
Waterville *(G-13473)*

GOVERNMENT, LEGISLATIVE BODIES: State & Local

Comanche County ....F.... 620 582-2933
Coldwater *(G-1054)*

GRADING SVCS

Haupt Construction Company ....F.... 913 686-4411
Spring Hill *(G-12085)*
Wildcat Construction Co Inc ....C.... 316 945-9408
Wichita *(G-16049)*

GRAIN & FIELD BEANS WHOLESALERS

Cargill Incorporated ....E.... 913 236-0346
Overland Park *(G-8517)*
Cargill Incorporated ....F.... 316 291-1939
Wichita *(G-13947)*
Central Soyfoods ....F.... 785 312-8638
Lawrence *(G-4781)*
CHS Inc ....D.... 620 241-4247
McPherson *(G-6948)*
Green Plains Cattle Co LLC ....D.... 620 624-6296
Kismet *(G-4630)*
Lange Company LLC ....F.... 620 456-2996
Conway Springs *(G-1143)*

Redwood Group LLC ....D.... 816 979-1786
Mission *(G-7137)*

GRANITE: Crushed & Broken

Apac-Kansas Inc ....F.... 620 392-5771
Hartford *(G-2726)*
Rocky Top Counter Top LLC ....G.... 316 262-0497
Wichita *(G-15475)*

GRANITE: Dimension

Trendstone LLC ....G.... 913 599-5492
Lenexa *(G-6191)*

GRANTMAKING FOUNDATIONS

Oak Ridge Youth Dev Corp ....E.... 913 788-5657
Kansas City *(G-4292)*
Trego Hospital Endowment Fndtn ....E.... 785 743-2182
Wakeeney *(G-13392)*

GRAPHIC ARTS & RELATED DESIGN SVCS

Copy Co Corporation ....E.... 785 823-2679
Salina *(G-10463)*
Greteman Group Inc ....F.... 316 263-1004
Wichita *(G-14517)*
Harvest Graphics LLC ....E.... 913 438-5556
Shawnee Mission *(G-11415)*
Infusion Design Incorporated ....E.... 913 422-0317
Bonner Springs *(G-555)*
Integrated Media Group LLC ....F.... 316 425-8333
Wichita *(G-14703)*
J2 Design Solutions LLC ....F.... 316 303-9460
Wichita *(G-14741)*
Last Chance Graphics Inc ....G.... 785 263-4470
Abilene *(G-44)*
Legends Printing & Graphics ....G.... 620 225-0020
Dodge City *(G-1396)*
Service Pak Inc ....D.... 913 438-3500
Lenexa *(G-6124)*
Terrell Publishing Co ....G.... 913 948-8226
Kansas City *(G-4464)*

GRAPHIC LAYOUT SVCS: Printed Circuitry

Pitsco Inc ....F.... 620 231-2424
Pittsburg *(G-9916)*

GRATINGS: Open Steel Flooring

Southwest Stl Fabrication LLC ....E.... 913 422-5500
Bonner Springs *(G-573)*

GREASES: Lubricating

Capital City Oil Inc ....E.... 785 233-8008
Topeka *(G-12428)*

GREETING CARDS WHOLESALERS

DCI Studios ....F.... 913 385-9550
Prairie Village *(G-10026)*

GRINDING SVC: Precision, Commercial Or Indl

Quality Tool Service Inc ....F.... 316 265-0048
Wichita *(G-15387)*
Sharpening Specialists LLC ....E.... 316 945-0593
Wichita *(G-15575)*

GROCERIES WHOLESALERS, NEC

American Bottling Company ....C.... 913 894-6777
Lenexa *(G-5645)*
Manildra Milling Corporation ....F.... 913 362-0777
Leawood *(G-5464)*
P-Americas LLC ....B.... 913 791-3000
Olathe *(G-7970)*
Thai Binh Supermarket ....F.... 316 838-8882
Wichita *(G-15755)*

GROCERIES, GENERAL LINE WHOLESALERS

Allied Sales and Marketing Inc ....F.... 316 617-2160
Wichita *(G-13674)*
American Fun Food Company Inc ....F.... 316 838-9329
Park City *(G-9600)*
Arts Mexican Products Inc ....F.... 913 371-2163
Kansas City *(G-3820)*

Cosentino Group Inc ....E.... 913 749-1500
Prairie Village *(G-10022)*
Dgs-Re LLC ....E.... 913 288-1000
Kansas City *(G-3971)*
Dillon Companies Inc ....D.... 620 275-0151
Garden City *(G-2148)*
Earp Meat Company ....C.... 913 287-3311
Edwardsville *(G-1497)*
Great Western Dining Svc Inc ....F.... 620 792-9224
Great Bend *(G-2585)*
Kms Inc ....E.... 316 264-8833
Wichita *(G-14868)*
McLane Foodservice Inc ....C.... 913 422-6100
Lenexa *(G-5992)*
Pallucca and Sons ....F.... 620 231-7700
Frontenac *(G-2062)*
Streeter Enterprises LLC ....F.... 785 537-0100
Manhattan *(G-6815)*
Sysco Corporation ....E.... 913 829-5555
Olathe *(G-8091)*
Sysco Kansas City Inc ....A.... 913 829-5555
Olathe *(G-8092)*

GROUP DAY CARE CENTER

Angel Little Learning Ctr Inc ....E.... 913 724-4442
Basehor *(G-372)*
Atchison Child Care Assn ....F.... 913 367-6441
Atchison *(G-207)*
Bugs Early Learning Ctr I ....F.... 913 254-0088
Olathe *(G-7565)*
Building Blocks Child Care Ctr ....F.... 620 767-8029
Council Grove *(G-1158)*
Building Blocks Child Dev Ctr ....E.... 913 888-7244
Shawnee Mission *(G-11191)*
Care A Lot Daycare ....F.... 785 628-2563
Hays *(G-2764)*
Childrens Center LLC ....F.... 913 432-5114
Roeland Park *(G-10220)*
Clay County Child Care Ctr Inc ....E.... 785 632-2195
Clay Center *(G-853)*
Community Day Care Center 1 ....E.... 620 275-5757
Garden City *(G-2130)*
Country Kids Day Care Inc ....E.... 913 888-9400
Shawnee Mission *(G-11269)*
Cradle To Cryons Childcare Ctr ....F.... 620 345-2390
Moundridge *(G-7181)*
Crazy Girls LLC ....F.... 913 495-9797
Lenexa *(G-5791)*
Emporia Community Daycare Ctr ....F.... 620 343-2888
Emporia *(G-1737)*
Good Shepherd Child Care Ctr ....F.... 620 429-4611
Columbus *(G-1076)*
Grace United Methodist Church ....E.... 913 859-0111
Olathe *(G-7738)*
Grannys ....E.... 913 837-5222
Louisburg *(G-6451)*
Great Bend Child Day Care Assn ....F.... 620 792-2421
Great Bend *(G-2573)*
Hadley Day Care Ctr Inc ....E.... 620 663-9622
Hutchinson *(G-3307)*
Happy House Day Care ....F.... 913 782-1115
Olathe *(G-7751)*
Jack Jill Prschl-Extended Care ....F.... 913 682-1222
Leavenworth *(G-5255)*
Kansas Association of Child ....E.... 785 823-3343
Salina *(G-10562)*
Kid Stop LLC ....F.... 913 422-9999
Shawnee *(G-10981)*
Kidcare Connection Inc ....E.... 316 944-6434
Wichita *(G-14856)*
Kiddi Kollege Inc ....F.... 913 814-7770
Overland Park *(G-8917)*
Kiddi Kollege Inc ....E.... 913 764-4423
Olathe *(G-7836)*
Kiddi Kollege Inc ....F.... 913 788-7060
Kansas City *(G-4175)*
Kiddi Kollege Inc ....E.... 913 649-4747
Shawnee Mission *(G-11530)*
Kiddi Kollege Inc ....F.... 913 780-0246
Olathe *(G-7837)*
Kids First Day Care Preschool ....E.... 620 231-4994
Frontenac *(G-2057)*
Kids Kampus ....E.... 620 241-8499
Mcpherson *(G-6983)*
Kindercare Education LLC ....F.... 913 631-6910
Shawnee Mission *(G-11531)*
Kindercare Education LLC ....F.... 316 721-0168
Wichita *(G-14858)*
Kindercare Education LLC ....E.... 316 733-2066
Andover *(G-99)*
Kindercare Education LLC ....F.... 316 684-4574
Wichita *(G-14859)*
Kindercare Education LLC ....F.... 316 775-7503
Augusta *(G-331)*
Kindercare Learning Ctrs LLC ....F.... 316 733-2066
Andover *(G-100)*
Kindercare Learning Ctrs LLC ....E.... 913 402-1024
Shawnee Mission *(G-11532)*
Kindercare Learning Ctrs LLC ....F.... 913 727-6267
Lansing *(G-4677)*
Kindercare Learning Ctrs LLC ....F.... 316 788-5925
Derby *(G-1256)*
Kindercare Learning Ctrs LLC ....F.... 913 492-3221
Shawnee Mission *(G-11533)*
Kindercare Learning Ctrs LLC ....F.... 785 539-7540
Manhattan *(G-6699)*
Kindercare Learning Ctrs LLC ....E.... 913 451-6066
Shawnee Mission *(G-11534)*
Learn & Grow Childcare Center ....F.... 316 777-0355
Mulvane *(G-7219)*
Little Bldg Blocks Daycare LLC ....F.... 913 856-5633
Gardner *(G-2354)*
Loving Arms Daycare Ctrs Inc ....F.... 785 238-2767
Junction City *(G-3722)*
Manhattan Day Care & Lrng Ctr ....F.... 785 776-5071
Manhattan *(G-6721)*
Mini Adventures ....F.... 913 334-6008
Kansas City *(G-4262)*
Munchkin Village ....F.... 620 577-2440
Independence *(G-3542)*
New Day Educare ....F.... 913 764-1353
Olathe *(G-7917)*
Shining Stars Daycare Center ....E.... 913 829-5000
Olathe *(G-8063)*
St Michaels Day School Inc ....E.... 913 432-1174
Shawnee Mission *(G-11890)*
Sunshine Day Care LLC ....F.... 620 221-1177
Winfield *(G-16176)*
Swansons Streamway Dog P ....F.... 913 422-8242
Shawnee Mission *(G-11915)*
Tender Hearts Inc ....F.... 913 962-2200
Shawnee Mission *(G-11925)*
Tender Hearts Inc ....F.... 913 788-2273
Kansas City *(G-4463)*
Todays Tomorrows Lrng Ctr LLC ....F.... 888 602-1815
Mulvane *(G-7228)*
Tree House Learning Center ....F.... 316 773-3335
Wichita *(G-15796)*
Womens Community Y ....F.... 913 682-6404
Leavenworth *(G-5308)*

GROUP FOSTER HOME

Creative Community Living S ....B.... 620 221-1119
Winfield *(G-16136)*
Saint Francis Cmnty Svcs Inc ....C.... 785 587-8818
Manhattan *(G-6796)*
Saint Francis Cmnty Svcs Inc ....D.... 785 243-4215
Concordia *(G-1128)*
Twin Vly Dvelopmental Svcs Inc ....E.... 785 353-2347
Beattie *(G-421)*
Twin Vly Dvelopmental Svcs Inc ....E.... 785 353-2347
Beattie *(G-422)*
Twin Vly Dvelopmental Svcs Inc ....F.... 785 353-2226
Beattie *(G-423)*

GROUP HOSPITALIZATION PLANS

United Omaha Life Insurance Co ....E.... 913 402-1191
Shawnee Mission *(G-11963)*

GUARD PROTECTIVE SVCS

Civil Air Patrol Inc ....E.... 620 275-6121
Garden City *(G-2127)*
Kansas State University ....E.... 785 532-6412
Manhattan *(G-6691)*

GUARD SVCS

Alert 360 ....C.... 913 599-3439
Lenexa *(G-5639)*
American Sentry Security Sys ....E.... 785 232-1525
Topeka *(G-12323)*
First State Bnk of St Charles ....F.... 913 469-5400
Leawood *(G-5404)*
Fishnet Security ....F.... 816 701-3315
Leawood *(G-5405)*
Free State Security Svcs LLC ....F.... 785 843-7073
Shawnee Mission *(G-11380)*
Security Portfolio X LP ....F.... 316 634-1115
Wichita *(G-15543)*
Williams Investigation & SEC ....E.... 620 275-1134
Garden City *(G-2315)*

GUIDED MISSILES/SPACE VEHICLE PARTS/AUX EQPT: Research/Devel

Torotel Products Inc ....C.... 913 747-6111
Olathe *(G-8116)*

GUN STOCKS: Wood

Bell and Carlson Incorporated ....E.... 620 225-6688
Dodge City *(G-1306)*

GUTTERS

Preferred Seamless Guttering ....G.... 620 663-7600
Hutchinson *(G-3414)*

GYMNASTICS INSTRUCTION

Acrobatic Acadmy Ftns/Educ Ctr ....E.... 316 721-2230
Wichita *(G-13608)*
Byrds Dance & Gymnastics Inc ....E.... 913 788-9792
Kansas City *(G-3883)*
Capital Area Gymnstics Emprium ....F.... 785 266-4151
Topeka *(G-12424)*
County of Johnson ....C.... 913 403-8069
Shawnee Mission *(G-11273)*
Diamond Gymnstics Dnce Academy ....E.... 913 851-7500
Stilwell *(G-12144)*
Emerald City Gymnastics Inc ....E.... 913 438-4444
Overland Park *(G-8678)*
Folgers Gymnastics Inc ....F.... 316 733-7525
Wichita *(G-14401)*
K D Sullivan Investments LLC ....F.... 785 460-0170
Colby *(G-1018)*
Kansas Gymnastics & Dance Ctr ....E.... 913 764-8282
Olathe *(G-7829)*
Lawrence Gymnastics Academy ....E.... 785 865-0856
Lawrence *(G-4968)*
Raeanns Fancy Footwork ....F.... 316 788-4499
Derby *(G-1267)*
Wichita Gymnastics Club Inc ....F.... 316 634-1900
Wichita *(G-16003)*

GYPSUM MINING

National Gympson ....F.... 620 248-3247
Sun City *(G-12217)*
New Ngc Inc ....C.... 620 886-5613
Medicine Lodge *(G-7069)*

GYPSUM PRDTS

Certainteed Gypsum Mfg Inc ....G.... 785 762-2994
Junction City *(G-3679)*
Georgia-Pacific LLC ....C.... 785 363-7767
Blue Rapids *(G-536)*

HAIR REPLACEMENT & WEAVING SVCS

Hair Club For Men Ltd Inc ....F.... 888 888-8986
Overland Park *(G-8783)*
Svetas Body Therapy LLC ....F.... 316 630-0400
Wichita *(G-15706)*

HAIRDRESSERS

All In Cut ....F.... 316 722-4962
Wichita *(G-13664)*
Beauty Brands LLC ....E.... 816 531-2266
Lenexa *(G-5695)*
Bijin For Hair ....D.... 913 671-7777
Shawnee Mission *(G-11165)*
Chez Belle ....F.... 316 682-7323
Wichita *(G-14003)*
Creative Hairlines Inc ....E.... 620 241-3535
McPherson *(G-6953)*
Executive Hills Style Shop ....F.... 913 451-1204
Shawnee Mission *(G-11355)*
First Class Hair ....F.... 316 721-2662
Wichita *(G-14373)*
Hair Affaire ....F.... 785 827-0445
Salina *(G-10529)*
Hair Experts ....E.... 785 776-4455
Manhattan *(G-6650)*
Hair Productions Inc ....F.... 785 273-2881
Topeka *(G-12658)*
Hair Shop & Retailing Center ....E.... 913 397-9888
Olathe *(G-7745)*
Hair Shop West Inc ....E.... 913 829-4868
Olathe *(G-7746)*

Hair Wear and Co .... F 785 625-2875
Hays (G-2824)
Karen Tobin .... F 913 341-1976
Shawnee Mission (G-11520)
Keith Shaw .... F 316 262-7297
Wichita (G-14841)
Krizmans Beauty Salons Inc .... F 913 648-6080
Prairie Village (G-10043)
Lulu Salon & Spa .... F 913 648-3658
Shawnee Mission (G-11583)
Mane Event .... F 785 827-1999
Salina (G-10590)
Mane Thing .... E 785 762-2397
Junction City (G-3723)
Oliver P Steinnagel Inc .... E 913 338-2266
Shawnee Mission (G-11696)
Perfect Touch Inc .... F 316 522-9205
Wichita (G-15281)
Salon Avanti .... F 913 829-2424
Olathe (G-8051)
Styling Studios .... E 913 685-8800
Shawnee Mission (G-11904)

HAND TOOLS, NEC: Wholesalers

Harbor Freight Tools Usa Inc .... F 316 269-2779
Wichita (G-14559)
Kc Tool LLC .... F 913 440-9766
Olathe (G-7833)
Mid Kansas Tool & Electric Inc .... F 785 825-9521
Salina (G-10600)

HANDBAGS: Women's

Too Cute Totes .... G 775 423-5907
Lenexa (G-6184)

HANDYMAN SVCS

Dick Construction Inc .... F 620 275-1806
Garden City (G-2147)

HANGARS & OTHER AIRCRAFT STORAGE FACILITIES

Emerald Aerospace Holdings LLC .... D 316 440-6966
Wichita (G-14274)

HARDWARE

Elec-Tron Inc .... D 316 522-3401
Wichita (G-14263)
Kmi Inc .... E 316 777-0146
Mulvane (G-7217)
Niece Products of Kansas Inc .... E 620 223-0340
Fort Scott (G-1994)
Vektek LLC .... C 620 342-7637
Emporia (G-1845)

HARDWARE & BUILDING PRDTS: Plastic

Balco Inc .... C 800 767-0082
Wichita (G-13798)
Etco Specialty Products Inc .... E 620 724-6463
Girard (G-2403)

HARDWARE STORES

Ackerman Supply Inc .... F 785 738-5733
Beloit (G-469)
Alternative Building Tech .... F 913 856-4536
Gardner (G-2325)
Bartels Inc .... F 316 755-1853
Valley Center (G-13336)
Berry Companies Inc .... E 316 838-3321
Wichita (G-13833)
Diebolt LLC .... E 620 496-2222
Iola (G-3598)
Dodge City Cooperative Exch .... E 620 225-4193
Dodge City (G-1344)
Gibson Products Co Salina Inc .... E 785 827-4474
Salina (G-10510)
Gibsons Ace Hardware .... E 785 632-3147
Clay Center (G-865)
Healy Cooperative Elevator Co .... E 620 398-2211
Healy (G-2966)
High Reach Equipment LLC .... F 316 942-5438
Wichita (G-14605)
Kanza Cooperative Association .... E 316 444-2141
Andale (G-78)
Newtons Inc .... F 620 336-2276
Cherryvale (G-811)
Orscheln Farm and Home LLC .... D 620 583-5043
Eureka (G-1897)
Orscheln Farm and Home LLC .... F 620 241-0707
McPherson (G-7012)
Orscheln Farm and Home LLC .... F 620 331-2551
Independence (G-3546)
Orscheln Farm and Home LLC .... F 785 825-1681
Salina (G-10624)
Orscheln Farm and Home LLC .... F 620 442-5760
Arkansas City (G-168)
Orscheln Farm and Home LLC .... F 785 762-4411
Junction City (G-3734)
Orscheln Farm and Home LLC .... F 913 367-2261
Atchison (G-254)
Orscheln Farm and Home LLC .... E 620 421-0555
Parsons (G-9715)
Orscheln Farm and Home LLC .... F 620 662-8867
Hutchinson (G-3397)
Orscheln Farm and Home LLC .... F 620 251-2950
Coffeyville (G-968)
Orscheln Farm and Home LLC .... F 785 838-3184
Lawrence (G-5050)
Orscheln Farm and Home LLC .... E 785 776-1476
Manhattan (G-6766)
Orscheln Farm and Home LLC .... F 316 321-4004
El Dorado (G-1589)
Orscheln Farm and Home LLC .... F 785 625-7316
Hays (G-2884)
Orscheln Farm and Home LLC .... E 785 242-3133
Ottawa (G-8296)
Orscheln Farm and Home LLC .... F 785 228-9688
Topeka (G-12955)
Piqua Farmers Coop Assn Incthe .... F 620 468-2535
Piqua (G-9801)
Quality Homes Inc .... E 402 248-6218
Summerfield (G-12216)
Skaggs Inc .... E 620 672-5312
Pratt (G-10148)
Suther Building Supply Inc .... F 785 336-2255
Seneca (G-10883)
Two-Bee Inc .... F 785 364-2162
Holton (G-3113)
Ulysses Standard Supply Inc .... F 620 356-4171
Ulysses (G-13327)
Waters Inc .... E 785 822-6540
Salina (G-10760)
Waters Inc .... E 620 343-2800
Emporia (G-1849)
Waters Inc .... E 785 537-1340
Manhattan (G-6847)
Waters Inc .... E 785 238-3114
Junction City (G-3767)
Waters Inc .... E 620 227-2900
Dodge City (G-1451)
Wurth/Service Supply Inc .... F 316 869-2159
Wichita (G-16078)

HARDWARE STORES: Builders'

J & S Tool and Fastener Inc .... F 913 677-2000
Kansas City (G-4114)
Locks & Pulls Inc .... F 913 381-1335
Overland Park (G-8967)
Rueschhoff Communications .... E 785 841-0111
Lawrence (G-5098)

HARDWARE STORES: Pumps & Pumping Eqpt

McCullough Enterprises Inc .... F 316 942-8118
Wichita (G-15024)
Robinson Supply LLC .... G 620 251-0490
Coffeyville (G-973)
Stenner Sales Company .... G 913 768-4114
New Century (G-7300)

HARDWARE STORES: Tools

Harbor Freight Tools Usa Inc .... F 316 269-2779
Wichita (G-14559)
Orscheln Farm and Home LLC .... F 620 930-3276
Medicine Lodge (G-7071)
Sharpening Specialists LLC .... E 316 945-0593
Wichita (G-15575)
Tractor Supply Company .... F 785 827-3300
Salina (G-10738)
Tractor Supply Company .... F 620 663-7607
Hutchinson (G-3465)
Woodcraft Supply LLC .... G 913 599-2800
Shawnee Mission (G-12016)

HARDWARE STORES: Tools, Power

Kuhn Co LLC .... E 316 788-6500
Derby (G-1257)
Patchen Electric & Indus Sup .... G 785 843-4522
Lawrence (G-5057)
Richmond Electric Inc .... G 316 264-2344
Wichita (G-15457)

HARDWARE WHOLESALERS

Blish-Mize Co .... C 913 367-1250
Atchison (G-218)
Bruna Brothers Implement LLC .... E 785 325-2232
Washington (G-13461)
CBS Manhattan LLC .... F 785 537-4935
Manhattan (G-6579)
Indian Hills Hardware Inc .... E 785 841-1479
Lawrence (G-4911)
Print Source Inc .... D 316 945-7052
Wichita (G-15348)
T W Lacy & Associates Inc .... F 913 706-7625
Prairie Village (G-10073)
Tsr LLC .... F 316 946-1527
Wichita (G-15814)
Wesco Aircraft Hardware Corp .... C 316 315-1200
Wichita (G-15949)

HARDWARE, WHOLESALE: Bolts

Nifast Corporation .... F 913 888-9344
Lenexa (G-6024)

HARDWARE, WHOLESALE: Builders', NEC

Blish-Mize Co .... E 913 367-1250
Atchison (G-217)
Engineered Door Products Inc .... F 316 267-1984
Wichita (G-14288)
Frank Colladay Hardware Co .... F 620 663-4477
Hutchinson (G-3292)
Locks & Pulls Inc .... F 913 381-1335
Overland Park (G-8967)

HARDWARE, WHOLESALE: Nuts

Infinity Fasteners Inc .... E 913 438-8547
Lenexa (G-5914)

HARDWARE, WHOLESALE: Power Tools & Access

Overland Tool & Machinery Inc .... E 913 599-4044
Shawnee (G-11007)
WW Grainger Inc .... E 913 492-8550
Lenexa (G-6237)

HARDWARE, WHOLESALE: Security Devices, Locks

Smallwood Lock Supply Inc .... F 913 371-5678
Kansas City (G-4425)

HARDWARE: Aircraft

Koehn Machine Inc .... G 316 282-2298
Newton (G-7372)
Mac Fasteners Inc .... E 785 242-2538
Ottawa (G-8287)

HARDWARE: Aircraft & Marine, Incl Pulleys & Similar Items

North American Aviation Inc .... E 316 744-6450
Park City (G-9639)

HARDWARE: Builders'

Dormakaba USA Inc .... F 913 831-3001
Kansas City (G-3975)
Dormakaba USA Inc .... G 316 267-6891
Wichita (G-14229)

HARNESS ASSEMBLIES: Cable & Wire

Anderson Industries Inc .... F 316 945-4488
Wichita (G-13705)
Celltron Inc .... B 620 783-1333
Galena (G-2070)
Electrex Inc .... C 620 662-4866
Hutchinson (G-3276)
Electronic Contrls Assembly Co .... G 913 780-0036
Olathe (G-7675)

Quality Intrcnnect Systems Inc ....E....... 620 783-5087
Galena *(G-2081)*
S and Y Industries Inc ....C....... 620 221-4001
Winfield *(G-16171)*

HARVESTING MACHINERY & EQPT WHOLESALERS

Bill Harmon ....E....... 620 275-9597
Garden City *(G-2110)*
Mikes Equipment Company ....F....... 620 543-2535
Buhler *(G-618)*
Quality Power Products Inc ....G....... 785 263-0060
Solomon *(G-12052)*

HEAD START CENTER, EXC IN CONJUNCTION WITH SCHOOL

Augusta Head Start ....F....... 316 775-3421
Augusta *(G-306)*
Child Start Inc ....E....... 316 522-8677
Wichita *(G-14006)*
Child Start Inc ....B....... 316 682-1853
Wichita *(G-14007)*
Child Start Inc ....D....... 316 682-1853
Wichita *(G-14008)*
Clay County Child Care Ctr Inc ....F....... 785 632-5399
Clay Center *(G-854)*
Community Child Care Center ....E....... 620 421-6550
Parsons *(G-9676)*
Community Childrens Center Inc ....F....... 785 842-2515
Lawrence *(G-4803)*
Dodge Cy Unified Schl Dst 443 ....D....... 620 227-1614
Dodge City *(G-1354)*
Early Chldhood Cnnection/Pre K ....E....... 785 726-2413
Ellis *(G-1642)*
Early Head Start Clay County ....F....... 877 688-5454
Clay Center *(G-861)*
Early Headstart Cmnty Action ....D....... 785 266-3152
Topeka *(G-12567)*
East Central Kansas Economic ....E....... 913 294-4880
Paola *(G-9554)*
Growing Futures Early Educ ....E....... 913 649-6057
Overland Park *(G-8780)*
Kansas Childrens Service Leag ....D....... 316 942-4261
Wichita *(G-14792)*
Kansas Childrens Service Leag ....F....... 785 274-3800
Topeka *(G-12765)*
Nek Cap Inc ....F....... 785 364-4798
Holton *(G-3107)*
Nek Cap Inc ....E....... 785 742-2222
Hiawatha *(G-3019)*
Nek Cap Inc ....F....... 913 367-7848
Atchison *(G-251)*
Nek Cap Inc ....F....... 913 651-5692
Leavenworth *(G-5276)*
Nek Cap Inc ....F....... 785 456-9165
Wamego *(G-13430)*
Southeast Kansas Community ....F....... 620 365-7189
Iola *(G-3634)*
Southeast Kansas Community ....F....... 620 795-2102
Oswego *(G-8236)*

HEALTH & ALLIED SERVICES, NEC

Center For Woman Hlth Wichita ....F....... 316 634-0060
Wichita *(G-13974)*
Ctr Imprvmnt Hmn Fnctnng Int ....E....... 316 682-3100
Wichita *(G-14140)*
Defy Medical Group LLC ....F....... 913 396-2888
Overland Park *(G-8647)*
Home Health Agency ....F....... 785 826-6600
Salina *(G-10546)*
Johnson Cnty Dept Hlth & Envmt ....D....... 913 826-1200
Olathe *(G-7813)*
Kansas Medical Assoc Inc ....F....... 316 733-4747
Andover *(G-97)*
Kdhe Ber Attn R Avila ....E....... 785 291-3121
Topeka *(G-12814)*
Maple Hills Healthcare Inc ....E....... 913 383-2001
Overland Park *(G-8985)*
Ncs Healthcare of Kansas LLC ....E....... 316 522-3449
Wichita *(G-15156)*
Rolling Hills Health and Rehab ....C....... 316 722-6916
Wichita *(G-15480)*
Sandhill Orthopaedic ....F....... 620 624-7400
Liberal *(G-6362)*
Tanglewood Hlth Rehabilitation ....E....... 785 273-0886
Topeka *(G-13139)*
Via Christi ....F....... 316 613-4931
Wichita *(G-15879)*

Wolters Kluwer Health Inc ....F....... 316 612-5000
Wichita *(G-16062)*

HEALTH & WELFARE COUNCIL

Alzheimrs Dsease Rltd Dsordrs ....F....... 913 381-3888
Shawnee Mission *(G-11100)*
Children & Family Services ....D....... 785 296-4653
Topeka *(G-12464)*
City of Wichita ....E....... 316 268-8351
Wichita *(G-14028)*
Economic & Empolyment Support ....D....... 785 296-4276
Topeka *(G-12570)*
Health Partnership Clinic Inc ....E....... 913 433-7583
Olathe *(G-7760)*
National Rural Health Assn ....F....... 913 220-2997
Leawood *(G-5500)*

HEALTH AIDS: Vaporizers

Splintek Inc ....E....... 816 531-1900
Lenexa *(G-6148)*

HEALTH CLUBS

24 Hour Fitness Usa Inc ....E....... 913 338-2442
Overland Park *(G-8329)*
24 Hour Fitness Usa Inc ....E....... 913 248-0724
Shawnee Mission *(G-11058)*
24 Hour Fitness Usa Inc ....E....... 913 829-4503
Olathe *(G-7501)*
Fit Physique ....E....... 316 721-2230
Wichita *(G-14379)*
Fitness Plus More LLC ....F....... 913 383-2636
Overland Park *(G-8725)*
Genesis Health Club Inc ....E....... 316 721-8938
Wichita *(G-14457)*
Genesis Health Club Inc ....E....... 316 945-8331
Wichita *(G-14458)*
Genesis Health Club Inc ....F....... 620 663-9090
Hutchinson *(G-3298)*
Genesis Hlth Clubs Emporia LLC ....B....... 620 343-6034
Emporia *(G-1761)*
Hartzler Lorenda ....E....... 785 749-2424
Lawrence *(G-4891)*
Healthridge Fitness Center LLC ....C....... 913 888-0656
Olathe *(G-7761)*
Hoover Bachman & Assoc Inc ....F....... 620 342-2348
Emporia *(G-1774)*
Life Time Fitness Inc ....C....... 913 492-4781
Lenexa *(G-5971)*
Life Time Fitness Inc ....C....... 913 239-9000
Overland Park *(G-8958)*
Maximus Fitness and Wellness ....F....... 785 232-3133
Topeka *(G-12867)*
Prairie Lf Ctr of Overland Pk ....F....... 913 764-5444
Olathe *(G-7998)*
Prairie Lf Ctr of Overland Pk ....E....... 913 648-8077
Overland Park *(G-9177)*
Quivira Athletic Club L C ....D....... 913 268-3633
Lenexa *(G-6086)*
Wood Valley Racquet Club Inc ....E....... 785 506-8928
Topeka *(G-13250)*
Young Mens Christian Associat ....C....... 316 685-2251
Wichita *(G-16096)*

HEALTH INSURANCE CARRIERS

Bcbsks ....E....... 785 291-7498
Topeka *(G-12367)*
Blue Cross Blue Sheld Kans Inc ....A....... 785 291-7000
Topeka *(G-12390)*
Healthcare Alliance Group LLC ....F....... 913 956-2080
Lenexa *(G-5894)*
Kammco Health Solutions Inc ....F....... 800 435-2104
Topeka *(G-12753)*
Kansas Medical Mutual Insur Co ....E....... 785 232-2224
Topeka *(G-12790)*
Rx Power ....E....... 913 696-0691
Shawnee Mission *(G-11817)*
United Omaha Life Insurance Co ....E....... 913 402-1191
Shawnee Mission *(G-11963)*

HEALTH MAINTENANCE ORGANIZATION: Insurance Only

Centene Corporation ....D....... 913 599-3078
Lenexa *(G-5738)*
Coventry Health Care Kans Inc ....C....... 800 969-3343
Overland Park *(G-8606)*
Coventry Health Care Kans Inc ....F....... 316 634-1222
Wichita *(G-14117)*

Humana Inc ....E....... 316 612-6820
Wichita *(G-14651)*
Humana Inc ....E....... 913 217-3300
Overland Park *(G-8834)*
Sunflower State Hlth Plan Inc ....C....... 877 644-4623
Overland Park *(G-9374)*
United Healthcare Services Inc ....D....... 888 340-9716
Overland Park *(G-9443)*
Unitedhealth Group Inc ....E....... 952 936-1300
Overland Park *(G-9445)*

HEALTH PRACTITIONERS' OFFICES, NEC

Dr Vernon Rowe ....E....... 913 894-1500
Lenexa *(G-5824)*
Edward J Lind II ....E....... 316 788-6963
Derby *(G-1242)*
Michael R Magee ....E....... 913 339-6551
Shawnee Mission *(G-11623)*

HEALTH SCREENING SVCS

Assured Occupational Solutions ....F....... 316 321-3313
El Dorado *(G-1530)*
Coliseum Imging Ventures I LLC ....F....... 913 338-3344
Overland Park *(G-8576)*
County of Geary ....E....... 785 762-5788
Junction City *(G-3684)*
Examinetics Inc ....C....... 913 748-2000
Overland Park *(G-8698)*
Examone World Wide Inc ....E....... 913 888-1770
Lenexa *(G-5840)*
Health Partnership Clinic Inc ....E....... 913 433-7583
Olathe *(G-7760)*
Marc A Asher Md Comprehensi ....E....... 913 945-9800
Overland Park *(G-8986)*

HEALTH SYSTEMS AGENCY

Compresults LLC ....F....... 913 310-9800
Fairway *(G-1906)*
County of Jefferson ....E....... 785 863-2447
Oskaloosa *(G-8222)*
Destiny Supports Inc ....F....... 620 272-0564
Garden City *(G-2146)*
Developmental Svcs NW Kans ....F....... 785 735-2262
Victoria *(G-13373)*
Heart To Heart Intl Inc ....E....... 913 764-5200
Lenexa *(G-5895)*
L & C Home Health Agency Inc ....F....... 785 465-7444
Colby *(G-1022)*
Quest Services Inc ....C....... 620 208-6180
Emporia *(G-1814)*
Southwind Hospice Inc ....F....... 620 672-7553
Pratt *(G-10152)*

HEARING AID REPAIR SVCS

Audiology Consultants Inc ....F....... 785 823-3761
Salina *(G-10412)*

HEARING TESTING SVCS

Central State Services ....F....... 316 613-3989
Wichita *(G-13986)*

HEAT TREATING SALTS

Kissner Group Holdings LP ....G....... 913 713-0600
Overland Park *(G-8920)*

HEAT TREATING: Metal

Bodycote Thermal Proc Inc ....E....... 316 943-3288
Wichita *(G-13862)*
Bodycote Thermal Proc Inc ....E....... 316 267-6264
Wichita *(G-13863)*
Ferroloy Inc ....E....... 316 838-0897
Wichita *(G-14358)*
Metal Finishing Company Inc ....E....... 620 326-7655
Wellington *(G-13516)*

HEATING & AIR CONDITIONING EQPT & SPLYS WHOLESALERS

Commercial Fltr Svc Knsas Cty ....G....... 913 384-5858
Kansas City *(G-3929)*
Daikin Applied Americas Inc ....F....... 913 492-8885
Shawnee Mission *(G-11290)*
Foley Group Inc ....F....... 913 342-3336
Kansas City *(G-4014)*
Goodman Manufacturing Co LP ....B....... 316 946-9145
Wichita *(G-14483)*

J M OConnor Inc ....F 913 438-7867
Shawnee Mission (G-11477)
Knipp Equipment Inc ....E 316 265-9655
Wichita (G-14871)
Lennox Industries Inc ....E 913 339-9993
Shawnee Mission (G-11564)
OConnor Company Inc ....E 316 267-2246
Wichita (G-15208)
Sandifer Engrg & Contrls Inc ....E 316 794-8880
Wichita (G-15516)
Style Crest Inc ....F 316 832-6303
Wichita (G-15678)
Washer Specialties Company ....E 316 263-8179
Wichita (G-15930)

HEATING & AIR CONDITIONING UNITS, COMBINATION

ABB Installation Products Inc ....D 913 755-3181
Osawatomie (G-8191)
Airxcel Inc ....B 316 832-3400
Wichita (G-13656)
Dunco Inc ....F 785 594-7137
Lawrence (G-4842)

HEATING APPARATUS: Steam

A/C Enterprises Inc ....G 620 767-5695
Council Grove (G-1157)

HEATING EQPT & SPLYS

Airtex Manufacturing Lllp ....C 913 583-3181
De Soto (G-1192)
Ernstings Incorporated ....G 620 564-2793
Ellinwood (G-1631)
Jorban-Riscoe Associates Inc ....E 913 438-1244
Lenexa (G-5932)
Kansas City Deaerator Inc ....F 913 312-5800
Overland Park (G-8894)
Vornado Air LLC ....D 316 733-0035
Andover (G-115)
Webster Combustion Tech LLC ....D 620 221-7464
Winfield (G-16179)

HEATING EQPT: Complete

Evcon Holdings Inc ....E 316 832-6300
Wichita (G-14311)

HEATING EQPT: Induction

MSI Automation Inc ....F 316 681-3566
Bel Aire (G-436)

HEATING SYSTEMS: Radiant, Indl Process

Heatron Inc ....C 913 651-4420
Leavenworth (G-5252)

HELP SUPPLY SERVICES

Advantage Tech Inc ....D 913 888-5050
Overland Park (G-8352)
APS Staffing Services Inc ....F 913 327-7605
Overland Park (G-8391)
Career Athletes LLC ....E 913 538-6259
Lenexa (G-5729)
Kleeb Services Inc ....F 913 253-7000
Overland Park (G-8922)
Kwik Staff LLC ....F 785 430-5806
Topeka (G-12825)
Manchester Inc ....F 913 262-0440
Overland Park (G-8983)
Squadbuilders Inc ....D 913 649-4401
Leawood (G-5559)
Starfire Enterprises Inc ....F 785 842-1111
Lawrence (G-5121)
Tdb Communications Inc ....C 913 327-7400
Lenexa (G-6168)
Team International Inc ....F 913 681-0740
Overland Park (G-9397)
Volt Management Corp ....D 913 906-9568
Overland Park (G-9471)
Yoh Services LLC ....F 913 648-4004
Overland Park (G-9518)

HELPING HAND SVCS, INCLUDING BIG BROTHER, ETC

Kansas Big Bros Big Ssters Inc ....D 316 263-3300
Wichita (G-14787)
Kansas Big Bros Big Ssters Inc ....F 785 843-7359
Lawrence (G-4931)
Kansas Big Bros Big Ssters Inc ....F 620 421-0472
Parsons (G-9695)

HIGHWAY & STREET MAINTENANCE SVCS

City of Liberal ....E 620 626-0135
Liberal (G-6292)
City of Overland Park ....E 913 895-6040
Overland Park (G-8556)
City of Topeka ....D 785 295-3803
Topeka (G-12474)
County of Dickinson ....F 785 263-3193
Abilene (G-21)
County of Kiowa ....F 620 723-2531
Greensburg (G-2673)
County of Labette ....E 620 784-5391
Altamont (G-72)
County of Morton ....E 620 593-4288
Elkhart (G-1618)
County of Russell ....E 785 483-4032
Russell (G-10270)
County of Sedgwick ....E 316 685-2035
Wichita (G-14112)
County of Stevens ....E 620 544-8782
Hugoton (G-3154)
Dustrol Inc ....D 316 536-2262
Towanda (G-13264)
Kansas Department Trnsp ....D 785 672-3113
Oakley (G-7478)
Kansas Department Trnsp ....B 785 823-3754
Salina (G-10564)
Kansas Department Trnsp ....D 620 583-5661
Eureka (G-1893)
Kansas Department Trnsp ....C 316 744-1271
Wichita (G-14796)
Ness County Engineers Office ....E 785 798-3350
Ness City (G-7264)
Recycling Enterprises Inc ....F 316 536-2262
Towanda (G-13266)
Surface Protection Svcs LLC ....F 316 322-5135
El Dorado (G-1606)
Wyandtte Cnty Unfied Gvernment ....E 913 573-8300
Kansas City (G-4554)

HIGHWAY BRIDGE OPERATION

County of Kingman ....F 620 532-5241
Kingman (G-4588)

HISTORICAL SOCIETY

American Overseas Schools Hist ....E 316 265-6837
Wichita (G-13693)
Burlingame Historical Preserva ....D 785 654-3561
Burlingame (G-622)
Douglas County Historical Soc ....F 785 841-4109
Lawrence (G-4840)
Executive Office of Kansas ....F 785 272-8681
Topeka (G-12587)
Historic Presrvtn Aliance of W ....D 316 269-9432
Wichita (G-14617)
Kansas Genealogical Socie ....E 620 225-1951
Dodge City (G-1386)
Kansas State Historical Soc ....F 785 272-8681
Topeka (G-12807)
Sunflower Chapter of The Ameri ....F 785 656-0329
Hays (G-2915)

HOBBY, TOY & GAME STORES: Arts & Crafts & Splys

D J Inc ....F 785 667-4651
Assaria (G-200)

HOBBY, TOY & GAME STORES: Ceramics Splys

Evans Industries Inc ....G 316 262-2551
Wichita (G-14310)

HOBBY, TOY & GAME STORES: Children's Toys & Games, Exc Dolls

U S Toy Co Inc ....E 913 642-8247
Leawood (G-5587)

HOBBY, TOY & GAME STORES: Dolls & Access

Doll Cradle ....F 913 631-1900
Shawnee Mission (G-11313)

HOBBY, TOY & GAME STORES: Toys & Games

Bruces Woodworks LLC ....F 913 441-1432
Bonner Springs (G-543)

HOLDING COMPANIES, NEC

Eldridge Holding LLC ....F 785 749-5011
Lawrence (G-4849)
Giant Kfn Holding Company LLC ....E 785 362-2532
Holton (G-3092)
Northwest Centre LLC ....F 316 262-3331
Wichita (G-15195)
Spoon Creek Holdings LLC ....F 913 375-2275
Olathe (G-8078)

HOLDING COMPANIES: Banks

Coronado Inc ....F 620 278-2161
Sterling (G-12115)
Cunningham Agency Inc ....F 913 795-2212
Mound City (G-7170)
First Nat Bncshres of Fredonia ....F 620 378-2151
Fredonia (G-2032)
Hnb Corporation ....D 620 442-4040
Arkansas City (G-160)
Holyrood Bancshares Inc ....F 785 252-3239
Holyrood (G-3116)
Intrust Financial Corporation ....E 316 383-1111
Wichita (G-14727)
Johnson State Bankshares Inc ....F 620 492-6200
Johnson (G-3657)
Peabody State Bancorp Inc ....F 620 983-2810
Peabody (G-9761)
Republic Bancshares Inc ....F 785 483-2300
Russell (G-10288)
Wheatland Investments Inc ....F 620 465-2225
Haven (G-2738)

HOLDING COMPANIES: Investment, Exc Banks

Beechcraft Holdings LLC ....E 316 676-7111
Wichita (G-13826)
Frontier Farm Credit Aca ....C 785 776-6955
Manhattan (G-6641)
Gjo Holdings Inc ....E 913 621-6611
Kansas City (G-4036)
Great Plains Ventures Inc ....F 316 684-1540
Wichita (G-14505)
Koch Business Holdings LLC ....F 316 828-8943
Wichita (G-14873)
M R Imaging Center LP ....F 316 268-6742
Wichita (G-14993)
Mariner Wealth Advisors LLC ....E 913 904-5700
Overland Park (G-8991)
Mtc Holding Corporation ....F 913 319-0300
Overland Park (G-9060)
Nations Holding Company ....E 913 383-8185
Prairie Village (G-10050)
Prairie Band LLC ....F 785 364-2463
Holton (G-3109)
Tech Investments III LLC ....D 816 674-9993
Mission Hills (G-7149)

HOLDING COMPANIES: Personal, Exc Banks

Bicknell Family Holding Co LLC ....E 913 387-2743
Overland Park (G-8447)
Developers and Management Inc ....E 316 682-6770
Wichita (G-14202)
EBY Group Inc ....A 913 782-3200
Olathe (G-7668)
Mrv Holding Company ....F 785 272-1398
Topeka (G-12918)
R L Dial Co Inc ....B 316 721-0108
Wichita (G-15404)

HOME CENTER STORES

Home Depot USA Inc ....C 913 789-8899
Merriam (G-7095)
Home Depot USA Inc ....F 785 217-2260
Topeka (G-12700)

Home Depot USA Inc ....C.... 316 681-0899
Wichita *(G-14628)*
Home Depot USA Inc ....C.... 316 773-1988
Wichita *(G-14629)*
Home Depot USA Inc ....C.... 785 749-2074
Lawrence *(G-4900)*
Home Depot USA Inc ....D.... 620 275-5943
Garden City *(G-2197)*
Home Depot USA Inc ....C.... 785 272-5949
Topeka *(G-12701)*
Home Depot USA Inc ....C.... 913 648-7811
Shawnee Mission *(G-11438)*
Lowes Home Centers LLC ....C.... 913 631-3003
Shawnee Mission *(G-11579)*
Lowes Home Centers LLC ....C.... 316 773-1800
Wichita *(G-14982)*
Lowes Home Centers LLC ....C.... 785 452-9303
Salina *(G-10585)*
Lowes Home Centers LLC ....C.... 620 513-2000
Hutchinson *(G-3359)*
Lowes Home Centers LLC ....C.... 316 684-3117
Wichita *(G-14983)*
Lowes Home Centers LLC ....C.... 913 397-7070
Olathe *(G-7866)*
Lowes Home Centers LLC ....C.... 785 273-0888
Topeka *(G-12852)*
Lowes Home Centers LLC ....C.... 316 206-0000
Derby *(G-1259)*
Lowes Home Centers LLC ....C.... 913 328-7170
Kansas City *(G-4207)*
Lowes Home Centers LLC ....C.... 913 261-1040
Roeland Park *(G-10227)*
Lowes Home Centers LLC ....C.... 316 206-1030
Wichita *(G-14984)*

HOME ENTERTAINMENT EQPT: Electronic, NEC

T & M Electronics ....G.... 785 537-1455
Manhattan *(G-6819)*

HOME FOR THE DESTITUTE

Cherished Friends LLC ....F.... 620 326-3700
Wellington *(G-13495)*

HOME FOR THE MENTALLY HANDICAPPED

Applewood Rehabilation Inc ....E.... 620 431-7300
Altoona *(G-75)*
Community Living Opportunities ....F.... 913 341-9316
Overland Park *(G-8582)*
Community Lving Opprtnties Inc ....E.... 913 499-8894
Overland Park *(G-8583)*
Community Lving Opprtnties Inc ....E.... 785 979-1889
Baldwin City *(G-357)*
Community Lving Opprtnties Inc ....E.... 913 341-9316
Lenexa *(G-5777)*
Community Lving Opprtnties Inc ....C.... 785 865-5520
Lawrence *(G-4804)*
Community Lving Opprtnties Inc ....F.... 785 832-2332
Lawrence *(G-4805)*
Community Lving Opprtnties Inc ....E.... 785 843-7072
Lawrence *(G-4806)*
Faith Village Inc ....D.... 913 856-4607
Gardner *(G-2343)*
Faith Village Inc ....D.... 913 906-5000
Olathe *(G-7701)*
Lakeside Terrace ....E.... 785 284-0005
Sabetha *(G-10315)*
Northview Developmental Svcs ....F.... 316 283-5170
Newton *(G-7400)*
RES-Care Kansas Inc ....D.... 620 793-8501
Great Bend *(G-2631)*
Tri-Valley Developmental Svcs ....D.... 620 223-3990
Fort Scott *(G-2012)*
Tri-Valley Developmental Svcs ....D.... 620 365-3307
Iola *(G-3637)*
Twin Rivers Developmental Supp ....D.... 620 402-6395
Arkansas City *(G-183)*

HOME FOR THE MENTALLY RETARDED

Kansas Dept For Aging & Disabi ....B.... 785 296-5389
Topeka *(G-12769)*
Lakemary Center Inc ....E.... 913 768-6831
Olathe *(G-7853)*

HOME FOR THE MENTALLY RETARDED, EXC SKILLED OR INTERMEDIATE

4-B Properties LLC ....E.... 785 364-4643
Holton *(G-3083)*
Applewood Rehabilation Inc ....E.... 620 431-7300
Altoona *(G-75)*
Community Lving Opprtnties Inc ....F.... 785 832-2332
Lawrence *(G-4805)*
Community Lving Opprtnties Inc ....E.... 785 843-7072
Lawrence *(G-4806)*
Developmental Svcs NW Kans Inc ....E.... 785 625-5678
Hays *(G-2785)*
Developmental Svcs NW Kans Inc ....C.... 785 625-2521
Hays *(G-2786)*
Developmental Svcs NW Kans Inc ....F.... 785 877-5154
Norton *(G-7443)*
Developmental Svcs NW Kans Inc ....F.... 785 483-3020
Russell *(G-10272)*
Faith Village Inc ....D.... 913 906-5000
Olathe *(G-7701)*
Lakemary Center Homes Inc ....F.... 913 557-4000
Paola *(G-9569)*
Martin Luther Homes Kansas Inc ....D.... 620 229-8702
Winfield *(G-16156)*
Mosaic ....E.... 785 472-4081
Ellsworth *(G-1679)*
Sheltered Living Inc ....E.... 785 233-2566
Topeka *(G-13068)*
Sheltered Living Inc ....F.... 785 266-8686
Topeka *(G-13069)*
Sunflower Supports Company ....C.... 785 267-3093
Topeka *(G-13122)*

HOME FOR THE PHYSICALLY HANDICAPPED

Big Lkes Developmental Ctr Inc ....D.... 785 776-9201
Manhattan *(G-6558)*
Futures Unlimited Inc ....E.... 620 326-8906
Wellington *(G-13501)*
Help Housing Corporation ....D.... 913 651-6810
Leavenworth *(G-5253)*
Twin Vly Dvelopmental Svcs Inc ....F.... 785 747-2611
Greenleaf *(G-2670)*

HOME FURNISHINGS WHOLESALERS

Crawford Supply Co ....F.... 785 434-4631
Plainville *(G-9984)*
Frank Colladay Hardware Co ....F.... 620 663-4477
Hutchinson *(G-3292)*
Interstate Flooring LLC ....C.... 913 573-0600
Kansas City *(G-4110)*
Sysco Kansas City Inc ....E.... 316 942-4205
Wichita *(G-15711)*

HOME HEALTH CARE SVCS

Aberdeen Village Inc ....E.... 913 599-6100
Olathe *(G-7507)*
Accessible Home Care ....F.... 785 493-0340
Salina *(G-10390)*
Adult Health Services Inc ....C.... 913 788-9896
Kansas City *(G-3786)*
Advanced Homecare MGT Inc ....E.... 620 662-9238
Hutchinson *(G-3193)*
Advoctes For Bhavioral Hlth PA ....F.... 316 630-8444
Wichita *(G-13632)*
Alegria Living & Healthcare ....D.... 785 665-7124
Overbrook *(G-8322)*
All Saints Home Care Inc ....F.... 316 755-1076
Wichita *(G-13665)*
Angel Arms ....F.... 620 241-1074
McPherson *(G-6936)*
Apria Healthcare LLC ....E.... 316 283-1936
Newton *(G-7310)*
APS Staffing Services Inc ....F.... 913 327-7605
Overland Park *(G-8391)*
Arbuthnots Inc ....E.... 785 527-2146
Belleville *(G-450)*
Archdiocese Kansas Cy In Kans ....E.... 913 621-5090
Kansas City *(G-3816)*
Arj Infusion Services Inc ....E.... 913 451-8804
Lenexa *(G-5661)*
Ascend Mdia Med Healthcare LLC ....F.... 913 469-1110
Overland Park *(G-8399)*
Ascension Via Christi ....F.... 620 231-3088
Pittsburg *(G-9812)*
Assisted Transportation Svcs ....F.... 785 291-2900
Topeka *(G-12342)*
Associated Homecare Inc ....C.... 316 320-0473
El Dorado *(G-1529)*
At Home Assisted Care ....E.... 785 473-7007
Wamego *(G-13403)*
At Home Assisted Care Inc ....F.... 785 473-7007
Manhattan *(G-6550)*
At Home Support Care Inc ....E.... 620 341-9350
Emporia *(G-1696)*
Axelacare Holdings Inc ....C.... 877 342-9352
Lenexa *(G-5678)*
Barber County Home Health Agcy ....F.... 620 886-3775
Medicine Lodge *(G-7057)*
Brookdale Snior Lving Cmmnties ....F.... 785 263-7800
Abilene *(G-18)*
C&L Management LLC ....E.... 913 851-4800
Overland Park *(G-8504)*
Caldwell Communicare ....D.... 620 845-6492
Caldwell *(G-656)*
Care 4 U Inc ....E.... 620 223-1411
Girard *(G-2395)*
Carecentrix Inc ....D.... 913 749-5600
Overland Park *(G-8515)*
Caregivers of KS Inc ....F.... 785 354-0767
Topeka *(G-12447)*
Caring Compassionate Care LLC ....F.... 785 215-8127
Topeka *(G-12450)*
Carondelet Home Care Services ....E.... 913 529-4800
Shawnee *(G-10924)*
Childrens Mercy Home Care ....E.... 913 696-8999
Kansas City *(G-3910)*
Childrens Mercy Hospital ....D.... 913 696-8000
Shawnee Mission *(G-11221)*
Choicecare LLC ....D.... 913 906-9880
Lenexa *(G-5754)*
Coffey County Hospital ....E.... 620 364-8861
Burlington *(G-629)*
Comforcare Senior Services ....E.... 913 906-9880
Lenexa *(G-5771)*
Comfort Keepers ....E.... 785 215-8330
Topeka *(G-12488)*
Community Healthcare Sys Inc ....C.... 785 889-4274
Onaga *(G-8173)*
Community Works Inc ....C.... 913 789-9900
Shawnee Mission *(G-11254)*
Compassionate Care Community ....E.... 785 783-8785
Topeka *(G-12495)*
Complete Home Health Care Inc ....F.... 316 260-5012
Wichita *(G-14080)*
County of Clay ....E.... 785 632-3193
Clay Center *(G-859)*
County of Kiowa ....D.... 620 723-3341
Greensburg *(G-2674)*
County of Saline ....F.... 785 826-6606
Salina *(G-10465)*
County of Sumner ....E.... 316 262-2686
Wellington *(G-13496)*
Craig Homecare ....E.... 785 798-4821
Ness City *(G-7258)*
Diversified Family Svcs LLC ....D.... 316 269-3368
Wichita *(G-14215)*
Dodge Cy Healthcare Group LLC ....F.... 620 225-8401
Dodge City *(G-1353)*
Enhanced Home Care LLC ....F.... 913 327-0000
Overland Park *(G-8682)*
Frax ....F.... 888 987-3729
Wichita *(G-14414)*
Garden Vly Retirement Vlg LLC ....C.... 620 275-9651
Garden City *(G-2184)*
Genoa Healthcare Kansas LLC ....F.... 785 783-0209
Topeka *(G-12634)*
Gentiva Health Services Inc ....A.... 913 814-2800
Overland Park *(G-8753)*
Golden Livingcenter Wellington ....F.... 620 326-7437
Wellington *(G-13506)*
Great Plains Ellinwood Inc ....E.... 620 564-2548
Ellinwood *(G-1634)*
Hand In Hand & Hospice ....F.... 620 340-6177
Emporia *(G-1766)*
Hands 2 Help ....D.... 785 832-2515
Lawrence *(G-4887)*
Harris Healthcare LLC ....F.... 316 721-4828
Wichita *(G-14564)*
Health In Sync Home Inc ....E.... 316 295-4692
Wichita *(G-14576)*
Health Management of Kansas ....D.... 620 431-7474
Chanute *(G-731)*
Health Management of Kansas ....D.... 620 251-1866
Coffeyville *(G-944)*
Health Management of Kansas ....D.... 620 429-3803
Columbus *(G-1078)*

Healthback of Wichita.................F 316 687-0340
Wichita *(G-14577)*
Heartland HM Hlth & Hospice PA ....D....... 316 788-7626
Wichita *(G-14584)*
Heartland Hospice Services LLC..........F 913 362-0044
Leawood *(G-5425)*
Heartland Hospice Services LLC..........E 785 271-6500
Topeka *(G-12679)*
Home Health Agency Hosp Dst............F 620 724-8469
Girard *(G-2412)*
Home Instead Senior Care ....E 316 612-7541
Wichita *(G-14631)*
Home Instead Senior Care ....E 785 272-6101
Topeka *(G-12702)*
Hospice Incorporated.........................D....... 316 265-9441
Wichita *(G-14637)*
Hospice of Graham County...................C 785 421-2121
Hill City *(G-3035)*
Hospice Preferred Choice Inc...............E 785 840-0820
Lawrence *(G-4903)*
Hospital District 1 of Dcknsn...............F 785 263-6630
Abilene *(G-39)*
Independence Inc...............................E 785 841-0333
Lawrence *(G-4910)*
Individual Support Systems Inc ....D....... 785 228-9443
Topeka *(G-12720)*
Infusion LLC.......................................F 316 686-1610
Wichita *(G-14693)*
Inspire Hospice LLC ....F 913 521-2727
Overland Park *(G-8854)*
Integral Care Provider Inc....................C....... 913 384-2273
Shawnee Mission *(G-11463)*
Integrated Behavioral Tech Inc.............E 913 662-7071
Basehor *(G-380)*
Integrated Behavioral Tech Inc.............D....... 913 662-7071
Basehor *(G-379)*
Integrity Home Care Inc.......................F 913 685-1616
Overland Park *(G-8855)*
Interim Healthcare Kansas City ....E 913 381-3100
Leawood *(G-5439)*
John Knox Village................................F 913 403-8343
Leawood *(G-5443)*
Kansas Masonic Home..........................C....... 316 269-7500
Wichita *(G-14814)*
Kindred Healthcare Oper LLC...............E 913 906-0522
Overland Park *(G-8919)*
Kuderx LLC..F 785 760-2298
Concordia *(G-1121)*
Lenere LLC...F 785 320-0208
Saint Marys *(G-10371)*
Lifespace Communities Inc ....C....... 913 383-2085
Shawnee Mission *(G-11570)*
Locamp LLC...F 913 287-4400
Kansas City *(G-4206)*
Marlene Schoenberger.........................E 785 625-8189
Ellis *(G-1650)*
Maxim Healthcare Services Inc ....C....... 913 381-8233
Overland Park *(G-8997)*
Medicalodges Inc.................................C....... 620 223-5085
Fort Scott *(G-1984)*
Mercy Home Health..............................F 620 223-8090
Fort Scott *(G-1988)*
MHS Home Health LLC..........................E 913 663-9930
Overland Park *(G-9019)*
Midland Care ....F 785 232-2044
Topeka *(G-12891)*
Midland Care Connection Inc ....C....... 785 232-2044
Topeka *(G-12892)*
Minds Matter LLC.................................F 866 429-6757
Overland Park *(G-9040)*
Missouri Hospice Holdings LLC ....F 913 905-0255
Leawood *(G-5487)*
Moore Enterprises Inc ....C....... 913 451-5900
Overland Park *(G-9052)*
Muve Health LLC..................................F 303 862-9215
Leawood *(G-5493)*
Newman Mem Hosp Foundation ....E 620 340-6161
Emporia *(G-1805)*
Newton William Memorial Hosp.............F 620 221-2916
Winfield *(G-16162)*
North Centl Kans Hm Hlth Agcy ....F 785 738-5175
Beloit *(G-496)*
Norton County Hospital.........................F 785 877-5745
Norton *(G-7459)*
Olathe Medical Center Inc....................E 913 791-4200
Olathe *(G-7940)*
Olathe Medical Center Inc....................E 913 791-4315
Olathe *(G-7941)*
Option Care Enterprises Inc ....E 913 599-3745
Overland Park *(G-9109)*

Peace of Mind......................................F 316 260-7046
Rose Hill *(G-10244)*
Pharmcare Hlth Specialists LLC............F 316 681-2181
Wichita *(G-15290)*
Prestige Home Care of Kansas..............F 913 680-0493
Leavenworth *(G-5279)*
Professional Home Health Svcs ....F 785 625-0055
Hays *(G-2891)*
Professional Orthc & Prosthtc...............E 785 375-7458
Manhattan *(G-6782)*
Progressive Care Prof Hm Care ....E 785 984-2290
Alton *(G-74)*
RES-Care Inc..E 913 281-1161
Kansas City *(G-4371)*
RES-Care Inc..E 620 421-2454
Parsons *(G-9731)*
RES-Care Inc..E 620 793-8501
Great Bend *(G-2630)*
RES-Care Inc..E 620 271-0176
Garden City *(G-2267)*
RES-Care Inc..E 785 899-2322
Goodland *(G-2482)*
RES-Care Inc..E 620 624-5117
Liberal *(G-6360)*
RES-Care Inc..E 316 283-5170
Newton *(G-7410)*
RES-Care Inc..C 620 221-4112
Winfield *(G-16168)*
Rescare Kansas Wichita ....F 316 651-2585
Wichita *(G-15446)*
Rooney Enterprises Corporation ....E 913 325-4770
Overland Park *(G-9257)*
Sacred Heart Home Care......................F 913 299-4515
Kansas City *(G-4395)*
Saint Raphael Home Care Inc...............E 316 269-5400
Wichita *(G-15509)*
Salina Regional Health Ctr Inc..............B 785 452-7000
Salina *(G-10688)*
Sisters Servants of Mary ....E 913 371-3423
Kansas City *(G-4423)*
Sleepcair Inc...E 913 438-8200
Lenexa *(G-6138)*
Sonodora Inc...E 316 494-2218
Wichita *(G-15615)*
Southeast KS AR AG Aging ....D....... 620 431-2980
Chanute *(G-765)*
Southern Care Inc ....E 913 906-9497
Topeka *(G-13081)*
Southview Homecare.............................F 913 837-5121
Louisburg *(G-6467)*
Southwind Hospice Inc ....F 620 672-7553
Pratt *(G-10152)*
Spectrum Health Foundation Inc...........D....... 913 831-2979
Kansas City *(G-4433)*
Spectrum Private Care Services............D....... 913 299-7100
Shawnee *(G-11032)*
St Catherine Hospital...........................F 620 272-2660
Garden City *(G-2287)*
Sunshine Horizons ....F 620 276-1787
Garden City *(G-2294)*
Sunshine Nursing Agency Inc ....E 620 276-8868
Garden City *(G-2295)*
Teakwood Investments LLC..................D....... 913 203-7444
Overland Park *(G-9395)*
There Is No Place Like Home................F 316 721-6001
Wichita *(G-15758)*
Thoughtful Care Inc...............................F 816 256-8200
Prairie Village *(G-10075)*
Trinity In-Home Care Inc.......................C....... 785 842-3159
Lawrence *(G-5146)*
True Home Care LLC ....E 316 776-4685
Wichita *(G-15808)*
Vintage Park At Tonganoxie LLC...........E 913 845-2204
Tonganoxie *(G-12272)*
Visiting Nurses Association...................D....... 785 843-3738
Lawrence *(G-5175)*
Vitalcore Hlth Strategies LLC ....F 785 246-6840
Topeka *(G-13227)*
Vitas Healthcare Corp Midwest ....E 913 722-1631
Overland Park *(G-9468)*
Vitas Healthcare Corporation ....E 913 722-1631
Lenexa *(G-6216)*

HOME IMPROVEMENT & RENOVATION CONTRACTOR AGENCY

Second Hand Enterprises Inc...............F 316 775-7627
Augusta *(G-343)*
Skilled Saws Inc....................................F 785 249-5084
Silver Lake *(G-12028)*

Thermal King Windows Inc....................E 913 451-2300
Shawnee Mission *(G-11928)*

HOMEFURNISHING STORES: Barbeque Grills

Waltons Inc...F 316 262-0651
Wichita *(G-15925)*

HOMEFURNISHING STORES: Cutlery

Dunns Custom Knives Inc ....G....... 785 584-6856
Rossville *(G-10251)*
Phantom Enterprises Inc.......................F 316 264-7070
Newton *(G-7405)*

HOMEFURNISHING STORES: Lighting Fixtures

Accent Lighting Inc...............................F 316 636-1278
Wichita *(G-13601)*
Accurate Electric Inc ....G....... 785 825-4010
Salina *(G-10391)*
Jims Electric Inc....................................F 785 460-2844
Colby *(G-1017)*
Rensen House of Lights Inc..................E 913 888-0888
Lenexa *(G-6103)*
Robert Wilson Co Inc............................E 913 642-1500
Overland Park *(G-9251)*
Western Chandelier Company...............F 913 685-2000
Overland Park *(G-9491)*

HOMEFURNISHING STORES: Mirrors

Olathe Glass Company Inc ....E 913 782-7444
Olathe *(G-7938)*

HOMEFURNISHING STORES: Window Furnishings

Schammerhorn Inc ....G....... 316 265-8659
Wichita *(G-15528)*
Window Flair Draperies ....G....... 913 722-6070
Shawnee *(G-11054)*

HOMEFURNISHING STORES: Window Shades, NEC

Pratt Glass Inc.......................................F 620 672-6463
Pratt *(G-10139)*

HOMEFURNISHINGS & SPLYS, WHOLESALE: Decorative

Home Depot USA Inc ....B 913 871-1221
Overland Park *(G-8824)*

HOMEFURNISHINGS, WHOL: Resilient Floor Coverings, Tile/Sheet

Atlantic Dev Corp of PA.........................F 316 267-2255
Wichita *(G-13762)*
Tile Shop LLC..F 913 631-8453
Shawnee *(G-11040)*

HOMEFURNISHINGS, WHOLESALE: Blinds, Vertical

King Industries Inc................................E 785 823-1785
Salina *(G-10575)*

HOMEFURNISHINGS, WHOLESALE: Carpets

Cap Carpet Inc.......................................E 316 262-3496
Wichita *(G-13936)*
Cap Carpet Inc.......................................F 785 273-1402
Topeka *(G-12422)*
Country Carpet Inc................................F 785 256-4800
Maple Hill *(G-6863)*
Designed Bus Intrors Tpeka Inc............F 785 233-2078
Topeka *(G-12553)*
Gardner Floor Covering Inc ....E 785 266-6220
Topeka *(G-12632)*
Image Flooring LLC ....D....... 314 432-3000
Lenexa *(G-5910)*
Rigdon Floor Coverings Inc...................E 913 362-9829
Kansas City *(G-4378)*
Schammerhorn Inc ....G....... 316 265-8659
Wichita *(G-15528)*

HOMEFURNISHINGS, WHOLESALE: Grills, Barbecue

LAd Global Enterprises Inc.................F 913 768-0888
Olathe *(G-7851)*
Pools Plus.................F 785 823-7665
Salina *(G-10636)*

HOMEFURNISHINGS, WHOLESALE: Kitchenware

Big W Industries Inc.................E 913 321-2112
Kansas City *(G-3860)*
R P Products Inc.................E 913 492-6380
Shawnee Mission *(G-11773)*
William Sonoma Store Inc.................E 316 636-5990
Wichita *(G-16051)*

HOMEFURNISHINGS, WHOLESALE: Mirrors/Pictures, Framed/Unframd

Olathe Glass Company Inc.................E 913 782-7444
Olathe *(G-7938)*
Petty Products Inc.................G 913 782-0028
Olathe *(G-7981)*

HOMEFURNISHINGS, WHOLESALE: Pottery

Ceramic Cafe.................F 913 383-0222
Overland Park *(G-8540)*

HOMEFURNISHINGS, WHOLESALE: Stainless Steel Flatware

Phantom Enterprises Inc.................F 316 264-7070
Newton *(G-7405)*

HOMEFURNISHINGS, WHOLESALE: Window Covering Parts & Access

Mel Stevenson & Associates Inc.................D 913 262-0505
Kansas City *(G-4232)*

HOMEFURNISHINGS, WHOLESALE: Window Shades

Sebring & Co.................F 913 888-8141
Overland Park *(G-9288)*

HOMEFURNISHINGS, WHOLESALE: Wood Flooring

Classic Floors & Design Center.................E 913 780-2171
Overland Park *(G-8561)*

HOMEMAKERS' SVCS

Always There Senior Care Inc.................D 316 946-9222
Wichita *(G-13681)*
D Kohake.................E 785 857-3854
Centralia *(G-698)*

HOMES FOR THE ELDERLY

Ala Operations LLC.................E 785 313-4059
Kansas City *(G-3795)*
American Baptist Estates Inc.................E 316 263-8264
Wichita *(G-13683)*
Atria Senior Living Inc.................E 785 234-6225
Topeka *(G-12353)*
Bickford Overland Park LLC.................E 913 782-3200
Shawnee Mission *(G-11162)*
Brad Carson.................F 620 856-3999
Baxter Springs *(G-400)*
Brandon Woods Retirement Cmnty.................C 785 838-8000
Lawrence *(G-4766)*
Brown Memorial Foundation.................E 785 263-2351
Abilene *(G-19)*
Cedars Inc.................E 620 241-7959
McPherson *(G-6943)*
Chaucer Estates LLC.................D 316 630-8111
Wichita *(G-14000)*
Cherry Vlg Assisted Self-Care.................F 620 793-5765
Great Bend *(G-2539)*
Congregational Home.................C 785 274-3350
Topeka *(G-12501)*
Country Acres Senior Residence.................F 316 773-3900
Wichita *(G-14107)*
Crawford Cnty Assistd Lvng Com.................F 620 724-6760
Girard *(G-2400)*
Dove Estates Senior Living.................E 316 550-6343
Goddard *(G-2436)*
Eagle Estates Inc.................E 620 331-1662
Independence *(G-3513)*
East Orlndo Hlth Rehab Ctr Inc.................D 913 383-9866
Shawnee Mission *(G-11326)*
Eb Group.................E 217 787-9000
Olathe *(G-7666)*
Fountain Villa Inc.................F 620 365-6002
Iola *(G-3602)*
Garden Vly Retirement Vlg LLC.................C 620 275-9651
Garden City *(G-2184)*
Guest Home Estates.................F 620 431-7115
Pittsburg *(G-9869)*
Kearny County Home For Aged.................E 620 355-7836
Lakin *(G-4652)*
Kenwood Plaza Inc.................F 620 549-6133
Saint John *(G-10354)*
Meadowlark Adult Care Home.................E 316 773-2277
Wichita *(G-15030)*
Medical Lodges Inc.................E 620 325-2244
Neodesha *(G-7244)*
Meridian Nursing Center Inc.................D 316 942-8471
Wichita *(G-15041)*
Omega Senior Living LLC.................A 316 260-9494
Wichita *(G-15215)*
Park Meadows Senior Living LLC.................D 913 901-8200
Overland Park *(G-9141)*
Prairie Elder Homes LLC.................F 913 257-5425
Overland Park *(G-9176)*
Prairie Wind Villa Assstant.................F 785 543-6180
Phillipsburg *(G-9795)*
Schowalter Villa.................E 620 327-0400
Hesston *(G-3000)*
Spectrum Retirement Shawnee KS.................E 913 631-0058
Shawnee Mission *(G-11882)*
St Johns Rest Home Inc.................D 785 735-2208
Hays *(G-2910)*
Sunrise Senior Living Inc.................D 913 262-1611
Prairie Village *(G-10070)*
Sunrise Senior Living LLC.................D 913 685-3340
Overland Park *(G-9376)*
Sunrise Senior Living Svcs Inc.................E 913 262-1611
Prairie Village *(G-10071)*
Tri City Assisted Living LLC.................D 913 782-3200
Olathe *(G-8120)*
Vintage Group Inc.................E 316 321-7777
El Dorado *(G-1612)*
Vintage Park At Ottawa LLC.................F 785 242-3715
Ottawa *(G-8320)*
Womens Chldren Shelter Linwood.................D 620 231-0415
Pittsburg *(G-9971)*

HOMES, MODULAR: Wooden

Countryside of Hays Inc.................G 785 625-6539
Hays *(G-2777)*

HOODS: Range, Sheet Metal

Labconco Corporation.................E 620 223-5700
Fort Scott *(G-1980)*
Weis Fire Safety Equip Co Inc.................F 785 825-9527
Salina *(G-10765)*

HOSE: Pneumatic, Rubber Or Rubberized Fabric, NEC

G T Sales & Manufacturing Inc.................D 316 943-2171
Wichita *(G-14434)*

HOSES & BELTING: Rubber & Plastic

HBD Industries Inc.................D 620 431-9100
Chanute *(G-730)*
Nance Manufacturing Inc.................E 316 942-8671
Wichita *(G-15146)*

HOSPITAL BEDS WHOLESALERS

Big Sur Waterbeds Inc.................F 316 944-6225
Wichita *(G-13848)*

HOSPITALS: Cancer

Cancer Center.................E 620 235-7900
Pittsburg *(G-9828)*
Cancer Center of Kansas PA.................F 620 399-1224
Wellington *(G-13494)*
Radiation Oncology.................E 913 588-3600
Kansas City *(G-4358)*

HOSPITALS: Children's

Childrens Hospital Association.................E 913 262-1436
Overland Park *(G-8547)*
Childrens Mercy Hospital.................B 913 234-8683
Olathe *(G-7593)*
Childrens Mercy Specialty Ctr.................D 816 234-3000
Overland Park *(G-8549)*

HOSPITALS: Hospital, Professional Nursing School

West Central Kansas Assn Inc.................C 785 483-3131
Russell *(G-10303)*

HOSPITALS: Maternity

Mary Elizabeth Maternity Home.................F 785 625-6800
Hays *(G-2869)*

HOSPITALS: Medical & Surgical

Adventist Health System/Sunbel.................A 913 676-2163
Shawnee Mission *(G-11081)*
Andover Spine & Health Ctr.................F 316 733-9555
Andover *(G-81)*
Ascension Arizona.................C 316 689-5360
Wichita *(G-13745)*
Ascension Via Christi.................A 620 231-6100
Pittsburg *(G-9811)*
Ascension Via Christi Hospital.................A 316 268-5880
Wichita *(G-13747)*
Ascension Via Christi Hospital.................F 316 721-9500
Wichita *(G-13749)*
Ascension Via Christi Hospital.................A 316 268-5040
Wichita *(G-13752)*
Atchison Hospital Association.................B 913 367-2131
Atchison *(G-209)*
Bob Wilson Mem Grant Cnty Hosp.................C 620 356-1266
Ulysses *(G-13284)*
Cah Acquisition Company 5 LLC.................E 620 947-3114
Hillsboro *(G-3043)*
Central Kansas Medical Center.................B 620 792-2511
Great Bend *(G-2529)*
Central Kansas Medical Center.................F 620 792-8171
Great Bend *(G-2530)*
Cheyenne County Hospital.................D 785 332-2104
Saint Francis *(G-10339)*
Childrens Mercy Hospital.................A 316 500-8900
Wichita *(G-14010)*
Childrens Mercy Hospital.................E 913 287-8800
Kansas City *(G-3911)*
Childrens Mercy Hospital.................E 913 696-5767
Shawnee Mission *(G-11220)*
Childrens Mercy Hospital.................B 913 696-8000
Overland Park *(G-8548)*
Childrens Mercy Hospital.................D 913 696-8000
Shawnee Mission *(G-11221)*
Citizens Medical Center Inc.................B 785 462-7511
Colby *(G-994)*
City of Wamego.................E 785 456-2295
Wamego *(G-13413)*
Clara Barton Hospital.................F 620 653-4191
Hoisington *(G-3060)*
Clara Barton Hospital.................D 620 653-2114
Hoisington *(G-3061)*
Clara Barton Hospital.................D 620 653-2114
Hoisington *(G-3062)*
Clay Center Fmly Physicians PA.................F 785 446-2226
Clyde *(G-905)*
Cloud County Health Center Inc.................C 785 243-1234
Concordia *(G-1106)*
Coffey County Hospital.................C 620 364-5655
Burlington *(G-628)*
Coffey County Hospital.................E 785 733-2744
Waverly *(G-13481)*
Coffey County Hospital.................E 620 364-8861
Burlington *(G-629)*
Coffey County Hospital.................E 620 364-5395
Burlington *(G-630)*
Coffey Health Systems.................D 620 364-5118
Burlington *(G-632)*
Coffeyvlle Rgional Med Ctr Inc.................B 620 251-1200
Coffeyville *(G-924)*
College Park Endoscopy Ctr LLC.................A 913 385-4400
Overland Park *(G-8577)*
Comanche Cnty Hosp Med Clinic.................E 620 582-2144
Coldwater *(G-1052)*
Comanche County.................E 620 582-2144
Coldwater *(G-1055)*
Community Memorial Healthcare.................C 785 562-2311
Marysville *(G-6884)*

Community Memorial Healthcare........F....... 785 363-7202
Blue Rapids *(G-535)*
County of Gove........C....... 785 754-3335
Quinter *(G-10181)*
County of Graham........E....... 785 421-5464
Hill City *(G-3031)*
County of Hamilton........E....... 620 384-7780
Syracuse *(G-12223)*
County of Kiowa........D....... 620 723-3341
Greensburg *(G-2674)*
County of Riley........E....... 785 539-3535
Manhattan *(G-6603)*
County of Sheridan........F....... 785 675-3281
Hoxie *(G-3136)*
County of Sherman........E....... 785 890-3625
Goodland *(G-2467)*
Decatur Health Systems Inc........D....... 785 475-2208
Oberlin *(G-7492)*
Edwards County Hospital........D....... 620 659-2732
Kinsley *(G-4616)*
Ellsworth County Medical Ctr........C....... 785 472-3111
Ellsworth *(G-1670)*
Emporia Physical Therapy........F....... 620 342-4100
Emporia *(G-1742)*
Foundation of Neosho Memorial........E....... 620 431-4000
Chanute *(G-729)*
Fresenius Medical Service........F....... 316 264-3115
Wichita *(G-14423)*
Geary County Hospital........B....... 785 238-4131
Junction City *(G-3694)*
Girard Medical Center........D....... 620 724-7288
Girard *(G-2407)*
Girard Medical Center........D....... 620 724-8291
Girard *(G-2408)*
Great Plains Hlth Aliance Inc........D....... 785 332-2104
Saint Francis *(G-10342)*
Great Plains Hlth Aliance Inc........D....... 785 284-2121
Sabetha *(G-10311)*
Great Plains Kiowa Co Inc........D....... 620 723-3341
Greensburg *(G-2676)*
Great Plains of Sabetha Inc........C....... 785 284-2121
Sabetha *(G-10312)*
Great Plains Smith Co Inc........C....... 785 282-6845
Smith Center *(G-12034)*
Greeley County Health Svcs Inc........C....... 620 376-4221
Tribune *(G-13270)*
Greenwood Cnty Hosp Foundation........C....... 620 583-5909
Eureka *(G-1888)*
Grisell Memorial Hospital Assn........D....... 785 731-2231
Ransom *(G-10193)*
Hamilton County Hospital........D....... 620 384-7461
Syracuse *(G-12227)*
Hanover Hospital & Clinic........D....... 785 337-2214
Hanover *(G-2712)*
Harper Hospital District 5........C....... 620 896-7324
Anthony *(G-127)*
Hays Medical Center Inc........F....... 785 623-5774
Hays *(G-2833)*
Hays Medical Center Inc........A....... 785 623-5000
Hays *(G-2834)*
Hays Medical Center Inc........A....... 785 623-6270
Hays *(G-2835)*
HCA Inc........C....... 620 365-1000
Iola *(G-3608)*
Health Care Inc........A....... 620 665-2000
Hutchinson *(G-3309)*
Heartland Health........A....... 785 985-2211
Troy *(G-13274)*
Hiawatha Hospital Association........F....... 785 742-2161
Hiawatha *(G-3010)*
Hodgeman County Health Center........C....... 620 357-8361
Jetmore *(G-3647)*
Hospital District 1........E....... 620 724-8291
Girard *(G-2413)*
Hospital District 1 Rice Cnty........C....... 620 257-5173
Lyons *(G-6484)*
Hospital District 3 Clark Cnty........D....... 620 635-2241
Ashland *(G-196)*
Hospital Dst 1 Marion Cnty........C....... 620 382-2177
Marion *(G-6873)*
Hospital Dst 1 of Rice Cnty........D....... 620 257-5173
Lyons *(G-6485)*
Hospital Dst 6 Harper Cnty........C....... 620 914-1200
Anthony *(G-128)*
Hutchnson Regional Med Ctr Inc........A....... 620 665-2000
Hutchinson *(G-3331)*
Jefferson County Mem Hosp Inc........D....... 913 774-4340
Winchester *(G-16110)*
Jewell County Hospital........D....... 785 378-3137
Mankato *(G-6859)*
Kansas City Orthoped........C....... 913 338-4100
Leawood *(G-5444)*
Kansas Heart Hospital LLC........C....... 800 574-3278
Wichita *(G-14805)*
Kansas Spine Spcialty Hosp LLC........C....... 316 462-5000
Wichita *(G-14824)*
Kansas Srgery Recovery Ctr LLC........C....... 316 634-0090
Wichita *(G-14825)*
Labette Health Foundation Inc........B....... 620 421-4881
Parsons *(G-9705)*
Labette Health Foundation Inc........F....... 620 922-3838
Coffeyville *(G-954)*
Lane County Hospital........D....... 620 397-5321
Dighton *(G-1287)*
Lawrence Memorial Hospital........E....... 785 505-5000
Lawrence *(G-4973)*
Lawrence Memorial Hospital End........F....... 785 840-3114
Lawrence *(G-4975)*
Lawrence Memorial Hospital End........F....... 785 505-3780
Lawrence *(G-4976)*
Lawrence Memorial Hospital End........A....... 785 505-3315
Lawrence *(G-4974)*
Lincoln County Hospital........D....... 785 524-4403
Lincoln *(G-6383)*
Lindsborg Community Hosp Assn........D....... 785 227-3308
Lindsborg *(G-6400)*
Medicine Lodge Memorial Hosp........C....... 620 886-3771
Medicine Lodge *(G-7067)*
Mercy & Truth Med Missions Inc........F....... 913 248-9965
Kansas City *(G-4235)*
Mercy Health........B....... 620 223-2200
Fort Scott *(G-1986)*
Mercy Hosp Fdn of Independence........F....... 620 331-2200
Independence *(G-3537)*
Mercy Hospital Columbus........F....... 620 429-2545
Columbus *(G-1083)*
Mercy Kansas Communities Inc........B....... 620 223-7075
Fort Scott *(G-1989)*
Mercy Kansas Communities Inc........B....... 620 332-3264
Independence *(G-3539)*
Mercy Kansas Communities Inc........F....... 913 352-8379
Pleasanton *(G-9999)*
Miami County Medical Ctr Inc........C....... 913 294-2327
Paola *(G-9572)*
Midwest Division - Oprmc LLC........A....... 913 541-5000
Shawnee Mission *(G-11632)*
Minneola Hospital District 2........F....... 620 885-4202
Bloom *(G-531)*
Minneola Hospital District 2........D....... 620 885-4238
Minneola *(G-7126)*
Mitchell Count Hospi Healt Sys........B....... 785 738-2266
Beloit *(G-493)*
Morton County Hospital........C....... 620 697-2141
Elkhart *(G-1623)*
Newton Healthcare Corporation........A....... 316 283-2700
Newton *(G-7393)*
Newton William Memorial Hosp........B....... 620 221-2300
Winfield *(G-16163)*
Norton County Hospital........F....... 785 877-3351
Norton *(G-7457)*
Norton County Hospital........F....... 785 877-3305
Norton *(G-7458)*
Norton County Hospital........F....... 785 877-5745
Norton *(G-7459)*
Nueterra Holdings LLC........E....... 785 776-5100
Manhattan *(G-6763)*
Olathe Medical Center Inc........E....... 913 791-4200
Olathe *(G-7940)*
On Call Mobile Therapies LLC........E....... 913 449-1679
Lenexa *(G-6036)*
Ottawa County Health Center........C....... 785 392-2044
Minneapolis *(G-7119)*
Overland Park Reg Med Staff Df........F....... 913 541-5000
Shawnee Mission *(G-11709)*
Overland Park Regional Hosp........E....... 913 541-5406
Overland Park *(G-9121)*
Overland Pk Rgonal Med Ctr Inc........A....... 913 541-0000
Overland Park *(G-9126)*
Phillips County Hospital........D....... 785 543-5226
Phillipsburg *(G-9792)*
Pinnacle Regional Hospital Inc........E....... 913 541-0230
Overland Park *(G-9169)*
Plainville Rural Hospital........C....... 785 434-2622
Plainville *(G-9990)*
Prime Health Servi-Saint John........F....... 913 680-6000
Leavenworth *(G-5280)*
Prime Healthcare Services Inc........A....... 913 596-4000
Kansas City *(G-4337)*
Prime Healthcare Services Inc........E....... 913 651-3542
Leavenworth *(G-5281)*
Promise Hosp Overland Pk Inc........D....... 913 275-5092
Overland Park *(G-9193)*
Providence Medical Center........F....... 913 596-4870
Kansas City *(G-4347)*
Ransom Memorial Hospital Chari........C....... 785 229-8200
Ottawa *(G-8308)*
Ransom Memorial Hospital Chari........B....... 785 229-8200
Ottawa *(G-8309)*
Rawlins County Health Center........D....... 785 626-3211
Atwood *(G-289)*
Resurrection Hospital Physn CL........E....... 785 483-3333
Russell *(G-10289)*
Riverbend Rgnal Hlthcare Fndti........B....... 913 367-2131
Atchison *(G-258)*
Rural Hlth Rsurces Jackson Inc........C....... 785 364-2116
Holton *(G-3110)*
Rush County Memorial Hospital........D....... 785 222-2545
La Crosse *(G-4637)*
Saint Lukes Cushing Hospital........B....... 913 684-1100
Leavenworth *(G-5288)*
Saint Lukes Hosp Garnett Inc........C....... 785 448-3131
Garnett *(G-2388)*
Saint Lukes South Hospital Inc........B....... 913 317-7000
Shawnee Mission *(G-11825)*
Saint Lukes South Hospital Inc........E....... 913 317-7514
Kansas City *(G-4396)*
Salina Regional Health Ctr Inc........A....... 785 452-7000
Salina *(G-10686)*
Salina Regional Health Ctr Inc........B....... 785 452-7000
Salina *(G-10688)*
Salina Regional Health Ctr Inc........D....... 785 452-4850
Salina *(G-10687)*
Salina Surgical Center LLC........D....... 785 827-0610
Salina *(G-10694)*
Satanta District Hosp & Long T........C....... 620 649-2761
Satanta *(G-10790)*
Scott County Hospital Inc........D....... 620 872-5811
Scott City *(G-10833)*
Shawnee Mission Med Ctr Inc........F....... 913 632-9800
Shawnee Mission *(G-11857)*
Shawnee Mission Med Ctr Inc........A....... 913 676-2000
Shawnee Mission *(G-11858)*
Sisters of Charity of Leavenwo........F....... 785 295-7800
Topeka *(G-13073)*
Sisters of Charity of Leavenwo........E....... 785 295-5310
Topeka *(G-13074)*
Sisters of Charity of Leavenwo........E....... 913 825-0500
Kansas City *(G-4422)*
Sisters St Joseph Wichita KS........E....... 316 686-7171
Wichita *(G-15598)*
South Cntl Kans Rgonal Med Ctr........C....... 620 442-2500
Arkansas City *(G-181)*
Southwest Medical Center........E....... 620 624-1651
Liberal *(G-6372)*
St Catherine Hospital........B....... 620 272-2222
Garden City *(G-2288)*
St Catherine Hospital........F....... 620 272-2519
Garden City *(G-2289)*
St Cathrine Hosp Dev Fundation........F....... 620 272-2222
Garden City *(G-2290)*
St Jhns Maude Norton Mem Hosp........D....... 620 429-2545
Columbus *(G-1087)*
St Lukes Health Corporation........C....... 913 250-1244
Lansing *(G-4693)*
Stanton County Hosp Aux Inc........C....... 620 492-6250
Johnson *(G-3662)*
Stevens County Hospital........C....... 620 544-8511
Hugoton *(G-3177)*
Stormont-Vail Healthcare Inc........C....... 785 270-4600
Topeka *(G-13103)*
Stormont-Vail Healthcare Inc........A....... 785 354-6000
Topeka *(G-13104)*
Stormont-Vail Healthcare Inc........B....... 785 584-6705
Rossville *(G-10256)*
Stormont-Vail Healthcare Inc........B....... 785 270-4820
Topeka *(G-13105)*
Stormont-Vail Healthcare Inc........B....... 785 270-8625
Topeka *(G-13106)*
Stormont-Vail Healthcare Inc........B....... 785 863-3417
Oskaloosa *(G-8230)*
Stormont-Vail Healthcare Inc........B....... 785 354-9591
Topeka *(G-13107)*
Stormont-Vail Healthcare Inc........B....... 785 231-1800
Topeka *(G-13108)*
Stormont-Vail Healthcare Inc........B....... 620 343-2900
Emporia *(G-1830)*
Stormont-Vail Healthcare Inc........B....... 785 537-2651
Manhattan *(G-6814)*
Stormont-Vail Healthcare Inc........B....... 785 273-8224
Topeka *(G-13109)*

Stormont-Vail Healthcare Inc...............B....... 785 354-6116
Topeka *(G-13110)*
Stormont-Vail Healthcare Inc...............B....... 785 354-5545
Topeka *(G-13111)*
Stormont-Vail Healthcare Inc...............B....... 785 270-8605
Topeka *(G-13112)*
Stormont-Vail Healthcare Inc...............E....... 785 354-5225
Topeka *(G-13113)*
Stormont-Vail Healthcare Inc...............F....... 785 836-7111
Carbondale *(G-685)*
Stormont-Vail Healthcare Inc...............E....... 785 456-2207
Wamego *(G-13442)*
Sumner County Hospital Dst 1.............D....... 620 845-6492
Caldwell *(G-662)*
Susan B Allen Memorial Hosp.............B....... 316 322-4510
El Dorado *(G-1607)*
Swope Health Services.........................F....... 816 922-7600
Kansas City *(G-4453)*
Taylor Mih Womens Clinic...................F....... 620 431-0340
Chanute *(G-767)*
Thi of Kans At Spclty Hosp LLC...........C....... 913 649-3701
Overland Park *(G-9405)*
Ukhs Great Bend LLC...........................E....... 620 792-8833
Great Bend *(G-2650)*
United States Dept of Army..................B....... 913 684-6000
Fort Leavenworth *(G-1943)*
United States Dept of Army..................A....... 785 239-7000
Fort Riley *(G-1953)*
University of Kansas............................C....... 913 588-5000
Kansas City *(G-4500)*
University of Kansas............................C....... 785 864-2700
Lawrence *(G-5163)*
University of Kansas Hosp Auth..........F....... 913 588-5000
Kansas City *(G-4506)*
University of Kansas Hospital..............C....... 913 588-8400
Shawnee Mission *(G-11968)*
Veterans Health Administration............A....... 785 350-3111
Topeka *(G-13222)*
Via Christi Health Inc...........................F....... 316 268-7000
Wichita *(G-15889)*
Via Christi Hospital...............................D....... 316 796-7000
Wichita *(G-15894)*
Via Chrsti Rhbltation Hosp Inc.............F....... 316 268-8040
Wichita *(G-15902)*
Wamego Hospital Association..............D....... 785 456-2295
Wamego *(G-13451)*
Wesley Medical Center LLC..................E....... 316 858-2610
Wichita *(G-15953)*
Western Plins Rgional Hosp LLC..........B....... 620 225-8400
Dodge City *(G-1456)*
Westley Woodlawn Hosp Emrgncy.......E....... 316 962-2000
Wichita *(G-15962)*
Wichita County Health Center..............D....... 620 375-2233
Leoti *(G-6263)*
Wichita County Health Center..............D....... 620 375-2233
Leoti *(G-6264)*
Wilson County Hospital.........................C....... 620 325-2611
Neodesha *(G-7250)*
Woodich John..E....... 620 332-3280
Independence *(G-3574)*

HOSPITALS: Medical School Affiliated With Nursing

Newman Mem Hosp Foundation...........B....... 620 343-6800
Emporia *(G-1803)*

HOSPITALS: Medical School Affiliated with Residency

HCA Hospital Svcs San Diego..............A....... 316 962-2000
Wichita *(G-14572)*
University of Kansas............................C....... 913 588-5238
Shawnee Mission *(G-11967)*

HOSPITALS: Medical School Affiliation

University of Kansas............................E....... 913 588-5133
Kansas City *(G-4499)*
University of Kansas............................C....... 316 293-2607
Wichita *(G-15856)*
University of Kansas Med Ctr...............F....... 913 588-6311
Kansas City *(G-4508)*
University of Kansas Med Ctr...............F....... 913 588-6805
Kansas City *(G-4509)*

HOSPITALS: Mental Retardation

Alegria Living & Healthcare..................D....... 785 665-7124
Overbrook *(G-8322)*
Golden Oaks Healthcare Inc................D....... 913 788-2100
Kansas City *(G-4039)*
Leisureterrace LLC...............................D....... 773 945-1000
Overland Park *(G-8953)*

HOSPITALS: Mental, Exc For The Mentally Retarded

Kansas Dept For Aging & Disabi..........D....... 913 755-7000
Osawatomie *(G-8195)*
Providence Living Center Inc...............D....... 785 233-0588
Topeka *(G-12993)*
South Cntl Mntal Hlth Cnsling..............E....... 316 321-6036
El Dorado *(G-1604)*
Turner House Clinic Inc........................E....... 913 342-2552
Kansas City *(G-4478)*

HOSPITALS: Orthopedic

Summit Surgical LLC............................E....... 620 663-4800
Hutchinson *(G-3455)*

HOSPITALS: Psychiatric

High Plains Mental Health Ctr...............F....... 785 625-2400
Hays *(G-2847)*
Kansas Dept For Aging & Disabi..........D....... 620 285-2131
Larned *(G-4706)*
Paul W Murphy MD................................E....... 316 686-6303
Wichita *(G-15271)*
Prairie View Inc.....................................B....... 316 284-6400
Newton *(G-7407)*
Prairie View Inc.....................................E....... 620 947-3200
Hillsboro *(G-3055)*
Psychiatric Associates...........................E....... 913 438-8221
Shawnee Mission *(G-11761)*
Stormont-Vail Healthcare Inc...............C....... 785 270-4600
Topeka *(G-13103)*

HOSPITALS: Rehabilitation, Alcoholism

Alcoholics Anonyms Bnnr Sprngs........F....... 913 441-3277
Bonner Springs *(G-539)*
Bills Friends AA Group..........................F....... 913 722-9801
Roeland Park *(G-10218)*
Center For Counseling & Cnsltn...........E....... 620 792-2544
Great Bend *(G-2526)*
Compass Behavioral Health.................E....... 620 227-8566
Dodge City *(G-1329)*
Dccca Inc...E....... 316 265-6011
Wichita *(G-14179)*
Guidance Center....................................E....... 913 367-1593
Atchison *(G-233)*
Mirror Inc...E....... 316 283-6743
Newton *(G-7389)*
New Chance Inc.....................................E....... 620 225-0476
Dodge City *(G-1412)*
Recovery Unlimited Inc..........................F....... 316 941-9948
Wichita *(G-15428)*
Tiyosaye Inc Higher Ground..................F....... 316 262-2060
Wichita *(G-15768)*
Valley Hope Association........................E....... 785 877-2421
Norton *(G-7463)*

HOSPITALS: Rehabilitation, Drug Addiction

A Clear Direction Inc..............................F....... 316 260-9101
Wichita *(G-13586)*
Adolescent Adult Fmly Recovery..........F....... 316 943-2051
Wichita *(G-13614)*
Comcare of Sedgwick County...............F....... 316 660-7550
Wichita *(G-14060)*
Cottonwood Springs LLC.......................F....... 913 353-3000
Olathe *(G-7618)*
Counseling Ctr For Butlr Cnty...............D....... 316 776-2007
El Dorado *(G-1552)*
For Central Kansas Foundation............D....... 785 825-6224
Salina *(G-10504)*
Four Cnty Mental Hlth Ctr Inc................C....... 620 251-8180
Coffeyville *(G-939)*
Horizons Mental Health Ctr Inc.............F....... 620 532-3895
Kingman *(G-4595)*
Livewell Northwest Kansas Inc.............F....... 785 460-8177
Colby *(G-1026)*
Pawnee Mental Health Svcs Inc............E....... 785 587-4344
Manhattan *(G-6770)*
Ralph Bharati MD PA.............................F....... 316 686-7884
Wichita *(G-15413)*
South Central Mntl Hlth CN...................F....... 316 775-5491
Augusta *(G-346)*
Valeo Behavioral Hlth Care Inc.............E....... 785 273-2252
Topeka *(G-13216)*
Valley Hope Association........................E....... 913 367-1618
Atchison *(G-269)*

HOSPITALS: Specialty, NEC

Ascension Via Christi Hospital..............C....... 316 634-3400
Wichita *(G-13751)*
Butler County Health Services..............D....... 316 320-4140
El Dorado *(G-1540)*
Centennial Healthcare Corp..................C....... 913 829-2273
Olathe *(G-7584)*
Childrens Mercy Hospital.......................D....... 913 696-8000
Shawnee Mission *(G-11221)*
Community Mntl Hlth Ctr Crwfd............E....... 620 724-8806
Girard *(G-2397)*
Encompass Health Corporation............D....... 913 649-3701
Shawnee Mission *(G-11337)*
Kansas Heart Hospital LLC...................C....... 800 574-3278
Wichita *(G-14805)*
Kansas Rehabilitation Hospital.............C....... 785 235-6600
Topeka *(G-12800)*
Lee Ann Britian Infant Dev Ctr...............E....... 913 676-2253
Shawnee Mission *(G-11556)*
Mercy Kansas Communities Inc...........B....... 620 223-7075
Fort Scott *(G-1989)*
Meridian Nursing Center Inc..................D....... 316 942-8471
Wichita *(G-15041)*
Parsons State Hosp Trining Ctr.............B....... 620 421-6550
Parsons *(G-9722)*
Sandpiper Healthcare and.....................C....... 316 945-3606
Wichita *(G-15517)*
Topeka Hospital LLC.............................F....... 785 295-8000
Topeka *(G-13177)*
Via Christi Rehabilitation Ctr.................C....... 316 634-3400
Wichita *(G-15896)*
Wesley Rehabilitation Hospital..............C....... 316 729-9999
Wichita *(G-15954)*

HOSPITALS: Substance Abuse

Cypress Recovery Inc...........................F....... 913 764-7555
Olathe *(G-7633)*

HOSTELS

Bethany College....................................D....... 785 227-3380
Lindsborg *(G-6393)*
Gli LLC...F....... 913 648-7858
Overland Park *(G-8757)*

HOT AIR BALLOONS & EQPT DEALERS

Old World Balloonery LLC.....................F....... 913 338-2628
Overland Park *(G-9097)*

HOTEL & MOTEL RESERVATION SVCS

Leisure Hotel Corporation......................E....... 620 275-5900
Garden City *(G-2224)*

HOTEL: Franchised

Apple Eght Hospitality MGT Inc............E....... 913 491-0010
Shawnee Mission *(G-11113)*
Comfort Suites.......................................F....... 620 672-9999
Pratt *(G-10102)*
Derrick Inn..E....... 785 798-3617
Ness City *(G-7261)*
Grand Prairie Ht & Convention..............C....... 620 669-9311
Hutchinson *(G-3303)*
Hpt Trs Ihg-2 Inc....................................F....... 316 634-6070
Wichita *(G-14645)*
Island Hospitality MGT LLC...................E....... 316 631-3773
Wichita *(G-14732)*
Krina Corporation..................................F....... 620 251-1034
Coffeyville *(G-953)*
KS City Marriott Overland Park.............E....... 913 338-8627
Overland Park *(G-8930)*
Lodging Enterprises Inc.........................E....... 620 326-8191
Wellington *(G-13512)*
Minter-Wilson Drilling Co Inc..................F....... 620 276-8269
Garden City *(G-2237)*
Nogales Hotel Company LLC................E....... 785 238-1454
Junction City *(G-3732)*
Paola Inn and Suites..............................F....... 913 294-3700
Paola *(G-9580)*
Swami Investment Inc...........................F....... 913 788-9929
Kansas City *(G-4451)*
Tps Leavenworth Lp..............................E....... 913 297-5400
Leavenworth *(G-5299)*

HOTELS & MOTELS

17th Street Properties LLC ....F.... 785 320-5440
Manhattan *(G-6525)*
Ambassador Hotel Wichita LLC ....E.... 316 239-7100
Wichita *(G-13682)*
Andrea Investments LLC ....E.... 785 823-1739
Salina *(G-10402)*
Beacon Hill Hotel Operator LLC ....F.... 316 260-9088
Wichita *(G-13823)*
Belmont Hotels LLC ....F.... 785 823-6939
Salina *(G-10422)*
Booth Hotel LLC ....F.... 620 331-1704
Independence *(G-3501)*
Bristol Hotel & Resorts Inc ....E.... 785 462-8787
Colby *(G-991)*
Bristol Hotel & Resorts Inc ....D.... 785 823-1739
Salina *(G-10431)*
Broadview Hsptlity Hldings LLC ....D.... 316 262-5000
Wichita *(G-13894)*
Cambridge Suites Hotel ....F.... 316 263-1061
Wichita *(G-13930)*
Candlewood Suites Hotel ....F.... 913 768-8888
Olathe *(G-7574)*
Cobblestoner Inn and Suites ....F.... 620 896-2400
Harper *(G-2717)*
Corporate East LLC ....F.... 620 356-5010
Ulysses *(G-13290)*
Corporate Hills LLC ....C.... 316 651-0333
Wichita *(G-14104)*
Dab of Lenexa KS II LLC ....E.... 913 492-4516
Lenexa *(G-5800)*
Drury Hotels Company LLC ....E.... 316 267-1961
Wichita *(G-14239)*
Drury Hotels Company LLC ....E.... 913 345-1500
Overland Park *(G-8662)*
Drury Hotels Company LLC ....E.... 913 236-9200
Shawnee Mission *(G-11319)*
Eldridge House Invest Ltd Ptnr ....E.... 785 749-5011
Lawrence *(G-4850)*
Extended Stay America ....F.... 316 652-8844
Wichita *(G-14324)*
Farmers Dream Inc ....F.... 785 562-5588
Marysville *(G-6888)*
Flint Hills Hospitality LLC ....F.... 785 320-7995
Manhattan *(G-6634)*
Fossil Creek Hotel & Suites ....E.... 785 483-4200
Russell *(G-10274)*
Four of Wichita Inc ....F.... 316 858-3343
Wichita *(G-14410)*
Grand Central Hotel Corp ....E.... 620 273-6763
Cottonwood Falls *(G-1154)*
Greenwich Hotel LLC ....E.... 316 925-5100
Wichita *(G-14512)*
Hardage Hotels I LLC ....F.... 913 491-3333
Shawnee Mission *(G-11409)*
Hospitality Oakley Group LLC ....F.... 785 671-1111
Oakley *(G-7476)*
Hotel At Old Town Inc ....E.... 316 267-4800
Wichita *(G-14640)*
Hpt Trs Ihg 2 Inc ....F.... 316 942-0400
Wichita *(G-14644)*
Hpt Trs Ihg-2 Inc ....F.... 913 469-5557
Shawnee Mission *(G-11442)*
Janki Inc ....F.... 620 225-7373
Dodge City *(G-1382)*
Merrifield Hotel Associates LP ....E.... 316 681-5100
Wichita *(G-15046)*
Midland Properties Inc ....F.... 913 677-5300
Mission Woods *(G-7151)*
Midwest Star Equities LLC ....F.... 620 225-3000
Dodge City *(G-1406)*
Minter-Wilson Drilling Co Inc ....E.... 620 275-7471
Garden City *(G-2238)*
Mokan Hospitality LLC ....E.... 913 541-9999
Olathe *(G-7907)*
Oak Tree and Pennys Diner ....F.... 785 562-1234
Marysville *(G-6904)*
Pillar Hotels and Resorts LLC ....E.... 785 271-6165
Topeka *(G-12974)*
Regency Midwest Ventures Limit ....E.... 785 273-8888
Topeka *(G-13004)*
Rl Heritage Inn of Kc LLC ....E.... 913 788-5650
Kansas City *(G-4377)*
Ruffin Riverfront Hotel LLC ....D.... 316 293-1234
Wichita *(G-15493)*
Senate Luxury Suites Inc ....F.... 785 233-5050
Topeka *(G-13057)*
Slawson Exploration Co Inc ....E.... 316 263-3201
Wichita *(G-15603)*
Summit Hotel Properties Inc ....E.... 785 826-1711
Salina *(G-10720)*
Sunset Inn ....F.... 316 321-9172
El Dorado *(G-1605)*
Swedish Country Inn ....F.... 785 227-2985
Lindsborg *(G-6406)*
Tucson Hotels LP ....C.... 785 431-7200
Topeka *(G-13201)*
Ventura Hotel Corp ....C.... 785 841-3100
Lawrence *(G-5173)*
Wichita Aloft ....F.... 316 744-1100
Wichita *(G-15972)*
Wichita Inn Suites Inc ....E.... 316 685-2233
Wichita *(G-16008)*
Wichita Residence Assoc LP ....E.... 316 263-1061
Wichita *(G-16020)*
Ww Kc Metcalf LLC ....F.... 913 956-0234
Leawood *(G-5602)*
Wyndham Garden ....F.... 316 269-2090
Wichita *(G-16080)*

HOTLINE

Augusta Crime Stoppers Inc ....E.... 316 775-0055
Augusta *(G-302)*
City of McPherson ....F.... 620 241-1122
McPherson *(G-6950)*
County of Seward ....F.... 620 626-0198
Liberal *(G-6297)*

HOUSEHOLD APPLIANCE REPAIR SVCS

Appliance Doctor Inc ....E.... 316 263-0005
Wichita *(G-13723)*

HOUSEHOLD APPLIANCE STORES

AAA Restaurant Supply LLC ....F.... 316 265-4365
Wichita *(G-13592)*
Bartels Inc ....F.... 316 755-1853
Valley Center *(G-13336)*
Liebert Brothers Electric Co ....F.... 620 251-0299
Coffeyville *(G-956)*
Lowes Home Centers LLC ....C.... 913 631-3003
Shawnee Mission *(G-11579)*
Lowes Home Centers LLC ....C.... 316 773-1800
Wichita *(G-14982)*
Lowes Home Centers LLC ....C.... 785 452-9303
Salina *(G-10585)*
Lowes Home Centers LLC ....C.... 620 513-2000
Hutchinson *(G-3359)*
Lowes Home Centers LLC ....C.... 316 684-3117
Wichita *(G-14983)*
Lowes Home Centers LLC ....C.... 913 397-7070
Olathe *(G-7866)*
Lowes Home Centers LLC ....C.... 785 273-0888
Topeka *(G-12852)*
Lowes Home Centers LLC ....C.... 316 206-0000
Derby *(G-1259)*
Lowes Home Centers LLC ....C.... 913 328-7170
Kansas City *(G-4207)*
Lowes Home Centers LLC ....C.... 913 261-1040
Roeland Park *(G-10227)*
Lowes Home Centers LLC ....C.... 316 206-1030
Wichita *(G-14984)*
Ricks Appliance Service Inc ....F.... 316 265-2866
Wichita *(G-15460)*
Two-Bee Inc ....F.... 785 364-2162
Holton *(G-3113)*
Walmart Inc ....B.... 316 636-5384
Wichita *(G-15924)*

HOUSEHOLD APPLIANCE STORES: Electric

Ott Electric Inc ....F.... 785 562-2641
Marysville *(G-6907)*
Skaggs Inc ....E.... 620 672-5312
Pratt *(G-10148)*

HOUSEHOLD APPLIANCE STORES: Electric Household Appliance, Sm

Mar-Beck Appliance Svc Co Inc ....E.... 913 322-4022
Lenexa *(G-5985)*

HOUSEHOLD APPLIANCE STORES: Electric Household, Major

Bhjllc Inc ....E.... 785 272-8800
Topeka *(G-12379)*
Factory Direct Appliance ....F.... 785 272-8800
Topeka *(G-12592)*
Schnell & Pestinger Inc ....F.... 785 738-3624
Beloit *(G-502)*

HOUSEHOLD APPLIANCE STORES: Fans, Electric

Rensen House of Lights Inc ....E.... 913 888-0888
Lenexa *(G-6103)*
Robert Wilson Co Inc ....E.... 913 642-1500
Overland Park *(G-9251)*

HOUSEHOLD ARTICLES: Metal

Lb Steel LLC ....B.... 785 862-1071
Topeka *(G-12836)*
Sinclair & Sons Custom Welding ....E.... 316 263-3500
Wichita *(G-15597)*

HOUSEHOLD FURNISHINGS, NEC

Golden Star Inc ....D.... 913 874-2178
Atchison *(G-231)*

HOUSEKEEPING & MAID SVCS

CD McCormick & Company Inc ....E.... 913 541-0106
Overland Park *(G-8531)*
Cleaning Authority of Central ....F.... 316 733-7890
Wichita *(G-14041)*
Cottagecare Inc ....F.... 913 469-8778
Overland Park *(G-8603)*
Cs Cleaners Inc ....F.... 785 825-8636
Salina *(G-10469)*
Grace of Wichita Ks LLC ....F.... 316 832-9009
Wichita *(G-14489)*
Have It Maid ....F.... 316 264-0110
Wichita *(G-14568)*
Housekeeping Unlimited ....E.... 785 842-2444
Lawrence *(G-4905)*
Merry Maids 391 ....F.... 785 273-3422
Topeka *(G-12884)*
Merry Maids Ltd Partnership ....E.... 913 403-0813
Overland Park *(G-9012)*
Merry Maids Ltd Partnership ....F.... 785 842-2410
Lawrence *(G-5023)*
Mini Maid Joco Incorporated ....F.... 913 894-2200
Lenexa *(G-6005)*
Residential Services Inc ....E.... 316 832-9058
Wichita *(G-15449)*

HOUSES: Boarding, Fraternity & Sorority

Delta Gamma ....F.... 785 830-9945
Lawrence *(G-4831)*

HOUSES: Fraternity & Sorority

Alpha CHI Omega ....F.... 785 843-7600
Lawrence *(G-4731)*
Beta Theta PHI ....F.... 785 843-9188
Lawrence *(G-4756)*

HOUSES: Fraternity Residential

Masonic Order ....E.... 785 625-3127
Hays *(G-2870)*

HOUSES: Rooming & Boarding

Hutchinson Community College ....F.... 620 665-3500
Hutchinson *(G-3320)*
Visiting Nurses Association ....D.... 785 843-3738
Lawrence *(G-5175)*

HOUSEWARE STORES

Urban Outfitters Inc ....E.... 785 331-2885
Lawrence *(G-5169)*

HOUSEWARES, ELECTRIC: Cooking Appliances

Select Brands Inc ....E.... 913 663-4500
Lenexa *(G-6123)*

HOUSEWARES, ELECTRIC: Fans, Floor

Vornado Air LLC ....D.... 316 733-0035
Andover *(G-115)*

HOUSEWARES, ELECTRIC: Waffle Irons

Big W Industries Inc ....E.... 913 321-2112
Kansas City *(G-3860)*

HOUSEWARES, ELECTRIC: Water Pulsating Devices

City of Topeka ....D 785 368-3851
Topeka *(G-12470)*

HOUSEWARES: Dishes, China

Pioneer - Ram Incorporated ....A 316 685-2266
Wichita *(G-15301)*

HOUSEWARES: Dishes, Plastic

Charloma Inc ....E 620 336-2124
Cherryvale *(G-801)*

HOUSING AUTHORITY OPERATOR

Och Regional Office ....E 913 599-6137
Shawnee Mission *(G-11694)*
Salina Housing Authority ....F 785 827-0441
Salina *(G-10676)*

HUMAN RESOURCE, SOCIAL WORK & WELFARE ADMINISTRATION SVCS

Kansas Department of Labor ....F 913 680-2200
Leavenworth *(G-5260)*
Kansas Dept For Aging & Disabi ....D 913 755-7000
Osawatomie *(G-8195)*
Kansas Dept For Chldren Fmlies ....C 913 651-6200
Leavenworth *(G-5261)*
Kansas Dept For Chldren Fmlies ....C 785 296-1368
Topeka *(G-12771)*
Kansas Dept For Chldren Fmlies ....E 785 296-3237
Topeka *(G-12772)*
Kansas Dept For Chldren Fmlies ....E 913 755-2162
Osawatomie *(G-8197)*
Kansas Dept For Chldren Fmlies ....F 620 241-3802
McPherson *(G-6981)*
Social and Rehabilitation Serv ....D 620 272-5800
Garden City *(G-2283)*

HUMANE SOCIETIES

Allen Cnty Anmal Rscue Fndtion ....F 620 496-3647
La Harpe *(G-4647)*
Caring Hands Humane Society ....F 316 284-0487
Newton *(G-7326)*
Great Plains Spca ....E 913 831-7722
Merriam *(G-7093)*
Helping Hands Humane Society ....E 785 233-7325
Topeka *(G-12683)*
Humane Soc of High Plains ....F 785 625-5252
Hays *(G-2851)*
Kansas Humane Soc Wichita Kans ....F 316 524-9196
Wichita *(G-14806)*
Pawnee County Humane Soc Inc ....F 620 285-8510
Larned *(G-4709)*

HUNTING CAMPS

Show ME Birds Hunting Resort ....F 620 674-8863
Baxter Springs *(G-413)*

HYDRAULIC EQPT REPAIR SVC

B & B Hydraulics Inc ....E 620 662-2552
Hutchinson *(G-3210)*
Herrs Machine ....G 785 325-2875
Washington *(G-13464)*
Kanamak Hydraulics Inc ....E 800 473-5843
Garden City *(G-2212)*
Kansas City Hydraulics Inc ....G 913 371-6151
Kansas City *(G-4145)*
Midway Manufacturing Inc ....E 620 659-3631
Kinsley *(G-4620)*
Northeast Kansas Hydraulics ....G 785 235-0405
Topeka *(G-12936)*

Hard Rubber & Molded Rubber Prdts

T & C Mfg & Operating Inc ....E 620 793-5483
Great Bend *(G-2646)*

ICE

Arctic Glacier Inc ....F 620 275-5751
Garden City *(G-2102)*
Arctic Glacier Texas Inc ....E 316 529-2173
Wichita *(G-13732)*
Berrys Arctic Ice LLC ....F 785 357-4466
Topeka *(G-12376)*
MidAmerican Sales Group ....G 913 689-8505
Overland Park *(G-9029)*
Pepsi Cola Btlg Co of Salina ....D 785 827-7297
Salina *(G-10633)*

ICE MAKING MACHINERY REPAIR SVCS

Ice-Masters Inc ....F 316 945-6900
Wichita *(G-14665)*

ICE WHOLESALERS

John G Levin ....E 785 234-5551
Topeka *(G-12746)*
Rods Food Stores Inc ....E 785 243-2035
Concordia *(G-1127)*

IGNEOUS ROCK: Crushed & Broken

Martin Marietta Materials Inc ....E 316 775-5458
Augusta *(G-334)*
Ngc Industries LLC ....F 620 248-3248
Sun City *(G-12218)*
South West Butler Quarry LLC ....F 316 775-1737
Augusta *(G-347)*

INDEMNITY PLANS HEALTH INSURANCE, EXC MEDICAL SVCS

Streamline Benefits Group LLC ....F 913 744-2900
Lenexa *(G-6155)*

INDL & PERSONAL SVC PAPER WHOLESALERS

Earp Meat Company ....C 913 287-3311
Edwardsville *(G-1497)*
Joe Smith Company ....E 620 231-3610
Pittsburg *(G-9883)*
McLane Company Inc ....E 913 492-7090
Shawnee Mission *(G-11609)*
National Fiber Supply LLC ....F 913 321-0066
Kansas City *(G-4280)*
Northview Development Services ....C 316 281-3213
Newton *(G-7399)*
Q4 Industries LLC ....F 913 894-6240
Overland Park *(G-9205)*
Shaughnsy-Knp-Hw-ppr Co St ....E 913 541-0080
Lenexa *(G-6129)*
Southwest Paper Company Inc ....E 316 838-7755
Wichita *(G-15631)*
Streeter Enterprises LLC ....F 785 537-0100
Manhattan *(G-6815)*
Sunflower Supply Company Inc ....E 620 783-5473
Galena *(G-2088)*
Universal Products Inc ....C 316 794-8601
Goddard *(G-2455)*
Veritiv Operating Company ....D 913 492-5050
Kansas City *(G-4517)*
Veritiv Operating Company ....F 785 862-2233
Topeka *(G-13219)*
Veritiv Operating Company ....E 316 522-3494
Wichita *(G-15874)*
Veritiv Operating Company ....F 620 231-2508
Pittsburg *(G-9955)*

INDL & PERSONAL SVC PAPER, WHOL: Bags, Paper/Disp Plastic

Central Bag Company ....E 913 250-0325
Leavenworth *(G-5215)*
Creative Mktg Unlimited Inc ....G 913 894-0077
Overland Park *(G-8611)*
Drafting Room Inc ....G 316 267-2291
Wichita *(G-14236)*

INDL & PERSONAL SVC PAPER, WHOLESALE: Paperboard & Prdts

Ken OKelly ....G 816 868-6028
Prairie Village *(G-10042)*

INDL & PERSONAL SVC PAPER, WHOLESALE: Press Sensitive Tape

Crown Packaging Corp ....E 913 888-1951
Shawnee Mission *(G-11283)*

INDL & PERSONAL SVC PAPER, WHOLESALE: Shipping Splys

Medina Logistics LLC ....D 785 506-4002
Topeka *(G-12880)*

INDL CONTRACTORS: Exhibit Construction

Display Studios Inc ....E 913 305-5948
Kansas City *(G-3974)*

INDL EQPT CLEANING SVCS

Trimac Industrial Systems LLC ....E 913 441-0043
Bonner Springs *(G-578)*

INDL EQPT SVCS

Adelphi Construction Lc ....D 913 384-5511
Shawnee Mission *(G-11075)*
Invena Corporation ....E 620 583-8630
Eureka *(G-1892)*
Machine Design Services Inc ....G 620 663-4949
South Hutchinson *(G-12060)*
Shannahan Crane & Hoist Inc ....F 816 746-9822
Kansas City *(G-4419)*
Squires Corporation ....F 316 944-0040
Wichita *(G-15650)*
Wes Material Handling Inc ....F 913 369-9375
Tonganoxie *(G-12273)*

INDL GASES WHOLESALERS

Compressed Gases Inc ....F 316 838-3222
Wichita *(G-14082)*
Matheson Tri-Gas Inc ....F 785 537-0395
Manhattan *(G-6734)*

INDL MACHINERY & EQPT WHOLESALERS

Ach Foam Technologies Inc ....D 913 321-4114
Kansas City *(G-3782)*
Asset Lifecycle LLC ....F 785 861-3100
Topeka *(G-12341)*
Associated Air Products Inc ....F 913 894-5600
Lenexa *(G-5670)*
Associated Eqp Sls Co LLC ....F 913 894-4455
Lenexa *(G-5671)*
Baader Linco Inc ....E 913 621-3366
Kansas City *(G-3836)*
Backwoods Equipment Company ....E 316 267-0350
Wichita *(G-13790)*
Berry Companies Inc ....D 316 838-3321
Wichita *(G-13835)*
Berry Companies Inc ....E 316 838-3321
Wichita *(G-13833)*
C W Mill Equipment Co Inc ....E 785 284-3454
Sabetha *(G-10308)*
Continental-Agra Equip Inc ....F 316 283-9602
Newton *(G-7334)*
Ernstmann Machine Co Inc ....G 316 943-5282
Wichita *(G-14303)*
Foley Equipment Company ....D 785 537-2101
Manhattan *(G-6637)*
Foley Industries Inc ....D 316 943-4211
Wichita *(G-14399)*
Fujifilm Sericol USA Inc ....C 913 342-4060
Kansas City *(G-4022)*
General Machinery & Sup Co Inc ....F 620 231-1550
Pittsburg *(G-9865)*
Hughes Machinery Company ....E 913 492-0355
Lenexa *(G-5906)*
Hughes Machinery Company ....G 316 612-0868
Wichita *(G-14649)*
I2 Asia LLC ....F 913 422-1600
Shawnee *(G-10972)*
Invena Corporation ....E 620 583-8630
Eureka *(G-1892)*
Jem International Inc ....F 913 441-4788
Shawnee *(G-10978)*
Kansas Truck Equipment Co Inc ....E 316 722-4291
Wichita *(G-14828)*
Mack McClain & Associates Inc ....F 913 339-6677
Olathe *(G-7871)*
Magnatech Engineering Inc ....G 913 845-3553
Tonganoxie *(G-12265)*
Murdock Companies Inc ....E 316 262-4476
Wichita *(G-15139)*
Murphy Tractor & Eqp Co Inc ....F 785 233-0556
Topeka *(G-12919)*
Northern Tool & Eqp Co Inc ....F 316 854-9422
Wichita *(G-15190)*

P B Hoidale Co Inc ..... F 316 942-1361
Wichita *(G-15250)*
Palmer Johnson Pwr Systems LLC ..... F 913 268-2941
Olathe *(G-7972)*
Pmti Inc ..... E 913 432-7500
Shawnee Mission *(G-11740)*
Praxair Distribution Inc ..... E 913 492-1551
Lenexa *(G-6069)*
Price Bros Equipment Co ..... E 316 265-9577
Wichita *(G-15340)*
Roberts Group Inc ..... G 913 381-3930
Overland Park *(G-9252)*
Salina Vortex Corp ..... C 785 825-7177
Salina *(G-10696)*
Sanden North America Inc ..... A 913 888-6667
Shawnee Mission *(G-11826)*
Sellers Companies Inc ..... E 785 823-6378
Salina *(G-10702)*
Sellers Equipment Inc ..... E 785 823-6378
Salina *(G-10703)*
Sellers Equipment Inc ..... E 316 943-9311
Wichita *(G-15556)*
Voestalpine Nortrak Inc ..... D 316 284-0088
Newton *(G-7424)*
W + D North America Inc ..... E 913 492-9880
Overland Park *(G-9474)*
Weber Manufacturing LLC ..... F 620 251-9800
Coffeyville *(G-985)*
Wes Material Handling Inc ..... F 913 369-9375
Tonganoxie *(G-12273)*
WW Grainger Inc ..... E 316 945-5101
Wichita *(G-16079)*

INDL MACHINERY REPAIR & MAINTENANCE

Accent Erection & Maint Co Inc ..... F 913 371-1600
Kansas City *(G-3780)*
Acsys Lasertechnik US Inc ..... G 847 468-5302
Lenexa *(G-5626)*
Berry Companies Inc ..... E 316 838-3321
Wichita *(G-13833)*
Ernstings Incorporated ..... G 620 564-2793
Ellinwood *(G-1631)*
Exline Inc ..... C 785 825-4683
Salina *(G-10489)*
General Electric Company ..... E 816 244-9672
Overland Park *(G-8751)*
High Plains Machine Works Inc ..... F 785 625-4672
Hays *(G-2845)*
Kansas Forklift Inc ..... F 316 262-1426
Wichita *(G-14802)*
Mame Inc ..... F 620 964-2156
Le Roy *(G-5198)*
Mid-American Machine & Eqp Inc ..... F 620 964-2156
Le Roy *(G-5199)*
Mid-Kansas Cylinder Head Inc ..... F 620 241-6800
McPherson *(G-7004)*
Premier Casting & Machine Svc ..... F 620 241-2040
McPherson *(G-7020)*
Schwabs Tinker Shop Intl Inc ..... G 620 624-7611
Liberal *(G-6363)*
T N T Machine Inc ..... F 316 440-6004
Wichita *(G-15714)*
Thompson Dehydrating Co Inc ..... F 785 272-7722
Topeka *(G-13160)*
Woofter Pump & Well Inc ..... F 785 675-3991
Hoxie *(G-3144)*

INDL PROCESS INSTRUMENTS: Boiler Controls, Power & Marine

Autoflame ..... G 620 229-8048
Wichita *(G-13772)*

INDL PROCESS INSTRUMENTS: Digital Display, Process Variables

Focalpoint Imaging LLC ..... G 620 325-2298
Neodesha *(G-7241)*

INDL PROCESS INSTRUMENTS: Fluidic Devices, Circuit & Systems

National-Spencer Inc ..... E 316 265-5601
Wichita *(G-15154)*

INDL SALTS WHOLESALERS

Clarke Enterprises LLC ..... E 913 601-3830
Kansas City *(G-3917)*

INDL SPLYS WHOLESALERS

Beaver Drill & Tool Company ..... F 913 384-2400
Kansas City *(G-3851)*
Chada Sales Inc ..... F 785 842-1199
Lawrence *(G-4783)*
Crown Packaging Corp ..... E 913 888-1951
Shawnee Mission *(G-11283)*
Fairbank Equipment Inc ..... E 316 943-2247
Wichita *(G-14333)*
Gates Corporation ..... A 620 365-4100
Iola *(G-3603)*
H & P Inc ..... G 785 263-4183
Abilene *(G-36)*
Hajoca Corporation ..... E 316 262-2471
Wichita *(G-14544)*
Ibt Inc ..... C 913 677-3151
Shawnee Mission *(G-11450)*
Inventory Sales Co ..... E 913 371-7002
Kansas City *(G-4111)*
Mem Industrial LLC ..... F 316 944-4400
Wichita *(G-15038)*
Menard Incorporated ..... F 620 364-3600
Burlington *(G-640)*
Mid-America Pump LLC ..... F 913 287-3900
Kansas City *(G-4244)*
O Ring Sales and Service Inc ..... F 913 310-0001
Lenexa *(G-6031)*
Southerncarlson Inc ..... F 316 942-1392
Wichita *(G-15625)*
Westheffer Company Inc ..... E 785 843-1633
Lawrence *(G-5183)*
Wichita Pump & Supply Company ..... F 316 264-8308
Wichita *(G-16019)*
Wilco Inc ..... F 316 943-9379
Wichita *(G-16047)*
WW Grainger Inc ..... E 316 945-5101
Wichita *(G-16079)*

INDL SPLYS, WHOL: Fasteners, Incl Nuts, Bolts, Screws, Etc

Domestic Fastener & Forge Inc ..... F 913 888-9447
New Century *(G-7280)*
Fastenal Company ..... F 316 283-2266
Newton *(G-7344)*
Fastenal Company ..... F 316 320-2223
El Dorado *(G-1561)*
Flinthills Trading Company ..... C 785 392-3017
Minneapolis *(G-7117)*
Supply Technologies LLC ..... E 913 982-4016
Lenexa *(G-6161)*
Wurth/Service Supply Inc ..... F 316 869-2159
Wichita *(G-16078)*

INDL SPLYS, WHOLESALE: Abrasives

Husqvrna Cnstr Pdts N Amer Inc ..... A 913 928-1000
Olathe *(G-7781)*

INDL SPLYS, WHOLESALE: Bearings

Applied Industrial Tech Inc ..... F 785 232-5508
Topeka *(G-12334)*
Headco Industries Inc ..... F 913 831-1444
Kansas City *(G-4072)*
Ibt Inc ..... F 913 428-4958
Kansas City *(G-4093)*
Manko Corporation ..... F 785 825-1301
Salina *(G-10591)*
Motion Industries Inc ..... E 316 265-9608
Wichita *(G-15133)*
Murdock Companies Inc ..... E 316 262-4476
Wichita *(G-15139)*
Timken Company ..... F 913 492-4848
Lenexa *(G-6181)*

INDL SPLYS, WHOLESALE: Bottler Splys

Ragland Specialty Printing ..... E 785 542-3058
Eudora *(G-1879)*

INDL SPLYS, WHOLESALE: Cordage

Great Lakes Polymer Tech LLC ..... E 208 324-2120
Kingman *(G-4593)*

INDL SPLYS, WHOLESALE: Electric Tools

Kc Tool LLC ..... F 913 440-9766
Olathe *(G-7833)*
WW Grainger Inc ..... E 913 492-8550
Lenexa *(G-6237)*

INDL SPLYS, WHOLESALE: Filters, Indl

Air Filter Plus Inc ..... E 785 542-3700
Eudora *(G-1869)*

INDL SPLYS, WHOLESALE: Fittings

Mize & Co Inc ..... E 620 532-3191
Kingman *(G-4607)*

INDL SPLYS, WHOLESALE: Hydraulic & Pneumatic Pistons/Valves

Austin A-7 Ltd ..... F 316 945-8892
Wichita *(G-13769)*
Tompkins Industries Inc ..... E 913 764-8088
Olathe *(G-8113)*

INDL SPLYS, WHOLESALE: Plastic Bottles

Koller Enterprises Inc ..... D 913 422-2027
Lenexa *(G-5957)*

INDL SPLYS, WHOLESALE: Rope, Exc Wire

Custom Rope A Div Williams ..... E 620 825-4196
Kiowa *(G-4623)*

INDL SPLYS, WHOLESALE: Rubber Goods, Mechanical

G T Sales & Manufacturing Inc ..... D 316 943-2171
Wichita *(G-14434)*
Lewis-Goetz and Company Inc ..... F 316 265-4623
Wichita *(G-14957)*

INDL SPLYS, WHOLESALE: Signmaker Eqpt & Splys

Glantz Holdings Inc ..... F 913 722-1000
Kansas City *(G-4037)*

INDL SPLYS, WHOLESALE: Springs

Big Springs Sports Center ..... E 785 887-6700
Lecompton *(G-5610)*
Wkcsc Inc ..... G 316 652-7113
Wichita *(G-16060)*

INDL SPLYS, WHOLESALE: Tools

Barrow Tooling Systems Inc ..... G 785 364-4306
Holton *(G-3085)*
Diteq Corporation ..... E 816 246-5515
Lenexa *(G-5821)*
Kuhn Co LLC ..... E 316 788-6500
Derby *(G-1257)*
Professional Sales Svcs Inc ..... F 316 941-4542
El Dorado *(G-1594)*
Total Tool Supply Inc ..... F 913 722-7879
Kansas City *(G-4471)*
Wilde Tool Co Inc ..... E 785 742-7171
Hiawatha *(G-3028)*

INDL SPLYS, WHOLESALE: Valves & Fittings

Bamford Fire Sprinkler Co Inc ..... E 913 432-6688
Shawnee Mission *(G-11145)*
Experitec Inc ..... F 913 894-4044
Shawnee Mission *(G-11356)*
Kenneth R Johnson Inc ..... E 913 599-1133
Lenexa *(G-5945)*
Missouri-Kansas Supply Co Inc ..... E 816 842-6513
Kansas City *(G-4263)*
V Mach Inc ..... E 913 894-2001
Shawnee Mission *(G-11971)*

INDL TOOL GRINDING SVCS

Barrow Tooling Systems Inc ..... G 785 364-4306
Holton *(G-3085)*

INDL TRUCK REPAIR SVCS

Randy Schwindt ..... F 785 391-2277
Utica *(G-13335)*
Rmvk Enterprises Inc ..... E 913 321-1915
Kansas City *(G-4382)*

INDUCTORS

Torotel Inc ..... E 913 747-6111
Olathe *(G-8115)*

INFORMATION BUREAU SVCS

Dodge City Public Library......E....... 620 225-0248
Dodge City *(G-1350)*
First Call For Help Ellis Cnty......E....... 785 623-2800
Hays *(G-2806)*
Unified School District 259......D....... 316 973-4200
Wichita *(G-15836)*

INFORMATION RETRIEVAL SERVICES

Blue Infotech Inc......F....... 816 945-2583
Leawood *(G-5341)*
Company Kitchen LLC......E....... 913 384-4900
Shawnee Mission *(G-11255)*
Elavon Inc......B....... 913 648-6444
Overland Park *(G-8672)*
Fusion Telecom Intl Inc......F....... 913 262-4638
Shawnee Mission *(G-11387)*
General Dynamics Info Tech Inc......E....... 785 832-0207
Lawrence *(G-4871)*
Hooper Holmes Inc......D....... 913 764-1045
Olathe *(G-7777)*
Kansas Info Consortium LLC......F....... 785 296-5059
Topeka *(G-12783)*
Marketing Technologies Inc......D....... 913 342-9111
Kansas City *(G-4218)*
Topeka Unified School Dst 501......E....... 785 438-4750
Topeka *(G-13190)*

INFORMATION SVCS: Consumer

County of Sedgwick......E....... 316 660-7060
Wichita *(G-14114)*

INFRARED OBJECT DETECTION EQPT

Advance Systems International......E....... 913 888-3578
Lenexa *(G-5631)*

INK OR WRITING FLUIDS

Nunik Engineering......F....... 913 384-0010
Shawnee Mission *(G-11691)*

INK: Letterpress Or Offset

Inland Industries Inc......G....... 913 492-9050
Bucyrus *(G-600)*

INK: Lithographic

Inkcycle Inc......D....... 913 894-8387
Shawnee *(G-10973)*

INK: Printing

Cartridge King of Kansas......E....... 620 241-7746
McPherson *(G-6941)*
Fujifilm Sericol USA Inc......C....... 913 342-4060
Kansas City *(G-4022)*
Hubergroup Usa Inc......F....... 913 262-2510
Kansas City *(G-4088)*
INX International Ink Co......D....... 913 441-0057
Edwardsville *(G-1504)*
Nazdar Company......F....... 913 422-1888
Shawnee *(G-11004)*

INK: Screen process

Nazdar Company......C....... 913 422-1888
Shawnee *(G-11003)*

INNS

Americas Best Value Inn......F....... 620 793-8486
Great Bend *(G-2507)*
Apple Tree Inn......F....... 620 331-5500
Independence *(G-3497)*
H Schwaller & Sons Inc......F....... 785 628-6162
Hays *(G-2822)*
Hospice Incorporated......E....... 316 283-1103
Newton *(G-7363)*
Lodging Enterprises LLC......F....... 785 852-4664
Sharon Springs *(G-10900)*
Ramada Conference Center Salin......F....... 785 823-1739
Salina *(G-10650)*
Relax Investments Inc......F....... 785 838-4242
Lawrence *(G-5092)*
Shreeji Investments Inc......F....... 785 838-4242
Lawrence *(G-5110)*
Single Tree Inn......E....... 620 356-1500
Ulysses *(G-13318)*

T M H Hotels Inc......E....... 316 669-6175
Wichita *(G-15713)*
Waterfront Assisted Living......F....... 316 945-3344
Wichita *(G-15936)*

INSECTICIDES

C5 Manufacturing LLC......E....... 620 532-3675
Kingman *(G-4584)*

INSPECTION & TESTING SVCS

Butler National Corporation......E....... 913 780-9595
Olathe *(G-7571)*
CP Engners Land Srveyors Inc......F....... 785 267-5071
Topeka *(G-12526)*
Cr Inspection Inc......D....... 620 544-2666
Hugoton *(G-3157)*
Dbi Inc......E....... 316 831-9323
Wichita *(G-14177)*
Great Plains Insptn & Lining......F....... 620 793-7090
Great Bend *(G-2584)*
Gsi Engineering Nthrn Div LLC......F....... 316 554-0725
Wichita *(G-14523)*
Kansas Crop Improvement Assn......F....... 785 532-6118
Manhattan *(G-6675)*
Kansas Grain Inspection Svc......F....... 785 827-3671
Salina *(G-10565)*
Kaw Valley Engineering Inc......E....... 785 762-5040
Junction City *(G-3714)*
Legacy Home Inspections......E....... 913 484-4157
Lenexa *(G-5965)*
Paragon Ndt LLC......E....... 316 927-4283
Wichita *(G-15260)*
T T Companies Inc......A....... 913 599-6886
Olathe *(G-8097)*

INSPECTION SVCS, TRANSPORTATION

Advance Systems International......E....... 913 888-3578
Lenexa *(G-5631)*
Advanced Infrared Systems......G....... 913 888-3578
Lenexa *(G-5633)*
Dodge City International Inc......E....... 620 225-4177
Dodge City *(G-1348)*

INSTRUMENT LANDING SYSTEMS OR ILS: Airborne Or Ground

Selex Es Inc......D....... 913 945-2600
Overland Park *(G-9293)*

INSTRUMENTS, MEASURING & CNTRL: Radiation & Testing, Nuclear

Radiation Oncology......E....... 913 588-3600
Kansas City *(G-4358)*

INSTRUMENTS, MEASURING & CNTRLG: Fatigue Test, Indl, Mech

Aviation Cnslting Engrg Sltons......G....... 316 265-8335
Maize *(G-6508)*

INSTRUMENTS, MEASURING & CNTRLG: Thermometers/Temp Sensors

Fireboard Labs LLC......G....... 816 945-2232
Olathe *(G-7710)*

INSTRUMENTS, MEASURING & CNTRLNG: Wind Direction Indicators

Tradewind Energy Inc......E....... 913 888-9463
Lenexa *(G-6188)*

INSTRUMENTS, MEASURING & CONTROLLING: Surveying & Drafting

Point Inc......F....... 913 928-2720
Olathe *(G-7989)*

INSTRUMENTS, MEASURING & CONTROLLING: Weather Tracking

Weather Metrics Inc......G....... 913 438-7666
Overland Park *(G-9486)*

INSTRUMENTS, OPTICAL: Test & Inspection

Viavi Solutions LLC......C....... 913 764-2452
Lenexa *(G-6213)*

INSTRUMENTS, SURGICAL & MEDICAL: Inhalation Therapy

O2 Corporation......F....... 316 634-1240
Wichita *(G-15202)*

INSTRUMENTS: Airspeed

Emerald Aerospace Services LLC......E....... 316 644-4284
Wichita *(G-14275)*

INSTRUMENTS: Analytical

Medical Positioning Inc......E....... 816 474-1555
Kansas City *(G-4229)*
Perkinelmer Inc......F....... 316 773-0055
Wichita *(G-15284)*
Pinnacle Technology Inc......E....... 785 832-8866
Lawrence *(G-5066)*
Thermo Fisher Scientific Inc......D....... 800 255-6730
Lenexa *(G-6178)*

INSTRUMENTS: Analyzers, Internal Combustion Eng, Electronic

Howard Electronic Instrs Inc......G....... 316 321-2800
El Dorado *(G-1568)*

INSTRUMENTS: Digital Panel Meters, Electricity Measuring

Design Concepts Inc......F....... 913 782-5672
Olathe *(G-7651)*

INSTRUMENTS: Electrolytic Conductivity, Laboratory

Sunlite Science & Technology......G....... 785 832-8818
Lawrence *(G-5130)*

INSTRUMENTS: Electron Test Tube

Steinlite Corporation......F....... 913 367-3945
Atchison *(G-262)*

INSTRUMENTS: Electronic, Analog-Digital Converters

Gateway Wireless Services LLC......F....... 316 264-0037
Wichita *(G-14451)*

INSTRUMENTS: Frequency Meters, Electrical, Mech & Electronic

Commercial Trade Services LLC......F....... 316 721-5432
Wichita *(G-14073)*
Ecs Inc International......F....... 913 782-7787
Lenexa *(G-5829)*

INSTRUMENTS: Indl Process Control

Emerson Electric Co......C....... 913 752-6000
Shawnee Mission *(G-11334)*
Kustom Signals Inc......C....... 620 431-2700
Chanute *(G-736)*
Pinnacle Technology Inc......E....... 785 832-8866
Lawrence *(G-5066)*
Ruskin Company......E....... 620 421-6090
Parsons *(G-9733)*
TEC Engineering Inc......E....... 316 259-8881
Wichita *(G-15723)*
Total Electric Inc......G....... 316 524-2642
Wichita *(G-15775)*

INSTRUMENTS: Measurement, Indl Process

Eurotech Inc......E....... 913 549-1000
Overland Park *(G-8693)*

INSTRUMENTS: Measuring & Controlling

Hail Signature Tech LLC......G....... 913 620-4928
Stilwell *(G-12150)*
Kohlman Systems Research Inc......F....... 785 843-4099
Lawrence *(G-4948)*
Networks International Corp......E....... 913 685-3400
Overland Park *(G-9078)*
Sands Level and Tool Company......D....... 620 325-2687
Neodesha *(G-7248)*
Siemens Industry Inc......E....... 316 267-5814
Wichita *(G-15584)*

Solid State Sonics & Elec....G.... 785 232-0497
Topeka (G-13080)

INSTRUMENTS: Measuring Electricity

Mid West Elc Transformers Inc....F.... 316 283-7500
Newton (G-7382)
Midamerica Meter....G.... 913 441-0790
Shawnee (G-10995)
Smiths Intrcnnect Americas Inc....C.... 913 342-5544
Kansas City (G-4429)
Viavi Solutions LLC....B.... 316 522-4981
Wichita (G-15905)

INSTRUMENTS: Measuring, Electrical Power

Steinlite Corporation....E.... 913 367-3945
Atchison (G-261)

INSTRUMENTS: Medical & Surgical

B/E Aerospace Inc....C.... 913 338-7292
Shawnee Mission (G-11142)
Bayer Healthcare LLC....E.... 913 268-2000
Shawnee Mission (G-11154)
Biomedical Devices of KS LLC....G.... 913 845-3851
Tonganoxie (G-12254)
Cardinal Health Inc....D.... 800 523-0502
Shawnee Mission (G-11202)
Disposable Instrument Co Inc....F.... 913 492-6492
Shawnee Mission (G-11310)
Entracare LLC....G.... 913 451-2234
Shawnee Mission (G-11343)
Hans Rudolph Inc....E.... 913 422-7788
Shawnee (G-10967)
Innara Health Inc....G.... 913 742-7770
Olathe (G-7793)
Ivy Animal Health Inc....E.... 913 310-7900
Lenexa (G-5924)
Nexus Medical LLC....D.... 913 451-2234
Shawnee Mission (G-11682)
Optimuz Manufacturing Inc....E.... 316 519-1354
Wichita (G-15229)
Schroer Manufacturing Company....C.... 913 281-1500
Kansas City (G-4404)

INSTRUMENTS: Radio Frequency Measuring

Legacy Technologies LLC....E.... 913 432-2020
Shawnee Mission (G-11559)

INSTRUMENTS: Telemetering, Indl Process

Harlan Hermanson....G.... 316 263-5958
Wichita (G-14560)

INSTRUMENTS: Test, Electronic & Electric Measurement

Technical Mfg Concepts Inc....E.... 913 764-1011
Olathe (G-8104)
Viavi Solutions LLC....C.... 913 764-2452
Lenexa (G-6213)

INSULATING BOARD, CELLULAR FIBER

Central Fiber LLC....E.... 785 883-4600
Wellsville (G-13541)

INSULATING COMPOUNDS

Stress Panel Manufacturers....G.... 620 347-8200
Arma (G-191)

INSULATION & CUSHIONING FOAM: Polystyrene

Ach Foam Technologies Inc....F.... 913 371-1973
Kansas City (G-3783)
Ach Foam Technologies Inc....D.... 913 321-4114
Kansas City (G-3782)
Future Foam Inc....D.... 316 283-8600
Newton (G-7350)

INSULATION: Fiberglass

Johns Manville Corporation....B.... 620 241-6260
McPherson (G-6979)
Owens Corning Sales LLC....B.... 419 248-8000
Kansas City (G-4305)
Premier Mechanical Pdts LLC....F.... 913 271-5002
Kansas City (G-4332)

INSURANCE ADVISORY SVCS

Genex Services LLC....E.... 913 310-0303
Lenexa (G-5872)
Prevail Strategies LLC....E.... 913 295-9500
Leawood (G-5526)
T & M Financial Inc....F.... 785 266-8333
Topeka (G-13129)

INSURANCE AGENCIES & BROKERS

Agrilogic Insurance Svcs LLC....F.... 913 982-2450
Overland Park (G-8359)
Berkley Risk ADM Co LLC....F.... 913 385-4960
Overland Park (G-8440)
Davis G Sam Insurance....F.... 913 451-1800
Shawnee Mission (G-11293)
Harlan C Parker Insurance Agcy....F.... 913 782-3310
Olathe (G-7752)
Keating & Associates Inc....E.... 785 537-0366
Manhattan (G-6698)
Medova Hlthcare Fncl Group LLC....E.... 316 616-6160
Wichita (G-15034)
Metropolitan Life Insur Co....E.... 913 234-4800
Overland Park (G-9016)
Metropolitan Life Insur Co....E.... 913 451-8282
Shawnee Mission (G-11621)
Metropolitan Life Insur Co....F.... 316 688-5600
Wichita (G-15061)
New York Life Insurance Co....F.... 316 262-0671
Wichita (G-15171)
Shelter Insurance....E.... 785 272-7181
Topeka (G-13067)
Sunburst Properties Inc....F.... 913 393-4747
Stilwell (G-12174)

INSURANCE AGENTS, NEC

American Academy Family Physcn....F.... 913 906-6000
Shawnee Mission (G-11101)
American Fidelity Assurance Co....D.... 785 232-8100
Topeka (G-12316)
American Trust Administrators....D.... 913 378-9860
Overland Park (G-8380)
Axa Advisors LLC....E.... 913 345-2800
Shawnee Mission (G-11137)
Axa Advisors LLC....E.... 316 263-5761
Wichita (G-13780)
Berkshire Risk Services LLC....E.... 913 433-7000
Overland Park (G-8441)
Blue Valley Insurance Agencies....F.... 785 337-2268
Hanover (G-2710)
C & T Enterprises Inc....E.... 913 782-1404
Olathe (G-7572)
Calvin Eddy & Kappelman Inc....E.... 785 843-2772
Lawrence (G-4774)
Cappers Insurance Service Inc....E.... 785 274-4300
Topeka (G-12441)
Charlson & Wilson Bonded Abstr....F.... 785 565-4800
Manhattan (G-6584)
Charlson Wilsin Insurance Agcy....F.... 785 537-1600
Manhattan (G-6585)
Cliff Tozier Insurance Agency....F.... 913 385-5000
Overland Park (G-8566)
Cobbs Allen & Hall Inc....E.... 913 267-5600
Overland Park (G-8571)
Colt Investments Inc....E.... 913 385-5010
Prairie Village (G-10020)
Comptech Group LLC....F.... 913 341-7600
Overland Park (G-8592)
Crop USA Hutson Insur Group....E.... 913 345-1515
Overland Park (G-8615)
D & K Insurance Services Inc....F.... 785 540-4133
Phillipsburg (G-9784)
Dee Jays Enterprises....F.... 620 227-3126
Dodge City (G-1340)
Dorothy Rush Realty Inc....F.... 620 442-7851
Arkansas City (G-153)
Eck Agency Inc....E.... 620 254-7222
Attica (G-277)
Elliott Insurance Inc....F.... 913 294-2110
Louisburg (G-6446)
Employers Mutual Casualty Co....E.... 913 663-0119
Overland Park (G-8679)
Employers Mutual Casualty Co....C.... 316 352-5700
Wichita (G-14279)
Farm Bur Property Cslty Insur....E.... 316 978-9950
Wichita (G-14340)
Federated Rural Elc Insur Exch....E.... 913 541-0150
Shawnee (G-10954)
Fee Insurance Group Inc....F.... 620 662-2381
Hutchinson (G-3283)
Frank E Seufert & Associates....F.... 785 456-2782
Wamego (G-13423)
G H C Associates Inc....F.... 785 243-1555
Concordia (G-1112)
Health and Benefit Systems LLC....E.... 913 642-1666
Leawood (G-5422)
Henry Scherer Crop Insurance....F.... 785 847-6843
Atchison (G-234)
Insurance Center Inc....E.... 316 321-5600
El Dorado (G-1571)
Insurance Designer Kansas City....F.... 913 451-3960
Shawnee Mission (G-11461)
Insurance Planning Inc....E.... 785 625-5605
Hays (G-2853)
Inter-Americas Insurance Corp....D.... 316 794-2200
Goddard (G-2443)
John C Gross III....F.... 620 223-2550
Fort Scott (G-1976)
John Jaco Inc....F.... 620 792-2541
Great Bend (G-2595)
Johnston Insurance Agency....E.... 913 396-0800
Shawnee Mission (G-11501)
Kansas Medical Mutual Insur Co....F.... 316 681-8119
Wichita (G-14815)
Keller Leopold Insurance LLC....F.... 620 276-7671
Garden City (G-2218)
Marysville Mutual Insurance Co....F.... 785 562-2379
Marysville (G-6901)
McInnes Group Inc....F.... 913 831-0999
Fairway (G-1913)
Med James Inc....D.... 913 663-5500
Overland Park (G-9005)
Missouri Livestock Mktg Assn....E.... 816 891-0502
Leawood (G-5488)
Newkirk Dennis & Buckles....F.... 620 331-3700
Independence (G-3543)
Oliver Insurance Agency Inc....F.... 913 341-1900
Overland Park (G-9099)
Parkway Insurance Agency Inc....F.... 913 385-5000
Shawnee Mission (G-11718)
Peoples/Commercial Insur LLC....F.... 785 271-8097
Topeka (G-12968)
Preferred Physicians Mdcl Rrg....E.... 913 262-2585
Overland Park (G-9179)
Professional Insurance Mgt....E.... 316 942-0699
Wichita (G-15362)
Provalue Insurance LLC....E.... 620 662-5406
Hutchinson (G-3417)
Relation Insurance Services....E.... 800 955-1991
Overland Park (G-9233)
Relation Insurance Services....F.... 800 955-1991
Overland Park (G-9234)
Renn & Company Inc....F.... 620 326-2271
Wellington (G-13523)
Risk Counselors Inc....F.... 620 221-1760
Winfield (G-16169)
Robert E Miller Insurance Agcy....E.... 816 333-3000
Leawood (G-5540)
SBS Insurance....F.... 785 336-2821
Seneca (G-10880)
Sims Insurance Services I....F.... 316 722-9977
Maize (G-6520)
Stephens Realestate Inc....D.... 785 841-4500
Lawrence (G-5122)
T S A Inc....F.... 913 322-2800
Prairie Village (G-10072)
Target Insurance Services LLC....E.... 913 384-6300
Overland Park (G-9391)
Tri-County Title & Abstract Co....F.... 913 682-8911
Leavenworth (G-5301)
Truck Insurance Mart Inc....F.... 913 441-0349
Edwardsville (G-1519)
Truck Insurance Mart Inc....F.... 620 654-3921
Galva (G-2096)
Truenorth Companies Lc....D.... 913 307-0838
Overland Park (G-9432)
Trustpoint Services Inc....F.... 620 364-5665
Burlington (G-644)
United States Aviation Underwr....F.... 316 267-1325
Wichita (G-15849)
W Ralph Wilkerson Jr Inc....C.... 913 432-4400
Shawnee Mission (G-11986)

INSURANCE BROKERS, NEC

Bankers and Investors Co....F.... 913 299-5008
Kansas City (G-3844)
Chris-Leef General Agency Inc....E.... 913 631-1232
Shawnee Mission (G-11222)
Cjd & Associates LLC....F.... 913 469-1188
Shawnee Mission (G-11235)

Ima Financial Group Inc .... F 316 267-9221
Wichita *(G-14672)*
Ima of Kansas Inc .... C 316 267-9221
Wichita *(G-14673)*
Kansas Department of Labor .... F 913 680-2200
Leavenworth *(G-5260)*
Lewer Agency Inc .... D 816 753-4390
Overland Park *(G-8954)*
Lockton Affinity LLC .... C 913 652-7500
Overland Park *(G-8968)*
Marino & Associates Inc .... F 816 478-1122
Leawood *(G-5466)*
Marsh & McLennan Agency LLC .... D 913 451-3900
Leawood *(G-5467)*
Virtus LLC .... E 816 919-2323
Overland Park *(G-9466)*

INSURANCE CARRIERS: Automobile

Bituminous Casualty Corp .... F 913 262-4664
Fairway *(G-1905)*
Ima Select LLC .... E 316 266-6203
Wichita *(G-14674)*

INSURANCE CARRIERS: Dental

Cigna Dental Health Kansas Inc .... F 913 339-4700
Overland Park *(G-8551)*
Delta Dental of Kansas Inc .... F 913 381-4928
Leawood *(G-5377)*
Delta Dental of Kansas Inc .... D 316 264-4511
Wichita *(G-14188)*

INSURANCE CARRIERS: Direct Accident & Health

American National Insurance Co .... E 913 722-2232
Shawnee Mission *(G-11106)*
Federated Mutual Insurance Co .... D 913 906-9363
Leawood *(G-5397)*
Health and Benefit Systems LLC .... E 913 642-1666
Leawood *(G-5422)*
Medicare Advisors 365 LLC .... F 866 956-0745
Lenexa *(G-5993)*
Mennonite Union Aid .... F 620 846-2286
Montezuma *(G-7159)*
New Drctons Bhavioral Hlth LLC .... C 816 237-2300
Overland Park *(G-9080)*

INSURANCE CARRIERS: Direct Product Warranty

Ima Financial Group Inc .... E 785 232-2202
Topeka *(G-12714)*

INSURANCE CARRIERS: Hospital & Medical

Blue Cross and Blue Shield of .... E 785 291-4180
Topeka *(G-12389)*
Blue Cross Blue Sheld Kans Inc .... D 316 269-1666
Wichita *(G-13858)*
Blue Cross Blue Sheld Kans Inc .... A 785 291-7000
Topeka *(G-12390)*
Heart of America Bone Marrow D .... F 913 901-3131
Shawnee Mission *(G-11420)*
New Drctons Bhavioral Hlth LLC .... C 816 237-2300
Overland Park *(G-9080)*

INSURANCE CARRIERS: Life

American Income Life Insurance .... E 402 699-3366
Overland Park *(G-8378)*
Arrowood Indemnity Company .... E 913 345-1776
Shawnee Mission *(G-11120)*
Clinical Reference Lab Inc .... B 913 492-3652
Lenexa *(G-5765)*
Financial Designs Inc .... F 913 451-4747
Overland Park *(G-8715)*
Foster Callanan Financial Svc .... E 866 363-9595
Topeka *(G-12624)*
Great Plains Annuity Marketing .... F 913 888-0488
Overland Park *(G-8772)*
Keller Leopold Insurance LLC .... F 620 276-7671
Garden City *(G-2218)*
Massachusetts Mutl Lf Insur Co .... E 913 234-0300
Overland Park *(G-8994)*
New York Life Insurance Co .... E 913 451-9100
Overland Park *(G-9081)*
New York Life Insurance Co .... D 913 906-4000
Leawood *(G-5501)*
Penn Mutual Life Insurance Co .... F 316 685-9296
Wichita *(G-15277)*
Penn Mutual Life Insurance Co .... F 913 322-9177
Leawood *(G-5519)*
Pinnacle Consulting Group LLC .... E 913 254-3030
Overland Park *(G-9168)*
Security Benefit Corporation .... C 785 438-3000
Topeka *(G-13052)*
Security Benefit Life Insur Co .... B 785 438-3000
Topeka *(G-13054)*
Unified Life Insur Co Texas .... E 913 685-2233
Shawnee Mission *(G-11960)*
United Services Auto Assn .... B 913 451-6100
Shawnee Mission *(G-11965)*
Waddell & Reed Inc .... E 785 537-4505
Manhattan *(G-6844)*
Waddell & Reed Fincl Svcs Inc .... B 913 236-2000
Overland Park *(G-9478)*
Zurich Agency Services Inc .... B 913 339-1000
Overland Park *(G-9530)*

INSURANCE CARRIERS: Pet, Health

Kansas Medical Mutual Insur Co .... F 316 681-8119
Wichita *(G-14815)*

INSURANCE CARRIERS: Property & Casualty

Armed Forces Insurance Exhange .... C 913 651-5000
Leavenworth *(G-5204)*
Bituminous Casualty Corp .... E 913 268-9176
Shawnee Mission *(G-11167)*
Federated Mutual Insurance Co .... D 913 906-9363
Leawood *(G-5397)*
First Excess Reinsurance Corp .... A 913 676-5524
Shawnee Mission *(G-11369)*
Great American Insurance Co .... D 785 840-1100
Lawrence *(G-4881)*
Liberty Mutual Insurance Co .... D 913 648-5900
Shawnee Mission *(G-11567)*
Old United Casualty Company .... E 913 432-6400
Shawnee Mission *(G-11695)*
Progressive Casualty Insur Co .... F 913 202-6600
Kansas City *(G-4344)*
W Ralph Wilkerson Jr Inc .... C 913 432-4400
Shawnee Mission *(G-11986)*
Zurich American Insurance Co .... D 913 339-1000
Overland Park *(G-9531)*

INSURANCE CARRIERS: Title

Chicago Title Insurance Co .... F 913 385-9307
Shawnee Mission *(G-11219)*
Chicago Title Insurance Co .... E 316 267-8371
Wichita *(G-14004)*
Lawyers Title of Kansas Inc .... F 785 271-9500
Topeka *(G-12835)*

INSURANCE CLAIM ADJUSTERS, NOT EMPLOYED BY INSURANCE COMPANY

Alternative Claims Services .... F 816 298-7506
Olathe *(G-7523)*
Farm Bureau Claims .... F 620 275-9195
Garden City *(G-2156)*
Heartland Adjustments Inc .... F 785 823-5100
Salina *(G-10539)*

INSURANCE CLAIM PROCESSING, EXC MEDICAL

Farm Bureau Mutl Insur Co Inc .... F 316 652-1800
Wichita *(G-14341)*

INSURANCE INFORMATION & CONSULTING SVCS

Assurance Partners LLC .... E 785 825-0286
Salina *(G-10411)*
Hokanson Lehman & Stevens .... F 913 338-2525
Leawood *(G-5430)*
Labone Inc .... A 913 888-1770
Lenexa *(G-5961)*
Lewis & Ellis Inc .... E 913 491-3388
Overland Park *(G-8955)*
Professional Benefit Cons .... F 913 268-0515
Shawnee Mission *(G-11754)*
Se2 LLC .... B 800 747-3940
Topeka *(G-13047)*

INSURANCE INFORMATION BUREAUS

Hooper Holmes Inc .... D 913 764-1045
Olathe *(G-7777)*
New Mountain Capital I LLC .... D 913 451-3222
Shawnee Mission *(G-11680)*

INSURANCE INSPECTION & INVESTIGATIONS SVCS

Auditing For Cmpliance Educatn .... F 913 648-8572
Shawnee Mission *(G-11133)*

INSURANCE LOSS PREVENTION SVCS

Overland Solutions Inc .... C 913 451-3222
Overland Park *(G-9127)*

INSURANCE RESEARCH SVCS

National Crop Insur Svcs Inc .... E 913 685-2767
Overland Park *(G-9070)*

INSURANCE: Agents, Brokers & Service

Advance Insurance Company Kans .... F 785 273-9804
Topeka *(G-12293)*
Agency Services Corp Kansas .... F 785 232-0561
Topeka *(G-12301)*
Albright Investment Company .... E 620 221-7653
Winfield *(G-16114)*
American Gen Lf Insur Co Del .... E 913 402-5000
Overland Park *(G-8377)*
American Home Life Insur Co .... E 785 235-6276
Topeka *(G-12318)*
American National Insurance Co .... E 913 722-2232
Shawnee Mission *(G-11106)*
American Senior Benefits .... E 785 273-8200
Topeka *(G-12322)*
Ameritrust Group Inc .... F 913 339-5000
Overland Park *(G-8381)*
Ascension Insur Holdings LLC .... B 800 955-1991
Overland Park *(G-8400)*
Automobile Club of Missouri .... F 316 942-0008
Wichita *(G-13774)*
Bankers Life & Casualty Co .... F 785 820-8815
Salina *(G-10420)*
Bituminous Casualty Corp .... F 913 262-4664
Fairway *(G-1905)*
Boulevard Insurance LLC .... F 785 865-0077
Overland Park *(G-8476)*
Bukaty Companies .... E 913 345-0440
Leawood *(G-5344)*
Burnham Builders .... F 620 343-2047
Emporia *(G-1713)*
Cbiz Benefits & Insur Svcs Inc .... F 913 234-1000
Leawood *(G-5350)*
CC Services Inc .... F 913 894-0700
Shawnee Mission *(G-11209)*
CC Services Inc .... F 913 381-1995
Overland Park *(G-8529)*
Central of Kansas Inc .... D 785 238-4114
Junction City *(G-3678)*
Century Health Solutions Inc .... F 785 233-1816
Topeka *(G-12459)*
Chubb US Holding Inc .... D 913 491-2000
Shawnee Mission *(G-11224)*
Claim Solution Inc .... E 913 322-2300
Shawnee Mission *(G-11236)*
CNA Financial Corporation .... D 913 661-2700
Overland Park *(G-8570)*
Creative One Marketing Corp .... C 913 814-0510
Leawood *(G-5363)*
Design Benefits .... F 316 729-7676
Wichita *(G-14200)*
Employers Reassurance Corp .... D 913 676-5200
Shawnee Mission *(G-11336)*
Farm and Family Insur Assoc .... E 785 823-5071
Salina *(G-10495)*
Farm Bureau Mutl Insur Co Inc .... C 785 587-6000
Manhattan *(G-6625)*
Farm Bureau Mutl Insur Co Inc .... F 620 275-9195
Garden City *(G-2157)*
Farmers & Drovers Bank .... E 620 767-2265
Council Grove *(G-1166)*
Farmers Alliance Mutl Insur Co .... A 620 241-2200
McPherson *(G-6963)*
Farmers Group Inc .... E 785 271-8088
Topeka *(G-12595)*
Farmers Group Inc .... E 785 267-4653
Topeka *(G-12596)*

Farmers Group Inc ... E ... 316 682-4500
Wichita *(G-14342)*
Farmers Group Inc ... E ... 316 263-4927
Wichita *(G-14343)*
Farmers Group Inc ... E ... 913 227-2000
Olathe *(G-7703)*
Farmers Group Inc ... E ... 913 227-3200
Olathe *(G-7704)*
Farmers National Bank ... F ... 785 543-6541
Phillipsburg *(G-9785)*
Financial Benefits of Kansas ... F ... 913 385-7000
Leawood *(G-5400)*
Financial Insurance Corp ... F ... 913 631-7441
Overland Park *(G-8716)*
First State Bank ... E ... 785 877-3341
Norton *(G-7447)*
Fmh Benefit Services Inc ... C ... 913 685-4740
Overland Park *(G-8731)*
Garden City Co-Op Inc ... F ... 620 275-6161
Garden City *(G-2170)*
Gerber Insurance Group ... F ... 913 649-7800
Prairie Village *(G-10031)*
Haas Wilkerson & Wohlberg Inc ... E ... 913 432-4400
Fairway *(G-1909)*
Hartford Fire Insurance Co ... D ... 913 693-8500
Shawnee Mission *(G-11414)*
Ima Inc ... B ... 316 267-9221
Wichita *(G-14671)*
Insurance Guys LLC ... F ... 316 775-0606
Augusta *(G-327)*
Kansas City Financial Group ... E ... 913 649-7447
Overland Park *(G-8895)*
Kansas Health Solutions Inc ... D ... 785 575-9393
Topeka *(G-12780)*
Kansas Hospital Association ... E ... 785 233-7436
Topeka *(G-12781)*
Kansas Mutual Insurance Co ... F ... 785 354-1076
Topeka *(G-12792)*
Keller RE & Insur Agcy ... F ... 620 792-2128
Great Bend *(G-2599)*
Kermit Cottrell Allstate Agcy ... E ... 785 843-2532
Lawrence *(G-4943)*
L J Gliem & Associates LLC ... E ... 913 557-9402
Overland Park *(G-8935)*
Madrigal & Associates Inc ... E ... 316 265-5680
Wichita *(G-15000)*
Max Share Fund Inc ... E ... 913 338-1100
Overland Park *(G-8996)*
Mitchell County Farm Bur Assn ... F ... 785 738-2551
Beloit *(G-494)*
Msaver Resources Llc ... E ... 913 663-4672
Overland Park *(G-9059)*
Mutualaid Exchange ... E ... 913 338-1100
Overland Park *(G-9065)*
Northwestern Mutual ... E ... 316 265-8139
Wichita *(G-15197)*
Parker Hafkins Insurance Inc ... F ... 620 225-2888
Dodge City *(G-1417)*
Peoples Bank ... F ... 620 582-2166
Coldwater *(G-1056)*
Ppm Services Inc ... E ... 913 262-2585
Overland Park *(G-9175)*
Prudential Insur Co of Amer ... E ... 913 327-1060
Shawnee Mission *(G-11759)*
Quest Capital Management Inc ... F ... 913 599-6422
Shawnee Mission *(G-11766)*
Ralph S Passman & Associates ... F ... 913 642-5432
Overland Park *(G-9221)*
Regional Insurance Service Co ... F ... 316 686-6553
Wichita *(G-15438)*
Reilly Company LLC ... D ... 913 682-1234
Leavenworth *(G-5284)*
Resnick Associates ... F ... 913 681-5454
Shawnee Mission *(G-11790)*
Rutter Cline Associates Inc ... F ... 620 276-8274
Garden City *(G-2271)*
Security Benefit Group Inc ... B ... 785 438-3000
Topeka *(G-13053)*
Smart Money Concepts Inc ... F ... 913 962-9806
Overland Park *(G-9318)*
St Paul Fire and Mar Insur Co ... B ... 913 469-2720
Shawnee Mission *(G-11891)*
Swiss RE Management US Corp ... F ... 913 676-5200
Overland Park *(G-9385)*
Tfwilson LLC ... E ... 913 327-0200
Shawnee Mission *(G-11927)*
Thrivent Financial For Luthera ... E ... 620 364-2177
Burlington *(G-643)*
United Agency Inc ... E ... 620 442-0400
Arkansas City *(G-187)*
Upland Mutual Insurance Inc ... F ... 785 762-4324
Junction City *(G-3761)*
USI Insurance Services LLC ... D ... 316 263-3211
Wichita *(G-15864)*
Waddell & Reed Inc ... F ... 913 491-9202
Leawood *(G-5593)*
Waddell & Reed Financial Inc ... D ... 913 236-2000
Overland Park *(G-9477)*
Willis North America Inc ... D ... 913 339-0800
Overland Park *(G-9495)*

INTEGRATED CIRCUITS, SEMICONDUCTOR NETWORKS, ETC

Leidos Inc ... G ... 913 317-5120
Shawnee Mission *(G-11560)*

INTERCOMMUNICATIONS SYSTEMS: Electric

Special Product Company ... E ... 972 208-1460
Lenexa *(G-6146)*
Special Product Company ... F ... 913 491-8088
Shawnee *(G-11031)*

INTERIOR DECORATING SVCS

Sewing Workshop ... F ... 785 357-6231
Topeka *(G-13061)*
Yaeger Architecture Inc ... E ... 913 742-8000
Lenexa *(G-6239)*

INTERIOR DESIGN SVCS, NEC

Arch Design Builders LLC ... E ... 913 599-5565
Overland Park *(G-8392)*
BKM Construction LLC ... F ... 913 297-0049
Leavenworth *(G-5212)*
Madden-Mcfarland Interiors Ltd ... E ... 913 681-2821
Leawood *(G-5462)*
Michael S Hundley Cnstr Inc ... F ... 913 367-7059
Atchison *(G-249)*

INTERIOR DESIGNING SVCS

Bailey Showroom 2 LLC ... F ... 913 432-9696
Shawnee Mission *(G-11144)*
D J Company ... F ... 316 685-3241
Wichita *(G-14158)*
Deans Designs Inc ... F ... 316 686-6674
Wichita *(G-14181)*
Design Central Inc ... F ... 785 825-4131
Salina *(G-10474)*
Designed Bus Intrors Tpeka Inc ... F ... 785 233-2078
Topeka *(G-12553)*
Facc Solutions Inc ... G ... 316 425-4040
Wichita *(G-14330)*
Glmv Architecture Inc ... E ... 316 265-9367
Wichita *(G-14472)*
Picture Perfect Interiors LLC ... F ... 913 829-3365
Overland Park *(G-9167)*
Therien & Company Inc ... F ... 415 956-8850
Plainville *(G-9993)*

INTERMEDIATE CARE FACILITY

Andbe Home Inc ... D ... 785 877-2601
Norton *(G-7441)*
Angel Arms ... F ... 620 245-0848
McPherson *(G-6935)*
Attica Hospital District 1 ... D ... 620 254-7253
Attica *(G-276)*
Brandon Woods Retirement Cmnty ... C ... 785 838-8000
Lawrence *(G-4766)*
Centennial Homestead Inc ... D ... 785 325-2361
Washington *(G-13462)*
Centrlia Cmmmity Hlth Care Svc ... D ... 785 857-3388
Centralia *(G-697)*
Cheyenne Lodge Inc ... E ... 785 439-6211
Jamestown *(G-3642)*
Coffey County Hospital ... E ... 785 733-2744
Waverly *(G-13481)*
Community Care Inc ... E ... 785 455-3522
Clifton *(G-900)*
Cornerstone Ridge Plaza ... E ... 316 462-3636
Wichita *(G-14103)*
County of Stevens ... D ... 620 544-2023
Hugoton *(G-3155)*
Cumbernauld Village Inc ... D ... 620 221-4141
Winfield *(G-16137)*
Douglass Medicalodges ... E ... 316 747-2157
Douglass *(G-1466)*
Evangelical Lutheran ... D ... 785 472-3167
Ellsworth *(G-1674)*
Evangelical Lutheran ... C ... 785 621-2499
Hays *(G-2802)*
Evangelical Lutheran ... C ... 785 332-3588
Saint Francis *(G-10341)*
Eventide Convalescent Center ... D ... 785 233-8918
Topeka *(G-12582)*
Fowler Nursing Home ... E ... 620 646-5215
Fowler *(G-2020)*
Frankfort Community Care Home ... D ... 785 292-4442
Frankfort *(G-2022)*
Friends Kansas Christn HM Inc ... C ... 316 283-6600
Newton *(G-7348)*
Frontline Management ... D ... 620 227-8551
Dodge City *(G-1363)*
Glenwood Estate Inc ... D ... 620 331-2260
Independence *(G-3523)*
Halstead Place Inc ... E ... 316 830-2424
Halstead *(G-2701)*
Health Management of Kansas ... C ... 620 251-5190
Coffeyville *(G-945)*
Hilltop Manor Inc ... C ... 620 298-2781
Cunningham *(G-1187)*
Infinia At Wichita Inc ... E ... 316 691-9999
Wichita *(G-14691)*
Jefferson County Mem Hosp Inc ... D ... 913 774-4340
Winchester *(G-16110)*
Kansas Masonic Home ... C ... 316 269-7500
Wichita *(G-14814)*
Kingman County Retirement Assn ... D ... 620 532-5801
Kingman *(G-4599)*
Lafayette Life Plan Inc ... D ... 785 742-7465
Hiawatha *(G-3015)*
Lakeview Village Inc ... A ... 913 888-1900
Lenexa *(G-5962)*
Leonardville Nursing Home Inc ... D ... 785 468-3661
Leonardville *(G-6249)*
Life Care Centers America Inc ... D ... 785 336-3528
Seneca *(G-10872)*
Life Care Centers America Inc ... D ... 620 364-2117
Burlington *(G-639)*
Lindsborg House 2 ... F ... 785 227-3652
Lindsborg *(G-6401)*
Linn Community Nursing Home ... D ... 785 348-5551
Linn *(G-6408)*
Living Center Inc ... D ... 620 665-2170
Hutchinson *(G-3355)*
Maria Villa Inc ... D ... 316 777-1129
Mulvane *(G-7220)*
Martin Luther Homes Kansas Inc ... D ... 620 229-8702
Winfield *(G-16156)*
Marysville Health Corporation ... D ... 785 562-2424
Marysville *(G-6899)*
McCrite Retirement Association ... C ... 785 267-2960
Topeka *(G-12868)*
Medicalodges Inc ... D ... 620 223-0210
Fort Scott *(G-1985)*
Medicalodges Inc ... D ... 620 231-0300
Pittsburg *(G-9902)*
Medicalodges Inc ... D ... 620 429-2134
Columbus *(G-1082)*
Medicalodges Inc ... D ... 620 583-7418
Eureka *(G-1894)*
Medicalodges Inc ... D ... 620 442-9300
Arkansas City *(G-165)*
Medicalodges Inc ... E ... 620 659-2156
Kinsley *(G-4619)*
Medicalodges Inc ... D ... 316 794-8635
Goddard *(G-2446)*
Medicalodges Inc ... D ... 316 755-1288
Valley Center *(G-13348)*
Midwest Division - Oprmc LLC ... A ... 913 541-5000
Shawnee Mission *(G-11632)*
Midwest Health Services Inc ... E ... 620 272-9800
Garden City *(G-2233)*
Midwest Health Services Inc ... E ... 785 537-1065
Manhattan *(G-6748)*
Midwest Health Services Inc ... E ... 785 776-1772
Manhattan *(G-6750)*
Mission Village Living Ctr Inc ... E ... 785 486-2697
Horton *(G-3131)*
Old Creek Senior Living ... E ... 785 272-2601
Topeka *(G-12945)*
Pine Village ... C ... 620 345-2901
Moundridge *(G-7196)*
Prairie Sunset Home Inc ... E ... 620 459-6822
Pretty Prairie *(G-10168)*
Presbyterian Manors Inc ... D ... 913 334-3666
Kansas City *(G-4333)*

Presbyterian Manors Inc ....D.... 785 825-1366
Salina *(G-10641)*
Presbyterian Manors Inc ....D.... 785 632-5646
Clay Center *(G-876)*
Presbyterian Manors Inc ....D.... 316 942-7456
Wichita *(G-15335)*
Protection Valley Manor Inc ....D.... 620 622-4261
Protection *(G-10176)*
Regal Estate ....E.... 305 751-4257
Independence *(G-3552)*
RES-Care Kansas Inc ....E.... 785 728-7198
Goodland *(G-2483)*
RES-Care Kansas Inc ....D.... 620 793-8501
Great Bend *(G-2631)*
Riordan Clinic Inc ....E.... 316 682-3100
Wichita *(G-15464)*
Riverview Estates Inc ....E.... 785 546-2211
Marquette *(G-6877)*
Rural Health Development Inc ....D.... 785 462-8295
Colby *(G-1037)*
Sabetha Manor Incorporated ....E.... 785 284-3411
Sabetha *(G-10329)*
Sunset Home Inc ....D.... 785 243-2720
Concordia *(G-1131)*
Sunset Manor Inc ....C.... 620 231-7340
Frontenac *(G-2066)*
Valley Springs ....F.... 785 256-7100
Auburn *(G-298)*
Via Christi Vlg Manhattan Inc ....C.... 785 539-7671
Manhattan *(G-6842)*
Villa St Francis Inc ....C.... 913 254-3264
Olathe *(G-8140)*
Vintage Park of Paola ....E.... 913 557-0202
Paola *(G-9594)*
Westview Mnor Healthcare Assoc ....D.... 316 788-3739
Derby *(G-1281)*
Westy Community Care Home Inc ....D.... 785 457-2806
Westmoreland *(G-13549)*
Wichita Cnty Long Term Rest Hm ....D.... 620 375-4600
Leoti *(G-6262)*
Windsor Nursing Home Assoc ....D.... 785 825-6757
Salina *(G-10771)*
Woodridge Estates LLC ....F.... 620 421-2431
Parsons *(G-9751)*

INTERNATIONAL AFFAIRS, GOVERNMENT: Foreign Missions

Hope Planting Intl Inc ....F.... 785 776-8523
Manhattan *(G-6659)*

INVENTOR

Invena Corporation ....E.... 620 583-8630
Eureka *(G-1892)*

INVENTORY COMPUTING SVCS

Monarch Inventories Services ....E.... 913 541-0645
Lenexa *(G-6011)*
Quality Inventory Services ....F.... 913 888-7700
Merriam *(G-7101)*
Retail Services Wis Corp ....E.... 913 831-6400
Shawnee Mission *(G-11791)*
Retail Services Wis Corp ....E.... 316 683-3289
Bel Aire *(G-439)*
Rgis LLC ....C.... 316 685-6233
Wichita *(G-15455)*

INVESTMENT ADVISORY SVCS

6 Meridian LLC ....F.... 316 776-4601
Wichita *(G-13582)*
Ameriprise Financial Svcs Inc ....E.... 913 451-2811
Shawnee Mission *(G-11109)*
Creative Planning Inc ....E.... 913 341-0900
Overland Park *(G-8612)*
David M King & Associates ....F.... 319 377-4636
Hays *(G-2782)*
Eveans Bash Klein Inc ....F.... 913 345-7000
Overland Park *(G-8694)*
Fidelity Investments Instituti ....E.... 913 345-8079
Leawood *(G-5398)*
Financial Counselors Inc ....F.... 816 329-1500
Leawood *(G-5401)*
First Horizon National Corp ....D.... 913 339-5400
Overland Park *(G-8720)*
Foresters Financial Svcs Inc ....E.... 913 310-0435
Leawood *(G-5408)*
Great Plains Trust Company ....F.... 913 831-7999
Overland Park *(G-8775)*
Insight Financial Services LLC ....F.... 913 402-2020
Overland Park *(G-8853)*
Kwmg LLC ....F.... 913 624-1841
Overland Park *(G-8933)*
Mariner LLC ....E.... 913 647-9700
Leawood *(G-5465)*
McDaniel Knutson Inc ....F.... 785 841-4664
Lawrence *(G-5017)*
Mitchell Capital Management Co ....F.... 913 428-3222
Leawood *(G-5489)*
Mutual Fund Store Inc ....E.... 913 338-2323
Shawnee Mission *(G-11660)*
Susan Pool ....F.... 316 266-6574
Wichita *(G-15704)*
Tortoise Capital Advisors LLC ....E.... 913 981-1020
Leawood *(G-5578)*
Trust Company of Manhattan ....F.... 785 537-7200
Manhattan *(G-6832)*
Waddell & Reed Inv MGT Co ....E.... 913 491-9202
Leawood *(G-5594)*

INVESTMENT BANKERS

Morgan Stanley & Co LLC ....F.... 316 383-8300
Wichita *(G-15127)*
Morgan Stanley & Co LLC ....F.... 785 749-1111
Lawrence *(G-5032)*
UBS Financial Services Inc ....E.... 316 612-6500
Wichita *(G-15828)*

INVESTMENT COUNSELORS

Devlin Management Inc ....F.... 316 634-1800
Wichita *(G-14204)*
Mutual Fund Store LLC ....F.... 913 319-8181
Overland Park *(G-9064)*
Waddell & Reed Inc ....A.... 913 236-2000
Shawnee Mission *(G-11987)*
Waddell & Reed Inc ....E.... 316 942-9010
Wichita *(G-15914)*
Waddell & Reed Inc ....F.... 785 263-7496
Abilene *(G-56)*
Waddell & Reed Inv Mgt Co ....E.... 913 236-2000
Shawnee Mission *(G-11988)*

INVESTMENT FIRM: General Brokerage

Financial Consultants America ....E.... 316 943-7307
Wichita *(G-14367)*
Prosperity Netwrk Advisors LLC ....E.... 913 451-4501
Overland Park *(G-9197)*
Wells Fargo Clearing Svcs LLC ....E.... 316 267-0300
Wichita *(G-15946)*

INVESTMENT FUNDS, NEC

Freestate Advisors LLC ....E.... 888 735-2724
Wichita *(G-14419)*

INVESTMENT FUNDS: Open-Ended

SBC Funding LLC ....A.... 785 438-3000
Topeka *(G-13037)*
Security Benefit Life Insur Co ....B.... 785 438-3000
Topeka *(G-13054)*

INVESTMENT OFFICES: Management, Closed-End

Bridge Capital Management LLC ....F.... 913 283-7804
Lenexa *(G-5712)*

INVESTMENT OFFICES: Money Market Mutual

Buffalo Balanced Fund Inc ....F.... 913 677-7778
Shawnee Mission *(G-11189)*
Buffalo Funds ....E.... 913 677-7778
Shawnee Mission *(G-11190)*
Ivy Funds Distributor Inc ....F.... 913 261-2800
Shawnee Mission *(G-11469)*
Ivy Funds VIP Small Cap Growth ....F.... 800 777-6472
Overland Park *(G-8866)*
Palmer Square Capital MGT LLC ....E.... 816 994-3201
Shawnee Mission *(G-11714)*
Tortoise Energy Independenc ....E.... 913 981-1020
Leawood *(G-5580)*
Waddell & Reed Fincl Svcs Inc ....B.... 913 236-2000
Overland Park *(G-9478)*

INVESTMENT OFFICES: Mutual Fund Sales, On Own Account

Rydex Fund Services Inc ....C.... 301 296-5100
Topeka *(G-13031)*
Tortoise Energy Capital Corp ....F.... 913 981-1020
Leawood *(G-5579)*

INVESTORS, NEC

Awg Acquisition LLC ....A.... 913 288-1000
Kansas City *(G-3831)*
Big Creek Investment Corp Inc ....G.... 620 431-3445
Chanute *(G-707)*
Brittany Court Inv Partner LP ....F.... 816 300-0685
Gardner *(G-2330)*
Cg Investments ....E.... 816 398-5862
Kansas City *(G-3907)*
Eighteen Capital Group ....F.... 866 799-5157
Leawood *(G-5385)*
GE Capital Montgomery Ward ....A.... 913 676-4100
Shawnee Mission *(G-11391)*
John T Arnold Associates Inc ....F.... 316 263-7242
Wichita *(G-14763)*
Midland Properties Inc ....F.... 913 677-5300
Mission Woods *(G-7151)*
Mkl Acquisitions LLC ....F.... 620 704-5228
Pittsburg *(G-9907)*
Prime SEC Svcs Borrower LLC ....F.... 630 410-0662
Lawrence *(G-5076)*
Resources Inv Advisors Inc ....E.... 913 338-5300
Leawood *(G-5538)*
S J Investments Inc of Topeka ....F.... 785 233-1568
Topeka *(G-13032)*
Stone Investment Inc ....E.... 913 367-0276
Atchison *(G-263)*
Vfs Acquisition Corp ....F.... 913 422-4088
Bonner Springs *(G-579)*

INVESTORS: Real Estate, Exc Property Operators

Cambridgen Inc ....E.... 913 384-3800
Overland Park *(G-8507)*
Capital City Investments Inc ....E.... 785 274-5600
Topeka *(G-12427)*
Dean Development Inc ....F.... 913 685-4100
Shawnee Mission *(G-11296)*
Licausi-Styers Company ....E.... 913 681-5888
Shawnee Mission *(G-11568)*
Midwest Legacy LLC ....F.... 316 518-9350
Park City *(G-9631)*

IRON & STEEL PRDTS: Hot-Rolled

Cromwell Builders Mfg ....F.... 785 949-2433
Carlton *(G-686)*

IRRIGATION EQPT WHOLESALERS

96 Agri Sales Inc ....F.... 316 661-2281
Mount Hope *(G-7202)*
Callaway Electric ....G.... 785 632-5588
Clay Center *(G-847)*
Gigot Agra Services Inc ....F.... 620 276-8444
Cheney *(G-792)*
Industrial Sales Company Inc ....E.... 913 829-3500
Olathe *(G-7787)*
Jies LLC ....F.... 620 668-5585
Copeland *(G-1149)*
Kanequip Inc ....F.... 785 632-3441
Clay Center *(G-869)*
Luka Irrigation Systems Inc ....E.... 913 248-0400
Shawnee *(G-10990)*
Minter-Wilson Drilling Co Inc ....E.... 620 275-7471
Garden City *(G-2238)*
Professnal Turf Pdts Ltd Prtnr ....E.... 913 599-1449
Lenexa *(G-6073)*
Stans Sprinkler Service Inc ....E.... 800 570-5932
Wichita *(G-15654)*
T & C Mfg & Operating Inc ....E.... 620 793-5483
Great Bend *(G-2646)*
Teeter Irrigation Inc ....F.... 620 276-8257
Garden City *(G-2297)*
Western Kansas Valley Inc ....F.... 785 852-4606
Sharon Springs *(G-10902)*
Western Sprinklers Inc ....F.... 785 462-6755
Colby *(G-1048)*
Woofter Cnstr & Irrigation Inc ....E.... 785 462-8653
Colby *(G-1049)*

JANITORIAL & CUSTODIAL SVCS

Bobs Janitorial Service & Sup..............C....... 785 271-6600
Topeka ***(G-12395)***
Buckingham Palace Inc..........................D....... 785 842-6264
Lawrence ***(G-4771)***
Buzz Building Maintenance Inc.............E....... 316 773-9860
Wichita ***(G-13922)***
C & S Maintenance Inc...........................E....... 913 227-9609
Overland Park ***(G-8503)***
Central Maintenance System.................E....... 913 621-6545
Kansas City ***(G-3901)***
City Wide Holding Company Inc...........C....... 913 888-5700
Lenexa ***(G-5757)***
City Wide Maintenance Co Inc..............C....... 913 888-5700
Lenexa ***(G-5758)***
Clean-Rite LLC...F....... 785 628-1945
Hays ***(G-2771)***
Cleaning Up LLC.......................................E....... 913 327-7226
Lenexa ***(G-5761)***
D&A Services Inc......................................D....... 316 943-8857
Wichita ***(G-14161)***
Ermc II LP...E....... 913 859-9621
Overland Park ***(G-8688)***
Fsig LLC..D....... 785 784-2566
Fort Riley ***(G-1948)***
Goodwill Wstn MO & Eastrn Kans.........F....... 785 331-3908
Lawrence ***(G-4875)***
Goodwill Wstn MO & Eastrn Kans.........E....... 913 768-9540
Olathe ***(G-7737)***
Hawk Wash Window Cleaning................F....... 785 749-0244
Lawrence ***(G-4893)***
Heartland Building Maintenance...........D....... 913 268-7132
Shawnee Mission ***(G-11422)***
Hutchinson Usd 308.................................F....... 620 615-5575
Hutchinson ***(G-3327)***
I B S Industries Inc..................................F....... 913 281-0787
Kansas City ***(G-4091)***
Jenkins Building Maintenance..............F....... 316 529-1263
Haysville ***(G-2949)***
Jones Janitorial Service..........................F....... 316 722-5520
Wichita ***(G-14770)***
Kc Cleaning Solutions..............................C....... 913 236-0040
Overland Park ***(G-8905)***
Landscapes Inc..E....... 316 262-7557
Wichita ***(G-14921)***
Majestic Franchising Inc..........................F....... 913 385-1440
Lenexa ***(G-5983)***
Mc Janitorial LLC.......................................F....... 913 780-0731
Olathe ***(G-7879)***
Modern Maintenance Inc..........................B....... 913 345-9777
Shawnee Mission ***(G-11651)***
Pioneer Janitorial LLC...............................E....... 785 379-5101
Topeka ***(G-12975)***
Prairie Cleaning Service............................E....... 785 539-4997
Manhattan ***(G-6778)***
Progreen Window Cleaning Inc..................F....... 913 387-3210
Lenexa ***(G-6075)***
Smart Way...F....... 913 764-3071
Olathe ***(G-8069)***
Source Building Services Inc....................F....... 913 341-7500
Overland Park ***(G-9329)***
Spotless Janitorial Services.....................E....... 316 682-2070
Wichita ***(G-15646)***
Superior Building Maintenance.................B....... 316 943-2347
Wichita ***(G-15692)***
T D C Ltd...E....... 913 780-9631
Olathe ***(G-8096)***
Tee Time Investments Inc..........................D....... 316 262-7900
Wichita ***(G-15727)***
Tidy Up Angels LLC...................................F....... 913 642-2006
Overland Park ***(G-9410)***
Tk & Company Inc of Kansas......................F....... 785 472-3226
Ellsworth ***(G-1682)***
Wilson Building Maintenance.....................C....... 316 264-0699
Wichita ***(G-16053)***
Xtreme Clean 88 LLC..................................F....... 913 451-9274
Overland Park ***(G-9514)***

JANITORIAL EQPT & SPLYS WHOLESALERS

City Wide Holding Company Inc...........C....... 913 888-5700
Lenexa ***(G-5757)***
Clean-Rite LLC...F....... 785 628-1945
Hays ***(G-2771)***
Edwards Chemicals Inc.............................F....... 913 365-5158
Elwood ***(G-1686)***
Emporia Wholesale Coffee Co..................C....... 620 343-7000
Emporia ***(G-1747)***
Four State Maintenance Sup Inc...............E....... 620 251-7033
Coffeyville ***(G-940)***
Hugos Industrial Supply Inc.....................E....... 620 331-4846
Independence ***(G-3526)***
Lafe T Williams & Assoc Inc....................F....... 316 262-0479
Wichita ***(G-14914)***
Southwest Paper Company Inc...............E....... 316 838-7755
Wichita ***(G-15631)***
Ultra-Chem Inc..C....... 913 492-2929
Shawnee Mission ***(G-11955)***
Waxene Products Company Inc................G....... 316 263-8523
Wichita ***(G-15938)***
Wilson Building Maintenance....................C....... 316 264-0699
Wichita ***(G-16053)***

JEWELRY REPAIR SVCS

Brimans Leading Jewelers Inc..................F....... 785 357-4438
Topeka ***(G-12408)***
Burnells Creative Gold Inc.........................G....... 316 634-2822
Wichita ***(G-13916)***
Mark Boose...G....... 785 234-4808
Topeka ***(G-12860)***
Noble House Jewelry Ltd............................F....... 913 491-4861
Overland Park ***(G-9090)***
Riddles Group Inc...D....... 620 371-6284
Dodge City ***(G-1424)***
Vernon Jewelers of Salina Inc...................F....... 785 825-0531
Salina ***(G-10751)***

JEWELRY STORES

File A Gem Inc..G....... 620 856-3800
Baxter Springs ***(G-407)***
Paco Designs Inc..G....... 913 541-1708
Shawnee Mission ***(G-11713)***
Riddles Group Inc...D....... 620 371-6284
Dodge City ***(G-1424)***

JEWELRY STORES: Precious Stones & Precious Metals

Brimans Leading Jewelers Inc..................F....... 785 357-4438
Topeka ***(G-12408)***
Burnells Creative Gold Inc.........................G....... 316 634-2822
Wichita ***(G-13916)***
D J Company..F....... 316 685-3241
Wichita ***(G-14158)***
Mark Boose...G....... 785 234-4808
Topeka ***(G-12860)***
Noble House Jewelry Ltd............................F....... 913 491-4861
Overland Park ***(G-9090)***
Tivol Plaza Inc...E....... 913 345-0200
Overland Park ***(G-9416)***
Vernon Jewelers of Salina Inc...................F....... 785 825-0531
Salina ***(G-10751)***

JEWELRY, PRECIOUS METAL: Pearl, Natural Or Cultured

Burnells Creative Gold Inc.........................G....... 316 634-2822
Wichita ***(G-13916)***

JEWELRY, PRECIOUS METAL: Settings & Mountings

Mark Boose...G....... 785 234-4808
Topeka ***(G-12860)***

JEWELRY, WHOLESALE

Dee Jays Enterprises...................................F....... 620 227-3126
Dodge City ***(G-1340)***
Ehlers Industries Inc...................................E....... 913 381-7884
Leawood ***(G-5384)***

JEWELRY: Decorative, Fashion & Costume

Swarovski North America Ltd....................G....... 913 599-3791
Overland Park ***(G-9381)***

JEWELRY: Precious Metal

James Avery Craftsman Inc.......................F....... 913 307-0419
Overland Park ***(G-8871)***
Paco Designs Inc..G....... 913 541-1708
Shawnee Mission ***(G-11713)***

JOB PRINTING & NEWSPAPER PUBLISHING COMBINED

Hall Publications Inc...................................G....... 785 232-8600
Topeka ***(G-12659)***
Lewis Legal News Inc..................................G....... 913 780-5790
Olathe ***(G-7860)***
NPS Sales Inc...G....... 913 406-1454
Olathe ***(G-7924)***
Parsons Publishing Company LLC..........E....... 620 421-2000
Parsons ***(G-9721)***
Winfield Publishing Co Inc.........................E....... 620 221-1100
Winfield ***(G-16189)***

JOB TRAINING & VOCATIONAL REHABILITATION SVCS

Class Ltd...D....... 620 231-3131
Pittsburg ***(G-9835)***
Class Ltd...C....... 620 429-1212
Columbus ***(G-1066)***
Class Ltd...D....... 620 421-2800
Parsons ***(G-9672)***
Heartland Works Inc...................................E....... 785 234-0500
Topeka ***(G-12681)***
Medicalodges Inc..D....... 316 755-1288
Valley Center ***(G-13348)***
New Beginnings Enterprise.........................F....... 620 583-6835
Eureka ***(G-1896)***
Northview Development Services.............C....... 316 281-3213
Newton ***(G-7399)***
RES-Care Kansas Inc...................................F....... 913 342-9426
Kansas City ***(G-4372)***
RES-Care Kansas Inc...................................D....... 620 793-8501
Great Bend ***(G-2631)***
Social and Rehabilitation Serv...................D....... 620 272-5800
Garden City ***(G-2283)***
Starkey Inc..C....... 316 942-4221
Wichita ***(G-15657)***
Sunflower Diversified Svcs Inc...................C....... 620 792-1325
Great Bend ***(G-2645)***
Unified School District 259.........................C....... 316 973-4000
Wichita ***(G-15833)***

JOB TRAINING SVCS

Curtis Klaassen..F....... 913 661-4616
Leawood ***(G-5366)***
Goodwill Wstn MO & Eastrn Kans.........E....... 785 228-9774
Topeka ***(G-12642)***
Goodwill Wstn MO & Eastrn Kans.........F....... 785 331-3908
Lawrence ***(G-4875)***
Goodwill Wstn MO & Eastrn Kans.........E....... 913 768-9540
Olathe ***(G-7737)***
Kansas Schl For Effective Lrng..................E....... 316 263-9620
Wichita ***(G-14822)***
Nemaha County Training Center...............F....... 785 300-1306
Sabetha ***(G-10321)***
Occk Inc..E....... 785 243-1977
Concordia ***(G-1125)***
Occk Inc..E....... 785 738-3490
Beloit ***(G-498)***
Occk Inc..C....... 785 827-9383
Salina ***(G-10617)***
Pryor Learning Solutions Inc......................E....... 913 967-8300
Shawnee Mission ***(G-11760)***

JOINTS: Expansion

Balco Inc...C....... 800 767-0082
Wichita ***(G-13798)***
Southwest Stl Fabrication LLC..................E....... 913 422-5500
Bonner Springs ***(G-573)***

JUNIOR COLLEGES

Hutchinson Community College...............F....... 620 665-3500
Hutchinson ***(G-3320)***

JUVENILE CORRECTIONAL FACILITIES

Corrections Kansas Department...............C....... 620 285-0300
Larned ***(G-4699)***
County of Sedgwick.....................................E....... 316 660-9775
Wichita ***(G-14110)***
Reno County Youth Services......................E....... 620 694-2500
Hutchinson ***(G-3425)***
Sedgwick Juvenile Field Svcs....................E....... 316 660-5380
Wichita ***(G-15550)***

KIDNEY DIALYSIS CENTERS

Bio-Mdcal Applcations Kans Inc.................F....... 913 498-1780
Overland Park ***(G-8449)***
Bio-Mdcal Applcations Kans Inc.................E....... 785 823-6460
Salina ***(G-10424)***
Bladon Dialysis LLC.....................................E....... 620 728-0440
Hutchinson ***(G-3216)***

Davita Healthcare Partners Inc ....E 316 773-1400
Maize *(G-6512)*
Davita Inc ....E 620 331-6117
Independence *(G-3511)*
Davita Inc ....E 913 660-8881
Lenexa *(G-5805)*
Fms Midwest Dialysis Ctrs LLC ....F 316 634-6760
Wichita *(G-14396)*
Fms Midwest Dialysis Ctrs LLC ....F 620 431-1239
Chanute *(G-728)*
Fms Midwest Dialysis Ctrs LLC ....F 316 729-5321
Wichita *(G-14397)*
Fresenius Med Care W Wllow LLC ....F 785 625-0033
Hays *(G-2813)*
Kenai Dialysis LLC ....E 913 649-2671
Overland Park *(G-8914)*
Nra-Ukmc Kansas LLC ....F 913 299-1044
Kansas City *(G-4290)*
Renal Trtmnt Centers-West Inc ....F 316 788-2899
Derby *(G-1268)*
Renal Trtmnt Centers-West Inc ....F 620 421-1081
Parsons *(G-9730)*
Renal Trtmnt Centers-West Inc ....F 316 263-9090
Wichita *(G-15443)*
Renal Trtmnt Centers-West Inc ....F 316 636-5719
Wichita *(G-15444)*
Renal Trtmnt Centers-West Inc ....F 620 331-6117
Independence *(G-3554)*
Renal Trtmnt Centers-West Inc ....E 316 684-3200
Wichita *(G-15445)*
Renal Trtmnt Centers-West Inc ....F 620 260-9852
Garden City *(G-2266)*
Salina County Medical Supply ....F 785 823-6416
Salina *(G-10670)*
Total Renal Care Inc ....E 785 235-1094
Topeka *(G-13194)*
Total Renal Care Inc ....E 785 841-0490
Lawrence *(G-5143)*
Total Renal Care Inc ....E 620 340-8043
Emporia *(G-1839)*
Total Renal Care Inc ....E 785 273-1824
Topeka *(G-13195)*
Total Renal Care Inc ....F 785 843-2000
Lawrence *(G-5144)*
Total Renal Care Inc ....E 913 287-5724
Kansas City *(G-4470)*
Windcreek Dialysis LLC ....E 913 294-8417
Paola *(G-9596)*
Wyandotte Central Dialysis LLC ....F 913 233-0536
Kansas City *(G-4552)*

KINDERGARTEN

Ancilla Center For Children ....F 913 758-6113
Leavenworth *(G-5202)*
Archdiocese Kansas Cy In Kans ....E 913 631-0004
Shawnee Mission *(G-11117)*
Early Childhood Dev Ctr ....E 620 544-4334
Hugoton *(G-3161)*
Happy House Day Care ....F 913 782-1115
Olathe *(G-7751)*
Little Learners Early Childho ....F 913 254-1818
Olathe *(G-7861)*

KITCHEN CABINET STORES, EXC CUSTOM

CCM Countertop & Cab Mfg LLC ....F 316 554-0113
Wichita *(G-13967)*
Guthridge/Nighswonger Corp ....F 316 264-7900
Wichita *(G-14529)*
Roys Custom Cabinets ....G 785 625-6724
Hays *(G-2902)*

KITCHEN CABINETS WHOLESALERS

Century Wood Products Inc ....G 913 839-8725
Olathe *(G-7587)*
Kc Cabinetwright Inc ....E 913 825-6555
Lenexa *(G-5939)*
Roys Custom Cabinets ....G 785 625-6724
Hays *(G-2902)*

KITCHENWARE STORES

Muckenthaler Incorporated ....F 620 342-5653
Emporia *(G-1799)*
R P Products Inc ....E 913 492-6380
Shawnee Mission *(G-11773)*

KNIVES: Agricultural Or indl

McM Manufacturing Inc ....G 785 235-1015
Topeka *(G-12872)*

LABELS: Paper, Made From Purchased Materials

Creative Mktg Unlimited Inc ....G 913 894-0077
Overland Park *(G-8611)*
GC Labels Inc ....F 913 897-6966
Stilwell *(G-12148)*
Lowen Corporation ....B 620 663-2161
Hutchinson *(G-3358)*
Lynn Tape & Label ....F 913 422-0484
Kansas City *(G-4210)*
Phenix Label Company Inc ....D 913 327-7000
Olathe *(G-7984)*

LABOR UNION

Construction & Gen Labor 1290 ....F 913 432-1903
Kansas City *(G-3934)*
I A M A W District Lodge 70 ....F 316 522-1591
Wichita *(G-14663)*
International Brotherhood ....E 913 371-2640
Kansas City *(G-4103)*
International Union United Au ....A 913 342-7330
Kansas City *(G-4109)*
International Union United Au ....C 620 251-2022
Coffeyville *(G-948)*
Kansas State Council of Fire ....F 620 662-1808
Hutchinson *(G-3347)*
National Assn Ltr Carriers ....E 620 378-3263
Coyville *(G-1183)*
National Assn Ltr Carriers ....E 620 257-3934
Lyons *(G-6495)*
National Assn Ltr Carriers ....F 785 232-6835
Topeka *(G-12923)*
Teamsters Union Local 795 ....F 316 683-2651
Wichita *(G-15722)*
Ufcw District Union Local 2 ....E 816 842-4086
Bel Aire *(G-442)*
United Steel Wrkrs of America ....F 785 234-5688
Topeka *(G-13210)*
United Steelworkers ....E 913 674-5067
Atchison *(G-268)*

LABORATORIES, TESTING: Food

Als Marshfield LLC ....F 620 225-4172
Dodge City *(G-1292)*
Veriprime Inc ....E 620 873-7175
Meade *(G-7055)*

LABORATORIES, TESTING: Forensic

Kruger Technologies Inc ....E 913 498-1114
Overland Park *(G-8929)*

LABORATORIES, TESTING: Hazardous Waste

Pace Analytical Services Inc ....D 913 599-5665
Lenexa *(G-6042)*

LABORATORIES, TESTING: Hydrostatic

Kansas State University ....E 620 421-4826
Parsons *(G-9697)*

LABORATORIES, TESTING: Metallurgical

Arrow Laboratory Inc ....F 316 267-2893
Wichita *(G-13736)*

LABORATORIES, TESTING: Pollution

Shaw Group Inc ....A 316 220-8020
Wichita *(G-15577)*

LABORATORIES, TESTING: Product Testing

Dvt LLC ....E 913 636-3056
Overland Park *(G-8667)*

LABORATORIES, TESTING: Product Testing, Safety/Performance

Metal Finishing Company Inc ....F 316 267-7289
Wichita *(G-15053)*

LABORATORIES, TESTING: Soil Analysis

Gsi Engineering Nthrn Div LLC ....F 316 554-0725
Wichita *(G-14523)*

LABORATORIES, TESTING: Veterinary

Antech Diagnostics Inc ....E 913 529-4392
Overland Park *(G-8388)*
K State Rabies Laboratory ....F 785 532-4472
Manhattan *(G-6668)*
Sdk Laboratories Inc ....E 620 665-5661
Hutchinson *(G-3439)*

LABORATORIES, TESTING: Water

Continental Analytical Svcs ....E 785 827-1273
Salina *(G-10461)*

LABORATORIES: Biological Research

Mriglobal - Kansas LLC ....A 816 753-7600
Manhattan *(G-6754)*

LABORATORIES: Biotechnology

Deciphera Pharmaceuticals LLC ....F 785 830-2100
Lawrence *(G-4830)*
Heartland Plant Innovations ....F 785 320-4300
Manhattan *(G-6652)*
Kcas LLC ....C 913 248-3000
Shawnee Mission *(G-11524)*
PRA International LLC ....F 913 345-5754
Lenexa *(G-6067)*
United Biosource LLC ....D 913 339-7000
Overland Park *(G-9442)*

LABORATORIES: Blood Analysis

Biodesix Inc ....E 913 583-9000
De Soto *(G-1195)*
Kansas Dialysis Services LLC ....D 785 234-2277
Topeka *(G-12774)*

LABORATORIES: Commercial Nonphysical Research

Deere & Company ....E 913 310-8100
Olathe *(G-7645)*
Glover Inc ....E 800 654-1511
Olathe *(G-7735)*
Harte-Hanks Inc ....B 913 312-8100
Shawnee Mission *(G-11413)*
National Opinion Research Ctr ....D 316 221-5800
Wichita *(G-15150)*

LABORATORIES: Dental

Dental Concepts Inc ....F 913 829-0242
Olathe *(G-7648)*
Dentek Inc ....E 913 262-1717
Lenexa *(G-5812)*
Interdent Inc ....E 913 248-8880
Lenexa *(G-5918)*
Legends Drive Dental Ctr LLC ....F 785 841-5590
Lawrence *(G-4992)*
Sokolov Dental Laboratory Inc ....E 913 262-5444
Shawnee Mission *(G-11879)*
Sunflower Dental Studio Inc ....F 785 354-1981
Topeka *(G-13118)*

LABORATORIES: Dental & Medical X-Ray

Central KS Medical Park PA ....F 620 793-5404
Great Bend *(G-2533)*
Dodge Cy Unified Schl Dst 443 ....D 620 227-7771
Dodge City *(G-1355)*
General Electric Company ....A 785 666-4244
Dorrance *(G-1464)*
Johnson County Imaging Ctr PA ....E 913 469-8998
Overland Park *(G-8878)*

LABORATORIES: Dental, Artificial Teeth Production

Sentage Corporation ....D 785 235-9293
Topeka *(G-13059)*
Sentage Corporation ....E 316 263-0284
Wichita *(G-15561)*

LABORATORIES: Dental, Crown & Bridge Production

Eurodent Dental Lab Inc ....F 913 685-9930
Shawnee Mission *(G-11347)*
Ful Tech Dental Lab Inc ....F 316 681-3546
Wichita *(G-14430)*

Jade Dental Lab Inc ....E 913 469-9500
Shawnee Mission *(G-11481)*
Kaylor Dental Laboratory Inc ....D 316 943-3226
Wichita *(G-14835)*
Medallion Dental Lab Inc ....F 913 642-0039
Prairie Village *(G-10047)*
Modern Methods ....F 316 686-6391
Wichita *(G-15120)*
Myrons Dental Laboratories ....E 800 359-7111
Kansas City *(G-4276)*
Root Laboratory Inc ....C 913 491-3555
Leawood *(G-5543)*
Steve Hnsens Prcision Dntl Lab ....E 913 432-6951
Shawnee Mission *(G-11898)*

LABORATORIES: Electronic Research

Solid State Sonics & Elec ....G 785 232-0497
Topeka *(G-13080)*

LABORATORIES: Environmental Research

University of Kansas ....D 785 864-1500
Lawrence *(G-5161)*

LABORATORIES: Medical

Ameripath Inc ....E 816 412-7003
Lenexa *(G-5653)*
Boyce Bynum Pathology Labs PC ....E 816 813-2792
Lenexa *(G-5709)*
Consultants In Neurology PA ....E 913 894-1500
Shawnee Mission *(G-11262)*
Diagnostic Imaging Center ....E 913 491-9299
Shawnee Mission *(G-11305)*
Hays Pathology Laboratories PA ....E 785 650-2700
Hays *(G-2837)*
Hutchinson Clinic PA ....A 620 669-2500
Hutchinson *(G-3319)*
Infectious Disease Cons PA ....E 316 264-3505
Wichita *(G-14689)*
Kansas Pathology Cons PA ....E 316 681-2741
Wichita *(G-14818)*
Kansas State University ....D 785 532-5650
Manhattan *(G-6688)*
Ksu Dprtment of Clncal Science ....D 785 532-5690
Manhattan *(G-6703)*
Kupi Rprdctive Endcrnology Lab ....E 913 588-6377
Kansas City *(G-4184)*
Mercy Kansas Communities Inc ....F 620 332-3215
Independence *(G-3538)*
Mid Star Lab Inc ....F 913 369-8734
Tonganoxie *(G-12268)*
New York Blood Center Inc ....E 785 233-0195
Topeka *(G-12926)*
Palmer Webber Macy ....E 785 823-7201
Salina *(G-10631)*
PH Enterprises Inc ....F 620 232-1900
Pittsburg *(G-9913)*
Quest Diagnostics Incorporated ....F 785 621-4300
Hays *(G-2894)*
Quest Diagnostics Incorporated ....F 913 768-1959
Olathe *(G-8015)*
Riordan Clinic Inc ....E 316 682-3100
Wichita *(G-15464)*
Ultrasound For Women LLC ....E 785 331-4160
Lawrence *(G-5149)*

LABORATORIES: Medical Pathology

Anatomical Pathology Services ....E 620 421-2424
Parsons *(G-9666)*
Cytocheck Laboratory LLC ....E 620 421-2424
Parsons *(G-9678)*
Laboratory Corporation America ....B 913 338-4070
Overland Park *(G-8938)*
Laboratory Corporation America ....C 316 636-2300
Wichita *(G-14910)*
Peterson Laboratory Svcs PA ....D 785 539-5363
Manhattan *(G-6774)*
South Central Pathology Lab PA ....F 316 689-5668
Wichita *(G-15618)*
Weber Palmer & Macy Chartered ....E 785 823-7201
Salina *(G-10763)*

LABORATORIES: Neurological

Kansas Spine Spcialty Hosp LLC ....C 316 462-5000
Wichita *(G-14824)*
Salina Regional Health Ctr Inc ....D 785 823-1032
Salina *(G-10685)*
Somnograph Inc ....D 316 925-4624
Wichita *(G-15612)*

LABORATORIES: Noncommercial Research

190th Medical Group ....D 785 861-4663
Topeka *(G-12274)*
American Cancer Socty Heartlnd ....F 316 265-3400
Wichita *(G-13688)*
Glover Inc ....E 800 654-1511
Olathe *(G-7735)*
Jewish Heritage Fndtn Greater ....E 913 981-8866
Leawood *(G-5442)*
Mitre Corporation ....E 913 946-1900
Leavenworth *(G-5271)*
South Central KS Econ Dev Dist ....E 316 262-7035
Wichita *(G-15617)*

LABORATORIES: Physical Research, Commercial

Alliance Monitoring Tech LLC ....F 316 263-7775
Wichita *(G-13670)*
Clinical Reference Lab Inc ....B 913 492-3652
Lenexa *(G-5765)*
Eaglepicher Technologies LLC ....F 620 232-3631
Pittsburg *(G-9854)*
Ez2 Technologies Inc ....E 913 498-8872
Leawood *(G-5393)*
Fairmount Technologies LLC ....F 316 978-3313
Wichita *(G-14335)*
Iqvua RDS Inc ....D 913 894-5533
Shawnee Mission *(G-11467)*
Iqvua RDS Inc ....D 913 708-6000
Overland Park *(G-8862)*
Paragon N D T & Finishes Inc ....E 316 945-5285
Wichita *(G-15259)*
PRA International ....D 913 410-2000
Lenexa *(G-6066)*
PRA Intrntional Operations Inc ....B 913 410-2000
Shawnee Mission *(G-11746)*
Secureaire Ltd Liability Co ....F 813 766-0400
Lenexa *(G-6122)*
Servi Tech Inc ....C 620 227-7509
Dodge City *(G-1429)*

LABORATORIES: Testing

Affiliated Medical Svcs Lab ....D 316 265-4533
Wichita *(G-13641)*
Aviation Cnslting Engrg Sltons ....G 316 265-8335
Maize *(G-6508)*
Clinical Reference Lab Inc ....B 913 492-3652
Lenexa *(G-5765)*
Great Plains Laboratory Inc ....D 913 341-8949
Overland Park *(G-8774)*
Heartland Health Labs Inc ....D 913 599-3636
Lenexa *(G-5897)*
Labone Inc ....A 913 888-1770
Lenexa *(G-5961)*
Laboratory Corporation America ....E 785 539-2537
Manhattan *(G-6707)*
Mid America Pathology Lab LLC ....E 913 341-6275
Overland Park *(G-9022)*
Pipeline Tstg Consortium Inc ....E 620 669-8800
Hutchinson *(G-3406)*
Progene Biomedical Inc ....F 913 492-2224
Lenexa *(G-6074)*
Quest Diagnostics Incorporated ....F 913 299-8538
Kansas City *(G-4353)*
Quest Diagnostics Incorporated ....F 913 982-2900
Shawnee Mission *(G-11767)*
Quest Diagnostics Incorporated ....F 316 634-1946
Wichita *(G-15391)*
Somnitech Inc ....E 913 498-8120
Overland Park *(G-9327)*
Synexis LLC ....F 816 399-0895
Overland Park *(G-9388)*

LABORATORIES: Testing

Als USA Inc ....E 913 281-9881
Kansas City *(G-3802)*
Certified Environmental Mgt ....E 785 823-0492
Salina *(G-10446)*
Clinical Reference Lab Inc ....B 913 492-3652
Lenexa *(G-5765)*
Colt Tech LLC ....G 913 839-8198
Olathe *(G-7600)*
County of Johnson ....F 913 432-3868
Shawnee Mission *(G-11270)*
Dbi Inc ....E 316 831-9323
Wichita *(G-14177)*
Dbi Inc ....E 913 888-2321
Lenexa *(G-5807)*

Identigen North America Inc ....F 785 856-8800
Lawrence *(G-4908)*
Idexx Laboratories Inc ....D 913 339-4550
Lenexa *(G-5909)*
K-State Diagnostic & Analyticl ....C 785 532-3294
Manhattan *(G-6669)*
Kcas LLC ....C 913 248-3000
Shawnee Mission *(G-11524)*
Ksu National Gas Machinery Lab ....F 785 532-2617
Manhattan *(G-6705)*
Lee Dental Laboratory ....F 913 599-3888
Shawnee *(G-10985)*
Meridian Analytical Labs LLC ....F 620 328-3222
Mound Valley *(G-7177)*
NTS Technical Systems ....F 316 832-1600
Wichita *(G-15198)*
Paragon N D T & Finishes Inc ....E 316 945-5285
Wichita *(G-15259)*
Professnal Toxicology Svcs Inc ....F 913 599-3535
Overland Park *(G-9189)*
Syntech Research Lab Svcs LLC ....E 913 378-0998
Stilwell *(G-12175)*

LABORATORY APPARATUS & FURNITURE

Labconco Corporation ....E 620 223-5700
Fort Scott *(G-1980)*
Schroer Manufacturing Company ....C 913 281-1500
Kansas City *(G-4404)*
T Kennel Systems Inc ....D 816 668-8995
Kansas City *(G-4454)*

LABORATORY CHEMICALS: Organic

Jacam Chemicals 2013 LLC ....C 620 278-3355
Sterling *(G-12123)*
Labone Inc ....G 913 577-1643
Shawnee Mission *(G-11545)*
Phytotech Labs Inc ....F 913 341-5343
Lenexa *(G-6056)*

LABORATORY EQPT, EXC MEDICAL: Wholesalers

Continental Equipment Company ....F 913 845-2148
Tonganoxie *(G-12258)*

LABORATORY EQPT: Chemical

Phytotech Labs Inc ....F 913 341-5343
Lenexa *(G-6056)*

LABORATORY INSTRUMENT REPAIR SVCS

McLaughlin Leasing Inc ....F 316 542-0303
Cheney *(G-794)*

LADDERS: Metal

Locknclimb LLC ....G 620 331-8247
Independence *(G-3534)*

LAMINATED PLASTICS: Plate, Sheet, Rod & Tubes

Mid America Products Inc ....C 913 856-6550
Gardner *(G-2355)*

LAMP & LIGHT BULBS & TUBES

Advanced Technologies Inc ....G 316 744-2285
Bel Aire *(G-427)*
Occk Inc ....C 785 827-9383
Salina *(G-10617)*
Pwi Inc ....E 316 942-2811
Wichita *(G-15380)*

LAMP BULBS & TUBES, ELEC: Lead-In Wires, From Purchased Wire

Cmt Inc ....C 785 762-4400
Junction City *(G-3683)*
Junction City Wire Harness LLC ....D 785 762-4400
Junction City *(G-3706)*

LAMP BULBS & TUBES, ELECTRIC: Light, Complete

Led Direct LLC ....G 913 912-3760
Kansas City *(G-4198)*

LAMPS: Fluorescent

Signify North America Corp..................D....... 785 826-5218
Salina *(G-10708)*

LAND SUBDIVIDERS & DEVELOPERS: Commercial

Licausi-Styers Company........................E....... 913 681-5888
Shawnee Mission *(G-11568)*
Mark IV Associates LLC..........................E....... 913 345-2120
Shawnee Mission *(G-11595)*
OS Companies Inc.................................E....... 316 265-5611
Wichita *(G-15238)*
Petersen Development Corp....................F....... 785 228-9494
Topeka *(G-12971)*
Quality Inv Prpts Land Co LLC...............F....... 913 312-5500
Overland Park *(G-9212)*
Summit Group of Salina KS LP...............F....... 785 826-1711
Salina *(G-10718)*

LAND SUBDIVIDERS & DEVELOPERS: Residential

John H Moffitt & Co Inc..........................E....... 913 491-6800
Shawnee Mission *(G-11491)*

LAND SUBDIVISION & DEVELOPMENT

Alvamar Inc..E....... 785 842-2929
Lawrence *(G-4732)*
Builders Development Inc........................E....... 316 684-1400
Wichita *(G-13913)*
Clark Investment Group..........................E....... 316 634-1112
Wichita *(G-14037)*
Corvias Military Living LLC....................F....... 785 717-2200
Fort Riley *(G-1947)*
General Financial Services Inc...............G....... 316 636-1070
Wichita *(G-14456)*
Haren & Laughlin Cnstr Co Inc...............E....... 913 495-9558
Lenexa *(G-5890)*
J A Peterson Enterprises Inc..................E....... 913 384-3800
Shawnee Mission *(G-11471)*
Jones & Jones Development LLC.............F....... 913 422-9477
Bonner Springs *(G-557)*
Kdc Construction Inc..............................F....... 913 677-1920
Leawood *(G-5447)*
Kessinger/Hunter & Company Lc..............C....... 816 842-2690
Shawnee Mission *(G-11529)*
Lodging Enterprises LLC.........................A....... 316 630-6300
Wichita *(G-14975)*
McCullough Development Inc..................E....... 888 776-3010
Manhattan *(G-6737)*
Midland Properties Inc...........................F....... 913 677-5300
Mission Woods *(G-7151)*
Nai Heartland Co....................................F....... 913 362-1000
Leawood *(G-5496)*
Prime Development Company..................F....... 316 634-0643
Wichita *(G-15344)*
Sheets Adams Realtors Inc......................F....... 620 241-3648
McPherson *(G-7026)*
Southwind Development Co.....................E....... 620 275-2117
Garden City *(G-2285)*
Turkey Creek Golf Course.......................F....... 620 241-8530
McPherson *(G-7032)*
Tutera Group Inc...................................E....... 913 851-0215
Shawnee Mission *(G-11951)*
Woodstone Inc.......................................F....... 913 685-2282
Shawnee Mission *(G-12018)*

LASER SYSTEMS & EQPT

Paragon Holdings Lc...............................E....... 620 343-0920
Emporia *(G-1811)*

LAUNDRIES, EXC POWER & COIN-OPERATED

Best Value Services LLC.........................D....... 316 440-1048
Wichita *(G-13839)*

LAUNDRY & DRYCLEANING SVCS, EXC COIN-OPERATED: Pickup

Band Box Corporation.............................E....... 785 272-6646
Topeka *(G-12361)*

LAUNDRY & GARMENT SVCS, NEC: Fur Cleaning, Repairing/Storage

Alaskan Fur Company Inc........................E....... 913 649-4000
Overland Park *(G-8365)*
Bayless Dry Cleaning Inc........................F....... 620 793-3576
Great Bend *(G-2517)*

LAUNDRY & GARMENT SVCS, NEC: Garment Alteration & Repair

Comet 1 H R Cleaners Inc.......................F....... 620 626-8100
Liberal *(G-6295)*
Scotch Industries Inc..............................E....... 785 843-8585
Lawrence *(G-5105)*
Something Different Inc..........................G....... 785 537-1171
Wamego *(G-13441)*
U S S A Inc..G....... 316 686-1653
Wichita *(G-15826)*

LAUNDRY & GARMENT SVCS, NEC: Garment Making, Alter & Repair

Mias Bridal & Tailoring LLC.....................F....... 913 764-9114
Olathe *(G-7890)*

LAUNDRY & GARMENT SVCS: Tailor Shop, Exc Custom/Merchant

Expert Alteration....................................G....... 913 322-2242
Westwood *(G-13553)*

LAUNDRY SVC: Wiping Towel Sply

Waxene Products Company Inc................G....... 316 263-8523
Wichita *(G-15938)*

LAUNDRY SVCS: Indl

Ameripride Services Inc..........................D....... 785 234-3475
Topeka *(G-12324)*
Aramark Unf & Career AP LLC.................D....... 316 262-5467
Wichita *(G-13726)*
N C K Commercial Laundry Inc................F....... 785 243-4432
Concordia *(G-1124)*
Penn Enterprises Inc..............................E....... 785 762-3600
Junction City *(G-3737)*
Unifirst Corporation................................F....... 316 264-2342
Wichita *(G-15837)*

LAWN & GARDEN EQPT

Century Partners LLC..............................F....... 913 642-2489
Olathe *(G-7586)*
Danville Industries..................................G....... 620 896-7126
Harper *(G-2719)*
First Start Rentl Sls Svc Inc....................G....... 620 343-0983
Emporia *(G-1756)*
Great Plains Manufacturing Inc...............C....... 785 263-2486
Abilene *(G-34)*
Harper Industries Inc..............................D....... 620 896-7381
Harper *(G-2723)*
Prohoe Mfg LLC.....................................F....... 785 987-5450
Munden *(G-7229)*

LAWN & GARDEN EQPT STORES

Excel Sales Inc.......................................F....... 620 327-4911
Hesston *(G-2990)*
Foster Unruh Inc....................................E....... 620 227-2165
Dodge City *(G-1362)*
J & W Equipment Inc...............................F....... 620 365-2341
Iola *(G-3614)*
Kaw Valley Industrial Inc.........................G....... 785 841-9751
Eudora *(G-1876)*
McConnell Machinery Co Inc...................F....... 785 843-2676
Lawrence *(G-5016)*
Pankratz Implement Co...........................E....... 620 662-8681
Hutchinson *(G-3399)*
Tractor Supply Company.........................F....... 785 827-3300
Salina *(G-10738)*
Tractor Supply Company.........................F....... 620 663-7607
Hutchinson *(G-3465)*

LAWN & GARDEN EQPT: Grass Catchers, Lawn Mower

Taylor Implement Co Inc..........................E....... 785 675-3272
Hoxie *(G-3143)*

LAWN & GARDEN EQPT: Lawnmowers, Residential, Hand Or Power

Moridge Manufacturing Inc......................B....... 620 345-6301
Moundridge *(G-7193)*

LAWN & GARDEN EQPT: Rollers

Lippert Components Inc..........................G....... 785 282-6366
Smith Center *(G-12037)*

LAWN & GARDEN EQPT: Tractors & Eqpt

Heritage Tractor Inc...............................E....... 785 235-5100
Topeka *(G-12686)*

LAWN MOWER REPAIR SHOP

Century Partners LLC..............................F....... 913 642-2489
Olathe *(G-7586)*
Excel Sales Inc.......................................F....... 620 327-4911
Hesston *(G-2990)*
Heritage Tractor Inc...............................E....... 785 235-5100
Topeka *(G-12686)*

LEASING & RENTAL SVCS: Cranes & Aerial Lift Eqpt

Belger Cartage Service Inc......................E....... 316 943-0101
Wichita *(G-13829)*
Building Erection Svcs Co Inc..................E....... 913 764-5560
Olathe *(G-7568)*
Duke Aerial Inc......................................F....... 785 494-8001
Saint George *(G-10346)*
Gerard Tank & Steel Inc..........................E....... 785 243-3895
Concordia *(G-1116)*
Midwest Crane and Rigging LLC..............E....... 913 747-5100
Olathe *(G-7894)*
Nesco Holdings Inc.................................G....... 913 287-0001
Kansas City *(G-4286)*
Panhandle Steel Erectors Inc..................F....... 620 271-9878
Garden City *(G-2247)*
Russell & Russell LLC............................F....... 785 827-4878
Salina *(G-10654)*
Wilkerson Crane Rental Inc.....................E....... 913 238-7030
Lenexa *(G-6230)*

LEASING & RENTAL SVCS: Oil Field Eqpt

Reinhardt Services Inc............................G....... 785 483-2556
Russell *(G-10287)*

LEASING & RENTAL SVCS: Oil Well Drilling

Trimble & Maclaskey Oil LLC...................F....... 620 836-2000
Gridley *(G-2691)*
U S Weatherford L P...............................D....... 620 624-6273
Liberal *(G-6377)*

LEASING & RENTAL: Computers & Eqpt

Evolv Solutions LLC................................E....... 913 469-8900
Shawnee Mission *(G-11352)*

LEASING & RENTAL: Construction & Mining Eqpt

AAF Fleet Service Inc.............................F....... 913 683-3816
Mc Louth *(G-6924)*
Berry Companies Inc...............................E....... 785 232-7731
Topeka *(G-12375)*
Cillessen Equipment Co LLC....................F....... 316 682-2400
Kechi *(G-4566)*
Crane Sales & Service Co Inc..................F....... 913 621-7040
Kansas City *(G-3944)*
Eby Corporation.....................................F....... 316 268-3500
Wichita *(G-14256)*
Ferco Inc...E....... 785 825-6380
Salina *(G-10500)*
Foley Equipment Company.......................D....... 785 537-2101
Manhattan *(G-6637)*
Foley Industries Inc................................D....... 316 943-4211
Wichita *(G-14399)*
Foley Supply LLC....................................E....... 316 944-7368
Wichita *(G-14400)*
High Reach Equipment LLC.....................F....... 316 942-5438
Wichita *(G-14605)*
Midwest Siding Incorporated...................E....... 785 825-5576
Salina *(G-10602)*
Road Builders Mchy & Sup Co.................D....... 913 371-3822
Kansas City *(G-4384)*
Sunbelt Rentals Inc.................................F....... 316 789-7000
Wichita *(G-15684)*

Trinity Sales LLC ...E ... 316 942-5555
Wichita *(G-15803)*
U-Haul Co of Kansas Inc ...D ... 913 287-1327
Kansas City *(G-4481)*
United Rentals North Amer Inc ...F ... 316 682-7368
Wichita *(G-15848)*

LEASING & RENTAL: Medical Machinery & Eqpt

American Homepatient Inc ...E ... 913 495-9545
Lenexa *(G-5649)*
Apria Healthcare LLC ...E ... 316 689-4500
Wichita *(G-13725)*
Apria Healthcare LLC ...F ... 785 272-8411
Topeka *(G-12335)*
Ascension Via Christi Home Med ...D ... 316 265-4991
Wichita *(G-13746)*
Broadway Home Medical Inc ...F ... 316 264-8600
Wichita *(G-13895)*
First Biomedical Inc ...E ... 800 962-9656
Lenexa *(G-5856)*
Health Care Inc ...A ... 620 665-2000
Hutchinson *(G-3309)*
Hutchinson Hlth Care Svcs Inc ...E ... 620 665-0528
Hutchinson *(G-3321)*

LEASING & RENTAL: Mobile Home Sites

American Rsdntial Cmmnties LLC ...F ... 785 776-4440
Manhattan *(G-6542)*
Bartos Enterprises Inc ...F ... 620 232-9813
Frontenac *(G-2053)*
Martin Mobile Home Park Inc ...F ... 620 275-4722
Garden City *(G-2228)*
Mid-America Mnfct Hsng Cmmnts ...D ... 913 441-0194
Kansas City *(G-4243)*
Southborough Partners ...F ... 316 529-3200
Wichita *(G-15621)*

LEASING & RENTAL: Office Machines & Eqpt

ABC Leasing Co Inc ...E ... 785 267-4555
Topeka *(G-12282)*
Century Business Technologies ...E ... 785 267-4555
Topeka *(G-12458)*
Midwest Office Technology ...E ... 913 894-9600
Overland Park *(G-9034)*
Ricoh Usa Inc ...E ... 316 262-7172
Wichita *(G-15461)*
Sta-Mot-Ks LLC ...E ... 913 894-9600
Overland Park *(G-9349)*

LEASING & RENTAL: Other Real Estate Property

Bent Tree Partners LLC ...F ... 417 206-7846
Galena *(G-2069)*
Blecha Enterprises LLC ...F ... 785 539-6640
Manhattan *(G-6563)*
Employers Mutual Casualty Co ...E ... 913 663-0119
Overland Park *(G-8679)*
Employers Mutual Casualty Co ...C ... 316 352-5700
Wichita *(G-14279)*
Fairleigh Ranch Corporation ...F ... 620 872-2111
Scott City *(G-10810)*
Home Town Real ...F ... 620 271-9500
Garden City *(G-2198)*
KS Commercial RE Svcs Inc ...F ... 785 272-2525
Topeka *(G-12824)*
Northstar Property Management ...F ... 316 689-8577
Wichita *(G-15194)*
Qae Acquisition Company LLC ...F ... 913 814-9988
Overland Park *(G-9206)*
Quality Technology Svcs NJ LLC ...F ... 913 814-9988
Overland Park *(G-9218)*
Reece & Nichols Realtors Inc ...F ... 913 247-3064
Spring Hill *(G-12097)*
Sheila M Burdett Agency LLC ...F ... 785 762-2451
Junction City *(G-3753)*
Walnut Ridge Group Inc ...F ... 620 232-3359
Pittsburg *(G-9961)*

LEASING & RENTAL: Trucks, Without Drivers

Garden City Travel Plaza LLC ...E ... 620 275-4404
Garden City *(G-2179)*
Mead Rental Center ...F ... 620 672-7718
Pratt *(G-10125)*
Midwest Bus Sales Inc ...E ... 913 422-1000
Bonner Springs *(G-562)*
Mike Groves Oil Inc ...F ... 620 442-0480
Arkansas City *(G-166)*
Paynes Inc ...F ... 620 231-3170
Frontenac *(G-2063)*
Penske Truck Leasing Co LP ...F ... 316 943-8500
Wichita *(G-15278)*
Penske Truck Leasing Co LP ...F ... 785 776-3139
Manhattan *(G-6772)*
Roberts Truck Ctr Holdg Co LLC ...D ... 316 262-8413
Park City *(G-9640)*
Santa Fe Market Inc ...F ... 785 594-7466
Baldwin City *(G-368)*
Stewart Truck Leasing Inc ...E ... 785 827-0336
Salina *(G-10716)*
U Haul Co Independent Dealers ...F ... 316 722-0216
Maize *(G-6522)*
U-Haul Co of Kansas Inc ...D ... 913 287-1327
Kansas City *(G-4481)*
U-Haul Co of Oregon ...F ... 913 780-4494
Olathe *(G-8130)*

LEASING & RENTAL: Utility Trailers & RV's

Ryder Truck Rental Inc ...E ... 913 888-5040
Shawnee Mission *(G-11818)*

LEASING: Laundry Eqpt

Jetz Service Co Inc ...F ... 785 354-7588
Topeka *(G-12744)*

LEASING: Passenger Car

Bob Allen Ford Inc ...D ... 913 381-3000
Overland Park *(G-8473)*
Bud Brown Automotive Inc ...D ... 913 393-8100
Olathe *(G-7564)*
Enterprise Leasing Co KS LLC ...C ... 913 383-1515
Shawnee Mission *(G-11340)*
Enterprise Leasing Co KS LLC ...F ... 913 262-8888
Shawnee Mission *(G-11342)*
Fleet Auto Rent Inc ...F ... 913 901-9900
Overland Park *(G-8727)*
Joe Self Chevrolet Inc ...C ... 316 689-4390
Wichita *(G-14760)*
Mel Hambelton Ford Inc ...C ... 316 462-3673
Wichita *(G-15035)*
Merchants Automotive Group Inc ...E ... 913 901-9900
Leawood *(G-5474)*
Noller Lincoln-Mercury Inc ...E ... 785 267-2800
Topeka *(G-12932)*
Oakley Motors Inc ...E ... 785 672-3238
Oakley *(G-7484)*
Ray Shepherd Motors Inc ...E ... 620 644-2625
Fort Scott *(G-2001)*
South Star Chrysler Inc ...F ... 785 242-5600
Ottawa *(G-8313)*

LEASING: Residential Buildings

Cof Residential Authority Inc ...F ... 785 242-5035
Ottawa *(G-8257)*
E State Management LLC ...F ... 785 312-9945
Lawrence *(G-4843)*
Fogelman Management Group LLC ...F ... 913 345-2888
Shawnee Mission *(G-11375)*
Timothy D White ...F ... 620 331-7060
Independence *(G-3565)*

LEASING: Shipping Container

Mobile Mini Inc ...F ... 316 838-2663
Park City *(G-9636)*

LEATHER GOODS, EXC FOOTWEAR, GLOVES, LUGGAGE/BELTING, WHOL

Berger Company ...F ... 913 367-3700
Atchison *(G-214)*

LEGAL & TAX SVCS

Thompson Tax & Associates LLC ...F ... 916 346-7829
Waverly *(G-13482)*
Unitedlex Corporation ...C ... 913 685-8900
Overland Park *(G-9446)*

LEGAL AID SVCS

Kansas Legal Services Inc ...E ... 620 227-7349
Dodge City *(G-1387)*
Kansas Legal Services Inc ...F ... 620 694-2955
Hutchinson *(G-3346)*
Kansas Legal Services Inc ...E ... 785 354-8531
Topeka *(G-12784)*
Kansas Legal Services Inc ...E ... 316 265-9681
Wichita *(G-14812)*
Kansas Legal Services Inc ...F ... 913 621-0200
Kansas City *(G-4156)*
Sharon Lee Family Health Care ...D ... 913 722-3100
Kansas City *(G-4420)*

LEGAL OFFICES & SVCS

Adams Brown Bran Ball Chrtered ...F ... 620 549-3271
Great Bend *(G-2500)*
Adams Brown Bran Ball Chrtered ...F ... 620 241-2090
McPherson *(G-6931)*
Administration Kansas Dept ...F ... 785 296-3017
Topeka *(G-12291)*
Barber Financial Group Inc ...F ... 913 393-1000
Lenexa *(G-5686)*
Brenton Financial Group Inc ...F ... 913 451-9072
Overland Park *(G-8483)*
County of Allen ...E ... 620 365-1425
Iola *(G-3597)*
Holman Hansen and Colvile PC ...E ... 913 648-7272
Leawood *(G-5431)*
Indigents Defense Svcs Kans Bd ...F ... 785 296-1833
Topeka *(G-12717)*
Indigents Defense Svcs Kans Bd ...F ... 785 296-6631
Topeka *(G-12718)*
Indigents Defense Svcs Kans Bd ...E ... 785 296-5484
Topeka *(G-12719)*
James S Willard ...F ... 785 267-0040
Topeka *(G-12737)*
Judiciary Court of The State ...D ... 785 233-8200
Topeka *(G-12751)*
Kansas Dept For Chldren Fmlies ...C ... 785 296-1368
Topeka *(G-12771)*
Kansas Medical Mutual Insur Co ...E ... 785 232-2224
Topeka *(G-12790)*
Ryan Condray and Wenger LLC ...F ... 785 632-5666
Clay Center *(G-880)*
Western Professional Assoc ...F ... 316 264-5628
Wichita *(G-15961)*
Wichita Bar Association ...F ... 316 263-2251
Wichita *(G-15980)*
Wilbert & Towner PA ...F ... 620 231-5620
Pittsburg *(G-9969)*
Work Comp Specialty Associates ...E ... 785 841-7751
Lawrence *(G-5191)*
Yeretsky & Maher LLC ...F ... 913 897-5813
Shawnee Mission *(G-12023)*

LEGAL SVCS: Administrative & Government Law

County of Johnson ...C ... 913 715-3300
Olathe *(G-7622)*
Hinkle Law Firm LLC ...D ... 316 267-2000
Wichita *(G-14616)*
Sunflwer Child Spport Svcs LLC ...F ... 785 623-4516
Hays *(G-2917)*

LEGAL SVCS: Bankruptcy Law

Charles Ritz Inc ...F ... 913 685-2600
Overland Park *(G-8542)*
Ofc of US Trustee ...F ... 316 269-6607
Wichita *(G-15210)*
Wagoner Bankruptcy Group PC ...F ... 913 422-0909
Olathe *(G-8145)*
William H Griffin ...F ... 913 677-1311
Roeland Park *(G-10231)*

LEGAL SVCS: Criminal Law

Bottaro Morefield & Kubin Lc ...F ... 913 948-8200
Leawood *(G-5342)*
Butler & Associates PA ...E ... 785 267-6444
Topeka *(G-12416)*
Case Mses Zimmerman Martin PA ...F ... 316 303-0100
Wichita *(G-13957)*
Jennifer Brunetti ...D ... 620 235-0100
Frontenac *(G-2056)*
Joseph & Hollander PA ...F ... 316 262-9400
Wichita *(G-14772)*

LEGAL SVCS: Debt Collection Law

Berman & Rabin PA ...F ... 913 649-1555
Overland Park *(G-8442)*

LEGAL SVCS: Divorce & Family Law

Simpson Lgback Lynch Norris PA ....E....... 913 342-2500
Overland Park *(G-9313)*

LEGAL SVCS: General Practice Attorney or Lawyer

Adrian & Pankratz PA ....F....... 316 283-8746
Newton *(G-7306)*
Arthur Green LLP ....F....... 785 537-1345
Manhattan *(G-6546)*
Ausemus Stnley R Esq Chartered ....F....... 620 342-8717
Emporia *(G-1697)*
Bangerter Rebein PA ....F....... 620 227-8126
Dodge City *(G-1301)*
Barbera & Watkins LLC ....F....... 913 677-3800
Overland Park *(G-8432)*
Beam-Ward Kruse Wilson ....F....... 913 339-6888
Overland Park *(G-8436)*
Bretz & Young Law Office ....F....... 620 662-3435
Hutchinson *(G-3221)*
Bruce Bruce & Lehman LLC ....F....... 316 722-3391
Wichita *(G-13900)*
Busch Johnson & Mank ....F....... 316 263-5661
Wichita *(G-13919)*
Calihan Brwn Burgrdt Wurst ....F....... 620 276-2381
Garden City *(G-2120)*
County of Butler ....F....... 316 322-4130
El Dorado *(G-1553)*
Dana Manweiler Milby PA ....F....... 316 267-8677
Wichita *(G-14164)*
Davis Ktchmark Eschens McCrght ....F....... 816 842-1515
Leawood *(G-5374)*
Davis Unrein Hummer McCalister ....F....... 785 354-1100
Topeka *(G-12549)*
Dennis P Wetta ....F....... 316 267-5293
Wichita *(G-14192)*
Duggan Shadwick Doerr Kurlbaum ....F....... 913 498-3536
Overland Park *(G-8664)*
Elder & Disability Law Firm PA ....F....... 913 338-5713
Overland Park *(G-8673)*
Eric K Johnson ....F....... 785 267-2410
Topeka *(G-12581)*
Evans & Mullinix PA ....E....... 913 962-8700
Shawnee Mission *(G-11348)*
Ferree Bunn OGrady & Rundberg ....F....... 913 381-8180
Shawnee Mission *(G-11366)*
Fisher Pttrson Syler Smith LLP ....E....... 785 232-7761
Topeka *(G-12615)*
Fleeson Ging Coulson Kitch LLC ....D....... 316 267-7361
Wichita *(G-14384)*
Foulston Siefkin LLP ....D....... 316 291-9514
Wichita *(G-14405)*
Foulston Siefkin LLP ....C....... 316 267-6371
Wichita *(G-14406)*
Foulston Siefkin LLP ....E....... 913 498-2100
Overland Park *(G-8735)*
Foulston Siefkin LLP ....F....... 785 233-3600
Topeka *(G-12625)*
Frank C Allison Jr ....E....... 913 648-2080
Shawnee Mission *(G-11378)*
Fred Spigarelli PA ....F....... 620 231-1290
Pittsburg *(G-9862)*
Gillian & Hayes LLP ....F....... 316 264-7321
Wichita *(G-14464)*
Gilliland & Hayes PA ....D....... 620 662-0537
Hutchinson *(G-3299)*
Gilliland & Hayes PA ....F....... 913 317-5100
Overland Park *(G-8755)*
Gilliland & Hayes PA ....F....... 316 264-7321
Wichita *(G-14465)*
Gilmore Shellenberger & Maxwel ....F....... 620 624-5599
Liberal *(G-6312)*
Glassman Bird Powell LLP ....F....... 785 625-6919
Hays *(G-2816)*
Greenleaf & Brooks Smith ....F....... 620 624-6266
Liberal *(G-6315)*
Hampton & Royce Lc ....E....... 785 827-7251
Salina *(G-10532)*
Hayford East ....F....... 316 267-6259
Wichita *(G-14571)*
Hite Fanning & Honeyman LLP ....E....... 316 265-7741
Wichita *(G-14619)*
Hutton & Hutton Law Firm ....E....... 316 688-1166
Wichita *(G-14659)*
Indigents Defense Svcs Kans Bd ....E....... 316 264-8700
Wichita *(G-14684)*
Kahrs Nelson Fanning Hite Kllg ....D....... 316 265-7741
Wichita *(G-14779)*
Kreamer Kincaid Taylor ....F....... 913 782-2350
Overland Park *(G-8927)*
Lathrop & Gage LLP ....D....... 913 451-5100
Shawnee Mission *(G-11548)*
Law Offices of M Steven Wagle ....F....... 316 264-4878
Wichita *(G-14935)*
Lee Wilson & Gurney ....F....... 316 685-2245
Wichita *(G-14944)*
Little & Miller Chartered Inc ....F....... 785 841-6245
Lawrence *(G-4999)*
Marilyn M Wilder ....F....... 316 283-8746
Newton *(G-7376)*
McAnany Van Cleave & Phillips ....F....... 913 371-3838
Kansas City *(G-4224)*
McCullough Wareheim & Labunker ....F....... 785 233-2323
Topeka *(G-12869)*
McPherson & Mcvey Law Offices ....F....... 620 793-3420
Great Bend *(G-2608)*
Michael J Unrein Atty ....F....... 785 354-1100
Topeka *(G-12888)*
Midwest Bioscience RES Pk LLC ....E....... 913 319-0300
Leawood *(G-5482)*
Monnat & Spurrier Chartered ....F....... 316 264-2800
Wichita *(G-15123)*
Norton Wssrman Jones Kelly LLC ....E....... 785 827-3646
Salina *(G-10614)*
Oswalt Arnold Oswald & Henry ....F....... 620 662-5489
Hutchinson *(G-3398)*
Palmer Leatherman & White LLP ....F....... 785 233-1836
Topeka *(G-12959)*
Parker & Hay LLP ....F....... 785 266-3044
Topeka *(G-12961)*
Parkview Joint Venture ....F....... 785 267-3410
Topeka *(G-12962)*
Payne and Jones Chartered ....D....... 816 960-3600
Shawnee Mission *(G-11720)*
Prochaska Howell Prochaska LLC ....F....... 316 683-9080
Wichita *(G-15356)*
Ray Hodge & Associates LLC ....F....... 316 269-1414
Wichita *(G-15420)*
Redmon Michael Law Office ....F....... 913 342-5917
Kansas City *(G-4366)*
Roger Fincher ....F....... 785 430-5770
Topeka *(G-13024)*
Sanders Warren & Russell LLP ....E....... 913 234-6100
Overland Park *(G-9278)*
Schlagel Kinzer LLC ....F....... 913 782-5885
Olathe *(G-8058)*
Shank & Hamilton PC ....F....... 816 471-0909
Shawnee Mission *(G-11849)*
Sharp McQueen Mckinley Mora ....E....... 620 624-2548
Liberal *(G-6368)*
Slape and Howard Chartered ....F....... 316 262-3445
Wichita *(G-15602)*
Smith Shay Farmer & Wetta LLC ....F....... 316 267-5293
Wichita *(G-15608)*
Smithyman & Zakoura Chartered ....F....... 913 661-9800
Shawnee Mission *(G-11876)*
Southeast Bancshares Inc ....E....... 620 431-1400
Chanute *(G-763)*
Stevens & Brand LLP ....E....... 785 843-0811
Lawrence *(G-5125)*
Stinson Lasswell & Wilson LLC ....F....... 316 264-9137
Wichita *(G-15673)*
Stinson Leonard Street LLP ....E....... 913 451-8600
Shawnee Mission *(G-11901)*
Topeka Attorneys ....F....... 785 267-2410
Topeka *(G-13168)*
Waldeck Matteuzzi & Sloan ....E....... 913 253-2500
Overland Park *(G-9479)*
Wallace Saunders Chartered ....F....... 316 269-2100
Wichita *(G-15922)*
Wallace Saunders Chartered ....C....... 913 888-1000
Shawnee Mission *(G-11990)*
Weary Davis LLC ....F....... 785 762-2210
Junction City *(G-3768)*
Wheeler & Mitchelson Chartered ....F....... 620 231-4650
Pittsburg *(G-9968)*
Williamson & Cubbison ....F....... 913 371-1930
Kansas City *(G-4545)*
Wise & Breymer ....F....... 620 241-0554
McPherson *(G-7044)*
Woner Glenn Reder Grant Riordn ....F....... 785 235-5371
Topeka *(G-13249)*
Woodard Hernandez Roth Day LLC ....E....... 316 263-4958
Wichita *(G-16063)*
Wright Henson Clark & Bakr LLP ....E....... 785 232-2200
Topeka *(G-13253)*
Young Bogle McCausland Wells ....F....... 316 265-7841
Wichita *(G-16089)*
Yoxall Antrim & Yoxall ....F....... 620 624-8444
Liberal *(G-6378)*

LEGAL SVCS: General Practice Law Office

Adam & McDonald PA ....F....... 913 647-0670
Shawnee Mission *(G-11074)*
Adams Jones Law Firm PA ....F....... 316 265-8591
Wichita *(G-13613)*
Alderson Alderson Weiler Co ....E....... 785 232-0753
Topeka *(G-12303)*
Beam-Ward Kruse Wilson Wright ....F....... 785 865-1558
Lawrence *(G-4752)*
Bever Dye Lc ....E....... 316 263-8294
Wichita *(G-13843)*
Blake & Uhlig P A ....E....... 913 321-8884
Kansas City *(G-3867)*
Bryan Lykins Hjtmnek Fncher PA ....F....... 785 428-4566
Topeka *(G-12412)*
Cavanaugh Biggs and Lemon PA ....F....... 785 440-4000
Topeka *(G-12452)*
City of Overland Park ....B....... 913 895-6080
Overland Park *(G-8554)*
Clark Mize Linville Chartered ....E....... 785 823-6325
Salina *(G-10456)*
Crpenter Charted ....F....... 785 357-5251
Topeka *(G-12533)*
Davis & Jack LLC ....F....... 316 945-8251
Wichita *(G-14175)*
Davis Ketchmark McCreight ....F....... 816 842-1515
Leawood *(G-5373)*
Depew Gllen Rthbun McInteer Lc ....F....... 316 262-4000
Wichita *(G-14196)*
Dowell & Sypher LLC ....E....... 913 451-8833
Shawnee Mission *(G-11317)*
Foulston Conlee Schmidt Emerso ....F....... 316 264-3300
Wichita *(G-14404)*
Franklin L Taylor PA ....F....... 913 782-2350
Overland Park *(G-8738)*
Garcia and Antosh LLP ....F....... 620 225-7400
Dodge City *(G-1364)*
Gates Shields Ferguson Swall H ....F....... 913 661-0222
Overland Park *(G-8747)*
Gilmore & Bell A Prof Corp ....F....... 316 267-2091
Wichita *(G-14466)*
Goodell Stratton Edmonds & P ....E....... 785 233-0593
Topeka *(G-12641)*
Hovey Williams LLP ....E....... 913 647-9050
Overland Park *(G-8831)*
Jackson Lewis PC ....E....... 913 982-5747
Overland Park *(G-8869)*
Justis Law Firm LLC ....F....... 913 955-3710
Overland Park *(G-8883)*
Kennedy & Willis ....F....... 316 263-4921
Wichita *(G-14849)*
Kennedy Brkley Yrnvich Wllmson ....F....... 785 825-4674
Salina *(G-10574)*
Klenda Austerman LLC ....E....... 316 267-0331
Wichita *(G-14867)*
Kutak Rock LLP ....E....... 316 609-7900
Wichita *(G-14901)*
Law Office of Pter A Jouras Jr ....F....... 913 677-1999
Fairway *(G-1912)*
Lewis Brsbois Bsgard Smith LLP ....D....... 316 609-7900
Wichita *(G-14956)*
Lyle Law LLC ....F....... 913 225-6463
Overland Park *(G-8976)*
Marietta Kellogg & Price ....F....... 785 825-5403
Salina *(G-10592)*
Martin Pringle Olivr Wallace ....D....... 316 265-9311
Wichita *(G-15013)*
Martindell Swearer Shaffer ....E....... 620 662-3331
Hutchinson *(G-3365)*
Mc Dowell Rice Smith Buchanan ....F....... 913 338-5400
Shawnee Mission *(G-11604)*
McAnany Van Cleave Phillips PA ....D....... 913 371-3838
Kansas City *(G-4225)*
McDonald Tinker Skaer Quinn ....E....... 316 440-4882
Wichita *(G-15028)*
Morris Laing Evans Brock ....F....... 785 232-2662
Topeka *(G-12912)*
Polsinelli PC ....E....... 913 451-8788
Shawnee Mission *(G-11742)*
Potts Law Firm LLP ....F....... 816 931-2230
Shawnee Mission *(G-11745)*
Reynold Fork Berkl Suter Rose ....E....... 620 663-7131
Hutchinson *(G-3427)*
Richeson Anderson Byrd ....F....... 785 242-1234
Ottawa *(G-8310)*
Robert A Kumin PC ....F....... 913 432-1826
Shawnee Mission *(G-11806)*

Roger A Riedmiller F 316 448-1028
Wichita *(G-15476)*
Rouse Frets White Goss Gentile E 913 387-1600
Overland Park *(G-9259)*
Scott Qinlan Willard Barns LLC F 785 267-0040
Topeka *(G-13044)*
Sloan Eisenbarth Glassman E 785 357-6311
Topeka *(G-13077)*
Snyder Law Firm LLC F 913 685-3900
Leawood *(G-5553)*
Spencer Fane Britt Browne LLP E 913 345-8100
Overland Park *(G-9334)*
Stinson Leonard Street LLP E 316 265-8800
Wichita *(G-15674)*
Thompson Ramsdell Qualseth PA F 785 841-4554
Lawrence *(G-5136)*
Timothy R Keenan F 620 793-7811
Great Bend *(G-2647)*
Vold & Morris LLC F 913 696-0001
Overland Park *(G-9470)*
Wallace Saunders Chartered D 913 888-1000
Overland Park *(G-9482)*
Watkins Calcara Rondeau Friede F 620 792-8231
Great Bend *(G-2658)*

LEGAL SVCS: Real Estate Law

Coffman Defries & Nothern F 785 234-3461
Topeka *(G-12484)*
Newberry Ungerer & Heckert LLP F 785 273-5250
Topeka *(G-12927)*
P C Southlaw C 913 663-7600
Overland Park *(G-9132)*

LEGAL SVCS: Specialized Law Offices, Attorney

Cornwell & Scheriff F 913 254-7600
Olathe *(G-7617)*
Couch Pierce King & Hoffmeiste F 913 451-8430
Overland Park *(G-8604)*
Finney County Attorneys Office F 620 272-3568
Garden City *(G-2161)*
Hutton & Hutton E 316 688-1166
Wichita *(G-14658)*
Manhattan-City F 785 587-8995
Manhattan *(G-6729)*
Michael W Ryan Atty F 785 632-5666
Clay Center *(G-873)*

LEGITIMATE LIVE THEATER PRODUCERS

Granada Theater F 785 842-1390
Lawrence *(G-4879)*
Lawrence Theatre Inc F 785 843-7469
Lawrence *(G-4988)*
Prior Productions Incorporated E 816 654-5473
Olathe *(G-8009)*
Topeka Civic Theatre & Academy F 785 357-5211
Topeka *(G-13172)*

LESSORS: Farm Land

Circle Land & Cattle Corp F 620 275-6131
Garden City *(G-2124)*

LESSORS: Landholding Office

Wallace Saunders Chartered C 913 888-1000
Shawnee Mission *(G-11990)*

LICENSE TAGS: Automobile, Stamped Metal

Elitegear4ucom LLC G 316 993-4398
Wichita *(G-14271)*

LIFE INSURANCE AGENTS

American Underwriters Lf Insur D 316 794-2200
Goddard *(G-2429)*
Waddell & Reed Inc A 913 236-2000
Shawnee Mission *(G-11987)*

LIFE INSURANCE CARRIERS

Employers Mutual Casualty Co E 913 663-0119
Overland Park *(G-8679)*
Employers Mutual Casualty Co C 316 352-5700
Wichita *(G-14279)*
Standard Insurance Company F 913 661-9241
Overland Park *(G-9352)*
United Omaha Life Insurance Co E 913 402-1191
Shawnee Mission *(G-11963)*

LIFE INSURANCE: Funeral

Hawks Funeral Home Inc F 620 442-0220
Arkansas City *(G-159)*

LIFE INSURANCE: Mutual Association

Ameritas Life Insurance Corp F 785 273-3504
Topeka *(G-12325)*

LIGHTING FIXTURES WHOLESALERS

Accent Lighting Inc F 316 636-1278
Wichita *(G-13601)*
Biehler Companies Inc D 316 529-0002
Wichita *(G-13847)*
Green Expectations Ldscpg Inc F 913 897-8076
Kansas City *(G-4049)*
Rensen House of Lights Inc E 913 888-0888
Lenexa *(G-6103)*
Robert Wilson Co Inc E 913 642-1500
Overland Park *(G-9251)*
Treescape Inc E 316 733-6388
Andover *(G-112)*
Western Chandelier Company F 913 685-2000
Overland Park *(G-9491)*

LIGHTING FIXTURES, NEC

Advanced Technologies Inc G 316 744-2285
Bel Aire *(G-427)*
Elecsys Corporation C 913 647-0158
Olathe *(G-7672)*
Flame Engineering Inc E 785 222-2873
La Crosse *(G-4633)*
Led2 Lighting Inc G 816 912-2180
Kansas City *(G-4199)*

LIGHTING FIXTURES: Fluorescent, Commercial

Fishing Lights Etc LLC G 785 621-2646
Hays *(G-2809)*

LIGHTING FIXTURES: Fluorescent, Residential

Fishing Lights Etc LLC G 785 621-2646
Hays *(G-2809)*

LIGHTING FIXTURES: Indl & Commercial

Advanced Technologies Inc G 316 744-2285
Bel Aire *(G-427)*
Lightwild Inc E 913 851-3000
Overland Park *(G-8959)*
Lw Holding Lc E 913 851-3000
Overland Park *(G-8975)*
Mges LLC G 913 334-6333
Kansas City *(G-4240)*
Pwi Inc E 316 942-2811
Wichita *(G-15380)*

LIGHTING FIXTURES: Motor Vehicle

Pwi Inc E 316 942-2811
Wichita *(G-15380)*

LIGHTING FIXTURES: Residential

Advanced Technologies Inc G 316 744-2285
Bel Aire *(G-427)*
Corbin Bronze Limited G 913 766-4012
Kansas City *(G-3940)*
Jensen Design Inc G 316 943-7900
Wichita *(G-14754)*

LIGHTING FIXTURES: Underwater

Fishing Lights Etc LLC G 785 621-2646
Hays *(G-2809)*

LIGHTING MAINTENANCE SVC

T W Lacy & Associates Inc F 913 706-7625
Prairie Village *(G-10073)*

LIME

Florence Rock Company LLC G 620 878-4544
Newton *(G-7346)*
Mk Minerals Inc G 785 989-4566
Wathena *(G-13477)*

Quikrete Companies Inc E 913 441-6525
Kansas City *(G-4355)*

LIMESTONE: Crushed & Broken

Ash Grove Cement Company C 913 451-8900
Overland Park *(G-8403)*
Bayer Construction Company Inc C 785 776-8839
Manhattan *(G-6553)*
Cornejo & Sons LLC E 620 336-3534
Cherryvale *(G-804)*
Hamm Inc E 785 597-5111
Perry *(G-9768)*
Johnson County Aggregates E 913 764-2127
Olathe *(G-7814)*
Marietta Martin Materials Inc E 620 736-2962
Severy *(G-10891)*
Martin Marietta Materials Inc G 913 390-8396
Olathe *(G-7875)*
Martin Marietta Materials Inc E 785 242-3232
Ottawa *(G-8289)*
Martin Marietta Materials Inc F 913 583-3311
De Soto *(G-1207)*
Mid-States Materials LLC G 785 887-6038
Scranton *(G-10839)*
Midwest Concrete Materials Inc C 785 776-8811
Manhattan *(G-6746)*
Nelson Quarries Inc E 620 496-2211
Gas *(G-2392)*
Norris Quarries LLC G 641 682-3427
Wichita *(G-15185)*
Wade Agricultural Products Inc G 913 757-2255
La Cygne *(G-4646)*

LIMESTONE: Cut & Shaped

U S Stone Industries LLC C 913 529-4154
Herington *(G-2982)*

LIMESTONE: Dimension

Hamm Inc G 785 597-5111
Perry *(G-9769)*
Mulberry Limestone Quarry Co F 620 764-3337
Mulberry *(G-7208)*

LIMESTONE: Ground

Ash Grove Aggregates Inc D 660 679-4128
Overland Park *(G-8402)*
Cornejo & Sons LLC D 620 231-8120
Pittsburg *(G-9846)*

LIMOUSINE SVCS

Agenda Usa Inc E 913 268-4466
Shawnee Mission *(G-11084)*
Crescent Limousines F 785 232-2236
Topeka *(G-12530)*
Extreme Limousine LLC F 913 831-2039
Shawnee *(G-10951)*
S&S Limousine LLC F 316 794-3340
Goddard *(G-2454)*
Stretch It Limousine Service F 913 269-1955
Shawnee Mission *(G-11903)*
Wheatland Enterprises Inc E 913 381-3504
Leawood *(G-5598)*
Wheatland Enterprises Inc E 816 756-1700
Leawood *(G-5599)*

LINEN SPLY SVC

Aramark Unf & Career AP LLC E 913 351-3534
Lansing *(G-4667)*
N C K Commercial Laundry Inc F 785 243-4432
Concordia *(G-1124)*

LINEN SPLY SVC: Non-Clothing

Unifirst Corporation F 785 825-8766
Salina *(G-10745)*

LINEN SPLY SVC: Uniform

Ameripride Services Inc D 785 234-3475
Topeka *(G-12324)*
Aramark Unf & Career AP LLC D 316 262-5467
Wichita *(G-13726)*
Cintas Corporation C 913 782-8333
Olathe *(G-7595)*
Excel Linen Supply E 816 842-6565
Kansas City *(G-3999)*
Hospital Linen Services Inc D 913 621-2228
Kansas City *(G-4085)*

Ineeda Laundry & Dry Cleaners......D....... 620 662-6450
Hutchinson *(G-3332)*
Unifirst Corporation......F....... 785 233-1550
Topeka *(G-13203)*
Whiteway Inc......D....... 816 842-6565
Kansas City *(G-4541)*

LIQUEFIED PETROLEUM GAS DEALERS

Berwick Cooperative Oil Co......F....... 785 284-2227
Sabetha *(G-10307)*
Cooperative Elevator & Sup Co......E....... 620 873-2161
Meade *(G-7047)*
Crossfaith Ventures Lc......E....... 620 662-8365
Hutchinson *(G-3251)*
Ferrell Companies Inc......D....... 913 661-1500
Overland Park *(G-8712)*
Wallis Oil Company......F....... 913 621-6521
Kansas City *(G-4530)*

LIQUEFIED PETROLEUM GAS WHOLESALERS

Crossfaith Ventures Lc......E....... 620 662-8365
Hutchinson *(G-3251)*
Ferrellgas Inc......F....... 913 661-1500
Overland Park *(G-8713)*
G H K Farms......F....... 785 462-6440
Colby *(G-1008)*
Geo Bit Exploration Inc......F....... 940 888-3134
Council Grove *(G-1168)*
Girton Propane Service Inc......D....... 785 632-6273
Clay Center *(G-866)*
John E Jones Oil Co Inc......F....... 785 425-6746
Stockton *(G-12182)*
L C McClain Inc......F....... 785 584-6151
Rossville *(G-10253)*
Propane Central......F....... 785 762-5160
Junction City *(G-3742)*

LIQUID CRYSTAL DISPLAYS

Elecsys International Corp......C....... 913 647-0158
Olathe *(G-7673)*

LITHOGRAPHIC PLATES

Ejrex Inc......D....... 620 421-6200
Parsons *(G-9683)*

LIVESTOCK WHOLESALERS, NEC

Anderson County Sales Co......F....... 785 448-3811
Garnett *(G-2369)*
Livestock Nutrition Center LLC......F....... 913 725-0300
Overland Park *(G-8963)*
Parsons Livestock Market Inc......E....... 620 421-2900
Parsons *(G-9720)*
Premiere Pork Inc......F....... 620 872-7073
Scott City *(G-10829)*

LOCKS

Schlage Lock Company LLC......C....... 888 805-9837
Olathe *(G-8057)*

LOCKS: Safe & Vault, Metal

SA Consumer Products Inc......G....... 888 792-4264
Leawood *(G-5544)*

LOCKSMITHS

Eichhorn Holdings LLC......F....... 785 843-1426
Lawrence *(G-4848)*
Outlaws Group LLC......F....... 913 381-5565
Shawnee Mission *(G-11704)*
Rueschhoff Communications......E....... 785 841-0111
Lawrence *(G-5098)*
Smallwood Lock Supply Inc......F....... 913 371-5678
Kansas City *(G-4425)*
Topeka Foundry and Ir Works Co......D....... 785 232-8212
Topeka *(G-13176)*

LOGGING

Black Jack Tree Lawn and Ldscp......G....... 785 865-8536
Baldwin City *(G-356)*
International Forest Pdts LLC......D....... 913 451-6945
Overland Park *(G-8857)*

LOGGING CAMPS & CONTRACTORS

Martin James......G....... 785 525-7761
Lucas *(G-6474)*

LOGGING: Timber, Cut At Logging Camp

Barns Timber Creek B & B......G....... 620 221-2797
Winfield *(G-16116)*

LOGGING: Wooden Logs

Newton Healthcare Corporation......A....... 316 283-2700
Newton *(G-7393)*

LOOSELEAF BINDERS

Leslie Company Inc......D....... 913 764-6660
Olathe *(G-7859)*

LOUDSPEAKERS

Martin-Logan Ltd......D....... 785 749-0133
Lawrence *(G-5012)*
Ms Electronics LLC......F....... 866 663-9770
Lenexa *(G-6015)*

LUBRICATING OIL & GREASE WHOLESALERS

Barton Solvents Inc......F....... 316 321-1540
El Dorado *(G-1534)*
Barton Solvents Inc......F....... 913 287-5500
Kansas City *(G-3847)*
Clean Harbors Wichita LLC......E....... 913 287-6880
Kansas City *(G-3919)*
Clean Harbors Wichita LLC......C....... 316 832-0151
Wichita *(G-14039)*
Farneys Inc......F....... 316 522-7248
Haysville *(G-2943)*
Fuchs Lubricants Co......D....... 913 422-4022
Kansas City *(G-4020)*
Industrial Sling Lbrcation Inc......F....... 913 294-3001
Olathe *(G-7788)*
Lubrication Engineers Inc......E....... 800 537-7683
Wichita *(G-14989)*
Parker Oil Co Inc......F....... 316 529-4343
Kansas City *(G-4313)*
Parker Oil Company Inc......F....... 913 596-6247
Kansas City *(G-4314)*
Robinson Oil Co Inc......F....... 620 275-4237
Garden City *(G-2268)*
Wallis Oil Company......F....... 913 621-6521
Kansas City *(G-4530)*

LUBRICATION SYSTEMS & EQPT

P B Hoidale Co Inc......F....... 913 438-1500
Shawnee *(G-11008)*

LUMBER & BLDG MATLS DEALER, RET: Electric Constructn Matls

Southwestern Electrical Co Inc......C....... 316 263-1264
Wichita *(G-15632)*

LUMBER & BLDG MATLS DEALER, RET: Garage Doors, Sell/Install

Delbert Chopp Co Inc......F....... 785 825-8530
Salina *(G-10472)*
EE Newcomer Enterprises Inc......B....... 816 221-0543
Olathe *(G-7671)*
Kansas Door Inc......F....... 620 793-7600
Great Bend *(G-2597)*
Overhead Door Company......E....... 316 265-4634
Wichita *(G-15240)*
Ray Anderson Co Inc......E....... 785 233-7454
Topeka *(G-13000)*
Raynor Gar Door Co Inc Kans Cy......F....... 913 422-0441
Shawnee Mission *(G-11779)*
Southwest Glass & Door Inc......F....... 620 626-7400
Liberal *(G-6369)*
Stoner Door & Dock Corporation......F....... 785 478-3074
Topeka *(G-13101)*
Superior Door Service Inc......F....... 913 381-1767
Kansas City *(G-4447)*

LUMBER & BLDG MATLS DEALERS, RET: Energy Conservation Prdts

Worldwide Energy Inc......F....... 913 310-0705
Lenexa *(G-6234)*

LUMBER & BLDG MATRLS DEALERS, RETAIL: Doors, Wood/Metal

Kansas Builders Supply Co Inc......F....... 913 831-1511
Shawnee Mission *(G-11508)*

LUMBER & BLDG MTRLS DEALERS, RET: Planing Mill Prdts/Lumber

McCray Lumber Company......E....... 913 780-0060
Olathe *(G-7882)*
McCray Lumber Company......D....... 913 321-8840
Kansas City *(G-4226)*

LUMBER & BLDG MTRLS DEALERS, RET: Windows, Storm, Wood/Metal

Custom Renovation......F....... 620 544-2653
Hugoton *(G-3158)*
Mid-Continent Thermal-Guard......E....... 316 838-4044
Wichita *(G-15079)*

LUMBER & BUILDING MATERIAL DEALERS, RETAIL: Roofing Material

Beacon Sales Acquisition Inc......D....... 913 262-7663
Shawnee Mission *(G-11155)*
Building Solutions LLC......F....... 620 225-1199
Dodge City *(G-1314)*
Metal Panels Inc......E....... 913 766-7200
Kansas City *(G-4236)*

LUMBER & BUILDING MATERIALS DEALER, RET: Door & Window Prdts

Champion Opco LLC......F....... 316 636-4200
Wichita *(G-13996)*
Cheney Door Co Inc......F....... 620 669-9306
Hutchinson *(G-3236)*
Duranotic Door Inc......F....... 913 764-3408
Olathe *(G-7661)*
Elco Manufacturing Inc......E....... 620 896-7333
Harper *(G-2720)*
Hi-Plains Door Systems Inc......F....... 785 462-6352
Colby *(G-1013)*
Lorac Company Inc......F....... 316 263-2565
Wichita *(G-14979)*
Martinek & Flynn Wholesale Inc......E....... 785 233-6666
Topeka *(G-12862)*
Miami Lumber Inc......F....... 913 294-2041
Paola *(G-9574)*
Mid-AM Building Supply Inc......F....... 316 942-0389
Wichita *(G-15073)*
Midland Exteriors LLC......F....... 785 537-5130
Manhattan *(G-6743)*
Midway Sales & Distrg Inc......F....... 785 537-4665
Manhattan *(G-6745)*
Rayers Bearden Stained GL Sup......F....... 316 942-2929
Wichita *(G-15421)*
Southard Corporation......E....... 620 793-5434
Great Bend *(G-2637)*
Tracker Door Systems LLC......G....... 913 585-3100
De Soto *(G-1214)*
Weathercraft Company N Platte......G....... 785 899-3064
Goodland *(G-2490)*
Window Design Company......G....... 785 582-2888
Silver Lake *(G-12030)*
Worldwide Windows......F....... 785 826-1701
Salina *(G-10773)*

LUMBER & BUILDING MATERIALS DEALER, RET: Masonry Matls/Splys

Dodge City Concrete Inc......F....... 620 227-3041
Dodge City *(G-1343)*
Midwest Cast Stone Kansas Inc......E....... 913 371-3300
Kansas City *(G-4250)*
Quikrete Companies Inc......E....... 913 441-6525
Kansas City *(G-4355)*

LUMBER & BUILDING MATERIALS DEALERS, RETAIL: Brick

Salina Concrete Products Inc ....F 316 943-3241
Wichita (G-15510)
Wilbert Funeral Services Inc................E........ 316 832-1114
Wichita (G-16046)

LUMBER & BUILDING MATERIALS DEALERS, RETAIL: Countertops

Global Stone LLC....................................G....... 913 310-9500
Olathe (G-7733)

LUMBER & BUILDING MATERIALS DEALERS, RETAIL: Flooring, Wood

Superior Hardwood Floors LLC.............G....... 316 554-9663
Wichita (G-15694)

LUMBER & BUILDING MATERIALS DEALERS, RETAIL: Paving Stones

Sturgis Materials Inc..............................E....... 913 371-7757
Kansas City (G-4442)

LUMBER & BUILDING MATERIALS DEALERS, RETAIL: Sand & Gravel

Eslinger Construction & Rdymx............F 620 659-2371
Kinsley (G-4617)

LUMBER & BUILDING MATERIALS DEALERS, RETAIL: Siding

Superior Home Improvements LLC.......G....... 620 225-3560
Dodge City (G-1437)

LUMBER & BUILDING MATERIALS DEALERS, RETAIL: Tile, Ceramic

Carpet Factory Outlet Inc......................E....... 913 261-6800
Kansas City (G-3892)
Metro Tile Contractors Inc ....E....... 913 381-7770
Lenexa (G-5996)

LUMBER & BUILDING MATLS DEALERS, RET: Concrete/Cinder Block

Augusta Rental Inc ....F 316 775-5050
Augusta (G-308)
Beran Icf Solutions LLC ....F 316 944-2131
Wichita (G-13832)
Tarbet Construction Co Inc....................F........ 620 356-2110
Ulysses (G-13321)

LUMBER: Hardwood Dimension & Flooring Mills

McCray Lumber Company ....E....... 913 780-0060
Olathe (G-7882)

LUMBER: Treated

Wood RE New Joco Inc..........................G....... 913 661-9663
Olathe (G-8159)
Wood Rot Pro..G....... 913 638-5732
Olathe (G-8160)

MACHINE PARTS: Stamped Or Pressed Metal

Center Industries Corporation..............C....... 316 942-8255
Wichita (G-13976)
Kearney Equipment LLC ....F 316 722-8710
Maize (G-6515)
Wkcsc Inc ....G....... 316 652-7113
Wichita (G-16060)

MACHINE SHOPS

2r Tool & Machine Inc............................G....... 620 902-5151
Chanute (G-700)
Aeromotive Inc.......................................F 913 647-7300
Shawnee Mission (G-11082)
Big Creek Investment Corp Inc.............G....... 620 431-3445
Chanute (G-707)
Continental Components LLC ....G....... 816 547-8325
Lenexa (G-5784)
Exline Inc ....C....... 785 825-4683
Salina (G-10489)
L & M Steel & Mfg..................................G....... 785 462-8216
Colby (G-1023)
Machining Programming Mfg Inc ....E....... 316 945-1227
Wichita (G-14998)
Mid-Continent Industries Inc ....F 316 283-9648
Newton (G-7384)
Nance Manufacturing Inc ....E....... 316 942-8671
Wichita (G-15146)
Natoma Leasing LLC ....D....... 785 877-3529
Norton (G-7452)
Natoma Realty LLC...............................D....... 785 877-3529
Norton (G-7454)
Williams Company Inc...........................F 785 873-3260
Whiting (G-13575)

MACHINE TOOL ACCESS: Cutting

Ach Foam Technologies Inc ....D 913 321-4114
Kansas City (G-3782)
Madill Carbide Inc ....F 316 263-9285
Wichita (G-14999)
Sharpening Specialists LLC ....E 316 945-0593
Wichita (G-15575)
Superior Tool Service Inc......................E 316 945-8488
Wichita (G-15700)

MACHINE TOOL ACCESS: Diamond Cutting, For Turning, Etc

D B Investments Inc...............................G....... 913 928-1000
Olathe (G-7635)

MACHINE TOOL ACCESS: Milling Machine Attachments

Universal Construction Pdts..................E 316 946-5885
Wichita (G-15853)

MACHINE TOOL ACCESS: Sockets

Alltite Inc..E 316 686-3010
Wichita (G-13678)

MACHINE TOOL ATTACHMENTS & ACCESS

Abbott Aluminum Inc..............................E 785 776-8555
Manhattan (G-6529)

MACHINE TOOLS & ACCESS

Midwest Precision Inc ....F....... 913 307-0211
Lenexa (G-6003)
Nibarger Tool Service Inc.......................G....... 316 262-6152
Wichita (G-15175)
Vektek LLC..C....... 620 342-7637
Emporia (G-1845)

MACHINE TOOLS, METAL CUTTING: Drilling & Boring

Straightline Hdd Inc ....D 620 802-0200
Hutchinson (G-3449)

MACHINE TOOLS, METAL CUTTING: Grind, Polish, Buff, Lapp

Nance Manufacturing Inc ....E 316 942-8671
Wichita (G-15146)

MACHINE TOOLS, METAL CUTTING: Plasma Process

Hornet Cutting Systems LLC ....E 316 755-3683
Valley Center (G-13343)

MACHINE TOOLS, METAL FORMING: Electroforming

S D M Die Cutting Equipment ....G....... 913 782-3737
Shawnee (G-11022)

MACHINE TOOLS, METAL FORMING: Pressing

Quality Record Pressings ....E 785 820-2931
Salina (G-10645)

MACHINE TOOLS: Metal Cutting

Acsys Lasertechnik US Inc....................G....... 847 468-5302
Lenexa (G-5626)
ADM Milling Co.......................................D 785 825-1541
Salina (G-10395)
Bazin Sawing & Drilling Llc....................F 913 764-0843
Louisburg (G-6440)
Steel Fabrications Inc.............................G....... 785 625-3075
Hays (G-2913)

MACHINE TOOLS: Metal Forming

Jorban-Riscoe Associates Inc ....E 913 438-1244
Lenexa (G-5932)
Marion Manufacturing Inc ....E 620 382-3751
Marion (G-6874)
Mockry & Sons Machine Co Inc.............E 316 788-7878
Derby (G-1263)

MACHINERY & EQPT FINANCE LEASING

Commercial Capital Company LLC ....E 913 341-0053
Lenexa (G-5774)
Medova Hlthcare Fncl Group LLC.........E 316 616-6160
Wichita (G-15034)

MACHINERY & EQPT, AGRICULTURAL, WHOL: Farm Eqpt Parts/Splys

Bruna Brothers Implement LLC.............E 785 325-2232
Washington (G-13461)
C & W Farm Supply Inc ....F 785 374-4521
Courtland (G-1179)
Crustbuster/Speed King Inc..................D 620 227-7106
Dodge City (G-1337)
Golden Plains AG Tech..........................G....... 785 462-6753
Colby (G-1009)
Keating Tractor & Eqp Inc......................E 620 624-1668
Liberal (G-6327)
Simpson Farm Enterprises Inc ....F 785 731-2700
Ransom (G-10195)

MACHINERY & EQPT, AGRICULTURAL, WHOL: Grain Elev Eqpt/Splys

Mid-Continent Industries Inc ....F 316 283-9648
Newton (G-7384)

MACHINERY & EQPT, AGRICULTURAL, WHOLESALE: Agricultural, NEC

Abilene Machine LLC..............................C....... 785 655-9455
Solomon (G-12046)
Foley Equipment Company....................C....... 785 266-5770
Topeka (G-12623)
Rhs Inc ....E 785 742-2949
Hiawatha (G-3023)
Unruh-Foster Inc.....................................E 620 846-2215
Montezuma (G-7161)
Upu Industries Inc..................................D....... 785 238-6990
Junction City (G-3762)

MACHINERY & EQPT, AGRICULTURAL, WHOLESALE: Dairy

Dairy Farmers America Inc ....B 816 801-6455
Kansas City (G-3953)

MACHINERY & EQPT, AGRICULTURAL, WHOLESALE: Farm Implements

AG Power Equipment Co ....F 785 852-4235
Sharon Springs (G-10894)
American Implement Inc ....E 620 275-4114
Garden City (G-2098)
American Implement Inc ....F 620 544-4351
Hugoton (G-3147)
American Implement Inc.........................E 620 697-2182
Elkhart (G-1617)
Beaver Valley Supply Co Inc..................E 800 982-1280
Atwood (G-281)
Bruna Brothers Implement LLC.............F 785 562-5304
Marysville (G-6881)
Carrico Implement Co Inc ....D....... 785 738-5744
Beloit (G-480)
Carrico Implement Co Inc......................F 785 472-4400
Ellsworth (G-1658)
Carrico Implement Co Inc ....E 785 625-2219
Hays (G-2765)
Colby A G Center LLC ....F 785 462-6132
Colby (G-995)
Foster Unruh Inc ....E 620 227-2165
Dodge City (G-1362)

Great Bend Farm Equipment Inc ....F 620 793-3509
Great Bend *(G-2578)*
Hoxie Implement Co Inc ....E 785 675-3201
Hoxie *(G-3139)*
J & W Equipment Inc ....F 620 365-2341
Iola *(G-3614)*
Jewell Implement Company Inc ....F 785 428-3261
Jewell *(G-3650)*
John Schmidt & Sons Inc ....E 316 445-2103
Mount Hope *(G-7205)*
Kalvesta Implement Co Inc ....F 620 855-3567
Kalvesta *(G-3771)*
Kanequip Inc ....F 620 225-0016
Dodge City *(G-1384)*
Kanequip Inc ....F 785 562-2377
Marysville *(G-6891)*
Kearney Equipment LLC ....F 316 722-8710
Maize *(G-6515)*
Kincheloe Inc ....F 620 672-6401
Pratt *(G-10123)*
Leoti Greentech Incorporated ....F 620 375-2621
Leoti *(G-6255)*
McLaughlin Leasing Inc ....F 316 542-0303
Cheney *(G-794)*
Oregon Trail Equipment LLC ....F 785 562-2346
Marysville *(G-6905)*
Pankratz Implement Co ....E 620 662-8681
Hutchinson *(G-3399)*
R & F Farm Supply Inc ....F 620 244-3275
Erie *(G-1864)*
R & H Implement Company Inc ....F 620 384-7421
Syracuse *(G-12230)*
Shepherds Truck & Tractor ....F 620 331-2970
Independence *(G-3560)*
Storrer Implement Inc ....F 620 365-5692
Iola *(G-3636)*
Straub International Inc ....F 620 662-0211
Hutchinson *(G-3451)*
Van-Wall Equipment Inc ....E 913 397-6009
Olathe *(G-8138)*

MACHINERY & EQPT, AGRICULTURAL, WHOLESALE: Garden, NEC

Frank Colladay Hardware Co ....F 620 663-4477
Hutchinson *(G-3292)*

MACHINERY & EQPT, AGRICULTURAL, WHOLESALE: Landscaping Eqpt

Glen-Gery Corporation ....G 913 281-2800
Kansas City *(G-4038)*

MACHINERY & EQPT, AGRICULTURAL, WHOLESALE: Lawn

Western Supply Co Inc ....E 620 663-9082
Hutchinson *(G-3486)*

MACHINERY & EQPT, AGRICULTURAL, WHOLESALE: Lawn & Garden

Century Partners LLC ....F 913 642-2489
Olathe *(G-7586)*
Landscape Outfitters LLC ....F 620 221-1108
Winfield *(G-16154)*
Lawrence Landscape Inc ....E 785 843-4370
Lawrence *(G-4972)*
Lightning Grounds Services Inc ....E 913 441-3900
Shawnee Mission *(G-11572)*
TLC Lawn Care Inc ....D 913 780-5296
Olathe *(G-8112)*
Treescape Inc ....E 316 733-6388
Andover *(G-112)*
Underground Specialists Inc ....F 620 276-3344
Garden City *(G-2305)*

MACHINERY & EQPT, AGRICULTURAL, WHOLESALE: Livestock Eqpt

Animal Health Intl Inc ....E 620 276-8289
Garden City *(G-2101)*
Hog Slat Incorporated ....F 580 338-5003
Liberal *(G-6321)*
Keesecker Agri Business Inc ....E 785 325-3134
Washington *(G-13466)*
Liberty Inc ....D 785 770-8788
Manhattan *(G-6713)*
Linn Post & Pipe Inc ....E 785 348-5526
Linn *(G-6409)*
Roto-Mix LLC ....G 620 872-1100
Scott City *(G-10830)*
Roto-Mix LLC ....E 620 653-7323
Hoisington *(G-3070)*
Zeitlow Distributing Co Inc ....F 620 241-4279
McPherson *(G-7045)*

MACHINERY & EQPT, AGRICULTURAL, WHOLESALE: Tractors

Bucklin Tractor & Impt Co Inc ....E 620 826-3271
Bucklin *(G-591)*
General Tech A Svcs & Pdts Co ....G 913 766-5566
Olathe *(G-7727)*
Kubota Tractor Corporation ....F 913 215-5298
Edgerton *(G-1486)*
McConnell Machinery Co Inc ....F 785 843-2676
Lawrence *(G-5016)*
Miller Welding Inc ....F 785 454-3425
Downs *(G-1472)*
Plp Inc ....E 620 532-3106
Kingman *(G-4610)*
Romans Outdoor Power Inc ....E 913 837-5225
Louisburg *(G-6466)*

MACHINERY & EQPT, INDL, WHOL: Brewery Prdts Mfrg, Commercial

Black Stag Brewery LLC ....D 785 764-1628
Lawrence *(G-4760)*

MACHINERY & EQPT, INDL, WHOL: Controlling Instruments/Access

Clarios ....E 316 721-2777
Wichita *(G-14034)*

MACHINERY & EQPT, INDL, WHOL: Meters, Consumption Registerng

Superior School Supplies Inc ....E 316 265-7683
Wichita *(G-15699)*

MACHINERY & EQPT, INDL, WHOLESALE: Conveyor Systems

Bedeschi Mid-West Conveyor LLC ....E 913 384-9950
Lenexa *(G-5696)*
Bl Brooks & Sons Inc ....G 913 829-5494
Olathe *(G-7553)*
Miniature Plastic Molding LLC ....G 316 264-2827
Wichita *(G-15112)*
Peerless Conveyor and Mfg Corp ....F 913 342-2240
Kansas City *(G-4318)*
U S Automation Inc ....G 913 894-2410
Shawnee Mission *(G-11953)*

MACHINERY & EQPT, INDL, WHOLESALE: Cranes

Wilkerson Crane Rental Inc ....E 913 238-7030
Lenexa *(G-6230)*

MACHINERY & EQPT, INDL, WHOLESALE: Engines & Parts, Diesel

Central Pwr Systems & Svcs LLC ....E 316 943-1231
Wichita *(G-13984)*
Central Pwr Systems & Svcs LLC ....F 785 462-8211
Colby *(G-992)*
Cummins Central Power LLC ....E 316 838-0875
Park City *(G-9615)*
Cummins Central Power LLC ....F 785 462-3945
Colby *(G-1002)*
Engquist Tractor Service Inc ....E 620 654-3651
McPherson *(G-6959)*
Foley Equipment Company ....C 785 266-5770
Topeka *(G-12623)*

MACHINERY & EQPT, INDL, WHOLESALE: Engines, Gasoline

Kansas City Power Products Inc ....F 913 321-7040
Kansas City *(G-4149)*
Kaw Valley Industrial Inc ....G 785 841-9751
Eudora *(G-1876)*
Medart Inc ....F 636 282-2300
Kansas City *(G-4227)*
Orscheln Farm and Home LLC ....F 785 825-1681
Salina *(G-10624)*
Orscheln Farm and Home LLC ....F 913 367-2261
Atchison *(G-254)*
Orscheln Farm and Home LLC ....F 785 625-7316
Hays *(G-2884)*
Teeter Irrigation Inc ....F 620 276-8257
Garden City *(G-2297)*

MACHINERY & EQPT, INDL, WHOLESALE: Engs/Transportation Eqpt

Cstk Inc ....E 913 233-7220
Overland Park *(G-8621)*
Velociti Inc ....E 913 233-7230
Kansas City *(G-4514)*

MACHINERY & EQPT, INDL, WHOLESALE: Fans

Air Capital Equipment Inc ....E 316 522-1111
Wichita *(G-13647)*
WW Grainger Inc ....E 913 492-8550
Lenexa *(G-6237)*

MACHINERY & EQPT, INDL, WHOLESALE: Food Manufacturing

Baader North America Corp ....F 913 621-3366
Kansas City *(G-3837)*
Hantover Inc ....C 913 214-4800
Overland Park *(G-8792)*

MACHINERY & EQPT, INDL, WHOLESALE: Food Product Manufacturng

Marlen Research Corp ....F 913 888-3333
Lenexa *(G-5987)*

MACHINERY & EQPT, INDL, WHOLESALE: Heat Exchange

AW Schultz Inc ....F 913 307-0399
Shawnee Mission *(G-11136)*
Blackmore and Glunt Inc ....F 913 469-5715
Shawnee Mission *(G-11168)*

MACHINERY & EQPT, INDL, WHOLESALE: Hoists

Shannahan Crane & Hoist Inc ....F 816 746-9822
Kansas City *(G-4419)*

MACHINERY & EQPT, INDL, WHOLESALE: Hydraulic Systems

Alltite Inc ....E 316 686-3010
Wichita *(G-13678)*
Austin A-7 Ltd ....F 316 945-8892
Wichita *(G-13769)*
B & B Hydraulics Inc ....E 620 662-2552
Hutchinson *(G-3210)*
Cross Manufacturing Inc ....D 785 625-2585
Hays *(G-2780)*
Cross Manufacturing Inc ....C 620 324-5525
Lewis *(G-6268)*
Eaton Corporation ....B 620 663-5751
Hutchinson *(G-3274)*
Fluidtech LLC ....E 913 492-3300
Lenexa *(G-5859)*
Fluidtech LLC ....E 913 492-3300
Lenexa *(G-5860)*
Fluidtech LLC ....F 913 492-3300
Lenexa *(G-5861)*
Hartfiel Automation Inc ....F 913 894-6545
Overland Park *(G-8797)*
Hyspeco Inc ....E 316 943-0254
Wichita *(G-14662)*
Innovative Fluid Power ....F 913 768-7008
Olathe *(G-7794)*
Kanamak Hydraulics Inc ....E 800 473-5843
Garden City *(G-2212)*
Northeast Kansas Hydraulics ....G 785 235-0405
Topeka *(G-12936)*
Precision Manifold Systems Inc ....E 913 829-1221
Olathe *(G-8001)*
Reintjes & Hiter Co Inc ....F 913 371-1872
Kansas City *(G-4368)*

MACHINERY & EQPT, INDL, WHOLESALE: Indl Machine Parts

Custom Mobile Equipment Inc ....E 785 594-7475
Baldwin City (G-358)

MACHINERY & EQPT, INDL, WHOLESALE: Instruments & Cntrl Eqpt

RE Pedrotti Company Inc.......................F 913 677-7754
Shawnee Mission (G-11781)

MACHINERY & EQPT, INDL, WHOLESALE: Lift Trucks & Parts

American Equipment Sales Inc ....F 785 843-4500
Lawrence (G-4734)
Arrow Acquisition LLC ....D....... 913 495-4869
Lenexa (G-5662)
Crown Equipment Corporation.............E....... 316 942-4400
Wichita (G-14136)
Heubel Material Handling Inc................F....... 316 941-4115
Wichita (G-14602)
Kansas Forklift Inc..................................F 316 262-1426
Wichita (G-14802)
Royal Tractor Company Inc ....E....... 913 782-2598
New Century (G-7296)
Tvh Parts Co...B 913 829-1000
Olathe (G-8125)
Wki Operations Inc ....F 316 838-0867
Dodge City (G-1462)

MACHINERY & EQPT, INDL, WHOLESALE: Machine Tools & Metalwork

Motion Industries Inc..............................E 316 265-9608
Wichita (G-15133)

MACHINERY & EQPT, INDL, WHOLESALE: Packaging

Crown Packaging Corp ....E....... 913 888-1951
Shawnee Mission (G-11283)
Raab Sales Inc...F 913 227-0814
Shawnee Mission (G-11775)

MACHINERY & EQPT, INDL, WHOLESALE: Paint Spray

Spray Equipment & Svc Ctr LLC ....E 316 264-4349
Wichita (G-15647)

MACHINERY & EQPT, INDL, WHOLESALE: Paper Manufacturing

Ryko Solutions Inc...................................F 913 451-3719
Lenexa (G-6115)

MACHINERY & EQPT, INDL, WHOLESALE: Petroleum Industry

McDonald Tank and Eqp Co Inc ....E....... 620 793-3555
Great Bend (G-2606)
P B Hoidale Co Inc ....F 913 438-1500
Shawnee (G-11008)

MACHINERY & EQPT, INDL, WHOLESALE: Pneumatic Tools

Global Systems Incorporated ....F 913 829-5900
Olathe (G-7734)
IAC Systems Inc..E 913 384-5511
Shawnee Mission (G-11449)
Industrial Accessories Company ....D 913 384-5511
Shawnee Mission (G-11455)
Schenck Process LLC ....C....... 785 284-2191
Sabetha (G-10331)

MACHINERY & EQPT, INDL, WHOLESALE: Power Plant Machinery

Locke Equipment Sales Co.....................E 913 782-8500
Olathe (G-7864)
Pentair Flow Technologies LLC............C....... 913 371-5000
Kansas City (G-4319)

MACHINERY & EQPT, INDL, WHOLESALE: Processing & Packaging

Harbor Freight Tools Usa Inc.................F 316 269-2779
Wichita (G-14559)
J-W Operating Company.........................F 620 626-7243
Liberal (G-6324)
Tractor Supply Company ....F 785 827-3300
Salina (G-10738)
Veritiv Operating Company....................C....... 913 667-1500
Kansas City (G-4516)

MACHINERY & EQPT, INDL, WHOLESALE: Propane Conversion

Ferrellgas Inc..F 913 661-1500
Overland Park (G-8713)
Ferrellgas Partners LP...........................D....... 913 661-1500
Overland Park (G-8714)

MACHINERY & EQPT, INDL, WHOLESALE: Safety Eqpt

Weis Fire & Safety Eqp LLC...................E 303 421-2001
Shawnee (G-11051)

MACHINERY & EQPT, INDL, WHOLESALE: Tanks, Storage

Tank Connection LLC ....F 620 423-0251
Parsons (G-9744)

MACHINERY & EQPT, INDL, WHOLESALE: Textile & Leather

Spsi Inc ....F 913 541-8304
Lenexa (G-6150)

MACHINERY & EQPT, INDL, WHOLESALE: Water Pumps

Hydro Rsrces - Mid Cntnent Inc ....D....... 620 277-2389
Garden City (G-2201)

MACHINERY & EQPT, INDL, WHOLESALE: Woodworking

Woodcraft Supply LLC ....G....... 913 599-2800
Shawnee Mission (G-12016)

MACHINERY & EQPT, WHOLESALE: Blades, Graders, Scrapers, Etc

Midwest Truck Equipment Inc ....F 316 744-2889
Park City (G-9633)
Welborn Sales Inc...................................F 785 823-2394
Salina (G-10766)

MACHINERY & EQPT, WHOLESALE: Concrete Processing

M6 Concrete Accessories Co Inc ....E....... 316 263-7251
Wichita (G-14995)

MACHINERY & EQPT, WHOLESALE: Construction, Cranes

American Crane & Tractor Parts............D....... 913 551-8223
Kansas City (G-3804)
Nesco Holdings Inc..................................G....... 913 287-0001
Kansas City (G-4286)
Wilkerson Crane Rental Inc ....E 913 238-7030
Lenexa (G-6230)

MACHINERY & EQPT, WHOLESALE: Construction, General

Baxter Mechanical Contractors.............F 913 281-6303
Kansas City (G-3849)
Berry Companies Inc...............................F 785 266-9509
Topeka (G-12373)
Berry Companies Inc...............................F 785 228-2225
Topeka (G-12374)
Berry Companies Inc...............................E 316 943-4246
Wichita (G-13834)
Berry Companies Inc...............................E 785 232-7731
Topeka (G-12375)
Berry Companies Inc...............................D....... 316 838-3321
Wichita (G-13835)
Berry Companies Inc...............................E 316 838-3321
Wichita (G-13833)
Crane Sales & Service Co Inc................F 913 621-7040
Kansas City (G-3944)
Ditch Witch Sales Inc..............................F 913 782-5223
Olathe (G-7657)
Foley Equipment Company....................E 620 225-4121
Dodge City (G-1361)
Foley Equipment Company....................E 785 825-4661
Salina (G-10503)
Foley Equipment Company....................F 620 792-5246
Great Bend (G-2566)
Foley Industries Inc ....D....... 316 943-4211
Wichita (G-14399)
Logan Contractors Supply Inc...............E 913 768-1551
Olathe (G-7865)
Mel Stevenson & Associates Inc...........D....... 913 262-0505
Kansas City (G-4232)
Midway Sales & Distrg Inc ....F 785 537-4665
Manhattan (G-6745)
Murphy Tractor & Eqp Co Inc ....F 620 227-3139
Dodge City (G-1408)
Murphy Tractor & Eqp Co Inc ....F 620 792-2748
Great Bend (G-2614)
Reed Company LLC................................E 785 456-7333
Wamego (G-13439)
Road Builders McHy & Sup Co..............F 913 371-3822
Kansas City (G-4383)
Road Builders Mchy & Sup Co ....D....... 913 371-3822
Kansas City (G-4384)
Rogers Contracting ....F 316 613-2002
Haysville (G-2958)
Sellers Equipment Inc ....E 316 943-9311
Wichita (G-15556)
United Rentals North Amer Inc..............F 913 696-5628
Olathe (G-8133)
Victor L Phillips Company ....F 316 854-1118
Wichita (G-15906)
Victor L Phillips Company ....F 785 380-0678
Topeka (G-13223)

MACHINERY & EQPT, WHOLESALE: Contractors Materials

Berry Companies Inc...............................F 620 277-2290
Garden City (G-2109)
Coneqtec Corp ....E 316 943-8889
Wichita (G-14088)
Easy Money Pawn Shop Inc...................G....... 316 687-2727
Wichita (G-14255)
Husqvrna Cnstr Pdts N Amer Inc ....A....... 913 928-1000
Olathe (G-7781)
Kanequip Inc ....F 785 632-3441
Clay Center (G-869)
KC Coring & Cutng Cnstr Inc.................F 316 832-1580
Wichita (G-14837)
Murphy Tractor & Eqp Co Inc ....E 855 246-9124
Park City (G-9638)
United Water Works Co ....E 913 287-1280
Kansas City (G-4491)
Universal Construction Pdts..................E 316 946-5885
Wichita (G-15853)
Vermeer Great Plains Inc.......................E 913 782-3655
Olathe (G-8139)
Wall-Ties & Forms Inc.............................C....... 913 441-0073
Shawnee (G-11049)

MACHINERY & EQPT, WHOLESALE: Drilling, Wellpoints

Environmental Mfg Inc ....E 785 587-0807
Manhattan (G-6621)

MACHINERY & EQPT, WHOLESALE: Graders, Motor

Weller Tractor Salvage Inc ....F 620 792-5243
Great Bend (G-2659)

MACHINERY & EQPT, WHOLESALE: Oil Field Eqpt

Buckeye Corporation...............................G....... 316 321-1060
El Dorado (G-1539)
Buckeye Corporation...............................G 785 483-3111
Russell (G-10267)
Francis Casing Crews Inc ....E 620 275-0443
Garden City (G-2166)
Mud-Co/Service Mud Inc ....F 620 672-2957
Pratt (G-10126)

Raymond Oil Company Inc ....F 316 267-4214
Wichita *(G-15422)*
U S Weatherford L P ....D 620 624-6273
Liberal *(G-6377)*

MACHINERY & EQPT, WHOLESALE: Road Construction & Maintenance

Foley Equipment Company ....C 785 266-5770
Topeka *(G-12623)*
Sellers Companies Inc ....E 785 823-6378
Salina *(G-10702)*
Sellers Equipment Inc ....E 785 823-6378
Salina *(G-10703)*
Shears Shop ....F 785 823-6201
Salina *(G-10706)*

MACHINERY & EQPT: Farm

A & B Machine Inc ....F 785 827-5171
Salina *(G-10387)*
Adrian Manufacturing Inc ....G 507 381-9746
Newton *(G-7307)*
Broce Manufacturing Co Inc ....G 620 227-8811
Dodge City *(G-1312)*
Bultman Company Inc Mfg ....F 620 544-8004
Hugoton *(G-3149)*
Buster Crust Inc ....D 620 227-7106
Dodge City *(G-1315)*
Buster Crust Inc ....E 620 385-2651
Spearville *(G-12070)*
Center Industries Corporation ....C 316 942-8255
Wichita *(G-13976)*
Cliffs Welding Shop Inc ....G 785 543-5895
Phillipsburg *(G-9780)*
Custom Metal Fabricators Inc ....E 785 258-3744
Herington *(G-2973)*
Express Scale Parts Inc ....E 913 441-4787
Lenexa *(G-5844)*
Grain Belt Supply Company Inc ....C 785 827-4491
Salina *(G-10514)*
Great Plains International LLC ....F 785 823-3276
Salina *(G-10516)*
Great Plains Manufacturing Inc ....C 785 263-2486
Abilene *(G-34)*
Great Plains Manufacturing Inc ....B 785 825-1509
Salina *(G-10519)*
Great Plains Manufacturing Inc ....E 785 373-4145
Tipton *(G-12248)*
Great Plains Manufacturing Inc ....G 785 472-3508
Ellsworth *(G-1675)*
Great Plains Manufacturing Inc ....G 785 823-2255
Salina *(G-10520)*
Great Plains Manufacturing Inc ....E 785 525-6128
Lucas *(G-6471)*
H C Davis Sons Mfg Co ....F 913 422-3000
Bonner Springs *(G-554)*
Hutchinson/Mayrath ....E 785 632-2161
Clay Center *(G-868)*
Inityaero Inc ....E 316 265-0603
Wichita *(G-14694)*
Ksi Conveyor Inc ....D 785 284-0600
Sabetha *(G-10314)*
Linn Post & Pipe Inc ....E 785 348-5526
Linn *(G-6409)*
Magnum ....E 913 783-4600
Hillsdale *(G-3059)*
Mega Manufacturing Inc ....E 620 663-1127
Hutchinson *(G-3371)*
Mid-Continent Industries Inc ....F 316 283-9648
Newton *(G-7384)*
Midwest Contracting & Mfg ....G 785 743-2026
WA Keeney *(G-13383)*
Midwest Mill Modernization ....F 620 583-6883
Eureka *(G-1895)*
Midwest Mixer Service LLC ....F 620 225-7150
Dodge City *(G-1405)*
Nance Manufacturing Inc ....E 620 842-3761
Anthony *(G-130)*
Rvc Enterprises Inc ....F 785 937-4386
Princeton *(G-10170)*
Schroer Manufacturing Company ....C 913 281-1500
Kansas City *(G-4404)*
Scoular Company ....E 785 823-6301
Salina *(G-10699)*
Shield Industries Inc ....E 620 662-7221
Hutchinson *(G-3441)*
Stinger Ltd ....E 620 465-2683
Burrton *(G-651)*
Triple C Manufacturing Inc ....E 785 284-3674
Sabetha *(G-10334)*

Usc LLC ....F 785 431-7900
Sabetha *(G-10336)*

MACHINERY CLEANING SVCS

Industrial Cleaning and Maint ....E 785 246-9262
Topeka *(G-12722)*

MACHINERY, COMMERCIAL LAUNDRY: Dryers, Incl Coin-Operated

Husqvarna US Holding Inc ....F 913 928-1000
Olathe *(G-7780)*

MACHINERY, FOOD PRDTS: Dairy & Milk

Engineered Systems & Eqp Inc ....D 620 879-5841
Caney *(G-667)*

MACHINERY, FOOD PRDTS: Flour Mill

Great Western Mfg Co Inc ....D 913 682-2291
Leavenworth *(G-5247)*
Norvell Company Inc ....E 620 223-3110
Fort Scott *(G-1995)*
Norvell Company Inc ....E 785 825-6663
Salina *(G-10615)*

MACHINERY, FOOD PRDTS: Processing, Poultry

Baader Linco Inc ....E 913 621-3366
Kansas City *(G-3836)*
Midwest B R D Inc ....F 785 256-6240
Topeka *(G-12894)*
Sterling Manufacturing Co Inc ....G 620 783-5234
Galena *(G-2087)*

MACHINERY, MAILING: Postage Meters

Pitney Bowes Inc ....D 913 681-5579
Shawnee Mission *(G-11736)*
Pitney Bowes Inc ....G 785 266-6750
Topeka *(G-12978)*

MACHINERY, METALWORKING: Assembly, Including Robotic

Encobotics Inc ....G 316 788-5656
Derby *(G-1245)*

MACHINERY, METALWORKING: Coiling

Bradbury Co Inc ....B 620 345-6394
Moundridge *(G-7178)*

MACHINERY, OFFICE: Dictating

Grabar Voice and Data Inc ....G 701 258-3528
Wichita *(G-14488)*

MACHINERY, OFFICE: Perforators

Cummins - Allison Corp ....G 913 894-2266
Lenexa *(G-5797)*

MACHINERY, PACKAGING: Packing & Wrapping

H&H Design & Manufacturing LLC ....F 620 421-9800
Parsons *(G-9691)*

MACHINERY, PAPER INDUSTRY: Converting, Die Cutting & Stampng

Wichita Bindery Inc ....E 316 262-3473
Wichita *(G-15981)*

MACHINERY, PRINTING TRADES: Bookbinding Machinery

Brackett Inc ....G 785 862-2205
Topeka *(G-12402)*

MACHINERY, PRINTING TRADES: Printing Trade Parts & Attchts

Baldwin Americas Corporation ....G 913 310-3258
Lenexa *(G-5683)*

MACHINERY, SEWING: Sewing & Hat & Zipper Making

Scriptpro LLC ....D 913 403-5260
Kansas City *(G-4409)*
SPX Cooling Technologies Inc ....C 913 782-1600
Olathe *(G-8079)*

MACHINERY, TEXTILE: Printing

Cliff Hix Engineering Inc ....E 620 232-3000
Pittsburg *(G-9836)*

MACHINERY, TEXTILE: Silk Screens

Signature Sportswear Inc ....D 620 421-1871
Wichita *(G-15591)*

MACHINERY, WOODWORKING: Cabinet Makers'

Kc Cabinetwright Inc ....E 913 825-6555
Lenexa *(G-5939)*

MACHINERY/EQPT, INDL, WHOL: Cleaning, High Press, Sand/Steam

DCS Sanitation Management Inc ....C 620 624-5533
Liberal *(G-6302)*
Hydrochem LLC ....E 316 321-7541
El Dorado *(G-1569)*
Oasis Car Wash Systems Inc ....E 620 783-1355
Galena *(G-2077)*
Pro Carwash Systems Inc ....F 316 788-9933
Derby *(G-1266)*

MACHINERY: Ammunition & Explosives Loading

Scientific Engineering Inc ....F 785 827-7071
Salina *(G-10698)*

MACHINERY: Automotive Maintenance

Standard Motor Products Inc ....B 620 331-1000
Independence *(G-3562)*
Stinger By Axe ....F 620 767-7555
Council Grove *(G-1177)*

MACHINERY: Automotive Related

Enco of Kansas Inc ....D 316 788-4143
Derby *(G-1244)*

MACHINERY: Bag & Envelope Making

W + D Machinery Co Inc ....E 913 492-9880
Overland Park *(G-9473)*

MACHINERY: Blasting, Electrical

L S Industries Inc ....E 316 265-7997
Wichita *(G-14907)*
Machine Works Inc ....E 316 265-7997
Wichita *(G-14997)*

MACHINERY: Boot Making & Repairing

Oasis Car Wash Systems Inc ....E 620 783-1355
Galena *(G-2077)*

MACHINERY: Clay Working & Tempering

Kratzer Industries ....G 620 824-6405
Geneseo *(G-2393)*

MACHINERY: Concrete Prdts

Dynamold Corporation ....F 785 667-4626
Assaria *(G-201)*

MACHINERY: Construction

Dymax Inc ....E 785 456-2705
Wamego *(G-13415)*
JR Custom Metal Products Inc ....C 316 263-1318
Wichita *(G-14776)*
Lynns Heavy Hauling LLC ....F 913 393-3863
Olathe *(G-7868)*
Peerless Conveyor and Mfg Corp ....F 913 342-2240
Kansas City *(G-4318)*
R & R Equipment Inc ....G 620 223-2450
Fort Scott *(G-2000)*

Rgs Industries Inc ....G.... 913 780-9033
Olathe *(G-8031)*
Roto-Mix LLC ....E.... 620 653-7323
Hoisington *(G-3070)*
Vernon L Goedecke Company Inc ....E.... 913 621-1284
Kansas City *(G-4518)*
Wsm Industries Inc ....E.... 913 492-9299
Lenexa *(G-6236)*

MACHINERY: Custom

Engineered Machine Tool Co ....F.... 316 942-6147
Wichita *(G-14289)*
Midwest B R D Inc ....F.... 785 256-6240
Topeka *(G-12894)*
Midwest Industries & Dev Ltd ....D.... 620 241-5996
McPherson *(G-7007)*
Rice Precision Mfg Inc ....E.... 785 594-2670
Baldwin City *(G-367)*
Thomas Manufacturing Inc ....F.... 620 724-6220
Girard *(G-2421)*

MACHINERY: Extruding

Hf Rubber Machinery Inc ....E.... 785 235-2336
Topeka *(G-12688)*

MACHINERY: Industrial, NEC

Topeka Metal Specialties ....E.... 785 862-1071
Topeka *(G-13181)*

MACHINERY: Jewelers

Glendo LLC ....E.... 620 343-1084
Emporia *(G-1763)*

MACHINERY: Kilns, Lumber

McLiney Lumber and Supply LLC ....F.... 913 766-7102
Prairie Village *(G-10046)*

MACHINERY: Labeling

Huhtamaki Inc ....B.... 913 583-3025
De Soto *(G-1202)*
Liberty Labels LLC ....G.... 620 223-2208
Fort Scott *(G-1981)*

MACHINERY: Metalworking

A & B Machine Inc ....F.... 785 827-5171
Salina *(G-10387)*
Concept Machinery Inc ....G.... 317 845-5588
Overland Park *(G-8594)*
Converting Technologies Inc ....F.... 316 722-6907
Goddard *(G-2433)*

MACHINERY: Milling

Haarslev Inc ....F.... 785 527-5641
Belleville *(G-457)*
Valley View Milling ....F.... 785 858-4777
Seneca *(G-10886)*

MACHINERY: Mining

AG Growth International Inc ....C.... 785 632-2161
Clay Center *(G-842)*
Atkinson Industries Inc ....D.... 620 231-6900
Pittsburg *(G-9816)*
Midwestern Metals Inc ....E.... 785 232-1582
Topeka *(G-12904)*
Rimpull Corporation ....C.... 913 782-4000
Olathe *(G-8036)*
Royal Tractor Company Inc ....E.... 913 782-2598
New Century *(G-7296)*

MACHINERY: Packaging

Magnum Systems Inc ....E.... 620 421-5550
Parsons *(G-9707)*
Performance Packg Group LLC ....E.... 913 438-2012
Shawnee Mission *(G-11727)*
Taylor Products Co Inc ....E.... 620 421-5550
Parsons *(G-9746)*
Tdi Global Solutions Inc ....F.... 877 834-6750
Meriden *(G-7082)*

MACHINERY: Paper Industry Miscellaneous

Buyrollscom Inc ....F.... 913 851-7100
Overland Park *(G-8500)*
Specialty Technology Inc ....F.... 620 241-6307
McPherson *(G-7027)*

MACHINERY: Pharmaciutical

Scriptpro LLC ....D.... 913 384-1008
Shawnee Mission *(G-11839)*

MACHINERY: Plastic Working

Aarons Repair & Supply Inc ....G.... 620 792-5361
Great Bend *(G-2499)*
American Maplan Corporation ....D.... 620 241-6843
McPherson *(G-6934)*
Converting Technologies Inc ....F.... 316 722-6907
Goddard *(G-2433)*
Femco Inc ....D.... 620 241-3513
McPherson *(G-6964)*

MACHINERY: Road Construction & Maintenance

Diteq Corporation ....E.... 816 246-5515
Lenexa *(G-5821)*
Neosho County Road and Bridge ....E.... 620 244-3855
Erie *(G-1861)*

MACHINERY: Robots, Molding & Forming Plastics

Miniature Plastic Molding LLC ....G.... 316 264-2827
Wichita *(G-15112)*

MACHINERY: Saw & Sawing

Husqvrna Cnstr Pdts N Amer Inc ....A.... 913 928-1000
Olathe *(G-7781)*

MACHINERY: Textile

Federal Prison Industries ....D.... 913 682-8700
Leavenworth *(G-5238)*
Hix Corporation ....D.... 620 231-8568
Pittsburg *(G-9876)*

MACHINISTS' TOOLS: Precision

Takako America Co Inc ....C.... 620 663-1790
Hutchinson *(G-3462)*

MAGAZINES, WHOLESALE

435 Magazine LLC ....F.... 913 469-6700
Overland Park *(G-8330)*
Florists Review Entps Inc ....E.... 785 266-0888
Topeka *(G-12620)*
Subscription Ink Co ....D.... 913 248-1800
Shawnee Mission *(G-11905)*

MAGNETS: Ceramic

Bunting Group Inc ....C.... 316 284-2020
Newton *(G-7325)*

MAGNETS: Permanent

Stouse LLC ....E.... 913 384-0014
Kansas City *(G-4441)*

MAIL PRESORTING SVCS

American Pre Sort Inc ....F.... 785 232-2633
Topeka *(G-12321)*

MAIL-ORDER HOUSE, NEC

Diligence Inc ....E.... 913 254-0500
New Century *(G-7279)*
Waxman Candles Inc ....G.... 785 843-8593
Lawrence *(G-5181)*

MAIL-ORDER HOUSES: Automotive Splys & Eqpt

Long Motor Corporation ....C.... 913 541-1525
Lenexa *(G-5978)*

MAIL-ORDER HOUSES: Cards

Victorian Paper Company ....D.... 913 438-3995
Lenexa *(G-6214)*

MAIL-ORDER HOUSES: Computer Eqpt & Electronics

Stallard Technologies Inc ....E.... 913 851-2260
Overland Park *(G-9351)*

MAIL-ORDER HOUSES: Fitness & Sporting Goods

Combat Brands LLC ....E.... 913 689-2300
Lenexa *(G-5770)*

MAIL-ORDER HOUSES: Food

Williams Foods Inc ....C.... 913 888-4343
Lenexa *(G-6231)*

MAIL-ORDER HOUSES: General Merchandise

Mediacorp LLC ....E.... 913 317-8900
Overland Park *(G-9006)*

MAIL-ORDER HOUSES: Gift Items

Hemslojd Inc ....G.... 785 227-2983
Lindsborg *(G-6399)*

MAIL-ORDER HOUSES: Novelty Merchandise

Stealth Technologies LLC ....F.... 913 228-2214
Olathe *(G-8082)*

MAILBOX RENTAL & RELATED SVCS

Jasper Investments Inc ....F.... 913 599-0899
Lenexa *(G-5928)*
Nadia Inc ....F.... 316 686-6190
Wichita *(G-15145)*
U P S Stores ....F.... 913 829-3750
Olathe *(G-8129)*
United Parcel Service Inc ....E.... 913 541-3700
Lenexa *(G-6201)*
Waisner Inc ....F.... 913 345-2663
Shawnee Mission *(G-11989)*

MAILING LIST: Compilers

Contemprary Communications Inc ....D.... 316 265-0879
Wichita *(G-14094)*

MAILING MACHINES WHOLESALERS

Avcorp Business Systems LLC ....E.... 913 888-0333
Overland Park *(G-8415)*
I M S of Kansas City Inc ....F.... 913 599-6007
Shawnee Mission *(G-11446)*

MAILING SVCS, NEC

Aegis Processing Solutions Inc ....D.... 785 232-0061
Topeka *(G-12300)*
Burdiss Lettershop Services Co ....F.... 913 492-0545
Overland Park *(G-8492)*
Consolidated Mailing Corp ....E.... 913 262-4400
Tonganoxie *(G-12257)*
Handy Mailing Service ....F.... 316 944-6258
Wichita *(G-14553)*
Kc Presort ....F.... 913 432-0866
Kansas City *(G-4165)*
Lexinet Corporation ....E.... 620 767-6346
Council Grove *(G-1170)*
Lionshare Marketing Inc ....F.... 913 631-8400
Lenexa *(G-5974)*
Marketing Concepts ....F.... 785 364-4611
Holton *(G-3104)*
Midpoint National Inc ....E.... 913 362-7400
Kansas City *(G-4248)*
Postal Presort Inc ....D.... 316 262-3333
Wichita *(G-15316)*
Southwest Pubg & Mailing Corp ....C.... 785 233-5662
Topeka *(G-13084)*
Step Two Investments LLC ....E.... 913 888-9000
Overland Park *(G-9357)*
U P S Stores ....F.... 913 829-3750
Olathe *(G-8129)*

MANAGEMENT CONSULTING SVCS: Administrative

Kansas Credit Union Assn ....E.... 316 942-7965
Wichita *(G-14795)*
Nonprofit Solutions Inc ....D.... 620 343-6111
Emporia *(G-1806)*
Pbp Management Group Inc ....E.... 316 262-2900
Wichita *(G-15274)*

MANAGEMENT CONSULTING SVCS: Automation & Robotics

Pioneer Automation Technology .... F 316 322-0123
El Dorado *(G-1591)*

MANAGEMENT CONSULTING SVCS: Banking & Finance

EAC Audit Inc .... F 785 594-6707
Baldwin City *(G-359)*
Kci Kansas Counselors Inc .... E 913 541-9704
Shawnee Mission *(G-11526)*
Nuesynergy Inc .... F 913 396-0884
Leawood *(G-5505)*

MANAGEMENT CONSULTING SVCS: Business

Accenture LLP .... C 913 319-1000
Overland Park *(G-8340)*
Advisory Associates Inc .... E 913 829-7323
Lenexa *(G-5635)*
Cartesian Inc .... E 913 345-9315
Overland Park *(G-8524)*
Geneva-Roth Ventures Inc .... E 913 825-1200
Shawnee Mission *(G-11394)*
Globalcom Solutions LLC .... F 785 832-8101
Lawrence *(G-4873)*
Gorham Gold Greenwich & Assoc .... F 913 981-4442
Overland Park *(G-8766)*
Hatcher Consultants Inc .... F 785 271-5557
Topeka *(G-12667)*
Heritage Group Lc .... F 316 261-5301
Wichita *(G-14594)*
HMS Holdings Corp .... E 785 271-9300
Topeka *(G-12695)*
Intellectual Growth Engrg .... F 913 210-8570
Shawnee *(G-10975)*
Kea Advisors .... F 913 832-6099
Lawrence *(G-4939)*
Mbs Inc .... F 913 393-2525
Olathe *(G-7878)*
Prime Concepts Group Inc .... F 316 942-1111
Wichita *(G-15343)*
Sterling Readiness Rounds LLC .... F 785 542-1405
Eudora *(G-1880)*
Telcon Associates Inc .... F 855 864-1571
Overland Park *(G-9400)*
Thats A Wrap LLC .... E 913 390-0035
Olathe *(G-8108)*
Tru8 Solutions LLC .... F 678 451-0264
Manhattan *(G-6831)*
Water Systems Engineering Inc .... F 785 242-5853
Ottawa *(G-8321)*

MANAGEMENT CONSULTING SVCS: Business Planning & Organizing

Advanced Resources LLC .... E 913 207-9998
Leawood *(G-5313)*
ASK Associates Inc .... E 785 841-8194
Lawrence *(G-4738)*
Greg Orscheln Trnsp Co .... E 913 371-1260
Lenexa *(G-5884)*
Level Five Solutions Inc .... F 913 400-2014
Stilwell *(G-12163)*
Onyx Meetings Inc .... F 913 381-1123
Overland Park *(G-9106)*
Pennington Co Fundraising LLC .... E 785 843-1661
Lawrence *(G-5060)*
Stepp and Rothwell .... F 913 345-4800
Overland Park *(G-9359)*

MANAGEMENT CONSULTING SVCS: Compensation & Benefits Planning

Axcet Hr Solutions Inc .... E 913 383-2999
Overland Park *(G-8420)*
CPI Qualified Plan Cons Inc .... B 620 793-8473
Great Bend *(G-2549)*
J L D J Inc .... F 785 625-6316
Hays *(G-2855)*

MANAGEMENT CONSULTING SVCS: Construction Project

CCL Construction Consultants .... E 913 491-0807
Overland Park *(G-8530)*
Conant Construction LLC .... F 620 408-6784
Dodge City *(G-1330)*
Enterprise Bus Solutions LLC .... F 913 529-4350
Lenexa *(G-5834)*
Manning Construction Co Inc .... E 913 390-1007
Olathe *(G-7873)*
Phillips Resource Network Inc .... E 913 236-7777
Shawnee Mission *(G-11732)*
Royal Mechanical Services Inc .... E 913 897-3436
Overland Park *(G-9260)*
Yaeger Architecture Inc .... E 913 742-8000
Lenexa *(G-6239)*
Ziegler Corporation .... F 785 841-4250
Lawrence *(G-5193)*

MANAGEMENT CONSULTING SVCS: Distribution Channels

Skutouch Solutions LLC .... F 913 538-5165
Lenexa *(G-6136)*

MANAGEMENT CONSULTING SVCS: Food & Beverage

Agenda Usa Inc .... E 913 268-4466
Shawnee Mission *(G-11084)*

MANAGEMENT CONSULTING SVCS: General

Excel Personnel Services Inc .... E 913 341-1150
Shawnee Mission *(G-11353)*
Leisure Hotels LLC .... F 913 905-1460
Lenexa *(G-5967)*
Professionals Business MGT Inc .... F 913 888-1444
Overland Park *(G-9188)*
Stratgic Knwldge Solutions Inc .... F 913 682-2002
Leavenworth *(G-5292)*
Xk Solutions Inc .... E 877 954-9656
Overland Park *(G-9513)*

MANAGEMENT CONSULTING SVCS: Hospital & Health

3c Healthcare Inc .... F 620 221-7850
Winfield *(G-16113)*
Advantage Medical Group .... F 785 749-0130
Lawrence *(G-4722)*
Communityworks Inc .... D 913 789-9900
Overland Park *(G-8584)*
Corridor Group Holdings LLC .... E 913 362-0600
Shawnee Mission *(G-11267)*
Genoa Healthcare Mass LLC .... E 913 680-1652
Leavenworth *(G-5245)*
Health Data Specialists LLC .... E 785 242-3419
Pomona *(G-10004)*
Healthcare Prfmce Group Inc .... D 316 796-0337
Spring Hill *(G-12086)*
Healthcare Revenue Group LLC .... F 913 717-4000
Stilwell *(G-12151)*
Kdjm Consulting Inc .... F 913 362-0600
Shawnee Mission *(G-11527)*
McMc LLC .... E 913 341-8811
Overland Park *(G-9003)*
Medova Hlthcare Fncl Group LLC .... E 316 616-6160
Wichita *(G-15034)*
Midland Professional Services .... E 785 840-9676
Lawrence *(G-5026)*
Midwest Division - Oprmc LLC .... A 913 541-5000
Shawnee Mission *(G-11632)*
Midwest Health Services Inc .... F 316 685-1587
Wichita *(G-15095)*
Regulatory Consultants Inc .... E 785 486-2882
Horton *(G-3133)*
Sisters St Joseph Wichita KS .... E 316 686-7171
Wichita *(G-15598)*
Vigilias LLC .... E 800 924-8140
Wichita *(G-15907)*

MANAGEMENT CONSULTING SVCS: Industrial

Garden Cy Ammonia Program LLC .... F 620 271-0037
Garden City *(G-2180)*

MANAGEMENT CONSULTING SVCS: Industrial Hygiene

Certified Environmental Mgt .... E 785 823-0492
Salina *(G-10446)*

MANAGEMENT CONSULTING SVCS: Industry Specialist

Advanced Medical Resources .... E 316 687-3071
Wichita *(G-13624)*
American Maplan Corporation .... D 620 241-6843
McPherson *(G-6934)*
CLC Group Inc .... C 316 636-5055
Wichita *(G-14038)*
Integrated Solutions Inc .... D 316 264-7050
Wichita *(G-14704)*
Proactive Solutions Inc .... E 913 948-8000
Shawnee Mission *(G-11753)*
Protiviti Inc .... F 913 685-6200
Overland Park *(G-9198)*
T T Companies Inc .... A 913 599-6886
Olathe *(G-8097)*
Terracon Consultants Inc .... E 316 262-0171
Wichita *(G-15730)*
Terracon Consultants Inc .... F 785 267-3310
Topeka *(G-13153)*
U S Automation Inc .... G 913 894-2410
Shawnee Mission *(G-11953)*

MANAGEMENT CONSULTING SVCS: Information Systems

High Quality Tech Inc .... G 316 448-3559
Wichita *(G-14604)*
Incisive Consultants LLC .... F 800 973-1743
Overland Park *(G-8840)*

MANAGEMENT CONSULTING SVCS: Maintenance

Kansas Rural Housing Service .... E 785 862-4877
Topeka *(G-12802)*
Medicalodges Cnstr Co Inc .... F 620 251-6700
Coffeyville *(G-961)*

MANAGEMENT CONSULTING SVCS: Planning

Culture Index LLC .... F 816 361-7575
Leawood *(G-5365)*
Fbd Consulting Inc .... F 913 319-8850
Overland Park *(G-8709)*

MANAGEMENT CONSULTING SVCS: Quality Assurance

NTS Technical Systems .... F 316 832-1600
Wichita *(G-15198)*
Selective Site Consultants Inc .... E 913 438-7700
Overland Park *(G-9292)*
TFT Global Inc .... F 519 842-4540
Kansas City *(G-4467)*

MANAGEMENT CONSULTING SVCS: Real Estate

Block Real Estate Services LLC .... F 816 412-8457
Overland Park *(G-8464)*
Chelepis & Associates Inc .... E 913 912-7113
Overland Park *(G-8544)*
Complex Property Advisers Corp .... F 913 498-0790
Overland Park *(G-8591)*
Ellis Grubb Martens Coml Group .... E 316 262-0000
Wichita *(G-14272)*
Integra Realty Resources .... E 913 236-4700
Shawnee Mission *(G-11462)*
Kessinger/Hunter & Company Lc .... C 816 842-2690
Shawnee Mission *(G-11529)*
Land Acquisitions Inc .... E 847 749-0675
Wichita *(G-14919)*
Lawing Financial Group Inc .... D 913 491-6226
Overland Park *(G-8948)*
Midland Properties Inc .... F 913 677-5300
Mission Woods *(G-7151)*
Slawson Exploration Co Inc .... E 316 263-3201
Wichita *(G-15603)*

MANAGEMENT CONSULTING SVCS: Restaurant & Food

Caenen Castle .... F 913 631-4100
Shawnee *(G-10922)*
Cro Magnon Repast LLC .... F 913 747-5559
Lenexa *(G-5793)*

Restaurant Purchasing Svcs LLC ....F 800 548-2292
Overland Park *(G-9237)*
Ross Consultants Inc ....E 213 926-2090
Overland Park *(G-9258)*

MANAGEMENT CONSULTING SVCS: Retail Trade Consultant

First Intermark Corporation ....E 620 442-2460
Arkansas City *(G-156)*

MANAGEMENT CONSULTING SVCS: Training & Development

Aib International Inc ....D 785 537-4750
Manhattan *(G-6537)*
American Management Assn Intl ....C 913 451-2700
Shawnee Mission *(G-11105)*
DVC Training Specialists LLC ....G 913 908-3393
Gardner *(G-2340)*
Franklin Covey Co ....G 800 819-1812
Overland Park *(G-8737)*
Higher Ground ....F 316 262-2060
Wichita *(G-14607)*
Leidos Inc ....G 913 317-5120
Shawnee Mission *(G-11560)*
Tiyosaye Inc Higher Ground ....F 316 262-2060
Wichita *(G-15768)*
Training Tech & Support Inc ....E 913 682-7048
Leavenworth *(G-5300)*

MANAGEMENT CONSULTING SVCS: Transportation

Mixon-Hill Inc ....F 913 239-8400
Shawnee Mission *(G-11648)*
Parsons Brnckrhoff Hldings Inc ....E 913 310-9943
Lenexa *(G-6043)*
Return Products Management Inc ....F 913 768-1747
Olathe *(G-8028)*

MANAGEMENT SERVICES

Agelix Consulting LLC ....E 913 708-8145
Overland Park *(G-8357)*
Allen Press Inc ....D 785 843-1234
Lawrence *(G-4729)*
American Multi-Cinema Inc ....C 913 213-2000
Leawood *(G-5322)*
Archer-Daniels-Midland Company ....D 785 825-1541
Salina *(G-10407)*
Arwood Waste Inc ....F 316 448-1576
Wichita *(G-13744)*
Butler National Corporation ....E 913 780-9595
Olathe *(G-7571)*
Capstone MGT & Dev Group Inc ....F 785 341-2494
Manhattan *(G-6576)*
Carson Development Inc ....F 913 499-1926
Overland Park *(G-8522)*
Centrinex LLC ....F 913 827-9600
Lenexa *(G-5739)*
City of Wichita ....E 316 942-4482
Wichita *(G-14025)*
Corvel Corporation ....E 913 253-7200
Overland Park *(G-8602)*
Cryo Management Inc ....E 913 362-9005
Prairie Village *(G-10023)*
Cullor Property Management LLC ....F 913 324-5900
Lenexa *(G-5796)*
Curo Management LLC ....E 316 771-0000
Wichita *(G-14143)*
Curo Management LLC ....D 316 722-3801
Wichita *(G-14145)*
Dalmark Management Group LLC ....F 816 272-0041
Leawood *(G-5368)*
Den Management Co Inc ....C 316 686-1964
Wichita *(G-14191)*
Dynamic Management Solutions ....E 785 456-1794
Wamego *(G-13416)*
Event Systems Inc ....F 316 641-1848
Wichita *(G-14314)*
Fidelity Management Corp ....E 316 291-5950
Wichita *(G-14365)*
Heartland Golf Dev II LLC ....F 913 856-7235
Mission Hills *(G-7143)*
Heartland Management Company ....F 785 233-6655
Topeka *(G-12680)*
Interntnal Mtr Coach Group Inc ....F 913 906-0111
Lenexa *(G-5920)*
Kansas Assc Home For Aged Inc ....F 785 233-7443
Topeka *(G-12758)*
Kcoe Isom LLP ....E 785 825-1561
Salina *(G-10572)*
Knight Enterprises Ltd ....E 785 843-5511
Lawrence *(G-4946)*
Koppers Recovery Resources LLC ....E 913 213-6127
Overland Park *(G-8926)*
L C Epoch Group ....C 855 753-7624
Overland Park *(G-8934)*
Lakemary Center Inc ....E 913 768-6831
Olathe *(G-7853)*
Latour Management Inc ....F 316 733-1922
Andover *(G-102)*
Lodging Enterprises LLC ....A 316 630-6300
Wichita *(G-14975)*
Macfarlane Group LLC ....E 913 825-1200
Shawnee Mission *(G-11589)*
Material Management Inc ....F 620 221-9060
Winfield *(G-16157)*
Midwest Bioscience RES Pk LLC ....E 913 319-0300
Leawood *(G-5482)*
Miq Logistics LLC ....C 913 696-7100
Overland Park *(G-9041)*
National Bd For Rspratory Care ....F 913 895-4900
Overland Park *(G-9069)*
Natural Gas Pipeline Amer LLC ....G 620 885-4505
Minneola *(G-7127)*
Osage Cnty Ecnmic Dev Corp Inc ....D 785 828-3242
Lyndon *(G-6478)*
Petl Management Corp Inc ....F 620 792-1717
Great Bend *(G-2622)*
PSI Services Inc ....C 913 895-4600
Olathe *(G-8011)*
Quality Technology Svcs LLC ....D 913 814-9988
Overland Park *(G-9217)*
Resource Service Solutions LLC ....E 913 338-5050
Lenexa *(G-6107)*
Retail Groc Assn Grter Kans Cy ....F 913 384-3830
Westwood *(G-13558)*
Saint Francis Cmnty Svcs Inc ....E 785 210-1000
Junction City *(G-3749)*
Sr Food and Beverage Co Inc ....D 913 299-9797
Kansas City *(G-4437)*
T W Lacy & Associates Inc ....F 913 706-7625
Prairie Village *(G-10073)*
Tetra Management Inc ....F 316 685-6221
Wichita *(G-15731)*
Tmfs Management LLC ....C 913 319-8100
Overland Park *(G-9417)*
Watco Supply Chain Svcs LLC ....F 479 502-3658
Great Bend *(G-2657)*
Young Management Corporation ....D 913 341-3113
Overland Park *(G-9519)*

MANAGEMENT SVCS, FACILITIES SUPPORT: Environ Remediation

Blackstone Environmental Inc ....F 913 495-9990
Stilwell *(G-12136)*
Cleaning By Lamunyon Inc ....F 785 632-1259
Clay Center *(G-855)*
Hydrogeologic Inc ....E 913 317-8860
Shawnee Mission *(G-11445)*
Remediation Services Inc ....E 800 335-1201
Independence *(G-3553)*
Sky Blue Inc ....D 785 842-9013
Lawrence *(G-5112)*

MANAGEMENT SVCS: Administrative

Adorers of Bld of Chrst ....F 316 942-2201
Wichita *(G-13615)*
Kickapoo Tribe In Kansas Inc ....C 785 486-2131
Horton *(G-3130)*
Liberal School District ....E 620 604-2400
Liberal *(G-6335)*
Medtrak Services LLC ....D 913 262-2187
Overland Park *(G-9008)*
Mosaic ....E 913 788-8400
Kansas City *(G-4267)*
Mosaic ....D 620 229-8702
Winfield *(G-16161)*
Mpp Co Inc ....F 913 895-0269
Shawnee Mission *(G-11656)*
Nustar Pipeline Oper Partnr LP ....F 316 773-9000
Wichita *(G-15200)*
T T Companies Inc ....A 913 599-6886
Olathe *(G-8097)*
University of Kansas Med Ctr ....E 913 945-5598
Westwood *(G-13562)*

MANAGEMENT SVCS: Business

Arthur Dogswell LLC ....D 620 231-7779
Frontenac *(G-2052)*
Ceva US Holdings Inc ....F 913 894-0230
Lenexa *(G-5747)*
Cushman Wkefield Solutions LLC ....C 316 721-3656
Colwich *(G-1093)*
Devlin Management Inc ....F 316 634-1800
Wichita *(G-14204)*
Eagle Case Management LLC ....E 913 334-9035
Kansas City *(G-3978)*
L D F Company ....E 316 636-5575
Wichita *(G-14905)*
Lrico Services LLC ....C 316 847-4800
Wichita *(G-14987)*
Mll Management Group Inc ....D 620 947-3608
Hillsboro *(G-3052)*
Plaza Belmont MGT Group II LLC ....B 913 381-7177
Shawnee Mission *(G-11738)*
Priority Logistics Inc ....E 913 991-7281
Overland Park *(G-9186)*
Profit Plus Bus Solutions LLC ....F 913 583-8440
De Soto *(G-1210)*
Reit Management & Research ....F 913 492-4375
Lenexa *(G-6099)*
Tsvc Inc ....C 913 599-6886
Olathe *(G-8124)*
Tyr Energy Inc ....F 913 754-5800
Overland Park *(G-9435)*
Young Management Group Inc ....F 913 213-3827
Overland Park *(G-9520)*

MANAGEMENT SVCS: Construction

Bettis Contractors Inc ....E 785 783-8353
Topeka *(G-12378)*
Black & Veatch Holding Company ....D 913 458-2000
Overland Park *(G-8457)*
Capital Performance MGT LLC ....E 913 381-1481
Leawood *(G-5346)*
Century Construction Sup LLC ....F 913 438-3366
Lenexa *(G-5741)*
Construction MGT Svcs Inc ....E 913 231-5736
Olathe *(G-7612)*
Davidson & Associates Inc ....E 913 271-6859
Leawood *(G-5372)*
Dondlinger Companies Inc ....D 316 945-0555
Wichita *(G-14228)*
GBA Builders Llc ....E 913 492-0400
Lenexa *(G-5870)*
Gunter Construction Company ....F 913 362-7844
Kansas City *(G-4059)*
Henderson Bldg Solutions LLC ....F 913 894-9720
Lenexa *(G-5899)*
Home Depot USA Inc ....E 913 888-9090
Shawnee Mission *(G-11437)*
J & K Contracting Lc ....F 785 238-3298
Junction City *(G-3702)*
Kansas Asphalt Inc ....D 877 384-2280
Bucyrus *(G-601)*
Kessinger/Hunter & Company Lc ....C 816 842-2690
Shawnee Mission *(G-11529)*
Manning Construction Co Inc ....E 913 390-1007
Olathe *(G-7873)*
R D H Electric Inc ....E 785 625-3833
Hays *(G-2895)*
Rf Construction Inc ....E 785 776-8855
Manhattan *(G-6791)*
Universal Construction Co Inc ....E 913 342-1150
Kansas City *(G-4494)*
Woofter Cnstr & Irrigation Inc ....E 785 462-8653
Colby *(G-1049)*

MANAGEMENT SVCS: Financial, Business

Firstsource Solutions USA Inc ....F 620 223-8200
Fort Scott *(G-1968)*
Westdale Asset Management Ltd ....D 913 307-5900
Lenexa *(G-6227)*

MANAGEMENT SVCS: Hospital

Adventist Health Mid-America ....C 913 676-2184
Shawnee Mission *(G-11080)*
Delmar Gardens of Overland Pk ....C 913 469-4210
Shawnee Mission *(G-11300)*
Deseret Health Group Llc ....B 620 662-0597
Hutchinson *(G-3262)*
Kansas Medical Insur Svcs Corp ....F 785 232-2224
Topeka *(G-12789)*

Mosaic....E....785 472-4081
Ellsworth *(G-1679)*
Nueterra DC Holdings LLC....E....913 387-0689
Leawood *(G-5506)*
Pulse Systems Inc....D....316 636-5900
Wichita *(G-15375)*
Saint Francis Cmnty Svcs Inc....F....620 326-6373
Wellington *(G-13526)*
Saint Francis Cmnty Svcs Inc....E....785 825-0541
Salina *(G-10658)*
Saint Francis Cmnty Svcs Inc....C....620 276-4482
Garden City *(G-2272)*
Saint Francis Cmnty Svcs Inc....E....785 825-0541
Salina *(G-10659)*
Saint Francis Cmnty Svcs Inc....E....785 452-9653
Salina *(G-10660)*
Saint Francis Cmnty Svcs Inc....F....316 831-0330
Wichita *(G-15507)*
Via Christi Health Inc....E....316 858-4900
Wichita *(G-15891)*
Western Plins Rgional Hosp LLC....F....620 225-8700
Dodge City *(G-1455)*

MANAGEMENT SVCS: Hotel Or Motel

Bristol Hotel & Resorts Inc....E....785 462-8787
Colby *(G-991)*
Bristol Hotel & Resorts Inc....D....785 823-1739
Salina *(G-10431)*
Channelview SW Hotel Inc....E....913 345-2111
Lenexa *(G-5752)*
Commercial Hotel Management Co....E....913 642-0160
Lenexa *(G-5775)*
Crestline Hotels & Resorts LLC....E....913 451-2553
Overland Park *(G-8613)*
Gaelic Management Inc....F....316 683-5150
Wichita *(G-14436)*
Innco Hospitality Inc....E....913 451-1300
Shawnee Mission *(G-11458)*
Leisure Hotel Corporation....D....913 905-1460
Lenexa *(G-5966)*
Lodgeworks Partners LP....D....316 681-5100
Wichita *(G-14974)*
Rhw Hotel Holdings Company LLC....F....913 451-1222
Shawnee Mission *(G-11798)*
Six Continents Hotels Inc....E....785 462-8787
Colby *(G-1041)*

MANAGEMENT SVCS: Industrial

Paradigm Liaison Services LLC....E....316 554-9225
Wichita *(G-15256)*
Pk Technology LLC....F....316 866-2955
Wichita *(G-15304)*

MANAGEMENT SVCS: Nursing & Personal Care Facility

Beverly Enterprises-Kansas LLC....E....316 683-7588
Wichita *(G-13844)*
Beverly Enterprises-Kansas LLC....E....913 351-1284
Lansing *(G-4669)*
Beverly Enterprises-Kansas LLC....E....785 449-2294
Eskridge *(G-1865)*
Centennial Healthcare Corp....C....913 829-2273
Olathe *(G-7584)*
Health Management of Kansas....D....620 431-7474
Chanute *(G-731)*
Health Management of Kansas....D....620 251-1866
Coffeyville *(G-944)*
Health Management of Kansas....D....620 429-3803
Columbus *(G-1078)*
Health Management of Kansas....C....620 251-5190
Coffeyville *(G-945)*
Health Management of Kansas....D....620 251-6545
Coffeyville *(G-946)*
Lamar Court....D....913 906-9696
Overland Park *(G-8941)*
Lutheran Home WA Keeney....E....785 743-5787
Wakeeney *(G-13389)*
Preferred Mental Health Mgt....F....316 262-0444
Wichita *(G-15328)*
Presbytrian Mnors of Md-Merica....E....316 685-1100
Wichita *(G-15336)*

MANAGEMENT SVCS: Personnel

Foster Design Inc....C....316 832-9700
Wichita *(G-14403)*
United States Dept of Army....E....913 684-2151
Fort Leavenworth *(G-1944)*

MANAGEMENT SVCS: Restaurant

Delight Tb Indiana LLC....B....561 301-6257
Wichita *(G-14187)*
L C Enterprises....F....316 682-3300
Wichita *(G-14904)*
Latour Management Inc....E....316 524-2290
Wichita *(G-14933)*
Sasnak Management Corporation....E....316 683-2611
Wichita *(G-15521)*
T-143 Inc....E....913 681-8313
Overland Park *(G-9390)*

MANPOWER POOLS

Manpowergroup Inc....F....316 946-0088
Wichita *(G-15005)*
Temporary Employment Corp....E....785 749-2800
Lawrence *(G-5134)*
Topeka Services Inc....F....785 228-7800
Lawrence *(G-5141)*

MANUFACTURED & MOBILE HOME DEALERS

Clayton Homes Inc....C....785 434-4617
Plainville *(G-9981)*

MANUFACTURING INDUSTRIES, NEC

Al Industries Prof Corp....F....918 401-9641
Wichita *(G-13645)*
Centurion Manufacturing....G....316 210-3504
Benton *(G-515)*
Dw Industries LLC....G....913 782-7575
Olathe *(G-7662)*
E C Manufacturing....D....913 825-3077
Shawnee *(G-10942)*
Kls Industries LLC....G....877 952-2548
Shawnee *(G-10983)*
Memory and Music Inc....F....913 449-4473
Overland Park *(G-9009)*
Orange Industries LLC....G....816 694-1919
Mission *(G-7134)*
Percision Mfg....G....913 362-9244
Shawnee *(G-11010)*
Sparker Industries Inc....G....913 963-5261
Bucyrus *(G-610)*
Warren Consulting Inc....E....620 727-2468
Hutchinson *(G-3481)*

MAPMAKING SVCS

Wilson Inc Engneers Architects....E....913 652-9911
Overland Park *(G-9496)*

MARBLE, BUILDING: Cut & Shaped

Artistic Marble LLC....F....316 944-8713
Wichita *(G-13743)*

MARINAS

North Shore Marina MGT LLC....G....785 453-2240
Quenemo *(G-10178)*

MARKETS: Meat & fish

Dillon Companies Inc....C....785 272-0661
Topeka *(G-12557)*
Dillon Companies Inc....D....785 823-9403
Salina *(G-10478)*
Queen-Morris Ventures LLC....C....913 383-2563
Shawnee Mission *(G-11765)*
Waggoner Enterprises Inc....E....620 465-3807
Yoder *(G-16196)*

MARKING DEVICES

E-Z Info Inc....F....913 367-5020
Atchison *(G-226)*
Wichita Stamp and Seal Inc....G....316 263-4223
Wichita *(G-16029)*

MARKING DEVICES: Embossing Seals & Hand Stamps

Snow Inc....G....785 869-2021
Lane *(G-4663)*

MARKING DEVICES: Postmark Stamps, Hand, Rubber Or Metal

Advance Business Supply....G....785 440-7826
Topeka *(G-12292)*
Superior Rbr Stamp & Seal Inc....G....316 682-5511
Wichita *(G-15698)*

MARTIAL ARTS INSTRUCTION

Fit Physique....E....316 721-2230
Wichita *(G-14379)*
Team Ko LLC....F....913 897-1300
Overland Park *(G-9398)*

MASQUERADE OR THEATRICAL COSTUMES STORES

L V S Inc....E....316 636-5005
Wichita *(G-14908)*

MASSAGE PARLOR & STEAM BATH SVCS

Courtland Day Spa....F....620 223-0098
Fort Scott *(G-1962)*
Images Salon & Day Spa....F....785 843-2138
Lawrence *(G-4909)*

MASSAGE PARLORS

Gram Enterprises Inc....E....913 888-3689
Lenexa *(G-5879)*
Herbs & More Inc....F....785 865-4372
Lawrence *(G-4895)*
Mane Thing....E....785 762-2397
Junction City *(G-3723)*

MASTIC ROOFING COMPOSITION

Quality Roofg Installation LLC....G....316 946-1068
Wichita *(G-15384)*

MATERIAL GRINDING & PULVERIZING SVCS NEC

Creason Corrugating McHy Inc....F....423 629-5532
Park City *(G-9613)*

MATERIALS HANDLING EQPT WHOLESALERS

Accent Erection & Maint Co Inc....F....913 371-1600
Kansas City *(G-3780)*
Adelphi Construction Lc....D....913 384-5511
Shawnee Mission *(G-11075)*
Berry Companies Inc....F....785 228-2225
Topeka *(G-12374)*
Berry Companies Inc....F....620 277-2290
Garden City *(G-2109)*
Beumer Kansas City LLC....E....816 245-7260
Overland Park *(G-8443)*
Hertel Tank Service Inc....G....785 628-2445
Hays *(G-2841)*
Key Equipment & Supply Co....F....913 788-2546
Kansas City *(G-4172)*
Lift Truck Center Inc....E....316 942-7465
Wichita *(G-14963)*
McLaughlin Leasing Inc....F....316 542-0303
Cheney *(G-794)*
Mid-West Conveyor Company....C....734 288-4400
Kansas City *(G-4247)*
Neighbors & Associates Inc....F....620 423-3010
Parsons *(G-9710)*
Overhead Door Company....E....316 265-4634
Wichita *(G-15240)*
Professional Fleet Svcs LLC....F....316 524-6000
Wichita *(G-15361)*
Southerncarlson Inc....F....316 942-1392
Wichita *(G-15625)*
Wiese Usa Inc....E....316 942-1600
Wichita *(G-16045)*

MATS & MATTING, MADE FROM PURCHASED WIRE

Balco Inc....C....800 767-0082
Wichita *(G-13798)*

MEAL DELIVERY PROGRAMS

Linn County Nutrition Project....F....913 795-2279
Mound City *(G-7172)*

Meals On Whls of Shwnee & Jeff ....E 785 354-5420
Topeka (G-12875)
Mid-America Nutrition Program............E 785 242-8341
Ottawa (G-8291)
Tonys Pizza..F 620 275-4626
Garden City (G-2299)

MEAT & MEAT PRDTS WHOLESALERS

Associated Wholesale Groc Inc ....A 913 288-1000
Kansas City (G-3825)
Flatland Food Distributors LLC ....F 316 945-5171
Wichita (G-14382)
Hormel Foods Corp Svcs LLC ....F 913 888-8744
Shawnee Mission (G-11440)
Qins International Inc ....E 913 342-4488
Kansas City (G-4350)
Seaboard Foods LLC.............................D 913 261-2600
Shawnee Mission (G-11842)
Swiss Burger Brand Meat Co.................F 316 838-7514
Wichita (G-15709)
Waltons Inc..F 316 262-0651
Wichita (G-15925)

MEAT CUTTING & PACKING

B&B Quality Meats LLC.........................G 620 285-8988
Larned (G-4694)
Browns Processing ....G 620 378-2441
Fredonia (G-2027)
Cargill Incorporated...............................E 785 743-2288
WA Keeney (G-13382)
Cargill Incorporated...............................F 316 291-1939
Wichita (G-13947)
Cargill Meat Solutions Corp..................E 620 225-2610
Dodge City (G-1317)
Cargill Mt Lgstics Sltions Inc.................F 620 225-2610
Dodge City (G-1318)
Diecks Inc..E 785 632-5550
Clay Center (G-860)
Ehresman Packing Co ....F 620 276-3791
Garden City (G-2152)
Elkhorn Valley Packing..........................E 620 326-3443
Wellington (G-13498)
Empirical Technology Inc......................C 620 277-2753
Holcomb (G-3074)
Farview Farms Meat Co.........................G 785 246-1154
Topeka (G-12597)
Indian Hills Meat and Plty Inc ....E 316 264-1644
Wichita (G-14683)
Jacksons Frozen Food Center..............G 620 662-4465
Hutchinson (G-3339)
Kensington Lockers Inc ....F 785 476-2834
Kensington (G-4577)
Kiowa Locker System LLC....................F 620 825-4538
Kiowa (G-4626)
Moran Meat Locker...............................G 620 237-4331
Moran (G-7163)
National Beef Packing Co LLC ....C 620 624-1851
Liberal (G-6349)
National Beef Packing Co LLC ....D 620 227-7135
Dodge City (G-1410)
Nordic Foods Inc...................................D 913 281-1167
Kansas City (G-4289)
Olpe Locker...G 620 475-3375
Emporia (G-1809)
OSI..G 316 688-5011
Wichita (G-15239)
Plankenhorn Inc ....F 620 276-3791
Garden City (G-2256)
S&S Quality Meats LLC ....D 620 342-6354
Emporia (G-1818)
Seaboard Foods LLC.............................D 913 261-2600
Shawnee Mission (G-11842)
Smithfield Foods Inc..............................F 785 762-3306
Junction City (G-3756)
Smokey Hill Meat Processing...............G 785 735-2278
Victoria (G-13377)
Stroot Locker Inc ....G 316 777-4421
Mulvane (G-7227)
Tyson Fresh Meats Inc ....D 620 277-2614
Holcomb (G-3082)
Tyson Fresh Meats Inc ....G 620 343-3640
Emporia (G-1843)
Waggoner Enterprises Inc ....E 620 465-3807
Yoder (G-16196)
Walnut Valley Packing LLC ....G 866 421-3595
El Dorado (G-1613)
Winchester Meat Processing................G 913 774-2860
Winchester (G-16111)

MEAT MARKETS

Bern Meat Plant Incorporated................F 785 336-2165
Bern (G-521)
Bichelmeyer Meats A Corp.....................F 913 342-5945
Kansas City (G-3859)
Duis Meat Processing Inc ....F 785 243-7850
Concordia (G-1109)
Fritzs Mt Superior Sausage LLC............G 913 381-4618
Shawnee Mission (G-11383)
Grinnell Locker Plant Inc........................F 785 824-3400
Grinnell (G-2693)
Kier Enterprises Inc...............................E 785 325-2150
Washington (G-13467)
Krehbiels Specialty Meats Inc ....E 620 241-0103
McPherson (G-6985)
Plankenhorn Inc.....................................F 620 276-3791
Garden City (G-2256)
Stroot Locker Inc ....G 316 777-4421
Mulvane (G-7227)
Winchester Meat Processing.................G 913 774-2860
Winchester (G-16111)

MEAT PRDTS: Bacon, Slab & Sliced, From Slaughtered Meat

Dold Foods LLC ....C 316 838-9101
Wichita (G-14221)
Sugar Creek Packing Co ....C 620 232-2700
Frontenac (G-2064)

MEAT PRDTS: Dried Beef, From Purchased Meat

Luthers Smokehouse Inc.......................G 620 964-2222
Le Roy (G-5197)

MEAT PRDTS: Meat By-Prdts, From Slaughtered Meat

APC Inc ....E 620 675-8691
Sublette (G-12197)

MEAT PRDTS: Pork, From Slaughtered Meat

Seaboard Corporation............................C 913 676-8800
Merriam (G-7103)
Seaboard Foods LLC.............................G 620 593-4353
Rolla (G-10233)

MEAT PRDTS: Prepared Pork Prdts, From Purchased Meat

Hams Pool Service LLC.........................G 913 927-0882
Overland Park (G-8789)

MEAT PRDTS: Sausages, From Purchased Meat

Fritzs Mt Superior Sausage LLC............G 913 381-4618
Shawnee Mission (G-11383)
Johnsonville LLC....................................C 785 364-3126
Holton (G-3102)
Smithfield Packaged Meats Corp ....A 316 942-8461
Wichita (G-15610)
Sugar Creek Packing Co ....C 620 232-2700
Frontenac (G-2064)

MEAT PROCESSED FROM PURCHASED CARCASSES

Alma Foods LLC ....F 785 765-3396
Alma (G-61)
Cargill Mt Lgstics Sltions Inc.................F 620 225-2610
Dodge City (G-1318)
Diecks Inc..E 785 632-5550
Clay Center (G-860)
Dold Foods LLC ....C 316 838-9101
Wichita (G-14221)
Empirical Technology Inc.......................C 620 277-2753
Holcomb (G-3074)
Grinnell Locker Plant Inc........................F 785 824-3400
Grinnell (G-2693)
Indian Hills Meat and Plty Inc ....E 316 264-1644
Wichita (G-14683)
Jacksons Frozen Food Center...............G 620 662-4465
Hutchinson (G-3339)
Kiowa Locker System LLC.....................F 620 825-4538
Kiowa (G-4626)
National Beef Packing Co LLC ....D 620 227-7135
Dodge City (G-1410)
Nordic Foods Inc....................................D 913 281-1167
Kansas City (G-4289)
Plankenhorn Inc ....F 620 276-3791
Garden City (G-2256)
S&S Quality Meats LLC ....D 620 342-6354
Emporia (G-1818)
Tyson Foods Inc.....................................B 620 663-6141
South Hutchinson (G-12067)
Tyson Fresh Meats Inc ....D 620 277-2614
Holcomb (G-3082)
Waggoner Enterprises Inc ....E 620 465-3807
Yoder (G-16196)
Winchester Meat Processing.................G 913 774-2860
Winchester (G-16111)

MEAT PROCESSING MACHINERY

Chad Equipment LLC ....F 913 764-0321
Olathe (G-7589)

MEATS, PACKAGED FROZEN: Wholesalers

Smithfield Packaged Meats Corp ....A 316 942-8461
Wichita (G-15610)

MEDIA: Magnetic & Optical Recording

Data Locker Inc ....G 913 310-9088
Overland Park (G-8636)
Magtek Inc ....F 913 451-1151
Lenexa (G-5981)

MEDICAL & DENTAL ASSISTANT SCHOOL

University of Kansas ....C 913 588-5238
Shawnee Mission (G-11967)

MEDICAL & HOSPITAL EQPT WHOLESALERS

Briovarx LLC ....F 913 307-9900
Lenexa (G-5716)
Karis Inc...F 620 260-9931
Garden City (G-2215)
LAd Global Enterprises Inc....................F 913 768-0888
Olathe (G-7851)
Lincare Inc...E 913 438-8200
Lenexa (G-5973)
Medical Eqp Solutions Inc ....F 816 241-3334
Leawood (G-5471)
Newman Mem Hosp Foundation ....F 620 343-1800
Emporia (G-1804)
Newman Mem Hosp Foundation ....B 620 343-6800
Emporia (G-1803)
Pharmacy Dist Partners LLC ....F 903 357-3391
Mission Hills (G-7147)
Sizewise Rentals LLC............................E 785 726-4371
Ellis (G-1653)

MEDICAL & SURGICAL SPLYS: Braces, Orthopedic

Arveda Llc..E 785 625-4674
Hays (G-2750)

MEDICAL & SURGICAL SPLYS: Limbs, Artificial

Hanger Prosthetics & ....G 913 498-1540
Shawnee Mission (G-11407)
Hanger Prosthetics & ....G 913 341-8897
Overland Park (G-8790)
Hanger Prosthetics & ....G 913 588-6548
Kansas City (G-4065)
Hanger Prosthetics & ....G 785 232-5382
Topeka (G-12664)

MEDICAL & SURGICAL SPLYS: Orthopedic Appliances

Acustep LLC...G 785 826-2500
Salina (G-10393)
Hanger Prsthetcs & Ortho Inc................F 316 685-1268
Wichita (G-14555)
Kansas Specialty Services Inc ....F 620 221-6040
Winfield (G-16151)
Knit-Rite Inc...D 913 279-6310
Kansas City (G-4178)
Scott Specialties Inc...............................C 785 527-5627
Belleville (G-466)
Zimmer Inc...G 913 888-1024
Lenexa (G-6242)

MEDICAL & SURGICAL SPLYS: Prosthetic Appliances

Emergency Services PA .... E 316 962-2239
Wichita (G-14276)
Turntine Oclar Prosthetics Inc .... E 913 962-6299
Shawnee Mission (G-11949)

MEDICAL & SURGICAL SPLYS: Respiratory Protect Eqpt, Personal

Dentec Safety Specialists .... F 905 953-9946
Lenexa (G-5811)

MEDICAL & SURGICAL SPLYS: Supports, Abdominal, Ankle, Etc

Cramer Products Inc .... F 913 856-7511
Gardner (G-2335)

MEDICAL & SURGICAL SPLYS: Technical Aids, Handicapped

Assistive Technology For Kans .... E 620 421-8367
Parsons (G-9667)

MEDICAL CENTERS

A M S Diagnostic LLC .... E 316 462-2020
Wichita (G-13590)
Community Memorial Healthcare .... E 785 562-3942
Marysville (G-6885)
Concentra Medical Centers .... F 913 894-6601
Lenexa (G-5783)
Days Inn Olathe Medical Center .... E 913 390-9500
Olathe (G-7642)
HCA Inc .... E 913 498-7409
Overland Park (G-8800)
Hoisington Homestead .... F 620 653-4121
Hoisington (G-3066)
Kansas Cardiovascular Assoc .... F 913 682-6950
Lansing (G-4676)
Kansas Rgnrtive Mdcine Ctr LLC .... F 785 320-4700
Manhattan (G-6676)
Medical Heights Medical Center .... E 620 227-3141
Dodge City (G-1403)
Occupational Hlth Partners LLC .... E 785 823-8381
Salina (G-10618)
Pma Andover .... E 316 733-1331
Andover (G-105)
St Francis Medical Clinic .... E 785 232-4248
Topeka (G-13095)
Surgicare of Wichita Inc .... D 316 685-2207
Wichita (G-15702)
Turner House Clinic Inc .... E 913 342-2552
Kansas City (G-4478)
University of Kansas .... A 913 677-1590
Fairway (G-1924)
University of Kansas .... E 913 588-5900
Kansas City (G-4497)
University of Kansas .... A 913 588-1443
Kansas City (G-4501)
University of Kansas Hospital .... C 913 588-5000
Kansas City (G-4507)
University of Kansas Med Ctr .... E 913 945-5598
Westwood (G-13562)
University of Kansas School of .... D 316 293-3432
Wichita (G-15858)
Veterans Health Administration .... A 316 685-2221
Wichita (G-15878)
Via Christi Health Inc .... D 316 685-0400
Wichita (G-15890)
Via Christi Health Inc .... E 316 858-4900
Wichita (G-15891)
Via Christi Hlth Partners Inc .... F 316 719-3240
Wichita (G-15892)
Via Chrsti Rvrside Med Ctr Inc .... C 316 689-5335
Wichita (G-15904)

MEDICAL EQPT REPAIR SVCS, NON-ELECTRIC

Broadway Home Medical Inc .... F 316 264-8600
Wichita (G-13895)
Merry X-Ray Chemical Corp .... E 858 565-4472
Overland Park (G-9013)

MEDICAL EQPT: Diagnostic

Fetal Well-Being LLC .... G 316 644-8919
Wichita (G-14359)

MEDICAL EQPT: Electromedical Apparatus

Relevium Labs Inc .... F 614 568-7000
Dodge City (G-1423)

MEDICAL EQPT: MRI/Magnetic Resonance Imaging Devs, Nuclear

M R I of Rock Creek .... E 913 351-4674
Lansing (G-4687)

MEDICAL EQPT: Pacemakers

Hearttraining LLC .... G 913 402-6012
Overland Park (G-8809)

MEDICAL EQPT: Sterilizers

Primus Sterilizer Company LLC .... E 620 793-7177
Great Bend (G-2624)

MEDICAL EQPT: X-Ray Apparatus & Tubes, Therapeutic

LSI International Inc .... E 913 894-4493
Kansas City (G-4208)

MEDICAL FIELD ASSOCIATION

American Academy Family Physcn .... F 913 906-6000
Shawnee Mission (G-11101)
American College of Clinical .... E 913 492-3311
Lenexa (G-5646)
Clinical Radiology Foundation .... F 913 588-6830
Kansas City (G-3920)
Community Care Netwrk Kans Inc .... E 785 233-8483
Topeka (G-12492)
Kansas Hospital Association .... E 785 233-7436
Topeka (G-12781)
Kansas Medical Society .... F 785 235-2383
Topeka (G-12791)
National Bd For Rspratory Care .... F 913 895-4900
Overland Park (G-9069)
Society of Teachers of Family .... F 913 906-6000
Shawnee Mission (G-11878)
University of Kansas .... E 316 293-2620
Wichita (G-15857)

MEDICAL HELP SVCS

Addiction and Prevention Svcs .... F 785 296-6807
Topeka (G-12287)
Carestaf Inc .... B 913 498-2888
Overland Park (G-8516)
County of Seward .... E 620 626-3275
Liberal (G-6299)
Kansas City Transcription Inc .... F 913 469-1000
Shawnee Mission (G-11512)
Maxim Healthcare Services Inc .... F 913 383-2220
Overland Park (G-8998)
MB Health Specialist Inc .... F 913 438-6337
Shawnee Mission (G-11603)
Ortho Innovations LLC .... F 913 449-8376
Overland Park (G-9115)
Winfield Area E M S .... E 620 221-2300
Winfield (G-16183)

MEDICAL INSURANCE CLAIM PROCESSING: Contract Or Fee Basis

Benefit Management LLC .... E 620 792-1779
Great Bend (G-2520)
Medplans Partners Inc .... D 620 223-8200
Shawnee Mission (G-11615)
Mobile Health Clinics LLC .... D 913 383-0991
Leawood (G-5490)

MEDICAL RESCUE SQUAD

Ellsworth County Ambulance .... E 785 472-3454
Ellsworth (G-1668)

MEDICAL SVCS ORGANIZATION

Compass Behavioral Health .... E 620 227-5040
Dodge City (G-1328)
Finney County Community Hlth .... F 620 765-1185
Garden City (G-2162)
Galichia Medical Group PA .... E 316 684-3838
Wichita (G-14438)
Greensburg Family Practice PA .... F 620 723-2127
Greensburg (G-2677)
Hospital Dst 1 of Rice Cnty .... F 620 278-2123
Sterling (G-12121)
Hutchinson Care Center LLC .... D 620 662-0597
Hutchinson (G-3318)
Icare Usa Inc .... F 919 624-9095
Kansas City (G-4094)
Kansas City Cancer Center LLC .... F 913 788-8883
Kansas City (G-4143)
Medical Center P A .... D 620 669-6690
Hutchinson (G-3368)
Medical Center P A .... E 620 669-9657
Hutchinson (G-3369)
Midwest Transplant Network Inc .... D 913 262-1668
Shawnee Mission (G-11637)
Salina Hlth Educatn Foundation .... D 785 825-7251
Salina (G-10674)
Tria Health LLC .... E 888 799-8742
Overland Park (G-9427)

MEDICAL TRAINING SERVICES

Assessment Tech Inst LLC .... B 800 667-7531
Leawood (G-5334)

MEDICAL X-RAY MACHINES & TUBES WHOLESALERS

Browns Medical Imaging .... F 913 888-6710
Lenexa (G-5719)
Merry X-Ray Chemical Corp .... E 858 565-4472
Overland Park (G-9013)

MEDICAL, DENTAL & HOSPITAL EQPT, WHOL: Dentists' Prof Splys

Steven Joseph Jr DDS .... F 316 262-5273
Wichita (G-15670)

MEDICAL, DENTAL & HOSPITAL EQPT, WHOL: Hosptl Eqpt/Furniture

Apria Healthcare LLC .... B 913 492-2212
Lenexa (G-5658)
Apria Healthcare LLC .... F 949 616-2606
Dodge City (G-1295)
Apria Healthcare LLC .... E 316 689-4500
Wichita (G-13725)

MEDICAL, DENTAL & HOSPITAL EQPT, WHOL: Surgical Eqpt & Splys

Finucane Enterprises Inc .... F 913 829-5665
De Soto (G-1199)

MEDICAL, DENTAL & HOSPITAL EQPT, WHOLESALE: Artificial Limbs

Hanger Prosthetics & .... G 913 588-6548
Kansas City (G-4065)

MEDICAL, DENTAL & HOSPITAL EQPT, WHOLESALE: Med Eqpt & Splys

Advanced Medical Dme LLC .... F 913 814-7464
Kansas City (G-3787)
Broadway Home Medical Inc .... F 316 264-8600
Wichita (G-13895)
Central Plins Rsprtory Med LLC .... F 785 527-8727
Belleville (G-455)
Cherub Medical Supply LLC .... F 913 227-0440
Shawnee (G-10928)
Concordnce Hlthcare Sltons LLC .... F 316 945-6941
Wichita (G-14086)
Contourmd Marketing Group LLC .... E 913 541-9200
Lenexa (G-5786)
Cramer Products Inc .... F 913 856-7511
Gardner (G-2335)
Ddi Holdings Inc .... E 913 371-2200
Kansas City (G-3962)
First Biomedical Inc .... E 800 962-9656
Lenexa (G-5856)
Jay Hatfield Mobility LLC .... F 785 452-9888
Wichita (G-14750)
Jay Hatfield Mobility LLC .... F 620 429-2636
Columbus (G-1079)
Kansas Specialty Services Inc .... F 620 221-6040
Winfield (G-16151)
Lincare Inc .... F 316 684-4689
Wichita (G-14965)
Medical Equipment Exchange .... F 913 451-2888
Shawnee Mission (G-11613)

Medical Positioning Inc ....E.... 816 474-1555
Kansas City (G-4229)
Medventures International Inc ....F.... 785 862-2300
Topeka (G-12881)
Peavey Corporation ....D.... 913 888-0600
Lenexa (G-6047)
Pulse Needlefree Systems Inc ....F.... 913 599-1590
Lenexa (G-6080)
Somnicare Inc ....E.... 913 498-1331
Overland Park (G-9326)
Spectrum Medical Equipment Inc ....F.... 913 831-2979
Kansas City (G-4434)
Spinal Simplicity LLC ....F.... 913 451-4414
Leawood (G-5558)
Stecklein Enterprises LLC ....F.... 785 625-2529
Hays (G-2912)
Suture Express Inc ....E.... 913 384-2220
Overland Park (G-9380)
Unimed II Inc ....C.... 913 533-2202
Stilwell (G-12177)
Vitalograph Inc ....E.... 913 888-4221
Lenexa (G-6215)

MEDICAL, DENTAL & HOSPITAL EQPT, WHOLESALE: Medical Lab

Carefore Medical Inc ....E.... 913 327-5445
Olathe (G-7578)
Line Medical Inc ....E.... 316 262-3444
Wichita (G-14967)

MEDICAL, DENTAL & HOSPITAL EQPT, WHOLESALE: Orthopedic

C A Titus Inc ....D.... 913 888-1024
Lenexa (G-5724)
Howmedica Osteonics Corp ....E.... 913 491-3505
Leawood (G-5432)

MEDICAL, DENTAL/HOSPITAL EQPT, WHOL: Tech Aids, Handicapped

Kansas Truck Equipment Co Inc ....E.... 316 722-4291
Wichita (G-14828)

MEDICAL, DENTAL/HOSPITAL EQPT, WHOL: Veterinarian Eqpt/Sply

Animal Health Intl Inc ....E.... 620 276-8289
Garden City (G-2101)
Centaur Inc ....G.... 913 390-6184
Olathe (G-7583)
Mwi Veterinary Supply Co ....F.... 913 422-3900
Edwardsville (G-1509)

MEMBER ORGS, CIVIC, SOCIAL & FRATERNAL: Bars & Restaurants

Kanbrews LLC ....F.... 913 499-6495
Overland Park (G-8887)

MEMBERSHIP HOTELS

Delta Omega of Delta Zeta Bldg ....E.... 785 625-3719
Hays (G-2784)

MEMBERSHIP ORGANIZATIONS, BUSINESS: Better Business Bureau

Kansas Electric Cooperatives ....E.... 785 478-4554
Topeka (G-12775)

MEMBERSHIP ORGANIZATIONS, BUSINESS: Contractors' Association

Bettis Contractors Inc ....E.... 785 783-8353
Topeka (G-12378)
Lawrence Home Builders Assn ....F.... 785 748-0612
Lawrence (G-4969)
Retail Groc Assn Grter Kans Cy ....F.... 913 384-3830
Westwood (G-13558)
Valiant Global Def Svcs Inc ....D.... 913 651-9782
Leavenworth (G-5304)

MEMBERSHIP ORGANIZATIONS, BUSINESS: Merchants' Association

I P H F H A Inc ....F.... 316 685-1200
Wichita (G-14664)
Midway Co-Op Association ....F.... 785 346-5401
Osborne (G-8211)
Midway Co-Op Association ....F.... 785 346-5451
Osborne (G-8212)
Ninnescah Sailing Association ....F.... 316 729-5757
Wichita (G-15181)

MEMBERSHIP ORGANIZATIONS, BUSINESS: Regulatory Association

Kcc Conservation District II ....F.... 316 630-4000
Wichita (G-14838)
Sac & Fox Gaming Commission ....F.... 785 467-8070
Powhattan (G-10009)

MEMBERSHIP ORGANIZATIONS, CIVIC, SOCIAL/FRAT: Boy Scout Org

Boys and Girls Club of Topeka ....E.... 785 234-5601
Topeka (G-12400)
Coronado Area Council Bsa ....F.... 785 827-4461
Salina (G-10464)
Jayhawk Area Cncl Bsa Cncl ....F.... 785 354-0291
Topeka (G-12739)
Quivira Cncil Boy Scuts Amer I ....E.... 316 264-4466
Wichita (G-15397)
SE Kansas Nture Ctr Schrmrhorn ....E.... 620 783-5207
Galena (G-2084)

MEMBERSHIP ORGANIZATIONS, CIVIC, SOCIAL/FRAT: Rec Assoc

Young Mens Christian Associa ....C.... 316 942-2271
Wichita (G-16091)

MEMBERSHIP ORGANIZATIONS, CIVIC, SOCIAL/FRAT: Social Assoc

Natio Assoc For The Advan of ....D.... 913 334-0366
Kansas City (G-4278)
Natio Assoc For The Advan of ....F.... 913 362-2272
Shawnee Mission (G-11670)
National Society Daughters Rev ....E.... 785 448-5959
Garnett (G-2384)
Optimist International ....E.... 316 744-0849
Wichita (G-15228)
Rosedale Development Assn Inc ....F.... 913 677-5097
Kansas City (G-4389)

MEMBERSHIP ORGANIZATIONS, CIVIC, SOCIAL/FRAT: Youth Orgs

Boys & Girls CLB Manhattan Inc ....D.... 785 539-1947
Manhattan (G-6567)
Boys & Girls Club of S Central ....E.... 316 687-5437
Wichita (G-13877)
Boys & Girls Clubs of America ....F.... 913 621-3260
Kansas City (G-3873)
Boys Girls Clubs Huthinson Inc ....F.... 620 665-7171
Hutchinson (G-3219)
Boys Grls CLB Lwrnce Lwrnce K ....D.... 785 841-5672
Lawrence (G-4763)
Corinth Scouts Inc ....E.... 913 236-8920
Roeland Park (G-10221)
Early Learning Center ....F.... 316 685-2059
Wichita (G-14252)
Emberhope Inc ....D.... 620 225-0276
Dodge City (G-1357)
Junction City Family YMCA Inc ....E.... 785 762-4780
Junction City (G-3704)
Paul Henson Family YMCA Inc ....E.... 913 642-6800
Prairie Village (G-10056)
Stilwell Venturing Crew ....F.... 913 306-2419
Stilwell (G-12173)
YMCA of Hutchinson Reno Cnty ....D.... 620 662-1203
Hutchinson (G-3494)
YMCA Topeaka Downtown Branch ....E.... 785 354-8591
Topeka (G-13256)
Young Mens Christian ....F.... 785 233-9815
Topeka (G-13258)
Young Mens Christian Assn ....E.... 620 275-1199
Garden City (G-2319)
Young Mens Christian Associa ....C.... 316 733-9622
Andover (G-118)
Young Mens Christian Associa ....C.... 316 219-9622
Wichita (G-16093)
Young Mens Christian Associa ....D.... 316 260-9622
Wichita (G-16094)
Young Mens Christian Associa ....C.... 316 942-5511
Wichita (G-16095)
Young Mens Christian Associa ....D.... 316 320-9622
El Dorado (G-1616)
Young Mens Christian Associat ....C.... 316 685-2251
Wichita (G-16096)
Young Mens Christian Associat ....C.... 620 545-7290
Viola (G-13380)
Young Mens Christian Gr Kansas ....D.... 913 642-6800
Shawnee Mission (G-12024)
Young Mens Christian Gr Kansas ....D.... 913 362-3489
Prairie Village (G-10088)
Young Mens Christian Gr Kansas ....C.... 913 393-9622
Olathe (G-8163)
Young Mens Christian Gr Kansas ....D.... 913 782-7707
Olathe (G-8164)
Young MNS Chrstn Assn of Sthwe ....E.... 620 275-1199
Garden City (G-2320)
Young MNS Chrstn Assn of Tpeka ....C.... 785 354-8591
Topeka (G-13259)
Young MNS Chrstn Assn Pttsburg ....D.... 620 231-1100
Pittsburg (G-9972)
Young MNS Chrstn Assn Slina Ka ....D.... 785 825-2151
Salina (G-10775)
Youthfront Inc ....D.... 913 262-3900
Westwood (G-13564)

MEMBERSHIP ORGANIZATIONS, NEC: Amateur Sports Promotion

Sports Car Club America Inc ....E.... 785 357-7222
Topeka (G-13091)
Wichita Rugby Foundation Inc ....E.... 316 262-6800
Wichita (G-16022)

MEMBERSHIP ORGANIZATIONS, NEC: Automobile Owner Association

AAA Allied Group Inc ....F.... 785 233-0222
Topeka (G-12281)
Automobile Club of Missouri ....F.... 913 248-1627
Shawnee Mission (G-11135)

MEMBERSHIP ORGANIZATIONS, NEC: Charitable

A Adopt Family Inc ....F.... 620 378-4458
Fredonia (G-2025)
Alpha Ministries ....F.... 785 597-5235
Perry (G-9765)
Called To Greatness Ministries ....E.... 785 749-2100
Lawrence (G-4773)
Casa of The Thirty-First Judic ....E.... 620 365-1448
Iola (G-3589)
Catholic Charities of Southwes ....F.... 620 227-1562
Dodge City (G-1319)
Citizens Savings & Loan Assn ....E.... 913 727-1040
Leavenworth (G-5218)
Council Grove Area Foundation ....F.... 620 767-6653
Council Grove (G-1160)
Elk County Development Corp ....E.... 620 325-3333
Neodesha (G-7239)
Elks Club ....F.... 785 263-1675
Abilene (G-26)
Foundation For A Christian Civ ....F.... 785 584-6251
Rossville (G-10252)
Heartstrings Cmnty Foundation ....F.... 913 649-5700
Shawnee Mission (G-11425)
Hope Planting Intl Inc ....F.... 785 776-8523
Manhattan (G-6659)
Interntnal Pnck Day Lberal Inc ....E.... 620 624-6423
Liberal (G-6323)
Johnson County Kansas Heritage ....E.... 913 481-3137
Olathe (G-7817)
Kanas Cattlemens Associate ....F.... 785 238-1483
Junction City (G-3711)
Kansas Health Foundation ....E.... 316 262-7676
Wichita (G-14804)
Kansas Schl For Effective Lrng ....E.... 316 263-9620
Wichita (G-14822)
Lake Region Resource Conservat ....E.... 785 242-2073
Ottawa (G-8282)
Legacy Community Foundation ....F.... 620 221-7224
Winfield (G-16155)
Leukemia & Lymphoma Soc Inc ....F.... 913 262-1515
Shawnee Mission (G-11566)
Lords Diner ....F.... 316 295-2122
Wichita (G-14980)
Neighborhood Network LLC ....E.... 913 341-9316
Lenexa (G-6020)
Opportunity Project Lrng Ctr ....E.... 316 522-8677
Wichita (G-15223)
Ozanam Pathways ....E.... 316 682-4000
Wichita (G-15245)

Parkinsons Exercise and ....F 913 276-4665
Leawood *(G-5514)*
Pastorserve Inc ....F 877 918-4746
Overland Park *(G-9144)*
Proud Anmal Lovers Shelter Inc ....F 620 421-0445
Parsons *(G-9726)*
Rural Water Dist 5 Sumner Cnty ....F 620 456-2350
Conway Springs *(G-1144)*
Salvation Army ....F 316 283-3190
Newton *(G-7413)*
Salvation Army ....F 620 663-3353
Hutchinson *(G-3437)*
Salvation Army ....F 620 225-4871
Dodge City *(G-1427)*
Salvation Army ....E 620 276-6622
Garden City *(G-2274)*
Salvation Army ....E 785 843-1716
Lawrence *(G-5101)*
Salvation Army ....F 785 233-9648
Topeka *(G-13033)*
Salvation Army ....F 620 343-3166
Emporia *(G-1821)*
Servant Chrstn Cmnty Fundation ....E 913 310-0279
Overland Park *(G-9296)*
South Central Tele Assn Inc ....E 620 930-1000
Medicine Lodge *(G-7074)*
Taylor Made Visions LLC ....F 913 210-0699
Kansas City *(G-4459)*
Tfi Family Services Inc ....C 620 342-2239
Emporia *(G-1836)*
Trash Mountain Project Inc ....F 785 246-6845
Topeka *(G-13197)*
Unbound ....C 913 384-6500
Kansas City *(G-4484)*
Wichita Ind Neighborhoods Inc ....E 316 260-8000
Wichita *(G-16007)*

MEMBERSHIP ORGANIZATIONS, NEC: Historical Club

National Socty of The Daughtrs ....F 620 356-2570
Ulysses *(G-13307)*
Onaga Historical Society ....E 785 889-7104
Onaga *(G-8178)*

MEMBERSHIP ORGANIZATIONS, NEC: Personal Interest

American Bonanza Society Inc ....F 316 945-1700
Wichita *(G-13685)*
Kaw Valley Rabbit Club ....F 913 764-1531
Olathe *(G-7831)*
National Soc Tole/Dec Pntr Inc ....F 316 269-9300
Wichita *(G-15153)*
Nationl Soc Daught AMR Rev ....E 620 457-8747
Pittsburg *(G-9910)*
Pride/Chapter Intl Assoc ....E 913 321-2733
Kansas City *(G-4336)*
Veterans Fgn Wars Post 9076 ....F 785 625-9940
Hays *(G-2924)*
Wichita Crime Stoppers Program ....E 316 267-2111
Wichita *(G-15992)*

MEMBERSHIP ORGANIZATIONS, NEC: Professional Golf Association

Golf Crse Superintendents Amer ....D 785 841-2240
Lawrence *(G-4874)*
Kansas City Compensation & Ben ....F 913 381-4458
Overland Park *(G-8892)*

MEMBERSHIP ORGANIZATIONS, PROF: Education/Teacher Assoc

Accreditation Council For Busi ....F 913 339-9356
Overland Park *(G-8342)*
American Assn Univ Women ....F 785 472-5737
Ellsworth *(G-1656)*
Command and General Staff ....F 913 651-0624
Fort Leavenworth *(G-1936)*
First Response ....F 913 557-2187
Paola *(G-9559)*
Kansas Assn of Schl Boards ....E 785 273-3600
Topeka *(G-12761)*
Kansas National Education Assn ....F 913 268-4005
Shawnee Mission *(G-11518)*
Kansas National Education Assn ....E 785 232-8271
Topeka *(G-12793)*
Olathe Unified School Dst 233 ....C 913 780-7880
Olathe *(G-7952)*
Society of Tchers Fmly Mdicine ....F 913 906-6000
Shawnee Mission *(G-11877)*
South Centl KS Educatn Svc Ctr ....F 620 584-3300
Clearwater *(G-897)*

MEMBERSHIP ORGANIZATIONS, PROFESSIONAL: Health Association

Advanced Health Care Corp ....C 913 890-8400
Overland Park *(G-8349)*
American Acdemy Fmly Physcians ....B 913 906-6000
Leawood *(G-5319)*
Cowley County Joint Board Hlth ....F 620 221-1430
Winfield *(G-16133)*
Kansas Fndtion For Med Care In ....E 785 273-2552
Topeka *(G-12777)*
Medical Society Sedgwick Cnty ....E 316 683-7557
Wichita *(G-15033)*
National Healthcareer Assn ....E 800 499-9092
Leawood *(G-5499)*
National Rural Health Assn ....F 913 220-2997
Leawood *(G-5500)*

MEMBERSHIP ORGANIZATIONS, REL: Christian & Reformed Church

Glenn Pk Christn Ch Preschool ....E 316 943-4283
Wichita *(G-14471)*
Hillcrest Chrstn Child Dev Ctr ....E 913 663-1997
Shawnee Mission *(G-11432)*
Salvation Army ....F 785 233-9648
Topeka *(G-13033)*

MEMBERSHIP ORGANIZATIONS, REL: Christian Reformed Church

Hillview Church of God Inc ....F 913 299-4406
Kansas City *(G-4080)*

MEMBERSHIP ORGANIZATIONS, REL: Churches, Temples & Shrines

Ashbury Church Pre School ....F 913 432-5573
Shawnee Mission *(G-11123)*
Mennonite Mission Network ....F 540 434-6701
Newton *(G-7379)*
Salvation Army ....F 620 343-3166
Emporia *(G-1821)*

MEMBERSHIP ORGANIZATIONS, REL: Covenant & Evangelical Church

Hillcrest Covenant Church ....E 913 901-2300
Shawnee Mission *(G-11433)*

MEMBERSHIP ORGANIZATIONS, RELIGIOUS: Baptist Church

American Baptist Church ....F 913 236-7067
Shawnee Mission *(G-11102)*
First Baptist Church Olathe ....F 913 764-7088
Olathe *(G-7711)*
Nall Ave Baptist Church ....E 913 432-4141
Prairie Village *(G-10049)*
One Hope United - Northern Reg ....E 785 827-1756
Salina *(G-10621)*
Sharon Baptist Church ....F 316 684-5156
Wichita *(G-15573)*

MEMBERSHIP ORGANIZATIONS, RELIGIOUS: Catholic Church

Catholic Diocese of Wichita ....E 316 269-3900
Wichita *(G-13963)*
Holy Name Catholic Church ....C 785 232-7744
Topeka *(G-12698)*

MEMBERSHIP ORGANIZATIONS, RELIGIOUS: Church Of God

Pawnee Avenue Church of God ....E 316 683-5648
Wichita *(G-15273)*

MEMBERSHIP ORGANIZATIONS, RELIGIOUS: Church Of The Nazarene

Shawnee Church of Nazarene ....F 913 631-5555
Shawnee Mission *(G-11850)*
Woodland Lakes Community Churc ....F 316 682-9522
Wichita *(G-16065)*

MEMBERSHIP ORGANIZATIONS, RELIGIOUS: Community Church

Antioch Church ....F 785 232-1937
Topeka *(G-12332)*

MEMBERSHIP ORGANIZATIONS, RELIGIOUS: Lutheran Church

Faith Evangelical Lutheran Ch ....E 316 788-1715
Derby *(G-1246)*
Hope Lutheran Church Shawnee ....E 913 631-6940
Shawnee Mission *(G-11439)*
Lord of Life Lutheran Church ....E 913 681-5167
Leawood *(G-5459)*

MEMBERSHIP ORGANIZATIONS, RELIGIOUS: Mennonite Church

Mennonite Church USA ....G 316 283-5100
Newton *(G-7378)*

MEMBERSHIP ORGANIZATIONS, RELIGIOUS: Methodist Church

Aldersgate Untd Meth Pre Schl ....E 913 764-2407
Olathe *(G-7516)*
Countryside United Methdst Ch ....F 785 266-7541
Topeka *(G-12516)*
East Heights United Methdst Ch ....E 316 682-6518
Wichita *(G-14253)*
Emmanuel United Methodist Ch ....F 785 263-3342
Abilene *(G-27)*
First United Methodist Church ....E 316 263-6244
Wichita *(G-14376)*
Grace United Methodist Church ....E 913 859-0111
Olathe *(G-7738)*
Kansas East Conference United ....E 913 631-2280
Shawnee Mission *(G-11516)*
Kansas East Conference United ....F 913 383-9146
Shawnee Mission *(G-11517)*
Senate United States ....F 620 227-2244
Dodge City *(G-1428)*
Woodland United Methodist Ch ....F 316 265-6669
Wichita *(G-16066)*

MEMBERSHIP ORGANIZATIONS, RELIGIOUS: Nonchurch

Salvation Army ....F 620 663-3353
Hutchinson *(G-3437)*
Salvation Army ....F 620 225-4871
Dodge City *(G-1427)*
Salvation Army ....E 620 276-6622
Garden City *(G-2274)*

MEMBERSHIP ORGANIZATIONS, RELIGIOUS: Presbyterian Church

Shawnee Presbyterian Church ....E 913 631-6689
Shawnee Mission *(G-11862)*

MEMBERSHIP ORGS, BUSINESS: Growers' Marketing Advisory Svc

Global Prairie Marketing LLC ....E 913 722-7244
Mission Hills *(G-7142)*

MEMBERSHIP ORGS, CIVIC, SOCIAL & FRAT: Comm Member Club

Caldwell Snior Ctizens Ctr Inc ....F 620 845-6926
Caldwell *(G-657)*
Roeland Park Community Center ....F 913 722-0310
Roeland Park *(G-10229)*
Salvation Army ....E 316 685-8699
Wichita *(G-15513)*

MEMBERSHIP ORGS, CIVIC, SOCIAL & FRAT: Dwelling-Related

Kings Court Investors ....F 913 764-7500
Olathe *(G-7840)*
Washburn Endowment Association ....E 785 670-4483
Topeka *(G-13231)*

MEMBERSHIP ORGS, CIVIC, SOCIAL & FRAT: Girl Scout

Central Knss Cncil of Grl Sct.................F 785 827-3679
Salina *(G-10442)*
Girl Scouts Kans Heartland Inc.............E 316 684-6531
Wichita *(G-14467)*
Girl Scts of Ne Kansas & NW MO..........F 816 358-8750
Topeka *(G-12637)*

MEMBERSHIP ORGS, CIVIC, SOCIAL & FRAT: Neighborhood Assoc

Rebuilding Together Shawnee/Jo.........F 913 558-5079
Shawnee *(G-11015)*

MEMBERSHIP ORGS, CIVIC, SOCIAL & FRATERNAL: Civic Assoc

Benevolent & P O of Elks 1404..............F 620 276-3732
Garden City *(G-2107)*
Downtown Shareholders..........................E 913 371-0705
Kansas City *(G-3976)*
Eudora Lion Club Foundation.................F 785 542-2315
Eudora *(G-1874)*
General Grnd Chpter Estrn Star............C 620 326-3797
Wellington *(G-13503)*
International Assn Lions Clubs............E 620 673-8081
Havana *(G-2728)*
International Assn Lions Clubs............E 785 388-2764
Abilene *(G-42)*
International Assn Lions Clubs............E 785 694-2278
Brewster *(G-584)*
International Association of..................E 785 842-8847
Lawrence *(G-4914)*
International Association of..................E 620 327-4271
Hesston *(G-2994)*
International Association of..................F 785 283-4746
Tescott *(G-12245)*
Interntional Forest Friendship..............E 913 367-1419
Atchison *(G-237)*
Kansas State High Schl Actvtie.............F 785 273-5329
Topeka *(G-12806)*
Kiwanis International Inc......................F 620 672-6257
Pratt *(G-10124)*
Kiwanis International Inc......................F 316 733-4984
Andover *(G-101)*
Kiwanis International Inc......................E 785 742-2596
Hiawatha *(G-3014)*
Kiwanis International Inc......................F 913 724-1120
Basehor *(G-383)*
Kiwanis International Inc......................F 913 727-1039
Lansing *(G-4678)*
Kiwanis International Inc......................F 620 365-3925
Iola *(G-3617)*
Kiwanis International Inc......................F 620 544-8445
Hugoton *(G-3169)*
Kiwanis International Inc......................F 785 238-4521
Junction City *(G-3716)*
Kiwanis International Inc......................F 785 462-6007
Colby *(G-1021)*
Kiwanis International Inc......................F 785 282-6680
Smith Center *(G-12035)*
Potwin Lions Club..................................F 620 752-3644
Potwin *(G-10008)*
Rotary International...............................F 913 299-0466
Kansas City *(G-4390)*
Soroptimist International......................E 316 321-0433
El Dorado *(G-1603)*
Wichita Chapter of Links Inc.................F 316 744-7873
Bel Aire *(G-443)*
Wichita Family Crisis Ctr Inc.................F 316 263-7501
Wichita *(G-15998)*

MEMBERSHIP ORGS, CIVIC, SOCIAL & FRATERNAL: Protection

Lake Region Resource Conservat.........E 785 242-2073
Ottawa *(G-8282)*
Soil Conservation Service USDA..........E 785 823-4500
Salina *(G-10712)*
The Nature Conservancy........................F 785 233-4400
Topeka *(G-13158)*
The Nature Conservancy........................F 316 689-4237
Wichita *(G-15757)*

MEMBERSHIP ORGS, CIVIC, SOCIAL & FRATERNAL: Singing Society

Sweet Adelines Intrntnl Chorus.............F 316 733-4467
Wichita *(G-15707)*

MEMBERSHIP ORGS, CIVIC, SOCIAL & FRATERNAL: University Club

Delta Gamma..F 785 830-9945
Lawrence *(G-4831)*
Delta Kappa Gamma Society.................E 620 793-3977
Great Bend *(G-2553)*
Delta Tau Delta Society.........................F 785 843-6866
Lawrence *(G-4832)*
Delta Upsilon House Corp.....................E 316 295-4320
Wichita *(G-14190)*
Epsilon Sigma Alpha Intl.......................E 620 331-1063
Independence *(G-3515)*
Lambda CHI Alpha Frternity Inc............D 785 843-1172
Lawrence *(G-4953)*
PI Beta PHI House Inc...........................F 785 539-1818
Manhattan *(G-6776)*
PI Kappa PHI House Mother..................D 785 856-1400
Lawrence *(G-5063)*
Upsilon Chapter Alpha PHI Intl.............E 785 233-7466
Topeka *(G-13212)*

MEMBERSHIP ORGS, CIVIC, SOCIAL/FRAT: Business Persons Club

Stone Croft Ministries Inc......................D 816 763-7800
Overland Park *(G-9365)*

MEMBERSHIP ORGS, CIVIC, SOCIAL/FRAT: Educator's Assoc

Deaf Cultural Ctr Foundation.................F 913 782-5808
Olathe *(G-7643)*
International Inst Christian S.................E 913 962-4422
Overland Park *(G-8858)*
Kansas National Education Assn..........F 913 268-4005
Shawnee Mission *(G-11518)*
Mid America Assc Computer Ed............F 785 273-3680
Topeka *(G-12889)*
Nacada The Glbl Comm For Acdm........E 785 532-3398
Manhattan *(G-6756)*

MEMBERSHIP ORGS, LABOR UNIONS/SIMILAR: Employees' Assoc

Empac Inc..F 316 265-9922
Wichita *(G-14278)*
Harvest America Corporation................E 913 342-2121
Overland Park *(G-8798)*
Kansas Assn of Pub Employees...........F 785 233-1956
Topeka *(G-12760)*
Kansas Pub Emplyee Rtrment Sys.......D 785 296-1019
Topeka *(G-12798)*

MEMBERSHIP ORGS, LABOR UNIONS: Collective Bargaining

International Brotherhood.......................F 913 281-5036
Kansas City *(G-4104)*

MEMBERSHIP ORGS, RELIGIOUS: Non-Denominational Church

World Impact Inc.....................................E 316 687-9398
Wichita *(G-16073)*

MEMBERSHIP ORGS, RELIGIOUS: Seventh Day Adventist Church

Association of Kansas Nebraska..........E 785 478-4726
Topeka *(G-12345)*

MEMBERSHIP SPORTS & RECREATION CLUBS

All American Indoor Sports...................D 913 888-5425
Shawnee Mission *(G-11093)*
Alvamar Inc..E 785 843-0196
Lawrence *(G-4733)*
Bobby TS Bar & Grill Inc........................F 785 537-8383
Manhattan *(G-6564)*
Central Station Club & Gr.......................F 620 225-1176
Dodge City *(G-1321)*
Challenger Sports Corp..........................E 913 599-4884
Lenexa *(G-5749)*
Club Rodeo LLC......................................F 316 613-2424
Wichita *(G-14044)*
Cowboy Inn LLC.....................................F 316 943-3869
Wichita *(G-14118)*
Coyotes Inc..E 785 842-2295
Lawrence *(G-4816)*
Darco Inc..E 620 221-7529
Winfield *(G-16138)*
Johnson Cnty Pk Recreation Dst..........E 913 438-7275
Shawnee Mission *(G-11495)*
Kansas City Racquet Club......................F 913 789-8000
Shawnee Mission *(G-11510)*
McDs Clubhouse 5..................................F 620 504-6044
McPherson *(G-6991)*
Olathe Soccer Club.................................F 913 764-4111
Olathe *(G-7949)*
Recreation Commission.........................F 620 223-0386
Fort Scott *(G-2002)*
Sherwood Lake Club Inc.........................F 785 478-3305
Topeka *(G-13070)*
Sublette Recreation Commission..........F 620 675-8211
Sublette *(G-12211)*
Sunflower Soccer Assn..........................F 785 233-9700
Topeka *(G-13121)*
Title Boxing LLC......................................C 913 438-4427
Lenexa *(G-6182)*
Title Boxing Club......................................F 785 856-2696
Lawrence *(G-5138)*
Title Boxing Club LLC..............................E 913 991-8285
Overland Park *(G-9415)*
Topeka Round Up Club Inc......................F 785 478-4431
Topeka *(G-13185)*
Town & Country Racquet Club...............E 620 792-1366
Great Bend *(G-2648)*
Tuckers Bar & Grill..................................F 785 235-3172
Topeka *(G-13200)*
Wichita Sports Forum..............................F 316 201-1414
Wichita *(G-16023)*
Young Mens Christian Associa...............D 316 945-2255
Wichita *(G-16092)*
Young MNS Chrstn Assn Slina Ka..........D 785 825-2151
Salina *(G-10775)*

MEN'S & BOYS' CLOTHING STORES

Urban Outfitters Inc..................................E 785 331-2885
Lawrence *(G-5169)*
Vf Outdoor Inc..D 913 384-4000
Shawnee Mission *(G-11976)*

MEN'S & BOYS' CLOTHING WHOLESALERS, NEC

Acres Inc...F 785 776-3234
Manhattan *(G-6532)*
Dri Duck Traders Inc................................F 913 648-8222
Overland Park *(G-8661)*
Realm Brands LLC....................................F 316 821-9700
Wichita *(G-15426)*

MEN'S & BOYS' SPORTSWEAR CLOTHING STORES

Epic Sports...C 316 612-0150
Bel Aire *(G-432)*
Kellys Corporate Apparel........................G 316 263-5858
Wichita *(G-14847)*
Maurices Incorporated.............................E 620 275-1210
Garden City *(G-2229)*
Tioga Territory Ltd....................................F 620 431-2479
Chanute *(G-770)*

MEN'S & BOYS' SPORTSWEAR WHOLESALERS

Its Greek To Me Inc..................................C 800 336-4486
Manhattan *(G-6666)*
Stardust Corporation................................F 913 894-1966
Kansas City *(G-4439)*

MEN'S SUITS STORES

Mias Bridal & Tailoring LLC.....................F 913 764-9114
Olathe *(G-7890)*

MENTAL HEALTH CLINIC, OUTPATIENT

Bert Nash Cmnty Mntal Hlth Ctr..............C 785 843-9192
Lawrence *(G-4755)*

Breakthrough CLB Sedgwick Cnty .... E 316 269-2534
Wichita *(G-13886)*
Center For Counseling & Cnsltn .... E 620 792-2544
Great Bend *(G-2526)*
Central Kansas Mental Hlth Ctr .... D 785 823-6322
Salina *(G-10441)*
Comcare of Sedgwick County .... E 316 660-1900
Wichita *(G-14059)*
Community Mntl Hlth Ctr Crwfd .... E 620 724-8806
Girard *(G-2397)*
Compass Behavioral Health .... D 620 275-0625
Garden City *(G-2132)*
Compass Behavioral Health .... F 620 872-5338
Scott City *(G-10808)*
Compass Behavioral Health .... E 620 227-5040
Dodge City *(G-1328)*
Compass Behavioral Health .... E 620 227-8566
Dodge City *(G-1329)*
Elizabeth Layton Center Inc .... D 785 242-3780
Ottawa *(G-8270)*
Family Svc Gdnce Ctr Tpeka Inc .... C 785 232-5005
Topeka *(G-12593)*
For Wyandot Center .... C 913 328-4600
Kansas City *(G-4017)*
For Wyandot Center .... D 913 362-0393
Kansas City *(G-4016)*
Four Cnty Mental Hlth Ctr Inc .... C 620 331-1748
Independence *(G-3520)*
Four Cnty Mental Hlth Ctr Inc .... F 620 325-2141
Neodesha *(G-7242)*
Four Cnty Mental Hlth Ctr Inc .... F 620 331-0057
Independence *(G-3521)*
Guidance Center .... E 913 367-1593
Atchison *(G-233)*
High Plains Mental Health Ctr .... C 785 628-2871
Hays *(G-2846)*
High Plains Mental Health Ctr .... F 785 543-5284
Phillipsburg *(G-9788)*
Horizons Mental Health Ctr Inc .... F 620 532-3895
Kingman *(G-4595)*
Horizons Mental Health Ctr Inc .... C 620 663-7595
Hutchinson *(G-3312)*
Integrated Behavioral Tech Inc .... D 913 662-7071
Basehor *(G-379)*
Integrated Behavioral Tech Inc .... E 913 662-7071
Basehor *(G-380)*
Iroquois Ctr For Humn Dev Inc .... E 620 723-2272
Greensburg *(G-2680)*
Kansas City Ctr For Anxty Trmt .... F 913 649-8820
Overland Park *(G-8893)*
Kansas Dept For Chldren Fmlies .... C 913 755-7000
Osawatomie *(G-8196)*
Kaw Valley Center .... F 913 334-0294
Kansas City *(G-4159)*
Kvc Health Systems Inc .... D 913 621-5753
Kansas City *(G-4186)*
Kvc Hospitals Inc .... E 913 322-4900
Olathe *(G-7846)*
Labette Center For Mental Inc .... F 620 421-9402
Parsons *(G-9702)*
Labette Ctr For Mntal Hlth Svc .... D 620 421-3770
Parsons *(G-9704)*
Mental Health Association .... E 913 281-2221
Kansas City *(G-4234)*
Mental Hlth Ctr of Est-Cntral .... E 620 343-2211
Emporia *(G-1794)*
Pawnee Mental Health Svcs Inc .... C 785 762-5250
Manhattan *(G-6769)*
Pawnee Mental Health Svcs Inc .... E 785 762-5250
Junction City *(G-3735)*
Pawnee Mental Health Svcs Inc .... E 785 587-4344
Manhattan *(G-6770)*
Prairie View Inc .... F 620 245-5000
McPherson *(G-7018)*
Saint Francis Acdmy Inc Atchsn .... E 913 367-5005
Atchison *(G-259)*
South Cntl Mntal Hlth Cnsling .... E 316 321-6036
El Dorado *(G-1604)*
Southeast Kans Mental Hlth Ctr .... D 620 473-2241
Humboldt *(G-3188)*
Southeast Kans Mental Hlth Ctr .... F 913 352-8214
Pleasanton *(G-10002)*
Southeast Kans Mental Hlth Ctr .... E 620 223-5030
Fort Scott *(G-2006)*
Southeast Kans Mental Hlth Ctr .... F 785 448-6806
Garnett *(G-2389)*
Southeast Kans Mental Hlth Ctr .... F 620 431-7890
Chanute *(G-764)*
Spring Rver Mntal Hlth Wllness .... D 620 848-2300
Riverton *(G-10213)*
Starkey Inc .... C 316 942-4221
Wichita *(G-15657)*
Stormont-Vail Healthcare Inc .... C 785 270-4600
Topeka *(G-13103)*
Veridian Behavorial Health .... E 785 452-4930
Salina *(G-10750)*
Vigilias LLC .... E 800 924-8140
Wichita *(G-15907)*
Wyandot Center For Community B .... E 913 233-3300
Kansas City *(G-4550)*
Wyandot Inc .... F 913 233-3300
Kansas City *(G-4551)*

MERCHANDISING MACHINE OPERATORS: Vending

Chilton Vending & Billd Inc .... F 316 262-3539
Wichita *(G-14011)*
Hutchinson Vending Company .... F 620 662-6474
Hutchinson *(G-3328)*
Premier Food Service Inc .... C 316 269-2447
Wichita *(G-15330)*
Schmidt Vending Inc .... F 785 354-7397
Topeka *(G-13038)*

METAL COMPONENTS: Prefabricated

L & M Steel & Mfg .... G 785 462-8216
Colby *(G-1023)*
Martinez Inc .... G 316 587-7814
Wichita *(G-15015)*

METAL CUTTING SVCS

Metal Cut To Length .... F 913 829-8600
Olathe *(G-7884)*

METAL DETECTORS

Dragnet Enterprises .... F 913 362-8378
Kansas City *(G-3977)*

METAL FABRICATORS: Architechtural

Architectural Cast Metals Inc .... G 785 221-6901
Topeka *(G-12337)*
Balco Inc .... C 800 767-0082
Wichita *(G-13798)*
Bradford Built Inc .... E 785 325-3300
Washington *(G-13460)*
Corbin Bronze Limited .... G 913 766-4012
Kansas City *(G-3940)*
Landwehr Manufacturing Company .... G 316 942-1719
Wichita *(G-14923)*
Mc Kinnes Iron & Metal Inc .... G 620 257-3821
Lyons *(G-6494)*
Tindle Construction Inc .... D 620 378-2046
Fredonia *(G-2047)*
Town & Country Sheetmetal Inc .... F 913 441-1208
Shawnee *(G-11041)*
Ultra Modern Pool & Patio Inc .... G 316 681-3011
Wichita *(G-15829)*
Unique Metal Fabrication Inc .... E 620 232-3060
Pittsburg *(G-9949)*

METAL FABRICATORS: Plate

Abbott Aluminum Inc .... E 785 776-8555
Manhattan *(G-6529)*
American Energy Products Inc .... G 913 351-3388
Lansing *(G-4666)*
Balco Inc .... C 800 767-0082
Wichita *(G-13798)*
Bmg of Kansas Inc .... D 620 327-4038
Hesston *(G-2985)*
Bradford Built Inc .... E 785 325-3300
Washington *(G-13460)*
Contech Engnered Solutions LLC .... E 785 234-1000
Topeka *(G-12504)*
Custom Metal Fabricators Inc .... E 785 258-3744
Herington *(G-2973)*
Eaton Corporation .... B 620 663-5751
Hutchinson *(G-3274)*
Hammersmith Mfg & Sales Inc .... G 913 338-0754
Overland Park *(G-8788)*
Hix Corporation .... D 620 231-8568
Pittsburg *(G-9876)*
Koch Rail LLC .... G 316 828-5500
Wichita *(G-14886)*
Marley Cooling Tower Co Inc .... G 913 664-7400
Overland Park *(G-8993)*
Oxwell Inc .... D 620 326-7481
Wellington *(G-13521)*
Redguard LLC .... C 316 554-9000
Wichita *(G-15431)*
SPX Cooling Technologies Inc .... C 913 782-1600
Olathe *(G-8079)*
Taylor Forge Engineered .... E 785 448-6803
Garnett *(G-2390)*
Wall-Ties & Forms Inc .... C 913 441-0073
Shawnee *(G-11049)*
We-Mac Manufacturing Co .... F 620 879-2187
Caney *(G-678)*

METAL FABRICATORS: Sheet

Adapa Incorporated .... F 785 862-2060
Topeka *(G-12286)*
B & B Airparts Inc .... C 316 946-0300
Wichita *(G-13784)*
Barnes & Dodge Inc .... E 913 321-6444
Lenexa *(G-5687)*
Bmg of Kansas Inc .... D 620 327-4038
Hesston *(G-2985)*
Bradford Built Inc .... E 785 325-3300
Washington *(G-13460)*
Central Steel Inc .... D 316 265-8639
Wichita *(G-13988)*
Centurion Industries Inc .... E 620 244-3201
Erie *(G-1857)*
Centurion Industries Inc .... B 620 378-4401
Fredonia *(G-2028)*
Contech Engnered Solutions LLC .... E 785 234-1000
Topeka *(G-12504)*
Curbs Plus Inc .... E 888 639-2872
El Dorado *(G-1554)*
Custom Metal Fabricators Inc .... E 785 258-3744
Herington *(G-2973)*
Daniel Todd Industries Inc .... G 913 780-0382
Olathe *(G-7641)*
Dayton Superior Corporation .... C 937 866-0711
Parsons *(G-9681)*
Db2 Services Inc .... F 913 677-2408
Kansas City *(G-3961)*
Debackers Inc .... E 785 232-6999
Topeka *(G-12550)*
Etco Specialty Products Inc .... E 620 724-6463
Girard *(G-2403)*
G & D Metals Inc .... G 316 303-9090
Wichita *(G-14431)*
General Repair & Supply Inc .... G 620 365-5954
Iola *(G-3604)*
Globe Engineering Co Inc .... C 316 943-1266
Wichita *(G-14476)*
Goodwill Wstn MO & Eastrn Kans .... E 785 228-9774
Topeka *(G-12642)*
Goodwill Wstn MO & Eastrn Kans .... F 785 331-3908
Lawrence *(G-4875)*
Goodwill Wstn MO & Eastrn Kans .... E 913 768-9540
Olathe *(G-7737)*
Grain Belt Supply Company Inc .... C 785 827-4491
Salina *(G-10514)*
H & R Parts Co Inc .... E 316 942-6984
Wichita *(G-14531)*
Hall Steel & Fabrication Inc .... G 316 263-4222
Wichita *(G-14547)*
Impresa Aerospace LLC .... D 316 942-9100
Wichita *(G-14679)*
JR Custom Metal Products Inc .... C 316 263-1318
Wichita *(G-14776)*
Kasa Companies Inc .... D 785 825-5612
Salina *(G-10569)*
Kemlee Manufacturing Inc .... D 620 783-5035
Galena *(G-2076)*
Lb Steel LLC .... B 785 862-1071
Topeka *(G-12836)*
Lippert Components Mfg Inc .... C 323 663-1261
North Newton *(G-7437)*
LMI Aerospace Inc .... C 316 943-6059
Wichita *(G-14972)*
Manufacturing Development Inc .... E 316 542-0182
Cheney *(G-793)*
Metalform Industries Inc .... F 316 945-6700
Wichita *(G-15058)*
Millett Industries .... G 913 752-3572
Overland Park *(G-9038)*
New Age Industrial Corp Inc .... C 785 877-5121
Norton *(G-7455)*
Oxwell Inc .... D 620 326-7481
Wellington *(G-13521)*
Progressive Manufacturing Co .... F 913 383-2239
Leawood *(G-5530)*
Quality Tech Metals .... E 316 945-4781
Wichita *(G-15386)*

R P M Smith Corporation ....F.... 913 888-0695
Lenexa *(G-6087)*
Reliance Steel & Aluminum Co ....D.... 316 636-4500
Wichita *(G-15440)*
Rppg Inc ....E.... 620 705-5100
Arkansas City *(G-176)*
SC Hall Industrial Svcs Inc ....E.... 316 945-4255
Wichita *(G-15525)*
Southwest and Associates Inc ....D.... 620 463-5631
Burrton *(G-650)*
Star Pipe Usa LLC ....C.... 281 558-3000
Coffeyville *(G-979)*
Starflite Manufacturing Co ....G.... 316 267-7297
Wichita *(G-15656)*
Tennison Brothers Inc ....F.... 316 263-7581
Wichita *(G-15729)*
Town & Country Guttering Inc ....F.... 913 441-0003
Shawnee Mission *(G-11935)*
Twin Oaks Industries Inc ....E.... 785 827-4839
Salina *(G-10743)*
U-Tek Cnc Solutions LLC ....F.... 888 317-6503
Hiawatha *(G-3026)*
Webco Manufacturing Inc ....D.... 913 764-7111
Olathe *(G-8149)*
Wholesale Sheet Metal Inc ....C.... 913 432-7100
Kansas City *(G-4543)*

METAL FABRICATORS: Structural, Ship

Trinity Steel and Pipe Inc ....F.... 620 396-8900
Weir *(G-13486)*

METAL FINISHING SVCS

Central Electropolishing Inc ....E.... 620 842-3701
Anthony *(G-122)*
Metal Finishing Co Inc ....G.... 316 267-7289
Wichita *(G-15050)*
Metal Finishing Company Inc ....F.... 316 267-7289
Wichita *(G-15053)*
Paragon N D T & Finishes Inc ....E.... 316 945-5285
Wichita *(G-15259)*
True Spec Finishes LLC ....G.... 620 254-7733
Attica *(G-280)*

METAL MINING SVCS

Triple J Machining LLC ....F.... 316 214-2414
Augusta *(G-349)*

METAL SERVICE CENTERS & OFFICES

A M Castle & Co ....E.... 316 943-0277
Wichita *(G-13588)*
Butterfly Supply Inc ....F.... 620 793-7156
Great Bend *(G-2525)*
Joseph T Ryerson & Son Inc ....E.... 316 942-6061
Wichita *(G-14774)*
Kemlee Manufacturing Inc ....D.... 620 783-5035
Galena *(G-2076)*
Rgs Industries Inc ....G.... 913 780-9033
Olathe *(G-8031)*
Rock Ridge Steel Company LLC ....F.... 913 365-5200
Elwood *(G-1690)*
Thyssenkrupp Materials NA Inc ....F.... 620 802-0900
Hutchinson *(G-3464)*

METAL SLITTING & SHEARING

Specialty Fabrication Inc ....F.... 316 264-0603
Wichita *(G-15636)*

METAL STAMPING, FOR THE TRADE

Bennett Tool & Die LLC ....D.... 913 371-4641
Kansas City *(G-3855)*
Neosho Small Parts LLC ....F.... 620 244-3263
Erie *(G-1862)*

METAL TREATING: Cryogenic

Metal Finishing Company Inc ....F.... 316 267-7289
Wichita *(G-15053)*

METALS SVC CENTERS & WHOLESALERS: Ferroalloys

Custom Alloy Sales 34p LLC ....D.... 913 471-4800
Prescott *(G-10166)*

METALS SVC CENTERS & WHOLESALERS: Nonferrous Sheets, Etc

SOS Metals Midwest LLC ....E.... 316 522-0101
Wichita *(G-15616)*

METALS SVC CENTERS & WHOLESALERS: Pipe & Tubing, Steel

Hajoca Corporation ....F.... 785 825-1333
Salina *(G-10531)*
Piping Alloys Inc ....E.... 913 677-3833
Lenexa *(G-6058)*
Teeter Irrigation Inc ....F.... 620 276-8257
Garden City *(G-2297)*
Welborn Sales Inc ....F.... 785 823-2394
Salina *(G-10766)*

METALS SVC CENTERS & WHOLESALERS: Sheets, Metal

Reliance Steel & Aluminum Co ....D.... 316 636-4500
Wichita *(G-15440)*
Wholesale Sheet Metal Inc ....C.... 913 432-7100
Kansas City *(G-4543)*

METALS SVC CENTERS & WHOLESALERS: Steel

Al Stevens Construction LLC ....F.... 913 897-0688
Overland Park *(G-8364)*
American Metals Supply Co Inc ....E.... 913 754-0616
Lenexa *(G-5651)*
AMI Metals Inc ....E.... 316 945-7771
Wichita *(G-13700)*
Brown Strauss Inc ....E.... 913 621-4000
Kansas City *(G-3879)*
Eagle Trailer Company Inc ....G.... 785 841-3200
Lawrence *(G-4844)*
Frank Black Pipe & Supply Co ....F.... 620 241-2582
McPherson *(G-6966)*
Hall Steel & Fabrication Inc ....G.... 316 263-4222
Wichita *(G-14547)*
L & M Steel & Mfg ....G.... 785 462-8216
Colby *(G-1023)*
Metalwest LLC ....D.... 913 829-8585
New Century *(G-7293)*
Midwest Iron & Metal Co Inc ....E.... 620 662-5663
Hutchinson *(G-3378)*
Norfolk Iron & Metal Co ....C.... 620 342-9202
Emporia *(G-1807)*
P K M Steel Service Inc ....D.... 785 827-3638
Salina *(G-10629)*
Phoenix Corporation ....E.... 913 321-5200
Kansas City *(G-4321)*
Pioneer Tank & Steel Inc ....G.... 620 672-2153
Pratt *(G-10133)*
Reliance Steel & Aluminum Co ....F.... 316 838-9351
Wichita *(G-15441)*
Royal Metal Industries Inc ....E.... 913 829-3000
Olathe *(G-8044)*
Salina Steel Supply Inc ....E.... 785 825-2138
Salina *(G-10692)*
Steel and Pipe Supply Co Inc ....C.... 785 587-5100
Manhattan *(G-6809)*
Steel and Pipe Supply Co Inc ....D.... 913 768-4333
New Century *(G-7299)*
Steel Building Sales LLC ....F.... 316 733-5380
Rose Hill *(G-10249)*
TW Metals Inc ....E.... 316 744-5000
Park City *(G-9650)*
Wessel Iron & Supply Inc ....F.... 620 225-0568
Dodge City *(G-1453)*
Wifco Steel Products Inc ....D.... 620 543-2827
Hutchinson *(G-3489)*

METALS SVC CTRS & WHOLESALERS: Aluminum Bars, Rods, Etc

Alcoa Inc ....C.... 620 665-5281
Hutchinson *(G-3195)*

METALWORK: Miscellaneous

Custom Rollforming Corp ....E.... 800 457-8837
Moundridge *(G-7182)*
Lane Myers Company Inc ....E.... 620 622-4310
Protection *(G-10175)*
Midwest Contracting & Mfg ....G.... 785 743-2026
WA Keeney *(G-13383)*

Performance Contracting Inc ....E.... 913 928-2800
Lenexa *(G-6054)*
Performance Contracting Inc ....E.... 913 928-2832
Lenexa *(G-6052)*
Southwest Stl Fabricators Inc ....E.... 913 422-5500
Bonner Springs *(G-574)*

METALWORK: Ornamental

Designer Palms Inc ....F.... 316 733-2284
Andover *(G-89)*

METERS: Liquid

Great Plains Industries Inc ....B.... 316 686-7361
Wichita *(G-14503)*

METERS: Magnetic Flow, Indl Process

Torotel Inc ....E.... 913 747-6111
Olathe *(G-8115)*

MGMT CONSULTING SVCS: Matls, Incl Purch, Handle & Invntry

Century Construction Sup LLC ....F.... 913 438-3366
Lenexa *(G-5741)*

MGT SVCS, FACIL SUPPT: Base Maint Or Provide Personnel

Kansas Asphalt Inc ....D.... 877 384-2280
Bucyrus *(G-601)*
Skookum Educational Programs ....C.... 785 307-8180
Fort Riley *(G-1950)*
Usd 383 Mnhttan Ogden Schl Dst ....D.... 785 587-2180
Manhattan *(G-6839)*

MICROCIRCUITS, INTEGRATED: Semiconductor

LSI Corporation ....E.... 316 201-2000
Wichita *(G-14988)*

MICROFILM EQPT

Salina Microfilm ....F.... 785 827-6648
Salina *(G-10680)*

MICROFILM SVCS

Casey Associates Inc ....F.... 913 276-3200
Lenexa *(G-5731)*
Imaging Solutions Company ....E.... 316 630-0440
Wichita *(G-14677)*
Salina Microfilm ....F.... 785 827-6648
Salina *(G-10680)*

MICROPROCESSORS

Research Concepts Inc ....F.... 913 422-0210
Lenexa *(G-6106)*

MICROWAVE COMPONENTS

Smiths Intrcnnect Americas Inc ....G.... 913 342-5544
Kansas City *(G-4428)*
Smiths Intrcnnect Americas Inc ....C.... 913 342-5544
Kansas City *(G-4429)*

MIDWIVES' OFFICES

For Women Only Inc ....F.... 913 541-9495
Leawood *(G-5407)*

MILLINERY STORES

Trainwreck Tees LLC ....G.... 620 224-2480
Fort Scott *(G-2011)*

MILLING: Cereal Flour, Exc Rice

ADM Milling Co ....E.... 620 442-5500
Arkansas City *(G-140)*
ADM Milling Co ....D.... 913 491-9400
Overland Park *(G-8348)*

MILLING: Grains, Exc Rice

ADM Milling Co ....D.... 620 442-6200
Arkansas City *(G-139)*
ADM Milling Co ....E.... 620 227-8101
Dodge City *(G-1289)*

Employee Codes: A=Over 500 employees, B=251-500
C=101-250, D=51-100, E=20-50, F=10-19, G=5-9

ADM Milling Co....D....785 825-1541
Salina *(G-10395)*
ADM Milling Co....E....785 263-1631
Abilene *(G-11)*
Fairview Mills LLC....F....785 336-2148
Elwood *(G-1687)*
Grain Craft Inc....B....913 890-6300
Leawood *(G-5417)*
Grain Craft Inc....E....913 262-1779
Kansas City *(G-4044)*

MILLWORK

Cabinetry & Mllwk Concepts Inc....F....785 232-1234
Topeka *(G-12417)*
Columbia Industries Inc....E....785 227-3351
Lindsborg *(G-6396)*
Doubrava Woodworking Inc....G....785 472-4204
Ellsworth *(G-1666)*
Grandview Products Co....D....620 336-2309
Cherryvale *(G-808)*
Hardwood Manufacturing LLC....F....620 463-2663
Burrton *(G-649)*
Hays Planing Mill Inc....G....785 625-6507
Hays *(G-2838)*
McCray Lumber Company....D....913 321-8840
Kansas City *(G-4226)*
Olathe Millwork LLC....G....913 738-8074
Olathe *(G-7947)*
Shawnee Woodwork Inc....E....785 354-1163
Topeka *(G-13065)*
Tischlerei-Fine Wdwkg LLC....F....785 404-3322
Salina *(G-10734)*
Weisbender Contracting Inc....G....785 776-5034
Manhattan *(G-6849)*
Wood Haven Inc....G....785 597-5618
Perry *(G-9775)*
Wooten Enterprises LLC....G....316 830-2328
Halstead *(G-2707)*

MINERAL WOOL

Certainteed Corporation....B....913 342-6624
Kansas City *(G-3906)*
Owens Corning Sales LLC....E....913 281-9495
Kansas City *(G-4304)*

MINERALS: Ground or Treated

A&M Products Manufacturing Co....E....913 592-4344
Spring Hill *(G-12074)*
Calvert Corporation....G....785 877-5221
Almena *(G-67)*
Koch Companies Pub Sector LLC....G....316 828-5500
Wichita *(G-14876)*
McShares Inc....E....785 825-2181
Salina *(G-10598)*
Reed Mineral Division....G....913 757-4561
La Cygne *(G-4642)*

MISC FINAN INVEST ACTIVITY: Mutual Fund, Ind Salesperson

Waddell & Reed Inc....F....913 491-9202
Leawood *(G-5593)*
Waddell & Reed Inc....E....785 537-4505
Manhattan *(G-6844)*
Waddell & Reed Inv MGT Co....E....913 491-9202
Leawood *(G-5594)*

MIXING EQPT

H C Davis Sons Mfg Co....F....913 422-3000
Bonner Springs *(G-554)*

MIXTURES & BLOCKS: Asphalt Paving

Apac-Kansas Inc....D....316 524-5200
Wichita *(G-13716)*
County of McPherson....E....620 241-0466
McPherson *(G-6952)*
CPB Materials LLC....G....316 833-1146
Haysville *(G-2938)*
Ergon Asphalt & Emulsions Inc....G....913 788-5300
Kansas City *(G-3995)*
Husqvrna Cnstr Pdts N Amer Inc....A....913 928-1000
Olathe *(G-7781)*
Mm Distribution LLC....G....800 689-2098
Douglass *(G-1467)*
Nk Asphalt Partners....G....316 828-5500
Wichita *(G-15182)*
Semcrude LP....F....620 234-5532
Stafford *(G-12109)*
Semmaterials LP....G....785 825-1535
Salina *(G-10704)*

MOBILE HOMES

Clayton Homes Inc....C....785 434-4617
Plainville *(G-9981)*

MOBILE HOMES WHOLESALERS

Clayton Homes Inc....C....785 434-4617
Plainville *(G-9981)*
Southside Homes Inc....F....316 522-7100
Wichita *(G-15626)*

MOBILE HOMES, EXC RECREATIONAL

Skyline Corporation....D....620 442-9060
Arkansas City *(G-180)*

MODELING SVCS

Mobile Health Clinics LLC....D....913 383-0991
Leawood *(G-5490)*

MOLDING COMPOUNDS

National Plastics Color Inc....C....316 755-1273
Valley Center *(G-13349)*

MOLDINGS: Picture Frame

Laminage Products Inc....G....316 267-5233
Wichita *(G-14916)*

MOLDS: Indl

Certified Water & Mold Restrtn....G....816 835-4959
Olathe *(G-7588)*
Dme Electronics....G....316 529-2441
Haysville *(G-2940)*
Sektam of Independence Inc....F....620 331-5480
Independence *(G-3558)*

MOLDS: Plastic Working & Foundry

Creative Paradise Inc....F....316 794-8621
Goddard *(G-2434)*
Kansas American Tooling Inc....F....620 241-4200
McPherson *(G-6980)*
Mastercraft Pattern Inc....G....620 231-3530
Pittsburg *(G-9900)*

MONTESSORI CHILD DEVELOPMENT CENTER

Agape Montessori School....E....913 768-0812
Olathe *(G-7513)*
Global Montessori Academy....F....816 561-4533
Prairie Village *(G-10032)*
Hillcrest Chrstn Child Dev Ctr....E....913 663-1997
Shawnee Mission *(G-11432)*
Little Tots Montessori Corp....F....913 602-7923
Kansas City *(G-4205)*
Russell Child Dev Ctr Inc....D....620 275-0291
Garden City *(G-2270)*
Wichita Montessori School....F....316 686-7265
Wichita *(G-16012)*

MONUMENTS & GRAVE MARKERS, WHOLESALE

Bell Memorials LLC....F....785 738-2257
Beloit *(G-474)*
Smith Monuments Inc....G....785 425-6762
Stockton *(G-12187)*
Suhor Industries Inc....A....620 421-4434
Overland Park *(G-9371)*
Wolf Memorial Co Inc....F....785 726-4430
Ellis *(G-1655)*

MOPS: Floor & Dust

Direct Mop Sales Inc....E....913 367-3087
Atchison *(G-224)*

MORTGAGE BANKERS

Albright Investment Company....E....620 221-7653
Winfield *(G-16114)*
Collateral RE Capitl LLC....F....913 677-2001
Mission Woods *(G-7150)*
First Horizon Bank....E....913 317-2000
Overland Park *(G-8719)*
M Squared Financial LLC....F....913 745-7000
Prairie Village *(G-10045)*
Security National Fincl Corp....B....620 241-3400
McPherson *(G-7025)*
Triad Capital Advisors Inc....F....816 561-7000
Fairway *(G-1922)*
Wells Fargo Home Mortgage Inc....E....405 475-2880
Wichita *(G-15948)*

MORTGAGE COMPANIES: Urban

Tru Home Solutions LLC....E....913 219-7547
Lenexa *(G-6192)*

MORTGAGE GUARANTEE INSURANCE

Reece and Nichols Realtors Inc....B....913 945-3704
Leawood *(G-5536)*

MOTEL

B and L Motels....E....913 451-5874
Overland Park *(G-8421)*
Bhakta LLC....F....620 532-3118
Kingman *(G-4583)*
Branding Iron Restaurant & CLB....E....620 624-7254
Liberal *(G-6286)*
Cottage House Hotel and Motel....F....620 767-6828
Council Grove *(G-1159)*
Cottonwood Inn....E....785 543-2125
Phillipsburg *(G-9783)*
Executives Inc....F....316 685-8131
Wichita *(G-14320)*
Extra Inn Inc....E....620 232-2800
Pittsburg *(G-9859)*
Four of Wichita Inc....E....316 943-2373
Wichita *(G-14407)*
Four of Wichita Inc....E....316 636-2022
Wichita *(G-14408)*
Four of Wichita Inc....E....316 634-2303
Wichita *(G-14409)*
Gateway Inn....D....620 624-0242
Liberal *(G-6311)*
Kan Tex Hospitality Inc....F....785 404-1870
Salina *(G-10561)*
Kansas Inn Limited Partnership....F....316 269-9999
Wichita *(G-14809)*
Kansas Investment Corporation....F....785 843-6611
Lawrence *(G-4933)*
Lake Perry Yacht & Marina LLC....F....785 783-4927
Perry *(G-9771)*
Leisure Hotel Corporation....E....913 250-1000
Lansing *(G-4685)*
Lenexa Hotel LP....D....913 217-1000
Lenexa *(G-5970)*
Lodge....F....785 594-0574
Baldwin City *(G-365)*
Mark 8 Inn Lc....F....316 265-4679
Wichita *(G-15008)*
P & A Investments....E....316 634-2303
Wichita *(G-15246)*
Rothfuss Motels....F....785 632-2148
Clay Center *(G-878)*
Rothfuss Motels....F....785 632-5611
Clay Center *(G-879)*
Sabetha Country Inn Inc....E....785 284-2300
Sabetha *(G-10327)*
Salina Red Coach Inn....F....785 825-2111
Salina *(G-10684)*
Sands Motor Inn....F....620 356-1404
Ulysses *(G-13317)*
Scotsman Inn West LLC....E....316 943-3800
Wichita *(G-15537)*
Service Oil Company....F....785 462-3441
Colby *(G-1040)*
Shamir Corp....E....785 266-8880
Topeka *(G-13062)*
Skyline Motel....F....620 431-1500
Chanute *(G-762)*
Summit Hospitality LLC....E....970 765-5690
Salina *(G-10719)*
Wamego Inn and Suites....F....785 458-8888
Wamego *(G-13452)*

MOTEL: Franchised

Fryslie Inc....F....620 672-6407
Pratt *(G-10116)*
Russells America Inn LLC....F....785 483-4200
Russell *(G-10298)*

MOTION PICTURE & VIDEO DISTRIBUTION

1038 Productions ... F ... 316 644-6883
Wichita *(G-13577)*
Arteyeview Productions ... F ... 316 737-7080
Wichita *(G-13740)*
Do Good Productions Inc ... F ... 913 400-3416
Leawood *(G-5379)*
F&F Productions Inc ... F ... 785 235-8300
Topeka *(G-12591)*
K&J Outdoor Products LLC ... F ... 816 769-6060
Cherryvale *(G-810)*
Leisure Time Products ... F ... 620 308-5224
Pittsburg *(G-9894)*
Mid America Printed ... F ... 913 432-2700
Merriam *(G-7100)*
Midwest Sports Productions LLC ... E ... 913 543-6116
Lenexa *(G-6004)*
Oasis Productions ... F ... 316 210-4488
Wichita *(G-15204)*
Over Cat Products LLC ... F ... 913 256-2126
Osawatomie *(G-8202)*
Purpose Productions ... F ... 913 620-3508
Kansas City *(G-4349)*
Santa Fe Products LLC ... F ... 913 362-6611
Overland Park *(G-9279)*
Yaco Productions ... F ... 913 669-7380
Kansas City *(G-4562)*

MOTION PICTURE & VIDEO PRODUCTION SVCS

Jack Wilson & Associates Inc ... F ... 785 856-4546
Lawrence *(G-4918)*
Nuvidia LLC ... F ... 913 599-5200
Lenexa *(G-6030)*

MOTOR HOMES

Zodiac Industries Inc ... E ... 620 783-5041
Galena *(G-2090)*

MOTOR REBUILDING SVCS, EXC AUTOMOTIVE

Zimmerman Electric Service ... G ... 620 431-2260
Chanute *(G-775)*

MOTOR SCOOTERS & PARTS

Burke Inc ... E ... 913 722-5658
Kansas City *(G-3880)*

MOTOR VEHICLE ASSEMBLY, COMPLETE: Autos, Incl Specialty

Custom Vinyl & Paint Inc ... G ... 316 651-6180
Wichita *(G-14147)*
Midwest Motorsports Inc ... E ... 913 334-0477
Kansas City *(G-4254)*

MOTOR VEHICLE ASSEMBLY, COMPLETE: Bus/Large Spclty Vehicles

Chance Rides Manufacturing Inc ... C ... 316 945-6555
Wichita *(G-13997)*
Diamond Coach Corporation ... D ... 620 795-2191
Oswego *(G-8233)*
New Horizons Rv Corp ... E ... 785 238-7575
Junction City *(G-3731)*

MOTOR VEHICLE ASSEMBLY, COMPLETE: Buses, All Types

Eldorado National Kansas Inc ... C ... 785 827-1033
Salina *(G-10486)*

MOTOR VEHICLE ASSEMBLY, COMPLETE: Fire Department Vehicles

Unruh Fire Inc ... G ... 316 772-5400
Sedgwick *(G-10854)*

MOTOR VEHICLE ASSEMBLY, COMPLETE: Military Motor Vehicle

Legacy Technologies LLC ... E ... 913 432-2020
Shawnee Mission *(G-11559)*

MOTOR VEHICLE ASSEMBLY, COMPLETE: Motor Buses

Collins Bus Corporation ... C ... 620 662-9000
Hutchinson *(G-3242)*

MOTOR VEHICLE ASSEMBLY, COMPLETE: Snow Plows

Henke Manufacturing Corp ... C ... 913 682-9000
Leavenworth *(G-5254)*

MOTOR VEHICLE ASSEMBLY, COMPLETE: Truck & Tractor Trucks

Brown Industries LLC ... D ... 785 842-6506
Lawrence *(G-4770)*

MOTOR VEHICLE ASSY, COMPLETE: Street Sprinklers & Sweepers

Sb Manufacturing Inc ... B ... 316 941-9591
Wichita *(G-15524)*

MOTOR VEHICLE DEALERS: Automobiles, New & Used

Allen Samuels Waco D C J Inc ... E ... 620 860-1869
Hutchinson *(G-3196)*
Autobody of Lawrence ... E ... 785 843-3055
Lawrence *(G-4744)*
Bme Inc ... E ... 785 274-5116
Topeka *(G-12391)*
Bob Allen Ford Inc ... D ... 913 381-3000
Overland Park *(G-8473)*
Boss Motors Inc ... F ... 785 562-3696
Marysville *(G-6880)*
Briggs Auto Group Inc ... E ... 785 776-3677
Manhattan *(G-6569)*
Bud Brown Automotive Inc ... D ... 913 393-8100
Olathe *(G-7564)*
Dept Lincoln Service ... E ... 316 928-7331
Wichita *(G-14197)*
Dick Edwards Ford Lincoln Merc ... D ... 785 320-4499
Junction City *(G-3687)*
Don Hattan Derby Inc ... E ... 316 744-1275
Derby *(G-1240)*
Doug Reh Chevrolet Inc ... E ... 620 672-5633
Pratt *(G-10109)*
E & J Rental & Leasing Inc ... F ... 316 721-0442
Wichita *(G-14249)*
Flint Hills Ford Inc ... E ... 785 776-4004
Manhattan *(G-6632)*
General Motors LLC ... A ... 913 573-7981
Kansas City *(G-4031)*
Great Western Tire of Dodge Cy ... F ... 620 225-1343
Dodge City *(G-1367)*
Happy Autos LLC ... F ... 785 621-4100
Hays *(G-2826)*
Hillsboro Ford Inc ... E ... 620 947-3134
Hillsboro *(G-3049)*
Joe Self Chevrolet Inc ... C ... 316 689-4390
Wichita *(G-14760)*
John Schmidt & Sons Inc ... E ... 316 445-2103
Mount Hope *(G-7205)*
Johnson County Investors Inc ... C ... 913 631-0000
Shawnee Mission *(G-11498)*
Kline Motors Inc ... F ... 620 221-2040
Winfield *(G-16153)*
Laird Noller Ford Inc ... C ... 785 235-9211
Topeka *(G-12828)*
Laird Noller Ford Inc ... E ... 785 264-2800
Topeka *(G-12829)*
Manweiler Chevrolet Co Inc ... F ... 620 653-2121
Hoisington *(G-3069)*
Mel Hambelton Ford Inc ... C ... 316 462-3673
Wichita *(G-15035)*
Midway Motors Inc ... D ... 620 241-7737
McPherson *(G-7005)*
Miles Automotive Inc ... D ... 785 843-7700
Lawrence *(G-5028)*
Murphy-Hoffman Company ... E ... 816 483-6444
Leawood *(G-5492)*
Noller Lincoln-Mercury Inc ... E ... 785 267-2800
Topeka *(G-12932)*
Oakley Motors Inc ... E ... 785 672-3238
Oakley *(G-7484)*
Olathe Ford Sales Inc ... E ... 913 782-0881
Olathe *(G-7936)*
Olathe Ford Sales Inc ... E ... 913 856-8145
Gardner *(G-2357)*
Olathe Ford Sales Inc ... E ... 913 829-1957
Olathe *(G-7937)*
Ray Shepherd Motors Inc ... E ... 620 644-2625
Fort Scott *(G-2001)*
Reedy Ford Inc ... E ... 620 442-4800
Arkansas City *(G-174)*
Riley Ford Mercury Co ... F ... 620 356-1206
Ulysses *(G-13315)*
Robert Brogden Buick Gmc Inc ... E ... 913 782-1500
Olathe *(G-8038)*
Schmidt Haven Ford Sales Inc ... F ... 620 465-2252
Haven *(G-2736)*
Shaw Motor Co Inc ... F ... 785 673-4228
Grainfield *(G-2496)*
South Star Chrysler Inc ... F ... 785 242-5600
Ottawa *(G-8313)*
Star Motors Ltd ... E ... 913 432-7800
Shawnee Mission *(G-11895)*
Wichita Kenworth Inc ... D ... 316 838-0867
Park City *(G-9655)*
Winfield Motor Company Inc ... E ... 620 221-2840
Winfield *(G-16187)*

MOTOR VEHICLE DEALERS: Cars, Used Only

Andrade Auto Sales Inc ... F ... 620 624-2400
Liberal *(G-6278)*
Butler Enterprises Inc ... F ... 913 262-9109
Shawnee Mission *(G-11192)*
Credit Motors Inc ... F ... 913 621-1206
Kansas City *(G-3945)*
Easy Credit Auto Sales Inc ... E ... 316 522-3279
Wichita *(G-14254)*
Enterprise Leasing Co KS LLC ... C ... 913 383-1515
Shawnee Mission *(G-11340)*
Johns Body Shop Inc ... F ... 620 225-2213
Dodge City *(G-1383)*
K D Sullivan Investments LLC ... F ... 785 460-0170
Colby *(G-1018)*
Merchants Automotive Group Inc ... E ... 913 901-9900
Leawood *(G-5474)*
Olathe Ford Sales Inc ... E ... 913 829-1957
Olathe *(G-7937)*
Pringle Auto Body & Sales Inc ... F ... 913 432-6361
Kansas City *(G-4339)*
Ritchey Motors LLC ... F ... 785 380-0222
Topeka *(G-13019)*
Wagner Auto Body & Sales Inc ... F ... 913 422-1955
Bonner Springs *(G-580)*

MOTOR VEHICLE DEALERS: Pickups & Vans, Used

Automotive Specialists Inc ... F ... 316 321-5130
El Dorado *(G-1532)*
Reed Company LLC ... E ... 785 456-7333
Wamego *(G-13439)*

MOTOR VEHICLE DEALERS: Pickups, New & Used

K Young Inc ... F ... 785 475-3888
Colby *(G-1019)*
Murphy-Hoffman Company ... F ... 913 441-6300
Kansas City *(G-4274)*

MOTOR VEHICLE DEALERS: Trucks, Tractors/Trailers, New & Used

American Equipment Sales Inc ... F ... 785 843-4500
Lawrence *(G-4734)*
Chuck Henry Sales Inc ... F ... 785 655-9430
Solomon *(G-12049)*
Diamond Intl Trcks Inc ... E ... 785 235-8711
Topeka *(G-12555)*
Dodge City International Inc ... E ... 620 225-4177
Dodge City *(G-1348)*
Easy Money Pawn Shop Inc ... G ... 316 687-2727
Wichita *(G-14255)*
Georgia Kenworth Inc ... E ... 816 483-6444
Leawood *(G-5411)*
Kansas Cy Freightliner Sls Inc ... E ... 913 780-6606
Olathe *(G-7828)*
Mitten Inc ... E ... 785 672-3062
Oakley *(G-7481)*
Omaha Truck Center Inc ... E ... 785 823-2204
Salina *(G-10620)*

Skymark Refuelers LLC.........D....... 913 653-8100
Kansas City (G-4424)
Southwest Sterling Inc.........E....... 816 483-6444
Leawood (G-5555)
Vernies Trux-N-Equip Inc.........G....... 785 625-5087
Hays (G-2923)
Weis Fire Safety Equip Co Inc.........F....... 785 825-9527
Salina (G-10765)
Williams Service Inc.........E....... 620 878-4225
Florence (G-1930)
Wilson Trailer Sales Kans Inc.........F....... 620 225-6220
Dodge City (G-1458)
Wki Operations Inc.........F....... 316 838-0867
Dodge City (G-1462)

MOTOR VEHICLE DEALERS: Vans, New & Used

Zodiac Industries Inc.........E....... 620 783-5041
Galena (G-2090)

MOTOR VEHICLE PARTS & ACCESS: Air Conditioner Parts

Timken Smo LLC.........B....... 620 223-0080
Fort Scott (G-2008)

MOTOR VEHICLE PARTS & ACCESS: Booster Cables, Jump-Start

Clore Automotive LLC.........E....... 913 310-1050
Lenexa (G-5766)

MOTOR VEHICLE PARTS & ACCESS: Brakes, Air

Haldex Brake Products Corp.........D....... 620 365-5275
Iola (G-3606)

MOTOR VEHICLE PARTS & ACCESS: Engines & Parts

Thunder Struck Inc.........E....... 785 200-6680
Abilene (G-54)

MOTOR VEHICLE PARTS & ACCESS: Fifth Wheels

Kalmar Solutions LLC.........B....... 785 242-2200
Ottawa (G-8279)

MOTOR VEHICLE PARTS & ACCESS: Frames

Youngs Products LLC.........D....... 620 431-2199
Chanute (G-774)

MOTOR VEHICLE PARTS & ACCESS: Manifolds

Precision Manifold Systems Inc.........E....... 913 829-1221
Olathe (G-8001)

MOTOR VEHICLE PARTS & ACCESS: Trailer Hitches

B & W Custom Truck Beds Inc.........C....... 800 810-4918
Humboldt (G-3181)

MOTOR VEHICLE PARTS & ACCESS: Wiring Harness Sets

Mize & Co Inc.........E....... 620 532-3191
Kingman (G-4607)

MOTOR VEHICLE RADIOS WHOLESALERS

Custom Rdo Communications Ltd.........F....... 816 561-4100
Leawood (G-5367)

MOTOR VEHICLE SPLYS & PARTS WHOLESALERS: New

Advance Stores Company Inc.........C....... 785 826-2400
Salina (G-10396)
Computer Distribution Corp.........E....... 785 354-1086
Topeka (G-12498)
Long Motor Corporation.........C....... 913 541-1525
Lenexa (G-5979)
OReilly Automotive Stores Inc.........F....... 316 729-7311
Wichita (G-15233)
OReilly Automotive Stores Inc.........F....... 316 686-5536
Wichita (G-15234)
OReilly Automotive Stores Inc.........F....... 913 287-2409
Kansas City (G-4296)
OReilly Automotive Stores Inc.........F....... 913 381-0451
Overland Park (G-9111)
OReilly Automotive Stores Inc.........E....... 913 764-8685
Olathe (G-7962)
S & W Supply Company Inc.........E....... 785 625-7363
Hays (G-2904)

MOTOR VEHICLE SPLYS & PARTS WHOLESALERS: Used

Jobbers Automotive Whse Inc.........D....... 316 267-4393
Wichita (G-14759)
S & W Supply Company Inc.........E....... 785 625-7363
Hays (G-2904)

MOTOR VEHICLES & CAR BODIES

Broce Manufacturing Co Inc.........G....... 620 227-8811
Dodge City (G-1312)
General Motors LLC.........A....... 913 573-7981
Kansas City (G-4031)
Wichita Body & Equipment Co.........G....... 316 522-1080
Haysville (G-2964)

MOTOR VEHICLES, WHOLESALE: Trailers for passenger vehicles

Brown Industries LLC.........D....... 785 842-6506
Lawrence (G-4770)

MOTOR VEHICLES, WHOLESALE: Trailers, Truck, New & Used

Contract Trailer Service Inc.........F....... 913 281-2589
Kansas City (G-3936)
Western Trailer Service Inc.........E....... 913 281-2226
Kansas City (G-4538)
Wilkens Manufacturing Inc.........D....... 785 425-7070
Stockton (G-12190)
Wilson Trailer Sales Kans Inc.........F....... 620 225-6220
Dodge City (G-1458)

MOTOR VEHICLES, WHOLESALE: Truck tractors

Hays Mack Sales and Svc Inc.........F....... 785 625-7343
Hays (G-2832)
Kansas Kenworth Inc.........E....... 785 823-9700
Salina (G-10566)
Moss Enterprises Inc.........E....... 620 277-2646
Garden City (G-2241)
Omaha Truck Center Inc.........E....... 785 823-2204
Salina (G-10619)

MOTOR VEHICLES, WHOLESALE: Trucks, commercial

Aeroswint.........F....... 785 391-2276
Utica (G-13334)
Bme Inc.........E....... 785 274-5116
Topeka (G-12391)
Chuck Henry Sales Inc.........F....... 785 655-9430
Solomon (G-12049)
Cstk Inc.........F....... 316 744-2061
Park City (G-9614)
Doonan Truck & Equipment Inc.........E....... 620 792-2491
Great Bend (G-2555)
Iowa Kenworth Inc.........E....... 816 483-6444
Leawood (G-5440)
J & D Equipment Inc.........E....... 913 342-1450
Kansas City (G-4113)
Kansas City Peterbilt Inc.........D....... 913 441-2888
Kansas City (G-4148)
Larrys Trailer Sales & Svc LLC.........F....... 316 838-1491
Wichita (G-14927)
Meyer Truck Center Inc.........F....... 913 764-2000
Olathe (G-7887)
Midwest Services & Towing Inc.........E....... 913 281-1003
Kansas City (G-4257)
North Carolina Kenworth Inc.........E....... 816 483-6444
Leawood (G-5503)
Olathe Ford Sales Inc.........E....... 913 782-0881
Olathe (G-7936)
Roberts Truck Ctr Holdg Co LLC.........D....... 316 262-8413
Park City (G-9640)
Rush Truck Centers Kansas Inc.........E....... 913 764-6000
Olathe (G-8047)
Tennessee Kenworth Inc.........E....... 816 483-6444
Leawood (G-5571)

MOTOR VEHICLES, WHOLESALE: Vans, commercial

Zodiac Industries Inc.........E....... 620 783-5041
Galena (G-2090)

MOTORCYCLE DEALERS

Clevlun Enterprises Inc.........F....... 913 631-1111
Shawnee Mission (G-11239)
K & N Motorcycles Corporation.........E....... 316 945-8221
Valley Center (G-13346)
Kaw Valley Industrial Inc.........G....... 785 841-9751
Eudora (G-1876)

MOTORCYCLE DEALERS

Big Twin Inc.........E....... 785 234-6174
Topeka (G-12381)
City Cycle Sales.........F....... 785 238-3411
Junction City (G-3681)
Mid-Continent Harley-Davidson.........F....... 316 440-5700
Park City (G-9630)
Oakley Motors Inc.........E....... 785 672-3238
Oakley (G-7484)

MOTORCYCLE DEALERS: All-Terrain Vehicle Parts & Access

Foster Unruh Inc.........E....... 620 227-2165
Dodge City (G-1362)
Kanequip Inc.........F....... 785 632-3441
Clay Center (G-869)
Straub International Inc.........F....... 620 672-2998
Pratt (G-10156)

MOTORCYCLE PARTS & ACCESS DEALERS

Frankenstein Trikes LLC.........G....... 913 352-6788
Pleasanton (G-9995)
Truett & Osborn Cycle Inc.........G....... 316 682-4781
Wichita (G-15811)

MOTORCYCLE PARTS: Wholesalers

Truett & Osborn Cycle Inc.........G....... 316 682-4781
Wichita (G-15811)

MOTORCYCLE REPAIR SHOPS

Big Twin Inc.........E....... 785 234-6174
Topeka (G-12381)
City Cycle Sales.........F....... 785 238-3411
Junction City (G-3681)
Clevlun Enterprises Inc.........F....... 913 631-1111
Shawnee Mission (G-11239)
Flint Hills Powersports Inc.........G....... 785 336-3901
Bern (G-522)
K & N Motorcycles Corporation.........E....... 316 945-8221
Valley Center (G-13346)
Kaw Valley Industrial Inc.........G....... 785 841-9751
Eudora (G-1876)
Mid-Continent Harley-Davidson.........F....... 316 440-5700
Park City (G-9630)
Romans Outdoor Power Inc.........E....... 913 837-5225
Louisburg (G-6466)
Truett & Osborn Cycle Inc.........G....... 316 682-4781
Wichita (G-15811)

MOTORCYCLES & RELATED PARTS

Cosentino Group II Inc.........G....... 913 422-2130
Shawnee (G-10935)
Holthaus Autohaus LLC.........G....... 785 467-3101
Fairview (G-1904)

MOTORS: Electric

Ametek Advanced Industries Inc.........D....... 316 522-0424
Wichita (G-13698)
Power Tech Electric Motors LLC.........G....... 913 888-4488
Overland Park (G-9173)

MOTORS: Generators

Clare Generator Service Inc.........F....... 785 827-3321
Salina (G-10453)
Welco Technologies.........G....... 316 941-0400
Wichita (G-15943)

MOVIE THEATERS, EXC DRIVE-IN

Acme Cinema Inc ...... E 620 421-4404
Parsons *(G-9663)*
AMC Entertainment Holdings Inc ...... D 913 213-2000
Leawood *(G-5317)*
American Multi-Cinema Inc ...... C 913 213-2000
Leawood *(G-5322)*
B & B Movie Theatres LLC ...... F 620 342-0900
Emporia *(G-1699)*
B & B Movie Theatres LLC ...... F 620 227-8100
Dodge City *(G-1299)*
B & B Movie Theatres LLC ...... F 620 669-8510
Hutchinson *(G-3211)*
Cinemark Usa Inc ...... C 913 789-7038
Shawnee Mission *(G-11226)*
Cooper Enterprises ...... F 620 225-4347
Dodge City *(G-1331)*
Dickinson Theatres ...... E 913 383-6114
Overland Park *(G-8654)*
Eastwynn Theatres Inc ...... E 913 213-2000
Leawood *(G-5382)*
Finch Theatres ...... F 785 524-4350
Lincoln *(G-6382)*
Gkc Michigan Theatres Inc ...... B 913 213-2000
Leawood *(G-5412)*
Glenwood Arts Theater ...... F 913 642-1132
Overland Park *(G-8756)*
Goodrich Quality Theaters Inc ...... F 620 232-2256
Pittsburg *(G-9867)*
Innovtive Cinema Solutions LLC ...... F 855 401-4567
Lenexa *(G-5916)*
Liberty Hall Inc ...... E 785 749-1972
Lawrence *(G-4995)*
Regal Cinemas Inc ...... E 925 757-0466
Leawood *(G-5537)*
State Theatre ...... E 620 285-3535
Larned *(G-4714)*
Vbc Enterprises LLC ...... E 316 789-0114
Derby *(G-1279)*
Warren Old Town Theatre Grill ...... E 316 262-7123
Wichita *(G-15926)*

MOVIE THEATERS: Drive-In

Cooper Enterprises ...... F 620 225-4347
Dodge City *(G-1331)*

MOVING SVC & STORAGE: Local

A Arnold of Kansas City LLC ...... E 913 829-8267
Olathe *(G-7503)*
Bailey Moving & Storage Co LLC ...... E 785 232-0521
Topeka *(G-12357)*
Coleman American Mvg Svcs Inc ...... E 913 631-1440
Shawnee Mission *(G-11246)*
Coleman American Mvg Svcs Inc ...... E 913 248-1766
Shawnee *(G-10930)*
Coleman American Mvg Svcs Inc ...... E 785 537-7284
Manhattan *(G-6593)*
James B Stddard Trnsf Stor Inc ...... E 913 727-3627
Leavenworth *(G-5256)*
Reliable Transfer & Storage ...... F 785 776-4887
Manhattan *(G-6790)*

MOVING SVC: Local

A&Atruck Rental/3 Men With ...... F 785 236-0003
Topeka *(G-12280)*
Bourbon Trucking LLC ...... E 785 428-3030
Jewell *(G-3649)*
Coleman American Moving Svcs ...... F 785 537-7284
Manhattan *(G-6592)*
Get A Move On Inc ...... E 316 729-4897
Wichita *(G-14461)*
Heartland Moving & Storage ...... F 316 554-0224
Wichita *(G-14586)*
Kings Moving & Storage Inc ...... E 785 238-7341
Junction City *(G-3715)*
Moving Kings LLC ...... E 913 882-2121
Overland Park *(G-9058)*
NL Wilson Moving Inc ...... E 913 652-9488
Olathe *(G-7923)*
Speedway Service Corporation ...... F 913 488-6695
Olathe *(G-8077)*

MOVING SVC: Long-Distance

A Arnold of Kansas City LLC ...... E 913 829-8267
Olathe *(G-7503)*
James B Stddard Trnsf Stor Inc ...... E 913 727-3627
Leavenworth *(G-5256)*
Studdard Moving & Storage Inc ...... E 913 341-4600
Leavenworth *(G-5293)*

MOWERS & ACCESSORIES

Desert Steel Corporation ...... F 316 282-2244
Wichita *(G-14199)*
Mojack Distributors LLC ...... F 877 466-5225
Wichita *(G-15121)*

MULTI-SVCS CENTER

Olathe Unified School Dst 233 ...... E 913 780-7002
Olathe *(G-7950)*
Salvation Army ...... E 785 233-9648
Topeka *(G-13034)*

MUSEUMS

Adjutant Generals Dept Kans ...... F 785 862-1020
Topeka *(G-12288)*
B-29 Museum Inc ...... F 620 282-1123
Pratt *(G-10099)*
City of Newton ...... E 316 283-3113
Newton *(G-7330)*
City of Salina ...... F 785 309-5775
Salina *(G-10450)*
Cosmosphere Inc ...... E 620 662-2305
Hutchinson *(G-3247)*
County of Franklin ...... E 785 242-1250
Ottawa *(G-8261)*
County of Johnson ...... F 913 715-2550
Overland Park *(G-8605)*
Dane G Hansen Memorial M ...... F 785 689-4848
Logan *(G-6423)*
Deaf Cultural Ctr Foundation ...... F 913 782-5808
Olathe *(G-7643)*
Docs Friends Inc ...... F 316 943-3246
Wichita *(G-14217)*
Exploration Place Inc ...... D 316 660-0600
Wichita *(G-14323)*
Fort Hays State University ...... E 785 628-4286
Hays *(G-2811)*
Great Plins Trnspration Museum ...... F 316 263-0944
Wichita *(G-14506)*
Greyhound Hall of Fame ...... F 785 263-3000
Abilene *(G-35)*
Historic Wichita Sedqwick Cnty ...... E 316 219-1871
Wichita *(G-14618)*
Kansas Firefighters Museum ...... F 316 264-5990
Wichita *(G-14799)*
Kansas Museum of Mltry Histry ...... F 316 775-1425
Augusta *(G-329)*
Kansas State University ...... E 785 532-7718
Manhattan *(G-6680)*
Kauffman Museum Association ...... F 316 283-1612
North Newton *(G-7436)*
Lanesfield Schl Historic Site ...... F 913 893-6645
Edgerton *(G-1487)*
Lecompton Historical Soc Inc ...... F 785 887-6260
Lecompton *(G-5611)*
Medicine Lodge Indian & Peace ...... F 620 886-9815
Medicine Lodge *(G-7066)*
Midwest Educational Center ...... F 785 776-1234
Manhattan *(G-6747)*
National AG Ctr & Hall Fame ...... F 913 721-1075
Bonner Springs *(G-565)*
National Archives and Rec ADM ...... D 785 263-6700
Abilene *(G-47)*
Pawnee Valley Scouts Inc ...... F 620 285-6427
Larned *(G-4710)*
Richard Allen Cultural Center ...... E 913 682-8772
Leavenworth *(G-5285)*
Rolling Hills Zoo Foundation ...... E 785 827-9488
Salina *(G-10652)*
Rooks County Historical Museum ...... F 785 425-7217
Stockton *(G-12185)*
Santa Fe Trail Association ...... F 620 285-2054
Larned *(G-4711)*
Seward County Historical Soc ...... E 620 624-7624
Liberal *(G-6366)*
Stafford County Historical ...... F 620 234-5664
Stafford *(G-12110)*
University of Kansas ...... C 785 864-2451
Lawrence *(G-5164)*
University of Kansas ...... D 785 864-4710
Lawrence *(G-5165)*

MUSEUMS & ART GALLERIES

Culture House Inc ...... E 913 393-3141
Olathe *(G-7629)*
Fisch Bowl Inc ...... F 316 200-5200
Wichita *(G-14377)*
Interntnal Sclpture Foundation ...... F 785 864-2599
Olathe *(G-7800)*
University of Kansas ...... C 785 864-4540
Lawrence *(G-5167)*

MUSIC SCHOOLS

Jim Starkey Music Center Inc ...... F 316 262-2351
Wichita *(G-14757)*

MUSICAL ENTERTAINERS

B & B Backyard ...... F 785 246-6348
Topeka *(G-12355)*

MUSICAL INSTRUMENT REPAIR

Hume Music Inc ...... F 816 474-1960
Stilwell *(G-12154)*
Jim Starkey Music Center Inc ...... F 316 262-2351
Wichita *(G-14757)*
Kansas City Strings Violin Sp ...... E 913 677-0400
Shawnee Mission *(G-11511)*
Manning Music Inc ...... F 785 272-1740
Topeka *(G-12857)*
Wichita Band Instrument Co ...... F 316 684-0291
Wichita *(G-15979)*

MUSICAL INSTRUMENTS & SPLYS STORES

Hume Music Inc ...... F 816 474-1960
Stilwell *(G-12154)*
Jim Starkey Music Center Inc ...... F 316 262-2351
Wichita *(G-14757)*
Manning Music Inc ...... F 785 272-1740
Topeka *(G-12857)*
Reuter Organ Co Inc ...... E 785 843-2622
Lawrence *(G-5094)*
Sparks Music Co ...... F 620 442-5030
Arkansas City *(G-182)*
Wichita Band Instrument Co ...... F 316 684-0291
Wichita *(G-15979)*

MUSICAL INSTRUMENTS & SPLYS STORES: String instruments

Kansas City Strings Violin Sp ...... E 913 677-0400
Shawnee Mission *(G-11511)*

MUSICAL INSTRUMENTS: Organs

Reuter Organ Co Inc ...... E 785 843-2622
Lawrence *(G-5094)*

NAIL SALONS

Beauty Brands LLC ...... E 913 663-4848
Shawnee Mission *(G-11157)*
California Nail Salon ...... F 316 942-5400
Wichita *(G-13927)*
Images Salon & Day Spa ...... F 785 843-2138
Lawrence *(G-4909)*
Nail Perfection LLC ...... F 913 722-0799
Roeland Park *(G-10228)*
Nail Pro ...... F 913 402-0882
Shawnee Mission *(G-11665)*
Nailery ...... F 913 599-2225
Overland Park *(G-9067)*
Nailery Too ...... F 913 599-3331
Shawnee Mission *(G-11666)*
Prim and Polished LLC ...... F 316 516-2537
Derby *(G-1265)*
Professional Hairstyling ...... F 913 888-3536
Lenexa *(G-6072)*
Royal Spa ...... F 316 681-0002
Wichita *(G-15488)*
Xiphium Hair Salon ...... F 913 696-1616
Leawood *(G-5603)*

NAMEPLATES

Barton Industries Inc ...... G 316 262-3171
Wichita *(G-13815)*

NATIONAL SECURITY FORCES

Dla Document Services ...... G 913 684-5591
Fort Leavenworth *(G-1937)*

NATIONAL SECURITY, GOVERNMENT: Army

Army & Air Force Exchange Svc ....E 785 239-4366
Fort Riley *(G-1945)*
U S Army Corps of Engineers ....D 785 537-7392
Manhattan *(G-6834)*
U S Army Corps of Engineers ....F 785 597-5144
Perry *(G-9774)*
U S Army Corps of Engineers ....F 785 453-2201
Vassar *(G-13372)*
United States Dept of Army ....D 785 240-0308
Fort Riley *(G-1952)*
United States Dept of Army ....B 913 684-2747
Fort Leavenworth *(G-1942)*
United States Dept of Army ....E 785 239-2385
Fort Riley *(G-1951)*
United States Dept of Army ....B 913 684-6000
Fort Leavenworth *(G-1943)*
United States Dept of Army ....E 913 684-2151
Fort Leavenworth *(G-1944)*
United States Dept of Army ....A 785 239-7000
Fort Riley *(G-1953)*

NATIONAL SECURITY, GOVERNMENT: National Guard

Adjutant Generals Dept Kans ....F 785 862-1020
Topeka *(G-12288)*

NATURAL GAS COMPRESSING SVC, On-Site

Archrock Inc ....E 620 241-8740
McPherson *(G-6937)*
Great Plins Gas Cmpression LLC ....C 620 544-3578
Hugoton *(G-3164)*

NATURAL GAS DISTRIBUTION TO CONSUMERS

Atmos Energy Corporation ....F 785 258-2300
Herington *(G-2970)*
Atmos Energy Corporation ....D 913 254-6300
Olathe *(G-7540)*
Black Hills/Kansas Gas ....E 605 721-1700
Lawrence *(G-4759)*
Black Hills/Kansas Gas ....F 605 721-1700
Garden City *(G-2112)*
Black Hills/Kansas Gas ....E 605 721-1700
Wichita *(G-13855)*
Black Hills/Kansas Gas ....F 605 721-1700
Dodge City *(G-1309)*
Black Hills/Kansas Gas ....F 605 721-1700
Liberal *(G-6284)*
Duke Energy Corporation ....F 620 855-6830
Cimarron *(G-824)*
Kinder Morgan Kansas Inc ....G 620 384-7830
Syracuse *(G-12228)*
Midwest Energy Inc ....F 620 872-2179
Scott City *(G-10822)*
Northern Natural Gas Company ....F 620 277-2364
Holcomb *(G-3076)*
Oneok Inc ....E 913 319-8600
Overland Park *(G-9104)*
Oneok Inc ....F 800 794-4780
Kansas City *(G-4295)*
Oneok Inc ....F 785 738-9700
Beloit *(G-499)*
Oneok Inc ....E 620 728-4303
Hutchinson *(G-3393)*
Oneok Inc ....D 785 431-4201
Topeka *(G-12947)*
Oneok Inc ....E 316 821-2722
Wichita *(G-15220)*
Oneok Energy Services Co II ....E 785 274-4900
Topeka *(G-12949)*
Southern Star Central Gas Pipe ....E 913 422-6304
Lenexa *(G-6142)*
Southern Star Central Gas Pipe ....E 785 448-4800
Welda *(G-13487)*
Sterling Energy Resources Inc ....F 913 469-9072
Overland Park *(G-9360)*
Williams Natural Gas Company ....F 913 422-4496
Shawnee Mission *(G-12011)*

NATURAL GAS LIQUIDS PRODUCTION

Oneok Inc ....E 620 562-4205
Bushton *(G-654)*
Oneok Field Services Co LLC ....F 620 248-3258
Pratt *(G-10128)*
Oneok Field Services Co LLC ....D 620 356-2231
Ulysses *(G-13309)*
Panhandle Eastrn Pipe Line LP ....E 620 624-7241
Liberal *(G-6353)*
Tri Resources Inc ....G 620 982-4568
Pawnee Rock *(G-9755)*

NATURAL GAS PRODUCTION

Natural Gas Pipeline Amer LLC ....G 620 885-4505
Minneola *(G-7127)*
One Gas Inc ....C 913 319-8617
Overland Park *(G-9103)*
Red Hills Resources Inc ....G 620 669-9996
Hutchinson *(G-3421)*

NATURAL GAS TRANSMISSION

ANR Pipeline Company ....F 620 723-2381
Greensburg *(G-2672)*
ANR Pipeline Company ....F 785 948-2670
Havensville *(G-2739)*
ANR Pipeline Company ....F 785 479-5814
Enterprise *(G-1853)*
Natural Gas Pipeline Amer LLC ....G 785 568-2231
Glasco *(G-2422)*
Northern Natural Gas Company ....E 620 675-2239
Kismet *(G-4631)*
Northern Natural Gas Company ....E 785 455-3311
Clifton *(G-902)*
Northern Natural Gas Company ....E 620 723-2151
Mullinville *(G-7210)*
Northern Natural Gas Company ....E 620 298-5111
Cunningham *(G-1188)*
Oneok Inc ....E 785 483-2501
Russell *(G-10283)*
Oneok Inc ....F 620 341-7054
Emporia *(G-1810)*
Oneok Inc ....D 785 431-4201
Topeka *(G-12947)*
Oneok Inc ....E 785 575-8554
Topeka *(G-12948)*
Oneok Inc ....E 620 792-0603
Great Bend *(G-2618)*
Oneok Inc ....F 620 669-2300
Hutchinson *(G-3394)*
Oneok Inc ....F 785 223-5408
Junction City *(G-3733)*
Oneok Inc ....E 620 672-6706
Pratt *(G-10127)*
Oneok Inc ....E 785 822-3522
Salina *(G-10622)*
Oneok Inc ....F 316 322-8131
El Dorado *(G-1587)*
Oneok Field Services Co LLC ....F 620 544-2179
Hugoton *(G-3174)*
Panhandle Eastrn Pipe Line LP ....E 620 465-2201
Haven *(G-2735)*
Panhandle Eastrn Pipe Line LP ....F 620 475-3226
Olpe *(G-8167)*
Panhandle Eastrn Pipe Line LP ....E 913 837-5163
Louisburg *(G-6461)*
Tallgrass Energy LP ....F 913 928-6060
Leawood *(G-5566)*
Tallgrass Energy Partners LP ....F 620 355-7122
Lakin *(G-4660)*
Tallgrass Interstate Gas Trans ....F 913 928-6060
Leawood *(G-5568)*
West Wichita Gas Gathering LLC ....F 970 764-6653
Cheney *(G-798)*

NATURAL GAS TRANSMISSION & DISTRIBUTION

Dcp Operating Company LP ....E 620 626-1201
Liberal *(G-6301)*
Edwards County Gas Company ....F 316 682-3022
Wichita *(G-14262)*
Evergy Kansas Central Inc ....D 785 575-1352
Topeka *(G-12584)*
Southern Star Central Gas Pipe ....E 620 657-2130
Satanta *(G-10791)*
Southern Star Central Gas Pipe ....F 620 257-7800
Lyons *(G-6498)*
Star Transport LLC ....E 913 396-5070
Overland Park *(G-9355)*
Tallgrass Energy Partners LP ....E 913 928-6060
Leawood *(G-5567)*

NATURAL GASOLINE PRODUCTION

Robinson Supply LLC ....G 620 251-0490
Coffeyville *(G-973)*
Southern Star Central Gas Pipe ....E 620 657-2130
Satanta *(G-10791)*
Woolsey Petroleum Corporation ....F 316 267-4379
Wichita *(G-16069)*

NATURAL RESOURCE PRESERVATION SVCS

Grassland Heritage Foundation ....F 913 856-4784
Olathe *(G-7740)*
Natural Rsource Protection Inc ....E 316 303-0505
Wichita *(G-15155)*

NAVIGATIONAL SYSTEMS & INSTRUMENTS

Airfield Technology Inc ....G 913 780-9800
Olathe *(G-7515)*
Garmin International Inc ....A 913 397-8200
Olathe *(G-7722)*

NEIGHBORHOOD DEVELOPMENT GROUP

Housing and Credit Counseling ....E 785 234-0217
Topeka *(G-12705)*

NEW & USED CAR DEALERS

Bradford Built Inc ....E 785 325-3300
Washington *(G-13460)*
Conklin Fangman Investment Co ....C 620 662-4467
Hutchinson *(G-3245)*
Perl Auto Center Inc ....F 620 251-4050
Coffeyville *(G-972)*

NEWSPAPERS, WHOLESALE

Ascension Via Christi Hospital ....F 316 268-6096
Wichita *(G-13750)*
Main Street Media Inc ....F 785 483-2116
Russell *(G-10281)*

NONDURABLE GOODS WHOLESALERS, NEC

K & F Distributors Inc ....F 316 213-2030
Kechi *(G-4570)*
Omc Distribution Center ....F 913 791-3592
Olathe *(G-7957)*

NOVELTIES, DURABLE, WHOLESALE

U S Toy Co Inc ....E 913 642-8247
Leawood *(G-5587)*

NOVELTIES: Plastic

Century Manufacturing Inc ....C 316 636-5423
Bel Aire *(G-430)*

NUCLEAR ELECTRIC POWER GENERATION

Wolf Creek Nuclear Oper Corp ....A 620 364-4141
Burlington *(G-645)*

NURSERIES & LAWN & GARDEN SPLY STORE, RET: Lawn/Garden Splys

Heritage Tractor Inc ....E 785 235-5100
Topeka *(G-12686)*
Skaggs Inc ....E 620 672-5312
Pratt *(G-10148)*
Tarwaters Inc ....E 785 286-2390
Topeka *(G-13143)*

NURSERIES & LAWN & GARDEN SPLY STORES, RETAIL

Hermes Nursery Inc ....E 913 441-2400
Shawnee Mission *(G-11429)*
Hongs Landscape & Nursery Inc ....F 316 687-3492
Wichita *(G-14635)*
Jacksons Greenhouse & Grdn Ctr ....F 785 232-3416
Topeka *(G-12735)*
Jerrys Nursery and Ldscpg Inc ....F 913 721-1444
Kansas City *(G-4122)*
Landscape Outfitters LLC ....F 620 221-1108
Winfield *(G-16154)*

NURSERIES & LAWN & GARDEN SPLY STORES, RETAIL: Fertilizer

AG Connection Sales Inc ....F 785 336-2121
Seneca *(G-10856)*

AG Valley Coop Non-Stock ....F 785 877-5131
Norton *(G-7440)*
Archer-Daniels-Midland Company ....F 620 657-3411
Satanta *(G-10776)*
Archer-Daniels-Midland Company ....F 620 872-2174
Scott City *(G-10804)*
Archer-Daniels-Midland Company ....F 785 671-3171
Oakley *(G-7471)*
Archer-Daniels-Midland Company ....G 785 694-2286
Brewster *(G-582)*
Dodge City Cooperative Exch ....F 620 227-8671
Dodge City *(G-1345)*
Farmers Cooperative Elev Co ....F 316 835-2261
Halstead *(G-2699)*
Farmers Union Coop Assn ....F 785 632-5632
Clay Center *(G-863)*
Frontier Ag Inc ....F 785 694-2281
Brewster *(G-583)*
Koch Industries Inc ....E 620 227-8631
Dodge City *(G-1395)*
MFA Enterprises Inc ....F 620 237-4668
Moran *(G-7162)*
Nemaha County Cooperative Assn ....F 785 456-6924
Belvue *(G-507)*

NURSERIES & LAWN & GARDEN SPLY STORES, RETAIL: Sod

Grass Pad Inc ....D 913 764-4100
Olathe *(G-7739)*

NURSERIES & LAWN & GARDEN SPLY STORES, RETAIL: Top Soil

Apac-Kansas Inc ....E 785 625-3459
Hutchinson *(G-3201)*

NURSERIES & LAWN/GARDEN SPLY STORE, RET: Lawnmowers/Tractors

American Implement Inc ....E 620 872-7244
Scott City *(G-10803)*
Berry Companies Inc ....F 620 277-2290
Garden City *(G-2109)*
Bruna Brothers Implement LLC ....E 785 325-2232
Washington *(G-13461)*
Bti Ness City ....E 785 798-2251
Ness City *(G-7253)*
Colby A G Center LLC ....F 785 462-6132
Colby *(G-995)*
Concordia Tractor Inc ....E 785 632-3181
Clay Center *(G-856)*
Concordia Tractor Inc ....F 785 263-3051
Abilene *(G-20)*
Easy Money Pawn Shop Inc ....G 316 687-2727
Wichita *(G-14255)*
Engels Sales & Service Center ....F 785 877-3391
Norton *(G-7444)*
Excel Industries Inc ....F 800 942-4911
Hesston *(G-2989)*
Kanequip Inc ....F 620 225-0016
Dodge City *(G-1384)*
Kanequip Inc ....F 785 632-3441
Clay Center *(G-869)*
Karls Tire & Auto Service Inc ....F 316 685-5338
Wichita *(G-14833)*
Plp Inc ....E 620 532-3106
Kingman *(G-4610)*
Romans Outdoor Power Inc ....F 620 331-2970
Independence *(G-3556)*
Romans Outdoor Power Inc ....E 913 837-5225
Louisburg *(G-6466)*

NURSERIES & LAWN/GARDEN SPLY STORES, RET: Garden Splys/Tools

Eastside Mkt Westside Mkt LLC ....G 785 532-8686
Manhattan *(G-6619)*
Gablers Nursery Inc ....F 913 642-4164
Shawnee Mission *(G-11389)*
Johnsons Garden Center Inc ....E 316 942-3751
Wichita *(G-14769)*
Riedel Garden Center ....F 785 628-2877
Hays *(G-2900)*

NURSERIES/LAWN/GARDEN SPLY STORES, RET: Hydroponic Eqpt/Sply

Total Turfcare Inc ....F 785 827-6983
Salina *(G-10735)*

NURSERIES/LAWN/GRDN SPLY STORE, RET: Nursery Stck, Seed/Bulb

Beachner Grain Inc ....F 620 244-3277
Erie *(G-1856)*
Bornholdt Plantland Inc ....F 620 662-0544
Hutchinson *(G-3218)*
Grass Pad Inc ....E 913 681-8948
Bucyrus *(G-597)*
Hillside Nursery Inc ....F 316 686-6414
Wichita *(G-14614)*
Loma Vista Garden Center Inc ....E 913 897-7010
Ottawa *(G-8284)*
Polansky Seed Inc ....F 785 527-2271
Belleville *(G-462)*
Star Seed Inc ....F 800 782-7311
Osborne *(G-8219)*
Stutzman Greenhouse Inc ....E 620 662-0559
Hutchinson *(G-3454)*
Tree Top Nursery and Landscape ....E 316 686-7491
Wichita *(G-15797)*

NURSERY & GARDEN CENTERS

Alternative Building Tech ....F 913 856-4536
Gardner *(G-2325)*
Blackburn Nursery Inc ....E 785 272-2707
Topeka *(G-12387)*
Chisholm Trail Country Str LLC ....F 316 283-3276
Newton *(G-7328)*
Hoffmanns Green Industries ....E 316 634-1500
Wichita *(G-14624)*
Kanequip Inc ....F 785 267-9200
Topeka *(G-12754)*
Prairie Hills Nursery Inc ....F 620 665-5500
Hutchinson *(G-3410)*
R & H Implement Company Inc ....F 620 384-7421
Syracuse *(G-12230)*
Treescape Inc ....E 316 733-6388
Andover *(G-112)*

NURSERY SCHOOLS

Basic Beginnings Educational ....F 316 721-7946
Wichita *(G-13818)*
Kindercare Learning Ctrs LLC ....E 316 721-0168
Wichita *(G-14860)*

NURSERY STOCK, WHOLESALE

Grass Pad Inc ....D 913 764-4100
Olathe *(G-7739)*
Hermes Nursery Inc ....E 913 441-2400
Shawnee Mission *(G-11429)*
Jerrys Nursery and Ldscpg Inc ....F 913 721-1444
Kansas City *(G-4122)*
Loma Vista Garden Center Inc ....E 913 897-7010
Ottawa *(G-8284)*

NURSING & PERSONAL CARE FACILITIES, NEC

Guest Home Estates ....F 620 431-7115
Pittsburg *(G-9869)*
Just In Time Adult Care ....F 913 371-3391
Kansas City *(G-4130)*
Woodland Hlth Ctr Oprtions LLC ....D 785 234-6147
Topeka *(G-13251)*

NURSING CARE FACILITIES: Skilled

Accredo Health Group Inc ....E 913 339-7100
Lenexa *(G-5622)*
Ahc of Overland Park LLC ....F 913 232-2413
Overland Park *(G-8360)*
America Care Quaker Hill Manor ....E 620 848-3797
Baxter Springs *(G-392)*
American Retirement Corp ....E 913 248-1500
Shawnee Mission *(G-11108)*
Andbe Home Inc ....D 785 877-2601
Norton *(G-7441)*
Apostolic Christian Home ....C 785 284-3471
Sabetha *(G-10305)*
Arkansas City Presbt Manor Inc ....F 620 442-8700
Arkansas City *(G-147)*
Arma Care Center LLC ....E 620 347-4103
Arma *(G-188)*
Augusta L Lakepoint L C ....F 316 733-8100
Wichita *(G-13768)*
Avita Assisted Living At Derby ....F 316 260-4447
Derby *(G-1221)*
Beaver Dam Health Care Center ....E 620 231-1120
Pittsburg *(G-9824)*
Beaver Dam Health Care Center ....D 316 321-4444
El Dorado *(G-1535)*
Beaver Dam Health Care Center ....D 913 422-5952
Edwardsville *(G-1495)*
Beaver Dam Health Care Center ....E 620 273-6369
Cottonwood Falls *(G-1151)*
Bethany HM Assn Lindsborg Kans ....C 785 227-2334
Lindsborg *(G-6394)*
Beverly Enterprises-Kansas LLC ....D 785 454-3321
Downs *(G-1468)*
Beverly Enterprises-Kansas LLC ....E 785 461-5417
Wakefield *(G-13398)*
Brandon Woods Retirement Cmnty ....C 785 838-8000
Lawrence *(G-4766)*
Brighton Place W Oper Co LLC ....E 785 232-1212
Topeka *(G-12407)*
Brookdale Overland Pk Glenwood ....F 913 385-2052
Overland Park *(G-8487)*
Brookdale Senior Living Commun ....E 785 628-1111
Hays *(G-2761)*
Brookdale Senior Living Commun ....E 913 894-6979
Shawnee Mission *(G-11183)*
Brookdale Senior Living Commun ....F 316 684-3100
Wichita *(G-13897)*
Brookdale Senior Living Commun ....F 785 263-7400
Abilene *(G-17)*
Brookdale Senior Living Commun ....E 620 342-1000
Emporia *(G-1708)*
Brookdale Senior Living Commun ....F 620 792-7000
Great Bend *(G-2522)*
Brookdale Senior Living Commun ....E 785 820-2991
Salina *(G-10432)*
Brookdale Senior Living Commun ....F 620 241-6600
Conway *(G-1133)*
Brookdale Senior Living Commun ....F 620 326-3031
Wellington *(G-13492)*
Brookdale Senior Living Commun ....E 620 225-7555
Dodge City *(G-1313)*
Buhler Sunshine Home Inc ....D 620 543-2251
Buhler *(G-614)*
Caregiver Support System ....E 214 207-7273
Marion *(G-6867)*
Catholic Diocese of Wichita ....E 316 269-3900
Wichita *(G-13963)*
Cedars Inc ....C 620 241-0919
McPherson *(G-6942)*
Centennial Healthcare Corp ....C 913 829-2273
Olathe *(G-7584)*
Cheney Golden Age Home Inc ....D 316 540-3691
Cheney *(G-789)*
City of Logan ....D 785 689-4227
Logan *(G-6421)*
City of Stockton ....E 785 425-6754
Stockton *(G-12181)*
CLC Bonner Springs ....D 913 441-2515
Bonner Springs *(G-545)*
Clearwtr Nrsing Rhabilitation ....F 620 584-2271
Clearwater *(G-889)*
College Hl Nrsing Rhbilitation ....E 316 685-9291
Wichita *(G-14057)*
Comfort Care Homes Inc ....E 316 685-3322
Wichita *(G-14063)*
Community Healthcare Sys Inc ....D 785 437-3734
Saint Marys *(G-10361)*
Congregational Home ....C 785 274-3350
Topeka *(G-12501)*
Country Place Senior Living ....F 785 336-6868
Seneca *(G-10860)*
Countryside Health Center ....E 785 234-6147
Topeka *(G-12515)*
County of Hamilton ....E 620 384-7780
Syracuse *(G-12223)*
County of Johnson ....C 913 894-8383
Olathe *(G-7621)*
County of Mitchell ....F 785 738-2266
Beloit *(G-482)*
County of Stevens ....D 620 544-2023
Hugoton *(G-3155)*
Cumbernauld Village Inc ....D 620 221-4141
Winfield *(G-16137)*
Delmar Gardens Lenexa Oper LLC ....D 913 492-1130
Lenexa *(G-5808)*
Delmar Gardens of Lenexa Inc ....C 913 492-1130
Lenexa *(G-5809)*
Deseret Health Group ....F 785 476-2623
Kensington *(G-4574)*
Deseret Hlth Rhab At Onaga LLC ....E 785 889-4227
Onaga *(G-8174)*

Dickinson County..................................D....... 785 263-1431
Abilene *(G-24)*
Diversicare Leasing Corp........................F........ 316 524-3211
Haysville *(G-2939)*
Diversicare Leasing Corp........................F....... 620 431-4940
Chanute *(G-724)*
Diversicare Leasing Corp........................F....... 620 767-5172
Council Grove *(G-1163)*
Diversicare of Hutchinson ....F....... 620 669-9393
Hutchinson *(G-3267)*
Diversicare of Larned LLC ....D....... 620 285-6914
Larned *(G-4701)*
Eagle Care Inc..F....... 785 227-2304
Lindsborg *(G-6397)*
Eaglecrest Operations LLC.........................F....... 785 272-1535
Topeka *(G-12566)*
East Orlndo Hlth Rehab Ctr Inc...................D....... 913 383-9866
Shawnee Mission *(G-11326)*
Enterprise Cmnty Nursing Hm....................E....... 785 263-8278
Enterprise *(G-1854)*
Evangelical Lutheran...................................C....... 620 663-1189
Hutchinson *(G-3280)*
Evangelical Lutheran...................................D....... 620 624-3832
Liberal *(G-6308)*
Evangelical Lutheran...................................D....... 785 472-3167
Ellsworth *(G-1674)*
Eventide Convalescent Center...................D....... 785 233-8918
Topeka *(G-12582)*
Five Star Quality Care-Ks LLC...................D....... 620 564-2337
Ellinwood *(G-1632)*
Five Star Senior Living Inc.........................D....... 913 648-4500
Leawood *(G-5406)*
Flint Hills Care Center ....D....... 620 342-3280
Emporia *(G-1757)*
Fountainview Nursing &..............................F....... 316 776-2194
Rose Hill *(G-10239)*
Fowler Nursing Home.................................E....... 620 646-5215
Fowler *(G-2020)*
Frankfort Community Care Home ....D....... 785 292-4442
Frankfort *(G-2022)*
Friends Kansas Christn HM Inc....................C....... 316 283-6600
Newton *(G-7348)*
Frontline Management................................D....... 620 227-8551
Dodge City *(G-1363)*
Garden Vly Retirement Vlg LLC...................C....... 620 275-9651
Garden City *(G-2184)*
Genesis Healthcare Corporation ....F....... 785 594-6492
Baldwin City *(G-362)*
Ggnsc Holdings LLC ....F....... 913 422-5832
Kansas City *(G-4033)*
Glencare/Cherryvale CA Ltd Pt....................E....... 620 336-2102
Cherryvale *(G-807)*
Golden Boomers Home................................F....... 316 730-3110
Wichita *(G-14481)*
Golden Lc Edwardsvill ....E....... 913 441-1900
Edwardsville *(G-1501)*
Golden Living Center...................................F....... 913 727-1284
Lansing *(G-4674)*
Golden Livingcenter Room 132b..................F....... 785 658-2505
Wilson *(G-16106)*
Good Samaritan Society ....C....... 620 663-1189
Hutchinson *(G-3302)*
Good Shepherd Villages Inc ....E....... 785 244-6418
Summerfield *(G-12214)*
Grace Grdns Assistd Lvng Fclty ....F....... 913 685-4800
Leawood *(G-5416)*
Grace Management Inc................................A....... 913 367-2655
Atchison *(G-232)*
Great Bend Manor.......................................D....... 620 792-2448
Great Bend *(G-2583)*
Greeley Cnty Hosp & Long TRM C ....D....... 620 376-4225
Tribune *(G-13268)*
Hays Medical Center Inc.............................A....... 785 623-5000
Hays *(G-2834)*
Health Management of Kansas....................C....... 620 251-5190
Coffeyville *(G-945)*
Heart Living Centers Colo LLC...................D....... 817 739-8529
Salina *(G-10537)*
Herington Opco LLC....................................F....... 785 789-4750
Herington *(G-2975)*
Heritage House Assisted Living ....F....... 620 473-3456
Humboldt *(G-3184)*
Highland Healthcare and.............................E....... 785 442-3217
Highland *(G-3029)*
Homestead Inc ....D....... 785 325-2361
Washington *(G-13465)*
Homestead of Augusta.................................D....... 316 775-1000
Augusta *(G-325)*
Hospice Care of Kansas...............................E....... 316 283-2116
McPherson *(G-6975)*
Hospice of Graham County..........................C....... 785 421-2121
Hill City *(G-3035)*
Hospice of Reno County Inc.........................F....... 620 669-3773
Hutchinson *(G-3313)*
Hospital District 2 Rice Cnty........................D....... 620 897-6266
Little River *(G-6419)*
Hre—Colorado Springs LLC ....D....... 817 739-8529
Salina *(G-10548)*
Hutch Good Samaritan Village ....E....... 620 663-1189
Hutchinson *(G-3316)*
Kansas Long Term Care Phys ....D....... 316 315-0145
Wichita *(G-14813)*
Kansas Masonic Home.................................C....... 316 269-7500
Wichita *(G-14814)*
Lane County Hospital..................................D....... 620 397-5321
Dighton *(G-1287)*
Lansing Care Rhbltion Ctr LLC ....D....... 913 727-1284
Lansing *(G-4679)*
Las Villas Del Norte ....D....... 760 741-1046
Junction City *(G-3720)*
Lawrence Memorial Hospital End.................A....... 785 505-3315
Lawrence *(G-4974)*
Lcrc...F....... 913 383-2085
Prairie Village *(G-10044)*
Leisure Homestead Association ....E....... 620 234-5208
Stafford *(G-12106)*
Leisure Homestead At St John.....................E....... 620 549-3541
Saint John *(G-10355)*
Leisure Operations LLC ....D....... 718 327-5762
Overland Park *(G-8952)*
Liberty Assisted Living Center....................E....... 785 273-0886
Topeka *(G-12842)*
Liberty Healthcare of Oklahoma..................D....... 785 823-7107
Salina *(G-10581)*
Liberty Terrace Care Center........................C....... 816 792-2211
Overland Park *(G-8956)*
Life Care Center Burlington.........................D....... 620 364-2117
Burlington *(G-638)*
Life Care Centers America Inc.....................F....... 423 472-9585
Overland Park *(G-8957)*
Life Care Centers America Inc.....................C....... 913 631-2273
Shawnee Mission *(G-11569)*
Life Care Centers America Inc.....................D....... 785 336-3528
Seneca *(G-10872)*
Life Care Services LLC................................C....... 785 762-2162
Junction City *(G-3721)*
Lifespace Communities Inc ....C....... 913 383-2085
Shawnee Mission *(G-11570)*
Linn Community Nursing Home...................D....... 785 348-5551
Linn *(G-6408)*
Logan County Manor...................................F....... 785 672-8109
Oakley *(G-7480)*
Long Term Care Specialists LLC...................F....... 620 326-0251
Wellington *(G-13513)*
Lsl of Derby Ks LLC....................................D....... 316 788-3739
Derby *(G-1260)*
Manhattan Rtrment Fndation Inc.................B....... 785 537-4610
Manhattan *(G-6727)*
Manor Care of Wichita Ks LLC ....F....... 316 684-8018
Wichita *(G-15004)*
Manor of Liberal Inc....................................D....... 620 624-0130
Liberal *(G-6339)*
Marysville Health Corporation.....................D....... 785 562-2424
Marysville *(G-6899)*
McCrite Retirement Association..................C....... 785 267-2960
Topeka *(G-12868)*
McPherson Care Center LLC ....E....... 620 241-5360
McPherson *(G-6993)*
Meade Hospital District...............................C....... 620 873-2146
Meade *(G-7052)*
Medicalodges Inc...D....... 620 429-4317
Columbus *(G-1081)*
Medicalodges Inc...D....... 316 755-1288
Valley Center *(G-13348)*
Medicalodges Inc...D....... 620 223-0210
Fort Scott *(G-1985)*
Medicalodges Inc...D....... 620 231-0300
Pittsburg *(G-9902)*
Medicalodges Inc...D....... 620 429-2134
Columbus *(G-1082)*
Medicalodges Inc...D....... 620 583-7418
Eureka *(G-1894)*
Mennonite Bethesda Society.......................D....... 620 367-2291
Goessel *(G-2458)*
Mennonite Frndship Communities...............C....... 620 663-7175
South Hutchinson *(G-12062)*
Meridian Nursing Center Inc........................D....... 316 942-8471
Wichita *(G-15041)*
Midland Care Connection Inc ....C....... 785 232-2044
Topeka *(G-12892)*
Midwest Health Services Inc........................C....... 785 440-0399
Topeka *(G-12897)*
Midwest Health Services Inc........................B....... 913 829-4663
Olathe *(G-7896)*
Midwest Health Services Inc........................E....... 913 894-0014
Lenexa *(G-6002)*
Midwest Health Services Inc........................E....... 913 663-3351
Leawood *(G-5484)*
Midwest Health Services Inc........................D....... 785 776-0065
Manhattan *(G-6749)*
Midwest Health Services Inc........................D....... 785 233-0544
Topeka *(G-12900)*
Midwest Health Services Inc........................C....... 620 276-7643
Garden City *(G-2234)*
Midwest Health Services Inc........................C....... 785 665-7124
Overbrook *(G-8326)*
Minneola Hospital District 2.........................D....... 620 885-4238
Minneola *(G-7126)*
New Hope Services.....................................F....... 620 231-9895
Pittsburg *(G-9911)*
Nhi of Chanute LLC ....D....... 620 431-4940
Chanute *(G-746)*
Nursing By Numbers LLC ....F....... 913 788-0566
Olathe *(G-7926)*
Oxford Grand Assisted Living.......................D....... 316 927-2007
Wichita *(G-15243)*
Parkside Homes Inc.....................................D....... 620 947-2301
Hillsboro *(G-3053)*
Pine Village..C....... 620 345-2901
Moundridge *(G-7196)*
Pinnacle Hlth Fclties Xviii LP.......................D....... 913 441-2515
Bonner Springs *(G-571)*
Pioneer Ridge Ind Living..............................F....... 785 749-6785
Lawrence *(G-5067)*
Pioneer Ridge Retirement Cmnty..................C....... 785 344-1100
Lawrence *(G-5068)*
Pleasant Valley Nursing LLC ....F....... 620 725-3154
Sedan *(G-10845)*
Prairie Mission Retirement Vlg.....................D....... 620 449-2400
Saint Paul *(G-10384)*
Pratt Health and Rehab ....D....... 620 672-6541
Pratt *(G-10140)*
Premier Living By Warden LLC ....E....... 316 945-2028
Wichita *(G-15331)*
Presbyterian Manors Inc ....E....... 620 225-4474
Dodge City *(G-1421)*
Presbyterian Manors Inc ....D....... 316 942-7456
Wichita *(G-15335)*
Presbyterian Manors Inc ....D....... 913 334-3666
Kansas City *(G-4333)*
Presbyterian Manors Inc ....D....... 785 825-1366
Salina *(G-10641)*
Presbyterian Manors Inc ....D....... 785 632-5646
Clay Center *(G-876)*
Prime Healthcare Services Inc......................A....... 913 596-4000
Kansas City *(G-4337)*
Providence Place Inc...................................F....... 913 596-4200
Kansas City *(G-4348)*
Rh Montgomery Properties Inc.....................E....... 785 445-3732
Russell *(G-10290)*
Rh Montgomery Properties Inc.....................D....... 913 837-2916
Louisburg *(G-6465)*
Rh Montgomery Properties Inc.....................D....... 620 725-3154
Sedan *(G-10846)*
Rh Montgomery Properties Inc.....................E....... 785 284-3411
Sabetha *(G-10324)*
Rh Montgomery Properties Inc.....................E....... 785 528-3138
Osage City *(G-8188)*
Richmond Healthcare...................................D....... 785 835-6135
Richmond *(G-10204)*
Rolling Hills Health Center..........................E....... 785 273-2202
Topeka *(G-13027)*
Royal Terrace Healthcare LLC ....D....... 913 829-2273
Olathe *(G-8045)*
Rush County Nursing Home Soc ....F....... 785 222-2574
La Crosse *(G-4638)*
Saint Lukes Hosp Garnett Inc.......................C....... 785 448-3131
Garnett *(G-2388)*
Salem Hospital Inc.......................................D....... 620 947-2272
Hillsboro *(G-3057)*
Sandpiper Healthcare and............................C....... 316 945-3606
Wichita *(G-15517)*
Seniortrust of Haysville LLC.........................C....... 316 524-3211
Haysville *(G-2959)*
Shawnee Gardens Health.............................C....... 913 631-2146
Shawnee *(G-11027)*
Shepherd of Plains Foundation....................E....... 620 855-3498
Cimarron *(G-836)*
Southwest Medical Center............................E....... 620 624-1651
Liberal *(G-6372)*

St Catherine Hospital.....F 620 272-2519
Garden City *(G-2289)*
St Johns Rest Home Inc.....D 785 628-3241
Hays *(G-2911)*
Stanton County Hosp Aux Inc.....C 620 492-6250
Johnson *(G-3662)*
Sunbrdge Asssted Lving Rsdnces.....D 913 385-2052
Shawnee Mission *(G-11907)*
Sunrise Senior Living Inc.....D 913 262-1611
Prairie Village *(G-10070)*
Sunrise Senior Living Inc.....D 913 307-0665
Lenexa *(G-6160)*
Sunrise Senior Living LLC.....D 913 685-3340
Overland Park *(G-9376)*
Sunrise Senior Living LLC.....D 913 906-0200
Leawood *(G-5564)*
Sunrise Senior Living Svcs Inc.....E 913 262-1611
Prairie Village *(G-10071)*
Sunset Home Inc.....D 785 243-2720
Concordia *(G-1131)*
Sunset Manor Inc.....C 620 231-7340
Frontenac *(G-2066)*
Survey Companies LLC.....E 620 862-5291
Haviland *(G-2742)*
Susan B Allen Memorial Hosp.....B 316 322-4510
El Dorado *(G-1607)*
Sweet Life At Rosehill.....C 913 962-7600
Overland Park *(G-9382)*
Thi of Kansas Indian Meadows.....E 913 649-5110
Overland Park *(G-9406)*
Topeka Adult Care Center.....F 785 233-7397
Topeka *(G-13164)*
Truecare Nursing Services LLC.....E 626 818-2420
Wichita *(G-15810)*
Tutera Group Inc.....D 913 381-6000
Shawnee Mission *(G-11952)*
Tutera Group Inc.....E 913 851-0215
Shawnee Mission *(G-11951)*
United Methodist Homes Inc.....B 785 478-9440
Topeka *(G-13206)*
Valley View Senior Life LLC.....D 316 733-1144
Junction City *(G-3763)*
Via Christi Vlg Pittsburg Inc.....E 620 235-0020
Pittsburg *(G-9956)*
Victory Hill Retirement Cmnty.....E 913 299-1166
Kansas City *(G-4520)*
Villa St Francis Inc.....C 913 254-3264
Olathe *(G-8140)*
Vintage Group Inc.....E 316 321-7777
El Dorado *(G-1612)*
Vintage Group Inc.....E 785 483-5882
Russell *(G-10302)*
Vintage Park Assisted Living.....F 785 456-8997
Wamego *(G-13447)*
Vitas Healthcare Corp Midwest.....E 913 722-1631
Overland Park *(G-9468)*
Vitas Healthcare Corporation.....E 913 722-1631
Lenexa *(G-6216)*
Waterfront Assisted Living.....F 316 945-3344
Wichita *(G-15936)*
Wathena Healthcare.....E 785 989-3141
Wathena *(G-13479)*
Wesley Retirement Community.....C 316 636-1000
Wichita *(G-15955)*
Wheat State Manor Inc.....D 316 799-2181
Whitewater *(G-13573)*
Wichita Cnty Long Term Rest Hm.....D 620 375-4600
Leoti *(G-6262)*
Windsor Place At-Home Care.....E 620 331-3388
Independence *(G-3573)*
Woodlawn Care and Rehab LLC.....F 316 691-9999
Wichita *(G-16067)*

NURSING HOME, EXC SKILLED & INTERMEDIATE CARE FACILITY

Carondelet Health.....D 913 345-1745
Overland Park *(G-8520)*
Carrington House LLC.....E 316 262-5516
Wichita *(G-13954)*
Cherry Village Benevolence.....D 620 792-2165
Great Bend *(G-2538)*
City of Stockton.....E 785 425-6754
Stockton *(G-12181)*
Clyde Development Inc.....E 785 446-2818
Clyde *(G-906)*
Comfort Care Homes Inc.....E 316 685-3322
Wichita *(G-14063)*
Dawson Place Inc.....E 785 421-3414
Hill City *(G-3032)*
Deaconess Long Term Care of MI.....C 785 242-5399
Ottawa *(G-8264)*
Deaconess Long Term Care of MI.....F 785 242-9378
Ottawa *(G-8265)*
Evangelical Lutheran.....C 620 663-1189
Hutchinson *(G-3280)*
Evangelical Lutheran.....D 785 475-2245
Oberlin *(G-7493)*
Evangelical Lutheran.....D 785 626-9015
Atwood *(G-284)*
Evangelical Lutheran.....C 785 625-7331
Hays *(G-2801)*
Evangelical Lutheran.....D 620 624-3832
Liberal *(G-6308)*
Evangelical Lutheran.....B 913 782-1372
Olathe *(G-7694)*
Evangelical Lutheran.....D 620 257-5163
Lyons *(G-6483)*
Evangelical Lutheran.....D 785 726-3101
Ellis *(G-1644)*
Evangelical Lutheran.....D 785 890-7517
Goodland *(G-2469)*
Evangelical Lutheran.....D 785 456-9482
Wamego *(G-13422)*
Evangelical Lutheran.....D 620 421-1110
Parsons *(G-9684)*
Evangelical Lutheran.....D 785 472-3167
Ellsworth *(G-1674)*
Evergreen Lving Innvations Inc.....D 913 477-8227
Olathe *(G-7695)*
Ggnsc Spring Hill LLC.....E 913 592-3100
Spring Hill *(G-12084)*
Heritage Healthcare Management.....F 785 899-0100
Goodland *(G-2477)*
Liberty Healthcare of Oklahoma.....D 785 823-7107
Salina *(G-10581)*
Lsl of Kansas LLC.....E 785 527-5636
Belleville *(G-461)*
Meade Hospital District.....C 620 873-2146
Meade *(G-7052)*
Meridian Nursing Center Inc.....D 316 942-8471
Wichita *(G-15041)*
Midwest Health Services Inc.....E 785 765-3318
Alma *(G-65)*
Midwest Health Services Inc.....E 785 945-3832
Valley Falls *(G-13368)*
Norton Retirement and Assisted.....E 785 874-4314
Norton *(G-7460)*
Nursing Home Legacy At Pk View.....E 620 356-3331
Ulysses *(G-13308)*
Overland Pk Nursing Rehab Ctr.....F 913 383-9866
Overland Park *(G-9125)*
Pioneer Community Care Inc.....E 620 582-2123
Coldwater *(G-1057)*
Presbyterian Manors Inc.....D 913 334-3666
Kansas City *(G-4333)*
Presbyterian Manors Inc.....D 785 632-5646
Clay Center *(G-876)*
Presbyterian Manors Inc.....E 620 421-1450
Parsons *(G-9725)*
Vintage Park At Hiawatha LLC.....F 785 742-4566
Hiawatha *(G-3027)*
Winfield Rest Haven Inc.....E 620 221-9290
Winfield *(G-16190)*

NUTRITION SVCS

Hope Planting Intl Inc.....F 785 776-8523
Manhattan *(G-6659)*

OFC/CLINIC OF MED DRS: Special, Phys Or Surgeon, Eye Or ENT

Central Kansas Ent Assoc PA.....E 785 823-7225
Salina *(G-10440)*
Eye Specialists.....F 785 628-8218
Hays *(G-2803)*
Fry Eye Surgery Center LLC.....E 620 276-7699
Garden City *(G-2169)*
Hunkeler Eye Institute PA.....F 913 338-4733
Shawnee Mission *(G-11443)*
Midwest Ear Nose Throat PA.....F 913 764-2737
Olathe *(G-7895)*
Otolaryngic Head/Neck Surgry.....E 913 588-6700
Kansas City *(G-4301)*
Trudi R Grin.....F 913 888-1888
Olathe *(G-8122)*

OFC/CLINIC OF MED DRS: Specl, Phys Or Surgeon, Occup & Indl

US Healthworks Medical Group.....E 913 495-9905
Lenexa *(G-6206)*
Wyandtte Occpational Hlth Svcs.....F 913 945-9740
Kansas City *(G-4557)*

OFC/CLINIC, MED DRS: Specl, Phys Or Surgeon, Infect Disease

Infectious Disease Cons PA.....E 316 264-3505
Wichita *(G-14689)*
Infectious Disease Consultants.....E 316 264-3505
Wichita *(G-14690)*

OFCS & CLINICS,MEDICAL DRS: Specl, Physician Or Surgn, ENT

Head & Neck Surgical Assoc.....F 913 663-5100
Leawood *(G-5421)*
Lawrence Otlryngology Assoc PA.....F 620 343-6600
Lawrence *(G-4981)*
S E K Otolaryngology PA.....F 620 232-7500
Pittsburg *(G-9933)*
Tallgrass Immediate Care LLC.....D 785 234-0880
Topeka *(G-13133)*
Thomas P Eyen.....F 913 663-5100
Shawnee Mission *(G-11929)*
Topeka Ear Nose & Throat.....F 620 340-0168
Topeka *(G-13175)*
Wichita Ear Clinic PA.....F 316 686-6608
Wichita *(G-15995)*

OFFICE CLEANING OR CHARRING SVCS

Air Capital Building Maint.....F 316 838-3828
Wichita *(G-13646)*

OFFICE EQPT WHOLESALERS

Bolen Office Supply Inc.....F 620 672-7535
Pratt *(G-10100)*
Central Office Svc & Sup Inc.....F 785 632-2177
Clay Center *(G-848)*
Consolidated Prtg & Sty Co Inc.....E 785 825-5426
Salina *(G-10460)*
Daniksco Office Interiors LLC.....F 316 491-2607
Park City *(G-9616)*
Digital Office Systems Inc.....E 316 262-7700
Wichita *(G-14211)*
Docuforce Inc.....F 316 636-5400
Wichita *(G-14218)*
Faimon Publications Inc.....F 620 364-5325
Burlington *(G-634)*
Gibbs Technology Company.....E 913 621-2424
Kansas City *(G-4034)*
Image Quest Inc.....E 316 686-3200
Wichita *(G-14676)*
Kingman Leader Courier.....G 620 532-3151
Kingman *(G-4602)*
Midwest Office Technologies.....E 785 272-7704
Topeka *(G-12903)*
Midwest Office Technology.....E 913 894-9600
Overland Park *(G-9034)*
Midwest Single Source Inc.....E 316 267-6333
Wichita *(G-15102)*
Office Works LLC.....F 785 462-2222
Colby *(G-1032)*
Ricoh Usa Inc.....E 785 272-0248
Topeka *(G-13017)*
Sta-Mot-Ks LLC.....E 913 894-9600
Overland Park *(G-9349)*

OFFICE EQPT, WHOL: Check Writing, Signing/Endorsing Mach

American Paper Products Inc.....F 913 681-5777
Shawnee Mission *(G-11107)*

OFFICE EQPT, WHOLESALE: Photocopy Machines

Century Business Systems Inc.....F 785 776-0495
Manhattan *(G-6583)*
Century Business Technologies.....E 785 267-4555
Topeka *(G-12458)*
Century Office Pdts Inc Topeka.....E 785 267-4555
Topeka *(G-12460)*
Copy Products Inc.....D 620 365-7611
Iola *(G-3596)*

Knighton Bus Solutions LLC ... E ... 913 747-2818
Overland Park (G-8924)
Konica Minolta Business Soluti ... E ... 913 563-1800
Lenexa (G-5958)
Logan Business Machines Inc ... E ... 785 233-1102
Topeka (G-12848)
Ricoh Usa Inc ... E ... 316 262-7172
Wichita (G-15461)
Ricoh Usa Inc ... E ... 316 558-5488
Valley Center (G-13351)
Ricoh Usa Inc ... C ... 913 890-5100
Shawnee Mission (G-11802)

OFFICE EQPT, WHOLESALE: Typewriters

Danikisco Office Interiors LLC ... F ... 620 259-8009
Hutchinson (G-3254)

OFFICE FURNITURE REPAIR & MAINTENANCE SVCS

Panel Systems Plus Inc ... E ... 913 321-0111
Kansas City (G-4309)

OFFICE SPLY & STATIONERY STORES

Shawnee Copy Center Inc ... F ... 913 268-4343
Shawnee Mission (G-11851)
Timber Creek Paper Inc ... F ... 316 264-3232
Wichita (G-15765)

OFFICE SPLY & STATIONERY STORES: Office Forms & Splys

Back Room Printing LLC ... G ... 620 873-2900
Meade (G-7046)
Blade Empire Publishing Co ... E ... 785 243-2424
Concordia (G-1103)
Central Office Svc & Sup Inc ... F ... 785 632-2177
Clay Center (G-848)
Golden Plains Publishers Inc ... G ... 620 855-3902
Cimarron (G-827)
Images ... G ... 785 827-0824
Salina (G-10549)
Liberal Office Machines Co ... G ... 620 624-5653
Liberal (G-6334)
McCarty Office Machines Inc ... F ... 620 421-5530
Parsons (G-9708)
Office Products Inc ... E ... 620 793-8180
Great Bend (G-2616)
Quality Printing and Off Sups ... F ... 913 491-6366
Lenexa (G-6084)
Roberts Hutch-Line Inc ... E ... 620 662-3356
Hutchinson (G-3428)
U P S Stores ... F ... 913 829-3750
Olathe (G-8129)
United Office Products Inc ... E ... 913 782-4441
Olathe (G-8132)

OFFICE SPLY & STATIONERY STORES: School Splys

Superior School Supplies Inc ... E ... 316 265-7683
Wichita (G-15699)

OFFICE SPLYS, NEC, WHOLESALE

Blade Empire Publishing Co ... E ... 785 243-2424
Concordia (G-1103)
Bolen Office Supply Inc ... F ... 620 672-7535
Pratt (G-10100)
Key Office Products Inc ... G ... 620 227-2101
Dodge City (G-1390)
McCartys ... G ... 620 251-6169
Coffeyville (G-957)
Midwest Office Technology ... E ... 913 894-9600
Overland Park (G-9034)
Office Works LLC ... F ... 785 462-2222
Colby (G-1032)
OfficeMax Incorporated ... E ... 913 667-5300
Edwardsville (G-1511)
Sta-Mot-Ks LLC ... E ... 913 894-9600
Overland Park (G-9349)
Topeka Blue Print & Sup Co Inc ... G ... 785 232-7209
Topeka (G-13169)
United Office Products Inc ... E ... 913 782-4441
Olathe (G-8132)

OFFICES & CLINICS DOCTORS OF MED: Intrnl Med Practitioners

Internal Medicine ... E ... 316 321-2100
El Dorado (G-1572)
University of Kansas ... D ... 913 588-2720
Kansas City (G-4504)
Vigilias LLC ... E ... 800 924-8140
Wichita (G-15907)

OFFICES & CLINICS DRS OF MED: Psychiatrists/Psychoanalysts

Marillac Center Inc ... E ... 816 508-3300
Overland Park (G-8990)

OFFICES & CLINICS OF DENTISTS: Dental Clinic

Accent Dental LLC ... F ... 620 231-2871
Pittsburg (G-9804)
Community Health Center of Sou ... F ... 620 856-2900
Baxter Springs (G-403)
Dental Innovation ... F ... 913 236-8899
Shawnee Mission (G-11301)
Derby Dental Care ... E ... 316 789-9999
Derby (G-1235)
Executive Hills Family Dental ... F ... 913 451-1606
Shawnee Mission (G-11354)
Gentle Dental Service Corp ... E ... 913 248-8880
Lenexa (G-5873)
Holton Dental ... F ... 785 364-3038
Holton (G-3096)
McPherson Dental Care LLC ... F ... 620 241-5000
McPherson (G-6997)
Morningstar Family Dental PA ... F ... 913 344-9990
Overland Park (G-9055)
Perfect Smiles Dental Care PA ... F ... 913 631-2677
Lenexa (G-6049)
Prairie Vista Dental LLC ... F ... 620 424-4311
Ulysses (G-13314)
R2 Center For Assisting LLC ... F ... 316 749-2097
Wichita (G-15408)
Rawlins Cnty Dntl Clinic Fund ... F ... 785 626-8290
Atwood (G-288)

OFFICES & CLINICS OF DENTISTS: Dental Clinics & Offices

First Care Clinic Inc ... E ... 785 621-4990
Hays (G-2807)
Pacific Dental Services LLC ... E ... 913 299-8860
Kansas City (G-4307)
Turner House Clinic Inc ... E ... 913 342-2552
Kansas City (G-4478)

OFFICES & CLINICS OF DENTISTS: Dental Surgeon

Douglas County Dntl Clinic Inc ... F ... 785 312-7770
Lawrence (G-4839)
Drs Alley and Brammer LC ... F ... 316 265-0856
Wichita (G-14238)
Manhattan Oral Surgery & ... F ... 785 477-4038
Manhattan (G-6725)
Mobilecare 2u LLC ... E ... 913 362-1112
Overland Park (G-9048)
Oral & Facial Surgery Assoc ... E ... 913 381-5194
Prairie Village (G-10054)
Oral & Facial Surgery Assoc ... E ... 913 782-1529
Olathe (G-7961)
Oral & Facial Surgery Assoc ... E ... 913 541-1888
Shawnee Mission (G-11700)
Oral and Facial Associate ... E ... 913 381-5194
Prairie Village (G-10055)
Steven L Thomas DDS ... F ... 913 451-7680
Shawnee Mission (G-11900)

OFFICES & CLINICS OF DENTISTS: Dentists' Office

Adams Dental Group PA ... F ... 913 621-3113
Kansas City (G-3784)
Allen K Kelley DDS PA ... F ... 785 841-5590
Lawrence (G-4728)
Ann Barber ... F ... 913 788-0800
Kansas City (G-3813)
Antoine E Wakim Inc ... F ... 316 721-4477
Wichita (G-13713)
Associates In Dentistry ... F ... 785 843-4333
Lawrence (G-4740)
Augusta Family Dentistry PA ... F ... 316 775-2482
Augusta (G-304)
Barden and Thompson LLC ... F ... 620 343-8000
Emporia (G-1702)
Bel-Air Dental Care Chartered ... E ... 913 649-0310
Prairie Village (G-10015)
Bob Durbin DDS ... F ... 785 267-5010
Topeka (G-12394)
Boynton Family Dental Arts LLC ... E ... 316 685-8881
Wichita (G-13876)
Briscoe Richard L DDS PA ... F ... 620 669-1032
Hutchinson (G-3224)
Bruce Speak ... F ... 785 267-6301
Topeka (G-12411)
Cambridge Family Dentistry ... F ... 316 687-2110
Wichita (G-13929)
Cascade Dental Care ... F ... 785 841-3311
Lawrence (G-4776)
Central Dental Center PA ... F ... 316 945-9845
Wichita (G-13979)
Chuck Pierson DDS PA ... E ... 316 634-1333
Wichita (G-14018)
Clay Center Family Dentistry ... F ... 785 632-3126
Clay Center (G-850)
Complete Dental Care ... F ... 913 469-5646
Olathe (G-7608)
Dalton L Hunt DDS ... F ... 620 543-2768
Buhler (G-615)
Dan A Burton DDS ... F ... 316 684-5511
Wichita (G-14163)
David Koepsel DDS LLC ... F ... 316 686-7395
Wichita (G-14173)
Dennis C McAllister DDS PA ... E ... 316 788-3736
Derby (G-1234)
Dental Associates ... E ... 785 539-7401
Manhattan (G-6612)
Dental Associates W Wichita PA ... E ... 316 942-5358
Wichita (G-14193)
Dental Corner ... E ... 316 681-2425
Wichita (G-14194)
Discover Dental Care ... F ... 913 268-1337
Shawnee Mission (G-11308)
Dlabal & Fellner Gen Denistry ... F ... 785 537-8484
Manhattan (G-6615)
Dodge City Dental ... F ... 620 225-2650
Dodge City (G-1347)
Douglas V Oxler DDS ... F ... 316 722-2596
Wichita (G-14231)
Dr Nick Rogers ... F ... 620 442-5660
Arkansas City (G-154)
Dr William E Hartman Assoc PA ... F ... 913 441-1600
Bonner Springs (G-550)
E Brent Nelson ... F ... 316 789-9999
Derby (G-1241)
Enchanted Smiles Eashetic ... E ... 785 246-6300
Topeka (G-12576)
Erik J Peterson DDS ... F ... 785 227-2299
Lindsborg (G-6398)
Gage Center Dental Group PA ... D ... 785 273-4770
Topeka (G-12631)
Gardner Dental Care ... F ... 913 856-7123
Gardner (G-2348)
Grace Dental ... F ... 913 685-9111
Overland Park (G-8767)
Grant D Ringler DDS Inc ... F ... 620 669-0835
Hutchinson (G-3304)
Grant Phipps DDS ... F ... 620 326-7983
Wellington (G-13507)
Greg Cohen DDS ... F ... 785 273-2350
Topeka (G-12649)
Heartland Dental Group ... F ... 913 682-1000
Leavenworth (G-5250)
Heath Family Dentistry ... F ... 785 234-5410
Topeka (G-12682)
Howell Matthew D Dr DDS PA ... F ... 316 260-6220
Andover (G-94)
Interdent Inc ... E ... 913 248-8880
Lenexa (G-5918)
James P Gertken DDS ... F ... 620 669-0411
Hutchinson (G-3341)
James R Kiene Jr DDS PA LLC ... F ... 913 825-9373
Shawnee Mission (G-11482)
Jerry R Lundgrin DDS ... F ... 785 825-5473
Salina (G-10554)
Joe Rosenberg DDS ... F ... 620 285-3886
Saint John (G-10353)
John C Patton DDS ... F ... 620 342-0673
Emporia (G-1780)

John Fales Dr F 913 782-2207
Olathe *(G-7811)*
Joseph P Steven DDS PA F 316 262-5273
Wichita *(G-14773)*
Joseph Wommack DDS F 620 421-0980
Parsons *(G-9694)*
Kc Smile PA F 913 491-6874
Overland Park *(G-8908)*
Kelly B Deeter DDS Chartered F 785 267-6120
Topeka *(G-12816)*
Kelly S Henrichs DDS F 620 225-6555
Dodge City *(G-1388)*
Kuhlman and Majors DDS F 316 652-0000
Wichita *(G-14898)*
Larry D Sheldon DDS F 913 782-7580
Olathe *(G-7855)*
Le John Minh DDS F 913 888-9399
Overland Park *(G-8949)*
Leawood Ctr For Dntl Exccllence F 913 491-4466
Shawnee Mission *(G-11553)*
Lee & Devlin DDS F 316 685-2309
Wichita *(G-14945)*
Lenexa Dental Group Chartered F 913 888-8008
Shawnee Mission *(G-11563)*
Lisa R Gonzales DDS P C F 913 299-3999
Shawnee *(G-10989)*
Lynne M Schopper DDS PA F 913 451-2929
Leawood *(G-5461)*
Mark H Armfield DDS F 316 775-5451
Augusta *(G-333)*
Mark Hungerford MD F 785 539-5949
Manhattan *(G-6731)*
Mark S Jensen DDS PA F 913 384-0600
Shawnee Mission *(G-11598)*
Mark Troilo DDS PA F 316 776-2144
Rose Hill *(G-10242)*
Michael A Dold DDS F 316 721-2024
Wichita *(G-15064)*
Michael P Harris Inc F 620 276-7623
Garden City *(G-2231)*
Miller Sullivan & Assoc DDS PA F 913 492-5052
Shawnee Mission *(G-11641)*
Murray Clary Anita C DDS F 785 272-6060
Topeka *(G-12921)*
Nevin K Waters DDS PA F 913 782-1330
Olathe *(G-7916)*
New Horizons Dental Care F 785 376-0250
Salina *(G-10612)*
Olathe Dental Care Center F 913 782-1420
Olathe *(G-7930)*
Olathe Family Dentistry PA F 913 829-1438
Olathe *(G-7932)*
Overland Park Dental F 913 383-2343
Shawnee Mission *(G-11706)*
Overland Park Dentistry PA F 913 647-8700
Shawnee Mission *(G-11707)*
Overland Park Smiles F 913 851-8400
Leawood *(G-5512)*
Palmer Family Dentistry F 316 453-6918
Haysville *(G-2954)*
Pediatric Dental Specialist PA F 913 829-0981
Olathe *(G-7978)*
Robert G Smith DDS Chartered F 913 649-5600
Shawnee Mission *(G-11807)*
Roger D Gausman DDS F 620 663-5044
Hutchinson *(G-3429)*
Roger L Stevens Dentist F 785 539-2314
Manhattan *(G-6794)*
Ronald G Higgins F 620 584-2223
Clearwater *(G-895)*
Ronald J Burgmeier DDS PA F 913 764-1169
Olathe *(G-8041)*
Salina Dental Arts F 785 823-2472
Salina *(G-10671)*
Salina Dental Associates PA F 785 827-4401
Salina *(G-10672)*
Scheer Dentistry PA F 316 636-1222
Wichita *(G-15529)*
Smith Ned E Jr DDS Ms Charter F 913 383-3233
Leawood *(G-5552)*
Stephen P Moore DDS F 316 681-3228
Wichita *(G-15662)*
Steven F Twietmeyer DDS F 316 942-3113
Wichita *(G-15668)*
Steven G Mitchell DDS F 913 492-9660
Lenexa *(G-6154)*
Steven J Pierce DDS PA F 913 888-2882
Shawnee Mission *(G-11899)*
Steven Joseph Jr DDS F 316 262-5273
Wichita *(G-15670)*
Todays Dentistry F 785 267-5010
Topeka *(G-13162)*
W Ross Greenlaw DMD F 207 374-5538
Overland Park *(G-9475)*
Webber Webber & Exon F 785 232-7707
Topeka *(G-13236)*
Wilkerson Anderson & Anderson E 785 843-6060
Lawrence *(G-5185)*
Wince Family Dental F 620 241-0266
McPherson *(G-7042)*
Ziegenhorn & Linneman DDS F 913 649-7500
Prairie Village *(G-10089)*

OFFICES & CLINICS OF DENTISTS: Endodontist

Michael J Randall F 913 498-3636
Leawood *(G-5478)*
Olathe Endodontics F 913 829-0060
Olathe *(G-7931)*

OFFICES & CLINICS OF DENTISTS: Group & Corporate Practice

Heartland Dental Group PA D 913 682-1000
Leavenworth *(G-5251)*

OFFICES & CLINICS OF DENTISTS: Oral Pathologist

Oral Mxilo Ofcial Srgery Assoc E 913 268-9500
Shawnee Mission *(G-11701)*

OFFICES & CLINICS OF DENTISTS: Pedodontist

Glenn V Hemberger DDS F 913 345-0331
Shawnee Mission *(G-11397)*

OFFICES & CLINICS OF DENTISTS: Periodontist

Edwards & Wilson Periodontides F 785 843-4076
Lawrence *(G-4847)*
Moxley &WAgle Dr F 316 685-2731
Wichita *(G-15136)*
Periodontist PA F 913 451-6158
Overland Park *(G-9156)*

OFFICES & CLINICS OF DENTISTS: Specialist, Maxillofacial

Faerber Surgical Arts F 913 469-8895
Shawnee Mission *(G-11358)*
Lawrence Oral Surgery F 785 843-5490
Lawrence *(G-4979)*

OFFICES & CLINICS OF DENTISTS: Specialist, Practitioners

First Dental E 620 225-5154
Dodge City *(G-1360)*
Lance Anderson DDS F 316 687-2104
Wichita *(G-14918)*

OFFICES & CLINICS OF DOCTORS OF MEDICINE: Allergist

Allergy & Asthma Care PA E 913 491-3300
Overland Park *(G-8368)*
Allergy Rhmtlogy Clnics Kc LLC F 913 338-3222
Overland Park *(G-8369)*
Asthma & Allergy Associates PA F 785 842-3778
Lawrence *(G-4741)*
Henry J Kanarek F 913 451-8555
Shawnee Mission *(G-11426)*
Topeka Allrgy Asthma Clinic PA F 785 273-9999
Topeka *(G-13166)*

OFFICES & CLINICS OF DOCTORS OF MEDICINE: Anesthesiologist

Advanced Anesthesia Assoc F 316 942-4519
Wichita *(G-13622)*
Advanced Pain Mdcine Assoc LLC F 316 942-4519
Wichita *(G-13626)*
Anesthesia Assoc Kans Cy PC C 913 428-2900
Overland Park *(G-8385)*
Anesthesia Associates Topeka E 785 235-3451
Topeka *(G-12327)*
Independence Anesthesia Inc F 913 707-5294
Lenexa *(G-5911)*
Kansas Prffsnl Anesthesia E 316 618-1515
Wichita *(G-14819)*
Mid Continent Anesthesiology E 316 789-8444
Wichita *(G-15068)*
Midwest Anesthesia Assoc PA E 913 642-4900
Leawood *(G-5481)*
PA Hays Anesthesiologist Assoc F 785 628-8300
Antonino *(G-136)*
Topeka Ansthsia Pain Trtmnt PA E 785 295-8000
Topeka *(G-13167)*
Wichita Ansthsiology Chartered D 316 686-1564
Wichita *(G-15973)*

OFFICES & CLINICS OF DOCTORS OF MEDICINE: Dermatologist

Advanced Dermatology and Skin E 785 537-4990
Manhattan *(G-6533)*
Christopher Moeller F 316 682-7546
Wichita *(G-14016)*
Dermatology & Skin Cancer Ctr F 913 451-7546
Shawnee Mission *(G-11302)*
Dermatology Clinic E 316 685-4395
Wichita *(G-14198)*
Dermatology Cons Midwest F 913 469-0110
Overland Park *(G-8650)*
Heartland Dermatology Center E 785 628-3231
Hays *(G-2840)*
Johnson County Dermatology F 913 764-1125
Olathe *(G-7816)*
Mark A McCune E 913 541-3230
Shawnee Mission *(G-11594)*
Mid Knsas Drmtology Clinic P A F 316 612-1833
Wichita *(G-15071)*
Multispecialty Kanza Group PA E 913 788-7099
Kansas City *(G-4272)*
Premier Dermatologic F 913 327-1117
Overland Park *(G-9180)*
Skin Renewal E 913 722-5551
Overland Park *(G-9315)*

OFFICES & CLINICS OF DOCTORS OF MEDICINE: Gastronomist

Endoscopic Associates LLC E 913 492-0800
Overland Park *(G-8680)*
Gastrointestinal Associates PA F 913 495-9600
Overland Park *(G-8746)*
Kansas Medical Clinic PA F 785 233-3553
Topeka *(G-12786)*
Kansas Medical Clinic PA F 785 233-3555
Topeka *(G-12787)*
Mark Molos F 913 962-2122
Shawnee Mission *(G-11596)*
Physicians Medical Clinics E 316 683-4334
Wichita *(G-15295)*
Physicians Medical Clinics F 316 687-2651
Wichita *(G-15296)*
Physicians Medical Clinics F 316 261-3130
Wichita *(G-15297)*
Physicians Medical Clinics C 316 721-4910
Wichita *(G-15298)*
Westglen Endoscopy Center LLC E 913 248-8800
Shawnee Mission *(G-12006)*

OFFICES & CLINICS OF DOCTORS OF MEDICINE: Group Health Assoc

Delaware Hghlnds Assistd Lvng F 913 721-1400
Kansas City *(G-3966)*
Pediatric Orthopedic Surgery F 913 451-0000
Prairie Village *(G-10057)*
Student Health Center Psu F 620 235-4452
Pittsburg *(G-9942)*

OFFICES & CLINICS OF DOCTORS OF MEDICINE: Gynecologist

Associates For Female Care PA F 913 299-2229
Kansas City *(G-3828)*
Associates In Womens Health PA F 316 283-4153
Newton *(G-7312)*
Center For Womens Health LLC F 316 634-0060
Wichita *(G-13975)*
College Hill Ob/Gyn Inc E 316 683-6766
Wichita *(G-14056)*
Comprehensive Womens Care F 913 643-0075
Shawnee Mission *(G-11257)*

Heartland Womens Group At Wes........E....... 316 962-7175
Wichita *(G-14589)*
Hodes & Nauser Mds PA........F....... 913 491-6878
Overland Park *(G-8821)*
Kansas City Womens Clinic PA........D....... 913 894-8500
Shawnee Mission *(G-11514)*
Ku Womens Hlth Specialty Ctrs........F....... 913 588-6200
Kansas City *(G-4183)*
Lincoln Ctr Obstrcs/Gynclgy PA........F....... 785 273-4010
Topeka *(G-12846)*
Mid-Kansas Womens Center PA........E....... 316 685-3081
Wichita *(G-15080)*
Mowery Clinic LLC........C....... 785 827-7261
Salina *(G-10608)*
Olathe Womens Center Inc........F....... 913 780-3388
Olathe *(G-7954)*
Rockhill Womens Care Inc........E....... 816 942-3339
Leawood *(G-5541)*
Sugar Scholl Magee Carriker........E....... 913 384-4990
Overland Park *(G-9370)*
Summit Surgical LLC........E....... 620 663-4800
Hutchinson *(G-3455)*
Ultrasound For Women LLC........E....... 785 331-4160
Lawrence *(G-5149)*
Wichita Ob Gyn Associates PA........E....... 316 685-0559
Wichita *(G-16014)*
Womens Care........E....... 913 384-4990
Overland Park *(G-9501)*
Womens Clinic Assoc PA........F....... 913 788-9797
Leavenworth *(G-5307)*
Womens Health Associates Inc........E....... 913 677-3113
Shawnee Mission *(G-12015)*
Womens Health Care Group........F....... 816 589-2121
Lawrence *(G-5190)*
Womens Health Care Group........E....... 913 438-0018
Lenexa *(G-6233)*

OFFICES & CLINICS OF DOCTORS OF MEDICINE: Hematologist

Cancer Center of Kansas PA........C....... 316 262-4467
Wichita *(G-13933)*

OFFICES & CLINICS OF DOCTORS OF MEDICINE: Nephrologist

Kansas Nphrology Physicians PA........E....... 316 263-7285
Wichita *(G-14816)*
Nephrology Associates Inc........F....... 913 381-0622
Olathe *(G-7915)*

OFFICES & CLINICS OF DOCTORS OF MEDICINE: Neurologist

Christopher B Geha........E....... 913 383-9099
Shawnee Mission *(G-11223)*
Consultants In Neurology PA........E....... 913 894-1500
Shawnee Mission *(G-11262)*
Headache & Pain Center PA........D....... 913 491-3999
Overland Park *(G-8801)*
John D Ebeling MD........F....... 785 232-3555
Topeka *(G-12745)*
Neurology Associates Kans LLC........F....... 316 682-5544
Wichita *(G-15163)*
Neurology Center of Wichita........F....... 316 686-6866
Wichita *(G-15164)*
Neurology Cons Chartered........F....... 913 632-9810
Shawnee Mission *(G-11678)*
Neurology Consultants Kans LLC........E....... 316 261-3220
Wichita *(G-15165)*

OFFICES & CLINICS OF DOCTORS OF MEDICINE: Neurosurgeon

Neurosurgery Kansas City PA........F....... 913 299-9507
Lenexa *(G-6023)*

OFFICES & CLINICS OF DOCTORS OF MEDICINE: Obstetrician

Associates In Womens Health PA........E....... 316 219-6777
Wichita *(G-13759)*
Center For Woman Health........F....... 913 491-6878
Shawnee Mission *(G-11210)*
Contemporary Womens Centre........F....... 913 345-2322
Overland Park *(G-8596)*
Dennis Knudsen Dr........F....... 620 624-3811
Liberal *(G-6303)*
For Women Only Inc........F....... 913 541-9495
Leawood *(G-5407)*
HCA Holdings Inc........D....... 620 365-1330
Iola *(G-3607)*
Johnson Cnty Ob-Gyn Chartered........E....... 913 236-6455
Shawnee Mission *(G-11494)*
Kansas Cy Ob Gyn Pysicians PC........F....... 913 648-1840
Overland Park *(G-8901)*
Lincoln Ctr Obstrcs/Gynclgy PA........E....... 785 273-4010
Topeka *(G-12845)*
Maternal Fetal Medicine Inc........F....... 316 962-7188
Wichita *(G-15018)*
Parris R David MD........E....... 620 223-8045
Fort Scott *(G-1997)*
Womans Place PA........F....... 620 662-2229
Hutchinson *(G-3491)*
Womens Health Svcs Kans Cy PC........F....... 816 941-2700
Leawood *(G-5601)*

OFFICES & CLINICS OF DOCTORS OF MEDICINE: Oncologist

Cancer Center of Kansas PA........F....... 620 399-1224
Wellington *(G-13494)*
Cancer Center of Kansas PA........F....... 620 421-2855
Parsons *(G-9670)*
Cancer Center of Kansas PA........F....... 620 629-6727
Liberal *(G-6290)*
Cancer Center of Kansas PA........D....... 316 262-4467
Wichita *(G-13932)*
Cancer Center of Kansas PA........F....... 620 431-7580
Chanute *(G-708)*
Kansas City Cancer Center LLC........F....... 913 788-8883
Kansas City *(G-4143)*
Kansas City Cancer Center LLC........E....... 913 541-4600
Overland Park *(G-8891)*
Lawrence Cancer Center........F....... 785 749-3600
Lawrence *(G-4959)*
Olathe Regional Oncology Ctr........F....... 913 768-7200
Olathe *(G-7948)*
Saint Frncis Radiation Therapy........E....... 316 268-5927
Wichita *(G-15508)*
Saint Joseph Oncology Inc........F....... 913 367-9175
Atchison *(G-260)*
Salina Regional Health Ctr Inc........D....... 785 452-4850
Salina *(G-10687)*

OFFICES & CLINICS OF DOCTORS OF MEDICINE: Ophthalmologist

Arla Jean Genstler MD PA........F....... 785 537-3400
Manhattan *(G-6544)*
Arla Jean Genstler MD PA........E....... 785 273-8080
Topeka *(G-12338)*
Bradley Kwapiszeski MD........F....... 913 362-3210
Shawnee Mission *(G-11178)*
Bruce Ochsner MD........E....... 316 263-6273
Wichita *(G-13901)*
Cavanaugh Eye Center PA........F....... 913 897-9200
Overland Park *(G-8527)*
Central Plains Eye Mds LLC........F....... 316 712-4970
Wichita *(G-13982)*
Cokingtin Eye Center PA........D....... 913 491-3737
Shawnee Mission *(G-11244)*
David B Lyon MD........E....... 913 261-2020
Leawood *(G-5371)*
Esther V Rettig........F....... 620 245-0556
McPherson *(G-6960)*
Eye Care PC........E....... 816 478-4400
Leawood *(G-5392)*
Fry Eye Associates........E....... 620 275-7248
Garden City *(G-2167)*
Fry Eye Associates........F....... 620 276-7699
Garden City *(G-2168)*
Heart America Eye Care PA........F....... 913 492-0021
Overland Park *(G-8804)*
K Craig Place MD........F....... 913 385-9009
Prairie Village *(G-10039)*
Kansas City Eye Clinic PA........E....... 913 341-3100
Shawnee Mission *(G-11509)*
Keil Vtrnary Ophthalmology LLC........F....... 785 331-4600
Overland Park *(G-8910)*
Leawood Family Care PA........F....... 913 338-4515
Leawood *(G-5453)*
Medical-Surgical Eye Care PA........E....... 913 299-8800
Kansas City *(G-4230)*
Mid America Eye Center Inc........E....... 913 384-1441
Prairie Village *(G-10048)*
Milton B Grin MD PA........E....... 913 829-5511
Olathe *(G-7901)*
Ophthalmic Services PA........F....... 913 498-2015
Overland Park *(G-9107)*
Parsons Eye Clinic PA........F....... 620 421-5900
Parsons *(G-9717)*
Reifschneider Eye Center PC........F....... 913 682-2900
Leavenworth *(G-5283)*
Richard A Orchards MD........F....... 785 841-2280
Lawrence *(G-5095)*
Sabates Eye Centers PC........F....... 913 261-2020
Shawnee Mission *(G-11822)*
Sabates Eye Centers PC........F....... 913 261-2020
Leawood *(G-5545)*
Sabates Eye Centers PC........E....... 913 469-8806
Shawnee Mission *(G-11823)*
Vision Green Group........E....... 620 663-7187
Hutchinson *(G-3479)*

OFFICES & CLINICS OF DOCTORS OF MEDICINE: Pathologist

Midwest Pathology Assoc LLC........F....... 913 341-6275
Overland Park *(G-9035)*
Via Christi Clinic PA........E....... 316 613-4680
Wichita *(G-15880)*

OFFICES & CLINICS OF DOCTORS OF MEDICINE: Pediatrician

Cottonwood Pediatrics........F....... 316 283-7100
Newton *(G-7335)*
Coventry Health Care Kans Inc........C....... 800 969-3343
Overland Park *(G-8606)*
Dennis M Cooley MD........E....... 785 235-0335
Topeka *(G-12551)*
Dr Vernon A Mills........F....... 913 772-6046
Leavenworth *(G-5234)*
Geary Community Hospital........F....... 785 762-5437
Junction City *(G-3692)*
Heartland Primary Care PA........E....... 913 299-3700
Kansas City *(G-4077)*
Johnson County Pediatrics........D....... 913 384-5500
Merriam *(G-7097)*
KU Childrens Ctr Foundation........E....... 913 588-6301
Kansas City *(G-4181)*
Ku Physicians Inc........F....... 913 588-3243
Kansas City *(G-4182)*
Lawrence Pediatrics PA........F....... 785 856-9090
Lawrence *(G-4983)*
Leawood Pediatrics LLC........F....... 913 825-3627
Leawood *(G-5454)*
Mid Kansas Pediatric Assoc PA........E....... 316 773-3100
Wichita *(G-15069)*
Mid Kansas Pediatric Assoc PA........E....... 316 634-0057
Wichita *(G-15070)*
Partners In Pediatrics PA........F....... 785 234-4624
Topeka *(G-12963)*
Pediatric Care Specialist PA........E....... 913 906-0900
Overland Park *(G-9151)*
Pediatric Partners........E....... 913 888-4567
Overland Park *(G-9152)*
Pediatric Professional Assn........E....... 913 541-3300
Shawnee Mission *(G-11723)*
Pediatrics Associates........E....... 785 235-0335
Topeka *(G-12967)*
Preferred Pediatrics PA........F....... 913 764-7060
Olathe *(G-8002)*
Premier Pediatrics PA........F....... 913 384-5500
Overland Park *(G-9182)*
Redbud Pediatrics LLC........F....... 316 201-1202
Wichita *(G-15430)*
Salina Pediatric Care........F....... 785 825-2273
Salina *(G-10681)*
Shawnee Mission Pediatrics PA........E....... 913 362-1660
Overland Park *(G-9305)*
Stormont Vale Hospital........E....... 785 273-8224
Topeka *(G-13102)*
Thomas E Moskow MD........E....... 785 273-8224
Topeka *(G-13159)*
Tyler Physicians PA........F....... 316 729-9100
Wichita *(G-15823)*
Village Pediatrics LLC........E....... 913 642-2100
Prairie Village *(G-10080)*

OFFICES & CLINICS OF DOCTORS OF MEDICINE: Psychiatric Clinic

Compass Behavioral Health........E....... 620 227-5040
Dodge City *(G-1328)*
Compass Behavioral Health........E....... 620 227-8566
Dodge City *(G-1329)*

OFFICES & CLINICS OF DOCTORS OF MEDICINE: Psychiatrist

Center For Counseling & Cnsltn ....E 620 792-2544
Great Bend *(G-2526)*
Comcare of Sedgwick County ....C 316 660-7700
Wichita *(G-14062)*
Morton County Hospital ....F 620 697-2175
Elkhart *(G-1624)*
Psychiatry Assoc Kans Cy PC ....E 913 385-7252
Shawnee Mission *(G-11762)*
Ralph Bharati MD PA ....F 316 686-7884
Wichita *(G-15413)*
Riverbend Rgnal Hlthcare Fndti ....B 913 367-2131
Atchison *(G-258)*
Shirley Alexander ....D 316 651-3621
Wichita *(G-15582)*
Stormont-Vail Healthcare Inc ....C 785 270-4600
Topeka *(G-13103)*

OFFICES & CLINICS OF DOCTORS OF MEDICINE: Radiologist

Anatomi Imaging ....F 316 858-4091
Wichita *(G-13701)*
Diagnostic Imaging Center ....E 913 491-9299
Shawnee Mission *(G-11304)*
Diagnostic Imaging Center ....F 913 344-9989
Olathe *(G-7652)*
Diagnostic Imaging Centers PA ....C 913 319-8450
Leawood *(G-5378)*
Kansas City Imaging Center ....F 913 667-5600
Kansas City *(G-4146)*
Kansas Imaging Consultants ....F 316 268-5000
Wichita *(G-14807)*
Kansas Imaging Consultants PA ....F 316 689-5043
Wichita *(G-14808)*
Leavenwrth-Knsas Cy Imaging PA ....E 913 651-6066
Overland Park *(G-8951)*
Manhattan Radiology LLP ....F 785 539-7641
Manhattan *(G-6726)*
Premier Open Mri Inc ....E 316 262-1103
Wichita *(G-15332)*
Radiologic Prof Svcs PA ....F 785 841-3211
Lawrence *(G-5086)*
Radiological Wichita Group PA ....E 316 685-1367
Wichita *(G-15410)*
Radiological Wichita Group PA ....F 316 681-1827
Wichita *(G-15411)*
Radiology Nuclear Medicine LLC ....E 785 234-3454
Topeka *(G-12997)*
United Rdlgy Group Chartered ....F 785 827-9526
Salina *(G-10747)*

OFFICES & CLINICS OF DOCTORS OF MEDICINE: Surgeon

Advanced Dermatologic Surgery ....F 913 661-1755
Shawnee Mission *(G-11078)*
Center For Same Day Surgery ....E 316 262-7263
Wichita *(G-13973)*
Cypress Surgery Center LLC ....D 316 634-0404
Wichita *(G-14152)*
Dale P Denning MD Facs ....F 785 856-8346
Lawrence *(G-4824)*
Deer Creek Surgery Center LLC ....F 913 897-0022
Overland Park *(G-8646)*
Endoscopy & Surgery Ctr Topeka ....F 785 354-1254
Topeka *(G-12577)*
Eye Surgery Center Wichita LLC ....E 316 681-2020
Wichita *(G-14328)*
Hays Orthopedic Clinic PA ....E 785 625-3012
Hays *(G-2836)*
Head & Neck Surgery Kans Cy PA ....E 913 599-4800
Leawood *(G-5420)*
Kansas Cy Gen Vscular Surgeons ....E 913 754-2800
Overland Park *(G-8899)*
Kansas Surgical Consultants ....E 316 685-6222
Wichita *(G-14826)*
Kansas Surgical Consultants ....E 316 219-9360
Wichita *(G-14827)*
Ku Midwest Ambulatory Svc Ctr ....E 913 588-8452
Shawnee Mission *(G-11539)*
Mid America Physicians Charter ....E 913 422-2020
Shawnee Mission *(G-11627)*
Midwest Surgery Center Lc ....F 316 683-3937
Wichita *(G-15104)*
Oral and Maxilla Facial Assoc ....E 316 634-1414
Wichita *(G-15230)*
Overland Park Surgery Ctr LLC ....D 913 894-7260
Overland Park *(G-9123)*
Physicians Surgery Center ....E 913 384-9600
Shawnee Mission *(G-11733)*
Premier Plastic Surgery ....F 913 782-0707
Olathe *(G-8003)*
South Kans Cy Surgical Ctr Lc ....E 913 901-9000
Overland Park *(G-9330)*
Steve Priddle ....E 785 776-1400
Manhattan *(G-6811)*
Surgery Center Olathe LLC ....F 913 829-4001
Olathe *(G-8089)*
Tallgrass Prairie Surgical ....E 785 234-9830
Topeka *(G-13136)*
Topeka Surgery Center Inc ....E 785 273-8282
Topeka *(G-13186)*
Vascular Surgery Associates PA ....F 913 262-9201
Shawnee *(G-11046)*
Wichita Srgical Specialists PA ....E 316 722-5814
Wichita *(G-16024)*
Wichita Srgical Specialists PA ....E 316 684-2838
Wichita *(G-16028)*

OFFICES & CLINICS OF DOCTORS OF MEDICINE: Surgeon, Plastic

Associated Plastic Surgeons PC ....F 913 451-3722
Shawnee Mission *(G-11126)*
Faerber Surgical Arts ....F 913 469-8895
Shawnee Mission *(G-11358)*
Monarch Plastic Surgery ....E 913 663-3838
Overland Park *(G-9049)*
Quinn Plastic Surgery Ctr LLC ....F 913 492-3443
Leawood *(G-5531)*
Surgery Center of Leawood LLC ....E 913 661-9977
Shawnee Mission *(G-11913)*
Wichita Srgical Specialists PA ....E 316 688-7500
Wichita *(G-16027)*

OFFICES & CLINICS OF DOCTORS OF MEDICINE: Urologist

Associated Urologist P A ....F 785 537-8710
Manhattan *(G-6549)*
Ayham J Farha MD ....E 316 636-6100
Wichita *(G-13783)*
Candlewood Medical Group PA ....F 785 539-0800
Manhattan *(G-6574)*
Kansas City Urology Care ....F 913 831-1003
Humboldt *(G-3186)*
Kansas City Urology Care ....E 913 338-5585
Overland Park *(G-8897)*
Kansas City Urology Care PA ....C 913 341-7985
Overland Park *(G-8898)*
Mid America Urology PC ....F 913 948-8365
Leawood *(G-5479)*
Salina Urology Associates PA ....F 785 827-9635
Salina *(G-10695)*
Urologic Surgery Associates PA ....F 913 438-3833
Shawnee Mission *(G-11969)*
Urology Associates Topeka PA ....F 785 233-4256
Topeka *(G-13213)*

OFFICES & CLINICS OF DOCTORS, MEDICINE: Gen & Fam Practice

Arnold Katz MD ....F 913 888-3231
Shawnee Mission *(G-11119)*
Ascension Via Christi Hospital ....E 316 687-1555
Wichita *(G-13748)*
Associates Family Medicine PA ....E 913 596-1313
Kansas City *(G-3827)*
Augusta Family Practice PA ....E 316 775-9191
Augusta *(G-305)*
Axtell Clinic P A ....D 316 283-2800
Newton *(G-7314)*
Carol J Feltheim ....D 913 469-5579
Overland Park *(G-8519)*
Central Care PA ....E 620 624-4700
Liberal *(G-6291)*
Central Kans Fmly Practice PA ....E 620 792-5341
Great Bend *(G-2527)*
Charles L Brroks MD ....F 913 248-8008
Shawnee Mission *(G-11217)*
Clay Center Fmly Physicians PA ....E 785 632-2181
Clay Center *(G-851)*
Coffeyvile Fmly Prctice Clinic ....E 620 251-1100
Coffeyville *(G-923)*
College Park Fmly Care Ctr Inc ....F 913 681-8866
Shawnee Mission *(G-11250)*
Communi
Blue Rap
Cotton ONe
Osage City
County of Ke
Lakin *(G-46*
Daniel J Geha
Leawood *(G-5*
Diabetes & Endo
Overland Park (
E M Specialist PA
Shawnee Mission
Edward J Lind II ....
Derby *(G-1242)*
Family Care Center 620 221-9500
Winfield *(G-16141)*
Family Center For Heal... Care ....E 785 462-6184
Colby *(G-1003)*
Family Medical Group PA ....E 913 299-9200
Kansas City *(G-4007)*
Family Medicine Associates PA ....F 785 830-0100
Lawrence *(G-4856)*
Family Medicine East Chartered ....E 316 689-6630
Wichita *(G-14338)*
Family Physicians Kansas LLC ....F 316 733-4500
Andover *(G-92)*
Family Practice Associates ....E 620 241-7400
McPherson *(G-6962)*
Family Practice Associates ....F 913 299-2100
Kansas City *(G-4008)*
Family Practice Associates ....F 913 438-2226
Lenexa *(G-5848)*
First Med PA ....E 785 865-5300
Lawrence *(G-4861)*
Flanner & Mc Bratney Mds PA ....F 913 651-3111
Lansing *(G-4673)*
Garden Surgical Assoc ....E 620 275-3740
Garden City *(G-2183)*
Gerstberger Medical Clinic ....F 620 356-2432
Ulysses *(G-13299)*
Greeley County Family Practice ....F 620 376-4251
Tribune *(G-13269)*
Grisell Memorial Hospital Assn ....D 785 731-2231
Ransom *(G-10194)*
Gupta Ganesh ....F 913 451-0000
Overland Park *(G-8782)*
Harder Family Practice PA ....F 316 775-7500
Augusta *(G-323)*
Hays Family Practice Center ....E 785 623-5095
Hays *(G-2829)*
Health Ministries Clinic Inc ....D 316 283-6103
Newton *(G-7358)*
Healthcore Clinic Inc ....E 316 691-0249
Wichita *(G-14578)*
Heartland Clinic ....F 785 263-4131
Abilene *(G-37)*
Hess Medical Services PA ....E 785 628-7495
Hays *(G-2842)*
Hillside Medical Office ....E 316 685-1381
Wichita *(G-14613)*
Holy Family Medical Assoc LLP ....E 316 682-9900
Wichita *(G-14627)*
Hospital Dst 1 of Rice Cnty ....F 620 278-2123
Sterling *(G-12121)*
Josie Norris MD ....F 785 232-6950
Topeka *(G-12749)*
Kansas Fmly Mdicine Foundation ....E 913 588-1900
Kansas City *(G-4155)*
Kimberly A Allman LLC ....F 316 733-3003
Andover *(G-98)*
Konza Prairie Cmnty Hlth Ctr ....F 785 238-4711
Junction City *(G-3718)*
Laurie D Fisher MD ....E 913 345-3650
Overland Park *(G-8947)*
Leavenworth Family Health Ctr ....F 913 682-5588
Lansing *(G-4684)*
Leawood Family Physicians ....F 913 451-4443
Shawnee Mission *(G-11554)*
Lowe Fryldnhoven Mds Chartered ....F 913 677-2508
Shawnee Mission *(G-11578)*
Merrill R Conant MD ....E 620 227-6550
Dodge City *(G-1404)*
Mid Kansas Family Practice ....E 620 327-2440
Hesston *(G-2997)*
Mid-Amrica Rhumatology Cons PA ....E 913 661-9980
Overland Park *(G-9027)*
Minneola Hospital District 2 ....F 620 885-4202
Bloom *(G-531)*
Moufarrij Nazih ....D 316 263-0296
Wichita *(G-15135)*

...dcenter ....F 316 777-0176
...224)
...non Kapln WMS MD ....F 913 599-3800
...a (G-6022)
...aha County Community Hlth ....F 785 284-2152
Sabetha (G-10320)
New Frontiers ....F 785 672-3261
Oakley (G-7482)
New Market Health Care LLC ....E 316 773-1212
Wichita (G-15168)
Newman Mem Hosp Foundation ....E 620 342-2521
Emporia (G-1802)
Olathe Family Practice PA ....E 913 782-3322
Olathe (G-7933)
Olathe Medical Services Inc ....F 913 782-3798
Lenexa (G-6034)
Olathe Medical Services Inc ....F 913 755-3044
Osawatomie (G-8200)
Olathe Medical Services Inc ....D 913 782-7515
Olathe (G-7943)
Overland Park Fmly Hlth Prtnr ....F 913 894-6500
Overland Park (G-9118)
P A Comcare ....E 785 392-2144
Minneapolis (G-7120)
P A Family Medcenters ....C 316 771-9999
Derby (G-1264)
Partners Family Practice LLC ....E 620 345-6322
Moundridge (G-7195)
Patrick A Blanchard MD ....F 785 456-8778
Wamego (G-13433)
Peter J Cristiano Dr ....F 913 682-5588
Lansing (G-4690)
Physician Office Partners LLC ....E 913 754-0467
Overland Park (G-9163)
Pma Twin Lakes Medical Off P A ....E 316 832-0465
Wichita (G-15311)
Pratt Family Practice ....E 620 672-7422
Pratt (G-10137)
Primary Care Associates LLC ....E 316 684-2851
Wichita (G-15342)
Pro Partners MD Holbrook ....E 913 451-4776
Leawood (G-5529)
Rick R Tague MD MPH ....F 785 228-2277
Topeka (G-13015)
Rural Hlth Rsurces Jackson Inc ....F 785 364-2126
Holton (G-3111)
Sharon Lee Family Health Care ....D 913 722-3100
Kansas City (G-4420)
Shawnee Mission Med Ctr Inc ....F 913 676-8400
Shawnee Mission (G-11860)
Smith County Family Practice ....F 785 282-6834
Smith Center (G-12042)
Southeast Family Healthcare ....F 316 612-1332
Wichita (G-15622)
Stonecreek Family Physicians ....E 785 587-4101
Manhattan (G-6813)
Stormont-Vail Healthcare Inc ....F 785 836-7111
Carbondale (G-685)
Stormont-Vail Healthcare Inc ....E 785 456-2207
Wamego (G-13442)
Sumner County Family Care Ctr ....E 620 326-3301
Wellington (G-13533)
Tanglewood Family Medical Ctr ....E 316 788-3787
Derby (G-1274)
Thomas C Klein MD ....D 316 682-7411
Wichita (G-15760)
Timothy M Koehler MD ....E 316 462-6220
Wichita (G-15767)
Via Christi Clinic PA ....F 316 789-8222
Derby (G-1280)
Warren Clinic ....D 785 337-2214
Hanover (G-2714)
Wheatland Medical Clinic PA ....F 316 524-9400
Wichita (G-15963)
Wichita Family Medicine Specia ....E 316 858-5800
Wichita (G-15999)
Wichita Srgical Specialists PA ....D 316 263-0296
Wichita (G-16025)
Winfield Medical Arts PA ....E 620 221-6100
Winfield (G-16186)

OFFICES & CLINICS OF DRS OF MED: Cardiologist & Vascular

Cardiology Cons Topeka PA ....E 785 233-9643
Topeka (G-12444)
Cardiovascular Cons Kans PA ....D 316 440-0845
Wichita (G-13945)
Cardiovascular Consultants Inc ....E 913 491-1000
Shawnee Mission (G-11203)
Cardivsclar Thrcic Surgeons PA ....F 785 270-8625
Topeka (G-12445)
Cedar Surgical LLC ....F 316 616-6272
Andover (G-86)
Cypress Heart ....E 316 858-5200
Wichita (G-14151)
Daniel A Tatpati MD ....F 316 689-6803
Wichita (G-14166)
Flint Hills Heart Vascular ....F 785 320-5858
Manhattan (G-6633)
Heart Ctr At Ovrland Pk Rgonal ....E 913 541-5374
Overland Park (G-8806)
Mid America Cardiology ....F 913 588-9549
Westwood (G-13556)
Mid America Crdiolgy Assoc PC ....E 913 588-9600
Westwood (G-13557)
Mid America Crdiolgy Assoc PC ....E 913 588-9600
Kansas City (G-4242)
Midwest Cardiology Associates ....F 913 894-9015
Lenexa (G-6000)
Midwest Cardiology Associates ....D 913 253-3045
Shawnee Mission (G-11631)
Olathe Medical Services Inc ....D 913 780-4900
Olathe (G-7942)
P A Heartland Cardiology ....F 316 773-5300
Wichita (G-15248)
P A Heartland Cardiology ....E 316 686-5300
Wichita (G-15249)
St Marys Hosp of Blue Sprng ....B 816 523-4525
Iola (G-3635)
University of Kansas ....E 913 588-6798
Kansas City (G-4496)
University of Kansas Hospital ....E 913 682-6950
Leavenworth (G-5303)
University of Kansas Med Ctr ....F 913 588-6311
Kansas City (G-4508)
Zepick Cardiology ....E 316 616-2020
Wichita (G-16101)

OFFICES & CLINICS OF DRS OF MED: Clinic, Op by Physicians

Abilene Family Physicians PA ....F 785 263-7190
Abilene (G-4)
Ark City Clinic P A ....E 620 442-2100
Arkansas City (G-143)
Arthritis and Rheumatology ....E 316 612-4815
Wichita (G-13741)
Ascension Via Christi ....D 620 231-6788
Pittsburg (G-9813)
Belleville Medical Clinic P A ....F 785 527-2217
Belleville (G-451)
Brookdale Snior Lving Cmmnties ....E 913 491-3681
Leawood (G-5343)
C & S Medical Clinic PA ....E 620 408-9700
Dodge City (G-1316)
Carondelet Orthpdc Srgns Sprts ....E 913 642-0200
Overland Park (G-8521)
Cheyenne County Hospital ....E 785 332-2682
Saint Francis (G-10340)
City of Wamego ....E 785 456-2295
Wamego (G-13413)
Coffey County Hospital ....E 620 364-5395
Burlington (G-630)
Comanche County ....F 620 582-2136
Coldwater (G-1053)
Community Health Center of Sou ....E 620 231-6788
Pittsburg (G-9840)
Community Health Center of Sou ....F 620 429-2101
Columbus (G-1069)
Community Healthcare Sys Inc ....E 785 364-3205
Holton (G-3086)
Community Healthcare Sys Inc ....F 785 889-4241
Onaga (G-8172)
Community Hlth Ctr Sthast Kans ....D 620 231-9873
Pittsburg (G-9841)
Community Physicians Clinic ....F 785 562-3942
Marysville (G-6887)
Compcare ....E 785 823-7470
Salina (G-10458)
Cotton Oneil Clinic Endoscopy ....E 785 270-4850
Topeka (G-12512)
County of Harvey ....F 316 283-1637
Newton (G-7337)
County of Shawnee ....C 785 368-2000
Topeka (G-12522)
Debakey Heart Clinic ....F 785 625-4699
Hays (G-2783)
Dodge City Med Ctr Chartered ....C 620 227-8506
Dodge City (G-1349)
El Dorado Clinic PA ....E 316 321-2010
El Dorado (G-1557)
Envision Inc ....E 316 440-1600
Wichita (G-14293)
Family Health Ctr Morris Cnty ....F 620 767-5126
Council Grove (G-1165)
Family Physicians Mgt Corp ....F 620 365-3115
Iola (G-3599)
Fandhill Orthpd & Spt Medicine ....F 620 275-8400
Garden City (G-2155)
First Care Clinic Inc ....E 785 621-4990
Hays (G-2807)
Flint Hills Cmnty Hlth Ctr Inc ....D 620 342-4864
Emporia (G-1758)
Garden Medical Clinic PA ....C 620 275-3702
Garden City (G-2182)
Great Bend Childrens Clinic PA ....E 620 792-5437
Great Bend (G-2574)
Haysville Family Medcenter ....F 316 858-4165
Haysville (G-2946)
Health Ministries Clinic Inc ....F 620 727-1183
Newton (G-7359)
Health Partnership Clinic Inc ....E 913 433-7583
Olathe (G-7760)
Heartland Dental Group PA ....D 913 682-1000
Leavenworth (G-5251)
Heartland Medical Clinic Inc ....F 785 841-7297
Lawrence (G-4894)
Hiawatha Hospital Association ....F 785 742-2161
Hiawatha (G-3010)
Hunter Health Clinic Inc ....D 316 262-2415
Wichita (G-14656)
Hutchinson Clinic PA ....A 620 669-2500
Hutchinson (G-3319)
Kansas City Bone & Joint Clini ....E 913 381-5225
Overland Park (G-8889)
Kansas Medical Clinic PA ....F 785 233-3555
Topeka (G-12788)
Kansas Orthopedic Center PA ....D 316 838-2020
Wichita (G-14817)
Kansas Univ Physicians Inc ....C 913 362-2128
Kansas City (G-4158)
Kickapoo Nation Health Center ....F 785 486-2154
Horton (G-3129)
Labette County Medical Center ....E 620 421-4880
Parsons (G-9703)
Lawrence Family Practice Ctr ....E 785 841-6540
Lawrence (G-4965)
Lawrence Occpational Hlth Svcs ....F 785 838-1500
Lawrence (G-4978)
Marysville Clinic ....F 785 562-2744
Marysville (G-6898)
Meade Rural Health Clinic ....F 620 873-2112
Meade (G-7053)
Medical Arts Clnic A Prof Assn ....E 620 343-2900
Emporia (G-1791)
Mercy Kansas Communities Inc ....F 913 352-8379
Pleasanton (G-9999)
Mosier Mosier Fmly Physicians ....F 785 539-8700
Manhattan (G-6751)
Nemaha Valley Community Hosp ....E 785 336-6107
Seneca (G-10877)
Newman Mem Hosp Foundation ....B 620 343-6800
Emporia (G-1803)
North Amdon Fmly Physicians PA ....F 316 838-8585
Wichita (G-15186)
P A Comcare ....E 785 825-8221
Salina (G-10627)
P A Comcare ....E 785 827-6453
Salina (G-10628)
Parallel Pkwy Emrgncy Physcans ....E 913 596-4000
Kansas City (G-4310)
Prairiestar Health Center Inc ....F 620 663-8484
Hutchinson (G-3413)
Prefered Medical Associates ....E 620 365-6933
Iola (G-3626)
Republic County Family ....F 785 527-2237
Belleville (G-465)
Scott County Hospital ....C 620 872-2187
Scott City (G-10832)
SE Kansas Orthopedic Clinic ....F 620 421-0881
Parsons (G-9736)
Shawnee Mission Corp Care LLC ....E 913 492-9675
Shawnee Mission (G-11855)
Shawnee Mission Med Ctr Inc ....E 913 422-2020
Shawnee (G-11028)
South Wichita Family Medicine ....F 316 524-4338
Wichita (G-15620)
Stormont-Vail Healthcare Inc ....E 785 354-5225
Topeka (G-13113)

Sunflower Prompt Care F 785 246-3733
Topeka *(G-13119)*
Tanglewood Family Med Ctr PA E 316 788-3787
Derby *(G-1273)*
Team Vision Surgery Center E 316 729-6000
Wichita *(G-15721)*
Ulysses Family Physicians C 620 356-1261
Ulysses *(G-13326)*
Veterans Health Administration B 785 826-1580
Salina *(G-10752)*
Veterans Health Administration B 620 423-3858
Parsons *(G-9748)*
Via Christi Clinic PA B 316 689-9111
Wichita *(G-15881)*
Via Christi Clinic PA F 316 945-5400
Wichita *(G-15882)*
Via Christi Clinic PA D 316 689-9111
Wichita *(G-15884)*
Via Christi Clinic PA E 316 689-9111
Wichita *(G-15885)*
Via Christi Clinic PA E 316 651-2252
Wichita *(G-15886)*
Via Christi Clinic PA F 316 733-6618
Andover *(G-113)*
Via Christi Medical Management F 316 268-8123
Wichita *(G-15895)*
Wellness Services Inc F 913 438-8779
Shawnee Mission *(G-12000)*
Womens Clinic Johnson County F 913 491-4020
Leawood *(G-5600)*
Womens Clinic Johnson County F 913 491-4020
Overland Park *(G-9502)*

OFFICES & CLINICS OF DRS OF MED: Em Med Ctr, Freestanding

County of Smith E 785 282-6924
Smith Center *(G-12033)*
Emergency Services of Kansas E 866 815-9776
Newton *(G-7340)*
First Point Urgent Care Inc F 913 856-1369
Gardner *(G-2344)*
P A Med Assist F 785 272-2161
Topeka *(G-12956)*

OFFICES & CLINICS OF DRS OF MED: Health Maint Org Or HMO

Nuehealth Management Svcs LLC D 913 387-0510
Leawood *(G-5504)*
Sisters of Charity of Leavenwo E 913 825-0500
Kansas City *(G-4422)*

OFFICES & CLINICS OF DRS OF MED: Physician/Surgeon, Int Med

Alexander C Davis F 913 888-5577
Shawnee Mission *(G-11092)*
Associate In Family Hlth Care E 913 727-1018
Lansing *(G-4668)*
Associates In Internal Medped F 913 393-4888
Olathe *(G-7537)*
Beloit Medical Center P A E 785 738-2246
Beloit *(G-477)*
El Dorado Intrnal Medicine LLC F 316 321-2100
El Dorado *(G-1558)*
Great Bend Internists PA E 620 793-8429
Great Bend *(G-2582)*
Health Professionals Winfield F 620 221-4000
Winfield *(G-16146)*
Internal Medicine Associates E 620 342-2521
Emporia *(G-1778)*
Internal Medicine Group PA E 785 843-5160
Lawrence *(G-4912)*
James L Ruhlen MD PA E 913 829-4001
Olathe *(G-7806)*
Kansas Cy Internal Medicine PA E 913 451-8500
Overland Park *(G-8900)*
Kent W Haverkamp MD E 785 267-0744
Topeka *(G-12818)*
Kuhns H Richard Jr Md El E 316 320-1917
El Dorado *(G-1581)*
Kyle Tipton MD LLC E 316 321-2100
El Dorado *(G-1582)*
Lawrence Internal Medicine PA E 785 842-7200
Lawrence *(G-4970)*
Marian Clinic Inc E 785 233-2800
Topeka *(G-12859)*
Medical Assoc Manhattan PA E 785 537-2651
Manhattan *(G-6739)*
Medical Plaza Consultants P C E 913 945-6900
Overland Park *(G-9007)*
Medical Specialist E 785 623-2312
Hays *(G-2871)*
Mid-Amrca Kdny Stn Assctn LLC F 913 766-1860
Leawood *(G-5480)*
Orthokansas PA E 785 843-9125
Lawrence *(G-5051)*
Pittsburg Internal Medcine PA F 620 231-1650
Pittsburg *(G-9921)*
PMa Medical Associates PA D 316 261-3100
Wichita *(G-15310)*
Pratt Intrnal Mdicine Group PA E 620 672-7417
Pratt *(G-10141)*
Primary Care Physcans Mnhattan E 785 537-4940
Manhattan *(G-6780)*
Quivira Internal Medicine E 913 541-3340
Shawnee Mission *(G-11769)*
Rheumatology Cons Chartered E 913 661-9990
Shawnee Mission *(G-11796)*
Rhulen & Morgan Prof Assn F 913 782-8300
Olathe *(G-8032)*
Richard F Sosinski E 785 843-5160
Lawrence *(G-5096)*
Shawnee Mission Med Ctr Inc E 913 789-1980
Shawnee Mission *(G-11859)*
Statland Clinic Ltd PA E 913 345-8500
Shawnee Mission *(G-11897)*
Steven Donnenwerth E 620 672-7422
Pratt *(G-10155)*
United Medical Group LLC C 913 287-7800
Kansas City *(G-4487)*
University of Kansas A 913 588-6000
Kansas City *(G-4505)*
Vello Kass MD E 316 283-3600
Newton *(G-7423)*
Via Christi Health Inc D 785 456-6288
Wamego *(G-13446)*
Wichita Nephrology Group PA E 316 263-5891
Wichita *(G-16013)*

OFFICES & CLINICS OF DRS OF MED: Physician/Surgeon, Phy Med

Vision Today Inc F 913 397-9111
Olathe *(G-8142)*
Volunteers With Heart Inc F 913 563-5100
Olathe *(G-8143)*
Wichita Physical Medicine P A F 316 729-1030
Wichita *(G-16017)*
Womens Health Group PA E 785 776-1400
Manhattan *(G-6856)*

OFFICES & CLINICS OF DRS OF MED: Specialist/Phy, Fertility

Midwest Reproductive Center PA F 913 780-4300
Olathe *(G-7897)*
Reproductive Rsrce Ctr of Grtr E 913 894-2323
Shawnee Mission *(G-11788)*
Rodney Lyles MD E 913 894-2323
Shawnee Mission *(G-11813)*

OFFICES & CLINICS OF DRS OF MEDICINE: Diabetes

Mid-America Diabetes Assoc PA E 316 687-3100
Mount Hope *(G-7206)*

OFFICES & CLINICS OF DRS OF MEDICINE: Geriatric

Charles I Davis MD PA F 913 648-8880
Overland Park *(G-8541)*

OFFICES & CLINICS OF DRS OF MEDICINE: Med Clinic, Pri Care

Abay Neuroscience Center PA E 316 609-2600
Wichita *(G-13595)*
Community Hlth Ctr In Cwley CN F 620 221-3350
Winfield *(G-16125)*
Cotton-Neil Clnic Revocable Tr D 785 354-9591
Topeka *(G-12513)*
County of Lincoln F 785 524-4474
Lincoln *(G-6380)*
Donald B Scrafford E 316 721-2701
Wichita *(G-14225)*
Encompass Medical Group PA E 913 495-2000
Lenexa *(G-5833)*
Health Options That Matter E 913 722-3100
Kansas City *(G-4073)*
Logan County Manor F 785 672-8109
Oakley *(G-7480)*
Midwest Pain Management F 620 664-6724
Hutchinson *(G-3380)*
Via Christi Clinic PA E 316 609-4440
Wichita *(G-15883)*
Via Christi Health Inc D 316 773-4500
Wichita *(G-15888)*
Wellington Fmly Pract Clinc E 620 399-1222
Wellington *(G-13539)*
Wesley Medical Center LLC E 316 962-2000
Wichita *(G-15952)*

OFFICES & CLINICS OF DRS OF MEDICINE: Med Insurance Assoc

Comptech Group LLC F 913 341-7600
Overland Park *(G-8592)*

OFFICES & CLINICS OF DRS OF MEDICINE: Physician, Orthopedic

Advanced Orthopedic Assoc Inc D 316 631-1600
Wichita *(G-13625)*
Advanced Orthpdcs & Sprts Med F 620 225-7744
Dodge City *(G-1290)*
Alan Moskowitz MD PC D 316 858-1900
Wichita *(G-13658)*
Associated Orthopedics P A F 913 541-8897
Lenexa *(G-5672)*
Central Kansas Orthpd Group F 620 792-4383
Great Bend *(G-2531)*
Dickson-Diveley Midwest Ortho D 913 319-7600
Shawnee Mission *(G-11306)*
Hand Center PA F 316 688-5656
Wichita *(G-14552)*
Ian S Kovach MD PHD E 620 672-1002
Pratt *(G-10121)*
Kevin Mosier MD F 620 421-0881
Parsons *(G-9699)*
Lawrence Orthpaedic Surgery PA E 785 843-9125
Lawrence *(G-4980)*
Mark S Humphrey MD F 913 541-8897
Shawnee Mission *(G-11597)*
Medical Administrative K U Med E 913 588-8400
Kansas City *(G-4228)*
Metropolitan Spine Rehab PA F 913 387-2800
Overland Park *(G-9018)*
Mid-America Orthopedics PA E 316 262-4886
Wichita *(G-15076)*
Mid-America Orthopedics PA E 316 440-1100
Wichita *(G-15077)*
Midwest Orthopedics PA E 913 362-8317
Shawnee Mission *(G-11636)*
Newton Surgery Ctr F 316 283-9977
Newton *(G-7396)*
Ortho 4-States Real Estate LLC F 417 206-7846
Galena *(G-2078)*
Orthopaedic MGT Svcs LLC D 913 319-7500
Shawnee Mission *(G-11703)*
Orthopdic Spcalists Four State E 620 783-4441
Galena *(G-2079)*
Orthopdic Spt Mdicine Cons LLC E 913 319-7534
Leawood *(G-5510)*
Orthopdic Spt Medicine Ctr LLP E 785 537-4200
Manhattan *(G-6767)*
Orthopedic & Spo F 913 319-7546
Leawood *(G-5511)*
Orthopedic & Sports Medicine E 316 219-8299
Wichita *(G-15237)*
Orthopedic Professional Assn F 913 788-7111
Kansas City *(G-4299)*
Paincare PA E 913 901-8880
Overland Park *(G-9136)*
Salina Sports Med &ORth Clinic F 785 823-7213
Salina *(G-10691)*
South Cntl Kans Bone Joint Ctr F 620 672-1002
Pratt *(G-10150)*
Southeast Kansas Orthpd Clinic F 620 421-0881
Parsons *(G-9740)*
Stateline Surgery Center LLC E 620 783-4072
Galena *(G-2086)*
Tallgrass Orthpdics Spt Mdcine F 785 228-9999
Topeka *(G-13134)*
Tallgrass Orthpdics Spt Mdcine E 785 228-4700
Topeka *(G-13135)*
Wichita Orthopaedic Assoc LLC E 316 838-2020
Wichita *(G-16015)*

Wichita Srgical Specialists PA ... E ... 316 631-1600
Wichita *(G-16026)*

OFFICES & CLINICS OF DRS OF MEDICINE: Pulmonary

Pulmonary Sleep Consultant ... F ... 316 440-1010
Wichita *(G-15374)*
Shawnee Mssion Plmnary Cons PA ... F ... 913 362-0300
Shawnee Mission *(G-11861)*

OFFICES & CLINICS OF DRS OF MEDICINE: Rheumatology

Arthritis RES Ctr Foundation ... E ... 316 263-2125
Wichita *(G-13742)*
Trustees Indiana University ... E ... 913 499-6661
Fairway *(G-1923)*

OFFICES & CLINICS OF DRS, MED: Specialized Practitioners

Mednax Inc ... F ... 913 599-1396
Shawnee Mission *(G-11614)*
William Unsderfer MD ... E ... 620 669-6690
Hutchinson *(G-3490)*

OFFICES & CLINICS OF HEALTH PRACTITIONERS: Coroner

County of Sedgwick ... E ... 316 660-4800
Wichita *(G-14109)*

OFFICES & CLINICS OF HEALTH PRACTITIONERS: Nutrition

Salina Regional Health Ctr Inc ... D ... 785 452-4850
Salina *(G-10687)*
Shc Services Inc ... C ... 913 652-9229
Overland Park *(G-9306)*

OFFICES & CLINICS OF HEALTH PRACTITIONERS: Occu Therapist

Kansas Specialty Services Inc ... F ... 620 221-6040
Winfield *(G-16151)*

OFFICES & CLINICS OF HEALTH PRACTITIONERS: Physical Therapy

Advance Rehabilitation LLC ... F ... 785 232-9805
Topeka *(G-12294)*
Advanced Therapy & Spt Med LLC ... F ... 620 792-7868
Great Bend *(G-2501)*
Andbe Home Inc ... D ... 785 877-2601
Norton *(G-7441)*
ARC Physica Thera Plus Limite ... E ... 913 831-2721
Shawnee Mission *(G-11116)*
Capper Foundation ... E ... 785 272-4060
Topeka *(G-12440)*
Consultants In Neurology PA ... E ... 913 894-1500
Shawnee Mission *(G-11262)*
Fandhill Orthpd & Spt Medicine ... F ... 620 275-8400
Garden City *(G-2155)*
Geary Rhabilitation Fitnes Ctr ... E ... 785 238-3747
Junction City *(G-3696)*
Health Adminisource LLC ... F ... 913 384-5600
Shawnee Mission *(G-11419)*
Mid-America Orthopedics PA ... E ... 316 440-1100
Wichita *(G-15077)*
Occupational Hlth Partners LLC ... E ... 785 823-8381
Salina *(G-10618)*
P A Therapyworks Inc ... E ... 785 749-1300
Lawrence *(G-5053)*
Physical Rsprtory Therapy Svcs ... E ... 785 742-7606
Hiawatha *(G-3022)*
Physical Rsprtory Therapy Svcs ... F ... 785 742-2131
Hiawatha *(G-3021)*
Salina Physical Therapy Clinic ... F ... 785 825-1361
Salina *(G-10682)*
Saltcreek Fitness & Rehab ... F ... 785 528-1123
Osage City *(G-8190)*
Select Medical Corporation ... F ... 316 687-4581
Wichita *(G-15552)*
Select Medical Corporation ... F ... 913 239-9539
Overland Park *(G-9290)*
Select Medical Corporation ... F ... 913 385-0075
Overland Park *(G-9291)*
Trumove Physical Therapy PA ... F ... 913 642-7746
Overland Park *(G-9433)*

Wilcox Advanced Physical ... F ... 316 942-5448
Wichita *(G-16048)*

OFFICES & CLINICS OF HEALTH PRACTITIONERS: Physiotherapist

Abilene Physcl Thrpy & Sprts ... F ... 785 263-3519
Abilene *(G-6)*
Bloom & Associates Therapy ... F ... 785 273-7700
Topeka *(G-12388)*
Rebound Physical Therapy ... E ... 785 271-5533
Topeka *(G-13003)*
Sports Rehab/Physl Thrpy Assoc ... E ... 913 663-2555
Overland Park *(G-9335)*

OFFICES & CLINICS OF HEALTH PRACTITIONERS: Psychotherapist

Family Therapy Inst Midwest ... F ... 785 830-8299
Lawrence *(G-4857)*

OFFICES & CLINICS OF HEALTH PRACTITIONERS: Speech Pathology

County of Saline ... F ... 785 826-6606
Salina *(G-10465)*
Dermatology & Skin Cancer Ctr ... F ... 913 451-7546
Shawnee Mission *(G-11302)*
Erin Is Hope Foundation Inc ... E ... 316 681-3204
Wichita *(G-14301)*

OFFICES & CLINICS OF HEALTH PRACTITIONERS: Speech Therapist

Bethany HM Assn Lindsborg Kans ... C ... 785 227-2334
Lindsborg *(G-6394)*

OFFICES & CLINICS OF HEALTH PRACTRS: Clinical Psychologist

Christian Psychological Svcs ... F ... 785 843-2429
Lawrence *(G-4788)*
Clinical Associates ... E ... 913 677-3553
Lenexa *(G-5762)*
Clinical Associates PA ... F ... 913 677-3553
Lenexa *(G-5763)*
Compass Behavioral Health ... E ... 620 227-8566
Dodge City *(G-1329)*
Counseling & Mediation Center ... F ... 316 269-2322
Wichita *(G-14106)*
Fss Psychiatric LLC ... F ... 913 677-0500
Leawood *(G-5409)*
Guidance Center ... E ... 913 367-1593
Atchison *(G-233)*
Horizons Mental Health Ctr Inc ... F ... 620 532-3895
Kingman *(G-4595)*
Prairie View Inc ... E ... 620 947-3200
Hillsboro *(G-3055)*
Unified School District 214 ... D ... 620 356-4577
Ulysses *(G-13328)*

OFFICES & CLINICS OF HLTH PRACTITIONERS: Reg/Practical Nurse

Allstaff Chartered ... E ... 620 792-4643
Great Bend *(G-2504)*
Associated Homecare Inc ... C ... 316 320-0473
El Dorado *(G-1529)*
Integral Care Provider Inc ... C ... 913 384-2273
Shawnee Mission *(G-11463)*
Moore Enterprises Inc ... C ... 913 451-5900
Overland Park *(G-9052)*
Via Chrsti HM Hlth Wichita Inc ... D ... 316 268-8588
Wichita *(G-15900)*

OFFICES & CLINICS OF OPTOMETRISTS: Group & Corporate

West Wichita Fmly Optometrist ... F ... 316 262-3716
Wichita *(G-15958)*

OFFICES & CLINICS OF OPTOMETRISTS: Special, Visual Training

Shea Vision Associates ... E ... 316 686-6071
Wichita *(G-15579)*

OFFICES & CLINICS OF OPTOMETRISTS: Specialist, Contact Lens

Branstetter & Associates ... F ... 316 788-9290
Derby *(G-1224)*
Cohake Deutscher and Hefner ... E ... 785 271-8181
Topeka *(G-12485)*
Drs Price Young Odle Horsch PA ... E ... 620 343-7120
Emporia *(G-1733)*
Jackson & Baalman ... F ... 316 722-6452
Wichita *(G-14743)*
Price & Young & Odle ... F ... 785 223-5777
Junction City *(G-3739)*
Price & Young & Odle ... F ... 913 780-3200
Olathe *(G-8005)*
Price & Young & Odle ... E ... 785 537-1118
Manhattan *(G-6779)*
Price & Young & Odle ... F ... 785 272-0707
Topeka *(G-12987)*
Wolf & Hatfield Inc ... F ... 620 227-3071
Dodge City *(G-1463)*

OFFICES & CLINICS OF OPTOMETRISTS: Specialist, Low Vision

Eye Association Overland Park ... F ... 913 339-9090
Overland Park *(G-8701)*

OFFICES & CLINICS OF OPTOMETRISTS: Specialist, Optometrists

Burlingame Vision Associates ... F ... 913 338-1948
Overland Park *(G-8493)*
Drake & Assoc Optometrists ... F ... 913 894-2020
Lenexa *(G-5825)*
Drs Dobbins & Letourneau ... F ... 785 843-5665
Lawrence *(G-4841)*
Eye Associates of Wichita ... F ... 316 943-0433
Wichita *(G-14326)*
Eye Care Associates ... F ... 316 685-1898
Wichita *(G-14327)*
Hopkins & Hopkins ... F ... 620 275-5375
Garden City *(G-2199)*
Kannarr Eye Care LLC ... F ... 620 235-1737
Pittsburg *(G-9886)*
Kuhlmann Roberts & Janasek ... E ... 316 681-0991
Wichita *(G-14900)*
Lentz & Baker Eye Care ... F ... 316 634-2020
Wichita *(G-14955)*
Mc Pherson Eye Care LLP ... F ... 620 241-2262
McPherson *(G-6990)*
Morrison Optometric Assoc PA ... F ... 785 462-8231
Colby *(G-1030)*
Norris & Kelly Drs ... F ... 913 682-2929
Leavenworth *(G-5277)*
Olathe Family Vision ... F ... 913 782-5993
Olathe *(G-7934)*
Olathe Family Vision ... F ... 913 254-0200
Olathe *(G-7935)*
Ron D Hansen Od Inc ... F ... 620 662-2355
Hutchinson *(G-3430)*
Stiles Glaucoma Cons P A ... F ... 913 897-9299
Overland Park *(G-9363)*
Tran Majher and Shaw Od PA ... E ... 316 686-6063
Wichita *(G-15786)*
Vincent Pennipede Od ... E ... 913 825-2600
Overland Park *(G-9464)*
Vincent Pennipede Od ... E ... 913 780-9696
Olathe *(G-8141)*
Wichita Fmly Vision Clinic PA ... F ... 316 722-1001
Wichita *(G-16002)*

OIL & GAS FIELD MACHINERY

FMC Technologies Inc ... E ... 913 214-4300
Lenexa *(G-5862)*
Invena Corporation ... E ... 620 583-8630
Eureka *(G-1892)*
Oilpure Technologies Inc ... G ... 913 906-0400
Leawood *(G-5508)*
Quality Connectionz Inc ... G ... 620 380-6262
Iola *(G-3628)*
Schwabs Tinker Shop Intl Inc ... G ... 620 564-2547
Ellinwood *(G-1636)*
Star Pipe Usa LLC ... C ... 281 558-3000
Coffeyville *(G-979)*
U S Weatherford L P ... F ... 620 624-9324
Liberal *(G-6376)*

OIL FIELD MACHINERY & EQPT

Ernstings Incorporated .... G 620 564-2793
Ellinwood *(G-1631)*
Harbison-Fischer Inc .... G 620 624-9042
Liberal *(G-6317)*
Parmac LLC .... E 620 251-5000
Coffeyville *(G-969)*
Precision International .... D 620 365-7255
Iola *(G-3625)*
Ridge Enterprises LLC .... G 620 491-2141
Kingman *(G-4613)*
Schwabs Tinker Shop Intl Inc .... G 620 624-7611
Liberal *(G-6363)*
Vulcan Machine & Repair .... G 620 796-2190
Great Bend *(G-2655)*
Wsi Holdings LLC .... E 785 421-2255
Hill City *(G-3038)*

OIL FIELD SVCS, NEC

Abes Oilfield Service LLC .... E 620 532-5551
Spivey *(G-12072)*
Albert G Hogoboom .... E 316 321-1397
El Dorado *(G-1527)*
Alliance Well Service Inc .... G 620 672-1065
Pratt *(G-10095)*
Alpha Services and Production .... G 620 624-8318
Liberal *(G-6277)*
B & B Oil Tools Co LLC .... G 785 673-4828
Grainfield *(G-2494)*
B&B Cooperative Ventures LLC .... E 620 364-1311
Burlington *(G-625)*
Baker Hghes Olfld Oprtions LLC .... C 785 650-0182
Hays *(G-2754)*
Baker Petrolite LLC .... D 620 793-3546
Great Bend *(G-2514)*
Basic Energy Services LLC .... G 620 624-2277
Liberal *(G-6283)*
Bogner Oil Field Service Inc .... G 620 276-9453
Garden City *(G-2114)*
Brackeen Line Cleaning Inc .... F 620 587-3351
Claflin *(G-839)*
Brians Hot Oil Service LLC .... G 620 629-5933
Liberal *(G-6287)*
Butler Bros Inc .... F 620 221-3570
Winfield *(G-16118)*
C&J Well Services Inc .... E 785 628-6395
Hays *(G-2763)*
Cgf Investments Inc .... E 316 691-4500
Wichita *(G-13994)*
Chase Tubing Testing .... G 620 356-4314
Ulysses *(G-13289)*
Chase Well Service Inc .... F 620 793-9556
Great Bend *(G-2535)*
Chem-Tech LLC .... G 785 625-1141
Hays *(G-2768)*
Cheyenne Oil Services Inc .... E 785 798-2282
Ness City *(G-7255)*
Chitos Well Service LLC .... F 785 434-4942
Plainville *(G-9979)*
D S & W Well Servicing Inc .... E 620 793-5838
Great Bend *(G-2551)*
DC Oilfield Services .... G 620 598-2643
Moscow *(G-7167)*
Elite Pipe Testing .... G 785 726-4366
Ellis *(G-1643)*
Ellinwood Tank Service Inc .... G 620 793-0246
Ellinwood *(G-1630)*
Express Well Service & Sup Inc .... E 785 735-9405
Victoria *(G-13375)*
Fischer Pipe Testing Inc .... F 785 726-3411
Ellis *(G-1645)*
Fischer Well Service Inc .... G 785 628-3837
Hays *(G-2808)*
Gabel Lease Service Inc .... G 785 798-3122
Ness City *(G-7263)*
Gary Gorby .... E 620 879-5243
Caney *(G-668)*
Geres .... G 620 276-6179
Garden City *(G-2187)*
H2 Oil Field Services .... G 620 792-7115
Great Bend *(G-2588)*
Hertel Tank Service Inc .... G 785 628-2445
Hays *(G-2841)*
Kansas Acid Inc .... G 785 625-5599
Hays *(G-2857)*
L & D Oilfield Service Inc .... G 620 624-3329
Liberal *(G-6330)*
L-K Wireline Inc .... G 785 625-6877
Hays *(G-2861)*
Log-Tech Inc .... F 785 625-3858
Hays *(G-2866)*
Lone Star Services LLC .... E 620 626-7100
Liberal *(G-6337)*
M & D Excavating Inc .... F 785 628-3169
Hays *(G-2867)*
MAI Excavating Inc .... G 785 483-3387
Russell *(G-10280)*
MBC Well Logging & Leasing .... G 620 873-2953
Meade *(G-7051)*
Mercury Wireline .... G 785 625-1182
Hays *(G-2872)*
Mid-West Oilfield Service .... G 620 930-2051
Medicine Lodge *(G-7068)*
Mikes Pipe Inspection Inc .... E 620 624-9245
Liberal *(G-6344)*
Monster Pump Operations Inc .... G 785 623-4488
Hays *(G-2875)*
Nichols Water Svc An Okla Corp .... F 620 624-5582
Liberal *(G-6350)*
Palmer Oil Inc .... E 620 275-2963
Garden City *(G-2246)*
Petroleum Property Services .... G 316 265-3351
Wichita *(G-15287)*
Petropower LLC .... G 316 361-0222
Wichita *(G-15288)*
Piqua Petro Inc .... G 620 468-2681
Piqua *(G-9802)*
Poe Well Service Inc .... F 785 475-3422
Oberlin *(G-7499)*
Professional Pulling Svc LLC .... F 785 625-8928
Hays *(G-2892)*
Q Consldated Oil Well Svcs LLC .... G 620 431-9210
Chanute *(G-757)*
Qes Pressure Pumping LLC .... E 620 431-9210
Chanute *(G-758)*
Qes Pressure Pumping LLC .... F 785 242-4044
Ottawa *(G-8307)*
Qes Pressure Pumping LLC .... F 785 672-8822
Oakley *(G-7486)*
Reinhardt Services Inc .... G 785 483-2556
Russell *(G-10287)*
S & G Water Service Inc .... G 620 246-5212
Nashville *(G-7230)*
Schankie Well Service Inc .... G 620 437-2595
Madison *(G-6504)*
Spivey Oil Field Service LLC .... E 620 532-5178
Spivey *(G-12073)*
Steves Electric Roustabout Co .... F 785 434-7590
Plainville *(G-9992)*
Swift Services Inc .... E 785 798-2380
Ness City *(G-7267)*
T & C Mfg & Operating Inc .... E 620 793-5483
Great Bend *(G-2646)*
T R Service & Rental .... F 620 672-9100
Pratt *(G-10158)*
Treco Inc .... D 620 356-4785
Ulysses *(G-13325)*
Trilobite Testing Inc .... E 785 625-4778
Hays *(G-2921)*
X-Pert Service Tools Inc .... G 785 421-5600
Hill City *(G-3039)*

OIL LEASES, BUYING & SELLING ON OWN ACCOUNT

Castle Resources Inc .... E 785 625-5155
Schoenchen *(G-10802)*
Ritchie Exploration Inc .... F 316 691-9500
Wichita *(G-15468)*
Younger Energy Company .... G 316 681-2542
Wichita *(G-16097)*

OILS & GREASES: Blended & Compounded

Clean Harbors Wichita LLC .... C 316 832-0151
Wichita *(G-14039)*
Fuchs Lubricants Co .... D 913 422-4022
Kansas City *(G-4020)*
Lubrication Engineers Inc .... E 316 529-2112
Wichita *(G-14990)*

OILS & GREASES: Lubricating

Bg Products Incorporated .... E 316 265-2686
Wichita *(G-13845)*
Bg Products Incorporated .... C 316 265-2686
El Dorado *(G-1537)*
Crossfaith Ventures Lc .... E 620 662-8365
Hutchinson *(G-3251)*
Kcg Inc .... E 913 438-4142
Lenexa *(G-5942)*
Kcg Inc .... G 913 888-0882
Lenexa *(G-5943)*
Koch Industries Inc .... F 620 662-6691
Hutchinson *(G-3352)*
Petronomics Mfg Group Inc .... E 620 663-8559
Hutchinson *(G-3405)*
Rs Used Oil Services Inc .... E 866 778-7336
Wichita *(G-15490)*

OILS: Lubricating

Nalco Company LLC .... F 785 885-4161
Natoma *(G-7232)*

OLD AGE ASSISTANCE

Alderbrook Village .... F 620 442-4400
Arkansas City *(G-141)*
Baptist Senior Ministries .... E 913 685-4800
Shawnee Mission *(G-11150)*
Dove Estates Senior Living .... E 316 550-6343
Goddard *(G-2436)*
Good Shepherd Villages Inc .... E 785 244-6418
Summerfield *(G-12214)*
Halstead Place Inc .... E 316 830-2424
Halstead *(G-2701)*
Homestead Assisted Living .... E 785 272-2200
Topeka *(G-12703)*
North Central Flint Hills Area .... E 785 323-4300
Manhattan *(G-6762)*
Senior Services Inc Wichita .... D 316 267-0302
Wichita *(G-15559)*
Southeast KS AR AG Aging .... D 620 431-2980
Chanute *(G-765)*
Thriver Services LLC .... F 913 955-2555
Lenexa *(G-6179)*
Via Christi Hope Inc .... E 316 858-1111
Wichita *(G-15893)*

ON-LINE DATABASE INFORMATION RETRIEVAL SVCS

Building Solutions LLC .... F 620 225-1199
Dodge City *(G-1314)*
Kansas African American Aff .... F 785 296-4874
Topeka *(G-12756)*

OPERATIVE BUILDERS: Condominiums

A G Spanos Development Inc .... F 913 663-2400
Overland Park *(G-8335)*

OPERATIVE BUILDERS: Cooperative Apartment

Rooks County Holdings LLC .... F 785 261-0455
Stockton *(G-12186)*

OPERATOR: Apartment Buildings

A G Spanos Development Inc .... F 913 663-2400
Overland Park *(G-8335)*
Anchor Properties Inc .... D 913 661-2250
Shawnee Mission *(G-11112)*
Archon Residential MGT LP .... F 913 631-2100
Shawnee Mission *(G-11118)*
Aspen Place Apartments .... F 913 856-8185
Gardner *(G-2328)*
Barrington Park Town Homes .... F 913 469-5449
Shawnee Mission *(G-11153)*
Bethany Home Cottage Complex .... F 785 227-2721
Lindsborg *(G-6395)*
Boulevard Apprtments Townhomes .... F 913 722-3171
Roeland Park *(G-10219)*
Builders Apartments Inc .... F 316 684-1400
Wichita *(G-13911)*
Chase Manhattan Apartment .... F 785 776-3663
Manhattan *(G-6586)*
Clark Investment Group .... E 316 634-1112
Wichita *(G-14037)*
Colorado Plaza Management .... F 785 776-7994
Manhattan *(G-6595)*
Double T Enterprises .... F 620 342-2655
Emporia *(G-1731)*
Eden West Inc .... E 913 384-3800
Shawnee Mission *(G-11327)*
Edr Lawrence Ltd Partnership .... F 785 842-0032
Lawrence *(G-4846)*
Evangelical Lthrn Good Smrtn .... D 785 456-9482
Wamego *(G-13421)*
Evangelical Lutheran .... D 785 472-3167
Ellsworth *(G-1674)*

Evergreen Apartments .... F 913 341-5572
Overland Park *(G-8695)*
First Management Inc .... F 785 232-5555
Topeka *(G-12614)*
Fogelman Management Group LLC .... F 913 345-2888
Shawnee Mission *(G-11375)*
Fort Leavenworth Frontier .... F 913 682-6300
Fort Leavenworth *(G-1939)*
Fox Ridge Coop Townhouses Inc .... F 785 273-0640
Topeka *(G-12626)*
Gateway Housing LP .... E 913 621-3840
Kansas City *(G-4026)*
Griffith Developement .... F 316 686-1831
Wichita *(G-14518)*
Hanover Rs Limited Partnership .... F 913 851-4200
Overland Park *(G-8791)*
Highlands Highpoint Village .... F 913 381-0335
Overland Park *(G-8814)*
Hill Investment & Rental Co .... F 785 537-9064
Manhattan *(G-6658)*
Hillcrest Apartment Bldg Co .... F 316 684-7204
Wichita *(G-14610)*
Ilm 1 Holding Inc .... E 316 687-3741
Wichita *(G-14670)*
J A Peterson Enterprises Inc .... F 913 642-9020
Shawnee Mission *(G-11472)*
J A Peterson Realty Co Inc .... F 913 631-2332
Shawnee Mission *(G-11474)*
J A Peterson Realty Co Inc .... F 785 842-1455
Lawrence *(G-4917)*
J A Peterson Realty Co Inc .... F 913 432-5050
Shawnee Mission *(G-11475)*
Kansas Masonic Home .... C 316 269-7500
Wichita *(G-14814)*
Lee Construction Co .... F 785 539-7961
Manhattan *(G-6711)*
Lodge of Overland Park LLC .... E 913 648-8000
Overland Park *(G-8969)*
M P M Services Inc .... F 785 841-5797
Lawrence *(G-5005)*
Maple Gardens Assoc Ltd Partnr .... E 316 722-7960
Wichita *(G-15007)*
McCullough Developement Inc .... E 785 776-3010
Manhattan *(G-6736)*
MD Associates 3 Inc .... F 913 831-2996
Shawnee Mission *(G-11611)*
Meadowbrook Apartments .... E 785 842-4200
Lawrence *(G-5020)*
Mkt Community Development Inc .... F 913 596-7310
Kansas City *(G-4264)*
Mt Hope Community Development .... D 316 667-2431
Mount Hope *(G-7207)*
Nfi Management Co Inc .... F 913 341-4411
Shawnee Mission *(G-11683)*
Nies Investments LP .... E 316 684-0161
Wichita *(G-15179)*
Nolan Real Estate Services Inc .... F 913 362-1920
Shawnee Mission *(G-11686)*
Npi Property Management Corp .... F 913 648-4339
Shawnee Mission *(G-11689)*
Quarters At Cambridge LP .... F 316 636-1277
Wichita *(G-15390)*
Rane Management .... F 620 663-3341
Pretty Prairie *(G-10169)*
Real Estate Corporation Inc .... F 913 642-5134
Prairie Village *(G-10062)*
Retreat of Shawnee Apartments .... F 913 624-1326
Shawnee Mission *(G-11792)*
Saratoga Capital Inc .... F 316 838-1972
Wichita *(G-15520)*
Sentinel Real Estate Corp .... F 913 451-8976
Overland Park *(G-9295)*
Sentinel Real Estate Corp .... F 316 265-9471
Wichita *(G-15562)*
Southeast Kansas Lutherans Inc .... F 620 331-8010
Independence *(G-3561)*
Summer Stone Duplexes .... F 316 636-9000
Wichita *(G-15681)*
Tiehen Group .... F 913 648-1188
Leawood *(G-5575)*
Waddell & Reed Inc .... F 785 233-6400
Topeka *(G-13229)*
Wathena Heights Apartments .... F 417 883-7887
Wathena *(G-13480)*
Winfield Walnut KS LLC .... D 216 520-1250
Winfield *(G-16191)*
Wood View Apartments LLC .... F 913 262-8733
Kansas City *(G-4549)*
Yarco Company Inc .... C 620 564-2180
Ellinwood *(G-1640)*

OPERATOR: Nonresidential Buildings

7600 College Partnr Ted Greene .... F 913 341-1000
Overland Park *(G-8332)*
Associates Gould-Evens .... E 785 842-3800
Lawrence *(G-4739)*
Bacm 2005-3 Main Woodlawn LLC .... E 316 291-8450
Wichita *(G-13791)*
Clark Investment Group .... E 316 634-1112
Wichita *(G-14037)*
Foley Industries Inc .... D 316 943-4211
Wichita *(G-14399)*
Gcb Holdings LLC .... D 785 841-5185
Lawrence *(G-4869)*
Health Care Inc .... A 620 665-2000
Hutchinson *(G-3309)*
Healthpeak Properties Inc .... F 316 733-2645
Wichita *(G-14579)*
Loyalty Properties LLC .... F 913 323-6850
Overland Park *(G-8971)*
Manhattan Medical Center Inc .... F 785 537-2651
Manhattan *(G-6724)*
March Inc .... E 913 449-7640
Overland Park *(G-8987)*
MD Associates 4 Inc .... F 913 831-2996
Shawnee Mission *(G-11612)*
Mid Amrica Prpts Pittsburg LLC .... F 620 232-1678
Frontenac *(G-2060)*
Omni Center LP .... F 316 268-9108
Wichita *(G-15218)*
Patrick Properties Services .... F 913 262-6824
Overland Park *(G-9146)*
Quality Tech Svcs Lenexa LLC .... E 913 814-9988
Overland Park *(G-9215)*
Sagar Inc .... E 620 241-5343
McPherson *(G-7024)*
Santa Fe Law Building .... F 913 648-3220
Shawnee Mission *(G-11832)*
United Wrlss Arina Mgrk Conf C .... F 620 371-7390
Dodge City *(G-1446)*
Vista Franchise Inc .... E 785 537-0100
Manhattan *(G-6843)*

OPHTHALMIC GOODS

Bushnell Holdings Inc .... G 913 981-1929
Olathe *(G-7570)*
Bushnell Holdings Inc .... C 913 752-3400
Overland Park *(G-8497)*
Duffens Opticals .... D 785 234-3481
Overland Park *(G-8663)*
Duffins-Langley Optical Co .... D 913 492-5379
Shawnee Mission *(G-11320)*
Essilor Laboratories Amer Inc .... D 800 397-2020
Overland Park *(G-8691)*

OPHTHALMIC GOODS WHOLESALERS

Duffins-Langley Optical Co .... D 913 492-5379
Shawnee Mission *(G-11320)*

OPHTHALMIC GOODS, NEC, WHOLESALE: Frames

Essilor Laboratories Amer Inc .... D 800 397-2020
Overland Park *(G-8691)*

OPHTHALMIC GOODS: Frames & Parts, Eyeglass & Spectacle

Criss Optical Mfg Co Inc .... G 316 529-0414
Wichita *(G-14131)*

OPTICAL GOODS STORES

Kuhlmann Roberts & Janasek .... E 316 681-0991
Wichita *(G-14900)*
Morrison Optometric Assoc PA .... F 785 462-8231
Colby *(G-1030)*
Sabates Eye Centers PC .... E 913 469-8806
Shawnee Mission *(G-11823)*
Sears Roebuck and Co .... C 785 826-4378
Salina *(G-10701)*

OPTICAL GOODS STORES: Contact Lenses, Prescription

Branstetter & Associates .... F 316 788-9290
Derby *(G-1224)*
Cohake Deutscher and Hefner .... E 785 271-8181
Topeka *(G-12485)*
Drs Dobbins & Letourneau .... F 785 843-5665
Lawrence *(G-4841)*
Eye Associates of Wichita .... F 316 943-0433
Wichita *(G-14326)*
Eye Association Overland Park .... F 913 339-9090
Overland Park *(G-8701)*
Flintells Eyecare .... E 620 343-7120
Emporia *(G-1760)*
Hopkins & Hopkins .... F 620 275-5375
Garden City *(G-2199)*
Jackson & Baalman .... F 316 722-6452
Wichita *(G-14743)*
Ron D Hansen Od Inc .... F 620 662-2355
Hutchinson *(G-3430)*
Southwind Eyecare .... F 620 662-2355
Hutchinson *(G-3444)*

OPTICAL GOODS STORES: Opticians

Awad Nicola .... E 913 381-6969
Overland Park *(G-8417)*
O H Gerry Optical Company .... E 913 362-8822
Overland Park *(G-9095)*
Price & Young & Odle .... F 785 223-5777
Junction City *(G-3739)*
Vision Today Inc .... F 913 397-9111
Olathe *(G-8142)*

OPTICAL INSTRUMENTS & LENSES

Bushnell Inc .... C 913 752-6178
Overland Park *(G-8498)*

OPTICAL SCANNING SVCS

Century Business Technologies .... E 785 267-4555
Topeka *(G-12458)*

OPTOMETRISTS' OFFICES

Bealmear Bowl Trrey Hoch Reves .... E 620 276-3381
Garden City *(G-2105)*
Brian Strange .... E 620 663-8700
Hutchinson *(G-3222)*
Chris O D Jacquinot .... F 620 235-1737
Pittsburg *(G-9831)*
Cole & Cooper PA .... F 785 823-6391
Salina *(G-10457)*
Daniel S Durrie Cokingtin LLC .... E 913 491-3330
Overland Park *(G-8633)*
Eye Care Associates .... F 785 823-7403
Salina *(G-10494)*
Fisher Ronald Od PA .... F 316 942-7496
Wichita *(G-14378)*
Flintells Eyecare .... E 620 343-7120
Emporia *(G-1760)*
Grene Vision Group LLC .... E 316 721-2701
Wichita *(G-14513)*
Grene Vision Group LLC .... E 316 722-8883
Wichita *(G-14514)*
Grene Vision Group LLC .... D 316 691-4444
Wichita *(G-14515)*
Grene Vision Group LLC .... D 316 684-5158
Wichita *(G-14516)*
Hawks Bsler Rgers Optmtrist PA .... F 913 341-4508
Shawnee Mission *(G-11416)*
Heartland Eye Care LLC .... E 785 235-3322
Topeka *(G-12678)*
Henry L Bumgardner Jr Od .... F 316 264-4648
Wichita *(G-14593)*
Lawrence Eyecare Associates .... F 785 841-2280
Lawrence *(G-4964)*
Lynn W ONeal .... F 785 841-2280
Lawrence *(G-5004)*
Milton B Grin MD PA .... E 913 829-5511
Olathe *(G-7901)*
Mosier Mosier Fmly Physicians .... F 785 539-8700
Manhattan *(G-6751)*
Patrick J Pirrote Od PA .... F 316 721-8877
Wichita *(G-15268)*
Physicians Optical .... F 913 829-5511
Olathe *(G-7985)*
Southwind Eyecare .... F 620 662-2355
Hutchinson *(G-3444)*
The Eye Doctors .... F 785 272-3322
Topeka *(G-13157)*

ORCHESTRAS & BANDS

Pride of Prairie Orchestra Inc .... E 785 460-5518
Colby *(G-1034)*

ORGANIZATIONS & UNIONS: Labor

American Federation ....F.... 785 267-0100
Topeka **(G-12315)**
Calvin Investments LLC ....F.... 785 266-8755
Topeka **(G-12419)**
Firefighters Bnfit Asn-Sedgwic ....E.... 316 660-3473
Park City **(G-9618)**
Go Local LLC ....E.... 913 231-3083
Overland Park **(G-8761)**
International Brotherhood of ....F.... 913 371-2640
Kansas City **(G-4105)**

ORGANIZATIONS, NEC

Active Prime Timers Inc ....F.... 785 272-0237
Topeka **(G-12285)**
International Association ....F.... 785 760-5005
Lawrence **(G-4913)**
Interntional Wheat Gluten Assn ....F.... 913 381-8180
Overland Park **(G-8859)**
Kansas City Regional ....F.... 913 661-1600
Leawood **(G-5445)**
Kansas Intrschlstc Athltc Admn ....D.... 316 655-8929
Wichita **(G-14810)**
Neosho County Fair Assn Inc ....E.... 620 433-0446
Erie **(G-1860)**
Teaching Parents Assn Inc ....F.... 316 347-9900
Wichita **(G-15720)**
Waldorf Association Lawrence ....F.... 785 841-8800
Lawrence **(G-5177)**

ORGANIZATIONS: Biotechnical Research, Noncommercial

Ventria Bioscience Inc ....F.... 785 238-1101
Junction City **(G-3764)**
Xenotech LLC ....C.... 913 438-7450
Kansas City **(G-4559)**

ORGANIZATIONS: Civic & Social

Blind Pig ....F.... 785 827-7449
Salina **(G-10426)**
City of Emporia ....E.... 620 340-6339
Emporia **(G-1720)**
Great Bend Foundation Inc ....F.... 620 792-4217
Great Bend **(G-2580)**
Independent Order Oddfellows ....E.... 785 456-9493
Wamego **(G-13425)**
Kansas Scholastic Press Assoc ....F.... 785 864-7612
Lawrence **(G-4936)**
Lawrence Public Lib Foundation ....D.... 785 843-3833
Lawrence **(G-4985)**
Manhattan Martin Luther King J ....E.... 785 410-4599
Manhattan **(G-6723)**
Marais Des Cygnes Chapter Daug ....E.... 913 898-3088
Parker **(G-9658)**
McPherson Family Ymca Inc ....D.... 620 241-0363
McPherson **(G-6999)**
Midian Shriners ....F.... 316 265-9676
Wichita **(G-15087)**
Scooters LLC ....F.... 785 284-2978
Sabetha **(G-10332)**
Servant Foundation ....E.... 913 310-0279
Overland Park **(G-9297)**
Shawns Foundations ....F.... 316 214-1070
Garfield **(G-2367)**
Wichita State Unvsity Almni As ....F.... 316 978-3290
Wichita **(G-16035)**

ORGANIZATIONS: Educational Research Agency

Edge Enterprises Inc ....E.... 785 749-1473
Lawrence **(G-4845)**

ORGANIZATIONS: Medical Research

MSI Automation Inc ....F.... 316 681-3566
Bel Aire **(G-436)**
Phoenix Medical Research Inc ....F.... 913 381-7180
Prairie Village **(G-10060)**

ORGANIZATIONS: Professional

Adams-Gabbert & Associates LLC ....F.... 913 735-4390
Overland Park **(G-8346)**
American Heart Association Ka ....E.... 785 272-7056
Topeka **(G-12317)**
American Heart Association Ka ....E.... 913 652-1913
Shawnee Mission **(G-11104)**
Association of National ....F.... 785 296-5474
Topeka **(G-12346)**
Astronomical Society Kansas Cy ....F.... 913 631-8413
Shawnee Mission **(G-11127)**
Child Health Corp America ....C.... 913 262-1436
Lenexa **(G-5753)**
Domestic Vlnce Assn of Cntl Ka ....F.... 785 827-5862
Salina **(G-10480)**
Firemans Relief Assoc Inc ....F.... 620 365-4972
Iola **(G-3601)**
Health Dpknsas Assn Lcal Depts ....F.... 785 271-8391
Topeka **(G-12672)**
Hillside Medical Office ....E.... 316 685-1381
Wichita **(G-14613)**
Job Board Network LLC ....F.... 913 238-1181
Overland Park **(G-8875)**
Kansas Assn of Insur Agents ....F.... 785 232-0561
Topeka **(G-12759)**
Kansas City Blues Society Inc ....F.... 913 660-4692
Olathe **(G-7824)**
Kansas Cnty Dst Attys Associat ....D.... 785 232-5822
Kansas City **(G-4153)**
Mental Health Association of ....D.... 316 685-1821
Wichita **(G-15039)**
Mental Health Association of ....B.... 316 651-5368
Wichita **(G-15040)**
Revisor of Statutes ....E.... 785 296-2321
Topeka **(G-13012)**
Salina Child Care Association ....E.... 785 827-6431
Salina **(G-10667)**
Topeka Unified School Dst 501 ....D.... 785 295-3750
Topeka **(G-13189)**
Wichita Area Assn of Realtors ....F.... 316 263-3167
Wichita **(G-15974)**

ORGANIZATIONS: Religious

94 5 Country Inc ....D.... 785 272-3456
Topeka **(G-12275)**
Catholic Charities of Salina ....F.... 785 825-0208
Salina **(G-10437)**
Central Knss Cncil of Grl Sct ....F.... 785 827-3679
Salina **(G-10442)**
Christs Care Pre-School ....F.... 620 662-1283
Hutchinson **(G-3237)**
East Kansas Quartly Cnfrce Fre ....G.... 785 272-1843
Topeka **(G-12568)**
Edwardslle Untd Mthdst Daycare ....F.... 913 422-5384
Edwardsville **(G-1498)**
Finney County Attorneys Office ....F.... 620 272-3568
Garden City **(G-2161)**
First United Methodist Church ....F.... 316 755-1112
Valley Center **(G-13342)**
Humankind Mnstries Wichita Inc ....E.... 316 264-9303
Wichita **(G-14652)**
International Inst Christian S ....E.... 913 962-4422
Overland Park **(G-8858)**
Pine Village ....C.... 620 345-2901
Moundridge **(G-7196)**
Prizm Incorporated ....F.... 785 456-1831
Wamego **(G-13436)**
Salvation Army ....F.... 620 276-4027
Garden City **(G-2273)**
Salvation Army ....F.... 316 283-3190
Newton **(G-7413)**
Salvation Army ....E.... 785 843-1716
Lawrence **(G-5101)**
Shawnee Hts Untd Methdst Ch ....E.... 785 379-5492
Tecumseh **(G-12243)**
Stone Croft Ministries Inc ....D.... 816 763-7800
Overland Park **(G-9365)**
USA Missions Church of God ....E.... 620 345-2532
Moundridge **(G-7201)**
Worship Woodworks Inc ....G.... 620 622-4568
Protection **(G-10177)**
Young Mens Christian Assoc At ....D.... 913 367-4948
Atchison **(G-272)**

ORGANIZATIONS: Research Institute

Crititech Inc ....F.... 785 841-7120
Lawrence **(G-4817)**
Kansas State University ....E.... 785 625-3425
Hays **(G-2858)**
University of Kansas ....A.... 913 588-4718
Kansas City **(G-4498)**
University of KS Medcl ....E.... 913 588-1261
Fairway **(G-1925)**
Via Christi Research ....E.... 316 291-4774
Wichita **(G-15897)**

ORGANIZATIONS: Scientific Research Agency

Kansas State University ....D.... 785 532-6011
Manhattan **(G-6686)**

ORGANIZATIONS: Veterans' Membership

American Legion ....F.... 620 241-0343
McPherson **(G-6933)**
American Legion Post 156 ....E.... 913 294-4676
Paola **(G-9539)**
American Legion Post 400 ....F.... 785 296-9400
Topeka **(G-12319)**
American Legion Post 95 Inc ....F.... 620 983-2048
Peabody **(G-9758)**
Argonna Post 180 Amercn Legion ....F.... 620 793-5912
Great Bend **(G-2511)**
Ball-Mccolm Post No 5 Inc ....E.... 620 342-1119
Emporia **(G-1701)**
Grahem-Hrbers VFW Post No 3084 ....D.... 785 213-6232
Valley Falls **(G-13363)**
Kansas Assc Home For Aged Inc ....F.... 785 233-7443
Topeka **(G-12758)**
Pearce Keller American Legion ....F.... 785 776-4556
Manhattan **(G-6771)**
Veterans Affairs Kans Comm On ....F.... 785 350-4489
Topeka **(G-13221)**
Veterans Fgn Wars Post 9076 ....F.... 785 625-9940
Hays **(G-2924)**
Wholmoor Amrcn Lgion Post 237 ....F.... 785 348-5370
Linn **(G-6413)**

ORTHODONTIST

Bulleigh Orthodontics ....E.... 913 962-7223
Shawnee **(G-10921)**
Emporia Orthodontics ....F.... 620 343-7275
Emporia **(G-1740)**
Fry Orthodontics Prairie Vlg ....E.... 913 387-2500
Prairie Village **(G-10030)**
Gary J Newman DDS PA ....F.... 785 273-1544
Topeka **(G-12633)**
Gina B Pinamonti DDS ....F.... 620 231-6910
Pittsburg **(G-9866)**
Gust Orothondtcs PA G Morrison ....F.... 620 662-3255
Hutchinson **(G-3306)**
Gust Orthodontics ....F.... 316 283-1090
Newton **(G-7354)**
Hamilton & Wilson DDS ....F.... 785 272-3722
Topeka **(G-12660)**
Hannah & Oltjen ....F.... 913 829-2244
Olathe **(G-7749)**
Hannah & Oltjen ....F.... 620 343-3000
Emporia **(G-1767)**
Hannah & Oltjen ....F.... 913 268-5559
Shawnee Mission **(G-11408)**
Hullings Jon G DDS Ms PA ....F.... 316 636-1980
Wichita **(G-14650)**
Jenkins & Leblanc PA ....E.... 913 378-9610
Prairie Village **(G-10038)**
John D Meschke DDS PA ....F.... 620 662-6667
Hutchinson **(G-3342)**
Michael F Cassidy DDS ....F.... 785 233-0582
Topeka **(G-12887)**
Michael S Klein DDS ....F.... 913 829-4466
Olathe **(G-7891)**
Michael Yowell DDS PA ....F.... 620 241-0842
McPherson **(G-7002)**
Oread Orthodontics ....F.... 785 856-2483
Lawrence **(G-5047)**
Orthodonics Thompson PC ....F.... 913 681-8300
Leawood **(G-5509)**
Orthodontics P A Young ....F.... 913 592-2900
Spring Hill **(G-12094)**
Orthosynetics Inc ....E.... 913 782-1663
Olathe **(G-7965)**
Ratzlaff Craig D Ratzlaff DDS ....F.... 316 722-7100
Wichita **(G-15419)**
Richard E Crowder DDS ....F.... 316 684-5184
Wichita **(G-15456)**
Rogers Duncan Dillehay DDS PA ....F.... 316 683-6518
Derby **(G-1270)**
Steven L Hechler DDS Ms ....F.... 913 345-0541
Overland Park **(G-9361)**
Thompson R Wayne DDS Inc ....F.... 913 631-0110
Shawnee Mission **(G-11930)**
William E Hoffman DDS ....F.... 913 663-2992
Shawnee Mission **(G-12007)**

OSCILLATORS

Caliber Electronics Inc .... E 913 782-7787
Olathe *(G-7573)*
Xsis Electronics Inc .... F 913 631-0448
Shawnee *(G-11056)*

OUTLETS: Electric, Convenience

Sterling Food Mart Inc .... G 620 278-3371
Hutchinson *(G-3446)*

OUTREACH PROGRAM

Community Foundation of Ellis .... F 785 726-2660
Ellis *(G-1641)*

PACKAGE DESIGN SVCS

A G I Inc .... F 913 281-5533
Shawnee Mission *(G-11063)*

PACKAGED FROZEN FOODS WHOLESALERS, NEC

Associated Wholesale Groc Inc .... A 913 288-1000
Kansas City *(G-3825)*
Earp Meat Company .... C 913 287-3311
Edwardsville *(G-1497)*
Foodbrands Sup Chain Svcs Inc .... C 913 393-7000
Olathe *(G-7717)*
Jacksons Frozen Food Center .... G 620 662-4465
Hutchinson *(G-3339)*

PACKAGING & LABELING SVCS

Ash Grove Materials Corp .... D 913 345-2030
Overland Park *(G-8404)*
Bar Code Systems .... F 913 894-6368
Shawnee Mission *(G-11151)*
Box Central Inc .... F 316 689-8484
Wichita *(G-13875)*
Huhtamaki Films Inc .... A 913 583-3025
De Soto *(G-1204)*
Kaw Valley Companies Inc .... F 913 596-9752
Kansas City *(G-4161)*

PACKAGING MATERIALS, WHOLESALE

Ambrose Packaging Inc .... E 913 780-5666
Olathe *(G-7525)*
Ambrose Sales Inc .... E 913 780-5666
Olathe *(G-7526)*
Express Scale Parts Inc .... E 913 441-4787
Lenexa *(G-5844)*
Greif Inc .... E 620 221-2330
Winfield *(G-16145)*
Lawrence Paper Company .... C 785 843-8111
Lawrence *(G-4982)*
Neff Sales Co Inc .... F 913 371-0777
Kansas City *(G-4285)*
Robbie Transcontinental Inc .... C 913 492-3400
Lenexa *(G-6110)*
Tdi Global Solutions Inc .... F 877 834-6750
Meriden *(G-7082)*
Tytan International LLC .... F 913 492-3222
Lenexa *(G-6196)*
Waxene Products Company Inc .... G 316 263-8523
Wichita *(G-15938)*

PACKAGING MATERIALS: Paper

Bagcraftpapercon I LLC .... C 620 856-4615
Baxter Springs *(G-395)*
Gunze Plas & Engrg Corp Amer .... D 913 829-5577
Olathe *(G-7743)*
Kendall Packaging Corporation .... E 620 231-9804
Pittsburg *(G-9891)*
Polynova (usa) LLC .... G 913 309-6977
Lenexa *(G-6062)*
Superior School Supplies Inc .... F 620 421-3190
Parsons *(G-9743)*

PACKAGING MATERIALS: Polystyrene Foam

Tasler Inc .... G 785 885-4533
Natoma *(G-7233)*

PACKING SVCS: Shipping

Jasper Investments Inc .... F 913 599-0899
Lenexa *(G-5928)*

PAINT & PAINTING SPLYS STORE

Dahmer Contracting Group LLC .... D 816 795-3332
Overland Park *(G-8630)*

PAINT STORE

Adelhardt Enterprises Inc .... F 620 672-6463
Pratt *(G-10093)*
Alternative Building Tech .... F 913 856-4536
Gardner *(G-2325)*
Andrew Inc .... F 316 267-3328
Wichita *(G-13708)*
Sherwin-Williams Company .... F 913 782-0126
Olathe *(G-8062)*
Ulysses Standard Supply Inc .... F 620 356-4171
Ulysses *(G-13327)*

PAINTING SVC: Metal Prdts

Pro-Kleen Inc .... E 316 775-6898
Augusta *(G-339)*

PAINTS & ADDITIVES

Master Pnt Indus Coating Corp .... F 316 283-3999
Newton *(G-7377)*
Superior Products Intl II Inc .... G 913 962-4848
Shawnee Mission *(G-11912)*

PAINTS & ALLIED PRODUCTS

AMBS and Associates Inc .... G 913 599-5939
Lenexa *(G-5644)*
Lorac Company Inc .... F 316 263-2565
Wichita *(G-14979)*
Paragon N D T & Finishes Inc .... E 316 945-5285
Wichita *(G-15259)*
PPG Industries Inc .... E 316 262-2456
Bel Aire *(G-438)*
PPG Industries Inc .... E 913 681-5573
Overland Park *(G-9174)*
Prosoco Inc .... D 785 865-4200
Lawrence *(G-5081)*
Vanberg Specialized Coatings .... G 913 948-9825
Lenexa *(G-6208)*

PAINTS, VARNISHES & SPLYS, WHOLESALE: Paints

Andrew Inc .... F 316 267-3328
Wichita *(G-13708)*
Blish-Mize Co .... C 913 367-1250
Atchison *(G-218)*
Master Pnt Indus Coating Corp .... F 316 283-3999
Newton *(G-7377)*
Sherwin-Williams Company .... F 913 782-0126
Olathe *(G-8062)*
Sunbelt Chemicals Inc .... F 972 296-3920
Shawnee *(G-11035)*

PAINTS: Asphalt Or Bituminous

Epro Services Inc .... F 316 262-2513
Wichita *(G-14298)*

PALLET REPAIR SVCS

Capital City Pallet Inc .... F 785 379-5099
Topeka *(G-12429)*

PALLETS

B J Best Buy Pallets .... G 785 488-2923
Solomon *(G-12047)*
Precision Pallet .... G 620 221-4066
Winfield *(G-16166)*
Triple T Pallets .... E 316 772-9155
Valley Center *(G-13357)*

PALLETS & SKIDS: Wood

Baco Corporation .... F 316 945-5300
Wichita *(G-13792)*
Burgess Manufacturing Inc .... E 316 838-5748
Wichita *(G-13915)*
Companion Industries Inc .... E 620 345-3277
Moundridge *(G-7180)*
Stinnett Timbers LLC .... G 620 363-4757
Kincaid *(G-4581)*

PALLETS: Wooden

Asset Lifecycle LLC .... F 785 861-3100
Topeka *(G-12341)*
Hoyt Pallet Co .... E 785 986-6785
Hoyt *(G-3145)*
Industrial Crating Inc .... E 620 449-2003
Saint Paul *(G-10381)*
Kansas Hardwoods Inc .... F 785 456-8141
Belvue *(G-506)*
Mrg Holdings Inc .... F 913 371-3555
Kansas City *(G-4269)*
Palleton of Kansas Inc .... F 620 257-3571
Lyons *(G-6496)*
Pratt Industries USA Inc .... D 316 838-0851
Wichita *(G-15323)*
R&R Pallet Garden City Inc .... E 620 275-2394
Garden City *(G-2262)*
Reardon Pallet Company Inc .... E 816 221-3300
Kansas City *(G-4363)*
Southwest Pallets .... G 620 275-4343
Garden City *(G-2284)*
Whiteleys Inc .... F 785 233-3801
Topeka *(G-13243)*
Wirths & Sons Inc .... F 316 838-0509
Wichita *(G-16059)*

PAPER & BOARD: Die-cut

Tabco Incorporated .... E 913 287-3333
Kansas City *(G-4457)*

PAPER CONVERTING

Central Fiber LLC .... E 785 883-4600
Wellsville *(G-13541)*
Partners Kan-Verting LLC .... G 913 894-2700
Lenexa *(G-6044)*
Roll Products Inc .... F 785 437-6000
Saint Marys *(G-10374)*

PAPER MANUFACTURERS: Exc Newsprint

International Paper Company .... E 316 943-1033
Wichita *(G-14709)*

PAPER, WHOLESALE: Printing

Southwest Paper Company Inc .... E 316 838-7755
Wichita *(G-15631)*
Timber Creek Paper Inc .... F 316 264-3232
Wichita *(G-15765)*

PAPER: Building, Insulating & Packaging

Illinois Tool Works Inc .... E 913 856-2546
Gardner *(G-2351)*

PAPER: Business Form

Kansas Business Forms LLC .... E 620 724-5234
Girard *(G-2414)*

PAPER: Coated & Laminated, NEC

Bagcraftpapercon I LLC .... C 620 856-4615
Baxter Springs *(G-395)*
Gary Bell .... G 785 233-6677
Holton *(G-3090)*
RGI Publications Inc .... E 913 829-8723
Olathe *(G-8030)*
Spectragraphics Inc .... E 913 888-6828
Lenexa *(G-6147)*

PAPER: Wrapping & Packaging

Million Packaging Inc .... E 913 402-0055
Overland Park *(G-9039)*

PAPERBOARD

Sonoco Products Company .... C 620 662-2331
Hutchinson *(G-3443)*

PAPERBOARD CONVERTING

Ken OKelly .... G 816 868-6028
Prairie Village *(G-10042)*

PARKING GARAGE

Car Park Inc .... E 316 265-0553
Wichita *(G-13942)*

PARKING LOTS

Apac-Kansas Inc....E....620 662-3307
Hutchinson *(G-3200)*
Central Plains Maintenance....D....316 945-4774
Wichita *(G-13983)*
Parking Systems Inc....F....913 345-9272
Shawnee Mission *(G-11717)*

PARKING LOTS & GARAGES

City of Newton....F....316 284-6083
Newton *(G-7329)*

PAROLE OFFICE

Corrections Kansas Department....F....620 792-3549
Great Bend *(G-2547)*
Corrections Kansas Department....E....620 341-3294
Emporia *(G-1726)*
Department Corrections Kansas....F....913 829-6207
Olathe *(G-7649)*
Supreme Court United States....E....785 295-2790
Topeka *(G-13126)*

PARTICLEBOARD: Laminated, Plastic

Laminate Works Inc....E....913 281-7474
Kansas City *(G-4194)*
Laminate Works Inc....D....913 800-8263
Lenexa *(G-5963)*
Laminate Works Kansas City LLC....G....913 281-7474
Kansas City *(G-4195)*

PARTITIONS & FIXTURES: Except Wood

Countertop Trends LLC....E....620 836-2311
Gridley *(G-2689)*
New Age Industrial Corp Inc....C....785 877-5121
Norton *(G-7455)*

PARTITIONS: Wood & Fixtures

Kesters Mdsg Display Intl....E....913 281-4200
Kansas City *(G-4171)*

PARTITIONS: Wood, Floor Attached

Alderman Acres Mfg Inc....F....620 251-4095
Coffeyville *(G-909)*

PARTS: Metal

CD Custom Enterprises LLC....F....316 804-4520
Newton *(G-7327)*
Twin Oaks Industries Inc....E....785 827-4839
Salina *(G-10743)*

PARTY & SPECIAL EVENT PLANNING SVCS

Ase Group Inc....F....913 339-9333
Leawood *(G-5333)*
Cec Entertainment Inc....E....913 648-4920
Overland Park *(G-8533)*
Cec Entertainment Inc....D....316 636-2225
Wichita *(G-13968)*
Ice Sports Kansas City LLC....E....913 441-3033
Shawnee Mission *(G-11451)*
Lawrence Gymnastics Academy....E....785 865-0856
Lawrence *(G-4968)*
Rekat Recreation Inc....E....785 272-1881
Topeka *(G-13007)*
Two Guys & A Grill....F....913 393-4745
Olathe *(G-8126)*

PATENT OWNERS & LESSORS

Mriglobal - Kansas LLC....A....816 753-7600
Manhattan *(G-6754)*

PATTERNS: Indl

Mastercraft Pattern Inc....G....620 231-3530
Pittsburg *(G-9900)*
Rapid Processing Solutions Inc....F....316 265-2001
Wichita *(G-15417)*

PAVERS

CPB Materials LLC....G....316 833-1146
Haysville *(G-2938)*

PAWN SHOPS

Abraham Jacob Gorelick....F....913 371-0459
Kansas City *(G-3779)*
Easy Money Pawn Shop Inc....G....316 687-2727
Wichita *(G-14255)*

PAYROLL SVCS

Automatic Data Processing Inc....C....515 875-3160
Wichita *(G-13773)*
Axcet Hr Solutions Inc....E....913 383-2999
Overland Park *(G-8420)*
Choices Network Inc....B....785 820-8018
Salina *(G-10447)*
County of Wallace....E....785 852-4282
Sharon Springs *(G-10896)*
Infosync Services Llc....B....316 685-1622
Wichita *(G-14692)*
Kennedy Mc Kee and Company LLP....F....620 227-3135
Dodge City *(G-1389)*
Paychex Inc....D....913 814-7776
Leawood *(G-5517)*
Paycor Inc....D....913 262-9484
Shawnee Mission *(G-11719)*
Payroll Plus....E....620 846-2658
Montezuma *(G-7160)*
Prescriptive Payroll Inc....F....316 247-3166
Wichita *(G-15337)*
Pro Pay LLC....E....913 826-6300
Salina *(G-10642)*
Syndeo Outsourcing LLC....E....316 630-9107
Wichita *(G-15710)*
Tax 911com Incorporated....F....913 712-8539
Olathe *(G-8102)*

PENSION & RETIREMENT PLAN CONSULTANTS

CPI Qualified Plan Cons Inc....B....620 793-8473
Great Bend *(G-2549)*
Demarche Associates Inc....D....913 384-4994
Overland Park *(G-8648)*
Demars Pnsion Cnslting Svcs In....E....913 469-6111
Overland Park *(G-8649)*
Great-West Financial Retiremen....A....847 857-3000
Overland Park *(G-8776)*
Mid West Pnsion Administrators....F....913 663-2777
Shawnee Mission *(G-11628)*
Nestegg Consulting Inc....F....316 383-1064
Wichita *(G-15158)*
Nolan Company....E....913 888-3500
Overland Park *(G-9091)*
Senio Livin Retir Commu LLC....C....913 534-8872
Overland Park *(G-9294)*
Tax Favored Benefits Inc....E....913 648-5526
Overland Park *(G-9392)*
Tic International Corporation....E....913 236-5490
Overland Park *(G-9409)*
True North Inc....F....316 266-6574
Wichita *(G-15809)*
Wells Fargo Clearing Svcs LLC....F....785 825-4636
Salina *(G-10767)*

PERFORMING ARTS CENTER PRODUCTION SVCS

McPherson Opera House Company....F....620 241-1952
McPherson *(G-7001)*

PERFUME: Perfumes, Natural Or Synthetic

Product Dev & Designers....F....913 783-4364
Paola *(G-9584)*

PERSONAL APPEARANCE SVCS

Friend That Cooks LLC....E....913 660-0790
Shawnee *(G-10959)*
Genesis Health Club Inc....E....316 945-8331
Wichita *(G-14458)*
Hair Shop & Retailing Center....E....913 397-9888
Olathe *(G-7745)*

PERSONAL CARE FACILITY

Asbury Park Inc....C....316 283-4770
Newton *(G-7311)*
Athletic & Rehabilitation Ctr....F....913 378-0778
Shawnee Mission *(G-11131)*
Bucklin Hospital District Inc....E....620 826-3202
Bucklin *(G-590)*
Buhler Sunshine Home Inc....D....620 543-2251
Buhler *(G-614)*
Catholic Charities of Northeas....E....913 621-5090
Overland Park *(G-8526)*
Cedars Inc....C....620 241-0919
McPherson *(G-6942)*
Cherry Village Benevolence....D....620 792-2165
Great Bend *(G-2538)*
Clp Healthcare Services Inc....D....620 232-9898
Pittsburg *(G-9837)*
Country Care Inc....D....913 773-5517
Easton *(G-1478)*
Country Place Senior Living....F....785 632-5052
Clay Center *(G-857)*
County of Atchison....E....913 367-1905
Atchison *(G-223)*
Dignity Care Home Inc....F....785 823-3434
Salina *(G-10477)*
Heart America Hospice Kans LLC....E....785 228-0400
Topeka *(G-12674)*
Heartland Assisted Living....E....913 248-6600
Shawnee *(G-10968)*
Heartland Hospice Services LLC....D....419 252-5743
Wichita *(G-14585)*
Homestead Health Center Inc....D....316 262-4473
Wichita *(G-14633)*
Hospice Incorporated....E....620 251-1640
Coffeyville *(G-947)*
Hospice Incorporated....E....620 229-8398
Winfield *(G-16147)*
Hospice Advantage LLC....F....913 859-9582
Overland Park *(G-8826)*
Hospice Care of Kansas LLC....E....316 721-8803
Wichita *(G-14638)*
Hospice of Salina Inc....F....785 825-1717
Salina *(G-10547)*
Hospice of The Prairie Inc....E....620 227-7209
Dodge City *(G-1375)*
Hospice Services Inc....F....785 543-2900
Phillipsburg *(G-9789)*
Kansas City Hospice Inc....E....816 363-2600
Overland Park *(G-8896)*
Maria Villa Inc....E....316 777-9917
Mulvane *(G-7221)*
Mennonite Frndship Communities....C....620 663-7175
Hutchinson *(G-3374)*
Midwest Health Services Inc....C....785 440-0500
Topeka *(G-12899)*
Morton County Hospital....C....620 697-2141
Elkhart *(G-1623)*
Multi Community Diversfd Svcs....F....785 227-2712
Lindsborg *(G-6405)*
Nicol Home Inc....E....785 568-2251
Glasco *(G-2423)*
Osborne Development Company....D....785 346-2114
Osborne *(G-8215)*
Park Wheatridge Care Center....E....620 624-0130
Liberal *(G-6355)*
Parkside Homes Inc....D....620 947-2301
Hillsboro *(G-3053)*
Saint Jude Hospice....F....785 742-3823
Hiawatha *(G-3024)*
Spring View Manor Inc....E....620 456-2285
Conway Springs *(G-1145)*
Wheat State Manor Inc....D....316 799-2181
Whitewater *(G-13573)*
Woodworth Enterprises Inc....E....620 236-7248
Chetopa *(G-818)*

PERSONAL CREDIT INSTITUTIONS: Auto Loans, Incl Insurance

Dominion Management Svcs Inc....F....571 408-4770
Wichita *(G-14222)*
Dominion Management Svcs Inc....F....703 765-2274
Wichita *(G-14223)*

PERSONAL CREDIT INSTITUTIONS: Consumer Finance Companies

Beneficial Kansas Inc....E....913 492-1383
Shawnee Mission *(G-11161)*
Capital Resources LLC....F....913 469-1630
Overland Park *(G-8511)*
Hsbc Finance Corporation....F....913 362-1400
Roeland Park *(G-10225)*
Qc Financial Services Inc....D....913 439-1100
Shawnee Mission *(G-11763)*

PERSONAL CREDIT INSTITUTIONS: Finance Licensed Loan Co's, Sm

Qc Holdings Inc....C....866 660-2243
Lenexa (G-6082)

PERSONAL CREDIT INSTITUTIONS: Financing, Autos, Furniture

Toyota Motor Credit Corp....F....913 661-6800
Shawnee Mission (G-11937)

PERSONAL CREDIT INSTITUTIONS: Licensed Loan Companies, Small

Capfusion LLC....E....816 888-5302
Prairie Village (G-10018)

PERSONAL DOCUMENT & INFORMATION SVCS

Walgreen Co....E....913 393-2757
Olathe (G-8146)

PERSONAL INVESTIGATION SVCS

National Screening Bureau LLC....F....316 263-4400
Wichita (G-15152)
Vend-Tech Enterprise LLC....E....316 689-6850
Wichita (G-15873)

PERSONAL SVCS

Lenexa Services Inc....D....913 541-0150
Shawnee (G-10987)
Regional Prvntion Ctr Wyndotte....F....913 288-7685
Kansas City (G-4367)

PEST CONTROL IN STRUCTURES SVCS

Betts Pest Control Inc....F....316 943-3555
Wichita (G-13840)
Central States Enterprises LLC....E....785 827-8215
Salina (G-10445)
General Pest Control LLC....F....620 855-7768
Cimarron (G-826)
Gunter Pest Management Inc....E....913 397-0220
Olathe (G-7742)
Hawks Interstate Pestmasters....E....316 267-8331
Wichita (G-14569)
Moxie Services LLC....E....913 416-1205
Lenexa (G-6013)
Schendel Services Inc....F....913 498-1811
Olathe (G-8056)
Schendel Services Inc....F....316 320-6422
Wichita (G-15530)

PEST CONTROL SVCS

Advance Termite & Pest Control....F....620 662-3616
Hutchinson (G-3192)
Augustine Exterminators Inc....E....913 362-4399
Overland Park (G-8413)
Browns Tree Service LLC....F....785 379-9212
Topeka (G-12410)
Edge Pest Control Kans Cy LLC....F....913 262-3343
Shawnee (G-10943)
Landscape Outfitters LLC....F....620 221-1108
Winfield (G-16154)
Orkin LLC....F....785 827-0314
Salina (G-10623)
Orkin LLC....F....913 492-4029
Lenexa (G-6038)
Parker Pest Control Inc....F....316 524-4311
Augusta (G-336)
Patton Termite & Pest Ctrl Inc....F....316 773-3825
Wichita (G-15270)
Plainjans Feedlot Service....F....620 872-5777
Scott City (G-10827)
Terminix Intl Co Ltd Partnr....E....913 696-0351
Lenexa (G-6176)
Terminix Intl Co Ltd Partnr....F....785 266-2600
Topeka (G-13152)
Terminix Intl Co Ltd Partnr....E....913 696-0351
Overland Park (G-9402)

PESTICIDES

Pbi-Gordon Corporation....D....816 421-4070
Shawnee (G-11009)
Pbi-Gordon Corporation....E....816 421-4070
Kansas City (G-4317)
Pbi-Gordon Corporation....E....620 848-3849
Galena (G-2080)

PESTICIDES WHOLESALERS

Alternative Building Tech....F....913 856-4536
Gardner (G-2325)
Schendel Services Inc....F....913 498-1811
Olathe (G-8056)

PET & PET SPLYS STORES

Barks N Bows Dog Grooming....G....785 823-1627
Salina (G-10421)
Joco Barking Club....E....913 558-2625
Overland Park (G-8876)
Kth Properties Corporation....E....316 941-1100
Wichita (G-14897)
R C Kennels....F....785 238-7000
Junction City (G-3747)

PET COLLARS, LEASHES, MUZZLES & HARNESSES: Leather

Kth Properties Corporation....E....316 941-1100
Wichita (G-14897)

PET FOOD WHOLESALERS

Hills Pet Nutrition Inc....B....800 255-0449
Topeka (G-12690)
Hills Pet Nutrition Sales Inc....E....785 354-8523
Topeka (G-12693)
Ziwi USA Incorporated....F....913 291-0189
Overland Park (G-9529)

PET SPLYS

All American Pet Brands Inc....G....913 951-4999
Shawnee (G-10907)
All Crtres Veterinary Hosp P A....F....316 721-3993
Wichita (G-13663)
Barks N Bows Dog Grooming....G....785 823-1627
Salina (G-10421)
Countryside Pet Clinic PA....E....316 733-8433
Andover (G-88)
El Paso Animal Clinic....F....316 788-1561
Derby (G-1243)
Ewy Animal Hosp Inc....G....785 823-8428
Salina (G-10487)
Fairview Mills LLC....E....785 336-2148
Seneca (G-10866)
Rokenn Enterprises Inc....G....785 523-4251
Delphos (G-1217)
Tr Sales & Distribution Inc....F....800 478-5468
Olathe (G-8118)
West Wichita Pet Clinic....F....316 722-0100
Wichita (G-15959)

PET SPLYS WHOLESALERS

Cosmic Pet LLC....E....316 941-1100
Wichita (G-14105)
Premium Nutritional Pdts Inc....F....913 962-8887
Shawnee Mission (G-11750)
Treatco Inc....D....316 265-7900
Wichita (G-15795)

PET-SITTING SVC: In-Home

Joco Barking Club....E....913 558-2625
Overland Park (G-8876)

PETROLEUM & PETROLEUM PRDTS, WHOL Svc Station Splys, Petro

P B Hoidale Co Inc....F....913 438-1500
Shawnee (G-11008)

PETROLEUM & PETROLEUM PRDTS, WHOLESALE Crude Oil

Great Salt Plins Midstream LLC....E....316 262-2819
Wichita (G-14507)
Kelly Maclaskey....E....316 321-9011
El Dorado (G-1578)
Mv Purchasing LLC....E....316 262-2819
Wichita (G-15143)
Tex-Ok-Kan Oil Field Svcs LLC....E....620 271-7310
Garden City (G-2298)

PETROLEUM & PETROLEUM PRDTS, WHOLESALE Diesel Fuel

Frontier Ag Inc....F....785 734-2331
Bird City (G-530)
Garden City Co-Op Inc....F....620 276-8903
Garden City (G-2171)

PETROLEUM & PETROLEUM PRDTS, WHOLESALE Engine Fuels & Oils

Central Valley AG Cooperative....C....785 738-2241
Beloit (G-481)
Golden Belt Coop Assn Inc....F....785 726-3115
Ellis (G-1646)

PETROLEUM & PETROLEUM PRDTS, WHOLESALE Fuel Oil

Farmers Cooperative Elev Co....F....316 835-2261
Halstead (G-2699)
Mackie Clemens Fuel Company....F....785 242-2177
Ottawa (G-8288)

PETROLEUM & PETROLEUM PRDTS, WHOLESALE Gases

Kinder Morgan Kansas Inc....G....620 384-7830
Syracuse (G-12228)

PETROLEUM & PETROLEUM PRDTS, WHOLESALE: Bulk Stations

Bartlett Cooperative Assn....E....620 226-3311
Bartlett (G-371)
Bennington Oil Co Inc....F....785 392-3031
Minneapolis (G-7113)
Berwick Cooperative Oil Co....F....785 284-2227
Sabetha (G-10307)
Brecheisens Stop 2 Shop Inc....E....620 392-5577
Hartford (G-2727)
Brown - Dupree Oil Co Inc....F....620 353-1874
Ulysses (G-13285)
Capital City Oil Inc....E....785 233-8008
Topeka (G-12428)
Clough Oil Company Inc....F....620 251-0521
Coffeyville (G-916)
Consumer Oil Company Inc....F....785 988-4459
Bendena (G-511)
Decatur Cooperative Assn....F....785 475-2234
Oberlin (G-7490)
Farmers Co-Operative Equity Co....F....620 739-4335
Isabel (G-3639)
Great Bend Cooperative Assn....E....620 793-3531
Great Bend (G-2576)
Haag Oil Co LLC....D....785 357-0270
Topeka (G-12656)
Hallauer Oil Co Inc....F....785 364-3140
Holton (G-3094)
Hampel Oil Inc....E....913 321-0139
Kansas City (G-4063)
Hampel Oil Distributors Inc....E....316 529-1162
Wichita (G-14549)
Hampel Oil Distributors Inc....F....800 530-5848
Wichita (G-14550)
Hoc Industries Inc....E....316 838-4663
Wichita (G-14620)
Jim Woods Marketing Inc....F....620 856-3554
Baxter Springs (G-410)
L C McClain Inc....F....785 584-6151
Rossville (G-10253)
Leavenworth County Coop Assn....F....913 727-1900
Lansing (G-4683)
Leiszler Oil Co Inc....E....785 632-5648
Manhattan (G-6712)
McCune Farmers Union Coop....F....620 632-4226
Mc Cune (G-6920)
Mike Groves Oil Inc....F....620 442-0480
Arkansas City (G-166)
Mulvane Cooperative Union Inc....F....316 777-1121
Mulvane (G-7223)
Nusser Oil Company Inc....E....620 697-4624
Elkhart (G-1625)
Parker Oil Co Inc....F....316 529-4343
Wichita (G-15264)
Rakies Oil LLC....F....620 442-2210
Arkansas City (G-171)
Robson Oil Co Inc....F....785 263-2470
Abilene (G-51)

Service Oil Company ....F 785 462-3441
Colby *(G-1040)*
Severy Cooperative Association ....F 620 736-2211
Severy *(G-10893)*
Stuhlsatz Service Inc ....F 316 531-2282
Garden Plain *(G-2322)*
Triplett Inc ....F 785 823-7839
Salina *(G-10742)*
Universal Motor Fuels Inc ....F 316 832-0151
Wichita *(G-15855)*
Wenger Oil Inc ....F 316 283-8795
Newton *(G-7427)*
World Fuel Services Inc ....C 913 643-2300
Overland Park *(G-9505)*

PETROLEUM BULK STATIONS & TERMINALS

Clark-Timmons Oil Company ....F 816 229-0228
Kansas City *(G-3916)*
Mitten Inc ....E 785 672-3062
Oakley *(G-7481)*
Semcrude LP ....F 620 234-5532
Stafford *(G-12109)*

PETROLEUM PRDTS WHOLESALERS

Andax Industries LLC ....E 785 437-0604
Saint Marys *(G-10358)*
Casillas Petroleum Corp ....E 620 276-3693
Satanta *(G-10778)*
Chc McPherson Refinery Inc ....E 620 793-3111
Great Bend *(G-2536)*
Clough Oil Company Inc ....E 620 251-0103
Coffeyville *(G-917)*
Collingwood Grain Inc ....D 785 899-3636
Goodland *(G-2466)*
Ferrellgas Partners LP ....D 913 661-1500
Overland Park *(G-8714)*
Garden City Co-Op Inc ....F 620 275-6161
Garden City *(G-2170)*
Johnson Cooperative Grn Co Inc ....F 620 492-6210
Johnson *(G-3654)*
Koch Carbon LLC ....E 316 828-5500
Wichita *(G-14875)*
Koch Industries Inc ....A 316 828-5500
Wichita *(G-14881)*
Koch Mineral Services LLC ....E 316 828-5500
Wichita *(G-14884)*
Lybarger Oil Inc ....F 785 448-5512
Garnett *(G-2381)*
Norton County Co-Op Assn Inc ....F 785 877-5900
Norton *(G-7456)*
Plains Marketing LP ....F 620 365-3208
Iola *(G-3624)*
Redwood Group LLC ....D 816 979-1786
Mission *(G-7137)*
Skyland Grain LLC ....F 620 492-2126
Johnson *(G-3660)*
Southern Plains Co-Op At Lewis ....E 620 324-5536
Lewis *(G-6270)*
T & E Oil Company Inc 1 ....E 620 663-3777
Hutchinson *(G-3460)*
Town and Country Food Mkts Inc ....E 316 942-7940
Wichita *(G-15779)*
Volz Oil Company - Kinsley Inc ....F 620 659-2979
Greensburg *(G-2685)*

PETS & PET SPLYS, WHOLESALE

Lawrence Feed & Farm Sup Inc ....F 785 843-4311
Lawrence *(G-4966)*
Pet Haven LLC ....F 316 942-2151
Wichita *(G-15285)*

PHARMACEUTICAL PREPARATIONS: Druggists' Preparations

Biomed Kansas Inc ....G 913 661-0100
Lenexa *(G-5705)*
Cydex Pharmaceuticals Inc ....F 913 685-8850
Lawrence *(G-4822)*
Genzada Pharmaceuticals LLC ....G 620 204-7150
Sterling *(G-12119)*
Rd2rx LLC ....F 816 754-8047
Lenexa *(G-6093)*

PHARMACEUTICAL PREPARATIONS: Medicines, Capsule Or Ampule

Diversified Sports Tech LLC ....G 949 466-2393
Baxter Springs *(G-404)*
Prescription Centre ....G 620 364-5523
Burlington *(G-641)*
Via Chrsti Rhbltation Hosp Inc ....G 316 946-1790
Wichita *(G-15903)*

PHARMACEUTICAL PREPARATIONS: Powders

Crititech Particle Engg ....F 785 841-7120
Lawrence *(G-4818)*

PHARMACEUTICAL PREPARATIONS: Solutions

Alixa Rx LLC ....G 913 307-8150
Lenexa *(G-5640)*

PHARMACEUTICAL PREPARATIONS: Water, Sterile, For Injections

Fagron Compounding Svcs LLC ....E 316 773-0405
Wichita *(G-14332)*

PHARMACEUTICALS

Aratana Therapeutics Inc ....D 913 353-1000
Leawood *(G-5329)*
Arconic Inc ....G 620 665-2932
Hutchinson *(G-3206)*
B F Ascher & Company Inc ....E 913 888-1880
Lenexa *(G-5680)*
Baxter Drug Inc ....G 620 856-5858
Baxter Springs *(G-396)*
Bayer Healthcare LLC ....E 913 268-2000
Shawnee Mission *(G-11154)*
Carefusion 213 LLC ....B 800 523-0502
Leawood *(G-5347)*
Celgene Corporation ....F 913 266-0300
Overland Park *(G-8534)*
Centaur Inc ....G 913 390-6184
Olathe *(G-7583)*
E I Du Pont De Nemours & Co ....F 302 774-1000
New Century *(G-7282)*
Elias Animal Health LLC ....G 913 492-2221
Olathe *(G-7676)*
Glaxosmithkline LLC ....E 316 214-4811
Wichita *(G-14470)*
Hospira Inc ....B 620 241-6200
McPherson *(G-6976)*
Ligand Pharmaceuticals Inc ....G 785 856-2346
Lawrence *(G-4996)*
Med Care of Kansas Inc ....F 785 295-8548
Topeka *(G-12876)*
Med Care of Kansas Inc ....G 785 295-8548
Topeka *(G-12877)*
Merck Sharp & Dohme Corp ....D 913 422-6001
De Soto *(G-1208)*
Norbrook Inc ....G 913 802-5050
Overland Park *(G-9093)*
OBrien Pharmacy ....F 913 322-0001
Shawnee Mission *(G-11693)*
Parnell Corporate Svcs US Inc ....E 913 274-2100
Leawood *(G-5515)*
Pfizer Inc ....C 913 897-3054
Leawood *(G-5521)*
Pharmion Corporation ....E 913 266-0300
Overland Park *(G-9161)*
Sparhawk Laboratories Inc ....D 913 888-7500
Lenexa *(G-6144)*
Teva Pharmaceuticals ....G 610 727-6055
Leawood *(G-5574)*

PHARMACIES & DRUG STORES

Biomed Kansas Inc ....G 913 661-0100
Lenexa *(G-5705)*
Dillon Companies Inc ....D 785 823-9403
Salina *(G-10478)*
Genoa Healthcare Mass LLC ....E 913 680-1652
Leavenworth *(G-5245)*
Hutchinson Clinic PA ....A 620 669-2500
Hutchinson *(G-3319)*
Queen-Morris Ventures LLC ....C 913 383-2563
Shawnee Mission *(G-11765)*
Via Christi Clinic PA ....E 316 689-9111
Wichita *(G-15885)*

Walmart Inc ....B 620 232-1593
Pittsburg *(G-9960)*

PHOTOCOPY MACHINE REPAIR SVCS

Canon Solutions America Inc ....G 913 323-5010
Overland Park *(G-8508)*
Century Office Pdts Inc Topeka ....E 785 267-4555
Topeka *(G-12460)*
Logan Business Machines Inc ....E 785 233-1102
Topeka *(G-12848)*
Perfect Output LLC ....D 913 317-8400
Overland Park *(G-9154)*

PHOTOCOPY SPLYS WHOLESALERS

Evolv Solutions LLC ....E 913 469-8900
Shawnee Mission *(G-11352)*
Images ....G 785 827-0824
Salina *(G-10549)*

PHOTOCOPYING & DUPLICATING SVCS

Administration Kansas Dept ....C 785 296-3001
Topeka *(G-12290)*
ARC Document Solutions ....E 316 264-9344
Wichita *(G-13727)*
ARC Document Solutions Inc ....E 816 300-6600
Kansas City *(G-3814)*
ARC Document Solutions Inc ....E 314 231-5025
Kansas City *(G-3815)*
ARC Document Solutions Inc ....E 316 264-9344
Wichita *(G-13728)*
Barker Printing and Copy Svcs ....G 785 233-5533
Topeka *(G-12365)*
Capitol LLC ....E 602 462-5888
Olathe *(G-7576)*
City Blue Print Inc ....D 316 265-6224
Wichita *(G-14023)*
Copy Center of Topeka Inc ....E 785 233-6677
Topeka *(G-12507)*
Copy Shoppe ....G 785 232-0403
Topeka *(G-12508)*
Documart Inc ....F 913 649-3800
Shawnee Mission *(G-11312)*
Docuplex Inc ....E 316 262-2662
Wichita *(G-14220)*
Evolv Solutions LLC ....E 913 469-8900
Shawnee Mission *(G-11352)*
Fedex Office & Print Svcs Inc ....F 913 239-9399
Overland Park *(G-8710)*
Fedex Office & Print Svcs Inc ....E 913 894-2010
Lenexa *(G-5850)*
Fedex Office & Print Svcs Inc ....E 316 636-5443
Wichita *(G-14350)*
Fedex Office & Print Svcs Inc ....F 316 682-1327
Wichita *(G-14351)*
Fedex Office & Print Svcs Inc ....F 785 537-7340
Manhattan *(G-6627)*
Fedex Office & Print Svcs Inc ....F 316 941-9909
Wichita *(G-14352)*
Fedex Office & Print Svcs Inc ....E 913 661-0192
Shawnee Mission *(G-11364)*
Fedex Office & Print Svcs Inc ....F 913 677-4488
Shawnee Mission *(G-11365)*
Fedex Office & Print Svcs Inc ....E 316 721-6529
Wichita *(G-14353)*
Fedex Office & Print Svcs Inc ....F 913 383-2178
Overland Park *(G-8711)*
Fedex Office & Print Svcs Inc ....E 785 272-2500
Topeka *(G-12603)*
Fedex Office & Print Svcs Inc ....F 913 393-0953
Olathe *(G-7707)*
Fedex Office & Print Svcs Inc ....F 913 780-6010
Olathe *(G-7708)*
Independent Oil & Gas Svc Inc ....G 316 263-8281
Wichita *(G-14680)*
Jet Digital Printing & Copies ....F 316 685-2679
Wichita *(G-14755)*
Optimation Holographics Inc ....E 785 233-6000
Topeka *(G-12950)*
Perfect Output LLC ....D 913 317-8400
Overland Park *(G-9154)*
Print Time Inc ....E 913 345-8900
Leawood *(G-5528)*
Proprint Incorporated ....G 785 272-0070
Topeka *(G-12992)*
Scanning America Inc ....D 785 749-7471
Lawrence *(G-5102)*
Shahrokhi Inc ....G 913 764-5775
Olathe *(G-8060)*

PHOTOFINISHING LABORATORIES

CVS Pharmacy Inc ....E 913 651-2323
Leavenworth *(G-5230)*
CVS Pharmacy Inc ....F 913 722-3711
Shawnee Mission *(G-11287)*
Ranieri Camera & Video Inc ....F 785 336-3719
Seneca *(G-10879)*
Steinle Inc ....C 620 421-3940
Parsons *(G-9741)*
Vizworx Inc ....E 316 691-4589
Wichita *(G-15910)*
Walgreen Co ....E 913 393-2757
Olathe *(G-8146)*
Walgreen Co ....E 785 628-1767
Hays *(G-2928)*
Walgreen Co ....E 316 652-9147
Wichita *(G-15917)*
Walgreen Co ....E 316 689-0866
Wichita *(G-15918)*
Walgreen Co ....E 316 729-6171
Wichita *(G-15919)*
Walgreen Co ....E 316 943-2299
Wichita *(G-15920)*
Walgreen Co ....E 913 814-7977
Overland Park *(G-9480)*
Walgreen Co ....E 913 829-3176
Olathe *(G-8147)*
Walgreen Co ....E 913 789-9275
Merriam *(G-7109)*
Walgreen Co ....E 316 218-0819
Andover *(G-116)*
Walgreen Co ....E 913 341-1725
Overland Park *(G-9481)*
Walgreen Co ....E 316 684-2828
Wichita *(G-15921)*
Walgreen Co ....E 785 841-9000
Lawrence *(G-5178)*
Walgreen Co ....E 785 832-8388
Lawrence *(G-5179)*
Walmart Inc ....C 785 899-2111
Goodland *(G-2489)*
Walmart Inc ....B 620 232-1593
Pittsburg *(G-9960)*

PHOTOFINISHING LABORATORIES

Dillon Companies Inc ....C 620 225-6130
Dodge City *(G-1341)*
Walmart Inc ....B 316 347-2092
Goddard *(G-2456)*
Wolfes Camera Shops Inc ....E 785 235-1386
Topeka *(G-13248)*

PHOTOGRAMMATIC MAPPING SVCS

Paradigm Alliance Inc ....E 316 554-9225
Wichita *(G-15255)*

PHOTOGRAPHIC EQPT & SPLYS

Canon Solutions America Inc ....G 913 323-5010
Overland Park *(G-8508)*

PHOTOGRAPHIC EQPT & SPLYS WHOLESALERS

Daymark Solutions Inc ....F 913 541-8980
Shawnee Mission *(G-11294)*
Fujifilm North America Corp ....F 816 914-5942
Kansas City *(G-4021)*
Meridianpro Inc ....E 620 421-1107
Parsons *(G-9709)*
Wolfes Camera Shops Inc ....E 785 235-1386
Topeka *(G-13248)*

PHOTOGRAPHIC EQPT & SPLYS, WHOL: Motion Picture Studio/Thtr

R E B Inc ....E 620 365-5701
Iola *(G-3630)*

PHOTOGRAPHIC EQPT & SPLYS, WHOLESALE: Printing Apparatus

Heartland Imaging Companies ....B 913 621-1211
Kansas City *(G-4076)*

PHOTOGRAPHIC EQPT & SPLYS: Toners, Prprd, Not Chem Plnts

Inkcycle Inc ....D 913 894-8387
Shawnee *(G-10973)*

PHOTOGRAPHIC SVCS

McKissick Enterprises LLC ....F 316 687-0272
Wichita *(G-15029)*

PHOTOGRAPHY SVCS: Commercial

Ranieri Camera & Video Inc ....F 785 336-3719
Seneca *(G-10879)*

PHOTOGRAPHY SVCS: Portrait Studios

Inter-State Studio & Pubg Co ....D 913 745-6700
Bonner Springs *(G-556)*
Lifetouch Inc ....E 316 262-6611
Wichita *(G-14962)*
Sears Roebuck and Co ....C 785 826-4378
Salina *(G-10701)*
Walmart Inc ....B 620 275-0775
Garden City *(G-2308)*

PHOTOGRAPHY SVCS: Still Or Video

Scholastic Photography Inc ....F 913 384-9126
Shawnee Mission *(G-11837)*
Tpp Acquisition Inc ....F 913 317-5591
Overland Park *(G-9421)*

PHYSICAL EXAMINATION & TESTING SVCS

U S X-Ray LLC ....F 913 652-0550
Lenexa *(G-6199)*

PHYSICAL EXAMINATION SVCS, INSURANCE

Hooper Holmes Inc ....D 913 764-1045
Olathe *(G-7777)*

PHYSICAL FITNESS CENTERS

Angus Inn Best Western Motel ....D 620 792-3541
Great Bend *(G-2509)*
Darco Inc ....E 620 221-7529
Winfield *(G-16138)*
Element Fitness ....D 913 268-3633
Shawnee Mission *(G-11331)*
Executive Mnor Leavenworth Inc ....F 785 234-5400
Topeka *(G-12586)*
Geary Rhabilitation Fitnes Ctr ....E 785 238-3747
Junction City *(G-3696)*
Genesis Health Clubs MGT LLC ....E 316 634-0094
Wichita *(G-14459)*
Get After It LLC ....F 402 885-0964
Manhattan *(G-6645)*
Inside Sports and Fitness LLC ....F 913 888-9247
Overland Park *(G-8849)*
Inside Sports and Fitness LLC ....F 913 894-4752
Overland Park *(G-8850)*
Jewish Cmnty Ctr Grter Kans Cy ....B 913 327-8000
Shawnee Mission *(G-11486)*
Junction City Family YMCA Inc ....E 785 762-4780
Junction City *(G-3704)*
Kansas State University ....F 785 532-6980
Manhattan *(G-6685)*
Lees Energy Connection ....F 913 682-3782
Leavenworth *(G-5267)*
Maximus Fitness and Wellness ....F 785 267-2132
Topeka *(G-12865)*
Memorial Hospital Fitness Ctr ....F 785 263-3888
Abilene *(G-46)*
Oprc Inc ....E 913 642-6880
Overland Park *(G-9108)*
Opti-Life East Wichita LLC ....D 316 927-5959
Wichita *(G-15224)*
Orangetheory Fitness ....F 316 440-4640
Wichita *(G-15231)*
R & D Fitness Inc ....E 913 722-2001
Shawnee Mission *(G-11770)*
Sagar Inc ....E 620 241-5343
McPherson *(G-7024)*
Steven Enterprises LLC ....C 316 681-3010
Wichita *(G-15667)*
Topeka Country Club ....D 785 232-2090
Topeka *(G-13173)*
Wichita State University ....E 316 978-3584
Wichita *(G-16032)*
Woodside Tennis & Health Club ....C 913 831-0034
Shawnee Mission *(G-12017)*
YMCA of Hutchinson Reno Cnty ....D 620 662-1203
Hutchinson *(G-3494)*
YMCA Topeaka Downtown Branch ....E 785 354-8591
Topeka *(G-13256)*
Young Mens Christian ....F 785 233-9815
Topeka *(G-13258)*
Young Mens Christian Assn ....E 620 275-1199
Garden City *(G-2319)*
Young Mens Christian Associa ....D 316 320-9622
El Dorado *(G-1616)*
Young Mens Christian Associa ....E 913 321-9622
Kansas City *(G-4564)*
Young Mens Christian Associa ....C 316 942-2271
Wichita *(G-16091)*
Young Mens Christian Associa ....C 316 219-9622
Wichita *(G-16093)*
Young Mens Christian Associa ....D 316 260-9622
Wichita *(G-16094)*
Young Mens Christian Associa ....C 316 942-5511
Wichita *(G-16095)*
Young Mens Christian Associat ....C 620 545-7290
Viola *(G-13380)*
Young Mens Christian Gr Kansas ....D 913 362-3489
Prairie Village *(G-10088)*
Young Mens Christian Gr Kansas ....C 913 393-9622
Olathe *(G-8163)*
Young Mens Christian Gr Kansas ....D 913 782-7707
Olathe *(G-8164)*
Young MNS Chrstn Assn of Tpeka ....C 785 354-8591
Topeka *(G-13259)*
Young MNS Chrstn Assn Pttsburg ....D 620 231-1100
Pittsburg *(G-9972)*

PHYSICAL FITNESS CLUBS WITH TRAINING EQPT

Bar Method West Plaza ....E 913 499-1468
Westwood *(G-13550)*
Capital Frsght Golf Fitnes LLC ....E 913 648-1600
Overland Park *(G-8509)*
Kristie Winters ....F 913 648-8946
Park *(G-9597)*
Nck Wellness Center Inc ....E 785 738-3995
Beloit *(G-495)*

PHYSICIANS' OFFICES & CLINICS: Medical

Bluestem Medical LLP ....F 785 754-2458
Quinter *(G-10179)*
College Park Fmly Care Ctr Inc ....C 913 469-5579
Shawnee Mission *(G-11249)*
College Park Fmly Care Ctr Inc ....D 913 492-8686
Lenexa *(G-5769)*
College Park Fmly Care Ctr Inc ....E 913 829-0505
Olathe *(G-7598)*
Community Memorial Hospital ....E 785 562-2311
Marysville *(G-6886)*
Ellsworth Medical Clinic Inc ....E 785 472-3277
Ellsworth *(G-1671)*
Heartland Cardiology LLC ....F 316 686-5300
Wichita *(G-14581)*
John P Gravino Do ....F 785 842-5070
Lawrence *(G-4927)*
Johnson County Imaging Ctr PA ....E 913 469-8998
Overland Park *(G-8878)*
Kevin J Stuever MD ....E 785 843-5160
Lawrence *(G-4944)*
Mallery Clinic LLC ....F 785 825-9024
Salina *(G-10589)*
Olathe Medical Services Inc ....F 913 782-8487
Olathe *(G-7944)*
Ottawa Fmly Physcans Chartered ....E 785 242-1620
Ottawa *(G-8297)*
Preferred Medical Associates ....E 316 733-1331
Andover *(G-106)*
Steven D Braun ....F 620 662-1212
Hutchinson *(G-3447)*
Sunflower Medical Group ....E 913 432-2080
Shawnee Mission *(G-11909)*
Sunflower Medical Group PA ....D 913 261-5800
Shawnee Mission *(G-11910)*
Sunflower Medical Group PA ....E 913 722-4240
Shawnee Mission *(G-11911)*
Tall Grass Prarie Surg Spclsts ....E 785 233-7491
Topeka *(G-13132)*
Tallgrass Prairie Surgical ....F 785 295-4500
Topeka *(G-13137)*
Topeka Urology Clinic PA ....F 785 232-1005
Topeka *(G-13191)*

Vitre-Retinal Cons Surgeons PA ....E 316 683-5611
Wichita *(G-15909)*

PHYSICIANS' OFFICES & CLINICS: Medical doctors

Ascension Via Christi Hospital ....A 316 268-5040
Wichita *(G-13752)*
Bio-Mdcal Applcations Kans Inc ....E 785 266-3087
Topeka *(G-12383)*
Birth & Women Center Inc ....F 785 232-6950
Topeka *(G-12385)*
Braham J Geha ....E 913 383-9099
Kansas City *(G-3875)*
Bruce Speak ....F 785 267-6301
Topeka *(G-12411)*
Burkey Richard L DPM P A ....F 620 793-7624
Great Bend *(G-2524)*
Captify Health Inc ....E 913 951-2600
Lenexa *(G-5728)*
Carondelet Home Care Services ....E 913 529-4800
Shawnee *(G-10924)*
Cedar Vale Rural Health Clinic ....F 620 758-2221
Cedar Vale *(G-693)*
Center For Rprductive Medicine ....E 316 687-2112
Wichita *(G-13972)*
Coffeyville Doctors Clinic P A ....E 620 251-7500
Coffeyville *(G-919)*
Cole & Cooper PA ....F 785 823-6391
Salina *(G-10457)*
College Park Fmly Care Ctr Inc ....E 913 438-6700
Shawnee Mission *(G-11248)*
Comcare of Sedgwick County ....B 316 660-7600
Wichita *(G-14061)*
Compassionate Family Care LLC ....F 913 744-4300
Lenexa *(G-5780)*
County of Finney ....E 620 272-3600
Garden City *(G-2134)*
County of Geary ....E 785 762-5788
Junction City *(G-3684)*
Dandurand Drug Company Inc ....E 316 685-2353
Wichita *(G-14165)*
Daniel Aires MD ....E 913 588-6050
Kansas City *(G-3955)*
Debra L Heidgen ....F 913 772-6046
Leavenworth *(G-5231)*
Drs Dobbins & Letourneau ....F 785 843-5665
Lawrence *(G-4841)*
Emergency Dept Physicians ....E 913 469-1411
Shawnee Mission *(G-11333)*
Emergency Services PA ....E 316 962-2239
Wichita *(G-14276)*
Ent Assctes Greater Kans Cy PC ....E 816 478-4200
Merriam *(G-7091)*
Eye Association Overland Park ....F 913 339-9090
Overland Park *(G-8701)*
Galichia Medical Group Kans PA ....C 316 684-3838
Wichita *(G-14439)*
Greeley Cnty Hosp & Long TRM C ....F 785 852-4230
Sharon Springs *(G-10898)*
Green Medical Group ....E 316 691-3937
Wichita *(G-14511)*
Hays Medical Center Inc ....F 785 623-5774
Hays *(G-2833)*
Healthcare Administrative Svcs ....E 816 763-5446
Overland Park *(G-8803)*
Howell Matthew D Dr DDS PA ....F 316 260-6220
Andover *(G-94)*
Hutchinson Clinic PA ....F 620 486-2985
Saint John *(G-10352)*
Ian F Yeats MD Chartered ....F 620 624-0142
Liberal *(G-6322)*
Jayhawk Primary Care Inc ....D 913 588-9000
Westwood *(G-13554)*
Jewell County Hospital ....D 785 378-3137
Mankato *(G-6859)*
Kansas Univ Physicians Inc ....B 913 742-7611
Shawnee *(G-10980)*
Kevin R McDonald ....F 785 628-6014
Hays *(G-2859)*
Kvc Behavioral Healthcare Inc ....D 620 820-7680
Parsons *(G-9701)*
Labette Health Foundation Inc ....F 620 922-3838
Coffeyville *(G-954)*
Lakepoint Family Physicians ....E 316 636-2662
Wichita *(G-14915)*
Lawrence Anaesthesia PA ....F 785 842-7026
Lawrence *(G-4958)*
Mercy Hlth Fndtion Sthstern PA ....F 620 223-2200
Fort Scott *(G-1987)*
Mid America Crdiolgy Assoc PC ....E 913 588-9554
Shawnee Mission *(G-11626)*
Mid America Crdiolgy Assoc PC ....E 913 588-9400
Overland Park *(G-9021)*
Mid America Polyclinic PA ....E 913 599-2440
Overland Park *(G-9023)*
Newton Healthcare Corporation ....A 316 283-2700
Newton *(G-7393)*
Norton County Hospital ....F 785 877-3305
Norton *(G-7458)*
Olathe Medical Services Inc ....F 913 764-0036
Olathe *(G-7945)*
Olathe Medical Services Inc ....E 913 782-1610
Olathe *(G-7946)*
Oral & Facial Surgery Assoc ....E 913 381-5194
Prairie Village *(G-10054)*
Oswego Medical Center LLC ....E 620 795-2386
Oswego *(G-8235)*
Partners In Primary Care ....E 913 335-6986
Kansas City *(G-4316)*
Partners In Primary Care ....E 913 815-5508
Olathe *(G-7973)*
Radiation Oncology ....E 913 588-3600
Kansas City *(G-4358)*
Renal Trtmnt Centers-West Inc ....F 316 263-9090
Wichita *(G-15443)*
Rogers Duncan Dillehay DDS PA ....F 316 683-6518
Derby *(G-1270)*
Saint Lukes Primary Care At ....D 913 317-7990
Overland Park *(G-9274)*
Salina Hlth Educatn Foundation ....D 785 825-7251
Salina *(G-10674)*
Somnitech Inc ....E 913 498-8120
Overland Park *(G-9327)*
Southwest Guidance Center ....F 620 624-8171
Liberal *(G-6370)*
Stephen Rohner Doctor Office ....F 316 687-0006
Wichita *(G-15663)*
Surgical Specialists PA ....F 316 945-7309
Wichita *(G-15701)*
Topeka Pathology Group PA ....F 785 354-6031
Topeka *(G-13183)*
United States Dept of Army ....B 913 684-2747
Fort Leavenworth *(G-1942)*
University of Kansas ....E 785 864-2277
Lawrence *(G-5158)*
Via Chrsti Rhbltation Hosp Inc ....G 316 946-1790
Wichita *(G-15903)*
Ward Parkway Medical Group ....F 913 383-9099
Shawnee Mission *(G-11992)*
Wellness Services Inc ....C 913 894-6600
Lenexa *(G-6225)*
West Central Kansas Assn Inc ....C 785 483-3131
Russell *(G-10303)*
Wichita Home Health Care Group ....F 316 219-0095
Wichita *(G-16005)*
Woodich John ....E 620 332-3280
Independence *(G-3574)*

PHYSICIANS' OFFICES & CLINICS: Osteopathic

Anesthia Assn Centl Kans PA ....E 785 827-2238
Salina *(G-10403)*
Coffeyvlle Fmly Prctice Clinic ....E 620 251-1100
Coffeyville *(G-923)*
Rita Oplotnik DO ....F 913 764-0036
Olathe *(G-8037)*
Ron J Marek Do PA ....F 316 462-1050
Wichita *(G-15481)*
St Francis Hospital ....E 785 945-3263
Valley Falls *(G-13369)*
Surgical Specialists PA ....F 316 945-7309
Wichita *(G-15701)*
Witchita Clinic Inc ....F 620 583-7436
Eureka *(G-1899)*

PICTURE FRAMES: Metal

Laminage Products Inc ....G 316 267-5233
Wichita *(G-14916)*

PICTURE FRAMES: Wood

Howell Mouldings LC ....E 913 782-0500
New Century *(G-7289)*

PICTURE FRAMING SVCS, CUSTOM

Prairiebrooke Arts Inc ....F 913 341-0333
Overland Park *(G-9178)*

PIECE GOODS, NOTIONS & DRY GOODS, WHOL: Binding, Textile

Berger Company ....F 913 367-3700
Atchison *(G-214)*

PIECE GOODS, NOTIONS & DRY GOODS, WHOL: Fabrics, Fiberglass

LAd Global Enterprises Inc ....F 913 768-0888
Olathe *(G-7851)*

PIECE GOODS, NOTIONS & DRY GOODS, WHOLESALE: Fabrics

John K Burch Company ....F 800 365-1988
Shawnee Mission *(G-11492)*

PIECE GOODS, NOTIONS & OTHER DRY GOODS, WHOLESALE: Fabrics

Classic Cloth Inc ....F 785 434-7200
Plainville *(G-9980)*
Designers Library Inc ....F 913 227-0010
Shawnee Mission *(G-11303)*
Spirit Industries Inc ....F 913 749-5858
Lawrence *(G-5115)*

PIECE GOODS, NOTIONS/DRY GOODS, WHOL: Drapery Mtrl, Woven

Sebring & Co ....F 913 888-8141
Overland Park *(G-9288)*

PIECE GOODS, NOTIONS/DRY GOODS, WHOL: Fabrics, Synthetic

Tell Industries LLC ....F 316 260-3297
Park City *(G-9649)*

PIECE GOODS, NOTIONS/DRY GOODS, WHOL: Sewing Splys/Notions

Ray Bechard Inc ....E 785 864-5077
Lawrence *(G-5087)*

PILOT CAR ESCORT SVCS

A S Escort ....F 620 655-6613
Liberal *(G-6272)*

PILOT SVCS: Aviation

Archein Aerospace LLC ....E 682 499-2150
Wichita *(G-13730)*
Flightsafety International ....F 316 612-5300
Wichita *(G-14388)*
Kansas Air Center Topeka Inc ....E 785 234-2602
Topeka *(G-12757)*

PIPE & FITTING: Fabrication

Bennett Rgers Pipe Coating Inc ....E 913 371-3880
Kansas City *(G-3854)*
CDI Industrial Mech Contrs Inc ....C 913 287-0334
Kansas City *(G-3898)*
Little Giant Fittings Company ....G 620 793-5399
Great Bend *(G-2603)*
Mid America Pipe Fabg Sup LLC ....C 620 827-6121
Scammon *(G-10796)*
Premier Mechanical Pdts LLC ....F 913 271-5002
Kansas City *(G-4332)*
Reintjes & Hiter Co Inc ....F 913 371-1872
Kansas City *(G-4368)*
Spears Manufacturing Co ....B 620 879-2131
Caney *(G-674)*
US Pipe Fabrication LLC ....F 785 242-6284
Ottawa *(G-8318)*

PIPE & FITTINGS: Cast Iron

Fastfittingscom ....G 913 709-4467
Overland Park *(G-8706)*

PIPE FITTINGS: Plastic

Fittings Export LLC ....G 620 364-2930
Burlington *(G-636)*
Formufit Lc ....G 913 782-0444
Lenexa *(G-5863)*
Spears Caney Inc ....C 620 879-2131
Caney *(G-673)*

Spears Manufacturing Co ....B 620 879-2131
Caney *(G-674)*

PIPE, CULVERT: Concrete

Forterra Concrete Products Inc ....E 913 422-3634
Shawnee *(G-10957)*

PIPE: Concrete

McPherson Concrete Pdts Inc ....D 620 241-1678
McPherson *(G-6995)*
Wichita Concrete Pipe Inc ....E 316 838-8651
Wichita *(G-15989)*

PIPE: Plastic

Formufit Lc ....G 913 782-0444
Lenexa *(G-5863)*
Mc Coy Company Inc ....C 913 342-1653
Kansas City *(G-4222)*
Vanguard Industries Inc ....G 620 241-6369
McPherson *(G-7037)*
Vanguard Piping Systems Inc ....C 620 241-6369
McPherson *(G-7038)*
Vanguard Plastics Inc ....C 620 241-6369
McPherson *(G-7039)*
Vinylplex Inc ....E 620 231-8290
Pittsburg *(G-9959)*
Werner Pipe Service Inc ....F 620 331-7384
Independence *(G-3572)*

PIPE: Plate Fabricated, Large Diameter

Optimus Industries LLC ....C 620 431-3100
Chanute *(G-751)*

PIPE: Sheet Metal

Trinity Steel and Pipe Inc ....F 620 396-8900
Weir *(G-13486)*

PIPELINE & POWER LINE INSPECTION SVCS

Welco Services Inc ....E 620 241-3000
McPherson *(G-7041)*

PIPELINE TERMINAL FACILITIES: Independent

Nebraska Transport Co Inc ....E 913 281-9991
Kansas City *(G-4284)*
Propak Logistics Inc ....D 913 213-3896
Kansas City *(G-4346)*

PIPELINES, EXC NATURAL GAS: Coal

Nowak Pipe Reaming Inc ....D 316 794-8898
Goddard *(G-2450)*

PIPELINES, EXC NATURAL GAS: Gasoline, Common Carriers

Tessenderlo Kerley Inc ....F 620 251-3111
Coffeyville *(G-982)*

PIPELINES: Crude Petroleum

CHS McPherson Refinery Inc ....B 620 241-2340
McPherson *(G-6949)*
Jayhawk Pipeline LLC ....F 620 241-9270
McPherson *(G-6978)*
Jayhawk Pipeline LLC ....E 620 938-2971
Chase *(G-783)*
Koch Pipeline Company LP ....F 620 834-2309
Conway *(G-1134)*
Koch Pipeline Company LP ....D 316 828-5511
Wichita *(G-14885)*
Magellan Pipeline Company LP ....E 913 647-8400
Kansas City *(G-4213)*
Magellan Pipeline Company LP ....F 913 647-8504
Kansas City *(G-4214)*
Minnesota Pipe Line Co LLC ....F 316 828-5500
Wichita *(G-15113)*
Panhandle Eastrn Pipe Line LP ....E 620 624-8661
Liberal *(G-6352)*
Panhandle Eastrn Pipe Line LP ....F 620 723-2185
Greensburg *(G-2683)*
Panhandle Eastrn Pipe Line LP ....E 913 906-1500
Overland Park *(G-9139)*
Plains Marketing LP ....F 620 365-3208
Iola *(G-3623)*
Plains Marketing LP ....F 785 483-3171
Russell *(G-10284)*
Semcrude LP ....F 620 234-5532
Stafford *(G-12109)*

PIPELINES: Natural Gas

Colorado Interstate Gas Co LLC ....F 620 355-7955
Lakin *(G-4648)*
Kinder Morgan Kansas Inc ....G 620 384-7830
Syracuse *(G-12228)*
Natural Gas Pipeline Amer LLC ....F 620 793-7118
Great Bend *(G-2615)*
Natural Gas Pipeline Amer LLC ....G 620 885-4505
Minneola *(G-7127)*
Oneok Inc ....F 913 599-8936
Ottawa *(G-8295)*
Oneok Inc ....F 620 241-0837
McPherson *(G-7011)*
Oneok Inc ....E 316 821-2722
Wichita *(G-15220)*
Rockies Express Pipeline LLC ....F 913 928-6060
Leawood *(G-5542)*
Tallgrass Development LP ....E 513 941-0500
Leawood *(G-5565)*
Tallgrass Energy Partners LP ....E 913 928-6060
Leawood *(G-5567)*
Tallgrass Operations LLC ....E 913 928-6060
Leawood *(G-5569)*

PIPELINES: Refined Petroleum

CHS Inc ....D 620 241-4247
McPherson *(G-6948)*
Kinder Mrgan Enrgy Partners LP ....F 785 543-6602
Phillipsburg *(G-9790)*
Kinder Mrgan Enrgy Partners LP ....F 620 834-2211
Windom *(G-16112)*
Koch Industries Inc ....F 316 321-6380
El Dorado *(G-1580)*
Magellan Pipeline Company LP ....F 913 310-7710
Shawnee Mission *(G-11590)*
Magellan Pipeline Company LP ....F 316 321-3730
El Dorado *(G-1585)*
Nustar Pipeline Oper Partnr LP ....F 316 321-3500
El Dorado *(G-1586)*
Phillips 66 ....F 316 821-2250
Wichita *(G-15292)*
Trailblazer Pipeline Co LLC ....F 913 928-6060
Leawood *(G-5582)*

PIPES & FITTINGS: Fiber, Made From Purchased Materials

Rickerson Pipe Lining LLC ....F 785 448-5401
Garnett *(G-2386)*

PIPES & TUBES

Steel Ventures LLC ....D 785 587-5100
Manhattan *(G-6810)*

PIPES & TUBES: Steel

Alexander Manufacturing Co Inc ....F 620 421-5010
Parsons *(G-9664)*
Contech Engnered Solutions LLC ....E 913 294-2131
Paola *(G-9549)*
Progressive Products Inc ....E 620 235-1712
Pittsburg *(G-9925)*
Werner Pipe Service Inc ....F 620 331-7384
Independence *(G-3572)*

PIPES: Steel & Iron

R & S Pipe Supply LLC ....F 785 448-5401
Garnett *(G-2385)*
US Pipe Fabrication LLC ....F 785 242-6284
Ottawa *(G-8318)*

PLANING MILLS: Millwork

Salina Planing Mill Inc ....E 785 825-0588
Salina *(G-10683)*

PLANNING & DEVELOPMENT ADMINISTRATION, GOVT: County Agency

County of McPherson ....E 620 241-0466
McPherson *(G-6952)*

PLANT CARE SVCS

Hoffmanns Green Industries ....E 316 634-1500
Wichita *(G-14624)*

PLANTS, POTTED, WHOLESALE

Alex R Masson Inc ....D 913 301-3281
Linwood *(G-6415)*
Arnolds Greenhouse Inc ....F 620 964-2463
Le Roy *(G-5195)*
Stutzman Greenhouse Inc ....E 620 662-0559
Hutchinson *(G-3454)*

PLASMAPHEROUS CENTER

Biomat Usa Inc ....F 785 233-0079
Topeka *(G-12384)*
Csl Plasma Inc ....E 785 749-5750
Lawrence *(G-4819)*
Csl Plasma Inc ....F 785 776-9177
Manhattan *(G-6607)*

PLASTIC WOOD

Howell Mouldings LC ....E 913 782-0500
New Century *(G-7289)*

PLASTICS FINISHED PRDTS: Laminated

Novation Iq LLC ....E 913 492-6000
Lenexa *(G-6029)*
Thermoformed Plastic Products ....G 316 214-9623
Wichita *(G-15759)*

PLASTICS MATERIAL & RESINS

Ach Foam Technologies Inc ....D 913 321-4114
Kansas City *(G-3782)*
DOT Green Bioplastics Inc ....F 620 273-8919
Emporia *(G-1730)*
DOT Green Bioplastics LLC ....G 785 889-4600
Onaga *(G-8175)*
North Amrcn Specialty Pdts LLC ....F 620 241-5511
McPherson *(G-7010)*
Sunbelt Chemicals Inc ....F 972 296-3920
Shawnee *(G-11035)*
Techmer Pm LLC ....E 316 943-1520
Wichita *(G-15725)*

PLASTICS MATERIALS, BASIC FORMS & SHAPES WHOLESALERS

Univar Solutions USA Inc ....F 913 621-7494
Kansas City *(G-4493)*

PLASTICS PROCESSING

Cope Plastics Inc ....F 785 267-0552
Topeka *(G-12506)*
Fabpro Oriented Polymers LLC ....F 620 532-5141
Kingman *(G-4590)*
Gemtech LLC ....E 913 782-3080
Olathe *(G-7726)*
Neodesha Plastics Inc ....E 620 325-3096
Neodesha *(G-7246)*
Osborne Industries Inc ....D 785 346-2192
Osborne *(G-8216)*
Rehrig Pacific Company ....E 913 585-1175
De Soto *(G-1211)*
Tramec Sloan LLC ....E 620 326-5007
Wellington *(G-13537)*

PLASTICS: Blow Molded

Western Inds Plastic Pdts LLC ....C 620 221-9464
Winfield *(G-16180)*
Western Industries Inc ....C 620 221-9464
Winfield *(G-16181)*

PLASTICS: Extruded

Quality Profile Services Inc ....E 620 767-6757
Council Grove *(G-1175)*
Reifenhauser Incorporated ....F 316 260-2122
Maize *(G-6518)*

PLASTICS: Finished Injection Molded

Certainteed Corporation ....C 316 554-9638
McPherson *(G-6945)*
Illinois Tool Works Inc ....G 800 262-7907
Shawnee Mission *(G-11453)*

PLASTICS: Injection Molded

Advanced Extrusions Co LLC ....F 620 241-2006
McPherson *(G-6932)*
Esslinger Manufacturing ....G 620 431-4338
Chanute *(G-726)*
Ferguson Production Inc ....C 620 241-2400
McPherson *(G-6965)*
Hayes Tooling & Plastics Inc ....F 913 782-0046
Olathe *(G-7757)*
Hayesbrand Molding Inc ....F 913 238-0424
Garnett *(G-2377)*
Heartland Plastics Inc ....G 316 775-2199
Augusta *(G-324)*
Hi-Line Plastics Inc ....D 913 782-3535
Olathe *(G-7767)*
Koller Enterprises Inc ....D 913 422-2027
Lenexa *(G-5957)*
Manufacturing Services Inc ....G 316 267-4111
Wichita *(G-15006)*
Mid America Products Inc ....C 913 856-6550
Gardner *(G-2355)*
Miniature Plastic Molding LLC ....G 316 264-2827
Wichita *(G-15112)*
Monarch Molding Inc ....G 620 767-5115
Council Grove *(G-1171)*
Monoflo International Inc ....G 785 242-2928
Ottawa *(G-8292)*
Neodesha Plastics Inc ....E 620 325-3096
Neodesha *(G-7245)*
Packerware LLC ....A 785 331-4236
Lawrence *(G-5055)*
Plastikon Industries Inc ....F 785 749-1630
Lawrence *(G-5070)*
Roberts Group Inc ....G 913 381-3930
Overland Park *(G-9252)*
Rutland Inc ....F 913 782-8862
Olathe *(G-8049)*
Wescon Plastics LLC ....C 855 731-6055
Wichita *(G-15951)*

PLASTICS: Molded

Criss Optical Mfg Co Inc ....G 316 529-0414
Wichita *(G-14131)*
GVL Polymers Inc ....F 320 693-8411
Hesston *(G-2991)*
Jem Industries Inc ....G 913 837-3202
Louisburg *(G-6452)*
Mid-States Laboratories Inc ....F 316 264-6758
Wichita *(G-15081)*
Mid-States Laboratories Inc ....F 316 262-7013
Wichita *(G-15082)*
North American Aviation Inc ....E 316 744-6450
Park City *(G-9639)*
Stm Inc ....E 316 775-2223
Augusta *(G-348)*
T & C Mfg & Operating Inc ....E 620 793-5483
Great Bend *(G-2646)*

PLASTICS: Polystyrene Foam

Buckley Industries Inc ....D 316 744-7587
Park City *(G-9606)*
Novation Iq LLC ....E 913 492-6000
Lenexa *(G-6029)*

PLASTICS: Thermoformed

Formation Plastics Inc ....E 785 754-3828
Hoxie *(G-3138)*
Lustercraft Plastics LLC ....F 316 942-8451
Wichita *(G-14991)*
Thermovac Inc ....G 620 431-3270
Chanute *(G-769)*

PLATEMAKING SVC: Color Separations, For The Printing Trade

Mid West Color Graphics Inc ....E 620 429-1088
Columbus *(G-1084)*

PLATES

Copy Center of Topeka Inc ....E 785 233-6677
Topeka *(G-12507)*
Printery Inc ....F 785 632-5501
Clay Center *(G-877)*

PLATING & POLISHING SVC

Ferroloy Inc ....E 316 838-0897
Wichita *(G-14358)*
Hampton Hydraulics Llc ....D 620 792-4368
Great Bend *(G-2590)*
Metal Finishing Co Inc ....E 316 267-7289
Wichita *(G-15051)*
Premier Processing ....F 316 425-3565
Wichita *(G-15333)*
Right Stuff Co ....G 913 722-4002
Prairie Village *(G-10064)*

PLATING SVC: Chromium, Metals Or Formed Prdts

Alternative Chrome Creations ....G 316 680-1209
Haysville *(G-2936)*
Ics Inc ....E 620 654-3020
McPherson *(G-6977)*
Industrial Chrome Inc ....D 785 235-3463
Topeka *(G-12721)*
Precision Industries Inc ....E 620 241-5010
McPherson *(G-7019)*
Specialty Technology Inc ....F 620 241-6307
McPherson *(G-7027)*

PLATING SVC: Electro

Chrome Plus International Inc ....F 316 944-3600
Wichita *(G-14017)*

PLATING SVC: NEC

C & R Plating Inc ....F 785 392-2626
Minneapolis *(G-7115)*
Isf LLC ....E 316 945-4040
Wichita *(G-14730)*
Thayer Aerospace Plating Inc ....C 316 522-5426
Wichita *(G-15756)*

PLAYGROUND EQPT

Backyard Adventures LLC ....E 620 308-6863
Pittsburg *(G-9821)*

PLEATING & STITCHING SVC

Express Yourself Digital ....G 620 724-8389
Girard *(G-2404)*
Gfsi LLC ....B 913 693-3200
Lenexa *(G-5875)*
United States Awards Inc ....E 620 231-8470
Pittsburg *(G-9951)*

PLUMBING & HEATING EQPT & SPLY, WHOL: Htg Eqpt/Panels, Solar

Design Concepts Inc ....F 913 782-5672
Olathe *(G-7651)*

PLUMBING & HEATING EQPT & SPLY, WHOLESALE: Hydronic Htg Eqpt

Ferguson Enterprises LLC ....F 785 354-4305
Topeka *(G-12604)*
Heating and Cooling Distrs Inc ....F 913 262-5848
Stilwell *(G-12152)*
Hughes Machinery Company ....G 316 612-0868
Wichita *(G-14649)*

PLUMBING & HEATING EQPT & SPLYS WHOLESALERS

Ambrose Sales Inc ....E 913 780-5666
Olathe *(G-7526)*
Frank Colladay Hardware Co ....F 620 663-4477
Hutchinson *(G-3292)*
K & K Industries Inc ....E 906 293-5242
Junction City *(G-3709)*
Kansas City Winnelson Co ....F 913 262-6868
Kansas City *(G-4152)*
Smith and Loveless Inc ....C 913 888-5201
Shawnee Mission *(G-11875)*
Superior Plumbing of Wichita ....F 316 684-8349
Wichita *(G-15696)*
Western Supply Co Inc ....E 620 663-9082
Hutchinson *(G-3486)*

PLUMBING & HEATING EQPT & SPLYS, WHOL: Fireplaces, Prefab

Evcon Holdings Inc ....E 316 832-6300
Wichita *(G-14311)*

PLUMBING & HEATING EQPT & SPLYS, WHOL: Pipe/Fitting, Plastic

Callaway Electric ....G 785 632-5588
Clay Center *(G-847)*
Fiber Glass Systems LP ....F 316 946-3900
Wichita *(G-14362)*
Harrington Industrial Plas LLC ....F 816 400-9438
Lenexa *(G-5892)*
Industrial Sales Company Inc ....E 913 829-3500
Olathe *(G-7787)*
United Pipe & Supply ....F 785 357-0612
Topeka *(G-13208)*
Vanguard Piping Systems Inc ....C 620 241-6369
McPherson *(G-7038)*

PLUMBING & HEATING EQPT & SPLYS, WHOL: Plumbing Fitting/Sply

Boettcher Supply Inc ....E 785 738-5781
Beloit *(G-479)*
Ferguson Enterprises LLC ....E 316 262-0681
Wichita *(G-14355)*
Ferguson Enterprises LLC ....D 913 752-5660
Lenexa *(G-5851)*
Hajoca Corporation ....E 316 262-2471
Wichita *(G-14544)*
Hajoca Corporation ....F 785 825-1333
Salina *(G-10531)*
Home Depot USA Inc ....E 913 310-0204
Overland Park *(G-8823)*
Johnson & White Sales Company ....F 913 390-9808
Olathe *(G-7812)*
Mack McClain & Associates Inc ....F 913 339-6677
Olathe *(G-7871)*
Mc Coy Company Inc ....C 913 342-1653
Kansas City *(G-4222)*
Mid-America Fittings LLC ....E 913 962-7277
Overland Park *(G-9024)*
Phoenix Supply Inc ....E 316 262-7241
Wichita *(G-15294)*
Salina Supply Company ....E 785 823-2221
Salina *(G-10693)*
Viega LLC ....F 678 447-1882
McPherson *(G-7040)*

PLUMBING & HEATING EQPT & SPLYS, WHOL: Water Purif Eqpt

American Wtr Purification Inc ....F 316 685-3333
Wichita *(G-13695)*
Dxp Enterprises Inc ....F 913 888-0108
Lenexa *(G-5827)*

PLUMBING & HEATING EQPT & SPLYS, WHOLESALE: Pwr Indl Boiler

Clarios ....E 785 827-6829
Salina *(G-10454)*
Hughes Machinery Company ....E 913 492-0355
Lenexa *(G-5906)*
Locke Equipment Sales Co ....E 913 782-8500
Olathe *(G-7864)*

PLUMBING & HEATING EQPT, WHOLESALE: Water Heaters/Purif

Power Chemicals Inc ....F 316 524-7899
Wichita *(G-15318)*

PLUMBING FIXTURES

Mc Coy Company Inc ....C 913 342-1653
Kansas City *(G-4222)*
Mid-America Fittings LLC ....E 913 962-7277
Overland Park *(G-9024)*
Vanguard Industries Inc ....G 620 241-6369
McPherson *(G-7037)*

PLUMBING FIXTURES: Plastic

Bultman Company Inc Mfg ....F 620 544-8004
Hugoton *(G-3149)*
Formufit Lc ....G 913 782-0444
Lenexa *(G-5863)*
KBK Industries LLC ....C 785 372-4331
Rush Center *(G-10260)*
Onyx Collection Inc ....B 785 456-8604
Belvue *(G-508)*
Vanguard Industries Inc ....G 620 241-6369
McPherson *(G-7037)*

PODIATRISTS' OFFICES

Associated Podiatrist PA ....E 913 321-0522
Kansas City *(G-3824)*
David B Laha MD Bpm ....F 913 338-4440
Overland Park *(G-8640)*
Foot Specialist Kansas City ....F 913 677-3600
Overland Park *(G-8733)*
Heart America Eye Care PA ....E 913 362-3210
Overland Park *(G-8805)*
Podiatry Associates PA ....F 913 432-5052
Shawnee Mission *(G-11741)*

POLICE PROTECTION

ADT 24 7 Alarm and Security ....D 620 860-0229
Pratt *(G-10094)*
City of Leavenworth ....F 913 682-1090
Leavenworth *(G-5221)*

POLICE PROTECTION: Local Government

City of Anthony ....G 620 842-5123
Anthony *(G-123)*
City of Overland Park ....C 913 895-6000
Shawnee Mission *(G-11231)*
City of Pittsburg ....D 620 308-6916
Pittsburg *(G-9834)*

POLICE PROTECTION: Sheriffs' Office

Redbud Village ....F 785 425-6312
Stockton *(G-12184)*

POLYETHYLENE RESINS

Flint Hlls Rsrces Longview LLC ....F 316 828-5500
Wichita *(G-14393)*
Rapid Processing Solutions Inc ....F 316 265-2001
Wichita *(G-15417)*

POLYSTYRENE RESINS

Zell-Metall Usa Inc ....F 913 327-0300
Lenexa *(G-6240)*

POLYURETHANE RESINS

McPu Polymer Engineering LLC ....G 620 231-4239
Pittsburg *(G-9901)*

POSTAL STATION SVC, CONTRACTED

Downtown Station ....D 316 267-7747
Wichita *(G-14235)*

POTASH MINING

Compass Minerals ....B 913 344-9200
Overland Park *(G-8585)*

POULTRY & POULTRY PRDTS WHOLESALERS

Cal-Maine Foods Inc ....D 620 938-2300
Chase *(G-782)*

POULTRY & SMALL GAME SLAUGHTERING & PROCESSING

Cal-Maine Foods Inc ....D 620 938-2300
Chase *(G-782)*
Cargill Incorporated ....E 785 743-2288
WA Keeney *(G-13382)*
Cargill Incorporated ....F 316 291-1939
Wichita *(G-13947)*
Indian Hills Meat and Plty Inc ....E 316 264-1644
Wichita *(G-14683)*
National Beef Packing Co LLC ....C 620 624-1851
Liberal *(G-6349)*
Simmons Prepared Foods Inc ....C 479 524-8151
Emporia *(G-1829)*

POWER MOWERS WHOLESALERS

Boettcher Supply Inc ....E 785 738-5781
Beloit *(G-479)*

POWER SUPPLIES: All Types, Static

Power Control Devices Inc ....E 913 829-1900
Olathe *(G-7995)*

POWER TOOLS, HAND: Drills & Drilling Tools

Bazin Sawing & Drilling Llc ....F 913 764-0843
Louisburg *(G-6440)*
Diteq Corporation ....E 816 246-5515
Lenexa *(G-5821)*

POWER TRANSMISSION EQPT WHOLESALERS

Headco Industries Inc ....F 913 831-1444
Kansas City *(G-4072)*
Simplex Time Recorder LLC ....E 316 686-6363
Wichita *(G-15595)*

POWER TRANSMISSION EQPT: Aircraft

Aerospace Products Company ....G 316 733-4440
Wichita *(G-13637)*
Pwi Inc ....E 316 942-2811
Wichita *(G-15381)*

POWER TRANSMISSION EQPT: Mechanical

Carlson Company Inc ....E 316 744-0481
Park City *(G-9608)*
Curtis Machine Company Inc ....D 620 227-7164
Dodge City *(G-1338)*
Ics Inc ....E 620 654-3020
McPherson *(G-6977)*

POWER TRANSMISSION EQPT: Vehicle

John Dere Cffeyville Works Inc ....B 620 251-3400
Coffeyville *(G-951)*

POWERED GOLF CART DEALERS

Kansas Golf and Turf Inc ....F 316 267-9111
Park City *(G-9622)*

PRECAST TERRAZZO OR CONCRETE PRDTS

Nips LLC ....G 913 592-2365
Spring Hill *(G-12092)*
Pappas Concrete Inc ....E 620 277-2127
Lakin *(G-4657)*
Pretech Corporation ....E 913 441-4600
Kansas City *(G-4334)*
Salina Concrete Products Inc ....E 785 827-7281
Salina *(G-10668)*

PREFABRICATED BUILDING DEALERS

Green Line Inc ....F 620 896-7372
Harper *(G-2722)*
Salina Building Systems Inc ....E 785 823-6812
Salina *(G-10666)*
Tuff Shed Inc ....F 913 541-8833
Shawnee Mission *(G-11947)*

PRERECORDED TAPE, CD & RECORD STORE: Record, Disc/Tape

Acoustic Sounds Inc ....E 785 825-8609
Salina *(G-10392)*

PRERECORDED TAPE, CD & RECORD STORES: Video Discs/Tapes

Family Video Movie Club Inc ....F 913 254-7219
Olathe *(G-7702)*

PRERECORDED TAPE, COMPACT DISC & RECORD STORES: Records

Half Price Bks Rec Mgzines Inc ....F 913 829-9959
Olathe *(G-7748)*

PRESCHOOL CENTERS

A Childs World Day Care Ctr ....F 785 863-2161
Oskaloosa *(G-8220)*
A Deere Place Inc ....F 913 727-5437
Lansing *(G-4665)*
Abilene Childcare Learning Ctr ....F 785 263-1799
Abilene *(G-2)*
Allen Preschool LLC ....E 913 451-1066
Shawnee Mission *(G-11096)*
Apple Tree Kid Day Out/Presch ....E 913 888-3702
Shawnee Mission *(G-11114)*
Ashbury Church Pre School ....F 913 432-5573
Shawnee Mission *(G-11123)*
Ashleys House Learning Center ....E 316 941-9877
Wichita *(G-13753)*
Board of Edcatn of Kans Cy Ks ....E 913 627-6550
Kansas City *(G-3870)*
Books & Blocks Academy Inc ....F 785 266-5150
Topeka *(G-12397)*
Bright Circle Montesorri Schl ....F 785 235-1033
Topeka *(G-12406)*
Century School Inc ....E 785 832-0101
Lawrence *(G-4782)*
Chase Childrens Services Inc ....F 620 273-6650
Strong City *(G-12192)*
Christs Care Pre-School ....F 620 662-1283
Hutchinson *(G-3237)*
Christs Kids Childcare ....F 620 654-4567
Galva *(G-2092)*
Church of Magdalen ....E 316 634-1572
Wichita *(G-14019)*
Clay Jars Childrens Center Inc ....F 785 379-9098
Tecumseh *(G-12238)*
Cornerstone Day Care Preschool ....F 620 257-5622
Lyons *(G-6481)*
Country Child Care Inc ....E 316 722-4500
Maize *(G-6510)*
Countryside United Methdst Ch ....F 785 266-7541
Topeka *(G-12516)*
Creativity Place Inc ....D 316 684-1860
Wichita *(G-14127)*
Creche Academy LLC ....F 785 484-3100
Meriden *(G-7079)*
Dandelion & Mudd Puddles Cdc ....E 913 825-0399
Shawnee *(G-10940)*
Dinosaur Den Child Dev Ctr ....F 913 780-2626
Olathe *(G-7656)*
Early Childhood Dev Ctr ....E 620 544-4334
Hugoton *(G-3161)*
First Baptist Church Olathe ....F 913 764-7088
Olathe *(G-7711)*
First United Methodist Church ....F 316 755-1112
Valley Center *(G-13342)*
Friends of Montessori Assn ....F 913 649-6160
Prairie Village *(G-10029)*
Futures Unlimited Inc ....E 620 326-8906
Wellington *(G-13501)*
Genesis School Inc ....E 913 845-9498
Tonganoxie *(G-12262)*
Glenn Pk Christn Ch Preschool ....E 316 943-4283
Wichita *(G-14471)*
Goddard School ....E 913 764-1331
Olathe *(G-7736)*
Goddard School ....E 913 451-1066
Shawnee Mission *(G-11398)*
Googols of Learning ....E 785 856-6002
Lawrence *(G-4876)*
Hays Area Children Center Inc ....E 785 625-3257
Hays *(G-2828)*
Headstart Program ....E 620 341-2260
Emporia *(G-1768)*
Hillcrest Covenant Church ....E 913 901-2300
Shawnee Mission *(G-11433)*
Hilltop Child Development Ctr ....E 785 864-4940
Lawrence *(G-4897)*
Hillview Church of God Inc ....F 913 299-4406
Kansas City *(G-4080)*
Holy Name Catholic Church ....C 785 232-7744
Topeka *(G-12698)*
Holy Name Church ....E 785 232-1603
Topeka *(G-12699)*
Hope Lutheran Church Shawnee ....E 913 631-6940
Shawnee Mission *(G-11439)*
Iola Pre Schl For Excptnl Chld ....F 620 365-6730
Iola *(G-3610)*
Ivy League Learning Center ....E 913 338-4060
Overland Park *(G-8867)*
Joyful Noise Academy ....E 316 688-5060
Wichita *(G-14775)*
Kansas Kids Daycare Preschool ....F 785 762-4338
Junction City *(G-3713)*
Kids At Heart Inc ....E 913 648-8577
Overland Park *(G-8918)*
Kids R Kids ....E 913 390-0234
Olathe *(G-7838)*
Knox Presbt Ch Child Dev Ctr ....F 913 888-0089
Overland Park *(G-8925)*
La Petite Academy Inc ....F 913 685-2800
Shawnee Mission *(G-11541)*

La Petite Academy Inc.......................E....... 913 441-5100
Shawnee Mission *(G-11542)*
La Petite Academy Inc.......................F....... 785 843-5703
Lawrence *(G-4951)*
La Petite Academy Inc.......................F....... 316 684-5916
Wichita *(G-14909)*
La Petite Academy Inc.......................F....... 785 273-9393
Topeka *(G-12827)*
La Petite Academy Inc.......................F....... 913 432-5053
Shawnee Mission *(G-11543)*
La Petite Academy Inc.......................F....... 913 764-2345
Olathe *(G-7848)*
La Petite Academy Inc.......................F....... 913 492-4183
Lenexa *(G-5960)*
La Petite Academy Inc.......................F....... 913 649-5773
Overland Park *(G-8936)*
La Petite Academy Inc.......................F....... 785 843-6445
Lawrence *(G-4952)*
La Petite Academy Inc.......................F....... 913 780-2318
Olathe *(G-7849)*
La Petite Academy Inc.......................F....... 913 469-1006
Overland Park *(G-8937)*
Learning Care Group Inc.......................E....... 913 851-7800
Shawnee Mission *(G-11552)*
Lets Grow Preschool.......................F....... 913 262-2261
Shawnee Mission *(G-11565)*
Little Learners Early Childho.......................F....... 913 254-1818
Olathe *(G-7861)*
Little Wnders Christn Day Care.......................E....... 913 393-3035
Olathe *(G-7862)*
Lord of Life Lutheran Church.......................E....... 913 681-5167
Leawood *(G-5459)*
Loving Arms Child Care Center.......................E....... 316 722-1912
Wichita *(G-14981)*
Mini Masters Lrng Academy LLC.......................F....... 785 862-0772
Topeka *(G-12905)*
Neighborhood Learning Ctr LLC.......................F....... 785 238-2321
Junction City *(G-3729)*
New Song Academy Inc.......................E....... 316 688-1911
Wichita *(G-15169)*
Olathe Unified School Dst 233.......................D....... 913 780-7410
Olathe *(G-7953)*
Old Mission United Methdst Ch.......................F....... 913 262-1040
Fairway *(G-1915)*
One of Kind Progressive Chld C.......................E....... 785 830-9040
Lawrence *(G-5045)*
Open Arms Lthran Child Dev Ctr.......................E....... 316 721-5675
Wichita *(G-15221)*
Open Arms Lthran Child Dev Ctr.......................E....... 913 856-4250
Gardner *(G-2358)*
Open Minds Child Dev Ctr LLC.......................F....... 913 703-6736
Olathe *(G-7958)*
Our Ladys Montessori School.......................F....... 913 403-9550
Kansas City *(G-4302)*
Pandarama Prschool Toddler Ctr.......................F....... 913 342-9692
Kansas City *(G-4308)*
Parkdale Pre-School Center.......................E....... 785 235-7240
Topeka *(G-12960)*
Peanut Co LLC.......................E....... 913 647-2240
Overland Park *(G-9150)*
Peppermint Pttys Mntssori Schl.......................F....... 913 631-9376
Shawnee Mission *(G-11725)*
Pioneer Pre School LLC.......................E....... 913 338-4282
Shawnee Mission *(G-11735)*
Plymouth Preschool Lrng Ctr.......................E....... 316 684-0222
Wichita *(G-15309)*
Primrose School.......................E....... 316 807-8622
Wichita *(G-15345)*
Princeton Childrens Center Wl.......................F....... 316 618-0275
Wichita *(G-15347)*
Rhum Wee Rockets Pre School.......................F....... 316 776-9330
Rose Hill *(G-10246)*
Rock Pre-K Center.......................F....... 785 266-2285
Topeka *(G-13023)*
Salvation Army.......................F....... 913 782-3640
Olathe *(G-8052)*
Salvation Army.......................F....... 913 782-3640
Olathe *(G-8053)*
Seaman Unified School Dst 345.......................E....... 785 286-7103
Topeka *(G-13048)*
Sharon Baptist Church.......................F....... 316 684-5156
Wichita *(G-15573)*
Shawnee Hts Untd Methdst Ch.......................E....... 785 379-5492
Tecumseh *(G-12243)*
Special Beginnings Inc.......................D....... 913 894-0131
Shawnee Mission *(G-11880)*
Special Beginnings Inc.......................D....... 913 393-2223
Olathe *(G-8075)*
St Agnes Montessori Pre School.......................E....... 913 262-2400
Westwood *(G-13560)*
Stepping Stones Inc.......................D....... 785 843-5919
Lawrence *(G-5123)*
Top Flight Kids Learning Ctr.......................E....... 913 768-4661
Olathe *(G-8114)*
Topeka Lutheran Schl Cntr For.......................E....... 785 272-1704
Lawrence *(G-5140)*
Trinity Daycare & Preschool.......................F....... 316 838-0909
Wichita *(G-15801)*
Tutor Time Lrng Systems Inc.......................E....... 316 721-0848
Wichita *(G-15818)*
We R Kids LLC.......................F....... 316 729-0172
Wichita *(G-15940)*
Wee Workshop Inc.......................E....... 913 681-2191
Stilwell *(G-12179)*
West Side Kids Day Out Program.......................F....... 913 764-0813
Olathe *(G-8151)*
Woodland United Methodist Ch.......................F....... 316 265-6669
Wichita *(G-16066)*
Word of Life Preschool.......................E....... 316 838-5683
Wichita *(G-16071)*
Young Mens Christian Associat.......................C....... 316 685-2251
Wichita *(G-16096)*

PRESS CLIPPING SVC

Luce Press Clippings Inc.......................D....... 785 232-0201
Topeka *(G-12853)*

PRIMARY FINISHED OR SEMIFINISHED SHAPES

Concordia Technologies LLC.......................E....... 785 262-4066
Concordia *(G-1108)*

PRINT CARTRIDGES: Laser & Other Computer Printers

Perfect Output LLC.......................D....... 913 317-8400
Overland Park *(G-9154)*

PRINTED CIRCUIT BOARDS

Avatar Engineering Inc.......................F....... 913 897-6757
Lenexa *(G-5676)*
Colt Tech LLC.......................G....... 913 839-8198
Olathe *(G-7600)*
Commtech Inc.......................F....... 316 636-1131
Wichita *(G-14075)*
Compass Controls Mfg Inc.......................E....... 913 213-5748
Lenexa *(G-5779)*
Elecsys Corporation.......................C....... 913 647-0158
Olathe *(G-7672)*
Electronic Contrls Assembly Co.......................G....... 913 780-0036
Olathe *(G-7675)*
Pivot-Digittron Inc.......................F....... 913 441-0221
Shawnee *(G-11012)*
Pwi Inc.......................E....... 316 942-2811
Wichita *(G-15380)*
S and Y Industries Inc.......................C....... 620 221-4001
Winfield *(G-16171)*
Vista Manufacturing Company.......................E....... 913 342-4939
Kansas City *(G-4521)*

PRINTERS' SVCS: Folding, Collating, Etc

Arrow Printing Company Inc.......................G....... 785 825-8124
Salina *(G-10409)*
My1stop LLC.......................F....... 316 554-9700
Fort Scott *(G-1992)*

PRINTERS: Magnetic Ink, Bar Code

American Marking Systems Inc.......................G....... 913 492-6028
Lenexa *(G-5650)*

PRINTING & BINDING: Books

Printing Services Inc.......................G....... 913 492-1500
Lenexa *(G-6070)*

PRINTING & EMBOSSING: Plastic Fabric Articles

Golden Sea Graphics Inc.......................G....... 785 747-2822
Greenleaf *(G-2669)*

PRINTING & ENGRAVING: Invitation & Stationery

CB Grduation Announcements LLC.......................E....... 785 776-5018
Manhattan *(G-6578)*
L V S Inc.......................E....... 316 636-5005
Wichita *(G-14908)*

PRINTING & ENGRAVING: Rolls, Textile Printing

Walson Ink Inc.......................G....... 785 537-7370
Manhattan *(G-6845)*

PRINTING & WRITING PAPER WHOLESALERS

Digital Printing Services Inc.......................F....... 913 492-1500
Lenexa *(G-5817)*
Veritiv Operating Company.......................D....... 913 492-5050
Kansas City *(G-4517)*
Ward-Kraft Inc.......................E....... 620 223-1104
Fort Scott *(G-2018)*
Westfall Newco LLC.......................E....... 844 663-5939
Hutchinson *(G-3487)*

PRINTING INKS WHOLESALERS

Fujifilm Sericol USA Inc.......................C....... 913 342-4060
Kansas City *(G-4022)*
INX International Ink Co.......................D....... 913 441-0057
Edwardsville *(G-1504)*
Nazdar Company.......................F....... 913 422-1888
Shawnee *(G-11004)*
Perfect Output LLC.......................D....... 913 317-8400
Overland Park *(G-9154)*

PRINTING MACHINERY

Hix Corporation.......................D....... 620 231-8568
Pittsburg *(G-9876)*
Inland Newspaper Mchy Corp.......................E....... 913 492-9050
Shawnee Mission *(G-11457)*
Nazdar Company.......................F....... 913 422-1888
Shawnee *(G-11004)*
R P M Smith Corporation.......................F....... 913 888-0695
Lenexa *(G-6087)*
Star Innovations II LLC.......................E....... 913 764-7738
New Century *(G-7298)*
Styers Equipment Company.......................F....... 913 681-5225
Overland Park *(G-9369)*

PRINTING MACHINERY, EQPT & SPLYS: Wholesalers

Barton Solvents Inc.......................F....... 316 321-1540
El Dorado *(G-1534)*
Fujifilm North America Corp.......................F....... 816 914-5942
Kansas City *(G-4021)*
Inland Industries Inc.......................G....... 913 492-9050
Bucyrus *(G-600)*
Inland Newspaper Mchy Corp.......................E....... 913 492-9050
Shawnee Mission *(G-11457)*
Sharpening Specialists LLC.......................E....... 316 945-0593
Wichita *(G-15575)*
Styers Equipment Company.......................F....... 913 681-5225
Overland Park *(G-9369)*

PRINTING TRADES MACHINERY & EQPT REPAIR SVCS

Styers Equipment Company.......................F....... 913 681-5225
Overland Park *(G-9369)*

PRINTING, COMMERCIAL: Business Forms, NEC

Professional Bank Forms.......................G....... 620 455-2205
Oxford *(G-9534)*

PRINTING, COMMERCIAL: Decals, NEC

Elitegear4ucom LLC.......................G....... 316 993-4398
Wichita *(G-14271)*
George Eschbaugh Advg Inc.......................E....... 785 658-2105
Wilson *(G-16105)*
R Miller Sales Co Inc.......................E....... 913 341-3727
Shawnee Mission *(G-11772)*

PRINTING, COMMERCIAL: Invitations, NEC

Copy Co Corporation.......................G....... 785 832-2679
Lawrence *(G-4811)*
Copy Co Corporation.......................E....... 785 823-2679
Salina *(G-10463)*
Mr PS Party Outlet Inc.......................F....... 785 537-1804
Manhattan *(G-6753)*

PRINTING, COMMERCIAL: Labels & Seals, NEC

Capital Label LLC ....G....... 785 291-9702
Topeka *(G-12433)*
GC Labels Inc ....F....... 913 897-6966
Stilwell *(G-12148)*
Kc Digical ....G....... 913 541-2688
Lenexa *(G-5940)*
Lynn Tape & Label ....F....... 913 422-0484
Kansas City *(G-4210)*
Print Tech Inc ....G....... 913 894-6644
Olathe *(G-8007)*

PRINTING, COMMERCIAL: Magazines, NEC

Mennonite Press Inc ....E....... 316 283-3060
Newton *(G-7380)*

PRINTING, COMMERCIAL: Menus, NEC

Iris Strgc Mktg Support Inc ....E....... 913 232-4825
Lenexa *(G-5923)*

PRINTING, COMMERCIAL: Promotional

Ragland Specialty Printing ....E....... 785 542-3058
Eudora *(G-1879)*
Resellers Edge LLC ....F....... 620 364-3398
Burlington *(G-642)*
Tmi Corp ....F....... 785 232-8705
Topeka *(G-13161)*

PRINTING, COMMERCIAL: Publications

Brileys Designs & Signs ....E....... 913 579-7533
Shawnee Mission *(G-11182)*

PRINTING, COMMERCIAL: Screen

4th Gneration Promotional Pdts ....G....... 913 393-0837
Olathe *(G-7502)*
Art Craft Printers & Design ....G....... 785 776-9151
Manhattan *(G-6545)*
B Scott Studio Inc ....G....... 316 321-1225
El Dorado *(G-1533)*
Creative Design TS Inc ....F....... 316 681-1868
Bel Aire *(G-431)*
Creative Signs & Design Inc ....G....... 785 233-8000
Topeka *(G-12528)*
D Rockey Holdings Inc ....E....... 816 474-9423
Kansas City *(G-3950)*
David Camp Inc ....C....... 913 648-0573
Overland Park *(G-8641)*
Epi Holdings Inc ....E....... 816 474-9423
Kansas City *(G-3992)*
Falcon Design and Mfg ....E....... 913 441-1074
Shawnee *(G-10953)*
Falcon Enterprises Inc ....C....... 727 579-1233
Wichita *(G-14336)*
Gone Logo Screen Printing ....G....... 785 625-3070
Hays *(G-2820)*
Goodwin Sporting Goods Inc ....G....... 785 625-2419
Hays *(G-2821)*
Graphic Impressions Inc ....E....... 620 663-5939
Hutchinson *(G-3305)*
Gregory A Scott Inc ....E....... 913 677-0414
Kansas City *(G-4053)*
Guerrilla Marketing Inc ....G....... 800 946-9150
Newton *(G-7353)*
Its Greek To Me Inc ....C....... 800 336-4486
Manhattan *(G-6666)*
Kellys Corporate Apparel ....G....... 316 263-5858
Wichita *(G-14847)*
Khaos Apparel LLC ....F....... 316 804-4900
Newton *(G-7370)*
Last Chance Graphics Inc ....G....... 785 263-4470
Abilene *(G-44)*
New Wave Enterprises Inc ....F....... 913 287-7671
Kansas City *(G-4287)*
Norton Enterprises ....G....... 620 221-1987
Winfield *(G-16164)*
Prairie Print Inc ....G....... 316 267-1950
Wichita *(G-15321)*
Prestige Graphics Inc ....F....... 316 262-3480
Wichita *(G-15338)*
Print Source Inc ....D....... 316 945-7052
Wichita *(G-15349)*
Rand Graphics Inc ....E....... 316 942-1125
Wichita *(G-15414)*
Sands Enterprises Inc ....G....... 316 942-8686
Wichita *(G-15518)*
Screen-It Grphics Lawrence Inc ....C....... 785 843-8888
Lawrence *(G-5107)*
Shirts Plus Inc ....F....... 316 788-1550
Derby *(G-1272)*
Simon & Simon Inc ....G....... 913 888-9889
Overland Park *(G-9311)*
Special Tee Graphics ....G....... 620 227-8160
Dodge City *(G-1434)*
Sterling Screen Printing Inc ....F....... 913 441-4411
Shawnee *(G-11034)*
Stewarts Sports & Awards ....G....... 620 241-5990
McPherson *(G-7028)*
Tioga Territory Ltd ....F....... 620 431-2479
Chanute *(G-770)*
Trainwreck Tees LLC ....G....... 620 224-2480
Fort Scott *(G-2011)*
U S Logo Inc ....F....... 316 264-1321
Wichita *(G-15824)*
U S S A Inc ....G....... 316 686-1653
Wichita *(G-15826)*
Universal Products Inc ....C....... 316 794-8601
Goddard *(G-2455)*

PRINTING, COMMERCIAL: Stationery, NEC

Printing Services Inc ....G....... 913 492-1500
Lenexa *(G-6070)*

PRINTING, COMMERCIAL: Tickets, NEC

Universal Manufacturing Co ....C....... 816 231-2771
Shawnee *(G-11044)*

PRINTING, LITHOGRAPHIC: Advertising Posters

Gill Bebco LLC ....E....... 816 942-3100
Lenexa *(G-5876)*

PRINTING, LITHOGRAPHIC: Calendars & Cards

Dimension Graphics Inc ....D....... 913 469-6800
Lenexa *(G-5820)*

PRINTING, LITHOGRAPHIC: Color

Pittcraft Printing Inc ....E....... 620 231-6200
Pittsburg *(G-9920)*

PRINTING, LITHOGRAPHIC: Decals

Award Decals Inc ....F....... 913 677-6681
Overland Park *(G-8418)*
Lowen Corporation ....G....... 620 663-2161
Hutchinson *(G-3357)*

PRINTING, LITHOGRAPHIC: Forms & Cards, Business

Envision Industries Inc ....D....... 316 267-2244
Wichita *(G-14296)*
Jfaonlinecom LLc ....G....... 316 554-1222
Wichita *(G-14756)*

PRINTING, LITHOGRAPHIC: Forms, Business

Rps Inc ....F....... 620 342-3026
Emporia *(G-1817)*

PRINTING, LITHOGRAPHIC: Maps

Black and Jensen Inc ....E....... 316 262-7277
Wichita *(G-13854)*

PRINTING, LITHOGRAPHIC: Offset & photolithographic printing

Screen Machine LLC ....F....... 785 762-3081
Junction City *(G-3750)*

PRINTING, LITHOGRAPHIC: On Metal

Copy Shoppe ....G....... 785 232-0403
Topeka *(G-12508)*
Food Trends Inc ....G....... 913 383-3600
Overland Park *(G-8732)*
Minneapolis Messenger Pubg Co ....G....... 785 392-2129
Minneapolis *(G-7118)*
Telescope Inc ....F....... 785 527-2244
Belleville *(G-467)*

PRINTING, LITHOGRAPHIC: Posters & Decals

Stouse LLC ....C....... 913 764-5757
New Century *(G-7301)*

PRINTING, LITHOGRAPHIC: Promotional

Express Print and Signs LLC ....E....... 785 825-8434
Salina *(G-10491)*

PRINTING, LITHOGRAPHIC: Publications

Roth K Christopherson ....G....... 316 269-2494
Wichita *(G-15485)*

PRINTING, LITHOGRAPHIC: Transfers, Decalcomania Or Dry

Pps Inc ....D....... 913 791-0164
Olathe *(G-7996)*

PRINTING: Books

Scholastic Book Fairs Inc ....F....... 913 599-5700
Shawnee Mission *(G-11836)*

PRINTING: Books

Adr Inc ....D....... 316 522-5599
Wichita *(G-13616)*
L & L Manufacturing Inc ....E....... 816 257-8411
Kansas City *(G-4187)*

PRINTING: Broadwoven Fabrics. Cotton

Spirit Industries Inc ....F....... 913 749-5858
Lawrence *(G-5115)*

PRINTING: Checkbooks

Deluxe Corporation ....C....... 913 888-3801
Lenexa *(G-5810)*

PRINTING: Commercial, NEC

Administration Kansas Dept ....D....... 785 296-3631
Topeka *(G-12289)*
Arrow Printing Company Inc ....G....... 785 825-8124
Salina *(G-10409)*
Baker Bros Printing Co Inc ....G....... 620 947-3520
Hillsboro *(G-3041)*
Blue Eagle Productions Inc ....F....... 816 225-2980
Overland Park *(G-8466)*
Bolen Office Supply Inc ....F....... 620 672-7535
Pratt *(G-10100)*
Brightmarks LLC ....E....... 913 338-1131
Lenexa *(G-5713)*
Coffeyville Printing Center ....G....... 620 251-6040
Coffeyville *(G-920)*
Custom Color Corp ....E....... 913 730-3100
Lenexa *(G-5798)*
Dataco Derex Inc ....F....... 913 438-2444
Leawood *(G-5370)*
Davies Communications Inc ....F....... 620 241-1504
McPherson *(G-6956)*
Daymark Solutions Inc ....F....... 913 541-8980
Shawnee Mission *(G-11294)*
Deluxe Corporation ....C....... 913 888-3801
Lenexa *(G-5810)*
Digital Lagoon Inc ....F....... 913 648-6900
Overland Park *(G-8656)*
Documart Inc ....F....... 913 649-3800
Shawnee Mission *(G-11312)*
Drafting Room Inc ....G....... 316 267-2291
Wichita *(G-14236)*
Drexel Technologies Inc ....E....... 913 371-4430
Lenexa *(G-5826)*
Edoc Printing ....G....... 913 469-0071
Shawnee Mission *(G-11328)*
Ejrex Inc ....D....... 620 421-6200
Parsons *(G-9683)*
Federal Prison Industries ....D....... 913 682-8700
Leavenworth *(G-5238)*
Fedex Office & Print Svcs Inc ....F....... 913 677-4488
Shawnee Mission *(G-11365)*
Fedex Office & Print Svcs Inc ....E....... 785 272-2500
Topeka *(G-12603)*
Fontastik Inc ....G....... 816 474-4366
Kansas City *(G-4015)*
Gary Bell ....G....... 785 233-6677
Holton *(G-3090)*

Genigraphics LLC ....F.... 913 441-1410
Shawnee *(G-10961)*
Gray County Printers ....G.... 620 855-2467
Cimarron *(G-828)*
Holderman Printing LLC ....G.... 913 557-6848
Paola *(G-9567)*
Iola Register Inc ....E.... 620 365-2111
Iola *(G-3611)*
Kelsey Construction Inc ....G.... 913 894-0330
Shawnee Mission *(G-11528)*
Kendall Packaging Corporation ....E.... 620 231-9804
Pittsburg *(G-9891)*
Kingston Printing & Design Inc ....F.... 785 690-7222
Eudora *(G-1878)*
Linn County Publishing Inc ....F.... 913 352-6235
Pleasanton *(G-9997)*
Lowen Corporation ....B.... 620 663-2161
Hutchinson *(G-3358)*
Marketing Technologies Inc ....D.... 913 342-9111
Kansas City *(G-4218)*
McCartys ....G.... 620 251-6169
Coffeyville *(G-957)*
Midwest Single Source Inc ....E.... 316 267-6333
Wichita *(G-15102)*
National Bd For Rspratory Care ....F.... 913 895-4900
Overland Park *(G-9069)*
Navrats Inc ....F.... 620 342-2092
Emporia *(G-1800)*
Niffie Printing Inc ....F.... 913 592-3040
Spring Hill *(G-12091)*
On Demand Technologies LLC ....F.... 913 438-1800
Overland Park *(G-9102)*
Perfect Output LLC ....D.... 913 317-8400
Overland Park *(G-9154)*
Pinnacle Plotting and Sup Lc ....G.... 913 766-1822
Shawnee *(G-11011)*
Pittcraft Printing Inc ....E.... 620 231-6200
Pittsburg *(G-9920)*
Print Time Inc ....E.... 913 345-8900
Leawood *(G-5528)*
Printing Inc ....E.... 316 265-1201
Wichita *(G-15350)*
Priority Envelope Inc ....E.... 913 859-9710
Lenexa *(G-6071)*
Professional Printing Kans Inc ....F.... 620 343-7125
Emporia *(G-1813)*
PSI Services Inc ....C.... 913 895-4600
Olathe *(G-8011)*
Quality Litho Inc ....E.... 913 262-5341
Kansas City *(G-4352)*
Quality Printing Inc ....G.... 620 421-0630
Parsons *(G-9727)*
Shire Signs LLC ....G.... 316 838-1362
Park City *(G-9643)*
Sign Solutions ....F.... 620 442-5649
Arkansas City *(G-179)*
Superior School Supplies Inc ....F.... 620 421-3190
Parsons *(G-9743)*
Tritats LLC ....G.... 913 219-5949
Overland Park *(G-9431)*
Witzkes Screen Printing ....G.... 913 839-8270
Olathe *(G-8156)*

PRINTING: Flexographic

Express Card and Label Co Inc ....E.... 785 233-0369
Topeka *(G-12589)*
Spectragraphics Inc ....E.... 913 888-6828
Lenexa *(G-6147)*
Tabco Incorporated ....E.... 913 287-3333
Kansas City *(G-4457)*

PRINTING: Gravure, Job

Superior Printing Co ....G.... 913 682-3313
Leavenworth *(G-5296)*

PRINTING: Gravure, Promotional

Ace Forms of Kansas Inc ....D.... 620 232-9290
Pittsburg *(G-9805)*

PRINTING: Gravure, Rotogravure

W/K Holding Company Inc ....F.... 620 223-5500
Fort Scott *(G-2016)*

PRINTING: Laser

Southwest Holding Corporation ....E.... 785 233-5662
Topeka *(G-13083)*

PRINTING: Letterpress

Abilene Printing Co Inc ....G.... 785 263-2330
Abilene *(G-7)*
Central Printing & Binding ....G.... 620 665-7251
Hutchinson *(G-3233)*
Garnett Publishing Inc ....F.... 785 448-3121
Garnett *(G-2373)*
Greeley County Republican ....G.... 620 376-4264
Tribune *(G-13271)*
Leroy Cook ....G.... 316 321-0844
El Dorado *(G-1583)*
Paper Graphics Inc ....G.... 620 276-7641
Garden City *(G-2248)*
Printery Inc ....F.... 785 632-5501
Clay Center *(G-877)*
Quality Printing & Gift Shop ....G.... 620 654-3487
Galva *(G-2095)*
Spangler Graphics LLC ....D.... 913 722-4500
Overland Park *(G-9332)*
Taylor Printing Inc ....G.... 620 672-3656
Pratt *(G-10159)*

PRINTING: Lithographic

Administration Kansas Dept ....D.... 785 296-3631
Topeka *(G-12289)*
Advocate Publishing Co Inc ....E.... 785 562-2317
Marysville *(G-6878)*
AG Press Inc ....D.... 785 539-7558
Manhattan *(G-6536)*
Baker Bros Printing Co Inc ....G.... 620 947-3520
Hillsboro *(G-3041)*
Bisel Inc ....G.... 785 842-2656
Lawrence *(G-4758)*
Blade Empire Publishing Co ....E.... 785 243-2424
Concordia *(G-1103)*
Brad Vignatelli ....G.... 913 541-9777
Lenexa *(G-5711)*
Brush Group LLC ....D.... 785 454-3383
Downs *(G-1470)*
Chanute Publishing Company ....A.... 620 431-4100
Chanute *(G-712)*
Cliff Hix Engineering Inc ....E.... 620 232-3000
Pittsburg *(G-9836)*
Cookbook Publishers Inc ....E.... 913 689-3038
Overland Park *(G-8598)*
D & B Print Shop Inc ....G.... 913 782-6688
Olathe *(G-7634)*
Deluxe Corporation ....C.... 913 888-3801
Lenexa *(G-5810)*
Dla Document Services ....G.... 913 684-5591
Fort Leavenworth *(G-1937)*
Ejrex Inc ....D.... 620 421-6200
Parsons *(G-9683)*
Federal Prison Industries ....D.... 913 682-8700
Leavenworth *(G-5238)*
Fedex Office & Print Svcs Inc ....E.... 785 272-2500
Topeka *(G-12603)*
Gatehuse Mdia Kans Hldings Inc ....F.... 316 321-6136
El Dorado *(G-1564)*
Go-Modern LLC ....G.... 785 271-1445
Topeka *(G-12639)*
Graphic Impressions Inc ....E.... 620 663-5939
Hutchinson *(G-3305)*
Graphics Four Inc ....G.... 913 268-0564
Shawnee *(G-10964)*
Graphics Systems Inc ....D.... 316 267-4171
Wichita *(G-14497)*
Guerrilla Marketing Inc ....G.... 800 946-9150
Newton *(G-7353)*
Harvest Graphics LLC ....E.... 913 438-5556
Shawnee Mission *(G-11415)*
High Plains Printing ....G.... 785 460-6350
Colby *(G-1015)*
Holderman Printing LLC ....G.... 913 557-6848
Garnett *(G-2378)*
Images ....G.... 785 827-0824
Salina *(G-10549)*
Independent Oil & Gas Svc Inc ....G.... 316 263-8281
Wichita *(G-14680)*
Iola Register Inc ....E.... 620 365-2111
Iola *(G-3611)*
Jdb Enterprises Inc ....G.... 316 263-2411
Wichita *(G-14752)*
Kelsey Construction Inc ....G.... 913 894-0330
Shawnee Mission *(G-11528)*
Key Office Products Inc ....G.... 620 227-2101
Dodge City *(G-1390)*
Koller Enterprises Inc ....D.... 913 422-2027
Lenexa *(G-5957)*
Lees Printing Company Inc ....G.... 913 371-0569
Kansas City *(G-4200)*
Legal Printing Company Inc ....G.... 913 369-1623
Bonner Springs *(G-559)*
Lowen Corporation ....B.... 620 663-2161
Hutchinson *(G-3358)*
Martin Dysart Enterprises Inc ....G.... 785 776-6731
Manhattan *(G-6732)*
McKissick Enterprises LLC ....F.... 316 687-0272
Wichita *(G-15029)*
Mennonite Church USA ....G.... 316 283-5100
Newton *(G-7378)*
Minuteman Press ....G.... 913 829-0300
Olathe *(G-7903)*
Morris Communications Co LLC ....D.... 620 231-2600
Pittsburg *(G-9908)*
Morris Communications Co LLC ....E.... 620 225-4151
Dodge City *(G-1407)*
Osage Graphics ....F.... 785 654-3939
Burlingame *(G-624)*
Patterson Advertising Agency ....G.... 785 232-0533
Topeka *(G-12964)*
Print Time Inc ....E.... 913 345-8900
Leawood *(G-5528)*
Printing Services Inc ....G.... 913 492-1500
Lenexa *(G-6070)*
Printing Solutions Kansas Inc ....G.... 785 841-8336
Lawrence *(G-5077)*
RGI Publications Inc ....E.... 913 829-8723
Olathe *(G-8030)*
Roberts Hutch-Line Inc ....E.... 620 662-3356
Hutchinson *(G-3428)*
Seaton Publishing Co Inc ....D.... 785 776-2200
Manhattan *(G-6798)*
Sky Printing and Pubg Inc ....G.... 913 362-9292
Shawnee Mission *(G-11873)*
Specialty Projects Corp Inc ....G.... 620 429-1086
Columbus *(G-1086)*
Superior Printing Co ....G.... 913 682-3313
Leavenworth *(G-5296)*
Wilbert Screen Printing Inc ....G.... 620 231-1730
Pittsburg *(G-9970)*
Winfield Publishing Co Inc ....E.... 620 221-1100
Winfield *(G-16189)*

PRINTING: Offset

A C Printing Co Inc ....G.... 913 780-3377
Olathe *(G-7504)*
Abilene Printing Co Inc ....G.... 785 263-2330
Abilene *(G-7)*
Ace Forms of Kansas Inc ....D.... 620 232-9290
Pittsburg *(G-9805)*
Adr Inc ....D.... 316 522-5599
Wichita *(G-13616)*
Arrow Printing Company Inc ....G.... 785 825-8124
Salina *(G-10409)*
Art Craft Printers & Design ....G.... 785 776-9151
Manhattan *(G-6545)*
Back Room Printing LLC ....G.... 620 873-2900
Meade *(G-7046)*
Barker Printing and Copy Svcs ....G.... 785 233-5533
Topeka *(G-12365)*
Burns Publishing Company Inc ....E.... 913 782-0321
Olathe *(G-7569)*
Caraway Printing Company Inc ....G.... 913 727-5223
Lansing *(G-4670)*
Cds Inc ....F.... 913 541-1166
Overland Park *(G-8532)*
Central Printing & Binding ....G.... 620 665-7251
Hutchinson *(G-3233)*
Chester Press Inc ....G.... 620 342-8792
Emporia *(G-1719)*
City Print Inc ....G.... 316 267-5555
Wichita *(G-14032)*
Consolidated Prtg & Sty Co Inc ....E.... 785 825-5426
Salina *(G-10460)*
Copy Center of Topeka Inc ....E.... 785 233-6677
Topeka *(G-12507)*
Copy Shop Inc ....G.... 316 262-8200
Wichita *(G-14100)*
Creative Printing Company Inc ....E.... 913 262-5000
Merriam *(G-7089)*
D P Enterprises Inc ....F.... 316 263-4234
Wichita *(G-14159)*
Davis Publications Inc ....F.... 785 945-6170
Valley Falls *(G-13362)*
Direct Mail Printers Inc ....F.... 316 263-1855
Wichita *(G-14213)*
Docuplex Inc ....E.... 316 262-2662
Wichita *(G-14220)*

Donnelley Financial LLC ....F 913 541-4099
Shawnee Mission *(G-11316)*
Fast Print ....G 316 688-1242
Wichita *(G-14344)*
Financial Printing Resource ....F 913 599-6979
Lenexa *(G-5852)*
Gary Bell ....G 785 233-6677
Holton *(G-3090)*
Golden Belt Printing II LLC ....F 620 793-6351
Great Bend *(G-2572)*
Graphic Images Inc ....F 316 283-3776
Newton *(G-7352)*
Greeley County Republican ....G 620 376-4264
Tribune *(G-13271)*
Happy Shirt Printing Co LLC ....G 785 371-1660
Lawrence *(G-4888)*
J-Con Reprographics Inc ....F 913 859-0800
Lenexa *(G-5927)*
Kansas Graphics Inc ....G 620 273-6111
Cottonwood Falls *(G-1155)*
Kopco Inc ....D 620 879-2117
Caney *(G-671)*
La Dow & Spohn Inc ....F 620 378-2541
Fredonia *(G-2037)*
Lawrence Printing and Design ....F 785 843-4600
Lawrence *(G-4984)*
Legends Printing & Graphics ....G 620 225-0020
Dodge City *(G-1396)*
Leroy Cook ....G 316 321-0844
El Dorado *(G-1583)*
Liberal Office Machines Co ....G 620 624-5653
Liberal *(G-6334)*
Linn County Publishing Inc ....F 913 352-6235
Pleasanton *(G-9997)*
Lockwood Company Inc ....E 913 367-0110
Atchison *(G-241)*
Louisburg Herald ....G 913 837-4321
Paola *(G-9570)*
Mainline Printing Inc ....D 785 233-2338
Topeka *(G-12856)*
McCormick-Armstrong Co Inc ....D 316 264-1363
Wichita *(G-15022)*
Mennonite Press Inc ....E 316 283-3060
Newton *(G-7380)*
Mid West Color Graphics Inc ....E 620 429-1088
Columbus *(G-1084)*
Midwestern Litho ....G 620 378-2912
Fredonia *(G-2040)*
Navrats Inc ....F 620 342-2092
Emporia *(G-1800)*
Northwestern Printers Inc ....F 785 625-1110
Hays *(G-2881)*
On Demand Technologies LLC ....F 913 438-1800
Overland Park *(G-9102)*
Paper Graphics Inc ....G 620 276-7641
Garden City *(G-2248)*
Par Forms Corporation ....F 620 421-0970
Parsons *(G-9716)*
Petersen Printing Inc ....G 620 275-7331
Garden City *(G-2252)*
Print Source Inc ....D 316 945-7052
Wichita *(G-15349)*
Printery Inc ....F 785 632-5501
Clay Center *(G-877)*
Printery Inc ....G 785 762-5112
Junction City *(G-3740)*
Printing Inc ....E 316 265-1201
Wichita *(G-15350)*
Printing Dynamics Inc ....G 816 524-0444
Olathe *(G-8008)*
Printingplus Inc ....G 316 269-3010
Wichita *(G-15351)*
Professional Graphics Inc ....F 913 663-3330
Shawnee Mission *(G-11755)*
Pronto Print ....G 785 823-2285
Salina *(G-10644)*
Proprint Incorporated ....G 785 272-0070
Topeka *(G-12992)*
Proprint Incorporated ....E 785 842-3610
Lawrence *(G-5080)*
Quad/Graphics Inc ....B 816 936-8536
Lenexa *(G-6083)*
Quality Litho Inc ....E 913 262-5341
Kansas City *(G-4352)*
Quality Printing & Gift Shop ....G 620 654-3487
Galva *(G-2095)*
Quality Printing Inc ....G 620 421-0630
Parsons *(G-9727)*
Ravin Printing LLC ....G 620 431-5830
Chanute *(G-759)*
Sekan Printing Company Inc ....E 620 223-5190
Fort Scott *(G-2003)*
Shahrokhi Inc ....G 913 764-5775
Olathe *(G-8060)*
Sharpe Printing Co Inc ....F 316 262-4041
Wichita *(G-15574)*
Shawnee Copy Center Inc ....F 913 268-4343
Shawnee Mission *(G-11851)*
Southwest Holding Corporation ....E 785 233-5662
Topeka *(G-13083)*
Spangler Graphics LLC ....D 913 722-4500
Overland Park *(G-9332)*
Super Speed Printing Inc ....F 316 283-5828
North Newton *(G-7439)*
Tarrant Enterprises Inc ....F 785 273-8503
Topeka *(G-13142)*
Taylor Printing Inc ....G 620 672-3656
Pratt *(G-10159)*
Topeka Blue Print & Sup Co Inc ....G 785 232-7209
Topeka *(G-13169)*
Valley Offset Printing Inc ....E 316 755-0061
Valley Center *(G-13360)*
Waynes Printing & Copying ....G 620 662-4655
Hutchinson *(G-3482)*
Wichita Press Inc ....G 316 945-5651
Wichita *(G-16018)*
Wooten Printing Co Inc ....G 316 265-8575
Wichita *(G-16070)*
Z3 Graphix Inc ....E 913 599-3355
Overland Park *(G-9525)*

PRINTING: Photo-Offset

Quality Printing and Off Sups ....F 913 491-6366
Lenexa *(G-6084)*

PRINTING: Screen, Broadwoven Fabrics, Cotton

CP Partnerships Inc ....F 785 625-7388
Hays *(G-2779)*
Express Print and Signs LLC ....E 785 825-8434
Salina *(G-10491)*
Guerrilla Marketing Inc ....G 800 946-9150
Newton *(G-7353)*
New Wave Enterprises Inc ....F 913 287-7671
Kansas City *(G-4287)*
Stewarts Sports & Awards ....G 620 241-5990
McPherson *(G-7028)*
Sun Creations Inc ....E 785 830-0403
Lawrence *(G-5127)*

PRINTING: Screen, Fabric

Finchers Findings Inc ....G 620 886-5952
Medicine Lodge *(G-7060)*
First Edition Inc ....G 620 232-6002
Pittsburg *(G-9861)*
Guerrilla Marketing Inc ....G 800 946-9150
Newton *(G-7353)*
Nill Brothers Silkscreen Inc ....F 913 384-4242
Kansas City *(G-4288)*
Screen-It Grphics Lawrence Inc ....C 785 843-8888
Lawrence *(G-5107)*
Seen Merchandising LLC ....F 913 233-1981
Shawnee *(G-11026)*
Sun Creations Inc ....E 785 830-0403
Lawrence *(G-5127)*
USA Inc ....F 785 825-6247
Salina *(G-10748)*

PRINTING: Screen, Manmade Fiber & Silk, Broadwoven Fabric

Sun Creations Inc ....E 785 830-0403
Lawrence *(G-5127)*

PRINTING: Thermography

Donmar Inc ....F 913 432-2700
Shawnee Mission *(G-11315)*
Shahrokhi Inc ....G 913 764-5775
Olathe *(G-8060)*

PRIVATE INVESTIGATOR SVCS

Blue Eagle Investigations Inc ....F 913 685-2583
Paola *(G-9542)*
Clarence M Kelley & Assoc of K ....D 913 647-7700
Shawnee *(G-10929)*
D & B Legal Services Inc ....D 913 362-8110
Prairie Village *(G-10024)*
Kansas Investigative Services ....F 316 267-1357
Wichita *(G-14811)*

PROBATION OFFICE

County of Barton ....F 620 793-1910
Great Bend *(G-2548)*
County of Reno ....E 620 665-7042
Hutchinson *(G-3249)*
County of Shawnee ....E 785 233-8856
Topeka *(G-12518)*
Fourth Judicial Dist Comnity C ....F 785 229-3510
Ottawa *(G-8273)*
Geary Corrections Center ....E 785 762-4679
Junction City *(G-3693)*
Sedgwick Juvenile Field Svcs ....E 316 660-5380
Wichita *(G-15550)*
United States Courts ADM ....D 913 735-2242
Kansas City *(G-4489)*

PROFESSIONAL EQPT & SPLYS, WHOLESALE: Analytical Instruments

Shimadzu Scientific Instrs Inc ....F 913 888-9449
Shawnee Mission *(G-11864)*

PROFESSIONAL EQPT & SPLYS, WHOLESALE: Bank

Guardian Business Services ....F 785 823-1635
Salina *(G-10524)*
Oppliger Banking Systems Inc ....E 913 829-6300
Olathe *(G-7959)*

PROFESSIONAL EQPT & SPLYS, WHOLESALE: Engineers', NEC

ARC Document Solutions ....E 316 264-9344
Wichita *(G-13727)*
Cretex ....E 785 863-3300
Oskaloosa *(G-8223)*

PROFESSIONAL EQPT & SPLYS, WHOLESALE: Law Enforcement

Baysinger Police Supply Inc ....F 316 262-5663
Wichita *(G-13821)*

PROFESSIONAL EQPT & SPLYS, WHOLESALE: Optical Goods

Bushnell Holdings Inc ....C 913 752-3400
Overland Park *(G-8497)*
Midwest Lens Inc ....F 913 894-1030
Shawnee Mission *(G-11634)*
O H Gerry Optical Company ....E 913 362-8822
Overland Park *(G-9095)*

PROFESSIONAL EQPT & SPLYS, WHOLESALE: Precision Tools

Kc Tool LLC ....F 913 440-9766
Olathe *(G-7833)*

PROFESSIONAL EQPT & SPLYS, WHOLESALE: Scientific & Engineerg

Professional Engrg Cons PA ....C 316 262-2691
Wichita *(G-15359)*

PROFESSIONAL EQPT & SPLYS, WHOLESALE: Theatrical

Kneisley Manufacturing Company ....F 620 365-6628
Iola *(G-3618)*

PROFESSIONAL INSTRUMENT REPAIR SVCS

Midwest Merchandising Inc ....C 913 428-8430
Overland Park *(G-9033)*
Total Tool Supply Inc ....F 913 722-7879
Kansas City *(G-4471)*

PROFESSIONAL SCHOOLS

Cleveland University - Kans Cy ....D 913 234-0600
Overland Park *(G-8565)*

PROFILE SHAPES: Unsupported Plastics

Kaman Composites - Wichita .... C 316 942-1241
Wichita *(G-14780)*

PROGRAM ADMIN, GOVT: Air, Water & Solid Waste Mgmt, Local

City of Waterville .... E 785 363-2367
Waterville *(G-13473)*

PROGRAM ADMIN, GOVT: Air, Water & Solid Waste Mgmt, State

Health and Envmt Kans Dept .... F 620 231-8540
Frontenac *(G-2055)*
Kansas State University .... E 620 275-9164
Garden City *(G-2214)*

PROGRAM ADMINISTRATION, GOVERNMENT: Social & Manpower, State

Kansas Dept For Aging & Disabi .... D 785 296-2917
Topeka *(G-12770)*
Kansas Dept For Chldren Fmlies .... D 620 421-4500
Parsons *(G-9696)*
Kansas Dept For Chldren Fmlies .... E 785 462-6769
Colby *(G-1020)*

PROGRAMMERS: Indl Process

Power Admin LLC .... G 800 401-2339
Olathe *(G-7994)*

PROGRAMS ADMIN, GOVT: Environmental Protection Agencies

County of Johnson .... F 913 432-3868
Shawnee Mission *(G-11270)*
Environmental Protection Agcy .... B 913 551-7118
Lenexa *(G-5835)*

PROMOTERS OF SHOWS & EXHIBITIONS

Skillpath Seminars Inc .... C 913 362-3900
Shawnee Mission *(G-11872)*

PROMOTION SVCS

Creative Mktg Unlimited Inc .... G 913 894-0077
Overland Park *(G-8611)*
Discovery Concepts Inc .... G 913 814-7100
Shawnee Mission *(G-11309)*
Raymarr Inc .... F 913 648-3480
Shawnee Mission *(G-11778)*
Spectrum Promotional Pdts Inc .... F 316 262-1199
Wichita *(G-15638)*

PROPERTY & CASUALTY INSURANCE AGENTS

Agri-Risk Services Inc .... F 913 897-1699
Stilwell *(G-12133)*

PROPERTY DAMAGE INSURANCE

Kansas Mutual Insurance Co .... F 785 354-1076
Topeka *(G-12792)*
Swiss RE America Holding Corp .... A 913 676-5200
Overland Park *(G-9384)*
United Services Auto Assn .... B 913 451-6100
Shawnee Mission *(G-11965)*
Westport Insurance Corporation .... C 913 676-5270
Overland Park *(G-9492)*
Zurich Agency Services Inc .... B 913 339-1000
Overland Park *(G-9530)*

PROTECTIVE FOOTWEAR: Rubber Or Plastic

Sid Bdeker Safety Shoe Svc Inc .... G 913 599-6463
Lenexa *(G-6134)*

PUBLIC ADDRESS SYSTEMS

Galaxy Audio Inc .... F 316 263-2852
Wichita *(G-14437)*

PUBLIC FINANCE, TAX & MONETARY POLICY OFFICES, GOVT: State

Treasurer Kansas State .... E 785 296-3171
Topeka *(G-13198)*

PUBLIC FINANCE, TAXATION & MONETARY POLICY OFFICES

Federal Deposit Insurance Corp .... E 316 729-0301
Wichita *(G-14346)*

PUBLIC HEALTH PROGRAM ADMINISTRATION, GOVERNMENT: County

County of Sedgwick .... E 316 660-9500
Wichita *(G-14113)*
County of Sherman .... E 785 890-3625
Goodland *(G-2467)*
Cowley County Joint Board Hlth .... F 620 442-3260
Arkansas City *(G-151)*

PUBLIC HEALTH PROGRAM ADMINISTRATION, GOVERNMENT: State

Health and Envmt Kans Dept .... E 620 272-3600
Garden City *(G-2192)*
Kans Dept Health and Envmt .... A 785 296-0461
Topeka *(G-12755)*

PUBLIC HEALTH PROGRAMS ADMINISTRATION SVCS

Administration Kansas Dept .... F 785 296-3017
Topeka *(G-12291)*
County of Johnson .... C 913 894-8383
Olathe *(G-7621)*
Kansas Dept For Chldren Fmlies .... C 913 755-7000
Osawatomie *(G-8196)*
Kindred Healthcare Oper LLC .... E 913 906-0522
Overland Park *(G-8919)*
Kvc Behavioral Healthcare Inc .... D 620 820-7680
Parsons *(G-9701)*

PUBLIC LIBRARY

Dodge City Public Library .... E 620 225-0248
Dodge City *(G-1350)*

PUBLIC ORDER & SAFETY ACTIVITIES, NEC

ADT 24 7 Alarm and Security .... D 620 860-0229
Pratt *(G-10094)*

PUBLIC RELATIONS & PUBLICITY SVCS

Frank Agency Inc .... D 913 648-8333
Overland Park *(G-8736)*
Morningstar Communications Co .... F 913 660-9630
Overland Park *(G-9054)*
Walz Tetrick Advertising Inc .... E 913 789-8778
Mission *(G-7140)*

PUBLIC RELATIONS SVCS

Cpg Communications Group LLC .... G 913 317-2888
Shawnee Mission *(G-11276)*
Family Ftres Edtorial Synd Inc .... E 913 722-0055
Shawnee Mission *(G-11360)*
Mennonite Mission Network .... F 540 434-6701
Newton *(G-7379)*
Pennington Co Fundraising LLC .... E 785 843-1661
Lawrence *(G-5060)*

PUBLIC WELFARE CENTER

Choices Network Inc .... B 785 820-8018
Salina *(G-10447)*
Social and Rehabilitation Serv .... D 620 272-5800
Garden City *(G-2283)*

PUBLISHERS: Book

Aircraft Bluebook .... C 913 967-1719
Shawnee Mission *(G-11088)*
Monaco & Associates Inc .... G 785 272-5501
Topeka *(G-12910)*
University of Kansas .... E 785 864-4154
Lawrence *(G-5166)*
University Press of Kansas .... E 785 864-4155
Lawrence *(G-5168)*

PUBLISHERS: Books, No Printing

Aapc Inc .... G 877 277-8254
Shawnee *(G-10905)*
Edwin Myers .... G 316 799-2112
Whitewater *(G-13570)*

PUBLISHERS: Catalogs

Glover Inc .... E 800 654-1511
Olathe *(G-7735)*

PUBLISHERS: Directories, NEC

Central Publishing Co Inc .... G 620 365-2106
Iola *(G-3591)*

PUBLISHERS: Magazines, No Printing

435 Magazine LLC .... F 913 469-6700
Overland Park *(G-8330)*
Advanstar Communications Inc .... E 913 871-3800
Shawnee Mission *(G-11079)*
Anthem Motorsports Inc .... F 913 894-6923
Leawood *(G-5328)*
Bank News Publications Inc .... F 913 261-7000
Roeland Park *(G-10217)*
Foil Stamping & Embossing Assn .... G 785 271-5816
Topeka *(G-12621)*
Good News Publishing Co Inc .... E 620 879-5460
Caney *(G-669)*
Interstate Publishers Inc .... F 913 341-4445
Prairie Village *(G-10036)*
McCall Pattern Company .... B 785 776-4041
Manhattan *(G-6735)*
Patient Resource Pubg LLC .... F 913 725-1000
Overland Park *(G-9145)*
Peterson Publications Inc .... G 785 271-5801
Topeka *(G-12972)*

PUBLISHERS: Maps

ARC Document Solutions .... E 316 264-9344
Wichita *(G-13727)*

PUBLISHERS: Miscellaneous

Aapc Inc .... G 877 277-8254
Shawnee *(G-10905)*
Anthem Media LLC .... E 913 894-6923
Leawood *(G-5327)*
AT&T Inc .... F 913 676-1136
Lenexa *(G-5673)*
Edwin Myers .... G 316 799-2112
Whitewater *(G-13570)*
Fontastik Inc .... G 816 474-4366
Kansas City *(G-4015)*
Franklin Covey Co .... G 800 819-1812
Overland Park *(G-8737)*
Good News Publishing Co Inc .... E 620 879-5460
Caney *(G-669)*
Gospel Publishers .... G 620 345-2532
Moundridge *(G-7183)*
Haynes Publishing Co .... G 785 475-2206
Oberlin *(G-7496)*
Master Teacher Inc .... E 785 539-0555
Manhattan *(G-6733)*
Nationwide Learning LLC .... C 785 862-2292
Topeka *(G-12925)*
Ogden Publications Inc .... C 785 274-4300
Topeka *(G-12943)*
Rockhurst University Continuin .... D 913 432-7755
Shawnee Mission *(G-11812)*
Tristar Publishing Inc .... G 913 491-4200
Overland Park *(G-9430)*
Viralnova LLC .... E 913 706-9710
Overland Park *(G-9465)*
Wichita State Sunflower Inc .... E 316 978-6917
Wichita *(G-16030)*

PUBLISHERS: Music Book & Sheet Music

Miracorp Inc .... G 913 322-8000
Lenexa *(G-6006)*

PUBLISHERS: Newspaper

City of Anthony .... G 620 842-5123
Anthony *(G-123)*
Gannett Co Inc .... C 785 832-6319
Lawrence *(G-4868)*
McGrath Publishing Company .... G 785 738-2424
Beloit *(G-492)*

Montgomery Communications Inc........D....... 785 762-5000
Junction City (G-3727)
Morris Communications Co LLC...........E....... 316 283-1500
Newton (G-7390)
Morris Communications Co LLC...........E....... 620 442-4200
Arkansas City (G-167)
Morris Communications Co LLC...........E....... 785 823-1111
Salina (G-10604)
Nor West Newspaper Inc........................G....... 785 332-3162
Saint Francis (G-10343)
Ottaway Amusement Co Inc.................G....... 316 529-0086
Onaga (G-8179)
Prairie Dog Press.................................F....... 785 669-2009
Almena (G-68)
Wichita State Sunflower Inc..................E....... 316 978-6917
Wichita (G-16030)

PUBLISHERS: Newspapers, No Printing

Abilene Rflctor Chronicle Pubg.............E....... 785 263-1000
Abilene (G-8)
Beloit Call...G....... 785 738-3537
Beloit (G-475)
Chanute Publishing Company...............A....... 620 431-4100
Chanute (G-712)
Cnhi LLC..E....... 620 421-9450
Parsons (G-9673)
Dan Diehl...G....... 785 336-2175
Seneca (G-10863)
Davis Publications Inc..........................F....... 785 945-6170
Valley Falls (G-13362)
Galena Sentinel Times...........................G....... 620 783-5034
Galena (G-2074)
Garnett Publishing Inc..........................F....... 785 448-3121
Garnett (G-2373)
Gatehouse Media Inc.............................G....... 913 367-0583
Atchison (G-229)
Greeley County Republican...................G....... 620 376-4264
Tribune (G-13271)
Harvey County Independent..................G....... 316 835-2235
Halstead (G-2702)
High Plains Publishers Inc....................D....... 620 227-7171
Dodge City (G-1372)
Labette Avenue.....................................F....... 620 795-2550
Oswego (G-8234)
Louisburg Herald..................................G....... 913 837-4321
Paola (G-9570)
Lyons Daily News.................................G....... 620 257-2368
Lyons (G-6489)
Marshall Publishing Inc.........................G....... 620 278-2114
Sterling (G-12125)
Miami County Publishing Co.................E....... 913 294-2311
Paola (G-9573)
Minneapolis Messenger Pubg Co..........G....... 785 392-2129
Minneapolis (G-7118)
Montgomery County Chronicle.............G....... 620 879-2156
Caney (G-672)
Montgomery County Media LLC...........E....... 620 331-3550
Independence (G-3541)
Mulvane News and Bandwagon............G....... 316 777-4233
Mulvane (G-7225)
Powls Publishing Company Inc.............F....... 785 364-3141
Holton (G-3108)
Tcv Publishing Inc................................G....... 316 681-1155
Wichita (G-15719)
Telescope Inc..F....... 785 527-2244
Belleville (G-467)
Times Sentinel Newspapers..................G....... 316 540-0500
Cheney (G-797)
Tri-County Newspapers Inc...................F....... 913 856-7615
Gardner (G-2366)
Western Kansas World Inc....................G....... 785 743-2155
Wakeeney (G-13396)
Wichita Business Journal Inc................F....... 316 267-6406
Wichita (G-15983)
Wilson County Citizen Inc....................G....... 620 378-4415
Fredonia (G-2049)

PUBLISHERS: Pamphlets, No Printing

McCall Pattern Company.......................B....... 785 776-4041
Manhattan (G-6735)
Premiere Marketing Group Inc..............G....... 913 362-9100
Overland Park (G-9183)

PUBLISHERS: Patterns, Paper

McCall Pattern Company.......................B....... 785 776-4041
Manhattan (G-6735)

PUBLISHERS: Periodical, With Printing

Mennonite Weekly Review Inc...............G....... 316 283-3670
Newton (G-7381)

PUBLISHERS: Periodicals, Magazines

Advocate Publishing Co Inc..................E....... 785 562-2317
Marysville (G-6878)
Century Marketing Inc..........................F....... 913 696-9758
Lenexa (G-5742)
Claflin Books & Copies.........................F....... 785 776-3771
Manhattan (G-6591)
East Kansas Quartly Cnfrce Fre............G....... 785 272-1843
Topeka (G-12568)
Herald and Banner Press......................F....... 913 432-0331
Overland Park (G-8811)
Informa Business Media Inc..................D....... 913 341-1300
Olathe (G-7789)
Kansas Electric Cooperatives...............E....... 785 478-4554
Topeka (G-12775)
Kansas Rest Hospitality Assn...............F....... 316 267-8383
Wichita (G-14821)
Morris Communications Co LLC...........E....... 620 442-4200
Arkansas City (G-167)
Morris Communications Co LLC...........D....... 785 295-1111
Topeka (G-12914)
Wichita State Sunflower Inc..................E....... 316 978-6917
Wichita (G-16030)

PUBLISHERS: Periodicals, No Printing

Hall Publications Inc............................G....... 785 232-8600
Topeka (G-12659)

PUBLISHERS: Shopping News

Chanute Publishing Company...............A....... 620 431-4100
Chanute (G-712)
Gatehuse Mdia Kans Hldings Inc..........F....... 316 321-6136
El Dorado (G-1564)
McGrath Publishing Company...............G....... 785 738-2424
Beloit (G-492)
Salina Journal Inc.................................C....... 785 823-6363
Salina (G-10678)

PUBLISHERS: Telephone & Other Directory

Hall Publications Inc............................G....... 785 232-8600
Topeka (G-12659)
Interstate Publishers Inc.......................F....... 913 341-4445
Prairie Village (G-10036)
K W Brock Directories Inc.....................C....... 620 231-4000
Pittsburg (G-9884)
RGI Publications Inc.............................E....... 913 829-8723
Olathe (G-8030)

PUBLISHERS: Trade journals, No Printing

National Publishers Group Inc..............F....... 316 788-6271
Haysville (G-2953)

PUBLISHING & BROADCASTING: Internet Only

Converg Media LLC..............................G....... 913 871-0453
Olathe (G-7613)
Squad It Services LLC.........................E....... 785 844-3114
Herington (G-2981)

PUBLISHING & PRINTING: Book Clubs

Schroff Development Corp....................F....... 913 262-2664
Shawnee Mission (G-11838)

PUBLISHING & PRINTING: Books

Cookbook Publishers Inc......................E....... 913 689-3038
Overland Park (G-8598)
Devore & Sons Inc................................E....... 316 267-3211
Wichita (G-14205)
Purplefrogintl.......................................G....... 816 510-0871
Shawnee (G-11014)
Terrell Publishing Co............................G....... 913 948-8226
Kansas City (G-4464)

PUBLISHING & PRINTING: Directories, NEC

Guest Communications Corp................E....... 913 888-1217
Shawnee Mission (G-11405)

PUBLISHING & PRINTING: Magazines: publishing & printing

Allen Press Inc.....................................D....... 785 843-1234
Lawrence (G-4729)
Cpg Communications Group LLC.........G....... 913 317-2888
Shawnee Mission (G-11276)
Family Media Group Inc........................E....... 913 815-6600
Overland Park (G-8703)
Feed-Lot Magazine Inc..........................G....... 620 397-2838
Dighton (G-1285)
Half Price Bks Rec Mgzines Inc............F....... 913 829-9959
Olathe (G-7748)
Multi-Media International LLC..............G....... 913 469-6800
Shawnee Mission (G-11659)

PUBLISHING & PRINTING: Newsletters, Business Svc

Propane Resources LLC.......................E....... 913 262-8345
Shawnee Mission (G-11756)

PUBLISHING & PRINTING: Newspapers

AG Press Inc...D....... 785 539-7558
Manhattan (G-6536)
Council Grove Republican....................G....... 620 767-5123
Council Grove (G-1161)
Dighton Herald......................................G....... 620 397-5347
Dighton (G-1284)
Faimon Publications Inc........................F....... 620 364-5325
Burlington (G-634)
Gatehouse Media LLC..........................D....... 913 682-0305
Leavenworth (G-5241)
Gatehouse Media LLC..........................E....... 620 326-3326
Wellington (G-13502)
Gatehouse Media LLC..........................F....... 620 241-2422
McPherson (G-6968)
Gatehouse Media LLC..........................E....... 913 682-0305
Leavenworth (G-5242)
Gatehuse Mdia Kans Hldings Inc..........F....... 316 321-6136
El Dorado (G-1564)
Harris Enterprises Group......................F....... 785 827-6035
Salina (G-10536)
Haynes Publishing Co...........................G....... 785 475-2206
Oberlin (G-7496)
Haynes Publishing Co...........................E....... 785 899-2338
Goodland (G-2475)
Haynes Publishing Co...........................F....... 785 462-3963
Colby (G-1011)
Hoch Publishing Co Inc.........................G....... 620 382-2165
Marion (G-6872)
Independent Oil & Gas Svc Inc.............G....... 316 263-8281
Wichita (G-14680)
Inland Industries Inc.............................G....... 913 492-9050
Bucyrus (G-600)
Iola Register Inc...................................E....... 620 365-2111
Iola (G-3611)
Kansas Newspaper Foundation.............E....... 785 271-5304
Topeka (G-12794)
Lee Enterprises Incorporated...............G....... 620 276-2311
Garden City (G-2223)
Lincoln Sentinel Republican.................G....... 785 524-4200
Lincoln (G-6384)
McClatchy Newspapers Inc...................D....... 816 234-4636
Shawnee Mission (G-11608)
Morris Communications Co LLC...........D....... 620 231-2600
Pittsburg (G-9908)
Morris Communications Co LLC...........E....... 620 225-4151
Dodge City (G-1407)
Morris Newspaper Corp Kansas...........E....... 620 792-1211
Great Bend (G-2613)
Mt Pleasant News Inc...........................F....... 913 492-9050
Shawnee Mission (G-11657)
Ottawa Herald Inc.................................E....... 785 242-4700
Ottawa (G-8298)
Rawlins County Sq Deal Pubg..............G....... 785 626-3600
Atwood (G-290)
Record Publications.............................G....... 913 362-1988
Kansas City (G-4365)
Russell Publishing Co...........................G....... 785 483-2116
Russell (G-10297)
Salina Journal Inc.................................C....... 785 823-6363
Salina (G-10678)
Senate United States............................F....... 620 227-2244
Dodge City (G-1428)
Smith County Pioneer...........................G....... 785 282-3371
Smith Center (G-12043)
University Daily Kansan.......................C....... 785 864-4358
Lawrence (G-5154)

Walker Publishing Inc G 913 352-6700
Pleasanton *(G-10003)*
White Corporation Inc E 620 342-4800
Emporia *(G-1851)*
Wichita Eagle Beacon Pubg Inc D 316 268-6000
Wichita *(G-15994)*
Willgrattten Publications LLC E 785 762-5000
Junction City *(G-3769)*
Wsu Sunflower Newspaper E 316 978-6900
Wichita *(G-16077)*

PUBLISHING & PRINTING: Shopping News

Abilene Rflctor Chronicle Pubg E 785 263-1000
Abilene *(G-8)*
Davies Communications Inc F 620 241-1504
McPherson *(G-6956)*

PUBLISHING & PRINTING: Technical Manuals

Linux New Media Usa LLC G 785 856-3080
Lawrence *(G-4998)*

PUBLISHING & PRINTING: Yearbooks

Herff Jones LLC D 913 432-8100
Edwardsville *(G-1502)*
Walsworth Publishing Co Inc E 800 265-6795
Overland Park *(G-9483)*

PUMP JACKS & OTHER PUMPING EQPT: Indl

Stenner Sales Company G 913 768-4114
New Century *(G-7300)*

PUMPS

Allegion S&S US Holding Co E 913 393-8629
Olathe *(G-7518)*
Eaton Corporation B 620 663-5751
Hutchinson *(G-3274)*
Fairbanks Morse Pump Corp B 630 859-7000
Kansas City *(G-4003)*
Fairbanks Morse Pump Corp F 913 371-5000
Kansas City *(G-4004)*
Grundfos CBS Inc G 281 994-2830
Overland Park *(G-8781)*
Hallowell Manufacturing LLC F 620 597-2552
Columbus *(G-1077)*
Schlumberger Technology Corp C 785 841-5610
Lawrence *(G-5103)*
Seals Inc G 913 438-1212
Shawnee Mission *(G-11844)*

PUMPS & PUMPING EQPT REPAIR SVCS

C & B Equipment Midwest Inc F 913 236-8222
Overland Park *(G-8502)*
Cook Pump Company E 620 251-0880
Coffeyville *(G-930)*
Gibson Industrial Controls Inc G 620 241-3551
McPherson *(G-6969)*
Jci Industries Inc F 316 942-6200
Wichita *(G-14751)*
Layne Christensen Company E 913 321-5000
Kansas City *(G-4196)*
Seals Inc G 913 438-1212
Shawnee Mission *(G-11844)*

PUMPS & PUMPING EQPT WHOLESALERS

C & B Equipment Midwest Inc F 316 262-5156
Wichita *(G-13924)*
Callaway Electric G 785 632-5588
Clay Center *(G-847)*
Darwin Industries Inc F 620 251-8438
Coffeyville *(G-932)*
Dxp Enterprises Inc F 913 888-0108
Lenexa *(G-5827)*
Gibson Industrial Controls Inc G 620 241-3551
McPherson *(G-6969)*
Hajoca Corporation F 785 825-1333
Salina *(G-10531)*
Jci Industries Inc F 316 942-6200
Wichita *(G-14751)*
Layne Christensen Company F 913 321-5000
Kansas City *(G-4197)*
Layne Christensen Company E 316 264-5365
Wichita *(G-14937)*
Seals Inc G 913 438-1212
Shawnee Mission *(G-11844)*

Thompson Pump Co E 913 788-2583
Kansas City *(G-4468)*
Western Hydro LLC F 620 277-2132
Garden City *(G-2310)*
Wichita Pump & Supply Company F 316 264-8308
Wichita *(G-16019)*

PUMPS: Measuring & Dispensing

Great Plains Industries Inc B 316 686-7361
Wichita *(G-14503)*
Scriptpro LLC D 913 384-1008
Shawnee Mission *(G-11839)*

PUMPS: Oil Well & Field

Cook Pump Company E 620 251-0880
Coffeyville *(G-930)*
Jacks Genuine Mfg Inc F 620 948-3000
Coffeyville *(G-950)*
Max Papay LLC F 620 873-5350
Meade *(G-7050)*
Star Pipe Usa LLC C 281 558-3000
Coffeyville *(G-979)*
Well Watch LLC G 785 798-0020
Ness City *(G-7268)*

PUMPS: Oil, Measuring Or Dispensing

Power Flame Incorporated C 620 421-0480
Parsons *(G-9724)*

PURCHASING SVCS

Associated Purch Svcs Corp F 913 327-8730
Overland Park *(G-8406)*
Ils National LLC F 913 888-9191
Olathe *(G-7785)*
University of Kansas D 785 864-8885
Lawrence *(G-5160)*

PURIFICATION & DUST COLLECTION EQPT

Mac Equipment Inc F 785 284-2191
Sabetha *(G-10317)*

PUSHCARTS & WHEELBARROWS

JM Tran-Sport LLC G 785 545-3756
Glen Elder *(G-2426)*

QUARTZ CRYSTALS: Electronic

Inficon Edc Inc D 913 888-1750
Overland Park *(G-8842)*

QUARTZITE: Crushed & Broken

Apac-Kansas Inc E 785 524-4413
Lincoln *(G-6379)*

QUILTING SVC & SPLYS, FOR THE TRADE

Prairie Point E 913 322-1222
Lenexa *(G-6068)*

RACE CAR DRIVER SVCS

Patterson Racing Inc F 316 775-7771
Augusta *(G-337)*

RACE TRACK OPERATION

B & H Motor Sports E 785 966-2575
Mayetta *(G-6914)*

RACETRACKS: Auto

Kansas Speedway Corporation E 913 328-3300
Kansas City *(G-4157)*
Thunder Hill Speedway LLC E 785 313-2922
Mayetta *(G-6919)*

RADAR SYSTEMS & EQPT

Kustom Signals Inc C 620 431-2700
Chanute *(G-736)*

RADIO & TELEVISION COMMUNICATIONS EQUIPMENT

AT&T Inc F 913 676-1136
Lenexa *(G-5673)*
Childrens Mercy Hospital D 913 696-8000
Shawnee Mission *(G-11221)*

Digital Ally Inc D 913 814-7774
Lenexa *(G-5816)*
Frank Communications Hays Inc G 785 623-1500
Hays *(G-2812)*
Lg Elctrnics Mbilecomm USA Inc E 913 234-3701
Leawood *(G-5457)*
Networks International Corp E 913 685-3400
Overland Park *(G-9078)*

RADIO & TELEVISION REPAIR

Custom Rdo Communications Ltd F 816 561-4100
Leawood *(G-5367)*
Northeast Kans Educatn Svc Ctr C 913 538-7250
Ozawkie *(G-9536)*
Paragon N D T & Finishes Inc E 316 945-5285
Wichita *(G-15259)*

RADIO BROADCASTING & COMMUNICATIONS EQPT

Ka-Comm Inc G 785 776-8177
Manhattan *(G-6672)*
Kustom Signals Inc C 620 431-2700
Chanute *(G-736)*
Overfield Corporation F 785 843-3434
Lawrence *(G-5052)*
Tfmcomm Inc G 785 841-2924
Lawrence *(G-5135)*

RADIO BROADCASTING STATIONS

94 5 Country Inc D 785 272-3456
Topeka *(G-12275)*
Alpha Media LLC F 785 823-1111
Salina *(G-10400)*
Alpha Media LLC F 785 272-3456
Topeka *(G-12310)*
American Media Investments Inc E 620 231-7200
Pittsburg *(G-9808)*
Bott Communications Inc F 913 642-7770
Shawnee Mission *(G-11176)*
CM Wind Down Topco Inc D 785 272-2122
Topeka *(G-12481)*
Community Broadcasting Inc F 913 642-7770
Overland Park *(G-8581)*
Cumulus Media Inc E 913 514-3000
Shawnee Mission *(G-11285)*
Davies Communications Inc F 620 241-1504
McPherson *(G-6956)*
Eagle Communications Inc F 785 625-5910
Hays *(G-2793)*
Eagle Communications Inc F 620 792-3101
Great Bend *(G-2557)*
Eagle Communications Inc F 785 726-3291
Hays *(G-2794)*
Eagle Communications Inc D 785 650-5349
Hays *(G-2795)*
Eagle Communications Inc F 785 587-0103
Manhattan *(G-6618)*
Eagle Communications Inc E 785 483-3244
Russell *(G-10273)*
Eagle Communications Inc E 620 662-4486
Hutchinson *(G-3272)*
Eagle Communications Inc F 785 825-4631
Salina *(G-10482)*
Emmis Communications Corp F 620 793-7868
Wichita *(G-14277)*
Emporias Radio Stations Inc F 620 342-1400
Emporia *(G-1749)*
Entercom Kansas City LLC C 913 744-3600
Shawnee Mission *(G-11338)*
EW Scripps Company E 316 436-1045
Wichita *(G-14317)*
Iheartcommunications Inc D 316 494-6600
Wichita *(G-14668)*
Iheartcommunications Inc D 316 832-9600
Wichita *(G-14669)*
Innovative Broadcasting Corp F 620 232-5993
Pittsburg *(G-9880)*
Iola Broadcasting Inc F 620 365-3151
Iola *(G-3609)*
K H U T F M Country Music E 620 662-4486
Hutchinson *(G-3344)*
K J H K 907 FM E 785 864-4745
Lawrence *(G-4928)*
K S A J Oldies D 785 823-1111
Salina *(G-10559)*
Kccv Am 760 E 913 642-7600
Shawnee Mission *(G-11525)*
Kggf K U S N Broadcasting Stn F 620 251-3800
Coffeyville *(G-952)*

Knck Inc ....F 785 243-1414
Concordia *(G-1120)*
Kvco ....E 785 243-4444
Concordia *(G-1122)*
Kxbz B 104 7 FM ....E 785 539-1047
Manhattan *(G-6706)*
M Rocking Radio Inc ....F 785 565-0406
Manhattan *(G-6716)*
M Rocking Radio Inc ....D 620 225-8080
Dodge City *(G-1400)*
M Rocking Radio Inc ....F 785 460-3306
Colby *(G-1027)*
Manhattan Broadcasting Co Inc ....E 785 776-1350
Manhattan *(G-6718)*
Morris Communications Co LLC ....E 785 823-1111
Salina *(G-10604)*
Morris Communications Co LLC ....D 785 272-3456
Topeka *(G-12913)*
Praise Network Inc ....F 785 694-2877
Brewster *(G-585)*
Q 1035 ....F 785 762-5525
Junction City *(G-3743)*
Radio Kansas ....E 620 662-6646
Hutchinson *(G-3418)*
Reyes Media Group Inc ....E 913 287-1480
Kansas City *(G-4375)*
Seaton Publishing Co Inc ....D 785 776-2200
Manhattan *(G-6798)*
Seward County Broadcasting Co ....F 620 624-3891
Liberal *(G-6364)*
Waitt Media Inc ....F 620 225-8080
Dodge City *(G-1448)*
Wichita State University ....E 316 978-6789
Wichita *(G-16033)*

RADIO REPAIR SHOP, NEC

Aircraft Instr & Rdo Co Inc ....E 316 945-9820
Wichita *(G-13651)*
Clark Enterprises 2000 Inc ....E 785 825-7172
Salina *(G-10455)*
Gateway Wireless Services LLC ....F 316 264-0037
Wichita *(G-14451)*
Ka-Comm Inc ....F 785 827-8555
Salina *(G-10560)*
Mobile Radio Service Inc ....F 620 793-3231
Great Bend *(G-2612)*
T V Hephner and Elec Inc ....F 316 264-3284
Wichita *(G-15715)*

RADIO, TELEVISION & CONSUMER ELECTRONICS STORES: TV Sets

Sparks Music Co ....F 620 442-5030
Arkansas City *(G-182)*

RADIO, TV & CONSUMER ELEC STORES: High Fidelity Stereo Eqpt

Radio Shop Inc ....F 316 265-1851
Wichita *(G-15409)*
Redi Systems Inc ....F 785 587-9100
Manhattan *(G-6788)*

RADIO, TV & CONSUMER ELECTRONICS: VCR & Access

Wolfes Camera Shops Inc ....E 785 235-1386
Topeka *(G-13248)*

RADIO, TV/CONSUMER ELEC STORES: Antennas, Satellite Dish

Cox Communications Inc ....F 620 227-3361
Dodge City *(G-1333)*

RAILROAD CAR CUSTOMIZING SVCS

Falcon Industries Inc ....F 620 289-4290
Tyro *(G-13276)*
Millennium Rail Inc ....F 620 231-2230
Pittsburg *(G-9905)*

RAILROAD CAR RENTING & LEASING SVCS

Watco Inc ....D 208 734-4644
Pittsburg *(G-9962)*
Watco Switching Inc ....D 620 231-2230
Pittsburg *(G-9965)*

RAILROAD CAR REPAIR SVCS

Gbw Railcar Services LLC ....E 844 364-7403
Coffeyville *(G-942)*
Gbw Railcar Services LLC ....E 888 968-4364
Overland Park *(G-8749)*
Gbw Railcar Services LLC ....D 620 325-3001
Neodesha *(G-7243)*
Gbw Railcar Services LLC ....E 866 785-4082
Atchison *(G-230)*
Greenbrier Companies Inc ....E 866 722-7068
Topeka *(G-12647)*
Greenbrier Railcar LLC ....E 913 342-0010
Kansas City *(G-4050)*
Gunderson Rail Services LLC ....F 913 827-3536
Osawatomie *(G-8194)*
Kansas City Railcar Svc Inc ....E 913 621-0326
Kansas City *(G-4150)*
Millennium Rail Inc ....F 620 231-2230
Pittsburg *(G-9905)*
Watco Inc ....D 208 734-4644
Pittsburg *(G-9962)*
Watco Switching Inc ....D 620 231-2230
Pittsburg *(G-9965)*

RAILROAD CARGO LOADING & UNLOADING SVCS

Carrier Logistics LLC ....E 913 681-2780
Olathe *(G-7579)*
Cowley County Council On Aging ....F 620 221-7020
Winfield *(G-16130)*
Intermodal Acquisition LLC ....B 708 225-2400
Edgerton *(G-1485)*
Interntnal Mtr Coach Group Inc ....F 913 906-0111
Lenexa *(G-5920)*
Mid Continent Transportation ....F 620 793-3573
Great Bend *(G-2610)*

RAILROAD EQPT

Aero Transportation Pdts Inc ....D 620 241-7010
Mc Pherson *(G-6930)*
Amsted Rail Company Inc ....D 913 956-2400
Overland Park *(G-8384)*
Amsted Rail Company Inc ....E 913 367-7200
Atchison *(G-204)*
Railroad Group ....G 913 375-1157
Kansas City *(G-4359)*
Voestalpine Nortrak Inc ....D 316 284-0088
Newton *(G-7424)*

RAILROAD EQPT & SPLYS WHOLESALERS

A & K Railroad Materials Inc ....D 913 375-1810
Kansas City *(G-3776)*
Amsted Rail Company Inc ....F 913 299-2223
Kansas City *(G-3808)*
Progress Rail Services Corp ....E 913 345-4807
Overland Park *(G-9191)*
Progress Rail Services Corp ....C 913 352-6613
Pleasanton *(G-10000)*

RAILROAD EQPT: Cars, Rebuilt

Millennium Rail Inc ....F 620 231-2230
Pittsburg *(G-9905)*

RAILROAD MAINTENANCE & REPAIR SVCS

LG Pike Construction Co Inc ....D 620 442-9150
Arkansas City *(G-164)*
Railserve Inc ....E 316 321-3816
El Dorado *(G-1595)*

RAILROAD SWITCHING & TERMINAL SVCS

Bakken Oil Express LLC ....F 316 630-0287
Wichita *(G-13797)*
Bnsf Railway Company ....D 620 896-2096
Harper *(G-2716)*
South Kansas and Okla RR Inc ....E 620 336-2291
Cherryvale *(G-813)*
South Kansas and Okla RR Inc ....F 620 221-3470
Winfield *(G-16173)*
Wichita Terminal Association ....F 316 262-0441
Wichita *(G-16038)*

RAILROADS: Long Haul

Alabama Southern Railroad LLC ....E 620 231-2230
Pittsburg *(G-9806)*
Ann Arbor Railroad Inc ....D 620 231-2230
Pittsburg *(G-9809)*
Austin Western Railroad ....E 620 231-2230
Pittsburg *(G-9817)*
B N S F Inc ....A 316 284-3260
Newton *(G-7316)*
Bnsf Railway Company ....C 316 284-3224
Newton *(G-7320)*
Bnsf Railway Company ....E 620 227-5977
Dodge City *(G-1310)*
Bnsf Railway Company ....F 913 551-4882
Kansas City *(G-3868)*
Bnsf Railway Company ....E 620 441-2276
Arkansas City *(G-148)*
Bnsf Railway Company ....D 913 893-4295
Edgerton *(G-1480)*
Bnsf Railway Company ....E 913 551-2604
Kansas City *(G-3869)*
Bnsf Railway Company ....C 620 203-2586
Emporia *(G-1706)*
Bnsf Railway Company ....D 785 435-7021
Topeka *(G-12392)*
Bnsf Railway Company ....D 620 429-3850
Columbus *(G-1061)*
Bnsf Railway Company ....F 913 888-5250
Shawnee Mission *(G-11173)*
Bnsf Railway Company ....B 785 435-2000
Topeka *(G-12393)*
Bnsf Railway Company ....C 620 399-4201
Wellington *(G-13491)*
Bnsf Railway Company ....D 817 352-1000
Shawnee Mission *(G-11174)*
Bnsf Railway Company ....E 316 708-4472
Augusta *(G-312)*
Burlington Nthrn Santa Fe LLC ....D 913 577-5521
Lenexa *(G-5721)*
Genesee & Wyoming Inc ....F 785 899-2307
Goodland *(G-2473)*
Great Northwest Railroad ....F 620 231-2230
Pittsburg *(G-9868)*
Kanawha River Railroad LLC ....E 620 231-2030
Pittsburg *(G-9885)*
Kansas & Oklahoma Railroad LLC ....F 620 231-2230
Pittsburg *(G-9887)*
Louisiana Southern Railroad ....F 620 235-7360
Pittsburg *(G-9895)*
South Kansas and Okla RR Inc ....E 620 336-2291
Cherryvale *(G-813)*
South Kansas and Okla RR Inc ....E 620 231-2230
Pittsburg *(G-9939)*
South Kansas and Okla RR Inc ....F 620 221-3470
Winfield *(G-16173)*
Union Pacific Railroad Company ....D 316 250-0260
McPherson *(G-7034)*
Union Pacific Railroad Company ....D 316 268-9446
Wichita *(G-15838)*
Union Pacific Railroad Company ....D 785 232-7814
Topeka *(G-13204)*
Union Pacific Railroad Company ....C 209 642-1032
Pratt *(G-10163)*
Watco Companies LLC ....C 575 745-2329
Pittsburg *(G-9963)*
Watco Companies LLC ....D 316 263-3113
Wichita *(G-15935)*
Watco Companies LLC ....D 620 336-2291
Cherryvale *(G-815)*
Watco Railroad Co Holdings ....F 620 231-2230
Pittsburg *(G-9964)*

RAILS: Steel Or Iron

Brown Industries LLC ....D 785 842-6506
Lawrence *(G-4770)*

REAL ESTATE AGENCIES & BROKERS

Associated Commercial Brks Co ....E 785 228-9494
Topeka *(G-12343)*
Carr Auction & Realestate ....E 620 285-3148
Larned *(G-4697)*
Chuck Krte Rlty Est Auctn Svcs ....E 316 775-2201
Augusta *(G-313)*
Commercial Real Estate News ....E 913 345-2378
Overland Park *(G-8580)*
Crown Realty of Kansas Inc ....F 785 242-7700
Ottawa *(G-8263)*
Destination Properties Inc ....F 913 583-1515
Overland Park *(G-8652)*
Duke Realty Corporation ....D 913 829-1453
New Century *(G-7281)*
Glenwood Estate Inc ....D 620 331-2260
Independence *(G-3523)*

Heartland Multiple Ll.....F 913 661-1600
Leawood *(G-5426)*
Home Town Real.....F 620 271-9500
Garden City *(G-2198)*
John C Gross III.....F 620 223-2550
Fort Scott *(G-1976)*
KB Properties of Kansas LLC.....E 316 292-3924
Wichita *(G-14836)*
Keller RE & Insur Agcy.....F 620 792-2128
Great Bend *(G-2599)*
Keybank Real Estate.....F 216 813-4756
Leawood *(G-5449)*
KS Commercial RE Svcs Inc.....F 785 272-2525
Topeka *(G-12824)*
Larry Theurer.....F 620 326-2715
Wellington *(G-13510)*
Little Creek Dairy.....E 785 348-5576
Linn *(G-6410)*
Maccallum Char RE Group.....F 913 782-8857
Olathe *(G-7870)*
McCullough Development Inc.....E 888 776-3010
Manhattan *(G-6737)*
McCurdy Auction LLC.....E 316 683-0612
Wichita *(G-15026)*
N J Investors Inc.....F 316 652-0616
Wichita *(G-15144)*
Real Estate Ctr Indpndence LLC.....F 620 331-7550
Independence *(G-3550)*
Reece & Nichols Alliance Inc.....D 913 451-4415
Shawnee Mission *(G-11784)*
Reece & Nichols Realtors Inc.....E 913 351-5600
Basehor *(G-387)*
Reece & Nichols Realtors Inc.....E 913 491-1001
Leawood *(G-5535)*
Reece and Nichols Realtors Inc.....B 913 945-3704
Leawood *(G-5536)*
Reib Inc.....F 620 662-0583
Hutchinson *(G-3422)*
Renn & Company Inc.....F 620 326-2271
Wellington *(G-13523)*
Risk Counselors Inc.....F 620 221-1760
Winfield *(G-16169)*
Ritchie Associates Inc.....E 316 684-7300
Wichita *(G-15466)*
Salina Homes.....F 785 820-5900
Salina *(G-10675)*
Stephens Realestate Inc.....D 785 841-4500
Lawrence *(G-5122)*
Timothy D White.....F 620 331-7060
Independence *(G-3565)*
Tom Jones Real Estate Company.....F 913 341-7777
Shawnee Mission *(G-11934)*
Trammell Crow Company.....F 913 722-1155
Prairie Village *(G-10076)*
Trustpoint Services Inc.....F 620 364-5665
Burlington *(G-644)*
United Agency Inc.....F 620 442-0400
Arkansas City *(G-187)*
Winbury Group of KC LLC.....F 785 865-5100
Lawrence *(G-5187)*
Woodstone Inc.....F 913 685-2282
Shawnee Mission *(G-12018)*

REAL ESTATE AGENCIES: Commercial

BA Karbank & Co LLP.....F 816 221-4488
Shawnee Mission *(G-11143)*
Bulk Industrial Group LLC.....F 913 362-6000
Prairie Village *(G-10017)*
Capital Realty LLC.....E 913 469-4600
Overland Park *(G-8510)*
Cbre Inc.....F 785 435-2399
Topeka *(G-12455)*
Circle C Country Supply Inc.....F 785 398-2571
Louisburg *(G-6443)*
Colliers Intl Neng LLC.....E 785 865-5100
Lawrence *(G-4798)*
Commercial Property Services.....F 316 688-5200
Wichita *(G-14071)*
Crossroads Shop Ctr LLC.....F 913 362-1999
Shawnee Mission *(G-11282)*
D D I Realty Services Inc.....F 913 685-4100
Overland Park *(G-8627)*
EBY Realty Group LLC.....E 913 782-3200
Olathe *(G-7669)*
Integra Realty Resources.....E 913 236-4700
Shawnee Mission *(G-11462)*
John T Arnold Associates Inc.....F 316 263-7242
Wichita *(G-14763)*
Kc Commercial Realty Group.....F 913 232-5100
Prairie Village *(G-10041)*
Kessinger/Hunter & Company Lc.....C 816 842-2690
Shawnee Mission *(G-11529)*
Lee & Associates Kansas Cy LLC.....F 913 890-2000
Leawood *(G-5455)*
Licausi-Styers Company.....E 913 681-5888
Shawnee Mission *(G-11568)*
Marcus Mllchap RE Inv Svcs Inc.....E 816 410-1010
Overland Park *(G-8989)*
Prism Real Estate Services LLC.....F 913 674-0438
Overland Park *(G-9187)*
Quality Group Companies LLC.....E 913 814-9988
Overland Park *(G-9211)*
Rubenstein Real Estate Co LLC.....F 913 362-1999
Shawnee Mission *(G-11815)*
Tiehen Group Inc.....F 913 648-1188
Leawood *(G-5576)*

REAL ESTATE AGENCIES: Leasing & Rentals

Dddi Commercial Inc.....F 913 685-4100
Shawnee Mission *(G-11295)*
Development Inc.....F 913 651-9717
Leavenworth *(G-5233)*
H Schwaller & Sons Inc.....F 785 628-6162
Hays *(G-2822)*
L L C Fun Services of K C.....F 913 441-9200
Shawnee *(G-10984)*
Montara LLC.....F 785 862-1030
Topeka *(G-12911)*
Prestige Property Co.....E 800 730-1249
Topeka *(G-12986)*
Rick Wayland & Associates.....F 316 524-0079
Wichita *(G-15458)*
SC Hall Industrial Svcs Inc.....E 316 945-4255
Wichita *(G-15525)*
Stoltz Realty Delaware Inc.....E 913 451-4466
Overland Park *(G-9364)*
Vic Regnier Builders Inc.....E 913 649-0123
Overland Park *(G-9463)*

REAL ESTATE AGENCIES: Rental

Clearview City Inc.....F 913 583-1451
De Soto *(G-1196)*
Connection At Lawrence.....E 785 842-3336
Lawrence *(G-4809)*
R & R Builders Inc.....D 913 682-1234
Leavenworth *(G-5282)*
Weigand-Omega Management Inc.....E 316 925-6341
Wichita *(G-15942)*
Wyncroft Hill Apartments.....F 913 829-1404
Olathe *(G-8162)*

REAL ESTATE AGENCIES: Residential

Albright Investment Company.....E 620 221-7653
Winfield *(G-16114)*
Astle Realty Inc.....F 620 662-0576
Hutchinson *(G-3208)*
Berkshire Hthway Frst Realtors.....F 785 271-2888
Topeka *(G-12371)*
Cek Real Estate Inc.....F 785 843-2055
Lawrence *(G-4778)*
Coldwell Banker Advantage.....D 913 345-9999
Overland Park *(G-8575)*
Coldwell Banker RE Corp.....E 620 331-2950
Independence *(G-3504)*
Coldwell Banker Regan Realtors.....E 913 631-2900
Shawnee Mission *(G-11245)*
Coldwell Bnkr Psternak Johnson.....F 620 331-5510
Independence *(G-3505)*
Crown Realty of Kansas Inc.....E 913 837-5155
Louisburg *(G-6444)*
David W Head.....D 913 402-0057
Overland Park *(G-8642)*
Diamond Partners Inc.....E 913 322-7500
Olathe *(G-7653)*
Dinning Beard Inc.....F 316 636-1115
Wichita *(G-14212)*
Dinning Beard Inc.....F 316 775-2201
Augusta *(G-317)*
Dorothy Rush Realty Inc.....F 620 442-7851
Arkansas City *(G-153)*
E F Hadel Realty Inc.....F 913 681-1600
Shawnee Mission *(G-11322)*
Faulkner Real Estate.....F 620 356-5808
Ulysses *(G-13295)*
Fishman and Co Realtors Inc.....F 913 782-9000
Overland Park *(G-8724)*
Fox Realty Inc.....F 316 681-1313
Wichita *(G-14412)*
G H C Associates Inc.....F 785 243-1555
Concordia *(G-1112)*
Gold Key Inc.....F 316 942-1925
Wichita *(G-14480)*
J B L Inc.....F 316 529-3100
Wichita *(G-14734)*
J P Weigand & Sons Inc.....C 316 686-3773
Wichita *(G-14738)*
J P Weigand & Sons Inc.....D 316 722-6182
Wichita *(G-14739)*
J P Weigand & Sons Inc.....E 316 788-5581
Derby *(G-1254)*
J P Weigand and Sons Inc.....F 620 663-4458
Hutchinson *(G-3338)*
J P Weigand and Sons Inc.....E 316 283-1330
Newton *(G-7367)*
JC Nchols Dnton Rbrts Rltors.....F 913 299-1600
Kansas City *(G-4121)*
Jim Bishop & Associates.....F 620 231-4370
Pittsburg *(G-9882)*
John H Moffitt & Co Inc.....E 913 491-6800
Shawnee Mission *(G-11491)*
Jury & Associates Inc.....E 913 642-5656
Shawnee Mission *(G-11504)*
Keller Williams Dave Neal.....F 316 681-3600
Wichita *(G-14842)*
Kirk & Cobb Realty.....E 785 272-5555
Topeka *(G-12823)*
Lawrence Realty Associates.....D 785 841-2727
Lawrence *(G-4986)*
Max RE Professional Inc.....F 620 227-3629
Dodge City *(G-1402)*
Mc Grew Realestate Inc.....F 785 843-2055
Lawrence *(G-5015)*
Mike Grbic Team Realtors Inc.....E 316 684-0000
Wichita *(G-15107)*
Miller & Midyett Realtor Inc.....F 785 843-8566
Lawrence *(G-5029)*
P F S Group Limited.....E 316 722-0001
Wichita *(G-15251)*
P K C Realty Company LLC.....C 913 491-1550
Overland Park *(G-9133)*
Partners Inc.....F 913 906-5400
Overland Park *(G-9143)*
Peterson Companies.....D 316 682-4903
Wichita *(G-15286)*
Preferred Land Company Inc.....F 316 634-1313
Wichita *(G-15326)*
Premier Realty LLC.....E 316 773-2707
Wichita *(G-15334)*
Prestige Real Estate.....F 785 242-1167
Ottawa *(G-8306)*
Prudential Henry & Burrows.....E 913 345-3000
Shawnee Mission *(G-11758)*
Prudential Kansas City Realty.....D 913 491-1550
Overland Park *(G-9200)*
RE Max Professionals L L C.....F 785 843-9393
Lawrence *(G-5089)*
Re/Max Excel.....F 785 856-8484
Lawrence *(G-5090)*
Reality Executives Center.....E 316 686-4111
Wichita *(G-15425)*
Realty Associates Inc.....F 785 827-0331
Salina *(G-10651)*
Realty Professionals LLC.....F 785 271-8400
Topeka *(G-13002)*
Realty World Alliance LLC.....E 316 688-0077
Wichita *(G-15427)*
Reece & Nichols Alliance Inc.....D 913 262-7755
Prairie Village *(G-10063)*
Reece & Nichols Alliance Inc.....D 913 782-8822
Olathe *(G-8022)*
Reece & Nichols Realtors Inc.....D 913 851-8082
Leawood *(G-5534)*
Reece & Nichols Realtors Inc.....E 913 620-3419
Overland Park *(G-9231)*
Reece & Nichols Realtors Inc.....E 913 307-4000
Shawnee *(G-11016)*
Reece & Nichols Realtors Inc.....E 913 339-6800
Shawnee Mission *(G-11785)*
Reilly Company LLC.....D 913 682-1234
Leavenworth *(G-5284)*
Rodrock & Associates Inc.....E 913 533-9980
Overland Park *(G-9254)*
Sharon Sigma Realtors LLC.....E 913 381-6794
Overland Park *(G-9304)*
Stewart Realty Co Inc.....F 620 223-6700
Fort Scott *(G-2007)*
Trail Wood Company Inc.....F 316 321-6500
El Dorado *(G-1610)*

Valley Realtors Inc ....F 785 233-4222
Topeka *(G-13218)*

REAL ESTATE AGENCIES: Selling

Farm & Ranch Realty Inc ....F 785 462-3904
Colby *(G-1004)*
Sheets Adams Realtors Inc ....F 620 241-3648
McPherson *(G-7026)*

REAL ESTATE AGENTS & MANAGERS

Avery Capital LLC ....F 913 742-3002
Overland Park *(G-8416)*
B&G Group LLC ....F 816 616-4034
Overland Park *(G-8422)*
Blackfin LLC ....F 816 985-4850
Kansas City *(G-3864)*
Block Real Estate Services LLC ....E 816 746-9922
Overland Park *(G-8465)*
Block Real Estate Services LLC ....E 816 412-8409
Lenexa *(G-5708)*
CSM-Csi Joint Venture ....D 913 227-9609
Overland Park *(G-8620)*
Devlin Partners LLC ....F 913 894-1300
Lenexa *(G-5814)*
Ebco Construction Group LLC ....F 866 297-2185
Olathe *(G-7667)*
Estates Unlimited Inc ....F 316 262-7600
Wichita *(G-14305)*
Executive Hills Management ....D 913 451-9000
Leawood *(G-5391)*
Facility Mgmt Svs Grp of Kc ....D 913 888-7600
Lenexa *(G-5846)*
Fairways of Ironhorse ....D 913 396-7931
Leawood *(G-5394)*
Green Hills Inc ....F 316 686-7673
Wichita *(G-14509)*
Joe Barns ....F 785 842-2772
Lawrence *(G-4924)*
Knickerbocker Properties Inc ....E 913 451-4466
Shawnee Mission *(G-11536)*
Land Acquisitions Inc ....E 847 749-0675
Wichita *(G-14919)*
Lenexa FDA Oc LLC ....D 913 894-9735
Lenexa *(G-5969)*
LLC Black Stone ....F 816 519-5650
Westwood *(G-13555)*
Mc Real Estate Service Inc ....F 913 451-4466
Shawnee Mission *(G-11605)*
Mission Place Ltd LP ....E 620 662-8731
Hutchinson *(G-3382)*
Omni Center II ....F 316 689-4256
Wichita *(G-15217)*
Price Brothers Realty Inc ....C 913 381-2280
Shawnee Mission *(G-11751)*
Reece & Nichols Realtors Inc ....F 913 247-3064
Spring Hill *(G-12097)*
Sandstone Creek Apartments ....F 913 402-8282
Shawnee Mission *(G-11828)*
Sheila M Burdett Agency LLC ....F 785 762-2451
Junction City *(G-3753)*
Town & Country Super Market ....E 620 653-2330
Hoisington *(G-3072)*
Xec Inc ....E 913 563-4260
Overland Park *(G-9511)*
Yarco Company Inc ....C 913 225-8733
Kansas City *(G-4563)*

REAL ESTATE APPRAISERS

Adamson and Associates ....F 913 722-5432
Shawnee *(G-10906)*
Adamson and Associates Inc ....E 913 722-5432
Overland Park *(G-8347)*
Appraisal Office Ford County ....F 620 227-4570
Dodge City *(G-1294)*
County of Riley ....F 785 537-6310
Manhattan *(G-6604)*
County of Shawnee ....E 785 233-2882
Topeka *(G-12519)*
Cushman & Wakefield III Inc ....F 913 440-0420
Overland Park *(G-8624)*
Midamerica Appraisals Inc ....F 620 231-0939
Pittsburg *(G-9904)*
Nations Title Agency ....E 913 341-2705
Prairie Village *(G-10051)*
Shaner Appraisals Inc ....F 913 451-1451
Overland Park *(G-9303)*
Sumner County Appraiser ....F 620 326-8986
Wellington *(G-13532)*

Tjk Inc ....F 785 841-0110
Lawrence *(G-5139)*

REAL ESTATE BOARDS

Kansas Real Estate Commission ....F 785 296-3411
Topeka *(G-12799)*

REAL ESTATE BROKERS: Manufactured Homes, On-Site

Antrim & Assoc ....F 316 267-2753
Wichita *(G-13714)*
Crown Realty of Kansas Inc ....E 913 782-1155
Olathe *(G-7628)*

REAL ESTATE INSURANCE AGENTS

Ellis Grubb Martens Coml Group ....E 316 262-0000
Wichita *(G-14272)*

REAL ESTATE INVESTMENT TRUSTS

Midwest Bioscience RES Pk LLC ....E 913 319-0300
Leawood *(G-5482)*
Qts Invstmnt Props Carpathia ....E 913 814-9988
Overland Park *(G-9209)*
Qts Realty Trust Inc ....E 913 814-9988
Overland Park *(G-9210)*
Quality Investment Properties ....F 913 814-9988
Overland Park *(G-9213)*
Reeble Inc ....D 620 342-0404
Emporia *(G-1816)*

REAL ESTATE MANAGERS: Cemetery

Newcomer Funeral Svc Group Inc ....F 785 233-6655
Topeka *(G-12928)*

REAL ESTATE OPERATORS, EXC DEVEL: Prprty, Auditorium/Theater

Kansas State University ....E 785 532-7600
Manhattan *(G-6687)*

REAL ESTATE OPERATORS, EXC DEVEL: Theater Bldg, Owner & Op

Midland Theater Foundation Inc ....F 901 501-6832
Coffeyville *(G-963)*

REAL ESTATE OPERATORS, EXC DEVELOPERS: Apartment Hotel

Fidelity Management Corp ....F 785 266-8010
Topeka *(G-12606)*
J A Peterson Realty Co Inc ....F 913 384-3800
Shawnee Mission *(G-11473)*
Jefferson Pointe Apartments ....F 913 906-9100
Shawnee Mission *(G-11483)*
Ledic Management Group LLC ....F 316 685-8768
Wichita *(G-14943)*
Louisberg Square Apartments ....F 913 381-4997
Overland Park *(G-8970)*
Malkin Properties LLC ....F 913 262-2666
Shawnee Mission *(G-11593)*
Oak Park Village ....F 913 888-1500
Lenexa *(G-6032)*
Park West Plaza LLC ....D 316 729-4114
Wichita *(G-15262)*
Parklane Towers Inc ....F 316 684-7247
Wichita *(G-15266)*
Parkway 4000 LP ....F 785 749-2555
Lawrence *(G-5056)*
Perserve At Overland Park ....F 913 685-3700
Overland Park *(G-9158)*
Price Brothers Realty Inc ....C 913 381-2280
Shawnee Mission *(G-11751)*
Waterwalk Wichita LLC ....E 316 201-1899
Wichita *(G-15937)*
Wiston Property Management ....F 913 383-8100
Shawnee Mission *(G-12014)*
Wyncroft Hill Apartments ....F 913 829-1404
Olathe *(G-8162)*

REAL ESTATE OPERATORS, EXC DEVELOPERS: Auditorium & Hall

City of Salina ....E 785 826-7200
Salina *(G-10449)*
Clonmel Community Club Inc ....E 620 545-7136
Clearwater *(G-890)*

Complete Music Inc ....E 913 432-1111
Leawood *(G-5357)*
Coyotes Inc ....E 785 842-2295
Lawrence *(G-4816)*

REAL ESTATE OPERATORS, EXC DEVELOPERS: Bank Building

Crossfirst Bankshares Inc ....C 913 754-9700
Overland Park *(G-8618)*
First National Bank ....F 785 366-7225
Hope *(G-3121)*

REAL ESTATE OPERATORS, EXC DEVELOPERS: Commercial/Indl Bldg

Builders Inc ....E 316 684-1400
Wichita *(G-13909)*
Builders Commercials Inc ....F 316 686-3107
Wichita *(G-13912)*
Chilton Vending & Billd Inc ....F 316 262-3539
Wichita *(G-14011)*
City Oil Company Inc ....E 913 321-1764
Kansas City *(G-3912)*
Cloverleaf Office Park ....F 913 831-3200
Shawnee Mission *(G-11240)*
Ellis Grubb Martens Coml Group ....E 316 262-0000
Wichita *(G-14272)*
Fugate Leasing Inc ....C 316 722-5670
Wichita *(G-14429)*
Great Plains Investments Ltd ....D 913 492-9880
Overland Park *(G-8773)*
Greenamyre Rentals Inc ....F 913 651-9717
Leavenworth *(G-5249)*
Inland Industries Inc ....G 913 492-9050
Bucyrus *(G-600)*
J A Peterson Enterprises Inc ....E 913 384-3800
Shawnee Mission *(G-11471)*
J A Peterson Realty Co Inc ....F 913 384-3800
Shawnee Mission *(G-11473)*
Kuhn Co LLC ....E 316 788-6500
Derby *(G-1257)*
L C Enterprises ....F 316 682-3300
Wichita *(G-14904)*
Landvest Corporation ....E 316 634-6510
Wichita *(G-14922)*
Mallon Family LLC ....F 620 342-6622
Emporia *(G-1789)*
Marc Gorges ....E 316 630-0689
Eastborough *(G-1476)*
Midwest Drywall Co Inc ....D 316 722-9559
Wichita *(G-15093)*
Nallwood Heights Corporation ....F 913 341-4880
Shawnee Mission *(G-11668)*
Parkview Joint Venture ....F 785 267-3410
Topeka *(G-12962)*
Price Brothers Realty Inc ....C 913 381-2280
Shawnee Mission *(G-11751)*
Ranch Mart Inc ....F 913 649-0123
Overland Park *(G-9223)*
Real Estate Corporation Inc ....F 913 642-5134
Prairie Village *(G-10062)*
Roach Building Co Inc ....F 785 233-9606
Topeka *(G-13021)*
Southwest Bowl ....F 785 272-1324
Topeka *(G-13082)*
Universal Motor Fuels Inc ....F 316 832-0151
Wichita *(G-15855)*
Weigand-Omega Associates Inc ....F 316 925-6341
Wichita *(G-15941)*
Woodland Lakes Community Churc ....F 316 682-9522
Wichita *(G-16065)*

REAL ESTATE OPERATORS, EXC DEVELOPERS: Property, Retail

All American Indoor Sports ....D 913 888-5425
Shawnee Mission *(G-11093)*
Calvin Investments LLC ....F 785 266-8755
Topeka *(G-12419)*

REAL ESTATE OPERATORS, EXC DEVELOPERS: Residential Hotel

Vintage Prk Assistd Lvng Rsdnc ....F 913 837-5133
Louisburg *(G-6468)*
Wesley Retirement Community ....C 316 636-1000
Wichita *(G-15955)*

REAL ESTATE OPERATORS, EXC DEVELOPERS: Retirement Hotel

Abilene Housing Inc ....F 785 263-1080
Abilene *(G-5)*
Active Prime Timers Inc ....F 785 272-0237
Topeka *(G-12285)*
Atriums Retirement Home ....D 913 381-9133
Shawnee Mission *(G-11132)*
Bloom Living Senior Apartments ....D 913 738-4335
Olathe *(G-7557)*
Brookdale Senior Living Inc ....E 913 345-9339
Overland Park *(G-8488)*
Cedars Inc ....C 620 241-0919
McPherson *(G-6942)*
Contemprary Hsing Altrntves of ....E 785 271-9594
Topeka *(G-12505)*
Cumbernauld Village Inc ....D 620 221-4141
Winfield *(G-16137)*
Delmar Gardens of Lenexa Inc ....E 913 492-8682
Shawnee Mission *(G-11299)*
Delmar Gardens of Lenexa Inc ....C 913 492-1130
Lenexa *(G-5809)*
Eaglecrest Retirement Cmnty ....E 785 309-1501
Salina *(G-10484)*
Emeritus Corporation ....D 620 663-9195
Hutchinson *(G-3279)*
Emporia Prsbt Mnor of Mid Amer ....D 620 412-2019
Emporia *(G-1743)*
Harvest Facility Holdings LP ....E 316 722-5100
Wichita *(G-14567)*
Harvest Facility Holdings LP ....E 785 228-0555
Topeka *(G-12665)*
Lakeview Village Inc ....A 913 888-1900
Lenexa *(G-5962)*
Liberty Assisted Living Center ....E 785 273-0886
Topeka *(G-12842)*
Liberty Assisted Living Center ....F 785 273-6847
Topeka *(G-12843)*
Lifespace Communities Inc ....C 913 383-2085
Shawnee Mission *(G-11570)*
Living Center Inc ....D 620 665-2170
Hutchinson *(G-3355)*
McCrite Retirement Association ....C 785 267-2960
Topeka *(G-12868)*
Medicalodges Inc ....D 913 367-2077
Atchison *(G-243)*
Parkwood Village ....E 620 672-5541
Pratt *(G-10130)*
Santa Marta Retirement Cmnty ....F 913 906-0990
Olathe *(G-8054)*
Spearville District Hospital ....F 620 385-2632
Spearville *(G-12071)*
Sunset Home Inc ....D 785 243-2720
Concordia *(G-1131)*
Wesley Towers Inc ....B 620 663-9175
Hutchinson *(G-3485)*
Windsor Estates Inc ....F 785 825-8183
Salina *(G-10770)*

REAL ESTATE OPERATORS, EXC DEVELOPERS: Shopping Ctr

Central Mall Realty Holdg LLC ....E 785 825-7733
Salina *(G-10443)*

REAL ESTATE OPERATORS, EXC DEVELOPERS: Shopping Ctr, Commnty

Warmack and Company LLC ....E 785 825-0122
Salina *(G-10758)*

REAL ESTATE OPS, EXC DEVELOPER: Residential Bldg, 4 Or Less

Builders Inc ....E 316 684-1400
Wichita *(G-13909)*
Greenamyre Rentals Inc ....F 913 651-9717
Leavenworth *(G-5249)*
O K Electric Work Inc ....G 620 251-2270
Coffeyville *(G-966)*
Riley Communities LLC ....D 785 717-2210
Fort Riley *(G-1949)*
Ritchie Associates Inc ....E 316 684-7300
Wichita *(G-15466)*
Woodland Lakes Community Churc ....F 316 682-9522
Wichita *(G-16065)*

REALTY INVESTMENT TRUSTS

Broadmoor One LLC ....D 316 683-0562
Wichita *(G-13893)*

RECORDING TAPE: Video, Blank

Nuvidia LLC ....F 913 599-5200
Lenexa *(G-6030)*

RECORDS & TAPES: Prerecorded

Acoustic Sounds Inc ....E 785 825-8609
Salina *(G-10392)*

RECOVERY SVC: Iron Ore, From Open Hearth Slag

Ram Metal Products Inc ....G 913 422-0099
Leawood *(G-5532)*

RECOVERY SVCS: Metal

Eureka Technology LLC ....G 913 557-9639
Paola *(G-9557)*

RECOVERY SVCS: Solvents

Safety-Kleen Systems Inc ....E 913 829-6677
Olathe *(G-8050)*
Safety-Kleen Systems Inc ....F 316 942-5001
Wichita *(G-15505)*

RECREATIONAL & SPORTING CAMPS

Alexander Camp ....E 620 342-1386
Emporia *(G-1694)*
Earth Rising Inc ....F 913 796-2141
Mc Louth *(G-6926)*
Kings Camp & Retreat Center ....E 316 794-2913
Goddard *(G-2444)*
Volley Ball Inc ....E 913 422-4070
Shawnee *(G-11048)*

RECREATIONAL DEALERS: Campers/Pickup Coaches Truck Mounted

Four Seasons Rv Acres Inc ....E 785 598-2221
Abilene *(G-32)*

RECREATIONAL VEHICLE DEALERS

Olathe Ford Sales Inc ....E 913 782-0881
Olathe *(G-7936)*

RECREATIONAL VEHICLE PARTS & ACCESS STORES

Adventure Rv and Truck Ctr LLC ....E 316 721-1333
Wichita *(G-13629)*
Redneck Inc ....E 316 263-6090
Wichita *(G-15432)*

RECREATIONAL VEHICLE REPAIRS

Adventure Rv and Truck Ctr LLC ....E 316 721-1333
Wichita *(G-13629)*
Four Seasons Rv Acres Inc ....E 785 598-2221
Abilene *(G-32)*
Olathe Ford Sales Inc ....E 913 856-8145
Gardner *(G-2357)*

RECYCLABLE SCRAP & WASTE MATERIALS WHOLESALERS

Bohm Farm & Ranch Inc ....E 785 823-0303
Salina *(G-10429)*
Solomon Transformers LLC ....B 785 655-2191
Solomon *(G-12054)*
SOS Metals Midwest LLC ....E 316 522-0101
Wichita *(G-15616)*
Stallard Technologies Inc ....E 913 851-2260
Overland Park *(G-9351)*

RECYCLING: Paper

Central Fiber LLC ....E 785 883-4600
Wellsville *(G-13541)*

REFERRAL SVCS, PERSONAL & SOCIAL PROBLEMS

Erc/Resource & Referral Inc ....F 785 357-5171
Topeka *(G-12580)*

REFINERS & SMELTERS: Aluminum

Custom Alloy Sales 34p LLC ....D 913 471-4800
Prescott *(G-10166)*
Tower Metal Products LP ....E 620 215-2622
Fort Scott *(G-2009)*

REFINERS & SMELTERS: Nonferrous Metal

Erman Corporation Inc ....E 913 287-4800
Kansas City *(G-3996)*
Shostak Iron and Metal Co Inc ....E 913 321-9210
Overland Park *(G-9309)*

REFINING: Petroleum

Chc McPherson Refinery Inc ....F 785 543-5246
Phillipsburg *(G-9779)*
Chc McPherson Refinery Inc ....E 620 793-3111
Great Bend *(G-2536)*
Chc McPherson Refinery Inc ....G 785 798-3684
Ness City *(G-7254)*
Coffeyville Resources LLC ....G 785 434-4832
Plainville *(G-9982)*
Coffeyville Resources LLC ....F 785 434-4832
Plainville *(G-9983)*
Coffeyville Resources LLC ....E 913 982-0500
Kansas City *(G-3923)*
Coffeyvlle Rsrces Ref Mktg LLC ....D 620 251-4252
Coffeyville *(G-926)*
Equilon Enterprises LLC ....F 913 648-0535
Shawnee Mission *(G-11346)*
Gerald A Wallace ....G 620 275-2484
Garden City *(G-2186)*
Hollyfrntier El Dorado Ref LLC ....B 316 321-2200
El Dorado *(G-1567)*
Koch Industries Inc ....E 316 828-8737
Wichita *(G-14882)*
Koch Industries Inc ....A 316 828-5500
Wichita *(G-14881)*
Koch Resources LLC ....E 316 828-5500
Wichita *(G-14887)*
Koch Supply & Trading LP ....F 316 828-5500
Wichita *(G-14890)*
Kpl South Texas LLC ....G 316 828-5500
Wichita *(G-14894)*
KS&t International Holdings LP ....A 316 828-5500
Wichita *(G-14896)*
Murphy USA Inc ....F 620 664-9479
Hutchinson *(G-3386)*
Murphy USA Inc ....F 620 227-5607
Dodge City *(G-1409)*
Oneok Hydrocarbon LP ....D 620 669-3759
Hutchinson *(G-3395)*
Phares Petroleum Inc ....G 316 682-3349
Wichita *(G-15289)*
Sinclair Companies ....D 785 799-3116
Home *(G-3120)*
Tpi Petroleum Inc ....D 913 831-3145
Shawnee Mission *(G-11938)*
Wynnewood Refining Company LLC ....D 913 982-0500
Kansas City *(G-4558)*

REFRACTORIES: Clay

Harbisonwalker Intl Inc ....E 913 888-0425
Lenexa *(G-5889)*

REFRACTORIES: Nonclay

Thermal Ceramics Inc ....E 620 343-2308
Emporia *(G-1837)*

REFRIGERATION & HEATING EQUIPMENT

Airtex Inc ....D 913 583-3181
De Soto *(G-1191)*
Everidge LLC ....C 316 733-1385
Andover *(G-91)*
Hussmann Corporation ....E 816 373-1274
Lenexa *(G-5907)*
SPX Cooling Technologies Inc ....B 913 664-7400
Overland Park *(G-9344)*
Trane US Inc ....D 785 272-3224
Topeka *(G-13196)*
Trane US Inc ....D 316 265-9655
Wichita *(G-15788)*

Trane US Inc ....C 417 863-2110
Lenexa *(G-6189)*
York International Corporation ....D 316 832-6300
Wichita *(G-16087)*

REFRIGERATION EQPT & SPLYS WHOLESALERS

Wichita Wholesale Supply Inc ....F 316 267-3629
Wichita *(G-16044)*
WW Grainger Inc ....E 913 492-8550
Lenexa *(G-6237)*

REFRIGERATION EQPT & SPLYS, WHOL: Refrig Units, Motor Veh

Cstk Inc ....E 913 233-7220
Overland Park *(G-8621)*
Larrys Trailer Sales & Svc LLC ....F 316 838-1491
Wichita *(G-14927)*
Velociti Inc ....E 913 233-7230
Kansas City *(G-4514)*

REFRIGERATION EQPT & SPLYS, WHOLESALE: Commercial Eqpt

Refrigeration Technologies ....F 316 542-0397
Cheney *(G-795)*
Weber Refrigeration & Htg Inc ....E 580 338-7338
Garden City *(G-2309)*

REFRIGERATION EQPT & SPLYS, WHOLESALE: Ice Making Machines

Tresko Inc ....E 913 631-6900
Shawnee Mission *(G-11941)*

REFRIGERATION REPAIR SVCS

Cstk Inc ....E 913 233-7220
Overland Park *(G-8621)*
Even Temp of Wichita Inc ....F 316 469-5321
Wichita *(G-14312)*
Temp-Con Inc ....D 913 768-4888
Olathe *(G-8106)*
Velociti Inc ....E 913 233-7230
Kansas City *(G-4514)*

REFRIGERATION SVC & REPAIR

Automated Control Systems Corp ....D 913 766-2336
Leawood *(G-5337)*
Murphy-Hoffman Company ....F 913 441-6300
Kansas City *(G-4274)*
Tresko Inc ....E 913 631-6900
Shawnee Mission *(G-11941)*

REFRIGERATOR REPAIR SVCS

Ricks Appliance Service Inc ....F 316 265-2866
Wichita *(G-15460)*

REFUSE SYSTEMS

Images ....G 785 827-0824
Salina *(G-10549)*
Itgs Shipping ....E 316 322-3000
El Dorado *(G-1574)*
Safety-Kleen (wt) Inc ....E 316 269-7400
Wichita *(G-15504)*
Sea Coast Disposal Inc ....E 785 784-5308
Junction City *(G-3751)*
United States Dept of Army ....E 785 239-2385
Fort Riley *(G-1951)*
Waste Connections Inc ....E 316 941-4320
Wichita *(G-15933)*
Waste Management of Kansas ....D 785 233-3541
Topeka *(G-13234)*
Waste Management of Kansas ....D 913 631-3300
Kansas City *(G-4531)*
Waste Management of Kansas ....F 785 238-3293
Junction City *(G-3766)*

REGULATION, LICENSING & INSPECTION, GOVT: Cml, Misc, State

Kansas Real Estate Commission ....F 785 296-3411
Topeka *(G-12799)*

REHABILITATION CENTER, OUTPATIENT TREATMENT

Advantage Medical Group ....F 785 749-0130
Lawrence *(G-4722)*
Ascension Via Christi ....E 620 232-0178
Pittsburg *(G-9814)*
Big Lkes Developmental Ctr Inc ....E 785 632-5357
Clay Center *(G-843)*
Brown Cnty Developmental Svcs ....E 785 742-2053
Hiawatha *(G-3004)*
Childrens Therapy Group ....F 913 383-9014
Mission *(G-7129)*
Developmental Svcs NW Kans Inc ....F 785 877-5154
Norton *(G-7443)*
Developmental Svcs NW Kans Inc ....F 785 483-6686
Russell *(G-10271)*
Douglass Medicalodges ....E 316 747-2157
Douglass *(G-1466)*
Key Rehabilitation Inc ....F 620 231-3887
Pittsburg *(G-9892)*
Midamerica Rehabilitation Ctr ....F 913 491-2432
Shawnee Mission *(G-11629)*
Midwest Health Services Inc ....E 316 835-4810
Halstead *(G-2703)*
Mosaic ....D 620 624-3817
Liberal *(G-6345)*
New Chance Inc ....E 620 225-0476
Dodge City *(G-1412)*
P A Therapyworks Inc ....E 785 749-1300
Lawrence *(G-5053)*
Performance Rehab LLC ....E 913 681-9909
Overland Park *(G-9155)*
Pinkerton Pain Therapy LLC ....F 417 649-6406
Olathe *(G-7987)*
Professional Renewal Center PA ....F 785 842-9772
Lawrence *(G-5079)*
Renew ....F 913 768-6606
Olathe *(G-8026)*
Salina Regional Health Ctr Inc ....B 785 452-7000
Salina *(G-10688)*
Select Medical Corporation ....F 316 261-8303
Wichita *(G-15553)*
Select Medical Corporation ....F 316 687-9227
Wichita *(G-15554)*
Shawnee Gardens Health ....C 913 631-2146
Shawnee *(G-11027)*
Shormán & Associates Inc ....E 913 341-8811
Shawnee Mission *(G-11866)*
Summitt Rest Care LLC ....F 620 624-5117
Liberal *(G-6373)*
Unxmed-Immediate Medical Care ....F 316 440-2565
Wichita *(G-15860)*
Via Christi Vlg Manhattan Inc ....C 785 539-7671
Manhattan *(G-6842)*
Via Chrsti Rehabilitation Hosp ....E 316 268-5000
Wichita *(G-15901)*

REHABILITATION CTR, RESIDENTIAL WITH HEALTH CARE INCIDENTAL

Class Ltd ....D 620 231-3131
Pittsburg *(G-9835)*
Class Ltd ....C 620 429-1212
Columbus *(G-1066)*
Mirror Inc ....F 913 248-1943
Shawnee Mission *(G-11642)*
Overland Park Seniorcare LLC ....E 913 491-1144
Shawnee Mission *(G-11710)*
Substance Abuse Cntr E Kansas ....E 913 362-0045
Kansas City *(G-4444)*
University of Kansas ....E 913 588-6798
Kansas City *(G-4496)*

REHABILITATION SVCS

Athletic & Rehabilitation Ctr ....F 913 378-0778
Shawnee Mission *(G-11131)*
Auspision LLC ....E 620 343-3685
Emporia *(G-1698)*
Class Ltd ....E 620 331-8604
Independence *(G-3503)*
Developmental Svcs NW Kans Inc ....F 785 483-6686
Russell *(G-10271)*
Judiciary Court of The State ....E 785 296-6290
Topeka *(G-12750)*
Kansas Dept For Chldren Fmlies ....E 913 755-2162
Osawatomie *(G-8197)*
Kansas Dept For Chldren Fmlies ....F 620 241-3802
McPherson *(G-6981)*

Legend Senior Living LLC ....C 316 337-5450
Wichita *(G-14953)*
Meridian Nursing Center Inc ....D 316 942-8471
Wichita *(G-15041)*
Salvation Army National Corp ....E 316 943-9893
Wichita *(G-15515)*
Select Medical Corporation ....F 913 385-0075
Overland Park *(G-9291)*
Summit Care Inc ....E 913 239-8777
Leawood *(G-5563)*

REINSURANCE CARRIERS: Accident & Health

Employers Mutual Casualty Co ....E 913 663-0119
Overland Park *(G-8679)*
Employers Mutual Casualty Co ....C 316 352-5700
Wichita *(G-14279)*
Scor Globl Lf USA Reinsurance ....E 913 901-4600
Leawood *(G-5549)*

REINSURANCE CARRIERS: Life

Scor Globl Lf USA Reinsurance ....E 913 901-4600
Leawood *(G-5549)*
Swiss RE America Holding Corp ....A 913 676-5200
Overland Park *(G-9384)*
Swiss Reinsurance America Corp ....A 913 676-5200
Overland Park *(G-9387)*

REINSURANCE CARRIERS: Surety

CNA Financial Corporation ....D 913 661-2700
Overland Park *(G-8570)*
Newcomer Funeral Svc Group Inc ....F 785 233-6655
Topeka *(G-12928)*

RENDERING PLANT

Central Kansas Rendering Inc ....G 620 792-2059
Great Bend *(G-2532)*
Darling Ingredients Inc ....E 620 276-7618
Garden City *(G-2142)*

RENT-A-CAR SVCS

Avis Budget Group Inc ....F 785 331-0658
Lawrence *(G-4745)*
Avis Rent A Car System Inc ....F 316 946-4882
Wichita *(G-13779)*
Avis Rental Car Systems ....B 785 749-1464
Lawrence *(G-4746)*
Budget Car Trck Rentl Wichita ....E 316 729-7979
Wichita *(G-13907)*
Budget Rent-A-Car of Kansas ....E 316 946-4891
Wichita *(G-13908)*
Central Kansas Auto Rental ....F 785 827-7237
Salina *(G-10439)*
Classic Enterprises Inc ....F 785 628-6700
Hays *(G-2769)*
E & J Rental & Leasing Inc ....F 316 721-0442
Wichita *(G-14249)*
Enterprise Leasing Co KS LLC ....E 913 254-0012
Olathe *(G-7686)*
Enterprise Leasing Co KS LLC ....F 913 262-8888
Shawnee Mission *(G-11342)*
Enterprise Leasing Co KS LLC ....C 913 383-1515
Shawnee Mission *(G-11340)*
Hertz Corporation ....E 620 342-6322
Emporia *(G-1769)*
Hertz Corporation ....E 913 962-1226
Shawnee Mission *(G-11430)*
Hertz Corporation ....E 316 689-3773
Wichita *(G-14597)*
Hertz Corporation ....E 913 341-1782
Overland Park *(G-8813)*
Hertz Corporation ....E 316 946-4860
Wichita *(G-14598)*
Hertz Corporation ....E 316 946-4860
Wichita *(G-14599)*
Hertz Corporation ....E 316 946-4860
Wichita *(G-14600)*
Hertz Corporation ....E 316 946-4860
Wichita *(G-14601)*
Hertz Corporation ....E 620 341-9656
Emporia *(G-1770)*
Hertz Corporation ....E 316 284-6084
Newton *(G-7361)*
Hertz Corporation ....E 913 696-0003
Lenexa *(G-5902)*
Hobart Transportation Co Inc ....F 785 267-4468
Topeka *(G-12696)*

Midwest Car Corporation .... F 316 946-4851
Wichita *(G-15089)*
National Rental (us) Inc .... E 316 946-4851
Wichita *(G-15151)*
Priceless .... F 785 625-7664
Hays *(G-2889)*

RENTAL CENTERS: Furniture

Basham Furniture Rental Inc .... F 316 263-5821
Wichita *(G-13816)*
Basham Home Store Inc .... F 316 263-5821
Wichita *(G-13817)*
Cort Business Services Corp .... E 913 888-0100
Overland Park *(G-8601)*
Transitions Group Inc .... F 913 327-0700
Lenexa *(G-6190)*
Transitions Group Inc .... F 316 263-5750
Wichita *(G-15792)*

RENTAL CENTERS: General

Big DS Rent All .... F 785 625-2443
Hays *(G-2758)*
Bli Rentals LLC .... E 620 342-7847
Emporia *(G-1704)*
Gerken Rent-All Inc .... F 913 294-3783
Paola *(G-9561)*
Rental Station LLC .... E 620 431-7368
Chanute *(G-760)*
United Rentals North Amer Inc .... F 785 838-4110
Lawrence *(G-5153)*
United Rentals North Amer Inc .... F 316 722-7368
Wichita *(G-15847)*

RENTAL CENTERS: Party & Banquet Eqpt & Splys

AAA Party Rental Inc .... F 816 333-1767
Lenexa *(G-5617)*
All Seasons Party Rental Inc .... C 816 765-1444
Kansas City *(G-3798)*
Kansas Rental Inc .... F 785 272-1232
Topeka *(G-12801)*

RENTAL CENTERS: Tools

Ahern Rentals Inc .... E 913 281-7555
Kansas City *(G-3792)*
Alltite Inc .... E 316 686-3010
Wichita *(G-13678)*
Anderson Rentals Inc .... F 785 843-2044
Lawrence *(G-4735)*
Foley Supply LLC .... E 316 944-7368
Wichita *(G-14400)*
Home Depot USA Inc .... C 913 789-8899
Merriam *(G-7095)*
Home Depot USA Inc .... F 785 217-2260
Topeka *(G-12700)*
Home Depot USA Inc .... C 316 681-0899
Wichita *(G-14628)*
Home Depot USA Inc .... C 316 773-1988
Wichita *(G-14629)*
Home Depot USA Inc .... C 785 749-2074
Lawrence *(G-4900)*
Home Depot USA Inc .... D 620 275-5943
Garden City *(G-2197)*
Home Depot USA Inc .... C 785 272-5949
Topeka *(G-12701)*
Home Depot USA Inc .... C 913 648-7811
Shawnee Mission *(G-11438)*
Sunflower Rents Inc .... F 785 233-9489
Topeka *(G-13120)*

RENTAL SVCS: Aircraft

Jrm Enterprises Inc .... E 785 404-1328
Salina *(G-10557)*
Lyddon Aero Center Inc .... F 620 624-1646
Liberal *(G-6338)*
Textron Aviation Inc .... A 316 676-7111
Salina *(G-10733)*
Yingling Aircraft Inc .... D 316 943-3246
Wichita *(G-16085)*

RENTAL SVCS: Audio-Visual Eqpt & Sply

Kent Business Systems Corp .... F 316 262-4487
Wichita *(G-14851)*

RENTAL SVCS: Business Machine & Electronic Eqpt

Pitney Bowes Inc .... D 913 681-5579
Shawnee Mission *(G-11736)*
Pitney Bowes Inc .... G 785 266-6750
Topeka *(G-12978)*
Styers Equipment Company .... F 913 681-5225
Overland Park *(G-9369)*

RENTAL SVCS: Child Restraint Seat, Automotive

Taylor Crane & Rigging Inc .... D 620 251-1530
Coffeyville *(G-981)*

RENTAL SVCS: Coin-Operated Machine

B & K Enterprises Inc .... F 785 238-3076
Junction City *(G-3670)*

RENTAL SVCS: Costume

Bday Parties .... F 913 961-1857
De Soto *(G-1193)*
L V S Inc .... E 316 636-5005
Wichita *(G-14908)*
U S Toy Co Inc .... E 913 642-8247
Leawood *(G-5587)*

RENTAL SVCS: Film Or Tape, Motion Picture

Duncans Movie Magic Inc .... E 785 266-3010
Topeka *(G-12562)*

RENTAL SVCS: Home Cleaning & Maintenance Eqpt

Maid Services Inc .... E 785 537-6243
Manhattan *(G-6717)*

RENTAL SVCS: Invalid Splys

Kingman Drug Inc .... F 620 532-5113
Kingman *(G-4600)*

RENTAL SVCS: Lawn & Garden Eqpt

Augusta Rental Inc .... F 316 775-5050
Augusta *(G-308)*

RENTAL SVCS: Live Plant

Hoffmanns Green Industries .... E 316 634-1500
Wichita *(G-14624)*

RENTAL SVCS: Musical Instrument

Hume Music Inc .... F 816 474-1960
Stilwell *(G-12154)*
Manning Music Inc .... F 785 272-1740
Topeka *(G-12857)*

RENTAL SVCS: Office Facilities & Secretarial Svcs

Riley Hotel Suites LLC .... E 785 539-2400
Manhattan *(G-6793)*

RENTAL SVCS: Oil Eqpt

T & C Tank Rental & Anchor Svc .... E 806 592-3286
Overland Park *(G-9389)*

RENTAL SVCS: Personal Items, Exc Recreation & Medical

Ctmd LLC .... E 316 686-6116
Wichita *(G-14139)*

RENTAL SVCS: Recreational Vehicle

Adventure Rv and Truck Ctr LLC .... E 316 721-1333
Wichita *(G-13629)*
Adventureland Rv Rentals Inc .... F 800 333-8821
Wichita *(G-13630)*

RENTAL SVCS: Sign

Hedges Neon Sales Inc .... G 785 827-9341
Salina *(G-10540)*
Mather Flare Rental Inc .... F 785 478-9696
Topeka *(G-12863)*

RENTAL SVCS: Stores & Yards Eqpt

Berry Companies Inc .... F 620 277-2290
Garden City *(G-2109)*
High Reach Equipment LLC .... F 316 942-5438
Wichita *(G-14605)*
Kanequip Inc .... F 785 632-3441
Clay Center *(G-869)*
Ryder Truck Rental Inc .... F 316 945-8484
Wichita *(G-15497)*
Ryder Truck Rental Inc .... E 913 492-4420
Lenexa *(G-6114)*

RENTAL SVCS: Trailer

Budget Car Trck Rentl Wichita .... E 316 729-7979
Wichita *(G-13907)*
K Young Inc .... F 785 475-3888
Colby *(G-1019)*
Mather Flare Rental Inc .... F 785 478-9696
Topeka *(G-12863)*
Mike Groves Oil Inc .... F 620 442-0480
Arkansas City *(G-166)*

RENTAL SVCS: Tuxedo

Dcm Wichita Inc .... F 800 662-9573
Towanda *(G-13263)*
Jims Formal Wear LLC .... E 785 825-1529
Salina *(G-10555)*
United Distributors Inc .... F 316 263-6181
Wichita *(G-15842)*

RENTAL SVCS: Vending Machine

K-State Union Corporation .... C 785 532-6575
Manhattan *(G-6671)*
United Distributors Inc .... F 316 712-2174
Wichita *(G-15841)*

RENTAL SVCS: Video Cassette Recorder & Access

Family Video Movie Club Inc .... F 913 254-7219
Olathe *(G-7702)*

RENTAL SVCS: Video Disk/Tape, To The General Public

B & B Cinemas .... F 785 242-0777
Ottawa *(G-8247)*
Blockbuster LLC .... F 913 438-3203
Shawnee Mission *(G-11169)*
Dicks Thriftway .... E 785 456-2525
Wamego *(G-13414)*
Family Video Movie Club Inc .... F 620 342-4659
Emporia *(G-1755)*
Family Video Movie Club Inc .... F 913 254-7219
Olathe *(G-7702)*
Family Video Movie Club Inc .... E 785 263-3853
Abilene *(G-30)*
Family Video Movie Club Inc .... E 785 478-0606
Topeka *(G-12594)*
Family Video Movie Club Inc .... F 785 762-2377
Junction City *(G-3689)*
Fugate Enterprises .... F 316 722-5670
Wichita *(G-14428)*
Major Video of Kansas Inc .... F 913 649-7137
Overland Park *(G-8980)*

RENTAL SVCS: Work Zone Traffic Eqpt, Flags, Cones, Etc

C-Hawkk Construction Inc .... F 785 542-1800
Eudora *(G-1872)*
Traffic Control Services Inc .... F 316 448-0402
Wichita *(G-15784)*

RENTAL: Passenger Car

Bob Allen Ford Inc .... D 913 381-3000
Overland Park *(G-8473)*
Elrac LLC .... F 913 642-9669
Overland Park *(G-8675)*
Enterprise Leasing Co KS LLC .... E 913 782-6381
Olathe *(G-7687)*
Enterprise Leasing Co KS LLC .... E 913 631-7663
Shawnee Mission *(G-11341)*
Enterprise Leasing Co KS LLC .... E 913 402-1322
Overland Park *(G-8684)*
Ray Shepherd Motors Inc .... E 620 644-2625
Fort Scott *(G-2001)*

RENTAL: Portable Toilet

AAA Portable Services LLC ......F 316 522-6442
Wichita *(G-13591)*
Nisly Brothers Inc ......E 620 662-6561
Hutchinson *(G-3391)*

RENTAL: Trucks, With Drivers

Transervice Logistics Inc ......D 785 493-4295
Salina *(G-10739)*

RENTAL: Video Tape & Disc

Kier Enterprises Inc ......E 785 325-2150
Washington *(G-13467)*
Liberty Hall Inc ......E 785 749-1972
Lawrence *(G-4995)*
Liberty Hall Inc ......F 785 749-1972
Lawrence *(G-4994)*
Regal Audio Video ......G 785 628-2700
Hays *(G-2898)*
Sparks Music Co ......F 620 442-5030
Arkansas City *(G-182)*

REPAIR SERVICES, NEC

Heartland Deisel Repair ......F 913 403-0208
Shawnee Mission *(G-11423)*

REPOSSESSION SVCS

Atlas Recovery Systems LLC ......F 913 281-7000
Overland Park *(G-8410)*
Crown Recovery Services LLC ......F 816 777-2366
Overland Park *(G-8619)*
Guardian Business Services ......F 785 823-1635
Salina *(G-10524)*

REPRODUCTION SVCS: Video Tape Or Disk

Real Media LLC ......F 913 894-8989
Overland Park *(G-9228)*
Trinity Animation Inc ......F 816 525-0103
Overland Park *(G-9428)*
Twa LLC ......E 913 599-5200
Lenexa *(G-6195)*

RESEARCH, DEVEL & TEST SVCS, COMM: Sociological & Education

Everhance LLC ......F 785 218-1406
Overland Park *(G-8696)*
Little Hse On Prrie Museum Inc ......F 559 202-8147
Independence *(G-3533)*

RESEARCH, DEVELOPMENT & TEST SVCS, COMM: Cmptr Hardware Dev

Netchemia LLC ......E 913 789-0996
Overland Park *(G-9074)*
On Demand Technologies LLC ......F 913 438-1800
Overland Park *(G-9102)*

RESEARCH, DEVELOPMENT & TEST SVCS, COMM: Research, Exc Lab

Northrop Grumman Systems Corp ......B 913 651-8311
Fort Leavenworth *(G-1940)*
Ryan Development Company LLC ......E 316 630-9223
Wichita *(G-15496)*

RESEARCH, DEVELOPMENT & TESTING SVCS, COMM: Agricultural

Kansas State University ......E 620 275-9164
Garden City *(G-2214)*
Kansas State University ......E 620 421-4826
Parsons *(G-9697)*
Veterinary Research and Cnslt ......F 785 324-9200
Hays *(G-2925)*

RESEARCH, DEVELOPMENT & TESTING SVCS, COMM: Natural Resource

Land Institute ......E 785 823-5376
Salina *(G-10578)*

RESEARCH, DEVELOPMENT & TESTING SVCS, COMM: Research Lab

Citoxlab Usa LLC ......D 913 850-5000
Stilwell *(G-12141)*

RESEARCH, DEVELOPMENT & TESTING SVCS, COMMERCIAL: Business

Kansas Health Institute ......E 785 233-5443
Topeka *(G-12779)*

RESEARCH, DEVELOPMENT & TESTING SVCS, COMMERCIAL: Economic

Dpra Incorporated ......F 785 539-3565
Manhattan *(G-6616)*
Kingman Cnty Ecnmic Dev Cncil ......A 620 532-3694
Kingman *(G-4598)*

RESEARCH, DEVELOPMENT & TESTING SVCS, COMMERCIAL: Education

American Indian Health Researc ......F 913 422-7523
Shawnee *(G-10910)*
Juniper Gardens Childrens Prj ......D 913 321-3143
Kansas City *(G-4128)*
Stratgic Knwldge Solutions Inc ......F 913 682-2002
Leavenworth *(G-5292)*

RESEARCH, DEVELOPMENT & TESTING SVCS, COMMERCIAL: Food

American Institute of Baking ......D 785 537-4750
Manhattan *(G-6541)*

RESEARCH, DEVELOPMENT & TESTING SVCS, COMMERCIAL: Medical

Altasciences Clinical Kans Inc ......D 913 696-1601
Overland Park *(G-8373)*
Biodesix Inc ......E 913 583-9000
De Soto *(G-1195)*
Revolutionary Bus Concepts Inc ......D 913 385-5700
Shawnee Mission *(G-11793)*

RESEARCH, DEVELOPMENT & TESTING SVCS, COMMERCIAL: Physical

Leidos Inc ......G 913 317-5120
Shawnee Mission *(G-11560)*
University of Kansas ......B 785 864-4780
Lawrence *(G-5162)*

RESEARCH, DVLPT & TEST SVCS, COMM: Mkt Analysis or Research

Business & Technology Inst ......E 620 235-4920
Pittsburg *(G-9827)*
Callahan Creek Inc ......D 785 838-4774
Lawrence *(G-4772)*
Data Source of Kansas LLC ......F 620 735-4353
Cassoday *(G-687)*
E T C Institute Inc ......E 913 747-0646
Olathe *(G-7663)*
Education Market Resources Inc ......E 913 390-8110
Olathe *(G-7670)*
On-Line Communications Inc ......C 316 831-0500
Wichita *(G-15219)*
Pivot International Inc ......E 913 312-6900
Lenexa *(G-6060)*
Research Partnership Inc ......E 316 263-6433
Wichita *(G-15447)*
Walz Tetrick Advertising Inc ......E 913 789-8778
Mission *(G-7140)*

RESEARCH, DVLPT & TESTING SVCS, COMM: Mkt, Bus & Economic

American Gvrnment Slutions LLC ......F 913 428-2550
Leawood *(G-5320)*
Lionshare Marketing Inc ......F 913 631-8400
Lenexa *(G-5974)*

RESEARCH, DVLPT & TESTING SVCS, COMM: Survey, Mktg

Savoy Rgls BHN Engnrng Lnd Sur ......E 316 264-8008
Wichita *(G-15523)*

RESERVATION SVCS

Standees Pv LLC ......D 913 601-5250
Prairie Village *(G-10069)*
Super 8 Forbes Landing ......F 785 862-2222
Topeka *(G-13123)*

RESIDENCE CLUB: Organization

Linn Valley Lake Property Assn ......E 913 757-4591
Linn Valley *(G-6414)*

RESIDENTIAL CARE FOR CHILDREN

Agape Center of Hope LLC ......F 316 393-7252
Wichita *(G-13643)*
Emberhope Inc ......C 316 529-9100
Newton *(G-7339)*
Emberhope Inc ......C 316 529-9100
Wichita *(G-14273)*
Emberhope Inc ......D 620 225-0276
Dodge City *(G-1357)*
Gps Kids Club ......F 620 282-2288
Hoisington *(G-3065)*
Hufford House ......D 620 225-0276
Dodge City *(G-1377)*
Kvc Behavioral Healthcare Inc ......D 913 322-4900
Olathe *(G-7844)*
Kvc Health Systems Inc ......E 316 796-5503
Wichita *(G-14902)*
Kvc Health Systems Inc ......D 913 322-4900
Olathe *(G-7845)*
Pratt County Achievement Place ......F 620 672-6610
Pratt *(G-10135)*
Tfi Family Services Inc ......D 620 342-2239
Emporia *(G-1834)*
Tfi Family Services Inc ......F 913 894-2985
Overland Park *(G-9404)*
Tfi Family Services Inc ......F 620 342-2239
Emporia *(G-1835)*
Tfi Family Services Inc ......F 620 431-0312
Chanute *(G-768)*
Tfi Family Services Inc ......D 785 232-1019
Topeka *(G-13155)*
Youth Crisis Shelter Inc ......E 620 421-6941
Parsons *(G-9752)*

RESIDENTIAL CARE FOR THE HANDICAPPED

Angel Square ......F 785 534-1080
Concordia *(G-1102)*
Choices Network Inc ......B 785 820-8018
Salina *(G-10447)*
Cof Training Services Inc ......D 785 242-5035
Ottawa *(G-8258)*
Johnson County Dev Support ......F 913 826-2626
Lenexa *(G-5931)*
Multi Community Diversfd Svcs ......F 620 241-6693
McPherson *(G-7009)*
Occk Inc ......E 785 243-1977
Concordia *(G-1125)*
Occk Inc ......E 785 738-3490
Beloit *(G-498)*
Occk Inc ......C 785 827-9383
Salina *(G-10617)*
Riverside Resources Inc ......D 913 651-6810
Leavenworth *(G-5287)*

RESIDENTIAL MENTAL HEALTH & SUBSTANCE ABUSE FACILITIES

Bethesda Lthran Cmmunities Inc ......C 913 906-5000
Olathe *(G-7551)*
Big Lkes Developmental Ctr Inc ......F 785 776-7748
Manhattan *(G-6559)*
Big Lkes Developmental Ctr Inc ......E 785 632-5357
Clay Center *(G-843)*
Big Lkes Developmental Ctr Inc ......F 785 776-0777
Manhattan *(G-6560)*
Brad Carson ......F 620 429-1011
Columbus *(G-1062)*
Bridge Hven Mmory Care Rsdents ......E 785 856-1630
Lawrence *(G-4767)*
Brookdale Senior Living Commun ......F 316 788-0370
Derby *(G-1226)*
Caney Guest Home Inc ......F 620 431-7115
Chanute *(G-709)*
Comfort Care Homes Kans Cy LLC ......F 913 643-0111
Prairie Village *(G-10021)*
Cottonwood Point Inc ......F 316 775-0368
Augusta *(G-315)*

County of Sedgwick ... E ... 316 660-9500
Wichita *(G-14113)*
Creative Community Living of E ... F ... 620 221-9431
Winfield *(G-16135)*
Douglass Medicalodges ... E ... 316 747-2157
Douglass *(G-1466)*
Evangelical Lutheran ... D ... 785 456-9482
Wamego *(G-13422)*
Family Crisis Center Inc ... F ... 620 793-9941
Great Bend *(G-2562)*
Gran Villa ... F ... 620 583-7473
Eureka *(G-1887)*
Homestead of Hays ... D ... 785 628-3200
Hays *(G-2850)*
Kc House of Hope ... F ... 913 262-8885
Overland Park *(G-8907)*
Larksfield Place ... E ... 316 636-1000
Wichita *(G-14925)*
Legend Senior Living LLC ... D ... 316 616-6288
Wichita *(G-14954)*
Marquis Place Concordia LLc ... E ... 785 243-2255
Concordia *(G-1123)*
Martin Luther Homes Kansas Inc ... D ... 620 229-8702
Winfield *(G-16156)*
Medicalodges Inc ... D ... 316 755-1288
Valley Center *(G-13348)*
Midwest Health Services Inc ... C ... 316 729-2400
Wichita *(G-15094)*
Midwest Health Services Inc ... E ... 785 776-1772
Manhattan *(G-6750)*
Midwest Health Services Inc ... E ... 620 272-9800
Garden City *(G-2233)*
Mirror Inc ... E ... 316 283-6743
Newton *(G-7389)*
New Hope Services ... F ... 620 231-9895
Pittsburg *(G-9911)*
Prairie View Inc ... B ... 316 284-6400
Newton *(G-7407)*
Presbyterian Manors Inc ... D ... 785 841-4262
Lawrence *(G-5074)*
Presbytrian Mnors of MD-Merica ... E ... 620 223-5550
Fort Scott *(G-1999)*
Residentialsoultion LLC ... E ... 913 268-2967
Shawnee *(G-11017)*
Rh Montgomery Properties Inc ... F ... 785 284-3418
Sabetha *(G-10325)*
Rose Villa Inc ... E ... 785 232-0671
Topeka *(G-13029)*
Saint Francis Academy Newton ... E ... 316 284-2477
Newton *(G-7412)*
Saint Francis Cmnty Svcs Inc ... C ... 620 276-4482
Garden City *(G-2272)*
Saint Francis Cmnty Svcs Inc ... E ... 785 825-0541
Salina *(G-10659)*
Saint Francis Cmnty Svcs Inc ... E ... 785 452-9653
Salina *(G-10660)*
Saint Francis Cmnty Svcs Inc ... F ... 316 831-0330
Wichita *(G-15507)*
Salvation Army ... D ... 913 232-5400
Kansas City *(G-4398)*
Silver Crest At Deercreek ... F ... 913 681-1101
Shawnee Mission *(G-11869)*
Silvercrest At College View Sr ... F ... 913 915-6041
Lenexa *(G-6135)*
Tfi LLC ... F ... 785 235-1524
Topeka *(G-13154)*
Town Village Leawood LLC ... E ... 913 491-3681
Shawnee Mission *(G-11936)*
Valeo Behavioral Health Care ... E ... 785 233-1730
Topeka *(G-13215)*
Visiting Nurses Association ... D ... 785 843-3738
Lawrence *(G-5175)*
Welstone ... F ... 913 788-6045
Shawnee Mission *(G-12004)*
West Wchita Asssted Living LLC ... F ... 316 361-2500
Wichita *(G-15957)*
Wheat State Manor Inc ... D ... 316 799-2181
Whitewater *(G-13573)*

RESIDENTIAL MENTALLY HANDICAPPED FACILITIES

Apostolic Christian Home ... C ... 785 284-3471
Sabetha *(G-10305)*
Compass Behavioral Health ... E ... 620 276-6470
Garden City *(G-2131)*
High Plains Mental Health Ctr ... F ... 785 543-5284
Phillipsburg *(G-9788)*
High Plains Mental Health Ctr ... E ... 785 462-6774
Colby *(G-1014)*
High Plains Mental Health Ctr ... F ... 785 625-2400
Hays *(G-2847)*
RES-Care Kansas Inc ... F ... 913 342-9426
Kansas City *(G-4372)*

RESIDENTIAL REMODELERS

All Things Exterior Inc ... E ... 785 738-5015
Beloit *(G-472)*
American Exteriors LLC ... F ... 913 712-9668
Mount Hope *(G-7203)*
Antrim & Assoc ... F ... 316 267-2753
Wichita *(G-13714)*
Arrow Renovation & Cnstr LLC ... E ... 913 703-3000
Olathe *(G-7534)*
Benchmark Enterprises ... F ... 785 537-4447
Manhattan *(G-6555)*
Four Corners Construction LLC ... G ... 620 662-8163
Hutchinson *(G-3290)*
Nies Construction Inc ... D ... 316 684-0161
Wichita *(G-15177)*
Nies Homes Inc ... F ... 316 684-0161
Wichita *(G-15178)*
PDQ Construction Inc ... F ... 785 842-6844
Topeka *(G-12966)*

RESINS: Custom Compound Purchased

Continental American Corp ... C ... 316 321-4551
El Dorado *(G-1550)*
J and J Plastics ... F ... 620 660-9048
Rosalia *(G-10234)*

RESORT HOTEL: Franchised

Absecon SW Hotel Inc ... E ... 913 345-2111
Lenexa *(G-5619)*

RESORT HOTELS

Double Tree Hilton ... F ... 316 945-5272
Wichita *(G-14230)*
Ep Resorts Inc ... E ... 970 586-5958
Olathe *(G-7689)*
Great Wolf Kansas Spe LLC ... B ... 913 299-7001
Kansas City *(G-4047)*
Great Wolf Lodge Kansas Cy LLC ... F ... 913 299-7001
Kansas City *(G-4048)*
Inntel Corporation of America ... E ... 316 684-3466
Wichita *(G-14696)*
Oread Hotel ... E ... 785 843-1200
Lawrence *(G-5046)*
Show ME Birds Hunting Resort ... F ... 620 674-8863
Baxter Springs *(G-413)*
Sunstar Wichita Inc ... E ... 316 943-2181
Wichita *(G-15690)*

RESPIRATORY THERAPY CLINIC

Physical Rsprtory Therapy Svcs ... F ... 785 742-2131
Hiawatha *(G-3021)*

REST HOME, WITH HEALTH CARE INCIDENTAL

Country Living Inc ... F ... 620 842-5858
Anthony *(G-125)*
Holiday Healthcare LLC ... E ... 620 343-9285
Emporia *(G-1773)*
Meade Hospital District ... C ... 620 873-2146
Meade *(G-7052)*
Mennonite Frndship Communities ... C ... 620 663-7175
South Hutchinson *(G-12062)*
Ottawa Retirement Plaza Inc ... E ... 785 242-1127
Ottawa *(G-8300)*

RESTAURANT RESERVATION SVCS

Wallabys Inc ... F ... 913 541-9255
Lenexa *(G-6221)*

RESTAURANTS:Full Svc, American

Elderslie LLC ... F ... 316 680-2637
Valley Center *(G-13341)*
Little Apple Brewing Company ... C ... 785 539-5500
Manhattan *(G-6714)*
Osage Hills Inc ... F ... 620 449-2713
Saint Paul *(G-10383)*
Side Pockets Inc ... F ... 913 888-7665
Shawnee Mission *(G-11867)*
Windmill Inn Inc ... F ... 785 336-3696
Seneca *(G-10888)*

RESTAURANTS:Full Svc, Chinese

China Palace ... F ... 620 365-3723
Iola *(G-3592)*

RESTAURANTS:Full Svc, Diner

Executive Mnor Leavenworth Inc ... F ... 785 234-5400
Topeka *(G-12586)*
Oak Tree and Pennys Diner ... F ... 785 562-1234
Marysville *(G-6904)*

RESTAURANTS:Full Svc, Ethnic Food

Janki Inc ... F ... 620 225-7373
Dodge City *(G-1382)*

RESTAURANTS:Full Svc, Family

Granite City Food & Brewry Ltd ... D ... 913 334-2255
Kansas City *(G-4045)*
Tins Inc ... E ... 785 842-1234
Lawrence *(G-5137)*

RESTAURANTS:Full Svc, Family, Chain

Capital City Corral Inc ... D ... 785 273-5354
Topeka *(G-12425)*
S S of Kansas Inc ... E ... 620 663-5951
Hutchinson *(G-3435)*
S S of Kansas Inc ... D ... 785 823-2787
Salina *(G-10657)*
Stockade Companies LLC ... D ... 620 669-9372
Hutchinson *(G-3448)*

RESTAURANTS:Full Svc, Family, Independent

Dodge Enteprise Inc ... E ... 620 227-2125
Dodge City *(G-1356)*
Fanchon Ballroom & Supper Club ... F ... 785 628-8154
Hays *(G-2804)*
Flint Oak ... E ... 620 658-4401
Fall River *(G-1927)*
Garden City Travel Plaza LLC ... E ... 620 275-4404
Garden City *(G-2179)*
Heritage Restaurant Inc ... E ... 316 524-7495
Wichita *(G-14596)*
Q Golden Billiards ... F ... 785 625-6913
Hays *(G-2893)*
Quality Inn ... D ... 620 663-4444
South Hutchinson *(G-12064)*
Riverside Recreation Assn ... F ... 785 332-3401
Saint Francis *(G-10344)*

RESTAURANTS:Full Svc, Lebanese

Latour Management Inc ... E ... 316 524-2290
Wichita *(G-14933)*

RESTAURANTS:Full Svc, Mexican

La Mesa Mexican Restaurant ... F ... 913 837-3455
Louisburg *(G-6454)*

RESTAURANTS:Full Svc, Steak

B & C Restaurant Corporation ... C ... 913 327-0800
Shawnee Mission *(G-11138)*
Bartos Enterprises Inc ... F ... 620 232-9813
Frontenac *(G-2053)*

RESTAURANTS:Limited Svc, Coffee Shop

Rule Properties LLC ... F ... 785 621-8000
Hays *(G-2903)*
Spice Merchant & Co ... F ... 316 263-4121
Wichita *(G-15639)*

RESTAURANTS:Limited Svc, Fast-Food, Chain

Brown Management Inc ... F ... 785 528-3769
Osage City *(G-8181)*

RESTAURANTS:Limited Svc, Food Bars

T-143 Inc ... E ... 913 681-8313
Overland Park *(G-9390)*

RESTAURANTS:Limited Svc, Grill

Blind Pig ... F ... 785 827-7449
Salina *(G-10426)*

Mayberrys Inc........F 620 793-9400
Great Bend *(G-2605)*
Olathe Billiards Inc........F 913 780-5740
Olathe *(G-7928)*
Two Guys & A Grill........F 913 393-4745
Olathe *(G-8126)*

RESTAURANTS:Limited Svc, Hamburger Stand

Npc Quality Burgers Inc........F 913 327-5555
Overland Park *(G-9094)*

RESTAURANTS:Limited Svc, Ice Cream Stands Or Dairy Bars

Culvers Frozen Custard........E 913 402-9777
Overland Park *(G-8623)*
Stanley Dairy Queen........E 913 851-1850
Shawnee Mission *(G-11892)*

RESTAURANTS:Limited Svc, Pizza

Tellers........D 785 843-4111
Lawrence *(G-5133)*

RESTAURANTS:Limited Svc, Pizzeria, Chain

Cec Entertainment Inc........E 913 648-4920
Overland Park *(G-8533)*
Cec Entertainment Inc........D....... 316 636-2225
Wichita *(G-13968)*
Coach and Four Bowling Lanes........F 785 472-5571
Ellsworth *(G-1663)*
Devlin Partners LLC........F 913 894-1300
Lenexa *(G-5814)*
Fugate Leasing Inc........C....... 316 722-5670
Wichita *(G-14429)*
J A Peterson Enterprises Inc........E 913 384-3800
Shawnee Mission *(G-11471)*
Papa Murphys Take N Bake........F 913 897-0008
Overland Park *(G-9140)*
Pizza Ranch........F 620 662-2066
Hutchinson *(G-3407)*

RESTAURANTS:Limited Svc, Pizzeria, Independent

Cheney Lanes Inc........F 316 542-3126
Cheney *(G-790)*

RESTAURANTS:Limited Svc, Sandwiches & Submarines Shop

Doc Grens Gourmet Salads Grill........F 316 636-8997
Wichita *(G-14216)*
Mr Goodcents Franchise Systems........E 913 583-8400
De Soto *(G-1209)*

RESTAURANTS:Limited Svc, Soft Drink Stand

Streeter Enterprises LLC........F 785 537-0100
Manhattan *(G-6815)*

RESTROOM CLEANING SVCS

Tapco Products Co........E 913 492-2777
Shawnee Mission *(G-11920)*

RETAIL BAKERY: Bread

Bagatelle Inc........E 316 684-5662
Wichita *(G-13793)*

RETAIL BAKERY: Doughnuts

Drubers Donut Shop........G....... 316 283-1206
Newton *(G-7338)*
Johnny Schwindt Inc........G....... 620 275-0633
Garden City *(G-2209)*
M & K Daylight Donuts........G....... 913 495-2529
Shawnee Mission *(G-11588)*

RETAIL FIREPLACE STORES

Jay Henges Enterprises Inc........E 913 764-4600
Olathe *(G-7808)*
Weber Refrigeration & Htg Inc........E 580 338-7338
Garden City *(G-2309)*

RETAIL LUMBER YARDS

E D Bishop Lumber Muncie Inc........F 913 441-2691
Bonner Springs *(G-552)*

RETAIL STORES, NEC

Crossroads Shop Ctr LLC........F 913 362-1999
Shawnee Mission *(G-11282)*

RETAIL STORES: Alarm Signal Systems

Atronic Alarms Inc........E 913 432-4545
Lenexa *(G-5674)*
Rueschhoff Communications........E....... 785 841-0111
Lawrence *(G-5098)*

RETAIL STORES: Alcoholic Beverage Making Eqpt & Splys

Butterfly Supply Inc........F 620 793-7156
Great Bend *(G-2525)*
O K Thompsons Tire Inc........E 785 738-2283
Beloit *(G-497)*

RETAIL STORES: Architectural Splys

Stueder Contractors Inc........E 620 792-6044
Great Bend *(G-2642)*

RETAIL STORES: Art & Architectural Splys

Inland Industries Inc........G....... 913 492-9050
Bucyrus *(G-600)*

RETAIL STORES: Audio-Visual Eqpt & Splys

AVI Systems Inc........E 913 495-9494
Lenexa *(G-5677)*

RETAIL STORES: Awnings

Home Stl Siding & Windows LLC........F 785 625-8622
Hays *(G-2849)*
Martinek & Flynn Wholesale Inc........E 785 233-6666
Topeka *(G-12862)*
Overhead Door Company........E 316 265-4634
Wichita *(G-15240)*

RETAIL STORES: Banners

Fastsigns Inc........G....... 913 649-3600
Overland Park *(G-8707)*
Hightech Signs LLC........E 913 894-4422
Kansas City *(G-4079)*

RETAIL STORES: Business Machines & Eqpt

Galaxie Business Equipment Inc........E 620 221-3469
Winfield *(G-16142)*
Imaging Solutions Company........E 316 630-0440
Wichita *(G-14677)*

RETAIL STORES: Canvas Prdts

Colby Supply & Mfg Co........F 785 462-3981
Colby *(G-999)*
Durasafe Products Inc........F 316 942-3282
Wichita *(G-14245)*
Screen Machine LLC........F 785 762-3081
Junction City *(G-3750)*

RETAIL STORES: Christmas Lights & Decorations

Biehler Companies Inc........D....... 316 529-0002
Wichita *(G-13847)*

RETAIL STORES: Communication Eqpt

Golden Wheat Inc........E 620 782-3341
Udall *(G-13277)*
Skc Communication Products LLC........C....... 913 422-4222
Shawnee Mission *(G-11870)*

RETAIL STORES: Cosmetics

Beauty Brands LLC........E 785 228-9778
Topeka *(G-12369)*
Beauty Brands LLC........E 913 663-4848
Shawnee Mission *(G-11157)*
Beauty Brands LLC........E 816 531-2266
Lenexa *(G-5695)*
Gdm Enterprises LLC........F 816 753-2900
Fairway *(G-1908)*

Gram Enterprises Inc........E 913 888-3689
Lenexa *(G-5879)*

RETAIL STORES: Decals

Graphic Impressions Inc........E 620 663-5939
Hutchinson *(G-3305)*
Lowen Corporation........B 620 663-2161
Hutchinson *(G-3358)*

RETAIL STORES: Electronic Parts & Eqpt

Rolling Hills Electric Coop........F 785 534-1601
Beloit *(G-501)*

RETAIL STORES: Engine & Motor Eqpt & Splys

ABB Motors and Mechanical Inc........F 816 587-0272
Lenexa *(G-5618)*
Advanced Engine Machine Inc........G....... 785 825-6684
Salina *(G-10397)*
Automotive Equipment Services........E 913 254-2600
Olathe *(G-7543)*
Computer Distribution Corp........E 785 354-1086
Topeka *(G-12498)*
Gems Inc........G....... 785 731-2849
Ransom *(G-10192)*

RETAIL STORES: Farm Eqpt & Splys

Bucklin Tractor & Impt Co Inc........E 620 826-3271
Bucklin *(G-591)*
Goodland Machine & Auto LLC........G....... 785 899-6628
Goodland *(G-2474)*
Lang Diesel Inc........F 785 462-2412
Colby *(G-1024)*
McCullough Enterprises Inc........F....... 316 942-8118
Wichita *(G-15024)*
Plp Inc........E 620 842-5137
Anthony *(G-132)*
Plp Inc........E 620 382-3794
Marion *(G-6875)*
Plp Inc........E 620 342-5000
Emporia *(G-1812)*
Plp Inc........C....... 620 664-5860
Hutchinson *(G-3408)*
Plp Inc........E 316 943-4261
Wichita *(G-15307)*
Radke Implement Inc........F 620 935-4310
Russell *(G-10286)*
Shield Industries Inc........E 620 662-7221
Hutchinson *(G-3441)*
Tractor Supply Company........F 785 827-3300
Salina *(G-10738)*
Zeitlow Distributing Co Inc........F 620 241-4279
McPherson *(G-7045)*

RETAIL STORES: Farm Machinery, NEC

K Young Inc........F 785 475-3888
Colby *(G-1019)*
Kanequip Inc........E 785 456-2041
Wamego *(G-13426)*

RETAIL STORES: Fire Extinguishers

Weis Fire Safety Equip Co Inc........F 785 825-9527
Salina *(G-10765)*

RETAIL STORES: Foam & Foam Prdts

Novation Iq LLC........E 913 492-6000
Lenexa *(G-6029)*

RETAIL STORES: Hair Care Prdts

Hair Shop & Retailing Center........E 913 397-9888
Olathe *(G-7745)*
Hair Shop West Inc........E 913 829-4868
Olathe *(G-7746)*

RETAIL STORES: Hearing Aids

Audiology Consultants Inc........F 785 823-3761
Salina *(G-10412)*
Central Kansas Ent Assoc PA........E 785 823-7225
Salina *(G-10440)*
Central State Services........F 316 613-3989
Wichita *(G-13986)*
Head & Neck Surgery Kans Cy PA........E 913 599-4800
Leawood *(G-5420)*
Hutchinson Clinic PA........A 620 669-2500
Hutchinson *(G-3319)*

Lawrence Otlryngology Assoc PA.........F 620 343-6600
Lawrence *(G-4981)*
Mid-States Laboratories Inc..................F 316 262-7013
Wichita *(G-15082)*

RETAIL STORES: Hospital Eqpt & Splys

Broadway Home Medical Inc ....F 316 264-8600
Wichita *(G-13895)*
Hutchinson Hlth Care Svcs Inc.............E 620 665-0528
Hutchinson *(G-3321)*

RETAIL STORES: Ice

Arctic Glacier Texas Inc ....E 316 529-2173
Wichita *(G-13732)*

RETAIL STORES: Medical Apparatus & Splys

Apria Healthcare LLC ....F 785 272-8411
Topeka *(G-12335)*
Ascension Via Christi Home Med...........D 316 265-4991
Wichita *(G-13746)*
Cokingtin Eye Center PA.......................D 913 491-3737
Shawnee Mission *(G-11244)*
Continental Equipment Company ....F 913 845-2148
Tonganoxie *(G-12258)*
Kansas Specialty Services Inc ....F 620 221-6040
Winfield *(G-16151)*
Lincare Inc...F 316 684-4689
Wichita *(G-14965)*
Perrys Inc...F 620 662-2375
Hutchinson *(G-3404)*
Relevium Labs Inc ....F 614 568-7000
Dodge City *(G-1423)*
Somnicare Inc ....E 913 498-1331
Overland Park *(G-9326)*

RETAIL STORES: Mobile Telephones & Eqpt

Cellco Partnership ....F 316 789-9911
Derby *(G-1228)*
Sprint Spectrum LP ....F 913 671-7007
Merriam *(G-7105)*
Wireless Lifestyle LLC...........................D 913 962-0002
Overland Park *(G-9499)*

RETAIL STORES: Monuments, Finished To Custom Order

Alderwoods (kansas) Inc.........................F 316 682-5575
Wichita *(G-13661)*
Bell Memorials LLC.................................F 785 738-2257
Beloit *(G-474)*
Los Primos Inc ....G 785 527-5535
Belleville *(G-460)*
Louis Dengel & Son Mortuary................F 785 242-2323
Ottawa *(G-8285)*
Smith Monuments Inc.............................G 785 425-6762
Stockton *(G-12187)*
Wolf Memorial Co Inc ....F 785 726-4430
Ellis *(G-1655)*

RETAIL STORES: Motors, Electric

Richmond Electric Inc ....G 316 264-2344
Wichita *(G-15457)*

RETAIL STORES: Orthopedic & Prosthesis Applications

Hanger Prosthetics & ....G 913 341-8897
Overland Park *(G-8790)*
Hanger Prosthetics & ....G 785 232-5382
Topeka *(G-12664)*
Scott Specialties Inc................................E 785 243-2594
Concordia *(G-1129)*
Scott Specialties Inc................................E 785 632-3161
Clay Center *(G-881)*

RETAIL STORES: Perfumes & Colognes

Bath & Body Works LLC ....F 620 338-8409
Dodge City *(G-1304)*

RETAIL STORES: Pet Food

All Crtres Veterinary Hosp P A..............F 316 721-3993
Wichita *(G-13663)*
Chisholm Trail Country Str LLC ....F 316 283-3276
Newton *(G-7328)*
El Paso Animal Clinic ....F 316 788-1561
Derby *(G-1243)*

Pawsh Wash ....F 785 856-7297
Lawrence *(G-5059)*
Petsmart Inc ....E 913 393-4111
Olathe *(G-7980)*
Petsmart Inc ....E 913 338-5544
Shawnee Mission *(G-11728)*
Petsmart Inc ....E 785 272-3323
Topeka *(G-12973)*
Petsmart Inc ....E 913 384-4445
Shawnee Mission *(G-11729)*

RETAIL STORES: Pet Splys

Alternative Building Tech........................F 913 856-4536
Gardner *(G-2325)*

RETAIL STORES: Pets

Guptons Pets & Supplies Inc.................E 316 682-8111
Wichita *(G-14528)*
Land of Paws LLC...................................F 913 341-1011
Shawnee Mission *(G-11547)*
Pet Haven LLC...F 316 942-2151
Wichita *(G-15285)*
Rokenn Enterprises Inc...........................G 785 523-4251
Delphos *(G-1217)*

RETAIL STORES: Photocopy Machines

Copy Products Inc ....D 620 365-7611
Iola *(G-3596)*

RETAIL STORES: Picture Frames, Ready Made

Pratt Glass Inc...F 620 672-6463
Pratt *(G-10139)*

RETAIL STORES: Plumbing & Heating Splys

Action Plumbing of Lawrence ....F 785 843-5670
Lawrence *(G-4718)*
American Energy Products Inc..............G 913 351-3388
Lansing *(G-4666)*
Armstrong Plumbing Inc ....F 316 942-9535
Wichita *(G-13734)*
Bills Plumbing Service LLC ....F 913 829-8213
Olathe *(G-7555)*
Ferguson Enterprises LLC.....................E 316 262-0681
Wichita *(G-14355)*
Ferguson Enterprises LLC.....................F 785 354-4305
Topeka *(G-12604)*
Frederick Plumbing & Heating...............F 316 262-3713
Wichita *(G-14416)*
Hajoca Corporation..................................F 785 825-1333
Salina *(G-10531)*
Plumbing Specialists Inc.........................E 316 945-8383
Wichita *(G-15308)*

RETAIL STORES: Religious Goods

Worship Woodworks Inc ....G 620 622-4568
Protection *(G-10177)*

RETAIL STORES: Rock & Stone Specimens

House of Rocks Inc..................................E 913 432-5990
Kansas City *(G-4086)*

RETAIL STORES: Sunglasses

Jackson & Baalman..................................F 316 722-6452
Wichita *(G-14743)*

RETAIL STORES: Telephone & Communication Eqpt

AT&T Mobility LLC ....E 913 254-0303
Olathe *(G-7539)*
Overfield Corporation..............................F 785 843-3434
Lawrence *(G-5052)*
Sprint Communications Inc ....A 855 848-3280
Overland Park *(G-9337)*
Sprint Spectrum LP ....F 785 537-3500
Manhattan *(G-6804)*

RETAIL STORES: Telephone Eqpt & Systems

S N C Inc ....E 620 665-6651
Hutchinson *(G-3434)*
Sprint Spectrum LP ....E 316 634-4900
Wichita *(G-15649)*
Teledata Communications LLC ....E 913 663-2010
Lenexa *(G-6175)*

Tpcks Inc ....F 785 776-4429
Manhattan *(G-6828)*

RETAIL STORES: Tents

Infinity Tents Inc.......................................E 913 820-3700
Kansas City *(G-4100)*

RETAIL STORES: Typewriters

Liberal Office Machines Co.....................G 620 624-5653
Liberal *(G-6334)*

RETAIL STORES: Typewriters & Business Machines

Bolen Office Supply Inc...........................F 620 672-7535
Pratt *(G-10100)*

RETAIL STORES: Water Purification Eqpt

Central Marketing Inc ....F 316 613-2404
Wichita *(G-13980)*
John G Levin ....E 785 234-5551
Topeka *(G-12746)*
Quality Water Inc......................................F 785 825-4912
Salina *(G-10647)*
Scheopners Water Cond LLC ....F 620 275-5121
Garden City *(G-2275)*
Wheatland Waters Inc..............................D 785 267-0512
Olathe *(G-8153)*
Wichita Water Conditioning Inc..............D 316 267-5287
Wichita *(G-16042)*

RETAIL STORES: Welding Splys

Airgas Usa LLC ....E 316 941-9162
Wichita *(G-13653)*
Wichita Welding Supply Inc....................F 316 838-8671
Wichita *(G-16043)*

RETIREMENT COMMUNITIES WITH NURSING

Apostolic Christian Home........................C 785 284-3471
Sabetha *(G-10305)*
Brookdale Senior Living Commun.........F 620 251-6270
Coffeyville *(G-914)*
Brookdale Senior Living Commun.........E 785 762-3123
Junction City *(G-3675)*
Brookdale Snior Lving Cmmnties ....E 316 630-0788
Wichita *(G-13898)*
Brookdale Snior Lving Cmmnties ....F 785 263-7800
Abilene *(G-18)*
Brookdale Snior Lving Cmmnties ....F 785 832-9900
Lawrence *(G-4769)*
Brookdale Snior Lving Cmmnties ....D 913 491-1144
Shawnee Mission *(G-11184)*
Brookdale Snior Lving Cmmnties ....E 913 491-3681
Leawood *(G-5343)*
Cumbernauld Village Inc ....D 620 221-4141
Winfield *(G-16137)*
Galena Medical Properties LLC.............F 620 783-4616
Galena *(G-2073)*
Gran Villas of Wamego ....E 785 456-8997
Wamego *(G-13424)*
Lcd Unlimited Inc.....................................F 316 721-4803
Wichita *(G-14938)*
Medicalodges Inc.....................................F 620 251-3705
Coffeyville *(G-959)*
Midwest Health Services Inc..................F 785 272-2200
Topeka *(G-12898)*
Park View ....E 620 424-2000
Ulysses *(G-13310)*
Presbyterian Manors Inc ....D 785 825-1366
Salina *(G-10641)*
Presbyterian Manors Inc ....D 316 942-7456
Wichita *(G-15335)*
Vintage Park At Osawatomie LLC ....F 913 755-2167
Osawatomie *(G-8206)*
Vintage Park of Lenexa LLC ....F 913 894-6979
Shawnee Mission *(G-11981)*

REUPHOLSTERY SVCS

Andrews and Abbey Riley LLC..............F 913 262-2212
Kansas City *(G-3811)*
De Leon Furniture Inc..............................F 913 342-9446
Kansas City *(G-3964)*

ROBOTS: Assembly Line

Robotzone LLC .... G 620 221-7071
Winfield *(G-16170)*

ROCK SALT MINING

Compass Minerals America Inc .... C 913 344-9100
Overland Park *(G-8587)*

ROLLING MILL MACHINERY

Bradbury Co Inc .... B 620 345-6394
Moundridge *(G-7178)*
Marion Manufacturing Inc .... E 620 382-3751
Marion *(G-6874)*
Utah Machine & Mill Supply .... G 801 364-2812
Park City *(G-9653)*

ROOFING MATERIALS: Asphalt

Davinci Roofscapes LLC .... E 913 599-0766
Lenexa *(G-5804)*
Parsons Aaron Painting LLC .... G 620 532-1076
Kingman *(G-4609)*
Tamko Building Products Inc .... D 620 429-1800
Columbus *(G-1088)*

ROOFING MATERIALS: Sheet Metal

Metal Panels Inc .... E 913 766-7200
Kansas City *(G-4236)*

ROOFING MEMBRANE: Rubber

Topps Products Inc .... F 913 685-2500
Bucyrus *(G-611)*

ROOMING & BOARDING HOUSES: Dormitory, Commercially Operated

College Park Univ Xing Fully .... F 785 539-0500
Manhattan *(G-6594)*
Kansas State University .... B 785 532-6376
Manhattan *(G-6681)*
Lbubs 2003-C5 Nismith Hall LLC .... F 785 832-8676
Lawrence *(G-4990)*

ROOMING & BOARDING HOUSES: Furnished Room Rental

Blue Valley Partners LP .... E 913 963-5534
Prairie Village *(G-10016)*

ROOMING & BOARDING HOUSES: Lodging House, Exc Organization

Leisure Hotel Corporation .... F 620 225-3924
Dodge City *(G-1397)*

RUBBER

Everseal Gasket Inc .... E 913 441-9232
Shawnee Mission *(G-11351)*

RUBBER PRDTS: Mechanical

Everseal Gasket Inc .... E 913 441-9232
Shawnee Mission *(G-11351)*
Moore Rubber Co Inc .... F 913 422-5679
Shawnee Mission *(G-11654)*

RUBBER PRDTS: Sponge

Novation Iq LLC .... E 913 492-6000
Lenexa *(G-6029)*

RUBBLE MINING

Rapid Rubble Removal .... G 785 862-8875
Topeka *(G-12998)*

SADDLERY STORES

Chisholm Trail Country Str LLC .... F 316 283-3276
Newton *(G-7328)*

SAFETY EQPT & SPLYS WHOLESALERS

Airgas Usa LLC .... E 785 823-8100
Salina *(G-10398)*
Conrad Fire Equipment Inc .... F 913 780-5521
Olathe *(G-7611)*
Hantover Inc .... C 913 214-4800
Overland Park *(G-8792)*
Midco Holdings LLC .... F 316 522-0900
Wichita *(G-15085)*
Superior Signals Inc .... E 913 780-1440
Olathe *(G-8088)*

SAFETY INSPECTION SVCS

Paragon Aerospace Services .... E 316 945-5285
Wichita *(G-15257)*
Radiofrquency Saftey Intl Corp .... E 620 825-4600
Kiowa *(G-4629)*
Rueschhoff Communications .... E 785 841-0111
Lawrence *(G-5098)*

SALES PROMOTION SVCS

Big Creek Investment Corp Inc .... G 620 431-3445
Chanute *(G-707)*

SALT

Cargill Incorporated .... D 620 663-2141
Hutchinson *(G-3229)*
Compass Minerals America Inc .... C 913 344-9100
Overland Park *(G-8586)*
Compass Minerals America Inc .... C 913 344-9100
Overland Park *(G-8587)*
Compass Minerals Group Inc .... C 913 344-9100
Overland Park *(G-8588)*
Compass Minerals Intl Inc .... C 913 344-9200
Overland Park *(G-8589)*
Hutchinson Salt Company Inc .... G 620 856-3332
Baxter Springs *(G-409)*
Hutchinson Salt Company Inc .... E 620 662-3341
Hutchinson *(G-3324)*
Independent Salt Company .... E 785 472-4421
Kanopolis *(G-3772)*
Morton Salt Inc .... F 620 669-0401
South Hutchinson *(G-12063)*
Southwest Salt Company LLC .... G 913 755-1955
Paola *(G-9588)*

SALT & SULFUR MINING

Searles Valley Minerals Inc .... E 913 344-9500
Overland Park *(G-9286)*

SALT MINING: Common

Compass Minerals Intl Inc .... C 913 344-9200
Overland Park *(G-8589)*
Hutchinson Salt Company Inc .... E 620 662-3341
Hutchinson *(G-3324)*
Namsco Inc .... D 913 344-9100
Shawnee Mission *(G-11669)*

SAND & GRAVEL

Associated Material & Sup Co .... F 316 721-3848
Wichita *(G-13756)*
Cornejo & Sons LLC .... G 620 455-3720
Oxford *(G-9532)*
Dodge City Sand Company Inc .... F 620 227-6091
Dodge City *(G-1351)*
Gravel & Concrete Inc .... G 620 422-3249
Nickerson *(G-7432)*
Hardrock Sand & Gravel LLC .... G 620 408-4030
Dodge City *(G-1369)*
Holliday Sand & Gravel Co LLC .... E 913 492-5920
Lenexa *(G-5905)*
OBrien Rock Company Inc .... D 620 449-2257
Saint Paul *(G-10382)*
Unruh Sand & Gravel .... G 620 582-2774
Coldwater *(G-1058)*

SAND MINING

Huber Sand Company .... F 620 275-7601
Garden City *(G-2200)*

SANITARY SVC, NEC

Frontr-Rrwhead Joint Ventr LLC .... E 913 461-3804
Olathe *(G-7719)*
Reconserve of Kansas Inc .... E 913 621-5619
Kansas City *(G-4364)*

SANITARY SVCS: Environmental Cleanup

Geocore LLC .... E 785 826-1616
Salina *(G-10509)*
Haz-Mat Response Inc .... E 913 782-5151
Olathe *(G-7759)*
Kans Dept Health and Envmt .... A 785 296-0461
Topeka *(G-12755)*
W R King Contracting Inc .... E 913 238-7496
Shawnee Mission *(G-11985)*

SANITARY SVCS: Hazardous Waste, Collection & Disposal

Emerald Transformer Ppm LLC .... E 620 251-6380
Coffeyville *(G-937)*
Waste Corporation Kansas LLC .... D 713 292-2400
Parsons *(G-9749)*

SANITARY SVCS: Liquid Waste Collection & Disposal

Healy Biodiesel Inc .... F 620 545-7800
Clearwater *(G-893)*
Hodges Farms & Dredging LLC .... F 620 343-0513
Lebo *(G-5606)*

SANITARY SVCS: Medical Waste Disposal

Enserv LLC .... F 316 283-5943
Newton *(G-7341)*
Stericycle Inc .... F 913 321-3928
Kansas City *(G-4440)*

SANITARY SVCS: Nonhazardous Waste Disposal Sites

Budget Equipment Inc .... E 316 284-9994
Newton *(G-7323)*
Pcdisposalcom LLC .... E 913 980-4750
New Century *(G-7295)*

SANITARY SVCS: Oil Spill Cleanup

Andax Industries LLC .... E 785 437-0604
Saint Marys *(G-10358)*

SANITARY SVCS: Refuse Collection & Disposal Svcs

Allied Waste Inds Ariz Inc .... F 620 336-3678
Cherryvale *(G-800)*
Best Value Services LLC .... D 316 440-1048
Wichita *(G-13839)*
Better Hauling Co .... F 316 943-5865
Valley Center *(G-13337)*
County of Shawnee .... D 785 233-4774
Topeka *(G-12517)*
Lies Trash Service LLC .... E 316 522-1699
Wichita *(G-14959)*
Premier Contracting Inc .... D 913 362-4141
Kansas City *(G-4330)*
Republic Services Inc .... E 620 336-3678
Cherryvale *(G-812)*
Republic Services Inc .... E 620 783-5841
Galena *(G-2082)*
Salina Iron & Metal Company .... E 785 826-9838
Salina *(G-10677)*
Superior Disposal Service Inc .... F 913 406-9460
Eudora *(G-1881)*
Waste Connections Kansas Inc .... E 785 827-3939
Salina *(G-10759)*
Waste Connections Kansas Inc .... E 316 838-4920
Wichita *(G-15934)*

SANITARY SVCS: Sanitary Landfill, Operation Of

County of Finney .... F 620 275-4421
Garden City *(G-2136)*
County of Reno .... E 620 694-2587
Hutchinson *(G-3248)*
County of Seward .... F 620 626-3266
Liberal *(G-6298)*
County of Trego .... E 785 743-6441
Wakeeney *(G-13386)*
Deffenbaugh Industries Inc .... A 913 631-3300
Kansas City *(G-3965)*
Hamm Inc .... E 785 597-5111
Perry *(G-9768)*
Johnson County Landfill .... E 913 631-8181
Shawnee Mission *(G-11499)*
N R Hamm Quarry Inc .... E 785 842-3236
Lawrence *(G-5035)*
Waste Management of Kansas .... F 785 246-0413
Topeka *(G-13235)*

SANITARY SVCS: Sewage Treatment Facility

City of Manhattan..........F 785 587-4555
Manhattan *(G-6588)*
Siemens Industry Inc..........E 620 252-4223
Coffeyville *(G-977)*

SANITARY SVCS: Waste Materials, Disposal At Sea

Howies Enterprises LLC..........F 785 776-8352
Manhattan *(G-6660)*

SANITARY SVCS: Waste Materials, Recycling

21st St Steel..........F 316 265-6661
Wichita *(G-13578)*
Allen and Sons Waste Svcs LLC..........F 316 558-8050
Wichita *(G-13668)*
Allmetal Recycling LLC..........D 316 558-9914
Wichita *(G-13675)*
Allmetal Recycling LLC..........D 316 838-9381
Wichita *(G-13676)*
Asset Lifecycle LLC..........F 785 861-3100
Topeka *(G-12341)*
Champlin Tire Recycling Inc..........E 785 243-3345
Concordia *(G-1105)*
Commercial Metals Company..........E 620 331-1710
Independence *(G-3507)*
Evergreen Pallet LLC..........E 316 821-9991
Park City *(G-9617)*
F & F Iron & Metal Co..........E 785 877-3830
Norton *(G-7445)*
Greenpoint Cnstr Dem Proc Ctr..........F 785 234-6000
Topeka *(G-12648)*
Laser Recycling Company..........F 785 865-4075
Lawrence *(G-4956)*
Lrm Industries Inc..........E 785 843-1688
Lawrence *(G-5001)*
National Fiber Supply LLC..........F 913 321-0066
Kansas City *(G-4280)*
Recall Secure Destruction Serv..........F 913 310-0811
Shawnee Mission *(G-11782)*
Reconserve of Kansas Inc..........E 913 621-5619
Kansas City *(G-4364)*
Resource Management Co Inc..........F 785 398-2240
Brownell *(G-589)*
Scrap Management Kansas Inc..........F 316 832-1198
Park City *(G-9641)*
Veolia Water North America Ope..........F 785 762-5855
Junction City *(G-3765)*
Wichita Material Recovery LLC..........F 316 303-9303
Wichita *(G-16011)*

SANITATION CHEMICALS & CLEANING AGENTS

ITW Dymon..........F 913 397-9889
Olathe *(G-7803)*
Prosoco Inc..........D 785 865-4200
Lawrence *(G-5081)*

SAVINGS & LOAN ASSOCIATIONS, NOT FEDERALLY CHARTERED

Golden Belt Banking & Sav Assn..........E 785 625-7345
Hays *(G-2818)*

SAVINGS INSTITUTIONS: Federally Chartered

Bankwest of Kansas..........F 785 462-7557
Colby *(G-989)*
First Independence Corporation..........E 620 331-1660
Independence *(G-3517)*
First Independence Corporation..........F 620 331-1660
Independence *(G-3518)*
Sunflower Bank National Assn..........F 785 537-0550
Manhattan *(G-6817)*

SAW BLADES

Diteq Corporation..........E 816 246-5515
Lenexa *(G-5821)*
Husqvrna Cnstr Pdts N Amer Inc..........A 913 928-1000
Olathe *(G-7781)*

SAWING & PLANING MILLS

Kansas Hardwoods Inc..........F 785 456-8141
Belvue *(G-506)*
McCray Lumber Company..........E 913 780-0060
Olathe *(G-7882)*
Timber Products Inc..........E 316 941-9381
Wichita *(G-15766)*

SAWS & SAWING EQPT

Husqvarna Chain Saws & Pwr Eqp..........G 785 263-7668
Abilene *(G-41)*
Kanequip Inc..........F 785 632-3441
Clay Center *(G-869)*
Kaw Valley Industrial Inc..........G 785 841-9751
Eudora *(G-1876)*
Mid Kansas Tool & Electric Inc..........F 785 825-9521
Salina *(G-10600)*

SAWS: Hand, Metalworking Or Woodworking

Barrow Tooling Systems Inc..........G 785 364-4306
Holton *(G-3085)*

SAWS: Portable

Masterpiece Engineering LLC..........E 928 771-2040
Olathe *(G-7877)*

SCAFFOLDING WHOLESALERS

Brandsafway Services LLC..........F 913 342-9000
Kansas City *(G-3876)*

SCALE REPAIR SVCS

Express Scale Parts Inc..........E 913 441-4787
Lenexa *(G-5844)*
Hammel Scale Kansas City Inc..........F 913 321-5428
Kansas City *(G-4062)*
Salina Scale Sales & Service..........F 785 827-4441
Salina *(G-10690)*

SCALES & BALANCES, EXC LABORATORY

Express Scale Parts Inc..........E 913 441-4787
Lenexa *(G-5844)*
Hydeman Company Inc..........G 913 384-2620
Kansas City *(G-4090)*
Northeast Kansas Hydraulics..........G 785 235-0405
Topeka *(G-12936)*
Schroer Manufacturing Company..........C 913 281-1500
Kansas City *(G-4404)*

SCANNING DEVICES: Optical

General Dynamics Info Tech Inc..........E 785 832-0207
Lawrence *(G-4871)*

SCHOOL BUS SVC

All Point Transportation LLC..........F 785 273-4730
Topeka *(G-12305)*
Apple Bus Company..........D 913 592-5121
Spring Hill *(G-12077)*
Derby Public Schools..........D 316 788-8450
Derby *(G-1237)*
Durham School Services L P..........E 913 755-3593
Osawatomie *(G-8192)*
Durham School Services L P..........E 620 331-7088
Independence *(G-3512)*
Easton Bus Service Inc..........D 913 682-2244
Leavenworth *(G-5235)*
First Student Inc..........C 785 841-3594
Lawrence *(G-4864)*
First Student Inc..........F 913 856-5650
Gardner *(G-2345)*
First Student Inc..........C 913 782-1050
Olathe *(G-7713)*
Junction CT-Ft Rly Mht Trnsinc..........F 785 762-2219
Junction City *(G-3707)*
National Express LLC..........E 913 837-4470
Louisburg *(G-6460)*
National Express LLC..........E 620 662-1299
Hutchinson *(G-3388)*
National Express LLC..........F 620 326-3318
Wellington *(G-13519)*
Pratt Unified 12th Dist Transp..........F 620 672-4590
Pratt *(G-10145)*
Unified School District 383..........D 785 587-2190
Manhattan *(G-6838)*

SCHOOL FOR PHYSICALLY HANDICAPPED, NEC

Futures Unlimited Inc..........E 620 326-8906
Wellington *(G-13501)*
Heartspring Inc..........B 316 634-8700
Wichita *(G-14590)*

SCHOOL FOR RETARDED, NEC

Lakemary Center Inc..........E 913 768-6831
Olathe *(G-7853)*
Rainbows United Inc..........E 316 684-7060
Wichita *(G-15412)*

SCHOOL SPLYS, EXC BOOKS: Wholesalers

Pitsco Inc..........C 620 231-0000
Pittsburg *(G-9914)*
Pitsco Inc..........F 800 835-0686
Pittsburg *(G-9915)*
Superior School Supplies Inc..........F 620 421-3190
Parsons *(G-9743)*
U S Toy Co Inc..........E 913 642-8247
Leawood *(G-5587)*

SCHOOLS: Elementary & Secondary

Creme De La Creme Kansas Inc..........E 913 451-0858
Shawnee Mission *(G-11279)*
Garden City Public Schools..........E 620 275-0291
Garden City *(G-2176)*
Genesis School Inc..........E 913 845-9498
Tonganoxie *(G-12262)*
Hesston Unified School Dst 460..........E 620 327-2989
Hesston *(G-2993)*
Shirley Marley Enterprises..........F 913 492-0004
Shawnee Mission *(G-11865)*
Southeast Kans Educatn Svc Ctr..........C 620 724-6281
Girard *(G-2418)*
Southwest Plins Rgonal Svc Ctr..........D 620 675-2241
Sublette *(G-12207)*
Unified School District 259..........D 316 973-4200
Wichita *(G-15836)*

SCHOOLS: Vocational, NEC

Big Lkes Developmental Ctr Inc..........F 785 776-7748
Manhattan *(G-6559)*
Big Lkes Developmental Ctr Inc..........E 785 632-5357
Clay Center *(G-843)*
Big Lkes Developmental Ctr Inc..........F 785 776-0777
Manhattan *(G-6560)*
Big Lkes Developmental Ctr Inc..........D 785 776-9201
Manhattan *(G-6558)*
Unified School District 259..........C 316 973-4000
Wichita *(G-15833)*

SCRAP & WASTE MATERIALS, WHOLESALE: Ferrous Metal

Advantage Metals Recycling LLC..........E 913 321-3358
Kansas City *(G-3789)*
Advantage Metals Recycling LLC..........E 620 342-1122
Emporia *(G-1692)*
Advantage Metals Recycling LLC..........F 785 232-5152
Topeka *(G-12297)*
Asner Iron and Metal Co..........F 913 281-4000
Kansas City *(G-3822)*
Boge Iron & Metal Co Inc..........E 316 263-8241
Wichita *(G-13868)*
Erman Corporation Inc..........E 913 287-4800
Kansas City *(G-3996)*
Garden City Iron & Metal..........F 620 277-0227
Garden City *(G-2173)*
Mc Kinnes Iron & Metal Inc..........G 620 257-3821
Lyons *(G-6494)*
Midwest Iron & Metal Co Inc..........E 620 662-5663
Hutchinson *(G-3378)*
Wessel Iron & Supply Inc..........F 620 225-0568
Dodge City *(G-1453)*
Wichita Iron & Metals Corp Inc..........E 316 267-3291
Wichita *(G-16009)*

SCRAP & WASTE MATERIALS, WHOLESALE: Metal

Advantage Metals Recycling LLC..........D 620 674-3800
Columbus *(G-1059)*
Advantage Metals Recycling LLC..........E 913 621-2711
Kansas City *(G-3788)*
Advantage Metals Recycling LLC..........E 816 861-2700
Kansas City *(G-3790)*
Advantage Metals Recycling LLC..........E 785 841-0396
Lawrence *(G-4723)*
Allmetal Recycling LLC..........D 316 838-9381
Wichita *(G-13676)*

F & F Iron & Metal Co....E....785 877-3830
Norton *(G-7445)*
Salina Iron & Metal Company....E....785 826-9838
Salina *(G-10677)*
Scrap Management LLC....F....913 573-1000
Kansas City *(G-4408)*
Shostak Iron and Metal Co Inc....E....913 321-9210
Overland Park *(G-9309)*

SCRAP & WASTE MATERIALS, WHOLESALE: Oil

Environmental Protection Agcy....B....913 551-7118
Lenexa *(G-5835)*

SCRAP & WASTE MATERIALS, WHOLESALE: Paper

Batliner Paper Stock Company....F....913 233-1367
Kansas City *(G-3848)*

SCRAP & WASTE MATERIALS, WHOLESALE: Paper & Cloth Materials

National Fiber Supply LLC....F....913 321-0066
Kansas City *(G-4280)*

SCREENS: Window, Metal

Arko Manufacturing Co Inc....G....316 838-7162
Wichita *(G-13733)*

SCREW MACHINE PRDTS

Timken Smo LLC....B....620 223-0080
Fort Scott *(G-2008)*
Wescon Controls LLC....C....316 942-7266
Wichita *(G-15950)*

SCREWS: Metal

Milacron Marketing Company LLC....D....620 241-1624
McPherson *(G-7008)*

SEARCH & NAVIGATION SYSTEMS

B/E Aerospace Inc....C....913 338-7292
Shawnee Mission *(G-11142)*
Brittain Machine Inc....E....316 942-8223
Wichita *(G-13892)*
Cooper Electronics Inc....E....913 782-0012
Olathe *(G-7615)*
Garmin International Inc....G....913 440-8462
New Century *(G-7285)*
Garmin International Inc....E....312 787-3221
Olathe *(G-7721)*
H M Dunn Company Inc....C....314 535-6684
Wichita *(G-14533)*
Learjet Inc....A....316 946-2000
Wichita *(G-14940)*
Lyons Manufacturing Co Inc....E....620 257-2331
Lyons *(G-6491)*
Numerical Control Support Inc....E....913 441-3500
Shawnee Mission *(G-11690)*
Peavey Corporation....D....913 888-0600
Lenexa *(G-6047)*
Rockwell Collins Inc....C....316 677-4808
Wichita *(G-15474)*
Sigma Tek Inc....E....316 775-6373
Augusta *(G-345)*
Telecommunication Systems Inc....E....913 593-9489
Overland Park *(G-9401)*

SEARCH & RESCUE SVCS

Pk Safety Services Inc....D....316 260-4141
Augusta *(G-338)*

SEATING: Bleacher, Portable

Heartland Leasing Services Inc....F....913 268-0069
Shawnee *(G-10969)*
Heartland Seating Inc....F....913 268-0069
Shawnee *(G-10970)*

SEATING: Stadium

Integrated Stadium Seating Inc....F....316 494-6514
Wichita *(G-14705)*

SEATING: Transportation

Seats Incorporated....G....913 686-3137
Spring Hill *(G-12098)*

SECONDARY SCHOOLS, NEC

Cowley College & Area....B....620 442-0430
Arkansas City *(G-150)*

SECRETARIAL & COURT REPORTING

Copy Center of Topeka Inc....E....785 233-6677
Topeka *(G-12507)*
Davis Publications Inc....F....785 945-6170
Valley Falls *(G-13362)*
Graphic Images Inc....F....316 283-3776
Newton *(G-7352)*

SECRETARIAL SVCS

Answer Link....F....620 662-4427
Hutchinson *(G-3199)*
Omni Center II....F....316 689-4256
Wichita *(G-15217)*
Transcription Unlimited Inc....E....816 350-3800
Shawnee *(G-11042)*

SECURE STORAGE SVC: Document

Access Info MGT Shred Svcs LLC....E....913 492-4581
Lenexa *(G-5620)*
Salina Microfilm....F....785 827-6648
Salina *(G-10680)*
Underground Vaults & Stor Inc....E....620 662-6769
Hutchinson *(G-3472)*
Underground Vaults & Stor Inc....F....316 838-2121
Wichita *(G-15831)*
Underground Vaults & Stor Inc....E....620 663-5434
Hutchinson *(G-3473)*

SECURITY & COMMODITY EXCHANGES

Cboe Bats LLC....E....913 815-7000
Lenexa *(G-5736)*

SECURITY CONTROL EQPT & SYSTEMS

4pc LLC....G....316 833-6906
Augusta *(G-299)*
Advance Systems International....E....913 888-3578
Lenexa *(G-5631)*
Advanced Infrared Systems....G....913 888-3578
Lenexa *(G-5633)*

SECURITY DEVICES

Prime SEC Svcs Borrower LLC....F....630 410-0662
Lawrence *(G-5076)*
Wilbur Inc....F....913 207-6535
Olathe *(G-8154)*

SECURITY EQPT STORES

ADT LLC....E....316 858-4300
Wichita *(G-13618)*
Williams Investigation & SEC....E....620 275-1134
Garden City *(G-2315)*

SECURITY GUARD SVCS

Clark Security Service....F....620 225-6577
Dodge City *(G-1324)*
Day & Zimmermann Kansas LLC....C....620 421-7400
Parsons *(G-9679)*
Diamond Security Lc....E....316 263-3883
Wichita *(G-14209)*
Eagle Security Inc....D....913 721-1360
Kansas City *(G-3979)*
Eagle Security Services....D....620 251-0085
Coffeyville *(G-935)*
Guardsmark LLC....C....316 440-6646
Wichita *(G-14525)*
Livewatch Security LLC....F....785 844-2130
Saint Marys *(G-10372)*
Orion Security Inc....D....913 385-5657
Overland Park *(G-9114)*
Rees Contract Service Inc....B....913 888-0590
Shawnee Mission *(G-11786)*
Rockwell Security LLC....F....913 362-3300
Shawnee *(G-11021)*
Securitas SEC Svcs USA Inc....C....316 838-2900
Wichita *(G-15540)*
Silva Security Service....E....316 942-7872
Wichita *(G-15594)*
Strawder Security Service....F....620 343-8392
Emporia *(G-1831)*
Total Security Solutions LLC....E....316 209-0436
Wichita *(G-15776)*

SECURITY PROTECTIVE DEVICES MAINTENANCE & MONITORING SVCS

Tech Electronics Kansas LLC....E....785 379-0300
Topeka *(G-13149)*

SECURITY SYSTEMS SERVICES

ACS Electronic Systems Inc....E....913 248-8828
Lenexa *(G-5625)*
ADT 24 7 Alarm and Security....D....620 860-0229
Pratt *(G-10094)*
ADT LLC....C....316 858-6628
Wichita *(G-13617)*
Advance Systems International....E....913 888-3578
Lenexa *(G-5631)*
Advanced Infrared Systems....G....913 888-3578
Lenexa *(G-5633)*
Alliance Monitoring Tech LLC....F....316 263-7775
Wichita *(G-13670)*
CAM-Dex Corporation....F....913 621-6160
Kansas City *(G-3885)*
Eichhorn Holdings LLC....F....785 843-1426
Lawrence *(G-4848)*
Foresite Msp LLC....E....800 940-4699
Overland Park *(G-8734)*
Overfield Corporation....F....785 843-3434
Lawrence *(G-5052)*
Prime SEC Svcs Borrower LLC....F....630 410-0662
Lawrence *(G-5076)*
Riskanalytics LLC....E....913 685-6526
Overland Park *(G-9243)*
S N C Inc....E....620 665-6651
Hutchinson *(G-3434)*
Sentinel Real Estate Corp....F....316 265-9471
Wichita *(G-15562)*
Siemens Industry Inc....E....316 946-4190
Wichita *(G-15585)*
Wanda America Inv Holdg Co Ltd....A....913 213-2000
Leawood *(G-5595)*
Westar Industries Inc....C....785 575-6507
Topeka *(G-13240)*

SECURITY UNDERWRITERS

Infinity Insur Solutions LLC....E....913 338-3200
Leawood *(G-5436)*
Waddell & Reed Inc....A....913 236-2000
Shawnee Mission *(G-11987)*

SEEDS & BULBS WHOLESALERS

Lone Pine AG Services Inc....F....785 887-6559
Lecompton *(G-5612)*

SELF-HELP ORGANIZATION, NEC

For Central Kansas Foundation....D....785 825-6224
Salina *(G-10504)*
Options Dom & Sexual Violenc....F....785 625-4202
Hays *(G-2883)*

SELF-PROPELLED AIRCRAFT DEALER

Executive Beechcraft Inc....E....913 782-9003
New Century *(G-7284)*

SEMICONDUCTORS & RELATED DEVICES

Integra Holdings Inc....D....316 630-6805
Wichita *(G-14698)*
Integra Technologies LLC....C....316 630-6800
Wichita *(G-14699)*
Telecommunication Systems Inc....E....913 593-9489
Overland Park *(G-9401)*

SEPARATORS: Metal Plate

Taylor Forge Engineered....C....785 867-2590
Paola *(G-9592)*

SEPTIC TANK CLEANING SVCS

Daves Pumping Service Inc....F....620 343-3081
Emporia *(G-1727)*

SEPTIC TANKS: Concrete

W H Debrick Co Inc................................F 913 294-3281
Paola *(G-9595)*

SERVICES, NEC

Service USA Inc.......................................E 913 543-3844
Leawood *(G-5550)*
Tucson Transformer & Appa.................F 620 227-5100
Dodge City *(G-1441)*

SEWAGE & WATER TREATMENT EQPT

General Tech A Svcs & Pdts Co..............G....... 913 766-5566
Olathe *(G-7727)*

SEWAGE FACILITIES

Carson Mobile HM Pk Sewer Dst...........D....... 785 537-6330
Manhattan *(G-6577)*
City of Leavenworth...............................F 913 682-1090
Leavenworth *(G-5221)*
City of Topeka...E 785 368-3860
Topeka *(G-12472)*
Johnson County Unified Wstwtr...........D....... 913 715-8500
Olathe *(G-7819)*
Operations Management Intl Inc...........E 913 367-5563
Atchison *(G-252)*
Ray Lindsey Co.......................................F 913 339-6666
Olathe *(G-8019)*
Utility Maintenance Contrs LLC.............F 316 945-8833
Wichita *(G-15867)*

SEWAGE TREATMENT SYSTEMS & EQPT

Hertel Tank Service Inc..........................G....... 785 628-2445
Hays *(G-2841)*

SEWER CLEANING & RODDING SVC

A 1 Sewer & Septic Service....................F 913 631-5201
Kansas City *(G-3777)*
David Cobler...F 785 234-3384
Topeka *(G-12547)*
P & W Incorporated.................................E 316 267-4277
Wichita *(G-15247)*
Reid Plumbing Heating & AC Inc...........F 785 537-2869
Manhattan *(G-6789)*

SEWING CONTRACTORS

Hoffmann Fabricating LLC......................F 316 262-6041
Wichita *(G-14623)*

SEWING MACHINE REPAIR SHOP

Sew Easy Sewing Center Inc.................F........ 913 341-1122
Overland Park *(G-9301)*

SEWING MACHINE STORES

Sew Easy Sewing Center Inc.................F........ 913 341-1122
Overland Park *(G-9301)*

SEWING MACHINES & PARTS: Household

Swiss Made Inc..F 913 341-6400
Overland Park *(G-9383)*

SHAPES & PILINGS, STRUCTURAL: Steel

Earth Contact Products LLC...................F 913 393-0007
Olathe *(G-7665)*
Maico Industries Inc...............................D....... 785 472-5390
Ellsworth *(G-1677)*
Pitt Steel LLC...G....... 620 231-8100
Pittsburg *(G-9919)*

SHEARS

Agra Axe International Inc.......................E 620 879-5858
Caney *(G-664)*

SHEET METAL SPECIALTIES, EXC STAMPED

Accu-Fab Inc..F 785 862-0100
Topeka *(G-12283)*
Kice Industries Inc...................................C 316 744-7148
Park City *(G-9625)*
Tartan Manufacturing Inc........................C 913 432-7100
Kansas City *(G-4458)*
Tk Metals Inc..G....... 913 667-3055
Lenexa *(G-6183)*
Tower Metal Works Inc............................E 785 256-4281
Maple Hill *(G-6865)*
Trieb Sheet Metal Co................................E 913 831-1166
Kansas City *(G-4474)*
Vista Manufacturing Company...............E 913 342-4939
Kansas City *(G-4521)*

SHEETING: Window, Plastic

Worldwide Windows.................................F 785 826-1701
Salina *(G-10773)*

SHELTERED WORKSHOPS

Achievement Svcs For Ne Kans..............E 913 367-2432
Atchison *(G-202)*
Big Lkes Developmental Ctr Inc.............E 785 632-5357
Clay Center *(G-843)*
Cof Training Services Inc.......................D....... 785 242-5035
Ottawa *(G-8258)*
Cof Training Services Inc.......................E 620 364-2151
Burlington *(G-627)*
Cof Training Services Inc.......................D....... 785 242-6064
Ottawa *(G-8259)*
Futures Unlimited Inc...............................E 620 326-8906
Wellington *(G-13501)*
Hetlinger Dvlopmental Svcs Inc.............E 620 342-1087
Emporia *(G-1771)*
Tri-Ko Inc...E 913 755-3025
Osawatomie *(G-8205)*
Tri-Valley Developmental Svcs..............D....... 620 223-3990
Fort Scott *(G-2012)*
Tri-Valley Developmental Svcs..............D....... 620 365-3307
Iola *(G-3637)*

SHELVING, MADE FROM PURCHASED WIRE

Lynk Inc...F 913 492-9202
Shawnee Mission *(G-11586)*

SHELVING: Office & Store, Exc Wood

E-Z Shelving Systems Inc........................F 913 384-1331
Shawnee Mission *(G-11324)*

SHIP BUILDING & REPAIRING: Offshore Sply Boats

North Shore Marina MGT LLC.................G....... 785 453-2240
Quenemo *(G-10178)*

SHIPPING AGENTS

Northwind Merchant Company................F........ 785 856-1183
Lawrence *(G-5042)*
Preferred Cartage Service Inc................D....... 620 276-8080
Garden City *(G-2259)*
U P S Stores...F 913 829-3750
Olathe *(G-8129)*
Yusen Logistics Americas Inc................E 913 768-4484
Olathe *(G-8165)*

SHOE MATERIALS: Counters

Vorona LLC...G....... 913 888-4646
Lenexa *(G-6217)*

SHOE MATERIALS: Quarters

French Quarter LLC..................................G....... 316 440-7004
Wichita *(G-14422)*

SHOE STORES

Sharks Investment Inc..............................F 785 841-8289
Lawrence *(G-5109)*
Urban Outfitters Inc..................................E 785 331-2885
Lawrence *(G-5169)*

SHOE STORES: Orthopedic

Tradehome Shoe Stores Inc....................G....... 785 539-4003
Manhattan *(G-6830)*

SHOPPING CENTERS & MALLS

Flint Hills Mall LLC...................................F 620 342-4631
Emporia *(G-1759)*
Forest City Enterprises Inc.....................E 785 539-3500
Manhattan *(G-6638)*
Melvin Simon & Associates Inc..............D....... 620 665-5307
Hutchinson *(G-3372)*
Mtc Development LLC.............................E 785 539-3500
Manhattan *(G-6755)*
Oak Park Mall...E 913 888-4400
Overland Park *(G-9096)*
Pauline Food Center................................F 785 862-2774
Topeka *(G-12965)*
Rainbow Village Management.................E 913 677-3060
Kansas City *(G-4361)*
Rubenstein Real Estate Co LLC..............F 913 362-1999
Shawnee Mission *(G-11815)*
Timothy D White.......................................F 620 331-7060
Independence *(G-3565)*
Town Center Plaza LLC............................F 913 498-1111
Leawood *(G-5581)*
Towne East Square...................................E 316 686-9672
Wichita *(G-15780)*
Washington Prime Group Inc..................E 316 945-9374
Wichita *(G-15931)*

SHOT PEENING SVC

Metal Finishing Company Inc..................F 316 267-7289
Wichita *(G-15053)*
Metal Improvement Company LLC.........E 620 326-5509
Wellington *(G-13517)*

SHOWER STALLS: Plastic & Fiberglass

Arlwin Mfg Co Inc.....................................F 785 282-6487
Smith Center *(G-12031)*
Charloma Inc...E 620 364-2701
Burlington *(G-626)*

SHUTTERS, DOOR & WINDOW: Metal

Tracker Door Systems LLC......................G....... 913 585-3100
De Soto *(G-1214)*
Wheatbelt Inc..G....... 620 947-2323
Hillsboro *(G-3058)*

SIDING & STRUCTURAL MATERIALS: Wood

Advantage Framing Systems Inc............E 913 592-4150
Spring Hill *(G-12075)*

SIDING, INSULATING: Impregnated, From Purchased Materials

Superior Home Improvements LLC........G....... 620 225-3560
Dodge City *(G-1437)*

SIGN LETTERING & PAINTING SVCS

Allsigns LLC..G....... 785 232-5512
Topeka *(G-12308)*

SIGN PAINTING & LETTERING SHOP

Creative Signs & Design Inc...................G....... 785 233-8000
Topeka *(G-12528)*

SIGNALS: Traffic Control, Electric

City Traffic Operation...............................F 785 368-3913
Topeka *(G-12477)*

SIGNALS: Transportation

Nu-Line Company Inc...............................F 316 942-0990
Wichita *(G-15199)*

SIGNS & ADVERTISING SPECIALTIES

Allsigns LLC..G....... 785 232-5512
Topeka *(G-12308)*
Artstudio Signs & Design........................F 620 663-3950
Hutchinson *(G-3207)*
Ballyhoo Banners.....................................G....... 913 385-5050
Lenexa *(G-5684)*
Bandy Enterprises Inc..............................F 785 462-3361
Colby *(G-988)*
Brileys Designs & Signs...........................E 913 579-7533
Shawnee Mission *(G-11182)*
Creative Signs & Design Inc...................G....... 785 233-8000
Topeka *(G-12528)*
Cvr Manufacturing Inc.............................G....... 620 763-2500
Galesburg *(G-2091)*
Excel Lighting LLC...................................G....... 816 461-4694
Kansas City *(G-3998)*
Express Print and Signs LLC...................E 785 825-8434
Salina *(G-10491)*
Fast Signs Inc..G....... 785 271-8899
Topeka *(G-12598)*
Fastsigns Inc...G....... 913 649-3600
Overland Park *(G-8707)*

Finch Sign Company Inc ....G....... 785 423-3213
Baldwin City (G-360)
George Eschbaugh Advg Inc ....E....... 785 658-2105
Wilson (G-16105)
Gleason & Son Signs Inc ....G....... 785 823-8615
Salina (G-10512)
Halfpricebannerscom Inc ....G....... 913 441-9299
Shawnee (G-10966)
Hasty Awards Inc ....D....... 785 242-5297
Ottawa (G-8278)
Hmong Manufacturing Inc ....E....... 913 371-2752
Kansas City (G-4083)
Hutch Sign ....G....... 620 663-6108
Hutchinson (G-3317)
K C Sign Express Inc ....G....... 913 432-2500
Shawnee Mission (G-11506)
Kansas Graphics Inc ....G....... 620 273-6111
Cottonwood Falls (G-1155)
Lowen Corporation ....B....... 620 663-2161
Hutchinson (G-3358)
Luminous Neon Inc ....G....... 785 842-4930
Lawrence (G-5002)
Luminous Neon Inc ....E....... 913 780-3330
Olathe (G-7867)
Midtown Signs LLC ....F....... 816 561-7446
Kansas City (G-4249)
Midwest Sign Company LLC ....F....... 913 568-7552
Kansas City (G-4258)
Next Led Signs LLC ....F....... 888 263-6530
Wichita (G-15174)
Occk Inc ....E....... 785 738-3490
Beloit (G-498)
Oversize Warning Products Inc ....G....... 620 792-5266
Great Bend (G-2620)
Print Source Inc ....D....... 316 945-7052
Wichita (G-15348)
Schurle Signs Inc ....G....... 785 832-9897
Lawrence (G-5104)
Selex Es Inc ....D....... 913 945-2600
Overland Park (G-9293)
Sign Solutions ....F....... 620 442-5649
Arkansas City (G-179)
Signs & Design LLC ....G....... 316 264-7446
Wichita (G-15592)
Signs By Shire Inc ....G....... 316 838-1362
Park City (G-9645)
Signs of Business Inc ....F....... 316 683-5700
Wichita (G-15593)
Simon & Simon Inc ....G....... 913 888-9889
Overland Park (G-9311)
Stouse LLC ....C....... 913 764-5757
New Century (G-7301)
Thomas Outdoor Advertising Inc ....G....... 785 537-2010
Manhattan (G-6825)
Tradenet Publishing Inc ....C....... 913 856-4070
Gardner (G-2365)
U S S A Inc ....G....... 316 686-1653
Wichita (G-15826)
Vital Sign Center ....G....... 913 262-4447
Kansas City (G-4522)
Wrap Factory ....G....... 913 667-3010
Edwardsville (G-1522)
X-Press Signs and Graphics LLC ....G....... 316 613-2360
Wichita (G-16083)
Young Sign Co Inc ....E....... 913 651-5432
Leavenworth (G-5310)

SIGNS & ADVERTISING SPECIALTIES: Scoreboards, Electric

Power Ad Company Inc ....E....... 785 823-9483
Salina (G-10638)

SIGNS & ADVERTISING SPECIALTIES: Signs

E-Z Info Inc ....F....... 913 367-5020
Atchison (G-226)
Graphics Systems Inc ....D....... 316 267-4171
Wichita (G-14497)
Hightech Signs LLC ....E....... 913 894-4422
Kansas City (G-4079)
Js Sign & Awning LLC ....G....... 785 776-8860
Manhattan (G-6667)
Millers Sign Shoppe LLC ....G....... 913 441-6883
Bonner Springs (G-563)
National Sign Company Inc ....F....... 785 242-4111
Ottawa (G-8293)
Northwest Awards & Signs ....G....... 785 621-2116
Hays (G-2880)

SIGNS & ADVERTSG SPECIALTIES: Displays/Cutouts Window/Lobby

File A Gem Inc ....G....... 620 856-3800
Baxter Springs (G-407)

SIGNS, ELECTRICAL: Wholesalers

K C Sign Express Inc ....G....... 913 432-2500
Shawnee Mission (G-11506)

SIGNS, EXC ELECTRIC, WHOLESALE

Ballyhoo Banners ....G....... 913 385-5050
Lenexa (G-5684)
Raymarr Inc ....F....... 913 648-3480
Shawnee Mission (G-11778)
Signs of Business Inc ....F....... 316 683-5700
Wichita (G-15593)
Sunburst Systems Inc ....F....... 913 383-9309
Kansas City (G-4446)
Traftec Inc ....F....... 913 621-2919
Kansas City (G-4472)

SIGNS: Electrical

Coffelt Sign Co Inc ....G....... 620 343-6411
Emporia (G-1724)
Commercial Sign Company Hay ....F....... 785 625-1765
Hays (G-2775)
Custom Neon & Vinyl Graphics ....G....... 785 233-3218
Topeka (G-12538)
Freestyle Sign Co Inc ....G....... 316 267-5507
Wichita (G-14420)
Luminous Neon Inc ....D....... 620 662-2363
Hutchinson (G-3360)
Luminous Neon Inc ....G....... 785 823-1789
Salina (G-10586)
Rise Vision USA Inc ....F....... 866 770-1150
Wichita (G-15465)
Rons Sign Co Inc ....E....... 316 267-8914
Wichita (G-15482)
Sign Here Inc ....G....... 913 856-0148
Gardner (G-2363)
Star Signs & Graphics Inc ....E....... 785 842-2881
Lawrence (G-5120)
Trimark Signworks Inc ....E....... 316 263-2224
Wichita (G-15800)
Welch Sign Co Inc ....G....... 913 831-4499
Shawnee Mission (G-11998)

SIGNS: Neon

Excell Art Sign Products LLC ....G....... 620 378-4477
Fredonia (G-2031)
Excellart Sign Products LLC ....F....... 913 764-2364
Olathe (G-7697)
Hedges Neon Sales Inc ....G....... 785 827-9341
Salina (G-10540)
Schurle Signs Inc ....F....... 785 485-2885
Riley (G-10209)
Sign House Inc ....E....... 785 827-2729
Salina (G-10707)
Young Hoins Service Group LLC ....F....... 913 772-0708
Leavenworth (G-5309)

SILK SCREEN DESIGN SVCS

Air Capitol Dial Inc ....F....... 316 264-2483
Wichita (G-13649)
Khaos Apparel LLC ....F....... 316 804-4900
Newton (G-7370)
Plainjans Feedlot Service ....F....... 620 872-5777
Scott City (G-10827)
Printery Inc ....F....... 785 632-5501
Clay Center (G-877)
Wilbert Screen Printing Inc ....G....... 620 231-1730
Pittsburg (G-9970)

SKATING RINKS: Roller

Carousel Skate Center Inc ....E....... 316 942-4505
Wichita (G-13953)
Entertainment Specialties ....F....... 620 342-3322
Emporia (G-1750)
Roller City Inc ....F....... 316 942-4555
Wichita (G-15477)
Sk8away Inc ....E....... 785 272-0303
Topeka (G-13075)
Skate South Inc ....F....... 316 524-7261
Wichita (G-15600)
Starlite Skate Center South ....F....... 785 862-2241
Topeka (G-13096)

SKILL TRAINING CENTER

Nickell Barracks Training Ctr ....E....... 785 822-1198
Salina (G-10613)

SLAUGHTERING & MEAT PACKING

Creekstone Farm Prem ....A....... 620 741-3100
Arkansas City (G-152)
Duis Meat Processing Inc ....F....... 785 243-7850
Concordia (G-1109)
Elkhorn Valley Packing Co ....D....... 620 896-2300
Harper (G-2721)
Kirby Meat Co Inc ....G....... 620 225-0031
Dodge City (G-1392)
National Beef Packing Co LLC ....F....... 800 449-2333
Liberal (G-6348)

SMOKE DETECTORS

Darrow Company ....G....... 800 525-6084
Overland Park (G-8635)

SNACK & NONALCOHOLIC BEVERAGE BARS

B & E Inc ....F....... 913 299-1110
Kansas City (G-3833)
Lynco Rec Inc ....F....... 620 231-2222
Pittsburg (G-9896)
Twin Fiddle Investment Co LLC ....E....... 316 788-2855
Derby (G-1277)

SNOW PLOWING SVCS

4t Total Lawn Inc ....E....... 913 888-0997
Shawnee Mission (G-11059)
Biehler Companies Inc ....D....... 316 529-0002
Wichita (G-13847)
Jojacs Landscape & Mowing ....F....... 316 945-3525
Haysville (G-2950)
Karcher Investments Inc ....F....... 785 452-2850
Salina (G-10568)
Signature Landscape LLC ....C....... 913 829-8181
Olathe (G-8066)
Total Lease Service Inc ....G....... 785 735-9520
Hays (G-2920)
True North Outdoor LLC ....E....... 913 322-1340
Kansas City (G-4476)
True North Services LLC ....E....... 888 478-9470
Shawnee Mission (G-11945)
Tuff Turf Inc ....F....... 913 362-4545
Shawnee Mission (G-11948)
Turf Management LLC ....F....... 785 410-0394
Manhattan (G-6833)
Willowridge Landscape Inc ....F....... 785 842-7022
Lawrence (G-5186)

SOAPS & DETERGENTS

ACS Iiiiii - Ks LLC ....F....... 316 683-3489
Wichita (G-13609)
Prosoco Inc ....D....... 785 865-4200
Lawrence (G-5081)
Vvf Kansas Services LLC ....C....... 913 529-2292
Kansas City (G-4525)

SOCIAL CHANGE ASSOCIATION

Heartland Hbtat For Hmnity Inc ....F....... 913 342-3047
Kansas City (G-4075)
Winfield Area Hbtat For Hmnity ....E....... 620 221-7298
Winfield (G-16184)

SOCIAL CLUBS

Field & Stream Club Inc ....F....... 785 233-4793
Topeka (G-12608)
Jewish Cmnty Ctr Grter Kans Cy ....B....... 913 327-8000
Shawnee Mission (G-11486)
Masonic Lodge ....F....... 620 662-7012
Hutchinson (G-3366)
Spirit/Boeing Employees Assn ....F....... 316 522-2996
Wichita (G-15645)
St Marys Literary Club ....E....... 785 437-6418
Saint Marys (G-10376)

SOCIAL SERVICES INFORMATION EXCHANGE

Alcoholics Anonymous ....F....... 316 684-3661
Wichita (G-13660)

Erc/Resource & Referral Inc ....F 785 357-5171
Topeka (G-12580)
United Methodist Open Door ....E 316 265-9371
Wichita (G-15844)

SOCIAL SERVICES, NEC

Saint Francis Community ....D 785 825-0541
Salina (G-10661)

SOCIAL SVCS CENTER

Armed Services YMCA of USA ....F 785 238-2972
Junction City (G-3668)
Breakthrough House Inc ....E 785 232-6807
Topeka (G-12404)
Catholic Charities of Salina ....F 785 825-0208
Salina (G-10437)
Catholic Chrties Nrthast Kans ....D 913 433-2100
Kansas City (G-3897)
Dandelion & Mudd Puddles Cdc ....E 913 825-0399
Shawnee (G-10940)
Disability Rights Ctr of Kans ....F 785 273-9661
Topeka (G-12559)
East Central Kansas Economic ....E 785 242-6413
Ottawa (G-8266)
Economic Opprtunity Foundation ....E 913 371-7800
Kansas City (G-3980)
Episcopal Social Services Inc ....E 316 269-4160
Wichita (G-14297)
Family Life Services Emporia ....F 620 342-2244
Emporia (G-1754)
Humankind Mnstries Wichita Inc ....E 316 264-9303
Wichita (G-14652)
Humankind Mnstries Wichita Inc ....F 316 264-8051
Wichita (G-14653)
Interntnal Rscue Committee Inc ....E 316 201-1804
Wichita (G-14710)
Jewish Family Services ....E 913 327-8250
Overland Park (G-8874)
Lets Help Inc ....E 785 234-6208
Topeka (G-12839)
Manhattan Emrgncy Shelter Inc ....F 785 537-3113
Manhattan (G-6722)
New Beginnings Inc ....F 620 966-0274
Hutchinson (G-3390)
Resource Center For Ind Living ....F 785 267-1717
Topeka (G-13010)
Salina Rescue Mission Inc ....F 785 823-3317
Salina (G-10689)
Senior Center ....E 316 835-2283
Halstead (G-2704)
Southeast Kans Mental Hlth Ctr ....F 913 352-8214
Pleasanton (G-10002)
Topeka Ind Lving Rsrce Ctr Inc ....E 785 233-4572
Topeka (G-13179)
Union Rescue Mission Inc ....E 316 687-4673
Wichita (G-15839)
Wichita Family Crisis Ctr Inc ....F 316 263-7501
Wichita (G-15998)

SOCIAL SVCS, HANDICAPPED

Brown Cnty Developmental Svcs ....E 785 742-2053
Hiawatha (G-3004)
Community Living Serv ....C 620 227-8803
Dodge City (G-1327)
Developmental Svcs NW Kans ....F 785 735-2262
Victoria (G-13373)
Disablty Spprts of The Grt Pln ....C 620 241-8411
McPherson (G-6957)
Donipan Cnty Svcs & Workskills ....E 913 365-5561
Elwood (G-1684)
Flinthills Services Inc ....D 316 321-2325
El Dorado (G-1562)
Independence Inc ....E 785 841-0333
Lawrence (G-4910)
Link Inc ....F 785 625-6942
Hays (G-2864)
Mission Project Inc ....F 913 777-6722
Shawnee Mission (G-11647)
Mosaic ....C 620 231-5590
Pittsburg (G-9909)
Prairie Ind Lving Resource Ctr ....F 620 663-3989
Hutchinson (G-3411)
Resource Center For Ind Living ....D 785 528-3105
Osage City (G-8187)
Sedgwick Cnty Dvlpmntl Dsablty ....E 316 660-7630
Wichita (G-15545)
Three Rivers Inc ....F 785 456-9915
Wamego (G-13444)

Tri-Valley Developmental Svcs ....D 620 365-3307
Iola (G-3637)

SOCIAL SVCS: Individual & Family

Abwa Management LLC ....E 913 732-5100
Overland Park (G-8338)
Alzheimrs Dsease Rltd Dsordrs ....F 913 381-3888
Shawnee Mission (G-11100)
American National Red Cross ....E 620 446-0966
Arkansas City (G-142)
Andrea Clark ....D 913 683-3061
Leavenworth (G-5203)
Arrowhead West Inc ....F 620 225-5177
Dodge City (G-1298)
Bethel Neighborhood Center ....F 913 371-8218
Kansas City (G-3858)
Cancer Council of Reno County ....F 620 665-5555
Hutchinson (G-3228)
Catholic Charities ....E 913 433-2061
Shawnee Mission (G-11206)
Catholic Charities of ....D 913 721-1570
Kansas City (G-3895)
Catholic Charities of Northeas ....E 913 621-5090
Overland Park (G-8526)
Catholic Chrties Fndtion Nrtha ....C 913 621-1504
Kansas City (G-3896)
Communities In School ....E 316 973-5110
Wichita (G-14077)
Community Action Inc ....E 785 235-9561
Topeka (G-12490)
Community Lving Opprtnties Inc ....C 785 865-5520
Lawrence (G-4804)
Counseling Ctr For Butlr Cnty ....D 316 776-2007
El Dorado (G-1552)
County of Decatur ....F 785 475-8113
Oberlin (G-7489)
County of Doniphan ....F 785 985-2380
Troy (G-13273)
County of Riley ....F 785 537-4040
Manhattan (G-6602)
Cowley Cnty Mntl Hlth & Cnslng ....D 620 442-4540
Winfield (G-16129)
Cowley County Crime Stoppers ....F 620 221-7777
Winfield (G-16131)
Dccca Inc ....F 785 830-8238
Lawrence (G-4828)
Developmental Svcs NW Kans Inc ....C 785 625-2521
Hays (G-2786)
El Centro Inc ....F 913 677-1115
Kansas City (G-3983)
Elizabeth B Ballard Comm Ctr ....F 785 842-0729
Lawrence (G-4851)
Emergency Assistance Sites ....F 913 782-3640
Olathe (G-7678)
Families Together Inc ....F 620 276-6364
Garden City (G-2154)
First Choice Support Services ....F 785 823-3555
Salina (G-10502)
Florence Crittenton Services ....E 785 233-0516
Topeka (G-12619)
Four Cnty Mental Hlth Ctr Inc ....C 620 251-8180
Coffeyville (G-939)
Franklin Cnty Cncer Foundation ....F 785 242-6703
Ottawa (G-8274)
Health and Envmt Kans Dept ....E 620 272-3600
Garden City (G-2192)
Health Management Strategies ....F 785 233-1165
Topeka (G-12673)
Heart Spport Group For Bttred ....F 620 275-5911
Garden City (G-2193)
Hutchnson Hosp Psychiatric Ctr ....E 620 665-2364
Hutchinson (G-3330)
Jewish Cmnty Ctr Grter Kans Cy ....B 913 327-8000
Shawnee Mission (G-11486)
Jones Foundation ....F 620 342-1714
Emporia (G-1781)
Junction City Family YMCA Inc ....E 785 762-4780
Junction City (G-3704)
Kansas Affordable Housing Corp ....E 316 942-4848
Wichita (G-14785)
Kansas Childrens Service Leag ....F 620 626-5339
Liberal (G-6326)
Kansas Childrens Service Leag ....D 620 276-3232
Garden City (G-2213)
Kansas Dept For Chldren Fmlies ....D 620 421-4500
Parsons (G-9696)
Kansas Laleche League Inc ....F 785 865-5919
Lawrence (G-4934)
Kansas Statewide Homeless ....F 785 354-4990
Lawrence (G-4937)

Lawrence Wmens Trnstnal Cre S ....F 785 865-3956
Lawrence (G-4989)
Maison De Naissance Foundation ....F 913 402-6800
Leawood (G-5463)
Marshall County Agcy On Aging ....F 785 562-5522
Marysville (G-6895)
Martin Luther Homes Kansas Inc ....D 620 229-8702
Winfield (G-16156)
Medical Assistance Progra ....F 785 842-0726
Lawrence (G-5021)
Medicalodges Inc ....C 620 223-5085
Fort Scott (G-1984)
Mha Residential Care Inc ....D 316 685-1821
Wichita (G-15063)
Occk Inc ....E 785 243-1977
Concordia (G-1125)
Occk Inc ....E 785 738-3490
Beloit (G-498)
Pawnee Mental Health Svcs Inc ....C 785 762-5250
Manhattan (G-6769)
Pawnee Mental Health Svcs Inc ....E 785 587-4344
Manhattan (G-6770)
Rainbows United Inc ....E 316 684-7060
Wichita (G-15412)
Restorative Justice Authority ....F 620 235-7118
Pittsburg (G-9927)
Ronald McDnald Hse Chrties Nrt ....F 785 235-6852
Topeka (G-13028)
Saint Francis Acdmy Inc Atchsn ....F 785 625-6651
Hays (G-2905)
Saint Francis Cmnty Svcs Inc ....C 785 462-6679
Colby (G-1039)
Saint Francis Cmnty Svcs Inc ....F 620 326-6373
Wellington (G-13526)
Saint Francis Cmnty Svcs Inc ....D 785 243-4215
Concordia (G-1128)
Saint Frncis Acdemy Hutchinson ....E 620 669-3734
Hutchinson (G-3436)
Saint Vincent Depaul Society ....D 620 421-8004
Parsons (G-9735)
Salvation Army ....F 620 343-3166
Emporia (G-1821)
South Central Mntl Hlth CN ....F 316 775-5491
Augusta (G-346)
Southeast Kans Mental Hlth Ctr ....E 620 365-5717
Iola (G-3633)
Southwest Guidance Center ....F 620 624-8171
Liberal (G-6370)
Sunporch of Smith Center ....F 785 506-6003
Smith Center (G-12044)
Tfi Family Services Inc ....F 620 231-0443
Pittsburg (G-9945)
Tfi Family Services Inc ....F 913 894-2985
Overland Park (G-9404)
Unified School District 259 ....F 316 683-3315
Wichita (G-15835)
United Methodist Western Kansa ....E 620 275-1766
Garden City (G-2307)
United Way of McPherson County ....E 620 241-5152
McPherson (G-7036)
Valeo Behavioral Health Care ....E 785 233-1730
Topeka (G-13215)
Via Chrsti HM Hlth Wichita Inc ....D 316 268-8588
Wichita (G-15900)
Villages Inc ....F 785 267-5900
Topeka (G-13224)
West Side Good Neighbor Center ....F 316 942-7349
Wichita (G-15956)
Womens Chldren Shelter Linwood ....D 620 231-0415
Pittsburg (G-9971)
YMCA Topeaka Downtown Branch ....E 785 354-8591
Topeka (G-13256)
Young Kansas Christian ....C 785 233-1750
Topeka (G-13257)
Young Mens Christian ....F 785 233-9815
Topeka (G-13258)
Young Mens Christian Assn ....E 620 275-1199
Garden City (G-2319)
Young Mens Christian Assoc At ....D 913 367-4948
Atchison (G-272)
Young Mens Christian Associa ....C 316 219-9622
Wichita (G-16093)
Young Mens Christian Associa ....D 316 320-9622
El Dorado (G-1616)
Young Mens Christian Associa ....D 316 260-9622
Wichita (G-16094)
Young Mens Christian Associa ....C 316 942-5511
Wichita (G-16095)
Young Mens Christian Associat ....C 620 545-7290
Viola (G-13380)

Young Mens Christian Gr Kansas ....D....... 913 362-3489
Prairie Village *(G-10088)*
Young Mens Christian Gr Kansas ....C....... 913 393-9622
Olathe *(G-8163)*
Young Mens Christian Gr Kansas ....D....... 913 782-7707
Olathe *(G-8164)*
Young MNS Chrstn Assn of Tpeka ....C....... 785 354-8591
Topeka *(G-13259)*
Young MNS Chrstn Assn Pttsburg ....D....... 620 231-1100
Pittsburg *(G-9972)*

SOCIAL WORKER

Counseling & Mediation Center ....F....... 316 269-2322
Wichita *(G-14106)*
Guidance Center ....E....... 913 367-1593
Atchison *(G-233)*

SOFT DRINKS WHOLESALERS

American Bottling Company ....F....... 620 223-6166
Fort Scott *(G-1954)*
Coca-Cola Company ....F....... 785 243-1071
Concordia *(G-1107)*
Coca-Cola Refreshments USA Inc ....B....... 913 492-8100
Shawnee Mission *(G-11243)*
Pepsi Cola Btlg Co of Salina ....D....... 785 827-7297
Salina *(G-10633)*
Pepsi-Cola Metro Btlg Co Inc ....E....... 620 227-8123
Dodge City *(G-1419)*
Pepsi-Cola Metro Btlg Co Inc ....F....... 620 624-0287
Liberal *(G-6357)*
Pepsi-Cola Metro Btlg Co Inc ....C....... 785 628-3024
Hays *(G-2886)*
Seneca Wholesale Company Inc ....F....... 785 336-2118
Seneca *(G-10882)*

SOFTWARE PUBLISHERS: Application

Daniel Zimmerman ....G....... 303 378-2511
Overland Park *(G-8634)*
Data Locker Inc ....G....... 913 310-9088
Overland Park *(G-8636)*
Ddsports Inc ....G....... 913 636-0432
Merriam *(G-7090)*
Financial Institution Tech Inc ....E....... 888 848-7349
Topeka *(G-12610)*
General Dynamics Info Tech Inc ....E....... 785 832-0207
Lawrence *(G-4871)*
Mgmttv Inc ....F....... 316 262-4678
Wichita *(G-15062)*
Microsoft Corporation ....A....... 913 323-1200
Overland Park *(G-9020)*
Mobile Reasoning Inc ....G....... 913 888-2600
Lenexa *(G-6010)*
Redivus Health ....G....... 816 582-5428
Olathe *(G-8021)*
Soleran Inc ....G....... 913 647-5900
Overland Park *(G-9324)*

SOFTWARE PUBLISHERS: Business & Professional

Advanced Technology Group Inc ....E....... 913 239-0050
Overland Park *(G-8350)*
Bowman Software Systems LLC ....D....... 318 213-8780
Overland Park *(G-8477)*
Euronet Worldwide Inc ....D....... 913 327-4200
Leawood *(G-5389)*
Hyland LLC ....B....... 440 788-5045
Olathe *(G-7783)*
Jayhawk Software ....G....... 620 365-8065
Iola *(G-3615)*
Kaliaperumal Mamalay ....G....... 816 210-1248
Overland Park *(G-8885)*
Lockpath Inc ....D....... 913 601-4800
Overland Park *(G-8966)*
LPI Information Systems ....G....... 913 381-9118
Overland Park *(G-8972)*
Mersoft Corporation ....E....... 913 871-6200
Leawood *(G-5476)*
Optileaf Incorporated ....G....... 855 678-4532
Wichita *(G-15226)*
Orion Communications Inc ....G....... 913 538-7110
Overland Park *(G-9112)*
Professional Data Services ....F....... 620 663-5282
Hutchinson *(G-3415)*
Touchnet Info Systems Inc ....D....... 913 599-6699
Lenexa *(G-6187)*
Touchpoint Dashboard LLC ....G....... 512 585-5975
Wichita *(G-15777)*

SOFTWARE PUBLISHERS: Education

Examfx Inc ....E....... 800 586-2253
Leawood *(G-5390)*

SOFTWARE PUBLISHERS: Home Entertainment

Art of Escape Ict ....G....... 316 768-2588
Wichita *(G-13739)*
Professional Software Inc ....G....... 316 269-4264
Wichita *(G-15366)*

SOFTWARE PUBLISHERS: NEC

Black Knight Fincl Svcs Inc ....G....... 913 693-0000
Leawood *(G-5340)*
Blue Infotech Inc ....F....... 816 945-2583
Leawood *(G-5341)*
Classone Software ....G....... 913 831-4976
Shawnee Mission *(G-11238)*
Control Systems Intl Inc ....D....... 913 599-5010
Shawnee Mission *(G-11264)*
Control Vision Corporation ....E....... 620 231-5816
Pittsburg *(G-9845)*
Datateam Systems Inc ....E....... 785 843-8150
Lawrence *(G-4826)*
Digital Ally Inc ....D....... 913 814-7774
Lenexa *(G-5816)*
Hyland Holdings LLC ....E....... 913 227-7000
Lenexa *(G-5908)*
Igt Global Solutions Corp ....E....... 785 861-7300
Topeka *(G-12713)*
J & M Industries Inc ....E....... 913 362-8994
Prairie Village *(G-10037)*
Jaray Software Inc ....G....... 316 267-5758
Wichita *(G-14747)*
Kana Software Inc ....C....... 913 802-6756
Overland Park *(G-8886)*
Making The Mark Inc ....G....... 913 402-8000
Shawnee Mission *(G-11592)*
Medforce Technologies Inc ....F....... 845 426-0459
Topeka *(G-12879)*
Netsmart Technologies Inc ....C....... 913 327-7444
Overland Park *(G-9076)*
Nortonlifelock Inc ....E....... 913 451-6710
Shawnee Mission *(G-11688)*
Oracle Systems Corporation ....D....... 913 663-3400
Shawnee Mission *(G-11699)*
PSI Services Inc ....C....... 913 895-4600
Olathe *(G-8011)*
PSI Services Inc ....F....... 843 520-2992
Olathe *(G-8010)*
Rpms LLC ....F....... 800 776-7435
Overland Park *(G-9261)*
S & T Telephone Coop Assn ....F....... 785 460-7300
Colby *(G-1038)*
Scott Specialties Inc ....E....... 785 243-2594
Concordia *(G-1129)*
Servicetitan Inc ....G....... 316 267-5758
Wichita *(G-15568)*
Systems Building Services LLC ....E....... 913 385-1496
Lenexa *(G-6165)*
Tbcsoft Inc ....G....... 785 272-5993
Topeka *(G-13144)*
Thunderhead Engrg Cons Inc ....F....... 785 770-8511
Manhattan *(G-6826)*
U Inc ....F....... 913 814-7708
Overland Park *(G-9436)*
Unitas Global LLC ....D....... 913 339-2300
Overland Park *(G-9441)*
Web Creations & Consulting LLC ....G....... 785 823-7630
Salina *(G-10762)*
Wellsky Corporation ....C....... 913 307-1000
Overland Park *(G-9490)*
Work Comp Specialty Associates ....E....... 785 841-7751
Lawrence *(G-5191)*

SOFTWARE TRAINING, COMPUTER

Computer Instruments Inc ....E....... 913 307-8850
Lenexa *(G-5782)*
Examfx Inc ....E....... 800 586-2253
Leawood *(G-5390)*
Nexlearn LLC ....E....... 316 265-2170
Wichita *(G-15172)*

SOLAR CELLS

Evonik Corporation ....A....... 316 529-9670
Haysville *(G-2942)*

SOUND REPRODUCING EQPT

X Tech Midwest Inc ....G....... 316 777-6648
Wichita *(G-16082)*

SOUVENIRS, WHOLESALE

Terrell Publishing Co ....G....... 913 948-8226
Kansas City *(G-4464)*

SOYBEAN PRDTS

Archer-Daniels-Midland Company ....C....... 913 782-8800
Olathe *(G-7532)*
Cargill Incorporated ....D....... 316 292-2719
Wichita *(G-13948)*
Cargill Incorporated ....D....... 316 292-2380
Wichita *(G-13946)*

SPACE VEHICLE EQPT

B/E Aerospace Inc ....C....... 913 338-7292
Shawnee Mission *(G-11142)*
Brittain Machine Inc ....E....... 316 942-8223
Wichita *(G-13892)*
Burnham Composites Inc ....E....... 316 946-5900
Wichita *(G-13918)*
Inityaero Inc ....E....... 316 265-0603
Wichita *(G-14694)*
Learjet Inc ....E....... 316 946-3001
Wichita *(G-14941)*
Numerical Control Support Inc ....E....... 913 441-3500
Shawnee Mission *(G-11690)*
Primus International Inc ....C....... 316 425-8105
Wichita *(G-15346)*
Triumph Strctres - Kans Cy Inc ....D....... 913 882-7200
Edgerton *(G-1491)*
Vermillion Incorporated ....D....... 316 524-3100
Wichita *(G-15875)*

SPAS

Bella Vita Salon & Day Spa Inc ....E....... 913 651-6161
Leavenworth *(G-5207)*
Egos Salon & Day Spa Inc ....F....... 785 272-1181
Topeka *(G-12573)*
Heartland Pool & Spa Svc Inc ....F....... 913 438-2909
Lenexa *(G-5898)*
James Mirabile ....E....... 913 888-7546
Overland Park *(G-8872)*
Par Exsalonce ....E....... 913 469-9532
Shawnee Mission *(G-11715)*
Refresh Medical Spa LLC ....F....... 913 681-6200
Overland Park *(G-9232)*
Rsvp Medspa LLC ....F....... 913 387-1104
Overland Park *(G-9262)*
Salon Dimarco and Day Spa ....F....... 785 843-0044
Lawrence *(G-5100)*
Salon One 19 & Spa ....F....... 913 451-7119
Leawood *(G-5546)*
Salon Progressions & Day Spa ....F....... 316 729-1980
Wichita *(G-15512)*
Ultimate Escape Day Spa LLC ....E....... 913 851-3385
Overland Park *(G-9438)*

SPEAKER SYSTEMS

Induction Dynamics LLC ....F....... 913 663-5600
Lenexa *(G-5912)*
Soundtube Entertainment Inc ....F....... 913 233-8520
Lenexa *(G-6141)*
Soundtube Entertainment Inc ....E....... 435 647-9555
Overland Park *(G-9328)*

SPECIALIZED LIBRARIES

Midwest Hstrcal Gnalogical Soc ....E....... 316 264-3611
Wichita *(G-15096)*

SPECIALTY FOOD STORES: Coffee

Spice Merchant & Co ....F....... 316 263-4121
Wichita *(G-15639)*

SPECIALTY FOOD STORES: Dried Fruit

Qins International Inc ....E....... 913 342-4488
Kansas City *(G-4350)*

SPECIALTY FOOD STORES: Health & Dietetic Food

Herbs & More Inc ....F....... 785 865-4372
Lawrence *(G-4895)*

SPECIALTY OUTPATIENT CLINICS, NEC

Comcare of Sedgwick County .... B 316 660-7600
Wichita *(G-14061)*
Cowley County Joint Board Hlth .... F 620 442-3260
Arkansas City *(G-151)*
Critical Care Systems Intl Inc .... E 913 789-5560
Shawnee Mission *(G-11281)*
Four Cnty Mental Hlth Ctr Inc .... C 620 251-8180
Coffeyville *(G-939)*
Freeman Srgcl Ctr Pttsbrg LLC .... F 620 231-9072
Pittsburg *(G-9864)*
Heart America Surgery Ctr LLC .... E 913 334-8935
Kansas City *(G-4074)*
Heartspring Inc .... B 316 634-8700
Wichita *(G-14590)*
Infectious Disease Cons PA .... E 316 264-3505
Wichita *(G-14689)*
McPherson Family Clinic .... E 785 861-8800
McPherson *(G-6998)*
Medical Center P A .... E 620 669-9657
Hutchinson *(G-3369)*
P A Comcare .... E 785 827-6453
Salina *(G-10628)*
Prairie View Inc .... B 316 284-6400
Newton *(G-7407)*
Rural Hlth Rsurces Jackson Inc .... C 785 364-2116
Holton *(G-3110)*
Rural Hlth Rsurces Jackson Inc .... F 785 364-2126
Holton *(G-3111)*
Saint Lukes Primary Care At .... D 913 317-7990
Overland Park *(G-9274)*
Salina Physical Therapy Clinic .... F 785 825-1361
Salina *(G-10682)*
Surgicare of Wichita Inc .... D 316 685-2207
Wichita *(G-15702)*
Valeo Behavioral Health Care .... E 785 233-1730
Topeka *(G-13215)*

SPECULATIVE BUILDERS: Multi-Family Housing

Builders Development Inc .... E 316 684-1400
Wichita *(G-13913)*
R & R Developers Inc .... F 785 762-2255
Junction City *(G-3746)*

SPECULATIVE BUILDERS: Single-Family Housing

B L Rieke & Associates Inc .... F 913 599-3393
Shawnee Mission *(G-11141)*
Don Klausmeyer Cnstr LLC .... E 316 554-0001
Wichita *(G-14224)*
Home Center Construction Inc .... E 620 231-5607
Pittsburg *(G-9877)*
Suther Building Supply Inc .... F 785 336-2255
Seneca *(G-10883)*
Woodstone Inc .... F 913 685-2282
Shawnee Mission *(G-12018)*

SPORTING & ATHLETIC GOODS: Basketball Eqpt & Splys, NEC

First Team Sports Inc .... G 620 663-6080
Hutchinson *(G-3289)*
Pro-Bound Sports LLC .... F 785 666-4207
Dorrance *(G-1465)*

SPORTING & ATHLETIC GOODS: Bowling Alleys & Access

Aj Investors LLC .... F 316 321-0580
El Dorado *(G-1526)*

SPORTING & ATHLETIC GOODS: Boxing Eqpt & Splys, NEC

Title Boxing LLC .... C 913 438-4427
Lenexa *(G-6182)*

SPORTING & ATHLETIC GOODS: Cases, Gun & Rod

Shawnee Mission Builders LLC .... G 913 631-7020
Shawnee Mission *(G-11854)*

SPORTING & ATHLETIC GOODS: Dumbbells & Other Weight Eqpt

Oswald Manufacturing Co Inc .... G 785 258-2877
Herington *(G-2980)*

SPORTING & ATHLETIC GOODS: Fencing Eqpt

American Fence and SEC Co Inc .... G 316 945-5001
Wichita *(G-13691)*

SPORTING & ATHLETIC GOODS: Fishing Bait, Artificial

Rusty S Baits & Lures .... F 620 842-5301
Anthony *(G-134)*

SPORTING & ATHLETIC GOODS: Hunting Eqpt

Herron Inc .... G 913 731-2507
Paola *(G-9566)*

SPORTING & ATHLETIC GOODS: Shooting Eqpt & Splys, General

Rnn Enterprises LLC .... F 913 499-1230
Overland Park *(G-9246)*

SPORTING & ATHLETIC GOODS: Targets, Archery & Rifle Shooting

DVC Training Specialists LLC .... G 913 908-3393
Gardner *(G-2340)*
Lake Garnett Sporting Club .... G 785 448-5803
Garnett *(G-2380)*

SPORTING & ATHLETIC GOODS: Team Sports Eqpt

Epic Sports .... C 316 612-0150
Bel Aire *(G-432)*

SPORTING & ATHLETIC GOODS: Trap Racks, Clay Targets

GP Traps LLC .... G 620 394-2341
Atlanta *(G-274)*

SPORTING & REC GOODS, WHOLESALE: Ammunition, Sporting

Abraham Jacob Gorelick .... F 913 371-0459
Kansas City *(G-3779)*

SPORTING & RECREATIONAL GOODS & SPLYS WHOLESALERS

Bushnell Holdings Inc .... C 913 752-3400
Overland Park *(G-8497)*
Don Coffey Company Inc .... F 913 764-2108
Olathe *(G-7659)*
Nill Bros Sporting Goods Inc .... F 913 345-8655
Overland Park *(G-9087)*
RC Sports Inc .... E 913 894-5177
Lenexa *(G-6092)*
USA Inc .... F 785 825-6247
Salina *(G-10748)*

SPORTING & RECREATIONAL GOODS, WHOL: Sharpeners, Sporting

Combat Brands LLC .... E 913 689-2300
Lenexa *(G-5770)*

SPORTING & RECREATIONAL GOODS, WHOL: Water Slides, Rec Park

Grand Prairie Ht & Convention .... C 620 669-9311
Hutchinson *(G-3303)*

SPORTING & RECREATIONAL GOODS, WHOLESALE: Athletic Goods

R T Sporting Goods Inc .... F 620 275-5507
Garden City *(G-2261)*

SPORTING & RECREATIONAL GOODS, WHOLESALE: Bowling

Jayhawk Bowling Sup & Eqp Inc .... F 785 842-3237
Lawrence *(G-4919)*
Lo-Mar Bowling Supply Inc .... F 785 483-2222
Russell *(G-10279)*

SPORTING & RECREATIONAL GOODS, WHOLESALE: Exercise

Mid States Health Products .... F 316 681-3611
Wichita *(G-15072)*

SPORTING & RECREATIONAL GOODS, WHOLESALE: Fishing

Ludwikoski & Associates Inc .... F 913 879-2224
Overland Park *(G-8974)*

SPORTING & RECREATIONAL GOODS, WHOLESALE: Fishing Tackle

Bills Outdoor Sports .... F 620 241-7130
McPherson *(G-6938)*
Glen Thurber .... E 785 233-9541
Topeka *(G-12638)*

SPORTING & RECREATIONAL GOODS, WHOLESALE: Golf

County of Johnson .... E 913 829-4653
Olathe *(G-7623)*

SPORTING & RECREATIONAL GOODS, WHOLESALE: Gymnasium

USA Gym Supply Inc .... G 620 792-2209
Great Bend *(G-2653)*

SPORTING CAMPS

Young Mens Christian Associa .... D 316 320-9622
El Dorado *(G-1616)*

SPORTING FIREARMS WHOLESALERS

Joe Bob Outfitters LLC .... F 785 639-7121
Hays *(G-2856)*

SPORTING GOODS

Carlsons Choke Tube/NW Arms .... F 785 626-3078
Atwood *(G-282)*
Rings and Cages Inc .... G 816 945-7772
Bucyrus *(G-607)*
Sports Nutz of Kansas Inc .... F 913 400-7733
Kansas City *(G-4436)*

SPORTING GOODS STORES, NEC

B & E Inc .... F 913 299-1110
Kansas City *(G-3833)*
Bell and Carlson Incorporated .... E 620 225-6688
Dodge City *(G-1306)*
Brock Maggard .... F 417 793-7790
Baxter Springs *(G-401)*
Buds Tire Service Inc .... F 785 632-2135
Clay Center *(G-846)*
Coleman Company Inc .... G 800 835-3278
Wichita *(G-14053)*
Goodwin Sporting Goods Inc .... G 785 625-2419
Hays *(G-2821)*
Midwest Merchandising Inc .... C 913 428-8430
Overland Park *(G-9033)*
Orscheln Farm and Home LLC .... F 785 228-9688
Topeka *(G-12955)*
RC Sports Inc .... E 913 894-5177
Lenexa *(G-6092)*
Screen Machine LLC .... F 785 762-3081
Junction City *(G-3750)*
Stewarts Sports & Awards .... G 620 241-5990
McPherson *(G-7028)*
Topeka Country Club .... D 785 232-2090
Topeka *(G-13173)*
USA Inc .... F 785 825-6247
Salina *(G-10748)*

SPORTING GOODS STORES: Firearms

Joe Bob Outfitters LLC .... F 785 639-7121
Hays *(G-2856)*

Range 54 LLC ......F 316 440-2854
Wichita *(G-15416)*

SPORTING GOODS STORES: Fishing Eqpt

Bills Outdoor Sports ......F 620 241-7130
McPherson *(G-6938)*

SPORTING GOODS STORES: Hunting Eqpt

Herron Inc ......G 913 731-2507
Paola *(G-9566)*

SPORTING GOODS STORES: Playground Eqpt

Epic Sports ......C 316 612-0150
Bel Aire *(G-432)*

SPORTING GOODS STORES: Pool & Billiard Tables

Chilton Vending & Billd Inc ......F 316 262-3539
Wichita *(G-14011)*

SPORTING GOODS STORES: Skating Eqpt

Ice Sports Kansas City LLC ......E 913 441-3033
Shawnee Mission *(G-11451)*
Sk8away Inc ......E 785 272-0303
Topeka *(G-13075)*
Skate South Inc ......F 316 524-7261
Wichita *(G-15600)*
Starlite Skate Center South ......F 785 862-2241
Topeka *(G-13096)*

SPORTING GOODS STORES: Specialty Sport Splys, NEC

Nill Bros Sporting Goods Inc ......F 913 345-8655
Overland Park *(G-9087)*
R T Sporting Goods Inc ......F 620 275-5507
Garden City *(G-2261)*

SPORTING GOODS STORES: Tennis Goods & Eqpt

Genesis Health Club Inc ......E 316 945-8331
Wichita *(G-14458)*
Genesis Health Clubs MGT LLC ......E 316 634-0094
Wichita *(G-14459)*

SPORTING GOODS: Archery

B P E Inc ......G 620 343-3783
Emporia *(G-1700)*
Magnus Inc ......G 620 793-9222
Great Bend *(G-2604)*

SPORTING GOODS: Hammocks & Other Net Prdts

Ponca Products Inc ......E 316 262-4051
Wichita *(G-15314)*

SPORTING/ATHLETIC GOODS: Gloves, Boxing, Handball, Etc

Combat Brands LLC ......E 913 689-2300
Lenexa *(G-5770)*

SPORTS APPAREL STORES

Custom Branded Sportswear Inc ......F 866 441-7464
Overland Park *(G-8625)*
Its Greek To Me Inc ......C 800 336-4486
Manhattan *(G-6666)*
Sharks Investment Inc ......F 785 841-8289
Lawrence *(G-5109)*
Shirts Plus Inc ......F 316 788-1550
Derby *(G-1272)*
Stewarts Sports & Awards ......G 620 241-5990
McPherson *(G-7028)*

SPORTS CLUBS, MANAGERS & PROMOTERS

Challenger Sports Corp ......E 913 599-4884
Lenexa *(G-5749)*
Diversified Sports Tech LLC ......G 949 466-2393
Baxter Springs *(G-404)*

SPORTS TEAMS & CLUBS: Baseball

T-Bones Baseball Club LLC ......F 913 328-2255
Kansas City *(G-4455)*

SPORTS TEAMS & CLUBS: Basketball

Wichita Hoops LLC ......F 316 440-4990
Bel Aire *(G-444)*

SPORTS TEAMS & CLUBS: Football

Ksu Football Operation ......D 785 532-6832
Manhattan *(G-6704)*

SPORTS TEAMS & CLUBS: Ice Hockey

Wichita Thnder Prof Hckey Team ......F 316 264-4625
Wichita *(G-16039)*

SPORTS TEAMS & CLUBS: Soccer

All American Indoor Sports ......F 913 599-4884
Shawnee Mission *(G-11094)*
All American Indoor Sports ......D 913 888-5425
Shawnee Mission *(G-11093)*
Olathe Soccer Club ......F 913 764-4111
Olathe *(G-7949)*
Sunflower Soccer Assn ......F 785 233-9700
Topeka *(G-13121)*

SPRAYING EQPT: Agricultural

Bestway Inc ......E 785 742-2949
Hiawatha *(G-3003)*
Kiser AG Service LLC ......G 785 689-4292
Logan *(G-6425)*
Schaben Industries Inc ......E 316 283-4444
Newton *(G-7415)*
Simpson Farm Enterprises Inc ......F 785 731-2700
Ransom *(G-10195)*
Tatge Manufacturing Inc ......G 785 965-7213
Ramona *(G-10189)*
Westheffer Company Inc ......E 785 843-1633
Lawrence *(G-5183)*

SPRINGS: Wire

Coil Springs Specialties LLC ......G 785 437-2025
Saint Marys *(G-10359)*

SPRINKLING SYSTEMS: Fire Control

Earth Designs Inc ......G 913 791-2858
Shawnee Mission *(G-11325)*
General Automatic Sprinkler Fl ......E 913 390-1105
Overland Park *(G-8750)*
Zeroburn LLC ......G 877 207-7100
Overland Park *(G-9526)*

STACKERS: Power

Scrommel Resource Management ......G 785 825-7771
Salina *(G-10700)*

STADIUM EVENT OPERATOR SERVICES

Kansas Coliseum Inc ......F 316 440-0888
Park City *(G-9621)*
Smg Holdings Inc ......E 785 235-1986
Topeka *(G-13078)*

STAFFING, EMPLOYMENT PLACEMENT

Atterro Inc ......F 913 338-3020
Overland Park *(G-8412)*
Healthstaff Dental LLC ......D 913 402-4334
Leawood *(G-5423)*
Kansas Personnel Services Inc ......C 785 272-9999
Topeka *(G-12796)*
Robert Half International Inc ......D 913 451-7600
Overland Park *(G-9247)*
Robert Half International Inc ......D 816 421-6623
Overland Park *(G-9248)*
Spencer Reed Group LLC ......E 913 722-7860
Shawnee Mission *(G-11884)*
Tarc Inc ......D 785 266-2323
Topeka *(G-13140)*
Vertical 1 Inc ......E 913 829-8100
Lenexa *(G-6210)*

STAINED GLASS ART SVCS

Rayers Bearden Stained GL Sup ......F 316 942-2929
Wichita *(G-15421)*

STAINLESS STEEL WARE

Vita Craft Corporation ......D 913 631-6265
Shawnee Mission *(G-11982)*

STAIRCASES & STAIRS, WOOD

Goddard Manufacturing Inc ......G 785 689-4341
Logan *(G-6424)*

STAMPINGS: Metal

Schroer Manufacturing Company ......C 913 281-1500
Kansas City *(G-4404)*
Vita Craft Corporation ......D 913 631-6265
Shawnee Mission *(G-11982)*

STARTERS: Motor

Dels Alternator & Starter Svc ......G 785 825-4466
Salina *(G-10473)*

STATE CREDIT UNIONS, NOT FEDERALLY CHARTERED

Communityamerica Credit Union ......C 913 905-7000
Lenexa *(G-5778)*
Communityamerica Credit Union ......F 913 397-6600
Olathe *(G-7605)*
Communityamerica Credit Union ......F 785 232-6900
Topeka *(G-12493)*
Dillon Credit Union ......F 620 669-8500
Hutchinson *(G-3264)*
Educational Credit Union ......F 785 267-4900
Topeka *(G-12572)*
First Choice Credit Union ......F 316 425-5712
Wichita *(G-14372)*
Fort Leavenworth Credit Union ......E 913 651-6575
Fort Leavenworth *(G-1938)*
Golden Plains Credit Union ......E 620 275-8187
Garden City *(G-2188)*
Golden Plains Credit Union ......F 620 624-8491
Liberal *(G-6314)*
Golden Plains Credit Union ......F 785 628-1007
Hays *(G-2819)*
Meritrust Credit Union ......F 785 579-5700
Junction City *(G-3725)*
Meritrust Credit Union ......D 316 683-1199
Wichita *(G-15042)*
Meritrust Credit Union ......F 316 219-7614
Derby *(G-1261)*
Meritrust Credit Union ......F 316 683-1199
Wichita *(G-15043)*
Meritrust Credit Union ......F 316 761-4645
Wichita *(G-15044)*
Meritrust Credit Union ......F 316 761-4645
Wichita *(G-15045)*
Mid American Credit Union ......E 316 779-0052
Wichita *(G-15067)*
Midwest Regional Credit Union ......F 913 755-2127
Kansas City *(G-4256)*
Quantum Credit Union ......F 316 263-5756
Wichita *(G-15389)*
Skyward Credit Union ......E 316 517-6578
Wichita *(G-15601)*
U S Central Credit Union ......B 913 227-6000
Lenexa *(G-6198)*

STATE SAVINGS BANKS, NOT FEDERALLY CHARTERED

Chisholm Trail State Bank ......E 316 744-1293
Park City *(G-9610)*
Silver Lake Bank ......E 785 232-0102
Topeka *(G-13072)*

STATIONARY & OFFICE SPLYS, WHOL: Albums, Scrapbooks/Binders

Amanda Blu & Co LLC ......F 913 381-9494
Olathe *(G-7524)*

STATIONARY & OFFICE SPLYS, WHOLESALE: Laser Printer Splys

Perfect Output LLC ......D 913 317-8400
Overland Park *(G-9154)*

STATIONARY & OFFICE SPLYS, WHOLESALE: Stationery

Consolidated Prtg & Sty Co Inc.............E....... 785 825-5426
Salina (G-10460)

STATIONERY & OFFICE SPLYS WHOLESALERS

Graphic Impressions Inc.......................E....... 620 663-5939
Hutchinson (G-3305)
Kansas Business Forms LLC...............E....... 620 724-5234
Girard (G-2414)
Million Packaging Inc............................E....... 913 402-0055
Overland Park (G-9039)
Polynova (usa) LLC...............................G....... 913 309-6977
Lenexa (G-6062)
Shawnee Copy Center Inc....................F....... 913 268-4343
Shawnee Mission (G-11851)
Superior Computer Supply Inc.............F....... 316 942-5577
Wichita (G-15693)

STATORS REWINDING SVCS

Ametek Advanced Industries Inc..........D....... 316 522-0424
Wichita (G-13698)
Richmond Electric Inc...........................G....... 316 264-2344
Wichita (G-15457)

STEEL & ALLOYS: Tool & Die

Oxwell Inc...D....... 620 326-7481
Wellington (G-13521)

STEEL FABRICATORS

American Metal Fabrication Inc............F....... 620 399-8508
Wellington (G-13489)
Bennett Tool & Die LLC.........................D....... 913 371-4641
Kansas City (G-3855)
CDI Industrial Mech Contrs Inc.............C....... 913 287-0334
Kansas City (G-3898)
Central Steel Inc....................................D....... 316 265-8639
Wichita (G-13988)
Ceo Enterprises Inc...............................F....... 913 432-8046
Shawnee Mission (G-11214)
Cook Pump Company............................E....... 620 251-0880
Coffeyville (G-930)
Custom Metal Fabricators Inc...............E....... 785 258-3744
Herington (G-2973)
Danny Axe..E....... 620 767-5211
Council Grove (G-1162)
Derby Trailer Technologies LLC...........F....... 316 788-3331
Derby (G-1239)
Electromech Technologies LLC...........B....... 316 941-0400
Wichita (G-14266)
Electromech Technologies LLC...........C....... 316 941-0400
Wichita (G-14267)
Ernest-Spencer Metals Inc....................E....... 785 242-8538
Ottawa (G-8271)
Fab Works LLC.......................................G....... 620 585-2626
Inman (G-3581)
Fcs Manufacturing.................................G....... 620 427-4200
Gridley (G-2690)
Genco Manufacturing............................G....... 785 448-2501
Garnett (G-2374)
Goodwill Wstn MO & Eastrn Kans.........F....... 785 331-3908
Lawrence (G-4875)
Goodwill Wstn MO & Eastrn Kans.........E....... 913 768-9540
Olathe (G-7737)
Grain Belt Supply Company Inc............C....... 785 827-4491
Salina (G-10514)
Hall Steel & Fabrication Inc..................G....... 316 263-4222
Wichita (G-14547)
Haven Steel Products Inc......................D....... 620 465-2573
Haven (G-2731)
Heckendorn Eqp Co of Kans.................G....... 620 983-2186
Peabody (G-9760)
Industrial Maint Topeka Inc..................E....... 785 842-6252
Topeka (G-12723)
Industrial Mtal Fbrication Inc................D....... 316 283-3303
Newton (G-7366)
Jarit Manufacturing Inc.........................G....... 785 448-2501
Garnett (G-2379)
Kasa Companies Inc..............................D....... 785 825-5612
Salina (G-10569)
Kdoll Koatings Inc.................................G....... 620 456-2588
Conway Springs (G-1142)
Kice Industries Inc.................................C....... 316 744-7148
Park City (G-9625)
M E H Inc...D....... 785 235-1524
Topeka (G-12855)
M-C Fabrication Inc................................D....... 913 764-5454
Olathe (G-7869)
Magna Tech Inc.......................................E....... 620 431-3490
Chanute (G-740)
Maico Industries Inc...............................D....... 785 472-5390
Ellsworth (G-1677)
Matsu Manufacturing Inc.......................C....... 620 331-8737
Independence (G-3536)
Mellies Products Inc...............................G....... 785 926-4331
Morganville (G-7165)
Metal Arts LLC.......................................F....... 316 942-7958
Wichita (G-15048)
Mid-West Conveyor Company...............C....... 734 288-4400
Kansas City (G-4247)
Midwestern Metals Inc...........................E....... 785 232-1582
Topeka (G-12904)
Mobile Mini Inc.......................................F....... 316 838-2663
Park City (G-9636)
Needham & Associates Inc....................G....... 913 385-5300
Lenexa (G-6019)
New Age Industrial Corp Inc..................C....... 785 877-5121
Norton (G-7455)
North Topeka Fabrication LLC...............E....... 785 233-4430
Topeka (G-12934)
Pittsburg Steel & Mfg Co Inc.................F....... 620 231-8100
Leawood (G-5522)
Popup Industries Inc..............................E....... 620 431-9196
Chanute (G-755)
Raptor Manufacturing Lc.......................E....... 316 201-1772
Wichita (G-15418)
Rgs Industries Inc..................................G....... 913 780-9033
Olathe (G-8031)
Shawnee Steel & Welding Inc................E....... 913 432-8046
Shawnee Mission (G-11863)
Southwest and Associates Inc..............D....... 620 463-5631
Burrton (G-650)
Specialty Fabrication Inc.......................F....... 316 264-0603
Wichita (G-15636)
Steel Fabrications Inc............................G....... 785 625-3075
Hays (G-2913)
Steve Johnson Companies....................F....... 316 722-2660
Wichita (G-15664)
TEC Fab Parts Inc..................................F....... 913 369-0882
Tonganoxie (G-12270)
Tindle Construction Inc.........................D....... 620 378-2046
Fredonia (G-2047)
Tran Aerospace Inc................................G....... 316 260-8808
Wichita (G-15787)
Twin Oaks Industries Inc......................E....... 785 827-4839
Salina (G-10743)
US Pipe Fabrication LLC.......................F....... 785 242-6284
Ottawa (G-8318)
Valmont Industries Inc...........................D....... 316 321-1201
El Dorado (G-1611)
Valmont Industries Inc...........................D....... 785 452-9630
Salina (G-10749)

STEEL MILLS

Bradken Inc..D....... 913 367-2121
Atchison (G-220)
Contech Engnered Solutions LLC.........E....... 785 234-1000
Topeka (G-12504)
Full Vision Inc..D....... 316 283-3344
Newton (G-7349)
Geo Form International Inc...................G....... 913 782-1166
Olathe (G-7728)
Oswald Manufacturing Co Inc...............G....... 785 258-2877
Herington (G-2980)
Reliance Steel & Aluminum Co.............D....... 316 636-4500
Wichita (G-15440)
Shostak Iron and Metal Co Inc..............E....... 913 321-9210
Overland Park (G-9309)
Specialty Fabrication Inc.......................F....... 316 264-0603
Wichita (G-15636)
Tartan Manufacturing Inc......................C....... 913 432-7100
Kansas City (G-4458)
Werner Pipe Service Inc........................F....... 620 331-7384
Independence (G-3572)

STEREOPHONIC EQPT REPAIR SVCS

Radio Shop Inc.......................................F....... 316 265-1851
Wichita (G-15409)

STONE: Cast Concrete

Architectural Cast Stone Inc.................E....... 316 262-5543
Wichita (G-13731)
Midwest Cast Stone Kansas Inc............E....... 913 371-3300
Kansas City (G-4250)
Salina Concrete Products Inc................F....... 316 943-3241
Wichita (G-15510)

STORE FIXTURES, EXC REFRIGERATED: Wholesalers

Sorella Group Inc...................................F....... 913 390-9544
Lenexa (G-6140)

STORE FRONTS: Prefabricated, Metal

Manko Window Systems Inc..................B....... 785 776-9643
Manhattan (G-6730)

STORES: Auto & Home Supply

Aeroswint...F....... 785 391-2276
Utica (G-13334)
Automotive Warehouse Company.........E....... 316 942-8285
Wichita (G-13777)
Dick Edwards Ford Lincoln Merc..........D....... 785 320-4499
Junction City (G-3687)
Engels Sales & Service Center.............F....... 785 877-3391
Norton (G-7444)
Fleetpride Inc...F....... 785 862-1540
Topeka (G-12617)
Hub Cap & Wheel Store Inc...................F....... 913 432-0002
Kansas City (G-4087)
Mel Hambelton Ford Inc.........................C....... 316 462-3673
Wichita (G-15035)
Motivational Tubing LLC.......................G....... 316 283-7301
Newton (G-7391)
OReilly Automotive Stores Inc..............F....... 316 729-7311
Wichita (G-15233)
OReilly Automotive Stores Inc..............F....... 913 621-6939
Kansas City (G-4297)
Poorman Auto Supply Inc.....................E....... 316 265-6284
Wichita (G-15315)
Romans Outdoor Power Inc...................E....... 913 837-5225
Louisburg (G-6466)
Sears Roebuck and Co..........................C....... 785 826-4378
Salina (G-10701)
Sparkle Auto LLC..................................F....... 620 272-9559
Garden City (G-2286)
Walmart Inc..B....... 316 636-5384
Wichita (G-15924)
Walmart Inc..B....... 620 275-0775
Garden City (G-2308)

STORES: Drapery & Upholstery

Kimple Inc..F....... 620 564-2300
Ellinwood (G-1635)
Vos Window & Door Inc..........................D....... 913 962-5227
Shawnee Mission (G-11984)

STOVES: Wood & Coal Burning

Cvr Manufacturing Inc............................G....... 620 763-2500
Galesburg (G-2091)

STRAPPING

Concordia Technologies LLC................E....... 785 262-4066
Concordia (G-1108)

STRAPS: Cotton Webbing

BWI of Ks Inc..E....... 316 831-0488
Wichita (G-13923)

STUDIOS: Artist

Gallery Xii Inc...E....... 316 267-5915
Wichita (G-14440)

STUDIOS: Artist's

B Scott Studio Inc..................................G....... 316 321-1225
El Dorado (G-1533)
Dell Ann Upp..F....... 785 473-7001
Manhattan (G-6611)

STUDIOS: Artists & Artists' Studios

Saint Francis Cmnty Svcs Inc...............D....... 785 476-3234
Kensington (G-4580)
Spideroak Inc...F....... 847 564-8900
Mission (G-7138)
University of Kansas..............................D....... 785 864-9520
Lawrence (G-5159)

STUDIOS: Sculptor's

Corbin Bronze Limited ....G....... 913 766-4012
Kansas City *(G-3940)*

SUBSTANCE ABUSE CLINICS, OUTPATIENT

Adolescent Adult Fmly Recovery ....F....... 316 943-2051
Wichita *(G-13614)*
Mirror Inc ....F....... 620 326-8822
Wellington *(G-13518)*
Mirror Inc ....F....... 316 283-7829
Newton *(G-7388)*
Valeo Behavioral Hlth Care Inc ....E....... 785 273-2252
Topeka *(G-13216)*

SUBSTANCE ABUSE COUNSELING

Higher Ground ....F....... 316 262-2060
Wichita *(G-14607)*
Miracles Inc ....F....... 316 303-9520
Wichita *(G-15114)*
Recovery For All Foundation ....F....... 316 322-7057
El Dorado *(G-1596)*
Substance Abuse Center Kansas ....D....... 316 267-3825
Wichita *(G-15680)*

SUNROOMS: Prefabricated Metal

Sunshine Rooms Inc ....F....... 316 838-0033
Wichita *(G-15689)*

SUPERMARKETS & OTHER GROCERY STORES

El Taquito Inc ....G....... 913 371-0452
Kansas City *(G-3984)*
Healy Cooperative Elevator Co ....E....... 620 398-2211
Healy *(G-2966)*
Leiszler Oil Co Inc ....E....... 785 632-5648
Manhattan *(G-6712)*
Queen-Morris Ventures LLC ....C....... 913 383-2563
Shawnee Mission *(G-11765)*
Thai Binh Supermarket ....F....... 316 838-8882
Wichita *(G-15755)*

SURGICAL APPLIANCES & SPLYS

B/E Aerospace Inc ....C....... 913 338-7292
Shawnee Mission *(G-11142)*
Burke Inc ....E....... 913 722-5658
Kansas City *(G-3880)*
Hanger Inc ....F....... 913 677-1488
Merriam *(G-7094)*
Hanger Prosthetics & ....G....... 316 609-3000
Wichita *(G-14554)*
LSI International Inc ....E....... 913 894-4493
Kansas City *(G-4208)*
Midwest Contracting & Mfg ....G....... 785 743-2026
WA Keeney *(G-13383)*
Pos-T-Vac LLC ....F....... 800 279-7434
Dodge City *(G-1420)*
Scott Specialties Inc ....E....... 785 632-3161
Clay Center *(G-881)*

SURVEYING & MAPPING: Land Parcels

Alpha Land Surveys Inc ....F....... 620 728-0012
Hutchinson *(G-3197)*
B G Consultants Inc ....E....... 785 537-7448
Manhattan *(G-6551)*
Central Kans Surveying Mapping ....F....... 620 792-2873
Great Bend *(G-2528)*
Cornerstone Rgnal Srveying LLC ....E....... 620 331-6767
Independence *(G-3508)*
CP Engners Land Srveyors Inc ....F....... 785 267-5071
Topeka *(G-12526)*
Dolan Technologies Corporation ....E....... 913 390-5156
Olathe *(G-7658)*
Garber Surveying Service PA ....F....... 620 241-4441
McPherson *(G-6967)*
Garmin International Inc ....A....... 913 397-8200
Olathe *(G-7722)*
Idea Center Inc ....F....... 785 320-2400
Manhattan *(G-6664)*
Infinity Insur Solutions LLC ....E....... 913 338-3200
Leawood *(G-5436)*
Kansas Biological Survey ....E....... 785 864-1505
Lawrence *(G-4932)*
Kaw Valley Engineering Inc ....F....... 316 440-4304
Wichita *(G-14834)*
Kaw Valley Engineering Inc ....E....... 785 762-5040
Junction City *(G-3714)*
Land Acquisitions Inc ....E....... 847 749-0675
Wichita *(G-14919)*
Landplan Engineering PA ....D....... 785 843-7530
Lawrence *(G-4954)*
McAfee Henderson Solutions Inc ....F....... 913 888-4647
Lenexa *(G-5991)*
Mkec Engineering Inc ....C....... 316 684-9600
Wichita *(G-15118)*
MTS Quanta LLC ....E....... 913 383-0800
Overland Park *(G-9061)*
Olsson Inc ....C....... 913 381-1170
Overland Park *(G-9100)*
Payne & Brockway P A ....E....... 913 782-4800
Olathe *(G-7976)*
Phelps Engineering Inc ....E....... 913 393-1155
Olathe *(G-7983)*
Ponzeryoungquist PA ....F....... 913 782-0541
Olathe *(G-7992)*
Schmitz King & Associates Inc ....F....... 913 397-6080
Shawnee *(G-11025)*
Schwab-Eaton PA ....E....... 785 539-4687
Manhattan *(G-6797)*
Shafer Kline & Warren Inc ....E....... 913 888-7800
Lenexa *(G-6126)*
Survey Companies LLC ....F....... 316 722-6916
Wichita *(G-15703)*
Surveying and Mapping LLC ....C....... 913 344-9933
Overland Park *(G-9379)*
Surveys Inc ....E....... 785 472-4456
Ellsworth *(G-1681)*

SURVEYING INSTRUMENTS WHOLESALERS

Sokkia Corporation ....E....... 816 322-0939
Olathe *(G-8071)*

SURVEYING SVCS: Aerial Digital Imaging

Focalpoint Imaging LLC ....G....... 620 325-2298
Neodesha *(G-7241)*

SURVEYING SVCS: Photogrammetric Engineering

Baughman Co PA ....E....... 316 262-7271
Wichita *(G-13820)*
Garber Surveying Service PA ....E....... 620 665-7032
Hutchinson *(G-3297)*
McAfee Henderson Solutions Inc ....F....... 913 888-4647
Lenexa *(G-5990)*

SVC ESTABLISHMENT EQPT & SPLYS WHOLESALERS

McAfee Enterprises LLC ....F....... 913 839-3328
Olathe *(G-7880)*

SVC ESTABLISHMENT EQPT, WHOL: Cleaning & Maint Eqpt & Splys

Hertel Tank Service Inc ....G....... 785 628-2445
Hays *(G-2841)*
Huber Inc ....F....... 316 267-0289
Wichita *(G-14646)*
T D C Ltd ....E....... 913 780-9631
Olathe *(G-8096)*

SVC ESTABLISHMENT EQPT, WHOL: Concrete Burial Vaults & Boxes

Wilbert Funeral Services Inc ....E....... 316 832-1114
Wichita *(G-16046)*

SVC ESTABLISHMENT EQPT, WHOL: Laundry/Dry Cleaning Eqpt/Sply

Ryan D&M Inc ....F....... 620 231-4559
Pittsburg *(G-9930)*

SVC ESTABLISHMENT EQPT, WHOLESALE: Beauty Parlor Eqpt & Sply

Ahn Marketing Incorporated ....F....... 913 342-2176
Kansas City *(G-3793)*
Haynes Salon and Supply Inc ....F....... 785 539-5512
Manhattan *(G-6651)*
Netzer Sales Inc ....F....... 913 599-6464
Shawnee Mission *(G-11676)*
TDS Allocation Co ....E....... 800 857-2906
Topeka *(G-13146)*
Wholesale Beauty Club Inc ....F....... 316 941-9500
Wichita *(G-15967)*
Wholesale Beauty Club Inc ....F....... 316 687-9890
Wichita *(G-15966)*

SVC ESTABLISHMENT EQPT, WHOLESALE: Firefighting Eqpt

Bamford Fire Sprinkler Co Inc ....E....... 913 432-6688
Shawnee Mission *(G-11145)*
Jayhawk Fire Sprinkler Co Inc ....E....... 913 422-3770
Olathe *(G-7809)*

SVC ESTABLISHMENT EQPT, WHOLESALE: Laundry Eqpt & Splys

Comet 1 H R Cleaners Inc ....F....... 620 626-8100
Liberal *(G-6295)*
Fabriclean Supply Kansas Lc ....F....... 913 492-1743
Lenexa *(G-5845)*

SVC ESTABLISHMENT EQPT, WHOLESALE: Sprinkler Systems

Blackburn Nursery Inc ....E....... 785 272-2707
Topeka *(G-12387)*
Keller Fire & Safety Inc ....D....... 913 371-8494
Kansas City *(G-4169)*
Raintree Inc ....E....... 913 262-7013
Shawnee Mission *(G-11776)*

SVC ESTABLISHMENT EQPT, WHOLESALE: Vacuum Cleaning Systems

AAA Restaurant Supply LLC ....F....... 316 265-4365
Wichita *(G-13592)*
Bhjllc Inc ....D....... 913 888-8028
Lenexa *(G-5701)*
Bhjllc Inc ....E....... 785 272-8800
Topeka *(G-12379)*

SVC ESTABLISHMENT EQPT, WHOLESALE: Vending Machines & Splys

Premier Food Service Inc ....C....... 316 269-2447
Wichita *(G-15330)*
Scriptpro USA Inc ....B....... 913 384-1008
Shawnee Mission *(G-11840)*
Treat America Limited ....B....... 913 384-4900
Shawnee Mission *(G-11940)*

SVC LEAGUE

Assistance League Wichita Inc ....C....... 316 687-6107
Wichita *(G-13754)*

SWEEPING COMPOUNDS

Waxene Products Company Inc ....G....... 316 263-8523
Wichita *(G-15938)*

SWIMMING INSTRUCTION

Wichita Swim Club ....E....... 316 683-1491
Wichita *(G-16036)*

SWIMMING POOL & HOT TUB CLEANING & MAINTENANCE SVCS

Banks Swimming Pool Company ....E....... 913 897-9290
Overland Park *(G-8431)*
Pool & Patio Inc ....F....... 913 888-2226
Shawnee Mission *(G-11743)*
Pool & Patio Supply Inc ....F....... 913 888-2226
Shawnee Mission *(G-11744)*
Pools Plus ....F....... 785 823-7665
Salina *(G-10636)*

SWIMMING POOL EQPT: Filters & Water Conditioning Systems

United Industries Inc ....F....... 620 278-3160
Sterling *(G-12131)*

SWIMMING POOL SPLY STORES

Pool & Patio Inc ....F....... 913 888-2226
Shawnee Mission *(G-11743)*
Pool & Patio Supply Inc ....F....... 913 888-2226
Shawnee Mission *(G-11744)*
Scp Distributors LLC ....F....... 913 660-0061
Lenexa *(G-6120)*

SWIMMING POOLS, EQPT & SPLYS: Wholesalers

Great Plains Supply Inc........F 913 492-1520
Shawnee Mission *(G-11400)*
Scp Distributors LLC........F 913 660-0061
Lenexa *(G-6120)*
United Industries Inc........F 620 278-3160
Sterling *(G-12131)*

SWITCHBOARDS & PARTS: Power

Standard Motor Products Inc........B 620 331-1000
Independence *(G-3562)*

SWITCHGEAR & SWITCHBOARD APPARATUS

TEC Engineering Inc........E 316 259-8881
Wichita *(G-15723)*
Total Electric Inc........G 316 524-2642
Wichita *(G-15775)*

SYMPHONY ORCHESTRA

Hutchinson Symphony Assn........F 620 543-2511
Hutchinson *(G-3325)*
Wichita Symphony Society........C 316 267-7658
Wichita *(G-16037)*

SYNTHETIC RESIN FINISHED PRDTS, NEC

Orbis Corporation........C 785 528-4875
Osage City *(G-8185)*

SYSTEMS ENGINEERING: Computer Related

Foresite Msp LLC........E 800 940-4699
Overland Park *(G-8734)*
Leidos Inc........G 913 317-5120
Shawnee Mission *(G-11560)*

SYSTEMS INTEGRATION SVCS

American Ctrl & Engrg Svc Inc........F 316 776-7500
Rose Hill *(G-10235)*
Computer Sciences Corporation........C 913 469-8700
Overland Park *(G-8593)*
Danco Systems Inc........F 913 962-0600
Shawnee *(G-10939)*
Dynamic Cmpt Sltons Topeka Inc........F 785 354-7000
Topeka *(G-12563)*
Networks Plus........E 785 825-0400
Manhattan *(G-6759)*
Results Technology Inc........E 913 928-8300
Overland Park *(G-9238)*
Triple-I Corporation........D 913 563-7227
Leawood *(G-5585)*

SYSTEMS INTEGRATION SVCS: Local Area Network

Access Group LLC........F 316 264-0270
Wichita *(G-13602)*
Networks Plus........E 785 825-0400
Salina *(G-10611)*

SYSTEMS SOFTWARE DEVELOPMENT SVCS

Allegiant Networks LLC........E 913 599-6900
Leawood *(G-5316)*
Balance Innovations LLC........D 913 599-1177
Lenexa *(G-5682)*
Convergeone Inc........C 913 307-2300
Overland Park *(G-8597)*
Covansys Corporation........C 913 469-8700
Shawnee Mission *(G-11275)*
Datasystem Solutions Inc........E 913 362-6969
Overland Park *(G-8638)*
Fireboard Labs LLC........G 816 945-2232
Olathe *(G-7710)*
Gorydz Inc........F 913 486-1665
Kansas City *(G-4040)*
Harris Computer Systems........D 785 843-8150
Lawrence *(G-4890)*
Kansas Info Consortium LLC........F 785 296-5059
Topeka *(G-12783)*
Netchemia LLC........E 913 789-0996
Overland Park *(G-9074)*
Quark Studios LLC........F 913 871-5154
Olathe *(G-8014)*
Regulatory Consultants Inc........E 785 486-2882
Horton *(G-3133)*
Sara Software Systems LLC........E 913 370-4197
Olathe *(G-8055)*
Softwarfare LLC........F 202 854-9268
Prairie Village *(G-10068)*

TABLE OR COUNTERTOPS, PLASTIC LAMINATED

Cabinet Shopof Basehor Inc........E 913 845-2182
Tonganoxie *(G-12255)*
Grandview Products Co Inc........C 620 421-6950
Parsons *(G-9688)*

TABULATING SVCS

General Dynamics Info Tech Inc........E 785 832-0207
Lawrence *(G-4871)*

TACKLES: Carpet

Baco Corporation........F 316 945-5300
Wichita *(G-13792)*

TAGS & LABELS: Paper

Kc Digical........G 913 541-2688
Lenexa *(G-5940)*
Stephanie Wilson........G 913 563-1240
Paola *(G-9591)*

TANK REPAIR SVCS

KBK Industries LLC........C 785 372-4331
Rush Center *(G-10260)*
McDonald Tank and Eqp Co Inc........E 620 793-3555
Great Bend *(G-2606)*

TANK TRUCK CLEANING SVCS

Armdat Inc........F 913 321-4287
Kansas City *(G-3819)*
Eagle Environmental Svcs LLC........E 316 944-2445
Wichita *(G-14250)*

TANKS & OTHER TRACKED VEHICLE CMPNTS

Atec Steel LLC........C 877 457-5352
Baxter Springs *(G-394)*

TANKS: Cryogenic, Metal

Air Products and Chemicals Inc........F 620 626-7062
Liberal *(G-6274)*

TANKS: For Tank Trucks, Metal Plate

Niece Products of Kansas Inc........E 620 223-0340
Fort Scott *(G-1994)*

TANKS: Lined, Metal

Harbison-Fischer Inc........G 620 624-9042
Liberal *(G-6317)*
KBK Industries LLC........C 785 372-4331
Rush Center *(G-10260)*

TANKS: Plastic & Fiberglass

Glass King Manufacturing Co........F 620 793-7838
Great Bend *(G-2570)*
McDonald Tank II........G 620 792-3661
Great Bend *(G-2607)*
Scientific Plastics Co Inc........E 913 432-0322
Kansas City *(G-4407)*

TANKS: Standard Or Custom Fabricated, Metal Plate

Double T Ind Inc........E 620 593-4357
Rolla *(G-10232)*
Glass King Manufacturing Co........F 620 793-7838
Great Bend *(G-2570)*
Hammersmith Mfg & Sales Inc........G 785 364-4140
Holton *(G-3095)*
Pioneer Tank & Steel Inc........G 620 672-2153
Pratt *(G-10133)*
Tank Wind-Down Corp........C 620 421-0200
Parsons *(G-9745)*
We-Mac Manufacturing Co........F 913 367-3778
Atchison *(G-270)*

TANKS: Storage, Farm, Metal Plate

Cromwell Builders Mfg........F 785 949-2433
Carlton *(G-686)*

TANNING SALON EQPT & SPLYS, WHOLESALE

Ultimate Tan........F 785 842-4949
Lawrence *(G-5148)*

TANNING SALONS

A Total Image........F 785 272-2855
Topeka *(G-12279)*
Ah Tannery Inc........F 913 772-1111
Leavenworth *(G-5200)*
Extreme Tanning Inc........F 316 712-0190
Wichita *(G-14325)*
Hair Shop West Inc........E 913 829-4868
Olathe *(G-7746)*
Hartzler Lorenda........E 785 749-2424
Lawrence *(G-4891)*
Jaafar Inc........F 913 269-5113
Olathe *(G-7805)*
Midas Touch Golden Tans........F 620 340-1011
Emporia *(G-1795)*
Perfect Touch Inc........F 316 522-9205
Wichita *(G-15281)*
Sharks Investment Inc........F 785 841-8289
Lawrence *(G-5109)*
Ultimate Tan........F 785 842-4949
Lawrence *(G-5148)*

TAPES: Pressure Sensitive

Graphics Systems Inc........D 316 267-4171
Wichita *(G-14497)*
Peavey Corporation........D 913 888-0600
Lenexa *(G-6047)*

TARPAULINS

Colby Supply & Mfg Co........F 785 462-3981
Colby *(G-999)*
Girard Tarps Inc........G 620 724-8909
Girard *(G-2410)*
USA Gym Supply........F 620 792-2800
Great Bend *(G-2652)*
USA Gym Supply Inc........G 620 792-2209
Great Bend *(G-2653)*

TARPAULINS, WHOLESALE

Long Shot Enterprises LLC........F 785 493-0171
Salina *(G-10584)*

TAX RETURN PREPARATION SVCS

AC Professional LLC........E 816 668-4760
Olathe *(G-7508)*
Bob Thornton........E 620 624-7691
Liberal *(G-6285)*
Dave Tarter........F 620 227-8031
Dodge City *(G-1339)*
H & R Block........F 316 321-6960
El Dorado *(G-1565)*
H & R Block........F 620 421-2850
Parsons *(G-9690)*
H & R Block Inc........F 785 271-0706
Topeka *(G-12654)*
H & R Block Tax Services LLC........F 316 775-7331
Augusta *(G-322)*
H & R Block Tax Services LLC........F 913 648-1040
Olathe *(G-7744)*
H & R Block Tax Services LLC........F 620 231-5563
Pittsburg *(G-9870)*
H & R Block Tax Services LLC........F 785 749-1649
Lawrence *(G-4884)*
H&R Block Inc........F 316 636-4009
Wichita *(G-14535)*
H&R Block Inc........F 316 267-8257
Wichita *(G-14536)*
H&R Block Inc........F 913 837-5418
Ottawa *(G-8276)*
H&R Block Inc........F 785 827-4253
Salina *(G-10527)*
H&R Block Inc........F 316 683-4211
Wichita *(G-14537)*
H&R Block Inc........E 913 788-7779
Kansas City *(G-4060)*
H&R Block Inc........F 620 793-9361
Great Bend *(G-2587)*

H&R Block Inc ....F 785 776-7531
Manhattan *(G-6649)*
H&R Block Inc ....E 316 283-1495
Newton *(G-7355)*
H&R Block Inc ....F 620 336-2750
Cherryvale *(G-809)*
H&R Block Inc ....F 913 788-5222
Kansas City *(G-4061)*
I 70 Tax Services LLC ....F 785 539-5240
Manhattan *(G-6663)*
J L D J Inc ....F 785 625-6316
Hays *(G-2855)*
Keller & Miller Cpas LLP ....F 620 275-6883
Garden City *(G-2217)*
Keller & Owens LLC ....E 913 338-3500
Overland Park *(G-8911)*
Kramer & Associates Cpas LLC ....F 913 680-1690
Leavenworth *(G-5263)*
Liberty Tax ....F 913 384-1040
Roeland Park *(G-10226)*
Liberty Tax Service ....F 316 219-4829
Wichita *(G-14958)*
Mize Houser & Company PA ....D 785 233-0536
Topeka *(G-12908)*
Paycor Inc ....D 913 262-9484
Shawnee Mission *(G-11719)*
R & J Salina Tax Service Inc ....E 785 827-1304
Salina *(G-10649)*
Sckats Inc ....F 620 662-2368
Hutchinson *(G-3438)*
Sharon Miller ....F 620 856-3377
Baxter Springs *(G-412)*
Shemar Inc ....F 620 342-5787
Emporia *(G-1827)*
Stephen M Criser ....E 316 685-1040
Wichita *(G-15661)*
Tax 911com Incorporated ....F 913 712-8539
Olathe *(G-8102)*
Thompson Tax & Associates LLC ....F 916 346-7829
Waverly *(G-13482)*
Topeka Income Tax Service Inc ....F 785 478-2833
Topeka *(G-13178)*
V G Electracon Inc ....F 913 780-9995
Olathe *(G-8137)*
Y & M Business Services LLC ....F 620 331-4600
Independence *(G-3575)*

TAXI CABS

American Cab Inc ....F 316 262-7511
Wichita *(G-13687)*
Bell Taxi and Trnsp Inc ....F 785 238-6161
Junction City *(G-3672)*
Best Cabs Inc ....F 316 838-2233
Wichita *(G-13836)*
Capitol City Taxi Inc ....F 785 267-3777
Topeka *(G-12435)*
Coffey County Trnsp Inc ....F 620 364-1935
Burlington *(G-631)*
Edward French Loy ....F 785 825-4646
Salina *(G-10485)*
Gorydz Inc ....F 913 486-1665
Kansas City *(G-4040)*
Lafarge North America Inc ....B 913 780-6809
Olathe *(G-7852)*
Sunflower Taxi Courier Svc LLC ....F 785 826-1881
Salina *(G-10727)*
Yellow Cab Taxi Tpeka Kans LLC ....E 785 357-4444
Topeka *(G-13254)*

TELECOMMUNICATION EQPT REPAIR SVCS, EXC TELEPHONES

Athena Communications Ltd ....F 913 599-3444
Overland Park *(G-8409)*
Communication Link LLC ....F 913 681-5400
Lenexa *(G-5776)*
Kansas Communications Inc ....E 913 402-2200
Lenexa *(G-5937)*
Satellite Engrg Group Inc ....E 913 324-6000
Overland Park *(G-9282)*
Spectrum Elite Corp ....G 913 579-7037
Olathe *(G-8076)*

TELECOMMUNICATION SYSTEMS & EQPT

AT&T Inc ....F 913 676-1136
Lenexa *(G-5673)*
Computerwise Inc ....F 408 389-8241
Olathe *(G-7609)*
Special Product Company ....E 972 208-1460
Lenexa *(G-6146)*
Special Product Company ....F 913 491-8088
Shawnee *(G-11031)*

TELECOMMUNICATIONS CARRIERS & SVCS: Wired

AT&T Corp ....A 316 268-3380
Wichita *(G-13760)*
AT&T Corp ....D 785 276-8514
Topeka *(G-12350)*
AT&T Corp ....D 316 383-0380
Wichita *(G-13761)*
AT&T Corp ....F 620 231-9941
Pittsburg *(G-9815)*
AT&T Corp ....D 620 665-1946
Hutchinson *(G-3209)*
AT&T Inc ....F 913 676-1136
Lenexa *(G-5673)*
AT&T Mobility LLC ....E 913 254-0303
Olathe *(G-7539)*
Cox Communications Inc ....D 785 236-1606
Manhattan *(G-6605)*
Cox Communications Inc ....D 785 233-3383
Topeka *(G-12523)*
Flint Telecom Group Inc ....F 913 815-1570
Overland Park *(G-8730)*
Knology Inc ....C 785 841-2100
Lawrence *(G-4947)*
Motorola Solutions Inc ....E 913 317-3020
Overland Park *(G-9057)*
Nex-Tech LLC ....C 785 625-7070
Hays *(G-2878)*
Payspot LLC ....D 913 327-4200
Leawood *(G-5518)*
Qwest Corporation ....D 913 851-9024
Overland Park *(G-9220)*
Rainbow Telecom Assn Inc ....F 785 548-7511
Everest *(G-1902)*
S & T Telephone Coop Assn ....F 785 460-7300
Colby *(G-1038)*
S & T Telephone Coop Assn ....E 785 890-7400
Goodland *(G-2485)*
Savage Holdings Inc ....F 913 583-1007
Lenexa *(G-6118)*
Southern Kansas Tele Co Inc ....E 620 584-2255
Clearwater *(G-899)*
Sprint Solutions Inc ....D 800 829-0965
Overland Park *(G-9341)*
Sprint Spectrum Holding Co LP ....A 800 829-0965
Shawnee Mission *(G-11885)*
Sprint Spectrum LP ....F 785 537-3500
Manhattan *(G-6804)*
Surewest Communications ....F 913 825-2882
Lenexa *(G-6162)*
United Telephone Assn Inc ....E 620 227-8641
Dodge City *(G-1443)*
Wilson Communication Co Inc ....F 785 658-2111
Wilson *(G-16107)*
Windstream Nuvox Kansas LLC ....E 913 747-7000
Shawnee Mission *(G-12012)*

TELECOMMUNICATIONS CARRIERS & SVCS: Wireless

Cricket Communications Inc ....F 913 341-2799
Overland Park *(G-8614)*
Informtion Cmmunications Group ....E 913 469-6767
Leawood *(G-5437)*
Pioneer Telephone Assn Inc ....C 620 356-3211
Ulysses *(G-13312)*
Sprint Communications Inc ....A 855 848-3280
Overland Park *(G-9337)*
Sprint Spectrum LP ....F 913 671-7007
Merriam *(G-7105)*
Walmart Inc ....C 316 945-2800
Wichita *(G-15923)*
Walmart Inc ....B 316 636-5384
Wichita *(G-15924)*

TELEMARKETING BUREAUS

Alorica Customer Care Inc ....A 215 441-2323
Lenexa *(G-5642)*
Answernet Inc ....F 785 301-2810
Hays *(G-2748)*
Blue Valley Tele-Marketing ....D 785 799-3500
Home *(G-3118)*
Blue Vly Tl-Communications Inc ....D 785 799-3311
Home *(G-3119)*
Convergys Corporation ....E 913 782-3333
Olathe *(G-7614)*
On-Line Communications Inc ....C 316 831-0500
Wichita *(G-15219)*
T W Lacy & Associates Inc ....F 913 706-7625
Prairie Village *(G-10073)*

TELEPHONE ANSWERING SVCS

Answer Link ....F 620 662-4427
Hutchinson *(G-3199)*
Answer Topeka Inc ....E 785 234-4444
Topeka *(G-12331)*
Answering Exchange Inc ....E 316 262-8282
Wichita *(G-13712)*
Johnson County Communications ....E 913 764-2876
Olathe *(G-7815)*

TELEPHONE EQPT INSTALLATION

Alea Communications LLC ....F 913 439-7391
Gardner *(G-2323)*
Computer Cable Connection Inc ....E 913 390-5141
Lenexa *(G-5781)*
Italk Telecontracting Inc ....F 816 436-8080
Mission *(G-7131)*
Johnson Cmmunications Svcs Inc ....F 913 681-5505
Stilwell *(G-12159)*
S N C Inc ....E 620 665-6651
Hutchinson *(G-3434)*
Wachter Tech Solutions Inc ....D 856 222-0643
Lenexa *(G-6220)*

TELEPHONE EQPT: NEC

Kgp Products Inc ....C 800 755-1950
New Century *(G-7291)*

TELEPHONE SET REPAIR SVCS

Networks Plus ....E 785 825-0400
Salina *(G-10611)*
S N C Inc ....E 620 665-6651
Hutchinson *(G-3434)*
Tpcks Inc ....F 785 776-4429
Manhattan *(G-6828)*

TELEPHONE SVCS

Eagle Environmental Svcs LLC ....E 316 944-2445
Wichita *(G-14250)*
Elanco Kc ....F 816 442-4114
Lenexa *(G-5830)*
Informtion Cmmunications Group ....E 913 469-6767
Leawood *(G-5437)*
Nex-Tech LLC ....F 785 421-4197
Hill City *(G-3037)*
One Power LLC ....E 913 219-5061
Shawnee Mission *(G-11697)*
South Central Tele Assn Inc ....E 620 930-1000
Medicine Lodge *(G-7074)*
South Central Wireless Inc ....E 620 930-1000
Medicine Lodge *(G-7075)*
Tmd Telecom Inc ....E 316 462-0400
Wichita *(G-15772)*

TELEPHONE: Fiber Optic Systems

Ciena Corporation ....G 913 402-4800
Shawnee Mission *(G-11225)*
S & S Underground LLC ....F 620 704-1397
Pittsburg *(G-9932)*

TELEPHONE: Sets, Exc Cellular Radio

Spectrum Elite Corp ....G 913 579-7037
Olathe *(G-8076)*

TELEVISION BROADCASTING STATIONS

Channel News Department ....F 316 292-1111
Wichita *(G-13999)*
Evening Telegram Company ....D 417 624-0233
Pittsburg *(G-9858)*
Gray Television Group Inc ....F 316 838-1212
Wichita *(G-14499)*
Gray Television Group Inc ....E 785 272-6397
Topeka *(G-12645)*
Iheartcommunications Inc ....D 316 494-6600
Wichita *(G-14668)*
Kansas Public Telecom Svc Inc ....E 316 838-3090
Wichita *(G-14820)*
Meredith Corporation ....C 913 677-5555
Fairway *(G-1914)*
Montgomery Communications Inc ....D 785 762-5000
Junction City *(G-3727)*

Nexstar Broadcasting Inc......F....... 785 582-4000
Topeka *(G-12931)*
Nexstar Broadcasting Inc......D....... 316 265-3333
Wichita *(G-15173)*
Nvt Wichita LLC......E....... 316 265-3333
Wichita *(G-15201)*
Schurz Communications Inc......C....... 316 838-1212
Wichita *(G-15535)*
Smoky Hills Public TV Corp......F....... 785 483-6990
Bunker Hill *(G-620)*
Sunflower Broadcasting Inc......D....... 316 838-1212
Wichita *(G-15687)*
Waitt Media Inc......F....... 785 462-3305
Colby *(G-1047)*
Washburn University of Topeka......E....... 785 670-1111
Topeka *(G-13233)*

TELEVISION REPAIR SHOP

Overland TV Inc......F....... 913 648-2222
Shawnee Mission *(G-11711)*
Repair Shack Inc......E....... 913 732-0514
Lenexa *(G-6105)*

TEMPORARY HELP SVCS

Adkore Staffing Group LLC......F....... 913 402-8031
Leawood *(G-5312)*
Ado Staffing Inc......F....... 785 842-1515
Lawrence *(G-4719)*
Aerotek Inc......F....... 913 905-3000
Overland Park *(G-8355)*
Aerotek Inc......E....... 316 448-4500
Wichita *(G-13640)*
Aerotek Inc......E....... 913 981-1970
Lenexa *(G-5636)*
Apprentice Personnel Inc......D....... 316 267-4781
Wichita *(G-13724)*
Arnold & Associates of Wichita......F....... 316 263-9283
Wichita *(G-13735)*
Asgn Incorporated......F....... 913 341-9100
Overland Park *(G-8401)*
Atterro Inc......F....... 913 338-3020
Overland Park *(G-8412)*
Excel Personnel Services Inc......E....... 913 341-1150
Shawnee Mission *(G-11353)*
Exhibit Arts LLC......E....... 316 264-2915
Wichita *(G-14321)*
Favorite Hlthcare Staffing Inc......C....... 913 383-9733
Overland Park *(G-8708)*
Favorite Hlthcare Staffing Inc......A....... 913 648-6563
Leawood *(G-5396)*
Grafton Inc......A....... 913 498-0701
Overland Park *(G-8768)*
Interim Healthcare Inc......C....... 785 272-1616
Topeka *(G-12726)*
Interim Healthcare Inc......E....... 620 663-2423
Hutchinson *(G-3335)*
Interim Healthcare Kansas City......E....... 913 381-3100
Leawood *(G-5439)*
John A Marshall Company......C....... 913 599-4700
Lenexa *(G-5929)*
Kansas Personnel Services Inc......C....... 785 272-9999
Topeka *(G-12796)*
Kelly Services Inc......A....... 913 451-1400
Overland Park *(G-8913)*
Nexus It Group Inc......F....... 913 815-1750
Overland Park *(G-9085)*
On Demand Employment Svcs LLC......F....... 913 371-3212
Kansas City *(G-4294)*
Pivot Companies LLC......F....... 800 581-6398
Overland Park *(G-9170)*
Premier Personnel Inc......D....... 785 273-9944
Topeka *(G-12983)*
Professional Drivers GA Inc......E....... 316 945-9700
Wichita *(G-15358)*
Rebel Staffing LLC......D....... 888 372-3302
Phillipsburg *(G-9798)*
Specialists Group LLC......F....... 316 267-7375
Wichita *(G-15635)*
Spencer Reed Group LLC......C....... 913 663-4400
Leawood *(G-5557)*
Trac Staffing Service Inc......F....... 913 341-1150
Shawnee Mission *(G-11939)*

TEN PIN CENTERS

AMF Bowling Centers Inc......E....... 913 451-6400
Overland Park *(G-8382)*
Army & Air Force Exchange Svc......E....... 785 239-4366
Fort Riley *(G-1945)*
B & E Inc......F....... 913 299-1110
Kansas City *(G-3833)*
Bobec Inc......E....... 913 248-1110
Shawnee Mission *(G-11175)*
Boulevard One Inc......E....... 316 636-9494
Wichita *(G-13873)*
Boulevard One Inc......E....... 316 722-5211
Wichita *(G-13874)*
Boyd & Boyd Inc......D....... 913 764-4568
Olathe *(G-7558)*
Coach and Four Bowling Lanes......F....... 785 472-5571
Ellsworth *(G-1663)*
Colby Bowl......F....... 785 460-2672
Colby *(G-996)*
Frazier Enterprises Inc......F....... 316 788-0263
Derby *(G-1247)*
Incred-A-Bowl LLC......D....... 913 851-1700
Overland Park *(G-8841)*
Junction City Bowl Inc......F....... 785 238-6813
Junction City *(G-3703)*
Kc Bowl Inc......F....... 913 299-1110
Kansas City *(G-4164)*
Lynco Rec Inc......F....... 620 231-2222
Pittsburg *(G-9896)*
Mayberrys Inc......F....... 620 793-9400
Great Bend *(G-2605)*
Mission Recreation Inc......E....... 913 782-0279
Olathe *(G-7906)*
Northrock Lanes Inc......E....... 316 636-5444
Wichita *(G-15192)*
Prairie Sports Inc......F....... 785 625-2916
Hays *(G-2887)*
Raymire Inc......F....... 620 275-4061
Garden City *(G-2263)*
Rekat Recreation Inc......D....... 785 272-1881
Topeka *(G-13008)*
Southwest Bowl......F....... 785 272-1324
Topeka *(G-13082)*
Spare Tyme LLC......F....... 620 225-2695
Dodge City *(G-1433)*
Tins Inc......E....... 785 842-1234
Lawrence *(G-5137)*
West Ridge Lanes Fmly Fun Ctr......E....... 785 273-3333
Topeka *(G-13239)*

TENT REPAIR SHOP

Girard Tarps Inc......G....... 620 724-8909
Girard *(G-2410)*

TENTS: All Materials

Infinity Tents Inc......E....... 913 820-3700
Kansas City *(G-4100)*

TERMINAL BOARDS

Elec-Tron Inc......D....... 316 522-3401
Wichita *(G-14263)*

TERMITE CONTROL SVCS

Midwest Pest Control LLC......F....... 316 681-3417
Wichita *(G-15098)*

TESTERS: Environmental

Aviation Cnslting Engrg Sltons......G....... 316 265-8335
Maize *(G-6508)*

TESTING SVCS

Mayhew Envmtl Training Assoc......E....... 800 444-6382
Lawrence *(G-5014)*
National Bd For Rspratory Care......F....... 913 895-4900
Overland Park *(G-9069)*
PSI Services Inc......F....... 843 520-2992
Olathe *(G-8010)*
PSI Services Inc......C....... 913 895-4600
Olathe *(G-8011)*
T T Companies Inc......A....... 913 599-6886
Olathe *(G-8097)*
XCEL NDT LLC......E....... 785 455-2027
Clifton *(G-903)*

TEXTILE & APPAREL SVCS

US Textiles LLC......F....... 913 660-0995
Shawnee Mission *(G-11970)*

TEXTILE FINISHING: Embossing, Cotton, Broadwoven

Kellys Corporate Apparel......G....... 316 263-5858
Wichita *(G-14847)*

TEXTILES: Flock

Hix Corporation......D....... 620 231-8568
Pittsburg *(G-9876)*

THEATER COMPANIES

Topeka Performing Arts Center......F....... 785 234-2787
Topeka *(G-13184)*

THEATRICAL PRODUCERS

Overbudget Productions......E....... 913 254-1186
Olathe *(G-7967)*

THEATRICAL PRODUCERS & SVCS

Actors LLC......E....... 316 263-0222
Wichita *(G-13610)*
Marysvlle Area Cmnty Thtre Inc......D....... 785 268-0420
Marysville *(G-6903)*
New Theatre Company......C....... 913 649-7469
Shawnee Mission *(G-11681)*
SNC Alarm Service......E....... 620 665-6651
Hutchinson *(G-3442)*
Ticket Solutions LLC......E....... 913 384-4751
Shawnee Mission *(G-11932)*

THEATRICAL PRODUCTION SVCS

Wichita Center For The Arts......F....... 316 315-0151
Wichita *(G-15985)*

THEATRICAL TALENT & BOOKING AGENCIES

Complete Music Inc......E....... 913 432-1111
Leawood *(G-5357)*

THEOLOGICAL SEMINARIES

World Impact Inc......E....... 316 687-9398
Wichita *(G-16073)*

THREAD: Embroidery

Team Threads......G....... 620 429-4402
Columbus *(G-1089)*

TILE: Brick & Structural, Clay

Salina Concrete Products Inc......F....... 316 943-3241
Wichita *(G-15510)*

TILE: Rubber

Davinci Roofscapes LLC......E....... 913 599-0766
Lenexa *(G-5804)*

TIMBER PRDTS WHOLESALERS

Lumber One LLC......E....... 913 583-9889
De Soto *(G-1206)*

TIMING DEVICES: Electronic

Pivot International Inc......E....... 913 312-6900
Lenexa *(G-6060)*

TIRE & TUBE REPAIR MATERIALS, WHOLESALE

Tech Inc......E....... 913 492-6440
Lenexa *(G-6171)*

TIRE CORD & FABRIC

Polymer Group Inc......C....... 620 532-5141
Kingman *(G-4611)*

TIRE DEALERS

Action Tire & Service Inc......F....... 913 631-9600
Shawnee Mission *(G-11072)*
American Tire Distributors......E....... 316 616-9600
Wichita *(G-13694)*
Becker Tire & Treading Inc......D....... 620 793-5414
Great Bend *(G-2519)*

Becker Tire & Treading Inc F 316 943-7979
Wichita *(G-13825)*
Berning Tire Inc F 913 422-3033
Bonner Springs *(G-541)*
Blue Valley Goodyear Service F 913 345-1380
Shawnee Mission *(G-11170)*
Bosleys Tire Service Co Inc E 316 524-8511
Wichita *(G-13871)*
Bridgestone Americas F 785 267-0074
Topeka *(G-12405)*
Bridgestone Ret Operations LLC F 913 782-1833
Olathe *(G-7561)*
Bridgestone Ret Operations LLC E 913 334-1555
Kansas City *(G-3878)*
Bridgestone Ret Operations LLC F 913 492-8160
Shawnee Mission *(G-11181)*
Bridgestone Ret Operations LLC F 316 684-2682
Wichita *(G-13889)*
Buds Tire Service Inc F 785 632-2135
Clay Center *(G-846)*
Bultman Company Inc Mfg F 620 544-8004
Hugoton *(G-3149)*
Burnett Automotive Inc F 913 681-8824
Overland Park *(G-8494)*
Burnett Automotive Inc F 785 539-8970
Manhattan *(G-6572)*
Central AG Wheel & Tire F 316 942-1408
Wichita *(G-13977)*
Chris Archer Group Inc E 316 945-4000
Wichita *(G-14014)*
Clingan Tires Incorporated E 620 624-5649
Liberal *(G-6294)*
D & D Tire Inc F 785 843-0191
Lawrence *(G-4823)*
Economy Mfg Co Inc E 620 725-3520
Sedan *(G-10842)*
Fowlers LLC F 785 475-3451
Oberlin *(G-7494)*
Goodyear Tire & Rubber Company F 785 266-3862
Topeka *(G-12643)*
Great Bend Cooperative Assn F 620 792-1281
Great Bend *(G-2577)*
Gregg Tire Co Inc F 785 233-4156
Topeka *(G-12651)*
Gregg Tire Co Inc F 785 233-4156
Topeka *(G-12652)*
Kansasland Tire Inc C 316 522-5434
Wichita *(G-14830)*
Kansasland Tire Inc F 785 243-2706
Concordia *(G-1119)*
Kansasland Tire Inc F 620 231-7210
Pittsburg *(G-9890)*
Kansasland Tire Inc F 316 744-0401
Park City *(G-9624)*
Karls Tire & Auto Service Inc F 316 685-5338
Wichita *(G-14833)*
Leroy Cooperative Assn Inc E 620 964-2225
Le Roy *(G-5196)*
Macconnell Enterprises LLC E 785 885-8081
Natoma *(G-7231)*
Mels Tire LLC F 620 342-8473
Emporia *(G-1792)*
O K Thompsons Tire Inc E 785 738-2283
Beloit *(G-497)*
Rakies Oil LLC F 620 442-2210
Arkansas City *(G-171)*
Shamrock Tire & Auto Service E 316 522-2297
Wichita *(G-15572)*
Shore Tire Co Inc E 913 541-9300
Lenexa *(G-6132)*
Super Oil Co Inc F 785 354-1410
Topeka *(G-13125)*
Superior Car Care Center LLC F 620 492-6856
Johnson *(G-3663)*
T & W Tire LLC E 316 683-8364
Wichita *(G-15712)*
T O Haas LLC F 620 662-0261
Hutchinson *(G-3461)*
Tire Town Inc E 913 682-3201
Leavenworth *(G-5298)*
Wiebe Tire & Automotive F 316 283-4242
Newton *(G-7429)*
Wiseman Discount Tire Inc F 620 231-5291
Frontenac *(G-2067)*

TIRE RECAPPING & RETREADING

Bridgestone Ret Operations LLC F 913 498-0880
Shawnee Mission *(G-11180)*
Bridgestone Ret Operations LLC E 316 315-0363
Wichita *(G-13887)*
Bridgestone Ret Operations LLC E 316 942-1332
Wichita *(G-13888)*
Bridgestone Ret Operations LLC F 913 831-9955
Overland Park *(G-8485)*
Bridgestone Ret Operations LLC F 913 299-3090
Kansas City *(G-3877)*
Bridgestone Ret Operations LLC F 913 393-2212
Olathe *(G-7560)*
Garden City Tire Center Inc F 620 276-7652
Garden City *(G-2178)*
Kistler Service Inc E 620 782-3611
Udall *(G-13278)*

TIRES & INNER TUBES

American Tire Distributors E 316 616-9600
Wichita *(G-13694)*

TIRES & TUBES WHOLESALERS

American Tire Distributors E 316 616-9600
Wichita *(G-13694)*
Burnett Automotive Inc F 913 681-8824
Overland Park *(G-8494)*
Burnett Automotive Inc F 785 539-8970
Manhattan *(G-6572)*
Camso Manufacturing Usa Ltd E 620 340-6500
Emporia *(G-1715)*
Chris Archer Group Inc E 316 945-4000
Wichita *(G-14014)*
D & D Tire Inc F 785 843-0191
Lawrence *(G-4823)*
O K Thompsons Tire Inc E 785 738-2283
Beloit *(G-497)*
O K Tire of Dodge City Inc F 620 225-0204
Dodge City *(G-1415)*
Shamrock Tire & Auto Service E 316 522-2297
Wichita *(G-15572)*
Shore Tire Co Inc E 913 541-9300
Lenexa *(G-6132)*
Super Oil Co Inc F 785 354-1410
Topeka *(G-13125)*
T O Haas LLC F 620 662-0261
Hutchinson *(G-3461)*
Tire Town Inc E 913 682-3201
Leavenworth *(G-5298)*
Wiebe Tire & Automotive F 316 283-4242
Newton *(G-7429)*

TIRES & TUBES, WHOLESALE: Automotive

Allied Oil & Tire Company F 316 530-5221
Wichita *(G-13673)*
Becker Tire & Treading Inc D 620 793-5414
Great Bend *(G-2519)*
Becker Tire & Treading Inc F 316 943-7979
Wichita *(G-13825)*
Bridgestone Ret Operations LLC F 913 393-2212
Olathe *(G-7560)*
Buds Tire Service Inc F 785 632-2135
Clay Center *(G-846)*
Carrolls LLC F 913 321-2233
Kansas City *(G-3893)*
Clingan Tires Incorporated E 620 624-5649
Liberal *(G-6294)*
Garden City Tire Center Inc F 620 276-7652
Garden City *(G-2178)*
Great Western Tire of Dodge Cy F 620 225-1343
Dodge City *(G-1367)*
Gregg Tire Co Inc F 785 233-4156
Topeka *(G-12651)*
Rakies Oil LLC F 620 442-2210
Arkansas City *(G-171)*

TIRES & TUBES, WHOLESALE: Truck

Bridgestone Americas F 785 267-0074
Topeka *(G-12405)*
Pomps Tire Service Inc F 913 621-5200
Kansas City *(G-4326)*

TIRES, USED, WHOLESALE

Easy Money Pawn Shop Inc G 316 687-2727
Wichita *(G-14255)*

TIRES: Agricultural, Pneumatic

Central AG Wheel & Tire F 316 942-1408
Wichita *(G-13977)*

TIRES: Auto

Premium Ventures LLC F 785 842-5500
Lawrence *(G-5073)*

TIRES: Indl Vehicles

Carlstar Group LLC E 913 667-1000
Kansas City *(G-3891)*

TITLE & TRUST COMPANIES

Chicago Title Insurance Co F 913 782-0041
Olathe *(G-7592)*
Fidelity National Fincl Inc F 913 422-5122
Leawood *(G-5399)*
First American Title Company E 316 554-2872
Wichita *(G-14370)*
Guardian Title & Trust Company E 620 223-3330
Wichita *(G-14524)*
Kansas Secured Title F 316 320-2410
El Dorado *(G-1576)*
Land Title Services Inc F 785 823-7223
Salina *(G-10579)*
Lawyers Title of Kansas Inc F 785 271-9500
Topeka *(G-12835)*
Metro Title Services LLC D 913 236-9923
Lenexa *(G-5997)*
Midwest Title Co Inc F 913 393-2511
Olathe *(G-7898)*
Moon Abstract Company F 620 342-1917
Overland Park *(G-9050)*
Nations Title Agency E 913 341-2705
Prairie Village *(G-10051)*
Reno County Abstract & Title F 620 662-5455
Hutchinson *(G-3423)*
Security 1st Title LLC E 620 842-3333
Anthony *(G-135)*
Security 1st Title LLC E 316 260-5634
Augusta *(G-344)*
Security 1st Title LLC E 316 267-8371
Wichita *(G-15542)*
Title Midwest Inc F 785 232-9110
Fairway *(G-1920)*
Tm Holdings Inc F 785 232-9110
Fairway *(G-1921)*
Tri-County Title & Abstract Co F 913 682-8911
Leavenworth *(G-5301)*

TITLE ABSTRACT & SETTLEMENT OFFICES

Accurate Title Company LLC F 913 338-0100
Overland Park *(G-8343)*
Capital Title Insurance Co Lc F 785 272-2900
Topeka *(G-12434)*
Chicago Title and Trust Co F 913 451-1200
Leawood *(G-5351)*
First American Title Company D 316 267-8371
Wichita *(G-14371)*
Kansas Secured Title Sedgwick F 316 262-8261
Wichita *(G-14823)*
Kansas Secured Ttle Inc F 785 232-9349
Topeka *(G-12804)*
Security 1st Title LLC F 620 442-7029
Arkansas City *(G-178)*
Security 1st Title LLC F 316 322-8164
El Dorado *(G-1601)*
Security 1st Title LLC E 316 722-2463
Wichita *(G-15541)*
Security 1st Title LLC F 620 326-7460
Wellington *(G-13527)*

TITLE INSURANCE AGENTS

First American Title Company E 316 554-2872
Wichita *(G-14370)*
Nations Title Agency E 913 341-2705
Prairie Village *(G-10051)*

TITLE INSURANCE: Real Estate

Chicago Title and Trust Co F 913 451-1200
Leawood *(G-5351)*
Chicago Title Insurance Co F 913 782-0041
Olathe *(G-7592)*
Chicago Title Insurance Co F 913 451-1200
Overland Park *(G-8546)*
Koehler Bortnick Team LLC E 913 239-2069
Leawood *(G-5452)*

TOBACCO & PRDTS, WHOLESALE: Chewing

Sunflower Supply Company Inc........E....... 620 783-5473
Galena *(G-2088)*

TOBACCO & PRDTS, WHOLESALE: Cigarettes

Kansas Candy & Tobacco Inc..............F....... 316 942-9081
Wichita *(G-14789)*

TOBACCO & TOBACCO PRDTS WHOLESALERS

Joe Smith Company..............................E....... 620 231-3610
Pittsburg *(G-9883)*
Philip Morris USA Inc..........................F....... 913 339-9317
Shawnee Mission *(G-11731)*
Wichita Tobacco & Candy Co...............F....... 316 264-2412
Wichita *(G-16040)*

TOILETRIES, COSMETICS & PERFUME STORES

Ahn Marketing Incorporated.................F....... 913 342-2176
Kansas City *(G-3793)*
Bath & Body Works LLC........................F....... 785 749-0214
Lawrence *(G-4751)*
Beauty Brands LLC...............................E....... 913 492-7900
Lenexa *(G-5694)*
Beauty Brands LLC...............................E....... 913 393-4800
Olathe *(G-7549)*
Prescription Centre..............................G....... 620 364-5523
Burlington *(G-641)*
Salon Brands..F....... 785 301-2984
Hays *(G-2906)*
Wholesale Beauty Club Inc...................F....... 316 687-9890
Wichita *(G-15966)*

TOILETRIES, WHOLESALE: Hair Preparations

C & W Operations Ltd............................C....... 913 438-6400
Shawnee Mission *(G-11196)*

TOLL ROAD OPERATIONS

Kansas Turnpike Authority....................E....... 620 326-5044
Wellington *(G-13508)*
Kansas Turnpike Authority....................F....... 785 266-9414
Topeka *(G-12808)*
Kansas Turnpike Authority....................D....... 316 682-4537
Wichita *(G-14829)*
Kansas Turnpike Authority....................E....... 316 321-0631
El Dorado *(G-1577)*

TOOL & DIE STEEL

Larue Machine Inc.................................F....... 620 431-3303
Chanute *(G-738)*
PDQ Tools and Equipment Inc.............G....... 913 492-5800
Shawnee Mission *(G-11721)*

TOOL REPAIR SVCS

T W Lacy & Associates Inc...................F....... 913 706-7625
Prairie Village *(G-10073)*

TOOLS: Carpenters', Including Levels & Chisels, Exc Saws

Sands Level and Tool Company...........D....... 620 325-2687
Neodesha *(G-7248)*

TOOLS: Hand

Great Plains Manufacturing Inc............C....... 785 263-2486
Abilene *(G-34)*
J&M Tools LLC.......................................G....... 785 608-3343
Topeka *(G-12733)*
Kraft Tool Company...............................C....... 913 422-4848
Shawnee Mission *(G-11538)*
Russell Steel Products Inc....................E....... 913 831-4600
Kansas City *(G-4391)*
Wilde Tool Co Inc...................................E....... 785 742-7171
Hiawatha *(G-3028)*

TOOLS: Hand, Masons'

Finishpro Tools LLC..............................E....... 913 631-0804
Olathe *(G-7709)*

TOOLS: Hand, Power

Alltite Inc...E....... 316 686-3010
Wichita *(G-13678)*
Broderson Manufacturing Corp............D....... 913 888-0606
Lenexa *(G-5718)*

TOOLS: Hand, Shovels Or Spades

Haivala Concrete Tools Inc...................G....... 316 263-1683
Wichita *(G-14543)*

TOURIST INFORMATION BUREAU

Wichita Convention Tourism Bur..........F....... 316 265-2800
Wichita *(G-15991)*

TOURIST LODGINGS

Earth Rising Inc......................................F....... 913 796-2141
Mc Louth *(G-6926)*
Inland Industries Inc..............................G....... 913 492-9050
Bucyrus *(G-600)*
Kcai LP...E....... 913 596-6000
Kansas City *(G-4166)*

TOWELS: Paper

Envision Inc..F....... 316 425-7123
Wichita *(G-14294)*
Envision Inc..E....... 316 267-2244
Kansas City *(G-3991)*

TOWERS, SECTIONS: Transmission, Radio & Television

US Tower Corp..E....... 785 524-9966
Lincoln *(G-6389)*

TOWING BARS & SYSTEMS

Magna Tech Inc.......................................E....... 620 431-3490
Chanute *(G-740)*

TOYS

Step2 Discovery LLC..............................E....... 620 232-2400
Pittsburg *(G-9940)*

TOYS & HOBBY GOODS & SPLYS, WHOL: Toy Novelties & Amusements

Continental American Corp..................C....... 316 321-4551
El Dorado *(G-1550)*

TOYS & HOBBY GOODS & SPLYS, WHOLESALE: Amusement Goods

Fun Services of Kansas City.................E....... 913 631-3772
Shawnee Mission *(G-11385)*

TOYS & HOBBY GOODS & SPLYS, WHOLESALE: Arts/Crafts Eqpt/Sply

Decorator and Craft Corp.....................D....... 316 685-6265
Wichita *(G-14184)*
Evans Industries Inc..............................G....... 316 262-2551
Wichita *(G-14310)*

TOYS, HOBBY GOODS & SPLYS WHOLESALERS

Starlite Mold Co......................................F....... 316 262-3350
Wichita *(G-15658)*

TOYS: Kites

Kansas Assn For Conserv & Envr........G....... 785 889-4384
Onaga *(G-8177)*

TRACTOR REPAIR SVCS

Kansas Kenworth Inc.............................E....... 785 823-9700
Salina *(G-10566)*
Shepherds Truck & Tractor...................F....... 620 331-2970
Independence *(G-3560)*

TRADE SHOW ARRANGEMENT SVCS

Skyline E3 Inc...F....... 913 599-4787
Lenexa *(G-6137)*

TRADERS: Commodity, Contracts

Koch Resources LLC.............................E....... 316 828-5500
Wichita *(G-14887)*
Seaboard Corporation..........................C....... 913 676-8800
Merriam *(G-7103)*

TRAFFIC CONTROL FLAGGING SVCS

City of Overland Park............................E....... 913 895-6040
Overland Park *(G-8556)*
Roadsafe Traffic Systems Inc...............D....... 316 778-2112
El Dorado *(G-1599)*
Roadsafe Traffic Systems Inc...............E....... 316 322-3070
El Dorado *(G-1600)*

TRAILER COACHES: Automobile

Custom Campers Inc.............................C....... 620 431-3990
Chanute *(G-723)*

TRAILER PARKS

Lamont Hill Resort Inc..........................E....... 785 828-3131
Vassar *(G-13371)*

TRAILERS & PARTS: Truck & Semi's

Bradford Built Inc...................................E....... 785 325-3300
Washington *(G-13460)*
Doonan Specialized Trailer LLC...........E....... 620 792-6222
Great Bend *(G-2554)*
Dunning Express Inc.............................E....... 785 806-3915
Elwood *(G-1685)*
Eagle Trailer Company Inc...................G....... 785 841-3200
Lawrence *(G-4844)*
Flint Hills Industries Inc........................G....... 620 947-3127
Hillsboro *(G-3048)*
High Plains Machine Works Inc............F....... 785 625-4672
Hays *(G-2845)*
Landoll Corporation...............................B....... 785 562-5381
Marysville *(G-6893)*
R B Manufacturing Company...............G....... 913 829-3233
Olathe *(G-8016)*
Roadruner Manufacturing LLC............G....... 785 586-2228
Levant *(G-6265)*
Sharp Manufacturing LLC.....................F....... 785 363-7336
Blue Rapids *(G-537)*
Sun Valley Inc...E....... 620 662-0101
Hutchinson *(G-3456)*
VT Hackney Inc......................................C....... 620 331-6600
Independence *(G-3571)*
Wabash National Corporation..............C....... 913 621-7298
Kansas City *(G-4527)*
Western Truck Equipment Co...............F....... 620 793-8464
Great Bend *(G-2662)*
William R Harris Trucking......................F....... 913 422-5551
Shawnee Mission *(G-12010)*

TRAILERS & TRAILER EQPT

Circle D Corporation Inc.......................E....... 620 947-2385
Hillsboro *(G-3044)*
Cromwell Builders Mfg..........................F....... 785 949-2433
Carlton *(G-686)*
Eagle Trailer Company Inc...................G....... 785 841-3200
Lawrence *(G-4844)*
Landoll Corporation...............................E....... 785 738-6613
Beloit *(G-490)*

TRAILERS OR VANS: Horse Transportation, Fifth-Wheel Type

Short Go Inc..D....... 620 223-2866
Fort Scott *(G-2004)*

TRAILERS: Bodies

Landoll Corporation...............................F....... 785 562-4780
Marysville *(G-6894)*
Unruh Fab Inc...E....... 316 772-5400
Sedgwick *(G-10853)*

TRAILERS: Bus, Tractor Type

Brown Industries LLC............................D....... 785 842-6506
Lawrence *(G-4770)*

TRANSFORMERS: Electronic

Pwi Inc...E....... 316 942-2811
Wichita *(G-15381)*
Torotel Products Inc...............................C....... 913 747-6111
Olathe *(G-8116)*

PRDT & SVC

TRANSFORMERS: Power Related

ABB Enterprise Software Inc.................D....... 913 317-1310
Overland Park *(G-8337)*
Aerospace Systems Cmpnents Inc.......D....... 316 686-7392
Wichita *(G-13638)*
Control Components Inc........................G....... 620 221-2343
Winfield *(G-16127)*
Emerald Transformer Kansas LLC........E....... 620 251-6380
Coffeyville *(G-936)*
Experitec Inc..F....... 913 894-4044
Shawnee Mission *(G-11356)*
Harpenau Power & Process Inc.............G....... 913 451-2227
Lenexa *(G-5891)*
Torotel Products Inc...............................C....... 913 747-6111
Olathe *(G-8116)*

TRANSFORMERS: Signaling Transformers, Electric

Quickertek Inc..G....... 316 691-1585
Wichita *(G-15394)*

TRANSFORMERS: Specialty

Everbrite Electronics Inc........................D....... 620 431-7383
Chanute *(G-727)*

TRANSFORMERS: Voltage Regulating

Solomon Transformers LLC..................B....... 785 655-2191
Solomon *(G-12054)*

TRANSLATION & INTERPRETATION SVCS

Propio Ls LLC...F....... 913 381-3143
Overland Park *(G-9196)*

TRANSPORTATION AGENTS & BROKERS

ASAP Transport Solutions LLC.............E....... 800 757-1178
Lenexa *(G-5666)*
Bruenger Trucking Company.................E....... 316 744-0494
Park City *(G-9605)*
Gold Star Transportation Inc...............E....... 913 341-0081
Overland Park *(G-8762)*
Kansota Transport Inc............................E....... 620 792-9100
Great Bend *(G-2598)*
Myfreightworld Tech Inc.........................E....... 913 677-6691
Leawood *(G-5495)*
P1 Transportation LLC...........................F....... 913 249-1505
Overland Park *(G-9134)*
Ryan Transportation Svc Inc.................C....... 800 860-7926
Overland Park *(G-9266)*

TRANSPORTATION ARRANGEMENT SVCS, PASSENGER: Airline Ticket

Jade Travel Center Inc............................F....... 785 273-1226
Topeka *(G-12736)*
Vidtronix LLC..F....... 913 441-9777
Shawnee *(G-11047)*

TRANSPORTATION BROKERS: Truck

Butler Transport Inc.................................C....... 913 321-0047
Kansas City *(G-3882)*
C L Nationwide Inc..................................F....... 913 492-5200
Shawnee Mission *(G-11198)*
D & L Transport LLC...............................D....... 913 402-4514
Overland Park *(G-8626)*
Dynamic Logistix LLC.............................E....... 913 274-3800
Overland Park *(G-8668)*
Greg Orscheln Trnsp Co.........................E....... 913 371-1260
Lenexa *(G-5884)*
Hannebaum Grain Co Inc.........................F....... 785 825-8205
Salina *(G-10534)*
J & H Transportation Inc.........................F....... 316 733-8200
Andover *(G-96)*
J&J Driveaway Systems LLC..................E....... 913 387-0158
Overland Park *(G-8868)*
Metro Companies Inc...............................D....... 316 838-3345
Wichita *(G-15059)*
Team Drive-Away Inc..............................C....... 913 825-4776
Olathe *(G-8103)*
Tiger Cool Express LLC..........................F....... 913 305-3510
Overland Park *(G-9411)*
Transportation Inc...................................E....... 785 242-3660
Ottawa *(G-8316)*

TRANSPORTATION CLEARINGHOUSE

Raudin McCormick Inc............................C....... 913 928-5000
Lenexa *(G-6090)*

TRANSPORTATION EPQT & SPLYS, WHOL: Aircraft Engs/Eng Parts

Pratt & Whitney Eng Svcs Inc.................G....... 316 945-9763
Wichita *(G-15322)*

TRANSPORTATION EPQT & SPLYS, WHOLESALE: Acft/Space Vehicle

Rockwell Collins Inc................................C....... 316 677-4808
Wichita *(G-15474)*
Yingling Aircraft Inc................................D....... 316 943-3246
Wichita *(G-16085)*

TRANSPORTATION EQPT & SPLYS WHOLESALERS, NEC

McFarlane Aviation Inc............................D....... 785 594-2741
Baldwin City *(G-366)*
Textron Aviation Inc.................................C....... 620 332-0228
Independence *(G-3564)*

TRANSPORTATION PROGRAM REGULATION & ADMIN, GOVT: State

Kansas Department Trnsp.......................D....... 620 583-5661
Eureka *(G-1893)*

TRANSPORTATION PROGRAMS REGULATION & ADMINISTRATION SVCS

County of Johnson....................................F....... 913 782-2210
Olathe *(G-7620)*
Kansas Department Trnsp.......................C....... 316 744-1271
Wichita *(G-14796)*
Kansas Department Trnsp.......................F....... 785 527-2520
Belleville *(G-458)*
Kansas Department Trnsp.......................D....... 785 672-3113
Oakley *(G-7478)*
Kansas Department Trnsp.......................E....... 316 321-3370
El Dorado *(G-1575)*
Kansas Department Trnsp.......................B....... 785 823-3754
Salina *(G-10564)*
Kansas Department Trnsp.......................E....... 785 486-2142
Horton *(G-3128)*

TRANSPORTATION SVCS, NEC

4g Express Inc..F....... 316 619-3888
Colwich *(G-1090)*
Anderson County Council........................F....... 785 448-4237
Garnett *(G-2368)*
Cardinal Logistics.....................................E....... 620 223-4903
Fort Scott *(G-1956)*
Fcg Inc...F....... 620 545-8300
Clearwater *(G-892)*
First Class Transportation.......................F....... 785 266-1331
Topeka *(G-12613)*
Flatlands Transportation Ict....................F....... 316 250-1280
Wichita *(G-14383)*
Flint Hills Area Trnsp Agcy Bd...............D....... 787 537-6345
Manhattan *(G-6630)*
Hallcon Corporation................................F....... 913 890-6105
Lenexa *(G-5887)*
KS Transit Inc..F....... 281 841-6078
Overland Park *(G-8931)*
PSI Transport LLC...................................E....... 785 675-3881
Hoxie *(G-3140)*
Sarik LLC..F....... 785 379-1235
Topeka *(G-13036)*
Sedgwick County Transportation............E....... 316 660-7070
Wichita *(G-15548)*
Western Transport....................................F....... 620 271-0540
Garden City *(G-2312)*

TRANSPORTATION SVCS: Airport

Extreme Limousine LLC...........................F....... 913 831-2039
Shawnee *(G-10951)*
Lafarge North America Inc......................B....... 913 780-6809
Olathe *(G-7852)*
Wheatland Enterprises Inc......................E....... 816 756-1700
Leawood *(G-5599)*

TRANSPORTATION SVCS: Bus Line, Interstate

Kincaid Coach Lines Inc..........................D....... 913 441-6200
Edwardsville *(G-1506)*

TRANSPORTATION SVCS: Commuter Bus Operation

Topeka Metropolitan Trnst Auth..............D....... 785 233-2011
Topeka *(G-13182)*

TRANSPORTATION SVCS: Maint Facilities, Vehicle Passenger

Fleet Services Topeka..............................E....... 785 368-3735
Topeka *(G-12616)*
Hutchinson Usd 308.................................F....... 620 615-5575
Hutchinson *(G-3327)*

TRANSPORTATION SVCS: Railroad Switching

RJ Crman Derailment Svcs LLC..............F....... 913 371-1537
Kansas City *(G-4381)*
Watco Inc..D....... 208 734-4644
Pittsburg *(G-9962)*

TRANSPORTATION SVCS: Railroad Terminals

Watco Transloading LLC..........................D....... 620 231-2230
Pittsburg *(G-9966)*

TRANSPORTATION SVCS: Railroad, Passenger

CTI Freight Systems Inc...........................F....... 913 236-7400
Bucyrus *(G-595)*

TRANSPORTATION SVCS: Railroads, Interurban

Railamerica Inc...D....... 785 543-6527
Phillipsburg *(G-9796)*

TRANSPORTATION SVCS: Railroads, Steam

American Refrigerated Ex Inc..................F....... 913 406-8562
Olathe *(G-7527)*

TRANSPORTATION SVCS: Rental, Local

Security Transport Service......................E....... 785 267-3030
Topeka *(G-13056)*

TRANSPORTATION: Air, Nonscheduled Passenger

Executive Airshare LLC...........................F....... 816 221-7200
Lenexa *(G-5842)*

TRANSPORTATION: Air, Scheduled Freight

United Parcel Service Inc.........................F....... 800 742-5877
Salina *(G-10746)*

TRANSPORTATION: Bus Transit Systems

City of Wichita..C....... 316 265-7221
Wichita *(G-14031)*
Railcrew Xpress LLC...............................A....... 913 928-5000
Lenexa *(G-6089)*
Renzenberger Inc......................................C....... 913 631-0450
Lenexa *(G-6104)*
Shuttle Bus General Pub Trnsp...............D....... 620 326-3953
Wellington *(G-13529)*
Yellowfin Transportation Inc...................F....... 913 645-4834
Shawnee *(G-11057)*

TRANSPORTATION: Bus Transit Systems

Ds Bus Lines Inc.......................................D....... 913 384-1190
Bonner Springs *(G-551)*
Durham School Services L P...................E....... 620 331-7088
Independence *(G-3512)*
Greyhound Lines Inc................................E....... 785 827-9754
Salina *(G-10523)*
Lansing Unified Schl Dst 469..................E....... 913 250-0749
Lansing *(G-4680)*
Yellowfin Transportation Inc...................F....... 913 645-4834
Shawnee *(G-11057)*

TRANSPORTATION: Deep Sea Domestic Freight

Koch Carbon LLC ....E 316 828-5500
Wichita *(G-14875)*

TRANSPORTATION: Deep Sea Foreign Freight

Koch Carbon LLC ....E 316 828-5500
Wichita *(G-14875)*
Seaboard Corporation ....C 913 676-8800
Merriam *(G-7103)*

TRANSPORTATION: Local Passenger, NEC

A & A Medical Trnsp Inc ....F 785 233-8212
Topeka *(G-12277)*
Developmental Svcs NW Kans Inc ....F 785 621-2078
Hays *(G-2787)*
Medi Coach LLC ....E 913 825-1945
Shawnee *(G-10993)*
Otl Logistics Inc ....D 816 918-7688
Basehor *(G-386)*
Renzenberger Inc ....C 913 631-0450
Lenexa *(G-6104)*
Yellowfin Transportation Inc ....F 913 645-4834
Shawnee *(G-11057)*

TRANSPORTATION: Transit Systems, NEC

Bell Taxi and Trnsp Inc ....F 785 238-6161
Junction City *(G-3672)*
County of Johnson ....F 913 782-2210
Olathe *(G-7620)*
Finney Cnty Committee On Aging ....E 620 272-3626
Garden City *(G-2160)*
First Student Inc ....D 913 422-8501
Lenexa *(G-5857)*
Flint Hlls Area Trnsp Agcy Inc ....E 785 537-6345
Manhattan *(G-6635)*
Mv Transportation Inc ....E 785 312-7054
Lawrence *(G-5034)*
Rnw Transit LLC ....F 785 285-0083
Sabetha *(G-10326)*
Southwest KS Coord Trans Counc ....E 620 227-8803
Dodge City *(G-1432)*
Tri-Valley Developmental Svcs ....D 620 223-3990
Fort Scott *(G-2012)*
Tri-Valley Developmental Svcs ....D 620 365-3307
Iola *(G-3637)*

TRAP ROCK: Dimension

Ash Grove Materials Corp ....D 913 345-2030
Overland Park *(G-8404)*

TRAPS: Stem

Hughes Machinery Company ....G 316 612-0868
Wichita *(G-14649)*

TRAVEL AGENCIES

AAA Allied Group Inc ....F 785 233-0222
Topeka *(G-12281)*
Automobile Club of Missouri ....F 316 942-0008
Wichita *(G-13774)*
Brennco Travel Services Inc ....F 913 660-0121
Shawnee Mission *(G-11179)*
City of Dodge City ....E 620 225-8186
Dodge City *(G-1323)*
Eidsons Florist ....F 913 721-2775
Kansas City *(G-3981)*
Hoover Stores Inc ....D 620 364-5444
Burlington *(G-637)*
Jade Travel Center Inc ....F 785 273-1226
Topeka *(G-12736)*
K C I Roadrunner Express Inc ....D 785 238-6161
Junction City *(G-3710)*
Loves Travel Stops ....F 785 263-3390
Abilene *(G-45)*
Loves Travel Stops ....F 620 872-5727
Scott City *(G-10820)*
Royal Caribbean Cruises Ltd ....A 316 554-5000
Wichita *(G-15487)*
Shorts Travel Management Inc ....E 319 234-5577
Overland Park *(G-9308)*

TRAVEL CLUBS

Automobile Club of Missouri ....F 316 942-0008
Wichita *(G-13774)*
Global Services Inc ....D 913 451-0960
Leawood *(G-5414)*
Loves Travel Stops ....E 785 726-2561
Ellis *(G-1649)*

TRAVEL TRAILER DEALERS

Boss Motors Inc ....F 785 562-3696
Marysville *(G-6880)*

TRAVEL TRAILERS & CAMPERS

Astro Truck Covers Inc ....D 785 448-5577
Ottawa *(G-8246)*
Bultman Company Inc Mfg ....F 620 544-8004
Hugoton *(G-3149)*
Lacy Rv Ranch Inc ....G 620 245-9608
McPherson *(G-6986)*
Nu-WA Industries Inc ....C 620 431-2088
Chanute *(G-748)*

TRAVELER ACCOMMODATIONS, NEC

7240 Shawnee Mission Hospitali ....E 913 217-7283
Overland Park *(G-8331)*
A Scampis Bar & Grill ....E 785 539-5311
Manhattan *(G-6527)*
Abilene Super Eight ....F 785 263-4545
Abilene *(G-9)*
AHP H6 Topeka ....E 785 273-0066
Topeka *(G-12302)*
Airport Red Coach Inn of Wichi ....D 316 942-5600
Wichita *(G-13655)*
Allen County Lodging LLC ....F 620 365-3030
Iola *(G-3586)*
Americal Inc ....F 785 890-7566
Goodland *(G-2461)*
AmericInn Motel & Suites ....F 913 367-4000
Atchison *(G-203)*
Angus Inn Best Western Motel ....D 620 792-3541
Great Bend *(G-2509)*
Apple Eght Hospitality MGT Inc ....E 913 338-3600
Overland Park *(G-8389)*
Apple Eght Hospitality MGT Inc ....E 316 636-4600
Wichita *(G-13722)*
Apple Eght Svcs Ovrland Pk Inc ....E 913 327-7484
Overland Park *(G-8390)*
Ascend Learning Holdings LLC ....F 800 667-7531
Leawood *(G-5332)*
Atchison Hospitality Group LLC ....F 913 674-0033
Atchison *(G-210)*
B & L Motels Inc ....F 785 628-8008
Hays *(G-2753)*
Bartlesville SW Hotel Inc ....D 913 345-2111
Lenexa *(G-5688)*
Belleville Super 8 Motel ....F 785 527-2112
Belleville *(G-452)*
Best Western Bricktown Lodge ....F 620 251-3700
Coffeyville *(G-912)*
Best Western of Manhattan ....F 785 537-8300
Manhattan *(G-6556)*
Best Western Red Coach Inn ....F 316 283-9120
Newton *(G-7319)*
Best Wstn Cntry Inn & Suites ....F 620 225-7378
Dodge City *(G-1307)*
Best Wstn K C Spdway Inn Sites ....F 913 334-4440
Kansas City *(G-3857)*
Bradley Hotel Wichita ....E 316 262-2841
Wichita *(G-13881)*
Brandon Hospitality LLC ....E 316 613-1995
Wichita *(G-13885)*
Bsrep II Ws Hotel Trs Sub LLC ....E 443 569-7053
Wichita *(G-13902)*
C & I LLC ....F 316 214-7308
Park City *(G-9607)*
C B H Consultants Inc ....E 620 624-9700
Liberal *(G-6289)*
Cave Inn LLC ....E 785 749-6010
Lawrence *(G-4777)*
Chaudhrys Investment Group ....F 913 856-8887
Gardner *(G-2332)*
Chaudhrys Investment Group Inc ....E 913 393-1111
Olathe *(G-7590)*
Cni Thl Propco Fe LLC ....E 785 271-6165
Topeka *(G-12482)*
Comfort Inn ....F 620 793-9000
Great Bend *(G-2544)*
Comfort Inn ....F 316 744-7711
Park City *(G-9611)*
Comfort Inn & Suites ....E 620 231-8800
Pittsburg *(G-9838)*
Comfort Inn and Suites ....E 316 804-4866
Newton *(G-7331)*
Comfort Inn Kansas City ....F 913 299-5555
Kansas City *(G-3926)*
Condor Hospitality Trust Inc ....F 620 232-1881
Pittsburg *(G-9843)*
Country Inn Suites ....F 316 634-3900
Wichita *(G-14108)*
Courtyard By Marriott ....F 785 309-1300
Salina *(G-10466)*
Courtyard By Marriott ....F 913 339-9900
Shawnee Mission *(G-11274)*
Courtyard Kansas City Olathe ....E 913 839-4500
Olathe *(G-7624)*
Courtyard-Old Town ....E 316 264-5300
Wichita *(G-14116)*
Crystal Hospitality LLC ....E 913 680-1500
Leavenworth *(G-5229)*
Dab of Lenexa KS I LLC ....E 605 275-9499
Lenexa *(G-5799)*
Darco Inc ....E 620 221-7529
Winfield *(G-16138)*
Darlene Coffey ....F 620 229-8888
Winfield *(G-16139)*
Days Inn ....F 785 823-9791
Salina *(G-10471)*
Days Inn Inc ....F 316 942-1717
Wichita *(G-14176)*
Days Inn of Overland Park ....F 913 341-0100
Leawood *(G-5375)*
Days Inn Suites Hutchinson LLC ....F 620 665-3700
Hutchinson *(G-3259)*
Derby Hotel Inc ....F 316 425-7900
Derby *(G-1236)*
Dodge Enteprise Inc ....E 620 227-2125
Dodge City *(G-1356)*
Douglas Webb Co LP ....F 316 685-3777
Wichita *(G-14232)*
Econo Lodge ....E 785 242-3400
Ottawa *(G-8268)*
Econo Lodge ....F 785 625-4839
Hays *(G-2797)*
Embassy Suites Olathe ....F 913 353-9280
Olathe *(G-7677)*
Eqh - Leavenworth LLC ....F 913 651-8600
Leavenworth *(G-5236)*
ESA P Prtfolio Oper Lessee LLC ....F 316 652-8844
Wichita *(G-14304)*
ESA P Prtfolio Oper Lessee LLC ....F 913 661-9299
Overland Park *(G-8689)*
ESA P Prtfolio Oper Lessee LLC ....F 913 541-4000
Lenexa *(G-5836)*
ESA P Prtfolio Oper Lessee LLC ....F 913 236-6006
Merriam *(G-7092)*
Executive Mnor Leavenworth Inc ....F 785 234-5400
Topeka *(G-12586)*
Fairfield Inn Suites Hutchinson ....F 620 259-8787
Hutchinson *(G-3281)*
Fairfield Inn By Marriott ....E 913 768-7000
Olathe *(G-7700)*
Fairfield Inn By Marrtt Wichta ....E 316 685-3777
Wichita *(G-14334)*
Ferguson Properties Inc ....E 785 625-3344
Hays *(G-2805)*
First Call Hospitality LLC ....E 913 345-2661
Shawnee Mission *(G-11368)*
Five Star Hotel Management ....F 316 686-7331
Wichita *(G-14380)*
Four Points By Sheraton ....F 785 539-5311
Manhattan *(G-6639)*
Frontier Lodging Concordia LLC ....F 785 243-2700
Concordia *(G-1111)*
Frontier Lodging Liberal LLC ....E 620 624-9700
Liberal *(G-6310)*
Gardner Hospitality LLC ....E 913 856-2100
Gardner *(G-2349)*
Gbk Ventures LLC ....F 620 603-6565
Great Bend *(G-2569)*
Hampton Inn ....F 316 636-5594
Wichita *(G-14551)*
Hampton Inn ....F 620 272-0454
Garden City *(G-2191)*
Hampton Inn ....F 785 460-2333
Colby *(G-1010)*
Hampton Inn ....E 913 328-1400
Kansas City *(G-4064)*
Hampton Inn ....F 785 228-0111
Topeka *(G-12663)*
Hampton Inn Hays-North I-70 ....F 785 621-4444
Hays *(G-2825)*

Hampton Inn Junction City F 785 579-4633
Junction City *(G-3698)*
Hampton Inn Suites F 620 604-0699
Liberal *(G-6316)*
Hampton Inns LLC E 785 823-9800
Salina *(G-10533)*
Hawthorn Suites F 913 344-8100
Overland Park *(G-8799)*
HCW Wichita Hotel LLC E 316 925-6600
Wichita *(G-14573)*
Heart America Management LLC E 913 397-0100
Olathe *(G-7762)*
Heart of America Inn Inc E 785 827-9315
Salina *(G-10538)*
Hedrick Exotic Animal Farm E 620 422-3245
Nickerson *(G-7433)*
Heritage Inn Wichita Opco LLC E 316 686-2844
Wichita *(G-14595)*
HI Hritg Inn Wchita Opco LLC E 316 686-3576
Wichita *(G-14603)*
Hi-Plains Motel & Restaurant F 620 375-4438
Leoti *(G-6254)*
Highland Lodging LLC F 620 792-2431
Great Bend *(G-2591)*
Hilltop Lodge C 785 738-2509
Beloit *(G-487)*
Hilton Garden Inn 23930 D 913 342-7900
Kansas City *(G-4081)*
Hit Portfolio I Hil Trs LLC E 816 464-5454
Overland Park *(G-8816)*
Hit Portfolio I Trs LLC F 913 451-2553
Overland Park *(G-8817)*
Holiday Inn & Suites F 620 508-6350
Pratt *(G-10120)*
Holiday Inn Ex Ht & Suites E 785 263-4049
Abilene *(G-38)*
Holiday Inn Ex Suites Topeka N F 785 861-7200
Topeka *(G-12697)*
Holiday Inn Express F 913 250-1000
Lansing *(G-4675)*
Holiday Inn Express F 785 625-8000
Hays *(G-2848)*
Holiday Inn Express F 785 890-9060
Goodland *(G-2478)*
Holiday Inn Express & Suites F 316 804-7040
Newton *(G-7362)*
Holiday Inn Express & Suites E 785 404-3300
Salina *(G-10544)*
Holiday Inn Express & Suites E 620 431-0817
Chanute *(G-732)*
Holiday Inn Express and Suites F 316 322-7275
El Dorado *(G-1566)*
Holiday Inn Express Village W F 913 328-1024
Kansas City *(G-4084)*
Hotel Clubs Corp Woods Inc D 913 451-6100
Overland Park *(G-8829)*
Hotel Wichita Greenwich F 316 681-1800
Wichita *(G-14641)*
Howard Johnson Express Inn F 316 943-8165
Wichita *(G-14643)*
Hulsing Hotels Kansas Inc D 785 841-7077
Lawrence *(G-4906)*
Hulsing Hotels Kansas Inc D 785 539-5311
Manhattan *(G-6662)*
Hyatt Corporation C 316 293-1234
Wichita *(G-14661)*
I Samco Investments Ltd D 913 345-2111
Shawnee Mission *(G-11447)*
Im Olathe LP E 913 829-6700
Olathe *(G-7786)*
Inn Hampton and Suites F 620 225-0000
Dodge City *(G-1378)*
Innworks Inc F 620 342-7567
Emporia *(G-1777)*
Jay Maa Ambe LLC E 785 554-1044
Kansas City *(G-4118)*
Jefferson St Ht Partners LLC D 785 234-5400
Topeka *(G-12742)*
Jnn LLC E 785 843-9100
Lawrence *(G-4923)*
Jrko LLC E 913 648-7858
Shawnee Mission *(G-11503)*
Junction City Lodging LLC E 785 579-5787
Junction City *(G-3705)*
K & S LLC D 620 275-7471
Garden City *(G-2211)*
Kandarpam Hotels LLC E 785 762-4200
Lenexa *(G-5935)*
Kansas Global Hotel LLC E 913 722-0800
Merriam *(G-7098)*

Kellogg Hospitality LLC E 316 942-5600
Wichita *(G-14845)*
Kinseth Hospitality Co Inc D 316 686-7131
Wichita *(G-14864)*
Knights Inn F 316 942-1341
Wichita *(G-14870)*
Ladiwalla Hospitality LLC F 316 773-1700
Wichita *(G-14911)*
Lake Pointe Hotel Co LLC F 913 451-1222
Shawnee Mission *(G-11546)*
Laquinta Inn and Suites F 913 648-5555
Overland Park *(G-8946)*
Laxminarayan Lodging Llc F 785 462-3933
Colby *(G-1025)*
Leisure Hotel Corporation D 913 905-1460
Lenexa *(G-5966)*
Leisure Hotel Corporation D 316 832-9387
Park City *(G-9627)*
Leisure Hotel Corporation F 620 225-3924
Dodge City *(G-1397)*
Leisure Hotel Corporation E 620 227-5000
Dodge City *(G-1398)*
Leisure Hotel Corporation E 620 275-5900
Garden City *(G-2224)*
Lenexa City Center Hotel Corp E 913 742-7777
Lenexa *(G-5968)*
Lenexa Hotel LP A 785 841-3100
Lawrence *(G-4993)*
Liberal Super 8 Motel E 620 624-8880
Liberal *(G-6336)*
Lighthouse Properties LLC E 785 825-2221
Salina *(G-10583)*
Lighthouse Properties LLC E 316 260-8844
Wichita *(G-14964)*
Lilken Lllp E 785 749-7555
Lawrence *(G-4997)*
Lodgeworks LP E 316 681-5100
Wichita *(G-14973)*
Lodgian Inc E 785 841-7077
Lawrence *(G-5000)*
Lodging Enterprises LLC A 316 630-6300
Wichita *(G-14975)*
Lq Management LLC E 913 492-5500
Lenexa *(G-5980)*
Maa Santoshi LLC E 620 665-9800
Hutchinson *(G-3361)*
Magers Lodgings Inc E 785 841-4994
Lawrence *(G-5006)*
Mark Randolf F 620 431-7788
Chanute *(G-742)*
Marriott International Inc B 913 451-8000
Shawnee Mission *(G-11600)*
Mclcv Courtyard By Marriott F 913 317-8500
Overland Park *(G-9002)*
Microtel Inn & Suites F 620 331-0088
Independence *(G-3540)*
Midas Lenexa LLC D 913 225-9955
Lenexa *(G-5999)*
Midwest Heritage Inn F 785 273-6800
Topeka *(G-12901)*
Motel 6 F 316 684-6363
Wichita *(G-15131)*
Motel 6 Operating LP F 316 945-8440
Wichita *(G-15132)*
Motel 6 Operating LP F 785 827-8397
Salina *(G-10607)*
Motel 6 Operating LP F 913 541-8558
Shawnee Mission *(G-11655)*
Motel 6 Operating LP F 785 537-1022
Manhattan *(G-6752)*
Motel 6 Operating LP F 785 273-2896
Topeka *(G-12915)*
Motel 6 Operating LP F 785 272-8283
Topeka *(G-12916)*
Motel 6 Operating LP F 620 343-1240
Emporia *(G-1798)*
Nebco Inc F 785 462-3943
Salina *(G-10610)*
News Publishing Co Inc D 785 628-1081
Hays *(G-2877)*
Olathe Hotels LLC F 913 829-6700
Olathe *(G-7939)*
Overland Park Development Corp D 913 234-2100
Overland Park *(G-9117)*
Overland Park Hospitality LLC E 913 312-0900
Shawnee Mission *(G-11708)*
Overland Park Hotel Assoc Lc C 913 888-8440
Overland Park *(G-9120)*
Oz Accommodations Inc F 913 894-8400
Overland Park *(G-9131)*

Park Hotels & Resorts Inc D 913 649-7060
Shawnee Mission *(G-11716)*
Park-Rn Overland Park LLC F 913 850-5400
Overland Park *(G-9142)*
Payal Hotels LLC F 785 579-5787
Junction City *(G-3736)*
Phillip G Ruffin F 316 942-7940
Wichita *(G-15291)*
Prairie Inn Inc E 316 283-3330
Newton *(G-7406)*
Pssk LLC F 620 277-7100
Garden City *(G-2260)*
Quality Inn F 785 784-5106
Junction City *(G-3744)*
Quality Inn F 785 770-8000
Manhattan *(G-6784)*
Quality Inn D 620 663-4444
South Hutchinson *(G-12064)*
Quality Suites Airport F 316 945-2600
Wichita *(G-15385)*
Rainbow Village Management E 913 677-3060
Kansas City *(G-4361)*
Red Coach Inn E 316 321-6900
El Dorado *(G-1597)*
Residence Inn By Marriott LLC C 316 686-7331
Wichita *(G-15448)*
Rest Easy LLC E 913 684-4091
Fort Leavenworth *(G-1941)*
Revocable Trust B 785 210-1500
Junction City *(G-3748)*
Rhw Hotel Holdings Company LLC F 913 451-1222
Shawnee Mission *(G-11798)*
Rhw Management Inc E 785 776-8829
Manhattan *(G-6792)*
Rhw Management Inc F 913 451-1222
Shawnee Mission *(G-11799)*
Rhw Management Inc E 913 768-7000
Olathe *(G-8033)*
Rhw Management Inc E 913 631-8800
Shawnee *(G-11019)*
Rhw Management Inc E 913 722-0800
Shawnee Mission *(G-11800)*
Rhw Management Inc F 913 397-9455
Olathe *(G-8034)*
Riley Hotel Suites LLC E 785 539-2400
Manhattan *(G-6793)*
Rockgate Management Company E 402 331-0101
Overland Park *(G-9253)*
Ruffin Hotel of Wichita LLC F 316 685-3777
Wichita *(G-15492)*
S & B Motels Inc E 785 899-7181
Goodland *(G-2484)*
S & B Motels Inc C 316 522-3864
Wichita *(G-15499)*
S & B Motels Inc F 785 823-8808
Salina *(G-10656)*
Sady Vijay Inc F 620 343-7750
Emporia *(G-1819)*
Sagar Inc D 620 241-5566
McPherson *(G-7022)*
Sagar Inc E 620 241-5343
McPherson *(G-7023)*
Sagar Inc E 620 241-5343
McPherson *(G-7024)*
Salina KS Lodging LLC E 785 827-1271
Salina *(G-10679)*
Sana Hospitality Corp F 620 342-7567
Emporia *(G-1822)*
Sand Dollar Hospitality 2 LLC E 913 299-4700
Kansas City *(G-4400)*
Schwartz Inc F 620 275-5800
Garden City *(G-2276)*
Select Hotels Group LLC E 913 491-9002
Overland Park *(G-9289)*
Settle Inn F 913 381-5700
Overland Park *(G-9300)*
SF Hotel Company LP D 316 681-5100
Wichita *(G-15569)*
Shawnee Inn Inc E 913 248-1900
Shawnee Mission *(G-11852)*
Shirconn Investments Inc F 913 390-9500
Olathe *(G-8064)*
Shree Ram Investments of Pltte F 913 948-9000
Olathe *(G-8065)*
Shree-Guru Investments Inc F 785 273-0003
Topeka *(G-13071)*
Shri Ram Corp F 248 477-3200
Lenexa *(G-6133)*
Shriji Inc F 785 242-9898
Ottawa *(G-8312)*

Si Overland Park LP..........D....... 913 345-2661
Overland Park (G-9310)
Six Continents Hotels Inc..........D....... 785 827-9000
Salina (G-10709)
Six Continents Hotels Inc..........D....... 620 792-2431
Great Bend (G-2636)
Six Continents Hotels Inc..........E....... 785 462-8787
Colby (G-1041)
Slawson Investment Corporation..........E....... 316 263-3201
Wichita (G-15604)
Sleep Inn & Suites..........F....... 620 223-2555
Fort Scott (G-2005)
Sleep Inn & Suites Parsons..........F....... 620 421-6126
Parsons (G-9738)
Sleep Inn and Suite..........F....... 620 688-6400
Coffeyville (G-978)
Sleep Inn and Suites 07..........F....... 620 805-6535
Garden City (G-2281)
Sleep Inn Inn & Suites..........F....... 785 625-2700
Hays (G-2908)
Sleep Inn Suite..........F....... 316 425-6077
Haysville (G-2960)
Sonar Sangam Inc..........F....... 316 529-4911
Wichita (G-15613)
Springhill Suites..........F....... 316 260-4404
Wichita (G-15648)
Starwood Htls & Rsrts Wrldwde..........B....... 888 625-4988
Wichita (G-15659)
Sterling Centrecorp Inc..........E....... 785 841-6500
Lawrence (G-5124)
Sterling Centrecorp Inc..........E....... 913 651-6000
Leavenworth (G-5291)
Sterling Centrecorp Inc..........F....... 785 242-7000
Ottawa (G-8314)
Sugarcat Hospitality Inc..........F....... 620 275-5800
Garden City (G-2292)
Summit Group of Salina KS LP..........F....... 785 826-1711
Salina (G-10718)
Summit Hotel Properties LLC..........F....... 620 341-9393
Emporia (G-1833)
Sunflower Partners Inc..........E....... 785 462-3933
Colby (G-1042)
Super 8 Hotel In Colby Kansas..........F....... 785 462-8248
Colby (G-1043)
Super 8 Motel..........F....... 913 721-3877
Bonner Springs (G-576)
Super 8 Motel..........E....... 785 743-6442
Wakeeney (G-13391)
Super 8 Motel..........F....... 316 945-5261
Wichita (G-15691)
Super 8 Motel..........F....... 620 421-8000
Parsons (G-9742)
Super 8 Motel of Beloit..........F....... 785 738-4300
Beloit (G-504)
Super 8 Motel of Concordia..........F....... 785 243-4200
Concordia (G-1132)
Super 8 Motel of Pratt Inc..........F....... 620 672-5945
Pratt (G-10157)
Swami Inc..........F....... 785 228-2500
Topeka (G-13128)
Tenth Street Ht Partners LLC..........F....... 785 233-5411
Topeka (G-13150)
Tenth Street Ht Partners LLC..........E....... 785 228-9500
Topeka (G-13151)
Tgc Greenwich Hotel LLC..........E....... 316 500-2660
Wichita (G-15754)
Tirupati Balaji LLC..........F....... 913 262-9600
Overland Park (G-9412)
Transitions Group Inc..........E....... 316 262-9100
Wichita (G-15791)
True North Hotel Group Inc..........F....... 913 341-4440
Shawnee Mission (G-11944)
Tucson Hotels LP..........C....... 785 210-1500
Junction City (G-3760)
Turnpike Investments Inc..........F....... 316 524-4400
Wichita (G-15816)
Tusar Inc..........E....... 316 522-1800
Wichita (G-15817)
V & R Motel LLC..........F....... 620 331-8288
Independence (G-3570)
Value Place Hotel..........F....... 913 831-1417
Shawnee Mission (G-11975)
Value Place Topeka..........F....... 785 271-8862
Overland Park (G-9459)
Vchp Wichita LLC..........E....... 316 685-1281
Wichita (G-15872)
Venture Hotels LLC..........E....... 620 231-1177
Pittsburg (G-9954)
W2005/Fargo Hotels (pool C)..........E....... 785 271-6165
Topeka (G-13228)
Wichita Airport Ht Assoc L P..........C....... 316 945-5272
Wichita (G-15971)
Wichita Arprt Hospitality LLC..........F....... 316 522-0008
Wichita (G-15977)
Wichita East Hotel Associates..........D....... 316 686-7131
Wichita (G-15996)
Wichita Hspttlity Holdings LLC..........E....... 316 685-1281
Wichita (G-16006)
Wingate Inns International Inc..........E....... 620 241-5566
McPherson (G-7043)
Wingate Inns International Inc..........E....... 316 733-8833
Andover (G-117)
Woods of Cherry Creek Inc..........F....... 913 491-3030
Overland Park (G-9504)
Woofter Woofter Stupka Inc..........E....... 785 460-6683
Colby (G-1050)
Wyndham International Inc..........E....... 913 383-2550
Overland Park (G-9509)
Wyndham International Inc..........F....... 316 729-5700
Wichita (G-16081)

TRAVELERS' AID

Infectious Disease Cons PA..........E....... 316 264-3505
Wichita (G-14689)

TROPHIES, NEC

Stewarts Sports & Awards..........G....... 620 241-5990
McPherson (G-7028)

TROPHIES, WHOLESALE

Jayhawk Trophy Company Inc..........G....... 785 843-3900
Lawrence (G-4921)

TROPHIES: Metal, Exc Silver

Hasty Awards Inc..........D....... 785 242-5297
Ottawa (G-8278)

TROPHY & PLAQUE STORES

Jayhawk Trophy Company Inc..........G....... 785 843-3900
Lawrence (G-4921)
Lee Reed Engraving Inc..........G....... 316 943-9700
Wichita (G-14949)
Simon & Simon Inc..........G....... 913 888-9889
Overland Park (G-9311)

TRUCK & BUS BODIES: Bus Bodies

Wichita Body & Equipment Co..........G....... 316 522-1080
Haysville (G-2964)

TRUCK & BUS BODIES: Truck Beds

B & W Custom Truck Beds Inc..........C....... 800 810-4918
Humboldt (G-3181)
Economy Mfg Co Inc..........E....... 620 725-3520
Sedan (G-10842)
R B Manufacturing Company..........G....... 913 829-3233
Olathe (G-8016)
Star Pipe Usa LLC..........C....... 281 558-3000
Coffeyville (G-979)
Western Truck Equipment Co..........F....... 620 793-8464
Great Bend (G-2662)

TRUCK & BUS BODIES: Truck, Motor Vehicle

Nesco Holdings Inc..........G....... 913 287-0001
Kansas City (G-4286)
Randy Schwindt..........F....... 785 391-2277
Utica (G-13335)
Unruh Fab Inc..........E....... 316 772-5400
Sedgwick (G-10853)
VT Hackney Inc..........C....... 620 331-6600
Independence (G-3571)

TRUCK & FREIGHT TERMINALS & SUPPORT ACTIVITIES

Core Carrier Corporation..........C....... 913 621-3434
Kansas City (G-3941)
Jts Transports Inc..........E....... 316 554-0706
Haysville (G-2951)

TRUCK BODIES: Body Parts

Big Creek Investment Corp Inc..........G....... 620 431-3445
Chanute (G-707)
Midwest Truck Equipment Inc..........F....... 316 744-2889
Park City (G-9633)

TRUCK BODY SHOP

Nesco Holdings Inc..........G....... 913 287-0001
Kansas City (G-4286)

TRUCK DRIVER SVCS

Sebes Hay LLC..........E....... 620 285-6941
Larned (G-4712)

TRUCK FINANCE LEASING

Murphy-Hoffman Company..........E....... 816 483-6444
Leawood (G-5492)

TRUCK GENERAL REPAIR SVC

Diamond Intl Trcks Inc..........E....... 785 235-8711
Topeka (G-12555)
Dodge City International Inc..........E....... 620 225-4177
Dodge City (G-1348)
Midwest Services & Towing Inc..........E....... 913 281-1003
Kansas City (G-4257)
Murphy-Hoffman Company..........E....... 816 483-6444
Leawood (G-5492)
Omaha Truck Center Inc..........E....... 785 823-2204
Salina (G-10620)
Professional Fleet Svcs LLC..........F....... 316 524-6000
Wichita (G-15361)
Southwest Sterling Inc..........E....... 816 483-6444
Leawood (G-5555)
Wichita Kenworth Inc..........D....... 316 838-0867
Park City (G-9655)
Williams Service Inc..........E....... 620 878-4225
Florence (G-1930)

TRUCK PAINTING & LETTERING SVCS

Aeroswint..........F....... 785 391-2276
Utica (G-13334)
Fastsigns Inc..........G....... 913 649-3600
Overland Park (G-8707)
Georgia Kenworth Inc..........E....... 816 483-6444
Leawood (G-5411)

TRUCK PARTS & ACCESSORIES: Wholesalers

Errol E Engel Inc..........E....... 785 625-3195
Hays (G-2800)
Fleetpride Inc..........F....... 785 862-1540
Topeka (G-12617)
Fleetpride Inc..........F....... 316 942-4227
Wichita (G-14385)
Fleetpride Inc..........D....... 800 362-2600
Wichita (G-14386)
Hays Mack Sales and Svc Inc..........F....... 785 625-7343
Hays (G-2832)
Inland Truck Parts Company..........F....... 913 492-7559
Olathe (G-7792)
Maupin Truck Parts Inc..........E....... 620 225-4433
Dodge City (G-1401)
Mikes Equipment Company..........F....... 620 543-2535
Buhler (G-618)
Omaha Truck Center Inc..........E....... 785 823-2204
Salina (G-10619)
Paynes Inc..........F....... 620 231-3170
Frontenac (G-2063)
Tennessee Kenworth Inc..........E....... 816 483-6444
Leawood (G-5571)
Truck Stuff Inc..........F....... 316 264-1908
Wichita (G-15807)
Vernies Trux-N-Equip Inc..........G....... 785 625-5087
Hays (G-2923)
Williams Service Inc..........E....... 620 878-4225
Florence (G-1930)

TRUCK STOPS

Garden City Travel Plaza LLC..........E....... 620 275-4404
Garden City (G-2179)
Mitten Inc..........E....... 785 672-3062
Oakley (G-7481)
Triplett Inc..........F....... 785 823-7839
Salina (G-10742)

TRUCKING & HAULING SVCS: Animal & Farm Prdt

Clayton J Befort..........F....... 785 625-7628
Hays (G-2770)
Marroquin Express Inc..........F....... 316 295-0595
Maize (G-6516)

Ramon E Guardiola................F....... 620 355-4266
Lakin *(G-4658)*

TRUCKING & HAULING SVCS: Baggage Transfer Svcs

Automotive Associates................E....... 620 231-6350
Pittsburg *(G-9818)*

TRUCKING & HAULING SVCS: Building Materials

Coomes Brothers Ltd................E....... 785 543-5896
Phillipsburg *(G-9782)*

TRUCKING & HAULING SVCS: Contract Basis

ABF Freight System Inc................F....... 316 943-1241
Wichita *(G-13598)*
Aci Motor Freight Inc................E....... 316 522-5559
Wichita *(G-13605)*
All Freight Systems Inc................E....... 913 281-1203
Kansas City *(G-3797)*
B & H Freight Line Inc................F....... 913 621-1840
Kansas City *(G-3834)*
Bestmark Express Inc................E....... 620 273-7018
Strong City *(G-12191)*
Butler Transport Inc................C....... 913 321-0047
Kansas City *(G-3882)*
Cargill Mt Lgstics Sltions Inc................E....... 877 596-4062
Wichita *(G-13949)*
Cargill Mt Lgstics Sltions Inc................F....... 620 225-2610
Dodge City *(G-1318)*
Chc McPherson Refinery Inc................E....... 620 793-3111
Great Bend *(G-2536)*
Chc McPherson Refinery Inc................G....... 785 798-3684
Ness City *(G-7254)*
Chc McPherson Refinery Inc................F....... 785 543-5246
Phillipsburg *(G-9779)*
Coomes Inc................D....... 785 543-2759
Phillipsburg *(G-9781)*
Coover Trucking Inc................F....... 620 244-3572
Erie *(G-1858)*
Core Carrier Corporation................C....... 913 621-3434
Kansas City *(G-3941)*
D & A Trucking Inc................F....... 620 465-3370
Haven *(G-2729)*
Darling Ingredients Inc................F....... 785 336-2535
Seneca *(G-10864)*
Debrick Truck Line Company................F....... 913 294-5020
Paola *(G-9551)*
Doll Truck Line................F....... 620 456-2519
Conway Springs *(G-1140)*
Doug Bradley Trucking Inc................D....... 785 826-9681
Salina *(G-10481)*
E S Wilson Transport Inc................F....... 785 263-9845
Abilene *(G-25)*
Emporia Freight and Dlvry Svc................F....... 785 862-1611
Topeka *(G-12575)*
Estes Express Lines................D....... 620 260-9580
Garden City *(G-2153)*
Estes Express Lines Inc................D....... 316 554-0864
Wichita *(G-14306)*
Estes Express Lines Inc................D....... 913 281-1723
Kansas City *(G-3997)*
Fedex Freight Corporation................C....... 800 872-7028
Edwardsville *(G-1500)*
Fedex Ground Package Sys Inc................C....... 800 463-3339
Olathe *(G-7706)*
GP Express Inc................F....... 620 223-1244
Fort Scott *(G-1974)*
Graham Ship By Truck Company................E....... 913 621-7575
Prairie Village *(G-10034)*
Groendyke Transport Inc................E....... 913 621-2200
Kansas City *(G-4055)*
J and S Trucking Inc................F....... 785 973-2768
Prairie View *(G-10011)*
Jack Cooper Transport Co Inc................C....... 913 321-8500
Kansas City *(G-4116)*
Jim Mitten Trucking Inc................F....... 785 672-3279
Oakley *(G-7477)*
John E Jones Oil Co Inc................F....... 785 425-6746
Stockton *(G-12182)*
Kenny Livingston Trucking Inc................F....... 785 598-2493
Abilene *(G-43)*
Knight-Swift Trnsp Hldings Inc................D....... 913 535-5155
Kansas City *(G-4177)*
Korte Trucking Inc................F....... 620 276-8873
Garden City *(G-2220)*
L B White Trucking Inc................E....... 620 326-8921
Wellington *(G-13509)*
Mast Trucking Inc................F....... 620 668-5121
Copeland *(G-1150)*
McAlister Transportation LLC................E....... 620 326-2491
Wellington *(G-13515)*
Metro Companies Inc................D....... 316 838-3345
Wichita *(G-15059)*
Midwest Express Corporation................F....... 913 573-1400
Lenexa *(G-6001)*
Mss Transport Inc................E....... 785 825-7291
Salina *(G-10609)*
Price Truck Line Inc................C....... 316 945-6915
Wichita *(G-15341)*
Price Truck Line Inc................E....... 913 596-9779
Kansas City *(G-4335)*
Price Truck Line Inc................F....... 785 232-1183
Topeka *(G-12988)*
Price Truck Line Inc................F....... 785 625-2603
Hays *(G-2888)*
Price Truck Line Inc................F....... 620 365-6626
Iola *(G-3627)*
Quality Carriers Inc................F....... 913 281-0901
Kansas City *(G-4351)*
R & L Carriers Inc................E....... 316 529-1222
Wichita *(G-15398)*
Ruan Trnsp MGT Systems Inc................E....... 785 274-6672
Topeka *(G-13030)*
RVB Trucking Inc................E....... 620 365-6823
Iola *(G-3631)*
Saia Motor Freight Line LLC................E....... 316 522-1786
Wichita *(G-15506)*
Skillett & Sons Incorporated................E....... 785 222-3611
La Crosse *(G-4639)*
Smart Truck Line Inc................F....... 785 353-2411
Beattie *(G-419)*
Transam Trucking Inc................A....... 913 782-5300
Olathe *(G-8119)*
Tsi Kansas Inc................E....... 785 632-5183
Clay Center *(G-884)*
Tyson Fresh Meats Inc................E....... 620 343-8010
Emporia *(G-1844)*
Wakeeney Truck Line Inc................F....... 785 743-6778
Wakeeney *(G-13394)*
West Plains Transport Inc................E....... 620 563-7665
Plains *(G-9978)*
Xpo Logistics Freight Inc................D....... 913 281-3535
Kansas City *(G-4560)*
Xpo Logistics Freight Inc................D....... 785 823-3926
Salina *(G-10774)*
Xpo Logistics Freight Inc................E....... 316 942-0498
Wichita *(G-16084)*
Yrc Enterprise Services Inc................F....... 913 696-6100
Overland Park *(G-9521)*
Yrc Inc................B....... 913 696-6100
Overland Park *(G-9523)*
Yrc Inc................B....... 620 856-2161
Baxter Springs *(G-416)*
Yrc Inc................B....... 913 696-6100
Kansas City *(G-4565)*

TRUCKING & HAULING SVCS: Farm To Market, Local

Bekemeyer Enterprises Inc................F....... 785 325-2274
Washington *(G-13459)*
Jantz Inc................F....... 620 345-2783
Moundridge *(G-7186)*

TRUCKING & HAULING SVCS: Furniture Moving & Storage, Local

Apartment Movers Inc................E....... 316 267-5300
Wichita *(G-13717)*
Gamoict Inc................F....... 316 262-2123
Wichita *(G-14443)*

TRUCKING & HAULING SVCS: Garbage, Collect/Transport Only

Better Hauling Co................F....... 316 943-5865
Valley Center *(G-13337)*
CD&h Inc................F....... 316 320-7187
El Dorado *(G-1544)*
Deffenbaugh Industries Inc................A....... 913 631-3300
Kansas City *(G-3965)*

TRUCKING & HAULING SVCS: Haulage & Cartage, Light, Local

Boyd Delivery Systems Inc................D....... 913 677-6700
Westwood *(G-13551)*
C & C Truck Line................F....... 785 243-3719
Concordia *(G-1104)*

TRUCKING & HAULING SVCS: Hazardous Waste

Eagle Environmental Svcs LLC................E....... 316 944-2445
Wichita *(G-14250)*

TRUCKING & HAULING SVCS: Heavy Machinery, Local

Double T Ind Inc................E....... 620 593-4357
Rolla *(G-10232)*
Ferco Inc................E....... 785 825-6380
Salina *(G-10500)*

TRUCKING & HAULING SVCS: Heavy, NEC

A-Plus Logistics LLC................E....... 316 945-5757
Park City *(G-9598)*
Albert G Hogoboom................E....... 316 321-1397
El Dorado *(G-1527)*
Belger Cartage Service Inc................E....... 316 943-0101
Wichita *(G-13829)*
Browns Super Service Inc................F....... 785 267-1080
Topeka *(G-12409)*
C & C Truck Line................F....... 785 243-3719
Concordia *(G-1104)*
Double T Ind Inc................E....... 620 593-4357
Rolla *(G-10232)*
J & J Martin Trucking................F....... 620 544-7976
Hugoton *(G-3166)*
James Mason Enterprises Inc................E....... 316 838-7399
Wichita *(G-14746)*
Lynns Heavy Hauling LLC................F....... 913 393-3863
Olathe *(G-7868)*
Michael Downey................F....... 316 540-6166
Maize *(G-6517)*
T & M Contracting Inc................F....... 913 393-1087
Olathe *(G-8094)*
Valley Moving Company LLC................F....... 785 456-2400
Wamego *(G-13445)*

TRUCKING & HAULING SVCS: Liquid Petroleum, Exc Local

CHS McPherson Refinery Inc................B....... 620 241-2340
McPherson *(G-6949)*
Freight Logistics Inc................F....... 316 719-2074
Wichita *(G-14421)*
V & M Transport Inc................E....... 620 662-7281
Hutchinson *(G-3478)*
Wtg Hugoton LP................E....... 620 544-4381
Hugoton *(G-3180)*
Wynne Transport Service Inc................E....... 316 321-3900
El Dorado *(G-1615)*

TRUCKING & HAULING SVCS: Liquid Transfer Svc

Girton Propane Service Inc................D....... 785 632-6273
Clay Center *(G-866)*
Wal-Mac Inc................F....... 620 356-3422
Ulysses *(G-13331)*

TRUCKING & HAULING SVCS: Liquid, Local

Brady Fluid Service Inc................F....... 620 275-5827
Garden City *(G-2116)*
Gorges Dairy Inc................F....... 620 545-7297
Viola *(G-13379)*
K & L Tank Truck Service Inc................F....... 620 277-0101
Garden City *(G-2210)*

TRUCKING & HAULING SVCS: Machinery, Heavy

Hoffman Inc................F....... 316 942-8011
Wichita *(G-14622)*
Passmore Bros Inc................E....... 620 544-2189
Hugoton *(G-3175)*

TRUCKING & HAULING SVCS: Mail Carriers, Contract

Macconnell Enterprises LLC .... E 785 885-8081
Natoma *(G-7231)*
Mail Contractors of America .... D 913 287-9811
Kansas City *(G-4215)*

TRUCKING & HAULING SVCS: Mobile Homes

Great Plains Mobile HM Movers .... F 620 463-2420
Burrton *(G-648)*

TRUCKING & HAULING SVCS: Petroleum, Local

Haag Oil Company LLC .... F 785 357-0270
Topeka *(G-12657)*
Studer Truck Line Inc .... F 785 353-2241
Beattie *(G-420)*
United Petro Transports Inc .... E 316 263-6868
Park City *(G-9651)*
Wynne Transport Service Inc .... E 316 321-3900
El Dorado *(G-1615)*

TRUCKING & HAULING SVCS: Trailer/Container On Flat Car

International Ex Trckg Inc .... E 913 621-1525
Kansas City *(G-4106)*

TRUCKING, AUTOMOBILE CARRIER

Cowan Systems LLC .... C 913 393-0110
Olathe *(G-7625)*
Gs Enterprises Inc .... F 913 543-7614
Kansas City *(G-4057)*
J&J Driveaway Systems LLC .... E 913 387-0158
Overland Park *(G-8868)*
Marten Transport Ltd .... B 913 535-5255
Kansas City *(G-4219)*
Pro-Tow LLC .... F 913 262-3300
Shawnee Mission *(G-11752)*

TRUCKING, DUMP

A-Plus Logistics LLC .... E 316 945-5757
Park City *(G-9598)*
Anderson & Sons Trucking Inc .... E 913 422-3171
Kansas City *(G-3809)*
Apex Trucking Inc .... E 316 943-0774
Park City *(G-9601)*
Bettys Trucking Incorporated .... F 913 583-3666
De Soto *(G-1194)*
Bingham Transportation Inc .... D 620 679-9810
Treece *(G-13267)*
Everetts Inc .... F 785 263-4172
Abilene *(G-28)*
Galen Blenn Trucking .... E 785 457-3995
Westmoreland *(G-13548)*
Herrmans Excavating Inc .... E 785 233-4146
Topeka *(G-12687)*
Kansas Trucking LLC .... F 913 586-5911
De Soto *(G-1205)*
Kenco Trucking Inc .... E 316 943-4881
Wichita *(G-14848)*
Mary Carr .... E 913 207-0900
Kansas City *(G-4221)*
Max Rieke & Brothers Inc .... D 913 631-7111
Shawnee *(G-10991)*
Prockish Trucking & Excavating .... F 785 456-7320
Louisville *(G-6470)*
SD & S Trucking LLC .... E 316 744-2318
Park City *(G-9642)*
Steve Hilker Trucking Inc .... E 620 855-3257
Cimarron *(G-837)*

TRUCKING, REFRIGERATED: Long-Distance

Ark City Warehouse Truckline .... F 620 442-7305
Arkansas City *(G-144)*
Brisk Transportation .... E 620 669-3481
Hutchinson *(G-3225)*
Red Line Inc .... F 620 343-1000
Emporia *(G-1815)*
Seaboard Transport LLC .... F 913 676-8800
Shawnee Mission *(G-11843)*
Thomas and Sons Trucking LLC .... E 785 454-3839
Downs *(G-1473)*

TRUCKING: Except Local

Accord Services Inc .... E 913 281-1879
Kansas City *(G-3781)*
ADM Trucking Inc .... F 785 899-6500
Goodland *(G-2459)*
Austin Trucking .... F 316 323-0313
Augusta *(G-310)*
B & B Redimix Inc .... F 785 543-5133
Phillipsburg *(G-9777)*
B C A /fry-wagner Inc .... E 573 499-0000
Lenexa *(G-5679)*
Bar K Bar Trucking Inc .... F 620 257-5118
Lyons *(G-6479)*
Beaver Express Service LLC .... E 316 946-5700
Wichita *(G-13824)*
Bennet Rogers Pipe Coating .... F 913 371-5288
Kansas City *(G-3853)*
Bills Frank Trucking Inc .... E 620 736-2875
Severy *(G-10889)*
Box Central Inc .... F 316 689-8484
Wichita *(G-13875)*
Briggs Trucking Inc .... E 620 699-3448
Reading *(G-10198)*
C & H Trucking LLC .... F 316 794-8282
Goddard *(G-2430)*
Cal Southern Transport Co .... E 785 232-4202
Topeka *(G-12418)*
Central Transport Intl Inc .... E 913 371-7500
Kansas City *(G-3904)*
Central Transport Intl Inc .... F 877 446-3795
Wichita *(G-13989)*
Central Trnsp Svcs Inc .... D 316 263-3333
Wichita *(G-13990)*
Century Van Lines Inc .... E 913 651-3600
Leavenworth *(G-5216)*
Clinton L Williams .... E 316 775-1300
Leon *(G-6246)*
Convoy Equipment Leasing LLC .... D 913 371-6500
Kansas City *(G-3937)*
D & R Trucking Co .... E 620 672-7713
Pratt *(G-10106)*
Dredge Transport Service Inc .... F 785 506-8285
Topeka *(G-12561)*
Dugan Truck Line LLC .... F 316 946-5985
Wichita *(G-14244)*
Eagel Transit Inc .... E 620 343-3444
Emporia *(G-1735)*
Everetts Inc .... F 785 263-4172
Abilene *(G-28)*
Federal Express Corporation .... F 800 463-3339
Manhattan *(G-6626)*
Fedex Freight Corporation .... D 800 426-0104
Wichita *(G-14348)*
Fedex Freight Corporation .... E 800 752-0047
Topeka *(G-12601)*
Fedex Freight Corporation .... F 800 541-2032
Salina *(G-10498)*
Freight Brokers America LLC .... A 913 438-4300
Overland Park *(G-8740)*
Fry-Wagner Systems Inc .... D 913 438-2925
Lenexa *(G-5867)*
G & R Trucking Inc .... F 620 356-4500
Ulysses *(G-13297)*
Graham Ship By Truck Co .... D 913 621-7500
Prairie Village *(G-10033)*
Great Plains Trucking Inc .... D 785 823-2261
Salina *(G-10522)*
Greg Smith Enterprises Inc .... E 913 543-7614
Kansas City *(G-4052)*
Groendyke Transport Inc .... E 316 755-1266
Wichita *(G-14520)*
Hadley Transit LLC .... F 620 726-5853
Burns *(G-647)*
Hnry Logistics Inc .... F 833 810-4679
Overland Park *(G-8819)*
Intercity Direct LLC .... F 913 647-7550
Lenexa *(G-5917)*
Irish Express Inc .... E 785 765-2500
Alma *(G-64)*
J Marquez Trucking .... F 620 335-5872
Ingalls *(G-3578)*
Jacam Carriers 2013 LLC .... F 620 278-3355
Sterling *(G-12122)*
Jack B Kelley Inc .... D 620 792-8205
Great Bend *(G-2594)*
Jantz Inc .... F 620 345-2783
Moundridge *(G-7186)*
Jesse Latham & Sons Inc .... F 785 361-4281
Republic *(G-10200)*
Jessee Trucking Incorporated .... E 620 389-2546
Columbus *(G-1080)*
Jim Ogrady Trucking .... F 620 624-5343
Liberal *(G-6325)*
K C I Roadrunner Express Inc .... D 785 238-6161
Junction City *(G-3710)*
Kansas Continental Express Inc .... F 620 343-7100
Emporia *(G-1786)*
Kindsvater Inc .... D 620 227-6191
Dodge City *(G-1391)*
Kings Moving & Storage Inc .... E 316 247-6528
Wichita *(G-14863)*
Kunshek Chat & Coal Inc .... E 620 231-8270
Pittsburg *(G-9893)*
Kustom Karriers LLC .... D 316 283-1060
Newton *(G-7374)*
Kw Trucking Inc .... E 785 346-5881
Osborne *(G-8210)*
Little Creek Trucking Inc .... F 316 778-1873
Benton *(G-518)*
Lone Star Services LLC .... E 620 626-7100
Liberal *(G-6337)*
Ludwig Truck Line Inc .... E 620 878-4243
Florence *(G-1929)*
Lvt Trucking Inc .... F 913 233-2111
Kansas City *(G-4209)*
M & A Barnett Trucking Inc .... F 785 673-4700
Grainfield *(G-2495)*
MAI Excavating Inc .... G 785 483-3387
Russell *(G-10280)*
Marroquin Express Inc .... F 316 295-0595
Maize *(G-6516)*
Marten Transport Ltd .... E 913 535-5259
Kansas City *(G-4220)*
Martin Trucking Inc .... E 620 544-4920
Hugoton *(G-3172)*
Mel Rick Inc .... F 785 284-3577
Sabetha *(G-10318)*
Michael Bennett Trucking Inc .... F 785 336-2942
Seneca *(G-10873)*
Midwest Bulk Inc .... E 316 831-9700
Wichita *(G-15088)*
Midwest Trnspt Specialists Inc .... D 913 281-1003
Kansas City *(G-4259)*
Mies & Sons Trucking Inc .... E 316 796-0186
Colwich *(G-1099)*
Miller Trucking Ltd .... E 785 222-3170
La Crosse *(G-4636)*
Mj Transportation Inc .... E 316 832-1321
Park City *(G-9635)*
N T S LLC .... E 913 281-5353
Kansas City *(G-4277)*
Nationwide Transportation and .... F 913 888-1685
Shawnee *(G-11002)*
P & B Trucking Inc .... F 316 283-6868
Newton *(G-7402)*
Penner Feed & Supply Inc .... F 620 585-6612
Inman *(G-3583)*
Penner Trucking Inc .... F 620 353-8475
Sublette *(G-12206)*
Pratt Industries USA Inc .... D 316 838-0851
Wichita *(G-15323)*
Professional Cargo Svcs Inc .... E 316 522-2224
Wichita *(G-15357)*
Propane Resources Trnsp Inc .... E 913 262-8345
Shawnee Mission *(G-11757)*
R&R Pallet Garden City Inc .... E 620 275-2394
Garden City *(G-2262)*
Riverside Transport Inc .... D 913 233-5500
Kansas City *(G-4380)*
Robson Oil Co Inc .... F 785 263-2470
Abilene *(G-51)*
Run-R-Way Express Co Inc .... F 785 346-2900
Portis *(G-10006)*
Sallee Inc .... D 620 227-3320
Dodge City *(G-1426)*
Schmuhl Brothers Inc .... E 913 422-1111
Kansas City *(G-4403)*
Smith Brothers Inc .... F 620 754-3958
Stark *(G-12112)*
Smith Transportation Inc .... F 913 543-7614
Kansas City *(G-4427)*
Snell Harvesting Inc .... F 620 564-3312
Ellinwood *(G-1637)*
Sourdough Express Incorporated .... F 907 452-1181
Medicine Lodge *(G-7072)*
Southern Plains Co-Op At Lewis .... E 620 324-5536
Lewis *(G-6270)*
Southwest Express Inc .... F 620 544-7500
Hugoton *(G-3176)*

State Tractor Trucking Inc ... F ... 913 287-3322
Shawnee *(G-11033)*
Studer Truck Line Inc ... F ... 785 353-2241
Beattie *(G-420)*
T S Keim Inc ... C ... 785 284-2147
Sabetha *(G-10333)*
Taylor Crane & Rigging Inc ... D ... 620 251-1530
Coffeyville *(G-981)*
Thomas Transfer & Stor Co Inc ... D ... 620 342-2321
Emporia *(G-1838)*
Thomas Transfer & Stor Co Inc ... E ... 800 835-3300
Wichita *(G-15761)*
Tim R Schwab Inc ... E ... 316 772-9055
Sedgwick *(G-10852)*
Time Inc ... F ... 816 288-5394
Olathe *(G-8109)*
Total Distribution System Inc ... D ... 913 677-2292
Westwood *(G-13561)*
Traditional Trucking Corp ... D ... 785 456-8604
Belvue *(G-509)*
Transwood Edwardsville66 ... E ... 913 745-1773
Kansas City *(G-4473)*
Triangle Trucking Inc ... D ... 785 827-5500
Salina *(G-10741)*
Trucking By George Inc ... F ... 620 879-2117
Caney *(G-677)*
U S Road Freight Express Inc ... E ... 316 942-9944
Wichita *(G-15825)*
United Petro Transports Inc ... E ... 316 263-6868
Park City *(G-9651)*
UPS Ground Freight Inc ... F ... 913 281-0055
Kansas City *(G-4510)*
Vernon Enterprises ... E ... 620 343-9111
Emporia *(G-1846)*
W W Mails Inc ... E ... 316 943-0703
Wichita *(G-15913)*
Wilson Transportation Inc ... F ... 913 851-7900
Overland Park *(G-9497)*
Yellow Frt Sys Employees CLB ... F ... 913 344-3000
Overland Park *(G-9516)*
Yrc Global ... F ... 913 696-6100
Overland Park *(G-9522)*
Yrc Worldwide Inc ... B ... 913 696-6100
Overland Park *(G-9524)*

TRUCKING: Local, With Storage

Air Capitol Dlvry & Whse LLC ... D ... 316 303-9005
Park City *(G-9599)*
Beelman Truck Co ... E ... 913 362-0553
Kansas City *(G-3852)*
Beltmann Group Incorporated ... E ... 913 888-9105
Lenexa *(G-5698)*
Century Van Lines Inc ... E ... 913 651-3600
Leavenworth *(G-5216)*
Diamond Transfer & Dist Co ... F ... 785 825-1531
Salina *(G-10476)*
Get A Move On Inc ... E ... 316 729-4897
Wichita *(G-14461)*
Kansas Van & Stor Criqui Corp ... E ... 785 266-6992
Topeka *(G-12809)*
Kings Moving & Storage Inc ... E ... 316 247-6528
Wichita *(G-14863)*
Kings Moving & Storage Inc ... E ... 785 238-7341
Junction City *(G-3715)*
M & S Trucks Inc ... F ... 620 842-3764
Anthony *(G-129)*
Midwest Trnspt Specialists Inc ... D ... 913 281-1003
Kansas City *(G-4259)*
Professional Moving & Storage ... E ... 785 842-1115
Lawrence *(G-5078)*
Schmuhl Brothers Inc ... E ... 913 422-1111
Kansas City *(G-4403)*
Studdard Moving & Storage Inc ... E ... 913 341-4600
Leavenworth *(G-5293)*
Studdard Relocation Svcs LLC ... E ... 816 524-2772
Leavenworth *(G-5294)*
Taylor Crane & Rigging Inc ... D ... 620 251-1530
Coffeyville *(G-981)*

TRUCKING: Local, Without Storage

Allied Services LLC ... D ... 620 783-5841
Galena *(G-2068)*
American Trucking Inc ... F ... 620 594-2481
Sawyer *(G-10794)*
Ash Grove Materials Corp ... D ... 913 345-2030
Overland Park *(G-8404)*
Black & Winsor Inc ... D ... 316 943-0703
Wichita *(G-13853)*
Briggs Trucking Inc ... E ... 620 699-3448
Reading *(G-10198)*
Butler Transport Inc ... C ... 913 321-0047
Kansas City *(G-3882)*
C & H Trucking LLC ... F ... 316 794-8282
Goddard *(G-2430)*
C Bar P Trucking Inc ... E ... 316 722-2019
Goddard *(G-2431)*
Classic Motor Freight LLC ... E ... 913 586-5911
Leawood *(G-5353)*
Coomes Inc ... D ... 785 543-2759
Phillipsburg *(G-9781)*
Cutting Edge Trucking Inc ... E ... 913 837-2249
Louisburg *(G-6445)*
D & A Trucking Inc ... F ... 620 465-3370
Haven *(G-2729)*
D Doubled Inc ... F ... 913 334-1075
Shawnee *(G-10938)*
Federal Express Corporation ... D ... 316 941-4438
Wichita *(G-14347)*
Feed Mercantile Transport Inc ... F ... 620 275-4158
Garden City *(G-2159)*
Fexp Inc ... E ... 785 336-2148
Seneca *(G-10867)*
Harris Quality Inc ... D ... 402 332-5857
Olathe *(G-7755)*
Hdb Construction Inc ... E ... 785 232-5444
Topeka *(G-12669)*
Hit Inc ... E ... 913 281-4040
Kansas City *(G-4082)*
J S Transportation LLC ... E ... 816 651-1827
Lenexa *(G-5926)*
Jack B Kelley Inc ... D ... 620 792-8205
Great Bend *(G-2594)*
Jack Cooper Transport Co Inc ... C ... 913 321-8500
Kansas City *(G-4116)*
K C I Roadrunner Express Inc ... D ... 785 238-6161
Junction City *(G-3710)*
Kansas City Coml Whsng Co ... E ... 913 287-3800
Kansas City *(G-4144)*
Knight Trucking LLC ... E ... 620 256-6525
Lebo *(G-5607)*
Korte Trucking Inc ... F ... 620 276-8873
Garden City *(G-2220)*
L & S Scott Inc ... F ... 785 643-1488
Salina *(G-10577)*
Long Island Grain Co Inc ... F ... 785 854-7431
Long Island *(G-6428)*
Lrm Industries Inc ... E ... 785 843-1688
Lawrence *(G-5001)*
Magna Tech Inc ... E ... 620 431-3490
Chanute *(G-740)*
Materials Transport Company ... B ... 913 345-2030
Shawnee Mission *(G-11602)*
Metro Companies Inc ... D ... 316 838-3345
Wichita *(G-15059)*
Michael Bennett Trucking Inc ... F ... 785 336-2942
Seneca *(G-10873)*
Midwest Concrete Materials Inc ... C ... 785 776-8811
Manhattan *(G-6746)*
Moonlite Trucking Inc ... F ... 620 767-5499
Council Grove *(G-1172)*
Mr PS Truckn Inc ... E ... 785 372-4371
Rush Center *(G-10262)*
Myfreightworld Carrier MGT Inc ... E ... 877 549-9438
Overland Park *(G-9066)*
New Image Concrete Design LLC ... F ... 913 489-1699
Shawnee *(G-11005)*
Nichols Water Svc An Okla Corp ... F ... 620 624-5582
Liberal *(G-6350)*
NTS LLC ... E ... 913 321-3838
Kansas City *(G-4291)*
Penner Trucking Inc ... F ... 620 353-8475
Sublette *(G-12206)*
Price Truck Line Inc ... F ... 785 625-2603
Hays *(G-2888)*
Quality Carriers Inc ... F ... 913 281-0901
Kansas City *(G-4351)*
Richman Helstrom Trucking Inc ... F ... 785 478-3186
Topeka *(G-13014)*
Rick Sauceda Trucking LLC ... F ... 913 231-8584
Centerville *(G-696)*
Riverside Transport Inc ... D ... 913 233-5500
Kansas City *(G-4380)*
Roady Trucking ... F ... 785 562-1221
Marysville *(G-6908)*
Ronald Carlile ... F ... 620 624-2632
Liberal *(G-6361)*
S Noble Trucking Inc ... F ... 620 704-0886
Mc Cune *(G-6922)*
S P D Transfer Service Lc ... F ... 913 321-0333
Shawnee Mission *(G-11820)*
Sallee Inc ... D ... 620 227-3320
Dodge City *(G-1426)*
Satchell Creek Express Inc ... E ... 316 775-1300
Augusta *(G-342)*
Schueman Transfer ... E ... 785 378-3114
Mankato *(G-6861)*
Scott Heller Trucking ... E ... 816 591-1638
Lenexa *(G-6119)*
T L C Trucking LLC ... F ... 620 277-0140
Holcomb *(G-3081)*
Tandem Truck Service Inc ... F ... 913 782-5454
Olathe *(G-8101)*
Taylor Crane & Rigging Inc ... D ... 620 251-1530
Coffeyville *(G-981)*
Terry Trucking & Wrecking LLC ... F ... 913 281-3854
Kansas City *(G-4465)*
Thomas and Sons Trucking LLC ... E ... 785 454-3839
Downs *(G-1473)*
Trans Services Inc ... E ... 913 592-3878
Spring Hill *(G-12102)*
Transwood Inc ... E ... 620 331-5699
Independence *(G-3567)*
Transwood Edwardsville66 ... E ... 913 745-1773
Kansas City *(G-4473)*
U S Road Freight Express Inc ... E ... 316 942-9944
Wichita *(G-15825)*
Unlimited Logistics LLC ... F ... 913 851-4900
Stilwell *(G-12178)*
Valley Trucking Trailer ... F ... 785 945-3554
Valley Falls *(G-13370)*
Wakeeney Truck Line Inc ... F ... 785 743-6778
Wakeeney *(G-13394)*
Warren Davidson Trucking ... F ... 785 625-5126
Hays *(G-2929)*
William R Harris Trucking ... F ... 913 422-5551
Shawnee Mission *(G-12010)*
Yrc Inc ... B ... 913 696-6100
Kansas City *(G-4565)*

TRUCKING: Long-Distance, Less Than Truckload

Elite Transportation LLC ... E ... 316 295-4829
Wichita *(G-14270)*
Fedex Freight Corporation ... F ... 800 752-0045
Cherryvale *(G-806)*
Fedex Freight Corporation ... F ... 888 399-4737
Great Bend *(G-2564)*
Old Dominion Freight Line Inc ... D ... 316 522-3562
Wichita *(G-15213)*
Old Dominion Freight Line Inc ... F ... 785 354-7336
Topeka *(G-12946)*
Old Dominion Freight Line Inc ... E ... 620 421-4121
Parsons *(G-9712)*
Old Dominion Freight Line Inc ... F ... 620 792-2006
Great Bend *(G-2617)*
USF Holland LLC ... C ... 913 287-1770
Kansas City *(G-4512)*
Wichita Southeast Kansas Trnst ... C ... 620 421-2272
Parsons *(G-9750)*
Yrc Worldwide Technologies Inc ... D ... 913 344-3000
Shawnee Mission *(G-12025)*

TRUCKS & TRACTORS: Industrial

Adapa Incorporated ... F ... 785 862-2060
Topeka *(G-12286)*
Adobe Truck & Equipment LLC ... G ... 913 498-9888
Olathe *(G-7510)*
Brierton Engineering Inc ... E ... 785 263-7711
Abilene *(G-16)*
Cargotec Holding Inc ... B ... 785 242-2200
Ottawa *(G-8251)*
Custom Metal Fabricators Inc ... E ... 785 258-3744
Herington *(G-2973)*
Kmw Ltd ... C ... 620 278-3641
Sterling *(G-12124)*
Mid-West Conveyor Company ... C ... 734 288-4400
Kansas City *(G-4247)*
R O Terex Corporation ... D ... 913 782-1200
Olathe *(G-8018)*
Rimpull Corporation ... C ... 913 782-4000
Olathe *(G-8036)*

TRUCKS, INDL: Wholesalers

K Young Inc ... F ... 785 475-3888
Colby *(G-1019)*

TRUCKS: Forklift

Crown Equipment Corporation ....E 316 942-4400
Wichita *(G-14136)*
Harper Trucks Inc ....C 316 942-1381
Wichita *(G-14563)*
Kalmar Solutions LLC ....B 785 242-2200
Ottawa *(G-8279)*
Landoll Corporation ....B 785 562-5381
Marysville *(G-6893)*
Royal Tractor Company Inc ....E 913 782-2598
New Century *(G-7296)*

TRUCKS: Indl

Bones Co Inc ....G 785 242-3070
Ottawa *(G-8250)*
General Delivery Inc ....F 913 281-6580
Kansas City *(G-4030)*

TRUSSES: Wood, Floor

Timber Roots ....G 316 755-3114
Valley Center *(G-13356)*

TRUSSES: Wood, Roof

Axtell Truss Manufacturing Inc ....G 785 736-2291
Axtell *(G-350)*
Central Kansas Truss Co Inc ....D 316 755-3114
Valley Center *(G-13339)*
Component Fabricators Inc ....G 785 776-5081
Manhattan *(G-6601)*
Indevco Inc ....D 913 236-7222
Shawnee Mission *(G-11454)*
Parker Truss & Stuff ....G 913 898-2775
Parker *(G-9660)*
Perfection Strl Components LLC ....E 316 942-8361
Wichita *(G-15282)*
Precision Truss Inc ....F 785 244-6456
Summerfield *(G-12215)*
St Joseph Truss Company Inc ....F 785 989-4496
Wathena *(G-13478)*
Wheeler Consolidated Inc ....E 785 733-2848
Waverly *(G-13483)*

TRUST COMPANIES: National With Deposits, Commercial

Condon National Bank ....E 620 251-5500
Coffeyville *(G-929)*
Exchange National Bank & Tr Co ....E 913 367-6000
Atchison *(G-227)*
First National Bank In Pratt ....E 620 672-6421
Pratt *(G-10113)*
First Option Bank and Trust ....F 913 294-3811
Osawatomie *(G-8193)*
Intrust Bank NA ....F 316 383-3350
Andover *(G-95)*
Intrust Bank NA ....F 316 383-3340
Augusta *(G-328)*
Intrust Bank NA ....F 316 321-1640
El Dorado *(G-1573)*
Intrust Bank NA ....F 785 565-5400
Manhattan *(G-6665)*
Intrust Bank NA ....F 316 383-1731
Wichita *(G-14714)*
Intrust Bank NA ....F 316 383-1816
Wichita *(G-14715)*
Intrust Bank NA ....F 316 383-1563
Wichita *(G-14716)*
Intrust Bank NA ....F 316 383-1342
Wichita *(G-14717)*
Intrust Bank NA ....F 316 383-1549
Wichita *(G-14718)*
Intrust Bank NA ....F 316 383-1096
Wichita *(G-14719)*
Intrust Bank NA ....F 316 383-1194
Wichita *(G-14720)*
Intrust Bank NA ....F 316 383-1960
Wichita *(G-14721)*
Intrust Bank NA ....F 316 383-1505
Wichita *(G-14722)*
Rcb Bank Service Inc ....D 620 442-4040
Arkansas City *(G-173)*
Southwest National Bank ....D 316 291-5299
Wichita *(G-15627)*
Southwest National Bank ....F 316 941-1335
Wichita *(G-15629)*
Southwest National Bank ....F 316 838-5741
Wichita *(G-15630)*
Sunflower Bank National Assn ....F 785 312-7274
Lawrence *(G-5128)*
Sunflower Bank National Assn ....F 316 652-1279
Wichita *(G-15686)*
Sunflower Bank National Assn ....F 785 827-5564
Salina *(G-10724)*
Sunflower Bank National Assn ....F 785 537-0550
Manhattan *(G-6817)*
Sunflower Bank National Assn ....F 785 825-6900
Salina *(G-10725)*
Sunflower Bank National Assn ....F 785 238-3177
Junction City *(G-3758)*
Sunflower Bank National Assn ....F 620 624-2063
Liberal *(G-6374)*
Sunflower Holdings Inc ....F 620 241-1220
McPherson *(G-7029)*

TRUST COMPANIES: State Accepting Deposits, Commercial

Alliance Bank ....E 785 271-1800
Topeka *(G-12307)*
Andover State Bank ....F 316 733-1375
Andover *(G-82)*
Arvest Bank ....F 417 627-8000
Pittsburg *(G-9810)*
Arvest Bank ....F 913 953-4070
Leawood *(G-5330)*
Arvest Bank ....F 913 953-4000
Overland Park *(G-8397)*
Arvest Bank ....F 913 279-3300
Gardner *(G-2327)*
Arvest Bank ....F 620 879-5811
Caney *(G-666)*
Bank of Blue Valley ....F 785 284-3433
Sabetha *(G-10306)*
Bank of Blue Valley ....E 913 338-1000
Overland Park *(G-8428)*
Bank of Blue Valley ....E 785 889-4211
Onaga *(G-8171)*
Bank of Cmmrce Tr of Wllngton ....F 620 326-7471
Wellington *(G-13490)*
Bank of Commerce ....E 620 431-1400
Chanute *(G-705)*
Bank of Hays ....F 785 621-2265
Hays *(G-2756)*
Bank of Labor ....E 913 321-4242
Shawnee *(G-10914)*
Bank of Labor ....E 913 321-4242
Kansas City *(G-3841)*
Bank of Labor ....E 913 321-4242
Kansas City *(G-3842)*
Bank of Labor ....E 913 321-6800
Kansas City *(G-3843)*
Bank of Protection Inc ....F 620 622-4224
Protection *(G-10173)*
Bank of Tescott ....F 785 283-4217
Tescott *(G-12244)*
Bank of Tescott ....F 785 227-8830
Lindsborg *(G-6392)*
Bank of Tescott ....E 785 825-1621
Salina *(G-10418)*
Bank of West ....F 316 292-5840
Wichita *(G-13807)*
Bank of West ....F 913 362-8900
Shawnee Mission *(G-11148)*
Bank of West ....F 620 225-4147
Dodge City *(G-1303)*
Bank of West ....F 316 292-5870
Wichita *(G-13808)*
Bank of West ....F 620 662-0543
Hutchinson *(G-3213)*
Bank of West ....F 316 729-7999
Wichita *(G-13809)*
Bank of West ....F 785 242-2804
Ottawa *(G-8248)*
Bank of West ....F 620 792-1771
Great Bend *(G-2515)*
Bank VI ....F 785 825-4321
Salina *(G-10419)*
Bendena State Bank ....F 785 988-4453
Bendena *(G-510)*
Bennington State Bank ....F 785 392-2136
Minneapolis *(G-7114)*
Bennington State Bank ....E 785 827-5522
Salina *(G-10423)*
Bennington State Bank ....F 785 456-1806
Wamego *(G-13405)*
Cbw Bank ....F 620 396-8221
Weir *(G-13485)*
Centera Bank ....F 620 675-8611
Sublette *(G-12200)*
Central Bank and Trust Co ....E 620 663-0666
Hutchinson *(G-3231)*
Central Bank of Midwest ....D 913 856-7715
Gardner *(G-2331)*
Central Bank of Midwest ....D 913 791-9288
Shawnee Mission *(G-11211)*
Citizens State Bank ....E 316 518-6621
Hugoton *(G-3152)*
Citizens State Bank ....F 785 363-2521
Waterville *(G-13472)*
Citizens State Bank and Tr Co ....E 785 742-2101
Hiawatha *(G-3006)*
Citizens State Bnk Tr Ellswrth ....E 785 472-3141
Ellsworth *(G-1660)*
City State Bank ....F 620 223-1600
Fort Scott *(G-1960)*
City State Bank ....F 620 223-1600
Fort Scott *(G-1961)*
Colwich Financial Corp ....E 316 796-1221
Colwich *(G-1092)*
Commercial Bank ....E 620 423-0770
Parsons *(G-9674)*
Commercial Bank ....F 620 423-0750
Independence *(G-3506)*
Community Bank ....F 620 624-6898
Liberal *(G-6296)*
Community Bank and Trust ....F 620 783-1395
Galena *(G-2072)*
Community State Bank ....F 620 251-1313
Coffeyville *(G-928)*
Corefirst Bank & Trust ....E 785 267-8900
Topeka *(G-12509)*
Corefirst Bank & Trust ....F 620 341-7420
Emporia *(G-1725)*
Corefirst Bank & Trust ....F 785 267-8900
Topeka *(G-12511)*
Douglas County Bank ....D 785 865-1000
Lawrence *(G-4836)*
Emprise Bank ....D 316 383-4400
Wichita *(G-14280)*
Emprise Bank ....F 316 776-9584
Rose Hill *(G-10238)*
Emprise Bank ....F 316 383-4301
Wichita *(G-14281)*
Emprise Bank ....F 316 775-4233
Augusta *(G-318)*
Emprise Bank ....F 316 794-2258
Goddard *(G-2437)*
Emprise Bank ....F 316 383-4498
Wichita *(G-14284)*
Emprise Bank ....F 785 838-2001
Lawrence *(G-4852)*
Enterprise Bank & Trust ....F 620 431-7070
Chanute *(G-725)*
Esb Financial ....E 620 342-3454
Emporia *(G-1751)*
Everest Bancshares Inc ....F 785 863-2267
Oskaloosa *(G-8225)*
Exchange Bank ....F 785 762-4121
Junction City *(G-3688)*
Farmers Bank & Trust ....F 785 626-3233
Atwood *(G-285)*
Farmers State Bank ....F 785 989-4431
Wathena *(G-13474)*
Farmers State Bank of Bucklin ....F 620 826-3231
Bucklin *(G-592)*
Farmers State Bank of Oakley ....F 785 672-3251
Oakley *(G-7474)*
Farmers State Bankshares Inc ....E 785 924-3311
Circleville *(G-838)*
Farmers State Bnk of Wstmrland ....E 785 457-3316
Westmoreland *(G-13547)*
Farmers State Bnk of Wstmrland ....F 785 889-4211
Onaga *(G-8176)*
Fidelity State Bank and Tr Co ....E 785 295-2100
Topeka *(G-12607)*
First Bancshares Inc ....E 913 371-1242
Kansas City *(G-4010)*
First Bank ....F 620 278-2161
Sterling *(G-12117)*
First Bank of Newton ....E 316 283-2600
Newton *(G-7345)*
First Business Bank ....F 913 681-2223
Leawood *(G-5402)*
First Commerce Bank ....F 785 562-5558
Marysville *(G-6889)*
First Kansas Bank ....E 620 653-4921
Hoisington *(G-3064)*

First Neodesha Bank F 620 325-2632
Neodesha *(G-7240)*
First Security Bank & Trust Co E 785 877-3313
Norton *(G-7446)*
First State Bank F 785 798-2212
Ness City *(G-7262)*
First State Bank F 785 675-3241
Hoxie *(G-3137)*
First State Bank & Trust D 913 845-2500
Tonganoxie *(G-12261)*
First State Bank & Trust E 785 749-0400
Lawrence *(G-4863)*
First State Bank & Trust E 785 597-5151
Perry *(G-9767)*
First State Bank & Trust F 913 724-2121
Basehor *(G-378)*
First State Bank (inc) E 785 654-2421
Burlingame *(G-623)*
First State Bank of Edna Inc E 620 922-3294
Edna *(G-1493)*
First State Bnk Tr of Larned F 620 285-6931
Larned *(G-4703)*
Goppert State Service Bank E 785 448-3111
Garnett *(G-2375)*
Great American Bank F 913 585-1131
De Soto *(G-1200)*
Guaranty State Bnk Tr Bloit Ka E 785 738-3501
Beloit *(G-485)*
Harris Bmo Bank National Assn F 913 441-7900
Shawnee Mission *(G-11411)*
Harris Bmo Bank National Assn F 620 231-2000
Pittsburg *(G-9871)*
Harris Bmo Bank National Assn F 913 693-1600
Leawood *(G-5419)*
Harris Bmo Bank National Assn F 913 254-6600
Olathe *(G-7754)*
Harris Bmo Bank National Assn F 620 235-7250
Pittsburg *(G-9872)*
Holton National Bank F 785 364-2166
Holton *(G-3098)*
Home Bank and Trust Company F 620 583-5516
Eureka *(G-1891)*
Home State Bank & Trust Co E 620 241-3732
McPherson *(G-6974)*
Industrial State Bank E 913 831-2000
Kansas City *(G-4099)*
Jamestown State Bank F 785 439-6224
Jamestown *(G-3643)*
Johnson State Bank E 620 492-6200
Johnson *(G-3656)*
Kansas State Bank E 785 364-2166
Holton *(G-3103)*
Kansas State Bank E 785 242-1011
Ottawa *(G-8280)*
Kansas State Bank F 785 665-7121
Overbrook *(G-8325)*
Kanza Bank E 620 532-5821
Kingman *(G-4596)*
Kanza Bank F 316 636-5821
Wichita *(G-14831)*
Kanza Bank F 316 773-7007
Wichita *(G-14832)*
Kaw Valley Bank E 785 232-2700
Topeka *(G-12810)*
Kaw Valley Bank F 785 272-8100
Topeka *(G-12811)*
Kaw Valley State Bank F 785 542-4200
Eudora *(G-1877)*
Kaw Valley State Bank & Tr Co F 785 456-2025
Wamego *(G-13428)*
Kendall State Bank F 785 945-3231
Valley Falls *(G-13366)*
KS Statebank E 785 762-5050
Junction City *(G-3719)*
KS Statebank E 785 587-4000
Manhattan *(G-6702)*
Legacy Bank D 316 796-1221
Wichita *(G-14950)*
Legacy Bank F 316 260-3755
Wichita *(G-14951)*
Legacy Bank E 316 260-3711
Wichita *(G-14952)*
Lyndon State Bank E 785 828-4411
Lyndon *(G-6477)*
Lyon County State Bank E 620 342-3523
Emporia *(G-1787)*
Lyons State Bank E 620 257-3775
Lyons *(G-6493)*
Olpe State Bank Inc F 620 475-3213
Olpe *(G-8166)*
Osawatomie Agency Inc F 913 294-3811
Paola *(G-9577)*
Peabody State Bank F 620 983-2181
Peabody *(G-9762)*
Peoples Bank E 620 672-5611
Pratt *(G-10132)*
Peoples Bank F 620 582-2166
Coldwater *(G-1056)*
Peoples Bank F 785 282-6682
Smith Center *(G-12039)*
Peoples Bank & Trust Co E 620 241-2100
McPherson *(G-7013)*
Rcb Bank F 620 860-7797
Hutchinson *(G-3420)*
Riley State Bank of Riley Kans F 785 485-2811
Riley *(G-10208)*
Rose Hill Bank E 316 776-2131
Rose Hill *(G-10247)*
Security Bank of Kansas City D 913 281-3165
Kansas City *(G-4412)*
Security Bank of Kansas City F 913 621-8423
Kansas City *(G-4413)*
Security Bank of Kansas City F 913 621-8465
Kansas City *(G-4414)*
Security Bank of Kansas City F 913 621-8462
Kansas City *(G-4415)*
Security Bank of Kansas City D 913 299-6200
Kansas City *(G-4416)*
Security Bank of Kansas City F 913 621-8430
Shawnee Mission *(G-11846)*
Security Bank of Kansas City F 913 384-3300
Fairway *(G-1919)*
Security State Bank D 620 872-7224
Scott City *(G-10834)*
State Bank of Canton F 620 628-4425
Canton *(G-683)*
State Bank of Kansas F 620 378-2114
Fredonia *(G-2045)*
State Bank of Spring Hill F 913 592-3326
Spring Hill *(G-12100)*
Stockgrowers State Bank E 800 772-2265
Ashland *(G-199)*
Stockgrowers State Bank F 785 256-4241
Maple Hill *(G-6864)*
Stockgrowers State Bank F 620 873-2123
Meade *(G-7054)*
Union State Bank E 620 442-5200
Arkansas City *(G-186)*
Union State Bank Inc E 785 468-3341
Olsburg *(G-8169)*
Union State Bank of Everest F 785 548-7521
Everest *(G-1903)*
United Bank & Trust E 785 562-4330
Marysville *(G-6912)*
Valley State Bank E 620 488-2211
Belle Plaine *(G-449)*
Valley View State Bank C 913 381-3311
Shawnee Mission *(G-11973)*
Valley View State Bank F 913 381-3311
Shawnee Mission *(G-11974)*
Western State Bank F 785 899-2393
Goodland *(G-2491)*
Wilson State Bank F 785 658-3441
Wilson *(G-16108)*

TRUST MANAGEMENT SVCS: Charitable

Community Fndtion Sthwest Kans F 620 225-0959
Dodge City *(G-1326)*
University of Kansas A 913 588-5436
Kansas City *(G-4502)*

TRUST MANAGEMENT SVCS: Educational

Washburn University Foundation E 785 670-4483
Topeka *(G-13232)*

TRUST MGMT SVCS: Priv Estate, Personal Invest/Vacation Fund

National Advisors Holdings Inc E 913 234-8200
Overland Park *(G-9068)*

TUBE & TUBING FABRICATORS

Specialty Fabrication Inc F 316 264-0603
Wichita *(G-15636)*

TUBES: Finned, For Heat Transfer

SPX Dry Cooling Usa LLC G 913 685-0009
Overland Park *(G-9346)*

TUBES: Fins

Cft LLC E 620 431-0885
Chanute *(G-710)*

TUBING: Flexible, Metallic

EC Manufacturing LLC C 913 825-3077
Paola *(G-9555)*

TURBINES & TURBINE GENERATOR SET UNITS, COMPLETE

GE Oil & Gas Compression D 785 823-9211
Salina *(G-10508)*

TURBINES & TURBINE GENERATOR SETS

Caterpillar Inc D 309 675-1000
Wamego *(G-13409)*
Siemens Energy Inc G 316 315-4534
Wichita *(G-15583)*

TURBINES & TURBINE GENERATOR SETS & PARTS

Accessible Technologies Inc D 913 338-2886
Lenexa *(G-5621)*

TURBINES: Hydraulic, Complete

Kanamak Hydraulics Inc E 800 473-5843
Garden City *(G-2212)*

TURBO-SUPERCHARGERS: Aircraft

Hiperformance LLC G 913 829-3400
New Century *(G-7287)*

TURKEY PROCESSING & SLAUGHTERING

Hybrid Turkeys LLC G 620 951-4705
Newton *(G-7365)*

TWINE PRDTS

Great Lakes Polymer Tech LLC C 620 532-5141
Kingman *(G-4591)*

TWINE: Binder & Baler

Great Lakes Polymer Tech LLC E 208 324-2120
Kingman *(G-4593)*

TYPESETTING SVC

Administration Kansas Dept D 785 296-3631
Topeka *(G-12289)*
Art Craft Printers & Design G 785 776-9151
Manhattan *(G-6545)*
Consolidated Prtg & Sty Co Inc E 785 825-5426
Salina *(G-10460)*
Cookbook Publishers Inc E 913 689-3038
Overland Park *(G-8598)*
Copy Center of Topeka Inc E 785 233-6677
Topeka *(G-12507)*
Davis Publications Inc F 785 945-6170
Valley Falls *(G-13362)*
Deluxe Corporation C 913 888-3801
Lenexa *(G-5810)*
Ejrex Inc D 620 421-6200
Parsons *(G-9683)*
Gary Bell G 785 233-6677
Holton *(G-3090)*
Graphic Images Inc F 316 283-3776
Newton *(G-7352)*
J-Con Reprographics Inc F 913 859-0800
Lenexa *(G-5927)*
Kelsey Construction Inc G 913 894-0330
Shawnee Mission *(G-11528)*
Kopco Inc D 620 879-2117
Caney *(G-671)*
Mennonite Press Inc E 316 283-3060
Newton *(G-7380)*
Mid West Color Graphics Inc E 620 429-1088
Columbus *(G-1084)*
Midwestern Litho G 620 378-2912
Fredonia *(G-2040)*
Par Forms Corporation F 620 421-0970
Parsons *(G-9716)*
Print Time Inc E 913 345-8900
Leawood *(G-5528)*
Printery Inc F 785 632-5501
Clay Center *(G-877)*

Proprint Incorporated..........E....... 785 842-3610
Lawrence *(G-5080)*
Quality Printing Inc..........G....... 620 421-0630
Parsons *(G-9727)*
Taylor Printing Inc..........G....... 620 672-3656
Pratt *(G-10159)*
Valley Offset Printing Inc..........E....... 316 755-0061
Valley Center *(G-13360)*

TYPESETTING SVC: Hand Composition

R Miller Sales Co Inc..........E....... 913 341-3727
Shawnee Mission *(G-11772)*

ULTRASONIC EQPT: Cleaning, Exc Med & Dental

Novatech LLC..........E....... 913 451-1880
Lenexa *(G-6028)*

UNIFORM SPLY SVCS: Indl

Unifirst Corporation..........F....... 785 233-1550
Topeka *(G-13203)*
Unifirst Corporation..........F....... 785 825-8766
Salina *(G-10745)*
Unifirst Corporation..........D....... 620 275-0231
Garden City *(G-2306)*

UNIFORM STORES

Deyno LLC..........F....... 785 551-8949
Lawrence *(G-4835)*
Something Different Inc..........G....... 785 537-1171
Wamego *(G-13441)*

UNISEX HAIR SALONS

A Total Image..........F....... 785 272-2855
Topeka *(G-12279)*
C & W Operations Ltd..........C....... 913 438-6400
Shawnee Mission *(G-11196)*
C & W Operations Ltd..........F....... 913 299-8820
Kansas City *(G-3884)*
C & W Operations Ltd..........F....... 913 268-1032
Shawnee Mission *(G-11197)*
Capelli Hair & Nail Salon..........F....... 785 271-6811
Topeka *(G-12423)*
Eastside Barbershop & Salon..........E....... 800 857-2906
Topeka *(G-12569)*
Eric Fisher Salon..........F....... 316 729-0777
Wichita *(G-14300)*
Gaia Inc..........F....... 785 539-2622
Manhattan *(G-6643)*
Geesu Inc..........F....... 913 648-0087
Shawnee Mission *(G-11392)*
Golden Key Salon..........F....... 316 744-0230
Bel Aire *(G-433)*
Great Clips..........F....... 913 727-1917
Leavenworth *(G-5246)*
Great Clips For Hair..........F....... 913 888-7447
Lenexa *(G-5883)*
Great Clips For Hair..........E....... 913 888-3400
Overland Park *(G-8770)*
Great Clips For Hair..........F....... 913 338-2580
Overland Park *(G-8771)*
Hair Connection..........F....... 316 685-7213
Wichita *(G-14541)*
Hair Cutting Company..........F....... 316 283-0532
Newton *(G-7356)*
Hair E Clips Ltd..........F....... 620 793-9050
Great Bend *(G-2589)*
Hair Force..........F....... 316 684-3361
Wichita *(G-14542)*
Hairem of Olathe LLC..........F....... 913 829-1260
Olathe *(G-7747)*
Haynes Salon and Supply Inc..........F....... 785 539-5512
Manhattan *(G-6651)*
Jhon-Josephsons Salon..........E....... 913 338-4443
Shawnee Mission *(G-11490)*
Midland Clippers..........F....... 913 962-7070
Shawnee Mission *(G-11630)*
Perfect Details Inc..........F....... 913 592-5022
Spring Hill *(G-12096)*
Regis Corporation..........F....... 316 685-5333
Wichita *(G-15439)*
Regis Salon Corp..........E....... 785 273-2992
Topeka *(G-13006)*
Ruth Grimsley..........F....... 913 393-1711
Olathe *(G-8048)*
Salon Brands..........F....... 785 301-2984
Hays *(G-2906)*
Salon Mission Inc..........E....... 913 642-8333
Overland Park *(G-9277)*
Salon Progressions & Day Spa..........F....... 316 729-1980
Wichita *(G-15512)*
Salon Ten O Seven..........E....... 785 628-6000
Hays *(G-2907)*
Sams Fantastic..........F....... 913 856-4247
Gardner *(G-2361)*
Stem 2 LLC..........E....... 913 236-9368
Merriam *(G-7106)*
Strands..........F....... 620 663-6397
Hutchinson *(G-3450)*
Supercuts Inc..........F....... 316 218-1400
Andover *(G-109)*
Wave Review Salon..........F....... 913 345-9252
Shawnee Mission *(G-11997)*

UNIVERSITY

Fort Hays State University..........E....... 785 628-4286
Hays *(G-2811)*
Friends University..........F....... 316 295-5638
Wichita *(G-14424)*
Kansas State University..........D....... 785 826-2646
Salina *(G-10567)*
Kansas State University..........F....... 785 532-6980
Manhattan *(G-6685)*
Kansas State University..........E....... 785 532-7718
Manhattan *(G-6680)*
Kansas State University..........B....... 785 532-6376
Manhattan *(G-6681)*
Kansas State University..........A....... 785 539-4971
Manhattan *(G-6682)*
Kansas State University..........E....... 785 532-5961
Manhattan *(G-6683)*
Kansas State University..........E....... 785 532-7600
Manhattan *(G-6687)*
Kansas State University..........E....... 785 625-3425
Hays *(G-2858)*
Kansas State University..........D....... 785 532-5650
Manhattan *(G-6688)*
Kansas State University..........E....... 785 532-5640
Manhattan *(G-6689)*
Kansas State University..........F....... 785 532-5813
Manhattan *(G-6690)*
Kansas State University..........E....... 785 532-6412
Manhattan *(G-6691)*
Kansas State University..........E....... 785 532-6506
Manhattan *(G-6692)*
Kansas State University..........C....... 785 532-5654
Manhattan *(G-6693)*
Kansas State University..........F....... 785 532-6804
Manhattan *(G-6695)*
Kansas State University..........E....... 785 532-6984
Manhattan *(G-6696)*
Trustees Indiana University..........E....... 913 499-6661
Fairway *(G-1923)*
Trustees of The Baker Univ..........E....... 785 354-5850
Topeka *(G-13199)*
University of Kansas..........D....... 785 864-1500
Lawrence *(G-5161)*
University of Kansas..........E....... 316 293-2620
Wichita *(G-15857)*
University of Kansas..........E....... 785 864-2277
Lawrence *(G-5158)*
University of Kansas..........D....... 785 864-8885
Lawrence *(G-5160)*
University of Kansas..........E....... 913 588-5900
Kansas City *(G-4497)*
University of Kansas..........C....... 913 588-5000
Kansas City *(G-4500)*
University of Kansas..........C....... 316 293-2607
Wichita *(G-15856)*
University of Kansas..........A....... 913 588-1443
Kansas City *(G-4501)*
University of Kansas..........C....... 785 864-2700
Lawrence *(G-5163)*
University of Kansas..........C....... 785 864-2451
Lawrence *(G-5164)*
University of Kansas..........D....... 785 864-4710
Lawrence *(G-5165)*
University of Kansas..........E....... 785 864-4154
Lawrence *(G-5166)*
University of Kansas..........C....... 785 864-4540
Lawrence *(G-5167)*
University of Kansas Hospital..........C....... 913 588-5000
Kansas City *(G-4507)*
Washburn University of Topeka..........E....... 785 670-1111
Topeka *(G-13233)*
Wichita State University..........E....... 316 978-6789
Wichita *(G-16033)*
Wichita State University..........E....... 316 978-3581
Wichita *(G-16034)*

UNSUPPORTED PLASTICS: Floor Or Wall Covering

Better Life Technology LLC..........F....... 913 894-0403
Lenexa *(G-5699)*

UPHOLSTERY WORK SVCS

Circle Enterprises Inc..........F....... 316 943-9834
Wichita *(G-14021)*
Design Central Inc..........F....... 785 825-4131
Salina *(G-10474)*

USED BOOK STORES

Half Price Bks Rec Mgzines Inc..........F....... 913 829-9959
Olathe *(G-7748)*

USED CAR DEALERS

Bme Inc..........E....... 785 274-5116
Topeka *(G-12391)*
Brenneman & Bremmeman Inc..........F....... 316 282-8834
Newton *(G-7321)*
Briggs Auto Group Inc..........E....... 785 776-3677
Manhattan *(G-6569)*
Conklin Fangman Investment Co..........C....... 620 662-4467
Hutchinson *(G-3245)*
Dick Edwards Ford Lincoln Merc..........D....... 785 320-4499
Junction City *(G-3687)*
Ghumms Auto Center LLC..........F....... 620 544-7800
Hugoton *(G-3163)*
K Young Inc..........F....... 785 475-3888
Colby *(G-1019)*
Mel Hambelton Ford Inc..........C....... 316 462-3673
Wichita *(G-15035)*
Midway Motors Inc..........D....... 620 241-7737
McPherson *(G-7005)*
Oakley Motors Inc..........E....... 785 672-3238
Oakley *(G-7484)*
South Star Chrysler Inc..........F....... 785 242-5600
Ottawa *(G-8313)*

USED CLOTHING STORES

Disabled American Veterens Str..........F....... 785 827-6477
Salina *(G-10479)*
Goodwill Wstn MO & Eastrn Kans..........F....... 785 331-3908
Lawrence *(G-4875)*
Goodwill Wstn MO & Eastrn Kans..........E....... 913 768-9540
Olathe *(G-7737)*
Goodwill Wstn MO & Eastrn Kans..........E....... 785 228-9774
Topeka *(G-12642)*

USED MERCHANDISE STORES: Building Materials

Glen-Gery Corporation..........G....... 913 281-2800
Kansas City *(G-4038)*

USED MERCHANDISE STORES: Furniture

Bud Palmer Auction..........E....... 316 838-4141
Wichita *(G-13905)*

USED MERCHANDISE STORES: Musical Instruments

Hume Music Inc..........F....... 816 474-1960
Stilwell *(G-12154)*
Manning Music Inc..........F....... 785 272-1740
Topeka *(G-12857)*

USED MERCHANDISE STORES: Office Furniture

Cort Business Services Corp..........E....... 913 888-0100
Overland Park *(G-8601)*

UTILITY PROGRAM ADMIN & REG, GOVT: Communications Comm

Spectrum Elite Corp..........G....... 913 579-7037
Olathe *(G-8076)*

UTILITY TRAILER DEALERS

Eagle Trailer Company Inc..........G....... 785 841-3200
Lawrence *(G-4844)*

PRDT & SVC

Landoll Corporation....E....785 738-6613
Beloit (G-490)
Miller Welding Inc....F....785 454-3425
Downs (G-1472)
Redneck Inc....E....316 263-6090
Wichita (G-15432)
Wilson Trailer Sales Kans Inc....F....620 225-6220
Dodge City (G-1458)

VACATION LODGES

Flint Oak....E....620 658-4401
Fall River (G-1927)
Masonic Lodge....F....620 662-7012
Hutchinson (G-3366)

VACUUM CLEANER REPAIR SVCS

Midwest Sewing & Vacuum Center....E....316 722-9737
Wichita (G-15101)

VACUUM CLEANER STORES

Midwest Sewing & Vacuum Center....E....316 722-9737
Wichita (G-15101)

VALET PARKING SVCS

Car Park Inc....E....316 265-0553
Wichita (G-13942)
E & J Rental & Leasing Inc....F....316 721-0442
Wichita (G-14249)

VALUE-ADDED RESELLERS: Computer Systems

High Touch Inc....D....316 462-4001
Wichita (G-14606)

VALVES & PARTS: Gas, Indl

J Huston Howery....G....316 945-0023
Wichita (G-14736)
J Huston Howery....F....316 945-0023
Wichita (G-14737)

VALVES & PIPE FITTINGS

Aerospace Systems Cmpnents Inc....D....316 686-7392
Wichita (G-13638)
Eaton Corporation....B....620 663-5751
Hutchinson (G-3274)
Kice Industries Inc....C....316 744-7148
Park City (G-9625)
Little Giant Fittings Company....G....620 793-5399
Great Bend (G-2603)
Mid-America Fittings LLC....E....913 962-7277
Overland Park (G-9024)
Progressive Products Inc....E....620 235-1712
Pittsburg (G-9925)
Salina Vortex Corp....C....785 825-7177
Salina (G-10696)
Triumph Group Operations Inc....D....620 326-5761
Wellington (G-13538)

VALVES: Aerosol, Metal

Ram Metal Products Inc....G....913 422-0099
Leawood (G-5532)

VALVES: Aircraft, Hydraulic

Great Bend Industries Inc....D....620 792-4368
Great Bend (G-2581)

VALVES: Gas Cylinder, Compressed

Associated Cylinder SE....G....951 776-9915
Kansas City (G-3823)

VALVES: Indl

Arrow Valve Co Inc....G....620 879-2126
Caney (G-665)
Forum Energy Tecnhologies....D....620 437-2440
Madison (G-6500)
Powerline Machine Works Inc....F....620 824-6204
Chase (G-786)
Salina Vortex Corp....C....785 825-7177
Salina (G-10696)
V Mach Inc....E....913 894-2001
Shawnee Mission (G-11971)
Waddles Manufacturing & Mch Co....G....785 825-6166
Salina (G-10756)

VALVES: Regulating, Process Control

Cashco Inc....C....785 472-4461
Ellsworth (G-1659)

VARIETY STORE MERCHANDISE, WHOLESALE

Gibson Products Co Salina Inc....E....785 827-4474
Salina (G-10510)
Gibsons Ace Hardware....E....785 632-3147
Clay Center (G-865)
Touch Enterprises LLC....E....913 638-2130
Olathe (G-8117)

VARIETY STORES

Abraham Jacob Gorelick....F....913 371-0459
Kansas City (G-3779)
Touch Enterprises LLC....E....913 638-2130
Olathe (G-8117)

VEGETABLE STANDS OR MARKETS

Qins International Inc....E....913 342-4488
Kansas City (G-4350)

VEHICLES FINANCE LEASING, EXC AUTOMOBILES & TRUCKS

Wki Operations Inc....F....316 838-0867
Dodge City (G-1462)

VEHICLES: All Terrain

Flint Hills Powersports Inc....G....785 336-3901
Bern (G-522)

VENDING MACHINE OPERATORS: Cigarette

Coin Machine Distributors Inc....F....316 652-0361
Wichita (G-14052)

VENDING MACHINE OPERATORS: Food

Memorial Union Corp Emporia....D....620 341-5901
Emporia (G-1793)
Wichita Canteen Company Inc....E....316 524-2254
Wichita (G-15984)

VENDING MACHINE REPAIR SVCS

Online Vend Mch Sls & Svc Inc....G....913 492-1097
Lenexa (G-6037)

VENDING MACHINES & PARTS

Online Vend Mch Sls & Svc Inc....G....913 492-1097
Lenexa (G-6037)

VENTILATING EQPT: Metal

Dandee Air Inc....F....620 663-4341
Hutchinson (G-3253)
Systemair Mfg Inc....E....913 752-6000
Lenexa (G-6164)

VENTURE CAPITAL COMPANIES

Central States Capital Markets....F....913 766-6565
Prairie Village (G-10019)
Medova Hlthcare Fncl Group LLC....E....316 616-6160
Wichita (G-15034)
Prias Prairie View LLC....F....816 437-9636
Overland Park (G-9185)

VESSELS: Process, Indl, Metal Plate

Sauder Custom Fabrication Inc....D....620 342-2550
Emporia (G-1823)

VETERANS AFFAIRS ADMINISTRATION SVCS

National Cemetery ADM....F....913 758-4105
Leavenworth (G-5273)
National Cemetery ADM....F....913 758-4105
Leavenworth (G-5274)
Veterans Health Administration....A....316 685-2221
Wichita (G-15878)

VETERANS' AFFAIRS ADMINISTRATION, GOVERNMENT: Federal

Veterans Health Administration....A....785 350-3111
Topeka (G-13222)
Veterans Health Administration....B....785 826-1580
Salina (G-10752)
Veterans Health Administration....B....620 423-3858
Parsons (G-9748)

VETERINARY PHARMACEUTICAL PREPARATIONS

Bayer Hlthcare Animal Hlth Inc....E....913 268-2731
Shawnee (G-10915)
Ivy Animal Health Inc....E....913 310-7900
Lenexa (G-5924)
Norbrook Inc....E....913 599-5777
Lenexa (G-6026)

VETERINARY PRDTS: Instruments & Apparatus

Ross Manufacturing Inc....G....785 332-3012
Saint Francis (G-10345)
Stannley Veterinary Clinic....E....913 897-2080
Shawnee Mission (G-11894)

VIALS: Glass

Sands Level and Tool Company....F....989 428-4141
Lenexa (G-6117)

VIDEO & AUDIO EQPT, WHOLESALE

Cytek Media Systems Inc....E....785 295-4200
Topeka (G-12542)
Kent Business Systems Corp....F....316 262-4487
Wichita (G-14851)
Magtek Inc....F....913 451-1151
Lenexa (G-5981)

VIDEO EQPT

Keywest Technology Inc....F....913 492-4666
Lenexa (G-5947)

VIDEO PRODUCTION SVCS

Something Different Media Prod....F....913 764-9500
Olathe (G-8072)

VIDEO REPAIR SVCS

Kent Business Systems Corp....F....316 262-4487
Wichita (G-14851)

VIDEO TAPE PRODUCTION SVCS

Complete Video Production....F....913 888-2383
Shawnee Mission (G-11256)
Kent Business Systems Corp....F....316 262-4487
Wichita (G-14851)

VISITING NURSE

Absolute Home Health Care....E....316 832-1347
Wichita (G-13600)
Advantaged Home Care....E....785 267-4433
Topeka (G-12298)
Advocate Home Specialty Care....D....785 456-8910
Wamego (G-13402)
Alternacare Infusion Phrm Inc....F....913 906-9260
Olathe (G-7522)
Angels At Home Care....F....785 271-4376
Topeka (G-12328)
Angels Care Home Health....F....316 636-4000
Wichita (G-13710)
Another Day Homecare Inc....F....913 599-2221
Lenexa (G-5655)
Carestaf Inc....B....913 498-2888
Overland Park (G-8516)
Continua Home Health LLC....F....913 905-0255
Leawood (G-5359)
Craig Resources Inc....E....316 264-9988
Wichita (G-14125)
Gentiva Health Services Inc....E....913 906-0522
Overland Park (G-8754)
Home Health of Kansas LLC....E....316 684-5122
Wichita (G-14630)
Hospice of Reno County Inc....E....620 665-2473
Hutchinson (G-3314)

Jills Helping Hands Inc ... D ... 785 622-4254
Lenora (G-6244)
Preferred Registry of Nurses ... F ... 785 456-8628
Wamego (G-13435)
Proactive Home Care Inc ... D ... 316 688-5511
Wichita (G-15355)
Progressive Home Health Care ... E ... 316 691-5050
Wichita (G-15371)
Via Chrsti HM Hlth Wichita Inc ... D ... 316 268-8588
Wichita (G-15900)

VISUAL COMMUNICATIONS SYSTEMS

Garmin International Inc ... A ... 913 397-8200
Olathe (G-7722)

VOCATIONAL REHABILITATION AGENCY

Arrowhead West Inc ... E ... 620 225-4061
Dodge City (G-1296)
Arrowhead West Inc ... E ... 620 227-8803
Dodge City (G-1297)
Arrowhead West Inc ... E ... 316 722-4554
Wichita (G-13738)
Arrowhead West Inc ... E ... 620 886-3711
Medicine Lodge (G-7056)
Arrowhead West Inc ... F ... 620 225-5177
Dodge City (G-1298)
Cottonwood Incorporated ... C ... 785 842-0550
Lawrence (G-4812)
Developmental Svcs NW Kans Inc ... E ... 785 626-3688
Atwood (G-283)
Developmental Svcs NW Kans Inc ... E ... 785 421-2851
Hill City (G-3033)
Goodwill Industries Ea ... E ... 316 789-8804
Derby (G-1248)
Goodwill Industries Ea ... E ... 620 343-3564
Emporia (G-1764)
Goodwill Industries Ea ... E ... 620 275-1007
Garden City (G-2190)
Kansas Elks Training ... B ... 316 383-8700
Wichita (G-14797)
Northview Developmental Svcs ... F ... 316 283-5170
Newton (G-7400)
Riverside Resources Inc ... D ... 913 651-6810
Leavenworth (G-5287)
Sunflower Diversified Svcs Inc ... D ... 620 792-1321
Great Bend (G-2643)
Sunflower Diversified Svcs Inc ... C ... 620 792-4087
Great Bend (G-2644)
Twin Rvers Dvlpmental Supports ... D ... 620 442-3575
Arkansas City (G-184)

VOCATIONAL TRAINING AGENCY

Developmental Services of Jack ... E ... 785 364-3534
Holton (G-3087)
Multi Community Diversfd Svcs ... F ... 620 241-6693
McPherson (G-7009)
Nemaha County Training Center ... E ... 785 336-6116
Seneca (G-10875)

VOICE LESSONS

Academy of Arts LLC ... F ... 913 441-7300
Shawnee Mission (G-11065)

WALL COVERING STORE

Sewing Workshop ... F ... 785 357-6231
Topeka (G-13061)

WALL COVERINGS WHOLESALERS

Design Materials Inc ... E ... 913 342-9796
Kansas City (G-3969)
Designed Bus Intrors Tpeka Inc ... F ... 785 233-2078
Topeka (G-12553)
Designers Library Inc ... F ... 913 227-0010
Shawnee Mission (G-11303)

WALLBOARD: Decorated, Made From Purchased Materials

Open Road Brands LLC ... F ... 316 337-7550
Wichita (G-15222)

WALLPAPER STORE

Unique Design Inc ... F ... 785 272-6044
Topeka (G-13205)

WAREHOUSING & STORAGE FACILITIES, NEC

Exhibit Arts LLC ... E ... 316 264-2915
Wichita (G-14321)
Helena Agri-Enterprises LLC ... E ... 620 275-9531
Garden City (G-2195)
Mass Medical Storage LLC ... F ... 913 438-8835
Lenexa (G-5988)
Medart Inc ... F ... 636 282-2300
Kansas City (G-4227)
Mini Warehouse Limited II ... F ... 785 273-4004
Topeka (G-12906)
Northern Natural Gas Company ... E ... 620 675-2239
Kismet (G-4631)
Northern Natural Gas Company ... E ... 785 455-3311
Clifton (G-902)
Northern Natural Gas Company ... E ... 620 723-2151
Mullinville (G-7210)
Northern Natural Gas Company ... F ... 620 277-2364
Holcomb (G-3076)
Northern Natural Gas Company ... E ... 620 298-5111
Cunningham (G-1188)
Pepsico Inc ... F ... 620 275-5312
Garden City (G-2249)
Target Corporation ... C ... 785 274-6500
Topeka (G-13141)
Taylor Crane & Rigging Inc ... D ... 620 251-1530
Coffeyville (G-981)

WAREHOUSING & STORAGE, REFRIGERATED: Cheese

Cookbook Publishers Inc ... D ... 913 706-6069
Shawnee Mission (G-11265)

WAREHOUSING & STORAGE, REFRIGERATED: Cold Storage Or Refrig

Americold Logistics LLC ... E ... 316 838-9317
Wichita (G-13696)
Americold Logistics LLC ... E ... 620 276-2304
Garden City (G-2100)
Browns Processing ... G ... 620 378-2441
Fredonia (G-2027)
Emporia Cold Storage Co ... F ... 620 343-8010
Emporia (G-1736)
Midwest Refrigerated Svcs LLC ... F ... 913 621-1111
Kansas City (G-4255)
Winchester Meat Processing ... G ... 913 774-2860
Winchester (G-16111)

WAREHOUSING & STORAGE, REFRIGERATED: Frozen Or Refrig Goods

Grinnell Locker Plant Inc ... F ... 785 824-3400
Grinnell (G-2693)
Kensington Lockers Inc ... F ... 785 476-2834
Kensington (G-4577)
Olpe Locker ... G ... 620 475-3375
Emporia (G-1809)
Waggoner Enterprises Inc ... E ... 620 465-3807
Yoder (G-16196)

WAREHOUSING & STORAGE: Automobile, Dead Storage

Standard Motor Products Inc ... B ... 913 441-6500
Edwardsville (G-1516)

WAREHOUSING & STORAGE: Farm Prdts

Central Prairie Co-Op ... F ... 620 278-2470
Sterling (G-12113)
Cropland Co-Op Inc ... F ... 620 649-2230
Satanta (G-10782)

WAREHOUSING & STORAGE: General

Archrock Inc ... E ... 620 241-8740
McPherson (G-6937)
Builders Inc ... F ... 316 522-6104
Wichita (G-13910)
Comprehensive Logistics Co Inc ... E ... 913 371-0770
Kansas City (G-3932)
Dd Traders Inc ... F ... 913 402-6800
Gardner (G-2337)
Flexcon Company Inc ... F ... 913 768-8669
Olathe (G-7714)
Garvey Public Warehouse Inc ... F ... 316 522-4745
Wichita (G-14450)
Hall Industrial Dev LLC ... F ... 316 264-7268
Wichita (G-14545)
Hayes Company LLC ... F ... 316 838-8000
Wichita (G-14570)
Kansas City Coml Whsng Co ... E ... 913 287-3800
Kansas City (G-4144)
Kustom Karriers LLC ... D ... 316 283-1060
Newton (G-7374)
Metro Park Warehouses Inc ... E ... 913 621-3116
Kansas City (G-4237)
Metro Park Warehouses Inc ... E ... 913 342-8141
Kansas City (G-4238)
Metro Park Warehouses Inc ... E ... 913 287-7366
Kansas City (G-4239)
Midpoint National Inc ... E ... 913 362-7400
Kansas City (G-4248)
Mud-Co/Service Mud Inc ... F ... 620 672-2957
Pratt (G-10126)
Smart Warehousing LLC ... E ... 913 888-3222
Edgerton (G-1489)
Southwest Pallets ... G ... 620 275-4343
Garden City (G-2284)
Standard Motor Products Inc ... B ... 913 441-6500
Edwardsville (G-1516)
TFT Global Inc ... F ... 519 842-4540
Kansas City (G-4467)
Unified School District 383 ... D ... 785 587-2850
Manhattan (G-6837)
United Warehouse Company ... D ... 316 712-1000
Park City (G-9652)
UPS Srvice Parts Logistics Inc ... A ... 800 451-4550
Overland Park (G-9449)
Vf Outdoor Inc ... D ... 913 384-4000
Shawnee Mission (G-11976)

WAREHOUSING & STORAGE: General

Advance Stores Company Inc ... C ... 785 826-2400
Salina (G-10396)
Aldi Inc ... B ... 913 768-1119
Olathe (G-7517)
American Eagle Outfitters Inc ... B ... 724 779-5209
Ottawa (G-8244)
Associated Wholesale Groc Inc ... A ... 913 288-1000
Kansas City (G-3825)
Associated Wholesale Groc Inc ... C ... 913 319-8500
Kansas City (G-3826)
Attic Management Group LLC ... F ... 913 269-4583
Olathe (G-7541)
Bayer Healthcare LLC ... E ... 913 268-2000
Shawnee Mission (G-11154)
Berger Company ... D ... 913 367-3700
Atchison (G-215)
Bold LLC ... F ... 620 663-3300
Hutchinson (G-3217)
Dillards Inc ... B ... 913 791-6400
Olathe (G-7654)
Exhibit Arts LLC ... E ... 316 264-2915
Wichita (G-14321)
Hummert International Inc ... F ... 785 234-5652
Topeka (G-12707)
Kubota Tractor Corporation ... F ... 913 215-5298
Edgerton (G-1486)
Lubrication Engineers Inc ... E ... 316 529-2112
Wichita (G-14990)
Meritex Enterprises Inc ... F ... 913 888-0601
Shawnee Mission (G-11617)
National Cold Storage Inc ... E ... 913 422-4050
Bonner Springs (G-566)
National Cold Storage Kc Inc ... E ... 913 422-4050
Bonner Springs (G-567)
Professional Cargo Svcs Inc ... E ... 316 522-2224
Wichita (G-15357)
Suther Feeds Inc ... F ... 785 292-4415
Frankfort (G-2024)
Watco Transportation Svcs LLC ... E ... 620 231-2230
Pittsburg (G-9967)

WAREHOUSING & STORAGE: Household Goods

Mixture LLC ... F ... 913 944-2441
Shawnee (G-10997)
Thomas Transfer & Stor Co Inc ... D ... 620 342-2321
Emporia (G-1838)

WAREHOUSING & STORAGE: Liquid

Magellan Midstream Partners LP ... F ... 620 834-2205
McPherson (G-6987)

WAREHOUSING & STORAGE: Miniwarehouse

Kuhn Co LLC ... E ... 316 788-6500
Derby *(G-1257)*

WAREHOUSING & STORAGE: Refrigerated

Arctic Glacier Texas Inc ... E ... 316 529-2173
Wichita *(G-13732)*

Berrys Arctic Ice LLC ... F ... 785 357-4466
Topeka *(G-12376)*

WAREHOUSING & STORAGE: Self Storage

Illinois Auto Electric Co ... F ... 913 543-7600
Edwardsville *(G-1503)*

International Code Council Inc ... F ... 913 888-0304
Shawnee Mission *(G-11464)*

Public Storage ... E ... 316 522-1162
Wichita *(G-15373)*

Ronald Carlile ... F ... 620 624-2632
Liberal *(G-6361)*

Security Storage Prpts LLC ... F ... 316 634-6510
Wichita *(G-15544)*

Wilbur Inc ... F ... 913 207-6535
Olathe *(G-8154)*

WARM AIR HEATING & AC EQPT & SPLYS, WHOLESALE Air Filters

Mac Equipment Inc ... F ... 785 284-2191
Sabetha *(G-10317)*

WARM AIR HEATING & AC EQPT & SPLYS, WHOLESALE Furnaces

Salina Supply Company ... E ... 785 823-2221
Salina *(G-10693)*

Wsm Industries Inc ... C ... 316 942-9412
Wichita *(G-16075)*

Wsm Investments Inc ... C ... 316 942-9412
Wichita *(G-16076)*

WARM AIR HEATING & AC EQPT & SPLYS, WHOLESALE Thermostats

Clarios ... D ... 913 307-4200
Shawnee Mission *(G-11237)*

Clarios ... F ... 785 267-0801
Topeka *(G-12478)*

Clarios ... E ... 316 721-2777
Wichita *(G-14034)*

WARM AIR HEATING/AC EQPT/SPLYS, WHOL Warm Air Htg Eqpt/Splys

A-1 Electric Inc ... F ... 620 431-7500
Chanute *(G-701)*

American Metals Supply Co Inc ... E ... 913 754-0616
Lenexa *(G-5651)*

Freeman Supply Inc ... F ... 620 662-2330
Hutchinson *(G-3294)*

Heating and Cooling Distrs Inc ... F ... 913 262-5848
Stilwell *(G-12152)*

Heaven Engineering LLC ... F ... 316 262-1244
Wichita *(G-14592)*

Jorban-Riscoe Associates Inc ... E ... 913 438-1244
Lenexa *(G-5932)*

Piping Contractors Kansas Inc ... F ... 785 233-4321
Topeka *(G-12976)*

Triangle Sales Inc ... E ... 913 541-1800
Shawnee Mission *(G-11942)*

Western Supply Co Inc ... E ... 620 663-9082
Hutchinson *(G-3486)*

WW Grainger Inc ... E ... 913 492-8550
Lenexa *(G-6237)*

WARRANTY INSURANCE: Home

R & R Builders Inc ... D ... 913 682-1234
Leavenworth *(G-5282)*

WASHERS

...wer Washers Unlimited ... G ... 316 262-9274
...hita *(G-15320)*

...H REPAIR SVCS

...nc ... E ... 913 345-0200
...k *(G-9416)*

WATER BOTTLES: Rubber

Longford Water Company LLC ... G ... 785 388-2233
Longford *(G-6432)*

WATER PURIFICATION EQPT: Household

Ameripure Water Company ... F ... 913 825-6600
Kansas City *(G-3806)*

Pentair Flow Technologies LLC ... C ... 913 371-5000
Kansas City *(G-4319)*

WATER SOFTENER SVCS

All-Pro Services Inc ... F ... 785 842-1402
Lawrence *(G-4727)*

David E Dishop ... F ... 614 861-5440
Wichita *(G-14172)*

Power Chemicals Inc ... F ... 316 524-7899
Wichita *(G-15318)*

Scheopners Water Cond LLC ... F ... 620 275-5121
Garden City *(G-2275)*

Walker Centrifuge Services LLC ... F ... 785 826-8265
Salina *(G-10757)*

WATER SOFTENING WHOLESALERS

David E Dishop ... F ... 614 861-5440
Wichita *(G-14172)*

John G Levin ... E ... 785 234-5551
Topeka *(G-12746)*

Mid-American Water & Plbg Inc ... E ... 785 537-1072
Manhattan *(G-6741)*

Wheatland Waters Inc ... D ... 785 267-0512
Olathe *(G-8153)*

WATER SPLY: Irrigation

Kc Irrigation Specialist ... F ... 913 406-0670
Leawood *(G-5446)*

Premier Landscaping Inc ... F ... 316 733-4773
Andover *(G-107)*

T-L Irrigation Co ... F ... 620 675-2253
Sublette *(G-12212)*

WATER SUPPLY

City of Conway Springs ... E ... 620 456-2345
Conway Springs *(G-1136)*

City of Dodge City ... F ... 620 225-8176
Dodge City *(G-1322)*

City of Garden City ... F ... 620 276-1291
Garden City *(G-2126)*

City of Great Bend ... F ... 620 793-4170
Great Bend *(G-2542)*

City of Lawrence ... E ... 785 832-7840
Lawrence *(G-4791)*

City of Leavenworth ... E ... 913 682-1513
Leavenworth *(G-5222)*

City of Salina ... E ... 785 826-7305
Salina *(G-10448)*

City of Sedan ... E ... 620 725-3193
Sedan *(G-10840)*

Coffey County District 2 ... F ... 620 836-4080
Gridley *(G-2688)*

Consoldated Rur Wtr Distirct 4 ... F ... 785 286-1729
Topeka *(G-12502)*

County of Ellsworth ... F ... 785 472-4486
Ellsworth *(G-1665)*

Dickinson County Rur Wtr Dst 1 ... F ... 785 388-2290
Talmage *(G-12237)*

Greenwood Cnty Rur Wtr Dst 1 ... F ... 620 583-7181
Eureka *(G-1889)*

Kansas City Bd Pub Utilities ... E ... 913 573-9280
Kansas City *(G-4135)*

Kansas City Bd Pub Utilities ... D ... 913 573-9700
Kansas City *(G-4140)*

Kansas City Bd Pub Utilities ... C ... 913 573-9000
Kansas City *(G-4134)*

Kansas City Bd Pub Utilities ... D ... 913 573-9300
Kansas City *(G-4137)*

Kansas City Bd Pub Utilities ... A ... 913 573-9143
Kansas City *(G-4141)*

McPherson Bd of Pub Utilities ... D ... 620 245-2515
McPherson *(G-6992)*

Mitchell County Rur Wtr Dst 2 ... F ... 785 545-3341
Glen Elder *(G-2427)*

Public Whl Wtr Sup Dst No 13 ... F ... 913 795-2503
Mound City *(G-7174)*

Rural Water Distribution 3 ... F ... 913 755-4503
Osawatomie *(G-8203)*

Rural Water Dst 3 Cowley Cnty ... F ... 620 442-7131
Arkansas City *(G-177)*

Rural Water Dst 7 Osage Cnty ... F ... 785 528-5090
Osage City *(G-8189)*

Water Dst No1 Jhnson Cnty Kans ... C ... 913 895-5500
Lenexa *(G-6222)*

Water Dst No1 Jhnson Cnty Kans ... D ... 913 895-5800
Kansas City *(G-4532)*

WATER TREATMENT EQPT: Indl

Aero-Mod Incorporated ... E ... 785 537-4995
Manhattan *(G-6535)*

Bio-Microbics Inc ... E ... 913 422-0707
Lenexa *(G-5704)*

Evoqua Water Technologies LLC ... E ... 913 422-7600
Overland Park *(G-8697)*

Fresh Kc Water Inc ... G ... 913 745-0002
Shawnee *(G-10958)*

Siemens Industry Inc ... E ... 913 683-9787
Lansing *(G-4692)*

Siemens Industry Inc ... E ... 785 762-7814
Junction City *(G-3754)*

Smith and Loveless Inc ... C ... 913 888-5201
Shawnee Mission *(G-11875)*

WATER: Pasteurized, Canned & Bottled, Etc

City of Spring Hill ... F ... 913 592-3781
Spring Hill *(G-12082)*

Water Depot Inc ... G ... 913 782-7277
Olathe *(G-8148)*

WATERPROOFING COMPOUNDS

Boyer Industries Corporation ... D ... 785 865-4200
Lawrence *(G-4762)*

Epro Services Inc ... F ... 316 262-2513
Wichita *(G-14298)*

Koch Materials LLC ... C ... 316 828-5500
Wichita *(G-14883)*

Professional Products of Kans ... G ... 316 522-9300
Wichita *(G-15365)*

Prosoco Inc ... D ... 785 865-4200
Lawrence *(G-5081)*

WEATHER FORECASTING SVCS

National Weather Service ... E ... 785 899-2360
Goodland *(G-2480)*

National Weather Service ... E ... 785 234-2592
Topeka *(G-12924)*

National Weather Service ... E ... 620 225-6514
Dodge City *(G-1411)*

WEDDING CHAPEL: Privately Operated

Unity Church of Overland Park ... E ... 913 649-1750
Shawnee Mission *(G-11966)*

WELDING & CUTTING APPARATUS & ACCESS, NEC

Pac Mig Inc ... G ... 316 269-3040
Mulvane *(G-7226)*

Pmti Inc ... E ... 913 432-7500
Shawnee Mission *(G-11740)*

WELDING EQPT & SPLYS WHOLESALERS

Air Products and Chemicals Inc ... E ... 620 624-8151
Liberal *(G-6273)*

Airgas Usa LLC ... E ... 785 823-8100
Salina *(G-10398)*

Airgas Usa LLC ... E ... 316 941-9162
Wichita *(G-13653)*

Denison Inc ... F ... 620 378-4148
Fredonia *(G-2030)*

Lampton Welding Supply Co Inc ... E ... 316 263-3293
Wichita *(G-14917)*

Matheson Tri-Gas Inc ... F ... 785 537-0395
Manhattan *(G-6734)*

Matheson Tri-Gas Inc ... F ... 316 554-9353
Wichita *(G-15019)*

Matheson Tri-Gas Inc ... F ... 785 493-8200
Salina *(G-10594)*

Matheson Tri-Gas Inc ... E ... 785 234-3424
Topeka *(G-12864)*

Miller Welding Inc ... F ... 785 454-3425
Downs *(G-1472)*

Pac Mig Inc ... G ... 316 269-3040
Mulvane *(G-7226)*

Praxair Inc ... E ... 620 657-2711
Satanta *(G-10789)*

Thompson Bros Supplies Inc ....E 620 251-1740
Coffeyville *(G-983)*
Wichita Welding Supply Inc ....F 316 838-8671
Wichita *(G-16043)*

WELDING EQPT & SPLYS: Resistance, Electric

Hi-Tech Weld Overlay Group LLC ....E 816 524-9010
Lenexa *(G-5903)*
Polaris Electronics Corp ....E 913 764-5210
Olathe *(G-7990)*

WELDING EQPT REPAIR SVCS

Airgas Usa LLC ....E 316 941-9162
Wichita *(G-13653)*

WELDING REPAIR SVC

A&R Custom Form & Fabricatio ....G....... 620 423-0170
Parsons *(G-9662)*
Anna M Kramer ....G....... 785 353-2205
Beattie *(G-417)*
B&B Welding ....G....... 620 253-1023
Dodge City *(G-1300)*
Built-So-Well ....G....... 785 537-5166
Manhattan *(G-6571)*
Central States Machining Wldg ....G....... 785 233-1376
Topeka *(G-12457)*
Central Welding & Machine LLC ....F 620 663-9353
Hutchinson *(G-3235)*
Ceo Enterprises Inc ....F 913 432-8046
Shawnee Mission *(G-11214)*
Cimarron Welding Inc ....G....... 620 855-3582
Cimarron *(G-821)*
Cliffs Welding Shop Inc ....G....... 785 543-5895
Phillipsburg *(G-9780)*
Earl Resse Welding ....G....... 620 624-6141
Liberal *(G-6306)*
G F Enterprises ....G....... 785 539-7113
Manhattan *(G-6642)*
General Repair & Supply Inc ....G....... 620 365-5954
Iola *(G-3604)*
Hammersmith Mfg & Sales Inc ....D....... 785 486-2121
Horton *(G-3126)*
Hammersmith Mfg & Sales Inc ....G....... 785 364-4140
Holton *(G-3095)*
Harrison Machine Shop & Wldg ....G....... 913 764-0730
Olathe *(G-7756)*
Harrods Blacksmith & Welding ....G....... 620 374-2323
Howard *(G-3134)*
Harvest AG Fabricating LLC ....G....... 620 345-8205
Moundridge *(G-7184)*
Independent Electric McHy Co ....E 913 362-1155
Kansas City *(G-4097)*
Koehn Customs ....G....... 316 304-7979
Montezuma *(G-7157)*
Larue Machine Inc ....F 620 431-3303
Chanute *(G-738)*
Leons Welding & Fabrication ....F 785 625-5736
Hays *(G-2863)*
Linders Welding Inc ....G....... 913 681-2394
Stilwell *(G-12164)*
Martin Welding ....G....... 620 545-7311
Clearwater *(G-894)*
Mc Intire Welding Inc ....E 785 823-5454
Salina *(G-10595)*
Mid Kansas Machine Inc ....E 620 241-2959
McPherson *(G-7003)*
Miller Welding Inc ....F 785 454-3425
Downs *(G-1472)*
Mlr Welding LLC ....G....... 785 203-1020
Hays *(G-2874)*
Neville Welding Inc ....E 620 532-3487
Kingman *(G-4608)*
Numerical Control Support Inc ....E 913 441-3500
Shawnee Mission *(G-11690)*
Premier Tillage Inc ....E 785 754-2381
Quinter *(G-10184)*
Pro-Weld LLC ....G....... 316 648-6316
Wichita *(G-15354)*
Progressive Manufacturing Co ....F 913 383-2239
Leawood *(G-5530)*
Randy Schwindt ....F 785 391-2277
Utica *(G-13335)*
Rons Welding & Pipeline Svcs ....G....... 620 935-4275
Russell *(G-10291)*
Schlotterbeck Machine Shop ....G....... 620 678-3210
Hamilton *(G-2708)*
Steel Fabrications Inc ....G....... 785 625-3075
Hays *(G-2913)*
Toms Machine & Welding Svc ....G....... 785 434-2800
Plainville *(G-9994)*
Turon Welding and Fabrication ....G....... 620 388-4458
Turon *(G-13275)*
Webco Manufacturing Inc ....D....... 913 764-7111
Olathe *(G-8149)*
Welco Services Inc ....E 620 241-3000
McPherson *(G-7041)*

WELDING SPLYS, EXC GASES: Wholesalers

Airgas Usa LLC ....E 785 823-8100
Salina *(G-10398)*
Airgas Usa LLC ....E 316 941-9162
Wichita *(G-13653)*
Matheson Tri-Gas Inc ....E 785 234-3424
Topeka *(G-12864)*

WELL CURBING: Concrete

First Imprssons Crbscaping LLC ....G....... 913 620-5164
Stilwell *(G-12147)*

WESTERN APPAREL STORES

Chisholm Trail Country Str LLC ....F 316 283-3276
Newton *(G-7328)*

WHEEL BALANCING EQPT: Automotive

Trail Worthy Inc ....G....... 316 337-5311
Halstead *(G-2705)*

WHEELCHAIR LIFTS

Easy Money Pawn Shop Inc ....G....... 316 687-2727
Wichita *(G-14255)*
Thyssenkrupp Elevator Corp ....F 316 529-2233
Wichita *(G-15764)*

WHEELCHAIRS

Rayes Inc ....D....... 785 726-4885
Ellis *(G-1651)*
Rayes Inc ....D....... 785 726-4885
Hays *(G-2897)*

WHEELS & PARTS

GKN Armstrong Wheels Inc ....E 316 943-3571
Wichita *(G-14469)*

WIG & HAIRPIECE STORES

Mane Event ....F 785 827-1999
Salina *(G-10590)*

WIGS, WHOLESALE

Hairuwear Inc ....E 954 835-2200
Lenexa *(G-5886)*

WINDMILLS: Electric Power Generation

Cimarron Wind Energy LLC ....G....... 561 691-7171
Cimarron *(G-822)*
West Wind Energy LLC ....F 785 387-2623
Otis *(G-8242)*

WINDOW & DOOR FRAMES

Humphrey Products Inc ....E 316 267-2201
Wichita *(G-14655)*
Mpressions ....G....... 913 897-4401
Stilwell *(G-12169)*
Peerless Products Inc ....B 620 223-4610
Fort Scott *(G-1998)*

WINDOW CLEANING SVCS

Clear View Inc ....E 785 286-2070
Topeka *(G-12480)*
Noonshine Window Cleaning Svc ....F 913 381-3780
Overland Park *(G-9092)*
Noonshine Window Cleaning Svc ....F 913 381-9666
Shawnee Mission *(G-11687)*

WINDOW FURNISHINGS WHOLESALERS

Window Flair Draperies ....G....... 913 722-6070
Shawnee *(G-11054)*

WINE & DISTILLED ALCOHOLIC BEVERAGES WHOLESALERS

Blacks Retail Liquor LLC ....F 913 281-1551
Kansas City *(G-3866)*
Southern Glazer SPI KS ....C....... 913 745-2900
Edwardsville *(G-1515)*

WINE CELLARS, BONDED: Wine, Blended

Emporia Winery LLC ....G....... 620 481-7129
Emporia *(G-1748)*

WIRE

Valent Arstrctres - Lenexa LLC ....E 913 469-6400
Shawnee Mission *(G-11972)*
Wkcsc Inc ....G....... 316 652-7113
Wichita *(G-16060)*

WIRE & WIRE PRDTS

Burlingame Wire Products Inc ....F 785 483-3138
Russell *(G-10268)*
Certainteed LLC ....E 620 241-5511
McPherson *(G-6946)*
Hydeman Company Inc ....G....... 913 384-2620
Kansas City *(G-4090)*
Lane Myers Company Inc ....E 620 622-4310
Protection *(G-10175)*
Print Source Inc ....D....... 316 945-7052
Wichita *(G-15348)*
Quality Steel & Wire Pdts Co ....G....... 913 888-2929
Lenexa *(G-6085)*
Wireco Worldgroup Inc ....E 816 270-4700
Prairie Village *(G-10084)*

WIRE MATERIALS: Copper

Vermillion Incorporated ....D....... 316 524-3100
Wichita *(G-15875)*

WIRE MATERIALS: Steel

A-1 Scaffold Mfg Inc ....E 785 621-5121
Hays *(G-2743)*
Emco Specialty Products Inc ....G....... 913 281-4555
Kansas City *(G-3986)*
Lane Myers Company Inc ....E 620 622-4310
Protection *(G-10175)*

WIRE: Communication

Vermillion Incorporated ....D....... 316 524-3100
Wichita *(G-15875)*

WIRE: Nonferrous

Essex Group Inc ....B 620 653-2191
Hoisington *(G-3063)*
Mize & Co Inc ....E 620 532-3191
Kingman *(G-4607)*
Schlumberger Technology Corp ....C....... 785 841-5610
Lawrence *(G-5103)*
Standard Motor Products Inc ....B 913 441-6500
Edwardsville *(G-1516)*
Superior Essex Inc ....E 620 653-2191
Hoisington *(G-3071)*

WOMEN'S & CHILDREN'S CLOTHING WHOLESALERS, NEC

Acres Inc ....F 785 776-3234
Manhattan *(G-6532)*
Baldwin LLC ....F 913 312-2375
Leawood *(G-5338)*
Dri Duck Traders Inc ....F 913 648-8222
Overland Park *(G-8661)*
Strasburg-Jarvis Inc ....B 913 888-1115
Shawnee Mission *(G-11902)*
Urban Outfitters Inc ....E 785 331-2885
Lawrence *(G-5169)*

WOMEN'S & GIRLS' SPORTSWEAR WHOLESALERS

Its Greek To Me Inc ....C....... 800 336-4486
Manhattan *(G-6666)*
Stardust Corporation ....F 913 894-1966
Kansas City *(G-4439)*

WOMEN'S CLOTHING STORES

Baldwin LLC .... F 913 312-2375
Leawood *(G-5338)*
Town Center Plaza LLC .... F 913 498-1111
Leawood *(G-5581)*
United Distributors Inc .... F 316 263-6181
Wichita *(G-15842)*
United Distributors Inc .... F 316 712-2174
Wichita *(G-15841)*
Urban Outfitters Inc .... E 785 331-2885
Lawrence *(G-5169)*

WOMEN'S CLOTHING STORES: Ready-To-Wear

American Eagle Outfitters Inc .... B 724 779-5209
Ottawa *(G-8244)*
Maurices Incorporated .... E 620 275-1210
Garden City *(G-2229)*
Shear Designers .... F 620 342-5393
Emporia *(G-1826)*

WOMEN'S SPORTSWEAR STORES

Tioga Territory Ltd .... F 620 431-2479
Chanute *(G-770)*

WOOD FENCING WHOLESALERS

Macs Fence Inc .... E 913 287-6173
Kansas City *(G-4211)*
Wichita Fence Co Inc .... F 316 838-1342
Park City *(G-9654)*

WOOD PRDTS: Engraved

Advance Business Supply .... G 785 440-7826
Topeka *(G-12292)*

WOOD PRDTS: Excelsior, Including Pads & Wrappers

Delmarva Pad Co .... F 620 665-9757
Hutchinson *(G-3261)*

WOOD PRDTS: Moldings, Unfinished & Prefinished

Woodwork Mfg & Sup Inc .... E 620 663-3393
Hutchinson *(G-3492)*

WOOD PRDTS: Mulch, Wood & Bark

Capital City Pallet Inc .... F 785 379-5099
Topeka *(G-12429)*
CS Carey LLC .... F 913 432-4877
Kansas City *(G-3947)*

WOOD PRDTS: Porch Work

Window Design Company .... G 785 582-2888
Silver Lake *(G-12030)*

WOOD PRDTS: Signboards

Sunburst Systems Inc .... F 913 383-9309
Kansas City *(G-4446)*
Universal Sign & Display LLC .... F 785 242-8111
Ottawa *(G-8317)*

WOOD PRODUCTS: Reconstituted

Maine Flame LLC .... G 913 208-9484
Spring Hill *(G-12088)*

WOODWORK & TRIM: Exterior & Ornamental

Innotech LLC .... G 913 888-4646
Lenexa *(G-5915)*

WOODWORK & TRIM: Interior & Ornamental

Westhoff Interiors Inc .... E 620 449-2900
Saint Paul *(G-10386)*

WOODWORK: Carved & Turned

Woodcraft Supply LLC .... G 913 599-2800
Shawnee Mission *(G-12016)*

WOVEN WIRE PRDTS, NEC

Wireco Wrldgroup US Hldngs Inc .... F 816 270-4700
Prairie Village *(G-10086)*

X-RAY EQPT & TUBES

Harry B Rusk Company Inc .... G 316 263-4680
Wichita *(G-14565)*

YARN: Manmade & Synthetic Fiber, Twisting Or Winding

Polymer Group Inc .... C 620 532-4000
Kingman *(G-4612)*

YARNS & THREADS: Non-Fabric Materials

Golden Star Inc .... D 913 874-2178
Atchison *(G-231)*

YOUTH CAMPS

Junction City Family YMCA Inc .... E 785 762-4780
Junction City *(G-3704)*
YMCA Topeaka Downtown Branch .... E 785 354-8591
Topeka *(G-13256)*
Young Mens Christian .... F 785 233-9815
Topeka *(G-13258)*
Young Mens Christian Assn .... E 620 275-1199
Garden City *(G-2319)*
Young Mens Christian Associa .... C 316 219-9622
Wichita *(G-16093)*
Young Mens Christian Associa .... D 316 260-9622
Wichita *(G-16094)*
Young Mens Christian Associa .... C 316 942-5511
Wichita *(G-16095)*
Young Mens Christian Associat .... C 620 545-7290
Viola *(G-13380)*
Young Mens Christian Gr Kansas .... D 913 362-3489
Prairie Village *(G-10088)*
Young Mens Christian Gr Kansas .... C 913 393-9622
Olathe *(G-8163)*
Young Mens Christian Gr Kansas .... D 913 782-7707
Olathe *(G-8164)*
Young MNS Chrstn Assn of Tpeka .... C 785 354-8591
Topeka *(G-13259)*
Young MNS Chrstn Assn Pttsburg .... D 620 231-1100
Pittsburg *(G-9972)*

ZOOLOGICAL GARDEN, NONCOMMERCIAL

City of Topeka .... E 785 368-9180
Topeka *(G-12468)*

ZOOS & BOTANICAL GARDENS

City of Garden City .... E 620 276-1250
Garden City *(G-2125)*

& SVC

1247